S0-BEP-505

2007 / 2008

SERVICES FINANCIERS AU CANADA

FINANCIAL SERVICES CANADA

2007-2008 / 10TH EDITION

2007 / 2008

SERVICES FINANCIERS AU CANADA

FINANCIAL SERVICES CANADA

GREY HOUSE PUBLISHING CANADA

Grey House Publishing Canada

PUBLISHER: Leslie Mackenzie
GENERAL MANAGER: Bryon Moore
EDITORIAL MANAGER: Robert Lang
ASSOCIATE EDITORS: Janet Hawtin; Jaime Adams
ADMINISTRATIVE ASSISTANT: Lisa Lazoren

Grey House Publishing

MARKETING DIRECTOR: Jessica Moody
PRODUCTION MANAGER: Karen Stevens
COMPOSITION: David Garoogian

Grey House Publishing Canada
20 Victoria Street, Second Floor
Toronto, ON M5C 2N8
866-433-4739
FAX 416-644-1904
www.greyhouse.ca
e-mail: info@greyhouse.ca

10th edition published 2007
Printed in Canada

ISBN: 978-1-59237-221-8

Table of Contents

Introduction

Welcome to the 10th edition of *Financial Services Canada*, the first edition of this important work published by Grey House Publishing Canada. This 2007/2008 edition of *Financial Services Canada* includes nearly 18,000 listings, categorized in nine chapters, including Banks, Investment Management Companies, Accounting Firms, Major Canadian Corporations and Government Departments. It profiles organizations that are not only headquartered in Canada, but also those of significance to the Canadian financial industry that may be headquartered elsewhere, with branches or divisions in Canada.

Financial Services Canada is one of five recently acquired Canadian directories previously published by Micromedia, a division of ProQuest, including *Canadian Almanac & Directory, Associations Canada, The Directory of Libraries in Canada,* and *Canadian Environmental Directory,* new editions of which will be available throughout 2007 and early 2008.

Over the years, *Financial Services Canada* has provided the most comprehensive picture of Canada's financial industry sector. This 2007/2008 Grey House Canada edition is no exception. Chapters include:

- **Banks & Depositories**
- **Non-depositories**
- **Investment Management**
- **Insurance Companies**
- **Accounting & Law**
- **Major Companies**
- **Government Agencies**
- **Associations**
- **Publications**

Each listing presents a detailed organization profile, including founding date, scope of activity, executive information, full addresses and complete contact information. The indexes offer a variety of ways to search not only for specific organizations, but also for specific categories of organizations.

Financial Services Canada is the most up-to-date source for names and contact numbers of industry professionals, senior executives, portfolio managers, financial advisors, top agency bureaucrats and elected representatives. This 10th edition includes 960 new entries and close to 2,000 new key contacts.

New Features

In addition to the current, comprehensive factual information offered in *Financial Services Canada*, we have made some important changes and additions:

- **Articles & Statistics** that highlight significant issues in the Canadian financial services community are included in various chapters. You'll find articles such as • *Competition in the Canadian Financial Services Sector* • *Operating Profits by Major Industry* • *Recent Trends in Corporate Finance* • *Quarterly Statistics for Enterprises.*
- **Bold Category Headers** now exist in each profile, making it easy to find data points such as *Former Name, Year Founded, Number of Employees, Profile, Executives, Partners,* and *Branches.*
- **Hundreds more Descriptions** appear throughout, especially in *Accounting & Law* and *Publication* sections.
- **Hundreds more Listings** have been added, especially in *Banks, Major Corporations, Accounting & Law,* and *Investment Management* sections.
- **New Typeface** makes all content easy to read.

Available in print and by subscription online via Grey House Publishing Canada at www.greyhouse.ca, *Financial Services Canada* is widely used as a valuable resource for financial executives, bankers, financial planners, sales and marketing professionals, lawyers and chartered accountants, government officials, investment dealers, journalists, librarians and reference specialists.

We acknowledge the valuable contribution of those individuals and organizations who have responded to our information gathering process throughout the year; your help and timely responses to our questionnaires, phone calls and faxes is greatly appreciated.

Every effort has been made to ensure the accuracy of the information included in this edition of *Financial Services Canada*. Do not hesitate to contact us with comments or if revisions are necessary.

Users' Guide

Financial Services Canada provides a single-source approach to identifying and researching Canadian financial services companies and organizations. The book is organized with the user in mind. Categorized listings and three easy-to-use indexes allow you to find an institution or contact by company name, location, name of a senior officer, or service offered.

The Nine Sections

Section 1 - Banks & Depository Institutions
The first section presents the Canadian banking, trust and cooperative industry in the following sub-sections: Domestic Banks (Schedule I), Foreign Banks (Schedule II), Foreign Bank Branches (Schedule III), Foreign Bank Representative Offices, Savings Banks, Trust Companies, and Credit Unions/Caisses Populaires. Within each sub-section, the entries are arranged alphabetically. Listings may include an institution's Canadian branches, arranged alphabetically by city or town.

Section 2 - Non-Depository Institutions
Information about non-deposit-taking financial institutions is split into the following sub-sections: Financing & Loan Companies, Bond Rating Agencies, Collection Agencies, Credit Card Companies, and Trustees in Bankruptcy. Companies are arranged alphabetically within each sub-section. Concise information about branch offices may also be featured.

Section 3 - Investment Management Firms
The following sub-sections are presented in this section: Financial Planning & Investment Management Companies, Holding & Other Investment Companies, Venture Capital Firms, Investment Dealers, Investment Fund Companies, Pension & Money Management Companies, and Stock Exchanges. Companies in this section often fall under more than one of the sub-sections. A list of investment funds offered by each investment fund company is given and, where available, the name of the fund manager is indicated. Stock Exchange listings include member firms in the financial sector.

Section 4 - Insurance Companies
The fourth section is a guide to the insurance industry in Canada. Companies are compiled alphabetically by name. Federally and provincially incorporated insurance companies, reinsurance companies, mutual benefit companies, fraternal benefit societies, reciprocal exchanges are presented. Class(es) of insurance offered by each company is given.

Section 5 - Accounting & Law
Accountants, Actuarial Consultants, and Law Firms are the subsections of Section 5. Major Canadian accounting and law firms are listed here. Where provided, details of lawyers' areas of financial practice are included, as well as their contact information.

Section 6 - Major Canadian Companies
Canada's major private, public, or Crown corporations are found in this section. For each company, key financial contacts and a brief description of the business are highlighted.

Section 7 - Government
The government section incorporates federal, provincial and territorial government contacts. A quick reference sub-section provides topical reference, enabling you to locate particular contacts by general subject. Main listings provide full departmental information. Detail is given to those ministries or departments that have a strong financial component.

Section 8 - Associations
This section focuses on associations and institutes for the financial services sector.

Section 9 - Publications
The Publications section is a list of leading publications which serve the financial services industry in Canada. Publication listings typically include the publisher, editor, frequency of publication, and a brief description of magazine content.

The Indexes

The **Alphabetical Index** sorts every main office entry in the directory alphabetically by name of company, government agency, or association. If searching for a specific company, but unsure of which section to check, begin here. The index directs you to the appropriate section and page number. When an office is listed in more than one section, each section, with its page number, is indicated.

The **Geographic Index** breaks down the location of financial institutions and their branches by town or city. Listings are arranged by province, followed by place names in alphabetical order. This index provides a quick and simple method of finding companies in any given place across Canada. The index supplies the section and page number to see the complete entry for each organization. When an institution has several locations in a single city, its name appears once after the city name. The section and page number refers to the beginning of the listing.

The **Executive Name Index** lists all officers, directors, and senior personnel alphabetically by surname. Executives are accompanied by their title and organization name. If an executive has multiple positions within a company, or has roles with several companies, all are given.

Mailing Lists

Most of the information in Financial Services Canada is in databases that can be sorted and combined to provide you with mailing labels by category or subject interest. Lists are provided in printed or electronic form (see details at the back of the book or phone Grey House Publishing Canada at 1-866-433-4739).

Abbreviations

AACCA	Associate of Association of Certified Accountants & Corporate Accountants (British)
AACI	Accredited Appraiser Canadian Institute
AAE	Associate of Accountants' & Executives' Corp. of Canada
AB	Bachelor of Arts, American (Artium Baccalaureus)
ACA	Associate of Institute of Chartered Accountants (Eng.)
ACFP	Associate Certificate in Financial Planning
ACInstM	- of the Institute of Marketing
ACIS	- of Chartered Institute of Secretaries (British)
Adm. A. Pl.Fin.	Administrateur agréé en planification financière
AFC	Accredited Financial Counsellor
AICB	Associate of the Institute of Canadian Bankers
AIIC	- of the Insurance Institute of Canada
APA	Member of the Institute of Accredited Public Accountants (British)
BA	Bachelor of Arts
BAA	- of Applied Arts
B.Acc.	- of Accountancy
B.Adm. (B.Admin.)	- of Administration
BASM	- of Arts, Master of Science
BBA	- of Business Administration
BCL	- of Civil Law (or Canon Law)
B.Com. (B. Comm.)	- of Commerce
B. en Sc. Com.	Bachelier en Science Commerciale
B. ès Sc.	- ès Sciences
BSA	Bachelor of Science in Accounting, or in Administration
B.Sc.	- of Science
BScA	Bachelier ès science appliquées
BScB	- en Bibliothéconomie
B.Sc.Com.	Bachelor of Commercial Science
CA	Chartered Accountant
C. Adm., F.P.	Chartered Administrator in Financial Planning
CAE	Certified Association Executive
CAE/c.a.é.	Chartered Account Executive
CAM	Certified Administrative Manager
CBV	Chartered Business Valuator
CEBS	Certified Employee Benefit Specialist
Cert. Bus. Admin.	Certificate in Business Administration
CFA	Chartered Financial Analyst
CFP	Chartered Financial Planner
CGA	Certified General Accountant
CH.F.C.	Chartered Financial Consultant
CIM	Certified Investment Manager
CLU	Chartered Life Underwriter
CM	Member, Order of Canada
CMA	Certified Management Accountant
CMC	Certified Management Consultant
CPA	Certified Public Accountant
CR (c.r.)	Conseiller de la Reine (Queen's Counsel)
CSC	Canadian Securities Course
D. en Ph.	Docteur en Philosophie
D.F.Sc.	Doctor of Financial Science (Laval)
Dipl. Bus. Admin.	Diploma Business Administration
Dr. jur. (Dr. Juris)	Doctor of Law
D.Sc.Fin.	- of Financial Science
FAE	Fellow of the Accountants' & Executives' Corporation of Canada
FAIA	- of the American Institute of Actuaries
FAIA	- of the Association of International Accountants
FCA	- of the Institute of Chartered Accountants (British)
FCAM	- of the Institute of the Certified Administrative Managers
FCBA	- of Canadian Bankers' Association
FCCA	- of the Association of Certified Accountants
FCCUI	- of the Canadian Credit Union Institute
FCI	- of the Canadian Credit Institute
FCIA	- of the Canadian Institute of Actuaries
FCII	- of the Chartered Insurance Institute (British)
FCIS	- of the Chartered Institute of Secretaries (British)
FCMA	- of the Society of Management Accountants of Canada
FCSI	- of the Canadian Securities Institute
FCUIC	- of the Credit Union Institute of Canada
FFA	- of the Faculty of Actuaries (Scotland)
FIA	- of the Institute of Actuaries (British)
FICB	- of the Institute of Canadian Bankers
FIIC	- of the Insurance Institute of Canada
FMA	Financial Management Advisor
FSA	Fellow of the Society of Actuaries (honorary)
FSMAC	- of the Society of Management Accountants of Canada
IA	Investment Advisor
IC	Investment Counsellor
JD	Doctor of Jurisprudence
JurM	Master of Jurisprudence
LL	License in Civil Law
LLB	Bachelor of Laws (Legum Baccalaureus)
LLD	Doctor of Laws (usually honorary)
LLL	Licence en droit
LLM	Master of Law
MA	Master of Arts
M.Acc.	- of Accountancy
MBA	Master in Business Administration
MCI	Member of the Credit Institute
MCInstM	- of the Canadian Institute of Marketing
M.Com.	Master of Commerce
MICIA	Member of Industrial, Commercial & Institutional Accountants
MP	Member of Parliament
MPP	Member of Provincial Parliament
M.Sc.	Master of Science
MTCI	Member of Trust Companies Institute
OC	Order of Canada
PC	Privy Councillor
PFC	Planificateur Financier Certifié
PFP	Personal Financial Planner
PhD	Doctor of Philosophy
Prof.	Professor
QC	Queen's Counsel
REBC	Registered Employee Benefits Consultant
RFP	Registered Financial Planner
RHU	Registered Health Underwriter
RPA	Registered Professional Accountant
SFC	Specialist in Financial Counselling

Competition in the Canadian Financial Services Sector

Canada's financial services sector is highly competitive – Canadians can choose a full range of financial products and services from a variety of suppliers. Increasing competitiveness in the market for financial products and services is attributable to at least three major developments:

- Many of the old barriers prohibiting financial institutions from competing in each other's business have disappeared over the past 15 years. For example, any Canadian life insurance company may now own a bank, a bank may own an investment dealer or a mutual fund company,etc.
- More recent changes to federal law and regulation have opened up new opportunities for foreign banks to operate in Canada, encouraged the start up of new banks with new ownership rules, and given certain non-bank financial institutions direct access to the payments system.
- Innovations in technology have enabled financial institutions to offer more products and services in new ways and have triggered the emergence of new types of competitors, such as monoline credit card issuers MBNA Canada and Capital One Bank.

What This Means for Consumers

For Canadian consumers, the growing number of financial services providers means an expanding array of products and services is available to suit their individual needs, at costs ranked among the most competitive in the world. While Canada's bank financial groups are leading players in the country's financial services sector, there are several thousand other financial services providers in Canada, making for a varied and dynamic marketplace.

The Competitors

Competitors in Canada's financial services sector include:

- Canada's six largest domestic banks
- 13 smaller domestic banks
- 49 foreign-owned bank subsidiaries/branches
- 29 trust companies
- 89 life insurance companies
- 1,300 credit unions and caisses populaires
- 180 investment dealers
- 61 mutual fund companies
- 58 pension fund managers
- Over 4000 independent financial, deposit and mortgage brokers

Also, the 2001 Statistics Canada Survey of Business Financing counts 3700 financing firms with assets of at least $5 million. Many of these competitors also offer select banking products and services, including taking deposits, making loans, and issuing credit cards.

Several large unregulated competitors participate in Canada's financial services market and offer products and services, which include residential and commercial mortgages, credit cards, motor vehicle financing and equipment leasing. These competitors include:

- GE Capital group of companies
- General Motors Acceptance Corporation
- Ford Credit
- CIT Group
- Dell Financial Services

In addition to these competing private sector institutions, numerous government agencies also offer financial services. At the federal level, the Business Development Bank of Canada, Farm Credit Canada and Export Development Canada offer various products and services. Provincial government savings and lending agencies include ATB Financial, Alberta's Agricultural Financial Services Corporation and Investissement Québec.

New Competitors

Changes to bank ownership laws in 2001 encouraged the establishment of new banks in communities across Canada. For example, small banks were allowed to have a single owner and medium-sized banks (up to $5 billion in equity) were allowed to have a controlling owner, which could be a commercial enterprise. Examples include:

- Western Financial Group, a holding company for a network of insurance agencies, created Bank West;
- The Wheaton Group, a chain of car dealerships, has received permission to launch a new bank called General Bank of Canada;
- Pacific and Western eTrust of Canada, a provincially-regulated trust company, has converted to a bank, Pacific and Western Bank of Canada; and
- Canadian Tire has established a banking subsidiary (Canadian Tire Bank), as has Loblaws (President's Choice Bank).

It is reasonable to expect the emergence of other new banks in the Canadian market in the months and years ahead.

In addition to start-up operations, the Canadian financial services marketplace is made increasingly competitive by transactions involving new and existing competitors. This provides even more options for Canadians. For example:

- GMAC Residential Funding of Canada, a subsidiary of General Motors Acceptance Corporation, has acquired Mortgage Intelligence, the largest independent mortgage brokerage in Canada.
- Union Bank of California, a subsidiary of UnionBanCal, the third largest bank in California,has established a foreign lending branch in Calgary to provide debt capital to oil and gas companies.
- Household Financial, including its 110 branches across Canada offering consumer loans, credit cards, auto finance and credit insurance, has been acquired by HSBC Holdings, the parent of HSBC Bank Canada.

Indicators of Competition

There are numerous indicators of strong competition within Canada's financial sector, not only amongst the six largest bank financial groups but also with the host of other financial services providers active in the marketplace. Key indicators include access, price and choice.

Interest rate spreads: The difference between the interest rate a financial institution charges on loans to its borrowing customers and the interest rate it pays to its depositing customers – the interest rate spread – is an excellent measure of financial sector competition. Competition results in narrowing interest rate spreads, allowing borrowers to access funds at close to the banks' cost of acquiring those funds. According to the World Economic Forum's 2004-2005 Global Competitiveness Report, interest rate spreads in Canada in 2003 are among the lowest in the Organisation for Economic Cooperation and Development (OECD) countries. The report shows that Canadian spreads are 1.5 percentage points lower than in Australia and almost 4.0 percentage points lower than in Germany, demonstrating strong competition in the Canadian financial sector.

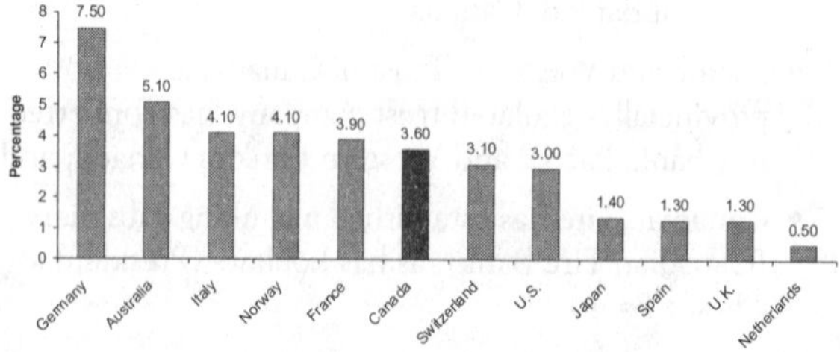

Source: World Economic Forum, The Global Competitveness Report, 2004-2005

Household financial assets: One way to measure the degree of competition for financial services business is to look at how Canadians manage their household financial assets. (Statistics Canada defines household financial assets to include cash, deposits, securities, mutual funds, life insurance and pensions – the current accounts, savings and investment holdings of Canadians). Statistics Canada's National Balance Sheet Accounts show that Canadians rely on a wide variety of Financial Institutions to manage their household financial assets. Twenty per cent of household financial assets are held by banks, 11 per cent by life insurance companies, and 69 per cent are held by other financial services providers such as pension and mutual funds, demonstrating a high level of competition in the Canadian marketplace.

Credit cards: The Canadian credit card market is one of the most competitive in the world, exemplifying the high degree of competition in Canada's financial services sector. With over 550 issuers of VISA or MasterCard and over 53 million credit cards in circulation, customers may choose from among standard cards that typically do not have an annual fee, premium cards that carry a variety of rewards and features, and low-rate cards for when the interest rate is a key consideration influencing card choice. For a more detailed examination of credit cards see Taking a Closer Look: Credit Cards on the CBA website at www.cba.ca.

Number of large competitors: Amongst the wide range of financial services providers in Canada are nine large, full-service financial groups. This is an impressive number for an economy of Canada's size. Three life insurance financial groups (Great West Lifeco/IGM Financial, Manulife Financial, Sun Life Financial) are in the top eight as measured by market capitalization, two of which are counted in the top five financial institutions operating in Canada. They offer similar suites of products and services as Canada's major bank financial groups, giving consumers a wide range of choice in their financial service providers.

Market Capitalization of Major Financial Groups ($ Billion at April 11, 2005)

Group	$ Billion
RBC Financial Group	$47.6
Manulife Financial + John Hancock	$47.4
Scotiabank	$39.9
IGM Financial + Great-West Lifeco	$34.1
TD Financial Group	$33.4
BMO Financial Group	$28.3
CIBC	$24.3
Sun Life Financial	$23.2
National Bank of Canada	$ 9.0

Reprinted with permission of the Canadian Bankers Association-www.cba.ca

CANADIAN BANKERS ASSOCIATION
Building a Better Understanding

Statistics of Growth and Progress in Canada

GROWTH STATISTICS: AGRICULTURE/FISHERIES

	POPULATION [1]	WHEAT	TOTAL CANADIAN CROPS [2]	FARM CASH RECEIPTS FOR TOTAL CROPS	FARM CASH RECEIPTS FOR LIVESTOCK & LIVESTOCK PRODUCTS [3]	SHIPMENTS, ESTIMATED VALUES OF GOODS OF OWN MANUFACTURING	FISHERIES LANDED VALUES
		('000 BUSHELS)	('000 ACRES)	($000,000)	($000,000)	($000,000)	($000,000)
1992	28,366,737 (IR)	1,097,806	100,905	8,551	11,388	7,502,142	1,400,322
1993	28,681,676 (IR)	1,000,387	102,612	9,046	12,300	7,361,334	1,424,056
1994	28,999,006 (IR)	842,154	102,771	11,543	12,514	7,458,679	1,699,372
1995	29,302,091 (IR)	918,197	102,553	13,114	12,704	7,856,580	1,782,957
1996	29,610,757 (ID)	1,095,008	100,567	14,016	13,857	8,228,177	1,565,642 (P)
1997	29,907,172 (ID)	892,846	110,319	14,103	14,627	8,177,141	1,634,285 (P)
1998	30,157,082 (ID)	884,866	100,832	13,822	14,443	8,619,947	1,610,678 (P)
1999	30,403,878 (ID)	990,598	100,902	13,218	15,163	8,756,324	1,924,589
2000	30,689,035 (ID)	975,014	100,727	13,062	17,090	9,068,182	2,061,194
2001	31,021,251 (PD)	755,722	100,016	13,591	18,964	9,876,082	-- -- --
2002	31,372,587 (PD)	595,143	99,791	14,455	18,191	10,005,411	-- -- --
2003	31,669,150 (PR)	865,402	99,485	13,431	16,167	10,984,470	-- -- --
2004	31,974,363 (PR)	950,204	99,715	14,500	17,173	11,534,465	-- -- --
2005	32,270,507 (PP)	983,821	99,006	13,500	18,462	12,402,725	-- -- --

1. Period from July 1 to June 30.
2. Includes grains, specialty crops, summerfallow and hay.
3. Total livestock and livestock products (including poultry & animals on fur farms).

Sources: Statistics Canada, Annual Demographic Statistics (cat. no. 91-213-XIB); Field Crop Reporting Series (cat. no. 22-002-XIB); Statistics Canada, CANSIM Tables 002-0001 & 304-0014, July 2006; Dept. of Fisheries & Oceans Canada

(IR) Revised intercensal estimates　(PD) Final Postcensal estimates　(PP) Preliminary Postcensal estimates
(ID) Final intercensal estimates　(PR) Updated Postcensal estimates　-- Not available

GROWTH STATISTICS: PRODUCTION OF SELECTED MINERALS/METALS

	PIG IRON PRODUCTION	CRUDE OIL & EQUIVALENT	COPPER	NICKEL	NATURAL GAS	IRON ORE	ZINC	ASBESTOS	CEMENT	VALUE OF TOTAL MINERAL PRODUCTION
	('000 metric tonnes)	('000 cubic metres)	('000 tonnes)	('000 tonnes)	('000 cubic metres)	('000 tonnes)	('000 tonnes)	('000 tonnes)	('000 tonnes)	($000,000)
1993	8,633	105,780	711.2	178.4	128,817	33,228	990.6	523	9,284	36,564
1994	8,106	110,452	591.0	142.0	138,856	36,416	976.4	531	10,457	41,150
1995	8,464	114,372	700.9	172.2	148,203	36,628	1,094.9	516	10,600	43,360
1996	8,638	117,621	652.5	182.4	153,578	34,400	1,162.8	506	11,003	49,678
1997	8,669	123,827	647.9	180.6	156,171	38,928	1,026.8	420	11,790	50,538
1998	8,936	128,401	690.7	197.9	160,651	36,586	991.5	321	12,168	44,339
1999	8,856	122,287	581.5	176.9	162,219	33,004	963.3	345	12,643	53,466
2000	8,904	127,769	621.7	181.2	167,794	35,247	935.7	310	12,753	83,854
2001	8,302	128,951	614.2	184.2	171,351	27,119	1,012.2	277	12,793	82,968
2002	8,670	136,970	584.2	179.7	172,197	30,969	924.1	241	13,081	76,951
2003	8,554	144,813	541.0	155.4	166,475	33,322	757.4	X	13,418	20,077*
2004 (R)	8,828	149,425	544.5	177.3	167,503	28,596	734.0	X	13,863	24,168*
2005 (P)	8,274	146,415	572.7	182.0	170,604	30,125	620.8	X	14,179	-- -- --

Standard Classification of Goods (SCG) code 7201.00.　* Excludes oil & gas as of 2003　-- Not available

Sources: Statistics Canada, Primary Iron & Steel (cat. no. 41-001-XIB) 1992-2004, and Steel, Tubular Products & Steel Wire (cat. no. 41-019); CANSIM Tables 152-0001, 152-0004, 303-0001 (1992-2003), & 303-0060; Statistics Canada, Manufacturing, Construction and Energy Division

(P) Preliminary　(R) Revised　X = suppressed to meet the confidentiality requirements of the Statistics Act

GROWTH STATISTICS: IMPORTS & EXPORTS

	TOTAL EXPORTS +	TOTAL IMPORTS	IMPORTS OF RAW SUGAR CANE	IMPORTS OF NATURAL RUBBER	IMPORTS OF RAW COTTON	IMPORTS OF CRUDE PETROLEUM
	($000,000)	($000,000)	('000 metric tonnes)	('000 kg)	('000 kg)	(cubic metres)
1993	187,515	169,953	997	61,418	46,063	32,957,060
1994	225,678	202,736	995	101,814	44,961	36,237,601
1995	262,266	225,552	919	115,606	50,347	39,866,227
1996	275,819	232,565	1,227	113,374	58,922	43,237,525
1997	298,072	272,946	1,051	129,752	56,644	51,849,518
1998	318,444	298,386	976	144,875	84,334	52,908,663
1999	355,420	320,408	27,569	137,949	52,227	45,866,143
2000	413,195	356,862	1,111	146,240	72,860	53,027,542
2001	404,085	343,127	1,141	130,073	71,696	52,785,900
2002	396,379	348,718	1,144	156,089	60,824	52,736,765
2003	380,756	335,250	1,413	140,147	72,029	54,281,684
2004	411,355	355,238	1,081	133,674	71,136	54,356,331
2005	435,641	379,577	1,247	142,470	48,005	56,805,800

1. HS code 1701.11　2. HS codes 4001.21, 4001.22, 4001.29　3. HS code 5201.00　4. HS code 2709.00

Sources: Statistics Canada, Exports by Commodity (cat. no. 65-004-XPB) & Imports by Commodity (cat. no. 65-007-XPB)

"Total exports +" equals Domestic Exports plus Re-Exports

GROWTH STATISTICS: TRANSPORT/TRANSPORTATION

	RAILWAY GROSS REVENUE	RAILWAY OPERATING EXPENSES	TONNE KILOMETRES REVENUE FREIGHT	MOTOR VEHICLE REGISTRATION
	($000,000)	($000,000)	('000,000)	('000)
1993	6,993	6,605	256,338	16,718
1994	7,510	6,677	288,432	16,972
1995	7,207	8,454	280,466	17,048
1996	7,180	6,775	282,482	17,183
1997	7,898	6,706	306,252	17,478
1998	7,584	6,912	298,695	17,988
1999	7,697	6,709	297,155	17,534
2000	8,088	6,412	319,382	17,882
2001	8,115	6,550	317,904	18,102
2002	8,209	6,616	320,555	18,617
2003	8,287	6,695	318,345	18,868
2004	8,855	6,980	336,482	19,081
2005	N/A	N/A	N/A	19.353

Sources: Statistics Canada, Rail in Canada, (cat. no. 52-216-XIB); Statistics Canada, CANSIM Tables 405-0001 (1992-1998) & 405-0004 (1999-2005) July 2006

GROWTH STATISTICS: FINANCIAL

		CHARTERED BANKS [1]					LIFE INSURANCE	FEDERAL FINANCE [2]		
	BANK OF CANADA NOTES IN CIRCULATION	ASSETS	LIABILITIES EXCLUDING CAPITAL RESERVES	DEMAND DEPOSITS	NOTICE DEPOSITS	TOTAL LOANS	NET AMOUNT LIFE INSURANCE IN FORCE DEC. 31 [3]	TOTAL GROSS REVENUE [4]	TOTAL GROSS EXPENDITURE [4]	NET DEBT [5]
	($000,000)	($000,000)	($000,000)	($000,000)	($000,000)	$000,000	($000,000)	($000,000)	($000,000)	($000,000)
1993	27,237	753,992	716,795	46,016	142,830	507,394	1,123,619	130,873	171,474	471,061
1994	28,329	841,037	799,279	51,370	140,282	550,444	1,234,746	129,277	169,709	513,219
1995	28,778	911,678	868,796	57,482	135,563	586,591	1,317,184	136,648	173,383	550,685
1996	29,109	1,104,828	1,059,219	68,564	145,589	674,913	1,357,310	142,553	175,765	578,718
1997	30,542	1,321,075	1,266,494	82,674	151,298	803,631	1,446,564	152,541	166,041	588,402
1998	32,638	1,432,114	1,371,371	98,684	152,832	840,929	1,467,479	165,179	160,672	581,581
1999	40,143	1,397,710	1,331,218	113,710	159,567	808,613	1,548,305	169,379	166,593	574,468
2000	36,775	1,550,016	1,476,705	125,453	182,649	884,556	1,606,497	180,336	173,337	561,733
2001	38,821	1,710,431	1,630,333	155,453	216,373	951,927	-- -- --	193,825	184,612	545,300
2002	-- -- --	-- -- --	-- -- --	-- -- --	-- -- --	-- -- --	-- -- --	192,288	184,941	534,690
2003	-- -- --	-- -- --	-- -- --	-- -- --	-- -- --	-- -- --	-- -- --	190,914	189,249	526,492
2004	-- -- --	-- -- --	-- -- --	-- -- --	-- -- --	-- -- --	-- -- --	199,107	196,992	523,648
2005	-- -- --	-- -- --	-- -- --	-- -- --	-- -- --	-- -- --	-- -- --	211,800	206,680	523,344

1. As of December of each year.
2. Based on the Financial Management System (FMS).
3. Compiled by the Office of the Superintentent of Financial Institutions Canada. Includes federally registered companies & societies. Does not include provincial companies and excludes annuities.
4. Fiscal Year ended March 31.
5. Fiscal Year ended March 31.

-- Not available

Source: Bank of Canada; Statistics Canada, CANSIM Tables 385-0002 & 383-0010, July 2006

GROWTH STATISTICS: INDUSTRIAL/TELEPHONE/POSTAL

	INDUSTRY PRICE INDEX, ALL MANUFACTURING INDUSTRIES	AVERAGE WEEKLY EARNINGS [1]	STRIKES AND LOCKOUTS: EMPLOYEES AFFECTED	STRIKES AND LOCKOUTS: DAYS NOT WORKED	TOTAL TELEPHONE ACCESS LINES	REVENUE FROM POSTAL OPERATIONS [2]
	(1997=100)	($CDN)	('000)	('000)	('000)	($000,000)
1993	86.8	583.15	102	1,517	16,716	4,118
1994	92.0	593.15	81	1,607	17,250	4,748
1995	98.9	598.90	149	1,583	17,763	4,953
1996	99.3	611.26	282	3,352	18,051	5,103
1997	100.0	623.63	258	3,610	18,660	5,088
1998	100.4	632.93	244	2,444	19,294	5,709
1999	102.2	640.71	159	2,446	19,806	5,638
2000	106.5	655.91	144	1,662	20,317	5,942
2001	107.6	667.27	224	2,240	20,805	4,441[3]
2002	107.6	680.93	--	--	20,301	6,154*
2003	106.2	690.57	--	--	20,068	6,344*
2004	109.5	706.03	--	--	--	6,651*
2005	111.2	728.17	--	--	--	6,945*

1.Average weekly earnings (SEPH), unadjusted for seasonal variation, all employees, including overtime, industrial aggregate excluding unclassified (NAICS)
2.Fiscal year ended March 31.
3.Represents 9 months of revenue — Canada Post's fiscal year now January - December.
* Fiscal year January - December data

-- Not available

Sources: Statistics Canada, CANSIM Tables 329-0038, 281-0027, 356-0001 (1992-1996), July 2005; Telecommunications Statistics (cat. no. 56-001); Statistics Canada, Public Institutions Division; Human Resources Development Canada

IMPORTS AND EXPORTS - CANADA 2005

Value of merchandise imported and exported during the twelve months ended December 31st, 2004.

COUNTRIES	IMPORTS ($000,000 Cdn.)	EXPORTS ($000,000 Cdn.)	COUNTRIES (cont.)	IMPORTS ($000,000 Cdn.)	EXPORTS ($000,000 Cdn.)	COUNTRIES (cont.)	IMPORTS ($000,000 Cdn.)	EXPORTS ($000,000 Cdn.)
Afghanistan	0.5	19.1	French Polynesia	1.8	15.8	Nigeria	176.6	111.4
Albania	1.3	5.8	French Southern Territories	0.0	0.3	Niue	0.1	0.0
Algeria	4,170.7	229.0	Gabon	1.4	10.9	Norfolk Island	0.0	0.1
American Samoa	0.7	1.3	Gambia	0.0	0.3	Norway	6,058.3	1,550.0
Andorra	0.1	0.1	Georgia	47.6	11.0	Oman	4.7	22.7
Angola	332.7	74.1	Germany	10,262.7	3,227.8	Pakistan	247.6	316.3
Anguilla	0.1	1.6	Ghana	29.1	94.3	Panama	44.7	60.1
Antarctica	0.6	2.1	Gibraltar	0.2	41.7	Papua New Guinea	2.9	6.7
Antigua & Barbuda	0.6	18.5	Greece	145.5	137.4	Paraguay	15.3	10.1
Argentina	452.5	174.3	Greenland	0.5	20.4	Peru	1,357.7	264.1
Armenia	1.8	5.1	Grenada	0.9	7.9	Philippines	921.4	365.6
Aruba	55.9	12.5	Guadaloupe	0.0	0.0	Pitcairn	0.0	0.3
Australia	1,746.8	1,634.7	Guam	0.1	4.4	Poland	532.7	266.7
Austria	1,290.3	450.7	Guatemala	207.3	173.0	Portugal	315.7	164.3
Azerbaijan	0.5	18.5	Guinea	28.7	8.5	Qatar	46.1	85.7
Bahamas	56.8	45.8	Guinea-Bissau	0.0	0.0	Reunion	0.0	0.0
Bahrain	7.6	28.0	Guyana	147.2	16.7	Romania	209.2	157.7
Bangladesh	490.1	102.2	Haiti	25.1	33.8	Russia	1,727.9	564.1
Barbados	7.1	61.3	Heard & McDonald Islands	0.0	0.1	Rwanda	0.4	2.3
Belarus	20.0	8.8	Honduras	129.8	44.3	Samoa (Western)	0.0	0.2
Belgium	1,792.4	2,275.1	Hong Kong	560.5	1,432.3	Sao Tome & Principe	0.1	0.0
Belize	9.6	7.2	Hungary	220.2	70.8	Saudi Arabia	1,723.5	436.5
Benin	0.0	3.8	Iceland	55.7	89.1	Senegal	0.6	23.8
Bermuda	17.7	78.8	India	1,787.5	1,082.4	Seychelles	3.1	0.9
Bhutan	0.0	0.1	Indonesia	955.5	688.9	Sierra Leone	2.4	4.5
Bolivia	24.8	16.0	Iran	44.5	274.2	Singapore	972.4	637.2
Bosnia-Herzegovina	2.7	2.4	Iraq	1,206.4	75.9	Slovakia	122.0	20.4
Botswana	1.0	6.3	Ireland	2,055.3	419.5	Slovenia	61.5	67.5
Bouvet Island	0.0	0.0	Israel	811.1	430.0	Solomon Islands	0.1	0.0
Brazil	3,143.4	1,103.0	Italy	4,576.0	1,915.8	Somalia	0.1	1.3
British Indian Ocean Territory	0.0	2.3	Jamaica	392.9	152.8	South Africa	699.1	452.6
Brunei Darussalam	3.4	3.2	Japan	14,783.8	9,126.8	Spain	1,200.9	1,194.5
Bulgaria	89.2	47.4	Jordan	8.7	121.8	Sri Lanka	109.1	121.3
Burkino Faso	0.2	15.2	Kazakhstan	36.8	115.9	St. Helena	0.1	0.0
Burundi	0.4	2.5	Kenya	16.0	40.5	St. Kitts & Nevis	7.9	6.0
Cambodia	131.5	2.4	Kiribati	0.0	0.1	St. Lucia	0.5	10.0
Cameroon	10.0	15.6	Korea, North	0.1	21.5	St. Pierre & Miquelon	0.0	17.8
Canada	3,543.5	0.0	Korea, South	5,374.7	2,805.9	St. Vincent & the Grenadines	0.1	7.6
Cape Verde	0.0	0.8	Kuwait	60.5	118.1	Sudan	80.4	112.4
Cayman Islands	0.4	24.8	Kyrgyzstan	21.5	4.3	Suriname	184.4	11.3
Central African Republic	0.2	0.3	Laos	7.0	0.8	Swaziland	3.9	3.8
Chad	0.0	5.9	Latvia	14.1	36.6	Sweden	2,293.7	462.9
Chile	1,662.8	411.7	Lebanon	10.8	47.4	Switzerland	2,125.6	1,068.5
China	29,498.5	7,060.3	Lesotho	14.5	0.3	Syria	21.8	64.6
Christmas Island	0.0	0.5	Liberia	13.4	4.3	Taiwan	3,894.5	1,344.2
Cocos (Keeling) Islands	0.1	0.1	Libya	91.4	84.8	Tajikistan	0.1	1.6
Colombia	582.4	446.9	Lithuania	512.4	31.2	Tanzania	159.2	32.6
Comoros	0.1	0.9	Luxembourg	88.7	72.8	Thailand	1,982.0	480.1
Congo	1.3	11.8	Macau	42.1	30.0	Togo	0.5	11.1
Congo, Dem. Rep. of	0.3	15.0	Macedonia	4.1	9.4	Tokelau	0.0	0.0
Cook Islands	0.4	0.4	Madagascar	14.3	0.9	Tonga	0.1	0.1
Costa Rica	355.7	85.0	Malawi	1.4	3.2	Trinidad & Tobago	237.1	159.2
Côte d'Ivoire	134.1	12.7	Malaysia	2,610.2	411.3	Tunisia	32.7	39.4
Croatia	25.4	20.4	Maldives	0.4	7.0	Turkey	636.9	468.7
Cuba	552.9	447.3	Mali	0.2	7.0	Turkmenistan	3.9	33.3
Cyprus	17.0	10.5	Malta	27.5	9.4	Turks & Caicos Islands	7.5	8.7
Czech Republic	303.7	140.6	Martinique	0.0	0.0	U.S. Minor Outlying Islands	14.2	10.4
Denmark	1,564.9	289.9	Mauritania	0.6	3.5	Uganda	3.1	10.0
Djibouti	0.0	2.0	Mauritius	5.8	2.1	Ukraine	296.3	81.7
Dominica	0.8	5.1	Mexico	14,585.2	3,255.0	United Arab Emirates	66.3	586.9
Dominican Republic	120.0	145.3	Moldova	20.0	1.1	United Kingdom	10,397.0	8,249.9
East Timor	0.8	0.1	Mongolia	157.9	14.3	United States	215,109.1	365,740.5
Ecuador	114.6	159.6	Montserrat	0.1	0.5	Uruguay	130.8	23.9
Egypt	142.0	311.3	Morocco	151.2	211.4	Uzbekistan	56.8	8.6
El Salvador	59.4	55.6	Mozambique	0.8	23.5	Vanuatu	4.7	1.1
Equatorial Guinea	547.3	2.5	Myanmar	11.1	0.4	Venezuela	1,828.0	686.4
Eritrea	0.0	1.6	Namibia	56.3	1.4	Vietnam	558.5	202.8
Estonia	51.1	28.5	Nauru	1.1	0.0	Virgin Islands (British)	2.7	3.5
Ethiopia	8.6	27.0	Nepal	12.6	5.8	Wallis & Futuna Islands	0.0	0.0
Falkland Islands	0.1	0.1	Netherlands	1,529.3	2,190.7	Western Sahara	0.0	0.0
Faroe Islands	8.2	2.4	Netherlands Antilles	1.5	20.4	Yemen	0.2	46.7
Fiji	7.2	9.2	New Caledonia	0.8	12.4	Yugoslavia	13.3	10.5
Finland	1,217.5	433.2	New Zealand	561.2	357.0	Zambia	0.4	16.6
France	4,990.2	2,534.5	Nicaragua	57.3	19.6	Zimbabwe	2.0	6.4
French Guiana	0.0	0.0	Niger	3.1	5.5			
						TOTAL	**380,691.2**	**435,834.2**

Source: Statistics Canada, International Trade Division.

SECTION 1

Banks & Depository Institutions

Included in this section:

Chartered banks in Canada are incorporated by letters patent. They are governed by the *Bank Act,* which establishes the legislative framework for Canada's banking system. The *Bank Act* provides for the incorporation of banks. The Office of the Superintendent of Financial Insitutions Canada regulates and supervises the Canadian financial system.

Domestic Banks, are federally regulated Canadian banks. The subsidiaries of **Foreign Banks** are federally regulated foreign banks. Both domestic and foreign banks have the same powers, restrictions and obligations under the *Bank Act*.

Foreign Bank Branches are federally regulated foreign bank branches. They are permitted to establish specialized, commercially-focused branches in Canada, in accordance with the *Bank Act.* Full service branches generally are not permitted to accept deposits of less than $150,000.

Foreign Bank Representative Offices are established by foreign banks in Canada. They act as a liaison between the foreign bank and its clients in Canada. These offices generally promote the services of the foreign bank, and do not accept deposits in Canada.

ATB Financial exemplifies a **Savings Bank** in Canada. In Alberta, ATB Financial operates under the authority of the *Alberta Treasury Branches Act* Chapter A-37.9, 1997 and *Treasury Branches Regulation* 187/97.

Trust Companies are regulated under the federal *Trust and Loan Companies Act* and operate under either provincial or federal legislation. The business of trust companies includes activities like those of a bank, plus fiduciary functions.

Credit Unions/Caisses Populaires are owned and controlled by their members. These cooperative financial institutions are regulated at the provincial level. Credit unions, in most provinces, must engage external auditors to prepare financial statements. An annual inspection of credit unions is conducted by their provincial regulatory body.

The national trade association and central finance facility for Canadian credit unions is Credit Union Central of Canada. It is regulated under the *Cooperative Credit Associations Act.* In Québec, Mouvement des caisses Desjardins du Québec consists of a network of caisses. Fédération des caisses Desjardins du Québec is a cooperative which supports Mouvement des caisses Desjardins du Québec.

Banks & Depository Institutions

Domestic Banks: Schedule I

Alterna Bank
400 Albert St., 3rd Fl.
Ottawa, ON K1R 5B2
613-560-0120
Fax: 613-560-0187
866-560-0120
questions@alterna.ca
www.alterna.ca
Former Name: CS Alterna Bank
Ownership: Wholly-owned subsidiary of Alterna Savings & Credit Union Limited.
Year Founded: 2000
Profile: Operating with cooperative principles in mind, Alterna Bank is a federally licensed bank that can operate anywhere in Canada. The bank offers a range of services, including chequing & savings accounts, mortgages, investment options, personal loans, credit card services, financial planning, & insurance.
Executives:
Carl Ramkerrysingh, Interim President/CEO; ceo_president@alterna.ca
Robyn Hall, Manager, Communications; robyn.hall@alterna.ca.
Branches:
Gatineau - Hôpital
160, boul de l'Hôpital
Gatineau, QC J8T 8J1 Canada
819-595-6980
Fax: 819-243-6611
MICR: 00016
Gatineau - Portage
142, promenade du Portage
Gatineau, QC J8X 2K3 Canada
819-595-6980
Fax: 613-560-6685
MICR: 00016
Kingston
CANEX Mall
PO Box 17000
29 Niagara Park
Kingston, ON K7K 7B4
613-544-6051
Fax: 613-541-1891
MICR: 00646
Nepean - Merivale Rd.
First Pro Viewmount Centre
1715 Merivale Rd.
Nepean, ON K2G 3K2
613-560-0100
Fax: 613-560-6381
MICR: 00646
Nepean - Robertson Rd.
Moodie Square Centre
90K Robertson Rd.
Nepean, ON K2H 5Z1
613-560-0100
Fax: 613-560-6359
MICR: 00646
North Bay
107 Shirreff Ave.
North Bay, ON P1B 7K8
705-472-9700
Fax: 705-472-9986
800-538-9907
MICR: 00646
Orleans
Place Centrum
210 Centrum Blvd.
Orleans, ON K1E 3V7
613-560-0100
Fax: 613-560-6365
MICR: 00646
Ottawa - Albert St.
400 Albert St.
Ottawa, ON K1R 5B2
613-560-0100
Fax: 613-560-0187
MICR: 00646
Ottawa - Bank St.
2300 Bank St.
Ottawa, ON K1V 8S1
613-560-0100
Fax: 613-560-0181
MICR: 00646
Ottawa - Riverside Dr.
Billings Bridge Plaza
2269 Riverside Dr.
Ottawa, ON K1H 8K2
613-560-0100
Fax: 613-560-0180
MICR: 00646
Ottawa - Sparks St.
61 Sparks St.
Ottawa, ON K1P 5A5
613-560-0100
Fax: 613-560-6360
MICR: 00646
Ottawa - St-Laurent Blvd.
St-Laurent Centre
1200 St-Laurent Blvd.
Ottawa, ON K1K 3B9
613-560-0100
Fax: 613-560-0137
MICR: 00646
Ottawa - Tunneys Pasture Driveway
R.H. Coats Bldg.
PO Box 3676
#1, 100 Tunneys Pasture Driveway
Ottawa, ON K1Y 4J8
613-560-0100
Fax: 613-560-0127
MICR: 00646
Pembroke
Rosewood Plaza
680 Pembroke St. East
Pembroke, ON K8A 3M2
613-735-5039
Fax: 613-735-5526
MICR: 00646
Toronto - Town Centre Ct.
200 Town Centre Ct.
Toronto, ON M1P 4X8
416-296-0248
Fax: 416-296-1967
MICR: 00646
Toronto - Yonge St.
4900 Yonge St.
Toronto, ON M2N 6A4
416-224-2575
Fax: 416-224-2578
MICR: 00646

The Bank of Nova Scotia(BNS)/ La Banque de Nouvelle-Écosse
Scotia Plaza
44 King St. West
Toronto, ON M5H 1H1
416-866-6161
Fax: 416-866-3750
Other Information: Telex: WUI6719400
email@scotiabank.com
www.scotiabank.com
Also Known As: Scotiabank
Ownership: Public
Year Founded: 1832
Number of Employees: 42,046
Assets: $357,000,000,000 Year End: 20051031
Stock Symbol: BNS
Profile: Scotiabank is a full-service financial institution which serves clients in personal, commercial, corporate & investment banking. Scotiabank Group employs over 55,000 people and, with its affiliates, operates in some 50 countries. Products & services offered by the international bank include personal, commercial, corporate & investment banking. Scotiabank trades on both the Toronto & New York Stock Exchanges.
Executives:
Richard Waugh, President/CEO
Barry Luter, Chief Executive Officer, Scotiabank (Ireland) Ltd.
Robert W. Chisholm, Vice-Chair, President/CEO, Domestic Banking & Wealth Management
Sarabjit (Sabi) S. Marwah, Vice-Chair, Group Treasurer
James McPhedran, Managing Director & Head, Private Client Group
Robert L. Brooks, Sr. Exec. Vice-President, Group Treasury
Deborah M. Alexander, Exec. Vice-President, General Counsel & Secretary
Peter C. Cardinal, Exec. Vice-President, Latin America
Alberta G. Cefis, Exec. Vice-President & Group Head, Global Transaction Banking
Sylvia D. Chrominska, Exec. Vice-President, Human Resources, Public, Corporate & Government Affair
Wendy Hannam, Exec. Vice-President, Domestic Branch Banking
Tim P. Hayward, Exec. Vice-President, Chief Administrative Officer, International Banking
Dieter W. Jentsch, Exec. Vice-President, Commercial Banking
Barbara Mason, Exec. Vice-President, Wealth Management
Kim B. McKenzie, Exec. Vice-President, Scotia intek
Robert H. Pitfield, Exec. Vice-President, International Banking
Jane Rowe, Exec. Vice-President, Domestic Personal Lending & Insurance
Luc A. Vanneste, Exec. Vice-President/CFO
Diane Giard, Sr. Vice-President, Québec & Eastern Ontario Region
David M. Poole, Sr. Vice-President, BC & Yukon Region
Brian Toda, Sr. Vice-President, Total Compensation Group
Stephen D. McDonald, Co-Chair & Co-CEO, Scotia Capital, Head, Global Corporate & Investment Banking
C. John Schumacher, Co-Chair & Co-CEO, Scotia Capital Inc., Head, Global Capital Markets
Brian J Porter, Chief Risk Officer
Directors:
Arthur R.A. Scace, QC, Chair
Ronald A. Brenneman
CEO, Petro-Canada
C.J. Chen
Sr. Partner, Rajah & Tann
N. Ashleigh Everett
President, Royal Canadian Securities Limited
John C. Kerr, CM.O.B.C., LL.D.
Chair, Lignum Ltd.
Michael J.L. Kirby
Senator
Laurent Lemaire
Exec. Vice-Chair, Cascades Inc.
John T. Mayberry
CEO, Dofasco Inc.
Barbara J. McDougall
Elizabeth Parr-Johnston, Ph.D.
President, Parr Johnston Economic & Policy Consultants
Alexis E. Rovzar de la Torre
Gerald W. Schwartz
Chair/CEO, Onex Corporation
Allan C. Shaw, OC C.M.LL.D
Chair/CEO, The Shaw Group Limited
Paul D. Sobey
President/CEO, Empire Company Limited
Honourary Directors:
Lloyd I. Barber
Malcolm R. Baxter
Bruce R. Birmingham
E. Kendall Cork
Graham Day
Peter C. Godsoe, O.C.
M. Keith Goodrich
Henry N.R. Jackman
Pierre J. Jeanniot, O.C.
John J. Jodrey
Gordon F. MacFarlane
Donald Maclaren
Gerald J. Maier
Malcolm H.D. McAlpine
Ian McDougall

The Bank of Nova Scotia(BNS)/ La Banque de Nouvelle-Écosse (continued)

William S. McGregor
David E. Mitchell, O.C.
David Morton
Helen A. Parker
Paul J. Phoenix
Robert L. Pierce, O.C.
David H. Race
Cedric E. Ritchie, O.C.
Thomas G. Rust
Isadore Sharp, O.C.
Marie Wilson, O.C.

Affiliated Companies:
Maple Trust Company
RoyNat Capital Inc.
Scotia Capital Inc.
Scotia Cassels Investment Counsel Limited
Scotia Discount Brokerage Inc.
Scotia Merchant Capital Corporation
Scotia Mortgage Corporation/SMC
Scotia Securities Inc.
Scotiabank Private Equity Investments
The Bank of Nova Scotia Trust Company

Branches:

Abbotsford
Ellwood Centre
#1, 31205 Maclure Rd.
Abbotsford, BC V2T 5E5 Canada
604-504-4150
MICR: 80960-002

Acton
36 Mill St. East
Acton, ON L7J 1H2 Canada
519-853-2420
MICR: 70102-002

Airdrie
#102, 304 Main St.
Airdrie, AB T4B 3C3 Canada
403-948-5995
MICR: 00109-002

Ajax - Harwood
Hardwood Place Mall
340 Harwood Ave. South
Ajax, ON L1S 2J1 Canada
905-683-4070
MICR: 32102-002

Ajax - Kingston
60 Kingston Rd. East
Ajax, ON L1Z 1G1 Canada
905-427-3244
MICR: 93682-002

Ajax - Westney
Westney Heights Plaza
15 Westney Rd. North
Ajax, ON L1T 1P4 Canada
905-427-3255
MICR: 24182-002

Albany
PO Box 38
Albany, PE C0B 1A0 Canada
902-855-2233
MICR: 50773-002

Alexandria
38 Alexandria Main St. North
Alexandria, ON K0C 1A0 Canada
613-525-1073
MICR: 50112-002

Alliston
13 Victoria St. West
Alliston, ON L9R 1S9 Canada
705-435-4344
MICR: 04986-002

Amherst - Albion
Amherst Centre
135 Albion St. South
Amherst, NS B4H 4A1 Canada
902-667-7521
MICR: 91413-002

Amherst - Victoria
79 Victoria St.
Amherst, NS B4H 3Z4 Canada
902-667-3328
MICR: 20073-002

Amherstburg
99 Richmond St.
Amherstburg, ON N9V 1G3 Canada
519-736-5491
MICR: 18812-002

Ancaster
The Meadowlands
851 Golf Links Rd.
Ancaster, ON L9K 1L5 Canada
905-304-4100
MICR: 18762-002

Angus
5 - 17 King St.
Angus, ON L0M 1B0 Canada
705-424-5761
MICR: 82222-002

Annapolis Royal
219 St. George St.
Annapolis Royal, NS B0S 1A0 Canada
902-532-2393
MICR: 60103-002

Antigonish
255 Main St.
Antigonish, NS B2G 2L6 Canada
902-863-4800
MICR: 40113-002

Arnprior
169 John St.
Arnprior, ON K7S 3H2 Canada
613-623-7314
MICR: 30106-002

Arrowwood
PO Box 29
Arrowwood, AB T0L 0B0 Canada
403-534-3836
MICR: 80119-002

Athabasca
4902 - 50th St.
Athabasca, AB T9S 1E3 Canada
780-675-2206
MICR: 60129-002

Aurora - Bayview
15420 Bayview Ave.
Aurora, ON L4G 3G8 Canada
905-727-1025
MICR: 14092-002

Aurora - Yonge
14720 Yonge St.
Aurora, ON L4G 7H8 Canada
905-727-1307
MICR: 10132-002

Avonlea
111 Main St.
Avonlea, SK S0H 0C0 Canada
306-868-2045
MICR: 10108-002

Avonmore
PO Box 99
25 Main St.
Avonmore, ON K0C 1C0 Canada
613-346-2102
MICR: 10116-002

Aylmer
42 Talbot St. East
Aylmer, ON N5H 1H4 Canada
519-773-8496
MICR: 05066-002

Azilda
PO Box 520
Notre Dame St.
Azilda, ON P0M 1B0 Canada
705-983-4201
MICR: 42242-002

Baie Verte
Hwy. 410
Baie Verte, NL A0K 1B0 Canada
709-532-8022
MICR: 80523-002

Bancroft
50 Hasting St. North
Bancroft, ON K0L 1C0 Canada
613-332-2040
MICR: 90142-002

Barrhead
PO Box 4440
5104 - 50th St.
Barrhead, AB T7N 1A3 Canada
780-674-8400
MICR: 40139-002

Barrie - Bayfield
580 Bayfield St.
Barrie, ON L4M 4Y5 Canada
705-726-3690
MICR: 85092-002

Barrie - Bayfield
Bayfield Mall
320 Bayfield St.
Barrie, ON L4M 3C1 Canada
705-721-1010
MICR: 15016-002

Barrie - Dunlop
BBC
1 Dunlop St. West
Barrie, ON L4M 4T2 Canada
705-726-0217
MICR: 60152-002

Barrie - Essa
Allandale Centre
25 Essa Rd.
Barrie, ON L4N 3K4 Canada
705-725-7100
MICR: 56622-002

Barrie - Mapleview
Molson Park
19 Mapleview Dr. West
Barrie, ON L4N 9H5 Canada
705-725-2670
MICR: 58172-002

Barrie - Minets Point
190 Minets Point Rd.
Barrie, ON L4N 4C3 Canada
705-725-7320
MICR: 44222-002

Bath
326 Main St.
Bath, NB E7J 1A2 Canada
506-278-5281
MICR: 30114-002

Bathurst
1300 St. Peter Ave.
Bathurst, NB E2A 3A6 Canada
506-548-9921
MICR: 60384-002

Bay Roberts
#199, 203 Conception Bay Hwy.
Bay Roberts, NL A0A 1G0 Canada
709-786-5310
MICR: 60533-002

Beachburg
Main St.
Beachburg, ON K0J 1C0 Canada
613-582-3344
MICR: 90126-002

Beardmore
PO Box 150
Beardmore, ON P0T 1G0 Canada
807-875-2015
MICR: 50187-002

Beaumont
5018 - 50th St.
Beaumont, AB T4X 1E5 Canada
780-929-8822
MICR: 71639-002

Bedford - Bedford
Bedford Place
1658 Bedford Hwy.
Bedford, NS B4A 2X9 Canada
902-420-4935
MICR: 71803-002

Bedford - Bedford
936 Bedford Hwy.
Bedford, NS B4A 3P1 Canada
902-420-3797
MICR: 00133-002

Beechy
Main St.
Beechy, SK S0L 0C0 Canada
306-859-2112
MICR: 70128-002

Belledune
3982 Main St.
Belledune, NB E8G 2P1 Canada
506-237-3131

MICR: 00224-002
Belleville - Front
Commercial Banking Centre
175 Front St.
Belleville, ON K8N 2Y9 Canada
613-967-6700
MICR: 40162-002
Belleville - North Front
North Front Centre
305 North Front St.
Belleville, ON K8P 3C3 Canada
613-962-3408
MICR: 55046-002
Belleville - North Front
Quinte Mall
390 North Front St.
Belleville, ON K8P 3E1 Canada
613-967-6750
MICR: 74302-002
Belleville - North Front
North Front Centre
305 North Front St.
Belleville, ON K8P 3C3 Canada
613-962-3408
MICR: 55046-002
Belmont
14104 Belmont Rd.
Belmont, ON N0L 1B0 Canada
519-644-0420
MICR: 20172-002
Blairmore
PO Box 537
Blairmore, AB T0K 0E0 Canada
403-562-8801
MICR: 31369-002
Blind River
PO Box 730
Blind River, ON P0R 1B0 Canada
705-356-2283
MICR: 00182-002
Bonavista
Church St.
Bonavista, NL A0C 1B0 Canada
709-468-1070
MICR: 40543-002
Boucherville
1070, rue Lionel-Daunais
Boucherville, QC J4B 8R6 Canada
450-655-1006
MICR: 20461-002
Bowmanville
Clarington Place
100 Clarington Blvd.
Bowmanville, ON L1C 4Z3 Canada
905-623-2122
MICR: 13862-002
Bracebridge
248-5 Manitoba St.
Bracebridge, ON P1L 2E1 Canada
705-645-2289
MICR: 80192-002
Bradford
76 Holland St. West
Bradford, ON L3Z 2B6 Canada
905-775-5311
MICR: 86082-002
Brampton - Advance
199 Advance Rd.
Brampton, ON L6T 4N2 Canada
905-790-5642
MICR: 17012-002
Brampton - Avondale
Avondale Shopping Centre
36 Avondale Blvd.
Brampton, ON L6T 1H3 Canada
905-790-2024
MICR: 31922-002
Brampton - Balmoral
Southgate Shopping Centre
700 Balmoral Dr.
Brampton, ON L6T 1X2 Canada
905-790-5635
MICR: 42762-002
Brampton - Hurontario
#301, 7700 Hurontario St.
Brampton, ON L6Y 4M3 Canada
905-453-7020
MICR: 77982-002
Brampton - Main
1 Main St. South
Brampton, ON L6Y 1M8 Canada
905-451-7330
MICR: 60202-002
Brampton - Mountainash
47 Mountainash Rd.
Brampton, ON L6R 1W4 Canada
905-790-7171
MICR: 93922-002
Brampton - Peel Centre
Bramalea City Centre
#322A, 25 Peel Centre Dr.
Brampton, ON L6T 3R5 Canada
905-790-5600
MICR: 73502-002
Brampton - Quarry Edge
66 Quarry Edge Dr.
Brampton, ON L6V 4K2 Canada
905-451-8865
MICR: 63552-002
Brampton - Queen
Brampton Business Banking Centre
#101, 284 Queen St.
Brampton, ON L6V 1C2 Canada
905-453-7602
MICR: 66662-002
Brampton - Steeles
Orion Gate
543 Steeles Ave. East
Brampton, ON L6W 4S2 Canada
905-453-7079
MICR: 72272-002
Brandon - 18th
Brandon Shoppers Mall
1570 - 18th St.
Brandon, MB R7A 5C5 Canada
204-729-3870
MICR: 10397-002
Brandon - Rosser
1003 Rosser Ave.
Brandon, MB R7A 0L5 Canada
204-729-3360
MICR: 80077-002
Brantford - Colborne
Business Banking Centre
170 Colborne St.
Brantford, ON N3T 2G6 Canada
519-751-5000
MICR: 40212-002
Brantford - Lynden
61 Lynden Rd.
Brantford, ON N3R 7J9 Canada
519-751-5030
MICR: 52282-002
Bridgetown
274 Granville St.
Bridgetown, NS B0S 1C0 Canada
902-665-4422
MICR: 80143-002
Bridgewater - Lahavre
Bridgewater Mall
PO Box 400
421 Lahavre St.
Bridgewater, NS B4V 2X6 Canada
902-543-8155
MICR: 71613-002
Bridgewater - Main Branch
Bridgewater Shopping Plaza
Bridgewater, NS B4V 3W3 Canada
902-543-8176
MICR: 90993-002
Brights Grove
6531 Waterworks Rd.
Brights Grove, ON N0N 1C0 Canada
519-869-4290
MICR: 76372-002
Brockville - King
7 King St. West
Brockville, ON K6V 3P7 Canada
613-342-0140
MICR: 00232-002
Brockville - Stewart
PO Box 218
329 Stewart Blvd.
Brockville, ON K6V 4W8 Canada
613-498-3020
MICR: 46862-002
Brooks
235 - 2nd St. West
Brooks, AB T1R 1B2 Canada
403-362-3491
MICR: 20149-002
Brossard - Lapinière
Champlain Mall Shopping Centre
2151, boul Lapinière
Brossard, QC J4W 2T5 Canada
450-672-4570
MICR: 31211-002
Brossard - Lepage
#5, 7240, Lepage
Brossard, QC J4Y 0B5 Canada
450-923-3003
MICR: 21691-002
Burgeo
PO Box 249
Burgeo, NL A0N 2H0 Canada
709-886-1400
MICR: 50963-002
Burin Bay Arm
PO Box 279
Burin Bay Arm, NL A0E 1G0 Canada
709-891-5200
MICR: 10553-002
Burlington - Brant
547 Brant St.
Burlington, ON L7R 4K5 Canada
905-637-5509
MICR: 80242-002
Burlington - Dundas
4519 Dundas St.
Burlington, ON L7M 5B4 Canada
905-332-4350
MICR: 87296-002
Nancy McMillan, Manager
Burlington - Lakeshore
Lakeside Shopping Plaza
5385 Lakeshore Rd. East
Burlington, ON L7L 1C8 Canada
905-637-5231
MICR: 82032-002
Burlington - New
4011 New St.
Burlington, ON L7L 1S8 Canada
905-637-5267
MICR: 03392-002
Burlington - Upper Middle
3505 Upper Middle Rd.
Burlington, ON L7M 4C6 Canada
905-332-2282
MICR: 95802-002
Burnaby - 10th
8691 - 10th Ave.
Burnaby, BC V3N 2S9 Canada
604-668-3765
MICR: 30460-002
Burnaby - East Broadway
Parkcrest Plaza
5901 East Broadway
Burnaby, BC V5B 2Y1 Canada
604-668-3729
MICR: 80630-002
Burnaby - East Hastings
6715 East Hastings St.
Burnaby, BC V5B 1S6 Canada
604-668-3717
MICR: 50450-002
Burnaby - East Hastings
4001 East Hastings St.
Burnaby, BC V5C 2J1 Canada
604-668-3725
MICR: 80580-002
Burnaby - Kingsway
4299 Kingsway St.
Burnaby, BC V5H 1Z5 Canada
604-668-3741

The Bank of Nova Scotia(BNS)/ La Banque de Nouvelle-Écosse (continued)

MICR: 40410-002
Burnaby - Kingsway
Mulberry Centre
7188 Kingsway
Burnaby, BC V5E 1G3 Canada
604-395-8023
MICR: 60400-002
Burnaby - Lougheed
Brentwood Shopping Centre
#26, 4567 Lougheed Hwy.
Burnaby, BC V5C 3Z6 Canada
604-656-1200
MICR: 62570-002
Burnaby - University
Cornerstone Bldg.
8972 University High St.
Burnaby, BC V5A 4Y6 Canada
604-294-6890
MICR: 72710-002
Caledonia
11 Argyle St. North
Caledonia, ON N3W 1B6 Canada
905-765-4427
MICR: 52662-002
Calgary - 162nd
#600, 2335 - 162nd Ave. SW
Calgary, AB T2Y 4S6 Canada
403-221-6968
MICR: 12559-002
Calgary - 17th
3820 - 17th Ave. SW
Calgary, AB T3E 0C2 Canada
403-221-6842
MICR: 10199-002
Calgary - 17th
Mount Royal
1401 - 17th Ave. SW
Calgary, AB T2T 0C6 Canada
403-221-6821
MICR: 70029-002
Barbara Van Weenan, Manager
Calgary - 17th
3320 - 17th Ave. SE
Calgary, AB T2A 0P9 Canada
403-221-6886
MICR: 20669-002
Calgary - 17th
1401 - 17th Ave. SW
Calgary, AB T2T 0C6 Canada
403-221-6821
MICR: 70029-002
Calgary - 18th
Glenmore Sq.
7740 - 18th St. SE
Calgary, AB T2C 2N5 Canada
403-221-6777
MICR: 21089-002
Calgary - 19th
Mayland Heights Shopping Plaza
#117, 817 - 19th St. NE
Calgary, AB T2E 4X5 Canada
403-221-6768
MICR: 20529-002
Calgary - 30th
Foothills Industrial Park
6303 - 30th St. SE
Calgary, AB T2C 1R4 Canada
403-221-6774
MICR: 11239-002
Calgary - 32nd
Horizon Sq.
#100, 3508 - 32 Ave. NE
Calgary, AB T1Y 6J2 Canada
403-221-6860
MICR: 91579-002
Calgary - 33rd
Marda Loop
2001 - 33rd Ave. SW
Calgary, AB T2T 1Z5 Canada
403-221-6838
MICR: 60079-002
Calgary - 5th
605 - 5th Ave. SW
Calgary, AB T2P 3H5 Canada
403-221-6629
MICR: 81299-002
Calgary - 61
MacLeod Centre
260 - 61 Ave. SW
Calgary, AB T2H 3A2 Canada
403-221-6814
MICR: 52639-002
Calgary - 68th
Monterey Sq.
#600, 2220 - 68th St. NE
Calgary, AB T1Y 6Y7 Canada
403-299-3090
MICR: 50609-002
Calgary - 7th
734 - 7th Ave. SW
Calgary, AB T2P 3P8 Canada
403-221-6530
MICR: 30189-002
Calgary - 8th
240 - 8th Ave. SW
Calgary, AB T2P 2N7 Canada
403-221-6401
MICR: 10009-002
Calgary - Anderson
Southcentre Mall
#24, 100 Anderson Rd. SE
Calgary, AB T2J 3V1 Canada
403-299-6030
MICR: 12419-002
Calgary - Beddington
Beddington Towne Centre
8120 Beddington Blvd. NW
Calgary, AB T3K 2A8 Canada
403-221-6896
MICR: 21329-002
Calgary - Brentwood NW
4110 Brentwood Rd. NW
Calgary, AB T2L 1K8 Canada
403-221-6804
MICR: 70599-002
Calgary - Centre
4805 Centre St. North
Calgary, AB T2E 2Z6 Canada
403-221-6850
MICR: 00729-002
Calgary - Centre
1303 Centre St. North
Calgary, AB T2E 2R6 Canada
403-221-6788
MICR: 30049-002
Calgary - Country Hills
Edgemont
#700, 5149 Country Hills Blvd. NW
Calgary, AB T3A 5K8 Canada
403-299-6221
MICR: 10819-002
Calgary - Country Hills
Country Hills Town Centre
#1000, 500 Country Hills Blvd. NE
Calgary, AB T3K 4Y7 Canada
403-226-7700
MICR: 02279-002
Calgary - Crowchild
Lakeview Plaza
6449 Crowchild Trail SW
Calgary, AB T3E 5R7 Canada
403-221-6846
MICR: 60459-002
Calgary - Falconridge
Castleridge Plaza
5075 Falconridge Blvd. NE
Calgary, AB T3J 3K9 Canada
403-299-6270
MICR: 82289-002
Calgary - Kensington
1204 Kensington Rd. NW
Calgary, AB T2N 3P5 Canada
403-974-7070
MICR: 92619-002
Calgary - MacLeod Trail
8706 MacLeod Trail South
Calgary, AB T2H 0M4 Canada
403-221-6874
MICR: 00539-002
Calgary - McKenzie Towne
McKenzie Towne Centre
55 McKenzie Towne Blvd. SE
Calgary, AB T2Z 3X8 Canada
403-221-6460
MICR: 52209-002
Calgary - Midlake
34 Midlake Blvd. SE
Calgary, AB T2X 2X7 Canada
403-221-6595
MICR: 01669-002
Calgary - Ranchlands
Ranchlands Shopping Centre
#171, 1829 Ranchlands Blvd. NW
Calgary, AB T3G 2A7 Canada
403-221-6810
MICR: 71829-002
Calgary - Richmond
4936 Richmond Rd. SW
Calgary, AB T3E 6K4 Canada
403-221-6834
MICR: 70979-002
Calgary - Southland
Braeside Shopping Plaza
1919 Southland Dr. SW
Calgary, AB T2W 0K1 Canada
403-221-6854
MICR: 30809-002
Calgary - Tuscany
#3015, 11300 Tuscany Blvd. NW
Calgary, AB T3L 2V7 Canada
403-221-6410
MICR: 92569-002
Calgary - Uxbridge
Bay 12, Stadium Shopping Centre
1941 Uxbridge Dr. NW
Calgary, AB T2N 2V2 Canada
403-221-6800
MICR: 20479-002
Calgary - Woodview
Woodbine Sq.
#205, 2525 Woodview Dr. SW
Calgary, AB T2W 4N4 Canada
403-221-6760
MICR: 01859-002
Cambridge - Christopher
115 Christopher Dr.
Cambridge, ON N1R 4S1 Canada
519-623-3210
MICR: 84822-002
Cambridge - Hespeler
BBC
544 Hespeler Rd.
Cambridge, ON N1R 6J8 Canada
519-740-4004
MICR: 33472-002
Cambridge - King
753 King St. East
Cambridge, ON N3H 3N8 Canada
519-653-7107
MICR: 94292-002
Cambridge - Main
72 Main St.
Cambridge, ON N1R 1V7 Canada
519-740-4050
MICR: 40352-002
Cambridge - Saginaw
Saginaw Sq.
95 Saginaw Pkwy.
Cambridge, ON N1T 1W2 Canada
519-740-2500
MICR: 08862-002
Campbell River
961 Alder St.
Campbell River, BC V9W 5C3 Canada
250-286-4350
MICR: 70730-002
Campbellton
157 Water St.
Campbellton, NB E3N 3L4 Canada
506-789-0120
MICR: 70094-002
Campbellville
36 Main St.
Campbellville, ON L0P 1B0 Canada
905-854-2261

MICR: 23432-002
Camrose
4801 - 50th St.
Camrose, AB T4V 1P4 Canada
780-672-9261
MICR: 60699-002
Cannington
10 Cameron St. West
Cannington, ON L0E 1E0 Canada
705-432-2341
MICR: 85126-002
Carbonear
92 Powell Dr.
Carbonear, NL A1Y 1B5 Canada
709-596-4680
MICR: 90563-002
Carleton Place
85 Bridge St.
Carleton Place, ON K7C 2V4 Canada
613-253-5400
MICR: 50146-002
Carp
438 Donald B. Munro Dr.
Carp, ON K0A 1L0 Canada
613-839-2800
MICR: 20156-002
Carrot River
2 Main St.
Carrot River, SK S0E 0L0 Canada
306-768-2763
MICR: 50138-002
Channel-Port-aux-Basques
Main St.
Channel-Port-aux-Basques, NL A0M 1C0 Canada
709-695-5630
MICR: 50583-002
Charlottetown - Grafton
143 Grafton St.
Charlottetown, PE C1A 1K9 Canada
902-566-5004
MICR: 30023-002
Charlottetown - St. Peter's
161 St. Peter's Rd.
Charlottetown, PE C1A 5P3 Canada
902-894-5013
MICR: 51003-002
Chatham - Grand
Thameslea Shopping Centre
635 Grand Ave. West
Chatham, ON N7L 1C5 Canada
519-354-5110
MICR: 45146-002
Chatham - King
213 King St. West
Chatham, ON N7M 1E6 Canada
519-354-5560
MICR: 50252-002
Chatham - Queen
420 Queen St.
Chatham, ON N7M 2J2 Canada
519-354-1940
MICR: 52332-002
Chelmsford
#1, 3454 Errington St.
Chelmsford, ON P0M 1L0 Canada
705-855-4552
MICR: 30262-002
Chester
2 Pleasant St.
Chester, NS B0J 1J0 Canada
902-275-3540
MICR: 10173-002
Chesterville
5 Main St.
Chesterville, ON K0C 1H0 Canada
613-448-2364
MICR: 10272-002
Chetwynd
5016 - 50th Ave.
Chetwynd, BC V0C 1J0 Canada
250-788-4900
MICR: 61770-002
Chilliwack
46059 Yale Rd.
Chilliwack, BC V2P 2M1 Canada
604-702-3250
MICR: 90100-002
Chipman
237 Main St.
Chipman, NB E4A 2H2 Canada
506-339-1820
MICR: 70144-002
Clarenville
Clarenville Shopping Centre
PO Box 9
Memorial Dr.
Clarenville, NL A5A 1N9 Canada
709-466-4601
MICR: 30593-002
Coaldale
1921 - 20th Ave.
Coaldale, AB T1M 1N2 Canada
403-345-4412
MICR: 51359-002
Cobden
Main St.
Cobden, ON K0J 1K0 Canada
613-646-2206
MICR: 80176-002
Cobourg - Elgin
Northumberland Mall
1111 Elgin St. West
Cobourg, ON K9A 5H7 Canada
905-373-7800
MICR: 95562-002
Cobourg - King
King George Ct.
68 King St. West
Cobourg, ON K9A 2M3 Canada
905-372-3361
MICR: 15156-002
Cochrane - 5th
200 - 5th Ave. West
Cochrane, AB T4C 1X3 Canada
403-932-8060
MICR: 51169-002
Cochrane - 6th
127 - 6th Ave.
Cochrane, ON P0L 1C0 Canada
705-272-4327
MICR: 70292-002
Cold Lake
5001 - 50th Ave.
Cold Lake, AB T9M 1P3 Canada
780-594-7121
MICR: 61549-002
Cole Harbour
Colby Village Shopping Centre
912 Cole Harbour Rd.
Cole Harbour, NS B2V 2J5 Canada
902-420-4958
MICR: 21873-002
Collingwood
247 Hurontario St.
Collingwood, ON L9Y 2M4 Canada
705-445-0580
MICR: 32342-002
Comox
Comox Plaza
#102, 1811 Comox Ave.
Comox, BC V9M 3L9 Canada
250-890-1100
MICR: 10850-002
Conception Bay South
PO Box 14093, Manuels Sta. Manuels
Conception Bay South, NL A1W 3J1 Canada
709-834-6280
MICR: 81463-002
Concord
Hwy. 7 & Keele St.
Concord, ON L4K 1B1 Canada
905-669-4610
MICR: 83022-002
Coquitlam - Barnet
Coquitlam Centre
2929 Barnet Hwy.
Coquitlam, BC V3B 5R5 Canada
604-927-7075
MICR: 51490-002
Coquitlam - Brunette
Maillardville
953 Brunette Ave.
Coquitlam, BC V3K 6S8 Canada
604-517-4380
MICR: 80200-002
Coquitlam - North
465 North Rd.
Coquitlam, BC V3K 3V9 Canada
604-933-3300
MICR: 41160-002
Corner Brook
Corner Brook Plaza
PO Box 1138
Corner Brook, NL A2H 6T2 Canada
709-637-4700
MICR: 61473-002
Corner Brook - Broadway
62 Broadway
Corner Brook, NL A2H 6H4 Canada
709-637-4720
MICR: 10603-002
Cornwall
#960, 17 Brookdale Ave. North
Cornwall, ON K6J 4P5 Canada
613-930-2565
MICR: 82982-002
Courtenay
392 - 5th St.
Courtenay, BC V9N 1K1 Canada
250-703-4800
MICR: 50120-002
Courtice
1500 King St. East
Courtice, ON L1E 2T5 Canada
905-404-4490
MICR: 95422-002
Cranbrook
524 Cranbrook St. North
Cranbrook, BC V1C 3R6 Canada
250-417-3075
MICR: 41640-002
Crapaud
PO Box 9
Crapaud, PE C0A 1J0 Canada
902-658-2778
MICR: 30783-002
Côte-St-Luc - Cavendish
Centre d'Achats Cavendish
5800, boul Cavendish
Côte Saint-Luc, QC H4W 2T5 Canada
514-482-3430
MICR: 42861-002
Dartmouth - Ilsley
Burnside Industrial Park
109 Ilsley Ave.
Dartmouth, NS B3B 1S8 Canada
902-420-3750
MICR: 32193-002
Dartmouth - Main
PO Box 2218
102 Main St.
Dartmouth, NS B2W 3Y4 Canada
902-420-3761
MICR: 70193-002
Dartmouth - Mic Mac
Mic Mac Mall
21 Mic Mac Blvd.
Dartmouth, NS B3A 4T4 Canada
902-420-4921
MICR: 91363-002
Dartmouth - Portland
91 - 93 Portland St.
Dartmouth, NS B2Y 3Y2 Canada
902-420-4940
MICR: 60053-002
Dartmouth - Wyse
112 Wyse Rd.
Dartmouth, NS B2Y 3Y8 Canada
902-420-3764
MICR: 90183-002
Dauphin
Dauphin Market Place Mall
1450 Main St. South
Dauphin, MB R7N 2H4 Canada
204-622-6260

The Bank of Nova Scotia(BNS)/ La Banque de Nouvelle-Écosse (continued)

MICR: 50047-002

Dawson Creek
10204 - 10th St.
Dawson Creek, BC V1G 3T4 Canada
250-784-1100
MICR: 30130-002

Deep River
Glendale Plaza
Deep River, ON K0J 1P0 Canada
613-584-3395
MICR: 10322-002

Deer Lake
12 Wights Rd.
Deer Lake, NL A8A 2H5 Canada
709-635-1133
MICR: 32243-002

Delta
1139 - 56th St.
Delta, BC V4L 2A2 Canada
604-948-4200
MICR: 82990-002

Dieppe
Champlain Place
477 Paul St.
Dieppe, NB E1A 4X5 Canada
506-862-0388
MICR: 10454-002

Digby
61 Water St.
Digby, NS B0V 1A0 Canada
902-245-2564
MICR: 50203-002

Doaktown
298 Main St.
Doaktown, NB E9C 1E2 Canada
506-365-7316
MICR: 40154-002

Dorchester
2095 Dorchester Rd.
Dorchester, ON N0L 1G2 Canada
519-268-7502
MICR: 46672-002

Dowling
Dowling Plaza
Hwy. 144
Dowling, ON P0M 1R0 Canada
705-855-9039
MICR: 33662-002

Drayton Valley
4603 - 50th St.
Drayton Valley, AB T7A 1J6 Canada
780-542-4454
MICR: 21279-002

Drumheller
Valley Plaza Shopping Centre
PO Box 2140
Drumheller, AB T0J 0Y0 Canada
403-823-5181
MICR: 10769-002

Duncan
435 Trunk Rd.
Duncan, BC V9L 2P5 Canada
250-715-3850
MICR: 71100-002

Dundas
University Plaza
24 Plaza Dr.
Dundas, ON L9H 4H4 Canada
905-627-9273
MICR: 90332-002

Earlton
16A - 10th St.
Earlton, ON P0J 1E0 Canada
705-563-2662
MICR: 02352-002

Edmonton - 118th
#166, 3210 - 118th Ave. NW
Edmonton, AB T5W 4W1 Canada
780-448-7788
MICR: 41319-002

Edmonton - 118th
8108 - 118th Ave. NW
Edmonton, AB T5B 0S1 Canada
780-448-7735
MICR: 10249-002

Edmonton - 137th
North City Centre
13232 - 137th Ave.
Edmonton, AB T5L 4Z6 Canada
780-448-7555
MICR: 42259-002

Edmonton - 160th
8140 - 160th Ave. NW
Edmonton, AB T5Z 3J8 Canada
780-448-7785
MICR: 90779-002

Edmonton - 170th
Terra Losa Centre
9740 - 170th St.
Edmonton, AB T5T 5L5 Canada
780-448-7500
MICR: 80689-002

Edmonton - 23rd
Heritage Village
11021 - 23rd Ave.
Edmonton, AB T6J 4V9 Canada
780-448-7820
MICR: 32219-002

Edmonton - 51st
Southgate
10835 - 51st Ave. NW
Edmonton, AB T6H 5T1 Canada
780-448-7776
MICR: 72439-002

Edmonton - 66th
Millwoods Town Centre
#119, 2331 - 66th St.
Edmonton, AB T6K 4B4 Canada
780-448-7960
MICR: 01289-002

Edmonton - 82nd
10537 - 82nd Ave.
Edmonton, AB T6E 4T5 Canada
780-448-7800
MICR: 40089-002

Edmonton - 90th
Ottewell Shopping Centre
6304 - 90th Ave.
Edmonton, AB T6B 0P2 Canada
780-448-7860
MICR: 80549-002

Edmonton - 97th
13150 - 97th St.
Edmonton, AB T5E 4C6 Canada
780-448-7756
MICR: 50229-002

Edmonton - Jasper
10050 Jasper Ave.
Edmonton, AB T5J 1V7 Canada
780-448-7600
MICR: 90019-002

Edmonton - Jasper
10709 Jasper Ave.
Edmonton, AB T5J 3N3 Canada
780-448-7890
MICR: 00489-002

Edmonton - Jasper
11508 Jasper Ave.
Edmonton, AB T5K 0M8 Canada
780-448-7928
MICR: 50039-002

Edmonton - Riverbend
540 Riverbend Sq. NW
Edmonton, AB T6R 2E3 Canada
780-448-7988
MICR: 72249-002

Edmonton - Wagner
8509 Wagner Rd.
Edmonton, AB T6E 5A7 Canada
780-448-7880
MICR: 81109-002

Edmonton - Westmount
232 Westmount Centre NW
Edmonton, AB T5M 3L7 Canada
780-413-4333
MICR: 02659-002

Edmundston
75 Canada Rd.
Edmundston, NB E3V 3K7 Canada
506-739-7358

MICR: 70524-002

Edson
402 - 50th St.
Edson, AB T7E 1T6 Canada
780-723-6001
MICR: 40279-002

Elliot Lake
151 Ontario Ave.
Elliot Lake, ON P5A 2T2 Canada
705-848-3667
MICR: 57422-002

Elmsdale
Elmsdale Shopping Centre
#3, 269 Hwy. 214
Elmsdale, NS B2S 1K1 Canada
902-883-7000
MICR: 62323-002

Emerson
30 Main St.
Emerson, MB R0A 0L0 Canada
204-373-2536
MICR: 20107-002

Estevan
1133 - 4th St.
Estevan, SK S4A 0W6 Canada
306-634-7272
MICR: 30668-002

Exeter
280 Main St.
Exeter, ON N0M 1S6 Canada
519-235-1142
MICR: 70342-002

Fergus
201 St. Andrews St. West
Fergus, ON N1M 2W8 Canada
519-787-2020
MICR: 51912-002

Fernie
502 - 3rd Ave.
Fernie, BC V0B 1M0 Canada
250-423-8440
MICR: 30890-002

Flin Flon
75 Main St.
Flin Flon, MB R8A 1J9 Canada
204-687-7140
MICR: 30767-002

Florenceville
325 Main St.
Florenceville, NB E7L 3G7 Canada
506-392-8020
MICR: 20164-002

Flowers Cove
44 Grenfell Ave.
Flowers Cove, NL A0K 2N0 Canada
709-456-2900
MICR: 40923-002

Fogo
PO Box 220
Fogo, NL A0G 2B0 Canada
709-266-2241
MICR: 90613-002

Fort Erie
200 Garrison Rd.
Fort Erie, ON L2A 5S6 Canada
905-871-5824
MICR: 14902-002

Fort McMurray - Franklin
9541 Franklin Ave.
Fort McMurray, AB T9H 3Z7 Canada
780-743-3386
MICR: 30569-002

Fort McMurray - Thickwood
331 Thickwood Blvd.
Fort McMurray, AB T9H 4V2 Canada
780-743-5838
MICR: 31419-002

Fort Nelson
PO Box 777
Fort Nelson, BC V0C 1R0 Canada
250-774-6151
MICR: 80770-002

Fort Saskatchewan

Market Sq.
10404 - 99th Ave.
Fort Saskatchewan, AB T8L 3W2 Canada
780-998-3711
MICR: 30759-002

Fort St. John
9915 - 100th St.
Fort St John, BC V1J 3Y3 Canada
250-262-5150
MICR: 10660-002

Fredericton - King
490 King St.
Fredericton, NB E3B 5A1 Canada
506-452-9800
MICR: 20024-002

Fredericton - Nashwaaksis
PO Box 3012, B Sta. B
Fredericton, NB E3A 5G8 Canada
506-458-9310
MICR: 80374-002

Fredericton - Regent
1111 Regent St.
Fredericton, NB E3B 3Z2 Canada
506-450-6477
MICR: 40964-002

Fredericton - Smythe
524 Smythe St.
Fredericton, NB E3B 5B4 Canada
506-458-8966
MICR: 20404-002

Gander
Elizabeth Drive Shopping Centre
PO Box 382
68 Elizabeth Dr.
Gander, NL A1V 1W8 Canada
709-256-1500
MICR: 70623-002

Gatineau - Buckingham
526, rue de Buckingham
Gatineau, QC J8L 2H1 Canada
819-986-3386
MICR: 00356-002

Gatineau - du Plateau
139, boul du Plateau
Gatineau, QC J9A 3G1 Canada
819-771-7071
MICR: 67686-002

Gatineau - l'Hôpital
Centre Ville
144, boul de l'Hôpital
Gatineau, QC J8T 7S7 Canada
819-243-6826
MICR: 71191-002

Gatineau - Maloney
381, boul Maloney est
Gatineau, QC J8P 1E3 Canada
819-663-7726
MICR: 90456-002

Gatineau - St-Joseph
Les Galeries de Hull
320, boul St-Joseph
Gatineau, QC J8Y 3Y8 Canada
819-770-5990
MICR: 40931-002

Georgetown
304 Guelph St.
Georgetown, ON L7G 4B1 Canada
905-877-6995
MICR: 14142-002

Glace Bay
125 Commercial St.
Glace Bay, NS B1A 5V1 Canada
902-849-3508
MICR: 10223-002

Glaslyn
202 Main St.
Glaslyn, SK S0M 0Y0 Canada
306-342-2042
MICR: 80168-002

Gloucester - City Park
Gloucester Centre
2400 City Park Dr.
Gloucester, ON K1J 1H6 Canada
613-748-6001
MICR: 50476-002

Gloucester - Ogilvie
Beacon Hill Shopping Centre
2339 Ogilvie Rd.
Gloucester, ON K1J 8M6 Canada
613-741-6265
MICR: 50526-002

Glovertown
Main St.
Glovertown, NL A0G 2L0 Canada
709-533-6100
MICR: 40873-002

Goderich
44 The Square
Goderich, ON N7A 3Z2 Canada
519-524-4010
MICR: 93062-002

Goulds
PO Box 820
Goulds, NL A1S 1G8 Canada
709-576-8008
MICR: 71373-002

Grand Bank
Water St.
Grand Bank, NL A0E 1W0 Canada
709-832-2400
MICR: 50633-002

Grand Bay-Westfield
110 River Valley Dr.
Grand Bay-Westfield, NB E5K 4V3 Canada
506-738-8491
MICR: 60764-002

Grand Falls
Grand Falls Shopping Mall
#270, 180 Madawaska Rd.
Grand Falls, NB E3Y 1A7 Canada
506-473-1220
MICR: 30544-002

Grand Falls-Windsor
26 Cromer Ave.
Grand Falls-Windsor, NL A2A 1X2 Canada
709-489-1700
MICR: 00893-002

Grand Manan
PO Box 908
Grand Manan, NB E5G 4M1 Canada
506-662-1860
MICR: 80184-002

Grande Prairie
9834 - 100th Ave.
Grande Prairie, AB T8V 0T8 Canada
780-532-9250
MICR: 20289-002

Gravenhurst
198 Muskoka Rd. North
Gravenhurst, ON P1P 1X2 Canada
705-687-2248
MICR: 43042-002

Greenwood
Greenwood Mall, K-Mart Plaza
Greenwood, NS B0P 1N0 Canada
902-765-6383
MICR: 02303-002

Guelph - Clair
15 Clair Rd. West
Guelph, ON N1L 0A6 Canada
519-837-3443
MICR: 26526-002

Guelph - Kortright
170 Kortright Rd. West
Guelph, ON N1G 4V7 Canada
519-821-2030
MICR: 12872-002

Guelph - Speedvale
338 Speedvale Ave. East
Guelph, ON N1E 1N5 Canada
519-766-8640
MICR: 00372-002

Guelph - Wyndham
St. George's Sq.
83 Wyndham St. North
Guelph, ON N1H 4E9 Canada
519-766-8600
MICR: 20362-002

Haileybury
478 Main St.
Haileybury, ON P0J 1K0 Canada
705-672-3357
MICR: 80382-002

Halifax - Chebucto
7171 Chebucto Rd.
Halifax, NS B3L 1N5 Canada
902-420-4962
MICR: 00273-002

Halifax - Coburg
6005 Coburg Rd.
Halifax, NS B3H 1Y8 Canada
902-420-4929
MICR: 70243-002

Halifax - Duke
Lower Mall, Scotia Sq.
5201 Duke St.
Halifax, NS B3J 2Y7 Canada
902-420-4971
MICR: 21063-002

Halifax - Dutch Village
3480 Dutch Village Rd.
Halifax, NS B3N 2R9 Canada
902-420-4967
MICR: 91603-002

Halifax - Hollis
CBC
1709 Hollis St.
Halifax, NS B3J 2M1 Canada
902-420-3567
MICR: 70003-002

Halifax - Lacewood
Clayton Park
255 Lacewood Dr.
Halifax, NS B3M 4G2 Canada
902-420-3590
MICR: 92213-002

Halifax - Quinpool
6169 Quinpool Rd.
Halifax, NS B3L 4T6 Canada
902-420-3757
MICR: 60293-002

Halifax - Spring Garden
5656 Spring Garden Rd.
Halifax, NS B3J 1H4 Canada
902-420-3787
MICR: 40303-002

Hamilton - Barton
Centre Mall
1227 Barton St. East
Hamilton, ON L8H 2V8 Canada
905-549-3521
MICR: 00422-002

Hamilton - Fennell
997A Fennell Ave. East
Hamilton, ON L8T 1R1 Canada
905-574-9010
MICR: 05256-002

Hamilton - James
600 James St. North
Hamilton, ON L8L 7Z2 Canada
905-523-2960
MICR: 60392-002

Hamilton - King St. East
924 King St. East
Hamilton, ON L8M 1B8 Canada
905-547-2311
MICR: 40402-002

Hamilton - King St. East
12 King St. East
Hamilton, ON L8N 4G9 Canada
905-528-7501
MICR: 60012-002

Hamilton - King St. West
999 King St. West
Hamilton, ON L8S 1K9 Canada
905-525-2640
MICR: 95216-002

Hamilton - Main
1396 Main St. East
Hamilton, ON L8K 1C1 Canada
905-548-5060
MICR: 20412-002

Hamilton - Queenston

The Bank of Nova Scotia(BNS)/ La Banque de Nouvelle-Écosse (continued)

686 Queenston Rd.
Hamilton, ON L8G 1A3 Canada
905-560-2200
MICR: 52092-002

Hamilton - Stone Church
1070 Stone Church Rd. East
Hamilton, ON L8W 3K8 Canada
905-575-6500
MICR: 74112-002

Hamilton - Upper James
630 Upper James St.
Hamilton, ON L9C 2Z1 Canada
905-575-6520
MICR: 60442-002

Hamilton - Upper James
1550 Upper James St.
Hamilton, ON L9B 1K3 Canada
905-575-3565
MICR: 25932-002

Hamilton - Upper Wentworth
859 Upper Wentworth St.
Hamilton, ON L9A 4W5 Canada
905-575-3333
MICR: 55236-002

Hamilton - Upper Wentworth
880 Upper Wentworth St.
Hamilton, ON L9A 5H2 Canada
905-318-0031
MICR: 27896-002

Hampton
#14, 454 Main St.
Hampton, NB E5N 6C1 Canada
506-832-1020
MICR: 60194-002

Hanover
County Fair Plaza
860 - 10th St.
Hanover, ON N4N 1S3 Canada
519-364-4410
MICR: 16022-002

Hantsport
49 Main St.
Hantsport, NS B0P 1P0 Canada
902-684-3241
MICR: 20313-002

Happy Valley-Goose Bay
45 Grenfell St.
Happy Valley-Goose Bay, NL A0P 1E0 Canada
709-897-3000
MICR: 11353-002

Hartland
390 Main St.
Hartland, NB E7P 2N2 Canada
506-375-4513
MICR: 70854-002

Hawkesbury
100 Main St. East
Hawkesbury, ON K6A 1A3 Canada
613-632-7052
MICR: 40196-002

Hearst
818 George St.
Hearst, ON P0L 1N0 Canada
705-362-4363
MICR: 33332-002

High River
#40, 30 - 3rd Ave. SE
High River, AB T1V 1N5 Canada
403-652-5808
MICR: 11429-002
Elaine P. Murley, Manager

Hillsborough
2839 Main St.
Hillsborough, NB E4H 2X6 Canada
506-734-2820
MICR: 20214-002

Hinton
432 Carmichael Lane
Hinton, AB T7V 1T4 Canada
780-865-3377
MICR: 80309-002

Hubbards
Main Rd.
Hubbards, NS B0J 1T0 Canada
902-857-3333
MICR: 00943-002

Hudson Bay
PO Box 70
119 Churchill St.
Hudson Bay, SK S0E 0Y0 Canada
306-865-2255
MICR: 60178-002

Humboldt
PO Box 700
542 Main St.
Humboldt, SK S0K 2A0 Canada
306-682-2678
MICR: 40188-002

Huntsville
70 King William St.
Huntsville, ON P1H 2A5 Canada
705-789-9631
MICR: 65276-002

Ingonish Beach
PO Box 10
Ingonish Beach, NS B0C 1L0 Canada
902-285-2555
MICR: 00323-002

Innisfail
4949 - 50th St.
Innisfail, AB T4G 1S7 Canada
403-227-3321
MICR: 60319-002

Kamloops - Summit
Sahali Shopping Centre
1201 Summit Dr.
Kamloops, BC V2C 6B8 Canada
250-314-5475
MICR: 81620-002

Kamloops - Tranquille
781 Tranquille Rd.
Kamloops, BC V2B 3J3 Canada
250-554-5625
MICR: 91330-002

Kamloops - Victoria
276 Victoria St.
Kamloops, BC V2C 2A2 Canada
250-314-3950
MICR: 10140-002

Kanata - Beaverbrook
2 Beaverbrook Rd.
Kanata, ON K2K 1L1 Canada
613-591-6644
MICR: 60426-002

Kanata - Campeau
8111 Campeau Dr.
Kanata, ON K2T 1B7 Canada
613-591-2020
MICR: 40576-002

Kanata - Eagleson
Bridlewood
701 Eagleson Rd.
Kanata, ON K2M 2G1 Canada
613-591-7545
MICR: 41376-002

Kanata - Hazeldean
482 Hazeldean Rd.
Kanata, ON K2L 1V4 Canada
613-831-2922
MICR: 00786-002

Kapuskasing
16 Circle St.
Kapuskasing, ON P5N 1T4 Canada
705-335-6071
MICR: 10462-002

Kelowna - Bernard
488 Bernard Ave.
Kelowna, BC V1Y 6N7 Canada
250-712-4055
MICR: 80150-002

Kelowna - Dilworth
Orchard Park Shopping Centre
#101, 1835 Dilworth Dr.
Kelowna, BC V1Y 6H1 Canada
250-717-2585
MICR: 11130-002

Kelowna - Hwy. 33
190 Hwy. 33 West
Kelowna, BC V1X 4K6 Canada
250-491-7000
MICR: 30650-002

Kelowna - Lakeshore
Lakeshore Centre
#100, 3275 Lakeshore Rd.
Kelowna, BC V1W 3S9 Canada
250-712-3075
MICR: 92080-002

Kemptville
139 Prescott St.
Kemptville, ON K0G 1J0 Canada
613-258-5961
MICR: 90472-002

Kenora
40 Main St. South
Kenora, ON P9N 1S7 Canada
807-468-6483
MICR: 90217-002

Kensington
54 Broadway St.
Kensington, PE C0B 1M0 Canada
902-836-3333
MICR: 10793-002

Kentville
47 Aberdeen St.
Kentville, NS B4N 3W4 Canada
902-678-2181
MICR: 90043-002

Keswick
Glenwoods Shopping Ctr.
443 The Queensway South
Keswick, ON L4P 2C9 Canada
905-476-4567
MICR: 15362-002

Kincardine
PO Box 1210
755 Queen St.
Kincardine, ON N2Z 1Z9 Canada
519-396-3328
MICR: 95646-002

Kindersley
200 Main St.
Kindersley, SK S0L 1S0 Canada
306-463-4683
MICR: 20198-002

Kingston - Gardiner's
660 Gardiner's Rd.
Kingston, ON K7M 3X9 Canada
613-389-6620
MICR: 24802-002

Kingston - Princess
#143, 145 Princess St.
Kingston, ON K7L 1A8 Canada
613-530-2010
MICR: 70482-002

Kingston - Princess
863 Princess St.
Kingston, ON K7L 5N4 Canada
613-542-2861
MICR: 30502-002

Kingston - Wellington
Commercial Banking Centre
168 Wellington St.
Kingston, ON K7L 4W8 Canada
613-544-3033
MICR: 25296-002

Kinistino
PO Box 520
Main St.
Kinistino, SK S0J 1H0 Canada
306-864-3644
MICR: 00208-002

Kitchener - Courtland
1144 Courtland Ave. East
Kitchener, ON N2C 2H5 Canada
519-579-3520
MICR: 44362-002

Kitchener - Doon Village
Doon Village Centre
Doon Village Rd.
Kitchener, ON N2P 1T6 Canada
519-895-7000
MICR: 68262-002

Kitchener - Highland

Highland Park
491 Highland Rd. West
Kitchener, ON N2M 5K2 Canada
519-741-1021
MICR: 45252-002

Kitchener - King
64 King St. West
Kitchener, ON N2G 3X1 Canada
519-571-6400
MICR: 70052-002

Kitchener - King
1258 King St. East
Kitchener, ON N2G 2N6 Canada
519-744-4417
MICR: 10512-002

Kitchener - Krug
501 Krug St.
Kitchener, ON N2B 1L3 Canada
519-745-6865
MICR: 72132-002

Kitimat
201 City Centre Mall
Kitimat, BC V8C 1T6 Canada
250-632-8420
MICR: 60160-002

La Scie
Shoe Cove Lane
La Scie, NL A0K 3M0 Canada
709-675-2435
MICR: 80524-002

Labrador City
500 Vanier Ave
Labrador City, NL A2V 2W7 Canada
709-944-3626
MICR: 60913-002
Patricia King, Manager

Lac La Biche
10202 - 101 Ave.
Lac La Biche, AB T0A 2C0 Canada
780-623-4445
MICR: 61929-002

Lacombe
5230 - 45th St., Bay 2
Lacombe, AB T4L 2A1 Canada
403-782-3321
MICR: 81679-002

Lanark
George St.
Lanark, ON K0G 1K0 Canada
613-259-2820
MICR: 90522-002

Langley - 96th
North Langley Centre
19989 - 96th Ave.
Langley, BC V1M 3C6 Canada
604-513-3275
MICR: 81760-002

Langley - Fraser
Willowbrook Shopping Centre
19705 Fraser Hwy.
Langley, BC V3A 7E9 Canada
604-514-5450
MICR: 22640-002

Langley - Main
Highland Village Shopping Centre
Langley, BC V3A 4R3 Canada
604-532-6750
MICR: 60780-002

Laval - Carrefour
#100, 3090, boul Le Carrefour
Laval, QC H7T 2J7 Canada
450-686-0960
MICR: 31591-002

Laval - Concorde
3019, boul de la Concorde ouest
Laval, QC H7E 2B5 Canada
450-661-4990
MICR: 90621-002

Laval - Corbusier
1600, boul Le Corbusier
Laval, QC H7S 1Y9 Canada
450-688-6110
MICR: 50641-002

Laval - Cure-Labelle
444, boul Cure-Labelle
Laval, QC H7P 4W7 Canada
450-625-2434
MICR: 21311-002

Laval - Laurentides
3000, boul des Laurentides
Laval, QC H7K 3G5 Canada
450-629-7304
MICR: 81331-002

Laval - Souvenir
3400, boul du Souvenir
Laval, QC H7V 3Z2 Canada
450-686-2211
MICR: 52761-002

Leamington
254 Erie St. South
Leamington, ON N8H 3C2 Canada
519-322-2811
MICR: 84442-002

Leduc
5419 - 50th St.
Leduc, AB T9E 6Z7 Canada
780-986-4441
MICR: 31179-002

Lethbridge - 13th
Westminster Shopping Plaza
425 - 13th St. North
Lethbridge, AB T1H 2S3 Canada
403-382-3355
MICR: 40659-002

Lethbridge - 3rd
702 - 3rd Ave. South
Lethbridge, AB T1J 0H6 Canada
403-382-3300
MICR: 00059-002

Lethbridge - 5th
2220 - 5th Ave. South
Lethbridge, AB T1J 4G6 Canada
403-382-3350
MICR: 20339-002

Lewisporte
Main St.
Lewisporte, NL A0G 3A0 Canada
709-535-3760
MICR: 80663-002

Lindsay
165 Kent St. West
Lindsay, ON K9V 4S2 Canada
705-324-2123
MICR: 63172-002

Linwood
5201 Ament Line
Linwood, ON N0B 2A0 Canada
519-698-2001
MICR: 70532-002

Listowel
190 Main St. East
Listowel, ON N4W 3H4 Canada
519-291-4010
MICR: 18242-002

Liverpool
183 Main St.
Liverpool, NS B0T 1K0 Canada
902-354-3432
MICR: 60343-002

Lloydminster
4802 - 50 Ave.
Lloydminster, AB T9V 0Y2 Canada
780-875-8801
MICR: 20099-002

London - Dundas
1880 Dundas St. East
London, ON N5W 3G2 Canada
519-455-5120
MICR: 20552-002

London - Fanshawe Park
109 Fanshawe Park Rd. East
London, ON N5X 3W1 Canada
519-660-6902
MICR: 54882-002

London - Hamilton
950 Hamilton Rd.
London, ON N5W 1A1 Canada
519-451-1880
MICR: 21972-002

London - Highbury
1250 Highbury Ave.
London, ON N5Y 6M7 Canada
519-451-4930
MICR: 41962-002

London - Oxford
Cherryhill Village Mall
301 Oxford St. West
London, ON N6H 1S6 Canada
519-642-5040
MICR: 00562-002

London - Queens
255 Queens Ave.
London, ON N6A 5R8 Canada
519-642-1156
MICR: 14562-002
Douglas M. Robertson, Manager

London - Richmond
750 Richmond St.
London, ON N6A 3H3 Canada
519-642-2829
MICR: 80572-002

London - Richmond
420 Richmond St.
London, ON N6A 3C9 Canada
519-642-5000
MICR: 00042-002

London - Richmond
Masonville Place
1680 Richmond St.
London, ON N6G 3Y9 Canada
519-667-9014
MICR: 55376-002

London - Southdale
639 Southdale Rd. East
London, ON N6E 3M2 Canada
519-686-0301
MICR: 73742-002

London - Springbank
Southcrest Shopping Centre
390 Springbank Dr.
London, ON N6J 1G9 Canada
519-471-7710
MICR: 42192-002

London - Wonderland South
Commissioners Court Plaza
580 Wonderland Rd. South
London, ON N6K 1L5 Canada
519-471-0812
MICR: 15396-002

Longueuil
2235, boul Roland-Therrien
Longueuil, QC J4N 1P2 Canada
450-647-4770
MICR: 00141-002

Lumby
1989 Vernon St.
Lumby, BC V0E 2G0 Canada
250-547-7810
MICR: 40170-002

Lytton
Main St.
Lytton, BC V0K 1Z0 Canada
250-455-3000
MICR: 20180-002

Mackenzie
PO Box 70
Mackenzie, BC V0J 2C0 Canada
250-997-3223
MICR: 00760-002

Maple Ridge
#100, 22529 Lougheed Hwy.
Maple Ridge, BC V2X 0L4 Canada
604-466-3575
MICR: 60830-002

Marathon
Marathon Centre Mall
#20, 2 Hemlo Dr.
Marathon, ON P0T 2E0 Canada
807-229-2600
MICR: 70557-002

Markdale
PO Box 616
25 Toronto St. North
Markdale, ON N0C 1H0 Canada

The Bank of Nova Scotia(BNS)/ La Banque de Nouvelle-Écosse (continued)

519-986-4011
MICR: 25486-002

Markham - Cochrane
York Commercial Banking Centre
625 Cochrane Dr.
Markham, ON L3R 9R9 Canada
905-470-5060
MICR: 77842-002

Markham - Hwy. 7
Markville Shopping Centre
5000 Hwy. 7 East
Markham, ON L3R 4M9 Canada
905-479-3544
MICR: 14696-002

Markham - Main
101 Main St. North
Markham, ON L3P 1X9 Canada
905-294-3113
MICR: 40592-002

Markham - Warden
Markham Town Sq.
8505 Warden Ave. & Hwy. 7
Markham, ON L3R 0Y8 Canada
905-940-6005
MICR: 75432-002

Markham - Woodbine
CBC
7321 Woodbine Ave.
Markham, ON L3R 3V7 Canada
905-940-6350
MICR: 84772-002

Marystown
Marystown Shopping Centre
PO Box 398
Marystown, NL A0E 2M0 Canada
709-279-4960
MICR: 70953-002

Mattawa
352 Main St.
Mattawa, ON P0H 1V0 Canada
705-744-5596
MICR: 00612-002

Maxville
4 Mechanic St.
Maxville, ON K0C 1T0 Canada
613-527-2980
MICR: 80622-002

Maynooth
PO Box 149
Maynooth, ON K0L 2S0 Canada
613-338-2025
MICR: 93732-002

McAdam
133 Saunders Rd.
McAdam, NB E6J 1L7 Canada
506-784-2234
MICR: 60244-002

McBride
Main St. & 3rd Ave.
McBride, BC V0J 2E0 Canada
250-569-2241
MICR: 00190-002

Meaford
PO Box 3398
5 Trowbridge St. West
Meaford, ON N4L 1A5 Canada
519-538-2060
MICR: 45476-002

Medicine Hat - 3rd
443 - 3rd St. SE
Medicine Hat, AB T1A 0G8 Canada
403-528-6260
MICR: 00349-002

Medicine Hat - Carry
#2, 83 Carry Dr. SE
Medicine Hat, AB T1B 3M5 Canada
403-528-6267
MICR: 71209-002

Melfort
218 Main St.
Melfort, SK S0E 1A0 Canada
306-752-2845
MICR: 80218-002

Middleton
PO Box 190
Middleton, NS B0S 1P0 Canada
902-825-4894
MICR: 30353-002

Midland - Hwy. 93
Huronia Mall
RR#2, Hwy. 93
Midland, ON L4R 4K4 Canada
705-526-0139
MICR: 95406-002

Midland - King
BBC
291 King St.
Midland, ON L4R 4L3 Canada
705-526-2237
MICR: 62182-002

Milo
PO Box 150
Milo, AB T0L 1L0 Canada
403-599-3792
MICR: 70359-002

Milton - Laurier
Laurier Centre
500 Laurier Ave.
Milton, ON L9T 4R3 Canada
905-876-1126
MICR: 68452-002

Milton - Main
244 Main St. East
Milton, ON L9T 1N8 Canada
905-875-2160
MICR: 10652-002

Milverton
1 Main St. South
Milverton, ON N0K 1M0 Canada
519-595-8141
MICR: 90662-002

Minto
11 King St.
Minto, NB E4B 3N6 Canada
506-327-1020
MICR: 30254-002

Miramichi - Henry
139 Henry St.
Miramichi, NB E1V 3M4 Canada
506-622-1461
MICR: 10074-002

Miramichi - Water
1707 Water St.
Miramichi, NB E1N 3A6 Canada
506-773-4473
MICR: 90134-002

Mission
PO Box 3580
33217 - 1st Ave.
Mission, BC V2V 4L1 Canada
604-820-5475
MICR: 60210-002

Mississauga - Airport
Airport Business Banking Centre
6725 Airport Rd.
Mississauga, ON L4V 1E5 Canada
905-678-2400
MICR: 60582-002

Mississauga - Britannia
1525 Britannia Rd. East
Mississauga, ON L4W 1S5 Canada
905-795-2900
MICR: 86462-002

Mississauga - Britannia
Heartland Town Centre
865 Britannia Rd. West
Mississauga, ON L5V 2X8 Canada
905-814-1655
MICR: 24042-002

Mississauga - City Centre
Square One Shopping Centre
100 City Centre Dr.
Mississauga, ON L5B 2C9 Canada
905-566-2247
MICR: 14746-002

Mississauga - Derry
3295 Derry Rd. West
Mississauga, ON L5N 7L7 Canada
905-824-3636
MICR: 35782-002

Mississauga - Dixie
4900 Dixie Rd.
Mississauga, ON L4W 2R1 Canada
416-695-8224
MICR: 84392-002

Mississauga - Dundas
1825 Dundas St. East
Mississauga, ON L4X 2X1 Canada
905-625-8010
MICR: 54122-002

Mississauga - Eglinton
1240 Eglinton Ave. West, Bldg. B16
Mississauga, ON L5V 1N3 Canada
905-858-7541
MICR: 26062-002

Mississauga - Eglinton
660 Eglinton Ave. West
Mississauga, ON L5R 3V2 Canada
905-568-4010
MICR: 54742-002

Mississauga - Eglinton
34 Eglinton Ave. West
Mississauga, ON L5R 3E7 Canada
905-568-3188
MICR: 18382-002

Mississauga - Erin Mills
Sheridan Centre
2225 Erin Mills Pkwy.
Mississauga, ON L5K 1T9 Canada
905-822-5354
MICR: 13482-002

Mississauga - Erin Mills
Erin Mills Town Centre
#R119, 5100 Erin Mills Pkwy.
Mississauga, ON L5M 4Z5 Canada
905-607-2055
MICR: 35832-002

Mississauga - Goreway
Westwood Mall
7205 Goreway Dr.
Mississauga, ON L4T 2T9 Canada
905-678-4300
MICR: 67082-002

Mississauga - Hurontario
4559 Hurontario St.
Mississauga, ON L4Z 3L9 Canada
905-712-0404
MICR: 67926-002

Mississauga - Kirwin
3295 Kirwin Ave.
Mississauga, ON L5A 4K9 Canada
905-276-5900
MICR: 13342-002

Mississauga - Lakeshore
1791 Lakeshore Rd. West
Mississauga, ON L5J 1J6 Canada
905-822-4262
MICR: 61952-002

Mississauga - Lakeshore
158 Lakeshore Rd. East
Mississauga, ON L5G 1E9 Canada
905-278-3358
MICR: 20842-002

Mississauga - North Service
Applewood Village
1077 North Service Rd.
Mississauga, ON L4Y 1A6 Canada
905-272-4244
MICR: 30122-002

Mississauga - Queen St. South
128 Queen St. South
Mississauga, ON L5M 1K8 Canada
905-826-1113
MICR: 21022-002

Mississauga - Robert Speck
West Metro Commercial Banking Centre
#100, 2 Robert Speck Pkwy.
Mississauga, ON L4Z 1H8 Canada
905-276-4540
MICR: 97832-002

Mississauga - South Service
Dixie Outlet Mall
1250 South Service Rd.
Mississauga, ON L5E 1V4 Canada

905-274-3681
MICR: 74716-002
Moncton - Main
780 Main St.
Moncton, NB E1C 8K7 Canada
506-857-3636
MICR: 00034-002
Moncton - Mountain
796 Mountain Rd.
Moncton, NB E1C 9M9 Canada
506-857-3646
MICR: 40394-002
Moncton - St. George St.
PO Box 747, Main Sta. Main
Moncton, NB E1C 8N3 Canada
506-857-3644
MICR: 50054-002
Moncton - Trinity
Wheeler Park
125 Trinity Dr.
Moncton, NB E1G 2J7 Canada
506-857-1497
MICR: 80804-002
Montague
21 Main St.
Montague, PE C0A 1R0 Canada
902-838-2252
MICR: 90803-002
Montréal - Chabanel
555, rue Chabanel ouest
Montréal, QC H2N 2H7 Canada
514-385-2400
MICR: 20081-002
Montréal - Côte-des-Neiges
5180, ch Côte-des-Neiges
Montréal, QC H3T 1X8 Canada
514-739-5508
MICR: 30171-002
Montréal - Côte-Vertu
3828, boul Côte-Vertu
Montréal, QC H4R 1P8 Canada
514-748-7751
MICR: 00471-002
Montréal - Décarie
7885, boul Décarie
Montréal, QC H4P 2H2 Canada
514-731-6844
MICR: 80051-002
Montréal - Frère-André
1170, place du Frère-André
Montréal, QC H3B 3C6 Canada
514-866-2286
MICR: 42721-002
Louise Brisson, Manager
Montréal - Greene
1326, av Greene
Montréal, QC H3Z 2B1 Canada
514-499-5622
MICR: 60251-002
Montréal - Jean-Talon
5094, rue Jean-Talon est
Montréal, QC H1S 1K7 Canada
514-376-4313
MICR: 62711-002
Richard Fontaine, Manager
Montréal - Langelier
Val Marie
8760, boul Langelier
Montréal, QC H1P 3C6 Canada
514-321-8788
MICR: 91231-002
Montréal - Les Galeries d'Anjou
7400, boul Les Galeries d'Anjou
Montréal, QC H1M 3M2 Canada
514-493-9408
MICR: 31401-002
Montréal - Lucerne
2380, ch Lucerne
Montréal, QC H3R 2J8 Canada
514-735-2261
MICR: 40071-002
Montréal - McGill College
Place Montréal Trust
1900, av McGill College
Montréal, QC H3A 3L2 Canada
514-499-4848
MICR: 02261-002
Montréal - Newman
7083, boul Newman
Montréal, QC H8N 1X1 Canada
514-365-3341
MICR: 00901-002
Montréal - Park
5185, av Park
Montréal, QC H2V 4G4 Canada
514-273-8800
MICR: 30031-002
Montréal - Provost
2480, rue Provost
Montréal, QC H8S 1P9 Canada
514-637-3581
MICR: 40691-002
Montréal - Queen Mary
5272, ch Queen Mary
Montréal, QC H3W 1X5 Canada
514-488-7000
MICR: 22301-002
Montréal - René-Lévesque
645, boul René-Lévesque ouest
Montréal, QC H3B 1S5 Canada
514-499-5672
MICR: 90191-002
Montréal - Rockland
Centre Commercial Rockland Inc.
#183, 2305, ch Rockland
Montréal, QC H3P 3E9 Canada
514-739-4758
MICR: 62851-002
Montréal - Sherbrooke ouest
5679, rue Sherbrooke ouest
Montréal, QC H4A 1W6 Canada
514-481-0406
MICR: 20271-002
Montréal - Sherbrooke ouest
Succursale Principale
1002, rue Sherbrooke ouest
Montréal, QC H3A 3L6 Canada
514-499-5432
MICR: 90001-002
Montréal - St-Charles
3064, rue St-Charles
Montréal, QC H9H 3B7 Canada
514-695-3670
MICR: 30981-002
Montréal - St-Jacques
437, rue St-Jacques
Montréal, QC H2Y 1P4 Canada
514-499-5950
MICR: 41301-002
Montréal - St-Jean
Place Scotia Pointe-Claire
620, boul St-Jean
Montréal, QC H9R 3K2 Canada
514-694-6500
MICR: 40451-002
Montréal - St-Laurent
3595, boul St-Laurent
Montréal, QC H2X 2T6 Canada
514-499-5712
MICR: 90241-002
Montréal - St-Michel
7740, boul St-Michel
Montréal, QC H2A 3A6 Canada
514-727-2881
MICR: 70441-002
Montréal - Transcanadienne
#E13, 6815, route Transcanadienne
Montréal, QC H9R 1C4 Canada
514-695-5230
MICR: 22251-002
Montréal - Van Horne
Van Horne Shopping Centre
4861, av Van Horne
Montréal, QC H3W 1J2 Canada
514-731-6883
MICR: 52811-002
Montréal - Wellington
4002, rue Wellington
Montréal, QC H4G 1V3 Canada
514-769-9695
MICR: 30411-002
Montréal - Westminster
5501, av Westminster
Montréal, QC H4W 2J2 Canada
514-489-3848
MICR: 40501-002
Moose Jaw
303 Main St. North
Moose Jaw, SK S6H 0W2 Canada
306-693-3691
MICR: 60038-002
Moosomin
1002 South Front St.
Moosomin, SK S0G 3N0 Canada
306-435-3857
MICR: 40808-002
Morell
PO Box 30
Morell, PE C0A 1S0 Canada
902-961-2019
MICR: 70813-002
Morinville
9927 - 100th St.
Morinville, AB T8R 1R4 Canada
780-939-2611
MICR: 81489-002
Morrisburg
37 Main St.
Morrisburg, ON K0C 1X0 Canada
613-543-2942
MICR: 70672-002
Mount Forest
202 Main St. South
Mount Forest, ON N0G 2L0 Canada
519-323-4100
MICR: 25346-002
Mount Pearl - Centennial
Shopping Centre
Centennial Sq.
Mount Pearl, NL A1N 2C1 Canada
709-576-7796
MICR: 21113-002
Mount Pearl - Topsail
760 Topsail Rd.
Mount Pearl, NL A1N 3J5 Canada
709-576-7222
MICR: 10843-002
Nackawic
#115, 135 Otis Dr.
Nackawic, NB E6G 1H1 Canada
506-575-2284
MICR: 20784-002
Nanaimo - Commercial
65 Commercial St.
Nanaimo, BC V9R 5G3 Canada
250-716-2300
MICR: 40220-002
Nanaimo - North Island
Nored Plaza
#101, 6750 North Island Hwy.
Nanaimo, BC V9V 1S3 Canada
250-390-5975
MICR: 31310-002
Nanaimo - Rutherford
Rutherford Village Shopping Centre
#166, 4750 Rutherford Rd.
Nanaimo, BC V9T 4K6 Canada
250-751-7700
MICR: 71530-002
Napanee
1 Dundas St. West
Napanee, ON K7R 1Z3 Canada
613-354-7401
MICR: 05546-002
Nepean - Merivale
1649 Merivale Rd.
Nepean, ON K2G 3K2 Canada
613-226-3983
MICR: 00166-002
Nepean - Richmond Rd.
Bells Corners
3750 Richmond Rd.
Nepean, ON K2H 5B9 Canada
613-829-2440
MICR: 70136-002

The Bank of Nova Scotia(BNS)/ La Banque de Nouvelle-Écosse (continued)

Nepean - Strandherd Dr.
Barrhaven Centre
3701 Strandherd Dr.
Nepean, ON K2J 4G8 Canada
613-825-3077
MICR: 51326-002

New Glasgow
Westside Shopping Centre
PO Box 544
New Glasgow, NS B2H 5E7 Canada
902-755-5757
MICR: 81083-002

New Glasgow - Provost
126 Provost St.
New Glasgow, NS B2H 5E5 Canada
902-755-6161
MICR: 10363-002

New Liskeard
35 Armstrong St.
New Liskeard, ON P0J 1P0 Canada
705-647-7366
MICR: 50682-002

New Minas
9121 Commercial St.
New Minas, NS B4N 3E6 Canada
902-681-6108
MICR: 41053-002

New Waterford
3421 Plummer Ave.
New Waterford, NS B1H 4K4 Canada
902-862-7116
MICR: 90373-002

New Westminster - Columbia
728 Columbia St.
New Westminster, BC V3M 1A9 Canada
604-668-2746
MICR: 60020-002

New Westminster - Sixth
445 Sixth St.
New Westminster, BC V3L 3B1 Canada
604-668-3758
MICR: 70250-002

Newmarket - Davis
1100 Davis Dr.
Newmarket, ON L3Y 8W8 Canada
905-830-5900
MICR: 87882-002

Newmarket - Main
258 Main St.
Newmarket, ON L3Y 3Z5 Canada
905-853-4985
MICR: 55442-002

Newmarket - Yonge
17900 Yonge St.
Newmarket, ON L3Y 8S1 Canada
905-853-7445
MICR: 30692-002

Newmarket - Yonge
16635 Yonge St.
Newmarket, ON L3Y 5V6 Canada
905-830-6964
MICR: 02642-002

Niagara Falls - Thorold Stone
6225 Thorold Stone Rd.
Niagara Falls, ON L2J 1A6 Canada
905-356-4495
MICR: 27052-002

Niagara Falls - Victoria
4800 Victoria Ave.
Niagara Falls, ON L2E 6S8 Canada
905-356-2426
MICR: 10702-002

Nipawin
200 - 1st Ave. West
Nipawin, SK S0E 1E0 Canada
306-862-4631
MICR: 50088-002

North Battleford
1102 - 101st St.
North Battleford, SK S9A 2Y3 Canada
306-445-8125
MICR: 60228-002

North Bay - Fisher
Northgate Plaza
1500 Fisher St.
North Bay, ON P1B 2H3 Canada
705-472-5680
MICR: 92122-002

North Bay - Lakeshore
Nipissing Plaza
390 Lakeshore Dr.
North Bay, ON P1A 2C7 Canada
705-474-0140
MICR: 01842-002

North Bay - Main
BBC
204 Main St. West
North Bay, ON P1B 2T7 Canada
705-494-4688
MICR: 70722-002

North Sydney
299 Commercial St.
North Sydney, NS B2A 3M1 Canada
902-794-4754
MICR: 70383-002

O'Leary
PO Box 70
O'Leary, PE C0B 1V0 Canada
902-859-2310
MICR: 50823-002

Oakville - Iroquois Shore
525 Iroquois Shore Rd.
Oakville, ON L6H 1M3 Canada
905-338-5005
MICR: 55202-002

Oakville - Lakeshore
207 Lakeshore Rd. East
Oakville, ON L6J 1H7 Canada
905-845-1625
MICR: 30742-002

Oakville - North Service
Oakville Town Centre
#B1, 300 North Service Rd.
Oakville, ON L6M 2R9 Canada
905-845-2424
MICR: 75622-002

Oakville - Speers
320 Speers Rd.
Oakville, ON L6K 3R9 Canada
905-338-5222
MICR: 26682-002

Oakville - Third Line
611 Third Line
Oakville, ON L6L 4A8 Canada
905-847-2778
MICR: 00752-002

Oakville - Trafalgar
Trafalgar Ridge
#1, 2391 Trafalgar Rd.
Oakville, ON L6H 6K7 Canada
905-257-4810
MICR: 73452-002

Oakville - Upper Middle
#10, 1500 Upper Middle Rd.
Oakville, ON L6M 3G3 Canada
905-847-0220
MICR: 23952-002

Okotoks
201 Southridge Dr.
Okotoks, AB T1S 2E1 Canada
403-938-4712
MICR: 91439-002

Olds
Garden Park Plaza
PO Box 3769, Main Sta. Main
Olds, AB T4H 1P5 Canada
403-556-3368
MICR: 50369-002

Orangeville
97 First St.
Orangeville, ON L9W 2E8 Canada
519-941-5544
MICR: 42432-002

Orillia - Mississaga
56 Mississauga St. East
Orillia, ON L3V 6K7 Canada
705-325-1341
MICR: 92312-002

Orillia - Monarch
West Ridge Place
3305 Monarch Dr.
Orillia, ON L3V 7Z4 Canada
705-325-2267
MICR: 23556-002

Orleans - Charlemagne
Charlemagne Plaza
#1, 470 Charlemagne Blvd.
Orleans, ON K4A 1S2 Canada
613-834-2400
MICR: 44016-002

Orleans - Innes
3888 Innes Rd.
Orleans, ON K1W 1K9 Canada
613-834-2029
MICR: 61176-002

Orleans - Place d'Orleans
110 Place d'Orleans Dr.
Orleans, ON K1C 2L9 Canada
613-824-6691
MICR: 60756-002

Oromocto
1024 Onondaga St.
Oromocto, NB E2V 1B8 Canada
506-357-8441
MICR: 80044-002

Osgoode
5677 Main St.
Osgoode, ON K0A 2W0 Canada
613-826-2003
MICR: 30486-002

Oshawa - Harmony
1367 Harmony Rd. North
Oshawa, ON L1H 7K5 Canada
905-404-6990
MICR: 95182-002

Oshawa - King
75 King St. West
Oshawa, ON L1H 8W7 Canada
905-723-1630
MICR: 80762-002

Oshawa - King
800 King St. West
Oshawa, ON L1J 2L5 Canada
905-404-6950
MICR: 37572-002

Ottawa - Alta Vista
2714 Alta Vista Dr.
Ottawa, ON K1V 7T4 Canada
613-731-3660
MICR: 20206-002

Ottawa - Bank
828 Bank St.
Ottawa, ON K1S 5B1 Canada
613-564-5333
MICR: 00216-002

Ottawa - Bank
186 Bank St.
Ottawa, ON K2P 1W6 Canada
613-564-5307
MICR: 00026-002

Ottawa - Bank
1145 Bank St.
Ottawa, ON K1S 3X4 Canada
613-564-5338
MICR: 50096-002

Ottawa - Bank
Southgate Shopping Centre
2515 Bank St.
Ottawa, ON K1V 8R9 Canada
613-738-4700
MICR: 31336-002

Ottawa - Baxter
Pinecrest Mall
1090 Baxter Rd.
Ottawa, ON K2C 4B1 Canada
613-829-8842
MICR: 10496-002

Ottawa - Carling
1427 Carling Ave.
Ottawa, ON K1Z 7L6 Canada
613-798-7001
MICR: 20396-002

Ottawa - Carling

1085 Carling Ave.
Ottawa, ON K1Y 4K4 Canada
613-798-2040
MICR: 70516-002
Ottawa - Carling
2121 Carling Ave.
Ottawa, ON K2A 1H2 Canada
613-798-2000
MICR: 60236-002
Ottawa - Colonel By
Carleton University
1125 Colonel By Dr.
Ottawa, ON K1S 5B6 Canada
613-564-5363
MICR: 00406-002
Ottawa - Earl Armstrong
Riverside South
655 Earl Armstrong Rd.
Ottawa, ON K1V 2G2 Canada
613-822-5332
MICR: 36566-002
Ottawa - Elgin
366 Elgin St.
Ottawa, ON K2P 1M8 Canada
613-564-5348
MICR: 10066-002
Ottawa - Heron
Herongate Mall
1670 Heron Rd.
Ottawa, ON K1V 0C2 Canada
613-526-1480
MICR: 00836-002
Ottawa - Main
65 Main St.
Ottawa, ON K1S 1B5 Canada
613-564-5355
MICR: 90266-002
Ottawa - McCarthy
3310 McCarthy Rd.
Ottawa, ON K1V 9S1 Canada
613-523-7750
MICR: 30726-002
Ottawa - Preston
425 Preston St.
Ottawa, ON K1S 4N3 Canada
613-564-5315
MICR: 70276-002
Ottawa - Richmond
388 Richmond Rd.
Ottawa, ON K2A 0E8 Canada
613-798-2070
MICR: 60046-002
Ottawa - Rideau
117 Rideau St.
Ottawa, ON K1N 5X4 Canada
613-564-5387
MICR: 20016-002
Ottawa - Ridgewood
Riverside Mall
751 Ridgewood Ave.
Ottawa, ON K1V 6MB Canada
613-521-5249
MICR: 00646-002
Ottawa - Somerset
661 Somerset St. West
Ottawa, ON K1R 5K3 Canada
613-564-5160
MICR: 50286-002
Ottawa - Sparks
118 Sparks St.
Ottawa, ON K1P 5T2 Canada
613-564-5100
MICR: 40006-002
Outlook
101A Saskatchewan Ave. East
Outlook, SK S0L 2N0 Canada
306-867-9991
MICR: 40238-002
Owen Sound
857 - 2nd Ave. East
Owen Sound, ON N4K 5P5 Canada
519-376-8480
MICR: 12062-002
Oxford
Main St.
Oxford, NS B0M 1P0 Canada
902-447-2035
MICR: 50393-002
Parksville
102 East Island Hwy.
Parksville, BC V9P 2H1 Canada
250-951-6125
MICR: 72090-002
Parry Sound
27 James St.
Parry Sound, ON P2A 1T6 Canada
705-746-5821
MICR: 60772-002
Peace River
10037 - 100th St.
Peace River, AB T8S 1S3 Canada
780-624-3490
MICR: 30379-002
Pemberton
PO Box 97
Pemberton, BC V0N 2L0 Canada
604-894-1050
MICR: 90670-002
Pembroke
PO Box 156, Main Sta. Main
81 Pembroke St. West
Pembroke, ON K8A 6X3 Canada
613-732-2826
MICR: 70086-002
Penetanguishene
135 Main St.
Penetanguishene, ON L9M 1L7 Canada
705-549-7466
MICR: 40782-002
Penticton - Main St.
401 Main St.
Penticton, BC V2A 6K3 Canada
250-770-7450
MICR: 50260-002
Penticton - Main St.
#101, 2050 Main St.
Penticton, BC V2A 6J9 Canada
250-770-3050
MICR: 43000-002
Perth
63 Foster St.
Perth, ON K7H 1R9 Canada
613-267-1717
MICR: 20792-002
Perth-Andover
#1, 728 Perth Main St.
Perth-Andover, NB E7H 2W7 Canada
506-273-2251
MICR: 90514-002
Petawawa
3468D Petawawa Blvd.
Petawawa, ON K8H 1X3 Canada
613-687-7580
MICR: 62786-002
Peterborough - Chemong
Portage Place Shopping Centre
1154 Chemong Rd.
Peterborough, ON K9H 7J6 Canada
705-749-0744
MICR: 45526-002
Peterborough - Clonsilla
Summit Plaza
780 Clonsilla Ave.
Peterborough, ON K9J 5Y3 Canada
705-748-5681
MICR: 04812-002
Peterborough - Hunter
111 Hunter St. West
Peterborough, ON K9H 7H5 Canada
705-748-2886
MICR: 00802-002
Petitcodiac
50 Main St.
Petitcodiac, NB E4Z 4M3 Canada
506-756-3313
MICR: 10264-002
Petrolia
4184 Petrolia St.
Petrolia, ON N0N 1R0 Canada
519-882-0410
MICR: 80812-002
Pickering - Brock
1020 Brock Rd.
Pickering, ON L1W 3H2 Canada
905-420-2146
MICR: 57612-002
Pickering - Kingston
#10, 705 Kingston Rd.
Pickering, ON L1V 6K3 Canada
905-420-1060
MICR: 15602-002
Pickering - Kingston
Pickering Town Centre
1355 Kingston Rd.
Pickering, ON L1V 1B8 Canada
905-420-7550
MICR: 64782-002
Picton
211 Main St.
Picton, ON K0K 2T0 Canada
613-476-3207
MICR: 60822-002
Pictou
Coleraine St.
Pictou, NS B0K 1H0 Canada
902-485-4378
MICR: 30403-002
Picture Butte
PO Box 190
Picture Butte, AB T0K 1V0 Canada
403-732-4632
MICR: 10389-002
Port Alberni
3777 - 10th Ave.
Port Alberni, BC V9Y 4W5 Canada
250-720-4400
MICR: 30270-002
Port Alice
PO Box 400
Port Alice, BC V0N 2N0 Canada
250-284-3311
MICR: 10280-002
Port Carling
11 Maple St.
Port Carling, ON P0B 1J0 Canada
705-765-6881
MICR: 40832-002
Port Colborne
105 Clarence St.
Port Colborne, ON L3K 3G2 Canada
905-834-7700
MICR: 34132-002
Port Coquitlam
#4100, 2850 Shaughnessy St.
Port Coquitlam, BC V3C 6K5 Canada
604-927-3225
MICR: 80820-002
Port Dover
407 Main St.
Port Dover, ON N0A 1N0 Canada
519-583-2000
MICR: 90852-002
Port Elgin
216 Goderich St.
Port Elgin, ON N0H 2C1 Canada
519-832-9034
MICR: 47092-002
Port Hardy
Port Hardy Shopping Centre
Port Hardy, BC V0N 2P0 Canada
250-949-6414
MICR: 90290-002
Port Hawkesbury
#18, 634 Reeves St.
Port Hawkesbury, NS B9A 3S4 Canada
902-625-2100
MICR: 30833-002
Port Hope
69 Walton St.
Port Hope, ON L1A 3W3 Canada
905-885-6311
MICR: 70862-002
Port Moody

The Bank of Nova Scotia(BNS)/ La Banque de Nouvelle-Écosse (continued)

2501 St. Johns St.
Port Moody, BC V3H 2B3 Canada
604-933-5100
MICR: 70300-002

Portage La Prairie
103 Saskatchewan Ave. East
Portage La Prairie, MB R1N 3B7 Canada
204-239-8630
MICR: 20057-002

Powassan
475 Main St.
Powassan, ON P0H 1Z0 Canada
705-724-2942
MICR: 50872-002

Powell River
7030 Alberni St.
Powell River, BC V8A 2C3 Canada
604-485-3175
MICR: 01230-002

Prince Albert
800 - 15th St. East
Prince Albert, SK S6V 8E3 Canada
306-764-3401
MICR: 10058-002

Prince George - Central
Spruceland Shopping Centre
675 Central St.
Prince George, BC V2N 2J9 Canada
250-960-4900
MICR: 70680-002

Prince George - Domano
College Heights
5051 Domano Blvd.
Prince George, BC V2N 5E1 Canada
250-906-3050
MICR: 02170-002

Prince George - Hart
Hart Shopping Centre
6541 Hart Hwy.
Prince George, BC V2K 3A4 Canada
250-962-4000
MICR: 90860-002

Prince George - Victoria
390 Victoria St.
Prince George, BC V2L 4X4 Canada
250-960-4700
MICR: 50310-002

Prince Rupert
348 - 3rd Ave. West
Prince Rupert, BC V8J 1L4 Canada
250-624-9126
MICR: 10710-002

Pugwash
PO Box 10
Water St.
Pugwash, NS B0K 1L0 Canada
902-243-2541
MICR: 10413-002

Quesnel
293 Reid St.
Quesnel, BC V2J 2M1 Canada
250-992-7021
MICR: 90720-002

Québec - René-Lévesque
2 Place Québec
#100, 900, boul René-Lévesque est
Québec, QC G1R 2B5 Canada
418-691-2600
MICR: 10041-002

Rama
5884 Rama Rd. South
Rama, ON L3V 6H6 Canada
705-327-5758
MICR: 94102-002

Ramea
PO Box 348
Ramea, NL A0M 1N0 Canada
709-625-2323
MICR: 21683-002
Louise Bourgeois, Manager

Red Deer - 50th Ave.
4421 - 50th Ave.
Red Deer, AB T4N 3Z5 Canada
403-340-4794
MICR: 50559-002

Red Deer - 50th Ave.
6704 - 50th Ave.
Red Deer, AB T4N 4E1 Canada
403-340-4787
MICR: 51409-002

Red Deer - 50th St.
5002 - 50th St.
Red Deer, AB T4N 1Y3 Canada
403-340-4780
MICR: 90399-002

Red Lake
Hwy. 105
Red Lake, ON P0V 2M0 Canada
807-727-2437
MICR: 50237-002

Regina - 11th
1980 - 11th Ave.
Regina, SK S4P 3M5 Canada
306-780-1200
MICR: 20008-002

Regina - 13th
2907 - 13th Ave.
Regina, SK S4T 1N8 Canada
306-780-1250
MICR: 80358-002

Regina - Albert
4110 Albert St.
Regina, SK S4S 3R8 Canada
306-780-1275
MICR: 20818-002

Regina - Albert
1504 Albert St.
Regina, SK S4P 2S4 Canada
306-780-1230
MICR: 20248-002

Regina - Albert
486 Albert St. North
Regina, SK S4R 3C1 Canada
306-780-1270
MICR: 20438-002

Regina - Sherwood
Regent Park Plaza
3835 Sherwood Dr.
Regina, SK S4R 4A8 Canada
306-780-1220
MICR: 70318-002

Regina - University Park
625 University Park Dr.
Regina, SK S4V 2V8 Canada
306-780-1285
MICR: 40378-002

Renfrew
215 Raglan St. South
Renfrew, ON K7V 4A4 Canada
613-432-5818
MICR: 30296-002

Richmond - Bridgeport
#104, 11911 Bridgeport Rd.
Richmond, BC V6X 1T5 Canada
604-668-2840
MICR: 71480-002

Richmond - McBean
5 McBean St.
Richmond, ON K0A 2Z0 Canada
613-838-2410
MICR: 10306-002

Richmond - No. 3 Rd.
Alderbridge Place
#112, 4940 No. 3 Rd.
Richmond, BC V6X 3A5 Canada
604-668-2830
MICR: 91470-002

Richmond - No. 3 Rd.
6300 No. 3 Rd.
Richmond, BC V6Y 2B3 Canada
604-668-2880
MICR: 50690-002

Richmond - Steveston
Ironwood Plaza
#3020, 11666 Steveston Hwy.
Richmond, BC V7A 5J3 Canada
604-717-7750
MICR: 51920-002

Richmond Hill - Bayview
9665 Bayview Ave.
Richmond Hill, ON L4C 9V4 Canada
905-770-6067
MICR: 74062-002

Richmond Hill - Hwy. 7
#38, 420 Hwy. 7 East
Richmond Hill, ON L4B 3K2 Canada
905-731-2381
MICR: 45922-002

Richmond Hill - Yonge
10355 Yonge St.
Richmond Hill, ON L4C 3C1 Canada
905-884-1107
MICR: 30882-002

Richmond Hill - Yonge
13311 Yonge St.
Richmond Hill, ON L4E 3L6 Canada
905-773-4311
MICR: 50732-002

Richmond Hill - Yonge
9325 Yonge St.
Richmond Hill, ON L4C 1V4 Canada
905-770-6000
MICR: 63982-002

Richmond Hill - Yonge
10909 Yonge St.
Richmond Hill, ON L4C 3E3 Canada
905-770-6100
MICR: 62752-002

Rockland
#B6, 2737 Laurier St.
Rockland, ON K4K 1A3 Canada
613-446-7131
MICR: 41186-002

Rosetown
218 Main St.
Rosetown, SK S0L 2V0 Canada
306-882-4206
MICR: 70698-002

Rothesay
10 Hampton Rd.
Rothesay, NB E2E 5K9 Canada
506-847-7575
MICR: 40444-002

Russell
PO Box 190
1116 Concession St.
Russell, ON K4R 1C9 Canada
613-445-2880
MICR: 90316-002

Sackville - Bridge
22 Bridge St.
Sackville, NB E4L 3N5 Canada
506-536-2480
MICR: 70334-002

Sackville - Sackville
518 Sackville Dr.
Sackville, NS B4C 2S9 Canada
902-864-2228
MICR: 80903-002

Saint John - King
Brunswick Sq.
39 King St.
Saint John, NB E2L 4J6 Canada
506-658-3365
MICR: 60004-002

Saint John - Main
35 Main St. West
Saint John, NB E2M 3M9 Canada
506-658-3360
MICR: 80234-002

Saint John - Main
365 Main St.
Saint John, NB E2L 4C3 Canada
506-658-3370
MICR: 30064-002

Saint John - Westmorland Rd.
533 Westmorland Rd.
Saint John, NB E2J 2G5 Canada
506-658-3200
MICR: 70664-002

Saint-Lambert
425, av Victoria
Saint-Lambert, QC J4P 2J1 Canada
450-465-3265

MICR: 42341-002
Salmon Arm
391 Hudson Ave.
Salmon Arm, BC V1E 4N6 Canada
250-833-3500
MICR: 30320-002
Sardis
#100, 45800 Promontory Rd.
Sardis, BC V2R 5Z5 Canada
604-847-2400
MICR: 02220-002
Peter Maguire, Manager
Sarnia - Exmouth
Northgate Shopping Ctr.
560 Exmouth St.
Sarnia, ON N7T 5P5 Canada
519-339-1300
MICR: 60962-002
Sarnia - Indian
Eastland Centre
238 Indian Rd. South
Sarnia, ON N7T 3W4 Canada
519-339-1330
MICR: 80952-002
Sarnia - North Christina
169 North Christina St.
Sarnia, ON N7T 7H9 Canada
519-336-5235
MICR: 10942-002
Saskatoon - 20th
West Side
306 - 20th St. West
Saskatoon, SK S7M 0X2 Canada
306-668-1540
MICR: 40048-002
Saskatoon - 22nd
2410 - 22nd St. West
Saskatoon, SK S7M 0V7 Canada
306-668-1565
MICR: 50328-002
Saskatoon - 2nd
CBC Main
111 - 2nd Ave. South
Saskatoon, SK S7K 1K6 Canada
306-668-1440
MICR: 00018-002
Saskatoon - 33rd
218 - 33rd St. West
Saskatoon, SK S7L 0V1 Canada
306-668-1500
MICR: 10348-002
Saskatoon - 8th
1004 - 8th St. East
Saskatoon, SK S7H 0R9 Canada
306-668-1480
MICR: 90068-002
Saskatoon - 8th
The Centre (East)
3510 - 8th St. East
Saskatoon, SK S7H 0W6 Canada
306-668-1600
MICR: 20628-002
Saskatoon - Circle
#12, 405 Circle Dr. East
Saskatoon, SK S7K 4B4 Canada
306-668-1460
MICR: 80648-002
Saskatoon - Midtown Plaza
Saskatoon, SK S7K 1J9 Canada
306-668-1515
MICR: 30338-002
Saskatoon - Primrose
Lawson Heights Mall
#A29, 134 Primrose Dr.
Saskatoon, SK S7K 5S6 Canada
306-668-1661
MICR: 30718-002
Saulnierville
PO Box 28
Saulnierville, NS B0W 2Z0 Canada
902-769-3234
MICR: 01073-002
Sault Ste Marie - Bay St. - Business Banking Centre
Station Mall
293 Bay St.
Sault Ste Marie, ON P6A 6W6 Canada
705-254-7660
MICR: 40972-002
Sault Ste Marie - Northern Ave.
294 Northern Ave.
Sault Ste Marie, ON P6B 4H6 Canada
705-254-1491
MICR: 62232-002
Selkirk
337 Main St.
Selkirk, MB R1A 1T3 Canada
204-785-4010
MICR: 80317-002
Sheet Harbour
PO Box 8
Sheet Harbour, NS B0J 3B0 Canada
902-885-2310
MICR: 50443-002
Shelburne
King St.
Shelburne, NS B0T 1W0 Canada
902-875-3115
MICR: 01883-002
Shellbrook
PO Box 190
21 Main St.
Shellbrook, SK S0J 2E0 Canada
306-747-2623
MICR: 70268-002
Shippagan
261 J.D. Gauthier Blvd.
Shippagan, NB E8S 1N5 Canada
506-336-2261
MICR: 50344-002
Sidney
2355 Beacon Ave.
Sidney, BC V8L 3S3 Canada
250-655-2250
MICR: 21550-002
Simcoe
54 Norfolk St. North
Simcoe, ON N3Y 3N6 Canada
519-426-7330
MICR: 92452-002
Smithers
Smithers Shopping Plaza
PO Box 2589
Smithers, BC V0J 2N0 Canada
250-877-4000
MICR: 41210-002
Smiths Falls
92 Lombard St.
Smiths Falls, ON K7A 4G5 Canada
613-284-4111
MICR: 20982-002
South Mountain
PO Box 50
South Mountain, ON K0E 1W0 Canada
613-989-2863
MICR: 50336-002
South Porcupine
Porcupine Plaza
Hwy. 101 East
South Porcupine, ON P0N 1K0 Canada
705-235-3383
MICR: 46052-002
Spanish
121 Front St.
Spanish, ON P0P 2A0 Canada
705-844-2161
MICR: 00992-002
Spiritwood
PO Box 40
236 Main St.
Spiritwood, SK S0J 2M0 Canada
306-883-2054
MICR: 50278-002
Springdale
PO Box 279
Juniper Rd.
Springdale, NL A0J 1T0 Canada
709-673-5368
MICR: 60723-002
Squamish
PO Box 129
38049 Cleveland Ave.
Squamish, BC V8B 0A1 Canada
604-892-2150
MICR: 10330-002
St Catharines - Geneva
Fairview Mall
285 Geneva St.
St Catharines, ON L2N 2G1 Canada
905-937-6325
MICR: 70912-002
St Catharines - Glendale
Pen Centre
#62, 221 Glendale Ave.
St Catharines, ON L2T 2K9 Canada
905-688-7731
MICR: 55566-002
St Catharines - Merritt
319 Merritt St.
St Catharines, ON L2T 1K3 Canada
905-227-6638
MICR: 40642-002
St Catharines - Ontario
Parkway Inn
327 Ontario St.
St Catharines, ON L2R 5L3 Canada
905-684-8333
MICR: 23572-002
St Catharines - St. Paul
185 St. Paul St.
St Catharines, ON L2R 6T3 Canada
905-684-2021
MICR: 10892-002
St Catharines - Welland
229 Welland Ave.
St Catharines, ON L2R 2P4 Canada
905-687-8841
MICR: 90902-002
St George
11 Main St.
St George, NB E5C 3H9 Canada
506-755-3374
MICR: 50294-002
St Isidore
4531 Ste. Catherine St.
St Isidore, ON K0C 2B0 Canada
613-524-2880
MICR: 70326-002
St Jacobs
1410 King St. North
St Jacobs, ON N0B 2N0 Canada
519-664-2201
MICR: 50922-002
St Marys
131 Queen St. East
St Marys, ON N4X 1B7 Canada
519-284-3840
MICR: 85696-002
St Thomas
472 Talbot St.
St Thomas, ON N5P 1C2 Canada
519-631-8660
MICR: 30932-002
St. Andrews
204 Water St.
St. Andrews, NB E5B 1B4 Canada
506-529-1140
MICR: 70284-002
St. Anthony
PO Box 100
St. Anthony, NL A0K 4S0 Canada
709-454-3553
MICR: 60673-002
St. John's - Avalon Mall
Avalon Mall Shopping Centre
PO Box 8801, A Sta. A
St. John's, NL A1B 3T2 Canada
709-576-1300
MICR: 10983-002
St. John's - Cornwall
2 Cornwall Ave.
St. John's, NL A1C 5J2 Canada
709-576-7654
MICR: 20693-002

The Bank of Nova Scotia(BNS)/ La Banque de Nouvelle-Écosse (continued)

St. John's - Elizabeth
21 Elizabeth Ave. East
St. John's, NL A1A 5B2 Canada
709-576-1988
MICR: 20883-002

St. John's - Rowan
Churchill Park
37 Rowan St.
St. John's, NL A1C 5J2 Canada
709-576-1199
MICR: 40683-002

St. John's - Torbay
Torbay Road Plaza
272 Torbay Rd.
St. John's, NL A1A 5B5 Canada
709-576-7805
MICR: 82263-002

St. John's - Water
Commercial Banking Centre
245 Water St.
St. John's, NL A1C 1B5 Canada
709-576-6000
MICR: 50013-002

St. Stephen
Milltown Blvd.
St. Stephen, NB E3L 2W9 Canada
506-466-1837
MICR: 90324-002

Steinbach
269 Main St.
Steinbach, MB R5G 1Y9 Canada
204-346-6150
MICR: 20727-002

Stellarton
Foord St.
Stellarton, NS B0K 1S0 Canada
902-755-1306
MICR: 20453-002

Stephenville
42 Queen St.
Stephenville, NL A2N 3A7 Canada
709-643-8400
MICR: 11213-002

Stittsville
1271 Stittsville Main St.
Stittsville, ON K2S 2E4 Canada
613-831-3115
MICR: 21196-002

Stoney Creek
155 Green Rd.
Stoney Creek, ON L8G 3X2 Canada
905-664-9377
MICR: 65656-002

Stouffville
6323 Main St.
Stouffville, ON L4A 1G5 Canada
905-640-3631
MICR: 61002-002

Stratford
1 Ontario St.
Stratford, ON N5A 6S9 Canada
519-272-8250
MICR: 41012-002

Strathroy
360 Caradoc St. South
Strathroy, ON N7G 2P6 Canada
519-245-4910
MICR: 67132-002

Sudbury - Algonquin
Algonquin Square
#14, 2040 Algonquin Rd.
Sudbury, ON P3E 4Z6 Canada
705-523-1424
MICR: 06486-002

Sudbury - Barrydowne
1094 Barrydowne Rd.
Sudbury, ON P3A 3V3 Canada
705-560-2700
MICR: 05322-002

Sudbury - Durham
Business Banking Ctr.
57 Durham St.
Sudbury, ON P3E 5B7 Canada
705-675-3361
MICR: 01032-002

Sudbury - Lorne
907 Lorne St.
Sudbury, ON P3C 4R6 Canada
705-673-4164
MICR: 83592-002

Summerside
PO Box 1595
274 Water St.
Summerside, PE C1N 2V5 Canada
902-436-2204
MICR: 00083-002

Surrey - 102nd
13551 - 102nd Ave.
Surrey, BC V3T 4X8 Canada
604-586-1300
MICR: 31120-002

Surrey - 108th
Fraser Heights Village
#201, 16033 - 108th Ave.
Surrey, BC V4N 1P2 Canada
604-586-3100
MICR: 82040-002

Surrey - 108th
Gateway Stn. Tower
#200, 13401 - 108th Ave.
Surrey, BC V3T 5T3 Canada
604-586-3126
MICR: 70060-002

Surrey - 120th
Strawberry Hill
7378 - 120th St.
Surrey, BC V3W 3M9 Canada
604-501-3325
MICR: 72140-002

Surrey - 138th
100 - 138th St.
Surrey, BC V3W 2P4 Canada
604-501-5353
MICR: 11650-002

Surrey - 152A
Fleetwood Sq.
#180, 8888 - 152A St.
Surrey, BC V3R 0V7 Canada
604-668-3000
MICR: 12070-002

Surrey - 175th
Cloverdale
5782 - 175th St.
Surrey, BC V3S 4T7 Canada
604-576-3550
MICR: 70110-002

Surrey - Guildford
Guilford Town Centre
2301 Guildford Town Centre
Surrey, BC V3R 7B9 Canada
604-586-3200
MICR: 50740-002

Surrey - King George
Redwood Sq.
#16, 3189 King George Hwy.
Surrey, BC V4P 1B8 Canada
604-541-0280
MICR: 81190-002

Surrey - Nordel
12040 Nordel Way
Surrey, BC V3W 1P6 Canada
604-501-7525
MICR: 51060-002

Sussex
635 Main St.
Sussex, NB E4E 7H5 Canada
506-432-3920
MICR: 20354-002

Sutton West
114 High St.
Sutton West, ON L0E 1R0 Canada
905-722-6591
MICR: 81042-002

Swift Current
280 Central Ave. North
Swift Current, SK S9H 0L2 Canada
306-773-8338
MICR: 80028-002

Sydney
258 Charlotte St.
Sydney, NS B1P 1C5 Canada
902-539-2110
MICR: 00463-002

Sydney Mines
765 Main St.
Sydney Mines, NS B1V 2Y4 Canada
902-736-6295
MICR: 80473-002

Tatamagouche
243 Main St.
Tatamagouche, NS B0K 1V0 Canada
902-657-2440
MICR: 60483-002

Tavistock
23 Woodstock St. South
Tavistock, ON N0B 2R0 Canada
519-655-2043
MICR: 05686-002

Tecumseh
21 Amy Croft Dr.
Tecumseh, ON N9K 1C7 Canada
519-735-4499
MICR: 27516-002

Temagami
Hwy. 11 North
Temagami, ON P0H 2H0 Canada
705-569-3625
MICR: 31062-002

Terrace
4602 Lakelse Ave.
Terrace, BC V8G 1R1 Canada
250-635-8500
MICR: 90340-002

The Pas
Opaskwayak
PO Box 10430
The Pas, MB R0B 2J0 Canada
204-627-5423
MICR: 10587-002

Thompson
35 Thompson Dr. North
Thompson, MB R8N 2B5 Canada
204-677-0730
MICR: 00257-002

Thornhill - Bathurst
#19, 7700 Bathurst St.
Thornhill, ON L4J 7Y3 Canada
905-731-8009
MICR: 65862-002

Thornhill - Steeles
#31, 800 Steeles Ave. West
Thornhill, ON L4J 7L2 Canada
905-738-6004
MICR: 83162-002

Thornhill - Steeles
2900 Steeles Ave. East
Thornhill, ON L3T 4X1 Canada
905-731-7388
MICR: 87122-002

Thornhill - Yonge
7681 Yonge St.
Thornhill, ON L3T 4A2 Canada
905-731-2080
MICR: 51052-002

Thorold
Pine St. Shopping Centre
PO Box 445
Thorold, ON L2V 4J6 Canada
905-227-5236
MICR: 35766-002

Thunder Bay - Hewitson
745 Hewitson St.
Thunder Bay, ON P7B 6B5 Canada
807-623-5626
MICR: 00687-002

Thunder Bay - Red River Rd.
225 Red River Rd.
Thunder Bay, ON P7B 1A7 Canada
807-343-5600
MICR: 70227-002

Thunder Bay - Victoria
501 Victoria Ave. East
Thunder Bay, ON P7C 1A8 Canada
807-624-5100

MICR: 10207-002
Tillsonburg
199 Broadway Ave.
Tillsonburg, ON N4G 3P9 Canada
519-688-6400
MICR: 34702-002
Timmins - Pine
BBC
1 Pine St. South
Timmins, ON P4N 7C9 Canada
705-268-8030
MICR: 11072-002
Timmins - Waterloo
100 Waterloo Rd.
Timmins, ON P4N 4X5 Canada
705-360-4440
MICR: 45492-002
Tisdale
1002 - 100th St.
Tisdale, SK S0E 1T0 Canada
306-873-2609
MICR: 70078-002
Toronto - Albion Rd.
1839 Albion Rd.
Toronto, ON M9W 5S8 Canada
416-675-8820
MICR: 53132-002
Toronto - Alton Towers Circle
250 Alton Towers Circle
Toronto, ON M1V 3Z4 Canada
416-297-6500
MICR: 05132-002
Toronto - Bamburgh Circle
#A114, 325 Bamburgh Circle
Toronto, ON M1W 3Y1 Canada
416-499-5773
MICR: 83642-002
Toronto - Bathurst St.
347 Bathurst St.
Toronto, ON M5T 2S7 Canada
416-866-6653
MICR: 71092-002
Toronto - Bathurst St.
3094 Bathurst St.
Toronto, ON M6A 2A1 Canada
416-784-3161
MICR: 30072-002
Toronto - Bay St.
392 Bay St.
Toronto, ON M5H 3K5 Canada
416-866-5700
MICR: 34272-002
Toronto - Bayview Ave.
Bayview Village Centre
2901 Bayview Ave.
Toronto, ON M2K 1E6 Canada
416-590-7910
MICR: 92072-002
Toronto - Bayview Ave.
1547 Bayview Ave.
Toronto, ON M4G 3B5 Canada
416-487-2826
MICR: 24596-002
Toronto - Bloor St. East
160 Bloor St. East
Toronto, ON M4W 1B9 Canada
416-515-2818
MICR: 51102-002
Toronto - Bloor St. West
1709 Bloor St. West
Toronto, ON M6P 4E5 Canada
416-760-2300
MICR: 82172-002
Toronto - Bloor St. West
2295 Bloor St. West
Toronto, ON M6S 1P1 Canada
416-760-2330
MICR: 31112-002
Toronto - Bloor St. West
1034 Bloor St. West
Toronto, ON M6H 1M3 Canada
416-538-5230
MICR: 63032-002
Toronto - Bloor St. West
332 Bloor St. West
Toronto, ON M5S 1W6 Canada
416-515-2850
MICR: 90092-002
Toronto - Bloor St. West
19 Bloor St. West
Toronto, ON M4W 1A3 Canada
416-515-2600
MICR: 91132-002
Toronto - Bloor St. West
2930 Bloor St. West
Toronto, ON M8X 1B6 Canada
416-236-1107
MICR: 81422-002
Toronto - Borough Dr.
Scarborough Town Centre
#211, 300 Borough Dr.
Toronto, ON M1P 4P5 Canada
416-296-5626
MICR: 84962-002
Toronto - Broadview Ave.
363 Broadview Ave.
Toronto, ON M4K 2M7 Canada
416-465-3531
MICR: 41152-002
Toronto - Brown's Line
388 Brown's Line
Toronto, ON M8W 3T8 Canada
416-503-6966
MICR: 52142-002
Toronto - College St.
440 College St.
Toronto, ON M5T 1T3 Canada
416-866-6083
MICR: 01172-002
Toronto - College St.
643 College St.
Toronto, ON M6G 1B7 Canada
416-537-2191
MICR: 81182-002
Toronto - Danforth Ave.
661 Danforth Ave.
Toronto, ON M4J 1L2 Canada
416-461-7541
MICR: 87916-002
Toronto - Danforth Ave.
1188 Danforth Ave.
Toronto, ON M4J 1M3 Canada
416-406-2246
MICR: 50062-002
Toronto - Danforth Ave.
2553 Danforth Ave.
Toronto, ON M4C 1L4 Canada
416-693-2333
MICR: 41202-002
Toronto - Danforth Ave.
649 Danforth Ave.
Toronto, ON M4K 1R2 Canada
416-465-2300
MICR: 21212-002
Toronto - Danforth Ave.
2072 Danforth Ave.
Toronto, ON M4C 1J6 Canada
416-425-8444
MICR: 01222-002
Toronto - Don Mills Rd.
789 Don Mills Rd.
Toronto, ON M3C 1T5 Canada
416-696-2042
MICR: 02022-002
Toronto - Don Mills Rd.
1500 Don Mills Rd.
Toronto, ON M3B 3K4 Canada
416-448-7020
MICR: 85282-002
Toronto - Dufferin St.
#49 & #50, 2700 Dufferin St.
Toronto, ON M6B 4J3 Canada
416-784-3200
MICR: 61242-002
Toronto - Dufferin St.
Yorkdale Shopping Centre
3401 Dufferin St.
Toronto, ON M6A 2T9 Canada
416-784-5124
MICR: 22152-002
Toronto - Dundas St. West
1616 Dundas St. West
Toronto, ON M6K 1V1 Canada
416-538-5255
MICR: 31252-002
Toronto - East Mall
Cloverdale Mall
250 The East Mall
Toronto, ON M9B 3Y8 Canada
416-233-5547
MICR: 21162-002
Toronto - Eglinton Ave. East
Eastown Plaza
2668 Eglinton Ave. East
Toronto, ON M1K 2S3 Canada
416-266-4446
MICR: 31302-002
Toronto - Eglinton Ave. East
880 Eglinton Ave. East
Toronto, ON M4G 2L2 Canada
416-696-2115
MICR: 11452-002
Toronto - Eglinton Ave. East
Golden Mile Supercentre
1880 Eglinton Ave. East
Toronto, ON M1L 2L9 Canada
416-285-2190
MICR: 91322-002
Toronto - Eglinton Ave. West
859 Eglinton Ave. West
Toronto, ON M6C 2B9 Canada
416-784-3100
MICR: 91272-002
Toronto - Eglinton Ave. West
2256 Eglinton Ave. West
Toronto, ON M6E 2L3 Canada
416-784-3184
MICR: 71282-002
Toronto - Eglinton Ave. West
438 Eglinton Ave. West
Toronto, ON M5N 1A2 Canada
416-932-2140
MICR: 51292-002
Toronto - Ellesmere Rd.
3 Ellesmere Rd.
Toronto, ON M1R 4B7 Canada
416-448-7000
MICR: 91652-002
Toronto - Finch Ave. West
845 Finch Ave. West
Toronto, ON M3J 2C7 Canada
416-665-8742
MICR: 92262-002
Toronto - Harbour Sq.
41 Harbour Sq.
Toronto, ON M5J 2G4 Canada
416-866-3393
MICR: 45872-002
Toronto - Islington Ave. North
2251 Islington Ave. North
Toronto, ON M9W 3W6 Canada
416-744-6100
MICR: 41582-002
Toronto - Jane St.
347 Jane St.
Toronto, ON M6S 3Z3 Canada
416-760-2310
MICR: 22202-002
Toronto - Keele St.
3809 Keele St.
Toronto, ON M3J 1N5 Canada
416-630-7114
MICR: 14332-002
Toronto - King St. West
720 King St. West
Toronto, ON M5V 2T3 Canada
416-866-3493
MICR: 37812-002
Toronto - King St. West
Aetna Centre
145 King St. West
Toronto, ON M5H 1J8 Canada
416-866-5870
MICR: 34322-002

The Bank of Nova Scotia(BNS)/ La Banque de Nouvelle-Écosse (continued)

Toronto - King St. West
Scotia Plaza
44 King St. West
Toronto, ON M5H 1H1 Canada
416-866-6430
MICR: 80002-002

Toronto - Kingston Rd.
1016 Kingston Rd.
Toronto, ON M4E 1T2 Canada
416-693-3969
MICR: 61382-002

Toronto - Kingston Rd.
2487 Kingston Rd.
Toronto, ON M1N 1V4 Canada
416-264-5160
MICR: 21402-002

Toronto - Kingston Rd.
4509 Kingston Rd.
Toronto, ON M1E 2N9 Canada
416-724-5200
MICR: 72322-002

Toronto - Kingston Rd.
Cliffcrest Plaza
3041 Kingston Rd.
Toronto, ON M1M 1P1 Canada
416-261-6149
MICR: 74856-002

Toronto - Lakeshore Blvd. West
2895 Lakeshore Blvd. West
Toronto, ON M8V 1J3 Canada
416-503-6930
MICR: 51482-002

Toronto - Lawrence Ave. East
2290 Lawrence Ave. East
Toronto, ON M1P 2P9 Canada
416-751-6500
MICR: 07906-002
Sue Facey, Manager

Toronto - Lawrence Ave. East
Cedarbrae Plaza
3475 Lawrence Ave. East
Toronto, ON M1H 1B2 Canada
416-439-2333
MICR: 71332-002

Toronto - Lawrence Ave. East
885 Lawrence Ave. East
Toronto, ON M3C 1P7 Canada
416-448-7050
MICR: 81232-002

Toronto - Lawrence Ave. East
2154 Lawrence Ave. East
Toronto, ON M1R 3A8 Canada
416-701-7272
MICR: 61432-002

Toronto - Lawrence Ave. West
1391 Lawrence Ave. West
Toronto, ON M6L 1A4 Canada
416-240-7600
MICR: 41442-002

Toronto - Markham Rd.
1137 Markham Rd.
Toronto, ON M1H 2Y5 Canada
416-439-6700
MICR: 32292-002

Toronto - McNicoll Ave.
3585 McNicoll Ave.
Toronto, ON M1V 2N3 Canada
416-297-7007
MICR: 16402-002

Toronto - Midland Ave.
Silverland Centre
3320 Midland Ave.
Toronto, ON M1V 5E6 Canada
416-292-6878
MICR: 74906-002

Toronto - O'Connor Dr.
802 O'Connor Dr.
Toronto, ON M4B 2S9 Canada
416-750-2005
MICR: 81612-002

Toronto - Overlea Blvd.
East York Town Centre
#2, 45 Overlea Blvd.
Toronto, ON M4H 1C3 Canada
416-421-3900
MICR: 64626-002

Toronto - Pape Ave.
1002 Pape Ave.
Toronto, ON M4K 3V9 Canada
416-696-2045
MICR: 31492-002

Toronto - Port Union Rd.
305 Port Union Rd.
Toronto, ON M1C 2L5 Canada
416-724-2255
MICR: 62422-002

Toronto - Queen St. East
79 Queen St. East
Toronto, ON M5C 1R8 Canada
416-866-6571
MICR: 71522-002

Toronto - Queen St. East
1046 Queen St. East
Toronto, ON M4M 1K4 Canada
416-465-5461
MICR: 31542-002

Toronto - Queen St. East
2080 Queen St. East
Toronto, ON M4E 1E1 Canada
416-693-3939
MICR: 81562-002

Toronto - Queen St. West
1464 Queen St. West
Toronto, ON M6K 1M2 Canada
416-538-5215
MICR: 51532-002

Toronto - Queen St. West
222 Queen St. West
Toronto, ON M5V 1Z3 Canada
416-866-6591
MICR: 40022-002

Toronto - Roncesvalles Ave.
203 Roncesvalles Ave.
Toronto, ON M6R 2L5 Canada
416-536-1196
MICR: 34496-002

Toronto - Sheppard Ave. East
2175 Sheppard Ave. East
Toronto, ON M2J 1W8 Canada
416-499-6400
MICR: 03012-002

Toronto - Sheppard Ave. East
4220 Sheppard Ave. East
Toronto, ON M1S 3B4 Canada
416-297-2460
MICR: 91082-002
Manuel Goncalves, Manager

Toronto - Sheppard Ave. East
Agincourt Mall
3850 Sheppard Ave. East
Toronto, ON M1T 3L4 Canada
416-291-3733
MICR: 74526-002

Toronto - Sheppard Ave. West
628 Sheppard Ave. West
Toronto, ON M3H 2S1 Canada
416-638-1955
MICR: 04796-002

Toronto - Spadina Ave.
110 Spadina Ave.
Toronto, ON M5V 2K4 Canada
416-866-6645
MICR: 41632-002

Toronto - Spadina Ave.
292 Spadina Ave.
Toronto, ON M5T 2E7 Canada
416-866-6633
MICR: 21642-002

Toronto - Spadina Rd.
416 Spadina Rd.
Toronto, ON M5P 2W4 Canada
416-932-1866
MICR: 51342-002

Toronto - St. Clair Ave. East
1 St. Clair Ave. East
Toronto, ON M4T 1Z3 Canada
416-515-8722
MICR: 61762-002

Toronto - St. Clair Ave. West
949 St. Clair Ave. West
Toronto, ON M6C 1C7 Canada
416-654-4343
MICR: 01602-002

Toronto - St. Clair Ave. West
1154 St. Clair Ave. West
Toronto, ON M6E 1B3 Canada
416-654-8906
MICR: 64816-002

Toronto - Steeles Ave. East
4723 Steeles Ave. East
Toronto, ON M1V 4S5 Canada
416-297-7835
MICR: 28472-002

Toronto - Tapscott Rd.
Malvern Town Centre
#57, 31 Tapscott Rd.
Toronto, ON M1B 4Y7 Canada
416-297-5077
MICR: 26492-002

Toronto - The Kingsway
Humbertown Centre
270 The Kingsway
Toronto, ON M9A 3T7 Canada
416-233-2136
MICR: 01362-002

Toronto - The Queensway
1037 The Queensway
Toronto, ON M8Z 6C7 Canada
416-503-3402
MICR: 81372-002

Toronto - The West Mall
Sherway Gardens
25 The West Mall
Toronto, ON M9C 1B8 Canada
416-621-8700
MICR: 94706-002

Toronto - Toryork Dr.
2 Toryork Dr.
Toronto, ON M9L 1X6 Canada
416-749-4900
MICR: 82362-002

Toronto - University Ave.
522 University Ave.
Toronto, ON M5G 1W7 Canada
416-866-3300
MICR: 14712-002

Toronto - Warden Ave.
Bridlewood Mall
2900 Warden Ave.
Toronto, ON M1W 2S8 Canada
416-497-7012
MICR: 34876-002

Toronto - Weston Rd.
1151 Weston Rd.
Toronto, ON M6M 4P3 Canada
416-240-7667
MICR: 71472-002

Toronto - Weston Rd.
1885 Weston Rd.
Toronto, ON M9N 1V9 Canada
416-240-7655
MICR: 51672-002

Toronto - Wilson Ave.
York Plaza
1603 Wilson Ave.
Toronto, ON M3L 1A5 Canada
416-244-1101
MICR: 44776-002

Toronto - Yonge St.
Centrepoint Mall
6464 Yonge St.
Toronto, ON M2M 3X4 Canada
416-590-7488
MICR: 31682-002

Toronto - Yonge St.
5075 Yonge St.
Toronto, ON M2N 6C6 Canada
416-590-7320
MICR: 91702-002

Toronto - Yonge St.
1867 Yonge St.
Toronto, ON M4S 1Y5 Canada
416-932-2160
MICR: 04382-002

Toronto - Yonge St.
2200 Yonge St.
Toronto, ON M4S 2C7 Canada
416-932-3033
MICR: 02162-002
Toronto - Yonge St.
5607 Yonge St.
Toronto, ON M2M 3S9 Canada
416-590-7500
MICR: 11692-002
Toronto - Yonge St.
3169 Yonge St.
Toronto, ON M4N 2K9 Canada
416-932-2144
MICR: 11742-002
Toronto - Yonge St.
555 Yonge St.
Toronto, ON M4Y 1Y5 Canada
416-515-2800
MICR: 83212-002
Toronto - Yonge St.
3446 Yonge St.
Toronto, ON M4N 2N2 Canada
416-485-7617
MICR: 94466-002
Tracadie-Sheila
Centre d'achats le Rond Point
3409, rue Principale
Tracadie, NB E1X 1C7 Canada
506-395-3321
MICR: 90704-002
Trail
Waneta Plaza
#118, 8100 Rock Island Hwy.
Trail, BC V1R 4N7 Canada
250-364-5000
MICR: 71670-002
Trenton - Dundas St. East
Trenton Town Centre
266 Dundas St. East
Trenton, ON K8V 5Z9 Canada
613-392-2881
MICR: 05736-002
Trenton - Dundas St. West
68 Dundas St. West
Trenton, ON K8V 3P3 Canada
613-392-2531
MICR: 21782-002
Truro - Inglis
7 Inglis St.
Truro, NS B2N 5C6 Canada
902-895-0591
MICR: 10033-002
Truro - Prince
589 Prince St.
Truro, NS B2N 5G7 Canada
902-895-7982
MICR: 01123-002
Twillingate
PO Box 39
Twillingate, NL A0G 4M0 Canada
709-884-2121
MICR: 20743-002
Upper Tantallon
3650 Hammonds Plains Rd.
Upper Tantallon, NS B3Z 4R3 Canada
902-826-2124
MICR: 52233-002
Uxbridge
Ashly Place
1 Douglas Rd., RR#1
Uxbridge, ON L9P 1M6 Canada
905-852-6138
MICR: 95612-002
Vancouver - 10th Ave.
4566 West 10th Ave.
Vancouver, BC V6R 2J1 Canada
604-221-3750
MICR: 22400-002
Vancouver - 12th Ave.
#130, 555 West 12th Ave.
Vancouver, BC V5Z 3X7 Canada
604-717-6700
MICR: 72520-002
Vancouver - 1st Ave.
#244, 2800 East 1st Ave.
Vancouver, BC V5M 4P1 Canada
604-668-2075
MICR: 52050-002
Vancouver - 41st Ave.
1576 West 41st Ave.
Vancouver, BC V6M 1X6 Canada
604-668-3707
MICR: 90480-002
Vancouver - 41st Ave.
2207 West 41st Ave.
Vancouver, BC V6M 2A3 Canada
604-668-3704
MICR: 30510-002
Vancouver - 41st Ave.
Oakridge Ctr.
650 West 41st Ave.
Vancouver, BC V5Z 2M9 Canada
604-668-3732
MICR: 80390-002
Vancouver - 49th Ave.
Killarney Square Shopping Plaza
2689 East 49th Ave.
Vancouver, BC V5S 1J9 Canada
604-668-3737
MICR: 60640-002
Vancouver - Broadway East
1695 East Broadway
Vancouver, BC V5N 1V9 Canada
604-668-3782
MICR: 40360-002
Vancouver - Broadway West
1801 West Broadway
Vancouver, BC V6J 1Y5 Canada
604-668-3768
MICR: 10090-002
Vancouver - Broadway West
2798 West Broadway
Vancouver, BC V6K 2G4 Canada
604-668-3775
MICR: 60350-002
Vancouver - Broadway West
1004 West Broadway
Vancouver, BC V6H 1E6 Canada
604-668-3778
MICR: 20370-002
Vancouver - Broadway West
1 West Broadway
Vancouver, BC V5Y 1P1 Canada
604-668-3789
MICR: 00380-002
Vancouver - Burrard St.
510 Burrard St.
Vancouver, BC V6C 3A8 Canada
604-718-1500
MICR: 01800-002
Vancouver - Burrard St.
970 Burrard St.
Vancouver, BC V6Z 2R4 Canada
604-668-2160
MICR: 11080-002
Vancouver - Cardero St.
591 Cardero St.
Vancouver, BC V6G 3L2 Canada
778-327-5085
MICR: 81950-002
James Darke, Manager
Vancouver - Dunbar St.
5659 Dunbar St.
Vancouver, BC V6N 1W5 Canada
604-668-3713
MICR: 00430-002
Vancouver - Fraser St.
6498 Fraser St.
Vancouver, BC V5W 3A5 Canada
604-668-3677
MICR: 50070-002
Vancouver - Georgia St. West - CBC & Main Branch
650 West Georgia St.
Vancouver, BC V6B 4P6 Canada
604-668-2094
MICR: 01420-002
Vancouver - Granville St.
2804 Granville St.
Vancouver, BC V6H 3J2 Canada
604-668-3771
MICR: 10470-002
Vancouver - Granville St.
8405 Granville St.
Vancouver, BC V6P 4Z9 Canada
604-668-3710
MICR: 70490-002
Vancouver - Keefer St.
#101, 268 Keefer St.
Vancouver, BC V6A 1X5 Canada
604-668-2163
MICR: 20040-002
Vancouver - Kingsway
2008 Kingsway
Vancouver, BC V5N 2T3 Canada
604-668-3785
MICR: 10520-002
Vancouver - Lonsdale Ave.
1357 Lonsdale Ave.
North Vancouver, BC V7M 2H7 Canada
604-981-7500
MICR: 40030-002
Vancouver - Lynn Valley Rd.
1246 Lynn Valley Rd.
North Vancouver, BC V7J 2A3 Canada
604-981-7550
MICR: 91280-002
Vancouver - Marine Dr.
1500 Marine Dr.
Vancouver, BC V7P 1T7 Canada
604-981-7570
MICR: 70540-002
Vancouver - Marine Dr.
1586 Marine Dr.
West Vancouver, BC V7V 1H8 Canada
604-981-7530
MICR: 60590-002
Vancouver - Park Royal South
Park Royal Shopping Centre
955 Park Royal South
West Vancouver, BC V7T 1A1 Canada
604-903-7400
MICR: 02550-002
Vancouver - Robson St.
1205 Robson St.
Vancouver, BC V6E 1C2 Canada
604-668-2190
MICR: 40550-002
Vanier
211 Montreal Rd.
Vanier, ON K1L 6C8 Canada
613-741-6540
MICR: 60186-002
Vankleek Hill
55 Main St.
Vankleek Hill, ON K0B 1R0 Canada
613-678-3224
MICR: 30346-002
Vaughan - Hwy. 27
8565 Hwy. 27
Vaughan, ON L4L 1A7 Canada
905-264-2300
MICR: 42952-002
Vaughan - Major MacKenzie Dr.
2810 Major MacKenzie Dr.
Vaughan, ON L6A 1R8 Canada
905-832-2109
MICR: 24562-002
Vernon - 27th
Village Green
4790 - 27th St.
Vernon, BC V1T 4Y6 Canada
250-260-5529
MICR: 61630-002
Vernon - 30th
3213 - 30th Ave.
Vernon, BC V1T 6M6 Canada
250-260-5500
MICR: 40600-002
Victoria - Aldersmith Pl.
Nelson Square
100 Aldersmith Pl.
Victoria, BC V9A 7M8 Canada
250-953-5470
MICR: 02410-002

The Bank of Nova Scotia(BNS)/ La Banque de Nouvelle-Écosse (continued)

Victoria - Cordova Bay Rd.
5144 Cordova Bay Rd.
Victoria, BC V8Y 2K5 Canada
250-658-6900
MICR: 82420-002

Victoria - Douglas St.
2669 Douglas St.
Victoria, BC V8W 2W4 Canada
250-953-2500
MICR: 90050-002

Victoria - Hillside Ave.
Hillside Shopping Centre
#76, 1644 Hillside Ave.
Victoria, BC V8T 2C5 Canada
250-953-5560
MICR: 40840-002

Victoria - Oak Bay Ave.
2212 Oak Bay Ave.
Victoria, BC V8R 1G3 Canada
250-953-8100
MICR: 20610-002

Victoria - Shelbourne St.
3609 Shelbourne St.
Victoria, BC V8P 4H1 Canada
250-953-8025
MICR: 00620-002

Victoria - Sooke Rd.
Hatley Park Shopping Centre
2230 Sooke Rd.
Victoria, BC V9B 1X1 Canada
250-391-3500
MICR: 21410-002

Victoria - Yates St. - CBC & Main Branch
702 Yates St.
Victoria, BC V8W 2T2 Canada
250-953-5400
MICR: 80010-002

Virden
190 Nelson St. West
Virden, MB R0M 2C0 Canada
204-748-2251
MICR: 10157-002

Wallaceburg
541 James St.
Wallaceburg, ON N8A 2P1 Canada
519-627-2268
MICR: 75002-002

Wasaga Beach
#1, 1263 Mosley St.
Wasaga Beach, ON L9Z 2Y7 Canada
705-429-0977
MICR: 34256-002

Waterloo - Erb St. West
Beechwood Centre
450 Erb St. West
Waterloo, ON N2J 1H4 Canada
519-883-5200
MICR: 64832-002

Waterloo - King St. North
569 King St. North
Waterloo, ON N2L 5Z7 Canada
519-884-2430
MICR: 07252-002

Waterloo - King St. South
Waterloo Square
75 King St. South
Waterloo, ON N2J 1P2 Canada
519-886-2500
MICR: 81802-002

Welland - East Main
38 East Main St.
Welland, ON L3B 3W3 Canada
905-734-7497
MICR: 41822-002

Welland - Lincoln St.
Lincoln Centre
354 Lincoln St.
Welland, ON L3B 4N4 Canada
905-732-4415
MICR: 42002-002

Welland - Niagara
440 Niagara St.
Welland, ON L3C 1L6 Canada
905-735-8750
MICR: 57372-002

Wellington
288 Main St.
Wellington, ON K0K 3L0 Canada
613-399-1375
MICR: 21832-002

Wesleyville
PO Box 10
Wesleyville, NL A0G 4R0 Canada
709-536-2500
MICR: 90753-002

Westbank
Westbank Towne Ctr.
#29, 2475 Dobbin Rd.
Westbank, BC V4T 2E9 Canada
250-768-6300
MICR: 91660-002

Westville
Main St.
Westville, NS B0K 2A0 Canada
902-396-4175
MICR: 20503-002

Weyburn
110 Government Rd.
Weyburn, SK S4H 0P1 Canada
306-842-6538
MICR: 50658-002

Whistler
#212, 2059 Lake Placid Rd.
Whistler, BC V0N 1B2 Canada
604-966-3230
MICR: 02790-002

Whitbourne
PO Box 99
Whitbourne, NL A0B 3K0 Canada
709-759-2720
MICR: 41483-002

Whitby - St. West
309 Dundas St. West
Whitby, ON L1N 2M6 Canada
905-668-9324
MICR: 14936-002

Whitby - Taunton Rd. West
160 Taunton Rd. West
Whitby, ON L1R 3H8 Canada
905-655-1441
MICR: 35212-002

Whitby - Winchester Rd. East
Brooklin Towne Centre
3 Winchester Rd. East
Whitby, ON L1M 2J7 Canada
905-655-2020
MICR: 37846-002

White Rock
15190 North Bluff Rd.
White Rock, BC V4B 3E5 Canada
604-541-3400
MICR: 01180-002

Whitehorse
212 Main St.
Whitehorse, YT Y1A 2B1 Canada
867-667-6231
MICR: 70920-002

Whitehorse
212 Main St.
Whitehorse, YT Y1A 2B1 Canada
867-667-6231
MICR: 70920-002

Wilberforce
PO Box 119
Wilberforce, ON K0L 3C0 Canada
705-448-2226
MICR: 93492-002

Williams Lake
24D South Second Ave.
Williams Lake, BC V2G 2V5 Canada
250-392-1700
MICR: 51110-002

Windsor
PO Box 428
Windsor, NS B0N 2T0 Canada
902-798-5742
MICR: 00513-002

Windsor - Dougall
3889 Dougall Ave.
Windsor, ON N9G 1X3 Canada
519-969-0251
MICR: 43612-002

Windsor - Huron Church
Ambassador Plaza
1570 Huron Church Rd.
Windsor, ON N9C 2L1 Canada
519-973-5380
MICR: 91892-002

Windsor - Ottawa
1357 Ottawa St.
Windsor, ON N8X 2E9 Canada
519-973-5355
MICR: 51862-002

Windsor - Ouellette Ave. - CBC
388 Ouellette Ave.
Windsor, ON N9A 6P1 Canada
519-973-5300
MICR: 71852-002

Windsor - Tecumseh
3745 Tecumseh Rd. East
Windsor, ON N8W 1H8 Canada
519-974-4500
MICR: 56382-002

Windsor - Tecumseh
East Park Ctr.
7041 Tecumseh Rd. East
Windsor, ON N8T 1E8 Canada
519-974-4530
MICR: 57802-002

Windsor - Wyandotte
Riverside Shopping Plaza
8400 Wyandotte St. East
Windsor, ON N8S 1T6 Canada
519-974-4570
MICR: 63362-002

Winkler
Southland Mall
Hwy. 32 & Hwy. 14
Winkler, MB R6W 2S2 Canada
204-325-9543
MICR: 00737-002

Winnipeg - Broadway
363 Broadway
Winnipeg, MB R3C 3N9 Canada
204-985-3002
MICR: 50377-002

Winnipeg - Corydon Ave.
623 Corydon Ave.
Winnipeg, MB R3M 0W3 Canada
204-985-3660
MICR: 30247-002

Winnipeg - Dakota St.
#14, 1500 Dakota St.
Winnipeg, MB R2N 3Y7 Canada
204-985-5125
MICR: 70607-002

Winnipeg - Dublin Ave.
Border Place
1648 Dublin Ave.
Winnipeg, MB R3H 0X5 Canada
204-985-3600
MICR: 40527-002

Winnipeg - Elizabeth Rd.
Windsor Park Shopping Ctr.
664 Elizabeth Rd.
Winnipeg, MB R2J 1A4 Canada
204-985-3650
MICR: 40147-002

Winnipeg - Killarney Ave.
#1, 9 Killarney Ave.
Winnipeg, MB R3T 3B1 Canada
204-985-5196
MICR: 20487-002

Winnipeg - Leila Ave.
Garden City Square
#2, 843 Leila Ave.
Winnipeg, MB R2V 3J7 Canada
204-985-3250
MICR: 60517-002

Winnipeg - Main St.
1425 Main St.
Winnipeg, MB R2W 3V3 Canada
204-985-3730
MICR: 90167-002

Winnipeg - Marion St.

235 Marion St.
Winnipeg, MB R2H 0T5 Canada
204-985-3750
MICR: 60137-002
Winnipeg - Nairn Ave.
1150 Nairn Ave.
Winnipeg, MB R2L 0Y5 Canada
204-985-3700
MICR: 40287-002
Winnipeg - Pembina Hwy.
1220 Pembina Hwy.
Winnipeg, MB R3T 2A8 Canada
204-985-3630
MICR: 00117-002
Winnipeg - Portage Ave.
3247 Portage Ave.
Winnipeg, MB R3K 0W5 Canada
204-985-3690
MICR: 80127-002
Winnipeg - Portage Ave.
Polo Park Shopping Ctr.
1485 Portage Ave.
Winnipeg, MB R3G 0W4 Canada
204-985-5510
MICR: 71407-002
Winnipeg - Portage Ave. - CBC & Main Branch
200 Portage Ave.
Winnipeg, MB R3C 2R7 Canada
204-985-3011
MICR: 30007-002
Winnipeg - Roblin Blvd.
4910 Roblin Blvd.
Winnipeg, MB R3R 0G7 Canada
204-985-3776
MICR: 90787-002
Winnipeg - Rothesay St.
Springfield Heights Shopping Ctr.
1169 Rothesay St.
Winnipeg, MB R2G 1T6 Canada
204-985-3670
MICR: 30387-002
Winnipeg - St. Mary's Rd.
Dakota Village Shopping Ctr.
1091 St. Mary's Rd.
Winnipeg, MB R2M 3T2 Canada
204-985-3117
MICR: 80267-002
Winnipeg - Waterloo St.
528 Waterloo St.
Winnipeg, MB R3N 0T1 Canada
204-985-3740
MICR: 90357-002
Woodbridge - Weston
#3, 7600 Weston Rd.
Woodbridge, ON L4L 8B7 Canada
905-850-1805
MICR: 47852-002
Woodstock
570 Main St.
Woodstock, NB E7M 2C3 Canada
506-328-3341
MICR: 00364-002
Woodstock - Dundas
485 Dundas St.
Woodstock, ON N4S 1C3 Canada
519-537-3473
MICR: 75796-002
Woodstock - Springbank
385 Springbank Ave. North
Woodstock, ON N4T 1R3 Canada
519-537-2900
MICR: 64212-002
Wynyard
229 Bosworth St.
Wynyard, SK S0A 4T0 Canada
306-554-2582
MICR: 10298-002
Yarmouth
389 Main St.
Yarmouth, NS B5A 4B1 Canada
902-742-7116
MICR: 40063-002
Yellowknife
#27, 5102 - 50th Ave.
Yellowknife, NT X1A 3S8 Canada
867-669-6000
MICR: 10629-002
Yorkton
#200, 277 Broadway St. East
Yorkton, SK S3N 3G7 Canada
306-783-8595
MICR: 90308-002

Bank West

c/o Western Financial Group
#103, 309 - 1st St. West
High River, AB T1V 1M5
403-652-2663
Fax: 403-652-2661
888-440-2265
info@bankwest.ca
www.bankwest.ca
Ownership: Owned by Western Financial Group
Year Founded: 2002
Number of Employees: 15
Assets: $50-100 million Year End: 20041231
Revenues: Under $1 million Year End: 20041231
Executives:
Doug Foster, President/CEO
Richard Brodeur, Sr. Vice-President, Banking & Credit
Ron Munaweera, Sr. Vice-President/CFO, Corporate Secretary
Directors:
Scott Tannas, Chair
Doug Foster
Lawrence Hanson
Harry Lively
Sharon Ranson
James Robb
Catherine A. Rogers
Craig Rothwell

BCP Bank Canada

1106 Dundas St. West
Toronto, ON M6J 1X2
416-588-8597
Fax: 416-588-8564
Former Name: SottoBank Canada; Sottomayor Bank Canada
Ownership: Part of BMO Financial Group.
Year Founded: 1990
Profile: BCP Bank Canada was purchased by BMO Financial Group in December 2006. Clients now have access to existing services, as well as the full range of BMO products. The bank provides both personal banking & business banking services. It is committed to the Portuguese-Canadian community it serves.

Executives:
Heather Grand, President/CEO
Maria de Lurdes, Vice-President
Branches:
Brampton
135 Main St. North
Brampton, ON L6X 1M9 Canada
905-457-9090
Fax: 905-457-9106
Hamilton
281 Barton St. East
Hamilton, ON L8L 2X4 Canada
905-521-5635
Fax: 905-521-8977
Mississauga
3643 Cawthra Rd. SE
Mississauga, ON L5A 2Y4 Canada
905-276-0926
Fax: 905-276-9844
Toronto - Dufferin St.
Dufferin Mall
#607, 900 Dufferin St.
Toronto, ON M6H 4B1 Canada
416-537-3312
Fax: 416-537-7588
Toronto - Dundas St. West - Main
1106 Dundas St. West
Toronto, ON M6J 1X2 Canada
416-588-8597
Fax: 416-588-8564
Toronto - Dupont St.
1502 Dupont St.
Toronto, ON M6P 3S1 Canada
416-533-7686
Fax: 416-533-1444
Toronto - Rogers Rd.
605 Rogers Rd.
Toronto, ON M6M 1B9 Canada
416-658-9292
Fax: 416-658-6587
Toronto - University Ave.
438 University Ave.
Toronto, ON M5G 2K8 Canada
416-596-8814
Fax: 416-596-8719

BMO Bank of Montréal(BMO)/ Banque de Montréal

119, rue St-Jacques ouest
Montréal, QC H2Y 1L6
514-877-7373
Fax: 514-877-7399
800-363-9992
feedback@bmo.com
www.bmo.com
Ownership: Public
Year Founded: 1817
Number of Employees: 34,000
Assets: $100 billion +
Revenues: $1-10 billion
Stock Symbol: BMO
Profile: BMO Bank of Montreal is the Canadian retail banking arm of BMO Financial Group. Canada's first bank, offers a broad range of financial products. Services include deposit accounts, loans, credit cards, insurance products & personal investment products. These services are offered across Canada & in the United States directly, & through BMO Nesbitt Burns, one of Canada's largest full-service investment firms, & Chicago-based subsidiary, Harris Bank, a major US mid-west financial institution. In Canada, there are over 900 branches and almost 2,000 automated banking machines.

Executives:
F. Anthony Comper, President/CEO
Lloyd F. Darlington, President/CEO, Technology & Solutions, Head, E-Business
Gilles G. Ouellette, President/CEO, Private Client Group
Robert W. Pearce, President/CEO, Personal & Commercial Client Group
William A. Downe, Deputy Chair
Ronald G. Rogers, Deputy Chair, Enterprise Risk & Portfolio Management
Karen E. Maidment, CFO, Chief Administrative Officer
Maurice A.D. Hudon, Sr. Exec. Vice-President, Group Development
Rose M. Patten, Sr. Exec. Vice-President, Human Resources, Head, Office of Strategic Management
Sherry S. Cooper, Exec. Vice-President, Global Economic Strategist
Joan T. Dea, Exec. Vice-President & Head, Strategic Management
Tom Flynn, Exec. Vice-President, Finance, Treasurer
Sandra L. Hanington, Exec. Vice-President, Customer Strategies & Marketing
Neil R. Macmillan, Exec. Vice-President, Investment Banking Group, Sr. Risk Officer
Robert L. McGlashan, Exec. Vice-President & Chief Risk Officer, Enterprise Risk & Portfolio Management
Dina Palozzi, Exec. Vice-President, Client Relations
Graham T. Parsons, Exec. Vice-President, Global Private Banking
Pamela J. Robertson, Exec. Vice-President, Personal & Commercial Delivery
Richard Egelton, Sr. Vice-President, Chief Economist
Ellen M. Costello, Vice-Chair & Head, Securitization & Credit Investment Management
Frederick J. Mifflin, Vice-Chair, Investment & Corporate Banking, Deputy Head
Michael R. P. Rayfield, Vice-Chair, Investment & Corporate Banking
Eric C. Tripp, Head, Equity Division
Barry K. Gilmour, Deputy Group Head/COO, Technology & Solutions
Tom V. Milroy, Global Head, Investment & Corporate Banking
Directors:
David A. Galloway, Chair
Robert M. Astley
Stephen E. Bachand
David R. Beatty, OBE
Robert Chevrier, CA, FCA
F. Anthony Comper
Martha Cook Piper
George A. Cope

BMO Bank of Montréal(BMO)/ Banque de Montréal (continued)

Ronald H. Farmer
Harold Kvisle
Eva Lee Kwok
Bruce H. Mitchell
Philip S. Orsino, FCA
J. Robert S. Prichard, O.C., O.Ont.
Jeremy H. Reitman
Guylaine Saucier, CM, FCA
Nancy C. Southern

Honourary Directors:
Charles F. Baird
Ralph M. Barford
Matthew W. Barrett, O.C.
Peter J.G. Bentley, O.C., L.L.D.
Claire P. Bertrand
Frederick S. Burbridge, O.C.
Pierre Côté, CM
C.William Daniel, O.C., LL.D.
Nathanael V. Davis
Graham R. Dawson
Louis A. Desrochers, CM, CR
A. John Ellis, O.C., L.L.D., O.R.S.
John F. Fraser, O.C., L.L.D.
Thomas M. Galt
J. Peter Gordon, O.C.
Richard M. Ivey, CC, Q.C.
Betty Kennedy, O.C., LLD
Ronald N. Mannix
Robert H. McKercher, Q.C.
Eric H. Molson
William D. Mulholland, LL.D.
Jerry E.A. Nickerson
Lucien G. Rolland, O.C.
Mary Alice Stuart, CM, O.Ont. LL.D.
Lorne C. Webster, CM

Affiliated Companies:
BCP Bank Canada
BMO InvestorLine Inc.
BMO Life Insurance Company
BMO Mutual Funds
BMO Nesbitt Burns Equity Partners Inc.
BMO Nesbitt Burns Inc.
BMO Trust Company
Bank of Montreal Capital Corporation/BMOCC
Bank of Montreal Mortgage Corporation
Jones Heward Investment Counsel Inc.

Branches:

100 Mile House
PO Box 10
#1220, 575 Hwy. 97 South
100 Mile House, BC V0K 2E0 Canada
250-395-2477
Fax: 250-395-4965
MICR: 0827-001

Abbotsford - South Fraser Way
32112 South Fraser Way
Abbotsford, BC V2T 1W4 Canada
604-853-8151
Fax: 604-853-7018
MICR: 0749-001

Abbotsford - South Fraser Way
33757 South Fraser Way
Abbotsford, BC V2S 2C3 Canada
604-854-8762
Fax: 604-854-3238
MICR: 0709-001

Acme
PO Box 206
102 Main St.
Acme, AB T0M 0A0 Canada
403-546-3953
Fax: 403-546-2606
MICR: 2503-001

Acton
21 Mill St. East
Acton, ON L7J 1G8 Canada
519-853-1100
Fax: 519-853-4134
MICR: 2301-001

Ajax - Harwood Ave. South - Main Office
154 Harwood Ave. South
Ajax, ON L1S 2H6 Canada
905-683-0140
Fax: 905-683-9247
MICR: 0300-001

Ajax - Westney Rd. North
Ajax Market Place
475 Westney Rd. North
Ajax, ON L1T 3H4 Canada
905-428-6881
Fax: 905-428-2477
MICR: 3969-001

Akwesasne
Peace Tree Trade Centre
167 Akwesasne International Rd.
Akwesasne, ON K6H 5R7 Canada
613-938-5634
Fax: 613-938-5638
MICR: 3862-001

Aldergrove
Safeway
27566 Fraser Hwy.
Aldergrove, BC V4W 3N5 Canada
604-607-7560
Fax: 604-607-7575
MICR: 3138-001

Alexandria
53 Main St.
Alexandria, ON K0C 1A0 Canada
613-525-2258
Fax: 613-525-4886
MICR: 2932-001

Alliston
2 Victoria St. West
Alliston, ON L9R 1S8 Canada
705-435-6208
Fax: 705-435-7978
MICR: 0301-001

Alma
530, rue Sacré-Coeur ouest
Alma, QC G8B 1L9 Canada
418-668-0186
Fax: 418-668-8891
MICR: 0190-001

Almonte
62 Mill St.
Almonte, ON K0A 1A0 Canada
613-256-3456
Fax: 613-256-5504
MICR: 0302-001

Alvinston
3238 River St.
Alvinston, ON N0N 1A0 Canada
519-898-2131
Fax: 519-898-2093
MICR: 2306-001

Amherstburg
243 Dalhousie St.
Amherstburg, ON N9V 1W8 Canada
519-736-2123
Fax: 519-736-0116
MICR: 0306-001

Amherstview
6 Speers Blvd.
Amherstview, ON K7N 1Z6 Canada
613-389-2934
Fax: 613-389-3855
MICR: 2982-001

Athens
20 Main St.
Athens, ON K0E 1B0 Canada
613-924-2602
Fax: 613-924-1143
MICR: 2309-001

Atlin
PO Box 100
Third St.
Atlin, BC V0W 1A0 Canada
250-651-7595
MICR: SA01-001

Aurora
15252 Yonge St.
Aurora, ON L4G 1N4 Canada
905-727-4228
Fax: 905-727-0176
MICR: 0303-001

Aylmer
3 Talbot St. East
Aylmer, ON N5H 1H3 Canada
519-773-9295
Fax: 519-765-1822
MICR: 2310-001

Baie-Comeau
321, boul Lasalle
Baie-Comeau, QC G4Z 2L5 Canada
418-296-2228
Fax: 418-296-8648
MICR: 0109-001

Banff
PO Box 1290
107 Banff Ave.
Banff, AB T1L 1B3 Canada
403-762-2275
Fax: 403-762-5340
MICR: 2510-001

Barrie - Bayfield St.
Georgian Mall
483 Bayfield St.
Barrie, ON L4M 4Z9 Canada
705-734-7930
Fax: 705-734-7954
MICR: 2305-001

Barrie - Duckworth St.
353 Duckworth St.
Barrie, ON L4M 5E2 Canada
705-734-7921
Fax: 705-734-7955
MICR: 2934-001

Barrie - Fred Grant St. - Main Office
6 Fred Grant St.
Barrie, ON L4M 3G6 Canada
705-734-7900
Fax: 705-734-7949
MICR: 2313-001

Barrie - Yonge St.
Allandale Marketplace
#1, 279 Yonge St.
Barrie, ON L4N 7T9 Canada
705-734-7960
Fax: 705-734-7967
MICR: 3872-001

Barrys Bay
19544 Opeongo Line
Barrys Bay, ON K0J 1B0 Canada
613-756-2693
Fax: 613-756-3798
MICR: 2311-001

Bathurst
201 Main St.
Bathurst, NB E2A 1A9 Canada
506-546-3358
Fax: 506-548-2356
MICR: 0105-001

Bay Roberts
Bay Roberts Mall
PO Box 520
Bay Roberts, NL A0A 1G0 Canada
709-786-2182
Fax: 709-786-7554
MICR: 1024-001

Beauval
PO Box 19
Beauval, SK S0M 0G0 Canada
306-288-2144
Fax: 306-288-2145
MICR: 3365-001

Bedford - Bedford Hwy.
Sobeys
961 Bedford Hwy.
Bedford, NS B4A 1A9 Canada
902-421-3331
Fax: 902-421-3921
MICR: 3664-001

Bedford - Dartmouth Rd.
21 Dartmouth Rd.
Bedford, NS B4A 3X7 Canada
902-421-3400
Fax: 902-421-3459
MICR: 3985-001

Belleville - Bell Blvd.
192 Bell Blvd.
Belleville, ON K8P 5L2 Canada
613-967-4315
Fax: 613-968-3118

MICR: 2917-001
Belleville - Front St. - Main Office
201 Front St.
Belleville, ON K8N 5A4 Canada
613-967-4300
Fax: 613-962-2422
MICR: 0043-001
Betsiamites
44, ch Messek
Betsiamites, QC G0H 1B0 Canada
418-567-9543
Fax: 418-567-9540
MICR: 3546-001
Blainville
280, de la Seigneurie ouest
Blainville, QC J7C 5A1 Canada
450-437-2030
Fax: 450-437-3319
MICR: 3778-001
Blenheim
39 Talbot St. West
Blenheim, ON N0P 1A0 Canada
519-676-5454
Fax: 519-676-8112
MICR: 0304-001
Bobcaygeon
75 Bolton St.
Bobcaygeon, ON K0M 1A0 Canada
705-738-2354
Fax: 705-738-5832
MICR: 0305-001
Boisbriand - Entreprises
Boisbriand IGA Extra
25, boul des Entreprises
Boisbriand, QC J7G 3K6 Canada
450-430-5490
Fax: 450-430-3192
MICR: 3201-001
Boisbriand - Grande-Cote
Les Terrasses Boisbriand
384, ch Grande-Cote
Boisbriand, QC J7G 1B1 Canada
450-437-7661
Fax: 450-437-0746
MICR: 2760-001
Bolton
Bolton Plaza
15 Allan Dr.
Bolton, ON L7E 2B5 Canada
905-857-0502
Fax: 905-857-8139
MICR: 2984-001
Bothwell
181 Main St.
Bothwell, ON N0P 1C0 Canada
519-695-2166
Fax: 519-695-3722
MICR: 2314-001
Botwood
PO Box 130
52 Water St.
Botwood, NL A0H 1E0 Canada
709-257-2957
Fax: 709-257-2628
MICR: 1001-001
Boucherville
Les Promenades Montarville
1001, boul de Montarville
Boucherville, QC J4B 6P5 Canada
450-641-1010
Fax: 450-641-9275
MICR: 2759-001
Bowmanville
PO Box 220
2 King St. West
Bowmanville, ON L1C 3K9 Canada
905-623-4411
Fax: 905-623-6175
MICR: 0307-001
Bracebridge
Bracebridge Plaza II
500 Hwy. 118 West
Bracebridge, ON P1L 1T4 Canada
705-645-5232
Fax: 705-645-2758
MICR: 0462-001
Bradford
North Bradford Centre
305 Barrie St.
Bradford, ON L3Z 2B1 Canada
905-775-9341
Fax: 905-775-8464
MICR: 3994-001
Brampton - Bramalea Rd. - Bramalea Main
69 Bramalea Rd.
Brampton, ON L6T 2W9 Canada
905-791-1685
Fax: 905-791-0239
MICR: 0470-001
Brampton - Brisdale Dr.
20 Brisdale Dr.
Brampton, ON L7A 2G8 Canada
905-495-4340
Fax: 905-495-4338
MICR: 3629-001
Brampton - Chinguacousy Rd.
Sobeys
8975 Chinguacousy Rd.
Brampton, ON L6V 1A1 Canada
905-796-2677
Fax: 905-796-5822
MICR: 3223-001
Brampton - Great Lakes Dr.
Trinity Commons A&P
20 Great Lakes Dr.
Brampton, ON L6R 2K7 Canada
905-791-1241
Fax: 905-791-5644
MICR: 3105-001
Brampton - Main St. South
Shopper's World
499 Main St. South
Brampton, ON L6Y 1N7 Canada
905-459-9330
Fax: 905-459-6602
MICR: 0489-001
Brampton - McLaughlin Rd.
10088 McLaughlin Rd.
Brampton, ON L7A 2X6 Canada
905-846-0215
Fax: 905-846-7988
MICR: 3625-001
Brampton - Peel Centre Dr.
Bramalea City Centre
25 Peel Centre Dr.
Brampton, ON L6T 3R5 Canada
905-793-4870
Fax: 905-793-4033
MICR: 0493-001
Brampton - Queen St. East - Main Office
56 Queen St. East
Brampton, ON L6V 4M8 Canada
905-451-5150
Fax: 905-451-5544
MICR: 2315-001
Brampton - Sandalwood Pkwy.
Heart Lake Town Centre
180 Sandalwood Pkwy.
Brampton, ON L6Z 1Y4 Canada
905-846-3834
Fax: 905-846-2732
MICR: 2679-001
Brampton - Vodden St. East
Centennial Mall
227 Vodden St. East
Brampton, ON L6V 1N2 Canada
905-457-1943
Fax: 905-457-9366
MICR: 2494-001
Brandon
1000 Rosser Ave.
Brandon, MB R7A 0L6 Canada
204-726-2800
Fax: 204-726-2813
MICR: 0028-001
Brantford - Colborne St
585 Colborne St., #A
Brantford, ON N3S 3M7 Canada
519-753-7329
Fax: 519-751-0524
MICR: 2333-001
Brantford - Market St. - Main Office
57 Market St.
Brantford, ON N3T 2Z6 Canada
519-756-2700
Fax: 519-756-2895
MICR: 0015-001
Brantford - St. Paul Ave.
421 St. Paul Ave.
Brantford, ON N3R 4N8 Canada
519-756-5269
Fax: 519-751-0523
MICR: 2317-001
Bridgewater
493 King St.
Bridgewater, NS B4V 1B3 Canada
902-543-2415
Fax: 902-543-1437
MICR: 0106-001
Brockville
1 Wall St.
Brockville, ON K6V 7K4 Canada
613-342-4418
Fax: 613-342-1996
MICR: 0046-001
Brooks
PO Box 1990
137 - 2nd St. West
Brooks, AB T1R 1C7 Canada
403-362-3375
Fax: 403-362-3613
MICR: 0617-001
Brossard - Lapiniere
Lapiniere IGA Extra
3260, boul Lapiniere
Brossard, QC J4Z 3L8 Canada
450-445-4719
Fax: 450-445-7472
MICR: 3224-001
Brossard - Lapiniere
2140, boul Lapiniere
Brossard, QC J4W 1L8 Canada
450-676-7791
Fax: 450-676-8733
MICR: 2199-001
Buchans
Main St.
Buchans, NL A0H 1G0 Canada
MICR: 1029-001
Burlington - Appleby Line
Millcroft Ultra Food & Drug
2010 Appleby Line
Burlington, ON L7L 1C8 Canada
905-335-5100
Fax: 903-335-5232
MICR: 3170-001
Burlington - Brant St. - Main Office
519 Brant St.
Burlington, ON L7R 2G6 Canada
905-637-8224
Fax: 905-333-0656
MICR: 2316-001
Burlington - Fairview St.
Woodview Place Ultra Mart
3365 Fairview St.
Burlington, ON L7N 3N9 Canada
905-634-2900
Fax: 905-634-2204
MICR: 3606-001
Burlington - Guelph Line
1505 Guelph Line
Burlington, ON L7P 3B6 Canada
905-336-2484
Fax: 905-336-1514
MICR: 2968-001
Burlington - Guelph Line
Burlington Mall
777 Guelph Line
Burlington, ON L7R 3N2 Canada
905-632-7000
Fax: 905-632-0995
MICR: 0478-001
Burlington - New St.

BMO Bank of Montréal(BMO)/ Banque de Montréal (continued)

Appleby Mall
5111 New St.
Burlington, ON L7L 1V2 Canada
905-639-0404
Fax: 905-639-6736
MICR: 2488-001

Burlington - Upper Middle Rd.
Walker Place
3505 Upper Middle Rd.
Burlington, ON L7M 4C6 Canada
905-336-3375
Fax: 905-336-1328
MICR: 3871-001

Burnaby - Austin Ave.
Lougheed Town Centre
#167A, 9855 Austin Ave.
Burnaby, BC V3J 1N4 Canada
604-665-3745
Fax: 604-665-3759
MICR: 2701-001

Burnaby - Austin Rd.
Lougheed Mall Safeway
9855 Austin Rd.
Burnaby, BC V1J 1N4 Canada
604-665-7081
Fax: 604-665-7088
MICR: 2643-001

Burnaby - East Hastings St.
4454 East Hastings St.
Burnaby, BC V5C 2K2 Canada
604-665-2520
Fax: 604-665-7555
MICR: 0727-001

Burnaby - Kingsway
4705 Kingsway
Burnaby, BC V5H 2C4 Canada
604-665-6639
Fax: 604-665-7586
MICR: 0728-001

Burnaby - Kingsway
Metrotown Centre
#268, 4820 Kingsway
Burnaby, BC V5H 4P1 Canada
604-665-3779
Fax: 604-665-3702
MICR: 3933-001

Burnaby - Lougheed Hwy.
Brentwood Town Centre
#72, 4567 Lougheed Hwy.
Burnaby, BC V5C 4A1 Canada
604-665-6660
Fax: 604-665-7193
MICR: 0752-001

Caledonia
322 Argyle St. South
Caledonia, ON N3W 1K8 Canada
905-765-4422
Fax: 905-765-1442
MICR: 2981-001

Calgary - Elbow Dr. SW - Southwood Corners
#345, 10233 Elbow Dr. SW
Calgary, AB T2W 1E8 Canada
403-234-3844
Fax: 403-503-7565
MICR: 0595-001

Calgary - 10th St. NW
Hillhurst Safeway
410 - 10th St. NW
Calgary, AB T2N 1V9 Canada
403-503-5300
Fax: 403-503-5306
MICR: 3187-001

Calgary - 11th Ave. SW
Downtown Safeway
813 - 11th Ave. SW
Calgary, AB T2R 0E6 Canada
403-503-7715
Fax: 403-503-7722
MICR: 3181-001

Calgary - 130th Ave. SE - South Trail Crossing
#210, 4307 - 130th Ave. SE
Calgary, AB T2Z 3V8 Canada
403-503-5555
Fax: 403-503-5577
MICR: 3301-001

Calgary - 14th Ave. NW
Northhill Safeway
#1846, 1632 - 14th Ave. NW
Calgary, AB T2N 1M7 Canada
403-503-5485
Fax: 403-503-5487
MICR: 3103-001

Calgary - 16th Ave. NW
Montgomery Safeway
5048 - 16th Ave. NW
Calgary, AB T3B 0N3 Canada
403-503-6200
Fax: 403-503-6206
MICR: 3258-001

Calgary - 17th Ave. SW
727 - 17th Ave. SW
Calgary, AB T2S 0B6 Canada
403-234-1823
Fax: 403-503-7676
MICR: 0512-001

Calgary - 1st St. SE
Telus Tower
411 - 1st St. SE
Calgary, AB T2G 4Y5 Canada
403-234-1800
Fax: 403-503-7169
MICR: 2512-001

Calgary - 32nd St. NE
Sunridge Spectrum Centre
#150, 2555 - 32nd St. NE
Calgary, AB T1Y 7J6 Canada
403-234-1715
Fax: 403-503-7291
MICR: 0676-001

Calgary - 34 Ave. SW
Garrison Woods Safeway
2425 - 34 Ave. SW
Calgary, AB T2T 6E3 Canada
403-503-6222
Fax: 403-503-6228
MICR: 3102-001

Calgary - 37th St. SW
Westbrook Shopping Centre
1200 - 37th St. SW
Calgary, AB T3C 1S2 Canada
403-234-2800
Fax: 403-503-7113
MICR: 2514-001

Calgary - 4th St. SW - Elbow Park
2302 - 4th St. SW
Calgary, AB T2S 1X2 Canada
403-234-1840
Fax: 403-503-7619
MICR: 0511-001

Calgary - 5th Ave. SW
Fifth Avenue Place
222 - 5th Ave. SW
Calgary, AB T2P 0L1 Canada
403-234-1810
Fax: 403-503-7150
MICR: 0677-001

Calgary - 7th Ave. SW - Main Office
340 - 7th Ave. SW
Calgary, AB T2P 0X4 Canada
403-234-3620
Fax: 403-503-7447
MICR: 0010-001

Calgary - 8th Ave. SW
Canadian Oxy Bldg.
635 - 8th Ave. SW
Calgary, AB T2P 3M3 Canada
403-234-1804
Fax: 403-503-7194
MICR: 2515-001

Calgary - 90th Ave. SW - Glenmore Landing
#D161, 1600 - 90th Ave. SW
Calgary, AB T2V 5A8 Canada
403-234-1879
Fax: 403-503-7050
MICR: 2499-001

Calgary - 9th Ave. SW
Gulf Canada Square
#235, 401 - 9th Ave. SW
Calgary, AB T2P 3C5 Canada
403-234-1815
Fax: 403-503-7220
MICR: 2789-001

Calgary - Anderson Rd. SE
#70, 100 Anderson Rd. SE
Calgary, AB T2J 3V1 Canada
403-234-1889
Fax: 403-503-7652
MICR: 2566-001

Calgary - Castleridge Blvd. NE
Castleridge Safeway
#50, 55 Castleridge Blvd. NE
Calgary, AB T3J 3J8 Canada
403-503-5900
Fax: 403-503-5907
MICR: 0671-001

Calgary - Centre St. NE
Beacon Safeway
#20, 1818 Centre St. NE
Calgary, AB T2E 2S6 Canada
403-503-5530
Fax: 403-503-5532
MICR: 3166-001

Calgary - Centre St. North - Beddington Village
8282 Centre St. North
Calgary, AB T3K 2X4 Canada
403-234-2851
Fax: 403-503-7501
MICR: 2547-001

Calgary - Charleswood Dr. NW
Brentwood Village Mall
3517 Charleswood Dr. NW
Calgary, AB T2L 2C1 Canada
403-234-2831
Fax: 403-503-7334
MICR: 2509-001

Calgary - Country Hills Blvd. NW - Panorama Hills
#206, 177 Country Hills Blvd. NW
Calgary, AB T3K 5M6 Canada
403-567-8991
Fax: 403-567-8990
MICR: 2622-001

Calgary - Crowfoot Way NW
Crowfoot Centre
101 Crowfoot Way NW
Calgary, AB T3G 2R2 Canada
403-234-2898
Fax: 403-503-7269
MICR: 0646-001

Calgary - Macleod Trail SW
Chinook Plaza
#301, 6100 Macleod Trail SW
Calgary, AB T2H 0K5 Canada
403-234-1848
Fax: 403-503-7540
MICR: 0526-001

Calgary - Memorial Dr. NE
Marlborough Town Square
#1185, 3800 Memorial Dr. NE
Calgary, AB T2A 2K2 Canada
403-234-2857
Fax: 403-503-7071
MICR: 0590-001

Calgary - Richmond Rd. SW
London Place West
#1, 5249 Richmond Rd. SW
Calgary, AB T3E 7C4 Canada
403-234-1886
Fax: 403-503-7129
MICR: 2634-001

Calgary - Shaganappi Trail NW
Calgary Market Mall
3625 Shaganappi Trail NW
Calgary, AB T3A 0E2 Canada
403-234-2840
Fax: 403-503-7313
MICR: 2500-001

Calgary - Shawville Blvd. SE
225 Shawville Blvd. SE
Calgary, AB T2Y 3H9 Canada
403-234-1875
Fax: 403-503-7241
MICR: 2641-001

Calgary - Shawville Blvd. SW

Shawnessy Safeway
70 Shawville Blvd. SW
Calgary, AB T2Y 2Z3 Canada
403-503-5459
Fax: 403-503-5461
MICR: 3108-001

Calgary - Stewart Green Dr. SW
Westhills Town Centre Safeway
200 Stewart Green Dr. SW
Calgary, AB T3H 3C8 Canada
403-503-7700
Fax: 403-503-7707
MICR: 3257-001

Calmar
4902 - 50th Ave.
Calmar, AB T0C 0V0 Canada
780-985-3606
Fax: 780-985-2330
MICR: 2521-001

Cambridge - Dundas St
142 Dundas St.
Cambridge, ON N1R 5P1 Canada
519-623-0440
Fax: 519-622-7543
MICR: 2340-001

Cambridge - Hespeler Rd.
600 Hespeler Rd.
Cambridge, ON N1R 8H2 Canada
519-624-1200
Fax: 519-624-1061
MICR: 0469-001

Cambridge - King St. East
807 King St. East
Cambridge, ON N3H 3P1 Canada
519-653-6296
Fax: 519-650-2303
MICR: 2395-001

Cambridge - Main St. - Main Office
44 Main St.
Cambridge, ON N1R 1V4 Canada
519-621-2550
Fax: 519-621-8873
MICR: 3053-001

Cambridge - Queen St. West
23 Queen St. West
Cambridge, ON N3C 1G2 Canada
519-658-9379
Fax: 519-658-0107
MICR: 3051-001

Campbell River
996 Shoppers Row
Campbell River, BC V9W 2C5 Canada
250-287-7437
Fax: 250-287-8830
MICR: 0796-001

Campbellford
66 Bridge St. East
Campbellford, ON K0L 1L0 Canada
705-653-3440
Fax: 705-653-1178
MICR: 0310-001

Camrose - 50th Ave.
4906 - 50th Ave.
Camrose, AB T4V 0S3 Canada
780-672-3327
Fax: 780-672-2451
MICR: 2517-001

Canmore
701 - 8th St.
Canmore, AB T1W 2V2 Canada
403-678-5568
Fax: 403-678-4979
MICR: 2543-001

Canso
PO Box 130
28 Main St.
Canso, NS B0H 1H0 Canada
902-366-2654
Fax: 902-366-3223
MICR: 0111-001

Canton-de-Granby
Granby IGA Extra
585, rue St. Hubert
Canton-de-Granby, QC J2H 1Y5 Canada
450-375-4245
Fax: 450-375-1315
MICR: 2640-001

Cap-Pelé
2680 Acadie Rd.
Cap-Pelé, NB E4N 1E5 Canada
506-577-4301
Fax: 506-577-1180
MICR: 0647-001

Carberry
PO Box 10
10 Main St.
Carberry, MB R0K 0H0 Canada
204-834-6360
Fax: 204-834-6367
MICR: 2506-001

Carnduff
PO Box 39
116 Broadway St.
Carnduff, SK S0C 0S0 Canada
306-482-3658
Fax: 306-482-3633
MICR: 2654-001

Carstairs
PO Box 489
1602 - 10th Ave.
Carstairs, AB T0M 0N0 Canada
403-337-3323
Fax: 403-337-3224
MICR: 2519-001

Castlegar
1990 Columbia Ave.
Castlegar, BC V1N 2W7 Canada
250-365-6488
Fax: 250-365-2744
MICR: 0707-001

Chambly - Bourgogne
1376, rue Bourgogne
Chambly, QC J3L 1Y3 Canada
450-658-8783
Fax: 450-658-5400
MICR: 2100-001

Chambly - Frechette
Chambly IGA Extra In-Store
3500, boul Frechette
Chambly, QC J3L 6Z6 Canada
450-447-4515
Fax: 450-447-7141
MICR: 3491-001

Channel-Port-aux-Basques
PO Box 1300
33 Main St.
Channel-Port-aux-Basques, NL A0M 1C0 Canada
709-695-5600
Fax: 709-695-7867
MICR: 1036-001

Charlottetown - Grafton St. - Main Office
105 Grafton St.
Charlottetown, PE C1A 1K9 Canada
902-892-2437
Fax: 902-566-4753
MICR: 0037-001

Charlottetown - University Ave.
Charlottetown Mall
670 University Ave.
Charlottetown, PE C1E 1H6 Canada
902-894-7021
Fax: 902-628-1372
MICR: 2157-001

Chatham - King St. West - Main Office
131 King St. West
Chatham, ON N7M 1E2 Canada
519-352-3060
Fax: 519-354-7859
MICR: 0039-001

Chatham - Queen St.
Queen Street Shopping Centre
835 Queen St.
Chatham, ON N7M 2K5 Canada
519-354-8111
Fax: 519-354-0450
MICR: 2582-001

Chatham - Richmond St.
550 Richmond St.
Chatham, ON N7M 1R3 Canada
519-352-5380
Fax: 519-352-5098
MICR: 0320-001

Chatham - St. Clair St.
North Maple Mall
801 St. Clair St. Extension
Chatham, ON N7M 5J7 Canada
519-354-8581
Fax: 519-354-1277
MICR: 2320-001

Chatham - Water St.
1710 Water St.
Chatham, NB E1N 1B4 Canada
506-773-5894
Fax: 506-778-2872
MICR: 0112-001

Chatsworth
PO Box 240
246 Garafraxa St.
Chatsworth, ON N0H 1G0 Canada
519-794-2100
Fax: 519-794-2124
MICR: 2319-001

Chicoutimi
Place du Saguenay
1324, boul Talbot
Chicoutimi, QC G7H 4B8 Canada
418-690-9005
Fax: 418-690-9035
MICR: 0258-001

Chilliwack - Lukakuck Way
Safeway
#200, 45610 Luckakuck Way
Chilliwack, BC V2R 1A2 Canada
604-824-5091
Fax: 604-824-5090
MICR: 3203-001

Chilliwack - Yale Rd.
PO Box 388
46115 Yale Rd.
Chilliwack, BC V2P 6K1 Canada
604-792-1971
Fax: 604-793-7255
MICR: 0705-001

Châteauguay - Anjou
179, boul d'Anjou
Châteauguay, QC J6J 2R3 Canada
450-699-3355
Fax: 450-699-4754
MICR: 0228-001

Châteauguay - Anjou
IGA Extra
90, boul d'Anjou
Châteauguay, QC J6K 1C3 Canada
450-699-3655
Fax: 450-669-8699
MICR: 3799-001

Clarenville
#102, 69 Manitoba Dr.
Clarenville, NL A5A 1K3 Canada
709-466-6180
Fax: 709-466-1050
MICR: 2765-001

Claresholm
PO Box 369
4901 - 1st St.
Claresholm, AB T0L 0T0 Canada
403-625-3366
Fax: 403-625-4043
MICR: 0513-001

Clinton
4 Victoria St.
Clinton, ON N0M 1L0 Canada
519-482-3905
Fax: 519-482-7767
MICR: 0323-001

Coaldale
PO Box 90
1722 - 20th Ave.
Coaldale, AB T1M 1M2 Canada
403-345-3077
Fax: 403-345-2188
MICR: 0509-001

Cobourg

BMO Bank of Montréal(BMO)/ Banque de Montréal (continued)

62 King St. West
Cobourg, ON K9A 2L9 Canada
905-372-6833
Fax: 905-372-2279
MICR: 0308-001

Cochrane
Safeway
304 - 5th Ave. West
Cochrane, AB T4C 2A5 Canada
403-851-2110
Fax: 403-851-2116
MICR: 2682-001

Collingwood
79 Hurontario St.
Collingwood, ON L9Y 2L9 Canada
705-445-3351
Fax: 705-445-3792
MICR: 0311-001

Concord
8400 Jane St.
Concord, ON L4K 4L8 Canada
905-660-6887
Fax: 905-660-6424
MICR: 3997-001

Cookshire
110, rue Principale est
Cookshire, QC J0B 1M0 Canada
819-875-3341
Fax: 819-875-1322
MICR: 0113-001

Coquitlam - Austin Ave.
1025 Austin Ave.
Coquitlam, BC V3K 3N9 Canada
604-665-3740
Fax: 604-936-0880
MICR: 0790-001

Coquitlam - The High St.
Coquitlam Town Centre
#1, 1161 The High St.
Coquitlam, BC V3B 7W3 Canada
604-665-3716
Fax: 604-944-4457
MICR: 0823-001

Corner Brook - West St. - Main Office
PO Box 220
1 West St.
Corner Brook, NL A2H 2Y6 Canada
709-637-6500
Fax: 709-637-6521
MICR: 1033-001

Corner Brook - Caribou Rd.
26 Caribou Rd.
Corner Brook, NL A2H 4W6 Canada
709-637-6565
Fax: 709-637-6588
MICR: 1030-001

Cornwall - Pitt St.
1328 Pitt St.
Cornwall, ON K6J 3T6 Canada
613-938-5656
Fax: 613-938-5627
MICR: 2321-001

Cornwall - Pitt St. - Main Office
159 Pitt St.
Cornwall, ON K6J 3P5 Canada
613-938-5617
Fax: 613-938-5695
MICR: 0312-001

Courtenay - Cliffe Ave.
Courtenay Safeway
1551 Cliffe Ave.
Courtenay, BC V9N 2K6 Canada
250-703-5356
Fax: 250-703-5358
MICR: 3680-001

Courtenay - England Ave.
585 England Ave.
Courtenay, BC V9N 2N2 Canada
250-334-3181
Fax: 250-338-4365
MICR: 0714-001

Cowansville
108, rue Principale
Cowansville, QC J2K 1J2 Canada
450-263-0555
Fax: 450-263-7170
MICR: 0116-001

Cranbrook - Baker St.
Safeway
1200 Baker St.
Cranbrook, BC V1C 1A8 Canada
250-426-1191
Fax: 250-426-1197
MICR: 3132-001

Cranbrook - Baker St.
934 Baker St.
Cranbrook, BC V1C 1A5 Canada
250-426-6621
Fax: 250-426-8781
MICR: 0722-001

Côte-St-Luc
6951, ch Côte-St-Luc
Côte Saint-Luc, QC H4V 1J2 Canada
514-877-9086
Fax: 514-877-9237
MICR: 0255-001

Dalhousie
PO Box 5155
400 William St.
Dalhousie, NB E8C 2X2 Canada
506-684-3339
Fax: 506-684-3657
MICR: 0118-001

Dartmouth - Cole Harbour Rd.
1086 Cole Harbour Rd.
Dartmouth, NS B2V 1E7 Canada
902-421-3636
Fax: 902-421-3671
MICR: 2747-001

Dartmouth - Ilsley Ave.
111 Ilsley Ave.
Dartmouth, NS B3B 1S8 Canada
902-421-3800
Fax: 902-421-3851
MICR: 3850-001

Dartmouth - Main St.
Westphal Sobeys
100 Main St.
Dartmouth, NS B2X 1R5 Canada
902-421-3338
Fax: 902-421-3904
MICR: 3638-001

Dartmouth - Micmac Blvd.
Micmac Mall
21 Micmac Blvd.
Dartmouth, NS B3A 4T4 Canada
902-421-3646
Fax: 902-421-3496
MICR: 0132-001

Dartmouth - Woodlawn Rd.
Staples Plaza
114 Woodlawn Rd.
Dartmouth, NS B2W 2S7 Canada
902-421-3678
Fax: 902-421-3681
MICR: 2159-001

Dauphin
320 Main St. North
Dauphin, MB R7N 1C6 Canada
204-638-4210
Fax: 204-638-3411
MICR: 0510-001

Davidson
PO Box 130
700 Railway St.
Davidson, SK S0G 1A0 Canada
306-567-3155
Fax: 306-567-5585
MICR: 0620-001

Dawson Creek
10124 - 10th St.
Dawson Creek, BC V1G 3T2 Canada
250-782-5811
Fax: 250-782-8239
MICR: 0711-001

Deep River
6 Ridge Rd.
Deep River, ON K0J 1P0 Canada
613-584-3341
Fax: 613-584-1005
MICR: 0314-001

Deer Lake
10 Pennell's Lane
Deer Lake, NL A84 1Y4 Canada
709-635-4575
Fax: 709-635-8157
MICR: 1031-001

Delhi
116 King St.
Delhi, ON N4B 1X8 Canada
519-582-2650
Fax: 519-582-4182
MICR: 2318-001

Delta - 56th St.
Tsawwassen Safeway
1143 - 56th St.
Delta, BC V4L 2A2 Canada
604-948-3620
Fax: 604-948-3626
MICR: 3118-001

Delta - 56th St.
Tsawwassen Shopping Centre
1206 - 56th St.
Delta, BC V4L 2A4 Canada
604-668-1412
Fax: 604-943-7410
MICR: 0787-001

Delta - Elliott St.
#120, 4857 Elliott St.
Delta, BC V4K 2X7 Canada
604-668-1408
Fax: 604-946-0938
MICR: 0704-001

Deux-Montagnes
1700, ch Oka
Deux-Montagnes, QC J7R 1M9 Canada
450-473-1509
Fax: 450-473-5800
MICR: 0241-001

Dieppe - Champlain St.
PO Box 4505
14 Champlain St.
Dieppe, NB E1A 1N3 Canada
506-853-5727
Fax: 506-853-5711
MICR: 2191-001

Dolbeau-Mistassini
1275, boul Wallberg
Dolbeau-Mistassini, QC G8L 1H3 Canada
418-276-2703
Fax: 418-276-8523
MICR: 0274-001

Drayton Valley
PO Box 6479
5109 - 50th St.
Drayton Valley, AB T7A 1R9 Canada
780-542-6030
Fax: 780-542-2330
MICR: 2632-001

Drumbo
19 Oxford St. West
Drumbo, ON N0J 1G0 Canada
519-463-5240
Fax: 519-463-5879
MICR: 2323-001

Drumheller
PO Box 1390
95 - 3rd Ave. West
Drumheller, AB T0J 0Y0 Canada
403-823-3336
Fax: 403-823-4165
MICR: 2530-001

Drummondville
1001, boul St-Joseph
Drummondville, QC J2C 2C4 Canada
819-472-1145
Fax: 819-472-5743
MICR: 0294-001

Dryden
21 King St.
Dryden, ON P8N 1B4 Canada
807-223-5307
Fax: 807-223-2710

MICR: 0318-001
Duncan
21 Station St.
Duncan, BC V9L 1M2 Canada
250-746-5161
Fax: 250-746-4483
MICR: 0708-001
Dundas
81 King St. West
Dundas, ON L9H 5E7 Canada
905-628-2283
Fax: 905-628-3133
MICR: 0316-001
Dunnville
207 Broad St. East
Dunnville, ON N1A 2X1 Canada
905-774-7551
Fax: 905-774-1411
MICR: 2324-001
Edmonton - 114th Ave. - Westmount Village
13370 - 114th Ave.
Edmonton, AB T5M 4B7 Canada
780-441-6561
Fax: 780-408-0280
MICR: 2533-001
Edmonton - 100 Ave. NW
West Point Centre North
17504 - 100 Ave. NW
Edmonton, AB T5S 2S2 Canada
780-441-6525
Fax: 780-408-0201
MICR: 2532-001
Edmonton - 101 St. NW - Main Office
PO Box 220
10199 - 101 St. NW
Edmonton, AB T5J 3Y4 Canada
780-428-7201
Fax: 780-408-0577
MICR: 0014-001
Edmonton - 104th Ave.
Oliver Square Safeway
11410 - 104th Ave.
Edmonton, AB T5K 2S5 Canada
780-408-0681
Fax: 780-408-0688
MICR: 3238-001
Edmonton - 106th Ave.
5024 - 106th Ave.
Edmonton, AB T6A 1E9 Canada
780-441-6518
Fax: 780-408-0009
MICR: 0522-001
Edmonton - 137th Ave.
Northgate Centre Safeway
9499 - 137th Ave.
Edmonton, AB T5E 5R9 Canada
780-408-0610
Fax: 780-408-0623
MICR: 3136-001
Edmonton - 137th Ave.
White Oaks Square
12240 - 137th Ave.
Edmonton, AB T5L 4Y4 Canada
780-441-6510
Fax: 780-408-0300
MICR: 2579-001
Edmonton - 150th St.
Lynnwood Shopping Centre
8706 - 150th St.
Edmonton, AB T5R 1E4 Canada
780-441-6538
Fax: 780-408-0262
MICR: 2539-001
Edmonton - 156th St.
Meadow Lark Safeway
8720 - 156th St.
Edmonton, AB T5R 5W9 Canada
780-408-0750
Fax: 780-408-0756
MICR: 3107-001
Edmonton - 170th St.
Wolf Willow Place
6833 - 170th St.
Edmonton, AB T5T 4W4 Canada
780-441-3722
Fax: 780-408-0250
MICR: 2633-001
Edmonton - 23rd Ave.
Terwillegar Gardens
14203 - 23rd Ave.
Edmonton, AB T6R 3E7 Canada
780-408-0830
Fax: 780-408-0840
MICR: 3741-001
Edmonton - 23rd Ave. - Heritage Lanes
10803 - 23rd Ave.
Edmonton, AB T6J 7B5 Canada
780-441-6521
Fax: 780-408-0099
MICR: 0678-001
Edmonton - 28th Ave. - Millwoods
6586 - 28th Ave.
Edmonton, AB T6L 6N3 Canada
780-441-3759
Fax: 780-408-0127
MICR: 2578-001
Edmonton - 75th St. NW
5340 - 75th St. NW
Edmonton, AB T6E 6S4 Canada
780-441-3751
Fax: 780-408-0156
MICR: 2544-001
Edmonton - 82nd Ave.
10802 - 82nd Ave.
Edmonton, AB T6E 2B3 Canada
780-441-6565
Fax: 780-408-0177
MICR: 0517-001
Edmonton - 87th Ave. - Windsor Park
11630 - 87th Ave.
Edmonton, AB T6G 0Y2 Canada
780-441-6580
Fax: 780-408-0140
MICR: 0593-001
Edmonton - 98 Ave.
Capilano Safeway
#1062, 5004 - 98 Ave.
Edmonton, AB T6A 0A1 Canada
780-408-0788
Fax: 780-408-0794
MICR: 3621-001
Edmonton - Bonnie Doon Shopping Centre NW
Bonnie Doon Shopping Centre
#102, Bonnie Doon Shopping Centre NW
Edmonton, AB T6C 4E3 Canada
780-441-6503
Fax: 780-408-0028
MICR: 0521-001
Edmonton - Kingsway NW
Kingsway Garden Mall
#208, Kingsway Garden Mall, Kingsway NW
Edmonton, AB T5G 3A6 Canada
780-441-6528
Fax: 780-408-0322
MICR: 0520-001
Edmonton - Londonderry Mall NW
Londonderry Mall
Londonderry Mall NW
Edmonton, AB T6C 3C8 Canada
780-441-6533
Fax: 780-408-0049
MICR: 0625-001
Edmonton - Manning Crossing
Manning Crossing Safeway
500 Manning Crossing
Edmonton, AB T5A 5A1 Canada
780-408-0655
Fax: 780-408-0662
MICR: 3264-001
Edmonton - Southgate Shopping Centre NW
Safeway, Southgate Shopping Centre
Southgate Shopping Centre NW
Edmonton, AB T6H 4M8 Canada
780-408-0668
Fax: 780-408-0675
MICR: 3263-001
Edmundston
50 Canada Rd.
Edmundston, NB E3V 1V3 Canada
506-735-3374
Fax: 506-739-6263
MICR: 0121-001
Eganville
266 Bridge St.
Eganville, ON K0J 1T0 Canada
613-628-2210
Fax: 613-628-2825
MICR: 2328-001
Elgin
28 Main St.
Elgin, ON K0G 1E0 Canada
613-359-5396
Fax: 613-359-6054
MICR: 2325-001
Elliot Lake
17 Mary Walk
Elliot Lake, ON P5A 1Z9 Canada
705-848-2211
Fax: 705-848-7824
MICR: 2404-001
Elmira
53 Arthur St. South
Elmira, ON N3B 2M6 Canada
519-669-5443
Fax: 519-669-4302
MICR: 3055-001
Elora
125 Geddes St.
Elora, ON N0B 1S0 Canada
519-846-5301
Fax: 519-846-9433
MICR: 2330-001
Enderby
PO Box 70
510 Cliff Ave.
Enderby, BC V0E 1V0 Canada
250-838-6421
Fax: 250-838-6582
MICR: 0710-001
Essex
38 Talbot St. North
Essex, ON N8M 1A4 Canada
519-776-7357
Fax: 519-776-5372
MICR: 2329-001
Estevan
1203 Fourth St.
Estevan, SK S4A 0W8 Canada
306-637-3149
Fax: 306-634-7788
MICR: 0630-001
Exeter
400 Main St.
Exeter, ON N0M 1S6 Canada
519-235-2860
Fax: 519-235-0888
MICR: 2331-001
Falher
PO Box 150
15 Main St.
Falher, AB T0H 1M0 Canada
780-837-2215
Fax: 780-837-2625
MICR: 0518-001
Fenelon Falls
39 Colborne St.
Fenelon Falls, ON K0M 1N0 Canada
705-887-2131
Fax: 705-887-1644
MICR: 0321-001
Finch
11 Main St.
Finch, ON K0C 1K0 Canada
613-984-2981
Fax: 613-984-2846
MICR: 2332-001
Forestburg
PO Box 340
4816 - 50th St.
Forestburg, AB T0B 1N0 Canada
780-582-3558
Fax: 780-582-4290
MICR: 2534-001
Fort Erie

BMO Bank of Montréal(BMO)/ Banque de Montréal (continued)

61 Jarvis St.
Fort Erie, ON L2A 5M6 Canada
905-871-4710
Fax: 905-871-0506
MICR: 0315-001

Fort McMurray
9920 Franklin Ave.
Fort McMurray, AB T9H 2K5 Canada
780-790-6992
Fax: 780-791-1826
MICR: 0628-001

Fort Saskatchewan
Fort Shoppers Mall
10420 - 98th Ave.
Fort Saskatchewan, AB T8L 2N6 Canada
780-998-4488
Fax: 780-998-1678
MICR: 2649-001

Fort Smith
PO Box 128
82 Breynat St.
Fort Smith, NT X0E 0P0 Canada
867-872-2001
Fax: 867-872-2243
MICR: 0995-001

Fort St. John - 100th St.
Safeway
9123 - 100th St.
Fort St John, BC V1J 1X6 Canada
250-261-2020
Fax: 250-261-2026
MICR: 3149-001

Fort St. John - 100th St.
10207 - 100th St.
Fort St John, BC V1J 3Y8 Canada
250-785-8356
Fax: 250-787-0314
MICR: 0785-001

Frankford
2 Mill St.
Frankford, ON K0K 2C0 Canada
613-398-6166
Fax: 613-398-8553
MICR: 2344-001

Fredericton - King St. - Main Office
505 King St.
Fredericton, NB E3B 1E7 Canada
506-453-0280
Fax: 506-453-0232
MICR: 0123-001

Fredericton - Main St. - Nashwaaksis
148 Main St.
Fredericton, NB E3A 1C8 Canada
506-453-0240
Fax: 506-453-0244
MICR: 2175-001

Fredericton - Prospect St.
1241 Prospect St. East
Fredericton, NB E3B 3B9 Canada
506-453-0250
Fax: 506-453-0257
MICR: 0626-001

Gananoque
101 King St. East
Gananoque, ON K7G 2V2 Canada
613-382-2177
Fax: 613-382-7302
MICR: 2339-001

Gander
265 Airport Blvd.
Gander, NL A1V 1Y9 Canada
709-651-4614
Fax: 709-256-2399
MICR: 1032-001

Gatineau - Hôpital
99, boul de l'Hôpital
Gatineau, QC J8T 7V1 Canada
819-246-2430
Fax: 819-246-0977
MICR: 2177-001

Gatineau - Portage
141, promenade du Portage
Gatineau, QC J8X 2K2 Canada
819-775-3710
Fax: 819-775-2927
MICR: 0020-001

Gatineau - St-Joseph
Les Galeries de Hull
320, boul St-Joseph
Gatineau, QC J8Y 3Y8 Canada
819-775-7930
Fax: 819-775-3066
MICR: 0275-001

Georgetown
Market Place
#24, 280 Guelph St.
Georgetown, ON L7G 4B1 Canada
905-877-5141
Fax: 905-873-1880
MICR: 2303-001

Gibsons
PO Box 160
431 Marine Dr.
Gibsons, BC V0N 1V0 Canada
604-886-2216
Fax: 604-886-3064
MICR: 0716-001

Glace Bay
37 Union St.
Glace Bay, NS B1A 2P6 Canada
902-849-5524
Fax: 902-849-1318
MICR: 0021-001

Glencoe
224 Main St.
Glencoe, ON N0L 1M0 Canada
519-287-2227
Fax: 519-287-3601
MICR: 2341-001

Goderich
128 Square St. East
Goderich, ON N7A 3Y5 Canada
519-524-7391
Fax: 519-524-8507
MICR: 0328-001

Gore Bay
68 Meredith St.
Gore Bay, ON P0P 1H0 Canada
705-282-2490
Fax: 705-282-3415
MICR: 2342-001

Granby - Principale
399, rue Principale
Granby, QC J2G 2W7 Canada
450-375-6748
Fax: 450-375-6713
MICR: 0177-001

Grand Bend
6 Ontario St.
Grand Bend, ON N0M 1T0 Canada
519-238-2381
Fax: 519-238-6120
MICR: 2337-001

Grand Falls
291 Broadway Blvd.
Grand Falls, NB E3Z 2K1 Canada
506-473-2933
Fax: 506-473-6107
MICR: 0129-001

Grand Falls-Windsor
PO Box 188
3 High St.
Grand Falls-Windsor, NL A2A 2J4 Canada
709-489-2268
Fax: 709-489-2115
MICR: 1004-001

Grande Prairie
10705 West Side Dr.
Grande Prairie, AB T8V 8E6 Canada
780-538-8150
Fax: 780-538-8164
MICR: 2538-001

Greenfield Park
Greenfield Park IGA Extra
300, rue Auguste
Greenfield-Park, QC J4V 3R4 Canada
450-462-4225
Fax: 450-462-8060
MICR: 3231-001

Grimsby
63 Main St. West
Grimsby, ON L3M 4H1 Canada
905-945-2201
Fax: 905-945-6363
MICR: 0326-001

Guelph - Speedvale Ave. West
146 Speedvale Ave. West
Guelph, ON N1H 1K4 Canada
519-824-5587
Fax: 519-763-6014
MICR: 2336-001

Guelph - St. George Sq. - Main Office
78 St. George Sq.
Guelph, ON N1H 6K9
519-824-3920
Fax: 519-824-7989
MICR: 0025-001

Guelph - Stone Rd.
Sone Rd. Mall
435 Stone Rd. West
Guelph, ON N1G 2X6
519-836-7400
Fax: 519-836-9512
MICR: 2931-001

Haliburton
194 Highland St.
Haliburton, ON K0M 1S0
705-457-1240
Fax: 705-457-1755
MICR: 0329-001

Halifax - George St. - Main Office
PO Box 100
5151 George St.
Halifax, NS B3J 2M3 Canada
902-421-3698
Fax: 902-421-3697
MICR: 0009-001

Halifax - Herring Cove Rd.
Spryfield Sobeys
297 Herring Cove Rd.
Halifax, NS B3P 1M2 Canada
902-421-5060
Fax: 902-421-5068
MICR: 3353-001

Halifax - Lacewood Dr.
Clayton Park Sobeys
287 Lacewood Dr.
Halifax, NS B3M 3Y7 Canada
902-421-3788
Fax: 902-421-3730
MICR: 3649-001

Halifax - Lacewood Dr.
360 Lacewood Dr.
Halifax, NS B3S 1M7 Canada
902-421-3688
Fax: 902-421-3784
MICR: 0176-001

Halifax - Mumford Rd.
6980 Mumford Rd.
Halifax, NS B3L 4W2 Canada
902-421-3773
Fax: 902-421-3855
MICR: 2189-001

Halifax - Quinpool Rd.
6371 Quinpool Rd.
Halifax, NS B3L 1A6 Canada
902-421-3748
Fax: 902-421-3703
MICR: 0133-001

Halifax - Spring Garden Rd.
5435 Spring Garden Rd.
Halifax, NS B3J 1G1 Canada
902-421-3798
Fax: 902-421-3491
MICR: 2754-001

Hamilton - Barton St. East
886 Barton St. East
Hamilton, ON L8L 3B7 Canada
905-526-2009
Fax: 905-543-1220
MICR: 0327-001

Hamilton - Bay St. South - Main Office
50 Bay St. South
Hamilton, ON L8P 4V9 Canada

905-526-2000
Fax: 905-526-2025
MICR: 0006-001

Hamilton - Fennell Ave. East
1128 Fennell Ave. East
Hamilton, ON L8T 1S5 Canada
905-526-2060
Fax: 905-388-2058
MICR: 2346-001

Hamilton - James St. North
303 James St. North
Hamilton, ON L8R 2L4 Canada
905-526-2016
Fax: 905-526-2076
MICR: 2353-001

Hamilton - Queenston Rd.
290 Queenston Rd.
Hamilton, ON L8K 1H1 Canada
905-526-2020
Fax: 905-543-1230
MICR: 2351-001

Hamilton - Upper Paradise Rd.
375 Upper Paradise Rd.
Hamilton, ON L9C 5C9 Canada
905-526-2066
Fax: 905-574-6404
MICR: 2922-001

Hamilton - Upper Wentworth St.
Kingfisher Square
920 Upper Wentworth St.
Hamilton, ON L9A 5C5 Canada
905-526-2055
Fax: 905-383-7792
MICR: 2919-001

Hanover
293 - 10th St.
Hanover, ON N4N 1P1 Canada
519-364-1350
Fax: 519-364-5562
MICR: 2349-001

Hawkesbury
280 Main St. East
Hawkesbury, ON K6A 2R4 Canada
613-632-7060
Fax: 613-632-7588
MICR: 2334-001

Hensall
99 King St.
Hensall, ON N0M 1X0 Canada
519-262-2524
Fax: 519-262-2324
MICR: 0331-001

High Level
PO Box 390
9910 - 100th Ave.
High Level, AB T0H 1Z0 Canada
780-926-3701
Fax: 780-926-4796
MICR: 2542-001

High River
PO Box 5220
121 - 1st St. West
High River, AB T1V 1M4 Canada
403-652-2378
Fax: 403-652-4078
MICR: 0634-001

Highgate
12 Main St.
Highgate, ON N0P 1T0 Canada
519-678-3363
Fax: 519-678-3210
MICR: 0338-001

Hudson
PO Box 610
54, rue Cameron
Hudson, QC J0P 1H0 Canada
450-458-5316
Fax: 450-458-7677
MICR: 0236-001

Huntingdon
PO Box 280
124, rue Châteauguay
Huntingdon, QC J0S 1H0 Canada
450-264-5342
Fax: 450-264-9492
MICR: 2111-001

Huntsville
15 Cann St.
Huntsville, ON P1H 2K8 Canada
705-789-8841
Fax: 705-789-9198
MICR: 2215-001

Ile-a-la-Crosse
PO Box 250
Ile-a-la-Crosse, SK S0M 1C0 Canada
306-833-3039
Fax: 306-833-3038
MICR: 3376-001

Ingersoll
104 Thames St. South
Ingersoll, ON N5C 2T4 Canada
519-485-2400
Fax: 519-485-6684
MICR: 0335-001

Ingleside
Ingleside Shopping Centre
PO Box 460
Ingleside, ON K0C 1M0 Canada
613-537-2245
Fax: 613-537-8447
MICR: 2357-001

Invermere
PO Box 850
1241 - 7th Ave.
Invermere, BC V0A 1K0 Canada
250-342-9268
Fax: 250-342-6598
MICR: 0828-001

Iroquois
Iroquois Shopping Plaza
23 Plaza Dr.
Iroquois, ON K0E 1K0 Canada
613-652-4848
Fax: 613-652-1170
MICR: 0342-001

Joliette
32, Place Bourget sud
Joliette, QC J6E 5E7 Canada
450-756-8038
Fax: 450-756-6501
MICR: 2106-001

Jonquière - Davis
2840, Place Davis
Jonquière, QC G7S 2C5 Canada
418-548-7133
Fax: 418-548-7135
MICR: 0104-001

Kamloops - Columbia St. West
Safeway
945 Columbia St. West
Kamloops, BC V2C 1L5 Canada
250-371-6470
Fax: 250-371-6476
MICR: 3122-001

Kamloops - Fortune Dr.
Fortune Shopping Centre Safeway
750 Fortune Dr.
Kamloops, BC V2B 2L2 Canada
250-554-5680
Fax: 250-554-5688
MICR: 3119-001

Kamloops - Fortune Dr.
Fortune Shopping Centre
#29, 750 Fortune Dr.
Kamloops, BC V2B 2L2 Canada
250-828-8805
Fax: 250-376-0521
MICR: 0806-001

Kamloops - Victoria St. - Main Office
210 Victoria St.
Kamloops, BC V2C 2A2 Canada
250-828-8847
Fax: 250-828-8832
MICR: 0720-001

Kelowna - Bernard Ave. - Main Office
294 Bernard Ave.
Kelowna, BC V1Y 6N4 Canada
250-861-1609
Fax: 250-861-6626
MICR: 0721-001

Kelowna - Dilworth Dr.
Orchard Place
1875 Dilworth Dr.
Kelowna, BC V1Y 9T1 Canada
250-861-1626
Fax: 250-861-8933
MICR: 0809-001

Kelowna - Harvey Ave.
Capri Centre
1141 Harvey Ave.
Kelowna, BC V1Y 6E8 Canada
250-861-1660
Fax: 250-979-1004
MICR: 0803-001

Kelowna - Lakeshore Rd.
Mission Park Centre
#16, 3155 Lakeshore Rd.
Kelowna, BC V1W 3S9 Canada
250-861-1651
Fax: 250-861-5644
MICR: 2738-001

Kenora
Bannister Centre
#100, 301 First Ave. South
Kenora, ON P9N 1W2 Canada
807-468-3105
Fax: 807-468-3125
MICR: 2354-001

Kentville
26 Aberdeen St.
Kentville, NS B4N 2N1 Canada
902-678-7303
Fax: 902-678-2779
MICR: 0138-001

Kincardine
PO Box 400
761 Queen St.
Kincardine, ON N2Z 2Y8 Canada
519-396-3335
Fax: 519-396-9694
MICR: 2355-001

Kingston - Bath Rd.
Financial Centre
42 Bath Rd.
Kingston, ON K7L 1H5 Canada
613-545-3037
Fax: 613-545-5802
MICR: 2356-001

Kingston - Front Rd.
704 Front Rd.
Kingston, ON K7M 4L5 Canada
613-384-6175
Fax: 613-384-6432
MICR: 2480-001

Kingston - Gardiner's Rd.
Cataraqui Town Centre
945 Gardiner's Rd.
Kingston, ON K7M 7H4 Canada
613-384-5276
Fax: 613-384-5091
MICR: 2476-001

Kingston - King St. East - Main Office
297 King St. East
Kingston, ON K7L 3B3 Canada
613-545-3005
Fax: 613-545-3124
MICR: 0016-001

Kingsville
2 Main St. East
Kingsville, ON N9Y 1A2 Canada
519-733-2351
Fax: 519-733-6504
MICR: 0347-001

Kitchener - Greenbrook Dr.
421 Greenbrook Dr.
Kitchener, ON N2M 4K1 Canada
519-885-8530
Fax: 519-743-0797
MICR: 3060-001

Kitchener - Highland Rd. West
875 Highland Rd. West
Kitchener, ON N2N 2Y2 Canada
519-749-3292
Fax: 519-576-3925
MICR: 3061-001

BMO Bank of Montréal(BMO)/ Banque de Montréal (continued)

Kitchener - Highland Rd. West
170 Highland Rd. West
Kitchener, ON N2M 3C2 Canada
519-885-9288
Fax: 519-741-8023
MICR: 2345-001

Kitchener - King St. East
1074 King St. East
Kitchener, ON N2G 2N2 Canada
519-885-9262
Fax: 519-581-5663
MICR: 0337-001

Kitchener - King St. West - Main Office
2 King St. West
Kitchener, ON N2G 1A3 Canada
519-885-9200
Fax: 519-581-6292
MICR: 0024-001

Kitchener - Weber St. East
Hi-Way Centre
1375 Weber St. East
Kitchener, ON N2A 3A7 Canada
519-885-9293
Fax: 519-748-1625
MICR: 0473-001

Kitchener - Westmount Rd. East
Laurentian Hills Shopping Centre
720 Westmount Rd. East
Kitchener, ON N2E 2M6 Canada
519-885-9285
Fax: 519-742-2787
MICR: 2969-001

Kitimat
374 City Centre
Kitimat, BC V8C 2G7 Canada
250-632-4604
Fax: 250-632-2901
MICR: 0723-001

Knowlton
PO Box 250
101, rue Lakeside
Knowlton, QC J0E 1V0 Canada
450-243-6109
Fax: 450-243-5248
MICR: 0137-001

Komoka
9952 Glendon Dr.
Komoka, ON N0L 1R0 Canada
519-657-4390
Fax: 519-657-7084
MICR: 2977-001

L'Assomption
PO Box 5093
290, boul l'Ange-Gardien
L'Assomption, QC J5W 1S1 Canada
450-589-4745
Fax: 450-589-3795
MICR: 0247-001

La Prairie
601, boul Taschereau
La Prairie, QC J5R 1V5 Canada
450-659-5407
Fax: 450-659-0959
MICR: 2105-001

Lachute
521, rue Principale
Lachute, QC J8H 1Y6 Canada
450-562-5241
Fax: 450-562-1432
MICR: 0139-001

Lacombe
5013 - 50th Ave.
Lacombe, AB T4L 1K4 Canada
403-782-3356
Fax: 403-782-4740
MICR: 2550-001

Ladysmith
370 Trans Canada Hwy.
Ladysmith, BC V9G 1T9 Canada
250-245-2286
Fax: 250-245-2201
MICR: 0835-001

Lancaster
193 Military Rd.
Lancaster, ON K0C 1N0 Canada
613-347-2474
Fax: 613-347-3241
MICR: 2358-001

Langley - 200th St.
#9, 6233 - 200th St.
Langley, BC V2Y 1A2 Canada
604-533-5900
Fax: 604-532-6711
MICR: 0807-001

Langley - Fraser Hwy.
Fraser Crossing Safeway
20871 Fraser Hwy.
Langley, BC V3A 4G7 Canada
604-532-6740
Fax: 604-532-6746
MICR: 2645-001

Langton
38 Queen St.
Langton, ON N0E 1G0 Canada
519-875-3277
Fax: 519-875-4468
MICR: 2360-001

Lansdowne
1136 Prince St.
Lansdowne, ON K0E 1L0 Canada
613-659-2118
Fax: 613-659-2122
MICR: 2359-001

Laval - Auteuil
957, boul d'Auteuil
Laval, QC H7E 5J7 Canada
450-661-4140
Fax: 450-661-5223
MICR: 2758-001

Laval - Carrefour
Le carrefour Laval
#P2, 3035, boul le Carrefour
Laval, QC H7T 1C8 Canada
450-682-6535
Fax: 450-682-3943
MICR: 2184-001

Laval - Corbusier
Centre Laval
#73, 1600, boul le Corbusier
Laval, QC H7S 1Y9 Canada
450-682-5533
Fax: 450-682-1298
MICR: 0231-001

Laval - Desserte ouest
Marché Crevier/IGA
550, Desserte ouest de l'Autoroute 13
Laval, QC H7X 3S9 Canada
450-969-3111
Fax: 450-969-1583
MICR: 3112-001

Laval - Labelle
1100, boul Labelle
Laval, QC H7V 2V5 Canada
450-682-6383
Fax: 450-682-4605
MICR: 0248-001

Laval - Laurentides
1722, boul des Laurentides
Laval, QC H7M 2P4 Canada
450-975-2920
Fax: 450-975-2934
MICR: 0281-001

Laval - Laval - Succ. Principale
Édifice Banque de Montréal
2, Place Laval
Laval, QC H7N 5N6 Canada
450-975-2805
Fax: 450-975-2890
MICR: 2786-001

Leamington
297 Erie St. South
Leamington, ON N8H 3A7 Canada
519-326-3228
Fax: 519-326-3318
MICR: 0344-001

Leduc - 50th Ave.
4706 - 50th Ave.
Leduc, AB T9E 6Y6 Canada
780-986-2281
Fax: 780-980-3438
MICR: 2552-001

Leduc - 50th St.
Safeway
6112 - 50th St.
Leduc, AB T9E 6N7 Canada
780-980-4390
Fax: 780-980-4395
MICR: 3117-001

Lethbridge - 13th St. North
230 - 13th St. North
Lethbridge, AB T1H 2R7 Canada
403-382-3271
Fax: 403-382-3255
MICR: 0529-001

Lethbridge - 4th Ave. South - Main Office
606 - 4th Ave. South
Lethbridge, AB T1J 0N7 Canada
403-382-3200
Fax: 403-382-3206
MICR: 0525-001

Lethbridge - Fairway Plaza Rd. South
Fairway Plaza Safeway
2750 Fairway Plaza Rd. South
Lethbridge, AB T1K 6Z3 Canada
403-317-7090
Fax: 403-317-7097
MICR: 3180-001

Lethbridge - University Dr.
West Lethbridge Safeway
#1, 550 University Dr.
Lethbridge, AB T1J 4T3 Canada
403-317-7070
Fax: 403-317-7077
MICR: 3262-001

Lindsay
16 William St. South
Lindsay, ON K9V 4S3 Canada
705-324-3521
Fax: 705-324-2943
MICR: 0340-001

Listowel
140 Main St. West
Listowel, ON N4W 1A1 Canada
519-291-4130
Fax: 519-291-5411
MICR: 2448-001

Little Current
29 Water St. East
Little Current, ON P0P 1K0 Canada
705-368-2260
Fax: 705-368-3238
MICR: 2361-001

Liverpool
PO Box 849
43 Market St.
Liverpool, NS B0T 1K0 Canada
902-354-3407
Fax: 902-354-4911
MICR: 0119-001

London - Boler Rd.
295 Boler Rd.
London, ON N6K 2K1 Canada
519-667-6191
Fax: 519-474-3624
MICR: 0319-001

London - Cherryhill Blvd.
101 Cherryhill Blvd.
London, ON N6H 4S4 Canada
519-667-6244
Fax: 519-667-6438
MICR: 2574-001

London - Commissioners Rd. East
Pond Mills Square
1200 Commissioners Rd. East
London, ON N5Z 4R3 Canada
519-667-6212
Fax: 519-668-1351
MICR: 2593-001

London - Dundas St.
270 Dundas St.
London, ON N6A 1H3 Canada
519-667-6129
Fax: 519-667-6431
MICR: 0348-001

London - Dundas St. East

1820 Dundas St. East
London, ON N5W 3E5 Canada
519-667-6234
Fax: 519-453-2294
MICR: 2364-001

London - Fanshawe Park Rd. East
101 Fanshawe Park Rd. East
London, ON N5X 3V9 Canada
519-667-6273
Fax: 519-667-6278
MICR: 3845-001

London - Hamilton Rd.
555 Hamilton Rd.
London, ON N5Z 1S5 Canada
519-667-6240
Fax: 519-667-6281
MICR: 2362-001

London - Highbury Ave.
1275 Highbury Ave.
London, ON N5Y 1B2 Canada
519-667-6171
Fax: 519-455-4889
MICR: 0455-001

London - Oxford St. West - Oakridge Branch
1182 Oxford St. West
London, ON N6H 4N2 Canada
519-667-6188
Fax: 519-473-6124
MICR: 0466-001

London - Southdale Rd. West
377 Southdale Rd. West
London, ON N6J 4G8 Canada
519-667-6195
Fax: 519-641-7122
MICR: 2915-001

London - Wellington Rd. South
338 Wellington Rd. South
London, ON N6C 4P6 Canada
519-667-6207
Fax: 519-667-6114
MICR: 0465-001

London - Wharncliffe Rd. South
457 Wharncliffe Rd. South
London, ON N6J 2M8 Canada
519-667-6224
Fax: 519-667-6398
MICR: 0468-001

London - Wonderland Rd. North
Sherwood Forest Mall
1225 Wonderland Rd. North
London, ON N6G 2V9 Canada
519-667-6183
Fax: 519-472-0916
MICR: 2463-001

Longueuil - Chambly
Place Desormeaux
2877, ch Chambly
Longueuil, QC J4L 1M8 Canada
450-463-3575
Fax: 450-463-4094
MICR: 0221-001

Longueuil - St-Charles ouest - Succ. Principale
279, rue St-Charles ouest
Longueuil, QC J4H 1E4 Canada
450-463-5008
Fax: 450-463-1200
MICR: 0143-001

Lower Sackville
779 Sackville Dr.
Lower Sackville, NS B4E 1R6 Canada
902-864-2422
Fax: 902-865-2263
MICR: 2194-001

Lucan
158 Main St.
Lucan, ON N0M 2J0 Canada
519-227-4473
Fax: 519-227-4275
MICR: 2365-001

Lucknow
630 Campbell St.
Lucknow, ON N0G 2H0 Canada
519-528-2824
Fax: 519-528-3736
MICR: 2366-001

Lunenburg
PO Box 369
12 King St.
Lunenburg, NS B0J 2C0 Canada
902-634-8875
Fax: 902-634-4148
MICR: 0142-001

Lévis - Président-Kennedy
Lévis IGA Extra In-Store
53, rte du Président-Kennedy
Lévis, QC G6V 6C7 Canada
418-835-5535
Fax: 418-835-4300
MICR: 3490-001

Lévis - Président-Kennedy
Les Promenade de Lévis
44, rte Président-Kennedy
Lévis, QC G6V 6C5 Canada
418-838-1600
Fax: 418-838-2646
MICR: 0141-001

Magog
498, rue Principale ouest
Magog, QC J1X 2A9 Canada
819-843-3317
Fax: 819-843-0470
MICR: 0146-001

Mahone Bay
PO Box 50
562 Main St.
Mahone Bay, NS B0J 2E0 Canada
902-624-8355
Fax: 902-624-9217
MICR: 0147-001

Manitowaning
15A Arthur St.
Manitowaning, ON P0P 1N0 Canada
705-859-3112
Fax: 705-859-3255
MICR: SF01-001

Maple
2535 Major Mackenzie Dr.
Maple, ON L6A 1C6 Canada
905-832-6336
Fax: 905-832-6764
MICR: 3995-001

Maple Creek
PO Box 1300
129 Jasper St.
Maple Creek, SK S0N 1N0 Canada
306-662-2631
Fax: 306-622-3842
MICR: 2671-001

Maple Ridge - Lougheed Hwy.
Safeway
#300, 20201 Lougheed Hwy.
Maple Ridge, BC V2X 2P6 Canada
604-460-9810
Fax: 604-460-9816
MICR: 3123-001

Maple Ridge - Lougheed Hwy.
22410 Lougheed Hwy.
Maple Ridge, BC V2X 2T6 Canada
604-463-2444
Fax: 604-463-4564
MICR: 0738-001

Maple Ridge - Lougheed Hwy.
Westridge Centre
20691 Lougheed Hwy.
Maple Ridge, BC V2X 2P9 Canada
604-465-5491
Fax: 604-465-1596
MICR: 0743-001

Markdale
PO Box 310
30 Main St.
Markdale, ON N0C 1H0 Canada
519-986-2270
Fax: 519-986-3844
MICR: 2369-001

Markham - 16th Ave.
Heritage Plaza
5970 - 16th Ave.
Markham, ON L3P 7R1 Canada
905-472-4890
Fax: 905-472-5540
MICR: 3993-001

Markham - John St.
#300, 2851 John St.
Markham, ON L3R 5R7 Canada
905-475-0831
Fax: 905-475-7153
MICR: 2949-001

Markham - Main St. North - Main Office
PO Box 28
86 Main St. North
Markham, ON L3P 1X8 Canada
905-294-1033
Fax: 905-294-6139
MICR: 2371-001

Markham - McCowan Rd.
Bur Oak & McCowan Sobeys
9580 McCowan Rd.
Markham, ON L3P 3J3 Canada
905-887-0207
Fax: 905-887-0387
MICR: 3269-001

Markham - Steeles Ave. East - Market Village
PO Box 120
4392 Steeles Ave. East
Markham, ON L3R 9V8 Canada
905-940-6211
Fax: 905-940-3621
MICR: 3975-001

Marystown
366 Ville Marie Dr.
Marystown, NL A0E 2M0 Canada
709-279-5499
Fax: 709-279-2000
MICR: 1026-001

Mascouche - Masson
Mascouche IGA Extra
65, montée Masson
Mascouche, QC J7K 3B4 Canada
450-474-2929
Fax: 450-474-2275
MICR: 3229-001

Mascouche - Masson
825, montée Mascouche
Mascouche, QC J7K 3B4 Canada
450-966-9090
Fax: 450-966-9094
MICR: 2744-001

Matane
315, av St-Jerome
Matane, QC G4W 3A8 Canada
418-562-6438
Fax: 418-562-5019
MICR: 0144-001

Meaford
26 Sykes St. North
Meaford, ON N4L 1V7 Canada
519-538-1430
Fax: 519-538-3138
MICR: 2370-001

Medicine Hat - 2nd St. SE - Main Office
606 - 2nd St. SE
Medicine Hat, AB T1A 0C9 Canada
403-529-8555
Fax: 403-529-6262
MICR: 0531-001

Medicine Hat - Division Ave. South
Division Ave. Safeway
615 Division Ave. South
Medicine Hat, AB T1A 2J9 Canada
403-504-2080
Fax: 403-504-2086
MICR: 3165-001

Medicine Hat - Dunmore Rd. SE
Carry Plaza
3215 Dunmore Rd. SE, #E
Medicine Hat, AB T1B 2H2 Canada
403-526-1114
Fax: 403-527-4576
MICR: 2672-001

Melville
141 - 3rd Ave. West
Melville, SK S0A 2P0 Canada

BMO Bank of Montréal(BMO)/ Banque de Montréal (continued)

306-728-5422
Fax: 306-728-5511
MICR: 2673-001

Merlin
2 Erie St. South
Merlin, ON N0P 1W0 Canada
519-689-4237
Fax: 519-689-7802
MICR: 0357-001

Midland
243 King St.
Midland, ON L4R 3M4 Canada
705-526-5491
Fax: 705-526-8844
MICR: 0343-001

Mildmay
70 Elora St.
Mildmay, ON N0G 2J0 Canada
519-367-2611
Fax: 519-367-5610
MICR: 2372-001

Mindemoya
PO Box 190
6103 Hwy. 542
Mindemoya, ON P0P 1S0 Canada
705-377-5391
Fax: 705-377-5655
MICR: 2373-001

Miramichi
185 Pleasant St.
Miramichi, NB E1V 1Y4 Canada
506-622-5802
Fax: 506-622-7584
MICR: 2152-001

Mississauga - 10th Line West
Sobeys
5602 - 10th Line West
Mississauga, ON L5M 7L9 Canada
905-567-0102
Fax: 905-567-0208
MICR: 3512-001

Mississauga - Argentia Rd.
Plaza One, Meadowvale Corporate Centre
2000 Argentia Rd.
Mississauga, ON L5N 1P7 Canada
905-826-5337
Fax: 905-826-1294
MICR: 2970-001

Mississauga - Bristol Rd. East
Sandalwood Square Shopping Centre
40 Bristol Rd. East
Mississauga, ON L4Z 3K8 Canada
905-568-3717
Fax: 905-568-3082
MICR: 3980-001

Mississauga - Burnhamthorpe Rd. West
South Common Mall
2146 Burnhamthorpe Rd. West
Mississauga, ON L5L 5Z5 Canada
905-820-7714
Fax: 905-820-3622
MICR: 0654-001

Mississauga - City Centre Dr.
Square One Shopping Centre
100 City Centre Dr.
Mississauga, ON L5B 2C9 Canada
905-277-0346
Fax: 905-277-0640
MICR: 0494-001

Mississauga - Crestlawn Dr.
1350 Crestlawn Dr.
Mississauga, ON L4W 1P8 Canada
905-625-7483
Fax: 905-625-7144
MICR: 2950-001

Mississauga - Derry Rd. West
3221 Derry Rd. West
Mississauga, ON L5N 7L7 Canada
905-785-2010
Fax: 905-785-2554
MICR: 3173-001

Mississauga - Dundas St. East
985 Dundas St. East
Mississauga, ON L4Y 2B9 Canada
905-279-6530
Fax: 905-279-6244
MICR: 0430-001

Mississauga - Dundas St. West
Westdale Mall
1151 Dundas St. West
Mississauga, ON L5C 1C6 Canada
905-270-2777
Fax: 905-272-5778
MICR: 2474-001

Mississauga - Dundas St. West
Woodchester Plaza
2458 Dundas St. West
Mississauga, ON L5K 1R8 Canada
905-822-8620
Fax: 905-822-6597
MICR: 2477-001

Mississauga - Eglinton Ave. West
Dominion Plus, Roseborough Centre
1240 Eglinton Ave. West
Mississauga, ON L5V 1N3 Canada
905-858-0447
Fax: 905-858-2017
MICR: 3607-001

Mississauga - Eglinton Ave. West - Erin Mills
2825 Eglinton Ave. West
Mississauga, ON L5M 6J5 Canada
905-569-3970
Fax: 905-569-3978
MICR: 3978-001

Mississauga - Goreway Dr.
7145 Goreway Dr.
Mississauga, ON L4T 2T5 Canada
905-671-0285
Fax: 905-673-6571
MICR: 2994-001

Mississauga - Lakeshore Rd. East
378 Lakeshore Rd. East
Mississauga, ON L5G 1H5 Canada
905-274-3438
Fax: 905-891-3375
MICR: 0353-001

Mississauga - Mavis Rd.
Heartland Town Centre
5800 Mavis Rd.
Mississauga, ON L5V 3B7 Canada
905-567-4443
Fax: 905-567-4171
MICR: 3632-001

Mississauga - Meadowvale Town Centre Circle
Meadowvale Town Centre
6780 Meadowvale Town Centre Circle
Mississauga, ON L5N 4B7 Canada
905-542-9533
Fax: 905-821-2923
MICR: 2670-001

Mississauga - Robert Speck Pkwy. - Main Office
1 Robert Speck Pkwy.
Mississauga, ON L4Z 3M3 Canada
905-949-4266
Fax: 905-949-8883
MICR: 3858-001

Mississauga - Royal Windsor Dr. - Clarkson
2057 Royal Windsor Dr.
Mississauga, ON L5J 1K5 Canada
905-822-8941
Fax: 905-822-5337
MICR: 2326-001

Mississauga - South Service Rd.
Dixie Value Mall
1250 South Service Rd.
Mississauga, ON L5E 1V4 Canada
905-278-5205
Fax: 905-278-5735
MICR: 2393-001

Mississauga - Twain Ave. - Meadowvale Village
735 Twain Ave.
Mississauga, ON L5W 1X1 Canada
905-564-0310
Fax: 905-564-5983
MICR: 3634-001

Mitchell
104 Ontario Rd.
Mitchell, ON N0K 1N0 Canada
519-348-8454
Fax: 519-348-4222
MICR: 2998-001

Moncton - Main St. - Main Office
633 Main St.
Moncton, NB E1C 9X9 Canada
506-853-5700
Fax: 506-853-5714
MICR: 0035-001

Moncton - Mountain Rd.
1633 Mountain Rd.
Moncton, NB E1G 1A5 Canada
506-853-5750
Fax: 506-853-5753
MICR: 3856-001

Mont-Saint-Hilaire
127, boul Sir-Wilfrid-Laurier
Mont-Saint-Hilaire, QC J3H 3N3 Canada
450-467-2814
Fax: 450-467-6881
MICR: 2140-001

Mont-Tremblant
845, rue de Saint-Jovite
Mont-Tremblant, QC J8E 3J8 Canada
819-425-2757
Fax: 819-425-9349
MICR: 2138-001

Montréal - Acadie
#10, 9150, boul de L'Acadie
Montréal, QC H4N 2T2 Canada
514-382-8060
Fax: 514-382-5840
MICR: 2116-001

Montréal - Atwater
Place Alexis Nihon
1500, av Atwater
Montréal, QC H3Z 1X5 Canada
514-846-0105
Fax: 514-846-3491
MICR: 0283-001

Montréal - Beaubien est
3251, rue Beaubien est
Montréal, QC H1X 1G4 Canada
514-877-2109
Fax: 514-877-2173
MICR: 0217-001

Montréal - Commerce
38, Place du Commerce
Montréal, QC H3E 1T8 Canada
514-768-5660
Fax: 514-768-7313
MICR: 0288-001

Montréal - Côte-des-Neiges
5145, ch de la Côte-des-Neiges
Montréal, QC H3T 1X9 Canada
514-341-2240
Fax: 514-341-7331
MICR: 0168-001

Montréal - Côte-Vertu
3300, boul Côte-Vertu
Montréal, QC H4R 2B7 Canada
514-877-1941
Fax: 514-877-7473
MICR: 3895-001

Montréal - Decarie
6521, boul Decarie
Montréal, QC H3W 3E3 Canada
514-343-5344
Fax: 514-343-0410
MICR: 0212-001

Montréal - Decarie
637, boul Decarie
Montréal, QC H4L 3L3 Canada
514-855-0501
Fax: 514-855-1852
MICR: 0193-001

Montréal - Donegani
33, av Donegani
Montréal, QC H9R 2V7 Canada
514-630-7874
Fax: 514-630-6313
MICR: 0224-001

Montréal - Dorval
274, av Dorval
Montréal, QC H9S 3H3 Canada

514-636-6300
Fax: 514-636-1770
MICR: 0226-001
Montréal - Fleury est
1769, rue Fleury est
Montréal, QC H2C 1T3 Canada
514-382-4525
Fax: 514-382-3845
MICR: 0262-001
Montréal - Galeries d'Anjou
7999, boul les Galeries d'Anjou
Montréal, QC HIM 1W9 Canada
514-354-2336
Fax: 514-354-3041
MICR: 0261-001
Montréal - Graham
1625, boul Graham
Montréal, QC H3R 1G7 Canada
514-341-1343
Fax: 514-341-0154
MICR: 0203-001
Montréal - Greene
1299, av Greene
Montréal, QC H3Z 2A6 Canada
514-846-1300
Fax: 514-846-1306
MICR: 0166-001
Montréal - Henri-Bourassa est
6025, boul Henri-Bourassa est
Montréal, QC H1G 2V2 Canada
514-322-7020
Fax: 514-322-5202
MICR: 0271-001
Montréal - Hymus ouest - Succ. Principale de Pointe-Claire
183, boul Hymus ouest
Montréal, QC H9R 1E9 Canada
514-630-5947
Fax: 514-630-9071
MICR: 2129-001
Montréal - Jean-Talon est
1805, rue Jean-Talon est
Montréal, QC H2E 1T4 Canada
514-877-8025
Fax: 514-877-8360
MICR: 0126-001
Montréal - Jean-Talon est
6455, rue Jean-Talon est
Montréal, QC H1S 3E8 Canada
514-255-1775
Fax: 514-255-5352
MICR: 3909-001
Montréal - Jean-Talon ouest
520, rue Jean-Talon ouest
Montréal, QC H3N 1R5 Canada
514-277-5551
Fax: 514-277-5008
MICR: 0140-001
Montréal - Lacordaire
9349, boul Lacordaire
Montréal, QC H1R 2B6 Canada
514-322-0235
Fax: 514-322-1456
MICR: 2171-001
Montréal - Langelier
St-Léonard IGA Extra
7150, boul Langelier
Montréal, QC H1S 2X6 Canada
514-254-3477
Fax: 514-254-5198
MICR: 3593-001
Montréal - Marcel-Laurin
Les Galeries St-Laurent
2133, boul Marcel-Laurin
Montréal, QC H4R 1K4 Canada
514-877-1973
Fax: 514-877-8418
MICR: 2183-001
Montréal - Masson
2831, rue Masson
Montréal, QC H1Y 1W8 Canada
514-877-1620
Fax: 514-877-1197
MICR: 0169-001
Montréal - Maurice-Duplessis
Place de la Rivière
7515, boul Maurice-Duplessis
Montréal, QC H1E 7N2 Canada
514-494-3188
Fax: 514-494-1662
MICR: 2628-001
Montréal - Metcalfe
Édifice Sun Life
1155, rue Metcalfe
Montréal, QC H3B 2V7 Canada
514-877-6801
Fax: 514-877-6942
MICR: 0153-001
Montréal - Monkland
5501, av Monkland
Montréal, QC H4A 1C8 Canada
514-877-9028
Fax: 514-877-8866
MICR: 0151-001
Montréal - Mont-Royal est
1101, av du Mont-Royal est
Montréal, QC H2J 1X9 Canada
514-521-6080
Fax: 514-521-7540
MICR: 2122-001
Montréal - Newman
7189, boul Newman
Montréal, QC H8N 2K3 Canada
514-363-3113
Fax: 514-363-6571
MICR: 0267-001
Montréal - Notre-Dame
998, rue Notre-Dame
Montréal, QC H8S 2B9 Canada
514-639-0707
Fax: 514-639-0919
MICR: 0038-001
Montréal - O'Brien
1845, boul O'Brien
Montréal, QC H4L 3W6 Canada
514-877-1733
Fax: 514-877-1764
MICR: 0219-001
Montréal - Peel
2005, rue Peel
Montréal, QC H3A 1T7 Canada
514-877-7320
Fax: 514-877-2117
MICR: 0158-001
Montréal - Queen Mary
5353, ch Queen Mary
Montréal, QC H3X 1V2 Canada
514-877-8186
Fax: 514-877-9578
MICR: 0125-001
Montréal - René-Lévesque ouest
Hydro-Québec
61, boul René-Lévesque ouest
Montréal, QC H2Z 1A3 Canada
514-877-8256
Fax: 514-877-1546
MICR: 2108-001
Montréal - René-Lévesque ouest
630, boul René-Lévesque ouest
Montréal, QC H3B 1S6 Canada
514-877-7146
Fax: 514-877-6923
MICR: 0230-001
Montréal - Rockland
Centre Rockland
#192, 2305, ch Rockland
Montréal, QC H3P 3E9 Canada
514-341-6113
Fax: 514-341-6533
MICR: 2145-001
Montréal - Salaberry
Les Galeries Normandie
2680, rue de Salaberry
Montréal, QC H3M 1L3 Canada
514-877-1955
Fax: 514-877-8358
MICR: 2113-001
Montréal - Salaberry
IGA Extra
11800, boul Salaberry
Montréal, QC H9B 2R8 Canada
514-685-2552
Fax: 514-685-1575
MICR: 3640-001
Montréal - Sherbrooke est
Centre Financier Point-aux-Trembles
#102, 13000, Sherbrooke est
Montréal, QC H1B 3W2 Canada
514-640-5959
Fax: 514-640-7607
MICR: 0269-001
Montréal - Sherbrooke est
Place Versailles
7275, rue Sherbrooke est
Montréal, QC H1N 1E9 Canada
514-352-7751
Fax: 514-352-8313
MICR: 0056-001
Montréal - Sherbrooke ouest
6405, rue Sherbrooke ouest
Montréal, QC H4B 1N3 Canada
514-877-9026
Fax: 514-877-9207
MICR: 0178-001
Montréal - Sherbrooke ouest
1601, rue Sherbrooke ouest
Montréal, QC H3H 1E2 Canada
514-846-0047
Fax: 514-846-1757
MICR: 0172-001
Montréal - Sherbrooke ouest
4817, rue Sherbrooke ouest
Montréal, QC H3Z 1G6 Canada
514-846-0304
Fax: 514-846-1344
MICR: 0136-001
Montréal - St-Charles
2867, boul St-Charles
Montréal, QC H9H 3B5 Canada
514-694-9900
Fax: 514-694-4488
MICR: 3672-001
Montréal - St-Hubert
6700, rue St-Hubert
Montréal, QC H2S 2M6 Canada
514-277-4454
Fax: 514-277-7266
MICR: 0218-001
Montréal - St-Jacques - Succ. Principale
119, rue St-Jacques
Montréal, QC H2Y 1L6 Canada
514-877-7373
Fax: 514-877-8118
MICR: 0001-001
Montréal - St-Laurent
5060, boul St-Laurent
Montréal, QC H2T 1R7 Canada
514-277-1060
Fax: 514-277-1878
MICR: 2120-001
Montréal - St-Pierre
Hôpital des Veterans
305, rue St-Pierre
Montréal, QC H9X 1Y9 Canada
514-457-3440
MICR: SG02-001
Montréal - Ste-Anne
93, rue Ste-Anne
Montréal, QC H9X 1L9 Canada
514-457-2430
Fax: 514-457-3927
MICR: 0161-001
Montréal - Ste-Catherine est
1700, rue Ste-Catherine est
Montréal, QC H2L 2J4 Canada
514-521-4181
Fax: 514-521-7343
MICR: 0157-001
Montréal - Ste-Catherine ouest
1205, rue Ste-Catherine ouest
Montréal, QC H3B 1K7 Canada
514-877-6850
Fax: 514-877-7037

BMO Bank of Montréal(BMO)/ Banque de Montréal (continued)

MICR: 2118-001

Montréal - Ste-Catherine ouest
670, rue Ste-Catherine ouest
Montréal, QC H3B 1C1 Canada
514-877-8010
Fax: 514-877-9663
MICR: 2127-001

Montréal - Sunnydale
3, ch Sunnydale
Montréal, QC H9B 1E1 Canada
514-684-6690
Fax: 514-684-7281
MICR: 0291-001

Montréal - Transcanadienne
Centre Fairview
6702, rte Transcanadienne
Montréal, QC H9R 1C4 Canada
514-630-0869
Fax: 514-630-4955
MICR: 0282-001

Montréal - Van Horne
1554, av Van Horne
Montréal, QC H2V 1L5 Canada
514-277-0404
Fax: 514-277-8038
MICR: 0124-001

Montréal - Verdun
5651, av Verdun
Montréal, QC H4H 1L6 Canada
514-766-0067
Fax: 514-766-5640
MICR: 0205-001

Montréal - Victoria
Stock Exchange, Tour de la Bourse
PO Box 22
800, Square Victoria
Montréal, QC H4Z 1A5 Canada
514-877-8180
Fax: 514-877-8531
MICR: 0243-001

Montréal - Westminster
101, av Westminster nord
Montréal, QC H4X 1Z3 Canada
514-877-9043
Fax: 514-877-9144
MICR: 0170-001

Moose Factory
107 Mcok-ki-june-i-beg
General Delivery
Moose Factory, ON P0L 1W0 Canada
705-658-6036
Fax: 705-658-6037
MICR: 3613-001

Moose Jaw
PO Box 550
48 High St. West
Moose Jaw, SK S6H 1S3 Canada
306-694-8130
Fax: 306-692-5155
MICR: 0029-001

Morris
PO Box 490
107 Main St.
Morris, MB R0G 1K0 Canada
204-746-2321
Fax: 204-746-8474
MICR: 2562-001

Morrisburg
Morrisburg Plaza
49 Main St.
Morrisburg, ON K0C 1X0 Canada
613-543-3756
Fax: 613-543-4238
MICR: 0358-001

Mount Forest
201 Main St.
Mount Forest, ON N0G 2L0 Canada
519-323-2130
Fax: 519-323-2767
MICR: 0345-001

Mount Pearl
Mount Pearl Sobeys In-Store
50 Old Placentia Rd.
Mount Pearl, NL A1N 4Y1 Canada
709-758-2831
Fax: 709-758-2842
MICR: 3641-001

Nain
General Delivery
Nain, NL A0P 1L0
709-922-2430
MICR: SH02-001

Nanaimo - Estevan Rd.
1533 Estevan Rd.
Nanaimo, BC V9S 3Y3 Canada
250-754-0564
Fax: 250-753-1365
MICR: 0793-001

Nanaimo - North Island Hwy.
#1, 6908 North Island Hwy.
Nanaimo, BC V9V 1P6 Canada
250-390-5086
Fax: 250-390-3574
MICR: 3820-001

Napanee
4 Dundas St. East
Napanee, ON K7R 1H6 Canada
613-354-3327
Fax: 613-354-6987
MICR: 2376-001

Napierville
PO Box 40
342, rue St-Jacques
Napierville, QC J0J 1L0 Canada
450-245-3386
Fax: 450-245-0065
MICR: 2147-001

Neepawa
PO Box 1210
436 Mountain Ave.
Neepawa, MB R0J 1H0 Canada
204-476-2357
Fax: 204-476-3640
MICR: 2570-001

Nelson
298 Baker St.
Nelson, BC V1L 4H3 Canada
250-352-5321
Fax: 250-352-9161
MICR: 0730-001

New Glasgow
99 Provost St.
New Glasgow, NS B2H 2P5 Canada
902-752-5440
Fax: 902-755-6665
MICR: 0182-001

New Westminster - 6th St.
Royal City Centre Safeway
#198, 610 - 6th St.
New Westminster, BC V3L 3C2 Canada
604-718-2200
Fax: 604-718-2206
MICR: 3186-001

New Westminster - 6th St.
#125, 610 - 6th St.
New Westminster, BC V3L 3C2 Canada
604-665-3770
Fax: 604-665-2724
MICR: 0731-001

Newmarket - Davis Dr.
404 Shopping Centre
1111 Davis Dr.
Newmarket, ON L3Y 8K3 Canada
905-853-2744
Fax: 905-853-6830
MICR: 3956-001

Newmarket - Main St. South - Main Office
231 Main St. South
Newmarket, ON L3Y 3Z4 Canada
905-895-4581
Fax: 905-898-3218
MICR: 0350-001

Newmarket - Yonge St.
Upper Canada Mall
PO Box 232
17600 Yonge St.
Newmarket, ON L3Y 4Z1 Canada
905-853-5116
Fax: 905-853-6517
MICR: 3999-001

Newmarket - Yonge St.
Yonge & Savage Dominion
16640 Yonge St.
Newmarket, ON L3Y 4V8 Canada
905-853-6404
Fax: 905-853-6406
MICR: 3156-001

Niagara Falls - Montrose Rd.
Niagara Square Shopping Centre
7555 Montrose Rd.
Niagara Falls, ON L2H 2E9 Canada
905-357-2300
Fax: 905-354-5488
MICR: 2996-001

Niagara Falls - Morrison St.
6841 Morrison St.
Niagara Falls, ON L2E 2G5 Canada
905-356-7561
Fax: 905-356-3260
MICR: 0490-001

Niagara Falls - Queen St. - Main Office
4365 Queen St.
Niagara Falls, ON L2E 2K9 Canada
905-358-7167
Fax: 905-356-5645
MICR: 0048-001

Niagara on the Lake
91 Queen St.
Niagara on the Lake, ON L0S 1J0 Canada
905-468-3227
Fax: 905-468-3677
MICR: 2991-001

Nipawin
PO Box 2046
101 - 1 Ave. East
Nipawin, SK S0E 1E0 Canada
306-862-4534
Fax: 306-862-5542
MICR: 0660-001

North Battleford
1152 - 101 St.
North Battleford, SK S9A 2Y7 Canada
306-445-2473
Fax: 306-445-1552
MICR: 0537-001

North Bay
154 Main St. East
North Bay, ON P1B 1A8 Canada
705-472-2620
Fax: 705-746-7517
MICR: 0359-001

North Vancouver - East 27th St.
Lynn Valley Safeway
1170 East 27th St.
North Vancouver, BC V7J 1S1 Canada
604-903-3151
Fax: 604-903-3157
MICR: 3617-001

North Vancouver - Edgemont Blvd.
3060 Edgemont Blvd.
North Vancouver, BC V7R 2N4 Canada
604-668-1225
Fax: 604-903-3130
MICR: 0745-001

North Vancouver - Lonsdale Ave.
1505 Lonsdale Ave.
North Vancouver, BC V7M 2J4 Canada
604-668-1292
Fax: 604-903-3090
MICR: 0744-001

North Vancouver - Main St.
1460 Main St.
North Vancouver, BC V7J 1C8 Canada
604-668-1261
Fax: 604-903-3003
MICR: 0754-001

North Vancouver - Marine Dr.
1120 Marine Dr.
North Vancouver, BC V7P 1S8 Canada
604-668-1243
Fax: 604-903-3050
MICR: 0740-001

North Vancouver - Mt. Seymour Rd.

Parkgate Village Safeway
1175 Mt. Seymour Rd.
North Vancouver, BC V7H 2Y4 Canada
604-924-4100
Fax: 604-924-4106
MICR: 3109-001

Northbrook
12265 Hwy. 41
Northbrook, ON K0H 2G0 Canada
613-336-2696
Fax: 613-336-9713
MICR: 3847-001

Norwich
30 Main St. West
Norwich, ON N0J 1P0 Canada
519-863-3022
Fax: 519-863-3692
MICR: 0364-001

Oakville - Dundas St. East
320 Dundas St. East
Oakville, ON L6H 6Z9 Canada
905-257-0904
Fax: 905-257-0187
MICR: 3318-001

Oakville - Lakeshore Rd. East - Main Office
159 Lakeshore Rd. East
Oakville, ON L6J 5C3 Canada
905-845-4274
Fax: 905-845-1311
MICR: 2382-001

Oakville - Leighland Ave.
Oakville Place
240 Leighland Ave.
Oakville, ON L6H 3H6 Canada
905-842-4212
Fax: 905-842-0464
MICR: 2472-001

Oakville - North Service Rd. West
Oakville Town Centre II
240 North Service Rd. West
Oakville, ON L6M 2Y5 Canada
905-849-6290
Fax: 905-845-3430
MICR: 3979-001

Ohsweken
PO Box 299
Ohsweken, ON N0A 1M0 Canada
519-445-4733
Fax: 519-445-0025
MICR: 3752-001

Okotoks
Safeway
610 Big Rock Lane
Okotoks, AB T1S 1B3 Canada
403-938-8545
Fax: 403-938-8552
MICR: 3239-001

Olds
PO Box 3710
5018 - 50th Ave.
Olds, AB T4H 1P5 Canada
403-556-3307
Fax: 403-556-3181
MICR: 2573-001

Orangeville
274 Broadway St.
Orangeville, ON L9W 1L1 Canada
519-941-6631
Fax: 519-942-3870
MICR: 2496-001

Orillia - Coldwater Rd. West
County Fair Plaza
285 Coldwater Rd. West
Orillia, ON L3V 3M1 Canada
705-325-1378
Fax: 705-327-1291
MICR: 2482-001

Orillia - Mississaga St. East - Main Office
1 Mississaga St. East
Orillia, ON L3V 1V4 Canada
705-326-6437
Fax: 705-326-1057
MICR: 2383-001

Oshawa - King St. East
East Mall Shopping Centre
600 King St. East
Oshawa, ON L1H 1G6 Canada
905-432-6734
Fax: 905-432-6739
MICR: 2905-001

Oshawa - King St. West
Oshawa Centre
PO Box 30570
419 King St. West
Oshawa, ON L1J 8L8 Canada
905-432-6740
Fax: 905-432-6775
MICR: 0352-001

Oshawa - Simcoe St. South - Main Office
PO Box 827
38 Simcoe St. South
Oshawa, ON L1H 7N1 Canada
905-432-6700
Fax: 905-432-6724
MICR: 0351-001

Oshawa - Taunton Rd. East
Five Points Mall A&P
285 Taunton Rd. East, #C
Oshawa, ON L1G 3V2 Canada
905-432-3383
Fax: 905-432-3316
MICR: 3354-001

Osoyoos
PO Box 357
8502 - 76th Ave.
Osoyoos, BC V0H 1V0 Canada
250-495-6511
Fax: 250-495-6255
MICR: 0735-001

Ottawa - Bank St.
2446 Bank St.
Ottawa, ON K1V 1A4 Canada
613-564-6376
Fax: 613-247-7708
MICR: 3874-001

Ottawa - Bank St.
1556 Bank St.
Ottawa, ON K1H 7Z4 Canada
613-564-6077
Fax: 613-521-3753
MICR: 2388-001

Ottawa - Beechwood Ave.
14 Beechwood Ave.
Ottawa, ON K1L 8B4 Canada
613-564-6085
Fax: 613-742-7825
MICR: 2455-001

Ottawa - Elgin St.
Place Bell Canada
160 Elgin St.
Ottawa, ON K2P 2C4 Canada
613-564-6037
Fax: 613-564-3629
MICR: 2486-001

Ottawa - Greenbank Rd.
250 Greenbank Rd.
Ottawa, ON K2H 8X4 Canada
613-564-6490
Fax: 613-596-5614
MICR: 2999-001

Ottawa - Hazeldean Rd.
Van Leeuwen Centre
#2, 420 Hazeldean Rd.
Ottawa, ON K2L 4B2 Canada
613-564-6426
Fax: 613-836-1067
MICR: 3981-001

Ottawa - Innes Rd.
2666 Innes Rd.
Ottawa, ON K1B 4Z5 Canada
613-564-6980
Fax: 613-824-5131
MICR: 0484-001

Ottawa - Kent St.
Place de Ville
112 Kent St.
Ottawa, ON K1P 5P2 Canada
613-564-6029
Fax: 613-564-6499
MICR: 2444-001

Ottawa - Laurier Ave. West
Capital Centre
269 Laurier Ave. West
Ottawa, ON K1P 5J9 Canada
613-564-6424
Fax: 613-564-6381
MICR: 0005-001

Ottawa - Merivale Rd.
1454 Merivale Rd.
Ottawa, ON K2E 5P1 Canada
613-564-6100
Fax: 613-226-2405
MICR: 2391-001

Ottawa - Montreal Rd.
1936 Montreal Rd.
Ottawa, ON K1J 6N2 Canada
613-564-6056
Fax: 613-742-6631
MICR: 0081-001

Ottawa - Montreal Rd.
470 Montreal Rd.
Ottawa, ON K1K 0V3 Canada
613-564-6071
Fax: 613-741-3844
MICR: 2387-001

Ottawa - Northside Rd.
60 Northside Rd.
Ottawa, ON K2H 5Z8 Canada
613-564-6976
Fax: 613-596-1194
MICR: 2312-001

Ottawa - Place d'Orleans Dr.
110 Place d'Orleans Dr.
Ottawa, ON K1C 2L9 Canada
613-564-6494
Fax: 613-841-2235
MICR: 2761-001

Ottawa - Prince of Wales Dr.
Rideau View Shopping Centre
1430 Prince of Wales Dr.
Ottawa, ON K2C 1N6 Canada
613-564-6111
Fax: 613-226-7285
MICR: 2976-001

Ottawa - Richmond Rd.
1315 Richmond Rd.
Ottawa, ON K2B 8J7 Canada
613-564-6247
Fax: 613-596-3924
MICR: 2755-001

Ottawa - Richmond Rd.
288 Richmond Rd.
Ottawa, ON K1Z 6X5 Canada
613-564-6096
Fax: 613-722-1999
MICR: 2386-001

Ottawa - Smyth Rd.
945 Smyth Rd.
Ottawa, ON K1G 1P5 Canada
613-564-6045
Fax: 613-523-5298
MICR: 2374-001

Ottawa - Strandherd Dr.
Barrhaven Town Centre
3775 Strandherd Dr., #A
Ottawa, ON K2J 4B1 Canada
613-825-2508
Fax: 613-825-7362
MICR: 3843-001

Ottawa - Wellington St.
1247 Wellington St.
Ottawa, ON K1Y 3A3 Canada
613-564-6090
Fax: 613-722-6665
MICR: 0356-001

Ottawa - Woodroffe Ave.
1381 Woodroffe Ave.
Ottawa, ON K2G 1V7 Canada
613-564-6984
Fax: 613-226-3899
MICR: 2442-001

Outlook

BMO Bank of Montréal(BMO)/ Banque de Montréal (continued)

PO Box 39
202 Franklin St.
Outlook, SK S0L 2N0 Canada
306-867-8689
Fax: 306-867-8057
MICR: 0540-001

Owen Sound
899 Second Ave. East
Owen Sound, ON N4K 2H2 Canada
519-376-4130
Fax: 519-371-4565
MICR: 0032-001

Paris
68 Grand River St. North
Paris, ON N3L 2M2 Canada
519-442-2291
Fax: 519-442-3829
MICR: 0360-001

Parksville
PO Box 910
220 West Island Hwy.
Parksville, BC V9P 2P3 Canada
250-248-5711
Fax: 250-248-3246
MICR: 0989-001

Pembroke
41 Pembroke St. West
Pembroke, ON K8A 5M5 Canada
613-735-0138
Fax: 613-735-4162
MICR: 2390-001

Penticton - Main St.
Safeway
#801, 1301 Main St.
Penticton, BC V2A 5E9 Canada
250-770-8820
Fax: 250-770-8828
MICR: 3270-001

Penticton - Main St. - Main Office
195 Main St.
Penticton, BC V2A 5A8 Canada
250-492-4240
Fax: 250-492-7879
MICR: 0736-001

Perth
30 Gore St. East
Perth, ON K7H 1H5 Canada
613-267-3220
Fax: 613-267-2904
MICR: 0361-001

Perth-Andover
686 Perth Main St.
Perth-Andover, NB E7H 2W7 Canada
506-273-2261
Fax: 506-273-2906
MICR: 0181-001

Peterborough - Chemong Rd.
Portage Place
1154 Chemong Rd.
Peterborough, ON K9H 7J6 Canada
705-745-1396
Fax: 705-745-2277
MICR: 2427-001

Peterborough - Lansdowne St. West
Lansdowne Place
645 Lansdowne St. West
Peterborough, ON K9J 7Y5 Canada
705-745-5714
Fax: 705-745-9608
MICR: 2678-001

Peterborough - Simcoe St. - Main Office
130 Simcoe St.
Peterborough, ON K9H 2H5 Canada
705-745-3201
Fax: 705-876-9611
MICR: 0017-001

Pickering - Kingston Rd.
#1, 726 Kingston Rd.
Pickering, ON L1V 1A9 Canada
905-839-3600
Fax: 905-839-1907
MICR: 3670-001

Pickering - Kingston Rd.
1298 Kingston Rd.
Pickering, ON L1V 3M9 Canada
905-839-8025
Fax: 905-839-0892
MICR: 2997-001

Picton
115 Main St.
Picton, ON K0K 2T0 Canada
613-476-2131
Fax: 613-476-7876
MICR: 0362-001

Ponoka
PO Box 4457
5101 - 50th Ave.
Ponoka, AB T4J 1S1 Canada
403-783-4401
Fax: 403-783-3270
MICR: 0544-001

Port Alberni - 3rd Ave.
PO Box 130
3100 - 3rd Ave.
Port Alberni, BC V9Y 4C8 Canada
250-723-2431
Fax: 250-724-2262
MICR: 0737-001

Port Alberni - Pacific Rim Hwy.
7585 Pacific Rim Hwy.
Port Alberni, BC V9Y 8Y5 Canada
250-724-7100
Fax: 250-724-0707
MICR: 3655-001

Port au Choix
PO Box 100
100 Main St.
Port au Choix, NL A0K 4C0 Canada
709-861-3508
Fax: 709-861-3053
MICR: 1039-001

Port Colborne
124 Clarence St.
Port Colborne, ON L3K 2G1 Canada
905-835-2232
Fax: 905-835-2220
MICR: 3177-001

Port Coquitlam - Shaughnessy St.
Shaughnessy Safeway
#1100, 2850 Shaughnessy St.
Port Coquitlam, BC V3C 6K9 Canada
604-927-4630
Fax: 604-927-4636
MICR: 3152-001

Port Coquitlam - Shaughnessy St. - Main Office
#102, 2564 Shaughnessy St.
Port Coquitlam, BC V3C 3G4 Canada
604-665-6665
Fax: 604-927-1910
MICR: 2707-001

Port Hawkesbury
#11, 634 Reeves St.
Port Hawkesbury, NS B9A 2R7 Canada
902-625-1250
Fax: 902-625-2287
MICR: 0239-001

Port Hope
70 Walton St.
Port Hope, ON L1A 1N3 Canada
905-885-4531
Fax: 905-885-0121
MICR: 3062-001

Port Moody
228 Ungless Way
Port Moody, BC V3H 4Y9 Canada
604-668-1322
Fax: 604-933-1955
MICR: 3855-001

Port Perry
Port Perry Plaza
1894 Scugog St.
Port Perry, ON L9L 1H7 Canada
905-985-8446
Fax: 905-985-9344
MICR: 2900-001

Portage la Prairie
1 Saskatchewan Ave. West
Portage La Prairie, MB R1N 0P4 Canada
204-239-8600
Fax: 204-239-8614
MICR: 0545-001

Powell River - Barnet St.
Safeway
7040 Barnet St.
Powell River, BC V8A 2A1 Canada
604-485-8580
Fax: 604-485-8586
MICR: 3204-001

Powell River - Marine Ave.
4729 Marine Ave.
Powell River, BC V8A 2L3 Canada
604-485-4221
Fax: 604-485-2282
MICR: 0781-001

Prescott
138 King St.
Prescott, ON K0E 1T0 Canada
613-925-2828
Fax: 613-925-0395
MICR: 2394-001

Prince Albert - 2nd Ave. West
2775 - 2nd Ave. West
Prince Albert, SK S6V 5E5 Canada
306-953-5252
Fax: 306-953-5222
MICR: 0659-001

Prince Albert - Central Ave. - Main Office
1200 Central Ave.
Prince Albert, SK S6V 4V8 Canada
306-953-5200
Fax: 306-953-5241
MICR: 0546-001

Prince George
1445 West Central St.
Prince George, BC V2M 5S5 Canada
250-565-8650
Fax: 250-565-8610
MICR: 0802-001

Prince Rupert
333 - 2nd Ave. West
Prince Rupert, BC V8J 3T1 Canada
250-624-9191
Fax: 250-627-7620
MICR: 0739-001

Qualicum Beach
#101, 661 Primrose St.
Qualicum Beach, BC V9K 2H5 Canada
250-752-1242
Fax: 250-752-2231
MICR: 3857-001

Quesnel
397 Reid St.
Quesnel, BC V2J 2M5 Canada
250-992-5577
Fax: 250-992-9893
MICR: 0747-001

Quispamsis
2A Landing Ct.
Quispamsis, NB E2E 4R2 Canada
506-847-7578
Fax: 506-848-6230
MICR: 2214-001

Québec - Grande Allee est - Succ. Principale
500, Grande Allee est
Québec, QC G1R 2J7 Canada
418-692-2500
Fax: 418-692-0410
MICR: 0007-001

Québec - Henri-Bourassa
8535, boul Henri-Bourassa
Québec, QC G1G 4E1 Canada
418-627-1700
Fax: 418-627-1136
MICR: 2173-001

Québec - Laurier
Place Laurier
2700, boul Laurier
Québec, QC G1V 2L8 Canada
418-577-1818
Fax: 418-577-1824
MICR: 0232-001

Québec - Lebourgneuf
Les Galeries de la Capitale
1600, boul Lebourgneuf
Québec, QC G2K 2M4 Canada

418-627-7446
Fax: 418-627-5091
MICR: 2193-001
Québec - Nordique
Beauport IGA Extra
969, rue Nordique
Québec, QC G1C 7S8 Canada
418-667-3135
Fax: 418-667-6155
MICR: 3764-001
Québec - Ste-Foy
1375, ch Ste-Foy
Québec, QC G1S 2N2 Canada
418-688-5800
Fax: 418-688-4671
MICR: 0184-001
Québec - Ste-Foy
Les Galeries Duplessis
3291, ch Ste-Foy
Québec, QC G1X 3V2 Canada
418-577-1848
Fax: 418-577-1867
MICR: 2125-001
Red Deer - 40th Ave.
3825 - 40th Ave.
Red Deer, AB T4N 2W4 Canada
403-340-4616
Fax: 403-340-4620
MICR: 0589-001
Red Deer - 50th Ave.
Port O'Call Mall Safeway
4408 - 50th Ave.
Red Deer, AB T4N 3Z8 Canada
403-309-4906
Fax: 403-309-4912
MICR: 3121-001
Red Deer - 50th Ave.
Bower Plaza
2325 - 50th Ave.
Red Deer, AB T4R 1M7 Canada
403-340-4626
Fax: 403-340-4621
MICR: 2621-001
Red Deer - Gaetz Ave. - Main Office
4903 Gaetz Ave.
Red Deer, AB T4N 4A6 Canada
403-340-4600
Fax: 403-340-4682
MICR: 0551-001
Regina - Albert St. North
Northgate Shopping Centre
305 Albert St. North
Regina, SK S4R 3C3 Canada
306-569-5733
Fax: 306-543-9960
MICR: 0675-001
Regina - Gordon Rd.
2705 Gordon Rd.
Regina, SK S4S 6H8 Canada
306-569-5720
Fax: 306-584-5511
MICR: 2675-001
Regina - Rochdale Blvd
5966 Rochdale Blvd.
Regina, SK S4X 4J7 Canada
306-569-5623
Fax: 306-545-8682
MICR: 3861-001
Regina - Scarth St. - Main Office
1800 Scarth St.
Regina, SK S4P 2G3 Canada
306-569-5640
Fax: 306-569-5757
MICR: 0013-001
Regina - Victoria Ave. East
Capital City Centre
1871 Victoria Ave. East
Regina, SK S4N 6E6 Canada
306-569-5725
Fax: 306-789-5228
MICR: 3800-001
Renfrew
236 Raglan St. South
Renfrew, ON K7V 1R1 Canada
613-432-4834
Fax: 613-432-7782
MICR: 0370-001
Repentigny - Brien
IGA Extra Repentigny In-Store
180, boul Brien
Repentigny, QC J9A 7E9 Canada
450-657-4600
Fax: 450-657-4745
MICR: 3191-001
Repentigny - Lafayette
#7, 125, rue de Lafayette
Repentigny, QC J6A 8K3 Canada
450-657-4636
Fax: 450-657-2016
MICR: 3876-001
Richmond - No. 3 Rd.
President Plaza
#100, 3880 - No. 3 Rd.
Richmond, BC V6X 2C1 Canada
604-668-1388
Fax: 604-668-1386
MICR: 3877-001
Richmond - No. 3 Rd. - Main Office
6088 - No. 3 Rd.
Richmond, BC V6Y 2B3 Canada
604-668-1575
Fax: 604-668-1173
MICR: 0782-001
Richmond Hill - Hwy. 7 East
Times Square
550 Hwy. 7 East
Richmond Hill, ON L4B 3Z4 Canada
905-707-8100
Fax: 905-707-8112
MICR: 3434-001
Richmond Hill - Major Mackenzie Dr. East
Bayview & Major Mackenzie Dominion
1070 Major Mackenzie Dr. East
Richmond Hill, ON L4S 1P3 Canada
905-884-2994
Fax: 905-884-0050
MICR: 3624-001
Richmond Hill - Spadina Rd.
1 Spadina Rd.
Richmond Hill, ON L4B 3M2 Canada
905-508-6611
Fax: 905-508-6615
MICR: 3846-001
Richmond Hill - Yonge St.
Hillcrest Mall
9350 Yonge St.
Richmond Hill, ON L4C 5G2 Canada
905-884-0333
Fax: 905-884-1273
MICR: 2211-001
Rimbey
PO Box 60
4948 - 50th Ave.
Rimbey, AB T0C 2J0 Canada
403-843-2002
Fax: 403-843-3085
MICR: 2581-001
Rimouski
85, av Rouleau
Rimouski, QC G5L 8M7 Canada
418-723-3307
Fax: 418-722-5019
MICR: 2131-001
Riverview
500 Coverdale Rd.
Riverview, NB E1B 3K2 Canada
506-853-5775
Fax: 506-853-7513
MICR: 0293-001
Rivière-du-Loup
PO Box 70
428, rue Lafontaine
Rivière-du-Loup, QC G5R 3B8 Canada
418-862-6961
Fax: 418-862-4397
MICR: 0122-001
Rocky Harbour
PO Box 119
Main St.
Rocky Harbour, NL A0K 4N0 Canada
709-458-2240
Fax: 709-458-2392
MICR: 2213-001
Rothesay
Fairvale Plaza Sobeys In-Store
PO Box 4787
#140, 142 Hampton Rd.
Rothesay, NB E2E 5X5 Canada
506-848-0640
Fax: 506-848-0646
MICR: 3456-001
Saint John - Fairville Blvd.
Lancaster Mall
621 Fairville Blvd.
Saint John, NB E2M 4X5 Canada
506-632-0225
Fax: 506-632-0281
MICR: 0253-001
Saint John - MacDonald St.
Loch Lomond Shopping Mall
120 MacDonald St.
Saint John, NB E2J 1M5 Canada
506-632-0221
Fax: 506-632-0232
MICR: 2153-001
Saint John - Market Sq. - Main Office
City Hall
15 Market Sq.
Saint John, NB E2L 1E8 Canada
506-632-0202
Fax: 506-632-0594
MICR: 0011-001
Saint John - Westmorland Rd.
McAllister Place Sobeys In-Store
519 Westmorland Rd.
Saint John, NB E2J 3W9 Canada
506-632-0212
Fax: 506-632-0242
MICR: 3455-001
Saint-Bruno
1560, rue Montarville
Saint-Bruno, QC J3V 3T7 Canada
450-653-3624
Fax: 450-653-4288
MICR: 0277-001
Saint-Constant
#13, 115, rue St-Pierre
Saint-Constant, QC J5A 2G9 Canada
450-632-8793
Fax: 450-632-9972
MICR: 0289-001
Saint-Georges - 1re est
11980, av 1e est
Saint-Georges, QC G5Y 2E1
418-228-8886
Fax: 418-228-4077
MICR: 0189-001
Saint-Georges - Lacroix
IGA Extra
8980, boul Lacroix
Saint-Georges, QC G5Y 5E2 Canada
418-228-7469
Fax: 418-228-7534
MICR: 2936-001
Saint-Hubert - Aéroport
Agence Spatiale Canadienne
6767, rte de l'Aéroport
Saint-Hubert, QC J3Y 8Y9 Canada
450-926-2350
Fax: 450-926-2827
MICR: SG04-001
Saint-Hubert - Cousineau
PO Box 100
7171, boul Cousineau
Saint-Hubert, QC J3Y 8N2 Canada
450-926-1122
Fax: 450-926-1414
MICR: 3881-001
Saint-Hyacinthe
2480, boul Casavant ouest
Saint-Hyacinthe, QC J2S 7R8 Canada

BMO Bank of Montréal(BMO)/ Banque de Montréal (continued)

450-773-9733
Fax: 450-774-2510
MICR: 0044-001

Saint-Lambert
500, av Victoria
Saint-Lambert, QC J4P 2J5 Canada
450-466-1666
Fax: 450-466-2463
MICR: 0192-001

Sainte-Adèle
555, boul Sainte-Adèle
Sainte-Adèle, QC J8B 1A7 Canada
450-229-3538
Fax: 450-229-9309
MICR: 2132-001

Sainte-Julie - Haut-Bois
Centre Commerciale Sainte-Julie
99, boul des Haut-Bois
Sainte-Julie, QC J3E 3J9 Canada
450-649-1589
Fax: 450-649-9052
MICR: 2196-001

Sainte-Julie - Principale
Marche IGA Faubourg Sainte-Julie
2055, rue Principale
Sainte-Julie, QC J3E 1W1 Canada
450-649-4250
Fax: 450-649-2336
MICR: 3188-001

Salaberry-de-Valleyfield
11, rue Nicholson
Salaberry-de-Valleyfield, QC J6T 4M4 Canada
450-373-1030
Fax: 450-373-7610
MICR: 0045-001

Salmon Arm
PO Box 1900
231 Transcanada Hwy.
Salmon Arm, BC V1E 4P9 Canada
250-832-7168
Fax: 250-832-6202
MICR: 0839-001

Salt Spring Island
116 Fulford-Ganges Rd.
Salt Spring Island, BC V8K 2S4 Canada
250-537-5524
Fax: 250-537-4955
MICR: 0715-001

Sarnia - Christina St. North - Main Office
215 Christina St. North
Sarnia, ON N7T 5V1 Canada
519-344-5822
Fax: 519-332-6568
MICR: 0042-001

Sarnia - Exmouth St.
435 Exmouth St.
Sarnia, ON N7T 5P1 Canada
519-344-2484
Fax: 519-344-4488
MICR: 2401-001

Sarnia - Lambton Mall Rd.
#117, 1362 Lambton Mall Rd.
Sarnia, ON N7S 5A1 Canada
519-542-8508
Fax: 519-542-7696
MICR: 0486-001

Saskatoon - 2nd Ave. North - Main Office
PO Box 290
101 - 2nd Ave. North
Saskatoon, SK S7K 3L4 Canada
306-934-5600
Fax: 306-934-5628
MICR: 0034-001

Saskatoon - 8th St. East
2122 - 8th St. East
Saskatoon, SK S7H 0V1 Canada
306-934-5725
Fax: 306-955-2218
MICR: 2680-001

Saskatoon - Central Ave.
804 Central Ave.
Saskatoon, SK S7N 2G6 Canada
306-934-5731
Fax: 306-955-3059
MICR: 0602-001

Saskatoon - Confederation Dr.
Confederation Mall
300 Confederation Dr.
Saskatoon, SK S7L 4R6 Canada
306-934-5737
Fax: 306-384-3720
MICR: 0618-001

Saskatoon - Preston Ave.
Market Mall
2325 Preston Ave.
Saskatoon, SK S7J 2G2 Canada
306-934-5720
Fax: 306-934-5773
MICR: 0557-001

Saskatoon - Primrose Dr.
Lawson Heights Mall
134 Primrose Dr.
Saskatoon, SK S7K 5S6 Canada
306-934-5745
Fax: 306-242-5256
MICR: 2691-001

Sault Ste Marie - Great Northern Rd.
Cambrian Mall
44 Great Northern Rd.
Sault Ste Marie, ON P6B 4Y5 Canada
705-254-7175
Fax: 705-254-6788
MICR: 2449-001

Sault Ste Marie - Korah Rd.
331 Korah Rd.
Sault Ste Marie, ON P6C 4H4 Canada
705-256-8486
Fax: 705-256-7593
MICR: 2436-001

Sault Ste Marie - Queen St. East - Main Office
556 Queen St. East
Sault Ste Marie, ON P6A 2A1 Canada
705-949-3221
Fax: 705-949-5423
MICR: 0041-001

Schreiber
PO Box 99
320 Scotia St.
Schreiber, ON P0T 2S0 Canada
807-824-2060
Fax: 807-824-2072
MICR: 0363-001

Sechelt
PO Box 100
5640 Cowrie St.
Sechelt, BC V0N 3A0 Canada
604-885-4121
Fax: 604-885-5886
MICR: 0748-001

Selkirk - Manitoba Ave.
Safeway
318 Manitoba Ave.
Selkirk, MB R1A 0Y7 Canada
204-482-1888
Fax: 204-482-1844
MICR: 3154-001

Selkirk - Manitoba Ave.
249 Manitoba Ave.
Selkirk, MB R1A 0Y4 Canada
204-482-1850
Fax: 240-482-1861
MICR: 0555-001

Sept-×les - Brochu
390, av Brochu
Sept-×les, QC G4R 2W6 Canada
418-962-9432
Fax: 418-968-8211
MICR: 0194-001

Sept-×les - Laure
Sept-×les IGA Extra
1010, boul Laure
Sept-×les, QC G4R 5P1 Canada
418-961-1538
Fax: 418-961-1660
MICR: 3242-001

Shediac
362 Main St.
Shediac, NB E4P 2E8 Canada
506-532-4411
Fax: 506-532-2216
MICR: 0196-001

Sherbrooke - Conseil
739, rue Conseil
Sherbrooke, QC J1G 1K8 Canada
819-822-5165
Fax: 819-822-5138
MICR: 0240-001

Sherbrooke - King ouest - Succ. Principale
2959, rue King ouest
Sherbrooke, QC J1L 1C7 Canada
819-822-5145
Fax: 819-822-5134
MICR: 0215-001

Sherbrooke - rue King ouest
Rock Forest IGA Extra In-Store
3950, rue King ouest
Sherbrooke, QC J1L 1P6 Canada
819-822-4285
Fax: 819-822-4389
MICR: 3492-001

Sherwood Park - Baseline Rd.
#300, 222 Baseline Rd.
Sherwood Park, AB T8H 1S8 Canada
780-464-3226
Fax: 780-467-3054
MICR: 2791-001

Sherwood Park - Ordze Ave.
145 Ordze Ave.
Sherwood Park, AB T8B 1M6 Canada
780-417-7272
Fax: 780-417-7262
MICR: 3740-001

Sherwood Park - Sherwood Dr.
Sherwood Mall Safeway
2020 Sherwood Dr.
Sherwood Park, AB T8A 3H9 Canada
780-417-7200
Fax: 780-417-7206
MICR: 2642-001

Sidney - Beacon Ave.
PO Box 2100
2461 Beacon Ave.
Sidney, BC V8L 3X7 Canada
250-656-7221
Fax: 250-656-5539
MICR: 2700-001

Siksika
Administration Complex
PO Box 1429
Hwy. #547
Siksika, AB T0J 3W0 Canada
403-734-3600
Fax: 403-734-3603
MICR: 3884-001

Simcoe
23 Norfolk St. South
Simcoe, ON N3Y 2V8 Canada
519-426-1860
Fax: 519-426-3765
MICR: 2396-001

Sioux Lookout
PO Box 639
61 Front St.
Sioux Lookout, ON P8T 1B1 Canada
807-737-1860
Fax: 807-737-3036
MICR: 2403-001

Smiths Falls
25 Beckwith St. South
Smiths Falls, ON K7A 2A9 Canada
613-283-4292
Fax: 613-283-9436
MICR: 2397-001

Springdale
PO Box 339
184 Main St.
Springdale, NL A0J 1T0 Canada
709-673-5170
Fax: 709-673-4983
MICR: 1025-001

Spruce Grove
#110, 16 Westway Rd.
Spruce Grove, AB T7X 3X3 Canada
780-962-4066
Fax: 780-962-0773

MICR: 2567-001
Squamish
PO Box 1549
38201 Cleveland Ave.
Squamish, BC V8B 0B1 Canada
604-892-3591
Fax: 604-892-2177
MICR: 0831-001
St Albans
PO Box 99
93 Main St.
St Albans, NL A0H 2E0 Canada
709-538-3405
Fax: 709-538-3111
MICR: 1038-001
St Albert - St. Albert Rd.
394 St. Albert Rd.
St Albert, AB T8N 5J9 Canada
780-458-8666
Fax: 780-460-8603
MICR: 2792-001
St Catharines - Bunting Rd.
366 Bunting Rd.
St Catharines, ON L2M 3Y6 Canada
905-641-7800
Fax: 905-937-0627
MICR: 3839-001
St Catharines - Glendale Ave.
228 Glendale Ave.
St Catharines, ON L2T 2K5 Canada
905-641-7874
Fax: 905-641-7893
MICR: 2485-001
St Catharines - King St. - Main Office
31 King St.
St Catharines, ON L2R 6W7 Canada
905-641-7837
Fax: 905-641-7854
MICR: 0033-001
St Catharines - Lakeshore Rd.
121 Lakeshore Rd.
St Catharines, ON L2N 2T7 Canada
905-641-7803
Fax: 905-937-1873
MICR: 2471-001
St Catharines - Welland Ave.
191 Welland Ave.
St Catharines, ON L2R 2P2 Canada
905-641-7878
Fax: 905-641-7899
MICR: 2399-001
St George Brant
9 Beverley St. West
St George Brant, ON N0E 1N0 Canada
519-448-1353
Fax: 519-448-3089
MICR: 2451-001
St Marys
136 Queen St. East
St Marys, ON N4X 1B3 Canada
519-284-2020
Fax: 519-284-1489
MICR: 0376-001
St Thomas - Elm St.
300 Elm St.
St Thomas, ON N5R 1J7 Canada
519-631-4260
Fax: 519-631-4224
MICR: 0453-001
St-Eustache
535, boul Arthur-Sauvé
Saint-Eustache, QC J7P 4X4 Canada
450-974-1010
Fax: 450-974-0329
MICR: 3849-001
St-Jean-sur-Richelieu
991, boul de Séminaire nord
St-Jean-sur-Richelieu, QC J3A 1K1 Canada
450-347-0391
Fax: 450-359-7439
MICR: 2137-001
St-Jérôme - Laurentides
511, boul des Laurentides
St-Jérôme, QC J7Z 4L9 Canada
450-432-4355
Fax: 450-432-6057
MICR: 2136-001
St-Jérôme - St-Georges
Marché Lord de Lafontaine IGA
2012, rue St-Georges
St-Jérôme, QC J7Y 1M8 Canada
450-436-3900
Fax: 450-436-2102
MICR: 3113-001
St-Jérôme - St-Georges
288, rue St-Georges
St-Jérôme, QC J7Z 5A6 Canada
450-432-4321
Fax: 450-432-8207
MICR: 2134-001
St-Romuald
835, 4e av
St-Romuald, QC G6W 5M6 Canada
418-834-3643
Fax: 418-834-3757
MICR: 0273-001
St. John's - Elizabeth Ave.
Howley Estates Sobeys In-Store
10 Elizabeth Ave.
St. John's, NL A1A 1W4 Canada
709-758-2126
Fax: 709-758-2128
MICR: 3647-001
St. John's - Elizabeth Ave. West
384 Elizabeth Ave. West
St. John's, NL A1B 1V2 Canada
709-758-2110
Fax: 709-758-2114
MICR: 1009-001
St. John's - Newfoundland Dr.
370 Newfoundland Dr.
St. John's, NL A1A 4A2 Canada
709-758-2100
Fax: 709-758-2104
MICR: 2190-001
St. John's - Ropewalk Lane
Ropewalk Lane Sobeys In-Store
45 Ropewalk Lane
St. John's, NL A1E 4P1 Canada
709-758-2160
Fax: 709-758-2167
MICR: 3689-001
St. John's - Topsail Rd.
Village Shopping Centre
PO Box 66
430 Topsail Rd.
St. John's, NL A1E 4N1 Canada
709-758-2140
Fax: 709-758-2145
MICR: 1035-001
St. John's - Water St. - Main Branch
238 Water St.
St. John's, NL A1C 1A9 Canada
709-758-2055
Fax: 709-758-2157
MICR: 1002-001
St. Jérôme - Grand Heron
St. Jérôme IGA Extra In-Store
1005 boul Grand Heron
St-Jérôme, QC J7Y 3P2 Canada
450-432-6141
Fax: 450-432-6629
MICR: 3779-001
St. Stephen
67 Milltown Blvd.
St. Stephen, NB E3L 1G4 Canada
506-466-3260
Fax: 506-466-3286
MICR: 0201-001
St. Thomas - Talbot St.
#43, 739 Talbot St.
St Thomas, ON N5P 1E3 Canada
519-631-9500
Fax: 519-633-9842
MICR: 2405-001
Ste-Agathe-des-Monts
#234, 40, boul Morin
Sainte-Agathe-des-Monts, QC J8C 2V6 Canada
819-326-1030
Fax: 819-326-1667
MICR: 2133-001
Ste-Thérèse
35, rue Blainville ouest
Sainte-Thérèse, QC J7E 1X1 Canada
450-437-6868
Fax: 450-437-5046
MICR: 2143-001
Stephenville
78 Main St.
Stephenville, NL A2N 1J3 Canada
709-643-8900
Fax: 709-643-9481
MICR: 1027-001
Stirling
7 Front St.
Stirling, ON K0K 3E0 Canada
613-395-3381
Fax: 613-395-2089
MICR: 0375-001
Stoney Creek
910 Queenston Rd.
Stoney Creek, ON L8G 1B5 Canada
905-662-4903
Fax: 905-578-2203
MICR: 2402-001
Stratford
73 Downie St.
Stratford, ON N5A 1W8 Canada
519-271-4910
Fax: 519-271-9403
MICR: 0031-001
Strathroy
630 Victoria St.
Strathroy, ON N7G 3C1 Canada
519-245-2990
Fax: 519-245-6322
MICR: 2957-001
Sudbury - Durham St. - Main Office
79 Durham St.
Sudbury, ON P3E 3M5 Canada
705-670-2235
Fax: 705-674-5012
MICR: 0377-001
Sudbury - LaSalle Blvd.
Sudbury Supermall Shopping Centre
1485 LaSalle Blvd.
Sudbury, ON P3A 5H7 Canada
705-566-3940
Fax: 705-566-3459
MICR: 2447-001
Sudbury - Long Lake Rd.
Four Corners Plaza
2017 Long Lake Rd.
Sudbury, ON P3E 4M8 Canada
705-522-2090
Fax: 705-522-6555
MICR: 2947-001
Summerland
PO Box 40
9902 Main St.
Summerland, BC V0H 1Z0 Canada
250-494-7831
Fax: 250-494-4377
MICR: 0775-001
Summerside
Country Fair Mall
455 Granville St. North
Summerside, PE C1N 4P7 Canada
902-436-9231
Fax: 902-436-1524
MICR: 0285-001
Sundre
PO Box 240
407 Main Ave. West
Sundre, AB T0M 1X0 Canada
403-638-3515
Fax: 403-638-2720
MICR: 0558-001
Surrey - 120 St.
7140 - 120 St.
Surrey, BC V3W 3M8 Canada
604-668-1560
Fax: 604-596-0328

BMO Bank of Montréal(BMO)/ Banque de Montréal (continued)

MICR: 0818-001

Surrey - 138th St.
Newton Safeway
7165 - 138th St.
Surrey, BC V3W 7T9 Canada
604-592-5890
Fax: 604-592-5896
MICR: 3686-001

Surrey - 152nd St.
Fleetwood Safeway
8860 - 152nd St.
Surrey, BC V3R 4E4 Canada
604-587-6830
Fax: 604-587-6836
MICR: 3131-001

Surrey - 16th Ave.
12810 - 16th Ave.
Surrey, BC V4A 1N4 Canada
604-536-2154
Fax: 604-536-2868
MICR: 0988-001

Surrey - 176A St.
5711 - 176A St.
Surrey, BC V3S 6S6 Canada
604-574-4152
Fax: 604-574-6872
MICR: 0706-001

Surrey - 24th Ave.
Peninsula Village Shopping Centre Safeway
#700, 15355 - 24th Ave.
Surrey, BC V4A 2H9 Canada
604-541-5662
Fax: 604-541-5697
MICR: 3120-001

Surrey - Guildford Town Centre
1883 Guildford Town Centre
Surrey, BC V3R 7B8 Canada
604-668-1589
Fax: 604-581-6317
MICR: 2737-001

Surrey - King George Hwy.
King George Hwy. Safeway
10355 King George Hwy.
Surrey, BC V3T 2W6 Canada
604-587-1030
Fax: 604-587-1036
MICR: 3114-001

Surrey - King George Hwy.
King's Cross Shopping Centre
#110, 7488 King George Hwy.
Surrey, BC V3W 0H9 Canada
604-668-1151
Fax: 604-599-0173
MICR: 0789-001

Surrey - King George Hwy.
10155 King George Hwy.
Surrey, BC V3T 5H9 Canada
604-668-1180
Fax: 604-588-6753
MICR: 0985-001

Sussex
9 Broad St.
Sussex, NB E4E 2J7 Canada
506-432-1920
Fax: 506-432-9270
MICR: 0292-001

Sutton West
Sutton West Shopping Centre
106 High St.
Sutton West, ON L0E 1R0 Canada
905-722-3293
Fax: 905-722-3585
MICR: 2466-001

Swift Current
213 Central Ave. North
Swift Current, SK S9H 0L3 Canada
306-773-4611
Fax: 306-773-3766
MICR: 0556-001

Sydney - Charlotte St. - Main Office
173 Charlotte St.
Sydney, NS B1P 1C4 Canada
902-562-9500
Fax: 902-562-9510
MICR: 0019-001

Sydney - Prince St.
493 Prince St.
Sydney, NS B1P 5L8 Canada
902-562-5586
Fax: 902-562-7462
MICR: 0245-001

Taber
5125 - 48th Ave.
Taber, AB T1G 1S9 Canada
403-223-3531
Fax: 403-223-8724
MICR: 0559-001

Tara
42 Yonge St.
Tara, ON N0H 2N0 Canada
519-934-2700
Fax: 519-934-3267
MICR: 2406-001

Tecumseh
13510 Tecumseh Rd.
Tecumseh, ON N8N 3N7 Canada
519-739-3280
Fax: 519-739-3402
MICR: 3547-001

Teeswater
PO Box 190
8 Clinton St.
Teeswater, ON N0G 2S0 Canada
519-392-6831
Fax: 519-392-6835
MICR: 2409-001

Terrace
4666 Lakelse Ave.
Terrace, BC V8G 1R4 Canada
250-615-6150
Fax: 250-635-6963
MICR: 0751-001

Terrebonne
Les Galeries de Terrebonne
#29, 1185, boul Moody
Terrebonne, QC J6W 3Z5 Canada
450-961-4143
Fax: 450-961-4374
MICR: 0298-001

Thamesville
PO Box 130
London Rd.
Thamesville, ON N0P 2K0 Canada
519-692-3931
Fax: 519-692-3214
MICR: 2407-001

Thorndale
190 King St.
Thorndale, ON N0M 2P0 Canada
519-461-0520
Fax: 519-461-1029
MICR: 0439-001

Thornhill - Bayview Ave. North
8218 Bayview Ave. North
Thornhill, ON L3T 2S2 Canada
905-881-2055
Fax: 905-881-7346
MICR: 2926-001

Thornhill - Promenade Circle
The Promenade
1 Promenade Circle
Thornhill, ON L4J 4P8 Canada
905-886-1860
Fax: 905-886-8766
MICR: 3920-001

Thorold
9 Pine St. North
Thorold, ON L2V 3Z9 Canada
905-641-7847
Fax: 905-227-1907
MICR: 0403-001

Thorsby
PO Box 210
4928 Hankin St.
Thorsby, AB T0C 2P0 Canada
780-789-3846
Fax: 780-789-2228
MICR: 0561-001

Thunder Bay - Arthur St. West
West Arthur St. Safeway
115 Arthur St. West
Thunder Bay, ON P7E 5P7 Canada
807-473-1410
Fax: 807-473-1437
MICR: 3645-001

Thunder Bay - Dawson Rd.
County Fair Plaza
1020 Dawson Rd.
Thunder Bay, ON P7B 5V1 Canada
807-766-1485
Fax: 807-766-1408
MICR: 0483-001

Thunder Bay - North Edward St.
Northwood Park Plaza
425 North Edward St.
Thunder Bay, ON P7C 4P7 Canada
807-473-1465
Fax: 807-473-1495
MICR: 0050-001

Thunder Bay - Red River Rd.
256 Red River Rd.
Thunder Bay, ON P7B 1A8 Canada
807-343-1450
Fax: 807-343-1430
MICR: 0036-001

Thunder Bay - Syndicate Ave. South - Main Office
Victoriaville Centre
PO Box 27002
101 Syndicate Ave. South
Thunder Bay, ON P7E 1C5 Canada
807-628-1400
Fax: 807-628-1411
MICR: 0022-001

Tilbury
PO Box 640
3 Queen St. North
Tilbury, ON N0P 2L0 Canada
519-682-2373
Fax: 519-682-0495
MICR: 2410-001

Tillsonburg
160 Broadway St.
Tillsonburg, ON N4G 3P8 Canada
519-842-6467
Fax: 519-842-4125
MICR: 0374-001

Timmins
27 Pine St. South
Timmins, ON P4N 2J9 Canada
705-264-5381
Fax: 705-268-9188
MICR: 0414-001

Tisdale
PO Box 1450
Tisdale, SK S0E 1T0 Canada
306-873-2626
Fax: 306-873-2800
MICR: 2685-001

Tofield
PO Box 240
5303 - 50th St.
Tofield, AB T0B 4J0 Canada
780-662-4091
Fax: 780-662-2420
MICR: 2596-001

Toronto - Albion Rd.
Shopper's World Albion
1530 Albion Rd.
Toronto, ON M9V 1B4 Canada
416-740-5705
Fax: 416-740-3769
MICR: 0474-001

Toronto - Bathurst St.
2953 Bathurst St.
Toronto, ON M6B 3B2 Canada
416-789-7915
Fax: 416-789-9519
MICR: 0424-001

Toronto - Bathurst St.
6172 Bathurst St.
Toronto, ON M2R 2A2 Canada
416-222-5496
Fax: 416-222-5444
MICR: 2469-001

Toronto - Bay St.
880 Bay St.
Toronto, ON M5S 1Z8 Canada
416-867-5190
Fax: 416-928-2008
MICR: 0442-001

Toronto - Bayview Ave.
1670 Bayview Ave.
Toronto, ON M4G 3C2 Canada
416-488-7298
Fax: 416-488-1710
MICR: 0383-001

Toronto - Bloor St. East
175 Bloor St. East
Toronto, ON M4W 3T5 Canada
416-867-6731
Fax: 416-929-2161
MICR: 0380-001

Toronto - Bloor St. West
Manulife Centre
55 Bloor St. West
Toronto, ON M4W 1A6 Canada
416-927-5915
Fax: 416-927-5376
MICR: 0389-001

Toronto - Bloor St. West
640 Bloor St. West
Toronto, ON M6G 1K9 Canada
416-533-8583
Fax: 416-533-2285
MICR: 2450-001

Toronto - Bloor St. West
1293 Bloor St. West
Toronto, ON M6H 1P1 Canada
416-531-3561
Fax: 416-531-6722
MICR: 0392-001

Toronto - Bloor St. West
2330 Bloor St. West
Toronto, ON M6S 1P3 Canada
416-769-4151
Fax: 416-769-0578
MICR: 0367-001

Toronto - Bloor St. West
Six Point Plaza
3835 Bloor St. West
Toronto, ON M9B 1K9 Canada
416-239-3903
Fax: 416-239-3651
MICR: 2335-001

Toronto - Bloor St. West
3022 Bloor St. West
Toronto, ON M8X 1C4 Canada
416-231-2255
Fax: 416-231-8232
MICR: 0368-001

Toronto - Bloor St. West
262 Bloor St. West
Toronto, ON M5S 1V9 Canada
416-867-4663
Fax: 416-921-6461
MICR: 0398-001

Toronto - Bridletowne Circle
2122 Bridletowne Circle
Toronto, ON M1W 2L1 Canada
416-497-2863
Fax: 416-497-8213
MICR: 2979-001

Toronto - Brimley Rd.
Chartwell Shopping Centre
2301 Brimley Rd.
Toronto, ON M1S 5B8 Canada
416-321-2070
Fax: 416-321-3276
MICR: 3974-001

Toronto - Brown's Line
863 Brown's Line
Toronto, ON M8W 3V7 Canada
416-259-3236
Fax: 416-251-0231
MICR: 0379-001

Toronto - College St.
568 College St.
Toronto, ON M6G 1B3 Canada
416-534-8441
Fax: 416-534-2891
MICR: 2412-001

Toronto - Danforth Ave.
Shoppers World Danforth Dominion
3003 Danforth Ave.
Toronto, ON M4C 1M9 Canada
416-699-4400
Fax: 416-699-4757
MICR: 3233-001

Toronto - Danforth Ave.
2810 Danforth Ave.
Toronto, ON M4C 1M1 Canada
416-698-1601
Fax: 416-693-6721
MICR: 2408-001

Toronto - Danforth Ave.
518 Danforth Ave.
Toronto, ON M4K 1P6 Canada
416-463-1177
Fax: 416-463-9895
MICR: 0400-001

Toronto - Dufferin St.
3169 Dufferin St.
Toronto, ON M6A 2S9 Canada
416-787-4564
Fax: 416-787-8422
MICR: 2377-001

Toronto - Dufferin St.
4800 Dufferin St.
Toronto, ON M3H 5S8 Canada
416-661-2101
Fax: 416-661-1408
MICR: 2464-001

Toronto - Dundas St. West
180 Dundas St. West
Toronto, ON M5G 1Z8 Canada
416-867-6810
Fax: 416-351-7855
MICR: 2210-001

Toronto - Dundas St. West
2859 Dundas St. West
Toronto, ON M6P 1Y9 Canada
416-767-3111
Fax: 416-767-5854
MICR: 0399-001

Toronto - Dupont St.
659 Dupont St.
Toronto, ON M6G 1Z5 Canada
416-534-3543
Fax: 416-534-3467
MICR: 2414-001

Toronto - Eglinton Ave. East
Markington Square Dominion Plus
3221 Eglinton Ave. East
Toronto, ON M1J 2H7
416-261-8331
Fax: 416-261-4433
MICR: 3355-001

Toronto - Eglinton Ave. East
2739 Eglinton Ave. East
Toronto, ON M1K 2S2 Canada
416-267-1157
Fax: 416-267-7571
MICR: 0450-001

Toronto - Eglinton Ave. West
898 Eglinton Ave. West
Toronto, ON M6C 2B6 Canada
416-787-4961
Fax: 416-787-8096
MICR: 0397-001

Toronto - Eglinton Ave. West
1901 Eglinton Ave. West
Toronto, ON M6E 2J5 Canada
416-781-5557
Fax: 416-789-2471
MICR: 0369-001

Toronto - Eringate Dr.
120 Eringate Dr.
Toronto, ON M9C 3Z8 Canada
416-621-7141
Fax: 416-621-5170
MICR: 0458-001

Toronto - Finch Ave. West
Finchdale Plaza
2546 Finch Ave. West
Toronto, ON M9M 2G3 Canada
416-749-9331
Fax: 416-748-2143
MICR: 2953-001

Toronto - Front St.
Front St. Market Dominion
80 Front St. East
Toronto, ON M5E 1T4 Canada
416-203-8110
Fax: 416-203-8116
MICR: 3174-001

Toronto - Islington Ave.
2428 Islington Ave.
Toronto, ON M9W 3X8 Canada
416-740-5664
Fax: 416-740-1720
MICR: 2440-001

Toronto - Keele St.
York University
4700 Keele St.
Toronto, ON M3J 1P3 Canada
416-665-4775
Fax: 416-665-8317
MICR: 3851-001

Toronto - Kennedy Rd.
2350 Kennedy Rd.
Toronto, ON M1T 3H1 Canada
416-291-7987
Fax: 416-291-7020
MICR: 2924-001

Toronto - Kennedy Rd.
Kennedy Park Shopping Centre
682 Kennedy Rd.
Toronto, ON M1K 2B5 Canada
416-265-1700
Fax: 416-265-7769
MICR: 0423-001

Toronto - King St. West
First Canadian Place
PO Box 3
100 King St. West
Toronto, ON M5X 1A3 Canada
416-867-5050
Fax: 416-867-6764
MICR: 0002-001

Toronto - King St. West
1211 King St. West
Toronto, ON M6K 1G3 Canada
416-533-8559
Fax: 416-516-3281
MICR: 0393-001

Toronto - King St. West
200 King St. West
Toronto, ON M5H 3T4 Canada
416-867-5268
Fax: 416-596-7700
MICR: 2418-001

Toronto - King St. West
6 King St. West
Toronto, ON M5H 1C3 Canada
416-867-5323
Fax: 416-867-7320
MICR: 2411-001

Toronto - Lakeshore Blvd. West
2194 Lakeshore Blvd. West
Toronto, ON M8V 1A2 Canada
416-251-3323
Fax: 416-251-3697
MICR: 0419-001

Toronto - Lakeshore Blvd. West
2448 Lakeshore Blvd. West
Toronto, ON M8V 1C8 Canada
416-251-3738
Fax: 416-251-9276
MICR: 2435-001

Toronto - Lavington Dr.
Martin Grove Gardens
5 Lavington Dr.
Toronto, ON M9R 2H1 Canada
416-247-8653
Fax: 416-247-4612
MICR: 0435-001

Toronto - Lawrence Ave. East

BMO Bank of Montréal(BMO)/ Banque de Montréal (continued)

5540 Lawrence Ave. East
Toronto, ON M1C 3B2 Canada
416-284-0157
Fax: 416-284-7753
MICR: 2458-001

Toronto - Lawrence Ave. East
3601 Lawrence Ave. East
Toronto, ON M1G 1P5 Canada
416-431-6607
Fax: 416-431-4312
MICR: 2461-001

Toronto - Lawrence Ave. East
877 Lawrence Ave. East
Toronto, ON M3C 2T3 Canada
416-447-8576
Fax: 416-449-5058
MICR: 0317-001

Toronto - Lawrence Ave. East
Westford Centre
2131 Lawrence Ave. East
Toronto, ON M1R 5G4 Canada
416-759-9366
Fax: 416-759-8337
MICR: 0425-001

Toronto - Leslie St.
4797 Leslie St.
Toronto, ON M2J 2K8 Canada
416-493-1090
Fax: 416-499-7112
MICR: 0457-001

Toronto - Livingston Rd.
71 Livingston Rd.
Toronto, ON M1E 1K7 Canada
416-266-4574
Fax: 416-266-0908
MICR: 2925-001

Toronto - McCowan Rd.
McCowan Square
1225 McCowan Rd.
Toronto, ON M1H 3K3
416-438-9900
Fax: 416-439-9507
MICR: 2986-001

Toronto - Overlea Blvd.
East York Town Centre
45 Overlea Blvd.
Toronto, ON M4H 1C3 Canada
416-421-0921
Fax: 416-421-6716
MICR: 0440-001

Toronto - Pharmacy Ave.
627 Pharmacy Ave.
Toronto, ON M1L 3H3 Canada
416-759-9371
Fax: 416-759-8140
MICR: 0417-001

Toronto - Queen St. East
1775 Queen St. East
Toronto, ON M4L 6S6 Canada
416-699-9351
Fax: 416-694-7972
MICR: 0394-001

Toronto - Queen St. East
711 Queen St. East
Toronto, ON M4M 1H1 Canada
416-461-0801
Fax: 416-461-7378
MICR: 0387-001

Toronto - Queen St. East
2 Queen St. East
Toronto, ON M5C 3G7 Canada
416-867-5596
Fax: 416-867-7769
MICR: 2487-001

Toronto - Queensway
Ontario Food Terminal
165 The Queensway
Toronto, ON M8Y 1H8 Canada
416-259-4697
Fax: 416-503-3591
MICR: 2379-001

Toronto - Queensway
1230 The Queensway
Toronto, ON M8Z 1R8 Canada
416-259-9691
Fax: 416-259-1818
MICR: 0416-001

Toronto - Rexdale Blvd.
155 Rexdale Blvd.
Toronto, ON M9W 5Z8 Canada
416-743-5905
Fax: 416-744-4251
MICR: 2416-001

Toronto - Royal York Rd.
1500 Royal York Rd.
Toronto, ON M9P 3B6 Canada
416-241-8687
Fax: 416-241-3557
MICR: 0438-001

Toronto - Sandhurst Circle
Woodside Square
1571 Sandhurst Circle
Toronto, ON M1V 1V2 Canada
416-299-3040
Fax: 416-299-6875
MICR: 2577-001

Toronto - Saturn Rd.
141 Saturn Rd.
Toronto, ON M9C 2S8 Canada
416-621-1532
Fax: 416-621-5441
MICR: 2492-001

Toronto - Sheppard Ave. East
2450 Sheppard Ave. East
Toronto, ON M2J 1X1 Canada
416-490-0089
Fax: 416-491-0036
MICR: 2465-001

Toronto - Sheppard Ave. East
4271 Sheppard Ave. East
Toronto, ON M1S 4G4 Canada
416-609-3388
Fax: 416-609-3392
MICR: 3992-001

Toronto - Sheppard Ave. West
1951 Sheppard Ave. West
Toronto, ON M3L 1Y8 Canada
416-743-0222
Fax: 416-743-5343
MICR: 0454-001

Toronto - Sheppard Ave. West
648 Sheppard Ave. West
Toronto, ON M3H 3W3 Canada
416-635-8210
Fax: 416-636-1976
MICR: 0436-001

Toronto - Spadina Ave.
291 Spadina Ave.
Toronto, ON M5T 2E6 Canada
416-867-4759
Fax: 416-591-7466
MICR: 3954-001

Toronto - Spadina Ave.
112 Spadina Ave.
Toronto, ON M5V 2K5 Canada
416-867-5310
Fax: 416-867-6568
MICR: 0418-001

Toronto - St. Clair Ave. West
1226 St. Clair Ave. West
Toronto, ON M6E 1B4 Canada
416-652-3444
Fax: 416-652-1388
MICR: 0396-001

Toronto - St. Clair Ave. West
2471 St. Clair Ave. West
Toronto, ON M6N 4Z5 Canada
416-762-8291
Fax: 416-762-9033
MICR: 0431-001

Toronto - University Ave.
700 University Ave.
Toronto, ON M5G 1X7 Canada
416-867-5330
Fax: 416-979-8899
MICR: 0420-001

Toronto - Weston Rd.
1939 Weston Rd.
Toronto, ON M9N 1W8 Canada
416-249-3387
Fax: 416-249-3438
MICR: 0410-001

Toronto - William Kitchen Rd.
Kennedy Commons Dominion
16 William Kitchen Rd.
Toronto, ON M1P 5B7 Canada
416-321-2170
Fax: 416-321-2959
MICR: 3605-001

Toronto - Wilson Ave.
North York Sheridan Mall
1700 Wilson Ave.
Toronto, ON M3L 1B2 Canada
416-247-6281
Fax: 416-247-7059
MICR: 0373-001

Toronto - Yonge St.
3320 Yonge St.
Toronto, ON M4N 2M4 Canada
416-488-8335
Fax: 416-488-1073
MICR: 2974-001

Toronto - Yonge St.
Northtown Dominion
5383 Yonge St.
Toronto, ON M2N 5R6 Canada
416-224-1370
Fax: 416-224-1304
MICR: 3151-001

Toronto - Yonge St.
Centerpoint Mall
6518 Yonge St.
Toronto, ON M2M 3X4 Canada
416-590-7880
Fax: 416-590-8940
MICR: 0459-001

Toronto - Yonge St.
Sheppard Centre
4841 Yonge St.
Toronto, ON M2N 5X2 Canada
416-590-7757
Fax: 416-223-6198
MICR: 2489-001

Toronto - Yonge St.
North York City Centre
5140 Yonge St.
Toronto, ON M2N 6L7 Canada
416-250-2950
Fax: 416-250-2955
MICR: 2429-001

Toronto - Yonge St.
2444 Yonge St.
Toronto, ON M4P 2H4 Canada
416-488-6608
Fax: 416-483-9403
MICR: 0384-001

Toronto - Yonge St.
5925 Yonge St.
Toronto, ON M2M 3V7 Canada
416-221-5561
Fax: 416-221-2823
MICR: 2439-001

Toronto - Yonge St.
2210 Yonge St.
Toronto, ON M4S 2B8 Canada
416-488-1145
Fax: 416-488-3703
MICR: 0443-001

Toronto - Yonge St.
1431 Yonge St.
Toronto, ON M4T 1Y9 Canada
416-920-9861
Fax: 416-920-5182
MICR: 0371-001

Toronto - Yorkgate Blvd.
Yorkgate Mall
1 Yorkgate Blvd.
Toronto, ON M3N 3A1 Canada
416-739-6000
Fax: 416-739-6902
MICR: 2937-001

Trail
1498 Bay Ave.
Trail, BC V1R 4B1 Canada

250-368-9141
Fax: 250-364-0399
MICR: 0755-001

Trenton
55 Dundas St. West
Trenton, ON K8V 3N9 Canada
613-392-9216
Fax: 613-392-0650
MICR: 0401-001

Trochu
PO Box 10
222 Main St.
Trochu, AB T0M 2C0 Canada
403-442-3822
Fax: 403-442-4392
MICR: 2597-001

Trois-Rivières - Forges
Centre les Rivières
4125, boul des Forges
Trois-Rivières, QC G8Y 1W1 Canada
819-372-4050
Fax: 819-372-4034
MICR: 2176-001

Trois-Rivières - Jean XXIII
5885, boul Jean XXIII
Trois-Rivières, QC G8Z 4N8 Canada
819-372-4042
Fax: 819-372-4045
MICR: 0026-001

Truro
507 Prince St.
Truro, NS B2N 1E8 Canada
902-895-5375
Fax: 902-895-1081
MICR: 0204-001

Tsuu T'ina
Tsuu T'ina Nation
9911 Chila Blvd. SW
Tsuu T'ina, AB T2W 6H6 Canada
403-234-1869
Fax: 403-503-7235
MICR: 3671-001

Tweed
225 Victoria St. North
Tweed, ON K0K 3J0 Canada
613-478-2120
Fax: 613-478-2098
MICR: 0402-001

Unionville
PO Box 141
100 Carlton Rd.
Unionville, ON L3R 1Z9 Canada
905-477-3505
Fax: 905-477-7223
MICR: 2592-001

Unity
PO Box 159
122 Main St.
Unity, SK S0K 4L0 Canada
306-228-4122
Fax: 306-228-2725
MICR: 2686-001

Upper Tantallon
Upper Tantallon Sobeys
3650 Hammonds Plains Rd.
Upper Tantallon, NS B3Z 4R3 Canada
902-826-2245
Fax: 902-826-3509
MICR: 3668-001

Val Caron
#2996, 1 Hwy. 69 North
Val Caron, ON P3N 1E3 Canada
705-897-4925
Fax: 705-897-4511
MICR: 2457-001

Valleyview
PO Box 330
5114 - 50th Ave.
Valleyview, AB T0H 3N0 Canada
780-524-3376
Fax: 780-524-2911
MICR: 0565-001

Vancouver - 41st Ave. West
2102 - 41st Ave. West
Vancouver, BC V6M 1Z2 Canada
604-668-1421
Fax: 604-668-1032
MICR: 0724-001

Vancouver - 4th Ave. West
3695 - 4th Ave. West
Vancouver, BC V6R 1P2 Canada
604-665-7144
Fax: 604-665-2696
MICR: 2714-001

Vancouver - Arbutus St.
Arbutus Shopping Centre
#108, 4255 Arbutus St.
Vancouver, BC V6J 4R1 Canada
604-668-1456
Fax: 604-668-1311
MICR: 0986-001

Vancouver - Burrard St. - Main Office
PO Box 49500
595 Burrard St.
Vancouver, BC V7X 1L7 Canada
604-665-2643
Fax: 604-665-6614
MICR: 0004-001

Vancouver - Commercial Dr.
2501 Commercial Dr.
Vancouver, BC V5N 4C1 Canada
604-665-2535
Fax: 604-665-7098
MICR: 2710-001

Vancouver - Davie St.
Davie St. Safeway
1641 Davie St.
Vancouver, BC V6G 1W1 Canada
604-668-1003
Fax: 604-668-1055
MICR: 3182-001

Vancouver - Denman St.
958 Denman St.
Vancouver, BC V6G 2M2 Canada
604-665-7235
Fax: 604-665-7115
MICR: 0757-001

Vancouver - Dunbar St.
4395 Dunbar St.
Vancouver, BC V6S 2G2 Canada
604-665-7093
Fax: 604-221-2555
MICR: 2721-001

Vancouver - East Broadway
Broadway & Commercial Safeway
1780 East Broadway
Vancouver, BC V5N 1W3 Canada
604-718-2380
Fax: 604-718-2385
MICR: 3124-001

Vancouver - East Hastings St.
2515 East Hastings St.
Vancouver, BC V5K 1Z2 Canada
604-665-6693
Fax: 604-665-5591
MICR: 2717-001

Vancouver - East Pender St. - Asian Banking Centre
168 East Pender St.
Vancouver, BC V6A 1T3 Canada
604-665-7225
Fax: 604-665-3600
MICR: 2712-001

Vancouver - Grandview Hwy.
3290 Grandview Hwy.
Vancouver, BC V5M 2G2 Canada
604-665-2514
Fax: 604-665-7549
MICR: 2720-001

Vancouver - Granville St.
2601 Granville St.
Vancouver, BC V6H 3H2 Canada
604-665-7307
Fax: 604-668-1569
MICR: 0760-001

Vancouver - Granville St.
8324 Granville St.
Vancouver, BC V6P 4Z7 Canada
604-668-1471
Fax: 604-665-7195
MICR: 2727-001

Vancouver - Kerr St.
Champlain Square
7150 Kerr St.
Vancouver, BC V5S 4W2 Canada
604-665-2510
Fax: 604-665-7353
MICR: 0838-001

Vancouver - Kingsway
Kingsway & Tyne Safeway
3410 Kingsway
Vancouver, BC V5R 5L4 Canada
604-718-2210
Fax: 604-718-2216
MICR: 3134-001

Vancouver - Main St.
8156 Main St.
Vancouver, BC V5X 3L6 Canada
604-668-1400
Fax: 604-668-1313
MICR: 0769-001

Vancouver - Oak St.
5755 Oak St.
Vancouver, BC V6M 2V7 Canada
604-668-1462
Fax: 604-668-1465
MICR: 2724-001

Vancouver - Victoria Dr.
5710 Victoria Dr.
Vancouver, BC V5P 2W6 Canada
604-665-2530
Fax: 604-665-2527
MICR: 0768-001

Vancouver - West 10th Ave.
10th & Sasamat Safeway
4575 West 10th Ave.
Vancouver, BC V6R 2J2 Canada
604-221-2870
Fax: 604-221-2878
MICR: 3798-001

Vancouver - West 10th Ave.
4502 - West 10th Ave.
Vancouver, BC V6R 2J1 Canada
604-665-7097
Fax: 604-221-2860
MICR: 0758-001

Vancouver - West 41st Ave.
Oakridge Shopping Centre Safeway
650 West 41st Ave.
Vancouver, BC V5Z 2M9 Canada
604-668-1010
Fax: 604-668-1013
MICR: 3234-001

Vancouver - West Broadway
2106 West Broadway
Vancouver, BC V6K 2C8 Canada
604-665-7148
Fax: 604-665-6611
MICR: 2713-001

Vancouver - West Broadway
#105, 777 West Broadway
Vancouver, BC V5Z 4J7 Canada
604-665-7179
Fax: 604-665-6670
MICR: 2715-001

Vancouver - West Georgia St.
#100, 401 West Georgia St.
Vancouver, BC V6B 5A1 Canada
604-665-7265
Fax: 604-665-7273
MICR: 2726-001

Vancouver - Western Pkwy.
University Marketplace
#105, 2142 Western Pkwy.
Vancouver, BC V6T 1V6 Canada
604-665-7076
Fax: 604-222-4500
MICR: 0811-001

Varennes
235, rue Langlois
Varennes, QC J3X 1R3 Canada
450-652-2921
Fax: 450-652-4720
MICR: 2146-001

Vegreville

BMO Bank of Montréal(BMO)/ Banque de Montréal (continued)

PO Box 189
5102 - 50th St.
Vegreville, AB T9C 1R2 Canada
780-632-2864
Fax: 780-632-6552
MICR: 2598-001

Vernon - 30th Ave. - Main Office
3200 - 30th Ave.
Vernon, BC V1T 2C5 Canada
250-549-4000
Fax: 250-549-4029
MICR: 0770-001

Vernon - 32nd St.
Vernon Square Mall Safeway
4300 - 32nd St.
Vernon, BC V1T 9H1 Canada
250-260-4801
Fax: 250-260-4808
MICR: 3141-001

Verona
6714 Hwy. 38
Verona, ON K0H 2W0 Canada
613-374-2213
Fax: 613-374-1182
MICR: 0404-001

Victoria - Cook St.
3481 Cook St.
Victoria, BC V8X 1B3 Canada
250-389-2430
Fax: 250-405-2265
MICR: 0772-001

Victoria - Douglas St. - Main Office
1225 Douglas St.
Victoria, BC V8W 2E6 Canada
250-389-2400
Fax: 250-405-2082
MICR: 0012-001

Victoria - Foul Bay Rd.
Oak Bay Shopping Centre Safeway
1950 Foul Bay Rd.
Victoria, BC V8R 5A7 Canada
250-405-5330
Fax: 250-405-5336
MICR: 3608-001

Victoria - Goldstream Ave.
#101, 735 Goldstream Ave.
Victoria, BC V9B 2X4 Canada
250-389-2485
Fax: 250-391-3537
MICR: 2704-001

Victoria - Menzies St.
230 Menzies St.
Victoria, BC V8V 2G7 Canada
250-389-2441
Fax: 250-405-2162
MICR: 0801-001

Victoria - Oak Bay Ave.
2219 Oak Bay Ave.
Victoria, BC V8R 1G4 Canada
250-389-2433
Fax: 250-405-2321
MICR: 2706-001

Victoria - Saanich Rd.
3451 Saanich Rd.
Victoria, BC V8X 1W6 Canada
250-389-2455
Fax: 250-405-2351
MICR: 0797-001

Victoria - Saanich Rd. West
4470 Saanich Rd. West
Victoria, BC V8Z 3E9 Canada
250-389-2478
Fax: 250-727-6920
MICR: 0783-001

Victoria - Shelbourne St.
3616 Shelbourne St.
Victoria, BC V8P 5J5 Canada
250-389-2460
Fax: 250-405-2183
MICR: 0830-001

Victoria - Tillicum Rd.
Tillicum Shopping Centre Safeway
#108, 3170 Tillicum Rd.
Victoria, BC V9A 6T2 Canada
250-405-8050
Fax: 250-405-8056
MICR: 3615-001

Victoriaville
51, rue Notre-Dame est
Victoriaville, QC G6P 3Z4 Canada
819-752-9763
Fax: 819-758-3699
MICR: 0211-001

Wabush
PO Box 10
Grenfell Dr.
Wabush, NL A0R 1B0 Canada
709-282-3231
Fax: 709-282-5122
MICR: 1022-001

Wainwright
422 - 10th St.
Wainwright, AB T9W 1P5 Canada
780-842-5890
Fax: 780-842-5611
MICR: 2601-001

Walkerton
131 Durham Rd.
Walkerton, ON N0G 2V0 Canada
519-881-0800
Fax: 519-881-0371
MICR: 2419-001

Wallaceburg
770 James St.
Wallaceburg, ON N8A 2P5 Canada
519-627-1685
Fax: 519-627-1457
MICR: 0406-001

Waskaganish
Neepsee Plaza
PO Box 150
Waskaganish, QC J0M 1R0 Canada
819-895-2177
Fax: 819-895-2179
MICR: 3633-001

Waterford
PO Box 160
9 Alice St.
Waterford, ON N0E 1Y0 Canada
519-443-8639
Fax: 519-443-8617
MICR: 0407-001

Waterloo - Glen Forrest Blvd.
730 Glen Forrest Blvd.
Waterloo, ON N2L 4K8 Canada
519-885-8410
Fax: 519-747-2019
MICR: 3056-001

Waterloo - King St. North
255 King St. North
Waterloo, ON N2J 4V2 Canada
519-885-9253
Fax: 519-885-9318
MICR: 2459-001

Waterloo - King St. South - Main Office
3 King St. South
Waterloo, ON N2J 3Z6 Canada
519-885-9250
Fax: 519-885-9280
MICR: 2423-001

Waterloo - Weber St. North
90 Weber St. North
Waterloo, ON N2J 3G8 Canada
519-885-8545
Fax: 519-885-7803
MICR: 3057-001

Watford
5282 Nauvoo Rd.
Watford, ON N0M 2S0 Canada
519-876-2120
Fax: 519-876-2736
MICR: 2424-001

Welland
Seaway Mall
800 Niagara St.
Welland, ON L3C 5Z4 Canada
905-735-7723
Fax: 905-732-6491
MICR: 2989-001

Wemindji
PO Box 30
#5, 30, ch Beaver
Wemindji, QC J0M 1L0 Canada
819-978-3588
Fax: 819-978-3590
MICR: 3437-001

West Lorne
226 Graham St.
West Lorne, ON N0L 2P0 Canada
519-768-1430
Fax: 519-768-2981
MICR: 2425-001

West Vancouver - Headland Dr.
Caulfield Village Shopping Centre
5377 Headland Dr.
West Vancouver, BC V7W 3C7 Canada
604-668-1213
Fax: 604-921-2988
MICR: 3953-001

West Vancouver - Marine Dr.
1434 Marine Dr.
West Vancouver, BC V7T 1B7 Canada
604-668-1207
Fax: 604-903-3149
MICR: 0778-001

West Vancouver - Park Royal South
959 Park Royal South
West Vancouver, BC V7T 1A1 Canada
604-668-1277
Fax: 604-903-2955
MICR: 2722-001

Westbank
#101, 3640 Gosset Rd.
Westbank, BC V4T 2N4 Canada
250-861-1670
Fax: 250-768-3247
MICR: 0779-001

Westlock
10603 - 100th Ave.
Westlock, AB T7P 2J4 Canada
780-349-3311
Fax: 780-349-6030
MICR: 2603-001

Westport
41 Main St.
Westport, ON K0G 1X0 Canada
613-273-2161
Fax: 613-273-2773
MICR: 2426-001

Wetaskiwin
5020 - 50th Ave.
Wetaskiwin, AB T9A 0S4 Canada
780-352-3317
Fax: 780-352-3870
MICR: 2605-001

Weyburn
Weyburn Square
110 Souris Ave. NE
Weyburn, SK S4H 2Z8 Canada
306-842-5417
Fax: 306-842-7736
MICR: 2600-001

Whitby - Brock St. North
3960 Brock St. North
Whitby, ON L1R 3E1 Canada
905-665-2740
Fax: 905-665-2770
MICR: 3190-001

Whitby - Dundas St. East
Whitby Mall
1615 Dundas St. East
Whitby, ON L1N 2L1 Canada
905-436-7700
Fax: 905-436-7343
MICR: 3941-001

White Rock
Semiahmoo Mall
1626 Martin Dr.
White Rock, BC V4A 6E7 Canada
604-531-5581
Fax: 604-541-5678
MICR: 0784-001

Whitehorse

111 Main St.
Whitehorse, YT Y1A 2A7 Canada
867-668-4200
Fax: 867-668-4501
MICR: 0998-001

Whitewood
PO Box 40
727 Lalonde St.
Whitewood, SK S0G 5C0 Canada
306-735-2683
Fax: 306-735-2621
MICR: 2688-001

Williams Lake
35 South 2nd Ave.
Williams Lake, BC V2G 3W3 Canada
250-392-4441
Fax: 250-392-6081
MICR: 0777-001

Winchester
510 Main St.
Winchester, ON K0C 2K0 Canada
613-774-2527
Fax: 613-774-2661
MICR: 0481-001

Windsor - Grand Marais Rd.
1399 Grand Marais Rd.
Windsor, ON N9E 1E2 Canada
519-973-3367
Fax: 519-969-3561
MICR: 2422-001

Windsor - Howard Ave.
Devonshire Mall
3100 Howard Ave.
Windsor, ON N8X 3Y8 Canada
519-973-3360
Fax: 519-972-1190
MICR: 2431-001

Windsor - Ouellette Ave. - Main Office
200 Ouellette Ave.
Windsor, ON N9A 6K9 Canada
519-973-3305
Fax: 519-973-3344
MICR: 0018-001

Windsor - Tecumseh Rd. East
2230 Tecumseh Rd. East
Windsor, ON N8Y 1E4 Canada
519-973-3390
Fax: 519-252-2737
MICR: 0405-001

Windsor - Tecumseh Rd. East
7995 Tecumseh Rd. East
Windsor, ON N8R 1A1 Canada
519-973-3403
Fax: 519-944-3749
MICR: 0446-001

Windsor - Tecumseh Rd. West
University Mall
2680 Tecumseh Rd. West
Windsor, ON N9B 3P9 Canada
519-973-3378
Fax: 519-252-6051
MICR: 2954-001

Windsor - Wyandotte St. East
8185 Wyandotte St. East
Windsor, ON N8S 1T4 Canada
519-973-3406
Fax: 519-945-4107
MICR: 2432-001

Wingham
55 Josephine St.
Wingham, ON N0G 2W0 Canada
519-357-1750
Fax: 519-357-1102
MICR: 2667-001

Winnipeg - Alpine Rd.
Niakwa Village Safeway
2 Alpine Rd.
Winnipeg, MB R2M 0Y5 Canada
204-985-2710
Fax: 204-985-2703
MICR: 3185-001

Winnipeg - Corydon Ave.
Tuxedo Park Shopping Centre
2025 Corydon Ave.
Winnipeg, MB R3P 0N5 Canada
204-985-2626
Fax: 204-985-2166
MICR: 0563-001

Winnipeg - Dakota St.
St. Vital Shopping Centre Safeway
850 Dakota St.
Winnipeg, MB R2M 5E9 Canada
204-985-2200
Fax: 204-985-2425
MICR: 3184-001

Winnipeg - Ellice Ave.
1780 Ellice Ave.
Winnipeg, MB R3H 0B5 Canada
204-985-2448
Fax: 204-985-2032
MICR: 0569-001

Winnipeg - Grant Ave.
Charleswood Centre
3900 Grant Ave.
Winnipeg, MB R3R 3C2 Canada
204-985-2571
Fax: 204-985-2179
MICR: 2683-001

Winnipeg - Henderson Hwy.
1108 Henderson Hwy.
Winnipeg, MB R2G 1L1 Canada
204-985-2904
Fax: 204-985-2152
MICR: 0536-001

Winnipeg - Jefferson Ave.
Jefferson & McPhillips Safeway
920 Jefferson Ave.
Winnipeg, MB R2P 1W1 Canada
204-985-2737
Fax: 204-985-2733
MICR: 3619-001

Winnipeg - Kenaston Blvd.
Lindenridge Safeway
1625 Kenaston Blvd.
Winnipeg, MB R3P 2M4 Canada
204-985-2826
Fax: 204-985-2846
MICR: 3116-001

Winnipeg - Lakewood Blvd.
Southdale Centre
#30, 31 Lakewood Blvd.
Winnipeg, MB R2J 2M8 Canada
204-985-2350
Fax: 204-985-2171
MICR: 2590-001

Winnipeg - Main St.
1468 Main St.
Winnipeg, MB R2W 3W1 Canada
204-985-2489
Fax: 204-985-2029
MICR: 2602-001

Winnipeg - Main St. - Main Office
PO Box 844
335 Main St.
Winnipeg, MB R3C 1C2 Canada
204-985-2611
Fax: 204-985-2099
MICR: 0003-001

Winnipeg - Marion St.
Marion Safeway
285 Marion St.
Winnipeg, MB R2H 0T8 Canada
204-985-2757
Fax: 204-985-2771
MICR: 3111-001

Winnipeg - McPhillips St.
1010 McPhillips St.
Winnipeg, MB R2X 2K5 Canada
204-985-2530
Fax: 204-985-2028
MICR: 0577-001

Winnipeg - McPhillips St.
1010 McPhillips St.
Winnipeg, MB R2X 2K5 Canada
204-985-2530
Fax: 204-985-2028
MICR: 0577-001

Winnipeg - Pembina Hwy.
Pembina Village Safeway
2155 Pembina Hwy.
Winnipeg, MB R3T 2H1 Canada
204-985-2160
Fax: 204-985-2167
MICR: 3609-001

Winnipeg - Pembina Hwy.
1188 Pembina Hwy.
Winnipeg, MB R3T 2A6 Canada
204-985-2496
Fax: 204-985-2004
MICR: 0578-001

Winnipeg - Pembina Hwy.
Fort Richmond Plaza
2860 Pembina Hwy.
Winnipeg, MB R3T 3L9 Canada
204-985-2225
Fax: 204-985-2177
MICR: 2615-001

Winnipeg - Portage Ave.
Polo Park Safeway
1485 Portage Ave.
Winnipeg, MB R3G 0W4 Canada
204-985-2888
Fax: 204-985-2910
MICR: 3135-001

Winnipeg - Portage Ave.
Courts of St. James
2727 Portage Ave.
Winnipeg, MB R3J 0R2 Canada
204-985-2514
Fax: 204-985-2168
MICR: 0584-001

Winnipeg - Portage Ave.
330 Portage Ave.
Winnipeg, MB R3C 0C4 Canada
204-985-2480
Fax: 204-985-2026
MICR: 0573-001

Winnipeg - Portage Ave.
3330 Portage Ave.
Winnipeg, MB R3K 0Z1 Canada
204-985-2555
Fax: 204-985-2025
MICR: 0653-001

Winnipeg - Regent Ave. West
Kildonan Crossing Shopping Centre Safeway
1615 Regent Ave. West
Winnipeg, MB R2C 5C6 Canada
204-985-2712
Fax: 204-985-2725
MICR: 3139-001

Winnipeg - Regent Ave. West
1565 Regent Ave. West
Winnipeg, MB R2C 3B3 Canada
204-985-2459
Fax: 204-985-2030
MICR: 2610-001

Wolfville
424 Main St.
Wolfville, NS B4P 1C9 Canada
902-542-2214
Fax: 902-542-9293
MICR: 0206-001

Woodbridge - Steeles Ave. West
3700 Steeles Ave. West
Woodbridge, ON L4L 8K8 Canada
905-856-5444
Fax: 905-856-7443
MICR: 2475-001

Woodbridge - Woodbridge Ave.
145 Woodbridge Ave.
Woodbridge, ON L4L 2S6 Canada
905-851-2226
Fax: 905-851-5951
MICR: 2433-001

Woodstock - Dundas St. - Main Office
534 Dundas St.
Woodstock, ON N4S 1C5 Canada
519-539-2057
Fax: 519-539-0887
MICR: 0047-001

Woodstock - Main St.
656 Main St.
Woodstock, NB E7M 2G9 Canada

BMO Bank of Montréal(BMO)/ Banque de Montréal (continued)

506-328-6631
Fax: 506-328-4134
MICR: 0207-001

Woodstock - Main St.
656 Main St.
Woodstock, NB E7M 2G9 Canada
506-328-6631
Fax: 506-328-4134
MICR: 0207-001

Woodville
87 King St.
Woodville, ON K0M 2T0 Canada
705-439-1125
Fax: 705-439-1123
MICR: 3873-001

Wynyard
PO Box 40
214 Bosworth St.
Wynyard, SK S0A 4T0 Canada
306-554-2546
Fax: 306-554-3455
MICR: 0697-001

Yarmouth
PO Box 189
354 Main St.
Yarmouth, NS B5A 4B2 Canada
902-742-9291
Fax: 902-742-1061
MICR: 0210-001

Yellowknife
PO Box 1799
#78, 5014 - 49th St.
Yellowknife, NT X1A 2P4 Canada
867-873-6261
Fax: 867-873-6621
MICR: 0997-001

Yorkton
15 Broadway St. East
Yorkton, SK S3N 0K2 Canada
306-782-8400
Fax: 306-782-8461
MICR: 0581-001

×le-Perrot
Marché d'alimentation IGA
110, boul Don Quichotte
×le-Perrot, QC J7V 6L7 Canada
514-425-3435
Fax: 514-425-5412
MICR: 3294-001

Bridgewater Bank

Also listed under: *Financing & Loan Companies*
#150, 926 - 5th Ave. SW
Calgary, AB T2P 0N7
403-232-6556
Fax: 403-233-2609
888-837-2326
www.bridgewaterfinancial.com
Former Name: Bridgewater Financial Services Ltd.
Ownership: Private. Wholly owned subsidiary of Alberta Motor Association.
Year Founded: 1997
Number of Employees: 80
Profile: Bridgewater is a mortgage banking company. It provides mortgages to Canadian homeowners & purchasers. Offices are located in the following cities: Halifax, Toronto, Ottawa, Victoria, Calgary & Edmonton.

Executives:
Peter L. O'Neill, Vice-President, General Manager
Gord Follett, Controller

Canadian Imperial Bank of Commerce(CIBC)/ Banque Canadienne Impériale de Commerce

Commerce Court
PO Box 1, Stn Commerce Court
Toronto, ON M5L 1A2
416-980-2211
Fax: 416-980-5028
800-465-2422
customer.care@cibc.com
www.cibc.com
Ownership: Public
Year Founded: 1858
Assets: $100 billion + Year End: 20041031
Revenues: $10-100 billion Year End: 20041031
Stock Symbol: CM
Profile: CIBC is a full-service financial institution with operations primarily in Canada & the United States, as well as in the West Indies, Europe & Asia. CIBC is ranked among the ten largest banks in North America by assets. The financial institution has almost nine million personal banking & business customers.

Executives:
Gerald T. McCaughey, President/CEO
Sonia A. Baxendale, Sr. Exec. Vice-President, CIBC Retail Markets
Ron Lalonde, Sr. Exec. Vice-President, Chief Administrative Office, Administration
S.R. (Steve) McGirr, Sr. Exec. Vice-President, Chief Risk Officer, Treasury & Risk Management
Brian G. Shaw, Sr. Exec. Vice-President, CIBC, Chair/CEO, CIBC World Markets
Richard E. Venn, Sr. Exec. Vice-President, Corporate Development
Tom D. Woods, Sr. Exec. Vice-President/CFO
Michael D. Woeller, Vice-Chair, Chief Information Officer
M.J. (Mike) Boluch, Exec. Vice-President, Technology & Operations
T.R. (Ted) Cadsby, Exec. Vice-President, Retail Distribution, CIBC World Markets
Michael G. Capatides, Exec. Vice-President & General Counsel, Legal & Compliance
Victor G. Dodig, Exec. Vice-President, Wealth Management
M. (Malcolm) Eylott, Exec. Vice-President, Global Operation, Technology
Michael G. Horrocks, Exec. Vice-President & Treasurer, Treasury & Risk Management
P. Ken M. Kilgour, Exec. Vice-President, Credit & Investment Portfolio Management
W.M (Walt) Macnee, Exec. Vice-President, Card Products
James R. McSherry, Exec. Vice-President & Managing Director, Commercial Banking, CIBC World Markets
John Orr, Exec. Vice-President, Amicus Division, CIBC Retail Markets
Joyce M. Phillips, Exec. Vice-President, Human Resources Administration
Pankaj P. Puri, Exec. Vice-President & Chief Privacy Officer
Bruce A. Renihan, Exec. Vice-President & Controller, Finance
G.C. (Grant) Westcott, Exec. Vice-President, Technology Infrastructure
S.J. (Stephen) Forbes, Sr. Vice-President, Communications & Public Affairs
R. (Raza) Hasan, Sr. Vice-President, Mortgages, Lending & Insurance, CIBC Retail Markets
T.S. (Tim) Moseley, Sr. Vice-President, Chief Compliance Officer
K.J. (Kevin) Patterson, Sr. Vice-President, Internal Audit & Corporate Security, Chief Auditor
Francesca Shaw, Sr. Vice-President & Chief Accountant, Finance
Michelle Caturay, Vice-President & Corporate Secretary
J.P. (John) Ferren, Vice-President, Investor Relations
Gary W. Brown, Managing Director & Head, US Region, CIBC World Markets
D.B. (David) Clifford, Managing Director, Merchant Banking & European Investment & Corporate Ban
David G. Leith, Managing Director, Canadian Investment & Corporate Banking, CIBC World Ma
P. (Phipps) Lounsbery, Managing Director, Global Debt Capital Markets, CIBC World Markets
MacCandlish D.R. (Donna), Ombudsman

Directors:
William A. Etherington, Chair
Brent S. Belzberg
President/CEO, Torquest Partners Inc.
Jalynn H. Bennett, CM
President, Jalynn H. Bennett & Associates Ltd.
Gary F. Colter, FCA
President, CRS Inc.
William L. Duke
Farmer
Ivan E.H. Duvar, P.Eng., LLD
President/CEO, MIJAC Inc.
A.L. Flood, CM
Margot A. Franssen, OC
President/CEO, Bibelot Inc.
Gordon D. Giffin
Sr. Partner, McKenna Long & Aldridge LLP
James A. Grant, P.C., Q.C., CM
Chair Emeritus, Stikeman Elliott LLP
Pat M. Hayles
President, PDA Inc.
Linda S. Hasenfratz
CEO, Linamar Corporation
John S. Lacey
Chair, Alderwoods Group Inc.
John P. Manley
Sr. Counsel, McCarthy Tétrault LLP
Gerald T. McCaughey
Charles Sirois, B.Fin., M.Fin., CM
Chair/CEO, Telesystem Ltd.
Stephen G. Snyder, B.Sc., MBA
President/CEO, TransAlta Corp.
Cynthia M. Trudell
Vice-President, Brunswick Corporation; President, Sea Ray Division
Ronald W. Tysoe
Vice-Chair, Federated Department Stores, Inc.

Affiliated Companies:
CIBC Asset Management Inc.
CIBC Capital Partners
CIBC Investor Services Inc.
CIBC Life Insurance Company Limited
CIBC Mellon Trust Company
CIBC Mortgages Inc./CMI
CIBC Securities Inc.
CIBC Trust Corporation
CIBC Wood Gundy
The CIBC World Markets Inc.

Branches:

100 Mile House
PO Box 98
325 Birch Ave.
100 Mile House, BC V0K 2E0 Canada
250-395-2292
Fax: 250-395-3639
MICR: 00550-010

Abbotsford - 32041 South Fraser Way
32041 South Fraser Way
Abbotsford, BC V2T 1W3 Canada
604-870-3123
Fax: 604-870-3085
MICR: 01920-010

Abbotsford - McCallum
2420 McCallum Rd.
Abbotsford, BC V2S 6R9 Canada
604-870-3101
Fax: 604-870-3036
MICR: 00420-010

Abbotsford - South Fraser Way
Westoaks Shopping Centre
32650 South Fraser Way
Abbotsford, BC V2T 4W2 Canada
604-870-3130
Fax: 604-870-3118
MICR: 08820-010

Acton
PO Box 239
31 Mill St. East
Acton, ON L7J 2M3 Canada
519-853-1853
Fax: 519-853-5234
MICR: 09552-010

Ajax - Harwood Ave. South
Ajax Shopping Centre
104 Harwood Ave. South
Ajax, ON L1S 2H6 Canada
905-683-5871
Fax: 905-683-6139
MICR: 01442-010

Ajax - Westney Rd. North
Westney Heights Plaza
15 Westney Rd. North
Ajax, ON L1T 1P4 Canada
905-683-1412
Fax: 905-683-1423
MICR: 02542-010

Alberton
PO Box 160
478 Main St.
Alberton, PE C0B 1B0 Canada
902-853-2102
Fax: 902-853-3723
MICR: 00383-010

Aldergrove

PO Box 652
3082 - 272nd St.
Aldergrove, BC V4W 3R7 Canada
604-857-7636
Fax: 604-856-2878
MICR: 04820-010

Alliston
35 Young St.
Alliston, ON L9R 1B5 Canada
705-435-4327
Fax: 705-435-3061
MICR: 06252-010

Altona
PO Box 180
2nd St. NE
Altona, MB R0G 0B0 Canada
204-324-6421
Fax: 204-324-1869
MICR: 00267-010

Amherst
PO Box 98
32 Church St.
Amherst, NS B4H 3Y9 Canada
902-667-3376
Fax: 902-667-0405
MICR: 00153-010

Amherstburg
PO Box 37
48 Richmond St.
Amherstburg, ON N9V 2Z2 Canada
519-736-2186
Fax: 519-736-8156
MICR: 09682-010

Amos
25 - 1re av ouest
Amos, QC J9T 3A5 Canada
819-732-3391
Fax: 819-732-0390
MICR: 00391-010

Ancaster - Golf Links Rd.
1015 Golf Links Rd.
Ancaster, ON L9K 1L6 Canada
905-304-4000
Fax: 905-304-4006
MICR: 09162-010

Ancaster - Wilson St. West
30 Wilson St. West
Ancaster, ON L9G 1N2 Canada
905-648-4441
Fax: 905-648-7962
MICR: 04062-010

Antigonish
185 Main St.
Antigonish, NS B2G 2B8 Canada
902-863-4740
Fax: 902-863-1995
MICR: 00143-010

Arborg
PO Box 490
282 Main St.
Arborg, MB R0C 0A0 Canada
204-376-5218
Fax: 204-376-2968
MICR: 00567-010

Armstrong
PO Box 220
2550 Pleasant Valley Blvd.
Armstrong, BC V0E 1B0 Canada
250-546-3104
Fax: 250-546-9331
MICR: 00560-010

Arnprior
75 Elgin St. West
Arnprior, ON K7S 3T9 Canada
613-623-4248
Fax: 613-623-9664
MICR: 00296-010

Asbestos
290, 1ere av
Asbestos, QC J1T 1Y7 Canada
819-879-5469
Fax: 819-879-6791
MICR: 00071-010

Ashern
PO Box 70
20 Main St.
Ashern, MB R0C 0E0 Canada
204-768-2727
Fax: 204-768-2383
MICR: 00367-010

Assiniboia
PO Box 669
237 Center St.
Assiniboia, SK S0H 0B0 Canada
306-642-6100
Fax: 306-642-3838
MICR: 00238-010

Athabasca
4819 - 50th St.
Athabasca, AB T9S 1C8 Canada
780-675-2247
Fax: 780-675-4499
MICR: 00279-010

Atikokan
PO Box 70
100 Main St. West
Atikokan, ON P0T 1C0 Canada
807-597-2742
Fax: 807-597-1069
MICR: 00297-010

Aurora - Yonge St.
Aurora Shopping Centre
14800 Yonge St.
Aurora, ON L4G 1N3 Canada
905-727-4248
Fax: 905-727-7601
MICR: 09942-010

Aurora - Yonge St.
15195 Yonge St.
Aurora, ON L4G 3H1 Canada
905-727-4248
Fax: 905-727-7352
MICR: 09042-010

Ayer's Cliff
PO Box 156
1110, rue Principal
Ayer's Cliff, QC J0B 1C0 Canada
819-838-4227
Fax: 819-838-5351
MICR: 00851-010

Aylmer
86 Talbot St. East
Aylmer, ON N5H 1H5 Canada
519-765-2540
Fax: 519-765-1524
MICR: 01982-010

Ayr
63 Stanley St.
Ayr, ON N0B 1E0 Canada
519-632-7462
Fax: 519-632-7194
MICR: 03752-010

Baie-Comeau - Lasalle
Les Galeries Baie-Comeau
300, boul Lasalle
Baie-Comeau, QC G4Z 2K2 Canada
418-296-6748
Fax: 418-296-3799
MICR: 00475-010

Banff
PO Box 820
98 Banff Ave.
Banff, AB T1L 1A8 Canada
403-762-3317
Fax: 403-762-7402
MICR: 00049-010

Barrie - Bayfield St.
363 Bayfield St.
Barrie, ON L4M 3C3 Canada
705-737-2411
Fax: 705-737-4897
MICR: 01142-010

Barrie - Dunlop St.
46 Dunlop St. East
Barrie, ON L4M 1A3 Canada
705-728-2459
Fax: 705-728-4618
MICR: 02042-010

Barrie - Mapleview Dr. West
33 Mapleview Dr. West
Barrie, ON L4N 9H5 Canada
705-721-0966
Fax: 705-721-8545
MICR: 03192-010

Barrington Passage
PO Box 10
3528 Hwy. #3
Barrington Passage, NS B0W 1G0 Canada
902-637-2212
Fax: 902-637-2673
MICR: 00353-010

Bathurst
#202, 270 Douglas Ave.
Bathurst, NB E2A 1M9 Canada
506-548-8838
Fax: 506-547-1949
MICR: 00074-010

Beamsville
PO Box 340
4961 King St. East
Beamsville, ON L0R 1B0 Canada
905-563-3286
Fax: 905-563-4316
MICR: 04572-010

Beaverlodge
PO Box 89
210 - 10th St.
Beaverlodge, AB T0H 0C0 Canada
780-354-2221
Fax: 780-354-8202
MICR: 00299-010

Beaverton
PO Box 70
339 Simcoe St. East
Beaverton, ON L0K 1A0 Canada
705-426-5815
Fax: 705-426-4302
MICR: 03642-010

Bedford - Bedford Hwy.
1600 Bedford Hwy.
Bedford, NS B4A 1E8 Canada
902-428-4712
Fax: 902-428-7225
MICR: 01003-010

Bedford - Principale
87, rue Principale
Bedford, QC J0J 1A0 Canada
405-248-3365
Fax: 405-248-4545
MICR: 00561-010

Belleville - Dundas St. East
Bayview Mall
470 Dundas St. East
Belleville, ON K8N 1G1 Canada
613-962-9257
Fax: 613-966-3405
MICR: 06942-010

Belleville - Front St.
237 Front St.
Belleville, ON K8N 2Z4 Canada
613-966-2641
Fax: 613-966-6879
MICR: 00042-010

Belleville - North Front St.
366 North Front St.
Belleville, ON K8P 5E6 Canada
613-969-8840
Fax: 613-969-8980
MICR: 04842-010

Beloeil
233, rue Duvernay
Beloeil, QC J3G 2M3 Canada
450-467-5557
Fax: 450-464-6862
MICR: 01651-010

Big River
PO Box 159
Big River, SK S0J 0E0 Canada
306-469-2124
Fax: 306-469-4409
MICR: 00838-010

Biggar

Canadian Imperial Bank of Commerce(CIBC)/ Banque Canadienne Impériale de Commerce (continued)

PO Box 10
301 Main St.
Biggar, SK S0K 0M0 Canada
306-948-3200
Fax: 306-948-5233
MICR: 00248-010

Binbrook
3011, Hwy. 56
Binbrook, ON L0R 1C0 Canada
905-692-4427
Fax: 905-692-3666
MICR: 07872-010

Birch Hills
PO Box 309
217 Bellamy
Birch Hills, SK S0J 0G0 Canada
306-749-3188
Fax: 306-749-2520
MICR: 00478-010

Blaine Lake
PO Box 100
118 Main St.
Blaine Lake, SK S0J 0J0 Canada
306-497-3610
Fax: 306-497-2572
MICR: 00588-010

Blainville
#104, 1083, boul Curé-Labelle
Blainville, QC J7C 3M9 Canada
450-433-2864
Fax: 450-433-5055
MICR: 01881-010

Blairmore
PO Box 325
12937 - 20th Ave.
Blairmore, AB T0K 0E0 Canada
403-562-2871
Fax: 403-562-2577
MICR: 09049-010

Blenheim
PO Box 490
27 Talbot St. West
Blenheim, ON N0P 1A0 Canada
519-676-5417
Fax: 519-676-0386
MICR: 02082-010

Bloomfield
PO Box 130
71 Main St.
Bloomfield, ON K0K 1G0 Canada
613-393-3150
Fax: 613-393-1657
MICR: 05842-010

Blyth
PO Box 160
442 Queen St.
Blyth, ON N0M 1H0 Canada
519-523-4247
Fax: 519-523-4213
MICR: 07852-010

Bobcaygeon
PO Box 430
93 Bolton St.
Bobcaygeon, ON K0M 1A0 Canada
705-738-2314
Fax: 705-738-5939
MICR: 05242-010

Bolton
PO Box 100
2 King St. East
Bolton, ON L7E 5T1 Canada
905-857-3665
Fax: 905-857-7331
MICR: 08052-010

Boucherville
#100, 130, boul de Mortagne
Boucherville, QC J4B 5M7 Canada
450-641-2021
Fax: 450-641-4196
MICR: 06071-010

Bowmanville
PO Box 99
2 King St. East
Bowmanville, ON L1C 3K8 Canada
905-623-3463
Fax: 905-623-3163
MICR: 04442-010

Boyle
PO Box 119
3rd St. & 4th Ave.
Boyle, AB T0A 0M0 Canada
780-689-3619
Fax: 780-689-2250
MICR: 05089-010

Bracebridge
245 Manitoba St.
Bracebridge, ON P1L 1S2 Canada
705-645-5213
Fax: 705-645-1853
MICR: 01242-010

Bradford
PO Box 910
49 Holland St. West
Bradford, ON L3Z 2B4 Canada
905-775-9304
Fax: 905-775-0321
MICR: 01042-010

Brampton - Bovaird Dr.
#1, 380 Bovaird Dr.
Brampton, ON L6Z 2S6 Canada
905-840-1057
Fax: 905-840-5874
MICR: 03952-010

Brampton - Bramalea Rd.
60 Bramalea Rd.
Brampton, ON L6T 2W8 Canada
905-791-1302
Fax: 905-791-1772
MICR: 03552-010

Brampton - Hurontario St.
Steeles Banking Centre
7940 Hurontario St.
Brampton, ON L6Y 0B8 Canada
905-454-0075
Fax: 905-454-2856
MICR: 01652-010

Brampton - Lisa St.
16 Lisa St.
Brampton, ON L6T 4W2 Canada
905-451-1497
Fax: 905-451-1915
MICR: 07612-010

Brampton - Main St. North
28 Main St. North
Brampton, ON L6V 1N6 Canada
905-451-3449
Fax: 905-450-0506
MICR: 01692-010

Brampton - North Park Dr.
930 North Park Dr.
Brampton, ON L6S 3Y5 Canada
905-791-3267
Fax: 905-791-8161
MICR: 00652-010

Brampton - Peter Robertson Blvd.
630 Peter Robertson Blvd.
Brampton, ON L6R 1T4 Canada
905-793-5644
Fax: 905-793-5437
MICR: 06032-010

Brandon - 9th St.
450 - 9th St.
Brandon, MB R7A 4B1 Canada
204-726-3007
Fax: 204-726-3012
MICR: 00877-010

Brandon - Rosser Ave.
803 Rosser Ave.
Brandon, MB R7A 0L1 Canada
204-726-3000
Fax: 204-727-8584
MICR: 00067-010

Brantford - King George Rd.
Brantford Mall
300 King George Rd.
Brantford, ON N3R 5L8 Canada
519-752-6529
Fax: 519-752-8922
MICR: 01472-010

Brantford - King George Rd.
2 King George Rd.
Brantford, ON N3R 5J7 Canada
519-756-2330
Fax: 519-759-6579
MICR: 07772-010

Brantford - Lynden Rd.
Lynden Park Mall
84 Lynden Rd.
Brantford, ON N3R 6B8 Canada
519-759-1250
Fax: 519-759-6208
MICR: 09472-010

Brantford - Market St.
PO Box 1056
34 Market St.
Brantford, ON N3T 5S7 Canada
519-752-5477
Fax: 519-752-1888
MICR: 00072-010

Brechin
PO Box 40
King St.
Brechin, ON L0K 1B0 Canada
705-484-5311
Fax: 705-484-0827
MICR: 06842-010

Bridgenorth
PO Box 119
871 Ward St.
Bridgenorth, ON K0L 1H0 Canada
705-292-9538
Fax: 705-292-6063
MICR: 08242-010

Bridgewater
PO Box 199
450 Lahave St.
Bridgewater, NS B4V 2W8 Canada
902-543-7377
Fax: 902-543-1840
MICR: 00253-010

Brighton
PO Box 100
48 Main St.
Brighton, ON K0K 1H0 Canada
613-475-2054
Fax: 613-475-1867
MICR: 08442-010

Brockville
98 King St. West
Brockville, ON K6V 3P9 Canada
613-342-6651
Fax: 613-342-7801
MICR: 00342-010

Bromont
89, boul Bromont
Bromont, QC J2L 2K5 Canada
450-534-3331
Fax: 450-534-2346
MICR: 01251-010

Brooklin
PO Box 130
50 Baldwin St.
Brooklin, ON L1M 1A2 Canada
905-655-8218
Fax: 905-655-4473
MICR: 04642-010

Brooks
431 Cassils Rd. West
Brooks, AB T1R 0W1 Canada
403-362-5511
Fax: 403-362-6048
MICR: 08049-010

Brossard
Place Portobello
#01, 7250, boul Taschereau ouest
Brossard, QC J4W 1M9 Canada
450-672-5880
Fax: 450-672-9793
MICR: 01241-010

Brussels
PO Box 20
36 King St.
Brussels, ON N0G 1H0 Canada

519-887-6521
Fax: 519-887-6785
MICR: 09652-010

Burford
PO Box 190
113 King St. East
Burford, ON N0E 1A0 Canada
519-449-2436
Fax: 519-449-5976
MICR: 05972-010

Burlington - Brant St.
575 Brant St.
Burlington, ON L7R 2G6 Canada
905-632-2221
Fax: 905-632-2424
MICR: 01062-010

Burlington - Dundas St.
3500 Dundas St.
Burlington, ON L7M 4B8 Canada
905-332-9755
Fax: 905-332-5740
MICR: 05162-010

Burlington - Fairview St.
4490 Fairview St.
Burlington, ON L7L 5P9 Canada
905-632-0747
Fax: 905-632-1075
MICR: 00262-010

Burlington - Fairview St.
Burlington Banking Centre
2400 Fairview St.
Burlington, ON L7R 2E4 Canada
905-632-5622
Fax: 905-632-5428
MICR: 04762-010

Burnaby - Austin Ave.
Lougheed Mall
#195, 9855 Austin Ave.
Burnaby, BC V3J 1N4 Canada
604-257-1175
Fax: 604-257-8055
MICR: 06910-010

Burnaby - East Hastings St.
4101 East Hastings St.
Burnaby, BC V5C 2J3 Canada
604-665-1090
Fax: 604-665-1078
MICR: 02000-010

Burnaby - Kingsway
4755 Kingsway
Burnaby, BC V5H 4W2 Canada
604-665-1379
Fax: 604-665-7614
MICR: 00410-010

Burnaby - Lougheed Hwy.
4567 Lougheed Hwy.
Burnaby, BC V5C 3Z6 Canada
604-665-1001
Fax: 604-665-1015
MICR: 05910-010

Burns Lake
Balmoral Plaza
PO Box 220
233 Balmoral Plaza, Hwy. 16
Burns Lake, BC V0J 1E0 Canada
250-692-3127
Fax: 250-692-3084
MICR: 01050-010

Caledon East
15968 Airport Rd. North
Caledon, ON L7C 1E8 Canada
905-584-4246
Fax: 905-584-9246
MICR: 07552-010

Caledonia
31 Argyle St.
Caledonia, ON N3W 1B6 Canada
905-765-4435
Fax: 905-765-6748
MICR: 07572-010

Calgary - 166th Ave.
2015 - 16th Ave. NW
Calgary, AB T2M 0M3 Canada
403-974-2734
Fax: 403-221-6146
MICR: 00319-010

Calgary - 16th Ave.
5032 - 16th Ave. NW
Calgary, AB T3B 0N3 Canada
403-974-2717
Fax: 403-221-6040
MICR: 00909-010

Calgary - 17th Ave.
1222 - 17th Ave. SW
Calgary, AB T2T 0B8 Canada
403-974-6371
Fax: 403-221-6216
MICR: 00209-010

Calgary - 17th Ave.
3619 - 17th Ave. SE
Calgary, AB T2A 0R8 Canada
403-974-6336
Fax: 403-221-6202
MICR: 00509-010

Calgary - 24th St.
Douglas Square
#228, 11520 - 24th St. SE
Calgary, AB T2Z 3E9 Canada
403-221-5067
Fax: 403-221-5061
MICR: 07209-010

Calgary - 3rd Ave.
Canterra Tower
400 - 3rd Ave. SW
Calgary, AB T2P 4H2 Canada
403-974-1691
Fax: 403-221-6004
MICR: 00109-010

Calgary - 4th St. NW
5609 - 4th St. NW
Calgary, AB T2K 1B3 Canada
403-974-6320
Fax: 403-221-6242
MICR: 03029-010

Calgary - 52nd St.
Eastport Centre
#2, 200 - 52nd St. NE
Calgary, AB T2A 4K8 Canada
403-974-6311
Fax: 403-221-6204
MICR: 06019-010

Calgary - 5th Ave.
Bow Valley Sq. 2
#110, 205 - 5th Ave. SW
Calgary, AB T2P 2W4 Canada
403-974-6326
Fax: 403-221-5951
MICR: 08009-010

Calgary - 7th Ave.
Elveden House
717 - 7th Ave. SW
Calgary, AB T2P 0Z3 Canada
403-974-2761
Fax: 403-221-5992
MICR: 00829-010

Calgary - 8th Ave.
CIBC Place Bankers Hall
PO Box 2585
309 - 8th Ave. SW
Calgary, AB T2P 2P2 Canada
403-974-1021
Fax: 403-221-5484
MICR: 00009-010

Calgary - 9th Ave.
1230 - 9th Ave. SE
Calgary, AB T2G 0T1 Canada
403-974-3729
Fax: 403-221-6210
MICR: 00229-010

Calgary - Anderson Rd.
PO Box 6197
100 Anderson Rd. SE
Calgary, AB T2J 3V1 Canada
403-974-2715
Fax: 403-221-6197
MICR: 07009-010

Calgary - Bow Trail SW
4623 Bow Trail SW
Calgary, AB T3C 2G6 Canada
403-974-3721
Fax: 403-221-6226
MICR: 00619-010

Calgary - Centre St. North
2318 Centre St. North
Calgary, AB T2E 2T7 Canada
403-974-6313
Fax: 403-221-6228
MICR: 00519-010

Calgary - Country Hills
#517, 388 Country Hills Blvd. NE
Calgary, AB T3K 5J6 Canada
403-226-7480
Fax: 403-226-7488
MICR: 02929-010

Calgary - Crowfoot Way
70 Crowfoot Way NW
Calgary, AB T3G 4C8 Canada
403-974-6317
Fax: 403-221-6200
MICR: 00809-010

Calgary - Falsbridge Gate
5224 Falsbridge Gate NE
Calgary, AB T3J 3G1 Canada
403-974-2787
Fax: 403-221-6270
MICR: 02309-010

Calgary - MacLeod Trail South
Chinook Station
6200 MacLeod Trail South
Calgary, AB T2H 0K6 Canada
403-974-2744
Fax: 403-221-6128
MICR: 00919-010

Calgary - Shaganappi Trail
Dalhousie Co-op Shopping Centre
5505 Shaganappi Trail NW
Calgary, AB T3A 1Z6 Canada
403-974-6347
Fax: 403-221-6222
MICR: 06029-010

Calgary - Shawville Blvd.
#200, 85 Shawville Blvd. SE
Calgary, AB T2Y 3W5 Canada
403-974-6322
Fax: 403-221-5038
MICR: 01319-010

Calgary - Southland Dr.
Oakridge Co-op Shopping Centre
#11, 2580 Southland Dr. SW
Calgary, AB T2V 4J8 Canada
403-974-6352
Fax: 403-221-6272
MICR: 08019-010

Calgary - Southport Rd.
10100 Southport Rd. SW
Calgary, AB T2W 3X4 Canada
403-974-6356
Fax: 403-221-6009
MICR: 01229-010

Calgary - Stewart Green
121 Stewart Green SW
Calgary, AB T3H 3C8 Canada
403-974-6338
Fax: 403-221-6211
MICR: 00329-010

Calgary - Sunridge Blvd.
3070 Sunridge Blvd. NE
Calgary, AB T1Y 7G6 Canada
403-221-6018
Fax: 403-221-6155
MICR: 07029-010

Calgary - Varsity Dr.
4625 Varsity Dr. NW
Calgary, AB T3A 0Z9 Canada
403-974-2708
Fax: 403-221-6045
MICR: 00929-010

Cambridge - Dundas St.
75 Dundas St.
Cambridge, ON N1R 6G5 Canada
519-623-0350
Fax: 519-623-9063
MICR: 02552-010

Cambridge - Hespeler Rd.

Canadian Imperial Bank of Commerce(CIBC)/ Banque Canadienne Impériale de Commerce (continued)

Cambridge Centre
PO Box 20061, John Galt Sta. John Galt
355 Hespeler Rd.
Cambridge, ON N1R 8C8 Canada
519-623-6110
Fax: 519-623-8193
MICR: 02452-010

Cambridge - King St. East
PO Box 3217, Preston Sta. Preston
567 King St. East
Cambridge, ON N3H 4S6 Canada
519-653-3244
Fax: 519-653-2821
MICR: 09052-010

Cambridge - Main St.
11 Main St.
Cambridge, ON N1R 5V5 Canada
519-621-5030
Fax: 519-621-5736
MICR: 00552-010

Campbell River
PO Box 430
952 Island Way
Campbell River, BC V9W 5B9 Canada
250-286-4300
Fax: 250-287-9815
MICR: 00140-010

Campbellton
131 Water St.
Campbellton, NB E3N 1B2 Canada
506-789-0050
Fax: 506-789-0054
MICR: 00034-010

Camrose
4901 - 50th St.
Camrose, AB T4V 1P9 Canada
780-672-4478
Fax: 780-672-1727
MICR: 00579-010

Canmore
#101, 730 - 8th St.
Canmore, AB T1W 2B6 Canada
403-609-6200
Fax: 403-678-4651
MICR: 08039-010

Canora
202 Main St.
Canora, SK S0A 0L0 Canada
306-563-5698
Fax: 306-563-6855
MICR: 00228-010

Canwood
PO Box 70
Main St. & 2nd
Canwood, SK S0J 0K0 Canada
306-468-2155
Fax: 306-468-2988
MICR: 00498-010

Capreol
PO Box 130
12 Young St.
Capreol, ON P0M 1H0 Canada
705-858-3708
Fax: 705-858-3514
MICR: 03992-010

Carbonear
Trinity Conception Square Mall
120 Colombus Dr.
Carbonear, NL A1Y 1B3 Canada
709-596-1670
Fax: 709-596-6015
MICR: 00563-010

Carleton Place
Carleton Place Mews
33 Lansdowne Ave.
Carleton Place, ON K7C 3S9 Canada
613-257-1880
Fax: 613-253-2822
MICR: 00886-010

Carlyle
PO Box 580
211 Main St.
Carlyle, SK S0C 0R0 Canada
306-453-6785
Fax: 306-453-2704
MICR: 01048-010

Carman
PO Box 40
25 First St. SW
Carman, MB R0G 0J0 Canada
204-745-2018
Fax: 204-745-6221
MICR: 00057-010

Castlegar
Castleaird Plaza
1801 Columbia Ave.
Castlegar, BC V1N 3Y2 Canada
250-365-3325
Fax: 250-365-6312
MICR: 05070-010

Cayuga
PO Box 40
22 Talbot St.
Cayuga, ON N0A 1E0 Canada
905-772-3378
Fax: 905-772-3008
MICR: 08772-010

Central Butte
211 Main St.
Central Butte, SK S0H 0T0 Canada
306-796-2060
Fax: 306-796-4515
MICR: 00548-010

Chambly
1455, boul de Perigny
Chambly, QC J3L 4K8 Canada
450-658-1723
Fax: 450-658-4983
MICR: 01061-010

Charlottetown - Queen St.
PO Box 99
151 Queen St.
Charlottetown, PE C1A 7K2 Canada
902-892-1284
Fax: 902-368-3262
MICR: 00083-010

Charlottetown - University Ave.
PO Box 1565
465 University Ave.
Charlottetown, PE C1A 7N3 Canada
902-892-3477
Fax: 902-566-2924
MICR: 00683-010

Chatham - King St. West
99 King St. West
Chatham, ON N7M 1C7 Canada
519-352-7150
Fax: 519-351-4238
MICR: 00282-010

Chatham - Richmond St.
445 Richmond St.
Chatham, ON N7M 1R2 Canada
519-352-7710
Fax: 519-352-1964
MICR: 08082-010

Chatham - St. Clair St.
PO Box 20010
426 St. Clair St.
Chatham, ON N7L 5K6 Canada
519-354-4200
Fax: 519-354-5619
MICR: 09982-010

Chemainus
PO Box 210
9760 Willow St.
Chemainus, BC V0R 1K0 Canada
250-246-3257
Fax: 250-246-2436
MICR: 00640-010

Chesley
PO Box 280
47 - 1st Ave. South
Chesley, ON N0G 1L0 Canada
519-363-3512
Fax: 519-363-3437
MICR: 01752-010

Chetwynd
PO Box 144
4757 - 51st St.
Chetwynd, BC V0C 1J0 Canada
250-788-9211
Fax: 250-788-9583
MICR: 01990-010

Chibougamau
489, 3e rue
Chibougamau, QC G8P 1N6 Canada
418-748-2695
Fax: 418-748-2145
MICR: 00891-010

Chicoutimi
204, rue Racine est
Chicoutimi, QC G7H 1R9 Canada
418-549-6774
Fax: 418-696-2628
MICR: 00375-010

Chilliwack
PO Box 220
9245 Young St.
Chilliwack, BC V2P 6J2 Canada
604-702-3130
Fax: 604-702-3131
MICR: 00120-010

Chisasibi
PO Box 60
Chisasibi, QC J0M 1E0 Canada
819-855-2803
Fax: 819-855-2226
MICR: 07091-010

Châteauguay
77-B, boul d'Anjou
Châteauguay, QC J6J 2R1 Canada
450-691-4151
Fax: 450-691-9691
MICR: 08051-010

Claremont
5006 Old Brock Rd. North
Claremont, ON L1Y 1B3 Canada
905-649-2091
Fax: 905-649-1634
MICR: 01842-010

Clarenville
240 Memorial Dr.
Clarenville, NL A5A 1N9 Canada
709-466-2334
Fax: 709-466-3135
MICR: 00573-010

Claresholm
PO Box 460
4821 - 1 St.
Claresholm, AB T0L 0T0 Canada
403-625-3331
Fax: 403-625-4845
MICR: 00249-010

Coaticook
20, rue Main est
Coaticook, QC J1A 1M9 Canada
819-849-6351
Fax: 819-849-9591
MICR: 00551-010

Coboconk
PO Box 120
Cameron & Albert Sts.
Coboconk, ON K0M 1K0 Canada
705-454-3373
Fax: 705-454-2484
MICR: 01742-010

Cobourg
PO Box 277
51 King St. West
Cobourg, ON K9A 4K8 Canada
905-372-4381
Fax: 905-372-2055
MICR: 04042-010

Cochrane
PO Box 1630
134 - 6th Ave.
Cochrane, ON P0L 1C0 Canada
705-272-4261
Fax: 705-272-3072
MICR: 07092-010

Colborne
PO Box 309
38 King St. West
Colborne, ON K0K 1S0 Canada

905-355-2011
Fax: 905-355-1506
MICR: 08542-010
Cold Lake
PO Box 2040
5105 - 50th Ave.
Cold Lake, AB T0A 1T0 Canada
780-594-7561
Fax: 780-594-2737
MICR: 07979-010
Collingwood
86 Hurontario St.
Collingwood, ON L9Y 2L8 Canada
705-445-2780
Fax: 705-445-1872
MICR: 06442-010
Comox
195 Port Augusta St.
Comox, BC V9N 3M9 Canada
250-890-6820
Fax: 250-339-6717
MICR: 03040-010
Concord - Keele St.
#302, 7501 Keele St.
Concord, ON L4K 1Y2 Canada
905-761-3235
Fax: 905-761-6505
MICR: 06432-010
Concord - Keele St.
8099 Keele St.
Concord, ON L4K 1Y6 Canada
905-669-4213
Fax: 905-669-3758
MICR: 04342-010
Coquitlam - Austin Ave.
PO Box 1235
1036 Austin Ave.
Coquitlam, BC V3J 6Z9 Canada
604-933-2166
Fax: 604-939-5638
MICR: 06920-010
Coquitlam - Clarke Rd.
Burquitlam Plaza
546 Clarke Rd.
Coquitlam, BC V3J 3X5 Canada
604-933-2133
Fax: 604-933-2105
MICR: 07020-010
Coquitlam - Lincoln Ave.
3000 Lincoln Ave.
Coquitlam, BC V3B 7L9 Canada
604-927-2767
Fax: 604-944-6388
MICR: 00920-010
Coquitlam - Parkway Blvd.
1410 Parkway Blvd., #E
Coquitlam, BC V3E 3J7 Canada
604-552-6360
Fax: 604-552-6363
MICR: 01420-010
Corner Brook
PO Box 578
9 Main St.
Corner Brook, NL A2H 6G2 Canada
709-637-1700
Fax: 709-634-1734
MICR: 00163-010
Cornwall - 14th St.
716 - 14th St. West
Cornwall, ON K6J 5T9 Canada
613-936-0102
Fax: 613-936-1997
MICR: 00146-010
Cornwall - Second St. West
PO Box 1269
1 Second St. West
Cornwall, ON K6H 5V3 Canada
613-932-3200
Fax: 613-932-0602
MICR: 00442-010
Coronach
PO Box 450
201 Centre St.
Coronach, SK S0H 0Z0 Canada
306-267-2245
Fax: 306-267-4575
MICR: 02078-010
Courtenay - Cliffe Ave.
825 Cliffe Ave.
Courtenay, BC V9N 2J8 Canada
250-338-6751
Fax: 250-338-7358
MICR: 00440-010
Courtenay - South Island Hwy.
Driftwood Mall
2785 South Island Hwy.
Courtenay, BC V9N 2L8 Canada
250-897-3770
Fax: 250-338-7227
MICR: 04940-010
Cowansville
175, rue Principale
Cowansville, QC J2K 3L9 Canada
450-263-2744
Fax: 450-263-9663
MICR: 00461-010
Cowessess
Cowessess First Nations
PO Box 70
104 Cowessess Mall
Cowessess, SK S0G 5L0 Canada
306-696-2497
Fax: 306-696-2410
MICR: 02308-010
Cranbrook
919 Baker St.
Cranbrook, BC V1C 1A4 Canada
250-489-8300
Fax: 250-489-8320
MICR: 00470-010
Creston
PO Box 550
1135 Canyon St.
Creston, BC V0B 1G0 Canada
250-428-9355
Fax: 250-428-3577
MICR: 00170-010
Crossfield
PO Box 70
1220 Railway St.
Crossfield, AB T0M 0S0 Canada
403-946-5686
Fax: 403-946-4580
MICR: 00949-010
Cudworth
PO Box 70
201 Main St.
Cudworth, SK S0K 1B0 Canada
306-256-3421
Fax: 306-256-3389
MICR: 00528-010
Côte-St-Luc
7005, ch Kildare
Côte-St-Luc, QC H4W 1C1 Canada
514-488-5161
Fax: 514-488-5928
MICR: 05031-010
Dartmouth - Cole Harbour
959 Cole Harbour Rd.
Dartmouth, NS B2V 1E5 Canada
902-428-7912
Fax: 902-428-4761
MICR: 00803-010
Dartmouth - Portland St.
Penhorn Mall
535 Portland St.
Dartmouth, NS B2Y 4B1 Canada
902-428-7913
Fax: 902-466-7047
MICR: 00513-010
Dartmouth - Portland St.
PO Box 309
56 Portland St.
Dartmouth, NS B2Y 3Y5 Canada
902-428-4884
Fax: 902-428-4989
MICR: 00303-010
Dartmouth - Wyse Rd.
162 Wyse Rd.
Dartmouth, NS B3A 1M6 Canada
902-428-7934
Fax: 902-463-1851
MICR: 00703-010
Dauphin
123 Main St. North
Dauphin, MB R7N 1C1 Canada
204-638-8045
Fax: 204-638-6402
MICR: 00277-010
Dawson
PO Box 1320
978, 2nd Ave.
Dawson, YT Y0B 1G0 Canada
867-993-5447
Fax: 867-993-5786
MICR: 00480-010
Dawson Creek
PO Box 599
10200 - 10th St.
Dawson Creek, BC V1G 4H6 Canada
250-782-4816
Fax: 250-782-3286
MICR: 01090-010
Delhi
172 Main St.
Delhi, ON N4B 2L9 Canada
519-582-0570
Fax: 519-582-4880
MICR: 07072-010
Delta - 112th St.
Nordel Place
8360 - 112th St.
Delta, BC V4C 7A2 Canada
604-501-7050
Fax: 604-591-5272
MICR: 02720-010
Delta - 48th Ave.
PO Box 160
5045 - 48th Ave.
Delta, BC V4K 3N6 Canada
604-940-7500
Fax: 604-946-9358
MICR: 04020-010
Delta - 56th St.
1197 - 56th St.
Delta, BC V4L 2A2 Canada
604-948-3201
Fax: 604-943-7787
MICR: 09920-010
Delta - 88th Ave.
Kennedy Heights Shopping Centre
11920 - 88th Ave.
Delta, BC V4C 3C8 Canada
604-501-7077
Fax: 604-596-2685
MICR: 01020-010
Deseronto
PO Box 303
352 Main St.
Deseronto, ON K0K 1X0 Canada
613-396-2120
Fax: 613-396-1556
MICR: 01292-010
Deux-Montagnes
569, 20ieme av
Deux-Montagnes, QC J7R 6B2 Canada
450-472-4610
Fax: 450-472-4200
MICR: 07081-010
Digby
Evangeline Shoppers' Mall
PO Box 1059
8791 Warwick St.
Digby, NS B0V 1A0 Canada
902-245-4754
Fax: 902-245-6334
MICR: 00543-010
Dinsmore
PO Box 248
Main St.
Dinsmore, SK S0L 0T0 Canada

Canadian Imperial Bank of Commerce(CIBC)/ Banque Canadienne Impériale de Commerce (continued)

306-846-2160
Fax: 306-846-2026
800-465-2422
MICR: 00638-010

Dominion City
PO Box 207
130 Waddell Ave.
Dominion City, MB R0A 0H0 Canada
204-427-2119
Fax: 204-427-2151
MICR: 00677-010

Dresden
PO Box 640
103 Main St.
Dresden, ON N0P 1M0 Canada
519-683-4434
Fax: 519-683-2208
MICR: 07082-010

Drumheller
PO Box 1420
105 - 3rd Ave. West
Drumheller, AB T0J 0Y0 Canada
403-823-5141
Fax: 403-823-4413
MICR: 00349-010

Drummondville
385, boul St-Joseph
Drummondville, QC J2C 2B1 Canada
819-478-1461
Fax: 819-478-5216
MICR: 08071-010

Dryden
35A Whyte Ave.
Dryden, ON P8N 1Z2 Canada
807-223-3211
Fax: 807-223-5809
MICR: 02097-010

Duncan
PO Box 190
116 Station St.
Duncan, BC V9L 3X3 Canada
250-701-4050
Fax: 250-746-7265
MICR: 00240-010

Dundalk
PO Box 70
31 Proton St. North
Dundalk, ON N0C 1B0 Canada
519-923-2242
Fax: 519-923-2969
MICR: 06852-010

Dundas
83 King St. West
Dundas, ON L9H 1V1 Canada
905-628-6371
Fax: 905-628-3170
MICR: 00662-010

Dunnville
PO Box 37
165 Lock St. East
Dunnville, ON N1A 2X1 Canada
905-774-7473
Fax: 905-774-5434
MICR: 04072-010

Durham
PO Box 110
106 Garafraxa St. North
Durham, ON N0G 1R0 Canada
519-369-2014
Fax: 519-369-3215
MICR: 02852-010

East Angus
30, rue Angus nord
East Angus, QC J0B 1R0 Canada
819-832-2433
Fax: 819-832-4634
MICR: 00351-010

Eastmain
Cree Nation Bldg.
PO Box 135
Eastmain, QC J0M 1W0 Canada
819-977-2062
Fax: 819-977-2066
MICR: 07191-010

Eckville
PO Box 60
5101 - 50th St.
Eckville, AB T0M 0X0 Canada
403-746-2231
Fax: 403-746-2005
MICR: 05039-010

Edmonton - North Town Mall SW
#170, North Town Mall SW
Edmonton, AB T5E 6C1 Canada
780-408-1092
Fax: 780-408-1085
MICR: 03869-010

Edmonton - 104th Ave.
Oliver Square
11504 - 104th Ave.
Edmonton, AB T5K 2S5 Canada
780-408-1183
Fax: 780-408-1199
MICR: 05059-010

Edmonton - 112th St.
College Plaza
8207 - 112th St.
Edmonton, AB T6G 2L9 Canada
780-432-1620
Fax: 780-439-2836
MICR: 09069-010

Edmonton - 118th Ave
8004 - 118th Ave.
Edmonton, AB T5B 0R8 Canada
780-474-9380
Fax: 780-471-2104
MICR: 00969-010

Edmonton - 118th Ave.
3924 - 118th Ave.
Edmonton, AB T5W 0Z9 Canada
780-408-1125
Fax: 780-408-1140
MICR: 00769-010

Edmonton - 137th Ave.
Palisades Sq. Shopping Centre
12720 - 137th Ave.
Edmonton, AB T5L 4Y8 Canada
780-408-1047
Fax: 780-408-1050
MICR: 00859-010

Edmonton - 170th St.
10058 - 170th St.
Edmonton, AB T5S 2G3 Canada
780-444-2340
Fax: 780-930-3551
MICR: 04959-010

Edmonton - 28th Ave.
6150 - 28th Ave.
Edmonton, AB T6L 6N4 Canada
780-408-1161
Fax: 780-408-1178
MICR: 06869-010

Edmonton - 50th St.
13610 - 50th St.
Edmonton, AB T5A 4Y3 Canada
780-473-3550
Fax: 780-472-2206
MICR: 02769-010

Edmonton - 82 Ave.
10431 - 82 Ave.
Edmonton, AB T6E 2A1 Canada
780-408-1262
Fax: 780-408-1260
MICR: 00159-010

Edmonton - 82nd Ave.
9903 - 82nd Ave.
Edmonton, AB T6E 1Z1 Canada
780-408-1002
Fax: 780-408-1000
MICR: 00459-010

Edmonton - 87th Ave.
Meadowlark Shopping Centre
15630 - 87th Ave.
Edmonton, AB T5R 5W9 Canada
780-408-1202
Fax: 780-408-1220
MICR: 06069-010

Edmonton - Gateway Blvd.
South Edmonton Banking Centre
4230 Gateway Blvd. NW
Edmonton, AB T6J 7K1 Canada
780-437-7139
Fax: 780-437-4616
MICR: 01859-010

Edmonton - Jasper Ave.
Commerce Place
10102 Jasper Ave.
Edmonton, AB T5J 1W5 Canada
780-429-7744
Fax: 780-429-7700
MICR: 00059-010

Edmonton - Riverbend Sq.
644 Riverbend Sq.
Edmonton, AB T6R 2E3 Canada
780-408-1246
Fax: 780-408-1258
MICR: 02169-010

Edmonton - Terrace Rd.
6130 Terrace Rd.
Edmonton, AB T6A 3Z1 Canada
780-408-1107
Fax: 780-408-1111
MICR: 05069-010

Edson
PO Box 6360
421 - 50th St.
Edson, AB T7E 1T8 Canada
780-723-6061
Fax: 780-723-5052
MICR: 00379-010

Elkhorn
PO Box 160
107 Richhill Ave. East
Elkhorn, MB R0M 0N0 Canada
204-845-2518
Fax: 204-845-2125
MICR: 00577-010

Elliot Lake
PO Box 128
37 Elizabeth Sq.
Elliot Lake, ON P5A 2J6 Canada
705-848-2266
Fax: 705-848-2701
MICR: 06092-010

Elm Creek
PO Box 9
30 Main St.
Elm Creek, MB R0G 0N0 Canada
204-436-2246
Fax: 204-436-2480
MICR: 00657-010

Embrun
210 Industriel St.
Embrun, ON K0A 1W1 Canada
613-443-2711
Fax: 613-443-5059
MICR: 00476-010

Emo
PO Box 270
Hwy. 71 & Hwy. 11
Emo, ON P0W 1E0 Canada
807-482-2770
Fax: 807-482-2092
MICR: 00987-010

Englehart
PO Box 639
3rd St. & 5th Ave.
Englehart, ON P0J 1H0 Canada
705-544-2208
Fax: 705-544-8468
MICR: 08092-010

Essex
PO Box 40
33 Talbot St. North
Essex, ON N8M 2Y1 Canada
519-776-5226
Fax: 519-776-4458
MICR: 01882-010

Estevan
PO Box 757
1138 - 4th St.
Estevan, SK S4A 2A6 Canada

306-634-4713
Fax: 306-634-9915
MICR: 00088-010

Eston
PO Box 309
102 Main St.
Eston, SK S0L 1A0 Canada
306-962-3613
Fax: 306-962-3626
MICR: 00128-010

Exeter
44 Thames Rd.
Exeter, ON N0M 1S3 Canada
519-235-1050
Fax: 519-235-1659
MICR: 03182-010

Fairview
PO Box 430
10118 - 110th St.
Fairview, AB T0H 1L0 Canada
780-835-2271
Fax: 780-835-2340
MICR: 00799-010

Farnham
323, rue Principal est
Farnham, QC J2N 1L5 Canada
450-293-5371
Fax: 450-293-8265
MICR: 00361-010

Fenelon Falls
PO Box 10
37 Colborne St.
Fenelon Falls, ON K0M 1N0 Canada
705-887-2660
Fax: 705-887-4912
MICR: 08342-010

Fergus
PO Box 83
301 St. Andrew St. West
Fergus, ON N1M 2W7 Canada
519-843-2250
Fax: 519-843-7390
MICR: 03052-010

Fernie
PO Box 550
501 - 2nd Ave.
Fernie, BC V0B 1M0 Canada
250-423-4426
Fax: 250-423-4811
MICR: 00970-010

Fisher Branch
PO Box 340
62 Tache St.
Fisher Branch, MB R0C 0Z0 Canada
204-372-6312
Fax: 204-372-8435
MICR: 00377-010

Flesherton
PO Box 40
13 Durham St.
Flesherton, ON N0C 1E0 Canada
519-924-2520
Fax: 519-924-3841
MICR: 08852-010

Flin Flon
89 Main St.
Flin Flon, MB R8A 1J9 Canada
204-687-6022
Fax: 204-687-8060
MICR: 00167-010

Fonthill
PO Box 1099
1461 Pelham St.
Fonthill, ON L0S 1E0 Canada
905-892-5738
Fax: 905-892-4044
MICR: 06672-010

Forest
PO Box 10
2 King St. West
Forest, ON N0N 1J0 Canada
519-786-2357
Fax: 519-786-2388
MICR: 05782-010

Fort Erie
85 Niagara Blvd.
Fort Erie, ON L2A 3G4 Canada
905-871-0990
Fax: 905-871-8593
MICR: 09072-010

Fort Frances
203 Scott St.
Fort Frances, ON P9A 1G8 Canada
807-274-5391
Fax: 807-274-5577
MICR: 00087-010

Fort Macleod
PO Box 580
163 Col. Macleod Blvd.
Fort MacLeod, AB T0L 0Z0 Canada
403-553-3334
Fax: 403-553-3899
MICR: 00239-010

Fort McMurray - Manning Ave.
8553 Manning Ave.
Fort McMurray, AB T9H 3N7 Canada
780-743-3312
Fax: 780-791-1827
MICR: 08089-010

Fort McMurray - Signal Rd.
Thickwood Shopping Plaza
121 Signal Rd.
Fort McMurray, AB T9H 4N7 Canada
780-791-1145
Fax: 780-743-6391
MICR: 05979-010

Fort Nelson
PO Box 157
5028 - 50th Ave. North
Fort Nelson, BC V0C 1R0 Canada
250-774-2555
Fax: 250-774-2723
MICR: 06090-010

Fort Qu'Appelle
PO Box 189
180 Broadway St.
Fort Qu'appelle, SK S0G 1S0 Canada
306-332-5619
Fax: 306-332-5073
MICR: 00178-010

Fort Saskatchewan
9903 - 101st St.
Fort Saskatchewan, AB T8L 1V6 Canada
780-998-2261
Fax: 780-998-1250
MICR: 01069-010

Fort Simpson
9909 - 97th Ave.
Fort Simpson, NT X0E 0N0 Canada
867-695-2284
Fax: 867-695-2383
MICR: 00999-010

Fort St. James
PO Box 309
470W Stuart Dr.
Fort St James, BC V0J 1P0 Canada
250-996-8256
Fax: 250-996-8393
MICR: 02050-010

Fort St. John
9959 - 100th Ave.
Fort St John, BC V1J 1Y4 Canada
250-785-8101
Fax: 250-785-4909
MICR: 03090-010

Fox Creek
PO Box 239
22 Commercial Ct.
Fox Creek, AB T0H 1P0 Canada
780-622-3894
Fax: 780-622-3082
MICR: 09089-010

Fraser Lake
PO Box 130
111 Chowsunket St.
Fraser Lake, BC V0J 1S0 Canada
250-699-6231
Fax: 250-699-8772
MICR: 01950-010

Fredericton - Main St.
Nashwaaksis Place
102 Main St.
Fredericton, NB E3A 9N6 Canada
506-458-9147
Fax: 506-452-9986
MICR: 00894-010

Fredericton - Queen St.
448 Queen St.
Fredericton, NB E3B 1B6 Canada
506-452-9100
Fax: 506-450-7922
MICR: 00014-010

Fredericton - Smythe St.
PO Box 446
1142 Smythe St.
Fredericton, NB E3B 3H5 Canada
506-458-8774
Fax: 506-450-8194
MICR: 00804-010

Gananoque
301 King St. East
Gananoque, ON K7G 1G6 Canada
613-382-4794
Fax: 613-382-8452
MICR: 06242-010

Gander
Fraser Mall
230 Airport Blvd.
Gander, NL A1V 1L7 Canada
709-651-3940
Fax: 709-651-3021
MICR: 00673-010

Gatineau - Portage
Place du Centre
200, promenade du Portage
Gatineau, QC J8X 4B7 Canada
819-771-7788
Fax: 819-771-0478
MICR: 00881-010

Gatineau - Principale
200, rue Principale
Gatineau, QC J9H 6J4 Canada
819-684-1602
Fax: 819-682-0663
MICR: 02981-010

Gatineau - Savane
Terrasses de la Savane
25, ch de la Savane
Gatineau, QC J8T 8A4 Canada
819-243-5144
Fax: 819-243-5685
MICR: 01981-010

Georgetown - Guelph St.
#14, 280 Guelph St.
Georgetown, ON L7G 4B1 Canada
905-877-1082
Fax: 905-877-7678
MICR: 02952-010

Georgetown - Main St. South
82 Main St. South
Georgetown, ON L7G 3E4 Canada
905-877-2109
Fax: 905-873-4760
MICR: 00752-010

Gibsons - Gibsons Way
PO Box 1100
#27, 900 Gibsons Way
Gibsons, BC V0N 1V0 Canada
604-886-4366
Fax: 604-886-3147
MICR: 07080-010

Gilbert Plains
PO Box 9
29 Main North
Gilbert Plains, MB R0L 0X0 Canada
204-548-2421
Fax: 204-548-2752
MICR: 00547-010

Gimli
PO Box 70
48 Centre St.
Gimli, MB R0C 1B0 Canada
204-642-8521
Fax: 204-642-7177
MICR: 00357-010

Canadian Imperial Bank of Commerce(CIBC)/ Banque Canadienne Impériale de Commerce (continued)

Glace Bay
PO Box 70
618 Main St.
Glace Bay, NS B1A 5V1 Canada
902-849-3531
Fax: 902-842-0787
MICR: 00033-010

Glencoe
PO Box 338
252 Main St.
Glencoe, ON N0L 1M0 Canada
519-287-2018
Fax: 519-287-3381
MICR: 05282-010

Gloucester
Gloucester Centre
#146, 1980 Ogilvie Rd.
Gloucester, ON K1J 9L3 Canada
613-747-2422
Fax: 613-747-1445
MICR: 00706-010

Goderich
24 The Square
Goderich, ON N7A 3Y7 Canada
519-524-8371
Fax: 519-524-8105
MICR: 07652-010

Golden
PO Box 229
520 - 9th Ave. North
Golden, BC V0A 1H0 Canada
250-344-2244
Fax: 250-344-6033
MICR: 00350-010

Granby - Principale
78, rue Principale
Granby, QC J2G 2T4 Canada
450-372-3345
Fax: 450-375-9775
MICR: 00371-010

Granby - Simonds
10, rue Simonds sud
Granby, QC J2G 7Z3 Canada
450-378-9016
Fax: 450-777-2243
MICR: 01661-010

Grand Falls - Windsor
PO Box 69
1 Church Rd.
Grand Falls-Windsor, NL A2A 2J3 Canada
709-489-0812
Fax: 709-489-6180
MICR: 00363-010

Grand Forks
PO Box 670
7310 - 2nd St.
Grand Forks, BC V0H 1H0 Canada
250-442-2181
Fax: 250-442-8622
MICR: 00570-010

Grand-Mère
575, 6ieme av
Grand-Mère, QC G9T 2H4 Canada
819-538-8674
Fax: 819-538-9191
MICR: 00581-010

Grande Cache
1309 Shoppers Park Mall
Grande Cache, AB T0E 0Y0 Canada
780-827-3725
Fax: 780-827-3222
MICR: 09079-010

Grande Prairie
9933 - 100th Ave.
Grande Prairie, AB T8V 0V1 Canada
780-538-8300
Fax: 780-538-8325
MICR: 00599-010

Grandview
PO Box 69
402 Main St.
Grandview, MB R0L 0Y0 Canada
204-546-2633
Fax: 204-546-3204
MICR: 00457-010

Greenwood
Greenwood Shopping Mall
PO Box 160
963 Central Ave.
Greenwood, NS B0P 1N0 Canada
902-765-3355
Fax: 902-765-2185
MICR: 00423-010

Grimsby
PO Box 248
27 Main St. West
Grimsby, ON L3M 4G5 Canada
905-945-2239
Fax: 905-945-2186
MICR: 02072-010

Grimshaw
PO Box 500
5401 - 50th St.
Grimshaw, AB T0H 1W0 Canada
780-332-4611
Fax: 780-332-1025
MICR: 00399-010

Guelph - Stone Rd.
374 Stone Rd. West
Guelph, ON N1G 4T8 Canada
519-824-6520
Fax: 519-824-6133
MICR: 09952-010

Guelph - Victoria Rd.
25 Victoria Rd. North
Guelph, ON N1E 5G6 Canada
519-823-1550
Fax: 519-823-1850
MICR: 01452-010

Guelph - Wyndham St.
St. George's Square
PO Box 578
59 Wyndham St.
Guelph, ON N1H 6K9 Canada
519-766-6400
Fax: 519-766-4815
MICR: 00052-010

Hafford
PO Box 430
Main St.
Hafford, SK S0J 1A0 Canada
306-549-2130
Fax: 306-549-2144
MICR: 00948-010

Hagersville
PO Box 160
2 King St. West
Hagersville, ON N0A 1H0 Canada
905-768-1131
Fax: 905-768-1868
MICR: 02772-010

Haliburton
PO Box 300
Highland & Maple Sts.
Haliburton, ON K0M 1S0 Canada
705-457-2751
Fax: 705-457-5167
MICR: 03242-010

Halifax - Barrington St.
PO Box 1665
1809 Barrington St.
Halifax, NS B3J 3A3 Canada
902-428-4750
Fax: 902-428-7972
MICR: 00003-010

Halifax - Parkland Dr.
Parkland Banking Centre
18 Parkland Dr.
Halifax, NS B3S 1T5 Canada
902-428-4701
Fax: 902-428-4984
MICR: 00503-010

Halifax - Quinpool Rd.
6429 Quinpool Rd.
Halifax, NS B3L 1A7 Canada
902-428-7943
Fax: 902-428-4593
MICR: 00403-010

Halifax - Spring Garden Rd.
5527 Spring Garden Rd.
Halifax, NS B3J 1G8 Canada
902-428-7950
Fax: 902-428-7988
MICR: 00103-010

Hamilton - Barton St.
879 Barton St. East
Hamilton, ON L8L 3B4 Canada
905-544-2874
Fax: 905-544-3684
MICR: 04862-010

Hamilton - Barton St.
The Centre Mall
1227 Barton St. East
Hamilton, ON L8H 2V4 Canada
905-547-1485
Fax: 905-549-1875
MICR: 03862-010

Hamilton - Fennell Ave.
997 Fennell Ave. East
Hamilton, ON L8T 1R1 Canada
905-389-2211
Fax: 905-389-3622
MICR: 04962-010

Hamilton - Greenhill Ave.
399 Greenhill Ave.
Hamilton, ON L8K 6N5 Canada
905-560-4477
Fax: 905-560-3109
MICR: 04562-010

Hamilton - King St. East
1882 King St. East
Hamilton, ON L8K 1V7 Canada
905-549-6523
Fax: 905-549-9245
MICR: 05962-010

Hamilton - King St. West
PO Box 89069, Westdale Sta. Westdale
1015 King St. West
Hamilton, ON L8S 4R5 Canada
905-572-3333
Fax: 905-528-5303
MICR: 00562-010

Hamilton - King St. West
Commerce Place
1 King St. West
Hamilton, ON L8P 1A4 Canada
905-572-3000
Fax: 905-572-3195
MICR: 00062-010

Hamilton - Mohawk Rd.
630 Mohawk Rd. West
Hamilton, ON L9C 1X6 Canada
905-385-3247
Fax: 905-385-7133
MICR: 03762-010

Hamilton - Parkdale Ave.
251 Parkdale Ave. North
Hamilton, ON L8H 5X6 Canada
905-549-1366
Fax: 905-549-9440
MICR: 08062-010

Hamilton - Upper James St.
673D Upper James St.
Hamilton, ON L9C 5R9 Canada
905-387-1382
Fax: 905-387-4090
MICR: 08862-010

Hamilton - Upper James St.
1550 Upper James St.
Hamilton, ON L9B 2L6 Canada
905-575-7557
Fax: 905-575-3424
MICR: 04972-010

Hanover
338 - 10th St.
Hanover, ON N4N 1P4 Canada
519-364-4341
Fax: 519-364-6756
MICR: 01152-010

Harbour Breton
PO Box 118
1 South Side Rd.
Harbour Breton, NL A0H 1P0 Canada

709-885-2277
Fax: 709-885-2065
MICR: 00663-010
Hardisty
PO Box 40
5123 - 50th St.
Hardisty, AB T0B 1V0 Canada
780-888-3546
Fax: 780-888-2337
MICR: 02079-010
Harriston
PO Box 339
40 Elora St. South
Harriston, ON N0G 1Z0 Canada
519-338-3944
Fax: 519-338-2327
MICR: 01252-010
Harrow
PO Box 340
25 King St. West
Harrow, ON N0R 1G0 Canada
519-738-2294
Fax: 519-738-3780
MICR: 08682-010
Havre-Saint-Pierre
PO Box 130
786, boul de l'Escale
Havre-Saint-Pierre, QC G0G 1P0 Canada
418-538-2711
Fax: 418-538-2821
MICR: 00185-010
Hawkesbury
PO Box 394
275 Main St. West
Hawkesbury, ON K6A 2S2 Canada
613-632-8517
Fax: 613-632-5518
MICR: 00696-010
Hay River
10A Gagnier St.
Hay River, NT X0E 1G1 Canada
867-874-6746
Fax: 867-874-2120
MICR: 05999-010
Hearst
PO Box 250
831 George St.
Hearst, ON P0L 1N0 Canada
705-362-4322
Fax: 705-362-8434
MICR: 01092-010
Hemmingford
500, rue Frontière
Hemmingford, QC J0L 1H0 Canada
450-247-2749
Fax: 450-247-3578
MICR: 02061-010
High Level
PO Box 330
10003 - 100th Ave.
High Level, AB T0H 1Z0 Canada
780-926-2211
Fax: 780-926-2696
MICR: 01899-010
High River
PO Box 5069
403 - 1st St. West
High River, AB T1V 1M3 Canada
403-652-2022
Fax: 403-652-3951
MICR: 00649-010
Hobbema
Maskwachees Mall
PO Box 264
Hwy. 2A South
Hobbema, AB T0C 1N0 Canada
780-585-2455
Fax: 780-585-2479
MICR: 01179-010
Holland
PO Box 209
118 Broadway St.
Holland, MB R0G 0X0 Canada
204-526-2048
Fax: 204-526-2262
MICR: 00757-010
Hope
PO Box 848
413 Wallace St.
Hope, BC V0X 1L0 Canada
604-869-9926
Fax: 604-869-7266
MICR: 05020-010
Hornepayne
PO Box 39
200 Front St.
Hornepayne, ON P0M 1Z0 Canada
807-868-2544
Fax: 807-868-2795
MICR: 05992-010
Howick
54, Colville
Howick, QC J0S 1G0 Canada
450-825-2252
Fax: 450-825-2220
MICR: 03051-010
Humboldt
PO Box 100
603 Main St.
Humboldt, SK S0K 2A0 Canada
306-682-2614
Fax: 306-682-5911
MICR: 00148-010
Huntingdon
154, rue Chateauguay
Huntingdon, QC J0S 1H0 Canada
450-264-5328
Fax: 450-264-6941
MICR: 00771-010
Huntsville
1 Main St. West
Huntsville, ON P1H 2C5 Canada
705-789-5585
Fax: 705-789-1938
MICR: 08942-010
Ignace
PO Box 130
328 Main St.
Ignace, ON P0T 1T0 Canada
807-934-2217
Fax: 807-934-6559
MICR: 01087-010
Ilderton
PO Box 70
13211 Ilderton Rd.
Ilderton, ON N0M 2A0 Canada
519-666-1820
Fax: 519-666-2217
MICR: 03682-010
Ingersoll
160 Thames St. South
Ingersoll, ON N5C 2T5 Canada
519-485-1420
Fax: 519-485-3069
MICR: 02782-010
Inuvik
PO Box 1250
134 MacKenzie Rd.
Inuvik, NT X0E 0T0 Canada
867-777-4539
Fax: 867-777-3491
MICR: 03999-010
Invermere
PO Box 218
1222 - 7th Ave.
Invermere, BC V0A 1K0 Canada
250-342-9237
Fax: 250-342-3896
MICR: 00370-010
Iqaluit
PO Box 2439
611 Queen Elizabeth II Way
Iqaluit, NU X0A 0H0 Canada
867-979-8663
Fax: 867-979-3027
MICR: 06899-010
Jarvis
PO Box 130
12 Talbot St. East
Jarvis, ON N0A 1J0 Canada
519-587-2253
Fax: 519-587-2173
MICR: 03872-010
Jasper
PO Box 789
416 Connaught Dr.
Jasper, AB T0E 1E0 Canada
780-852-3391
Fax: 780-852-3020
MICR: 00479-010
Joliette
10, rue Sainte-Anne
Joliette, QC J6E 4Y8 Canada
450-759-2110
Fax: 450-759-2094
MICR: 01081-010
Kamloops - East Trans-Canada Hwy.
#95, 1967 East Trans-Canada Hwy.
Kamloops, BC V2C 4A4 Canada
250-314-3100
Fax: 250-374-5218
MICR: 02950-010
Kamloops - Tranquille Rd.
North Hills Shopping Centre
#6, 700 Tranquille Rd.
Kamloops, BC V2B 3H9 Canada
250-554-5700
Fax: 250-376-6114
MICR: 07050-010
Kamloops - Victoria St.
PO Box 60
304 Victoria St.
Kamloops, BC V2C 5K3 Canada
250-314-3188
Fax: 250-828-8640
MICR: 00050-010
Kanata
Centrum Banking Centre
445 Kanata Ave.
Kanata, ON K2T 1K5 Canada
613-592-1800
Fax: 613-592-9725
MICR: 00486-010
Kapuskasing
2 Circle St.
Kapuskasing, ON P5N 1T3 Canada
705-335-2218
Fax: 705-335-8720
MICR: 00392-010
Kelowna - Bernard Ave.
328 Bernard Ave.
Kelowna, BC V1Y 6N5 Canada
250-763-6611
Fax: 250-861-1517
MICR: 00160-010
Kelowna - Harvey Ave.
Orchard Park Banking Centre
2107 Harvey Ave.
Kelowna, BC V1Y 9X4 Canada
250-470-1650
Fax: 250-862-8684
MICR: 06060-010
Kelowna - Pandosy St.
3039 Pandosy St.
Kelowna, BC V1Y 1W3 Canada
250-470-1670
Fax: 250-762-7399
MICR: 01060-010
Kelvington
PO Box 310
202 Main St.
Kelvington, SK S0A 1W0 Canada
306-327-4737
Fax: 306-327-4461
MICR: 00298-010
Kemptville
PO Box 1000
116 Prescott St.
Kemptville, ON K0G 1J0 Canada
613-258-3491
Fax: 613-258-1543
MICR: 00596-010
Kenora
111 Main St. South
Kenora, ON P9N 1T1 Canada

Canadian Imperial Bank of Commerce(CIBC)/ Banque Canadienne Impériale de Commerce (continued)

807-468-8933
Fax: 807-468-4226
MICR: 00787-010

Kentville
PO Box 458
10 Webster St.
Kentville, NS B4N 3X3 Canada
902-678-7371
Fax: 902-678-2165
MICR: 00433-010

Keremeos
PO Box 99
530 - 7th Ave.
Keremeos, BC V0X 1N0 Canada
250-499-5515
Fax: 250-499-2944
MICR: 00760-010

Keswick
24 The Queensway South
Keswick, ON L4P 1Y9 Canada
905-476-4362
Fax: 905-476-6857
MICR: 05642-010

Killaloe
PO Box 130
157 Queen St.
Killaloe, ON K0J 2A0 Canada
613-757-2910
Fax: 613-757-2733
MICR: 00306-010

Killarney
PO Box 370
522 Broadway Ave.
Killarney, MB R0K 1G0 Canada
204-523-4686
Fax: 204-523-4512
MICR: 00157-010

Kincardine
PO Box 29
822 Queen St.
Kincardine, ON N2Z 2Y6 Canada
519-396-7515
Fax: 519-396-7647
MICR: 05252-010

Kindersley
PO Box 1149
201 Main St.
Kindersley, SK S0L 1S0 Canada
306-463-4601
Fax: 306-463-2414
MICR: 00048-010

King City
PO Box 57
2208 King Rd.
King City, ON L7B 1G3 Canada
905-833-5362
Fax: 905-833-6011
MICR: 05742-010

Kingston - Bagot St.
PO Box 1088
256 Bagot St.
Kingston, ON K7L 4Y5 Canada
613-546-8000
Fax: 613-546-8020
MICR: 00542-010

Kingston - Bath Rd.
Kingston Banking Centre
117 Bath Rd.
Kingston, ON K7L 1H2 Canada
613-544-4320
Fax: 613-544-0097
MICR: 06542-010

Kingston - Gardiners Rd.
785 Gardiners Rd.
Kingston, ON K7M 7H8 Canada
613-384-2514
Fax: 613-384-2924
MICR: 05342-010

Kingston - Main St.
PO Box 10
655 Main St.
Kingston, NS B0P 1R0 Canada
902-765-3351
Fax: 902-765-8703
MICR: 00123-010

Kingsville
1 Main St. East
Kingsville, ON N9Y 1A1 Canada
519-733-2379
Fax: 519-733-8311
MICR: 03382-010

Kirkland Lake
PO Box 817
10 Government Rd. West
Kirkland Lake, ON P2N 3K4 Canada
705-567-5201
Fax: 705-567-9183
MICR: 00992-010

Kitchener - Frederick St.
385 Frederick St.
Kitchener, ON N2H 2P2 Canada
519-744-4151
Fax: 519-744-5892
MICR: 06052-010

Kitchener - King St.
PO Box 2547
1 King St. East
Kitchener, ON N2G 2K4 Canada
519-742-4432
Fax: 519-570-5525
MICR: 00152-010

Kitchener - Ottawa St.
1020 Ottawa St. North
Kitchener, ON N2A 3Z3 Canada
519-896-2272
Fax: 519-896-2279
MICR: 02352-010

Kitchener - Strasberg Rd.
Laurentian Banking Centre
249 Strasburg Rd., #C
Kitchener, ON N2E 1B6 Canada
519-578-2450
Fax: 519-578-0034
MICR: 08252-010

Kitimat
291 City Centre
Kitimat, BC V8C 1T6 Canada
250-632-8610
Fax: 250-632-2529
MICR: 00580-010

Knowlton
PO Box 900
308, ch de la Knowlton
Knowlton, QC J0E 1V0 Canada
450-243-6115
Fax: 450-243-4165
MICR: 01961-010

Kuujjuaq
PO Box 450
Kuujjuaq, QC J0M 1C0 Canada
819-964-2724
Fax: 819-964-2494
MICR: 00485-010

La Prairie
1020, boul Taschereau
La Prairie, QC J5R 1W6 Canada
450-659-5421
Fax: 450-444-3153
MICR: 01031-010

La Ronge - La Ronge
PO Box 420
1220 La Ronge Ave.
La Ronge, SK S0J 1L0 Canada
306-425-6700
Fax: 306-425-3646
MICR: 00938-010

La Ronge - Sooneyawi Kumik Reserve
PO Box 1799
La Ronge, SK S0J 1L0 Canada
306-425-6727
Fax: 306-425-6723
MICR: 01138-010

La Sarre
317, Principale
La Sarre, QC J9Z 1Z4 Canada
819-333-2374
Fax: 819-333-3465
MICR: 00591-010

Labrador City
Carol Lake Shopping Centre
208 Humber Ave.
Labrador City, NL A2V 1L1 Canada
709-944-2606
Fax: 709-944-3392
MICR: 00165-010

Lac La Biche
PO Box 446
10126 - 101st Ave.
Lac La Biche, AB T0A 2C0 Canada
780-623-4418
Fax: 780-623-1818
MICR: 00979-010

Lachute
Carrefour d'Argenteuil
505, rue Bethany
Lachute, QC J8H 4A6 Canada
450-562-7971
Fax: 450-562-1988
MICR: 08081-010

Lacolle
10, de l'Église sud
Lacolle, QC J0J 1J0 Canada
450-246-3852
Fax: 450-246-4505
MICR: 00951-010

Lacombe
5002 - 50th Ave.
Lacombe, AB T4L 2L1 Canada
403-782-4501
Fax: 403-782-7825
MICR: 05939-010

Ladysmith
PO Box 40
540 - 1st Ave.
Ladysmith, BC V0R 2E0 Canada
250-245-2265
Fax: 250-245-5602
MICR: 00540-010

Lakefield
PO Box 29
37 Queen St.
Lakefield, ON K0L 2H0 Canada
705-652-3311
Fax: 705-652-5242
MICR: 04942-010

Lamont
PO Box 30
5112 - 50th Ave.
Lamont, AB T0B 2R0 Canada
780-895-2033
Fax: 780-895-2139
MICR: 00889-010

Langley - 200 St.
6189 - 200th St.
Langley, BC V2Y 1A2 Canada
604-532-6660
Fax: 604-530-8433
MICR: 01320-010

Langley - Fraser Hwy.
20457 Fraser Hwy.
Langley, BC V3A 4G3 Canada
604-532-6606
Fax: 604-534-6321
MICR: 00720-010

Langton
PO Box 40
37 Queen St.
Langton, ON N0E 1G0 Canada
519-875-4465
Fax: 519-875-4723
MICR: 05572-010

Laval - Daniel-Johnson
Tours Triomphe II
2540, boul Daniel-Johnson
Laval, QC H7T 2S3 Canada
450-687-0735
Fax: 450-687-7347
MICR: 01331-010

Laval - Laurentides
2165, boul des Laurentides
Laval, QC H7M 4M2 Canada
450-662-6215
Fax: 450-662-6364
MICR: 03421-010

Laval - Samson
4641 boul Samson
Laval, QC H7W 2H5 Canada
450-688-7810
Fax: 450-688-7555
MICR: 06021-010
Laval - Samson
31, boul Samson
Laval, QC H7X 3S5 Canada
450-689-3858
Fax: 450-689-1824
MICR: 08121-010
Laval - St-Martin est
2495, boul St-Martin est
Laval, QC H7E 4X6 Canada
450-663-3971
Fax: 450-663-8930
MICR: 03021-010
Leader
PO Box 309
136 - 1st Ave. West
Leader, SK S0N 1H0 Canada
306-628-3857
Fax: 306-628-4390
MICR: 00278-010
Leamington
69 Erie St.
Leamington, ON N8H 3B2 Canada
519-326-6141
Fax: 519-326-4793
MICR: 07782-010
Lebel-sur-Quévillon
Centre d'Achat Allard
PO Box 370
Lebel-sur-Quévillon, QC J0Y 1X0 Canada
819-755-4888
Fax: 819-755-4494
MICR: 05091-010
Leduc
5003 - 50th Ave.
Leduc, AB T9E 6V9 Canada
780-986-8444
Fax: 780-986-1849
MICR: 01979-010
Lethbridge - 13th St.
PO Box 1150
515 - 13th St. North
Lethbridge, AB T1J 4A5 Canada
403-382-2080
Fax: 403-382-2097
MICR: 00839-010
Lethbridge - 4th Ave.
PO Box 1150
701 - 4th Ave. South
Lethbridge, AB T1J 4A5 Canada
403-382-2000
Fax: 403-320-0282
MICR: 00039-010
Lewisporte
PO Box 490
170 Main St.
Lewisporte, NL A0G 3A0 Canada
709-535-0670
Fax: 709-535-6465
MICR: 00273-010
Lillooet
PO Box 790
649 Main St.
Lillooet, BC V0K 1V0 Canada
250-256-4221
Fax: 250-256-7216
MICR: 00850-010
Lindsay
66 Kent St. West
Lindsay, ON K9V 2Y2 Canada
705-324-2183
Fax: 705-324-2568
MICR: 00942-010
Listowel
105 Main St. West
Listowel, ON N4W 1A2 Canada
519-291-1920
Fax: 519-291-5283
MICR: 02652-010
Lloydminster
PO Box 110
4915 - 50th St.
Lloydminster, SK S9V 0X9 Canada
306-825-2422
Fax: 306-825-9783
MICR: 00068-010
Logan Lake
PO Box 130
Opal Dr.
Logan Lake, BC V0K 1W0 Canada
250-523-5810
Fax: 250-523-6622
MICR: 06950-010
London - Adelaide St.
1088 Adelaide St. North
London, ON N5Y 2N1 Canada
519-661-8190
Fax: 519-661-8261
MICR: 04882-010
London - Baseline Rd.
1 Baseline Rd. East
London, ON N6C 5Z8 Canada
519-661-8333
Fax: 519-661-8153
MICR: 09782-010
London - Clarke Rd.
380 Clarke Rd.
London, ON N5W 6E7 Canada
519-451-1780
Fax: 519-451-2553
MICR: 05482-010
London - Fanshawe Rd. East
97 Fanshawe Rd. East
London, ON N5X 2S7 Canada
519-661-8182
Fax: 519-661-8188
MICR: 06182-010
London - Hyde Park Rd.
Oxford & Hyde Park Banking Centre
780 Hyde Park Rd.
London, ON N6H 5W9 Canada
519-471-1160
Fax: 519-471-7245
MICR: 04582-010
London - Oxford St. East
1299 Oxford St. East
London, ON N5Y 4W5 Canada
519-452-7400
Fax: 519-452-1709
MICR: 08382-010
London - Oxford St. East
228 Oxford St. East
London, ON N6A 1T7 Canada
519-661-8110
Fax: 519-661-0875
MICR: 01682-010
London - Wellington Rd. South
White Oaks Mall
1105 Wellington Rd. South
London, ON N6E 1V4 Canada
519-681-4260
Fax: 519-681-4473
MICR: 07382-010
London - Wellington St.
#177, 355 Wellington St.
London, ON N6A 3N7 Canada
519-661-8000
Fax: 519-661-8045
MICR: 00082-010
London - Wonderland Rd. South
983 Wonderland Rd. South
London, ON N6K 2V9 Canada
519-649-0660
Fax: 519-649-0610
MICR: 01182-010
Longlac
PO Box 30
120 Forestry Rd.
Longlac, ON P0T 2A0 Canada
807-876-2288
Fax: 807-876-2797
MICR: 06892-010
Longueuil - Chambly
#105, 1401, ch de Chambly
Longueuil, QC J4J 3X6 Canada
514-677-5242
Fax: 514-677-7170
MICR: 00231-010
Longueuil - Saint-Charles
190, rue Saint-Charles ouest
Longueuil, QC J4H 1C9 Canada
450-677-2867
Fax: 450-677-8627
MICR: 00901-010
Loon Lake
PO Box 10
Main St.
Loon Lake, SK S0M 1L0 Canada
306-837-2112
Fax: 306-837-4535
MICR: 00568-010
Lower Sackville
PO Box 344, Dartmouth Sta. Dartmouth
745 Sackville Dr.
Lower Sackville, NS B4C 2T2 Canada
902-869-3400
Fax: 902-865-9424
MICR: 00713-010
Lucky Lake
PO Box 39
Lucky Lake, SK S0L 1Z0 Canada
306-858-2031
Fax: 306-858-2212
MICR: 00328-010
Lundar
PO Box 270
21 Main St.
Lundar, MB R0C 1Y0 Canada
204-762-5471
Fax: 204-762-5154
MICR: 00477-010
Lunenburg
PO Box 130
4 King St.
Lunenburg, NS B0J 2C0 Canada
902-634-4469
Fax: 902-634-8610
MICR: 00323-010
Lévis
5300, boul de la Rive-Sud
Lévis, QC G6V 4Z2 Canada
418-837-0286
Fax: 418-833-9624
MICR: 00495-010
Magog
431, rue Principale ouest
Magog, QC J1X 2B2 Canada
819-843-6531
Fax: 819-843-9285
MICR: 00151-010
Maidstone
PO Box 10
205 Main St.
Maidstone, SK S0M 1M0 Canada
306-893-2671
Fax: 306-893-2233
MICR: 00378-010
Manitouwadge
PO Box 10
Huron St. & Barker St.
Manitouwadge, ON P0T 2C0 Canada
807-826-3201
Fax: 807-826-1208
MICR: 07892-010
Mankota
PO Box 150
Main St.
Mankota, SK S0H 2W0 Canada
306-478-2224
Fax: 306-478-2311
MICR: 00698-010
Manotick
Manotick Mews
PO Box 880
1160 Beaverwood Rd.
Manotick, ON K4M 1A7 Canada
613-692-2546
Fax: 613-692-2125
MICR: 00276-010
Mansonville

Canadian Imperial Bank of Commerce(CIBC)/ Banque Canadienne Impériale de Commerce (continued)

PO Box 60
291, rue Principale
Mansonville, QC J0E 1X0 Canada
450-292-3316
Fax: 450-292-4284
MICR: 03061-010

Maple
PO Box 577
10037 Keele St.
Maple, ON L6A 1S5 Canada
905-832-4162
Fax: 905-832-5282
MICR: 02742-010

Maple Creek
PO Box 160
204 Jasper St.
Maple Creek, SK S0N 1N0 Canada
306-662-2533
Fax: 306-662-4220
MICR: 00798-010

Maple Ridge
11909 - 224 St.
Maple Ridge, BC V2X 6B2 Canada
604-466-2500
Fax: 604-463-1423
MICR: 02020-010

Markham - Hwy. 48
9275 Hwy. 48 North
Markham, ON L6E 1A2 Canada
905-471-8081
Fax: 905-471-8735
MICR: 02432-010

Markham - Hwy. 7 East
Markville Shopping Centre
5000 Hwy. 7 East
Markham, ON L3R 4M9 Canada
905-477-5783
Fax: 905-477-2151
MICR: 02342-010

Markham - Kennedy Rd.
7220 Kennedy Rd.
Markham, ON L3R 7P2 Canada
905-479-2077
Fax: 905-479-9583
MICR: 03232-010

Markham - Woodbine Ave.
7125 Woodbine Ave.
Markham, ON L3R 1A3 Canada
905-475-6754
Fax: 905-475-3817
MICR: 02242-010

Markham - Woodbine Ave.
Bldg. C
#29, 9255 Woodbine Ave
Markham, ON L6C 1Y9 Canada
905-887-2923
Fax: 905-887-2913
MICR: 06232-010

Matheson
PO Box 100
429 Fifth Ave.
Matheson, ON P0K 1N0 Canada
705-273-2868
Fax: 705-273-2115
MICR: 05092-010

Meadow Lake
PO Box 250
202 Centre St.
Meadow Lake, SK S9X 1L6 Canada
306-236-4485
Fax: 306-236-4496
MICR: 00168-010

Medicine Hat - 3rd St.
501 - 3rd St. SE
Medicine Hat, AB T1A 0H2 Canada
403-528-6100
Fax: 403-526-8927
MICR: 00449-010

Medicine Hat - 8th St. NW
21 - 8th St. NW
Medicine Hat, AB T1A 6N9 Canada
403-528-6156
Fax: 403-528-6165
MICR: 06039-010

Medicine Hat - Dunmore Rd. SE
Medicine Hat Mall
#113, 3292 Dunmore Rd. SE
Medicine Hat, AB T1B 2R4 Canada
403-528-6145
Fax: 403-526-8035
MICR: 05949-010

Melfort
PO Box 1210
117 Main St.
Melfort, SK S0E 1A0 Canada
306-752-2881
Fax: 306-752-4499
MICR: 00188-010

Merritt
PO Box 459
2002 Quilchena Ave.
Merritt, BC V1K 1B8 Canada
250-378-2296
Fax: 250-378-2842
MICR: 03050-010

Miami
PO Box 70
449 Norton Ave.
Miami, MB R0G 1H0 Canada
204-435-2468
Fax: 204-435-2527
MICR: 00647-010

Midland
274 King St.
Midland, ON L4R 3M3 Canada
705-526-2256
Fax: 705-526-0908
MICR: 05042-010

Milestone
PO Box 88
137 Main St.
Milestone, SK S0G 3L0 Canada
306-436-2202
Fax: 306-436-2188
MICR: 00538-010

Milk River
PO Box 210
201 Main St. North
Milk River, AB T0K 1M0 Canada
403-647-3838
Fax: 403-647-2718
MICR: 00749-010

Mill Bay
Mill Bay Banking Centre
801 Deloume Rd.
Mill Bay, BC V0R 2P1 Canada
250-743-8400
Fax: 250-743-1347
MICR: 01140-010

Milton
PO Box 187
147 Main St. East
Milton, ON L9T 4N9 Canada
905-878-2321
Fax: 905-875-2470
MICR: 01052-010

Milverton
PO Box 460
2 Main St. North
Milverton, ON N0K 1M0 Canada
519-595-8111
Fax: 519-595-8969
MICR: 01852-010

Minden
PO Box 120
95 Main St.
Minden, ON K0M 2K0 Canada
705-286-2991
Fax: 705-286-6063
MICR: 01542-010

Miramichi
Miramichi Mall
408 King George Hwy.
Miramichi, NB E1V 1L4 Canada
506-622-0950
Fax: 506-622-6841
MICR: 00904-010

Mission
PO Box 3220
33165 - 1st Ave.
Mission, BC V2V 4J4 Canada
604-820-6070
Fax: 604-826-0515
MICR: 00220-010

Mississauga - Airport Rd.
6543 Airport Rd.
Mississauga, ON L4V 1E4 Canada
905-677-2212
Fax: 905-677-9407
MICR: 03722-010

Mississauga - Bristol Rd. East
30 Bristol Rd. East
Mississauga, ON L4Z 3K8 Canada
905-568-4755
Fax: 905-568-3222
MICR: 04822-010

Mississauga - City Centre Dr.
Mississauga City Centre
#105, 1 City Centre Dr.
Mississauga, ON L5B 1M2 Canada
905-566-2072
Fax: 905-279-1605
MICR: 03022-010

Mississauga - Creditview Rd.
6085 Creditview Rd.
Mississauga, ON L5V 2A8 Canada
905-567-6953
Fax: 905-567-6404
MICR: 05432-010

Mississauga - Creditview Rd.
4040 Creditview Rd.
Mississauga, ON L5C 3Y8 Canada
905-896-8860
Fax: 905-896-1381
MICR: 04022-010

Mississauga - Dixie Rd.
4141 Dixie Rd.
Mississauga, ON L4W 1V5 Canada
905-625-2047
Fax: 905-625-5478
MICR: 05222-010

Mississauga - Dixie Rd.
5330 Dixie Rd.
Mississauga, ON L4W 1E3 Canada
905-624-9801
Fax: 905-624-0757
MICR: 06322-010

Mississauga - Dixie Rd.
6266 Dixie Rd.
Mississauga, ON L5T 1A7 Canada
905-670-1946
Fax: 905-676-8138
MICR: 06122-010

Mississauga - Dundas St. East
PO Box 39
5 Dundas St. East
Mississauga, ON L5A 2Z2 Canada
905-270-2353
Fax: 905-566-4454
MICR: 02722-010

Mississauga - Dundas St. East
1161 Dundas St. East
Mississauga, ON L4Y 2C5 Canada
905-270-2773
Fax: 905-896-4933
MICR: 01722-010

Mississauga - Dundas St. West
3125 Dundas St. West
Mississauga, ON L5L 3R8 Canada
905-607-8701
Fax: 905-607-8857
MICR: 06422-010

Mississauga - Erin Mills Pkwy.
4099 Erin Mills Pkwy.
Mississauga, ON L5L 3P9 Canada
905-820-0169
Fax: 905-820-3879
MICR: 03122-010

Mississauga - Erin Mills Pkwy.
#B-129, 5100 Erin Mills Pkwy.
Mississauga, ON L5M 4Z5 Canada
905-569-6010
Fax: 905-569-3777

MICR: 04922-010
Mississauga - Goreway Dr.
Westwood Shopping Mall
7205 Goreway Dr.
Mississauga, ON L4T 2T9 Canada
905-677-3796
Fax: 905-677-3287
MICR: 01322-010
Mississauga - Lakeshore Rd. East
35 Lakeshore Rd. East
Mississauga, ON L5G 1C9 Canada
905-278-6112
Fax: 905-278-5088
MICR: 00422-010
Mississauga - Lakeshore Rd. West
1745 Lakeshore Rd. West
Mississauga, ON L5J 1J4 Canada
905-822-3757
Fax: 905-822-6161
MICR: 05722-010
Mississauga - Lorne Park Rd.
1150 Lorne Park Rd.
Mississauga, ON L5H 3A5 Canada
905-278-6125
Fax: 905-278-2911
MICR: 06822-010
Mississauga - Meadowvale Town Centre Circle
Meadowvale Town Centre
6677 Meadowvale Town Centre Circle
Mississauga, ON L5N 2R5 Canada
905-826-7062
Fax: 905-826-4058
MICR: 08222-010
Mississauga - Mississauga Rd.
Manulife Corporate Park
6711 Mississauga Rd.
Mississauga, ON L5N 2W3 Canada
905-826-3771
Fax: 905-826-1404
MICR: 03922-010
Mississauga - Queensway West
33 Queensway West
Mississauga, ON L5B 1B5 Canada
905-270-7918
Fax: 905-270-8345
MICR: 02222-010
Mississauga - Skymark Ave.
2800 Skymark Ave.
Mississauga, ON L4W 5A6 Canada
905-629-3935
Fax: 905-629-4126
MICR: 07152-010
Mitchell
PO Box 160
95 Ontario Rd.
Mitchell, ON N0K 1N0 Canada
519-348-8421
Fax: 519-348-4281
MICR: 03652-010
Moncton - Main St.
759 - 761 Main St.
Moncton, NB E1C 1E5 Canada
506-859-3717
Fax: 506-859-6026
MICR: 00024-010
Moncton - Main St.
1141 Main St.
Moncton, NB E1C 1H8 Canada
506-858-1633
Fax: 506-858-1640
MICR: 00044-010
Moncton - Mountain Rd.
655 Mountain Rd.
Moncton, NB E1C 2P4 Canada
506-859-3710
Fax: 506-859-3702
MICR: 00404-010
Montague
PO Box 250
532 Main St. North
Montague, PE C0A 1R0 Canada
902-838-2134
Fax: 902-838-2756
MICR: 00483-010
Montréal - 45e av
6, 45e av
Montréal, QC H8T 2L7 Canada
514-637-6754
Fax: 514-637-0204
MICR: 00911-010
Montréal - Beaconsfield
448, boul Beaconsfield
Montréal, QC H9W 4B9 Canada
514-697-5000
Fax: 514-697-6482
MICR: 03001-010
Montréal - Beaumont
1254, av Beaumont
Montréal, QC H3P 3E5 Canada
514-343-3309
Fax: 514-343-3835
MICR: 00601-010
Montréal - Bernard ouest
1195, av Bernard ouest
Montréal, QC H2V 1V5 Canada
514-278-3111
Fax: 514-278-8162
MICR: 00131-010
Montréal - Bélanger est
5931, rue Bélanger est
Montréal, QC H1T 1G8 Canada
514-254-3591
Fax: 514-254-5578
MICR: 05021-010
Montréal - Cathcart
Carré Phillips
600, rue Cathcart
Montréal, QC H3B 1K8 Canada
514-876-2114
Fax: 514-876-8649
MICR: 00021-010
Montréal - Chabanel
343, rue Chabanel ouest
Montréal, QC H2N 2G1 Canada
514-388-7900
Fax: 514-383-1224
MICR: 08041-010
Montréal - Côte-des-Neiges
5501, ch de la Côte-des-Neiges
Montréal, QC H3T 1Y8 Canada
514-342-4360
Fax: 514-342-3634
MICR: 00931-010
Montréal - Côte-Vertu
249, ch de la Côte-Vertu
Montréal, QC H4N 1C8 Canada
514-334-3405
Fax: 514-334-3709
MICR: 05011-010
Montréal - Côte-Vertu
Place-Vertu
3131, ch de la Côte-Vertu
Montréal, QC H4R 1Y8 Canada
514-334-4336
Fax: 514-334-0006
MICR: 01131-010
Montréal - Decarie
8000, boul Décarie
Montréal, QC H4P 2S4 Canada
514-342-6729
Fax: 514-731-2615
MICR: 00241-010
Montréal - Fleury est
1605, rue Fleury est
Montréal, QC H2C 1S9 Canada
514-388-9288
Fax: 514-388-0676
MICR: 08001-010
Montréal - Granby
3315, av de Granby
Montréal, QC H1N 2Z7 Canada
514-254-6622
Fax: 514-254-6205
MICR: 01011-010
Montréal - Henri-Bourassa est
5373, boul Henri-Bourassa est
Montréal, QC H1G 2T1 Canada
514-322-4010
Fax: 514-322-4649
MICR: 01021-010
Montréal - Jean-Talon est
4149, rue Jean-Talon est
Montréal, QC H1S 1J6 Canada
514-725-4761
Fax: 514-725-4331
MICR: 00301-010
Montréal - Jean-Talon est
7171, rue Jean-Talon est
Montréal, QC H1M 3N2 Canada
514-355-0503
MICR: 01321-010
Montréal - Langelier
8550, boul Langelier
Montréal, QC H1P 2Z4 Canada
514-326-9101
Fax: 514-326-0622
MICR: 01121-010
Montréal - Newman
Carrefour Angrignon
7077, boul Newman
Montréal, QC H8N 1X1 Canada
514-365-0592
Fax: 514-365-4907
MICR: 04031-010
Montréal - René-Lévesque ouest
Complexe Guy-Favreau
200, boul René-Lévesque ouest
Montréal, QC H2Z 1X4 Canada
514-286-4000
Fax: 514-286-4051
MICR: 01141-010
Montréal - René-Lévesque ouest
PO Box 6003, A Sta. A
1155, boul René-Lévesque ouest
Montréal, QC H3B 3Z4 Canada
514-876-2323
Fax: 514-876-3594
MICR: 00001-010
Montréal - Saint-Charles
2959, boul Saint-Charles
Montréal, QC H9H 3B5 Canada
514-694-3026
Fax: 514-694-5801
MICR: 01231-010
Montréal - Saint-Charles
Centre Bonanza
3725, boul Saint-Charles
Montréal, QC H9H 4M2 Canada
514-630-4999
Fax: 514-630-0916
MICR: 01431-010
Montréal - Saint-Jacques
265, rue Saint-Jacques ouest
Montréal, QC H2Y 1M6 Canada
514-845-2119
Fax: 514-845-2106
MICR: 00031-010
Montréal - Sherbrooke ouest
1006, rue Sherbrooke ouest
Montréal, QC H3A 2S2 Canada
514-288-5999
Fax: 514-288-5565
MICR: 01201-010
Montréal - Sherbrooke ouest
7355, rue Sherbrooke ouest
Montréal, QC H4B 1S1 Canada
514-481-7007
Fax: 514-481-7819
MICR: 00831-010
Montréal - Sherbrooke ouest
4854, rue Sherbrooke ouest
Montréal, QC H3Z 1H1 Canada
514-482-4999
Fax: 514-482-4760
MICR: 00221-010
Montréal - Somerled
6595, av Somerled
Montréal, QC H4V 1T1 Canada
514-481-5576
Fax: 514-481-5949
MICR: 00631-010
Montréal - Sources
Centennial Plaza
3343P, boul des Sources
Montréal, QC H9B 1Z8 Canada

Canadian Imperial Bank of Commerce(CIBC)/ Banque Canadienne Impériale de Commerce (continued)

514-683-1257
Fax: 514-683-8960
MICR: 03921-010

Montréal - Transcanada
Complexe Pointe-Claire
#120, 6341, route Transcanada
Montréal, QC H9R 5A5 Canada
514-697-1227
Fax: 514-697-1221
MICR: 00941-010

Moose Jaw - Main St.
PO Box 400
602 Main St. North
Moose Jaw, SK S6H 4P1 Canada
306-691-4438
Fax: 306-692-3342
MICR: 00038-010

Moose Jaw - Main St.
PO Box 400
204 Main St. North
Moose Jaw, SK S6H 4P1 Canada
306-691-4444
Fax: 306-694-2004
MICR: 00028-010

Moosonee
PO Box 68
Wabun Rd. & 1st Ave.
Moosonee, ON P0L 1Y0 Canada
705-336-2997
Fax: 705-336-2236
MICR: 08992-010

Morden
302 Stephen St.
Morden, MB R6M 1T5 Canada
204-822-4441
Fax: 204-822-3841
MICR: 01077-010

Mount Pearl
50 Commonwealth Ave.
Mount Pearl, NL A1N 1W8 Canada
709-576-8904
Fax: 709-576-8803
MICR: 00863-010

Murray River
PO Box 69
9327 Main St.
Murray River, PE C0A 1W0 Canada
902-962-3119
Fax: 902-962-3751
MICR: 00583-010

Nackawic
#118, 135 Otis Dr.
Nackawic, NB E6G 1H1 Canada
506-575-2264
Fax: 506-575-2891
MICR: 00294-010

Naicam
PO Box 160
100 Centre St.
Naicam, SK S0K 2Z0 Canada
306-874-2036
Fax: 306-874-2291
MICR: 00778-010

Nakusp
PO Box 160
402 Broadway St.
Nakusp, BC V0G 1R0 Canada
250-265-3696
Fax: 250-265-4050
MICR: 00670-010

Nanaimo - Island Hwy.
Country Club Mall Wellington
#123, 3200 Island Hwy.
Nanaimo, BC V9T 1W1 Canada
250-756-3400
Fax: 250-758-0178
MICR: 09040-010

Nanaimo - Island Hwy.
6570 Island Hwy.
Nanaimo, BC V9V 1K8 Canada
250-756-3430
Fax: 250-390-1915
MICR: 01240-010

Nanaimo - Terminal Ave.
Port Place Shopping Centre
#66, 650 Terminal Ave. South
Nanaimo, BC V9R 5E2 Canada
250-716-2060
Fax: 250-753-4362
MICR: 00040-010

Nanton
PO Box 459
1919 - 20th Ave.
Nanton, AB T0L 1R0 Canada
403-646-2201
Fax: 403-646-2972
MICR: 00549-010

Napanee
450 Centre St.
Napanee, ON K7R 1P8 Canada
613-354-3323
Fax: 613-354-7609
MICR: 09242-010

Neepawa
PO Box 399
380 Mountain Ave.
Neepawa, MB R0J 1H0 Canada
204-476-2371
Fax: 204-476-2896
MICR: 00247-010

Nelson
459 Baker St.
Nelson, BC V1L 4H7 Canada
250-352-8700
Fax: 250-352-7175
MICR: 00270-010

Nepean - Merivale Rd.
Merivale Mall
1642 Merivale Rd.
Nepean, ON K2G 4A1 Canada
613-226-1080
Fax: 613-226-1830
MICR: 00986-010

Nepean - Robertson Rd.
Bells Corners
120 Robertson Rd.
Nepean, ON K2H 5Z1 Canada
613-820-0300
Fax: 613-820-3203
MICR: 00586-010

Nepean - Strandherd Rd.
Barrhaven Town Centre
3777 Strandherd Rd.
Nepean, ON K2J 4B1 Canada
613-825-1553
Fax: 613-825-8179
MICR: 01086-010

New Glasgow
162 Provost St.
New Glasgow, NS B2H 2R1 Canada
902-752-2573
Fax: 902-755-4900
MICR: 00053-010

New Hamburg
50 Huron St.
New Hamburg, ON N3A 1J2 Canada
519-662-1170
Fax: 519-662-1759
MICR: 05752-010

New Liskeard
PO Box 400
6 Armstrong St.
New Liskeard, ON P0J 1P0 Canada
705-647-6877
Fax: 705-647-5539
MICR: 00592-010

New Westminster - 6th St.
554 - 6th St.
New Westminster, BC V3L 3B5 Canada
604-665-7953
Fax: 604-665-7933
MICR: 00520-010

Newcastle
72 King St. West
Newcastle, ON L1B 1H7 Canada
905-987-5481
Fax: 905-987-3259
MICR: 02842-010

Newmarket - Davis Dr.
54 Davis Dr.
Newmarket, ON L3Y 2M7 Canada
905-895-1105
Fax: 905-895-5964
MICR: 02642-010

Newmarket - Harry Walker Pkwy.
15 Harry Walker Pkwy.
Newmarket, ON L3Y 7B3 Canada
905-898-5545
Fax: 905-895-7477
MICR: 07312-010

Newmarket - Yonge St.
16715 Yonge St.
Newmarket, ON L3X 1X4 Canada
905-830-9182
Fax: 905-830-9185
MICR: 04152-010

Niagara Falls - Huggins St.
6225 Huggins St.
Niagara Falls, ON L2J 1H2 Canada
905-356-1345
Fax: 905-356-1370
MICR: 02872-010

Niagara Falls - Lundy's Lane
6345 Lundy's Lane
Niagara Falls, ON L2G 1T8 Canada
905-354-7494
Fax: 905-354-7638
MICR: 01072-010

Niagara Falls - Montrose Rd.
Niagara Square Shopping Centre
7555 Montrose Rd.
Niagara Falls, ON L2H 2E9 Canada
905-357-2171
Fax: 905-357-0587
MICR: 03272-010

Niagara Falls - Queen St.
PO Box 117
4514 Queen St.
Niagara Falls, ON L2E 6S8 Canada
905-354-7461
Fax: 905-354-7171
MICR: 00472-010

Niagara on the Lake
111 Garrison Village Dr., RR#3
Niagara on the Lake, ON L0S 1J0 Canada
905-468-2396
Fax: 905-468-5504
MICR: 07672-010

Nobleton
PO Box 220
Hwy. 27
Nobleton, ON L0G 1N0 Canada
905-859-0814
Fax: 905-859-5888
MICR: 04952-010

Norman Wells
#9 Town Square
Norman Wells, NT X0E 0V0 Canada
867-587-2131
Fax: 867-587-2792
MICR: 01799-010

Norquay
PO Box 40
103 Main St.
Norquay, SK S0A 2V0 Canada
306-594-2033
Fax: 306-594-2575
MICR: 00688-010

North Battleford
1262 - 101st St.
North Battleford, SK S9A 2Y9 Canada
306-445-6122
Fax: 306-445-7009
MICR: 00078-010

North Bay - Algonquin Ave.
PO Box 215
1236 Algonquin Ave.
North Bay, ON P1B 8H2 Canada
705-472-2310
Fax: 705-472-6422
MICR: 02092-010

North Bay - Main St.
195 Main St. West
North Bay, ON P1B 2T6 Canada

705-474-8900
Fax: 705-474-4336
MICR: 00792-010

North Vancouver - Lonsdale Ave.
1601 Lonsdale Ave.
North Vancouver, BC V7M 2J5 Canada
604-981-2402
Fax: 604-981-2444
MICR: 01800-010

North Vancouver - Lynn Valley Rd.
Lynn Valley Centre
1199 Lynn Valley Rd.
North Vancouver, BC V7J 3H2 Canada
604-981-2467
Fax: 604-981-2465
MICR: 04900-010

Norwich
PO Box 280
15 Main St. West
Norwich, ON N0J 1P0 Canada
519-863-2016
Fax: 519-863-3301
MICR: 09772-010

Oakville - Lakeshore Rd.
PO Box 1000
197 Lakeshore Rd. East
Oakville, ON L6J 5E8 Canada
905-845-4327
Fax: 905-338-1041
MICR: 00162-010

Oakville - Maple Grove Dr.
Maple Grove Village Shopping Centre
#5, 511 Maple Grove Dr.
Oakville, ON L6J 6X8 Canada
905-844-1720
Fax: 905-844-8478
MICR: 06962-010

Oakville - Rebecca St.
Hopedale Mall
1515 Rebecca St.
Oakville, ON L6L 5G8 Canada
905-827-9802
Fax: 905-827-3611
MICR: 07962-010

Oakville - Speers Rd.
600 Speers Rd.
Oakville, ON L6K 2G3 Canada
905-845-7359
Fax: 905-845-1843
MICR: 01662-010

Oakville - Upper Middle Rd. East
Upper Oakville Shopping Centre
1011 Upper Middle Rd. East
Oakville, ON L6H 4L2 Canada
905-842-2351
Fax: 905-842-7621
MICR: 09662-010

Oakville - Upper Middle Rd. West
1500 Upper Middle Rd. West
Oakville, ON L6M 3G3 Canada
905-825-2810
Fax: 905-825-1396
MICR: 02262-010

Okotoks
300 Village Lane
Okotoks, AB T1S 1Z6 Canada
403-938-4474
Fax: 403-938-3648
MICR: 09039-010

Olds
4513 - 52nd Ave., Bay 4
Olds, AB T4H 1M8 Canada
403-556-6958
Fax: 403-556-1530
MICR: 01939-010

Oliver
PO Box 610
35848 - 97th St.
Oliver, BC V0H 1T0 Canada
250-498-3454
Fax: 250-498-2245
MICR: 00360-010

Onoway
PO Box 219
4817 - 50 St.
Onoway, AB T0E 1V0 Canada
780-967-2211
Fax: 780-967-4545
MICR: 01079-010

Orangeville
2 First St.
Orangeville, ON L9W 2C4 Canada
519-941-0521
Fax: 519-951-2063
MICR: 07052-010

Orillia - Laclie St.
394 Laclie St.
Orillia, ON L3V 4P5 Canada
705-325-5931
Fax: 705-325-3913
MICR: 07242-010

Orillia - Mississauga St.
One Mississauga St. West
Orillia, ON L3V 3A5 Canada
705-325-4441
Fax: 705-326-1104
MICR: 00642-010

Orleans - 10th Line Rd.
Centre Fallingbrook
1675 - 10th Line Rd.
Orleans, ON K1E 3P6 Canada
613-837-8464
Fax: 613-837-3013
MICR: 01006-010

Orleans - Orleans Blvd.
Orleans Gardens
1615 Orleans Blvd.
Orleans, ON K1C 7E2 Canada
613-830-9234
Fax: 613-830-4943
MICR: 01106-010

Ormstown
63, rue Lambton
Ormstown, QC J0S 1K0 Canada
450-829-2365
Fax: 450-829-3945
MICR: 00871-010

Orono
PO Box 29
5284 Main St.
Orono, ON L0B 1M0 Canada
905-983-5304
Fax: 905-983-5274
MICR: 04742-010

Oshawa - King St. West
Oshawa Shopping Centre
419 King St. West
Oshawa, ON L1J 2K5 Canada
905-576-9560
Fax: 905-576-5277
MICR: 07542-010

Oshawa - Rossland Rd. East
555 Rossland Rd. East
Oshawa, ON L1K 1K8 Canada
905-579-5913
Fax: 905-576-4009
MICR: 02142-010

Oshawa - Rossland Rd. West
500 Rossland Rd. West
Oshawa, ON L1J 3H2 Canada
905-436-6512
Fax: 905-436-0440
MICR: 02942-010

Oshawa - Simcoe St.
PO Box 460
2 Simcoe St. South
Oshawa, ON L1H 7L5 Canada
905-571-5927
Fax: 905-571-3797
MICR: 00142-010

Oshawa - Wilson Rd. North
Taunton & Wilson Banking Centre
1371 Wilson Rd. North
Oshawa, ON L1K 2Z5 Canada
905-720-4552
Fax: 905-720-3410
MICR: 04142-010

Osoyoos
PO Box 900
8516 Main St.
Osoyoos, BC V0H 1V0 Canada
250-495-6502
Fax: 250-495-2544
MICR: 02060-010

Ottawa - Bank St.
84 Bank St.
Ottawa, ON K1P 5N4 Canada
613-564-8713
Fax: 613-564-4697
MICR: 00186-010

Ottawa - Bank St.
#B20, 1800 Bank St.
Ottawa, ON K1V 0W3 Canada
613-737-0450
Fax: 613-737-2021
MICR: 00386-010

Ottawa - Carling Ave.
829 Carling Ave.
Ottawa, ON K1S 2E7 Canada
613-564-8650
Fax: 613-564-4634
MICR: 00406-010

Ottawa - Carling Ave.
Carlingwood Shopping Centre
2121 Carling Ave.
Ottawa, ON K2A 1S3 Canada
613-725-3093
Fax: 613-725-3465
MICR: 00206-010

Ottawa - Lorry Greenberg Dr.
4 Lorry Greenberg Dr.
Ottawa, ON K1G 5H6 Canada
613-739-9168
Fax: 613-739-3670
MICR: 01206-010

Ottawa - Rideau St.
41 Rideau St.
Ottawa, ON K1N 5W8 Canada
613-564-8750
Fax: 613-564-4690
MICR: 00016-010

Ottawa - Riverside Dr. East
Billings Bridge Plaza
PO Box 39029
2217 Riverside Dr. East
Ottawa, ON K1H 1A1 Canada
613-736-6010
Fax: 613-736-6016
MICR: 00086-010

Ottawa - Sparks St.
119 Sparks St.
Ottawa, ON K1P 5B5 Canada
613-564-8600
Fax: 613-564-7145
MICR: 00006-010

Ottawa - St. Laurent Blvd.
St. Laurent Shopping Centre
PO Box 46
1200 St. Laurent Blvd.
Ottawa, ON K1K 3B8 Canada
613-744-0841
Fax: 613-744-2207
MICR: 00496-010

Owen Sound
PO Box 188
999 - 2nd Ave. East
Owen Sound, ON N4K 5P3 Canada
519-376-3050
Fax: 519-376-2530
MICR: 04052-010

Palmerston
PO Box 40
262 Main St.
Palmerston, ON N0G 2P0 Canada
519-343-2127
Fax: 519-343-3898
MICR: 08752-010

Paris
88 Grand River St. North
Paris, ON N3L 2M2 Canada
519-442-7837
Fax: 519-442-6444
MICR: 05672-010

Canadian Imperial Bank of Commerce(CIBC)/ Banque Canadienne Impériale de Commerce (continued)

Parkhill
PO Box 10
244 Main St.
Parkhill, ON N0M 2K0 Canada
519-294-6291
Fax: 519-294-0259
MICR: 04782-010

Parksville
PO Box 370
130 Morison Ave.
Parksville, BC V9P 2G5 Canada
250-951-4000
Fax: 250-248-2427
MICR: 00740-010

Parrsboro
PO Box 338
37 Main St.
Parrsboro, NS B0M 1S0 Canada
902-254-2066
Fax: 902-254-2305
MICR: 00343-010

Parry Sound
36 Seguin St.
Parry Sound, ON P2A 1B4 Canada
705-746-9395
Fax: 705-746-6313
MICR: 08042-010

Peace River
PO Box 6149
10010 - 100th St.
Peace River, AB T8S 1S1 Canada
780-624-5450
Fax: 780-624-4376
MICR: 00099-010

Pefferlaw
PO Box 70
Pefferlaw, ON L0E 1N0 Canada
705-437-1920
Fax: 705-437-1401
MICR: 08742-010

Pembroke
172 Pembroke St.
Pembroke, ON K8A 5M8 Canada
613-735-4173
Fax: 613-735-6494
MICR: 00806-010

Penticton - Main St.
Cherry Lane Shopping Centre
#112, 2111 Main St.
Penticton, BC V2A 6W6 Canada
250-770-3368
Fax: 250-492-7288
MICR: 07060-010

Penticton - Main St.
295 Main St.
Penticton, BC V2A 5B1 Canada
250-770-3333
Fax: 250-492-2869
MICR: 00060-010

Perth
Perth Mews Shopping Mall
80 Dufferin St.
Perth, ON K7H 3A7 Canada
613-267-1645
Fax: 613-267-2362
MICR: 00906-010

Peterborough - George St.
399 George St. North
Peterborough, ON K9H 3R3 Canada
705-743-3573
Fax: 705-743-9303
MICR: 00242-010

Peterborough - Monaghan Rd.
825 Monaghan Rd.
Peterborough, ON K9J 5K2 Canada
705-742-0445
Fax: 705-742-5584
MICR: 09442-010

Petrolia
PO Box 1360
4130 Petrolia St.
Petrolia, ON N0N 1R0 Canada
519-882-1357
Fax: 519-882-3418
MICR: 06282-010

Pickering - Glenanna Rd.
Hwy. 2 & Glenanna Banking Centre
1895 Glenanna Rd.
Pickering, ON L1V 7K1 Canada
905-839-1198
Fax: 905-839-7338
MICR: 07942-010

Pickering - Kingston Rd.
#1, 376 Kingston Rd.
Pickering, ON L1V 1A4 Canada
905-509-2560
Fax: 905-509-1094
MICR: 01932-010

Picton
PO Box 110
272 Main St.
Picton, ON K0K 2T0 Canada
613-476-3258
Fax: 613-476-2264
MICR: 06042-010

Pincher Creek
PO Box 998
762 Main St.
Pincher Creek, AB T0K 1W0 Canada
403-627-3361
Fax: 403-627-5375
MICR: 03049-010

Pitt Meadows
19130 Lougheed Hwy.
Pitt Meadows, BC V3Y 2H6 Canada
604-465-2555
Fax: 604-465-2389
MICR: 01220-010

Plattsville
PO Box 97
47 Albert St.
Plattsville, ON N0J 1S0 Canada
519-684-7414
Fax: 519-684-7707
MICR: 07752-010

Ponoka
PO Box 4310
5002 - 50th St.
Ponoka, AB T4J 1R7 Canada
403-783-5581
Fax: 403-783-8400
MICR: 00079-010

Port Alberni
2995 - 3rd Ave.
Port Alberni, BC V9Y 2A6 Canada
250-720-2300
Fax: 250-723-0665
MICR: 00340-010

Port Colborne
56 Clarence St.
Port Colborne, ON L3K 3E9 Canada
905-834-3671
Fax: 905-834-5976
MICR: 06572-010

Port Coquitlam
#A101, 1475 Prairie Ave.
Port Coquitlam, BC V3B 1T3 Canada
604-927-2737
Fax: 604-941-0516
MICR: 05920-010

Port Elgin
PO Box 130
635 Goderich St.
Port Elgin, ON N0H 2C0 Canada
519-832-9065
Fax: 519-832-2170
MICR: 08652-010

Port Hardy
PO Box 9
7085 Market St.
Port Hardy, BC V0N 2P0 Canada
250-949-6333
Fax: 250-949-6540
MICR: 01940-010

Port Hope
185 Toronto Rd.
Port Hope, ON L1A 3V5 Canada
905-885-6321
Fax: 905-885-0124
MICR: 03942-010

Port McNeill
PO Box 340
1596 Broughton Blvd.
Port McNeill, BC V0N 2R0 Canada
250-956-3351
Fax: 250-956-4382
MICR: 07040-010

Port Perry
PO Box 749
145 Queen St.
Port Perry, ON L9L 1A6 Canada
905-985-4444
Fax: 905-985-9471
MICR: 03442-010

Port Rowan
PO Box 70
1007 Bay St.
Port Rowan, ON N0E 1M0 Canada
519-586-3561
Fax: 519-586-3992
MICR: 01672-010

Port-Cartier
54, Portage des Mousses
Port-Cartier, QC G5B 1C6 Canada
418-766-5391
Fax: 418-766-8950
MICR: 00275-010

Portage La Prairie
7 Saskatchewan Ave. East
Portage La Prairie, MB R1N 0L8 Canada
204-857-6856
Fax: 204-239-6104
MICR: 00077-010

Powell River
Town Centre Mall
#71, 7100 Alberni St.
Powell River, BC V8A 5K9 Canada
604-485-3150
Fax: 604-485-9842
MICR: 00280-010

Prince Albert
1132 Central Ave.
Prince Albert, SK S6V 4V6 Canada
306-764-6692
Fax: 306-763-0036
MICR: 00058-010

Prince George - 3rd Ave.
PO Box 9
1410 - 3rd Ave.
Prince George, BC V2L 3G2 Canada
250-614-6444
Fax: 250-614-6478
MICR: 00650-010

Prince George - Central St.
Spruceland Shopping Centre
783 Central St.
Prince George, BC V2M 3C7 Canada
250-614-6450
Fax: 250-563-2310
MICR: 03950-010

Prince George - Massey Dr.
Pine Centre
#233, 3055 Massey Dr.
Prince George, BC V2N 2S9 Canada
250-614-6400
Fax: 250-564-0542
MICR: 08950-010

Prince Rupert
500 - 3rd Ave. West
Prince Rupert, BC V8J 1L8 Canada
250-627-1771
Fax: 250-624-5162
MICR: 00180-010

Princeton
PO Box 430
226 Bridge St.
Princeton, BC V0X 1W0 Canada
250-295-3225
Fax: 250-295-3866
MICR: 00460-010

Provost
PO Box 60
5102 - 50th St.
Provost, AB T0B 3S0 Canada

780-753-2241
Fax: 780-753-6073
MICR: 00389-010

Qualicum Beach
PO Box 69
686 Memorial Ave.
Qualicum Beach, BC V9K 1S7 Canada
250-752-4300
Fax: 250-752-5618
MICR: 00940-010

Quesnel
318 Reid St.
Quesnel, BC V2J 2M4 Canada
250-992-2104
Fax: 250-992-3038
MICR: 05950-010

Québec - 1e av
4250, 1e av
Québec, QC G1H 2S5 Canada
418-623-1579
Fax: 418-623-3467
MICR: 00105-010

Québec - Maguire
1270, av Maguire
Québec, QC G1T 1Z3 Canada
418-681-3529
Fax: 418-681-2352
MICR: 00045-010

Québec - Quatre-Bourgeois
2880, ch des Quatre-Bourgeois
Québec, QC G1V 4X7 Canada
418-653-8328
Fax: 418-653-4341
MICR: 00135-010

Québec - René Lévesque est
Place CIBC
91, boul René Lévesque est
Québec, QC G1R 2A9 Canada
418-529-2101
Fax: 418-529-4386
MICR: 00005-010

Québec - Sainte-Anne
La Canardière
2485, boul Sainte-Anne
Québec, QC G1J 1Y4 Canada
418-666-3184
Fax: 418-666-7066
MICR: 00055-010

Québec - Wilfrid-Hamel
Place Fleur-de-Lys
552, boul Wilfrid-Hamel
Québec, QC G1M 3E5 Canada
418-529-0667
Fax: 418-524-1386
MICR: 00115-010

Radisson
PO Box 70
Radisson, SK S0K 3L0 Canada
306-827-2044
Fax: 306-827-2277
MICR: 00658-010

Radville
PO Box 9
133 Main St.
Radville, SK S0C 2G0 Canada
306-869-2267
Fax: 306-869-3117
MICR: 00458-010

Rainy River
PO Box 189
120 - 4th St.
Rainy River, ON P0W 1L0 Canada
807-852-3234
Fax: 807-852-4498
MICR: 00487-010

Rankin Inlet
PO Box 10
Rankin Inlet, NU X0C 0G0 Canada
867-645-2863
Fax: 867-645-2573
MICR: 02799-010

Red Deer - 22nd St.
Gaetz Ave. & 22nd St. Banking Centre
#4, 5111 - 22nd St.
Red Deer, AB T4R 2K1 Canada
403-340-4500
Fax: 403-340-4565
MICR: 00339-010

Red Deer - Gaetz Ave.
#1, 6721 Gaetz Ave.
Red Deer, AB T4N 4C9 Canada
403-340-4549
Fax: 403-340-4563
MICR: 06939-010

Red Lake
PO Box 306
155 Howey St.
Red Lake, ON P0V 2M0 Canada
807-727-2688
Fax: 807-727-3339
MICR: 00497-010

Redcliff
11 - 3rd St. SE
Redcliff, AB T0J 2P0 Canada
403-548-3921
Fax: 403-548-3462
MICR: 06049-010

Redvers
PO Box 70
17 Broadway Ave.
Redvers, SK S0C 2H0 Canada
306-452-4100
Fax: 306-452-6005
MICR: 00268-010

Redwater
PO Box 40
4934 - 49th St.
Redwater, AB T0A 2W0 Canada
780-942-3561
Fax: 780-942-2001
MICR: 06079-010

Regina - Albert St.
3950 Albert St.
Regina, SK S4S 3R1 Canada
306-359-8473
Fax: 306-584-7553
MICR: 00608-010

Regina - Gordon Rd.
Southland Mall
2801 Gordon Rd.
Regina, SK S4S 6H7 Canada
306-359-8458
Fax: 306-584-5989
MICR: 05008-010

Regina - Hamilton St.
1800 Hamilton St.
Regina, SK S4P 4K7 Canada
306-359-8585
Fax: 306-359-8682
MICR: 00008-010

Regina - McCarthy Blvd. North
Normanview Crossing
322 McCarthy Blvd. North
Regina, SK S4R 7M2 Canada
306-359-8512
Fax: 306-359-8568
MICR: 08008-010

Regina - Park St.
2032 Park St.
Regina, SK S4N 2G6 Canada
306-359-8558
Fax: 306-359-8559
MICR: 02008-010

Regina - University Park Dr.
University Park Mall
258 University Park Dr.
Regina, SK S4V 1A3 Canada
306-359-8777
Fax: 306-359-8697
MICR: 01208-010

Repentigny
500, boul Iberville
Repentigny, QC J6A 6H9 Canada
450-581-0830
Fax: 450-654-5423
MICR: 01181-010

Revelstoke
PO Box 110
200 Mackenzie Ave.
Revelstoke, BC V0E 2S0 Canada
250-837-2151
Fax: 250-837-9499
MICR: 00750-010

Richmond
120, rue Principale nord
Richmond, QC J0B 2H0 Canada
819-826-3724
Fax: 819-826-3538
MICR: 01071-010

Richmond - Blundell Rd.
Garden City Shopping Centre
#200, 9100 Blundell Rd.
Richmond, BC V6Y 1K3 Canada
604-665-1385
Fax: 604-665-6147
MICR: 01500-010

Richmond - No. 1 Rd.
#1, 8751 No. 1 Rd.
Richmond, BC V7C 1V2 Canada
604-257-8007
Fax: 604-277-1545
MICR: 03900-010

Richmond - No. 3 Rd.
Three West Centre
6011 - No. 3 Rd.
Richmond, BC V6Y 2B2 Canada
604-665-6106
Fax: 604-273-4267
MICR: 00900-010

Richmond - Perth St.
Richmond Plaza
PO Box 878
6179 Perth St.
Richmond, ON K0A 2Z0 Canada
613-838-3200
Fax: 613-838-3204
MICR: 00376-010

Richmond Hill - Major MacKenzie East
650 Major MacKenzie Dr. East
Richmond Hill, ON L4C 1J9 Canada
905-884-8100
Fax: 905-884-8362
MICR: 06742-010

Richmond Hill - West Beaver Creek Rd.
300 West Beaver Creek Rd.
Richmond Hill, ON L4B 3B1 Canada
905-886-1370
Fax: 905-866-1250
MICR: 08642-010

Richmond Hill - Yonge St.
South Hill Shopping Centre
9335 Yonge St.
Richmond Hill, ON L4C 1V4 Canada
905-884-4460
Fax: 905-884-0311
MICR: 02442-010

Richmond Hill - Yonge St.
10520 Yonge St.
Richmond Hill, ON L4C 3C7 Canada
905-884-8162
Fax: 905-884-3055
MICR: 08842-010

Ridgetown
PO Box 910
43 Main St. West
Ridgetown, ON N0P 2C0 Canada
519-674-5452
Fax: 519-674-5208
MICR: 02882-010

Ridgeway
PO Box 160
310 Ridge Rd.
Ridgeway, ON L0S 1N0 Canada
905-894-1030
Fax: 905-894-6023
MICR: 05072-010

Rimouski
70, rue St-Germain est
Rimouski, QC G5L 7J9 Canada
418-723-4941
Fax: 418-721-6621
MICR: 00385-010

Riverview

Canadian Imperial Bank of Commerce(CIBC)/ Banque Canadienne Impériale de Commerce (continued)

Riverview Mall
720 Coverdale Rd.
Riverview, NB E1B 3L8 Canada
506-859-3703
Fax: 506-859-4561
MICR: 00794-010

Rocky Mountain House
PO Box 609
5003 - 50th St.
Rocky Mountain House, AB T4T 1A5 Canada
403-845-3357
Fax: 403-845-6950
MICR: 00539-010

Rockyford
PO Box 10
201 Main St.
Rockyford, AB T0J 2R0 Canada
403-533-3818
Fax: 403-533-2493
MICR: 04049-010

Rosemère
299, boul Labelle
Rosemère, QC J7A 2H7 Canada
450-437-0550
Fax: 450-437-0736
MICR: 04081-010

Rosthern
PO Box 100
1001 - 6th St.
Rosthern, SK S0K 3R0 Canada
306-232-8300
Fax: 306-232-4755
MICR: 00398-010

Rothesay
83C Hampton Rd.
Rothesay, NB E2E 2K3 Canada
506-847-7528
Fax: 506-849-5962
MICR: 00994-010

Rouleau
PO Box 160
101 Main St.
Rouleau, SK S0G 4H0 Canada
306-776-2244
Fax: 306-776-2435
MICR: 00558-010

Rouyn-Noranda - Principale
180, rue Principale
Rouyn-Noranda, QC J9X 4P8 Canada
819-762-3531
Fax: 819-797-9216
MICR: 00091-010

Saanichton
#C7819 East Saanich Rd.
Saanichton, BC V8M 2B4 Canada
250-544-5080
Fax: 250-652-5443
MICR: 05930-010

Saint John - Consumers Rd.
First Westmorland Shopping Centre
70 Consumers Rd.
Saint John, NB E2J 4Z3 Canada
506-633-7750
Fax: 506-633-4467
MICR: 00694-010

Saint John - King St.
44 King St.
Saint John, NB E2L 1G4 Canada
506-632-1110
Fax: 506-632-9007
MICR: 00004-010

Saint John - Main St. West
1 Main St. West
Saint John, NB E2M 3M9 Canada
506-635-1520
Fax: 506-635-5884
MICR: 00504-010

Saint-Bruno
1445, rue Roberval
Saint-Bruno, QC J3V 5J1 Canada
450-653-2427
Fax: 450-653-5748
MICR: 04051-010

Saint-Chrysostome
559, rang Notre Dame
Saint-Chrysostome, QC J0S 1R0 Canada
450-826-4941
Fax: 450-826-0565
MICR: 04071-010

Saint-Georges
11620, 1re av
Saint-Georges, QC G5Y 2C8 Canada
418-228-8869
Fax: 418-228-7680
MICR: 00465-010

Saint-Hubert - Cousineau
Carrefour Saint-Hubert
5950, boul Cousineau
Saint-Hubert, QC J3Y 7R9 Canada
450-443-6363
Fax: 450-443-5363
MICR: 01401-010

Saint-Hyacinthe - Girouard
1605, rue Girouard ouest
Saint-Hyacinthe, QC J2S 2Z9 Canada
450-261-1010
Fax: 450-261-1020
MICR: 00261-010

Saint-Hyacinthe - Laframboise
2755, rue Laframboise
Saint-Hyacinthe, QC J2S 4Y9 Canada
450-261-1027
Fax: 450-261-1030
MICR: 08061-010

Saint-Lambert - Victoria
1485, av Victoria
Saint-Lambert, QC J4R 1R5 Canada
450-671-1905
Fax: 450-671-9780
MICR: 00441-010

Sainte-Julie
#136, 1700, ch, du-Fer-a-Cheval
Sainte-Julie, QC J3E 1G2 Canada
450-922-1825
Fax: 450-922-3187
MICR: 01381-010

Salaberry-de-Valleyfield
15, Ave. du Centenaire
Salaberry-de-Valleyfield, QC J6S 6V7 Canada
450-373-7777
Fax: 450-377-5760
MICR: 01051-010

Salisbury
3155 Main St.
Salisbury, NB E4J 2K3 Canada
506-372-9344
Fax: 506-372-9976
MICR: 00094-010

Salmon Arm
PO Box 10
310 Alexander
Salmon Arm, BC V1E 4N2 Canada
250-833-3334
Fax: 250-832-4494
MICR: 00250-010

Salt Spring Island
120 Fulford-Ganges Rd.
Salt Spring Island, BC V8K 2S4 Canada
250-537-2035
Fax: 250-537-2299
MICR: 08030-010

Sarnia - Exmouth St.
478 Exmouth St.
Sarnia, ON N7T 5P3 Canada
519-336-2276
Fax: 519-336-2576
MICR: 06882-010

Sarnia - London Rd.
1170 London Rd.
Sarnia, ON N7S 1P4 Canada
519-337-0373
Fax: 519-337-0374
MICR: 04382-010

Sarnia - North Front St.
190 North Front St.
Sarnia, ON N7T 5S3 Canada
519-332-4466
Fax: 519-332-0769
MICR: 00582-010

Saskatoon - 21st St. East
201 - 21st St. East
Saskatoon, SK S7K 0B8 Canada
306-668-3488
Fax: 306-668-3378
MICR: 00018-010

Saskatoon - 8th St. East
3124 - 8th St. East
Saskatoon, SK S7H 0W2 Canada
306-668-3230
Fax: 306-668-3227
MICR: 00818-010

Saskatoon - Broadway Ave.
1814 Broadway Ave.
Saskatoon, SK S7H 2B7 Canada
306-668-3388
Fax: 306-668-3389
MICR: 00418-010

Saskatoon - Circle Dr. East
320 Circle Dr. East
Saskatoon, SK S7K 0T6 Canada
306-668-3466
Fax: 306-668-3437
MICR: 00518-010

Saskatoon - Confederation Dr.
307 Confederation Dr.
Saskatoon, SK S7L 5C3 Canada
306-668-3465
Fax: 306-668-3463
MICR: 01018-010

Sault Ste Marie - Churchill Blvd.
150 Churchill Blvd.
Sault Ste Marie, ON P6A 3Z9 Canada
705-253-2341
Fax: 705-253-7792
MICR: 09992-010

Sault Ste Marie - Great Northern Rd.
Cambrian Mall
44 Great Northern Rd.
Sault Ste Marie, ON P6B 4Y5 Canada
705-949-0297
Fax: 705-949-4023
MICR: 01792-010

Sault Ste Marie - Queen St.
530 Queen St. East
Sault Ste Marie, ON P6A 2A1 Canada
705-254-6633
Fax: 705-759-1586
MICR: 00192-010

Schomberg
PO Box 130
184 Main St.
Schomberg, ON L0G 1T0 Canada
905-939-8511
Fax: 905-939-8756
MICR: 04652-010

Seaforth
PO Box 339
44 Main St. South
Seaforth, ON N0K 1W0 Canada
519-527-0100
Fax: 519-527-2859
MICR: 06752-010

Sechelt
PO Box 1520
#101, 5530 Wharf St.
Sechelt, BC V0N 3A0 Canada
604-740-3389
Fax: 604-740-3387
MICR: 07710-010

Selkirk - Main St.
369 Main St.
Selkirk, MB R1A 1T7 Canada
204-482-2910
Fax: 204-482-7095
MICR: 00947-010

Selkirk - Main St.
PO Box 70
1 Main St.
Selkirk, ON N0A 1P0 Canada
905-776-2542
MICR: 03972-010

Senneterre

PO Box 608
780, 10ieme av
Senneterre, QC J0Y 2M0 Canada
819-737-2345
Fax: 819-737-8567
MICR: 03091-010

Sept-×les
400, av Brochu
Sept-×les, QC G4R 2W6 Canada
418-962-9734
Fax: 418-968-2506
MICR: 00075-010

Shaunavon
PO Box 1146
396 Centre St.
Shaunavon, SK S0N 2M0 Canada
306-297-2621
Fax: 306-297-3023
MICR: 00998-010

Shawinigan
559, 5ieme rue
Shawinigan, QC G9N 1E7 Canada
819-537-1844
Fax: 819-536-7003
MICR: 00181-010

Shawinigan - Sud
1497, 5ieme av
Shawinigan-Sud, QC G9P 1M4 Canada
819-536-4451
Fax: 819-536-7979
MICR: 00281-010

Shedden
PO Box 70
134 North Talbot Rd.
Shedden, ON N0L 2E0 Canada
519-764-2520
Fax: 519-764-2080
MICR: 05582-010

Shelburne
PO Box 70
146 Water St.
Shelburne, NS B0T 1W0 Canada
902-875-2388
Fax: 902-875-3161
MICR: 00223-010

Sherbrooke - King ouest
450, rue King ouest
Sherbrooke, QC J1H 1R4 Canada
819-562-2422
Fax: 819-564-0233
MICR: 00061-010

Sherbrooke - Portland
Carrefour de l'Estrie
3050, boul Portland
Sherbrooke, QC J1L 1K1 Canada
819-569-9911
Fax: 819-569-8878
MICR: 09051-010

Sherwood Park - Baseline Rd.
Lakeland Ridge
#160, 590 Baseline Rd.
Sherwood Park, AB T8H 1Y4 Canada
780-417-7677
Fax: 780-417-7670
MICR: 02159-010

Sherwood Park - Sherwood Dr.
#250, 1020 Sherwood Dr.
Sherwood Park, AB T8A 2G4 Canada
780-417-7600
Fax: 780-464-0442
MICR: 04069-010

Sidney
2339 Beacon Ave.
Sidney, BC V8L 1W9 Canada
250-655-2132
Fax: 250-656-3982
MICR: 01930-010

Simcoe
5 Norfolk St. South
Simcoe, ON N3Y 2V8 Canada
519-426-4630
Fax: 519-426-3971
MICR: 00972-010

Sioux Lookout
PO Box 189
50 Front St.
Sioux Lookout, ON P8T 1A3 Canada
807-737-2331
Fax: 807-737-1463
MICR: 00387-010

Smithers
PO Box 1059
1222 Main St.
Smithers, BC V0J 2N0 Canada
250-877-5061
Fax: 250-847-3517
MICR: 06050-010

Smiths Falls
PO Box 189
51 Beckwith St. North
Smiths Falls, ON K7A 2B4 Canada
613-283-3584
Fax: 613-283-1774
MICR: 00096-010

Smithville
PO Box 130
124 Griffin St. North
Smithville, ON L0R 2A0 Canada
905-957-3037
Fax: 905-957-0510
MICR: 03372-010

Smoky Lake
PO Box 10
49 Wheatland Ave.
Smoky Lake, AB T0A 3C0 Canada
780-656-3736
Fax: 780-656-3009
MICR: 00879-010

Sombra
PO Box 10
3461 St. Clair Pkwy.
Sombra, ON N0P 2H0 Canada
519-892-3471
Fax: 519-892-3040
MICR: 01582-010

Sooke
PO Box 459
6679 Sooke Rd.
Sooke, BC V0S 1N0 Canada
250-642-1650
Fax: 250-542-6011
MICR: 00830-010

Sorel-Tracy
#100, 215, boul Fiset
Sorel-Tracy, QC J3P 3P3 Canada
450-742-4581
Fax: 450-742-7815
MICR: 00471-010

Souris
PO Box 219
91 Main St.
Souris, PE C0A 2B0 Canada
902-687-2014
Fax: 902-687-3008
MICR: 00283-010

South Porcupine
PO Box 310
90 Golden Ave.
South Porcupine, ON P0N 1H0 Canada
705-235-5833
Fax: 705-235-4200
MICR: 08892-010

Southampton
PO Box 220
147 High St.
Southampton, ON N0H 2L0 Canada
519-797-3226
Fax: 519-797-3199
MICR: 03852-010

Sparwood
PO Box 36
105 Greenwood Mall
Sparwood, BC V0B 2G0 Canada
250-425-6215
Fax: 250-425-4418
MICR: 03070-010

Springhill
PO Box 730
41 Main St.
Springhill, NS B0M 1X0 Canada
902-597-3741
Fax: 902-597-3839
MICR: 00133-010

Spruce Grove
100 McLeod Ave.
Spruce Grove, AB T7X 2H8 Canada
780-962-2290
Fax: 780-962-1223
MICR: 07089-010

St Albert - Hebert Rd.
Gateway Village
#100, 10 Hebert Rd.
St Albert, AB T8N 5T8 Canada
780-460-3203
Fax: 780-460-3210
MICR: 03769-010

St Albert - Sir Winston Churchill
29 Sir Winston Churchill Ave.
St Albert, AB T8N 0G3 Canada
780-459-5528
Fax: 780-459-4419
MICR: 04969-010

St Catharines - 4th Ave.
Ridley Heights
#11, 100 - 4th Ave.
St Catharines, ON L2S 3P3 Canada
905-641-8080
Fax: 905-641-8863
MICR: 01272-010

St Catharines - Geneva St.
Fairview Mall
285 1/2 Geneva St.
St Catharines, ON L2N 2G1 Canada
905-937-6819
Fax: 905-937-3593
MICR: 06972-010

St Catharines - Glendale Ave.
The Pen
221 Glendale Ave. West
St Catharines, ON L2T 2K9 Canada
905-685-6920
Fax: 905-685-7969
MICR: 05472-010

St Catharines - King St.
PO Box 30
#41, 45 King St.
St Catharines, ON L2R 6S2 Canada
905-688-4442
Fax: 905-641-0976
MICR: 00172-010

St Catharines - Lakeshore Rd.
33 Lakeshore Rd.
St Catharines, ON L2N 7B3 Canada
905-937-3177
Fax: 905-937-1866
MICR: 04272-010

St Catharines - Niagara St.
442 Niagara St.
St Catharines, ON L2M 4W3 Canada
905-934-3508
Fax: 905-934-9247
MICR: 07972-010

St Clements
PO Box 329
3575 Lobsinger Line
St Clements, ON N0B 2M0 Canada
519-699-4414
Fax: 519-699-6103
MICR: 06952-010

St Paul
PO Box 189
5001 - 50th Ave.
St Paul, AB T0A 3A0 Canada
780-645-3371
Fax: 780-645-5568
MICR: 00189-010

St Thomas
PO Box 159
440 Talbot St.
St Thomas, ON N5P 3T7 Canada
519-631-1280
Fax: 519-633-5353

Canadian Imperial Bank of Commerce(CIBC)/ Banque Canadienne Impériale de Commerce (continued)

MICR: 03082-010
St Walburg
PO Box 278
23 Main St.
St Walburg, SK S0M 2T0 Canada
306-248-3641
Fax: 306-248-3952
MICR: 00368-010
St-Eustache
367, boul Arthur-Sauvé
St-Eustache, QC J7P 2B1 Canada
450-472-6016
Fax: 450-491-7388
MICR: 00981-010
St-Ferdinand
544, rue Principale
St-Ferdinand, QC G0N 1N0 Canada
418-428-3742
Fax: 418-428-9274
MICR: 05071-010
St-Jean-sur-Richelieu - Dorchester
640, rue Dorchester
St-Jean-sur-Richelieu, QC J3B 5A4 Canada
450-348-7315
Fax: 450-348-4767
MICR: 06051-010
St-Jean-sur-Richelieu - Pierre Caisse
Carrefour Richelieu
#10, 600, rue Pierre Caisse
St-Jean-sur-Richelieu, QC J3A 1M1 Canada
450-348-1123
Fax: 450-348-6296
MICR: 01151-010
St-Jean-sur-Richelieu - Richelieu
170, rue Richelieu
St-Jean-sur-Richelieu, QC J3B 6X4 Canada
450-347-5571
Fax: 450-347-2985
MICR: 00051-010
St-Jérôme
Centre d'achats St-Jérôme
1950, boul Labelle
St-Jérôme, QC J7Y 1S1 Canada
450-438-3525
Fax: 450-431-3268
MICR: 00481-010
St. John's - Hamlyn Rd.
15 Hamlyn Rd.
St. John's, NL A1E 2E2 Canada
709-576-8909
Fax: 709-576-8700
MICR: 00473-010
St. John's - Kenmount Rd.
48 Kenmount Rd.
St. John's, NL A1B 1W3 Canada
709-576-8877
Fax: 709-576-8956
MICR: 01163-010
St. John's - Rowan St.
Churchill Sq.
PO Box 23090
#8, 10 Rowan St.
St. John's, NL A1B 2X1 Canada
709-576-8777
Fax: 709-576-8811
MICR: 00763-010
St. John's - Torbay Rd.
Torbay Mall
PO Box 21129
141 Torbay Rd.
St. John's, NL A1A 5B2 Canada
709-576-8555
Fax: 709-576-8801
MICR: 00373-010
St. John's - Water St.
Atlantic Place
PO Box 30
215 Water St.
St. John's, NL A1C 5J9 Canada
709-576-8800
Fax: 709-576-8948
MICR: 00063-010
St. Stephen
Charlotte Shopping Mall
210 King St.
St. Stephen, NB E3L 2E2 Canada
506-466-3050
Fax: 506-466-0920
MICR: 00194-010
Stanstead
34, rue Principale
Stanstead, QC J0B 3E5 Canada
819-876-2441
Fax: 819-876-5686
MICR: 02051-010
Steinbach
205 Main St.
Steinbach, MB R5G 1Y5 Canada
204-326-3458
Fax: 204-326-3201
MICR: 00867-010
Stettler
PO Box 790
5100 - 50th St.
Stettler, AB T0C 2L0 Canada
403-742-4451
Fax: 403-742-8201
MICR: 07049-010
Stonewall
PO Box 10
356 Main St.
Stonewall, MB R0C 2Z0 Canada
204-467-5551
Fax: 204-467-8037
MICR: 00257-010
Stoney Creek - Barton St. East
393 Barton St. East
Stoney Creek, ON L8E 2L2 Canada
905-664-6433
Fax: 905-664-3354
MICR: 05762-010
Stoney Creek - Centennial Pkwy. North
Eastgate Square
75 Centennial Pkwy. North
Stoney Creek, ON L8E 5B2 Canada
905-561-3600
Fax: 905-561-0752
MICR: 03662-010
Stoney Creek - Hwy. 8
146 Hwy. 8
Stoney Creek, ON L8G 1C2 Canada
905-664-4436
Fax: 905-664-5867
MICR: 02962-010
Stony Plain
5100 - 50th St.
Stony Plain, AB T7Z 1T4 Canada
780-963-2267
Fax: 780-963-3426
MICR: 00679-010
Stouffville
6311 Main St.
Stouffville, ON L4A 1G5 Canada
905-640-1811
Fax: 905-640-1631
MICR: 00842-010
Stoughton
PO Box 150
312 Main St.
Stoughton, SK S0G 4T0 Canada
306-457-2233
Fax: 306-457-2209
MICR: 00438-010
Stratford
30 Downie St.
Stratford, ON N5A 1W5 Canada
519-271-0920
Fax: 519-271-4036
MICR: 00252-010
Strathmore
PO Box 2010
334 - 2nd St.
Strathmore, AB T1P 1K1 Canada
403-934-3328
Fax: 403-934-4896
MICR: 04939-010
Strathroy
52 Front St. West
Strathroy, ON N7G 1X7 Canada
519-245-2560
Fax: 519-245-5738
MICR: 09082-010
Sudbury - Cedar St.
PO Box 8, B Sta. B
116 Cedar St.
Sudbury, ON P3E 4N3 Canada
705-673-4195
Fax: 705-671-1740
MICR: 00692-010
Sudbury - Lasalle Blvd.
New Sudbury Shopping Centre
1349 Lasalle Blvd.
Sudbury, ON P3A 1Z2 Canada
705-566-2458
Fax: 705-566-5848
MICR: 03892-010
Sudbury - Regent St. South
Southridge Mall
1933 Regent St. South
Sudbury, ON P3E 5R2 Canada
705-522-3866
Fax: 705-522-6191
MICR: 03692-010
Summerland
PO Box 839
9920 Main St.
Summerland, BC V0H 1Z0 Canada
250-404-4000
Fax: 250-494-4186
MICR: 04060-010
Summerside
245 Water St.
Summerside, PE C1N 1B5 Canada
902-436-2255
Fax: 902-436-4868
MICR: 00183-010
Sunderland
PO Box 160
74 River St.
Sunderland, ON L0C 1H0 Canada
705-357-3197
Fax: 705-357-3580
MICR: 07742-010
Surrey - 120 St.
7420 - 120 St.
Surrey, BC V3W 3M9 Canada
604-501-5750
Fax: 604-501-5730
MICR: 03620-010
Surrey - 16th Ave.
Ocean Park Shopping Centre
12893 - 16th Ave.
Surrey, BC V4A 1N5 Canada
604-541-4533
Fax: 604-541-4544
MICR: 02620-010
Surrey - 176th St.
5699 - 176th St.
Surrey, BC V3S 4C5 Canada
604-575-6011
Fax: 604-576-8237
MICR: 07820-010
Surrey - Guildford
1294 Guildford Town Centre
Surrey, BC V3R 7B7 Canada
604-586-2303
Fax: 604-581-0418
MICR: 08920-010
Surrey - Hwy. 10
Panorama Village
#101, 15149 Hwy. 10
Surrey, BC V3S 1B6 Canada
604-574-8220
Fax: 604-574-8222
MICR: 03120-010
Surrey - King George Hwy.
Newton Crossing
7188 King George Hwy.
Surrey, BC V3W 5A3 Canada
604-501-7075
Fax: 604-591-9949
MICR: 00620-010

Surrey - King George Hwy.
10166 King George Hwy.
Surrey, BC V3T 2W4 Canada
604-586-2242
Fax: 604-586-2277
MICR: 03820-010

Sutton
PO Box 249
5, rue Principal sud
Sutton, QC J0E 2K0 Canada
450-538-2234
Fax: 450-538-1133
MICR: 00861-010

Swift Current
PO Box 488
307 Central Ave. North
Swift Current, SK S9H 3W3 Canada
306-773-3138
Fax: 306-773-1717
MICR: 00198-010

Sydney - Dorchester St.
15 Dorchester St.
Sydney, NS B1P 5Y9 Canada
902-562-6420
Fax: 902-539-3477
MICR: 00023-010

Sydney - Keltic Dr.
Cape Breton Plaza
11 Keltic Dr.
Sydney, NS B1S 1P4 Canada
902-539-7782
Fax: 902-539-5075
MICR: 00443-010

Sylvan Lake
5007 - 50th St.
Sylvan Lake, AB T4S 1M5 Canada
403-887-2237
Fax: 403-887-4640
MICR: 00939-010

Taber
5124 - 48th Ave
Taber, AB T1G 1R9 Canada
403-223-3551
Fax: 403-223-8689
MICR: 00139-010

Tamworth
PO Box 39
Country Rd #4
Tamworth, ON K0K 3G0 Canada
613-379-2995
Fax: 613-379-5303
MICR: 09842-010

Tavistock
PO Box 130
38 Woodstock St. South
Tavistock, ON N0B 2R0 Canada
519-655-2313
Fax: 519-655-3018
MICR: 09752-010

Tecumseh
13 Amy Croft Dr.
Tecumseh, ON N9K 1C7 Canada
519-735-2171
Fax: 519-735-7327
MICR: 03482-010

Terrace
#101, 4717 Lakelse Ave.
Terrace, BC V8G 1R5 Canada
250-615-5600
Fax: 250-635-4129
MICR: 03080-010

Terrace Bay
PO Box 339
14 Simcoe Plaza
Terrace Bay, ON P0T 2W0 Canada
807-825-3244
Fax: 807-825-9779
MICR: 09892-010

Terrebonne
1212, boul des Seigneurs
Terrebonne, QC J6W 3W4 Canada
450-964-6530
Fax: 450-471-8094
MICR: 01341-010

The Pas
PO Box 2580
333 Edwards St.
The Pas, MB R9A 1M3 Canada
204-623-3439
Fax: 204-623-7914
MICR: 00777-010

Thedford
PO Box 100
83 Main St.
Thedford, ON N0M 2N0 Canada
519-296-4968
Fax: 519-296-5717
MICR: 03982-010

Thessalon
PO Box 130
203 Main St.
Thessalon, ON P0R 1L0 Canada
705-842-2119
Fax: 705-842-3927
MICR: 01992-010

Thetford-Mines
147, rue Notre-Dame ouest
Thetford Mines, QC G6G 1J4 Canada
418-338-5191
Fax: 418-338-5857
MICR: 00271-010

Thompson
225 Mystery Lake Rd.
Thompson, MB R8N 1Z8 Canada
204-677-2359
Fax: 204-778-8519
MICR: 00767-010

Thornhill - Centre St.
Centre at New Westminster
#1, 1118 Centre St.
Thornhill, ON L4J 7R9 Canada
905-881-4142
Fax: 905-881-3475
MICR: 09542-010

Thornhill - John St.
Thornhill Square
300 John St.
Thornhill, ON L3T 5W4 Canada
905-889-7168
Fax: 905-886-4397
MICR: 00812-010

Thornhill - Yonge St.
7765 Yonge St.
Thornhill, ON L3T 2C4 Canada
905-889-5487
Fax: 905-889-8203
MICR: 09012-010

Thornhill - Yonge St.
7027 Yonge St.
Thornhill, ON L3T 2A5 Canada
905-889-4654
Fax: 905-889-0492
MICR: 04912-010

Thorold
15 Front St. North
Thorold, ON L2V 1X3 Canada
905-227-3955
Fax: 905-227-1225
MICR: 02572-010

Thunder Bay - Memorial Ave.
1038 Memorial Ave.
Thunder Bay, ON P7B 4A3 Canada
807-624-3850
Fax: 807-623-3673
MICR: 00687-010

Thunder Bay - Red River Rd.
832 Red River Rd.
Thunder Bay, ON P7B 1K2 Canada
807-768-3800
Fax: 807-767-4665
MICR: 04087-010

Thunder Bay - South Cumberland
2 South Cumberland St.
Thunder Bay, ON P7B 2T2 Canada
807-343-3710
Fax: 807-343-5771
MICR: 00097-010

Thunder Bay - Victoria Ave.
600 Victoria Ave. East
Thunder Bay, ON P7C 1A9 Canada
807-624-3680
Fax: 807-623-9158
MICR: 00187-010

Thunder Bay - West Arthur St.
127 West Arthur St.
Thunder Bay, ON P7E 5P7 Canada
807-474-3600
Fax: 807-475-8561
MICR: 00897-010

Thunder Bay - West Arthur St.
Thunder Bay Mall
1101 West Arthur St.
Thunder Bay, ON P7E 5S2 Canada
807-474-3833
Fax: 807-475-7234
MICR: 02087-010

Tilbury
PO Box 670
4 Queen St. North
Tilbury, ON N0P 2L0 Canada
519-682-2100
Fax: 519-682-1493
MICR: 04982-010

Tillsonburg
200 Broadway
Tillsonburg, ON N4G 5A7 Canada
519-842-7331
Fax: 519-842-3047
MICR: 03072-010

Timmins
PO Box 350
236 Third Ave.
Timmins, ON P4N 7E2 Canada
705-264-4234
Fax: 705-268-9044
MICR: 00492-010

Tofino
PO Box 91
301 Campbell St.
Tofino, BC V0R 2Z0 Canada
250-725-3321
Fax: 250-725-3311
MICR: 03940-010

Toronto - Albion Rd.
1530 Albion Rd.
Toronto, ON M9V 1B4 Canada
418-741-2102
Fax: 418-741-3383
MICR: 03522-010

Toronto - Alness St.
700 Alness St.
Toronto, ON M3J 2H5 Canada
416-661-3131
Fax: 416-661-4405
MICR: 03322-010

Toronto - Alton Towers Circle
250 Alton Towers Circle
Toronto, ON M1V 3Z4 Canada
416-293-4278
Fax: 416-293-0480
MICR: 02232-010

Toronto - Avenue Rd
1703 Avenue Rd.
Toronto, ON M5M 3Y3 Canada
416-789-1150
Fax: 416-789-7031
MICR: 09812-010

Toronto - Avenue Rd.
2040 Avenue Rd.
Toronto, ON M5M 4A6 Canada
416-485-9127
Fax: 416-485-5957
MICR: 06812-010

Toronto - Bathurst St.
4927 Bathurst St.
Toronto, ON M2R 1X8 Canada
416-222-1147
Fax: 416-222-0759
MICR: 06912-010

Toronto - Bay St.
595 Bay St.
Toronto, ON M5G 2C2 Canada
416-861-3801
Fax: 416-980-3377
MICR: 05702-010

Canadian Imperial Bank of Commerce(CIBC)/ Banque Canadienne Impériale de Commerce (continued)

Toronto - Bay St.
790 Bay St.
Toronto, ON M5G 1N8 Canada
416-980-2428
Fax: 416-980-2494
MICR: 07902-010

Toronto - Bay St.
Main Branch - Commerce Court, Commerce Court West, Concourse West
199 Bay St.
Toronto, ON M5L 1A2 Canada
416-980-7777
MICR: 00002-010

Toronto - Bayview Ave.
3315 Bayview Ave.
Toronto, ON M2K 1G4 Canada
416-223-2211
Fax: 416-223-6348
MICR: 05712-010

Toronto - Bayview Ave.
1529 Bayview Ave.
Toronto, ON M4G 3B5 Canada
416-485-9110
Fax: 416-485-0330
MICR: 04812-010

Toronto - Bayview Ave.
Bayview Village Centre
2901 Bayview Ave.
Toronto, ON M2K 1E6 Canada
416-224-1491
Fax: 416-224-5466
MICR: 02712-010

Toronto - Bloor St. West
1129 Bloor St. West
Toronto, ON M6H 1M7 Canada
416-533-1565
Fax: 416-533-0617
MICR: 01902-010

Toronto - Bloor St. West
892 Bloor St. West
Toronto, ON M6H 1L1 Canada
416-534-6492
Fax: 416-534-8486
MICR: 01802-010

Toronto - Bloor St. West
2219 Bloor St. West
Toronto, ON M6S 1N5 Canada
416-763-5124
Fax: 416-763-8807
MICR: 09622-010

Toronto - Bloor St. West
2990 Bloor St. West
Toronto, ON M8X 1B9 Canada
416-239-1200
Fax: 416-239-9280
MICR: 07722-010

Toronto - Bloor St. West
2 Bloor St. West
Toronto, ON M4W 2G7 Canada
416-980-4430
Fax: 416-980-3884
MICR: 00502-010

Toronto - Bloor St. West.
532 Bloor St. West
Toronto, ON M5S 1Y3 Canada
416-535-6625
Fax: 416-535-3902
MICR: 03702-010

Toronto - Brimley Rd.
2359 Brimley Rd.
Toronto, ON M1S 3L6 Canada
416-291-4023
Fax: 416-291-4527
MICR: 06532-010

Toronto - Burnhamthorpe Rd.
Burnhamthorpe Mall
666 Burnhamthorpe Rd.
Toronto, ON M9C 2Z4 Canada
416-621-1929
Fax: 416-621-1353
MICR: 07522-010

Toronto - Carlton St.
245 Carlton St.
Toronto, ON M5A 2L2 Canada
416-980-6179
Fax: 416-861-5119
MICR: 04802-010

Toronto - Church St.
436 Church St.
Toronto, ON M5B 2A4 Canada
416-980-2280
Fax: 416-861-5281
MICR: 04502-010

Toronto - College St.
641 College St.
Toronto, ON M6G 1B5 Canada
416-535-2538
Fax: 416-861-3237
MICR: 08902-010

Toronto - College St.
268 College St.
Toronto, ON M5T 1S1 Canada
416-861-3730
Fax: 416-980-6470
MICR: 00402-010

Toronto - Danforth Ave.
90 Danforth Ave.
Toronto, ON M4K 1N1 Canada
416-463-5624
Fax: 416-463-7672
MICR: 03602-010

Toronto - Danforth Ave.
557 Danforth Ave.
Toronto, ON M4K 1P7 Canada
416-461-2450
Fax: 416-461-1296
MICR: 03902-010

Toronto - Danforth Ave.
1586 Danforth Ave.
Toronto, ON M4C 1H6 Canada
416-461-7383
Fax: 416-461-6589
MICR: 00532-010

Toronto - Danforth Ave.
3003 Danforth Ave.
Toronto, ON M4C 1M9 Canada
416-698-7583
Fax: 416-698-7144
MICR: 07932-010

Toronto - Danforth Ave.
2083 Danforth Ave.
Toronto, ON M4C 1K1 Canada
416-638-3179
Fax: 416-698-8753
MICR: 00732-010

Toronto - Danforth Rd.
450 Danforth Rd.
Toronto, ON M1K 1C6 Canada
416-698-5983
Fax: 416-698-6608
MICR: 00432-010

Toronto - Don Mills Rd.
3931 Don Mills Rd.
Toronto, ON M2H 2S7 Canada
416-491-7669
Fax: 416-491-5309
MICR: 04532-010

Toronto - Dufferin St.
2866 Dufferin St.
Toronto, ON M6B 3S6 Canada
416-781-5610
Fax: 416-781-1527
MICR: 00312-010

Toronto - Dufferin St.
3303 Dufferin St.
Toronto, ON M6A 2T7 Canada
416-789-7246
Fax: 416-789-9548
MICR: 01912-010

Toronto - Dundas St. West
2340 Dundas St. West
Toronto, ON M6P 4A9 Canada
416-535-6080
Fax: 416-535-9821
MICR: 06022-010

Toronto - Dundas St. West
4914 Dundas St. West
Toronto, ON M9A 1B5 Canada
416-231-2850
Fax: 416-231-8433
MICR: 04622-010

Toronto - Dundas St. West
483 Dundas St. West
Toronto, ON M5T 1H1 Canada
416-980-8594
Fax: 416-980-6986
M!CR: 04612-010

Toronto - Eglinton Ave. East
660 Eglinton Ave. East
Toronto, ON M4G 2K2 Canada
416-485-6671
Fax: 416-485-6996
MICR: 02012-010

Toronto - Eglinton Ave. East
2705 Eglinton Ave. East
Toronto, ON M1K 2S2 Canada
416-266-5314
Fax: 416-266-6624
MICR: 01032-010

Toronto - Eglinton Ave. East
1 Eglinton Ave. East
Toronto, ON M4P 3A1 Canada
416-980-4655
Fax: 416-980-8660
MICR: 00212-010

Toronto - Eglinton Ave. West
1150 Eglinton Ave. West
Toronto, ON M6C 2E2 Canada
416-781-5240
Fax: 416-781-8441
MICR: 05012-010

Toronto - Eglinton Ave. West
West Side Mall
2400 Eglinton Ave. West
Toronto, ON M6M 1S6 Canada
416-651-5244
Fax: 416-651-3999
MICR: 03422-010

Toronto - Ellesmere Rd.
1100 Ellesmere Rd.
Toronto, ON M1P 2X3 Canada
416-291-8588
Fax: 416-291-6317
MICR: 01732-010

Toronto - Ellesmere Rd.
2870 Ellesmere Rd.
Toronto, ON M1E 4B8 Canada
416-284-0471
Fax: 416-284-7935
MICR: 07632-010

Toronto - Ellesmere Rd.
1575 Ellesmere Rd.
Toronto, ON M1P 2Y3 Canada
416-438-6563
Fax: 416-438-7521
MICR: 05732-010

Toronto - Finch Ave. East
3420 Finch Ave. East
Toronto, ON M1W 2R6 Canada
416-499-2382
Fax: 416-499-9929
MICR: 09532-010

Toronto - Finch Ave. West
2340 Finch Ave. West
Toronto, ON M9M 2C7 Canada
416-749-6062
Fax: 416-749-5891
MICR: 04322-010

Toronto - Gerrard St. East
Gerrard Square
1000 Gerrard St. East
Toronto, ON M4M 3G6 Canada
416-466-1147
Fax: 416-466-5518
MICR: 01702-010

Toronto - Guildwood Pkwy.
95 Guildwood Pkwy.
Toronto, ON M1E 1P1 Canada
416-267-6602
Fax: 416-267-0993
MICR: 06932-010

Toronto - Humber College Blvd.

Etobicoke General Hospital
89 Humber College Blvd.
Toronto, ON M9V 4B8 Canada
416-749-4116
Fax: 416-744-0508
MICR: 01122-010

Toronto - Islington Ave.
1500 Islington Ave.
Toronto, ON M9A 3L8 Canada
416-239-3097
Fax: 416-239-0442
MICR: 02822-010

Toronto - Islington Ave.
2973 Islington Ave.
Toronto, ON M9L 2K7 Canada
416-749-0416
Fax: 416-749-6637
MICR: 05422-010

Toronto - Jane St.
3863 Jane St.
Toronto, ON M3N 2K1 Canada
416-630-2047
Fax: 416-638-1708
MICR: 07422-010

Toronto - Jane St.
2516 Jane St.
Toronto, ON M3L 1S1 Canada
416-742-4807
Fax: 416-742-6109
MICR: 05522-010

Toronto - Keele St.
3940 Keele St.
Toronto, ON M3J 1P2 Canada
416-661-6014
Fax: 416-661-2634
MICR: 09522-010

Toronto - Keele St.
3324 Keele St.
Toronto, ON M3M 2H7 Canada
416-630-0953
Fax: 416-631-7341
MICR: 05322-010

Toronto - King St. West
1200 King St. West
Toronto, ON M6K 1G4 Canada
416-531-4693
Fax: 416-531-3050
MICR: 08802-010

Toronto - Kingston Rd.
915 Kingston Rd.
Toronto, ON M4E 1S4 Canada
416-694-0144
Fax: 416-694-3087
MICR: 02032-010

Toronto - Kingston Rd.
2973 Kingston Rd.
Toronto, ON M1M 1P1 Canada
416-261-0915
Fax: 416-261-0344
MICR: 08932-010

Toronto - Kingston Rd.
2472 Kingston Rd.
Toronto, ON M1N 1V3 Canada
416-266-4261
Fax: 416-266-7630
MICR: 03032-010

Toronto - Kipling Ave.
2291 Kipling Ave.
Toronto, ON M9W 4L6 Canada
416-742-8081
Fax: 416-742-5909
MICR: 01922-010

Toronto - Laird Dr.
180 Laird Dr.
Toronto, ON M4G 3V7 Canada
416-421-3845
Fax: 416-421-0486
MICR: 00612-010

Toronto - Lakeshore Blvd. West
2935 Lakeshore Blvd. West
Toronto, ON M8V 1J5 Canada
416-251-3794
Fax: 416-251-2536
MICR: 00222-010

Toronto - Lawrence Ave. East
Cedarbrae Mall
3453 Lawrence Ave. East
Toronto, ON M1H 1B2 Canada
416-431-1849
Fax: 416-431-1925
MICR: 03932-010

Toronto - Lawrence Ave. East
939 Lawrence Ave. East
Toronto, ON M3C 1P9 Canada
416-445-6862
Fax: 416-445-3574
MICR: 00132-010

Toronto - Lawrence Ave. East
2300 Lawrence Ave. East
Toronto, ON M1P 2R3 Canada
416-759-1044
Fax: 416-759-9031
MICR: 02932-010

Toronto - Lawrence Ave. West
504 Lawrence Ave. West
Toronto, ON M6A 1A1 Canada
416-789-5357
Fax: 416-789-9535
MICR: 07012-010

Toronto - Lawrence Ave. West
1400 Lawrence Ave. West
Toronto, ON M6L 1A7 Canada
416-235-2387
Fax: 416-235-2425
MICR: 02622-010

Toronto - Lebovic Ave.
Eglinton Town Centre
2 Lebovic Ave.
Toronto, ON M1L 4V9 Canada
416-757-6780
Fax: 416-757-2264
MICR: 08732-010

Toronto - Leslie St.
1865 Leslie St.
Toronto, ON M3B 2M4 Canada
416-447-4397
Fax: 416-447-7632
MICR: 04712-010

Toronto - Lloyd Manor Rd.
201 Lloyd Manor Rd.
Toronto, ON M9B 6H6 Canada
416-233-3316
Fax: 416-233-1409
MICR: 02122-010

Toronto - Montezuma Trail
141 Montezuma Trail
Toronto, ON M1V 1K4 Canada
416-291-7960
Fax: 416-291-7917
MICR: 08532-010

Toronto - Morningside Ave.
Morningside Mall
255 Morningside Ave.
Toronto, ON M1E 3E6 Canada
416-284-6142
Fax: 416-284-7774
MICR: 06832-010

Toronto - Oakwood Ave.
364 Oakwood Ave.
Toronto, ON M6E 2W2 Canada
416-651-5548
Fax: 416-651-3150
MICR: 08012-010

Toronto - Old Kingston Rd.
371 Old Kingston Rd.
Toronto, ON M1C 1B7 Canada
416-282-1477
Fax: 416-282-6485
MICR: 00832-010

Toronto - Ossington Ave.
235 Ossington Ave.
Toronto, ON M6J 2Z8 Canada
416-588-3478
Fax: 416-588-5957
MICR: 07102-010

Toronto - Pape Ave.
1037 Pape Ave.
Toronto, ON M4K 3W1 Canada
416-425-6013
Fax: 416-425-9023
MICR: 08402-010

Toronto - Queen St. East
1 Queen St. East
Toronto, ON M5C 2W5 Canada
416-980-3085
Fax: 416-980-5765
MICR: 00902-010

Toronto - Queen St. West
378 Queen St. West
Toronto, ON M5V 2A2 Canada
416-980-6911
Fax: 416-971-8482
MICR: 01002-010

Toronto - Queen St. West
205 Queen St. West
Toronto, ON M5V 1Z5 Canada
416-861-3735
Fax: 416-980-4471
MICR: 00602-010

Toronto - Queen St. West
378 Queen St. West
Toronto, ON M5V 2A2 Canada
416-980-6911
Fax: 416-971-8482
MICR: 01002-010

Toronto - Ravel Rd.
143 Ravel Rd.
Toronto, ON M2H 1T1 Canada
416-493-4538
Fax: 416-493-5087
MICR: 07712-010

Toronto - Rexdale Blvd.
136 Rexdale Blvd.
Toronto, ON M9W 1P6 Canada
416-743-8292
Fax: 416-743-7736
MICR: 05022-010

Toronto - Rexdale Blvd.
291 Rexdale Blvd.
Toronto, ON M9W 1R8 Canada
416-743-4223
Fax: 416-743-1745
MICR: 05922-010

Toronto - Roncesvalles Ave.
209 Roncesvalles Ave.
Toronto, ON M6R 2L5 Canada
416-533-1713
Fax: 416-533-6153
MICR: 01822-010

Toronto - Royal York Rd.
1500 Royal York Rd.
Toronto, ON M9P 3B6 Canada
416-249-5013
Fax: 416-249-3947
MICR: 04522-010

Toronto - St. Clair Ave. West
2161 St. Clair Ave. West
Toronto, ON M6N 1K5 Canada
416-762-7522
Fax: 416-762-3266
MICR: 00822-010

Toronto - St. Clair Ave. West
1164 St. Clair Ave. West
Toronto, ON M6E 1B3 Canada
416-652-1152
Fax: 416-658-5932
MICR: 07602-010

Toronto - St. Clair Ave. West
535 St. Clair Ave. West
Toronto, ON M6C 1A3 Canada
416-653-1791
Fax: 416-653-7665
MICR: 02802-010

Toronto - St. Clair Ave. West
1 St. Clair Ave. West
Toronto, ON M4V 1K7 Canada
416-980-4170
Fax: 416-861-5603
MICR: 00112-010

Toronto - The Queensway
Queensway & Atomic Banking Centre
#1580, 1582 The Queensway
Toronto, ON M8Z 1V1 Canada
416-255-4483
Fax: 416-259-4109

Canadian Imperial Bank of Commerce(CIBC)/ Banque Canadienne Impériale de Commerce (continued)

MICR: 00322-010
Toronto - Toronto St.
1 Toronto St.
Toronto, ON M5C 2V6 Canada
416-980-2772
Fax: 416-980-5764
MICR: 00302-010
Toronto - University Ave.
100 University Ave.
Toronto, ON M5J 1V6 Canada
416-980-3580
Fax: 416-980-4629
MICR: 04902-010
Toronto - University Ave.
460 University Ave.
Toronto, ON M5G 1V1 Canada
416-980-2260
Fax: 416-980-2528
MICR: 04702-010
Tottenham
PO Box 550
55 Queen St. South
Tottenham, ON L0G 1W0 Canada
905-936-4228
Fax: 905-936-3176
MICR: 04452-010
Trail
1298 Bay Ave.
Trail, BC V1R 4A6 Canada
250-368-2100
Fax: 250-368-2110
MICR: 00070-010
Treherne
PO Box 10
Railway Ave. & Broadway St.
Treherne, MB R0G 2V0 Canada
204-723-2407
Fax: 204-723-2469
MICR: 00557-010
Trenton
91 Dundas St. West
Trenton, ON K8V 3P4 Canada
613-394-3364
Fax: 613-394-2819
MICR: 07042-010
Trois-Rivières - Forges
379, rue des Forges
Trois-Rivières, QC G9A 2H4 Canada
819-374-4685
Fax: 819-379-3079
MICR: 00081-010
Trois-Rivières - Récollets
#540, 4520, boul des Récollets
Trois-Rivières, QC G9A 4N2 Canada
819-375-7779
Fax: 819-375-6724
MICR: 00781-010
Truro
813 Prince St.
Truro, NS B2N 1G7 Canada
902-895-5341
Fax: 902-893-1712
MICR: 00043-010
Turtleford
PO Box 70
225 Main St.
Turtleford, SK S0M 2Y0 Canada
306-845-2066
Fax: 306-845-2733
MICR: 00488-010
Tweed
PO Box 460
256 Victoria St. North
Tweed, ON K0K 3J0 Canada
613-478-2145
Fax: 613-478-1252
MICR: 03342-010
Ucluelet
PO Box 160
212 Main St.
Ucluelet, BC V0R 3A0 Canada
250-726-7701
Fax: 250-726-7619
MICR: 02040-010
Unionville
4360 Hwy. 7
Unionville, ON L3R 1L9 Canada
905-477-2540
Fax: 905-477-8397
MICR: 01642-010
Unity
PO Box 509
210 Main St.
Unity, SK S0K 4L0 Canada
306-228-2652
Fax: 306-228-2515
MICR: 00668-010
Uxbridge
PO Box 220
49 Brock St. West
Uxbridge, ON L9P 1M7 Canada
905-852-3347
Fax: 905-852-4659
MICR: 05542-010
Val Caron
2975 Hwy. 69 North
Val Caron, ON P3N 1E1 Canada
705-897-1080
Fax: 705-897-1083
MICR: 04192-010
Val-d'Or
824, 3e av
Val-d'Or, QC J9P 1T1 Canada
819-825-8830
Fax: 819-825-1427
MICR: 00191-010
Valemount
PO Box 160
1221 - 5th Ave.
Valemount, BC V0E 2Z0 Canada
250-566-4483
Fax: 250-566-9703
MICR: 08050-010
Vancouver - Burrard St.
Commerce Place
400 Burrard St.
Vancouver, BC V6C 3A6 Canada
604-665-1645
Fax: 604-665-1225
MICR: 00010-010
Vancouver - Cambie St.
5710 Cambie St.
Vancouver, BC V5Z 3A6 Canada
604-665-1511
Fax: 604-665-1580
MICR: 01910-010
Vancouver - Dunbar St.
4306 Dunbar St.
Vancouver, BC V6S 2G3 Canada
604-665-7697
Fax: 604-665-7612
MICR: 06010-010
Vancouver - East Broadway
1704 East Broadway
Vancouver, BC V5N 1W3 Canada
604-665-1894
Fax: 604-665-1823
MICR: 04700-010
Vancouver - East Hastings St.
2602 East Hastings St.
Vancouver, BC V5K 1Z6 Canada
604-665-6860
Fax: 604-665-6885
MICR: 03010-010
Vancouver - Fraser St.
6204 Fraser St.
Vancouver, BC V5W 3A1 Canada
604-482-2625
Fax: 604-327-5964
MICR: 00810-010
Vancouver - Grandview Hwy.
2890 Grandview Hwy.
Vancouver, BC V5M 2C9 Canada
604-665-1672
Fax: 604-665-1680
MICR: 03800-010
Vancouver - Granville St.
2904 Granville St.
Vancouver, BC V6H 3J7 Canada
604-665-7606
Fax: 604-665-7609
MICR: 03000-010
Vancouver - Granville St.
8450 Granville St.
Vancouver, BC V6P 4Z7 Canada
604-257-1120
Fax: 604-266-3652
MICR: 01010-010
Vancouver - Kingsway
3298 Kingsway
Vancouver, BC V5R 2K4 Canada
604-665-1288
Fax: 604-665-7695
MICR: 00910-010
Vancouver - Kingsway
1427 Kingsway
Vancouver, BC V5N 2R6 Canada
604-665-1089
Fax: 604-665-1023
MICR: 00600-010
Vancouver - Main St.
#1/F, 501 Main St.
Vancouver, BC V6A 2V2 Canada
604-665-2071
Fax: 604-665-2915
MICR: 00710-010
Vancouver - Main St.
4493 Main St.
Vancouver, BC V5V 3R2 Canada
604-665-7607
Fax: 604-665-7608
MICR: 06810-010
Vancouver - University Blvd.
5796 University Blvd.
Vancouver, BC V6T 1K6 Canada
604-221-3550
Fax: 604-224-5781
MICR: 05800-010
Vancouver - Victoria Dr.
5705 Victoria Dr.
Vancouver, BC V5P 3W2 Canada
604-482-2697
Fax: 604-325-4665
MICR: 08010-010
Vancouver - Victoria Dr.
High Value Centre
5653 Victoria Dr.
Vancouver, BC V5P 3W2 Canada
604-482-2667
Fax: 604-321-1852
MICR: 07610-010
Vancouver - West 10th Ave.
4489 West 10th Ave.
Vancouver, BC V6R 2H8 Canada
604-221-3535
Fax: 604-224-6293
MICR: 04810-010
Vancouver - West 41st Ave.
Kerrisdale Banking Centre
2288 West 41st Ave.
Vancouver, BC V6M 1Z8 Canada
604-257-1177
Fax: 604-263-7264
MICR: 06000-010
Vancouver - West Broadway
2896 West Broadway
Vancouver, BC V6K 2G7 Canada
604-665-6191
Fax: 604-665-1842
MICR: 04010-010
Vancouver - West Broadway
796 West Broadway
Vancouver, BC V5Z 1G8 Canada
604-665-2995
Fax: 604-665-1829
MICR: 02800-010
Vancouver - West Georgia St.
1036 West Georgia St.
Vancouver, BC V6E 3C7 Canada
604-665-1472
Fax: 604-665-1499
MICR: 00500-010
Vanderhoof

PO Box 130
2391 Burrard St.
Vanderhoof, BC V0J 3A0 Canada
250-567-2241
Fax: 250-567-4390
MICR: 00450-010
Vaudreuil-Dorion
Centre D'achat Vaudreuil
2555, rue Dutrisac
Vaudreuil-Dorion, QC J7V 7E6 Canada
450-424-0131
Fax: 450-424-0729
MICR: 03981-010
Vaughan - Hwy. 27
8535 Hwy. 27, RR#3
Vaughan, ON L4L 1A7 Canada
905-264-6184
Fax: 905-264-6504
MICR: 06132-010
Vaughan - Steeles Ave. West
800 Steeles Ave. West
Vaughan, ON L4J 7L2 Canada
905-660-3476
Fax: 905-660-9546
MICR: 06312-010
Vauxhall
PO Box 389
426 - 2nd Ave. North
Vauxhall, AB T0K 2K0 Canada
403-654-2123
Fax: 403-654-4041
MICR: 01049-010
Vegreville
PO Box 1410
4826 - 50th St.
Vegreville, AB T9C 1S6 Canada
780-632-2868
Fax: 780-632-4666
MICR: 02979-010
Vermillon
4940 - 50th Ave.
Vermilion, AB T9X 1A4 Canada
780-853-5351
Fax: 780-853-5987
MICR: 00179-010
Vernon - 27th St.
Village Green Mall
#234, 4900 - 27th St.
Vernon, BC V1T 7G7 Canada
250-260-6310
Fax: 250-545-9833
MICR: 08060-010
Vernon - 30th Ave.
3201 - 30th Ave.
Vernon, BC V1T 2C6 Canada
250-260-6300
Fax: 250-549-4948
MICR: 00260-010
Victoria - Douglas St.
1175 Douglas St.
Victoria, BC V8W 2E1 Canada
250-356-4439
Fax: 250-356-4372
MICR: 00090-010
Victoria - Douglas St.
Mayfair Shopping Centre
#326, 3147 Douglas St.
Victoria, BC V8Z 6E3 Canada
250-356-4262
Fax: 250-356-4363
MICR: 05030-010
Victoria - Goldstream Ave.
#9, 310 Goldstream Ave.
Victoria, BC V9B 2W3 Canada
250-391-2190
Fax: 250-478-5441
MICR: 00430-010
Victoria - Hillside Ave.
Hillside Centre
#29, 1644 Hillside Ave.
Victoria, BC V8T 2C5 Canada
250-356-4238
Fax: 250-356-4332
MICR: 00930-010
Victoria - Oak Bay Ave.
2224 Oak Bay Ave.
Victoria, BC V8R 1G5 Canada
250-356-4335
Fax: 250-356-4390
MICR: 00630-010
Victoria - Shelbourne St.
3970 Shelbourne St.
Victoria, BC V8N 3E2 Canada
250-356-4467
Fax: 250-356-4478
MICR: 04930-010
Victoria - Tillicum Rd.
2925 Tillicum Rd.
Victoria, BC V9A 2A6 Canada
250-356-4451
Fax: 250-356-4380
MICR: 02930-010
Victoriaville - Perreault
21, rue Perreault
Victoriaville, QC G6P 8H1 Canada
819-758-8216
Fax: 819-758-9556
MICR: 01771-010
Vineland
Heritage Village
4100 Victoria Ave.
Vineland, ON L0R 2C0 Canada
905-562-3127
Fax: 905-562-4751
MICR: 05172-010
Virden
PO Box 1000
204 Nelson St.
Virden, MB R0M 2C0 Canada
204-748-1236
Fax: 204-748-1050
MICR: 00047-010
Vulcan
PO Box 179
205 Centre St.
Vulcan, AB T0L 2B0 Canada
403-485-2201
Fax: 403-485-2385
MICR: 00739-010
Wadena
PO Box 250
98 Main St. North
Wadena, SK S0A 4J0 Canada
306-338-2501
Fax: 306-338-2303
MICR: 00258-010
Walkerton
PO Box 1450
302 Durham St. East
Walkerton, ON N0G 2V0 Canada
519-881-3380
Fax: 519-881-2491
MICR: 06652-010
Wallaceburg
802 Dufferin Ave. East
Wallaceburg, ON N8A 2V3 Canada
519-627-0741
Fax: 519-627-0927
MICR: 08782-010
Waterdown
PO Box 680
9 Hamilton St. North
Waterdown, ON L0R 2H0 Canada
905-689-6685
Fax: 905-689-2766
MICR: 01762-010
Waterloo
PO Box 380
5457, rue Foster
Waterloo, QC J0E 2N0 Canada
450-539-2567
Fax: 450-539-4780
MICR: 00761-010
Waterloo - King St. North
Conestoga Mall
550 King St. North
Waterloo, ON N2L 5W6 Canada
519-884-9230
Fax: 519-884-1050
MICR: 04252-010
Waterloo - King St. North
PO Box 97
27 King St. North
Waterloo, ON N2J 3Z6 Canada
519-886-2960
Fax: 519-746-2708
MICR: 00452-010
Waterloo - Lincoln Rd.
315 Lincoln Rd.
Waterloo, ON N2J 4H7 Canada
519-884-9290
Fax: 519-884-2273
MICR: 05452-010
Waterloo - University Ave.
Campus Centre Bldg.
PO Box 112
200 University Ave.
Waterloo, ON N2L 3G0 Canada
519-884-4760
Fax: 519-884-8880
MICR: 06552-010
Waterville
PO Box 15
168, rue Principale sud
Waterville, QC J0B 3H0 Canada
819-837-2474
Fax: 819-837-2001
MICR: 02071-010
Watson
PO Box 40
106 Main St.
Watson, SK S0K 4V0 Canada
306-287-3797
Fax: 306-287-3560
MICR: 00288-010
Watson Lake
PO Box 99
Watson Lake, YT Y0A 1C0 Canada
867-536-7495
Fax: 867-536-7412
MICR: 00680-010
Welland - Fitch St.
Welland Plaza
200 Fitch St.
Welland, ON L3C 4V9 Canada
905-735-1450
Fax: 905-735-6160
MICR: 03472-010
Welland - King St.
22 King St.
Welland, ON L3B 3H2 Canada
905-735-5653
Fax: 905-732-1463
MICR: 00872-010
Welland - Niagara St.
Seaway Mall
800 Niagara St.
Welland, ON L3C 5Z4 Canada
905-735-7744
Fax: 905-735-6354
MICR: 02372-010
Wellesley
PO Box 220
1207 Queens Bush Rd.
Wellesley, ON N0B 2T0 Canada
519-656-2070
Fax: 519-656-3375
MICR: 09852-010
West Vancouver - 17th St.
225 - 17th St.
West Vancouver, BC V7V 4T1 Canada
604-981-2528
Fax: 604-981-2521
MICR: 08910-010
West Vancouver - Park Royal South
Park Royal Shopping Centre
1031 Park Royal South
West Vancouver, BC V7T 1A1 Canada
604-981-2558
Fax: 604-981-2550
MICR: 08410-010
Westbank
PO Box 26016
Hwy. 97 South & Elliott Rd.
Westbank, BC V4T 2G3 Canada

Canadian Imperial Bank of Commerce(CIBC)/ Banque Canadienne Impériale de Commerce (continued)

250-768-5138
Fax: 250-768-5129
MICR: 09060-010

Wetaskiwin
5213 - 50th Ave.
Wetaskiwin, AB T9A 0S7 Canada
780-352-3355
Fax: 780-361-5315
MICR: 00089-010

Weyburn
PO Box 310
76 - 3rd St. NE
Weyburn, SK S4H 2K1 Canada
306-848-3737
Fax: 306-842-6333
MICR: 00098-010

Whitby - Brock St. North
PO Box 87
101 Brock St. North
Whitby, ON L1N 5R7 Canada
905-668-3352
Fax: 905-668-2033
MICR: 03042-010

Whitby - Garden St.
3050 Garden St.
Whitby, ON L1R 2G7 Canada
905-666-2237
Fax: 905-666-4445
MICR: 00892-010

Whitby - Thickson Rd. South
80 Thickson Rd. South
Whitby, ON L1N 7T2 Canada
905-430-1801
Fax: 905-430-1896
MICR: 07342-010

White Rock
15177 North Bluff Rd.
White Rock, BC V4A 6G3 Canada
604-541-4525
Fax: 604-541-4507
MICR: 02920-010

Whitecourt
PO Box 507
5103 - 50th St.
Whitecourt, AB T7S 1N6 Canada
780-778-2268
Fax: 780-778-5310
MICR: 00779-010

Whitehorse
110 Main St.
Whitehorse, YT Y1A 2A8 Canada
867-667-2534
Fax: 867-668-2995
MICR: 00080-010

Wilkie
PO Box 819
37 Main St.
Wilkie, SK SOK 4W0 Canada
306-843-2255
Fax: 306-843-2077
MICR: 00348-010

Williams Lake
220 Oliver St.
Williams Lake, BC V2G 1M1 Canada
250-392-2351
Fax: 250-392-5351
MICR: 00150-010

Windsor
PO Box 39
66 Gerrish St.
Windsor, NS B0N 2T0 Canada
902-798-5786
Fax: 902-798-3786
MICR: 00233-010

Windsor
85, rue Principal nord
Windsor, QC J1S 2C5 Canada
819-845-2726
Fax: 819-845-5929
MICR: 00161-010

Windsor - Devonshire Rd.
415 Devonshire Rd.
Windsor, ON N8Y 2L5 Canada
519-254-5191
Fax: 519-254-5743
MICR: 00382-010

Windsor - Dougall Ave.
Gateway Plaza
3168 Dougall Ave.
Windsor, ON N9E 1S6 Canada
519-969-8720
Fax: 519-969-2494
MICR: 03782-010

Windsor - Howard Ave.
Devonshire Shopping Centre
3100 Howard Ave.
Windsor, ON N8X 3Y8 Canada
519-969-5932
Fax: 519-969-5025
MICR: 05382-010

Windsor - Huron Church Rd.
1550 Huron Church Rd.
Windsor, ON N9C 3Z3 Canada
519-252-4463
Fax: 519-252-7064
MICR: 06582-010

Windsor - Malden Rd.
5870 Malden Rd.
Windsor, ON N9H 1S4 Canada
519-969-3712
Fax: 519-969-4942
MICR: 06382-010

Windsor - Ottawa St.
1395 Ottawa St.
Windsor, ON N8X 2E9 Canada
519-256-3441
Fax: 519-256-6830
MICR: 00682-010

Windsor - Ouellette Ave.
PO Box 180
100 Ouellette Ave.
Windsor, ON N9A 6K5 Canada
519-977-7000
Fax: 519-977-7411
MICR: 00182-010

Windsor - Tecumseh Rd. East
6800 Tecumseh Rd. East
Windsor, ON N8T 1E6 Canada
519-948-5295
Fax: 519-948-4263
MICR: 07582-010

Windsor - Tecumseh Rd. East
1600 Tecumseh Rd. East
Windsor, ON N8W 1C5 Canada
519-254-9221
Fax: 519-254-0171
MICR: 01082-010

Windsor - Tecumseh Rd. East
710 Tecumseh Rd. East
Windsor, ON N8X 2S2 Canada
519-252-6561
Fax: 519-252-3983
MICR: 09382-010

Windsor - Walker Rd.
3295 Walker Rd.
Windsor, ON N8W 3R7 Canada
519-969-9370
Fax: 519-969-3108
MICR: 02582-010

Windsor - Wyandotte St. East
5690 Wyandotte St. East
Windsor, ON N8S 1M3 Canada
519-944-7300
Fax: 519-944-0130
MICR: 07682-010

Winfield
#6, 10051 Hwy. 97 North
Winfield, BC V4V 1P6 Canada
250-766-2551
Fax: 250-776-2454
MICR: 03060-010

Wingham
PO Box 310
14 Victoria St. East
Wingham, ON N0G 2W0 Canada
519-357-1661
Fax: 519-357-1361
MICR: 05652-010

Winkler
PO Box 1690
309 Main St.
Winkler, MB R6W 4B5 Canada
204-325-4301
Fax: 204-325-2244
MICR: 00177-010

Winnipeg - Empress St.
Empress & Ellice Banking Centre
895 Empress St.
Winnipeg, MB R3G 3P8 Canada
204-944-5868
Fax: 204-944-6984
MICR: 00507-010

Winnipeg - Grant Ave.
Grant Park Shopping Centre
1120 Grant Ave.
Winnipeg, MB R3M 2A6 Canada
204-944-5063
Fax: 204-475-2338
MICR: 01007-010

Winnipeg - Henderson Hwy.
739 Henderson Hwy.
Winnipeg, MB R2K 2K5 Canada
204-944-6999
Fax: 204-667-0917
MICR: 00137-010

Winnipeg - Henderson Hwy.
River East Banking Centre
1433 Henderson Hwy.
Winnipeg, MB R2G 1N3 Canada
204-944-6415
Fax: 204-334-3887
MICR: 00837-010

Winnipeg - Lakewood Blvd.
Southdale Mall Shopping Centre
35 Lakewood Blvd.
Winnipeg, MB R2J 2M8 Canada
204-944-6525
Fax: 204-254-7363
MICR: 00927-010

Winnipeg - Main St.
1658 Main St.
Winnipeg, MB R2V 1Y9 Canada
204-944-5039
Fax: 204-334-3776
MICR: 00627-010

Winnipeg - Main St.
One Lombard Place
PO Box 814
375 Main St.
Winnipeg, MB R3C 2P3 Canada
204-944-6963
Fax: 204-944-5820
MICR: 00007-010

Winnipeg - Marion St.
119 Marion St.
Winnipeg, MB R2H 0T2 Canada
204-944-5027
Fax: 204-235-1186
MICR: 00207-010

Winnipeg - McPhillips St.
Seven Oaks
2260 McPhillips St.
Winnipeg, MB R2V 4W1 Canada
204-944-5042
Fax: 204-944-6878
MICR: 00717-010

Winnipeg - Pembina Hwy.
Fort Richmond Square
#10, 2866 Pembina Hwy.
Winnipeg, MB R3T 2J1 Canada
204-944-5119
Fax: 204-269-4828
MICR: 00807-010

Winnipeg - Pembina Hwy.
1160 Pembina Hwy.
Winnipeg, MB R3T 2A4 Canada
204-944-6578
Fax: 204-287-8721
MICR: 00427-010

Winnipeg - Portage Ave.
3369 Portage Ave.
Winnipeg, MB R3K 0W9 Canada
204-944-6029
Fax: 204-831-6060

MICR: 00917-010
Winnipeg - Regent Ave. West
Crossroads Shopping Centre
1586 Regent Ave. West
Winnipeg, MB R2C 3B4 Canada
204-944-5900
Fax: 204-663-8966
MICR: 00937-010
Winnipeg - Roblin Blvd.
3408 Roblin Blvd.
Winnipeg, MB R3R 0C7 Canada
204-944-6557
Fax: 204-837-3720
MICR: 02007-010
Winnipeg - St. Mary Ave.
CityPlace
#87, 333 St. Mary Ave.
Winnipeg, MB R3C 4A5 Canada
204-944-5057
Fax: 204-942-4735
MICR: 00107-010
Winnipeg - St. Mary's Rd.
St. Vital Centre
1545 St. Mary's Rd.
Winnipeg, MB R2M 3V8 Canada
204-944-6803
Fax: 204-254-1621
MICR: 04007-010
Woodbridge
Piazza del Sole Banking Centre
#2, 7850 Weston Rd.
Woodbridge, ON L4L 9N8 Canada
905-851-7003
Fax: 905-851-7213
MICR: 08152-010
Woodstock - Connell St.
Carleton Shopping Mall
#5, 370 Connell St.
Woodstock, NB E7M 5G9 Canada
506-328-8858
Fax: 506-328-2365
MICR: 00494-010
Woodstock - Dundas St.
656 Dundas St.
Woodstock, ON N4S 1E3 Canada
519-537-5544
Fax: 519-537-6915
MICR: 04752-010
Woodstock - Dundas St.
PO Box 305
441 Dundas St.
Woodstock, ON N4S 7X6 Canada
519-537-6221
Fax: 519-537-3147
MICR: 00852-010
Yarmouth
PO Box 68
317 Main St.
Yarmouth, NS B5A 4B1 Canada
902-742-7855
Fax: 902-749-2130
MICR: 00243-010
Yellowknife
PO Box 430
5001 - 50th Ave.
Yellowknife, NT X1A 2N3 Canada
867-873-4452
Fax: 867-873-4730
MICR: 02099-010
Yorkton
PO Box 939
30 Second Ave. North
Yorkton, SK S3N 2X1 Canada
306-782-2408
Fax: 306-782-2044
MICR: 00898-010
×le-Perrot
#145, 25, boul Don Quichotte
×le-Perrot, QC J7V 7X4 Canada
514-453-2828
Fax: 514-453-8591
MICR: 04201-010

Canadian Tire Financial Services Ltd.(CTAL)

Also listed under: *Financial Planning*

PO Box 2000
Welland, ON L3B 5S3
905-735-3131
Fax: 905-735-8962
800-464-9166
www.ctfs.com
Ownership: Wholly owned subsidiary of Canadian Tire Corporation Limited
Year Founded: 1966
Number of Employees: 1,300
Profile: Canadian Tire Financial Services offers a variety of financial products, primarily branded credit cards, that give Canadian Tire customers a choice of payment options, as well as increased loyalty rewards.

Executives:
Tom Gauld, President
Mary Turner, Vice-President, Customer Service & Operations

Canadian Western Bank(CWB)/ Banque Canadienne de l'Ouest

#2300, 10303 Jasper Ave.
Edmonton, AB T5J 3X6
780-423-8888
Fax: 780-423-8897
comments@cwbank.com
www.cwbank.com
Also Known As: Canada's Western Bank
Ownership: Widely held Canadian corporation
Year Founded: 1984
Number of Employees: 1,000
Assets: $1-10 billion Year End: 20041031
Revenues: $100-500 million Year End: 20041031
Stock Symbol: CWB
Profile: Canadian Western Bank offers financial services, loan arrangements & features on deposit products. Its trust arm, Canadian Western Trust, specializes in the administration of self-directed retirement products & offers deposit & mortgage lending services. Canadian Western Bank is the largest Schedule 1 chartered bank headquartered in & regionally focused on Western Canada.

Executives:
Larry M. Pollock, President/CEO
Tracey C. Ball, CA, CFO & Exec. Vice-President
William J. Addington, Exec. Vice-President
Donald C. Kemp, Sr. Vice-President
Jack C. Wright, Sr. Vice-President
William A. Book, Vice-President, Northern Alberta Region
David R. Gillespie, Vice-President & Chief Inspector, Internal Auditor
Michael Halliwell, Vice-President & Regional Manager, Prairies
Gail Harding, Vice-President, General Counsel & Corporate Secretary
David R. Pogue, Vice-President, Corporate Development
Raymond L. Young, Vice-President, Real Estate Lending
R. Graham Gilbert, Ombudsman
Directors:
Jack C. Donald, Chair
Charles R. Allard
Albrecht W.A. Bellstedt
Partner, Milner Fenerty
Jordan L. Golding
Allan W. Jackson
Wendy A. Leaney
Robert A. Manning
President, Cathton Holding Ltd.
Gerald A.B. McGavin
Howard E. Pechet
President, Mayfield Investments Ltd.
Robert L. Phillips
Larry M. Pollock
Alan M. Rowe
Sr. Vice-President & CFO, Crown Life Insurance Company
Arnold Shell
Affiliated Companies:
Canadian Direct Insurance Incorporated
Canadian Western Trust Co./CWT
Valiant Trust Company
Branches:
Calgary - 32 Ave. NE
2810 - 32 Ave. NE
Calgary, AB T1Y 5J4 Canada
403-250-8838
Glen Eastwood, Manager
Calgary - 4th St. SW
606 - 4th St. SW
Calgary, AB T2P 1T1 Canada
403-262-8700
MICR: 03039-030
Doug Crook, Manager
Calgary - Barlow Trail SE
6127 Barlow Trail SE
Calgary, AB T2C 4W8 Canada
403-252-2299
Chris Minke, Manager
Calgary - MacLeod Trail SW
6606 MacLeod Trail SW
Calgary, AB T2H 0K6 Canada
403-269-9882
MICR: 03129-030
Lew Christie, Manager
Coquitlam
#310, 101 Schoolhouse St.
Coquitlam, BC V3K 4X8 Canada
604-540-8829
David McCosh, Manager
Courtenay
#200, 470 Puntledge Rd.
Courtenay, BC V9N 3R1 Canada
250-334-8888
MICR: 00600-030
Alan Dafoe, Manager
Cranbrook
2009 - 5th St. South
Cranbrook, BC V1C 1K6 Canada
250-426-1140
Mike Eckersley, Manager
Edmonton - 100th Ave.
17603 - 100th Ave.
Edmonton, AB T5S 2M1 Canada
780-484-7407
MICR: 03049-030
Kevin MacMillen, Manager
Edmonton - 104 St.
7933 - 104 St.
Edmonton, AB T6E 4C9 Canada
780-433-4286
MICR: 03119-030
Donna Austin, Manager
Edmonton - Jasper Ave.
11350 Jasper Ave.
Edmonton, AB T5K 0L8 Canada
780-424-4846
MICR: 03029-030
Keith Wilkes, Manager
Edmonton - Jasper Ave.
10303 Jasper Ave., Main Fl.
Edmonton, AB T5J 3N6 Canada
780-423-8801
Jake Muntain, Manager
Edmonton - South Commons
2142 - 99 St.
Edmonton, AB T6N 1L2 Canada
780-988-8607
Wayne Dosman, Manager
Grande Prairie
11226 - 100 Ave.
Grande Prairie, AB T8V 7L2 Canada
780-831-1888
David Harvey, Manager
Kelowna - Bertram
1674 Bertram St.
Kelowna, BC V1Y 9G4 Canada
250-862-8008
MICR: 00340-030
Ron Baker, Manager
Kelowna - Harvey Ave.
#101, 1505 Harvey Ave.
Kelowna, BC V1Y 6G1 Canada
250-860-0088
Jim Kitchin, Manager
Langley
#100, 19915 - 64 Ave.
Langley, BC V2Y 1G9 Canada
604-539-5088
Craig Martin, Manager
Lethbridge
744 - 4th Ave. South
Lethbridge, AB T1J 0N8 Canada
403-328-9199

Canadian Western Bank(CWB)/ Banque Canadienne de l'Ouest (continued)

MICR: 03079-030
Donald Grummett, Manager

Nanaimo
#101, 6475 Metral Dr.
Nanaimo, BC V9T 2L9 Canada
250-390-0088
Fax: 250-390-0099
MICR: 00360-030
Russ Burke, Manager

Prince George
300 Victoria St.
Prince George, BC V2L 4X4 Canada
250-612-0123
MICR: 00390-030
David Duck, Manager

Red Deer
4822 - 51 Ave.
Red Deer, AB T4N 4H3 Canada
403-341-4000
MICR: 03059-030
Don Odell, Manager

Regina
McCallum Hill Centre II
#100, 1881 Scarth St.
Regina, SK S4P 4K9 Canada
306-757-8888
MICR: 00418-030
Trent Bobinski, Manager

Saskatoon
244 - 2nd Ave. South
Saskatoon, SK S7K 1K9 Canada
306-477-8888
MICR: 00408-030
Ron Kowalenko, Manager

St. Albert
#300, 700 St. Albert Rd.
St Albert, AB T8N 7A5 Canada
780-458-4001
MICR: 03099-030
Ward Fleming, Manager

Surrey
#1, 7548 - 120 St.
Surrey, BC V3W 3N1 Canada
604-591-1898
Richard Howard, Manager

Vancouver - Burrard St.
#100, 666 Burrard St.
Vancouver, BC V6C 2X8 Canada
604-688-8711
MICR: 00350-030
Rob Berzins, Manager

Vancouver - Burrard St. - Deposit Processing Centre
666 Burrard St., 22nd Fl.
Vancouver, BC V6C 2X8 Canada
604-443-5175
800-663-1000

Vancouver - Burrard St. - Regional Office
666 Burrard St., 22nd Fl.
Vancouver, BC V6C 2X8 Canada
604-669-0081

Vancouver - West Broadway
#110, 1333 West Broadway
Vancouver, BC V6H 4C1 Canada
604-730-8818
MICR: 00370-030
Jules Mihalyi, Manager

Victoria
1201 Douglas St.
Victoria, BC V8W 2E6 Canada
250-383-1206
MICR: 00390-030
Gerry Laliberté, Manager

Winnipeg
230 Portage Ave.
Winnipeg, MB R3C 0B1 Canada
204-956-4669
MICR: 00207-030
Robert Bean, Manager

Yorkton
#45, 277 Broadway St. East
Yorkton, SK S3N 3G7 Canada
306-782-1002
MICR: 00428-030
Barb Apps, Manager

Citizens Bank of Canada

#401, 815 West Hastings St.
Vancouver, BC V6C 1B4
604-682-7171
Fax: 604-708-7790
888-708-7800
service@citizensbank.ca
www.citizensbank.ca
Ownership: Subsidiary of Vancouver City Savings Credit Union
Year Founded: 1997
Number of Employees: 120
Executives:
Ian J. Warner, President/CEO
Directors:
Dave Mowat, Chair
Chris Dobrzanski
Mobina Jaffer
Greg McDade
Essop Mia
Ian Warner
Alexandra Wilson
Roger Woodward
Affiliated Companies:
Citizens Trust Company

Dundee Bank of Canada(DBC)

1 Adelaide St. East, 20th Fl.
Toronto, ON M5C 2V9
Fax: 416-849-1700
866-884-3434
support@dbc.ca
www.dbc.ca
Former Name: Dundee Wealth Bank
Ownership: Member of Dundee Financial Group (DFG), a division of Dundee Wealth Management Inc.
Year Founded: 2006
Profile: The Schedule I bank offers an alternative source of banking services through financial & investment advisors. Services are tailored for use by professional advisors with their clients and include investment savings & cheqing accounts, GICs & mortgages.

Executives:
Greg Reed, President/CEO

First Nations Bank of Canada

224 - 4th Ave. South
Saskatoon, SK S7K 5M5
306-931-2409
Fax: 306-955-6811
888-454-3622
service@firstnationsbank.com
www.firstnationsbank.com
Ownership: Private
Year Founded: 1996
Number of Employees: 35
Assets: $100-500 million Year End: 20051031
Revenues: $5-10 million Year End: 20051031
Executives:
Arden Buskell, President/COO
Cheryl Foster, Treasurer
Directors:
Arden Buskell
Paul Douglas
Christopher D. Dyrda
Urban Joseph
Keith Martell
Bill Namagoose
Kerry A. Peacock
Mark Wedge
Branches:

Chisasibi
General Delivery
Chisasibi, QC J0M 1E0 Canada
819-855-3458
Fax: 819-855-3496
888-825-3458

Wallaceburg - Walpole Island
#1 Thunderbird Plaza
RR#3
Wallaceburg, ON N8A 4K9 Canada
519-627-1657
Fax: 519-627-1432
800-647-7347
Pat Auger, Contact

Whitehorse
200 Main St.
Whitehorse, YT Y1A 2A9 Canada
867-668-8100
Fax: 867-668-4982

Winnipeg
360 Broadway
Winnipeg, MB R3C 0T6 Canada
204-988-1380
Fax: 204-988-1388
866-519-5898
Greg Cox, Manager

General Bank of Canada(GBC)

c/o LeMarchand Mansion
#006, 11523 - 100 Ave.
Edmonton, AB T5K 0J8
780-443-5626
Fax: 780-443-5628
877-443-5620
info@generalbank.ca
www.generalbank.ca
Ownership: Parent company is Firstcan Management Inc.
Year Founded: 2005
Profile: The Schedule I bank's core products are automobile loans & Guaranteed Investment Certificates. General Bank of Canada partners with franchised automotive retailers to bring clients automobile loans. GICs are provided to investors throughout Canada by a network of independent deposit brokers.

Executives:
Gord Mooney, Chief Operating Officer; 780-732-5041
Karen Becker, Chief Financial Officer; 780-732-5042
Marley Begg, Director, Dealer Services; 780-732-5043
Scott Bryant, Sr. Manager, Credit; 780-732-5046

Laurentian Bank of Canada/ Banque Laurentienne du Canada

1981, av McGill College
Montréal, QC H3A 3K3
514-522-1846
Fax: 514-284-3396
800-522-1846
Other Information: Telebanking Service/Customer Services: 1-877-522-1846
courrier@banquelaurentienne.ca
www.laurentianbank.com
Ownership: Public
Year Founded: 1846
Number of Employees: 3,373
Assets: $10-100 billion Year End: 20051031
Revenues: $500m-1 billion Year End: 20051031
Stock Symbol: LB
Profile: The Laurentian Bank offers a full range of financial services to individuals & corporate clients.
Executives:
Raymond McManus, President/CEO; 514-284-7967
Robert Cardinal, Sr. Exec. Vice-President/CFO; 514-284-4500
Bernard Piché, Sr. Exec. Vice-President, Treasury, Capital Markets & Brokerage; 514-284-4500; picheb@blcmf.com
Réjean Robitaille, Sr. Exec. Vice-President/COO; 514-284-4500
Luc Bernard, Exec. Vice-President, Retail Financial Services; 514-284-4500; luc.bernard@banquelaurentienne.ca
François Desjardins, Exec. Vice-President; 416-865-5900
Lorraine Pilon, Exec. Vice-President, Corporate Affairs & Human Resources, Secretary; 514-284-4500
André Scott, Exec. Vice-President, Commercial Financial Services; 514-284-4500; andre.scott@banquelaurentienne.ca

Dana Ades-Landy, Sr. Vice-President, Commerical Banking, Québec (National Accounts); 514-284-4500
Yassir Berbiche, Sr. Vice-President & Treasurer, Corporate Treasury; 514-284-4500
Louise Bourassa, Sr. Vice-President, Administrative Services; 514-284-4500
Denise Brisebois, Sr. Vice-President, Human Resources; 514-284-4500
Philippe Duby, Sr. Vice-President, Real Estate, Chief Information Officer; 514-284-4500; philippe.duby@banquelaurentienne.ca
Paul Hurtubise, Sr. Vice-President, Real Estate Financing; 416-865-5757; paul.hurtubise@laurentianbank.ca
Louis Marquis, Sr. Vice-President, Credit; 514-284-4500; louis.marquis@banquelaurentienne.ca
Pierre Minville, Sr. Vice-President, Integrated Risk Management, Mergers & Acquisitions; 514-284-4500

Marc Paradis, Sr. Vice-President, Strategic Planning & Control; 514-284-4500; marc.paradis2@banquelaurentienne.ca
Marcel Beaulieu, Vice-President, Product Management; 514-284-4500
Jean-François Doyon, Vice-President, Internal Audit & Corporate Security; 514-284-4500
Richard Fabre, Vice-President, Retail Financial Services, North Shore, Downtown Montréal & West of Québec; 514-849-7998; richard.fabre@banquelaurentienne.ca
William Galbraith, Vice-President, Commercial Banking, Ontario; 905-564-7745; william.galbraith@laurentianbank.ca
Mario Galella, Vice-President, Retail Financial Services, North & West Montréal; 514-721-3236; mario.galella@banquelaurentienne.ca
Michel Garneau, Vice-President, Retail Financial Services, Québec, Eastern Québec & Mauricie; 418-692-1489
Michel Gendron, Vice-President, National Accounts, Commercial Banking; 514-284-4500
Rick C. Lane, Vice-President, Real Estate Financing, Ontario; 416-865-5763; rick.lane@laurentianbank.ca
Chantale Lauzon, Vice-President, Taxation; 514-284-4500
André Lopresti, Vice-President, Chief Accountant; 514-284-4500

Claude Sasseville, Vice-President, Retail Financial Services, East of Montréal & South Shore; 514-729-7880

Directors:

L. Denis Desautels, Chair; 613-562-5800
Pierre Michaud, Vice-Chair; 514-849-8508
Lise Bastarache; 450-659-7533
Jean Bazin; 514-878-8804
Richard Bélanger; 418-266-3300
Eve-Lyne Biron; 514-866-5005
Pierre Genest; 418-652-2731
Georges Hébert; 514-255-3454
Veronica S. Maidman; 416-227-5377
Raymond McManus; 514-284-7967
Carmand Normand; 514-287-7373
Dominic J. Taddeo; 514-283-7042
Jonathan I. Wener; 514-842-8636

Affiliated Companies:

B2B Trust
LBC Trust
Laurentian Bank Securities Inc.
Laurentian Trust of Canada Inc.

Branches:

Alma
500, rue Sacré-Coeur ouest
Alma, QC G8B 1M1 Canada
800-522-1846

Amos
1, 1ère av ouest
Amos, QC J9T 1T7 Canada

Baie-Comeau
600, boul Lafleche
Baie-Comeau, QC G5C 2X8 Canada
800-522-1846

Beloeil
706, boul Laurier
Beloeil, QC J3G 4J6 Canada

Blainville - Curé-Labelle
1356, boul du Curé-Labelle
Blainville, QC J7C 2P2 Canada

Blainville - Seigneurie est
#2, 9, boul de la Seigneurie est
Blainville, QC J7C 4G6

Boisbriand - Faubourg
2250, boul du Faubourg
Boisbriand, QC J7H 1S3

Boucherville
999, boul Montarville
Boucherville, QC J4B 6R2 Canada

Brossard
1635, boul Rome
Brossard, QC J4W 3B1 Canada

Campbell's Bay
148, rue Front
Campbell's Bay, QC J0X 1K0 Canada

Chambly
1495, rue Brassard
Chambly, QC J3L 5W3 Canada

Chibougamau
530, 3e rue
Chibougamau, QC G8P 1N9 Canada

Chicoutimi
#100, 1611, boul Talbot
Chicoutimi, QC G7H 4C3 Canada
800-522-1846

Châteauguay
111, boul St-Jean-Baptiste
Châteauguay, QC J6K 3B1 Canada

Dolbeau-Mistassini
1372, boul Wallberg
Dolbeau-Mistassini, QC G8L 1H1 Canada

Drummondville
571, boul St-Joseph
Drummondville, QC JC2 2B6 Canada
800-522-1846

Fort-Coulonge
532, rue Baume
Fort-Coulonge, QC J0X 1V0 Canada

Gatineau - Hôpital
139, boul de l'Hôpital
Gatineau, QC J8T 8A3 Canada
800-522-1846

Gatineau - Plateau
#109, 75, boul du Plateau
Gatineau, QC J9A 3G1 Canada

Gatineau - St-Joseph
770, boul St-Joseph
Gatineau, QC J8Y 4B8 Canada

Granby
40, rue Évangéline
Granby, QC J2G 8K1 Canada
800-522-1846

Grand-Mère
531, 6e av
Grand-Mère, QC G9T 2H4 Canada

Greenfield-Park
3700, boul Taschereau
Greenfield-Park, QC J4V 2H8 Canada

Grenville
240, rue Principale
Grenville, QC J0V 1J0

Joliette
373, rue Notre-Dame
Joliette, QC J6E 3H5 Canada
800-252-1846

Jonquière
3460, boul St-François
Jonquière, QC G7X 8L3 Canada
800-522-1846

La Baie
1220, av du Port
La Baie, QC G7B 1W4 Canada

La Prairie
995, boul Taschereau
La Prairie, QC J5R 1W7 Canada

Lachute
470, rue Principale
Lachute, QC J8H 1Y3

Laval - Chomedy
Édifice C
#1, 928 autoroute Chomedy
Laval, QC H7X 3S9 Canada

Laval - Curé-Labelle
233, boul Curé-Labelle
Laval, QC H7L 2Z9 Canada

Laval - Dagenais ouest
3387, boul Dagenais ouest
Laval, QC H7P 1V5 Canada

Laval - Laurentides
510, boul des Laurentides
Laval, QC H7G 2V4 Canada

Laval - Montrose
750, rue Montrose
Laval, QC H7E 3M4 Canada

Laval - Notre-Dame
3870, boul Notre-Dame
Laval, QC H7V 1R9 Canada

Laval - René-Lévesque
1899, boul René-Lévesque
Laval, QC H7M 5E2 Canada

Laval - Saint-Martin ouest
1995, boul Saint-Martin ouest
Laval, QC H7S 1N2 Canada

Laval - Samson
4600, boul Samson
Laval, QC H7W 2H3 Canada
514-522-1846

Longueuil - Chambly
2836, ch Chambly
Longueuil, QC J4L 1M9 Canada

Longueuil - Saint-Charles
4, rue Saint-Charles est
Longueuil, QC J4H 1A9 Canada

Maniwaki
111, boul Desjardins
Maniwaki, QC J9E 2C9 Canada
800-522-1846

Mascouche
848, montée Masson
Mascouche, QC J7K 2L7 Canada

Mont-Laurier
476, rue de la Madone
Mont-Laurier, QC J9L 1S5 Canada
800-522-1846

Montréal - Amiens
4135, rue d'Amiens
Montréal, QC H1H 2G3 Canada

Montréal - Beaubien est
6593, rue Beaubien est
Montréal, QC H1M 1B1 Canada

Montréal - Beaubien est - Entrepreneurship
4945, rue Beaubien est
Montréal, QC H1T 1V1 Canada

Montréal - Bélanger est
5900, rue Bélanger est
Montréal, QC H1T 1G7 Canada

Montréal - Bélanger est
4155, rue Bélanger est
Montréal, QC H1T 1A2 Canada

Montréal - Chabanel ouest
290, rue Chabanel ouest
Montréal, QC H2N 1G5 Canada

Montréal - Champlain
8262, boul Champlain
Montréal, QC H8P 1B5 Canada

Montréal - Crémazie est
#1100, 255, boul Crémazie
Montréal, QC H2M 1M2 Canada

Montréal - Darlington
6225, av Darlington
Montréal, QC H3S 2J2 Canada

Montréal - Dorval
325, av Dorval
Montréal, QC H9S 3H6 Canada

Montréal - Décarie
865, boul Décarie
Montréal, QC H4L 3M2 Canada

Montréal - Décarie
5159, boul Décarie
Montréal, QC H3W 3C2

Montréal - Fleury est
885, rue Fleury est
Montréal, QC H2C 1P3 Canada

Montréal - Fleury est
2200, rue Fleury est
Montréal, QC H2B 1K4 Canada

Montréal - Henri-Bourassa est
5501, boul Henri-Bourassa est
Montréal, QC H1G 2T4 Canada

Montréal - Hochelaga
8595, rue Hochelaga
Montréal, QC H1L 2M2 Canada

Montréal - Jacques-Bizard
136, boul Jacques-Bizard
Montréal, QC H9C 2T9 Canada

Montréal - Jarry est
4725, rue Jarry est
Montréal, QC H1R 1X7 Canada

Montréal - Jarry est
7050, rue Jarry est
Montréal, QC H1J 1G4 Canada

Montréal - Jarry ouest
790, rue Jarry ouest
Montréal, QC H3N 1G6 Canada

Montréal - Jean-Talon est
5355, rue Jean-Talon est
Montréal, QC H1S 1L4 Canada

Montréal - Jean-Talon est
10, rue Jean-Talon est
Montréal, QC H2R 1S3 Canada

Montréal - Jean-Talon ouest

Laurentian Bank of Canada/ Banque Laurentienne du Canada (continued)

555, rue Jean-Talon ouest
Montréal, QC H3N 1R6 Canada
Montréal - Joseph-Renaud
6651, boul Joseph-Renaud
Montréal, QC H1K 3V3 Canada
Montréal - Lajeunesse
9095, rue Lajeunesse
Montréal, QC H2M 1S1 Canada
Montréal - Langelier
8410, boul Langelier
Montréal, QC H1P 2C2 Canada
Montréal - Lorimier
6500, av de Lorimier
Montréal, QC H2G 2P6 Canada
Montréal - Léger
6525, boul Léger
Montréal, QC H1G 6K1 Canada
Montréal - Masson
2937, rue Masson
Montréal, QC H1Y 1X5 Canada
Montréal - Maurice-Duplessis
8646, boul Maurice-Duplessis
Montréal, QC H1E 3L1 Canada
Montréal - McGill College
1981, av McGill College, 1e étage
Montréal, QC H3A 3K3 Canada
Montréal - McGill College
Tour Banque Laurentienne
#132, 1981, av McGill College
Montréal, QC H3A 3K3 Canada
Montréal - Monk
6270, boul Monk
Montréal, QC H4E 3H7 Canada
Montréal - Mont-Royal est
1100, av du Mont-Royal est
Montréal, QC H2J 1X8 Canada
Montréal - Newman
8787, boul Newman
Montréal, QC H8R 1Y9 Canada
Montréal - Notre-Dame ouest
1675, rue Notre-Dame ouest
Montréal, QC H8S 2E5 Canada
Montréal - Ontario est
3720, rue Ontario est
Montréal, QC H1W 1R9 Canada
Montréal - Papineau
7705, av Papineau
Montréal, QC H2E 2H4
Montréal - Parc
5059, av du Parc
Montréal, QC H2V 4E9 Canada
Montréal - Poirier
1430, rue Poirier
Montréal, QC H4L 1H3 Canada
Montréal - René-Lévesque ouest
1100, boul René-Lévesque ouest
Montréal, QC H3B 4C2
Montréal - Saint-Denis
8090, rue Saint-Denis
Montréal, QC H2R 2G1 Canada
Montréal - Saint-Jacques
4080, rue Saint-Jacques
Montréal, QC H4C 1J2 Canada
Montréal - Saint-Jacques
391, rue Saint-Jacques
Montréal, QC H2Y 1N9 Canada
Montréal - Saint-Jean
4057, montée Saint-Jean
Montréal, QC H2G 2R4 Canada
Montréal - Saint-Laurent
3730, boul Saint-Laurent
Montréal, QC H2X 2V8 Canada
Montréal - Saint-Michel
7182, boul Saint-Michel
Montréal, QC H2A 2Z4 Canada
Montréal - Saint-Michel
8930, boul Saint-Michel
Montréal, QC H1Z 3G4 Canada
Montréal - Sainte-Catherine est
936, rue Sainte-Catherine est
Montréal, QC H2L 2E7 Canada
Montréal - Salaberry
2490, rue de Salaberry
Montréal, QC H3M 1K9 Canada

Montréal - Sauvé ouest
1805, rue Sauvé ouest
Montréal, QC H4N 3B8 Canada
Montréal - Sherbrooke est
801, rue Sherbrooke est
Montréal, QC H2L 1K7 Canada
Montréal - Sherbrooke est
6615, rue Sherbrooke est
Montréal, QC H1N 1C7 Canada
Montréal - Sherbrooke est
12050, rue Sherbrooke est
Montréal, QC H1B 1C7 Canada
Montréal - Sherbrooke ouest
5651, rue Sherbrooke ouest
Montréal, QC H4A 1W6 Canada

Montréal - Sherbrooke ouest
4848, rue Sherbrooke ouest
Montréal, QC H3Z 1G8 Canada
Montréal - Shevchenko
1291, boul Shevchenko
Montréal, QC H8N 1N8 Canada
Montréal - Somerled
6640, av Somerled
Montréal, QC H4V 1T2 Canada
Montréal - Sources
3500, boul des Sources
Montréal, QC H9B 1Z9 Canada
Montréal - Van Horne
1447, av Van Horne
Montréal, QC H2V 1K9 Canada
Montréal - Van Horne
4790, av Van Horne
Montréal, QC H3W 1H7 Canada
Montréal - Verdun
5501, av Verdun
Montréal, QC H4H 1K9 Canada
Montréal - Viau
8945, boul Viau
Montréal, QC H1R 2V4 Canada
Montréal - Wellington
4214, rue Wellington
Montréal, QC H4G 1W2 Canada
514-522-1846
Montréal - Westminster
5479, av Westminster
Montréal, QC H4X 2A4 Canada
Murdochville
601, 5e rue
Murdochville, QC G0E 1W0 Canada
800-522-1846
New Carlisle
168, boul Gérard D. Lévesque
New Carlisle, QC G0C 1Z0 Canada
New Richmond
PO Box 10
228, boul Perron
New Richmond, QC G0C 2B0 Canada
Nicolet
92, Place du 21 Mars
Nicolet, QC J3T 1E9 Canada
Ottawa
#9, 1021 Cyrille Rd.
Ottawa, ON K1J 7S3 Canada
Paspébiac
120, boul Gérard D. Lévesque
Paspébiac, QC G0C 2K0 Canada
Port-Daniel
PO Box 70
10, rte 132
Port-Daniel, QC G0C 2N0 Canada
Québec - Bourgogne
999, rue de Bourgogne
Québec, QC G1W 4S6 Canada
800-252-1846
Québec - Carrefour
3323, rue du Carrefour
Québec, QC G1C 7E1 Canada
800-522-1846
Québec - Charest est
510, boul Charest est
Québec, QC G1K 3J3 Canada
Québec - Charles Albanel
1221, rue Charles Albanel
Québec, QC G1X 4Y5 Canada

Québec - Galeries
5401, boul des Galeries
Québec, QC G2K 1N4 Canada
800-522-1846
Québec - Grande Allée
#30, 580, Grande Allée est
Québec, QC G1R 2K2 Canada
800-522-1846
Québec - Henri-Bourassa
8000, boul Henri-Bourassa
Québec, QC G1G 4C7 Canada
800-522-1846
Québec - Laurier
Place de la Cité
#25, 2600, boul Laurier
Québec, QC G1V 4T3 Canada
800-522-1846
Québec - Laurier
Place Laurier
#2287, 2700, boul Laurier
Québec, QC G1V 2L8 Canada
Québec - Ste-Foy
1275, ch Ste-Foy
Québec, QC G1S 4S5 Canada

Québec - Wilfrid-Hamel ouest
#112, 3930, boul Wilfrid-Hamel ouest
Québec, QC G1P 2J2 Canada
800-522-1846
Repentigny - Iberville
150, boul Iberville
Repentigny, QC J6A 5M2 Canada
Repentigny - Iberville
910, boul Iberville, #A
Repentigny, QC J5Y 2P9
Rimouski
320, rue St-Germain est
Rimouski, QC G5L 1C2 Canada
800-522-1846
Roberval
#101, 773, boul St-Joseph
Roberval, QC G8H 2L4 Canada
Rock Forest
4857, boul Bourque
Rock Forest, QC J1N 1E8 Canada
Rosemère
401, boul Labelle
Rosemère, QC J7A 3T2 Canada
Rouyn-Noranda
24, rue Perreault est
Rouyn-Noranda, QC J9X 3C2 Canada
800-522-1846
Roxboro
10451, boul Gouin ouest
Roxboro, QC H8Y 1W9 Canada
Saint-Bruno
1354, rue Roberval
Saint-Bruno, QC J3V 5J2 Canada
Saint-Constant
400, rte 132
Saint-Constant, QC J5A 2L8 Canada
Saint-Hubert - Cousineau
#200, 6250, boul Cousineau
Saint-Hubert, QC J3Y 8X9 Canada
Saint-Hubert - Payer
5925, boul Payer
Saint-Hubert, QC J3Y 6W6 Canada
Saint-Hyacinthe
5915, rue Martineau
Saint-Hyacinthe, QC J2R 2H6 Canada
Saint-Lambert
400, av Victoria
Saint-Lambert, QC J4P 2H8 Canada
Sainte-Marie
16, rue Notre-Dame nord
Sainte-Marie, QC G6E 3Z5 Canada
Salaberry-de-Valleyfield
187, rue Victoria
Salaberry-de-Valleyfield, QC J6T 1A7 Canada
Sept-×les
770, boul Laure
Sept-×les, QC G4R 1Y5 Canada
800-522-1846
Sherbrooke

2637, rue King ouest
Sherbrooke, QC J1J 2H3 Canada
800-522-1846
Sorel-Tracy
831, rte Marie Victorin
Sorel-Tracy, QC J3R 1L1 Canada
St-Eustache
250, boul Arthur-Sauvé
St-Eustache, QC J7R 2H9 Canada
St-Georges
#35, 11400 - 1ère av
St-Georges, QC G5Y 5S4 Canada
800-252-1846
St-Jean-sur-Richelieu
605, rue Pierre-Caisse
St-Jean-sur-Richelieu, QC J3A 1P1 Canada
St-Jérôme
900, boul Grignon
St-Jérôme, QC J7Y 3S7 Canada
800-522-1846
St-Raymond
300, rue Saint-Joseph
St-Raymond, QC G3L 1J6 Canada
800-522-1846
Ste-Thérèse
95, boul Labelle
Sainte-Thérèse, QC J7E 2X6 Canada
Terrebonne
1035, boul des Seigneurs
Terrebonne, QC J6W 3W5 Canada

Thetford Mines
#101, 222, boul Frontenac ouest
Thetford Mines, QC G6G 6N7 Canada
Trois-Rivières - Forges
4450, boul des Forges
Trois-Rivières, QC G8Y 1W5 Canada
Trois-Rivières - Forges
425, rue des Forges
Trois-Rivières, QC G9A 5H5 Canada
Val-d'Or
872, 3e av
Val-d'Or, QC J9P 1T1 Canada
800-522-1846
Vaudreuil-Dorion
43, Cité des Jeunes
Vaudreuil-Dorion, QC J7V 8C1 Canada
Victoriaville
403, boul Jutras est
Victoriaville, QC G6P 7H4 Canada
800-252-1846
×le-Perrot
88, boul Don Quichotte
×le-Perrot, QC J7V 6L7 Canada

Manulife Bank of Canada

PO Box 1602, Waterloo Stn. Waterloo
#500MA, 500 King St. North
Waterloo, ON N2J 4C6
519-747-7000
877-765-2265
manulife_bank@manulife.com
www.manulifebank.ca
Ownership: Private. Wholly-owned subsidiary of Manulife Financial.
Year Founded: 1993
Number of Employees: 200+
Assets: $1-10 billion
Profile: Serving clients in all provinces & territories, Manulife Bank provides the following services: bank accounts, investments, loans, mortgages, & credit cards. In 2007, the bank opened an office in Halifax.

Executives:
J. Roman Fedchyshyn, President/CEO
Douglas Myers, Vice-President/CFO
Lynne Alex, Vice-President, Human Resources

National Bank of Canada(NBC)/ Banque Nationale du Canada(BNC)

National Bank Tower
600, rue de La Gauchetière ouest
Montréal, QC H3B 4L2
514-394-6081
Fax: 514-394-8434
www.nbc.ca
Former Name: The Provincial Bank of Canada; The Mercantile Bank of Canada
Ownership: Public
Year Founded: 1859
Number of Employees: 17,070
Stock Symbol: NA
Stock Exchange Membership: Natural Gas Exchange
Profile: National Bank of Canada provides comprehensive financial services to consumers, small- & medium-sized enterprises & large corporations. It also offers a full array of banking & investment services.

Executives:
Luc Paiement, Co-President/Co-CEO, National Bank Financial Group
Richard Pascoe, Co-President/Co-CEO, National Bank Financial Group
Réal Raymond, President/CEO, National Bank
Louis Vachon, Chief Operating Officer
Patricia Curadeau-Grou, Exec. Sr. Vice-President, Risk Management
Gisèle Desrochers, Exec. Sr. Vice-President, Human Resources & Operations
Tony P. Meti, Exec. Sr. Vice-President, Commercial Banking & International
Michel Tremblay, Exec. Sr. Vice-President, Personal Banking & Wealth Management
Brian A. Davis, Exec. Vice-President, Corporate Development & Governance
Pierre Desbiens, Sr. Vice-President, Sales & Personal Banking
Pierre Dubreuil, Sr. Vice-President, Greater Montréal & Southern Québec
Pierre Fitzgibbon, Sr. Vice-President, Finance, Technology & Corporate Affairs
Charles Guay, Sr. Vice-President, Altamira, NB Funds Inc., SVP Mutual Funds
Alice Keung, Sr. Vice-President, Information Technology
Michel Labonté, Sr. Vice-President, Special Projects
Oliver H. Lecat, Sr. Vice-President, Internal Audit
Réjean Lévesque, Sr. Vice-President, Operation Review Program
Denis Pellerin, Sr. Vice-President, Operational & Market Risk Management
James S. Porter, Sr. Vice-President & Managing Director, Central-Atlantic & Western Canada, Head, National Business Development for Individual In
Jean-Luc Alimondo, Vice-President, Europe/Middle East/Africa
Richard Barriault, Vice-President, Taxation
Guy Beno(140t, Vice-President, Montérégie & Central Quebec
Pierre Blais, Vice-President, Government Banking
Jean Blouin, Vice-President, Deposit Solutions & Credit
Martin-Pierre Boulianne, Vice-President, Assistant Secretary
Yves G. Breton, Vice-President, National Bank Brokerage, NnB Direct Brokerage
Jean-François Bureau, Vice-President, Credit & Specialized Products
Vincent Butkiewicz, Vice-President, Financial Markets
Jean-Paul Caron, Vice-President, Corporate Affairs
Linda Caty, Vice-President, Corporate Secretary
Sylvie R. Chagnon, Vice-President, Regional, Laval & North Shore
Gilles Choquet, Vice-President, Specialized Networks - Credit
René Collette, Vice-President, Atlantic Canada
Suzanne Côté, Vice-President, Legal Affairs
France Croteau, Vice-President, Regional, Québec & East of Québec
Jean Dagenais, Vice-President & Chief Accountant
France David, Vice-President, Basel Accord & Risk Analysis
Danny Dery, Vice-President, Regional, West of Montréal Island
Diane Déry, Vice-President, Québec & Eastern Québec
Yvan Desrosiers, Vice-President, Natbank
Lévis Doucet, Vice-President, Montréal
Nicole Dumont, Vice-President, Business Solution INC.
Pascal Duquette, Vice-President, Natbank Investment Management Inc.
Michel Faubert, Vice-President, Operations Optimization
Luc Fredette, Vice-President, Credit, Canada
Christine Ghalbouni, Vice-President, Internal Audit
Clément Gignac, Vice-President & Chief Economist
Eric Girard, Vice-President, Internal Fund Manager
Rubina Havlin, Vice-President, Electronic Payment Solutions
Brigitte Hébert, Vice-President, Information Technology
Jacynthe Hotte, Vice-President, Operational Risks
Lynn Jeanniot, Vice-President, Human Resources
D. William Kennedy, Vice-President, Special Loans
Raymond H. Keroack, Vice-President, Laval/North Shore/Abitibi-Témiscamingue
Marc Knuepp, Vice-President, Administration, Altamira & National Bank Funds
Pierrette Lacroix, Vice-President, Market Risk
Éric Laflamme, Vice-President, National Bank Trust Inc. & Natcan Trust Company Inc.
Jean-Pierre Lambert, Vice-President, Montérégie/Eastern Townships
Jacques Latendresse, Vice-President, Nassau
Yannik Laurin, Vice-President, Québec & Eastern Québec
Michelle Leduc, Vice-President, Retail Credit
Beno(140t Loranger, Vice-President, Alternative Networks
Beno(140t Marcotte, Vice-President, Coordination - Wealth Management Advisory Services
André Mondor, Vice-President, Montréal
Renaud Nadeau, Vice-President, Wealth Management
Jacques Naud, Vice-President, Ontario & Western Canada
Martin Ouellet, Vice-President & Treasurer
Guy Oullette, Vice-President, Regional, South Shore
David Pinsonneault, Vice-President, Specialized Groups
Paolo Pizzuto, Vice-President, Sales & Service Strategies
Roland Provost, Vice-President, Drummond/Bois-Francs/Mauricie
Chantale Reid, Vice-President, Network Support
Nicole Rondou, Vice-President, Compliance
Sylvie Roy, Vice-President, Marketing & Public Affairs
France Roy Maffeï, Vice-President, Customer Relationship Centres
Lili J. Shain, Vice-President, National Accounts, Ontario
Vincent Sofia, Vice-President, Asia
John W. Swendsen, Vice-President, Western Canada & Energy
Marc Taillon, Vice-President, Saguenay
Pierre Therrien, Vice-President, Private Banking Québec
Peter D. Thompson, Vice-President, Outaouais/Ontario
Benoit Villeneuve, Vice-President, Finance
Jimmy Villeneuve, Vice-President, Organizational Performance, Premises & Material Resour
Kathleen Zicat, Vice-President, Laval/Northern & Western Québec

Directors:
Jean Douville, Chair
Lawrence S. Bloomberg
Pierre Bourgie
President/CEO, Société Financière Bourgie Inc.
Gérard Coulombe
Chair & Sr. Partner, Desjardins Ducharme Stein Monast
Bernard Cyr
President, Cyr Holdings Inc.
Shirley A. Dawe
President, Shirley Dawe Associates Inc.
Nicole Diamond-Gélinas
President & General Manager, Aspasie Inc.
Marcel Dutil
Chair & CEO, The Canam Manac Group Inc.
Jean Gaulin
Paul Gobeil
Vice-Chair, Métro Inc.; Chair, Export Development Canada
Réal Raymond
Roseann Runte
President, Old Dominion University
Marc P. Tellier

Affiliated Companies:
Alter Moneta
Assurance-Vie Banque Nationale
CanCap Preferred Corporation
NATCAN Trust Company
National Bank Direct Brokerage Inc.
National Bank Financial Inc.
National Bank Securities Inc.
National Bank Trust

Administration Offices:
Toronto
#200, 150 York St.
Toronto, ON M5H 3A9 Canada
416-864-9080
Fax: 416-864-7819

Branches:
Acton Vale
1056, rue St-André
Acton Vale, QC J0H 1A0 Canada
450-546-3284
Fax: 450-546-3797
MICR: 0400-1
Alfred

National Bank of Canada(NBC)/ Banque Nationale du Canada(BNC) (continued)

PO Box 10
270 Telegraph St.
Alfred, ON K0B 1A0 Canada
613-679-2202
Fax: 613-679-4328
MICR: 1125-1

Alliston
PO Box 269
5 Victoria St. West
Alliston, ON L9R 1S9 Canada
705-435-2816
Fax: 705-435-5939
MICR: 0860-1

Alma
560, rue Sacré-Coeur ouest
Alma, QC G8B 1L9 Canada
418-668-7977
Fax: 418-668-2272
MICR: 0635-1

Amos
101, 1re av ouest
Amos, QC J9T 1V1
819-727-9391
Fax: 819-727-9358
MICR: 0200-1

Amqui
#72, 30, boul Saint-Beno(140t est
Amqui, QC G5J 2B7 Canada
418-629-4416
Fax: 418-629-5927
MICR: 1364-1

Asbestos
277, 1ère av
Asbestos, QC J1T 1Y6 Canada
819-879-5471
Fax: 819-879-6280
MICR: 1127-1

Aurora
St. Andrews Village
2 Orchard Heights Blvd.
Aurora, ON L4G 3W3 Canada
905-727-3686
Fax: 905-727-3162
MICR: 0378-1

Baie-Comeau - Lasalle
283, boul Lasalle
Baie-Comeau, QC G4Z 1T2 Canada
418-296-3307
Fax: 418-296-2861
MICR: 0645-1

Baie-Comeau - Puyjalon
921, rue de Puyjalon
Baie-Comeau, QC G5C 1N3 Canada
418-589-3781
Fax: 418-589-7585
MICR: 0656-1

Baie-Saint-Paul
11, rue St-Jean-Baptiste
Baie-Saint-Paul, QC G3Z 1M1 Canada
418-435-2250
Fax: 418-435-2771
MICR: 1134-1

Barrie - Bayfield St.
487 Bayfield St.
Barrie, ON L4M 4Z9 Canada
705-726-0340
Fax: 705-726-5373
MICR: 0869-1

Barrie - Dunlop St. East
64 Dunlop St. East
Barrie, ON L4M 1A3 Canada
705-726-9311
Fax: 705-726-9320
MICR: 0657-1

Bathurst
#3, 219 Main St.
Bathurst, NB E2A 1A9 Canada
506-548-9916
Fax: 506-549-3423
MICR: 1135-1

Beauceville
630B, boul Renault
Beauceville, QC G5X 1M6 Canada
418-774-9868
Fax: 418-774-9887
MICR: 0283-1

Beauharnois
465, rue Ellice
Beauharnois, QC J6N 1X6 Canada
450-429-3544
Fax: 450-429-3525
MICR: 0201-1

Bedford
84, rue Principale
Bedford, QC J0J 1A0 Canada
450-248-3361
Fax: 450-248-3802
MICR: 0772-1

Belle River
PO Box 160
555 Notre Dame St.
Belle River, ON N0R 1A0 Canada
519-728-1410
Fax: 519-728-3144
MICR: 1139-1

Beloeil
180, boul Sir Wilfrid Laurier
Beloeil, QC J3G 4G7 Canada
450-467-0231
Fax: 450-467-9768
MICR: 0273-1

Beresford
879, rue Principale
Beresford, NB E8K 1R3 Canada
506-542-1400
Fax: 506-542-1288
MICR: 1015-1

Berthierville
PO Box 209
777, Notre-Dame
Berthierville, QC J0K 1A0 Canada
450-836-3771
Fax: 450-836-1979
MICR: 0202-1

Blainville
973, boul Curé-Labelle
Blainville, QC J7C 2L8 Canada
450-430-8320
Fax: 450-430-8003
MICR: 1374-1

Boisbriand
938, boul de la Grande-Allée
Boisbriand, QC J7G 1W5 Canada
450-430-0131
Fax: 450-430-0404
MICR: 1023-1

Boucherville - Fort St-Louis
650, boul du Fort St-Louis
Boucherville, QC J4B 1S9 Canada
450-655-3120
Fax: 450-655-6653
MICR: 0214-1

Boucherville - Montarville
1000, boul de Montarville
Boucherville, QC J4B 5V9 Canada
450-449-2619
Fax: 450-449-3020
MICR: 1323-1

Bouctouche
123, boul Irving
Bouctouche, NB E4S 3K2 Canada
506-743-5526
Fax: 506-743-5528
MICR: 0040-1

Bourget
3779 Champlain St.
Bourget, ON K0A 1E0 Canada
613-487-2454
Fax: 613-487-3864
MICR: 0326-1

Bracebridge
102 Manitoba St.
Bracebridge, ON P1L 1S1 Canada
705-645-3031
Fax: 705-645-3032
MICR: 0863-1

Brampton - McLaughlin Rd. South
4 McLaughlin Rd. South
Brampton, ON L6Y 3B2 Canada
905-455-3333
Fax: 905-455-2174
MICR: 0335-1

Brampton - Quarry Edge Dr.
58 Quarry Edge Dr.
Brampton, ON L6V 4K2 Canada
905-452-7474
Fax: 905-452-1962
MICR: 1048-1

Brossard - Grande-Allée
5645, boul Grande-Allée
Brossard, QC J4Z 3G3 Canada
450-656-1650
Fax: 450-656-3270
MICR: 1041-1

Brossard - Taschereau
Carrefour Pelletier
8200, boul Taschereau
Brossard, QC J4X 2S6 Canada
450-923-1000
Fax: 450-923-9558
MICR: 1032-1

Burlington
3315 Fairview St.
Burlington, ON L7N 3N9 Canada
905-634-5528
Fax: 905-634-0028
MICR: 0328-1

Bécancour
1600, boul Bécancour
Bécancour, QC G9H 3T9 Canada
819-298-2202
Fax: 819-298-4206
MICR: 1195-1

Cabano
130, rue Commerciale
Cabano, QC G0L 1E0 Canada
418-854-2801
Fax: 418-854-1467
MICR: 0235-1

Calgary
301 - 6th Ave. SW
Calgary, AB T2P 4M9 Canada
403-294-4900
Fax: 403-294-4965
MICR: 1405-1

Campbellton
116 Roseberry St.
Campbellton, NB E3N 2G9 Canada
506-753-7691
Fax: 506-789-0430
MICR: 1154-1

Cap-aux-Meules
425, ch Principal
Cap-aux-Meules, QC G4T 1E3 Canada
418-986-2335
Fax: 418-986-5885
MICR: 0605-1

Cap-Pelé
2661, ch Acadie, #F
Cap-Pelé, NB E4N 1C2 Canada
506-577-4344
Fax: 506-577-4317
MICR: 1390-1

Caraquet
25, boul St-Pierre ouest
Caraquet, NB E1W 1B8 Canada
506-727-3495
Fax: 506-727-7456
MICR: 1150-1

Carleton
PO Box 148
554, boul Perron
Carleton, QC G0C 1J0 Canada
418-364-3319
Fax: 418-364-3283
MICR: 0659-1

Casselman
PO Box 336
90, boul Lafléche
Casselman, ON K0A 1M0 Canada
613-764-2824
Fax: 613-764-0060
MICR: 0301-1

Chambly

1295, boul de Périgny
Chambly, QC J3L 1W7 Canada
450-658-4374
Fax: 450-658-0361
MICR: 1340-1

Chandler
PO Box 760
79, rue Commerciale ouest
Chandler, QC G0C 1K0 Canada
418-689-2271
Fax: 418-689-6958
MICR: 0607-1

Charlottetown
132 Kent St.
Charlottetown, PE C1A 1N2 Canada
902-892-7443
Fax: 902-628-1471
MICR: 1037-1

Charny
8032, av des Églises
Charny, QC G6X 1X7 Canada
418-832-2966
Fax: 418-832-0320
MICR: 0521-1

Chibougamau
525, 3e rue
Chibougamau, QC G8P 1N8 Canada
418-748-2673
Fax: 418-748-7074
MICR: 0652-1

Chicoutimi - Racine est
432, rue Racine est
Chicoutimi, QC G7H 7R7 Canada
418-545-0590
Fax: 418-693-0172
MICR: 1155-1

Chicoutimi - Tadoussac
2169, boul de Tadoussac
Chicoutimi, QC G7G 4X2 Canada
418-543-0396
Fax: 418-549-1100
MICR: 0024-1

Chicoutimi - Talbot
1180, boul Talbot
Chicoutimi, QC G7H 4B6 Canada
418-545-1655
Fax: 418-545-1097
MICR: 0671-1

Châteauguay - Anjou
99, boul d'Anjou
Châteauguay, QC J6J 2R2 Canada
450-692-1990
Fax: 450-698-1847
MICR: 0276-1

Clair
775, rue Principale
Clair, NB E7A 2H5 Canada
506-992-2128
Fax: 506-992-0930
MICR: 1225-1

Coaticook
137, rue Child
Coaticook, QC J1A 2B2 Canada
819-849-2795
Fax: 819-849-9373
MICR: 0403-1

Collingwood
108 Hurontario St.
Collingwood, ON L9Y 2L8 Canada
705-445-1020
Fax: 705-445-1035
MICR: 0867-1

Contrecoeur
4889, boul Marie-Victorin
Contrecoeur, QC J0L 1C0 Canada
450-587-2005
Fax: 450-587-8484
MICR: 0099-1

Cowansville
402, rue du Sud
Cowansville, QC J2K 2X7 Canada
450-263-3577
Fax: 450-263-4821
MICR: 0402-1

Daveluyville
374, rue Principale
Daveluyville, QC G0Z 1C0 Canada
819-367-2373
Fax: 819-367-3342
MICR: 1449-1

Delson
35, boul Georges-Gagné
Delson, QC J5B 2E4 Canada
450-638-1601
Fax: 450-638-5052
MICR: 1375-1

Dieppe
#1604, 200 Champlain St.
Dieppe, NB E1A 1P1 Canada
506-859-2212
Fax: 506-858-1344
MICR: 1348-1

Disraéli
145, rue Champoux
Disraéli, QC G0N 1E0 Canada
418-449-2414
Fax: 418-449-1669
MICR: 1165-1

Dolbeau-Mistassini - Saint-Michel
193, boul Saint-Michel
Dolbeau-Mistassini, QC G8L 5Y7 Canada
418-276-0404
Fax: 418-276-9392
MICR: 0637-1

Dolbeau-Mistassini - Wallberg
1201, boul Wallberg
Dolbeau-Mistassini, QC G8L 1H3 Canada
418-276-0383
Fax: 418-276-8605
MICR: 0642-1

Donnacona
Centre d'achat Donnacona
325, rue de l'Église
Donnacona, QC G3M 2A2 Canada
418-285-2902
Fax: 418-285-0017
MICR: 1376-1

Drummondville - Marchand
150, rue Marchand
Drummondville, QC J2C 4N1 Canada
819-477-9494
Fax: 819-477-0181
MICR: 1358-1

Drummondville - Mercure
1700, boul Mercure
Drummondville, QC J2B 3N4 Canada
819-477-8344
Fax: 819-477-4816
MICR: 1472-1

Drummondville - St-Joseph
595, boul St-Joseph
Drummondville, QC J2C 2B6 Canada
819-475-2428
Fax: 819-477-4804
MICR: 1166-1

Dégelis
389, av Principale
Dégelis, QC G5T 1L3 Canada
418-853-2945
Fax: 418-853-2418
MICR: 0036-1

Edmonton
9 Sir Winston Churchill Sq. NW
Edmonton, AB T5J 5B5 Canada
780-424-4771
Fax: 780-425-5774
MICR: 1413-1

Edmundston - Hébert
180, boul Hébert
Edmundston, NB E3V 2S7 Canada
506-735-8881
Fax: 506-735-7056
MICR: 1309-1

Edmundston - Église
111, rue de l'Église
Edmundston, NB E3V 1J9 Canada
506-735-8426
Fax: 506-735-5097
MICR: 1175-1

Farnham
280, rue Principale est
Farnham, QC J2N 1L6 Canada
450-293-3615
Fax: 450-293-7325
MICR: 0204-1

Ferme-Neuve
103, 12e rue
Ferme-Neuve, QC J0W 1C0 Canada
819-587-3121
Fax: 819-587-4980
MICR: 1387-1

Forestville
PO Box 8
7, 1ère av
Forestville, QC G0T 1E0 Canada
418-587-2281
Fax: 418-587-4315
MICR: 0653-1

Fredericton
PO Box 414
551 King St.
Fredericton, NB E3B 1E7 Canada
506-458-8129
Fax: 506-457-1611
MICR: 1206-1

Gaspé
#39, 26, Montée de Sandy Beach
Gaspé, QC G4X 2A9 Canada
418-368-2226
Fax: 418-368-6714
MICR: 0609-1

Gatineau - Casino
1, boul du Casino
Gatineau, QC J8Y 6W3 Canada
819-770-6229
Fax: 819-770-6975
MICR: 0819-1

Gatineau - Gréber
Place Farmer
68, boul Gréber
Gatineau, QC J8T 3P8 Canada
819-561-0500
Fax: 819-561-6932
MICR: 1253-1

Gatineau - l'Hôpital
492, boul de l'Hôpital
Gatineau, QC J8V 2P4 Canada
819-243-4889
Fax: 819-243-7216
MICR: 1257-1

Gatineau - Maclaren
101, rue Maclaren
Gatineau, QC J8L 1J9 Canada
819-986-8525
Fax: 819-986-3585
MICR: 1228-1

Gatineau - Maloney est
405, boul Maloney est
Gatineau, QC J8P 6Z8 Canada
819-663-5359
Fax: 819-663-8352
MICR: 1360-1

Gatineau - Park
21, rue Park
Gatineau, QC J9H 4J6 Canada
819-684-5321
Fax: 819-684-1356
MICR: 1126-1

Gatineau - St-Joseph
428, boul St-Joseph
Gatineau, QC J8Y 3Y7 Canada
819-770-1437
Fax: 819-770-5636
MICR: 0486-1

Gatineau - St-Joseph
Centre Paul Cardinal
#200, 920, boul St-Joseph
Gatineau, QC J8Z 1S9 Canada
819-772-4931
Fax: 819-595-3464
MICR: 1020-1

Gatineau - St-Joseph
#101, 259, boul St-Joseph
Gatineau, QC J8Y 6T1 Canada

National Bank of Canada(NBC)/ Banque Nationale du Canada(BNC) (continued)

819-771-3227
Fax: 819-771-5395
MICR: 0558-1

Granby
193, rue Principale
Granby, QC J2G 2V5 Canada
450-372-5859
Fax: 450-372-5509
MICR: 0205-1

Grand-Mère
600, 6e av
Grand-Mère, QC G9T 2H5 Canada
819-538-1646
Fax: 819-538-1298
MICR: 0408-1

Grande-Anse
357 Acadie St.
Grande-Anse, NB E8N 1C6 Canada
506-732-5761
Fax: 506-732-1199
MICR: 0059-1

Grande-Rivière
PO Box 700
99, rue Grande-Allée est
Grande-Rivière, QC G0C 1V0 Canada
418-385-2229
Fax: 418-385-4186
MICR: 1443-1

Gravenhurst
395 Muskoka Rd. South
Gravenhurst, ON P1P 1J4 Canada
705-687-2212
Fax: 705-687-2214
MICR: 0870-1

Greenfield-Park
3224, boul Taschereau
Greenfield-Park, QC J4V 2H3 Canada
450-672-8110
Fax: 450-672-5810
MICR: 1236-1

Hamilton - Main St. East
447 Main St. East
Hamilton, ON L8N 1K1 Canada
905-524-2464
Fax: 905-524-0466
MICR: 1300-1

Hamilton - Upper James St. South
891 Upper James St. South
Hamilton, ON L9C 7N1 Canada
905-383-3383
Fax: 905-383-5988
MICR: 1302-1

Hawkesbury
203 Main St. East
Hawkesbury, ON K6A 1A1 Canada
613-632-7067
Fax: 613-632-0445
MICR: 0303-1

Hudson
468, rue Principale
Hudson, QC J0P 1H0 Canada
450-458-5351
Fax: 450-458-0530
MICR: 0458-1

Joliette
979, boul Firestone
Joliette, QC J6E 2W4 Canada
450-759-0742
Fax: 450-753-9931
MICR: 1350-1

Jonquière - Davis
1923, rue Davis
Jonquière, QC G7S 3B7 Canada
418-548-3161
Fax: 418-548-3255
MICR: 0641-1

Jonquière - Harvey est
3880, boul Harvey est
Jonquière, QC G7X 8R6 Canada
418-547-5701
Fax: 418-547-3184
MICR: 0267-1

Kingston
328 King St. East
Kingston, ON K7L 3B4 Canada
613-542-7200
Fax: 613-542-7514
MICR: 0873-1

Kitchener
851 Fischer Hallman Rd.
Kitchener, ON N2M 5N8 Canada
519-744-8402
Fax: 519-741-8041
MICR: 0359-1

L'Ancienne-Lorette
1366, rue Saint-Jacques
L'Ancienne-Lorette, QC G2E 2X1 Canada
418-872-3787
Fax: 418-872-1494
MICR: 1028-1

L'Annonciation
348, rue Principale nord
L'Annonciation, QC J0T 1T0 Canada
819-275-2202
Fax: 819-275-2573
MICR: 0254-1

L'Assomption
352, boul de L'Ange Gardien
L'Assomption, QC J5W 1S5 Canada
450-589-4772
Fax: 450-589-0551
MICR: 1213-1

La Baie
662, rue Victoria
La Baie, QC G7B 3M6 Canada
418-544-6841
Fax: 418-544-0563
MICR: 0602-1

La Guadeloupe
PO Box 115
350, 14e av
La Guadeloupe, QC G0M 1G0 Canada
418-459-6441
Fax: 418-459-6946
MICR: 0529-1

La Malbaie
316, rue St-Étienne
La Malbaie, QC G5A 1T8 Canada
418-665-6487
Fax: 418-665-7714
MICR: 1211-1

La Plaine
5333, boul Laurier
La Plaine, QC J7M 1W1 Canada
450-477-3302
Fax: 450-477-3304
MICR: 0047-1

La Pocatière
Carrefour
#800, 625, 1re rue
La Pocatière, QC G0R 1Z0 Canada
418-856-3194
Fax: 418-856-3409
MICR: 0636-1

La Prairie
Place La Citière
50, boul Taschereau ouest
La Prairie, QC J5R 4V3 Canada
450-444-4520
Fax: 450-444-9688
MICR: 0472-1

La Sarre
255, 3e rue est
La Sarre, QC J9Z 3N7 Canada
819-333-2207
Fax: 819-333-3572
MICR: 0253-1

La Tuque
325, rue St-Joseph
La Tuque, QC G9X 3P3 Canada
819-523-5635
Fax: 819-523-8024
MICR: 0412-1

Lac Mégantic
5271, rue Frontenac
Lac-Mégantic, QC G6B 1H2 Canada
819-583-0183
Fax: 819-583-2747
MICR: 1216-1

Lac-Etchemin
222, 2e av
Lac-Etchemin, QC G0R 1S0 Canada
418-625-2661
Fax: 418-625-2662
MICR: 1283-1

Lachenaie - Gascon
2135, ch Gascon
Lachenaie, QC J6X 4H2 Canada
450-964-4859
Fax: 450-964-9686
MICR: 0046-1

Lachenaie - Pionnieres
322, Montée des Pionnieres
Lachenaie, QC J6V 1H4 Canada
450-654-1958
Fax: 450-654-9652
MICR: 1026-1

Lachute
569, rue Principale
Lachute, QC J8H 1Y6 Canada
450-562-8864
Fax: 450-562-1907
MICR: 1210-1

Lacolle
60, rte 202
Lacolle, QC J0J 1J0 Canada
450-246-4166
Fax: 450-246-2427
MICR: 0028-1

Lameque
29, rue Principale
Lamèque, NB E8T 1M9 Canada
506-344-2274
Fax: 506-344-7422
MICR: 1308-1

Laurier-Station
Galerie Laurier
170, boul Laurier
Laurier-Station, QC G0S 1N0 Canada
418-728-2812
Fax: 418-728-2866
MICR: 1286-1

Laval - Chomedey
Manoir Le Corbusier
1000, boul Chomedey
Laval, QC H7V 3X8 Canada
450-682-9959
MICR: 1138-2

Laval - Concorde
3131, boul de la Concorde est
Laval, QC H7E 4W4 Canada
450-661-4132
Fax: 450-661-0507
MICR: 1174-1

Laval - Curé Labelle
201, boul Curé-Labelle
Laval, QC H7V 2R9 Canada
450-687-9980
Fax: 450-687-8916
MICR: 1138-1

Laval - Dagenaie
3123, boul Dagenais ouest
Laval, QC H7P 1T8 Canada
450-625-2451
Fax: 450-625-1220
MICR: 0401-1

Laval - Daniel-Johnson
2500, boul Daniel-Johnson
Laval, QC H7T 2P6 Canada
450-686-7030
Fax: 450-686-2332
MICR: 1086-1

Laval - Daniel-Johnson
#115, 2500, boul Daniel-Johnson
Laval, QC H7T 2P6 Canada
450-682-3200
Fax: 450-682-0104
MICR: 0535-1

Laval - Laurentides
2175, boul des Laurentides
Laval, QC H7K 2J3 Canada
450-669-9208
Fax: 450-669-6844
MICR: 0009-1

Laval - Laurentides

61, boul des Laurentides
Laval, QC H7G 2S9 Canada
450-669-7184
Fax: 450-669-9324
MICR: 0464-1

Laval - Lévesque
5313, boul Lévesque est
Laval, QC H7C 1N6 Canada
450-661-5010
Fax: 450-661-0387
MICR: 0244-1

Laval - Moulin
1235, montée du Moulin
Laval, QC H7A 3V6 Canada
450-665-0692
Fax: 450-665-0227
MICR: 1091-1

Laval - Place Laval
1, Place Laval
Laval, QC H7N 1A1 Canada
450-667-3031
Fax: 450-667-9707
MICR: 1190-1

Laval - Sainte-Rose
226, boul Sainte-Rose
Laval, QC H7L 1L6 Canada
450-625-1904
Fax: 450-625-1338
MICR: 0438-1

Laval - Sainte-Rose
4265, boul Sainte-Rose
Laval, QC H7R 1V5 Canada
450-627-5171
Fax: 450-627-2890
MICR: 1373-1

Laval - Samson
47, boul Samson
Laval, QC H7X 3R8 Canada
450-689-2120
Fax: 450-689-8006
MICR: 0480-1

Laval - St-Martin
1200, boul St-Martin ouest
Laval, QC H7S 2E4 Canada
450-668-8331
Fax: 450-668-3608
MICR: 0499-1

Laval - St-Martin
3770, boul St-Martin ouest
Laval, QC H7T 1B1 Canada
450-681-1655
Fax: 450-681-9820
MICR: 1177-1

Laval-des-Rapides
405, boul Cartier ouest
Laval-des-Rapides, QC H7N 2K8 Canada
450-687-8690
Fax: 450-687-1532
MICR: 1170-1

Lavaltrie
234, rue St-Antoine nord
Lavaltrie, QC J5T 2G3 Canada
450-586-4221
Fax: 450-586-0327
MICR: 1389-1

Le Gardeur
24, rue Rivest
Le Gardeur, QC J5Z 2J1
450-582-5664
Fax: 450-582-6534
MICR: 0066-1

Les Côteaux
250, rte 338
Les Côteaux, QC J7X 1E4 Canada
450-267-3594
Fax: 450-267-4561
MICR: 1394-1

London
465 Richmond St.
London, ON N6A 5P4 Canada
519-432-8371
Fax: 519-432-4964
MICR: 1427-1

Longueuil - Chambly
Place Desormeaux
2877, ch Chambly
Longueuil, QC J4L 1M8 Canada
450-670-4180
Fax: 450-670-3807
MICR: 0218-1

Longueuil - Fernand-Lafontaine
2099, boul Fernand-Lafontaine
Longueuil, QC J4G 2J4 Canada
450-651-9401
Fax: 450-651-0563
MICR: 0209-1

Longueuil - St-Charles
160, rue St-Charles ouest
Longueuil, QC J4H 1C9 Canada
450-651-7200
Fax: 450-651-0511
MICR: 0762-1

Lorraine
95, boul de Gaulle
Lorraine, QC J6Z 3R8 Canada
450-621-9223
Fax: 450-621-6425
MICR: 0495-1

Louiseville
160, rue St-Laurent
Louiseville, QC J5V 1J9 Canada
819-228-5511
Fax: 819-228-8053
MICR: 1368-1

Lévis
49B, route du Président Kennedy
Lévis, QC G6V 6C3 Canada
418-833-8020
Fax: 418-833-1076
MICR: 1221-1

Magog
165, rue Principale ouest
Magog, QC J1X 2A7 Canada
819-843-6524
Fax: 819-843-4255
MICR: 0413-1

Malartic
PO Box 3030
660, rue Royale
Malartic, QC J0Y 1Z0 Canada
819-757-3651
Fax: 819-757-3465
MICR: 0017-1

Maniwaki
252, rue Notre-Dame
Maniwaki, QC J9E 2J8 Canada
819-449-3181
Fax: 819-449-4543
MICR: 1231-1

Maple
#1, 9505 Keele St.
Maple, ON L6A 1W3 Canada
905-832-5978
Fax: 905-832-8036
MICR: 0363-1

Marieville
#1, 491, rue Ste-Marie
Marieville, QC J3M 1M4 Canada
450-460-4436
Fax: 450-460-3628
MICR: 0211-1

Markham - Carlton Rd.
528 Carlton Rd.
Markham, ON L3R 0C6 Canada
905-940-0734
Fax: 905-940-2007
MICR: 0374-1

Markham - McCowan Rd.
7380 McCowan Rd.
Markham, ON L3S 3H8 Canada
905-513-0520
Fax: 905-513-1335
MICR: 0362-1

Mascouche
Terrasses Mascouche
#4, 1100, Montée Masson
Mascouche, QC J7K 2L8 Canada
450-966-0303
Fax: 450-966-0700
MICR: 1027-1

Matane
750, ave. du Phare ouest
Matane, QC G4W 3W8 Canada
418-562-1205
Fax: 418-566-2163
MICR: 0619-1

Memramcook
139 St-Thomas St.
Memramcook, NB E4K 2N8 Canada
506-758-2558
Fax: 506-758-2702
MICR: 1310-1

Midland - King St.
248 King St.
Midland, ON L4R 3M3 Canada
705-526-4296
Fax: 705-526-4298
MICR: 0875-1

Midland - RR#2
Mountainview Mall
PO Box 51
RR#2
Midland, ON L4R 4K4 Canada
705-526-2273
Fax: 705-526-2274
MICR: 0876-1

Mississauga - Britannia Rd. West
1201 Britannia Rd. West
Mississauga, ON L5V 1N2 Canada
905-858-2390
Fax: 905-858-3140
MICR: 0371-1

Mississauga - Burnhamthorpe Rd. West
#100, 350 Burnhamthorpe Rd. West
Mississauga, ON L5B 3J1 Canada
905-272-4680
Fax: 905-272-5499
MICR: 0324-1

Mississauga - Eglinton Ave. East
Delaware Square
295 Eglinton Ave. East
Mississauga, ON L4Z 3X6 Canada
905-568-1476
Fax: 905-568-4449
MICR: 0341-1

Mississauga - Winston Churchill Blvd.
3100 Winston Churchill Blvd.
Mississauga, ON L5L 2V7 Canada
905-569-3911
Fax: 905-569-6803
MICR: 0353-1

Moncton - Main St. South
#201, 735 Main St. South
Moncton, NB E1C 1E5 Canada
506-858-1340
Fax: 506-859-2201
MICR: 1035-1

Moncton - Moncton University
Taillon Bldg., Moncton University
PO Box 12
Moncton, NB E1A 3E9 Canada
506-859-2218
Fax: 506-859-2203
MICR: 1436-1

Moncton - Mountain Rd.
1566 Mountain Rd.
Moncton, NB E1G 1A2 Canada
506-859-2260
Fax: 506-858-1322
MICR: 1331-1

Mont-Joli
1511, boul Jacques-Cartier
Mont-Joli, QC G5H 2V5 Canada
418-775-8867
Fax: 418-775-9670
MICR: 0621-1

Mont-Laurier
497, rue du Pont
Mont-Laurier, QC J9L 3K2 Canada
819-623-1505
Fax: 819-623-6018
MICR: 0212-1

Mont-Saint-Hilaire

National Bank of Canada(NBC)/ Banque Nationale du Canada(BNC) (continued)

Sir Wilfrid
365, boul Laurier
Mont-Saint-Hilaire, QC J3H 6A2 Canada
450-467-9349
Fax: 450-467-5802
MICR: 0255-1

Mont-Tremblant - Curé-Deslauriers
PO Box 2568
160, Curé-Deslauriers
Mont-Tremblant, QC J8E 1B1 Canada
819-425-8444
Fax: 819-425-6888
MICR: 1438-1

Montebello
509, rue Notre-Dame
Montebello, QC J0V 1L0 Canada
819-423-6321
Fax: 819-423-5650
MICR: 0437-1

Montmagny
1, place de l'Église
Montmagny, QC G5V 2L9 Canada
418-248-2255
Fax: 418-248-4487
MICR: 0622-1

Montréal - 4e
9700, 4e rue
Montréal, QC H1C 1T2 Canada
514-648-3845
Fax: 514-648-8586
MICR: 0197-1

Montréal - Beaubien
2303, rue Beaubien est
Montréal, QC H2G 1N1 Canada
514-728-3603
Fax: 514-728-9781
MICR: 0172-1

Montréal - Beaubien
5100, rue Beaubien est
Montréal, QC H1T 1V7 Canada
514-254-6083
Fax: 514-254-9325
MICR: 1159-1

Montréal - Beaubien
6405, rue Beaubien est
Montréal, QC H1M 1B1 Canada
514-255-5702
Fax: 514-255-4221
MICR: 1085-1

Montréal - Bernard
1285, av Bernard ouest
Montréal, QC H2V 1V8 Canada
514-274-7531
Fax: 514-274-2290
MICR: 0150-1

Montréal - Boisé
Sanctuaire du Mont-Royal
6100, rue du Boisé
Montréal, QC H3S 2W1 Canada
514-738-8296
Fax: 514-738-7861
MICR: 1029-1

Montréal - Bord du Lac
312, ch du Bord du Lac
Montréal, QC H9S 4L5 Canada
514-697-6230
Fax: 514-697-8545
MICR: 0120-1

Montréal - Bélanger
1695, rue Bélanger est
Montréal, QC H2G 1B1 Canada
514-729-3287
Fax: 514-729-3145
MICR: 0171-1

Montréal - Canora
1319, ch Canora
Montréal, QC H3P 2J5 Canada
514-735-6391
Fax: 514-735-4572
MICR: 0076-1

Montréal - Casino
1, av du Casino
Montréal, QC H3C 4W7 Canada
514-861-7151
Fax: 514-861-7165
MICR: 0815-1

Montréal - Centrale
7685, rue Centrale
Montréal, QC H8P 1L7 Canada
514-365-5200
Fax: 514-365-6703
MICR: 0177-1

Montréal - Chabanel
235, rue Chabanel ouest
Montréal, QC H2N 1G3 Canada
514-381-9991
Fax: 514-381-4097
MICR: 1080-1

Montréal - Charleroi
4983, rue de Charleroi
Montréal, QC H1G 2Z2 Canada
514-325-3003
Fax: 514-325-1579
MICR: 1188-1

Montréal - Chatillon
8200, av de Chatillon
Montréal, QC H1K 1P2 Canada
514-353-6261
Fax: 514-353-9367
MICR: 0139-1

Montréal - Commerce
48, Place du Commerce
Montréal, QC H3E 0A1
MICR: 1115-1

Montréal - Côte-des-Neiges
5355, Côte-des-Neiges
Montréal, QC H3T 1Y4 Canada
514-340-9550
Fax: 514-340-9641
MICR: 1133-1

Montréal - Côte-Vertu
185, ch Côte-Vertu
Montréal, QC H4N 1C8 Canada
514-331-2633
Fax: 514-331-4391
MICR: 1194-1

Montréal - Desjardins
PO Box 246, Place Desjardins Sta. Place Desjardins
2, complexe Desjardins
Montréal, QC H5B 1B4 Canada
514-281-9650
Fax: 514-282-1331
MICR: 1096-1

Montréal - Dorval
185, av Dorval
Montréal, QC H9S 3G6 Canada
514-636-6422
Fax: 514-636-1432
MICR: 0188-1

Montréal - Décarie
1000, boul Décarie
Montréal, QC H4L 3M5 Canada
514-331-9180
Fax: 514-331-5780
MICR: 0184-1

Montréal - Fleury est
1201, rue Fleury est
Montréal, QC H2C 1R2 Canada
514-387-2513
Fax: 514-387-8462
MICR: 0181-1

Montréal - Fleury est
1795, rue Fleury est
Montréal, QC H2C 1T3 Canada
514-382-8262
Fax: 514-382-9571
MICR: 0192-1

Montréal - Gauchetière ouest
Niveau A
600, rue de la Gauchetière ouest
Montréal, QC H3B 4L2 Canada
514-394-4385
Fax: 514-394-8258
MICR: 0001-1

Montréal - Gauchetière ouest
#340, 895, rue de la Gauchetière ouest
Montréal, QC H3B 4G1 Canada
514-871-9631
Fax: 514-871-8812
MICR: 0082-1

Montréal - Gouin est
1635, boul Gouin est
Montréal, QC H2C 1C2 Canada
514-388-1761
Fax: 514-388-0932
MICR: 0192-2

Montréal - Gouin ouest
5990, boul Gouin ouest
Montréal, QC H4J 1E6 Canada
514-334-5510
Fax: 514-334-5265
MICR: 1121-1

Montréal - Henri-Bourassa
265, boul Henri-Bourassa est
Montréal, QC H3L 1C1 Canada
514-387-6291
Fax: 514-387-7136
MICR: 0182-1

Montréal - Hochelaga
8775, rue Hochelaga
Montréal, QC H1L 2N1 Canada
514-354-0322
Fax: 514-351-5928
MICR: 0131-1

Montréal - Jean-Talon est
4111, boul Jean-Talon est
Montréal, QC H1S 1J5 Canada
514-729-2819
Fax: 514-729-4951
MICR: 0186-1

Montréal - Jean-Talon est
5281, rue Jean-Talon est
Montréal, QC H1S 1L2 Canada
514-376-0301
Fax: 514-729-9856
MICR: 0155-1

Montréal - Jean-Talon est
Complexe LeBaron
6010, rue Jean-Talon est
Montréal, QC H1S 3A9 Canada
514-255-2850
Fax: 514-255-1643
MICR: 1082-1

Montréal - Jean-Talon ouest
855, rue Jean-Talon ouest
Montréal, QC H3N 1S5 Canada
514-279-8506
Fax: 514-279-5820
MICR: 11521-1

Montréal - Lacordaire
8450, boul Lacordaire
Montréal, QC H1R 2A5 Canada
514-325-4706
Fax: 514-325-3917
MICR: 1197-1

Montréal - Langelier
8020, boul Langelier
Montréal, QC H1P 3K1 Canada
514-327-4133
Fax: 514-327-0859
MICR: 1178-1

Montréal - Langelier
8020, boul Langelier
Montréal, QC H1P 3K1 Canada
514-327-4133
Fax: 514-327-0859
MICR: 0527-1

Montréal - Laurier
1074, av Laurier ouest
Montréal, QC H2V 2K8 Canada
514-273-5909
Fax: 514-273-9704
MICR: 1116-1

Montréal - Léger
6425, boul Léger
Montréal, QC H1G 1L4 Canada
514-327-1611
Fax: 514-327-0815
MICR: 1084-1

Montréal - Marcel-Laurin
1130, rue Marcel-Laurin
Montréal, QC H4R 1J7 Canada
514-332-4220
Fax: 514-332-9632
MICR: 1083-1

Montréal - Masson
2890, rue Masson
Montréal, QC H1Y 1W9 Canada
514-376-4711
Fax: 514-376-4006
MICR: 0135-1

Montréal - Maurice-Duplessis - Rivières-des-Plaines
8599, boul Maurice-Duplessis
Montréal, QC H1E 4H7 Canada
514-648-3444
Fax: 514-648-9078
MICR: 0179-1

Montréal - Monk
6800, boul Monk
Montréal, QC H4E 3J3 Canada
514-767-9907
Fax: 514-767-7290
MICR: 0108-1

Montréal - Mont-Royal
2100, av Mont-Royal est
Montréal, QC H2H 1J8 Canada
514-521-6900
Fax: 514-521-6867
MICR: 0107-1

Montréal - Newman
8449, boul Newman
Montréal, QC H8N 2Y7 Canada
514-367-0112
Fax: 514-367-4325
MICR: 0079-1

Montréal - Notre-Dame
1000, rue Notre-Dame
Montréal, QC H8S 2C2 Canada
514-637-5831
Fax: 514-637-3069
MICR: 0038-1

Montréal - Notre-Dame ouest
3611, rue Notre-Dame ouest
Montréal, QC H4C 1P6 Canada
514-935-5246
Fax: 514-935-4128
MICR: 0126-1

Montréal - Ontario est
3785, rue Ontario est
Montréal, QC H1W 1S3 Canada
514-523-3101
Fax: 514-523-4633
MICR: 0102-1

Montréal - Ontario est
2290, rue Ontario est
Montréal, QC H2K 1V8 Canada
514-527-9837
Fax: 514-527-0194
MICR: 0110-1

Montréal - Parc
5070, av du Parc
Montréal, QC H2V 4G1 Canada
514-273-1791
Fax: 514-273-3975
MICR: 0137-1

Montréal - Pierrefonds
14965, boul de Pierrefonds
Montréal, QC H9H 4M5 Canada
514-626-7330
Fax: 514-626-2237
MICR: 0125-1

Montréal - Place d'Armes
Rez-de-chausée
500, Place d'Armes
Montréal, QC H2Y 2W3 Canada
514-394-6642
Fax: 514-394-6182
MICR: 1460-1

Montréal - Provencher
8730, boul Provencher
Montréal, QC H1R 3N7 Canada
514-729-1886
Fax: 514-729-4418
MICR: 0098-1

Montréal - Queen Mary
5469, ch Queen Mary
Montréal, QC H3X 1V4 Canada
514-481-0341
Fax: 514-481-2492
MICR: 0173-1

Montréal - Saint-Michel
10212, boul Saint-Michel
Montréal, QC H1H 5H1 Canada
514-382-3980
Fax: 514-382-8861
MICR: 1169-1

Montréal - Saint-Michel
8995, boul Saint-Michel
Montréal, QC H1Z 3G3 Canada
514-381-5381
Fax: 514-381-7382
MICR: 1162-1

Montréal - Salaberry
2119, rue de Salaberry
Montréal, QC H3M 1K8 Canada
514-334-2663
Fax: 514-334-6681
MICR: 0158-1

Montréal - Sherbrooke est
5880, rue Sherbrooke est
Montréal, QC H1N 1B5 Canada
514-253-1793
Fax: 514-253-8875
MICR: 1187-1

Montréal - Sherbrooke est
12675, rue Sherbrooke est
Montréal, QC H1A 3W7 Canada
514-642-5550
Fax: 514-642-5609
MICR: 0070-1

Montréal - Sherbrooke ouest
1140, rue Sherbrooke ouest
Montréal, QC H3B 2S1 Canada
514-281-9621
Fax: 514-281-5585
MICR: 0073-1

Montréal - Sources
3627, boul des Sources
Montréal, QC H9B 2K4 Canada
514-684-5670
Fax: 514-684-0798
MICR: 0090-1

Montréal - Sources
1868, boul des Sources
Montréal, QC H9R 5R2 Canada
514-697-7794
Fax: 514-697-5103
MICR: 0067-1

Montréal - St-Charles
3918, boul St-Charles
Montréal, QC H9H 3C6 Canada
514-624-5421
Fax: 514-624-7089
MICR: 1033-1

Montréal - St-Denis
4506, rue St-Denis
Montréal, QC H2J 2L3 Canada
514-281-9610
Fax: 514-281-3185
MICR: 0114-1

Montréal - St-Denis
8091, rue St-Denis
Montréal, QC H2R 2G2 Canada
514-381-2391
Fax: 514-381-9155
MICR: 0159-1

Montréal - St-Hubert
3501, rue St-Hubert
Montréal, QC H2L 3Z8 Canada
514-526-4905
Fax: 514-526-5425
MICR: 0154-1

Montréal - St-Hubert
6420, rue St-Hubert
Montréal, QC H2S 2M2 Canada
514-273-5813
Fax: 514-273-8365
MICR: 1101-1

Montréal - St-Jean
4319, boul St-Jean
Montréal, QC H9H 2A4 Canada
514-620-2064
Fax: 514-620-4542
MICR: 1098-1

Montréal - St-Laurent
3850, boul St-Laurent
Montréal, QC H2W 1X6 Canada
514-281-9600
Fax: 514-499-9537
MICR: 1108-1

Montréal - St-Laurent
6875, boul St-Laurent
Montréal, QC H2S 3C9 Canada
514-279-8588
Fax: 514-279-7158
MICR: 0130-1

Montréal - St-Laurent
8595, boul St-Laurent
Montréal, QC H2P 2M9 Canada
514-381-7223
Fax: 514-381-7428
MICR: 0194-1

Montréal - Ste-Catherine est
Place Dupuis
801, Ste-Catherine est
Montréal, QC H2L 4M4 Canada
514-281-9630
Fax: 514-281-0167
MICR: 1109-1

Montréal - Ste-Catherine ouest
4084, rue Ste-Catherine ouest
Montréal, QC H3Z 1P2 Canada
514-933-1186
Fax: 514-933-0726
MICR: 1070-1

Montréal - University
2100, rue University
Montréal, QC H3A 2T3 Canada
514-281-9620
Fax: 514-281-5126
MICR: 1095-1

Montréal - Vincent-d'Indy
1, av Vincent-d'Indy
Montréal, QC H2V 4N7 Canada
514-739-3265
Fax: 514-739-9342
MICR: 0550-1

Montréal - Wellington
4014, rue Wellington
Montréal, QC H4G 1V3 Canada
514-766-2391
Fax: 514-766-6955
MICR: 1114-1

Métabetchouan-Lac-à-La-Croix
93, rue St-André
Métabetchouan-Lac-a-la-Croi, QC G8G 1V5 Canada
418-349-8803
Fax: 418-349-8716
MICR: 0620-1

Neguac
954 Principale St.
Néguac, NB E9G 1N7 Canada
506-776-8308
Fax: 506-776-3421
MICR: 1322-1

Nepean
Moodie Mall
1 Stafford Rd.
Nepean, ON K2H 9N5 Canada
613-596-3372
Fax: 613-596-1177
MICR: 1050-1

Newmarket
72 Davis Dr.
Newmarket, ON L3Y 2M7 Canada
905-898-5554
Fax: 905-898-5561
MICR: 0878-1

Nicolet
1639, Louis-Fréchette
Nicolet, QC J3T 2A7 Canada
819-293-4531
Fax: 819-293-6806
MICR: 0258-1

Normandin
1056, rue St-Cyrille
Normandin, QC G8M 4J2 Canada
418-274-2815
Fax: 418-274-4169
MICR: 0230-1

National Bank of Canada(NBC)/ Banque Nationale du Canada(BNC) (continued)

Norton
140, rte 124
Norton, NB E5T 1B9 Canada
506-839-2019
Fax: 506-839-2665
MICR: 1240-1

Notre-Dame-du-Lac
PO Box 100
689, rue Commerciale
Notre-Dame-du-Lac, QC G0L 1X0 Canada
418-899-6755
Fax: 418-899-0131
MICR: 1444-1

Oakville
2828 Kingsway Dr.
Oakville, ON L6J 7M2 Canada
905-829-2001
Fax: 905-829-4476
MICR: 0346-1

Orangeville
163 First St.
Orangeville, ON L9W 3J8 Canada
519-941-8781
Fax: 519-941-8789
MICR: 0880-1

Orillia
44 Mississauga St. East
Orillia, ON L3V 6S1 Canada
705-325-4451
Fax: 705-325-4453
MICR: 0881-1

Orleans
5929 Jeanne d'Arc Ave. North
Orleans, ON K1C 6V8 Canada
613-830-9327
Fax: 613-830-2708
MICR: 1244-1

Oshawa
575 Thornton Rd. North
Oshawa, ON L1J 8L5 Canada
905-433-8718
Fax: 905-433-3844
MICR: 0365-1

Ottawa - Baseline Rd.
780 Baseline Rd.
Ottawa, ON K2C 3V8 Canada
613-723-0937
Fax: 613-723-0489
MICR: 0314-1

Ottawa - O'Connor St.
Metropolitan Centre
#205, 50 O'Connor St.
Ottawa, ON K1P 6L2 Canada
613-236-7966
Fax: 613-236-0882
MICR: 1235-1

Ottawa - Rideau St.
242 Rideau St.
Ottawa, ON K1N 5Y3 Canada
613-241-9110
Fax: 613-241-1204
MICR: 1005-1

Papineauville
256, rue Papineau
Papineauville, QC J0V 1R0 Canada
819-427-6251
Fax: 819-427-8212
MICR: 1259-1

Paspébiac
PO Box 370
23, boul Gerard D.-Levésque
Paspébiac, QC G0C 2K0 Canada
418-752-2258
Fax: 418-752-5420
MICR: 0298-1

Pembroke
131 Pembroke St. West
Pembroke, ON K8A 6Y6 Canada
613-732-2801
Fax: 613-732-7696
MICR: 1261-1

Peterborough
421 George St. North
Peterborough, ON K9H 3R4 Canada
705-743-5558
Fax: 705-743-5699
MICR: 1419-1

Petit-Rocher
557 Principale St.
Petit-Rocher, NB E8J 1J7 Canada
506-783-4234
Fax: 506-783-4237
MICR: 1263-1

Pickering
1848 Liverpool Rd.
Pickering, ON L1V 1W3 Canada
905-831-4140
Fax: 905-831-9484
MICR: 0331-1

Pierreville
PO Box 218
61, rue Georges
Pierreville, QC J0G 1J0 Canada
450-568-2816
Fax: 450-568-0821
MICR: 1260-1

Plessisville
PO Box 83
1754, rue St-Calixte
Plessisville, QC G6L 1R3 Canada
819-362-7341
Fax: 819-362-2704
MICR: 0239-1

Pont-Rouge
173, rue Dupont
Pont-Rouge, QC G3H 1N4 Canada
418-873-4408
Fax: 418-873-3959
MICR: 0032-1

Portneuf
215, 1ère av.
Portneuf, QC G0A 2Y0 Canada
418-286-3325
Fax: 418-286-4771
MICR: 0415-1

Princeville
100, rue St-Jacques ouest
Princeville, QC G6L 4Y6 Canada
819-364-5245
Fax: 819-364-2261
MICR: 0294-1

Quyon
1137, Clarendon
Quyon, QC J0X 2V0 Canada
819-458-2357
Fax: 819-647-5113
MICR: 0776-1

Québec - 18e
1510, 18e rue
Québec, QC G1J 1Z5 Canada
418-647-6127
Fax: 418-647-6233
MICR: 1223-1

Québec - 1ère
4605, 1ère av
Québec, QC G1H 2T1 Canada
418-628-1331
Fax: 418-623-3820
MICR: 1167-1

Québec - 3e
498, 3e av
Québec, QC G1L 2W1 Canada
418-647-6170
Fax: 418-529-9248
MICR: 0237-1

Québec - Chaudière
1100, boul de la Chaudière
Québec, QC G1Y 0A1 Canada
418-651-1715
Fax: 418-651-2385
MICR: 0224-1

Québec - Etna
1451, rue de L'Etna
Québec, QC G3K 2S1 Canada
418-847-7069
Fax: 418-847-7763
MICR: 1379-1

Québec - Galeries
Galeries de la Capitale
5800, boul des Galeries
Québec, QC G2K 2K7 Canada
418-622-8284
Fax: 418-622-5319
MICR: 0010-1

Québec - Grand Allée ouest
Jardins Mérici
801, Grand Allée ouest
Québec, QC G1S 1C1 Canada
418-684-0385
Fax: 418-684-0386
MICR: 1065-1

Québec - Henri-Bourassa
4000, boul Henri-Bourassa
Québec, QC G1G 3Y8 Canada
418-623-9831
Fax: 418-623-7704
MICR: 0611-1

Québec - Henri-Bourassa
8500, boul Henri-Bourassa
Québec, QC G1G 5X1 Canada
418-628-8565
Fax: 418-622-6016
MICR: 1266-1

Québec - Laurier
2535, boul Laurier
Québec, QC G1V 4M3 Canada
418-653-6533
Fax: 418-652-7771
MICR: 1073-1

Québec - Laurier
Place de la Cité
#156, 2600, boul Laurier
Québec, QC G1V 4T3 Canada
418-652-7000
Fax: 418-652-7110
MICR: 1272-1

Québec - Ormière
9550, Place de l'Ormière
Québec, QC G2B 3Z6 Canada
418-842-9219
Fax: 418-842-7382
MICR: 0284-1

Québec - Place d'Orléans
5, rue Place d'Orléans
Québec, QC G1E 4Z3 Canada
418-661-8488
Fax: 418-661-7309
MICR: 1136-1

Québec - Principale
100, rue Principale
Québec, QC J0C 1L0 Canada
819-396-2426
Fax: 819-396-0508
MICR: 1290-1

Québec - Proulx
230, av Proulx
Québec, QC G1M 1W7 Canada
418-684-0374
Fax: 418-684-0376
MICR: 0601-1

Québec - Père-Lelièvre
Place Duberger
2300, boul Père-Lelièvre
Québec, QC G1P 2X5 Canada
418-684-0300
Fax: 418-684-0307
MICR: 1077-1

Québec - Quatre-Bourgeois
3440, ch des Quatre-Bourgeois
Québec, QC G1W 4T3 Canada
418-651-7520
Fax: 418-651-4183
MICR: 0259-1

Québec - Racine
280, rue Racine
Québec, QC G2B 1E6 Canada
418-842-9281
Fax: 418-842-1684
MICR: 1214-1

Québec - Raymond
900, boul Raymond
Québec, QC G1B 3G3 Canada

418-661-8772
Fax: 418-661-7654
MICR: 1072-1

Québec - René-Lévesque est
Place de la Capitale
150, boul René-Lévesque est
Québec, QC G1R 2B2 Canada
418-647-6100
Fax: 418-647-6213
MICR: 1075-1

Québec - Saint-Joseph est
700, rue Saint-Joseph est
Québec, QC G1K 3C3 Canada
418-649-0481
Fax: 418-649-9195
MICR: 0223-1

Québec - Ste-Foy
1385, ch Ste-Foy
Québec, QC G1S 2N2 Canada
418-684-0328
Fax: 418-684-0329
MICR: 1064-1

Québec - Ste-Foy
Plaza Laval
2750, ch Ste-Foy
Québec, QC G1V 1V6 Canada
418-651-9852
Fax: 418-651-0490
MICR: 0655-1

Québec - Ste-Foy
Centre Innovation
2360, ch Ste-Foy
Québec, QC G1V 4H2 Canada
418-658-1674
Fax: 418-658-1527
MICR: 1055-1

Rawdon
3664, rue Queen
Rawdon, QC J0K 1S0 Canada
450-834-2563
Fax: 450-834-7356
MICR: 0271-1

Repentigny - Brien
Galerie Rive-Nord
100, boul Brien
Repentigny, QC J6A 5N4 Canada
450-585-8111
Fax: 450-585-1368
MICR: 1097-1

Repentigny - Iberville
1124, boul Iberville
Repentigny, QC J5Y 3M6 Canada
450-654-0471
Fax: 450-654-1215
MICR: 1092-1

Repentigny - Notre-Dame
Place Repentigny
155, rue Notre-Dame
Repentigny, QC J6A 5L3 Canada
450-585-5900
Fax: 450-585-0790
MICR: 1160-1

Richibucto
25 boul Cartier
Richibucto, NB E4W 3W7 Canada
506-523-4428
Fax: 506-523-7354
MICR: 1252-1

Richmond
#180, 4040 #3 Rd
Richmond, BC V6X 2C2 Canada
604-821-1899
Fax: 604-821-1707
MICR: 0395-1

Richmond
60, rue Principale nord
Richmond, QC J0B 2H0 Canada
819-826-3731
Fax: 819-826-3940
MICR: 0777-1

Richmond Hill - 16 Ave.
883 - 16 Ave.
Richmond Hill, ON L4B 3E5 Canada
905-731-1743
Fax: 905-731-9584
MICR: 0347-1

Richmond Hill - West Pearce St.
Capital Centre
1 West Pearce St.
Richmond Hill, ON L4B 3K3 Canada
905-882-6094
Fax: 905-882-9435
MICR: 0379-1

Richmond Hill - Yonge St.
9737 Yonge St.
Richmond Hill, ON L4C 1V7 Canada
905-737-0314
Fax: 905-737-9541
MICR: 1410-1

Rigaud
535, ch de la Mairie
Rigaud, QC J0P 1P0 Canada
450-451-5301
Fax: 450-451-5276
MICR: 0416-1

Rimouski - Cathédrale
186, av de la Cathédrale
Rimouski, QC G5L 5H9 Canada
418-723-3394
Fax: 418-725-4203
MICR: 0262-1

Rimouski - Jessop
415, boul Jessop
Rimouski, QC G5L 1N3 Canada
418-724-4119
Fax: 418-723-7612
MICR: 1200-1

Rivière-du-Loup
Édifice Plaza Thériault
295A, boul Armand-Thériault
Rivière-du-Loup, QC G5R 5H3 Canada
418-862-7248
Fax: 418-862-2431
MICR: 0629-1

Roberval
840, boul St-Joseph
Roberval, QC G8H 2L7 Canada
418-275-2062
Fax: 418-275-1201
MICR: 0631-1

Rockland
PO Box 700
1624 Laurier St.
Rockland, ON K4K 1L4 Canada
613-446-5113
Fax: 613-446-6491
MICR: 1275-1

Rogersville
11089 Main St.
Rogersville, NB E4Y 2L9 Canada
506-775-6144
Fax: 506-775-1105
MICR: 1332-1

Rouyn-Noranda - Lac - Principale
132, av du Lac
Rouyn-Noranda, QC J9X 4N5 Canada
819-764-9425
Fax: 819-764-9767
MICR: 0297-1

Roxboro
10458, boul Gouin ouest
Roxboro, QC H8Y 1X1 Canada
514-683-0505
Fax: 514-683-6804
MICR: 0097-1

Saint John
71 King St.
Saint John, NB E2L 1G5 Canada
506-634-1234
Fax: 506-634-8440
MICR: 1011-1

Saint-Basile-le-Grand
33, rue Robert
Saint-Basile-le-Grand, QC J3N 1L7 Canada
450-653-7801
Fax: 450-653-2940
MICR: 1388-1

Saint-Bruno
1452, rue Roberval
Saint-Bruno, QC J3V 5J2 Canada
450-653-3643
Fax: 450-653-9238
MICR: 0203-1

Saint-Constant
210, rue Ste-Catherine
Saint-Constant, QC J5A 2J4 Canada
450-638-4020
Fax: 450-638-5474
MICR: 1019-1

Saint-Césaire
#2064, rte 112
Saint-Césaire, QC J0L 1T0 Canada
450-469-0632
Fax: 450-469-0335
MICR: 0022-1

Saint-Hyacinthe - Casavant ouest
2109, boul Casavant ouest
Saint-Hyacinthe, QC J2S 7E5 Canada
450-773-8773
Fax: 450-774-2885
MICR: 0050-1

Saint-Hyacinthe - Cascades
1955, rue des Cascades
Saint-Hyacinthe, QC J2S 8K9 Canada
450-773-5474
Fax: 450-773-6829
MICR: 0044-1

Saint-Jacques
83, rue St-Jacques
Saint-Jacques, QC J0K 2R0 Canada
450-839-3654
Fax: 450-839-3614
MICR: 0216-1

Saint-Lambert
564, av Victoria
Saint-Lambert, QC J4P 2J5 Canada
450-671-6142
Fax: 450-671-0658
MICR: 0219-1

Saint-Lin-Laurentides
1086, rue St-Isidore
Saint-Lin-Laurentides, QC J5M 2V5 Canada
450-439-2014
Fax: 450-439-7807
MICR: 1212-1

Saint-Léonard - Principale
692, rue Principale
Saint-Léonard, NB E7E 2H6 Canada
506-423-6389
Fax: 506-423-1989
MICR: 1006-1

Saint-Pie
224, rue Notre-Dame
Saint-Pie, QC J0H 1W0 Canada
450-772-2412
Fax: 450-772-6837
MICR: 0388-1

Saint-Quentin
245 Canada St.
Saint-Quentin, NB E8K 1K2 Canada
506-235-2936
Fax: 506-235-2122
MICR: 1307-1

Saint-Rémi
830, rue Notre-Dame
Saint-Rémi, QC J0L 2L0 Canada
450-454-4661
Fax: 450-454-5785
MICR: 0222-1

Saint-Sauveur
6, rue de la Gare
Saint-Sauveur, QC J0R 1R0 Canada
450-227-8445
Fax: 450-227-3799
MICR: 0461-1

Sainte-Adèle
1063, boul de Sainte-Adèle
Sainte-Adèle, QC J8B 2N4 Canada
450-229-3529
Fax: 450-229-9443
MICR: 1314-1

Sainte-Agathe-des-Monts
48, rue Principale est
Sainte-Agathe-des-Monts, QC J8C 1J6 Canada

National Bank of Canada(NBC)/ Banque Nationale du Canada(BNC) (continued)

819-326-2211
Fax: 819-326-9339
MICR: 1280-1

Sainte-Anne-des-Plaines
477, boul Ste-Anne
Sainte-Anne-des-Plaines, QC J0N 1H0 Canada
450-478-2231
Fax: 450-478-5953
MICR: 1215-1

Sainte-Julie
1033, boul Armand-Frappier
Sainte-Julie, QC J3E 3R5 Canada
450-649-1141
Fax: 450-649-8170
MICR: 1079-1

Sainte-Marie
160, rue Notre-Dame nord
Sainte-Marie, QC G6E 3Z9 Canada
418-387-2333
Fax: 418-387-6581
MICR: 0240-1

Sainte-Martine
236, rue St-Joseph
Sainte-Martine, QC J0S 1V0 Canada
450-427-2015
Fax: 450-427-0419
MICR: 0241-1

Salaberry-de-Valleyfield - Mgr Langlois
1396, boul Mgr Langlois
Salaberry-de-Valleyfield, QC J6S 1E3 Canada
450-371-4560
Fax: 450-371-1410
MICR: 0053-1

Salaberry-de-Valleyfield - Sainte-Cécile
57, rue Sainte-Cécile
Salaberry-de-Valleyfield, QC J6T 1L6 Canada
450-373-2992
Fax: 450-373-9288
MICR: 0045-1

Saskatoon
116 - 2nd Ave. South
Saskatoon, SK S7K 1K5 Canada
306-244-0662
Fax: 306-665-8802
MICR: 0327-1

Sayabec
PO Box 219
1, rue Keable
Sayabec, QC G0J 3K0 Canada
418-536-5421
Fax: 418-536-3633
MICR: 1447-1

Sept-×les
350, rue Smith
Sept-×les, QC G4R 3X2 Canada
418-962-7091
Fax: 418-968-0725
MICR: 1237-1

Shawinigan - 5e
792, 5e rue
Shawinigan, QC G9N 1E9 Canada
819-536-2595
Fax: 819-536-2173
MICR: 1352-1

Shawinigan - St-Marc
2082, rue St-Marc
Shawinigan, QC G9N 2J2 Canada
819-536-2511
Fax: 819-536-4787
MICR: 0758-1

Shawville
PO Box 400
347, rue Principale
Shawville, QC J0X 2Y0 Canada
819-647-2264
Fax: 819-647-7037
MICR: 0775-1

Shediac
342 Main St.
Shediac, NB E4P 2E7 Canada
506-532-4468
Fax: 506-533-3808
MICR: 1311-1

Sherbrooke - King est
578, rue King est
Sherbrooke, QC J1G 1B5 Canada
819-346-8448
Fax: 819-346-3952
MICR: 0466-1

Sherbrooke - King ouest
1405, rue King ouest
Sherbrooke, QC J1J 2C1 Canada
819-569-9783
Fax: 819-569-8400
MICR: 1370-1

Sherbrooke - Laval
PO Box 191
81, rue Laval
Sherbrooke, QC J1C 0P9 Canada
819-846-2735
Fax: 819-846-0165
MICR: 0055-1

Sherbrooke - Mi-Vallon
#100, 1300, boul Mi-Vallon
Sherbrooke, QC J1N 3B9 Canada
819-564-1644
Fax: 819-564-7420
MICR: 1393-1

Sherbrooke - Portland
3075, boul de Portland
Sherbrooke, QC J1L 2Y7 Canada
819-563-4011
Fax: 819-563-9340
MICR: 0510-1

Sherbrooke -12e
3001, 12e av nord, 5e étage
Sherbrooke, QC J1H 5N4 Canada
819-566-4422
Fax: 819-566-8783
MICR: 0056-1

Shippagan
229 J.D. Gauthier Blvd.
Shippagan, NB E8S 1N2 Canada
506-336-2266
Fax: 506-336-0081
MICR: 1248-1

Sorel-Tracy - Marie-Victorin
655, rte Marie-Victorin
Sorel-Tracy, QC J3R 1K9 Canada
450-742-5925
Fax: 450-746-5861
MICR: 0450-1

Sorel-Tracy - Roi
58, rue du Roi
Sorel-Tracy, QC J3P 4M7 Canada
450-742-5687
Fax: 450-742-7624
MICR: 0049-1

St-Agapit
1142, rue Principale
St-Agapit, QC G0S 1Z0 Canada
418-888-3913
Fax: 418-888-3611
MICR: 1299-1

St-Alexandre-d'Iberville
433A, rue St-Denis
St-Alexandre-d'Iberville, QC J0J 1S0 Canada
450-346-3182
Fax: 450-346-8832
MICR: 0443-1

St-Alexis-des-Monts
82, rue Notre-Dame
St-Alexis-des-Monts, QC J0K 1V0 Canada
819-265-2021
Fax: 819-265-4071
MICR: 0761-1

St-André-Avellin
#110, 20, rue Principale
St-André-Avellin, QC J0V 1W0 Canada
819-983-7317
Fax: 819-983-1747
MICR: 1281-1

St-Anselme
133, rue Principale
St-Anselme, QC G0R 2N0 Canada
418-885-4445
Fax: 418-885-8207
MICR: 1282-1

St-Augustin-de-Desmaures
421, rte 138
St-Augustin-de-Desmaures, QC G3A 2S7 Canada
418-878-5898
Fax: 418-878-5188
MICR: 0673-1

St-Charles-de-Bellechasse
2774, av Royale
St-Charles-de-Bellechass, QC G0R 2T0 Canada
418-887-3355
Fax: 418-887-6226
MICR: 1494-1

St-Clet
624, route 201
St-Clet, QC J0P 1S0 Canada
450-456-3241
Fax: 450-456-0028
MICR: 1285-1

St-Damien-de-Buckland
141, rue Commerciale
St-Damien-de-Buckland, QC G0R 2Y0 Canada
418-789-2317
Fax: 418-789-2771
MICR: 1480-1

St-Donat-de-Montcalm
PO Box 98
400, rue Principale
St-Donat-de-Montcalm, QC J0T 2C0 Canada
819-424-2033
Fax: 819-424-4607
MICR: 0014-1

St-Eustache - Arthur-Sauvé
539, boul Arthur-Sauvé
St-Eustache, QC J7P 4X5 Canada
450-472-8772
Fax: 450-472-7983
MICR: 1351-1

St-Eustache - St. Eustache
91, rue St-Eustache
St-Eustache, QC J7R 2L3 Canada
450-472-2320
Fax: 450-472-2413
MICR: 0249-1

St-Félicien
1121, boul Sacré-Coeur
St-Félicien, QC G8K 1P9 Canada
418-679-0822
Fax: 418-679-9340
MICR: 0281-1

St-Félix-de-Valois
4541, rue Principale
St-Félix-de-Valois, QC J0K 2M0 Canada
450-889-5501
Fax: 450-889-8649
MICR: 1384-1

St-Gabriel-de-Brandon
57, rue St-Gabriel
St-Gabriel-de-Brandon, QC J0K 2N0 Canada
450-835-3411
Fax: 450-835-4399
MICR: 0231-1

St-Georges
11458, 1ère av est
St-Georges, QC G5Y 2C7 Canada
418-228-8828
Fax: 418-228-9171
MICR: 0269-1

St-Germain-de-Grantham
273, rue Notre-Dame
St-Germain-de-Grantham, QC J0C 1K0 Canada
819-395-4289
Fax: 819-395-4873
MICR: 1455-1

St-Henri-de-Lévis
235, rue Commerciale
St-Henri-de-Lévis, QC G0R 3E0 Canada
418-882-2264
Fax: 418-882-5984
MICR: 1495-1

St-Hubert - Cousineau
6250, boul Cousineau
St-Hubert, QC J3Y 8X9 Canada
450-656-1112
Fax: 450-656-3489
MICR: 1013-1

St-Jean-Chrysostome

892, rue Commerciale
St-Jean-Chrysostome, QC G6Z 2E2 Canada
418-839-9803
Fax: 418-839-5989
MICR: 0624-1

St-Jean-Port-Joli
PO Box 760
48, av de Gaspé est
St-Jean-Port-Joli, QC G0R 3G0 Canada
418-598-3325
Fax: 418-598-7009
MICR: 0394-1

St-Jean-sur-Richelieu - 1ère
540 - 1ère rue
St-Jean-sur-Richelieu, QC J2X 3B4 Canada
450-347-0344
Fax: 450-347-1368
MICR: 0443-1

St-Jean-sur-Richelieu - St-Luc
#1, 310, boul St-Luc
St-Jean-sur-Richelieu, QC J2W 2M6 Canada
450-359-9765
Fax: 450-359-9859
MICR: 0025-1

St-Jean-sur-Richelieu - Séminaire
400, boul du Séminaire nord
St-Jean-sur-Richelieu, QC J3B 5L2 Canada
450-348-6131
Fax: 450-349-5001
MICR: 1203-1

St-Joseph-de-Beauce
875, av du Palais
St-Joseph-de-Beauce, QC G0S 2V0 Canada
418-397-5757
Fax: 418-397-5204
MICR: 0285-1

St-Joseph-du-Lac
21, rue Principale
St-Joseph-du-Lac, QC J0N 1M0 Canada
450-472-2980
Fax: 450-472-2257
MICR: 1292-1

St-Jérôme - Grignon
#34, 900, boul Grignon
St-Jérôme, QC J7Y 3S7 Canada
450-432-5209
Fax: 450-432-7849
MICR: 1477-1

St-Jérôme - St-Georges
265, rue St-Georges
St-Jérôme, QC J7Z 5A1 Canada
450-436-3314
Fax: 450-436-6644
MICR: 1313-1

St-Lazare-de-Vaudreuil
1811, ch Ste-Angélique
St-Lazare-de-Vaudreuil, QC J7T 2X9 Canada
450-424-2757
Fax: 450-424-6465
MICR: 1385-1

St-Léonard-d'Aston
63, rue Principale
St-Léonard-d'Aston, QC J0C 1M0 Canada
819-399-2224
Fax: 819-399-3448
MICR: 0048-1

St-Marc-des-Carrières
PO Box 117
805, av Bona-Dussault
St-Marc-des-Carrières, QC G0A 4B0 Canada
418-268-8758
Fax: 418-268-5071
MICR: 0687-1

St-Nicolas - Marie-Victorin
845, rue Marie-Victorin
St-Nicolas, QC G7A 3S8 Canada
418-831-0621
Fax: 418-831-5176
MICR: 0051-1

St-Nicolas - Pont
465, boul du Pont
St-Nicolas, QC G7A 2N9 Canada
418-831-7724
Fax: 418-831-4156
MICR: 0042-1

St-Pamphile
56, rue Principale nord
St-Pamphile, QC G0R 3X0 Canada
418-356-5521
Fax: 418-356-5808
MICR: 0397-1

St-Pascal
PO Box 69
500, rue Taché
St-Pascal, QC G0L 3Y0 Canada
418-492-6320
Fax: 418-492-6254
MICR: 1294-1

St-Prosper
2655, 20e av
St-Prosper, QC G0M 1Y0 Canada
418-594-8214
Fax: 418-594-6061
MICR: 1450-1

St-Raymond
202, av St-Michel
St-Raymond, QC G3L 3W7 Canada
418-337-6731
Fax: 418-337-8821
MICR: 0421-1

St-Romuald
2195, boul de la Rive-Sud
St-Romuald, QC G6W 2S5 Canada
418-839-0641
Fax: 418-839-8240
MICR: 1234-1

St-Tite
530, rue Notre-Dame
St-Tite, QC G0X 3H0 Canada
418-365-5145
Fax: 418-365-7404
MICR: 0759-1

Ste-Anne-de-Beaupré
10516, boul Ste-Anne
Ste-Anne-de-Beaupré, QC G0A 3C0 Canada
418-827-3764
Fax: 418-827-8104
MICR: 0632-1

Ste-Anne-de-la-Pérade
177, rue Principale
Ste-Anne-de-la-Pérade, QC G0X 2J0 Canada
418-325-2077
Fax: 418-325-3364
MICR: 0760-1

Ste-Anne-des-Monts
1, boul Ste-Anne est
Ste-Anne-des-Monts, QC G4V 1M4 Canada
418-763-2241
Fax: 418-763-9148
MICR: 0647-1

Ste-Claire
92, boul Bégin
Ste-Claire, QC G0R 2V0 Canada
418-883-3354
Fax: 418-883-3850
MICR: 0383-1

Ste-Croix
6169, rue Principale
Ste-Croix, QC G0S 2H0 Canada
418-926-3270
Fax: 418-926-2260
MICR: 0524-1

Ste-Thérèse
206, boul Curé-Labelle
Ste-Thérèse, QC J7E 2X7 Canada
450-430-2077
Fax: 450-430-8504
MICR: 1042-1

Sturgeon Falls
205 King St.
Sturgeon Falls, ON P2B 1R8 Canada
705-753-0330
Fax: 705-753-5483
MICR: 0311-1

Sudbury
2 Lisgar St.
Sudbury, ON P3E 3L6 Canada
705-673-9555
Fax: 705-673-2674
MICR: 0315-1

Summerside
290 Water St.
Summerside, PE C1N 1B8 Canada
902-436-9121
Fax: 902-436-1719
MICR: 1304-1

Trois-Rivière - Forges
3920, boul des Forges
Trois-Rivières, QC G8Y 1V7 Canada
819-376-6433
Fax: 819-376-4950
MICR: 0675-1

Tecumseh
12321 Tecumseh Rd. East
Tecumseh, ON N8N 1M5 Canada
519-735-2168
Fax: 519-735-7355
MICR: 1319-1

Terrebonne
1080, boul des Seigneurs
Terrebonne, QC J6W 3W4 Canada
450-471-3768
Fax: 450-492-7449
MICR: 1315-1

Thetford Mines - Frontenac ouest
365, boul Frontenac ouest
Thetford Mines, QC G6G 6K2 Canada
418-338-6131
Fax: 418-338-9133
MICR: 0427-1

Thetford Mines - Notre-Dame ouest
94, rue Notre-Dame ouest
Thetford Mines, QC G6G 1J3 Canada
418-338-6123
Fax: 418-338-3478
MICR: 0389-1

Tilbury
PO Box 610
18 Queen St. South
Tilbury, ON N0P 2L0 Canada
519-682-1616
Fax: 519-682-2401
MICR: 1317-1

Timmins
151 Algonquin Blvd. East
Timmins, ON P4N 1A6 Canada
705-267-7991
Fax: 705-268-3541
MICR: 0300-1

Toronto - College St.
747 College St.
Toronto, ON M6G 1C5 Canada
416-537-3182
Fax: 416-537-3011
MICR: 1422-1

Toronto - Danforth Ave.
629 Danforth Ave.
Toronto, ON M4K 1R2 Canada
416-461-0271
Fax: 416-461-5779
MICR: 1249-1

Toronto - Dundas St. West
468 Dundas St. West
Toronto, ON M5T 1G9 Canada
416-977-6812
Fax: 416-977-5705
MICR: 1421-1

Toronto - Finch Ave. East
4040 Finch Ave. East
Toronto, ON M1S 4V5 Canada
416-321-6276
Fax: 416-321-6470
MICR: 0333-1

Toronto - Kingston Rd.
1089 Kingston Rd.
Toronto, ON M1N 1N6 Canada
416-690-8065
Fax: 416-690-5295
MICR: 0369-1

Toronto - Martin Grove Rd.
2200 Martin Grove Rd.
Toronto, ON M9V 5H9 Canada
416-744-2910
Fax: 416-744-9786
MICR: 0382-1

National Bank of Canada(NBC)/ Banque Nationale du Canada(BNC) (continued)

Toronto - Sheppard Ave. East
2002 Sheppard Ave. East
Toronto, ON M2J 5B3 Canada
416-496-8237
Fax: 416-496-1300
MICR: 0336-1

Toronto - St. Clair Ave. West
1295 St. Clair Ave. West
Toronto, ON M6E 1C2 Canada
416-654-8890
Fax: 416-654-9622
MICR: 1297-1

Toronto - Wilson Ave.
343 Wilson Ave.
Toronto, ON M3H 1T1 Canada
416-633-0161
Fax: 416-633-9153
MICR: 0879-1

Toronto - York St.
150 York St., Main Fl.
Toronto, ON M5H 3S5 Canada
416-864-7791
Fax: 416-864-7784
MICR: 1417-11

Tracadie-Sheila
3503, rue Principale
Tracadie-Sheila, NB E1X 1G5 Canada
506-395-2281
Fax: 506-395-5552
MICR: 1362-1

Trois-Pistoles
41, rue Notre-Dame ouest
Trois-Pistoles, QC G0L 4K0 Canada
418-851-2071
Fax: 418-851-4701
MICR: 0639-1

Trois-Rivières - Barkoff
305, rue Barkoff
Trois-Rivières, QC G8T 2A5 Canada
819-376-3735
Fax: 819-379-4178
MICR: 0457-1

Trois-Rivières - Forges
324, rue des Forges
Trois-Rivières, QC G9A 2G8 Canada
819-378-2771
Fax: 819-378-5676
MICR: 0026-1

Trois-Rivières - Jean XXIII
5620, rue Jean XXIII
Trois-Rivières, QC G8Z 4B1 Canada
819-378-4815
Fax: 819-372-5423
MICR: 0065-1

Trois-Rivières - St-Maurice
778, rue St-Maurice
Trois-Rivières, QC G9A 3P6 Canada
819-375-4747
Fax: 819-375-9766
MICR: 1437-1

Témiscaming
PO Box 790
306, ch Kipawa
Témiscaming, QC J0Z 3R0 Canada
819-627-3361
Fax: 819-627-1482
MICR: 0770-1

Val-d'Or
842, 3e av
Val-d'Or, QC J9P 1T1 Canada
819-825-3460
Fax: 819-825-5722
MICR: 0444-1

Valcourt
1030, rue St-Joseph
Valcourt, QC J0E 2L0 Canada
450-532-3414
Fax: 450-532-3410
MICR: 0442-1

Vancouver
Two Bentall Tower
555 Burrard St.
Vancouver, BC V7X 1M7 Canada
604-661-5500
Fax: 604-661-5509
MICR: 1402-1

Vanier
355 Montréal Rd.
Vanier, ON K1L 6B1 Canada
613-744-1020
Fax: 613-744-6932
MICR: 1201-1

Vankleek Hill
38 Main St.
Vankleek Hill, ON K0B 1R0 Canada
613-678-3324
Fax: 613-678-5908
MICR: 0309-1

Varennes
2020, boul René-Gaultier
Varennes, QC J3X 1N9 Canada
450-652-3924
Fax: 450-652-7640
MICR: 1326-1

Vaudreuil-Dorion - Harwood
378, boul Harwood
Vaudreuil-Dorion, QC J7V 7H4 Canada
450-455-5761
Fax: 450-455-1076
MICR: 0428-1

Vaudreuil-Dorion - St-Charles
585, av St-Charles
Vaudreuil-Dorion, QC J7V 8P9 Canada
450-424-3758
Fax: 450-424-5962
MICR: 1025-1

Verchères
627, boul Marie-Victorin
Verchères, QC J0L 2R0 Canada
450-583-3356
Fax: 450-583-5231
MICR: 1327-1

Victoriaville
174, rue Notre-Dame est
Victoriaville, QC G6P 4A1 Canada
819-758-3136
Fax: 819-758-3219
MICR: 0229-1

Wakefield
PO Box 130
741, ch de la Rivière
Wakefield, QC J0X 3G0 Canada
819-459-2323
Fax: 819-459-3165
MICR: 0429-1

Warwick
77, rue Hôtel de Ville
Warwick, QC J0A 1M0 Canada
819-358-2001
Fax: 819-358-2030
MICR: 0280-1

Waterloo
PO Box 370
5140 Foster
Waterloo, QC J0E 2N0 Canada
450-539-0484
Fax: 450-539-4959
MICR: 0773-1

Welland
469 Main St. East
Welland, ON L3B 3X7 Canada
905-735-4633
Fax: 905-735-9285
MICR: 0305-1

Windsor
155 rue St-Georges
Windsor, QC J1S 1J7 Canada
819-845-5481
Fax: 819-845-9167
MICR: 1337-1

Windsor - Grand Marais Rd. West
1301 Grand Marais Rd. West
Windsor, ON N9E 1E2 Canada
519-969-1560
Fax: 519-969-3330
MICR: 1333-1

Windsor - Malden Rd.
5841 Malden Rd.
Windsor, ON N9H 1S3 Canada
519-969-1686
Fax: 519-969-1612
MICR: 0380-1

Windsor - Ottawa St.
1599 Ottawa St.
Windsor, ON N8X 2G3 Canada
519-256-3488
Fax: 519-256-2592
MICR: 1334-1

Windsor - Riverside Dr. West
1 Riverside Dr. West, Ground Fl.
Windsor, ON N9A 5K3 Canada
519-258-3581
Fax: 519-258-7146
MICR: 1018-1

Windsor - Tecumseh Rd. East
5060 Tecumseh Rd. East
Windsor, ON N8T 1C1 Canada
519-944-2211
Fax: 519-944-0629
MICR: 1207-1

Winnipeg
179 Provencher Blvd.
Winnipeg, MB R2H 0G4 Canada
204-233-4983
Fax: 204-237-1716
MICR: 0503-1

Yamachiche
680, rue Ste-Anne
Yamachiche, QC G0X 3L0 Canada
819-296-3743
Fax: 819-296-3833
MICR: 0757-1

×le-Perrot
60, boul Don Quichotte
×le-Perrot, QC J7V 6L7 Canada
514-453-7142
Fax: 514-425-2099
MICR: 0433-1

Commercial Banking Centres:

Alma
560, rue Sacré-Coeur ouest
Alma, QC G8B 5V6 Canada
MICR: 6801-4

Amos
101, av 1ère ouest
Amos, QC J9T 1V1 Canada
MICR: 6702-2

Amqui
#72, 30, Saint-Beno(140t est
Amqui, QC G5J 2B7
MICR: 0818-1

Baie-Comeau
921, rue de Puyjalon
Baie-Comeau, QC G5C 1N3 Canada
MICR: 6801-7

Barrie
#401, 85 Bayfield St.
Barrie, ON L4M 3A7 Canada
705-734-3863
Fax: 705-734-7601
MICR: 6022-1

Bathurst
#3, 219 Main St.
Bathurst, NB E2A 1A9 Canada
506-548-3420
Fax: 506-548-5630
MICR: 6902-1

Burlington
5500 North Service Rd., 2nd Fl.
Burlington, ON L7P 5H7 Canada
905-332-4338
Fax: 905-332-7734
MICR: 6028-1

Calgary
#2700, 530 - 8th Ave. SW
Calgary, AB T2P 3S8 Canada
MICR: 6683-1

Cap-aux-Meules
425, ch Principale
Cap-aux-Meules, QC G4T 1E3
MICR: 0818-1

Caraquet
25, boul St-Pierre
Caraquet, NB E1W 1B8 Canada

506-727-3495
Fax: 506-858-1348
MICR: 6904-1
Casselman
90 boul Lafléche
Casselman, ON K0A 1M0 Canada
MICR: 6035-1
Charlottetown
132 Kent St.
Charlottetown, PE C1A 7L1 Canada
902-892-7443
Fax: 902-628-1471
MICR: 6903-2
Chicoutimi
1180, boul Talbot, 2e étage
Chicoutimi, QC G7H 4B6 Canada
418-690-8505
Fax: 418-545-8578
MICR: 6801-1
Coaticook - Child - Centre Agricole
137, rue Child
Coaticook, QC J1A 2B2
MICR: 0947-1
Dolbeau-Mistassini
1201, boul Wallberg
Dolbeau-Mistassini, QC G8L 1H3 Canada
MICR: 6801-6
Donnacona
325, rte de l'Église
Donnacona, QC G3M 2A2
MICR: 0890-1
Drummondville - Marchand - Centre Agricole
150, rue Marchand
Drummondville, QC J2C 4N1
MICR: 0949-1
Drummondville - St-Joseph
595, boul St-Joseph, 2e étage
Drummondville, QC J2C 2B6 Canada
819-477-9553
Fax: 819-474-7760
MICR: 6708-1
Edmonton
9 Sir Winston Churchill Sq.
Edmonton, AB T5J 5B5 Canada
MICR: 6684-1
Edmundston
111, rue de l'Église
Edmundston, NB E3V 1J9 Canada
506-735-8426
Fax: 506-735-5097
MICR: 6900-1
Gaspé
Carrefour Gaspé
#26, 39, montée de Sandy Beach
Gaspé, QC G4X 2A9
MICR: 6804-4
Gatineau
#200, 920, boul St-Joseph
Gatineau, QC J8Z 1S9 Canada
819-595-2551
Fax: 819-595-2403
MICR: 6701-1
Granby
424, rue Principale
Granby, QC J2G 2W8 Canada
450-375-8755
Fax: 450-372-3037
MICR: 6051-1
Iberville - 1ère - Centre Agricole
540, 1ère rue, 2e étage
Iberville, QC J2X 3B4
MICR: 0443-1
Joliette
#200, 985, boul Firestone
Joliette, QC J6E 5G1 Canada
MICR: 6710-1
La Pocatière
625, 1ère rue
La Pocatière, QC G0R 1Z0
MICR: 0890-1
Laurier-Station
170, boul Laurier
Laurier-Station, QC G0S 1N0
MICR: 0890-1
Laval
Les Tours Triomphe
#200, 2500, boul Daniel-Johnson
Laval, QC H7T 2P6 Canada
450-686-7110
Fax: 450-686-7102
MICR: 6605-1
London
435 Richmond St.
London, ON N6A 5P4 Canada
519-432-8371
Fax: 519-432-4964
MICR: 0747-1
Longueil
#400, 555, boul Roland-Therrien
Longueuil, QC J4H 4E7 Canada
MICR: 6604-1
Lévis
49B, rte. Kennedy, 2e étage
Lévis, QC G6V 6C3 Canada
418-837-6466
Fax: 418-837-7057
MICR: 6808-1
Mississauga
#216, 350 Burnhamthorpe Rd. West
Mississauga, ON L5B 3J1 Canada
MICR: 0768-1
Moncton
#301, 735 Main St.
Moncton, NB E1C 1E5 Canada
506-858-1320
Fax: 506-858-1348
MICR: 6901-1
Mont-Joli
1511, boul Jacques-Cartier
Mont-Joli, QC G5H 2V5
MICR: 0817-1
Mont-Laurier
497, rue du Pont
Mont-Laurier, QC J9L 3K2 Canada
MICR: 6045-1
Mont-Tremblant - St-Jovite
1104, rue de St-Jovite
Mont-Tremblant, QC J8E 3J9 Canada
819-425-2791
Fax: 819-425-3161
MICR: 0462-1
Montréal - Armes
500, Place d' Armes, 17e étage
Montréal, QC H2Y 2W3 Canada
MICR: 6602-1
Montréal - Gauchetière ouest
600, de la Gauchetière ouest
Montréal, QC H3B 4L2
MICR: 0755-1
Montréal - Langelier
#502, 8000, boul Langelier
Montréal, QC H1P 3K2
MICR: 6601-1
Montréal - Sources
#420, 1868, boul des Sources
Montréal, QC H9R 5R2 Canada
514-630-8006
Fax: 514-630-5046
MICR: 6607-1
Nicolet - Louis-Fréchette - Centre Agricole
1639, boul Louis-Fréchette
Nicolet, QC J3T 2A7
MICR: 4566-1
Normandin
1056, rue Saint-Cyrille
Normandin, QC G8M 4J2
MICR: 0836-1
Notre-Dame-du-Lac
689, rue Commerciale
Notre-Dame-du-Lac, QC G0L 1X0
MICR: 1817-1
Ottawa - O'Connor St.
#205, 50 O'Connor St.
Ottawa, ON K1P 6L2 Canada
MICR: 6008-1
Québec - Galeries
#200, 5800, boul des Galeries
Québec, QC G2K 2K7 Canada
MICR: 6805-1
Québec - René-Lévesque est
#1830, 150, boul René-Lévesque est
Québec, QC G1R 5B1 Canada
MICR: 0739-1
Regina
#34, 395 Park St.
Regina, SK S4N 5B2 Canada
306-525-9161
Fax: 306-525-9904
MICR: 6686-1
Richmond Hill
#201, 1 West Pearce St.
Richmond Hill, ON L4B 1H1 Canada
905-882-6095
Fax: 905-882-6338
MICR: 6013-1
Rimouski
184, de la Cathédrale, 2nd Fl.
Rimouski, QC G5L 5H9 Canada
418-723-3226
Fax: 418-725-3375
MICR: 6806-1
Rivière-du-Loup
Edifice Plaza Thériault
295A, boul Thériault
Rivière-du-Loup, QC G5R 5H3 Canada
MICR: 6806-2
Rouyn-Noranda
132, av du Lac
Rouyn-Noranda, QC J9X 3C2 Canada
MICR: 6702-4
Saint John
71 King St.
Saint John, NB E2L 1G5 Canada
506-634-1234
Fax: 506-634-8440
MICR: 6903-3
Saint-Georges
11485, 1ère av est
Saint-Georges, QC G5Y 2C7 Canada
418-227-1974
Fax: 418-227-4401
MICR: 6808-9
Saint-Hyacinthe
#2500, 1355, Gauvin
Saint-Hyacinthe, QC J2S 8W7 Canada
450-773-9337
Fax: 450-773-1354
800-463-0616
MICR: 6706-1
Saint-Rémi - Notre-Dame - Centre Agricole
832, rue Notre-Dame, 2e étage
Saint-Rémi, QC J0L 2L0
MICR: 0927-1
Sainte-Marie
160, rue Notre-Dame nord
Sainte-Marie, QC G6E 3Z9 Canada
MICR: 6808-6
Sainte-Martine - Saint-Joseph - Centre Agricole
236, rue Saint-Joseph
Sainte-Martine, QC J0S 1V0
MICR: 0821-1
Sainte-Thérèse
260, curé Labelle
Sainte-Thérèse, QC J7E 2X7 Canada
450-437-5506
Fax: 450-437-4814
MICR: 6030-1
Saskatoon
116 Second Ave.
Saskatoon, SK S7K 1K5 Canada
306-244-0662
Fax: 306-665-8802
MICR: 6685-1
Sherbrooke
3075, boul Portland, 1e étage
Sherbrooke, QC J1L 2Y7 Canada
819-564-1489
Fax: 819-564-1487
MICR: 6705-1
St-Clet - Centre Agricole
624, rte 201
St-Clet, QC J0P 1S0
MICR: 1560-1
St-Eustache

National Bank of Canada(NBC)/ Banque Nationale du Canada(BNC) (continued)

539, Arthur-Sauvé
St-Eustache, QC J7P 4X5 Canada
450-661-8526
Fax: 450-472-7983
MICR: 6030-3

St-Félicien
1121, boul Sacré-Coeur
St-Félicien, QC G8K 1P9 Canada
MICR: 0894-1

St-Jean-sur-Richelieu
400, boul du Séminaire nord
St-Jean-sur-Richelieu, QC J3B 5L2 Canada
450-348-1964
Fax: 450-348-2511
MICR: 6707-1

St-Jérôme
#101, 55, Castonguay
St-Jérôme, QC J7Y 2H9 Canada
450-565-1804
Fax: 450-565-3497
MICR: 6043-1

Terrebonne
2135, ch Gascon
Terrebonne, QC J6X 4H2 Canada
819-492-5664
Fax: 819-964-6882
MICR: 6046-1

Thetford Mines
365, boul Smith sud
Thetford Mines, QC G6G 6K2
MICR: 0427-1

Timmins
151 Algonquin Blvd. East
Timmins, ON P4N 1C5 Canada
705-267-7991
Fax: 705-268-3541
MICR: 0300-1

Toronto - King St. West - National Accounts
#820, 130 King St. West
Toronto, ON M5X 1E3
MICR: 0741-1

Toronto - University Ave.
481 University Ave., 5th Fl.
Toronto, ON M5G 2E9 Canada
MICR: 745-1

Tracadie-Sheila
PO Box 3652
3503, rue Principale
Tracadie-Sheila, NB E1X 1G5 Canada
506-395-2281
Fax: 506-395-5552
MICR: 6904-3

Trois-Rivières
#460, 1500, rue Royal
Trois-Rivières, QC G9A 6E6 Canada
819-376-6633
Fax: 819-378-5298
MICR: 6709-1

Val-d'Or
888 - 3e av, 3e étage
Val-d'Or, QC J9P 5E6 Canada
819-825-0104
Fax: 819-825-8291
MICR: 6702-1

Vancouver
Bentall Tower 2
#200, 555 Burrard St.
Vancouver, BC V7X 1M7 Canada
MICR: 6682-1

Vaudreuil-Dorion
#305, 585, av St-Charles
Vaudreuil-Dorion, QC J7V 8P9 Canada
450-424-6446
Fax: 450-424-6648
MICR: 6052-1

Vaughan
#301, 3901 Hwy.7
Vaughan, ON L4L 8L5 Canada
MICR: 6023-1

Victoriaville
174, rue Notre-Dame est
Victoriaville, QC G6P 9C3 Canada
MICR: 6704-1

Ville-Marie
13, rue Ste-Anne
Ville-Marie, QC J9V 2B6 Canada
819-629-2404
Fax: 819-629-3517
MICR: 0242-1

Windsor - Riverside Dr. West
#690, 1 Riverside Dr. West
Windsor, ON N9A 5K3 Canada
519-256-2361
Fax: 519-256-1253
MICR: 6003-1

Windsor - Saint-Georges - Centre Agricole
155, rue Saint-Georges
Windsor, QC J1S 1J7
MICR: 0947-1

Winnipeg
#2101, 360 Main St.
Winnipeg, MB R3C 3Z3 Canada
MICR: 6009-1

National Bank of Greece (Canada)/ Banque Nationale de Grèce (Canada)

1170, Place du Frère André
Montréal, QC H3B 3C6
514-954-1522
Fax: 514-954-1224
800-954-1005
www.nbgbank.com
Ownership: Foreign
Year Founded: 1971
Number of Employees: 255
Executives:
Nicholas Avgoustakis, CEO
Michael Antoniades, Sr. Vice-President
Don Bellows, Vice-President/CFO
Henry Crochetière, Vice-President, Human Resources
Ted Dandoulakis, Vice-President & Chief Credit Officer
Vassilios Giannis, Vice-President, Legal & Corporate Affairs
Chrys Kostopoulos, Vice-President & Chief Administration Officer
Jim Lekas, Vice-President, Sales & Marketing, President, NBG Bank Foundation
John Dellis, Asst. Vice-President Information System & Technolo
George Fragias, Asst. Vice-President & Chief Auditor
Branches:

Hamilton
#12, 880 Upper Wentworth St.
Hamilton, ON L9A 5H2 Canada
905-318-0031
Fax: 905-318-2660

Laval
3400, boul du Souvenir
Laval, QC H7V 3Z2 Canada
450-686-2211
Fax: 450-686-9354

Mississauga
4559 Hurontario St.
Mississauga, ON L4Z 3L9 Canada
905-712-0404
Fax: 905-712-0408

Montréal - Frère André - Downtown Branch
1170, Place du Frère André
Montréal, QC H3B 3C6 Canada
514-866-2286
Fax: 514-866-8768

Montréal - Frère André - NBG Bank Commercial Foreign Exchange
1170, Place du Frère André
Montréal, QC H3B 3C6 Canada
Fax: 514-866-2816
888-683-3371

Montréal - Frère André - NBG Cambio
1170, Place du Frère André
Montréal, QC H3B 3C6 Canada
514-866-2286
Fax: 514-866-8768

Montréal - Jean-Talon ouest
852, rue Jean-Talon ouest
Montréal, QC H3N 1S4 Canada
514-273-4233
Fax: 514-273-2111
Peter Caloudis, Vice-President & Regional Manager

Montréal - Jean-Talon ouest
5094, rue Jean-Talon ouest
Montréal, QC H1S 1K7 Canada
514-376-4313
Fax: 514-376-2324

Montréal - Parc
5801, av du Parc
Montréal, QC H2V 4H4 Canada
514-273-1301
Fax: 514-273-7165

Montréal - St-Jean
4010, boul St-Jean
Montréal, QC H7G 1X1 Canada
514-624-3303
Fax: 514-624-3313

Toronto - Danforth Ave.
661 Danforth Ave.
Toronto, ON M4J 1L2 Canada
416-461-7541
Fax: 416-461-8636

Toronto - Danforth Ave. - NBG Bank Commercial Foreign Exchange
#330, 658 Danforth Ave.
Toronto, ON M4J 5B9 Canada
416-466-3611
Fax: 416-466-1557

Toronto - Danforth Ave. - Ontario Regional Office
671 Danforth Ave.
Toronto, ON M4J 1L2 Canada
416-463-1807
Fax: 416-463-2015
Nicolas Patiniotis, Asst. Vice-President & Regional Manager

Toronto - Lawrence Ave. East
2290 Lawrence Ave. East
Toronto, ON M1P 2P9 Canada
416-751-6500
Fax: 416-751-8058

Pacific & Western Bank of Canada

#2002, 140 Fullarton St.
London, ON N6A 5P2
519-645-1919
Fax: 519-645-2060
866-979-1919
www.pwbank.com
Ownership: Parent company is Pacific & Western Credit Corp., a public company.
Year Founded: 1979
Number of Employees: 61
Assets: $1,000,000,000 Year End: 20051031
Revenues: $5,200,000 Year End: 20051031
Stock Symbol: PWC
Executives:
David Taylor, President/CEO
Barry Walter, Sr. Vice-President/CFO
John W. Asma, Sr. Vice-President & Treasurer
Richard H.L. Jankura, Sr. Vice-President
Jonathan F.P. Taylor, Sr. Vice-President
Brian Conley, Vice-President, Credit & Administration
Ross Duggan, Vice-President, Lending Operations
Barbara E.M. Hale, Vice-President, General Counsel & Corporate Secretary
Tel Matrundola, Vice-President, Public & Government Relations
Bruce Schruder, Vice-President, Marketing & Promotion
Directors:
Doug Gough, Chair
David Bratton
Arnold Hillier
Thomas Hoskin
William Mitchell
Frank Newbould
Paul Oliver
Scott Ritchie
David Taylor
Branches:

Calgary
#250, 441 - 5th Ave. SW
Calgary, AB T2P 2V1 Canada
403-265-5913
Fax: 403-265-5826
888-666-5913

Saskatoon
#950, 410 - 22nd St. East
Saskatoon, SK S7K 5T6 Canada

306-244-1868
Fax: 206-244-4649
800-213-4282
Toronto
357 Bay St., 8th Fl.
Toronto, ON M5H 2T7 Canada
Fax: 416-203-8588
866-787-9936

President's Choice Bank
439 King St. West, 5th Fl.
Toronto, ON M5V 1K4
416-204-2600
888-723-8881
www.banking.pcfinancial.ca
Profile: President's Choice Bank offers the following consumer banking services: accounts, mortgages, savings & investments, mutual funds, borrowing, & the President's Choice Financial MasterCard.

Executives:
Kevin Lengyell, Vice-President, Finance
Affiliated Companies:
PC Financial Insurance Agency

Royal Bank of Canada(RBC)
200 Bay St.
Toronto, ON M5J 2S5
416-974-5151
Fax: 416-955-7800
www.rbc.com
Also Known As: RBC Financial Group
Year Founded: 1869
Number of Employees: 70,000
Assets: $100 billion + Year End: 20061031
Stock Symbol: RY
Profile: The Royal Bank is Canada's largest bank in terms of assets.

Executives:
David P. O'Brien, Chair
Gordon M. Nixon, President/CEO
Janice Fukakusa, Chief Financial Officer
Barbara G. Stymiest, Chief Operating Officer
Peter Armenio, Group Head, RBC U.S. & International Personal & Business
Elisabetta Bigsby, Group Head, Human Resources & Transformation
Martin J. Lippert, Group Head, Global Technology & Operations
W. James Westlake, Group Head, RBC Canadian Personal & Business
Charles M. Winograd, Group Head, RBC Capital Markets
Directors:
W. Geoffrey Beattie
President, The Woodbridge Company Limited; Deputy Chair, The Thomson Corporation
George A. Cohon, OC, O.Ont
Founder, McDonald's Restaurants of Canada Limited
Douglas T. Elix
Sr. Vice-President & Group Executive, Sales & Distribution, IBM Corporation
John T. Ferguson, FCA
Chair, Princeton Developments Ltd.
Paule Gauthier, P.C., O.C., O.Q. Q.C.
Sr. Partner, Desjardins Ducharme L.L.P. Attorneys
Timothy J. Hearn
President/CEO & Chair, Imperial Oil Limited
Alice D. Laberge
Jacques Lamarre, OC
President/CEO, SNC-Lavalin Group Inc.
Brandt C. Louie, FCA
President/CEO, H.Y. Louie Co. Limited; Chair/CEO, London Drugs Limited
Michael H. McCain
President & CEO, Maple Leaf Foods Inc.
Gordon M. Nixon
David P. O'Brien
Chair, EnCana Corporation
Robert B. Peterson
J. Pedro Reinhard
Cecil W. Sewell Jr.
Kathleen P. Taylor
President, Worldwide Business Operations, Four Seasons Hotels Inc.
Victor L. Young, OC
Affiliated Companies:
RBC Asset Management Inc. - RBC Funds
RBC Capital Markets
RBC Dexia Investor Services
RBC Direct Investing
RBC Dominion Securities Inc.
RBC Insurance
The Royal Trust Company
Branches:
100 Mile House
PO Box 700
200 Birch
100 Mile House, BC V0K 2E0 Canada
250-395-7460
Fax: 250-395-2957
MICR: 04120-003
Abbey
Wayne & Cathedral
Abbey, SK S0N 0A0 Canada
306-587-2635
Fax: 306-587-2370
MICR: 00118-003
Abbotsford - South Fraser Way
33780 South Fraser Way
Abbotsford, BC V2S 5M4 Canada
604-853-2212
Fax: 604-853-9602
MICR: 00080-003
Abbotsford - South Fraser Way
31975 South Fraser Way
Abbotsford, BC V2T 1V5 Canada
604-855-5349
Fax: 604-850-0193
MICR: 01040-003
Abbotsford - South Fraser Way
Seven Oaks Shopping Centre
#142, 32900 South Fraser Way
Abbotsford, BC V2S 5A1 Canada
604-853-8384
Fax: 604-853-6648
MICR: 01050-003
Airdrie
100 Main St.
Airdrie, AB T4B 2B7 Canada
403-948-1130
Fax: 403-948-1146
MICR: 00319-003
Ajax - Harwood
2 Harwood Ave. South
Ajax, ON L1S 7L8 Canada
905-683-2291
Fax: 905-683-1897
MICR: 00042-003
Ajax - Westney
#2, 955 Westney Rd. South
Ajax, ON L1S 3K7 Canada
905-683-1321
Fax: 905-683-7483
MICR: 01292-003
Aldergrove
27510 Fraser Hwy.
Aldergrove, BC V4W 3N5 Canada
604-857-6160
Fax: 604-856-8753
MICR: 00160-003
Alexandria
440 Main St. South
Alexandria, ON K0C 1A0 Canada
613-525-3885
Fax: 613-525-5307
MICR: 00062-003
Alma
510, rue Sacré Coeur ouest
Alma, QC G8B 1L9 Canada
418-662-8510
Fax: 418-662-6766
MICR: 00041-003
Almonte
443 Ottawa St.
Almonte, ON K0A 1A0 Canada
613-256-3625
Fax: 613-256-3342
MICR: 00082-003
Amherst
103 Victoria St. East
Amherst, NS B4H 1X9 Canada
902-667-7275
Fax: 902-667-8180
MICR: 00113-003
Amherstburg
400 Sandwich St. South
Amherstburg, ON N9V 3L4 Canada
519-736-6466
Fax: 519-736-8305
MICR: 00732-003
Ancaster
59 Wilson St. West
Ancaster, ON L9G 1N1 Canada
905-648-4411
Fax: 905-648-8271
MICR: 00102-003
Ancienne-Lorette
1875, rue Notre-Dame
L'Ancienne-Lorette, QC G2E 4K1 Canada
418-872-3366
Fax: 418-872-6507
MICR: 09191-003
Annapolis Royal
248 St George St.
Annapolis Royal, NS B0S 1A0 Canada
902-532-2371
Fax: 902-532-7341
MICR: 00223-003
Antigonish
236 Main St.
Antigonish, NS B2G 2C2 Canada
902-863-4411
Fax: 902-863-0008
MICR: 00333-003
Apsley
PO Box 509
135 Burleigh St.
Apsley, ON K0L 1A0 Canada
705-656-4421
Fax: 705-656-1078
MICR: 00162-003
Arnprior
91 John St. North
Arnprior, ON K7S 2N4 Canada
613-623-6526
Fax: 613-623-0261
MICR: 00182-003
Arthur
199 George St.
Arthur, ON N0G 1A0 Canada
519-848-2532
Fax: 519-848-3995
MICR: 00202-003
Assiniboia
106 - 1st Ave. West
Assiniboia, SK S0H 0B0 Canada
306-642-5966
Fax: 306-642-3183
MICR: 00158-003
Atikokan
112 Main St. West
Atikokan, ON P0T 1C0 Canada
807-597-6905
Fax: 807-597-1396
MICR: 00222-003
Aurora - Bayview
15420 Bayview Ave.
Aurora, ON L4G 7J1 Canada
905-841-2800
Fax: 905-841-2341
MICR: 04030-003
Aurora - Yonge
Aurora Heights Plaza
15408 Yonge St.
Aurora, ON L4G 1N9 Canada
905-841-2020
Fax: 905-841-7721
MICR: 00232-003
Aylmer
7 Talbot St. West
Aylmer, ON N5H 1J6 Canada
519-773-4817
Fax: 519-765-1360
MICR: 00242-003
Ayton

Royal Bank of Canada(RBC) (continued)

Louisa St.
Ayton, ON N0G 1C0 Canada
519-665-7702
Fax: 519-665-2038
MICR: 00262-003

Baddeck
496 Chebucto St.
Baddeck, NS B0E 1B0 Canada
902-295-2224
Fax: 902-295-1299
MICR: 00553-003

Baie-Comeau
327, boul A. Lasalle
Baie-Comeau, QC G4Z 2L5 Canada
418-296-3368
Fax: 418-296-1508
MICR: 00221-003

Balcarres
106 Main St.
Balcarres, SK S0G 0C0 Canada
306-334-2592
Fax: 306-334-2343
MICR: 00558-003

Barrie - Bayfield
53 Bayfield St.
Barrie, ON L4M 3A6 Canada
705-734-4400
Fax: 705-734-2632
MICR: 00302-003

Barrie - Mapleview
99 Mapleview Dr. West
Barrie, ON L4N 9H7 Canada
705-725-7830
Fax: 705-725-7842
MICR: 00292-003

Barrie - Wellington St. West
Wellington Square
128 Wellington St. West
Barrie, ON L4N 8J6 Canada
705-725-7800
Fax: 705-725-7823
MICR: 00322-003

Barrie - Yonge
649 Yonge St.
Barrie, ON L4N 4E7 Canada
705-792-1990
Fax: 705-792-1117
MICR: 09409-003

Barrington Passage
Route 3
Barrington Passage, NS B0W 1G0 Canada
902-637-2040
Fax: 902-637-2593
MICR: 00663-003

Bath
375 Main St.
Bath, ON K0H 1G0 Canada
613-352-7294
Fax: 613-352-7472
MICR: 00342-003

Bathurst
230 Main St.
Bathurst, NB E2A 1A8 Canada
506-547-1020
Fax: 506-547-1025
MICR: 00114-003

Beamsville
4310 Ontario St.
Beamsville, ON L0R 1B0 Canada
905-563-8296
Fax: 905-563-6181
MICR: 00362-003

Beauharnois
385, rue Ellice
Beauharnois, QC J6N 1X5 Canada
450-429-3504
Fax: 450-429-6108
MICR: 00431-003

Beausejour
602 Park Ave. East
Beausejour, MB R0E 0C0 Canada
204-268-1766
Fax: 204-268-3889
MICR: 00267-003

Bedford
1597 Bedford Hwy.
Bedford, NS B4A 1E7 Canada
902-421-8844
Fax: 902-835-1776
MICR: 00883-003

Beeton
12 Main St.
Beeton, ON L0G 1A0 Canada
905-729-2296
Fax: 905-729-4229
MICR: 00382-003

Belle River
549 Notre-Dame St. North
Belle River, ON N0R 1A0 Canada
519-728-3413
Fax: 519-728-4526
MICR: 02222-003

Belleville - Front
241 Front St.
Belleville, ON K8N 2Z6 Canada
613-966-5020
Fax: 613-962-0485
MICR: 00402-003

Belleville - North Front
246 North Front St.
Belleville, ON K8P 3C2 Canada
613-969-6101
Fax: 613-966-9310
MICR: 00392-003

Beloeil
600, boul Sir Wilfrid Laurier
Beloeil, QC J3G 4J2 Canada
450-536-2000
Fax: 450-536-2020
MICR: 00501-003

Berthierville
31, rue Iberville
Berthierville, QC J0K 1A0 Canada
450-836-3741
Fax: 450-836-1271
MICR: 00531-003

Berwick
195 Commercial St.
Berwick, NS B0P 1E0 Canada
902-538-8025
Fax: 902-538-7885
MICR: 00993-003

Biggar
303 Main St.
Biggar, SK S0K 0M0 Canada
306-948-5001
Fax: 306-948-3655
MICR: 00618-003

Birtle
743 Main St.
Birtle, MB R0M 0C0 Canada
204-842-3313
Fax: 204-842-3395
MICR: 00527-003

Blainville
780, boul Curé Labelle
Blainville, QC J7C 2K5 Canada
450-433-1140
Fax: 450-433-7872
MICR: 00941-003

Blairmore
12713 - 20th Ave.
Blairmore, AB T0K 0E0 Canada
403-562-2881
Fax: 403-562-8486
MICR: 1109-003

Blenheim
181 Chatham St.
Blenheim, ON N0P 1A0 Canada
519-676-8101
Fax: 519-676-8991
MICR: 00332-003

Blind River
1 Woodward Ave.
Blind River, ON P0R 1B0 Canada
705-356-2212
Fax: 705-356-7872
MICR: 00422-003

Boissevain
388 South Railway St.
Boissevain, MB R0K 0E0 Canada
204-534-7293
Fax: 204-534-6429
MICR: 00657-003

Bolton
8 Queen St. North
Bolton, ON L7E 5T4 Canada
905-951-2540
Fax: 905-951-2617
MICR: 00892-003

Bonnyville
#104, 5028 - 50th Ave.
Bonnyville, AB T9N 2G8 Canada
780-826-2092
Fax: 780-826-5918
MICR: 01119-003

Boucherville
141, boul de Mortagne
Boucherville, QC J4B 6G4 Canada
450-655-6710
Fax: 450-655-3471
MICR: 00901-003

Bouctouche
15 Irving Blvd.
Bouctouche, NB E4S 3J4 Canada
506-743-2401
Fax: 506-743-2414
MICR: 00224-003

Bowmanville
55 King St. East
Bowmanville, ON L1C 1N4 Canada
905-623-4471
Fax: 905-623-0665
MICR: 00432-003

Bracebridge
37 Manitoba St.
Bracebridge, ON P1L 1T6 Canada
705-645-3001
Fax: 705-645-1184
MICR: 00442-003

Bradford
PO Box 340
26 Holland St.
Bradford, ON L3Z 2A9 Canada
905-775-3396
Fax: 905-775-3104
MICR: 00462-003

Brampton - Bramalea Rd.
50 Bramalea Rd.
Brampton, ON L6T 2W8 Canada
905-792-5000
Fax: 905-792-1546
MICR: 00472-003

Brampton - County Court Blvd.
209 County Court Blvd.
Brampton, ON L6W 4P5 Canada
905-796-6200
Fax: 905-796-8897
MICR: 08932-003

Brampton - Main St. North
1 Main St. North
Brampton, ON L6X 1M8 Canada
905-874-4800
Fax: 905-874-4835
MICR: 00482-003

Brampton - Main St. South
Brampton Shopping Centre
160 Main St. South
Brampton, ON L6W 2E1 Canada
905-796-5050
Fax: 905-796-5066
MICR: 00502-003

Brampton - McLaughlin
10098 McLaughlin Rd.
Brampton, ON L7A 2X6 Canada
905-495-4497
Fax: 905-495-4487
MICR: 09970-003

Brampton - Peel Centre Dr.
Bramalea City Centre
#146, 25 Peel Centre Dr.
Brampton, ON L6T 3R5 Canada
905-790-7120
Fax: 905-790-7142

MICR: 00792-003
Brampton - Queen
235 Queen St. East
Brampton, ON L6W 2B5 Canada
905-796-5075
Fax: 905-796-5089
MICR: 00492-003
Brampton - Sandalwood Pkwy. East
Heart Lake Plaza
164 Sandalwood Pkwy. East
Brampton, ON L6Z 3S4 Canada
905-840-1644
Fax: 905-840-7084
MICR: 08382-003
Brampton - Sunnymeadow
7 Sunnymeadow Blvd.
Brampton, ON L6R 1W7 Canada
905-790-2011
Fax: 905-790-2030
MICR: 00512-003
Brandon - 18th St.
661 - 18 St.
Brandon, MB R7A 5B3 Canada
204-726-3116
Fax: 204-726-0787
MICR: 00797-003
Brandon - Rosser Ave.
740 Rosser Ave.
Brandon, MB R7A 0K9 Canada
204-726-3100
Fax: 204-726-9290
MICR: 00787-003
Brantford - Colborne
22 Colborne St
Brantford, ON N3T 2G2 Canada
519-758-2056
Fax: 519-758-2080
MICR: 00522-003
Brantford - Lynden
95 Lynden Rd.
Brantford, ON N3R 7J9 Canada
519-758-2500
Fax: 519-758-2517
MICR: 01312-003
Brentwood Bay
1185 Verdier Ave.
Brentwood Bay, BC V8M 1R2 Canada
250-356-3337
Fax: 250-652-3218
MICR: 00200-003
Bridgetown
3 Queen St.
Bridgetown, NS B0S 1C0 Canada
902-665-4483
Fax: 902-665-4352
MICR: 01103-003
Bridgewater
565 King St.
Bridgewater, NS B4V 1B3 Canada
902-543-7161
Fax: 902-543-0184
MICR: 01213-003
Brighton
75 Main St.
Brighton, ON K0K 1H0 Canada
613-475-0951
Fax: 613-475-4089
MICR: 00812-003
Brockville - King
80 King St. West
Brockville, ON K6V 3P9 Canada
613-345-1471
Fax: 613-345-3858
MICR: 00582-003
Brockville - Parkedale
1000 Islands Mall
Parkedale Ave.
Brockville, ON K6V 3G9 Canada
613-342-4122
Fax: 613-342-2525
MICR: 00852-003
Brooks
PO Box 40
220 - 2nd St. West
Brooks, AB T1R 1B2 Canada
403-362-5586
Fax: 403-362-8252
MICR: 01439-003
Brossard - Lapinière
Mail Champlain
2151 Lapinière
Brossard, QC J4W 2T5 Canada
450-923-6150
Fax: 450-923-6199
MICR: 08523-003
Brossard - Taschereau
Place Portobello
#2, 7250, boul Taschereau
Brossard, QC J4W 1M9 Canada
450-923-5130
Fax: 450-923-5143
MICR: 00541-003
Bruce Mines
9202 Hwy. 17
Bruce Mines, ON P0R 1C0 Canada
705-785-3432
Fax: 705-785-3752
MICR: 00622-003
Burks Falls
189 Ontario St.
Burks Falls, ON P0A 1C0 Canada
705-382-2906
Fax: 705-382-2927
MICR: 00642-003
Burlington - Brant
#3, 2201 Brant St.
Burlington, ON L7P 3N8 Canada
905-335-1611
Fax: 905-335-2142
MICR: 00752-003
Burlington - Lakeshore
2003 Lakeshore Rd.
Burlington, ON L7R 1A1 Canada
905-634-1891
Fax: 905-634-1127
MICR: 00662-003
Burlington - Mainway
3030 Mainway
Burlington, ON L7M 1A3 Canada
905-335-1530
Fax: 905-335-9924
MICR: 00712-003
Burlington - New
3535 New St.
Burlington, ON L7N 3W2 Canada
905-639-7440
Fax: 905-639-4542
MICR: 00742-003
Burlington - Plains Rd. East
15 Plains Rd. East
Burlington, ON L7T 2B8 Canada
905-637-5658
Fax: 905-637-2567
MICR: 00702-003
Burlington - William O'Connell Blvd.
2025 William O'Connell Blvd.
Burlington, ON L7M 4E4 Canada
905-332-1566
Fax: 905-332-3666
MICR: 08272-003
Burnaby - Bainbridge
2840 Bainbridge Ave.
Burnaby, BC V5A 3W7 Canada
604-665-8500
Fax: 604-420-3468
MICR: 00750-003
Burnaby - East Hastings St.
4382 East Hastings St.
Burnaby, BC V5C 2J9 Canada
604-665-5900
Fax: 604-665-5910
MICR: 00400-003
Burnaby - East Hastings St.
6570 East Hastings St.
Burnaby, BC V5B 1S2 Canada
604-665-5925
Fax: 604-665-5935
MICR: 00440-003
Burnaby - Kingsway
4370 Kingsway
Burnaby, BC V5H 4G9 Canada
604-665-3800
Fax: 604-665-5239
MICR: 00320-003
Burnaby - Kingsway
7299 Kingsway
Burnaby, BC V5E 1G7 Canada
604-665-8352
Fax: 604-522-7057
MICR: 00480-003
Burnaby - Kingsway
Kingsway Plaza
5010 Kingsway
Burnaby, BC V5H 2E4 Canada
604-665-3850
Fax: 604-665-8625
MICR: 00490-003
Burns Lake
354 Yellowhead Hwy #16
Burns Lake, BC V0J 1E0 Canada
250-692-7111
Fax: 250-692-7381
MICR: 00560-003
Cabri
120 Centre St.
Cabri, SK S0N 0J0 Canada
306-587-2635
Fax: 306-587-2370
MICR: 00778-003
Cache Creek
1047 South Trans-Canada Hwy.
Cache Creek, BC V0K 1H0 Canada
250-457-6287
Fax: 250-457-6620
MICR: 00640-003
Calgary - 10th St. NW
417 - 10th St. NW
Calgary, AB T2N 1W1 Canada
403-292-2160
Fax: 403-292-8901
MICR: 01989-003
Calgary - 130th
South Trail Crossing
#46, 4307 - 130 Ave. SE
Calgary, AB T2Z 3V8 Canada
403-257-7105
Fax: 403-257-7320
MICR: 06892-003
Calgary - 18th
#800, 8338 - 18th St. SE
Calgary, AB T2C 4E4 Canada
403-292-2166
Fax: 403-292-8241
MICR: 02869-003
Calgary - 32nd
1333 - 32nd Ave. NE
Calgary, AB T2E 7Z5 Canada
403-292-2340
Fax: 403-291-5071
MICR: 02089-003
Calgary - 49th
807 - 49th Ave. SW
Calgary, AB T2S 1G8 Canada
403-292-8271
Fax: 403-292-8973
MICR: 02649-003
Calgary - 4th Ave. SW
Sun Life Plaza
#110, 144 - 4th Ave. SW
Calgary, AB T2P 3N4 Canada
403-292-2212
Fax: 403-292-1704
MICR: 01639-003
Calgary - 4th St. NW
5602 - 4th St. NW
Calgary, AB T2K 1B2 Canada
403-292-8251
Fax: 403-292-3672
MICR: 02189-003
Calgary - 4th St. SW
Rideau Park
2215 - 4th St. SW
Calgary, AB T2S 1X1 Canada

Royal Bank of Canada(RBC) (continued)

403-292-3900
Fax: 403-292-3035
MICR: 04508-003

Calgary - 52nd
Village Square Shopping Centre
#100, 2640 - 52nd St. NE
Calgary, AB T1Y 3R6 Canada
403-292-3355
Fax: 403-292-3185
MICR: 02169-003

Calgary - 58th
411 - 58th Ave. SE
Calgary, AB T2H 0P5 Canada
403-292-8200
Fax: 403-292-3065
MICR: 02699-003

Calgary - 5th
Bow Valley Sq.
255 - 5th Ave. SW
Calgary, AB T2P 3G6 Canada
403-292-2048
Fax: 403-292-2182
MICR: 02319-003

Calgary - 8th Ave. SW
740 - 8th Ave. SW
Calgary, AB T2P 1H2 Canada
403-292-2110
Fax: 403-292-2143
MICR: 02539-003

Calgary - 8th Ave. SW
339 - 8th Ave. SW
Calgary, AB T2P 1C4 Canada
403-292-3311
Fax: 403-292-3766
MICR: 00009-003

Calgary - Bow Trail
3810 Bow Trail SW
Calgary, AB T3C 2E7 Canada
403-292-2414
Fax: 403-292-3580
MICR: 01549-003

Calgary - Braeside
Brae Centre
11480 Braeside Dr. SW
Calgary, AB T2W 4X8 Canada
403-292-2640
Fax: 403-292-3814
MICR: 02159-003

Calgary - Canyon Meadows Dr. SE
Deer Valley Shopping Centre
#5, 1221 Canyon Meadows Dr. SE
Calgary, AB T2J 6G2 Canada
403-292-8336
Fax: 403-292-3557
MICR: 00629-003

Calgary - Centre St. NE
Beddington Heights
8220 Centre St. NE
Calgary, AB T3K 1J7 Canada
403-292-8292
Fax: 403-292-8940
MICR: 01509-003

Calgary - Centre St. North
Lambda Instore Banking
1423 Centre St. North
Calgary, AB T2E 2R8 Canada
403-292-3235
Fax: 403-292-3413
MICR: 04528-003

Calgary - Country Hills Blvd. NW
Royal Oak Centre
#1000, 8888 Country Hills Blvd. NW
Calgary, AB T3G 5T4 Canada
403-509-2940
Fax: 403-509-2948
MICR: 06498-003

Calgary - Country Village Rd.
Coventry Hills Centre
#100, 130 Country Village Rd.
Calgary, AB T3K 6B8 Canada
403-509-2710
Fax: 403-509-2711
MICR: 09219-003

Calgary - Crowfoot Way NW
Crowfoot Centre
75 Crowfoot Way NW
Calgary, AB T3G 2R2 Canada
403-292-8386
Fax: 403-292-2177
MICR: 02949-003

Calgary - Fairmount
9919 Fairmount Dr. SE
Calgary, AB T2J 0S3 Canada
403-292-8320
Fax: 403-292-3652
MICR: 01819-003

Calgary - Falsbridge Dr. NE
McKnight Village
5445 Falsbridge Dr. NE
Calgary, AB T3J 3C7 Canada
403-292-2400
Fax: 403-292-2413
MICR: 01309-003

Calgary - Lake Bonavista Dr. SE
755 Lake Bonavista Dr. SE
Calgary, AB T2J 0N3 Canada
403-299-5040
Fax: 403-271-7632
MICR: 09099-003

Calgary - Memorial Dr. SE
#1, 5269 Memorial Dr. SE
Calgary, AB T2A 4V1 Canada
403-292-2424
Fax: 403-204-1695
MICR: 02109-003

Calgary - Northland
Northland Plaza
#220, 4820 Northland Dr. NW
Calgary, AB T2L 2L3 Canada
403-292-2477
Fax: 403-292-2411
MICR: 01259-003

Calgary - Northmount Dr. NW
Northmount Village
#17, 728 Northmount Dr. NW
Calgary, AB T2K 3K2 Canada
403-292-2440
Fax: 403-299-5147
MICR: 01659-003

Calgary - Richmond Rd. SW
Glamorgan Shopping Centre
3919A Richmond Rd. SW
Calgary, AB T3E 4P2 Canada
403-292-2492
Fax: 403-292-3596
MICR: 01879-003

Calgary - Shawville Blvd. SE
Shawnessy Centre
#144, 250 Shawville Blvd. SE
Calgary, AB T2Y 2Z7 Canada
403-292-2651
Fax: 403-292-8989
MICR: 02299-003

Calgary - Strathcona Blvd. SW
Strathcona Sq.
#100, 555 Strathcona Blvd. SW
Calgary, AB T3H 2Z9 Canada
403-292-3605
Fax: 403-292-3916
MICR: 02349-003

Callander
5 Main St. North
Callander, ON P0H 1H0 Canada
705-752-1804
Fax: 705-752-4861
MICR: 01352-003

Cambridge - Dundas St. South
311 Dundas St. South, RR#1
Cambridge, ON N1T 1P8 Canada
519-740-4460
Fax: 519-740-4464
MICR: 04366-003

Cambridge - Hespeler Rd.
541 Hespeler Rd.
Cambridge, ON N1R 6J2 Canada
519-623-1012
Fax: 519-623-0077
MICR: 01632-003

Cambridge - Jamieson
100 Jamieson Pkwy.
Cambridge, ON N3C 4B3 Canada
519-658-6850
Fax: 519-658-6436
MICR: 00592-003

Cambridge - King
637 King St. East
Cambridge, ON N3H 3N7 Canada
519-653-2388
Fax: 519-653-8846
MICR: 04002-003

Cambridge - Main St.
73 Main St.
Cambridge, ON N1R 1V9 Canada
519-621-8810
Fax: 519-621-0167
MICR: 01622-003

Cambridge Bay
4 Kamotik Rd.
Cambridge Bay, NU X0B 0C0 Canada
867-983-2007
Fax: 867-983-2754
MICR: 06527-003

Campbell River
1290 Shoppers Row
Campbell River, BC V9W 2C8 Canada
250-286-5500
Fax: 250-286-3971
MICR: 00720-003

Campbellford
15 Doxsee Ave. North
Campbellford, ON K0L 1L0 Canada
705-653-2210
Fax: 705-653-2675
MICR: 00802-003

Campbellton
161 Roseberry St.
Campbellton, NB E3N 2H2 Canada
506-789-1650
Fax: 506-759-9650
MICR: 00334-003

Camrose
5102 - 50 Ave.
Camrose, AB T4V 0S7 Canada
780-672-7751
Fax: 780-672-2462
MICR: 02979-003

Candiac
201, boul de l'Industrie
Candiac, QC J5R 6A6 Canada
450-659-9681
Fax: 450-659-6442
MICR: 00641-003

Canmore
1000 Railway Ave.
Canmore, AB T1W 1P4 Canada
403-678-3180
Fax: 403-678-3190
MICR: 01297-003

Cardston
204 Main St.
Cardston, AB T0K 0K0 Canada
403-653-3321
Fax: 403-653-3307
MICR: 03089-003

Cargill
Main St.
Cargill, ON N0G 1J0 Canada
519-366-2242
Fax: 519-366-2217
MICR: 00822-003

Carleton Place
93 Bridge St.
Carleton Place, ON K7C 2V4 Canada
613-257-3800
Fax: 613-257-8873
MICR: 00842-003

Carlyle
PO Box 250
131 Main St.
Carlyle, SK S0C 0R0 Canada
306-453-6788
Fax: 306-453-6048
MICR: 00998-003

Carman

25 Main St. South
Carman, MB R0G 0J0 Canada
204-745-2015
Fax: 204-745-6216
MICR: 00897-003

Casselman
650 Principale St.
Casselman, ON K0A 1M0 Canada
613-764-5259
Fax: 613-764-3893
MICR: 00266-003

Chambly
15, Place Chambly
Chambly, QC J3L 2Y7 Canada
450-658-8753
Fax: 450-658-1579
MICR: 00741-003

Chandler
36, boul René-Levésque
Chandler, QC G0C 1K0 Canada
418-689-2225
Fax: 418-689-5453
MICR: 00761-003

Chapleau
33 Birch St.
Chapleau, ON P0M 1K0 Canada
705-864-0570
Fax: 705-864-0888
MICR: 00862-003

Charlottetown - Queen
83 Queen St.
Charlottetown, PE C1A 4A8 Canada
902-892-2405
Fax: 902-628-6527
MICR: 05054-003

Charlottetown - University
335 University Ave.
Charlottetown, PE C1A 4M6 Canada
902-892-0104
Fax: 902-892-1453
MICR: 05064-003

Chase
746 Shuswap Ave.
Chase, BC V0E 1M0 Canada
250-679-3215
Fax: 250-679-8113
MICR: 00880-003

Chatham - Keil
171 Keil Dr. South
Chatham, ON N7M 3H3 Canada
519-354-4340
Fax: 519-354-3829
MICR: 00902-003

Chatham - King
190 King St. West
Chatham, ON N7M 1E6 Canada
519-354-1680
Fax: 519-354-7905
MICR: 00882-003

Chelmsford
3420 Errington St.
Chelmsford, ON P0M 1L0 Canada
705-855-9081
Fax: 705-855-2360
MICR: 00912-003

Cheticamp
15374 Cabot Trail Rd.
Cheticamp, NS B0E 1H0 Canada
902-224-2040
Fax: 902-224-1066
MICR: 01323-003

Chicoutimi
106, rue Racine est
Chicoutimi, QC G7H 1R1 Canada
418-693-4500
Fax: 418-693-4545
MICR: 00921-003

Chilliwack - Main St.
9296 Main St.
Chilliwack, BC V2P 4M5 Canada
604-792-1384
Fax: 604-702-3035
MICR: 00960-003

Chilliwack - Vedder Rd.
Vedder Crossing Plaza
#23, 6014 Vedder Rd.
Chilliwack, BC V2R 5M4 Canada
604-824-4725
Fax: 604-824-4726
MICR: 01420-003

Church Point
1729 Hwy. 1
Church Point, NS B0W 1M0 Canada
902-769-2412
Fax: 902-769-0189
MICR: 01433-003

Churchill
203 Laverendrye Ave.
Churchill, MB R0B 0E0 Canada
204-675-8894
Fax: 204-675-2738
MICR: 01697-003

Châteauguay
Regional Shopping Centre
#455, 200, boul d'Anjou
Châteauguay, QC J6K 1C5 Canada
450-691-2720
Fax: 450-691-6588
MICR: 00781-003

Clarks Harbour
Main St.
Clarks Harbour, NS B0W 1P0 Canada
902-745-2191
Fax: 902-745-1729
MICR: 01543-003

Clearwater
Brookfield Mall
Clearwater, BC V0E 1N0 Canada
250-674-2231
Fax: 250-674-2551
MICR: 01090-003

Clifford
12 Elora St.
Clifford, ON N0G 1M0 Canada
519-327-8031
Fax: 519-327-8829
MICR: 00962-003

Climax
214 Main St.
Climax, SK S0N 0N0 Canada
306-297-2641
MICR: 01328-003

Clinton
68 Victoria St.
Clinton, ON N0M 1L0 Canada
519-482-3926
Fax: 519-482-5845
MICR: 00982-003

Coaticook
77, rue Wellington
Coaticook, QC J1A 2H6 Canada
819-849-9144
Fax: 819-849-7880
MICR: 01061-003

Cobourg
66 King St. West
Cobourg, ON K9A 2L9 Canada
905-372-2101
Fax: 905-372-3204
MICR: 01002-003

Cochrane
130 - 1st Ave. West
Cochrane, AB T4C 1A5 Canada
403-932-2231
Fax: 403-932-4396
MICR: 03199-003

Coldbrook
6615 Hwy. 1
Coldbrook, NS B4R 1B6 Canada
902-679-7141
Fax: 902-679-0769
MICR: 07153-003

Collingwood
280 Hurontario St.
Collingwood, ON L9Y 2M3 Canada
705-446-3000
Fax: 705-446-3001
MICR: 01012-003

Comber
6307 Main St.
Comber, ON N0P 1J0 Canada
519-687-3010
Fax: 519-687-3920
MICR: 01022-003

Conception Bay South
#100, 681 Conception Bay Hwy.
Conception Bay South, NL A1X 3G7 Canada
709-834-6160
Fax: 709-834-8511
MICR: 9353-003

Concord
#100, 3300 Hwy. 7
Concord, ON L4K 4M3 Canada
905-738-3200
Fax: 905-738-3217
MICR: 00192-003

Consort
5003 - 50th St.
Consort, AB T0C 1B0 Canada
403-577-3565
Fax: 403-577-3025
MICR: 03309-003

Cookstown
11 Queen St.
Cookstown, ON L0L 1L0 Canada
705-458-4331
Fax: 705-458-1368
MICR: 01042-003

Coquitlam - Barnet Hwy.
Town Centre
2885 Barnet Hwy.
Coquitlam, BC V3B 1C1 Canada
604-927-5555
Fax: 604-942-3021
MICR: 01260-003

Coquitlam - Como Lake Rd.
Como Lake Village Shopping Centre
1962 Como Lake Rd.
Coquitlam, BC V3J 3R3 Canada
604-927-5633
Fax: 604-937-7924
MICR: 01240-003

Coquitlam - North Rd.
439 North Rd.
Coquitlam, BC V3K 3V9 Canada
604-927-5653
Fax: 604-939-8365
MICR: 01200-003

Corner Brook
66 West St.
Corner Brook, NL A2H 2Z3 Canada
709-639-4000
Fax: 709-634-8909
MICR: 09103-003

Cornwall - Pitt
300 Pitt St.
Cornwall, ON K6J 3P9 Canada
613-930-2500
Fax: 613-930-2557
MICR: 01082-003

Cornwall - Second
The Mall
1380 Second St. East
Cornwall, ON K6H 2B8 Canada
613-932-6740
Fax: 613-932-9823
MICR: 01092-003

Corunna
348 Lyndock St.
Corunna, ON N0N 1G0 Canada
519-862-1456
Fax: 519-862-3002
MICR: 01102-003

Courtenay
Comox Valley
1015 Ryan Rd.
Courtenay, BC V9N 3R6 Canada
250-334-6150
Fax: 250-338-6569
MICR: 01280-003

Courtice
1405 King St. East
Courtice, ON L1E 2J6 Canada

Royal Bank of Canada(RBC) (continued)

905-576-5521
Fax: 905-576-5858
MICR: 03692-003

Cowansville
420, rue du Sud
Cowansville, QC J2K 2X7 Canada
450-266-3850
Fax: 450-266-3855
MICR: 01131-003

Craik
201 - 3rd St.
Craik, SK S0G 0V0 Canada
306-734-2672
Fax: 306-734-5230
MICR: 01548-003

Cranbrook
2 Cranbrook St.
Cranbrook, BC V1C 3P6 Canada
250-426-7291
Fax: 250-426-5740
MICR: 1360-003

Creston
1008 Canyon St.
Creston, BC V0B 1G0 Canada
250-402-6810
Fax: 250-428-3500
MICR: 01440-003

Cross Lake
#1068, Communications Bldg.
Cross Lake, MB R0B 0J0 Canada
204-676-6650
Fax: 204-676-6656
MICR: 00767-003

Crystal City
213 Broadway St.
Crystal City, MB R0K 0N0 Canada
204-873-2468
Fax: 204-873-2303
MICR: 01047-003

Cut Knife
114 Broad St.
Cut Knife, SK S0M 0N0 Canada
306-398-4983
Fax: 306-398-2268
MICR: 01768-003

Côte-St-Luc
5755, boul Cavendish
Côte-St-Luc, QC H4W 2X8 Canada
514-874-2226
Fax: 514-874-2311
MICR: 02891-003

Dalhousie
388 William St.
Dalhousie, NB E8C 2X2 Canada
506-684-1820
Fax: 506-684-2712
MICR: 00554-003

Dartmouth - Brownlow
#100, 202 Brownlow Ave.
Dartmouth, NS B3B 1T5 Canada
902-421-8825
Fax: 902-421-8897
MICR: 01793-003

Dartmouth - Cole Harbour
1022 Cole Harbour Rd.
Dartmouth, NS B2V 1E7 Canada
902-421-8889
Fax: 902-421-6117
MICR: 01833-003

Dartmouth - Portland
44 Portland St.
Dartmouth, NS B2Y 1H3 Canada
902-421-8800
Fax: 902-421-8841
MICR: 01763-003

Dartmouth - Tacoma
Tacoma Centre
40 Tacoma Dr.
Dartmouth, NS B2W 3E5 Canada
902-421-8863
Fax: 902-462-4866
MICR: 01943-003

Dauphin
202 Main St. North
Dauphin, MB R7N 1C4 Canada
204-638-4920
Fax: 204-638-7367
MICR: 01177-003

Dawson Creek
10324 - 10th St.
Dawson Creek, BC V1G 3T6 Canada
250-782-9441
Fax: 250-782-6813
MICR: 01680-003

Delisle
300 First St. West
Delisle, SK S0L 0P0 Canada
306-493-2292
Fax: 306-493-2442
MICR: 01878-003

Deloraine
102 North Railway Ave.
Deloraine, MB R0M 0M0 Canada
204-747-3012
Fax: 204-747-3217
MICR: 01187-003

Delta - 120th
Scottsdale Mall
7157 - 120th St.
Delta, BC V4E 2A9 Canada
604-665-0484
Fax: 604-596-8013
MICR: 02810-003

Delta - 48th
5231 - 48th Ave.
Delta, BC V4K 1W4 Canada
604-940-3251
Fax: 604-946-1820
MICR: 02800-003

Delta - 56th
1281 - 56th St.
Delta, BC V4L 2A6 Canada
604-948-2450
Fax: 604-943-4586
MICR: 05400-003

Delta - 84th
11170 - 84th St.
Delta, BC V4C 2L7 Canada
604-665-0380
Fax: 604-596-8648
MICR: 01730-003

Devon
39 Athabasca Ave.
Devon, AB T9G 1G5 Canada
780-987-3368
Fax: 780-987-4600
MICR: 03419-003

Didsbury
1911 - 20th St.
Didsbury, AB T0M 0W0 Canada
403-335-3328
Fax: 403-335-9368
MICR: 03529-003

Digby
51 Water St.
Digby, NS B0V 1A0 Canada
902-245-4771
Fax: 902-245-6812
MICR: 02093-003

Dolbeau-Mistassini
1300, boul Wallberg
Dolbeau-Mistassini, QC G8L 3L8 Canada
418-276-2750
Fax: 418-276-8708
MICR: 01201-003

Drayton
23 Main St.
Drayton, ON N0G 1P0 Canada
519-638-3061
Fax: 519-638-2140
MICR: 01222-003

Drayton Valley
5001 - 51st Ave.
Drayton Valley, AB T7A 1R9 Canada
780-542-5371
Fax: 780-542-3932
MICR: 03639-003

Drumheller
PO Box 2580
110 - 3rd Ave. West
Drumheller, AB T0J 0Y0 Canada
403-823-4414
Fax: 403-823-8667
MICR: 03649-003

Drummondville
1125, boul St-Joseph
Drummondville, QC J2C 2C8 Canada
819-478-6305
Fax: 819-478-6339
MICR: 01341-003

Dryden
40 King St.
Dryden, ON P8N 2Y7 Canada
807-223-5251
Fax: 807-223-4034
MICR: 01242-003

Dubreuilville
23 Pine St.
Dubreuilville, ON P0S 1K0 Canada
705-884-2833
Fax: 705-884-2470
MICR: 01252-003

Duncan
395 Trunk Rd.
Duncan, BC V9L 2P4 Canada
250-746-2400
Fax: 250-746-2406
MICR: 01760-003

Dundas
70 King St. West
Dundas, ON L9H 1T8 Canada
905-627-3577
Fax: 905-627-5571
MICR: 01262-003

Dunnville
163 Queen St.
Dunnville, ON N1A 1H6 Canada
905-774-7421
Fax: 905-774-8741
MICR: 01282-003

Durham
108 Garafraxa St. South
Durham, ON N0G 1R0 Canada
519-369-2512
Fax: 519-369-3673
MICR: 01302-003

Dutton
206 Main St.
Dutton, ON N0L 1J0 Canada
519-762-2060
Fax: 519-762-3312
MICR: 01322-003

Duvernay
3100, boul Concorde
Duvernay, QC H7E 2B8 Canada
450-661-7771
Fax: 450-661-5693
MICR: 01411-003

Edmonton - 101st
Manulife Place
10180 - 101st St.
Edmonton, AB T5J 3S4 Canada
780-448-6680
Fax: 780-425-1941
MICR: 04739-003

Edmonton - 103A
16909 - 103A Ave.
Edmonton, AB T5P 4Y5 Canada
780-448-6980
Fax: 780-448-6984
MICR: 1599-003

Edmonton - 104th
Old Sq. West
11604 - 104th Ave.
Edmonton, AB T5K 2T7 Canada
780-448-6340
Fax: 780-448-6181
MICR: 05179-003

Edmonton - 111th
Southgate Shopping Centre
111th St. & 51st Ave.
Edmonton, AB T6H 4M6 Canada

780-448-6470
Fax: 780-448-6248
MICR: 04359-003
Edmonton - 118th
4000 - 118th Ave. NW
Edmonton, AB T5W 1A1 Canada
780-448-6690
Fax: 780-448-6115
MICR: 05229-003
Edmonton - 137th
Manning Crossing
129 - 137th Ave.
Edmonton, AB T5A 5A1 Canada
780-448-6940
Fax: 780-448-6121
MICR: 05429-003
Edmonton - 137th
Northgate Centre
#1032, 9499 - 137 Ave.
Edmonton, AB T5E 5R8 Canada
780-448-6300
Fax: 780-448-6065
MICR: 04629-003
Edmonton - 142nd
9102 - 142nd St.
Edmonton, AB T5R 0M7 Canada
780-448-6995
Fax: 780-448-6189
MICR: 05399-003
Edmonton - 23rd
11010 - 23rd Ave. NW
Edmonton, AB T6J 7J7 Canada
780-448-6370
Fax: 780-448-6120
MICR: 04089-003
Edmonton - 40th
#A121, 14711 - 40th Ave.
Edmonton, AB T6R 1N1 Canada
780-448-6119
Fax: 780-448-6129
MICR: 04219-003
Edmonton - 51st
9042 - 51st Ave.
Edmonton, AB T6E 5X4 Canada
780-448-6845
Fax: 780-448-6162
MICR: 04529-003
Edmonton - 66th
Mill Woods Town Centre
2633 - 66th St. NW
Edmonton, AB T6K 4E8 Canada
780-448-6360
Fax: 780-448-6214
MICR: 04349-003
Edmonton - 82nd
10843 - 82nd Ave.
Edmonton, AB T6E 2B2 Canada
780-448-6900
Fax: 780-448-6116
MICR: 04509-003
Edmonton - 82nd
Bonnie Doon Shopping Centre
#150A, 82nd Ave. & 83rd St.
Edmonton, AB T6C 4E3 Canada
780-448-6955
Fax: 780-448-6140
MICR: 04409-003
Edmonton - 87th
Meadowlark Centre
15710 - 87th Ave.
Edmonton, AB T5R 5W9 Canada
780-448-6965
Fax: 780-448-6167
MICR: 04329-003
Edmonton - 91st
Lake District
16745 - 91st St.
Edmonton, AB T5Z 2W7 Canada
780-448-6055
Fax: 780-448-6063
MICR: 03869-003
Edmonton - Jasper
10107 Jasper Ave.
Edmonton, AB T5J 1W9 Canada
780-448-6611
Fax: 780-448-6459
MICR: 03749-003
Edmonton - Kingsway
Kingsway Mews
10567 Kingsway Ave.
Edmonton, AB T5H 4K1 Canada
780-448-6450
Fax: 780-448-6114
MICR: 05029-003
Edmonton - St. Albert Trail
13647 St. Albert Trail NW
Edmonton, AB T5L 5E7 Canada
780-409-7660
Fax: 780-409-7666
MICR: 04620-003
Edmundston
48 rue St. François
Edmundston, NB E3V 1E3 Canada
506-735-5518
Fax: 506-735-1404
MICR: 00774-003
Edson
124 - 50th St.
Edson, AB T7E 1V4 Canada
780-723-6683
Fax: 780-723-7686
MICR: 05439-003
Elliot Lake
2 Saskatchewan Rd.
Elliot Lake, ON P5A 1Z1 Canada
705-461-1922
Fax: 705-461-1760
MICR: 01342-003
Elmira
6 Church St. West
Elmira, ON N3B 1M3 Canada
519-669-1555
Fax: 519-669-3559
MICR: 01362-003
Elmsdale
178 Hwy. 214
Elmsdale, NS B2S 1H7 Canada
902-883-2261
Fax: 902-883-1610
MICR: 02203-003
Elrose
Main & First
Elrose, SK S0L 0Z0 Canada
306-378-3300
Fax: 306-378-4040
MICR: 02098-003
Embro
112 Commissioner St.
Embro, ON N0J 1J0 Canada
519-475-4106
Fax: 519-475-6027
MICR: 01402-003
Embrun
936 Notre Dame St.
Embrun, ON K0A 1W0 Canada
613-443-2210
Fax: 613-443-1484
MICR: 01422-003
Erickson
34 Main St.
Erickson, MB R0J 0P0 Canada
204-636-7711
Fax: 204-636-2264
MICR: 01437-003
Erin
152 Main St.
Erin, ON N0B 1T0 Canada
519-833-1008
Fax: 519-833-7264
MICR: 01442-003
Espanola
115 Tudhope St.
Espanola, ON P5E 1S6 Canada
705-869-3241
Fax: 705-869-5302
MICR: 01482-003
Essex
161 Talbot St. North
Essex, ON N8M 2C6 Canada
519-776-5217
Fax: 519-776-6263
MICR: 01472-003
Esterhazy
436 Main St.
Esterhazy, SK S0A 0X0 Canada
306-745-3948
Fax: 306-745-2770
MICR: 02208-003
Estevan
1202 - 4th St.
Estevan, SK S4A 0W9 Canada
306-637-4800
Fax: 306-634-9923
MICR: 02318-003
Evansburg
5119 - 50th St.
Evansburg, AB T0E 0T0 Canada
780-727-3566
Fax: 780-727-2952
MICR: 05509-003
Exeter
226 Main St. South
Exeter, ON N0M 1S7 Canada
519-235-2111
Fax: 519-235-0525
MICR: 01492-003
Eyebrow
34 Main St.
Eyebrow, SK S0H 1L0 Canada
306-759-5203
Fax: 306-759-2052
MICR: 02428-003
Fairview
10201 - 110th St.
Fairview, AB T0H 1L0 Canada
780-835-2235
Fax: 780-835-4717
MICR: 05619-003
Fenwick
795 Canboro Rd.
Fenwick, ON L0S 1C0 Canada
905-892-5704
Fax: 905-892-8281
MICR: 01522-003
Fergus
100 St. Andrew St. East
Fergus, ON N1M 1P8 Canada
519-843-2590
Fax: 519-843-6677
MICR: 1542-003
Fillmore
PO Box 10
29 Main St.
Fillmore, SK S0G 1N0 Canada
306-848-3900
Fax: 306-722-3607
MICR: 2538-003
Fisherville
8 Erie Ave. North
Fisherville, ON N0A 1G0 Canada
905-779-3474
Fax: 905-779-3778
MICR: 01552-003
Flin Flon
94 Main St.
Flin Flon, MB R8A 1K1 Canada
204-687-7551
Fax: 204-687-8163
MICR: 01567-003
Foam Lake
405 Main St.
Foam Lake, SK S0A 1A0 Canada
306-272-3393
Fax: 306-272-4119
MICR: 02648-003
Fonthill
33 - 35 Hwy. 20 East
Fonthill, ON L0S 1E0 Canada
905-892-7641
Fax: 905-892-7661
MICR: 08562-003
Foremost
120 Main St.
Foremost, AB T0K 0X0 Canada

Royal Bank of Canada(RBC) (continued)
403-867-3500
Fax: 403-867-2232
MICR: 05729-003
Forest
35 King St. West
Forest, ON N0N 1J0 Canada
519-786-2131
Fax: 519-786-6431
MICR: 07372-003
Fort Erie
67 Jarvis St.
Fort Erie, ON L2A 5M9 Canada
905-871-5800
Fax: 905-871-9094
MICR: 01562-003
Fort Frances
343 Scott St.
Fort Frances, ON P9A 1H1 Canada
807-274-7758
Fax: 807-274-8775
MICR: 01592-003
Fort McMurray - Manning Ave.
8540 Manning Ave.
Fort McMurray, AB T9H 5G2 Canada
780-743-3327
Fax: 780-743-1002
MICR: 07489-003
Fort McMurray - Millennium Dr.
106 Millennium Dr.
Fort McMurray, AB T9K 2S8 Canada
780-792-5455
Fax: 780-792-5449
MICR: 06231-003
Fort Saskatchewan
9916 - 102nd St.
Fort Saskatchewan, AB T8L 2C3 Canada
780-998-3721
Fax: 780-998-9198
MICR: 05839-003
Fort St. James
#55, 496 Stuart Dr.
Fort St. James, BC V0J 1P0 Canada
250-996-7111
Fax: 250-996-7720
MICR: 01860-003
Fort St. John
10312 - 100th St.
Fort St. John, BC V1J 3Z1 Canada
250-787-0681
Fax: 250-787-0691
MICR: 01920-003
Fredericton - Brookside Dr.
Brookside Mall
#1A, 435 Brookside Dr.
Fredericton, NB E3A 8V4 Canada
506-450-2300
Fax: 506-450-2304
MICR: 00824-003
Fredericton - Prospect St. East
Shopping Mall
1150 Prospect St. East
Fredericton, NB E3B 3C1 Canada
506-458-0817
Fax: 506-453-1336
MICR: 00934-003
Fredericton - Queen St.
504 Queen St.
Fredericton, NB E3B 5G1 Canada
506-453-1710
Fax: 506-452-0193
MICR: 00884-003
Gander
78 Elizabeth Dr.
Gander, NL A1V 1J8 Canada
709-256-1600
Fax: 709-651-3274
MICR: 09153-003
Gatineau - Aylmer
Place Grande Rivière
203, rue Aylmer
Gatineau, QC J9H 6H4 Canada
819-685-9490
Fax: 819-685-0126
MICR: 04585-003
Gatineau - Maloney
1100, boul Maloney ouest
Gatineau, QC J8T 6G3 Canada
819-243-9500
Fax: 819-243-9510
MICR: 01581-003
Gatineau - Saint-Louis
#1, 2310, rue Saint-Louis
Gatineau, QC J8T 5L7 Canada
819-243-9588
Fax: 819-243-9570
MICR: 08661-003
Gatineau - St-Joseph
Le Village Place Cartier
425, boul St-Joseph
Gatineau, QC J8Y 3Z8 Canada
819-773-2030
Fax: 819-770-2070
MICR: 01711-003
Georgetown - Guelph St.
232 Guelph St.
Georgetown, ON L7G 4B1 Canada
905-877-2244
Fax: 905-877-8844
MICR: 01672-003
Georgetown - Main St. South
83 Main St. South
Georgetown, ON L7G 3E5 Canada
905-877-5181
Fax: 905-877-7729
MICR: 01642-003
Geraldton
109 Main St.
Geraldton, ON P0T 1M0 Canada
807-854-0691
Fax: 807-854-0225
MICR: 01662-003
Gibsons
Sunnycrest Shopping Plaza
PO Box 310
#33, 900 Gibsons Way
Gibsons, BC V0N 1V0 Canada
604-886-5400
Fax: 604-886-3974
MICR: 02000-003
Glace Bay
41 Union St.
Glace Bay, NS B1A 2P6 Canada
902-849-5571
Fax: 902-849-7188
MICR: 02313-003
Glenboro
614 Railway Ave.
Glenboro, MB R0K 0X0 Canada
204-827-2729
Fax: 204-827-2899
MICR: 01957-003
Goderich
158 The Square
Goderich, ON N7A 3Z2 Canada
519-524-2626
Fax: 519-524-5833
MICR: 01682-003
Granby
195, rue Principale
Granby, QC J2G 2V7 Canada
450-375-8100
Fax: 450-375-8123
MICR: 01651-003
Grand Falls
305 Broadway Blvd.
Grand Falls, NB E3Z 2K3 Canada
506-473-9745
Fax: 506-473-9749
MICR: 01104-003
Grand Falls-Windsor
Exploits Valley Mall
19 Cromer Ave.
Grand Falls-Windsor, NL A2A 2K5 Canada
709-489-8750
Fax: 709-489-8762
MICR: 09203-003
Grand Valley
43 Main St.
Grand Valley, ON L0N 1G0 Canada
519-928-2070
Fax: 519-928-5330
MICR: 01722-003
Grande Prairie
9815 - 98th St.
Grande Prairie, AB T8V 2E4 Canada
780-538-6500
Fax: 780-538-6568
MICR: 05949-003
Gravenhurst
398 Muskoka Rd. North
Gravenhurst, ON P1P 1G3 Canada
705-687-3436
Fax: 705-687-4015
MICR: 01742-003
Grimsby
Grimsby Shopping Centre
24 Livingston Ave.
Grimsby, ON L3M 1K7 Canada
905-945-2236
Fax: 905-945-2305
MICR: 01752-003
Guelph - Gordon
987 Gordon St.
Guelph, ON N1G 4W3 Canada
519-821-5610
Fax: 519-821-5191
MICR: 03956-003
Guelph - Silvercreek
117 Silvercreek Pkwy. North
Guelph, ON N1H 3T2 Canada
519-767-4750
Fax: 519-767-4763
MICR: 01772-003
Guelph - Wyndham
74 Wyndham St. North
Guelph, ON N1H 4E6 Canada
519-824-6800
Fax: 519-824-1723
MICR: 01762-003
Gull Lake
1188 Conrad Ave.
Gull Lake, SK S0N 1A0 Canada
306-672-4143
Fax: 306-672-4089
MICR: 02868-003
Guysborough
Main St.
Guysborough, NS B0H 1N0 Canada
902-533-3604
Fax: 902-533-2360
MICR: 02423-003
Hagersville
30 Main St. South
Hagersville, ON N0A 1H0 Canada
905-768-3335
Fax: 905-768-3511
MICR: 01802-003
Halifax - Almon
5805 Almon St.
Halifax, NS B3K 1T7 Canada
902-421-8338
Fax: 902-421-6181
MICR: 02533-003
Halifax - George
Royal Centre
5161 George St.
Halifax, NS B3J 1M7 Canada
902-421-8330
Fax: 902-421-0897
MICR: 00003-003
Halifax - Herring Cove
339 Herring Cove Rd.
Halifax, NS B3R 1V5 Canada
902-421-8494
Fax: 902-421-8867
MICR: 06113-003
Halifax - Lacewood
Clayton Park
271 Lacewood Dr.
Halifax, NS B3M 4K3 Canada
902-421-8435
Fax: 902-421-8349
MICR: 05783-003
Halifax - Mumford

Halifax Shopping Centre
7001 Mumford Rd.
Halifax, NS B3L 2H8 Canada
902-421-8445
Fax: 902-454-4925
MICR: 03353-003
Halifax - Quinpool
6390 Quinpool Rd.
Halifax, NS B3L 4N2 Canada
902-421-8420
Fax: 902-421-8933
MICR: 03303-003
Halifax - Spring Garden
5466 Spring Garden Rd.
Halifax, NS B3J 4S2 Canada
902-421-8177
Fax: 902-425-8275
MICR: 03413-003
Hamilton - Barton
The Centre Mall
1227 Barton St. East
Hamilton, ON L8H 7J3 Canada
905-548-5700
Fax: 905-547-2481
MICR: 01942-003
Hamilton - Concession
555 Concession St.
Hamilton, ON L8V 1A8 Canada
905-388-7552
Fax: 905-388-1361
MICR: 01882-003
Hamilton - King
2132 King St. East
Hamilton, ON L8K 1W6 Canada
905-547-2404
Fax: 905-547-2540
MICR: 01952-003
Hamilton - King St. West
Stelco Tower, Lloyd D. Jackson Square
100 King St. West
Hamilton, ON L8P 1A2 Canada
905-521-2000
Fax: 905-525-1051
MICR: 01822-003
Hamilton - Locke
65 Locke St. South
Hamilton, ON L8P 4A3 Canada
905-572-4900
Fax: 905-572-4909
MICR: 01962-003
Hamilton - Main St. East
730 Main St. East
Hamilton, ON L8M 1K9 Canada
905-549-2446
Fax: 905-549-4935
MICR: 01982-003
Hamilton - Main St. West
1845 Main St. West
Hamilton, ON L8S 1J2 Canada
905-521-2021
Fax: 905-521-2213
MICR: 02072-003
Hamilton - Mohawk
Harvard Square Shopping Centre
801 Mohawk Rd. West
Hamilton, ON L9C 6C2 Canada
905-388-8550
Fax: 905-388-8890
MICR: 02112-003
Hamilton - Rymal
St. Elizabeth Village
393 Rymal Rd.
Hamilton, ON L9B 1V2 Canada
905-385-6988
Fax: 905-385-6113
MICR: 02244-003
Hamilton - Upper Gage Ave.
810 Upper Gage Ave.
Hamilton, ON L8V 4L8 Canada
905-575-4911
Fax: 905-575-4488
MICR: 01922-003
Hamilton - Upper James
752 Upper James St.
Hamilton, ON L9C 3A2 Canada
905-389-2291
Fax: 905-389-2210
MICR: 02042-003
Hamilton - Upper James
1642 Upper James St.
Hamilton, ON L9B 1K4 Canada
905-388-4223
Fax: 905-388-9662
MICR: 04202-003
Hamiota
43 Fourth St. SE
Hamiota, MB R0M 0T0 Canada
204-764-2722
Fax: 204-764-2786
MICR: 02087-003
Hanley
113 Lincoln St.
Hanley, SK S0G 2E0 Canada
306-544-2921
Fax: 306-544-2278
MICR: 02978-003
Hanmer
Valley Plaza Shopping Centre
Hwy. 69 North
Hanmer, ON P3P 1J6 Canada
705-969-4463
Fax: 705-969-3353
MICR: 02052-003
Hanna
102 - 2nd Ave. West
Hanna, AB T0J 1P0 Canada
403-854-3355
Fax: 403-854-2687
MICR: 06169-003
Hanover
287 - 10th St.
Hanover, ON N4N 1P1 Canada
519-364-3580
Fax: 519-364-6451
MICR: 02062-003
Happy Valley - Goose Bay
36 Grenfell St.
Happy Valley-Goose Bay, NL A0P 1E0 Canada
709-896-6510
Fax: 709-896-9578
MICR: 09801-003
Harriston
31 Elora St.
Harriston, ON N0G 1Z0 Canada
519-338-3034
Fax: 519-338-3520
MICR: 02082-003
Harvey Station
1941 Rte. 3
Harvey Station, NB E6K 1K3 Canada
506-366-9020
Fax: 506-366-3183
MICR: 01214-003
Hastings
19 Front St.
Hastings, ON K0L 1Y0 Canada
705-696-2302
Fax: 705-696-3232
MICR: 02102-003
Hawkesbury
400 Spence Ave.
Hawkesbury, ON K6A 2Y3 Canada
613-632-8568
Fax: 613-632-5720
MICR: 02152-003
Hay River
77 Woodland Dr.
Hay River, NT X0E 1G1 Canada
867-874-6547
Fax: 867-874-2248
MICR: 09859-003
Hearts Content
230-236 Main Rd.
Hearts Content, NL A0B 1Z0 Canada
709-583-2860
Fax: 709-583-2033
MICR: 09253-003
High Prairie
5117 - 49th St.
High Prairie, AB T0G 1E0 Canada
780-523-3381
Fax: 780-523-5312
MICR: 06279-003
High River
102 - 3rd Ave. West
High River, AB T1V 1M4 Canada
403-652-2351
Fax: 403-652-3784
MICR: 06389-003
Hillsburgh
97 Main St.
Hillsburgh, ON N0B 1Z0 Canada
519-855-4922
Fax: 519-855-4191
MICR: 02142-003
Hinton
874 Carmichael Lane
Hinton, AB T7V 1Y6 Canada
780-865-3344
Fax: 780-865-7611
MICR: 06609-003
Holyrood
396 Conception Bay, Rte. 60
Holyrood, NL A0A 2R0 Canada
709-229-1220
Fax: 709-229-7067
MICR: 09303-003
Houston
3232 West Yellowhead Hwy. 16
Houston, BC V0J 1Z0 Canada
250-845-2218
Fax: 250-845-3111
MICR: 02240-003
Humboldt
703 Main St.
Humboldt, SK S0K 2A0 Canada
306-682-2567
Fax: 306-682-4143
MICR: 03178-003
Hunter River
Rte. 2
Hunter River, PE C0A 1N0 Canada
902-964-2002
Fax: 902-964-2464
MICR: 05104-003
Huntsville
22 Main St.
Huntsville, ON P1H 2C9 Canada
705-788-7000
Fax: 705-788-7019
MICR: 02162-003
Imperial
300 Royal St.
Imperial, SK S0G 2J0 Canada
306-963-2030
Fax: 306-963-2770
MICR: 03198-003
Indian Head
PO Box 850
501 Grand Ave.
Indian Head, SK S0G 2K0 Canada
306-695-2278
Fax: 306-695-2377
MICR: 03308-003
Ingersoll
156 Thames St. South
Ingersoll, ON N5C 2T4 Canada
519-485-3710
Fax: 519-485-4021
MICR: 02182-003
Innisfail
4962 - 52nd St.
Innisfail, AB T4G 1S7 Canada
403-227-3307
Fax: 403-227-4311
MICR: 06829-003
Innisfil
902 Lockhart Rd.
Innisfil, ON L9S 4V2 Canada
705-436-3141
Fax: 705-436-7735
MICR: 00272-003
Invermay
218 Main St. North
Invermay, SK S0A 1M0 Canada

Royal Bank of Canada(RBC) (continued)
306-593-2083
Fax: 306-338-3717
MICR: 03418-003

Inverness
15794 Central Ave.
Inverness, NS B0E 1N0 Canada
902-258-2776
Fax: 902-258-3533
MICR: 03523-003

Iqaluit
#922, Igluvut Bldg.
Iqaluit, NU X0A 0H0 Canada
867-979-8700
Fax: 867-979-4845
MICR: 09851-003

Iron Bridge
22172 Hwy. 17 West
Iron Bridge, ON P0R 1H0 Canada
705-843-2260
Fax: 705-843-2755
MICR: 02232-003

Iroquois
53 Plaza Dr.
Iroquois, ON K0E 1K0 Canada
613-652-4861
Fax: 613-652-2029
MICR: 02242-003

Iroquois Falls
160 Main St.
Iroquois Falls, ON P0K 1G0 Canada
705-232-4076
Fax: 705-232-7211
MICR: 00122-003

Ituna
503 Main St.
Ituna, SK S0A 1N0 Canada
306-795-2661
Fax: 306-795-2224
MICR: 03528-003

Joliette
375, boul Manseau
Joliette, QC J6E 3C9 Canada
450-752-6300
Fax: 450-752-6333
MICR: 01901-003

Jonquière
Place du Marquis
3750, boul du Royaume
Jonquière, QC G7X 0A4 Canada
418-547-5711
Fax: 418-547-1112
MICR: 01971-003

Kamloops - Columbia
Sahali Shopping Centre
#175, 945 Columbia St. West
Kamloops, BC V2C 1L5 Canada
250-374-8334
Fax: 250-374-9322
MICR: 02360-003

Kamloops - Fortune
789 Fortune Dr.
Kamloops, BC V2B 2L3 Canada
250-376-8822
Fax: 250-376-1862
MICR: 03520-003

Kamloops - Victoria
186 Victoria St.
Kamloops, BC V2C 5R3 Canada
250-371-1500
Fax: 250-372-1045
MICR: 02320-003

Kanata - Hazeldean
500 Hazeldean Rd.
Kanata, ON K2L 2B5 Canada
613-831-2981
Fax: 613-831-2990
MICR: 04356-003

Kanata - March
360 March Rd.
Kanata, ON K2K 2T5 Canada
613-592-5793
Fax: 613-592-7728
MICR: 00726-003

Keewatin
815 Ottawa St.
Keewatin, ON P0X 1C0 Canada
807-547-2218
Fax: 807-547-3167
MICR: 02302-003

Kelowna - Cooper
Orchard Plaza
1840 Cooper Rd.
Kelowna, BC V1Y 8K5 Canada
250-860-3727
Fax: 250-861-8913
MICR: 02440-003

Kelowna - Ellis
#102, 1665 Ellis St.
Kelowna, BC V1Y 2B3 Canada
250-868-4100
Fax: 250-763-4265
MICR: 02400-003

Kelowna - Hwy. 33
Plaza 33
#48, 301 Hwy. 33 West
Kelowna, BC V1X 1X8 Canada
250-765-7761
Fax: 250-491-2800
MICR: 05000-003

Kelowna - Pandosy
3036 Pandosy St.
Kelowna, BC V1Y 1W2 Canada
250-763-1101
Fax: 250-861-8936
MICR: 02450-003

Kemptville
#26, 2600 County Rd.
Kemptville, ON K0G 1J0 Canada
613-258-1434
Fax: 613-258-1409
MICR: 04910-003

Kenora
144 Main St. South
Kenora, ON P9N 1S9 Canada
807-468-8921
Fax: 807-468-6247
MICR: 02322-003

Kentville
63 Webster St.
Kentville, NS B4N 1H4 Canada
902-679-3850
Fax: 902-679-1698
MICR: 03633-003

Kerrobert
446 Pacific St.
Kerrobert, SK S0L 1R0 Canada
306-834-2651
Fax: 306-834-5020
MICR: 03638-003

Keswick
#8, 24018 Woodbine Ave.
Keswick, ON L4P 3E9 Canada
905-476-7220
Fax: 905-476-7516
MICR: 05714-003

Killarney
533 Broadway Ave
Killarney, MB R0K 1G0 Canada
204-523-4642
Fax: 204-523-7144
MICR: 2097-003

Kimberley
375 Wallinger Ave.
Kimberley, BC V1A 1Z3 Canada
250-427-4821
Fax: 250-427-3022
MICR: 02560-003

Kinburn
3803 Loggers Way
Kinburn, ON K0A 2H0 Canada
613-832-2323
Fax: 613-832-4115
MICR: 02342-003

Kincardine
757 Queen St.
Kincardine, ON N2Z 2Y8 Canada
519-396-3481
Fax: 519-396-9618
MICR: 02362-003

Kindersley
401 Main St.
Kindersley, SK S0L 1S0 Canada
306-463-5330
Fax: 306-463-2091
MICR: 03668-003

Kingston - Bath
1646 Bath Rd.
Kingston, ON K7M 4X6 Canada
613-389-4770
Fax: 613-389-2744
MICR: 02402-003

Kingston - Princess
65 Princess St.
Kingston, ON K7L 1A6 Canada
613-549-2441
Fax: 613-549-4654
MICR: 02382-003

Kingston - Princess
823 Princess St.
Kingston, ON K7L 1G6 Canada
613-546-3628
Fax: 613-546-3411
MICR: 02422-003

Kingsville
11 Division St. North
Kingsville, ON N9Y 1C7 Canada
519-733-2333
Fax: 519-733-3131
MICR: 02442-003

Kirkland Lake
30 Government Rd. West
Kirkland Lake, ON P2N 3H7 Canada
705-567-5386
Fax: 705-567-9440
MICR: 02462-003

Kitchener - Duke
32 Duke St. West
Kitchener, ON N2H 3W4 Canada
519-575-2300
Fax: 519-575-2315
MICR: 02482-003

Kitchener - Fairway
600 Fairway Rd. South
Kitchener, ON N2C 1X3 Canada
519-894-2100
Fax: 519-894-2275
MICR: 02512-003

Kitchener - Highland
413 Highland Rd. West
Kitchener, ON N2M 3C6 Canada
519-575-2280
Fax: 519-575-2281
MICR: 02552-003

Kitchener - Ottawa
1020 Ottawa St. North
Kitchener, ON N2A 3Z3 Canada
519-894-5580
Fax: 519-894-5114
MICR: 02502-003

Kitimat
378 City Centre
Kitimat, BC V8C 1T6 Canada
250-639-9281
Fax: 250-632-3386
MICR: 02640-003

Kleinburg
8 Nashville Rd.
Kleinburg, ON L0J 1C0 Canada
905-893-1611
Fax: 905-893-2862
MICR: 02542-003

La Sarre
59, 5e av est
La Sarre, QC J9Z 1L1 Canada
819-339-6000
Fax: 819-339-6011
MICR: 02211-003

Lac Du Bonnet
14 Park North
Lac Du Bonnet, MB R0E 1A0 Canada
204-345-8616
Fax: 204-345-6582
MICR: 02217-003

Lacombe

5022 - 50th Ave.
Lacombe, AB T4L 2L1 Canada
403-782-3326
Fax: 403-782-6250
MICR: 07049-003

Ladysmith
527 First Ave.
Ladysmith, BC V9G 1A7 Canada
250-245-7111
Fax: 250-245-7144
MICR: 02820-003

Lake Cowichan
75 Cowichan Lake Rd.
Lake Cowichan, BC V0R 2G0 Canada
250-749-6693
Fax: 250-749-6351
MICR: 08720-003

Lakefield
50 Queen St.
Lakefield, ON K0L 2H0 Canada
705-652-6713
Fax: 705-652-6720
MICR: 02562-003

Langenburg
120 - 2nd St.
Langenburg, SK S0A 2A0 Canada
306-743-2627
Fax: 306-743-2650
MICR: 03658-003

Langley - 204th
Walnut Grove
#105, 8843 - 204th St.
Langley, BC V1M 2K4 Canada
604-882-2200
Fax: 604-882-0412
MICR: 02830-003

Langley - 40th
Brookswood Mall
20059 - 40th Ave.
Langley, BC V3A 2W2 Canada
604-532-6300
Fax: 604-530-3407
MICR: 02900-003

Langley - Willowbrook
19888 Willowbrook Dr.
Langley, BC V2Y 1K9 Canada
604-533-6800
Fax: 604-534-6813
MICR: 02880-003

Lanigan
c/o Carlton Trail Shopping Centre
Lanigan, SK S0K 2M0 Canada
306-365-2012
Fax: 306-365-3393
MICR: 03748-003

Laval - Curé-Labelle
St. Martin Shopping Centre
965, boul Curé-Labelle
Laval, QC H7V 2V6 Canada
450-686-3446
Fax: 450-686-3456
MICR: 00991-003

Laval - Curé-Labelle
560, boul Curé-Labelle
Laval, QC H7L 4V6 Canada
450-625-2300
Fax: 450-625-2348
MICR: 02621-003

Laval - Dagenais
Place Fabreville
3557, boul Dagenais ouest
Laval, QC H7P 1V8 Canada
450-625-6906
Fax: 450-625-0792
MICR: 02271-003

Laval - Laurentides
1806, boul des Laurentides
Laval, QC H7M 2Y5 Canada
450-667-9150
Fax: 450-667-4054
MICR: 02291-003

Laval - Le Carrefour
3100, boul Le Carrefour
Laval, QC H7T 2K7 Canada
450-686-3400
Fax: 450-686-3437
MICR: 02301-003

Laval - Samson
Ste Dorothée
5, boul Samson
Laval, QC H7X 3S5 Canada
450-689-2060
Fax: 450-689-2295
MICR: 05970-003

Leamington
35 Talbot St. West
Leamington, ON N8H 1M3 Canada
519-322-2821
Fax: 519-322-2127
MICR: 02642-003

Leduc
10 Leduc Towne Centre
Leduc, AB T9E 7K6 Canada
780-986-2266
Fax: 780-986-4449
MICR: 07159-003

Lemberg
332 Main St.
Lemberg, SK S0A 2B0 Canada
306-335-2248
Fax: 306-728-4607
MICR: 03968-003

Lethbridge - 2A
Centre Village Mall
1240 - 2A Ave. North
Lethbridge, AB T1H 0E4 Canada
403-382-3860
Fax: 403-380-3346
MICR: 07319-003

Lethbridge - 4th
614 - 4th Ave. South
Lethbridge, AB T1J 0N7 Canada
403-382-3800
Fax: 403-382-3844
MICR: 07269-003

Lethbridge - Mayor Magrath
1139 Mayor Magrath Dr.
Lethbridge, AB T1K 2P9 Canada
403-382-3880
Fax: 403-380-3699
MICR: 07379-003

Lindsay
189 Kent St. West
Lindsay, ON K9V 5G6 Canada
705-324-6151
Fax: 705-324-2690
MICR: 02662-003

Lions Head
10 Webster St.
Lions Head, ON N0H 1W0 Canada
519-793-3125
Fax: 519-793-3906
MICR: 02682-003

Listowel
175 Wallace Ave. North
Listowel, ON N4W 1K8 Canada
519-291-1590
Fax: 519-291-5601
MICR: 02702-003

Lively
Walden Plaza
Lively, ON P3Y 1J1 Canada
705-692-3606
Fax: 705-692-3355
MICR: 02712-003

Liverpool
209 Main St.
Liverpool, NS B0T 1K0 Canada
902-354-5717
Fax: 902-354-7406
MICR: 03963-003

Lloydminster
4716 - 50th Ave.
Lloydminster, AB T9V 0W4 Canada
780-871-5800
Fax: 780-871-5829
MICR: 04238-003

Lockeport
25A Beech St.
Lockeport, NS B0T 1L0 Canada
902-656-2212
Fax: 902-656-3303
MICR: 04073-003

London - Adelaide
1530 Adelaide St. North
London, ON N5X 1K4 Canada
519-661-1137
Fax: 519-661-1188
MICR: 02772-003

London - Boler
Bryon Village
440 Boler Rd.
London, ON N6K 4L2 Canada
519-641-5000
Fax: 519-641-5010
MICR: 02732-003

London - Dundas
1670 Dundas St. East
London, ON N5W 3C7 Canada
519-457-5700
Fax: 519-457-5710
MICR: 02762-003

London - Fanshawe
Richmond North Centre
96 Fanshawe Park Rd. East
London, ON N5X 4C5 Canada
519-660-4200
Fax: 519-660-4233
MICR: 07482-003

London - Huron
621 Huron St. East
London, ON N5Y 4J7 Canada
519-661-1144
Fax: 519-661-1449
MICR: 02752-003

London - Main
Lambeth
2550 Main St.
London, ON N6P 1R1 Canada
519-652-3523
Fax: 519-652-0318
MICR: 02602-003

London - Richmond
383 Richmond St.
London, ON N6A 3C4 Canada
519-661-1180
Fax: 519-661-1100
MICR: 02722-003

London - Wellington
White Oaks Mall
1105 Wellington Rd. South
London, ON N6E 1V4 Canada
519-681-4440
Fax: 519-681-7293
MICR: 02972-003

London - Wharncliffe
515 Wharncliffe Rd. South
London, ON N6J 2N1 Canada
519-661-1153
Fax: 519-661-1219
MICR: 02882-003

London - Wonderland
Sherwood Forest Mall
1225 Wonderland Rd. North
London, ON N6G 2V9 Canada
519-472-6882
Fax: 519-472-2158
MICR: 02852-003

London - Wonderland
851 Wonderland Rd. South
London, ON N6K 4T2 Canada
519-472-0910
Fax: 519-472-7598
MICR: 09047-003

Longueuil - Chambly
2068, rue de Chambly
Longueuil, QC J4J 3Y7 Canada
450-442-5570
Fax: 450-442-5577
MICR: 01831-003

Longueuil - St-Charles

Royal Bank of Canada(RBC) (continued)

Old Longueuil
#101, 43, rue St-Charles ouest
Longueuil, QC J4H 1C5 Canada
450-442-5611
Fax: 450-442-5619
MICR: 03411-003

Longueuil - St. Laurent
Place Longueuil
825, boul St. Laurent ouest
Longueuil, QC J4K 2V1 Canada
450-442-5580
Fax: 450-442-5588
MICR: 01851-003

Louisbourg
7509 Main St.
Louisbourg, NS B1C 1H8 Canada
902-733-2012
Fax: 902-733-3150
MICR: 04183-003

Lower Sackville
790 Sackville Dr.
Lower Sackville, NS B4E 1R7 Canada
902-869-3060
Fax: 902-421-8481
MICR: 03653-003

Lumsden
325 James St. North
Lumsden, SK S0G 3C0 Canada
306-731-3311
Fax: 306-731-2906
MICR: 04298-003

Lunenburg
84 Pelham St.
Lunenburg, NS B0J 2C0 Canada
902-634-8861
Fax: 902-634-4299
MICR: 04293-003

Luseland
405 Grand Ave.
Luseland, SK S0L 2A0 Canada
306-372-5002
Fax: 306-372-4232
MICR: 04408-003

Lévis
5415, boul de la Rive sud
Lévis, QC G6V 4Z3 Canada
418-838-3640
Fax: 418-838-3655
MICR: 02431-003

Mackenzie
#119, 403 Mackenzie Blvd.
Mackenzie, BC V0J 2C0 Canada
250-997-3213
Fax: 250-597-5836
MICR: 02890-003

Macklin
4816 - 50th St.
Macklin, SK S0L 2C0 Canada
306-753-2045
Fax: 306-753-2339
MICR: 04518-003

Mallorytown
4 Quabbin Rd.
Mallorytown, ON K0E 1R0 Canada
613-923-5218
Fax: 613-923-5058
MICR: 02942-003

Manitou
Main & Ellis St.
Manitou, MB R0G 1G0 Canada
204-242-2882
Fax: 204-242-2105
MICR: 02477-003

Manotick
5539 Main St.
Manotick, ON K4M 1A2 Canada
613-692-5400
Fax: 613-692-0659
MICR: 02962-003

Maple
9791 Jane St.
Maple, ON L6A 3N9 Canada
905-832-4300
Fax: 905-832-4799
MICR: 07472-003

Maple Ridge - 207th
Meadow Ridge Shopping Centre
11910 - 207th St.
Maple Ridge, BC V2X 1X7 Canada
604-467-3822
Fax: 604-467-6959
MICR: 02920-003

Maple Ridge - 224th
11855 - 224th St.
Maple Ridge, BC V2X 6B1 Canada
604-463-6271
Fax: 604-466-7063
MICR: 02080-003

Markham - Main
47 Main St. North
Markham, ON L3P 1X3 Canada
905-294-2920
Fax: 905-294-3439
MICR: 02982-003

Markham - Woodbine
9231 Woodbine Ave.
Markham, ON L3R 0K1 Canada
905-513-8508
Fax: 905-513-8536
MICR: 01334-003

Markham - Woodbine
7481 Woodbine Ave.
Markham, ON L3R 2W1 Canada
905-474-4010
Fax: 905-474-1942
MICR: 03012-003

Maryfield
115 Main St.
Maryfield, SK S0G 3K0 Canada
306-646-2100
Fax: 306-646-2284
MICR: 04628-003

Massey
195 Sauble St.
Massey, ON P0P 1P0 Canada
705-865-2400
Fax: 705-864-3271
MICR: 3002-003

McCreary
516 Burrows Rd.
McCreary, MB R0J 1B0 Canada
204-835-2226
Fax: 204-835-2628
MICR: 02607-003

Meadow Lake
130 Centre St.
Meadow Lake, SK S9X 1L4 Canada
306-236-5623
Fax: 306-236-4222
MICR: 04738-003

Medicine Hat - 13th
2901 - 13th Ave. SE
Medicine Hat, AB T1A 3R1 Canada
403-528-6440
Fax: 403-527-7749
MICR: 07619-003

Medicine Hat - 3rd
580 - 3rd St. SE
Medicine Hat, AB T1A 0H3 Canada
403-528-6400
Fax: 403-529-0557
MICR: 07599-003

Melbourne
6570 Longwoods Rd.
Melbourne, ON N0L 1W0 Canada
519-289-2111
Fax: 519-289-0132
MICR: 03022-003

Melfort
201 Main St.
Melfort, SK S0E 1A0 Canada
306-752-2863
Fax: 306-752-3386
MICR: 04848-003

Melita
85 Main St.
Melita, MB R0M 1L0 Canada
204-522-3268
Fax: 204-522-3118
MICR: 02737-003

Melville
303 Main St.
Melville, SK S0A 2P0 Canada
306-728-4553
Fax: 306-728-4607
MICR: 04958-003

Merrickville
125 Main St. East
Merrickville, ON K0G 1N0 Canada
613-269-4781
Fax: 613-269-3894
MICR: 03042-003

Merritt
2090 Quilchena Ave.
Merritt, BC V1K 1B8 Canada
250-378-5196
Fax: 250-378-6070
MICR: 02940-003

Metcalfe
8220 Victoria St.
Metcalfe, ON K0A 2P0 Canada
613-821-2021
Fax: 613-821-4467
MICR: 03062-003

Meteghan
Rte. 1
Meteghan, NS B0W 2J0 Canada
902-645-2410
Fax: 902-645-3824
MICR: 04513-003

Middle Musquodoboit
12332 Hwy. 224
Middle Musquodoboit, NS B0N 1X0 Canada
902-384-2020
Fax: 902-384-3277
MICR: 04623-003

Middleton
6 Commercial St.
Middleton, NS B0S 1P0 Canada
902-825-3417
Fax: 902-825-2242
MICR: 04733-003

Midland
271 King St.
Midland, ON L4R 3M4 Canada
705-526-4221
Fax: 705-526-6252
MICR: 03082-003

Mill Bay
#110, 2690 Mill Bay Rd.
Mill Bay, BC V0R 2P1 Canada
250-743-4229
Fax: 250-743-5910
MICR: 02970-003

Milton - Ontario
55 Ontario St. South
Milton, ON L9T 2M3 Canada
905-875-0600
Fax: 905-875-1780
MICR: 03092-003

Milton - Steeles
1240 Steeles Ave. East
Milton, ON L9T 6R1 Canada
905-875-1772
Fax: 905-875-1631
MICR: 09971-003

Minnedosa
61 Main St.
Minnedosa, MB R0J 1E0 Canada
204-867-2733
Fax: 204-867-3261
MICR: 02997-003

Miramichi - Pleasant
PO Box 396
335 Pleasant St.
Miramichi, NB E1V 3M5 Canada
506-622-2153
Fax: 506-622-5311
MICR: 01544-003

Miramichi - Water
Chatham Town Centre
1780 Water St.
Miramichi, NB E1N 1B6 Canada
506-778-1130
Fax: 506-778-1139

MICR: 00484-003
Mission
33114 - 1st Ave.
Mission, BC V2V 1G4 Canada
604-820-4700
Fax: 604-826-5804
MICR: 03040-003
Mississauga - Airport
6205 Airport Rd.
Mississauga, ON L4V 1E1 Canada
905-671-6262
Fax: 905-671-6264
MICR: 02952-003
Mississauga - Argentia
2965 Argentia Rd.
Mississauga, ON L5N 0A2 Canada
905-858-8843
Fax: 905-858-8892
MICR: 09987-003
Mississauga - Bloor
1125 Bloor St. East
Mississauga, ON L4Y 2N6 Canada
905-897-8160
Fax: 905-897-8700
MICR: 03102-003
Mississauga - City Centre
33 City Centre Dr.
Mississauga, ON L5B 2N5 Canada
905-897-8261
Fax: 905-897-1463
MICR: 03132-003
Mississauga - Dixie
4141 Dixie Rd.
Mississauga, ON L4W 1V5 Canada
905-624-0152
Fax: 905-624-6087
MICR: 03232-003
Mississauga - Dixie
6240 Dixie Rd.
Mississauga, ON L5T 1A6 Canada
905-564-5740
Fax: 905-564-5709
MICR: 03252-003
Mississauga - Dundas
2 Dundas St. West
Mississauga, ON L5B 1H3 Canada
905-897-8130
Fax: 905-897-8222
MICR: 01062-003
Mississauga - Eglinton
#B4, 1240 Eglinton Ave. West
Mississauga, ON L5V 1N3 Canada
905-567-7202
Fax: 905-567-7422
MICR: 00364-003
Mississauga - Financial
6880 Financial Dr.
Mississauga, ON L5N 7Y5 Canada
905-286-7100
Fax: 905-286-7111
MICR: 03212-003
Mississauga - Glen Erin
6040 Glen Erin Dr.
Mississauga, ON L5N 3M4 Canada
905-542-7430
Fax: 905-542-7299
MICR: 00354-003
Mississauga - Goreway
Westwood Shopping Mall
7205 Goreway Dr.
Mississauga, ON L4T 2T9 Canada
905-671-6340
Fax: 905-671-6361
MICR: 03032-003
Mississauga - Hurontario
#B2, 4557 Hurontario St.
Mississauga, ON L4Z 3M2 Canada
905-712-8388
Fax: 905-712-8396
MICR: 03372-003
Mississauga - Lakeshore
1730 Lakeshore Rd. West
Mississauga, ON L5J 1J5 Canada
905-822-1648
Fax: 905-822-7250
MICR: 00942-003
Mississauga - Lakeshore
220 Lakeshore Rd. West
Mississauga, ON L5H 1G6 Canada
905-274-3180
Fax: 905-274-0598
MICR: 02612-003
Mississauga - Matheson
#1, 700 Matheson Blvd.
Mississauga, ON L5R 3T2 Canada
905-712-5000
Fax: 905-712-5022
MICR: 00143-003
Mississauga - Milverton
25 Milverton Dr.
Mississauga, ON L5R 3G2 Canada
905-568-1800
Fax: 905-568-3403
MICR: 08802-003
Mississauga - Queen
189 Queen St. South
Mississauga, ON L5M 1L4 Canada
905-542-5200
Fax: 905-542-5234
MICR: 04942-003
Moncton - Main
Blue Cross Centre
644 Main St.
Moncton, NB E1C 1E2 Canada
506-857-0316
Fax: 506-859-6218
MICR: 01374-003
Moncton - Mountain
1845 Mountain Rd.
Moncton, NB E1G 4R3 Canada
506-870-3700
Fax: 506-870-3701
MICR: 02374-003
Moncton - Mountain
719 Mountain Rd.
Moncton, NB E1C 2P4 Canada
506-857-3122
Fax: 506-859-6230
MICR: 01434-003
Mont-Tremblant
759, rue de Saint-Jovite
Mont-Tremblant, QC J8E 3J8 Canada
819-429-6380
Fax: 819-429-6378
MICR: 06419-003
Montmagny
72, rue Palais de Justice
Montmagny, QC G5V 1P5 Canada
418-248-1707
Fax: 418-248-2295
MICR: 02461-003
Montréal - 45e av
53 - 45e av
Montréal, QC H8T 2L8 Canada
514-637-2592
Fax: 514-637-5793
MICR: 02071-003
Montréal - Beaubien
1951, rue Beaubien est
Montréal, QC H2G 1M2 Canada
514-722-4628
Fax: 514-722-8489
MICR: 02781-003
Montréal - Cavendish
5755, boul Cavendish
Montréal, QC H4W 2X8 Canada
514-874-2226
Fax: 514-874-2311
MICR: 02891-003
Montréal - Commerce
Centre d'achat du village
40, Place du Commerce
Montréal, QC H3E 1J6 Canada
514-762-3170
Fax: 514-762-3199
MICR: 08971-003
Montréal - Complexe Desjardins
5, Complexe Desjardins
Montréal, QC H5B 1B4 Canada
514-874-5277
Fax: 514-874-5195
MICR: 02931-003
Montréal - Crémazie
Place Crémazie
#27, 50, av Crémazie ouest
Montréal, QC H2P 1A2 Canada
514-385-4100
Fax: 514-385-4104
MICR: 05501-003
Montréal - Côte St-Luc
7031, ch Côte St-Luc
Montréal, QC H4V 1J2 Canada
514-874-5244
Fax: 514-874-3137
MICR: 03021-003
Montréal - Côte Vertu
Place Vertu
#1F, 3131, boul de la Côte Vertu
Montréal, QC H4R 1Y8 Canada
514-856-8900
Fax: 514-856-8944
MICR: 03051-003
Montréal - Côte-des-Neiges
5700, Côte-des-Neiges
Montréal, QC H3T 2A6 Canada
514-340-3130
Fax: 514-340-3131
MICR: 02941-003
Montréal - Dollard
Newman Plaza
#38, 2101, av Dollard
Montréal, QC H8N 1S2 Canada
514-368-5610
Fax: 514-368-5611
MICR: 02091-003
Montréal - Dorval
Dorval Shopping Centre
316, av Dorval
Montréal, QC H9S 3H7 Canada
514-636-7656
Fax: 514-636-4440
MICR: 01271-003
Montréal - Décarie
800, boul Décarie
Montréal, QC H4L 3L5 Canada
514-748-7200
Fax: 514-748-7085
MICR: 08011-003
Montréal - Décarie
1165, boul Décarie
Montréal, QC H4L 3M8 Canada
514-748-2033
Fax: 514-748-2037
MICR: 08081-003
Montréal - Gouin est
Résidence les Cascades
3461, boul Gouin est
Montréal, QC H1H 1B2 Canada
514-328-8266
Fax: 514-328-8270
MICR: 06651-003
Montréal - Gouin ouest
13135, boul Gouin ouest
Montréal, QC H8Z 1X1 Canada
514-624-2100
Fax: 514-624-1930
MICR: 07111-003
Montréal - Graham
1427, boul Graham
Montréal, QC H3P 3M9 Canada
514-340-3080
Fax: 514-340-3090
MICR: 06781-003
Montréal - Guy
2157, rue Guy
Montréal, QC H3H 2L9 Canada
514-874-8966
Fax: 514-874-2241
MICR: 05981-003
Montréal - Jean Talon est
4286, rue Jean-Talon est
Montréal, QC H1S 1J7 Canada
514-722-3568
Fax: 514-722-3104

Royal Bank of Canada(RBC) (continued)
MICR: 04541-003
Montréal - Jean Talon est
Place Carillon
7155, rue Jean Talon est
Montréal, QC H1M 3A4 Canada
514-493-5800
Fax: 514-493-5815
MICR: 05575-003
Montréal - Jean-Talon est
Tour Jean-Talon
#210, 600 rue Jean-Talon est
Montréal, QC H2R 3A8 Canada
514-495-5940
Fax: 514-495-5960
MICR: 05261-003
Montréal - Joseph Renaud
6680, boul Joseph Renaud
Montréal, QC H1K 3V4 Canada
514-493-5900
Fax: 514-493-5910
MICR: 00081-003
Montréal - Laurier
351, av Laurier ouest
Montréal, QC H2V 2K4 Canada
514-495-5900
Fax: 514-495-5921
MICR: 03661-003
Montréal - Léo Pariseau
Place du Parc
#100, 300, rue Léo Pariseau
Montréal, QC H2X 4B3 Canada
514-874-6901
Fax: 514-874-2337
MICR: 03631-003
Montréal - Maurice-Duplessis
7945, Maurice-Duplessis
Montréal, QC H1E 1M5 Canada
514-494-7977
Fax: 514-494-1164
MICR: 03041-003
Montréal - Monkland
5701, av Monkland
Montréal, QC H4A 1E7 Canada
514-874-3433
Fax: 514-874-3428
MICR: 03901-003
Montréal - Mont Royal
1801, av Mont Royal est
Montréal, QC H2H 1J2 Canada
514-599-2100
Fax: 514-599-2122
MICR: 03981-003
Montréal - Newman
Place Angrignon
7191, boul Newman
Montréal, QC H8N 2K3 Canada
514-368-0996
Fax: 514-368-0708
MICR: 03451-003
Montréal - Pie IX
10611, boul Pie IX
Montréal, QC H1H 4A3 Canada
514-328-8230
Fax: 514-328-8240
MICR: 06621-003
Montréal - Queen Mary
5185, rue Queen Mary
Montréal, QC H3W 1Y1 Canada
514-874-6681
Fax: 514-874-8532
MICR: 04701-003
Montréal - Royalmount
5500, av Royalmount
Montréal, QC H4P 1H7 Canada
514-340-3003
Fax: 514-340-3017
MICR: 6941-003
Montréal - Saint-Jean
3610, boul Saint-Jean
Montréal, QC H9G 1X1 Canada
514-624-6700
Fax: 514-624-6850
MICR: 01211-003
Montréal - Saint-Jean
321, boul Saint-Jean
Montréal, QC H9R 3J1 Canada
514-630-5222
Fax: 514-630-5220
MICR: 07171-003
Montréal - Saint-Jean
610, boul Saint-Jean
Montréal, QC H9R 3K2 Canada
514-630-8400
Fax: 514-630-8430
MICR: 07191-003
Montréal - Salaberry
Les Galeries Normandie
2560, rue de Salaberry
Montréal, QC H3M 1L3 Canada
514-856-8950
Fax: 514-856-8966
MICR: 03221-003
Montréal - Sherbrooke est
5100, boul Sherbrooke est
Montréal, QC H1V 3R9 Canada
514-257-3002
Fax: 514-257-3004
MICR: 03461-003
Montréal - Sherbrooke est
12675, rue Sherbrooke est
Montréal, QC H1A 3W7 Canada
514-644-3030
Fax: 514-644-3025
MICR: 08561-003
Montréal - Sherbrooke ouest
1100, rue Sherbrooke ouest
Montréal, QC H3A 1G7 Canada
514-874-8730
Fax: 514-874-6962
MICR: 04461-003
Montréal - Sherbrooke ouest
6051, rue Sherbrooke ouest
Montréal, QC H4A 1Y2 Canada
514-874-5027
Fax: 514-874-8487
MICR: 06061-003
Montréal - Sherbrooke ouest
4849, rue Sherbrooke ouest
Montréal, QC H3Z 1G6 Canada
514-874-8483
Fax: 514-874-2955
MICR: 09311-003
Montréal - Somerled
6510, av Somerled
Montréal, QC H4V 1S8 Canada
514-874-3447
Fax: 514-874-2188
MICR: 06141-003
Montréal - Sources
Galeries des Sources
3075, boul Sources
Montréal, QC H9B 1Z6 Canada
514-684-0202
Fax: 514-684-1471
MICR: 01141-003
Montréal - Sources
4400, boul Sources
Montréal, QC H8Y 3B7 Canada
514-684-8110
Fax: 514-684-4724
MICR: 07671-003
Montréal - St-Charles
Place Grilli
3535, boul St-Charles
Montréal, QC H9H 5B9 Canada
514-630-8455
Fax: 514-630-8454
MICR: 02755-003
Montréal - St-Jacques
360, rue St-Jacques ouest
Montréal, QC H2Y 1P6 Canada
514-874-2959
Fax: 514-874-5619
MICR: 05341-003
Montréal - St-Joseph
Instore Banking
3600, rue St-Joseph est
Montréal, QC H1X 1W6 Canada
514-257-6585
Fax: 514-257-8808
MICR: 07135-003
Montréal - St. Charles
Beaconsfield Shopping Centre
#23D, 50, boul St. Charles
Montréal, QC H9W 2X3 Canada
514-630-5260
Fax: 514-630-5250
MICR: 00361-003
Montréal - Ste-Catherine
1140, rue Ste-Catherine ouest
Montréal, QC H3B 1H7 Canada
514-874-3043
Fax: 514-874-5199
MICR: 05101-003
Montréal - Van Horne
2835, av Van Horne
Montréal, QC H3S 1P6 Canada
514-340-3030
Fax: 514-340-3040
MICR: 06221-003
Montréal - Van Horne
4851, av Van Horne
Montréal, QC H3W 1J2 Canada
514-340-3050
Fax: 514-340-3060
MICR: 06301-003
Montréal - Van Horne
1307, av Van Horne
Montréal, QC H2V 1K7 Canada
514-495-5904
Fax: 514-495-5907
MICR: 07091-003
Montréal - Viau
8689, boul Viau
Montréal, QC H1R 2T9 Canada
514-328-8280
Fax: 514-328-8290
MICR: 08111-003
Montréal - Ville Marie
1, Place Ville Marie, Main Fl.
Montréal, QC H3C 3B5 Canada
514-874-7222
Fax: 514-874-6365
MICR: 00001-003
Montréal - Wellington
4370, rue Wellington
Montréal, QC H4G 1W4 Canada
514-762-3100
Fax: 514-762-3106
MICR: 09151-003
Montréal - Westminster
26, av Westminster nord
Montréal, QC H4X 1Z2 Canada
514-874-3451
Fax: 514-874-2830
MICR: 06701-003
Montréal - Westmount
1, carré Westmount
Montréal, QC H3Z 2P9 Canada
514-874-5793
Fax: 514-874-2927
MICR: 09231-003
Moorefield
46 McGivern St.
Moorefield, ON N0G 2K0 Canada
519-638-3011
Fax: 519-638-9952
MICR: 03122-003
Moose Jaw - High
52 High St. West
Moose Jaw, SK S6H 1S3 Canada
306-691-4100
Fax: 306-692-0899
MICR: 05178-003
Moose Jaw - Main
Town & Country Mall
1235 Main St. North
Moose Jaw, SK S6H 6M4 Canada
306-691-4200
Fax: 306-692-7058
MICR: 05188-003
Moosomin

633 Main St.
Moosomin, SK S0G 3N0 Canada
306-435-3387
Fax: 306-435-3083
MICR: 05288-003

Morden
289 Stephen St.
Morden, MB R6M 1V2 Canada
204-822-4405
Fax: 204-822-5943
MICR: 03257-003

Morinville
9921 - 102 St.
Morinville, AB T8R 1E7 Canada
780-939-4331
Fax: 780-939-5601
MICR: 07929-003

Mount Brydges
22466 Adelaide Rd.
Mount Brydges, ON N0L 1W0 Canada
519-264-1112
Fax: 519-264-1920
MICR: 03142-003

Mount Pearl
45 Commonwealth Ave.
Mount Pearl, NL A1N 1W7 Canada
709-576-4443
Fax: 709-576-4676
MICR: 09243-003

Musquodoboit Harbour
#1, 7907 Hwy. 7
Musquodoboit Harbour, NS B0J 2L0 Canada
902-889-2626
Fax: 902-889-3525
MICR: 04903-003

Nanaimo - Commercial
205 Commercial St.
Nanaimo, BC V9R 5G8 Canada
250-741-3500
Fax: 250-741-3535
MICR: 03120-003

Nanaimo - Island
Brooks Landing
#110, 2000 Island Hwy. North
Nanaimo, BC V9S 5W3 Canada
250-758-7381
Fax: 250-758-2317
MICR: 03160-003

Nanaimo - Island
Woodgrove Shopping Centre
#49, 6631 Island Hwy. North
Nanaimo, BC V9T 4T7 Canada
250-390-4311
Fax: 250-390-2154
MICR: 03180-003

Napanee
36 Dundas St. East
Napanee, ON K7R 1H8 Canada
613-354-2107
Fax: 613-354-6913
MICR: 03182-003

Navan
3435 Trim Rd.
Navan, ON K4B 1M8 Canada
613-835-2300
Fax: 613-835-3332
MICR: 03202-003

Neepawa
101 Davidson St.
Neepawa, MB R0J 1H0 Canada
204-476-3321
Fax: 204-476-3817
MICR: 03277-003

Nelson
401 Baker St.
Nelson, BC V1L 4H7 Canada
250-354-4111
Fax: 250-354-4115
MICR: 03200-003

Nepean - Centrepointe
117 Centrepointe Dr.
Nepean, ON K2G 5X3 Canada
613-727-8130
Fax: 613-727-0706
MICR: 00084-003

Nepean - Merivale
1460 Merivale Rd.
Nepean, ON K2E 5P2 Canada
613-224-8660
Fax: 613-224-8903
MICR: 00496-003

Nepean - Moodie
Bells Corners
303 Moodie Dr.
Nepean, ON K2H 9R4 Canada
613-721-9300
Fax: 613-721-4659
MICR: 00372-003

Nepean - Strandherd
3131 Standherd Dr.
Nepean, ON K2J 5N1 Canada
613-825-5061
Fax: 613-825-3217
MICR: 09277-003

New Germany
Hwy. 10
New Germany, NS B0R 1E0 Canada
902-644-2730
Fax: 902-644-2694
MICR: 04953-003

New Glasgow
91 Provost St.
New Glasgow, NS B2H 2P5 Canada
902-755-7700
Fax: 902-755-3584
MICR: 05063-003

New Hamburg
29 Huron St.
New Hamburg, ON N3A 1K1 Canada
519-662-1263
Fax: 519-662-3094
MICR: 03282-003

New Hazelton
Hwy. 16 Hagwilget Village
New Hazelton, BC V0J 2J0 Canada
250-842-2424
Fax: 250-842-6361
MICR: 02160-003

New Liskeard
5 Armstrong St.
New Liskeard, ON P0J 1P0 Canada
705-647-6891
Fax: 705-647-5822
MICR: 03302-003

New Minas
9256 Commercial St.
New Minas, NS B4N 4A9 Canada
902-681-8333
Fax: 902-681-1523
MICR: 05103-003

New Waterford
3414 Plummer Ave.
New Waterford, NS B1H 1Z3 Canada
902-862-6443
Fax: 902-862-3593
MICR: 05173-003

New Westminster
626 Sixth Ave.
New Westminster, BC V3M 6Z2 Canada
604-665-0375
Fax: 604-525-9427
MICR: 03280-003

Newboro
24 Drummond St.
Newboro, ON K0G 1P0 Canada
613-272-2600
Fax: 613-272-3431
MICR: 03242-003

Newbury
22886 Hagerty Rd.
Newbury, ON N0L 1Z0 Canada
519-693-4371
Fax: 519-693-4218
MICR: 03262-003

Newcastle
1 Wheelhouse Dr.
Newcastle, ON L1B 1B9 Canada
905-623-1187
Fax: 905-623-1188
MICR: 00692-003

Newmarket - Davis
1181 Davis Dr. East
Newmarket, ON L3Y 7V1 Canada
905-895-1246
Fax: 905-895-3601
MICR: 03322-003

Newmarket - Yonge
17770 Yonge St.
Newmarket, ON L3Y 8P4 Canada
905-895-5551
Fax: 905-895-7340
MICR: 03342-003

Niagara Falls - Cummington
8170 Cummington Sq. West
Niagara Falls, ON L2G 6V9 Canada
905-295-4301
Fax: 905-295-3463
MICR: 00922-003

Niagara Falls - Lundy
6518 Lundy's Lane
Niagara Falls, ON L2G 1T6 Canada
905-356-7313
Fax: 905-356-7861
MICR: 03382-003

Niagara Falls - Portage
3499 Portage Rd.
Niagara Falls, ON L2J 2K5 Canada
905-354-5673
Fax: 905-354-5728
MICR: 03392-003

Niagara Falls - Queen St.
4491 Queen St.
Niagara Falls, ON L2E 2L4 Canada
905-357-3001
Fax: 905-357-3009
MICR: 03362-003

Niagara on the Lake
234 Mary St.
Niagara on the Lake, ON L0S 1J0 Canada
905-468-3288
Fax: 905-468-5354
MICR: 03412-003

Nipawin
118 - 1st Ave. West
Nipawin, SK S0E 1E0 Canada
306-862-9888
Fax: 306-862-2332
MICR: 05538-003

Nipigon
157 Railway St.
Nipigon, ON P0T 2J0 Canada
807-887-3137
Fax: 807-887-2932
MICR: 03422-003

North Battleford
1101 - 101 St.
North Battleford, SK S9A 0Z5 Canada
306-937-5000
Fax: 306-446-4488
MICR: 05618-003

North Bay - Main
105 Main St. West
North Bay, ON P1B 8G8 Canada
705-472-5470
Fax: 705-472-1090
MICR: 03442-003

North Bay - Stockdale
925 Stockdale Rd., Main Fl.
North Bay, ON P1B 9N5 Canada
705-494-7100
Fax: 705-494-7155
MICR: 03452-003

North Gower
6683 - 4th Line Rd.
North Gower, ON K0A 2T0 Canada
613-489-3385
Fax: 613-489-2239
MICR: 03462-003

North Sydney
291 Commercial St.
North Sydney, NS B2A 1B9 Canada
902-794-4751
Fax: 902-794-9093
MICR: 05283-003

North Vancouver - Edgemont

Royal Bank of Canada(RBC) (continued)

Edgemont Village
3145 Edgemont Blvd.
North Vancouver, BC V7R 2N7 Canada
604-981-6533
Fax: 604-985-2608
MICR: 03840-003

North Vancouver - Lonsdale
1789 Lonsdale Ave.
North Vancouver, BC V7M 2J6 Canada
604-981-7800
Fax: 604-981-7849
MICR: 04000-003

North Vancouver - Lynn Valley
1501 Lynn Valley Rd.
North Vancouver, BC V7J 2B1 Canada
604-981-7880
Fax: 604-981-7888
MICR: 02960-003

North Vancouver - North Dollarton
Dollarton Village
477 North Dollarton Hwy.
North Vancouver, BC V7G 1M9 Canada
604-929-3464
Fax: 604-929-8479
MICR: 03920-003

Norway House
PO Box 444
Norway House, MB R0B 1B0 Canada
204-359-3486
Fax: 204-359-3481
MICR: 05879-003

Norwood
2369 County Rd. 45
Norwood, ON K0L 2V0 Canada
705-639-5371
Fax: 705-639-2522
MICR: 03482-003

Oakville - Hays
Oak Park
309 Hays Blvd.
Oakville, ON L6H 6Z3 Canada
905-338-2933
Fax: 905-257-6622
MICR: 01532-003

Oakville - Lakeshore Rd. East
279 Lakeshore Rd. East
Oakville, ON L6J 1H9 Canada
905-845-4224
Fax: 905-845-6252
MICR: 03502-003

Oakville - Lakeshore Rd. West
2329 Lakeshore Rd. West
Oakville, ON L6L 1H2 Canada
905-469-2399
Fax: 905-469-2383
MICR: 2782-003

Oakville - North Service
220 North Service Rd. West
Oakville, ON L6M 2Y3 Canada
905-849-4414
Fax: 905-849-4229
MICR: 08982-003

Oakville - Speers
1005 Speers Rd.
Oakville, ON L6L 2X5 Canada
905-842-2360
Fax: 905-842-7151
MICR: 03592-003

Oakville - Third Line
2501 Third Line, #A
Oakville, ON L6M 5A9 Canada
905-469-8807
Fax: 905-469-6010
MICR: 07412-003

Oakville - Winston Churchill
2460 Winston Churchill Blvd.
Oakville, ON L6H 6J5 Canada
905-829-8665
Fax: 905-829-8733
MICR: 00932-003

Odessa
147 Main St.
Odessa, ON K0H 2H0 Canada
613-386-7391
Fax: 613-386-1095
MICR: 03542-003

Ogema
103 Main St.
Ogema, SK S0C 1Y0 Canada
306-459-2212
Fax: 306-459-2855
MICR: 05728-003

Ohsweken - Six Nations Of The Grand River
Iroquois Village Plaza, Six Nations Of The Grand River
PO Box 279
Ohsweken, ON N0A 1M0 Canada
519-445-4141
Fax: 519-445-4772
MICR: 01144-003

Okotoks
1 McRae St.
Okotoks, AB T1S 1A4 Canada
403-938-4416
Fax: 403-938-3527
MICR: 08039-003

Olds
5026 - 51st St.
Olds, AB T4H 1P6 Canada
403-556-6941
Fax: 403-556-2845
MICR: 08049-003

Oliver
36024 - 97th St.
Oliver, BC V0H 1T0 Canada
250-498-3437
Fax: 250-498-6177
MICR: 04080-003

Orangeville
136 Broadway Ave.
Orangeville, ON L9W 1J9 Canada
519-941-2610
Fax: 519-941-2095
MICR: 03562-003

Orillia
40 Peter St. South
Orillia, ON L3V 5B1 Canada
705-326-6417
Fax: 705-326-5019
MICR: 03582-003

Orleans - Centrum
211 Centrum Blvd.
Orleans, ON K1E 3X1 Canada
613-830-1010
Fax: 613-830-1130
MICR: 02124-003

Orleans - Jeanne d'Arc
6505 Jeanne d'Arc Blvd.
Orleans, ON K1C 2R1 Canada
613-837-1570
Fax: 613-837-7266
MICR: 03742-003

Oromocto
287 Restigouche Rd.
Oromocto, NB E2V 2H2 Canada
506-446-3060
Fax: 506-446-3069
MICR: 01644-003

Oshawa - King St. East
549 King St. East
Oshawa, ON L1H 1G3 Canada
905-728-2559
Fax: 905-728-2577
MICR: 03632-003

Oshawa - King St. West
500 King St. West
Oshawa, ON L1J 2K9 Canada
905-579-8300
Fax: 905-579-7658
MICR: 09077-003

Oshawa - Simcoe St. North
27 Simcoe St. North
Oshawa, ON L1G 4R7 Canada
905-723-8511
Fax: 905-723-1582
MICR: 03622-003

Oshawa - Simcoe St. North
1050 Simcoe St. North
Oshawa, ON L1G 4W5 Canada
905-576-6010
Fax: 905-576-6028
MICR: 03672-003

Oshawa - Taunton
800 Taunton Rd. East
Oshawa, ON L1H 7K5 Canada
905-576-5660
Fax: 905-576-6881
MICR: 09847-003
Douglas Allan, President

Ottawa - Bank St.
745 Bank St.
Ottawa, ON K1S 3V3 Canada
613-564-4591
Fax: 613-564-2111
MICR: 00116-003

Ottawa - Bank St.
1535 Bank St.
Ottawa, ON K1H 7Z1 Canada
613-733-8850
Fax: 613-733-4350
MICR: 00226-003

Ottawa - Bank St.
99 Bank St.
Ottawa, ON K1P 6B9 Canada
613-564-4563
Fax: 613-564-2750
MICR: 00236-003

Ottawa - Carling
Westgate Shopping Centre
1309 Carling Ave.
Ottawa, ON K1Z 7L3 Canada
613-798-4450
Fax: 613-728-0851
MICR: 01326-003

Ottawa - Carling
2121 Carling Ave.
Ottawa, ON K2A 1H2 Canada
613-725-3145
Fax: 613-725-3808
MICR: 09057-003

Ottawa - Elgin
200 Elgin St.
Ottawa, ON K2P 1L5 Canada
613-564-4706
Fax: 613-564-4735
MICR: 00576-003

Ottawa - Montréal Rd.
551 Montréal Rd.
Ottawa, ON K1K 0V1 Canada
613-749-4579
Fax: 613-749-4580
MICR: 00666-003

Ottawa - Riverside
Billings Bridge
2269 Riverside Dr.
Ottawa, ON K1H 8K2 Canada
613-731-4920
Fax: 613-731-4510
MICR: 00776-003

Ottawa - Sparks
90 Sparks St.
Ottawa, ON K1P 5T6 Canada
613-564-3100
Fax: 613-564-2118
MICR: 00006-003

Ottawa - St. Laurent
1930 St. Laurent Blvd.
Ottawa, ON K1G 1A4 Canada
613-739-4333
Fax: 613-739-5992
MICR: 00886-003

Ottawa - Sussex
Lester B. Pearson Bldg
125 Sussex Dr.
Ottawa, ON K1A 0G2 Canada
613-564-2005
Fax: 613-789-4796
MICR: 01016-003

Ottawa - Wellington
1145 Wellington St.
Ottawa, ON K1Y 2Y9 Canada
613-722-8351
Fax: 613-722-1786
MICR: 01216-003

Otterville

202 Main St. East
Otterville, ON N0J 1R0 Canada
519-879-6553
Fax: 519-879-6905
MICR: 03642-003

Outlook
119 Saskatchewan Ave. East
Outlook, SK S0L 2N0 Canada
306-867-8604
Fax: 306-867-8520
MICR: 05828-003

Owen Sound
900 - 2nd Ave. East
Owen Sound, ON N4K 5P5 Canada
519-376-2570
Fax: 519-376-2766
MICR: 03662-003

Oxbow
302 Main St.
Oxbow, SK S0C 2B0 Canada
306-483-2995
Fax: 306-483-5130
MICR: 05838-003

Paisley
574 Queen St. South
Paisley, ON N0G 2N0 Canada
519-353-5693
Fax: 519-353-5690
MICR: 03682-003

Pakenham
2534 County Rd. 29
Pakenham, ON K0A 2X0 Canada
613-624-5243
Fax: 613-624-5570
MICR: 03702-003

Paradise
Personal Banking Centre
1314 Topsail Rd
Paradise, NL A1L 1N9 Canada
709-782-2740
Fax: 709-782-2742
MICR: 09003-003

Parksville - South Alberni Hwy.
PO Box 429
152 South Alberni, Hwy. 9
Parksville, BC V9P 2G5 Canada
250-248-8321
Fax: 250-248-5572
MICR: 04130-003

Parrsboro
188 Main St.
Parrsboro, NS B0M 1S0 Canada
902-254-2051
Fax: 902-254-2864
MICR: 05393-003

Parry Sound
70 Joseph St.
Parry Sound, ON P2A 2G5 Canada
705-746-2144
Fax: 705-746-8814
MICR: 03732-003

Peace River
10036 - 100 St.
Peace River, AB T8S 1S8 Canada
780-624-1650
Fax: 780-624-2822
MICR: 08059-003

Peguis
Peguis First Nations
Peguis, MB R0C 3J0 Canada
204-645-2584
Fax: 204-645-5103
MICR: 03767-003

Pembroke
48 Pembroke St. West
Pembroke, ON K8A 5M6 Canada
613-735-0601
Fax: 613-735-1813
MICR: 03722-003

Penticton - Main St.
302 Main St.
Penticton, BC V2A 5C3 Canada
250-490-4400
Fax: 250-492-2426
MICR: 04160-003

Penticton - Main St.
Apple Plaza
#132, 1848 Main St.
Penticton, BC V2A 5H3 Canada
250-770-3000
Fax: 250-492-4998
MICR: 04180-003

Perth
44 Gore St. East
Perth, ON K7H 1H7 Canada
613-267-2277
Fax: 613-267-5144
MICR: 03762-003

Petawawa
3435B Petawawa Blvd.
Petawawa, ON K8H 1X4 Canada
613-687-6226
Fax: 613-687-5960
MICR: 03710-003

Peterborough - Chemong
806 Chemong Rd.
Peterborough, ON K9H 5Z6 Canada
705-743-0545
Fax: 705-743-9361
MICR: 03752-003

Peterborough - George
401 George St. North
Peterborough, ON K9H 3R4 Canada
705-876-3520
Fax: 705-745-2132
MICR: 03782-003

Peterborough - Lansdowne
198 Lansdowne St. East
Peterborough, ON K9J 7N9 Canada
705-743-4303
Fax: 705-743-4441
MICR: 03932-003

Peterborough - Park
823 Park St. South
Peterborough, ON K9J 3T9 Canada
705-743-4241
Fax: 705-743-4664
MICR: 03802-003

Petrolia
4186 Petrolia St.
Petrolia, ON N0N 1R0 Canada
519-882-2160
Fax: 519-882-1517
MICR: 08122-003

Pickering
#5, 1340 Kingston Rd.
Pickering, ON L1V 3M9 Canada
905-839-5152
Fax: 905-839-1808
MICR: 03832-003

Pictou
25 Water St.
Pictou, NS B0K 1H0 Canada
902-485-4352
Fax: 902-485-6990
MICR: 05503-003

Pierson
68 Railway Ave.
Pierson, MB R0M 1S0 Canada
204-634-2351
Fax: 204-634-2503
MICR: 03517-003

Pincher Creek
PO Box 760
732 Main St.
Pincher Creek, AB T0K 1W0 Canada
403-627-4441
Fax: 403-627-2005
MICR: 08149-003

Pincourt
101, boul Cardinal-Léger
Pincourt, QC J7V 3Y3 Canada
514-453-2294
Fax: 514-453-9528
MICR: 07121-003

Pine Falls
One Linden St.
Pine Falls, MB R0E 1M0 Canada
204-367-2213
Fax: 204-367-8313
MICR: 03647-003

Placentia
Placentia Mall
61 Blockhouse Rd.
Placentia, NL A0B 2Y0 Canada
709-227-0060
Fax: 709-227-2016
MICR: 09403-003

Plantagenet
295 Water St.
Plantagenet, ON K0B 1L0 Canada
613-673-5167
Fax: 613-673-4872
MICR: 03822-003

Plaster Rock
199 Main St.
Plaster Rock, NB E7G 2G8 Canada
506-356-2674
Fax: 506-356-1139
MICR: 01654-003

Ponoka
5031 - 51st St.
Ponoka, AB T4J 1R7 Canada
403-783-4417
Fax: 403-783-8080
MICR: 08189-003

Ponteix
249 Centre St.
Ponteix, SK S0N 1Z0 Canada
306-625-3569
Fax: 306-625-3620
MICR: 06168-003

Port Alberni
2925 - 3rd Ave.
Port Alberni, BC V9Y 2A6 Canada
250-723-9411
Fax: 250-723-9400
MICR: 04240-003

Port Colborne
59 Clarence St.
Port Colborne, ON L3K 3G1 Canada
905-835-1153
Fax: 905-835-2468
MICR: 03882-003

Port Coquitlam - Coast Meridian
3361 Coast Meridian Rd.
Port Coquitlam, BC V3B 3N6 Canada
604-927-5520
Fax: 604-941-5402
MICR: 04330-003

Port Coquitlam - Shaughnessy
2581 Shaughnessy St.
Port Coquitlam, BC V3C 3G3 Canada
604-927-5500
Fax: 604-941-2280
MICR: 04320-003

Port Dover
308 Main St.
Port Dover, ON N0A 1N0 Canada
519-583-0941
Fax: 519-583-2576
MICR: 03902-003

Port Hawkesbury
327 Granville St.
Port Hawkesbury, NS B9A 2M5 Canada
902-625-1170
Fax: 902-625-0186
MICR: 05613-003

Port Hope
85 Walton St.
Port Hope, ON L1A 1N4 Canada
905-885-6306
Fax: 905-885-4371
MICR: 03922-003

Port Lambton
4352 St. Clair Pkwy.
Port Lambton, ON N0P 2B0 Canada
519-677-5671
Fax: 519-677-4029
MICR: 03942-003

Port Moody
218 Newport Dr.
Port Moody, BC V3H 5B9 Canada
604-927-5683
Fax: 604-552-5030

Royal Bank of Canada(RBC) (continued)
MICR: 04400-003
Port Perry
210 Queen St.
Port Perry, ON L9L 1B9 Canada
905-985-7316
Fax: 905-985-0741
MICR: 03962-003
Portage la Prairie
140 Saskatchewan Ave. East
Portage La Prairie, MB R1N 0L1 Canada
204-856-2500
Fax: 204-239-6581
MICR: 03777-003
Porters Lake
Lakeview Shopping Centre
#6, 5228 Hwy. 7
Porters Lake, NS B3E 1J8 Canada
902-827-2930
Fax: 902-827-3880
MICR: 05563-003
Portland
32 Colborne St.
Portland, ON K0G 1V0 Canada
613-272-2881
Fax: 613-272-2919
MICR: 03972-003
Powell River
#101, 7035 Barnet St.
Powell River, BC V8A 1Z9 Canada
604-485-7991
Fax: 604-485-5968
MICR: 04480-003
Prescott
302 King St. West
Prescott, ON K0E 1T0 Canada
613-925-2861
Fax: 613-925-1242
MICR: 03982-003
Prince Albert - 2nd Ave.
2880 - 2nd Ave. West
Prince Albert, SK S6V 5Z4 Canada
306-953-5750
Fax: 306-763-4190
MICR: 06288-003
Prince Albert - Central Ave.
1135 Central Ave.
Prince Albert, SK S6V 4V7 Canada
306-953-5700
Fax: 306-953-5766
MICR: 06278-003
Prince George - Massey
Pine Centre Mall
#101, 3055 Massey Dr.
Prince George, BC V2N 2S9 Canada
250-960-4540
Fax: 250-562-5852
MICR: 04540-003
Prince George - Victoria
550 Victoria St.
Prince George, BC V2L 2K1 Canada
250-960-4530
Fax: 250-562-9822
MICR: 04530-003
Prince Rupert
#301, 500 West 2nd Ave.
Prince Rupert, BC V8J 3T6 Canada
250-627-1751
Fax: 250-627-1684
MICR: 04640-003
Qualicum Beach
133 West 2nd Ave.
Qualicum Beach, BC V9K 1T1 Canada
250-752-6981
Fax: 250-752-3247
MICR: 04670-003
Quesnel
201 St. Laurent
Quesnel, BC V2J 2C8 Canada
250-992-2127
Fax: 250-992-2134
MICR: 04720-003
Quispamsis
Super Valu Mall
175 Hampton Rd.
Quispamsis, NB E2E 4Y7 Canada
506-849-5555
Fax: 506-849-5550
MICR: 01904-003
Québec - 1ere
4250, 1ere av
Québec, QC G1H 2S5 Canada
418-624-3444
Fax: 418-624-3477
MICR: 00775-003
Québec - Cambronne
490, rue Cambronne
Québec, QC G1E 6X1 Canada
418-821-6800
Fax: 418-821-6822
MICR: 04175-003
Québec - Charest est
Charles R. Rochette
575, boul Charest est
Québec, QC G1K 3J2 Canada
418-648-6868
Fax: 418-648-6933
MICR: 7137-003
Québec - d'Youville
700, Place d'Youville
Québec, QC G1R 3P2 Canada
418-692-6800
Fax: 418-692-6884
MICR: 00005-003
Québec - Grande Allée est
St.Patrick
#100, 140 Grande Allée est
Québec, QC G1R 5M8 Canada
418-648-6894
Fax: 418-648-6994
MICR: 00115-003
Québec - Jean-Gauvin
839, rte Jean-Gauvin
Québec, QC G1X 4V9 Canada
418-872-7045
Fax: 418-872-7355
MICR: 00095-003
Québec - Jean-Gauvin
839 rte. Jean-Gauvin
Québec, QC G1X 4V9 Canada
418-872-7045
Fax: 418-872-7355
MICR: 00095-003
Québec - Laurier
Place Ste-Foy
#2450, 2, boul Laurier
Québec, QC G1V 2L1 Canada
418-654-2454
Fax: 418-654-2455
MICR: 00335-003
Québec - Lebourgneuf
1260, boul Lebourgneuf
Québec, QC G2K 2G2 Canada
418-624-3484
Fax: 418-624-3488
MICR: 00651-003
Rankin Inlet
PO Box 220
Rankin Inlet, NU X0C 0G0 Canada
867-645-3260
Fax: 867-645-3261
MICR: 06887-003
Rawdon
3591, rue Queen
Rawdon, QC J0K 1S0 Canada
450-834-5476
Fax: 450-834-4702
MICR: 07311-003
Red Deer - Gaetz
#1, 6791 Gaetz Ave.
Red Deer, AB T4N 4C9 Canada
403-340-7290
Fax: 403-340-7318
MICR: 08249-003
Red Deer - Molly Banister
Bower Place
4900 Molly Banister Dr.
Red Deer, AB T4R 1N9 Canada
403-340-7275
Fax: 403-342-7750
MICR: 08319-003
Red Deer - Ross
4943 Ross St.
Red Deer, AB T4N 1Y1 Canada
403-340-7200
Fax: 403-340-7315
MICR: 08259-003
Regina - 11th
2002 - 11th Ave.
Regina, SK S4P 0J3 Canada
306-780-2400
Fax: 306-780-2468
MICR: 00008-003
Regina - 7 North
2441 - 7 Ave. North
Regina, SK S4R 0K4 Canada
306-780-2811
Fax: 306-775-0492
MICR: 06508-003
Regina - Albert
3816 Albert St.
Regina, SK S4S 3R3 Canada
306-780-2691
Fax: 306-586-9533
MICR: 06718-003
Regina - Broad
1246 Broad St.
Regina, SK S4R 1Y3 Canada
306-780-2721
Fax: 306-780-2726
MICR: 06828-003
Regina - Rochdale
6250 Rochdale Blvd.
Regina, SK S4X 4K8 Canada
306-780-2267
Fax: 306-780-2272
MICR: 08755-003
Regina - Victoria East
950 Victoria Ave. East
Regina, SK S4N 7A9 Canada
306-780-2861
Fax: 306-780-2886
MICR: 07218-003
Renfrew
182 Raglan St. South
Renfrew, ON K7V 1R1 Canada
613-432-4881
Fax: 613-432-9690
MICR: 04022-003
Repentigny
447, rue Leclerc
Repentigny, QC J6A 8J4 Canada
450-581-0854
Fax: 450-581-0829
MICR: 03111-003
Revelstoke
123 Mackenzie Ave.
Revelstoke, BC V0E 2S0 Canada
250-837-5133
Fax: 250-837-9229
MICR: 04760-003
Richibucto
#1, 9393 Main St.
Richibucto, NB E4W 4B6 Canada
506-523-4491
Fax: 506-523-1098
MICR: 01764-003
Richmond - Ackroyd
#1950, 8171 Ackroyd Rd.
Richmond, BC V6X 3K1 Canada
604-668-4997
Fax: 604-665-8363
MICR: 03880-003
Richmond - Airport
Vancouver International Airport
Level 3, South APO 23913
Richmond, BC V7B 1Y1 Canada
604-668-4438
Fax: 604-668-4455
MICR: 05500-003
Richmond - Cambie
#1, 11600 Cambie Rd.
Richmond, BC V6X 1L5 Canada
604-665-6900
Fax: 604-665-5805
MICR: 04960-003

Richmond - Moncton
3740 Moncton St.
Richmond, BC V7E 3A4 Canada
604-668-4355
Fax: 604-277-9395
MICR: 05200-003

Richmond - No. 3 Rd.
6400 - No. 3 Rd.
Richmond, BC V6Y 2C2 Canada
604-665-3200
Fax: 604-665-5863
MICR: 04800-003

Richmond - No. 3 Rd.
#125, 10111 - No. 3 Rd.
Richmond, BC V7A 1W6 Canada
604-668-4333
Fax: 604-277-7513
MICR: 04880-003

Richmond - Westminster
Terra Nova Personal Financial Centre
#140, 3671 Westminster Hwy.
Richmond, BC V7C 5V2 Canada
604-656-2818
Fax: 604-656-2823
MICR: 08088-003

Richmond Hill - East Beaver Creek
Hwy 404 & 7
260 East Beaver Creek Rd.
Richmond Hill, ON L4B 3M3 Canada
905-764-4400
Fax: 905-764-4388
MICR: 06032-003

Richmond Hill - Major MacKenzie
1450 Major MacKenzie Dr. East
Richmond Hill, ON L4S 0A1 Canada
905-884-1802
Fax: 905-884-1454
MICR: 09998-003

Richmond Hill - Yonge
South Hill Shopping Centre
9325 Yonge St.
Richmond Hill, ON L4C 0A8 Canada
905-780-8100
Fax: 905-737-2849
MICR: 08552-003

Richmond Hill - Yonge
12935 Yonge St.
Richmond Hill, ON L4E 0G7 Canada
905-313-2030
Fax: 905-313-2055
MICR: 09999-003

Richmond Hill - Yonge St.
Bldg. A
11000 Yonge St.
Richmond Hill, ON L4C 3E4 Canada
905-884-1138
Fax: 905-884-2024
MICR: 04062-003

Ridgetown
One Main St. East
Ridgetown, ON N0P 2C0 Canada
519-674-5468
Fax: 519-674-2759
MICR: 04082-003

Ridgeway
385 Ridge Rd.
Ridgeway, ON L0S 1N0 Canada
905-894-1100
Fax: 905-894-5743
MICR: 04102-003

Rimouski
1, rue St. Germain est
Rimouski, QC G5L 1A1 Canada
418-725-6000
Fax: 418-725-6031
MICR: 07381-003

Ripley
41 Queen St.
Ripley, ON N0G 2R0 Canada
519-395-3101
Fax: 519-395-4323
MICR: 04122-003

Riverview
Pine Glen Mall
121 Pine Glen Rd.
Riverview, NB E1B 1V5 Canada
506-856-7300
Fax: 506-856-7318
MICR: 01784-003

Roberval
893, boul St-Joseph
Roberval, QC G8H 2L8 Canada
418-275-1302
Fax: 418-275-6736
MICR: 07451-003

Roblin
179 Main St. West
Roblin, MB R0L 1P0 Canada
204-937-2128
Fax: 204-937-8093
MICR: 04167-003

Rockland
2864 Laurier St.
Rockland, ON K4K 1L7 Canada
613-446-7702
Fax: 613-446-7719
MICR: 04104-003

Rockwood
118 Main St.
Rockwood, ON N0B 2K0 Canada
519-856-2055
Fax: 519-856-2110
MICR: 04142-003

Rodney
244 Furnival Rd.
Rodney, ON N0L 2C0 Canada
519-785-0170
Fax: 519-785-0076
MICR: 04162-003

Rosemère
Les Jardins Rosemère
395, Grande Côte
Rosemère, QC J7A 1K8 Canada
450-621-5660
Fax: 450-621-1244
MICR: 07591-003

Rosetown
213 Main St.
Rosetown, SK S0L 2V0 Canada
306-882-4221
Fax: 306-882-3610
MICR: 07268-003

Rouyn-Noranda
Les Promenades du Cuivre
100, rue du Terminus ouest
Rouyn-Noranda, QC J9X 6H7 Canada
819-763-4030
Fax: 819-763-4040
MICR: 07661-003

Russell
181 Main St. North
Russell, MB R0J 1W0 Canada
204-773-2141
Fax: 204-773-3516
MICR: 04427-003

Sackville
103 Main St.
Sackville, NB E4L 4B1 Canada
506-536-1030
Fax: 506-536-1121
MICR: 01874-003

Saint John - Fairville
Westwind Place
800 Fairville Blvd.
Saint John, NB E2M 5T4 Canada
506-635-1030
Fax: 506-635-0681
MICR: 01264-003

Saint John - King
100 King St.
Saint John, NB E2L 1G4 Canada
506-632-8080
Fax: 506-634-7665
MICR: 00004-003

Saint John - Lansdowne
111 Lansdowne Ave.
Saint John, NB E2K 2Z9 Canada
506-634-8220
Fax: 506-632-0707
MICR: 01984-003

Saint John - Westmorland
McAllister Place
515 Westmorland Rd.
Saint John, NB E2J 3W9 Canada
506-633-7680
Fax: 506-633-7089
MICR: 02014-003

Saint-Bruno
30, boul Clairevue ouest
Saint-Bruno, QC J3V 1P8 Canada
450-653-7846
Fax: 450-653-5356
MICR: 07721-003

Saint-Constant
#800, 564 Hwy. 132
Saint-Constant, QC J5A 2S6 Canada
450-635-5260
Fax: 450-635-3496
MICR: 09985-003

Saint-Hyacinthe
Les Galeries
1050, boul Casavant ouest
Saint-Hyacinthe, QC J2S 8B9 Canada
450-771-3833
Fax: 450-771-3831
MICR: 07811-003

Saint-Lambert
Carrefour Victoria
635, av Victoria
Saint-Lambert, QC J4P 3R4 Canada
450-923-5320
Fax: 450-923-5333
MICR: 07941-003

Saint-Sauveur
#H-1, 75, rue de la Gare
Saint-Sauveur, QC J0R 1R6 Canada
450-227-4683
Fax: 450-227-5301
MICR: 08211-003

Sainte-Agathe-des-Monts
61, rue St-Vincent
Sainte-Agathe-des-Monts, QC J8C 2A5 Canada
819-326-2001
Fax: 819-326-2928
MICR: 07711-003

Salaberry-de-Valleyfield
169, rue Victoria
Salaberry-de-Valleyfield, QC J6T 1A5 Canada
450-373-6424
Fax: 450-373-7519
MICR: 08921-003

Salmon Arm
PO Box 670
340 Alexander St. NE
Salmon Arm, BC V1E 4N8 Canada
250-832-8071
Fax: 250-832-4668
MICR: 04990-003

Sarnia - Lakeshore
1125 Lakeshore Rd.
Sarnia, ON N7V 2V5 Canada
519-542-7774
Fax: 519-542-7852
MICR: 04342-003

Sarnia - London
1349 London Rd.
Sarnia, ON N7S 1P6 Canada
519-542-3431
Fax: 519-542-7902
MICR: 04312-003

Sarnia - North Christina
230 North Christina St.
Sarnia, ON N7T 5V2 Canada
519-332-6800
Fax: 519-332-3688
MICR: 04322-003

Saskatoon - 1st
154 - 1st Ave. South
Saskatoon, SK S7K 1K2 Canada
306-933-3400
Fax: 306-933-3587
MICR: 07378-003

Royal Bank of Canada(RBC) (continued)

Saskatoon - 8th
2802 - 8th St. East
Saskatoon, SK S7H 0V9 Canada
306-933-3655
Fax: 306-933-3625
MICR: 07758-003

Saskatoon - Ave. C
2030 Ave. C North
Saskatoon, SK S7L 1M2 Canada
306-933-3510
Fax: 306-933-3663
MICR: 07388-003

Saskatoon - Broadway
842 Broadway Ave.
Saskatoon, SK S7N 1B6 Canada
306-933-3571
Fax: 306-933-3585
MICR: 07598-003

Saskatoon - Central
705 Central Ave.
Saskatoon, SK S7N 2S4 Canada
306-933-3560
Fax: 306-933-3624
MICR: 07408-003

Saskatoon - College
1402 College Dr.
Saskatoon, SK S7N 0W7 Canada
306-933-3535
Fax: 306-933-3542
MICR: 07488-003

Saskatoon - Lenore
#1, 123 Lenore Dr.
Saskatoon, SK S7K 7H9 Canada
306-933-3770
Fax: 306-933-3771
MICR: 07418-003

Saskatoon - Worobetz
#15, 15 Worobetz Pl.
Saskatoon, SK S7L 6R4 Canada
306-933-3586
Fax: 306-933-3570
MICR: 07748-003

Sauble Beach
632 Main St.
Sauble Beach, ON N0H 2G0 Canada
519-422-1472
Fax: 519-422-3124
MICR: 02122-003

Sault Ste Marie - Queen
602 Queen St. East, 2nd Fl.
Sault Ste Marie, ON P6A 2A4 Canada
705-759-7000
Fax: 705-759-1370
MICR: 04362-003

Sault Ste Marie - Second Line
312 Second Line West
Sault Ste Marie, ON P6C 2J5 Canada
705-254-1442
Fax: 705-946-3134
MICR: 04392-003

Sault Ste Marie - Wellington
298 Wellington St. West
Sault Ste Marie, ON P6A 1H7 Canada
705-254-4381
Fax: 705-946-3135
MICR: 04402-003

Sault Ste Marie - Wellington
1496 Wellington St. East
Sault Ste Marie, ON P6A 2R1 Canada
705-254-6495
Fax: 705-946-3136
MICR: 04442-003

Scotland
284 Oakland St.
Scotland, ON N0E 1R0 Canada
519-446-2252
Fax: 519-446-1176
MICR: 04602-003

Sechelt
Trail Bay Mall
#100, 5760 Teredo St.
Sechelt, BC V0N 3A0 Canada
604-740-5100
Fax: 604-885-7935
MICR: 05010-003

Selkirk
#7, 366 Main St.
Selkirk, MB R1A 1T6 Canada
204-482-3608
Fax: 204-482-4801
MICR: 05467-003

Sept-×les
440, rue Brochu
Sept-×les, QC G4R 2W8 Canada
418-962-9858
Fax: 418-962-1476
MICR: 08291-003

Sexsmith
9921 - 100th St.
Sexsmith, AB T0H 3C0 Canada
780-568-3852
Fax: 780-568-4062
MICR: 08479-003

Sharbot Lake
1043 Elizabeth St.
Sharbot Lake, ON K0H 2P0 Canada
613-279-3191
Fax: 613-279-2173
MICR: 04622-003

Shaunavon
304 Centre St.
Shaunavon, SK S0N 2M0 Canada
306-297-2641
Fax: 306-297-3354
MICR: 07818-003

Shawinigan
1, La Plaza de la Mauricie
Shawinigan, QC G9N 7C1 Canada
819-539-6995
Fax: 819-539-8755
MICR: 08371-003

Shawville
341, rue Main
Shawville, QC J0X 2Y0 Canada
819-647-2258
Fax: 819-647-2091
MICR: 08391-003

Shelburne
123 Owen Sound St.
Shelburne, ON L0N 1S0 Canada
519-925-2023
Fax: 519-925-5030
MICR: 04642-003

Sherbrooke - King
Place des Congrès
#101, 2665, rue King ouest
Sherbrooke, QC J1L 2G5 Canada
819-823-4200
Fax: 819-823-4213
MICR: 05585-003

Sherbrooke - King
763 King St. East
Sherbrooke, QC J1G 1C6 Canada
819-823-4288
Fax: 819-823-4290
MICR: 08541-003

Sherbrooke - Main St.
6 Main St.
Sherbrooke, NS B0J 3C0 Canada
902-522-2800
Fax: 902-522-2867
MICR: 05943-003

Sherbrooke - Queen
131, rue Queen
Sherbrooke, QC J1M 1J7 Canada
819-823-4299
Fax: 819-823-4292
MICR: 02391-003

Sherwood Park
#160, 390 Baseline Rd.
Sherwood Park, AB T8H 1X1 Canada
780-449-7700
Fax: 780-449-7722
MICR: 05489-003

Shoal Lake
Station Rd.
Shoal Lake, MB R0J 1Z0 Canada
204-759-2474
Fax: 204-759-2111
MICR: 05597-003

Shubenacadie
2824 Main St.
Shubenacadie, NS B0N 2H0 Canada
902-758-2295
Fax: 902-758-4249
MICR: 06053-003

Sidney
2464 Beacon Ave.
Sidney, BC V8L 1X6 Canada
250-356-3340
Fax: 250-656-6932
MICR: 05030-003

Simcoe
55 Norfolk St. South
Simcoe, ON N3Y 2W1 Canada
519-428-3800
Fax: 519-426-6136
MICR: 04662-003

Slave Lake
204 Main St. North
Slave Lake, AB T0G 2A0 Canada
780-849-8100
Fax: 780-849-8112
MICR: 08589-003

Smithers
1106 Main St.
Smithers, BC V0J 2N0 Canada
250-847-4405
Fax: 250-847-4454
MICR: 05040-003

Smiths Falls
31 Beckwith St. North
Smiths Falls, ON K7A 2B2 Canada
613-283-7660
Fax: 613-283-9486
MICR: 04702-003

Smithville
185 Griffin St. North
Smithville, ON L0R 2A0 Canada
905-957-2522
Fax: 905-957-2576
MICR: 04722-003

Smooth Rock Falls
28 Second Ave.
Smooth Rock Falls, ON P0L 2B0 Canada
705-338-2794
Fax: 705-338-2357
MICR: 04742-003

Snow Lake
81 Balsam St.
Snow Lake, MB R0B 1M0 Canada
204-358-7711
Fax: 204-358-2119
MICR: 05727-003

Somerset
309 - 3rd St.
Somerset, MB R0G 2L0 Canada
204-744-2242
Fax: 204-744-2390
MICR: 05857-003

Sooke
#118, 6660 Sooke Rd.
Sooke, BC V0S 1N0 Canada
250-356-3355
Fax: 250-642-2214
MICR: 05050-003

Souris
47 Crescent Ave. West
Souris, MB R0K 2C0 Canada
204-483-2181
Fax: 204-483-2716
MICR: 05987-003

Southey
165 Keats St.
Southey, SK S0G 4P0 Canada
306-726-2031
Fax: 306-726-4607
MICR: 07928-003

Sparwood
Greenwood Shopping Centre
#86, 101 Red Cedar Dr.
Sparwood, BC V0B 2G0 Canada
250-425-3360
Fax: 250-425-0077
MICR: 05080-003

Spencerville
29 Bennett St.
Spencerville, ON K0E 1X0 Canada
613-658-3032
Fax: 613-658-3369
MICR: 04782-003
Spirit River
4601 - 50 St.
Spirit River, AB T0H 3G0 Canada
780-864-3734
Fax: 780-864-4106
MICR: 08699-003
Spruce Grove
112 King St.
Spruce Grove, AB T7X 3B4 Canada
780-962-2872
Fax: 780-962-1963
MICR: 08719-003
Squamish
PO Box 770
38100 - 2nd Ave.
Squamish, BC V8B 0A6 Canada
604-892-3555
Fax: 604-892-1534
MICR: 05120-003
St Albert
Inglewood Sq.
#24, 11 Bellerose Dr.
St Albert, AB T8N 5E1 Canada
780-460-3100
Fax: 780-458-3901
MICR: 08399-003
St Catharines - Hartzel
108 Hartzel Rd.
St Catharines, ON L2P 1N4 Canada
905-688-3350
Fax: 905-688-1981
MICR: 04252-003
St Catharines - Martindale
211 Martindale Rd.
St Catharines, ON L2S 3V7 Canada
905-641-0307
Fax: 905-641-5765
MICR: 09082-003
St Catharines - Scott
Grantham Shopping Plaza
380 Scott St.
St Catharines, ON L2M 3W4 Canada
905-934-4303
Fax: 905-934-5557
MICR: 04242-003
St Catharines - St. Paul
89-91 St. Paul St.
St Catharines, ON L2R 6X2 Canada
905-641-0553
Fax: 905-641-0339
MICR: 04222-003
St Marys
PO Box 460
133 Queen St. East
St Marys, ON N4X 1B3 Canada
519-284-1600
Fax: 519-284-4428
MICR: 04262-003
St Peters
9955 Grenville St.
St Peters, NS B0E 3B0 Canada
902-535-2001
Fax: 902-535-2881
MICR: 05833-003
St Thomas - Talbot
367 Talbot St.
St Thomas, ON N5P 1B7 Canada
519-631-7220
Fax: 519-631-6753
MICR: 04282-003
St Thomas - Talbot
East End
1099 Talbot St. East
St Thomas, ON N5P 1G4 Canada
519-631-7369
Fax: 519-631-6628
MICR: 04302-003
St-Eustache
430, boul Arthur Sauvé
St-Eustache, QC J7R 6V6 Canada
450-472-1570
Fax: 450-472-9185
MICR: 07751-003
St-Félicien
1110, boul Sacré Coeur
St-Félicien, QC G8K 1A2 Canada
418-679-0725
Fax: 418-679-2367
MICR: 07741-003
St-Georges
12095, 1e av est
St-Georges, QC G5Y 2E2 Canada
418-227-7901
Fax: 418-227-1495
MICR: 07731-003
St-Jean-sur-Richelieu
135, rue Richelieu
St-Jean-sur-Richelieu, QC J3B 6X7 Canada
450-358-6000
Fax: 450-358-6060
MICR: 07871-003
St-Jérôme
#100, 460, boul Labelle
St-Jérôme, QC J7Z 5L3 Canada
450-569-5500
Fax: 450-569-5511
MICR: 07841-003
St. John's - Elizabeth Ave
65 Elizabeth Ave.
St. John's, NL A1A 1W8 Canada
709-576-4545
Fax: 709-576-4677
MICR: 09503-003
St. John's - Freshwater
337 Freshwater Rd.
St. John's, NL A1B 3N4 Canada
709-576-4577
Fax: 709-576-4866
MICR: 09573-003
St. John's - Topsail
664 Topsail Rd.
St. John's, NL A1E 2E2 Canada
709-576-4606
Fax: 709-576-4115
MICR: 09603-003
St. John's - Water
226 Water St.
St. John's, NL A1C 1A9 Canada
709-576-4222
Fax: 709-576-4985
MICR: 09453-003
St. Stephen
26 Milltown Blvd.
St. Stephen, NB E3L 1G3 Canada
506-466-2127
Fax: 506-466-9141
MICR: 02094-003
Stayner
7307, Hwy. 26
Stayner, ON L0M 1S0 Canada
705-428-2843
Fax: 705-428-6921
MICR: 04812-003
Ste Rose du Lac
644 Central Ave.
Ste Rose du Lac, MB R0L 1S0 Canada
204-447-2892
Fax: 204-447-3106
MICR: 05337-003
Ste-Thérèse-de-Blainville
60, rue Turgeon
Ste-Thérèse-de-Blainville, QC J7E 3H4 Canada
450-433-2202
Fax: 450-433-2281
MICR: 08221-003
Steinbach
288 Main St.
Steinbach, MB R5G 1Y8 Canada
204-326-3416
Fax: 204-346-5428
MICR: 06117-003
Stellarton
254 Foord St.
Stellarton, NS B0K 1S0 Canada
902-752-1523
Fax: 902-755-6572
MICR: 06163-003
Stephenville
73 Main St.
Stephenville, NL A2N 1H9 Canada
709-643-8300
Fax: 709-643-9549
MICR: 09703-003
Stettler
4920 - 51st St.
Stettler, AB T0C 2L0 Canada
403-742-2382
Fax: 403-742-1355
MICR: 08919-003
Stewiacke
267 George St.
Stewiacke, NS B0N 2J0 Canada
902-639-2246
Fax: 902-639-2489
MICR: 06273-003
Stittsville
1615 Main St.
Stittsville, ON K2S 1A3 Canada
613-836-4044
Fax: 613-836-6106
MICR: 04842-003
Stonewall
340 Main St.
Stonewall, MB R0C 2Z0 Canada
204-467-5544
Fax: 204-467-5575
MICR: 06147-003
Stoney Creek - King
42 King St. East
Stoney Creek, ON L8G 1K1 Canada
905-664-6554
Fax: 905-664-1810
MICR: 04862-003
Stoney Creek - Paramount
1050 Paramount Dr.
Stoney Creek, ON L8J 1P8 Canada
905-573-8101
Fax: 905-573-8820
MICR: 02034-003
Stoney Creek - Queenston
917 Queenston Rd.
Stoney Creek, ON L8G 1B8 Canada
905-664-6412
Fax: 905-664-6898
MICR: 04882-003
Stouffville
#1-2, 28 Sandiford Dr.
Stouffville, ON L4A 7X5 Canada
905-640-2800
Fax: 905-640-2717
MICR: 00150-003
Strasbourg
109 Mountain St.
Strasbourg, SK S0G 4V0 Canada
306-725-3500
Fax: 306-725-3110
MICR: 08148-003
Stratford - Downie
33 Downie St.
Stratford, ON N5A 1W6 Canada
519-271-6880
Fax: 519-271-5361
MICR: 04902-003
Stratford - Ontario
966 Ontario St.
Stratford, ON N5A 3K1 Canada
519-271-8210
Fax: 519-271-5670
MICR: 04912-003
Strathmore
202 - 2nd Ave.
Strathmore, AB T1P 1K3 Canada
403-934-3351
Fax: 403-934-4870
MICR: 09029-003
Strathroy

Royal Bank of Canada(RBC) (continued)

38 Front St. West
Strathroy, ON N7G 1X4 Canada
519-245-1420
Fax: 519-245-5115
MICR: 04922-003

Sturgeon Falls
170 King St.
Sturgeon Falls, ON P2B 1R5 Canada
705-753-1010
Fax: 705-753-4430
MICR: 04962-003

Sudbury - Durham
72 Durham St., 3rd Fl.
Sudbury, ON P3E 4N7 Canada
705-688-4700
Fax: 705-674-3109
MICR: 04982-003

Sudbury - Lasalle
1720 Lasalle Blvd.
Sudbury, ON P3A 2A1 Canada
705-566-1710
Fax: 705-566-6078
MICR: 04992-003

Sudbury - Regent
243 Regent St. South
Sudbury, ON P3C 4C6 Canada
705-674-2175
Fax: 705-674-0303
MICR: 05002-003

Sudbury - Regent
1879 Regent St. South
Sudbury, ON P3E 3Z7 Canada
705-522-7170
Fax: 705-522-5995
MICR: 05052-003

Summerland
7519 Prairie Valley Rd.
Summerland, BC V0H 1Z4 Canada
250-494-6036
Fax: 250-494-3088
MICR: 05130-003

Summerside
222 Water St.
Summerside, PE C1N 2V5 Canada
902-436-4237
Fax: 902-888-3929
MICR: 05204-003

Sundridge
15 John St.
Sundridge, ON P0A 1Z0 Canada
705-384-5311
Fax: 705-384-7804
MICR: 05022-003

Surrey - 10 Hwy.
Sullivan Square
15365 - 10 Hwy.
Surrey, BC V3S 0X9 Canada
604-575-3350
Fax: 604-575-3371
MICR: 5840-003

Surrey - 120th St.
Scott Town
9490 - 120th St.
Surrey, BC V3V 4B9 Canada
604-665-8992
Fax: 604-586-3565
MICR: 03600-003

Surrey - 128 St.
Ocean Park Plaza
#60, 1658 - 128 St.
Surrey, BC V4A 3V3 Canada
604-541-4488
Fax: 604-541-4499
MICR: 08610-003

Surrey - 152nd St.
#150, 10470 - 152nd St.
Surrey, BC V3R 0Y3 Canada
604-665-6765
Fax: 604-588-6921
MICR: 03610-003

Surrey - 152nd St.
3002 - 152nd St.
Surrey, BC V4P 3N7 Canada
604-542-3110
Fax: 604-542-3111
MICR: 4695-003

Surrey - 56th Ave.
17931 - 56th Ave.
Surrey, BC V3S 1E2 Canada
604-576-5550
Fax: 604-574-7135
MICR: 01110-003

Surrey - 72nd Ave.
13681 - 72nd Ave.
Surrey, BC V3W 2P2 Canada
604-665-8414
Fax: 604-594-2482
MICR: 05220-003

Surrey - Fraser Hwy.
#307, 15988 Fraser Hwy.
Surrey, BC V4N 0X8 Canada
604-501-7175
Fax: 604-599-1608
MICR: 03620-003

Surrey - King George Hwy.
King George Centre
10201 King George Hwy.
Surrey, BC V3T 2W6 Canada
604-665-8940
Fax: 604-586-3535
MICR: 03680-003

Sussex
664 Main St.
Sussex, NB E4E 7H9 Canada
506-432-1620
Fax: 506-432-1644
MICR: 02204-003

Swan River
502 Main St. East
Swan River, MB R0L 1Z0 Canada
204-734-3427
Fax: 204-734-4917
MICR: 06177-003

Swift Current
261 - 1st Ave. NW
Swift Current, SK S9H 0N1 Canada
306-778-4100
Fax: 306-773-5881
MICR: 08258-003

Sydenham
4395 Mill St.
Sydenham, ON K0H 2T0 Canada
613-376-3616
Fax: 613-376-6999
MICR: 05042-003

Sydney
Prince St. Plaza
325 Prince St.
Sydney, NS B1P 5K6 Canada
902-567-8570
Fax: 902-539-5431
MICR: 06603-003

Taber
4818 - 53rd St.
Taber, AB T1G 1W4 Canada
403-223-4481
Fax: 403-223-1626
MICR: 09179-003

Tecumseh
13281 Tecumseh Rd. East
Tecumseh, ON N8N 3T4 Canada
519-979-2444
Fax: 519-979-2866
MICR: 08842-003

Terrace
4640 Lakelse Ave.
Terrace, BC V8G 1R2 Canada
250-635-8000
Fax: 250-635-4625
MICR: 05440-003

Terrebonne
1100, boul Moody
Terrebonne, QC J6W 3K9 Canada
450-964-4000
Fax: 450-964-4016
MICR: 02221-003

Thamesford
110 Dundas St.
Thamesford, ON N0M 2M0 Canada
519-285-3127
Fax: 519-285-3491
MICR: 05062-003

The Pas
301 Edwards Ave.
The Pas, MB R9A 1L1 Canada
204-623-3427
Fax: 204-623-6504
MICR: 06247-003

Thetford Mines
129, rue Notre-Dame ouest
Thetford Mines, QC G6G 1J4 Canada
418-335-7536
Fax: 418-335-6612
MICR: 08641-003

Thompson
23 Selkirk Ave.
Thompson, MB R8N 0M5 Canada
204-778-7367
Fax: 204-778-4257
MICR: 06377-003

Thornhill - Centre
1136 Centre St.
Thornhill, ON L4J 3M8 Canada
905-764-2655
Fax: 905-764-2756
MICR: 05076-003

Thornhill - Green Lane
#1, 8 Green Lane
Thornhill, ON L3T 7P7 Canada
905-764-5006
Fax: 905-764-6402
MICR: 00324-003

Thornhill - Yonge
Bay Hill Mews
8165 Yonge St.
Thornhill, ON L3T 2C6 Canada
905-881-1742
Fax: 905-881-9695
MICR: 05072-003

Thorold
52 Front St. South
Thorold, ON L2V 3Y7 Canada
905-227-5262
Fax: 905-227-1657
MICR: 05082-003

Three Hills
PO Box 430
501 Main St.
Three Hills, AB T0M 2A0 Canada
403-443-5531
Fax: 403-443-7538
MICR: 09249-003

Thunder Bay - Alloy
#100, 1159 Alloy Dr.
Thunder Bay, ON P7B 6M8 Canada
807-684-8300
Fax: 807-345-0847
MICR: 09870-003

Thunder Bay - Frederica
201 Frederica St. West
Thunder Bay, ON P7E 3W1 Canada
807-473-1760
Fax: 807-475-7487
MICR: 07782-003

Thunder Bay - Hodder
449 Hodder Ave.
Thunder Bay, ON P7A 1V2 Canada
807-343-1890
Fax: 807-683-8469
MICR: 03862-003

Thunder Bay - Memorial
282 Memorial Ave.
Thunder Bay, ON P7B 3Y2 Canada
807-343-1850
Fax: 807-345-9651
MICR: 05092-003

Thunder Bay - North Edward
504 North Edward St.
Thunder Bay, ON P7C 4P9 Canada
807-473-1700
Fax: 807-475-8675
MICR: 03852-003

Thunder Bay - Red River

214 Red River Rd.
Thunder Bay, ON P7B 1A6 Canada
807-343-1800
Fax: 807-345-3995
MICR: 03842-003

Thunder Bay - River
Grandview Mall
640 River St.
Thunder Bay, ON P7A 3S4 Canada
807-343-1870
Fax: 807-345-0948
MICR: 03872-003

Thunder Bay - Victoria
620 Victoria Ave. East
Thunder Bay, ON P7C 1A9 Canada
807-626-1733
Fax: 807-623-1165
MICR: 01602-003

Tilbury
PO Box 1210
85 Queen St. North
Tilbury, ON N0P 2L0 Canada
519-682-1271
Fax: 519-682-0347
MICR: 5152-003

Tillsonburg
121 Broadway St.
Tillsonburg, ON N4G 3P7 Canada
519-842-7321
Fax: 519-842-7506
MICR: 05102-003

Timmins
The 101 Mall, 38 Pine St. North
Timmins, ON P4N 6K6 Canada
705-267-7171
Fax: 705-264-2940
MICR: 05112-003

Tisdale
1102 - 100th St.
Tisdale, SK S0E 1T0 Canada
306-873-3581
Fax: 306-873-2256
MICR: 08288-003

Tobermory
7371 Hwy. 6
Tobermory, ON N0H 2R0 Canada
519-596-2775
Fax: 519-596-2727
MICR: 06862-003

Torbay
1296 Torbay Rd.
Torbay, NL A1K 1K5 Canada
709-437-5361
Fax: 709-437-1037
MICR: 09563-003

Toronto - Albion
1104 Albion Rd.
Toronto, ON M9V 1A8 Canada
416-749-3200
Fax: 416-749-3044
MICR: 05142-003

Toronto - Avenue
1635 Avenue Rd.
Toronto, ON M5M 3X8 Canada
416-785-5810
Fax: 416-785-5223
MICR: 07212-003

Toronto - Bathurst
2788 Bathurst St.
Toronto, ON M6B 3A3 Canada
416-781-3561
Fax: 416-781-0999
MICR: 05192-003

Toronto - Bathurst
4401 Bathurst St.
Toronto, ON M3H 3R9 Canada
416-632-7900
Fax: 416-632-7914
MICR: 06622-003

Toronto - Bathurst
5968 Bathurst St.
Toronto, ON M2R 1Z1 Canada
416-663-7620
Fax: 416-663-8445
MICR: 05172-003

Toronto - Bay
200 Bay St., Main Fl.
Toronto, ON M5J 2J5 Canada
416-974-3940
Fax: 416-974-8837
MICR: 00002-003

Toronto - Bayview
1554 Bayview Ave.
Toronto, ON M4G 3B6 Canada
416-974-3609
Fax: 416-974-8769
MICR: 05272-003

Toronto - Bayview
2514 Bayview Ave.
Toronto, ON M2L 1A9 Canada
415-510-3080
Fax: 416-510-3099
MICR: 5282-003

Toronto - Bloor St. East
2 Bloor St. East
Toronto, ON M4W 1A8 Canada
416-974-2746
Fax: 416-974-8349
MICR: 06702-003

Toronto - Bloor St. West
2947 Bloor St. West
Toronto, ON M8X 1B8 Canada
416-239-7771
Fax: 416-239-1384
MICR: 05362-003

Toronto - Bloor St. West
Bloor West Village
2329 Bloor St. West
Toronto, ON M6S 1P1 Canada
416-766-7296
Fax: 416-766-2909
MICR: 05382-003

Toronto - Bloor St. West
972 Bloor St. West
Toronto, ON M6H 1L6 Canada
416-535-3153
Fax: 416-535-0734
MICR: 05342-003

Toronto - Broadview
739 Broadview Ave.
Toronto, ON M4K 2P6 Canada
416-461-3503
Fax: 416-461-3631
MICR: 05452-003

Toronto - College
429 College St.
Toronto, ON M5T 1T2 Canada
416-974-2137
Fax: 416-974-3905
MICR: 05442-003

Toronto - College
833 College St.
Toronto, ON M6H 1A1 Canada
416-534-1168
Fax: 416-534-5500
MICR: 05462-003

Toronto - College
#130, 101 College St.
Toronto, ON M5G 1L7 Canada
416-542-1508
Fax: 416-542-1602
MICR: 08099-003

Toronto - Coxwell
253 Coxwell Ave.
Toronto, ON M4L 3B4 Canada
416-461-5070
Fax: 416-461-4235
MICR: 05482-003

Toronto - Coxwell
1043 Coxwell Ave.
Toronto, ON M4C 3G4 Canada
416-421-1651
Fax: 416-421-8185
MICR: 05502-003

Toronto - Danforth
2780 Danforth Ave.
Toronto, ON M4C 1M1 Canada
416-699-3993
Fax: 416-699-3453
MICR: 05522-003

Toronto - Danforth
650 Danforth Ave.
Toronto, ON M4K 1R3 Canada
416-465-5404
Fax: 416-465-5538
MICR: 06222-003

Toronto - Danforth
2076 Danforth Ave.
Toronto, ON M4C 1J6 Canada
416-425-1100
Fax: 416-425-1612
MICR: 06662-003

Toronto - Dixon
235 Dixon Rd.
Toronto, ON M9P 2M5 Canada
416-247-6125
Fax: 416-247-1446
MICR: 05582-003

Toronto - Don Mills
1090 Don Mills Rd.
Toronto, ON M3C 3R6 Canada
416-510-5400
Fax: 416-391-5938
MICR: 06142-003

Toronto - Dufferin
2765 Dufferin St.
Toronto, ON M6B 3R6 Canada
416-789-7637
Fax: 416-789-0427
MICR: 05602-003

Toronto - Dundas St. West
4860 Dundas St. West
Toronto, ON M9A 1B5 Canada
416-239-8175
Fax: 416-239-3863
MICR: 05662-003

Toronto - Dundas St. West
500 Dundas St. West
Toronto, ON M5T 1G9 Canada
416-974-5580
Fax: 416-974-7954
MICR: 06752-003

Toronto - Eglinton Ave. East
2043 Eglinton Ave. East
Toronto, ON M1L 2M9 Canada
416-751-2600
Fax: 416-751-7810
MICR: 05762-003

Toronto - Eglinton Ave. West
880 Eglinton Ave. West
Toronto, ON M6C 2B6 Canada
416-789-7405
Fax: 416-787-5898
MICR: 05722-003

Toronto - Eglinton Ave. West
473 Eglinton Ave. West
Toronto, ON M5N 1A7 Canada
416-481-1400
Fax: 416-481-1228
MICR: 00139-003

Toronto - Finch
1510 Finch Ave. East
Toronto, ON M2J 4Y6 Canada
416-491-0050
Fax: 416-491-2717
MICR: 05592-003

Toronto - Gerrard
997 Gerrard St. East
Toronto, ON M4M 1Z4 Canada
416-778-8318
Fax: 416-778-8319
MICR: 05842-003

Toronto - Grangeway
111 Grangeway Ave.
Toronto, ON M1H 3E9 Canada
416-289-5600
Fax: 416-431-5350
MICR: 05752-003

Toronto - Jane
1732 Jane St.
Toronto, ON M9N 2S4 Canada
416-247-6163
Fax: 416-247-8252
MICR: 05812-003

Toronto - Jane

Royal Bank of Canada(RBC) (continued)

901 Jane St.
Toronto, ON M6N 4C6 Canada
416-766-6864
Fax: 416-766-4553
MICR: 05952-003

Toronto - Jane
4720 Jane St. North
Toronto, ON M3N 2L2 Canada
416-661-6363
Fax: 416-661-4309
MICR: 05892-003

Toronto - Keele
2766 Keele St.
Toronto, ON M3M 2G2 Canada
416-636-2030
Fax: 416-636-2044
MICR: 05902-003

Toronto - Keele
3336 Keele St.
Toronto, ON M3J 1L5 Canada
416-636-3805
Fax: 416-636-3802
MICR: 5882-003

Toronto - Kennedy
1421 Kennedy Rd.
Toronto, ON M1P 2L6 Canada
416-288-6800
Fax: 416-288-6821
MICR: 05922-003

Toronto - King
1005 King St. West
Toronto, ON M6K 3M8 Canada
416-974-5771
Fax: 416-974-5882
MICR: 00034-003

Toronto - Kingston
936 Kingston Rd.
Toronto, ON M4E 1S7 Canada
416-698-7109
Fax: 416-698-4616
MICR: 05992-003

Toronto - Kingston
4410 Kingston Rd.
Toronto, ON M1E 2N5 Canada
416-284-1624
Fax: 416-284-1601
MICR: 06002-003

Toronto - Kingston
3090 Kingston Rd.
Toronto, ON M1M 1P1 Canada
416-266-7600
Fax: 416-266-7906
MICR: 06022-003

Toronto - Kingsway
Humbertown Centre
270 The Kingsway
Toronto, ON M9A 3T7 Canada
416-239-3961
Fax: 416-239-1307
MICR: 09067-003

Toronto - La Rose
140 La Rose Ave.
Toronto, ON M9P 1B2 Canada
416-247-6215
Fax: 416-247-2325
MICR: 06112-003

Toronto - Lakeshore Blvd. West
Marina Del Rey
2275 Lakeshore Blvd. West
Toronto, ON M8V 3Y3 Canada
416-503-1250
Fax: 416-503-1262
MICR: 00864-003

Toronto - Lakeshore Blvd. West
3609 Lakeshore Blvd. West
Toronto, ON M8W 1P5 Canada
416-259-3226
Fax: 416-259-0900
MICR: 06102-003

Toronto - Lawrence Ave. East
3091 Lawrence Ave. East
Toronto, ON M1H 1A1 Canada
416-431-7002
Fax: 416-431-2000
MICR: 06172-003

Toronto - Lawrence Ave. East
1919 Lawrence Ave. East
Toronto, ON M1R 2Y6 Canada
416-752-8900
Fax: 416-752-8670
MICR: 06182-003

Toronto - Markham
789 Markham Rd.
Toronto, ON M1H 2Y1 Canada
416-439-3031
Fax: 416-289-0352
MICR: 06202-003

Toronto - O'Connor
803 O'Connor Dr.
Toronto, ON M4B 2S7 Canada
416-759-3730
Fax: 416-759-3719
MICR: 06442-003

Toronto - Overlea
65 Overlea Blvd.
Toronto, ON M4H 1P1 Canada
416-425-5250
Fax: 416-425-3829
MICR: 06192-003

Toronto - Queen
2175 Queen St. East
Toronto, ON M4E 1E5 Canada
416-698-5244
Fax: 416-698-5370
MICR: 06262-003

Toronto - Queens Quay
#120, 207 Queens Quay West
Toronto, ON M5J 1A7 Canada
416-955-2777
Fax: 416-955-2991
MICR: 00059-003

Toronto - Queensway
1233 The Queensway
Toronto, ON M8Z 1S1 Canada
416-253-8465
Fax: 416-253-9461
MICR: 06302-003

Toronto - Rexdale
129 Rexdale Blvd.
Toronto, ON M9W 1P4 Canada
416-743-8666
Fax: 416-743-8669
MICR: 06342-003

Toronto - Roncesvalles
235 Roncesvalles Ave.
Toronto, ON M6R 2L6 Canada
416-537-5232
Fax: 416-537-5116
MICR: 06352-003

Toronto - Rylander
75 Rylander Blvd.
Toronto, ON M1B 5M5 Canada
416-724-2560
Fax: 416-724-2567
MICR: 09242-003

Toronto - Sandhurst Circle
1571 Sandhurst Circle
Toronto, ON M1V 1V2 Canada
416-292-6701
Fax: 416-292-9592
MICR: 05942-003

Toronto - Sheppard Ave. East
4022 Sheppard Ave. East
Toronto, ON M1S 3B4 Canada
416-293-1136
Fax: 416-293-8864
MICR: 06462-003

Toronto - Sheppard Ave. East
5080 Sheppard Ave. East
Toronto, ON M1S 4N3 Canada
416-291-0188
Fax: 416-291-0665
MICR: 06492-003

Toronto - Spadina Ave.
648 Spadina Ave.
Toronto, ON M5S 2H7 Canada
416-974-5950
Fax: 416-974-8793
MICR: 05802-003

Toronto - Spadina Rd.
414 Spadina Rd.
Toronto, ON M5P 2W2 Canada
416-974-7170
Fax: 416-974-6486
MICR: 01412-003

Toronto - St. Clair Ave. West
10 St. Clair Ave. West
Toronto, ON M4V 1L4 Canada
416-974-7840
Fax: 416-974-8462
MICR: 06402-003

Toronto - St. Clair Ave. West
935 St. Clair Ave. West
Toronto, ON M6C 1C7 Canada
416-654-4333
Fax: 416-654-4135
MICR: 06422-003

Toronto - Steeles Ave. East
1545 Steeles Ave. East
Toronto, ON M2M 3Y7 Canada
416-512-4680
Fax: 416-512-4698
MICR: 06512-003

Toronto - Steeles Ave. East
4751 Steeles Ave. East
Toronto, ON M1V 4S5 Canada
416-412-6900
Fax: 416-412-6961
MICR: 03172-003

Toronto - Summerhill
436 Summerhill Ave.
Toronto, ON M4W 2E4 Canada
416-974-2450
Fax: 416-974-2433
MICR: 05302-003

Toronto - University
443 University Ave.
Toronto, ON M5G 2H6 Canada
416-974-2159
Fax: 416-974-0023
MICR: 06542-003

Toronto - Victoria Park
2786 Victoria Park Ave.
Toronto, ON M2J 4A8 Canada
416-491-2173
Fax: 416-491-6463
MICR: 06532-003

Toronto - Warden
2900 Warden Ave.
Toronto, ON M1W 2S8 Canada
416-497-1230
Fax: 416-497-7627
MICR: 06832-003

Toronto - West Mall
290 The West Mall
Toronto, ON M9C 1C6 Canada
416-622-1790
Fax: 416-622-5991
MICR: 06572-003

Toronto - West Mall
401 The West Mall
Toronto, ON M9C 5J5 Canada
416-695-7025
Fax: 416-695-7135
MICR: 05422-003

Toronto - Weston
1906 Weston Rd.
Toronto, ON M9N 1W2 Canada
416-241-1195
Fax: 416-241-5816
MICR: 06582-003

Toronto - Westway
415 The Westway
Toronto, ON M9R 1H5 Canada
416-249-3371
Fax: 416-249-3654
MICR: 06612-003

Toronto - Wynford Heights
34 Wynford Heights Cres.
Toronto, ON M3C 1K7 Canada
416-447-7030
Fax: 416-447-7546
MICR: 06672-003

Toronto - Yonge

3224 Yonge St.
Toronto, ON M4N 2L2 Canada
416-974-3600
Fax: 416-974-2492
MICR: 05562-003

Toronto - Yonge
2346 Yonge St.
Toronto, ON M4P 2W7 Canada
416-974-3500
Fax: 416-974-6150
MICR: 06722-003

Toronto - Yonge
468 Yonge St.
Toronto, ON M4Y 1X3 Canada
416-974-7763
Fax: 416-974-7760
MICR: 06742-003

Toronto - Yonge
Dynasty Towers
5460 Yonge St.
Toronto, ON M2N 6K7 Canada
416-512-4646
Fax: 416-512-4658
MICR: 06762-003

Toronto - Yonge
2559 Yonge St.
Toronto, ON M4P 2J1 Canada
416-974-3575
Fax: 416-974-0136
MICR: 06802-003

Toronto - Yonge
5001 Yonge St.
Toronto, ON M2N 6P6 Canada
416-512-4600
Fax: 416-512-4601
MICR: 02874-003

Tottenham
2 Queen St. South
Tottenham, ON L0G 1W0 Canada
905-936-3481
Fax: 905-936-5511
MICR: 07522-003

Trenton
112 Dundas St. West
Trenton, ON K8V 3P3 Canada
613-392-1211
Fax: 613-392-1822
MICR: 07542-003

Trinity
Rte. 230
Trinity, NL A0C 2S0 Canada
709-464-2260
Fax: 709-464-3886
MICR: 09753-003

Trois-Rivières - Barkoff
Galeries du Cap
300, rue Barkoff
Trois-Rivières, QC G8T 2A3 Canada
819-691-3620
Fax: 819-691-3626
MICR: 00721-003

Trois-Rivières - Forges
Les Rivières
4125, boul des Forges
Trois-Rivières, QC G8Y 1W1 Canada
819-691-3900
Fax: 819-691-3916
MICR: 08811-003

Trois-Rivières - Recollets
3105, boul des Recollets
Trois-Rivières, QC G8Z 6M1 Canada
819-691-4150
Fax: 819-691-4170
MICR: 05971-003

Truro - Prince
940 Prince St.
Truro, NS B2N 1H5 Canada
902-893-4343
Fax: 902-893-7166
MICR: 06823-003

Turner Valley
104 Main St.
Turner Valley, AB T0L 2A0 Canada
403-933-4364
Fax: 403-933-3843
MICR: 09359-003

Unionville
#10, 4261 Hwy. 7
Unionville, ON L3R 1L5 Canada
905-940-5205
Fax: 905-940-5208
MICR: 08112-003

Val Caron
#30, 3140 Hwy. 69 North
Val Caron, ON P3N 1G3 Canada
705-897-4903
Fax: 705-897-2933
MICR: 07572-003

Val-d'Or
689, 3e av
Val-d'Or, QC J9P 1S7 Canada
819-824-5150
Fax: 819-824-3253
MICR: 08851-003

Vancouver - 10th
4501 West 10th Ave.
Vancouver, BC V6R 2J2 Canada
604-665-5950
Fax: 604-228-8924
MICR: 07600-003

Vancouver - 41st
2208 West 41st Ave.
Vancouver, BC V6M 1Z8 Canada
604-665-0550
Fax: 604-665-0540
MICR: 06800-003

Vancouver - 41st
Oakridge Centre
650 West 41st Ave.
Vancouver, BC V5Z 2M9 Canada
604-665-0100
Fax: 604-665-0624
MICR: 07360-003

Vancouver - 4th
2395 West 4th Ave.
Vancouver, BC V6K 1P2 Canada
604-665-0199
Fax: 604-665-0587
MICR: 05560-003

Vancouver - 57th
531 West 57th Ave.
Vancouver, BC V6P 1R8 Canada
604-665-0555
Fax: 604-324-9527
MICR: 05790-003

Vancouver - Arbutus
3076 Arbutus St.
Vancouver, BC V6J 3Z2 Canada
604-665-0155
Fax: 604-665-0562
MICR: 05520-003

Vancouver - Broadway
1497 West Broadway
Vancouver, BC V6H 1H7 Canada
604-665-5700
Fax: 604-665-3145
MICR: 05680-003

Vancouver - Broadway
398 West Broadway
Vancouver, BC V5Y 1R2 Canada
604-665-8650
Fax: 604-665-0473
MICR: 05600-003

Vancouver - Commercial
1715 Commercial Dr.
Vancouver, BC V5N 4A4 Canada
604-665-8050
Fax: 604-665-8370
MICR: 05920-003

Vancouver - Denman
945 Denman St.
Vancouver, BC V6G 2M3 Canada
604-665-4189
Fax: 604-665-8046
MICR: 06000-003

Vancouver - Dunbar
4205 Dunbar St.
Vancouver, BC V6S 2G1 Canada
604-665-5972
Fax: 604-224-8726
MICR: 06080-003

Vancouver - Fraser
6505 Fraser St.
Vancouver, BC V5X 3T4 Canada
604-665-0882
Fax: 604-321-4790
MICR: 06160-003

Vancouver - Georgia
Vancouver Royal Centre
1025 West Georgia St.
Vancouver, BC V6E 3N9 Canada
604-665-6991
Fax: 604-665-0867
MICR: 00010-003

Vancouver - Granville
8585 Granville St.
Vancouver, BC V6P 4Z9 Canada
604-665-0500
Fax: 604-665-0520
MICR: 06520-003

Vancouver - Hastings
685 West Hastings St.
Vancouver, BC V6B 1N9 Canada
604-665-6766
Fax: 604-665-4460
MICR: 06550-003

Vancouver - Hastings
2381 Hastings St. East
Vancouver, BC V5L 1V6 Canada
604-665-8000
Fax: 604-665-3160
MICR: 06640-003

Vancouver - Howe
982 Howe St.
Vancouver, BC V6Z 1N9 Canada
604-665-5138
Fax: 604-665-5811
MICR: 06720-003

Vancouver - Kingsway
3318 Kingsway
Vancouver, BC V5R 5K7 Canada
604-665-3888
Fax: 604-665-5861
MICR: 06840-003

Vancouver - MacDonald
2490 MacDonald St.
Vancouver, BC V6K 3Z1 Canada
604-665-0342
Fax: 604-665-0584
MICR: 07680-003

Vancouver - Main
400 Main St.
Vancouver, BC V6A 2T5 Canada
604-665-5240
Fax: 604-665-6315
MICR: 07120-003

Vancouver - Main
4095 Main St.
Vancouver, BC V5V 3P5 Canada
604-665-3111
Fax: 604-665-8077
MICR: 07200-003

Vancouver - Oak
3935 Oak St.
Vancouver, BC V6H 2M7 Canada
604-665-0341
Fax: 604-665-0573
MICR: 06820-003

Vancouver - Pacific
Yaletown
1195 Pacific Blvd.
Vancouver, BC V6Z 2R8 Canada
604-668-8200
Fax: 604-668-7799
MICR: 08280-003

Vancouver - Renfrew
1716 Renfrew St.
Vancouver, BC V5M 3H8 Canada
604-665-8040
Fax: 604-665-8074
MICR: 07440-003

Vancouver - Victoria
6490 Victoria Dr.
Vancouver, BC V5P 3X7 Canada

Royal Bank of Canada(RBC) (continued)
604-665-3266
Fax: 604-324-6704
MICR: 07760-003
Vanderhoof
2517 Burrard St.
Vanderhoof, BC V0J 3A0 Canada
250-567-4776
Fax: 250-567-9468
MICR: 07840-003
Varennes
1950, rue René Gaultier
Varennes, QC J3X 1P5 Canada
450-652-0693
Fax: 450-652-7690
MICR: 08991-003
Vaudreuil-Dorion
#30, 585, av St-Charles
Vaudreuil-Dorion, QC J7V 8P9 Canada
450-455-4321
Fax: 450-455-4340
MICR: 00077-003
Vernon - 27th
Village Green Mall
#105, 4900 - 27th St.
Vernon, BC V1T 7G7 Canada
250-558-4320
Fax: 250-545-2465
MICR: 07950-003
Vernon - 30th
3131 - 30th Ave.
Vernon, BC V1T 2C4 Canada
250-558-4300
Fax: 250-545-7194
MICR: 07920-003
Vernon - Hwy. 6
Polson Place
2306 Hwy. 6
Vernon, BC V1T 7E3 Canada
250-558-4310
Fax: 250-542-1372
MICR: 07930-003
Victoria - Burnside
306 West Burnside Rd.
Victoria, BC V8Z 1M1 Canada
250-356-4675
Fax: 250-356-4694
MICR: 08160-003
Victoria - Cook
304 Cook St.
Victoria, BC V8V 3X6 Canada
250-356-4600
Fax: 250-356-4682
MICR: 08040-003
Victoria - Douglas
1079 Douglas St.
Victoria, BC V8W 2C5 Canada
250-356-4500
Fax: 250-356-3111
MICR: 08000-003
Victoria - Douglas
1501 Douglas St.
Victoria, BC V8W 2G4 Canada
250-356-4630
Fax: 250-356-4648
MICR: 08080-003
Victoria - Esquimalt
#65, 1153 Esquimalt Rd.
Victoria, BC V9A 3N7 Canada
250-356-4670
Fax: 250-356-4683
MICR: 01810-003
Victoria - Kelly
#100, 800 Kelly Rd.
Victoria, BC V9B 5T6 Canada
250-391-1000
Fax: 250-391-1036
MICR: 08300-003
Victoria - Oak Bay
2255 Oak Bay Ave.
Victoria, BC V8R 1G4 Canada
250-356-3455
Fax: 250-370-1198
MICR: 08340-003
Victoria - Royal Oak
Broadmead Village
#600, 777 Royal Oak Dr.
Victoria, BC V8X 4V1 Canada
250-356-4756
Fax: 250-356-3424
MICR: 08060-003
Victoria - Shelbourne
3970 Shelbourne St.
Victoria, BC V8N 3E2 Canada
250-356-4626
Fax: 250-477-9351
MICR: 08370-003
Victoria - Sooke
#507, 1913 Sooke Rd.
Victoria, BC V9B 1V9 Canada
250-356-3338
Fax: 250-478-6182
MICR: 01120-003
Victoriaville
118, rue Notre-Dame est
Victoriaville, QC G6P 3Z6 Canada
819-751-6130
Fax: 819-751-6144
MICR: 09181-003
Virden
229 - 7th Ave. South
Virden, MB R0M 2C0 Canada
204-748-2145
Fax: 204-748-1080
MICR: 06397-003
Wadena
105 Main St.
Wadena, SK S0A 4J0 Canada
306-338-2548
Fax: 306-338-3717
MICR: 08538-003
Wainwright
401 - 10 St.
Wainwright, AB T9W 1N9 Canada
780-842-3338
Fax: 780-842-4511
MICR: 09389-003
Wallaceburg
552 James St. East
Wallaceburg, ON N8A 2N9 Canada
519-627-1484
Fax: 519-627-0024
MICR: 07582-003
Warkworth
36 Main St.
Warkworth, ON K0K 3K0 Canada
705-924-2831
Fax: 705-924-3455
MICR: 07602-003
Waterdown
304 Dundas St. East
Waterdown, ON L0R 2H0 Canada
905-689-6655
Fax: 905-689-3332
MICR: 07662-003
Waterloo - Erb
Beechwood
420 Erb St. West
Waterloo, ON N2L 6H6 Canada
519-747-1761
Fax: 519-747-0369
MICR: 09037-003
Waterloo - King
#70, 74 King St. South
Waterloo, ON N2J 1N8 Canada
519-747-8335
Fax: 519-747-8336
MICR: 07682-003
Waterloo - King
248 King St. North
Waterloo, ON N2J 2Y7 Canada
519-747-8320
Fax: 519-747-8321
MICR: 07702-003
Waterloo - Weber
585 Weber St. North
Waterloo, ON N2V 1V8 Canada
519-747-8360
Fax: 519-747-8361
MICR: 07712-003
Waterloo - Westmount
50 Westmount Rd. North
Waterloo, ON N2L 2R5 Canada
519-747-8300
Fax: 519-747-8301
MICR: 07692-003
Watrous
202 Main St.
Watrous, SK S0K 4T0 Canada
306-946-3391
Fax: 306-946-2111
MICR: 08698-003
Wawa
72 Broadway Ave.
Wawa, ON P0S 1K0 Canada
705-856-2261
Fax: 705-856-4960
MICR: 07722-003
Wawanesa
147 - 4th St.
Wawanesa, MB R0K 2G0 Canada
204-824-2049
Fax: 204-824-2145
MICR: 06767-003
Wawota
107 Main St.
Wawota, SK S0G 5A0 Canada
306-739-2561
Fax: 306-739-2458
MICR: 08808-003
Welland - East Main
41 East Main St.
Welland, ON L3B 5P4 Canada
905-735-7910
Fax: 905-735-7103
MICR: 07742-003
Welland - Niagara
571 Niagara St.
Welland, ON L3C 1L7 Canada
905-735-1511
Fax: 905-735-8110
MICR: 07792-003
West Pubnico
Rte. 335
West Pubnico, NS B0W 3S0 Canada
902-762-2205
Fax: 902-762-3030
MICR: 07213-003
West Vancouver - Marine
1705 Marine Dr.
West Vancouver, BC V7V 1J5 Canada
604-981-6550
Fax: 604-922-9832
MICR: 08400-003
West Vancouver - Marine
2403 Marine Dr.
West Vancouver, BC V7V 1L3 Canada
604-981-6580
Fax: 604-981-6247
MICR: 08440-003
West Vancouver - Park Royal
672 Park Royal North
West Vancouver, BC V7T 1H9 Canada
604-981-6500
Fax: 604-981-5001
MICR: 08480-003
Westbank
3650 Gosset Rd.
Westbank, BC V4T 2N4 Canada
250-768-5176
Fax: 250-768-4522
MICR: 08380-003
Westlock
10427 - 100th Ave.
Westlock, AB T7P 2J2 Canada
780-349-3378
Fax: 780-349-6142
MICR: 09399-003
Westville
1813 Main St.
Westville, NS B0K 2A0 Canada
902-396-4121
Fax: 902-396-5508
MICR: 07263-009
Wetaskiwin

4916 - 50th Ave.
Wetaskiwin, AB T9A 3P8 Canada
780-352-6011
Fax: 780-352-3794
MICR: 09459-003

Weyburn
220 Souris Ave.
Weyburn, SK S4H 0C5 Canada
306-848-3900
Fax: 306-842-1464
MICR: 08918-003

Weymouth
Rte. 1
Weymouth, NS B0W 3T0 Canada
902-837-5136
Fax: 902-837-7636
MICR: 07373-003

Wheatley
10 Talbot St. East
Wheatley, ON N0P 2P0 Canada
519-825-4616
Fax: 519-825-7232
MICR: 07822-003

Whistler
#101, 4000 Whistler Way
Whistler, BC V0N 1B4 Canada
604-938-5800
Fax: 604-932-7073
MICR: 08500-003

Whitby - Brock
307 Brock St. South
Whitby, ON L1N 4K3 Canada
905-665-7200
Fax: 905-665-7202
MICR: 07842-003

Whitby - Rossland
714 Rossland Rd.
Whitby, ON L1N 9L3 Canada
905-665-1500
Fax: 905-665-1519
MICR: 06962-003

Whitby - Taunton
40 Taunton Rd. East
Whitby, ON L1R 0A1 Canada
905-655-2999
Fax: 905-655-2997
MICR: 00024-003

Whitby - Victoria
1761 Victoria St. East
Whitby, ON L1N 9W4 Canada
905-571-7823
Fax: 905-571-5434
MICR: 09837-003

White River
204 Elgin St.
White River, ON P0M 3G0 Canada
807-822-2345
Fax: 807-822-2638
MICR: 07862-003

White Rock
1588 Johnston Rd.
White Rock, BC V4B 3Z7 Canada
604-665-8125
Fax: 604-531-7828
MICR: 08580-003

Whitecourt
5117 - 50th Ave.
Whitecourt, AB T7S 1A1 Canada
780-778-6895
Fax: 780-778-4805
MICR: 08229-003

Whitehorse
4110 - 4th Ave.
Whitehorse, YT Y1A 4N7 Canada
403-667-6416
Fax: 403-668-7410
MICR: 09950-003

Whycocomagh
72 Village Rd.
Whycocomagh, NS B0E 3M0 Canada
902-756-2600
Fax: 902-756-3500
MICR: 07483-003

Wiarton
577 Berford St.
Wiarton, ON N0H 2T0 Canada
519-534-1040
Fax: 519-534-1731
MICR: 07882-003

Wilkie
114 - 2nd Ave. East
Wilkie, SK S0K 4W0 Canada
306-843-2611
Fax: 306-843-2090
MICR: 09028-003

Williams Lake
51 Fourth Ave. North
Williams Lake, BC V2G 4S1 Canada
250-398-2500
Fax: 250-398-5833
MICR: 08640-003

Winchester
481 Main St.
Winchester, ON K0C 2K0 Canada
613-774-2290
Fax: 613-774-2799
MICR: 07902-003

Windsor - Dougall
3854 Dougall Ave.
Windsor, ON N9G 1X2 Canada
519-972-3373
Fax: 519-972-5707
MICR: 08152-003

Windsor - Howard
Devon Plaza
2669 Howard Ave.
Windsor, ON N8X 3X2 Canada
519-966-1410
Fax: 519-966-0328
MICR: 07942-003

Windsor - Huron Church
1600 Huron Church Rd.
Windsor, ON N9C 3Z3 Canada
519-256-3485
Fax: 519-256-0216
MICR: 07952-003

Windsor - Ouellette
245 Ouellette Ave.
Windsor, ON N9A 7J2 Canada
519-253-4281
Fax: 519-255-8608
MICR: 07922-003

Windsor - Tecumseh
2614 Tecumseh Rd. East
Windsor, ON N8W 1G2 Canada
519-945-1193
Fax: 519-945-3832
MICR: 08022-003

Windsor - Water
111 Water St.
Windsor, NS B0N 2T0 Canada
902-798-5721
Fax: 902-798-0366
MICR: 07593-003

Windsor - Wyandotte
4635 Wyandotte St. East
Windsor, ON N8Y 1H6 Canada
519-944-7200
Fax: 519-944-0409
MICR: 08002-003

Windsor - Wyandotte
8135 Wyandotte St. East
Windsor, ON N8S 1T4 Canada
519-944-5977
Fax: 519-944-0418
MICR: 08052-003

Windthorst
133 Railway Ave.
Windthorst, SK S0G 5G0 Canada
306-224-2024
Fax: 306-224-2142
MICR: 09138-003

Winkler
225 Main St.
Winkler, MB R6W 4B3 Canada
204-325-4371
Fax: 204-325-9163
MICR: 06907-003

Winnipeg - Corydon
Corydon Village Mall
#100, 1700 Corydon Ave.
Winnipeg, MB R3N 0K1 Canada
204-988-5750
Fax: 204-488-9728
MICR: 07287-003

Winnipeg - Ellice
Ellice Centre
#130, 1395 Ellice Ave.
Winnipeg, MB R3G 0G3 Canada
204-988-6565
Fax: 204-783-2942
MICR: 05137-003

Winnipeg - Goulet
125 Goulet St.
Winnipeg, MB R2H 0R6 Canada
204-988-5760
Fax: 204-231-2527
MICR: 04627-003

Winnipeg - Grant
1219 Grant Ave.
Winnipeg, MB R3M 1Z1 Canada
204-988-4321
Fax: 204-452-1316
MICR: 07437-003

Winnipeg - Henderson
Northdale Shopping Centre
963 Henderson Hwy.
Winnipeg, MB R2K 2M3 Canada
204-988-6268
Fax: 204-654-1346
MICR: 01357-003

Winnipeg - Henderson
1795 Henderson Hwy.
Winnipeg, MB R2G 1P3 Canada
204-988-6473
Fax: 204-663-2150
MICR: 07497-003

Winnipeg - London
517 London St.
Winnipeg, MB R2K 2Z4 Canada
204-988-6530
Fax: 204-669-6197
MICR: 01307-003

Winnipeg - Main
1846 Main St.
Winnipeg, MB R2V 3H2 Canada
204-988-5830
Fax: 204-338-8591
MICR: 06827-003

Winnipeg - Main
540 Main St.
Winnipeg, MB R3B 1C4 Canada
204-988-4010
Fax: 204-942-1890
MICR: 07817-003

Winnipeg - McPhillips
2350 McPhillips St.
Winnipeg, MB R2V 4J6 Canada
204-988-6035
Fax: 204-339-7599
MICR: 06807-003

Winnipeg - McPhillips
Northgate Shopping Centre
1399 McPhillips St.
Winnipeg, MB R2V 3C4 Canada
204-988-5840
Fax: 204-338-8474
MICR: 06857-003

Winnipeg - Osborne
669 Osborne St.
Winnipeg, MB R3L 2B8 Canada
204-988-5790
Fax: 204-477-5493
MICR: 07947-003

Winnipeg - Pembina
#26, 2855 Pembina Hwy.
Winnipeg, MB R3T 2H5 Canada
204-988-6062
Fax: 204-269-0052
MICR: 08067-003

Winnipeg - Pembina
1300 Pembina Hwy.
Winnipeg, MB R3T 2B4 Canada

Royal Bank of Canada(RBC) (continued)

204-988-6410
Fax: 204-475-2528
MICR: 01827-003

Winnipeg - Portage
3297 Portage Ave.
Winnipeg, MB R3K 0W7 Canada
204-988-5870
Fax: 204-832-9876
MICR: 02147-003

Winnipeg - Portage
1863 Portage Ave.
Winnipeg, MB R3J 0H1 Canada
204-988-5860
Fax: 204-889-4546
MICR: 04817-003

Winnipeg - Portage
885 Portage Ave.
Winnipeg, MB R3G 0P3 Canada
204-988-4242
Fax: 204-783-5108
MICR: 08197-003

Winnipeg - Portage
333 Portage Ave.
Winnipeg, MB R3C 2C3 Canada
204-988-4068
Fax: 204-942-5772
MICR: 08327-003

Winnipeg - Portage
220 Portage Ave.
Winnipeg, MB R3C 0A5 Canada
204-988-4000
Fax: 204-956-1314
MICR: 00007-003

Winnipeg - Regent
1532 Regent Ave. West
Winnipeg, MB R2C 3B4 Canada
204-988-5800
Fax: 204-663-0762
MICR: 04687-003

Winnipeg - Roblin
5128 Roblin Blvd.
Winnipeg, MB R3R 0G9 Canada
204-988-5900
Fax: 204-896-3657
MICR: 08567-003

Winnipeg - Sargent
588 Sargent Ave.
Winnipeg, MB R3E 0A1 Canada
204-988-6370
Fax: 204-786-5615
MICR: 09107-003

Winnipeg - St Marys
1550 St. Marys Rd.
Winnipeg, MB R2M 5M9 Canada
204-988-6300
Fax: 204-988-6316
MICR: 08577-003

Winnipeg - St. Anne
167 St. Anne's Rd.
Winnipeg, MB R2M 2Z7 Canada
204-988-4113
Fax: 204-988-3560
MICR: 05207-003

Winnipeg - Vermillion
Southdale Sq.
111 Vermillion Rd.
Winnipeg, MB R2J 4A9 Canada
204-988-6590
Fax: 204-254-7365
MICR: 03757-003

Winona
1282 Hwy. 8
Winona, ON L8E 5R1 Canada
905-643-4116
Fax: 905-643-4905
MICR: 08042-003

Wolfville
437 Main St.
Wolfville, NS B4P 1E1 Canada
902-542-2221
Fax: 902-542-4639
MICR: 07703-003

Woodbridge - Marycroft
211 Marycroft Rd.
Woodbridge, ON L4L 4T8 Canada
905-856-3800
Fax: 905-856-3731
MICR: 08282-003

Woodbridge - Rutherford
#2, 4101 Rutherford Rd.
Woodbridge, ON L4L 1A6 Canada
905-850-3080
Fax: 905-850-3687
MICR: 05633-003

Woodbridge - Woodbridge
131 Woodbridge Ave.
Woodbridge, ON L4L 2S6 Canada
905-851-2284
Fax: 905-851-5377
MICR: 08062-003

Woodstock - Dundas
452 Dundas St.
Woodstock, ON N4S 1C1 Canada
519-537-5574
Fax: 519-537-8839
MICR: 08082-003

Woodstock - Main
540 Main St.
Woodstock, NB E7M 2C3 Canada
506-325-7630
Fax: 506-328-6470
MICR: 02314-003

Woodstock - Springbank
Springbank Shopping Centre
218 Springbank Ave.
Woodstock, ON N4S 7R3 Canada
519-539-8536
Fax: 519-539-6319
MICR: 08102-003

Yarmouth
399 Main St.
Yarmouth, NS B5A 1G3 Canada
902-742-2496
Fax: 902-742-2399
MICR: 07813-003

Yellowknife
#1, 4920 - 52nd St.
Yellowknife, NT X1A 3T1 Canada
867-873-5961
Fax: 867-873-5488
MICR: 09879-003

Yorkton
78 Broadway St. East
Yorkton, SK S3N 0K9 Canada
306-786-3200
Fax: 306-786-7711
MICR: 09248-003

Sears Bank Canada

222 Jarvis St.
Toronto, ON M5B 2B8
416-941-3606
Fax: 416-941-2325
800-265-3675
scb@sears.ca
www.sears.ca

Ownership: Wholly owned subsidiary of Sears Canada Inc.
Profile: A federally regulated bank, Sears Canada Bank was established to offer financial products & services consistently across Canada. In late 2005, its credit card portfolio will be purchased by JPMorgan Chase & Co.

Executives:
G. Bruce Clark, CEO

The Toronto-Dominion Bank

TD Centre
PO Box 1
Toronto, ON M5K 1A2
416-982-8222
866-222-3456
www.td.com

Also Known As: TD Bank; TD Canada Trust
Ownership: Public
Year Founded: 1855
Number of Employees: 51,000
Stock Symbol: TD
Executives:
W. Edmund Clark, President/CEO
John M. Thompson, Chair
Bharat B. Masrani, Vice-Chair, Chief Risk Officer
Fredric J. Tomczyk, Vice-Chair, Corporate Operations
T. Christian Armstrong, Exec. Vice-President, Acting President TD Waterhouse USA
Theresa L. Currie, Exec. Vice-President, Human Resources
Paul C. Douglas, Exec. Vice-President, Commercial Banking
Michael A. Foulkes, Exec. Vice-President, TD U.K. Brokerage
Brian J. Haier, Exec. Vice-President, Retail Distribution
Colleen M. Johnston, Exec. Vice-President/CFO
Michael W. MacBain, Exec. Vice-President, President, TD Securities
Robert F. MacLellan, Exec. Vice-President, Chief Investment Officer
Daniel A. Marinangeli, Exec. Vice-President, Corporate Development
Christopher A. Montague, Exec. Vice-President, General Counsel
John G. See, Exec. Vice-President, Discount Brokerage & Financial Planning
Alain P. Thibault, Exec. Vice-President, Property & Casualty Insurance, CEO, Td Meloche Monnex inc.
Diane E. Walker, Exec. Vice-President, Chief Administrative Officer, TD Waterhouse USA
Robert E. Dorrance, Group Head, Wholesale Banking, Chairman & CEO TD Securities
Vice Chair TD Bank Financial Group
Bernard T. Dorval, Group Head, Business Banking & Insurance, Co-Chair Chair, TD Canada Trust
William H. Hatanaka, Group Head, Wealth Management, Chair/CEO TD Waterhouse Canada
Timothy D. Hockey, Group Head, Personal Banking, Co-Chair, TD Canada Trust
William J. Ryan, Group Head, US Personnal & Commercial Banking, Chair, CEO & President TD Banknorth
Vice Chair TD BAnk Financial Group
Peter J. Verrill, Sr. Exec. Vice President, COO, TD Banknorth
Riaz E. Admed, Sr. Vice-President, Corporate Development
Sinan O. Akdeniz, Sr. Vice-President, Operations
Rod F. Ashtaryeh, Sr. Vice-President, U.S. Media Communications
Robert M. Aziz, Sr. Vice-President, Legal
Cathy L. Backman, Sr. Vice-President, e-Bank
Joan D. Beckett, Sr. Vice-President, Retail Distribution, GTA Suburban Region
Warren W. Bell, Sr. Vice-President, Human Resources
J. Thomas Bradley, Jr., Sr. Vice-President, Institutional Services, TD Waterhouse USA
John A. Capozzolo, Sr. Vice-President, Retail Distribution, Ontario Central Region
Mark R. Chauvin, Sr. Vice-President, Credit Risk Management
Paul M. Clark, Sr. Vice-President, Small Business Banking & Merchant Services
James E. Coccimiglio, Sr. Vice-President, GTA Commercial Banking
John F. Coombs, Sr. Vice-President, Credit Management
Barbara I. Cromb, Sr. Vice-President, Corporate Development
Susan A. Cummings, Sr. Vice President, Human Resources, Richmond Hill
John T. Davies, Sr. Vice-President, Enterprise Technology Solutions
Alan H. Desnoyers, Sr. Vice-President, Commercial Banking, Québec District
Suzanne Deuel, Sr. Vice-President, Operational Risk & Insurance Management, Risk Manageme
Alexandra P. Dousmanis-Curtis, Sr. Vice-President, Retail Distribution, Ontario South-West Region
Lisa A. Driscoll-Biggs, Sr. Vice President, Retail Distribution, Atlantic Region
Donald E. Drummond, Sr. Vice-President, TD Economics
Christopher D. Dyrda, Sr. Vice-President, Commercial Banking, Western District
David M. Fisher, Sr. Vice-President & Ombudsman
William R. Fulton, Sr. Vice-President, Private Client Services
William Gazzard, Sr. Vice-President, Compliance
Philip D. Ginn, Sr. Vice-President, Computing Services
Robert A. Hamilton, Sr. Vice-President, NatWest Stockbrokers
Janet M. Hawkins, Sr. Vice-President, Marketing, TD Waterhouse USA
Charles A. Hounsell, Sr. Vice-President, Retail Distribution
Paul W. Huyer, Sr. Vice-President, Finance
Martine M. Irman, Sr. Vice-President, Global Foreign Exchange & Money Markets
Alan J. Jette, Sr. Vice-President, Treasury & Balance Sheet Management
Sean E. Kilburn, Sr. Vice-President, TD Life Group
Paul N. Langill, Sr. Vice-President, Finance, Wholesale Banking

David W. McCaw, Sr. Vice-President, Human Resources
Christine Marchildon, Sr. Vice-President, Retail Distribution, Québec Region
Jason A. Marks, Sr. Vice-President, Energy Trading & International Proprietary Equity Trad
Margo M. McConvey, Sr. Vice-President, Core Banking & Term Products
Ronald J. McInnis, Sr. Vice-President, Retail Distribution, Ontario North & East Regions
Damian McNamee, Sr. Vice-President, Finance, Canadian Personal & Commercial Banking
Nico Meijer, Sr. Vice-President, Global Risk & Management Strategy
Patrick B. Meneley, Sr. Vice-President, Investment Banking
Dominic J. Mercuri, Sr. Vice-President & Chief Marketing Officer
David I. Morton, Sr. Vice-President, Sales & Service, Commercial Banking
Brendan O'Halloran, Sr. Vice-President, TD Securities USA
Gerard J. O'Mahoney, Sr. Vice-President, Operations, TD Waterhouse
Dwight P. O'Neill, Sr. Vice-President, Chief Risk Officer, Personal Banking
Barbara F. Palk, Sr. Vice-President, TD Asset Management
Kerry A. Peacock, Sr. Vice-President, Corporate & Public Affairs

John R. Pepperell, Sr. Vice-President, TD Asset Management
David P. Picket, Sr. Vice-President, Practice Management
Timothy P. Pinnington, Sr. Vice President, TD Mutual Funds
Suzanne E. Poole, Sr. Vice-President, Retail Distribution, Pacific Region
Robbie J. Pryde, Sr. Vice-President, Institutional Equities
S. Kenneth Pustai, Sr. Vice-President, Human Resources
Chakravarthi Raghunathan, Sr. Vice-President, Trading Risk
Satish C. Rai, Sr. Vice-President, Investment Advice, TD Waterhouse
Lisa A. Reikman, Sr. Vice-President, Commercial National Accounts
Michael E. Reilly, Sr. Vice-President, Investment Advice, TD Waterhouse
Heather D. Ross, Sr. Vice President, Retail Transformation
Richard J. Rzasa, Sr. Vice-President, Technology Solutions, TD Waterhouse USA
Rudy J. Sankovic, Sr. Vice-President, Finance, Wealth Management
Bruce M. Shirreff, Sr. Vice-President, Real Estate Secured Lending & Credit Administration
J. David Sloan, Sr. Vice-President, Audit
R. Iain Strump, Sr. Vice-President, Retail Distribution, Prairie Region
Ian B. Struthers, Sr. Vice President, Commercial Banking, Ontario District
Steven L. Tennyson, Sr. Vice-President & Chief Information Officer
Paul I. Verwymeren, Sr. Vice-President, Commercial Credit Risk Management
Paul J. Vessey, Sr. Vice President, Commercial Credit Risk Management
Alan E. Wheable, Sr. Vice-President, Taxation
Kevin J. Whyte, Sr. Vice-President, Technology Solutions
M. Suellen Wiles, Sr. Vice-President, Retail Distribution, GTA Central Region

Directors:

William E. Bennett
Corporate Director & former President, Director & CEO, Draper & Kramer Inc.
Hugh J. Bolton
Chair, EPCOR Utilities Inc.
John L. Bragg
Chair, President & Co-CEO, Oxford Frozen Foods Limited & Chair, Bragg Communicat
W. Edmund Clark
Marshall A. Cohen
Counsel, Cassels Brock & Blackwell
Wendy K. Dobson
Professor & Director, Institute for International Business, Joseph L. RotmanScho
Darren Entwhistle
President/CEO, TELUS Corp.
Donna M. Hayes
Publisher & CEO, Harlequin Enterprises Limited
Henry H. Ketcham
President/CEO & Chair, West Fraser Timber Co. Ltd.
Pierre H. Lessard
President/CEO, METRO Inc.
Harold H. Mackay
Sr. Business Law Partner, MacPherson, Leslie & Tyerman LLP
Brian F. MacNeill
Chair, Petro-Canada
Roger Phillips
Corporate Director & Retired President/CEO, IPSCO Inc.
Wilbur J. Prezzano
Corporate Director & Retired Vice-Chair, Eastman Kodak Co.

William J. Ryan
Chair, President & CEO Banknorth Group, Inc.
Helen K. Sinclair
CEO, BankWorks Trading Inc.
John M. Thompson, Chairman

Affiliated Companies:

Canada Trust Income Investments/CTII
First Nations Bank of Canada
Meloche Monnex Inc.
TD Capital
TD Mortgage Corporation/TDMC

Branches:

Abbotsford - South Fraser Way
32817 South Fraser Way
Abbotsford, BC V2S 2A6 Canada
604-870-2200
MICR: 9032-004

Abbotsford - South Fraser Way
#1, 32435 South Fraser Way
Abbotsford, BC V2T 1X4 Canada
604-850-5921
MICR: 0115-004

Abbotsford - Sumas Way
2130 Sumas Way
Abbotsford, BC V2S 2C7 Canada
604-870-3950
MICR: 9064-004

Airdrie
Tower Lane Mall, Bay D-118
505 Main St. South
Airdrie, AB T4B 2B7 Canada
403-948-5974
MICR: 8030-004

Ajax - Bayly St. West
75 Bayly St. West
Ajax, ON L1S 7K7 Canada
905-428-3211
MICR: 0545-004

Ajax - Westney Rd. North
15 Westney Rd. North
Ajax, ON L1T 1P4 Canada
905-686-1218
MICR: 0536-004

Aldergrove
Algergrove Mall
#880, 26310 Fraser Hwy.
Aldergrove, BC V4W 2Z7 Canada
604-607-3660
MICR: 9035-004

Alliston
PO Box 490
6 Victoria St. West
Alliston, ON L9R 1S8 Canada
705-435-6215
Fax: 705-435-0436
MICR: 2040-004

Amherst
PO Box 38
136 Victoria St.
Amherst, NS B4H 3Y6 Canada
902-667-5143
MICR: 4845-004

Amherstburg
89 Richmond St.
Amherstburg, ON N9V 1G2 Canada
519-736-9125
MICR: 0720-004

Ancaster - Golf Links Rd.
977 Golf Links Rd.
Ancaster, ON L9K 1K1 Canada
905-648-7222
MICR: 2047-004

Ancaster - Wilson St. West
98 Wilson St. West
Ancaster, ON L9G 1N3 Canada
905-648-1805
MICR: 0202-004

Arnprior
Arnprior Shopping Centre
375 Daniel St. South
Arnprior, ON K7S 3K6 Canada
613-623-6577
MICR: 2055-004

Arthur
156 George St.
Arthur, ON N0G 1A0 Canada
519-848-3934
MICR: 2050-004

Assiniboia
PO Box 700
300 Centre St.
Assiniboia, SK S0H 0B0 Canada
306-642-3391
MICR: 7032-004

Atikokan
PO Box 580
100 East Main St.
Atikokan, ON P0T 1C0 Canada
807-597-2706
MICR: 6032-004

Aurora - Bayview Ave.
Aurora Centre
#9, 15440 Bayview Ave.
Aurora, ON L4G 7J1 Canada
905-841-4177
MICR: 1044-004

Aurora - Yonge St.
15255 Yonge St.
Aurora, ON L4G 1N5 Canada
905-727-2220
MICR: 1038-004

Aurora - Yonge St.
14845 Yonge St.
Aurora, ON L4G 6H8 Canada
905-727-4123
MICR: 0506-004

Bancroft
PO Box 580
25 Hasting St. North
Bancroft, ON K0L 1C0 Canada
613-332-3550
MICR: 2064-004

Barrhead
PO Box 4599
5037 - 50th St.
Barrhead, AB T7N 1A5 Canada
780-674-2216
MICR: 8032-004

Barrie - Ardagh Rd.
53 Ardagh Rd.
Barrie, ON L4N 9B5 Canada
705-722-5767
MICR: 2082-004

Barrie - Bayfield St.
534 Bayfield St.
Barrie, ON L4M 5A2 Canada
705-721-6005
MICR: 2078-004

Barrie - Cundles Rd. East
201 Cundles Rd. East
Barrie, ON L4M 4S5 Canada
705-728-7878
MICR: 2023-004

Barrie - Dunlop St. East
66 Dunlop St. East
Barrie, ON L4M 4T3 Canada
705-721-6001
MICR: 2072-004

Barrie - Mapleview Dr.
60 Mapleview Dr.
Barrie, ON L4N 9H6 Canada
705-734-2287
MICR: 0182-004

Barrie - Yonge St.
320 Yonge St.
Barrie, ON L4N 4C8 Canada
705-722-5010
MICR: 2083-004

Barrie - Yonge St.

The Toronto-Dominion Bank (continued)

624 Yonge St.
Barrie, ON L4N 4E6 Canada
705-726-5594
MICR: 2079-004

Bathurst
117 Main St.
Bathurst, NB E2A 1A6 Canada
506-546-8444
MICR: 5020-004

Beaverton
PO Box 560
370 Simcoe St.
Beaverton, ON L0K 1A0 Canada
705-426-7345
MICR: 2084-004

Bedford
1475 Bedford Hwy.
Bedford, NS B4A 3Z5 Canada
902-835-7400
MICR: 0537-004

Belleville - Front St.
202 Front St.
Belleville, ON K8N 2Z2 Canada
613-967-2222
MICR: 2088-004

Belleville - North Front St.
143 North Front St.
Belleville, ON K8P 3B5 Canada
613-966-3347
MICR: 2092-004

Birch River
PO Box 250
137 - 3rd St.
Birch River, MB R0L 0E0 Canada
204-236-4461
MICR: 6124-004

Blainville
259, boul de la Seigneurie
Blainville, QC J7C 4N3 Canada
450-437-1128
MICR: 4204-004

Bolton
12684 Hwy. 50
Bolton, ON L7E 1L9 Canada
905-857-4000
MICR: 2113-004

Bonnyville
4919 - 50th Ave.
Bonnyville, AB T9N 2G9 Canada
780-826-8800
MICR: 8048-004

Boucherville
#200, 575, ch de Touraine
Boucherville, QC J4B 5E4 Canada
450-449-5151
MICR: 4565-004

Bowmanville - Hwy. 2
PO Box 189
2379 Hwy. 2
Bowmanville, ON L1C 5A4 Canada
905-623-2514
MICR: 2104-004

Bowmanville - King St. East
188 King St. East
Bowmanville, ON L1C 1P1 Canada
905-697-1722
MICR: 0779-004

Bracebridge
205 Manitoba St.
Bracebridge, ON P1L 1S3 Canada
705-645-2266
MICR: 2112-004

Bradford
Holland Marsh Square
PO Box 1449
188 Holland St. West
Bradford, ON L3Z 1H7 Canada
905-775-9661
MICR: 2110-004

Brampton - Airport Rd.
10990 Airport Rd.
Brampton, ON L6R 0E1 Canada
905-791-6230
MICR: 1140-004

Brampton - Brickyard Way
130 Brickyard Way
Brampton, ON L6V 4N1 Canada
902-451-1355
MICR: 0310-004

Brampton - Cottrelle Blvd.
3978 Cottrelle Blvd.
Brampton, ON L9P 2R1 Canada
905-794-5453
MICR: 1179-004

Brampton - Dixie Rd.
8125 Dixie Rd.
Brampton, ON L6T 2J9 Canada
905-793-6666
MICR: 2116-004

Brampton - Great Lakes Dr.
90 Great Lakes Dr.
Brampton, ON L6R 2K7 Canada
905-790-8557
MICR: 0184-004

Brampton - Hurontario St.
7686 Hurontario St.
Brampton, ON L6Y 5B5 Canada
905-457-3201
MICR: 0136-004

Brampton - Mountainash Rd.
Springdale Square Shopping Centre
55 Mountainash Rd.
Brampton, ON L6R 1W3 Canada
905-790-2770
MICR: 1185-004

Brampton - Peel Centre Dr.
100 Peel Centre Dr.
Brampton, ON L6T 4G8 Canada
902-793-4880
MICR: 0089-004

Brampton - Queen St. East
1 Queen St. East
Brampton, ON L6W 2A7 Canada
905-451-4750
MICR: 2120-004

Brampton - Queen St. East
295A Queen St. East
Brampton, ON L6W 3W9 Canada
905-451-4280
MICR: 1180-004

Brampton - Sandalwood Pkwy. East
150 Sandalwood Pkwy. East
Brampton, ON L6Z 1Y5 Canada
905-840-0988
MICR: 2117-004

Brampton - Steeles Ave. West
College Plaza
545 Steeles Ave. West
Brampton, ON L6Y 4E7 Canada
905-454-3540
MICR: 2124-004

Brampton - Worthington Ave.
5 Worthington Ave.
Brampton, ON L7A 2Y7 Canada
905-495-2986
MICR: 2122-004

Brandon - Rosser Ave.
903 Rosser Ave.
Brandon, MB R7A 0L3 Canada
204-729-2600
MICR: 0039-004

Branpton - Hurontario Rd.
#F1, 10908 Hurontario Rd.
Brampton, ON L7A 3R9 Canada
905-495-0236
MICR: 2073-004

Brantford - Colborne St. East
661 Colborne St. East
Brantford, ON N3S 3M8 Canada
519-759-3084
MICR: 2176-004

Brantford - Fairview Dr.
444 Fairview Dr.
Brantford, ON N3R 2X8 Canada
519-756-3620
MICR: 0341-004

Brantford - King George Rd.
39 King George Rd.
Brantford, ON N3R 5K2 Canada
519-756-3160
MICR: 0224-004

Brantford - Market St.
70 Market St.
Brantford, ON N3T 2Z7 Canada
519-756-4020
MICR: 0340-004

Brantford - Shellard Lane
#1, 230 Shellard Lane
Brantford, ON N3T 5L5 Canada
519-752-6026
MICR: 2194-004

Bridgewater
PO Box 55
1 Old Bridge St.
Bridgewater, NS B4V 2W6 Canada
902-543-7777
MICR: 5350-004

Brockville - King St. West
133 King St. West
Brockville, ON K6V 6Z1 Canada
613-345-1815
MICR: 0352-004

Brockville - Stewart Blvd.
125 Stewart Blvd.
Brockville, ON K6V 4W4 Canada
613-345-1810
MICR: 2188-004

Brooks
1040 - 2nd St. West
Brooks, AB T1R 0N8 Canada
403-362-6333
MICR: 8050-004

Brossard
#5, 9782, boul Leduc
Brossard, QC J4Y 0B3 Canada
450-656-2961
MICR: 4481-004

Brossard - Lapinière
#100, 2220, boul Lapinière
Brossard, QC J4W 1M2 Canada
450-443-4311
MICR: 0511-004

Brossard - Milan
6825, boul Milan
Brossard, QC J4Z 2B5 Canada
450-676-7912
MICR: 4484-004

Brossard - Taschereau
#400, 8330, boul Taschereau
Brossard, QC J4X 1C2 Canada
450-465-1500
MICR: 4478-004

Burford
128 King St.
Burford, ON N0E 1A0 Canada
519-449-2406
MICR: 2200-004

Burlington - Appleby Line
#G1, 2000 Appleby Line
Burlington, ON L7L 6M6 Canada
905-332-2240
MICR: 2221-004

Burlington - Brant St.
2201 Brant St.
Burlington, ON L7P 3N8 Canada
905-335-2444
MICR: 0342-004

Burlington - Brant St.
510 Brant St.
Burlington, ON L7R 2G7 Canada
905-639-8921
MICR: 0080-004

Burlington - Fairview St.
4031 Fairview St.
Burlington, ON L7L 2A4 Canada
905-681-1050
MICR: 2212-004

Burlington - Guelph Line
701 Guelph Line
Burlington, ON L7R 3M7 Canada
905-632-6161
MICR: 0062-004

Burlington - Guelph Line
500 Guelph Line
Burlington, ON L7R 3M4 Canada

905-639-0252
MICR: 0343-004
Burlington - Guelph Line
1505 Guelph Line
Burlington, ON L7P 3B6 Canada
905-335-1990
MICR: 0168-004
Burlington - New St.
5000 New St.
Burlington, ON L7L 1V1 Canada
905-639-3561
MICR: 0162-004
Burlington - Plains Rd. East
596 Plains Rd. East
Burlington, ON L7T 2E7 Canada
905-632-7050
MICR: 0239-004
Burlington - Walkers Line
2931 Walkers Line
Burlington, ON L7M 4M6 Canada
905-332-3550
MICR: 2228-004
Burnaby - Canada Way
3710 Canada Way
Burnaby, BC V5G 1G4 Canada
604-654-3995
MICR: 9462-004
Burnaby - Hastings St.
4298 Hastings St.
Burnaby, BC V5C 2J6 Canada
604-291-6000
MICR: 0393-004
Burnaby - Kingsway
4630 Kingsway
Burnaby, BC V5H 4L9 Canada
604-654-3935
MICR: 9463-004
Burnaby - Kingsway
4994 Kingsway
Burnaby, BC V5H 2E2 Canada
604-437-0814
MICR: 0091-004
Burnaby - Kingway Ave.
7155 Kingsway Ave.
Burnaby, BC V5E 2V1 Canada
604-482-2474
MICR: 9529-004
Burnaby - Rumble St.
5201 Rumble St.
Burnaby, BC V5J 2B7 Canada
604-654-3930
MICR: 9702-004
Burnaby - Willingdon Ave.
1933 Willingdon Ave.
Burnaby, BC V5C 5J3 Canada
604-654-3939
MICR: 9656-004
Calgary - 130th Ave. SE
#20, 4307 - 130th Ave. SE
Calgary, AB T2Z 3V8 Canada
403-257-7120
MICR: 0690-004
Calgary - 14 St. NW
3400 - 14 St. NW
Calgary, AB T2K 1H9 Canada
403-284-2206
MICR: 0228-004
Calgary - 14th Ave. NW
North Hill Shopping Centre
#1810, 1632 - 14th Ave. NW
Calgary, AB T2N 1M7 Canada
403-299-3443
MICR: 8068-004
Calgary - 17 Ave. SW
1029 - 17 Ave. SW
Calgary, AB T2T 0A9 Canada
403-244-5541
MICR: 0171-004
Calgary - 17th Ave. SE
#3013, 3200 - 17th Ave. SE
Calgary, AB T2B 0X6 Canada
403-299-3429
MICR: 8180-004
Calgary - 32 Ave. NW
4880 - 32 Ave. NW
Calgary, AB T3A 4N7 Canada
403-299-3255
MICR: 8067-004
Calgary - 32nd Ave. NE
3545 - 32 Ave. NE
Calgary, AB T1Y 6M6 Canada
403-291-2712
MICR: 0293-004
Calgary - 34th St. NE
2045 - 34th St. NE
Calgary, AB T1Y 6Z2 Canada
403-292-1254
MICR: 8181-004
Calgary - 3rd St. SW
751 - 3rd St. SW
Calgary, AB T2P 4K8 Canada
403-294-3362
MICR: 0220-004
Calgary - 58th Ave. SE
500 - 58th Ave. SE
Calgary, AB T2H 0P6 Canada
403-292-2710
MICR: 8065-004
Calgary - 5th Ave. SW
340 - 5th Ave. SW
Calgary, AB T2P 0L3 Canada
403-292-1100
MICR: 8060-004
Calgary - 7th Ave. SW
Toronto-Dominion Square
#180, 317 - 7th Ave. SW
Calgary, AB T2P 3Y9 Canada
403-292-1221
MICR: 8062-004
Calgary - 8th Ave. SW
Medical Centre Bldg
902 - 8th Ave. SW
Calgary, AB T2P 1H8 Canada
403-292-1440
MICR: 8076-004
Calgary - 90th Ave. SW
1600 - 90th Ave. SW
Calgary, AB T2V 5A8 Canada
403-252-5352
MICR: 0258-004
Calgary - Beddington Blvd. NW
8118 Beddington Blvd. NW
Calgary, AB T3K 2R6 Canada
403-275-4033
MICR: 0290-004
Calgary - Brentwood Rd. NW
3630 Brentwood Rd. NW
Calgary, AB T2L 1K8 Canada
403-282-9377
MICR: 0291-004
Calgary - Castleridge Blvd. NE
#109, 77 Castleridge Blvd. NE
Calgary, AB T3J 4J8 Canada
403-293-6994
MICR: 0608-004
Calgary - Centre St.
305 Centre St.
Calgary, AB T2G 2B9 Canada
403-292-1830
MICR: 8189-004
Calgary - Centre St. North
1216 Centre St. North
Calgary, AB T2E 2R4 Canada
403-230-2207
MICR: 0205-004
Calgary - Country Hills Blvd.
450 Country Hills Blvd.
Calgary, AB T3K 5A5 Canada
403-226-7300
MICR: 8063-004
Calgary - Crowfoot Cres. NW
260 Crowfoot Cres. NW
Calgary, AB T3G 3N5 Canada
403-299-3418
MICR: 8098-004
Calgary - Dalhousie Dr.
#303, 5005 Dalhousie Dr.
Calgary, AB T3A 5R8 Canada
403-543-7280
MICR: 0780-004
Calgary - Deer Ridge Dr. SE
14927 Deer Ridge Dr. SE
Calgary, AB T2J 7C4 Canada
403-271-3506
MICR: 0595-004
Calgary - Hamptons Dr. NW
1000 Hamptons Dr. NW
Calgary, AB T3A 6A7 Canada
403-208-8686
MICR: 0183-004
Calgary - Lake Bonavista Dr. SE
755 Lake Bonavista Dr. SE
Calgary, AB T2J 0N3 Canada
403-299-3400
MICR: 8075-004
Calgary - MacLeod Trail SE
8330 MacLeod Trail SE
Calgary, AB T2H 2V2 Canada
403-259-8889
MICR: 0397-004
Calgary - Macleod Trail SE
10816 Macleod Trail SE
Calgary, AB T2J 5N8 Canada
403-271-0202
MICR: 0104-004
Calgary - MacLeod Trail SW
#5490, 6455 MacLeod Trail SW
Calgary, AB T2H 0K3 Canada
403-292-2747
MICR: 8072-004
Calgary - MacLeod Trail SW
#200, 9737 MacLeod Trail SW
Calgary, AB T2J 0P6 Canada
403-299-3475
MICR: 8074-004
Calgary - Memorial Dr. SE
4415 Memorial Dr. SE
Calgary, AB T2A 6A4 Canada
403-273-3424
MICR: 0172-004
Calgary - Millrise Blvd. SW
#6000, 150 Millrise Blvd. SW
Calgary, AB T2Y 5G7 Canada
413-254-6724
MICR: 8055-004
Calgary - Sarcee Trail NW
11410 Sarcee Trail NW
Calgary, AB T3R 0A1 Canada
403-531-8880
MICR: 8018-004
Calgary - Shawville Blvd. SE
69 Shawville Blvd. SE
Calgary, AB T2Y 3P3 Canada
403-215-5670
MICR: 0826-004
Calgary - Signal Hill Centre SW
5717 Signal Hill Centre SW
Calgary, AB T3H 3P8 Canada
403-217-7000
MICR: 8080-004
Calgary - Signal Hill Centre SW
5627 Signal Hill Centre SW
Calgary, AB T3H 3P8 Canada
403-249-9113
MICR: 0169-004
Cambridge - Cedar St.
Westgate Shopping Centre
#1, 130 Cedar St.
Cambridge, ON N1S 1W4 Canada
519-621-2800
MICR: 2452-004
Cambridge - Franklin Blvd.
200 Franklin Blvd.
Cambridge, ON N1R 5S2 Canada
519-622-1010
MICR: 0165-004
Cambridge - Franklin Blvd.
960 Franklin Blvd.
Cambridge, ON N1R 8R3 Canada
519-622-6108
MICR: 2650-004
Cambridge - Hespeler Rd.
425 Hespeler Rd.
Cambridge, ON N1R 6J2 Canada

The Toronto-Dominion Bank (continued)

519-623-4770
MICR: 0092-004

Cambridge - Holiday Inn Dr.
180 Holiday Inn Dr.
Cambridge, ON N3C 3K1 Canada
519-658-5752
MICR: 0656-004

Cambridge - King St. East
699 King St. East
Cambridge, ON N3H 3N7 Canada
519-653-2363
MICR: 0071-004

Cambridge - Main St.
81 Main St.
Cambridge, ON N1R 1W1 Canada
519-621-7730
Fax: 519-621-3131
MICR: 2448-004

Campbell River
1400 Island Hwy.
Campbell River, BC V9W 8C9 Canada
250-286-5450
MICR: 9038-004

Campbellford
43 Front St. South
Campbellford, ON K0L 1L0 Canada
705-653-4600
MICR: 2222-004

Campbellton
123 Water St.
Campbellton, NB E3N 1B2 Canada
506-753-5058
MICR: 4857-004

Camrose
4888 - 50th St.
Camrose, AB T4V 1P7 Canada
780-672-7795
MICR: 8184-004

Cardston
PO Box 370
240 Main St.
Cardston, AB T0K 0K0 Canada
403-653-4451
MICR: 8192-004

Carman
PO Box 729
3 First Ave. SW
Carman, MB R0G 0J0 Canada
204-745-2083
MICR: 6146-004

Charlottetown - Queen St.
PO Box 726
192 Queen St.
Charlottetown, PE C1A 7L3 Canada
902-629-2265
MICR: 5680-004

Charlottetown - University Ave.
695 University Ave.
Charlottetown, PE C1E 1E5 Canada
902-569-2819
MICR: 5683-004

Chatham
255 King St. West
Chatham, ON N7M 1E6 Canada
519-354-0681
MICR: 0011-004

Chatham
345 St. Clair St.
Chatham, ON N7L 3J8 Canada
519-354-8730
MICR: 0042-004

Chesterville
PO Box 520
9 Queen St. East
Chesterville, ON K0C 1H0 Canada
613-448-2316
MICR: 2258-004

Chetwynd
PO Box 720
5300 North Access Rd.
Chetwynd, BC V0C 1J0 Canada
250-788-7600
MICR: 8020-004

Chicoutimi
#100, 255, rue Racine est
Chicoutimi, QC G7H 7L2 Canada
418-549-0412
MICR: 4048-004

Chilliwack - Luckakuck Way
#51, 45585 Luckakuck Way
Chilliwack, BC V2R 1A1 Canada
604-824-5150
MICR: 9056-004

Chilliwack - Yale Rd.
46017 Yale Rd.
Chilliwack, BC V2P 2M1 Canada
604-795-9166
MICR: 0274-004

Châteauguay
114, boul St-Jean-Baptiste
Châteauguay, QC J6K 3A9 Canada
450-691-7860
MICR: 4044-004

Cobourg
PO Box 70
1 King St. West
Cobourg, ON K9A 4K2 Canada
905-372-5471
MICR: 2272-004

Cold Lake - 50th Ave.
PO Box 69
5202 - 50th Ave.
Cold Lake, AB T9M 1P1 Canada
780-594-4477
MICR: 8832-004

Coldwater
PO Box 100
7 Coldwater Rd.
Coldwater, ON L0K 1E0 Canada
705-686-3331
MICR: 2280-004

Collingwood
104 Hurontario St.
Collingwood, ON L9Y 2L8 Canada
705-445-4881
MICR: 2288-004

Copper Cliff
PO Box 818
2 Serpentine St.
Copper Cliff, ON P0M 1N0 Canada
705-682-4457
MICR: 2304-004

Coquitlam - Austin Ave.
1022 Austin Ave.
Coquitlam, BC V3K 3P3 Canada
604-939-7331
MICR: 0736-004

Coquitlam - Como Lake Ave.
1980C Como Lake Ave.
Coquitlam, BC V3J 3R3 Canada
604-933-4930
MICR: 9076-004

Coquitlam - Johnson St.
1140 Johnson St.
Coquitlam, BC V3B 7G5 Canada
604-927-5700
MICR: 9324-004

Coquitlam - North Rd.
#400, 329 North Rd.
Coquitlam, BC V3K 3V8 Canada
604-933-4900
MICR: 9070-004

Corner Brook
1 Mount Bernard Ave.
Corner Brook, NL A2H 6Y5 Canada
709-637-1076
MICR: 5771-004

Cornwall - 9th St. East
61 - 9th St. East
Cornwall, ON K6H 6R3 Canada
613-932-0204
MICR: 2312-004

Cornwall - Water St. East
1 Water St. East
Cornwall, ON K6H 6M2 Canada
613-933-1433
MICR: 0137-004

Coronation
PO Box 129
4901 Royal St.
Coronation, AB T0C 1C0 Canada
403-578-3855
MICR: 8224-004

Courtenay
#A, 789 Ryan Rd.
Courtenay, BC V9N 3R6 Canada
250-703-4300
MICR: 9075-004

Cranbrook
1101 Baker St.
Cranbrook, BC V1C 1A7 Canada
250-417-3025
MICR: 9079-004

Creemore
PO Box 10
181 Mill St.
Creemore, ON L0M 1G0 Canada
705-466-2018
MICR: 2320-004

Dartmouth - Forest Hill Pkwy.
6 Forest Hills Pkwy.
Dartmouth, NS B2W 6E4 Canada
902-420-8186
MICR: 5370-004

Dartmouth - Portland St.
590 Portland St.
Dartmouth, NS B2W 6B7 Canada
902-434-4010
MICR: 0364-004

Dartmouth - Portland St.
97 Portland St.
Dartmouth, NS B2Y 1H5 Canada
902-420-8120
MICR: 5380-004

Dauphin
424 Main St. North
Dauphin, MB R7N 1C8 Canada
204-622-2900
MICR: 6154-004

Dawson Creek
1040 - 102nd Ave.
Dawson Creek, BC V1G 2B8 Canada
250-784-6300
MICR: 8024-004

Delhi
121 King St.
Delhi, ON N4B 1X9 Canada
519-582-0510
MICR: 0082-004

Deloraine
PO Box 368
104 Broadway St. South
Deloraine, MB R0M 0M0 Canada
204-747-2277
MICR: 6156-004

Delta
PO Box 54
54 King St.
Delta, ON K0E 1G0 Canada
613-928-2561
MICR: 2330-004

Delta - 120th St.
7317 - 120th St.
Delta, BC V4C 6P5 Canada
604-591-1500
MICR: 0275-004

Delta - 120th St.
8109 - 120th St.
Delta, BC V4C 6P7 Canada
604-501-4540
MICR: 9080-004

Delta - 48th Ave.
5154 - 48th Ave.
Delta, BC V4K 1W3 Canada
604-940-4600
MICR: 9160-004

Delta - 56 St.
1323 - 56 St.
Delta, BC V4L 2A6 Canada
604-943-4677
MICR: 0574-004

Dorchester

PO Box 189
4206 Catherine St.
Dorchester, ON N0L 1G0 Canada
519-268-7376
MICR: 2360-004
Drayton Valley
#1, 5505 - 50 St.
Drayton Valley, AB T7A 1W2 Canada
780-542-3773
MICR: 8211-004
Dresden
PO Box 460
412 St. George St.
Dresden, ON N0P 1M0 Canada
519-683-4496
MICR: 2368-004
Drummondville
1900, boul St-Joseph
Drummondville, QC J2B 1R2 Canada
819-477-5551
MICR: 4052-004
Dryden
30 Princess St.
Dryden, ON P8N 1C6 Canada
807-223-5237
MICR: 6068-004
Duncan
488 Robertson St.
Duncan, BC V9L 4X9 Canada
250-701-4000
MICR: 0678-004
Dundas - King St. West
PO Box 8586
82 King St. West
Dundas, ON L9H 1T9 Canada
905-627-3559
MICR: 0081-004
Dundas - Osler Dr.
119 Osler Dr.
Dundas, ON L9H 6X4 Canada
905-627-3548
Fax: 905-628-0005
MICR: 2370-004
Dunnville
163 Lock St. East
Dunnville, ON N1A 1J6 Canada
905-774-7491
MICR: 0120-004
Edmonton - 178th St. NW
#120, 6655 - 178 St. NW
Edmonton, AB T5T 4J5 Canada
780-448-8360
MICR: 8318-004
Edmonton - 101st St.
10205 - 101 St.
Edmonton, AB T5J 2Y8 Canada
780-448-8000
MICR: 8238-004
Edmonton - 104th Ave. NW
11550 - 104 Ave. NW
Edmonton, AB T5K 2S5 Canada
780-423-2374
MICR: 0223-004
Edmonton - 111 St. NW
2325 - 111 St. NW
Edmonton, AB T6J 5E5 Canada
780-438-3013
MICR: 0296-004
Edmonton - 111th Ave.
16317 - 111th Ave.
Edmonton, AB T5M 2S2 Canada
780-448-8570
MICR: 8630-004
Edmonton - 118th Ave.
6527 - 118th Ave.
Edmonton, AB T5W 1G5 Canada
780-448-8750
MICR: 8688-004
Edmonton - 142 Ave.
12645 - 142 Ave.
Edmonton, AB T5X 5Y8 Canada
780-472-2400
MICR: 0716-004
Edmonton - 142nd St.
Crestwood Shopping Centre
9604 - 142nd St.
Edmonton, AB T5N 4B2 Canada
780-448-8765
MICR: 8248-004
Edmonton - 156 St. NW
8705 - 156 St. NW
Edmonton, AB T5R 1Y5 Canada
780-483-2515
MICR: 0238-004
Edmonton - 38th Ave.
38th Ave. & Millwoods Rd.
Edmonton, AB T6K 3L6 Canada
780-462-4625
MICR: 0154-004
Edmonton - 42nd Ave.
9622 - 42nd Ave.
Edmonton, AB T6E 5Y4 Canada
780-448-8520
MICR: 8250-004
Edmonton - 50 St. NW
13318 - 50 St. NW
Edmonton, AB T5A 4Z8 Canada
780-456-8578
MICR: 0681-004
Edmonton - 51st Ave.
Pleasantview Shopping Centre
11016 - 51st Ave.
Edmonton, AB T6H 0L4 Canada
780-448-8399
MICR: 8326-004
Edmonton - 76 Ave.
11202 - 76 Ave.
Edmonton, AB T6G 0K1 Canada
780-448-8435
MICR: 8432-004
Edmonton - 82 Ave. NW
8140 - 82 Ave. NW
Edmonton, AB T6C 0Y4 Canada
780-468-6817
MICR: 0225-004
Edmonton - 93 St. NW
13703 - 93 St. NW
Edmonton, AB T5E 5V6 Canada
780-475-6671
MICR: 0226-004
Edmonton - 97th St. NW
16535 - 97 St. NW
Edmonton, AB T5X 6A9 Canada
780-448-8415
MICR: 8325-004
Edmonton - 98 Ave.
Capilano Mall
5004 - 98 Ave.
Edmonton, AB T6A 0A1 Canada
780-448-8620
MICR: 8244-004
Edmonton - Calgary Trail South
4108 Calgary Trail South
Edmonton, AB T6J 6Y6 Canada
780-434-6481
MICR: 0203-004
Edmonton - Groat Rd.
11210 Groat Rd.
Edmonton, AB T5M 4E7 Canada
780-448-8300
MICR: 8336-004
Edmonton - Hewes Way
2505 Hewes Way
Edmonton, AB T6L 6W6 Canada
780-448-8135
MICR: 8333-004
Edmonton - James Mowatt Trail
93 James Mowatt Trail
Edmonton, AB T6W 1S4 Canada
780-448-8668
MICR: 8204-004
Edmonton - Jasper Ave.
11704 Jasper Ave.
Edmonton, AB T5K 0N3 Canada
780-448-8480
MICR: 8304-004
Edmonton - Londonderry Mall
36 Londonderry Mall
Edmonton, AB T5C 3C8 Canada
780-448-8630
MICR: 8312-004
Edmonton - Parsons Rd. SW
880 Parsons Rd. SW
Edmonton, AB T6X 0B4 Canada
781-448-8330
MICR: 8206-004
Edmonton - Riverbend Sq. NW
490 Riverbend Sq. NW
Edmonton, AB T6R 2E3 Canada
780-438-3221
MICR: 0559-004
Edmonton - Stony Plain Rd.
Jasper Gates Square
14941 Stony Plain Rd.
Edmonton, AB T5P 4W1 Canada
780-448-8808
MICR: 8254-004
Edmonton - Whyte Ave.
10864 Whyte Ave.
Edmonton, AB T6E 2B3 Canada
780-448-8450
MICR: 8368-004
Edmundston
14 Court St.
Edmundston, NB E3V 1S2 Canada
506-735-8843
MICR: 4848-004
Elk Point
PO Box 100
4830 - 50 St.
Elk Point, AB T0A 1A0 Canada
780-724-8085
MICR: 8816-004
Elliot Lake
17 Nova Scotia Walk
Elliot Lake, ON P5A 2J7 Canada
705-461-9203
MICR: 2384-004
Elmira
41 Arthur St.
Elmira, ON N3B 2M6 Canada
519-669-5496
MICR: 2392-004
Elmvale
7 Queen St. West
Elmvale, ON L0L 1P0 Canada
705-322-1772
MICR: 2400-004
Elora
PO Box 69
192 Geddes St.
Elora, ON N0B 1S0 Canada
519-846-5305
MICR: 2402-004
Erin
PO Box 369
125 Main St.
Erin, ON N0B 1T0 Canada
519-833-9675
MICR: 2204-004
Espanola
115 Centre St.
Espanola, ON P5E 1S4 Canada
705-869-3051
MICR: 2406-004
Essex
34 Talbot St. North
Essex, ON N8M 1A4 Canada
519-776-6453
MICR: 2021-004
Estevan
1305 - 4th St.
Estevan, SK S4A 0X1 Canada
306-634-4707
MICR: 7128-004
Fernie
PO Box 1110
391 - 2nd Ave.
Fernie, BC V0B 1M0 Canada
250-423-2100
MICR: 9083-004
Fleurimont
156, ch Duplessis
Fleurimont, QC J1E 3C7 Canada

The Toronto-Dominion Bank (continued)

819-565-2812
MICR: 4930-004

Fonthill
PO Box 489
1439 South Pelham St.
Fonthill, ON L0S 1E0 Canada
905-892-2689
MICR: 2424-004

Forest
PO Box 569
15 King St. East
Forest, ON N0N 1J0 Canada
519-786-2185
MICR: 2428-004

Fort Erie
450 Garrison Rd.
Fort Erie, ON L2A 1N2 Canada
905-871-7361
MICR: 2430-004

Fort Frances
200 Scott St.
Fort Frances, ON P9A 1G7 Canada
807-274-3241
MICR: 6040-004

Fort McMurray
#504, 8600 Franklin Ave.
Fort McMurray, AB T9H 4G8 Canada
780-743-2261
MICR: 8828-004

Fort St. John
10155 - 100 St.
Fort St John, BC V1J 3Y6 Canada
250-262-5000
MICR: 8028-004

Fredericton - Prospect St.
1211 Prospect St.
Fredericton, NB E3B 3B9 Canada
506-459-1300
MICR: 5090-004

Fredericton - Westmorland St.
77 Westmorland St.
Fredericton, NB E3B 6Z3 Canada
506-458-8228
MICR: 5080-004

Gananoque
PO Box 100
100 King St. East
Gananoque, ON K7G 2V2 Canada
613-382-2191
MICR: 2456-004

Gander
92 Elizabeth Dr.
Gander, NL A1V 1W7 Canada
709-651-3620
MICR: 4650-004

Garson
PO Box 310
3060 Falconbridge Hwy.
Garson, ON P3L 1P6 Canada
705-693-2218
MICR: 3724-004

Gaspé
134, rue de la Reine
Gaspé, QC G0C 1R0 Canada
418-368-3311
MICR: 4064-004

Gatineau - Paiment
750, montee Paiement
Gatineau, QC J8R 4A3 Canada
819-669-6313
MICR: 4051-004

Gatineau - Plateau
125, boul du Plateau
Gatineau, QC J9A 3G1 Canada
819-771-7202
MICR: 4089-004

Gatineau - Principale
181, rue Principale
Gatineau, QC J9H 3N2 Canada
819-682-5375
MICR: 4028-004

Gatineau - Savane
25, ch de la Savane
Gatineau, QC J8T 8A4 Canada
819-243-7040
MICR: 4072-004

Gatineau - St-Joseph
349, boul St-Joseph
Gatineau, QC J8Y 3Z4 Canada
819-770-5672
MICR: 4088-004

Georgetown
231 Guelph St.
Georgetown, ON L7G 4A8 Canada
905-877-6981
MICR: 2472-004

Georgetown
29 Main St. South
Georgetown, ON L7G 3G2 Canada
905-877-2266
MICR: 0070-004

Geraldton
PO Box 670
300 Main St.
Geraldton, ON P0T 1M0 Canada
807-854-1014
Fax: 807-854-1080
MICR: 6064-004

Gloucester - Innes Rd.
2608 Innes Rd.
Gloucester, ON K1B 4Z6 Canada
613-824-9600
MICR: 3283-004

Gloucester - Montreal Rd.
1648 Montreal Rd.
Gloucester, ON K1J 6N5 Canada
613-745-6533
MICR: 0794-004

Goderich
39 Victoria St. South
Goderich, ON N7A 3H4 Canada
519-524-2682
MICR: 0519-004

Granby
867, rue Principale
Granby, QC J2G 2Y9 Canada
450-372-5497
MICR: 4080-004

Grand Bend
#24, 81 Crescent St.
Grand Bend, ON N0M 1T0 Canada
519-238-8435
MICR: 2484-004

Grande Prairie - West Side Dr.
10704 West Side Dr.
Grande Prairie, AB T8V 8E6 Canada
780-538-8100
MICR: 8836-004

Gravelbourg
PO Box 119
501 Main St.
Gravelbourg, SK S0H 1X0 Canada
306-648-3135
MICR: 7176-004

Gravenhurst
PO Box 460
210 Muskoka Rd.
Gravenhurst, ON P1P 1H5 Canada
705-687-6601
MICR: 2488-004

Grenfell
PO Box 279
740 Desmond St.
Grenfell, SK S0G 2B0 Canada
306-697-2300
MICR: 7192-004

Grimsby
20 Main St. East
Grimsby, ON L3M 4G5 Canada
905-945-9256
MICR: 2492-004

Guelph - Clair Rd. West
9 Clair Rd. West
Guelph, ON N1L 0A6 Canada
519-763-2123
MICR: 2506-004

Guelph - Edinburgh Rd.
496 Edinburgh Rd.
Guelph, ON N1G 4Z1 Canada
519-821-2200
MICR: 2500-004

Guelph - Eramosa Rd.
350 Eramosa Rd.
Guelph, ON N1E 2M9 Canada
519-763-2020
MICR: 0516-004

Guelph - Kortright Rd. West
200 Kortright Rd. West
Guelph, ON N1G 4X8 Canada
519-763-3111
MICR: 0728-004

Guelph - Silvercreek Pkwy. North
170 Silvercreek Pkwy. North
Guelph, ON N1H 7P7 Canada
519-824-8100
MICR: 0088-004

Guelph - Woolwich St.
666 Woolwich St.
Guelph, ON N1H 7G5 Canada
519-836-0270
MICR: 0131-004

Guelph - Wyndham St.
34 Wyndham St.
Guelph, ON N1H 4E5 Canada
519-824-1121
MICR: 0018-004

Halifax - Barrington St.
PO Box 427
1785 Barrington St.
Halifax, NS B3J 2P8 Canada
902-420-8040
MICR: 5420-004

Halifax - Bayers Rd.
7071 Bayers Rd.
Halifax, NS B3L 2C2 Canada
902-496-6767
MICR: 5421-004

Halifax - Lacewood Dr.
278 Lacewood Dr.
Halifax, NS B3M 3N8 Canada
902-420-8500
MICR: 5423-004

Halifax - Quinpool Rd.
6239 Quinpool Rd.
Halifax, NS B3L 1A4 Canada
902-422-7471
MICR: 0036-004

Halifax - Spring Garden Rd.
5415 Spring Garden Rd.
Halifax, NS B3J 3J1 Canada
902-496-0800
MICR: 4959-004

Hamilton - Barton St. East
1227 Barton St. East
Hamilton, ON L8H 2V4 Canada
905-549-1352
MICR: 0102-004

Hamilton - Fennell Ave. East
1119 Fennell Ave. East
Hamilton, ON L8T 1S2 Canada
905-387-9500
MICR: 0178-004

Hamilton - Fennell Ave. East
550 Fennell Ave. East
Hamilton, ON L8V 4S9 Canada
905-387-3831
MICR: 0160-004

Hamilton - James St. South
194 James St. South
Hamilton, ON L8P 3A7 Canada
905-527-2906
MICR: 2536-004

Hamilton - King St. East
1900 King St. East
Hamilton, ON L8K 1W1 Canada
905-545-7903
MICR: 0237-004

Hamilton - King St. East
46 King St. East
Hamilton, ON L8N 3K7 Canada
905-521-2452
MICR: 0015-004

Hamilton - King St. West

PO Box 57148
100 King St. West
Hamilton, ON L8P 4W9 Canada
905-527-3626
MICR: 2512-004

Hamilton - King St. West
938 King St. West
Hamilton, ON L8S 1K8 Canada
905-523-5111
MICR: 0346-004

Hamilton - Mall Rd.
65 Mall Rd.
Hamilton, ON L8V 5B3 Canada
905-574-4393
MICR: 2606-004

Hamilton - Mohawk Rd. West
781 Mohawk Rd. West
Hamilton, ON L9C 7B7 Canada
905-575-9221
MICR: 0250-004

Hamilton - Upper James St.
830 Upper James St.
Hamilton, ON L9C 3A4 Canada
905-387-9330
MICR: 0191-004

Hamilton - Upper James St.
1565 Upper James St.
Hamilton, ON L9B 1K2 Canada
905-318-5539
MICR: 2522-004

Hanna
PO Box 609
602 - 2nd Ave. West
Hanna, AB T0J 1P0 Canada
403-854-4461
MICR: 8837-004

Hanover - 10th St.
297 - 10th St.
Hanover, ON N4N 1P1 Canada
519-364-5200
MICR: 0372-004

Harrow
PO Box 670
29 King St. East
Harrow, ON N0R 1G0 Canada
519-738-2216
MICR: 2640-004

Havelock
PO Box 40
40 Ottawa St. West
Havelock, ON K0L 1Z0 Canada
705-778-3375
MICR: 2648-004

Hawkesbury
PO Box 639
258 Main St. East
Hawkesbury, ON K6A 3C8 Canada
613-632-7077
MICR: 2652-004

High Prairie
PO Box 939
4831 - 51st Ave.
High Prairie, AB T0G 1E0 Canada
780-523-4591
MICR: 8840-004

High River
PO Box 5083
315 Macleod Trail
High River, AB T1V 1M3 Canada
403-652-2921
MICR: 8830-004

Huntsville
38 Main St. East
Huntsville, ON P1H 2C8 Canada
705-789-4434
Fax: 705-789-1480
MICR: 2664-004

Ingersoll - Thames St. South
195 Thames St. South
Ingersoll, ON N5C 2T6 Canada
519-485-6010
MICR: 0503-004

Innisfil - Innisfil Beach Rd.
1054 Innisfil Beach Rd.
Innisfil, ON L9S 4T9 Canada
705-436-5176
MICR: 2236-004

Innisfil - Yonge St. North
#7, 7975 Yonge St. North
Innisfil, ON L9S 1L2 Canada
705-431-2046
MICR: 3668-004

Jasper
PO Box 1360
606 Patricia St.
Jasper, AB T0E 1E0 Canada
780-852-6270
Fax: 780-852-5186
MICR: 8842-004

Kamloops - East Trans-Canada Hwy.
#8, 2121 East Trans-Canada Hwy.
Kamloops, BC V2C 5P9 Canada
250-314-5100
MICR: 9146-004

Kamloops - Notre Dame Dr.
500 Notre Dame Dr.
Kamloops, BC V2C 6T6 Canada
250-314-3000
MICR: 0790-004

Kamloops - Tranquille Rd.
700 Tranquille Rd.
Kamloops, BC V2B 3H9 Canada
250-376-7774
MICR: 0698-004

Kamloops - Victoria St.
#102, 301 Victoria St.
Kamloops, BC V2C 2A3 Canada
250-314-5035
MICR: 0276-004

Kamsack
PO Box 699
357 - 3rd Ave.
Kamsack, SK S0A 1S0 Canada
306-542-2633
MICR: 7256-004

Kanata - Eagleson Rd.
#28, 457 Eagleson Rd.
Kanata, ON K2L 1V1 Canada
613-592-8400
MICR: 3295-004

Kanata - Eagleson Rd.
#100, 700 Eagleson Rd.
Kanata, ON K2M 2G9 Canada
613-592-7918
MICR: 3249-004

Kanata - Earl Grey Dr.
110 Earl Grey Dr.
Kanata, ON K2T 1B7 Canada
613-599-8020
MICR: 3282-004

Kelowna - Ellis St.
#100, 1633 Ellis St.
Kelowna, BC V1Y 2A8 Canada
250-763-4241
MICR: 0277-004

Kelowna - Harvey Ave.
#150, 1950 Harvey Ave.
Kelowna, BC V1Y 8J8 Canada
250-762-4142
MICR: 0204-004

Kelowna - Hwy. 33 West
#47, 301 Hwy. 33 West
Kelowna, BC V1X 1X8 Canada
250-491-5130
MICR: 9364-004

Kelowna - Hwy. 97 North
#700, 2339 Hwy. 97 North
Kelowna, BC V1X 4H9 Canada
250-712-3350
MICR: 9155-004

Kelowna - K.L.O Rd.
#16, 605 K.L.O Rd.
Kelowna, BC V1Y 8E7 Canada
250-860-7765
MICR: 0715-004

Kelowna - Yates Rd.
532 Yates Rd.
Kelowna, BC V1V 2V8 Canada
250-870-5300
MICR: 9153-004

Kenora
108 Main St. South
Kenora, ON P9N 1S9 Canada
807-467-3456
MICR: 6072-004

Kentville
42 Webster St.
Kentville, NS B4N 3X1 Canada
902-678-2131
MICR: 5391-004

Kincardine
665 Philip Pl.
Kincardine, ON N2Z 2E3 Canada
519-396-3314
MICR: 2690-004

Kindersley
PO Box 880
217 Main St.
Kindersley, SK S0L 1S0 Canada
306-463-2661
MICR: 7264-004

King City
2200 King Rd.
King City, ON L7B 1A6 Canada
905-833-2900
MICR: 1061-004

Kingston - Bayridge Dr.
741 Bayridge Dr.
Kingston, ON K7P 1T5 Canada
613-384-7200
MICR: 2700-004

Kingston - Gardiners Rd.
750 Gardiners Rd.
Kingston, ON K7M 3X9 Canada
613-384-1553
MICR: 0190-004

Kingston - Gore Rd.
Pittburgh Towns
235 Gore Rd.
Kingston, ON K7L 5H6 Canada
613-549-6132
MICR: 2693-004

Kingston - Princess St.
1062 Princess St.
Kingston, ON K7L 1H2 Canada
613-546-2666
MICR: 2728-004

Kingston - Princess St.
94 Princess St.
Kingston, ON K7L 1A5 Canada
613-549-8770
MICR: 0139-004

Kipling
PO Box 390
529 Main St.
Kipling, SK S0G 2S0 Canada
306-736-2531
MICR: 7272-004

Kirkland Lake
PO Box 486
12 Government Rd. West
Kirkland Lake, ON P2N 3J5 Canada
705-567-5247
MICR: 2744-004

Kitchener - Belmont Ave. West
693 Belmont Ave. West
Kitchener, ON N2M 1P1 Canada
519-885-8515
MICR: 0072-004

Kitchener - Fischer Hallman Rd.
#200, 1187 Fischer Hallman Rd.
Kitchener, ON N2E 4H9 Canada
517-744-5238
MICR: 2855-004

Kitchener - Highland Rd. West
272 Highland Rd. West
Kitchener, ON N2M 3C5 Canada
519-749-3277
MICR: 2760-004

Kitchener - Highland Rd. West
875 Highland Rd. West
Kitchener, ON N2N 2Y2 Canada
519-885-8549
MICR: 0395-004

Kitchener - King St. West

The Toronto-Dominion Bank (continued)

381 King St. West
Kitchener, ON N2G 1B8 Canada
519-579-2160
MICR: 2752-004

Kitchener - King St. West
55 King St. West
Kitchener, ON N2G 4W1 Canada
519-742-2614
MICR: 0067-004

Kitchener - Kingsway Dr.
2960 Kingsway Dr.
Kitchener, ON N2C 1X1 Canada
519-885-8520
MICR: 0076-004

Kitchener - Ottawa St. North
1005 Ottawa St. North
Kitchener, ON N2A 1H2 Canada
519-885-8540
MICR: 0078-004

Kitchener - Pioneer Dr.
#1, 123 Pioneer Dr.
Kitchener, ON N2P 1K8 Canada
519-885-8555
MICR: 0111-004

Kitchener - Strasburg Rd.
700 Strasburg Rd.
Kitchener, ON N2E 2M2 Canada
519-885-8433
MICR: 0174-004

Kyle
PO Box 100
118 Centre St.
Kyle, SK S0L 1T0 Canada
306-375-5500
MICR: 7288-004

Lacombe
5116 - 51 Ave.
Lacombe, AB T4L 2A9 Canada
403-782-6687
MICR: 8843-004

Lafleche
PO Box 70
42 Main St.
Lafleche, SK S0H 2K0 Canada
306-472-3137
MICR: 7320-004

Langenburg
139 Kaiser William
Langenburg, SK S0A 2A0 Canada
306-743-2691
Fax: 306-743-2606
MICR: 7336-004

Langley - 200th St.
#300, 7150 - 200th St.
Langley, BC V2Y 3B9 Canada
604-539-3990
MICR: 9193-004

Langley - 204th St.
#3, 5501 - 204th St.
Langley, BC V3A 5N8 Canada
604-514-5160
MICR: 9186-004

Langley - 210th St.
#201, 8840 - 210th St.
Langley, BC V1M 2Y2 Canada
604-513-6200
MICR: 9188-004

Langley - 48 Ave.
#400, 22259 - 48 Ave.
Langley, BC V3A 8T1 Canada
604-514-5150
MICR: 9190-004

Langley - Willowbrook Dr.
19711 Willowbrook Dr.
Langley, BC V2Y 2T6 Canada
604-514-5155
MICR: 9194-004

Lasalle
1190 Front Rd.
Lasalle, ON N9J 1Z9 Canada
519-734-7801
MICR: 2800-004

Laval - Carrefour
3080, boul Carrefour
Laval, QC H7T 2R5 Canada
450-973-5400
MICR: 4440-004

Laval - Chomedey
1120, aut Chomedy, #A13 Desserte ouest
Laval, QC H7X 4C9 Canada
450-969-2772
MICR: 4383-004

Laval - Laurentides
2146, boul des Laurentides
Laval, QC H7M 2R5 Canada
450-629-2838
MICR: 4307-004

Laval - Normandie
326, ch de la Normandie
Laval, QC H7G 2A8 Canada
450-663-4970
MICR: 4292-004

Laval - Notre-Dame
4865, boul Notre-Dame
Laval, QC H7W 1V3 Canada
450-688-4610
Fax: 450-688-3651
MICR: 4486-004

Laval - Val-des-Brises
5880, boul de Val-des-Brises
Laval, QC H7E 0A5 Canada
450-665-3477
MICR: 4303-004

Leamington - Erie St. South
PO Box 129
274 Erie St. South
Leamington, ON N8H 3C5 Canada
519-326-5753
MICR: 2808-004

Leduc
4915 - 50th Ave.
Leduc, AB T9E 6W7 Canada
780-986-2237
MICR: 8844-004

Lethbridge - 4th Ave. South
#156, 200 - 4th Ave. South
Lethbridge, AB T1J 4C9 Canada
403-381-5000
MICR: 8848-004

Lethbridge - Mayor Magrath Dr. South
2033 Mayor Magrath Dr. South
Lethbridge, AB T1K 2S2 Canada
403-381-5030
MICR: 0680-004

Levack
PO Box 70
51 Levack Dr.
Levack, ON P0M 2C0 Canada
705-966-3477
MICR: 2816-004

Lindsay
81 Kent St. West
Lindsay, ON K9V 2Y3 Canada
705-324-3573
MICR: 2824-004

Little Current
2 Robinson St. West
Little Current, ON P0P 1K0 Canada
705-368-3110
MICR: 2405-004

Lively
PO Box 9
617 Main St.
Lively, ON P3Y 1M2 Canada
705-692-3623
MICR: 2832-004

Lloydminster
4918 - 50th Ave.
Lloydminster, AB T9V 0W6 Canada
780-871-5885
MICR: 8864-004

London - Adelaide St. North
1030 Adelaide St. North
London, ON N5Y 2M9 Canada
519-673-6435
MICR: 0703-004

London - Clarke Rd.
155 Clarke Rd.
London, ON N5W 5C9 Canada
519-453-3980
MICR: 2934-004

London - Commissioners Rd. East
1086 Commissioners Rd. East
London, ON N5Z 4W8 Canada
519-649-2371
MICR: 0510-004

London - Commissioners Rd. West
1260 Commissioners Rd. West
London, ON N6K 1C7 Canada
519-473-0671
MICR: 0108-004

London - Dundas St.
687 Dundas St.
London, ON N5W 2Z5 Canada
519-673-6041
MICR: 0008-004

London - Dundas St.
1920 Dundas St.
London, ON N5V 3P1 Canada
519-451-1911
MICR: 0240-004

London - Dundas St.
220 Dundas St.
London, ON N6A 1H3 Canada
519-663-1560
MICR: 0001-004

London - Dundas St.
275 Dundas St.
London, ON N6A 4S4 Canada
519-663-1500
MICR: 0101-004

London - Ernest Ave.
1420 Ernest Ave.
London, ON N6E 2H8 Canada
519-686-6812
MICR: 0114-004

London - Fanshawe Park Rd.
608 Fanshawe Park Rd.
London, ON N5X 1L1 Canada
519-660-4340
MICR: 2933-004

London - Hamilton Rd.
972 Hamilton Rd.
London, ON N5W 1V6 Canada
519-451-9340
MICR: 2932-004

London - Huron St.
1314 Huron St.
London, ON N5Y 4V2 Canada
519-451-0453
MICR: 0053-004

London - Main St.
2478 Main St.
London, ON N6P 1R2 Canada
519-652-3254
MICR: 2796-004

London - Oxford St. West
1213 Oxford St. West
London, ON N6H 1V8 Canada
519-471-5500
MICR: 0040-004

London - Oxford St. West
215 Oxford St. West
London, ON N6H 1S5 Canada
519-673-6491
MICR: 0110-004

London - Richmond St.
1663 Richmond St.
London, ON N6G 2N3 Canada
519-660-8169
MICR: 0256-004

London - Richmond St.
1137 Richmond St.
London, ON N6A 3K6 Canada
519-673-6021
MICR: 0021-004

London - Wellington Rd.
353 Wellington Rd.
London, ON N6C 4P8 Canada
519-673-3095
MICR: 0236-004

London - Wellington Rd. South
1067 Wellington Rd. South
London, ON N6E 2H5 Canada
519-686-4471

MICR: 2860-004
London - Wonderland Rd. North
1055 Wonderland Rd. North
London, ON N6G 2Y9 Canada
519-473-1710
MICR: 0066-004
London - Wonderland Rd. South
795 Wonderland Rd. South
London, ON N6K 3C2 Canada
519-472-1314
MICR: 0109-004
London - Wortley Rd.
191 Wortley Rd.
London, ON N6C 3P8 Canada
519-673-6011
MICR: 0012-004
Longueuil - Chambly
2665, ch Chambly
Longueuil, QC J4L 1M3 Canada
450-647-5243
MICR: 4418-004
Longueuil - Roland-Therrien Centreville
2155, boul Roland-Therrien
Longueuil, QC J4N 1P2 Canada
450-448-8850
MICR: 4120-004
Lower Sackville
752 Sackville Dr.
Lower Sackville, NS B4E 1R7 Canada
902-864-3515
MICR: 4950-004
Lucan
285 Main St.
Lucan, ON N0M 2J0 Canada
519-227-4446
Fax: 519-227-1743
MICR: 2940-004
Lunenburg
36 King St.
Lunenburg, NS B0J 2C0 Canada
902-634-8809
MICR: 0367-004
MacTier
14 Front St.
MacTier, ON P0C 1H0 Canada
705-375-2160
MICR: 2951-004
Madoc
PO Box 130
18 St. Lawrence St. West
Madoc, ON K0K 2K0 Canada
613-473-4245
MICR: 2968-004
Malartic
PO Box 70
692, av Royale
Malartic, QC J0Y 1Z0 Canada
819-757-3626
MICR: 4128-004
Maple - Major MacKenzie Dr.
2933 Major MacKenzie Dr.
Maple, ON L6A 3N9 Canada
905-832-2000
MICR: 3003-004
Maple Ridge - Dewdney Trunk Rd.
20398 Dewdney Trunk Rd.
Maple Ridge, BC V2X 3E3 Canada
604-460-2925
MICR: 9103-004
Maple Ridge - Lougheed Hwy.
#560, 22709 Lougheed Hwy.
Maple Ridge, BC V2X 2V5 Canada
604-466-6800
MICR: 9104-004
Marathon
PO Box 10
10 Peninsula Rd.
Marathon, ON P0T 2E0 Canada
807-229-1691
MICR: 6080-004
Markdale
PO Box 320
5 Toronto St. North
Markdale, ON N0C 1H0 Canada
519-986-3211
MICR: 2984-004
Markham - Hwy 7
5762 Hwy. 7
Markham, ON L3P 1A8 Canada
905-294-2152
MICR: 1996-004
Markham - Kennedy Rd.
7077 Kennedy Rd.
Markham, ON L3R 0N8 Canada
905-946-8824
MICR: 0532-004
Markham - Main St. North
231 Main St. North
Markham, ON L3P 1Y6 Canada
905-294-3207
MICR: 1313-004
Markham - Markham Rd.
7670 Markham Rd.
Markham, ON L3S 4S1 Canada
905-294-7788
MICR: 1289-004
Markham - McCowan Rd.
8545 McCowan Rd.
Markham, ON L3P 1W9 Canada
905-471-4200
MICR: 0206-004
Markham - McCowan Rd.
9600 McCowan Rd.
Markham, ON L3P 8M1 Canada
905-927-1716
MICR: 1439-004
Markham - Warden Ave.
8601 Warden Ave.
Markham, ON L3R 2L6 Canada
905-940-9505
Fax: 905-940-9509
MICR: 1991-004
Markham - Warden Ave.
7080 Warden Ave.
Markham, ON L3R 5Y2 Canada
905-475-7598
MICR: 1882-004
Markham - Woodbine Ave.
7085 Woodbine Ave.
Markham, ON L3R 1A3 Canada
905-475-6291
Fax: 905-475-0858
MICR: 1277-004
Markham - Woodbine Ave.
9255 Woodbine Ave.
Markham, ON L6C 1Y9 Canada
905-887-2811
MICR: 0798-004
Markham - Wooten Way North
3 Wooten Way North
Markham, ON L3P 2Y2 Canada
905-294-5913
MICR: 1997-004
Marmora
PO Box 220
36 Forsyth St.
Marmora, ON K0K 2M0 Canada
613-472-2241
MICR: 3000-004
Marwayne
#9, 1st Ave. & 38 Centre St.
Marwayne, AB T0B 2X0 Canada
780-847-8185
MICR: 8880-004
Marystown
McGettigan Blvd. & Columbia Dr.
Marystown, NL A0E 2M0 Canada
709-279-1102
Fax: 709-279-4136
MICR: 5770-004
Mayerthorpe
PO Box 210
4930 - 50th St.
Mayerthorpe, AB T0E 1N0 Canada
780-786-2204
MICR: 8896-004
Meaford
PO Box 849
53 Sykes St. North
Meaford, ON N4L 1V9 Canada
519-538-3390
MICR: 3008-004
Medicine Hat - 3rd St. SE
601 - 3rd St. SE
Medicine Hat, AB T1A 0H4 Canada
403-528-6300
MICR: 8928-004
Medicine Hat - Southview Dr. SE
1311 Southview Dr. SE
Medicine Hat, AB T1B 4M1 Canada
403-528-6340
MICR: 8930-004
Melfort
PO Box 3340
1121 Main St. North
Melfort, SK S0E 1A0 Canada
306-752-5767
MICR: 7412-004
Midland
PO Box 278
283 King St.
Midland, ON L4R 4K8 Canada
705-526-5475
Fax: 705-526-4498
MICR: 3032-004
Millbrook - King St. East
23 King St. East
Millbrook, ON L0A 1G0 Canada
705-932-3090
MICR: 3041-004
Milton - Kennedy Circle
1040 Kennedy Circle
Milton, ON L9T 0C6 Canada
905-875-3834
MICR: 3058-004
Milton - Main St.
310 Main St.
Milton, ON L9T 1P4 Canada
905-878-5561
MICR: 3044-004
Milton - Main St. East
252 Main St. East
Milton, ON L9T 1N8 Canada
905-878-2834
MICR: 0065-004
Minden
PO Box 60
14 South Water St.
Minden, ON K0M 2K0 Canada
705-286-1300
MICR: 3042-004
Miramichi
PO Box 513
360 Pleasant St.
Miramichi, NB E1V 3M6 Canada
506-622-9040
MICR: 5040-004
Mission
#140, 32555 London Ave.
Mission, BC V2V 6M7 Canada
604-820-5600
MICR: 9208-004
Mississauga - Airport Rd.
6575 Airport Rd.
Mississauga, ON L4V 1E5 Canada
905-677-4145
MICR: 1035-004
Mississauga - Bristol Rd. West
728 Bristol Rd. West
Mississauga, ON L5R 4A3 Canada
905-501-1716
MICR: 1293-004
Mississauga - Burnhamthorpe Rd. West
800 Burnhamthorpe Rd. West
Mississauga, ON L5C 2R9 Canada
905-270-0252
MICR: 1202-004
Mississauga - Burnhamthorpe Rd. West
2200 Burnhamthorpe Rd. West
Mississauga, ON L5L 5Z5 Canada
905-820-7100
MICR: 0230-004

The Toronto-Dominion Bank (continued)

Mississauga - Central Pkwy. West
1177 Central Pkwy. West
Mississauga, ON L5C 4P3 Canada
905-896-3188
MICR: 1868-004

Mississauga - City Centre Dr.
100 City Centre Dr.
Mississauga, ON L5B 2C9 Canada
905-270-9102
MICR: 0093-004

Mississauga - Clayhill Rd.
3037 Clayhill Rd.
Mississauga, ON L5B 4L2 Canada
905-949-6565
MICR: 1878-004

Mississauga - Creditview Rd.
6085 Creditview Rd.
Mississauga, ON L5V 2A8 Canada
905-542-3112
MICR: 1870-004

Mississauga - Derry Rd.
3285 Derry Rd.
Mississauga, ON L5N 7L7 Canada
905-824-8225
MICR: 1594-004

Mississauga - Dixie Rd.
4141 Dixie Rd.
Mississauga, ON L4W 1V5 Canada
905-625-8400
MICR: 1741-004

Mississauga - Dundas St. East
1145 Dundas St. East
Mississauga, ON L4Y 2C3 Canada
905-273-4500
MICR: 1340-004

Mississauga - Dundas St. West
1151 Dundas St. West
Mississauga, ON L5C 1C6 Canada
905-279-5810
MICR: 1880-004

Mississauga - Dundas St. West
2400 Dundas St. West
Mississauga, ON L5K 2R8 Canada
905-823-3652
MICR: 1037-004

Mississauga - Eglinton Ave. West
2955 Eglinton Ave. West
Mississauga, ON L5M 6J3 Canada
905-569-3400
MICR: 1305-004

Mississauga - Goreway Dr.
7205 Goreway Dr.
Mississauga, ON L4T 2T9 Canada
905-677-8903
MICR: 1862-004

Mississauga - Hurontario St.
#C-10, 4555 Hurontario St.
Mississauga, ON L4Z 3M1 Canada
905-507-0870
MICR: 1309-004

Mississauga - Hurontario St.
2580 Hurontario St.
Mississauga, ON L5B 1N5 Canada
905-277-9474
MICR: 0064-004

Mississauga - Lakeshore Rd. West
254 Lakeshore Rd. West
Mississauga, ON L5H 1G6 Canada
905-278-2444
MICR: 0535-004

Mississauga - McLaughlin Rd.
7060 McLaughlin Rd.
Mississauga, ON L5W 1W7 Canada
905-565-7220
MICR: 1597-004

Mississauga - Meadowvale Town Centre Circle
6760 Meadowvale Town Centre Circle
Mississauga, ON L5N 4B7 Canada
905-826-2712
MICR: 0159-004

Mississauga - Meyerside Dr.
1500 Meyerside Dr.
Mississauga, ON L5T 1V4 Canada
905-565-4160
MICR: 1274-004

Mississauga - Milverton Dr.
20 Milverton Dr.
Mississauga, ON L5R 3G2 Canada
905-568-3600
MICR: 1275-004

Mississauga - Mississauga Valley Blvd.
1585 Mississauga Valley Blvd.
Mississauga, ON L5A 3W9 Canada
905-275-0991
MICR: 0311-004

Mississauga - North Service Rd.
1077 North Service Rd.
Mississauga, ON L4Y 1A6 Canada
905-279-5827
MICR: 1036-004

Mississauga - Queen St. South
168 Queen St. South
Mississauga, ON L5M 1K8 Canada
905-542-9290
MICR: 0521-004

Mississauga - Rathburn Rd. East
925 Rathburn Rd. East
Mississauga, ON L4W 4C3 Canada
905-848-3390
MICR: 0334-004

Mississauga - Southdown Rd.
1052 Southdown Rd.
Mississauga, ON L5J 2Y8 Canada
905-855-7000
MICR: 0593-004

Mississauga - Tenth Line West
5626 Tenth Line West
Mississauga, ON L5M 7L9 Canada
905-286-5762
MICR: 1579-004

Mississauga - Truscott Dr.
2425 Truscott Dr.
Mississauga, ON L5J 2B4 Canada
905-822-4501
MICR: 1618-004

Mitchell
PO Box 430
31 Ontario St.
Mitchell, ON N0K 1N0 Canada
519-348-8452
Fax: 519-348-8047
MICR: 3048-004

Moncton - Main St.
860 Main St.
Moncton, NB E1C 1G2 Canada
506-853-4370
MICR: 5161-004

Montmartre
PO Box 180
100 Central Ave.
Montmartre, SK S0G 3M0 Canada
306-424-2400
MICR: 7416-004

Montréal - Bernard
1000, av Bernard
Montréal, QC H2V 1T8 Canada
514-289-0328
MICR: 4240-004

Montréal - Brunswick
317, boul Brunswick
Montréal, QC H9R 5M7 Canada
514-695-7124
Fax: 514-695-7280
MICR: 4382-004

Montréal - Cavendish
5800, boul Cavendish
Montréal, QC H4W 2T5 Canada
514-369-2622
MICR: 4312-004

Montréal - Chabanel ouest
433, rue Chabanel ouest
Montréal, QC H2N 2J3 Canada
514-289-1580
MICR: 4280-004

Montréal - Côte-des-Neiges
5900, ch de la Côte-des-Neiges
Montréal, QC H3S 1Z5 Canada
514-289-1488
MICR: 4808-004

Montréal - Côte-Vertu
3131, boul de la Côte-Vertu
Montréal, QC H4R 1Y8 Canada
514-337-2772
MICR: 0361-004

Montréal - De Bleury
1401, rue De Bleury
Montréal, QC H3A 2H6 Canada
514-289-8424
MICR: 4256-004

Montréal - Décarie
901, boul Décarie
Montréal, QC H4L 3M3 Canada
514-744-5889
MICR: 4320-004

Montréal - Décarie
8200, boul Décarie
Montréal, QC H4P 2P5 Canada
514-289-0390
MICR: 4336-004

Montréal - Greene
1289, av Greene
Montréal, QC H3Z 2A4 Canada
514-289-0379
MICR: 4772-004

Montréal - Herron
890, ch Herron
Montréal, QC H9S 1B3 Canada
514-631-6754
MICR: 4368-004

Montréal - Hymus
203, boul Hymus
Montréal, QC H9R 1E9 Canada
514-697-3833
MICR: 0360-004

Montréal - Jean Talon est
5070, rue Jean-Talon est
Montréal, QC H1S 1K6 Canada
514-593-6060
MICR: 0558-004

Montréal - Jean-Talon ouest
478, rue Jean-Talon ouest
Montréal, QC H3N 1R3 Canada
514-273-8680
MICR: 4400-004

Montréal - Laird
1201, boul Laird
Montréal, QC H3P 2S9 Canada
514-289-0352
MICR: 4432-004

Montréal - Langelier
7373, boul Langelier
Montréal, QC H1S 1V7 Canada
514-259-4608
MICR: 4276-004

Montréal - Léger
5872, boul Léger
Montréal, QC H1G 5X5 Canada
514-322-2783
MICR: 4446-004

Montréal - Maisonneuve ouest
999, boul de Maisonneuve ouest
Montréal, QC H3A 3L4 Canada
514-847-4300
MICR: 0527-004

Montréal - Maurice Duplessis
9111, Maurice Duplessis
Montréal, QC H1E 6M3 Canada
514-494-1550
MICR: 4482-004

Montréal - Newman
8450, rue Newman
Montréal, QC H8N 1Y5 Canada
514-363-4200
MICR: 4420-004

Montréal - O'Brien
1825, boul O'Brien
Montréal, QC H4L 3W6 Canada
514-956-0909
MICR: 0530-004

Montréal - Pierrefonds
11701, boul Pierrefonds
Montréal, QC H9A 1A1 Canada
514-684-4900
MICR: 4608-004

Montréal - Queen Mary

5409, ch Queen Mary
Montréal, QC H3X 1V1 Canada
514-489-9381
MICR: 0359-004
Montréal - Remembrance
2942, ch Remembrance
Montréal, QC H8S 1X8 Canada
514-634-7124
MICR: 4444-004
Montréal - René-Lévesque ouest
800, boul René-Lévesque ouest
Montréal, QC H3B 1X9 Canada
514-861-9781
MICR: 0017-004
Montréal - Sherbrooke
1130, rue Sherbrooke ouest
Montréal, QC H3A 2M9 Canada
514-289-1496
MICR: 4758-004
Montréal - Sherbrooke est
2959, rue Sherbrooke est
Montréal, QC H1W 1B2 Canada
514-289-0357
MICR: 4456-004
Montréal - Sherbrooke est
7920, rue Sherbrooke est
Montréal, QC H1L 1A5 Canada
514-351-0420
MICR: 4288-004
Montréal - Sherbrooke ouest
1130, rue Sherbrooke ouest
Montréal, QC H3A 2M9 Canada
514-289-1496
MICR: 4758-004
Montréal - Sherbrooke ouest
6100, rue Sherbrooke ouest
Montréal, QC H4A 1Y3 Canada
514-481-3767
MICR: 0515-004
Montréal - Sherbrooke ouest
5002, rue Sherbrooke ouest
Montréal, QC H3Z 1H4 Canada
514-489-9337
MICR: 4768-004
Montréal - Somerled
6505, av Somerled
Montréal, QC H4V 1S7 Canada
514-483-4878
Fax: 514-483-6902
MICR: 4784-004
Montréal - Sources
4499, boul des Sources
Montréal, QC H8Y 3C1 Canada
514-684-1114
MICR: 0525-004
Montréal - Sources
3339, boul des Sources
Montréal, QC H9B 1Z8 Canada
514-683-0391
MICR: 4350-004
Montréal - St-Charles
3662, boul St-Charles
Montréal, QC H9H 3C3 Canada
514-694-9790
MICR: 4384-004
Montréal - St-Hubert
6930, rue St-Hubert
Montréal, QC H2S 2M6 Canada
514-289-0372
MICR: 4624-004
Montréal - St-Jacques
PO Box 6009
500, rue St-Jacques
Montréal, QC H2Y 1S1 Canada
514-289-0799
MICR: 4160-004
Montréal - St-Jean
265A, boul St-Jean
Montréal, QC H9R 3J1 Canada
418-695-2590
Fax: 418-695-2958
MICR: 4824-004
Montréal - St-Laurent
3590, boul St-Laurent
Montréal, QC H2X 2V3 Canada
514-289-1385
MICR: 4720-004
Montréal - St-Louis
2065, rue St-Louis
Montréal, QC H4M 1P1 Canada
514-744-3443
MICR: 4736-004
Montréal - Ste-Catherine ouest
1601, rue Ste-Catherine ouest
Montréal, QC H3H 1L8 Canada
514-289-1536
MICR: 4576-004
Montréal - University
2001, rue University
Montréal, QC H3A 2A6 Canada
514-289-0711
MICR: 4794-004
Montréal - Van Horne
1555, rue Van Horne
Montréal, QC H2V 1L6 Canada
514-278-2711
MICR: 4800-004
Montréal - Verdun
5290, av Verdun
Montréal, QC H4H 1K1 Canada
514-768-5455
MICR: 4816-004
Montréal - Viau
8940, boul Viau
Montréal, QC H1R 2V3 Canada
514-727-9861
MICR: 4528-004
Montréal - Victoria
5499, av Victoria
Montréal, QC H3W 2P9 Canada
514-735-0233
Fax: 514-735-0718
MICR: 4822-004
Montréal - Westminster
5500, av Westminster
Montréal, QC H4W 2J1 Canada
514-482-5469
MICR: 0654-004
Moose Jaw
145 Main St. North
Moose Jaw, SK S6H 0V9 Canada
306-691-4610
MICR: 7432-004
Mount Albert
PO Box 1010
19132 Centre St.
Mount Albert, ON L0G 1M0 Canada
905-473-2427
MICR: 3056-004
Mount Forest
PO Box 160
174 Main St. South
Mount Forest, ON N0G 2L0 Canada
519-323-1250
MICR: 3064-004
Mount Pearl
PO Box 479
18 Centennial St.
Mount Pearl, NL A1N 2C4 Canada
709-758-5030
MICR: 4651-004
Nakina
PO Box 114
114 Quebec St.
Nakina, ON P0T 2H0 Canada
807-329-5935
MICR: 6083-004
Nanaimo - Boundary Cres.
1588 Boundary Cres.
Nanaimo, BC V9S 5K8 Canada
250-716-2600
MICR: 9228-004
Nanaimo - North Terminal Ave.
1-1150 North Terminal Ave.
Nanaimo, BC V9S 5L6 Canada
250-754-7731
MICR: 0043-004
Nanaimo - Turner Rd.
5777 Turner Rd.
Nanaimo, BC V9T 6L8 Canada
250-390-1248
MICR: 0594-004
Napanee
24 Dundas St. East
Napanee, ON K7R 1H6 Canada
613-354-2137
MICR: 3072-004
Nepean - Bayshore Dr.
100 Bayshore Dr.
Nepean, ON K2B 8C1 Canada
613-726-6411
MICR: 5926-004
Nepean - Merivale Rd.
1642 Merivale Rd.
Nepean, ON K2G 4A1 Canada
613-226-2224
MICR: 0353-004
Nepean - Merivale Rd.
1547 Merivale Rd.
Nepean, ON K2G 4V3 Canada
613-224-1188
MICR: 3293-004
Nepean - Stafford Rd. West
245 Stafford Rd. West
Nepean, ON K2H 9E8 Canada
613-726-1045
MICR: 3286-004
Nepean - Strandherd Dr.
3671 Strandherd Dr.
Nepean, ON K2J 4G8 Canada
613-825-3472
MICR: 2831-004
Nepean - Strandherd Dr.
#100, 3191 Strandherd Dr.
Nepean, ON K2J 5N1 Canada
613-823-2110
MICR: 3409-004
New Dundee
110 Queen St. North
New Dundee, ON N0B 2E0 Canada
519-696-2205
MICR: 3080-004
New Glasgow
PO Box 578
156 Riverside Pkwy.
New Glasgow, NS B2H 5E7 Canada
902-755-0068
MICR: 5440-004
New Hamburg
PO Box 2700
114 Huron St.
New Hamburg, ON N3A 1J3 Canada
519-662-3100
MICR: 0244-004
New Liskeard
Timiskaming Sq.
PO Box 182
New Liskeard, ON P0J 1P0 Canada
705-647-6749
MICR: 0768-004
New Westminster
573 - 6th St.
New Westminster, BC V3L 3B9 Canada
604-654-5394
MICR: 9272-004
Newmarket - Davis Dr.
130 Davis Dr.
Newmarket, ON L3Y 2N1 Canada
905-898-6831
MICR: 0307-004
Newmarket - Davis Dr.
1155 Davis Dr.
Newmarket, ON L3Y 7V1 Canada
905-830-9650
MICR: 0542-004
Newmarket - Davis Dr.
615 Davis Dr.
Newmarket, ON L3Y 2R2 Canada
905-898-2700
MICR: 3637-004
Newmarket - Yonge St.
#1, 16655 Yonge St.
Newmarket, ON L3X 1V6 Canada
905-836-2777
MICR: 3102-004

The Toronto-Dominion Bank (continued)

Newmarket - Yonge St.
18154 Yonge St.
Newmarket, ON L3Y 4V8 Canada
905-836-2690
MICR: 3076-004

Niagara Falls - Dorchester Rd.
5900 Dorchester Rd.
Niagara Falls, ON L2G 5S9 Canada
905-357-1930
MICR: 0151-004

Niagara Falls - Montrose Rd.
3930 Montrose Rd.
Niagara Falls, ON L2H 3C9 Canada
905-374-2000
MICR: 3116-004

Niagara Falls - Portage Rd.
3643 Portage Rd.
Niagara Falls, ON L2J 2K8 Canada
905-356-6934
MICR: 0124-004

Niagara Falls - Queen St.
4463 Queen St.
Niagara Falls, ON L2E 2L2 Canada
905-354-7453
MICR: 0123-004

Nobleton
PO Box 338
13305 Hwy. 27
Nobleton, ON L0G 1N0 Canada
905-859-0871
MICR: 3085-004

North Battleford
1147 - 101st St.
North Battleford, SK S9A 0Z5 Canada
306-445-7221
MICR: 7474-004

North Bay - Cassells St.
2031 Cassells St.
North Bay, ON P1B 4E1 Canada
705-474-3421
MICR: 3110-004

North Bay - Lakeshore Dr.
300 Lakeshore Dr.
North Bay, ON P1A 3V2 Canada
705-474-1724
MICR: 0156-004

North Bay - Main St. East
240 Main St. East
North Bay, ON P1B 1B1 Canada
705-472-4370
MICR: 3120-004

North Vancouver - Brooksbank Ave.
#1020, 333 Brooksbank Ave.
North Vancouver, BC V7J 3S8 Canada
604-981-2375
MICR: 0743-004

North Vancouver - Edgemont Blvd.
3190 Edgemont Blvd.
North Vancouver, BC V7R 2N9 Canada
604-981-5650
MICR: 9465-004

North Vancouver - Lonsdale Ave.
1400 Lonsdale Ave.
North Vancouver, BC V7M 2J1 Canada
604-981-5600
MICR: 9640-004

North Vancouver - Marine Dr.
1315 Marine Dr.
North Vancouver, BC V7P 3E5 Canada
604-984-4282
MICR: 0377-004

Oakville - Upper Middle Rd. East
1011 Upper Middle Rd. East
Oakville, ON L6H 4L1 Canada
905-849-1340
MICR: 3133-004

Oakville - Dundas St. West
498 Dundas St. West
Oakville, ON L6H 6Y3 Canada
905-257-0558
MICR: 3171-004

Oakville - Iroquois Rd.
321 Iroquois Rd.
Oakville, ON L6H 1M3 Canada
905-845-6621
MICR: 3138-004

Oakville - Lakeshore Rd. East
282 Lakeshore Rd. East
Oakville, ON L6J 5B2 Canada
905-845-7181
MICR: 0063-004

Oakville - Lakeshore Rd. West
2221 Lakeshore Rd. West
Oakville, ON L6L 1H1 Canada
905-847-5454
MICR: 0398-004

Oakville - North Service Rd. West
231 North Service Rd. West
Oakville, ON L6M 3R2 Canada
905-815-8565
MICR: 0714-004

Oakville - Rebecca St.
1515 Rebecca St.
Oakville, ON L6L 5G8 Canada
905-827-1107
MICR: 3140-004

Oakville - Trafalgar Rd.
2325 Trafalgar Rd.
Oakville, ON L6H 6N9 Canada
905-257-0255
MICR: 0564-004

Oakville - Upper Middle Rd. West
1424 Upper Middle Rd. West
Oakville, ON L6M 3G3 Canada
905-847-6692
MICR: 0217-004

Oakville - Westoak Trails Blvd.
2993 Westoak Trails Blvd.
Oakville, ON L6M 5E4 Canada
905-874-6993
MICR: 3125-004

Olds
PO Box 3840
4817 - 50th Ave.
Olds, AB T4H 1P5 Canada
403-556-3925
MICR: 8934-004

Orangeville - Broadway Ave.
89 Broadway Ave.
Orangeville, ON L9W 1K2 Canada
519-941-1850
MICR: 3160-004

Orangeville - Centennial Rd.
225 Centennial Rd.
Orangeville, ON L9W 5K9 Canada
519-938-5502
MICR: 2996-004

Orangeville - First St.
150 First St.
Orangeville, ON L9W 3T7 Canada
519-941-4880
MICR: 0166-004

Orillia - Monarch Dr.
3300 Monarch Dr.
Orillia, ON L3V 8A2 Canada
705-327-7900
MICR: 3170-004

Orillia - Peter St. North
39 Peter St. North
Orillia, ON L3V 4Y8 Canada
705-329-4828
MICR: 0596-004

Orleans - Innes Rd.
4422 Innes Rd.
Orleans, ON K4A 3W3 Canada
613-837-1899
MICR: 0563-004

Orleans - Jeanne D'Arc Blvd. North
6489 Jeanne D'Arc Blvd. North
Orleans, ON K1C 2R1 Canada
613-824-0603
MICR: 0271-004

Orleans - Mer Bleue Rd.
2012 Mer Bleue Rd.
Orleans, ON K1W 1K9 Canada
613-837-6564
MICR: 3316-004

Orleans - St Joseph Blvd.
2325 St Joseph Blvd.
Orleans, ON K1C 1E7 Canada
613-837-7588
MICR: 3315-004

Orleans - Watters Rd.
910 Watters Rd.
Orleans, ON K4A 3R1 Canada
613-824-1164
MICR: 2916-004

Oromocto
PO Box 158
1025 Bliss St.
Oromocto, NB E2V 2G5 Canada
506-357-9871
MICR: 5200-004

Oshawa - King St. East
601 King St. East
Oshawa, ON L1H 1G3 Canada
905-579-1617
MICR: 3200-004

Oshawa - King St. East
1300 King St. East
Oshawa, ON L1H 8J4 Canada
905-436-5111
MICR: 3203-004

Oshawa - King St. West
PO Box 247
4 King St. West
Oshawa, ON L1H 7L3 Canada
905-576-6281
MICR: 3184-004

Oshawa - Ritson Rd. North
1211 Ritson Rd. North
Oshawa, ON L1G 8B9 Canada
905-576-0880
MICR: 0526-004

Oshawa - Simcoe St. South
455 Simcoe St. South
Oshawa, ON L1H 4J7 Canada
905-728-7510
MICR: 3216-004

Oshawa - Stevenson Rd.
22 Stevenson Rd.
Oshawa, ON L1J 5L9 Canada
905-436-9331
MICR: 0391-004

Ottawa - Bank St.
1596 Bank St.
Ottawa, ON K1H 7Z5 Canada
613-526-1850
MICR: 0229-004

Ottawa - Bank St.
1158 Bank St.
Ottawa, ON K1S 3X8 Canada
613-783-6220
MICR: 3248-004

Ottawa - Bank St.
2470 Bank St.
Ottawa, ON K1V 8S2 Canada
613-526-2128
MICR: 0533-004

Ottawa - Carling Ave.
1800 Carling Ave.
Ottawa, ON K2A 1E2 Canada
613-728-1802
MICR: 0268-004

Ottawa - Carling Ave.
1309 Carling Ave.
Ottawa, ON K1Z 7L3 Canada
613-728-2681
MICR: 0164-004

Ottawa - Elgin St.
263 Elgin St.
Ottawa, ON K2P 1L8 Canada
613-783-6260
MICR: 3292-004

Ottawa - Kilborn Ave.
1785 Kilborn Ave.
Ottawa, ON K1H 6N1 Canada
613-521-6292
MICR: 0557-004

Ottawa - Laurier Ave. West
427 Laurier Ave. West
Ottawa, ON K1R 7Y2 Canada
613-783-6200
MICR: 3290-004

Ottawa - Laurier Ave. West

170 Laurier Ave. West
Ottawa, ON K1P 5V5 Canada
613-598-4707
MICR: 0035-004

Ottawa - Meadowlands Dr. East
888 Meadowlands Dr. East
Ottawa, ON K2C 3R2 Canada
613-226-7353
MICR: 3270-004

Ottawa - Montréal Rd.
562 Montréal Rd.
Ottawa, ON K1K 0T9 Canada
613-783-6210
MICR: 3312-004

Ottawa - O'Connor St.
45 O'Connor St.
Ottawa, ON K1P 1A4 Canada
613-782-1201
MICR: 0354-004

Ottawa - Pretoria Ave.
5 Pretoria Ave.
Ottawa, ON K1S 5L6 Canada
613-238-1234
MICR: 0249-004

Ottawa - Richmond Rd.
337 Richmond Rd.
Ottawa, ON K2A 0E7 Canada
613-728-1768
MICR: 3360-004

Ottawa - Richmond Rd.
PO Box 6010
1480 Richmond Rd.
Ottawa, ON K2B 6S1 Canada
613-726-6330
MICR: 5938-004

Ottawa - Rideau St.
400 Rideau St.
Ottawa, ON K1N 5Z1 Canada
613-783-6230
MICR: 3324-004

Ottawa - Riverside Dr.
#1, 2269 Riverside Dr.
Ottawa, ON K1H 8K2 Canada
613-731-4220
MICR: 3250-004

Ottawa - Scott St.
1620 Scott St.
Ottawa, ON K1Y 4S7 Canada
613-729-3331
MICR: 0513-004

Ottawa - St Laurent Blvd.
PO Box 41
1200 St Laurent Blvd.
Ottawa, ON K1K 3B8 Canada
613-745-1588
MICR: 3314-004

Ottawa - Wellington St.
1236 Wellington St.
Ottawa, ON K1K 3A4 Canada
613-722-4247
MICR: 3344-004

Owen Sound
PO Box 308
901 - 2nd Ave. East
Owen Sound, ON N4K 5P5 Canada
519-376-6510
MICR: 3376-004

Oyen
PO Box 60
118 Main St.
Oyen, AB T0J 2J0 Canada
403-664-3601
MICR: 8944-004

Paris
53 Grand River St. North
Paris, ON N3L 2M3 Canada
519-442-2201
MICR: 3384-004

Parksville
PO Box 906
115 Alberni Hwy.
Parksville, BC V9P 2G9 Canada
250-248-7329
MICR: 0679-004

Parry Sound
55 James St.
Parry Sound, ON P2A 1T6 Canada
705-746-5846
MICR: 3392-004

Peace River
7816 - 100 Ave.
Peace River, AB T8S 1M5 Canada
780-624-2652
MICR: 8952-004

Pembroke
150 Pembroke St. West
Pembroke, ON K8A 5M8 Canada
613-732-2847
MICR: 3400-004

Penetanguishene
Village Square Mall
#117, 2 Poyntz St.
Penetanguishene, ON L9M 1M2 Canada
705-549-7485
MICR: 3408-004

Penticton - Main St.
390 Main St.
Penticton, BC V2A 5C3 Canada
250-770-2300
MICR: 9288-004

Penticton - Main St.
#130, 2210 Main St.
Penticton, BC V2A 5H8 Canada
250-770-2333
MICR: 9285-004

Perth
PO Box 38
70 Gore St. East
Perth, ON K7H 3E2 Canada
613-267-6042
MICR: 3410-004

Petawawa
PO Box 159
3507 Petawawa Blvd.
Petawawa, ON K8H 2X2 Canada
613-687-5561
MICR: 3412-004

Peterborough - George St. North
Peterborough Square
340 George St. North
Peterborough, ON K9H 7E8 Canada
705-745-5777
MICR: 3432-004

Peterborough - Lansdowne St. West
1096 Lansdowne St. West
Peterborough, ON K9J 1Z9 Canada
705-742-6558
MICR: 0606-004

Peterborough - Monaghan Rd.
830 Monaghan Rd.
Peterborough, ON K9J 5K3 Canada
705-748-6634
MICR: 3434-004

Petrolia
4201 Petrolia Line
Petrolia, ON N0N 1R0 Canada
519-882-0320
MICR: 3448-004

Pickering - Kingston Rd.
1355 Kingston Rd.
Pickering, ON L1V 1B8 Canada
905-831-2873
MICR: 1805-004

Pickering - Liverpool Rd.
1794 Liverpool Rd.
Pickering, ON L1V 1V9 Canada
905-831-6114
MICR: 0272-004

Pickering - Oklahoma Dr.
750 Oklahoma Dr.
Pickering, ON L1W 3G9 Canada
905-420-8855
MICR: 0747-004

Pickering - Whites Rd.
1822 Whites Rd.
Pickering, ON L1V 4M1 Canada
905-420-8312
MICR: 1802-004

Picton
PO Box 2280
164 Main St.
Picton, ON K0K 2T0 Canada
613-476-3205
MICR: 3450-004

Pilot Mound
PO Box 328
125 Broadway Ave.
Pilot Mound, MB R0G 1P0 Canada
204-825-2636
MICR: 6188-004

Port Alberni
3008 - 3rd Ave. South
Port Alberni, BC V9Y 2A5 Canada
250-720-4810
MICR: 9320-004

Port Colborne
148 Clarence St.
Port Colborne, ON L3K 3G5 Canada
905-835-2437
Fax: 905-834-7768
MICR: 3464-004

Port Coquitlam - Lougheed Hwy.
#11, 2755 Lougheed Hwy.
Port Coquitlam, BC V3B 5Y9 Canada
604-464-2322
MICR: 0234-004

Port Coquitlam - Prairie Ave.
Prairie Mall
1492 Prairie Ave.
Port Coquitlam, BC V3B 5M8 Canada
604-552-8120
MICR: 9323-004

Port Elgin
PO Box 430
723 Goderich St.
Port Elgin, ON N0H 2C0 Canada
519-832-2035
MICR: 3476-004

Port Hawkesbury
PO Box 482
#6, 298 Reeves St.
Port Hawkesbury, NS B9A 2B4 Canada
902-625-0086
MICR: 4956-004

Port Hope
113 Walton St.
Port Hope, ON L1A 1N4 Canada
905-885-6361
MICR: 0314-004

Port Perry
165 Queen St.
Port Perry, ON L9L 1B8 Canada
905-985-8435
MICR: 2054-004

Portage La Prairie
102 Saskatchewan Ave. West
Portage La Prairie, MB R1N 0M1 Canada
204-857-8761
MICR: 6190-004

Preeceville
PO Box 289
24 Main St.
Preeceville, SK S0A 3B0 Canada
306-547-3231
MICR: 7496-004

Prescott
PO Box 1300
100 King St. West
Prescott, ON K0E 1T0 Canada
613-925-4244
MICR: 3496-004

Prince Albert
#107, 2805 - 6th Ave. East
Prince Albert, SK S6V 6Z6 Canada
306-953-8230
MICR: 7508-004

Prince George - Massey Dr.
#186, 3055 Massey Dr.
Prince George, BC V2N 2J9 Canada
250-612-6000
MICR: 0752-004

Prince George - O'Grady Rd.
5902 O'Grady Rd.
Prince George, BC V2N 7A2 Canada

The Toronto-Dominion Bank (continued)

250-906-3000
MICR: 9333-004

Prince George - Victoria St.
400 Victoria St.
Prince George, BC V2L 2J7 Canada
250-614-2950
MICR: 9336-004

Prince Rupert
Rupert Sq. Shopping Centre
#236, 500 West 2nd Ave.
Prince Rupert, BC V8J 3T6 Canada
250-627-1767
MICR: 9340-004

Quesnel
321 Reid St.
Quesnel, BC V2J 2M5 Canada
250-992-2167
MICR: 9352-004

Quispamsis
PO Box 21012
184 Hampton Rd.
Quispamsis, NB E2E 4Z4 Canada
506-848-6010
MICR: 5234-004

Québec - Claire-Fontaine
1150, rue de Claire-Fontaine
Québec, QC G1R 5G4 Canada
418-522-5684
MICR: 4832-004

Québec - Gradins
5685, boul des Gradins
Québec, QC G2J 1V1 Canada
418-624-2966
MICR: 4874-004

Québec - Henri-Bourassa
8425, boul Henri-Bourassa
Québec, QC G1G 4E1 Canada
418-628-1422
MICR: 4040-004

Québec - Ormière
9445, boul de l'Ormière
Québec, QC G2B 3K7 Canada
418-843-8542
MICR: 4876-004

Québec - Quatre-Bourgeois
3400, ch des Quatre-Bourgeois
Québec, QC G1W 2L3 Canada
418-653-8393
MICR: 4902-004

Red Deer - 19th St.
#500, 5001 - 19th St.
Red Deer, AB T4R 3R1 Canada
403-342-4700
MICR: 0221-004

Red Deer - 50th Ave.
6320 - 50 Ave.
Red Deer, AB T4N 4C6 Canada
403-346-7711
MICR: 0025-004

Red Deer - Gaetz Ave.
4902 Gaetz Ave.
Red Deer, AB T4N 4A8 Canada
403-340-7400
MICR: 8960-004

Regina - Albert St.
4240 Albert St.
Regina, SK S4S 3R9 Canada
306-780-0406
MICR: 7632-004

Regina - Hamilton St.
1904 Hamilton St.
Regina, SK S4P 3N5 Canada
306-780-0212
MICR: 7544-004

Regina - Rochdale Blvd.
#E, 4011 Rochdale Blvd.
Regina, SK S4X 4P7 Canada
306-780-0395
MICR: 7629-004

Regina - Victoria Ave. East
#107, 2223 Victoria Ave. East
Regina, SK S4N 6E4 Canada
306-780-0360
MICR: 7596-004

Renfrew
PO Box 246
270 Raglan St. South
Renfrew, ON K7V 4A4 Canada
613-432-3682
MICR: 3512-004

Repentigny
#145, 100, boul Brien
Repentigny, QC J6A 5N4 Canada
450-582-1881
MICR: 4888-004

Revelstoke
PO Box 1390
406 - 1 St. West
Revelstoke, BC V0E 2S0 Canada
250-837-6900
MICR: 9360-004

Richmond - Francis Rd.
3960 Francis Rd.
Richmond, BC B7C 1J7 Canada
604-277-6080
MICR: 0212-004

Richmond - No. 2 Rd.
#145, 8100 No. 2 Rd.
Richmond, BC V7C 5J9 Canada
604-241-4233
MICR: 0762-004

Richmond - No. 3 Rd.
10151 - No. 3 Rd.
Richmond, BC V7A 4R6 Canada
604-606-0700
MICR: 9725-004

Richmond - No. 3 Rd.
5991 - No. 3 Rd.
Richmond, BC V6X 3Y6 Canada
604-654-3180
MICR: 9720-004

Richmond - No. 3 Rd.
6380 No. 3 Rd.
Richmond, BC V6Y 2B3 Canada
604-278-7735
MICR: 0152-004

Richmond - No. 3 Rd.
#626, 5300 No. 3 Rd.
Richmond, BC V6X 2X9 Canada
604-273-0821
MICR: 0281-004

Richmond - Sexsmith Rd.
Continental Centre
#2100, 3799 Sexsmith Rd.
Richmond, BC V6X 3Z9 Canada
604-654-8878
MICR: 9713-004

Richmond Hill - Bayview Ave.
9019 Bayview Ave.
Richmond Hill, ON L4B 3M6 Canada
905-771-0925
MICR: 1083-004

Richmond Hill - Bayview Ave.
10381 Bayview Ave.
Richmond Hill, ON L4C 0R9 Canada
905-508-6627
MICR: 1074-004

Richmond Hill - Hwy. 7 East
500 Hwy. 7 East
Richmond Hill, ON L4B 1J1 Canada
905-764-7730
MICR: 1085-004

Richmond Hill - Hwy. 7 East
#55, 550 Hwy. 7 East
Richmond Hill, ON L4B 3Z4 Canada
905-886-1728
MICR: 0868-004

Richmond Hill - Yonge St.
10909 Yonge St.
Richmond Hill, ON L4C 3E3 Canada
905-508-4511
MICR: 1060-004

Richmond Hill - Yonge St.
9350 Yonge St.
Richmond Hill, ON L4C 5G2 Canada
905-883-1393
MICR: 1999-004

Richmond Hill - Yonge St.
10395 Yonge St.
Richmond Hill, ON L4C 3C2 Canada
905-770-7200
MICR: 0569-004

Richmond Hill - Yonge St.
8889 Yonge St.
Richmond Hill, ON L4C 6Z1 Canada
905-707-6639
MICR: 1097-004

Riverview
502 Coverdale Rd.
Riverview, NB E1B 3K4 Canada
506-859-2500
MICR: 4851-004

Rocanville
PO Box 149
128 Ellice St.
Rocanville, SK S0A 3L0 Canada
306-645-2110
MICR: 7640-004

Rosetown
PO Box 70
118 Main St.
Rosetown, SK S0L 2V0 Canada
306-882-2646
MICR: 7656-004

Rouyn-Noranda
130, av Principale
Rouyn-Noranda, QC J9X 4P5 Canada
819-762-0977
MICR: 4896-004

Saint John - Chipman Hill
44 Chipman Hill
Saint John, NB E2L 2A9 Canada
506-634-1870
MICR: 5240-004

Saint John - Main St. West
78 Main St. West
Saint John, NB E2M 3N3 Canada
506-635-1220
MICR: 5248-004

Saint-Lambert - Victoria
572, av Victoria
Saint-Lambert, QC J4P 2J5 Canada
450-923-1015
MICR: 4820-004

Salmon Arm
391 Alexander Ave.
Salmon Arm, BC V1E 4P9 Canada
250-833-1350
MICR: 9366-004

Sarnia - Cathcart Blvd.
693 Cathcart Blvd.
Sarnia, ON N7V 2N6 Canada
519-332-5571
MICR: 3616-004

Sarnia - Christina St. North
357 Christina St. North
Sarnia, ON N7T 5V6 Canada
519-332-0550
MICR: 0023-004

Sarnia - London Rd.
1210 London Rd.
Sarnia, ON N7S 1P4 Canada
519-383-8320
MICR: 3624-004

Saskatoon - 2nd Ave. South
170 - 2nd Ave. South
Saskatoon, SK S7K 1K5 Canada
306-975-1700
MICR: 0030-004

Saskatoon - 4th Ave. South
224 - 4th Ave. South
Saskatoon, SK S7K 5M5 Canada
306-955-3622
MICR: 7601-004

Saskatoon - 8th St. East
3020 - 8th St. East
Saskatoon, SK S7H 0W2 Canada
306-975-7260
MICR: 7736-004

Saskatoon - Attridge Dr.
970 Attridge Dr.
Saskatoon, SK S7S 1N3 Canada
306-955-6592
MICR: 7666-004

Saskatoon - Primrose Dr.

#242, 234 Primrose Dr.
Saskatoon, SK S7K 6Y6 Canada
306-975-7330
MICR: 7740-004
Sault Ste Marie - Bay St.
Station Tower
421 Bay St.
Sault Ste Marie, ON P6A 1V3 Canada
705-254-6424
MICR: 3644-004
Sault Ste Marie - Great Northern Rd.
44 Great Northern Rd.
Sault Ste Marie, ON P6B 4Y5 Canada
705-254-7355
MICR: 0355-004
Sault Ste Marie - Second Line West
275 Second Line West
Sault Ste Marie, ON P6C 6C5 Canada
705-942-2330
MICR: 3652-004
Seaforth
PO Box 520
56 Main St. South
Seaforth, ON N0K 1W0 Canada
519-527-1460
MICR: 3656-004
Seeleys Bay
161 Main St.
Seeleys Bay, ON K0H 2N0 Canada
613-387-3891
MICR: 3660-004
Selkirk
396 Main St.
Selkirk, MB R1A 1V1 Canada
204-482-2800
MICR: 6204-004
Shelburne
PO Box 219
100 Main St.
Shelburne, ON L0N 1S0 Canada
519-925-3832
MICR: 3664-004
Sherbrooke
2815, rue King ouest
Sherbrooke, QC J1L 1C1 Canada
819-821-4252
MICR: 4928-004
Sherwood Park - Ordze Ave.
139 Ordze Ave.
Sherwood Park, AB T8B 1M6 Canada
780-449-1612
MICR: 0541-004
Sherwood Park - Sherwood Dr.
2020 Sherwood Dr.
Sherwood Park, AB T8A 3H9 Canada
780-449-9300
MICR: 8972-004
Sidney
2406 Beacon Ave.
Sidney, BC V8L 1X4 Canada
250-655-5244
MICR: 0721-004
Simcoe - Norfolk St. North
46 Norfolk St. North
Simcoe, ON N3Y 5C6 Canada
519-426-2942
MICR: 0083-004
Simcoe - Queensway Dr. East
135 Queensway Dr. East
Simcoe, ON N3Y 4M5 Canada
519-426-9230
MICR: 0155-004
Smiths Falls
15 Beckwith St. North
Smiths Falls, ON K7A 2B2 Canada
613-283-0956
MICR: 3676-004
Sorel-Tracy
1005, rte Marie-Victorin
Sorel-Tracy, QC J3R 1L5 Canada
450-742-2769
MICR: 4936-004
South Porcupine
90 Bruce Ave.
South Porcupine, ON P0N 1H0 Canada
705-235-3305
MICR: 3680-004
Spruce Grove
#10, 100 Campsite Rd.
Spruce Grove, AB T7X 4B8 Canada
780-962-0404
MICR: 8975-004
St Albert - Inglewood Dr.
11 Inglewood Dr.
St Albert, AB T8N 5E2 Canada
780-460-3550
MICR: 8967-004
St Albert - St Albert Rd.
#40, 101 St Albert Rd.
St Albert, AB T8N 6L5 Canada
780-458-3515
MICR: 0177-004
St Catharines - Geneva St.
270 Geneva St.
St Catharines, ON L2N 2E8 Canada
905-937-6220
MICR: 3536-004
St Catharines - Glendale Ave.
240 Glendale Ave.
St Catharines, ON L2T 2L2 Canada
905-684-8710
MICR: 0024-004
St Catharines - Lakeshore Rd.
37 Lakeshore Rd.
St Catharines, ON L2N 2T2 Canada
905-646-4141
MICR: 0261-004
St Catharines - Queen St.
PO Box 458
31 Queen St.
St Catharines, ON L2R 6V9 Canada
905-685-8455
MICR: 3520-004
St Catharines - Scott St.
364 Scott St.
St Catharines, ON L2M 3W4 Canada
905-934-6226
MICR: 0126-004
St Marys
PO Box 669
4 Church St. North
St Marys, ON N4X 1B4 Canada
519-284-2070
MICR: 3584-004
St Paul
PO Box 908
4901 - 50th Ave.
St Paul, AB T0A 3A0 Canada
780-645-7000
MICR: 8968-004
St Thomas - Talbot St.
378 Talbot St.
St Thomas, ON N5P 1B8 Canada
519-631-7071
MICR: 0002-004
St Thomas - Wellington St.
417 Wellington St.
St Thomas, ON N5R 5J5 Canada
519-633-4641
MICR: 0100-004
St-Jean-sur-Richelieu - St-Jacques
46, rue St-Jacques
St-Jean-sur-Richelieu, QC J3B 2J7 Canada
450-347-3708
MICR: 4912-004
St-Jérôme - Grand-Héron
1015, boul du Grand-Héron
St-Jérôme, QC J7Y 3P2 Canada
450-432-9779
MICR: 4920-004
St. John's - Elizabeth Ave.
80 Elizabeth Ave.
St. John's, NL A1A 1W7 Canada
709-758-1850
MICR: 0502-004
St. John's - Kenmount Rd.
PO Box 8275
58 Kenmount Rd.
St. John's, NL A1B 1W2 Canada
709-758-5040
MICR: 4663-004
St. John's - Water St.
TD Place
140 Water St.
St. John's, NL A1C 6H6 Canada
709-758-5000
MICR: 5800-004
Stayner
7269 Hwy. 26
Stayner, ON L0M 1S0 Canada
705-428-2016
MICR: 3688-004
Ste-Marthe-sur-le-Lac
#47, 2801, Promenades
Ste-Marthe-sur-le-Lac, QC J0N 1P0 Canada
450-472-9675
MICR: 4610-004
Steinbach
299 Main St.
Steinbach, MB R5G 1Z2 Canada
204-326-9881
MICR: 6212-004
Stettler
PO Box 1433
4902 - 50th St.
Stettler, AB T0C 2L0 Canada
403-742-3464
MICR: 8971-004
Stittsville
1270 Main St.
Stittsville, ON K2S 2A9 Canada
613-831-8700
MICR: 3281-004
Stonewall
333 Main St.
Stonewall, MB R0C 2Z0 Canada
204-467-7820
MICR: 6215-004
Stoney Creek - Hwy. 8
267 Hwy. 8
Stoney Creek, ON L8G 1E4 Canada
905-662-5824
MICR: 0350-004
Stoney Creek - King St. East
54 King St. East
Stoney Creek, ON L8G 1K2 Canada
905-664-4424
MICR: 3696-004
Stoney Creek - Queenston Rd.
800 Queenston Rd.
Stoney Creek, ON L8G 1A7 Canada
905-664-6510
MICR: 0090-004
Stoney Creek - Rymal Rd. East
2285 Rymal Rd. East
Stoney Creek, ON L8J 2V8 Canada
905-573-8991
MICR: 2284-004
Stouffville - Main St.
5887 Main St.
Stouffville, ON L4A 1N2 Canada
905-640-4000
MICR: 3700-004
Stratford - Downie St.
41 Downie St.
Stratford, ON N5A 1W7 Canada
519-271-4160
MICR: 0054-008
Stratford - Ontario St.
832 Ontario St.
Stratford, ON N5A 3K1 Canada
519-272-2090
MICR: 3708-004
Strathroy
360 Caradoc St. South
Strathroy, ON N7G 2P6 Canada
519-245-4020
MICR: 0775-004
Sudbury - Elm St.
43 Elm St.
Sudbury, ON P3E 4R7 Canada
705-669-4000
MICR: 3712-004
Sudbury - Frood St.

The Toronto-Dominion Bank (continued)

402 Frood St.
Sudbury, ON P3C 4Z8 Canada
705-669-4000
MICR: 3710-004

Sudbury - LaSalle Blvd.
2208 LaSalle Blvd.
Sudbury, ON P3A 2A8 Canada
705-566-2313
MICR: 3716-004

Sudbury - Paris St.
1935 Paris St.
Sudbury, ON P3E 3C6 Canada
705-522-2370
MICR: 3736-004

Summerside
120 Harbour Dr.
Summerside, PE C1N 5Y8 Canada
902-888-5450
MICR: 5720-004

Surrey - 101 Ave.
15190 - 101 Ave.
Surrey, BC V3R 7V4 Canada
604-586-2055
MICR: 9276-004

Surrey - 152nd St.
#100, 2429 - 152nd St.
Surrey, BC V4P 1N4 Canada
604-541-6600
MICR: 9016-004

Surrey - 64th Ave.
#108, 17755 - 64th Ave.
Surrey, BC V3S 1Z2 Canada
604-575-3560
MICR: 9028-004

Surrey - 72 Ave.
13650 - 72 Ave.
Surrey, BC V3W 2P3 Canada
604-572-8188
MICR: 0547-004

Surrey - 96th Ave.
12898 - 96th Ave.
Surrey, BC V3V 6A8 Canada
604-586-2075
MICR: 9274-004

Surrey - Fraser Hwy.
#601, 15960 Fraser Hwy.
Surrey, BC V3S 2W5 Canada
604-501-8900
MICR: 0175-004

Surrey - King George VI Hwy.
10435 King George VI Hwy.
Surrey, BC V3T 2W7 Canada
604-586-2000
MICR: 9280-004

Sussex
620 Main St.
Sussex, NB E4E 5L4 Canada
506-433-7000
MICR: 5260-004

Sutton
PO Box 550
20865 Dalton Rd.
Sutton, ON L0E 1R0 Canada
905-722-3234
MICR: 3740-004

Swan River
PO Box 430
501 Main St.
Swan River, MB R0L 1Z0 Canada
204-734-4544
MICR: 6220-004

Swift Current
PO Box 876
185 Central Ave. North
Swift Current, SK S9H 0K9 Canada
306-773-3158
MICR: 7784-004

Sydney
292 Charlotte St.
Sydney, NS B1P 1C7 Canada
902-539-3640
MICR: 0371-004

Terrace
4633 Lakelse Ave.
Terrace, BC V8G 1R3 Canada
250-635-8900
MICR: 9380-004

Teulon
PO Box 109
96 Main St.
Teulon, MB R0C 3B0 Canada
204-886-4020
MICR: 6236-004

The Pas
PO Box 479
302 Edwards Ave.
The Pas, MB R9A 1K6 Canada
204-623-3464
MICR: 6244-004

Thompson
City Centre Mall
300 Mystery Lake Rd.
Thompson, MB R8N 0M2 Canada
204-677-6080
MICR: 6252-004

Thornbury
4 Bruce St. South
Thornbury, ON N0H 2P0 Canada
519-599-2622
MICR: 3744-004

Thornhill - Bathurst St.
#2, 9200 Bathurst St.
Thornhill, ON L4J 8W1 Canada
905-707-7663
MICR: 1215-004

Thornhill - Centre St.
1054 Centre St.
Thornhill, ON L4J 3M8 Canada
905-889-8400
MICR: 0640-004

Thornhill - Clark Ave. West
441 Clark Ave. West
Thornhill, ON L4J 6W7 Canada
905-889-6204
MICR: 1214-004

Thornhill - Dufferin St.
#11, 8707 Dufferin St.
Thornhill, ON L4J 0A2 Canada
905-660-0017
MICR: 1471-004

Thornhill - Steeles Ave. East
2900 Steeles Ave. East
Thornhill, ON L3T 4X1 Canada
905-881-8090
MICR: 0315-004

Thornhill - Steeles Ave. West
#1, 100 Steeles Ave. West
Thornhill, ON L4J 7Y1 Canada
905-882-0300
MICR: 0531-004

Thornhill - Yonge St.
7967 Yonge St.
Thornhill, ON L3T 2C4 Canada
905-881-3252
MICR: 0316-004

Three Hills
PO Box 250
508 Main St.
Three Hills, AB T0M 2A0 Canada
403-443-5521
MICR: 8974-004

Thunder Bay - Arthur St. West
595 Arthur St. West
Thunder Bay, ON P7E 5R5 Canada
807-474-4310
MICR: 0663-004

Thunder Bay - Dawson Rd.
1090 Dawson Rd.
Thunder Bay, ON P7B 5V1 Canada
807-768-3100
MICR: 6092-004

Thunder Bay - Memorial Ave.
1039 Memorial Ave.
Thunder Bay, ON P7B 4A4 Canada
807-626-1565
MICR: 6053-004

Thunder Bay - Red River Rd.
231 Red River Rd.
Thunder Bay, ON P7B 5E8 Canada
807-346-3175
MICR: 6088-004

Tillsonburg
200 Broadway St.
Tillsonburg, ON N4G 5A7 Canada
519-842-8401
MICR: 0308-004

Timmins
PO Box 10
6 Pine St. South
Timmins, ON P4N 7C5 Canada
705-264-1305
MICR: 3760-004

Toronto - Adelaide St. West
141 Adelaide St. West
Toronto, ON M5H 3L5 Canada
416-982-8768
MICR: 1992-004

Toronto - Albion Rd.
972 Albion Rd.
Toronto, ON M9V 1A7 Canada
416-743-8121
MICR: 1824-004

Toronto - Avenue Rd.
1677 Avenue Rd.
Toronto, ON M5M 3Y3 Canada
416-789-7941
MICR: 0252-044

Toronto - Avenue Rd.
165 Avenue Rd.
Toronto, ON M5R 2S4 Canada
416-944-4160
MICR: 1040-004

Toronto - Avenue Rd.
1677 Avenue Rd.
Toronto, ON M5M 3Y3 Canada
416-789-7941
MICR: 0252-004

Toronto - Bathurst St.
3757 Bathurst St.
Toronto, ON M3H 3M5 Canada
416-630-3700
MICR: 1080-004

Toronto - Bathurst St.
6209 Bathurst St.
Toronto, ON M2R 2A5 Canada
416-229-4433
MICR: 1076-004

Toronto - Bathurst St.
3114 Bathurst St.
Toronto, ON M6A 2A1 Canada
416-789-7311
MICR: 0328-004

Toronto - Bay St.
394 Bay St.
Toronto, ON M5H 2Y3 Canada
416-982-4007
MICR: 1216-004

Toronto - Bay St.
777 Bay St.
Toronto, ON M5G 2C8 Canada
416-982-4364
MICR: 1224-004

Toronto - Bay St.
161 Bay St.
Toronto, ON M5J 2T2 Canada
416-361-5400
MICR: 0500-004

Toronto - Bayview Ave.
3275 Bayview Ave.
Toronto, ON M2K 1G4 Canada
416-223-6310
MICR: 1084-004

Toronto - Bayview Ave.
1511 Bayview Ave.
Toronto, ON M4G 4E2 Canada
416-440-0537
MICR: 0255-004

Toronto - Bayview Ave.
2518 Bayview Ave.
Toronto, ON M2L 1A9 Canada
416-444-4457
MICR: 0337-004

Toronto - Bloor St. East
420 Bloor St. East
Toronto, ON M4W 1H4 Canada
416-944-6294

MICR: 1168-004
Toronto - Bloor St. West
574 Bloor St. West.
Toronto, ON M6G 1K1 Canada
416-534-9211
MICR: 0132-004
Toronto - Bloor St. West
3868 Bloor St. West
Toronto, ON M9B 1L3 Canada
416-236-1095
MICR: 0235-004
Toronto - Bloor St. West
2322 Bloor St. West
Toronto, ON M6S 1P2 Canada
416-766-9200
MICR: 0375-004
Toronto - Bloor St. West
77 Bloor St. West
Toronto, ON M5S 1M2 Canada
416-944-4115
MICR: 1104-004
Toronto - Bloor St. West
2440 Bloor St. West
Toronto, ON M6S 1P9 Canada
416-763-2441
MICR: 1144-004
Toronto - Bloor St. West
2972 Bloor St. West
Toronto, ON M8X 1B9 Canada
416-231-3444
MICR: 0326-004
Toronto - Bloor St. West
3300 Bloor St. West
Toronto, ON M8X 2W8 Canada
416-236-4380
Fax: 416-237-0468
MICR: 1136-004
Toronto - Bloor St. West
4335 Bloor St. West
Toronto, ON M9C 2A5 Canada
416-621-8321
MICR: 0050-004
Toronto - Borough Dr.
#36, 300 Borough Dr.
Toronto, ON M1P 4P5 Canada
416-279-0588
MICR: 1795-004
Toronto - Bremner Blvd.
363 Bremner Blvd.
Toronto, ON M5V 3V4 Canada
MICR: 1228-004
Toronto - Brimley Rd.
2098 Brimley Rd.
Toronto, ON M1S 5X1 Canada
416-609-9888
MICR: 1175-004
Toronto - Brown's Line
430 Brown's Line
Toronto, ON M8W 3T9 Canada
416-255-8193
Fax: 416-251-7955
MICR: 1192-004
Toronto - Burnhamthorpe Rd.
327 Burnhamthorpe Rd.
Toronto, ON M9B 2A2 Canada
416-234-6246
MICR: 1200-004
Toronto - Burnhamthorpe Rd.
666 Burnhamthorpe Rd.
Toronto, ON M9C 2Z4 Canada
416-622-6130
MICR: 0331-004
Toronto - College St.
623 College St.
Toronto, ON M6G 1B4 Canada
416-538-3400
MICR: 0677-004
Toronto - Coxwell Ave.
1050 Coxwell Ave.
Toronto, ON M4C 3G5 Canada
416-425-8334
MICR: 1232-004
Toronto - Danforth Ave.
3060 Danforth Ave.
Toronto, ON M4C 1N2 Canada
416-698-2871
MICR: 0032-004
Toronto - Danforth Ave.
480 Danforth Ave.
Toronto, ON M4K 1P4 Canada
416-465-4681
MICR: 1256-004
Toronto - Danforth Ave.
890 Danforth Ave.
Toronto, ON M4J 1L9 Canada
416-466-1161
MICR: 1248-004
Toronto - Danforth Ave.
2080 Danforth Ave.
Toronto, ON M4C 1J9 Canada
416-425-6137
MICR: 1268-004
Toronto - Danforth Ave.
1684 Danforth Ave.
Toronto, ON M4C 1H6 Canada
416-466-2317
MICR: 0374-004
Toronto - Don Mills Rd.
1470 Don Mills Rd.
Toronto, ON M3B 2X9 Canada
416-445-3000
MICR: 1284-004
Toronto - Don Mills Rd.
3555 Don Mills Rd.
Toronto, ON M2H 3N3 Canada
416-498-3331
MICR: 1282-004
Toronto - Dufferin St.
3401 Dufferin St.
Toronto, ON M6A 2T9 Canada
416-789-0541
MICR: 0338-004
Toronto - Dufferin St.
3140 Dufferin St.
Toronto, ON M6A 2T1 Canada
416-785-7230
MICR: 1993-004
Toronto - Dundas St. West
413 Dundas St. West
Toronto, ON M5T 1G6 Canada
416-977-2300
MICR: 0246-004
Toronto - Dundas St. West
501 Dundas St. West
Toronto, ON M5T 1H1 Canada
416-982-2111
MICR: 1328-004
Toronto - Dundas St. West
1140 Dundas St. West
Toronto, ON M6J 1X2 Canada
416-531-4671
MICR: 1336-004
Toronto - Dundas St. West
3422 Dundas St. West
Toronto, ON M6S 2S1 Canada
416-763-4661
MICR: 1354-004
Toronto - Dundas St. West
4242 Dundas St. West
Toronto, ON M8X 1Y6 Canada
416-234-6245
MICR: 1344-004
Toronto - Dupont St.
657 Dupont St.
Toronto, ON M6G 1Z4 Canada
416-531-9955
MICR: 1360-004
Toronto - Dupont St.
1245 Dupont St.
Toronto, ON M6H 2A6 Canada
416-537-2608
MICR: 1304-004
Toronto - Eglinton Ave. East
2428 Eglinton Ave. East
Toronto, ON M1K 2P7 Canada
416-751-3810
MICR: 1488-004
Toronto - Eglinton Ave. East
878 Eglinton Ave. East
Toronto, ON M4G 2L1 Canada
416-425-6360
MICR: 1416-004
Toronto - Eglinton Ave. East
2428 Eglinton Ave. East
Toronto, ON M1K 2P7 Canada
416-751-3810
MICR: 1488-004
Toronto - Eglinton Ave. West
472 Eglinton Ave. West
Toronto, ON M5N 1A6 Canada
416-481-5171
MICR: 0031-004
Toronto - Eglinton Ave. West
1886 Eglinton Ave. West
Toronto, ON M6E 2J6 Canada
416-785-7742
MICR: 0607-004
Toronto - Eglinton Ave. West
846 Eglinton Ave. West
Toronto, ON M6C 2B7 Canada
416-787-1841
MICR: 1376-004
Toronto - Eglinton Ave. West
2623 Eglinton Ave. West
Toronto, ON M6M 1T6 Canada
416-653-2790
MICR: 1408-004
Toronto - Eglinton Sq.
15 Eglinton Sq.
Toronto, ON M1L 2K1 Canada
416-751-8530
MICR: 1440-004
Toronto - Ellesmere Rd.
1900 Ellesmere Rd.
Toronto, ON M1H 2V6 Canada
416-438-2901
Fax: 416-438-6332
MICR: 1790-004
Toronto - Ellesmere Rd.
85 Ellesmere Rd.
Toronto, ON M1R 4B7 Canada
416-441-2041
MICR: 0324-004
Toronto - Evans Ave.
689 Evans Ave.
Toronto, ON M9C 1A2 Canada
416-695-8788
MICR: 0573-004
Toronto - Finch Ave. East
648 Finch Ave. East
Toronto, ON M2K 2E6 Canada
416-225-7791
MICR: 0153-004
Toronto - Finch Ave. West
2574 Finch Ave. West
Toronto, ON M9M 2G3 Canada
416-748-7311
MICR: 1458-004
Toronto - Glencairn Ave.
500 Glencairn Ave.
Toronto, ON M6B 1Z1 Canada
416-785-8711
MICR: 0522-004
Toronto - Hanna Ave.
61 Hanna Ave.
Toronto, ON M6K 3N7 Canada
416-536-2371
MICR: 1637-004
Toronto - Islington Ave.
1048 Islington Ave.
Toronto, ON M8Z 4R6 Canada
416-236-2591
MICR: 0231-004
Toronto - Islington Ave.
1498 Islington Ave.
Toronto, ON M9A 3L7 Canada
416-239-4352
MICR: 0251-004
Toronto - Jane St.
1746 Jane St.
Toronto, ON M9N 2S9 Canada
416-244-1121
MICR: 1472-004
Toronto - Jane St.

The Toronto-Dominion Bank (continued)
2709 Jane St.
Toronto, ON M3L 1S3 Canada
416-748-7317
MICR: 1476-004
Toronto - Keele St.
2390 Keele St.
Toronto, ON M6M 4A5 Canada
416-249-7286
MICR: 1580-004
Toronto - Keele St.
York University
3931 Keele St.
Toronto, ON M3J 1N6 Canada
416-631-7411
MICR: 1480-004
Toronto - King St. West
55 King St. West
Toronto, ON M5K 1A2 Canada
416-982-2322
MICR: 1025-004
Toronto - King St. West
PO Box 1
55 King St. West, 2nd Fl.
Toronto, ON M5K 1A2 Canada
416-982-2322
MICR: 1020-004
Toronto - Kingston Rd.
4411 Kingston Rd.
Toronto, ON M1E 2N3 Canada
416-283-0733
MICR: 0544-004
Toronto - Kingston Rd.
1448 Kingston Rd.
Toronto, ON M1N 1R6 Canada
416-699-9369
MICR: 1536-004
Toronto - Kingston Rd.
3115 Kingston Rd.
Toronto, ON M1M 1P3 Canada
416-264-2585
MICR: 0253-004
Toronto - Kipling Ave.
1735 Kipling Ave.
Toronto, ON M9R 2Y8 Canada
416-247-6251
MICR: 1544-004
Toronto - Kipling Ave.
2038 Kipling Ave.
Toronto, ON M9W 4K1 Canada
416-745-9940
MICR: 1552-004
Toronto - Kipling Ave.
2700 Kipling Ave. North
Toronto, ON M9V 4P2 Canada
416-748-6900
MICR: 1550-004
Toronto - Kipling Ave.
1735 Kipling Ave.
Toronto, ON M9R 2Y8 Canada
416-247-6251
MICR: 1544-004
Toronto - Lake Shore Blvd. West
2814 Lake Shore Blvd. West
Toronto, ON M8V 1H7 Canada
416-259-7645
MICR: 1576-004
Toronto - Lake Shore Blvd. West
3567 Lake Shore Blvd. West
Toronto, ON M8W 1P4 Canada
416-252-1166
MICR: 1560-004
Toronto - Lake Shore Blvd. West
2472 Lake Shore Blvd. West
Toronto, ON M8V 1C9 Canada
416-253-9298
MICR: 0538-004
Toronto - Lapsley Rd.
49 Lapsley Rd.
Toronto, ON M1B 1K1 Canada
416-293-3683
MICR: 1029-004
Toronto - Lawrence Ave. East
939 Lawrence Ave. East
Toronto, ON M3C 1P8 Canada
416-445-6601
MICR: 0241-004
Toronto - Lawrence Ave. East
1846 Lawrence Ave. East
Toronto, ON M1R 2Y4 Canada
416-751-8312
MICR: 0192-004
Toronto - Lawson Rd.
285 Lawson Rd.
Toronto, ON M1C 2J6 Canada
416-283-6828
MICR: 0590-004
Toronto - Leslie St.
5875 Leslie St.
Toronto, ON M2H 1J8 Canada
416-493-5528
MICR: 1590-004
Toronto - Markham Rd.
680 Markham Rd.
Toronto, ON M1H 2A7 Canada
416-439-5534
MICR: 0329-004
Toronto - Marlee Ave.
246 Marlee Ave.
Toronto, ON M6B 3H7 Canada
416-789-2947
MICR: 1592-004
Toronto - McCowan Rd.
697 McCowan Rd.
Toronto, ON M1J 1K2 Canada
416-431-4810
MICR: 1584-004
Toronto - Moore Ave.
321 Moore Ave.
Toronto, ON M4G 3T6 Canada
416-421-2034
MICR: 1595-004
Toronto - Morningside Ave.
255 Morningside Ave.
Toronto, ON M1E 3E6 Canada
416-281-6701
MICR: 1512-004
Toronto - O'Connor Dr.
801 O'Connor Dr.
Toronto, ON M4B 2S7 Canada
416-757-1361
MICR: 0575-004
Toronto - Overlea Blvd.
45 Overlea Blvd.
Toronto, ON M4H 1C3 Canada
416-421-1221
MICR: 1828-004
Toronto - Pape Ave.
991 Pape Ave.
Toronto, ON M4K 3V6 Canada
416-696-9605
MICR: 0540-004
Toronto - Port Union Rd.
271 Port Union Rd.
Toronto, ON M1C 2L3 Canada
416-286-3313
MICR: 1857-004
Toronto - Provost Dr.
50 Provost Dr.
Toronto, ON M2K 2X6 Canada
416-224-2983
MICR: 1929-004
Toronto - Queen St. East
2044 Queen St. East
Toronto, ON M4E 1C9 Canada
416-691-2141
MICR: 0392-004
Toronto - Queen St. East
904 Queen St. East
Toronto, ON M4M 1J3 Canada
416-461-2429
MICR: 1672-004
Toronto - Queen St. East
1809 Queen St. East
Toronto, ON M4L 3Y3 Canada
416-686-3633
MICR: 1660-004
Toronto - Queen St. West
443 Queen St. West
Toronto, ON M5V 2B1 Canada
416-982-2535
Fax: 416-982-6434
MICR: 1704-004
Toronto - Queen St. West
686 Queen St. West
Toronto, ON M6J 1E7 Canada
416-982-8631
MICR: 1636-004
Toronto - Queen St. West
1435 Queen St. West
Toronto, ON M6R 1A1 Canada
416-533-7979
MICR: 1640-004
Toronto - Queensway
742 The Queensway
Toronto, ON M8Y 1H6 Canada
416-253-7227
MICR: 1736-004
Toronto - Queensway
1315 The Queensway
Toronto, ON M8Z 1S8 Canada
416-259-9281
MICR: 1728-004
Toronto - Renforth Dr.
460 Renforth Dr.
Toronto, ON M9C 2N2 Canada
416-621-6243
MICR: 1740-004
Toronto - Rexdale Blvd.
500 Rexdale Blvd.
Toronto, ON M9W 6K5 Canada
416-674-5516
MICR: 0262-004
Toronto - Roncesvalles Ave.
382 Roncesvalles Ave.
Toronto, ON M6R 2M9 Canada
416-536-2300
MICR: 0543-004
Toronto - Royal York Rd.
1440 Royal York Rd.
Toronto, ON M9P 3B1 Canada
416-243-0855
MICR: 0193-004
Toronto - Sandhurst Circle
1571 Sandhurst Circle
Toronto, ON M1V 1V2 Canada
416-298-2320
MICR: 0330-004
Toronto - Sheppard Ave. East
1800 Sheppard Ave. East
Toronto, ON M2J 5A7 Canada
416-493-0020
MICR: 1450-004
Toronto - Sheppard Ave. East
3477 Sheppard Ave. East
Toronto, ON M1T 3K6 Canada
416-291-9566
MICR: 1033-004
Toronto - Sheppard Ave. East
312 Sheppard Ave. East
Toronto, ON M2N 3B4 Canada
416-224-5512
MICR: 0265-004
Toronto - Sheppard Ave. East
#218, 1800 Sheppard Ave. East
Toronto, ON M2J 5A7 Canada
416-491-0567
MICR: 0087-004
Toronto - Sheppard Ave. West
580 Sheppard Ave. West
Toronto, ON M3H 2S1 Canada
416-633-1550
MICR: 1800-004
Toronto - Spadina Rd.
443 Spadina Rd.
Toronto, ON M5P 2W3 Canada
416-322-3708
MICR: 0507-003
Toronto - St. Clair Ave. West
510 St. Clair Ave. West
Toronto, ON M6C 1A2 Canada
416-653-3507
MICR: 1760-004
Toronto - St. Clair Ave. West

870 St. Clair Ave. West
Toronto, ON M6C 1C1 Canada
416-652-5780
MICR: 0571-004

Toronto - St. Clair Ave. West
1347 St. Clair Ave. West
Toronto, ON M6E 1C3 Canada
416-654-6655
MICR: 0658-004

Toronto - St. Clair East
2 St. Clair Ave. East
Toronto, ON M4T 2V4 Canada
416-944-4054
MICR: 1968-004

Toronto - Steeles Ave.
#1, 1881 Steeles Ave.
Toronto, ON M3H 5Y4 Canada
416-736-0222
MICR: 0321-004

Toronto - Steeles Ave. West
4999 Steeles Ave. West
Toronto, ON M9L 1R4 Canada
416-741-4900
MICR: 1459-004

Toronto - Summerhill Ave.
408 Summerhill Ave.
Toronto, ON M4W 2E4 Canada
416-944-6977
MICR: 1087-004

Toronto - The Links Rd.
29 The Links Rd.
Toronto, ON M2P 1T7 Canada
416-226-0484
MICR: 0051-004

Toronto - Underhill Dr.
61 Underhill Dr.
Toronto, ON M3A 2J8 Canada
416-447-6486
MICR: 1292-004

Toronto - University Ave.
465 University Ave.
Toronto, ON M5G 1W8 Canada
416-982-8710
MICR: 1832-004

Toronto - Victoria Park Ave.
2561 Victoria Park Ave.
Toronto, ON M1T 1A4 Canada
416-491-2727
MICR: 1844-004

Toronto - Warden Ave.
2565 Warden Ave.
Toronto, ON M1W 2H5 Canada
416-498-8155
MICR: 0197-004

Toronto - Wellesley St. East
65 Wellesley St. East
Toronto, ON M4Y 1G7 Canada
416-944-4135
MICR: 1220-004

Toronto - Weston Rd.
1979 Weston Rd.
Toronto, ON M9N 1W8 Canada
416-247-8276
MICR: 0335-004

Toronto - Westway
418 The Westway
Toronto, ON M9R 1H6 Canada
416-244-6151
MICR: 0748-004

Toronto - William Kitchen Rd.
26 William Kitchen Rd.
Toronto, ON M1P 5B7 Canada
416-292-2201
MICR: 0327-004

Toronto - Wilson Ave.
1050 Wilson Ave.
Toronto, ON M3K 1G6 Canada
416-633-1060
MICR: 1872-004

Toronto - Wilson Ave.
1601 Wilson Ave.
Toronto, ON M3L 1A5 Canada
416-248-4135
MICR: 1864-004

Toronto - Wincott Dr.
250 Wincott Dr.
Toronto, ON M9R 2R5 Canada
416-241-5248
MICR: 0048-004

Toronto - Yonge St.
110 Yonge St.
Toronto, ON M5C 1T4 Canada
416-869-6262
MICR: 0010-004

Toronto - Yonge St.
5928 Yonge St.
Toronto, ON M2M 3V9 Canada
416-221-3406
MICR: 1924-004

Toronto - Yonge St.
1148 Yonge St.
Toronto, ON M4W 2M1 Canada
416-944-4145
MICR: 1967-004

Toronto - Yonge St.
2263 Yonge St.
Toronto, ON M4P 2C6 Canada
416-932-1500
MICR: 1928-004

Toronto - Yonge St.
3174 Yonge St.
Toronto, ON M4N 2L1 Canada
416-487-5305
MICR: 1952-004

Toronto - Yonge St.
3415 Yonge St.
Toronto, ON M4N 2M8 Canada
416-487-1537
MICR: 1984-004

Toronto - Yonge St.
4841 Yonge St.
Toronto, ON M2N 5X2 Canada
416-223-0030
MICR: 1976-004

Toronto - Yonge St.
5650 Yonge St.
Toronto, ON M2M 4G3 Canada
416-250-5855
MICR: 1970-004

Toronto - Yonge St.
5400 Yonge St.
Toronto, ON M2N 5R5 Canada
416-225-5767
MICR: 0233-004

Toronto - Yonge St.
2453 Yonge St.
Toronto, ON M4P 2H6 Canada
416-481-4435
MICR: 0057-004

Toronto - Yonge St.
1955 Yonge St.
Toronto, ON M4S 1Z6 Canada
416-481-4423
MICR: 0320-004

Toronto - York Mills Rd.
808 York Mills Rd.
Toronto, ON M3B 1X8 Canada
416-445-6171
MICR: 1988-004

Trail
#100, 1199 Bay Ave.
Trail, BC V1R 4A4 Canada
250-368-2551
MICR: 9384-004

Trenton
PO Box 218
8 Dundas St. West
Trenton, ON K8V 5R2 Canada
613-392-9271
MICR: 3768-004

Truro
22 Inglis Pl.
Truro, NS B2N 4B4 Canada
902-893-9423
MICR: 5371-004

Unionville
4681 Hwy. 7
Unionville, ON L3R 1M6 Canada
905-475-9960
MICR: 0339-004

Uxbridge
PO Box 280
1 Brock St. West
Uxbridge, ON L9P 1P6 Canada
905-852-3324
MICR: 3776-004

Val-d'Or
PO Box 970
814, 3e av
Val-d'Or, QC J9P 4P8 Canada
819-825-4123
MICR: 4972-004

Vancouver - 10th Ave. West
4597 - 10th Ave. West
Vancouver, BC V6R 2J2 Canada
604-224-6388
MICR: 0751-004

Vancouver - Broadway East
2396 Broadway East
Vancouver, BC V5N 1X1 Canada
604-654-3980
MICR: 9692-004

Vancouver - Broadway West
805 Broadway West
Vancouver, BC V5Z 1K1 Canada
604-874-2122
MICR: 0568-004

Vancouver - Broadway West
3396 Broadway West
Vancouver, BC V6R 2B2 Canada
604-731-3123
MICR: 0269-004

Vancouver - Burrard St.
1200 Burrard St.
Vancouver, BC V6Z 2C7 Canada
604-654-3572
MICR: 9448-004

Vancouver - Cambie St.
3401 Cambie St.
Vancouver, BC V5Z 2W7 Canada
604-654-3135
MICR: 9456-004

Vancouver - Davie St.
1690 Davie St.
Vancouver, BC V6G 1V9 Canada
604-683-5644
MICR: 0060-004

Vancouver - Dunbar Ave.
4200 Dunbar Ave.
Vancouver, BC V6S 2E9 Canada
604-654-6888
MICR: 9835-004

Vancouver - Dunsmuir St.
1055 Dunsmuir St.
Vancouver, BC V7X 1P3 Canada
604-659-2070
MICR: 0216-004

Vancouver - East Hastings St.
2497 East Hastings St.
Vancouver, BC V5K 1Y8 Canada
604-654-3990
MICR: 9544-004

Vancouver - Fraser St.
3245 Fraser St.
Vancouver, BC V5V 4B8 Canada
604-654-8640
MICR: 9466-004

Vancouver - Fraser St.
6499 Fraser St.
Vancouver, BC V5W 3A6 Canada
604-327-4366
MICR: 0566-004

Vancouver - Granville St.
2801 Granville St.
Vancouver, BC V6H 3J2 Canada
604-654-3775
MICR: 9520-004

Vancouver - Granville St.
8005 Granville St.
Vancouver, BC V6P 4Z5 Canada
604-257-7830
MICR: 9697-004

Vancouver - Hamilton St.
1001 Hamilton St.
Vancouver, BC V6B 5T4 Canada

The Toronto-Dominion Bank (continued)
605-482-2780
MICR: 9651-004
Vancouver - Kingsway
3363 Kingsway
Vancouver, BC V5R 5K6 Canada
604-654-3975
MICR: 9624-004
Vancouver - Kingsway
1995 Kingsway
Vancouver, BC V5N 2T1 Canada
604-879-5045
MICR: 0556-004
Vancouver - Main St.
450 Main St.
Vancouver, BC V6A 2T4 Canada
604-682-6701
MICR: 0044-004
Vancouver - West 41st Ave.
511 West 41st Ave.
Vancouver, BC V5Z 2M7 Canada
604-267-7675
MICR: 0034-004
Vancouver - West 41st Ave.
2198 West 41st Ave.
Vancouver, BC V6M 1Z1 Canada
604-261-1301
MICR: 0047-004
Vancouver - West Georgia St.
700 West Georgia St.
Vancouver, BC V7Y 1A2 Canada
604-654-3665
MICR: 9400-004
Vancouver - West King Edward Ave.
900 West King Edward Ave.
Vancouver, BC V5Z 2E2 Canada
604-654-3720
MICR: 9608-004
Vaudreuil-Dorion - Cite des Jeunes
40, boul Cité des Jeunes
Vaudreuil-Dorion, QC J7V 9L5 Canada
450-424-1124
MICR: 4823-004
Vaughan - Major Mackenzie Dr.
Bldg. D
3737 Major Mackenzie Dr.
Vaughan, ON L4H 0A2 Canada
905-417-5054
MICR: 3026-004
Vaughan - Rutherford Rd.
5100 Rutherford Rd.
Vaughan, ON L4H 2J2 Canada
905-893-2811
MICR: 1891-004
Vaughan - Rutherford Rd.
Bldg. B
3255 Rutherford Rd.
Vaughan, ON L4K 5Y5 Canada
905-761-5390
MICR: 3022-004
Vaughan - Steeles Ave. West
#100, 2300 Steeles Ave. West
Vaughan, ON L4K 5X6 Canada
905-660-6068
MICR: 1482-004
Vegreville
5033 - 50 St.
Vegreville, AB T9C 1R6 Canada
780-632-2891
MICR: 8976-004
Vermilion
5002 - 50th Ave.
Vermilion, AB T9X 1A2 Canada
780-853-5327
MICR: 8984-004
Vernon - 32nd St.
3300 - 32nd St.
Vernon, BC V1T 5M8 Canada
250-260-5725
MICR: 9880-004
Vernon - Anderson Way
5000 Anderson Way
Vernon, BC V1T 9V2 Canada
250-550-1250
MICR: 9886-004
Victoria - Blanshard St.
3530 Blanshard St.
Victoria, BC V8X 1W3 Canada
250-356-4121
MICR: 9956-004
Victoria - Cadboro Bay Rd.
2000 Cadboro Bay Rd.
Victoria, BC V8R 5G5 Canada
250-592-8111
MICR: 0259-004
Victoria - Douglas St.
1080 Douglas St.
Victoria, BC V8W 2C3 Canada
250-356-4018
MICR: 9900-004
Victoria - Fairfield Rd.
1568 Fairfield Rd.
Victoria, BC V8S 1G1 Canada
250-953-6033
MICR: 9984-004
Victoria - Jacklin Rd.
#136, 2945 Jacklin Rd.
Victoria, BC V9B 5E3 Canada
250-391-3450
MICR: 9915-004
Victoria - Oak Bay Ave.
#107, 2187 Oak Bay Ave.
Victoria, BC V8R 1G1 Canada
250-953-6044
MICR: 9992-004
Victoria - Quadra St.
4000 Quadra St.
Victoria, BC V8X 1K2 Canada
250-953-6011
MICR: 9986-004
Victoria - Royal Oak Dr.
811 Royal Oak Dr.
Victoria, BC V8X 3T3 Canada
250-727-2232
MICR: 0753-004
Victoria - Shelbourne St.
3675 Shelbourne St.
Victoria, BC V8P 4H1 Canada
250-405-5260
MICR: 0287-004
Victoria - Wilson St.
#100, 184 Wilson St.
Victoria, BC V9A 7N6 Canada
250-405-6100
MICR: 9919-004
Walkerton
PO Box 878
1304 Yonge St.
Walkerton, ON N0G 2V0 Canada
519-881-0160
MICR: 3780-004
Wallaceburg
#1 Thunderbird Plaza
RR#3
Wallaceburg, ON N8A 4K9 Canada
519-627-1657
MICR: 3739-004
Wallaceburg - James St.
PO Box 100
402 James St.
Wallaceburg, ON N8A 4L5 Canada
519-627-1681
MICR: 3792-004
Wasaga Beach - 45th St. South
30 - 45th St. South
Wasaga Beach, ON L9Z 0A6 Canada
705-429-5322
MICR: 3807-004
Wasaga Beach - Mosley St.
862 Mosley St.
Wasaga Beach, ON L9Z 2H2 Canada
705-429-6166
MICR: 3804-004
Waterdown
PO Box 82100
255 Dundas St. East
Waterdown, ON L0R 2M0 Canada
905-689-8772
MICR: 3810-004
Waterloo - Columbia St. West
450 Columbia St. West
Waterloo, ON N2T 2W1 Canada
519-883-4701
MICR: 3659-004
Waterloo - Erb St. West
460 Erb St. West
Waterloo, ON N2T 1N5 Canada
519-885-8586
MICR: 0270-004
Waterloo - King St. North
550 King St. North
Waterloo, ON N2L 5W6 Canada
519-885-8485
MICR: 0163-004
Waterloo - King St. South
15 King St. South
Waterloo, ON N2J 1N9 Canada
519-725-3630
MICR: 3814-004
Waterloo - University Ave. East
68 University Ave. East
Waterloo, ON N2J 2V8 Canada
519-746-6933
Fax: 519-746-2701
MICR: 3822-004
Waterloo - Weber St. North
576 Weber St. North
Waterloo, ON N2L 5C6 Canada
519-884-4710
MICR: 3823-004
Waterloo - Westmount Rd. North
50 Westmount Rd. North
Waterloo, ON N2L 2R5 Canada
519-885-8550
MICR: 0085-004
Welland - Main St. East
144 Main St. East
Welland, ON L3B 3W6 Canada
905-735-0120
MICR: 0129-004
Welland - Niagara St. North
845 Niagara St. North
Welland, ON L3C 1M4 Canada
905-732-2461
MICR: 3824-004
West Vancouver - Marine Dr.
1645 Marine Dr.
West Vancouver, BC V7V 1J2 Canada
604-981-5680
MICR: 9664-004
West Vancouver - Park Royal North
632 Park Royal North
West Vancouver, BC V7T 1H9 Canada
604-926-5484
MICR: 0086-004
Westbank
#501, 2330 Hwy. 97
Westbank, BC V4T 2P3 Canada
250-768-6500
MICR: 9151-004
Westlock
Site #1, 10227 - 96 St.
Westlock, AB T7P 2R3 Canada
780-349-4441
MICR: 8994-004
Wetaskiwin
5002 - 50th Ave.
Wetaskiwin, AB T9A 0S4 Canada
780-361-5200
Fax: 780-361-5205
MICR: 8996-004
Weyburn
PO Box 280
101 - 2nd St.
Weyburn, SK S0K 0T7 Canada
306-842-7414
MICR: 7890-004
Whistler
#138, 4370 Lorimer Rd.
Whistler, BC V0N 1B4 Canada
604-905-5500
MICR: 9987-004
Whitby - Dundas St. West
404 Dundas St. West
Whitby, ON L1N 2M7 Canada

905-665-1800
MICR: 3843-004
Whitby - Garden St.
3050 Garden St.
Whitby, ON L1R 2G7 Canada
905-430-0983
MICR: 3745-004
Whitby - Taunton Rd. West
110 Taunton Rd. West
Whitby, ON L1R 3H8 Canada
905-655-6627
MICR: 3849-004
Whitby - Thickson Rd. South
80 Thickson Rd. South
Whitby, ON L1N 7T2 Canada
905-666-9933
MICR: 0273-004
White Rock
15110 North Bluff Rd.
White Rock, BC V4B 3E5 Canada
604-541-7100
MICR: 9993-004
Whitehorse
200 Main St.
Whitehorse, YT Y1A 2A9 Canada
403-668-8100
MICR: 9996-004
Wiarton
PO Box 790
585 Berford St.
Wiarton, ON N0H 2T0 Canada
519-534-2100
MICR: 3846-004
Williams Lake
101 - 2nd Ave. North
Williams Lake, BC V2G 1Z5 Canada
250-305-2975
MICR: 9994-004
Windsor - Dougall Ave.
3281 Dougall Ave.
Windsor, ON N9E 1S8 Canada
519-972-9555
MICR: 3884-004
Windsor - Grand Marais Rd. West
1550 Grand Marais Rd. West
Windsor, ON N9E 4L1 Canada
519-972-1991
MICR: 0378-004
Windsor - Howard Ave.
3100 Howard Ave.
Windsor, ON N8X 3Y8 Canada
519-969-0182
MICR: 0084-004
Windsor - Malden Rd.
5990 Malden Rd.
Windsor, ON N9H 1S8 Canada
519-250-1446
MICR: 0125-004
Windsor - Ottawa St.
1407 Ottawa St.
Windsor, ON N8X 2G1 Canada
519-256-6363
MICR: 0524-004
Windsor - Ouellette Ave.
PO Box 39
596 Ouellette Ave.
Windsor, ON N9A 6J8 Canada
519-973-7770
MICR: 3880-004
Windsor - Tecumseh Blvd.
189 Tecumseh Blvd.
Windsor, ON N8X 1E8 Canada
519-253-4623
MICR: 3888-004
Windsor - Tecumseh Rd. East
7404 Tecumseh Rd. East
Windsor, ON N8T 1E9 Canada
519-944-8822
MICR: 3864-004
Windsor - Tecumseh Rd. East
3900 Tecumseh Rd. East
Windsor, ON N8W 1J3 Canada
519-944-1300
MICR: 3896-004
Windsor - Tecumseh Rd. East
13300 Tecumseh Rd. East
Windsor, ON N8N 4R8 Canada
519-735-0010
MICR: 0505-004
Windsor - Victoria Ave.
305 Victoria Ave.
Windsor, ON N9A 4M7 Canada
519-252-4434
MICR: 3890-004
Windsor - Wyandotte St. East
5790 Wyandotte St. East
Windsor, ON N8S 1M5 Canada
519-944-4355
MICR: 0514-004
Windsor - Wyandotte St. West
2110 Wyandotte St. West
Windsor, ON N9B 1J9 Canada
519-253-0033
MICR: 3904-004
Wingham
PO Box 420
228 Josephine St.
Wingham, ON N0G 2W0 Canada
519-357-2770
MICR: 3936-004
Winnipeg - Broadway
360 Broadway
Winnipeg, MB R3C 0T6 Canada
204-988-1380
MICR: 6201-004
Winnipeg - Corydon Ave.
1460 Corydon Ave.
Winnipeg, MB R3N 0J5 Canada
204-988-2265
MICR: 6460-004
Winnipeg - Corydon Ave.
1114 Corydon Ave.
Winnipeg, MB R3M 0Y9 Canada
204-985-4400
MICR: 0501-004
Winnipeg - Corydon Ave.
2030 Corydon Ave.
Winnipeg, MB R3P 0N2 Canada
204-985-4620
MICR: 0512-004
Winnipeg - Henderson Hwy.
#10, 1128 Henderson Hwy.
Winnipeg, MB R2G 3Z7 Canada
204-985-4550
MICR: 0379-004
Winnipeg - Keewatin St.
850 Keewatin St.
Winnipeg, MB R2R 0Z5 Canada
204-988-2481
MICR: 6974-004
Winnipeg - Kenaston Blvd.
1723 Kenaston Blvd.
Winnipeg, MB R3Y 1V5 Canada
204-988-2951
MICR: 6641-004
Winnipeg - McPhillips
#7, 1375 McPhillips
Winnipeg, MB R2V 3V1 Canada
204-985-4560
MICR: 0399-004
Winnipeg - McPhillips St.
2305 McPhillips St.
Winnipeg, MB R2V 3E1 Canada
204-988-2457
MICR: 6508-004
Winnipeg - Notre Dame Ave.
648 Notre Dame Ave.
Winnipeg, MB R3B 1S9 Canada
204-988-2983
MICR: 6620-004
Winnipeg - Osborne St.
120 Osborne St.
Winnipeg, MB R3L 1Y5 Canada
204-988-2947
MICR: 6780-004
Winnipeg - Pembina Hwy.
1305 Pembina Hwy.
Winnipeg, MB R3T 2B6 Canada
204-988-2446
MICR: 6644-004
Winnipeg - Pembina Hwy.
2799 Pembina Hwy.
Winnipeg, MB R3T 2H5 Canada
204-988-2446
MICR: 6546-004
Winnipeg - Portage Ave.
3260 Portage Ave.
Winnipeg, MB R3K 0Z1 Canada
204-988-2402
MICR: 6980-004
Winnipeg - Portage Ave.
PO Box 896
201 Portage Ave.
Winnipeg, MB R3C 2T2 Canada
204-988-2811
MICR: 6330-004
Winnipeg - Regent Ave.
#800, 1615 Regent Ave.
Winnipeg, MB R2C 5C6 Canada
204-988-2700
MICR: 6548-004
Winnipeg - Regent Ave. West
200 Regent Ave. West
Winnipeg, MB R2C 1R2 Canada
204-988-2465
MICR: 6972-004
Winnipeg - Roblin Blvd.
6650 Roblin Blvd.
Winnipeg, MB R3R 1X1 Canada
204-988-2605
MICR: 6634-004
Winnipeg - St Mary's Rd.
1631 St. Mary's Rd., #A
Winnipeg, MB R2N 1Z4 Canada
204-988-2630
MICR: 6977-004
Winnipeg - St. Anne's Rd.
270 St. Anne's Rd.
Winnipeg, MB R2M 3A4 Canada
204-988-2600
MICR: 6612-004
Winnipeg - St. Mary Ave.
444 St. Mary Ave.
Winnipeg, MB R3C 3T1 Canada
204-988-2846
MICR: 6792-004
Wolseley
602 Front St.
Wolseley, SK S0G 5H0 Canada
306-698-2501
MICR: 7912-004
Woodbridge - Hwy. 7
4499 Hwy. 7
Woodbridge, ON L4L 9A9 Canada
905-851-5556
Fax: 905-851-2153
MICR: 1890-004
Woodbridge - Martin Grove Rd.
7766 Martin Grove Rd.
Woodbridge, ON L4L 2C7 Canada
905-851-3975
MICR: 1885-004
Woodbridge - Weston Rd.
9200 Weston Rd.
Woodbridge, ON L4H 2P8 Canada
905-832-8872
MICR: 1898-004
Woodbridge - Woodbridge Ave.
124 Woodbridge Ave.
Woodbridge, ON L4L 2S7 Canada
905-851-8581
MICR: 1887-004
Woodstock - Dundas St.
400 Dundas St.
Woodstock, ON N4S 1B9 Canada
519-539-4886
MICR: 0227-004
Woodstock - Dundas St.
539 Dundas St.
Woodstock, ON N4S 1C6 Canada
519-539-2003
MICR: 0309-004
Woodstock - Main St.
685 Main St.
Woodstock, NB E7M 2E1 Canada

The Toronto-Dominion Bank (continued)

506-328-8847
MICR: 4854-004

Wyoming
PO Box 160
596 Broadway St.
Wyoming, ON N0N 1T0 Canada
519-845-3379
MICR: 3952-004

Yarmouth
PO Box 218
360 Main St.
Yarmouth, NS B5A 4B2 Canada
902-742-3561
MICR: 5490-004

Yellowknife
Yukon Centre
#18, 4910 - 50th Ave.
Yellowknife, NT X1A 3S5 Canada
867-873-5891
MICR: 8998-004

Yorkton
63 Broadway St. East
Yorkton, SK S3N 0K6 Canada
306-786-4800
MICR: 7944-004

Commercial Banking Centres:

Abbotsford
32817 South Fraser Way
Abbotsford, BC V2S 2A6 Canada
604-872-2207

Barrie
50 Dunlop St. East
Barrie, ON L4M 4T3 Canada
705-727-7425

Brampton
8125 Dixie Rd.
Brampton, ON L6T 2J9 Canada
905-793-6666

Brantford
70 Market St., 2nd Fl.
Brantford, ON N9T 2Z7 Canada
519-759-4020

Burlington
5515 North Service Rd.
Burlington, ON L7L 5H7 Canada
905-336-6644

Burnaby
1933 Willingdon Ave.
Burnaby, BC V5C 5J3 Canada
604-654-3026

Calgary
Calgary Place, Tower 2
355 - 4th Ave. SW, 4th Fl.
Calgary, AB T2P 1H9 Canada
403-292-1101

Cambridge
1165 Franklin Blvd., #H
Cambridge, ON N1R 8E1 Canada
519-621-4167

Charlottetown
101 Kent St.
Charlottetown, PE C1A 1N3 Canada
902-629-2254

Collingwood
104 Hurontario St.
Collingwood, ON L9Y 2L8 Canada
705-445-5247

Edmonton
#2601 TD Tower
10088 - 102nd Ave.
Edmonton, AB T5J 2Z1 Canada
780-448-8156

Guelph
55 Cork St. East, 2nd Fl.
Guelph, ON N1H 2W7 Canada
519-822-7030

Halifax
1785 Barrington St.
Halifax, NS B3J 2P8 Canada
902-420-8060

Hamilton
Jackson Sq.
100 King St. West
Hamilton, ON L8P 1A2 Canada
905-521-6519

Huntsville
38 Main St. East
Huntsville, ON P1H 2C8 Canada
705-78 -434

Kamloops
#102, 301 Victoria St.
Kamloops, BC V2C 2A3 Canada
250-314-5053

Kelowna
#310, 1633 Ellis St.
Kelowna, BC V1Y 2A8 Canada
250-470-3050

Kingston
94 Princess St., 3rd Fl.
Kingston, ON K7L 4X1 Canada
613-227-2323

Kitchener
381 King St. West
Kitchener, ON N2G 1B8 Canada
519-579-2168

London
Canada Trust Tower
275 Dundas St., 9th Fl., Tower A
London, ON N6B 3L1 Canada
519-675-4155

Midland
283 King St.
Midland, ON L4R 4K8 Canada
705-526-5475

Mississauga - Milverton Dr.
20 Milverton Dr.
Mississauga, ON L5R 3G2 Canada
905-890-4177

Mississauga - Milverton Dr. - Real Estate
20 Milverton Dr.
Mississauga, ON L5R 3G2 Canada
905-890-4177

Moncton
1199 Main St.
Moncton, NB E1C 1H9 Canada
506-853-4366

Montréal
#200, 999, boul de Maisonneuve ouest
Montréal, QC H3A 3L4 Canada
514-289-8316

Nanaimo
#1, 1150 North Terminal
Nanaimo, BC V9S 5L6 Canada
250-716-2629

Newmarket
16655 Yonge St.
Newmarket, ON L3X 1V6 Canada
905-836-1570

North Bay
133 Main St. West
North Bay, ON P1B T26 Canada
705-472-4370

Oshawa
2 King St. East, 2nd Fl.
Oshawa, ON L1H 7L3 Canada
905-576-6264

Ottawa
World Exchange Tower
#240, 45 O'Connor St.
Ottawa, ON K1P 1A4 Canada
613-783-6104

Owen Sound
901 - 2nd Ave. East
Owen Sound, ON N4K 2H5 Canada
519-376-6510

Peterborough
340 George St. North
Peterborough, ON K9H 7E8 Canada
705-745-5722

Prince George
400 Victoria St., 3rd Fl.
Prince George, BC V2L 2J7 Canada
250-614-2985

Regina
1904 Hamilton St., 2nd Fl.
Regina, SK S4P 3N5 Canada
306-780-0228

Richmond Hill - Hwy. 7 East
500 Hwy. 7 East, 3rd Fl.
Richmond Hill, ON L4B 1J1 Canada
905-771-2297

Richmond Hill - Hwy. 7 East - Beaver Creek Real Estate
500 Hwy. 7, East, 3rd Fl.
Richmond Hill, ON L4B 1J1 Canada
905-771-2313

Saint John
#200, 44 Chipman Hill
Saint John, NB E2L 2A9 Canada
506-634-1870

Sarnia
1210 London Rd.
Sarnia, ON N7S 1P4 Canada
519-383-7287

Saskatoon
170 - 2nd Ave., 3rd Fl.
Saskatoon, SK S7K 1K5 Canada
306-975-7223

Sault Ste Marie
421 Bay St.
Sault Ste Marie, ON P6A 1X3 Canada
705-254-6424

St Catharines
40 Queen St.
St Catharines, ON L2R 6V9 Canada
905-685-7644

St. John's
140 Water St., 2nd Fl.
St. John's, NL A1C 6H6 Canada
709-758-5125

Stratford
42 Downie St.
Stratford, ON N5A 6T1 Canada
519-572-8266

Sudbury
Commerce Court
43 Elm St.
Sudbury, ON P3E 4P8 Canada
705-669-4030

Surrey
10435 King George VI Hwy.
Surrey, BC V3T 4X1 Canada
604-586-2010

Thunder Bay
1039 Memorial Ave.
Thunder Bay, ON P7B 4A4 Canada
807-626-1570

Toronto - Don Mills Rd.
1470 Don Mills Rd., 3rd Fl.
Toronto, ON M3B 2X9 Canada
416-445-6442

Toronto - King St. West - Toronto Commercial Centre
TD Tower
55 King St. West, 3rd Fl.
Toronto, ON M5K 1A2 Canada
416-982-8521

Toronto - Queensway
1315 The Queensway
Toronto, ON M8Z 1S8 Canada
416-259-9281

Toronto - Rexdale Blvd.
140 Rexdale Blvd.
Toronto, ON M9W 1P6 Canada
416-474-2422

Toronto - Sheppard Ave. East
3477 Sheppard Ave. East
Toronto, ON M1T 3K6 Canada
416-291-8737

Toronto - St. Clair Ave. East
2 St. Clair Ave. East
Toronto, ON M4T 2V4 Canada
416-944-4044

Toronto - Wellington St. West - Commercial National Accounts
CP Tower
100 Wellington St. West, 26th Fl.
Toronto, ON M5K 1A2 Canada
888-339-6673

Vancouver - West Georgia St.
Pacific Centre
700 West Georgia St.
Vancouver, BC V7Y 1A2 Canada
604-654-3503

Vancouver - West Georgia St. - BC Real Estate

Pacific Centre
700 West Georgia St.
Vancouver, BC V7Y 1A2 Canada
604-654-4745
Vaughan
200, 2300 Steeles Ave. West
Vaughan, ON L4K 5X6 Canada
905-660-5915
Victoria
#440, 1070 Douglas St.
Victoria, BC V8W 2C4 Canada
250-356-4010
Windsor
#400, 4250 Rhodes Dr.
Windsor, ON N8W 5C2 Canada
519-945-2411

Winnipeg
201 Portage Ave.
Winnipeg, MB R3C 2T2 Canada
204-988-2538
Woodbridge
4499 Hwy. 7
Woodbridge, ON L4L 9A9 Canada
905-264-6720

Ubiquity Bank of Canada

Also listed under: *Financing & Loan Companies*
#303, 32071 South Fraser Way
Abbotsford, BC V2T 1W3
888-881-0188
contact@ubiquitybank.ca
www.ubiquitybank.ca
Ownership: Private.
Year Founded: 2004
Assets: $100-500 million Year End: 20061031
Revenues: Under $1 million Year End: 20061031
Executives:
Bruce Howell, President/CEO, CFO
Peter J. Wright, Exec. Vice-President/COO
Roger Payer, General Manager & Corporate Secretary; 604-557-5000; rpayer@ubiquitybank.ca
Directors:
Maurice Mourton, Chair
John Allen, Vice-Chair
Geoffrey Thompson, 2nd Vice-Chair
Trevor Hildebrand
Bruce Howell
Karen Laing
Karl Noordam
William Rogers
Tim Spiegel
Peter J. Wright

Foreign Banks: Schedule II

Amex Bank of Canada

Also listed under: *Credit Card Companies*
101 McNabb St.
Markham, ON L3R 4H8
800-668-2639
Other Information: TTY/TDD: 1-866-549-6426
www.americanexpress.com/canada
Ownership: Wholly-owned subsidiary of American Express Travel Related Services Company, Inc., New York, USA.
Year Founded: 1853
Number of Employees: 3,700
Profile: Amex Bank of Canada & Amex Canada Inc. are the operating names for American Express in Canada. The Bank issues American Express cards in Canada, while Amex Canada Inc. operates the corporate travel, travel services network & travellers cheque divisions in Canada.

Executives:
Beth Horowitz, President/CEO
Francisco Da Rocha Campos (Xiko), Vice-President, Consumer & Small Business Products

Bank of China (Canada)

The Exchange Tower
PO Box 356
#2730, 130 King St. West
Toronto, ON M5X 1E1
416-362-2991
Fax: 416-362-3047
Ownership: Wholly owned subsidiary of the Bank of China Limited, Beijing, China.
Year Founded: 1992
Number of Employees: 85
Assets: $100-500 million Year End: 20051231
Revenues: $10-50 million Year End: 20051231
Profile: The following services are offered: trade services; personal banking; commercial banking; Canada-China business banking; & global remittance services.

Executives:
Dashu Zhu, President/CEO
Fei Lu, Exec. Vice-President
Albert Shum, Exec. Vice-President
Branches:
Toronto - Dundas St. West
396 Dundas St. West
Toronto, ON M5T 1G7 Canada
416-971-8806
Chunhua Gu, Branch Contact
Toronto - Midland Ave.
#33, 3300 Midland Ave.
Toronto, ON M1V 4A1 Canada
416-297-7921
Queenie Leung, Branch Contact
Vancouver
Four Bentall Centre
1025 Dunsmuir St.
Vancouver, BC V7X 1L3 Canada
604-683-1088
Jijun Zhang, Branch Contact

The Bank of East Asia (Canada)

East Asia Centre
#102-103, 350 Hwy. 7 East
Richmond Hill, ON L4B 3N2
905-882-8182
Fax: 905-882-5220
Other Information: (852) 3608 0200 (Phone, Overseas Branch Operations & Development Department in Hong Kong)
info@hkbea.com, OsEnquiry@hkbea.com
www.hkbea.com
Ownership: Private. Member of The Bank of East Asia Group, Hong Kong.
Year Founded: 1991
Profile: Full retail banking services are provided.

Executives:
Cedric Ng Chun-ki, General Manager
Affiliated Companies:
East Asia Securities Inc.
Branches:
Markham
Pacific Mall
#88B, 4300 Steeles Ave. East
Markham, ON L3R 0Y5 Canada
905-940-2218
Fax: 905-940-3030
Clarence Cho Ying-kwong, Branch Manager
Mississauga
#GR05, 25 Watline Ave.
Mississauga, ON L4Z 2Z1 Canada
905-890-2388
Fax: 905-890-8800
Michael Leung Kit-ming, Branch Manager
Richmond Hill
East Asia Centre
#102-103, 350 Hwy. 7 East
Richmond Hill, ON L4B 3N2 Canada
905-882-8182
Fax: 905-882-5220
Perry So Tsze-kwan, Branch Manager
Toronto
Dynasty Centre
#38, 8 Glen Watford Dr.
Toronto, ON M1S 2B9 Canada
416-298-6883
Fax: 416-298-6880
Jack Chan Kuok-meng, Branch Manager
Vancouver - Cambie St.
3396 Cambie St.
Vancouver, BC V5Z 2W5
604-709-9668
Fax: 604-709-9660
Vancouver - No. 3 Rd.
6740 No. 3 Rd.
Richmond, BC V6Y 2C2 Canada
604-278-9668
Fax: 604-276-8606
Peter Choi Ping-chung, Branch Manager

Bank of Tokyo-Mitsubishi UFJ (Canada)

#1700, South Tower, Royal Bank Plaza
PO Box 42
Toronto, ON M5J 2J1
416-865-0220
Fax: 416-865-0196
www.bk.mufg.jp/english
Ownership: Foreign. Part of The Bank of Tokyo-Mitsubishi UFJ, Ltd., Tokyo,Japan.
Year Founded: 1996
Profile: The Bank of Tokyo-Mitsubishi & UFJ Bank integrated in 2006 to become Bank of Tokyo-Mitsubishi UFJ (Canada).

Executives:
Yoshio Furuhashi, President/CEO
Branches:
Montréal
Tour de la Banque Nationale
#2780, 600, rue de la Gauchetière ouest
Montréal, QC H3B 4L8 Canada
514-875-9261
Fax: 514-875-9392
Vancouver
Park Place
#950, 666 Burrard St.
Vancouver, BC V6C 3L1 Canada
604-691-7300
Fax: 604-689-8990
Yukio Tagawa, Exec. Vice-President & General Manager

BNP Paribas (Canada)

1981, av McGill College
Montréal, QC H3A 2W8
514-285-6000
Fax: 514-285-6278
bnp.canada@americas.bnpparibas.com
www.bnpparibas.ca
Former Name: Banque Nationale de Paris (Canada)
Ownership: Foreign. Wholly owned subsidiary of BNP Paribas, Paris, France
Year Founded: 1961
Number of Employees: 240
Assets: $2,590,052,000
Profile: In Canada since 1961, BNP Paribas provides specialized financial services, derivatives & investment products. Clients include medium & large sized companies with local & international activities.

Executives:
Edward N. Speal, President/CEO
Eric Vigne, Sr. Vice-President & General Secretary
Marise Chenier-Jetté, Vice-President, Manager, Legal Department
Jamie Goodall, Managing Director
Daniel Grenier, Managing Director, Capital Markets
Frédéric Mayrand, Director & Head, Foreign Exchange Sales
Yves Pichette, Director & Head, Interest Rate Derivatives Sales
Branches:
Québec
#350, 925 ch Saint-Louis
Québec, QC G1S 1C1 Canada
418-684-7575
MICR: 00025-250
Bernard Kennepohl, Manager
Toronto
Royal Trust Tower, TD Centre
PO Box 31
#4100, 77 King St. West
Toronto, ON M5K 1N8 Canada
416-360-8040
Fax: 416-947-3541
MICR: 00032-250
Vancouver
Three Bentall Centre
PO Box 49334
#1733, 595 Burrard St.
Vancouver, BC V7X 1L4 Canada
604-688-2212
Fax: 604-688-4613
MICR: 00040-250

Citibank Canada

Citigroup Place
#1100, 123 Front St. West
Toronto, ON M5J 2M3
416-947-5500
Fax: 416-947-5387
www.citibank.com/canada
Ownership: Wholly owned indirect subsidiary of Citibank, N.A.
Year Founded: 1982
Number of Employees: 5,000+
Profile: Citibank is a Schedule II bank which serves consumer & corporate customers. The bank offers corporate & investment banking, private banking, retail banking, consumer finance, investment, leasing & credit cards. It is a member of Citigroup.

Executives:
Martin Johansson, Chair/CEO
Stephen Stobie, Chief Financial Officer
Christine Discola, Vice-President, Human Resources
Offices:
Calgary - Family Maintenance Support Orders & Support Provisions
Canterra Tower
#4301, 400 - 3rd Ave. SW
Calgary, AB T2P 4H2
Montréal - Family Maintenance Support Orders & Support Provisions
#2450, 630, boul René-Lévesque ouest
Montréal, QC H3B 1S6
Toronto - Commercial Cards
PO Box 4099, A Sta. A
Toronto, ON M5C 2V6 Canada
416-369-6399
Fax: 416-369-4878
888-834-2484
Toronto - Credit Cards
PO Box 4087, A Sta. A
Toronto, ON M5W 2R6 Canada
416-947-2900
Fax: 416-369-4863
800-387-1616
www.kidsfutures.ca, www.petro-points.com
Toronto - Front St. - CitiPhone Banking Centre
Citigroup Place
#1700, 123 Front St.
Toronto, ON M5W 2M3 Canada
416-947-4100
Fax: 416-947-5498
800-387-9292
Toronto - Front St. - Family Maintenance Support Orders & Support Provisions
Citigroup Place
#1700, 123 Front St. West
Toronto, ON M5J 2M3
Vancouver - Family Maintenance Support Orders & Support Provisions
Bentall 5
#1228, 550 Burrard St.
Vancouver, BC V6C 2B5

CTC Bank of Canada(CTCB)

1518 West Broadway
Vancouver, BC V6J 1W8
604-683-3882
Fax: 604-683-3723
service@ctcbank.com
www.ctcbank.com
Ownership: Private. Part of Chinatrust Commercial Bank.
Profile: Part of the Taiwanese bank, CTCB Canada offers a full range of financial services.

Executives:
Joseph Chou, Canadian Contact
Branches:
Richmond
#120, 8191 Westminster Hwy.
Richmond, BC V6X 1A7
604-233-1261
Fax: 604-273-1251

Habib Canadian Bank

#1B, 918 Dundas St. East
Mississauga, ON L4Y 4H9
905-276-5300
Fax: 905-276-5400
habibcanadian@on.aibn.com
www.habibcanadian.com
Ownership: Private. Foreign. Wholly owned by Habib Bank of AG Zurich, Switzerland.
Year Founded: 1967
Assets: $50-100 million
Revenues: $1-5 million
Profile: A wholly owned subsidiary of Habib Bank AG Zurich, the bank provides a comprehensive range of commercial and personal banking services. Products are designed to cover the needs of all its customers, from small savers to the larger international corporations.

Executives:
Muslim Hassan, CEO; 905-276-5300
Robert Budd, CFO, Zonal Compliance; 905-276-5300
Adil Mavalwala, Chief Manager, Trade Finance Dept.; 905-276-5300

HSBC Bank Canada

#300, 885 West Georgia St.
Vancouver, BC V6C 3E9
604-525-4722
Fax: 604-641-1849
888-310-4722
info@hsbc.ca
www.hsbc.ca
Ownership: Subsidiary of HSBC Holdings plc, London, UK.
Year Founded: 1981
Assets: $10-100 billion
Stock Symbol: HSB.PR.A; HSB.PR.C
Profile: HSBC Bank Canada is a major international bank in Canada. The member of the HSBC Group is a full-service financial services provider.

Executives:
Lindsay Gordon, President/CEO
Graham McIsaac, Chief Financial Officer
Sean O'Sullivan, Chief Operating Officer
Jeff Dowle, Exec. Vice-President
Jon Hountalas, Exec. Vice-President, Commercial Banking
Jim Mahaffy, Exec. Vice-President, Corporate & Institutional Banking
Brad Meredith, Exec. Vice-President, Corporate Investment Banking & Markets
Tracy Redies, Exec. Vice-President, Personal Financial Services

Directors:
Martin Glynn, Chair
James Cleave, Vice-Chair
Peter Eng
Lindsay Gordon
Nancy Hughes Anthony
Robert Martin
Samuel Minzberg
Ross Smith
Affiliated Companies:
HSBC Capital (Canada) Inc.
HSBC Investments (Canada) Limited
HSBC Securities Canada Inc.
HSBC Trust Company (Canada)
Branches:
Abbotsford
32412 South Fraser Way
Abbotsford, BC V2T 1X3 Canada
604-853-7411
MICR: 10670-006
Aurora
#9C, 150 Hollidge Blvd.
Aurora, ON L4G 8A3
905-940-4722
MICR: 10372-006
Barrie
#436, 406 Bryne Dr.
Barrie, ON L4N 9R1 Canada
705-726-6403
MICR: 10172-006
Brampton
312 Queen St. East
Brampton, ON L6V 1C2 Canada
905-451-5363
MICR: 10292-006
Brossard
#C15, 8080, boul Taschereau
Brossard, QC J4X 1C2 Canada
450-672-3766
MICR: 10131-006
Burlington
2500 Appleby Line
Burlington, ON L7L 0A2
888-310-4722
MICR: 10342-006
Burnaby - Kingsway
5210 Kingsway
Burnaby, BC V5H 2E9 Canada
604-438-6411
MICR: 10140-006
Burnaby - Kingsway
#2829, 4500 Kingsway, 2nd Fl.
Burnaby, BC V5H 2A9 Canada
604-668-4510
MICR: 10730-006
Calgary - 130th Ave. SE
#602, 4600 - 130th Ave. SE
Calgary, AB T2Z 0C2
MICR: 10159-006
Calgary - 3rd Ave. SE
Opulence Centre
#212, 111 - 3rd Ave. SE
Calgary, AB T2G 0B7 Canada
403-233-8303
MICR: 10129-006
Calgary - 58th Ave. SE
347 - 58th Ave. SE
Calgary, AB T2H 0P3 Canada
403-253-4003
MICR: 10019-006
Calgary - 8th Ave. SW
407 - 8th Ave. SW
Calgary, AB T2P 1E5 Canada
403-261-8910
MICR: 10029-006
Calgary - Crowfoot Cres. NW
Crowfoot Centre
95 Crowfoot Cres. NW
Calgary, AB T3G 2L5 Canada
403-208-8800
MICR: 10009-006
Campbell River
1000 Shoppers Row
Campbell River, BC V9W 2C8 Canada
250-286-0011
MICR: 10650-006
Chicoutimi
1444, boul Talbot
Chicoutimi, QC G7H 4B7 Canada
418-693-4690
MICR: 10191-006
Chilliwack
#100B, 45850 Yale Rd.
Chilliwack, BC V2P 2N9 Canada
604-795-9181
MICR: 10660-006
Concord
#1-2, 9222 Keele St.
Concord, ON L4K 5A3
905-940-4722
MICR: 10592-006
Coquitlam - North Rd.
#1, 405 North Rd.
Coquitlam, BC V3K 3V9 Canada
604-939-8366
MICR: 10170-006
Coquitlam - Pinetree Way
Henderson Place
#1001, 1163 Pinetree Way
Coquitlam, BC V3B 8A9 Canada
604-468-1678
MICR: 10300-006
Cranbrook
928 Baker St.
Cranbrook, BC V1C 1A5 Canada
250-426-7221
MICR: 10360-006
Edmonton - 101st St.
10250 - 101st St.
Edmonton, AB T5J 3P4 Canada
780-428-1144
MICR: 10099-006
Edmonton - 105 Ave. NW
Pacific Rim Mall
#118, 9700 - 105 Ave. NW
Edmonton, AB T5H 4J1 Canada

780-424-3591
MICR: 10139-006
Edmonton - Calgary Trail South
#104, 5241 Calgary Trail South
Edmonton, AB T6H 5G8 Canada
780-435-3411
MICR: 10039-006
Edmonton - Jasper Ave.
10561 Jasper Ave.
Edmonton, AB T5J 1Z4 Canada
780-423-3563
MICR: 10329-006
Fredericton
520 King St.
Fredericton, NB E3B 6G3 Canada
506-452-0011
MICR: 10024-006
Halifax
1801 Hollis St.
Halifax, NS B3J 3N4 Canada
902-423-8352
MICR: 10093-006
Hamilton
40 King St. East
Hamilton, ON L8N 1A3 Canada
905-525-8730
MICR: 10322-006
Kamloops
380 Victoria St.
Kamloops, BC V2C 2A5 Canada
250-372-7141
MICR: 10460-006
Kanata
Gateway Business Park
#101, 320 March Rd.
Kanata, ON K2K 2E3 Canada
613-591-9929
MICR: 10041-006
Kelowna - Bernard Ave.
384 Bernard Ave.
Kelowna, BC V1Y 6N5 Canada
250-763-3939
MICR: 10430-006
Kelowna - Cooper Rd.
Orchard Plaza
1950 Cooper Rd.
Kelowna, BC V1Y 8K5 Canada
250-762-2811
MICR: 10250-006
Kingston
914 Princess St.
Kingston, ON K7L 1H1 Canada
613-549-5800
MICR: 10132-006
Kitchener
281 King St. West
Kitchener, ON N2G 1B1 Canada
519-745-9403
MICR: 10252-006
Langley
20045 Langley Bypass
Langley, BC V3A 8R6 Canada
604-530-5331
MICR: 10690-006
Laval
#100, 3030, boul Le Carrefour
Laval, QC H7T 2P5 Canada
450-687-6920
MICR: 10121-006
Lethbridge
817 - 4th Ave. South
Lethbridge, AB T1J 0P3 Canada
403-327-8521
MICR: 10079-006
London
285 King St.
London, ON N6B 3M6 Canada
519-439-1631
MICR: 10352-006
Longueuil
430, rue St-Charles ouest
Longueuil, QC J4H 1G2 Canada
450-674-4991
MICR: 10221-006
Maple Ridge
11955 - 224th St.
Maple Ridge, BC V2X 6B4 Canada
604-467-1131
MICR: 10700-006
Markham - Steeles Ave. East
Mandarin Centre
#133, 3636 Steeles Ave.
Markham, ON L3R 1K6 Canada
905-940-4722
MICR: 10302-006
Markham - Steeles Ave. East
Market Village
4390 Steeles Ave. East
Markham, ON L3R 9V7 Canada
905-513-8801
MICR: 10112-006
Markham - Steeles Ave. East
Markham Gateway Centre
3000 Steeles Ave. East
Markham, ON L3R 4T9 Canada
905-475-3777
MICR: 10482-006
Medicine Hat
602 - 3rd St. SE
Medicine Hat, AB T1A 0H5 Canada
403-527-1151
MICR: 10319-006
Mississauga - Dundas St. East
Chinese Centre
#B7-4, 888 Dundas St. East
Mississauga, ON L4Y 4G6 Canada
905-277-5300
MICR: 10072-006
Mississauga - Hurontario St.
City Centre
4550 Hurontario St.
Mississauga, ON L5R 4E4 Canada
905-568-3666
MICR: 10052-006
Mississauga - The Chase
Chase Square
#18, 1675 The Chase
Mississauga, ON L5M 5Y7 Canada
905-308-0115
MICR: 10082-006
Montréal - Acadie
Marché Centrale
8999, boul L'Acadie
Montréal, QC H4N 3K1 Canada
MICR: 10061-006
Montréal - Jean Talon est
5095, rue Jean Talon est
Montréal, QC H1S 3G4 Canada
MICR: 10381-006
Montréal - Jean Talon est
5095, rue Jean Talon est
Montréal, QC H1S 3G4
MICR: 10571-006
Montréal - McGill College
#150, 2001, av McGill College
Montréal, QC H3A 1G1 Canada
MICR: 10001-006
Montréal - René-Lévesque ouest
88, boul René-Lévesque ouest
Montréal, QC H2Z 1A2 Canada
514-393-1626
MICR: 10021-006
Montréal - René-Lévesque ouest
#100, 500, boul René-Lévesque ouest
Montréal, QC H2Z 1W7 Canada
514-866-2841
MICR: 10251-006
Montréal - St-Jean
#110, 1000, boul St-Jean
Montréal, QC H9R 5P1 Canada
514-697-8831
MICR: 10071-006
Nanaimo
#101, 6551 Aulds Rd.
Nanaimo, BC V9T 6K2 Canada
250-390-0668
MICR: 10620-006
New Westminster
504 - 6th St.
New Westminster, BC V3L 3B4 Canada
604-524-9751
MICR: 10180-006
North Vancouver - Edgemont Blvd.
3131 Edgemont Blvd.
North Vancouver, BC V7R 2N7 Canada
604-980-6388
MICR: 10260-006
North Vancouver - Lonsdale Ave.
1577 Lonsdale Ave.
North Vancouver, BC V7M 2J2 Canada
604-903-7000
MICR: 10500-006
Oakville
#102A, 271 Cornwall Rd.
Oakville, ON L6J 7Z5 Canada
MICR: 10182-006
Ottawa
31 Queen St.
Ottawa, ON K1P 0A1 Canada
613-238-5656
MICR: 10031-006
Pender Island
RR#1
Pender Island, BC V0N 2M0 Canada
250-629-6516
MICR: 10610-006
Penticton
201 Main St.
Penticton, BC V2A 5B1 Canada
250-492-2704
MICR: 10350-006
Port Coquitlam
Poco Place
#41, 2755 Lougheed Hwy.
Port Coquitlam, BC V3B 5Y9 Canada
604-464-6444
MICR: 10710-006
Prince George
#110, 299 Victoria St.
Prince George, BC V2L 5B8 Canada
250-564-9800
MICR: 10400-006
Québec
2795, boul Laurier
Québec, QC G1V 4M7 Canada
418-656-6941
MICR: 10171-006
Red Deer
#108, 4909 - 49th Ave.
Red Deer, AB T4N 1V1 Canada
403-343-2344
MICR: 10059-006
Regina
1874 Scarth St.
Regina, SK S4P 4B3 Canada
306-791-8770
MICR: 10128-006
Richmond - Hazelbridge Way
Aberdeen Centre
#1160, 4151 Hazelbridge Way
Richmond, BC V6X 4J7 Canada
604-270-8711
MICR: 10070-006
Richmond - No. 3 Rd.
Fortuna House
6168 No. 3 Rd.
Richmond, BC V6Y 2B3 Canada
604-276-8700
MICR: 10290-006
Richmond - No. 3 Rd.
6800 No. 3 Rd.
Richmond, BC V6Y 2C4 Canada
604-273-1961
MICR: 10120-006
Richmond - No. 3 Rd.
Parker Place Mall
#1010, 4380 No. 3 Rd.
Richmond, BC V6X 3V7 Canada
604-270-8711
MICR: 10570-006
Richmond Hill - Hwy. 7 East
#111, 330 Hwy. 7 East
Richmond Hill, ON L4B 3P8 Canada
905-881-7007
MICR: 10122-006

HSBC Bank Canada (continued)

Richmond Hill - Major Mackenzie Dr. East
#27J, 1070 Major Mackenzie Dr. East
Richmond Hill, ON L4S 1P3 Canada
905-770-2230
MICR: 10332-006

Saint John
7 Market Sq.
Saint John, NB E2L 5C8 Canada
506-632-8110
MICR: 10084-006

Saskatoon
321 - 21st St. East
Saskatoon, SK S7K 0C1 Canada
306-244-2331
MICR: 10138-006

Sault Ste Marie
601 Queen St. East
Sault Ste Marie, ON P6A 2A6 Canada
705-946-2011
MICR: 10102-006

Sherbrooke
2785, rue King ouest
Sherbrooke, QC J1L 1X6 Canada
819-566-8393
MICR: 10401-006

St Catharines
43 Church St.
St Catharines, ON L2R 7E1 Canada
905-688-0903
MICR: 10212-006

St. John's
PO Box 818
205 Water St.
St. John's, NL A1C 5L7 Canada
709-722-8000
MICR: 10043-006

Surrey - 120th St.
#101, 7500 - 120th St.
Surrey, BC V3W 3N1 Canada
604-590-3141
MICR: 10200-006

Surrey - 135th St.
10388 - 135th St.
Surrey, BC V3T 2W6 Canada
604-584-1371
MICR: 10130-006

Surrey - 152nd St.
#410, 3099 - 152nd St.
Surrey, BC V4P 3K1
888-310-4722
MICR: 10680-006

Surrey - 16th Ave.
12894 - 16th Ave.
Surrey, BC V4A 1N7
888-310-4722
MICR: 10680-006

Thunder Bay
955 Alloy Dr.
Thunder Bay, ON P7B 5Z8 Canada
807-343-6300
Fax: 807-345-7504
MICR: 10057-006

Timmins
190 - 3rd Ave.
Timmins, ON P4N 1C8 Canada
705-267-6405
MICR: 10542-006

Toronto - Adelaide St. East
One Financial Place
1 Adelaide St. East
Toronto, ON M5C 2V9 Canada
416-366-0858
MICR: 10532-006

Toronto - Attwell Dr.
Skyway Business Park
170 Attwell Dr.
Toronto, ON M9W 5Z5 Canada
416-675-7102
MICR: 10142-006

Toronto - Bloor St. West
#100M, 150 Bloor St. West
Toronto, ON M5S 2Y5 Canada
416-968-7622
MICR: 10362-006

Toronto - Eglinton Ave. East
#1, 1940 Eglinton Ave. East
Toronto, ON M1L 4R1 Canada
416-752-8910
MICR: 10282-006

Toronto - Eglinton Ave. West
20 Eglinton Ave. West
Toronto, ON M4K 1K8 Canada
905-940-4722
MICR: 10232-006

Toronto - Milliken Blvd.
Milliken Square
15 Milliken Blvd.
Toronto, ON M1V 1V3 Canada
416-321-8017
MICR: 10042-006

Toronto - Sheppard Ave. East
Oriental Centre
#102, 4438 Sheppard Ave. East
Toronto, ON M1S 1V2 Canada
MICR: 10022-006

Toronto - Spadina Ave.
Chinatown Centre
#101N, 222 Spadina Ave.
Toronto, ON M5T 3A2 Canada
416-348-8888
MICR: 10422-006

Toronto - Spadina Rd.
#106, 446 Spadina Rd.
Toronto, ON M5P 3M2 Canada
416-489-2288
MICR: 10312-006

Toronto - St. Clair Ave. West
1241 St. Clair Ave. West
Toronto, ON M6E 1B8 Canada
416-654-1920
MICR: 10642-006
Anthony Consentino, Branch Manager

Toronto - Victoria Park Ave.
3640 Victoria Park Ave.
Toronto, ON M2H 3B2 Canada
416-756-2333
MICR: 10032-006

Toronto - Wilson Ave.
693 Wilson Ave.
Toronto, ON M3K 1E3 Canada
905-940-4722
MICR: 10562-006

Toronto - Yonge St.
5160 Yonge St.
Toronto, ON M2N 6L9 Canada
905-940-4722
MICR: 10192-006

Toronto - York Mills Rd.
#100, 300 York Mills Rd.
Toronto, ON M2L 2Y5 Canada
416-385-7638
MICR: 10202-006

Toronto - York St.
70 York St.
Toronto, ON M5J 1S9 Canada
416-868-8000
MICR: 10002-006

Trois-Rivières
1182, rue Royale
Trois-Rivières, QC G9A 4J1 Canada
819-375-7341
MICR: 10321-006

Unionville
#5B, 8390 Kennedy Rd.
Unionville, ON L3R 0W4 Canada
905-479-8076
MICR: 10682-006

Vancouver - Cambie St.
5812 Cambie St.
Vancouver, BC V5Z 3A8 Canada
604-325-1868
MICR: 10220-006

Vancouver - Denman St.
1010 Denman St.
Vancouver, BC V6G 2M5 Canada
604-683-8189
MICR: 10100-006

Vancouver - East Hastings St.
2590 East Hastings St.
Vancouver, BC V5K 1Z3 Canada
604-253-1531
MICR: 10050-006

Vancouver - Fraser St.
6373 Fraser St.
Vancouver, BC V5W 3A3 Canada
604-324-2481
MICR: 10060-006

Vancouver - Granville St.
2735 Granville St.
Vancouver, BC V6H 3J1 Canada
604-668-4715
MICR: 10030-006

Vancouver - Granville St.
5688 Granville St.
Vancouver, BC V6M 3C5 Canada
604-267-6382
MICR: 10230-006

Vancouver - Granville St.
8118 Granville St.
Vancouver, BC V6P 4Z4 Canada
604-266-8087
MICR: 10380-006

Vancouver - Kingsway
3366 Kingsway
Vancouver, BC V5R 5K6 Canada
604-430-3261
MICR: 10160-006

Vancouver - Main St.
Wayfoong House
608 Main St.
Vancouver, BC V6A 2V3 Canada
604-683-9611
MICR: 10320-006

Vancouver - Pacific Blvd.
1196 Pacific Blvd.
Vancouver, BC V6Z 2X7 Canada
604-605-8718
MICR: 10210-006

Vancouver - West 10th Ave.
4480 West 10th Ave.
Vancouver, BC V6R 2H9 Canada
604-228-1421
MICR: 10150-006

Vancouver - West 41st. Ave.
2164 West 41st Ave.
Vancouver, BC V6M 1Z1 Canada
604-261-4251
MICR: 10110-006

Vancouver - West Broadway St.
601 West Broadway St.
Vancouver, BC V5Z 4C2 Canada
604-668-4735
MICR: 10090-006

Vancouver - West Georgia St.
#108, 1188 West Georgia St.
Vancouver, BC V6E 4A2 Canada
604-687-7441
MICR: 10240-006

Vancouver - West Georgia St. - Main Branch
885 West Georgia St.
Vancouver, BC V6C 3G1 Canada
604-685-1000
MICR: 10020-006

Vancouver - West Hastings St.
999 West Hastings St.
Vancouver, BC V6C 1M3 Canada
604-895-7100
MICR: 10280-006

Vaughan
#37D, 7398 Yonge St.
Vaughan, ON L4J 8J2 Canada
905-771-8727
MICR: 10162-006

Vernon
3321 - 30th Ave.
Vernon, BC V1T 2C9 Canada
250-542-3345
MICR: 10420-006

Victoria - Fort St.
752 Fort St.
Victoria, BC V8W 1H2 Canada
250-388-5511
MICR: 10600-006

Victoria - Jacklin Rd.

2968 Jacklin Rd.
Victoria, BC V9B 0A3
250-391-5000
MICR: 10640-006
Victoria - Oak Bay Ave.
2154 Oak Bay Ave.
Victoria, BC V8R 1E9 Canada
250-592-5423
MICR: 10580-006
Victoria - Vernon Ave.
#100, 771 Vernon Ave.
Victoria, BC V8X 5A7 Canada
250-388-6465
MICR: 10610-006
West Vancouver
1578 Marine Dr.
West Vancouver, BC V7V 1H8 Canada
604-922-3311
MICR: 10510-006
Whitby
1200 Dundas St.
Whitby, ON L1N 2K5 Canada
905-666-2300
MICR: 10092-006
White Rock
1493 Johnston Rd.
White Rock, BC V4B 3Z4 Canada
604-531-8366
MICR: 10680-006
Windsor
190 University Ave. West
Windsor, ON N9A 5N9 Canada
519-256-5591
MICR: 10262-006
Debbie Peltier, Manager, Personal Financial Services
Winnipeg
#110, 330 St. Mary Ave.
Winnipeg, MB R3C 3Z5 Canada
MICR: 10317-006
Woodbridge - Hsy. 7 - Community Banking Centre
#200, 4500 Hwy. 7
Woodbridge, ON L4L 4Y7
MICR: 10522-006
Woodbridge - Hwy. 7
#135, 4500 Hwy. 7
Woodbridge, ON L4L 4Y7 Canada
905-850-2288
MICR: 10522-006
Lucy Pittiglio, Branch Manager

ICICI Bank Canada

Exchange Tower
PO Box 58
#2130, 130 King St. West
Toronto, ON M5X 1B1
888-424-2422
customercare.ca@icicibank.com
www.icicibank.ca
Ownership: Wholly-owned subsidiary of ICICI Bank Limited, Mumbai, India.
Profile: The full-service direct bank offers personal, corporate, commercial, investment & treasury & trade services.

Executives:
Hari Panday, President/CEO
Sriram H. Iyer, Sr. Vice-President/COO
Piyush Bhatia, Vice-President, Commercial, Corporate & Investment Banking
Atul Chandra, Vice-President/CFO
Anthony Nelson, Vice-President, Credit, Credit Risk Officer
Directors:
K.V. Kamath, Chair
Madan Bhayana
Sonjoy Chatterjee
Chanda Kochhar
Robert G. Long
Hari Panday
David P. Smith
John Thompson
Branches:
Brampton
Bartley's Square
1 Bartley Bull Pkwy.
Brampton, ON L6W 3T7 Canada
905-456-3700
Surrey
#303, 9288 - 120th St.
Surrey, BC V3V 4B8
604-951-9989
Toronto - Gerrard St. East
1404 Gerrard St. East
Toronto, ON M4L 1Z4
416-466-6196
Toronto - King St.
Exchange Tower
#2130, 130 King St. West
Toronto, ON M5X 1B1 Canada
416-360-0909
Toronto - Steeles Ave. East
#1, 5631 Steeles Ave. East
Toronto, ON M1V 5P6 Canada
416-298-9222
Vancouver
569 Howe St.
Vancouver, BC V6C 2C2
604-646-4160

ING Bank of Canada

111 Gordon Baker Rd.
Toronto, ON M2H 3R1
416-758-5344
Fax: 416-756-2422
800-464-3473
Other Information: 1-866-464-3473 (Toll Free, French service)
clientservices@ingdirect.ca
www.ingdirect.ca
Also Known As: ING DIRECT
Ownership: Wholly owned subsidiary of ING Group, Netherlands
Year Founded: 1997
Number of Employees: 850+
Assets: $10-100 billion
Profile: ING DIRECT Canada has over 1.4 million clients, employs over 850 people and has over $22 billion in assets

Directors:
Arkadi Kuhlmann, Chair
Michael R. Bell
Johanne Brossard
Paul Cantor
Claude Dussault
Dick Harryvan
Michiel R. Leenders
Eileen A. Mercier
W. Ross Walker
Branches:
Calgary
Petex Building
600 - 6th Ave. SW
Calgary, AB T2P 0S5
403-539-5520
888-464-3232
Montréal
1248, rue Peel
Montréal, QC H3B 2T6
514-396-2233
866-464-4277
Vancouver
466 Howe St.
Vancouver, BC V6C 2X1
604-732-1028
888-464-3232

J.P. Morgan Bank Canada

South Tower, Royal Bank Plaza
PO Box 80
#1800, 200 Bay St.
Toronto, ON M5J 2J2
416-981-9200
Fax: 416-981-9176
www.jpmorgan.com
Profile: The bank provides wholesale financial services. Its clients include corporations, institutional investors, hedge funds, governments & affluent individuals in more than 100 countries.

Korea Exchange Bank of Canada(KEBOC)

Madison Centre
#103, 4950 Yonge St.
Toronto, ON M2N 6K1
416-222-5200
Fax: 416-222-5822
www.kebcanada.com
Year Founded: 1981
Number of Employees: 90
Profile: Korea Exchange Bank of Canada offers the following services: investment, bill payment, loan, export & import, credit card, & remittance.

Executives:
See Mok Kim, Vice-President, Business Operations Department
Branches:
Burnaby - Kingsway
#100, 4900 Kingsway
Burnaby, BC V2H 2E3 Canada
604-432-1984
Fax: 604-432-1964
Burnaby - North Rd.
202A, 4501 North Rd.
Burnaby, BC V3N 4R7 Canada
604-432-1984
Fax: 604-432-1964
Mississauga
West Tower, Sussex Centre
#120, 90 Burnhamthorpe Rd. West
Mississauga, ON L5B 3C3 Canada
905-272-3130
Fax: 905-272-3430
Thornhill
#5, 7670 Yonge St.
Thornhill, ON L4J 1W1 Canada
905-707-7001
Fax: 905-707-0171
Toronto
627 Bloor St. West
Toronto, ON M6G 1K8 Canada
416-533-8593
Fax: 416-531-1047
Vancouver
590 Robson St.
Vancouver, BC V3B 2B7
604-609-2700
Fax: 604-609-2777

MBNA Canada Bank

1600 James Naismith Dr.
Ottawa, ON K1B 5N8
613-907-4800
Fax: 613-907-3501
800-404-1319
Other Information: 1-877-862-7759 (Toll Free for card applications); 1-800-872-5758 (TTY/TTD)
www.mbna.com/canada
Ownership: Private. MBNA Corporation, Wilmington, Delaware, USA.
Year Founded: 1997
Profile: Loans, credit cards & insurance are among the services offered.

Executives:
Joseph DeSantis, CEO
Debra Armstrong, President

Mega International Commercial Bank (Canada)

Madison Centre
#1002, 4950 Yonge St.
Toronto, ON M2N 6K1
416-947-2800
Fax: 416-947-9964
megato@ipoline.com
www.megabank.com.tw
Former Name: International Commercial Bank of Cathay (Canada)
Ownership: Wholly-owned subsidiary of Mega International Commercial Bank Co., Ltd., Taipei City, Taiwan.
Profile: Mega International Commercial Bank Co., Ltd. was formed by the merger of The International Commercial Bank of China Co. Ltd. & Chiao Tung Bank Co. Ltd. in August 2006.

Branches:
Richmond
6111 No. 3 Rd.
Richmond, BC V6Y 2B1
604-273-3107
Fax: 604-273-3187
Toronto
241 Spadina Ave.
Toronto, ON M5T 1G6
416-597-8545
Fax: 416-597-6526
Vancouver

Mega International Commercial Bank (Canada) (continued)
#1250, 1095 West Pender St.
Vancouver, BC V6E 2M6
604-689-5650
Fax: 604-689-5625

Mizuho Corporate Bank (Canada)(MHCB)

PO Box 29
#1102, 100 Yonge St.
Toronto, ON M5C 2W1
416-874-0222
Fax: 416-367-3452
800-668-5917
www.mizuhocbk.co.jp/english
Former Name: Mizuho Bank (Canada)
Ownership: Foreign. Part of Mizuho Corporate Bank, Ltd., Tokyo, Japan.
Year Founded: 2000
Profile: The bank provides solutions to the diverse & sophisticated needs of customers, in the areas of both finance & business strategies. Mihuzo focuses its efforts on serving major corporations, financial institutions & their group companies, public sector entities, & overseas corporations, including subsidiaries of Japanese corporations.

Executives:
Juni Kumazaki, President/CEO
S.F. Luk, Group Vice-President, Risk Management
Campbell McLeish, Sr. Vice-President

Société Générale (Canada)

#1800, 1501, av McGill College
Montréal, QC H3A 3M8
514-841-6000
Fax: 514-841-6250
www.socgen.com
Ownership: Wholly-owned subsidiary of Société Générale Group, Paris, France.
Year Founded: 1974
Profile: The Schedule II bank provides services in the areas of retail banking, specialized financial services, corporate & investment banking, & global investment management services.

Executives:
Edouard-Malo Henry, President
Branches:
Calgary
#3206, 450 - 1st St. SW
Calgary, AB T2P 5H1 Canada
ed.more@sgcib.com
Michel Hurtubise, Managing Director, Corporate Investment Banking
Toronto
#1002, 100 Yonge St.
Toronto, ON M5C 2W1 Canada
416-364-2864
Fax: 416-364-1879

State Bank of India (Canada)

#1600, Royal Bank Plaza, North Tower
PO Box 81, Royal Bank Stn. Royal Bank
200 Bay St.
Toronto, ON M5J 2J2
416-865-0414
Fax: 416-865-1735
800-668-8947
sbican@sbicanada.com
www.sbicanada.com
Ownership: Subsidiary of State Bank of India
Year Founded: 1982
Number of Employees: 45
Assets: $100-500 million
Revenues: $1-5 million
Executives:
Shailesh Verma, President/CEO; 416-865-0414; pandceo@sbicanada.com
Ajai Sahore, Vice-President, Credit; 416-865-0414; vpcredit@sbicanada.com
Ajay Tandon, Vice-President; 416-865-0414; nris@sbicanada.com
R. Vijayendran, Vice-President, Operations; 416-865-0414; vpopc@sbicanada.com
Leena Ancheril, Asst. Vice-President, Trade Finance; 416-865-0414; elcee@sbicanada.com
Biresh Kumar, Asst. Vice-President, Dealing Operations; 416-865-0414; avpdo@sbicanada.com
Atam Prakash Chugh, Asst. Vice-President, Accounts; 416-865-0414; accts@sbicanada.com
Govind Subbanna, Asst. Vice-President, Credit; 416-865-0414; avpcredi@sbicanada.com
Varinder Thareja, Asst. Vice-President, Operations; 416-865-0414; avpops@sbicanada.com
Branches:
Mississauga
Dixie Place
#100, 1450 Meyerside Dr.
Mississauga, ON L5T 2N5 Canada
905-565-8959
Fax: 905-565-5967
sbicmiss@sbicanada.com
Sanjiv Katyal, Vice-President & Manager
Surrey
9368 - 120 St.
Surrey, BC V3V 4B9 Canada
604-583-3363
Fax: 604-583-3324
J.K. Dubey, Vice-President/Manager
Toronto
3471 Sheppard Ave. East
Toronto, ON M1T 3K5 Canada
416-754-0039
Fax: 416-754-0489
scarborough@sbicanada.com
Michael Wilson, Branch Manager
Vancouver
6433 Fraser St.
Vancouver, BC V5W 3A6 Canada
604-731-6635
Fax: 604-731-5268
S.V. Prasadu, Vice-President/Manager

Sumitomo Mitsui Banking Corporation of Canada

#1400, Ernst & Young Tower
PO Box 172, TD Centre Stn. TD Centre
Toronto, ON M5K 1H6
416-368-4766
Fax: 416-367-3565
www.smbc.co.jp/aboutus/english
Former Name: Sakura Bank (Canada); The Sumitomo Bank of Canada
Ownership: Private. Foreign. Wholly owned subsidiary of Sumitomo Mitsui Banking Corporation, Tokyo, Japan.
Year Founded: 2001
Number of Employees: 32
Profile: The corporation offers a broad range of financial services centered on banking. It is also engaged in leasing, securities, credit cards, investments, mortgage securitization, venture capital, & other credit related businesses.

Executives:
Minami Aida, President/CEO

UBS Bank (Canada)

***Also listed under:** Financial Planning; Investment Management*

#800, 154 University Ave.
Toronto, ON M5H 3Z4
416-343-1800
Fax: 416-343-1900
800-268-9709
www.ubs.com/canada
Also Known As: UBS Canada
Ownership: Foreign. Public.
Year Founded: 1856
Number of Employees: 70,000
Assets: $100 billion + Year End: 20051231
Revenues: $10-100 billion Year End: 20051231
Stock Symbol: UBS
Profile: UBS Bank is a wealth management, financial planning & investment solutions services company.

Executives:
Grant Rasmussen, CEO & Managing Director
Sharon Ashton, Contact, Products Group
Anurag Deep, Contact, Finance
Balan Gunaratnam, Contact, Information Technology
Graeme Harris, Contact, Corporate Communications
Branches:
Calgary
#600, 326 - 11th Ave. SW
Calgary, AB T2R 0C5 Canada
403-532-2180
Beat Meier, Director
Montréal
#2710, 600, boul Maisonneuve ouest
Montréal, QC H3A 3J2 Canada
514-845-8828
Karel Nemel, Director
Vancouver
PO Box 24
#650, 999 West Hastings St.
Vancouver, BC V6C 2W2 Canada
604-669-5570
800-305-5181
Martine Cunliffe, Director

Foreign Banks: Schedule III

ABN AMRO Bank N.V., Canada Branch

Toronto-Dominion Centre
PO Box 114, T-D Centre Stn. T-D Centre
#1500, 79 Wellington St. West, 15th Fl.
Toronto, ON M5K 1G8
416-367-0850
Fax: 416-367-7937
Other Information: canada.jobs@abnamro.com (Employment Enquiries); 416-367-7943 (Business & Commercial Fax); 416-367-7937 (Corporate & Institutional Fax)
canada.branch@abnamro.com
www.abnamro.ca
Ownership: Branch of ABN AMRO Bank N.V.
Year Founded: 1824
Profile: In 2002, the Bank in Canada moved from subsidiary to branch status. It now operates as a Schedule III Chartered bank. The Canadian locations have access to a global network of ABN AMRO offices. A wide range of financial services is offered to corporate, institutional, business & commercial clients.

Executives:
Giles Meikle, Chair
Lawrence J. Maloney, Country Executive Officer
Affiliated Companies:
ABN AMRO Asset Management Canada Limited
Offices:
Burlington
5515 North Service Rd., 2nd Fl.
Burlington, ON L7L 6G4 Canada
905-331-2000
Fax: 905-331-2020
Brent Keenan, Group Vice-President
Montréal
#2810, 600 de Maisonneuve ouest
Montréal, QC H3A 3J2 Canada
514-284-1133
Fax: 514-284-2357
Michel Hylands, Sr. Vice-President
Vancouver
PO Box 49127
#2373, 595 Burrard St.
Vancouver, BC V7X 1J1 Canada
604-484-7175
Fax: 604-484-7165
Paul Dunstan, Sr. Vice-President

Bank of America, National Association

#2700, 200 Front St. West
Toronto, ON M5V 3L2
416-349-4100
Fax: 416-349-4278
800-387-1729
www.bankofamerica.com
Profile: Bank of America is one of the world's largest financial institutions, serving individual consumers, small & middle market businesses & large corporations with a full range of banking, investing, asset management & other financial & risk-management products & services.

Capital One Bank (Canada Branch)

***Also listed under:** Credit Card Companies*
#1300, 5650 Yonge St.
Toronto, ON M2M 4G3
Fax: 416-228-5113
800-481-3239
Other Information: Customer Relations Address: PO Box 503, Stn. D, Toronto, ON M1R 5L1; Payment Address: PO Box 501, Stn. D, Toronto, ON M1R 5S4
ombudsman@capitalone.com
www.capitalone.ca
Ownership: Foreign. Part of Capital One Services, Inc., McLean, VA, USA.

Profile: The international financial services company is known in the credit card marketplace, for pioneering low introductory rates, balance transfers, & fixed rate products in North America.

Executives:
William Cilluffo, President
Ian Cunningham, Chief Operating Officer
Robert Livingston, Chief Marketing Officer
Ramona Tobler, Chief People Officer
Felix Wu, Chief Financial Officer
Scott Wilson, Ombudsman

Comerica Bank

South Tower, Royal Bank Plaza
PO Box 61
#2210, 200 Bay St.
Toronto, ON M5J 2J2
416-646-4797
Fax: 416-367-6435
www.comerica.com
Ownership: Foreign. Branch of Comerica Bank, Detroit, Michigan, USA.
Profile: The Canada branch is engaged in the following activities: cash management, corporate banking, trade services & treasury.

Credit Suisse, Toronto Branch

PO Box 301, First Canadian Pl. Stn. First Canadian Pl.
#3000, 1 First Canadian Pl.
Toronto, ON M5X 1C9
416-352-4500
Fax: 416-352-4680
www.csfb.com
Ownership: Part of Credit Suisse Group, Zurich, Switzerland.
Profile: Investment banking services are offered.

Executives:
Bruce Wetherly, Principal Agent; bruce.wetherly@csfb.com
Branches:
Montréal
#3935, 1250, boul René-Lévesque ouest
Montréal, QC H3B 4W8 Canada
514-933-8774
Fax: 514-933-7699

Deutsche Bank AG

Commerce Court West
PO Box 263
#4700, 199 Bay St.
Toronto, ON M5L 1E9
416-682-8000
Fax: 416-682-8383
deutsche.bank@db.com
www.db.com
Ownership: Foreign. Branch of Deutsche Bank AG, Frankfurt, Germany.

Dexia Crédit Local S.A. Canada

PO Box 201
#1620, 800, du carré Victoria
Montréal, QC H4A 1E3
514-868-1200
webmaster@dexia.com
www.dexia.com
Ownership: Branch of Dexia Crédit Local, Paris, France.
Profile: Dexia was formed in 1996 with the alliance of Crédit Communal de Belgique & Crédit Local de France.

Fifth Third Bank

20 Bay St., 12th Fl.
Toronto, ON M5J 2N8
416-216-4638
www.53.com
Ownership: Foreign. Branch of Fifth Third Bank, Cincinnati, Ohio, USA

First Commercial Bank

#100, 5611 Cooney Rd.
Richmond, BC V6X 3J6
604-207-9600
Fax: 604-207-9638
www.firstbank.com
Ownership: Foreign. Branch of First Commercial Bank, Taiwan.

Profile: Caters to small businesses and consumers who wish to take advantage of a local bank that offers all of the services that are expected from a larger organization

HSBC Bank USA, National Association

70 York St., 4th Fl.
Toronto, ON M5J 1S9
www.us.hsbc.com, www.hsbc.ca

JPMorgan Chase Bank, National Association

South Tower, Royal Bank Plaza
PO Box 80
#1800, 200 Bay St.
Toronto, ON M5J 2J2
416-981-9200
Fax: 416-981-9175
888-430-9844
www.jpmorganchase.com
Former Name: The Chase Manhattan Bank; Morgan Guaranty Trust Co. of New York
Ownership: Branch of J.P. Morgan Chase & Co. Inc., Chicago, IL, USA.
Profile: Leader in investment banking, financial services for consumers, small business and commercial banking, financial transaction processing, asset management, and private equity

Executives:
John Rodrigue, Ombudsman; 800-265-3675; John.P.Rodrigue@chase.com

Maple Bank GmbH

c/o Maple Financial Group Inc., Maritime Life Tower, TD Centre
PO Box 328
#3450, 79 Wellington St. West
Toronto, ON M5K 1K7
416-350-8200
Fax: 416-350-8226
info@maplefinancial.com
www.maplebank.com
Former Name: First Marathon Bank GmbH
Ownership: Subsidiary of Maple Financial Group Inc.
Profile: The Toronto branch is engaged in securities finance & wholesale lending.

Executives:
Paul Lishman, General Manager; plishman@maplefinancial.com

Mellon Bank, N.A., Canada Branch

PO Box 16
#1710, 95 Wellington St. West
Toronto, ON M5J 2N7
416-860-0777
www.mellon.com
Ownership: Foreign. Branch of Mellon Financial Corp., Pittsburgh, PA, USA.
Year Founded: 1983
Profile: The Canada Branch offers treasury services for Mellon's corporate customers doing business in Canada. Mellon Canada is part of Mellon Working Capital Solutions.

Executives:
John P. Rehob, Principal Officer

National City Bank - Canada Branch

The Exchange Tower
PO Box 462
#2140, 130 King St. West
Toronto, ON M5X 1E4
416-361-1744
Fax: 416-361-0085
www.nationalcity.com
Ownership: owned by National City Bank, Cleveland, Ohio
Year Founded: 1845
Number of Employees: 5
Profile: A broad range of financial services are offered to large- & medium-sized corporations. Services include credit, syndicated lending & asset-based wholesale banking. It is affiliated with National City Commercial Capital Corporation.

Executives:
G. William Hines, Sr. Vice-President & Principal Officer; 416-361-1744; william.hines@nationalcity.com
Kenneth G. Argue, Vice-President, Operations; 416-361-1744; kenneth.argue@nationalcity.com
Andrew Riddell, Vice-President, Relationship Manager; 416-361-1744; andrew.riddell@nationalcity.com
Caroline Stade, Vice-President, Relationship Manager; 416-361-1744; caroline.stade@nationalcity.com

Ohio Savings Bank, Canadian Branch

Centre Tower, Clarica Centre
#3110, 3300 Bloor St. West
Toronto, ON M8X 2X3
800-696-2222
www.ohiosavings.com
Ownership: Foreign. Branch of Ohio Savings Bank, Cleveland, OH, USA.

Rabobank Nederland

Royal Trust Tower
#4520, 77 King St. West
Toronto, ON M5K 1E7
416-941-9777
Fax: 416-941-9750
www.rabobank.com
Former Name: Rabobank Canada
Ownership: Cooperative. Foreign. Branch of Rabobank Nederland, Netherlands
Year Founded: 2001
Number of Employees: 14
Assets: $1-10 billion Year End: 20051231
Profile: The Dutch-based cooperative financial institution operates as a wholesale bank, serving corporate clients in the food & agriculture sectors.

Executives:
Govert Verstralen, General Manager, Principal Officer; 416-941-0271; govert.verstralen@rabobank.com
Peter Greenberg, Head, Corporate Banking; 416-941-0284; peter.greenberg@rabobank.com

State Street Bank & Trust Company - Canada

Also listed under: *Trust Companies*
#1100, 30 Adelaide St. East
Toronto, ON M5C 3G6
416-362-1100
Fax: 416-956-2525
888-287-8639
www.statestreet.com
Former Name: State Street Trust Company Canada
Ownership: State Street Corporation
Year Founded: 1990
Number of Employees: 700
Profile: World's leading provider of financial services to institutional investors. Range of services spans the entire investment spectrum, including research, investment management, trading services and investment servicing

Branches:
Montréal
#1100, 770, rue Sherbrooke ouest
Montréal, QC H3A 1G1 Canada
514-282-2400
Fax: 514-282-2439

U.S. Bank National Association - Canada Branch

Adelaide Centre
#2300, 120 Adelaide St. West
Toronto, ON M5H 1T1
877-332-7461
www.usbankcanada.com
Ownership: Part of U.S. Bank, Minneapolis, MN, USA.
Profile: The Canada branch focuses upon the business of corporate payment systems.

Executives:
Kevin Jephcott, Vice-President, Sales, Relationship Management & Marketing; 416-306-3507; kevin.jephcott@usabank.com

Union Bank of California, N.A.

#730, 440 - 2 Ave. SW
Calgary, AB T2P 5E9
403-264-2700
Fax: 403-264-2770
www.uboc.com
Ownership: Parent Union BanCal Corporation
Year Founded: 1864
Stock Symbol: UB
Profile: Union Bank is among the 25 largest banks in the United States, based on assets. The bank has 321 branch offices; two international offices; and facilities in other states

Executives:
Karen Anderson, Vice-President
James Chepyha, Vice-President; james.chepyha@uboc.com

United Overseas Bank Limited(UOB)
Vancouver Centre
PO Box 11616
#1680, 650 West Georgia St.
Vancouver, BC V6B 4N9
604-662-7055
Fax: 604-662-3356
UOB.Vancouver@uobgroup.com
www.uobgroup.com
Ownership: Foreign. Branch of United Overseas Bank Limited, Singapore.
Year Founded: 1987
Profile: UOB's vast network of over 500 offices around the world comprises 72 offices in Singapore and over 450 offices in Australia, Brunei, Canada, China, France, Hong Kong, Indonesia, Japan, Malaysia, Myanmar, Philippines, South Korea, Taiwan, Thailand, United Kingdom, USA and Vietnam

WestLB AG
North Tower, Royal Bank Plaza
PO Box 41
#2301, 200 Bay St.
Toronto, ON M5J 2J1
416-216-5000
Fax: 416-216-5020
info@westlb.de
www.westlb.com
Ownership: Foreign. Branch of WestLB AG, Düsseldorf, Germany.
Profile: The commercial bank operates on an international scale.

Foreign Banks Representative Offices

Allied Irish Banks, p.l.c.(AIB)
20 Bay St., 12th Fl.
Toronto, ON M5J 2N8
www.aib.ie
Ownership: Foreign. Office of Allied Irish Banks p.l.c., Dublin, Ireland.
Profile: Corporate banking services are offered, including structured finance & lending services.

American Express Bank Ltd.
#1350, 1090 West Georgia St.
Vancouver, BC V6E 3V7
Ownership: Foreign. Office of American Express Bank, New York, NY, USA.

Banco Comercial dos Açores
836 Dundas St. West
Toronto, ON M6J 1V5
416-603-0802
Fax: 416-603-8892
www.bca.pt

Banco Espirito Santo e Comercial de Lisboa, SA
860C College St.
Toronto, ON M6H 1A2
416-530-1700
www.bes.pt
Ownership: Private

Banco Santander Totta, SA
1110 Dundas St. West
Toronto, ON M6J 1X2
416-538-7111
www.santandertotta.pt

Bank Hapoalim B.M.
#2105, 4950 Yonge St.
Toronto, ON M2N 6K1
416-398-4250
Fax: 416-398-4246
www.bankhapoalim.com
Branches:
Montréal
1, Place Alexis Nihon
#1470, 3400, boul de Maissoneuve ouest
Montréal, QC H3Z 3B8 Canada
514-935-1128
Fax: 514-935-1129

Bank Leumi Le-Israel, B.M.
#400, 1 carré Westmount
Montréal, QC H3Z 2P9
514-931-4457
Fax: 514-931-5240
bllmtl@sprint.ca
english.leumi.co.il
Ownership: Office of Bank Leumi Le-Israel, B.M., Tel Aviv, Israel.
Year Founded: 1902
Assets: $10-100 billion
Revenues: $100-500 million
Branches:
Toronto
#2220, 5140 Yonge St.
Toronto, ON M2N 6L7 Canada
416-594-0681
Fax: 416-594-0801
blltor@bellnet.ca

Bank of Cyprus, Canada Representative Office
#302, 658 Danforth Ave.
Toronto, ON M4J 5B9
416-461-5570
Fax: 416-461-6062
888-529-2265
info@bankofcyprus.ca
www.bankofcyprus.ca
Ownership: Office of the Bank of Cyprus Group, Cyprus.
Year Founded: 1997
Profile: The representative office serves mostly the Greek & Greek-Cypriot community. It is a link between customers & branches in Greece, Cyprus, Australia, United Kingdom and the Channel Islands.

Bank of Ireland Asset Management (U.S.) Limited
#2460, 1800, av McGill College
Montréal, QC H3A 3J6
514-849-6868
Fax: 514-849-8118
canada@biam.boi.ie
www.biam.ie
Year Founded: 1987
Executives:
Padraig Connolly, Chief Representative & Vice-President, Client Services; padraig.connolly@biam.boi.ie
Branches:
Toronto
#2500, 1 Dundas St. West
Toronto, ON M5G 1Z3 Canada
416-777-0004
Fax: 416-777-0034
canada@biam.boi.ie

Bank of Punjab Ltd.
#337, 1515 Britannia Rd. East
Mississauga, ON L4W 4K1
905-696-0943

Bank of Valletta p.l.c., Canada Representative Office
West Tower
#625, 3300 Bloor St. West, 6th Fl.
Toronto, ON M8X 2X2
416-234-2265
Fax: 416-234-2281
800-567-2265
bovcanada@bov.com
www.bov.com
Executives:
Emmanuel Ciappara, Chief Representative

Bank Vontobel AG
#1760, 999 West Hastings St.
Vancouver, BC V6C 2W2
604-688-1122
Fax: 604-688-1123
www.vontobel.com
Ownership: Office of Bank Vontobel AG, Zürich, Switzerland.

Banque Centrale Populaire du Maroc
#1514, 1010 rue Sherbrooke ouest
Montréal, QC H3A 2R7
514-281-1855
Fax: 514-281-1974
gbpmaroc@qc.aira.com
www.bp.co.ma

Baring Asset Management Inc.
#1703, 150 King St. West
Toronto, ON M5H 1J9
416-599-1835
Fax: 416-599-0373
randall.o'leary@baring-asset.com
www.baring-asset-can.com
Ownership: Private
Year Founded: 1977
Executives:
Randall O'Leary, Managing Director, Canada

Bayerische Landesbank
#2060, 1501, av McGill College
Montréal, QC H3A 3M8
514-985-0047
Fax: 514-985-3459
info.montreal@bayernlb.com
www.bayernlb.de
Ownership: Foreign. Part of Bayerische Landesbank (BayernLB), Munich, Germany.

Caixa Economica Montepio Gual
1286 Dundas St. West
Toronto, ON M6J 1X7
416-588-7776
Fax: 416-588-0030
montepiocavaco@on.aibn.com
www.montepio.pt

Calyon
#1900, 2000, av McGill College
Montréal, QC
Ownership: Office of Credit Agricole Group, Paris, France.
Year Founded: 2004

Centurion Bank of Punjab, Ltd.
#337, 1515 Britannia Rd. East
Mississauga, ON L4W 4K1
905-696-0943
Fax: 905-696-0976
nri.services@centurionbop.co.in
www.centurionbop.co.in
Ownership: Office of Centurion Bank of Punjab, India.

Crédit Libanais S.A.L. Representative Office (Canada)
Place du Canada
#1325, 1010, rue de la Gauchetière ouest
Montréal, QC H3B 2N2
514-866-6688
Fax: 514-866-6220
800-864-5512
info@creditlibanais.com
www.creditlibanais.com
Ownership: Office of Credit Libanais S.A.L., Beirut, Lebanon.
Executives:
Malek G. Badro, Branch Manager

Cyprus Popular Bank Ltd.
484 Danforth Ave., 2nd Fl.
Toronto, ON M4K 1P6
416-466-8180
Fax: 416-466-9609
877-524-5422
laiki.toronto@laiki.com, laikiebank@laiki.com
www.laiki.com
Also Known As: Laiki Bank
Ownership: Office of Laiki Group, Cyprus.
Profile: The Canadian representative office of Laiki Group is one of five operated around the world. Activities include the provision of information about banking products & services offered by the following branches: Cyprus Popular Bank in Cyprus & the United Kingdom; Laiki Bank (Hellas) S.A. in Greece; Laiki Bank (Australia) Ltd. in Australia; & Laiki Bank a.d. in Serbia.
Executives:
Dimitris Maras, Manager, Canada
Patti Papadakis, Administrator
Helen Zoubanioti, Representative
Branches:
Montréal
5724, av du Parc
Montréal, QC H2V 4H1 Canada
514-495-8118
Fax: 514-495-9746
laiki.montreal@laiki.com
Eftyhia Mourelatos, Representative

Glitnir banki hf
#810, 1718 Argyle St.
Halifax, NS B3J 3N6
902-429-3113
Fax: 902-422-0288
glitnir@glitnir.is
www.glitnir.is
Ownership: Office of Glitnir, Iceland.
Year Founded: 2006
Profile: Part of Glitnir Corporate & Investment Banking, Region Americas & Asia, the Canadian representative office focuses upon the seafood industry, as well as the sustainable energy, food & offshore supply vessel industries.

Executives:
Magnús Bjarnason, Managing Director, Asia & Americas; magnus.bjarnason@glitnir.is
Jonathan Logan, Executive Director, Asia & Americas; jonathan.logan@glitnir.is
Joe Fillmore, Director & Chief Representative, Glitnir Halifax Office; joe.fillmore@glitnirbank.com

Jamaica National Overseas (Canada) Ltd.
1672 Eglinton Ave. West
Toronto, ON M6E 2H2
416-784-2075
Fax: 416-784-2076
800-462-9003
info@jnocanada.com, rosbourne@jnocanada.com, sstamp@jnocanada.com
www.jnbs.com
Ownership: Office of Jamaica National Building Society, Kingston Jamaica.
Profile: Part of Jamaica National Building Society, the Canadian office facilitates money transfers from Canada.

Japan Bank for International Cooperation - Toronto Liaison Office(JBIC)
Exchange Tower
PO Box 493, 2 First Canadian Pl. Stn. 2 First Canadian Pl.
#3660, 130 King St. West
Toronto, ON M5X 1E5
416-865-1700
Fax: 416-865-0124
www.jbic.go.jp/english
Ownership: Office of Japan Bank for International Cooperation, Tokyo, Japan.

JCB International (Canada) Ltd.
Also listed under: *Credit Card Companies*
#510, 1030 West Georgia St. W
Vancouver, BC V6E 2Y3
604-689-8110
Fax: 604-689-8101
www.jcbinternational.com
Ownership: Office of JCB International Co., Ltd., Tokyo, Japan
Year Founded: 1961

JS Trasta komercbanka
#800, St. Clair Ave. East
Toronto, ON M4T 2T5
416-644-4941
Fax: 416-644-4946
canada@tkb.lv, info@tkb.lv
www.tkb.lv
Ownership: Office of JS Trasta komercbanka, Riga, Latvia.

Landsbanki Islands hf
George Mitchell House
5112 Prince St.
Halifax, NS B3J 1L3
902-576-3100
info@landsbanki.is
www.landsbanki.is
Ownership: Office of Landsbanki Islands hf, Reykjavik, Iceland.

Olafur Thorsteinsson, Head, Canada Representative Office

Lebanese Canadian Bank, s.a.l.
#1837, 1, Place Ville-Marie
Montréal, QC H3B 5K9
514-871-3999
Fax: 514-871-2079
Other Information: Alternative Phone Numbers: 514-871-1905; 514-871-1913; 514-871-1926
www.lebcanbank.com
Executives:
Imad Assio, Principal Representative

National Bank of Pakistan
#210, 175 Commerce Valley Dr. West
Thornhill, ON L3T 7P6
905-707-0244
Fax: 905-707-1040
chiefrep@nbpcanada.com, enquiries@nationalbank.com.pk
www.nbp.com.pk
Ownership: Office of National Bank of Pakistan, Karachi, Pakistan.

Schroder Investment Management North America Limited - Canadian Representative Office
Also listed under: *Financial Planning*
Canada Trust Tower, BCE Place
#4720, 161 Bay St.
Toronto, ON M5J 2S1
416-360-1200
Fax: 416-360-1202
www.schroders.com/ca
Former Name: Schroder Investment Management Canada Limited
Ownership: Office of Schroders plc, London, UK.
Profile: The Canadian office offers a wide range of investment products. Its global presence provides an integrated international research ability.

Stanford International Bank Ltd.(SIBL)
#3010, 1800, av McGill College
Montréal, QC H3A 3J6
514-985-3600
SIBprivate@stanfordeagle.com
www.stanfordinternational.com
Ownership: Office of Stanford International Bank Ltd., St. Johns, Antigua, West Indies.
Year Founded: 2004
Profile: A member of the Stanford Financial Group, the SIBL representative office is authorized to promote Bank products & services, as well as the products & services of Stanford affiliates.

Executives:
Alain Lapointe, Sr. Vice-President, Representative Office, Montréal

UBS AG
PO Box 3
#650, 999 West Hastings St.
Vancouver, BC V6C 2W2
604-691-8061
Fax: 604-691-8098
www.ubs.com
Ownership: Office of UBS AG, Zurich, Switzerland.

Victoria Mutual Building Society - Canadian Representative Office(VMBS)
Nortown Plaza
#14, 875 Eglinton Ave. West
Toronto, ON M6C 3Z9
416-652-8652
Fax: 416-652-5266
800-465-6500
vmbscanada@direct.com, manager@vmbs.com
www.vmbs.com
Ownership: Office of Victoria Mutual Building Society, Kingston, Jamaica.
Executives:
Denise Sinclair, Chief Representative
Branches:
Toronto
#101, 801 Eglinton Ave. West
Toronto, ON N5N 1E3
416-783-8627
Fax: 416-783-8024
877-783-8627
vmbs@bellnet.ca
Michael Steele, General Manager

Westdeutsche Landesbank Girozentrale
North Tower, Royal Bank Plaza
PO Box 41
#2301, 200 Bay St.
Toronto, ON M5J 2J1
416-216-5000
Fax: 416-216-5020
info@westlb.de
www.westlb.de
Also Known As: WestLB
Ownership: Office of Westdeutsche Landesbank Girozentrale, Düsseldorf, Germany
Profile: The Canadian office focuses upon structured finance/project finance, asset securitization, loan syndications & global financial markets.
Executives:
Alik Kassner, Executive Director; alik_kassner@westlb.com
Robert Dyck, Director; robert_dyck@westlb.com

Savings Banks

ATB Financial
ATB Place
9888 Jasper Ave. NW
Edmonton, AB T5J 1P1
780-408-7000
Fax: 780-422-4178
800-332-8383
atbinfo@atb.com
www.atb.com
Former Name: Alberta Treasury Branches
Ownership: Crown. 100% owned by the Provincial Government of Alberta
Year Founded: 1938
Number of Employees: 3,500
Assets: $10-100 billion
Profile: ATB Financial, with assets over $18 billion, is a full-service financial institution based in Edmonton, AB. With over half a million customers, ATB provides both personal & business financial services. Services are provided across the province through a network of branches, agencies, automated banking machines, telephone & internet banking, & a Customer Contact Centre located in Calgary.
Executives:
Robert Normand, President/CEO
Amolak Grewal, Chief Operating Officer
Jim McKillop, Chief Financial Officer
Bob Mann, Exec. Vice-President, Credit
Craig W. Warnock, Exec. Vice-President, Treasurer
Michael Baker, Sr. Vice-President, Personal & Business Financial Services
Ken Casey, Sr. Vice-President, Retail Banking Delivery
Sheldon Dyck, Sr. Vice-President, Investor Services
Ian Wild, Sr. Vice-President, Corporate Financial Services
Bob Ascah, Vice-President, Government Relations, Research & Analysis
Sharon Bell, Vice-President, Marketing
Peter Bolton, Vice-President, Direct Sales
Sandy Chipchar, Vice-President, Human Resources
Kerry Day, Vice-President, Legal & Corporate Compliance
Bruce Edgelow, Vice-President, Energy
Bill Fanous, Vice-President, Internal Audit
Shelly Flint, Vice-President, Mastercard
Lukasz Forys, Vice-President, Global Financial Markets
Mario Frison, Vice-President, Commercial
Jay Hamblin, Vice-President, Asset Management
Chris Hopfner, Vice-President, Credit Process
Keith Hughes, Vice-President, North Region
Kim Irving, Vice-President, South Region
Ed Knash, Vice-President, Agri-Industry
Dwayne Mann, Vice-President, Commercial Credit
Chet Niemczyk, Vice-President, Computer Operations
Dean Ozanne, Vice-President, Central Services
Robert B. G. (Rob) Smith, Vice-President, Central Region
Ray Wells, Vice-President, Retail Credit
Directors:
Robert (Bob) Splane, Chair
Robert G. Brawn
Gary Campbell
Robert C. (Bob) Clark
Arthur Froelich
John (Jack) Halpin
Brian R. Heidecker
Brian Hesje
Linda Hohol
Bern Kotelko
Brian McCook
Norm (Skip) McDonald
Al O'Brien
Branches & Agencies:
Acadia Valley
Main St.
Acadia Valley, AB T0J 0A0 Canada

ATB Financial (continued)
403-972-3805
Fax: 403-972-2263
Airdrie
404 Main St.
Airdrie, AB T4B 3C3 Canada
403-948-5989
Fax: 403-948-5990
Alberta Beach
4824 - 50 Ave.
Alberta Beach, AB T0H 0A0 Canada
780-924-2211
Fax: 780-924-2211
Alder Flats
General Delivery
Alder Flats, AB T0C 0A0 Canada
780-388-3889
Fax: 780-388-3075
Alix
4914 - 50 St.
Alix, AB T0C 0B0
403-747-2444
Fax: 403-747-2444
Alliance
215 Main St.
Alliance, AB T0B 0A0
780-879-3653
Fax: 780-879-2477
Amisk
5004 - 1st St.
Amisk, AB T0B 0B0
780-856-3751
Fax: 780-856-2243
Andrew
5026 - 51st St.
Andrew, AB T0B 0C0 Canada
780-365-3834
Fax: 780-365-3800
Athabasca
4910 - 50 St.
Athabasca, AB T9S 1E3 Canada
780-675-2258
Fax: 780-675-2240
Banff
317 Banff Ave.
Banff, AB T1L 1B2 Canada
403-762-8505
Fax: 403-762-4984
Barons
109 Main St.
Barons, AB T0L 0G0
403-757-2125
Fax: 403-757-2125
Barrhead
5141 - 50th St.
Barrhead, AB T7N 1A4 Canada
780-674-2241
Fax: 780-674-8466
Bashaw
4909 - 50 St.
Bashaw, AB T0B 0H0 Canada
780-372-3030
Fax: 780-372-3677
Bassano
308 - 2nd Ave.
Bassano, AB T0J 0B0
403-641-3041
Fax: 403-641-3042
Bawlf
105 Railway Ave.
Bawlf, AB T0B 0J0 Canada
780-377-3770
Fax: 780-373-3776
Beaumont
5000 - 50 St.
Beaumont, AB T4X 1E6 Canada
780-929-7777
Fax: 780-929-1205

Beaverlodge
302 - 10th St.
Beaverlodge, AB T0H 0C0 Canada
780-354-2235
Fax: 780-354-2238
Benalto
4918 - 50 Ave.
Benalto, AB T0M 0H0 Canada
403-746-3775
Fax: 403-746-3776
Berwyn
5010 - 51 St.
Berwyn, AB T0H 0E0 Canada
780-338-3838
Fax: 780-338-3839
Big Valley
52 Main St.
Big Valley, AB T0J 0G0 Canada
403-876-2515
Fax: 403-876-2515
Black Diamond
122 Centre Ave. West
Black Diamond, AB T0L 0H0 Canada
403-933-4357
Fax: 403-933-4360
Blackie
106 Aberdeen St.
Blackie, AB T0L 0J0 Canada
403-684-0023
Fax: 403-684-0019
Blairmore
13219 - 20 Ave.
Blairmore, AB T0K 0E0 Canada
403-562-8223
Fax: 403-562-2277
Blue Ridge
312 Main St.
Blue Ridge, AB T0E 0B0 Canada
780-648-3980
Fax: 780-648-2057
Bon Accord
4909 - 50 St.
Bon Accord, AB T0A 0K0 Canada
780-921-3762
Fax: 780-921-3695
Bonanza
9 Main St.
Bonanza, AB T0H 0K0 Canada
780-353-3044
Fax: 780-353-3919
Bonnyville
4902 - 50 Ave. West
Bonnyville, AB T9N 2G3 Canada
780-826-3024
Fax: 780-826-4669
Bow Island
128 - 5 Ave. West
Bow Island, AB T0K 0G0 Canada
403-545-2204
Fax: 403-545-2208
Bowden
2020 - 20 Ave.
Bowden, AB T0M 0K0 Canada
403-224-2180
Fax: 403-224-2931
Boyle
5115 - 3rd St.
Boyle, AB T0A 0M0 Canada
780-689-4099
Fax: 780-689-4011
Bragg Creek
7 River Dr. South
Bragg Creek, AB T0L 0K0 Canada
403-949-3513
Fax: 403-949-3537
Breton
4923 - 50th Ave.
Breton, AB T0C 0P0 Canada
780-696-3664
Fax: 780-696-2426
Brooks
219 - 2 St. West
Brooks, AB T1R 1B5 Canada
403-362-3351
Fax: 403-362-3342
Bruce
Main St.
Bruce, AB T0B 0R0 Canada
780-688-3366
Fax: 780-688-3390
Bruderheim
4904 Queen St.
Bruderheim, AB T0B 0S0 Canada
780-796-3616
Fax: 780-796-3919
Calgary - 16th Ave. NW
217 - 16th Ave. NW
Calgary, AB T2M 0H5 Canada
403-974-5222
Fax: 403-276-9625
Calgary - 16th Ave. NW - North Hill Business Hub
217 - 16th Ave. NW
Calgary, AB T2M 0H5
403-974-5275
Fax: 403-276-9625

Calgary - 17th Ave. SE
3620 - 17th Ave. SE
Calgary, AB T2A 0R9 Canada
403-297-6507
Fax: 403-235-2829
Calgary - 17th Ave. SW
1110 - 17 Ave. SW
Calgary, AB T2T 0B4 Canada
403-974-5380
Fax: 403-974-5383
Calgary - 24 St. SE
#200, 11488 - 24 St. SE
Calgary, AB T2Z 4C9 Canada
403-920-3000
Fax: 403-920-3017
Calgary - 2nd St. SW
Fifth Avenue Place
420 - 2nd St. SW
Calgary, AB TP2 3K4 Canada
403-297-2009
Fax: 403-297-2016
Calgary - 32nd St. NE
#600, 2555 - 32nd St. NE
Calgary, AB T1Y 7J6 Canada
403-974-5240
Fax: 403-974-5274
Calgary - 34 Ave. SW
2140 - 34 Ave. SW
Calgary, AB T2T 5P6 Canada
403-297-7163
Fax: 403-246-4362
Calgary - 6th Ave. SW
#100, 801- 6th Ave. SW
Calgary, AB T2P 3W2 Canada
403-297-6206
Fax: 403-297-5314
Calgary - 8 Ave. SW
239 - 8 Ave. SW
Calgary, AB T2P 1B9 Canada
403-974-5700
Fax: 403-974-5741
Calgary - 8 Ave. SW - Stephen Ave. Business Hub
239 - 8 Ave. SW
Calgary, AB T2P 1B9
403-974-5701
Fax: 403-974-5288
Calgary - 85th St. SW
#202, 917 - 85th St. SW
Calgary, AB T3H 5Z9
403-663-4545
Fax: 403-663-4566
Calgary - Brentwood Rd NW
Brentwood Village Shopping Centre
3630 Brentwood Rd. NW
Calgary, AB T2L 1K8 Canada
403-297-8164
Fax: 403-282-7063
Calgary - Country Hills Blvd. NE
#800, 388 Country Hills Blvd. NE
Calgary, AB T3K 5J6 Canada
403-226-7377
Fax: 403-226-7391
Calgary - Crowfoot Cres. NW
480 Crowfoot Cres. NW
Calgary, AB T3G 5H7 Canada
403-974-5767
Fax: 403-974-5768
Calgary - Glenmore Trail SE - Business Financial Services Centre

303 - 3200 Glenmore Trail SE
Calgary, AB T2C 4V7 Canada
403-974-8078
Fax: 403-974-8095
Calgary - Heritage Meadows Way SE
#1200, 33 Heritage Meadows Way SE
Calgary, AB T2H 3B8
403-974-3599
Fax: 403-974-3717
Calgary - Macleod Trail SW
Chinook Centre
#264, 6455 Macleod Trail SW
Calgary, AB T2H 0K3 Canada
403-297-6503
Fax: 403-253-3347
Calgary - McKenzie Towne Ave.
48 McKenzie Towne Ave.
Calgary, AB T2Z 3S7
403-974-6048
Fax: 403-974-6064
Calgary - Rockyvalley Dr. NW
#3000, 11595 Rockyvalley Dr. NW
Calgary, AB T3G 5Y6
403-208-4070
Fax: 403-208-4082
Calgary - Sarcee Trail SW
11680 Sarcee Trail NW
Calgary, AB T3R 0A1
403-974-8989
Fax: 403-974-8969
Calgary - Shawville Blvd. SE
#100, 303 Shawville Blvd. SE
Calgary, AB T2Y 3W6 Canada
403-297-2831
Fax: 403-974-8577
Calgary - Stewart Green SW
601 Stewart Green SW
Calgary, AB T3H 3C8 Canada
403-297-3900
Fax: 403-686-1548

Calgary - Symons Valley Rd. NW
12012 Symons Valley Rd. NW
Calgary, AB T3P 0A3
403-974-3441
Fax: 403-974-3470
Calmar
4905 - 50 Ave.
Calmar, AB T0C 0V0 Canada
780-985-2103
Fax: 780-985-2104
Camrose
4877 - 50 St.
Camrose, AB T4V 1P6 Canada
780-672-3331
Fax: 780-672-5444
Canmore
#104, 1240 Railway Ave.
Canmore, AB T1W 1P4 Canada
403-678-6868
Fax: 403-678-6169
Carbon
407 Caradoc Ave.
Carbon, AB T0M 0L0 Canada
403-572-3434
Fax: 403-572-3339
Cardston
24 - 2 Ave. West
Cardston, AB T0K 0K0 Canada
403-653-3394
Fax: 403-653-3396
Carmangay
119 Carmen St.
Carmangay, AB T0L 0N0 Canada
403-643-3595
Fax: 403-643-2007
Caroline
5039 - 50 Ave.
Caroline, AB T0M 0M0 Canada
403-722-3830
Fax: 403-722-3832
Carseland
104 Main St.
Carseland, AB T0J 0M0 Canada
403-934-3826
Fax: 403-934-3949
Carstairs
103 - 10 Ave. North
Carstairs, AB T0M 0N0 Canada
403-337-3345
Fax: 403-337-3348
Castor
4913 - 50 Ave.
Castor, AB T0C 0X0 Canada
403-882-3110
Fax: 403-882-3118
Cereal
211 Main St.
Cereal, AB T0J 0N0 Canada
403-326-3818
Fax: 403-326-3800
Champion
118 Main St.
Champion, AB T0L 0R0 Canada
403-897-3781
Fax: 403-897-3781
Chauvin
216 Main St.
Chauvin, AB T0B 0V0 Canada
780-858-3881
Fax: 780-858-2125
Chipman
4919 - 50 St.
Chipman, AB T0B 0W0 Canada
780-363-3982
Fax: 780-363-2386
Claresholm
115 - 49 Ave. West
Claresholm, AB T0L 0T0 Canada
403-625-4451
Fax: 403-625-4453
Clive
5110 - 50 St.
Clive, AB T0C 0Y0 Canada
403-784-3411
Fax: 403-784-3471
Coaldale
1821 - 20 Ave.
Coaldale, AB T1M 1N1 Canada
403-345-2611
Fax: 403-345-2613
Cochrane
280 - 5th Ave. West
Cochrane, AB T4C 2G4 Canada
403-932-3117
Fax: 403-932-6487
Cold Lake
6501 - 51st St.
Cold Lake, AB T9M 1C8 Canada
780-594-7149
Fax: 780-594-4780
Compeer
Main St.
Compeer, AB T0C 1A0 Canada
403-552-3791
Fax: 403-552-3791

Consort
4911 - 50th St.
Consort, AB T0C 1B0 Canada
403-577-3800
Fax: 403-577-3665
Coronation
5026 Victoria Ave.
Coronation, AB T0C 1C0 Canada
403-578-4101
Fax: 403-578-4106
Coutts
101 Centre Ave.
Coutts, AB T0K 0N0 Canada
403-344-3644
Fax: 403-344-3645
Crossfield
1214 Railway St.
Crossfield, AB T0M 0S0 Canada
403-946-4345
Fax: 403-946-4347
Czar
4927 - 50 St.
Czar, AB T0B 0Z0 Canada
780-867-0008
Fax: 780-857-2208
Daysland
5033 - 50 St.
Daysland, AB T0B 1A0 Canada
780-374-3524
Fax: 780-374-3660
Delburne
2207 - 20 St.
Delburne, AB T0M 0V0 Canada
403-749-3633
Fax: 403-749-3633
Delia
207 Main St.
Delia, AB T0J 0W0 Canada
403-364-2701
Fax: 403-364-2702
Devon
#102 - 14 Athabasca Ave.
Devon, AB T9G 1G2 Canada
780-987-5683
Fax: 780-987-5683
Didsbury
1820 - 20 St.
Didsbury, AB T0M 0W0 Canada
403-335-3386
Fax: 403-335-3982
Donalda
5015 Main St.
Donalda, AB T0B 1H0 Canada
403-883-0000
Fax: 403-883-2417
Drayton Valley
5117 - 51 Ave.
Drayton Valley, AB T7A 1S2 Canada
780-542-4406
Fax: 780-542-4400
Drumheller
#300, 650 South Railway Ave. East
Drumheller, AB T0J 0Y0 Canada
403-823-5161
Fax: 403-823-4938
Duchess
103 Centre St.
Duchess, AB T0J 0Z0 Canada
403-378-4330
Fax: 403-378-4330
Eaglesham
4914 - 50 St.
Eaglesham, AB T0H 1H0 Canada
780-359-2246
Fax: 780-359-2246
Eckville
5108 - 50 St.
Eckville, AB TOM OXO Canada
403-746-3145
Fax: 403-746-3316
Edberg
48 Main St.
Edberg, AB T0B 1J0 Canada
780-877-3969
Fax: 780-877-3969
Edgerton
5024 - 50 St.
Edgerton, AB T0B 1K0 Canada
780-755-3200
Fax: 780-755-2204
Edmonton - 102 Ave.
City Centre
#127D, 10200 - 102 Ave.
Edmonton, AB T5J 4B7 Canada
780-422-2897
Fax: 780-422-8378
Edmonton - 104 Ave.
11366 - 104 Ave.
Edmonton, AB T5K 2W9 Canada
780-422-4800
Fax: 780-422-4203
Edmonton - 104 St.
8008 - 104 St.
Edmonton, AB T6E 4E2 Canada

ATB Financial (continued)
780-427-4162
Fax: 780-433-4165

Edmonton - 118 Ave.
8804 - 118 Ave.
Edmonton, AB T5B 0T4 Canada
780-427-4171
Fax: 780-479-5340
Edmonton - 137 Ave.
13304 - 137 Ave.
Edmonton, AB T5L 4Z6 Canada
780-427-7353
Fax: 780-456-4151
Edmonton - 23 Ave. NW
14236 - 23rd Ave. NW
Edmonton, AB T6R 3A8 Canada
780-408-7660
Fax: 780-408-7679
Edmonton - 23rd Ave.
5331 - 23rd Ave.
Edmonton, AB T6L 7G4 Canada
780-422-2600
Fax: 780-462-2557
Edmonton - 97 St.
16775 - 97 St.
Edmonton, AB T5X 6A7 Canada
780-408-7400
Fax: 780-408-7413
Edmonton - 97 St. NW
12703 - 97 St. NW
Edmonton, AB T5E 4C1 Canada
780-422-9438
Fax: 780-473-0117
Edmonton - 97 St. NW - Killarney Business Hub
12703 - 97 St. NW
Edmonton, AB T5E 4C1
780-422-9438
Fax: 780-473-0117
Edmonton - 99 St. NW
2103 - 99 St. NW
Edmonton, AB T6N 1L4 Canada
780-408-7800
Fax: 780-408-7822
Edmonton - Calgary Trail
4234 Calgary Trail
Edmonton, AB T6J 6Y8 Canada
780-408-7433
Fax: 780-408-7451
Edmonton - Calgary Trail - Business Hub
4234 Calgary Trail
Edmonton, AB T6Y 6Y8
780-408-7433
Fax: 780-408-7451
Edmonton - James Mowatt Trail
1003 James Mowatt Trail
Edmonton, AB T6W 1S4
780-408-6430
Fax: 780-408-6435
Edmonton - Jasper Ave.
ATB Place
#100, 9888 Jasper Ave.
Edmonton, AB T5T 1P1 Canada
780-408-7500
Fax: 780-408-7523
Edmonton - Jasper Ave. - Business Hub
ATB Place
9888 Jasper Ave., 2nd Fl.
Edmonton, AB T5J 1P1
780-408-7527
Fax: 780-422-9687
Edmonton - Lessard Rd.
18358 Lessard Rd.
Edmonton, AB T6M 2W8 Canada
780-408-8044
Fax: 780-408-8049
Edmonton - Manning Crossing
350 Manning Crossing NW
Edmonton, AB T5A 5A1 Canada
780-422-6003
Fax: 780-478-5883
Edmonton - Stony Plain Rd.
Jasper Place
15548 Stony Plain Rd.
Edmonton, AB T5P 3Z2 Canada
780-427-8300
Fax: 780-422-5410
Edmonton - Stony Plain Rd.
17107 Stony Plain Rd.
Edmonton, AB T5S 2M9 Canada
780-408-7474
Fax: 780-408-7477
Edmonton - Stony Plain Rd. - Business Hub
Jasper Place
15548 Stony Plain Rd.
Edmonton, AB T5P 2Z2
780-408-6589
Fax: 780-422-5410
Edson
313 - 50 St.
Edson, AB T7E 1T8 Canada
780-723-5571
Fax: 780-723-5570
Elk Point
4925 - 50 St.
Elk Point, AB T0A 1A0 Canada
780-724-3883
Fax: 780-724-4461
Elnora
206 Main St.
Elnora, AB T0M 0Y0 Canada
403-773-3923
Fax: 403-773-2220

Enchant
115 Centre St.
Enchant, AB T0K 0V0 Canada
403-739-3768
Fax: 403-739-3810
Evansburg
4913 - 50th Ave.
Evansburg, AB T0E 0T0 Canada
780-727-3766
Fax: 780-727-4013
Fairview
11012 - 102 Ave.
Fairview, AB T0H 1L0 Canada
780-835-4932
Fax: 780-835-4935
Falher
General Delivery
Falher, AB T0H 1M0 Canada
780-837-2218
Fax: 780-837-2810
Fawcett
General Delivery
Fawcett, AB T0G 0Y0 Canada
780-954-2516
Fax: 780-954-2519
Ferintosh
314 Main St.
Ferintosh, AB T0B 1M0 Canada
780-877-3965
Fax: 780-877-2404
Foremost
201 Main St.
Foremost, AB T0K 0X0 Canada
403-867-2069
Fax: 403-867-2048
Forestburg
General Delivery
Forestburg, AB T0B 1N0 Canada
780-582-3745
Fax: 780-582-3947
Fort Assiniboine
33 State Ave.
Fort Assiniboine, AB T0G 1A0 Canada
780-584-3995
Fax: 780-584-3995
Fort Macleod
221 Macleod Blvd.
Fort MacLeod, AB T0L 0Z0 Canada
403-553-4444
Fax: 403-553-4447
Fort McMurray - Haineault St.
11 Haineault St.
Fort McMurray, AB T9H 1R8 Canada
780-790-3300
Fax: 780-791-2451
Fort McMurray - Thickwood
330 Thickwood Blvd.
Fort McMurray, AB T9K 1Y1 Canada
780-790-6940
Fax: 780-790-3340
Fort Saskatchewan
9964 - 99th Ave.
Fort Saskatchewan, AB T8L 4G8 Canada
780-998-5161
Fax: 780-998-7010
Fort Vermilion
Main St.
Fort Vermilion, AB T0H 1N0 Canada
780-927-3781
Fax: 780-927-3075
Fox Creek
55C Kaybob Dr.
Fox Creek, AB T0H 1P0 Canada
780-622-2006
Fax: 780-622-2007
Galahad
109 Sir Galahad St.
Galahad, AB T0B 1R0 Canada
780-583-3755
Fax: 780-583-2142
Gibbons
4740 - 50 Ave.
Gibbons, AB T0A 1N0
780-923-9650
Fax: 780-923-9648
Gleichen
345 Greisbach St.
Gleichen, AB T0J 1N0 Canada
403-734-1070
Fax: 403-734-1072
Glendon
203 Railway Ave. NE
Glendon, AB TOA 1P0 Canada
780-635-4140
Fax: 780-635-4149
Glenwood
60 Main Ave.
Glenwood, AB T0K 2R0 Canada
403-626-3483
Fax: 403-626-3486
Grande Cache
2700 Pine Plaza
Grande Cache, AB T0E 0Y0 Canada
780-827-3606
Fax: 780-827-2997

Grande Prairie - 106A Ave.
9907 - 106A Ave.
Grande Prairie, AB T8V 8E9 Canada
780-539-7450
Fax: 780-538-5404
Grande Prairie - 106A St. - Business Hub
9907 - 106A St.
Grande Prairie, AB T8V 8E9
780-539-7450
Fax: 780-538-5100
Grande Prairie - 99 St.
11507 - 99 St.
Grande Prairie, AB T8V 2H6 Canada
780-538-5225
Fax: 780-538-2968
Granum
210 Railway Ave.
Granum, AB T0L 1A0 Canada
403-687-3794
Fax: 403-687-3983
Grassland
Main St.
Grassland, AB T0A 1V0 Canada
780-525-2837
Fax: 780-525-3583
Grimshaw
5216 - 50 St.
Grimshaw, AB T0H 1W0 Canada
780-332-4637
Fax: 780-332-4640
Halkirk
101 Railway Ave.
Halkirk, AB T0C 1M0 Canada
403-884-4633
Fax: 403-884-4632

Hanna
232 - 2nd Ave. West
Hanna, AB T0J 1P0 Canada
403-854-4404
Fax: 403-854-4407

Hardisty
5032 - 50 St.
Hardisty, AB T0B 1V0 Canada
780-888-0000
Fax: 780-888-2408

Hay Lakes
11 Main St.
Hay Lakes, AB T0B 1W0 Canada
780-878-3337
Fax: 780-878-3338

Heisler
202A Main St.
Heisler, AB T0B 2A0 Canada
780-889-3981
Fax: 780-889-3900

High Level
10102 - 100 Ave.
High Level, AB T0H 1Z0 Canada
780-926-2221
Fax: 780-926-2175

High Prairie
5201/03 - 49th St.
High Prairie, AB T0G 1E0 Canada
780-523-5201
Fax: 780-523-5204

Hines Creek
114 - 10 St.
Hines Creek, AB T0H 2A0 Canada
780-494-2152
Fax: 780-494-2204

Hinton
207 Pembina Ave.
Hinton, AB T7V 2B3 Canada
780-865-2294
Fax: 780-865-2385

Holden
5015 - 50 St.
Holden, AB T0B 2C0 Canada
780-688-3865
Fax: 780-668-3870

Hythe
10026 - 101 Ave.
Hythe, AB T0H 2C0 Canada
780-356-3823
Fax: 780-356-3853

Innisfail
4962 - 50 St.
Innisfail, AB T4G 1S7 Canada
403-227-3350
Fax: 403-227-1336

Innisfree
5116 - 50 Ave.
Innisfree, AB T0B 2G0 Canada
780-592-2083
Fax: 780-592-2087

Irma
4924 - 50 St.
Irma, AB T0B 2H0 Canada
780-754-3607
Fax: 780-754-2443

Irricana
224 - 2nd St.
Irricana, AB T0M 1B0 Canada
403-935-4261
Fax: 403-935-4261

Irvine
85 South Railway Ave.
Irvine, AB T0J 1V0 Canada
403-834-2670
Fax: 403-834-2671

Islay
4940 - 50 St.
Islay, AB T0B 2J0 Canada
780-744-6688
Fax: 780-744-6680

Jasper
404 Patricia St.
Jasper, AB T0E 1E0 Canada
780-852-3297
Fax: 780-852-3717

Killam
4940 - 50 St.
Killam, AB T0B 2L0 Canada
780-385-3751
Fax: 780-385-2413

Kinuso
347 Main St.
Kinuso, AB T0G 1K0 Canada
780-775-2061
Fax: 780-775-2061

Kitscoty
4912 - 50 St.
Kitscoty, AB T0B 2P0 Canada
780-846-2440
Fax: 780-846-2440

La Crete
10102 - 100th Ave.
La Crete, AB T0H 2H0 Canada
780-928-3777
Fax: 780-928-3039

Lac La Biche
10039 - 101st. St.
Lac La Biche, AB T0A 2C0 Canada
780-623-4446
Fax: 780-623-3869

Lacombe
4720 - 51st Ave.
Lacombe, AB T4L 2J5 Canada
403-782-3550
Fax: 403-782-3967

Lake Louise
101A Lake Louise Dr.
Lake Louise, AB T0L 1E0 Canada
403-522-3678
Fax: 403-522-3867

Lamont
5130 - 50th Ave.
La Crete, AB T0B 2R0 Canada
780-895-2261
Fax: 780-895-2267

Leduc
4821 - 50 Ave.
Leduc, AB T9E 6X6 Canada
780-986-2226
Fax: 780-986-7897

Lethbridge - 6th St.
319 - 6 St. South
Lethbridge, AB T1J 2C7 Canada
403-381-5431
Fax: 403-327-3311

Lethbridge - Mayor Magrath Dr. South
601 Mayor Magrath Dr. South
Lethbridge, AB T1J 4M5 Canada
403-382-4388
Fax: 403-327-3799

Lethbridge - Mayor Magrath Dr. South - Business Hub
601 Mayor Magrath Dr. South
Lethbridge, AB T1J 4M5
403-382-4388
Fax: 403-327-3799

Linden
104 Central Ave. East
Linden, AB T0M 1J0 Canada
403-546-3993
Fax: 403-546-3997

Lloydminster
7001 - 44 St.
Lloydminster, AB T9V 2X1 Canada
780-875-8901
Fax: 780-875-8903

Lomond
112 Railway Ave.
Lomond, AB T0L 1G0 Canada
403-792-3663
Fax: 403-792-3663

Magrath
82 - 1 Ave. SW
Magrath, AB T0K 1J0 Canada
403-758-3345
Fax: 403-758-3347

Mallaig
Main St.
Mallaig, AB T0A 2K0 Canada
780-635-3966
Fax: 780-635-2106

Manning
General Delivery
Manning, AB T0H 2M0 Canada
780-836-3301
Fax: 780-836-3304

Mannville
#2, 4906 - 50 Ave.
Mannville, AB T0B 2W0 Canada
780-763-3555
Fax: 780-763-3557

Marwayne
27 Railway Ave.
Marwayne, AB T0B 2X0 Canada
780-847-2110
Fax: 780-847-2112

Mayerthorpe
4910 - 50 St.
Mayerthorpe, AB T0E 1N0 Canada
780-786-2207
Fax: 780-786-2575

McLennan
General Delivery
McLennan, AB T0H 2L0 Canada
780-324-3975
Fax: 780-324-3861

Medicine Hat - 2nd St. SE
536 - 2 St. SE
Medicine Hat, AB T1A 0C6 Canada
403-504-3000
Fax: 403-526-1606

Medicine Hat - 2nd St. SE - Business Hub
536 - 2nd St. SE
Medicine Hat, AB T1A 0C6
403-504-3000
Fax: 403-526-1606

Medicine Hat - Carry Drive
50 Carry Dr. SE
Medicine Hat, AB T1B 4E1 Canada
403-504-2000
Fax: 403-526-1033

Milk River
140 Main St. NE
Milk River, AB T0K 1M0 Canada
403-647-3532
Fax: 403-647-3635

Millarville
1 Main St.
Millarville, AB T0L 1K0 Canada
403-931-3626
Fax: 403-931-2124

Millet
5004 - 51 Ave.
Millet, AB T0C 1Z0 Canada
780-387-4633
Fax: 780-387-4168

Minburn
5009 - 50 St.
Minburn, AB T0B 3B0 Canada
780-593-3999
Fax: 780-593-3999

Mirror
5019 - 50 Ave.
Mirror, AB T0B 3C0 Canada
403-788-3056
Fax: 403-788-3252

Morinville
10006 - 103rd St.
Morinville, AB T8R 1R7
780-939-2821
Fax: 780-939-6779

Morrin
103 Main St.
Morrin, AB T0J 2B0 Canada
403-772-2435
Fax: 403-772-2435

Mulhurst Bay
5606 Lakeshore Dr.
Mulhurst Bay, AB T0C 2C0 Canada
780-389-3688
Fax: 780-389-3559

Mundare

ATB Financial (continued)

Main St.
Mundare, AB T0B 3H0 Canada
780-764-3786
Fax: 780-764-3786

Myrnam
5020 - 49 St.
Myrnam, AB T0B 3K0 Canada
780-366-3911
Fax: 780-366-3814

Nampa
9810 - 100 Ave.
Nampa, AB T0H 2R0 Canada
780-322-3747
Fax: 780-322-2245

Nanton
2202 - 20 St.
Nanton, AB T0L 1R0 Canada
403-646-2207
Fax: 403-646-2206

New Norway
126 Main St.
New Norway, AB T0B 3L0 Canada
780-855-3762
Fax: 780-855-3764

New Sarepta
5063 Centre Ave.
New Sarepta, AB T0B 3M0 Canada
780-941-2363
Fax: 780-941-3716

Newbrook
General Delivery
Newbrook, AB T0A 2P0 Canada
780-576-3966
Fax: 780-576-2272

Nobleford
110 King St.
Nobleford, AB T0L 1S0 Canada
403-824-3372
Fax: 403-824-3272

Okotoks
#131, 31 Southridge Dr.
Okotoks, AB T1S 2N3 Canada
403-938-7232
Fax: 403-938-7247

Olds
4901 - 50 Ave.
Olds, AB T4H 1P5 Canada
403-556-3232
Fax: 403-556-3288

Onoway
4809 - 50 St.
Onoway, AB T0E 1V0 Canada
780-967-2201
Fax: 780-967-2203

Oyen
200 Main St.
Oyen, AB T0J 2J0 Canada
403-664-3553
Fax: 403-664-3856

Paradise Valley
109 Main St.
Paradise Valley, AB T0B 3R0 Canada
780-745-2626
Fax: 780-745-2620

Peace River
9904 - 100 Ave.
Peace River, AB T8S 1S2 Canada
780-618-3299
Fax: 780-618-3293

Peers
General Delivery
Peers, AB T0E 1W0 Canada
780-693-3948
Fax: 780-693-3959

Picture Butte
330 Highway Ave.
Picture Butte, AB T0K 1V0 Canada
403-732-5611
Fax: 403-732-5613

Pincher Creek
769 Main St.
Pincher Creek, AB T0K 1W0 Canada
403-627-3304
Fax: 403-627-3306

Plamondon
General Delivery
Plamondon, AB T0A 2T0 Canada
780-798-3783
Fax: 780-798-2409

Ponoka
5018 - 48th Ave.
Ponoka, AB T4J 1R7 Canada
403-783-3301
Fax: 403-783-3305

Provost
5013 - 50 St.
Provost, AB T0B 3S0 Canada
780-753-2247
Fax: 780-753-2240

Radway
Main St.
Radway, AB T0A 2V0 Canada
780-736-2229
Fax: 780-736-2226

Rainbow Lake
2 Park Plaza
Rainbow Lake, AB T0H 2Y0 Canada
780-956-3777
Fax: 780-956-3649

Raymond
69A Broadway St. North
Raymond, AB T0K 2S0 Canada
403-752-4511
Fax: 403-752-4514

Red Deer - 51 St.
First Red Deer Place
#100, 4911 - 51 St.
Red Deer, AB T4N 6V4 Canada
403-340-5130
Fax: 403-343-1577

Red Deer - 59 St.
4919 - 59 St.
Red Deer, AB T4N 6C9 Canada
403-340-5384
Fax: 403-342-0515

Red Deer - 59 St. - Business Hub
4919 - 59 St.
Red Deer, AB T4N 6C9
403-342-0515
Fax: 403-342-0515

Red Deer - Molly Banister Dr.
Bower Mall
4999 Molly Banister Dr.
Red Deer, AB T4R 3B9 Canada
403-357-3023
Fax: 403-357-3002

Red Earth Creek
249 Hwy. 88
Red Earth Creek, AB T0G 1X0 Canada
780-649-1200
Fax: 780-649-1206

Redcliff
205 Broadway Ave. NE
Redcliff, AB T0J 2P0 Canada
403-548-7166
Fax: 403-548-7419

Redwater
4832 - 50 Ave.
Redwater, AB T0A 2W0 Canada
780-942-4545
Fax: 780-942-4560

Rimbey
5037 - 50 Ave.
Rimbey, AB T0C 2J0 Canada
403-843-2291
Fax: 403-843-3025

Rocky Mountain House
4515 - 52 St.
Rocky Mountain House, AB T4T 1A6 Canada
403-845-2811
Fax: 403-845-5458

Rockyford
PO Box 160
218 Main St.
Rockyford, AB T0J 2R0 Canada
403-533-3771
Fax: 403-533-3772

Rolling Hills
117 - 1st Ave.
Rolling Hills, AB T0J 2S0
403-964-3912
Fax: 403-964-3672

Rosemary
510 Centre St.
Rosemary, AB T0J 2W0 Canada
403-378-4120
Fax: 403-378-4120

Rycroft
4635 - 50 St.
Rycroft, AB T0H 3A0 Canada
780-765-3624
Fax: 780-765-3059

Ryley
5021 - 50 St.
Ryley, AB T0B 4A0 Canada
780-663-3513
Fax: 780-663-3514

Sangudo
5003 - 50 St.
Sangudo, AB T0E 2A0 Canada
780-785-2265
Fax: 780-785-2261

Sedgewick
4837 - 47 St.
Sedgewick, AB T0B 4C0 Canada
780-384-3639
Fax: 780-384-2728

Sexsmith
9905 - 100 St.
Sexsmith, AB T0H 3C0 Canada
780-568-4055
Fax: 780-568-3614

Sherwood Park - Baseline Rd.
#100, 550 Baseline Rd.
Sherwood Park, AB T8H 2G8 Canada
780-464-4444
Fax: 780-449-3416

Sherwood Park - Baseline Rd. - Business Hub
#100, 550 Baseline Rd.
Sherwood Park, AB T8H 2G8
780-718-2177
Fax: 780-449-3406

Sherwood Park - Wye Rd.
210 Wye Rd.
Sherwood Park, AB T8B 1N1 Canada
780-449-3636
Fax: 780-464-1032

Slave Lake
301 Main St.
Slave Lake, AB T0G 2A0 Canada
780-849-3911
Fax: 780-849-3922

Smoky Lake
50 Wheatland Ave.
Smoky Lake, AB T0A 3C0 Canada
780-656-3833
Fax: 780-656-3995

Spirit River
4518 - 50 St.
Spirit River, AB T0H 3G0 Canada
780-864-3650
Fax: 780-864-3740

Spruce Grove
16 McLeod Ave.
Spruce Grove, AB T7X 3Y1 Canada
780-962-6000
Fax: 780-962-0695

St Albert - St. Albert Rd.
350, 700 St. Albert Rd.
St Albert, AB T8N 7A5 Canada
780-460-4960
Fax: 780-460-4965

St Albert - Tudor Glen Market
5515 Tudor Glen Market
St Albert, AB T8N 3V4 Canada
780-459-1221
Fax: 780-459-4385

St Paul
4801 - 50 Ave.
St Paul, AB T0A 3A0 Canada
780-645-4406
Fax: 780-645-6857

Standard
811 The Broadway
Standard, AB T0J 3G0 Canada
403-644-3757
Fax: 403-644-2433

Stavely
5001 - 50 Ave.
Stavely, AB T0L 1Z0
403-549-2239
Fax: 403-549-2039

Stettler
5007 - 51 St.
Stettler, AB T0C 2L0 Canada
403-742-4466
Fax: 403-742-1616

Stirling
218 - 4 Ave.
Stirling, AB T0K 2E0 Canada
403-756-3964
Fax: 403-756-3963

Stony Plain
5014 - 50 St.
Stony Plain, AB T7Z 1T2 Canada
780-963-2214
Fax: 780-963-3533

Strathmore
#109, 100 Ranch Market
Strathmore, AB T1P 0A8 Canada
403-934-5293
Fax: 403-934-5351

Strome
5103 - 50 St.
Strome, AB T0B 4H0 Canada
780-376-3550
Fax: 780-376-2333

Sundre
304 Main Ave. West
Sundre, AB T0M 1X0 Canada
403-638-4312
Fax: 403-638-4059

Swan Hills
4916 Plaza Ave.
Swan Hills, AB T0G 2C0 Canada
780-333-4587
Fax: 780-333-2715

Sylvan Lake
150 Pelican Pl.
Sylvan Lake, AB T4S 1M5 Canada
403-887-2102
Fax: 403-887-4402

Taber
5317 - 48 Ave.
Taber, AB T1G 1S7 Canada
403-223-8941
Fax: 403-223-8945

Tangent
Main St.
Tangent, AB T0H 3J0 Canada
780-359-2220
Fax: 780-359-2220

Thorhild
710 - 1st St.
Thorhild, AB T0A 3J0 Canada
780-378-3935
Fax: 780-398-2251

Thorsby
4816 - 50 St.
Thorsby, AB T0C 2P0 Canada
780-789-3885
Fax: 780-789-3608

Three Hills
211 Main St.
Three Hills, AB T0M 2A0 Canada
403-443-5571
Fax: 403-443-5578

Tilley
111 Centre St.
Tilley, AB T0J 3K0 Canada
403-377-2275
Fax: 403-377-2276

Tofield
5120 - 50 St.
Tofield, AB T0B 4J0 Canada
780-662-3773
Fax: 780-662-3701

Torrington
101 - 1 Ave.
Torrington, AB T0M 2B0 Canada
403-631-2267
Fax: 403-631-2267

Trochu
201 Main St.
Trochu, AB T0M 2C0 Canada
403-442-4200
Fax: 403-442-4206

Two Hills
5009 - 50 Ave. South
Two Hills, AB T0B 4K0 Canada
780-657-3391
Fax: 780-657-3394

Valleyview
4805A - 50 Ave.
Valleyview, AB T0H 3N0 Canada
780-524-3965
Fax: 780-524-3967

Vauxhall
514 - 2 Ave. North
Vauxhall, AB T0K 2K0 Canada
403-654-2512
Fax: 403-654-2345

Vegreville
4931 - 50 St.
Vegreville, AB T9C 1R1 Canada
780-632-2340
Fax: 780-632-2995

Vermilion
5014 - 50 Ave.
Vermilion, AB T9X 1A2 Canada
780-853-4080
Fax: 780-853-3113

Veteran
107 Waterloo St.
Veteran, AB T0C 2S0 Canada
403-575-3920
Fax: 403-575-3920

Viking
5211 - 50th St.
Viking, AB T0B 4N0 Canada
780-336-3209
Fax: 780-336-2044

Vilna
5112 - 50 St.
Vilna, AB T0A 3L0 Canada
780-636-3666
Fax: 780-636-3666

Vulcan
212 Centre St.
Vulcan, AB T0L 2B0 Canada
403-485-2271
Fax: 403-485-2274

Wabamun
5123 - 52 St.
Wabamun, AB T0E 2K0 Canada
780-892-7927
Fax: 780-892-7927

Wabasca
991 Mistassiniy Rd. South
Wabasca, AB T0G 2K0 Canada
780-891-3680
Fax: 780-891-3847

Wainwright
509 - 10 St.
Wainwright, AB T9W 1P1 Canada
780-842-3355
Fax: 780-842-4442

Wandering River
Main St.
Wandering River, AB T0A 3M0 Canada
780-771-2032
Fax: 780-771-2034

Wanham
Main St.
Wanham, AB T0H 3P0 Canada
780-694-3770
Fax: 780-694-2255

Warburg
5035 - 52 St.
Warburg, AB T0C 2T0 Canada
780-848-2876
Fax: 780-848-2461

Warner
304 - 2nd St.
Warner, AB T0K 2L0 Canada
403-642-2032
Fax: 403-642-2112

Waskatenau
5040 - 50 St.
Waskatenau, AB T0A 3P0 Canada
780-358-2260
Fax: 780-358-2260

Wembley
9931 - 100 Ave.
Wembley, AB T0H 3S0 Canada
780-766-2511
Fax: 780-766-2599

Westerose
30 Village Dr.
Westerose, AB T0C 2V0 Canada
780-586-3803
Fax: 780-586-3801

Westlock
10532 - 100 Ave.
Westlock, AB T7P 2J9 Canada
780-349-4481
Fax: 780-349-4471

Wetaskiwin
5202 - 50 Ave.
Wetaskiwin, AB T9A 0S8 Canada
780-352-7300
Fax: 780-352-0907

Whitecourt
5015 - 50 St.
Whitecourt, AB T7S 1P2 Canada
780-778-2442
Fax: 780-778-2535

Wildwood
5115 - 50 St.
Wildwood, AB T0E 2M0 Canada
780-325-3837
Fax: 780-325-2036

Willingdon
5015 - 50 St.
Willingdon, AB T0B 4R0 Canada
780-367-2881
Fax: 780-367-2890

Winfield
12 - 2 Ave. East
Winfield, AB T0C 2X0 Canada
780-682-2447
Fax: 780-682-2354

Worsley - Highway Dr.
808 Highway Dr.
Worsley, AB T0H 3W0 Canada
780-685-3013
Fax: 780-685-2021

Worsley - Main St.
Main St.
Worsley, AB T0H 3W0 Canada
780-685-2977
Fax: 780-685-2978

Youngstown
216 Main St.
Youngstown, AB T0J 3P0 Canada
403-779-3828
Fax: 403-779-3900

Trust Companies

AGF Trust Company
Toronto-Dominion Centre
66 Wellington St. West, 31st Fl.
Toronto, ON M5K 1E9
416-216-5353
800-244-8457
trust@agf.com
www.agf.com/mortgages
Ownership: Wholly owned subsidiary of AGF Management Limited.
Year Founded: 1988
Executives:
Blake C. Goldring, Chair/CEO

AGF Trust Company (continued)
Mario R. Causarano, President/COO
Directors:
Blake C. Goldring, Chair
Douglas L. Derry
W. Robert Farquarson
Walter A. Keyser
David A. King
Donald G. Lang
William Morneau
Winthrop H. Smith

All Nations Trust Company
#208, 345 Yellowhead Hwy.
Kamloops, BC V2H 1H1
250-828-9770
Fax: 250-372-2585
800-663-2959
antco@antco.bc.ca
www.antco.bc.ca
Ownership: Private
Year Founded: 1984
Number of Employees: 13
Executives:
Ruth Williams, CEO
Denise Birdstone, President
Nelson Leon, Vice-President
Julia Dick, Treasurer
Directors:
Denise Birdstone, Chair
Archie Deneault
Dianne Francois
Greg Gabriel
Barbara Huston
Joyce Kenoras, Secretary
Latricia Nicholas
Tracey Simon
Byron Spinks
Gary Swite

B2B Trust
130 Adelaide St. West
Toronto, ON M5H 3P5
416-947-7427
Fax: 416-947-9476
800-263-8349
www.b2b-trust.com
Former Name: Sun Life Trust Company
Ownership: Private. Subsidiary of Laurentian Bank of Canada, Montréal, QC.
Year Founded: 1991
Number of Employees: 258
Assets: $1-10 billion Year End: 20051031
Revenues: $50-100 million Year End: 20051031
Executives:
François Desjardins, President/CEO; 416-865-5900; francois.desjardins@b2b-trust.com
Marc Paradis, Chief Financial Officer; 514-284-4500; marc.paradis@banquelaurentienne.ca
Patricia Barry, Vice-President, Marketing; 416-865-5737; tricia.barry@b2b-trust.com
Diane Lafresnaye, Vice-President, Finance; 416-865-5767; diane.lafresnaye@b2b-trust.com
Al Spadaro, Vice-President, Business Development; 416-865-5662; al.spadaro@b2b-trust.com
Eva Stamadianos, Vice-President, Human Resources, Chief Risk Officer; 416-865-5668; eva.stamadianos@b2b-trust.com

Lorraine Pilon, Secretary; 514-284-4500
Directors:
Raymond McManus, Chair; 514-284-7967
Robert Cardinal; 514-284-4500
François Desjardins; 416-865-5900
Bernard Piché; 514-284-4500
Lorraine Pilon; 514-284-4500
Réjean Robitaille; 514-284-4500
André Scott; 514-284-4500
Branches:
Montréal - Deposit Agent Centre
#520, 555, rue Chabanel ouest
Montréal, QC H2N 2H8 Canada
514-284-7055
Fax: 514-284-4067
800-361-5681
Toronto - Deposit Agent Service Centre
130 Adelaide St. West, 4th Fl.
Toronto, ON M5H 3P5 Canada
416-947-5145
Fax: 416-864-9053
800-461-9938

The Bank of Nova Scotia Trust Company
Scotia Plaza
44 King St. West
Toronto, ON M5H 1H1
416-866-6161
Fax: 416-866-3750
Also Known As: Scotiatrust
Ownership: Private. Subsidiary of Bank of Nova Scotia
Year Founded: 1993
Number of Employees: 450
Executives:
Rick Waugh, President/CEO

BMO Trust Company
First Canadian Place
100 King St. West
Toronto, ON M5X 1A3
416-867-6784
AATinvestmentservices@bmo.com
www.advisorsadvantagetrust.com
Former Name: The Trust Company of Bank of Montréal
Also Known As: Advisor's Advantage Trust
Ownership: Wholly owned subsidiary of Bank of Montréal. Member of BMO Financial Group.
Executives:
Gilles G. Ouellette, President
Offices:
Montréal - Advisor's Advantage Trust - Québec, Atlantic Provinces & Eastern Ontario
129, rue St-Jacques, 1e étage
Montréal, QC H2Y 1L6 Canada
514-877-5739
Fax: 514-877-5782
Toronto - Advisor's Advantage Trust National Office
55 Bloor St. West, 19th Fl.
Toronto, ON M4W 3N5 Canada
416-927-4786
877-469-2020

BNY Trust Company of Canada
#1101, 4 King St. West
Toronto, ON M5H 1B6
www.bankofny.com
Ownership: Wholly owned subsidiary of the Bank of New York Company Inc.
Year Founded: 2001

The Canada Trust Company
Toronto Dominion Centre
PO Box 1, TD Centre Stn. TD Centre
55 King St. West, 12th Fl.
Toronto, ON M5K 1A2
888-222-3456
www.tdcanadatrust.com
Year Founded: 1855
Profile: The Canada Trust Company offers personal & small business financial services, including a range of home mortgages & rate plans. In 2005, it continued as a federally incorporated trust company, following the amalgamation of The Canada Trust Company and Canada Trustco Mortgage Company.
Executives:
J.G. Dent, President
Bernard T. Dorval, Co-Chair
Timothy D. Hockey, Co-Chair

Canadian Western Trust Co.(CWT)
#600, 750 Cambie St.
Vancouver, BC V6B 0A2
604-685-2081
Fax: 604-669-6069
800-663-1124
informationservices@cwt.ca
www.cwt.ca
Ownership: Wholly owned subsidiary of Canadian Western Bank
Executives:
Adrian Baker, Vice-President/COO
Bernie Ward, Director, Sales, Corporate & Group Services
Peter Laing, Regional Sales Director, Pacific Region; 604-699-4855; peter.laing@cwt.ca
Thaidra Walsh, Regional Sales Director, Prairie Region; 403-291-5268; thaidra.walsh@cwt.ca
Joe Woitas, Regional Sales Director, Central Region; 204-947-5590; joseph.woitas@cwt.ca

CIBC Mellon Trust Company
320 Bay St., 4th Fl.
Toronto, ON M5H 4A6
416-643-5000
Fax: 416-643-6409
www.cibcmellon.ca
Ownership: Parent companies are Canadian Imperial Bank of Commerce & Mellon Financial Corporation
Year Founded: 1978
Number of Employees: 350
Assets: $500m-1 billion
Executives:
Thomas C. MacMillan, President/CEO
C. Paul Marchand, Chief Officer, Risk, Compliance & Anti-Money Laundering
Mark Hemingway, Sr. Vice-President, General Counsel
David Linds, Sr. Vice-President
Helen Polatajko, Sr. Vice-President, CIO
John Riviere, Sr. Vice-President/CFO
Rob Shier, Sr. Vice-President, COO
James Slater, Sr. Vice-President
Rajesh Uttamchandani, Sr. Vice-President, Human Resources
Margaret Barrett, Vice-President
Savie Fiorini, Vice-President
Catherine Goetz, Vice-President
Catherine Lewis, Vice-President
Stephen MacDonald, Vice-President, Finance
Ursula McDonald, Vice-President
Laurel Savoy, Vice-President
James Gould, Secretary
Michel Longpré, Asst. Secretary
Elizabeth Earle, Asst. Secretary
Tedford C. Mason, Asst. Secretary
Shawn Murphy, Asst. Secretary
Linda Whitfield, Asst. Secretary
Directors:
Richard E. Venn, Chair
Kevin J.E. Adolphe
James D. Aramanda
Victor G. Dodig
Jeffrey S. Graham
Thomas C. MacMillan
Jacqueline Moss
James P. Palermo
Branches:
Calgary
The Dome Tower
#600, 333 - 7th Ave. SW
Calgary, AB T2P 2Z1 Canada
403-232-2400
David Planden, Executive Director, Western Canada
Halifax
Centennial Bldg.
1660 Hollis St., 4th Fl.
Halifax, NS B3J 1V7 Canada
902-420-3222
Paula Morrison, Director & Regional Manager, Eastern Canada
London
150 Dufferin Ave.
London, ON N6A 5N6 Canada
519-873-2218
Cathy Lewis, Vice-President, Pension Benefit Payments
Montréal
2001, rue University, 16e étage
Montréal, QC H3A 2A6 Canada
514-285-3600
Michel Longpré, Asst. Vice-President
Toronto
320 Bay St., 6th Fl.
Toronto, ON M5H 4A6 Canada
416-643-5000
Laurel Savoy, Vice-President, Eastern Region
Vancouver
#1600, 1066 West Hasting St.
Vancouver, BC V6E 3X1 Canada
604-688-4330
Van Bot, Sr. Manager, Client Relations

CIBC Trust Corporation
#900, 55 Yonge St.
Toronto, ON M5E 1J4
800-465-3863
www.cibc.com
Executives:
Sonia A. Baxendale, Sr. Exec. Vice-President, CIBC Retail Markets

Citizens Trust Company
#401, 815 West Hastings St.
Vancouver, BC V6B 1B4
604-682-7171
Fax: 604-708-7790
800-663-1435
www.citizensbank.ca
Executives:
Ian J. Warner, President

Clarica Trustco Company
PO Box 1601, Waterloo Stn. Waterloo
227 King St. South
Waterloo, ON N2J 4C5
888-864-5463
service@clarica.com
www.clarica.ca
Former Name: Mutual Trust Co.
Ownership: Subsidiary of Sun Life Assurance Company of Canada
Year Founded: 1918

Community Trust Company
2271 Bloor St. West
Toronto, ON M6S 1P1
416-763-2291
Fax: 416-763-2444
officepresident@communitytrust.ca
Ownership: Private
Year Founded: 1975
Profile: The federally regulated & chartered trust company is a full service financial institution. Its prime focus is mortgage lending.
Executives:
Roman Humeniuk, President

Computershare Trust Company of Canada
100 University Ave., 11th Fl.
Toronto, ON M5J 2Y1
416-263-9200
Fax: 416-263-9261
800-663-9097
www.computershare.com
Former Name: Montreal Trust
Ownership: Public. Listed on the Australian Stock Exchange
Year Founded: 2000
Number of Employees: 1,400
Revenues: $1-5 million
Profile: Computershare (ASX: CPU) is the world's leading financial services & technology provider to the global securities industry in its provision of services & solutions to listed companies, investors, employees, exchanges & other financial institutions. With a unique range of integrated services, Computershare provides specialized records management for company share registers & employee share & stock option plans, document design & communication, strategic investor relations & market intelligence & a variety of sophisticated trading technologies for financial markets. Computershare is the largest provider of global shareholder & employee management services - administering more than 90 million shareholder accounts for over 13,000 corporations across 21 countries on 5 continents. Founded in Australia in 1978, Computershare today employs almost 10,000 people worldwide. Georgeson Shareholder Canada (416-862-8088) is a Computershare Company. It provides proxy solicitation & other shareholder response services, including information agent services, asset reunification, small shareholder programs, mutual fund services & depositary services.
Executives:
Wayne Newling, President; 416-263-9201
Alan Vesprini, Exec. Vice-President, Business Development
Rachael Cronin, Vice-President, Document Services; 905-771-4411
Lindsay Horwood, Vice-President, General Counsel; 416-263-9206
Margot Jordan, Vice-President, Client Services; 416-263-9514
Robert Mackenzie, Vice-President, Product Management; 416-263-9204
Terry Martinuk, Vice-President, Compliance; 416-263-9302
Stuart Swartz, Vice-President, Corporate Trust Services; 416-263-9346
Matthew Cox, Controller; 416-263-9215
Offices:
Calgary
530 - 8th Ave. SW, 6th Fl.
Calgary, AB T2P 3S8 Canada
403-267-6800
Fax: 403-267-6529
Halifax
Purdy's Wharf Tower II
#2008, 1969 Upper Water St.
Halifax, NS B3J 3R7 Canada
902-420-3557
Fax: 902-420-2764
Montréal
#700, 1500, rue University
Montréal, QC H3A 3S8 Canada
514-982-7888
Fax: 514-982-7635
David Nugent, Vice-President & Director, Employee Plans
Vancouver
510 Burrard St., 2nd Fl.
Vancouver, BC V6C 3B9 Canada
604-661-9400
Fax: 604-661-9401
Winnipeg
830 - 201 Portage Ave.
Winnipeg, MB R3B 3K6 Canada
204-940-4600
Fax: 204-940-4608

The Effort Trust Company
242 Main St. East
Hamilton, ON L8N 1H5
905-528-8956
Fax: 905-528-8182
www.efforttrust.ca
Ownership: Private. Wholly owned subsidiary of Effort Corporation.
Year Founded: 1978
Number of Employees: 100
Assets: $100-500 million
Revenues: $10-50 million
Profile: The company places particular emphasis on asset administration, including income-producing real estate.
Executives:
Thomas J. Weisz, President/CEO; tweisz@efforttrust.ca
Arthur Weisz, Chair
Gerald Asa, Vice-President & Secretary
David Horwood, Asst. Vice-President
Branches:
Toronto
#30, 980 Yonge St.
Toronto, ON M4W 3V8 Canada
416-924-4680
Eric Weisz, Managing Director, Toronto

The Equitable Trust Company
#700, 30 St. Clair Ave. West
Toronto, ON M4V 3A1
416-515-7000
Fax: 416-515-7001
mortgage@equitabletrust.com
www.equitabletrust.com
Ownership: Wholly-owned subsidiary of Equitable Group Inc.
Year Founded: 1970
Profile: Equitable Trust is a federally regulated financial institution which provides mortgage financing. Its main business is residential first mortgage financing. Clients are purchasers of single family dwellings & multi-unit residential buildings. The company conducts business in southwestern Ontario, with a focus on the greater Toronto area.
Executives:
Geoffrey Bledin, President/CEO
Stephen Coffey, Sr. Vice-President/CFO
John Harry, Vice-President, Credit & Risk Management
Kimberley Kukulowicz, Vice-President, Mortgage Services
Tamara Malozewski, Vice-President, Finance
Robert McMillian, Vice-President, Deposit Services
Tim Storus, Vice-President & General Counsel, Chief Compliance Officer & Corporate Secretary
Nicholas Strube, Treasurer

Equity Transfer & Trust Company
#400, 200 University Ave.
Toronto, ON M5H 4H1
416-361-0152
Fax: 416-361-0470
866-393-4891
Other Information: newbusiness@equitytransfer.com (New Business); investor@equitytransfer.com (Investor Inquiries); clientservices@equitytransfer.com (Client Services) info@equitytransfer.com, trustservices@equitytransfer.com
www.equitytransfer.com
Ownership: Wholly owned subsidiary of Grey Horse Capital Corporation.
Year Founded: 1990
Profile: The company provides services to small & mid-cap public companies. In August 2006, the company registered to do business in Ontario.

Fiduciary Trust Company of Canada
Also listed under: *Financial Planning*
#3100, 350 Seventh Ave. SW
Calgary, AB T2P 3N9
403-543-3950
Fax: 403-543-3955
800-574-3822
www.fiduciarytrust.ca
Former Name: Bissett & Associates Investment Management Ltd.
Year Founded: 1982
Profile: With regulatory approval, Fiduciary Trust Company of Canada was established in 2004.

Fiducie Desjardins/ Desjardins Trust
Also listed under: *Investment Fund Companies*
CP 34, Desjardins Stn. Desjardins
1, Complexe Desjardins
Montréal, QC H5B 1E4
514-286-9441
Fax: 514-286-1131
800-361-6840
Other Information: 514-286-3225 (Business Centre Phone); 514-286-3100 (Asset Custody Service Phone); 514-499-8440 (Immigrant Investors Program Phone)
info@immigrantinvestor.com
www.fiduciedesjardins.com
Ownership: Part of the Desjardins Group.
Year Founded: 1963
Number of Employees: 850
Profile: Desjardins Trust offers the following services: trust services, asset custody services, Guaranteed Investment Certificates, & the Immigrant Investors Program. The trust company is responsible for the trust activities of the Desjardins caisses. Trust services are provided to both individuals & businesses. Business clientele includes pension funds, life insurance companies, full service brokers, portfolio managers, associations, plus private, public, parapublic & cooperative businesses. The company's activities also include the wholesale & distribution of mutual funds & private management services.
Executives:
Bertrand Laferrière, President
Marc Audet, Vice-President, Immigrant Investor Program
François Gagnon, Vice-President, Custody Services
Affiliated Companies:
Northwest Mutual Funds Inc.
Desjardins:
Québec Balanced Fund
RRSP Eligible; Inception Year: 1997; Fund Managers: Fiera Capital
Canadian Balanced Fund
RRSP Eligible; Inception Year: 1986; Fund Managers: Alliance Bernstein
Canadian Bond Fund
RRSP Eligible; Inception Year: 1959; Fund Managers: Fiera Capital
Dividend Fund
RRSP Eligible; Inception Year: 1994; Fund Managers: Fiera Capital
Environment Fund
RRSP Eligible; Inception Year: 1990; Fund Managers: Fiera Capital
Canadian Small Cap Equity Fund
RRSP Eligible; Inception Year: 1994; Fund Managers: Fiera Capital

Fiducie Desjardins/ Desjardins Trust (continued)

Money Market Fund
RRSP Eligible; Inception Year: 1989; Fund Managers:
Desjardins Investment Management
Global Equity Value Fund
RRSP Eligible; Inception Year: 1959; Fund Managers:
Alliance Bernstein
Short Term Income Fund
RRSP Eligible; Inception Year: 1965; Fund Managers:
Fiera Capital
American Equity Value Fund
RRSP Eligible; Inception Year: 2004; Fund Managers:
Alliance Bernstein
Select Canadian Balanced Fund
RRSP Eligible; Inception Year: 1999; Fund Managers:
Northwest Mutual Funds
Select Canadian Equity Fund
RRSP Eligible; Inception Year: 1999; Fund Managers:
AIM Trimark
Ethical Canadian Balanced Fund
RRSP Eligible; Inception Year: 2000; Fund Managers:
Ethical Funds
Dividend T FundInception Year: 2002; Fund Managers:
Fiera Capital
Québec T FundInception Year: 2002; Fund Managers:
Fiera Capital
Canadian Equity Value FundInception Year: 2002; Fund Managers:
Alliance Bernstein
Global Science & Technology FundInception Year: 2001; Fund Managers:
Alliance Bernstein
CI Canadian Investment Fund
RRSP Eligible; Inception Year: 2004; Fund Managers:
CI Mutual Funds
Fidelity True North Fund
RRSP Eligible; Inception Year: 2004; Fund Managers:
Fidelity Investment Canada
Fidelity Canadian Growth Company Fund
RRSP Eligible; Inception Year: 2004; Fund Managers:
Fidelity Investment Canada
Fidelity International Portfolio Fund
RRSP Eligible; Inception Year: 2004; Fund Managers:
Fidelity Investment Canada
Alternative Invesments Fund
RRSP Eligible; Inception Year: 2004; Fund Managers:
Montrusco Bolton
Global Equity Value T FundInception Year: 2004; Fund Managers:
Alliance Bernstein
Overseas Equity Value Fund
RRSP Eligible; Inception Year: 1998; Fund Managers:
Alliance Bernstein
Select Global Equity Fund
RRSP Eligible; Inception Year: 1999; Fund Managers:
Fidelity Investment Canada
Enhanced Bond Fund
RRSP Eligible; Inception Year: 2004; Fund Managers:
Alliance Bernstein
Select American Equity Fund
RRSP Eligible; Inception Year: 1999; Fund Managers:
AGF
CI Value Trust Corporate Class Fund
RRSP Eligible; Inception Year: 2004; Fund Managers:
CI Mutual Funds
Fidelity Small Cap America Fund
RRSP Eligible; Inception Year: 2004; Fund Managers:
Fidelity Investment Canada
Canadian Equity Fund
RRSP Eligible; Inception Year: 1959; Fund Managers:
Fiera Capital
Alternative Investment T FundInception Year: 2004; Fund Managers:
Montrusco Bolton

Branches:
Montréal
Tour est
PO Box 991, Desjardins Sta. Desjardins
2, complexe Desjardins, 22e étage
Montréal, QC H5B 1C1 Canada
514-286-3498
Fax: 514-286-3145
888-252-5332
Ottawa
#1650, 20 Laurier Ave. West
Ottawa, ON K1P 5Z9 Canada
613-567-2885
Fax: 613-567-4225
866-567-2885
Québec
#1100, 2875, boul Laurier
Québec, QC G1V 2M2 Canada
418-653-7922
Fax: 418-651-0371
800-653-7922

Home Trust Company

Also listed under: *Credit Card Companies*
#2300, 145 King St. West
Toronto, ON M5H 1J8
416-360-4663
Fax: 416-360-0401
800-990-7881
inquiry@hometrust.ca
www.hometrust.ca
Ownership: Public. Principal subsidiary of Home Capital Group Inc.
Year Founded: 1977
Number of Employees: 296
Assets: $1-10 billion Year End: 20050930
Revenues: $100-500 million Year End: 20050930
Stock Symbol: HCG
Profile: Federally regulated trust company carrying on business across Canada.

Executives:
Gerald M. Soloway, President/CEO; 416-775-5001; gerald.soloway@hometrust.ca
Nick Kyprianou, Sr. Vice-President/COO; 416-775-5012; nick.kyprianou@hometrust.ca
Brian Mosko, Sr. Vice-President; 416-775-5061; brian.mosko@hometrust.ca
Chris Ahlvik, Vice-President
Cathy A. Sutherland, Treasurer; 905-688-3131; cathy.sutherland@hometrust.ca
Sharron Hatton, Corporate Secretary; 416-775-5007; sherry.hatton@hometrust.ca

Directors:
William G. Davis, P.C., C.C, Q.C., Chair
Norman F. Angus
William A. Dimma
Janet L. Ecker
Harvey F. Kolodny
Nick Kyprianou
John Marsh
Robert A. Mitchell
Gerald M. Soloway
Warren K. Walker

Branches:
Calgary
#720, 5920 MacLeod Trail South
Calgary, AB T2H 0K2 Canada
403-244-2432
Fax: 403-244-6542
866-235-2432
prairiesbranch@hometrust.ca
Emilio Fuoco, Sr. Manager, Mortgages
Halifax
Duke Tower
#1205, 5251 Duke St.
Halifax, NS B3J 1P3 Canada
902-422-4387
Fax: 902-422-8891
888-306-2421
maritimesbranch@hometrust.ca
Scott Congdon, Regional Manager, Mortgage Lending
St Catharines
PO Box 1554
#100, 15 Church St.
St Catharines, ON L2R 7J9 Canada
905-688-3131
Fax: 905-688-0534
888-771-9913
stcatharinesbranch@hometrust.ca
Cathy A. Sutherland, Vice-President, Finance
Vancouver
#1288, 200 Granville St.
Vancouver, BC V6C 1S4 Canada
604-484-4663
Fax: 604-484-4664
866-235-3080
vancouverbranch@hometrust.ca
Jason Humeniuk, Branch Manager

HSBC Trust Company (Canada)

620, 885 West Georgia St.
Vancouver, BC V6C 3E9
604-641-1122
Fax: 604-641-1138
888-887-3388
www.hsbc.ca
Ownership: Private. Wholly owned subsidiary of HSBC Bank Canada
Year Founded: 1972
Number of Employees: 28

Branches:
Edmonton
#9F, 10250 - 101 St.
Edmonton, AB T5J 3P4 Canada
780-409-7066
Fax: 780-409-4206
Toronto - Victoria Park Ave.
3640 Victoria Park Ave., #G/F
Toronto, ON M2H 3B2 Canada
416-756-1236
Fax: 416-756-0210
Toronto - York St.
#600, 70 York St.
Toronto, ON M5J 1S9 Canada
416-868-8186
Fax: 416-868-8381
Victoria
752 Fort St.
Victoria, BC V8W 1H2 Canada
604-641-1199
Fax: 604-641-1138

IBT Trust Company (Canada)

PO Box 231, First Canadian Place Stn. First Canadian Place
#2800, 100 King St. West
Toronto, ON M5X 1C8
416-363-6427
Fax: 416-861-8989
Other Information: 416-861-8983 (Sales phone)
www.ibtco.com
Ownership: Subsidiary of Investors Bank & Trust, Boston, MA
Year Founded: 1993

Industrial Alliance Trust Inc.

1080, Grande Allée ouest
Québec, QC G1K 7M3
418-684-5000
www.inalco.com
Former Name: Industrial-Alliance Trust Company
Year Founded: 2000
Profile: In 2005, the formerly Québec incorporated company continued as a federally incorporated trust company.

Executives:
Yvon Charest, President

Investors Group Trust Co. Ltd./ La Compagnie de Fiducie du Groupe Investors Ltée

One Canada Centre
447 Portage Ave.
Winnipeg, MB R3C 3B6
Fax: 204-956-7688
888-746-6344
www.investorsgroup.com
Ownership: Subsidiary of Investors Group Inc.
Year Founded: 1968

Executives:
Gregory D. Tretiak, President/CEO
Roger George Joseph Blanchette, Vice-President, Finance, Compliance Officer
Brian V. Jones, Vice-President
Donna L. Janovcik, Secretary
Manfred Proch, Director, Trust Administration, Asst. Secretary
B.J. Reid, Treasurer
Carole D.M. Tetreault, Manager, Financial Services

Directors:
Dale A.F. Parkinson, Chair
Richard Elliot Archer
Jean-Claude Bachand
Sylvie Bernier
Otto Lang
Gregory D. Tretiak
Wayne Stanley Walker
William Warren

Laurentian Trust of Canada Inc.
1981, av McGill College
Montréal, QC H3A 3K3
514-284-4500
Fax: 514-284-3396
mail@laurentianbank.ca
www.laurentianbank.com
Ownership: Private. Wholly owned subsidiary of the Laurentian Bank of Canada.
Year Founded: 1939
Assets: $500m-1 billion Year End: 20051031
Revenues: $10-50 million Year End: 20051031
Executives:
Réjean Robitaille, President/CEO; 514-284-4500
Marc Paradis, Chief Financial Officer; 514-284-4500; marc.paradis2@banquelaurentienne.ca
Luc Bernard, Sr. Vice-President, Trust Services; 514-284-4500; luc.bernard@banquelaurentienne.ca
Marcel Beaulieu, Vice-President, Trust Services; 514-284-4500
Lorraine Pilon, Vice-President, Legal Affairs, Secretary; 514-284-4500
Richard Guay, General Manager; 514-284-7077; richard.guay@banquelaurentienne.ca
Directors:
Raymond McManus, Chair; 514-284-7967
Robert Cardinal; 514-284-4500
Marc Paradis; 514-284-4500
Bernard Piché; 514-284-4500
Lorraine Pilon; 514-284-4500
Réjean Robitaille; 514-284-4500
André Scott; 514-284-4500
Branches:
Montréal
425, boul de Maisonneuve ouest, 1e étage
Montréal, QC H3A 3G5 Canada
514-284-7077
Fax: 514-284-4685

LBC Trust
130 Adelaide St. West
Toronto, ON M5H 3P5
800-522-1846
www.laurentianbank.ca
Ownership: Wholly-owned subsidiary of Laurentian Bank
Executives:
François Desjardins, President

Legacy Private Trust
PO Box 1
#800, 1 Toronto St.
Toronto, ON M5C 2V6
416-868-0001
Fax: 416-868-6541
Other Information: 416-868-4205 (Corporate Secretary Phone)
Ownership: Private
Year Founded: 2002
Profile: Legacy Private Trust is a federally regulated trust company.
Executives:
James Barton Love, Chair/CEO
Robert L. Wilson, President

M.R.S. Trust Company
#2100, 777 Bay St.
Toronto, ON M5G 2N4
416-964-0028
Fax: 416-413-1723
800-387-2087
Other Information: mortgages@mrs.com (Email MRS Mortgages); 888-677-5363 (Mortgage Toll-Free); 416-926-0570 (Mortgage Information Phone)
accounthelp@mrs.com
www.mackenziefinancial.com
Former Name: Mackenzie Trust Company
Also Known As: MRS Trust
Ownership: Subsidiary of Mackenzie Financial Corporation.
Year Founded: 1979
Profile: The federally regulated trust company provides fiduciary services for all MRS Inc. accounts. It also acts as trustee on registered products offered by its parent company, Mackenzie Financial Corporation. A variety of deposit & lending products & services are offered by MRS Trust.
Executives:
Allan Warren, President/CEO
Branches:
Calgary
#3810, 855 - 2nd St. SW
Calgary, AB T2J 4J8 Canada
403-264-8400

Maple Trust Company/ Compagnie Maple Trust
TD Waterhouse Tower, Toronto-Dominion Centre
PO Box 349
#3500, 79 Wellington St. West
Toronto, ON M5K 1K7
416-350-7400
Fax: 416-350-7441
800-307-8341
Other Information: 416-350-7488 (Client Services Hotline); 416-350-7498 (Client Services Fax); MTMortgageAdministration@mapletrust.com (Mortgage Email) MTTrustServices@mapletrust.com, MTDepositServices@mapletrust.com
www.mapletrust.com
Former Name: London Trust and Savings Corporation
Ownership: Private. Member of the Scotiabank Group.
Year Founded: 1999
Assets: $1-10 billion
Profile: The fully licensed trust company focuses on residential mortgage lending & deposit products. It was purchased by Scotiabank in 2006.
Executives:
John Webster, President/CEO
Barbara Chiarantano, Vice-President
James Smith, Vice-President

Mennonite Trust Limited
PO Box 40
3005 Central Ave.
Waldheim, SK S0K 4R0
306-945-2080
Fax: 306-945-2225
mtl@sasktel.ca
www.mennonitetrust.com
Year Founded: 1917
Executives:
Tim Redekopp, General Manager

NATCAN Trust Company
National Bank
1100, rue University, 12e étage
Montréal, QC H3B 2G7
514-871-7633
Fax: 514-871-7580
800-235-5566
Ownership: Wholly owned by National Bank Acquisition Holding Inc.
Profile: A range of financial products & services are offered by the federally incorporated trust company.
Executives:
Eric Laflamme, President/CEO

National Bank Trust/ Trust Banque National
1100, rue University, 10e étage
Montréal, QC H3B 2G7
514-871-7240
800-463-6643
www.nbc.ca
Branches:
Brossard
#1400, 8200, boul Taschereau
Brossard, QC J4X 2S6 Canada
450-923-1000
Fax: 450-923-9558
Gatineau
#101, 259, boul St-Joseph
Gatineau, QC J8Y 6T1 Canada
819-771-3227
Fax: 819-771-5395
Laval
2500, boul Daniel-Johnson
Laval, QC H7T 2P6 Canada
450-682-3200
Fax: 450-682-0104
Montréal - Boisé
Centre Commercial du Sanctuaire
6100, av du Boisé
Montréal, QC H3S 2W1 Canada
514-738-8296
Fax: 514-738-7861
Montréal - Langelier
8020, boul Langelier
Montréal, QC H1P 3K1 Canada
514-327-4133
Fax: 514-327-0859
Montréal - Vincent-d'Indy
1, av Vincent-d'Indy
Montréal, QC H2V 4N7 Canada
514-739-3265
Fax: 514-739-9342
Rimouski - Cathedrale
186, av de la Cathedrale
Rimouski, QC G5L 5H9 Canada
418-723-3394
Fax: 418-725-4203
Rimouski - Jessop
415, boul Jessop
Rimouski, QC G5L 1N3 Canada
418-724-4119
Fax: 418-723-7612

Northern Trust Company, Canada
PO Box 526
#1510, 145 King St. West
Toronto, ON M5H 1J8
416-365-7161
Fax: 416-365-9484
www.ntrs.com
Ownership: Subsidiary of Northern Trust Company, Chicago, USA
Number of Employees: 31
Profile: The Northern Trust Company, Canada was the first foreign-owned trust company to be granted full trust powers in Canada. It provides a full range of trustee, custody, participant service, & relationship management to the Canadian market.
Executives:
Robert Baillie, President/CEO, Canadian Office

Oak Trust Company
One London Place
#2410, 255 Queens Ave.
London, ON N6A 5R8
519-433-6629
Fax: 519-433-6652
Other Information: 519-979-2338 (Windsor/Essex Phone)
www.oaktrust.ca
Year Founded: 2004
Profile: Oak Trust is an independent federally chartered trust company. The company's activities include estate settlement, trust administration & wealth management services.
Executives:
J. Christopher Scarff, President
Mitch Schurmans, Vice-President
Bryan Head, Trust Consultant; bhead@oaktrust.ca
Dave Shaw, Trust Consultant; dshaw@oaktrust.ca
Directors:
Ross Batson, Chair
J. Anthony Boeckh
William T. Dodds
Richard Jankura
Stan Martin
J. Christopher Scarff
Mitchell P. Schurmans
John Thompson

Olympia Trust Company
#2300, 125 - 9th Ave. SW
Calgary, AB T2G 0P6
403-261-0900
Fax: 403-265-1455
800-727-4493
info@olympiatrust.com
www.olympiatrust.com
Ownership: Wholly owned subsidiary of Olympia Financial Group Inc.
Profile: The Alberta based non-depository institution offers services in the following areas: private health services plan administration, self-adminnistered plans, corporate services (registrar & transfer agent services), & foreign exchange.
Executives:
Richard Barnowski, Vice-President, Olympia Transfer Services & Eastern Operations
Randy Gregory, Vice-President, Corporate & Shareholder Services

Olympia Trust Company (continued)
Lori Martai, Vice-President, Registered Plans; lmartai@olympiatrust.com
Sangita Prasad, Assistant Vice-President, Client Services
Lynn Crichton, Manager, Registered Plans; crichtonl@olympiatrust.com
Craig Skauge, Manager, Business Development, Registered Plans; craigs@olympiatrust.com
Gail Williams, Manager, Operations
Kelly Revol, Sr. Administrator, Mortgages; revolk@olympiatrust.com
Branches:
Belcarra
Belcarra, BC
604-936-3792
Fax: 604-936-3667
888-987-7477
Shirley MacDonald, Regional Manager, Sales
Calgary - 9th Ave. SE
#2300, 125 - 9th Ave. SE
Calgary, AB T2G 0P6
403-261-8460
Fax: 403-261-7512
Daniel Gillis, Regional Manager, Sales
Calgary - Bermuda Rd. NW
96 Bermuda Rd. NW
Calgary, AB T3K 1E6
403-275-4453
Gerry G. Hefflick, Regional Manager, Sales
Calgary - Edmonton Trail NE
2202 Edmonton Trail NE
Calgary, AB T2E 3M5
403-230-3824
Fax: 403-230-3886
Wayne Wiebe, Regional Manager, Sales
Calgary - Hospital Dr. NW
#304, 3031 Hospital Dr. NW
Calgary, AB T2N 2T8
403-521-5222
Fax: 403-521-5229
Harvey Kachmarski, Regional Manager, Sales
Calgary - Midlake Pl. SE
7 Midlake Pl. SE
Calgary, AB T2X 1J2
403-809-1135
John Comeau, Regional Manager, Sales
Cranbrook
#202, 135 - 10 Ave. South
Cranbrook, BC V1C 2N1
250-426-4949
Fax: 250-417-3939
Al Dyck, Regional Manager, Sales
Delta
#462, 7231 - 120th St.
Delta, BC V4C 6P5
604-592-2990
Fax: 604-507-5574
Doug McChesney, Regional Manager, Sales
Edmonton - 99 St.
#460, 10123 - 99 St.
Edmonton, AB T5J 3H1 Canada
780-496-9713
Fax: 780-408-3382
866-289-3015
Art Merrick, Regional Manager, Sales
Edmonton - Kingsway Ave.
11630 Kingsway Ave.
Edmonton, AB T5G 0X5
780-496-7744
Fax: 780-496-7755
Robert Frost, Regional Manager, Sales
Estevan
2035 Mayfair Bay
Estevan, SK S4A 1X7
306-634-6073
Fax: 306-421-0240
William M. Martin, Regional Manager, Sales
Grande Prairie
202, 9914 - 109 Ave.
Grande Prairie, AB T8V 1R6
780-532-2991
Fax: 780-532-2796
Lane Smith, Regional Manager, Sales
Kelowna
#200, 1789 Harvey Ave.
Kelowna, BC V1Y 6G4
250-448-8428
Fax: 250-448-8429
866-752-7135
fxadmin@olympiatrust.com
Lethbridge
PO Box 1481
Lethbridge, AB T1J 4K2
403-320-8677
Fax: 403-328-9071
Clifford Rau, Regional Manager, Sales
Nanaimo
#1, 6421 Apple Cross Rd.
Nanaimo, BC V9V 1N1
250-390-1995
Fax: 250-390-1941
Mel M. Zulak, Regional Manager, Sales
North Vancouver
#604, 718-333 Brooksbank Ave.
North Vancouver, BC V7J 3V8
604-727-1904
Fax: 604-677-6582
Daniel Van Blerk, Regional Manager, Sales
Provost
PO Box 920
Provost, AB T0B 3S0
403-350-3435
Fax: 780-753-4961
Brian Kemp, Regional Manager, Sales
Regina
1236 Degelman Dr.
Regina, SK S4N 7N4
306-751-0766
Fax: 306-751-0724
Kim Shaheen, Regional Manager, Sales
Saskatoon
37 McLellan Ave.
Saskatoon, SK S7H 3K7
306-651-3880
Fax: 306-374-3655
866-651-3880
Richard Buzik, Regional Manager, Sales
Sidney
2444 Beacon Ave.
Sidney, BC V8L 1X6
250-656-1154
Fax: 250-656-7262
George Abram, Regional Manager, Sales
Surrey
#562, 800-15355 - 24th Ave
Surrey, BC V4A 2H9
778-908-3343
866-869-6973
Michael H. Campany, Regional Manager, Sales
Vancouver
Cathedral Place
#1900, 925 West Georgia St.
Vancouver, BC V6C 3L2
604-408-7774
Fax: 604-669-8111
866-752-7135
fxadmin@olympiatrust.com
Winnipeg - Lombard Ave.
#303, 93 Lombard Ave.
Winnipeg, MB R3B 3B1
204-949-0990
Fax: 204-943-5989
888-588-2845
Rick Yates, Regional Manager, Sales
Winnipeg - St. Mary's Rd.
2942 St. Mary's Rd.
Winnipeg, MB R2N 4J6
204-975-5032
Fax: 204-253-4064
877-528-3816
Chris Leroux, Regional Manager, Sales

Pacific Corporate Trust Company
510 Burrard St., 2nd Fl.
Vancouver, BC V6C 3B9
604-689-9853
Fax: 604-689-8144
pacific@pctc.com
www.pctc.com
Former Name: Pacific Corporate Services Limited
Ownership: Private
Year Founded: 1981
Profile: Security transfer services are provided for venture capital corporations which issue publicly traded securities.
Executives:
Marc Castonguay, CEO, Vice-President
Bill Brolly, Vice-President
Branches:
Toronto
100 University Ave., 11th Fl.
Toronto, ON M5J 2Y1 Canada
Fax: 416-263-9394
877-288-6822

Peace Hills Trust Company
Samson Mall, Samson Cree Nation Reserve
PO Box 60
Hobbema, AB T0C 1N0
780-585-3013
Fax: 780-585-2216
pht@peacehills.com
www.peacehills.com
Ownership: Private
Year Founded: 1981
Number of Employees: 120
Assets: $100-500 million Year End: 20041231
Revenues: $10-50 million Year End: 20041231
Profile: Peace Hills Trust provides financial services to the First Nations & their members, corporations, institutions & associations both on & off reserve. Financial services are also offered to non-native clientele.
Executives:
W.W. Hannay, President/CEO
G.T. Kinsella, C.A., Exec. Vice-President/CFO
David Boisvert, Vice-President, Credit
Directors:
Robert Louie, Chair
Ray Ahenakew
Thoma Amgwerd
Florence Buffalo
Victor S. Buffalo
Ted Fontaine
W.W. Hannay
Stewart Paul
Boyd Robertson
Rose Saddleback
Robert Swampy
Gerry Webber
Marvin Yellowbird
Branches:
Calgary
8408 Elbow St. SW
Calgary, AB T2V 1K7 Canada
403-299-9730
Fax: 403-299-9749
Stephen Buffalo, Regional Manager
Edmonton
Peace Hills Trust Tower
10011 - 109th St.
Edmonton, AB T5J 3S8 Canada
780-421-1229
Fax: 780-425-1005
Harold Baram, Asst. Vice-President, Northern Alberta Region
Fort Qu'Appelle
298 Broadway St. West
Fort Qu'appelle, SK S0G 1S0 Canada
306-332-2230
Fax: 306-332-1886
Bob Fahlman, Regional Manager
Fredericton
150 Cliffe St.
Fredericton, NB E3A 0A1 Canada
506-455-3430
Fax: 506-455-3405
Brayden Nichols, Regional Manager
Hobbema
Samson Mall
PO Box 60
Hobbema, AB T0C 1N0 Canada
780-585-3013
Fax: 780-585-2216
Leslie Calhoun, Regional Manager
Kelowna
515 Hwy. #97 South
Kelowna, BC V1Z 3J2 Canada

250-769-9081
Fax: 250-769-9082
Scott Baldwin, Regional Manager
Saskatoon
103C Packham Ave.
Saskatoon, SK S7N 4K4 Canada
306-955-8600
Fax: 306-955-0344
Kelly Bitternose, Regional Manager
Winnipeg
244 Portage Ave.
Winnipeg, MB R3C 0B1 Canada
204-943-8093
Fax: 204-943-8251
Brian Bender, Asst. Vice-President, Manitoba Region

Peoples Trust Company

Also listed under: *Financing & Loan Companies*
888 Dunsmuir St., 14th Fl.
Vancouver, BC V6C 3K4
604-683-2881
Fax: 604-331-3469
people@peoplestrust.com
www.peoplestrust.com
Ownership: Private
Year Founded: 1985
Profile: The financial institution is engaged in mortgage lending, mortgage investing & deposit services. The lending business consists of mostly conventional & insured loans. Properties are multi-family residential properties in urban centers. Investing services focus upon mortgage banking for institutional investors, plus long term RRSP & GIC products.

Executives:
Frank A. Renou, President/CEO
Derek Peddlesden, Exec. Vice-President/COO
Barrie M. Battley, Sr. Vice-President
Dennis Aitken, Vice-President, Mortgages, Regional Manager, Prairies
Dennis Dineen, Vice-President, Commercial Mortgages
Jim Dysart, Vice-President, Mortgages, Regional Manager, Ontario
Brian Kennedy, Vice-President, Mortgages, Regional Manager, British Columbia
Kathleen Klassen, Vice-President, Finance, Treasurer
Aleta Brown, Assistant Vice-President, Mortgage Banking Administration
Chris Hudson, Assistant Vice-President, Mortgages, Prairies
Bruce Martinuik, Assistant Vice-President, Mortgages, British Columbia
Jeanette Curtis, Sr. Manager, Deposit Services
John Nation, Sr. Manager, Mortgage Administration
Tom Wollner, Manager, Residential Mortgages
Directors:
Eskander Ghermezian, Chair
Howard Anson
Michael Andrews
Andrew Bury
David Ghermezian
Peter Hindmarch-Watson
Jonathan A. Levin
Frank A. Renou
Michael Terrell
Keith Thompson
Derek Woods
Branches:
Calgary
#955, 808 - 4th Ave. SW
Calgary, AB T2P 3E8 Canada
403-237-8975
Fax: 403-266-5002
Toronto
#1801, 130 Adelaide St. West
Toronto, ON M5H 3P5 Canada
416-368-3266
Fax: 416-368-3328
Vancouver - Dunsmuir St.
#750, 888 Dunsmuir St.
Vancouver, BC V6C 3K4 Canada
604-685-1068
Fax: 604-683-2787
Vancouver - Dunsmuir St. - Investment Centre
#750, 888 Dunsmuir St.
Vancouver, BC V6C 3K4
604-683-2881
Fax: 604-683-5110

RBC Dexia Investor Services Trust

Royal Trust Tower, Toronto Dominion Centre
77 King St. West, 35th Fl.
Toronto, ON M5W 1P9
416-955-5907
www.rbcdexia-is.com
Ownership: Wholly-owned subsidiary of RBC Dexia Investor Services
Year Founded: 2006
Profile: The creation of the Trust in 2006 incorporated the institutional investor services division of RBC Global Services.

ResMor Trust Company

Also listed under: *Financing & Loan Companies*
#400, 555 - 4th Ave. SW
Calgary, AB T2P 3E7
403-539-4920
Fax: 403-539-4921
866-333-7030
www.resmor.com
Former Name: Equisure Trust Company
Ownership: Private. ResMor Capital Corporation.
Year Founded: 1964
Number of Employees: 195
Assets: $100-500 million Year End: 20041231
Revenues: $10-50 million Year End: 20041231
Executives:
James P. Clayton, President/CEO; 403-539-4901; jclayton@resmor.com
K. Gerry Wagner, Vice-President/CFO; 403-539-4902; gwagner@resmor.com
Directors:
Harold Allsopp
Cody T. Church
James P. Clayton
Ronald A. Jackson
Lorne H. Jacobson
Donald Potvin
Peter Valentine
K. Gerry Wagner
Branches:
Calgary
#400, 555 - 4 Ave. SW
Calgary, AB T2P 3E7 Canada
403-534-1920
Fax: 403-538-4965

The Royal Trust Company

Also listed under: *Financial Planning*
Royal Bank
1, Place Ville-Marie, 6e étage sud
Montréal, QC H3B 2B2
514-874-7222
800-668-1990
Other Information: 866-553-5585 (Eastern Canada Toll Free); 888-299-5290 (Western Canada Toll Free); 866-474-4344 (Québec Toll Free); tradvmtl@rbc.com (Québec Email) tradvtor@rbc.com (East), tradvcal@rbc.com (West)
www.rbc.com
Ownership: Part of RBC Financial Group.
Year Founded: 1899
Profile: The trust company is engaged in securities custody & investment management. Clients include individuals, families & businesses. Its services are part of RBC Investments, Wealth Management Division & RBC Global Services.

Executives:
M. George Lewis, President

Standard Life Trust Company

#206, 1245, rue Sherbrooke ouest
Montréal, QC H3G 1G3
888-841-6633
www.standardlife.ca
Former Name: Bonaventure Trust Company of Canada
Ownership: Private
Year Founded: 1825
Profile: The federally incorporated trust company also accepts deposits.

Executives:
Joseph Iannicelli, President/CEO
Branches:
Toronto
121 King St.
Toronto, ON M3H 3T9 Canada
416-367-2424
Fax: 416-367-2426

State Street Bank & Trust Company - Canada

Also listed under: *Foreign Banks: Schedule III*
#1100, 30 Adelaide St. East
Toronto, ON M5C 3G6
416-362-1100
Fax: 416-956-2525
888-287-8639
www.statestreet.com
Former Name: State Street Trust Company Canada
Ownership: State Street Corporation
Year Founded: 1990
Number of Employees: 700
Profile: World's leading provider of financial services to institutional investors. Range of services spans the entire investment spectrum, including research, investment management, trading services and investment servicing

Branches:
Montréal
#1100, 770, rue Sherbrooke ouest
Montréal, QC H3A 1G1 Canada
514-282-2400
Fax: 514-282-2439

Sun Life Financial Trust Inc.

PO Box 1601, Waterloo Stn. Waterloo
227 King St. South
Waterloo, ON N2J 4C5
800-786-5433
www.sunlife.com
Profile: In 2005, Sun Life Financial Trust Inc. continued as a federally incorporated trust company.

Executives:
Dikran Ohannessian, President

Trimark Trust/ Fiducie Trimark

#900, 5140 Yonge St.
Toronto, ON M2N 6X7
416-590-0036
800-631-7008
inquiries@aimtrimark.com
www.aimtrimark.com
Former Name: Bayshore Trust
Ownership: AIM Trimark Investments, Toronto, ON.
Year Founded: 1977
Profile: Trimark Trust is a federally incorporated trust company.

Executives:
Arthur S. Labatt, President

The Trust Company of London Life

One Canada Centre
447 Portage Ave.
Winnipeg, MB R3C 3B6
204-956-8470
Profile: This is a federally incorporated trust company.

Executives:
Gregory D. Tretiak, President

Valiant Trust Company

#600, 750 Cambie St.
Vancouver, BC V6B 0A2
604-699-4880
Fax: 604-681-3067
877-699-4880
inquiries@valianttrust.com
www.valianttrust.com
Ownership: Subsidiary of Canadian Western Bank
Executives:
Adrian Baker, President; 604-699-4801; adrian.baker@cwt.ca
Bob Morris, Managing Director; 604-699-4881; bob.morris@valianttrust.com
Janet M. Brown, Director, Client Services; 604-699-4879; janet.brown@valianttrust.com
Dianna Reimer, Director, Operations; 604-699-4886; dianna.reimer@valianttrust.com
Terry Pask, Director, Business Development; 604-699-4882; terry.pask@valianttrust.com
Branches:
Calgary
#310, 606 - 4th St. SW
Calgary, AB T2P 1T1

Valiant Trust Company (continued)
402-233-2801
Fax: 403-233-2857
866-313-1872
inquiries@valianttrust.com
Matt Colpitts, General Manager
Edmonton
#2300, 10303 Jasper Ave.
Edmonton, AB T5J 3X6
780-441-2267
Fax: 780-441-2247
888-441-2267
inquiries@valianttrust.com
Julia Molloy, Manager, Relationship

Western Pacific Trust Company
#500, 1130 West Pender St.
Vancouver, BC V6E 4A4
604-683-0455
Fax: 604-669-6978
www.westernpacifictrust.com
Ownership: Public
Year Founded: 1964
Profile: Affiliated with Futureworth Financial Planners Corp.

Executives:
Victor Lee, President/CEO; dmercier@westernpacifictrust.com
Alison Alfer, Manager, Communications; aalfer@westernpacifictrust.com
Directors:
Anthony Liscio, B.Sc, DDS, Chair
J. Cowan McKinney, CA, Deputy Chair
Stephanie Green, FCA
Victor Lee, MBA
Daniel Kostiuk, LL.B.

Credit Unions/Caisses Populaires

1st Choice Savings & Credit Union Ltd.
PO Box 1237
1320 - 3 Ave. South
Lethbridge, AB T1J 4A4
403-320-4600
Fax: 403-329-6434
contact@1stchoicesavings.ca
www.1stchoicesavings.ca
Former Name: St. Patrick's Credit Union Ltd.; Southland Credit Union
Ownership: Public
Year Founded: 2001
Number of Employees: 90
Assets: $100-500 million
Executives:
Gerry Jensen, CEO; 403-380-1930; gjensen@1stchoicesavings.ca
Lynn Corbett, Vice-President, Human Resources; 403-320-4636; lcorbett@1stchoicesavings.ca
Brian Kinahan, Vice-President, Lending; 403-320-4065; bkinahan@1stchoicesavings.ca
Darrel Koskewich, Vice-President, Operations & Marketing; 403-320-4646; dkoskewich@1stchoicesavings.ca
Jason Sentes, Vice-President, Finance; 403-329-7625; jsentes@1stchoicesavings.ca
Branches:
Cardston
70 - 3rd Ave. West
Cardston, AB T0K 0K0 Canada
403-320-4600
Fax: 403-653-4194
Ken Secretan, Branch Manager
Lethbridge
45 Fairmont Blvd. South
Lethbridge, AB T1K 1T1 Canada
403-320-4600
Fax: 403-320-8192
Denise Clarke, Branch Manager
Lethbridge
300 - 3 St. South
Lethbridge, AB T1J 1Y9 Canada
403-320-4600
Fax: 403-327-1019
Sandra Habetler, Branch Manager
Lethbridge
1320 - 3 Ave. South
Lethbridge, AB T1J 4A4 Canada
403-320-4600
Fax: 403-329-6434
Barb Wolstoncroft, Branch Manager
Magrath
81 West Harker Ave.
Magrath, AB T0K 1J0 Canada
403-320-4600
Fax: 403-758-3717
Patrick Bilyk, Branch Manager
Taber
5227 - 48 Ave.
Taber, AB T1G 1S8 Canada
403-320-4600
Fax: 403-223-2498
Eric Jensen, Branch Manager

3M Employees' (London) Credit Union Limited
1840 Oxford St. East
London, ON N6A 4T1
519-452-6765
Fax: 519-452-6023
cuca-corporate@mmm.com
www.3mcreditunion.com
Executives:
Sam Cornelisse, President

Acadian Credit Union
PO Box 250
15089 Cabot Trail
Cheticamp, NS B0E 1H0
902-224-2055
Fax: 902-224-3510
877-477-7724
www.acadiancreditu.ca
Former Name: Cheticamp Credit Union
Year Founded: 1936
Number of Employees: 12
Executives:
Denis H. Larade, General Manager; dlarade@acadian.creditu.net
Branches:
LeMoyne
PO Box 40
13101 Cabot Trail
Grand Etang, NS B0E 1L0 Canada
902-224-2015
Fax: 902-224-1102
866-364-2136
Lynn Cormier, Manager

ACE Credit Union Limited
PO Box 3030
#100, 2055 Albert St.
Regina, SK S4P 2T8
306-337-1700
Fax: 306-337-1719
info@ace.cu.sk.ca
www.acecreditunion.com
Year Founded: 1973
Executives:
Gail Peterson, General Manager; 306-337-1701; gail.peterson@ace.cu.sk.ca

Adjala Credit Union Limited
PO Box V1
7320 St James Lane
Colgan, ON L0G 1W0
905-936-2761
Fax: 905-936-6391
Year Founded: 1946

Advance Savings Credit Union
47 Main St.
Petitcodiac, NB E4Z 4L9
506-756-3331
Fax: 506-756-8596
www.royal-cu.com
Former Name: Royal Credit Union; Trico Credit Union
Year Founded: 2006
Executives:
Don Roper, CEO; drcroper@advancesavings.ca
Janice Rice, COO; jrice@advancesavings.ca
Directors:
Tony Baker, President
Gerald Gogan, Vice-President
Iona McCully, Secretary
Branches:
Moncton - Record
10 Record St.
Moncton, NB E1C 0B2 Canada
506-853-1880
Fax: 506-853-7536
Derek Ellard, Branch Manager
Moncton - St George
960 St George Blvd.
Moncton, NB E1E 3Y3 Canada
506-857-3188
Fax: 506-384-6710
Nic Maltais, Branch Manager
Port Elgin
9 East Main St.
Port Elgin, NB E4M 2X8 Canada
506-538-2213
Fax: 506-538-7354
Mike Tubrett, Branch Manager
Riverview
620 Coverdale Rd.
Riverview, NB E1B 3K6 Canada
506-386-2830
Fax: 506-386-2833
Gary Wright, Branch Manager
Salisbury
3118 Main St.
Salisbury, NB E4J 2L6 Canada
506-372-4950
Fax: 506-372-8596
Nadine Brown, Branch Manager

Advantage Credit Union
PO Box 1657
118 Main St.
Melfort, SK S0E 1A0
306-752-2744
Fax: 306-752-1919
www.advantagecu.com
Former Name: Melfort Credit Union Ltd.
Ownership: Private.
Year Founded: 1943
Number of Employees: 130
Assets: $100-500 million Year End: 20051231
Revenues: $100-500 million Year End: 20051231
Profile: An affiliated company is ACU Insurance Services Inc.
Executives:
Jim Thiessen, CEO
Don Hawes, Vice-President, Finance
Laurie Kennedy, Vice-President, Organizational Development
Murray Yeadon, Vice-President, Relationship Services
Branches:
Englefeld
PO Box 40
Englefeld, SK S0K 1N0 Canada
306-287-4242
Fax: 306-287-3720
Don Bohay, Manager, Business Development
Gronlid
PO Box 44
Gronlid, SK S0E 0W0 Canada
306-277-6250
Fax: 306-277-2122
Brenda Rolles, Manager, Business Development
Kinistino
PO Box 334
Kinistino, SK S0J 1H0 Canada
306-864-6230
Fax: 306-864-2448
Kendall Knutson, Manager, Business Development
Lake Lenore
PO Box 189
Lake Lenore, SK S0K 2J0 Canada
306-368-2315
Fax: 306-368-2225
Shelly Kunz, Manager, Business Development
Melfort
PO Box 1657
Melfort, SK S0E 1A0 Canada
306-752-2744
Fax: 306-752-1919
Sandra Boyle, Manager, Business Development
Naicam
PO Box 459
Naicam, SK S0K 2Z0 Canada

306-874-6250
Fax: 306-874-2212
Greg Wacholtz, Manager, Business Development
Spalding
PO Box 70
Spalding, SK S0K 4C0 Canada
306-872-2050
Fax: 306-872-2100
Marion Olsen, Manager, Business Development
St. Brieux
PO Box 190
St Brieux, SK S0K 3V0 Canada
306-275-4444
Fax: 306-275-4511
Eldon Kralkay, Manager, Business Development
Star City
PO Box 36
113 - 4th St.
Star City, SK S0E 1P0 Canada
306-863-2420
Fax: 306-863-2777
Brenda Rolles, Manager, Business Development
Watson
PO Box 190
Watson, SK S0K 4V0 Canada
306-287-3730
Fax: 306-287-4222
Brad Gaetz, Manager, Business Development
Weldon
PO Box 130
Weldon, SK S0J 3A0 Canada
306-887-2330
Fax: 306-887-2091
Kendall Knutson, Manager, Business Development

Affinity Credit Union

1515 - 20th St. West
Saskatoon, SK S7M 0Z5
306-382-1177
Fax: 306-382-7600
info@affinity.cu.sk.ca
www.affinitycu.com
Former Name: St. Mary's Credit Union Limited
Ownership: Member-owned
Year Founded: 1949
Number of Employees: 37
Assets: $100-500 million
Revenues: $5-10 million
Executives:
Randy Ottenbreit, President
Ed Cechanowicz, 1st Vice-President
Lois Herback, 2nd Vice-President
Directors:
Karl Baumgardner
Larry Doetzel
Stewart Elder
Joanne Griffith
Audrey Horkoff
Patrick Melin
Evan Olsen
Ralph Schidlowsky
John Waddington
Branches:
Aberdeen
PO Box 100
207 Main St. North
Aberdeen, SK S0K 0A0 Canada
306-253-3440
Bulyea
PO Box 97
Ashley St.
Bulyea, SK S0G 0L0 Canada
306-725-4811
Hague
PO Box 432
302 Main St.
Hague, SK S0K 1X0 Canada
306-225-2166
Kamsack
316 - 3rd Ave. South
Kamsack, SK S0A 1S0 Canada
306-542-2672
Laird
220B Main St.
Laird, SK S0K 2H0 Canada
306-223-4450
Norquay
PO Box 477
24 Main St.
Norquay, SK S0A 2V0 Canada
306-594-2225
Osler
PO Box 208
228 Willow Drive
Osler, SK S0K 3A0 Canada
306-239-4623
Pelly
PO Box 340
24 Main St.
Pelly, SK S0A 2Z0 Canada
306-595-2116
Regina
3418 Hill Ave.
Regina, SK S4S 0W9 Canada
306-791-9622
Regina
2101 Scarth St.
Regina, SK S4P 2H9 Canada
306-791-9611
Rosthern
PO Box 176
2003 - 6th St.
Rosthern, SK S0K 3R0 Canada
306-232-5522
Saskatoon
124 - 3rd Ave. North
Saskatoon, SK S7K 5E5 Canada
306-653-9600
Saskatoon
1515 - 20th St. West
Saskatoon, SK S7M 0Z5 Canada
306-382-1177
Sedley
PO Box 156
121 Broadway St.
Sedley, SK S0G 4K0 Canada
306-885-2112
Semans
PO Box 84
Main St.
Semans, SK S0A 3S0 Canada
306-524-2030
Simpson
PO Box 40
408 George St.
Simpson, SK S0G 4K0 Canada
306-836-2130
St Isidore de Bellevue
PO Box 69
200A Grenier Cresc.
St Isidore de Bellevue, SK S0K 3Y0 Canada
306-423-5225
Strasbourg
PO Box 488
208 Mountain St.
Strasbourg, SK S0G 4V0 Canada
306-725-3132
Togo
PO Box 90
175 Main St.
Togo, SK S0A 4E0 Canada
306-597-2151
Watrous
PO Box 790
210 Main St.
Watrous, SK S0K 4T0 Canada
306-946-3312

Agassiz Credit Union Ltd.

430 Stephen St.
Morden, MB R6M 1T6
204-822-4485
Fax: 204-822-6155
admin@agassizcu.mb.ca
www.agassizcu.mb.ca
Ownership: Member-owned
Executives:
Ken Lofgren, CEO
Branches:
Dominion City
PO Box 37
122 Waddell Ave.
Dominion City, MB R0A 0H0 Canada
204-427-2444
Fax: 204-427-2004
vcul@escape.ca
MICR: 61127-879
Mitzi Borodenko, Account Manager
Manitou
330 Main St.
Manitou, MB R0G 1G0 Canada
204-242-2756
Fax: 204-242-3141
MICR: 60657-879
Ed Giesbrecht, Manager, West Region
Miami
517 Norton St.
Miami, MB R0G 1H0 Canada
204-435-2161
Fax: 204-435-2072
MICR: 30577-879
Shelly Bartley, Account Manager
Morris
PO Box 730
100 Main St.
Morris, MB R0G 1K0 Canada
204-746-2391
Fax: 204-746-2243
MICR: 90977-879
Jeff Samson, Manager, East Region

Air-Toronto Credit Union

#1434, 50 Bay St.
Toronto, ON M5J 2X3
416-359-9685
airtoronto@bellnet.ca
Year Founded: 1959

Airline Financial Credit Union Limited

#120, 5955 Airport Rd.
Mississauga, ON L4V 1R9
905-673-7262
Fax: 905-676-8437
800-392-5005
airline@airlinecreditunion.ca
www.airlinecreditunion.ca
Former Name: Airline (Malton) Credit Union Limited.
Number of Employees: 10
Assets: $31,000,000

Aldergrove Credit Union

2941 - 272nd St.
Aldergrove, BC V4W 3R3
604-856-7724
Fax: 604-856-2565
www.aldergrovecu.ca
Executives:
Neil Ranson, General Manager
Shel Gould, Branch Manager
Branches:
Abbotsford
5824 Riverside St.
Abbotsford, BC V4X 1V1 Canada
604-826-1201
Fax: 604-826-1240
Brent Janzen
Abbotsford - Mt. Lehman Centre
#100, 3224 Mt. Lehman Rd.
Abbotsford, BC V4X 2M9 Canada
604-857-0654
Fax: 604-857-0659
Carla Desmond
Aldergrove - Otter Co-op
3528 - 248th St.
Aldergrove, BC V4W 1Y7 Canada
604-856-2558
Fax: 604-856-0210
Lynn Spencer
Langley
22242 - 48th Ave.
Langley, BC V3A 3N5 Canada
604-534-9477
Fax: 604-534-0272
Harvey Spiess

All Trans Financial Credit Union Limited
Administration Ctr.
#707, 3250 Bloor St. West
Toronto, ON M8X 2X9
416-231-8400
Fax: 416-231-8296
info@alltrans.com
www.alltrans.com
Year Founded: 1993
Number of Employees: 18
Executives:
Michael Alexander, CEO
G. Turgeon, CFO
Branches:
Clarica Center
East Tower
#100, 3250 Bloor St. West
Toronto, ON M5R 3G9 Canada
416-533-1090
Fax: 416-538-9655
clarica@alltrans.com
K. Nanhu, Pavilion Money Manager
London
450 Highbury Ave. North
London, ON N5W 5L2 Canada
519-453-2480
Fax: 519-453-0556
london@alltrans.com
C. Buckingham, Pavilion Money Manager
Toronto
Ol Canada Kipling
777 Kipling Ave.
Toronto, ON M8Z 5Z4 Canada
416-232-3389
Fax: 416-233-5020
David Shivgulam, Mobile Money Manager
Toronto - TTC Hillcrest Yards
Operations Bldg.
1138 Bathurst St.
Toronto, ON M5R 3H2 Canada
K. Philip, Mobile Money Manager

Alliance Credit Union
1177 Portage Ave.
Winnipeg, MB R3G 0T2
204-927-0460
Fax: 204-927-0461
mail@alliancecu.ca
www.alliancecu.ca
Former Name: Adanac Credit Union Ltd; Communicators Credit Union; Progress Vera Credit Union
Year Founded: 2001
Branches:
Winnipeg - Maples Branch
#101, 930 Jefferson Ave.
Winnipeg, MB R2P 1W1 Canada
204-927-0450
Fax: 204-927-0451

Alterna Savings & Credit Union Limited
400 Albert St.
Ottawa, ON K1R 5B2
613-560-0100
Fax: 613-560-0177
877-560-0100
Other Information: 416/252-5621 (Toronto phone)
query@alterna.ca
www.alterna.ca
Former Name: Civil Service Co-operative Credit Society Ltd.
Ownership: Member-owned
Year Founded: 2005
Number of Employees: 600+
Assets: $1-10 billion
Profile: Formed April 1, 2005 by the merger of Ottawa-based Civil Service Co-operative Credit Society Ltd. & Toronto-based Metro Credit Union, member-owned Alterna Savings provides a range of financial products & services.

Executives:
Gary M. Seveny, President/CEO
Directors:
Donald Altman
Ginette Bethell
Penny Bethke
Mary-Lu Brennan
Ted Brown
Bill Burleigh
Earl Campbell
Johanne Charbonneau
Pierre J.A. Choquette
Gail Di Cintio
James G. Frank
Fred Gorbet
David N. Kinsman
Mel Lang
Jeff May
Richard J. Neville
Richard Ranger
John Richmond
Douglas Thwaites
Anna Tosto
Affiliated Companies:
Alterna Bank
Branches:
Bolton
1 Queensgate Blvd.
Bolton, ON L7E 2X7 Canada
416-252-5621
Fax: 905-857-7153
Brampton
Howden Plaza
375 Howden Blvd.
Brampton, ON L6S 4L6 Canada
416-252-5621
Kingston - CFB Kingston
CANEX Mall
PO Box 17000
29 Niagara Park
Kingston, ON K7K 7B4 Canada
613-544-6051
Fax: 613-541-1891
Mississauga - Derry Rd.
2829 Derry Rd. East
Mississauga, ON L4T 1A5 Canada
416-252-5621
Mississauga - Queen St.
113 Queen St. South
Mississauga, ON L5M 1K7 Canada
416-252-5621
Nepean - Bells Corners
Moodie Square Centre
90K Robertson Rd.
Nepean, ON K2H 5Z1 Canada
613-560-0100
Fax: 613-560-6359

Nepean - Merivale Rd.
First Pro Viewmount Centre
1715 Merivale Rd.
Nepean, ON K2G 3K2 Canada
613-560-0100
Fax: 613-560-6381
North Bay
107 Shirreff Ave.
North Bay, ON P1B 7K8 Canada
705-472-9700
Fax: 705-472-9986
800-538-9907
Orleans
Place Centrum
210 Centrum Blvd.
Orleans, ON K1E 3V7 Canada
613-560-0100
Fax: 613-560-6365
Ottawa - Albert St.
400 Albert St.
Ottawa, ON K1R 5B2 Canada
613-560-0100
Fax: 613-560-0177
Ottawa - Billings Bridge
2269 Riverside Dr.
Ottawa, ON K1H 8K2 Canada
613-560-0100
Fax: 613-560-0180
Ottawa - South Keys
2300 Bank St.
Ottawa, ON K1V 8S1 Canada
613-560-0100
Fax: 613-560-0181
Ottawa - Sparks St.
61 Sparks St.
Ottawa, ON K1P 5A5 Canada
613-560-0100
Fax: 613-560-6360
Ottawa - St. Laurent Shopping Centre
1200 St. Laurent Blvd
Ottawa, ON K1K 3B9 Canada
613-560-0100
Fax: 613-560-0137
Ottawa - Tunney's Pasture
R.H. Coats Bldg.
Ottawa, ON K1Y 4J8 Canada
613-560-0100
Fax: 613-560-0127
Pembroke
Rosewood Plaza
680 Pembroke St. East
Pembroke, ON K8A 3M2 Canada
613-735-5039
Fax: 613-735-5526
Toronto - Bay St.
800 Bay St.
Toronto, ON M5S 3A9 Canada
416-252-5621
Toronto - Danforth Ave.
1577 Danforth Ave.
Toronto, ON M4C 1H7 Canada
416-252-5621
Toronto - Keele St., York University Campus
York Lanes Mall
#18, 4700 Keele St.
Toronto, ON M3J 1P3 Canada
416-252-5621
Toronto - Lakeshore Blvd.
3001 Lakeshore Blvd. West
Toronto, ON M8V 1J8 Canada
416-252-5621
Toronto - Progress Ave.
#D4, 410 Progress Ave.
Toronto, ON M1P 5J1 Canada
416-252-5621
Toronto - Town Centre Ct.
200 Town Centre Ct.
Toronto, ON M1P 4X8 Canada
416-296-0248
Fax: 416-296-1967
Toronto - Victoria St.
#158, 350 Victoria St.
Toronto, ON M5B 2K3 Canada
416-252-5621
Toronto - Yonge St.
4900 Yonge St.
Toronto, ON M2N 6A4 Canada
416-224-2575
Fax: 416-224-2578
Corporate Office:
Toronto
165 Attwell Dr.
Toronto, ON M9W 5Y5 Canada
416-252-5621

Altona Credit Union Limited
PO Box 299
129 - 3rd Ave. NE
Altona, MB R0G 0B0
204-324-6437
Fax: 204-324-1466
info@altonacu.mb.ca
www.altonacu.mb.ca
Number of Employees: 39
Branches:
Emerson
PO Box 186
13 Main St.
Emerson, MB R0A 0S0 Canada
204-373-2195
Fax: 204-373-2392

Anishinabek Nation Credit Union(ANCU)
7 Shingwauk St.
Garden River, ON P6A 6Z8
705-942-7655
Fax: 705-942-7613
866-775-2628
allan@ancu.ca
www.ancu.ca

Profile: ANCU offers standard financial services, plus trust services, securities, mutual funds & stock brokerage through alliances with Cooperative Trust Company & Credential Securities.

Apex Credit Union Limited

Crandell Bldg.
#106G, 1301 - 16th Ave. NW
Calgary, AB T2M 0L4
403-974-8640
Fax: 403-282-3099
www.apexcreditunion.com
Ownership: Member-owned
Number of Employees: 15
Branches:
Downtown
#101, 407 - 2nd Street SW
Calgary, AB T2P 2Y3 Canada
403-974-8390
Fax: 403-262-4887
ghowe@alberta-cu.com
North Central
Crandell Bldg.
#106G, 1301 - 16th Ave. NW
Calgary, AB T2M 0L4 Canada
403-974-8640
Fax: 403-282-3099
mpaston@alberta-cu.com
Northwest
Science Theatres
#48, 2500 University Dr. NW
Calgary, AB T2N 1N4 Canada
403-220-7335
Fax: 403-220-0726
sredstone@alberta-cu.com
Southwest
#156E, 4825 Richard Rd. SW
Calgary, AB T3E 6K6 Canada
403-974-8646
Fax: 403-249-8151
lbarr@alberta-cu.com

Apple Community Credit Union

406 North Cumberland St.
Thunder Bay, ON P7A 4P8
807-345-8153
Fax: 807-343-9271
info@applecu.com
www.applecu.com
Ownership: Private

Arctic Credit Union Ltd.

800 Central Ave., 9th Fl.
Prince Albert, SK S6V 6Z2
306-922-8252
Former Name: Arctic Savings & Credit Union Ltd.
Year Founded: 1939

Arnstein Community Credit Union Limited

PO Box 104
Port Loring, ON P0H 1Y0
705-757-2662
Fax: 705-757-2662
b.whitmell@thot.net
Year Founded: 1962
Executives:
Bud Whitmell, Treasurer & General Manager

Assiniboine Credit Union Limited

PO Box 2
200 Main St.
Winnipeg, MB R3C 2G1
204-958-8588
Fax: 204-942-3549
www.assiniboine.mb.ca
Ownership: Member-owned
Year Founded: 1943
Number of Employees: 220
Assets: $1-10 billion Year End: 20061000
Executives:
Al Morin, President/CEO
Mona Forsen, Sr. Vice-President/COO
Garry Mitchell, Vice-President/CFO
Gerry Campbell, Vice-President, Sales & Service
Branches:
Winnipeg - Broadway
640 Broadway
Winnipeg, MB R3C 0X3 Canada
204-958-8588
Fax: 204-779-7915
Winnipeg - Henderson Hwy.
655 Henderson Hwy
Winnipeg, MB R2K 2J6 Canada
204-958-8588
Fax: 204-669-0141
Winnipeg - Kennedy St. - Medical Arts Branch
233 Kennedy St.
Winnipeg, MB R3C 0L7 Canada
204-958-8588
Fax: 204-947-1926
Winnipeg - Main St.
PO Box 2
200 Main St.
Winnipeg, MB R3C 2G1 Canada
204-958-8588
Winnipeg - Main St. - Rivergrove
2567 Main St.
Winnipeg, MB R2V 4W3 Canada
Winnipeg - McPhillips St. - Garden City Branch
2211 McPhillips St.
Winnipeg, MB R2V 3M5 Canada
204-958-8588
Fax: 204-661-2825
Winnipeg - Pembina Hwy. - Fort Richmond Branch
2800 Pembina Hwy.
Winnipeg, MB R3T 5P3 Canada
204-958-8588
Fax: 204-269-6501
Winnipeg - Portage Ave. - St. James Branch
2565 Portage Ave.
Winnipeg, MB R3R 0P4 Canada
204-958-8588
Fax: 204-888-1354
Winnipeg - Regent Ave. West
1609 Regent Ave. West
Winnipeg, MB R2C 3B3 Canada
204-958-8588
Fax: 204-663-5952
Winnipeg - Roblin Blvd. - Charleswood Branch
5930 Roblin Blvd.
Winnipeg, MB R3R 0H3 Canada
204-958-8588
Fax: 204-895-3978
Winnipeg - St. Mary's Rd.
1033 St. Mary's Rd.
Winnipeg, MB R2M 3S8 Canada
204-958-8588
Fax: 204-257-8801

Astra Credit Union Limited

1907 Portage Ave.
Winnipeg, MB R3J 0H9
204-982-1470
Fax: 204-889-6203
877-278-7228
astra@astracu.mb.ca
www.astracu.mb.ca
Year Founded: 1958
Assets: $100-500 million
Executives:
Ian Dark, CEO
Branches:
Winnipeg - Crestview
#140, 3393 Portage Ave.
Winnipeg, MB R3K 2G7 Canada
Winnipeg - Keewatin
1038 Keewatin St.
Winnipeg, MB R2R 2E2 Canada
Winnipeg - Kenaston
1855 Grant Ave.
Winnipeg, MB R3N 1Z2 Canada
Winnipeg - Mcleod
844 Mcleod Ave.
Winnipeg, MB R2G 2T7 Canada
Winnipeg - St. Vital
#10, 200 Meadowood Dr.
Winnipeg, MB R2M 5G3 Canada

Austin Credit Union

PO Box 205
24 - 2nd Ave.
Austin, MB R0H 0H0
204-637-2202
Fax: 204-637-2204
products@austincu.mb.ca
www.austincreditunion.com
Year Founded: 1949
Number of Employees: 36
Executives:
Liana DeGraeve, Branch Manager
Branches:
Gladstone - Commercial/Agri Centre
PO Box 534
16 Dennis St. West
Gladstone, MB R0J 0T0 Canada
204-385-6026
Fax: 204-385-6030
Lynn Hayward, Manager
Gladstone - Member Services Centre
PO Box 534
14 Dennis St. East
Gladstone, MB R0J 0T0 Canada
204-385-6020
Fax: 204-385-6025
Lynn Hayward, Manager
MacGregor
PO Box 458
30 Hampton St. East
MacGregor, MB R0H 0R0 Canada
204-685-5620
Fax: 204-685-5626
Tammy Davey, Branch Manager
Plumas
PO Box 63
112 Burrows Ave.
Plumas, MB R0J 1P0 Canada
204-386-2462
Fax: 204-386-2252
Carol Walker, Account Manager
Portage La Prairie - Agriculture/Commercial Centre
1800 Saskatchewan Ave. West
Portage La Prairie, MB R1N 0N9 Canada
204-239-7024
Fax: 204-239-0034
Roy Shields, Senior Account Manager

Auto Workers (Ajax) Credit Union Limited

PO Box 21115
290 Harwood Ave. South
Ajax, ON L1S 2J1
905-683-0791
Fax: 905-683-6047
Year Founded: 1968

Auto Workers' Community Credit Union Limited

322 King St. West
Oshawa, ON L1J 2J9
905-728-5187
Fax: 905-728-8727
800-268-8771
information@awccu.com
www.awccu.com
Ownership: Private. Cooperative
Year Founded: 1938
Number of Employees: 70
Revenues: $100-500 million
Executives:
Brent Reid, CEO; 905-728-5444; breid@awccu.com
Branches:
Bowmanville
221 King St. East
Bowmanville, ON L1C 1P7 Canada
Chris Chapman, Branch Manager

Battle River Credit Union Ltd.

5007 - 51 St.
Camrose, AB T4V 1S6
780-672-1175
Fax: 780-672-5996
comegrowthus@battlerivercreditunion.com
www.battlerivercreditunion.com
Ownership: Member-owned
Year Founded: 1949
Number of Employees: 110
Assets: $100-500 million Year End: 20050930
Revenues: $1-5 million Year End: 20050930
Executives:
Alan Fielding, President

Battle River Credit Union Ltd. (continued)
Steve Friend, Sr. Vice-President, Operations
Joe Mohan, Vice-President, Operations
Mickey Mohan, Vice-President, Operations
Arlene Stauffer, Vice-President, Finance & Administration
Terry Kelly, General Manager
Branches:
Alliance
PO Box 180
201 Main St.
Alliance, AB T0B 0A0 Canada
780-879-3644
Fax: 780-879-3838
Dave Sheets, Manager
Camrose - 51 St. (City Centre)
5005 - 51 St.
Camrose, AB T4V 1S5 Canada
780-672-9221
Fax: 780-672-9230
Jerry Hansen, Manager
Camrose - 65 St. (West End)
4705 - 65 St.
Camrose, AB T4V 3M5 Canada
780-672-8893
Fax: 780-672-8895
Matt Danko, Manager
Castor
PO Box 60
5002 - 50 Ave.
Castor, AB T0C 0X0 Canada
403-882-3950
Fax: 403-882-3555
Kevin Johnson, Manager
Daysland
PO Box 130
5004 - 50 St.
Daysland, AB T0B 1A0 Canada
780-374-3951
Fax: 780-374-3736
Yvonne Schell, Manager
Killam
PO Box 39
5004 - 50 St.
Killam, AB T0B 2L0 Canada
780-385-3731
Fax: 780-385-2406
Melody Rott, Manager
Sedgewick
PO Box 127
4838 - 47 St.
Sedgewick, AB T0B 4C0 Canada
780-384-3912
Fax: 780-384-3938
Tom Moore, Manager
Stettler
PO Box 1357
4911 - 51 St.
Stettler, AB T0C 2L0 Canada
403-742-2331
Fax: 403-742-2255
Steve Davies, Manager
Two Hills
4916 - 47 Ave.
Two Hills, AB T0B 4K0 Canada
780-657-3321
Fax: 780-657-2036
Jason Terlesky, Manager
Vegreville
PO Box 1315
4917 - 51 Ave.
Vegreville, AB T9C 1S5 Canada
780-632-3998
Fax: 780-632-4080
Rory Sperling, Manager
Viking
PO Box 215
5302 - 50 St.
Viking, AB T0B 4N0 Canada
780-336-4944
Fax: 780-336-3181
Gerard Durand, Manager

Battlefords Credit Union
PO Box 638
1202 - 102nd St.
North Battleford, SK S9A 2Y7
306-446-7000
Fax: 306-445-6086
webmail@bcufinancial.ca
www.battlefordscreditunion.com
Year Founded: 1952
Number of Employees: 122
Assets: $100-500 million
Revenues: $10-50 million
Executives:
Brian Maunula, CEO
Branches:
Battleford
PO Box 160
131 - 22nd St. West
Battleford, SK S0M 0E0 Canada
306-446-7000
Fax: 306-937-3498
Glaslyn
PO Box 186
101 Main St.
Glaslyn, SK S0M 0Y0 Canada
306-342-2145
Hafford
PO Box 338
Main St.
Hafford, SK S0J 1A0 Canada
306-549-6310
Leoville
PO Box 100
38 Main St.
Leoville, SK S0J 1N0 Canada
306-984-2222
Medstead
403 - 1st Ave.
Medstead, SK S0M 1W0 Canada
306-342-4649

Meota
PO Box 249
300 Main St.
Meota, SK S0M 1X0 Canada
306-446-7000
Shell Lake
PO Box 38
204 Main St.
Shell Lake, SK S0J 2G0 Canada
306-427-2144
Vawn
PO Box 22
Vawn, SK S0M 2V0 Canada
306-397-2885
Fax: 306-397-2213

Bay Credit Union Limited
142 Algoma St. South
Thunder Bay, ON P7B 3B8
807-345-7612
Fax: 807-345-8939
1-877-249-7076
www.baycreditunion.com

Bay St Lawrence Credit Union
PO Box 112
3020 Bay St. Lawrence Rd.
Dingwall, NS B0C 1G0
902-383-2003
Year Founded: 1937
Number of Employees: 1
Executives:
Annette Gosse, Manager

Bayshore Credit Union Ltd.
PO Box 878
191 North Front St.
Belleville, ON K8N 5B5
613-966-5550
Fax: 613-966-9523
www.bayshorecu.com
Branches:
Frankford
PO Box 120
34 South Trent St.
Frankford, ON K0K 2C0 Canada
613-398-6103
Fax: 613-398-6930
Trenton
#101, 266 Dundas St E.
Trenton, ON K8V 6Z9 Canada
613-394-4872
Fax: 613-394-6267

Bayview Credit Union
54 Loch Lomond Dr.
Saint John, NB E2J 1X7
506-634-8585
Fax: 506-652-2536
bayviewc@nb.aibn.com
www.bayviewnb.com
Year Founded: 1938
Number of Employees: 85
Executives:
Bob Marshall, CEO
Anna Florczynski, Finance Manager
Ginny Hourihan, Human Resources Manager
Vern MacInnis, Credit Manager
Jan O'Connor-George, Operations Manager
Greg Pinfold, IT Manager
Directors:
Norma Kelly, President
Liz Chisholm, Vice-President
Shirley Coleman, Secretary
Randy Allaby
Tom Bishop
John Clarke
Larry Gallant
Paul O'Leary
Lois Vincent
Branches:
Hampton
550 Main St.
Hampton, NB E5N 6C3 Canada
506-832-3469
Fax: 506-832-4226
Shawn Leonard, Branch Manager
Rothesay - Kennebecasis Valley
59 Marr Rd.
Rothesay, NB E2E 5Y8 Canada
506-847-8443
Brian Thorne, Branch Manager
Saint John - Hospital Branch
Saint John Regional Hospital
PO Box 2100
Saint John, NB E2L 4L2 Canada
506-648-6600
Fax: 506-648-6605
Mike Bartlett, Manager
Saint John - Oak Hall Branch
57 King St.
Saint John, NB E2L 1G5 Canada
506-634-7910
Fax: 506-634-7449
Cathy Barry, Branch Manager
Saint John - West
46 Main St. West
Saint John, NB E2M 3N1 Canada
506-635-8193
Fax: 506-635-3017
Joan McGarvey, Branch Manager
Sussex
582 Main St.
Sussex, NB E4E 7H8 Canada
506-433-5005
Fax: 506-433-5134
Terry Craig, Branch Manager

BCU Financial
PO Box 638
1202 - 102nd St.
North Battleford, SK S9A 2Y7
306-446-7000
Fax: 306-445-5359
www.bcufinancial.ca
Ownership: Member-owned
Executives:
Jerome Bru, President
Branches:
Meadow Lake
105 - 3rd Ave. West
Meadow Lake, SK S9X 1T4 Canada
306-236-5619
Fax: 306-236-6167

Beaubear Credit Union
PO Box 764
376 Water St.
Miramichi, NB E1V 3V4
506-622-4532
Fax: 506-622-9329
beaubear@beaubear.creditu.net
www.beaubear.ca
Executives:
George Greenwood, General Manager
Betty Holland, Branch Manager
Branches:
Newcastle
PO Box 764
112 Newcastle Blvd.
Miramichi, NB E1V 3V4 Canada
506-622-4532
Fax: 506-622-9329
John Strong, Branch Manager

Beaumont Credit Union Limited
5007 - 50th Ave.
Beaumont, AB T4X 1E7
780-929-8561
Fax: 780-929-2999
cberube@alberta-cu.com
www.beaumontcu.com
Former Name: St Vital & Beaumont Savings & Credit Union
Ownership: Private
Year Founded: 1946
Number of Employees: 32
Assets: $1-5 million Year End: 20051031
Revenues: $1-5 million Year End: 20051031
Profile: Offers services which include RRSPs; RRIFs; mutual funds; consumer, commercial & farm loans; personal, commercial & agricultural accounts; MasterCard products.
Executives:
Camille Bérubé, General Manager; 780-929-1399
Cindy Bennett, Manager, Deposit Services; 780-929-1380
Ian Reid, Manager, Lending Services; 780-929-1377
Directors:
Reuben Hickman, President
Dan Chalifoux, 1st Vice-President
Barb Willis, 2nd Vice-President
Pierre Daigneault
Stan Gerber
Marc Gobeil
David Rudzki
Case Watson

Beautiful Plains Credit Union
PO Box 99
239 Hamilton St.
Neepawa, MB R0J 1H0
204-476-3341
Fax: 204-476-3609
bpcunion@mb.sympatico.ca
www.bpcu.mb.ca
Year Founded: 1955
Executives:
Greg Fleck, General Manager
Warren McLeod, Manager, Loans
Don Palmer, Manager, Operations
Gord Sylvester, Manager, Wealth Management & Business Development
Directors:
Keith Jury, President
Marjorie Marciski, Vice-President
Marg Loucks, Secretary
Bruce Bremner
Darlene Csversko
Ron Jesson
Greg McConnell
Branches:
Glenella
PO Box 57
70 - 2nd St. West
Glenella, MB R0J 0V0 Canada
204-352-4475
Fax: 204-352-2212
Carol Turko, Office Manager

Bengough Credit Union Ltd.
PO Box 70
Bengough, SK S0C 0K0
306-268-2930
Fax: 306-268-2622
info@bengough.cu.sk.ca
www.bengough.cu.sk.ca
Year Founded: 1943
Number of Employees: 10
Executives:
Collin Giblett, General Manager
Branches:
Kayville
PO Box 18
Kayville, SK S0H 2C0 Canada
306-475-2712

Bergengren Credit Union
257 Main St.
Antigonish, NS B2G 2C1
902-863-6600
Fax: 902-863-3031
888-273-3488
info@bergengrencu.com
www.bergengrencu.com
Year Founded: 1933
Number of Employees: 51
Directors:
Kevin Bekkers, Chair
Branches:
St. Andrews
PO Box 66
St Andrews, NS B0H 1X0 Canada
902-863-3877
Fax: 902-863-4074

Blackville Credit Union
128 Main St.
Blackville, NB E9B 1P1
506-843-2219
Fax: 506-843-6773
Year Founded: 1936
Executives:
Kathleen Coughlan, Manager; kcoughlan@bcu.creditu.net

Bow Valley Credit Union Limited
PO Box 8540
Canmore, AB T1W 2V3
403-678-9760
Fax: 403-678-5412
www.bowvalleycu.com
Ownership: Member-owned
Executives:
Larry Bohn, General Manager; lbohn@bowvalleycu.com
Branches:
Airdrie
104 - 1st Ave. NE
Airdrie, AB T4B 2B7 Canada
403-948-6737
Fax: 403-948-6056
Ken J. Koob, Branch Manager
Banff
216 Banff Ave.
Banff, AB T1L 1A8 Canada
403-762-3368
Fax: 403-762-5872
Bryan Gerrie, Branch Manager
Canmore
810 - 8th St.
Canmore, AB T1W 2B7 Canada
403-678-5549
Fax: 403-678-5120
Bryan Gerrie, Branch Manager
Cochrane
PO Box 874
212 - 5th Ave. West
Cochrane, AB T4C 1X3 Canada
403-932-3277
Fax: 403-932-6468
Todd Phillips, Branch Manager

Brewers Warehousing Employees (Hamilton) Credit Union Limited
c/o Beer Store
673 Upper James St.
Hamilton, ON L9C 5R9
905-574-7652

Brewers Warehousing Employees (Kitchener) Credit Union Limited
53 Filbert St.
Kitchener, ON N2H 1Y1
519-576-7324

Brook Street Credit Union
PO Box 713
38 Brook St.
Corner Brook, NL A2H 6G7
709-634-4632
Fax: 709-634-4247
866-273-4632
brookstreet@brookstreet.creditu.net
www.brookstreetcreditunion.com
Ownership: Private
Year Founded: 1963
Number of Employees: 7
Assets: $5-10 million
Executives:
Bill Dawson, General Manager; wdawson@brookstreet.creditu.net
Diane Poole, Assistant Manager; dianep@brookstreet.creditu.net
Holley Simmonds, Business Manager; hsimmonds@brookstreet.creditu.net
Directors:
Frank Loder
Addison Pieroway
David Simon
Barry Simms
Dean Stickland
Victoria Stokes
Steve Thorne
Brian Warren

Bruno Savings & Credit Union Ltd.
PO Box 158
511 Main St.
Bruno, SK S0K 0S0
306-369-2901
Fax: 306-369-2225

Budd Automotive Employees (Kitchener) Credit Union Limited
PO Box 1060, C Stn. C
1011 Homer Watson Blvd.
Kitchener, ON N2G 4G5
519-748-5070
Year Founded: 1968

Buduchnist Credit Union
2280 Bloor St. West
Toronto, ON M6S 1N9
416-763-6883
Fax: 416-763-4512
800-461-5941
info@buduchnist.com
www.buduchnist.com
Year Founded: 1952
Branches:
Hamilton
239 Kenilworth Ave. North
Hamilton, ON L5H 4S4 Canada
905-545-7776
Fax: 905-545-9662
877-859-8877
Mississauga
1891 Rathburn Rd. East
Mississauga, ON L4W 3Z3 Canada
905-238-1273
Fax: 905-238-1526
Ottawa
913 Carling Ave.
Ottawa, ON K1Y 4E3 Canada
613-722-7075
Fax: 613-722-4206
800-561-1682
Toronto - East
221 Milner Ave.
Toronto, ON M1S 4P4 Canada
416-299-7291
Toronto - West
2280 Bloor St. West
Toronto, ON M6S 1N9 Canada

Buduchnist Credit Union (continued)
416-763-6883
Fax: 416-763-4512
800-461-5941

Buffalo Credit Union Limited
#100, 275 Broadway
Winnipeg, MB R3C 4M6
204-944-8738
Fax: 204-956-2451
866-334-3365
info@buffalocu.com
www.buffalocu.com
Year Founded: 1949
Number of Employees: 17
Executives:
Hugh O'Hare, CEO
Debra Zier-Vogel, CFO
Branches:
HSC
653 William Ave.
Winnipeg, MB R3A 0K1 Canada
204-944-8738
Fax: 204-786-0645
800-561-1467

Bulkley Valley Credit Union
PO Box 3637
3872 - 1st Ave.
Smithers, BC V0J 2N0
250-847-3255
Fax: 250-847-3012
infoadmin@bvcu.com
www.bvcu.com
Executives:
W.D. (Dave) Stene, CEO
Branches:
Burns Lake - Lakes District
Lake View Mall
PO Box 1029
Hwy. 16
Burns Lake, BC V0J 1E0 Canada
250-692-7761
Fax: 250-692-3661
infolakes@bvcu.com
Ron Hooper, Branch Manager
Hazeltons'
PO Box 159
4646 - 10th Ave.
New Hazelton, BC V0J 2J0 Canada
250-842-2255
Fax: 250-842-2121
infohaz@bvcu.com
Tamia Hatler, Branch Manager
Houston & District
PO Box 1480
2365 Copeland Ave.
Houston, BC V0J 1Z0 Canada
250-845-7117
Fax: 250-845-2783
infohous@bvcu.com
Tanya Hackle, Branch Manager
Smithers
PO Box 3729
3894 - 1st Ave.
Smithers, BC V0J 2N0 Canada
250-847-3255
Fax: 250-847-2818
infosmi@bvcu.com
Cindy Stucklberger, Branch Manager

Caisse Centrale Desjardins du Québec
#2822, 1, Complexe Desjardins
Montréal, QC H5B 1B3
514-281-7070
Fax: 514-281-7083
bernard.bellerose@ccd.desjaradins.com
www.desjardins.com
Ownership: Subsidiary of Fédération des Caisses Desjardins du Québec
Year Founded: 1979
Number of Employees: 250
Assets: $10-100 billion Year End: 20041231
Revenues: $100-500 million Year End: 20041231
Executives:
Jean-Guy Langelier, President/COO
André Bellefeuille, Exec. Sr. Vice-President
Jacques Descoteaux, Sr. Vice-President, Capital Markets
Huu Trung Nguyen, Sr. Vice-President, Administration & International
Michel Paradis, Sr. Vice-President, Integrated Risk Management
Christian St-Arnaud, Sr. Vice-President, Financing & Banking Services
Alain Francoeur, Vice-President, Financing & Banking Services
Sylvain Gascon, Vice-President, Financing & Banking Services
Jacques Landry, Vice-President & General Manager, International Services Centre
General Manager, Desjardins International
Gilles Lapierre, Vice-President, Legal & Corporate Affairs, Asst. Secretary of the Board
Pierre Pelletier, Vice-President, Financing & Banking Services
Directors:
Jacques Baril
Jean-Guy Bureau
Louise Charbonneau
Alban D'Amours
André Gagné
Raymond Gagné
André Lachapelle
André Lafortune
Madeleine Lapierre
Marcel Lauzon
Olivier Lavoie
Pierre Leblanc
Daniel Mercier
Jacqueline Mondy
Denis Paré
Clément Samson
Richard Sarrazin
André Shatskoff
Sylvie St-Pierre Babin
Pierre Tardif
International Service Centres:
Montréal
#1810, 300, rue Léo-Pariseau
Montréal, QC H2X 4B3 Canada
800-707-2305
Québec
#140, 5600, boul des Galeries
Québec, QC G2K 2H6 Canada
866-634-5775
Trois-Rivières
PO Box 1000
2000, boul de Récollets
Trois-Rivières, QC G9Z 5K3 Canada
819-374-3594
Regional Offices:
Chicoutimi - Saguenay/Lac St-Jean
#200, 1700, boul Talbot
Chicoutimi, QC G7H 7Z4 Canada
418-543-1718
Gatineau - Outaouais
#100, 880, boul de la Carrière
Gatineau, QC J8Y 6T5 Canada
819-778-1400
877-441-1400
Québec
#140, 5600, boul de Galeries
Québec, QC G2K 2H5 Canada
866-835-1881
Saint-Lambert
2051, rue Victoria
Saint-Lambert, QC J4S 1H1 Canada
450-672-4116
Sherbrooke - Estrie
#110, 1845, rue King ouest
Sherbrooke, QC J1J 2E4 Canada
819-821-3220
800-481-3220

Caisse Horizon Credit Union Ltd.
PO Box 147
Girouxville, AB T0H 1S0
780-323-4600
Fax: 780-323-4545
866-758-6466
www.chorizoncu.ca
Ownership: Member-owned
Year Founded: 1956
Number of Employees: 18
Profile: A credit union offering all financial services.
Executives:
Rene George, General Manager
Branches:
Falher
PO Box 538
Falher, AB T0H 1M0 Canada
780-837-2227
Fax: 780-837-3456
Tom Allan, Branch Manager
High Prairie
PO Box 1380
High Prairie, AB T0G 1E0 Canada
780-536-2667
Fax: 780-536-2626
La Crete
PO Box 2170
La Crete, AB T0H 2H0 Canada
780-928-4441
Fax: 780-928-4420
La Glace
PO Box 110
La Glace, AB T0H 2J0 Canada
780-568-2409
Fax: 780-568-4601
Manning
PO Box 70
Manning, AB T0H 2M0 Canada
780-836-3371
Fax: 780-836-3703
St Isidore
PO Box 1129
St Isidore, AB T0H 3B0 Canada
780-624-1182

Caisse populaire de Saulnierville
RR#1
Saulnierville, NS B0W 2Z0
902-769-2574
Fax: 902-769-3555
Year Founded: 1953
Executives:
Anna LeBlanc, Manager

Cambrian Credit Union Ltd.
Also listed under: *Financing & Loan Companies*
225 Broadway
Winnipeg, MB R3C 5R4
204-925-2600
Fax: 204-231-1306
ccuinfo@cambrian.mb.ca
www.cambrian.mb.ca
Ownership: Member-owned
Year Founded: 1959
Number of Employees: 225
Assets: $1-10 billion Year End: 20051231
Revenues: $50-100 million Year End: 20051231
Executives:
Tom Bryk, President/CEO
Bruce Fink, Sr. Vice-President/CFO
Jim Grapentine, Sr. Vice-President/COO
Connie Clarke, Vice-President, Systems & Administration
Directors:
Paul Holden, Chair
Rose Marie Couture, 1st Vice-Chair
Shauna MacKenzie-Sykes, 2nd Vice-Chair
Branches:
Selkirk
282 Main St.
Selkirk, MB R1A 2P3 Canada
204-482-1810
Fax: 204-482-1818
Margaret Kubas, Manager, Retail Sales & Services
Winnipeg - Henderson Hwy.
1336 Henderson Hwy.
Winnipeg, MB R2G 1M8 Canada
204-925-2630
Fax: 204-334-7913
Bernice McClintock, Manager, Retail Sales & Services
Winnipeg - Marion St.
255 Marion St.
Winnipeg, MB R2H 0T8 Canada
204-925-2620
Fax: 204-233-9599
John Coutris, Manager, Retail Sales & Services
Winnipeg - McPhillips St.

2136 McPhillips St.
Winnipeg, MB R2V 3C8 Canada
204-925-2640
Fax: 204-694-7238
David Gregg, Manager, Retail Sales & Services
Winnipeg - Pembina Hwy.
735 Pembina Hwy.
Winnipeg, MB R3M 2L8 Canada
204-925-2670
Fax: 204-478-1430
David Ross, Manager, Retail Sales & Services
Winnipeg - Pembina Hwy.
2251 Pembina Hwy.
Winnipeg, MB R3T 2H1 Canada
204-925-2660
Fax: 204-269-2368
Lorne Warren, Manager, Retail Sales & Services
Winnipeg - Portage Ave.
#1, 3421 Portage Ave.
Winnipeg, MB R3K 2C9 Canada
204-925-2748
Fax: 204-889-9946
Cindy Gerry, Manager, Retail Sales & Services
Winnipeg - Regent Ave.
#100, 855 Regent Ave. West
Winnipeg, MB R2C 0R1 Canada
204-925-2755
Fax: 204-669-6762
David Durant, Manager, Retail Sales & Services
Winnipeg - St. Mary's Rd.
1602 St. Mary's Rd.
Winnipeg, MB R2M 3W5 Canada
204-925-2680
Fax: 204-254-6536
Craig Fardoe, Manager, Retail Sales & Services
Winnipeg - Vermillion Rd.
#190, 115 Vermillion Rd.
Winnipeg, MB R2J 4A9 Canada
204-925-2690
Fax: 204-257-2390
Cheryl Jones, Manager, Retail Sales & Services
Winnipeg - Wall St.
910 Wall St.
Winnipeg, MB R3G 2V2 Canada
204-925-2650
Fax: 204-775-4419
Glenn Solar, Manager, Retail Sales & Services

Campbell's Employees' (Toronto) Credit Union Limited

60 Birmingham St.
Toronto, ON M8V 2B8
416-251-1117
Fax: 416-253-8669

Canada Safeway Limited Employees Savings & Credit Union

1822 - 10th Ave. SW
Calgary, AB T3C 0J8
403-261-5681
Fax: 403-261-5748
877-723-2653
info@safewaycucalgary.com
www.safewaycucalgary.com
Ownership: Member-owned
Year Founded: 1952
Number of Employees: 12
Executives:
Cliff Roberts, General Manager

Canada Sand Papers Employees' (Plattsville) Credit Union Limited

28 Albert St.
Plattsville, ON N0J 1S0
519-684-7441
Fax: 519-684-7210
savageo@execulink.com
Year Founded: 1954

Canadian Alternative Investment Cooperative

#111, 146 Laird Dr.
Toronto, ON M4G 3V7
416-467-7797
Fax: 416-467-8946
866-241-2242
caic@caic.ca
www.caic.ca
Year Founded: 1984
Executives:
Mary Halder, President

Canadian General Tower Employees (Galt) Credit Union Limited

Cambridge Place
#117, 73 Water St. North
Cambridge, ON N1R 7L6
519-623-2211
Fax: 519-623-2051
Ownership: Private
Number of Employees: 3
Executives:
Lois James, Manager

Canadian Transportation Employees' Credit Union Ltd.

PO Box 4
600 Ferguson Ave. North
Hamilton, ON L8L 4Z9
905-523-7385
Fax: 905-523-7556
Number of Employees: 3
Executives:
Gary Clairmont, General Manager

Capital Credit Union

30 Hughes
Fredericton, NB E3A 2W3
506-458-9145
Fax: 506-459-0106
syork@capital.creditu.net
www.capitalcu.nb.ca
Year Founded: 1949
Executives:
Owen C. Taylor, CEO; otaylor@capital.creditu.net
Branches:
Stanley
41 Limekiln Rd.
Stanley, NB E6B 2K5 Canada
506-367-2010
Fax: 506-367-2027
sforeman@capital.creditu.net
Karen Armstrong, Branch Manager

Carleton Pioneer Credit Union

#1, 106 Richmond St.
Woodstock, NB E7M 2N9
506-328-8120
Fax: 506-328-3445
cpcu@nb.sympatico.ca
www.woodstocknb.ca/carletonpioneercreditunion.htm
Year Founded: 1938
Number of Employees: 9
Executives:
Eric Smith, Manager
Branches:
Centreville
787 Central St.
Centreville, NB E7K 3E6 Canada
506-276-3221
Fax: 506-276-3275
rcalhoun@cpcu.creditu.net
Rhonda Calhoun, Manager

Carpathia Credit Union

952 Main St., 3rd Fl.
Winnipeg, MB R2W 3P4
204-989-7400
Fax: 204-589-2529
info@carpathiacu.mb.ca
www.carpathiacu.mb.ca
Ownership: Member-owned
Year Founded: 1940
Number of Employees: 53
Assets: $100-500 million
Revenues: $5-10 million
Executives:
Walter Dlugosh, Acting CEO
Roman Hrabowych, Vice-President, Credit
Brian Petrynko, Vice-President, Sales & Marketing
Directors:
Roman Zubach, President
Mark Karpa, Vice-President
Patricia Kmet, Secretary
Ken Bielak
George Chuchman
Bohoan Halkewycz
Demyan Hyworon
Donna Korban
Noella Pylypowich
Branches:
Winnipeg - Henderson Hwy.
1341A Henderson Hwy.
Winnipeg, MB R2G 1M5 Canada
204-989-7400
Fax: 204-338-8893
Ted Sims, Branch Manager
Winnipeg - Main St.
950 Main St.
Winnipeg, MB R2W 3P4 Canada
204-989-7400
Fax: 204-989-7404
Jaroslawa Middleton, Branch Manager
Winnipeg - McPhillips St.
#80, 2200 McPhillips St.
Winnipeg, MB R2V 3P4 Canada
204-989-7400
Fax: 204-697-1664
Victoria Pestrak, Branch Manager

Casera Credit Union

1300 Plessis Rd.
Winnipeg, MB R2C 2Y6
204-958-6300
Fax: 204-222-6766
www.transconacu.mb.ca
Also Known As: Transcona Credit Union
Year Founded: 1951
Executives:
Brent Thomas, CEO
Directors:
Dave Abel, President
Branches:
Winnipeg - Kilkare Ave. East.
#8, 630 Kilkare Ave. East
Winnipeg, MB R2C 0P8 Canada
204-958-6320
Fax: 204-222-6807

Castlegar Savings Credit Union

#100, 630 - 17th St.
Castlegar, BC V1N 4G7
250-365-7232
Fax: 250-365-2913
cscu@cascu.com
www.cascu.com
Ownership: Member-owned
Number of Employees: 50
Directors:
Bruce Gerrand, Director
Ed Rohn, Director
Branches:
Slocan Park
PO Box 39
Slocan Park, BC V0G 2E0 Canada
250-226-7212
Fax: 250-226-7351
cscu@cascu.com

Cataract Savings & Credit Union Limited

7172 Dorchester Rd.
Niagara Falls, ON L2G 5V6
905-357-5222
www.cataractsavings.on.ca
Year Founded: 1949
Executives:
David Benny, General Manager
Branches:
Niagara Falls
6289 Huggins St.
Niagara Falls, ON L2J 1H2 Canada
905-356-4467

CBC (Nfld) Credit Union Ltd.

PO Box 12010, A Stn. A
29-31 Pippy Place
St. John's, NL A1B 3T8
709-576-5407
Fax: 709-576-5409
cbccreditunion@cbccu.ca

CBC (Nfld) Credit Union Ltd. (continued)
www.cbccu.ca
Year Founded: 1965
Number of Employees: 3
Executives:
Margaret Harvey, Manager; mharvey@cbccu.ca

CCB Employees' Credit Union Limited
46 Overlea Blvd.
Toronto, ON M4H 1B6
416-424-6280
Fax: 416-701-1944
Year Founded: 1973
Number of Employees: 2
Revenues: Under $1 million

CCEC Credit Union
2250 Commercial Dr.
Vancouver, BC V5N 5P9
604-254-4100
Fax: 604-254-6558
866-254-4100
info@ccec.bc.ca
www.ccec.bc.ca
Ownership: Cooperative
Year Founded: 1976

Central Credit Union Limited
PO Box 279
512 Main St.
O'Leary, PE C0B 1V0
902-859-2266
Fax: 902-859-3219
central.cu@central.creditu.net
www.peicreditunions.com/oleary/
Ownership: Member-owned
Year Founded: 1969
Number of Employees: 17
Profile: We serve over 5,400 Islanders from the communities of O'Leary, Coleman, Elmsdale & surrounding areas.

Executives:
Stephen Rogers, President
Roger Young, General Manager
Shirley Betts, Privacy Officer

Church River Credit Union
305 Burnt Church Rd.
Burnt Church, NB E9G 4C8
506-776-3247
Executives:
Carole Kilbride, Manager

Churchbridge Savings & Credit Union
PO Box 260
103 Vincent Ave. East
Churchbridge, SK S0A 0M0
306-896-2544
Fax: 306-896-2325
info@churchbridge.cu.sk.ca
www.churchbridgecu.ca
Year Founded: 1945
Number of Employees: 15
Assets: $10-50 million
Executives:
Perry Wishlow, General Manager
Branches:
Langenburg
PO Box 187
106 Carl Ave. East
Langenburg, SK S0A 2A0 Canada
306-743-5212
Fax: 306-743-2908

City Plus Credit Union Ltd.
Municipal Bldg.
PO Box 2100, M Stn. M
#8130, 800 MacLeod Trail SE, 5th Fl.
Calgary, AB T2P 2M5
403-268-2626
Fax: 403-268-4886
main@cpcu.ca
www.cpcu.ca
Former Name: Calgary Civic Employees Credit Union Limited
Ownership: Private
Year Founded: 1942
Number of Employees: 5
Executives:
Z. Zalusky, President

Branches:
Highland Park
Lower Level
#231, 37 Ave. NE
Calgary, AB T2E 8J2 Canada
403-230-0640
Fax: 403-230-0692

City Savings & Credit Union Ltd.
6002 Yonge St.
Toronto, ON M2M 3V9
416-225-7716
Fax: 416-225-7772
info@citysavingscu.com
www.citysavingscu.com
Number of Employees: 15
Executives:
Raymond B. Wood, CEO
Debbie Odea, Operations Manager

Civic Credit Union Ltd.
433 Main St.
Winnipeg, MB R3B 1B3
204-942-5149
Fax: 204-957-7935
info@civiccu.mb.ca
www.civiccu.mb.ca
Ownership: Member-owned
Year Founded: 1943
Branches:
Regent Ave.
1536 Regent Ave. West
Winnipeg, MB R2C 3B4 Canada
204-654-9307
St. James St.
937 St. James St.
Winnipeg, MB R3H 0X2 Canada
204-988-4600
Fax: 204-988-4620
info@civiccu.mb.ca
Winnipeg Sq.
Shops of Winnipeg Square
Winnipeg, MB R3C 3Z8 Canada
204-944-8290
Fax: 204-944-8341

CN (London) Credit Union Limited
#301, 205 York St.
London, ON N6A 1B1
519-667-2326
Fax: 519-434-5687
info@cncu.ca
www.cncu.ca
Year Founded: 1945
Number of Employees: 4
Executives:
David Lucier, General Manager

CNR Employees (Lakehead Terminal) Credit Union Limited
417 Fort William Rd.
Thunder Bay, ON P7B 2Z5
807-344-4096
Fax: 807-346-0595

Coady Credit Union
32 West Ave.
Glace Bay, NS B1A 6E9
902-849-7610
Fax: 902-842-0911
Year Founded: 1933

Coast Capital Savings Credit Union
15117 - 101 Ave.
Surrey, BC V3R 8P7
604-517-7000
Fax: 604-517-7405
888-517-7000
info@coastcapitalsavings.com
www.coastcapitalsavings.com
Year Founded: 2000
Number of Employees: 2,000+
Assets: $1-10 billion
Profile: Acquired Surrey Metro Savings in June, 2002.

Executives:
Lloyd Craig, President/CEO
Lawrie Ferciuson, Vice-President, Marketing

Directors:
Bill Wellburn, Chair
Bob Garnett, 1st Vice-Chair
Karen Kesteloo, 2nd Vice-Chair
Christine Brodie
Daniel Burns
Frank Harper
Ken Martin
Gordon Munn
Mary Jane Stenberg
Doug Stone
Elizabeth Rhett Woods
Branches:
Abbotsford
2611 Clearbrook Rd.
Abbotsford, BC V2T 2Y6 Canada
604-852-7000
Fax: 604-852-7015
Chilliwack
#1, 45480 Luckakuck Way
Chilliwack, BC V2R 2X5 Canada
604-824-4444
Fax: 604-824-4405
Tammi Wallace, Branch Manager
Coquitlam
1175 Johnson St.
Coquitlam, BC V3B 7K1 Canada
604-517-7000
Fax: 604-941-8805
Coquitlam - Westwood Mall
#103, 3000 Lougheed Hwy.
Coquitlam, BC V3B 1C5 Canada
604-953-5720
Fax: 604-953-5722

Delta - North Delta
8445 - 120 St.
Delta, BC V4C 6R2 Canada
604-517-7000
Fax: 604-517-7875
Delta - Tsawwassen
#7, 5506 - 12th Ave.
Tsawwassen, BC V4M 4C2 Canada
604-517-7000
Fax: 604-948-5436
Duncan - Beverly Corners
2755 Beverly St.
Duncan, BC V9L 6X2 Canada
Fax: 250-701-4107
888-517-7000
Fort Langley
PO Box 282
9140 Glover Rd.
Fort Langley, BC V1M 2R6 Canada
604-517-7000
Fax: 604-517-7295
Langley - Brookswood
4145 - 200th St.
Langley, BC V3A 1K8 Canada
604-517-7000
Fax: 604-517-7275
Langley - Fraser Hwy.
20550 Fraser Hwy.
Langley, BC V3A 4G2 Canada
604-517-7000
Fax: 604-517-7225
Langley - Walnut Grove
20991 - 88th Ave.
Langley, BC V1M 2C9 Canada
604-517-7000
Fax: 604-517-7285
Mill Bay
2734A Barry Rd.
Mill Bay, BC V0R 2P2 Canada
Fax: 250-701-4117
888-517-7000
Nanaimo - Longwood Station
2 - 5765 Turner Rd.
Nanaimo, BC V9T 6L8 Canada
Fax: 250-760-1309
888-517-7000
Pitt Meadows - Meadowtown
320 - 19800 Lougheed Hwy.
Pitt Meadows, BC V3Y 2W1 Canada

604-517-7000
Fax: 604-953-5701
Richmond - Blundell
7960 No. 2 Rd.
Richmond, BC V7C 3L9 Canada
604-517-7000
Fax: 604-272-4104
Richmond - Broadmoor
#124, 10111 No. 3 Rd.
Richmond, BC V7A 1W6 Canada
604-517-7000
Fax: 604-272-6505
Richmond - Cambie
11911 Cambie Rd.
Richmond, BC V6X 1L6 Canada
604-517-7000
Fax: 604-273-5727
Richmond - Centre
6253 No. 3 Rd.
Richmond, BC V6Y 2B5 Canada
604-517-7000
Fax: 604-273-9157
Richmond - Ironwood
#1070, 11660 Steveston Hwy.
Richmond, BC V7A 1N6 Canada
604-517-7000
Fax: 604-271-9688
Richmond - Steveston
3960 Chatham St.
Richmond, BC V7E 2Z5 Canada
604-517-7000
Fax: 604-272-5093
Richmond - Terra Nova
#100, 3679 Westminster Hwy.
Richmond, BC V7C 5V2 Canada
604-517-7000
Fax: 604-207-8873
Saanichton - Central Saanich
#201, 7860 Wallace Dr.
Saanichton, BC V8M 2H8 Canada
250-483-7000
Fax: 250-652-1223
Sidney
2297 Beacon Ave.
Sidney, BC V8L 1W9 Canada
250-483-7000
Fax: 250-655-1621
Sooke
#101, 6661 Sooke Rd.
Sooke, BC V0S 1N0 Canada
250-483-7000
Fax: 250-642-4940
Surrey - Central City
2672 Central City, Upper Level East 134A St.
Surrey, BC V3T 2W1 Canada
604-517-7000
Fax: 604-517-7855

Surrey - Clayton Crossing
#101, 18737 Fraser Hwy.
Surrey, BC V3S 8E7 Canada
604-517-7000
Fax: 604-953-5741
Surrey - Cloverdale
17730 - Hwy. #10
Surrey, BC V3S 1C7 Canada
604-517-7000
Fax: 604-517-7205
Surrey - Fleetwood
#102, 9014 - 152nd St.
Surrey, BC V3R 4E7 Canada
604-517-7000
Fax: 604-517-7195
Surrey - Guildford
1110 Guildford Town Centre
Surrey, BC V3R 7B7 Canada
604-517-7000
Fax: 604-517-7995
Surrey - Newton
13764 - 72nd Ave.
Surrey, BC V3W 2P4 Canada
604-517-7000
Fax: 604-517-7885
Surrey - Ocean Park
1680 - 128 St.
Surrey, BC V4A 3V3 Canada
604-517-7000
Fax: 604-517-7345
Surrey - Peninsula Village
#640, 15355 - 24th Ave.
Surrey, BC V4A 2H9 Canada
604-517-7000
Fax: 604-517-7335
Surrey - Semiahmoo
#103, 1797 - 152nd St.
Surrey, BC V4A 4N3 Canada
604-517-7000
Fax: 604-536-6322
Surrey - Strawberry Hill
12091 - 72nd Ave.
Surrey, BC V3W 2M1 Canada
604-517-7000
Fax: 604-517-7325
Surrey - Sunshine Hills
#100, 6350 - 120th St.
Surrey, BC V3X 3K1 Canada
604-517-7000
Fax: 604-572-7667
Vancouver - Georgia St.
1075 West Georgia St.
Vancouver, BC V6E 3C9 Canada
604-517-7000
Fax: 604-682-0122
Victoria - Admirals Walk
1499 Admirals Walk
Victoria, BC V9A 2P8 Canada
250-483-7000
Fax: 250-388-7794
Victoria - Bay Centre
#212, 1150 Douglas St.
Victoria, BC V8W 3M9 Canada
250-483-7000
Fax: 250-385-4117
Victoria - Broadmead
#150, 777 Royal Oak Dr.
Victoria, BC V8X 4V1 Canada
250-483-7000
Fax: 250-479-7505
Victoria - Canwest Mall
#120, 2945 Jacklin Rd.
Victoria, BC V9B 5E3 Canada
250-483-7000
Fax: 250-474-6315
Victoria - Colwood
1911 Sooke Rd.
Victoria, BC V9B 1V8 Canada
250-483-7000
Fax: 250-474-0701
Victoria - James Bay
239 Menzies St.
Victoria, BC V8V 2G6 Canada
250-483-7000
Fax: 250-382-5107
Victoria - Oak Bay
2067 Cadboro Bay Rd.
Victoria, BC V8R 5G4 Canada
250-483-7000
Fax: 250-595-1443
Victoria - Shelbourne
3750 Shelbourne St.
Victoria, BC V8P 4H4 Canada
250-483-7000
Fax: 250-477-0947
Victoria - Tillicum Mall
#169, 3170 Tillicum Rd.
Victoria, BC V9A 7C9 Canada
250-483-7000
Fax: 250-361-3921
West Vancouver
1702 Marine Dr.
West Vancouver, BC V7V 1J3 Canada
604-517-7000
Fax: 604-926-0366

White Rock
15241 Thrift Ave.
White Rock, BC V4B 2K9 Canada
604-517-7000
Fax: 604-517-7955

Coastal Community Credit Union

#21, 13 Victoria Cres.
Nanaimo, BC V9R 5B9
250-741-3200
888-741-1010
www.cccu.ca
Ownership: Member-owned
Year Founded: 1946
Number of Employees: 525
Assets: $1-10 billion
Revenues: $10-50 million
Profile: Coastal Community Credit Union is a full-service financial institution serving the communities of Alert Bay, Campbell River, Comox, Courtenay, Gabriola, Nanaimo, Nanoose Bay, Parkville, Port Alberni, Port Hardy, Qualicum Beach, Sointula, Tofino & Ucluelet. Services include retirement services, chequing & savings accounts, term deposits, GICs, loans & mortgages, credit cards & home banking. Financial planning, brokerage & insurance services are offered through its various subsidiaries.

Executives:
Garth Sheane, CEO
Directors:
Richard Allen
Mary Ashley
Evelyn Clark
Judy Fraser
Sharon Fisher
Susanne Jakobsen
Richard Kerton
Doug Lang
John Newall, Chair
Ron Philip
Gail Preus
Norm Reynolds
Robert Smits
Ray Stokes
Cheryl Tellier
Administration Offices:
Campbell River
920 Alder St.
Campbell River, BC V9W 2P8 Canada
250-286-3243
Fax: 250-286-2728
888-517-1133
Comox
#305, 1797 Comox Ave.
Comox, BC V9M 3L9 Canada
250-703-4100
Fax: 250-703-4219
800-532-8686
Branches:
Alert Bay
30 Maple St.
Alert Bay, BC V0N 1A0 Canada
250-974-5527
Fax: 250-974-5445
Campbell River - Discovery Harbour
1354 Island Hwy.
Campbell River, BC V9W 8C9 Canada
250-286-6205
Fax: 250-286-0145
Campbell River - Willow Point Express Centre
#1, 2204 South Island Hwy.
Campbell River, BC V9W 1C3 Canada
250-923-0862
Fax: 250-923-0863
Chemainus
9781 Willow St.
Chemainus, BC V0R 1K0 Canada
250-246-4704
Fax: 250-246-3690
Comox
#202, 1797 Comox Ave.
Comox, BC V9M 3L9 Canada
250-703-4100
Fax: 250-703-4239
Courtenay - 4th St.
291 - 4th St.
Courtenay, BC V9N 1G7 Canada
250-703-4100
Fax: 250-703-4109

Courtenay - Ryan Rd.

Coastal Community Credit Union (continued)
1045 Ryan Rd.
Courtenay, BC V9N 3R6 Canada
250-703-4100
Fax: 250-703-4169
Gabriola Island
#7, 580 North Rd.
Gabriola, BC V0R 1X0 Canada
250-247-8521
Fax: 250-247-8520
Nanaimo - Bowen Rd.
2350 Labieux Rd.
Nanaimo, BC V9T 3M6 Canada
250-729-2550
Fax: 250-729-2556
Nanaimo - Hammond Bay
6365 Hammond Bay Rd.
Nanaimo, BC V9T 5Y1 Canada
250-390-8900
Fax: 250-390-8939
Nanaimo - Harbourfront Plaza
#111, 59 Wharf St.
Nanaimo, BC V9R 2X3 Canada
250-741-3100
Fax: 250-741-3135
Nanaimo - Southgate
#111, 50 Tenth St.
Nanaimo, BC V9R 6L1 Canada
250-741-1233
Fax: 250-741-1683
Nanoose Bay
#2, 2451 Collins Cres.
Nanoose Bay, BC V9P 9J9 Canada
250-468-7624
Fax: 250-468-7200
Parksville - Alberni Hwy.
140 Alberni Hwy.
Parksville, BC V9P 2G6 Canada
250-248-3275
Fax: 250-248-4300
Parksville - Wembley Mall
Wembley Mall
#16, 826 West Island Hwy.
Parksville, BC V9P 2B7 Canada
250-248-3293
Fax: 250-248-4780
Port Alberni
PO Box 520
3009 - 4th Ave.
Port Alberni, BC V9Y 7M9 Canada
250-723-8101
Fax: 250-723-2157
Port Hardy
8755 Granville St.
Port Hardy, BC V0N 2P0 Canada
250-949-7471
Fax: 250-949-9997
Qualicum Beach
118 West 2nd Ave.
Qualicum Beach, BC V9K 1S7 Canada
250-852-9244
Fax: 250-752-1119
Sointula
185 - 1st St.
Sointula, BC V0N 3E0 Canada
250-973-6723
Fax: 250-973-6543
Ucluelet
1566 Peninsula Rd.
Ucluelet, BC V0R 3A0 Canada
250-726-7785
Fax: 250-726-1285

Coastal Financial Credit Union
2 Collins St.
Yarmouth, NS B5A 3C3
902-742-7322
Fax: 902-742-7476
rdoucette@coastalfinancial.ca
www.coastalfinancial.ca
Ownership: Member-owned
Year Founded: 2001
Number of Employees: 53
Assets: $50-100 million
Executives:
Rick Doucette, General Manager
Phyllis Amirault, Manager, Operations
Directors:
Irvin Surette, President
Raymond Doucette, 1st Vice-Chair
Raymond Surette, 2nd Vice-Chair
Claude d'Entremont, Secretary
John Armstrong
Danielle Boudreau
Yvon Boudreau
Pat Dempsey
Dave Marling
Ricky Muise
Charles Pothier
Diane Walker
Branches:
Pubnico - Argyle
PO Box 70
3703 Hwy. 3
Pubnico, NS B0W 2W0 Canada
902-643-2484
Fax: 902-643-2018
Muriel d'Entrement, Manager
Tusket
PO Box 130
59 Van Norden Rd.
Tusket, NS B0W 3M0 Canada
902-648-2322
Fax: 902-648-2131
Tom Moulaison, Manager
Wedgeport
PO Box 330
2776 Hwy. 334
Wedgeport, NS B0W 3P0 Canada
902-663-2525
Fax: 902-663-4723
Philip O. Atkinson, Manager
West Pubnico
PO Box 166
9, ch de l'Eglise
West Pubnico, NS B0W 2M0 Canada
902-762-2372
Fax: 902-762-3011
Kevin Cooke, Manager
Yarmouth
PO Box 490
371 Main St.
Yarmouth, NS B5A 4B4 Canada
902-742-2123
Fax: 902-742-0092
Linda Cain, Manager
Yarmouth - East Pubnico
683 Hwy. #3, RR#1
Yarmouth, NS B0W 2A0 Canada
902-762-2617
Fax: 902-762-3224
Darryl LeBlanc, Manager

Codroy Valley Credit Union
PO Box 29
Doyles, NL A0N 1J0
709-955-2402
Fax: 709-955-3081
www.codroyvalleycu.com
Executives:
Harry Coates, President
Gordon Aucoin, Vice-President
Gary O'Brian, Secretary
Cory Munden, General Manager
Madonna Hynes, Branch Manager
Branches:
Cartyville - McKays
PO Box 130
Cartyville, NL A0N 1G0 Canada
709-645-2512
Fax: 709-645-2886
Rhoda Pumphrey, Branch Manager
Grand Bay East
PO Box 680
27 Grand Bay Rd.
Grand Bay East, NL A0N 1K0 Canada
709-695-7000
Fax: 709-695-7014
St-Georges
178 Main St.
St-Georges, NL A0N 1Z0 Canada
709-647-2000
Fax: 709-647-2002

College Hill Credit Union
c/o University of New Brunswick, McConnell Hall
PO Box 4400
#107, 19 Bailey Dr.
Fredericton, NB E3B 5A3
506-455-3535
www.unb.ca/facilities/chcu

Columbia Valley Credit Union
PO Box 720
511 Main St
Golden, BC V0A 1H0
250-344-2282
Fax: 250-344-2117
888-298-1777
cvcu@cvcu.bc.ca
www.cvcu.bc.ca
Number of Employees: 18

Common Wealth Credit Union
Atrium Centre
PO Box 1410
5012 - 49 St.
Lloydminster, AB S9V 1K4
780-875-4434
Fax: 780-875-4578
877-606-6333
www.commonwealthcu.net
Former Name: Border Credit Union Limited
Ownership: Member-owned
Year Founded: 1955
Number of Employees: 298
Assets: $1,200,000,000 Year End: 20050831
Revenues: $1-10 billion Year End: 20050831
Profile: The credit union also offers the following services: financing, loan services, financial planning & investment management.
Executives:
Jeff Mulligan, President/CEO
Pierre Amyotte, Sr. Vice-President, Strategy & Innovation
Eric Dillon, Sr. Vice-President, Member Service
Ken Sutherland, Sr. Vice-President, Business & Marketing Development
Brian Weiss, Sr. Vice-President, Finance
Kathy Bootsman, Vice-President, Infrastructure & Standards
Don Coomber, Vice-President, Entreprise Risk Management
Marcel Fizell, Vice-President, Credit
Allan Gabert, Vice-President, Business Banking
Steve Till-Rogers, Vice-President, Information Services
Directors:
Douglas Hastings, Chair
Rene Dumas
Gerald Holmen
John Lamb
Merv Loewen
Dagmar Mehlsen
Greg Preston
Juergen Schwenk
Barry Smith
Alison Starke
Branches:
Athabasca
4914 - 49 St.
Athabasca, AB T9S 1C2 Canada
780-675-2976
Fax: 780-675-9131
Brian Hall, Branch Manager
Barrhead
4929 - 50 Ave.
Barrhead, AB T7N 1A4 Canada
780-674-3345
Fax: 780-674-6287
Kathy Stocking, Manager, Lending
Dewberry
PO Box 42
Dewberry, AB T0B 1G0 Canada
780-847-3838
Fax: 780-847-2130
Linda Romanchuk, Manager, Personal Banking
Edmonton - Roper Rd.
7203 Roper Rd.
Edmonton, AB T6B 3J4 Canada

780-471-4306
Fax: 780-471-4488
Marilyn Norman, Branch Manager
Edmonton - West End
14909 - 121A Ave.
Edmonton, AB T5V 1P3 Canada
780-455-9500
Fax: 780-455-9540
Barbara Bourassa, Manager, Personal Banking
Fairview
PO Box 459
10300 - 110 St.
Fairview, AB T0H 1L0 Canada
780-835-2914
Fax: 780-835-4214
Patrick Watkins, Branch Manager
Grande Prairie
9902 - 100 Ave.
Grande Prairie, AB T8V 0T9 Canada
780-532-3710
Fax: 780-538-3985
Robin Chambers, Manager, Lending
Grimshaw
PO Box 410
5211 - 50 St.
Grimshaw, AB T0H 1W0 Canada
780-332-2226
Fax: 780-332-4501
Bernadette Wearden, Branch Manager
Kitscoty
PO Box 390
Kitscoty, AB T0B 2P0 Canada
780-846-2875
Fax: 780-846-2082
John Mason, Contact
Provost
PO Box 669
Provost, AB T0B 3S0 Canada
780-753-6288
Fax: 780-753-3330
Debbie Bishop, Branch Manager
Westlock
Town Centre Mall
#2, 9936 - 106 St.
Westlock, AB T7P 2K2 Canada
780-349-4497
Fax: 780-349-3069
Loretta Keller, Supervisor, Member Service
Whitecourt
PO Box 1020
5016 - 50 St.
Whitecourt, AB T7S 1N9 Canada
780-778-3911
Fax: 780-778-5221
Laurie Higgins, Manager, Lending

Communication Technologies Credit Union Limited
Eaton Centre
PO Box 501
#102, 220 Yonge St.
Toronto, ON M5B 2H1
416-598-1197
Fax: 416-598-0171
800-209-7444
member_services@comtechcu.com
www.comtechcu.com
Ownership: Member-owned
Number of Employees: 14
Assets: $50-100 million
Executives:
Louise Spence, Branch Manager
Branches:
Brampton - Nortel
8200 Dixie Rd.
Brampton, ON L6T 4B8 Canada
905-863-5659
Fax: 905-863-5594
brampton_branch@comtechcu.com
Lorraine McAulay, Representative, Financial Service
Mississauga - Bell Mobility
5099 Creekbank Rd.
Mississauga, ON L4W 5N2 Canada
905-625-6662
Fax: 905-625-6682
creekbank@comtechcu.com
Lynn Wine, Branch Manager
Nepean - Nortel
3500 Carling Ave.
Nepean, ON K2H 8E8 Canada
613-763-4310
Fax: 613-763-4307
Ron Conlin, Branch Manager

Community Credit Union Ltd.
164 Main St.
Grunthal, MB R0A 0R0
204-434-6338
Fax: 204-434-9074
grunthal@communitycu.mb.ca
www.communitycu.mb.ca
Ross Ballantine, CEO
Branches:
Sprague Credit Union
PO Box 89
Sprague, MB R0A 1Z0 Canada
204-437-2371
Fax: 204-437-2139
sprague@communitycu.mb.ca
Vita Credit Union
PO Box 88
100 - 1st St. West
Vita, MB R0A 2K0 Canada
204-425-3351
Fax: 204-425-7705
vita@communitycu.mb.ca

Community Credit Union of Cumberland Colchester Ltd.
PO Box 578
33 Prince Arthur St.
Amherst, NS B4H 4B8
902-667-7541
Fax: 902-667-1779
www.communitycreditunion.ns.ca
Former Name: Amherst Credit Union; Colchester Credit Union
Year Founded: 1999
Number of Employees: 45
Assets: $50-100 million
Revenues: $1-5 million
Executives:
Bruce Cowie, General Manager
Debbie Smith-Donkin, Manager, Operations & Administration
John Chisholm, Manager, Truro
Edith Doyle, Manager, Amherst
Directors:
Howard Welch, Chair; 902-647-7689
Darrell Jones, Past Chair; 902-667-7682
Irene Caswell, Vice-Chair; 902-667-8947
Charlotte MacVicar, Secretary; 902-668-2459
Branches:
Bass River
Bass River Plaza
Bass River, NS B0M 1B0 Canada
902-647-2424
Fax: 902-647-2533
866-318-2424
John Chisholm, Officer-in-Charge
Truro
347 Willow St.
Truro, NS B2N 5A6 Canada
902-893-7134
Fax: 902-897-4655
866-893-7134
John Chisholm, Manager

Community First Credit Union Limited
289 Bay St.
Sault Ste Marie, ON P6A 1W7
705-942-1000
Fax: 705-946-2363
www.communityfirst-cu.com
Year Founded: 1948
Profile: Merged with Timmins Regional Credit Union to serve Province of Ontario as Community First Credit Union Limited in 2006.
Executives:
Aldo Greco, CEO
Greg Peres, CFO
Branches:
Timmins
146 Cedar St. South
Timmins, ON P4N 2G8 Canada
705-267-6481
Fax: 705-268-4648
Trunk Rd.
535 Trunk Rd.
Sault Ste Marie, ON P6A 3T1 Canada
705-942-1000
Fax: 705-946-2364
Pat Mancuso, Branch Manager

Community Savings Credit Union
Central City Tower
#1600, 13450 - 102nd Ave., 16th Fl.
Surrey, BC V3T 5X3
604-654-2000
Fax: 604-586-5156
888-963-2000
www.comsavings.com
Former Name: IWA & Community Credit Union
Year Founded: 1944
Number of Employees: 500
Profile: With 12,000 members, Community Savings offers chequing & savings accounts, term deposits, mutual funds, loans & mortgages, card products, travellers cheques & safety deposit boxes at locations in central & southern Alberta.
Executives:
Bruce Cook, President/CEO
Directors:
Colleen Jordan, Chair
Ken Isomura, Vice-Chair
David Tones, Sec.-Treas.
Ken Bauder
Marie Decaire
Phillip Legg
Trevor Oram
Dale Sagmoen
Jagdip Singh Sivia
Dave Wilson
Branches:
New Westminster
1188 - 8th Ave.
New Westminster, BC V3M 2R6 Canada
604-654-2000
Fax: 604-654-2050

Port Coquitlam
#100, 1125 Nicola Ave.
Port Coquitlam, BC V3B 8B2 Canada
Fax: 604-464-5986
Surrey
#900, 7380 King George Hwy.
Surrey, BC V3W 5A5 Canada
Fax: 604-592-2265
Vancouver
5108 Joyce St.
Vancouver, BC V5R 4H1 Canada
604-654-2000
Fax: 604-654-2130
Victoria
#103, 2750 Quadra St.
Victoria, BC V8T 4E8 Canada
250-385-8431
Fax: 250-385-8679

Concentra Financial Corporate Banking
PO Box 3030
2055 Albert St.
Regina, SK S4P 3G8
306-566-7440
Fax: 306-566-7401
Other Information: Email: concentra-corporatebankingadministrators@concentrafinancial.ca
www.concentrafinancial.ca
Former Name: CUCORP Financial Services
Ownership: Private
Year Founded: 1997
Revenues: $1-10 billion
Executives:
Marty Meloche, Sr. Vice-President; 306-566-7403; marty.meloche@cucorp.ca
Hugh Balkwill, Vice-President, Relationship Management
Daniel Johnson, Vice-President; 306-566-1339; david.smith@cucorp.ca

Conexus Credit Union
1960 Albert St.
Regina, SK S4P 2T4
306-780-1750
800-667-7477
information@conexuscu.com
www.conexuscu.com
Former Name: Assiniboia Credit Union Ltd.
Profile: Conexus is Saskatchewan's largest & Canada's 6th largest credit union. Conexus has more than $3 billion in assets & more than 167,000 members; 1000 staff & sales professionals are here to serve you. Our credit unions provide personalized service at 48 branches across the province.

Directors:
Dennis Anderson, Chair
Crystal Asmussen
Don Blocka
Loretta Elford
Norbert Fries
Ed Gebert
Carol Glasser
Laverne Goodsman
Randy Grimsrud
Glenn Hepp
Sherry Knight
Wes Kolosky
Arnold Leatherdale
Maurice Nekurak
Peter Nicholson
Gerald Unger

Branches:

Abernethy
Main St.
Abernethy, SK S4V 2Z3 Canada
306-333-2131

Assiniboia
400 Centre St.
Assiniboia, SK S0H 0B0 Canada
306-642-3343

Bethune
460 Main St.
Bethune, SK S0G 0H0 Canada
306-638-2200

Central Butte
PO Box 100
Main St.
Central Butte, SK S0H 0T0 Canada
306-796-2133

Chamberlain
415 Hwy. 11
Chamberlain, SK S0G 0R0 Canada
306-638-4700

Chaplin
PO Box 180
416 - 4th St.
Chaplin, SK S0H 0V0 Canada
306-395-2215

Coronach
126 Centre St.
Coronach, SK S0H 0Z0 Canada
306-267-2171

Cudworth
PO Box 580
200 Main St.
Cudworth, SK S0K 1B0 Canada
306-256-3446

Cupar
111 Stanley St.
Cupar, SK S0G 0Y0 Canada
306-723-4424

Domremy
PO Box 250
200 - 1st Ave.
Domremy, SK S0K 1G0 Canada
306-423-5335
Fax: 306-423-5299

Duck Lake
PO Box 70
220 Front St.
Duck Lake, SK S0K 1J0 Canada
306-467-5220
Fax: 306-467-4511

Fort Qu'Appelle
PO Box 279
102 Broadway St. East
Fort Qu'appelle, SK S0G 1S0 Canada
306-332-5606

Guernsey
PO Box 1
117 Francis St.
Drake, SK S0K 1H0 Canada
306-363-2011

Holdfast
PO Box 10
815 Main St.
Holdfast, SK S0G 2H0 Canada
306-488-4000
Fax: 306-488-4225

Humboldt
724 Main St.
Humboldt, SK S0K 2A0 Canada
306-682-2696

La Ronge
120 Boardman St.
La Ronge, SK S0J 1L0 Canada
306-425-6800
Fax: 306-425-3856

Lanigan
34 Downing Dr. West
Lanigan, SK S0K 2M0 Canada
306-365-3084

Lemberg
326 Main St.
Lemberg, SK S0A 2B0 Canada
306-335-2316

Limerick
PO Box 760
Main St.
Limerick, SK S0H 2P0 Canada
306-263-2002

Lumsden
PO Box 800
370 James St.
Lumsden, SK S0G 3C0 Canada
306-731-3322

Meath Park
PO Box 10
Railway Ave.
Meath Park, SK S0J 1T0 Canada
306-929-2125
Fax: 306-929-3191

Middle Lake
PO Box 99
112 Main St.
Middle Lake, SK S0K 2X0 Canada
306-367-2163

Moose Jaw - High
80 High St. West
Moose Jaw, SK S6H 4P4 Canada
306-691-4800
Darrell Foster, Manager, Lending

Moose Jaw - South Hill
335 - 4th Ave. SW
Moose Jaw, SK S6H 4P4 Canada
306-691-4800

Moosomin
714 Main St.
Moosomin, SK S0G 3N0 Canada
306-435-3374

Mossbank
316 Main St.
Mossbank, SK S0H 3G0 Canada
306-354-2320

Prince Albert - City Centre
40 - 10th St. East
Prince Albert, SK S6V 6P2 Canada
306-953-6100
Fax: 306-763-4757

Prince Albert - South Hill
2800 - 2nd Ave. West
Prince Albert, SK S6V 5Z4 Canada
306-953-6100

Regina - 5th Ave.
3433 - 5th Ave
Regina, SK S4T 0M1 Canada
306-780-1831

Regina - Conexus Crossing
1040 North Pasqua St.
Regina, SK S4X 4V3 Canada

Regina - Connexus Plaza
1801 Hamilton St.
Regina, SK S4P 4B4 Canada
306-780-0130

Regina - North Albert
265 Albert St. North
Regina, SK S4R 3C2 Canada
306-780-1878

Regina - Sherwood Place
1960 Albert St.
Regina, SK S4P 2T4 Canada
306-780-1750

Regina - South Albert
4540 Albert St.
Regina, SK S4S 6B4 Canada
306-780-1866

Regina - Wallace
904 Victoria Ave.
Regina, SK S4P 4M1 Canada
306-780-1711
Marianne Engel, Manager

Regina - West Landing
570 University Park Dr.
Regina, SK S4V 2Z3 Canada
306-780-1800

Rocanville
123 Ellice St.
Rocanville, SK S0A 3L0 Canada
306-645-2177

Smeaton
PO Box 178
Railway Ave.
Smeaton, SK S0J 2J0 Canada
306-426-2035
Fax: 306-426-2251

Southey
205 Keats St.
Southey, SK S0G 4P0 Canada
306-726-2044

Spy Hill
200 Main St.
Spy Hill, SK S0A 3W0 Canada
306-534-2100

St. Benedict
PO Box 130
120 Centre St.
St. Benedict, SK S0K 3T0 Canada
306-289-2125

Viceroy
Main St.
Viceroy, SK S0H 4H0 Canada
306-268-4559

Wakaw
PO Box 550
219 - 1st St.
Wakaw, SK S0K 4P0 Canada
306-233-6250
Fax: 306-233-4730

Wawota
400 Railway Ave.
Wawota, SK S0G 5A0 Canada
306-739-2553

Whitewood
602 - 3rd Ave.
Whitewood, SK S0G 5C0 Canada
306-735-2681

Wilcox
501 Railway Ave.
Wilcox, SK S0G 5E0 Canada
306-732-2110

Willow Bunch
22 - 5th St. East
Willow Bunch, SK S0H 4K0 Canada
306-473-2301

Young
PO Box 160
109 Main St.
Young, SK 306-259-2122 S0K 4Y0

Credit Union Atlantic
PO Box 1105
#350, 7105 Chebucto Pl.
Halifax, NS B3J 2X1
902-492-6500
Fax: 902-492-6501
800-474-4282
cua@cua.com
www.cua.com
Year Founded: 1948
Number of Employees: 81
Executives:
James Baillie, President/CEO
John Blue, Vice-President, Lending Services
Peter Bellworthy, Vice-President, Business Development & Branch Support
Lynda Coe, Vice-President, Finance
Directors:
John Hawrylak, Chair
Allan Billard
Dennis d'Entremont
Bruce Frazee
Roswell James
Jim Johnson
Doreen E. Malone
David Ness
Ralph Settle
Eloise Surette
Walter Thompson
Len Wilson
Branches:
Dartmouth - Cumberland Dr.
3 Cumberland Dr.
Dartmouth, NS B2V 2T6 Canada
902-492-6610
Fax: 902-492-6616
Dariene Shortell, Manager
Dartmouth - Pleasant St.
#1, 380 Pleasant St.
Dartmouth, NS B2Y 3S5 Canada
902-492-6590
Pam Mountan, Manager
Dartmouth - Wyse Rd.
135 Wyse Rd.
Dartmouth, NS B3A 4K9 Canada
902-492-6570
Fax: 902-492-6574
Susan Chawner, Manager
Halifax - Mumford Rd.
Shopping Centre Annex
6954 Mumford Rd.
Halifax, NS B3L 4V9 Canada
902-492-6690
Darlene Young, Manager
Halifax - Spring Garden Rd.
5670 Spring Garden Rd.
Halifax, NS B3J 1H6 Canada
902-492-6580
Fax: 902-492-6586
Lynne Campbell, Manager
Halifax - Young St.
6080 Young St.
Halifax, NS B3K 5L2 Canada
902-492-6550
Fax: 902-492-6558
Steve MacDonald, Manager

Credit Union Central Alberta Limited
#350N, 8500 MacLeod Trail SE
Calgary, AB T2H 2N1
403-258-5900
Fax: 403-253-7720
email@albertacentral.com
www.albertacentral.com
Ownership: Private
Year Founded: 1968
Number of Employees: 250
Executives:
James Scopick, President/CEO
Barry Johnson, Exec. Vice-President
Graham Wetter, Sr. Vice-President & General Counsel
Don Gregorski, Vice-President, Payment Services
Paul Rossmann, Vice-President, Administration
Dick Williams, Vice-President, Financial Services
Pat Dolan, Asst. Vice-President, Treasury
Anne Gillespie, Asst. Vice-President, Controller
Judy Hammond, Asst. Vice-President, Payment Services
Mark McLeod, Asst. Vice-President, Audit Services
Karen Niven, Asst. Vice-President, Electronic Payments
Susan Greenaway, Corporate Secretary
Directors:
G. Penny Reeves, Chair
Rene Dumas, First Vice-Chair
Rod Banman, Second Vice-Chair
Nigel Teucher, Secretary
Marcel Chorel
Ray Coates
Terry Cooper
Cam Durham
Bruno Friesen
Randy Harper
Dave Munro
Greg Nail
Bill Purdy

Credit Union Central of British Columbia
1441 Creekside Dr.
Vancouver, BC V6J 4S7
604-734-2511
Fax: 604-737-5085
info@cucbc.com, switch@cucbc.com
www.cucbc.com, www.peoplebeforeprofits.ca
Ownership: Cooperative
Year Founded: 1944
Number of Employees: 350
Assets: $1-10 billion
Revenues: $100-500 million
Executives:
Rowland Kelly, Interim President/CEO
Kim Andres, Vice-President, Credit Union Development
Linda Archer, Vice-President, Human Resources & Marketing
Richard J. Thomas, Vice-President, Trade Services, Corporate Secretary
Mervin Zabinsky, Vice-President, Technology & Payment Services
Directors:
Daniel A. Burns, Chair
Lorne Myhra, Vice-Chair
Christine Brodie
Valerie Gauvin
Pearl Graham
Henry Jansen
Ed MacIntosh
Catherine McCreary
Ross Montgomery
Jay Strong
Michael Tarr

Credit Union Central of Canada(CUCC)
#500, 300 The East Mall
Toronto, ON M9B 6B7
416-232-1262
Fax: 416-232-9196
cucc@cucentral.com
www.cucentral.ca
Ownership: Owned by the provincial credit union centrals
Year Founded: 1953
Profile: CUCC is a national trade association & central finance facility for credit unions in Canada. It is also affiliated with The Co-Operators Group & Concentra Financial.

Affiliated Companies:
Credential Financial Inc.
The CUMIS Group Limited

Credit Union Central of Manitoba
PO Box 9900, Main Stn. Main
Winnipeg, MB R3C 3E2
204-985-4700
Fax: 204-957-0849
cuinfo@creditunion.mb.ca
www.creditunion.mb.ca
Former Name: Cooperative Credit Society of Manitoba Ltd.
Ownership: Member-owned
Year Founded: 1950
Number of Employees: 100
Assets: $1-10 billion
Revenues: $83,000,000
Profile: Central financial institution & trade association for Manitoba credit unions.

Executives:
Garth Manness, CEO; 204-985-4808; gmanness@creditunion.mb.ca
Mike Safiniuk, Treasurer & Manager, Finance & Administration; 204-985-4818; msafiniuk@creditunion.mb.ca
Dale Ward, Corporate Secretary & Manager, Marketing & Development Services; 204-985-4792; dward@creditunion.mb.ca
Brian Peto, Divisional Manager, HR & Consulting; 204-985-4732; brian.peto@creditunion.mb.ca
Directors:
Russ Fast, Chair
Sandy Wallace, 1st Vice-Chair
Wayne McLeod, 2nd Vice-Chair

Credit Union Central of New Brunswick
663 Pinewood Rd.
Riverview, NB E1B 5R6
506-857-8184
Fax: 506-857-9431
800-332-3320
comment@cucnb.ca
www.creditunion.nb.ca
Also Known As: New Brunswick Credit Union Federation
Ownership: Public
Year Founded: 1950
Number of Employees: 300
Profile: Financial & regulatory services & credit unions.

Executives:
Gerard Adams, CEO
Donna Baranowski, Vice-President, Vision & Strategy
Barry R. Veno, Vice-President, Corporate Development
Kim Walker, Controller
Directors:
Tony Baker
Bill Brown
Frank Carroll
Robert Christie
Vance Craig
Marc Griffiths
Garth Lawson
Bobbi McNutt
Kevin Murphy
Charlie Parker
Paul Emile Rioux
Jacqueline Robichaud-Hebert
Branches:
Bathurst
Consolidated Bathurst Credit Union
PO Box 1022
480 St. Peter Ave.
Bathurst, NB E2A 3N3 Canada
Kimberly Harvey, Manager
Blackville
Blackville Credit Union
128 Main St.
Blackville, NB E9B 1P1 Canada
Kathleen Coughlan, Manager
Burnt Church
Church River Credit Union
305 Burnt Church Rd.
Burnt Church, NB E9G 4C8 Canada
Carole Kilbride, Manager
Dalhousie
Dalhousie Industrial Credit Union
422 William St.
Dalhousie, NB E8C 2X2 Canada
Kevin Murphy, Manager
Fredericton - Capital Credit Union
30 Hughes St.
Fredericton, NB E3A 2W3 Canada
Perry MacPherson, Manager
Fredericton - College Hill Credit Union
PO Box 4400
Fredericton, NB E3B 5A3 Canada
Brenda Mersereau, Manager
Fredericton - NBTA Credit Union
PO Box 752
650 Montgomery St.
Fredericton, NB E3B 5R6 Canada
Judy Jewett, Manager
Fredericton - York Credit Union
494 Queen St.
Fredericton, NB E3B 1B6 Canada
Dennis Williams, Manager
Fredericton Junction

Credit Union Central of New Brunswick (continued)

Citizens Credit Union
179 Sunbury Dr.
Fredericton Junction, NB E5L 1R5 Canada
Nedra Dionne, Manager

Lords Cove
Deer Island Credit Union
PO Box 10
193 Hwy. 772
Lord's Cove, NB E5V 1H9 Canada
George Kline, Manager

McAdam
McAdam Credit Union
110 Saunders Rd.
McAdam, NB E6J 1L2 Canada
Marjery Nichol, Manager

Miramichi
Beaubear Credit Union
PO Box 764
52 Nelson St.
Miramichi, NB E1V 3V4 Canada
George Greenwood, Manager

Moncton
Moncton Civic Credit Union
473 St. George St.
Moncton, NB E1C 1Y2 Canada
Margaret Gould, Manager

Moncton - Omista Credit Union
#1, 1192 Mountain Rd.
Moncton, NB E1C 2T6 Canada
Paul Dugas, Manager

Moncton - Public Service Employees Credit Union
PO Box 92
141 Weldon St.
Moncton, NB E1C 8R9 Canada
Jeanette Holmden, Manager

Moncton - Trico Credit Union
10 Record St.
Moncton, NB E1C 0B2 Canada
Don Roper, Manager

Petitcodiac
Royal Credit Union
47 Main St.
Petitcodiac, NB E4Z 4L9 Canada
Shirley Perkins, Manager

Rexton
Rexton Credit Union
PO Box 390
5 Brait St.
Rexton, NB E4W 1V9 Canada
Garth Lawson, Manager

Saint John - Bayview Credit Union
54 Loch Lomond Rd.
Saint John, NB E2J 1X7 Canada
Brian Thorne, Manager

Saint John - Prosper Credit Union
72 Germain St.
Saint John, NB E2L 2E7 Canada
Sandra Hamilton, Manager

Shippagan
Caisse populaire Shippagan
PO Box 370
212, boul J.D.-Gaultier
Shippagan, NB E8S 1P5 Canada
R.S. Charbonneau, Président

St. Stephen
Charlotte County Credit Union
#107, 73 Milltown Blvd.
St Stephen, NB E3L 1G5 Canada
Leo Ryan, Manager

Woodstock
Carleton Pioneer Credit Union
#1, 106 Richmond St.
Woodstock, NB E7M 2N9 Canada
Eric Smith, Manager

Credit Union Central of Nova Scotia

PO Box 9200
6074 Lady Hammond Rd.
Halifax, NS B3K 5N3
902-453-0680
Fax: 902-455-2437
www.ns-credit-unions.com

Executives:
Bernie O'Neil, President/CEO

Directors:
David MacLean, Chair

Credit Union Central of Ontario

2810 Matheson Blvd. East
Mississauga, ON L4W 4X7
905-238-9400
Fax: 905-238-8691
Other Information: Toll Free: 1-800-661-6813, ext.212
#customerservice@cuco.on.ca
www.ontariocreditunions.com
Assets: $10-100 billion

Executives:
Howard Bogach, President/CEO
Phillip Braginetz, COO
Norm Davidson, Vice-President, Information Technology Services, CIO
Jim MacDonald, CFO & Corporate Secretary
Susan McNulty, Sr. Vice-President, Payments & Banking Services
Steve Van Buskirk, Sr. Vice-President, Trade
Mike Howard, Vice-President, Treasury
Marie Parker, Vice-President, Human Resources
Daniel Atlin, Director, Public Affairs
Wayne Ballard, Director, Development & Projects
Pam Brewster, Director, Corporate Administration
Peter Collins, Director, Credit & Lending Operations
Gary Gratton, Director, Technical Services
Linda Jeffery, Director, Treasury Services
Paul Martinello, Director, Systems Development
Julie McPhee, Director, Operations
André Schroer, Director, Commercial Lending & Product Development
Sadhana Sharma, Director, Quantitative Risk
Dorothy Watson, Director, Member Relations & Member Service
Ron Smith, Controller
Sharmann Grad, Coordinator, Management

Directors:
Scott Kennedy, Chair
Alan Marentette, Vice-Chair
Sheena Lucas, 2nd Vice-Chair
Howard Bogach
Tim Bossence
Janet Grantham
Sean Jackson
George Joyce
Ron Koppmann
Wayne Lee
Nadia Martin
Jack Morneau
Ian Russell
Dave Sitaram
Jack Smit

Credit Union Central of Prince Edward Island

PO Box 968
281 University Ave.
Charlottetown, PE C1A 7M4
902-566-3350
Fax: 902-368-3534
dturner@cucpei.creditu.net
www.peicreditunions.com
Ownership: Private
Year Founded: 1936
Number of Employees: 11
Assets: $50-100 million
Revenues: $5-10 million
Profile: The Credit Union Central of Prince Edward Island acts as an administration & coordinating organization to the province's 10 credit unions. Membership is restricted to these 10 credit unions.

Executives:
Gerard T. Dougan, CEO; gtdougan@cucpei.creditu.net

Affiliates:
Consolidated Credit Union - Borden/Carleton
PO Box 119
Port Borden, PE C0B 1X0 Canada
902-855-2066
Fax: 902-855-2171

Consolidated Credit Union - Summerside
305 Water St.
Summerside, PE C1N 1C1 Canada
902-436-9218
Fax: 902-436-7979
srogers@consolidated.creditu.net

Evangeline Credit Union - Tyne Valley
PO Box 8
Tyne Valley, PE C0B 2C0 Canada
902-831-2900
Fax: 902-831-2902

Evangeline Credit Union - Wellington Station
37 Mill Rd.
Wellington Station, PE C0B 2E0 Canada
902-854-2595
Fax: 902-854-3210
evangeline@evangeline.creditu.net

Malpeque Bay Credit Union Limited
PO Box 428
1 Commercial St.
Kensington, PE C0B 1M0 Canada
902-836-3030
Fax: 902-836-5659
malpeque@mb.creditu.net

Metro Credit Union - Charlottetown
PO Box 681
281 University Ave.
Charlottetown, PE C1A 7L3 Canada
902-892-4107
Fax: 902-368-3567

Metro Credit Union - Stratford
10 Kinlock Rd.
Stratford, PE C1B 1R1 Canada
902-569-6900
Fax: 902-569-6901

Montague Credit Union Ltd.
PO Box 760
77 Main St.
Montague, PE C0A 1R0 Canada
902-838-3636
Fax: 902-838-2691

Morell Credit Union Limited
PO Box 59
Morell, PE C0A 1S0 Canada
902-961-2735
Fax: 902-961-3485

Souris Credit Union
PO Box 159
Souris, PE C0A 2B0 Canada
902-687-2721
Fax: 902-687-3510

Stella Maris Credit Union
PO Box 130
North Rustico, PE C0A 1X0 Canada
902-963-2543
Fax: 902-963-3450
smaris@stellamaris.creditu.net

Tignish Credit Union
PO Box 40
Tignish, PE C0B 2B0 Canada
902-882-2303
Fax: 902-882-3733

Credit Union Central of Saskatchewan

PO Box 3030
2055 Albert St.
Regina, SK S4P 3G8
306-566-1200
Fax: 306-566-1372
mediarelations@cucs.com
www.saskcu.com
Ownership: Private
Year Founded: 1941
Number of Employees: 260

Executives:
Sid Bildfell, CEO

Creston & District Credit Union

PO Box 215
140 - 11th Ave. North
Creston, BC V0B 1G0
250-428-5351
Fax: 250-428-5302
cdcu@cdcu.com
www.cdcu.com
Ownership: Credit Union Central, BC
Year Founded: 1951

Executives:
Lorne Eckersley, President
Carole Materi, Vice-President
Gerrie Campbell, Secretary

Directors:

Rand Archibald
Betty Martin
Mike Ramaradhya
Jim Ryckman

Croatian (Toronto) Credit Union Limited

1165 Bloor St. West
Toronto, ON M6H 1M9
416-532-4006
Fax: 416-532-0846
Year Founded: 1958

Crocus Credit Union

1016 Rosser Ave.
Brandon, MB R7A 0L6
204-729-4800
Fax: 204-729-4818
info@crocuscu.mb.ca
www.crocuscu.mb.ca
Ownership: Cooperative. Member-owned.
Year Founded: 1952
Number of Employees: 15
Assets: $50-100 million Year End: 20060930
Revenues: $1-5 million Year End: 20060930
Executives:
Arnie J. Guist, CEO
Neal Boyce, Manager, Office
Tom Maxwell, Manager, Loans

Crosstown Credit Union

171 Donald St.
Winnipeg, MB R3C 1M4
204-942-1277
Fax: 204-947-3108
cu@crosstowncu.mb.ca
www.crosstowncu.mb.ca
Ownership: Member-owned
Year Founded: 1944
Number of Employees: 41
Executives:
Jascha Boge, President
Helen Kasdorf, Vice-President
Directors:
Jocelyn Bartel
Henry Dyck
Esther Epp
Alan J. Janzen
Ron Koslowsky
Henry Thiessen
John Zacharias
Branches:
Donald St.
171 Donald St.
Winnipeg, MB R3C 1M4 Canada
204-947-1243
Fax: 204-942-6948
171donald@crosstowncu.mb.ca
Henderson Hwy.
1200 Henderson Hwy.
Winnipeg, MB R2G 1L6 Canada
204-338-0365
Fax: 204-334-4998
1200henderson@crosstowncu.mb.ca
Portage Ave.
1250 Portage Ave.
Winnipeg, MB R3G 0T6 Canada
204-783-7081
Fax: 204-783-4535
1250portage@crowstowncu.mb.ca
St. Anne's Rd.
515 St. Anne's Rd.
Winnipeg, MB R2M 3E7 Canada
204-954-9892
Fax: 204-956-4154
515stannes@crosstowncu.mb.ca

Crown Cork & Seal Employees Credit Union Limited

7250 Keele St.
Concord, ON L4K 1Z8
905-660-2537
ccsecu@on.aibn.com
Year Founded: 1955
Number of Employees: 2

Cut Knife Credit Union Ltd.

PO Box 308
205 Broad St.
Cut Knife, SK S0M 0N0
306-398-2544
Fax: 306-398-2744
Mitch.Rokochy@cutknife.cu.sk.ca
Year Founded: 1960
Number of Employees: 7

Cypress Credit Union Ltd.

PO Box 1060
115 Jasper St.
Maple Creek, SK S0N 1N0
306-662-2683
Fax: 306-662-3859
877-353-6311
contactus@cypresscu.sk.ca
www.cypresscu.sk.ca
Directors:
Andy Brown
Cliff Brown
Barry Elderkin
Gordon Freitag
Joan Kuntz
Graham Market
Laird Murray
Mel Sharp
Branches:
Consul
PO Box 56
Railway Ave.
Consul, SK S0N 0P0 Canada
306-299-2002
Fax: 306-299-2197
Fox Valley
PO Box 88
Fox Valley, SK S0N 0V0 Canada
306-666-2022
Fax: 306-669-2128
Richmound
PO Box 30
Richmound, SK S0N 2E0 Canada
306-669-2011
Fax: 306-669-2039
Theresa Fauth, Branch Supervisor
Tompkins
PO Box 220
1 - 2nd St.
Tompkins, SK S0N 2S0 Canada
306-622-2200
Fax: 306-622-2139

Cypress River Credit Union

PO Box 9
133 Railway Ave.
Cypress River, MB R0K 0P0
204-743-2181
Fax: 204-743-2245
info@cypressrivercu.mb.ca
www.cypressrivercu.mb.ca
Year Founded: 1960
Executives:
Tim Klassen, General Manager
Branches:
Baldur
PO Box 208
205 Elizabeth Ave. East
Baldur, MB R0K 0B0 Canada
204-535-5000
Fax: 204-535-5009

Dana Canada Employees' (Ontario) Credit Union Limited

PO Box 85
Hayes Rd.
Thorold, ON L2V 3Y7
905-227-6645
Fax: 905-227-4103
dccu@sympatico.ca
Year Founded: 1951

Dauphin Plains Credit Union

505 Main St. North
Dauphin, MB R7N 1E1
204-622-4500
Fax: 204-622-4530
info@dauphinplainscu.mb.ca
www.dauphinplainscu.mb.ca
Year Founded: 1940
Number of Employees: 35
Executives:
Ron Hedley, General Manager
Branches:
Gilbert Plains
36 Main St. North
Gilbert Plains, MB R0L 0X0 Canada
204-548-3000
Fax: 204-548-3010
Winnipegosis
PO Box 460
228 - 1st St. North
Winnipegosis, MB R0L 2G0 Canada
204-656-5050
Fax: 204-656-5060

Desjardins Credit Union

Also listed under: *Credit Card Companies; Non-Depository Institutions*
East Tower, Whitby Mall
1615 Dundas St. East, 3rd Fl.
Whitby, ON L1N 2L1
905-743-5790
Fax: 905-743-6156
888-283-8333
www.desjardins.com
Ownership: Member-owned
Year Founded: 2002
Number of Employees: 235
Assets: $1-10 billion Year End: 20050700
Revenues: $50-100 million Year End: 20050700
Executives:
Alfred Pfeiffer, President/COO
Jacques Luys, Vice-President, Operations
Trung Nguyen, Sec.-Treas.
Vincent Brossard, Manager, Legal & Corporate Affairs
Karen Deering, Manager, Communication & Marketing
John Laughlin, Manager, Information Technology
Bruno Poirier, Acting Manager, Finance & Control
Peter Roberts, Manager, Head Office Administration
Directors:
Thomas Blais
Deborah J. Findlay
Paul E. Garfinkel
Michael Howlett
Jean-Guy Langelier
Heather Nicol
Trung Nguyen
Hubert Thibault
Pierre Tougas
Branches:
Aylmer
34 Talbot St. West
Aylmer, ON N5H 1J7 Canada
519-765-1286
Fax: 519-765-1690
Brantford
171 Colborne St.
Brantford, ON N3T 6C9 Canada
519-753-4131
Fax: 519-753-7121
Guelph
153 Wyndham St. North
Guelph, ON N1H 4E9 Canada
519-821-2101
Fax: 519-821-2990
Hamilton - Barton St.
Central Mall
1227 Barton St. East
Hamilton, ON L8H 2V4 Canada
905-547-6202
Fax: 905-547-4748
Hamilton - King St.
Lloyd D. Jackson Square
2 King St. West
Hamilton, ON L8P 1A1 Canada
905-528-6391
Fax: 905-528-8103
London - Richmond St.

Desjardins Credit Union (continued)

353 Richmond St.
London, ON N6A 3C2 Canada
519-432-1197
Fax: 519-432-7896

London - Richmond St.
University Community Centre, University of Western Ontario
#73, 1151 Richmond St.
London, ON N6A 3K7 Canada
519-850-2550
Fax: 519-850-2553

Mississauga
214 Queen St. South
Mississauga, ON L5M 1L5 Canada
905-821-7345
Fax: 905-821-8128

Ottawa
171 Sparks St.
Ottawa, ON K1P 5B9 Canada
613-239-1469
Fax: 613-239-1482

Owen Sound
825 - 2nd Ave. East
Owen Sound, ON N4K 5P3 Canada
519-376-6025
Fax: 519-376-1041

Pembroke
40 Pembroke St. West
Pembroke, ON K8A 6X3 Canada
613-732-7821
Fax: 613-732-3830

Seaforth
49 Main St. South
Seaforth, ON N0K 1W0 Canada
519-527-0210
Fax: 519-527-2512

St Catharines
106 King St.
St Catharines, ON L2R 3H8 Canada
905-688-4661
Fax: 905-688-0320

St Marys
PO Box 100
134 Queen St.
St Marys, ON N4X 1A9 Canada
519-284-2260
Fax: 519-284-2622

Sudbury
#105, 159 Cedar St.
Sudbury, ON P3E 6A5 Canada
705-671-9525
Fax: 705-671-2501

Thunder Bay
#102, 189 Red River Rd.
Thunder Bay, ON P7B 1A2 Canada
807-345-6686
Fax: 807-345-6438

Toronto - Bay St.
375 Bay St.
Toronto, ON M5H 2V5 Canada
416-363-7282
Fax: 416-363-0896

Toronto - Broadview Ave.
838 Broadview Ave.
Toronto, ON M4K 2R1 Canada
416-463-1117
Fax: 416-463-7773

Toronto - Danforth Ave.
2031 Danforth Ave.
Toronto, ON M4C 1J8 Canada
416-698-8320
Fax: 416-698-9131

Toronto - St. Clair Ave.
26 St. Clair Ave. East
Toronto, ON M4T 1L7 Canada
416-925-3887
Fax: 416-925-3874

Toronto - University Ave.
439 University Ave.
Toronto, ON M5G 1Y8 Canada
416-593-1763
Fax: 416-593-6936

Toronto - Wellesley St.
56 Wellesley St. West
Toronto, ON M5S 2S3 Canada
416-928-6468
Fax: 416-928-2757

Walkerton
PO Box 308
244 Durham St.
Walkerton, ON N0G 2V0 Canada
519-881-3321
Fax: 519-881-3797

Windsor
545 Ouellette Ave.
Windsor, ON N9A 4J3 Canada
519-254-4324
Fax: 519-254-6270

Woodstock
396 Dundas St. East
Woodstock, ON N4S 1B7 Canada
519-537-8194
Fax: 519-537-8844

Desjardins Gestion d'actifs/ Desjardins Asset Management

Also listed under: *Credit Card Companies; Non-Depository Institutions*

95 St Clair Ave. West
Toronto, ON M4V 1N7
Affiliated Companies:
Gestion Fiera Capital

Diamond North Credit Union

PO Box 2074
Nipawin, SK S0E 1E0
306-862-4651
Fax: 306-862-9611
877-881-2020
Other Information: 306/862-2370 (Loans)
contactus@diamondnorthcu.com
www.diamondnorthcu.com, www.nipawincu.com
Year Founded: 2006
Assets: $100-500 million
Profile: Carrot River & District Credit Union, Nipawin Credit Union, White Fox Savings & Credit Union, & Zenon Park Credit Union amalgamated to become Diamond North Credit Union in 2006. The credit union has a membership of 12,000.

Branches:

Arborfield
PO Box 265
108 Main St.
Arborfield, SK S0E 0A0 Canada
306-769-8581
Fax: 306-769-4114

Aylsham
PO Box 143
Aylsham, SK S0E 0C0 Canada
306-862-2121

Carrot River
PO Box 639
10 Main St.
Carrot River, SK S0E 0L0 Canada
306-768-3103
Fax: 306-768-3113

Choiceland
PO Box 39
100 Railway Ave. West
Choiceland, SK S0J 0M0 Canada
306-428-2152
Fax: 306-428-4244

White Fox
PO Box 310
125 Railway Ave.
White Fox, SK S0J 3B0 Canada
306-276-2142
Fax: 306-276-2595

Zenon Park
PO Box 160
735 Main St.
Zenon Park, SK S0E 1W0 Canada
306-767-2434
Fax: 306-767-2224

Dodsland & District Credit Union Ltd.

PO Box 129
Dodsland, SK S0L 0V0
306-356-2155
Fax: 306-356-2202
james.duncan@dodsland.cu.sk.ca
www.dodslandcreditunion.com
Year Founded: 1961
Number of Employees: 7
Executives:
James Duncan, General Manager

Dominion Credit Union

94 Commercial St.
Dominion, NS B1G 1B4
902-849-8648
Fax: 902-842-0273
Year Founded: 1934
Executives:
Rina Gouthro, Manager

Domtar Newsprint Employees (Trenton) Credit Union Limited

PO Box 254
Trenton, ON K8V 5R5
613-392-2426
Fax: 613-392-6851
ldwannamaker@sympatico.ca
Executives:
Larry Wannamaker, General Manager

DUCA Financial Services Credit Union Ltd.

5290 Yonge St.
Toronto, ON M2N 5P9
416-223-8502
Fax: 416-223-2575
866-900-3822
duca.info@duca.com
www.duca.com
Former Name: Duca Community Credit Union Limited
Ownership: Member-owned
Year Founded: 1954
Number of Employees: 100
Assets: $500m-1 billion
Revenues: $10-50 million
Profile: Established to serve the Greater Toronto Area, Duca is a full service credit union. Services include: savings & chequing accounts; term deposits; RRSPs; RRIFs; RESPs; mortgage & personal loans, commercial credit & current accounts; insurance services & mutual funds.

Executives:
Jack Vanderkooy, President/CEO
Branches:

Bowmanville
200 King St. East
Bowmanville, ON L1C 1P3 Canada
905-623-6343
Fax: 905-623-1634
bowmanville@duca.com

Brampton
7900 McLaughlin Rd. South
Brampton, ON L6Y 5A7 Canada
905-453-1971
Fax: 905-453-7766
brampton@duca.com

Burlington
2017 Mount Forest Dr.
Burlington, ON L7P 1H4 Canada
905-315-7981
Fax: 905-315-8034
burlington@duca.com

Etobicoke
1451 Royal York Rd.
Toronto, ON M9P 3B2 Canada
416-245-2413
Fax: 416-245-4433
etobicoke@duca.com

Newmarket
17310 Yonge St.
Newmarket, ON L3Y 7R8 Canada
905-898-4543
Fax: 905-895-9228
newmarket@duca.com

Orangeville
16 Broadway
Orangeville, ON L9W 1J4 Canada
519-941-8211
Fax: 519-941-8217
orangeville@duca.com

Richmond Hill
9174 Yonge St.
Richmond Hill, ON L4C 7A1 Canada

905-764-3893
Fax: 905-764-5433
richmondhill@duca.com
Toronto
5290 Yonge St.
Toronto, ON M2N 5P9 Canada
416-223-8502
Fax: 416-223-2575
duca.info@duca.com
Toronto
245 Eglinton Ave. East
Toronto, ON M4P 3B7 Canada
416-485-0789
Fax: 416-485-3875
toronto@duca.com
Toronto
2184 Kipling Ave.
Toronto, ON M9W 4K9 Canada
416-747-1791
Fax: 416-747-7698
rexdale@duca.com
Toronto
#107, 1265 Morningside Ave.
Toronto, ON M1B 3V9 Canada
416-724-2957
Fax: 416-724-0822
scarborough@duca.com
Whitby
1818 Dundas St. East
Whitby, ON L1N 2L4 Canada
905-728-4658
Fax: 905-728-4249
whitby@duca.com

Dufferin Credit Union

PO Box 130
71st Ave. SW
Carman, MB R0G 0J0
204-745-2043
Fax: 204-745-3917
info@dufferincu.mb.ca
www.dufferincu.mb.ca
Year Founded: 1964
Number of Employees: 8
Assets: $23,000,000
Executives:
Richard Dyck, General Manager

Dundalk District Credit Union Limited

PO Box 340
79 Proton St. North
Dundalk, ON N0C 1B0
519-923-2400
Fax: 519-923-2950
diannek@dundalkdistrictcreditunion.ca
www.dundalkdistrictcreditunion.ca
Year Founded: 1943
Number of Employees: 11
Assets: $10-50 million
Revenues: Under $1 million
Executives:
Dianne Keating, General Manager
Directors:
Leonard Black, President; 519-923-6811
Ross Johnson, Vice-President; 519-538-3515

Dunnville & District Credit Union Ltd.

208 Broad St. East
Dunnville, ON N1A 1G2
905-774-7559
Fax: 905-774-4662
Ownership: Member owned
Number of Employees: 7
Executives:
Don Ecker, Branch Manager

Dysart Credit Union Ltd.

PO Box 39
110 Main St.
Dysart, SK S0G 1H0
306-432-2211
donjeworski@sasktel.net
Year Founded: 1960

Eagle River Credit Union

PO Box 29
8 Branch Rd.
L'Anse au Loup, NL A0K 3L0
709-927-5524
Fax: 709-927-5018
877-377-3728
aobrien@eagleriver.creditu.net
www.eaglerivercu.com
Year Founded: 1984
Number of Employees: 40
Assets: $10-50 million
Revenues: Under $1 million
Executives:
Bert Belben, President
Dennis Normore, Vice-President
Alvina O'Brien, General Manager
Jeannette Yetman, Recording Secretary
Directors:
Terry Casey
Lisa Davis
Darcy Hancock
Milton Hancock
Heather Normore
Shawn Warren
Branches:
Cartwright
PO Box 12
1 Back Rd.
Cartwright, NL A0K 1V0 Canada
709-938-7438
Fax: 709-938-7380
866-938-1468
sdyson@eagleriver.creditu.net
Sonya Dyson, Branch Manager
Happy Valley-Goose Bay - Labrador Savings
PO Box 57, C Sta. C
368 Hamilton River Rd.
Happy Valley-Goose Bay, NL AOP 1C0 Canada
709-896-8352
Fax: 709-896-5935
877-896-8352
gstewart@eagleriver.creditu.net
Greg Stewart, Branch Manager
L'Anse au Loup
PO Box 29
8 Branch Rd.
L'Anse au Loup, NL A0K 3L0 Canada
709-927-5522
Fax: 709-927-5759
jpye@eagleriver.creditu.net
Jamie Pye, Branch Manager
Marys Harbour
PO Box 133
#10, 12 Hillview Rd.
Marys Harbour, NL A0K 3P0 Canada
709-921-6345
866-991-6354
srumbolt@eagleriver.creditu.net
Sandra Rumbolt, Branch Manager
Port Saunders - Tri-Town
PO Box 322
104 Rte. 430
Port Saunders, NL A0K 4H0 Canada
709-861-9188
Fax: 709-861-9189
866-861-9188
tbiggin@eagleriver.creditu.net
Tobi Biggin, Branch Manager
St. Anthony - White Hills
PO Box 695
1 West St.
St. Anthony, NL A0K 4S0 Canada
709-454-8800
Fax: 709-454-2138
866-554-8800
fhowell@eagleriver.creditu.net
Frances Howell, Branch Manager

East Coast Credit Union

Admin. Office
305 Granville St.
Port Hawkesbury, NS B9A 2M5
902-625-5610
www.eastcoastcreditu.ca
Year Founded: 2003
Number of Employees: 104
Assets: $100-500 million
Executives:
Douglas Hastings, CEO; 902-295-1753; dhastings@eastcoast.creditu.net
Branches:
Baddeck
PO Box 527
521 Chebucto St.
Baddeck, NS B0E 1B0 Canada
902-295-3477
Fax: 902-295-2981
Theresa MacDonald, Manager
D'Escousse - North Isle Madame
PO Box 552
9 Cap LaRonde Rd.
D'Escousse, NS B0E 1K0 Canada
902-226-2722
Fax: 902-226-9743
Patricia Poirier, Manager
Havre Boucher
PO Box 182
12512 Hwy. 4
Havre Boucher, NS B0H 1P0 Canada
902-234-2523
Fax: 902-234-2445
Sheri Taylor-Wood, Manager
Inverness
PO Box 29
15886 Central Ave.
Inverness, NS B0E 1N0 Canada
902-258-2045
Fax: 902-258-3762
Tanya Forance, Manager
L'Ardoise
42 School Rd.
L'Ardoise, NS B0E 1S0 Canada
902-587-2414
Fax: 902-587-2493
Andrée Sampson, Manager
Louisdale
PO Box 626
340 Main St.
Louisdale, NS B0E 1V0 Canada
902-345-2015
Fax: 902-345-2284
Blair Samson, Manager
Mabou
PO Box 35
11627 Main St.
Mabou, NS B0E 1X0 Canada
902-945-2003
Fax: 902-945-2176
Tena Young, Manager
Margaree
General Delivery, 1168 East Margaree Rd.
Margaree, NS B0E 1Y0 Canada
902-235-2659
Fax: 902-235-2683
Patricia LeBlanc, Manager
Mulgrave
PO Box 220
428A Main St.
Mulgrave, NS B0E 2G0 Canada
902-747-3142
Fax: 902-747-2444
Wilma Spencer, Manager
North East Margaree
PO Box 10
1601 West Big Intervale Rd.
Margaree Centre, NS B0E 1Z0 Canada
902-248-2401
Fax: 902-248-2693
Carol Hart, Office Supervisor
Port Hawkesbury
299 Reeves St.
Port Hawkesbury, NS B9A 2B6 Canada
902-625-0190
Fax: 902-625-3889
Wanda MacLean, Manager
Port Hood
PO Box 128
138 Main St.
Port Hood, NS B0E 2W0 Canada

East Coast Credit Union (continued)
902-787-3246
Fax: 902-787-2525
Isabel Gillis, Manager
St Peters
PO Box 361
10001 Grenville St.
St Peters, NS B0E 3B0 Canada
902-535-3101
Fax: 902-535-2295
Janie Vickers, Manager

East Kootenay Community Credit Union

924 Baker St.
Cranbrook, BC V1C 1A5
250-426-6666
Fax: 250-426-0879
866-960-6666
reception@ekccu.com
www.ekccu.com
Number of Employees: 30
Executives:
Jody Burk, CEO
Directors:
Don Holt, Chair
Ron Boese, Vice-Chair
Ed Berukoff
Cindy Corrigan
Jean Ann Debrecenni
Imelda Engels
Dean McKerracher
Mike Pang
Jean Samis
Branches:
Cranbrook
920 Baker St.
Cranbrook, BC V1C 1A5 Canada
250-426-6666
Fax: 250-426-7370
Diane Baher, Senior Manager
Elkford
Elkford Square
PO Box 189
Elkford, BC V0B 1H0 Canada
250-865-4661
Fax: 250-865-7537
Cindy Hesje, Assistant Manager
Fernie
PO Box 1440
1601 - 9th Ave.
Fernie, BC V0B 1M0 Canada
250-423-9222
Fax: 250-423-9223
866-423-9222
Andy Aichholz, Sr. Manager

EasternEdge Credit Union

PO Box 2110
10 Factory Lane
St. John's, NL A1C 5H6
709-739-2920
Fax: 709-739-3728
800-716-7283
www.easternedgecu.com
Former Name: NewTel Credit Union
Year Founded: 1976
Assets: $10-50 million
Executives:
Cynthia Strickland, Manager; 709-739-3800
Claude Howell, Assistant Manager
Donna Careen, Loan Officer
Directors:
Steve Blackwood, President
Ephram Laing, Vice-President
Mary Stowe, Secretary
Derrick Andrews
Keith Healey
Patricia Lindahl
Kim Mercer
Paul Newman
Paul Summers

Eckville District Savings & Credit Union Ltd.

PO Box 278
Eckville, AB T0M 0X0
403-746-2288
Fax: 403-746-3737
info@eckvillecu.com
www.eckvillecu.com
Ownership: Private
Year Founded: 1943
Number of Employees: 9
Executives:
Mitch Krecsy, General Manager
Directors:
Richard Anderson
Peter Baker
Heather Bott
Ron Marcinek
Sheron Moss
Ken Purnell
Garth Yeomans

Edson Savings & Credit Union

PO Box 6118
4912 - 2nd Ave.
Edson, AB T7E 1T6
780-723-4468
Fax: 780-723-7973
edsoncu@alberta-cu.com
www.edsoncu.com
Year Founded: 1940
Directors:
Jean Dann
Brenda Gogowich
Calvin Hill
Jack Lawrence
Peter Serdiak
Fred Shaw
Wally Snow
Laura Leigh White

Electragas Credit Union

c/o Nova Scotia Power Inc.
PO Box 910
Halifax, NS B3J 2W5
902-454-6843
Fax: 902-453-5161
Executives:
David Nevitt, Manager

Electric Employees Credit Union

10 Lanceleve Cres.
Albert Bridge, NS B1K 3J3
902-564-9707
Fax: 902-564-0956
Executives:
Dave du Chene, Manager

Employees of Dofasco (Hamilton) Credit Union Limited

Gate #17
PO Box 2460
1721 Burlington St. East
Hamilton, ON L8N 3J5
905-549-6506
Fax: 905-548-9216
www.edcu.ca
Year Founded: 1954
Number of Employees: 10
Assets: $25,000,000
Executives:
Kathy Zebruck, General Manager

Enderby & District Credit Union

703 Mill St.
Enderby, BC V0E 1V0
250-838-6841
Fax: 250-838-9756
info@enderbycreditunion.com
www.enderbycreditunion.com

Entegra Credit Union

Corporate Head Office
1335 Jefferson Ave.
Winnipeg, MB R2P 1S7
204-949-7744
Fax: 204-949-5865
info@entegra.ca
www.entegra.ca
Former Name: Holy Spirit Credit Union
Year Founded: 1960
Number of Employees: 47
Assets: $100-500 million
Executives:
Gordon Kirkwood, CEO
Directors:
Edward Plezia, President
Fier Tulleken, Vice-President
Ken Dudeck, Secretary
Gary Keam
Ed Kolodziej
Ryan Wirth
Jerzy Zielinski
Branches:
Disraeli & BBC
121 Disraeli Freeway
Winnipeg, MB R3B 2Z5 Canada
Jefferson Ave.
1335 Jefferson Ave.
Winnipeg, MB R2P 1S7 Canada
204-949-7744
Fax: 204-949-5865
Selkirk
303 Selkirk Ave.
Winnipeg, MB R2W 2L8 Canada
204-949-7744
Fax: 204-949-5865

Envision Credit Union

6470 - 201st St.
Langley, BC V2Y 2X4
604-539-7300
Fax: 604-539-7315
www.envisionfinancial.ca
Also Known As: Envision Financial
Ownership: Member-owned
Year Founded: 1946
Number of Employees: 779
Assets: $1-10 billion
Revenues: $100-500 million
Executives:
Gord Huston, President/CEO; 604-539-7333; ghuston@envisionfinancial.ca
Jeff Connery, Chief Investment Officer; 604-539-7375; jconnery@envisionfinancial.ca
Tim Wasilieff, Chief Operating Officer; 604-539-7411; twasilieff@envisionfinancial.ca
Thomas Webster, Chief Financial Officer; 604-539-7356; twebster@envisionfinancial.ca
Fred Bobye, Sr. Vice-President, Human Resources; 604-539-7337; fbobye@envisionfinancial.ca
Bev Brown, Sr. Vice-President, Sales & Service; 604-539-7336; bbrown@envisionfinancial.ca
Barry Delaney, Sr. Vice-President, Strategy & Governance; 604-539-7335; bdelaney@envisionfinancial.ca
John Dundas, Sr. Vice-President, Marketing & Communications; 403-520-6805; jdundas@1stCalgary.com
Directors:
Terry Enns, Chair
Ken Voth, Vice-Chair
Lois Wilkinson, Secretary
Alex Copland
Kevin Demers
Henry Jansen
David Letkemann
Don Murray
Shawn Neumann
Sally O'Sullivan
Peter Scherle
Myrna Webster
Branches:
Abbotsford - Minter St.
2670 Minter St.
Abbotsford, BC V2T 3K2 Canada
604-557-7250
Fax: 604-557-7251
Nilde West, Branch Manager
Abbotsford - South Fraser Way
32711 South Fraser Way
Abbotsford, BC V2T 3S3 Canada
604-557-7450
Fax: 604-557-7451
Michele Potoroka, Manager, Insurance Services
Abbotsford - Sumas Way
2090 Sumas Way
Abbotsford, BC V2S 2C7 Canada

604-557-7480
Fax: 604-557-7481
Pat Wenger, Branch Manager
Aldergrove
27030A Fraser Hwy.
Aldergrove, BC V4W 3L6 Canada
604-557-7530
Fax: 604-857-1113
Crystal Lanz, Manager, Insurance Services
Chilliwack - Cheam Ave.
45840 Cheam Ave.
Chilliwack, BC V2P 1N8 Canada
604-703-7600
Fax: 604-703-7601
Ruth Maccan, Branch Manager
Chilliwack - Luckakuck Way
45410 Luckakuck Way
Chilliwack, BC V2R 3S9 Canada
604-703-7680
Fax: 604-703-7681
Mark Redman, Branch Manager
Chilliwack - Yarrow Central Rd.
42206 Yarrow Central Rd.
Chilliwack, BC V2R 5E4 Canada
604-703-7660
Fax: 604-703-7661
Chilliwack - Yarrow Central Rd. - Insurance Services
42313 Yarrow Central Rd.
Chilliwack, BC V2R 5E4 Canada
604-703-7656
Fax: 604-823-6716

Coquitlam
Sunwood Square
#600, 3025 Lougheed Hwy.
Coquitlam, BC V3B 6S2 Canada
604-539-5900
Fax: 604-539-5901
Yolanda Fequet, Branch Manager
Delta - 120th St.
8393 - 120th St.
Delta, BC V4C 6R1 Canada
604-501-4220
Fax: 604-501-4202
Sidhu Suki, Manager, Insurance Services
Delta - 120th St.
6955 - 120th St.
Delta, BC V4E 2A8 Canada
604-501-4240
Fax: 604-501-4204
Josh Hoskins, Branch Manager
Delta - 56th St.
1319E - 56th St.
Delta, BC V4L 2A6 Canada
604-501-4230
Fax: 604-501-4203
Reggie Sahota, Branch Manager
Delta - Ladner Trunk Rd.
5125 Ladner Trunk Rd.
Delta, BC V4K 1W2 Canada
604-501-4219
Fax: 604-501-4218
Tracy Gillan, Manager, Insurance Services
Delta - Ladner Trunk Rd.
5155 Ladner Trunk Rd.
Delta, BC V4K 1W4 Canada
604-501-4210
Fax: 604-501-4201
Tracy Yolland, Branch Manager
Hope - Commission St.
243 Commission St.
Hope, BC V0X 1L0 Canada
604-860-7800
Fax: 604-860-7801
Nancy Schultz, Manager, Insurance
Hope - Commission St.
231 Commision St.
Hope, BC V0X 1L0 Canada
604-860-7810
Fax: 604-861-7811
Marlene Fehlauer, Branch Manager
Kelowna - Carrington Rd.
#201, 3550 Carrington Rd.
Kelowna, BC V4T 2Z1 Canada
250-212-5722
Julie Clitheroe, Branch Manager
Kelowna - Dougall Rd. North
c/o Don Tobbe Insurance Associates Ltd.
#102, 200 Dougall Rd. North
Kelowna, BC V1X 3K5 Canada
250-765-0068
Fax: 250-765-7763
Grant Stobbe, Manager
Kitimat - Wakashan Ave.
954 Wakashan Ave.
Kitimat, BC V8C 2G3 Canada
250-639-9391
Fax: 250-639-9500
Wendy Kraft, Branch Manager
Kitimat - Wakashan Ave.
956 Wakashan Ave.
Kitimat, BC V8C 2G3 Canada
250-632-7165
Fax: 250-632-6053
888-632-9915
Amanda Chaulk, Manager, Insurance
Langley - 64th Ave.
20193 - 64th Ave.
Langley, BC V2Y 1M9 Canada
604-592-7230
Fax: 604-592-7231
Terry D. Jones, Branch Manager
Langley - Fraser Hwy.
20627 Fraser Hwy.
Langley, BC V3A 4G4 Canada
604-592-7190
Fax: 604-592-7191
Kay Gandham, Branch Manager
Mission - London Ave.
#120, 32555 London Ave.
Mission, BC V2V 6M7 Canada
604-557-7510
Fax: 604-557-7511
Carla Posein, Branch Manager
Smithers
c/o R.W. Claderwood Insurance Services Ltd.
PO Box 730
1175 Main St.
Smithers, BC Canada
250-847-3224
Fax: 250-847-3268

Smithers - Main St.
c/o Pioneer Agencies Ltd.
1142 Main St.
Smithers, BC Canada
250-847-2405
Fax: 250-847-3264
Summerland
c/o McBain Insurance Agency Ltd.
PO Box 779
3601 Victoria Rd. North
Summerland, BC VOH 1Z0 Canada
250-494-6781
Fax: 250-494-9464
Surrey - 152nd St.
3061 - 152nd St.
Surrey, BC V4P 3K1 Canada
604-501-4270
Fax: 604-501-4207
Nikki Barrett, Branch Manager
Surrey - 152nd St.
c/o White Rock Insurance
1959 - 152nd St.
Surrey, BC V4A 9E3 Canada
604-501-4279
Fax: 604-501-4278
Kusum (Kay) Mbaso, Manager, Insurance Services
Surrey - Fraser Hwy.
15355 Fraser Hwy.
Surrey, BC V3R 3P3 Canada
604-501-4280
Fax: 604-501-4208
James Co, Branch Manager

Equity Financial Services
#3, 400 Eastern Ave.
Toronto, ON M4M 1B9
416-463-3173
Fax: 416-465-9984
1-800-263-9793
info@equityfs.ca
www.equitycreditunion.ca
Former Name: Unilever Employees Credit Union Limited; Equity Credit Union
Tom Dimson, General Manager

Erickson Credit Union Limited
PO Box 100
24 Main St. West
Erickson, MB R0J 0P0
204-636-7771
Fax: 204-636-2498
info@ericksoncu.mb.ca
www.ericksoncu.mb.ca
Ownership: Member-owned
Year Founded: 1952

Eriksdale Credit Union Limited
PO Box 99, Railway Stn. Railway
Eriksdale, MB R0C 0W0
204-739-2137
Fax: 204-739-5409
info@eriksdalecu.mb.ca
www.eriksdalecu.mb.ca
Ownership: Member-owned
Year Founded: 1972
Number of Employees: 28
Executives:
Craig Hughson, General Manager
Branches:
Ashern
PO Box 580
Ashern, MB R0C 0E0 Canada
204-768-2733
Fax: 204-768-3499
Moosehorn
PO Box 190
Moosehorn, MB R0C 2E0 Canada
204-768-2437
Fax: 204-768-2378

Espanola & District Credit Union Limited
91 Centre St.
Espanola, ON P5E 1S4
705-869-3001
www.espanolacu.com
Year Founded: 1958
Branches:
Gore Bay
47 Meredith St.
Gore Bay, ON P0P 1H0 Canada
705-282-2511
Little Current
3 Manitowaning Rd.
Little Current, ON P0P 1K0 Canada
705-368-3222

Estonian (Toronto) Credit Union Limited
958 Broadview Ave.
Toronto, ON M4K 2R6
416-465-4659
Fax: 416-465-8442
866-844-3828
estonian.info@estoniancu.com
www.estoniancu.com
Year Founded: 1954
Number of Employees: 12
Executive(s):
Tarmo Lõbu, CEO & President

ETCU Financial
1 East Mall Cres.
Toronto, ON M9B 6G8
416-622-8500
Fax: 416-622-0610
877-337-8500
www.etcu.com
Former Name: Etobicoke Teachers' Credit Union Limited
Year Founded: 1951
Executives:
R.M. (Bob) Lockwood, CEO
Gary A. Lockwood, Credit Manager
Directors:
Earl Hogben, Chair

ETCU Financial (continued)
Brent Bailey
Bernie Burley
John Gardiner
Catherine Lewis
David Lewis
Stan Shack
David West
John Woolfrey

Ethelbert Credit Union
109 Railway Ave.
Ethelbert, MB R0L 0T0
204-742-3529
Branches:
Pine River
1st Ave.
Pine River, MB R0L 1M0 Canada
204-263-2166

Etobicoke Aluminum Employees' Credit Union Limited
15 Browns Line
Toronto, ON M8W 3S3
416-253-2319
Fax: 416-253-2396
Number of Employees: 1
Executives:
Richard Pollitt, General Manager

Fairview & District Savings & Credit Union Ltd.
PO Box 459
10300 - 110 St.
Fairview, AB T0H 1L0
780-835-2914
Fax: 780-835-4214

Fédération des caisses Desjardins du Québec
100, av des Commandeurs
Lévis, QC G6V 7N5
418-835-8444
Former Name: Fédération des Caisses Populaires Desjardins du Québec
Ownership: Private
Number of Employees: 450
Executives:
Alban D'Amours, Président, Chef de la direction du MCD
Bertrand Laferrière, Président/Chef de l'exploitation
Stéphane Achard, 1er Vice-président Marchés des entreprises
Pauline D'Amboise, Secrétaire générale du MCD
Pierre Brossard, 1er Vice-président exécutif du MCD
Monique F. Leroux, 1re Vice-présidente exécutive, Chef de la direction financière du MCD
Jean Brunet, 1er Vice-président, Ressources humaines
Normand Desautels, 1er Vice-président, Région de l'ouest
Jacques Dignard, 1er Vice-président, Ressources humaines du MCD
Serge Dufresne, 1er Vice-président, Caisses de groupes
Daniel Gauvin, 1er Vice-président, Chef de la gestion intégrée des risques du MCD
Richard Halley, 1er Vice-président, Efficacité opérationnelle, Technologies de l'information
Marc Jean, 1er Vice-président, Planification et Coopération, Adjoint au président et chef de l'exploitation
Marc Laplante, 1er Vice-président, Finance et crédit
Michel Latour, 1er Vice-président Région du centre
Liliane Laverdière, 1re Vice-présidente, Région de l'est
Louise Le Brun, 1re Vice-présidente, Opérations et administration
Pierre Moran, 1er Vice-président, Marché des particuliers
Bruno Morin, 1er Vice-président, Fonds de placement et Services fiduciaires
Pierre Tougas, 1er Vice-président, Caisses populaires de l'Ontario
Marcel Pepin, 1er Vice-président, Planification stratégique, Développement des affaires pancanadiennes du MCD
Affiliated Companies:
Caisse Centrale Desjardins du Québec
Desjardins Capital de risque
Desjardins Credit Union
Desjardins Financial Security
Desjardins Gestion d'actifs
Desjardins Groupe d'assurances générales inc
Fédération des caisses populaires acadiennes ltée
Fédération des caisses populaires de l'Ontario
Fédération des caisses populaires du Manitoba
Valeurs mobilières Desjardins inc/VMD

Affiliates:
Caisse d'économie du Rail
935, rue de la Gauchetière ouest
Montréal, QC H3B 2M9 Canada
514-399-5000
Fax: 514-399-7073
MICR: 815-92267
Caisse d'économie Canipco
74, rue Main
Gatineau, QC J8P 5J1 Canada
819-663-5324
Fax: 819-663-0805
MICR: 815-92258
Caisse d'économie des employés de la C.I.P. La Tuque
288, rue St-Joseph
La Tuque, QC G9X 1K8 Canada
819-523-2741
Fax: 819-523-9973
MICR: 815-92260
Caisse d'économie Desjardins de l'Éducation
#100, 7100, rue Jean-Talon est
Montréal, QC H1M 3S3 Canada
514-351-7295
Fax: 514-351-1268
MICR: 815-92204
Caisse d'économie Desjardins de la Culture
#200, 465, rue McGill
Montréal, QC H2Y 2H1 Canada
514-285-8873
Fax: 514-285-4445
MICR: 815-92262
Caisse d'économie Desjardins de la Vallée de l'Amiante
PO Box 158
222, rue Simoneau
Thetford Mines, QC G6G 5S5 Canada
418-338-4641
Fax: 418-338-6422
MICR: 815-92066
Caisse d'économie Desjardins de Sept-×les
500, av Arnaud
Sept-×les, QC G4R 3B5 Canada
418-962-7241
Fax: 418-962-0369
MICR: 815-92135
Caisse d'économie Desjardins des Cantons
560, rue Bowen sud
Sherbrooke, QC J1G 2E3 Canada
819-566-1181
Fax: 819-566-0390
MICR: 815-92096
Caisse d'économie Desjardins des employées et employés du Ministère de la Défense Nationale (Québec)
Centre commercial CANEX
190, rue Dubé
Courcelette, QC G0A 1R1 Canada
418-844-3787
Fax: 418-844-3241
MICR: 815-92158
Caisse d'économie Desjardins des employés d'Alcoa-Manic-McCormick
10, av Roméo Vézina
Baie-Comeau, QC G4Z 2W2 Canada
418-296-1519
Fax: 418-296-5145
MICR: 815-92075
Caisse d'économie Desjardins des Employés de Ville de Laval
3009, boul Industriel
Laval, QC H7L 3W9 Canada
450-975-8583
Fax: 450-975-8591
MICR: 815-92277
Caisse d'économie Desjardins des employés du C.N.
935, rue de la Gauchetière ouest
Montréal, QC H3B 2M9 Canada
514-399-5119
Fax: 514-399-4585
MICR: 815-92219
Caisse d'économie Desjardins des Employés du Réseau de la santé du Saguenay, Lac-St-Jean, Charlevoix, Québec
350, rue Racine est
Chicoutimi, QC G7H 1S6 Canada
418-549-6088
Fax: 418-549-1822
MICR: 815-92076
Caisse d'économie Desjardins des employés en Télécommunication
1050, rue Côte du Beaver Hall, 3e étage
Montréal, QC H2Z 1S4 Canada
514-393-9552
Fax: 514-393-1454
MICR: 815-92239
Caisse d'économie Desjardins des travailleurs unis
PO Box 117
302, 545, boul Crémazie est
Montréal, QC H2M 2V1 Canada
514-255-2973
Fax: 514-255-3919
MICR: 815-92154
Caisse d'économie Desjardins du personnel de la Métallurgie et du Papier (Centre-du-Québec et Mauricie)
#100, 190, rue Fusey
Trois-Rivières, QC G8T 2V8 Canada
819-379-9596
Fax: 819-379-2035
MICR: 815-92007
Caisse d'économie Desjardins du personnel du réseau de la santé
#102, 2100, boul de Maisonneuve est
Montréal, QC H2K 4S1 Canada
514-522-4773
Fax: 514-522-4775
MICR: 815-92278
Caisse d'économie Desjardins du personnel municipal (QC)
#100, 600, boul Pierre-Bertrand
Québec, QC G1M 3W5 Canada
418-691-6089
Fax: 418-691-7643
MICR: 815-92019
Caisse d'économie Desjardins Hydro
Niveau Mezzanine
75, boul René-Lévesque ouest
Montréal, QC H2Z 1A3 Canada
514-289-3500
Fax: 514-289-3498
MICR: 815-92012
Caisse d'économie Desjardins Laurentide
PO Box 518
100, 1re rue
Grand-Mère, QC G9T 5L3 Canada
819-538-6644
Fax: 819-538-3573
MICR: 815-92056
Caisse d'économie Desjardins Le Cha(140non
#150, 2175, boul De Maisonneuve est
Montréal, QC H2K 4S3 Canada
514-598-1931
Fax: 514-598-2496
MICR: 815-92105
Caisse d'économie Desjardins Marie-Victorin
950, rte Marie-Victorin
Sorel-Tracy, QC J3R 1L3 Canada
450-742-3791
Fax: 450-746-9425
MICR: 815-92188
Caisse d'économie Desjardins Strathcona
#3, 17035, boul Brunswick
Montréal, QC H9H 5G6 Canada
514-426-5111
Fax: 514-856-5703
MICR: 815-92238
Caisse d'économie Desjardins Sûreté du Québec
#101, 2100, boul de Maisonneuve est
Montréal, QC H2K 4S1 Canada
514-526-7714
Fax: 514-526-4288
MICR: 815-92150
Caisse d'économie Deux-Montagnes
PO Box 171
Deux-Montagnes, QC J7R 4K6 Canada
450-473-6065
MICR: 815-92272
Caisse d'économie Employés de Domglas Inc.
2376, rue Wellington
Montréal, QC H3K 1X6 Canada
514-932-9088
Fax: 514-932-4090
MICR: 815-92020
Caisse d'économie employés de la S.T.C.U.M.

8635, boul Saint-Laurent
Montréal, QC H2P 2M9 Canada
514-382-0430
Fax: 514-382-0439
MICR: 815-92011
Caisse d'économie Henri-Bourassa
#1, 636, rue de la Madone
Mont-Laurier, QC J9L 1S9 Canada
819-623-4014
Fax: 819-623-4813
MICR: 815-92176
Caisse d'économie Hodelau
1525, rue Principale nord
L'Annonciation, QC J0T 1T0 Canada
819-275-2118
Fax: 819-275-3812
MICR: 815-92140
Caisse d'économie Honoré-Mercier
#102, 315, rue MacDonald
St-Jean-sur-Richelieu, QC J3B 8J3 Canada
450-348-9214
Fax: 450-348-9217
MICR: 815-92182
Caisse d'économie Laurentienne
34, rue Préfontaine est
Sainte-Agathe-des-Monts, QC J8C 1S1 Canada
819-326-2700
Fax: 819-326-6724
MICR: 815-92116
Caisse d'économie Lituaniens de Montréal-Litas
1475, rue de Sève
Montréal, QC H4E 2A8 Canada
514-766-5827
Fax: 514-766-1349
MICR: 815-92233
Caisse d'économie Or Blanc
608, boul Simoneau
Asbestos, QC J1T 4P8 Canada
819-879-5404
Fax: 819-879-6680
caisse.t92099@desjardins.com
MICR: 815-92099
Caisse d'économie polonaise du Québec
5355, rue Sherbrooke ouest
Montréal, QC H4A 1V7 Canada
514-845-3534
Fax: 514-845-3021
MICR: 815-92229
Caisse d'économie Portugais de Montréal
4244, boul St-Laurent
Montréal, QC H2W 1Z3 Canada
514-842-8077
Fax: 514-842-7930
MICR: 815-92166
Caisse d'économie solidaire Desjardins
#500, 155, boul Charest est
Québec, QC G1K 3G6 Canada
418-647-1527
Fax: 418-647-2051
MICR: 815-92276
Caisse d'économie St-Luc
5901, av Westminster
Côte Saint-Luc, QC H4W 2J9 Canada
514-483-7059
Fax: 514-483-8910
caisse.t92008@desjardins.com
MICR: 815-92008
Caisse d'Économie des employées et employés de Gaz Métropolitan
1717, rue du Havre
Montréal, QC H2K 2X3 Canada
514-598-3261
Fax: 514-598-3269
MICR: 815-92177
Caisse d'Économie Desjardins (Saguenay-Lac-Saint-Jean)
PO Box 1097
1936, boul Mellon
Jonquière, QC G7S 4K7 Canada
418-548-4683
Fax: 418-548-5747
MICR: 815-92067
Caisse d'Économie Desjardins des Pompiers, des Cols bleus et des Cols blancs (Montréal, Longueuil, Repentigny)
2600, boul Saint-Joseph est
Montréal, QC H1Y 2A4 Canada
514-526-4971
Fax: 514-526-0767
MICR: 815-92001
Caisse Desjardins Notre-Dame de Bellerive
120, rue Alexandre
Salaberry-de-Valleyfield, QC J6S 3K4 Canada
450-373-4055
Fax: 450-373-0436
MICR: 815-30080
Caisse Desjardins Atwater-Centre
2100, rue Centre
Montréal, QC H3K 1J4 Canada
514-380-8000
Fax: 514-935-8584
MICR: 815-30001
Caisse Desjardins Cap-Martin de Charlevoix
PO Box 9
118, rue Principale
St-Irénée, QC G0T 1V0 Canada
418-452-3285
Fax: 418-452-8228
MICR: 815-20314
Caisse Desjardins Cité-du-Nord de Montréal
205, rue Jarry est
Montréal, QC H2P 1T6 Canada
514-382-6096
Fax: 514-382-2741
MICR: 815-30219
Caisse Desjardins d'Amos
PO Box 670
2, rue Principale nord
Amos, QC J9T 3X2 Canada
819-732-3327
Fax: 819-732-1465
MICR: 815-80012
Caisse Desjardins d'Arvida-Kénogami
PO Box 1130
1970, boul Mellon
Jonquière, QC G7S 4K7 Canada
418-548-7123
Fax: 418-548-4234
MICR: 815-70026
Caisse Desjardins de Beauce-Centre
825, av du Palais
Saint-Joseph-de-Beauce, QC G0S 2V0 Canada
418-397-5238
Fax: 418-397-4630
MICR: 815-20048
Caisse Desjardins de Beauport
PO Box 85068
799, rue Clemenceau
Québec, QC G1E 6B3 Canada
418-660-3119
Fax: 418-661-5294
MICR: 815-20049
Caisse Desjardins de Beloeil
830, rue Laurier
Beloeil, QC J3G 4K4 Canada
450-467-2809
Fax: 450-467-5149
MICR: 815-90040
Caisse Desjardins de Bienville
6700, rue St-Georges
Lévis, QC G6V 4H3 Canada
418-833-3733
Fax: 418-833-3969
MICR: 815-20020
Caisse Desjardins de Boucherville
1071, boul de Montarville
Boucherville, QC J4B 6R2 Canada
450-655-9041
Fax: 450-641-1605
MICR: 815-30329
Caisse Desjardins de Broughton
232, av du Collège
East Broughton, QC G0N 1G0 Canada
418-427-3551
Fax: 418-427-3775
MICR: 815-20033
Caisse Desjardins de Béarn-Fabre-Lorrainville
PO Box 232
1, rue Notre-Dame ouest
Lorrainville, QC J0Z 2R0 Canada
819-625-2145
Fax: 819-625-2724
MICR: 815-30053
Caisse Desjardins de Chomedey
3075, boul Cartier
Laval, QC H7V 1J4 Canada
450-688-0900
Fax: 450-688-1704
MICR: 815-30449
Caisse Desjardins de Clermont
149, boul Notre-Dame
Clermont, QC G4A 1E7 Canada
418-439-3982
Fax: 418-439-3984
MICR: 815-20163
Caisse Desjardins de Drummondville
50, rue Notre-Dame, 2e étage
Drummondville, QC J2C 2K3 Canada
819-474-2524
Fax: 819-471-4184
MICR: 815-90104
Caisse Desjardins de Duberger
2620, rue Darveau
Québec, QC G1P 3V5 Canada
418-687-2520
Fax: 418-687-5975
MICR: 815-20448
Caisse Desjardins de Gatineau
655, boul St-René ouest
Gatineau, QC J8T 8M4 Canada
819-568-5368
Fax: 819-568-9063
MICR: 815-30126
Caisse Desjardins de Granby-Haute-Yamaska
30, rue Saint-Antoine sud
Granby, QC J2G 6W3 Canada
450-770-5353
Fax: 450-372-5596
MICR: 815-90052
Caisse Desjardins de Jonquière
PO Box 991
2358, rue St-Dominique
Jonquière, QC G7X 7W8 Canada
418-695-1850
Fax: 418-695-4479
MICR: 815-70009
Caisse Desjardins de l'Ile de Hull
41, rue Victoria
Gatineau, QC J8X 2A1 Canada
819-777-4373
Fax: 819-777-2364
MICR: 815-30038
Caisse Desjardins de l'Ile-d'Orléans
PO Box 39
1136, ch Royal
St-Pierre-Ile-d'Orléans, QC G0A 4E0 Canada
418-828-1501
Fax: 418-828-2126
MICR: 815-20231
Caisse Desjardins de L'Ile-Des-Soeurs
#150, 14, Place du Commerce
Montréal, QC H3E 1T5 Canada
514-762-5094
Fax: 514-762-5715
MICR: 815-30541
Caisse Desjardins de L'Islet
339, boul Nilus-Leclerc
L'Islet, QC G0R 2C0 Canada
418-247-5031
Fax: 418-247-7160
MICR: 815-20225
Caisse Desjardins de l'ouest de la Mauricie
PO Box 145
75, av St-Laurent
Louiseville, QC J5V 2L6 Canada
819-228-9422
Fax: 819-228-2977
MICR: 815-10106
Caisse Desjardins de l'ouest de la Montérégie
823, boul St-Jean-Baptiste
Mercier, QC J6R 1E4 Canada
450-698-2204
Fax: 450-698-0159
MICR: 815-30086
Caisse Desjardins de l'Érable

Fédération des caisses Desjardins du Québec (continued)
PO Box 187
1658, rue St-Calixte
Plessisville, QC G6L 2Y7 Canada
819-362-3236
Fax: 819-362-8751
MICR: 815-20105

Caisse Desjardins de L'×le-Perrot
#1, 100, boul Don Quichotte
×le-Perrot, QC J7V 6L7 Canada
514-453-3025
Fax: 514-453-6877
MICR: 815-30328

Caisse Desjardins de La Chevrotière
1075, boul Bona-Dussault
Saint-Marc-des-Carrières, QC G0A 4B0 Canada
418-268-3521
Fax: 418-268-3660
MICR: 815-20085

Caisse Desjardins de la Nouvelle-Acadie
PO Box 120
4, rue Beaudry
Saint-Jacques, QC J0K 2R0 Canada
450-839-7211
Fax: 450-839-2823
MICR: 815-00007

Caisse Desjardins de La Rive-Nord du Saguenay
2212, rue Roussel
Chicoutimi, QC G7G 1W7 Canada
418-549-4273
Fax: 418-549-5688
MICR: 815-70053

Caisse Desjardins de la Seigneurie de Ramezay
385, rue Couture
Sainte-Hélène-de-Bagot, QC J0H 1M0 Canada
450-791-2476
Fax: 450-791-2143
MICR: 815-90024

Caisse Desjardins de la Vallée de l'Or
602, 3e av
Val-d'Or, QC J9P 1S5 Canada
819-825-2843
Fax: 819-825-7083
MICR: 815-80009

Caisse Desjardins de la Vallée de Saint-Sauveur
218, rue Principale
Saint-Sauveur, QC J0R 1R0 Canada
450-227-3712
Fax: 450-227-8780
MICR: 815-30389

Caisse Desjardins de la Vallée-des-Forts
#100, 145, boul St-Joseph
St-Jean-sur-Richelieu, QC J3B 1W5 Canada
450-359-5933
Fax: 450-359-0956
caisse.t30204@desjardins.com
MICR: 815-30204

Caisse Desjardins de la Vallée-du-Saint-Maurice
350, 5e av
Grand-Mère, QC G9T 2M1 Canada
819-538-1621
Fax: 819-538-0002
MICR: 815-10023

Caisse Desjardins de Lac-St-Charles
444, rue Jacques-Bédard
Québec, QC G3G 1P9 Canada
418-849-4437
Fax: 418-849-7941
MICR: 815-20382

Caisse Desjardins de Lauzon
7777, boul de la Rive-Sud
Lévis, QC G6V 6Z1 Canada
418-833-5701
Fax: 418-833-5709
MICR: 815-20080

Caisse Desjardins de Longueuil
1, rue St-Charles ouest
Longueuil, QC J4H 1C4 Canada
450-646-9811
Fax: 450-646-2618
MICR: 815-30200

Caisse Desjardins De Lorimier
2050, boul Rosemont
Montréal, QC H2G 1T1 Canada
514-376-7676
Fax: 514-274-3192
MICR: 815-30015

Caisse Desjardins de Lyster - Inverness - Val-Alain
635, rue Laurier
Lyster, QC G0S 1V0 Canada
819-389-5777
Fax: 819-389-5636
MICR: 815-20183

Caisse Desjardins de Maizerets
1650, ch de la Canardière
Québec, QC G1J 2C9 Canada
418-661-8441
Fax: 418-661-9292
MICR: 815-20179

Caisse Desjardins de Marieville
1344, rue du Pont
Marieville, QC J3M 1G2 Canada
450-460-2134
Fax: 450-460-2807
MICR: 815-90033

Caisse Desjardins de Mercier-Rosemont
5790, av Pierre-de-Coubertin
Montréal, QC H1N 1R4 Canada
514-254-4586
Fax: 514-254-4730
MICR: 815-30401

Caisse Desjardins de Mont-Laurier
601, rue de la Madone
Mont-Laurier, QC J9L 1S8 Canada
819-623-4400
Fax: 819-623-5476
MICR: 815-30117

Caisse Desjardins de Rimouski
PO Box 880
100, rue Julien-Rehel
Rimouski, QC G5L 7C9 Canada
418-723-3368
Fax: 418-722-9527
MICR: 815-60003

Caisse Desjardins de Rivière-des-Prairies
8300, boul Maurice-Duplessis
Montréal, QC H1E 3A3 Canada
514-648-5800
Fax: 514-648-0380
MICR: 815-30519

Caisse Desjardins de Rouyn-Noranda
130, rue Perreault est
Rouyn-Noranda, QC J9X 3C4 Canada
819-762-0966
Fax: 819-762-3903
MICR: 815-30167

Caisse Desjardins de Saint-Antoine-des-Laurentides
663, boul St-Antoine
Saint-Jérome, QC J7Z 3B8 Canada
450-436-5331
Fax: 450-436-5229
MICR: 815-30448

Caisse Desjardins de Saint-Boniface
130, rue Guillemette
Saint-Boniface-de-Shawiniga, QC G0X 2L0 Canada
819-535-3940
Fax: 819-535-2205
MICR: 815-10136

Caisse Desjardins de Saint-Hubert
2400, boul Gaétan-Boucher
Saint-Hubert, QC J3Y 5B7 Canada
450-443-0047
Fax: 450-443-6705
MICR: 815-30087

Caisse Desjardins de Salaberry-de-Valleyfield
222, rue Alphonse-Desjardins
Salaberry-de-Valleyfield, QC J6S 5J4 Canada
450-377-4177
Fax: 450-377-4267
MICR: 815-30029

Caisse Desjardins de Shawinigan-Sud
2500, 5e av
Shawinigan-Sud, QC G9P 1P6 Canada
819-537-6607
Fax: 819-537-6604
MICR: 815-10001

Caisse Desjardins de Sherbrooke-Est
2, rue Bowen sud
Sherbrooke, QC J1G 2C5 Canada
819-565-9991
Fax: 819-565-5584
MICR: 815-50037

Caisse Desjardins de Sillery — Saint-Louis-de-France
1394, av Maguire
Québec, QC G1T 1Z3 Canada
418-681-3566
Fax: 418-681-1049
MICR: 815-20272

Caisse Desjardins de St-Georges
10555, boul Lacroix
St-Georges, QC G5Y 1K2 Canada
418-228-8824
Fax: 418-228-8866
MICR: 815-20157

Caisse Desjardins de St-Léonard
8050, boul Lacordaire
Montréal, QC H1R 2A2 Canada
514-324-5252
Fax: 514-321-0748
MICR: 815-30381

Caisse Desjardins de St-Pierre Apôtre
257, rue de Gentilly ouest
Longueuil, QC J4H 1Z5 Canada
450-646-3605
Fax: 450-646-4718
MICR: 815-30360

Caisse Desjardins de St-Romuald
2160, boul de la Rive-Sud
Saint-Romuald, QC G6W 2S6 Canada
418-839-7501
Fax: 418-839-2794
MICR: 815-20207

Caisse Desjardins de Ste-Foy
2600, boul Laurier
Québec, QC G1V 4T3 Canada
418-658-4871
Fax: 418-658-4878
866-658-5888
MICR: 815-20480

Caisse Desjardins de Tracadièche
751, boul Perron
Carleton, QC G0C 1J0 Canada
418-364-3337
Fax: 418-364-7441
MICR: 815-40018

Caisse Desjardins de Trois-Rivières
PO Box 967
1200, rue Royale
Trois-Rivières, QC G9A 5K2 Canada
819-376-1200
Fax: 819-375-4802
877-375-4987
MICR: 815-10101

Caisse Desjardins de Tétreaultville
2775, rue des Ormeaux
Montréal, QC H1L 4X6 Canada
514-351-1916
Fax: 514-351-1303
MICR: 815-30185

Caisse Desjardins de Vaudreuil-Dorion
455, av St-Charles
Vaudreuil-Dorion, QC J7V 2N4 Canada
450-455-7901
Fax: 450-455-9623
MICR: 815-30271

Caisse Desjardins de Woburn
475, rue St-Augustin
Woburn, QC G0Y 1R0 Canada
819-544-2131
Fax: 819-544-9191
MICR: 815-50079

Caisse Desjardins des Berges de Roussillon
296, voie de la Desserte
Saint-Constant, QC J5A 2C9 Canada
450-632-2820
Fax: 450-632-2303
MICR: 815-30415

Caisse Desjardins des Chutes Montmorency
4, rue Vachon
Québec, QC G1C 2V2 Canada
418-663-3581
Fax: 418-663-1904
MICR: 815-20029

Caisse Desjardins des Hauts-Reliefs (Frontenac)
5824, boul Frontenac est
Thetford Mines, QC G6H 4H7 Canada

418-338-6021
Fax: 418-338-6025
MICR: 815-20397

Caisse Desjardins des Monts et rivières
PO Box 146
22, rue de L'Église
Matapédia, QC G0J 1V0 Canada
418-865-2955
Fax: 418-865-2853
MICR: 815-60043

Caisse Desjardins des Métaux blancs
535, 1re av
Asbestos, QC J1T 3Y3 Canada
819-879-7167
Fax: 819-879-5735
MICR: 815-50047

Caisse Desjardins des Plateaux de Sherbrooke
2185, rue King ouest
Sherbrooke, QC J1J 2G2 Canada
819-566-0050
Fax: 819-564-6862
MICR: 815-50030

Caisse Desjardins des policiers et policières de Montréal
460, rue Gilford
Montréal, QC H2J 1N3 Canada
514-849-3761
Fax: 514-849-6804
MICR: 819-92004

Caisse Desjardins des Rivières
53, 2e av
Forestville, QC G0T 1E0 Canada
418-587-4441
Fax: 418-587-4578
MICR: 815-20432

Caisse Desjardins des Rivières Boyer et Etchemin
730, rte Bégin
Saint-Anselme, QC G0R 2N0 Canada
418-885-4421
Fax: 418-885-8042
MICR: 815-20034

Caisse Desjardins des Versants-Nord de Sherbrooke
5001, boul Bourque
Sherbrooke, QC J1N 2K6 Canada
819-564-8233
Fax: 819-564-8407
MICR: 815-50009

Caisse Desjardins du Quartier-Chinois
988, rue Clark
Montréal, QC H2Z 1J9 Canada
514-866-8888
Fax: 514-866-1389
MICR: 815-30588

Caisse Desjardins du Carrefour Minier
PO Box 368, Black Lake Sta. Black Lake
815, rue St-Désiré
Thetford Mines, QC G6H 2J4 Canada
418-423-7501
Fax: 418-423-5139
MICR: 815-20274

Caisse Desjardins du Grand-Coteau
933A, boul Armand-Frappier
Sainte-Julie, QC J3E 2N2 Canada
450-649-1155
Fax: 450-649-8841
MICR: 815-30066

Caisse Desjardins du Haut Shawinigan
2843, av Beaudry-Leman
Shawinigan, QC G9N 3H7 Canada
819-539-9494
Fax: 819-539-8300
MICR: 815-10071

Caisse Desjardins du Lac des Deux-Montagnes
100, rue Notre-Dame
Oka, QC J0N 1E0 Canada
450-472-5200
Fax: 450-479-8581
MICR: 815-30164

Caisse Desjardins du Lac des Nations de Sherbrooke
1146, rue King ouest
Sherbrooke, QC J1H 1S2 Canada
819-563-5080
Fax: 819-563-0747
MICR: 815-50086

Caisse Desjardins du Lac-Memphrémagog
230, rue Principale ouest
Magog, QC J1X 2A5 Canada
819-843-3328
Fax: 819-843-2892
MICR: 815-50066

Caisse Desjardins du Marigot de Laval
250, boul de la Concorde est
Laval, QC H7N 2E4 Canada
450-663-6020
Fax: 450-663-8443
MICR: 815-30522

Caisse Desjardins du Mont-Saint-Bruno
1649, rue Montarville
Saint-Bruno, QC J3V 3T8 Canada
450-653-3646
Fax: 450-461-0380
MICR: 815-30046

Caisse Desjardins du Mont-St-Hilaire
330, boul Sir-Wilfrid-Laurier
Mont-Saint-Hilaire, QC J3H 3N9 Canada
450-464-2383
Fax: 450-464-1519
MICR: 815-90011

Caisse Desjardins du parc Sir-G.-É.-Cartier de Montréal
4545, rue Notre-Dame ouest
Montréal, QC H4C 1S3 Canada
514-935-1123
Fax: 514-932-5199
MICR: 815-30227

Caisse Desjardins du personnel de l'Administration et des Services Publics
1035, rue de la Chevrotière
Québec, QC G1R 5X4 Canada
418-643-2540
Fax: 418-528-2459
866-246-2540
MICR: 815-20184

Caisse Desjardins du Quartier-Latin de Montréal
1255, rue Berri
Montréal, QC H2L 4C6 Canada
514-849-3581
Fax: 514-849-7019
MICR: 815-30008

Caisse Desjardins du Sault-au-Récollet
2612, boul Henri-Bourassa est
Montréal, QC H2B 1V6 Canada
514-382-2742
Fax: 514-382-4933
MICR: 815-30403

Caisse Desjardins du Vieux-Moulin (Beauport)
2500, ch du Petit Village
Québec, QC G1C 1V6 Canada
418-667-4440
Fax: 418-667-0072
MICR: 815-20075

Caisse Desjardins Godefroy
4265, boul de Port-Royal
Bécancour, QC G9H 1Z3 Canada
819-233-2333
Fax: 819-233-2890
MICR: 815-10024

Caisse Desjardins l'Ardoise
303, rue Collège nord
Richmond, QC J0B 2H0 Canada
819-826-6555
Fax: 819-826-3743
MICR: 815-50081

Caisse Desjardins Lachine/Saint-Pierre
1625, rue Notre-Dame
Montréal, QC H8S 2E5 Canada
514-637-4691
Fax: 514-637-9060
MICR: 815-30295

Caisse Desjardins Laviolette
4505, boul des Récollets
Trois-Rivières, QC G9A 5V2 Canada
819-697-2345
Fax: 819-378-0040
MICR: 815-10049

Caisse Desjardins Les Estacades
670, boul Thibeau
Trois-Rivières, QC G8T 6Z8 Canada
819-378-4029
Fax: 819-378-7761
MICR: 815-10006

Caisse Desjardins Les Méandres
312, boul l'Ange-Gardien
L'Assomption, QC J5W 1S3 Canada
450-588-6000
Fax: 450-589-7578
MICR: 815-30153

Caisse Desjardins Les Salines
3050, boul Laframboise
Saint-Hyacinthe, QC J2S 4Z4 Canada
450-778-7421
Fax: 450-773-1474
caisse.t90063@desjardins.com
MICR: 815-90063

Caisse Desjardins Mistouk
112, rue Mistouk
Alma, QC G8E 2J2 Canada
418-347-3343
Fax: 418-347-5776
MICR: 815-70037

Caisse Desjardins Saint-Joseph de Hull
215, boul St-Joseph
Gatineau, QC J8Y 3X6 Canada
819-776-6335
Fax: 819-776-5328
MICR: 815-30092

Caisse Desjardins Samuel-De Champlain
PO Box 26
945, rue Notre-Dame
Champlain, QC G0X 1C0 Canada
819-295-3948
Fax: 819-295-5231
MICR: 815-10009

Caisse Desjardins Thérèse-de Blainville
37, rue Turgeon
Sainte-Thérèse, QC J7E 3H2 Canada
450-430-6550
Fax: 450-430-0085
MICR: 815-30022

Caisse populaire Berthier-sur-Mer
47, rue Principale est
Berthier-sur-Mer, QC G0R 1E0 Canada
418-259-7795
Fax: 418-259-7796
MICR: 815-20339

Caisse Populaire Canadienne Italienne
6999, boul St-Laurent
Montréal, QC H2S 3E1 Canada
514-270-4124
Fax: 514-270-2247
MICR: 815-30606

Caisse populaire Châteauguay
65, rue Principale
Châteauguay, QC J6K 1E9 Canada
450-692-6751
Fax: 450-692-7329
MICR: 815-30171

Caisse populaire Contrecoeur
PO Box 309
4956, rue Legendre
Contrecoeur, QC J0L 1C0 Canada
450-587-2023
Fax: 450-587-5436
MICR: 815-30291

Caisse populaire de Cabano
103, rue Commerciale
Cabano, QC G0L 1E0 Canada
418-854-2120
Fax: 418-854-2208
MICR: 815-60038

Caisse populaire de Frampton
143, rue Principale
Frampton, QC G0R 1M0 Canada
418-479-2012
Fax: 418-479-5640
MICR: 815-20318

Caisse populaire de Hérouxville
1160, rue St-Pierre
Hérouxville, QC G0X 1J0 Canada
418-365-7571
Fax: 418-365-4248
MICR: 815-10086

Caisse populaire de l'Ange-Gardien
101, rue Canrobert
L'Ange-Gardien, QC J0E 1E0 Canada

Fédération des caisses Desjardins du Québec (continued)

450-293-3691
Fax: 450-293-3272
MICR: 815-90006

Caisse populaire de l'Enseignement du Grand-Portage
PO Box 338
#300, 506, rue Lafontaine
Rivière-du-Loup, QC G5R 3Y9 Canada
418-862-9905
Fax: 418-862-4444
MICR: 815-20471

Caisse populaire de La Prairie
450, boul Taschereau
La Prairie, QC J5R 1V1 Canada
450-659-5431
Fax: 450-444-5431
MICR: 815-30325

Caisse populaire de La Tabatière
6, rue Desjardins
La Tabatière, QC G0G 1T0 Canada
418-773-2259
Fax: 418-773-2612
MICR: 815-20475

Caisse populaire de Lac-à-la-Tortue
PO Box 99
680, 98e rue
Lac-à-la-Tortue, QC G0X 1L0 Canada
819-538-1633
Fax: 819-538-4431
MICR: 815-10059

Caisse populaire de Maskinongé
PO Box 59
62, rue St-Aimé
Maskinongé, QC J0K 1N0 Canada
819-227-2351
Fax: 819-227-2022
MICR: 815-10035

Caisse Populaire de Notre Dame du Mont Carmel
3960, rue Mgr Béliveau
Notre-Dame-du-Mont-Carmel, QC G0X 3J0 Canada
819-374-6380
Fax: 819-374-6187
MICR: 815-10037

Caisse populaire de Notre-Dame de Fatima
6318, rue Salaberry
Lac-Mégantic, QC G6B 1J1 Canada
819-583-2380
Fax: 819-583-2658
cpfatima@megantic.net
MICR: 815-50106

Caisse populaire de Notre-Dame-du-Chemin
900, av des Érables
Québec, QC G1R 2M5 Canada
418-687-1844
Fax: 418-687-4059
MICR: 815-20093

Caisse populaire de Parent
PO Box 247
77, rue de l'Église
Parent, QC G0X 3P0 Canada
819-667-2518
Fax: 819-667-2617
MICR: 815-10162

Caisse populaire de Précieux-Sang
7425, rte du Missouri
Bécancour, QC G9H 3H7 Canada
819-294-6620
Fax: 819-294-1270
MICR: 815-10046

Caisse populaire de Rougemont
991, rue Principale
Rougemont, QC J0L 1M0 Canada
450-469-3164
Fax: 450-469-3724
MICR: 815-90073

Caisse populaire de Saint-Alexis des Monts
41, rue Richard
Saint-Alexis-des-Monts, QC J0K 1V0 Canada
819-265-2052
Fax: 819-265-3521
MICR: 815-10070

Caisse populaire de Saint-Claude
306, boul de la Concorde ouest
Laval, QC H7N 5B2 Canada
450-663-5050
Fax: 450-663-5485
MICR: 815-30524

Caisse populaire de Saint-Hyacinthe
1697, rue Girouard ouest
Saint-Hyacinthe, QC J2S 2Z9 Canada
450-773-9751
Fax: 450-773-6426
MICR: 815-90044

Caisse populaire de Saint-Séverin de Proulxville
40, rue St-François
Proulxville, QC G0X 2B0 Canada
418-365-7585
Fax: 418-365-3370
MICR: 815-10068

Caisse populaire de Saint-Urbain
207A, rue Principale
Saint-Urbain-Premier, QC J0S 1Y0 Canada
450-427-2119
Fax: 450-427-3075
MICR: 815-30115

Caisse populaire de St-André
PO Box 98
141, rue Principale
Saint-André-de-Kamouraska, QC G0L 2H0 Canada
418-493-2176
Fax: 418-493-2524
MICR: 815-20013

Caisse populaire de St-Charles
PO Box 236
2807, av Royale
Saint-Charles-de-Bellechass, QC G0R 2T0 Canada
418-887-6631
Fax: 418-887-3397
MICR: 815-20067

Caisse populaire de St-Charles sur Richelieu
14, rue de l'Union
Saint-Charles-sur-Richelieu, QC J0H 2G0 Canada
450-584-2275
Fax: 450-584-3568
MICR: 815-90009

Caisse populaire de St-Dominique de Bagot
1199, rue Principale
St-Dominique de Bagot, QC J0H 1L0 Canada
450-773-1359
Fax: 450-773-5489
MICR: 815-90055

Caisse populaire de St-Fortunat
152, rue Principale
Saint-Fortunat, QC G0P 1G0 Canada
819-344-5548
Fax: 819-344-2067
MICR: 815-50082

Caisse populaire de St-Honoré de Shenley
PO Box 40
476, rue Principale
Saint-Honoré-de-Shenley, QC G0M 1V0 Canada
418-485-6341
Fax: 418-485-6302
MICR: 815-20012

Caisse populaire de St-Jean Baptiste de Rouville
3221, rue Principale
St Jean Baptiste, QC J0L 2B0 Canada
450-467-7227
Fax: 450-467-9368
MICR: 815-90023

Caisse populaire de St-Léon-le-Grand
679, rue Principale
Saint-Léon-le-Grand, QC J0K 2W0 Canada
819-228-3151
Fax: 819-228-8855
MICR: 815-10163

Caisse populaire de St-Mathieu
1, rue Du Moulin
St-Mathieu-de-Rioux, QC G0L 3T0 Canada
418-738-2024
Fax: 418-738-2047
MICR: 815-60011

Caisse populaire de St-Pierre-les-Becquets
320, rue Marie-Victorin
Saint-Pierre-les-Becquets, QC G0X 2Z0 Canada
819-263-2861
Fax: 819-263-2787
MICR: 815-10088

Caisse populaire de St-Rodrigue
4765, 1re av
Québec, QC G1H 2T3 Canada
418-623-9878
Fax: 418-623-3472
MICR: 815-20385

Caisse populaire de St-Sylvère
756, rue Principale
Saint-Sylvère, QC G0Z 1H0 Canada
819-285-2633
Fax: 819-285-2437
MICR: 815-10072

Caisse populaire de St-Tite
400, rue Notre-Dame
Saint-Tite, QC G0X 3H0 Canada
418-365-7591
Fax: 418-365-3889
MICR: 815-10081

Caisse populaire de Ste Agathe de Lotbinière
PO Box 100
222, rue St-Pierre
Sainte-Agathe-de-Lotbinière, QC G0S 2A0 Canada
418-599-2841
Fax: 418-599-2940
MICR: 815-20071

Caisse populaire de Ste-Angèle-de-Laval
14825, boul Bécancour
Bécancour, QC G9H 2L2 Canada
819-222-5606
Fax: 819-222-5662
MICR: 815-10003

Caisse populaire de Ste-Madeleine
1040, rue St-Simon
Sainte-Madeleine, QC J0H 1S0 Canada
450-795-3323
Fax: 450-795-6932
MICR: 815-90071

Caisse populaire de Verchères
6, rue Provost
Verchères, QC J0L 2R0 Canada
450-583-3337
Fax: 450-583-6362
MICR: 815-30336

Caisse populaire de Waterloo
PO Box 200
4990, rue Foster
Waterloo, QC J0E 2N0 Canada
450-539-1023
Fax: 450-539-3362
MICR: 815-90058

Caisse populaire des Sources
45, boul Brunswick
Montréal, QC H9B 1P7 Canada
514-683-1390
Fax: 514-683-1041
MICR: 815-30356

Caisse populaire Desjardins du Sud des Bois-Francs
172, rue St-Louis
Warwick, QC J0A 1M0 Canada
819-358-3200
Fax: 819-358-3246
MICR: 815-10062

Caisse populaire Desjardins Allard-Saint-Paul
2645, rue Allard
Montréal, QC H4E 2L7 Canada
514-765-3577
Fax: 514-765-0061
MICR: 815-30279

Caisse populaire Desjardins Beauharnois
555, rue Ellice
Beauharnois, QC J6N 1X8 Canada
450-225-0335
Fax: 450-225-2537
MICR: 815-30040

Caisse populaire Desjardins Bellevue de Québec
1351, ch Ste-Foy
Québec, QC G1S 2N2 Canada
418-681-7878
Fax: 418-681-1337
MICR: 815-20186

Caisse populaire Desjardins Belvédère
999, av Murray
Québec, QC G1S 3B4 Canada
418-688-1010
Fax: 418-688-7262
MICR: 815-20278

Caisse Populaire Desjardins Centre de Lotbinière

94, rue Principale
Saint-Flavien, QC G0S 2M0 Canada
418-728-2001
Fax: 418-728-4921
MICR: 815-20205

Caisse populaire Desjardins Centre du Bas-Richelieu
498, ch Ste-Victoire
Sainte-Victoire-de-Sorel, QC J0G 1T0 Canada
450-746-4646
Fax: 450-782-2971
MICR: 815-90053

Caisse populaire Desjardins Centre-est du Témiscamingue
PO Box 25
11, rue Principale
Laverlochère, QC J0Z 2P0 Canada
819-765-3261
Fax: 819-765-2276
MICR: 815-30071

Caisse populaire Desjardins Chapeau
PO Box 10
110, rue King
Chapeau, QC J0X 1M0 Canada
819-689-5252
Fax: 819-689-2723
MICR: 815-30188

Caisse populaire Desjardins Charles-LeMoyne
477, av Victoria
Saint-Lambert, QC J4P 2J1 Canada
450-671-3733
Fax: 450-671-1725
MICR: 815-30397

Caisse populaire Desjardins Christ-Roi de Châteauguay
169, boul Maple
Châteauguay, QC J6J 3R1 Canada
450-691-6616
Fax: 450-691-8777
MICR: 815-30345

Caisse populaire Desjardins Cité de Shawinigan
PO Box 21006
1795, av St-Marc
Shawinigan, QC G9N 8M7 Canada
819-536-2621
Fax: 819-536-2577
MICR: 815-10084

Caisse populaire Desjardins d'Acton Vale
1100, rue St-André
Acton Vale, QC J0H 1A0 Canada
450-546-2706
Fax: 450-546-4131
MICR: 815-90021

Caisse populaire Desjardins d'Alma
PO Box 367
600, rue Collard ouest
Alma, QC G8B 5V8 Canada
418-669-1414
Fax: 418-669-1466
MICR: 815-70014

Caisse populaire Desjardins d'Anjou
7000, boul Joseph Renaud
Montréal, QC H1K 3V5 Canada
514-493-1285
Fax: 514-493-0610
MICR: 815-30424

Caisse populaire Desjardins d'Argenteuil
570, rue Principale
Lachute, QC J8H 1Y7 Canada
450-562-8888
Fax: 450-562-1397
MICR: 815-30284

Caisse populaire Desjardins d'Aylmer
375, ch d'Aylmer
Gatineau, QC J9H 1A5 Canada
819-684-4952
Fax: 819-684-6698
MICR: 815-30371

Caisse populaire Desjardins d'Hochelaga-Maisonneuve
3871, rue Ontario est
Montréal, QC H1W 1S7 Canada
514-255-4477
Fax: 514-527-0652
MICR: 815-30327

Caisse populaire Desjardins d'Outremont
1145, av Bernard
Montréal, QC H2V 1V4 Canada
514-274-8221
Fax: 514-274-9405
MICR: 815-30208

Caisse populaire Desjardins de Baie-Comeau
267, boul Lasalle
Baie-Comeau, QC G4Z 1S7 Canada
418-296-3339
Fax: 418-296-0183
MICR: 815-20284

Caisse populaire Desjardins de Beauceville
620, boul Renault
Beauceville, QC G5X 3P1 Canada
418-774-3647
Fax: 418-774-2345
MICR: 815-20074

Caisse populaire Desjardins de Beaujeu-Hemmingford
3, rue de l'Église nord
Lacolle, QC J0J 1J0 Canada
450-246-3891
Fax: 450-246-3661
MICR: 815-30407

Caisse populaire Desjardins de Beaurivage
400, rue Principale
Saint-Narcisse-de-Beaurivag, QC G0S 1W0 Canada
418-475-6686
Fax: 418-475-4030
MICR: 815-20120

Caisse populaire Desjardins de Bedford
24, rue Rivière
Bedford, QC J0J 1A0 Canada
450-248-4351
Fax: 450-248-3922
MICR: 815-90051

Caisse populaire Desjardins de Berthier-et-des-Iles
PO Box 900
670, rue Montcalm
Berthierville, QC J0K 1A0 Canada
450-836-6221
Fax: 450-836-1295
MICR: 815-00022

Caisse populaire Desjardins de Blanc-Sablon
PO Box 69
1056, boul Dr. Camille Marcoux
Lourdes-de-Blanc-Sablon, QC G0G 1W0 Canada
418-461-2020
Fax: 418-461-2325
MICR: 815-20416

Caisse populaire Desjardins de Bois-Franc—Cartierville
5890, boul Gouin ouest
Montréal, QC H4J 1E4 Canada
514-334-6006
Fax: 514-334-1775
caisse.t30355@desjardins.com
MICR: 815-30355

Caisse populaire Desjardins de Brandon
119, rue Pacifique
Saint-Gabriel-de-Brandon, QC J0K 2N0 Canada
450-835-3421
Fax: 450-835-3428
MICR: 815-00039

Caisse populaire Desjardins de Breakeyville
35, rue du Ruisseau
Sainte-Hélène-de-Breakeyvil, QC G0S 1E2 Canada
418-832-4684
Fax: 418-832-2580
MICR: 815-20388

Caisse populaire Desjardins de Brome-Missisquoi
101, rue Principale
Cowansville, QC J2K 1J3 Canada
450-263-1393
Fax: 450-263-8475
MICR: 815-90027

Caisse populaire Desjardins de Brossard
#100, 1850, av Panama
Brossard, QC J4W 3C6 Canada
450-671-3720
Fax: 450-671-2431
MICR: 815-30435

Caisse populaire Desjardins de Bécancour
8310, rue Désormeaux
Bécancour, QC G9H 2X2 Canada
819-294-2594
Fax: 819-294-2595
MICR: 815-10095

Caisse populaire Desjardins de Cap-Rouge
1111, boul de la Chaudière
Québec, QC G1Y 3T4 Canada
418-651-5487
Fax: 418-651-6806
MICR: 815-20426

Caisse populaire Desjardins de Cavignac
171, rue St-Germain
Saint-Hugues, QC J0H 1N0 Canada
450-794-2121
Fax: 450-794-2977
MICR: 815-90062

Caisse populaire Desjardins de Charlemagne
60, rue Sacré-Coeur
Charlemagne, QC J5Z 1W5 Canada
450-581-4740
Fax: 450-581-3160
MICR: 815-30248

Caisse populaire Desjardins de Charlesbourg
PO Box 87126
155, 76e rue est
Québec, QC G1G 5E1 Canada
418-626-1146
Fax: 418-626-1607
MICR: 815-20030

Caisse populaire Desjardins de Chibougamau
519, 3e rue
Chibougamau, QC G8P 1N8 Canada
418-748-6461
Fax: 418-748-7337
MICR: 815-80035

Caisse populaire Desjardins de Chicoutimi
PO Box 1180
245, rue Racine est
Chicoutimi, QC G7H 5G7 Canada
418-549-3224
Fax: 418-549-3234
MICR: 815-70001

Caisse populaire Desjardins de Cranbourne
PO Box 69
390, rue Langevin
Saint-Odilon, QC G0S 3A0 Canada
418-464-2381
Fax: 418-464-4310
MICR: 815-20294

Caisse Populaire Desjardins de Côte-des-Neiges
5480, ch de la Côte-des-Neiges
Montréal, QC H3T 1Y5 Canada
514-735-1574
Fax: 514-735-2996
MICR: 815-30289

Caisse populaire Desjardins de Daveluyville
PO Box 250
360, rue Principale
Daveluyville, QC G0Z 1C0 Canada
418-367-2301
Fax: 418-367-3457
MICR: 815-10010

Caisse populaire Desjardins de Dolbeau-Mistassini
1200, boul Wallberg
Dolbeau-Mistassini, QC G8L 1H1 Canada
418-276-3291
Fax: 418-276-8790
MICR: 815-70020

Caisse populaire Desjardins de Donnacona
260, rue de l'Église
Donnacona, QC G3M 1Z3 Canada
418-285-2525
Fax: 418-285-3013
MICR: 815-20117

Caisse populaire Desjardins de East Angus
46, rue Hôtel de Ville
East Angus, QC J0B 1R0 Canada
819-832-4916
Fax: 418-832-2962
MICR: 815-50060

Caisse populaire Desjardins de Farnham
200, rue Desjardins est
Farnham, QC J2N 1P9 Canada
450-293-3613
Fax: 450-293-6912
MICR: 815-90057

Caisse populaire Desjardins de Fatima
623, ch des Caps
Fatima, QC G4T 2S9 Canada

Fédération des caisses Desjardins du Québec (continued)

418-986-2360
Fax: 418-986-6045
MICR: 815-40043

Caisse populaire Desjardins de Fort Coulonge
PO Box 70
175, rue Principale
Fort-Coulonge, QC J0X 1V0 Canada
819-683-2451
Fax: 819-683-3842
MICR: 815-30216

Caisse populaire Desjardins de Gentilly
1780, av des Hirondelles
Bécancour, QC G9H 4L7 Canada
819-298-2844
Fax: 819-298-3011
MICR: 815-10021

Caisse populaire Desjardins de Grantham-Wickham
242, rue Ste-Thérèse
Saint-Germain-de-Grantham, QC J0C 1K0 Canada
819-395-4228
Fax: 819-395-4522
MICR: 815-10022

Caisse populaire Desjardins de Hauterive
990, boul Laflèche
Baie-Comeau, QC G5C 2W9 Canada
418-589-3734
Fax: 418-589-7237
MICR: 815-20408

Caisse populaire Desjardins de Havre-aux-Maisons
PO Box 30
38, ch Central
Havre-aux-Maisons, QC G4T 5G9 Canada
418-969-2266
Fax: 418-969-2913
MICR: 815-40027

Caisse populaire Desjardins de Havre-St-Pierre
1072, rue Dulcinée
Ha@vre-Saint-Pierre, QC G0G 1P0 Canada
418-538-2123
Fax: 418-538-2854
MICR: 815-20147

Caisse populaire Desjardins de Jean-Talon-Papineau
2295, rue Jean Talon est
Montréal, QC H2E 1V6 Canada
514-376-7691
Fax: 514-374-9090
MICR: 815-30009

Caisse populaire Desjardins de Joliette
575, rue Notre-Dame
Joliette, QC J6E 3H8 Canada
450-759-2422
Fax: 450-759-8241
MICR: 815-00026

Caisse populaire Desjardins de Kennebec
1324, rue Principale
Saint-Côme-Linière, QC G0M 1J0 Canada
418-685-3078
Fax: 418-685-3081
MICR: 815-20026

Caisse populaire Desjardins de Kildare
PO Box 58
999, rte 343
Saint-Ambroise-de-Kildare, QC J0K 1C0 Canada
450-752-0602
Fax: 450-756-0106
MICR: 815-00001

Caisse populaire Desjardins de l'Anse (Portneuf)
3, rue Gérard-Morisset
Cap-Santé, QC G0A 1L0 Canada
418-285-2434
Fax: 418-285-4711
MICR: 815-20214

Caisse Populaire Desjardins de l'Anse de La Pocatière
308, 4e av
La Pocatière, QC G0R 1Z0 Canada
418-856-2340
Fax: 418-856-9778
MICR: 815-20052

Caisse populaire Desjardins de l'Anse-St-Jean
243, rue St-Jean-Baptiste
L'Anse-Saint-Jean, QC G0V 1J0 Canada
418-272-2550
Fax: 418-272-3199
MICR: 815-70052

Caisse populaire Desjardins de l'Envolée
PO Box 1200
13845, boul du Curé-Labelle
Mirabel, QC J7J 1A1 Canada
450-430-4603
Fax: 450-430-2858
MICR: 815-30266

Caisse populaire Desjardins de l'Est de Drummond
PO Box 430
330, rue Notre-Dame
Bon-Conseil, QC J0C 1A0 Canada
819-336-2600
Fax: 819-336-2731
MICR: 815-10042

Caisse populaire Desjardins de l'Est de l'Abitibi
PO Box 458
740, 9e av
Senneterre, QC J0Y 2M0 Canada
819-737-2247
Fax: 819-737-8816
MICR: 815-80001

Caisse populaire Desjardins de l'Estuaire (Charlevoix)
PO Box 87
417, rue St-Laurent
Saint-Siméon, QC G0T 1X0 Canada
418-638-2493
Fax: 418-638-5390
MICR: 815-20280

Caisse populaire Desjardins de l'Héritage des Basques
80, rue Notre-Dame ouest
Trois-Pistoles, QC G0L 4K0 Canada
418-851-2173
Fax: 418-851-1223
MICR: 815-60039

Caisse populaire Desjardins de l'Iles-aux-Coudres
29, ch de la Traverse
Isle-aux-Coudres, QC G0A 3J0 Canada
418-438-2555
Fax: 418-438-2159
MICR: 815-20298

Caisse populaire Desjardins de l'Industrie
PO Box 545
179, rue St-Pierre sud
Joliette, QC J6E 7N2 Canada
450-756-1664
Fax: 450-756-1235
MICR: 815-00034

Caisse populaire Desjardins de L'Isle-aux-Grues
178, ch du Roi
L'Isle-aux-Grues, QC G0R 1PO Canada
418-248-5789
Fax: 418-248-5789
MICR: 815-20079

Caisse populaire Desjardins de La Baie
361, rue Albert
La Baie, QC G7B 3L5 Canada
418-544-7365
Fax: 418-544-0392
MICR: 815-70019

Caisse populaire Desjardins de la Baie-de-Gaspé
80, rue Jacques-Cartier
Gaspé, QC G4X 2V2 Canada
418-368-5555
Fax: 418-368-2368
MICR: 815-40025

Caisse populaire Desjardins de la Basse-Lièvre
PO Box 2720
104, rue Maclaren est
Gatineau, QC J8L 2X1 Canada
819-986-5182
Fax: 819-986-1377
MICR: 815-30429

Caisse populaire Desjardins de la Chaudière
1001, rte Lagueux
Saint-Étienne-de-Lauzon, QC G6J 1J9 Canada
418-831-3586
Fax: 418-831-5304
MICR: 815-20372

Caisse populaire Desjardins de la Feuille d'Or
1061, rue Principale
Saint-Thomas, QC J0K 3L0 Canada
450-755-4165
Fax: 450-755-6541
MICR: 815-00020

Caisse populaire Desjardins de la Forêt enchantée
51, rue Ste-Anne
Ville-Marie, QC J9V 2B6 Canada
819-629-2446
Fax: 819-629-2998
MICR: 815-30050

Caisse populaire Desjardins de la Haute Matawinie
100, rue Saint-Maurice ouest
Saint-Michel-des-Saints, QC J0K 3B0 Canada
450-833-6321
Fax: 450-833-5711
MICR: 815-00027

Caisse populaire Desjardins de la Haute-Beauce
387, 14e av
La Guadeloupe, QC G0M 1G0 Canada
418-459-3474
Fax: 418-459-3121
MICR: 815-20130

Caisse populaire Desjardins de la Haute-Chaudière
PO Box 99
146, rue de l'Église
Saint-Gédéon-de-Beauce, QC G0M 1T0 Canada
418-582-3323
Fax: 418-582-6417
MICR: 815-20018

Caisse populaire Desjardins de La Haute-Gaspésie
10, 1re av est
Sainte-Anne-des-Monts, QC G4V 1A3 Canada
418-763-2214
Fax: 418-763-2424
MICR: 815-40035

Caisse populaire Desjardins de la Haute-Gatineau
#29, 100, rue Principale sud
Maniwaki, QC J9E 3L4 Canada
819-449-1432
Fax: 819-449-4322
MICR: 815-30312

Caisse populaire Desjardins de la Maison de Radio-Canada
1400, boul René-Lévesque est
Montréal, QC H2L 2M2 Canada
514-597-2695
Fax: 514-597-2050
MICR: 815-30484

Caisse populaire Desjardins de La Malbaie
130, rue John-Nairne
La Malbaie, QC G5A 1Y1 Canada
418-665-4443
Fax: 418-665-4888
MICR: 815-20032

Caisse populaire Desjardins de la Mitis
PO Box 70
10, rue St-Jean Baptiste
Price, QC G0J 1Z0 Canada
418-775-7058
Fax: 418-775-8273
MICR: 815-60095

Caisse populaire Desjardins de la Moraine
PO Box 68
1470, rue Notre-Dame
Saint-Maurice, QC G0X 2X0 Canada
819-374-3024
Fax: 819-374-2994
MICR: 815-10080

Caisse populaire Desjardins de la Ouareau
3690, rue Queen
Rawdon, QC J0K 1S0 Canada
450-834-5446
Fax: 450-834-2939
MICR: 815-00030

Caisse populaire Desjardins de la Petite-Nation
105, rue Principale
Saint-André-Avellin, QC J0V 1W0 Canada
819-983-7313
Fax: 819-983-2001
MICR: 815-30463

Caisse populaire Desjardins de la Pointe de Ste-Foy
3455, boul Neilson
Québec, QC G1W 2W2 Canada
418-653-0515
Fax: 418-653-2180
MICR: 815-20465

Caisse populaire Desjardins de la Rivière du Sud
PO Box 160
526, ch St-François ouest
St-François-de-la-Rivière-d, QC G0R 3A0 Canada

418-259-7786
Fax: 418-259-7787
MICR: 815-20227
Caisse populaire Desjardins de la Rivière du Chêne (Lotbinière)
PO Box 279
100, 16e av
Deschaillons-sur-Saint-Laur, QC G0S 1G0 Canada
819-292-2707
Fax: 819-292-2807
MICR: 815-20212
Caisse Populaire Desjardins de la Rivière Noire
1390, rue Principale
St-Valérien, QC J0H 2B0 Canada
450-549-2418
Fax: 450-549-2697
MICR: 815-90019
Caisse populaire Desjardins de la Rivière Ouelle
7, rue Caron
Saint-Pacôme, QC G0L 3X0 Canada
418-852-2812
Fax: 418-852-3071
MICR: 815-20199
Caisse populaire Desjardins de la Région-Ouest-de-Mégantic
4749, rue Laval
Lac-Mégantic, QC G6B 1C8 Canada
819-583-1911
Fax: 819-583-0897
MICR: 815-50021
Caisse populaire Desjardins de la Saint-François
1832, rue Galt est
Sherbrooke, QC J1G 3H8 Canada
819-566-2515
Fax: 819-566-0425
MICR: 815-50124
Caisse populaire Desjardins de La Sarre
66, 5e av est
La Sarre, QC J9Z 1K9 Canada
819-333-5424
Fax: 819-333-3181
MICR: 815-80011
Caisse populaire Desjardins de la Seigneurie Sainte-Marie
182, rue Ste-Anne
Sainte-Anne-de-la-Pérade, QC G0X 2J0 Canada
418-325-2822
Fax: 418-325-2756
MICR: 815-10002
Caisse populaire Desjardins de la Seigneurie des Grondines
PO Box 116
300, boul de la Montagne
Saint-Casimir, QC G0A 3L0 Canada
418-339-2265
Fax: 418-339-3149
MICR: 815-20148
Caisse populaire Desjardins de la Vallée de l'Etchemin
PO Box 160
508, rue Principale
Standon, QC G0R 4L0 Canada
418-642-5471
Fax: 418-642-2031
MICR: 815-20046
Caisse populaire Desjardins de la Vallée des Lacs
PO Box 58
121, rue St-Joseph
Squatec, QC G0L 4H0 Canada
418-855-2049
Fax: 418-855-2571
MICR: 815-60017
Caisse populaire Desjardins de la Vallée du Gouffre
2, rue St-Jean Baptiste
Baie-Saint-Paul, QC G3Z 1L7 Canada
418-435-2228
Fax: 418-435-6834
MICR: 815-20297
Caisse populaire Desjardins de Labelle-Nominingue
7531, boul Curé-Labelle
Labelle, QC J0T 1H0 Canada
819-686-2282
Fax: 819-686-3758
MICR: 815-30413
Caisse Populaire Desjardins de Lac Mistissini
#200, 136, rue Amanda
Mistissini, QC G0W 1C0 Canada
418-923-3289
Fax: 418-923-2224
MICR: 815-80054
Caisse populaire Desjardins de Lac-au-Saumon
PO Box 280
15, rue Rioux
Lac-au-Saumon, QC G0J 1M0 Canada
418-778-5835
Fax: 418-778-3157
MICR: 815-60033
Caisse populaire Desjardins de Lac-à-la-Croix
380, rue St-Jean
Métabetchouan-Lac-a-la-Croi, QC G8G 2J5 Canada
418-349-2812
Fax: 418-349-8428
MICR: 815-70022
Caisse populaire Desjardins de Langevin
PO Box 380
111, rue de la Caisse
Sainte-Justine, QC G0R 1Y0 Canada
418-383-3062
Fax: 418-383-5561
MICR: 815-20174
Caisse populaire Desjardins de Lanoraie
392, rue Notre-Dame
Lanoraie, QC J0K 1E0 Canada
450-887-2355
Fax: 450-887-2912
MICR: 815-00023
Caisse populaire Desjardins de LaSalle
Centre service Cavelier-de-LaSalle
2223, av Dollard
Montréal, QC H8N 1S2 Canada
514-366-6231
Fax: 514-366-0480
MICR: 815-30422
Caisse populaire Desjardins de Laterrière
5812, boul Talbot
Laterrière, QC G7N 1W1 Canada
418-678-1233
Fax: 418-678-1599
MICR: 815-70013
Caisse populaire Desjardins de Lavaltrie
PO Box 81
1000, rue Notre-Dame
Lavaltrie, QC J5T 4A9 Canada
450-586-1766
Fax: 450-585-2205
MICR: 815-00038
Caisse populaire Desjardins de Lebel-sur-Quévillon
PO Box 220
45, Place Quévillon
Lebel-sur-Quévillon, QC J0Y 1X0 Canada
819-755-4863
Fax: 819-755-3631
MICR: 815-80007
Caisse populaire Desjardins de Les Écureuils
984, rue Notre Dame
Donnacona, QC G3M 1J5 Canada
418-285-0505
Fax: 418-285-0480
MICR: 815-20111
Caisse populaire Desjardins de Limoilou
3174, 1re av
Québec, QC G1L 3P7 Canada
418-628-0155
Fax: 418-628-9395
MICR: 815-20366
Caisse populaire Desjardins de Loretteville
9850, boul l'Ormière
Québec, QC G2B 3L1 Canada
418-842-1918
Fax: 418-842-0173
MICR: 815-20137
Caisse populaire Desjardins de Lévis
Centre Financier Galeries Chagnon
1200, boul Alphonse-Desjardins
Lévis, QC G6V 6Y8 Canada
418-833-5515
Fax: 418-833-6583
MICR: 815-20083
Caisse populaire Desjardins de Lévrard
219, rue Principale
Sainte-Cécile-de-Lévrard, QC G0X 2M0 Canada
819-263-2103
Fax: 819-263-2823
MICR: 815-10116
Caisse populaire Desjardins de Maria
PO Box 190
554, boul Perron est
Maria, QC G0C 1Y0 Canada
418-759-3456
Fax: 418-759-3801
MICR: 815-40001
Caisse populaire Desjardins de Masham-Luskville
88, rue Principale est
Sainte-Cécile-de-Masham, QC J0X 2W0 Canada
819-456-2461
Fax: 819-456-2482
MICR: 815-30107
Caisse populaire Desjardins de Matane
PO Box 248
300, rue Bon Pasteur
Matane, QC G4W 3N2 Canada
418-562-2646
Fax: 418-562-6232
MICR: 815-60024
Caisse populaire Desjardins de Milot
531, rue Levesque
Saint-Ludger-de-Milot, QC G0W 2B0 Canada
418-373-2571
Fax: 418-373-2350
MICR: 815-70054
Caisse populaire Desjardins de Mingan-Anticosti
PO Box 40
998, ch du Roi
Longue-Pointe-de-Mingan, QC G0G 1V0 Canada
418-949-2882
Fax: 418-949-2025
MICR: 815-20321
Caisse populaire Desjardins de Mirabel
8000, rue St-Jacques
Mirabel, QC J7N 2B7 Canada
450-475-8110
Fax: 450-475-7857
MICR: 815-30196
Caisse populaire Desjardins de Mont-Joli
PO Box 128
1553, boul Jacques Cartier
Mont-Joli, QC G5H 3K9 Canada
418-775-7253
Fax: 418-775-5116
MICR: 815-60004
Caisse populaire Desjardins de Mont-Tremblant
470, rue Charbonneau
Mont-Tremblant, QC J8E 3H4 Canada
819-425-8624
Fax: 819-425-8628
MICR: 815-30113
Caisse populaire Desjardins de Montcalm
915, 12e av
Saint-Lin-Laurentides, QC J5M 2W1 Canada
450-439-3615
Fax: 450-439-6853
MICR: 815-00008
Caisse populaire Desjardins de Montmagny
143, rue St-Jean-Baptiste est
Montmagny, QC G5V 1K4 Canada
418-248-4884
Fax: 418-248-8241
MICR: 815-20108
Caisse populaire Desjardins de Montréal-Nord
11000, boul St-Vital
Montréal, QC H1H 4T6 Canada
514-322-9310
Fax: 514-322-0763
MICR: 815-30513
Caisse populaire Desjardins de Neuville
757, rue des Érables
Neuville, QC G0A 2R0 Canada
418-876-2838
Fax: 418-876-3405
MICR: 815-20200
Caisse populaire Desjardins de New Richmond
carrefour Baie-des-Chaleurs
120, boul Perron ouest
New Richmond, QC G0C 2B0 Canada
418-392-4489
Fax: 418-392-6365
MICR: 815-40008
Caisse populaire Desjardins de Nicolet
181, rue Notre-Dame
Nicolet, QC J3T 1V8 Canada

Fédération des caisses Desjardins du Québec (continued)
819-293-4567
Fax: 819-293-8569
caisse.t10038@desjardins.com
MICR: 815-10038
Caisse populaire Desjardins de Notre-Dame-de-Grâce
3830, boul Décarie
Montréal, QC H4A 3J7 Canada
514-482-9366
Fax: 514-482-2933
MICR: 815-30226
Caisse populaire Desjardins de Notre-Dame-du-Laus
PO Box 130
104, rue Principale
Notre-Dame-du-Laus, QC J0X 2M0 Canada
819-767-2257
Fax: 819-767-2102
MICR: 815-30269
Caisse populaire Desjardins de Pentecôte
PO Box 68
4359, rte Jacques-Cartier
Rivière-Pentecôte, QC G0H 1R0 Canada
418-799-2277
Fax: 418-799-2355
MICR: 815-20399
Caisse populaire Desjardins de Petit-Saguenay
PO Box 69
61, rue Dumas
Petit-Saguenay, QC G0V 1N0 Canada
418-272-2066
Fax: 418-272-2471
MICR: 815-70050
Caisse populaire Desjardins de Pintendre
730, rte du Président-Kennedy
Pintendre, QC G6C 1E2 Canada
418-837-0268
Fax: 418-833-4562
MICR: 815-20371
Caisse populaire Desjardins de Pohénégamook
1034, rue Principale
Pohenegamook, QC G0L 1J0 Canada
418-859-2691
Fax: 418-859-2430
MICR: 815-60056
Caisse populaire Desjardins de Pointe-aux-Trembles
13120, rue Sherbrooke est
Montréal, QC H1A 3W2 Canada
514-640-5200
Fax: 514-640-5156
MICR: 815-30209
Caisse populaire Desjardins de Pointe-Bleue
1838, rue Ouiatchouan
Mashteuiatsh, QC G0W 2H0 Canada
418-275-0655
Fax: 418-275-0519
MICR: 815-70075
Caisse populaire Desjardins de Pont-Rouge
10, rue de la Fabrique
Pont-Rouge, QC G3H 3J6 Canada
418-873-2531
Fax: 418-873-3572
MICR: 815-20139
Caisse populaire Desjardins de Port-Cartier
Les Galeries des Iles
8, boul des Iles
Port-Cartier, QC G5B 2J4 Canada
418-766-3032
Fax: 418-766-5745
MICR: 815-20378
Caisse populaire Desjardins de Québec
550, rue Saint-Jean
Québec, QC G1R 1P6 Canada
418-522-6806
Fax: 418-522-2365
MICR: 815-20031
Caisse populaire Desjardins de Repentigny
477, rue Notre-Dame
Repentigny, QC J6A 2T6 Canada
450-585-5555
Fax: 450-585-9980
MICR: 815-30514
Caisse populaire Desjardins de Richelieu - St-Mathias
1111, 3e rue
Richelieu, QC J3L 3Z2 Canada
450-658-0649
Fax: 450-658-9824
MICR: 815-90065
Caisse populaire Desjardins de Rivière-du-Loup
298, boul Thériault
Rivière-du-Loup, QC G5R 4C2 Canada
418-862-7255
Fax: 418-862-7292
MICR: 815-20135
Caisse populaire Desjardins de Rivière-Portneuf
PO Box 68
292, rue Principale
Portneuf-sur-Mer, QC G0T 1P0 Canada
418-238-2088
Fax: 418-238-5318
MICR: 815-20459
Caisse populaire Desjardins de Rivière-Rouge
550, rue Principale nord
L'Annonciation, QC J0T 1T0 Canada
819-275-2472
Fax: 819-275-3268
MICR: 815-30326
Caisse populaire Desjardins de Rivière-Éternité
416, rue Principale
Rivière-Éternite, QC G0V 1P0 Canada
418-272-2447
Fax: 418-272-3357
MICR: 815-70065
Caisse populaire Desjardins de Rosemont
2597, rue Beaubien est
Montréal, QC H1Y 1G4 Canada
514-728-4531
Fax: 514-728-2719
MICR: 815-30140
Caisse populaire Desjardins de Royal-Roussillon
11, 7e av ouest
Macamic, QC J0Z 2S0 Canada
819-782-4676
Fax: 819-782-4332
MICR: 815-80006
Caisse populaire Desjardins de Saint-Césaire
1201 av St-Paul
Saint-Césaire, QC J0L 1T0 Canada
514-469-4913
Fax: 514-469-3838
MICR: 815-90032
Caisse populaire Desjardins de Saint-Damase
111, rue Principale
Saint-Damase, QC J0H 1J0 Canada
450-797-3353
Fax: 450-797-3519
MICR: 815-90010
Caisse populaire Desjardins de Saint-Eustache/Deux-Montagnes
575, boul Arthur-Sauvé
Saint-Eustache, QC J7P 4X5 Canada
450-473-6875
Fax: 450-473-1343
MICR: 815-30511
Caisse populaire Desjardins de Saint-Jean-sur-Richelieu
75, rue St-Jacques
St-Jean-sur-Richelieu, QC J3B 2J8 Canada
450-347-5553
Fax: 450-347-8201
MICR: 815-30290
Caisse populaire Desjardins de Saint-Jérôme
100, Place du Curé-Labelle
Saint-Jérome, QC J7Z 1Z6 Canada
450-436-5335
Fax: 450-436-8455
MICR: 815-30023
Caisse populaire Desjardins de Saint-Laurent
1460, rue de l'Église
Montréal, QC H4L 2H6 Canada
514-748-8821
Fax: 514-748-7893
MICR: 815-30202
Caisse populaire Desjardins de Saint-Martin
140, 1re av est
Saint-Martin, QC G0M 1B0 Canada
418-382-5391
Fax: 418-382-3422
MICR: 815-20003
Caisse populaire Desjardins de Saint-Michel
8127, boul St-Michel
Montréal, QC H1Z 3E3 Canada
514-725-2275
Fax: 514-725-9160
MICR: 815-30211
Caisse populaire Desjardins de Saint-Moïse et de Saint-Noël
PO Box 43
104, rue Principale
Saint-Moïse, QC G0J 2Z0 Canada
418-776-2187
Fax: 418-776-2485
MICR: 815-60057
Caisse populaire Desjardins de Saint-Pascal
PO Box 176
#620, 12, rue Taché
Saint-Pascal, QC G0L 3Y0 Canada
418-492-2509
Fax: 418-492-9044
MICR: 815-20119
Caisse populaire Desjardins de Saint-Prime
589, rue Principale
Saint-Prime, QC G8J 1S9 Canada
418-251-2212
Fax: 418-251-2966
MICR: 815-70023
Caisse populaire Desjardins de Sainte-Agathe-des-Monts
77, rue Principale est
Sainte-Agathe-des-Monts, QC J8C 1J5 Canada
819-326-2883
Fax: 819-326-8500
MICR: 815-30190
Caisse populaire Desjardins de Sainte-Jeanne-d'Arc-de-Roberval
385, rue François-Bilodeau
Boulanger, QC G0W 1E0 Canada
418-276-2556
Fax: 418-276-2582
MICR: 815-70030
Caisse populaire Desjardins de Sayabec
PO Box 100
2, rue St-Arthur
Sayabec, QC G0J 3K0 Canada
418-536-5415
Fax: 418-536-3479
MICR: 815-60022
Caisse populaire Desjardins de Sept-×les
760, boul Laure
Sept-×les, QC G4R 1Y4 Canada
418-962-9448
Fax: 418-968-2305
MICR: 815-20335
Caisse populaire Desjardins de St-Agapit - St-Gilles
PO Box 220
1076, av Bergeron
Saint-Agapit, QC G0S 1Z0 Canada
418-888-3902
Fax: 418-888-3072
MICR: 815-20115
Caisse populaire Desjardins de St-Alexandre
PO Box 67
487, av de l'École
Saint-Alexandre-de-Kamouras, QC G0L 2G0 Canada
418-495-2420
Fax: 418-495-2041
MICR: 815-20172
Caisse populaire Desjardins de St-Antonin
1, rue Jean
Saint-Antonin, QC G0L 2J0 Canada
418-862-3793
Fax: 418-862-4524
MICR: 815-20004
Caisse populaire Desjardins de St-Apollinaire et de Tilly
11, rue Industrielle
Saint-Apollinaire, QC G0S 2E0 Canada
418-881-3949
Fax: 418-881-2874
MICR: 815-20253
Caisse populaire Desjardins de St-Augustin Dalmas
742, rue Principale
Dalmas, QC G0W 1K0 Canada
418-374-2161
Fax: 418-374-2628
MICR: 815-70031
Caisse populaire Desjardins de St-Augustin-de-Desmaures
330, rte 138
Saint-Augustin-de-Desmaures, QC G3A 1G8 Canada

418-878-2180
Fax: 418-878-4907
MICR: 815-20089

Caisse populaire Desjardins de St-Basile
310, rue de l'Église
Saint-Basile, QC G0A 3G0 Canada
418-329-2822
Fax: 418-329-2810
MICR: 815-20203

Caisse populaire Desjardins de St-Bernard
PO Box 28
1497, rue St-Georges
Saint-Bernard, QC G0S 2G0 Canada
418-475-6651
Fax: 418-475-4118
MICR: 815-20181

Caisse populaire Desjardins de St-Camille
87, rue Desrivières
Saint-Camille, QC J0A 1G0 Canada
819-828-2590
Fax: 819-828-3578
MICR: 815-50025

Caisse populaire Desjardins de St-Cyprien
PO Box 117
126, rue Principale
Saint-Cyprien, QC G0L 2P0 Canada
418-963-3223
Fax: 418-963-6340
MICR: 815-60054

Caisse populaire Desjardins de St-Dominique
1165, av Bourlamaque
Québec, QC G1R 2P9 Canada
418-529-9204
Fax: 418-529-7164
MICR: 815-20246

Caisse populaire Desjardins de St-Eugène-d'Argentenay
PO Box 100
493, rue Principale
Saint-Eugène-d'Argentenay, QC G0W 1B0 Canada
418-276-0045
Fax: 418-276-7547
MICR: 815-70034

Caisse populaire Desjardins de St-Fabien
PO Box 308
20, 7e av
Saint-Fabien, QC G0L 2Z0 Canada
418-869-2112
Fax: 418-869-3404
MICR: 815-60049

Caisse populaire Desjardins de St-Félicien - La Doré
PO Box 6
1297, boul Sacré-Coeur
St-Félicien, QC G8K 2P8 Canada
418-679-1381
Fax: 418-679-9329
MICR: 815-70006

Caisse populaire Desjardins de St-Félix-de-Valois
4950, rue Principale
Saint-Félix-de-Valois, QC J0K 2M0 Canada
450-889-8321
Fax: 450-889-8517
MICR: 815-00015

Caisse populaire Desjardins de St-Jean-de-Matha
75, rue Lessard
Saint-Jean-de-Matha, QC J0K 2S0 Canada
450-886-9311
Fax: 418-886-5195
MICR: 815-00040

Caisse populaire Desjardins de St-Juste-du-Lac
PO Box 10
26, ch Principal
Saint-Juste-du-Lac, QC G0L 3R0 Canada
418-899-6617
Fax: 418-899-0123
MICR: 815-60085

Caisse populaire Desjardins de St-Nicolas
815, rte Marie-Victorin
Saint-Nicolas, QC G7A 3S6 Canada
418-831-9103
Fax: 418-831-8883
MICR: 815-20310

Caisse populaire Desjardins de St-Pie-de-Bagot
65, rue St-François
Saint-Pie, QC J0H 1W0 Canada
450-772-2454
Fax: 450-772-5023
MICR: 815-90037

Caisse populaire Desjardins de St-Raymond
225, av St-Maxime
Saint-Raymond, QC G3L 3W2 Canada
418-337-2218
Fax: 418-337-6270
MICR: 815-20116

Caisse populaire Desjardins de St-Roch-de-l'Achigan
PO Box 270
40, rue Dr. Wilfrid Locat nord
Saint-Roch-de-l'Achigan, QC J0K 3H0 Canada
450-588-2513
Fax: 450-588-6537
MICR: 815-00006

Caisse populaire Desjardins de St-Rédempteur
PO Box 1960
103, 16e rue
St-Rédempteur, QC G6K 1N7 Canada
418-831-2674
Fax: 418-831-4625
MICR: 815-20037

Caisse populaire Desjardins de St-Séverin
900, rue des Lacs
Saint-Séverin-de-Beauce, QC G0N 1V0 Canada
418-426-2221
Fax: 418-426-2820
MICR: 815-20077

Caisse populaire Desjardins de St-Valérien
PO Box 40
35, rue Principale
Saint-Valérien-de-Rimouski, QC G0L 4E0 Canada
418-736-4862
Fax: 418-736-5861
MICR: 815-60012

Caisse populaire Desjardins de St-Éloi
PO Box 2
280, rue Principale
Saint-Éloi, QC G0L 2V0 Canada
418-898-2252
Fax: 418-898-3952
MICR: 815-60002

Caisse populaire Desjardins de Stanstead
484, rue Dufferin
Stanstead, QC J0B 3E0 Canada
819-876-7551
Fax: 819-876-5663
MICR: 815-50044

Caisse populaire Desjardins de Ste-Anne du Lac
14, rue St-François-Xavier
Sainte-Anne-du-Lac, QC J0W 1V0 Canada
819-586-2755
Fax: 819-586-2277
MICR: 815-30230

Caisse populaire Desjardins de Ste-Catherine-de-Hatley
25, ch de la Montagne
Sainte-Catherine-de-Hatley, QC J0B 1W0 Canada
819-843-5993
Fax: 819-843-1110
MICR: 815-50023

Caisse populaire Desjardins de Ste-Hénédine-Ste-Marguerite
PO Box 39
79, rue Langevin
Sainte-Hénédine, QC G0S 2R0 Canada
418-935-3536
Fax: 418-935-3039
MICR: 815-20110

Caisse populaire Desjardins de Ste-Julienne
2590, rue Yvan-Varin
Sainte-Julienne, QC J0K 2T0 Canada
450-831-2711
Fax: 450-831-4232
MICR: 815-00035

Caisse populaire Desjardins de Ste-Louise
PO Box 2094
537, rue Principale
Sainte-Louise, QC G0R 3K0 Canada
418-354-2595
Fax: 418-354-2111
MICR: 815-20286

Caisse populaire Desjardins de Ste-Luce - Luceville
60, rue St-Laurent
Sainte-Luce, QC G0K 1P0 Canada
418-739-4141
Fax: 418-739-4102
MICR: 815-60080

Caisse populaire Desjardins de Ste-Rosalie (Bagot)
4880, rue des Seigneurs est
Saint-Hyacinthe, QC J2R 1Z5 Canada
450-799-3205
Fax: 450-799-2232
MICR: 815-90029

Caisse populaire Desjardins de Ste-Thècle - St-Adelphe
250, rue Masson
Sainte-Thècle, QC G0X 3G0 Canada
418-289-2972
Fax: 418-289-2314
MICR: 815-10076

Caisse populaire Desjardins de Thetford-Mines
PO Box 819
375, rue Labbé
Thetford Mines, QC G6G 5V3 Canada
418-338-3591
Fax: 418-334-1330
MICR: 815-20008

Caisse populaire Desjardins de Trois-Saumons
PO Box 458
8, av de Gaspé est
Saint-Jean-Port-Joli, QC G0R 3G0 Canada
418-598-3026
Fax: 418-598-1393
MICR: 815-20124

Caisse populaire Desjardins de Témiscaming
PO Box 1025
467, rue Kipawa
Témiscaming, QC J0Z 3R0 Canada
819-627-3396
Fax: 819-627-3965
MICR: 815-30486

Caisse populaire Desjardins de Tête-à-la Baleine
PO Box 9
Tête-à-la-Baleine, QC G0G 2W0 Canada
418-242-2061
Fax: 418-242-2921
MICR: 815-20425

Caisse populaire Desjardins de Université Laval
Pavillon Alphonse-Desjardins, Cité universitaire
Québec, QC G1K 7P4 Canada
418-656-2358
Fax: 418-656-0224
MICR: 815-20439

Caisse populaire Desjardins de Vallée-Jonction
PO Box 96
325, rue Principale
Vallée-Jonction, QC G0S 3J0 Canada
418-253-5493
Fax: 418-253-5170
MICR: 815-20076

Caisse populaire Desjardins de Varennes
#100, 50, rue de La Gabelle
Varennes, QC J3X 2J4 Canada
450-652-0607
Fax: 450-652-4148
MICR: 815-30229

Caisse populaire Desjardins de Verdun
5035, rue de Verdun
Montréal, QC H4G 1N5 Canada
514-766-8591
Fax: 514-766-8407
MICR: 815-30240

Caisse populaire Desjardins de Verdun
5035, rue de Verdun
Montréal, QC H4G 1N5 Canada
514-766-8591
Fax: 514-766-8407
MICR: 815-30240

Caisse populaire Desjardins de Viger
PO Box 7
10, rue Taché ouest
Saint-Hubert-Rivière-du-Lou, QC G0L 3L0 Canada
418-497-3901
Fax: 418-497-2844
MICR: 815-60055

Caisse populaire Desjardins de Villeray
8164, rue St-Hubert
Montréal, QC H2P 1Z2 Canada
514-270-7221
Fax: 514-270-8857

Fédération des caisses Desjardins du Québec (continued)
MICR: 815-30370
Caisse populaire Desjardins de Vimont-Auteuil
1890, boul des Laurentides
Vimont, QC H7M 2P9 Canada
450-669-2694
Fax: 450-669-5699
MICR: 815-30512
Caisse populaire Desjardins de Waswanipi
5, rte 113
Waswanipi, QC J0Y 3C0 Canada
819-753-2576
Fax: 819-723-2665
MICR: 815-80056
Caisse populaire Desjardins de Weedon
225, 2e av
Weedon, QC J0B 3J0 Canada
819-877-2155
Fax: 819-877-2557
MICR: 815-50034
Caisse populaire Desjardins de Windsor
77, rue St-Georges
Windsor, QC J1S 2K5 Canada
819-845-2707
Fax: 819-845-4811
MICR: 815-50119
Caisse populaire Desjardins des Abénakis
159, boul Bégin
Sainte-Claire, QC G0R 2V0 Canada
418-883-3373
Fax: 418-883-3487
MICR: 815-20021
Caisse populaire Desjardins des Affluents
9009, boul du Centre-Hospitalier
Charny, QC G6X 1L4 Canada
418-839-8819
Fax: 418-832-7923
MICR: 815-20202
Caisse populaire Desjardins des Cascades
PO Box 21026
1105, rue Frigon
Shawinigan, QC G9N 8M7 Canada
819-539-6923
Fax: 819-539-8674
MICR: 815-10056
Caisse populaire Desjardins des Champs et des bois
PO Box 9
700, rue du Couvent
Sainte-Hélène-de-Kamouraska, QC G0L 3J0 Canada
418-492-6415
Fax: 418-492-1186
MICR: 815-20047
Caisse populaire Desjardins des Cinq-Cantons
PO Box 340
535, rue St-Alphonse
Saint-Bruno, QC G0W 2L0 Canada
418-343-3403
Fax: 418-343-2819
MICR: 815-70016
Caisse populaire Desjardins des Deux Rives
PO Box 40
17, rue Ste-Anne
Sainte-Perpétue, QC J0C 1R0 Canada
819-336-6101
Fax: 819-336-6860
MICR: 815-10048
Caisse populaire Desjardins des Frontières
PO Box 117
24, rue de l'Église nord
Rivière-Bleue, QC G0L 2B0 Canada
418-893-7203
Fax: 418-893-7138
MICR: 815-60025
Caisse populaire Desjardins des Grandes-Seigneuries
PO Box 399
373, rue St-Jacques
Napierville, QC J0J 1L0 Canada
450-245-3391
Fax: 450-245-0213
MICR: 815-30368
Caisse populaire Desjardins des Hautes-Terres (L'Islet)
#100, 366, rue Principale sud
Sainte-Perpétue-de-l'Islet, QC G0R 3Z0 Canada
418-359-2226
Fax: 418-359-3524
MICR: 815-20313
Caisse populaire Desjardins des Hauts-Boisés
50, rue Bibeau
Cookshire, QC J0B 1M0 Canada
819-875-3325
Fax: 819-875-5657
MICR: 815-50045
Caisse populaire Desjardins des Hauts-Phares
PO Box 250
54, montée Morris
Gaspé, QC G4X 5M6 Canada
418-269-3305
Fax: 418-269-3445
MICR: 815-40028
Caisse populaire Desjardins des Horizons
PO Box 330
560, rue St-Jean
Wotton, QC J0A 1N0 Canada
819-828-2626
Fax: 819-828-2698
MICR: 815-50032
Caisse populaire Desjardins des Laurentides
1395, av de la Rivière-Javne
Québec, QC G2N 1R9 Canada
418-849-4425
Fax: 418-849-3973
877-866-3426
MICR: 815-20315
Caisse populaire Desjardins des Mille-Iles
4433, boul de la Concorde est
Laval, QC H7C 1M4 Canada
450-661-7274
Fax: 450-661-7855
MICR: 815-30469
Caisse populaire Desjardins des Moissons
810, rue Notre-Dame
Saint-Rémi, QC J0L 2L0 Canada
450-454-4645
Fax: 450-454-6474
MICR: 815-30026
Caisse populaire Desjardins des Monts de Bellechasse
PO Box 40
2, rue du Plateau
Armagh, QC G0R 1A0 Canada
418-466-2124
Fax: 418-466-3021
MICR: 815-20082
Caisse populaire Desjardins des Moulins et du Vieux-Nord
122, rue St-Lambert
Sherbrooke, QC J1C 0N8 Canada
819-846-2766
Fax: 819-846-3241
MICR: 815-50061
Caisse populaire Desjardins des Pays-d'en-Haut
893, boul Sainte-Adèle
Sainte-Adèle, QC J8B 2N1 Canada
450-229-2901
Fax: 450-229-2902
MICR: 815-30020
Caisse populaire Desjardins des Plaines boréales
1032, rue St-Cyrille
Normandin, QC G8M 4H5 Canada
418-274-2916
Fax: 418-274-7031
MICR: 815-70061
Caisse populaire Desjardins des Quatre-Vents
104, av Louisbourg
Bonaventure, QC G0C 1E0 Canada
418-534-2001
Fax: 418-534-4229
MICR: 815-40002
Caisse populaire Desjardins des Ramées
1278, ch de La Vernière
L'Étang-du-Nord, QC G4T 3E6 Canada
418-986-2319
Fax: 418-986-5883
MICR: 815-40026
Caisse populaire Desjardins des Seigneuries de Soulanges
20, rue Principale
Coteau-du-Lac, QC J0P 1B0 Canada
450-763-5500
Fax: 450-763-0937
MICR: 815-30439
Caisse populaire Desjardins des Sept-Chutes
PO Box 180
1611, rue Principale
Saint-Côme, QC J0K 2B0 Canada
450-883-2252
Fax: 450-883-0574
MICR: 815-00004
Caisse populaire Desjardins des Trois-Lacs
415, rue Principale
Dégelis, QC G5T 1L4 Canada
418-853-2110
Fax: 418-853-3823
MICR: 815-60061
Caisse populaire Desjardins des Trois-Vallées
206, rue Principale
Huberdeau, QC J0T 1G0 Canada
819-687-3312
Fax: 819-687-8294
MICR: 815-30224
Caisse populaire Desjardins des Versants du Mont-Comi
PO Box 10
24, rue Principale est
Saint-Anaclet, QC G0K 1H0 Canada
418-723-6798
Fax: 418-725-4850
MICR: 815-60029
Caisse populaire Desjardins des Verts-Sommets de l'Estrie
PO Box 140
155, rue Child
Coaticook, QC J1A 2S9 Canada
819-849-9822
Fax: 819-849-6500
MICR: 815-50007
Caisse populaire Desjardins Domaine St-Sulpice
8955, av André-Grasset
Montréal, QC H2M 2E9 Canada
514-381-9323
Fax: 514-381-2674
MICR: 815-30453
Caisse populaire Desjardins du Bas-Saint-François
PO Box 6
191, rue Léveillée
Saint-François-du-Lac, QC J0G 1M0 Canada
450-568-3108
Fax: 450-568-0168
MICR: 815-10142
Caisse populaire Desjardins du Bassin-de-Chambly
455, boul Brassard
Chambly, QC J3L 4V6 Canada
450-658-0691
Fax: 450-658-9089
MICR: 815-30168
Caisse populaire Desjardins du Bic
157, rue Ste-Cécile
Le Bic, QC G0L 1B0 Canada
418-736-4373
Fax: 418-736-5419
MICR: 815-60001
Caisse populaire Desjardins du Canton d'Aston
501, rue Beaudoin
Saint-Léonard-d'Aston, QC J0C 1M0 Canada
819-399-2000
Fax: 819-399-2006
MICR: 815-10031
Caisse populaire Desjardins du Centre d'Ahuntsic
1050, rue Fleury est
Montréal, QC H2C 1P7 Canada
514-388-3434
Fax: 514-383-0596
MICR: 815-30166
Caisse populaire Desjardins du Centre de Bellechasse
87, rue Principale
Saint-Raphaël, QC G0R 4C0 Canada
418-243-2066
Fax: 418-243-2828
MICR: 815-20247
Caisse populaire Desjardins du Centre de la Nouvelle-Beauce
275, av Marguerite-Bourgeoys
Sainte-Marie, QC G6E 3Y9 Canada
418-387-5456
Fax: 418-387-8498
MICR: 815-20106
Caisse populaire Desjardins du Centre-sud Gaspésien
PO Box 1387
163, rue Commerciale ouest
Chandler, QC G0C 1K0 Canada

418-689-3351
Fax: 418-689-4531
MICR: 815-40023

Caisse populaire Desjardins du Centre-Ville de Québec
135, rue Saint-Vallier ouest
Québec, QC G1K 1J9 Canada
418-687-2810
Fax: 418-529-6704
MICR: 815-20100

Caisse populaire Desjardins du Christ-Roi (Joliette)
PO Box 484
100, rue Juge Guibault
Saint-Charles-Borromée, QC J6E 3Z9 Canada
450-759-0165
Fax: 450-759-6883
MICR: 815-00014

Caisse populaire Desjardins du Coeur-des-vallées
PO Box 589
63, ch Montréal est
Gatineau, QC J8M 1K7 Canada
819-986-3364
Fax: 819-986-1906
MICR: 815-30430

Caisse populaire Desjardins du Collège de Lévis
9, rue Mgr-Gosselin
Lévis, QC G6V 5K1 Canada
418-837-2648
Fax: 418-837-7592
MICR: 815-20312

Caisse populaire Desjardins du Fleurdelisé
129, rue Yamaska
Saint-Denis-sur-Richelieu, QC J0H 1K0 Canada
450-787-3026
Fax: 450-787-2822
563
MICR: 815-90007

Caisse populaire Desjardins du Granit
PO Box 40
201, rue Principale
Lambton, QC G0M 1H0 Canada
418-486-3000
Fax: 418-486-3001
MICR: 815-20237

Caisse populaire Desjardins du Haut-Pays de la Neigette
674, rte des Pionniers
Rimouski, QC G5N 5P3 Canada
418-735-2074
Fax: 418-735-2543
MICR: 815-60020

Caisse populaire Desjardins du Lac-Aylmer
572, av Jacques-Cartier
Disraéli, QC G0N 1E0 Canada
418-449-2652
Fax: 418-449-2097
MICR: 815-50098

Caisse populaire Desjardins du Littoral de Bellechasse
PO Box 68
76, rue Principale
Saint-Michel-de-Bellechasse, QC G0R 3S0 Canada
418-884-3101
Fax: 428-884-2867
MICR: 815-20144

Caisse populaire Desjardins du Littoral gaspésien
PO Box 428
73, rue Grande-Allée est
Grande-Rivière, QC G0C 1V0 Canada
418-385-2247
Fax: 418-385-2257
MICR: 815-40029

Caisse populaire Desjardins du Mont-Bellevue de Sherbrooke
1100, rue Galt ouest
Sherbrooke, QC J1H 2A4 Canada
819-566-4363
Fax: 819-566-6550
MICR: 815-50012

Caisse populaire Desjardins du Mont-Royal
435, av du Mont-Royal est
Montréal, QC H2J 1W2 Canada
514-288-5249
Fax: 514-288-7536
MICR: 815-30197

Caisse populaire Desjardins du Moulin des Mères
PO Box 89009, Saint-Émilie Sta. Saint-Émilie
1680, av Lapierre
Québec, QC G3E 1S9 Canada
418-842-1214
Fax: 418-842-1259
MICR: 815-20463

Caisse populaire Desjardins du Nord de la Beauce
PO Box 70
106, rte du Vieux Moulin
St-Isidore, QC G0S 2S0 Canada
418-882-5678
Fax: 418-882-5637
MICR: 815-20070

Caisse populaire Desjardins du Nord de Laval
396, boul Curé-Labelle
Laval, QC H7L 4T7 Canada
450-622-8130
Fax: 450-628-1065
MICR: 815-30339

Caisse populaire Desjardins du Nord du Lac-Abitibi
PO Box 330
59, rue Principale
Dupuy, QC J0Z 1X0 Canada
819-783-2488
Fax: 819-783-3013
MICR: 815-80019

Caisse populaire Desjardins du Nord-Ouest du Témiscamingue
PO Box 128
24, rue Ontario
Notre-Dame-du-Nord, QC J0Z 3B0 Canada
819-723-2265
Fax: 819-723-2558
MICR: 815-30043

Caisse populaire Desjardins Du Parc et Villeray
PO Box 127
91, rue St-Jean Baptiste
L'Isle-Verte, QC G0L 1K0 Canada
418-898-2061
Fax: 418-898-2039
MICR: 815-60019

Caisse populaire Desjardins du Parc régional des Appalaches
PO Box 148
305, 4e av
Saint-Paul-de-Montminy, QC G0R 3Y0 Canada
418-469-2733
Fax: 418-469-2747
MICR: 815-20438

Caisse populaire Desjardins du Passage
405, boul Thibeau
Trois-Rivières, QC G8T 6Y6 Canada
819-376-4447
Fax: 819-376-7705
MICR: 815-10137

Caisse populaire Desjardins du Petit-Pré
7973, av Royale
Château-Richer, QC G0A 1N0 Canada
418-822-1818
Fax: 418-824-3443
MICR: 815-20185

Caisse populaire Desjardins du Piémont Laurentien
1638, rue Notre-Dame
L'Ancienne-Lorette, QC G2E 3B6 Canada
418-872-1445
Fax: 418-872-1435
MICR: 815-20088

Caisse populaire Desjardins du Plateau des Appalaches
PO Box 340
2880, 25e av
Saint-Prosper-de-Dorchester, QC G0M 1Y0 Canada
418-594-8227
Fax: 418-594-8840
MICR: 815-20006

Caisse populaire Desjardins du Portage
234, rue Gauvin
Saint-Louis-du-Ha-Ha, QC G0L 3S0 Canada
418-854-2434
Fax: 418-854-0739
MICR: 815-60106

Caisse populaire Desjardins du Rivage et des Monts
PO Box 483
248, rue Thibault
Matane, QC G4W 3P5 Canada
418-562-3674
Fax: 418-562-7467
MICR: 815-60124

Caisse populaire Desjardins du Royaume de l'érable
9, rte 271 sud
Saint-Éphrem-de-Beauce, QC G0M 1R0 Canada
418-484-2804
Fax: 418-484-2302
MICR: 815-20090

Caisse populaire Desjardins du Saguenay-St-Laurent
PO Box 159
11, rue Sirois
Les Escoumins, QC G0T 1K0 Canada
418-233-2965
Fax: 418-233-2669
MICR: 815-20420

Caisse populaire Desjardins du Sud de l'Etchemin
223, 2e av
Lac-Etchemin, QC G0R 1S0 Canada
418-625-3739
Fax: 418-625-3743
MICR: 815-20017

Caisse populaire Desjardins du Sud de l'Islet
112, rue Principale nord
Saint-Pamphile, QC G0R 3X0 Canada
418-356-3336
Fax: 418-356-2140
MICR: 815-20325

Caisse populaire Desjardins du Suro(140t-Sud
8, rue Prince
Huntingdon, QC J0S 1H0 Canada
450-264-5371
Fax: 450-264-6543
MICR: 815-30426

Caisse populaire Desjardins du Terroir basque
PO Box 279
71, rue Principale nord
Saint-Jean-de-Dieu, QC G0L 3M0 Canada
418-963-2716
Fax: 418-963-6890
MICR: 815-60028

Caisse populaire Desjardins du Vallon
2615, boul Masson
Québec, QC G1P 1J5 Canada
418-871-8301
Fax: 418-871-1690
MICR: 815-20359

Caisse populaire Desjardins du Village Huron
155, rue Aimé-Romain
Wendake, QC G0A 4V0 Canada
418-843-0242
Fax: 418-843-8087
MICR: 815-20464

Caisse populaire Desjardins Dusablé
665, rue York
Saint-Barthélémy, QC J0K 1X0 Canada
450-885-3161
Fax: 450-885-3276
MICR: 815-00037

Caisse populaire Desjardins Est du Haut-Saint-Laurent
PO Box 28
12, rue Bridge
Ormstown, QC J0S 1K0 Canada
450-825-2255
Fax: 450-829-2766
MICR: 815-30375

Caisse populaire Desjardins Ferme-Neuve
155, 12e rue
Ferme-Neuve, QC J0W 1C0 Canada
819-587-3123
Fax: 819-587-7002
MICR: 815-30161

Caisse populaire Desjardins Gracefield
PO Box 99
32, rue Principale
Gracefield, QC J0X 1W0 Canada
819-463-2849
Fax: 819-463-4538
MICR: 815-30177

Caisse populaire Desjardins Immaculée-Conception
1685, rue Rachel est
Montréal, QC H2J 2K6 Canada
514-524-3551
Fax: 514-524-8758
MICR: 815-30504

Caisse populaire Desjardins l'Ouest de Laval
440, autoroute Chomedey
Laval, QC H7X 3S9 Canada
450-962-1800
Fax: 450-689-1532
MICR: 815-30419

Fédération des caisses Desjardins du Québec (continued)

Caisse populaire Desjardins La porte des Anciens-Maires
5325, boul Laurier ouest
Saint-Hyacinthe, QC J2S 3V6 Canada
450-773-5015
Fax: 450-773-4307
MICR: 815-90068

Caisse populaire Desjardins La Sablière
132, boul Antonio Barrette
Notre-Dame-des-Prairies, QC J6E 1E5 Canada
450-756-8061
Fax: 450-756-2144
MICR: 815-00048

Caisse populaire Desjardins Le Manoir
820, Montée Masson
Mascouche, QC J7K 3B6 Canada
450-474-2474
Fax: 450-474-5774
MICR: 815-00028

Caisse populaire Desjardins Mer et montagnes
PO Box 38
2, rue du Couvent
Grande-Vallée, QC G0E 1K0 Canada
418-393-2100
Fax: 418-393-2532
MICR: 815-40015

Caisse populaire Desjardins Mont-Rose-Saint-Michel
4565, rue Jean-Talon est
Montréal, QC H1S 3H6 Canada
514-725-5050
Fax: 513-725-8643
MICR: 815-30261

Caisse populaire Desjardins Mont-Ste-Anne
9751, boul Ste-Anne
Sainte-Anne-de-Beaupré, QC G0A 3C0 Canada
418-827-3768
Fax: 418-827-8571
MICR: 815-20194

Caisse populaire Desjardins Morilac
1120, av des Cascades
Valcourt, QC J0E 2L0 Canada
450-532-3112
Fax: 450-532-3128
MICR: 815-50020

Caisse populaire Desjardins Nicolas-Juchereau
PO Box 249
11, rue Desjardins
Mont-Carmel, QC G0L 1W0 Canada
418-498-3184
Fax: 418-498-3389
MICR: 815-20005

Caisse populaire Desjardins Pierre-Boucher
2401, boul Roland-Therrien
Longueuil, QC J4N 1C5 Canada
450-468-7411
Fax: 450-468-1509
MICR: 815-30446

Caisse populaire Desjardins Pierre-De Saurel
PO Box 39
93, rue du Prince
Sorel-Tracy, QC J3P 5N6 Canada
450-746-7000
Fax: 450-746-5636
MICR: 815-90016

Caisse populaire Desjardins Pointe-Platon de Lotbinière
6276, rue Principale
Sainte-Croix, QC G0S 2H0 Canada
418-926-3240
Fax: 418-926-3105
MICR: 815-20096

Caisse populaire Desjardins Provost de Lachine
910, rue Provost
Montréal, QC H8S 1M9 Canada
514-634-8954
Fax: 514-634-8416
MICR: 815-30323

Caisse populaire Desjardins Préfontaine-Hochelaga
3211, rue Rachel est
Montréal, QC H1W 1A3 Canada
514-521-2102
Fax: 514-256-8151
MICR: 815-30529

Caisse populaire Desjardins Saint-Donat de Montcalm
470, rue Principale
Saint-Donat-de-Montcalm, QC J0T 2C0 Canada
819-424-2563
Fax: 819-424-1443
MICR: 815-00050

Caisse populaire Desjardins Saint-Donat de Montréal
6406, rue Sherbrooke est
Montréal, QC H1N 3P6 Canada
514-259-6931
Fax: 514-255-1688
MICR: 815-30395

Caisse populaire Desjardins Saint-Faustin
630, rue Principale
Saint-Faustin-Lac-Carré, QC J0T 1J3 Canada
819-688-2739
Fax: 819-688-6797
MICR: 815-30235

Caisse populaire Desjardins Saint-Jean-de-la-Croix
170, rue St-Zotique est
Montréal, QC H2S 1K8 Canada
514-273-4431
Fax: 514-273-2560
MICR: 815-30530

Caisse populaire Desjardins Sainte-Geneviève de Pierrefonds
15000, boul Pierrefonds
Montréal, QC H9H 4G2 Canada
514-620-3000
Fax: 514-620-9373
MICR: 815-30388

Caisse populaire Desjardins Sainte-Scholastique
9975, rue St-Vincent
Mirabel, QC J7N 2Y3 Canada
450-258-2401
Fax: 450-258-4149
MICR: 815-30510

Caisse populaire Desjardins Sieur-d'Iberville
730, boul Iberville
St-Jean-sur-Richelieu, QC J2X 3Z9 Canada
450-357-5000
Fax: 450-357-5067
MICR: 815-90042

Caisse populaire Desjardins Sieur-de-Roberval
841, boul St-Joseph
Roberval, QC G8H 2L6 Canada
418-275-0182
Fax: 418-275-5160
MICR: 815-70004

Caisse populaire Desjardins St-Adolphe de Dudswell
189, rue Principale
Marbleton, QC J0B 2L0 Canada
819-887-6824
Fax: 819-887-6855
MICR: 815-50054

Caisse populaire Desjardins St-Albert
1245, rue Principale
Saint-Albert, QC J0A 1E0 Canada
819-353-3400
Fax: 819-353-3419
MICR: 815-10093

Caisse populaire Desjardins St-Camille - St-Just - St-Magloire
PO Box 190
124, rue Principale
Saint-Camille-de-Bellechass, QC G0R 2S0 Canada
418-595-2994
Fax: 418-595-2190
MICR: 815-20419

Caisse populaire Desjardins St-Simon-Apôtre de Montréal
8940, rue De Reims
Montréal, QC H2N 1T6 Canada
514-388-5303
Fax: 514-388-0443
MICR: 815-30414

Caisse populaire Desjardins St-Victor de Montréal
9540, rue Hochelaga
Montréal, QC H1L 2R2 Canada
514-493-4404
Fax: 514-493-6239
MICR: 815-30338

Caisse populaire Desjardins Terrebonne
513, rue Masson
Terrebonne, QC J6W 2Z2 Canada
450-471-3735
Fax: 450-471-7313
MICR: 815-30321

Caisse populaire Desjardins Ukrainienne de Montréal
3250, rue Beaubien est
Montréal, QC H1X 3C9 Canada
514-727-9456
Fax: 514-727-5886
MICR: 815-30347

Caisse populaire Desjardins Vallée de la Kiamika
100, boul St-François sud
Lac-des-Écorces, QC J0W 1H0 Canada
819-585-2521
Fax: 819-585-3982
MICR: 815-30274

Caisse populaire Desjardins Vallée de la Matapédia
15, rue du Pont
Amqui, QC G5J 2P4 Canada
418-629-2271
Fax: 418-629-1400
MICR: 815-60010

Caisse populaire Dorval-Pointe-Claire
625, ch Bord-du-Lac-Lakeshore
Montréal, QC H9S 2B5 Canada
514-426-1156
Fax: 514-631-9627
MICR: 815-30364

Caisse populaire Kahnawake
Kahnawake Services Complex
PO Box 1987
Kahnawake, QC J0L 1B0 Canada
450-638-5464
Fax: 450-638-3411
MICR: 815-30539

Caisse populaire Kamouraska
PO Box 8
83, av Morel
Kamouraska, QC G0L 1M0 Canada
418-492-2065
Fax: 418-492-5439
MICR: 815-20460

Caisse populaire La Présentation
802, rue Principale
La Présentation, QC J0H 1B0 Canada
450-796-3441
Fax: 450-796-1689
MICR: 815-90025

Caisse populaire La Tuque
341, rue St-Joseph
La Tuque, QC G9X 1L3 Canada
819-523-2791
Fax: 819-523-2972
MICR: 815-10103

Caisse populaire Les Grands Boulevards
1535, boul St-Martin ouest
Laval, QC H7S 1N1 Canada
450-668-4000
Fax: 450-668-7981
MICR: 815-30399

Caisse populaire Longue-Pointe
8025, rue Notre-Dame est
Montréal, QC H1L 3K9 Canada
514-353-4030
Fax: 514-353-9566
MICR: 815-30212

Caisse populaire Place Desjardins
PO Box 244, Desjardins Sta. Desjardins
#5, 100, Promenade
Montréal, QC H5B 1B4 Canada
514-281-7101
Fax: 514-281-6232
MICR: 815-30500

Caisse populaire Riviera
3175, boul de Tracy
Sorel-Tracy, QC J3R 5M7 Canada
450-746-5669
Fax: 450-742-8133
MICR: 815-90076

Caisse populaire Saint-André-Apôtre
223, rue Fleury ouest
Montréal, QC H3L 1T8 Canada
514-384-4912
Fax: 514-384-4411
MICR: 815-30340

Caisse populaire Saint-Camille de Montréal-Nord
5200, rue Charleroi
Montréal, QC H1G 3A1 Canada
514-324-8402
Fax: 514-324-1344
MICR: 815-30473

Caisse populaire Saint-Martin de Laval

4114, boul Saint-Martin ouest
Laval, QC H7T 1C1 Canada
450-688-6940
Fax: 450-688-3100
MICR: 815-30231
Caisse populaire Saint-Stanislas de Montréal
1350, rue Gilford
Montréal, QC H2J 1R7 Canada
514-524-7521
Fax: 514-524-2807
MICR: 815-30012
Caisse populaire St-Ambroise
1250, rue Beaubien est
Montréal, QC H2S 1T9 Canada
514-274-9343
Fax: 514-274-2240
MICR: 815-30145
Caisse populaire St-Hubert de Audet
PO Box 67
238, rue Principale
Audet, QC G0Y 1A0 Canada
819-583-3114
Fax: 819-583-5661
MICR: 815-50041
Caisse populaire St-Joseph-de-Bordeaux
1558, rue Viel
Montréal, QC H3M 1G5 Canada
514-334-1022
Fax: 514-334-8194
MICR: 815-30132
Caisse populaire St-Louis de France
3160, boul Thibeau
Trois-Rivières, QC G8T 1G5 Canada
819-375-4462
Fax: 819-375-2893
MICR: 815-10124
Caisse populaire St-Paul-l'Ermite
#2, 515, boul Lacombe
Le Gardeur, QC J5Z 1P5 Canada
450-585-3240
Fax: 450-585-9368
MICR: 815-30502
Caisse populaire St-Raymond de Hull
53, boul St-Raymond
Gatineau, QC J8Y 1R8 Canada
819-777-2721
Fax: 819-777-6502
MICR: 815-30423
Caisse populaire St-Zacharie
726, 15e rue
Saint-Zacharie, QC G0M 2C0 Canada
418-593-6401
Fax: 418-593-6411
MICR: 815-20015
Caisse populaire Ste-Geneviève
90, rue de l'Église
Sainte-Geneviève-de-Batisca, QC G0X 2R0 Canada
418-362-2717
Fax: 418-362-2910
MICR: 815-10025
Caisse populaire Ville-Émard
6000, boul Monk
Montréal, QC H4E 3H6 Canada
514-766-7713
Fax: 514-766-4595
MICR: 815-30090
Caisse économie Desjardins des employé(e)s du Secteur industriel (Montréal)
5705, rue Sherbrooke est
Montréal, QC H1N 1A8 Canada
514-253-0610
Fax: 514-253-9971
MICR: 815-92003
La Caisse Populaire de Laflèche
3355, boul Grande-Allée
Saint-Hubert, QC J4T 2T2 Canada
450-678-4150
Fax: 450-678-0330
MICR: 815-30301
La Caisse populaire de Ragueneau
550, rte 138
Ragueneau, QC G0H 1S0 Canada
418-567-4300
MICR: 815-20103
La Caisse populaire de St-Antoine-sur-Richelieu
PO Box 210
16, rue Marie-Rose
Saint-Antoine-sur-Richelieu, QC J0L 1R0 Canada
450-787-3125
Fax: 450-787-3852
MICR: 815-90003
La Caisse populaire de St-Liboire
151, rue Gabriel
Saint-Liboire, QC J0H 1R0 Canada
450-793-4491
Fax: 450-793-4905
MICR: 815-90004
La Caisse populaire de St-Théodore-d'Acton
1698, rue Principale
Saint-Théodore-d-Acton, QC J0H 1Z0 Canada
450-546-3219
Fax: 450-546-4605
MICR: 815-90002
La Caisse populaire Desjardins du Sud de l'Abitibi-Ouest
PO Box 25
108, rue Principale
Palmarolle, QC J0Z 3C0 Canada
819-787-2451
Fax: 819-787-2683
MICR: 815-80003
La Caisse populaire Sainte-Catherine
PO Box 39
2, rue Laurier
Ste-Catherine-de-la-J-Carti, QC G0A 3M0 Canada
418-875-2744
Fax: 418-875-2478
MICR: 815-20154

Fédération des caisses populaires acadiennes ltée

CP 5554
295, boul St-Pierre ouest
Caraquet, NB E1W 1B7
506-726-4202
acadievie@acadie.net.
www.acadie.com
Year Founded: 1946
Number of Employees: 227
Executives:
Yves Duguay, CFP,A.V.A,C.Fin.A., Directeur
Affiliates:
Caisse populaire Acadie - Bertrand
685, boul des Acadiens
Bertrand, NB E1W 1G7 Canada
506-726-1920
Fax: 506-726-1925
cp.acadie@acadie.com
Caisse populaire Acadie - Grande-Anse
PO Box 1004
313, rue Acadie
Grande-Anse, NB E8N 2T9 Canada
506-732-2350
Fax: 506-732-2355
cp.acadie@acadie.com
MICR: 865-00334
Caisse populaire Acadie - Maisonnette
PO Box 59
1614, rue Châtillon
Maisonnette, NB E8N 1T7 Canada
506-727-1885
Fax: 506-727-0906
cp.acadie@acadie.com
Caisse populaire Atholville - Val d'Amours - Atholville
230, rue Notre-Dame
Atholville, NB E3N 3Z8 Canada
506-789-1400
Fax: 506-789-1600
cp.atholvalda@acadie.com
MICR: 865-00054
Caisse populaire Atholville - Val-D'Amour
1992, ch McKendrick
Val-D'Amour, NB E3N 5K6 Canada
506-789-9545
Fax: 506-759-9821
cp.atholvalda@acadie.com
Caisse Populaire Beauséjour - Fredericton
198, rue Regent
Fredericton, NB E3B 3W7 Canada
506-458-8828
Fax: 506-457-9492
cp.beausejour@acadie.com
MICR: 865-00044
Caisse populaire Beauséjour - Moncton
305, rue St-Georges
Moncton, NB E1C 1W8 Canada
506-870-6000
Fax: 506-857-9763
cp.beausejour@acadie.com
MICR: 865-00044
Caisse populaire Beauséjour - Moncton
35 Morton Ave.
Moncton, NB E1A 3H8 Canada
506-870-6000
Fax: 506-853-7383
cp.beausejour@acadie.com
Caisse populaire Chaleur - Bathurst - Main
325, rue Main
Bathurst, NB E2A 1B1 Canada
506-548-4457
Fax: 506-548-5778
cp.chaleur@acadie.com
Caisse populaire Chaleur - Allardville
291, rte 160
Allardville, NB E8L 1J1 Canada
506-725-2959
Fax: 506-725-2207
cp.chaleur@acadie.com
Caisse populaire Chaleur - Bathurst - St-Pierre
1215, rue St-Pierre
Bathurst, NB E2A 3A2 Canada
506-546-8620
Fax: 506-546-9394
cp.chaleur@acadie.com
MICR: 865-00694
Caisse populaire de Baie Sainte-Anne
5572, ch 117
Baie-Sainte-Anne, NB E9A 1E8 Canada
506-228-3219
Fax: 506-228-3537
cp.baiesainte-anne@acadie.com
MICR: 865-00064
Caisse populaire de Beresford
816, rue Principale
Beresford, NB E8K 2G4 Canada
506-542-9200
Fax: 506-542-2153
cp.beresford@acadie.com
MICR: 865-00154
Caisse populaire de Caraquet
82, boul St-Pierre ouest
Caraquet, NB E1W 1B6 Canada
506-726-1133
Fax: 506-726-1144
cp.caraquet@acadie.com
MICR: 865-00194
Caisse populaire de la Péninsule - Bas-Caraquet
8236, rue St-Paul
Bas-Caraquet, NB E1W 6E2 Canada
506-727-2600
Fax: 506-727-9129
cp.peninsule@acadie.com
MICR: 865-00534
Caisse populaire de la Péninsule - Inkerman
838, rue 113
Inkerman, NB E8P 1C9 Canada
506-336-2211
Fax: 506-336-8253
cp.peninsule@acadie.com
Caisse populaire de la Péninsule - Pokemouche
11445, rue 11
Pokemouche, NB E8P 1J2 Canada
506-727-2576
Fax: 506-727-0120
cp.peninsule@acadie.com
Caisse populaire de la Péninsule - Saint-Simon
48, ch LeBouthillier
Saint-Simon, NB E8P 1Z7 Canada
506-727-4475
Fax: 506-727-3673
cp.peninsule@acadie.com
Caisse populaire de Saint-Basile - Rivière-Verte
79, rue Principale
Rivière-Verte, NB E7C 2T7 Canada
506-263-8420
Fax: 506-263-1130
cp.st-basile@acadie.com

Fédération des caisses populaires acadiennes ltée (continued)

Caisse populaire de Saint-Basile - Saint-Basile
200, rue Principale
Saint-Basile, NB E7C 1H6 Canada
506-263-1020
Fax: 506-263-1021
cp.st-basile@acadie.com
MICR: 865-00684

Caisse populaire de Sheila
PO Box 4120, B Sta. B
4178, rue Principale
Tracadie-Sheila, NB E1X 1G4 Canada
506-393-8400
Fax: 506-393-8404
cp.sheila@acadie.com
MICR: 865-00954

Caisse populaire de St-Sauveur
1920, rue 160
Saint-Sauveur, NB E8L 1N4 Canada
506-725-2072
Fax: 506-725-5835
cp.saint-sauveur@acadie.com
MICR: 865-00904

Caisse populaire de Tracadie
PO Box 3037, bureau-chef Sta. bureau-chef
3353, boul Dr. Victor-Leblanc
Tracadie-Sheila, NB E1X 1G5 Canada
506-395-6395
Fax: 506-393-1510
866-622-4773
cp.tracadie@acadie.com
MICR: 865-01004

Caisse populaire de Tracadie - Sainte Rose
2001, ch 355
Sainte Rose, NB E1X 2W6 Canada
506-395-3301
Fax: 506-395-5926
cp.tracadie@acadie.com

Caisse populaire des Fondateurs - Petit-Rocher
566, rue Principale
Petit-Rocher, NB E8J 1R2 Canada
506-783-4241
Fax: 506-783-3883
cp.desfondateurs@acadie.com
MICR: 865-00504

Caisse populaire des Fondateurs - Pointe-Verte
415, rue Principale
Pointe-Verte, NB E8J 2S5 Canada
506-783-4284
Fax: 506-783-4600
cp.desfondateurs@acadie.com

Caisse populaire des Iles - Sainte-Marie-Saint-Raphaël
8, rue de l'Église
Sainte-Marie-Saint-Raphaël, NB E8T 1N8 Canada

Caisse populaire des Iles-Lamèque
PO Box 2069
71, rue Principale
Lamèque, NB E8T 3N5 Canada
506-344-1500
Fax: 506-344-1515
800-686-6060
cp.desiles@acadie.com
MICR: 865-00404

Caisse populaire Dieppe - Champlain
251, rue Champlain
Dieppe, NB E1A 1P2 Canada
506-857-9217
Fax: 506-852-3523
cp.dieppe@acadie.com
MICR: 865-00664

Caisse populaire Dieppe - Scoudouc
3105, ch 132
Scoudouc, NB E4P 2Z9 Canada
506-857-9217
Fax: 506-532-2369
cp.dieppe@acadie.com

Caisse populaire Fondateurs - Robertville
1725, rte 322
Robertville, NB E8K 2T6 Canada
506-783-4226
Fax: 506-783-2605
cp.desfondateurs@acadie.com

Caisse populaire Haut-Madawaska - Clair
821, rue Principale
Clair, NB E7A 2H7 Canada
506-992-2158
Fax: 506-992-3478
cp.haut-madawaska@acadie.com
MICR: 865-00224

Caisse populaire Haut-Madawaska - Lac Baker
5442, rue Centrale
Lac Baker, NB E7A 1H7 Canada
506-992-2154
Fax: 506-992-2360
cp.haut-madawaska@acadie.com

Caisse populaire Haut-Madawaska - Saint-François
1982A, rue Commerciale
St-François, NB E7A 1S6 Canada
506-992-2103
Fax: 506-992-3666
cp.haut-madawaska@acadie.com

Caisse populaire Haut-Madawaska - Saint-Hilaire
2272, rue Centrale
St-Hilaire, NB E3V 4W1 Canada
506-258-6511
Fax: 506-258-3561
cp.haut-madawaska@acadie.com

Caisse populaire Kedgwick
51, rue Notre-Dame
Kedgwick, NB E8B 1H5 Canada
506-284-2238
Fax: 506-284-9040
cp.kedgwick@acadie.com
MICR: 865-00374

Caisse populaire Kent Nord - Acadieville
4016, ch 480
Acadieville, NB E4Y 2B7 Canada
506-775-2422
Fax: 506-775-6587
cp.kentnord@acadie.com

Caisse populaire Kent Nord - Pointe-Sapin
3274, ch 117
Pointe-Sapin, NB E9A 1T2 Canada
506-876-4901
Fax: 506-876-9809
cp.kentnord@acadie.com

Caisse populaire Kent Nord - Saint-Ignace
1859, ch Saint-Ignace sud
Saint-Ignace, NB E4X 2H5 Canada
506-876-3669
Fax: 506-876-2742
cp.kentnord@acadie.com

Caisse populaire Kent Nord - St-Louis
10512, rue Principale
Saint-Louis-de-Kent, NB E4X 1G6 Canada
506-876-2464
Fax: 506-876-4778
cp.kentnord@acadie.com
MICR: 865-00804

Caisse populaire Kent-Beauséjour - Bouctouche
196, boul Irving
Bouctouche, NB E4S 3L7 Canada
506-743-2423
Fax: 506-743-6388
cp.kent-beausejour@acadie.com

Caisse populaire Kent-Beauséjour - Sainte-Anne
7681, rte 134
Sainte-Anne-de-Kent, NB E4S 1E6 Canada
506-743-1330
Fax: 506-743-8759
cp.kent-beausejour@acadie.com

Caisse populaire Kent-Beauséjour - Sainte-Marie
1546, rte 525
Sainte-Marie-de-Kent, NB E4S 2H8 Canada
506-955-3777
Fax: 506-955-3768
cp.kent-beausejour@acadie.com
MICR: 865-00834

Caisse populaire Kent-Beauséjour - St-Paul
6519, rte 515
St-Paul, NB E4T 3P6 Canada
506-955-3880
Fax: 506-955-3092
cp.kent-beausejour@acadie.com

Caisse populaire Kent-Centre - Richibouctou Village
4029, rte 505
Richibouctou Village, NB E4W 1N4 Canada
506-523-9133
Fax: 506-523-9628
cp.kent-centre@acadie.com

Caisse populaire Kent-Centre - Richibucto
39, boul Cartier
Richibucto, NB E4W 3W6 Canada
506-523-9171
Fax: 506-523-9096
cp.kent-centre@acadie.com
MICR: 865-00574

Caisse populaire Kent-Centre - Rogersville
20, rue Boucher
Rogersville, NB E4Y 1X5 Canada
506-775-2387
Fax: 506-775-0826
cp.kent-centre@acadie.com

Caisse populaire Kent-Sud - Cocagne
PO Box 1006
1913, ch 535
Cocagne, NB E4R 1N6 Canada
506-576-6666
Fax: 506-576-6400
cp.kent-sud@acadie.com
MICR: 865-00234

Caisse populaire Kent-Sud - Grande-Digue
432, ch 530
Grande-Digue, NB E4R 5K3 Canada
506-532-2200
Fax: 506-532-6554
cp.kent-sud@acadie.com

Caisse populaire Kent-Sud - Notre-Dame
3800, ch 115
Notre-Dame, NB E4V 2H9 Canada
506-576-7753
Fax: 506-576-7196
cp.kent-sud@acadie.com

Caisse populaire Kent-Sud - St-Antoine
4490, rue Principale
Saint-Antoine, NB E4V 1P9 Canada
506-525-2197
Fax: 506-525-9535
cp.kent-sud@acadie.com

Caisse Populaire La Vallée - Drummond
1413, rue Tobique
Drummond, NB E3Y 2P6 Canada
506-473-2339
Fax: 506-473-2274
cp.lavallee@acadie.com

Caisse populaire La Vallée - Grand-Sault
181, boul Broadway
Grand-Sault, NB E3Z 2J8 Canada
506-473-3660
Fax: 506-473-9020
cp.lavallee@acadie.com
MICR: 865-00364

Caisse populaire La Vallée - Notre Dame de Lourdes
250, ch Notre-Dame de Lourdes
Notre Dame de Lourdes, NB E7E E3E Canada
506-445-2091
Fax: 506-445-2265
cp.lavallee@acadie.com

Caisse populaire La Vallée - Saint-Georges
91, rue Tobique
Grand-Sault, NB E3Y 1B9 Canada
506-473-1485
Fax: 506-473-6266
cp.lavallee@acadie.com

Caisse populaire La Vallée - Saint-Léonard Ville
683, rue Principale
Saint-Léonard, NB E7E 2J4 Canada
506-423-6386
Fax: 506-423-1200
cp.lavallee@acadie.com

Caisse populaire La Vallée - St-André
492, rue de l'Église
Saint-André, NB E3Y 2Y6 Canada
506-473-1041
Fax: 506-473-3604
cp.lavallee@acadie.com

Caisse populaire le lien d'or - Pont Landry
454, ch Georges
Pont Landry, NB E1X 2T8 Canada
506-395-5828
Fax: 506-395-2823
cp.leliendor@acadie.com

Caisse populaire le lien d'or - St-Isidore
3922, boul des Fondateurs
St-Isidore, NB E8M 1C2 Canada

506-358-6348
Fax: 506-358-1822
cp.leliendor@acadie.com
MICR: 865-00744
Caisse populaire Madawaska - Edmundston
85, ch Canada
Edmundston, NB E3V 1V6 Canada
506-735-4708
Fax: 506-735-4131
cp.madawaska@acadie.com
MICR: 865-00304
Caisse populaire Madawaska - Saint-Jacques
214, rue Principale
Saint-Jacques, NB E7B 1W6 Canada
506-737-1133
Fax: 506-735-0059
cp.madawaska@acadie.com
Caisse populaire Madawaska - Ste-Anne du Madawaska
88, rue Principale
Sainte-Anne-de-Madawaska, NB E7E 1B6 Canada
506-445-2077
Fax: 506-445-1020
cp.madawaska@acadie.com
Caisse populaire Memramcook - Centrale
587, rue Centrale
Memramcook, NB E4K 3R5 Canada
506-758-2505
Fax: 506-758-9469
cp.memramcook@acadie.com
MICR: 865-00434
Caisse populaire Memramcook - Pré-d'en-Haut
986, rue Pré-d'en-Haut
Memramcook, NB E4K 1L1 Canada
506-758-9329
Fax: 506-758-8911
cp.memramcook@acadie.com
Caisse populaire Notre-Dame de Grâce
26, rue Churchill
Moncton, NB E1C 7H7 Canada
506-858-8218
Fax: 506-858-8674
cp.nddegrace@acadie.com
MICR: 865-00464
Caisse populaire Néguac - Lagacéville
1892, St-Wilfred
Néguac, NB E9G 1S1 Canada
506-776-8313
Fax: 506-776-1129
cp.neguac@acadie.com
Caisse populaire Néguac - Néguac
617, rue Principale
Néguac, NB E9G 1S1 Canada
506-776-8313
Fax: 506-776-3487
cp.neguac@acadie.com
MICR: 865-00444
Caisse populaire Néguac - Rivière du Portage
5720, rue 11
Rivière-du-Portage, NB E9H 1X1 Canada
506-394-1929
Fax: 506-394-1924
cp.neguac@acadie.com
Caisse populaire Néguac - Tabusintac
4172, rue 11
Tabusintac, NB E9G 1S1 Canada
506-776-8313
Fax: 506-779-4775
cp.neguac@acadie.com
Caisse populaire Paquetville
1095, rue du Parc
Paquetville, NB E8R 1J1 Canada
506-764-1930
Fax: 506-764-1929
cp.paquetville@acadie.com
MICR: 865-00494
Caisse populaire Restigouche - Balmoral
PO Box 2569
1744, av des Pionniers
Balmoral, NB E8E 2W7 Canada
506-826-9840
Fax: 506-826-9846
cp.restigouche@acadie.com
Caisse populaire Restigouche - Campbellton
PO Box 900
14, rue Roseberry
Campbellton, NB E3N 3H3 Canada
506-753-5025
Fax: 506-753-6177
cp.restigouche@acadie.com
MICR: 865-00184
Caisse populaire Restigouche Est - Eel River
239, rue Principale
Eel River Crossing, NB E8E 1S4 Canada
506-826-2761
Fax: 506-826-9193
cp.restigoucheest@acadie.com
MICR: 865-00324
Caisse populaire Restigouche-Est - Charlo
PO Box 2010
330, rue Chaleur
Charlo, NB E8E 2W8 Canada
506-684-5604
Fax: 506-684-5197
cp.restigoucheest@acadie.com
Caisse populaire Restigouche-Est - Dalhousie
374, rue Adélaïde
Dalhousie, NB E8C 1A5 Canada
506-684-8060
Fax: 506-684-2528
cp.restigoucheest@acadie.com
Caisse populaire Restigouche-Est - Dundee
440, rte 280
Dundee, NB E8E 1Y9 Canada
506-826-9835
Fax: 506-826-9837
cp.restigoucheest@acadie.com
Caisse populaire République - Baker Brook
3851, rue Principale
Baker Brook, NB E7A 2A1 Canada
506-258-3220
Fax: 506-258-3330
cp.republique@acadie.com
Caisse populaire République - Edmundston - Rice
24, rue Rice
Edmundston, NB E3V 3P1 Canada
506-735-9060
Fax: 506-735-3340
cp.republique@acadie.com
Caisse populaire République - Edmundston - Victoria
Bureau enregistré
232, rue Victoria
Edmundston, NB E3V 2H9 Canada
506-735-4715
Fax: 506-737-1300
cp.republique@acadie.com
MICR: 865-00484
Caisse populaire St-Quentin
205, rue Canada
Saint-Quentin, NB E8A 1J9 Canada
506-235-2976
Fax: 506-235-2735
cp.saint-quentin@acadie.com
MICR: 865-00874
Caisse populaire Sud-Est - Cap-Pelé
2588, ch Acadie ouest
Cap-Pelé, NB E4N 1E3 Canada
506-532-6609
Fax: 506-577-6033
cp.sud-est@acadie.com
Caisse Populaire Sud-Est - Haute-Aboujagane
907, ch 933
Haute-Aboujagane, NB E4P 5P9 Canada
506-532-6609
Fax: 506-532-2021
cp.sud-est@acadie.com
Caisse populaire Sud-Est - Shediac
339, rue Main
Shediac, NB E4P 2B1 Canada
506-532-6609
Fax: 506-532-8242
cp.sud-est@acadie.com
Caisse populaire Sud-Est -Grand-Barachois
1363, ch 133
Grand-Barachois, NB E4P 8C8 Canada
506-532-6609
Fax: 506-532-3007
cp.sud-est@acadie.com
MICR: 865-00104

Fédération des caisses populaires de l'Ontario
214 Montreal Rd.
Ottawa, ON K1L 8L8
613-746-3276
Fax: 613-746-6035
800-423-3276
Affiliates:
Caisse populaire Azilda Inc.
PO Box 550
43 Notre-Dame St.
Azilda, ON P0M 1B0 Canada
705-983-4274
Fax: 705-983-2360
MICR: 829-00313
Caisse populaire d'Alfred Limitée
PO Box 231
499 St-Philippe St.
Alfred, ON K0B 1A0 Canada
613-679-2221
Fax: 613-679-4720
MICR: 829-00137
Caisse populaire d'Earlton Limitée
PO Box 130
29 10th St.
Earlton, ON P0J 1E0 Canada
705-563-2573
Fax: 705-563-2198
MICR: 829-00203
Caisse Populaire de Cochrane Limitée
PO Box 1868
187 - 5th Ave.
Cochrane, ON P0L 1C0 Canada
705-272-4258
Fax: 705-272-2936
MICR: 829-00211
Caisse populaire de Coniston Inc.
PO Box 170
24 Amanda St.
Coniston, ON P0M 1M0 Canada
705-694-4743
Fax: 705-694-3340
MICR: 829-00335
Caisse populaire de Cornwall Inc.
#100, 840 Pitt St.
Cornwall, ON K6J 3S2 Canada
613-932-4989
Fax: 613-932-4240
MICR: 829-00147
Caisse populaire de Hawkesbury Ltée
PO Box 215
480 Principale St. East
Hawkesbury, ON K6A 2R8 Canada
613-632-7024
Fax: 613-632-4358
MICR: 829-00139
Caisse populaire de la Vallée inc.
255 Main St. South
Alexandria, ON K0C 1A0 Canada
613-525-2141
Fax: 613-525-2153
MICR: 829-00145
Caisse populaire de New Liskeard Limitée
PO Box 1555
138 Whitewood Ave.
New Liskeard, ON P0J 1P0 Canada
705-647-8135
Fax: 705-647-8439
MICR: 829-00201
Caisse populaire de Tecumseh Inc.
St-Clair Shopping Center
13470 Tecumseh St. East
Tecumseh, ON N8N 3N7 Canada
519-735-6069
Fax: 519-735-4985
MICR: 829-00403
Caisse populaire Lasalle Inc. (Sudbury, Oshawa, Toronto, Lafontaine, Perkinsfield)
1380 Lasalle Blvd.
Sudbury, ON P3A 1Z6 Canada
705-566-3644
Fax: 705-566-3658
MICR: 829-00303
Caisse populaire Nolin de Sudbury Incorporée
531 Notre-Dame Ave.
Sudbury, ON P3C 5L1 Canada

Fédération des caisses populaires de l'Ontario (continued)
705-674-4234
Fax: 705-674-5972
MICR: 829-00337
Caisse populaire Nouvel-Horizon Inc.
PO Box 600
859 Notre-Dame St.
Embrun, ON K0A 1W0 Canada
613-443-2992
Fax: 613-443-3714
MICR: 829-00153
Caisse populaire Orléans Inc.
2591 St-Joseph Blvd.
Orleans, ON K1C 1G4 Canada
613-824-6363
Fax: 613-824-5307
MICR: 829-00127
Caisse populaire Pointe-aux-Roches Limitée
PO Box 100
6900 Tecumseh Rd.
Pointe aux Roches, ON N0R 1N0 Canada
519-798-3026
Fax: 519-798-5718
MICR: 829-00407
Caisse populaire Rideau d'Ottawa Inc.
147 Rideau St.
Ottawa, ON K1N 5X4 Canada
613-241-1316
Fax: 613-241-4634
MICR: 829-00107
Caisse populaire St-Jacques de Hanmer
4477 Notre-Dame St.
Hanmer, ON P3P 1X6 Canada
705-969-2052
Fax: 705-969-5185
MICR: 829-00311
Caisse populaire Trillium Inc.
1173 Cyrville Rd.
Ottawa, ON K1J 7S6 Canada
613-745-2123
Fax: 613-745-2723
MICR: 829-00123
Caisse populaire Val Caron Limitée
3077 Hwy 69 North
Val Caron, ON P3N 1R8 Canada
705-897-6701
Fax: 705-897-4532
MICR: 829-00309
Caisse populaire Vermillon
PO Box 968
29 Main St. West
Chelmsford, ON P0M 1L0 Canada
705-855-9018
Fax: 705-855-0180
MICR: 829-00339
Caisse populaire Vision Inc.
99 Beechwood Ave.
Ottawa, ON K1M 1L7 Canada
613-745-0071
Fax: 613-747-8510
MICR: 829-00103
Caisse populaire Welland Limitée
59 Empire St.
Welland, ON L3B 2L3 Canada
905-735-3453
Fax: 905-732-0362
MICR: 829-00501

Fédération des caisses populaires du Manitoba

#200, 605 Des Meurons St.
Winnipeg, MB R2H 2R1
204-237-8988
Fax: 204-233-6405
federation@caisse.biz
www.caisse.biz
Ownership: Member-owned
Year Founded: 1937
Number of Employees: 240
Branches:
Haywood
9, rue Main est
Haywood, MB R0G 0W0 Canada
204-379-2368
Fax: 204-379-2368
Ile des Chenes
PO Box 700
478 Main St.
Ile des Chenes, MB R0A 0T0 Canada
204-878-3765
Fax: 204-878-3724
La Broquerie
PO Box 29
130 Main St.
La Broquerie, MB R0A 0W0 Canada
204-424-5238
Fax: 204-424-5077
Raymond Cormier, General Manager
Laurier
PO Box 61
115, rue Burrows
Laurier, MB R0J 1A0 Canada
204-447-2412
Fax: 204-447-3124
laurier@caisse.biz
Letellier
PO Box 266
32, rue First est
Letellier, MB R0G 1C0 Canada
204-737-2350
Fax: 204-737-2690
Lorette
PO Box 89
1238 Dawson Rd.
Lorette, MB R0A 0Y0 Canada
204-878-2791
Fax: 204-878-2065
Marquette
Marquette, MB R0H 0V0 Canada
204-375-6646
Notre-Dame de Lourdes
PO Box 248
151, av Notre Dame
Notre Dame de Lourdes, MB R0G 1M0 Canada
204-248-2332
Fax: 204-248-2281
lourdes@caisse.biz
Rathwell
Rathwell, MB R0G 1S0 Canada
204-749-2101
Fax: 204-749-2101
Richer
Dawson Rd.
Richer, MB R0E 1S0 Canada
204-422-8227
Fax: 204-422-8503
South Junction
PO Box 40
South Junction, MB R0A 1Y0 Canada
204-437-2345
Fax: 204-437-2824
St Adolphe
PO Box 160
385, ch St. Mary's
St Adolphe, MB R5A 1A1 Canada
204-883-2258
Fax: 204-883-2060
St Francois Xavier
1063 Hwy. 26
St Francois Xavier, MB R4L 1A5 Canada
204-864-2676
Fax: 204-864-2651
St Jean Baptiste
PO Box 99
178 Caron St.
St Jean Baptiste, MB R0G 2B0 Canada
204-758-3372
Fax: 204-758-3379
St Joseph
13 Morin St.
St Joseph, MB R0G 2C0 Canada
204-737-2695
Fax: 204-737-2059
St Laurent
St Laurent, MB R0C 2S0 Canada
204-646-2382
Fax: 204-646-2914
St Leon
59 Main St.
St Leon, MB R0G 2E0 Canada
204-744-2067
St Malo
PO Box 58
92, av de la Grotte
St Malo, MB R0A 1T0 Canada
204-347-5533
Fax: 204-347-5261
provencher@caisse.biz
St Pierre Jolys
PO Box 298
505 Jolys Ave.
St Pierre Jolys, MB R0A 1V0 Canada
204-433-7601
Fax: 204-433-7846
St-Claude
PO Box 245
76, rue Main
St-Claude, MB R0G 1Z0 Canada
204-379-2332
Fax: 204-379-2356
saintclaude@caisse.biz
St. Georges
PO Box 18
2 MacDougall Ave.
St. Georges, MB R0E 1V0 Canada
204-367-8268
Fax: 204-367-4766
Ste Agathe
PO Box 54
145 Pembina Trail
Ste Agathe, MB R0G 1Y0 Canada
204-882-2345
Fax: 204-882-2157
Ste Anne
130, av Centrale
Ste Anne, MB R5H 1J3 Canada
204-422-8896
Fax: 204-422-9994
laverendrye@caisse.biz
Winnipeg - Dakota
#1, 875 Dakota St.
Winnipeg, MB R2M 5S5 Canada
204-257-2400
Fax: 204-257-2040
Winnipeg - Lakewood
36 Lakewood Blvd.
Winnipeg, MB R2J 2M6 Canada
204-257-3360
Fax: 204-257-3007
Winnipeg - Marion
159 Marion St.
Winnipeg, MB R2H 0T3 Canada
204-237-4505
Fax: 204-233-5530
Winnipeg - Provencher
185, boul Provencher
Winnipeg, MB R2H 0G4 Canada
204-237-8874
Fax: 204-233-5383
saintboniface@caisse.biz
Élie
PO Box 36
10, rue Main est
Elie, MB R0H 0H0 Canada
204-353-2283
Fax: 204-353-2101
elie@caisse.biz

Fiberglas Employees (Guelph) Credit Union Limited

PO Box 3603
247 York Rd.
Guelph, ON N1E 3G4
519-824-2212
Fax: 519-824-1390
fiberglascu@bellnet.ca
Year Founded: 1953
Number of Employees: 1
Executives:
Mary Lou Eidt, Treasurer/Manager

First Calgary Savings & Credit Union Limited

#200, 510 - 16th Ave. NE
Calgary, AB T2E 1K4
403-230-2783
Fax: 403-276-6338
info@1stcalgary.com
www.1stcalgary.com

Ownership: Member-owned
Year Founded: 1987
Assets: $1-10 billion
Executives:
Dave Gregory, President/CEO
Rod Bannan, Sr. Vice-President, Credit Services
John Dundas, Sr. Vice-President, Marketing & Strategic Planning
Paul Kelly, Sr. Vice-President, CFO
Jackie Barber, Vice-President, Human Resources
Debbie Pratt, Vice-President, Sales & Services
Directors:
Mark McLoughlin, Chair
Bruno Friessen, Vice-Chair
Mark Lehman, Board Secretary
Ken Bolstad
Gary Cerantola
Jeannette Kirchner
Colleen Janssen Hood
Judy Morris
Ron Zeiger
Branches:
Beddington Heights
8220 Centre St. North
Calgary, AB T3K 1J7 Canada
403-275-7722
Fax: 403-295-9580
Brentwood
3570 Brentwood Rd. NW
Calgary, AB T2L 1K8 Canada
403-289-8436
Fax: 403-220-9522
Calgary - 7th Ave. SW
TD Square
#116, 317 - 7th Ave. SW
Calgary, AB T2P 2Y9 Canada
403-269-4850
Fax: 403-269-1153
Conventry Hills
#500, 130 Country Village Rd. NE
Calgary, AB T3K 6E8 Canada
403-503-8088
Fax: 403-503-8089
Crowfoot Towne Centre
800 Crowfoot Way NW
Calgary, AB T3G 4S3 Canada
403-547-6000
Fax: 403-547-6004
Dalhousie
#735, 5005 Dalhousie Dr. NW
Calgary, AB T3A 5R8 Canada
403-286-3630
Fax: 403-247-4633
Macleod Trail
8906 Macleod Trail South
Calgary, AB T2H 0M4 Canada
403-253-4431
Fax: 403-253-8003

Northgate Village
455 - 36 St. NE
Calgary, AB T2A 5K3 Canada
403-272-8821
Fax: 403-248-5139
Oakridge
#70, 2580 Southland Dr. SW
Calgary, AB T2V 4J8 Canada
403-281-2258
Fax: 403-281-2983
Shawnessy
#100, 70 Shawville Blvd. SE
Calgary, AB T2Y 2Z3 Canada
403-531-5100
Fax: 403-531-5104
Signal Hill
5735 Signal Hill Centre SW
Calgary, AB T3H 3P8 Canada
403-246-2245
Fax: 403-686-2529
South Trail
#400, 4915 - 130 Ave. SE
Calgary, AB T2Z 4J2 Canada
403-503-8090
Fax: 403-503-8091
Taradale
#100, 6520 Falconridge Blvd. NE
Calgary, AB T3J 3W6 Canada
403-503-8028
Fax: 403-503-8030
Trans Canada
510 - 16th Ave. NE
Calgary, AB T2E 1K4 Canada
403-230-1451
Fax: 403-276-5299
Village Square
#116, 2640 - 52nd St. NE
Calgary, AB T1Y 3R6 Canada
403-285-0700
Fax: 403-285-2441

FirstOntario Credit Union Limited

688 Queensdale Ave. East
Hamilton, ON L8V 1M1
905-387-0770
888-283-7835
contact@firstontariocu.com
www.firstontariocu.com
Former Name: Avestel Family Savings Credit Union Limited; Family Savings & Credit Union Limited
Year Founded: 1940
Number of Employees: 300
Assets: $500m-1 billion
Executives:
John Lahey, CEO
Barry Doan, Vice-President/CFO
Ron Choma, Vice-President, Commercial Services
Tim Tiernay, Vice-President, Human Resources
Carol Mayer, Operations & Technology, Vice-President
Louise Taylor-Green, Vice-President, Retail Services
Lloyd Smith, Vice-President, Treasury & Corporate Services
Directors:
Ken Bolton
Alan Bratton
Ron Fleet
Sandra Gribben
Murray McDiarmid
Val Narduzzi
Otto Penner, Chair
Brian Power
Catherine Rogers
Sandy Shaw
Eve Sigfrid
Branches:
Burlington
Cumberland Square Plaza
3300 Fairview St.
Burlington, ON L7N 3N7 Canada
905-333-5775
Connie Figueiredo, Branch Manager
Burlington
PO Box 730
895 Brant St.
Burlington, ON L7R 2J6 Canada
905-632-1470
Tanja Foss-Pedersen, Branch Manager
Cayuga
5 Talbot St. East
Cayuga, ON N0A 1E0 Canada
905-722-3501
Dorothy Biggar, Branch Manager
Hamilton - Central
928 Barton St. East.
Hamilton, ON L8L 3C3 Canada
905-549-4101
Karen Dore, Branch Manager
Hamilton - Mountain
486 Upper Sherman Ave.
Hamilton, ON L8V 3L8 Canada
905-389-5533
Kristan Gray, Branch Manager
Hamilton - West
Dundurn Place
50 Dundurn St. South
Hamilton, ON L8P 4W3 Canada
905-522-8202
Susan Hoag, Branch Manager
Niagara Falls
3969 Montrose Rd.
Niagara Falls, ON L2H 3A1 Canada
905-685-5555
Laurie Ryan Hill, Branch Manager
Oakville
338 Kerr St.
Oakville, ON L6K 3B5 Canada
Ilona McCoppen, Branch Manager
Simcoe
140 Queensway East
Simcoe, ON N3Y 4Y7 Canada
519-428-0800
Carolyn Mulholland, Branch Manager
St Catharines - Grantham Ave.
486 Grantham Ave.
St Catharines, ON L2M 3J7 Canada
905-685-5555
Alison Watt, Branch Manager
St Catharines - Niagara St.
PO Box 982
148 Niagara St.
St Catharines, ON L2R 6Z4 Canada
905-685-5555
Laurie Coletti-White, Branch Manager
St Catharines - Ontario St.
600 Ontario St.
St Catharines, ON L2N 4N7 Canada
905-685-5555
Janice Cheel, Branch Manager
St Catharines - Pelham Rd.
215 Pelham Rd.
St Catharines, ON L2N 4N2 Canada
905-685-5555
Nancy Cain, Branch Manager
Stoney Creek
95 Hwy. 8
Stoney Creek, ON L8G 1C1 Canada
Davina MacDonald, Branch Manager
Thorold
35 Albert St. West
Thorold, ON L2V 2G4 Canada
905-685-5555
Lucy Cino, Branch Manager
Tillsonburg
157 Broadway
Tillsonburg, ON N4G 3P7 Canada
519-842-8416
Kim McDonald, Branch Manager
Welland
840 Niagara St.
Welland, ON L3C 1M3 Canada
905-685-5555
Rob Cetaratti, Branch Manager

FirstSask Credit Union

309 - 22nd St. East
Saskatoon, SK S7K 0G7
306-934-4000
Fax: 306-934-4019
888-863-6237
questions@firstsask.ca
www.firstsask.ca
Former Name: Saskatoon Credit Union
Ownership: Member-owned
Year Founded: 2007
Number of Employees: 270
Assets: $500m-1 billion
Revenues: $1-5 million
Profile: Langham Credit Union Limited, Shellbrook Credit Union Limited & Saskatoon Credit Union (2002) merged in Jan. 2007. FirstSask Credit Union is 100% owned by more than 56,000 members.
Executives:
George Keter, CEO
Lise de Moissac, Vice-President, Finance & Administration
Gordon Hamilton, Vice-President, Human Resources
Kurt Holfeuer, Vice-President, Technology
Linda Moulin, Vice-President, Community Development
Serese Selanders, Vice-President, Retail Operations
Directors:
Elwood Harvey, President
Kearney Healy, 1st Vice-President
Gayl Basler, 2nd Vice-President
Michelle Beveridge
Robert Hackett
John Lagimodiere
Cheryl Loadman
Norman Sheehan

FirstSask Credit Union (continued)
Paul Wilkinson
Branches:
Langham
PO Box 30
302 Main St.
Langham, SK S0K 2L0 Canada
Fax: 306-283-4141
Langham - Borden
PO Box 60
107 Shepard St.
Borden, SK S0K 0N0 Canada
306-997-2097
Fax: 306-997-2080
Langham - Dalmeny
PO Box 389
115 - 3rd St.
Dalmeny, SK S0K 1E0 Canada
306-254-2082
Fax: 306-254-2688
Langham - Hepburn
PO Box 130
402 Main St.
Hepburn, SK S0K 1Z0 Canada
306-947-4660
Fax: 306-947-4662
Langham - Martensville
PO Box 490
#6, 7 Centennial Dr.
Martensville, SK S0K 2T0 Canada
306-975-9855
Fax: 306-975-9856
Langham - Waldheim
PO Box 250
3001 Central Ave.
Waldheim, SK S0K 4R0 Canada
306-945-5558
Fax: 306-945-5561
Saskatoon - 8th St. East
2201 - 8th St. East
Saskatoon, SK S7H 0V2 Canada
Fax: 306-934-5493
Saskatoon - Broadway Ave.
912 Broadway Ave.
Saskatoon, SK S7N 1B7 Canada
Fax: 306-934-5491
Saskatoon - Commercial Services Centre
#300, 310 - 20th St. East
Saskatoon, SK S7K 0A7 Canada
Fax: 306-934-5487
Saskatoon - Fairhaven
3315C Fairlight Dr.
Saskatoon, SK S7M 3Y5 Canada
Fax: 306-934-5496
Saskatoon - Main
309 - 22nd St. East
Saskatoon, SK S7K 0G7 Canada
Fax: 306-934-5490
Saskatoon - River Heights
7 Assiniboine Dr.
Saskatoon, SK S7K 1H1 Canada
Fax: 306-934-5495
Saskatoon - Westview
1624 - 33rd St. West
Saskatoon, SK S7L 0X3 Canada
Fax: 306-934-5494
Shellbrook
31 Main St.
Shellbrook, SK S0J 2E0 Canada
Fax: 306-747-3161
Shellbrook - Canwood
PO Box 8
Canwood, SK S0J 0K0 Canada
306-468-2325
Fax: 306-468-2121
Shellbrook - Leask
PO Box 370
Leask, SK S0J 1M0 Canada
306-466-5500
Fax: 306-466-5505
Shellbrook - Marcelin
PO Box 220
Marcelin, SK S0J 1R0 Canada
306-226-2112
Fax: 306-226-2050
Warman
204 Central St. West
Warman, SK S0K 4S0 Canada
Fax: 306-934-1034

Flin Flon Credit Union
36 Main St.
Flin Flon, MB R8A 1J6
204-687-6620
www.flinfloncu.mb.ca
Year Founded: 1940
Number of Employees: 3
Executives:
Diane Harris, General Manager
Directors:
Rob Gourley, President
Reuben Hagan, Vice-President
Tom Fehr, Secretary
Frank Fieber
Darren Grant
Donald Scott
Larry Scully

Foam Lake Savings & Credit Union Ltd.
PO Box 160
326 Main St.
Foam Lake, SK S0A 1A0
306-272-3385
Fax: 306-272-4948
info@foamlake.cu.sk.ca
www.foamlake.cu.sk.ca
Year Founded: 1941
Executives:
Andrey Reynolds, CFO; audrey.reynolds@foamlake.cu.sk.ca
Kent McMann, General Manager;
kent.mcmann@foamlake.cu.sk.ca
Randy Lamb, Manager, Loans; randy.lamb@foamlake.cu.sk.ca

Food Family Credit Union
2044 Danforth Ave.
Toronto, ON M4C 1J6
416-424-4798
Fax: 416-424-4760
800-267-3663
info@foodfamilycreditunion.com
www.foodfamilycreditunion.com
Year Founded: 1964
Number of Employees: 3
Assets: $11,000,000 Year End: 20041031
Executives:
Lance Porter, CEO

Forget Credit Union Ltd.
General Delivery
Stoughton, SK S0C 0X0
306-457-2747
Year Founded: 1950

Fort Erie Community Credit Union Limited
1201 Garrison Rd.
Fort Erie, ON L2A 1N8
905-994-1201
Fax: 905-994-1897
info@forteriecu.com
www.forteriecu.com
Executives:
Rebecca Havill, General Manager
Patti Carpenter, Loan Officer
Branches:
Jarvis
201 Jarvis St.
Fort Erie, ON L2A 2S7 Canada
905-871-1552
Fax: 905-871-9585
Denice Green, Loan Officer

Fort York Community Credit Union Limited
Sunnyside East
#207, 30 The Queensway
Toronto, ON M6R 1B5
416-530-6474
Fax: 416-530-6763
fyinfo@fortyork.com
www.fortyork.com
Year Founded: 1950
Executives:
Colette Coulter, General Manager
Directors:
Roger Harris, President
Dan Greene, Vice-President
Linda Watton, Secretary
Sandra Elgie
Cas Kelly
George Larter
Dwight Lyons

Frontline Financial Credit Union
365 Richmond Rd.
Ottawa, ON K2A 0E7
613-729-4312
Fax: 613-729-5075
www.911cu.com
Former Name: Ottawa Fire Fighters' Credit Union Ltd.
Year Founded: 1948
Branches:
Hydro Branch
3025 Albion Rd. North
Ottawa, ON K1V 9V9 Canada
613-523-8675
Fax: 613-523-7856
Regional Health
1053 Carling Ave.
Ottawa, ON K1Y 4E9 Canada
613-761-4737
Fax: 613-761-5335

G & F Financial Group
Also listed under: *Financial Planning; Insurance Companies*
7375 Kingsway
Burnaby, BC V3N 3B5
604-517-5100
Fax: 604-659-4025
www.gffg.com
Former Name: Gulf & Fraser Fishermen's Credit Union
Year Founded: 1941
Number of Employees: 175
Assets: $500m-1 billion Year End: 20041231
Revenues: $1-5 million Year End: 20041231
Executives:
Richard Davies, CEO
Bill Kiss, CFO
Ken McBain, COO
Directors:
Ed MacIntosh, Chair
Vince Fiamango, 1st Vice-Chair
Aubrey Searle, 2nd Vice-Chair
Joe Boroevich
Lewis Bublé
Christine Dacre
Brian Hamaguchi
Jim Heeps
Howard Normann
Vila Nova Carvalho
Kevin Riley
Jayne Roberts
John Secord
Al Wagner
Gary Williamson
Mercedes Wong
Branches:
Burnaby - Kingsway (South)
7375 Kingsway
Burnaby, BC V3N 3B5 Canada
604-521-2315
Fax: 604-521-8759
Burnaby - Southpoint Dr.
Podium B
6911 Southpoint Dr.
Burnaby, BC V3N 4X8 Canada
604-528-8383
Fax: 604-528-8386
800-663-0248
New Westminster
760 - 6th St.
New Westminster, BC V3L 3C7 Canada
604-526-2122
Fax: 604-522-6614
Port Coquitlam
#400, 2748 Lougheed Hwy.
Port Coquitlam, BC V3B 6P2 Canada
604-941-8300
Fax: 604-941-8307
Richmond - Chatham St. (Steveston)

3471 Chatham St.
Richmond, BC V7E 2Y9 Canada
604-271-5911
Fax: 604-271-6033
Richmond - Westminster Hwy. (Richmond Centre)
7971 Westminster Hwy.
Richmond, BC V6X 1A4 Canada
604-278-0220
Fax: 604-278-1572
Surrey - Fraser Hwy. (Fleetwood)
Fleetwood Park Village
#101, 15910 Fraser Hwy.
Surrey, BC V3S 2W4 Canada
604-599-6177
Fax: 604-599-6179
Surrey - Nordel Way
#101, 12020 Nordel Way
Surrey, BC V3W 1P6 Canada
604-507-8688
Fax: 604-507-8684
Vancouver - 41st Ave.
2735 East 41st Ave.
Vancouver, BC Canada
604-437-4774
Fax: 604-437-1174
Vancouver - Hastings St.
803 East Hastings St.
Vancouver, BC V6A 1R8 Canada
604-254-9811
Fax: 604-254-0215
Vancouver - Main St.
2949 Main St.
Vancouver, BC V5T 3G4 Canada
604-879-7131
Fax: 604-879-7397

Ganaraska Financial Services Group
17 Queen St.
Port Hope, ON L1A 2Y8
905-885-8134
Fax: 905-885-8298
info@ganaraskacu.com
www.ganaraskacu.com
Former Name: Ganaraska Credit Union
Year Founded: 1945
Branches:
Cobourg
57 Albert St.
Cobourg, ON K9A 2P8 Canada
905-372-8753
Fax: 905-372-0238
cobourg@ganaraskacu.com

Gateway Credit Union
PO Box 88
Rose Valley, SK S0E 1M0
306-322-2261
Fax: 306-322-4426
info@gateway.cu.sk.ca
www.gatewaycu.ca
Former Name: Rose Valley Credit Union Ltd.
Ownership: Member-owned
Year Founded: 1954
Number of Employees: 6
Dave Lyster, General Manager
Branches:
Archerwill
PO Box 220
Archerwill, SK S0E 0B0 Canada
306-323-2115
Fax: 306-323-2019
Bjorkdale
PO Box 60
Bjorkdale, SK S0E 0E0 Canada
306-886-2107
Fax: 306-886-4340

Genfast Employees Credit Union Limited
Bldg. 5
PO Box 1690
225 Henry St.
Brantford, ON N3T 5V7
519-754-4400
Fax: 519-750-1428
Ownership: Private
Number of Employees: 1
Executives:
Marg Woodrow, Treas./Manager

Glace Bay Central Credit Union
598 Main St.
Glace Bay, NS B1A 4X8
902-849-7512
Fax: 902-842-9201
www.glacebaycentralcreditunion.com
Year Founded: 1932
Executives:
Patricia Morrison, Manager
Directors:
Kelly Sparrow, President
Branches:
Reserve Mines
Tompkins Place
2249 Sydney Rd.
Reserve Mines, NS B1E 1J9 Canada
902-849-4583
Fax: 902-849-4583
Jackie Murray, Office Supervisor

Goderich Community Credit Union Limited
PO Box 66
39 St. David St.
Goderich, ON N7A 3Y5
519-524-8366
Fax: 519-524-1329
reception@gccu.on.ca
www.gccu.on.ca
Ownership: Member-owned
Year Founded: 1954
Number of Employees: 3
Executives:
Sandy Wilson, CEO; sandy@gccu.on.ca
Directors:
Lawrence Lassaline, Chair

Goodsoil Credit Union Limited
PO Box 88
Goodsoil, SK S0M 1A0
306-238-2033
Fax: 306-238-4441
Ownership: Member-owned
Year Founded: 1946
Number of Employees: 7
Assets: $10-50 million
Revenues: Under $1 million
Profile: Offers services that include interest-bearing chequing, savings, term deposits, youth accounts, Heritage '55, NISA, RRSPs, RRIFs, loans (commercial, agricultural & consumer), RESPs, mutual funds & a MasterCard product line.

Goodyear Employees (Bowmanville) Credit Union Limited
371 Orange Cres.
Oshawa, ON L1G 5X2
905-623-2606
Fax: 905-432-7590
Year Founded: 1966
Number of Employees: 1
Executives:
Del Rudman, General Manager

Govan Credit Union Ltd.
PO Box 280
Govan, SK S0G 1Z0
306-484-2177
govancreditunion@govan.cu.sk.ca
www.govancreditunion.ca
Year Founded: 1940

Grand Forks District Savings Credit Union
PO Box 2500
447 Market Ave.
Grand Forks, BC V0H 1H0
250-442-5511
Fax: 250-442-5644
info@gfdscu.com
www.gfdscu.com
Year Founded: 1949
Executives:
Cathy Manson, CEO

Grandview Credit Union
405 Main St.
Grandview, MB R0L 0Y0
204-546-5200
Fax: 204-546-5219
info@grandviewcu.mb.ca
www.grandviewcu.mb.ca

Greater Vancouver Community Credit Union
1801 Willingdon Ave.
Burnaby, BC V5C 5R3
604-298-3344
Fax: 604-421-8949
info@gvccu.com
www.gvccu.com
Branches:
Burnaby - Brentwood
1801 Willingdon Ave.
Burnaby, BC V5C 5R3 Canada
604-298-3344
Fax: 604-298-3417
brentwood@gvccu.com
Burnaby - Lougheed Plaza
9608 Cameron St.
Burnaby, BC V3J 1M2 Canada
604-421-3456
Fax: 604-420-5526
burnaby@gvccu.com
Surrey
#1, 10090 - 152nd St.
Surrey, BC V3R 4G5 Canada
604-584-4434
Fax: 604-584-6038
surrey@gvccu.com
Allen Ferrier, Manager
Vancouver - Cambie
#100, 4088 Cambie St.
Vancouver, BC V5Z 2X8 Canada
604-876-7101
Fax: 604-876-0892
vancouver@gvccu.com
Richard Rochard, Manager

Greater Victoria Savings Credit Union
1001 Blanshard St.
Victoria, BC V8W 2H4
250-388-4408
Fax: 250-384-4232
letters@victoriasavings.com
www.gvscu.com
Year Founded: 1940
Executives:
Dick Chadwick, Branch Manager; dchadwick@victoriasavings.com
Branches:
Goldstream - Langford
716 Goldstream Ave.
Victoria, BC V9B 2X3 Canada
250-474-3191
Fax: 250-474-1583
Maureen Erichsen, Branch Manager
Scott
3055 Scott St., Unit A
Victoria, BC V8R 4J9 Canada
250-595-1124
Fax: 250-595-8942
Lorna Paterson, Branch Manager

Grey Bruce Health Services Credit Union Ltd.
1939 - 8 Ave. East
Owen Sound, ON N4K 3C4
519-376-9336
creditunion@mbts.com
Former Name: Health Centre (Owen Sound) Employees Credit Union Limited
Year Founded: 1967

GSW (Fergus) Credit Union Limited
599 Hill St. West
Fergus, ON N1M 2X1
519-843-1616
Fax: 519-787-5533
Year Founded: 1951
Number of Employees: 2
Executives:
Sandra Beirnes, General Manager

Hald-Nor Community Credit Union Limited
PO Box 2135
22 Caithness St. East
Caledonia, ON N3W 2G6
905-765-4071
Fax: 905-765-0485
caledonia@hald-nor.on.ca
www.hald-nor.on.ca
Ownership: Member-owned
Year Founded: 1954
Assets: $50-100 million Year End: 20041231
Executives:
Ralph Luimes, CEO
John Henderson, Chair
Branches:
Cayuga
PO Box 308
18 Talbot St. East
Cayuga, ON N0A 1E0 Canada
905-772-3376
Fax: 905-772-0776
cayuga@hald-nor.on.ca
Hagersville
PO Box 337
15 King St. East
Hagersville, ON N0A 1H0 Canada
905-768-3347
Fax: 905-768-0456
hagers@hald-nor.on.ca
Simcoe
440 Norfolk St. South
Simcoe, ON N3Y 2X3 Canada
519-426-5930
Fax: 519-426-5939
simcoe@hald-nor.on.ca

Halifax Civic Credit Union
6070 Lady Hammond Rd.
Halifax, NS B3K 2R6
902-455-5489
Fax: 902-453-5491
info@hccu.ns.ca
www.hccu.ns.ca
Year Founded: 1938

Hamilton Community Credit Union Limited
698 King St. East
Hamilton, ON L8M 1A3
905-529-9445
Fax: 905-529-9016
hccu@sympatico.ca
www.hccu.on.ca
Number of Employees: 15
Executives:
Ken Kay, General Manager
Branches:
Mohawk Rd.
499 Mohawk Rd. East
Hamilton, ON L8V 2J4 Canada
905-383-3395
Fax: 905-383-5580
Diane Moat, Branch Manager

Health Care Credit Union Ltd.
PO Box 5375
800 Commissioners Rd. East
London, ON N6A 4G5
519-685-8353
Fax: 519-685-8153
creditunion@lhsc.on.ca
www.lhsc.on.ca/cr_union/
Year Founded: 1949

Healthcare & Municipal Employees Credit Union(HMECU)
209 Limeridge Rd. East
Hamilton, ON L9A 2S6
905-575-8888
Fax: 905-575-3104
866-808-2888
www.hmecu.com
Number of Employees: 9
Profile: Services the employees (& families) of Healthcare & Local Government in the cities of Hamilton, Brantford & Burlington.
Executives:
Charles Collura, CEO
Douglas Mann, CFO
Laurie Ryan-Hill, Branch Manager
Branches:
Brantford
368 Colborne St.
Brantford, ON N3S 3N3 Canada
519-756-6942
Fax: 519-756-9811
Lena Graves, Branch Manager
Burlington
426 Brant St.
Burlington, ON L7R 3Z6 Canada
905-335-7650
Fax: 905-639-8414
Elizabeth Galoni, Manager
Hamilton - West
#100, 1685 Main St.
Hamilton, ON L8S 1G5 Canada
905-526-7244
Fax: 905-526-0334
Elizabeth Galoni, Branch Manager

Heartland Credit Union
PO Box 1060
295 Main St.
Winkler, MB R6W 4B1
204-325-4351
Fax: 204-325-5752
800-264-2926
heartlandcu@hcu.mb.ca
www.hcu.mb.ca
Ownership: Member-owned
Year Founded: 2002
Executives:
Robert Jones, CEO
Ray Braun, COO
Rouben Schulz, CFO
James Funk, Manager, Financial Planning
Branches:
Gretna
PO Box 340
542 Hespeler Ave.
Gretna, MB R0G 0V0 Canada
204-327-5822
Fax: 204-327-5735
Wes Schroeder, Branch Manager
Plum Coulee
PO Box 380
257 Main St.
Plum Coulee, MB R0G 1R0 Canada
204-829-3655
Fax: 204-829-3734
Brad Penner, Branch Manager

Hir-Walk Employees' (Windsor) Credit Union Limited
2072 Riverside Dr. East
Windsor, ON N8Y 4S5
519-561-5543
Fax: 519-971-5744
hir-walker.credit@bellnet.ca
Year Founded: 1949
Number of Employees: 4
Executives:
Frank Ouellette, General Manager

Hobart Employees' (Owen Sound) Credit Union Limited
PO Box 278
Owen Sound, ON N4K 5P5
519-376-8886
Fax: 519-376-2955

Holy Angel's & St. Anne's Parish (St Thomas) Credit Union Limited
PO Box 20125
St Thomas, ON N5P 4H4
519-633-1710
Fax: 519-633-4024
LPHoffer@AOL.com

Holy Name Parish (Pembroke) Credit Union Limited
667 Front St.
Pembroke, ON K8A 6J4
613-732-3181
Fax: 613-732-1903
Ownership: Member-owned
Year Founded: 1942
Number of Employees: 3
Assets: Under $1 million
Revenues: Under $1 million

Horizon Credit Union
PO Box 1900
136 - 3rd Ave. East
Melville, SK S0A 2P0
306-728-5425
Fax: 306-728-4520
866-522-1880
Other Information: Telephone Banking: 306/728-1880
info@horizon.cu.sk.ca
www.horizon.cu.sk.ca
Former Name: Melville District Credit Union Ltd.; Aspen Prairie Credit Union Ltd.
Ownership: Co-operative. Member-owned
Year Founded: 1949
Number of Employees: 49
Branches:
Grayson
PO Box 56
Grayson, SK S0A 1E0 Canada
306-794-2155
Fax: 306-794-2253
Grenfell
PO Box 670
Grenfell, SK S0G 2B0 Canada
306-697-2803
Fax: 306-697-2911
Melville
PO Box 1900
Melville, SK S0A 2P0 Canada
306-728-5425
Fax: 306-728-4520
Neudorf
PO Box 160
Neudorf, SK S0A 2T0 Canada
306-748-2255
Fax: 306-748-2212
Wolseley
PO Box 98
Wolseley, SK S0G 5H0 Canada
306-698-2252
Fax: 306-698-2750

Hudson Bay Credit Union Ltd.
PO Box 538
208 Churchill St.
Hudson Bay, SK S0E 0Y0
306-865-2209
Fax: 306-865-2381
info@hudsonbay.cu.sk.ca
www.hudsonbaycu.com
Year Founded: 1954
Number of Employees: 17
Assets: $42,000,000
Revenues: $2,240,000
Executives:
Dave Lyster, General Manager

Industrial Savings & Credit Union Ltd.
PO Box 97
Hwy 16A & 17 St.
Edmonton, AB T5J 2G9
780-410-5502
Fax: 780-410-5391
Year Founded: 1964

Inglewood Savings & Credit Union
1328 - 9th Ave. SE
Calgary, AB T2G 0T3
403-265-5396
Fax: 403-265-1326
manager@inglewoodcu.com
www.inglewoodcu.com
Ownership: Member-owned
Year Founded: 1938
Profile: We are the oldest Credit Union in the Province of Alberta with assets over twelve million dollars & 1,500 members.

Integris Credit Union
1532 - 6th Ave.
Prince George, BC V2L 5B5

250-612-3456
Fax: 250-612-3450
www.integriscu.ca
Former Name: Prince George Savings Credit Union; Nechako Valley Credit Union; Quesnel & District Credit Union
Year Founded: 2004
Profile: A locally owned, full-service financial institution.

Executives:
Brian Bentley, CEO
Lorne Calder, CFO
Ken Dickson, COO
Sandra Rees, Sr. Manager, HR & Training
Directors:
Dave Oleskiw, Chair
Keith Brain, 1st Vice-Chair
Gerry ten Wolde, 2nd Vice-Chair
LeRoy Vossler, Corporate Secretary
Curtis Boucher
Steeve Cooley
Henry Eenkooren
Stephen Johnson
Jessie Maisonneuve
Allan Miller
Gene Mitran
Wendy Schmidt
Al Seto
Bruce Steele
Peter Valk
Branches:
Clinton
PO Box 549
1507 Hwy. 97 North
Clinton, BC V0K 1K0 Canada
250-459-2173
Fax: 250-459-2174

Fort St. James
PO Box 1360
602 Stuart Dr.
Fort St James, BC V0J 1P0 Canada
250-996-8667
Prince George
Parkwood Place Shopping Centre
#103, 1600 - 15th Ave.
Prince George, BC V2L 3X3 Canada
250-612-3456
Prince George - Ahbau & 5th
#205, 513 Ahbau St.
Prince George, BC V2M 3R8 Canada
250-612-3456
Fax: 250-612-3555
Quesnel
253 Reid St.
Quesnel, BC N2J 2M1 Canada
250-992-9216
Vanderhoof
PO Box 628
186 West Columbia St.
Vanderhoof, BC V0J 3A0 Canada
250-567-4737

Interior Savings Credit Union

#300, 678 Bernard Ave.
Kelowna, BC V1Y 6P3
250-762-4355
Fax: 250-762-9581
info@interiorsavings.com
www.interiorsavings.com
Ownership: Member owned
Assets: $100-500 million
Executives:
Barry Meckler, President/CEO
Kathy Stevenson, Sr. Vice-President, Finance
Dave Prince, Vice-President, Human Resources
Bob Peressini, Vice-President, Credit
Directors:
Elmer Epp, Chair
Wendy Caban
Roland Cacchioni
Ron Edward
Pauline Fleming
Don Grant
Jeff Holm
Bianca Iafrancesco
Gordon Matthews
Ross Parkin
Leroy Wagner
Branches:
Ashcroft
PO Box 580
201 Railway Ave.
Ashcroft, BC V0K 1A0 Canada
250-453-2219
Fax: 250-453-9080
Barriere
PO Box 860
621 Barriere Town Rd.
Barriere, BC V0E 1E0 Canada
250-672-9736
Fax: 250-672-5131
Chase
PO Box 81
814 Shuswap Ave.
Chase, BC V0E 1M0 Canada
250-679-8831
Fax: 250-679-3022
Clearwater
Brookfield Shopping Centre
PO Box 2587
RR#2
Clearwater, BC V0E 1N0 Canada
250-674-3111
Fax: 250-674-2666
Kamloops - St. Paul St.
444 St. Paul St.
Kamloops, BC V2C 2J6 Canada
250-374-3361
Fax: 250-374-8155
Kamloops - Summit Dr.
#370, 1210 Summit Dr.
Kamloops, BC V2C 6M1 Canada
250-314-1210
Fax: 250-314-3925
Kamloops - Tranquille Dr.
#100, 430 Tranquille Rd.
Kamloops, BC V2B 3H1 Canada
250-376-5544
Fax: 250-376-5379
Kamloops - Valleyview
#7, 101 East Trans Canada Hwy.
Kamloops, BC V2C 4A6 Canada
250-374-6676
Fax: 250-374-6645

Kelowna - Bernard Ave.
#101, 678 Bernard Ave.
Kelowna, BC V1Y 6P3 Canada
250-869-8300
Fax: 250-862-4839
Kelowna - Glenmore
385 Glenmore Rd.
Kelowna, BC V1V 2H3 Canada
250-762-2262
Fax: 250-762-8871
Kelowna - Mission
595 KLO Rd.
Kelowna, BC V1Y 8E7 Canada
250-763-8144
Fax: 250-862-4851
Kelowna - Orchard Centre
2071 Harvey Ave.
Kelowna, BC V1Y 8M1 Canada
250-860-7400
Fax: 250-868-9522
Kelowna - Rutland Rd.
185 Rutland Rd. South
Kelowna, BC V1X 2Z3 Canada
250-469-6575
Fax: 250-765-2846
Lake Country
#30, 9522 Main St.
Lake Country, BC V4V 2L9 Canada
250-766-3663
Fax: 250-766-3624
Lillooet
PO Box 1540
674 Main St.
Lillooet, BC V0K 1V0 Canada
250-256-4238
Fax: 250-256-4904
Merritt
PO Box 1349
1959 Voght St.
Merritt, BC V1K 1B8 Canada
250-378-5181
Fax: 250-378-9598
Okanagan Falls
PO Box 449
4929 - 9th Ave.
Okanagan Falls, BC V0H 1R0 Canada
250-497-8204
Fax: 250-497-8099
Oliver
PO Box 1080
35853 - 97th St.
Oliver, BC V0H 1T0 Canada
250-498-3457
Fax: 250-498-6288
Osoyoos
9145 Main St.
Osoyoos, BC V0H 1V0 Canada
250-495-8027
Fax: 250-495-2967
Vernon
4301 - 32nd St.
Vernon, BC V1T 9G8 Canada
250-545-1234
Fax: 250-542-7336
Westbank
3718 Elliott Rd.
Westbank, BC V4T 2H7 Canada
250-469-6550
Fax: 250-768-2459

Island Savings Credit Union

***Also listed under:** Financing & Loan Companies*
#300, 499 Canada Ave.
Duncan, BC V9L 1T7
250-748-4728
Fax: 250-748-8831
info@iscu.com
www.iscu.com
Ownership: Member-owned
Year Founded: 1951
Number of Employees: 300
Assets: $500m-1 billion
Executives:
Pam Marchant, CEO
Directors:
Sheila Service, Chair
Branches:
Brentwood Bay
#1, 7103 West Saanich Rd.
Brentwood Bay, BC V8M 1R1 Canada
250-544-4041
Fax: 250-544-0656
Cedar
Cedar Village Sq.
1830 Cedar Rd.
Cedar, BC V9X 1H9 Canada
250-722-7073
Fax: 250-722-7348
Chemainus
PO Box 120
#1, 2592 Legion St.
Chemainus, BC V0R 1K0 Canada
250-246-3273
Fax: 250-246-2821

Duncan
89 Evans Ave.
Duncan, BC V9L 1P5 Canada
250-746-4181
Fax: 250-746-4175
Ladysmith
370 Trans Canada Hwy., #A, RR#2
Ladysmith, BC V0R 2E0 Canada
250-245-0456
Fax: 250-245-5429
Lake Cowichan
PO Box 889
38 King George St. North
Lake Cowichan, BC V0R 2G0 Canada
250-749-6631
Fax: 250-749-3260

Island Savings Credit Union (continued)
Mill Bay
#38, 2720 Mill Bay Rd.
Mill Bay, BC V0R 2P0 Canada
250-743-5534
Fax: 250-743-7500
Nanaimo
Woodgrove Ctr.
#97, 6631 Island Hwy. North
Nanaimo, BC V9T 4T7 Canada
250-390-7070
Fax: 250-390-3417
Salt Spring Island
PO Box 350
124 McPhillips St.
Salt Spring Island, BC V8K 2T5 Canada
250-537-5587
Fax: 250-537-4623
Shawnigan Lake
PO Box 165
1765 Shawnigan-Mill Bay Rd.
Shawnigan Lake, BC V0R 2W0 Canada
250-743-5395
Fax: 250-743-0710
Victoria - Douglas
Mayfair Shopping Centre
#189, 3147 Douglas St.
Victoria, BC V8Z 6E3 Canada
250-358-4476
Fax: 250-384-3398
Victoria - Douglas & Broughton
933 Douglas St.
Victoria, BC V8W 2C2 Canada
250-385-4728
Fax: 250-360-1461
Victoria - Jacklin
2917 Jacklin Rd.
Victoria, BC V9B 3Y6 Canada
250-474-7262
Fax: 250-474-7219

Kakabeka Falls Community Credit Union Limited
115 Clergue St.
Kakabeka Falls, ON P0T 1W0
807-475-4276
Fax: 807-475-5990
kakabeka@tbaytel.net
www.kakabekacu.com
Executives:
Barbara Maxwell, Manager, Operations; barbaram@tbaytel.net
Branches:
Thunder Bay - Slate River
Rosslyn Rd., RR#6
Thunder Bay, ON P7C 5N5 Canada
807-939-2666
Fax: 807-939-2600
kbbranch@tbaytel.net

Kawartha Credit Union Limited
PO Box 116
1054 Monaghan Rd.
Peterborough, ON K9J 6Y5
705-743-3643
Fax: 705-749-1890
info@kawarthacu.com
www.kawarthacu.com
Year Founded: 1952
Executives:
Rob Wellstood, CEO
Cathy Martin, Branch Manager
Directors:
Carl Silvestri, Chair
Earl Robbins, Vice-Chair
Harvey Spry, Secretary
Branches:
Bancroft
PO Box 249
90C Hastings St.
Bancroft, ON K0L 1C0 Canada
613-332-2813
Fax: 613-332-2820
Sharon Rattle, Branch Manager
Bracebridge
#3, 295 Wellington St.
Bracebridge, ON P1L 1P3 Canada
705-645-9405
Fax: 705-645-4597
Robyn Specht-Kilroy, Branch Manager
Burks Falls
PO Box 548
186 Ontario St.
Burks Falls, ON P0A 1C0 Canada
705-382-2364
Fax: 705-382-1048
Amy Marshall, Branch Manager
Cobourg
2 King St. West
Cobourg, ON K9A 2L9 Canada
905-372-4331
Fax: 905-372-4332
Dana Farrell, Branch Manager
Coe Hill
Wollaston Municipal Bldg.
Coe Hill, ON K0L 1P0 Canada
613-337-5707
Sharon Rattle, Branch Manager
Emsdale
2 Church St.
Emsdale, ON P0A 1J0 Canada
705-636-7834
Fax: 705-636-7054
Amy Marshall, Branch Manager
Huntsville
110 North Kinton Ave.
Huntsville, ON P1H 0A9 Canada
705-789-7378
Fax: 705-789-1227
Tim Whitmore, Branch Manager
Keene
1107 Heritage Line
Keene, ON K0L 2G0 Canada
705-295-4455
Fax: 705-295-4452
Dan McNamee, Asst. Branch Manager
Lindsay
401 Kent St. West
Lindsay, ON K9V 2Y2 Canada
705-324-1978
Fax: 705-324-2388
Al MacKay, Branch Manager
Magnetawan
28 Church St.
Magnetawan, ON P0A 1P0 Canada
705-387-3763
Fax: 705-387-0943
Amy Marshall, Branch Manager
Parry Sound
1 Church St.
Parry Sound, ON P2A 1Y2 Canada
705-746-9061
Fax: 705-746-4898
psmcu@psmcu.com
Debbie McMurray, Branch Manager
Peterborough - Chemong
1091 Chemong Rd.
Peterborough, ON K9J 5L4 Canada
705-743-1402
Fax: 705-743-1188
Karen Woodman, Branch Manager
Peterborough - Lansdowne Place Mall
645 Lansdowne St. West
Peterborough, ON K9J 7Y7 Canada
705-743-1630
Fax: 705-743-5665
Steve Self, Branch Manager
South River
PO Box 460
83 Ottawa Ave. East
South River, ON P0A 1X0 Canada
705-386-0088
Fax: 705-386-0605
Dawn Pringle, Branch Manager
Trenton
107 Dundas St. West
Trenton, ON K8V 3P4 Canada
613-392-7200
Fax: 613-392-6358
Therese Touchette, Branch Manager

Kellogg Employees Credit Union Limited
PO Box 5517
100 Kellogg Lane
London, ON N6A 4P9
519-452-6414
Fax: 519-452-6316
kelloggcu@kelloggcu.com
www.kelloggcu.com
Year Founded: 1953
Number of Employees: 3
Revenues: $10-50 million
Executives:
Shelly Orcutt, Manager; 519-452-6321; shelly@kellogcu.com
Jennifer Palmer, Member Services Officer; 519-452-6322; jenn@kellogcu.com
Karen Ming, Representative, Member Service; 519-452-6414; karen@kelloggcu.com
Directors:
Peter Polischuk, President
Laraine Wotring, Vice-President
Henry Bartoch
Angela Elliott
Al Gibson
Lois Gosney

Kelvington Credit Union Ltd.
PO Box 459
Kelvington, SK S0A 1W0
306-327-4728
Fax: 306-327-5100
info@kelvington.cu.sk.ca
www.kelvingtoncu.com
Year Founded: 1943
Pieter McNair, General Manager
Branches:
Hendon
PO Box 88
Hendon, SK S0E 0X0 Canada
306-338-3211
Fax: 306-338-3211

Kenaston Credit Union Ltd.
PO Box 70
607 - 3rd St.
Kenaston, SK S0G 2N0
306-252-2160
garth.lewis@kenaston.cu.sk.ca
www.kenaston.cu.sk.ca
Executives:
Garth Lewis, General Manager

Kenora District Credit Union Limited
PO Box 2200
101 Park St.
Kenora, ON P9N 3X8
807-467-4400
Fax: 807-468-6452
www.kdcu.on.ca
Branches:
Keewatin
601 Ottawa St.
Keewatin, ON P0X 1C0 Canada
807-547-2751
Fax: 807-547-3004
Kenora
510 - 9th St. North
Kenora, ON P9N 2S8 Canada
807-467-4420
Fax: 807-468-9289

Kerrobert Credit Union Ltd.
PO Box 140
437 Pacific Ave.
Kerrobert, SK S0L 1R0
306-834-2611
Fax: 306-834-5558
info@kerrobert.cu.sk.ca
www.kerrobert.cu.sk.ca
Year Founded: 1963
Branches:
Major
General Delivery
Major, SK S0L 2H0 Canada
306-834-5424
Fax: 306-834-1118

Khalsa Credit Union (Alberta) Limited
#604, 4656 Westwinds Dr. NE
Calgary, AB T3J 3Z5
403-285-0707
Fax: 403-285-0771
khalsacu@telusplanet.net
Year Founded: 1995
Number of Employees: 3
Assets: $1-5 million Year End: 20061114
Revenues: $1-5 million Year End: 20061114
Executives:
Gurvinder K. Hundal, Manager

King-York Newsmen Toronto Credit Union Limited
444 Front St. West
Toronto, ON M5V 2S9
416-585-5110
Fax: 416-585-3498
credit-union@globeandmail.ca
Ownership: Private
Year Founded: 1955
Assets: $1-5 million
Revenues: $1-5 million
Executives:
Gerard Ter Hofstede, President

Kootenay Savings Credit Union
#300, 1199 Cedar Ave.
Trail, BC V1R 4B8
250-368-2686
Fax: 250-368-5203
info@kscu.com
www.kscu.com
Ownership: Member-owned
Year Founded: 1969
Number of Employees: 208
Assets: $500m-1 billion
Executives:
Brent Tremblay, President/CEO
Directors:
Forrest Drinnan, Chair
Judy Aldridge, 1st Vice-Chair
Nick Ogloff, 2nd Vice-Chair
Shehzad Bharmal
Helga Boker
Walter Bottcher
David Gentles
John Loo
Keith Smyth
Phyllis Stone
Branches:
Castlegar
1016 - 4th St.
Castlegar, BC V1N 2B2 Canada
250-365-3375
Fax: 250-365-2228
Edgewater
PO Box 39
5759 Sinclair St.
Edgewater, BC V0A 1E0 Canada
250-347-9473
Fax: 250-347-9362
Fruitvale
PO Box 790
1945 Main St.
Fruitvale, BC V0G 1L0 Canada
250-367-9223
Fax: 250-367-7741
Invermere
1028 - 7th St.
Invermere, BC V0A 1K0 Canada
250-342-6961
Fax: 250-342-6963
Kaslo
PO Box 478
437 Front St.
Kaslo, BC V0G 1M0 Canada
250-353-2217
Fax: 250-353-2272
Kimberley
200 Wallinger Ave.
Kimberley, BC V1A 1Z1 Canada
250-427-2288
Fax: 250-427-4488
Nakusp
PO Box 690
502 Broadway St.
Nakusp, BC V0G 1R0 Canada
250-265-3605
Fax: 250-265-3838
New Denver
PO Box 128
411 - 6th Ave.
New Denver, BC V0G 1S0 Canada
250-358-2217
Fax: 250-358-7166
Salmo
PO Box 242
619 Hwy. 6
Salmo, BC V0G 1Z0 Canada
250-357-2281
Fax: 250-357-2230
South Slocan
2804 Hwy. 3A, RR#1
South Slocan, BC V0G 2G0 Canada
250-359-7221
Fax: 250-359-7199
800-910-7221
Trail
1199 Cedar Ave.
Trail, BC V1R 4B8 Canada
250-368-2647
Fax: 250-368-3754
Trail - Waneta Plaza
#134, 8100 Hwy. 3B
Trail, BC V1R 4N7 Canada
250-368-8291
Fax: 250-368-8805
Trail - Warfield
890 Schofield Hwy.
Trail, BC V1R 2G9 Canada
250-368-6421
Fax: 250-368-8786

Korean (Toronto) Credit Union Limited
703 Bloor St. West
Toronto, ON M6G 1L5
416-535-4511
Fax: 416-535-9323
ktcul@rogers.com
Executives:
Harold Yu, General Manager

Korean Catholic Church Credit Union Limited
849 Don Mills Rd., 2nd Fl.
Toronto, ON M3C 1W1
416-447-7788
Fax: 416-447-5297
kcccu@on.aibn.com
Executives:
Francis. Jung, General Manager

Krek Slovenian Credit Union Ltd.
747 Brown's Line
Toronto, ON M8W 3V7
416-252-6527
Fax: 416-252-2092
main@krek.ca
www.krek.ca
Former Name: John E. Krek's Slovenian (Toronto) Credit Union Limited
Ownership: Private
Year Founded: 1953
Number of Employees: 17
Assets: $50-100 million Year End: 20060930
Executives:
Joseph Cestnik, General Manager
Roman Vojska, Manager, Finance
Branches:
Manning Ave.
#100, 611 Manning Ave.
Toronto, ON M6G 2W1 Canada
416-532-4746
Fax: 416-532-5134

L'Alliance des caisses populaires de l'Ontario limitée
PO Box 3500
1870 Bond St.
North Bay, ON P1B 4V6
705-474-5634
Fax: 705-474-5326
support@acpol.com
www.caissealliance.com
Ownership: Member-owned.
Year Founded: 1979
Number of Employees: 240
Assets: $500m-1 billion
Revenues: $10-50 million
Executives:
Philippe Boissonneault, President
Norman St. Amour, Vice-President
Lucie Moncion, General Manager
Robert Verreault, Secretary
Jocelyn St. Pierre, Treasurer
Directors:
Yves Bourassa
Bobby Prévost
Affiliates:
Caisse populaire d'Alban limitée
PO Box 40
21 Delemare Rd.
Alban, ON P0M 1A0 Canada
705-857-2082
Fax: 705-857-3181
Stéphane Methot, General Manager
Caisse populaire de Bonfield limitée
230 Yonge St.
Bonfield, ON P0H 1E0 Canada
705-776-2831
Fax: 705-776-1023
Darlene Hotte, General Manager
Caisse populaire de Field limitée
PO Box 3
8, Grande Allée St.
Field, ON P0H 1M0 Canada
705-758-6581
Fax: 705-758-9010
Pierre Leclair, General Manager
Caisse populaire de Hearst limitée
PO Box 698
908 Prince St.
Hearst, ON P0L 1N0 Canada
705-362-4308
Fax: 705-372-1987
Robert Verreault, General Manager
Caisse populaire de Mattawa limitée
PO Box 519
370 Main St.
Mattawa, ON P0H 1V0 Canada
705-744-5561
Fax: 705-744-5168
René Maheu, General Manager
Caisse populaire de Mattice limitée
PO Box 178
249 King St.
Mattice, ON P0L 1T0 Canada
705-364-4441
Fax: 705-364-2013
Huguette Vallée, General Manager
Caisse populaire de North Bay limitée
630 Cassells St.
North Bay, ON P1B 4A2 Canada
705-474-5650
Fax: 705-474-5687
nvoyer321@acpol.com
www.caissenorthbay.com
Norman St. Amour, General Manager
Caisse populaire de Verner limitée
PO Box 119
1 Principale St. East
Verner, ON P0H 2M0 Canada
705-594-2388
Fax: 705-594-9423
Serge Caron, General Manager
Caisse populaire Kapuskasing limitée
36 Riverside Dr.
Kapuskasing, ON P5N 1A6 Canada
705-335-6161
Fax: 705-335-2707
cpka@caissekap.on.ca
Isabelle Albert, General Manager
Caisse Populaire Noëlville limitée

L'Alliance des caisses populaires de l'Ontario limitée (continued)

PO Box 100
87 St David St. North
Noelville, ON P0M 2N0 Canada
705-898-2350
Fax: 705-898-3265
Hubert Nadeau, General Manager

Caisse populaire St-Charles Borromée limitée
15 King St.
St Charles, ON P0M 2W0 Canada
705-867-2002
Fax: 705-867-5710
Bobby Prévost, President

Caisse populaire Sturgeon Falls limitée
241 King St.
Sturgeon Falls, ON P2B 1S1 Canada
705-753-2970
Fax: 705-753-2986
Jean Louiseize, General Manager

La Caisse populaire de Timmins limitée
45 Mountjoy St. North
Timmins, ON P4N 8H7 Canada
705-268-9724
Fax: 705-268-6858
Jocelyn St-Pierre, General Manager

Ladysmith & District Credit Union

PO Box 430
330 First Ave.
Ladysmith, BC V9G 1A3
250-245-2247
Fax: 250-245-5913
info@ldcu.ca
www.ldcu.ca
Year Founded: 1944
Directors:
Brian Childs, President
Ted Girard, Vice-President
Tim Richards, Secretary
Joan Adair
Ralph Harding
Marie Polachek
Rob Viala

LaFleche Credit Union Ltd.

105 Main St.
Lafleche, SK S0H 2K0
306-472-5215
Fax: 306-472-5545
info@lafleche.cu.sk.ca
www.laflechecu.com
Ownership: Member-owned
Year Founded: 1938
Number of Employees: 14
Assets: $10-50 million
Executives:
Ben Filson, President
Loretta Eastley Halushka, Vice-President
Bruce Anderson, Treasurer
Carmen Ellis, Scretary
Directors:
Loratta Eastley, Vice-President
Debbie Ash
Clem Boisvert
Raymond Clermont
Ben Filson
Jim Hribnak
Marilyn Lamont
Dean Layman
Guy Monette
Branches:
Glentworth
PO Box 128
Centre St.
Glentworth, SK S0H 1V0 Canada
306-266-4821
Tracy Johnson, Manager

Lake View Credit Union

800 - 102nd Ave.
Dawson Creek, BC V1G 2B2
250-782-4871
Fax: 250-782-5828
www.lakeviewcreditunion.com
Ownership: Private
Number of Employees: 36
Directors:
Joseph Judge, Chair
Dennis Abbot
Erwin Hollingshead
Larry Loroff
Diana Mattson
Ruth Veiner
Heather Weather
Branches:
Chetwynd
PO Box 925
4729 - 51st St.
Chetwynd, BC V0C 1J0 Canada
250-788-9227
Fax: 250-788-9237
Tumbler Ridge
PO Box 970
245 Main St.
Tumbler Ridge, BC V0C 2W0 Canada
250-242-4871
Fax: 250-242-4544

Lakeland Credit Union

PO Box 8057
5016 - 50 Ave.
Bonnyville, AB T9N 2J3
780-826-3377
Fax: 780-826-6322
info@lakelandcreditunion.com
www.lakelandcreditunion.com
Executives:
Joanne Williamson
Branches:
Cold Lake
PO Box 1110
5217 - 50th Ave.
Cold Lake, AB T9M 1P3 Canada
780-594-4011
Fax: 780-594-2646
coldlake@lakelandcreditunion.com

Lakewood Credit Union Ltd.

346 - 2nd St. South
Kenora, ON P9N 1G5
807-468-9811
Fax: 807-468-3500
lakewoodcu@norcomcable.ca
www.lakewoodcu.on.ca
Ownership: Member-owned
Year Founded: 1954
Number of Employees: 34
Profile: Full-service financial institution.

Executives:
Randy Crerar, CEO
Directors:
Jim Rivington, Chair
Branches:
Ear Falls
PO Box 987
#4, 30 Spruce St.
Ear Falls, ON P0V 1T0 Canada
807-222-2240
Fax: 807-222-2233
earfalls@lakewoodcu.on.ca
Mary Hovorka, Branch Manager
Nestor Falls
General Delivery
Hwy. 71
Nestor Falls, ON P0X 1K0 Canada
807-484-2201
Fax: 807-484-2604
nestorfalls@lakewoodcu.on.ca
Debra Ducharme, Manager
Sioux Narrows
PO Box 397
Hwy. 71
Sioux Narrows, ON P0X 1N0 Canada
807-226-5500
Fax: 807-226-5636
siouxnarrows@lakewoodcu.on.ca

Lambton Financial Credit Union Ltd.

1295 London Rd.
Sarnia, ON N7S 1P6
519-542-0483
Fax: 519-542-3778
866-380-8008
www.lambtonfinancial.ca
Former Name: Polysar Lambton Credit Union Limited
Ownership: Private
Year Founded: 1947
Number of Employees: 48
Assets: $100-500 million
Revenues: $5-10 million
Executives:
John Hassenstein, General Manager; john@lambtonfinancial.ca
Sue Dupont, Manager, Administration; sue@lambtonfinancial.ca

Bob Ferris, Manager, Financial Services/Marketing; bob@lambtonfinancial.ca
Directors:
Shaun Larocque, Chair
Bryan Bouck, Vice-Chair
Herman Meixnec, Secretary
Vicki Bouman
Louis D'Alimonte
Neal Levitt
Clare MacDonald
Gary Matthews
Brad Taylor
Branches:
Brigden
2394 Jane St.
Brigden, ON N0N 1B0 Canada
519-864-1026
Mark Hoffman, Branch Manager
Port Lambton
4348 St Clair Pkwy.
Port Lambton, ON N0P 2B0 Canada
519-677-5652
Brenda Dennis, Branch Manager
Sarnia
300 Huron Blvd.
Sarnia, ON N7T 7J4 Canada
519-344-9538
Eileen Spowatt, Branch Manager

Landis Credit Union Ltd.

PO Box 220
Landis, SK S0K 2K0
306-658-2152
Fax: 306-658-2153
owen.nicklin@landis.cu.sk.ca
www.landis.cu.sk.ca
Year Founded: 1942
Number of Employees: 4
Assets: $5-10 million
Revenues: Under $1 million
Executives:
Owen Nicklin, General Manager

Lasco Employees' (Whitby) Credit Union Limited

1801 Hopkins St. South
Whitby, ON L1N 5T1
905-668-8811
Fax: 905-668-2807

Latvian Credit Union

4 Credit Union Dr.
Toronto, ON M4A 2N8
416-922-2551
Fax: 416-922-2758
www.kredsab.ca
Ownership: Member owned
Number of Employees: 12
Profile: Personal loans, car loans, line of credit loans, mortgage loans, home equity loans, reverse mortgages, savings accounts, US savings accounts, personal chequing accounts, term deposits, RRSP deposits, payroll deposits, electronic funds transfer, preauthorized payments, money transfers to Latvia.

Executives:
Andris Lagzdins, Manager; lagzdins@kredsab.ca
Directors:
Aleksandris Budrevics, Vice-Chair
Branches:
Hamilton
16 Queen St.
Hamilton, ON L8R 2T8 Canada
905-527-4344
Mara Leja

Lear Seating Canada Employees' (Kitchener) Credit Union Ltd.
PO Box 758
530 Manitou Dr.
Kitchener, ON
519-895-3213

Legacy Savings & Credit Union Ltd.
215 - 12 Ave. SE
Calgary, AB T2G 1A2
403-265-6050
Fax: 403-265-8010
admin@legacysavings.com
www.legacysavings.com
Executives:
Rod Anderson, General Manager
Robbie Allenhack, Manager, Financial Services
Directors:
Pat Rickards, President
Garry Riggs, Vice-President
Orson Abbott
Doug Chibry
James D. Phillips
Harry Vince
Robert Weselosky

Lethbridge Legion Savings & Credit Union Ltd.
324 Mayor Magrath Dr.
Lethbridge, AB T1J 3L7
403-327-6417
Fax: 403-317-0122
Year Founded: 1958

Libro Financial Group
167 Central Ave., 2nd Fl.
London, ON N6A 1M6
519-672-0124
Fax: 519-672-7831
800-265-5935
service@libro.ca
www.libro.ca
Former Name: St. Willibrod Credit Union Limited; St. Willibrod Community Credit Union Limited
Ownership: 47,000 owners
Year Founded: 1951
Number of Employees: 300
Assets: $1-10 billion Year End: 20060831
Revenues: $500m-1 billion Year End: 20060831
Profile: Full financial services are provided.

Executives:
Jack Smit, President/CEO
Harry Joosten, Vice-President, Owner Relations, Corporate Secretary
Branches:
Arkona
PO Box 2
7130 Arkona Rd.
Arkona, ON N0M 1B0 Canada
519-828-3971
Fax: 519-828-3900
800-561-7541

Blenheim
PO Box 675
11 Talbot St. West
Blenheim, ON N0P 1A0 Canada
519-676-8104
Fax: 519-676-0911
London - Central Ave.
167 Central Ave., 1st Fl.
London, ON N6A 1M6 Canada
519-673-4130
Fax: 519-642-1589
London - Dundas St. East
1867 Dundas St. East
London, ON N5W 3G1 Canada
519-451-2200
Fax: 519-451-2167
London - Richmond St.
1703 Richmond St.
London, ON N5X 3Y2 Canada
519-673-6928
Fax: 519-642-1873
London - Wellington Rd. South
841 Wellington Rd. South
London, ON N6E 3R5 Canada
519-686-1291
Fax: 519-686-9347
Sarnia
1315 Exmouth St.
Sarnia, ON N7S 3Y1 Canada
519-542-5578
Fax: 519-542-3008
St Thomas
8 Southside St.
St Thomas, ON N5R 3R6 Canada
519-631-6195
Fax: 519-631-6196
Stratford
391 Huron St.
Stratford, ON N5A 5T6 Canada
519-271-4883
Fax: 519-271-3431
Strathroy
72 Front St. West
Strathroy, ON N7G 1X7 Canada
519-245-1261
Fax: 519-245-6391
Waterloo
55 Northfield Dr. East
Waterloo, ON N2K 3T6 Canada
519-744-1031
Fax: 519-744-4011
Watford
PO Box 550
5307 Nauvoo Rd.
Watford, ON N0M 2S0 Canada
519-876-2748
Fax: 519-876-2116
800-425-8855
Wingham
8 Alfred St.
Wingham, ON N0G 2W0 Canada
519-357-2311
Fax: 519-357-3822

Lintlaw Credit Union Ltd.
PO Box 190
212 Main St.
Lintlaw, SK S0A 2H0
306-325-2118
Fax: 306-325-4311
Year Founded: 1940

LIUNA Local 183 Credit Union Limited
#108, 1263 Wilson Ave.
Toronto, ON M3M 3G2
416-242-6643
Fax: 416-242-7852

London Civic Employees' Credit Union Limited
343 Dundas St.
London, ON N6B 1V5
519-661-4563
Fax: 519-663-9369
memberservices@lcecu.com
www.lcecu.com
Ownership: Private
Year Founded: 1948
Executives:
Tom Jolliffe, CEO
Jean Gillespie, Sr. Financial Services Officer
Directors:
Lyle McLean, Chair
Kim Darling, Vice-Chair
Brenda Harwood
Paul Hearse
Jim Morton
Shelley Popovich
Lou Rivard

London Diesel Employees' Credit Union Limited
#4B, 525 First St.
London, ON N5V 1Z5
519-451-9580
Fax: 519-451-1831
london_diesel@yahoo.com
Year Founded: 1951

London Fire Fighters' Credit Union Limited
400 Horton St. East
London, ON N6B 1L7
519-661-5635
Fax: 519-661-5635
info@lfdcreditunion.com
www.lfdcreditunion.com
Ownership: Private
Number of Employees: 2
Executives:
Nellie Stronach, Manager

Macklin Credit Union Ltd.
PO Box 326
4809 Herald St.
Macklin, SK S0L 2C0
306-753-2333
Fax: 306-753-2676
info@macklin.cu.sk.ca
www.macklin.cu.sk.ca
Number of Employees: 13
Executives:
Reni Ostlund, General Manager
Directors:
Arnold Rolheiser, President
Linda Gramlich, Vice-President
Dennis Knox
Linda McKinnon
Wally Reschny
Michael Schachtel
Ron Veller
Art Wagner

Macleod Savings & Credit Union Ltd.
PO Box 1659
5018 - 2nd St. West
Claresholm, AB T0L 0T0
403-625-2179
Fax: 403-625-4413
admin@macleodcu.com
www.macleodcu.com
Ownership: Member-owned
Year Founded: 1941
Number of Employees: 35
Assets: $50-100 million
Branches:
Claresholm
PO Box 1056
134 - 50th Ave. West
Claresholm, AB T0L 0T0 Canada
403-625-4401
Fax: 403-625-4612
Fort Macleod
PO Box 940
2209 - 2nd Ave.
Fort MacLeod, AB T0L 0Z0 Canada
403-553-4414
Fax: 403-553-2473
Nanton
PO Box 548
2014 - 21 Ave.
Nanton, AB T0L 1R0 Canada
403-646-2610
Fax: 403-646-2717
Vulcan
PO Box 305
110 - 2 Ave.
Vulcan, AB T0L 2B0 Canada
403-485-2268
Fax: 403-485-2691

Main-à-Dieu Credit Union
#3, 2886 Louis-Main-A-Dieu Rd.
Main-à-Dieu, NS B1C 1X5
902-733-2555
Fax: 902-733-2301
Ownership: Members
Year Founded: 1935
Number of Employees: 2
Assets: $1-5 million Year End: 20051031
Revenues: Under $1 million Year End: 20051031
Executives:
Annette Phillips, Manager/Treasurer
Directors:
Theresa Boone; 902-733-2776
Frances Forgeron; 902-733-2871
Elizabeth McDougall; 902-733-2803
Mary Price; 902-733-2813
Keven Spencer; 902-733-3030

Main-à-Dieu Credit Union (continued)
Roberta Wadden; 902-733-2670

Mankota Credit Union
Main St.
Mankota, SK S0H 2W0
306-478-2284
Fax: 306-478-2277
info@mankota.cu.sk.ca
www.mankotacu.com
Number of Employees: 7
Lynda Anderson, General Manager

Mariposa Community Credit Union Limited
PO Box 129
2 King St. South
Little Britain, ON K0M 2C0
705-786-3524
Fax: 705-786-3568
mccu.littlebritain@sympatico.ca
www3.sympatico.ca/mccu.kinmount/
Ownership: Private
Year Founded: 1995
Number of Employees: 6
Executives:
Bob MacMorran, Acting General Manager
Branches:
Kinmount
PO Box 69
Main St.
Kinmount, ON K0M 2A0 Canada
705-488-9963
Fax: 705-488-9965
mccu.kinmount@sympatico.ca
Sue Strong, Branch Supervisor

McMaster Savings & Credit Union Ltd.
Westdale Village
1005 King St. West
Hamilton, ON L8S 1L3
905-522-2903
Fax: 905-522-4467
maccuwest@cogeco.net
www.maccu.com
Ownership: Member-owned
Year Founded: 1936
Branches:
Hamilton - Barton Village
654 Barton St. East
Hamilton, ON L8L 3A2 Canada
905-545-0269
Fax: 905-545-4511
bartoncu@maccu.com
Hamilton - Rymal Rd.
905 Rymal Rd. East
Hamilton, ON L8W 3Z5 Canada
905-388-0102
Fax: 905-388-3669
Mount Hope
PO Box 222
3200 Homestead Dr.
Mount Hope, ON L0R 1W0 Canada
905-679-8655
Fax: 905-679-8650
mscu@mountaincable.net

Me-Dian Credit Union
#102, 338 Broadway
Winnipeg, MB R3C 0T3
204-943-9111
Fax: 204-942-3698

Media Group Financial Credit Union Limited
369 York St.
London, ON N6A 4G1
519-667-4505
Fax: 519-667-5522
creditunion@mediagroupfinancial.ca
www.mediagroupfinancial.ca
Profile: Members are employees of The London Free Press, Bowes Publishers Ltd., Corus Entertainment Inc., The Blackburn Group, The A-Channel or CHUM Radio - BOB FM, & their families.
Executives:
Sandra Manship, Assistant Manager & Secretary
Directors:
Jara Kral, President
Jeff Kadlecik, Vice-President
Patty Blastock
Wanda Latuszak
Ben Phay

The Medical-Dental Financial, Savings & Credit Limited
c/o Credential, Ontario Regl. Office
#200, 3430 South Service Rd.
Burlington, ON L7N 3T9
905-632-9200
Fax: 905-632-0032

Member Savings Credit Union
55 Lakeshore Blvd. East
Toronto, ON M5E 1A4
416-864-2461
Fax: 416-864-6858
888-560-2218
membercu@membercu.com
www.membercu.com
Year Founded: 1949
Assets: $50-100 million
Executives:
Sharon Kent, General Manager; sharon@membercu.com
Susan Tustin, Manager, Operations; susan@membercu.com
Lila James, Loan Officer; lila@membercu.com
Branches:
Allstream
#1412, 200 Wellington St. West
Toronto, ON M5V 3C7 Canada
416-345-3175
Fax: 416-345-2044
karyn@membercu.com
Karyn Smith, Branch Manager
Honeywell Employees Branch
35 Dynamic Dr.
Toronto, ON M1V 4Z9 Canada
416-332-3330
Fax: 416-332-3332
lisa@membercu.com
Lisa Churcher, Administrator

MemberOne Credit Union Ltd.
PO Box 35
200 Front St. West, Concourse Level
Toronto, ON M5V 3K2
416-344-4070
Fax: 416-344-4069
info@memberone.ca
www.memberone.ca
Former Name: WCB Credit Union Limited
Executives:
Lenore Turgeon, General Manager
Tracy Patten, Asst. General Manager

Mendham-Burstall Credit Union
PO Box 69
Mendham, SK S0N 1P0
306-628-3257
Fax: 306-628-4284
mendham@sasktel.net
Ownership: Member-owned
Assets: $10-50 million
Revenues: Under $1 million
Executives:
Randy Schneider, General Manager
Branches:
Burstall
PO Box 130
Burstall, SK S0N 0H0 Canada
306-679-2280
Fax: 306-679-2120

Mennonite Savings & Credit Union (Ontario) Limited
1265 Strasburg Rd.
Kitchener, ON N2R 1S6
519-746-1010
Fax: 519-746-1045
888-672-6728
info@mscu.com
www.mscu.com
Ownership: Member-owned
Year Founded: 1964
Number of Employees: 96
Assets: $500m-1 billion
Revenues: $50-100 million
Profile: Credit Union is affiliated with Meritas Financial Inc.
Executives:
Nick Driedger, CEO
Michael Fewkes, CIO, Risk Manager
John Klassen, COO
Karl Braun, Manager, Member Relations
Pam McCartney, Manager, Human Resources
Branches:
Elmira
25 Hampton St.
Elmira, ON N3B 1L6 Canada
519-669-1529
Fax: 519-699-3292
Ben Doan, Branch Manager
Kitchener
50 Kent Ave.
Kitchener, ON N2G 3R1 Canada
519-576-7220
Fax: 519-576-9188
Bruce Fretz, Branch Manager
Leamington
243 Erie St. South
Leamington, ON N8H 3C1 Canada
519-326-8601
Fax: 519-326-4659
John Dean, Branch Manager
Milverton
#2, 12 Main St. South
Milverton, ON N0K 1M0 Canada
519-595-8796
Fax: 519-595-8799
Marion Good, Branch Manager
New Hamburg
#M, 100 Mill St.
New Hamburg, ON N0B 2G0 Canada
519-662-3550
Fax: 519-662-1102
Michelle Horst, Branch Manager
Waterloo
53 Bridgeport Rd., East
Waterloo, ON N2J 2J7 Canada
519-746-1770
Fax: 519-747-4109
Yvonne Martin, Branch Manager

Meridian Credit Union
Maclean-Hunter Bldg., College Park
777 Bay St., 26th Fl.
Toronto, ON M5G 2C8
416-597-4400
Fax: 416-597-5068
866-592-2226
www.meridiancu.ca
Former Name: HEPCOE Credit Union Limited
Ownership: Member-owned
Year Founded: 2005
Number of Employees: 1,000
Assets: $1-10 billion
Profile: Meridian Credit Union launched April 4, 2005, following member & shareholder approval of the amalgamation between HEPCOE Credit Union & NIAGARA Credit Union. Meridian becomes Ontario's largest & Canada's third largest credit union with 220,000 members, $4.6 billion in assets & a network of 43 branches & 8 commercial banking centres in communities across the Niagara region, the Greater Toronto Area & central Ontario.
Directors:
Don Ariss
Mark Basciano
Bruno Bellissimo
Judy Brisson
Alan Caslin
Bill Falk
Henry Koop
Erv Krause
John D. Kwekkeboom
Donna Lailey
Brian McAteer
Bob Pesant
Kevin Sherwood
Kevin Thompson
Karl Wettstein
Helen Young
Branches:
Aurora

297 Wellington St. East
Aurora, ON L4G 1G3 Canada
905-727-1191
Fax: 905-727-6357
Ann Boyle, Manager

Barrie
18 Collier St.
Barrie, ON L4M 5E1 Canada
705-728-5191
Fax: 705-728-9170
Victoria Boseley, Manager

Beamsville
4520 Ontario St.
Beamsville, ON L0R 1B5 Canada
905-563-0822
Fax: 905-563-1040
Brock Warriner, Manager

Bowmanville
320 Holt Rd. South, RR#2
Bowmanville, ON L1C 3K3 Canada
905-623-7973
Fax: 905-623-2648
Karen Van Alstyne, Manager

Collingwood
171 Marie St.
Collingwood, ON L9Y 3K3 Canada
705-445-9200
Fax: 705-445-6801
Lynda Wilson, Manager

Fergus
120 MacQueen Blvd.
Fergus, ON N1M 3T8 Canada
519-843-5451
Fax: 519-787-1620
Sylvain Painchaud, Manager

Fonthill
1401 Pelham St.
Fonthill, ON L0S 1E0 Canada
905-892-2626
Fax: 905-892-4421
Tom Naylor, Manager

Fort Erie
#14, 450 Garrison Rd.
Fort Erie, ON L2A 1N2 Canada
905-994-8181
Fax: 905-994-8383
Denise Faraday, Manager

Grimsby
155 Main St. East
Grimsby, ON L3M 1P2 Canada
905-945-2930
Fax: 905-945-6552
Ted Barnes, Manager

Guelph - Speedvale
200 Speedvale Ave. West
Guelph, ON N1H 6N3 Canada
519-822-1072
Fax: 519-822-5162
Sylvain Painchaud, Manager

Guelph - Stone
Stone Square
370 Stone Rd. West
Guelph, ON N1G 4V9 Canada
519-837-2233
Fax: 519-837-3295
Rita Pizzo, Manager, Accounts

Hanover
255 - 10 St.
Hanover, ON N4N 1P5 Canada
519-364-3473
Fax: 519-364-5462
Michele Hettrick, Manager

Kincardine
818 Durham St.
Kincardine, ON N2Z 3B9 Canada
519-395-3122
Fax: 519-395-4146
kincardine@hepcoe.com
Michele Hettrick, Manager

Mississauga - Clarkson
970 Southdown Rd.
Mississauga, ON L5J 2Y4 Canada
905-855-0951
Fax: 905-855-8375
Elena Howard-Jung, Manager

Nanticoke
34 Haldimand Rd. 55
Nanticoke, ON N0A 1L0 Canada
519-587-2241
Fax: 519-587-4243
Jacque James, Manager

Niagara Falls - Dunn
6175 Dunn St.
Niagara Falls, ON L2G 2P4 Canada
905-358-5045
Fax: 905-358-0798
Amy Hart, Manager

Niagara Falls - Portage
4780 Portage Rd.
Niagara Falls, ON L2E 6A8 Canada
905-356-2275
Fax: 905-357-9634
Tracy Barry-De Paz, Manager

Orangeville
#1, 190 Broadway
Orangeville, ON L9W 1K3 Canada
519-940-9943
Fax: 519-940-9243
Barbara Gardiner, Branch Manager

Orillia
73 Mississauga St.
Orillia, ON L3V 6K5 Canada
705-325-2287
Fax: 705-325-8679
Kathi Shropshire, Branch Manager

Owen Sound
1594 - 16th Ave. East
Owen Sound, ON N4K 5N3 Canada
519-371-7355
Fax: 519-371-9713
Mark Ostland, Branch Manager

Penetanguishene
7 Poyntz St.
Penetanguishene, ON L9M 1M3 Canada
705-549-3191
Fax: 705-549-5884
Maureen Reid, Manager

Pickering - Kingston
#25, 1550 Kingston Rd.
Pickering, ON L1V 1C3 Canada
905-831-1121
Fax: 905-420-0864
Tony Pelosi, Manager

Pickering - Montgomery Park
1675 Montgomery Park Rd.
Pickering, ON L1V 2R5 Canada
905-837-2580
Fax: 905-837-1690
Tony Pelosi, Manager

Port Colborne
43 Clarence St.
Port Colborne, ON L3K 3G1 Canada
905-834-6764
Fax: 905-835-2840
Deborah Crowe, Manager

Port Elgin
626 Goderich St.
Port Elgin, ON N0H 2C0 Canada
519-832-9011
Fax: 519-389-4613
Erin Zorzi, Manager

Richmond Hill
9050 Yonge St.
Richmond Hill, ON L4C 9S6 Canada
905-882-5225
Fax: 905-882-8297
James Ecker, Manager

St Catharines - Fourth Ave.
111 Fourth Ave.
St Catharines, ON L2S 3P5 Canada
905-688-6563
Fax: 905-688-1015
Leslie Grivich, Manager

St Catharines - Lake St.
531 Lake St.
St Catharines, ON L2N 4H6 Canada
905-937-7111
Fax: 905-937-1311
Brian Berton, Manager

St Catharines - Scott St.
Scott St.
St Catharines, ON L2M 3W4 Canada
905-934-9561
Fax: 905-937-7995
Todd Horton, Manager

Stevensville
2763 Stevensville Rd.
Stevensville, ON L0S 1S0 Canada
905-382-3126
Fax: 905-382-2011
Frank Hannaway, Manager

Toronto - Bay
Trinity Square
#160S, 483 Bay St.
Toronto, ON M5G 2E1 Canada
416-591-0293
Fax: 416-348-9042
Doug Bray, Manager

Toronto - Ellesmere
1501 Ellesmere Rd.
Toronto, ON M1P 4T6 Canada
416-438-9231
Fax: 416-438-9346
Parm Persaud, Manager

Toronto - Kipling
800 Kipling Ave.
Toronto, ON M8Z 5S4 Canada
416-231-6329
Fax: 416-231-3222
Tim Josefik, Manager

Toronto - Morningside
797 Milner Ave.
Toronto, ON M1B 3C3 Canada
416-281-5111
Fax: 416-281-5012
Nick Tsiogas, Manager

Toronto - TeleOntario
700 University Ave., 25th Fl.
Toronto, ON M5G 1X6 Canada
416-204-7816
Fax: 416-204-7820
Sue Bennison, Senior Manager

Toronto - University
Hydro Place
700 University Ave., Lower Concourse
Toronto, ON M5G 1X6 Canada
416-597-1050
Fax: 416-971-9412
Doug Bray, Branch Manager

Vineland
3370 King St.
Vineland, ON L0R 2C0 Canada
905-562-7373
Fax: 905-562-4907
Wendy Cox, Manager

Virgil
1567 Niagara Stone Rd.
Virgil, ON L0S 1T0 Canada
905-468-2131
Fax: 905-468-4894
Gary Iggulden, Manager

Wainfleet
Hwy. 3
Wainfleet, ON L0S 1V0 Canada
905-899-3951
Fax: 905-899-1236
Lori Heemskerk, Manager

Wasaga Beach
707 River Rd. West
Wasaga Beach, ON L0L 2P0 Canada
705-429-9824
Fax: 705-429-9827
Dale Gamble, Manager

Welland
610 Niagara St. North
Welland, ON L3C 1L8 Canada
905-732-7372
Fax: 905-732-2558
Geri Morrone, Manager

Whitby
4061 Thickson Rd. North
Whitby, ON L1R 2X3 Canada
905-655-6336
Fax: 905-655-1371

Meridian Credit Union (continued)

Corporate Office:
St Catharines Corporate Head Office
75 Corporate Park Dr.
St Catharines, ON L2S 3W3 Canada
905-988-1000
Fax: 905-988-9326
866-592-2226

Midale Credit Union Ltd.
PO Box 418
211 Main St.
Midale, SK S0C 1S0
306-458-2222
Fax: 306-458-2329
bob.harris@midale.cu.sk.ca
www.midale.cu.sk.ca
Executives:
Robert Harris, General Manager
Directors:
Dave Piper, President

Milestone Credit Union Ltd.
PO Box 144
118 Main St.
Milestone, SK S0G 3L0
306-436-2002
Fax: 306-436-2114
info@milestone.cu.sk.ca
Former Name: Milestone Savings & Credit Union Ltd.

Minnedosa Credit Union
PO Box 459
60 Main St.
Minnedosa, MB R0J 1E0
204-867-6350
Fax: 204-867-6391
877-663-7228
www.minnedosacu.mb.ca
Year Founded: 1947
Number of Employees: 20
Executives:
Don Farr, General Manager
Carol Taylor, Manager, Member Services
Harvey Wedgewood, Manager, Loans
Directors:
Ray Morgan, President
Marc Chisholm, Vice-President
Ron Kingdon, Secretary
Ed Bilcowski
Debby Charles
Barb Cook
Pat Heuchert
Barry McNabb
Derek Turner

Minton-Gladmar Credit Union Ltd.
PO Box 79
Minton, SK S0C 1T0
306-969-2141
Fax: 306-969-2237

Miracle Credit Union Ltd.
#22, 86 Guided Crt.
Toronto, ON M9V 4K6
416-740-7553
Fax: 416-740-3767
miracle@on.aibn.com

Mitchell & District Credit Union Limited
105 Ontario Rd.
Mitchell, ON N0K 1N0
519-348-8448
Fax: 519-348-8009
mitchell@mitchellcu.ca
www.mitchellcu.ca
Ownership: Private
Year Founded: 1960
Number of Employees: 33
Assets: $50-100 million Year End: 20050930
Revenues: $1-5 million Year End: 20050930
Executives:
Beth Bruesch, CEO
Branches:
Sebringville
268 Huron Rd.
Sebringville, ON N0K 1X0 Canada
519-393-6670
sebringville@mitchellcu.ca
Pat Ruston, Branch Supervisor
Shakespeare
6 Huron Rd.
Shakespeare, ON N0B 2P0 Canada
519-625-8400
shakespeare@mitchellcu.ca
Mary Pines, Branch Supervisor
Stratford
1067 Ontario St.
Stratford, ON N5A 6W6 Canada
519-271-9083
stratford@mitchellcu.ca
Kevin Quipp, Branch Manager

Molson Brewery Employees Credit Union Limited
1 Carlingview Dr.
Toronto, ON M9W 5E5
416-675-8710
Fax: 416-213-0518
dmccurdy@bellnet.ca
Year Founded: 1956
Number of Employees: 2

Moore Employees' Credit Union Limited
6100 Vipond Dr.
Mississauga, ON L5T 2X1
416-241-7132
sylvia_murphy@ca.moore.com
Year Founded: 1962

Motor City Community Credit Union Limited
6701 Tecumseh Rd. East
Windsor, ON N8T 1E8
519-944-7333
Fax: 519-944-9765
info@mcccu.com
www.mcccu.com
Ownership: Member-owned
Assets: $100-500 million
Executives:
Randal Dupuis, CEO; 519-944-7333
Directors:
Charles Pope, President
Elizabeth Van der Pol, Vice-President
Wayne Lessard, Secretary
Carl Banks
Margaret Galad
Archie Glajch
Joe Graziano
Arunas Januska
John Joynt
Marc Moore
Barbara Nahnybida
Rita Pennesi
Paul White
Branches:
Windsor - City Hall Square
189 City Hall Sq.
Windsor, ON N9A 5W5 Canada
519-252-0123
Fax: 519-252-3543
Windsor - Erie St.
895 Erie St. East
Windsor, ON N9A 3Y7 Canada
519-977-6939
Fax: 519-256-9040
Windsor - Tecumseh Rd.
1405 Tecumseh Rd. West
Windsor, ON N8B 1T7 Canada
519-256-2396
Fax: 519-256-2397
Windsor - Walker
1375 Walker Rd.
Windsor, ON N8Y 2N9 Canada
519-258-0021
Fax: 519-258-2289

Mount Lehman Credit Union
5889 Mount Lehman Rd.
Mount Lehman, BC V4X 1V7
604-856-7761
Fax: 604-856-1429
info@mtlehman.com
www.mtlehman.com
Year Founded: 1942
Number of Employees: 12

Mountain View Credit Union Ltd.
PO Box 3752
4920 - 50 Ave.
Olds, AB T4H 1P5
403-556-3306
Fax: 403-556-1050
mvcu@alberta-cu.com
www.mountainviewcreditunion.ca
Ownership: Member-owned
Number of Employees: 1977
Assets: $100-500 million
Branches:
Beiseker
PO Box 440
237 - 6 St.
Beiseker, AB T0M 0G0 Canada
403-947-3993
Fax: 403-947-3227
Carbon
PO Box 398
645 Glengarry St.
Carbon, AB T0M 0L0 Canada
403-572-3594
Fax: 403-572-3011
Cremona
PO Box 166
102 Railway Ave.
Cremona, AB T0M 0R0 Canada
403-637-3771
Fax: 403-637-3900
Crossfield
PO Box 800
1301 Railway Ave.
Crossfield, AB T0M 0S0 Canada
403-946-0572
Fax: 403-946-0587
Delia
PO Box 209
302 Main St.
Delia, AB T0J 0W0 Canada
403-364-2671
Fax: 403-364-2671
Didsbury
PO Box 970
2003 - 20 St.
Didsbury, AB T0M 0W0 Canada
403-335-3335
Fax: 403-335-9599
Linden
PO Box 82
209 Central Ave. East
Linden, AB T0M 1J0 Canada
403-546-6798
Fax: 403-546-6731
Morrin
PO Box 160
104 Main St.
Morrin, AB T0J 2B0 Canada
403-772-3773
Fax: 403-772-2422
Olds
PO Box 3770
4920 - 50 Ave.
Olds, AB T4H 1P5 Canada
403-556-3304
Fax: 403-556-8161
Sundre
PO Box 483
117 Centre St. North
Sundre, AB T0M 1X0 Canada
403-638-4040
Fax: 403-638-2066

Mouvement des caisses Desjardins du Québec
Also listed under: *Financing & Loan Companies; Insurance Companies*
100, av des Commandeurs
Lévis, QC G6V 7N5
418-835-8444
Fax: 418-833-5873
www.desjardins.com
Ownership: Private.
Year Founded: 1901

Number of Employees: 38,000
Assets: $10-50 million Year End: 20051231
Profile: The Mouvement offers a complete range of financial services to its five million members & clients. The Mouvement comprises two sectors: 1) the co-operative sector & 2) the corporate sector, which is controlled by the co-operative sector. In Québec, 618 caisses make up the core of the co-operative sector. They are grouped together in the Fédération des caisses Desjardins du Québec.
Executives:
Alban D'Amours, Président, Chef de la direction du MCD
Germain Carrières, Président, Chef de l'exploitation de VMD
Gérard Guilbault, Président, Chef de l'exploitation de DGA
François Joly, Président, Chef de l'exploitation de DSF
Bertrand Laferrière, Président, Chef de l'exploitation de la FCDQ

Jean-Guy Langelier, Président/Chef, l'exploitation de la CCD, Chef de la trésorerie du MCD
J. Martineau, Président, Chef de l'exploitation de DGAG
Louis L. Roquet, Président, Chef de l'exploitation de DCR
Pierre Brossard, 1er Vice-président exécutif à la direction du MCD
Jacques Dignard, 1er Vice-président, Ressources humaines du MCD
Daniel Gauvin, 1er Vice-président, Chef de la gestion intégrée des risques du MCD
Monique F. Leroux, 1re Vice-présidente exécutive, Chef de la direction financière du MCD
Marcel Pepin, 1er Vice-président, Planification stratégique, Développement des affaires pancanadiennes du MCD
Pauline D'Amboise, Secrétaire, Comité de direction stratégique du MCD
Affiliated Companies:
Fiducie Desjardins
Fédération des caisses Desjardins du Québec

Mozart Savings & Credit Union Limited
PO Box 96
Mozart, SK S0A 2S0
306-554-2808
Fax: 306-554-2839
mozart@sasktel.net
Year Founded: 1940
Number of Employees: 3

Municipal Employees (Chatham) Credit Union Limited
301 Delaware Ave.
Chatham, ON N7L 2W9
519-354-9182
Year Founded: 1954
Number of Employees: 2
Assets: $1-5 million
Revenues: Under $1 million

Nasco Employees' Credit Union Limited
PO Box 2450
602 Kenilworth Ave. North
Hamilton, ON L8N 3J4
905-544-3311
Fax: 905-544-5449
nascocu@nascocu.ca
Year Founded: 1946
Number of Employees: 2
Executives:
Chris Skarupa, President; skarupac@steelcar.com
Jeanne Foster, Manager; jfoster@nascocu.ca

NCR Employees' Credit Union Ltd.
6865 Century Ave.
Mississauga, ON L5N 2E2
905-819-4000
Year Founded: 1949

Nelson & District Credit Union
PO Box 350
501 Vernon St.
Nelson, BC V1L 5R2
250-352-7207
Fax: 250-352-9663
877-352-7207
personalservice@nelsoncu.com
www.nelsoncu.com
Number of Employees: 50
Executives:
Doug Stoddart, General Manager
Directors:
John Malakoff, Chair
Michael Bandroft
Andy Chute
John Edwards
Linda MacDermid
Christine McCandlish
Gordon Player
Bernie Swendson
Lorne Westnedge
Branches:
Crawford Bay - East Shore
PO Box 98
16030 Hwy. 3A
Crawford Bay, BC V0B 1E0 Canada
250-227-9221
Fax: 250-227-9533
Allan Turberfield, Branch Manager
Rossland
PO Box 489
2071 Columbia Ave.
Rossland, BC V0G 1Y0 Canada
250-362-7393
Fax: 250-362-9011

New Brunswick Teachers' Association Credit Union
PO Box 752
650 Montgomery St.
Fredericton, NB E3B 5R6
506-452-1724
Fax: 506-452-1732
800-565-5626
nbtacu@nbnet.nb.ca
www.nbtacu.nb.ca
Ownership: Private
Year Founded: 1971
Number of Employees: 12
Assets: $10-50 million Year End: 20050930
Executives:
Judy Jewett, General Manager; jjewett@nbtacu.creditu.net
Jackie Jardine, Asst. Manager; jjardine@nbtacu.creditu.net
Directors:
Bobbie McNutt, President
Paul Munro, 1st Vice-President
Donna Cormier, 2nd Vice-President
Jeannie Matthews, Corporate Secretary
Eileen Hansen
Ken McIntyre
Pat O'Brien
Wayne Tomilson

New Community Credit Union
321 - 20th St. West
Saskatoon, SK S7M 0X1
306-653-1300
Fax: 306-653-4711
info@newcommunity.cu.sk.ca
www.newcommunitycu.com
Former Name: New Community Savings & Credit Union Ltd.
Year Founded: 1939
Executives:
Bill Zerebesky, General Manager
Darren Doepker, Manager, Loans; darren.doepker@newcommunity.cu.sk.ca
Directors:
Gord Trischuk, President
David Lalach, Vice-President
Annette Pshebylo, Secretary
Gord Klimek
Stan Hawryliw
Elaine Koshman
Rosanne Maluk
Eugene May

New Glasgow Credit Union
175 Victoria St.
New Glasgow, NS B2H 4V3
902-752-3102
Fax: 902-755-5777
Executives:
Norris G. Robinson, Manager

New Ross Credit Union
PO Box 32
56 Forties Rd.
New Ross, NS B0J 2M0
902-689-2949
Fax: 902-689-2597
www.newrosscreditunion.ca/
Year Founded: 1956
Executives:
Michael Wilcox, General Manager
Branches:
Chester Basin
PO Box 69
50 Hwy. 12
Chester Basin, NS B0J 1K0 Canada
902-275-3509
Fax: 902-275-2590
Michael Wilcox, General Manager

New Waterford Credit Union
3462 Plummer Ave.
New Waterford, NS B1H 1Z6
902-862-6453
Fax: 902-862-9206
www.newwaterfordcreditunion.com
Year Founded: 1934
Number of Employees: 14
Assets: $10-50 million
Executives:
Bruce MacDonald, Manager
Cheryl Angione, Supervisor, Accounting & Human Resources
Harvey Leblanc, Manager, Operations

Niverville Credit Union
PO Box 430
62 Main St.
Niverville, MB R0A 1E0
204-388-4747
Fax: 204-388-9970
info@nivervillecu.mb.ca
www.nivervillecu.mb.ca
Year Founded: 1949
Branches:
Landmark
PO Box 57
207 Main St.
Landmark, MB R0A 0X0 Canada
204-355-4035
Fax: 204-355-4800

Nokomis Credit Union Ltd.
PO Box 339
209 Main St.
Nokomis, SK S0G 3R0
306-528-2100
1-866-656-6474
Fax: 306-528-2200
info@nokomis.cu.sk.ca
www.nokomiscreditunion.com
Former Name: Nokomis Savings & Credit Union Ltd.
Year Founded: 1940
Executives:
Kerry Gray, General Manager

North Peace Savings & Credit Union
10344 - 100th St.
Fort St John, BC V1J 3Z1
250-787-0361
Fax: 250-787-9704
800-561-7849
members@northpeacesavings.com
www.northpeacesavings.com
Ownership: Private
Number of Employees: 53
Executives:
Gerald Paddock, General Manager
Directors:
Eberhard Bauer, Chair
Chris Maundrell, Vice-Chair
Branches:
Fort Nelson
Northern Rockies Plaza
5420 - 50th Ave. North
Fort Nelson, BC V0C 1R0 Canada
250-774-5215
Fax: 250-774-5216
Hudson's Hope
10050 Beattie Dr.
Hudson's Hope, BC V0C 1V0 Canada

North Peace Savings & Credit Union (continued)
250-783-5217
Fax: 250-783-5467

North Shore Credit Union
1112 Lonsdale Ave., 3rd Fl.
North Vancouver, BC V7M 2H2
604-982-8000
Fax: 604-985-6810
880-713-6728
www.nscu.ca
Year Founded: 1941
Executives:
Christopher Catliff, President/CEO
William Keen, CFO/Vice-President, Finance
Fred Cook, CIO
Marni Johnson, Vice-President, Human Resources & Communications
Doug Smith, Vice-President, Corporate Affairs
Mike Watson, Vice-President, Retail Banking
Directors:
Naomi Yamamoto, Chair
Susan Adams
Ron Davies
Neil McAskill
Sandford Osler
Greg Prewitt
Ninna Sherwood
Steve Tapp
Branches:
Burnaby
4403 Hastings St.
Burnaby, BC V5C 2K1 Canada
604-982-8000
Fax: 604-713-3033
MICR: 00260-809
Andy Sulentic, Manager
North Vancouver - Edgemont Village
3059 Edgemont Blvd.
North Vancouver, BC V7R 2N5 Canada
604-982-8000
Fax: 604-903-2444
MICR: 05380-809
North Vancouver - Lonsdale
1100 Lonsdale Ave.
North Vancouver, BC V7M 2H3 Canada
604-982-8000
Fax: 604-903-2500
MICR: 05310-809
Sue Godey, Manager
North Vancouver - Lynn Valley
#110, 1200 Lynn Valley Rd.
North Vancouver, BC V7J 2A2 Canada
604-982-8000
Fax: 604-903-2300
MICR: 05320-809
Graham Pearce, Manager
North Vancouver - Marine Drive
1080 Marine Dr.
North Vancouver, BC V7P 1S5 Canada
604-982-8000
Fax: 604-903-2400
MICR: 05340-809
Arlene Mooney, Manager
North Vancouver - Seymour
3730 Mt. Seymour Pkwy.
North Vancouver, BC V7G 1C3 Canada
604-982-8000
Fax: 604-713-2333
MICR: 05390-809
Andrea Conn, Manager
Pemberton
PO Box 952
#2, 7438 Prospect St.
Pemberton, BC V0N 2L0 Canada
604-982-8000
Fax: 604-894-1004
MICR: 00240-809
Nick Papoutsis, Manager
Squamish
#102, 40147 Glenalder Pl.
Squamish, BC V0N 3G0 Canada
604-982-8200
Fax: 604-989-2901
MICR: 00250-809
Alan Haigh, Manager
Vancouver - Melville
#110, 1100 Melville St.
Vancouver, BC V6E 4A6 Canada
604-982-8000
Fax: 604-713-3073
MICR: 00200-809
Brian Williams, Manager
West Vancouver - Park Royal
815 Main St.
West Vancouver, BC V7T 2Z3 Canada
604-982-8000
Fax: 604-903-2600
MICR: 05330-809
Arlene Mooney, Manager
Whistler
#101, 4321 Village Gate Blvd.
Whistler, BC V0N 1B4 Canada
604-982-8000
Fax: 604-905-4300
MICR: 05350-809
Azmir Jawa, Manager
Whistler - Nesters
7003 Nesters Rd.
Whistler, BC V0N 1B7 Canada
604-982-8000
Fax: 604-905-4333
MICR: 00230-809
Nick Papoutsis, Manager

North Valley Credit Union Limited
PO Box 1389
516 Main St.
Esterhazy, SK S0A 0X0
306-745-6615
Fax: 306-745-2858
www.northvalleycu.com
Former Name: Esterhazy Credit Union Limited
Ownership: Member-owned
Year Founded: 1998
Number of Employees: 14
Executives:
Roy Spence, General Manager/CEO; roy.spence@northvalley.cu.sk.ca
Jeffrey Bisschop, Manager, Loans
Directors:
Donna Overland, President
Vern Arndt, 1st Vice-President
Mark Johnson, 2nd Vice-President
Morris Croswell
Ralph May
George Ohnander
Robert Unchelenko
Douglas Ward
Iiona Zambel
Branches:
Stockholm
PO Box 130
116 Ohlen St.
Stockholm, SK S0A 3Y0 Canada
306-793-2171
Fax: 306-793-2013

North West Credit Union Ltd.
PO Box 310
504 Buffalo St.
Buffalo Narrows, SK S0M 0J0
306-235-4414
Fax: 306-235-4485
Year Founded: 1990
Number of Employees: 6
Assets: $5-10 million

North York Community Credit Union Limited
5799 Yonge St.
Toronto, ON M2M 3V3
416-223-7556
Fax: 416-223-0601
nyccu.info@nyccu.com
www.nyccu.com
Year Founded: 1955
Number of Employees: 20
Assets: $52,000,000
Executives:
Don Caldwell, Manager, Member Relations

Northern Credit Union
***Also listed under:** Financial Planning*
681 Pine St.
Sault Ste Marie, ON P6B 3G2
705-253-9868
Fax: 705-949-1056
www.northerncu.com
Year Founded: 1957
Number of Employees: 208
Assets: $100-500 million Year End: 20041200
Executives:
Al Suraci, President/CEO; al.suraci@northerncu.com
Brent Chevis, CFO; brent.chevis@northerncu.com
Michael Evetts, Vice-President, Human Resources; michael.evetts@northerncu.com
Duane Fecteau, Vice-President, Sales & Service; duane.fecteau@northerncu.com
Dan O'Connor, Director, Commercial Credit; dan.oconnor@northerncu.com
Michael Imbeau, Area Director, Eastern Region; michael.imbeau@northerncu.com
Sina Kicz, Area Director, Central Region; sina.kicz@northerncu.com
Jeff Ringler, Area Director, North Region; jeff.ringler@northerncu.com
Mary Thillman, Area Director, Western Region; mary.thillman@northerncu.com
Fraser Carlyle, Manager, Marketing; fraser.carlyle@northerncu.com
Bill Smith, Manager, Consumer Credit; bill.smith@northerncu.com
Directors:
Geoff Shaw, Chair
Keir Kitchen, Vice-Chair
Tony Andreacchi
Paul Beaulieu
Jack Cleverdon
Rob deBortoli
John Fogarty
Dave Kilgour
John Mangone
David Porter
Billie Rheault
Ed Robb
Michael Walz
Branches:
Arnprior
PO Box 280
100 Madawaska Blvd.
Arnprior, ON K7S 1S7 Canada
613-623-3103
Fax: 613-623-5357
Wayne Lavallee, Branch Manager
Barrys Bay
PO Box 1028
19630 Opeongo Line
Barrys Bay, ON K0J 1B0 Canada
613-756-3097
Fax: 613-756-1902
Diane Prince, Branch Manager
Capreol
PO Box 668
10 Vaughan St.
Capreol, ON P0M 1H0 Canada
705-858-1711
Fax: 705-858-2162
George Lalonde, Branch Manager
Chapleau
PO Box 719
106 Birch St.
Chapleau, ON P0M 1K0 Canada
705-864-1841
Fax: 705-864-2747
Ingrid Doyon, Branch Manager
Coniston
PO Box 59
110 Second Ave.
Coniston, ON P0M 1M0 Canada
705-694-4741
Fax: 705-694-5868
Claudette Strom, Branch Manager
Deep River
Glendale Plaza
PO Box 306
Deep River, ON K0J 1P0 Canada

613-584-3355
Fax: 613-584-4440
Kevin Schilling, Branch Manager
Eganville
PO Box 10
237 John St.
Eganville, ON K0J 1T0 Canada
613-628-2244
Fax: 613-628-1628
Sylvie Hanniman, Branch Manager
Elliot Lake
289 Hillside Dr. South
Elliot Lake, ON P5A 1N7 Canada
705-848-7129
Fax: 705-848-5040
Robert Irving, Branch Manager
Englehart
PO Box 689
50 Fourth Ave.
Englehart, ON P0J 1H0 Canada
705-544-2248
Fax: 705-544-2542
Guy Boileau, Branch Manager
Garson
PO Box 359
3555 Falconbridge Hwy.
Garson, ON P3L 1S7 Canada
705-693-3411
Fax: 705-693-0788
Richard Campbell, Branch Manager
Hornepayne
PO Box 160
84 Front St.
Hornepayne, ON P0M 1Z0 Canada
807-868-2471
Fax: 807-868-2898
Albena Liebigt, Branch Manager
Kirkland Lake
PO Box 972
13 Government Rd. West
Kirkland Lake, ON P2N 3L1 Canada
705-567-3254
Fax: 705-567-5056
Neil Lloyd, Branch Manager
North Bay
525 Main St. East
North Bay, ON P1B 1B7 Canada
705-476-3500
Fax: 705-474-3674
Linda Blackall, Branch Manager
Pembroke
432 Boundary Rd. East
Pembroke, ON K8A 6L1 Canada
613-732-9967
Fax: 613-732-3474
Steve Hartmann, Branch Manager
Red Rock
65 Salls St.
Red Rock, ON P0T 2P0 Canada
807-886-2247
Fax: 807-886-2248
Jackie Brewer, Branch Manager
Richards Landing
PO Box 128
Richard St.
Richards Landing, ON P0R 1J0 Canada
705-246-3081
Fax: 705-246-3335
Tammy Ambeault, Branch Manager
Sault Ste Marie - 2nd Line
612 Second Line West
Sault Ste Marie, ON P6C 2K7 Canada
705-942-2333
Fax: 705-942-7355
Debbie Fabbro, Branch Manager
Sault Ste Marie - Bay St.
480 Bay St.
Sault Ste Marie, ON P6A 6Y9 Canada
705-942-2344
Fax: 705-942-7062
Betty Rusnell, Branch Manager
Sault Ste Marie - McNabb St.
PO Box 2200
264 McNabb St.
Sault Ste Marie, ON P6A 5N9 Canada
705-949-2644
Fax: 705-949-2988
Debbie Kempny, Branch Manager
Sudbury
532 Kathleen St.
Sudbury, ON P3C 2N2 Canada
705-674-9822
Fax: 705-674-5076
Hazel Turcotte, Branch Manager
Thessalon
186 Main St.
Thessalon, ON P0R 1L0 Canada
705-842-3916
Fax: 705-842-2685
Robin MacDonald, Branch Manager
Thunder Bay - Frederica St.
111 West Frederica St.
Thunder Bay, ON P7E 3V8 Canada
807-475-5817
Fax: 807-475-7103
Mary Thillman, Area Director
Thunder Bay - Red River Rd.
697 Red River Rd.
Thunder Bay, ON P7B 1J3 Canada
807-767-1300
Fax: 807-768-1898
Susan Olynick, Branch Manager
Timmins
70 Mountjoy St. North
Timmins, ON P4N 4V7 Canada
705-267-6846
Fax: 705-264-1742
Leo Morin, Branch Manager
Wawa
14 Mission Rd.
Wawa, ON P0S 1K0 Canada
705-856-2322
Fax: 705-856-2961
Bill Chapman, Branch Manager

Northern Lights Credit Union Limited
PO Box 876
97 Duke St.
Dryden, ON P8N 2Z5
807-223-5358
Fax: 807-223-8650
kimf@nlcu.on.ca
www.nlcu.on.ca
Number of Employees: 57
Branches:
Fort Frances
601 Mowat Ave.
Fort Frances, ON P9A 1Z2 Canada
807-274-3217
Fax: 807-274-2755
marlat@nlcu.on.ca
Rainy River
PO Box 122
302 Atwood Ave.
Rainy River, ON P0W 1L0 Canada
807-852-3840
Fax: 807-852-1490
orestg@nlcu.on.ca
Sioux Lookout
PO Box 429
42 King St.
Sioux Lookout, ON P8T 1A5 Canada
807-737-1567
Fax: 807-737-2136
janicef@nlcu.on.ca
Thunder Bay - Amber
PO Box 20021
1201 Amber Dr.
Thunder Bay, ON P7E 6P2 Canada
807-345-1407
Fax: 807-344-1804
shelleyb@nlcu.on.ca
Thunder Bay - James
1500 James St. South
Thunder Bay, ON P7E 6N7 Canada
807-345-1407
Fax: 807-577-7022
shelleyb@nlcu.on.ca
Vermilion Bay
PO Box 57
Hwy. 17
Vermilion Bay, ON P0V 2V0 Canada
807-227-2134
Fax: 807-227-2772
ritaco@nlcu.on.ca

Northern Savings Credit Union
138 Third Ave. West
Prince Rupert, BC V8J 1K8
250-627-7571
Fax: 250-624-8297
www.northsave.com
Ownership: Member-owned
Executives:
Michael J. Tarr, President/CEO
Directors:
Brian Nesbitt, Chair
Branches:
Masset
PO Box 94
Masset, BC V0T 1M0 Canada
250-626-5231
Fax: 250-626-5498
Queen Charlotte
PO Box 38
Queen Charlotte, BC V0T 1S0 Canada
250-559-4407
Fax: 250-559-4729
Terrace & District Credit Union
4650 Lazelle Ave.
Terrace, BC V8G 1S6 Canada
250-635-7282
Fax: 250-635-2713
Sheila Monette
Terrace Community
4702 Lazelle Ave.
Terrace, BC V8G 1T2 Canada
250-638-7822
Fax: 250-638-7842

Northland Savings & Credit Union Limited
10 Cain Ave.
Kapuskasing, ON P5N 1S9
705-335-2348
Fax: 705-337-1070
kapcu@ntl.sympatico.ca
www.northlandcredit.com
Ownership: Member-owned
Year Founded: 1939
Executives:
André Filion, Manager
Directors:
Claude Ouellette, President
Linda Semczyszyn, Vice-President
Angela Ratte, Secretary
Martin Buller
Ken Campbell
Leslie Sigouin
Gerry Touchette
Branches:
Smooth Rock Falls
153 - 5th Ave.
Smooth Rock Falls, ON P0L 2B0 Canada
705-338-2697
Fax: 705-338-4104
Jeanette Cloutier, Manager

Northridge Savings & Credit Union Ltd.
9 Second Ave. North
Sudbury, ON P3B 3L7
705-566-8540
Fax: 705-566-8480
www.northridgesavings.com
Executives:
Erik Jokinen, General Manager
Tess McLaughlin, Branch Manager
Directors:
Patrick McNally, President
Gerry Labelle, Vice-President
Bette Choquette, Secretary
Ron Abreu
Anna Frattini
Barry Haneberry
Lisa LaCroix
Vally LaFlamme

Northridge Savings & Credit Union Ltd. (continued)
E. Robert Unger
Branches:
Sudbury
1250 Lasalle Blvd.
Sudbury, ON P3A 1Y7 Canada
705-566-2931
Fax: 705-566-2368
Pat Brady, Manager

Nova Scotia Postal Employees Credit Union

PO Box 8153, A Stn. A
6175 Almon St.
Halifax, NS B3K 5L9
902-453-1145
Fax: 902-453-0370
800-665-1145
ask@inovacreditunion.coop
www.nspostalcreditunion.com
Executives:
W.G. (Willy) Robinson, General Manager; 902-453-8870; wrobinson@inovacreditunion.coop
Phil Smith, Asst. Manager; 902-453-8871; psmith@inovacreditunion.coop

Oak Bank Credit Union

PO Box 217
686 Main St.
Oakbank, MB R0E 1J0
204-444-7200
Fax: 204-444-3513
info@oakbankcu.mb.ca
www.oakbankcu.mb.ca
Year Founded: 1946
Branches:
East St Paul
3187 Birds Hill Rd.
East St Paul, MB R2E 1G6 Canada
204-654-8100
Fax: 204-663-7517
info@oakbankcu.mb.ca

Ogema District Credit Union Ltd.

PO Box 339
Ogema, SK S0C 1Y0
306-459-2266
info@ogema.cu.sk.ca
www.ogema.cu.sk.ca
Year Founded: 1950
Branches:
Pangman
PO Box 158
125 Mergens St.
Pangman, SK S0C 2C0 Canada
306-442-2102

Omista Credit Union

151 Cornhill St.
Moncton, NB E1C 6L3
506-857-3222
Fax: 506-857-2235
cornhillstreet@omista.com
www.omista.com
Ownership: Member-owned
Executives:
Paul Innes, Branch Manager
Branches:
Heritage Court
#109, 95 Foundry St.
Moncton, NB E1C 5H7 Canada
506-857-9772
Fax: 506-857-1385
heritage@omista.creditu.net
Patty Barton, Branch Manager
Mountain Rd.
1192 Mountain Rd.
Moncton, NB E1C 2T6 Canada
506-858-7206
Fax: 506-859-7697
mountain@omista.creditu.net
Roxanne Archibald

ONR Employees' (North Bay) Credit Union Limited

555 Oak St. East
North Bay, ON P1B 9E5
705-472-1100
Fax: 705-472-0651
onrcu@ontc.on.ca
Year Founded: 1950

Ontario Civil Service Credit Union Limited

#1, 18 Grenville St.
Toronto, ON M4Y 3B3
416-314-6772
Fax: 416-314-1289
memberassistance@mycreditunion.ca
www.mycreditunion.ca
Ownership: Cooperative
Year Founded: 1945
Number of Employees: 60
Assets: $100-500 million
Revenues: $5-10 million
Executives:
J.A. Mahoney, President/CEO
P.K. Leak, Vice-President/CFO
Directors:
R. Redford, Chair
J. Collins
E. Kay-Zorowski
T. Kilpatrick
Sandra Lane
M. MacDonald
J. MacMillan
Gloria Marshall
R. Waterman
Branches:
Hamilton
Twin Pines Bldg.
PO Box 826
100 West 5th St.
Hamilton, ON L9C 3M8 Canada
905-389-7915
Fax: 905-389-3700
Micci McLarnon, Manager
Kingston
#102, 471 Counter St.
Kingston, ON K7M 6Z6 Canada
613-545-4343
Fax: 613-545-4333
Cindy Kane, Manager
North Bay
2125 Algonquin Ave.
North Bay, ON P1B 4Z3 Canada
705-495-3810
Sandra Gauthier, Manager
Orillia
Huronia Regional Centre
PO Box 365
700 Memorial Ave., Cottage C.
Orillia, ON L3V 6J8 Canada
Fax: 705-329-6048
Kathy Varey, Manager
Oshawa
33 King St. West
Oshawa, ON L1H 1A1 Canada
905-433-5303
Fax: 905-433-5441
Richelle Harwood, Manager
Peterborough
441 Water St.
Peterborough, ON K9H 3M2 Canada
705-755-2059
Fax: 705-755-2060
Jan Jamieson, Manager
Toronto - Yonge St.
5700 Yonge St., Mezzanine Level
Toronto, ON M2M 4K2 Canada
416-314-6772
Fax: 416-314-1289

Ontario Educational Credit Union Limited

PO Box 360
#101, 6435 Edwards Blvd.
Mississauga, ON L5T 2P7
905-795-1637
Fax: 905-795-0625
800-463-3602
www.oecu.on.ca
Year Founded: 1962
Number of Employees: 8
Profile: Open to all active or retired educational employees & their families throughout Ontario.
Directors:
Douglas McKee, President
Robert Murphy, Secretary
Jim Challiz
Dale Green
John Kostoff
Wayne McNally
Al Schmid
Paul Schmidt
Peter Worth
Branches:
Barrie
PO Box 13
#8B, 48 Alliance Blvd.
Barrie, ON L4M 5K3 Canada
705-737-5622
Fax: 705-737-9946
800-292-7202
F. Dougan, Representative, Member Service

Ontario Provincial Police Association Credit Union Limited

123 Ferris Lane
Barrie, ON L4M 2Y1
705-726-5656
Fax: 705-726-1449
800-461-4288
gd@oppacu.com
www.oppacu.com
Also Known As: O.P.P.A Credit Union
Year Founded: 1971
Executives:
Bryan Neely, CEO

Operating Engineers Credit Union

#205, 4333 Ledger Ave.
Burnaby, BC V5G 3T3
604-291-8831
Fax: 604-291-8987
creditunion@iuoe115.com
www.iuoe115.org/members/credit_union.html
Ownership: Member-owned

Oregon Employees Credit Union Limited

505 Edinburgh Rd. North
Guelph, ON N1H 6L4
519-822-6870

Osoyoos Credit Union

PO Box 360
8312 Main St.
Osoyoos, BC V0H 1V0
250-495-6522
Fax: 250-495-3363
800-882-1966
contact@osoyooscreditunion.com
www.osoyooscreditunion.com
Ownership: Member-owned
Year Founded: 1946
Number of Employees: 20

Ottawa Police Credit Union Limited

#206, 474 Elgin St., 2nd Fl.
Ottawa, ON K2P 2J6
613-236-1222
Fax: 613-567-3760
www.opcu.com
Former Name: Ottawa-Carleton Police Credit Union Limited
Ownership: Private.
Year Founded: 1955
Number of Employees: 5
Revenues: $10-50 million Year End: 20051231
Executives:
Kathryn Potter, Contact; 613-236-1222; kpotter@opcu.com

Ottawa Women's Credit Union Limited

Co-operative House
271 Bank St.
Ottawa, ON K2P 1X5
613-233-7711
Fax: 613-233-6413
info@owcu.on.ca
www.owcu.on.ca
Profile: OWCU is the only financial institution operated by & for women in Canada.

Pace Savings & Credit Union Limited

#1, 8111 Jane St.
Vaughan, ON L4K 4L7

905-738-8900
Fax: 905-738-8283
pace.info@pacecu.com
www.pacecu.com
Ownership: Member-owned
Year Founded: 1984
Assets: $272,492,163
Revenues: $9,363,703
Profile: Pace Savings provides full personal financial services of a banking cooperative. Membership is open to people who reside or work in Peel Region as well as businesses operating in the area.

Executives:
Larry Smith, CEO
Branches:
Brampton
Peel Region Bldg.
10 Peel Centre Dr.
Brampton, ON L6T 4B9 Canada
905-791-3877
Fax: 905-791-7974
brampton@pacecu.com
Burlington
#E109, 676 Appleby Line
Burlington, ON L7L 5Y1 Canada
905-333-8913
Fax: 905-333-8914
burlington@pacecu.com
Hamilton
55 Bay St. North, Ground Fl.
Hamilton, ON L8R 3P7 Canada
905-523-0986
Fax: 905-523-8923
federalbranch@pacecu.com
Markham
#1, 411 Manhattan Dr.
Markham, ON L3P 7P4 Canada
905-477-4311
Fax: 905-477-5922
Markham - Steeles
3600 Steeles Ave. East
Markham, ON L3R 2T4 Canada
905-474-1885
Fax: 905-474-9926
steelesbranch@pacecu.com
Markham - Woodbine
7537 Woodbine Ave.
Markham, ON L3R 2W1 Canada
905-479-5900
Fax: 905-479-5990
800-433-9122
inajjar@pacecu.com
Mississauga
#109, 550 Matheson Dr.
Mississauga, ON L5R 4B8 Canada
905-566-7223
Fax: 905-566-8737
mathesonbranch@pacecu.com
Stouffville
6245 Main St.
Stouffville, ON L4A 8A1 Canada
905-640-2811
Fax: 905-640-7713
stouffvillebranch@pacecu.com
Toronto - Consumers
#101, 505 Consumers Rd.
Toronto, ON M2J 4V8 Canada
416-493-0314
Fax: 416-493-1715
consumersbranch@pacecu.com
Toronto - Don Mills
844 Don Mills Rd.
Toronto, ON M3C 1V7 Canada
416-448-5611
Fax: 416-448-4727
celesticabranch@pacecu.com
Uxbridge
99 Brock St. West
Uxbridge, ON L9P 1P5 Canada
905-852-3388
Fax: 905-852-5108
uxbridgebranch@pacecu.com

Parama Lithuanian Credit Union Limited
1573 Bloor St. West
Toronto, ON M6P 1A6
416-532-1149
Fax: 416-532-5595
info@parama.ca
www.parama.net
Year Founded: 1952
Number of Employees: 30
Assets: $100-500 million
Executives:
Linas Zubrickas, General Manager
Branches:
Toronto
2975 Bloor St. West
Toronto, ON M8X 1C1 Canada
416-207-9239
Fax: 416-207-9401

Pedeco (Brockville) Credit Union Limited
2337 Parkedale Ave.
Brockville, ON K6V 5W5
613-342-4436
Fax: 613-342-6584
cmacdonald@ripnet.com
Year Founded: 1952
Executives:
Cathy MacDonald, General Manager

PenFinancial Credit Union
247 East Main St.
Welland, ON L3B 3X1
905-735-4801
Fax: 905-735-2983
www.penfinancial.com
Former Name: St Catharines Civic Employees' Credit Union Ltd.
Year Founded: 1951
Number of Employees: 57
Assets: $100-500 million
Profile: Result of a merger between Atlas & Civic and St. Catharines Civic Credit Unions.

Directors:
Larry Bousfield, Chair
Branches:
St Catharines - Bunting Rd.
#2, 300 Bunting Rd.
St Catharines, ON L2M 7X3 Canada
905-685-7737
Fax: 905-685-1672
Cindy Cwiertniewski, Branch Manager
St Catharines - Lake St.
82 Lake St.
St Catharines, ON L2R 5X5 Canada
905-688-2044
Fax: 905-688-9611
St Catharines - Seaway Office
508 Glendale Ave.
St Catharines, ON L2M 6P9 Canada
905-688-0717
Fax: 905-688-3222
Rhonda Maver, Branch Manager
St Catharines - St. David's Rd.
Heritage Office/Commercial Ctr.
#9, 640 St. David's Rd.
St Catharines, ON L2T 4E6 Canada
905-641-2662
Fax: 905-641-3110
Carm Mancini, Branch Manager
Welland - Hospital Office
115 Maclean Pl., 2nd Floor
Welland, ON L3B 5X9 Canada
905-732-1757
Fax: 905-732-3199

Peterborough Community Credit Union Limited
PO Box 1600
167 Brock St.
Peterborough, ON K9J 7S4
705-748-4481
Fax: 705-748-5520
www.pboccu.com
Year Founded: 1939
Executives:
Leon Butterworth, General Manager; leon@pboccu.com

Peterborough Industrial Credit Union
890 High St.
Peterborough, ON K9J 5R2
705-743-4651
Fax: 705-743-9889
info@picu.ca
www.picu.ca

Pierceland Credit Union Ltd.
PO Box 10
181 Main St.
Pierceland, SK S0M 2K0
306-839-2071
Fax: 306-839-2292
info@pierceland.cu.sk.ca
Year Founded: 1941
Number of Employees: 8

Pincher Creek Credit Union Ltd.
PO Box 1660
750 Kettles St.
Pincher Creek, AB T0K 1W0
403-627-4431
Fax: 403-627-5331
www.pinchercreek-creditunion.com
Ownership: Member-owned
Year Founded: 1944
Number of Employees: 10
Executives:
Vicki French, General Manager; vicki@pinchercreek-creditunion.com

Plainsview Credit Union
PO Box 150
600 Main St.
Kipling, SK S0G 2S0
306-736-2549
Fax: 306-736-8290
info1@plainsview.cu.sk.ca
www.plainsview.com
Branches:
Arcola
PO Box 240
Arcola, SK S0C 0G0 Canada
306-455-4200
Fax: 306-455-4206
Glenavon
PO Box 30
Glenavon, SK S0G 1Y0 Canada
306-429-2074
Fax: 306-429-2075
Indian Head
PO Box 310
Indian Head, SK S0G 2K0 Canada
306-695-2261
Fax: 306-695-2741
Kennedy
PO Box 125
Kennedy, SK S0G 2R0 Canada
306-538-2030
Fax: 306-538-2115
Montmartre
PO Box 240
Montmartre, SK S0G 3M0 Canada
306-424-2303
Fax: 306-424-2888
Odessa
PO Box 68
Odessa, SK S0G 3S0 Canada
306-957-2141
Fax: 306-957-2075
Qu'Appelle
PO Box 210
Qu'Appelle, SK S0G 4A0 Canada
306-699-2866
Fax: 306-699-2506
Riceton
PO Box 40
Riceton, SK S0G 4E0 Canada
306-738-2010
Fax: 306-738-4437
Sintaluta
PO Box 56
Sintaluta, SK S0G 4N0 Canada
306-727-2044
Fax: 306-727-2232

Plainsview Credit Union (continued)
Vibank
PO Box 68
Vibank, SK S0G 4Y0 Canada
306-762-2166
Fax: 306-762-4423

The Police Credit Union Ltd.
#303, 3650 Victoria Park Ave.
Toronto, ON M2H 3P7
416-226-3353
Fax: 416-226-1565
800-561-2557
callcentre@tpcu.on.ca
www.tpcu.on.ca
Ownership: Member-owned
Year Founded: 1946
Executives:
David Merrifield, Branch Manager
Branches:
Mississauga - Peel
85 Aventura Ct., #C
Mississauga, ON L5T 2Y6 Canada
905-795-2286
Fax: 905-795-2280
Bess Kominos-Estrela, Manager
Newmarket
18025 Yonge St.
Newmarket, ON L3Y 8C9 Canada
905-836-4998
Fax: 905-836-4766
877-242-8728
Len Wright, Manager
Pickering
962 Kingston Rd.
Pickering, ON L1V 1B3 Canada
905-839-2693
Fax: 905-839-5332
888-354-8728
Wayne Murray, Manager
Toronto - College St.
#101, 40 College St.
Toronto, ON M5G 2J3 Canada
416-961-2107
Fax: 416-962-5451
David Merrifield, Manager

Polish Alliance (Brant) Credit Union Limited
126 Albion St.
Brantford, ON N3T 3M6
519-756-1070
Fax: 519-756-9885
pabcu@execulink.com
Year Founded: 1957
Number of Employees: 3
Assets: $5-10 million Year End: 20041100
Revenues: Under $1 million Year End: 20041100

Porcupine Credit Union Ltd.
PO Box 189
150 McAllister Ave.
Porcupine Plain, SK S0E 1H0
306-278-2181
Fax: 306-278-2944
info@porcupine.cu.sk.ca
www.porcupine.cu.sk.ca
Year Founded: 1946

Portuguese Canadian (Toronto) Credit Union Ltd.
1168 Dundas St. West
Toronto, ON M6J 1X4
416-533-9245
Fax: 416-533-2578
inforequest@pccufinancial.com
www.pccufinancial.com
Year Founded: 1966
Executives:
Antonio Carvalho, CEO
Directors:
David J.M. Rendeiro, Chair

Powell River Credit Union Financial Group
Also listed under: *Financial Planning*
4721 Joyce Ave.
Powell River, BC V8A 3B5
604-485-6206
Fax: 604-485-7112
800-393-6733
www.prcu.com
Year Founded: 1939
Number of Employees: 46
Assets: $100-500 million
Revenues: $5-10 million
Profile: Affiliates include Powell River Insurance Services Ltd. & Athena CUSO Management Ltd.
Executives:
David B. Craigen, CEO; 604-483-8680; dave-craigen@prcu.com
Shehzad Somji, CFO
Frank Oldale, Chief Technology Officer
Sandra Phillips, Manager, Sales, Marketing & Branch Operations
Directors:
Shawn Gullette, President
Patricia Salomi, Vice-President
Gail Curtis, Secretary
Ken Barton
Peter Dowding
Carl Floe
David Northrop
Carol Roberts
Sharon Sawyer
Branches:
Van Anda
1207 Marble Bay
Van Anda, BC V0N 3K0 Canada
604-486-7851
Fax: 604-486-7671
Jane Waterman, Manager

Prairie Centre Credit Union
PO Box 940
Rosetown, SK S0L 2V0
306-882-2693
Fax: 306-882-3326
comments@pccu.ca
www.pccu.ca
Ownership: Cooperative
Year Founded: 1993
Number of Employees: 75
Assets: $100-500 million
Revenues: $5-10 million
Executives:
Al Meyer, CEO; al.meyer@pccu.ca
Tim Askin, Vice-President, Corporate Services; tim.askin@pccu.ca
Kent Jesse, Vice-President, Sales & Marketing
Branches:
Beechy
PO Box 8
Beechy, SK S0L 0C0 Canada
306-859-2262
Fax: 306-859-2203
beechy@pccu.ca
Kirsten Spence, Manager, Business Development
Dinsmore
PO Box 130
Dinsmore, SK S0L 0T0 Canada
306-846-2052
Fax: 306-846-4422
Terry Bencharski, Manager, Business Development
Eatonia
PO Box 399
Eatonia, SK S0L 0Y0 Canada
306-967-1212
Fax: 306-967-1213
eatonia@pccu.ca
Barb Derbawka, Manager, Business Development
Elbow
PO Box 100
Elbow, SK S0H 1J0 Canada
306-854-2118
Fax: 306-854-2248
elbow@pccu.ca
Tyler Pisiak, Manager, Business Development
Elrose
PO Box 39
Elrose, SK S0L 0Z0 Canada
306-378-2535
Fax: 306-378-2330
elrose@pccu.ca
Tracy Cafferata, Manager, Business Development
Eston
PO Box 129
Eston, SK S0L 1A0 Canada
306-962-3634
Fax: 306-962-3375
eston@pccu.ca
Craig Ekstrand, Manager, Business Development
Harris
PO Box 40
Harris, SK S0L 1K0 Canada
306-656-4466
Fax: 306-656-4433
harris@pccu.ca
Scott Ousdahl, Manager, Business Development
Kyle
PO Box 220
Kyle, SK S0L 1T0 Canada
306-375-2213
Fax: 306-375-2218
kyle@pccu.ca
Lynn Kerr, Manager, Business Development
Loreburn
PO Box 68
Loreburn, SK S0H 2S0 Canada
306-644-2118
Fax: 306-644-2150
loreburn@pccu.ca
Tyler Pisiak, Manager, Business Development
Outlook
PO Box 339
Outlook, SK S0L 2N0 Canada
306-867-9911
Fax: 306-867-9877
outlook@pccu.ca
Susan Forsberg, Manager, Business Development
Rosetown
PO Box 940
Rosetown, SK S0L 2V0 Canada
306-882-2693
Fax: 306-882-3326
rosetown@pccu.ca
Scott Ousdahl, Manager, Business Development

Prairie Diamond Credit Union
PO Box 819
123 Garfield St.
Davidson, SK S0G 1A0
306-567-2931
Fax: 306-567-5503
info@prairiediamond.cu.sk.ca
www.prairiediamond.com
Year Founded: 1994
Branches:
Tugaske
PO Box 130
114 Ogema St.
Tugaske, SK S0H 4B0 Canada
306-759-2303
Fax: 306-759-2729

Prairie Pride Credit Union
PO Box 37
Alameda, SK S0C 0A0
306-489-2131
Fax: 306-489-2188
info@prairiepride.cu.sk.ca
www.prairiepridecu.com
Former Name: Gainsborough Credit Union Ltd.
Year Founded: 2001
Number of Employees: 9
Directors:
Wayne Smith, President
David Widenmaier, 1st Vice-President
Lori Henderson, 2nd Vice-President
Daryl Harrison
Ken Ludtke
Melanie Meredith
Elaine Morgan
Sheri Patton
Ken Young
Branches:
Alida
PO Box 9
Alida, SK S0C 0B0 Canada
306-443-2225
Fax: 306-443-2410
Carievale

PO Box 16
Carievale, SK S0C 0P0 Canada
306-928-2044
Fax: 306-928-2210
Gainsborough
PO Box 210
Gainsborough, SK S0C 0Z0 Canada
306-685-2212
Fax: 306-685-2242

Prime Savings Credit Union
1005 King St. East
Hamilton, ON L8M 1C6
905-547-8150
Fax: 905-549-8558
www.primecu.com
Former Name: Industrial Family (Hamilton) Credit Union Ltd.
Executives:
Birk Cadman, General Manager
Margaret Grant, Manager, Loans
Branches:
Hamilton
132 Melvin Ave.
Hamilton, ON L8H 2J8 Canada
905-544-1139
Fax: 905-544-9356

Ingersoll
PO Box 1005
300 Ingersoll St.
Ingersoll, ON N5C 4A6 Canada
519-425-3172
Fax: 519-425-3174
London
31 Firestone Blvd.
London, ON N5W 5V7 Canada
519-459-8190
Fax: 519-452-3599

Princess Credit Union
22 Fraser Ave.
Sydney Mines, NS B1V 2B7
902-736-9204
Fax: 902-736-2887
Executives:
Brian McGean, Manager

Prosper Credit Union
72 Germain St.
Saint John, NB E2L 2E7
506-634-6913
Fax: 506-635-1384
800-222-9757
prosper@nb.sympatico.ca
www.prospercu.nb.ca
Year Founded: 1939
Number of Employees: 4
Executives:
Sandra Hamilton, Manager
Doreen Bordage, Loan Officer
Directors:
Richard Little, President
Wilson Peacock, Vice-President
Roger Schwartz, Secretary
Ken Cunningham
Gregory Lisson
Neil London
Jack MacDonald
Irene Maillet
Bernice Martin
Gerald McRae
Dale Parkhill
Cathy Thornton

Prosperity ONE Credit Union
44 Main St. East
Milton, ON L9T 1N3
905-878-4168
Fax: 905-878-5500
info@prosperityone.ca
www.prosperityone.ca
Former Name: Halton Community Credit Union
Year Founded: 1957
Number of Employees: 36
Assets: $50-100 million
Executives:
Peter Buwalda, CEO
Mike Shepherd, CAO
Directors:
Gord Krantz, Chair
Jennifer Boere, Vice-Chair
Katherine Clarke
Brad Clements
Pauline Gladstone
Andrew Kocher
John Lamberink
Sharon O'Driscoll
John Stieva
Branches:
Acton
350 Queen St.
Acton, ON L7J 1R2 Canada
519-853-0911
Fax: 519-853-4443
Burlington
3625 Mainway
Burlington, ON L7M 1A9 Canada
905-319-2220
Fax: 905-319-2212

Georgetown
187 Guelph St.
Georgetown, ON L7G 4A1 Canada
905-877-6926
Fax: 905-877-3863

Province House Credit Union Ltd.
PO Box 1083
1724 Granville St.
Halifax, NS B3J 2X1
902-424-5712
Fax: 902-424-3662
888-484-0880
info@provincehouse.com
www.provincehouse.com

Provincial Alliance Credit Union Limited
1201 Wilson Ave.
Toronto, ON M3M 1J8
416-235-4373
Fax: 416-235-4225
877-235-4606
pcscu@idirect.com
www.cuonline.on.ca
Year Founded: 1953
Number of Employees: 24
Executives:
Neil D. Arnold, CEO
Jenny Alleway, Manager, Loans
Lina DiGiovanni, Manager, Operations
Branches:
London
659 Exeter Rd.
London, ON N6E 1L3 Canada
519-873-4197
Fax: 519-873-4199
Donna Dixon, Branch Manager
St Catharines
301 St. Paul St.
St Catharines, ON L2R 3R7 Canada
905-704-2020
Fax: 905-704-2023
Anne White, Branch Supervisor
Thunder Bay - James St. South
405 James St. South
Thunder Bay, ON P7E 2V6 Canada
807-626-5666
Fax: 807-475-4035
tbcscu@tbaytel.net
Lorna Ball, Area Manager
Thunder Bay - St. Paul St.
56 St. Paul St.
Thunder Bay, ON P7A 4S6 Canada
807-346-2810
Fax: 807-345-9137
Heidi Liimatainen, Branch Manager

Public Service Credit Union Ltd.
403 Empire Ave.
St. John's, NL A1E 1W6
709-579-8210
Fax: 709-579-8233
800-563-6755
pscuadmin@pscu.creditu.net
www.pscu.ca
Ownership: Cooperative
Year Founded: 1936
Number of Employees: 18
Assets: $26,594,600
Revenues: $2,050,578
Executives:
Owen Taylor, General Manager; octaylor@pscu.creditu.net
Brian Quilty, Manager, Finance; bquilty@pscu.creditu.net
Sharon Tucker, Manager, Credit & Operations
Directors:
Doug Dewling, Chair
George Smith, Vice-Chair
Sheila Murphy, Secretary
Sam Connors, Member-at-Large
Barry Darby
Joseph Duggan
Velma Green
Myles Haydon
Tom Lawrence

Public Service Employees Credit Union
141 Weldon St.
Moncton, NB E1C 5W1
506-853-8881
Fax: 506-856-8492
www.psecreditunion.ca
Executives:
Jeannette Holmden, General Manager
Trish Carter, Manager, Operations

Quadra Credit Union
PO Box 190
657 Harper Rd.
Quathiaski Cove, BC V0P 1N0
250-285-3327
Fax: 250-285-2225
www.quadracu.com
Executives:
Steven Halliday, General Manager
Branches:
Mansons Landing - Cortes Island
PO Box 218
Mansons Landing, BC V0P 1K0 Canada
250-935-6617
Fax: 250-935-6514

Quill Lake Credit Union Ltd.
PO Box 520
Quill Lake, SK S0A 3E0
306-383-4155
Fax: 306-383-2622
www.quilllake.cu.sk.ca
Year Founded: 1946
Executives:
Guy Martin, General Manager; guy.martin@quilllake.cu.sk.ca
Joe Buller, Manager, Loans
Directors:
Brent Lowes, President
Paul Foley, Vice-President
Werner Block
Gordon Friesen
Glen Gilbertson
Mike Humenny
Mickey Ochitwa
Guy Thevenot
Garnet Zerbin
Branches:
Jansen
PO Box 60
Jansen, SK S0K 2B0 Canada
306-364-2057
Fax: 306-364-2144
Donna Krause, Loans Officer
Rose Valley
RR#1
Rose Valley, SK S0E 1M0 Canada
306-323-4519
Fax: 306-323-2118
Valerie Nivon, Service Rep.

QuintEssential Credit Union Limited
293 Sidney St.
Belleville, ON K8P 3Z4
613-966-4111
Fax: 613-966-8909
info@qcu.ca
www.qcscu.com
Executives:
Ron Koppmann, President
Branches:
Trenton
PO Box 278
251 RCAF Rd.
Trenton, ON K8V 5R5 Canada
613-394-3361
Fax: 613-394-4903
vhamilton@qcu.ca
www.qcscu.com
Don Lockey, Vice-President

Radville Credit Union Ltd.
PO Box 279
201 Main St.
Radville, SK S0C 2G0
306-869-2215
Fax: 306-869-2891
info@radville.cu.sk.ca
www.radville.cu.sk.ca
Year Founded: 1943
Executives:
Ted Struthers, General Manager

Railway Employees' (Sarnia) Credit Union Limited
431 Russell St. South
Sarnia, ON N7T 3N1
519-336-0093
Fax: 519-336-6945
info@recu.ca
www.recu.ca

Raymore Savings & Credit Union Ltd.
PO Box 460
121 Main St.
Raymore, SK S0A 3J0
306-746-2160
Fax: 306-746-5811
866-612-2300
info@raymore.cu.sk.ca
www.raymorecu.com
Year Founded: 1949
Branches:
Punnichy
PO Box 100
124 Main St.
Punnichy, SK S0A 3C0 Canada
306-835-2000
Fax: 306-835-2550
866-612-2300

RBW Employees' (Owen Sound) Credit Union Limited
2049 - 20th St.
Owen Sound, ON N4K 5R2
519-376-8330
Fax: 519-376-1164
Number of Employees: 1

Reddy Kilowatt Credit Union Ltd.
Newfoundland Power Bldg.
PO Box 8910
50 Duffy Pl.
St. John's, NL A1B 3P6
709-737-5624
Fax: 709-737-2937
800-409-2887
rkcu@reddykilowatt.creditu.net
www.reddyk.net
Year Founded: 1956
Number of Employees: 6
Executives:
Michelle Ward, General Manager
Ursula Maloney, Asst. Manager
Directors:
Robert Picks, President
Brian Walsh, Vice-President
Glenn Samms, Secretary
Ron Clark
Ronald Crane
Ted French
Kevin Mahar
Robert Pike
Wade White

Resurrection Parish (Toronto) Credit Union Limited
3 Resurrection Rd.
Toronto, ON M9A 5G1
416-532-3400
Fax: 416-532-4816
rpcul@rpcul.com
www.rpcul.com
Number of Employees: 13
Executives:
Rita Norvaisa, General Manager
Branches:
Mississauga
2185 Stavebank Rd.
Mississauga, ON L5C 1T3 Canada
905-566-0006
Fax: 905-566-1554

Rexton Credit Union
PO Box 390
5 Brait St.
Rexton, NB E4W 1V9
506-523-8020
Fax: 506-523-8190
rexton@rexton.creditu.net
www.rextoncreditunion.ca
Ownership: Member-owned
Year Founded: 1939
Number of Employees: 13
Assets: $10-50 million
Revenues: $1-5 million
Executives:
Garth K. Lawson, General Manager; glawson@rexton.creditu.net

River City Credit Union Ltd.
11715A - 108 Ave.
Edmonton, AB T5H 1B8
780-496-3482
Fax: 780-496-3477
rivercity@alberta-cu.com
www.river-citycu.com
Former Name: Edmonton Civic Employees Credit Union Ltd.
Executives:
Dave Munro, CEO
Branches:
Edmonton - 106A St.
11840 - 106A St.
Edmonton, AB T5G 2S4 Canada
780-496-8754
Fax: 780-471-1509
Edmonton - 58 Ave.
8620 - 58 Ave.
Edmonton, AB T6E 5G3 Canada
780-944-5616
Fax: 780-477-2358

Rochdale Credit Union Limited
943 Dundas St.
Woodstock, ON N4S 1H2
519-539-4813
Fax: 519-539-8667
rochdale@rcu.com
www.rcu.com
Year Founded: 1942
Executives:
Steve Mumford, General Manager; smumford@rcu.com
Ron Davidson, Manager, Credit; rdavidson@rcu.com
Ruth Wood, Manager, Marketing; rwood@rcu.com
Branches:
Ingersoll
108 Thames St. South
Ingersoll, ON N5C 2T4 Canada
519-485-1270
Fax: 519-485-6136
Sylvie Tiffin, Branch Manager
Norwich
48 Main St. West
Norwich, ON N0J 1P0 Canada
519-863-3401
Fax: 519-863-2649
Pat Pike, Branch Manager

Rocky Credit Union Ltd.
PO Box 1420
5035 - 49 St.
Rocky Mountain House, AB T4T 2A3
403-845-2861
Fax: 403-845-7295
rockycu@alberta-cu.com
www.rockycreditunion.com
Ownership: Public
Year Founded: 1944
Number of Employees: 40
Assets: $114,100,000
Revenues: $5,060,000
Executives:
Scott Campbell, General Manager; scampbell@alberta-cu.com
Michelle Andrishak, Manager, Finance & Control; mandrishak@alberta-cu.com
Angie French, Manager, Lending Services; afrench@alberta-cu.com
Tammy Young, Manager, Deposit Services; tyoung@alberta-cu.com

Rorketon & District Credit Union
691 Main St.
Rorketon, MB R0L 1R0
204-732-2448
Fax: 204-732-2275
Year Founded: 1961

Rosenort Credit Union Limited
PO Box 339
23 Main St.
Rosenort, MB R0G 1W0
204-746-2355
Fax: 204-746-2541
800-265-7925
info@rcu.mb.ca
www.rcu.mb.ca
Year Founded: 1940
Assets: $50-100 million
Executives:
Gary Friesen, General Manager; gfriesen@rcu.mb.ca
Allen Friesen, Manager, Loans

Rossignol Credit Union
PO Box 278
Brooklyn, NS B0J 1H0
902-354-2021
Ownership: Private
Year Founded: 1937
Number of Employees: 1
Assets: $1-5 million
Revenues: Under $1 million
Profile: This is a closed-shop credit union. A potential member must be an employee of Bowater to join.
Executives:
Elva Smith, Manager

Royglenor Savings & Credit Union Ltd.
Royal Alexander Hospital, Community Services Centre
#174, 10240 Kingsway Ave.
Edmonton, AB T5H 3V9
780-474-7724
Fax: 780-474-9043
www.royglenorcu.ca
Year Founded: 1956

St Gregor Credit Union Ltd.
PO Box 128
2 Main St.
St Gregor, SK S0K 3X0
306-366-2116
Fax: 306-366-2032
Executives:
Alan Kiefer, General Manager
Branches:
Annaheim
PO Box 65
Annaheim, SK S0K 0G0 Canada
306-598-2044
Fax: 306-598-4440

St Josaphat's Parish (Toronto) Credit Union Limited
12 Parkman Ave.
Toronto, ON M6P 3R5

416-536-2643
Fax: 416-536-4989
stjos@pathcom.com
Year Founded: 1950
Executives:
George Mareczko, General Manager

St. Joseph's Credit Union
PO Box 159
3552 Hwy. 206
Petit de Grat, NS B0E 2L0
902-226-2288
Fax: 902-226-9855
866-876-3192
www.stjosephscreditu.ca
Year Founded: 1936
Number of Employees: 12
Executives:
Michael Boudreau, Generel Manager

St Mary's (Toronto) Credit Union Limited
832 Bloor St. West
Toronto, ON M6G 1M2
416-537-2163
Fax: 416-537-7730
smcu@stmarys-cu.com
www.stmarys-cu.com
Year Founded: 1950
Branches:
Bellwoods
304 Bellwoods Ave.
Toronto, ON M6J 2P4 Canada
416-504-8355

St. Mary's Paperworkers Credit Union
75 Huron St.
Sault Ste Marie, ON P6A 5P4
705-541-2438
Fax: 705-942-6427
baile_s@stmarys-paper.com
Ownership: Private. Closed Bond.
Year Founded: 1953
Number of Employees: 1
Assets: Under $1 million
Revenues: Under $1 million
Executives:
Debbie Rydall, Manager

St. Stanislaus & St. Casimir's Polish Parishes Credit Union Ltd.
220 Roncesvalles Ave.
Toronto, ON M6R 2L7
416-537-2181
Fax: 416-536-8525
info@polcu.com
www.polcan.com
Former Name: Polish (St Catharines) Credit Union Limited
Year Founded: 1951
Number of Employees: 3
Executives:
Stenia Baran, Branch Manager
Branches:
Guelph
#18, 500 Willow Rd.
Guelph, ON N1H 8G4 Canada
519-837-1077
Fax: 519-837-8354
Danuta Walaszczyk, Branch Manager
Hamilton
709 Barton St. East
Hamilton, ON L8L 3A5 Canada
905-545-5537
Fax: 905-548-6899
Bozena Bratos, Branch Manager
Kitchener
215 Highland Rd. West
Kitchener, ON N2M 3C1 Canada
519-745-6393
Fax: 519-570-0386
Mary Koebel, Branch Manager
London - Polish (London) Credit Union Limited
383 Horton St.
London, ON N6B 1L6 Canada
519-672-1712
Fax: 519-672-6287
polcan@polcu.com
www.polcan.com
Miroslawa Wasinski, Manager
Mississauga - Dixie Rd.
3621 Dixie Rd.
Mississauga, ON L4Y 4H3 Canada
905-629-0365
Fax: 905-629-9515
Lucyna Jankowicz, Branch Manager
Mississauga - Dundas St. East
1900 Dundas St. East
Mississauga, ON L4X 2Z4 Canada
905-277-0772
Fax: 905-277-1492
Andrzej Pitek, Branch Manager
Mississauga - Parkerhill Rd.
3015 Parkerhill Rd.
Mississauga, ON L5B 4B2 Canada
905-272-5777
Fax: 905-272-5125
Mila Kolch, Branch Manager
Oakville
40 John St.
Oakville, ON L6K 1G8 Canada
905-339-0283
Fax: 905-339-0348
Anita Ryzynska, Branch Manager
Oshawa
50 Richmond St. East
Oshawa, ON L1G 7C7 Canada
905-432-2200
Fax: 905-432-1699
Elzbieta Plusa, Branch Manager
Ottawa
379 Waverley St.
Ottawa, ON K2P 0W4 Canada
613-230-6220
Fax: 613-230-6532
Malgorzata Lachowicz, Branch Manager
St Catharines
44 1/2 Facer St.
St Catharines, ON L2M 5H6 Canada
905-646-1900
Fax: 905-646-1920
Halina Pieczonka, Branch Manager
Toronto - Bloor St. West
2987 Bloor St. West
Toronto, ON M8X 1C1 Canada
416-236-1225
Fax: 416-236-4581
Ryszard Palka, Branch Manager
Toronto - Denison Ave.
12 Denison Ave.
Toronto, ON M5T 2M4 Canada
416-703-0996
Fax: 416-703-0994
Krystyna Dziadkowiec, Branch Manager
Toronto - Lakeshore Blvd. West
3055 Lakeshore Blvd. West
Toronto, ON M8V 1K6 Canada
416-503-9463
Fax: 416-503-9459
Stefan Holda, Branch Manager
Toronto - Middlefield Rd.
625 Middlefield Rd.
Toronto, ON M1V 5B8 Canada
416-754-1854
Fax: 416-754-4427
Malgorzata Sheikhan, Branch Manager
Windsor
924 Ottawa St.
Windsor, ON N8X 2E1 Canada
519-971-8295
Fax: 519-971-8654
Anthony Blak, Branch Manager

Sandhills Credit Union
PO Box 249
Leader, SK S0N 1H0
306-628-3687
Fax: 306-628-3674
info@sandhills.cu.sk.ca
www.sandhillscu.com
Ownership: Member-owned
Branches:
Prelate
PO Box 119
112 Main St.
Prelate, SK S0N 2B0 Canada
306-673-2311
Fax: 306-673-2294

Sandy Lake Credit Union
PO Box 129
102 Main St.
Sandy Lake, MB R0J 1X0
204-585-2609
Fax: 204-585-2163
slcunion@slcu.mb.ca
www.slcu.mb.ca

Sanford Credit Union
7 Mellow St.
Sanford, MB R0G 2J0
204-736-2373
Fax: 204-736-4108
info@sanfordcu.mb.ca
www.sanfordcu.mb.ca/
Year Founded: 1950
Executives:
David Domes, General Manager
Branches:
Oak Bluff
Oak Bluff General Store
PO Box 36
Oak Bluff, MB R0G 1N0 Canada
204-895-0005
Fax: 204-837-1845

Saskatoon City Employees Credit Union
222 - 3rd Ave. North
Saskatoon, SK S7K 0J5
306-975-3280
Fax: 306-975-7806
www.scecu.com
Former Name: Saskatoon City Employee Credit Union Ltd.
Year Founded: 1947
Number of Employees: 9
Assets: $10-50 million Year End: 20060900
Revenues: $1-5 million Year End: 20060900
Executives:
Robert Voth, General Manager
Directors:
Maria Besenski, President

Saugeen Community Credit Union Limited
PO Box 708
118 Queen St. South
Durham, ON N0G 1R0
519-369-2931
Fax: 519-369-2994
durhamcu@saugeencreditunion.com
www.saugeencreditunion.com
Executives:
Wayne Cargoe, General Manager
Branches:
Chesley
115 - 1st Ave.
Chesley, ON N0G 1L0 Canada
519-363-6188
Fax: 519-363-6108
chesleycu@saugeencreditunion.com
Jeff Vandervoort, Branch Manager
Elmwood
6 Main St.
Elmwood, ON N0G 1S0 Canada
519-363-2305
Fax: 519-363-0091
elmwoodcu@saugeencreditunion.com
Donna Love, Branch Manager
Holstein
109 Grey Rd.
Holstein, ON N0G 2A0 Canada
519-334-3460
holsteincu@saugeencreditunion.com

Scarborough Hospitals Employees' Credit Union Ltd.
#504, 3050 Lawrence Ave. East
Toronto, ON M10 2T7
416-438-2911
Fax: 416-431-8131
fran.carolyn@sympatico.ca

Scarborough Hospitals Employees' Credit Union Ltd. (continued)
Year Founded: 1964

Sceptre Credit Union Ltd.

PO Box 30
122 Kingsway St.
Sceptre, SK S0N 2H0
306-623-4363
sceptre.cu@sk.sympatico.ca

Servus Credit Union

#300, 8723 - 82 Ave.
Edmonton, AB T6C 0Y9
780-496-2000
Fax: 780-468-5220
877-496-2151
Other Information: TTY 780-450-9647
info@servuscu.ca
www.servuscu.ca
Former Name: Capital City Savings & Credit Union Limited
Ownership: Member-owned
Number of Employees: 700
Assets: $1,700,000,000
Revenues: $68,000,000
Profile: Servus Credit Union is a member-owned financial institution providing full financial services to 181,000 member-owners from 50 service locations in 27 Alberta communities. With $3.2 billion in assets, Servus Credit Union is the largest credit union in Alberta. We are also one of Canada's 50 Best Managed Companies.
Executives:
Harry Buddle, President/CEO
Gordon Gamble, Executive Vice-President
Garth Warner, Sr. Vice-President, Operations
Ian Glassford, CFO
Yves Auger, CIO
Kirk Harline, Vice-President & Controller
Craig King, Vice-President, Business Banking
Gary Repchuk, Vice-President, Business Development & Innovation
Dennis Horrigan, Vice-President, Direct Banking
Ray Duchesneau, Vice-President, Eastern Operations
Melissa Baddeley, Vice-President, Human Resources
Gail Stepanik-Keber, Vice-President, Marketing
Dave Ball, Vice-President, Risk Management & Corporate Services
Caroline Ziober, Vice-President, Urban Branches
Doug Forsyth, Vice-President, Western Operations
Directors:
Peter Galloway, Chair
Karen Anderson, Board Secretary
Taras Nohas, Vice-Chair
Penny Reeves, Exec. Member
Fernande Bergeron
Cheryl Budzinski
Chris Burt
Bruce Collingwood
Remi Cyr
Peter Elzinga
Elson Keown
Mavis McKay
Bob Porozni
Bill Purdy
Denis Richer
Branches:
Andrew
5011 - 51 St.
Andrew, AB T0B 0C0 Canada
780-365-3594
Fax: 780-365-2111
Calgary - Canada Place
Canada Place Bldg.
#101, 407 - 2 St. SW
Calgary, AB T2P 2Y3 Canada
403-509-2225
Fax: 403-294-0852
Calgary - SAIT
Crandell Bldg.
#G106, 1301 - 16 Ave. NW
Calgary, AB T2M 2Y3 Canada
403-240-4892
Fax: 403-240-4936
Devon
6 Superior St.
Devon, AB T9G 1E8 Canada
780-987-4422
Fax: 780-987-4425
Drayton Valley
5217 - 50 St.
Drayton Valley, AB T8A 1S3 Canada
780-542-2922
Fax: 780-542-1558
Edmonton - 107 Ave.
10303 - 107 Ave.
Edmonton, AB T5H 0V7 Canada
780-496-2133
Fax: 780-425-1354
Edmonton - Beverly
4230 - 118 Ave.
Edmonton, AB T5W 1A4 Canada
780-496-2155
Fax: 780-474-8344
Edmonton - Bonnie Doon
#100, 8723 - 82 Ave.
Edmonton, AB T6L 0Y9 Canada
780-496-2001
Fax: 780-465-6258
Edmonton - Callingwood
#420, 6655 - 178 St.
Edmonton, AB T5T 4J5 Canada
780-496-2148
Fax: 780-483-0191
Edmonton - Capilano
#1100, Capilano Mall
50 St. & 98 Ave.
Edmonton, AB T6A 0A1 Canada
780-496-2244
Fax: 780-465-7948
Edmonton - City Centre
#201D, 10200 - 102 Ave.
Edmonton, AB T5J 4B7 Canada
780-496-2074
Fax: 780-428-6966
Edmonton - Clearwater
15345 - 97 St.
Edmonton, AB T5X 5V3 Canada
780-415-4240
Fax: 780-415-4246
Edmonton - Clover Bar
14404 Miller Blvd.
Edmonton, AB T5J 2H7 Canada
780-471-0417
Fax: 780-471-0495
Edmonton - Delton
12809 - 82 St.
Edmonton, AB T5E 2S9 Canada
780-496-2100
Fax: 780-476-9114
Edmonton - Garrison Edmonton
PO Box 389
Falaise Ave. & Hwy. 28A
Lancaster Park, AB T0A 2H0 Canada
780-973-7100
Fax: 780-973-4622
Edmonton - Inglecroft
11245 - 124 St.
Edmonton, AB T5M 0J9 Canada
780-496-2177
Fax: 780-453-3860
Edmonton - Jasper Ave. BBC
11311 Kingsway Ave.
Edmonton, AB T5K 0L1 Canada
780-496-2276
Fax: 780-425-6256
Edmonton - Millwoods
2857 Millwoods Rd.
Edmonton, AB T6K 4A9 Canada
780-496-2200
Fax: 780-463-7518
Edmonton - Namao Centre
16517 - 97 St.
Edmonton, AB T5X 6B1 Canada
780-496-2255
Fax: 780-478-3407
Edmonton - Palisades
13106 - 137 Ave.
Edmonton, AB T5L 4Z6 Canada
780-496-2222
Fax: 780-456-9614
Edmonton - Petroleum Plaza
10747 - 100 Ave.
Edmonton, AB T5J 2W3 Canada
780-415-4200
Fax: 780-415-4209
Edmonton - Safecu
11635 - 160 St.
Edmonton, AB T5M 3Z3 Canada
780-413-3334
Fax: 780-452-7867
Edmonton - Southgate
#47, Southgate Mall
111 St. & 51 Ave.
Edmonton, AB T6H 4M6 Canada
780-496-2277
Fax: 780-438-0347
Edmonton - Southside BBC
4504 - 99 St.
Edmonton, AB T6E 5H5 Canada
780-496-2265
Fax: 780-428-9382
Edmonton - Terwillegar Heights
2315 Rabbit Hill Rd.
Edmonton, AB T6R 3K8 Canada
780-496-2296
Fax: 780-989-0900
Edmonton - Westgate
#148, 17010 - 90 Ave.
Edmonton, AB T5T 1L6 Canada
780-496-2300
Fax: 780-487-7913
Elk Point
4934 - 50 Ave.
Elk Point, AB T0A 1A0 Canada
780-724-4099
Fax: 780-724-4029
Entwistle
5002 - 50 Ave.
Entwistle, AB T0E 0S0 Canada
780-727-3593
Fax: 780-727-3900
Fort McMurray
9804 Morrison St.
Fort McMurray, AB T9H 5B8 Canada
780-799-7800
Fax: 780-799-7801
Fort Saskatchewan
#104, 9839 - 104 St.
Fort Saskatchewan, AB T8L 2E5 Canada
780-992-6920
Fax: 780-992-1733
Gibbons
4616 - 50 Ave.
Gibbons, AB T0A 1N0 Canada
780-923-3397
Fax: 780-923-3432
Grande Cache
305 Shoppers Park Mall
Grand Cache, AB T0E 0Y0 Canada
780-827-2156
Fax: 780-827-2896
Hinton
#1, 108 Athabasca Ave.
Hinton, AB T7V 2A5 Canada
780-865-4000
Fax: 780-865-5885
Jasper
PO Box 807
615 Patricia St.
Jasper, AB T0E 1E0 Canada
780-852-1175
Fax: 780-852-1197
Lac La Biche
10209 - 101 Ave.
Lac La Biche, AB T0A 2C0 Canada
780-623-8121
Fax: 780-623-8035
Lamont
4707 - 51 St.
Lamont, AB T0B 2R0 Canada
780-895-5920
Fax: 780-895-2064
Leduc
5203 - 50 Ave.
Leduc, AB T9E 6T2 Canada

780-980-4790
Fax: 780-986-2210
Legal
PO Box 99
4836 - 50 Ave.
Legal, AB T0G 1L0 Canada
780-961-3951
Fax: 780-961-3968
Morinville
PO Box 3035
10226 - 100 Ave.
Morinville, AB T8R 1P9 Canada
780-939-4120
Fax: 780-939-4897
Mundare
PO Box 631
5104 - 50 St.
Mundare, AB T0B 3H0 Canada
780-764-8800
Fax: 780-764-2573
Myrnam
5016 - 49 St.
Myrnam, AB T0B 3K0 Canada
780-366-3751
Fax: 780-366-2662
Plamondon
101 Main St.
Plamondon, AB T0A 2T0 Canada
780-798-3877
Fax: 780-798-2083
Sangudo
4927 - 50 St.
Sangudo, AB T0E 2A0 Canada
780-785-2891
Fax: 780-785-2296
Sherwood Park
800 Bethel Dr.
Sherwood Park, AB T8H 2N4 Canada
780-449-7760
Fax: 780-464-9842
Spruce Grove
PO Box 5124
202 Main St.
Spruce Grove, AB T7X 3A3 Canada
780-962-7000
Fax: 780-962-1249
St Albert
565 St. Albert Rd.
St Albert, AB T8N 6G5 Canada
780-460-3260
Fax: 780-458-2159
St Paul
4738 - 50 Ave.
St Paul, AB T0A 3A0 Canada
780-645-3357
Fax: 780-645-2955
Stony Plain
4904 - 48 St.
Stony Plain, AB T7Z 1L8 Canada
780-963-2870
Fax: 780-963-2070
Wabamun
5112 - 52 St.
Wabamun, AB T0E 2K0 Canada
780-892-2647
Fax: 780-892-2613

Sharons Credit Union
1055 Kingsway
Vancouver, BC V5V 3C7
604-873-6490
Fax: 604-873-6498
sharons@sharonscu.ca
www.sharonscu.ca
Year Founded: 1988
Number of Employees: 30
Assets: $100-500 million
Branches:
Burnaby
#185, 5665 Kingsway
Burnaby, BC V5H 2G4 Canada
604-435-6606
Fax: 604-435-6605
Coquitlam
#202, 403 North Rd.
Coquitlam, BC V3K 3V8 Canada
604-936-5058
Fax: 604-936-5023
Surrey
10541 King George Hwy.
Surrey, BC V3T 2X1 Canada
604-582-7272
Fax: 604-582-7209

Shaunavon Credit Union
399 Centre St.
Shaunavon, SK S0N 2N0
306-297-2635
Fax: 306-297-3137
shaunavon.cu@sasktel.net
www.shaunavoncu.sk.ca
Ownership: Member-owned
Year Founded: 1944
Executives:
Chuck Gartner, General Manager
Branches:
Admiral
PO Box 127
Admiral, SK S0N 0B0 Canada
306-297-6367
Fax: 306-297-2670
Bracken
PO Box 119
Bracken, SK S0N 0G0 Canada
306-293-2134
Fax: 306-293-2070
Val Marie
PO Box 180
Val Marie, SK S0N 2T0 Canada
306-298-2010
Fax: 306-298-2069

Shell Employees Credit Union Limited
PO Box 100, M Stn. M
Calgary, AB T2P 2H5
403-691-3817
Fax: 403-262-4009
Other Information: Toll Free: 1-877-582-6222 (AB only)
shellcu@shellcu.com
www.shellcu.com
Ownership: Member-owned
Year Founded: 1953

Sheridan Park Credit Union Ltd.
2251 Speakman Dr.
Mississauga, ON L5K 1B2
905-823-1263
Fax: 905-823-8661
spcu@primus.ca
www.spcu.ca

Smiths Falls Community Credit Union Limited
16 Beckwith St. North
Smiths Falls, ON K7A 2B1
613-283-3835
Fax: 613-283-9623
Year Founded: 1951

So-Use Credit Union
2265 Bloor St. West
Toronto, ON M6S 1P1
416-763-5575
Fax: 416-761-9604
800-322-9274
so-use.info@so-use.com
www.so-use.com
Year Founded: 1950
Executives:
Narc Sirard, CEO
Directors:
Walter Chewchuk, Chair
Dennis Hunt, Vice-Chair
Branches:
Mississauga
#1, 512 Bristol Rd. West
Mississauga, ON L5R 3Z1 Canada
905-568-9890
Fax: 905-568-9893

SOC Savings & Credit Union Ltd.
Eau Claire Place I
525 - 3 Ave. SW
Calgary, AB T2P 0G4
403-509-4078
Fax: 403-509-4299

South Calgary Savings & Credit Union Limited
4810 - 16th St. SW
Calgary, AB T2T 4J5
403-243-5224
Fax: 403-287-9189
Ownership: Member-owned

South Interlake Credit Union Ltd.
233 Main St.
Selkirk, MB R1A 1S1
204-785-7625
Fax: 204-785-7649
www.sicu.mb.ca
Ownership: Member-owned
Year Founded: 1944
Number of Employees: 106
Assets: $100-500 million
Executives:
Ed Bergen, CEO
Directors:
Rob Cox, Chair
Steven Fosty, Secretary
Branches:
Beausejour - Park Ave.
613 Park Ave.
Beausejour, MB R0E 0C0 Canada
204-268-3778
Fax: 204-268-4447
Curtis Fines, Branch Manager
Inwood
Main St.
Inwood, MB R0C 1P0 Canada
204-278-3580
Lac Du Bonnet
2 Park Ave.
Lac du Bonnet, MB R0E 1A0 Canada
204-345-9777
Fax: 204-345-9774
Zane Hunter, Branch Manager
Pinawa
PO Box 10
Burrows Rd.
Pinawa, MB R0E 1L0 Canada
204-753-5200
Fax: 204-753-5219
Charlene Fitkowsky, Branch Manager
Pine Falls
11 Linden St.
Pine Falls, MB R0E 1M0 Canada
204-367-4477
Fax: 204-367-9141
Debbie Cairns, Branch Manager
Selkirk
233 Main St.
Selkirk, MB R1A 1S1 Canada
204-785-7600
Fax: 204-785-7624
Kerry Hendry, Branch Manager
Stonewall
410 Centre Ave.
Stonewall, MB R0C 2Z0 Canada
204-467-5574
Fax: 204-467-5962
Ward Wilton, Branch Manager
Teulon
PO Box 90
76 Main St.
Teulon, MB R0C 3B0 Canada
204-886-2881
Fax: 204-886-9141
Derek Christian, Branch Manager
Whitemouth
250 Railway Ave.
Whitemouth, MB R0E 2G0 Canada
204-348-2359
Fax: 204-348-2361
Michael Bjarnarson, Branch Manager

Southlake Regional Health Centre Employees' Credit Union Limited
596 Davis Dr.
Newmarket, ON L0G 1V0
905-895-4521
Fax: 905-853-2218
Former Name: York County Hospital Employees' (Newmarket) Credit Union Limited
Number of Employees: 1

Southwest Credit Union Limited
PO Box 1090
198 - 1st Ave. NE
Swift Current, SK S9H 3X3
306-778-1700
Fax: 306-773-3381
800-381-5502
www.swcu.sk.ca
Ownership: Member-owned
Year Founded: 1993
Number of Employees: 200
Assets: $420,000,000 Year End: 20041231
Revenues: $25,000,000 Year End: 20041231
Executives:
Fred Townley-McKay, CEO
Pat Friesen, Vice-President, Marketing & Communication
Earl Hanson, Vice-President, Wealth Management
Jim Velichka, Vice-President, Finance
Susan Woods, Vice-President, Human Resources
Corinne Brown, Exec. Assistant to CEO
Directors:
Mike Davis, Chair
Russ Siemens, 1st Vice-President
Andrey Yee, 2nd Vice-President
Gordon Lightfoot, Past President
Gerry Gauvin
Betty Goddard
Patricia Martinson
Joanne Matsalla
Jeff Turcotte
Branches:
Cabri
PO Box 410
201 Centre St.
Cabri, SK S0N 0J0 Canada
306-587-2612
Fax: 306-587-2680
Climax
PO Box 90
Climax, SK S0N 0N0 Canada
306-293-2890
Fax: 306-293-2885
Coderre
PO Box 39
Coderre, SK S0H 0X0 Canada
306-394-2000
Fax: 306-394-2066
Frontier
104 - 1st Ave. West
Frontier, SK S0N 0W0 Canada
306-296-2200
Fax: 306-296-2034
Gravelbourg
PO Box 90
Gravelbourg, SK S0H 1X0 Canada
306-648-3171
Fax: 306-648-2949
Gull Lake
PO Box 178
1371 Conrad Ave.
Gull Lake, SK S0N 1A0 Canada
306-672-3821
Fax: 306-672-3224
Hazlet
PO Box 127
Hazlet, SK S0N 1E0 Canada
306-678-2000
Fax: 306-678-2239
Hodgeville
PO Box 64
Hodgeville, SK S0H 2B0 Canada
306-677-2388
Fax: 306-677-2289
Lancer
PO Box 120
Lancer, SK S0N 1G0 Canada
306-689-2221
Fax: 306-689-2988
Pennant Station
PO Box 95
Pennant Station, SK S0N 1X0 Canada
306-626-3201
Fax: 306-626-3668
Ponteix
PO Box 388
Ponteix, SK S0N 1Z0 Canada
306-625-3522
Fax: 306-625-3723
Shamrock
PO Box 100
Shamrock, SK S0H 3W0 Canada
306-648-3592
Fax: 306-648-2756
Swift Current
PO Box 1090
198 - 1st Ave. NE
Swift Current, SK S9H 3X3 Canada
306-778-1700
Fax: 306-773-1634

Southwest Regional Credit Union
1205 Exmouth St.
Sarnia, ON N7S 1W7
519-383-8001
Fax: 519-383-8841
info@southwestcu.com
www.southwestcu.com
Year Founded: 1989
Number of Employees: 30
Executives:
Tony Doucette, General Manager
Patty Levack, Branch Manager; 519-353-0750
Branches:
Corunna
411 Lyndock St.
Corunna, ON N0N 1G0 Canada
519-862-1421
Fax: 519-862-1423
Darragh Ginn, Branch Manager
Wallaceburg
County Fair Mall
60 McNaughton Ave.
Wallaceburg, ON N8A 1R9 Canada
519-627-6744
Fax: 519-627-3275
Elanor VanLandeghem, Branch Manager
Wyoming
618 Broadway St.
Wyoming, ON N0N 1T0 Canada
519-845-3362
Fax: 519-845-0731
Rick Swales, Branch Manager

Spalding Savings & Credit Union Ltd.
111 Centre St.
Spalding, SK S0K 4C0
306-872-2050
Fax: 306-872-2100
Year Founded: 1941

Spiritwood Credit Union Ltd.
PO Box 129
Spiritwood, SK S0J 2M0
306-883-2250
877-288-1414
contactus@spiritwood.cu.sk.ca
www.spiritwoodcu.com
Ownership: Member-owned
Year Founded: 1938

Spruce Credit Union
879 Victoria St.
Prince George, BC V2L 2K7
250-562-5415
sprucecu@cucbc.com
www.sprucecu.bc.ca
Number of Employees: 30
Assets: $50-100 million

Squamish Credit Union
PO Box 1940
38085 - 2nd St.
Squamish, BC V0N 3G0
604-892-5288
Fax: 604-892-5287
877-892-5288
squamishsavings.com
Ownership: Private
Executives:
Bill Brumpton, General Manager
Branches:
Garibaldi Highlands
PO Box 939
#1, 1900 Garibaldi Way
Garibaldi Highlands, BC V0N 1T0 Canada
604-898-1883
Fax: 604-898-4046
866-898-1883

Stanco Credit Union Ltd.
Chevron Plaza, Room 759
500 - 5 Ave. SW
Calgary, AB T2P 0L7
403-234-5300
Fax: 403-234-5823
info@stancocu.com
www.stancocu.com
Number of Employees: 1
Assets: $1-5 million
Revenues: Under $1 million

Standard Tube Employees' (Woodstock) Credit Union Limited
273 Ingersoll Ave.
Woodstock, ON N4S 4W7
519-537-8121
Fax: 519-537-8099
stucrun@execulink.com
Year Founded: 1948

Starbuck Credit Union
16 Main St.
Starbuck, MB R0G 2P0
204-735-2394
Fax: 204-735-2278
866-398-9642
info@starbuckcreditunion.com
www.starbuckcreditunion.com
Year Founded: 1940
Assets: $50-100 million
Executives:
Greg Goldsborough, President
Ray Ullenboom, Vice-President
Dennis James Hedley, General Manager
Directors:
Les Brooker
Neil Frantz
Henry Holtmann
Stuart Janke
Ralph Rasmussen
Branches:
Headingley
5240 Portage Ave.
Headingley, MB R4H 1E1 Canada
204-735-4021
Fax: 204-953-2333

Starnews Credit Union Limited
1 Yonge St.
Toronto, ON M5E 1E5
416-366-5534
Fax: 416-366-6225
877-782-7639
staff@starnewscu.com
www.starnewscu.com
Branches:
Woodbridge
One Century Place
Woodbridge, ON L4R 8R2 Canada
905-850-7978

State Farm (Toronto) Credit Union Limited
333 First Commerce Dr.
Aurora, ON L4G 8A4
905-750-4100
Fax: 905-750-4487

Year Founded: 1968

Steel Centre Credit Union
340 Prince St.
Sydney, NS B1P 5K9
902-562-5559
Fax: 902-539-6024
www.sccu.ca
Year Founded: 1993
Executives:
Gary Forsey, Manager

Steinbach Credit Union
305 Main St.
Steinbach, MB R5G 1B1
204-326-3495
Fax: 204-326-5621
800-728-6440
scu@scu.mb.ca
www.scu.mb.ca
Ownership: Member-owned
Year Founded: 1941
Number of Employees: 280
Assets: $1-10 billion Year End: 20041231
Revenues: $50-100 million Year End: 20041231
Executives:
Glenn Friesen, CEO
Brian Esau, Chief Operating Officer
Don Loewen, Chief Financial Officer
Robert Dueck, Manager, Special Services
James Gesselin, Manager, Lending
Lynette Gillen, Manager, Wealth Management
Sharon McMahon, Manager, Human Resources
Kevin Sitka, Manager, Marketing
Directors:
Ted Falk, President
Russ Fast, Vice-President
Reg Penner, 2nd Vice-President
Alan Barkman
Carl Doerksen
Abe Hiebert
Doris Martens
Sieg Peters
Bryan Rempel
Branches:
Winnipeg
2100 McGillivray Blvd.
Winnipeg, MB R3Y 1X2 Canada
204-222-2100
Fax: 204-487-0204
Murray Rempel, Manager

Stelco Finishing Works Credit Union Limited
1013 King St. East
Hamilton, ON L8M 1C9
905-547-8724
Fax: 905-547-4742
stelcocu@stelcocu.ca
www.stelcocu.ca

Stoughton Credit Union Ltd.
PO Box 420
Stoughton, SK S0G 4T0
306-457-2443
Fax: 306-457-2511
info@stoughton.cu.sk.ca
www.stoughtoncu.com
Year Founded: 1960
Number of Employees: 9
Assets: $10-50 million
Revenues: $1-5 million
Branches:
Kisbey
PO Box 250
Kisbey, SK S0G 1L0 Canada
306-462-2220
Fax: 306-462-2031

Strathclair Credit Union
PO Box 246
Strathclair, MB R0J 2C0
204-365-4700
Fax: 204-365-4710
info@strathclaircu.mb.ca
www.strathclaircu.mb.ca
Executives:
Brad Ross, General Manager
Branches:
Newdale
PO Box 215
Newdale, MB R0J 1J0 Canada
204-365-4700
Fax: 204-849-4301
Kathy Woodley, Representative, Member Services
Oakburn
PO Box 297
Oakburn, MB R0J 1L0 Canada
204-365-4700
Fax: 204-234-3104
Linda Wasilka, Office Supervisor
Shoal Lake
PO Box 129
Shoal Lake, MB R0J 1Z0 Canada
204-365-4700
Fax: 204-759-4207
Belinda Nowell, Branch Manager
Strathclair
PO Box 246
Strathclair, MB R0J 2C0 Canada
204-365-4700
Fax: 204-365-4710
Susan Mervyn, Branch Manager

Strathfiner Credit Union Ltd.
PO Box 1020
Edmonton, AB T5J 2M1
780-449-8295
Fax: 780-449-8174
sfcu@datanet.ab.ca
Ownership: Member-owned. Closed bond.
Year Founded: 1954
Number of Employees: 1
Assets: $1-5 million Year End: 20060930
Revenues: Under $1 million Year End: 20060930
Executives:
Andrew Bissell, President
Fred Tauber, Vice-President
Lorraine Ball, General Manager
Directors:
Don Bevan
Bernard Garneau
Randy Hoy
Glenn Mabbutt
Don Riddell
Russ White

Sudbury Regional Credit Union
Also listed under: *Financing & Loan Companies*
PO Box 662
1 Gribble St.
Copper Cliff, ON P0M 1N0
705-682-0645
Fax: 705-682-1348
888-444-2601
info@sudburycu.com
www.sudburycu.com
Ownership: Member-owned
Year Founded: 1951
Number of Employees: 43
Assets: $100-500 million Year End: 20060930
Revenues: Under $1 million Year End: 20060930
Executives:
William Falcioni, CEO; 705- 68- 064
Michael Moore, Manager, Operations; 705-682-0641
Suzie O'Neill, Manager, Human Resources
Rheal Paquette, Manager, Information & Technology
Douglas Yeo, Manager, Credit; 705-682-0641
Gary Blondin, Administrator, Credit Services
Mimi Wiseman, Controller; 705-682-0641
Directors:
George Joyce, President
Ted Joiner, Vice-President
Susan MacDonald, Secretary
Jenny Parisotto, Youth Director
Mara Storey, Youth Director
Kate Barber
John Cochrane
John Gouchie
Al Hickey
R.A. (Sandy) MacDonald
Joseph Marcuccio
Marvin Saunders
Rick Stickles
Branches:
Copper Cliff
PO Box 662
1 Gribble St.
Copper Cliff, ON P0M 1N0 Canada
705-682-0645
Fax: 705-682-1348
Jocelyne Akey, Supervisor
Levack
37 Levack Dr.
Levack, ON P0M 2C0 Canada
705-966-3451
Fax: 705-966-3747
Carol Nerpin, Supervisor
Sudbury - Barrydowne Rd.
1048 Barrydowne Rd.
Sudbury, ON P3A 3V3 Canada
705-560-5872
Fax: 705-560-2232
Patrick Tarini, Branch Manager
Sudbury - Bouchard St.
Regency Mall
469 Bouchard St.
Sudbury, ON P3E 2K8 Canada
705-522-5550
Fax: 705-522-8944
Mike DeNoble, Manager, Branch & Commercial Accounts
Sudbury - Lisgar St.
50 Lisgar St.
Sudbury, ON P3E 3L8 Canada
705-674-7526
Fax: 705-674-3253
Robert Rachkoloski, Branch Manager

Summerland & District Credit Union
PO Box 750
13601 Victoria Rd. North
Summerland, BC V0H 1Z0
250-494-7181
Fax: 250-494-4261
www.sdcu.com
Year Founded: 1944
Number of Employees: 39
Executives:
Len Grant, Chair
Al Eden, Vice-Chair
Directors:
Roy Cansdale
Tony Clare
Basil Cogill
Lorrie Forde
James Hopkins
Bev Skinner
John Waycott

Sunnybrook Credit Union Limited
c/o Sunnybrook & Women's College Health Services Centre
#CB02, 2075 Bayview Ave.
Toronto, ON M4N 3M5
416-480-4467
Fax: 416-480-5908
info@sunnybrookcu.com
www.sunnybrookcu.com
Year Founded: 1950
Directors:
Marian Lorenz, Chair
Greg Baker, Vice-Chair

Sunshine Coast Credit Union
Also listed under: *Financial Planning*
PO Box 799
985 Sunshine Coast Hwy.
Gibsons, BC V0N 1V0
604-886-2122
Fax: 604-886-0797
administration@sunshineccu.net
www.sunshineccu.com
Ownership: Member-owned
Year Founded: 1941
Number of Employees: 83
Assets: $100-500 million
Revenues: $100-500 million
Profile: A full-service community credit union. Affiliated with SunCu Financial Services Ltd.
Executives:
Dale Eichar, CEO

Sunshine Coast Credit Union (continued)
Rick Cooney, Manager, Operations & Development
Directors:
Brian Beecham, Chair
Karen Archer, 1st Vice-Chair
Bernard Bennett, 2nd Vice-Chair
Stan Anderson
Timothy Anderson
Harris Cole
Elfriede Hofmann
Robert Miller
Margaret Penney
Branches:
Gibsons
PO Box 715
985 Gibsons Coast Way
Gibsons, BC V0N 1V0 Canada
604-886-8121
Fax: 604-886-4831
gibsonsbranch@sunshineccu.com
Madeira Park
PO Box 28
12887 Madeira Park Rd.
Madeira Park, BC V0N 2H0 Canada
604-883-9531
Fax: 604-883-9475
penderbranch@sunshineccu.com
Sechelt
5655 Teredo St.
Sechelt, BC V0N 3A0 Canada
604-885-3255
Fax: 604-885-3278
secheltbranch@sunshineccu.com

Superior Credit Union Limited
318 South Syndicate Ave.
Thunder Bay, ON P7E 1E3
807-624-2255
info@supercu.com
www.supercu.com
Year Founded: 1997
Branches:
Marathon
21 Stevens Ave.
Marathon, ON P0T 2E0 Canada
807-229-1231
Schreiber
303 Scotia St.
Schreiber, ON P0T 2S0 Canada
807-824-2500
Thunder Bay - Arundel St.
320B Arundel St.
Thunder Bay, ON P7A 1L3 Canada
807-346-6710
Thunder Bay - North Court St.
29 North Court St.
Thunder Bay, ON P7A 4T4 Canada
807-346-6715

Sydenham Community Credit Union Limited
32 Front St. East
Strathroy, ON N7G 1Y4
519-245-2530
Fax: 519-245-0167
info@sydenhamccu.on.ca
www.sydenhamccu.on.ca
Year Founded: 1957
Executives:
Janet Grantham, CEO; mking@sydenhamccu.on.ca
Branches:
Ailsa Craig
PO Box 190
160 Main St.
Ailsa Craig, ON N0M 1A0 Canada
519-293-3947
Fax: 519-293-3454
ailsacraig@sydenhamccu.on.ca
Elva McLachlin, Branch Manager
London
4562 Colonel Talbot Rd.
London, ON N6P 1B1 Canada
519-652-5721
800-384-6587
lambeth@sydenhamccu.on.ca
Teri Lynn Witherspoon, Branch Manager
Mount Brydges
22478 Adelaide Rd.
Mount Brydges, ON N0L 1W0 Canada
519-264-9708
Fax: 519-264-9181
mountbrydges@sydenhamccu.on.ca
Patricia Rastin, Manager
Parkhill
PO Box 338
260 Main St.
Parkhill, ON N0M 2K0 Canada
519-294-6277
Fax: 519-294-0521
parkhill@sydenhamccu.on.ca
Bob Drouillard, Branch Manager
Strathroy
32 Front St. East
Strathroy, ON N7G 1Y4 Canada
519-245-2530
Fax: 519-245-6728
strathroy@sydenhamccu.on.ca
Rick Pikul, Manager

Sydney Credit Union
PO Box 1386
95 Townsend St.
Sydney, NS B1P 6K3
902-562-5593
Fax: 902-539-8448
sydney@sydney.creditu.net
www.sydneycreditunion.com
Ownership: Member-owned
Year Founded: 1935
Directors:
Kevin MacAdam, President
Dorothy Blanchard, Vice-President
John MacEachern, Secretary
Doreen Burke
Sandy Burke
Darrell Kyte
Lawrence MacDonald
Gerard MacKinnon
Jim MacLean
Branches:
Sydney River
1164 Kings Rd.
Sydney, NS B1S 1C9 Canada
902-539-1684
Fax: 902-567-1155

Taiwanese - Canadian Toronto Credit Union Limited
***Also listed under:** Financing & Loan Companies*
#305, 3636 Steeles Ave. East
Markham, ON L3R 1K9
905-944-0981
Fax: 905-944-0982
tcu@on.aibn.com
www.tctcu.com
Ownership: Member-owned
Year Founded: 1978
Number of Employees: 5
Assets: $5-10 million Year End: 20050930
Revenues: Under $1 million Year End: 20050930
Profile: Offers a full range of financial services to Ontario residents of Taiwan origin.
Executives:
Tony Y.C. Liao, President
Tina Wang, Vice-President
Grace Liaw, Treasurer, Manager

Talka Lithuanian Credit Union Limited
830 Main St. East
Hamilton, ON L8M 1L6
905-544-7125
Fax: 905-544-7126
Former Name: Talka Hamilton Credit Union
Year Founded: 1955
Executives:
Ray Sakalas, Branch Manager

Teachers Credit Union
75 James St. South
Hamilton, ON L8P 2Y9
905-525-8090
Fax: 905-525-7422
877-427-1281
www.teacherscu.on.ca
Former Name: Hamilton Teachers Credit Union Limited
Ownership: Private
Executives:
Beryl Roberto, President/CEO
Betty Gruba, Exec. Vice-President
Branches:
Ancaster
21 Stone Church Rd.
Ancaster, ON L9K 1S4 Canada
905-304-7022
Fax: 905-304-0128
866-507-7022
Brantford
#25, 27 King George Rd.
Brantford, ON N3R 5J8 Canada
519-752-1090
Fax: 519-752-0967
877-752-1090
Hamilton - Mountain
990 Upper Wentworth St.
Hamilton, ON L9A 5E9 Canada
905-318-1113
Fax: 905-318-8327
877-318-1113

Teachers Plus Credit Union
36 Brookshire Ct.
Bedford, NS B4A 4E9
902-477-5664
Fax: 902-477-4108
800-565-3103
info@teachersplus.ca
www.teachersplus.ca
Former Name: Nova Scotia Teachers Credit Union
Year Founded: 1956
Number of Employees: 11
Assets: $10-50 million
Profile: To be the financial institution of choice for Nova Scotia teachers.
Executives:
Cameron MacDonald, Manager
Darrell Jollimore, Manager, Financial Services

Thamesville Community Credit Union
84 London Rd.
Thamesville, ON N0P 2K0
519-692-3855
Fax: 519-692-9532
info@thamesvilleccu.ca
www.thamesvilleccu.ca
Ownership: Member-owned
Year Founded: 1955
Profile: The credit union provides a full range of financial services to over 2,800 members.
Executives:
David Ford, CEO
Branches:
Dutton
207 Main St.
Dutton, ON N0L 1J0 Canada
519-762-6650
Fax: 519-762-6629
info@thamesvilleccu.ca
Wardsville
1789 Longwoods Rd.
Wardsville, ON N0L 2N0 Canada
519-693-9936
Fax: 519-693-9937
info@thamesvilleccu.ca

Thorold Community Credit Union
63 Front St. South
Thorold, ON L2V 3Z3
905-227-1106
Fax: 905-227-1109
www.thoroldcu.com
Executives:
Morley Snary, General Manager

Thunder Bay Elevators Employees' Credit Union Limited
417 Fort William Rd.
Thunder Bay, ON P7B 2Z5
807-345-2471
Fax: 807-344-0829

Year Founded: 1953

Tiger Hills Credit Union
PO Box 163
197 Broadway
Treherne, MB R0G 2V0
204-723-3250
Fax: 204-723-3255
thcuinfo@tigerhillscu.mb.ca
www.tigerhillscu.mb.ca
Branches:
Holland
PO Box 99
110 Broadway St. North
Holland, MB R0G 0X0 Canada
204-526-6470
Fax: 204-526-6474

Tisdale Credit Union Ltd.
PO Box 455
Tisdale, SK S0E 1T0
306-873-2616
Fax: 306-873-4322
info@tisdale.cu.sk.ca
www.tisdalecu.com
Ownership: Private. Member-owned
Year Founded: 1943
Number of Employees: 30
Assets: $100-500 million
Revenues: $1-5 million
Executives:
Betty Bauhuis, CEO; betty.bauhuis@tisdale.cu.sk.ca
Stan Bentz, Manager, Retail Specialty Services
Bryan Furber, Manager, Finance & Technology
Linda Schulz, Manager, Retail Relationship Services

Toronto Catholic School Board Employees' Credit Union Ltd.
80 Sheppard Ave. East
Toronto, ON M2N 6E8
416-229-5315
Fax: 416-512-3427
tcsbecu-info@tcsbecu.com
www.mssbecu.com
Former Name: Metropolitan Separate School Board Employees Credit Union Limited
Ownership: Private
Year Founded: 1972
Number of Employees: 7
Assets: $10-50 million
Directors:
Horace Moore, President
Lewis Thomas, Vice-President

The Toronto Electrical Utilities Credit Union Limited
14 Carlton St.
Toronto, ON M5B 1K5
416-542-2522
teucu@teucu.com
www.teucu.com
Ownership: Member-owned
Year Founded: 1941
Number of Employees: 8
Profile: The credit union serves the employees of Toronto Hydro & the Plant Electrical Engineering Department of the Toronto Transit Commission.

Executives:
Diane Kocet, General Manager
Service Centres:
Toronto - Commissioners St.
500 Commissioners St.
Toronto, ON M4M 3N7 Canada
Fax: 416-542-2631

Toronto Municipal Employees' Credit Union Limited
City Hall
PO Box 30
100 Queen St. West, Main Fl.
Toronto, ON M5H 2N2
416-392-6868
Fax: 416-392-6895
www.tmecu.com
Year Founded: 1940
Branches:
Toronto - Etobicoke
2 Civic Centre Ct.
Toronto, ON M9C 5A3 Canada
416-622-9300
Fax: 416-622-2002

Tri-Island Credit Union
PO Box 580
1 Rink Rd.
Twillingate, NL A0G 4M0
709-884-2704
Fax: 709-884-2026
www.triislandcu.com
Year Founded: 1986
Number of Employees: 10
Executives:
Kathy Roberts, Branch Manager
Lucy Wheeler, Financial Manager
Steven Anstey, Loans Officer
Branches:
Twillingate
PO Box 344
184 Rd. to the Isles
Twillingate, NL A0G 4E0 Canada
709-629-3514
Mary Lou Small, Branch Manager

Turtle Mountain Credit Union
356 South Railway St.
Boissevain, MB R0K 0E0
204-534-2421
Fax: 204-534-6310
Former Name: Boissevain Credit Union Ltd.
Branches:
Minto
South Railway St. West
Minto, MB R0K 1M0 Canada
204-776-2330

Turtleford Credit Union Ltd.
PO Box 370
208 Main St.
Turtleford, SK S0M 2Y0
306-845-2105
Fax: 306-845-3035

Twin Oak Credit Union Ltd.
PO Box 463
1045 Industry St.
Oakville, ON L6J 5A8
905-845-3441
Fax: 905-845-2155
877-894-6625
industry@twinoakcu.com
www.twinoakcu.com
Year Founded: 1954
Number of Employees: 11
Assets: $10-50 million
Executives:
Linda Flemington, General Manager
Directors:
Bill Van Gaal, President
Ken Watman, Secretary
Mary Cardamone
Brian Cargill
Gail Luyben-Powers
Paul Taggart
Paul Vayda
Branches:
Brampton
2150 Steeles Ave. East
Brampton, ON L6T 1A7 Canada
905-790-0344
Fax: 905-790-0366
877-889-4662
brampton@twinoakcu.com

Ukrainian (St Catharines) Credit Union Limited(USCCU)
118 Niagara St.
St Catharines, ON L2R 4L4
905-684-5062
Fax: 905-684-3098
bruce@hroshi.com
www.hroshi.com
Year Founded: 1946
Executives:
Bruce Fulcher, General Manager
Directors:
Stephen Dominick, Chair
Robert Diakow, Vice-Chair
Andrey Bourak, Secretary
Peter Diakow
Kathryn Hryb
Diane Kusiak
Bryan Magwood
Nestor Siolkowsky
Ola Tkaczyk

Unigasco Credit Union Limited
40 Keil Dr. South
Chatham, ON N7M 3G8
519-436-4590
Fax: 519-436-5451
800-592-9592
www.unigasco.com
Year Founded: 1952
Number of Employees: 23
Executives:
Tim Bossence, General Manager
Patricia Marchand, Manager, Credit
Bruce Ross, Manager, Financial Services

Union Bay Credit Union
PO Box 158
313 McLeod Rd.
Union Bay, BC V0R 3B0
250-335-2122
Fax: 250-335-2131
www.unionbaycreditunion.com
Ownership: Member-owned
Year Founded: 1944
Executives:
Bryan Fisher, CEO
Sharon McGarvey, COO
Branches:
Bowser
PO Box 83
#1, 6996 West Island Hwy.
Bowser, BC V0R 1G0 Canada
250-757-8146
Fax: 250-757-8185
Leslie Stringer, Manager
Hornby Island
4325 Shingle Spit Rd.
Hornby Island, BC V0R 1Z0 Canada
250-335-2326
Fax: 250-335-2370

United Employees Credit Union Limited
964 Eastern Ave.
Toronto, ON M4L 1A6
416-461-9257
Fax: 416-461-8141
infounited@unitedcu.com
www.unitedcu.com
Year Founded: 1946
Number of Employees: 10
Executives:
Dwight Batke, General Manager
Branches:
London - McCormick's Employees (London) Credit Union Limited
1156 Dundas St. East
London, ON N5W 5Y4 Canada
519-455-8700
Fax: 519-455-1891
Mississauga
4567 Dixie Rd.
Mississauga, ON L4W 1S2 Canada
905-625-6973
Fax: 905-625-5895
Toronto
789 Don Mills Rd., 2nd Fl.
Toronto, ON M3C 1T9 Canada
416-429-3000
Fax: 416-463-1828

Unity Credit Union Ltd.
PO Box 370
120 - 2nd Ave. East
Unity, SK S0K 4L0
306-228-2688
Fax: 306-228-2185

Unity Credit Union Ltd. (continued)
info@unity.cu.sk.ca
www.unity.cu.sk.ca
Year Founded: 1941
Number of Employees: 31
Assets: $50-100 million
Revenues: $1-5 million
Branches:
Tramping Lake
PO Box 99
Tramping Lake, SK S0K 4H0 Canada
306-755-2131
Fax: 306-755-2122

Unity Savings & Credit Union Limited

Central Management Support Office, Bayridge Centre West
775 Strand Blvd.
Kingston, ON K7P 2S7
613-389-9965
unityone@unitysavings.com
www.unitysavings.com
Number of Employees: 23
Executives:
Mark Michener, CEO
Branches:
Maitland
PO Box 611
1400 County Rd. #2
Maitland, ON K0E 1P0 Canada
613-348-4223
Fax: 613-348-4245
maitland@unitysavings.com
Mary Haddow, Manager
Offices:
Brockville
2211 Parkedale Ave.
Brockville, ON K6V 6B2 Canada
613-342-6365
Fax: 613-342-9091
brockvil@unitysavings.com
Pierre Marcotte, Eastern Region Manager
Cornwall
1360 Marleau Ave.
Cornwall, ON K6H 2W8 Canada
613-938-7452
Fax: 613-938-8870
cornwall@unitysavings.com
Jim Coolen, Branch Manager
Kingston - Brock St. - Health Care Office
Hotel Dieu Hospital
166 Brock St.
Kingston, ON K7L 5G2 Canada
613-544-0038
Fax: 613-547-9776
healthca@unitysavings.com
Marrianne Hawkins, Branch Manager
Kingston - Front Rd.
455 Front Rd.
Kingston, ON K7L 4Z6 Canada
613-542-2313
Fax: 613-542-0026
frontrd@unitysavings.com
Cathy Fobert, Branch Manager
Kingston - Portsmouth Ave.
Kingston (St. Lawrence) Campus
100 Portsmouth Ave.
Kingston, ON K7L 5A6 Canada
613-544-5400
Fax: 613-545-3923
Kingston - Princess St.
850 Princess St.
Kingston, ON K7L 1G3 Canada
613-546-4209
Fax: 613-546-0613
888-809-8766
princess@unitysavings.com
Dan Devito, Branch Manager
Kingston - Princess St. - Credential Securities Inc. Office
850 Princess St., 2nd Fl.
Kingston, ON K7L 1G3 Canada
613-546-5567
Fax: 613-546-0613
fobert@unitysavings.com
Michael Fobert, Investment Advisor
Kingston - Strand Blvd. - Education Family Office
Bayridge Centre West
775 Strand Blvd.
Kingston, ON K7P 2S7 Canada
613-389-7721
Fax: 613-389-4186
800-504-6894
edfam@unitysavings.com
Bev Stubbert, Branch Manager
Napanee
136 Richmond Blvd.
Napanee, ON K7R 3Z7 Canada
613-354-6678
Fax: 613-354-6679
800-667-9348
napanee@unitysavings.com
Debra Kerr, Branch Manager
Smiths Falls
#101, 270 Brockville St.
Smiths Falls, ON K7A 5L4 Canada
613-284-1169
Fax: 613-284-0832
smithsfalls@unitysavings.com
Jim Coolen, Manager

University Hospitals Staff Credit Union Ltd.

8440 - 112 St.
Edmonton, AB T6G 2B7
780-407-8151
Fax: 780-407-7557
chauah@telus.net
Year Founded: 1949
Number of Employees: 3
Assets: $5-10 million
Revenues: Under $1 million
Executives:
Donna McAra, Manager

Utilities Employees' (Windsor) Credit Union Limited

4545 Rhodes Dr.
Windsor, ON N8W 5T1
519-945-5141
Fax: 519-945-0347

Valley Credit Union

PO Box 70
5682 Hwy. #1
Waterville, NS B0P 1V0
902-538-4510
Fax: 902-538-4529
www.valleycreditunion.com
Year Founded: 1994
Branches:
Bridgetown
PO Box 428
279 Granville St.
Bridgetown, NS B0S 1C0 Canada
902-665-2545
Fax: 902-665-2991
Gary Olsvik, Branch Manager
Caledonia - North Queens
PO Box 41
Caledonia, NS B0T 1B0 Canada
902-682-2016
Fax: 902-682-2957
Gary Olsvik, Branch Manager
Canning
PO Box 10
969 Seminary Ave.
Canning, NS B0P 1H0 Canada
902-582-7655
Fax: 902-582-7986
Harley Robicheau, Manager
Greenwood
Southgate Court
PO Box 1540
780 Central Ave.
Greenwood, NS B0P 1N0 Canada
902-765-3342
Fax: 902-765-3934
David Morse, Manager
Hantsport
PO Box 292
24 William St.
Hantsport, NS B0P 1P0 Canada
902-684-3274
Fax: 902-684-3705
Linda Shay, Manager
Middleton
PO Box 1319
32 Commercial St.
Middleton, NS B0S 1P0 Canada
902-825-6876
Fax: 902-825-5701
Cindy Tidman, Manager
New Minas
9202 Commercial St.
New Minas, NS B4N 3E8 Canada
902-681-6884
Fax: 902-681-3814
Janet MacLeod, Manager
Waterville
PO Box 70
5680 Hwy. #1
Waterville, NS B0P 1V0 Canada
902-538-3905
Fax: 902-538-4509
Dwight Doherty, Manager

Valley First Financial Group

184 Main St., 3rd Fl.
Penticton, BC V2A 8G7
250-490-2720
Fax: 250-490-2721
800-567-8111
info@valleyfirst.com
www.valleyfirst.com
Also Known As: Valley Field Credit Union
Year Founded: 2001
Assets: $500m-1 billion
Executives:
Harley Biddlecombe, President/CEO
Jackie Horton, Vice-President, Corporate Administration & Human Resources
Directors:
Colleen Lister, Chair
Terry Flannigan, Vice-Chair
Wayne Becker
Kevin Campbell
Peter Foodikoff
Stewart Ladyman
Lanny Martiniuk
Ramesh Rikhi
Lawrence Stevens
Branches:
Armstrong
PO Box 400
2575 Patterson Ave.
Armstrong, BC V0E 1B0 Canada
250-546-3191
Fax: 250-546-3115
Kamloops
180 Seymour St.
Kamloops, BC V2C 2E3 Canada
250-374-4924
Fax: 250-374-5710
Kelowna - Bernard Ave.
507 Bernard Ave.
Kelowna, BC V1Y 6N9 Canada
250-860-1900
Fax: 250-860-4148
Kelowna - Cooper Rd.
Orchard Plaza
1860 Cooper Rd.
Kelowna, BC V1Y 8K5 Canada
250-763-6117
Fax: 250-763-1557
Kelowna - Glenmore Rd.
401 Glenmore Rd.
Kelowna, BC V1V 1Z6 Canada
250-861-9500
Fax: 250-861-4515
Kelowna - Gordon Dr.
#101, 2395 Gordon Dr.
Kelowna, BC V1W 3X7 Canada
250-862-8822
Fax: 250-862-3630
Keremeos
PO Box 250
704 - 7th Ave.
Keremeos, BC V0X 1N0 Canada

250-499-5524
Fax: 250-499-5133

Lumby
PO Box 1029
2109 Shuswap Ave.
Lumby, BC V0E 2G0 Canada
250-547-8847
Fax: 250-547-8873

Oliver
Oliver Place Mall
PO Box 340
Oliver, BC V0H 1T0 Canada
250-498-6277
Fax: 250-498-6232

Peachland
PO Box 24
#24, 5500 Clements Cres.
Peachland, BC V0H 1X5 Canada
250-767-9200
Fax: 250-767-9119

Penticton - Head Office
#135, 2111 Main St.
Penticton, BC V2A 6W6 Canada
250-493-7773
Fax: 250-493-2203

Penticton - Main St.
184 Main St.
Penticton, BC V2A 8G7 Canada
250-490-2700
Fax: 250-490-2705

Penticton - Skaha Lake Rd.
Peachtree Square
2897 Skaha Lake Rd.
Penticton, BC V2A 9B8 Canada
250-492-0210
Fax: 250-492-5337

Princeton
PO Box 190
114 Tapton Ave.
Princeton, BC V0X 1W0 Canada
250-295-3171
Fax: 250-295-7577

Vernon
3322 - 31st Ave.
Vernon, BC V1T 2H5 Canada
250-558-5266
Fax: 250-558-5277

Van Tel/Safeway Credit Union

#2010, 4330 Kingsway
Burnaby, BC V5H 4G8
604-656-6200
Fax: 604-656-6167
800-663-1557
info@vantelsafeway.com
www.vantelsafeway.com
Former Name: Van Tel Credit Union
Year Founded: 1940
Number of Employees: 70+
Assets: $100-500 million
Executives:
Nancy Mathers, CEO
Directors:
Steve Lougheed, Chair
Mike Aubert, 1st Vice-Chair
Rick Bonneville, 2nd Vice-Chair
Karen Whitfield, Secretary
Mando De Cario
Elizabeth Fletcher
Kim Griffith
Anne Hay
Derek Lee
Greg Ryan
Branches:

Burnaby - Kingsway - Financial Service Centre
Telus Bldg.
3777 Kingsway, 6th Fl.
Burnaby, BC V5H 3Z7 Canada
604-656-6287
Fax: 604-656-6299
800-663-1557

Burnaby - Royal Oak Ave.
6632 Royal Oak Ave.
Burnaby, BC V5H 3P6 Canada
604-656-6285
Fax: 604-431-9011
800-663-1557

New Westminster
1625 - 6th Ave.
New Westminster, BC V3M 1Z7 Canada
604-520-9239
Fax: 604-520-9298

Surrey
#1D, 15251 - 101 Ave.
Surrey, BC V3R 9V8 Canada
604-581-1773
Fax: 604-584-0103
800-663-1557

Vancouver - PNG
#17, 200 Granville St.
Vancouver, BC V6C 1S4 Canada
604-605-2575
Fax: 604-605-2368
800-663-1557

Victoria
890 Short St.
Victoria, BC V8X 2V5 Canada
250-385-0112
Fax: 250-385-3253
800-663-1557

Vancouver City Savings Credit Union

PO Box 2120, Terminal Stn. Terminal
183 Terminal Ave.
Vancouver, BC V6B 5R8
604-877-7000
Fax: 604-877-7639
888-826-2489
vc_editor@vancity.com
www.vancity.com
Also Known As: VanCity Credit Union
Year Founded: 1946
Number of Employees: 1,600
Assets: $8,202,820,000
Profile: Vancity serves the people of the Lower Mainland & the Fraser Valley. It provides chequing & savings accounts, loans & mortages, trust, business & brokerage services & professional investment counselling.

Executives:
Dave Mowat, CEO
Directors:
Elaine Duvall, Chair
Reva Dexter, Vice-Chair
Lisa Barrett
Doreen Braverman
Ian Gill
Catherine McCreary
Patrice Pratt
Doug Soo
Affiliated Companies:
Citizens Bank of Canada
Branches:

Abbotsford
32675 South Fraser Way
Abbotsford, BC V2T 1X9 Canada

Burnaby - Hastings St.
4302 Hastings St.
Burnaby, BC V5C 2J9 Canada

Burnaby - Kingsway
5064 Kingsway
Burnaby, BC V5H 2E7 Canada

Burnaby - McKay Ave.
#120A, 6100 McKay Ave.
Burnaby, BC V5H 4L6 Canada

Burnaby - North Rd.
3977 North Rd.
Burnaby, BC V3J 1S2 Canada

Burnaby - Rosser Ave.
#106, 1901 Rosser Ave.
Burnaby, BC V5C 6R6 Canada

Chilliwack
45617 Luckakuck Way
Chilliwack, BC V2R 1A3 Canada

Coquitlam
#20, 2991 Lougheed Hwy.
Coquitlam, BC V3B 6J6 Canada

Coquitlam
1013 Brunette Ave.
Coquitlam, BC V3K 1E6 Canada

Delta
7211 - 120th St.
Delta, BC V4C 6P5 Canada

Langley
#100, 20055 Willowbrook Dr.
Langley, BC V2Y 2T5 Canada

Maple Ridge
22824 Lougheed Hwy.
Maple Ridge, BC V2X 2V6 Canada

Mission
#150, 32555 London Ave.
Mission, BC V2V 6V9 Canada

North Vancouver
1290 Marine Dr.
North Vancouver, BC V7P 1T2 Canada

North Vancouver
#712, 2601 Westview Dr.
North Vancouver, BC V7N 3X4 Canada

North Vancouver
1370 Main St.
North Vancouver, BC V7J 1C6 Canada

Port Coquitlam
#130, 2325 Ottawa St.
Port Coquitlam, BC V3B 8A4 Canada

Surrey - 101st Ave.
#108, 15175 - 101st Ave.
Surrey, BC V3R 7Z1 Canada

Surrey - 152nd St.
#104, 1790 - 152nd St.
Surrey, BC V4A 7Z7 Canada

Surrey - 96th Ave.
12820 - 96th Ave.
Surrey, BC V3V 6A8 Canada

Surrey - King George Hwy.
7555 King George Hwy.
Surrey, BC V3W 5A8 Canada

Surrey - King George Hwy.
10293 King George Hwy.
Surrey, BC V3T 2W6 Canada

Vancouver - 41st Ave. West
2380 - 41st Ave. West
Vancouver, BC V6M 2A4 Canada

Vancouver - 4th Ave. West
2233 - 4th Ave. West
Vancouver, BC V6K 1N9 Canada

Vancouver - Cambie St.
5594 Cambie St.
Vancouver, BC V5Z 3Y5 Canada

Vancouver - Commercial Dr.
1675 Commercial Dr.
Vancouver, BC V5L 3Y3 Canada

Vancouver - Dunbar St.
4445 Dunbar St.
Vancouver, BC V6S 2G4 Canada

Vancouver - East Hastings St.
2510 East Hastings St.
Vancouver, BC V5K 1Z3 Canada

Vancouver - East Pender St.
188 East Pender St.
Vancouver, BC V6A 1T3 Canada

Vancouver - Fraser St.
6288 Fraser St.
Vancouver, BC V5W 3A9 Canada

Vancouver - Granville St.
8615 Granville St.
Vancouver, BC V6P 5A2 Canada

Vancouver - Kingsway
3305 Kingsway
Vancouver, BC V5R 5K6 Canada

Vancouver - Main St.
4205 Main St.
Vancouver, BC V5V 3P8 Canada

Vancouver - Robson St.
1680 Robson St.
Vancouver, BC V6G 1C7 Canada

Vancouver - Terminal Ave.
#100, 183 Terminal Ave.
Vancouver, BC V6A 4G2 Canada

Vancouver - Victoria Dr.
5590 Victoria Dr.
Vancouver, BC V5P 3W1 Canada

Vancouver - West 10th Ave.
501 West 10th Ave.
Vancouver, BC V5Z 1K9 Canada

Vancouver City Savings Credit Union (continued)

Vancouver - West Broadway
3395 West Broadway
Vancouver, BC V6R 2B1 Canada

Vancouver - West Pender St.
898 West Pender St.
Vancouver, BC V6C 1J8 Canada

Victoria
3075 Douglas St.
Victoria, BC V8T 4N3 Canada

West Vancouver
1402 Marine Dr.
West Vancouver, BC V7T 1B7 Canada

Vanguard Credit Union

Also listed under: *Financing & Loan Companies; Investment Management*

PO Box 490
47 Main St.
Rossburn, MB R0J 1V0
204-859-5010
Fax: 204-859-5020
info@vanguardcu.mb.ca
www.vanguardcu.mb.ca

Ownership: Member-owned
Year Founded: 1947
Number of Employees: 92
Assets: $100-500 million Year End: 20051231
Revenues: $5-10 million Year End: 20051231

Executives:
Ian Gerrard, CEO
Guy Huberdeau, President
Kathy Brooks, Vice-President, Human Resources
Phil Corney, Vice-President, Credit & Corporate Development
Jean Hogarth, Vice-President, Finance
Betty-Ann Slon, Vice-President, Relationships & Marketing

Directors:
William Antonow
Don Armitage
Morley Butler
Rodney Cairns
Debbie Jensen
Darlene Lowes
Florence Pushka
Ron Sangster
Ed Slywchuk
Brent Strachan
Blaine Woodhouse

Branches:

Angusville
PO Box 40
239 Main St.
Angusville, MB R0J 0A0 Canada
204-773-2949
Fax: 204-773-3223
angusville@vanguardcu.mb.ca

Binscarth
PO Box 70
18 Russell St.
Binscarth, MB R0J 0G0 Canada
204-532-2000
Fax: 204-532-2255
binscarth@vanguardcu.mb.ca

Birtle
PO Box 267
681 Main St.
Birtle, MB R0M 0C0 Canada
204-842-5381
Fax: 204-842-3217
birtle@vanguardcu.mb.ca
Lucille Fulton, Manager

Brandon
Vanguard Business Centre, #B
824 - 18th St.
Brandon, MB R7A 5B7 Canada
204-571-3850
Fax: 204-571-3859
brandon@vanguardcu.mb.ca

Foxwarren
PO Box 191
75 First St. South
Foxwarren, MB R0J 0R0 Canada
204-847-3000
Fax: 204-847-3003
foxwarren@vanguardcu.mb.ca
Lucille Fulton, Manager

Hamiota
PO Box 430
50 Maple Ave. East
Hamiota, MB R0M 0T0 Canada
204-764-6230
Fax: 204-764-6240
hamiota@vanguardcu.mb.ca
Todd Hunter, Manager

Kenton
PO Box 160
308 Woodworth Ave.
Kenton, MB R0M 0Z0 Canada
204-838-2446
Fax: 204-838-2499
kenton@vanguardcu.mb.ca
Blair Fordyce, Manager

McAuley
PO Box 52
318 Railway Ave. North
McAuley, MB R0M 1H0 Canada
204-722-2035
Fax: 204-722-2289
mcauley@vanguardcu.mb.ca
Blair Fordyce, Manager

Miniota
PO Box 250
105 North Railway Ave.
Miniota, MB R0M 1M0 Canada
204-567-3838
Fax: 204-567-3555
miniota@vanguardcu.mb.ca
Blair Fordyce, Manager

Oak Lake
PO Box 279
162 North Railway St.
Oak Lake, MB R0M 1P0 Canada
204-855-2243
Fax: 204-855-2737
oaklake@vanguardcu.mb.ca
Blair Fordyce, Manager

Oak River
PO Box 29
17 North Railway St.
Oak River, MB R0K 1T0 Canada
204-566-2184
Fax: 204-566-2123
oakriver@vanguardcu.mb.ca
Todd Hunter, Manager

Rossburn
PO Box 490
47 Main St.
Rossburn, MB R0J 1V0 Canada
204-859-5025
Fax: 204-859-5039
rossburn@vanguardcu.mb.ca
Lucille Fulton, Manager

Russell
PO Box 117
447 Main St. North
Russell, MB R0J 1W0 Canada
204-773-7030
Fax: 204-773-7044
russell@vanguardcu.mb.ca

St Lazare
PO Box 190
241 Main St. South
St Lazare, MB R0M 1Y0 Canada
204-683-2466
Fax: 204-683-2295
stlazare@vanguardcu.mb.ca
Lucille Fulton, Manager

VANTIS Credit Union

#200, 900 Harrow St. East
Winnipeg, MB R3M 3Y7
204-452-8144
Fax: 204-477-0552
800-432-1950
info@vantis.mb.ca
www.vantis.mb.ca

Former Name: Decibel Credit Union; Hy-Line Credit Union
Ownership: Member-owned
Year Founded: 2002
Number of Employees: 142
Assets: $377,000,000
Revenues: $1,300,000

Executives:
Michel Audette, President/CEO; 204-478-8206
Jeff Bevaal, Vice-President, Finance, CFO
Phil Deutscher, Vice-President, COO
Lynda Parisian, Vice-President, Corporate Development & Information Technology
Val Breakenridge, Director, Human Resources
Henley Cunningham, Director, Member Services
Susan Iwanski, Director, Marketing
Marcel Rainville, Director, Commercial

Directors:
Wilbur Coates, Chair
Brent Reed, Vice-Chair
Peter Voth, Secretary
Ed Berard
Ted Boguski
Jules Champagne
Jules Garneau
Vern Laing
John Maksimow
Cheryl Reid

Branches:

Gillam
Gillam Shopping Centre
Gillam, MB R0B 0L0 Canada
204-652-2002
Kim Hildebrand, Manager

Thompson
City Centre Mall
300 Mystery Lake Rd.
Thompson, MB R8N 0M2 Canada
204-677-0850
Lynne Tate, Manager

Winnipeg - Graham Ave.
PO Box 25
#100, 200 Graham Ave.
Winnipeg, MB R3C 4L5 Canada
204-987-2520
Fax: 204-987-2523
Mladen Bukvic, Manager

Winnipeg - Harrow St. East
900 Harrow St. East
Winnipeg, MB R3M 3Y7 Canada
204-452-8144
Ken Curtis, Manager

Winnipeg - Pembina Hwy.
3525 Pembina Hwy.
Winnipeg, MB R3V 1A5 Canada
204-987-8020
Line Thurston, Manager

Winnipeg - Pembina Hwy.
2750 Pembina Hwy.
Winnipeg, MB R3T 2H8 Canada
204-987-8010
Stuart Roche, Manager

Winnipeg - Scurfield Blvd.
155 Scurfield Blvd.
Winnipeg, MB R3Y 1C6 Canada
204-987-7790
Paula Nelson, Manager

Winnipeg - St. James St.
694 St. James St.
Winnipeg, MB R3G 3J7 Canada
204-987-2525
Peter Jonker, Manager

Vermilion Credit Union Ltd.

5019 - 50 Ave.
Vermilion, AB T9X 1A7
780-853-2822
Fax: 780-853-4361
info@vermilioncu.com
www.vermilioncu.com

Branches:

Mannville
PO Box 609
5023 - 50 St.
Mannville, AB T0B 2WO Canada
780-763-6455
Fax: 780-763-6451

Vernon & District Credit Union

Also listed under: *Financing & Loan Companies; Investment Management*

3108 - 33rd Ave.
Vernon, BC V1T 2N7
250-545-9251
Fax: 250-545-8166
888-339-8328
info@vdcu.com
www.vdcu.com
Ownership: Co-operative. Member-owned.
Year Founded: 1944
Number of Employees: 54
Assets: $100-500 million Year End: 20051200
Revenues: $10-50 million Year End: 20051200
Profile: The credit union employs 45 full-time equivalent staff.

Executives:
Glenn Benischek, CEO; 250-545-9251; gbenischek@vantageone.net
Luby Pow, Chief Operating Officer; 250-545-9251; lpow@vantageone.net
Rheisa Campbell, Chief Financial Officer; 250- 97-6; rcampbell@vantageone.net
Directors:
Simo Korpisto, Chair; 250-542-5525
Don Main, Vice-Chair; 250-542-6209
Affiliated Companies:
VantageOne Capital Inc.
VantageOne Financial Corporation

Victory Community Credit Union
#102, 2100 Lawrence Ave. West
Toronto, ON M9N 3W3
416-243-0686
Fax: 416-243-9614
creditunion@vccu.com
www.vccu.com
Year Founded: 1948
Number of Employees: 3
Revenues: $5-10 million

Victory Credit Union
PO Box 340
41 Water St.
Windsor, NS B0N 2T0
902-798-3323
Fax: 902-798-1255
www.victorycreditunion.ca
Ownership: Cooperative
Number of Employees: 30
Revenues: $10-50 million Year End: 20061024
Executives:
Helen Deveau, General Manager
Wanda Lake, Supervisor, Accounting Services
Jim Riley, Assistant Manager; jriley@victory.creditu.net
Branches:
Kennetcook
PO Box 8, Comp. 8, 6206 Hwy. 354
Kennetcook, NS B0N 1P0 Canada
902-362-2594
Fax: 902-362-2150
Corey Rogers, Branch Manager
Newport - Hwy. 215 - Kempt Shore Branch
5986 Hwy. 215, RR#1
Newport, NS B0N 2A0 Canada
902-633-2361
Fax: 902-633-2278
Helen Lake, Branch Manager
Newport - Hwy.14 - Brooklyn Branch
PO Box 40
7763 Hwy. 14
Newport, NS B0N 2A0 Canada
902-757-2525
Fax: 902-757-1766
Helen Lake, Branch Manager
Windsor
PO Box 340
14 Water St.
Windsor, NS BON 2T0 Canada
902-798-5726
Fax: 902-798-4425
Glyn Hennigar, Branch Manager

Virden Credit Union
PO Box 1660
220 - 7th Ave. South
Virden, MB R0M 2C0
204-748-2907
Fax: 204-748-1081
virden@virdencu.mb.ca
www.virdencu.mb.ca
Year Founded: 1940
Number of Employees: 58
Assets: $100-500 million
Branches:
Melita
PO Box 128
106 Main St. South
Melita, MB R0M 1L0 Canada
204-522-3272
Fax: 204-522-3497
melita@virdencu.mb.ca
Reston
129 - 4th St. North
Reston, MB R0M 1X0 Canada
204-877-3991
Fax: 204-877-3505
reston@virdencu.mb.ca
Waskada
PO Box 145
Railway Ave. East
Waskada, MB R0M 2E0 Canada
204-673-2774
Fax: 204-673-2213
waskada@virdencu.mb.ca

Virtual One Credit Union Ltd.
3040 Bloor St. West
Toronto, ON M8X 1C4
416-243-0323
Fax: 416-243-1417
877-990-9916
info_cu@virtualonecu.com
www.virtualonecu.com
Year Founded: 1946
Assets: $50-100 million
Profile: The credit union is a full service financial institution which serves over 7,100 members.

Executives:
David Bird, President/CEO
Cameron Clark, Chief Financial Officer
Elsa Mueller, Vice-President, Lending Services
Burdett Williams, Branch Manager
Directors:
George Robertshaw, Chair
Ray Barker, Vice-Chair
Marg Oke, Corporate Secretary
Barry Carson
Ray Eaton
Brian George
Robert Griffin
Stu Irvine
George McLean
Shirley Parizeau
Branches:
Guelph
107 Woodlawn Rd. West
Guelph, ON N1H 1B4 Canada
519-822-3441
Fax: 519-822-0315
Toronto - CBC Branch
25 John St.
Toronto, ON M5W 1E6 Canada
416-205-3716
Fax: 416-205-2288
877-990-2455
info_cu@virtualonecu.com
Toronto - Molson Brewery
1 Carlingview Dr.
Toronto, ON M9W 5E5 Canada
416-675-1786
Fax: 416-213-0518
Toronto - Quebecor World
2250 Islington Ave.
Toronto, ON M9W 3W4 Canada
416-743-8920
Fax: 416-744-8959
info_cu@virtualonecu.com

Wainwright Credit Union
Administration Office
502 - 10 St.
Wainwright, AB T9W 1P4
780-842-9184
Fax: 780-842-2855
www.wainwright-cu.com
Ownership: Member-owned
Year Founded: 1943
Number of Employees: 84
Assets: $100-500 million Year End: 20041031
Revenues: $10-50 million Year End: 20041031
Executives:
Ken Morris, President/CEO
Doug Hoffman, Vice-President, Corporate Services
Brad Hopfauf, Vice-President, Branch Services
Ray Styranka, Vice-President, Credit
Directors:
Daryl Carson, Chair
Affiliated Companies:
Planwright Financial Ltd.
Branches:
Chauvin
PO Box 219
121 Main St.
Chauvin, AB T0B 0V0 Canada
780-858-3751
Fax: 780-858-3553
Valerie Gramlich, Branch Manager
Consort
PO Box 88
5014 - 50th St.
Consort, AB T0C 1B0 Canada
403-577-2650
Fax: 403-577-2665
Amy Gertsma, Manager, Business Development
Coronation
PO Box 353
5000 Windsor St.
Coronation, AB T0C 1C0 Canada
403-578-4444
Fax: 403-578-4446
Amy Gertsma, Manager, Business Development
Edgerton
PO Box 119
5005 - 50th St.
Edgerton, AB T0B 1K0 Canada
780-755-4064
Fax: 780-755-3888
Glenda Lapierre, Branch Manager
Hardisty
PO Box 258
#1, 4802 - 49 St.
Hardisty, AB T0B 1V0 Canada
780-888-2883
Fax: 780-888-2840
Amy Gertsma, Manager, Business Development
Hughenden
PO Box 10
21 McTavish
Hughenden, AB T0B 2E0 Canada
780-856-6070
Fax: 780-856-3504
Jerome Clavelle, Branch Manager
Irma
PO Box 9
5004 - 50 St.
Irma, AB T0B 2H0 Canada
780-754-4001
Fax: 780-754-3777
Tim Parchewsky, Branch Manager
Wainwright
502 - 10th St.
Wainwright, AB T9W 1P4 Canada
780-842-3391
Fax: 780-842-3546
Don Parker, Branch Manager

Wallace Barnes Employees' Credit Union Limited
3100 Mainway Dr.
Burlington, ON L7M 1A3
905-335-6688
Fax: 905-336-1336
Ownership: Private
Year Founded: 1943
Number of Employees: 1
Assets: Under $1 million Year End: 20041004
Revenues: Under $1 million Year End: 20041004
Executives:

Wallace Barnes Employees' Credit Union Limited (continued)
George Kartalianakis, General Manager
Directors:
Mike Flaherty
Mark Gamble
John Johnstone
Cao Ong
Jack Tooney

Westminster Savings Credit Union

Corporate Centre
#108, 960 Quayside Dr.
New Westminster, BC V3M 6G2
604-517-0100
Fax: 604-528-3812
www.wscu.com
Ownership: Member-owned
Year Founded: 1944
Number of Employees: 357
Assets: $1-10 billion Year End: 20041231
Revenues: $50-100 million Year End: 20041231
Executives:
Barry W. Forbes, President/CEO
Directors:
Mike Betts
Bev Briscoe
Bill Brown
Michael Edwards
John Goldsmith
Doug King
Emmet McGrath
J. Ross Montgomery
Meredith Pue
Langley
#1, 20831 Fraser Hwy.
Langley, BC V3A 4G7 Canada
Branches:
Coquitlam - Austin Ave.
1101 Austin Ave.
Coquitlam, BC V3K 3P4 Canada
604-931-7555
Fax: 604-931-7599
Coquitlam - Lougheed Hwy.
Sunwood Square
#290, 3025 Lougheed Hwy.
Coquitlam, BC V3B 6S2 Canada
604-464-7112
Fax: 604-464-7110
Maple Ridge - Lougheed Hwy.
#200, 20201 Lougheed Hwy.
Maple Ridge, BC V2X 2P6 Canada
604-460-7275
Fax: 604-460-7285
Maple Ridge - Lougheed Hwy. - Main
22565 Lougheed Hwy.
Maple Ridge, BC V2X 2V2 Canada
604-466-2200
Fax: 604-466-2496
New Westminster - 6th St.
#100, 601 - 6th St.
New Westminster, BC V3L 3C1 Canada
604-525-3411
Fax: 604-525-3419
New Westminster - Quayside Rd. - Commercial
#103, 960 Quayside Rd.
New Westminster, BC V3M 6G2 Canada
604-528-3803
Fax: 604-525-8702

Port Coquitlam
#6108, 2850 Shaughnessy St.
Port Coquitlam, BC V3C 6K5 Canada
604-942-6691
Fax: 604-942-1410
Surrey
#500, 7488 King George Hwy.
Surrey, BC V3W 0H9 Canada
604-599-8277
Fax: 604-599-5919
Ashif Somani, Branch Manager
Surrey - Cloverdale Community
18722 Fraser Hwy.
Surrey, BC V3S 8E7 Canada
White Rock
1608 - 152nd St.
White Rock, BC V4A 4N2 Canada
604-538-6944
Fax: 604-538-9233

Westoba Credit Union Limited

1020 Princess Ave.
Brandon, MB R7A 0P8
204-729-2050
Fax: 204-729-8852
www.westoba.com
Ownership: Member-owned
Year Founded: 1963
Number of Employees: 200
Assets: $500m-1 billion Year End: 20041231
Revenues: $10-50 million Year End: 20041231
Profile: Credit union is affiliated with Westoba Financial Services Limited.
Executives:
Wayne McLeod, President/CEO
R. Brown, Vice-President, Business Development
Brian Deutscher, Vice-President & Manager, Marketing & Human Resources
A. Foldant, Vice-President, Information & Technology
Bruce Kahler, Vice-President, Finance
H. Monita, Vice-President, Lending Services
Branches:
Brandon - 1st St.
602 - 1st St.
Brandon, MB R7A 6K5 Canada
204-729-2070
Fax: 204-728-0486
Don Cataford, Manager
Brandon - Princess Ave.
1020 Princess Ave.
Brandon, MB R7A 0P8 Canada
204-729-2060
Fax: 204-729-8872
Kevin Bower, Manager
Brandon - Victoria Ave.
3300 Victoria Ave.
Brandon, MB R7B 0N2 Canada
204-729-2080
Fax: 204-725-2823
Don Pringle, Manager
Bruxelles
PO Box 100
Bought St.
Bruxelles, MB R0G 0G0 Canada
204-526-6400
Fax: 204-526-6409
Linda Sundell, Manager
Carberry
PO Box 609
47 Main St.
Carberry, MB R0K 0H0 Canada
204-843-6300
Fax: 204-834-6309
Kerry Mcleod, Manager
Cartwright
PO Box 309
North Railway St. East
Cartwright, MB R0K 0L0 Canada
204-529-5600
Fax: 204-529-5609
Jim Hawkins, Manager
Glenboro
PO Box 6
106 Broadway
Glenboro, MB R0K 0X0 Canada
204-827-6300
Fax: 204-827-6309
Glen Tosh, Manager
Killarney
PO Box 1030
110 Finlay St.
Killarney, MB R0K 1G0 Canada
204-523-5300
Fax: 204-523-5339
Theresa Wright, Manager
La Riviere
PO Box 101
503 Broadway
La Riviere, MB R0G 1A0 Canada
204-242-2777
Fax: 204-242-2648
Betty Fargey, Manager
Ninette
PO Box 98
227 Queen St. North
Ninette, MB R0K 1R0 Canada
204-528-5400
Fax: 204-528-5409
Ross Coombs, Manager
Pilot Mound
PO Box 49
19 Railway St. South
Pilot Mound, MB R0G 1P0 Canada
204-825-6300
Fax: 204-825-6309
Keith Norrie, Manager
Rivers
PO Box 298
504 - 2nd Ave.
Rivers, MB R0K 1X0 Canada
204-328-6330
Fax: 204-328-6339
Randy Kuz, Manager
Shilo
Bldg. L25, CANEX Mall, CFB Shilo
PO Box 68
Shilo, MB R0K 2A0 Canada
204-765-6350
Fax: 204-765-6359
Cindy Evans, Manager
Souris
PO Box 126
104 - 1st St. South
Souris, MB R0K 2C0 Canada
204-483-6300
Fax: 204-483-6309
Budd Harder, Manager
Swan Lake
PO Box 125
Lorne Ave. West
Swan Lake, MB R0G 2S0 Canada
204-836-6500
Fax: 204-836-6509
Linda Sundell, Manager
The Pas
261 Fischer Ave.
The Pas, MB R9A 1L3 Canada
204-627-6300
Fax: 204-627-6309
Audrey Halvorsen, Manager

Weyburn Credit Union Limited

PO Box 1117
221 Coteau Ave.
Weyburn, SK S4H 2L3
306-842-6641
Fax: 306-842-6620
800-667-8842
info@weyburn.cu.sk.ca
www.weyburn.cu.sk.ca
Ownership: Member-owned
Year Founded: 1944
Number of Employees: 80
Assets: $1-5 million Year End: 20061000
Revenues: $1-5 million Year End: 20061000
Executives:
Don Shumlich, CEO; 306-842-9513
Tyson Balog, Exec. Manager, Deposit & Member Services; 306-842-9522
Randy Geisler, Exec. Manager, Lending; 306-842-9519
Robert Hippe, Exec. Manager, Finance; 306-842-9521
Mel Hoffman, Exec. Manager, Development; 306-842-9511
Colin Ovans, Exec. Manager, Wealth Management; 306-842-9555
Branches:
Lang
PO Box 130
Lang, SK S0G 2W0 Canada
306-464-2020
Greg Happ, Manager, Business Relations
Yellow Grass
PO Box 218
Yellow Grass, SK S0G 5J0 Canada
306-465-4200
Jeff Hayward, Manager, Business Relations

Weymouth Credit Union
PO Box 411
4569 Hwy. #1
Weymouth, NS B0W 3T0
902-837-4089
Profile: Phone & fax numbers are alike.

Executives:
George Churchill, Acting Manager

William S. Gibson Employees' Credit Union (Mt. Dennis) Limited
1551 Weston Rd.
Toronto, ON M6M 4Y4
416-246-6704

Williams Lake & District Credit Union
139 North 3rd Ave.
Williams Lake, BC V2G 2A5
250-392-4135
Fax: 250-392-4361
info@wldcu.com
www.wldcu.com
Year Founded: 1952
Number of Employees: 12
Branches:
100 Mile House
PO Box 1781
107 Cariboo Hwy. North
100 Mile House, BC V0K 2E0 Canada
250-395-4094
Fax: 250-395-5314
Bella Coola
PO Box 214
621 Cliff St.
Bella Coola, BC V0T 1C0 Canada
250-799-5328
Fax: 250-799-5352

Windsor Family Credit Union
2800 Tecumseth Rd East
Windsor, ON N8W 1G4
519-974-3100
Fax: 519-974-4077
info@windsorfamily.com
www.windsorfamily.com
Branches:
Lasalle
5932 Malden Rd. Plaza
Windsor, ON N9H 1S4 Canada
519-974-3100
Fax: 519-974-6126
Tecumseh
13158 Tecumseh Rd. East
Windor, ON N8N 3T6 Canada
519-974-3100
Fax: 519-979-4654
Windsor East - Riverside
1100 Lauzon Rd.
Windsor, ON N8S 3M9 Canada
Windsor South
3077 Dougall Ave.
Windsor, ON N9E 1S3 Canada
519-974-3100
Fax: 519-250-5977

Windsor-Essex County Catholic Parishes Credit Union Ltd.
2275 Wellesley Ave.
Windsor, ON N8W 2G1
519-256-7555
Fax: 519-256-6524
cathcu@mnsi.net

Winnipeg Police Credit Union Ltd.
300 William Ave.
Winnipeg, MB R3A 1P9
204-944-1033
Fax: 204-949-0821
www.policecu.mb.ca
Year Founded: 1949
Executives:
Michael Taylor, CGA, General Manager
Directors:
Lawrence Klippenstein, President
Allan Galbraith, Vice-President

York Credit Union
494 Queen St.
Fredericton, NB E3B 1B6
506-458-8844
Fax: 506-452-8496
membersfirst@york.creditu.net
www.yorkcu.nb.ca
Year Founded: 1953
Executives:
Dennis Williams, General Manager
Branches:
Oromocto
PO Box 20015
Oromocto, NB E2V 2R6 Canada
506-357-8686
Fax: 506-357-9948

Your Credit Union Limited
14 Chamberlain Ave
Ottawa, ON K1S 1V9
613-238-8001
Fax: 613-238-2149
800-379-7757
info@yourcu.com
www.yourcu.com
Branches:
Cardinal - Trillium
2112 Dundas St.
Cardinal, ON K0E 1E0 Canada
613-657-3657
Fax: 613-657-3657
kmacdonald@yourcu.com
Kelly MacDonald, General Manager
Cornwall - Second St. West - Howard Smith
321 Second St. West
Cornwall, ON K6J 1G8 Canada
613-932-7350
Fax: 613-932-5310
877-932-7350
dmacmillan@yourcu.com
Doug MacMillan, General Manager
Cornwall - Second St. West - United Counties
321 Second St. West
Cornwall, ON K6J 1G8 Canada
613-933-7737
Fax: 613-933-2756
dgordon@yourcu.com
Deborah Gordon, General Manager
Long Sault - Howard Smith
Long Sault Shopping Centre
PO Box 119
Long Sault, ON K0C 1P0 Canada
613-534-8381
Fax: 613-534-3863
cwoods@yourcu.com
Cindy Woods, Branch Supervisor
Nepean - Education
261 Centrepointe Dr.
Nepean, ON K2G 6E8 Canada
613-225-5654
Fax: 613-225-7674
griendeau@yourcu.com
Gilles Riendeau, Branch Manager
Ottawa - Baxter Rd. - Ottawa Citizen
1101 Baxter Rd.
Ottawa, ON K2C 3M4 Canada
613-596-3556
Fax: 613-596-3620
kmacdonald@yourcu.com
Kelly MacDonald, General Manager
Ottawa - Chamberlain Ave. - Education
14 Chamberlain Ave.
Ottawa, ON K1S 1V9 Canada
613-238-8001
Fax: 613-238-2149
800-379-7757
amcnamara@yourcu.com
Andrew McNamara, General Manager
Ottawa - Laurier Ave. West - Municipal
City of Ottawa
110 Laurier Ave. West
Ottawa, ON K1P 1J1 Canada
613-233-8977
Fax: 613-233-9706
tcole@yourcu.com
Terry Cole, General Manager
Ottawa - St. Laurent Blvd. - Municipal
OC Transpo
1500 St. Laurent Blvd.
Ottawa, ON K1G 0Z8 Canada
613-842-3622
Fax: 613-741-3784
lsmith@yourcu.com
Lorraine Smith, Branch Supervisor
Williamsburg - Trillium
12348 County Rd.
Williamsburg, ON K0C 1H0 Canada
613-535-9900
Fax: 613-535-9920
kmacdonald@yourcu.com
Kelly MacDonald, General Manager

Your Neighbourhood Credit Union Ltd.
5415 Tecumseh Rd. East
Windsor, ON N8T 1C5
519-258-3890
Fax: 519-945-5933
info@yncu.com
www.yncu.com
Former Name: Windsor & Essex Educational Credit Union
Year Founded: 1953
Branches:
Lasalle
5844 Malden Rd.
Lasalle, ON N9H 1S4 Canada
519-258-3890
Fax: 519-250-1304

SECTION 2

Non-Depository Institutions

Included in this section:

Financing & Loan Companies include the following different types of firms: mortgage, venture capital, merchant banks, investment, leasing, consumer financing and resource development capital. Loan companies are incorporated under the federal *Trust and Loan Companies Act* and/or corresponding provincial legislation. Organizations listed in this sub-section grant loans and extend financing to individuals and/or business operations. Services offered range from residential mortgage loans to business ventures.

Bond Rating Companies are a small, but important part of the finance industry. They rate the riskiness of corporate, municipal and government issued securities and give each security a rating.

Collection Agencies include consumer and commercial collection services, court representation services, credit reporting services and bailiffs.

Credit Card Companies are institutions which issue credit cards. In Canada, banks, credit unions, caisses populaires and retailers are also principal issuers.

Trustees in Bankruptcy include those firms specializing in bankruptcy services. Licensed bankruptcy trustees are regulated by the Office of the Superintendent of Bankruptcy Canada.

Non-Depository Institutions

Financing & Loan Companies

1000 Islands Community Development Corporation

#3, 3 Market St. West
Brockville, ON K6V 7L2
613-345-6216
Fax: 613-345-2391
800-431-6015
ticdc@ticdc.ca
www.ticdc.ca
Ownership: Government run program
Year Founded: 1990
Number of Employees: 4
Profile: Servicing nine municipalities in Leeds County & Eastern Ontario, the corporation offers loan guarantees, equity investments & community economic development project management.

Executives:
Tom Russell, Executive Director; tom.russell@ticdc.ca
Kim Benson, Investment Manager; kim.benson@ticdc.ca
Patty Broad-Melchers, Office Administrator; patti.broad-melchers@ticdc.ca
Susan Fournier, CED Officer; susan.fournier@ticdc.ca

16-37 Community Futures Development Corporation

#204, 4630 Lazelle Ave.
Terrace, BC V8G 1S6
250-635-5449
Fax: 250-635-2698
800-663-6398
info@1637cfdc.bc.ca
www.1637cfdc.bc.ca
Number of Employees: 8
Profile: Federal government initiative founded in 1988 to assist communities with their economic development by providing quality business and support services to entrepreneurs and small business. CFDCs are independent, non-profit Corporations run by a volunteer Board of Directors and supported by staff. Involved in lending, leveraging, business counselling, community economic development planning, advising and facilitating.

Executives:
Roger Leclerc, General Manager
Jocelyn Galloway, Manager, Financial Services; jocelyn@1637cfdc.bc.ca

Aberdeen Gould

#401, 55 St. Clair Ave. West
Toronto, ON M4V 2Y7
416-488-2887
Fax: 416-488-1233
info@aberdeengould.com
www.aberdeengould.com
Ownership: Private
Revenues: $1-5 million
Profile: The organization is a private investment equity partnership.

Executives:
Roger Rosmus, President
Steven Broude, Associate
Louis Hébert, CBV, Sr. Advisor

ACC Farmers Financial

#101, 90 Stone Rd. West
Guelph, ON N1G 5L3
519-766-0544
Fax: 519-766-9775
888-278-8807
agcorp@accfinancial.ca
www.accfarmersfinancial.ca
Former Name: Agricultural Commodity Corporation
Ownership: Non-profit
Year Founded: 1992
Number of Employees: 5
Profile: ACC is comprised of eight grain and oilseed organizations, seven horticultural organizations and the Ontario Federation of Agriculture. Livestock producers also sit on ACC's Board of Directors.

Executives:
Brian M. Hughes, General Manager/CEO
Brian Stover, Treasurer
Marilyn Webb, Secretary
Directors:
Brian Wiley, Chair
Fred Wagner, 1st Vice-Chair
Brad Oakley, 2nd Vice-Chair

Accord Business Credit Inc.

77 Bloor St. West
Toronto, ON M5S 1M2
416-961-0007
Fax: 416-961-9443
800-967-0015
sales@accordcredit.com
www.accordcredit.com
Ownership: Subsidiary of Accord Financial Corp.
Year Founded: 1978
Number of Employees: 45
Assets: $10-50 million Year End: 20041231
Revenues: $10-50 million Year End: 20041231
Stock Symbol: ACD
Profile: Offers a full range of flexible, cost-effective credit guarantee and receivables management services to help businesses over the long term.

Executives:
Mark Perna, President
Fred Fishman, Vice-President, Finance, Treasurer
Jim Bates, Vice-President, Ontario
Jean-Paul Lafontaine, Vice-President, Québec
Roy Owens, Vice-President/CIO
Peter Luk, Asst. Vice-President & Manager, Credit
Clive Swain, Asst. Vice-President & Manager, Credit
Peter Wong, Asst. Vice-President, Manager, Credit
Directors:
H. Thomas Beck
Austin C. Beutel
Ken Hitzig
John D. Lamont
Gerald S. Levinson
Mark Perna
Frank D. White
Branches:
Montréal
#310, 1440, rue Ste-Catherine ouest
Montréal, QC H3G 1R8 Canada
514-866-2711
Fax: 514-954-1836
Jean-Paul Lafontaine, Vice-President

Accord Financial Corp.

#1803, 77 Bloor St. West
Toronto, ON M5S 1M2
416-961-0007
Fax: 416-961-9443
800-967-0015
info@accordfinancial.com
www.accordfinancial.com
Former Name: Delta Star Resources Inc.
Ownership: Public
Year Founded: 1978
Number of Employees: 115
Stock Symbol: ACD
Profile: Accord Financial services small & medium-sized companies by providing capital to assist these firms in growth. The company is also affiliated with Accord Financial, Inc., #102, 25 Woods Lake Rd., Greenville, SC 29607.

Executives:
Ken Hitzig, President/CEO
Stuart Adair, Chief Financial Officer & Treasurer
Directors:
H. Thomas Beck
Austin C. Beutel
Robert J. Beutel
Ben Evans
Jeremy Hitzig
Ken Hitzig
John D. Lamont
Frank D. White
Affiliated Companies:
Accord Business Credit Inc.
Montcap Financial Corporation

Accurate Leasing Ltd.

#401, 1661 Portage Ave.
Winnipeg, MB R3J 3T7
204-772-2213
Fax: 204-783-5920
800-595-1477
sales@accurateleasing.com
www.accurateleasing.com
Ownership: Private
Year Founded: 1994
Number of Employees: 18
Profile: Equipment leasing services are offered across Canada.

Branches:
Calgary
4620 Manilla Rd. SE
Calgary, AB T2G 3T7 Canada
403-203-4680
Fax: 403-203-4679
Edmonton
10215 - 178 St.
Edmonton, AB T5S 1M3 Canada
780-414-1543
Fax: 780-444-7412

ACF Equity Atlantic

Purdy's Wharf Tower II
#1204, 1969 Upper Water St.
Halifax, NS B3J 3R7
902-492-5164
Fax: 902-421-1808
acf@acf.ca
www.acf.ca
Ownership: Private
Year Founded: 1996
Number of Employees: 3
Profile: ACF Equity Atlantic manages a $30 million venture capital fund that is available to businesses in Atlantic Canada.

Executives:
Peter Forton, President/CEO
David Wilson, Vice-President

Acorn Partners

#708, 350 Sparks St.
Ottawa, ON K1R 7S8
613-563-4588
Fax: 613-563-4689
info@acornpartners.com
www.acornpartners.com
Also Known As: 2811472 Canada Inc.
Ownership: Private
Year Founded: 1992
Number of Employees: 5
Profile: Acorn Partners finances Small & Medium-Sized Enterprises (SMEs)in the business-to-business sector of the market, when other avenues are either not possible or not desirable.

Executives:
Peter Kemball, CEO
R. Andy Chen, Sr. Account Manager

Aeonian Capital Corporation

#2150, 250 - 6th Ave. SW
Calgary, AB T2P 3H7
403-237-7766
Fax: 403-237-6027
information@aeonian.com
Ownership: Private
Number of Employees: 3
Profile: Private merchant banking and investment company which works closely with the management of companies in which it maintains core investments.

Executives:

Aeonian Capital Corporation (continued)
C. Alan Smith, President

Agriculture Financial Services Corporation(AFSC)
Also listed under: *Federal & Provincial*
5718 - 56 Ave.
Lacombe, AB T4J 1R5
403-782-3000
Fax: 403-782-4226
www.afsc.ca
Ownership: Crown corporation
Year Founded: 1972
Number of Employees: 700
Assets: $1-10 billion Year End: 20060331
Revenues: $500m-1 billion Year End: 20060331
Profile: Provincial crown corporation with a private sector Board of Directors that provides farmers, agribusinesses and other small businesses loans, crop insurance and farm income disaster assistance.

Executives:
Brad Klak, President & Managing Director; 403-782-8309; brad.klak@afsc.ca
Richard Bell, Vice-President, Lending; 403-782-8335; richard.bell@afsc.ca
Merle Jacobson, Vice-President, Insurance Operations; 403-782-8229; merle.jacobson@afsc.ca
Krish Krishnaswamy, Vice-President, Finance; 403-782-8284; krish.krishnaswamy@afsc.ca
Directors:
Lynn Dechant
Gene Dextrase
Harry Haney
Barry Holmes
Brad Klak
Joe Makowecki
Barry Mehr
Gerard Oosterhuis
Wayne Wagner
Gail Surkan
Insurance & Lending Offices:
Airdrie
909 Irricana Rd.
Airdrie, AB T4A 2G6 Canada
403-948-8543
Fax: 403-948-1418
Athabasca
Provincial Bldg.
#100, 4903 - 50th St.
Athabasca, AB T9S 1E2 Canada
780-675-4007
Fax: 780-675-3827
Barrhead
Provincial Bldg.
6203 - 49 St., Main Fl.
Barrhead, AB T7N 1A4 Canada
780-674-8282
Fax: 780-674-8362
Brooks
Provincial Bldg.
220 - 4 Ave. West
Brooks, AB T1R 0B1 Canada
403-362-1262
Fax: 403-362-8078
Calgary - 8th St. NE - District Office
Deerfoot Atrium Bldg. North
#150, 6815 - 8th St. NE
Calgary, AB T2E 7H7 Canada
403-297-6261
Fax: 403-297-8461
Camrose - 52 St. - Regional Office
PO Box 5000, M Sta. M
4910 - 52 St.
Camrose, AB T4V 4E8 Canada
780-679-1340
Fax: 780-679-1323
Cardston
Provincial Bldg.
PO Box 1228
576 Main St.
Cardston, AB T0K 0K0 Canada
403-653-5154
Fax: 403-653-5156
Claresholm
Provincial Bldg.
109 - 46 Ave. West
Claresholm, AB T0L 0T0 Canada
403-625-3534
Fax: 403-625-2862
Drumheller
PO Box 2319
#100, 515 Hwy. 10 East
Drumheller, AB T0J 0Y0 Canada
403-823-1684
Fax: 403-823-5083
Fairview - 109 St. - Regional Office
Provincial Bldg.
PO Box 1188
10209 - 109 St., 2nd Fl.
Fairview, AB T0H 1L0 Canada
780-835-4975
Fax: 780-835-5834
Falher
M.D. Bldg.
Main St.
Falher, AB T0H 1M0 Canada
780-837-2521
Fax: 780-837-8223
Fort Vermilion
Agriculture Canada Experimental Farm
Fort Vermilion, AB T0H 1N0 Canada
780-927-4209
Fax: 780-927-3838
Grande Prairie - 99 St.
Provincial Bldg.
10320 - 99 St.
Grande Prairie, AB T8V 6J4 Canada
780-538-5220
Fax: 780-532-2560
Grimshaw
5306 - 50th St.
Grimshaw, AB T0H 1W0 Canada
780-332-4494
Fax: 780-332-1044
Hanna
Provincial Bldg.
401 Centre St.
Hanna, AB T0J 1P0 Canada
403-854-5525
Fax: 403-854-2590
Lamont
5014 - 50 Ave.
Lamont, AB T0B 2R0 Canada
780-895-2266
Fax: 780-895-7755
Leduc - Sparrow Dr.
6547 Sparrow Dr.
Leduc, AB T9E 7C7 Canada
780-986-4088
Fax: 780-986-1085
Lethbridge
County of Lethbridge Bldg.
#200, 905 - 4th Ave. South
Lethbridge, AB T1J 0P4 Canada
403-381-5474
Fax: 403-382-4527
Medicine Hat
Provincial Bldg.
#107, 346 - 3rd St. SE
Medicine Hat, AB T1A 0G7 Canada
403-529-3600
Fax: 403-528-5264
Olds
Provincial Bldg.
#101, 5030 - 50th St.
Olds, AB T4H 1S1 Canada
403-556-4334
Fax: 403-556-4255
Ponoka
PO Box 4426
5110 - 49 Ave.
Ponoka, AB T4J 1R5 Canada
403-783-7071
Fax: 403-783-7079
Red Deer - 51st St. - Regional Office
Provincial Bldg.
#302, 4920 - 51st St.
Red Deer, AB T4N 6K8 Canada
403-340-5326
Fax: 403-340-7004
Rimbey
Provincial Bldg.
5025 - 55 St.
Rimbey, AB T0C 2J0 Canada
403-843-4516
Fax: 403-843-4516
Smoky Lake
Provincial Bldg.
108 Wheatland Ave.
Smoky Lake, AB T0A 3C0 Canada
780-656-3644
Fax: 780-656-3669
Spirit River
Provincial Bldg.
4602 - 50 St., 1st Fl.
Spirit River, AB T0H 3G0 Canada
780-864-3896
Fax: 780-864-2529
Stettler
Provincial Bldg.
4705 - 49 Ave.
Stettler, AB T0C 2L0 Canada
403-742-7536
Fax: 403-742-7911
Stony Plain
Provincial Bldg.
4709 - 44 Ave.
Stony Plain, AB T7Z 1N4 Canada
780-963-0600
Fax: 780-963-1251
Strathmore
325 - 3 Ave.
Strathmore, AB T1P 1B4 Canada
403-934-3616
Fax: 403-934-5018
Taber
Provincial Bldg.
5011 - 49 Ave.
Taber, AB T1G 1V9 Canada
403-223-7900
Fax: 403-223-7985
Three Hills
Provincial Bldg.
160 - 3 Ave. South
Three Hills, AB T0M 2A0 Canada
403-443-8515
Fax: 403-443-7519
Vegreville
Vinet's Village Mall
#138, 4925 - 50th Ave.
Vegreville, AB T9C 1S6 Canada
780-632-5431
Fax: 780-632-3385
Vermilion
Provincial Bldg.
4701 - 52 St.
Vermilion, AB T9X 1J9 Canada
780-853-8266
Fax: 780-853-1982
Vulcan
101 - 1 St. South
Vulcan, AB T0L 2B0 Canada
403-485-2766
Fax: 403-485-2947
Wainwright
Provincial Bldg.
810 - 14th Ave.
Wainwright, AB T9W 1R2 Canada
780-842-7547
Fax: 780-842-4948
Westlock
Provincial Bldg. #2
10003 - 100th St.
Westlock, AB T9P 2E8 Canada
780-349-4544
Fax: 780-349-2484
Offices:
Calgary - 8th St. NE
Deerfoot Atrium Bldg. North
#170, 6815 - 8th St. NE
Calgary, AB T2E 7H7 Canada
Fax: 403-297-4136
Castor

PO Box 719
4902 - 50th Ave.
Castor, AB T0C 0X0 Canada
403-882-3770
Fax: 403-882-2746
Edmonton
JG O'Donoghue Bldg.
10209 - 113 St.
Edmonton, AB T6H 5T6 Canada
780-427-2140
Fax: 780-422-9738
Edson
PO Box 7110
4924 - 1 Ave.
Edson, AB T7E 1V4 Canada
780-723-8233
Fax: 780-723-8575
Fairview
PO Box 159
Fairview, AB T0H 1L0 Canada
Foremost
218 Main St.
Foremost, AB T0K 0X0 Canada
403-867-3666
Fax: 403-867-2038
Fort McMurray
#102, 9816 Hardin St.
Fort McMurray, AB T9H 4K3 Canada
780-791-5875
Fax: 780-791-7257
Grande Prairie - 102 St.
Provincial Bldg.
#1128, 9909 - 102 St.
Grande Prairie, AB T8V 6J4 Canada
780-538-5220
Fax: 780-532-5531
High Prairie
PO Box 1259
High Prairie, AB T0G 1E0 Canada
780-523-6529
High Prairie - 53 Ave.
Provincial Bldg.
5226 - 53 Ave.
High Prairie, AB T0G 1E0 Canada
780-523-6507
Fax: 780-523-6569
High River
129 - 4 Ave. SW
High River, AB T1V 1M4 Canada
403-652-8313
Fax: 403-652-8306
Lacombe - 56 Ave. - District Office
5718 - 56 Ave.
Lacombe, AB T4L 1B1 Canada
403-782-6800
Fax: 403-782-6753
Leduc - 50 St.
4301 - 50 St.
Leduc, AB T9E 7H3 Canada
Manning
116 - 4 Ave. SW
Manning, AB T0H 2M0 Canada
780-836-3573
Fax: 780-836-2844
Oyen
212 Main St.
Oyen, AB T0J 2J0 Canada
403-664-3677
Fax: 403-664-2687
Peace River
PO Box 900
#23, 9809 - 98th Ave.
Peace River, AB T8S 1J5 Canada
780-624-6387
Fax: 780-624-6493
Provost
Provincial Bldg.
5419 - 44 St.
Provost, AB T0B 3S0 Canada
780-753-2150
Fax: 780-753-2876
Sedgewick
Flagstaff County Bldg.
4902 - 50 St.
Sedgewick, AB T0B 4C0 Canada
780-384-3880
Fax: 780-384-2156
St Paul
Provincial Bldg.
5025 - 49 Ave.
St Paul, AB T0A 3A4 Canada
780-645-6221
Fax: 780-645-2848
Thorhild
County Administration Bldg.
PO Box 400
801 - 1 St.
Thorhild, AB T0A 3J0 Canada
780-398-3933
Fax: 780-398-2087
Valleyview
Provincial Bldg.
5112 - 50 Ave.
Valleyview, AB T0H 3N0 Canada
780-524-3838
Fax: 780-524-4565

Alberta Indian Investment Corp.(AIIC)

Development Bldg.
PO Box 180
Enoch, AB T7X 3Y3
780-470-3600
Fax: 780-470-3605
888-308-6789
info@aiicbusiness.org
www.aiicbusiness.org
Ownership: AB First Nation.
Year Founded: 1987
Profile: As a First Nation owned investment company, AIIC provides a range of services to First Nation businesses, including the provision of direct business loans & equity investments.

Executives:
Rocky Sinclair, General Manager; rockys@aiicbusiness.org
Eugene Whiskeyjack, Sr. Manager, Business Loans; eugenew@aiicbusiness.org
Jeremy Makokis, Manager, Business Loans; jeremym@aiicbusiness.org
Errol Wilson, Manager, Business Loans; errolw@aiicbusiness.org

Alliance NumériQC

Bell MediaSphere
#300, 335, boul de Maisonneuve est
Montréal, QC H2X 1K1
514-848-7177
Fax: 514-848-7133
alliance@numeriqc.ca
www.numeriqc.ca
Former Name: Consortium Multimédia CESAM
Profile: The Alliance is the business network for the multi-media & digital content industry in Québec.

Executives:
Gilles Bertrand, General Manager

Alter Moneta

#550, 101, boul Roland-Therrien
Longueuil, QC J4H 4B9
450-679-0990
Fax: 450-679-5649
contact@altermoneta.com
www.altermoneta.com
Former Name: NBC Export Development Corporation Inc.
Ownership: Wholly owned subsidiary of the National Bank of Canada
Year Founded: 1988
Number of Employees: 40
Executives:
Alain Savard, President
Branches:
Mississauga
#115, 5935 Airport Rd.
Mississauga, ON L4V 1W5 Canada
905-672-1023
Fax: 905-672-1893

Amisk Inc.

Also listed under: *Holding & Other Investment Companies*
#101, 3633, rue Panet
Jonquière, QC G7X 8T7
418-546-1156
Fax: 418-546-0004
robert.taylor@amisk.qc.ca
www.amisk.qc.ca
Ownership: Public. Major shareholder Pan-O-Lac, 53.8% interest.
Year Founded: 1986
Number of Employees: 3
Assets: $10-50 million
Revenues: $1-5 million
Stock Symbol: AS.A
Profile: The investment company has principal investments in the following companies: Soccrent (8% interest), a venture capital firm which takes an equity position or makes loans to companies in the province of Québec; Panneaux MDF La Baie Inc. (12% interest), a medium density fibre panel producer in La Baie, Québec; Groupe Nova Inc. (13.125% interest), a hardwood flooring manufacturer in La Baie; & Scierie E. Tremblay (50% interest), a sawmill in Saint-Bruno d'Alma.

Executives:
Robert Taylor, General Manager
Directors:
Richard Harvey, President
Aimé Boudreau
Michel Dochesne; 418-669-9000
Pierre-Maurice Gagnon
Yvan Gagnon; 418-696-0666
Colette Gauthier
Germain Laroche
Jean-Robert Larouche
Normand Roy
Jean-Louis Vigneault; 418-542-5666

Ander Morris Mortgage Brokers

#1, 2453 Yonge St.
Toronto, ON M4P 2E8
416-488-2973
Fax: 416-488-2973
Ownership: Private
Year Founded: 1956
Number of Employees: 1
Assets: Under $1 million
Profile: Provides financial, legal & mortgage services. Also provides real estate loans.

Executives:
Morris Ander, Sole Proprietor

Anishinabe Mazaska Capital Corporation(AMCC)

#811, 294 Portage Ave.
Winnipeg, MB R3C 0B9
204-940-5000
Fax: 204-940-5003
800-665-8935
info.amcc@shawcable.com
www.amcc.mb.ca
Year Founded: 1990
Profile: The corporation's services include commercial financing for aboriginal business.

Executives:
Errol Wilson, General Manager
Directors:
Joe Malcolm
Carl Roberts
Larry Soldiers
John Thunder

Apeetogosan (Métis) Development Inc.(AMDI)

#302, 12308 - 111th Ave.
Edmonton, AB T5M 2N4
780-452-7951
Fax: 780-454-5997
800-252-7963
office@apeetogosan.ab.ca
www.apeetogosan.ab.ca
Profile: To contact the Calgary branch, phone the following toll free number: 1-877-800-5603. Apeetogosan was incorporated in 1984 as an initiative of the MNAA to create an economic developmental tool to provide small business loans and advisory services to Métis entrepreneurs.

Executives:
George Vass, Manager
Branches:
Bonnyville

NON-DEPOSITORY INSTITUTIONS

Apeetogosan (Métis) Development Inc.(AMDI) (continued)
5102 - 51 St.
Bonnyville, AB T9N 2H9 Canada
780-826-6008
866-849-4660
Slave Lake
PO Box 1787
Slave Lake, AB T0G 2A0 Canada
Fax: 780-849-2890
866-849-4660

Aquarian Industries International Ltd.
391 Campbell St.
Winnipeg, MB R3N 1B6
204-489-1214
Fax: 204-489-7372
aquarian@mb.sympatico.ca
Also Known As: Aquarian Capital Corp.
Ownership: Private.
Year Founded: 1968
Number of Employees: 4
Profile: Main structure of the corporation is based on Global Business Development, Strategic Partnerships, International Trade, Technology Transfers, Feasibility Analysis, Capital Funding & Environmental Technologies, Consulting & Agricultural Innovations.

Executives:
Norm Burns, President

Argosy Partners - The Shotgun Fund & The Succession Fund
Also listed under: *Pension & Money Management Companies; Investment Management*
#760, 141 Adelaide St. West
Toronto, ON M5H 3L5
416-367-3617
Fax: 416-367-3895
info@shotgunfund.com
www.shotgunfund.com, www.successionfund.com
Ownership: Private
Year Founded: 1999
Number of Employees: 6
Assets: $50-100 million Year End: 20060930
Profile: Argosy Partners manages several private equity limited partnerships. The Shotgun Fund will buy equity positions in private companies from departing shareholders during shareholder disputes. The fund will move quickly when a shotgun clause is activated. The Succession Fund provides equity financing for family business ownership change, management buyouts, & entrepreneurs who want to take \Chips off the Table\"". The Fund will take secondary equity positions in profitable private companies. Argosy Partners is also affiliated with The Bridge Fund.""

Executives:
Larry Klar, Partner
Jim Ambrose, Partner
Richard Reid, Partner
Directors:
Robert Cross
Pierre Gagnon
Craig Graham
Donald Jackson
John Kettlewell
Warren Kettlewell
Robert Rubinoff

Associated Mortgage Funds Inc.
Manulife Place
#1905, 10180 - 101 St.
Edmonton, AB T5J 3S4
780-421-8844
Fax: 780-426-2863
financing@abg.ca; mortgage@abg.ca; info@abg.ca
www.abg.ca
Also Known As: Associated Business Group
Ownership: Private
Year Founded: 1987
Number of Employees: 5
Profile: Associated Mortgage Funds Inc. provides commercial & residential mortgages for construction & acquisition, including high ratio.

Executives:
Hugh Burgess, President/CEO

Atkins Strauss Financial Corporation
#509, 4576 Yonge St.
Toronto, ON M2N 6N4
416-223-3355
Fax: 416-223-9692
800-409-7111
Number of Employees: 3
Executives:
Michael Kichuk, Contact

Augen Capital Corp.
#905, 120 Adelaide St. West
Toronto, ON M5H 1T1
416-777-2007
Fax: 416-777-2008
info@augencc.com
www.augencc.com
Ownership: Major shareholder J. David Mason (18% interest)
Year Founded: 1994
Number of Employees: 2
Stock Symbol: AUG
Profile: The merchant bank specializes in the financing of & investment in very early stage resource companies.

Executives:
J. David Mason, CEO, Chair
Timothy S. Hoar, Asst. Corporate Secretary
Directors:
Bill Allen
Stan Bharti
Gerald P. McCarvill
Hugh Squair

Axis Capital Corp.
#325, 126 York St.
Ottawa, ON K1N 1T1
613-236-6006
Fax: 416-203-6630
info@axisfunds.com
www.axisfunds.com
Former Name: StartingStartups Capital Corp.
Year Founded: 2000
Executives:
Doug Hewson, Managing Partner
Peter Low, Managing Partner
Greg McElheran, Partner
Directors:
Calvin Stiller, Chair/Co-Founder

Bancorp Financial Services Inc.
Also listed under: *Holding & Other Investment Companies*
#1420, 1090 West Georgia St.
Vancouver, BC V6E 3V7
604-608-2717
Fax: 604-609-7107
info@bancorpfinancial.com
www.bancorpfinancial.com
Year Founded: 1975
Profile: The company specializes in real estate lending & mortgage fund managing.

Branches:
Victoria
#101, 4420 Chatterton Way
Victoria, BC V8X 5J2
250-479-3999
Fax: 250-479-4494

Bank of Montreal Capital Corporation(BMOCC)
302 Bay St., 7th Fl.
Toronto, ON M5X 1A1
416-867-7247
Fax: 416-867-4108
bmocc@bmo.com
www.bmo.com/bmocc
Ownership: Subsidiary of the Bank of Montreal
Year Founded: 1996
Number of Employees: 20
Assets: $100-500 million
Profile: The corporation specializes in providing investments of up to $10 million. From offices strategically located across the country to serve industry from coast-to-coast, BMO Capital Corp. is a market-leading provider of subordinated debt, mezzanine finance & quasi-equity. Services include the following: working capital for growth; management buyout/leveraged buyout/minority buyout; acquisitions; service companies lacking hard asset support; joint ventures/strategic alliances; capital expenditures/expansion; & new geographic markets.

Executives:
Steve Somerville, President/CEO; 416-643-4352
Eric Ehgotez, Managing Director; 416-643-4388
Claude Miron, Managing Director, Québec & Atlantic Canada; 514-877-1879; claude.miron@bmo.com
Mary Ellen Neilson, Managing Director, Western Canada; 403-234-1847; mary.neilson@bmo.com
Bruce Wylie, Managing director; 416-867-2736; bruce.wylie@bmo.com
Branches:
Calgary
First Canadian Centre
350 - 7th Ave. SW, 9th Fl.
Calgary, AB T2P 3N9 Canada
Edmonton
10199 - 101 St., 5th Fl.
Edmonton, AB T5J 3Y4 Canada
Montréal
105, Saint-Jacques, 3e étage
Montréal, QC H2Y 1L6 Canada
Vancouver
595 Burrard St., 6th Fl.
Vancouver, BC V7X 1L7 Canada

Bank of Montreal Mortgage Corporation
First Canadian Place
350 - 7 Ave. SW
Calgary, AB T2P 3N9
403-503-7033
Fax: 403-503-7035
Ownership: Private
Year Founded: 1981
Number of Employees: 18
Assets: $10-100 billion
Revenues: $1-10 billion
Profile: Real Estate Loans; Mortgage Banker and Loan Correspondent.

Executives:
Susan Brown, Vice-President

Bayshore Capital Corporation
Royal Bank Plaza, South Tower
#3200, 200 Bay St.
Toronto, ON M5J 2J4
416-214-6851
Fax: 416-214-9895
info@bayshorecapital.com
www.bayshorecapital.com
Ownership: Private
Year Founded: 1989
Profile: Bayshore Capital finances and builds companies that create value at the intersection of financial services and information technologies. They assemble their portfolio from a variety of sources, including acquisitions of ongoing businesses, participation in strategic partnerships/joint ventures and capital injections into promising start-ups.

Executives:
Andrew Brown, President/Co-Founder
Henry Wolfond, Chair/Co-Founder
John P. Bujouves

BC Pacific Capital Corporation
Royal Centre
PO Box 11179
#2050, 1055 West Georgia St.
Vancouver, BC V6E 3R5
604-669-3141
Fax: 604-687-3419
bcpcc@direct.ca
Ownership: Major shareholder Trilon Financial Corp. holds 42.3% of the class A & 32.3% of the class B shares
Year Founded: 1969
Number of Employees: 4
Assets: $200,000,000
Stock Symbol: BPQ
Profile: BC Pacific Capital provides management services to corporations encountering financial difficulties, considering merger or acquisition initiatives, or requiring operational evaluations. It also invests in undervalued companies, primarily in the natural resource, real estate & financial services areas.

Executives:
Brian G. Kenning, President

Bruce M. McKay, Secretary
Directors:
Brian G. Kenning, Chair
Howard J. Kellough
Brian D. Lawson
Frank N.C. Lochan
Terrence A. Lyons
Bruce M. McKay

BCE Capital Inc.
#1400, 21 St. Clair Ave. E
Toronto, ON M4T 1L8
416-408-0700
Fax: 416-585-9749
www.bcecapital.com
Also Known As: BCEC
Ownership: Private. Wholly owned by BCE Inc.
Year Founded: 1990
Number of Employees: 8
Profile: Venture capital firm.

Executives:
Gary Rubinoff, President & Managing Director; 416-815-0001; grubinoff@bcecapital.com
Joe Catalfamo, Managing Director; 416-408-0300; jcatalfamo@bcecapital.com
Branches:
Ottawa
Tower B
#610, 555 Legget Drive.
Ottawa, ON K2K 2X3 Canada
613-725-1939
Fax: 613-725-9040
David McCarthy, Managing Director

Beaver River Community Futures Development Corporation
PO Box 2678
106 - 1st St. East
Meadow Lake, SK S9X 1Z6
306-236-4422
Fax: 306-236-5818
great.lakes@sasktel.net
www.beaverriver.ca
Ownership: Non-profit
Year Founded: 1988
Profile: Serves 46 communities in northwest Saskatchewan, in an area covering 120,000 square kilometers. Works as partners with businesses and their communities to provide services that instruct and inform, as well as provide leadership and support of local initiatives.

Bentall Capital
#330, 55 University Ave.
Toronto, ON M5J 2H7
416-681-3400
Fax: 416-681-3405
www.bentallcapital.com
Profile: The real estate advisory & service organization serves institutional & private investors. Investment management, asset & property services, leasing, development & merchant banking are provided.

Executives:
Gary Whitelaw, President/CEO; gwhitelaw@bentall.com
Andy Clydesdale, President/COO, Bentall Retail Services
Stuart Wanlin, Exec. Vice-President, Bentall Retail Services, Eastern Region
Brad Allen, Sr. Vice-President, Development & Construction, Eastern Canada
Michael Dobrijevic, Sr. Vice-President, Development & Leasing
Diane MacDiarmid, Sr. Vice-President, Human Resources
Don McLean, Sr. Vice-President, Sun Life Portfolio Manager
Barry Meyer, Sr. Vice-President, Finance & Administration
John St. Onge, Sr. Vice-President, Shopping Centres
Robert Blacklock, Vice-President, Development, Eastern Canada
Scott Gannon, Vice-President, Finance & Administration
Carl Gomez, Vice-President, Research
Kevin Haverty, Vice-President, Leasing, Bentall Real Estate Services
Steven Michniewicz, Vice-President, Operations, Retail Services Eastern Canada
Affiliated Companies:
Bentall Investment Management
Regional Offices:
Calgary - Western
#301, 240 - 4 Ave. SW
Calgary, AB T2P 4H4 Canada
403-303-2400
Fax: 403-303-2450
Randy Magnussen, Sr. Vice-President & General Manager, Western Canada
Montréal - Québec
#55, 1155, rue Metcalfe
Montréal, QC H3B 2V6 Canada
514-393-8820
Fax: 514-393-9820
Mario Bédard, Vice-President, Québec
Ottawa
#300, 45 O'Connor
Ottawa, ON K1P 1A4 Canada
613-230-3002
Fax: 613-563-3217
Dan Gray, Vice-President, Leasing
Toronto - Eastern
#500, 10 Carlson Ct.
Toronto, ON M9W 6L2 Canada
416-674-7707
Fax: 416-674-7738
Cheryl Gray, Sr. Vice-President, Property Management, Eastern Canada
Vancouver - Burrard St. - BC Real Estate Services
One Bentall Centre
#770, 505 Burrard St.
Vancouver, BC V7X 1M8 Canada
604-661-5670
Fax: 604-661-5866
Darcy Brabbins, Vice-President, Operations, BC Region
Vancouver - Dunsmuir St. - BC
Four Bentall Centre
PO Box 49001
#1800, 1055 Dunsmuir St.
Vancouver, BC V7X 1B1 Canada
604-661-5000
Fax: 604-661-5055
Lawrence Neilson, CFO

Black Mountain Capital Corp.
PO Box 28051
Vancouver, BC V6C 3T7
604-689-7533
Fax: 604-683-9681
isf@mercury.ca
Former Name: Mercury Partners & Company Inc.
Ownership: Public
Year Founded: 1954
Number of Employees: 5
Assets: $5-10 million
Revenues: $1-5 million
Stock Symbol: MYP.U, BMM.U
Profile: Mercury Partners & Company is a publicly traded financial services company engaged in merchant banking & private equity activities. Operations are located in Canada & the United States. Mercury's investment objective is to acquire influential ownership in companies, & through direct involvement bring about the change required to realize the strategic value of the companies. Affiliated companies are Mercury Digital Labs Inc. & Mercury Corporate Finance.

Executives:
Tom S. Kusumoto, President
Tian Kusumoto, Secretary; 604-689-9161
Directors:
Alex Blodgett
Lance Eng
Tom S. Kusumoto
Tian Kusumoto
Greg MacRae
Matthew B Walker

BMO Nesbitt Burns Equity Partners Inc.
PO Box 150
1 First Canadian Place, 6th Fl.
Toronto, ON M5X 1H3
416-359-6464
Fax: 416-359-4411
corporate.bmo.com/equitypartners/default.asp
Year Founded: 1996
Executives:
Georges Soaré, Managing Director
Robert S. Levine, Associate

Bombardier Capital Limited
800, boul René-Lévesque ouest
Montréal, QC H3B 1Y8
514-861-9481
Fax: 514-861-2746
www.bombardier.com
Year Founded: 1972
Executives:
Brian Peters, President/COO

Bridgewater Bank
***Also listed under:** Domestic Banks: Schedule I*
#150, 926 - 5th Ave. SW
Calgary, AB T2P 0N7
403-232-6556
Fax: 403-233-2609
888-837-2326
www.bridgewaterfinancial.com
Former Name: Bridgewater Financial Services Ltd.
Ownership: Private. Wholly owned subsidiary of Alberta Motor Association.
Year Founded: 1997
Number of Employees: 80
Profile: Bridgewater is a mortgage banking company. It provides mortgages to Canadian homeowners & purchasers. Offices are located in the following cities: Halifax, Toronto, Ottawa, Victoria, Calgary & Edmonton.

Executives:
Peter L. O'Neill, Vice-President, General Manager
Gord Follett, Controller

Brightspark Ventures L.P.
#506, 4711 Yonge St.
Toronto, ON M2N 6K8
416-488-1999
Fax: 416-488-1988
info@brightspark.com
www.brightspark.com
Profile: Works closely with entrepreneurs to develop and build market-leading software companies.

Executives:
Tony Davis, Managing Partner
Sophie Forest, Managing Partner
Mark Skapinker, Managing Partner
Steven Bloom, CFO
Salim Teja, Vice-President, Ventures
Branches:
Montréal Office
#300, 481, rue Viger ouest
Montréal, QC H2Z 1G6 Canada
514-448-2238
Fax: 514-396-4354
info@brightspark.com

Brome Financial Corporation
#700, 550, rue Sherbrooke ouest
Montréal, QC H3A 1B9
514-842-2975
Fax: 514-842-2050
888-878-9485
brome@bromeinc.com
www.bromeinc.com
Ownership: Joint ownership between firm management & the Fonds de solidarité des travailleurs du Québec & Laurentian Bank of Canada
Year Founded: 1994
Number of Employees: 50
Profile: Offers services to small and medium sized businesses experiencing strong growth, seasonal peaks or transition or turnaround period searching for cash flow solutions.

Executives:
Michel Gratton, President

Bronwyn Management Services Ltd.
#21, 4801 Steeles Ave. West
Toronto, ON M9L 2W1
416-746-2522
Fax: 416-746-8124
etsero@pathcom.com
Ownership: Private
Year Founded: 1978
Number of Employees: 2

Brookfield Asset Management Inc.
BCE Place
PO Box 762

Brookfield Asset Management Inc. (continued)
#300, 181 Bay St.
Toronto, ON M5J 2T3
416-363-9491
Fax: 416-363-2856
enquiries@brascancorp.com
www.brookfield.com
Former Name: Brascan Corporation; EdperBrascan Corporation

Year Founded: 1970
Number of Employees: 50,000
Stock Symbol: BAM
Profile: Focussed on property, power & infrastructure assets, Brookfield Asset Management has over US$50 billion of assets under management. Co-listed on the Toronto & New York stock exchanges, its symbol is BAM.
Executives:
Bruce Flatt, Managing Partner, President/CEO
Barry Blattman, Managing Partner, U.S. Operations
Jeff Blidner, Managing Partner
Richard Clark, Managing Partner, Commercial Properties
Bryan Davis, Managing Partner, Sr. Vice-President, Finance
Joe Freedman, Managing Partner
Harry Goldgut, Managing Partner, CEO, Power Generation
Clifford Lai, Managing Partner, Public Markets & Distribution
Brian Lawson, Managing Partner & CFO
Richard Legault, Managing Partner, President, Brookfield Power

Cyrus Madon, Managing Partner, Bridge Lending Fund & restructuring Groups
Marcelo Marinho, Managing Partner, President, Brazil Operations
George Myhal, Managing Partner, COO
Sam Pollock, Managing Partner, Private Equity
Bruce Robertson, Managing Partner, Public Markets & Distribution
Scott Parsons, President, European Real Estate
Lori Pearson, Sr. Vice-President, Human Resources
Katherine C. Vyse, Sr. Vice-President, Investor Relations & Communications
Directors:
Jack L. Cockwell, Group Chair
Robert J. Harding, Chair
James J. Blanchard
J. Trevor Eyton
J. Bruce Flatt
James K. Gray
David W. Kerr
Philip B. Lind
Roy MacLaren
Frank J. McKenna
Jack M. Mintz
George S. Taylor

Business Development Bank of Canada(BDC)/ Banque de développement du Canada

BDC Bldg.
#400, 5, Place Ville Marie
Montréal, QC H3B 5E7
514-283-5904
Fax: 514-283-2872
888-463-6232
info@bdc.ca
www.bdc.ca
Ownership: Crown corporation wholly owned by Government of Canada
Year Founded: 1944
Number of Employees: 1,400
Assets: $1-10 billion Year End: 20040331
Revenues: $100-500 million Year End: 20040331
Profile: BDC's mission is to help create & develop Canadian small & medium-sized businesses, through timely & relevant financial & consulting services. Key services include financing, venture capital, subordinate financing, consulting, & BDC Connex. Long-term loan financing is designed particularly to support start-ups & innovation strategies & to offer equipment financing for modernization purposes. Venture capital covers every stage of a company's development cycle, from seed through expansion, with a focus on early-stage & fast-growing businesses in 4 target sectors: 1) life sciences, 2) telecommunications, 3) information technology & 4) advanced technologies. Subordinate financing is a hybrid instrument, combining elements of both debt financing & equity financing, which is offered to more mature businesses with excellent growth potential. Customized business consulting services are delivered through a national network of professional consultants & designed to help Canadian entrepreneurs maximize their management savvy. BDC Connex offers Canadian entrepreneurs a variety of online services & handles all BDC alliances & partnerships, such as the partnership agreements with Community Futures Development Corporations.
Executives:
Jean-René Halde, President/CEO
Paul Buron, Exec. Vice-President/CFO
Edmée Métivier, Exec. Vice-President, Financing & Consulting
Jacques Simoneau, Exec. Vice-President, Investments
Mary Karamanos, Sr. Vice-President, Human Resources
Daniel Martel, Sr. Vice-President, Credit & Risk Management
Clément Albert, Vice-President, Treasurer
Richard Morris, Vice-President, Audit & Inspection
Directors:
Cedric E. Ritchie, Chair
Trevor Adey
Christiane Bergevin
Cynthia Bertolin
Stan Bracken-Horrocks
Cindy Chan
Léandre Cormier
Louis J. Duhamel
Terry B. Grieve
Jean-René Halde
John M. Hyshka
Leo Ledohowski
Andrina Lever
Kelvin Ng
Valerie Payn
Branches:
Barrie
PO Box 876
151 Ferris Lane
Barrie, ON L4M 4Y6 Canada
705-739-0444
Fax: 705-739-0467
Bathurst
Harbourview Place
#205, 275 Main St.
Bathurst, NB E2A 4W1 Canada
506-548-7360
Fax: 506-548-7381
Brampton
52 Queen St. East
Brampton, ON L6V 1A2 Canada
905-450-1088
Fax: 905-450-7514
Brandon
940 Princess Ave.
Brandon, MB R7A 0P6 Canada
204-726-7570
Fax: 204-726-7555
Bridgewater
Eastside Plaza
PO Box 540
450 LaHave St.
Bridgewater, NS B4V 2X6 Canada
902-527-5501
Fax: 902-527-5611
Burlington
#101, 4145 North Service Rd.
Burlington, ON L7L 6A3 Canada
905-315-9590
Fax: 905-315-9243
Calgary - 32 Ave. NE
#100, 1935 - 32 Ave. NE
Calgary, AB T2E 7C8 Canada
403-292-5590
Fax: 403-292-6651
Calgary - 7th Ave. SW
Barclay Centre
#110, 444 - 7th Ave. SW
Calgary, AB T2P 0X8 Canada
403-292-5600
Fax: 403-292-6616
Campbell River
#101, 901 Island Hwy.
Campbell River, BC V9W 2C2 Canada
250-286-5811
Fax: 250-286-5830
Charlottetown
BDC Place
111 Kent St.
Charlottetown, PE C1A 1N3 Canada
902-566-7454
Fax: 902-566-7459
Chicoutimi
#210, 345, rue des Saguenéens
Chicoutimi, QC G7H 6K9 Canada
418-698-5668
Fax: 418-698-5678
Corner Brook
Fortis Tower
4 Herald Ave., 1st Fl.
Corner Brook, NL A2H 4B4 Canada
709-637-4515
Fax: 709-637-4522
Cranbrook
205 Cranbrook St. North
Cranbrook, BC V1C 3R1 Canada
250-417-2201
Fax: 250-417-2213
Drummondville
1010, boul René-Lévesque
Drummondville, QC J2C 5W4 Canada
819-478-4951
Fax: 819-478-5864
Edmonton - Calgary Trail NW
Huntington Galleria
#201, 4628 Calgary Trail NW
Edmonton, AB T6H 6A1 Canada
780-495-7200
Fax: 780-495-7198
Edmonton - Jasper Ave.
First Edmonton Place
#200, 10665 Jasper Ave.
Edmonton, AB T5J 3S9 Canada
780-495-2277
Fax: 780-495-6616
Edmundston
Carrefour Assomption
#405, 121, rue de l'Église
Edmundston, NB E3V 1J9 Canada
506-739-8311
Fax: 506-735-0019
Fort St. John
#7, 10230 - 100th St.
Fort St John, BC V1J 3Y9 Canada
250-787-0622
Fax: 250-787-9423
Fredericton
The Barker House
PO Box 754
#504, 570 Queen St.
Fredericton, NB E3B 5B4 Canada
506-452-3030
Fax: 506-452-2416
Gatineau
#104, 259, boul St-Joseph
Gatineau, QC J8Y 6T1 Canada
819-953-4038
Fax: 819-997-4435
Granby
619, rue Principale
Granby, QC J2G 2Y1 Canada
450-372-5202
Fax: 450-372-2423
Grand Falls-Windsor
PO Box 744
42 High St.
Grand Falls-Windsor, NL A2A 2M4 Canada
709-489-2181
Fax: 709-489-6569
Grande Prairie
Windsor Court
#102, 9835 - 101 Ave.
Grande Prairie, AB T8V 5V4 Canada
403-532-8875
Fax: 403-539-5130
Halifax
Cogswell Tower, Scotia Square
#1400, 2000 Barrington St.
Halifax, NS B3J 2Z7 Canada
902-426-7850
Fax: 902-426-6783
Hamilton
#101, 25 Main St. West
Hamilton, ON L8P 1H1 Canada

905-572-2954
Fax: 905-572-4282
Kamloops
205 Victoria St.
Kamloops, BC V2C 2A1 Canada
250-851-4900
Fax: 250-851-4925
Kelowna
313 Bernard St.
Kelowna, BC V1Y 6N6 Canada
250-470-4812
Fax: 250-470-4832
Kenora
227 - 2nd St. South
Kenora, ON P9N 1G1 Canada
807-467-3535
Fax: 807-467-3533
Kingston
Plaza 16
PO Box 265
16 Bath Rd.
Kingston, ON K7L 4V8 Canada
613-545-8636
Fax: 613-545-3529
Kitchener
Commerce House Bldg.
#110, 50 Queen St. North
Kitchener, ON N2H 6P4 Canada
519-571-6676
Fax: 519-571-6685
Langley
#101B, 6424 - 200th St.
Langley, BC V2Y 2T3 Canada
604-532-5150
Fax: 604-532-5166
Laval
#100, 2525, boul Daniel-Johnson
Laval, QC H7T 1S8 Canada
450-973-6868
Fax: 450-973-6860
Lethbridge
520 - 5th Ave. South
Lethbridge, AB T1J 0T8 Canada
403-382-3182
Fax: 403-382-3162

London
380 Wellington St.
London, ON N6A 5B5 Canada
519-675-3101
Fax: 519-645-5450
Longueuil
#100, 550, ch Chambly
Longueuil, QC J4H 3L8 Canada
450-928-4120
Fax: 450-928-4127
Markham
3130 Hwy. 7
Markham, ON L3R 5A1 Canada
905-305-6867
Fax: 905-305-1969
Mississauga
#100, 4310 Sherwoodtowne Blvd.
Mississauga, ON L4Z 4C4 Canada
905-566-6499
Fax: 905-566-6425
Moncton
766 Main St.
Moncton, NB E1C 1E6 Canada
506-851-6120
Fax: 506-851-6033
Montréal - Sherbrooke est
6068, rue Sherbrooke est
Montréal, QC H1N 1C1 Canada
514-283-5858
Fax: 514-496-7535
Montréal - Côte-Vertu
#160, 3100, boul Côte-Vertu
Montréal, QC H4R 2J8 Canada
514-496-7500
Fax: 514-496-7510
Montréal - Jean-Talon est
6347, rue Jean-Talon est
Montréal, QC H1S 3E7 Canada
514-251-2818
Fax: 514-251-2758
Montréal - Place Ville-Marie
Le 5 Place Ville-Marie
#12525, 5, Place Ville-Marie, Plaza Level
Montréal, QC H3B 2G2 Canada
514-496-7966
Fax: 514-496-7974
Montréal - Saint-Jean
#110, 755, boul Saint-Jean
Montréal, QC H9R 5M9 Canada
514-697-8014
Fax: 514-697-3160
Nanaimo
#500, 6581 Aulds Rd.
Nanaimo, BC V9T 6J6 Canada
250-390-5757
Fax: 250-390-5753
North Bay
222 McIntyre St. West
North Bay, ON P1B 2Y8 Canada
705-495-5700
Fax: 705-495-5707
North Vancouver
#6, 221 West Esplanade
North Vancouver, BC V7M 3J3 Canada
604-666-7703
Fax: 604-666-1957
Oshawa
17 King St. East, Ground Fl.
Oshawa, ON L1H 1A8 Canada
905-725-3366
Fax: 905-725-6018
Ottawa
Manulife Place
55 Metcalfe St., Ground Fl.
Ottawa, ON K1P 6L5 Canada
613-995-0234
Fax: 613-995-9045
Peterborough
Peterborough Sq. Tower
PO Box 1419
340 George St. North, 4th Fl.
Peterborough, ON K9J 7H6 Canada
705-750-4801
Fax: 705-750-4808
Prince George
#100, 177 Victoria St.
Prince George, BC V2L 5R8 Canada
250-561-5323
Fax: 250-561-5512
Québec
1134, ch Saint-Louis
Québec, QC G1S 1E5 Canada
418-648-3972
Fax: 418-648-5525
Red Deer
#107, 4815 - 50th Ave.
Red Deer, AB T4N 4A5 Canada
403-340-4255
Fax: 403-340-4243
Regina
Bank of Canada Bldg.
#320, 2220 - 12th Ave.
Regina, SK S4P 0M8 Canada
306-780-6478
Fax: 306-780-7516
Rimouski
391, boul Jessop
Rimouski, QC G5L 1M9 Canada
418-722-3304
Fax: 418-722-3362
Rouyn-Noranda
#301, 139, boul Québec
Rouyn-Noranda, QC J9X 6M8 Canada
819-764-6701
Fax: 819-764-5472
Saint John
53 King St.
Saint John, NB E2L 1G5 Canada
506-636-4751
Fax: 506-636-3892
Saskatoon
135 - 21st St. East
Saskatoon, SK S7K 0B4 Canada
306-975-4822
Fax: 306-975-5955
Sault Ste Marie
153 Great Northern Rd.
Sault Ste Marie, ON P6B 4Y9 Canada
705-941-3030
Fax: 705-941-3040
Sept-×les
#305, 106, rue Napoléon
Sept-×les, QC G4R 3L7 Canada
418-968-1420
Fax: 418-962-2956
Sherbrooke
2532, rue King ouest
Sherbrooke, QC J1J 2E8 Canada
819-564-5700
Fax: 819-564-4276
St Catharines
PO Box 1193
#100, 39 Queen St.
St Catharines, ON L2R 7A7 Canada
905-988-2874
Fax: 905-988-2890
St-Jérôme
#102, 55, rue Castonguay
Saint-Jérome, QC J7Y 2H9 Canada
450-432-7111
Fax: 450-432-8366
St. John's
Atlantic Place
215 Water St., Main Fl.
St. John's, NL A1C 5K4 Canada
709-772-5505
Fax: 709-772-2516
Stratford
516 Huron St.
Stratford, ON N5A 5T7 Canada
519-271-3054
Fax: 519-271-8472
Sudbury
#10, 233 Brady Sq.
Sudbury, ON P3B 4H5 Canada
705-670-6482
Fax: 705-670-6387
Surrey
London Station
#160, 10362 King George Hwy.
Surrey, BC V3T 2W5 Canada
604-586-2410
Fax: 604-586-2430
Sydney
PO Box 726
225 Charlotte St.
Sydney, NS B1P 6H7 Canada
902-564-7700
Fax: 902-564-3975
Terrace
3233 Emerson St.
Terrace, BC V8G 5L2 Canada
250-615-5300
Fax: 250-615-5320
Thunder Bay
#102, 1136 Alloy Dr.
Thunder Bay, ON P7B 6M9 Canada
807-346-1795
Fax: 807-346-1790
Timmins
#105, 119 Pine St. South
Timmins, ON P4N 2K3 Canada
705-267-6456
Fax: 705-268-5437
Toronto - King St. West
#100, 150 King St. West
Toronto, ON M5H 1J9 Canada
416-952-6094
Fax: 416-954-5009
Toronto - Milner Ave.
Metro East Corporate Centre
#112, 305 Milner Ave.
Toronto, ON M1B 3V4 Canada
416-954-0709
Fax: 416-954-0716
Toronto - Yonge St.

Business Development Bank of Canada(BDC)/ Banque de développement du Canada (continued)

PO Box 2
#G6, 5700 Yonge St.
Toronto, ON M2M 4K2 Canada
416-952-8419
Fax: 416-973-0032
Trois-Rivières
1660, rue Royale
Trois-Rivières, QC G9A 4K3 Canada
819-371-5215
Fax: 819-371-5220
Truro
PO Box 1378
622 Prince St.
Truro, NS B2N 5N2 Canada
902-895-6377
Fax: 902-893-7957
Vancouver
BDC Tower, One Bentall Centre
PO Box 6
505 Burrard St., Main Fl.
Vancouver, BC V7X 1V3 Canada
604-666-7850
Fax: 604-666-7859
Victoria
990 Fort St.
Victoria, BC V8V 3K2 Canada
250-363-0161
Fax: 250-363-8029
Whitehorse
2090A - 2nd Ave.
Whitehorse, YT Y1A 1B6 Canada
403-633-7510
Fax: 403-667-4058
Williams Lake
266 Oliver St.
Williams Lake, BC V2G 1M1 Canada
250-305-4004
Fax: 250-305-4006
Windsor
#604, 500 Ouellette Ave.
Windsor, ON N9A 1B3 Canada
519-257-6808
Fax: 519-257-6811
Winnipeg
#1100, 155 Carlton St.
Winnipeg, MB R3C 3H8 Canada
204-983-7900
Fax: 204-983-0870
Woodbridge
#600, 3901 Hwy. 7 West
Woodbridge, ON L4L 8L5 Canada
905-264-0623
Fax: 905-264-2122
Yellowknife
4912 - 49th St.
Yellowknife, NT X1A 1P3 Canada
867-873-3565
Fax: 867-873-3501
Subordinate Financing:
Calgary - Western Canada Region
Barclay Centre
#110, 444 - 7th Ave. SW
Calgary, AB T2P 0X8 Canada
403-292-5600
Fax: 403-292-6616
Halifax - Atlantic & Ontario Region
Cogswell Tower
#1400, 2000 Barrington St.
Halifax, NS B3J 2Z7 Canada
902-426-7850
Fax: 902-426-7850
London - Atlantic & Ontario Region
380 Wellington St.
London, ON N6A 5B5 Canada
Fax: 519-645-5024
Montréal - St-Laurent/South Shore Region
Le 5 Place Ville-Marie
#12525, 5, Place Ville-Marie, Plaza Level
Montréal, QC H3B 2G2 Canada
514-496-7966
Fax: 514-496-7974
Ottawa - Atlantic & Ontario Region
Manulife Place
55 Mecalfe St., Ground Fl.
Ottawa, ON K1P 6L5 Canada
Fax: 613-995-9045
Toronto - Greater Toronto Region
#100, 150 King St. West
Toronto, ON M5H 1J9 Canada
416-952-6094
Fax: 416-954-5009
Vancouver - Western Canada Region
BDC Tower - Bentall Centre
PO Box 6
#1, 505 Burrard St., Main Fl.
Vancouver, BC V7X 1V3 Canada
604-666-7850
Fax: 604-666-7859

Business Development Centre West

#6, 205 - 1st St. East
Cochrane, AB T4C 1X6
403-932-5220
Fax: 403-932-6824
877-603-2329
bdcwest@nucleus.com
www.bdcwest.com
Ownership: Private
Profile: Cooperates with communities to enhance sustainable community development.

Executives:
Patti-Jay Callaghan, General Manager

C.A. Bancorp Inc.

The Exchange Tower
#2805, 130 King St. West
Toronto, ON M5X 1A4
416-214-5985
Fax: 416-364-2398
866-388-5985
info@cabancorp.com
www.cabancorp.com
Year Founded: 2005
Stock Symbol: BKP
Profile: A Toronto-based merchant bank, C.A. Bancorp provides a range of transactions with a variety of both public & private companies. It trades on the TSX-Venture Exchange.

Executives:
John F. Driscoll, Chair
Mark Gardhouse, President
Paolo de Luca, Chief Financial Officer
Mark MacDonald, Managing Director
Kevin Cohen, Manager, Corporate Affairs, General Counsel
Greg Walker, Sr. Associate

Cafa Corporate Finance

#200, 4269, rue Sainte-Catherine ouest
Montréal, QC H3Z 1P7
514-989-5508
Fax: 514-989-5941
info@cafa.ca
www.cafa.ca
Ownership: Private
Year Founded: 1986
Number of Employees: 6
Profile: Cafa Corporate Finance is an investment banking firm specializing in mergers, acquisitions & corporate finance.

Executives:
Jacques Gagnier, Founding Partner
John Gubany, Founding Partner
Pierre Girard, Partner
Christian Tylko, Partner

CAI Capital Corporation

Also listed under: *Holding & Other Investment Companies*
#200, 3429, rue Drummond
Montréal, QC H3G 1X6
514-849-1642
Fax: 514-849-1788
info@caifunds.com
www.caifunds.com
Year Founded: 1990
Stock Symbol: KCC
Profile: CAI is engaged in merchant banking activities.

Executives:
David M. Culver, Founding Partner
Mark P. Culver, Founding Partner
Leslie B. Daniels, Managing Partner
Peter M. Gottsegen, Managing Partner
Tracey L. McVicar, Managing Partner
Tim J. Patterson, Managing Partner
Mark B. Piotrowski, Managing Partner
Peter G. Restler, Managing Partner
Manfred W. Yu, Managing Partner
Craig A. Skolnick, CFO
Branches:
Toronto
Royal Bank Plaza, South Tower
#2320, 200 Bay St.
Toronto, ON M5J 2J1 Canada
416-306-9810
Fax: 416-306-9816
Vancouver
PO Box 11137, Royal Centre Sta. Royal Centre
#2028, 1155 West Georgia St.
Vancouver, BC V6E 3P3 Canada
604-694-2525
Fax: 604-694-2524

Calcap Merchant Banking Services Ltd.

#500, 34 St. Patrick St.
Toronto, ON M5T 1V1
416-597-8500
Fax: 416-597-1123
info@calcap.ca
www.calcap.ca
Ownership: Private
Year Founded: 1999
Number of Employees: 17
Assets: $5-10 million
Revenues: $5-10 million
Profile: Private independent fund.

Executives:
Wayne Albo, Partner
Christine Legein, Partner

Cambrian Credit Union Ltd.

Also listed under: *Credit Unions/Caisses Populaires*
225 Broadway
Winnipeg, MB R3C 5R4
204-925-2600
Fax: 204-231-1306
ccuinfo@cambrian.mb.ca
www.cambrian.mb.ca
Ownership: Member-owned
Year Founded: 1959
Number of Employees: 225
Assets: $1-10 billion Year End: 20051231
Revenues: $50-100 million Year End: 20051231
Executives:
Tom Bryk, President/CEO
Bruce Fink, Sr. Vice-President/CFO
Jim Grapentine, Sr. Vice-President/COO
Connie Clarke, Vice-President, Systems & Administration
Directors:
Paul Holden, Chair
Rose Marie Couture, 1st Vice-Chair
Shauna MacKenzie-Sykes, 2nd Vice-Chair
Branches:
Selkirk
282 Main St.
Selkirk, MB R1A 2P3 Canada
204-482-1810
Fax: 204-482-1818
Margaret Kubas, Manager, Retail Sales & Services
Winnipeg - Henderson Hwy.
1336 Henderson Hwy.
Winnipeg, MB R2G 1M8 Canada
204-925-2630
Fax: 204-334-7913
Bernice McClintock, Manager, Retail Sales & Services
Winnipeg - Marion St.
255 Marion St.
Winnipeg, MB R2H 0T8 Canada
204-925-2620
Fax: 204-233-9599
John Coutris, Manager, Retail Sales & Services
Winnipeg - McPhillips St.
2136 McPhillips St.
Winnipeg, MB R2V 3C8 Canada
204-925-2640
Fax: 204-694-7238

David Gregg, Manager, Retail Sales & Services
Winnipeg - Pembina Hwy.
735 Pembina Hwy.
Winnipeg, MB R3M 2L8 Canada
204-925-2670
Fax: 204-478-1430
David Ross, Manager, Retail Sales & Services
Winnipeg - Pembina Hwy.
2251 Pembina Hwy.
Winnipeg, MB R3T 2H1 Canada
204-925-2660
Fax: 204-269-2368
Lorne Warren, Manager, Retail Sales & Services
Winnipeg - Portage Ave.
#1, 3421 Portage Ave.
Winnipeg, MB R3K 2C9 Canada
204-925-2748
Fax: 204-889-9946
Cindy Gerry, Manager, Retail Sales & Services
Winnipeg - Regent Ave.
#100, 855 Regent Ave. West
Winnipeg, MB R2C 0R1 Canada
204-925-2755
Fax: 204-669-6762
David Durant, Manager, Retail Sales & Services
Winnipeg - St. Mary's Rd.
1602 St. Mary's Rd.
Winnipeg, MB R2M 3W5 Canada
204-925-2680
Fax: 204-254-6536
Craig Fardoe, Manager, Retail Sales & Services
Winnipeg - Vermillion Rd.
#190, 115 Vermillion Rd.
Winnipeg, MB R2J 4A9 Canada
204-925-2690
Fax: 204-257-2390
Cheryl Jones, Manager, Retail Sales & Services
Winnipeg - Wall St.
910 Wall St.
Winnipeg, MB R3G 2V2 Canada
204-925-2650
Fax: 204-775-4419
Glenn Solar, Manager, Retail Sales & Services

Canada Overseas Investments Limited(COIL)
Royal Bank South Tower
PO Box 62
#2910, 200 Bay St
Toronto, ON M5J 2J2
416-865-0266
Fax: 416-865-1910
Ownership: Private
Year Founded: 1956
Number of Employees: 3
Profile: Venture capital company.

Executives:
Michael Koerner, President

Canadian Capital Leasing Inc.
#711, 701 Evans Ave.
Toronto, ON M9C 1A3
416-207-9400
Fax: 416-207-9373
866-207-4465
mreid@leasingcanada.com
www.leasingcanada.com
Ownership: Private
Year Founded: 1989
Number of Employees: 7
Executives:
Murray Sutherland, President; msutherland@leasingcanada.com
Larry Siemon, Director; lsiemon@leasingcanada.com
Martin Reid, Manager, Operations; mreid@leasingcanada.com

Canadian Corporate Funding Limited(CCFL)
Also listed under: *Pension & Money Management Companies*
#2140, Canadian Pacific Tower
PO Box 86, T-D Centre Stn. T-D Centre
Toronto, ON M5K 1G8
416-977-1450
Fax: 416-977-6764
info@ccfl.com
www.ccfl.com
Ownership: Private
Year Founded: 1979
Number of Employees: 26
Profile: Affiliated companies are CCFL Advisory Services & CCFL Mezzanine Partners.

Executives:
Richard Kinlough, Co-President, CCFL Mezzanine Partners; rkinlough@ccfl.com
Robert Olsen, Co-President, CCFL Mezzanine Partners; rolsen@ccfl.com
Philip J. Mauchel, Sr. Vice-President, CCFL Mezzanine Partners; pmauchel@ccfl.com
Nagib Premji, Vice-President, CCFL Mezzanine Partners; npremji@ccfl.com
Patrick Trainor, Sr. Manager, CCFL Mezzanine Partners; ptrainor@ccfl.com
Directors:
Paul Lowenstein, Chair; plowenstein@ccfl.com
Branches:
Montréal
#2210, 1010, rue Sherbrooke ouest
Montréal, QC H3A 2R7 Canada
514-287-9884
Fax: 514-287-9030

Canadian Home Income Plan(CHIP)
45 St. Clair Ave. West
Toronto, ON M4V 1K9
Fax: 416-925-9938
800-563-2447
info@chip.ca
www.chip.ca
Ownership: Public. Subsidiary of Home Equity Income Trust
Year Founded: 1986
Stock Symbol: HEQ.UN
Profile: The Plan provides Canadian seniors with a reverse mortgage program. An affiliated company is Home Equity Mortgage Corporation.

Executives:
Steven Ranson, President/CEO
Gary Kirnkler, Sr. Vice-President & CFO
Greg Bandler, Sr. Vice-President, Marketing & Sales
Scott Cameron, Vice-President, Finance
Wendy Dryden, Vice-President, Marketing
Barry Ferguson, Vice-President, Sales
Neil Sider, Vice-President, Information Technology

Canadian Medical Discoveries Fund Inc.
#3740, 181 Bay St.
Toronto, ON M5J 2T3
416-601-2440
Fax: 416-601-2434
866-299-7929
info@cmdf.com
www.cmdf.com
Year Founded: 1994
Profile: The venture capital investment fund focuses on the life sciences industry.

Executives:
Andrew A. McKay, CEO
Steven J. Hawkins, President, COO/CFO
Jacques Ippersiel, Vice-President, Finance
Dale Patterson, Vice-President, Regulatory Affairs
Directors:
Gordon A. McMillan, Chair
Michèle Demers
Branches:
Toronto
100 International Blvd.
Toronto, ON M9W 6J6 Canada
416-213-4686
Fax: 416-213-4684

Canadian Venture Capital Corporation(CVCC)
12 Maple Ave.
Toronto, ON M4W 2T6
416-364-2557
Fax: 416-364-6765
Ownership: Private
Year Founded: 1974
Assets: $10-50 million Year End: 20051231
Profile: The corporation is engaged in venture capital & turnaround financing.

Executives:
James F. Stewart, President/CEO

Cantrell Capital Corp.
Also listed under: *Holding & Other Investment Companies*
#201, 1682 West 7th Ave.
Vancouver, BC V6J 4S6
604-681-9100
Fax: 604-681-9101
Ownership: Public
Year Founded: 1986
Stock Symbol: CLJ
Directors:
Arthur Lyons, President
Louise E. Bastien
Russell Crum
Thomas H. Reissner

Capda Capital Corporation
#400, 500, rue Sherbrooke ouest
Montréal, QC H3A 3C6
514-284-1004
Fax: 514-242-1852
aaudet@bromeinc.com
Ownership: Private
Year Founded: 1990
Executives:
André Audet, Principal

Capital Canada Limited
PO Box 58
#2308, 150 King St. West
Toronto, ON M5H 1J9
416-598-7700
Fax: 416-598-4306
www.capitalcanada.com
Ownership: Private
Year Founded: 1975
Number of Employees: 14
Executives:
Robert Foster, President/CEO; foster@capitalcanada.com
Glenn Bowman, Partner; glenn@capitalcanada.com
Jack Steckel, Partner; jack@capitalcanada.com
Elisa Sacratini, Controller & CFO
Benjamin Andrews, Vice-President

Carfinco Inc.
#300, 4245 - 97h St.
Edmonton, AB T6E 5Y7
780-413-7549
Fax: 780-450-1134
888-486-4356
carfinco@carfinco.com
www.carfinco.com
Former Name: Canadian Automotive Finance Corporation; Canadian Automotive Repair Finance Corporation
Ownership: Public. Parent is Carfinco Income Fund.
Year Founded: 1997
Number of Employees: 34
Stock Symbol: CFN.UN
Profile: Automotive financing is provided.

Executives:
T.A. Graf, President/CEO; 780-413-7549; tgraf@carfinco.com
T.S.F. Graf, Vice-President & CFO
R.G. Hewson, Vice-President, Marketing

Cavendish Investing Ltd.
Canterra Tower
#4615, 400 - 3rd Ave. SW
Calgary, AB T2P 4H2
403-269-6795
Fax: 403-265-2887
Ownership: Private
Executives:
Richard Bonnycastle, President/Chair

CCC Creative Capital Corp.
1446 Glenaire Cres.
Kelowna, BC V1Y 3N1
250-717-1910
Fax: 209-725-4500
creativecap@home.com
Year Founded: 1996
Profile: CCC Creative Capital services public companies.

Executives:
Jason Shepherd, President

CDP Capital - Technology Ventures
Also listed under: *Pension & Money Management Companies*

CDP Capital - Technology Ventures (continued)
1000, place Jean-Paul-Riopelle
Montréal, QC H2Z 2B3
514-842-3261
Fax: 514-847-2628
technologyventures@cdpcapital.com
Former Name: Capital Technologies CDPQ Inc.
Ownership: Subsidiary of Caisse de dépôt et placement du Québec
Year Founded: 1995
Number of Employees: 32

Central Plains Inc.
56 Royal Rd. North
Portage La Prairie, MB R1N 1V1
204-856-5000
Fax: 204-856-5006
888-947-2332
info@centralplains.ca
www.centralplains.ca
Ownership: Owned by membership.
Year Founded: 1968
Profile: The organization is a non-profit, community-based, regional economic development agency. Services are provided to individuals interested in starting a business, businesses interested in expansion or relocation, industries searching for a location, & local governments with regional economic development projects.

Executives:
Ron Roteliuk, Executive Director
Bryan Spencer, Manager, Business & Projects
Georgette Hutlet, Officer, Community
Directors:
Tom Kelly, President

Centre for Business & Economic Development
#2, 450 Hume St.
Collingwood, ON L9Y 1W6
705-445-8410
Fax: 705-444-6082
877-876-7908
info@centreforbusiness.ca
www.centreforbusiness.ca
Former Name: Georgian Triangle Economic Development Corporation
Ownership: Government owned
Year Founded: 1985

Centre for Business Development
5013 - 49 St.
Red Deer, AB T4N 3X1
403-342-2055
Fax: 403-347-6980
888-343-2055
cbd@rdcbd.com
www.rdcbd.com
Former Name: Red Deer & District Business Development Corporation
Number of Employees: 5
Profile: The Centre promotes community economic development & long-term job creation through high-risk financing & training for entrepreneurs in the west-central Alberta region.

Executives:
Kathy Lineham, General Manager; kathy@rdcbd.com
Morley Belle, Sr. Business Analyst; morley@rdcbd.com

Century Services Inc.
#410, 999 West Broadway
Vancouver, BC V5Z 1K5
604-602-0622
Fax: 604-602-0627
dchan@centuryservices.com
www.centuryservices.com
Ownership: Private
Year Founded: 1983
Number of Employees: 50
Assets: $10-50 million
Revenues: $50-100 million
Executives:
Dean Chan, Regional Manager

Champlain Consulting Associates Ltd.
***Also listed under:** Financial Planning; Investment Management*

PO Box 103, H Stn. H
#5, 1254, rue MacKay
Montréal, QC H3G 2K5
514-931-9336
Fax: 514-371-1565
866-931-9336
ron@champlainconsulting.com
www.champlainconsulting.com
Ownership: Private
Year Founded: 1969
Profile: Acting as financial consultant &/or investment banker, the company provides strategic, creative business planning & innovative sourcing of financing for mid-sized companies, whose needs typically range from $1,000,000 - $50,000,000. Ranging from secured debt to venture capital, all industry sectors & stages of development are covered. Geographic experience includes the following: Canada, USA, Bahamas, Caribbean, Western Europe, & Israel.

Executives:
Ronald Raisman, President/CEO;
ron@champlainconsulting.com

Chinook Community Futures Development Corporation
5324 - 48th Ave.
Taber, AB T1G 1S2
403-223-2984
Fax: 403-223-2096
admin@biz-help.ca
www.biz-help.ca
Ownership: Government owned
Year Founded: 1995
Number of Employees: 4
Profile: Financing to small businesses in the Chinook region of South Central Alberta is provided..

CIBC Capital Partners
BCE Place
PO Box 500
161 Bay St.
Toronto, ON M5J 2S8
416-594-7443
Fax: 416-594-8037
Executives:
Amanda Clark, Executive Director
Paul Choy, Associate

CIBC Mortgages Inc.(CMI)
PO Box 115, Commerce Cout Stn. Commerce Cout
#700, 33 Yonge St.
Toronto, ON M5E 1G4
416-865-0411
Fax: 416-865-1866
800-352-8515
www.cibc.com
Executives:
W.E. Gettings, President

CIT Group Inc. - Canada
#700, 207 Queens Quay West
Toronto, ON M5J 1A7
416-507-2400
Fax: 416-594-5995
877-639-2687
www.cit.com
Former Name: Tyco Capital Corporation
Also Known As: CIT Canada
Ownership: Public. CIT Group Inc., Livingston, NJ, USA.
Year Founded: 1908
Number of Employees: 600+
Stock Symbol: CIT
Profile: Products & services include corporate finance, equipment financing & vendor financing. Clients include transportation, construction, energy & consumer products industries.

Executives:
Jeffrey Peek, Chair/CEO
Tom Hallman, Vice-Chair, Specialty Finance
Rick Wolfert, Vice-Chair, Commerical Finance
J. Daryl MacLellan, President, CIT Canada
Affiliated Companies:
CIT Group Securities (Canada) Inc.

CitiFinancial Canada, Inc.
201 Queens Ave.
London, ON N6A 1J1
519-672-4220
Fax: 519-672-0739
800-995-2274
comments.ca@citifinancial.com
www.citifinancial.ca
Former Name: The Associates Financial Services of Canada
Ownership: Public. Owned by Citigroup.
Year Founded: 1912
Stock Symbol: C
Profile: The company provides commercial & consumer financial services in Canada. There are approximately 316 branches.

Executives:
Scott Wood, President, Country Manager
Jeff Low, Sr. Vice-President, Human Resources
Serge Beriault, Vice-President, Retail Sales
Dan Hillier, Vice-President, Risk Management
Frank Leblanc, Vice-President, Real Estate
Affiliated Companies:
London & Midland General Insurance Company

Clairvest Group Inc.
#1700, 22 St. Clair Ave. East
Toronto, ON M4T 2S3
416-925-9270
Fax: 416-925-5753
www.clairvest.com
Ownership: Public
Year Founded: 1987
Stock Symbol: CVG
Profile: Clairvest Group is a merchant bank that forms investment partnerships with public & private entrepreneurial corporations. The company invests its own capital, plus that of third party investors, as manager of Clairvest Equity Partners Limited Partnership.

Executives:
B. Jeffrey Parr, Co-CEO, Managing Director
Kenneth B. Rotman, Co-CEO, Managing Director
John Fisher, Managing Director
Michael Wagman, Managing Director
David Sturdee, Principal
Heather G. Crawford, CFO
Michael Castellarin, Vice-President
Mitch Green, Vice-President
Kamal Pastakia, Vice-President
Lana Reiken, Vice-President, Finance, Corporate Secretary
Directors:
Joseph Heffernan, Chair
H. Thomas Beck
Michael Bregman
Sydney C. Cooper
Gerald R. Heffernan
G. John Krediet
Philip S. Orsino
B. Jeffrey Parr
Joseph L. Rotman, Founder
Kenneth B. Rotman
Lionel H. Schipper
Isadore Sharp

Clearlink Capital Corporation(MFP)
2281 North Sheridan Way
Mississauga, ON L5K 2S3
905-855-2500
Fax: 905-403-4882
800-433-5553
www.clearlink.com
Former Name: FP Financial Services Ltd.; MFP Technology Services Ltd.
Ownership: Public
Year Founded: 1984
Number of Employees: 200
Stock Symbol: MFP
Profile: Provider of innovative financial solutions in technology & equipment leasing, & equipment trading

Executives:
Fraser R. Berrill, President/CEO
Robert D. Wright, Sr. Vice-President/CFO
Michael A. Flanagan, Sr. Vice-President, Sales & Trading
R. Brian Stevens, Vice-President, Debt Placement & Treasury Services
Robin Wilkinson, Vice-President
Karen Britton, General Counsel & Corporate Secretary
Directors:
K. Sahi, Chair
Fraser R. Berrill
Catherine (Kelly) Butt

Melvin M. Hawkrigg
Samuel J.B. Pollock
Ian Sutherland
J. Peter Wolfraim

Column Financial, Inc.
PO Box 301, First Canadian Pl. Stn. First Canadian Pl.
#3000, 1 First Canadian Pl.
Toronto, ON M5X 1C9
416-352-4740
Fax: 416-352-4741
www.columnfinancial.com
Ownership: Part of Credit Suisse Group, Zurich, Switzerland.
Year Founded: 1993
Profile: Column is a commercial real estate loan business. Loans are funded directly by Column.

Executives:
Pamela Spackman, President; pamela.spackman@colfin.com

The Commercial Capital Corporation
#2020, 150 King St. West
Toronto, ON M5H 1J9
416-599-4206
Fax: 416-599-9250
contact@commercialcapital.ca
www.commercialcapital.ca
Ownership: Private
Year Founded: 1975
Number of Employees: 15
Profile: Investment banking.

Executives:
William F. Rogers, President
William J. Farrell, Sr. Vice-President
Robert D. Bird, Vice-President
Lori Smith, Vice-President
Christine Legein, Vice-President

Community Futures Development Corporation of the Caribou-Chilcotin
266 Oliver St.
Williams Lake, BC V2G 1M1
250-392-3626
Fax: 250-392-4813
Other Information: Toll Free: 1-888-879-5399
doug@cfdccariboo.com
www.cfdccariboo.com
Ownership: Government owned
Year Founded: 1983
Number of Employees: 8
Profile: A federal agency established to assist small businesses in the Williams Lake, 100 Mile & Bella Coola area.

Executives:
Doug Frankiw, General Manager

Community Futures Development Corporation of Central Island
420 Albert St.
Nanaimo, BC V9R 2V7
250-753-6414
Fax: 250-753-0722
877-753-6414
info@cfnanaimo.org
www.cfnanaimo.org
Ownership: Government owned
Year Founded: 1975
Number of Employees: 10
Profile: Independent, non-profit organization consisting of volunteers and staff who are committed to fostering economic development and sustainable employment within the Central Vancouver Island Region.

Executives:
Sherree Walter, Executive Director; 250-713-7470; sherree@cfnanaimo.org

Community Futures Development Corporation of Central Kootenay
#201, 514 Vernon St.
Nelson, BC V1L 4E7
250-352-1933
Fax: 250-352-5926
cfdcck@futures.bc.ca
www.futures.bc.ca
Year Founded: 1984
Number of Employees: 9
Profile: Specializes in commercial lending, business counselling, training & self employment programs. Has a business resource library.

Executives:
Doreen Smecher

Community Futures Development Corporation of Fraser Fort George
1566 - 7 Ave.
Prince George, BC V2L 3P4
250-562-9622
Fax: 250-562-9119
general@cfdc.bc.ca
www.cfdc.bc.ca
Ownership: Community owned
Year Founded: 1987
Number of Employees: 10
Assets: $1-5 million
Revenues: $1-5 million
Profile: CFDC is a proactive, locally autonomous, not-for-profit organization that is working to mobilize the community to achieve a stronger, more sustainable future.

Executives:
Don Zurowski, General Manager
Bud Sweany, Operations Manager

Community Futures Development Corporation of North Okanagan
#102, 3105 - 33rd St.
Vernon, BC V1T 9P7
250-545-2215
Fax: 250-545-6447
info@futuresbc.com
www.futuresbc.com
Year Founded: 1984
Profile: Keeping pace with the changing world requires that we constantly re-examine the social, cultural & economic structures that make up our way of life. Given the enormous challenges facing us today, it is critical that we work together in the process of building strong & vital communities. Community economic development is a unique way to help communities take a leadership role in defining their future & achieving sustained development. The organization assists the citizens of the North Okanagan to achieve significant improvements in permanent employment & sustainable development.

Directors:
Don Main, Chair

Community Futures Development Corporation of Strathcona
#200, 580 Duncan Ave
Courtenay, BC V9N 2M7
250-338-4417
Fax: 250-338-4452
877-338-2775
cfdcs@crcn.net
www.strathfutures.bc.ca
Year Founded: 1988
Number of Employees: 8
Executives:
Marc Crane, General Manager
Branches:
Campbell River
PO Box 160
900 Alder St., West Wing
Campbell River, BC V9W 5A7 Canada
250-830-0999
Fax: 250-830-1189
877-338-2775

Community Futures Development Corporation of Central Okanagan
Landmark III
#110, 1632 Dickinson Ave.
Kelowna, BC V1Y 7T2
250-868-2132
Fax: 250-868-2173
info@cfdcco.bc.ca
www.cfdcco.bc.ca
Ownership: Non-profit
Year Founded: 1990
Number of Employees: 13
Profile: CFDC is a community organization that contributes to the social and economic well being of the Central Okanagan by providing small business owners and aspiring entrepreneurs access to services tailored to individual needs. From financing to training programs, CFDC is a full support centre for new and existing businesses.

Executives:
Eric Greer, General Manager

Community Futures Development Corporation of Alberni Clayoquot
Also listed under: *Financial Planning*
4757 Tebo Ave.
Port Alberni, BC V9Y 8A9
250-724-1241
Fax: 250-724-1028
877-724-1241
info@cfdcac.ca
www.cfdcac.ca
Ownership: Non-profit
Number of Employees: 9

Community Futures Development Corporation of Boundary Area
245 South Copper St.
Greenwood, BC V0H 1J0
250-445-6618
Fax: 250-445-6765
gw@boundarycf.com
www.boundarycf.com
Ownership: Non-profit
Year Founded: 1992
Number of Employees: 12
Branches:
Grand Forks
1647 Central Ave.
Grand Forks, BC V0H 1H0 Canada
250-442-2722
Fax: 250-442-5311
gf@boundarycf.com

Community Futures Development Corporation of Central Interior First Nations
#215, 345 Yellowhead Hwy.
Kamloops, BC V2H 1H1
250-828-9833
Fax: 250-828-9972
info@cfdcofcifn.com
www.cfdcofcifn.com
Ownership: Non-profit
Number of Employees: 9
Executives:
Geri Collins, General Manager

Community Futures Development Association of British Columbia
Marine Bldg.
#880, 355 Burrard St.
Vancouver, BC V6C 2G8
604-685-2332
Fax: 604-681-6575
info@communityfutures.ca
www.communityfutures.ca/provincial/bc/
Year Founded: 1992
Profile: To promote, coordinate & facilitate community economic development initiatives; to foster a better understanding of the Community Futures program; to serve as a catalyst in promoting strong partnerships between key stakeholders involved in the community economic development process.

Executives:
Simon Cumming, Managing Director

Community Futures Development Corporation of Greater Trail
843 Rossland Ave.
Trail, BC V1R 4S0
250-364-2595
Fax: 250-364-2728
info@communityfutures.com
www.communityfutures.com
Ownership: Non-profit
Year Founded: 1987
Number of Employees: 6

Community Futures Development Corporation of Nicola Valley
PO Box 159
2099 Quilchena Ave.
Merritt, BC V1K 1B8

Community Futures Development Corporation of Nicola Valley (continued)
250-378-3923
Fax: 250-378-3924
info@cfdcnicolavalley.ca
www.cfdcnicolavalley.ca
Year Founded: 1989
Number of Employees: 10
Profile: Assists the residents of the Valley to initiate and generate solutions to common economic problems.
Executives:
Patrick Lindsay, Manager

Community Futures Development Corporation of Howe Sound
PO Box 2539
37760 - 2nd Ave.
Squamish, BC V0N 3G0
604-892-5467
Fax: 604-892-5227
info@cfdchs.com
www.cfdchs.com
Number of Employees: 6
Executives:
Jeff Dawson, General Manager; jeff.dawson@cfdchs.com

Community Futures Development Corporation of Mt. Waddington
PO Box 458
#8, 311 Hemlock St.
Port McNeill, BC V0N 2R0
250-956-2220
Fax: 250-956-2221
info@rdmw.bc.ca
www.rdmw.bc.ca
Ownership: Non-profit
Number of Employees: 13
Executives:
Greg Fletchet, Administrator

Community Futures Development Corporation of Nadina
PO Box 236
3232 Hwy. 16
Houston, BC V0J 2N0
250-845-2522
Fax: 250-845-2528
800-556-5539
general.mail@cfdcnadina.ca
www.cfdcnadina.ca
Ownership: Non-profit
Year Founded: 1994
Number of Employees: 9
Executives:
Jerry Botti, General Manager; jerry.botti@cfdcnadina.ca
Branches:
Burns Lake
PO Box 1559
153 Francois Lake Dr.
Burns Lake, BC V0J 1E0 Canada
250-692-7722
Fax: 250-692-7719
Smithers
PO Box 2319
#200, 3848 - 3 Ave.
Smithers, BC VOJ 2N0 Canada
250-847-1389
Fax: 250-847-1860

Community Futures Development Corporation of the North Cariboo
679 Hwy. 97 South
Quesnel, BC V2J 4C7
250-747-1212
Fax: 250-747-1270
877-747-2332
www.cfquesnel.com
Ownership: Non-profit
Number of Employees: 12
Profile: Activities include: identifying and supporting initiatives to diversify the local economy; information resources and counseling support for businesses; financial assistance in the form of loans for business; the development of entrepreneurial skills and values.
Executives:
Greg Lawrence, General Manager

Community Futures Development Corporation of North Fraser
32386 Fletcher Ave.
Mission, BC V2V 5T1
604-826-6252
Fax: 604-826-0052
888-826-6252
cfcd@northfraser.org
www.northfraser.org
Number of Employees: 30
Profile: Business development company.
Branches:
Surrey
#202, 7380 King George Hwy.
Surrey, BC V3W 5A5 Canada
604-590-3710
smccallum@northfraser.org

Community Futures Development Corporation of Okanagan-Similkameen
#102, 3115 Skaha Lake Rd.
Penticton, BC V2A 6G5
250-493-2566
Fax: 250-493-7966
877-493-5566
info@cfdcokanagan.com
www.cfdcokanagan.com
Number of Employees: 8
Executives:
Mary Ellen Heidt, General Manager
Directors:
Milton Cook, Chair
Karen Davy, Vice-Chair
Jaymie Atkinson
Jane Coady
Jack Lank
Rory McIvor
Jack Minor
Roy Phillips
Jeff Rowe
Barb Sheppard
George Stayberg
Junior Thom
Stewart Wells

Community Futures Development Corporation of Peace Liard
904 - 102nd Ave.
Dawson Creek, BC V1G 2B7
250-782-8748
Fax: 250-782-8770
877-296-5888
www.communityfutures.biz
Ownership: Private.
Profile: Services include a self-employment benefits program, business loans, business planning, workshops related to business skills & economic development activities. Loans associated with economic development are the Arts & Culture Events Loans.
Executives:
Sue Kenny, General Manager; skenny@communityfutures.biz
Debbie Fynn, Manager, Self Employment Program; dfynn@communityfutures.biz
Paul DeCosta, Administrator, Loans; pdecosta@communityfutures.biz
Faith Kruk, Administrator, Finance & Accounting; fkruk@communityfutures.biz
Gloria Cleve, Coordinator, Communications & Special Projects; gcleve@communityfutures.biz
Branches:
Fort St. John
#106, 9907 - 99th Ave.
Fort St John, BC V1J 1V1 Canada
250-785-6794
Fax: 250-782-8770
877-296-5888

Community Futures Development Corporation of the Powell River Region
4717 Marine Ave., 2nd Fl.
Powell River, BC V8A 2L2
604-485-7901
Fax: 604-485-4897
cfdcprr@aisl.bc.ca
www.cfdcpowellriver.com
Ownership: Non-profit
Year Founded: 1988
Number of Employees: 6
Executives:
Pam Krompocker, General Manager

Community Futures Development Corporation of Revelstoke
PO Box 2398
204 Campbell Ave.
Revelstoke, BC V0E 2S0
250-837-5345
Fax: 250-837-4223
cfdc@revelstoke.net
www.revelstokecc.bc.ca/rcdc
Year Founded: 1985
Number of Employees: 5
Revenues: $5-10 million
Executives:
Darryl Willoughby, General Manager

Community Futures Development Corporation of the SE Region of BC
110A Slater Rd. NW
Cranbrook, BC V1C 5C8
250-489-4356
Fax: 250-489-1886
800-661-2293
info@keytoyourfuture.net
www.keytoyourfuture.net
Ownership: Private
Number of Employees: 11
Executives:
Rob Gay, General Manager

Community Futures Development Corporation of Stuart-Nechako
PO Box 1078
2750 Burrard Ave.
Vanderhoof, BC V0J 3A0
250-567-5219
Fax: 250-567-5224
800-266-0611
cfdcsn@telus.net
www.cfdcsn.ca
Year Founded: 1994
Number of Employees: 7
Profile: Provides a range of economic and business development programs and services to meet the needs of Stuart Nechako region.
Executives:
Keith Federink, General Manager

Community Futures Development Corporation of the Sunshine Coast
PO Box 128
#205, 5710 Teredo St.
Sechelt, BC V0N 3A0
604-885-1959
Fax: 604-885-2707
877-886-2332
info@communityfutures.org
www.communityfutures.org
Ownership: Non-profit
Year Founded: 1987
Number of Employees: 8
Assets: $1-5 million
Revenues: $1-5 million
Executives:
Al Mulholland, Executive Director; al.mulholland@communityfutures.org

Community Futures Development Corporation of Thompson Country
#101, 286 St Paul St.
Kamloops, BC V2C 6G4
250-828-8772
Fax: 250-828-6861
877-335-2950
info@communityfutures.net
www.communityfutures.net
Year Founded: 1987
Number of Employees: 11
Profile: Educator centre for small businesses. Offers a wide range of services including the Self-Employment Benefits Program, the Skills Development Employment Benefits

Program, the Abilities to Business Program, and business loans for start-up or expansion.

Executives:
Phil Lindsay, General Manager
Directors:
C. Wyld, Chair

Community Futures Partners of Saskatchewan
PO Box 1545
Saskatoon, SK S7K 3R3
306-260-2390
Fax: 306-665-5740
tom@cfsask.ca
www.cfsask.ca
Ownership: Non-profit
Profile: Provides economic development services to rural, northern and remote areas of Saskatchewan.

Executives:
Tom Kennedy, Executive Director

Community Futures Partners of Manitoba, Inc.
#559, 167 Lombard Ave.
Winnipeg, MB R3B 0V3
204-943-2905
Fax: 204-956-9363
info@cfpm.mb.ca
www.cfpm.mb.ca
Ownership: Non-profit
Year Founded: 1997

Community Futures Tawatinaw Region
#201, 10619 - 100 Ave.
Westlock, AB T7P 2J4
780-349-2903
Fax: 780-349-6542
info@tcfdc.ab.ca
www.tcfdc.ab.ca
Former Name: Tawatinaw Community Futures Development Corporation
Ownership: Private
Year Founded: 1988
Number of Employees: 4

Community Futures West Yellowhead
221 Pembina Ave.
Hinton, AB T7V 2B3
780-865-1224
Fax: 780-865-1227
800-263-1716
info@wycfdc.ab.ca
www.wycfdc.ab.ca
Former Name: West Yellowhead Community Futures Development Corporation
Year Founded: 1990
Profile: The organization serves entrepreneurs in the west central Alberta area. Services include: technical assistance to those developing a business plan, a self employment program & loans to entrepreneurs who cannot access capital through conventional means.

Executives:
Marc Butikofer, Executive Director;
marc.butikofer@wycfdc.ab.ca
Directors:
Gordon Frentz, Chair

Community Futures Wild Rose
PO Box 2159
#101, 331 - 3rd Ave.
Strathmore, AB T1P 1K2
403-934-6488
Fax: 403-934-6492
888-881-9675
wildrose@wildrose.ab.ca
www.gowildrose.com
Former Name: Wild Rose Economic Development Corporation
Year Founded: 1989
Number of Employees: 10
Profile: The not-for-profit organization provides services to assist local entrepreneurs & residents in the Wild Rose region of Alberta.

Concord Mortgage Group Ltd.
#680, 404 - 6th Ave. SE
Calgary, AB T2P 0R9
403-290-1990
Fax: 403-269-1853
concord@telusplanet.net
Ownership: Private
Year Founded: 1977
Number of Employees: 5
Profile: Placement is offered of commercial, residential, multifamily mortgages & personal loans, as well as placement of unconventional or non-bankable financing. Residential, commercial, business, investment & interim financing are offered.

Executives:
Frank P. Hickey, President

Concordat Mortgage Financial Corporation
#4, 525 Park Rd. North
Brantford, ON N3R 7K8
519-751-0624
Fax: 519-751-1532
Ownership: Private
Year Founded: 1992
Number of Employees: 1
Profile: The corporation is a mortgage brokerage firm.

Executives:
Mary Ranieri, President; 519-751-0624

Congress Financial Corporation (Canada)
#1500, 141 Adelaide St. West
Toronto, ON M5H 3L9
416-364-6080
Fax: 416-364-6068
800-441-2793
congress@congressfinancial.com
www.congressfinancial.com
Ownership: Foreign
Year Founded: 1994
Number of Employees: 30
Profile: Congress Financial Corporation is an asset-based lender, specializing in refinancing, buyouts, turnarounds & cross border transactions (Canada/US/UK). Congress provides operating, term cashflow as well as tradename loans.

Executives:
Wayne R. Ehgoetz, President;
wehgoetz@congressfinancial.com
David G. Phillips, Sr. Vice-President;
dphillips@congressfinancial.com
Branches:
Montréal
#2022, 1, Place Ville-Marie
Montréal, QC H3B 2C4 Canada
514-394-0088
Fax: 514-395-2094
Steve Sharpe, Vice-président
Vancouver
#500, 666 Burrard St.
Vancouver, BC V6C 3P6 Canada
Stephen Parker, Vice-President

Consolidated Firstfund Capital Corp.
Also listed under: *Holding & Other Investment Companies*
#304, 837 West Hastings St.
Vancouver, BC V6C 3N6
604-683-6611
Fax: 604-662-8524
wngrant@telus.net
www.firstfund.ca
Ownership: Major shareholder William N. Grant (72.2% interest)
Year Founded: 1984
Number of Employees: 5
Assets: \$1-5 million Year End: 20041231
Revenues: \$1-5 million Year End: 20041231
Stock Symbol: FFP
Profile: The venture capital company is engaged in the tourism & hospitality industry. It is also engaged in financial consulting related to merchant banking & venture capital activities in Canada & the United States. Wholly owned subsidiaries are as follows: Costar Marketing Corp., Goldstar Resort Destinations, Inc.

Executives:
William N. Grant, President/CEO
Robert H. Grant, Vice-President
W. Douglas Grant, Vice-President/CFO
James W.F. Tutton, Vice-President, Real Estate, Secretary
Directors:
Robert H. McClelland, Chair
Robert H. Grant
William N. Grant
James W.F. Tutton

Continental Corporation(CBOC)
Also listed under: *Pension & Money Management Companies*
#402, 4 King St. West
Toronto, ON M5H 1B6
416-867-9079
Fax: 416-867-1961
Former Name: Prairie Capital Inc; ATI Corporation
Ownership: Public. Major shareholder is The Coastal Group (48.1% interest directly & indirectly held)
Year Founded: 1962
Number of Employees: 3
Stock Symbol: CTL
Profile: The company holds a portfolio of medium- to long-term investments, participates in privately placed debt & equity issues, & provides cash management services & short-term financing facilities.

Executives:
Gordon Flatt, President
Lori Tange, Vice-President, Finance, Corporate Secretary
Directors:
J. Ian Flatt, Chair
Roy E. Collins
Gordon Flatt

Corpfinance International Limited
229 Niagara St.
Toronto, ON [TJ 2L5
416-364-6191
Fax: 416-364-1012
info@corpfinance.ca
www.corpfinance.ca
Ownership: Private
Year Founded: 1984
Number of Employees: 25
Assets: \$1-10 billion Year End: 20041231
Profile: Corpfinance International Limited is one of a group of companies within CFI group. Other companies include CFI Capital, CFI Trust & CFI Infrastructure Opportunities Fund. The organizations provide customized medium & long-term structured & infrastructure debt & equity financing solutions. Clients include public & private corporations.

Executives:
Kevin Andrews, President/CEO
Christopher J. Ball, Exec. Vice-President
John L. Burns, Sr. Vice-President & General Counsel
Frank Vihant, CA, Sr. Vice-President, Corpfinance International Limited
Eugene J. Wolski, Sr. Vice-President, Credit & Operations
Peter Heffernan, Vice-President
Jacques Huot, Vice-President
Eric Skillins, Vice-President

Crown Investments Corporation of Saskatchewan(CIC)
#400, 2400 College Ave.
Regina, SK S4P 1C8
306-787-6851
Fax: 306-787-8125
www.cicorp.sk.ca
Executives:
Tom Waller, President & CEO
Directors:
Pat Atkinson, Chair
Maynard Sonntag, Chair
Eric Cline
Eldon Lautermilch
Frank Quennell
Henry Van Mulligan
Information Services Corporation of Saskatchewan
Investment Saskatchewan Inc.
Saskatchewan Development Fund Corporation
Saskatchewan Government Growth Fund Management Corporation
Saskatchewan Government Insurance
Saskatchewan Opportunities Corporation
Saskatchewan Power Corporation
Saskatchewan Telecommunications
Saskatchewan Telecommunications
Saskatchewan Transportation Company
Saskatchewan Water Corporation
SaskEnergy Incorporated

Crown Investments Corporation of Saskatchewan(CIC) (continued)
Branches:
Saskatoon
#204, 15 Innovation Pl.
Saskatoon, SK S7N 2X8 Canada
306-933-6259
Fax: 306-933-7706

Crowsnest Pass Business Development Corporation

PO Box 818
Blairmore, AB T0K 0E0
403-562-8858
Fax: 403-562-7252
cnpbdc@telusplanet.net
www.telusplanet.net/public/cnpbdc/cnpbdc.htm
Number of Employees: 4
Profile: The corporation is affiliated with Community Futures Development Corporations & Western Economic Diversification.

Executives:
Shar Lazzarotto, Manager

CYR Mortgages & Investment Corporation
Thornhill Square Mall
#308, 300 John St.
Thornhill, ON L3T 5W4
905-731-1111
Fax: 905-731-6860
rmalkah@rogers.com
Ownership: Private
Year Founded: 1975
Profile: Cyr Mortgages & Investment Corporation finances all types of real estate investments across Canada, including industrial, commercial, residential, special purpose & business loans.

Executives:
Rena Malkah, Partner

DaimlerChrysler Financial Canada
DaimlerChrysler Canada Inc. Headquarters
1 Riverside Dr. West
Windsor, ON N8Y 4R8
519-973-2000
www.chryslerfinancialcanada.ca
Former Name: DaimlerChrysler Financial Services; Chrysler Credit Canada Ltd.
Ownership: Foreign, wholly owned subsidiary of Chrysler Financial Corporation, U.S.A.
Number of Employees: 300
Branches:
Calgary
#1200, 13131 Lake Fraser Dr. SE
Calgary, AB T2J 7E8 Canada
403-255-5600
888-613-3331
Mississauga
2425 Matheson Blvd. East, 3rd Fl.
Mississauga, ON L4W 5N7 Canada
905-629-6000
800-263-6920
Montréal - Côte-Vertu
#400, 3100, boul de la Côte-Vertu
Montréal, QC H4R 2J8 Canada
514-339-2370
Fax: 514-339-9989
800-363-0397

Dakota Ojibway Community Futures Development Corporation
4820 Portage Ave.
Headingley, MB R4H 1C8
204-988-5373
Fax: 204-988-5365
info@docfdc.mb.ca
www.docfdc.mb.ca
Ownership: Non-profit
Number of Employees: 4
Executives:
Kim Bullard, General Manager
Directors:
Francis Elk, Chair
Gus Higheagle, Vice-Chair
Ken Chalmers
Marvin Daniels
Keith Henry
Stan Myran
Lawrence Walker

Däna Näye Ventures(DNV)
409 Black St.
Whitehorse, YT Y1A 2N2
867-668-6925
Fax: 867-668-3127
800-661-0448
dnv@dananaye.com
www.dananaye.yk.net
Ownership: Private. Aboriginal-owned & operated.
Year Founded: 1985
Assets: $5-10 million Year End: 20050331
Revenues: $1-5 million Year End: 20050331
Profile: Däna Näye Ventures is a Yukon-based Aboriginal-owned institution that provides developmental financial & advisory services to Yukon entrepreneurs. As an Aboriginal Capital Corporation, funds are available to Aboriginal entrepreneurs & Aboriginal controlled small businesses. However, the company also has other loan funds, which are available to non-Aboriginal entrepreneurs as well. The Yukon Venture Group, a division of DNV, makes equity & quasi-equity investments in qualifying Aboriginal small businesses. DNV also delivers the Self-Employment Program, under contract to Human Resources & Skills Development Canada, & is an external delivery organization for the Aboriginal Business Canada (ABC) program, under contract to Industry Canada. DNV also provides bookkeeping services, administrative training & support to First Nation organizations, computer & entrepreneurial development training, as well as assistance with feasibility studies & business plans.

Executives:
Elaine Chambers, General Manager
Wayne McLennan, Manager, Financial Services
Sarah Steinberg, Manager, Finance & Administration
Blayne Epp, Officer, Loans
Kim Solonick, Officer, Youth Services & Business Support
Khêtäwk Louise Parker, Coordinator, Self Employment
Directors:
Louise Clethero, Chair
May Brodhagen
Richard (Dick) Dickson
Helen Holway

Desjardins Capital de risque/ Desjardins Venture Capital
***Also listed under:** Holding & Other Investment Companies*
CP 760, Desjardins Stn. Desjardins
#1717, 2, Complexe Desjardins
Montréal, QC H5B 1B8
514-281-7131
Fax: 514-281-7808
Other Information: Toll Free: 1-866-866-7000, poste 7131
www.dcrdesjardins.com
Former Name: Investissement Desjardins
Ownership: Private. Owned by Desjardins Cooperative Group
Year Founded: 1974
Number of Employees: 40
Executives:
Louis L. Roquet, President/CEO
Lucien Bergevin, Adjoint au président et Premier vice président, Ressources humaines, Administration et Réseau
Marie-Claude Boisvert, 1re vice-présidente, Chef de la direction financière
Sylvie Audet, Vice-présidente, Planification et communications
Roger Durand, Vice-président principal, Investissement régional
Ronald Gravel, Vice-président, Développement des affaires coopératives
Catherine Lenfant, Vice-présidente, Finances et évaluation du protefeuille
Fabrice Lucherini, Vice-président, Sciences de la vie, Technologie de l'information et Télécommunications
Claude Rhéaume, Vice-président, Gestion conseil
Gérald St-Aubin, Vice-président, Développement de marché

Drumheller Regional Business Development Centre Corp.
181 North Railway Ave.
Drumheller, AB T0J 0Y0
403-823-7703
Fax: 403-823-7753
info@cfdcdrumheller.com
www.cfdcdrumheller.com
Number of Employees: 10
Profile: Assesses the viability of business ideas, helps to build personal credit, as well as creates financial, marketing, and business plans.

Executives:
Wayne Hove, General Manager; w.hove@cfdcdrumheller.com

DS Marcil Inc.
Royal Bank Plaza, North Tower, 4th Fl.
PO Box 50
200 Bay St.
Toronto, ON M5J 2W7
416-842-8900
Fax: 416-842-8910
Ownership: DS Dominion Securities & Royal Bank Corporation (RBC)
Number of Employees: 22
Executives:
Douglas McGregor, President
Carolyn A. Blair, Vice-President & Regional Director
Rick Matheson, Vice-President & Director
Branches:
Calgary
Bankers Hall West
888 - 3rd St. SW
Calgary, AB T2P 5C5 Canada
403-299-6976
Fax: 403-299-6996
Montréal
#300, 1, Place Ville-Marie
Montréal, QC H3B 4R8 Canada
514-878-7230
Fax: 514-878-7235

East Algoma Community Futures Development Corporation
Lakewood Place
PO Box 398
#106, 1 Industrial Park Rd. East
Blind River, ON P0R 1B0
705-356-1152
Fax: 705-356-1711
888-227-3569
info@eastalgomacfdc.ca
www.eastalgomacfdc.ca
Former Name: Community Development Centre for East Algoma
Executives:
Shawn Heard, General Manager

East Central Development Corporation
PO Box 727
601 Edmonton St.
Broadview, SK S0G 0K0
306-696-2443
Fax: 306-696-2508
ecdc@sasktel.net
www.eastcentral.sk.ca
Ownership: Non-profit
Year Founded: 1985
Number of Employees: 3
Revenues: $360,000
Profile: The corporation provides small business financing & technical assistance in Saskatchewan.

Executives:
Elroy Trithardt, General Manager

East Parkland Community & Business Development Corporation
PO Box 250
Mirror, AB T0B 3C0
403-788-2212
Fax: 403-788-2199
888-788-2829
info@eastparkland.com
www.eastparkland.com
Year Founded: 1988
Number of Employees: 7
Profile: Affiliated with Western Economic Diversification.

Executives:
Don Moulton, General Manager
Branches:
Red Deer
200 Central Block
Red Deer, AB T4N 6C2 Canada
403-342-2068
Fax: 403-346-9761
888-371-8800
epsea@telusplanet.net

Elgin Community Futures Development Corporation
300 South Edgeware Rd.
St Thomas, ON N5P 4L1
519-633-7597
Fax: 519-633-5070
admin@elgincfdc.ca
www.elgincfdc.on.ca
Ownership: Non-profit.
Year Founded: 1986
Number of Employees: 7
Profile: The community based organization provides human & financial resources. It services new & existing businesses in Elgin County. Local economic development is also supported by the corporation. Egin CFDC is funded by the Industry Canada branch of the Federal Government.

Executives:
Helen LeFrank, General Manager
Anne Kenny, Officer, Economic Development
Donna Lunn, Officer, Community Development

ELNOS Corp. for Business Development
31 Nova Scotia Walk, 3rd Fl.
Elliot Lake, ON P5A 1Y6
705-848-0229
Fax: 705-848-1539
800-256-7299
www.elnos.com
Former Name: Elliot Lake & North Shore Corp. for Business Development
Ownership: Private
Year Founded: 1993
Number of Employees: 3
Profile: The community-based investment company provides flexible financing to ventures across Canada that will result in some business activity in the region around Elliot Lake in Northern Ontario.

Executives:
William Woods, Manager

Enercana Capital Ltd.
3911 Trasimene Cr. SW
Calgary, AB T3E 2J6
403-685-1888
Fax: 403-685-1880
www.enercana.com
Ownership: Private
Profile: Combined experience is offered in the following areas: corporate finance, merchant banking, global joint venturing & financial advice for North American, Asian & European companies & institutions. Enercana has hands-on experience in business, finance, marketing & technology in local & international markets. It provides comprehensive business & technical research by applying the latest in information technology tools, including access to the world's most sophisticated commercial databases.

Executives:
Barclay Hambrook, President

Entre-Corp Business Development Centre Ltd.
#202, 556 - 4th St. SE
Medicine Hat, AB T1A 0K8
403-528-2824
Fax: 403-527-3596
888-528-2824
business@entre-corp.com
www.entre-corp.com
Year Founded: 1988
Number of Employees: 15
Profile: Service includes financing & loan for small businesses to a maximum of $100,000. An affiliate is Community Futures of Alberta.

The Equicom Group Inc.
#530, 20 Toronto St.
Toronto, ON M5C 2B8
416-815-0700
Fax: 416-815-0080
info@equicomgroup.com
www.equicomgroup.com
Year Founded: 1996
Profile: Provides a full suite of corporate services to North American technology, life sciences & high growth companies.

Executives:
Barry Hildred, President & CEO
Hector Corkum, Sr. Vice-President
Jason Hogan, Exec. Vice-President
Martti Kangas, Sr. Vice-President
Scott Kelly, Sr. Vice-President
Dave Mason, Sr. Vice-President
Mike Polansky, Sr. Vice-President
Jo-Ann Archibald, Vice-President
Lawrence Chamberlain, Vice-President
Joanna Longo, Vice-President
James Smith, Vice-President
W. Bruce Wigle, Vice-President
Branches:
Calgary
#600, 205 5th Ave. SW
Calgary, AB T2P 2V7 Canada
403-538-4787
Fax: 403-266-2453
Montréal
#2160, 1155, Metcalfe
Montréal, QC H3B 2V6 Canada
514-844-7997
Fax: 514-844-2261

Essra Industries Inc.
***Also listed under:** Holding & Other Investment Companies*
#218, 10458 Mayfield Rd.
Edmonton, AB T5P 4P4
780-484-3794
Fax: 780-484-4230
esstragroup@dsm.ca
Ownership: Public
Year Founded: 1996
Stock Symbol: ESS
Profile: Esstra owns 6 buildings with 122 luxury rental townhomes in Eagan, Minnesota. The wholly owned subsidiary is Waterford Apartments Corp.

Executives:
Peter G. Dickson, President/CEO/CFO
Sharon Lewis, Secretary
Directors:
Peter G. Dickson
Glenn Stogryn

Execucor Financial Limited
#706, 505 Consumers Rd.
Toronto, ON M2J 4V8
416-498-5017
Fax: 416-498-6165
888-393-2826
info@execucor.com
www.execucor.com
Ownership: Private
Year Founded: 1983
Number of Employees: 4
Profile: A branch office is located in Kitchener, Ontario.

Executives:
Eric Edward Knight, President/CEO; eric.knight@execucor.com

Fairbanx Corp.
2940 Bloor St. W
Toronto, ON M8X 1B6
416-574-4788
Fax: 416-239-7315
877-386-3255
hmca@fairbanx.com
www.fairbanx.com
Number of Employees: 5
Profile: Specializes in providing factoring services to a wide range of businesses across Canada.

Executives:
Henry Mahdy, President

Farm Credit Canada(FCC)/ Financement agricole Canada(FAC)
PO Box 4320
1800 Hamilton St.
Regina, SK S4P 4L3
306-780-8100
Fax: 306-780-5456
888-332-3301
communications@fcc-fac.ca
www.fcc-fac.ca
Year Founded: 1959
Number of Employees: 1100+
Assets: $7,200,000,000 Year End: 20050331
Revenues: $548,500,000 Year End: 20050331
Profile: The FCC is Canada's largest agricultural long-term lender, offering flexible financial solutions to primary producers and agribusinesses.

Executives:
John J. Ryan, President/CEO
Moyez Somani, Exec. Vice-President/CFO
Greg Stewart, Exec. Vice-President, Operations
Greg Honey, Sr. Vice-President, Human Resources
Paul MacDonald, Sr. Vice-President, CIO
Lyndon Carlson, Vice-President, Market & Product Development
Kellie Garrett, Vice-President, Strategy, Knowledge & Reputation
Rick Hoffman, Vice-President & Controller
Mike Hoffort, Vice-President, Partners & Channel
Sophie MacDonald, Vice-President, Enterprise Integration & Innovation
Corinna Mitchell-Beaudin, Vice-President, Portfolio Managment
Donald Stevens, Vice-President & Treasurer
André Tétreault, Vice-President, Credit Risk
Ross Topp, Vice-President, Audit & Integrated Risk
Greg Willner, General Counsel & Corporate Secretary
Branches:
Abbotsford
#200, 1520 McCallum Rd.
Abbotsford, BC V2S 8A3 Canada
604-870-2417
Fax: 604-870-2431
Alma
640, rue Côté ouest
Alma, QC G8B 7S8 Canada
418-668-2411
Fax: 418-668-0636
Arborg
Interlake Mall
PO Box 460
145 Sunset Blvd.
Arborg, MB R0C 0A0 Canada
204-376-5291
Fax: 204-376-5710
Assiniboia
PO Box 1060
229 - 1st Ave. West
Assiniboia, SK S0H 0B0 Canada
306-642-5282
Fax: 306-642-4676
Barrhead
PO Box 4680
5002 - 50th St.
Barrhead, AB T7N 1A6 Canada
780-674-4744
Fax: 780-674-3610
Barrie
#2, 301 Bryne Dr.
Barrie, ON L4M 4S8 Canada
705-728-2235
Fax: 705-728-2494
Brandon
3000 G Victoria Ave.
Brandon, MB R7B 3Y3 Canada
204-726-7595
Fax: 204-726-7635
Calgary
#320, 3636 - 23rd St.
Calgary, AB T2E 8Z5 Canada
403-292-6100
Fax: 403-292-6121
Campbellford
PO Box 60
71 Front St. North
Campbellford, ON K0L 1L0 Canada
705-653-1760
Fax: 705-653-3326
Camrose
#200, 4918 - 51st St.
Camrose, AB T4V 1S3 Canada
780-672-2486
Fax: 780-672-4990
Carlyle
PO Box 430
109 Railway Ave. West
Carlyle, SK S0C 0R0 Canada
306-453-2595
Fax: 306-453-2299
Carman

Farm Credit Canada(FCC)/ Financement agricole Canada(FAC) (continued)

#5, 82 - 4th Ave. SE
Carman, MB R0G 0J0 Canada
204-745-6759
Fax: 204-745-3768

Charlottetown
#110, 420 University Ave.
Charlottetown, PE C1A 7Z5 Canada
902-566-7067
Fax: 902-566-7805

Chatham
#203, 405 Riverview Dr., RR#5
Chatham, ON N7M 5J5 Canada
519-380-8810
Fax: 519-380-8818

Clinton
282 Huron St. West
Clinton, ON N0M 1L0 Canada
519-482-5115
Fax: 519-482-5116

Dauphin
1450 Main St. South
Dauphin, MB R7N 3H4 Canada
204-622-4050
Fax: 204-622-4059

Dawson Creek
#1, 705 - 103rd Ave.
Dawson Creek, BC V1G 4W8 Canada
250-782-1346
Fax: 250-782-2476

Drumheller
PO Box 849
375 - 3rd St. West
Drumheller, AB T0J 0Y0 Canada
403-823-4111
Fax: 403-823-4118

Drummondville
#5, 400, rue Cormier
Drummondville, QC J2C 7L9 Canada
819-478-2561
Fax: 819-478-1782

Duncan
#301, 2700 Beverly St.
Duncan, BC V9L 5C7 Canada
250-715-2304
Fax: 250-715-2305

Edmonton
#1200, 10250 - 101 St.
Edmonton, AB T5J 3P4 Canada
780-495-4488
Fax: 780-495-5665

Embrun
PO Box 2407
735B Notre-Dame St.
Embrun, ON K0A 1W1 Canada
613-443-2138
Fax: 613-443-2855

Essex
39 Maidstone Ave. East
Essex, ON N8M 2J3 Canada
519-776-4219
Fax: 519-776-6890

Falher
PO Box 29
105 Main St. SW
Falher, AB T0H 1M0 Canada
780-837-2333
Fax: 780-837-3450

Gatineau
#100, 85, rue Bellehumeur
Gatineau, QC J8T 8B7 Canada
819-953-7226
Fax: 819-953-6979

Granby
#770, 1, rue Principale
Granby, QC J2G 2Y7 Canada
450-378-4050
Fax: 450-378-3176

Grand Falls
63B Industrial Rd.
Grand Falls, NB E3Y 3V1 Canada
506-473-3853
Fax: 506-473-2009

Grande Prairie
#102, 10712 - 100th St.
Grande Prairie, AB T8V 3X8 Canada
780-532-4790
Fax: 780-538-3575

Guelph
1030 Gordon St.
Guelph, ON N1G 4X5 Canada
519-824-6360
Fax: 519-826-2170

Humboldt
PO Box 937
640 - 10th St.
Humboldt, SK S0K 2A0 Canada
306-682-3902
Fax: 306-682-4383

Joliette
899, rue Papineau
Joliette, QC J6E 2L6 Canada
450-753-7855
Fax: 450-753-4651

Kanata
309 Leggett Dr.
Kanata, ON K2K 3A3 Canada
613-271-7640
Fax: 613-271-8978

Kelowna
#200, 1634 Harvey Ave.
Kelowna, BC V1Y 6G2 Canada
250-470-5050
Fax: 250-470-5061

Kentville
#203, 49 Cornwallis St.
Kentville, NS B4N 2E3 Canada
902-679-5722
Fax: 902-679-5756

Kindersley
PO Box 310
404C - 12th Ave. East
Kindersley, SK S0L 1S0 Canada
306-463-5320
Fax: 306-463-3435

Kingston
Frontenac Mall
#201, 1300 Bath Rd.
Kingston, ON K7M 4X4 Canada
613-545-8357
Fax: 613-546-4576

Leduc
6052 - 47th St.
Leduc, AB T9E 8L4 Canada
780-980-4320
Fax: 780-980-4325

Lethbridge
#400, 220 - 3rd Ave. South
Lethbridge, AB T1J 0G9 Canada
403-382-3137
Fax: 403-382-3195

Lindsay
152 Angeline St. North
Lindsay, ON K9V 4X2 Canada
705-324-5773
Fax: 705-324-6653

Listowel
PO Box 39
975 Wallace Ave. North
Listowel, ON N4W 1M6 Canada
519-291-3450
Fax: 519-291-4117

London
417 Exeter Rd.
London, ON N6E 2Z3 Canada
519-681-1130
Fax: 519-681-3304

Medicine Hat
1375 - 22nd St. SE
Medicine Hat, AB T1A 7V3 Canada
403-526-3747
Fax: 403-527-9759

Moncton
#200, 1133 St. George Blvd.
Moncton, NB E1E 4E1 Canada
506-851-6595
Fax: 506-851-6613

Moose Jaw
1216 Main St. North
Moose Jaw, SK S6H 3L1 Canada
306-693-4077
Fax: 306-692-2202

Morden
PO Box 998
401B North Railway St.
Morden, MB R6M 1S8 Canada
204-822-7350
Fax: 204-822-7360

Mount Pearl
Research Station
PO Box 68
Brookfield Rd.
Mount Pearl, NL A1N 2C1 Canada
709-772-4635
Fax: 709-772-4482

Neepawa
PO Box 236
41 Main St. West
Neepawa, MB R0J 1H0 Canada
204-476-7330
Fax: 204-476-7339

North Battleford
#201, 1301 - 101st St.
North Battleford, SK S9A 0Z9 Canada
306-446-1700
Fax: 306-445-1005

North Bay
#5, 593 Main St. East
North Bay, ON P1B 1B7 Canada
705-494-4229
Fax: 705-494-4231

Olds
#3, 5304 - 46th St.
Olds, AB T4H 1B8 Canada
403-556-8177
Fax: 403-556-2490

Owen Sound
#8, 1050 - 2nd Ave. East
Owen Sound, ON N4K 2H7 Canada
519-376-6338
Fax: 519-376-8968

Portage La Prairie
PO Box 1058
2370 Sissons Dr.
Portage La Prairie, MB R1N 3C5 Canada
204-239-8470
Fax: 204-239-8475

Prince Albert
#104, 2805 - 6th Ave. East
Prince Albert, SK S6V 6Z6 Canada
306-953-8562
Fax: 306-953-8575

Québec
#300, 979, av Bourgogne
Québec, QC G1W 2L4 Canada
418-648-5133
Fax: 418-648-4286

Red Deer
#1, 7710 - 50th Ave.
Red Deer, AB T4P 2A5 Canada
403-340-4200
Fax: 403-340-4227

Regina - Hamilton St. - Customer Service Centre
1800 Hamilton St.
Regina, SK S4P 4L3 Canada
306-780-8900
Fax: 306-780-8919

Regina - Hamilton St. - FCC Corp. DFC
1800 Hamilton St.
Regina, SK S4P 4L3 Canada
306-780-8100
Fax: 306-780-5167

Regina - Research Dr. - AG Expert
#170, 10 Research Dr.
Regina, SK S4S 7S7 Canada
306-721-7999
Fax: 306-721-1981

Regina - Victoria Ave. East
#201, 2180 Victoria Ave. East
Regina, SK S4N 7B9 Canada
306-780-5616
Fax: 306-780-5611

Rivière-du-Loup
298, boul Thériault
Rivière-du-Loup, QC G5R 4C2 Canada
418-862-7631
Fax: 418-862-8164
Rock-Forest
#203, 4300, boul Bourque
Rock Forest, QC J1N 2A6 Canada
819-564-5512
Fax: 819-564-5514
Rosetown
PO Box 1118
217 Railway Ave. East
Rosetown, SK S0L 2V0 Canada
306-882-2231
Fax: 306-882-3066
Saint-Hyacinthe
#1006, 1050, boul Casavant ouest
Saint-Hyacinthe, QC J2S 8B9 Canada
450-771-7080
Fax: 450-771-7456
Salaberry-de-Valleyfield
#105, 2055, boul Hébert
Salaberry-de-Valleyfield, QC J6S 5Y5 Canada
450-371-1772
Saskatoon
#301, 2100 - 8th St. East
Saskatoon, SK S7H 0V1 Canada
306-975-4248
Fax: 306-975-4864

Simcoe
65 Queensway East
Simcoe, ON N3Y 4M5 Canada
519-426-3312
Fax: 519-426-5106
St-Jean-sur-Richelieu
#101, 200, rue MacDonald
St-Jean-sur-Richelieu, QC J3B 8J6 Canada
450-348-3849
Fax: 450-348-1271
St-Jérôme
#235, 500, boul Des Laurentides
Saint-Jérome, QC J7Z 4M2 Canada
450-438-2119
Steinbach
PO Box 21650
#D6, 284 Reimer Ave.
Steinbach, MB R5G 1B3 Canada
204-326-9400
Fax: 204-346-6374
Stettler
PO Box 600
4910A - 51st St.
Stettler, AB T0C 2L0 Canada
403-742-3165
Fax: 403-742-1972
Stony Plain
#200, 72 Boulder Blvd.
Stony Plain, AB T7Z 1V7 Canada
780-963-6547
Fax: 780-963-9634
Stratford
516 Huron St.
Stratford, ON N5A 5T7 Canada
519-271-0460
Fax: 519-271-4053
Summerside
#1, 500 Granville St.
Summerside, PE C1N 5Y1 Canada
902-432-6525
Fax: 902-432-6528
Sussex
PO Box 4751
29 Milk Bd Rd.
Sussex, NB E4E 5L9 Canada
506-432-9135
Fax: 506-432-9137
Swift Current
#10, 1071 Central Ave. North
Swift Current, SK S9H 4Z1 Canada
306-773-2991
Fax: 306-778-3695
Tisdale
PO Box 820
803 - 100th St.
Tisdale, SK S0E 1T0 Canada
306-873-4511
Fax: 306-873-5457
Trois-Rivières
#108, 4720, boul Royal
Trois-Rivières, QC G9A 4N1 Canada
819-371-5351
Fax: 819-371-5355
Truro
PO Box 1408
#101, 640 Prince St.
Truro, NS B2N 1G4 Canada
902-893-6867
Fax: 902-893-6880
Vegreville
PO Box 340
#138, 4925 - 50th Ave.
Vegreville, AB T9C 1R3 Canada
780-632-2858
Fax: 780-632-6760
Vermilion
#102, 5102 - 50th Ave.
Vermilion, AB T9X 1B1 Canada
780-853-5738
Fax: 780-853-5562
Victoriaville
#10, 650, boul Jutras est
Victoriaville, QC G6S 1E1 Canada
819-751-0048
Fax: 819-751-0049
Vineland
4134 Victoria Ave.
Vineland, ON L0R 2C0 Canada
905-562-7355
Fax: 905-562-3839
Virden
PO Box 760
585 - 7th Ave. South
Virden, MB R0M 2C0 Canada
204-748-4150
Fax: 204-748-4169
Walkerton
PO Box 428
1315 Yonge St.
Walkerton, ON N0G 2V0 Canada
519-881-1490
Fax: 519-881-3484
Westlock
PO Box 370
#19, 10030 - 106th St.
Westlock, AB T7P 2K4 Canada
780-349-3202
Fax: 780-349-4910
Weyburn
609 Railway Ave.
Weyburn, SK S4H 0A9 Canada
306-842-3559
Fax: 306-842-3951

Woodstock - Connell St.
#1, 267 Connell St.
Woodstock, NB E7M 1L2 Canada
506-328-8427
Fax: 506-328-0961
Woodstock - Princess St.
ABACUS House
#2, 514 Princess St.
Woodstock, ON N4S 4B9 Canada
519-539-9839
Fax: 519-539-3459
Wyoming
Reece's Corners
4475 London Line, RR#1
Wyoming, ON N0N 1T0 Canada
519-845-3309
Fax: 519-845-0651
Yorkton
120 Smith St. East
Yorkton, SK S3N 3V3 Canada
306-783-9431
Fax: 306-786-7610

First Citizens Mortgage Corporation

#206, 20641 Logan Ave.
Langley, BC V3A 7R3
604-533-8288
Fax: 604-533-1987
bobw@firstcitizensmortgage.com
www.firstcitizensmortgage.com
Ownership: Private
Year Founded: 1969
Number of Employees: 8
Profile: First Citizens Mortgage Corporation is a provincially licensed mortgage broker, dealing mainly in B residential & commercial mortgages.

Executives:
R.W. Williams, President

First Data Loan Company, Canada

2630 Skymark Ave., 5th Fl.
Mississauga, ON L4W 5A4
905-605-3113
Profile: The federally incorporated company is also eligible to accept deposits.

Flagship Capital Partners Inc.

#400, 2300 Yonge St.
Toronto, ON M4P 1E4
416-545-1010
Fax: 416-545-1011
Former Name: Ashton Royce Capital Corporation
Ownership: Private
Year Founded: 1989
Number of Employees: 12
Profile: The private merchant bank specializes in unique investment opportunities for high net worth individuals. Typically, investments take advantage of Canadian income tax incentives. Affiliated companies are FACES Inc., Media Ventures Productions Limited Partnership & The Completion Guaranters.

Executives:
George Aprile

Fonds de développement Emploi-Montréal inc(FDEM)

#100, 5703, rue Sherbrooke est
Montréal, QC H1N 3M1
514-253-4667
Fax: 514-253-5128
guymarion@fdem.qc.ca
www.fdem.qc.ca
Ownership: Private
Year Founded: 1988
Number of Employees: 2
Executives:
Jean Gauthier, President
Jacques Roy, Vice-President
Guy Marion, Director General

Fonds de solidarité des travailleurs du Québec(FTQ)

Also listed under: Investment Fund Companies
#200, 545, boul Crémazie est
Montréal, QC H2M 2W4
514-383-8383
Fax: 514-850-4845
800-361-5017
www.fondsftq.com
Ownership: Public.
Year Founded: 1983
Number of Employees: 400
Assets: $1-10 billion
Revenues: $1-10 billion
Profile: The Fund finances primarily the growth of viable innovative companies that create permanent jobs. The Fund also makes investments directly or through its development fund network in the following types of projects: start-up, expansion, IPO, consolidation, mergers, acquisitions, & export.

Executives:
Henri Massé, Chair
Pierre Genest, CEO, Solidarity Fund QFL
Yvon Bolduc, Exec. Vice-President, Investments
Pierre Leblanc, Exec. Vice-President, Human Resources
Denis Leclerc, Sr. Vice-President, Shareholder Services & Development
Michel Pontbriand, Sr. Vice-President, Finance
Janie C. Béïque, Vice-President, Legal Affairs
René Roy, Secretary of the Board

Fonds de solidarité des travailleurs du Québec(FTQ) (continued)

QFL:
Québec Solidarity Fund
RRSP Eligible; Inception Year: 1984;
Fonds régionaux de solidarité:
Chibougamau
432B, 3e rue
Chibougamau, QC G8P 1N7 Canada
418-748-8180
Fax: 418-748-7121
888-748-8180
www.ndq.fondsreg.com
Raymond Grenier, Directeur régional
Gaspé
185, boul York est
Gaspé, QC G4X 2L1 Canada
418-368-7346
Fax: 418-368-4028
800-404-7429
mcayouette@gas.fondsreg.com
www.gas.fondsreg.com
Marc Cayouette, Directeur régional
Gatineau
#315, 259, boul St-Joseph
Gatineau, QC J8Y 6T1 Canada
819-778-2995
Fax: 819-778-2998
www.out.fondsreg.com
Michel Parent, Directeur régional
Joliette
284, rue Beaudry nord
Joliette, QC J6E 6A6 Canada
450-755-3992
Fax: 450-755-6560
888-755-3992
www.lan.fondsreg.com
Yves Landry, Directeur régional
Jonquière
#130, 2679, boul du Royaume
Jonquière, QC G7S 5T1 Canada
418-699-1485
Fax: 418-699-1187
888-699-1485
www.sls.fondsreg.com
Andrée Girard, Directrice régionale
Laval
#606, 3030, boul Le Carrefour
Laval, QC H7T 2P5 Canada
450-978-3344
Fax: 450-978-3313
info@lav.fondsreg.com
www.lav.fondsreg.com
Denis Bernier, Directeur régional
Lévis
#104B, 5790, boul Étienne-Dallaire
Lévis, QC G6V 8V6 Canada
418-837-1040
Fax: 418-837-3093
abelanger@cha.fondsreg.com
www.cha.fondsreg.com
Jean Roy, Directeur régional
Montréal
#610, 545, boul Crémazie est
Montréal, QC H2M 2V1 Canada
514-845-3233
Fax: 514-845-0625
dblanchard@mtl.fondsreg.com
www.mtl.fondsreg.com
Michel Parent, Directeur régional
Québec
#130, 5050, boul des Gradins
Québec, QC G2J 1P8 Canada
418-624-2773
Fax: 418-624-8975
www.que.fondsreg.com
Jean Roy, Directeur régional
Rimouski
#601, 2, rue Saint-Germain est
Rimouski, QC G5L 8T7 Canada
418-721-3565
Fax: 418-721-3564
888-456-3565
www.bsl.fondsreg.com
Marc Cayouette, Directeur régional
Rouyn-Noranda
#300, 75, boul Québec
Rouyn-Noranda, QC J9X 7A2 Canada
819-762-7422
Fax: 819-762-8335
www.abt.fondsreg.com
Raymond Grenier, Directeur régional
Sept-×les
#101, 818, boul Laure
Sept-×les, QC G4R 1Y8 Canada
418-968-3784
Fax: 418-962-2988
800-792-2488
www.cot.fondsreg.com
Marc Cayouette, Directeur régional
Sherbrooke
#140, 2100, rue King ouest
Sherbrooke, QC J1J 2E8 Canada
819-829-2220
Fax: 819-829-2263
www.est.fondsreg.com
Luc Pinard, Directeur régional
St-Jean-sur-Richeleau
#109, 923, boul du Séminaire nord
St-Jean-sur-Richelieu, QC J3A 1B6 Canada
450-359-3776
Fax: 450-359-3363
888-359-8939
www.mon.fondsreg.com
Luc Pinard, Directeur régional
St-Jérôme
333, rue Parent
Saint-Jérome, QC J7Z 2A2 Canada
450-569-6658
Fax: 450-569-6630
www.lau.fondsreg.com
Denis Bernier, Directeur régional
Trois-Rivières
#205, 7080, boul Marion
Trois-Rivières, QC G9A 6G4 Canada
819-370-3368
Fax: 819-370-1512
www.mcq.fondsreg.com
Yves Landry, Directeur régional

Ford Credit Canada Limited

The Canadian Rd.
Oakville, ON L6J 5C7
905-845-2511
Fax: 905-845-8244
www.fordcredit.ca
Ownership: Ford Motor Credit Company
Number of Employees: 520
Assets: $1-10 billion
Revenues: $1-5 million

Fort McMurray Regional Business Development Centre(FMRBDC)

#102, 9816 Hardin St.
Fort McMurray, AB T9H 4K3
780-791-0330
Fax: 780-791-0086
fmrbdc@altech.ab.ca
www.fmrbdc.com
Also Known As: Community Futures of Fort McMurray
Ownership: Non-profit
Year Founded: 1988
Number of Employees: 3
Assets: $1-5 million
Revenues: Under $1 million
Profile: The centre provides financing to a maximum of $125,000 to local ventures, $25,000 to youth entrepreneurs & $125,000 to entrepreneurs with disabilities.

Executives:
Randy Edison, General Manager
Directors:
Dan Sorenson, Chair
Aqueel Ahmad
Doug Bruce
Marie Cheecham
Joyce Dene
Kristen Everett
Collin Feser
Leo Jacobs
Steve Jani
Dale Mountain
Harold Turner
Don Pugh

Frobisher Financial Corporation

#903, 275 Sparks St.
Ottawa, ON K1R 7X9
613-232-8712
Fax: 613-230-8116
www.frobisher.com
Year Founded: 1998
Number of Employees: 3
Executives:
Brian Bradfield, General Manager

FutureCorp Cowichan

135 Third St.
Duncan, BC V9L 1R9
250-746-1004
Fax: 250-746-8819
cfdc@futurecorp.ca
www.futurecorp.ca
Former Name: Cowichan Region Community Futures Development Corporation
Year Founded: 1989
Profile: Community-driven and volunteer-based community economic development organization.

Executives:
Joanna Winter, General Manager

Gardhouse, Financial Counselling

***Also listed under:** Financial Planning*
PO Box 399
41 Louisa St. West
Thornbury, ON N0H 2P0
519-599-6535
Fax: 519-599-6536
800-665-8250
gardhouse@on.aibn.com
Former Name: Gardhouse + Gardhouse, Financial Counselling Practice
Ownership: Private
Year Founded: 1986
Number of Employees: 3
Executives:
R. Larry Gardhouse, CFP, RFP
Bev Gardhouse, Office Administrator

GC-Global Capital Corp.

#1400, 55 York St.
Toronto, ON M5J 1R7
416-488-7760
Fax: 416-483-1516
www.gcglobalcapital.ca
Former Name: A&E Capital Funding Inc
Ownership: Public
Year Founded: 1979
Number of Employees: 3
Assets: $10-50 million Year End: 20060930
Revenues: $1-5 million Year End: 20060930
Stock Symbol: GDE.A
Profile: The merchant bank focuses on providing a range of investment banking services to small & mid-cap companies in North America, in both public & private markets. Primarily bridge loan services are provided.

Executives:
Jason G. Ewart, Chief Executive Officer; jewart@gcglobalcapital.ca
Christopher A. Carmichael, Chief Financial Officer
Directors:
Gordon D. Ewart, Chair
William Atkinson
Mark J. Busgang
Jason G. Ewart
Hubert R. Marleau
Kent Smith
Branches:
Vancouver
#1103, 1166 Alberni St.
Vancouver, BC V6E 3Z3 Canada
604-688-3410
Fax: 604-683-2235

GE Capital Solutions

#1401, 1, Place Ville-Marie
Montréal, QC H3B 2B2

514-397-5300
Fax: 514-397-1506
866-317-4323
info@cefca.capital.ge.com
Former Name: GE Capital Canada Equipment Financing
Ownership: Private
Executives:
Patrick Palerme, President/CEO
Christian De Broux, Sr. Vice-President, Risk Management
Paul DeMarchi, Sr. Vice-President, National Programs Group
Josée Gravel, Sr. Vice-President, Legal
René Jolicoeur, Sr. Vice-President, Human Resources
Peter Ringler, Sr. Vice-President
Stéphane Therrien, Sr. Vice-President, Chief Commercial Officer

Gina Van Herck, Sr. Vice-President, Finance
Geoff Best, Sr. Regional Vice-President
François Nantel, Sr. Regional Vice-President
Jean-François Bertrand, Vice-President, Capital Markets
Carlo Fargnoli, Vice-President, Credit Controls & Processes
Philippe Lapeyre, Vice-President, Risk Management
Claude Perrier, Vice-President, Operations
Curtis Wennberg, Vice-President, Marketing
Branches:
Burlington
5500 North Service Rd., 8th Fl.
Burlington, ON L7L 6W6 Canada
Calgary
#2120, 530 - 8 Ave. SW
Calgary, AB T2P 3S8 Canada
Chicoutimi
#510, 255, rue Racine est
Chicoutimi, QC G7H 7L2 Canada
Dartmouth
#204, 239 Brownlow Ave.
Dartmouth, NS B3B 2B2 Canada
Edmonton
#404, 10525 - 170th St.
Edmonton, AB T5P 4W2 Canada
Grande Prairie
#205, 9804 - 100 Ave.
Grande Prairie, AB T8V 0T8 Canada
Kamloops
#202, 1967 Transcanada Hwy.
Kamloops, BC V2C 4A4 Canada
London
#112, 1069 Wellington Rd. South
London, ON N6E 2H6 Canada
Mississauga
2300 Meadowvale Blvd.
Mississauga, ON L5N 5P9 Canada
Montréal
#1401, 1, Place Ville Marie
Montréal, QC H3B 2B2 Canada
Nanaimo
201 Selby St.
Nanaimo, BC V9R 2R2 Canada
Ottawa
3030 Conroy Rd., 2nd Fl.
Ottawa, ON K1G 6C2 Canada
Prince George
#805, 299 Victoria St.
Prince George, BC V2L 5B8 Canada
Québec
#410, 3075, ch des Quatre-Bourgeois
Québec, QC G1W 4Y9 Canada
Saskatoon
#1, 3314 Millar Ave.
Saskatoon, SK S7K 7G9 Canada

St. John's
#603, 140 Water St.
St. John's, NL A1C 6H6 Canada
Sudbury
#4, 754 Falconbridge Rd.
Sudbury, ON P3A 5X5 Canada
Vancouver
#1050, 400 Burrard St.
Vancouver, BC V6C 3A6 Canada

Gedir Consultants Inc.
311 Mallin Cres.
Saskatoon, SK S7K 7X3
306-668-7575
Fax: 306-933-2466
jgedir@continuity.ca
Also Known As: Continuity Resources Group Inc.
Ownership: Private
Profile: The company provides a business advisory service to growth-oriented companies, designing innovative solutions to help owners/managers transfer the business from one generation to the next. Services include business succession, corporate finance & retirement compensation.

Executives:
Jerry Gedir, President

Geko Mortgage Services
#711, 2727 Yonge St.
Toronto, ON M4N 3R6
416-932-8245
Ownership: Private
Year Founded: 1984
Profile: Home mortgages & real estate loans.

General Motors Acceptance Corporation of Canada, Limited(GMAC)
#2800, 3300 Bloor St. West
Toronto, ON M8X 2X5
416-234-6600
Fax: 416-234-6614
800-463-7483
www.gmacfs.com
Also Known As: GMAC of Canada
Ownership: Private. Wholly owned by General Motors Acceptance Corporation, Detroit, Michigan.
Year Founded: 1953
Profile: The company is engaged in automotive financial services to & through General Motors Dealers in Canada. The Commercial Services Division provides receivables management & working capital solutions, with products such as traditional factoring, trade receivable credit guarantees, receivable inventory & term loans.

Executives:
Thomas E. Dickerson, President
Dennis De Braga, Sr. Vice-President & Canadian Sales Manager, Commercial Finance Services Division
Affiliated Companies:
Motors Insurance Corporation

Gestion Estrie Capital Inc.
1524, rue Maçon
Sherbrooke, QC J1N 1V5
819-822-4244
Fax: 819-564-8014
m4beaudoin@yahoo.fr
Ownership: Private
Year Founded: 1988
Number of Employees: 2
Executives:
Mario Beaudoin, Director General

GMAC Commercial Finance(GMAC CF)
#2300, 800, boul René-Lévesque ouest
Montréal, QC H3B 1X9
514-397-9240
Fax: 514-397-1133
www.gmaccf.com
Year Founded: 1999
Profile: GMAC CF provides loan facilities to a variety of middle market clients in diverse industries.

Executives:
Kevin Freer, Vice-President, Structured Finance
Branches:
Toronto
#1314, 150 York St.
Toronto, ON M5H 3S5 Canada
416-365-9555
www.gmaccf.com

GMAC Residential Funding of Canada
West Tower
#920, 3300 Bloor St. West
Toronto, ON M8X 2X2
866-536-7702
www.gmacresidentialfunding.ca
Ownership: GMAC Residential Funding Corporation, Minneapolis, USA.
Profile: GMAC Residential Funding of Canada is part of the General Motors family. The company is a mortgage lender & private issuer of securities, which is licensed to lend in ten provinces. It offers consumers a wide variety of conventional, subprime & Alt-A mortgage products.

Executives:
Lee Goderstad, President
Don Allan, COO, Sr. Financial Officer

GMS Mortgage Investments Corporation
439 Dundas St.
London, ON N6B 1W1
519-438-5645
Fax: 519-434-7287
Year Founded: 1955

Graff & Associates
30 Hazelton Ave.
Toronto, ON M5R 2E2
416-920-2711
Fax: 416-920-0815
cecgraff@inforamp.net
Profile: Graff & Associates provides strategic business planning, consulting & market research services for businesses.

Executives:
Jonathan Graff, Manager, Business Planning

Grand Erie Business Centre
#207, 11 Argyle St. North
Caledonia, ON N3W 1B6
905-765-5005
Fax: 905-765-5750
877-646-6606
connect@granderie.com
www.granderie.com
Former Name: Grand Erie Community Development Corp.
Ownership: Non-profit community-based
Year Founded: 1989
Number of Employees: 3
Executives:
Wayne Knox, Business Consultant
Robin Ramage, Business Consultant

Greater Peterborough Business Development Centre Inc., A Community Futures Development Corporation(CFDC)
351 Charlotte St.
Peterborough, ON K9J 2W1
705-745-5434
Fax: 705-745-2369
comdev@cdc.on.ca
www.cdc.on.ca
Also Known As: Community Futures
Year Founded: 1985
Number of Employees: 5
Profile: The Community Futures Development Corporation operates as a private lender, when conventional financing is not available. It supports small business development, through flexible financing & client counselling services. It is affiliated with the Ontario Association of Community Futures Development Corporations.

Executives:
Judy Heffernan, Chief Administrative Officer, General Manager

Greenstone Community Futures Development Corporation
#228, 35 Main St.
Flin Flon, MB R8A 1J7
204-687-6967
Fax: 204-687-4456
greencom@mts.net
greenstone.mb.ca
Ownership: Non-profit. Funded by federal government
Year Founded: 1986

Greenstone Venture Partners
#777, 1111 West Hastings St.
Vancouver, BC V6E 2J3
604-717-1977
Fax: 604-717-1976
info@greenstonevc.com
www.greenstonevc.com
Executives:
Brent Holliday, Partner
Livia Mahler, Partner
Rich Osborn, Partner

NON-DEPOSITORY INSTITUTIONS

Grenville Community Futures Corporation
PO Box 309
#405, 197 Water St.
Prescott, ON K0E 1T0
613-925-4275
Fax: 613-925-3758
877-925-4275
info@grenvillecfdc.com
www.grenvillecfdc.com
Former Name: Grenville Community Development Centre
Ownership: Non-profit. Funded by federal government
Year Founded: 1990
Number of Employees: 7
Profile: The corporation provides economic development & financial services to the town of Prescott & the townships of Augusta, Edwardsburgh/Cardinal, & North Grenville.

Executives:
Heather Lawless, Executive Director
Charlotte McArthur, Officer, Financial Administration
Mike O'Keefe, Officer, Business Development
Elaine Deschambault, Administrator, Self-Employment Benefit Program
Ben Tekamp, Consultant, Small Business

GrowthWorks Capital Ltd.
Also listed under: *Investment Fund Companies*
#2600, 1055 West Georgia St.
Vancouver, BC V6E 3R5
Fax: 604-688-9039
866-688-3430
info@growthworks.ca
www.growthworks.ca
Ownership: Private
Year Founded: 1999
Number of Employees: 90
Assets: $500m-1 billion
Profile: GrowthWorks means affiliates of GrowthWorks Ltd. It includes the manager of the Working Opportunity Fund (EVCC) Ltd., GrowthWorks WV Management Ltd., manager of GrowthWorks Canadian Fund Ltd. & GrowthWorks Commercialization Fund Ltd., & GrowthWorks Atlantic Ltd., manager of GrowthWorks Atlantic Venture Fund Ltd. GrowthWorks Capital Ltd., is a venture capital company. It manages the Working Opportunity Funds.

Executives:
David Levi, President/CEO
Craig Fookes, CFO & Vice-President, Finance
Donna Bridgeman, Sr. Vice-President, Corporate Affairs, Vice-President, Investments
Jim Charlton, Sr. Vice-President, Investments
Peter Fortin, Sr. Vice-President, Investments
Murray Munro, Sr. Vice-President, National Sales, Marketing & Government Relations
Carol Crow, Vice-President, Human Resources
Alex Irwin, Sr. Counsel
GrowthWorks:
Working Opportunity Commercialization 05 Fund
RRSP Eligible; Inception Year: 2005;
Working Opportunity Commercialization 06 Fund
RRSP Eligible; Inception Year: 2006;
Working Opportunity Balanced Series 1 Fund
RRSP Eligible; Inception Year: 1991;
Working Opportunity Balanced Series 2 Fund
RRSP Eligible; Inception Year: 2004;
Working Opportunity Diversified Fund
RRSP Eligible; Inception Year: 2006;
Working Opportunity Financial Fund
RRSP Eligible; Inception Year: 2006;
Working Opportunity Growth Series 1 Fund
RRSP Eligible; Inception Year: 2000;
Working Opportunity Growth Series 2 Fund
RRSP Eligible; Inception Year: 2004;
Working Opportunity Income Fund
RRSP Eligible; Inception Year: 2006;
Working Opportunity Resources Fund
RRSP Eligible; Inception Year: 2006;
Branches:
Halifax
Purdy's Wharf Tower 1
1959 Upper Water St., 14th Fl.
Halifax, NS B3J 3N2 Canada
902-492-5164
Fax: 902-421-1808
Saskatoon
#830, 410 - 22nd St. East
Saskatoon, SK S7K 5T6 Canada
306-242-1023
Fax: 306-242-9959
Brad Munro, Vice-President, Investments
Toronto
#3504, 20 Queen St.
Toronto, ON M5H 3R3 Canada
416-934-7777
Fax: 416-929-0901

GrowthWorks WV Management Ltd.
Also listed under: *Investment Fund Companies*
#3504, 20 Queen St. West
Toronto, ON M5H 3R3
416-934-7777
Fax: 416-929-4390
800-463-1652
info@growthworks.ca
www.growthworks.ca
Former Name: Working Ventures Funds
Also Known As: GrowthWorks WV Funds
Year Founded: 1990
Assets: $500m-1 billion
Executives:
Les Lyall, Sr. Vice-President
GrowthWorks:
Canadian Fund
RRSP Eligible; Inception Year: 1990;
Canadian (CAVI) Fund
RRSP Eligible; Inception Year: 2005;
Canadian (CSTGF) Fund
RRSP Eligible; Inception Year: 2005;
Canadian Balanced I Fund
RRSP Eligible; Inception Year: 2003;
Canadian Balanced II Fund
RRSP Eligible; Inception Year: 2003;
Canadian Diversified I Fund
RRSP Eligible; Inception Year: 2003;
Canadian Diversified II Fund
RRSP Eligible; Inception Year: 2003;
Canadian Financial I Fund
RRSP Eligible; Inception Year: 2003;
Canadian Financial II Fund
RRSP Eligible; Inception Year: 2003;
Canadian Fund Ltd. (FOF Growth) Fund
RRSP Eligible; Inception Year: 2006;
Canadian Fund Ltd. (FOF Traditional) Fund
RRSP Eligible; Inception Year: 2006;
Canadian Growth I Fund
RRSP Eligible; Inception Year: 2003;
Canadian Growth II Fund
RRSP Eligible; Inception Year: 2003;
Canadian Income I Fund
RRSP Eligible; Inception Year: 2003;
Canadian Income II Fund
RRSP Eligible; Inception Year: 2003;
Canadian Resources I Fund
RRSP Eligible; Inception Year: 2003;
Canadian Resources II Fund
RRSP Eligible; Inception Year: 2003;
Commercialization 505 Fund
RRSP Eligible; Inception Year: 2005;
Commercialization 506 Fund
RRSP Eligible; Inception Year: 2005;
Branches:
Ottawa
#900, 275 Slater St.
Ottawa, ON K1P 5H9 Canada
613-567-3225
Saskatoon
#830, 410 - 22nd St. East
Saskatoon, SK S7K 5T6 Canada
306-242-1023
Toronto
#3504, 20 Queen St. West
Toronto, ON M5H 3R3 Canada
416-934-7777
800-463-1652

GTI Capital
Also listed under: *Pension & Money Management Companies*
#200, 255, rue St. Jacques
Montréal, QC H2Y 1M6
514-845-3800
Fax: 514-845-3810
info@gticapital.com
www.gticapital.com
Ownership: Private
Year Founded: 1992
Number of Employees: 12
Assets: $100-500 million
Profile: Venture capital.
Executives:
Bernard Hamel, Chair & Sr. General Partner
Roger Jenkins, Sr. General Partner
Jean-Francois Couturier, General Partner
Jean Desjardins, Partner
François Veilleux, CFO
Joanne Bessette, Controller

Hargan-Global Ventures Inc.
Computer Methods Bldg.
4850 Keele St., 1st Fl.
Toronto, ON M3J 3K1
416-923-0660
Fax: 416-495-9750
info@harganglobal.com
www.harganglobal.com
Also Known As: Hargan Capital Inc.
Ownership: Private
Year Founded: 1997
Profile: The venture capital firm invests in early-stage entrepreneurial companies.

Executives:
Sam Ifergan, President/CEO
Leo Nochomovitz, CFO
Directors:
Michael Aron
Harry Hart
Sam Ifergan

Heartland Community Futures Development Corporation
11 - 2nd St. NE
Portage La Prairie, MB R1N 1R8
204-239-0135
Fax: 204-239-0176
877-472-7122
heartland@heartlandcfdc.com
www.heartlandcfdc.com
Ownership: Private
Number of Employees: 5
Profile: Provides business development services and community economic development services for rural Manitoba.

Executives:
Barb Kitching, General Manager

Hebrew Free Loan Association of Montréal
#202, 6525, boul Décarie
Montréal, QC H3W 3E3
514-733-7128
Fax: 514-733-3698
info@hflamtl.org
Year Founded: 1911
Number of Employees: 4
Profile: Interest-free loans to the community.

Executives:
Jack Noodelman, President
Nicky Madoff, Executive Director
Directors:
Morrie Cohen, Chair

Highwood Business Development Corporation(HBDC)
#3, 28 - 12 Ave. SE
High River, AB T1V 1T2
403-652-3700
Fax: 403-652-7022
info@hbdc.net
www.hbdc.net
Ownership: Government funded
Number of Employees: 10
Branches:
Okotoks
#200, 5 Elizabeth St.
Okotoks, AB T1S 2C1 Canada
403-995-4151
Fax: 403-995-3760

Homeguard Funding Ltd.
Also listed under: *Financial Planning; Investment Management*

83 Dawson Manor Blvd.
Newmarket, ON L3X 2H5
905-895-1777
Fax: 905-895-9073
800-225-1777
homeguard@homeguardfunding.com
www.homeguardfunding.com
Ownership: Private
Year Founded: 1983
Number of Employees: 26
Revenues: $2,400,000
Profile: Homeguard provides mortgage services in York Region & its surrounding areas. The company specializes in helping first time home buyers. It has servied over 45,000 borrowers since its establishment.

Executives:
Wayne A. Sudsbury, President; waynesudsbury@homeguardfunding.com
William R. Eves, Exec. Vice-President; billeves@homeguardfunding.com
Sheilah A. Sudsbury, Sec.-Treas.
Ralph M. Larin, Manager, Area Sales
Branches:
Bancroft
Bancroft, ON K0L 1C0
613-332-5852
877-403-6639
Paul B. Cameron, Regional Manager, Kawartha Region
Cameron
Cameron Rd., General Delivery
Cameron, ON K0M 1G0 Canada
705-359-2066
888-887-1915
Paul B. Cameron, Regional Manager, Kawartha Region
Mississauga
5659 McAdam Rd.
Mississauga, ON L4Z 1N9 Canada
905-568-9255
Ron Butler, Regional Manager, Mississauga Region
Pefferlaw
3 Quinn Rd.
Pefferlaw, ON L0E 1N0 Canada
705-437-3293
Waterloo
78 King St. North
Waterloo, ON N2J 2X4 Canada
519-746-5547
Stephen Jennings, Regional Manager, Kitchener-Waterloo

Honda Canada Finance Inc.
#400, 3650 Victoria Park Ave.
Toronto, ON M2H 3P7
416-754-2323
Fax: 416-754-2327
800-387-5399
www.honda.ca
Number of Employees: 100
Profile: Provides financing & leasing services for dealers of Honda & Acura automobiles.

Branches:
Boucherville
1750, rue Eiffel
Boucherville, QC J4B 7W1 Canada
450-641-9062
Fax: 450-641-067
800-463-6374
Richmond
#110, 13711 International Pl.
Richmond, BC V6V 2Z8 Canada
604-278-1200
Fax: 604-278-6627
800-667-6784

HSBC Capital (Canada) Inc.
PO Box 1016
#1100, 885 West Georgia St.
Vancouver, BC V6C 3E8
604-631-8088
Fax: 604-631-8073
hsbc_capital@hsbc.com
www.hsbc.ca/capital
Former Name: Wardley Canada Inc.
Ownership: Wholly owned subsidiary of HSBC Bank Canada which is wholly owned by HSBC Holdings plc of London
Year Founded: 1988
Number of Employees: 21
Executives:
David F. Mullen, CEO, Head of Private Equity, North America; 604-631-8094; dave_mullen@hsbc.ca
Simon D. Koch, CFO, Director, Merchant Banking; 604-631-8080; simon_koch@hsbc.com
Neil Johansen, Managing Director, Merchant Banking; 604-631-8095; neil_johansen@hsbc.ca
Daniel G. Jacques, Director, Merchant Banking; 604-631-8092; dan_jacques@hsbc.ca
Robert K. Withers, Director, Merchant Banking; 604-631-8090; rob_withers@hsbc.ca
Michael Berkson, Associate Director, Merchant Banking; 604-631-8082; michael_berkson@hsbc.ca
Paul Rowe, Associate Director, Merchant Banking; 604-631-8093; paul_rowe@hsbc.ca
Branches:
Toronto
70 York St., 7th Fl.
Toronto, ON M5J 1S9 Canada
416-864-2897
Fax: 416-868-0067
John Philp, Managing Director, Merchant Banking

Huron Business Development Corporation(HBDC)
PO Box 1120
138 Main St. South
Seaforth, ON N0K 1W0
519-527-0305
Fax: 519-527-2245
jniesen@smallbusinesshuron.ca
www.smallbusinesshuron.ca
Ownership: Non-profit. Community Futures Development Corporation.
Year Founded: 1993
Number of Employees: 15
Assets: $1-5 million Year End: 20050119
Revenues: Under $1 million Year End: 20050119
Profile: HBDC assists small businesses operating within Huron County, Ontario through the provision of mentoring, counselling, business planning, export development & financing services.

Executives:
Pamela Stanley, President; 519-482-9914; stanley-pam@hotmail.com
Donna Taylor, Vice-President; 519-482-9475; adtaylor@tcc.on.ca
Rick Hundey, Treasurer; 519-235-2072; jrhundey@sympatico.ca

Bonnie Lafontaine, Secretary; 519-524-6988; b.lafontaine@sympatico.ca
Paul Nichol, Manager, Economic Development; pnichol@smallbusinesshuron.ca
Jim Niesen, Manager, Business & Loans; jniesen@smallbusinesshuron.ca

Hydro-Québec CapiTech Inc.
1000, Sherbrooke ouest, 16e étage
Montréal, QC H3A 3G4
514-289-4783
Fax: 514-289-5420
hqcapitech@hydro.qc.ca
www.hqcapitech.com
Ownership: Hydro-Québec
Year Founded: 1998
Number of Employees: 18
Executives:
Jacques Simoneau, President/CEO
Robert Baril, Treasurer
Directors:
Elie Saheb, Chair
Michael M. Avedesian
Roger A. Blais
Robert Brouillette
Bernard Coupal
Armand Couture
Daniel Leclair
Lorraine Maheu
Serge Y. Piotte
Jacques Simoneau

i Trade Finance Inc.
#173, 75 Bayley St. West
Ajax, ON L1S 7K7
416-492-7773
Fax: 416-492-7749
877-734-7773
info@itfi.net
www.itfi.net
Ownership: Private
Year Founded: 1999
Executives:
Parker Gallant, President/CEO; pgallant@itfi.net
Anne Aurelius, Exec. Vice-President; aaurelius@itfi.net

Integrated Private Debt Corp.
Also listed under: *Pension & Money Management Companies*
#2200, 130 Adelaide St. West
Toronto, ON M5H 3P5
416-367-2044
Fax: 416-367-2594
probson@iamgroup.ca
www.iamgroup.com
Former Name: First Treasury Corporation
Ownership: Public. Subsidiary of Integrated Asset Management

Year Founded: 1987
Number of Employees: 15
Assets: $500m-1 billion Year End: 20041201
Stock Symbol: IAM-X
Executives:
John F.K. Robertson, President
Ben Bacigalupi, Managing Director
Donald Bangay, Managing Director
B. Frank Duffy, Managing Director
Michael LeClair, Managing Director
Philip S. Robson, Managing Director
Doug Zinkiewich, Managing Director
Nushi Kazemian, Associate Director
Vanessa B.Z. Luce, Controller
Directors:
Stephen Johnson
Victor Koloshuk
John F.K. Robertson
Branches:
Calgary
3116 - 4th St NW
Calgary, AB T2M 3A4 Canada
403-283-0152
Fax: 403-283-0165

Inter-Act Management Inc.
#5090, 3080 Yonge St.
Toronto, ON M4N 3N1
416-489-1900
Fax: 416-489-1977
www.interactmanagement.com
Former Name: Inter-Act Venture Fund Inc.
Executives:
Marc Ladouceur, Managing Director
Vic Casale, Managing Director

The Interface Group Ltd.
#245, 180 Renfrew Dr.
Markham, ON L3R 9Z2
905-475-5701
Fax: 905-475-8688
800-387-0860
ifg@interfacefinancial.com
www.interfacefinancial.com
Also Known As: The Interface Financial Group
Ownership: Private
Year Founded: 1970
Number of Employees: 7
Assets: Under $1 million
Revenues: $1-5 million
Profile: The Interface Group, an invoice discounter/factor, provides short-term working capital for small businesses ($10,000 - $1 million).

Executives:
John T. Sheehy, Chair; jsheehy@interfacefinancial.com
David T. Banfield, President; dbanfield@interfacefinancial.com
Branches:
Calgary - Edgebrook Green
48 Edgebrook Green NW
Calgary, AB T3A 4N2 Canada
403-241-9695
Daryl Turko, Franchise Owner
Calgary - Woodbrook Ct.

The Interface Group Ltd. (continued)
20 Woodbrook Ct. SW
Calgary, AB T2W 4G1 Canada
403-251-4191
Kewal Khakh, Franchise Owner
Cochrane
#203B, 205 Ross Ave.
Cochrane, AB T4C 1S9 Canada
403-932-9835
Marion Minogue, Franchise Co-Owner
Cole Harbour
PO Box 21038, Cole Harbour RPO Sta. Cole Harbour RPO
Cole Harbour, NS B2W 6B2 Canada
902-462-6361
Philip P. Emin, Franchise Owner
Edmonton
18417 - 76A Ave.
Edmonton, AB T5T 6A7 Canada
780-489-4348
Charlene Sinclair, Franchise Owner
Exeter
83 Andrew St.
Exeter, ON N0M 1S1 Canada
519-235-3622
John Hayman, Franchise Owner
Kamloops
#205, 444 Victoria St.
Kamloops, BC V2C 2A7 Canada
250-377-4996
Karl Stegemann, Franchise Owner
Lynden
PO Box 101
26 Lynden Rd.
Lynden, ON L0R 1T0 Canada
905-570-4894
John Cloke, Franchise Owner
Mississauga
5190 Shuttle Dr.
Mississauga, ON L4W 4J8 Canada
905-629-8555
David Franklin, Franchise Owner
Oakville - Maple Grove Dr.
PO Box 61051
511 Maple Grove Dr.
Oakville, ON L6J 6X0 Canada
905-338-2420
Mike Swartz, Franchise Owner
Oakville - Rambler Ct.
294 Rambler Ct.
Oakville, ON L6H 3A6 Canada
416-236-8180
Chris Ng, Franchise Owner
Parry Sound
Lake Forest Dr., RR#3
Parry Sound, ON P2A 2W9 Canada
705-342-1946
Mark Fisher, Franchise Owner
Regina
1735 Sinclair St. East
Regina, SK S4V 1G7 Canada
306-789-1081
Barry Bean, Franchise Co-Owner
Richmond
9611 Seacote Rd.
Richmond, BC V7A 4A2 Canada
604-271-8586
Timothy N. Novak, Franchise Owner
Richmond Hill
#100, 60 Laverock Ave.
Richmond Hill, ON L4C 4J6 Canada
905-883-6034
Bruce Tennant, Franchise Owner
St Catharines
#118, 210 Glendale Ave.
St Catharines, ON L2T 3Y6 Canada
905-680-9990
Nick Paoliello, Franchise Co-Owner
Surrey
3621 - 156A St.
Surrey, BC V3S 0L4 Canada
604-542-2705
James C. Sinclair, Franchise Owner
Thornhill
184 Clark Ave.
Thornhill, ON L3T 1T5 Canada
905-482-9377
Mario D'Avino, Franchise Owner
Thunder Bay
874 Tungsten St.
Thunder Bay, ON P7B 6J3 Canada
807-344-8899
Levino Tittaferrante, Franchise Owner
Toronto - Eglinton Ave.
#201, 600 Eglinton Ave. East
Toronto, ON M4P 1P3 Canada
416-932-9281
Patrick O'Reilly, Franchise Owner
Vernon
360 Northwind Dr.
Vernon, BC V1H 1X1 Canada
250-549-4839
Drew Johnson, Franchise Owner
Victoria
#333, 1900 Mayfair Dr.
Victoria, BC V8P 1P9 Canada
250-595-7494
David M. Griffiths, Franchise Owner
West Vancouver
1225 Sinclair St.
West Vancouver, BC V7V 3W3 Canada
604-925-3748
Hugh Roberts, Franchise Owner
Franchise Owners:
Toronto - Birchmount Rd.
#702, 544 Birchmount Rd.
Toronto, ON M1K 1P3 Canada
416-269-8631
Gobind Modi, Franchise Owner

Interface International
1517 Lawson Ave. West
Vancouver, BC V7V 2C8
604-922-9300
Fax: 604-922-9300
info@interfaceweb.com
www.interfaceweb.com
Executives:
David G.M. Smith, Principal

Interfinance Mortgage Merchants Inc.
#206, 85 Scarsdale Rd.
Toronto, ON M3B 2R2
416-445-4890
Fax: 416-445-7552
info@interfinance.ca
www.interfinance.ca
Ownership: Private
Year Founded: 1975
Profile: Interfinance Mortgage Merchants specializes in financing residential, commercial & investment properties. It represents numerous domestic, foreign & private lenders.
Executives:
Amar Kaushal, President
Shayam Kaushal, Vice-President
Kiran Kaushal, Sec.-Treas.

Invesco Mortgage Inc.
#400, 7015 MacLeod Trail South
Calgary, AB T2H 2K6
403-252-7882
Fax: 403-255-0435
invescomortgage@shaw.ca
www.invescomortgage.com
Year Founded: 1980
Profile: Invesco Mortgage Ltd. is a direct lender, lending on equity in real estate.
Executives:
Lee Ellison, President

Investissement Québec(IQ)/ Québec Investment
#500, 393, ch Saint-Jacques
Montréal, QC H2Y 1N9
Fax: 514-873-5786
866-870-0437
www.investquebec.com
Ownership: Public
Year Founded: 1973
Number of Employees: 360
Profile: Provides consulting and financing services to support expansion projects in Québec.
Executives:
Jacques Daoust, Chairman
Branches:
Chandler
#10A, 500, av Daigneault
Chandler, QC G0C 1K0 Canada
Drummondville
1406, rue Michaud
Drummondville, QC J2C 7V3 Canada
Gatineau
4, rue Taschereau
Gatineau, QC J8Y 2V5 Canada
Jonquière
3950, boul Harvey, 2e étage
Jonquière, QC G7X 8L6 Canada
Laval
#801, 3030, boul Le Carrefour
Laval, QC H7T 2P5 Canada
Longueuil
#310, 1010, rue Sérigny
Longueuil, QC J4K 5G7 Canada
Montréal - Côte-Vertu
#210, 3300, boul de la Côte-Vertu
Montréal, QC H4R 2B7 Canada
Montréal - Jean-Talon est
#1250, 7100, rue Jean-Talon est
Montréal, QC H1M 3S3 Canada
Québec
#500, 1200, route de l'Église
Québec, QC G1V 5A3 Canada
Rimouski
#100, 70, rue St-Germain est, 3e étage
Rimouski, QC G5L 7J9 Canada
418-727-3582
Fax: 418-727-3686
Rouyn-Noranda
170, rue Principale
Rouyn-Noranda, QC J9X 4P7 Canada
Saint-Georges
#303, 11535, 1e av
Saint-Georges, QC GSY 7H5 Canada
Sept-×les
454, av Arnaud
Sept-×les, QC G4R 3A9 Canada
Sherbrooke
#3.10, 200, rue Belvédère nord
Sherbrooke, QC J1H 4A9 Canada
Trois-Rivières
100, rue Laviolette
Trois-Rivières, QC G9A 5S9 Canada

The Investment Exchange
#103, 3553 - 31 St. NW
Calgary, AB T2L 2K7
403-299-1770
Fax: 403-208-2965
info@theinvestmentexchange.com
www.tinvex.com
Year Founded: 1986

Invis
#600, 701 Evans Ave.
Toronto, ON M9C 1A3
416-622-6363
Fax: 416-622-5300
888-468-4734
www.invis.ca
Number of Employees: 50
Executives:
Andrew Moor, President/CEO
A. Cameron Strong, CFO & Chief Privacy Officer
Fiona Campbell, Vice-President, Eastern Canada
Gord Dahlen, Vice-President, Western Canada
Offices:
Brossard
#607, 1850, Panama
Brossard, QC J4W 3C6 Canada
450-466-4066
Fax: 450-466-4699
888-243-8699
Calgary
821A - 14 St. NW
Calgary, AB T2N 2A4 Canada
403-508-7800
Fax: 403-508-7807
Dartmouth

#307, 73 Tacoma Dr.
Dartmouth, NS B2W 3Y6 Canada
902-435-6140
Fax: 902-462-7452
800-536-8594
Langley
#200, 20434 - 64th Ave.
Langley, BC V2Y 1N5 Canada
604-532-4700
Fax: 604-532-4719
866-844-6847

IPS Industrial Promotion Services Ltd.
Also listed under: *Holding & Other Investment Companies*
#720, 60 Columbia Way
Markham, ON L3R 0C9
905-475-9400
Fax: 905-475-5003
info@ipscanada.com
www.ipscanada.com
Also Known As: IPS Canada
Ownership: Private. Foreign. IPS, Geneva, Switzerland.
Year Founded: 1979
Profile: Part of the Aga Khan Fund for Economic Development, IPS Canada is a venture capital & investment company. It is engaged in promoting, developing, supporting & managing industrial & related projects in North America.

Executives:
Nizar Alibhai, President

Island Savings Credit Union
Also listed under: *Credit Unions/Caisses Populaires*
#300, 499 Canada Ave.
Duncan, BC V9L 1T7
250-748-4728
Fax: 250-748-8831
info@iscu.com
www.iscu.com
Ownership: Member-owned
Year Founded: 1951
Number of Employees: 300
Assets: $500m-1 billion
Executives:
Pam Marchant, CEO
Directors:
Sheila Service, Chair
Branches:
Brentwood Bay
#1, 7103 West Saanich Rd.
Brentwood Bay, BC V8M 1R1 Canada
250-544-4041
Fax: 250-544-0656
Cedar
Cedar Village Sq.
1830 Cedar Rd.
Cedar, BC V9X 1H9 Canada
250-722-7073
Fax: 250-722-7348
Chemainus
PO Box 120
#1, 2592 Legion St.
Chemainus, BC V0R 1K0 Canada
250-246-3273
Fax: 250-246-2821
Duncan
89 Evans Ave.
Duncan, BC V9L 1P5 Canada
250-746-4181
Fax: 250-746-4175
Ladysmith
370 Trans Canada Hwy., #A, RR#2
Ladysmith, BC V0R 2E0 Canada
250-245-0456
Fax: 250-245-5429
Lake Cowichan
PO Box 889
38 King George St. North
Lake Cowichan, BC V0R 2G0 Canada
250-749-6631
Fax: 250-749-3260
Mill Bay
#38, 2720 Mill Bay Rd.
Mill Bay, BC V0R 2P0 Canada
250-743-5534
Fax: 250-743-7500
Nanaimo
Woodgrove Ctr.
#97, 6631 Island Hwy. North
Nanaimo, BC V9T 4T7 Canada
250-390-7070
Fax: 250-390-3417
Salt Spring Island
PO Box 350
124 McPhillips St.
Salt Spring Island, BC V8K 2T5 Canada
250-537-5587
Fax: 250-537-4623
Shawnigan Lake
PO Box 165
1765 Shawnigan-Mill Bay Rd.
Shawnigan Lake, BC V0R 2W0 Canada
250-743-5395
Fax: 250-743-0710
Victoria - Douglas
Mayfair Shopping Centre
#189, 3147 Douglas St.
Victoria, BC V8Z 6E3 Canada
250-358-4476
Fax: 250-384-3398
Victoria - Douglas & Broughton
933 Douglas St.
Victoria, BC V8W 2C2 Canada
250-385-4728
Fax: 250-360-1461
Victoria - Jacklin
2917 Jacklin Rd.
Victoria, BC V9B 3Y6 Canada
250-474-7262
Fax: 250-474-7219

J.L. Albright Venture Partners(JLAVP)
Canada Trust Tower, BCE Place
PO Box 215
#4440, 161 Bay St.
Toronto, ON M5J 2S1
416-367-2440
Fax: 416-367-4604
info@jlaventures.com
www.jlaventures.com
Ownership: Private
Year Founded: 1996
Number of Employees: 7
Profile: Venture capital.

Partners:
John Albright
Tawfia Arafat
Stuart Lombard
Rick Segal

JD Factors Corporation/ Corporation D'Affacturage JD
#110, 5975 Whittle Rd.
Mississauga, ON L4Z 3N1
905-501-5000
Fax: 905-501-0395
800-263-0664
www.jdfactors.com
Former Name: Riviera Finance Inc.
Ownership: Private
Year Founded: 1985
Number of Employees: 18
Profile: The company provides factoring & commercial finance.

Executives:
Tina Capobianco, Manager

Jefferson Partners Capital Limited
260 Queen St. West, 4th Fl.
Toronto, ON M5V 1Z8
416-367-1533
Fax: 416-367-5827
info@jefferson.com
www.jefferson.com
Ownership: Private
Year Founded: 1993
Number of Employees: 9
Profile: Jefferson Partners is a venture capital organization that invests in emerging private & public companies.

Executives:
Jonathan Black, Venture Partner
David Folk
Penny Hung
Jack Kiervin
Byron Lee
Ian Locke
Lynda Ting

Kee West Financial Group Inc.
Also listed under: *Holding & Other Investment Companies*
#502, 5920 MacLeod Trail South
Calgary, AB T2H 0K2
403-255-4643
Fax: 403-255-6892
www.keewestfinancial.com
Ownership: Private. Division of Kee West Financial Group Inc.
Year Founded: 1978
Number of Employees: 5
Profile: The mortgage banking company provides financing services in Canada, the United States & Mexico. It specializes in commercial real estate lending. Services also include private residential mortgage financing, mortgage transfers & refinances.

Executives:
Lorne Keetbaas, President

Kempenfelt Capital Inc.
#5, 301 Bryne Dr.
Barrie, ON L4N 8V4
705-725-0070
Fax: 705-725-9915
877-725-0070
info@kempcap.com
www.kempcap.com
Year Founded: 1996
Number of Employees: 7
Profile: Leasing, commercial merger & acquisition consulting are offered.

Executives:
Ken Bailey, President; kbailey@kempcap.com

Key Equipment Finance
#600, 1122 International Blvd.
Burlington, ON L7L 6Z8
905-319-8000
Fax: 905-319-0222
888-968-2539
www.kefonline.com
Former Name: Leasetec Canada Ltd.
Ownership: Branch of Key Equipment Finance, Superior, CO USA.
Year Founded: 1979
Number of Employees: 40
Profile: The affiliate of KeyCorp partners with technology & capital asset equipment vendors. It provides lease financing to business customers & financing solutions related to equipment acquisitions to corporate & commercial clients.

Executives:
John Alfieri, Vice-President, Corporate Accounts
Shaun Danton, Vice-President, Syndications
David G. Timms, Vice-President, Division Counsel
Glen Wilson, Vice-President, Sales
Martin Davies, Sr. Account Executive, Vendor Financing
Casey Hrabchuk, Account Executive, Commercial Financing
Branches:
Calgary
Bow Valley Square II
#600, 205 - 5th Ave. SW
Calgary, AB T2P 2V7 Canada
403-538-5445
Casey Hrabchuk, Account Executive, Commercial Financing

Kingsway Investments Ltd.
#1510, 105 Main St. East
Hamilton, ON L8N 1G6
905-526-6300
Fax: 905-526-7200
888-606-0200
Ownership: Private
Year Founded: 1992
Number of Employees: 2
Executives:
Ray Khanna, President

Kitayan Community Futures Development Corporation
PO Box 442
Island Lake, MB R0B 0T0

Kitayan Community Futures Development Corporation (continued)
204-456-2072
Fax: 204-456-2596
800-898-1974
dbone@kitayan.ca
www.kitayan.ca
Year Founded: 1994
Executives:
Daryl Bone, General Manager
Branches:
Winnipeg
#345, 260 St. Mary Ave.
Winnipeg, MB R3C 0M6 Canada
204-982-2170
Fax: 204-943-3412

Kopas & Burritt Financial Agents Limited
#1111, 30 St. Clair Ave. West
Toronto, ON M4V 3A1
416-975-1161
Fax: 416-975-0422
Ownership: Private
Year Founded: 1929
Profile: The company's activities include mortgages.

Lac La Biche Regional Community Development Corporation
Community Futures Centre
PO Box 2188
10106 - 102 Ave.
Lac La Biche, AB T2A 2C0
780-623-2662
Fax: 780-623-2671
877-623-9696
rcdc@telusplanet.net
rcdc-rerc.com
Ownership: Private
Year Founded: 1986
Number of Employees: 6
Assets: $1-5 million
Revenues: Under $1 million

Lakeland Community Development Corporation
PO Box 8114
#201, 5006 - 50 Ave.
Bonnyville, AB T9N 2J4
780-826-3858
Fax: 780-826-7330
info@lcdc.ab.ca
www.lcdc.ab.ca
Year Founded: 1990
Number of Employees: 4
Profile: Assists with small and medium-sized business development and community economic development.
Executives:
Phyllis Maki, General Manager

Lambridge Capital Partners Inc.
Sun Life Place
#1870, 10123 - 99th St.
Edmonton, AB T5J 3H1
780-424-3570
Fax: 780-443-4283
slamphier@lcpcapital.com
www.lcpcapital.com
Executives:
Stephen J. Lamphier, CEO
Brian Taitinger, Managing Director
Paul A. Chalifoux, Director, Infrastructure Management

Lamont-Two Hills Business Development Corporation
PO Box 547
5109 - 51 St.
Two Hills, AB T0B 4K0
780-657-3512
Fax: 780-657-2359
lthbdc@telusplanet.net
www.centraleastalberta.com
Ownership: Non-profit
Year Founded: 1988
Number of Employees: 8
Executives:
Bernice Sambor, Manager

Latitude Partners Inc.
223 Avenue Rd.
Toronto, ON M5R 2J3
416-513-9090
Fax: 416-513-9339
info@latitudepartners.com
www.latitudepartners.com
Profile: Private equity and strategic advisory firm focused on the technology sector.
Executives:
Tom Eisenhauer, Managing Partner
Don Bent, Partner & CFO
Kevin Clay, Partner

League Savings & Mortgage Company
PO Box 8900
6074 Lady Hammond Rd.
Halifax, NS B3K 5M5
902-453-4220
Fax: 902-454-3116
800-668-2879
lsmhalifax@lsm.ca
www.lsm.ca
Ownership: Parent: Credit Union Central of Nova Scotia
Year Founded: 1966
Number of Employees: 55
Profile: Investment & loan company.
Executives:
Bernie O'Neil, President/CEO
Branches:
Moncton
PO Box 29103
1633 Mountain Rd.
Moncton, NB E1G 4R3 Canada
506-384-7000
Fax: 506-384-7077
800-363-7909
lsmmoncton@lsm.ca
Sydney
PO Box 668
235 Charlotte St.
Sydney, NS B1P 6H7 Canada
902-539-8222
Fax: 902-539-8630
800-285-5641
lsmsydney@lsm.ca

Leasebank Capital Corporation
Briarwood Business Park
#200, 410 North Service Rd. East
Oakville, ON L6H 5R2
905-338-3954
Fax: 905-248-3292
877-909-8007
info@leasebank.com
www.leasebank.com
Year Founded: 1995
Executives:
Thomas A. Howse, Managing Director

Lesser Slave Lake Community Development Corporation
PO Box 2100
Slave Lake, AB T0G 2A0
780-849-3232
Fax: 780-849-3360
800-622-7128
cdc1@telusplanet.net
www.lslcdcorp.ab.ca
Ownership: Non profit.
Year Founded: 1986
Number of Employees: 6
Assets: $1-5 million Year End: 20051201
Revenues: Under $1 million Year End: 20051201
Profile: Corporation is affiliated with Community Futures Organizations throughout Canada.
Executives:
Terry Kurucz, Executive Director

Lethbridge & District Business Development Centre Association
2626 South Parkside Dr.
Lethbridge, AB T1K 0C4
403-320-6044
Fax: 403-327-8476
email@ldbdca.com
www.ldbdca.com
Number of Employees: 5

Liquid Capital Corp.
#400, 5734 Yonge St.
Toronto, ON M2M 4E7
416-222-5599
Fax: 416-222-0166
877-228-0800
info@liquidcapitalcorp.com
www.liquidcapitalcorp.com
Ownership: Private
Year Founded: 1999
Assets: $1-5 million
Revenues: $1-5 million
Executives:
Sol Roter, President
Brian Bimbaum, Vice-President
Barnett Gordon, Secretary
Licensees:
Liquid Capital Advantage Corp.
Medicine Hat, AB Canada
403-502-3326
Fax: 403-526-4001
Dean Weinkauf
Liquid Capital Affiliates Ltd.
252 Barrett Dr.
Red Deer, AB T4R 1J4 Canada
403-314-1118
dulsifer@liquidcapitalcorp.com
Don Ulsifer
Liquid Capital Alberta Corp.
25 Ashmore Close
Red Deer, AB T4R 2R7 Canada
403-342-0006
Fax: 403-342-0552
gangl@liquidcapitalcorp.com
Travis Gangl
Liquid Capital Associates
#2, 3210 Dufferin St.
Toronto, ON M6A 2T1 Canada
416-781-9100
Fax: 416-922-6552
fischer@liquidcapitalcorp.com
Tom Fischer
Liquid Capital Central Corp.
#1105, 141 Adelaide St. West
Toronto, ON M5H 3L5 Canada
416-214-2653
Fax: 416-214-0054
pscott@trinitywood.com
Peter Scott
Liquid Capital Commerce Inc.
#403, 151 Robinson St.
Oakville, ON L6J 7N3 Canada
905-844-4531
Fax: 905-844-6804
haley@liquidcapitalcorp.com
Nick Haley
Liquid Capital Funding Corp.
30 The Masters Dr.
Ottawa, ON K1V 9Y4 Canada
613-224-5926
877-375-4120
sproule@liquidcapitalcorp.com
Rob Sproule
Liquid Capital Investments Corp.
10 Headdon Gate, #5
Richmond Hill, ON L4C 8Z3 Canada
905-770-3874
Fax: 905-508-7704
lblack@liquidcapitalcorp.com
Lenny Black
Liquid Capital LAeRS PLC
PO Box 4703, Main Sta. Main
Vancouver, BC V6B 4A4 Canada
604-484-6017
866-432-3539
laersplc@liquidcapitalcorp.com
Liquid Capital Metro Inc.
38 - 22146 South Cooking Lake Rd.
Sherwood Park, AB T8E 1G9 Canada
780-922-3643
Fax: 780-922-8370
rmetro@lcfactors.com
Ron Metro
Liquid Capital Newfoundland

57 Kinder Dr.
Paradise, NL A1L 2G9 Canada
709-781-2274
Fax: 709-781-2275
dallen@liquidcapitalcorp.com
Don Allen

Liquid Capital North
#1, 1191 Lansing Ave.
Sudbury, ON P3A 4C4 Canada
705-521-1313
Fax: 705-523-6295
fitzgerald@liquidcapitalcorp.com
Kevin Fitzgerald

Liquid Capital Pacific Corp.
14247 - 86 Ave.
Surrey, BC V3W 0S6 Canada
604-591-5252
Fax: 604-591-8191
877-326-3332
deffa@liquidcapitalcorp.com
Dan A. Effa

Liquid Capital Partners Ltd.
44 Laura Lee Lane
Lower Sackville, NS B4C 4E3 Canada
902-252-3999
Fax: 902-252-2998
msaunders@liquidcapitalcorp.com
Mark Saunders

Liquid Capital Prairie Corp.
#6, 300 Confederation Dr.
Saskatoon, SK S7L 4R6 Canada
306-668-2358
Fax: 306-668-2356
watts@liquidcapitalcorp.com
Wayne Watts

Liquid Capital Resource Corp.
4 Rochon Way
Kanata, ON K2W 1A2 Canada
613-839-7906
Fax: 613-839-7907
milne@liquidcapitalcorp.com
Peter Milne

Liquid Capital Rockyview Inc.
132 Cougarstone Sq. SW
Calgary, AB T3H 5J4 Canada
403-503-1233
Fax: 403-503-1235
jperdomo@liquidcapitalcorp.com
Judy Perdomo

Liquid Capital Smart Solutions Ltd.
63 Midlake Pl. SE
Calgary, AB T2X 1J2 Canada
403-201-0041
Fax: 403-451-1532
smart@liquidcapitalcorp.com
Jack Smart

Liquid Capital Solutions Inc.
#257, 3219 Yonge St.
Toronto, ON M4N 2L3 Canada
905-737-5969
Fax: 905-737-4120
arbour@liquidcapitalcorp.com
Anne Arbour

Liquid Capital Vanguard Corp.
#400, 5734 Yonge St.
Toronto, ON M2M 4E7 Canada
416-222-5599
Fax: 416-222-0166
gordon@liquidcapitalcorp.com
Barnett Gordon

Liquid Capital West Ltd.
4356 - 37B Ave.
Edmonton, AB T6L 7B4 Canada
780-450-3519
Fax: 780-450-3667
buchner@liquidcapitalcorp.com
Glen Buchner

Liquid Capital West Ontario Ltd.
MBE
#124, 525 Highland Rd. West
Kitchener, ON N2M 5P4 Canada
519-749-8844
Fax: 519-576-7102
rayburn@liquidcapitalcorp.com
John Rayburn

Martin Charney Corp.
#400, 5734 Yonge St.
Toronto, ON M2M 4E7 Canada
905-709-7518
Fax: 905-709-3307
martincharney@rogers.com
Martin Charney

Western Liquid Capital
3933 Parkway Dr.
Vancouver, BC V6L 3C9 Canada
604-738-1940
Fax: 604-648-9950
friedland@liquidcapitalcorp.com
Steve Friedland

Lloydminister Region Community Futures Development Corporation

#5, 4010 - 50 Ave.
Lloydminster, AB T9V 1B2
780-875-5458
Fax: 780-875-8026
comfutur@telusplanet.net
www.lloydcfdc.ca

London Acceptance Corporation

3205 Canterbury Dr.
Surrey, BC V3S 0J4
604-542-4226
Fax: 604-542-9226
info@londonacceptance.com
www.londonacceptance.com
Ownership: Private
Year Founded: 1978
Number of Employees: 4
Profile: London Acceptance Corporation is a home equity mortgage lender.

Executives:
Robert E. Lindley, President

Lozinski Financial Services Ltd.

Bell Mews Plaza
#238, 39 Robertson Rd.
Ottawa, ON K2H 8R2
613-721-6843
Fax: 613-596-6445
jlozinski@bellnet.ca
www.lozinski.com
Ownership: Private
Year Founded: 1989
Number of Employees: 6
Profile: Mortgage broker.

Executives:
Armand Legault; alegault@sympatico.ca
John Lozinski
Donna Mahoney; donna.mahoney@sympatico.ca
Karen McLeish; karen.mcleish@lozinski.com
Leslie Porowski; leslie.porowski@lozinski.com

Mackenzie Economic Development Corp.

PO Box 210
100065-100 St.
High Level, AB T0H 1Z0
780-926-4233
Fax: 780-926-2162
888-922-4233
info@medc.ab.ca
www.medc.ab.ca
Year Founded: 1989
Number of Employees: 5
Assets: $1-5 million
Revenues: Under $1 million
Profile: The coporation is a not-for-profit community futures organization.

Executives:
Mike Osborn, General Manager
Tony Walker, Business Analyst

Mandate National Mortgage Corporation

#505, 1195 West Broadway
Vancouver, BC V6H 3X5
604-731-2899
Fax: 604-734-5546
866-432-4949
mandate@telus.net
Ownership: Public
Year Founded: 1939
Number of Employees: 4
Assets: $10-50 million Year End: 20041231
Revenues: $1-5 million Year End: 20041231
Profile: The mortgage investment company has a portfolio of residential & other mortgages which is managed by Mandate Management Corporation.

Executives:
Alan E.R. Long, President/CEO
Directors:
Richard W. Gasten, Secretary
John LaVan
Alan E.R. Long
Andrew H. McLaren
Rob Parrish
Douglas Wark
Mandate:
Mortgage Fund
RRSP Eligible; Inception Year: 0;

Manitoba Agricultural Services Corporation - Insurance Corporate Office(MASC)

Also listed under: *Federal & Provincial*
#400, 50 - 24th St. NW
Portage La Prairie, MB R1N 3V9
204-239-3499
Fax: 204-239-3401
mailbox@masc.mb.ca
www.masc.mb.ca
Former Name: Manitoba Crop Insurance Corporation; Manitoba Agricultural Credit Corporation
Ownership: Crown corporation.
Year Founded: 1960
Number of Employees: 0
Profile: In 2005, the Manitoba Agricultural Credit Corporation & the Manitoba Crop Insurance Corporation merged to create the Manitoba Agricultural Services Corporation. The corporation offers the following insurance programs: production, forage, hail, fall frost, wildlife damage compensation, & young farmer crop plan credit.

Executives:
Neil Hamilton, President/CEO
Directors:
John Plohman, Chair
Walter Kolisnyk, Vice-Chair
Frieda Krpan, Vice-Chair
Anders Bruun
Frank Fiarchuk
Wilfred Harder
Carol Masse
Harry Sotas
Sandy Yanick
Branches:

Altona
PO Box 1209
67 - 2nd St. NE
Altona, MB R0G 0B0 Canada
204-324-2800
Fax: 204-324-2803
altona.insurance@masc.mb.ca

Beausejour
Provincial Government Building
PO Box 50
Beausejour, MB R0E 0C0 Canada
204-268-6001
Fax: 204-268-6060
beausejour.insurance@masc.mb.ca

Birtle
PO Box 39
726 Main St.
Birtle, MB R0M 0C0 Canada
204-842-7700
Fax: 204-824-7705
birtle.insurance@masc.mb.ca

Carman
PO Box 490
65 - 3rd Ave. NE
Carman, MB R0G 0J0 Canada
204-745-5600
Fax: 204-745-5605
carman.insurance@masc.mb.ca

Dauphin
Provincial Government Building
27 - 2nd Ave. SW
Dauphin, MB R7N 3E5 Canada

NON-DEPOSITORY INSTITUTIONS

Manitoba Agricultural Services Corporation - Insurance Corporate Office(MASC) (continued)

204-622-2017
Fax: 204-622-2076
dauphin.insurance@masc.mb.ca

Deloraine
PO Box 529
101 Finlay Ave. East
Deloraine, MB R0M 0M0 Canada
204-747-2050
Fax: 204-747-2889
deloraine.insurance@masc.mb.ca

Fisher Branch
PO Box 359
Fisher Branch, MB R0C 0Z0 Canada
204-372-6619
Fax: 204-372-6554
fisher.insurance@masc.mb.ca

Glenboro
PO Box 250
103 Broadway St.
Glenboro, MB R0K 0X0 Canada
204-827-8870
Fax: 204-827-8875
glenboro.insurance@masc.mb.ca

Grandview
PO Box 236
221 Roland Ave.
Grandview, MB R0L 0Y0 Canada
204-546-5010
Fax: 204-546-5015
grandview.insurance@masc.mb.ca

Hamiota
PO Box 50
221 Elm St.
Hamiota, MB R0M 0T0 Canada
204-764-3000
Fax: 204-764-3014
hamiota.insurance@masc.mb.ca

Neepawa
PO Box 1179
41 Main St. East
Neepawa, MB R0J 1H0 Canada
204-476-7050
Fax: 204-476-7094
neepawa.insurance@masc.mb.ca

Portage La Prairie
#200, 50 - 24th St. NW
Portage La Prairie, MB R1N 3V7 Canada
204-239-3499
Fax: 204-239-3401
portage.insurance@masc.mb.ca

Sanford
PO Box 7
8 Main St.
Sanford, MB R0G 2J0 Canada
204-736-5010
Fax: 204-736-5015
sanford.insurance@masc.mb.ca

Somerset
PO Box 190
279 Carlton St.
Somerset, MB R0G 2L0 Canada
204-744-4062
Fax: 204-744-4060
somerset.insurance@mascmb.ca

Souris
PO Box 610
95 - 1st St. North
Souris, MB R0K 2C0 Canada
204-483-5060
Fax: 204-483-5065
souris.insurance@masc.mb.ca

St Pierre Jolys
PO Box 249
466 Sabourin St. South
St Pierre Jolys, MB R0A 1V0 Canada
204-433-7298
Fax: 204-433-3282
stpierre.insurance@masc.mb.ca

Stonewall
PO Box 277
383 Main St.
Stonewall, MB R0C 2Z0 Canada
204-467-4710
Fax: 204-467-4715
stonewall.insurance@masc.mb.ca

Swan River
PO Box 1108
120 - 6th Ave. North
Swan River, MB R0L 1Z0 Canada
204-734-9326
Fax: 204-734-2685
swan.insurance@masc.mb.ca

Virden
PO Box 1570
247 Wellington St. West
Virden, MB R0M 2C0 Canada
204-748-4280
Fax: 204-748-4284
virden.insurance@masc.mb.ca

Manitoba Agricultural Services Corporation - Lending Corporate Office(MASC)

#100, 1525 First St. South
Brandon, MB R7A 7A1
204-726-6850
Fax: 204-726-6849
mailbox@masc.mb.ca
www.masc.mb.ca

Former Name: Manitoba Agricultural Credit Corporation; Manitoba Crop Insurance Corporation
Ownership: Crown corporation.
Year Founded: 1960
Profile: In 2005, the Manitoba Agricultural Credit Corporation & the Manitoba Crop Insurance Corporation merged to create the Manitoba Agricultural Services Corporation. To assist Manitoba rural entrepreneurs & agricultural producers, direct lending & loan guarantee programs are offered. Programs include the following: direct lending, young farmer rebate, stocker loans, comprehensive refinancing, & BSE recovery loan.

Branches:

Arborg
PO Box 2000
317 River Rd.
Arborg, MB ROC OAO
204-376-3305
Fax: 204-376-3311
arborg.lending@masc.mb.ca

Ashern
PO Box 260
43 Railway Ave.
Ashern, MB ROC OEO
204-768-2686
ashern.lending@masc.mb.ca

Beausejour
PO Box 50
20 - 1st St. South
Beausejour, MB ROE OCO
204-268-6016
Fax: 204-268-6060
beausejour.lending@masc.mb.ca

Brandon
#100, 1525 First St. South
Brandon, MB R7A 7A1
204-726-6018
Fax: 204-726-6849
brandon.lending@masc.mb.ca

Carman
PO Box 758
65 - 3rd Ave. NE
Carman, MB R0G 0J0
204-745-5621
Fax: 204-745-5605
carman.lending@masc.mb.ca

Dauphin
27 - 2nd Ave. SW
Dauphin, MB R7N 3E5
204-622-2016
Fax: 204-622-2076
dauphin.lending@masc.mb.ca

Killarney
PO Box 190
411 Broadway Ave.
Killarney, MB ROK 1GO
204-523-5270
Fax: 204-523-5272
killarney.lending@masc.mb.ca

Lundar
PO Box 40
9 Main St.
Lundar, MB ROC 1Y0
204-762-5649
lundar.lending@masc.mb.ca

Melita
PO Box 609
139 Main St.
Melita, MB ROM 1L0
204-522-3443
Fax: 204-522-8054
melita.lending@masc.mb.ca

Morris
PO Box 100
229 Main St. South
Morris, MB ROG 1K0
204-746-7506
Fax: 204-746-2932
morris.lending@masc.mb.ca

Neepawa
PO Box 550
41 Main St. East
Neepawa, MB ROJ 1H0
204-476-7026
Fax: 204-476-7094
neepawa.lending@masc.mb.ca

Portage La Prairie
#200, 50 - 24th St. NW
Portage La Prairie, MB R1N 3V7
204-239-3357
Fax: 204-239-3401
portage.lending@masc.mb.ca

Roblin
PO Box 820
117 - 2nd Ave. NW
Roblin, MB ROL 1P0
204-937-6470
Fax: 204-937-6479
roblin.lending@masc.mb.ca

Shoal Lake
Burlington Building
PO Box 130
4th Ave.
Shoal Lake, MB ROJ 1Z0
204-759-4064
Fax: 204-759-4069
shoal.lending@masc.mb.ca

St Pierre Jolys
PO Box 249
466 Sabourin St. South
St Pierre Jolys, MB ROA 1V0
204-433-7298
Fax: 204-433-3282
stpierre.lending@masc.mb.ca

Steinbach
PO Box 760
284 Reimer Ave.
Steinbach, MB R5G 1M6
204-346-6092
Fax: 204-326-4309
steinbach.lending@masc.mb.ca

Stonewall
293 Main St.
Stonewall, MB ROC 2Z0
204-467-8391
stonewall.lending@masc.mb.ca

Swan River
PO Box 1138
120 - 6th Ave. North
Swan River, MB ROL 1Z0
204-734-3172
Fax: 204-734-5271
swan.lending@masc.mb.ca

Teulon
PO Box 70
77 Main St.
Teulon, MB ROC 3BO
204-886-4412
Fax: 204-886-4415
teulon.lending@masc.mb.ca

Virden
PO Box 580
247 Wellington St. West
Virden, MB ROM 2C0
204-748-4779
Fax: 204-748-4775
virden.lending@masc.mb.ca

Manvest Inc.
PO Box 2510, M Stn. M
#1600, 530 - 8th Ave. SW
Calgary, AB T2P 3M7
403-231-7650
Fax: 403-231-7688
info@manvest.com
www.manvest.com
Year Founded: 1978
Profile: Private equity investment company

Executives:
William P. Robinson, President
Tim Heavenor, Vice-President
Troy Pearce, Vice-President

Maple Financial Group Inc.
Also listed under: *Financial Planning*
PO Box 328
#3500, 79 Wellington St. West
Toronto, ON M5K 1K7
416-350-8200
Fax: 416-350-8222
info@maplefinancial.com
www.maplefinancial.com
Ownership: Private
Year Founded: 1986
Number of Employees: 400
Assets: $19,000,000,000
Directors:
Bill Fung, Chair
Tom Higgins
Neil Petroff
Simon Ruddick
Jean Turmel
Affiliated Companies:
Maple Bank GmbH
Maple Securities Canada Ltd.
Maple Trade Finance Inc.

Maple Trade Finance Inc.
#701, 5475 Spring Garden Rd.
Halifax, NS B3J 3T2
902-444-5566
Fax: 902-860-2386
info@MapleTradeFinance.ca
www.mapletradefinance.ca

MCAN Mortgage Corporation
Also listed under: *Financial Planning*
#400, 200 King St. West
Toronto, ON M5H 3T4
416-591-5214
Fax: 416-598-4142
800-387-4405
mcanexecutive@mcanmortgage.com
www.mcanmortgage.com
Former Name: MCAP Inc.; MTC Mortgage Investment Corporation
Ownership: Public.
Year Founded: 1991
Number of Employees: 12
Assets: $100-500 million Year End: 20051231
Revenues: $10-50 million Year End: 20051231
Stock Symbol: MKP
Profile: MCAN Mortgage is a mortgage investment corporation.

Executives:
Blaine Welch, President/CEO; 416-591-2726; bwelch@mcanmortgage.com
Michael Misener, Vice-President, Investments; 416-591-5205; mmisener@mcanmortgage.com
Tammy Oldenburg, Vice-President/CFO; 416-847-3542; toldenberg@mcanmortgage.com
Kevin Dwarte, Asst. Vice-President, Investments, Privacy Officer, Chief Anti-Money Laudering Officer, Business Contintuity/Disaster Recovery Coordinator; 416-591-2721; kdwarte@mcanmortgage.com
Derek Sutherland, Asst. Vice-President, Chief Compleance Officer, Risk Officer & Treasurer; 416-591-5535; dsutherland@mcanmortgage.com
John Tyas, Controller; 416-847-3489; jtyas@mcanmortgage.com
Sylvia Pinto, Corporate Secretary; 416-591-5214; spinto@mcanmortgage.com
Directors:
Ian Sutherland, Chair; 705-835-1542
David G. Broadhurst; 416-350-8228
Raymond Doré; 416-591-2713
Brian Johnson; 306-546-8008
David MacIntosh; 519-725-7537
Derek Norton; 416-591-2746
Jean Pinard; 450-538-3268
Robert A. Stuebing; 416-591-2712
Blaine Welch; 416-591-2726

MCAP Financial Corporation
#400, 200 King St. West
Toronto, ON M5H 3T4
416-598-2665
Fax: 416-598-7837
800-387-4405
www.mcap.com
Ownership: Private
Year Founded: 1997
Number of Employees: 87
Assets: $10-50 million
Revenues: $10-50 million
Profile: MCAP is a major provider of mortgage management services for borrowers & corporate investors. It lends to the commercial & construction mortgage markets of Canada. The company owns MCAP Securities Inc., which pools, scrutinizes & syndicates mortgage investments, & MTC Leasing Inc.

Executives:
Raymond Doré, Chair/CEO
Steve Marker, President/COO
Derek Norton, Sr. Vice-President
Blaine Welch, Sr. Vice-President
Lorne S. Jenkins, Vice-President/CFO
Susan R. Doré, Secretary
Affiliated Companies:
MCAP Service Corporation

MCAP Service Corporation
PO Box 351, C Stn. C
Kitchener, ON N2G 3Y9
519-743-8773
Fax: 519-743-2677
800-922-0220
service@mcap.com
www.mcap.com
Ownership: Private
Year Founded: 1988
Number of Employees: 320
Assets: $10-100 billion
Revenues: $50-100 million
Executives:
Derek Norton, CEO; 416-598-2665; derek.norton@mcap.com
Steven Maker, President/COO; 416-598-2665; steve.maker@mcap.com
Jeff Armstrong, Vice-President, Residential Credit; 416-598-2665; jeff.armstrong@mcap.com
Gordon Herridge, Vice-President/CFO & Corporate Secretary, Executive; 416-588-2665; gord.herridge@mcap.com
Robert May, Vice-President, Technology Architecture; 519-743-8773; bob.may@mcap.com
Cheryl Preston, Vice-President, National Servicing; 519-743-8773; cheryl.preston@mcap.com
Jack Shapiro, Vice-President, Marketing & Communication; 416-598-2665; jack.shapiro@mcap.com
John Thompson, Vice-President, Product Development; 416-598-2665; john.thompson@mcap.com
Directors:
Cindy Brooks; 519-888-2797
Robert Floyd; 519-888-3429
Gail Kassie; 905-764-0254
Derek Norton; 416-598-2665
Robert Sadokierski; 905-770-7883
Branches:
Edmonton
#1312, 10235 - 101 St.
Edmonton, AB T5J 3J8 Canada
780-414-0911
Fax: 780-429-1652
800-265-2624

Halifax
#522, 2000 Barrington St.
Halifax, NS B3J 3K1 Canada
902-422-1920
Fax: 902-423-2410
800-310-8984

Kitchener
#200, 101 Frederick St.
Kitchener, ON N2H 6R2 Canada
519-743-8773
Fax: 519-743-2677
Montréal
#1510, 1550 Metcalf St.
Montréal, QC H3A 1X6 Canada
514-282-8038
Fax: 514-849-9264
800-363-1655
Toronto
#400, 200 King St. West.
Toronto, ON M5H 3T4 Canada
416-598-2665
Fax: 416-598-7837

McKenna Gale Capital Inc.
Also listed under: *Pension & Money Management Companies*
#1220, 145 King St. West
Toronto, ON M5H 1J8
416-364-8884
Fax: 416-364-8444
info@mckennagale.com
www.mckennagale.com
Executives:
Robert Gale, Managing Director; bgale@mckennagale.com
Kevin McKenna, Managing Director; kmckenna@mckennagale.com
Stephen Stewart, Managing Director; sstewart@mckennagale.com
Gary Wade, Managing Director
T. Craig Ferguson, Principal; cferguson@mckennagale.com
Jeffrey A. Sujitno, Principal; jsujitno@mckennagale.com
Mark A. Shulgan, Vice-President; mshulgan@mckennagale.com

MDS Capital Corporation(MDSCC)
Also listed under: *Pension & Money Management Companies*
100 International Blvd.
Toronto, ON M9W 6J6
416-675-7661
Fax: 416-213-4232
info@mdscapital.com
www.mdscapital.com
Ownership: Private.
Year Founded: 1988
Number of Employees: 25
Assets: $100-500 million
Revenues: $10-50 million
Profile: The venture capital company supplies development capital for emerging health & life sciences companies with innovative technologies. In addition to its Canadian locations, MDS Capital has two branches in the USA. The Boston/Cambridge office is situated at Suite 1800, 245 First St., Cambridge MA, 02142. The second American office is located at Suite 315, 435 Tasso St., Palo Alto, CA, 94301-1552.

Executives:
Peter van der Velden, CEO
Stephen L. Cummings, Chief Financial Officer
Michael Callaghan, Managing Director
Richard Lockie, Managing Director
Brian Underdown, Managing Director
Directors:
Jim Garner, Chair
Peter M. de Auer
Peter Brent
Richard W. Johnston
James G. Oborne
R. Anthony Pullen
Peter van der Velden
Branches:
Montréal
#502, 1550 rue Metcalfe
Montréal, QC H3A 1X6 Canada
514-844-3637
Fax: 514-844-5607
Daniel Hetu, Manager
Toronto
#343, 20 Bay St., 11th Fl.
Toronto, ON M5J 2N8 Canada
647-435-9376
Peter van der Velden, CEO

Mercantile Bancorp Limited
Also listed under: *Holding & Other Investment Companies*

Mercantile Bancorp Limited (continued)
#1508, 999 West Hastings St.
Vancouver, BC V6C 2W2
604-685-5765
Fax: 604-685-2755
www.mercantilebancorp.com
Year Founded: 1989
Profile: The merchant investor invests in & assists in the management of industrial, service & consumer products companies in western Canada.

Executives:
Donald Steele, President
Bruno Kristensen, Manager

Mercator Investments Limited
BCE Place
PO Box 201
#4520, 181 Bay St.
Toronto, ON M5J 2T3
416-865-0003
Fax: 416-865-9699
info@mercatorinvest.com
www.mercatorinvest.com
Profile: Private independent fund, venture capital company.

Executives:
Peter A. Allen, President

Meridian Community Futures Development Corporation
PO Box 2167
Kindersley, SK S0L 1S0
306-463-1850
Fax: 306-463-1855
888-919-3800
meridian.business@sasktel.net
www.meridiancfdc.ca
Ownership: Non-profit

Meyers Norris Penny(MNP)
Also listed under: *Accountants*
715 - 5th Ave. SW, 7th Fl.
Calgary, AB T2P 2X6
403-444-0150
Fax: 403-444-0199
www.mnp.ca
Year Founded: 1945
Number of Employees: 1300
Revenues: $100-500 million
Profile: MNP is a leading Western Canadian chartered accountancy & business advisory firm. In addition to traditional accounting services like taxation & assurance, MNP offers business services including corporate financing, human resource consulting, business & strategic planning, succession planning, valuations support, information technology consulting, self-employment training & agricultural advisory services.

Executives:
Daryl Ritchie, CA, CEO; 403-444-0190; daryl.ritchie@mnp.ca
Kelly Bernakevitch, Exec. Vice-President, Operations; 306-978-6302; kelly.bernakevitch@mnp.ca
Ted Poppitt, Exec. Vice-President, Practice Development; 403-444-0192; ted.poppitt@mnp.ca
Laurel Wood, CA, Exec. Vice-President, Advisory Services; 403-444-0177; laurel.wood@mnp.ca
Cheryl Lemieux, Vice-President, Finance & Administration; 403-444-0164; cheryl.lemieux@mnp.ca
Jeff Llewellyn, Vice-President, Taxation Services; 403-444-0176; jeff.llewellyn@mnp.ca
Randy Mowat, Vice-President, Marketing & Practice Development; 403-537-7669; randy.mowat@mnp.ca
Phil O'Brien-Moran, Vice-President, Information Technology; 204-571-7658; phil.obrienmoran@mnp.ca
Bob Twerdun, Vice-President, Human Capital; 403-444-0162; bob.twerdun@mnp.ca

Affiliated Companies:
Tamarack Capital Advisors Inc.

Full Time Offices:

Abbotsford
#300, 2975 Gladwin Rd.
Abbotsford, BC V2T 5T4 Canada
604-853-9471
Fax: 604-850-3672
Darrell P. Tracey, Contact

Arborg
349 Main St.
Arborg, MB R0C 0A0 Canada
204-376-2479
Jim Dangerfield

Baldur
211 Elizabeth St. West
Baldur, MB R0K 0B0 Canada
204-535-2205
Fax: 204-523-4538
Ron Schultz

Big River
PO Box 280
Big River, SK S0J 0E0 Canada
306-665-6766
Fax: 306-665-9910
Tom Plishka

Boissevain
PO Box 837
400 South Railway St.
Boissevain, MB R0K 0E0 Canada
204-534-2270
Fax: 204-534-2388
Julee Galvin

Bow Island
#6, 604 Centre St.
Bow Island, AB T0K 0G0 Canada
403-545-6309
Fax: 403-320-5066
Harry Gross

Brandon
1401 Princess Ave.
Brandon, MB R7A 7L7 Canada
204-727-0661
Fax: 204-726-1543
800-446-0890
Jeff Cristall

Brooks
247 - 1st St. West
Brooks, AB T1R 1C1 Canada
403-362-8909
Fax: 403-362-6869
877-500-5696
Randy Dykin

Calgary
#600, 808 - 4th Ave. SW
Calgary, AB T2P 3E8 Canada
403-263-3385
Fax: 403-269-8450
Durell Wiley

Campbell River
#201, 990 Cedar St.
Campbell River, BC V9W 7Z8 Canada
250-287-2131
Fax: 250-287-2134
800-450-9977

Carberry
46 Main St.
Carberry, MB R0K 0H0 Canada
204-834-2125
Fax: 204-834-3340
Tim Dekker

Carlyle
204 Main St.
Carlyle, SK S0C 0R0 Canada
306-453-6121
Fax: 306-453-6007
Heather Farfard

Caroline
PO Box 550
Caroline, AB T0M 0M0 Canada
403-722-3059
Fax: 403-722-2359
Gary Porter

Chilliwack
#1, 45780 Yale Rd.
Chilliwack, BC V2P 2N4 Canada
604-792-1915
Fax: 604-795-6526
800-444-4070
Darrell P. Tracey

Coleman
8509 - 19th Ave.
Coleman, AB T0K 0M0 Canada
800-207-8584
Kris Holbeck

Courtenay
467 Cumberland Rd.
Courtenay, BC V9N 2C5 Canada
250-338-5464
Fax: 250-338-0609
800-445-9988
info@huxham.com
Ben Vanderhorst

Dauphin
PO Box 6000
32 - 2nd Ave. SW
Dauphin, MB R7N 2V5 Canada
204-638-6767
Fax: 204-638-8634
877-500-0790
Gerry Musey

Deloraine
207 North Railway West
Deloraine, MB R0M 0M0 Canada
204-747-3111
Fax: 204-747-2989
Julee Galvin

Drumheller
365 - 2nd St. East
Drumheller, AB T0J 0Y0 Canada
403-823-7800
Fax: 403-823-8914
877-932-3387
Jeff Hall

Edmonton
West Tower
#500, 14310 - 111 Ave.
Edmonton, AB T5M 3Z7 Canada
780-451-4406
Fax: 780-454-1908
800-661-7778
Gordon Reid

Estevan
Wicklow Centre
#306, 1133 - 4th St.
Estevan, SK S4A 0W6 Canada
306-634-8447
Fax: 306-634-8448
Brian Drayton

Fairview
R&R Insurance Bldg.
Main St.
Fairview, AB T0H 1C0 Canada
780-835-3363
Rick Bisson

Foremost
102 - 2 Ave. West
Foremost, AB T0K 0X0 Canada
403-382-3688
Fax: 403-320-5066
Ed Stromsmoe

Fort McMurray
9707 Main St.
Fort McMurray, AB T9H 1T5 Canada
780-791-9000
Fax: 780-791-9047
Pat Olivier

Gladstone
24 Dennis St. West
Gladstone, MB R0J 0T0 Canada
204-385-0660
David Henlisia

Glenboro
604 Railway Ave.
Glenboro, MB R0K 0X0 Canada
204-827-2009
Fax: 204-523-4538
877-500-0760
Ron Schultz

Grande Prairie
214 Place
9909 - 102 St., 7th Fl.
Grande Prairie, AB T8V 2V4 Canada
780-831-1700
Fax: 780-539-9600
888-831-2870
Bridget Henniger

Hope
PO Box 1689
388 Wallace St.
Hope, BC V0X 1L0 Canada

604-869-9599
Fax: 604-869-3044
800-969-6060
Keith Britz, Contact
Hudson Bay
103 Churchill St.
Hudson Bay, SK S0E 0Y0 Canada
306-865-3783
Fax: 306-865-3319
Rhonda Lovell
Humboldt
701 - 9th St.
Humboldt, SK S0K 2A0 Canada
306-682-2673
Fax: 306-682-5910
877-500-0789
Larry Rode
Innisfail
4923 - 5th St.
Innisfail, AB T4G 1S7 Canada
403-227-3763
Fax: 403-227-2388
Sandra Steele
Kenora
101 Chipman St.
Kenora, ON P9N 1V7 Canada
807-468-3338
Fax: 807-468-1418
Joseph Fregeau
Killarney
501 Broadway Ave.
Killarney, MB R0K 1G0 Canada
204-523-4633
Fax: 204-523-4538
877-500-0760
Carla Beaudry
La Ronge
PO Box 1079
1309 La Ronge Ave.
La Ronge, SK S0J 1L0 Canada
306-425-2215
Fax: 306-425-3882
Gordon John
Lacombe
#5, 5265 - 45th St.
Lacombe, AB T4L 2A2 Canada
403-782-7790
Fax: 403-782-7703
Gerald Wasylyshen
Leduc
#200, 5019 - 49th Ave.
Leduc, AB T9E 6T5 Canada
780-986-2626
Fax: 780-986-2621
Deborah A. Sarnecki
Lethbridge
3425 - 2nd Ave. South
Lethbridge, AB T1J 4V1 Canada
403-329-1552
Fax: 403-329-1540
Gordon Tait
Lloydminster
103 Resource Centre
5704 - 44th St.
Lloydminster, AB T9V 2A1 Canada
780-875-9855
Fax: 780-875-9640
Ralph Cormack
Maple Creek
42 Pacific Ave.
Maple Creek, SK S0N 1N0 Canada
306-662-3127
Dena Weiss
Medicine Hat
666 - 4 St. SE
Medicine Hat, AB T1A 7G5 Canada
403-527-4441
Fax: 403-526-6218
877-500-0786
Michael Keck, Managing Partner
Melfort
609 Main St.
Melfort, SK S0E 1A0 Canada
306-752-5800
Fax: 306-752-5933
877-500-0787
John Harder
Melita
133 Main St. South
Melita, MB R0M 1L0 Canada
204-522-3333
Murray Gray
Milk River
PO Box 119
Milk River, AB T0K 1M0 Canada
403-647-3882
Fax: 403-320-5066
Don Hornford
Minnedosa
32 Main St. South
Minnedosa, MB R0J 1E0 Canada
204-867-2048
Marvin Beaumont
Moosomin
PO Box 670
715 Main St.
Moosomin, SK S0G 3N0 Canada
306-435-3347
Fax: 306-435-2494
877-500-0784
Layne McFarlane
Naicam
304 - 2nd Ave. North
Naicam, SK S0K 2Z0 Canada
306-874-2045
Bruce Ramstead
Nanaimo
PO Box 514
96 Wallace St.
Nanaimo, BC V9R 5L5 Canada
250-753-8251
Fax: 250-754-3999
877-340-3330
Lucie Gosselin
Neepawa
251 Davidson St.
Neepawa, MB R0J 1H0 Canada
204-476-2326
Fax: 204-476-3663
877-500-0795
Marvin Beaumont
Oyen
215B Main St.
Oyen, AB T0J 2J0 Canada
403-527-4441
Fax: 403-526-6218
Ronald Anderson
Peace River
PO Box 6030
10012 - 101st St.
Peace River, AB T8S 1S1 Canada
780-624-3252
Fax: 780-624-8758
Bill Hirtle
Pincher Creek
PO Box 1060
697 Main St.
Pincher Creek, AB T0K 1W0 Canada
403-627-3313
Fax: 403-627-5259
800-207-8584
Rita Kilkenny
Portage La Prairie
14 Tupper St. South
Portage La Prairie, MB R1N 1W6 Canada
204-239-6117
Fax: 204-857-3972
ronaldk@mnp.ca
Jerry Lupkowski
Preeceville
17 - 1st Ave. NW
Preeceville, SK S0A 3B0 Canada
306-547-3357
Fax: 306-865-3319
Rhonda Lovell
Prince Albert
25 - 11th St. East
Prince Albert, SK S6V 0Z8 Canada
306-764-6873
Fax: 306-763-0766
reidg@mnp.ca
Garth Busch
Radville
210 Main St.
Radville, SK S0C 2G0 Canada
306-869-4140
Fax: 306-869-4149
Blair Kotz
Red Deer
#102, 4922 - 53 St.
Red Deer, AB T4N 2E9 Canada
403-346-8878
Fax: 403-341-5599
877-500-0779
Tim Dekker
Redvers
PO Box 337
15 Broadway St.
Redvers, SK S0C 2H0 Canada
306-452-3382
Fax: 306-452-6458
Roy Olsen
Regina
#900, 2010 - 11th Ave.
Regina, SK S4P 0J3 Canada
306-790-7900
Fax: 306-790-7990
877-500-0780
Don Stewart
Rimbey
PO Box 317
4714A - 50th Ave.
Rimbey, AB T0C 2J0 Canada
403-843-4666
Fax: 403-843-4616
Chris Simpson
Roblin
PO Box 878
206 Main St.
Roblin, MB R0L 1P0 Canada
204-937-8019
Fax: 204-937-8067
Kelly Brook, Contact
Rocky Mountain House
PO Box 2138
5004 - 50th St.
Rocky Mountain House, AB T4T 1B6 Canada
403-845-2422
Fax: 403-845-3794
Gary Porter
Russell
227 Main St. North
Russell, MB R0J 1W0 Canada
204-773-2225
Fax: 204-773-3950
John Orisko
Saskatoon
366 - 3rd Ave. South
Saskatoon, SK S7K 1M5 Canada
306-665-6766
Fax: 306-665-9910
877-500-0778
David Kunaman
Ste Rose du Lac
635 Central Ave.
Ste Rose du Lac, MB R0L 1S0 Canada
204-447-2177
Fax: 204-447-3135
Tere Stykalo
Steinbach
316A Main St.
Steinbach, MB R5G 1Z1 Canada
204-326-9816
Fax: 204-326-9586
Alyson Kennedy
Swift Current
140 - 2nd Ave. NW
Swift Current, SK S9H 0P2 Canada
306-773-8375
Fax: 306-773-7735
877-500-0762
Al Lightfoot
Virden

Meyers Norris Penny(MNP) (continued)
233 Queen St. West
Virden, MB R0M 2C0 Canada
204-748-1340
Fax: 204-748-3294
Tom Kirkup
Wainwright
711 - 10 St.
Wainwright, AB T9W 1P3 Canada
780-842-4171
Fax: 780-842-4169
877-500-0763
Don Isaman
Wawota
111 Main St.
Wawota, SK S0G 5A0 Canada
306-739-2757
David Ablass
Weyburn
8 - 4th St. NE
Weyburn, SK S4H 0X7 Canada
306-842-8915
Fax: 306-842-1966
Sean Wallace
Winnipeg
#500, 1661 Portage Ave.
Winnipeg, MB R3J 3T7 Canada
204-775-4531
Fax: 204-783-8329
877-500-0795
Wayne McWhirter

Mirlaw Investments Ltd.
#1010, 1134, rue Ste-Catherine ouest
Montréal, QC H3B 1H4
514-861-9671
Fax: 514-866-4882
Ownership: Private
Year Founded: 1968
Number of Employees: 6
Executives:
S. Karkoukly, President

MMV Financial Inc.
95 Wellington St. West, 22nd Fl.
Toronto, ON M5J 2N7
416-977-9718
Fax: 416-591-1393
www.mmvf.com
Former Name: MM Venture Partners
Year Founded: 1998
Profile: The private independent fund specializes in venture debt financing.

Executives:
Minhas Mohamed, CEO
Ron Patterson, Exec. Vice-President
Brian F. Faughnan, Sr. Vice-President
Brian Hendry, Sr. Vice-President, Finance
Jacques Perreault, Sr. Vice-President
Nathan R. Gibb, Vice-President

Montcap Financial Corporation
#1510, 3500, boul de Maisonneuve ouest
Montréal, QC H3Z 3C1
514-932-8223
Fax: 514-932-0076
800-231-2977
info@montcap.com
www.montcap.com
Ownership: Public. Subsidiary of Accord Financial Corp.
Year Founded: 1990
Number of Employees: 38
Stock Symbol: ACD
Executives:
Fred Moss, President
Cynthia Aboud, Regional Vice-President, Business Development; caboud@montcap.com
Harold Shapiro, Regional Vice-President, Business Development; 416-961-6620; hshapiro@montcap.com
Matthew Levinson, Vice-President, Operations; mlevinson@montcap.com
Branches:
Toronto
77 Bloor St. West, 18th Fl.
Toronto, ON M5S 1M2 Canada
416-961-6620
800-701-9170
Harold Shapiro, Regional Vice-President

Morbank Financial Inc.
#1200, 635 - 8th Ave. SW
Calgary, AB T2P 3M3
403-205-4110
Fax: 403-264-9270
877-969-9899
morbank@shaw.ca
www.morbank.ca
Executives:
John Tiberio, CFO
Judy Christianson, Mortgage Administrator

Morrison Financial Services Limited
#15, 156 Duncan Mill Rd.
Toronto, ON M3B 3N2
416-391-3535
Fax: 416-391-4843
davidm@mfsl.net
Ownership: Private
Year Founded: 1987
Profile: The company is engaged in asset-based financing, factoring & mezzanine debt, as well as other services.

Executives:
David Morrison, President

Mortgage Corp Financial Services Inc.
Courtleigh Place
450 Main St. West
North Bay, ON P1B 2V2
705-494-9911
Fax: 705-494-9912
dan@mortgagecorponline.com
www.mortgagecorponline.com
Ownership: Private
Year Founded: 1992
Profile: Mortgage brokerage firm.

Executives:
Daniel R. Sauve, President

Mosaic Venture Partners
#200, 65 Front St. East
Toronto, ON M5E 1B9
416-367-2888
Fax: 416-367-8146
info@mosaicvp.com
www.mosaicvp.com
Ownership: Private
Year Founded: 1997
Executives:
Vernon Lobo, Managing Director
Dave Samuel, Managing Director
Frank Cotter, Venture Partner

Mouvement des caisses Desjardins du Québec
Also listed under: *Credit Unions/Caisses Populaires; Insurance Companies*
100, av des Commandeurs
Lévis, QC G6V 7N5
418-835-8444
Fax: 418-833-5873
www.desjardins.com
Ownership: Private.
Year Founded: 1901
Number of Employees: 38,000
Assets: $10-50 million Year End: 20051231
Profile: The Mouvement offers a complete range of financial services to its five million members & clients. The Mouvement comprises two sectors: 1) the co-operative sector & 2) the corporate sector, which is controlled by the co-operative sector. In Québec, 618 caisses make up the core of the co-operative sector. They are grouped together in the Fédération des caisses Desjardins du Québec.

Executives:
Alban D'Amours, Président, Chef de la direction du MCD
Germain Carrières, Président, Chef de l'exploitation de VMD
Gérard Guilbault, Président, Chef de l'exploitation de DGA
François Joly, Président, Chef de l'exploitation de DSF
Bertrand Laferrière, Président, Chef de l'exploitation de la FCDQ

Jean-Guy Langelier, Président/Chef, l'exploitation de la CCD, Chef de la trésorerie du MCD
J. Martineau, Président, Chef de l'exploitation de DGAG
Louis L. Roquet, Président, Chef de l'exploitation de DCR
Pierre Brossard, 1er Vice-président exécutif à la direction du MCD
Jacques Dignard, 1er Vice-président, Ressources humaines du MCD
Daniel Gauvin, 1er Vice-président, Chef de la gestion intégrée des risques du MCD
Monique F. Leroux, 1re Vice-présidente exécutive, Chef de la direction financière du MCD
Marcel Pepin, 1er Vice-président, Plantification stratégique, Développement des affaires pancanadiennes du MCD
Pauline D'Amboise, Secrétaire, Comité de direction stratégique du MCD
Affiliated Companies:
Fiducie Desjardins
Fédération des caisses Desjardins du Québec

MWI & Partners
BCE Place
PO Box 200
#2800, 161 Bay St.
Toronto, ON M5J 2S1
416-369-3981
Fax: 416-369-3986
Ownership: Private
Year Founded: 1996
Number of Employees: 5
Assets: $110,000,000 Year End: 20040930
Profile: Private merchant bank & private equity fund.

Executives:
John B. Breen, Managing Partner
R. Geoffrey Browne, Managing Partner
Alan S. Wearing, Managing Partner
Jennifer Kerr, Associate

National Apparel Bureau
Also listed under: *Collection Agencies*
#200, 294, rue Saint-Paul ouest
Montréal, QC H2Y 2A3
514-845-8135
Fax: 514-499-8468
800-361-2171
bureau@nabq.com
www.nabq.com
Ownership: Private
Year Founded: 1934
Number of Employees: 10
Executives:
B.C. Lafford, President

National Leasing Group Inc.
1558 Wilson Pl.
Winnipeg, MB R3T 0Y4
204-954-9000
800-665-1326
manitoba@nationalleasing.com
www.nationalleasing.com
Ownership: Private. The Megill Stephenson Company; Crocus Investments; Clarica Life; Employee Ownership
Year Founded: 1987
Number of Employees: 175
Branches:
Brossard
#201, 4, Place du Commerce
Brossard, QC J4W 3B3 Canada
450-923-8599
Fax: 450-923-4012
877-353-3389
info@cbnational.com
Calgary
7370 Sierra Morena Blvd. SW
Calgary, AB T3H 4H9 Canada
403-640-0343
800-561-6275
calgary@nationalleasing.com
Edmonton
11420 - 142nd St.
Edmonton, AB T5M 1V1 Canada
780-448-9239
800-897-3477
edmonton@nationalleasing.com
Halifax
5426 Portland Pl.
Halifax, NS B3K 1R1 Canada
902-468-5680
Fax: 902-468-5689
800-930-7555

atlantic@nationalleasing.com
London
#403, 1326 Huron St.
London, ON N5V 2E2 Canada
519-451-6979
Fax: 519-451-6723
877-383-1039
london@nationalleasing.com
Mississauga
#200, 4296 Village Centre Ct.
Mississauga, ON L4Z 1S2 Canada
905-281-3622
Fax: 905-279-2303
877-242-2202
mississauga@nationalleasing.com
Ottawa
#248, 99 - 5th Ave.
Ottawa, ON K1S 5P5 Canada
613-729-3830
Fax: 613-729-7984
877-312-7872
ottawa@nationalleasing.com
Quispamsis
2 Clarwood Dr.
Quispamsis, NB E2E 4K1 Canada
506-848-0020
Fax: 506-849-6540
800-930-7555
atlantic@nationalleasing.com
Regina
971 Dorothy St.
Regina, SK S4X 0W2 Canada
306-249-6544
888-315-6455
saskatchewan@nationalleasing.com
Saskatoon
#8B-505, 3120 - 8th St. East
Saskatoon, SK S7H 0W2 Canada
306-249-6544
888-315-6544
saskatchewan@nationalleasing.com
St. John's
PO Box 942
20 Sauve
St. John's, NL A1N 3C9 Canada
709-747-8464
Fax: 709-747-8465
800-930-7555
atlantic@nationalleasing.com
Vancouver
#720, 999 West Broadway
Vancouver, BC V5Z 1K5 Canada
604-659-7100
800-565-6338
bc@nationalleasing.com

Native Venture Capital Co. Ltd.

27 Artist View Pointe
Calgary, AB T3Z 3N3
403-208-5380
Fax: 403-208-5390
Ownership: Private
Year Founded: 1982
Number of Employees: 3
Profile: The company is engaged in equity investments with aboriginal businesses in Western Canada.

Executives:
Milt Pahl, President/CEO

NEICOM Developments

12 Main St. North
Riverton, MB R0C 2R0
204-378-5106
Fax: 204-378-5192
800-378-5106
neicom@mts.net
www.neicom.mb.ca
Ownership: Private
Year Founded: 1986
Number of Employees: 5
Executives:
Tammy Hudyma, General Manager

Newsask Community Futures Development Corporation

Tisdale Civic Centre
903 - 99th Ave.
Tisdale, SK S0E 1T0
306-873-4449
Fax: 306-873-4645
888-586-9855
newsask.community.fut.dev@sasktel.net
www.newsaskcfdc.ca
Ownership: Non-profit
Number of Employees: 5
Profile: To foster job creation through business creation and expansion.

Niagara Regional Mortgage Services Inc.

49 Dorothy St.
Welland, ON L3B 3V6
905-734-1338
Fax: 905-734-1470
nrm@iaw.on.ca
www.nrms.yp.ca
Year Founded: 1992
Number of Employees: 4
Profile: Mortgage financing is provided.

NISCO Network Investment Services Co. Ltd.

535 Falkland Rd.
Victoria, BC V8S 4L6
250-472-8530
Fax: 250-472-8540
800-661-2889
nisco@nisco.ca
www.nisco.ca
Ownership: Private
Profile: Underwriting financial services company that arranges financial solutions for businesses.

Executives:
Chris Carruthers

Nishnawbe Aski Development Fund

106 Centennial Sq., 2nd. Fl.
Thunder Bay, ON P7E 1H3
807-623-5397
Fax: 807-622-8271
800-465-6821
hyesno@nadf.org
www.nadf.org
Ownership: Private
Year Founded: 1984
Number of Employees: 18
Assets: $5-10 million
Revenues: $1-5 million
Profile: The aboriginal financial institution is affiliated with Neegani Investment Management Inc.

Executives:
Harvey Yesno, President/CEO
Guiseppe Buoncore, Sr. Exec. Assistant; cmartin@nadf.org
Branches:
Timmins
PO Box 1720
Timmins, ON P4N 7W9 Canada
705-268-3940
Fax: 705-268-4034
800-461-9858

North Central Community Futures Development Corporation

PO Box 1208
Thompson, MB R8N 1P1
204-677-1490
Fax: 204-778-5672
888-847-7878
ncd@northcentraldevelopment.ca
www.northcentraldevelopment.ca
Ownership: Non-profit
Profile: Endeavours to bring together to support, develop, and promote communities, individuals, organizations, business and other appropriate stakeholders within the north central region (of Manitoba) to encourage self reliance and viability of the social and economic quality of life.

North Red Community Futures Development Corporation

18 Main St.
Selkirk, MB R1A 1P5
204-482-2020
Fax: 204-482-2033
800-894-2621
info@northredcfdc.com
www.triplescfdc.mb.ca
Former Name: Triple S Community Futures Development Corporation
Ownership: Non-profit
Year Founded: 1985
Number of Employees: 5

Northern Securities Inc.

Also listed under: *Investment Dealers*
PO Box 35
#1800, 150 York St.
Toronto, ON M5H 3S5
416-644-8100
Fax: 416-644-0270
info@northernsi.com
www.northernsi.com
Former Name: St. James Securities Inc.
Ownership: Private. Wholly owned subsidiary of Northern Financial Corporation
Stock Exchange Membership: Canadian Trading & Quotation System Inc, Toronto Stock Exchange, TSX Venture Exchange
Profile: The independent full service investment bank & brokerage firm provides the following services: retail & institutional distribution, equity research, online trading, online public offerings, online private placements, corporate finance, mergers & acquisitions, & financial restructuring. Clients are both retail & institutional, including small capitalization companies.

Executives:
Vic Alboini, President/CEO & Chair
Doug Chornoboy, Sr. Vice-President/CFO
Chris Shaule, Sr. Vice-President & Head, Private Client Group
Ann Krallisch, Director, Business Development
Richard Pinkerton, Managing Director, Investment Banking
Paul A. Thornton, Vice-President, Private Client Group
Frederick Vance, Vice-President, Chief Compliance Officer
Branches:
Bamfield
61 Scotts Lane
Bamfield, BC V0R 1B0
250-728-3494
Brandon
#5, 1711 Kirkcaldy Dr.
Brandon, MB R7A 0B9
204-728-7866
Fax: 204-728-9448
866-720-7866
Calgary
Standard Life Tower
#1940, 639 Fifth Ave. SW
Calgary, AB T2P 0M9
403-398-7390
Fax: 403-313-5642
866-966-1234
Edmonton
Manulife Place
#1150, 10180 - 101 St.
Edmonton, AB T5J 3S4
780-425-0080
Fax: 780-425-0088
866-485-0080
Kamloops
Kamloops, BC
250-377-6900
Fax: 250-377-6949
877-377-6901
Kelowna
#153, 3151 Lakeshore Rd.
Kelowna, BC V1W 3S9
Fax: 250-764-0379
888-764-4037
Lantzville
7810 Aats Rd.
Lantzville, BC V0R 2H0
250-714-6243
Fax: 250-390-3480
Montréal
Place Montréal
#2530, 1800, av McGill College
Montréal, QC H3A 3J6

Northern Securities Inc. (continued)
514-288-4644
Fax: 514-288-5996
Ottawa
#600, 255 Albert St.
Ottawa, ON K1P 6A9
613-751-4447
Fax: 613-751-4467
Vancouver
One Bentall Centre
#2050, 505 Burrard St.
Vancouver, BC V7X 1M6
604-668-1800
Fax: 604-668-1816

Northwest Community Futures Development Corporation
761C - 106 St.
North Battleford, SK S9A 1V9
306-446-3200
Fax: 306-445-8076
877-446-2332
info@northwestcf.com
www.northwestcf.com
Ownership: Non-profit
Number of Employees: 3
Executives:
Pat Redl, General Manager

Northwood Mortgage Ltd.
#501, 9050 Yonge St.
Richmond Hill, ON L4C 9S6
416-969-8130
Fax: 905-889-2237
info@northwoodmortgage.com
www.northwoodmortgage.com
Ownership: Private
Year Founded: 1990
Profile: Residential, commercial & industrial mortgage financing is provided, using lending criteria less restrictive than financial institutions.
Executives:
Art Appelberg, President; 416-969-8130

NORTIP Community Business Development Corporation
Also listed under: *Financial Planning*
PO Box 140
Plum Point, NL A0K 4A0
709-247-2040
Fax: 709-247-2630
gloria.toope@cbdc.ca
www.cbdc.ca
Ownership: Private
Year Founded: 1991
Executives:
Gloria Toope, Chair
Richard May, Executive Director; rmay@nortin.cbdc.ca

Nuu Chah Nulth Economic Development Corporation
PO Box 1384
7563 Pacific Rim Hwy.
Port Alberni, BC V9Y 7M2
250-724-3131
Fax: 250-724-9967
866-444-6332
nedc@island.net
www.nedc.info
Former Name: Nuu Chah Nulth Community Futures Development Corporation
Ownership: Non-profit
Year Founded: 1984
Number of Employees: 8
Executives:
Al Little, Manager
Branches:
Campbell River
918 Island Hwy.
Campbell River, BC V9W 2C3 Canada
250-286-3155
Fax: 250-286-3156

Oncap Investment Partners
BCE Place, Canada Trust Tower
PO Box 220
161 Bay St., 48th Fl.
Toronto, ON M5J 2S1
416-214-4300
Fax: 416-214-6106
oncap@oncap.com
www.oncap.com
Year Founded: 1999
Profile: Established by Onex Corp., it invests in small-capitalization North American-based companies.
Executives:
Greg Baylin
Mark Gordon
Michael Lay
Ed Rieckelman
Jeremy Thompson

OPG Ventures Inc.
700 University Ave.
Toronto, ON M5G 1X6
416-592-2555
Fax: 416-592-8677
877-592-2555
opgventures@opg.com
www.opg.com/index.asp
Ownership: Ontario Power Generation Inc.
Year Founded: 2001
Profile: Provides equity capital to entrepreneurial companies developing new power generation and energy technologies.

Orillia Area Community Development Corp.
PO Box 2525
22 Peter St. South
Orillia, ON L3V 7A3
705-325-4903
Fax: 705-325-6817
mparker@orilliacdc.com
www.orilliacdc.com
Ownership: Non-profit
Year Founded: 1984
Number of Employees: 5
Assets: $1-5 million
Revenues: Under $1 million
Profile: Small business counselling services & financing up to $150,000 are provided.
Executives:
Donna Hewitt, General Manager
Christine Jarvis, Loans Officer

Paccar Financial Services Ltd
Markborough Place
#500, 6711 Mississauga Rd. North
Mississauga, ON L5N 4J8
905-858-2670
Fax: 905-858-2972
800-263-4754
www.paccarfinancial.com
Ownership: Private
Year Founded: 1956
Number of Employees: 40
Profile: Provides loans and financing for commercial trucking industry.

Parkland Community Futures Development Corporation
PO Box 516
421 Main St.
Grandview, MB R0L 0Y0
204-546-5100
Fax: 204-546-5107
888-987-2332
reception@pcfdc.mb.ca
pcfdc.mb.ca
Year Founded: 1991
Number of Employees: 5
Assets: $1-5 million
Revenues: Under $1 million
Executives:
Greg Tertesky, General Manager; 204-546-5103; greg@pcfdc.mb.ca

Peace Country Development Corporation
9816 - 98 Ave.
Peace River, AB T8S 1J5
780-624-1161
Fax: 780-624-1308
800-396-4605
admin@peacecountry-cfdc.com
www.peacecountry-cfdc.com
Ownership: Private. Non-profit.
Year Founded: 1994
Number of Employees: 7
Revenues: $1-5 million
Executives:
Randy Hodgkinson, Manager, Business Development
Joanne Shannon, Director, Youth Connections

Penfund Partners, Inc.
Also listed under: *Pension & Money Management Companies*
#1720, 390 Bay St.
Toronto, ON M5H 2Y2
416-865-0707
Fax: 416-364-4149
www.penfund.com
Also Known As: Penfund
Year Founded: 1979
Profile: Assets under management are $200 million..
Executives:
John Bradlow, Contact
Richard Bradlow, Contact
Adam Breslin, Contact
Barry Yontef, Contact

Peoples Trust Company
Also listed under: *Trust Companies*
888 Dunsmuir St., 14th Fl.
Vancouver, BC V6C 3K4
604-683-2881
Fax: 604-331-3469
people@peoplestrust.com
www.peoplestrust.com
Ownership: Private
Year Founded: 1985
Profile: The financial institution is engaged in mortgage lending, mortgage investing & deposit services. The lending business consists of mostly conventional & insured loans. Properties are multi-family residential properties in urban centers. Investing services focus upon mortgage banking for institutional investors, plus long term RRSP & GIC products.
Executives:
Frank A. Renou, President/CEO
Derek Peddlesden, Exec. Vice-President/COO
Barrie M. Battley, Sr. Vice-President
Dennis Aitken, Vice-President, Mortgages, Regional Manager, Prairies
Dennis Dineen, Vice-President, Commercial Mortgages
Jim Dysart, Vice-President, Mortgages, Regional Manager, Ontario
Brian Kennedy, Vice-President, Mortgages, Regional Manager, British Columbia
Kathleen Klassen, Vice-President, Finance, Treasurer
Aleta Brown, Assistant Vice-President, Mortgage Banking Administration
Chris Hudson, Assistant Vice-President, Mortgages, Prairies
Bruce Martinuik, Assistant Vice-President, Mortgages, British Columbia
Jeanette Curtis, Sr. Manager, Deposit Services
John Nation, Sr. Manager, Mortgage Administration
Tom Wollner, Manager, Residential Mortgages
Directors:
Eskander Ghermezian, Chair
Howard Anson
Michael Andrews
Andrew Bury
David Ghermezian
Peter Hindmarch-Watson
Jonathan A. Levin
Frank A. Renou
Michael Terrell
Keith Thompson
Derek Woods
Branches:
Calgary
#955, 808 - 4th Ave. SW
Calgary, AB T2P 3E8 Canada
403-237-8975
Fax: 403-266-5002
Toronto
#1801, 130 Adelaide St. West
Toronto, ON M5H 3P5 Canada
416-368-3266
Fax: 416-368-3328

Vancouver - Dunsmuir St.
#750, 888 Dunsmuir St.
Vancouver, BC V6C 3K4 Canada
604-685-1068
Fax: 604-683-2787
Vancouver - Dunsmuir St. - Investment Centre
#750, 888 Dunsmuir St.
Vancouver, BC V6C 3K4
604-683-2881
Fax: 604-683-5110

PFS Paramount Financial Services
#2300 - 2850 Shaughnessy St.
Port Coquitlam, BC H4T 1X4
604-552-4392
Fax: 604-648-9532
pfsali@aol.com
Ownership: Division of Paramount Holdings Ltd.
Profile: The organization provides lending & brokerage services in the areas of commercial mortgages, business capital & loans, plus equipment financing.

PHH Arval
#400, 2233 Argentia Rd.
Mississauga, ON L5N 2X7
905-286-5300
Fax: 905-286-5302
800-665-9744
www.phharval.com
Ownership: Private. Owned by Cendant Corp.
Executives:
Michael Goddard, Sr. Vice-President & General Manager
Branches:
Calgary
Sun Life Plaza II
#2100, 140 - 4th Ave. SW
Calgary, AB T2P 3N3 Canada
403-262-8980
David Graham, Vice-President, Western Region
Montréal
#104, 6363, rte Transcanadienne
Montréal, QC H4T 1Z9 Canada
514-744-7250
Fax: 514-744-9559
Vancouver
PO Box 12116
#930, 555 West Hastings St.
Vancouver, BC V6B 4N6 Canada
604-681-5426
Fax: 604-681-3715

Pinetree Capital Corp.
Exchange Tower
#2500, 130 King St. West
Toronto, ON M5X 1A9
416-941-9600
Fax: 416-941-1090
info@pinetreecapital.com
www.pinetreecapital.com
Ownership: Public
Year Founded: 1992
Stock Symbol: PNP
Profile: Pinetree Capital is focused on becoming the first to fund emerging growth companies. By investing strategically in early stage companies that have solid proprietary technology, they commit both financial & human resources.

Executives:
Sheldon Inwentash, Chair/CEO
Larry Goldberg, Exec. Vice-President/CFO
Richard Patricio, Vice-President, Legal & Corporate Affairs

Pinnacle Private Capital
***Also listed under:** Holding & Other Investment Companies*
#410, 2431 - 37th Ave NE
Calgary, AB T2E 6Y7
403-250-3188
Fax: 403-735-9181
info@pinnacle-capital.com
www.pinnacle-capital.com
Former Name: Agilis Corporation
Ownership: Private.
Year Founded: 2001
Profile: The capital management organization provides venture capital & support for existing portfolio companies or beginning entrepreneurs.
Executives:
Kevin Starozik, CEO
Don Broadhead, Chief Financial Officer

Prescott-Russell Community Development Corp.
519 Main St. East
Hawkesbury, ON K6A 1B3
613-632-0918
Fax: 613-632-7385
sdcpr@hawk.igs.net
www.sdcpr.on.ca
Ownership: Non-profit
Year Founded: 1986
Number of Employees: 6
Executives:
Daniel Gigault, General Manager

Primaxis Technology Ventures Inc.
Heritage Bldg., MaRS Centre
#230, 101 College St.
Toronto, ON M5G 1L7
416-673-8188
Fax: 416-977-3403
kerri.golden@primaxis.com
www.primaxis.com
Year Founded: 1998
Profile: The early stage venture capital fund invests in the physical & engineering sciences.

Executives:
Ilse Treurnicht, CEO
Kerri Golden, Vice-President
Tony Redpath, Vice-President

Prince Albert & District Community Futures Development Corporation
#1, 1499 - 10th Ave. East
Prince Albert, SK S6V 7S6
306-763-8125
Fax: 306-763-8127
888-388-0822
info@pacf.ca
www.pacf.ca
Ownership: Non-profit
Profile: Community-based organization that offers economic development assistance to entrepreneurial individuals.

Executives:
Wayne Cameron, General Manager
Pierre Leblanc, Loans Manager

Priveq Capital Funds
***Also listed under:** Pension & Money Management Companies; Investment Management*
#711, 1500 Don Mills Rd.
Toronto, ON M3B 3K4
416-447-3330
Fax: 416-447-3331
www.priveq.ca
Also Known As: Priveq
Ownership: Private
Year Founded: 1994
Number of Employees: 8
Assets: $37,000,000
Profile: Priveq provides tailor-made $3-$7 million of equity to growing companies. As an equity partner, it provides capital, strategic direction & business financial assistance to entrepreneurs & business owners to further enhance their company's value & provide superior returns for all stakeholders.

Executives:
Bradley W. Ashley, Managing Partner
Kevin B. Melnyk, Partner

Propulsion Ventures Inc.
1250, boul René-Lévesque ouest, 38e étage
Montréal, QC H3B 4W8
514-397-8450
Fax: 514-397-8451
info@propulsionventures.com
www.propulsionventures.com
Former Name: Telesystem Software Ventures Ltd. Partnership; Telesoft Ventures Inc.
Ownership: Private
Year Founded: 1995
Number of Employees: 8
Assets: $100-500 million
Profile: With over $125,000,000 of capital under management, Propulsion Ventures is one of Canada's largest venture-capital firms devoted to the software industry.

Executives:
François Gaouette, Managing Partner; 514-397-8456
Beno(140t Hogue, Managing Partner; 514-397-8453
Robert Talbot, Managing Partner; 514-397-8455

Pyxis Capital Inc.
#402, 4 King St. West
Toronto, ON M5H 1B6
416-867-9079
Fax: 416-867-1961
Former Name: Graystone Corporation; First Chicago Investment Corporation; Canadian Northstar Corporation
Ownership: Public
Year Founded: 1978
Number of Employees: 4
Stock Symbol: FCH.A, FCH.B, FCH.E
Profile: The company is engaged in merchant banking & investment activities in Canada.

Executives:
Andrew Kim, President
Carol Mendoza, Controller, Corporate Secretary
Directors:
J. Ian Flatt, Chair
Gordon Flatt, Vice-Chair
Roger D. Garon
Winston Wong

The REACH Corporation (A Community Futures Corporation)
PO Box 310
4612 McDougall Dr.
Smoky Lake, AB T0A 3C0
780-656-2110
Fax: 780-656-2106
866-282-8391
reach@reachcor.ca
www.reachcor.ca
Former Name: St. Paul/Smoky Lake Business & Community Development Corporation
Ownership: Private. Shareholders: Counties of St. Paul & Smokey Lake; Towns of St. Paul, Elk Point, Smoky Lake; Villages of Waskatenau & Vilna
Year Founded: 1988
Number of Employees: 5
Executives:
Paul Pelletier, General Manager; 780-645-5782
Branches:
St Paul
PO Box 1484
5101 - 50 St.
St Paul, AB T0A 3A4 Canada
780-645-5782
Fax: 780-645-1811
Dick Millar, Contact

Regional Financial Services Limited
#201, 1450 Hopkins St.
Whitby, ON L1N 2C3
905-665-8811
Fax: 905-430-9100
rfinancial@on.aibn.com
Ownership: Private
Year Founded: 1978
Executives:
Lucian Michaels, President
Barry Michaels, Sec.-Treas.

Research Capital Corporation
***Also listed under:** Investment Dealers*
Commerce Court West
PO Box 368
#4500, 199 Bay St.
Toronto, ON M5L 1G2
416-860-7600
Fax: 416-860-7671
contact@researchcapital.com
www.researchcapital.com
Ownership: Employee-owned.
Year Founded: 1921
Number of Employees: 300
Stock Exchange Membership: Canadian Trading & Quotation System Inc, Montreal Exchange, Toronto Stock Exchange, TSX Venture Exchange
Profile: The integrated investment dealer includes investment banking services that focus upon small to mid-cap growth companies & growth investors. The full service firm's public

Research Capital Corporation (continued)

venture capital group specializes in IPOs & small and micro-cap public company financings. Sales & trading professionals provide services to institutional investors. Research analysts offer coverage of growth companies. The private client division serves high-net worth investors.

Executives:
Ian G. Griffin, Honourary Chair; ian.griffin@researchcapital.com
Patrick G. Walsh, Chair/CEO; patrick.walsh@researchcapital.com
Geoffrey G. Whitlam, President; geoff.whitlam@researchcapital.com
Andrew Selbie, COO & Exec. Vice-President, Finance; andrew.selbie@researchcapital.com
Greg Finkle, Exec. Vice-President, Managing Director
David Hetherington, Branch Manager; david.hetherington@researchcapital.com

Branches:
Brantford
127 Charing Cross St.
Brantford, ON N3R 2J2 Canada
519-751-1311
Fax: 519-751-2629
800-516-9085
Caledonia
159 Haddington St.
Caledonia, ON N3W 1G1
905-765-0335
Fax: 905-765-0069
800-422-7032
Calgary
Sun Life Plaza II
#1330, 140 - 4 Ave. SW
Calgary, AB T2P 3N3 Canada
403-265-7400
Fax: 403-237-5951
Barb Richardson, Branch Manager
Delta
4337 River Rd. West
Delta, BC V4K 1R9
604-628-4463
866-300-2001
James H. Ross, Sr. Managing Director
Meaford
40 Gray Ave.
Meaford, ON N4L 1C4
519-538-3725
888-241-1103
Mississauga
2470 Oak Row Cres.
Mississauga, ON L5L 1P4
416-860-7628
Fax: 416-860-6798
Montréal
#100, 4, Place Ville-Marie
Montréal, QC H3B 2E7 Canada
514-399-1500
Fax: 514-399-1540
Donald Stevenson, Branch Manager
Pickering
560 Park Cres.
Pickering, ON L1W 2C9
905-839-8557
Fax: 905-839-2011
Regina
2400 College Ave., 5th Fl.
Regina, SK S4P 1C8
306-566-7550
Fax: 306-565-3718
Surrey
#412, 1787 - 154th St.
Surrey, BC V4A 4S1
604-662-1862
Fax: 604-662-1855
Terra Cotta
25589 Credit View Rd., RR#1
Terra Cotta, ON L7C 3G8
905-838-5070
Fax: 905-838-5069
Thornhill
44 Valleyview Rd.
Thornhill, ON L3T 6Y9
905-881-7980
Fax: 905-881-1759
800-282-8996
Toronto - Avoca Ave.
#903, 38 Avoca Ave.
Toronto, ON M4T 2B9
416-975-0262
Fax: 416-975-4042
Toronto - Douglas Cres.
35 Douglas Cres.
Toronto, ON M4W 2E6
416-323-6856
Fax: 416-923-8089
877-883-8885
Toronto - Lowther Ave.
#310, 4 Lowther Ave.
Toronto, ON M5R 1C6
416-920-9027
Fax: 416-920-4718
800-559-5537
Toronto - Minho Blvd.
24 Minho Blvd.
Toronto, ON M6G 4B3
416-537-7618
Fax: 416-537-9873
Toronto - Shaftesbury Ave.
42 Shaftesbury Ave.
Toronto, ON M4T 1A2
416-920-0684
Fax: 416-920-0685
888-211-0709
Toronto - Victoria Park Ave.
73 Victoria Park Ave.
Toronto, ON M4E 3S2
416-690-3732
Fax: 416-690-3729
866-860-4190
Toronto - Woodcrest Dr.
45 Woodcrest Dr.
Toronto, ON M9A 4J3
416-245-6128
Fax: 416-245-9867
888-866-1296
Vancouver
Four Bentall Centre
PO Box 49356
#564, 1055 Dunsmuir St.
Vancouver, BC V7X 1L4 Canada
604-662-1800
Fax: 604-662-1850
David Fawkes, Branch Manager
Victoria
4400 Meadowood Pl.
Victoria, BC V8X 4V7
250-658-8955
G. Peter Taylor, President
Whitby
62 Bluebell Cres.
Whitby, ON Whitby
416-860-7621
Fax: 905-665-7278
800-495-7749

ResMor Trust Company

***Also listed under:** Trust Companies*
#400, 555 - 4th Ave. SW
Calgary, AB T2P 3E7
403-539-4920
Fax: 403-539-4921
866-333-7030
www.resmor.com
Former Name: Equisure Trust Company
Ownership: Private. ResMor Capital Corporation.
Year Founded: 1964
Number of Employees: 195
Assets: $100-500 million Year End: 20041231
Revenues: $10-50 million Year End: 20041231

Executives:
James P. Clayton, President/CEO; 403-539-4901; jclayton@resmor.com
K. Gerry Wagner, Vice-President/CFO; 403-539-4902; gwagner@resmor.com

Directors:
Harold Allsopp
Cody T. Church
James P. Clayton
Ronald A. Jackson
Lorne H. Jacobson
Donald Potvin
Peter Valentine
K. Gerry Wagner

Branches:
Calgary
#400, 555 - 4 Ave. SW
Calgary, AB T2P 3E7 Canada
403-534-1920
Fax: 403-538-4965

Reynolds & Reynolds (Canada) Limited

PO Box 22
#700, 3 Robert Speck Pkwy.
Mississauga, ON L4Z 6G5
905-267-6000
Fax: 905-267-6101
877-473-9665
www.reyrey.com
Ownership: The Reynolds and Reynolds Company, Ohio

Executives:
Pierre Blais, Vice-President & General Manager

Branches:
Montréal
11075 Louis H. Lafontaine
Montréal, QC H1J 2Z4 Canada
514-355-7552
Fax: 514-355-7514
800-461-3570

Romspen Investment Corporation(RIC)

#300, 162 Cumberland St.
Toronto, ON M5R 3N5
416-966-1100
Fax: 416-966-1161
800-494-0389
info@romspen.com
www.romspen.com
Former Name: Romspen Management Services Limited
Also Known As: Romspen
Ownership: Private
Year Founded: 1992
Number of Employees: 18
Profile: Romspen Investment Corporation originates & manages a private syndicated portfolio of mortgages & income-producing commercial properties.

Executives:
Sheldon Esbin, President
Arthur Resnick, Vice-President

RoyNat Capital Inc.

Scotia Plaza
40 King St. West, 26th Fl.
Toronto, ON M5H 1H1
416-933-2730
Fax: 416-933-2783
info@roynat.com
www.roynatcapital.com
Ownership: Subsidiary of the Bank of Nova Scotia
Year Founded: 1962
Number of Employees: 150
Assets: $1-10 billion
Revenues: $100-500 million

Executives:
Earl Lande, President/CEO
Michel Desloges, Sr. Vice-President, Corporate Support Services & Controller; 416-933-2776
Keith Moorse, Sr. Vice-President, Risk Management; 416-933-2662
John Carusone, Vice-President, Information Technology
Don McLauchlin, Vice-President, Relationship Marketing; 416-933-2671
Iain Munro, Vice-President, Head of Structured Finance & Syndications
James Webster, Vice-President, Equity; 416-933-2665

District Offices:
Calgary
Scotia Centre
#3900, 700 - 2nd St. SW
Calgary, AB T2P 2W2 Canada
403-269-7755
Fax: 403-269-7701
Russ Andrew, Director & District Manager
Drummondville
#400, 150, rue Marchand
Drummondville, QC J2C 4N1 Canada
819-477-3801
Fax: 819-474-6423

Michel Ruest, Director & Distict Manager
Edmonton
Scotia Place
10060 Jasper Ave.
Edmonton, AB T5J 3R8 Canada
403-413-4361
Fax: 403-426-3456
Jason Barr, Director & District Manager
Kitchener
Frederick Tower
#605, 101 Frederick St.
Kitchener, ON N2H 6R2 Canada
519-742-8367
Fax: 519-742-1300
Brian K. Hunter, Director & District Manager, Western Ontario

Longueuil
Place Montérégie
#440, 101, boul Roland-Therrien
Longueuil, QC J4H 4B9 Canada
450-670-9210
Fax: 450-670-6921
Pierre Martin, Director & District Manager
Mississauga
#406, 201 City Centre Dr.
Mississauga, ON L5B 2T4 Canada
905-276-1025
Fax: 905-276-5726
Norm Stevenson, Director, Metro West
Montréal
Scotia Tower
#1100, 1002 rue Sherbrooke ouest
Montréal, QC H3A 3L6 Canada
514-987-1234
Fax: 514-987-1227
Alain Bonneterre, Director & District Manager
Ottawa
#220, 99 Bank St.
Ottawa, ON K1P 6B9 Canada
613-236-7185
Fax: 613-236-0646
Douglas R. Stewart, Director & District Manager
Québec
#230, 801, ch St-Louis
Québec, QC G1S 1C1 Canada
418-683-2177
Fax: 418-682-3527
Michel Ruest, Director & District Manager
Saskatoon
#505, 111 - 2 Ave. South
Saskatoon, SK S7K 1K6 Canada
306-665-8334
Fax: 306-244-7760
Ward Headrick, Sr. Associate, Merchant Banking
Sudbury
#403, 30 Cedar St.
Sudbury, ON P3E 1A4 Canada
705-673-3621
Fax: 705-673-4007
Denis Goupil, Manager, Merchant Banking
Toronto
PO Box 35
#1000, 5160 Yonge St.
Toronto, ON M2N 6L9 Canada
416-229-4221
Fax: 416-229-4760
Ken S. Karmona, Director & District Manager
Vancouver
PO Box 11570
#2320, 650 West Georgia St.
Vancouver, BC V6B 4N8 Canada
604-717-6760
Fax: 604-717-6761
Derek Strong, Director & District Manager
Windsor
#402, 380 Ouellette Ave.
Windsor, ON N9A 6T3 Canada
519-254-6408
Fax: 519-254-4425
Cameron Lee, Director, South Western Ontario
Winnipeg
#401, 200 Portage Ave.
Winnipeg, MB R3C 3X2 Canada
204-985-3072
Fax: 204-985-5530

Britt Karlson, Director & District Manager
Regional Offices:
Burlington
5500 North Service Rd., 2nd Fl.
Burlington, ON L7L 6W6 Canada
905-335-9540
Fax: 905-335-5255
Philip M. Heinrich, Director & District Manager
Calgary
Scotia Centre
#3900, 700 - 2 St. SW
Calgary, AB T2P 2W2 Canada
403-269-7755
Fax: 403-269-7701
Wray Stannard, Regional Vice-President
Dartmouth
#310, 238A Brownlow Ave.
Dartmouth, NS B3B 2B4 Canada
902-429-3500
Fax: 902-423-5607
John Maxwell, Director, District Manager
Mississauga
#406, 201 City Centre Dr.
Mississauga, ON L5B 2T4 Canada
905-276-1025
Fax: 905-276-5726
Jeffrey Chernin, Regional Vice-President
Moncton
#410, 644 Main St.
Moncton, NB E1C 1E2 Canada
506-857-9757
Fax: 506-853-8101
John Maxwell, Director & District Manager
Montréal
Scotia Tower
#1105, 1002, rue Sherbrooke ouest
Montréal, QC H3A 3L6 Canada
514-987-4949
Fax: 514-987-4908
Guy Perreault, Regional Vice-President
Toronto - King St. West - Ontario Region
Scotia Plaza
40 King St. West, 26th Fl.
Toronto, ON M5H 1H1 Canada
416-933-2730
Fax: 416-933-2930
Barry Vallier, Vice-President, Risk Management
Toronto - King St. West - Ontario Risk Management
Scotia Plaza
40 King St. West, 26th Fl.
Toronto, ON M5H 1H1 Canada
416-933-2765
Fax: 416-933-2930
Barry Vallier, Vice-President, Risk Management
Toronto - Yonge St. - Ontario East Region
PO Box 35
#1000, 5160 Yonge St.
Toronto, ON M2N 6L9 Canada
416-229-4221
Fax: 416-229-1870
Richard Icanemy, Regional Vice-President

RPG Receivables Purchase Group Inc.

#300, 221 Lakeshore Rd. East
Oakville, ON L6J 1H7
905-338-8777
Fax: 905-842-0242
800-837-0265
inquiry@rpgreceivables.com
www.rpgreceivables.com
Year Founded: 1995
Number of Employees: 3

Saskatchewan Government Growth Fund Management Corporation

#400, 2400 College Ave.
Regina, SK S4P 1C8
306-787-6851
Fax: 306-787-0294
www.sggfmc.com
Year Founded: 1989
Profile: Fund manager is Crown Capital Partners Inc. in Regina.

Executives:
Don Axtell, President/CEO

Saskatchewan Indian Equity Foundation Inc.

202 Joseph Okemasis Dr.
Saskatoon, SK S7N 1B1
306-955-4550
Fax: 306-373-4969
www.sief.sk.ca
Ownership: Private. Federation of Saskatchewan Indian Nations & 74 bands.
Year Founded: 1982
Number of Employees: 9
Assets: $10-50 million
Revenues: $1-5 million
Profile: SIEF's work with the Aboriginal people of Saskatchewan has assisted in the creation of jobs & economic growth for First Nations people & has enabled them to successfully own & operate their own businesses. Through its services, SIEF promotes economic self-sufficiency of the First Nations people of Saskatchewan.

Executives:
Therese McIlmoyl, General Manager
Jasmine Bear, Financial Controller
Branches:
North Battleford
1192 - 102nd St.
North Battleford, SK S9A 1E9 Canada
306-446-7486
Fax: 306-446-7447
Caroline Maze, Manager
Regina
1925 Rose St.
Regina, SK S4P 3P1 Canada
306-522-2770
Fax: 306-522-2812
Sharon Sugar, Manager

Sasknative Economic Development Corporation

#108, 219 Robin Cres.
Saskatoon, SK S7L 6M8
306-477-4350
Fax: 306-373-2512
snedco@sk.sympatico.ca
Ownership: Non-profit
Number of Employees: 7

Savers Mortgage Inc.

#501, 3100 Steeles Ave. West
Concord, ON L4K 1R3
416-493-1983
Fax: 416-493-6898
Other Information: 905/454-2000
youreapproved@saversmortgage.com
www.saversmortgage.com
Year Founded: 1982
Number of Employees: 7
Profile: Mortgage banker/broker.

Scotia Merchant Capital Corporation

Scotia Plaza
40 King St. West, 38th Fl.
Toronto, ON M5W 2X6
416-862-3000
Fax: 416-862-3054
smc@scotiamarkets.com
www.scotiamerchantcapital.com
Ownership: Private
Executives:
Andrew Brenton, Managing Partner
Jeffrey Cole, Partner
Todd Hryhorzcuk, Partner
Garth Davis, Partner

Scotia Mortgage Corporation(SMC)

44 King St. West
Toronto, ON M5H 1H1
416-288-4111
Fax: 416-701-7599
www.scotiabank.com
Ownership: Wholly owned subsidiary of The Bank of Nova Scotia.
Number of Employees: 60
Assets: $1-10 billion
Executives:
Alberta G. Cefis, President/CEO

SD&G Community Futures Development Corporation
26 Pitt St.
Cornwall, ON K6J 3P2
613-932-4333
Fax: 613-932-0596
info@sdgcdc.on.ca
www.sdgcdc.on.ca
Former Name: SD & G Economic Development
Year Founded: 1987
Number of Employees: 3
Profile: Private, non-profit development agency. Assists with the relocation and expansion processes of organizations.

Executives:
James de Pater, Executive Director

Services Financiers FBN/ NBF Financial Services
1155, Metcalfe, 5e étage
Montréal, QC H3B 4S9
514-879-5354
Fax: 514-879-3614
Other Information: Toll Free: Can. 1-800-361-8838, 1-800-361-9522
daniel.simard@fbn.ca
www.nbffinancialservices.com
Profile: Wholly owned subsidiary of National Bank Financial. Specializes in the management of corporate group insurance plans and estate planning for individuals and business owners.

Settlement Investment Corp.
18012 - 107 Ave.
Edmonton, AB T5S 2J5
780-488-5656
Fax: 780-488-5811
Other Information: Toll Free (AB only): 1-800-661-9902
www.settlementinvestcorp.com
Ownership: Private. Owned by Settlement Sooniyaw Corp.
Year Founded: 1986
Number of Employees: 5
Assets: $1-5 million Year End: 20040331
Revenues: $1-5 million Year End: 20040331
Executives:
Randall Hardy, Chair
Allan Wells, Vice-Chair
Alex McGillivray, Treasurer
Keith Heron, Secretary

Shuswap Community Futures Development Corporation(CFDCS)
PO Box 1930
#101, 160 Harbourfront Dr. NE
Salmon Arm, BC V1E 4P9
250-803-0156
Fax: 250-803-0157
info@futureshuswap.com
www.futureshuswap.com
Ownership: Non-profit
Year Founded: 1985
Number of Employees: 12
Profile: The organization is funded through Western Economic Diversification. It provides business guidance & support in Shuswap communities. The following loan funds are administered: Community Futures Investment Fund, Youth Entrepreneur Investment Fund, Forest Community Business Loan Fund, Entrepreneurs with Disabilities Fund & GrowthStart.

Executives:
Dave Andrews, General Manager
Kaija Isherwood, Business Development Officer
Geri Byrne, Coordinator, Self-Employment
Tanja Carlson, Coordinator, Marketing & Development
Cheryl Niemi, Coordinator, Employment Wage Subsidy

Skypoint Capital Corporation
Tower B
#830, 555 Legget Dr.
Kanata, ON K2K 2X3
613-271-1500
Fax: 613-271-1505
info@skypointcorp.com
www.skypointcorp.com
Former Name: Venture Coaches
Year Founded: 1998
Executives:
Peter Charbonneau, General Partner; pcharbonneau@skypointcorp.com
Andrew M. Katz, General Partner; akatz@skypointcorp.com
Leo Lax, General Partner; llax@skypointcorp.com
Larry Perron, Partner; lperron@skypointcorp.com
Ann Gordon, Vice-President, Operations, CFO; agordon@skypointcorp.com

Smart Seed Equity
#408, 1066 Hamilton St.
Vancouver, BC V6B 2R9
604-649-4980
Fax: 604-685-7892
www.smartseed.net
Former Name: Smart Seed Fund
Executives:
Alnoor Kassam, General Partner
Shaheen Tejani, General Partner
Peter B. Inman, Managing Partner
Kristen Collinson, Director, Operations

SMEDA Business Development Corporation
#104, 9817 - 101 Ave.
Grande Prairie, AB T8V 0X6
780-814-5340
Fax: 780-532-0553
smeda@smeda.com
www.smeda.com
Number of Employees: 10
Executives:
Holly Sorgen, Manager
Branches:
Grande Prairie
Centre 2000
11330 - 106 St.
Grande Prairie, AB T8V 7X9 Canada

SNC-Lavalin Capital Inc.
455, boul René-Lévesque ouest
Montréal, QC H2Z 1Z3
514-393-1000
Fax: 514-866-3116
montreal@snclavalincapital.com
www.snclavalincapital.com
Revenues: $10-50 million
Profile: Services include integrated project financing & financial modelling.

Denise Marion; denise.marion@snclavalincapital.com
Branches:
Toronto
2200 Lake Shore Blvd. West
Toronto, ON M8V 1A4 Canada
416-252-8877
Fax: 416-252-9774
toronto@snclavalincapital.com
Vancouver
1075 West Georgia St.
Vancouver, BC V6E 3C9 Canada
604-605-4944
Fax: 604-622-7688
vancouver@snclavalincapital.com

Société d'aide au développement des collectivités (BSQ) inc(SADC BSQ)
CP 308
674, 11e av
Senneterre, QC J0Y 2M0
819-737-2211
Fax: 819-737-8888
sadc_bsq@ciril.qc.ca
www.reseau-sadc.qc.ca/sadcbsq/
Year Founded: 1985
Number of Employees: 5
Profile: The venture capital company operates in Quebec only.

Executives:
Marc Hardy, Directeur général
Marie Laporte, Coordonnatrice au développement

Société d'Aide au Développement des Collectivés de la MRC de Rivière-du-Loup
#201, 646, rue Lafontaine
Rivière-du-Loup, QC G5R 3C8
418-867-4272
Fax: 418-867-8060
sadc@mrc-rdl.qc.ca
www.mrc-rdl.qc.ca
Year Founded: 1990
Number of Employees: 8
Profile: The venture capital company operates in Quebec only.
Executives:
Gilles Goulet, Directeur général

Société d'Aide au Développement des Collectivités Centre-de-la-Mauricie
812, av des Cèdres
Shawinigan, QC G9N 1P2
819-537-5107
Fax: 819-537-5109
info@sadccm.ca
www.sadccm.ca
Former Name: Groupe Forces Inc.
Year Founded: 1984
Number of Employees: 10
Profile: Participates in regional economic development of the region. Its mandate is to create jobs in Centre-de-la-Mauricie.

Executives:
Simon Charlebois, Directeur général

Société d'Aide au Développement du Rocher-Percé inc
CP 186
129, boul René-Lévesque ouest
Chandler, QC G0C 1K0
418-689-5699
Fax: 418-689-5556
sadc@globetrotter.qc.ca
www.reseau-sadc.qc.ca/perce/
Former Name: Société d'Aide au Développement de Pabok Inc.

Year Founded: 1997
Number of Employees: 6
Executives:
Andrée Roy, Directrice générale
Jocelyne McInnis, Agent de développement

Société d'Aide au Développement de la Collectivité de Portneuf Inc.
299, 1re ave.
Portneuf, QC G0A 2Y0
418-286-4422
Fax: 418-286-3737
sadcpor9@globetrotter.net
www.sadcportneuf.qc.ca
Year Founded: 1995
Profile: Promotes the economic development and initiatives in the region by investing in local enterprises.

Société d'Aide au Développement des Collectivités des Laurentides Inc.
#230, 1332, boul Sainte-Adèle
Sainte-Adèle, QC J8B 2N5
450-229-3001
Fax: 450-229-6928
info@sadclaurentides.org
www.sadclaurentides.org
Ownership: Non-profit. Funded by federal government

Société de crédit commercial autochtone/ Native Commercial Credit Corporation
#265, 101, Place Chef Michel Laveau
Wendake, QC G0A 4V0
418-842-0972
Fax: 418-842-8925
800-241-0972
administration@socca.qc.ca
www.socca.qc.ca
Year Founded: 1992
Number of Employees: 8
Executives:
Jean Vincent, Président-directeur général
Martin Légaré, Directeur, Comptes

Société financière GMAC - Canada/ GMAC Commercial Credit Corporation - Canada
#2300, 800, boul Réne-Lévesque ouest
Montréal, QC H3B 1X9
514-397-9600
Fax: 514-397-1133
www.gmaccf.com
Former Name: Société de Crédit Commercial GMAC - Canada; Corporation Financière BNY - Canada
Ownership: Wholly owned subsidiary of GMAC Financial Services
Year Founded: 1994
Number of Employees: 55

Profile: The company offers a complete range of asset-based products & services including: factoring (credit protection, collection services, accounts receivable bookkeeping); inventory & accounts receivable financing; fixed asset funding; letters of credit programs; debt restructuring; & acquisition financing.

Branches:
Montréal
#2300, 800, boul Réne-Lévesque ouest
Montréal, QC H3B 1X9 Canada
514-397-9600
John L. Waxlax, Exec. Vice-President & Managing Director
Toronto
#1314, 150 York St.
Toronto, ON M5H 3S5 Canada
416-365-9555
Michael J. Mann, Sr. Vice-President & Regional Manager

Société Innovatech du sud du Québec

#20, 2100, rue King ouest
Sherbrooke, QC J1J 2E8
819-820-3305
Fax: 819-820-3320
isq@isq.qc.ca
www.isq.qc.ca
Ownership: Owned by Government of Québec
Year Founded: 1995
Number of Employees: 5
Assets: $50-100 million
Revenues: Under $1 million
Profile: The organization is a venture capital firm.

Executives:
Daniel Poisson, President/CEO
Jean-Jacques Caron, Vice-President, Investment; 819-820-3341

Directors:
Bruno Plante; 819-820-3388

Société Innovatech Québec et Chaudière-Appalaches

10, rue Pierre-Olivier-Chauveau
Québec, QC G1R 4J3
418-528-9770
Fax: 418-528-9783
866-605-1676
info@innovatechquebec.com
www.innovatechquebec.com
Ownership: Government owned
Year Founded: 1994
Number of Employees: 18
Profile: Venture capital company.

Executives:
Francine Laurent, Présidente-directrice-générale, Présidente du conseil
Chantal Brunet, Vice-Présidente; 418-528-9774; cbrunet@innovatechquebec.com
Directors:
Francine Bonicalzi, Chair
Louise Bédard
Chantal Blouin
René Drouin
Robert Dufour
Régis Labeaume
Fernand Labrie
Francine Laurent
Gaston Ouellet

South Central Community Futures Development Corporation

PO Box 1087
131 - 3rd Ave.
Assiniboia, SK S0H 0B0
306-642-5558
Fax: 306-694-1728
Other Information: Self Employment Program: 1-800-329-1479
sccfdc@sasktel.net
www.sccfdc.ca
Ownership: Non-profit
Year Founded: 1994
Profile: Programs offered include business services, such as counseling & access to capital, self-employment, disabilities & community economic development.

Executives:
Les Mielke, CEO

Branches:
Moose Jaw
88 Saskatchewan St. East
Moose Jaw, SK S6H 0V4 Canada
306-692-6525
Fax: 306-694-1728
800-329-1479
Candi Galbraith, Business Development Officer

South Pacific Minerals Corp.

#2007, 1177 West Hastings St.
Vancouver, BC V6E 2K3
604-662-8183
Fax: 604-602-1606
888-662-8182
info@southpacificminerals.com
www.southpacificminerals.com
Former Name: Fraserfund Financial Corp.; FraserFund Venture Capital (VCC) Corporation
Ownership: Public.
Year Founded: 1985
Stock Symbol: SPZ
Profile: Fraserfund Financial Corp. became South Pacific Minerals Corp.in Feb. 2005.

Executives:
Graham Harris, Chair/CEO & Vice-President, Finance
Directors:
Mark Bailey
Graham Harris
Peter A. McNeil
Teresa Piorun
Larry Reaugh
Robert Schafer

Southeast Community Futures Development Corporation(SCFDC)

#200, 208 Edmonton St.
Winnipeg, MB R3C 1R7
204-943-1656
Fax: 204-943-1735
scfdc@mb.sympatico.ca
www.seed.mb.ca
Ownership: Private
Year Founded: 1979
Profile: Part of the Southeast Resource Development Council.

Southwest Alberta Business Development Centre

PO Box 1568
659 Main St.
Pincher Creek, AB T0K 1W0
403-627-3020
Fax: 403-627-3035
800-565-4418
swabdc@telusplanet.net
www.swbizdev.com
Ownership: Not-for-profit society
Year Founded: 1992
Number of Employees: 4
Assets: $1-5 million
Revenues: Under $1 million
Profile: Assist in the creation of additional permanent private sector employment through the provision of advisory and investment services to small businesses.

Executives:
Chuck Lee, Manager; swabdc@telusplanet.net
Directors:
Sharon Quinton, Chair
Harlan Cahoon, Vice-Chair
Robert Bernard, Treasurer

Spire Sharwood Financial Inc.

Also listed under: *Financial Planning; Investment Management*

#100, 8 King St. East
Toronto, ON M5C 1B5
416-869-1598
Fax: 416-366-4892
info@sharwood.com
www.spiresharwood.com
Former Name: Sharwood Inc.; Sharwood & Company Limited; Sharwood Bioventures Inc.
Ownership: Private
Year Founded: 1976
Number of Employees: 10
Executives:
Timothy Gray, President/CEO
Gordon R. Sharwood, Chair
Michael Caven, Managing Director
Jeffrey Kahn, Managing Director
Jim McMinn, Managing Director
Stephen Sloan, Managing Director

SpringBank TechVentures Fund

#1, 160 MacLaurin Dr.
Calgary, AB T3Z 3S4
403-685-8001
Fax: 403-685-8002
email@sbtechventures.com
www.sbtechventures.com
Year Founded: 2000
Profile: Venture capital fund focused on venture and private equity investments in companies developing the enabling technologies, infrastructure and services to support the growth sectors of information, communications and technology.

Executives:
Shawn Abbot, Principal
Andrew Kyle, Principal
Barry Poffenroth, Principal
Barb Richardson, Principal

Sterling Centrecorp Inc.

#1, 2851 John St.
Markham, ON L3R 5R7
905-477-9200
Fax: 905-477-7390
info@sterlingcentrecorp.com
www.sterlingcentrecorp.com
Former Name: Samoth Capital Corporation; Sterling Financial Corporation
Ownership: Major shareholder Viceroy Trust, a trust for the benefit of Peter H. Thomas & his family, (16% interest)
Year Founded: 1944
Stock Symbol: SCF
Profile: The company is engaged in investment real estate services in the shopping centre/retail sector.

Executives:
A. David Kosoy, Co-CEO
John W.S. Preston, Co-CEO
Robert S. Green, President/COO
Henry Berezinczki, President, Sterling Centrecorp Inc., Western Division
Brian D. Kosov, Exec. Vice-President/COO, Southeastern Division
Carol Taccone, Exec. Vice-President & CFO
Richard Levinsky, President, Centrecorp Levinsky Realty Inc.
Marcus Bertagnolli, Vice-President, Real Estate Finance
Tracy M. Butler, Vice-President, Legal Department
Brett Glanfield, Vice-President, Property Management
Daniel J. Kumer, Vice-President, Acquisitions & Business Development
Stephen Preston, Managing Director, Texas Region
Gilbert J. Weiss, Legal Counsel
Directors:
A. David Kosoy, Co-Chair
John W.S. Preston, Co-Chair
David G.R. Bloom
Peter A. Burnim
Robert S. Green
Neil Hasson
Bernard Kraft
Ralph Lean
Stewart J.L. Robertson

Stonebridge Financial Corporation/ Stonebridge Financière

Also listed under: *Financial Planning*
#1201, Adelaide St. East
Toronto, ON Toronto
416-364-3001
Fax: 416-364-1557
info@stonebridge.ca
www.stonebridge.ca
Ownership: Canada Life Assurance Co., Manufacturers Life Insurance Co. & Industrial Alliance Insurance & Financial Services Inc., hold minority equity.
Year Founded: 1998
Profile: The company is engaged in structuring financings in the institutional market. The following financing services are provided: project finance, bulk lease finance, structured finance, advisory services & administrative services. A variety of domestic & international industries are served. Stonebridge

Stonebridge Financial Corporation/ Stonebridge Financière (continued)

specializes in the energy, infrastructure, environment & healthcare sectors.

Executives:
Denis Bourassa, MBA, Partner; dbourassa@stonebridge.ca
Robert M. Colliver, CFA, Partner; rcolliver@stonebridge.ca
Darrell Salter, Managing Director, Corporate & Portfolio Administration
John Estey, Director, Lease Financing
Jim Cahill, Vice-President, Structured & Project Financing
Rhea Dechaine, Manager, Lease Financing
Directors:
Richard Drouin, Chair
Denis Bourassa
Robert Colliver
Marc Dorion
Laurie Harding
Richard Legault
Branches:
Montréal
#2350, 1000, rue Sherbrooke ouest
Montréal, QC H3A 3G4
514-842-5001
Fax: 514-842-0557

Sudbury Regional Credit Union

***Also listed under:** Credit Unions/Caisses Populaires*
PO Box 662
1 Gribble St.
Copper Cliff, ON P0M 1N0
705-682-0645
Fax: 705-682-1348
888-444-2601
info@sudburycu.com
www.sudburycu.com
Ownership: Member-owned
Year Founded: 1951
Number of Employees: 43
Assets: $100-500 million Year End: 20060930
Revenues: Under $1 million Year End: 20060930
Executives:
William Falcioni, CEO; 705- 68- 064
Michael Moore, Manager, Operations; 705-682-0641
Suzie O'Neill, Manager, Human Resources
Rheal Paquette, Manager, Information & Technology
Douglas Yeo, Manager, Credit; 705-682-0641
Gary Blondin, Administrator, Credit Services
Mimi Wiseman, Controller; 705-682-0641
Directors:
George Joyce, President
Ted Joiner, Vice-President
Susan MacDonald, Secretary
Jenny Parisotto, Youth Director
Mara Storey, Youth Director
Kate Barber
John Cochrane
John Gouchie
Al Hickey
R.A. (Sandy) MacDonald
Joseph Marcuccio
Marvin Saunders
Rick Stickles
Branches:
Copper Cliff
PO Box 662
1 Gribble St.
Copper Cliff, ON P0M 1N0 Canada
705-682-0645
Fax: 705-682-1348
Jocelyne Akey, Supervisor
Levack
37 Levack Dr.
Levack, ON P0M 2C0 Canada
705-966-3451
Fax: 705-966-3747
Carol Nerpin, Supervisor
Sudbury - Barrydowne Rd.
1048 Barrydowne Rd.
Sudbury, ON P3A 3V3 Canada
705-560-5872
Fax: 705-560-2232
Patrick Tarini, Branch Manager
Sudbury - Bouchard St.
Regency Mall
469 Bouchard St.
Sudbury, ON P3E 2K8 Canada
705-522-5550
Fax: 705-522-8944
Mike DeNoble, Manager, Branch & Commercial Accounts
Sudbury - Lisgar St.
50 Lisgar St.
Sudbury, ON P3E 3L8 Canada
705-674-7526
Fax: 705-674-3253
Robert Rachkoloski, Branch Manager

Sun Country Community Futures Development Corporation

PO Box 1480
310 Railway Ave.
Ashcroft, BC V0K 1A0
250-453-9165
Fax: 250-453-9500
800-567-9911
vision@cfdcsuncountry.bc.ca
www.cfdcsuncountry.bc.ca
Ownership: Non-profit
Year Founded: 1988
Number of Employees: 6
Profile: Non-profit community economic development organization that exists to assist rural areas experiencing slow economic growth.

Executives:
Debbie Arnott, General Manager

Sunrise Community Futures Development Corporation

PO Box 353
405 Coteau Ave.
Weyburn, SK S4H 2K1
306-842-8803
Fax: 306-842-4069
800-699-0533
sunrise.cfdc@sasktel.net
www.sunrisecommunityfutures.com
Ownership: Non-Profit
Year Founded: 1997
Number of Employees: 4
Executives:
Terry Kurucz, General Manager
Branches:
Estevan
Wicklow Centre
#303, 1133 - 4th St.
Estevan, SK S4A 0W6 Canada
306-634-8300

Super Six Community Futures Development Corporation

TBJ Mall
PO Box 68
Main St.
Ashern, MB R0C 0E0
204-768-3351
Fax: 204-768-3489
888-496-8932
supersix@supersix.mb.ca
www.supersix.mb.ca
Ownership: Private
Year Founded: 1986
Number of Employees: 4
Executives:
Henry Sikora, General Manager

Taiwanese - Canadian Toronto Credit Union Limited

***Also listed under:** Credit Unions/Caisses Populaires*
#305, 3636 Steeles Ave. East
Markham, ON L3R 1K9
905-944-0981
Fax: 905-944-0982
tcu@on.aibn.com
www.tctcu.com
Ownership: Member-owned
Year Founded: 1978
Number of Employees: 5
Assets: $5-10 million Year End: 20050930
Revenues: Under $1 million Year End: 20050930
Profile: Offers a full range of financial services to Ontario residents of Taiwan origin.

Executives:
Tony Y.C. Liao, President
Tina Wang, Vice-President
Grace Liaw, Treasurer, Manager

Tamarack Capital Advisors Inc.

715 - 5 Ave. SW, 7th Fl.
Calgary, AB T2P 2X6
403-444-0150
Fax: 403-539-6250
888-314-1011
info@tamarackcapital.ca
www.tamarackcapital.ca
Former Name: Tamarack Group Ltd.
Ownership: Private. Subsidiary of Meyers Norris Penny Chartered Accountants.
Year Founded: 1991
Number of Employees: 50
Executives:
Laural Wood, President; shelleyl@mnp.ca
Ron Hymers, Sr. Vice-President & Managing Director; wepplerr@mnp.ca
Kathy Reich, Sr. Vice-President
Juneyt Tirmandi, Sr. Vice-President
Branches:
Edmonton
#500 West Tower
14310 - 111th Ave.
Edmonton, AB T5M 3Z7 Canada
780-451-4406
Fax: 780-454-1908
Keven Spitzmacher
Saskatoon
#400, 128 - 4th Ave.
Saskatoon, SK S7K 1M8 Canada
306-244-6779
Fax: 306-242-7844
Christopher Doll
Vancouver
#1380, 200 Granville St.
Vancouver, BC V6C 1S4 Canada
604-685-8504
Fax: 604-685-8594
Charles Addison
Winnipeg
#500, 1661 Portage Ave.
Winnipeg, MB R3J 3T7 Canada
204-775-4531
Fax: 204-783-8329
Ben Kelly

Targeted Strategies Limited

#100A, 3550 Taylor St.
Saskatoon, SK S7H 5H9
306-477-5770
Fax: 306-477-7199
800-505-5503
planning@targetedstrategies.com
www.targetedstrategies.com
Former Name: Targeted Investments Limited
Ownership: Private
Year Founded: 1996
Number of Employees: 11
Assets: Under $1 million
Revenues: $1-5 million
Profile: The company creates financial solutions for business owners designed to meet the needs of business enhancement & succession, while ensuring the optimization & effective organization of personal wealth.

Executives:
Garnet Morris, Principal
Michelle Knaus, General Manager

TCE Capital Corporation

#707, 505 Consumers Rd.
Toronto, ON M2J 4V8
416-497-7400
Fax: 416-497-3139
800-465-0400
money@tcecapital.com
www.tcecapital.com
Ownership: Private
Year Founded: 1992
Number of Employees: 12
Assets: $10-50 million Year End: 20061000
Revenues: $5-10 million Year End: 20061000
Profile: TCE Capital provides fast, flexible funding for growing Canadian businesses.

TD Capital
Toronto-Dominion Bank Tower, 10th Fl.
66 Wellington St. West
Toronto, ON M5K 1A2
416-307-8470
Fax: 416-982-5045
www.tdcapital.com
Former Name: TD Capital Group
Year Founded: 1968
Number of Employees: 40
Assets: $3,000,000,000
Executives:
Robert F. MacLellan, President; rob.maclellan@td.com
J.T. Gabel, CFO; mel.gabel@tdsecurities.com
Frank Gawlina, Vice-President & Director, Finance; frank.gawlina@tdcapital.com
John G. Dryden, Managing Director; peinvestors@tdcapital.com
Paul R. Henry, Managing Director; paul.henry@tdcapital.com
Canadian Private Equity Part:
Stephen J. Dent, Managing Director & Co-Head; steve.dent@tdcapital.com
Joseph P. Wiley, Managing Director & Co-Head; joe.wiley@tdcapital.com
William A. Lambert, Managing Director; bill.lambert@tdcapital.com
David S. McCann, Managing Director; david.mccann@tdcapital.com
Kevin E. Godwin, Vice-President & Director; kevin.godwin@tdcapital.com
John T. Loh, Vice-President & Director; john.loh@tdcapital.com
Michael R. Mazan, Vice-President & Director; michael.mazan@tdcapital.com
Michael J. Salamon, Vice-President & Director; michael.salamon@tdcapital.com
William C. Stevens, Vice-President & Director; william.stevens@tdcapital.com
Thecla Sweeney, Vice-President; thecla.sweeney@tdcapital.com
Mezzanine Partners:
Ian M. Kidson, Managing Director & Co-Head; ian.kidson@tdcapital.com
Tom J. Rashotte, Managing Director & Co-Head; tom.rashotte@tdcapital.com
Paul Liebowitz, Vice-President & Director; paul.liebowitz@tdcapital.com
Jonathan Kay, Vice-President; jonathan.kay@tdcapital.com
Daniel Klass, Vice-President; daniel.klass@tdcapital.com
Michael A. Koen, Vice-President; michael.koen@tdcapital.com
Private Equity Investors (Fu:
John V. Greenwood, Managing Director; john.greenwood@tdcapital.com
Stuart D. Waugh, Managing Director
Michael Flood, Vice-President & Director; michael.flood@tdcaptial.com
David C. Austin, Vice-President; david.austin@tdcapital.com
Jeff Pentland, Vice-President; jeff.pentland@tdcapital.com
Melissa Watson McJannet, Vice-President; melissa.mcjannet@tdcapital.com
Ventures Partners:
Paul L. Ciriello, Group Head & Managing Director; paul.ciriello@tdcapital.com
James Goldinger, Vice-President & Director; james.goldinger@tdcapital.com
Richard Grinnel, Vice-President & Director; richard.grinnel@tdcapital.com

TD Mortgage Corporation(TDMC)
Toronto-Dominion Centre
PO Box 1, TD Stn. TD
55 King St. West
Toronto, ON M5K 1A2
416-982-8594
Fax: 416-944-6650
Former Name: Tordom Corporation
Ownership: Wholly owned subsidiary of the TD Bank
Year Founded: 1971
Assets: $26,591,453,000
Executives:
Bruce M. Shirreff, Chair, President & CEO
Susan Clifford, Controller
Affiliated Companies:
The Canada Trust Company
Branches:
Thornhill
#2, 9200 Bathurst St.
Thornhill, ON L4J 8W1 Canada
905-707-7663
MICR: 1215-004

TELUS Ventures
3777 Kingsway, 12th Fl.
Burnaby, BC V5H 3Z7
604-432-2150
Fax: 604-438-0325
venturesinfo@telus.com
www.telus.com/ventures
Year Founded: 2001
Executives:
Mathew George, Vice-President, Portfolio Management

Textron Financial Canada Funding Corp.
#800, 1959 Upper Water St.
Halifax, NS B3J 2X2
401-621-4255
Fax: 401-621-5040
Ownership: Textron Financial Corporation, Providence, RI, USA.
Stock Symbol: TXT:NYSE

Textron Financial Canada Ltd.
5515 North Service Rd., 2nd Fl.
Burlington, ON L7L 6G4
905-331-8325
Fax: 866-803-2159
877-395-5368
csharp@textronfinancial.com
www.textronfinancial.com
Ownership: Textron Inc.
Profile: Services include asset-based lending, vendor finance programs & factoring, equipment financing & leasing, term loans & golf course & resort financing.
Executives:
Chris Sharp, Vice-President & General Manager
Affiliated Companies:
Textron Financial Canada Funding Corp.

Transport Financial Services Ltd.
Also listed under: *Accountants*
105 Bauer Pl.
Waterloo, ON N2L 6B5
519-886-8070
Fax: 519-886-5214
800-461-5970
www.tfsgroup.com/tfs
Ownership: Private
Year Founded: 1974
Offices:
Oshawa
PO Box 264
#27, 1300 King St. East
Oshawa, ON L1H 8J4 Canada
905-432-8070
Fax: 905-432-8071
frang@tfsgroup.com
Fran Graham, Manager

Travelers Financial Group
#500, 4180 Lougheed Hwy.
Burnaby, BC V5C 6A7
604-293-0202
Fax: 604-473-3816
877-293-0202
jcase@travelersfinancial.com
www.travelersfinancial.com
Ownership: Private
Year Founded: 1972
Number of Employees: 60
Assets: $50-100 million
Revenues: $100-500 million
Profile: The following services are provided: term lending, asset-based leasing & financing on all capital equipment; prime & non-prime auto leasing; corporate financial services; & consumer acceptance & factoring.
Executives:
Dennis Holmes, Chair & Director
Jim Case, CEO
Bruce Wilson, CFO
Gary Thompson, Exec. Vice-President
Branches:
Calgary
#210, 2850 Glenmore Trail SE
Calgary, AB T2C 2E7 Canada
403-296-0180
Fax: 403-296-0194
877-703-7739
Edmonton
#104, 10525 - 170th St.
Edmonton, AB T5P 4W2 Canada
780-413-8440
Fax: 403-413-8727
877-703-7739
Mississauga
#750, 2 Robert Speck Pkwy
Mississauga, ON L4Z 1H8 Canada
905-306-2795
Fax: 905-306-7542

Treaty Seven Economic Development Corporation
#300, 6011 - 1A St. SW
Calgary, AB T2H 0G5
403-251-9242
Fax: 403-251-9750
info@t7edc.com
www.t7edc.com
Year Founded: 1993
Number of Employees: 10
Profile: An affiliate is Treaty Seven Tribal Council.
Executives:
Jim Russell, General Manager

Trellis Capital Corporation
#1302, 330 Bay St.
Toronto, ON M5H 2S8
416-398-2299
Fax: 416-398-1799
selby@trelliscapital.com
www.trelliscapital.com
Profile: Trellis Capital Corporation provides growth capital to proprietary technology companies in the following sectors: industrial, manufacturing, alternative energy & information technology infrastructures. Included are companies that have developed unique materials. The companies must gain competitive edge through development, or original use of technology in their products or services.
Executives:
Sunil Selby, Managing Partner
Dominic Talalla, Managing Partner

Tri-Star Equity Capital Partners Inc.
416-480-2715
Fax: 416-878-0401
tristarequitycapital@rogers.com
Executives:
Scott Sutherland, Sr. Partner; scottsutherland@sympatico.ca

Trian Equities Ltd.
#210, 4240 Manor St.
Burnaby, BC V5G 1B2
604-412-0166
Fax: 604-412-0117
Year Founded: 1985
Profile: The venture capital company invests in businesses in Canada & the United States.
Executives:
Raymond A. McLean, President/CEO
David Gadhia, Secretary

Tribal Resources Investment Corp.
344 - 2nd Ave. West
Prince Rupert, BC V8J 1G6
250-624-3535
Fax: 250-624-3883
800-665-3201
trico@citytel.net
www.tricorp.ca
Also Known As: TRICORP
Year Founded: 1990
Number of Employees: 9
Executives:
Frank Parnell, President/CEO

Tribal Wi-Chi-Way Win Capital Corporation
#203, 400 St. Mary Ave.
Winnipeg, MB R3C 4K5

Tribal Wi-Chi-Way Win Capital Corporation (continued)
204-943-0888
Fax: 204-946-5318
800-568-8488
info@twcc.mb.ca
www.twcc.mb.ca
Year Founded: 1993
Number of Employees: 8
Profile: Capital for aboriginal businesses is provided.
Executives:
Alan Park, CEO

Triple R Community Futures Development Corporation
PO Box 190
220 Main St.
Morris, MB R0G 1K0
204-746-6180
Fax: 204-746-2035
Other Information: Toll Free (MB only): 1-800-275-6611
tripler@triplercfdc.mb.ca
www.triplercfdc.mb.ca/
Executives:
Ian Goodall-George, CEO/Community Development Manager

Ubiquity Bank of Canada
Also listed under: *Domestic Banks: Schedule I*
#303, 32071 South Fraser Way
Abbotsford, BC V2T 1W3
888-881-0188
contact@ubiquitybank.ca
www.ubiquitybank.ca
Ownership: Private.
Year Founded: 2004
Assets: $100-500 million Year End: 20061031
Revenues: Under $1 million Year End: 20061031
Executives:
Bruce Howell, President/CEO, CFO
Peter J. Wright, Exec. Vice-President/COO
Roger Payer, General Manager & Corporate Secretary; 604-557-5000; rpayer@ubiquitybank.ca
Directors:
Maurice Mourton, Chair
John Allen, Vice-Chair
Geoffrey Thompson, 2nd Vice-Chair
Trevor Hildebrand
Bruce Howell
Karen Laing
Karl Noordam
William Rogers
Tim Spiegel
Peter J. Wright

Ulnooweg Development Group Inc.
PO Box 1259
Truro, NS B2N 5N2
902-893-7379
Fax: 902-893-0353
888-766-2376
thoskin@ulnooweg.ca
www.ulnooweg.ca
Year Founded: 1985
Number of Employees: 16
Assets: $5-10 million
Revenues: $1-5 million
Executives:
Todd Hoskin, CEO
Kendra Arsenault, General Manager
Branches:
Eel River Bar First Nation
#211, 11 Main St.
Eel River Bar First Nation, NB E8C 1A1 Canada
506-684-6295
Fax: 506-684-6333
Fredericton
Kchikhusis Commercial Center
PO Box R14
150 Cliffe St.
Fredericton, NB E3A 2T1 Canada
506-455-9334
Fax: 506-444-7582
888-248-2200
St. John's
58 Lemarchant Rd.
St. John's, NL A1C 6K1 Canada
709-726-3750
Fax: 709-726-3742

VanCity Community Business Solutions Centre
183 Terminal Ave.
Vancouver, BC V6A 4B6
604-709-6930
Fax: 604-871-5404
888-826-2489
peerlending@vancity.com
www.vancity.com/peerlending
Former Name: VanCity Micro-Credit Department
Year Founded: 1997
Number of Employees: 5
Profile: The Centre provides self-employed people, particularly women, youth & new Canadians, access to credit for their micro-businesses. Through the Advice & Business Loans to Entrepreneurs with Disabilities (ABLED) program, it also provides advice & loans to entrepreneurs who have a temporary or permanent disability

Vanguard Credit Union
Also listed under: *Credit Unions/Caisses Populaires; Investment Management*
PO Box 490
47 Main St.
Rossburn, MB R0J 1V0
204-859-5010
Fax: 204-859-5020
info@vanguardcu.mb.ca
www.vanguardcu.mb.ca
Ownership: Member-owned
Year Founded: 1947
Number of Employees: 92
Assets: $100-500 million Year End: 20051231
Revenues: $5-10 million Year End: 20051231
Executives:
Ian Gerrard, CEO
Guy Huberdeau, President
Kathy Brooks, Vice-President, Human Resources
Phil Corney, Vice-President, Credit & Corporate Development
Jean Hogarth, Vice-President, Finance
Betty-Ann Slon, Vice-President, Relationships & Marketing
Directors:
William Antonow
Don Armitage
Morley Butler
Rodney Cairns
Debbie Jensen
Darlene Lowes
Florence Pushka
Ron Sangster
Ed Slywchuk
Brent Strachan
Blaine Woodhouse
Branches:
Angusville
PO Box 40
239 Main St.
Angusville, MB R0J 0A0 Canada
204-773-2949
Fax: 204-773-3223
angusville@vanguardcu.mb.ca
Binscarth
PO Box 70
18 Russell St.
Binscarth, MB R0J 0G0 Canada
204-532-2000
Fax: 204-532-2255
binscarth@vanguardcu.mb.ca
Birtle
PO Box 267
681 Main St.
Birtle, MB R0M 0C0 Canada
204-842-5381
Fax: 204-842-3217
birtle@vanguardcu.mb.ca
Lucille Fulton, Manager
Brandon
Vanguard Business Centre, #B
824 - 18th St.
Brandon, MB R7A 5B7 Canada
204-571-3850
Fax: 204-571-3859
brandon@vanguardcu.mb.ca
Foxwarren
PO Box 191
75 First St. South
Foxwarren, MB R0J 0R0 Canada
204-847-3000
Fax: 204-847-3003
foxwarren@vanguardcu.mb.ca
Lucille Fulton, Manager
Hamiota
PO Box 430
50 Maple Ave. East
Hamiota, MB R0M 0T0 Canada
204-764-6230
Fax: 204-764-6240
hamiota@vanguardcu.mb.ca
Todd Hunter, Manager
Kenton
PO Box 160
308 Woodworth Ave.
Kenton, MB R0M 0Z0 Canada
204-838-2446
Fax: 204-838-2499
kenton@vanguardcu.mb.ca
Blair Fordyce, Manager
McAuley
PO Box 52
318 Railway Ave. North
McAuley, MB R0M 1H0 Canada
204-722-2035
Fax: 204-722-2289
mcauley@vanguardcu.mb.ca
Blair Fordyce, Manager
Miniota
PO Box 250
105 North Railway Ave.
Miniota, MB R0M 1M0 Canada
204-567-3838
Fax: 204-567-3555
miniota@vanguardcu.mb.ca
Blair Fordyce, Manager
Oak Lake
PO Box 279
162 North Railway St.
Oak Lake, MB R0M 1P0 Canada
204-855-2243
Fax: 204-855-2737
oaklake@vanguardcu.mb.ca
Blair Fordyce, Manager
Oak River
PO Box 29
17 North Railway St.
Oak River, MB R0K 1T0 Canada
204-566-2184
Fax: 204-566-2123
oakriver@vanguardcu.mb.ca
Todd Hunter, Manager
Rossburn
PO Box 490
47 Main St.
Rossburn, MB R0J 1V0 Canada
204-859-5025
Fax: 204-859-5039
rossburn@vanguardcu.mb.ca
Lucille Fulton, Manager
Russell
PO Box 117
447 Main St. North
Russell, MB R0J 1W0 Canada
204-773-7030
Fax: 204-773-7044
russell@vanguardcu.mb.ca
St Lazare
PO Box 190
241 Main St. South
St Lazare, MB R0M 1Y0 Canada
204-683-2466
Fax: 204-683-2295
stlazare@vanguardcu.mb.ca
Lucille Fulton, Manager

VantageOne Capital Inc.
3205 - 32nd St.
Vernon, BC V1T 5M7
250-260-4527
Fax: 250-260-4525
877-260-4527

lease@vdcu.com
www.vdcu.com/vantageonecapital
Ownership: Wholly-owned subsidiary of Vernon & District Credit Union, Vernon, BC.

VenGrowth Capital Management

Also listed under: *Investment Fund Companies*
#200, 145 Wellington St. West
Toronto, ON M5J 1H8
416-971-6656
Fax: 416-971-6519
800-382-7720
info@vengrowth.com
www.vengrowth.com
Ownership: Public
Year Founded: 1994
Profile: Labour-sponsored investment fund.

Executives:
Michael S. Cohen, Managing General Partner
Douglas Michael, General Partner, CFO
Peter Carrescia, General Partner
Jay Heller, General Partner
Mark Janoska, General Partner
Graham Matthews, General Partner
Peter Seeligsohn, General Partner
VenGrowth:
Investment II Fund
RRSP Eligible; Inception Year: 2000; Fund Managers:
Allen Lupyrypa
R. EarlStorie
Patrick DiPietro
David Ferguson
Luc Margengère
Graham McBride
Advanced Life Sciences Fund
RRSP Eligible; Inception Year: 2002; Fund Managers:
Luc Margengère
JeffCourtney
Investment I Fund
RRSP Eligible; Inception Year: 1995; Fund Managers:
Allen Lupyrypa
R. EarlStorie
Patrick DiPietro
David Ferguson
Luc Margengère
Graham McBride
Traditional Industries Fund
RRSP Eligible; Inception Year: 2003; Fund Managers:
Graham McBride
AllenLupyrypa
R. Earl Storie
Michael Wolfe
Gavin Muranake
Vengrowth:
Investment III Diversified Fund
RRSP Eligible; Inception Year: 2004; Fund Managers:
Allen Lupyrypa
R. EarlStorie
Patrick DiPietro
David Ferguson
Luc Margengère
Graham McBride
Cash Management Fund
RRSP Eligible; Inception Year: 2006; Fund Managers:
TD Asset Management

Ventures Community Futures Development Corporation

Deneschuk Homes Bldg.
PO Box 1180
Hwy. 10 East
Yorkton, SK S3N 2X3
306-782-0255
Fax: 306-783-2590
877-782-0255
info@venturescfdc.com
www.venturescfdc.com
Profile: Helps people develop the knowledge, experience, and attitudes that enable them to pursue their entrepreneurial goals.

Executives:
Corinne Lubiniecki, General Manager; 306-782-1299

Ventures West Management Inc.

#500, 1066 West Hastings St.
Vancouver, BC V6E 3X1
604-688-9495
Fax: 604-687-2145
info@ventureswest.com
www.ventureswest.com
Ownership: Private
Year Founded: 1968
Profile: The private venture capital investment group operates nationally. It invests in biotechnology, communications, energy technology & information technology.

Executives:
Robin Louis, Chair
Ted Anderson, President
Howard Riback, CFO
David Berkowitz, Sr. Vice-President
Barry Gekiere, Sr. Vice-President
Nancy Harrison, Sr. Vice-President
San Znaimer, Sr. Vice-President
Robin Axon, Vice-President
Maha Katabi, Vice-President
Pardeep Sangha, Vice-President
Marc Wickhan, Vice-President
Branches:
Montréal
1155, boul René-Lévesque, 25e étage
Montréal, QC H3B 2K4 Canada
514-395-0777
Fax: 514-395-8757
info@ventureswest.com
Toronto
#1200, 20 Adelaide St. East
Toronto, ON M5C 2T6 Canada
416-861-0700
Fax: 416-861-0866

Vernon & District Credit Union

Also listed under: *Credit Unions/Caisses Populaires; Investment Management*
3108 - 33rd Ave.
Vernon, BC V1T 2N7
250-545-9251
Fax: 250-545-8166
888-339-8328
info@vdcu.com
www.vdcu.com
Ownership: Co-operative. Member-owned.
Year Founded: 1944
Number of Employees: 54
Assets: $100-500 million Year End: 20051200
Revenues: $10-50 million Year End: 20051200
Profile: The credit union employs 45 full-time equivalent staff.

Executives:
Glenn Benischek, CEO; 250-545-9251; gbenischek@vantageone.net
Luby Pow, Chief Operating Officer; 250-545-9251; lpow@vantageone.net
Rheisa Campbell, Chief Financial Officer; 250- 97-6; rcampbell@vantageone.net
Directors:
Simo Korpisto, Chair; 250-542-5525
Don Main, Vice-Chair; 250-542-6209
Affiliated Companies:
VantageOne Capital Inc.
VantageOne Financial Corporation

Visions North Community Futures Development Corporation

PO Box 810
711 La Ronge Ave.
La Ronge, SK S0J 1L0
306-425-2612
Fax: 306-425-2205
visions@sasktel.net
www.visionsnorth.com
Ownership: Non-profit corporation
Year Founded: 1988
Number of Employees: 3
Profile: Financial assistance offered includes the following funds: Challenge Fund, Forestry Fund, Investment Fund, & the Youth Investment Fund. In addition, the corporation offers services such as technical services, business plan development, statistical information, resource materials, business counselling & feasibility studies.

Executives:
Jean Powell, Executive Administrator
Bill Hogan, General Manager

W.A. Robinson & Associates Ltd.

Also listed under: *Financial Planning; Investment Management*

The Simonett Bldg.
PO Box 208
14216 Hwy. 38
Sharbot Lake, ON K0H 2P0
613-279-2116
Fax: 613-279-3130
877-279-2116
wayne.robinson@robinsonsgroup.com
www.robinsonsgroup.com
Ownership: Private
Year Founded: 1980
Number of Employees: 22
Assets: $1,000,000 Year End: 20041130
Revenues: $1-5 million Year End: 20041130
Profile: Services include business financing, mortgages, financial planning, corporate & transition planning & money management. Affiliated companies are Pillar Financial Services Inc. & Lake District Realty Corporation.

Executives:
Wayne A. Robinson, CFA, President, Financial Planner, Investment Counsel & Portfolio Man; wayne.robinson@robinsonsgroup.com
David Robinson, Controller
Karen Bertram, Portfolio Administrator
Alison Robinson, Broker, Lake District Realty Corporation

Waterfront Capital Corporation

2489 Bellevue Ave.
West Vancouver, BC V7V 1E1
604-922-2030
Fax: 604-922-2037
888-888-9122
Other Information: Toll Free US: 1-888-888-9123
information@waterfrontgroup.com
www.waterfrontgroup.com
Year Founded: 1987
Number of Employees: 5
Stock Symbol: WCC
Profile: The investment/merchant bank makes investments for capital appreciation, as well as providing general management services, public & shareholder relation services & investment services for a fee. The company invests primarily in securities of industrial companies & enterprises.

Executives:
Bruce Morley, President
Sharon Constable, Vice-President, Administration, Corporate Secretary
Directors:
Sharon Constable
Bruce E. Morley
Stuart R. Ross

Wellington Financial LP

BCE Place
#2520, 161 Bay St.
Toronto, ON M5J 2S1
416-682-6002
Fax: 416-682-1160
aolah@wellingtonfund.com
www.wellingtonfund.com
Ownership: Private
Year Founded: 2000
Number of Employees: 8
Profile: The company is a debt provider. It offers operating lines, term loans & venture debt. Limited partners include Canadian institutional investors, such as life insurance companies, pension funds & money managers.

Executives:
Mark R. McQueen, President/CEO
Mark Usher, Partner
Kul Mani, Vice-President
Mark Wilk, Vice-President
Jason Nardari, Manager, Investment
Craig Netterfield, Manager, Investment
Amy Olay, Manager, Marketing
Directors:
Kenneth B. Rotman, Chair

Wellington West Corporate Finance
#300, 200 Waterfront Dr.
Winnipeg, MB R3B 3P1
204-925-5142
Fax: 204-942-4636
800-461-6314
info@wellwest.ca
wellingtonwest.com
Executives:
Charlie Spiring, Chair/CEO
John Rothwell, President
Blaine Coates, CFO

Wells Fargo Financial Corporation Canada
3 Concorde Gate, 4th Fl.
Toronto, ON M3C 3N7
416-382-5555
Fax: 905-755-7703
financial.wellsfargo.com/tcc/en/index.html
Former Name: Trans Canada Credit
Ownership: Wholly owned subsidiary of Wells Fargo Financial
Year Founded: 1940
Profile: The company is principally engaged in the consumer finance business in Canada.

Branches:
Abbotsford
#5, 53324 South Fraser Way
Abbotsford, BC V2S 4N8 Canada
604-853-5477
Amherst
147 Albion St. South
Amherst, NS B4H 2X2 Canada
902-667-3814
Antigonish
#42, 133 Church St.
Antigonish, NS B2G 2E3 Canada
902-863-4020
Barrie
#1, 10 Anne St. South
Barrie, ON L4N 2C6 Canada
705-728-5903
Bay Roberts
Bay Centre Mall
#1, 226 C.B. Hwy.
Bay Roberts, NL A0A 1G0 Canada
709-786-3141
Brampton - Gillingham Dr.
#407, 40 Gillingham Dr.
Brampton, ON L6X 4X7 Canada
905-451-7140
Brampton - Queen St.
253 Queen St. East
Brampton, ON L6W 2B8 Canada
905-453-1290
Brandon
714 - 18th St.
Brandon, MB R7A 5B5 Canada
204-727-0771
Bridgewater
557 King St.
Bridgewater, NS B4V 1B3 Canada
902-543-6331
Burlington - Plains Rd.
#5, 645 Plains Rd. East
Burlington, ON L7T 4J5 Canada
905-632-3994
Burlington - South Service Rd.
3380 South Service Rd.
Burlington, ON L7N 3J5 Canada
905-632-6225
Burnaby
#301, 3701 East Hastings
Burnaby, BC B5C 2H6 Canada
604-294-8944
Calgary - 17th Ave.
2935 - 17th Ave. SE
Calgary, AB T2A 0P7 Canada
403-273-6711
Calgary - 32nd Ave. NE
#114, 1725 - 32nd Ave. NE
Calgary, AB T2E 7C8 Canada
403-250-9009
Calgary - 42nd Ave.
#222, 855 - 42nd Ave.
Calgary, AB T2G 1Y8 Canada
403-214-4380
Calgary - Crowfoot Cres.
#316, Crowfoot Business Centre
400 Crowfoot Cres. NW
Calgary, AB T6G 5H6 Canada
403-241-2910
Calgary - MacLeod Trail SW
4315 MacLeod Trail SW
Calgary, AB T2G 0A3 Canada
403-243-2703
Cambridge
#4A, 534 Hespeler Rd.
Cambridge, ON N1R 6J7 Canada
519-621-8340
Campbell River
1275 Cypress St., #A
Campbell River, BC V9W 2Z3 Canada
250-287-8885
Campbellton
83 Roseberry St.
Campbellton, NB E3N 3G7 Canada
506-753-7791
Carbonear
127 Columbus Dr.
Carbonear, NL A1Y 1B6 Canada
709-596-1890
Channel-Port-aux-Basques
62 Main St.
Channel-Port-aux-Basques, NL A0M 1C0 Canada
709-695-5880
Charlottetown
#13.3, 449 University Ave.
Charlottetown, PE C1A 8K3 Canada
902-368-1814
Chilliwack
PO Box 353
Chilliwack, BC V2P 6J4 Canada
604-703-0602
Clarenville
124 Manitoba Dr.
Clarenville, NL A5A 1K7 Canada
709-466-7525
Corner Brook
#11, 1 Mount Bernard Ave.
Corner Brook, NL A2H 6G1 Canada
709-639-8994
Courtenay
#113, 750 Comox Rd.
Courtenay, BC V9N 3P6 Canada
250-879-1600
Cranbrook
100B Cranbrook St. North
Cranbrook, BC B1C 3P9 Canada
250-417-2663
Dartmouth - Main St.
#6, 100 Main St.
Dartmouth, NS B2V 1R5 Canada
902-434-1050
Dartmouth - Portland St.
535 Portland St.
Dartmouth, NS B2Y 4B1 Canada
902-469-2557
Delta
7909 - 120th St.
Delta, BC V4C 6P6 Canada
604-595-8190
Digby
#2, 507 Hwy. 303
Digby, NS B0V 1A0 Canada
902-245-5850

Edmonton - 107 Ave.
12220 - 107 Ave.
Edmonton, AB T5M 4A8 Canada
780-452-2720
Edmonton - 170 St.
10836 - 170 St.
Edmonton, AB T5S 2H7 Canada
780-483-7783
Edmonton - 99 St.
3841 - 99 St. NW
Edmonton, AB T6E 6H6 Canada
780-438-3058
Edmonton - Calgary Trail
#918, 5555 Calgary Trail NW
Edmonton, AB T6H 5P9 Canada
780-483-9494
Edmonton - Calgary Trail
#1250, 555 Calgary Trail
Edmonton, AB T6H 5P9 Canada
780-430-9328
Edmonton - Victoria Trail
14027 Victoria Trail
Edmonton, AB T5Y 2B6 Canada
780-822-2020
Edmundston
PO Box 94
180, boul Hebert
Edmundston, NB E3V 3K7 Canada
506-739-6216
Florenceville
#1, 317 Main St.
Florenceville, NB E1V 3G6 Canada
506-392-5504
Fort St John
10351 - 100 St.
Fort St John, BC V1J 3Z2 Canada
250-785-6193
Fredericton
1033 Prospect St.
Fredericton, NB E3B 3B9 Canada
506-458-1908
Gander
282 Airport Blvd.
Gander, NL A1V 1W7 Canada
709-256-4031
Gatineau
1134, boul St-René ouest
Gatineau, QC J8T 7P7 Canada
819-243-1140
Granby
184, rue Principale
Granby, QC J2G 2V6 Canada
450-372-4824
Grand Falls-Windsor
28 Cromer Ave.
Grand Falls-Windsor, NL A2A 1X2 Canada
709-489-6608
Grande Prairie
#102, 10027 - 101 Ave.
Grande Prairie, AB T8V 0X9 Canada
780-532-2374
Guelph
#12, 304 Stone Rd.
Guelph, ON N1G 3C4 Canada
519-836-3331
Halifax - Chain Lake Dr.
#11, 155 Chain Lake Dr.
Halifax, NS B3S 1B3 Canada
902-450-6307
Halifax - Mumford Rd.
#R32, 6960 Mumford Rd.
Halifax, NS B3L 4P1 Canada
902-455-1501
Hamilton - Ottawa St.
215 Ottawa St. North
Hamilton, ON L8H 3Z4 Canada
905-549-4176
Hamilton - Upper James St.
#8, 1171 Upper James St.
Hamilton, ON L9C 3B2 Canada
905-318-7238
Happy Valley-Goose Bay
358 Hamilton River Rd.
Happy Valley-Goose Bay, NL A0P 1C0 Canada
709-896-7260

Kamloops
231 Seymour
Kamloops, BC V2C 2E7 Canada
250-372-8861
Kelowna
#175, 2463 Hwy. 97
Kelowna, BC V1X 4J2 Canada
250-762-2878
Kentville
395 Main St.
Kentville, NS B4N 3X7 Canada

902-678-7347
Kingston
16 Bath Rd.
Kingston, ON K7L 1C4 Canada
613-549-4330
Kitchener
#6, 825 Weber St. East
Kitchener, ON N2H 1H5 Canada
519-743-2643
Labrador City
201 Humber Ave.
Labrador City, NL A1V 2Y3 Canada
709-944-6607
Laval - Cure-Labelle
#2101, boul Cure-Labelle
Laval, QC H7T 1L4 Canada
450-688-7502
Laval - Place Laval
#310, 2, Place Laval
Montréal, QC H7N 5N6 Canada
450-663-8999
Lethbridge
1020 - 3rd Ave. South
Lethbridge, AB T1J 0J4 Canada
403-328-8876
Liverpool
154 Main St.
Liverpool, NS B0T 1K0 Canada
902-354-3491
London - Dundas St.
#4, 1790 Dundas St. East
London, ON N5W 3E5 Canada
519-455-5050
London - Wellington Rd.
310 Wellington Rd. South
London, ON N6C 4P4 Canada
519-434-8416
Longueuil
1081, ch Chambly
Longueuil, QC J4H 3M7 Canada
450-670-8740
Lower Sackville
585 Sackville Dr.
Lower Sackville, NS B4C 2S4 Canada
902-865-3974
Lévis
124, route de Président Kennedy
Lévis, QC G6V 6C9 Canada
418-833-4222
Marystown
234 Ville Marie Dr.
Marystown, NL A0E 2M0 Canada
709-279-4007
Miramichi
#103, 2436 King George Hwy.
Miramichi, NB E1V 6V9 Canada
506-622-1384
Mississauga - Dundas St.
#3, 2273 Dundas St.
Mississauga, ON L5K 2L8 Canada
905-828-1711
Mississauga - Dundas St. East
#107, 1090 Dundas St. East
Mississauga, ON L4Y 2B8 Canada
905-279-2266
Mississauga - Standish Ct.
#400, 55 Standish Ct.
Mississauga, ON L5R 4J4 Canada
905-755-7064
Fax: 905-755-7108
Moncton
1126 Mountain Rd.
Moncton, NB E1C 2T9 Canada
506-857-8920
Montague
PO Box 1119
518C Main St.
Montague, PE C0A 1R0 Canada
902-838-3367
Montréal - Beaubien
#100, 6520, rue Beaubien
Montréal, QC H1M 1A9 Canada
514-251-0910
Montréal - Newman
7737, boul Newman
Montréal, QC H8N 1X7 Canada
514-363-0401
Montréal - Papineau
#220, 10345 Papineau
Montréal, QC H2B 2A3 Canada
514-285-6644
Montréal - St Jean-Baptiste
1528, boul St Jean-Baptiste
Montréal, QC H1B 4A4 Canada
514-645-9281
Mount Pearl
961 Topsail Rd., #D
Mount Pearl, NL A1N 3K1 Canada
709-368-0141
Nanaimo
#2, 4180 Island Hwy. North
Nanaimo, BC V9T 1W6 Canada
250-758-1450
Nepean
#12, 3657 Richmond Rd.
Nepean, ON K2H 8X3 Canada
613-829-0591
New Glasgow
PO Box 68
610 East River Rd.
New Glasgow, NS B2H 2S4 Canada
902-752-8318
North Bay
217 Main St. East
North Bay, ON P1B 1B2 Canada
705-472-3690
Oshawa
#3, 843 King St. West
Oshawa, ON L1J 2L4 Canada
905-728-4628
Ottawa - Bank St.
1500 Bank St.
Ottawa, ON K1H 7Z2 Canada
613-731-4264
Ottawa - Bank St.
#1, 2430 Bank St.
Ottawa, ON K1V 0T7 Canada
613-738-3336
Ottawa - St. Laurent Blvd.
#3, 1020 St Laurent Blvd.
Ottawa, ON K1K 4S2 Canada
613-738-3336
Owen Sound
1545 - 16th St. East
Owen Sound, ON N4K 5N3 Canada
519-376-0560
Pembroke
179 Pembroke St. East
Pembroke, ON K8A 3J6 Canada
613-732-9935
Penticton
#104, 575 Main St.
Penticton, BC V2A 5C6 Canada
250-492-3841
Peterborough
1840 Lansdowne St. West
Peterborough, ON K9K 2M9 Canada
705-472-3854
Pickering
#9, 1550 Kingston Rd.
Pickering, ON L1V 1C3 Canada
905-831-4100
Placentia
Placentia Mall
Placentia, NL A0B 2Y0 Canada
709-227-3675
Port Au Choix
47 Fishers St.
Port au Choix, NL A0K 4C0 Canada
709-861-3282

Port Coquitlam
#106, 2748 Lougheed Hwy.
Port Coquitlam, BC V3B 6P2 Canada
604-941-6711
Port Hawkesbury
#3, 902 Reeves St.
Port Hawkesbury, NS B9A 2S3 Canada
902-625-5227
Prince Albert
#5, 150 - 32nd St. West
Prince Albert, SK S6V 7H7 Canada
306-764-3333
Prince George
444 - 9th Ave.
Prince George, BC V2L 5N9 Canada
250-563-3688
Québec
#235, 3291, ch Ste-Foy
Québec, QC G1X 3V2 Canada
418-651-8556
Québec - Charest
#128, 1415, boul Charest ouest
Québec, QC G1N 4N7 Canada
418-688-1284
Québec - d'Estimauville
#100, 1870, av d'Estimauville
Québec, QC G1V 5B1 Canada
418-661-8411
Québec - Marais
#165, 355, rue Marais
Québec, QC G1M 3N8 Canada
418-687-1168
Red Deer
3440B - 50th Ave.
Red Deer, AB T4N 3Y4 Canada
403-346-3301
Regina - Albert St.
345A Albert St.
Regina, SK S4R 2N6 Canada
306-924-2255
Regina - Broad St.
1438 Broad St.
Regina, SK S4R 1Y9 Canada
306-522-1635
Rimouski
391, boul Jessop
Rimouski, QC G5L 1M9 Canada
418-723-2267
Saint John - Crown St.
70 Crown St.
Saint John, NB E2L 2X7 Canada
506-634-8522
Saint John - Lansdowne
87 Lansdowne Ave.
Saint John, NB E2K 3A1 Canada
506-635-2976
Sarnia
580 Murphy Rd., #F
Sarnia, ON N7S 5V4 Canada
519-336-2237
Saskatoon
2409 - 22nd St. West
Saskatoon, SK S7M 0V8 Canada
306-978-4485
Sault Ste Marie
499 Queen St. East
Sault Ste Marie, ON P6A 1Z9 Canada
705-946-4146
Sherbrooke
2524, rue King ouest
Sherbrooke, QC J1J 2E8 Canada
819-569-9061
Sorel-Tracy
279, boul Fiset
Sorel-Tracy, QC J3P 3P9 Canada
450-743-3303
Springdale
166 Main St.
Springdale, NL A0J 1T0 Canada
709-673-3891
St Catharines
#3, 525 Welland Ave.
St Catharines, ON L2M 6P3 Canada
905-682-9242

St-Jean-sur-Richelieu
#116, 315, rue MacDonald
St-Jean-sur-Richelieu, QC J3B 8J3 Canada
450-348-3805
St-Jerome
500, boul des Laurentides
Saint-Jérome, QC J7Z 4M2 Canada
450-436-8810

Wells Fargo Financial Corporation Canada (continued)

St. Anthony
110 West St.
St. Anthony, NL A0K 4S0 Canada
709-454-2250

St. John's
342 Freshwater Rd.
St. John's, NL A1B 1C2 Canada
709-722-2600

St. Stephen
76 Milltown Blvd.
St Stephen, NB E3L 2X1 Canada
506-466-3055

Stephenville
PO Box 333
43 Main St.
Stephenville, NL A2N 2Z5 Canada
709-643-2520

Sudbury - Elm St.
#100, 66 Elm St.
Sudbury, ON P3C 1R8 Canada
705-675-8355

Sudbury - Paris St.
1865 Paris St., #A
Sudbury, ON P3E 3C5 Canada
705-523-2800

Summerside
#2, 674 Water St. East
Summerside, PE C1N 4J1 Canada
902-436-1043

Surrey - 104 Ave.
#103, 13889 - 104 Ave.
Surrey, BC V3S 3K8 Canada
604-581-4487

Surrey - 152 St.
#202, 6355 - 152 St.
Surrey, BC B3S 3K8 Canada
604-595-8580

Surrey - Fraser Hwy.
#150, 19475 Fraser Hwy.
Surrey, BC V3S 6K7 Canada
604-534-9281

Sussex
#3, 654 Main St.
Sussex, NB E4E 7H9 Canada
902-433-1221

Sydney
1067 Kings Rd.
Sydney, NS B1S 1C6 Canada
902-567-0800

Terrace
4548 Lakelse Ave.
Terrace, BC V8G 1P8 Canada
250-635-6310

Terrebonne
Place Terreborne
587, boul des Seigneurs
Terrebonne, QC J6W 1T5 Canada
450-964-5792

Thornhill
#5-6, 398 Steeles Ave. West
Thornhill, ON L4J 6X3 Canada
905-882-1466

Thunder Bay
#101, 116 Waterford St.
Thunder Bay, ON P7B 5R1 Canada
807-625-1450

Timmins
30 Pine St. South
Timmins, ON P4N 7E7 Canada
705-264-4373

Toronto - Danforth Ave.
#6, 1577 Danforth Ave.
Toronto, ON M4C 1H7 Canada
416-693-2200

Toronto - Keele St.
#15A, 2355 Keele St.
Toronto, ON M6M 4A2 Canada
416-235-2665

Toronto - Kingston Rd.
#6, 3785 Kingston Rd.
Toronto, ON M1J 3M4 Canada
416-267-8256

Toronto - Lawrence Ave.
#2, 1967 Lawrence Ave. East
Toronto, ON M1R 2Z2 Canada
416-752-2160

Toronto - Milner Ave.
#310, 305 Milner Ave.
Toronto, ON M1B 3V4 Canada
416-291-9522

Toronto - Queens' Plate Dr.
#4A, 200 Queens' Plate Dr.
Toronto, ON M9W 6Y9 Canada
416-741-4310

Toronto - Queensway
773L The Queensway
Toronto, ON M8Z 6A9 Canada
416-253-4949

Toronto - Sheppard Ave.
#204, 3850 Sheppard Ave. East
Toronto, ON M1T 3L4 Canada
416-291-4468

Trenton
PO Box 604
43 Front St.
Trenton, ON K8V 5R7 Canada
613-392-9241

Trois-Rivières
5671, boul Jean XXIII
Trois-Rivières, QC 68Z 4B4 Canada
819-379-2040

Truro
PO Box 205
10 Esplanade St.
Truro, NS B2N 5C1 Canada
902-893-9468

Vancouver
5712 Tyne St.
Vancouver, BC V5R 4L6 Canada
604-438-7111

Vaudreuil-Dorion
379, boul Harwood
Vaudreuil-Dorion, QC J7V 7W1 Canada
450-424-0442

Vernon
#117, 3101 Hwy. 6
Vernon, BC V1T 9H6 Canada
250-260-4900

Victoria
#117, 877 Goldstream Ave.
Victoria, BC V1T 2X8 Canada
250-391-6023

Welland
545 Niagara St. North
Welland, ON L3C 1L7 Canada
905-732-1336

Williams Lake
131 - 2nd Ave. North
Williams Lake, BC V2G 1Z5 Canada
250-392-4401

Windsor - Dougall Ave.
2467 Dougall Ave.
Windsor, ON N8X 1T3 Canada
519-250-0020

Windsor - Wentworth Pl.
105 Wentworth Pl.
Windsor, NS B0N 2T0 Canada
902-798-8341

Winnipeg - Kingsbury
#4, 1099 Kingsbury Ave.
Winnipeg, MB R2P 2P9 Canada
204-694-3522

Winnipeg - Portage
#2, 2609 Portage Ave.
Winnipeg, MB R3J 0P6 Canada
204-885-6200

Winnipeg - Regent
#4, 1575 Regent Ave. West
Winnipeg, MB R2C 3B3 Canada
204-661-8593

Woodbridge
#5, 4140 Steeles Ave. West
Woodbridge, ON L4L 4V3 Canada
905-851-6363

Woodstock
#2, 365 Connell St.
Woodstock, NB E7M 5G5 Canada
506-328-6651

Yarmouth
302 Main St.
Yarmouth, NS B5A 1E4 Canada
902-742-2481

West Oak Capital Group Inc.

#1400, 400 Burrard St.
Vancouver, BC V6C 3G2
604-689-1749
Fax: 604-643-1760
westoak@direct.ca
Ownership: Private
Year Founded: 1990
Number of Employees: 3
Profile: The venture capital investment firm is affiliated with West Oak Resource Crop., Public Filmworks & Global Cable Systems Inc.

Executives:
Stuart W. Rogers, President

Western America Capital Inc.

Also listed under: *Holding & Other Investment Companies*
#1500, 10025 - 102A Ave.
Edmonton, AB T5J 2Z2
780-498-9171
Fax: 780-496-9172
info@wacapital.com
www.wacapital.com
Ownership: Private
Year Founded: 1987
Number of Employees: 200
Profile: Acquisitions & venture capital.

Executives:
Richard D. Caron, CEO, Director
Don P. Caron, President, Director

WestFactor Capital Inc.

1693 Brentwood St.
Parksville, BC V9P 2Y6
604-688-2210
888-427-4527
info@westfactor.ca
www.westfactor.ca
Ownership: Private
Year Founded: 2002
Number of Employees: 1
Assets: Under $1 million Year End: 20041101
Revenues: Under $1 million Year End: 20041101
Executives:
Bev Harrison, President; bev@westfactor.ca

Wheat Belt Community Futures Development Corporation

141 Rosser Ave.
Brandon, MB R7A 0J6
204-726-1513
Fax: 204-727-5832
888-347-4342
bdc@wheatbelt.mb.ca
www.wheatbelt.mb.ca
Ownership: Non-profit
Year Founded: 1987
Number of Employees: 8
Profile: Community-based, volunteer-driven organization, which strengthens the economy of southwestern Manitoba by operating a Business Development Centre, and by cooperating with individuals, communities and other agencies to encourage community economic development.

Executives:
Roger Guy, Executive Director

White Horse Plains Community Futures Development Corp.

56 Royal Rd. North
Portage La Prairie, MB R1N 1V1
204-856-5000
Fax: 204-856-5006
info@whpcfdc.ca
www.whpcfdc.ca
Also Known As: Community Futures White Horse Plains
Year Founded: 1997
Profile: The corporation assists small businesses, individuals who wish to start a business, & local communities in the White Horse Plains region of Manitoba.

Executives:
Ron Roteliuk, Executive Director
Bryan Spencer, Manager, Business & Projects
Georgette Hutlet, Officer, Community Development
Directors:
Jim Knight, Chair

Whitecastle Investments Limited
#1010, 22 St. Clair Ave. East
Toronto, ON M4T 2S3
416-961-5355
Fax: 416-961-3232
info@whitecapvp.com
www.whitecastleinvestments.com
Ownership: Private
Year Founded: 1959
Profile: The private investment company specializes in venture capital through its wholly owned division, Whitecap Venture Partners & public equity investing. Whitecap VP specializes in emerging technologies including telecom & software sectors.

Executives:
Carey J. Diamond, President/CEO
David Fillier, Vice-President, Finance
Directors:
A. Ephraim Diamond, Chair

Wifleur Inc.
#900, 30 St. Clair Ave. West
Toronto, ON M4V 3A1
416-927-2000
Fax: 416-927-2013
Year Founded: 1995
Executives:
David Posluns, Managing Director

XDL Intervest Capital Corp.
#901, 30 St. Clair Ave. West
Toronto, ON M4V 3A1
416-250-6500
Fax: 416-250-6330
info1@xdl.com
Former Name: XDL Capital Corp.
Year Founded: 1999
Executives:
Dennis Bennie, CEO
David Latner, Principal

The Yellowhead East Business Development Corporation
PO Box 249
5028 - 50th Ave.
Sangudo, AB T0E 2A0
780-785-2900
Fax: 780-785-3337
800-556-0328
yebdc@yebdc.ab.ca
www.yebdc.ab.ca
Year Founded: 1989
Number of Employees: 18
Executives:
Roxanne Harper, Manager
Robyn Youell, Asst. Manager

Bond Rating Companies

Dominion Bond Rating Service Limited(DBRS)
#700, 181 University Ave.
Toronto, ON M5H 3M7
416-593-5577
Fax: 416-593-8432
info@dbrs.com
www.dbrs.com
Ownership: Private
Year Founded: 1976
Number of Employees: 50
Profile: Full-service rating agency that provides credit ratings on issuers of commercial paper, bonds, long/short term debt, and preferred shares, as well as asset-backed securities. Also offers industry analysis, rating reports, and ratings indices for issuers and investors throughout the world.

Executives:
David Schroeder, Chief Operating Officer
Rory Buchalter, Exec. Vice-President
Chris Diceman, Exec. Vice-President
Bob Maxwell, Exec. Vice-President
Esther M. Muith, Exec. Vice-President
Huston Loke, Group Managing Director
Paul Holman, Managing Director
Kam Hon, Managing Director, Industrials

Fitch Ratings
#2500, 120 Adelaide St. West
Toronto, ON M5H 1T1
416-703-4824
Fax: 416-367-1954
www.fitchratings.com
Ownership: FIMALAC, Paris
Number of Employees: 1,200
Profile: As the international rating agency, Fitch Ratings is fully committed to serving capital market participants by providing the highest quality ratings & research.

Executives:
Stephen Shevdey, Contact

Moody's Canada Inc.
#1400, 70 York St.
Toronto, ON M5J 2T3
416-214-1635
Fax: 416-214-3869
hilary.parks@moodys.com
www.moodys.com
Ownership: Wholly owned subsidiary of Moody's Investors Service, New York
Year Founded: 1993
Number of Employees: 5
Profile: Major Canadian provider of independent credit ratings, research & financial information to the capital markets.

Executives:
Hilary J. Parkes, Representative Director

Société canadienne d'information sur le crédit/ Credit Information Company of Canada Ltd.
2954, boul Laurier
Québec, QC G1V 4T2
418-659-5797
Fax: 418-659-4346
800-400-7388
admin@infocredit.qc.ca
www.info-credit.net
Ownership: Foreign. Principal shareholder is Canamerican Credit Bureau
Year Founded: 1986
Number of Employees: 21
Profile: Affiliated companies are Québec Credit Bureau & English Name & Credit Information Company of Canada Ltd. Offices are located in Montréal, 514/399-9921 & Québec City, 418/659-5797.

Executives:
Jean-François St-Laurent, President

Standard & Poor's Canadian Ratings
The Exchange Tower
#1100, 130 King St. West
Toronto, ON M5X 1E5
416-507-2500
Fax: 416-507-2507
www.standardandpoors.com
Ownership: Public. A division of the McGraw-Hill Companies
Year Founded: 1860
Number of Employees: 1,500
Stock Symbol: MHP
Profile: Standard & Poor's is a pre-eminent global provider of independent financial analysis & information. Independent insight, analysis & information are provided to the financial community to help it determine value in the marketplace.

Executives:
Vickie A. Tillman, Exec. Vice-President
Thomas Connell, Managing Director; 416-507-2501; thomas_connell@standardandpoors.com
Valerie Blair, Director, Public Finance; 416-507-2536; valerie_blair@standardandpoors.com
Gregory Chang, Director, Ratings Origination; 416-507-2541; gregory_chang@standardandpoors.com
Mark Mettrick, Director, Corporate Ratings; mark_mettrick@standardandpoors.com
Maria Rabiasz, Director, Structured Finance; 416-507-2542; maria_rabiasz@standardandpoors.com

Strategic Analysis Corporation(SAC)
***Also listed under:** Financial Planning*
PO Box 2003
#1400, 20 Eglinton Ave. West
Toronto, ON M4R 1K8
416-489-3603
Fax: 416-489-8762
877-214-5641
info@strategicanalysis.ca
www.strategicanalysis.ca
Former Name: SAC The Solvency Analysis Corp.
Year Founded: 1979
Number of Employees: 9
Profile: SAC is a capital markets research firm with emphasis on the Dow Jones, S&P 500 & TSE 300 indices. The company publishes monthly valuation charts for each market, sector & individual stock for client use. SAC also provides a credit rating service covering the corporations on the TSE 300 index.

Executives:
C. Ross Healy, Chair/CEO

Collection Agencies

A1 Commercial Bailiffs Inc.
18932 - 62 Ave.
Surrey, BC V3S 7W1
604-576-8022
Fax: 604-576-2322
repos@axion.net
Ownership: Private
Year Founded: 1991

AAA Credit & Recovery Services Inc.
#304, 250 Consumers Rd.
Toronto, ON M2J 4V6
416-496-2225
Fax: 416-496-2226
888-223-4214
Ownership: Private
Year Founded: 1995
Number of Employees: 17
Assets:
Branches:
Burnaby
#183, 4664 Lougheed Hwy.
Burnaby, BC V5C 9T5 Canada
604-298-8857
Montréal - Côte-de-Liesse
7000, ch de la Côte-de-Liesse
Montréal, QC H4T 1E7 Canada
514-739-2900

ABC Professional Bailiffs Ltd.
#12103, 555 West Hastings St.
Vancouver, BC V6B 4N6
604-682-0337
Fax: 604-676-2782
info@probailiffs.com
www.probailiffs.com
Executives:
Douglas Kavanagh; doug@probailiffs.com

Absolute Bailiffs Service Inc.
405 Brunette Ave.
New Westminster, BC V3L 3E9
604-522-2773
Fax: 604-522-2633
absolutebailiffs@telus.net
Ownership: Private
Year Founded: 1992
Number of Employees: 5
Assets: Under $1 million
Revenues: Under $1 million
Executives:
Terry Bohn, President

Accurate Effective Bailiffs Ltd.
6139 Trapp Ave.
Burnaby, BC V3N 2V3
604-526-3737
Fax: 604-526-3716
800-227-5882
info@accurateeffectivebailiffs.com
www.accurateeffectivebailiffs.com
Former Name: Accurate Bailiff & Collection Agency Ltd.
Year Founded: 1971
Number of Employees: 45

Accurate Effective Bailiffs Ltd. (continued)
Profile: Performs seizures and repossessions under The Personal Property Security Act, Rent Distress Act, Leases, Repairers Liens, etc.

Action Collections & Receivables Management
#408, 2970 Lake Shore Blvd. West
Toronto, ON M8V 1J7
416-503-9633
Fax: 416-503-9458
collectionsmgr@actioncollections.com
www.actioncollections.com
Ownership: Private
Year Founded: 1986
Number of Employees: 7
Profile: Services include commercial collections, domestically & in the USA.
Executives:
John M. Canal, President; 416-503-9633

Active Bailiff Service Ltd.
8540 Greenall Ave.
Burnaby, BC V5J 3M6
604-434-2448
Fax: 604-437-7322
877-434-7376
info@activebailiff.com
www.activebailiff.com
Ownership: Private
Year Founded: 1955
Number of Employees: 12
Profile: Active Bailiff is a member of the BC Bailiff Association & the American Recovery Association.

Advanced Collection Services Ltd.
#200, 2840 Nanaimo St.
Victoria, BC V8T 4W9
250-388-0700
Fax: 250-388-0755
800-668-1383
len@advancedcollectionservices.com
www.advancedcollectionservices.com

Agence de Recouvrement Carlauson Inc.
#202, 400, boul Maloney est
Gatineau, QC J8P 1E6
819-669-4747
Fax: 819-669-2181
carlauson@qc.aira.com
Ownership: Private
Year Founded: 1986
Executives:
Carl G. Simpson, President

Agence de Recouvrement des Laurentides
136-A, rue Labelle
Saint-Jérôme, QC J7Z 5K7
450-431-5300
Fax: 450-431-6756
Year Founded: 1995

Agence de Recouvrement M. McGrath Québec Ltée
CP 79068
#103, 365A, boul St-Joseph
Gatineau, QC J8Y 6V2
819-778-0908
Fax: 819-778-1796
800-267-4124
collection@mcgrathquebec.com
www.mcgrathquebec.com
Ownership: Private. Parent is M. McGrath Canada Limited.
Year Founded: 1953
Number of Employees: 5
Profile: Provides full collection services for accounts receivable along with skip tracing services to assist with locating debtors and assets.
Executives:
Kalifa Goita, Président

Agence de Recouvrement Marathon
#240, 1145, boul Lebourgneuf
Québec, QC G2K 2K8
418-623-4763
Fax: 418-623-7630
800-667-2111
marathon@marathon-ltd.com
www.marathon-ltd.com/anglais/faccueil.htm
Year Founded: 1989
Profile: Provides commercial credit advisory services.

Agence de Recouvrement Ogilvie(ARO)
#700, 1001, Sherbrooke est
Montréal, QC H2L 1L3
514-322-1414
Fax: 514-322-5554
877-322-1414
manager.montreal@aro.ca
www.aro.ca
Former Name: Agence de Recouvrement ARO Inc.
Year Founded: 1994
Number of Employees: 232
Profile: International collection agency with 3 collection centers throughout Canada.
Branches:
Hamilton
#1, 70 Frid St.
Hamilton, ON L8P 4M4 Canada
905-667-5050
Fax: 905-667-5051
866-667-5050
manager.hamilton@aro.ca
Kelowna
#111, 565 Bernard Ave.
Kelowna, BC V1K 8R4 Canada
250-762-7070
Fax: 250-762-4111
877-250-7070
manager.kelowna@aro.ca

Agence de Recouvrement Optimum Inc.
#301, 1551, rue Montarville
Saint-Bruno, QC J3V 3T8
450-653-0304
Fax: 450-653-5266

Alberta Credit Repair
Bay 309
9612 Franklin
Fort McMurray, AB T9H 2J9
780-790-5711
Fax: 780-791-7496
jim@albertacreditrepair.ca

All Canada Collect
#23, 1100 Deasness Dr.
London, ON N6E 1N9
519-672-7100
Fax: 519-645-0701
800-439-6575
Number of Employees: 16

All Island Bailiff Ltd.
PO Box 1312
Parksville, BC V9P 2H3
250-951-0139
Fax: 250-951-0113
888-351-1115
islandbail@shaw.ca
Former Name: Statcom Bailiff Service Ltd.
Executives:
Daryl Hnatiuk, Manager

Allied International Credit Corp.
#26, 16635 Yonge St.
Newmarket, ON L3X 1V6
905-470-8181
Fax: 905-470-8155
sales@aiccorp.com
www.aiccorp.com
Ownership: Private
Profile: Provides a full range of debt collection and accounts receivable management programs.
Executives:
David Rae, President/CEO
David Gallagher, Exec. Vice-President
Tom McCausland, Sr. Vice-President, Operations
Steve Meschino, Vice-President, Information Systems
Winston Gurdyal, Finance Consultant
Branches:
Montreal
#705, 1000, St-Antoine ouest
Montréal, QC H3C 3R7 Canada
514-868-9718
Fax: 514-868-0195
Vancouver
#400, 1200 West 73rd Ave.
Vancouver, BC V6P 6G5 Canada
604-606-3200
Fax: 604-606-3225

Allphaze Credit Management & Consultants
PO Box 69066, Kensington Stn. Kensington
Edmonton, AB T6V 1G7
780-424-5963
Fax: 780-429-6327
Former Name: Commercial Credit Consultants
Executives:
Donna Bernard, President

Amalgamated Collection Services Inc.
#6, 101 King St.
St Catharines, ON L2R 3H6
905-641-1540
Fax: 905-641-1546
collect@niagara.com
Year Founded: 1997
Profile: Registered and bonded collection agency with experience in receivable management.

Andwell Collection Services Ltd.
28 - 8th Ave. South
Cranbrook, BC V1C 2K3
250-489-5440
Fax: 250-489-5844
andwell@telus.net

ARC Accounts Recovery Corporation
4240 Glanford Ave.
Victoria, BC V8Z 4B8
250-953-6900
Fax: 250-953-6999
888-254-1998
general_inquiries@arc.ca
www.arc.ca
Ownership: Private
Year Founded: 1988
Profile: ARC Accounts Recovery Corporation is a collection agency providing accounts receivable management.
Executives:
Dave McMillan, Exec. Vice-President
Lionel Pollard, Sr. Vice-President, National Recoveries
Neil Dickenson, Asst. Vice-President
Branches:
Burlington
#204, 777 Guelph Line
Burlington, ON L7R 3N2 Canada
905-639-6990
Fax: 905-639-0553
888-629-5396
Burnaby
#404, 6400 Roberts St.
Burnaby, BC V5G 4C9 Canada
604-606-2500
Fax: 604-606-2520
888-255-0265
Laval
#430, 2 Place Laval
Laval, QC H7N 5N6 Canada
450-973-1222
Fax: 450-669-3033
888-256-7415
Moncton
50 Assumption Blvd.
Moncton, NB E1C 0C5 Canada
506-384-7392
Fax: 506-384-7531
888-525-6184
Victoria
4240 Glanford Ave.
Victoria, BC V8Z 4B8 Canada
250-953-6900
Fax: 250-953-6999
888-254-1998

Aspen Bailiffs & Process Servers Inc.
PO Box 3043
Kamloops, BC V2C 6B7

250-828-2112
Fax: 250-828-1570
Ownership: Private
Executives:
Arlene Hollister, Contact

Associated Bailiffs & Process Servers
515C Lawrence Ave.
Kelowna, BC V1Y 6L8
250-860-3132
Fax: 250-860-1323
Former Name: Associated Bailiffs (1988) Inc.
Ownership: Private
Executives:
Gregg Booth, Contact; gregg_booth@telus.net

Associated Credit & Collection Agencies Inc.
#605, 345, av Victoria
Montréal, QC H3Z 2N2
514-483-6223
Fax: 514-483-3755
800-561-8921
info@acacollect.com
www.acacollect.com
Former Name: Associated Collection Agencies Inc.
Year Founded: 1980
Profile: Accounts receivable management and collections.

Branches:
Mississauga
#900, 201 City Centre Dr.
Mississauga, ON L5B 2T4 Canada
905-275-4787
Fax: 905-275-4306
800-561-8921
info@acacollect.com

Association Provinciale de Crédit-PAC(ACP)/ Provincial Association of Credit(PAC)
#201, 404, boul Décarie
Montréal, QC H4L 5E6
514-744-2314
Fax: 514-744-9766
800-210-9882
credit.pac@videotron.net
www.mart-info.com/credit.pac/
Ownership: Private
Year Founded: 1995
Number of Employees: 8
Executives:
Claude Archambault, President

Bond Street Collections Inc.
#209, 370 Steeles Ave. West
Thornhill, ON L4J 6X1
905-886-9422
Fax: 905-886-9423
888-877-2663
newclients@bondstreetcollections.ca
www.bondstreetcollections.ca
Former Name: Bond Street Collections & Consulting
Year Founded: 1994

Business Prospects
#101B, 1120 - 53rd Ave. NE
Calgary, AB T2E 6N9
403-275-2232
Fax: 403-274-6500

C.A.R.D. Bailiffs & Adjustments Inc.
PO Box 8473, T Stn. T
Ottawa, ON K1G 3H9
613-748-6919
Fax: 613-749-9248
888-748-6911
craig@cardbailiffs.ca
Executives:
Craig Danford, Contact

Canada Bonded Attorney
c/o Carma Financial Services Corporation
1280 Courtneypark Dr. E
Mississauga, ON L5T 1N6
905-283-3100
Fax: 905-283-3105
800-974-8845
salesteam@carmafinancial.com
www.carmafinancial.com
Ownership: Carma Financial Services Corporation, Mississauga, ON.
Year Founded: 1911
Profile: The collection agency offers a commercial & retail debt recovery system.

Executives:
John L. Smith, President

Canada Collections Inc.
PO Box 304
#202, 96 Clyde Ave.
Mount Pearl, NL A1N 4S2
709-747-8800
Fax: 709-747-8845
877-687-3275

Canada Legal Referral Inc.
51 Toro Rd., 2nd Fl.
Toronto, ON M3J 2A4
416-373-4300
Fax: 416-373-4301
800-241-0560
info@canlegal.net
www.canlegal.net
Year Founded: 1995
Executives:
Mark Teicher, Contact

Canadian Credit
4819 - 48 Ave.
Red Deer, AB T4N 3T2
403-341-4433
Fax: 403-341-4498
866-713-3555
simco@telusplanet.net
Ownership: Private
Year Founded: 1975
Number of Employees: 3
Assets: Under $1 million
Revenues: Under $1 million
Profile: An affiliated company is Simco Developments Ltd.

Executives:
Darryl Sim, General Manager

Caroline Amireault
39, rue Leblanc
L'Épiphanie, QC J5X 3Y3
450-588-7555
Fax: 450-588-3246
888-877-4444
camireault@qc.aira.com
Ownership: Private
Year Founded: 1999
Number of Employees: 3

Cash Flow Recoveries Inc.
945 Richmond Rd., Unit D
Ottawa, ON K2B 8B9
613-235-6177
Fax: 613-235-8834
Ownership: Private
Year Founded: 1998
Executives:
M.R. Janet Morin, President

CBV Collection Services Ltd.
#100, 814 Richards St.
Vancouver, BC V6B 3A7
604-687-4559
Fax: 604-661-7926
888-311-1121
vancouver@cbvcollections.com
www.cbvcollections.com
Former Name: Concord Collection Agencies
Executives:
K.F. Downie, President/CEO
R.W. (Bob) Richards, Exec. Vice-President/COO
Debbie Hayhow, Vice-President, Client Services
Alex Buhler, Director, Information Technology
Kathy MacLeod, Director, Administration, Compliance & Privacy
Sandra McLaren, Controller, Manager, Human Resources
Raymond Leather, Branch Manager, Prairie Region
Gary Sandhu, Branch Manager, Pacific Region
Pina Santangelo, Manager
Branches:
Calgary
#1100, 800 - 5th Ave. SW
Calgary, AB T2P 3T6 Canada
403-543-0500
Fax: 403-263-3581
888-311-1121
calgary@cbvcollections.com
Laval
#320, 2, Place Laval
Laval, QC H7N 5N6 Canada
450-972-1611
Fax: 450-975-1702
montreal@cbvcollections.com
Toronto
#900, 2200 Yonge St.
Toronto, ON M4S 2C6 Canada
416-482-9323
Fax: 416-482-9359
888-311-1121
toronto@cbvcollections.com
Winnipeg
#242, 240 Graham Ave.
Winnipeg, MB R3C 0J7 Canada
204-944-8633
Fax: 204-956-5699
888-311-1121
mgarbett@cbvcollections.com

CCC Consumer Credit Counselling (1993) Ltd.
#204, 6125 Sussex Ave.
Burnaby, BC V5H 4G1
604-435-7800
Fax: 604-435-7810
800-565-4515
info@iamdebtfree.com
www.iamdebtfree.com
Ownership: Private

CGC Collection Group of Canada Inc.
#600, 2550 Victoria Park Ave.
Toronto, ON M2J 5A9
416-491-1313
Fax: 416-491-0860
sales@collectiongroup.com
www.collectiongroup.com
Year Founded: 1984
Profile: Commercial collection agency that specializes in corporate debt recovery and total accounts receivable solutions.

City Collection & Bailiff Service Inc.
#200, 1355 Main St.
Winnipeg, MB R2W 3T7
204-982-2190
Fax: 204-663-2664
Ownership: Private
Executives:
Sandy McCoy, Manager

City Collection Company Ltd.
#600, 515 West Hastings St.
Vancouver, BC V6B 0B2
604-909-3966
Fax: 604-909-5960
www.impark.com
Executives:
John Laires, Sr. Vice-President, Western Canada & West Coast

CMC Credit Management Corp.
#201, 465 East Broadway
Vancouver, BC V5T 1W9
604-877-2380
Fax: 604-877-2399
888-877-2330
info@creditmanagementcorp.com
www.creditmanagementcorp.com
Year Founded: 1996
Profile: Specializes in the recovery of open, recurring receivables.

Coast Credit Recovery Group Ltd.
19517 - 96 Ave.
Surrey, BC V4N 4C5
604-580-7376
Fax: 604-580-2275
877-580-7376
terry@repobc.ca
Ownership: Private
Year Founded: 1989

NON-DEPOSITORY INSTITUTIONS

Coast Credit Recovery Group Ltd. (continued)
Number of Employees: 10
Profile: Collateral recovery company.

Collect Com Credit Inc.
#100, 3680 Victoria Park Ave.
Toronto, ON M2H 3K1
416-916-9162
Fax: 416-916-9163
866-916-9162
ccc@collectcom.com
www.collectcom.com
Ownership: Private. Parent is Collect Com Group Inc.
Year Founded: 1990
Number of Employees: 75
Assets: $1-5 million Year End: 20051231
Revenues: $5-10 million Year End: 20051231
Executives:
Aaron Taylor, President/CEO; 416-916-9142; ataylor@collectcom.com
Elliott Ocopnick, Exec. Vice-President/CFO; 416-916-9152; eocopnick@collectcom.com
Alex Warren, Vice-President, Operations; 416-916-9149; awarren@collectcom.com
Directors:
Elliott Ocopnick
Aaron Taylor

Collection Consultants
#750, 130 Slater St.
Ottawa, ON K1P 6E2
613-222-6923
800-401-6953
info@collection-consultants.com
www.collection-consultants.com
Ownership: Private
Year Founded: 1995
Branches:
Gatineau
#105, 10 rue Noël
Gatineau, QC J8Z 3G5 Canada
819-772-4250

Toronto
#1801, 1 Yonge St.
Toronto, ON M5E 1W7 Canada
416-214-0911
800-401-6953

Collection Corp.
#105, 16 Bath Rd.
Kingston, ON K7L 4W5
613-548-7777
Fax: 613-542-1439
800-567-9235
kingston@collectcorp.com
Year Founded: 1982
Number of Employees: 35
Executives:
Leigh Anderson, Vice-President, Regional Operations

The Collection Network of Ontario Inc.
99 Ferris Line
Barrie, ON L4M 2Y1
705-739-4665
Fax: 705-739-9199
Ownership: Private
Number of Employees: 30

Collection Recovery Systems
73 Centre St.
Oshawa, ON L1H 4A1
905-434-6186
Fax: 905-434-6825
pscott@collectionrecovery.com
www.collectionrecovery.ca
Also Known As: 706974 Ontario Inc.
Ownership: Private
Year Founded: 1987
Number of Employees: 9
Assets: Under $1 million Year End: 20040331
Revenues: Under $1 million Year End: 20040331
Profile: The organization provides collection agency services.
Executives:
Paul Scott, President

Collection Service of Windsor Ltd.
PO Box 1209
860 University Ave. West
Windsor, ON N9A 5R9
519-256-3421
Fax: 519-256-4616

Collections Canada
111A Rideau St.
Ottawa, ON K1N 8S4
613-241-8420
Fax: 613-241-1653
800-267-4124
Former Name: CCS Credit Collection Service Canada Inc.

Collectrite Cornwall Inc.
135 Augustus St.
Cornwall, ON K6H 5V5
613-932-9301
Fax: 613-932-3348
800-463-9692
collectrite@cogeco.net
Former Name: Retail Collection Agency (Brockville) Ltd.
Executives:
Simon Pierre, Contact

Collectrite of Hamilton Ltd.
#400, 20 Jackson St. West
Hamilton, ON L8P 1L2
905-525-7300
Fax: 905-525-1890
877-266-6686
info@collectritehamilton.com
www.collectritehamilton.com
Year Founded: 1975
Number of Employees: 13
Profile: Provides adjustment and collection services.

Commercial & Consumer Recovery Inc.(CCR Inc.)
#212B, 3425 Harvester Rd.
Burlington, ON L7N 3N1
905-634-1227
Fax: 905-634-3198
800-661-3915
ccrinc@ccrcollections.com
www.ccrcollections.com
Ownership: Private
Year Founded: 1990
Number of Employees: 5
Revenues: Under $1 million

Commercial Credit Adjusters
#800, 259 Portage Ave.
Winnipeg, MB R3B 2A9
204-958-5850
Fax: 204-958-5859
866-958-5850
collect@cca.ca
www.cca.ca
Ownership: Private
Year Founded: 1991
Number of Employees: 80
Assets: $1-5 million
Revenues: $5-10 million
Executives:
Kevin DeBlaere, President; kevin@cca.ca
Bonnie Gilmore, CFO; bonnie@cca.ca
Directors:
Claudette DeBlaere
Dennis DeBlaere
Kevin DeBlaere
Bonnie Gilmore
Branches:
Calgary
#612, 500 Country Hills Blvd.
Calgary, AB T3K 5K3 Canada
866-958-5850
Sandi Roe, Manager
Edmonton
#503, 10080 Jasper Ave.
Edmonton, AB T5J 1V9 Canada
866-958-5850
Joanne McGill, Manager

Common Collection Agency Inc.
#205, 11 Progress Ave.
Toronto, ON M1P 4S7
416-297-7077
Fax: 416-297-7439
888-851-8699
sales@commoncollections.com
www.commoncollections.com
Year Founded: 1962
Profile: Provider of accounts receivable management services.

Commonwealth Bailiffs Ltd.
19670 - 8th Ave.
Langley, BC V2Z 1W1
604-534-2082
Fax: 604-533-0030
Profile: Services include debt collections, process serving, rent distress, and repossessions.

Comret Credit Inc.
#501, 701 Evans Ave.
Toronto, ON M9C 1A2
416-232-1921
Fax: 416-236-2249
info@comretcredit.com
www.comretcredit.com
Executives:
Chris McAleer, President

Consumer Bailiffs Inc.
#A1, 44335 Yale Rd.
Chilliwack, BC V2R 4H2
604-795-7337
Fax: 604-795-7334
877-795-7337
consumerbailiffs@shaw.ca
www.consumerbailiffs.ca, www.repobc.ca
Ownership: Private.
Year Founded: 2000
Number of Employees: 7
Assets: Under $1 million
Revenues: Under $1 million
Profile: The company is engaged in the following activities: collections services, repossessions, lien filing & searching, process serving, rent distress, carfax searches, & commercial seizures.
Executives:
Judi Bruce, Owner; 604-795-7337; judi@repobc.ca

Corporate Collections
PO Box 68072
28 Crowfoot Terrace NW
Calgary, AB T3G 3N8
403-547-4423
Fax: 403-547-4768
Year Founded: 1996
Executives:
Warren Gramlich, President

CP Collection Platforms Inc.
#211, 402 Pender St. West
Vancouver, BC V6B 21T6
604-688-0223
Fax: 604-688-1444

Credex Collection Corp.
#103, 5510 - 192nd St.
Surrey, BC V3S 8E5
604-575-0780
Fax: 604-575-0702
800-263-6334
info@credex.ca
www.credex.ca
Year Founded: 1991
Profile: Services include debt recovery, lease portfolio administration, and accounts receivable management.

Credifax Atlantic Ltd.
Burnside Industrial Park
#4, 21 Williams Ave.
Dartmouth, NS B3B 1X3
902-450-5070
Fax: 902-450-5220
reports@credifax.com
www.credifax.com
Year Founded: 1997
Executives:
Rodger D. Noel, President

Crédit Belle-Chasse inc
10824, rue St-Hubert
Montréal, QC H2C 2J2
514-383-0036
Fax: 514-383-0966
Ownership: Private
Executives:
Michel Hamel, President

Credit Bureau Collections (Chatham) Limited
231 William St. South
Chatham, ON N7M 4T2
519-352-0400
Fax: 519-352-0402
Ownership: Private
Year Founded: 1935
Executives:
Gerald Bellinger, President

Credit Bureau Collections Ltd.
PO Box 337
110 Dunlop St. East
Barrie, ON L4M 4T5
705-722-3441
Fax: 705-722-5434
800-207-0841
collections@cbcollections.com
www.cbcollections.com
Ownership: Private
Year Founded: 1983
Profile: Financial collection services are provided for consumer & commercial accounts across Canada. It also offers process serving, court representation & skip tracing services.

Executives:
Dan Herbert, President
Branches:
Peterborough
#5, 1434 Chemong Rd.
Peterborough, ON K9J 6X2 Canada
705-742-5441
Fax: 705-742-8861

Credit Bureau Collections-Algoma District
#201, 262 Queen St. East
Sault Ste Marie, ON P6A 1Y7
705-254-7525
Fax: 705-256-5065
Former Name: Credit Bureau of Sault Ste Marie Ltd.

Credit Bureau of Cumberland Ltd.
11 Princess St.
Amherst, NS B4H 1W5
902-667-7900
Year Founded: 1965
Executives:
Blanche Thorburn, Contact

Credit Bureau of Ottawa & Hull/ Bureau de Crédit d'Ottawa & Hull
368 Slater St.
Ottawa, ON K1R 5C1
613-236-0251
Fax: 613-230-4425

Credit Bureau of Peel Collections
#201, 7895 Tranmere
Mississauga, ON L5S 1V9
905-670-7575
Fax: 905-670-7069
800-725-8964

Credit Bureau of Sarnia Ltd.
302 Christina St. North
Sarnia, ON N7T 5V5
519-336-6111
Fax: 519-336-3771
Profile: Provides adjustment and collection services.

Credit Bureau of St Thomas
55 Curtis St.
St Thomas, ON N5P 1H9
519-631-1050
Fax: 519-633-4691
Year Founded: 1959
Executives:
Wallace Herbert, Manager

Credit Bureau of Vernon Ltd.
#1, 3316A - 30th Ave.
Vernon, BC V1T 2C3
250-545-5351
Fax: 250-545-3377
888-628-3328
collect@bccreditbureau.com
www.bccreditbureau.com
Also Known As: B.C. Credit Burau, Credit Bureau of Kelowna, Kamloops
Year Founded: 1977
Profile: The licensed & bonded collection agency serves the interior of British Columbia. It specializes in the recovery of delinquent accounts.

Executives:
Richard G. Hunt, Contact

Credit Collections Ontario Ltd.
#7, 140 Welland Ave.
St Catharines, ON L2R 2N6
905-641-5086
Fax: 905-641-0795
888-646-6815
cco@creditcollectionsontario.com
www.creditcollectionsontario.com
Ownership: Private
Year Founded: 1994

Credit Consultants Ltd.
11 Scarfe Ct.
Dartmouth, NS B3B 1W4
902-468-5950
Fax: 902-468-7661

Credit Control Services Inc.
835 Topsail Rd.
Mount Pearl, NL A1N 3J6
709-368-8300
Fax: 709-368-8340
ccs@nf.aibn.com

Credit Counselling Society of British Columbia
Columbia SkyTrain Station Bldg.
#330, 435 Columbia St.
New Westminster, BC V3L 5N8
604-527-8999
Fax: 604-527-8008
888-527-8999
info@nomoredebts.org
www.nomoredebts.org
Year Founded: 1996
Number of Employees: 30
Profile: The society is engaged in credit counselling.

Executives:
Scott Hannah, Exec. Director; scott@nomoredebts.org
Branches:
Abbotsford
Abbotsford Community Services Bldg.
2420 Montrose Ave.
Abbotsford, BC V2S 3S9 Canada
Kelowna
Stewart Centre Bldg.
#230, 1855 Kirschner Rd.
Kelowna, BC V1Y 4N7 Canada
Nanaimo
201 Selby St.
Nanaimo, BC V9R 2R2 Canada
New Westminster
Columia SkyTrain Station Bldg.
#330, 435 Columbia St.
New Westminster, BC V3L 5N8 Canada
Penticton
Penticton & District Community Resources Society Bldg.
60 Calgary Ave.
Penticton, BC V2A 2T6 Canada

Surrey
Guildford Office Park Bldg.
#303, 15225 - 104 Ave.
Surrey, BC V3R 6Y8 Canada
Vancouver
#600, 890 West Pender St.
Vancouver, BC V6C 1J9 Canada
Vernon
North Okanagan Employment Enhancement Society Bldg.
#102, 3201 - 30th St.
Vernon, BC V1T 9G9 Canada
Victoria
James Bay Community Project Bldg.
547 Michigan St.
Victoria, BC V8V 1S5 Canada
Winnipeg
#200, 5 Donald St.
Winnipeg, MB R3L 2T4 Canada

Crédit Destination
#201, 145, Montée de Liesse
Montréal, QC H4T 1T9
514-840-8140
Fax: 514-840-9006
800-208-2189
info@creditdestination.com
www.creditdestination.com/ccrcanada.htm
Ownership: Private
Number of Employees: 13
Profile: Services include credit seminars, accounts receivable outsourcing, collections, credit manual development and consultations.

Crédit Mobile
#210, 3221, autoroute 440 ouest
Laval, QC H7P 5P2
450-681-3170
Fax: 450-681-5418
Year Founded: 1997
Executives:
Jason Dugas, President

Credit Network Inc.
91 Geneva St.
St Catharines, ON L2R 4M9
905-684-1324
Fax: 905-688-4820
Ownership: Private
Executives:
Nathalie Thibeault, General Manager

Crédit Protection ED Ltée
#114, 560, Henri-Bourassa ouest
Montréal, QC H3L 1P4
514-723-1010
Fax: 514-723-3600
800-833-3564
info@cpl.ca
www.cpl.ca
Ownership: Private
Year Founded: 1979
Profile: Services include recovering unpaid accounts.

Crédit Recouvrement Granby Agence de Recouvrement S E N C
221, rue Principale
Granby, QC J2G 2V7
450-372-5838
Fax: 450-372-8468
Former Name: Crédit Collection de Granby Inc
Year Founded: 1999

Credit Recovery Ltd.
PO Box 146, C Stn. C
55 Bond St.
St. John's, NL A1C 5H5
709-753-8810
Fax: 709-753-8820
877-539-9714
Number of Employees: 8

Credit Risk Management Canada
#202, 148 York St.
London, ON N6A 1A9
519-672-7100
Fax: 519-645-0701
800-267-0490
Former Name: Credit Bureau of Stratford Collections Ltd.
Year Founded: 1970
Number of Employees: 22
Profile: Services provided include collection, credit reporting, and employee screening and testing.

Executives:
Doug Forster, President

Credit Risk Management Canada (continued)

Branches:
Stratford
PO Box 96
90 Erie St.
Stratford, ON N5A 6S8 Canada
519-271-6211
Fax: 519-271-5725
800-267-0490

Crédit-Bail SPAR Leasing Inc.

#220, 4405, ch du Bois-Franc
Montréal, QC H4S 1A8
514-748-6787
Fax: 514-748-7053
info@sparleasing.com
www.sparleasing.com
Former Name: Groupe Financier Spar Inc.
Ownership: Private
Year Founded: 1989
Number of Employees: 13
Profile: Provides the following services: commercial credit reporting, property title search, commercial collection, A/R management outsourcing, US business reports, corporate searches, PPSA search and registration.

Executives:
Alan Chaput, General Manager

Creditcollect Ltd.

#105, 279 Weber St. North
Waterloo, ON N2J 3H8
519-747-8114

D & B Canada

5770 Hurontario St.
Missisauga, ON L5R 3G5
905-568-6000
Fax: 905-568-6197
800-463-6362
cic@dnb.com
www.dnb.ca
Former Name: Dun & Bradstreet Canada
Ownership: Public. Parent Dun & Bradstreet Corporation
Year Founded: 1841
Stock Symbol: DNB
Executives:
Patrick Manley, Vice-President, Finance; 905-568-5772; manleyp@dnb.com
Tony Milina, Vice-President, Sales; 905-568-6334; milinat@dnb.com

D&A Collection Corporation

131 Brunel Rd.
Mississauga, ON L4Z 1X3
905-507-8889
Fax: 905-507-6566
sales@dacollection.com
Ownership: Private
Year Founded: 1988
Number of Employees: 70
Profile: Provides adjustment and collection services.

Executives:
Manny Cabral, Manager

D&B Companies of Canada Ltd.

#200, 1000 Centre St. NE
Calgary, AB T2E 7W6
403-276-5546
Fax: 403-230-4209
800-661-1038
Executives:
Andy Cook, Contact

Diligent Bailiff Services Ltd.

567 Rougemount Dr.
Pickering, ON L1W 2C1
416-283-8444
Fax: 416-283-6654
888-295-6552
wayne@diligentbailiff.com
Executives:
Wayne Cook, Contact

Dixon Commercial Investigators (1982) Inc.

PO Box 670
91 Geneva St.
St Catharines, ON L2R 6W8
905-688-0447
Fax: 905-688-6491
800-388-0641
dixon@dixoncommercial.ca
www.dixoncommercial.com
Year Founded: 1956
Profile: Locations: Brantford, 519/751-3909; Etobicoke: 416/259-2792; Georgetown: 905/702-8921; Hamilton: 905/389-0822; Kitchener: 519/749-7029; London: 519/663-9472; Newmarket: 905/895-6427; Oshawa: 905/438-9313; Ottawa: 613/564-0154; Toronto: 416/777-2224; Windsor: 519/253-6559

Drico Recovery Services Ltd.

817 Denman St.
Vancouver, BC V6G 2L7
604-669-6661
Fax: 604-684-0329
Ownership: Private
Year Founded: 1996
Executives:
Ian Bailey, President

Duncan Bailiff & Collections

#101, 360 Festubert St.
Duncan, BC V9L 3S9
250-748-4461
Fax: 250-748-6421
duncanbailiffs@cvnet.net
Former Name: T. Stang & Associates Ltd.
Year Founded: 1990
Profile: Services include repossessions & rent distresses.

Executives:
Sally Stang, Manager

The Echo Group

#400, 1, Place Laval
Laval, QC H7N 1A1
514-335-3246
Fax: 514-334-7731
800-363-2809
service@groupecho.com
www.groupecho.com
Former Name: Agence de Recouvrement CF
Profile: Offers personalised credit information, collection and training services.

Branches:
Calgary - Creditfax of Canada
#614, 7620 Elbow Dr.
Calgary, AB T2V 1K2 Canada
403-201-2433
Fax: 403-201-2535
877-402-6115
Chicoutimi
100 rue Colinette
Chicoutimi, QC G7H 5A8 Canada
418-543-3246
Fax: 418-543-7390
800-667-4879
serviceQc@groupecho.com
Edmonton - Credifax of Canada
#310, 10335 - 172 St.
Edmonton, AB T5S 1K9 Canada
780-414-6104
Fax: 780-444-2545
888-221-3970
serviceWest@groupecho.com
Lower Sackville
#204, 405 Sackville Dr.
Lower Sackville, NS B4C 2R9 Canada
902-869-2006
Fax: 902-865-5336
877-775-8777
serviceatlantic@groupecho.com
Mississauga
#202, 6790 Century Ave.
Mississauga, ON L5N 2V8 Canada
905-567-3008
Fax: 905-542-1471
877-665-5515
serviceon@groupecho.com
Québec
#235, 455, rue Marais
Québec, QC G1M 3A2 Canada
418-681-1545
Fax: 418-681-3989
800-667-4879
serviceqc@groupecho.com
Rimouski
#215, 133, Julien-Réhel
Rimouski, QC G5L 9B1 Canada
418-723-3335
Fax: 418-724-9853
800-463-3235
serviceRm@groupecho.com

Elite Bailiff Services Ltd.

Also listed under: *Trustees in Bankruptcy*
20473 Logan Ave.
Langley, BC V3A 4L8
604-539-9900
Fax: 604-539-5678
info@elitebailiff.com
www.elitebailiff.com
Ownership: Private
Year Founded: 1979
Profile: Specializes in commercial credit services.

Envoy Bailiff & Collection Services Ltd.

#100, 4240 Glanford Ave.
Victoria, BC V8Z 0A1
250-474-7376
Fax: 250-474-7360
envoybailiffs@envoybailiffs.ca
Ownership: Private.
Number of Employees: 8
Executives:
David Becker, Contact

Executive Collections Inc.

#211, 402 West Pender St.
Vancouver, BC V6B 1T6
604-688-0600
Fax: 604-688-1444
Former Name: Gateway Collections Inc
Executives:
Douglas Appleton

Federal Credit & Consulting (Saskatchewan) Corp.

2636 Victoria Ave. East.
Regina, SK S4N 6M5
306-569-9668
Fax: 306-924-6777
Ownership: Private
Executives:
Dave Seitz, General Manager

Financial Debt Recovery Ltd.

#10, 40 West Wilmot St.
Richmond Hill, ON L4B 1H8
905-771-6000
Fax: 905-771-6005
800-763-3328
info@fdr.on.ca
www.fdr.on.ca
Ownership: Private
Year Founded: 1991
Number of Employees: 100
Profile: The company is focuses on collection services for accounts at the second and third level of placement. In addition to its Montréal branch, there is also a USA branch, situated at #200, 433 Main St., Buffalo, NY, 14202. To reach the Buffalo location, the toll-freee number is 1-888-256-0167.

Executives:
Nicholas A. Papeo, President, General Manager; 905-771-6000; nicholasp@fdr.on.ca
Peter Cuypers, Vice-President; 905-771-6000; pcuypers@fdr.on.ca
Branches:
Montréal
#920, 1117, rue Ste-Catherine ouest
Montréal, QC H3B 1H9 Canada
514-285-1003
Fax: 514-285-1904
877-651-9259

First Financial Underwriting Services (Canada) Inc.

919 Ellesmere Rd., 3rd Fl.
Toronto, ON M1P 2W7

416-750-7388
Fax: 416-750-7386
888-750-7388
customer-services@firstfin.com
www.firstfin.com
Year Founded: 1991
Profile: Inspection services.

Fort Bailiffs Ltd.
#1, 631 Fort St.
Victoria, BC V8W 1G1
250-382-9163
Fax: 250-386-8131
Year Founded: 1980
Executives:
Daniel Bjur

Fraser Collection Services Limited
#200, 3071 - 5 Rd.
Richmond, BC V6X 2T4
604-273-4671
Fax: 604-273-3875
fraserc@frasercollections.com
www.frasercollections.com
Ownership: Private
Year Founded: 1967
Profile: Engaged in recovering debts, mainly in corporate and commercial areas and primarily in Western Canada.

Gallard's Collection Service Ltd.
#215, 895 Fort St.
Victoria, BC V8W 1H7
250-383-0412
Fax: 250-383-4523
877-570-1110
Year Founded: 1957
Executives:
Robert Gallard, President

GB Collection Agency
#109, 100 Main St. E
Hamilton, ON L8N 3W4
905-546-1212
Fax: 905-546-1505
gbcollection@cogeco.net
www.gbcollection.ca
Ownership: Private
Year Founded: 2005
Profile: Services include collection, credit recovery. Specializes in consumer and commercial accounts receivables.

Executives:
Steve Bobko, President
Greg Maitinsky, Vice-President

Georgia Bailiff Service Ltd.
208 Broadwell Rd.
Salt Spring Island, BC V8K 1H3
250-537-1884
Ownership: Private
Year Founded: 1993

Gestion Credere inc
1543, 7e rue
Chertsey, QC J0K 3K0
450-882-4848
Fax: 450-882-3113
800-675-9203
ouellette.nathalie@videotron.ca
Ownership: Private
Year Founded: 1994
Profile: Collection agency & credit bureau.

Executives:
Nathalie Ouellette, President

Global Credit & Collection
#800, 15 Wertheim Ct.
Richmond Hill, ON L4B 3H7
905-764-6639
Fax: 905-764-9419
Former Name: York Region Collection Services Ltd.

Golden Choice Credit Reporting Agency Ltd.
#605, 11 Holland Ave.
Ottawa, ON K1Y 4S1
613-728-3971
Fax: 613-728-3892

Halton Bailiff Services
#601, 420 Main St. East
Milton, ON L9T 5G3
905-876-3332
Fax: 905-876-0414
800-262-2172
neilem@globalserve.net
Executives:
Neil Emerson, Contact

Havers, Dillon & Associates Ltd.
#2, 117 East 15th St.
North Vancouver, BC V7L 2P7
604-980-9321
Fax: 604-980-0641
Executives:
Bob Webber

Herr & Co. Bailiffs Inc.
PO Box 580
St Thomas, ON N5P 3V6
519-878-1830
Fax: 519-631-9789
jamesherrbailiff@sympatico.ca
Year Founded: 1997
Executives:
Jim Herr, President
David Herr, Contact

Impact Credit Recoveries Ltd.
PO Box 34241
1610 - 37th St. SW
Calgary, AB T3C 3W2
403-571-4760
Fax: 403-571-4769
Year Founded: 1995
Number of Employees: 2
Executives:
Douglas Moody, Owner

Infocrédit
#300, 440, rue Ste-Hélène
Montréal, QC H2Y 2K7
514-842-5600
Fax: 514-842-5696
800-850-3509
infocredit@videotron.ca
www.infocredit.net.ms
Ownership: Private
Year Founded: 1953
Executives:
Jean Pierre Campeau, President

International Credit Assistance Ltd.
#205, 31549 South Fraser Way
Abbotsford, BC V2T 1T8
604-854-3328
Fax: 604-854-3538
info@internetcollections.com
www.internetcollections.com
Ownership: Private
Year Founded: 1989
Number of Employees: 4
Revenues: Under $1 million
Executives:
Darry Taylor

J. McMillan Bailiff & Collection Ltd.
102 Doric Ave.
Nanaimo, BC V9R 3N2
250-753-7729
Fax: 250-753-7739
877-686-2929
jmbc@shaw.ca
www.jmcmillanbailiff.shawbiz.ca
Year Founded: 1998
Profile: Services include debt collection, process serving, skip tracing, and bailiff service.

Kay Bailiff & Adjustment Inc.
405 Midwest Rd.
Toronto, ON M1P 3A6
416-292-2221
Fax: 416-288-1161
Executives:
Peter Warmington

Keltic Collections Ltd.
#3, 46 Inglis Pl.
Truro, NS B2N 5B6
902-895-1675
Fax: 902-895-5633
800-653-4539
info@kelticcollections.ca
www.kelticcollections.ca
Ownership: Private
Year Founded: 1969
Number of Employees: 6
Executives:
Vincent Neary, President; vneary@kelticcollections.ca

Kent County Bailiff Services
PO Box 1935
98 Regent St.
Blenheim, ON N0P 1A0
519-676-4928
Fax: 519-676-1505

Les Agences de Collection Association Inc.
#605, 345, av Victoria
Montréal, QC H3Z 2N2
514-483-6223
Fax: 514-483-3755
Ownership: Private
Year Founded: 1986

Lincoln Collection Agencies Limited
PO Box 23026
St Catharines, ON L2R 7P6
905-688-2351
Fax: 905-688-2358
ddunbar@lcacanada.com
www.lcacanada.com
Ownership: Private
Year Founded: 1955
Number of Employees: 3
Assets: Under $1 million
Revenues: Under $1 million
Profile: The collection agency's activities include court representation services, & commercial & retail collections. Past due accounts receivable are located & collected.

Executives:
Dennis M. Dunbar, President; dennis@lcacanada.com

Lower Mainland Bailiffs
#400, 525 Seymour St.
Vancouver, BC V6B 3H7
604-681-6444
Fax: 604-681-6404
lmbctd@hotmail.com
Executives:
Ric Hayward, Manager

Loyalist Collection Services Inc.
PO Box 22081
199 Front St.
Belleville, ON K8N 5H5
613-968-7798
Fax: 613-968-8080
loyalist@on.aibn.com
Ownership: Private
Year Founded: 1994
Number of Employees: 3
Executives:
Dave Walker, General Manager

M. McGrath Canada Limited
PO Box 469
111A Rideau St.
Ottawa, ON K1N 8S4
613-241-8420
Fax: 613-241-1653
800-267-4124
collections@mcgrathcanada.com
www.mcgrathcanada.com
Ownership: Private
Year Founded: 1953
Affiliated Companies:
Agence de Recouvrement M. McGrath Québec Ltée

Marathon Commercial Credit Consultant
#240, 1145, boul Lebourgneuf
Québec, QC G2K 2K8

Marathon Commercial Credit Consultant (continued)
418-623-4763
Fax: 418-623-7630
800-667-2111
marathon@marathon-ltd.com
www.marathon-ltd.com
Ownership: Private
Year Founded: 1989
Profile: Services include credit reports, inquiries, establishing credit policies, consumer & commercial investigations, risk evaluation and recommendations, courses in commercial credit management, managing accounts receivable, commercial credit consulting, credit consulting for the construction industry, and credit consulting for export.

Medicine Hat Collection Agencies
#202, 1601 Dunmore Rd. SE
Medicine Hat, AB T1A 1Z8
403-527-7299
Fax: 403-529-1805

MGD Collections & Paralegal Services
#319, 93 West St., 2nd Fl.
Corner Brook, NL A2H 2Y6
709-634-0430
Fax: 709-634-0435
Profile: Collection and paralegal services.

MJR Collection Services Limited
#17-18, 7033 Telford Way
Mississauga, ON L5S 1V4
905-671-4151
Fax: 905-671-2225
genoff@mjrcollections.com
www.mjrcollections.com
Profile: Financial recovery service.

National Apparel Bureau
Also listed under: *Financing & Loan Companies*
#200, 294, rue Saint-Paul ouest
Montréal, QC H2Y 2A3
514-845-8135
Fax: 514-499-8468
800-361-2171
bureau@nabq.com
www.nabq.com
Ownership: Private
Year Founded: 1934
Number of Employees: 10
Executives:
B.C. Lafford, President

NCO Financial Services Inc.
#210, 6700 Century Ave.
Mississauga, ON L5N 6A4
905-819-4270
Fax: 905-819-4289
www.ncogroup.com
Former Name: Financial Collection Agencies (International) Inc.

Also Known As: NCO
Ownership: NCO Financial Systems Inc., US
Year Founded: 1964
Number of Employees: 600
Profile: Services include collection of accounts receivable on a contingency fee basis & management of account receivable portfolios.

Nor-Don Collection Network
#1111, 325 Milner Ave.
Toronto, ON M1B 5N1
416-412-3070
Fax: 416-412-3042
800-636-4879
www.ncn.ca
Ownership: Private
Number of Employees: 280
Revenues: $10-50 million
Profile: Debt collection services are provided to both business & government.
Executives:
Paul Morags, President/CEO
Tom Rossi, Vice-President, National Collection Operations
Barry L. Kryha, CFO
John Van Dam, Director, Information Technology
Branches:
Calgary
#202, 1409 Edmonton Trail NE
Calgary, AB T2E 3K8 Canada
403-276-7243
Fax: 403-230-3835
Edmonton
#300, 10250 - 101 St.
Edmonton, AB T5J 3P4 Canada
403-426-5800
Fax: 403-426-6254
Montréal
#400, 50, boul Cremazie
Montréal, QC H2P 2R3 Canada
514-383-5711
Fax: 514-383-3616
New Westminster
#409, 555 - 6th St.
New Westminster, BC V3L 5H1 Canada
604-540-1200
Fax: 604-540-1220
Winnipeg
#230, 530 Kenaston Blvd.
Winnipeg, MB R3N 1Z4 Canada
204-488-2445
Fax: 204-488-3406

Normand Pinard Inc.
3079, rue Milleret
Québec, QC G1X 1N1
418-658-7627
Fax: 418-658-9344
877-658-0407
info@creditpinard.com
www.creditpinard.com
Ownership: Private
Executives:
Normand Pinard, Owner

North Central Bailiffs Ltd.
2706 Jasper St.
Prince George, BC V2L 5B2
250-564-4900
Fax: 250-563-2024
headoffice@northcentralbailiffs.bc.ca
www.northcentralbailiffs.bc.ca
Executives:
Don McPhail, Manager
Offices:
Fort St. John
9831 - 98A Ave.
Fort St John, BC V1J 6W7 Canada
250-787-1696
Fax: 250-787-1650
markw@northcentralbailiffs.bc.ca
Mark White, Branch Manager
Kamloops
#7, 452 Dene Dr.
Kamloops, BC V2B 7K6 Canada
250-377-4148
Fax: 250-377-4149
northcentralbailiffskamloops@shaw.ca
Gary Granoff, Branch Manager
Kelowna
3953 Hwy. 97 North
Kelowna, BC V1X 5C4 Canada
250-491-1033
Fax: 250-491-1073
ncbkel@cnx.net
Don McPhail, Branch Manager
Terrace
#202, 4546 Park Ave.
Terrace, BC V8G 1V4 Canada
250-635-0115
Fax: 250-635-0185
kim@northcentralbailiffs.bc.ca
Kim Patten, Branch Manager
Williams Lake
PO Box 4868
Williams Lake, BC V2G 2V8 Canada
250-392-6200
Fax: 250-392-2927
garyb@northcentralbailiffs.bc.ca
Gary Batty, Branch Manager

Okanagan Court Bailiffs Inc.
3130 - 30 Ave.
Vernon, BC V1T 2C2
250-549-2727
Fax: 250-260-6070
bailiff@junction.net

Okanagan Credit Counsellors Ltd.
#202, 1755 Springfield Rd.
Kelowna, BC V1Y 5V5
250-763-5757
Fax: 250-763-5747
800-330-8944
info@debtmenders.ca
www.debtmenders.ca
Ownership: Private
Year Founded: 1992

Ontario Credit Collections Ltd.
PO Box 2292, B Stn. B
London, ON N6A 4E3
519-685-6499
Fax: 519-685-9557
Ownership: Private
Year Founded: 1989
Executives:
Brian Hynds, Manager

P & G Applied Bailiff Services Inc.
345 Christina St. North
Sarnia, ON N7T 5V6
519-337-4368
Fax: 519-337-4368

Partners in Credit
#503, 1 West Pearce St.
Richmond Hill, ON L4B 3K3
905-886-0555
Fax: 905-886-5784
888-730-6333
info@partnersincredit.com
www.partnersincredit.com
Ownership: Private. A Division of The Fiore Group Ltd.
Executives:
Vincent S. Fiore, President

PCM Collections Limited
#205, 180 Park Ave.
Thunder Bay, ON P7B 6J4
807-345-3368
Fax: 807-345-4308
Number of Employees: 4
Executives:
Donna Withenshaw, President

Peter Courneya Collection Services
#202, 1674 Hyde Park Rd.
London, ON N6H 5L7
519-641-3715
Fax: 519-641-3258
Ownership: Private
Year Founded: 1998
Number of Employees: 3
Executives:
Peter Courneya, President

Pinpoint Credit Solutions
#203, 206 Laird Dr.
Toronto, ON M4G 3W4
416-421-0086
Fax: 416-421-4288
800-368-0327
pinpointcredit@pinpointcredit.com
Ownership: Private
Year Founded: 1999
Number of Employees: 10
Profile: The company is also a skip tracing agency.
Executives:
Brenda L. Giles, President

Polar Collection Services Inc.
PO Box 1048
20 Nelson Rd.
Thompson, MB R8N 1N7
204-677-4520
Fax: 204-778-7160
Former Name: Credit Bureau of Northern Manitoba
Ownership: Private

Porcupine Credit Corporation 2001 Ltd.
PO Box 908
21 Cedar St. North
Timmins, ON P4N 7H2
705-264-5288
Fax: 705-560-2074
cbureau@ntl.sympatico.ca

Portfolio Management Solutions Inc.
#700, 200 Queens Ave.
London, ON N6A 1J3
519-432-0075
Fax: 519-964-3106
info@portfoliomci.com
Former Name: Ontario Commercial Collections Inc.
Ownership: Private
Year Founded: 1998
Profile: Provides adjustment and collection services.

Executives:
Gerry Coffin, President/CEO

Poulin Jacques
1200, av Galilée
Québec, QC G1P 4E3
418-681-3206
Fax: 418-683-2479
Year Founded: 1990
Number of Employees: 1

Prince George Bailiffs (1988) Inc.
575 Wainwright St.
Prince George, BC V2M 2C6
250-563-6778
Fax: 250-564-0411
Year Founded: 1988
Executives:
Eileen Milliken, Manager

Professional Collection Services Inc.
#200, 152 James St. South
Hamilton, ON L8P 3A2
905-523-8477
Fax: 905-523-5660
Year Founded: 1993
Executives:
Michael A. Losak, President

Profile Crédit
80, rue Fleury ouest
Montréal, QC H3L 1T2
514-385-3635
Fax: 514-385-9325
800-267-2774
info@profilecredit.com
www.profilecredit.com
Ownership: Private

Progressive Collection Services Ltd.
#3, 996 Main St.
Penticton, BC V2A 5E4
250-490-9924
Fax: 250-490-9750
800-458-3213
procoll@shaw.com
Former Name: Alexander Francis James
Year Founded: 1996
Number of Employees: 4

Quality Credit Services Limited
#105, 111 Granton Dr.
Richmond Hill, ON L4B 1L5
905-762-0740
Fax: 905-762-9410
800-655-9564
www.qualityinvestigative.com/credit/cgc/AboutHome.html
Profile: National consumer and commercial credit reporting agency that specializes in providing in-depth credit reports catered to industries such as credit, property management, banking, legal, insurance and franchises.

Executives:
Jim Marley, Manager

Renaissance Collection Agency Inc.
#720, 110 King St. West
Hamilton, ON L8P 4S6
905-523-1110
Fax: 905-523-0202
bkonow@bellnet.ca
Ownership: Private.
Year Founded: 1997
Executives:
Bill Konow, Manager

Rent Check Credit Bureau
#805, 80 Richmond St. West
Toronto, ON M5H 2A4
416-365-7060
Fax: 416-365-1987
800-661-7312
marketing@rentcheckcorp.com
www.rentcheckcorp.com
Ownership: Private
Year Founded: 1976
Profile: Rent Check Credit is a credit reporting agency & landlord services bureau. It also provides paralegal & corporate services.

Branches:
Ottawa
#304 Tower A
555 Legget Dr.
Ottawa, ON K2K 2X3 Canada
613-254-7167
Fax: 613-622-7855
brenda@rentcheckcorp.com
Sudbury
114 Pine St., 2nd Fl.
Sudbury, ON P3C 1X1 Canada
705-671-1221
Fax: 705-670-1752
shelley@rentcheckcorp.com

Revin Bailiffs Inc.
#3, 134 Norfinch Dr.
Toronto, ON M3N 1X7
416-749-7386
Fax: 416-749-1930
866-749-7386
revinbailiffs@on.aibn.com
Ownership: Private
Year Founded: 2000
Number of Employees: 5
Assets: Under $1 million
Revenues: Under $1 million
Executives:
Brian Revin, Owner
Nolan B. Revin, Bailiff

St Catharines Credit Corporation Limited
PO Box 186
26 Queen St., 2nd Fl.
St Catharines, ON L2R 6S7
905-688-9855
Fax: 905-688-9606
Also Known As: Credit Bureau Collections
Ownership: Private
Executives:
David Alexander, Vice-President

Schel Management Credit
#310, 8944 - 182 St. NW
Edmonton, AB T5T 2E3
780-481-1299
Fax: 780-481-1674
smc@schel.com
www.schel.com
Ownership: Schel Management Inc.
Year Founded: 1977
Number of Employees: 5
Executives:
Larry Heschel, President; larry@schel.com
Greg Shewchuk, Sec.-Treas.; gslaw@schel.com

Security Recovery Group Inc.
#200, 103 Richmond St. East
Toronto, ON M5C 1N9
416-955-4650
Fax: 416-955-4654
sales@srgi.net
www.securityrecoverygroup.com
Ownership: Private
Year Founded: 1996

Sterling Bailiffs Inc.
55 Irondale Dr.
Toronto, ON M9L 2S6
416-701-1322
Fax: 416-701-0005
877-888-7376
bailiff@sterbail.com
www.sterbail.com
Ownership: Private
Year Founded: 1991
Number of Employees: 10
Revenues: Under $1 million
Profile: Services include landlord distraints, vehicle and equipment recovery, skip tracing, storage, and complete auction and liquidation services.

Executives:
Stephen Wagman, President; steve@sterbail.com
Earl Boero, Vice-President; earl@sterbail.com

Terminal Bailiffs & Collectors
#107, 1475 Fairview Rd.
Penticton, BC V2A 7W5
250-493-2618
Fax: 250-493-8992
tbcbailiff@shaw.ca
Also Known As: 681471 BD Ltd.
Number of Employees: 3
Executives:
Jim Hanon, Manager

Torlon Credit Recovery Ltd.
#301, 120 Wellington St.
London, ON N6B 2K6
519-642-3300
Fax: 519-432-3202
torloncreditrecovery@on.aibn.com
Ownership: Private
Year Founded: 1997
Executives:
Lawrence W. Crawford, President

Total Credit Recovery Limited
225 Yorkland Blvd.
Toronto, ON M2J 4Y7
416-774-4000
Fax: 416-774-4001
800-267-2482
webmaster@totalcrediting.com
www.totalcrediting.com
Ownership: Private
Year Founded: 1980
Number of Employees: 550
Profile: Specializes in accounts receivable management, collections and call centre services.

Branches:
Edmonton - Prairies, NWT & Nunavut
#1090, 10250 - 101 St.
Edmonton, AB T5J 3P4 Canada
780-423-1515
Fax: 780-423-1616
Laval
#295, 4455, Autouroute Laval (440) ouest
Laval, QC H7P 4W6 Canada
450-680-1800
Fax: 450-680-1900
Moncton - New Brunswick, Newfoundland & Labrador
#208, 272 St. Georges St.
Moncton, NB E1C 1W6 Canada
506-853-0553
Fax: 506-853-7117
Richmond - BC & Yukon
#205, 6011 Westminster Hwy.
Richmond, BC V7C 4V4 Canada
604-231-1500
Fax: 604-231-1570

Trans Union du Canada Inc.
#370, 1, Place Laval
Laval, QC H7N 1A1
514-335-0374
Fax: 877-713-3393
800-363-2809
www.groupecho.com
Year Founded: 1960
Profile: Offers personalised credit information, collection and training services.

Trans Union du Canada Inc. (continued)
Affiliated Companies:
Credit Recovery Ltd.

Trend Collection & Bailiff Services Ltd.
264B - 10 St.
Brandon, MB R7A 4E8
204-726-0813
Fax: 204-726-0828
Ownership: Private
Year Founded: 1986
Number of Employees: 2
Assets: Under $1 million
Revenues: Under $1 million
Executives:
Judy Smith, President

U-Sue
#207, 614 - 6th Ave. SW
Calgary, AB T2P 0S4
403-216-0036
Fax: 403-216-0039
u-sue@telus.net
Profile: U-Sue is a small claims court agent.

Unik Collectrite Inc.
1581 Laurier St.
Rockland, ON K4K 1L6
613-446-5131
Fax: 613-446-6916
Former Name: Unik Collection Agency Ltd.
Year Founded: 1975
Number of Employees: 4

United Collection Agency NAB Inc.
294, St-Paul ouest, 2e étage
Montréal, QC H2Y 2A3
514-842-6126
Fax: 514-499-8468
Executives:
John Thomson, General Manager

Vanco Recovery Network Inc.
#612, 602 West Hastings St.
Vancouver, BC V6B 1P1
604-718-5151
Fax: 604-718-5144
info@vanco.bc.ca
www.vanco.bc.ca
Year Founded: 1979
Profile: Fully bonded and licensed collection agency.

Vancouver Credit Collection Inc.
#204, 9527 - 120th St.
Delta, BC V4C 6S3
604-588-7796
Fax: 604-588-7785
Ownership: Private.
Year Founded: 1993
Number of Employees: 2
Executives:
Nitya Nand, Manager
Nirmala Nand, Secretary

Vancouver Island Bailiffs Ltd.
#1, 2937 Kilpatrick Ave.
Courtenay, BC V9N 7S7
250-338-5913
Fax: 250-337-8501
pbinnes@mail.island.net
Executives:
Peter Innes, Manager

Vanguard Collection Agencies Ltd.
#201, 16220 Stony Plain Rd.
Edmonton, AB T5P 4A4
780-486-1011
Fax: 780-486-1163
800-487-1163
vca-edmonton@vanguardcollection.com
www.vanguardcollection.com
Ownership: Private
Year Founded: 1958
Number of Employees: 13
Assets: $1-5 million
Revenues: $1-5 million
Executives:
Don Bridgewater, Manager, Collections

Branches:
Burnaby
#29, 9912 Lougheed Hwy.
Burnaby, BC V3J 1N2 Canada
604-420-4664
Fax: 604-420-4280
Les Meachum, Contact
Calgary
1071 - 26 St. NE
Calgary, AB T2A 6K8 Canada
403-569-0001
Fax: 403-235-4334
John Koopmans, Contact

Veri-Cheque Ltd.
19 East Wilmot St.
Richmond Hill, ON L4B 1A3
905-709-0927
Fax: 905-709-0952
800-268-3284
info@vericheque.com
www.vericheque.com
Year Founded: 1978
Profile: The company is a credit authority to industries in the following businesses: computer, apparel, food & general merchandise.

Executives:
Ron Renwick, President
Branches:
Montréal
3454, rue Sainte-Catherine est
Montréal, QC H1W 2E2 Canada
514-282-0089
Fax: 514-282-6791
Vancouver
#314, 475 Howe St.
Vancouver, BC V6C 2B3 Canada
604-682-6733
Fax: 604-682-6223

Vernon Bailiffs Inc.
3130 - 31st Ave.
Vernon, BC V1T 2H1
250-545-6088
Fax: 250-545-2813
bailiff@junction.net
Ownership: Private
Number of Employees: 10
Executives:
Wayne MacGregor, Manager

Wiggins Adjustments Ltd.
19985 - 68th Ave.
Langley, BC V2Y 2W5
604-530-0211
Fax: 604-530-4977
888-376-6611
Ownership: Private
Profile: Provides adjustment and collection services.

Executives:
Larry Fraser, Manager

Windsor Credit Bureau
850 University Ave. West
Windsor, ON N9A 6R2
519-253-4481
Fax: 519-253-4405
Ownership: Private
Year Founded: 1922
Number of Employees: 6
Executives:
Don Larkin, Owner
Ken Severn, Owner

Windsor Investigation Services Ltd.
#1213, 5060 Tecumseh Rd. East
Windsor, ON N8T 1C1
519-966-0000
Fax: 519-250-0435
800-580-9967
pi@windsorinvestigation.com
www.windsorinvestigation.com
Ownership: Private
Year Founded: 1994
Profile: Specializes in insurance claims and covert video surveillance.

Woodstock-Oxford Collections Inc.
PO Box 155
13 Light St.
Woodstock, ON N4S 6G7
519-539-8196
Fax: 519-539-4991
866-622-6161
thecreditbureau@execulink.com
Former Name: Woodstock & Oxford County Collection Inc.
Year Founded: 1945
Number of Employees: 5
Executives:
John Hardman, President

Credit Card Companies

Amex Bank of Canada
***Also listed under:** Foreign Banks: Schedule II*
101 McNabb St.
Markham, ON L3R 4H8
800-668-2639
Other Information: TTY/TDD: 1-866-549-6426
www.americanexpress.com/canada
Ownership: Wholly-owned subsidiary of American Express Travel Related Services Company, Inc., New York, USA.
Year Founded: 1853
Number of Employees: 3,700
Profile: Amex Bank of Canada & Amex Canada Inc. are the operating names for American Express in Canada. The Bank issues American Express cards in Canada, while Amex Canada Inc. operates the corporate travel, travel services network & travellers cheque divisions in Canada.

Executives:
Beth Horowitz, President/CEO
Francisco Da Rocha Campos (Xiko), Vice-President, Consumer & Small Business Products

Capital One Bank (Canada Branch)
***Also listed under:** Foreign Banks: Schedule III*
#1300, 5650 Yonge St.
Toronto, ON M2M 4G3
Fax: 416-228-5113
800-481-3239
Other Information: Customer Relations Address: PO Box 503, Stn. D, Toronto, ON M1R 5L1; Payment Address: PO Box 501, Stn. D, Toronto, ON M1R 5S4
ombudsman@capitalone.com
www.capitalone.ca
Ownership: Foreign. Part of Capital One Services, Inc., McLean, VA, USA.
Profile: The international financial services company is known in the credit card marketplace, for pioneering low introductory rates, balance transfers, & fixed rate products in North America.

Executives:
William Cilluffo, President
Ian Cunningham, Chief Operating Officer
Robert Livingston, Chief Marketing Officer
Ramona Tobler, Chief People Officer
Felix Wu, Chief Financial Officer
Scott Wilson, Ombudsman

Capital One Financial Corporation
Customer Relations
PO Box 503, D Stn. D
Toronto, ON M1R 5L1
800-481-3239
www.capitalone.ca/canada/
Year Founded: 1988
Profile: Capital One has offered Canadian consumers a range of competitive MasterCard credit cards since 1996.

Executives:
Richard D. Fairbank, Chair/CEO
William Cilluffo, President
Ian Cunningham, COO
Robert Livingston, Chief Marketing Officer
Ramona Tobler, Chief Human Resources Officer
Felix Wu, CFO
Scott Wilson, Ombudsman
Affiliated Companies:
Capital One Bank (Canada Branch)

Desjardins Credit Union
***Also listed under:** Credit Unions/Caisses Populaires; Non-Depository Institutions*

East Tower, Whitby Mall
1615 Dundas St. East, 3rd Fl.
Whitby, ON L1N 2L1
905-743-5790
Fax: 905-743-6156
888-283-8333
www.desjardins.com
Ownership: Member-owned
Year Founded: 2002
Number of Employees: 235
Assets: $1-10 billion Year End: 20050700
Revenues: $50-100 million Year End: 20050700
Executives:
Alfred Pfeiffer, President/COO
Jacques Luys, Vice-President, Operations
Trung Nguyen, Sec.-Treas.
Vincent Brossard, Manager, Legal & Corporate Affairs
Karen Deering, Manager, Communication & Marketing
John Laughlin, Manager, Information Technology
Bruno Poirier, Acting Manager, Finance & Control
Peter Roberts, Manager, Head Office Administration
Directors:
Thomas Blais
Deborah J. Findlay
Paul E. Garfinkel
Michael Howlett
Jean-Guy Langelier
Heather Nicol
Trung Nguyen
Hubert Thibault
Pierre Tougas
Branches:
Aylmer
34 Talbot St. West
Aylmer, ON N5H 1J7 Canada
519-765-1286
Fax: 519-765-1690
Brantford
171 Colborne St.
Brantford, ON N3T 6C9 Canada
519-753-4131
Fax: 519-753-7121
Guelph
153 Wyndham St. North
Guelph, ON N1H 4E9 Canada
519-821-2101
Fax: 519-821-2990
Hamilton - Barton St.
Central Mall
1227 Barton St. East
Hamilton, ON L8H 2V4 Canada
905-547-6202
Fax: 905-547-4748
Hamilton - King St.
Lloyd D. Jackson Square
2 King St. West
Hamilton, ON L8P 1A1 Canada
905-528-6391
Fax: 905-528-8103
London - Richmond St.
353 Richmond St.
London, ON N6A 3C2 Canada
519-432-1197
Fax: 519-432-7896
London - Richmond St.
University Community Centre, University of Western Ontario
#73, 1151 Richmond St.
London, ON N6A 3K7 Canada
519-850-2550
Fax: 519-850-2553
Mississauga
214 Queen St. South
Mississauga, ON L5M 1L5 Canada
905-821-7345
Fax: 905-821-8128
Ottawa
171 Sparks St.
Ottawa, ON K1P 5B9 Canada
613-239-1469
Fax: 613-239-1482
Owen Sound
825 - 2nd Ave. East
Owen Sound, ON N4K 5P3 Canada
519-376-6025
Fax: 519-376-1041
Pembroke
40 Pembroke St. West
Pembroke, ON K8A 6X3 Canada
613-732-7821
Fax: 613-732-3830
Seaforth
49 Main St. South
Seaforth, ON N0K 1W0 Canada
519-527-0210
Fax: 519-527-2512
St Catharines
106 King St.
St Catharines, ON L2R 3H8 Canada
905-688-4661
Fax: 905-688-0320
St Marys
PO Box 100
134 Queen St.
St Marys, ON N4X 1A9 Canada
519-284-2260
Fax: 519-284-2622
Sudbury
#105, 159 Cedar St.
Sudbury, ON P3E 6A5 Canada
705-671-9525
Fax: 705-671-2501
Thunder Bay
#102, 189 Red River Rd.
Thunder Bay, ON P7B 1A2 Canada
807-345-6686
Fax: 807-345-6438
Toronto - Bay St.
375 Bay St.
Toronto, ON M5H 2V5 Canada
416-363-7282
Fax: 416-363-0896
Toronto - Broadview Ave.
838 Broadview Ave.
Toronto, ON M4K 2R1 Canada
416-463-1117
Fax: 416-463-7773

Toronto - Danforth Ave.
2031 Danforth Ave.
Toronto, ON M4C 1J8 Canada
416-698-8320
Fax: 416-698-9131
Toronto - St. Clair Ave.
26 St. Clair Ave. East
Toronto, ON M4T 1L7 Canada
416-925-3887
Fax: 416-925-3874
Toronto - University Ave.
439 University Ave.
Toronto, ON M5G 1Y8 Canada
416-593-1763
Fax: 416-593-6936
Toronto - Wellesley St.
56 Wellesley St. West
Toronto, ON M5S 2S3 Canada
416-928-6468
Fax: 416-928-2757
Walkerton
PO Box 308
244 Durham St.
Walkerton, ON N0G 2V0 Canada
519-881-3321
Fax: 519-881-3797
Windsor
545 Ouellette Ave.
Windsor, ON N9A 4J3 Canada
519-254-4324
Fax: 519-254-6270
Woodstock
396 Dundas St. East
Woodstock, ON N4S 1B7 Canada
519-537-8194
Fax: 519-537-8844

Desjardins Gestion d'actifs/ Desjardins Asset Management

Also listed under: *Credit Unions/Caisses Populaires; Non-Depository Institutions*
95 St Clair Ave. West
Toronto, ON M4V 1N7

Affiliated Companies:
Gestion Fiera Capital

Diners Club International

PO Box 4454, A Stn. A
Toronto, ON M5W 4B1
416-369-6313
800-363-3333
www.dinersclubnorthamerica.com
Former Name: Diners Club/En Route
Ownership: Public. Citigroup
Year Founded: 1992
Number of Employees: 200
Assets: $100-500 million
Revenues: $50-100 million
Profile: Diners Club offers cardmembers and corporate clients its expertise in managing their business travel and entertainment expenses worldwide.
Executives:
Yvon Dallaire, Managing Director, Canada

Home Trust Company

Also listed under: *Trust Companies*
#2300, 145 King St. West
Toronto, ON M5H 1J8
416-360-4663
Fax: 416-360-0401
800-990-7881
inquiry@hometrust.ca
www.hometrust.ca
Ownership: Public. Principal subsidiary of Home Capital Group Inc.
Year Founded: 1977
Number of Employees: 296
Assets: $1-10 billion Year End: 20050930
Revenues: $100-500 million Year End: 20050930
Stock Symbol: HCG
Profile: Federally regulated trust company carrying on business across Canada.
Executives:
Gerald M. Soloway, President/CEO; 416-775-5001; gerald.soloway@hometrust.ca
Nick Kyprianou, Sr. Vice-President/COO; 416-775-5012; nick.kyprianou@hometrust.ca
Brian Mosko, Sr. Vice-President; 416-775-5061; brian.mosko@hometrust.ca
Chris Ahlvik, Vice-President
Cathy A. Sutherland, Treasurer; 905-688-3131; cathy.sutherland@hometrust.ca
Sharron Hatton, Corporate Secretary; 416-775-5007; sherry.hatton@hometrust.ca
Directors:
William G. Davis, P.C., C.C, Q.C., Chair
Norman F. Angus
William A. Dimma
Janet L. Ecker
Harvey F. Kolodny
Nick Kyprianou
John Marsh
Robert A. Mitchell
Gerald M. Soloway
Warren K. Walker
Branches:
Calgary
#720, 5920 MacLeod Trail South
Calgary, AB T2H 0K2 Canada
403-244-2432
Fax: 403-244-6542
866-235-2432
prairiesbranch@hometrust.ca
Emilio Fuoco, Sr. Manager, Mortgages
Halifax
Duke Tower
#1205, 5251 Duke St.
Halifax, NS B3J 1P3 Canada
902-422-4387
Fax: 902-422-8891
888-306-2421
maritimesbranch@hometrust.ca
Scott Congdon, Regional Manager, Mortgage Lending
St Catharines
PO Box 1554
#100, 15 Church St.
St Catharines, ON L2R 7J9 Canada

Home Trust Company (continued)
905-688-3131
Fax: 905-688-0534
888-771-9913
stcatharinesbranch@hometrust.ca
Cathy A. Sutherland, Vice-President, Finance
Vancouver
#1288, 200 Granville St.
Vancouver, BC V6C 1S4 Canada
604-484-4663
Fax: 604-484-4664
866-235-3080
vancouverbranch@hometrust.ca
Jason Humeniuk, Branch Manager

JCB International (Canada) Ltd.

Also listed under: *Foreign Banks Representative Offices*
#510, 1030 West Georgia St. W
Vancouver, BC V6E 2Y3
604-689-8110
Fax: 604-689-8101
www.jcbinternational.com
Ownership: Office of JCB International Co., Ltd., Tokyo, Japan
Year Founded: 1961

MasterCard Canada

The Exchange Tower
PO Box 52
#1060, 130 King St. West
Toronto, ON M5X 1B1
416-365-6655
Fax: 416-365-6670
www.mastercard.com/canada
Ownership: Private. MasterCard International Inc.
Year Founded: 1992
Profile: MasterCard is a global payments solutions company, which serves financial institutions, consumers & businesses in over 210 countries & territories. It manages payment card brands including MasterCard, Maestro & Cirrus. Services support members' credit, deposit access, electronic cash, business-to-business & related payment programs.

Executives:
Kevin J. Stanton, President
Oliver Manahan, Director, Emerging Technology
Daniel O. Monehin, Director, Finance
Jeff Stroud, Director, Emerging Technology, Chip Centre of Excellence
William Giles, Vice-President, Emerging Technology
Pete Kaulbach, Vice-President, Market Development
Brian Lang, Vice-President, Corporate Payments Solutions
Craig Penney, Vice-President, Strategy Integration & Planning

Tammy Scott, Vice-President, Canada Brand Building
Sal Soyer, Vice-President, Segment Leader, Sales & Account Management
Colin Wright, Vice-President, Acceptance & Merchant Development
Luke Pollard, Leader, Client Business, Canada

Visa Canada Association

Scotia Bank Plaza
#3710, 40 King St. West
Toronto, ON M5H 3Y2
416-367-8472
Fax: 416-860-8891
www.visa.com
Ownership: Visa International
Number of Employees: 60
Profile: The 23 member financial institutions of Visa Canada Association have issued more than 26 million VISA cards.

Executives:
Derek Fry, President
Tim Wilson, Sr. Vice-President, Strategy, Finance & Administration
Rachel Brandes, Vice-President, Finance, Chief Financial Officer

Trustees in Bankruptcy

A. Farber & Partners Inc.

#300, 1200 Sheppard Ave. East
Toronto, ON M2K 2R8
416-496-1200
Fax: 416-496-9651
800-267-7733
info@afarber.com
www.afarber.com
Ownership: Private.
Year Founded: 1979
Number of Employees: 68
Profile: The organization is involved in corporate finance turnarounds. Affiliated companies are Klem Farber Corporate Finance Inc., Farber Turnaround Management Inc. & Farber CFO Resources Inc.

Executives:
Alan Farber, President
Branches:
Alliston
46 Wellington St. West
Alliston, ON L9R 1Z5 Canada
705-434-0448
Barrie
#1A, 580 Bryne Dr.
Barrie, ON L4N 9P6 Canada
705-725-1466
Brampton
#333, 284 Queen St. East
Brampton, ON L6VW 1C2 Canada
905-459-9582
Collingwood
#9-10, 275 First St.
Collingwood, ON L3V 6H3 Canada
705-444-7319
Dundas
#106, 89 King St. West
Dundas, ON L9H 1V1 Canada
905-308-9999
Hamilton
57 John St. South
Hamilton, ON L8N 2B9 Canada
905-308-9999
Keswick
#200, 449 The Queensway South
Keswick, ON L4P 2E1 Canada
905-476-7782
Markham
#302, 305 Renfrew Dr.
Markham, ON L3R 9S8 Canada
905-415-2613
Midland
295 King St.
Midland, ON L4R 3M5 Canada
705-529-0791
Mississauga
#502, 3025 Hurontario St.
Mississauga, ON L5A 2H1 Canada
905-270-9233

Newmarket
#217, 16775 Yonge St.
Newmarket, ON L3Y 8J4 Canada
905-895-6968
Orillia
27 Peter St. North
Orillia, ON L3V 6J8 Canada
705-329-3347
Stoney Creek
#1A, 8 King St. West
Stoney Creek, ON L8G 1G8 Canada
905-308-9999
Toronto - Burnhamthorpe Rd.
#506, 555 Burnhamthorpe Rd.
Toronto, ON M9C 2Y3 Canada
416-743-0671
Toronto - Danforth Ave.
2600 Danforth Ave., 2nd Fl.
Toronto, ON M4C 1L3 Canada
416-496-3283
Toronto - Ellesmere Rd.
#330, 2100 Ellesmere Rd.
Toronto, ON M1H 3B7 Canada
416-431-5327
Toronto - Rexdale Blvd.
Bank of Montreal Bldg.
#705, 155 Rexdale Blvd.
Toronto, ON M9W 5Z8 Canada
416-743-0671
Toronto - Sheppard Ave. West
#4, 1150 Sheppard Ave. West
Toronto, ON M1H 3B7 Canada
416-496-3288
Toronto - York St.
#1600, 150 York St.
Toronto, ON M5H 3S5 Canada
416-496-3288
Wasaga Beach
940 Mosley St.
Wasaga Beach, ON L9Z 2G9 Canada
705-444-7319

A. John Page & Associates Inc.

#447, 100 Richmond St. West
Toronto, ON M5H 3K6
416-364-4894
Fax: 416-364-4869
info@ajohnpage.com
www.ajohnpage.com
Ownership: Private
Year Founded: 1994

Abakhan & Associates Inc.

#1120, 625 West Howe St.
Vancouver, BC V6C 2T6
604-689-4255
Fax: 604-689-4277
877-308-8877
info@abakhan.com
www.abakhan.com
Ownership: Private
Number of Employees: 10
Executives:
George Abakhan, President
Philip McCourt, Sr. Vice-President
Rick Hamilton, Sr. Manager
Richard Robinson, Sr. Manager
Branches:
Victoria
#414, 1207 Douglas St.
Victoria, BC V8W 2E7 Canada
250-995-3122
Fax: 250-483-1003
866-995-3122
victoria@abakhan.com

Aberback Lapointe & Associés Inc., Syndic

1080, côte du Beaver Hall
Montréal, QC H2Z 1S8
514-395-0570
Fax: 514-395-0571
800-265-0570
info@aberbacklapointe.com
www.aberbacklapointe.com
Ownership: Private
Year Founded: 1994
Profile: An affiliated company is Martin & Associés, Gestionnaires.

Branches:
Drummondville
492, rue Lindsay
Drummondville, QC J2B 1H1 Canada
819-472-7085
Granby
89, Mont-Royal
Granby, QC J2H 2K2 Canada
450-777-4397
Longueuil
#200, 3065, ch Chambly
Longueuil, QC J4L 1N3 Canada
450-674-3906
Montréal - Jean-Talon
#204, 2348, Jean-Talon est
Montréal, QC H2E 1V7 Canada
Montréal - Lakeshore
273, rue Lakeshore, #F
Montréal, QC H9S 4L1 Canada
514-426-4994
St-Jérôme
#2-3, 255, rue de Martigny ouest
Saint-Jérome, QC J7Y 2G4 Canada
Ste-Agathe-des-Monts
124, rue St-Vincent
Sainte-Agathe-des-Monts, QC J8C 2B1 Canada
819-321-2844

Adamson & Associates Inc.

142 Centre St.
St Thomas, ON N5R 3A3

519-633-8185
Fax: 519-633-0912
mail@adamsonassoc.com
www.adamsonassoc.com
Ownership: Private
Number of Employees: 6
Profile: Full service firm of insolvency practitioners serving the Southwestern Ontario corridor. Provides a full range of insolvency and restructuring services to both individuals and businesses.

Executives:
John Adamson, Trustee
Branches:
St. Thomas
924 Oxford St. East
London, ON N5Y 3J9 Canada
519-451-2122
Fax: 519-633-0912
mail@adamsonassoc.com
Waterloo
279 Weber St. North
Waterloo, ON N2J 3H8 Canada
519-744-6696
Fax: 519-633-0912
mail@adamsonassoc.com
Windsor
430 Pelissier St.
Windsor, ON N9A 4K9 Canada
519-971-8519
Fax: 519-633-0912
888-332-8911
mail@adamsonassoc.com

Alan Lawson Fisher Inc.

50 Colborne St. East
Oshawa, ON L1G 1L9
905-433-2166
Fax: 905-433-0979
bankruptcy.oshawa@lawsonfisher.com
www.lawsonfisher.com
Ownership: Private
Number of Employees: 8
Profile: Services include assistance with: proposals for consumers, professionals & businesses, personal bankruptcies, business bankruptcies & receiverships, and budget & financial counselling.

Executives:
Andy Fisher
John A. Fisher
Branches:
Ajax
#6, 144 Old Kingston Rd. West
Ajax, ON L1T 2Z9 Canada
905-427-1833
Fax: 905-683-3428
bankruptcy.ajax@lawsonfisher.com
Belleville
525 Dundas St. East, 2nd Fl.
Belleville, ON K8N 1G4 Canada
613-962-2455
Fax: 613-969-0210
bankruptcy.belleville@lawsonfisher.com
Lindsay
6 Albert St. N
Lindsay, ON K9V 4J1 Canada
705-878-3509
Fax: 705-324-0060
h.robinson-3142@on.aibn.com
Napanee
58 Dundas St. East
Napanee, ON K7R 1H8 Canada
613-354-1128
Fax: 613-969-0210
bankruptcy.napanee@lawsonfisher.com
Peterborough
#303, 159 King St.
Peterborough, ON K9J 2R8 Canada
705-745-2741
Fax: 705-745-0406
bankruptcy.peterborough@lawsonfisher.com
Picton
290 Main St. E
Picton, ON K0K 2T0 Canada
613-476-5472
Fax: 613-969-0210
bankruptcy.oshawa@lawsonfisher.com
Trenton
290 Dundas St. West
Trenton, ON K8V 3S1 Canada
613-392-1248
Fax: 613-969-0210
bankruptcy.trenton@lawsonfisher.com

Alexander G. May Inc.

#204, 737 Carnarvon St.
New Westminster, BC V3M 5X1
604-524-9988
Fax: 604-524-0187
info@bankruptcypersonal.com
Ownership: Private
Year Founded: 1988
Profile: Provides bankruptcy services.

Executives:
Alexander G. May

Appel & CIE Inc.

#900, 1, carré Westmount
Montréal, QC H3Z 2P9
514-932-4115
Fax: 514-932-6766
appel@appel.ca
Ownership: Private
Number of Employees: 20
Executives:
Stuart Freedman, Manager

BDO Dunwoody LLP

***Also listed under:* Accountants**
Royal Bank Plaza, South Tower
200 Bay St., 30th Fl.
Toronto, ON M5J 2J8
416-865-0111
Fax: 416-367-3912
national@bdo.ca
www.bdo.ca
Ownership: Private
Year Founded: 1921
Number of Employees: 1,965
Revenues: $214,000,000
Profile: Canada's sixth-largest accounting firm concentrates on the special needs of independent business & community-based organizations. The firm provides a full range of comprehensive business advisory services.

Executives:
Gilles Chaput, CEO
R.J. Berry, COO
Directors:
Dianne McMullen, Chair, Policy Board
Walter Flasza, Member, Policy Board
Kenneth Grower, Member, Policy Board
Anne McArel, Member, Policy Board
Kurt Oelschlagel, Member, Policy Board
Offices:
Abbotsford
#100, 2890 Garden St.
Abbotsford, BC V2T 4W7 Canada
604-853-6677
Fax: 604-853-4876
abbotsford@bdo.ca
Ben Baartman, Partner
Alexandria
55 Anik St.
Alexandria, ON K0C 1A0 Canada
613-525-1585
Fax: 613-525-1436
alexandria@bdo.ca
Pierre Vaillancourt, Partner
Alfred
PO Box 539
497 St-Philippe St.
Alfred, ON K0B 1A0 Canada
613-679-1332
Fax: 613-679-1801
alfred@bdo.ca
Alliston
#13, 169 Dufferin St. South
Alliston, ON L9R 1E6 Canada
705-435-5585
Fax: 705-435-5587
alliston@bdo.ca
Doug Holmes, Partner
Altona
26 Centre Ave. East
Altona, MB R0G 0B0 Canada
204-324-8653
Fax: 204-324-1629
altona@bdo.ca
Robert Martins, Partner
Barrie
#300, 300 Lakeshore Dr.
Barrie, ON L4N 0B4 Canada
705-726-6331
Fax: 705-722-6588
barrie@bdo.ca
Joe Hilton, Manager
Boissevain
372 South Railway St.
Boissevain, MB R0K 0E0 Canada
204-534-6935
boissevain@bdo.ca
Tony DeVligere, Partner & Trustee
Bracebridge
#239, 1 Manitoba St.
Bracebridge, ON P1L 1S2 Canada
705-645-5215
Fax: 705-645-8125
bracebridge@bdo.ca
Murray Maw, Managing Partner
Brandon
117 - 10th St.
Brandon, MB R7A 4E7 Canada
204-727-0671
Fax: 204-726-4580
brandon@bdo.ca
Tony DeVliegere, Partner & Trustee
Brantford
#110B, 325 West St.
Brantford, ON N3R 3V6 Canada
519-759-8320
Fax: 519-759-8421
brantford@bdo.ca
Bill H. Kavelman, Partner
Calgary
#1900, 801 - 6 Ave. SW
Calgary, AB T2P 3W2 Canada
403-266-5608
Fax: 403-233-7833
calgary@bdo.ca
Richard Edwards, Partner/Sr. Vice-President
Cambridge
764 King St. East
Cambridge, ON N3H 3N9
519-653-7126
Fax: 519-653-8218
cambridge@bdo.ca
Don Laird, Chartered Accountant
Cardston
259 Main St.
Cardston, AB T0K OKO Canada
403-653-4137
cardson@bdo.ca
Charlottetown
PO Box 2158
91 Water St.
Charlottetown, PE C1A 8B9 Canada
902-892-5365
Fax: 902-892-0383
Chatham
375 St. Clair St.
Chatham, ON N7L 3K3 Canada
519-354-1560
Fax: 519-354-9346
chatham@bdo.ca
Rick Elliott, Partner
Cobourg
PO Box 627
204 Division St.
Cobourg, ON K9A 4L3 Canada
905-372-6863
Fax: 905-372-6650
cobourg@bdo.ca
Michael Machon, Partner
Collingwood
#202, 186 Hurontario St.
Collingwood, ON L9Y 3Z5 Canada

NON-DEPOSITORY INSTITUTIONS

BDO Dunwoody LLP (continued)

705-445-4421
Fax: 705-445-6691
collingwood@bdo.ca
Pierre Vaillancourt, Partner

Cornwall
PO Box 644
113 Second St. East
Cornwall, ON K6H 5T3 Canada
613-932-8691
Fax: 613-932-7591
cornwall@bdo.ca
Pierre Vaillencourt, Partner

Cranbrook
#200, 35 - 10 Ave. South
Cranbrook, BC V1C 2M9 Canada
250-426-4285
Fax: 250-426-8886
cranbrook@bdo.ca
Harley Lee, Partner

Dryden
37 King St.
Dryden, ON P8N 3G3 Canada
807-223-5321
Fax: 807-223-2978
dryden@bdo.ca
Doug Hannah, Partner

Edmonton
First Edmonton Pl.
#1000, 10665 Jasper Ave. NW
Edmonton, AB T5J 3S9 Canada
780-423-4353
Fax: 780-424-2110
edmonton@bdo.ca
Orest Bilous, Partner

Embrun
PO Box 128
991 Limoges Rd.
Embrun, ON K0A 1W0 Canada
613-443-5201
Fax: 613-443-2538
embrun@bdo.ca
Pierre Bourgon, Partner

Essex
180 Talbot St. South
Essex, ON N8M 1B6 Canada
519-776-6488
Fax: 519-776-6090
essex@bdo.ca
Mike McCreight, Partner

Fort Frances
375 Scott St.
Fort Frances, ON P9A 1H1 Canada
807-274-9848
Fax: 807-274-5142
fortfrances@bdo.ca
Marie Allan, Partner

Golden
PO Box 1709
#205, 421 - 9th Ave. North
Golden, BC V0A 1H0 Canada
250-344-5845
Fax: 250-344-7131
golden@bdo.ca
John Wilkey, Partner

Grande Prairie
Grande Prairie Place
9909 - 102 St., 5th Fl.
Grande Prairie, AB T8V 2V4 Canada
780-539-7075
Fax: 780-538-1890
grandeprairie@bdo.ca
Don Blonke, Partner

Guelph
#201, 660 Speedvale Ave. West
Guelph, ON N1K 1E5 Canada
519-824-5410
Fax: 519-824-5497
877-236-4835
Dan Cremasco, Partner

Hamilton
#2, 505 York Blvd.
Hamilton, ON L8R 3K4 Canada
905-525-6800
Fax: 905-525-6566
888-236-2383
hamilton@bdo.ca
Rino H. Bellavia, Partner

Hanover
485 - 10th St.
Hanover, ON N4N 1R2 Canada
519-364-3790
Fax: 519-364-5334
hanover@bdo.ca
John Hunt, Partner

Huntsville
PO Box 5484
2 Elm St.
Huntsville, ON P1H 2K8 Canada
705-789-4469
Fax: 705-789-1079
huntsville@bdo.ca
Bill McDonnell

Kamloops
#300, 272 Victoria St.
Kamloops, BC V2C 1Z6 Canada
250-372-9505
Fax: 250-374-6323
kamloops@bdo.ca
Bill Callandar, Partner

Kelowna
Landmark Technology Centre
#300, 1632 Dickson Ave.
Kelowna, BC V1Y 7T2 Canada
250-763-6700
Fax: 250-763-4457
kelowna@bdo.ca
Kevin Berry, Partner

Kenora
#300, 301 First Ave. South
Kenora, ON P9N 4E9 Canada
807-468-5531
Fax: 807-468-9774
kenora@bdo.ca
Jim Corbett, Partner

Kincardine
970 Queen St.
Kincardine, ON N2Z 2Y2 Canada
519-396-3425
Fax: 519-396-9829
kincardine@bdo.ca
Steven Watson, Partner

Kitchener
#401, 305 King St. West
Kitchener, ON N2G 1B9 Canada
519-576-5220
Fax: 519-576-5471
kitchenerwaterloo@bdo.ca
Dean Elliott, Partner

Langley
#220, 19916 - 64th Ave.
Langley, BC V2Y 1A2 Canada
604-534-8691
Fax: 604-534-8900
langley@bdo.ca
Ken Baker, Partner

Lethbridge
Southland Terrace
#200, 220 - 3rd Ave. South
Lethbridge, AB T1J 0G9 Canada
403-328-5292
Fax: 403-328-9534
lethbridge@bdo.ca
Jim Berezan, Partner

Lindsay
PO Box 358
165 Kent St. West
Lindsay, ON K9V 4S3 Canada
705-324-3579
Fax: 705-324-0774
lindsay@bdo.ca
Paul Allen, Partner

London
Station Park
#201, 252 Pall Mall St.
London, ON N6A 5P6 Canada
519-672-8940
Fax: 519-672-5562
london@bdo.ca
Ed Ramsay, Partner

MacGregor
78 Hampton St.
MacGregor, MB R0H 0R0 Canada
204-685-2323
Fax: 204-685-2341
macgregor@bdo.ca
Bernard Lapchuk, Partner

Manitou
330 Main St.
Manitou, MB R0G 1G0 Canada
204-242-2637
manitou@bdo.ca
Ron Westfall, Partner

Markham
#400, 60 Columbia Way
Markham, ON L3R 0C9 Canada
905-946-1066
Fax: 905-946-9524
markham@bdo.ca
Mohammad Ashraf, Partner

Minnedosa
39 Main St. South
Minnedosa, MB R0J 1E0 Canada
204-867-2957
minnedosa@bdo.ca
Jeanne Mills, Partner

Mississauga
4255 Sherwoodtowne Blvd.
Mississauga, ON L4Z 1Y5 Canada
905-270-7700
Fax: 905-671-7915
mississauga@bdo.ca
Glenn Agro, Partner

Mitchell
PO Box 792
11 Victoria St.
Mitchell, ON N0K 1N0 Canada
519-348-8412
Fax: 519-348-4300
mitchell@bdo.ca
Coralee J. Foster, Partner

Montréal
Westmount Premier
#600, 4150, rue Ste-Catherine ouest
Montréal, QC H3Z 2Y5 Canada
514-931-0841
Fax: 514-931-9491
montreal@bdo.ca
Pierre Lussier, Regional Managing Partner

Morden
133 - 7th St.
Morden, MB R6M 1S3 Canada
204-822-5486
Fax: 204-822-4828
morden@bdo.ca
Sam Andrew, Partner

Mount Forest
PO Box 418
191 Main St. South
Mount Forest, ON N0G 2L0 Canada
519-323-2351
Fax: 519-323-3661
mountforest@bco.ca
Kevin Drier, Partner

Nakusp
PO Box 1078
220 Broadway St.
Nakusp, BC V0G 1R0 Canada
250-265-4750
Fax: 250-837-7170
nakusp@bdo.ca
Ken Davidson, Partner

Newmarket
Gates of York Plaza
#2, 17310 Yonge St.
Newmarket, ON L3Y 7R8 Canada
905-898-1221
Fax: 905-898-0028
866-275-8836
newmarket@bdo.ca
Michael Jones, Partner

North Bay
PO Box 20001
142 Main St. West
North Bay, ON P1B 9N1 Canada

705-495-2000
Fax: 705-495-2001
800-461-6324
northbay@bdo.ca
Jack Campbell, Partner
Oakville
151 Randall St.
Oakville, ON L6J 1P5 Canada
905-844-3206
Fax: 905-844-7513
oakville@bdo.ca
Jim Booth, Partner
Orangeville
77 Broadway Ave., 2nd Fl.
Orangeville, ON L9W 1K1 Canada
519-941-0681
Fax: 519-941-8272
orangeville@bdo.ca
James Blackwell, Partner
Orillia
PO Box 670
19 Front St. North
Orillia, ON L3V 6K5 Canada
705-325-1386
Fax: 705-325-6649
orillia@bdo.ca
Ross Mitchell, Regional Managing Partner
Oshawa
Oshawa Executive Centre
#502, 419 King St. West
Oshawa, ON L1J 2K5 Canada
905-576-3430
Fax: 905-436-9138
oshawa@bdo.ca
Nigel Allen, Partner
Ottawa
#204, 260 Centrum Blvd
Ottawa, ON K1E 3P4 Canada
613-837-3300
Fax: 613-837-7733
800-754-1579
ottawa@bdo.ca
Daniel Suprenant, Partner
Owen Sound
PO Box 397
1717 - 2nd Ave. East
Owen Sound, ON N4K 5P7 Canada
519-376-6110
Fax: 519-376-4741
owensound@bdo.ca
Steve Lowe, Partner
Penticton
#102, 100 Front St.
Penticton, BC V2A 1H1 Canada
250-492-6020
Fax: 250-492-8110
penticton@bdo.ca
Michael Bovin, Partner
Peterborough
PO Box 1018
#202, 201 George St. North
Peterborough, ON K9J 7A5 Canada
705-742-4271
Fax: 705-742-3420
888-369-6600
peterborough@bdo.ca
Bill Gordanier, Partner
Petrolia
PO Box 869
4495 Petrolia Line
Petrolia, ON N0N 1R0 Canada
519-882-3333
Fax: 519-882-2703
petrolia@bdo.ca
Doug Johnston, Partner
Picture Butte
339 Highway Ave.
Picture Butte, AB T0K 1V0 Canada
403-732-4469
Fax: 403-732-5701
picturebutte@bdo.ca
Phillip Wever, Sr. Manager
Port Elgin
PO Box 1390
625 Mill St.
Port Elgin, ON N0H 2C0 Canada
519-832-2049
Fax: 519-832-5659
portelgin@bdo.ca
Mike Bolton, Partner
Portage La Prairie
480 Saskatchewan Ave. West
Portage La Prairie, MB R1N 0M4 Canada
204-857-2856
Fax: 204-239-1664
portagelaprairie@bdo.ca
John Chapman, Partner
Red Deer
4719 - 48 Ave., 3rd Fl.
Red Deer, AB T4N 3T1 Canada
403-346-1566
Fax: 403-343-3070
reddeer@bdo.ca
James Scott, Partner
Red Lake
PO Box 234
207 Discovery Centre
Red Lake, ON P0V 2M0 Canada
807-727-3227
Fax: 807-727-1172
redlake@bdo.ca
Revelstoke
PO Box 2100
#202, 103 - 1st St. East
Revelstoke, BC V0E 2S0 Canada
250-837-5225
Fax: 250-837-7170
revelstoke@bdo.ca
Ken Davidson, Partner
Ridgetown
211 Main St. East
Ridgetown, ON N0P 2C0 Canada
519-674-5418
Fax: 519-674-5410
ridgetown@bdo.ca
Rick Elliott, Partner
Rockland
#5, 2784 Laurier St.
Rockland, ON K4K 1A2 Canada
613-446-6497
Fax: 613-446-7117
rockland@bdo.ca
Judith Gratton, Partner
Salmon Arm
#201, 571 - 6th St. NE
Salmon Arm, BC V1E 1R6 Canada
250-832-7171
Fax: 250-832-2429
salmonarm@bdo.ca
Doug Adams, Partner
Sarnia
PO Box 730
250 Christina St. North
Sarnia, ON N7T 7V3 Canada
519-336-9900
Fax: 519-332-4828
sarnia@bdo.ca
Don Dafoe, Partner
Sault Ste Marie
PO Box 1109
747 Queen St. East
Sault Ste Marie, ON P6A 5N7 Canada
705-945-0990
Fax: 705-942-7979
ssm@bdo.ca
Thom Ambeault, Partner
Selkirk
378 Main St.
Selkirk, MB R1A 1T8 Canada
204-482-5626
Fax: 204-482-4969
selkirk@bdo.ca
Bill Findlater, Partner
Sicamous
PO Box 392
314 Finlayson St.
Sicamous, BC V0E 2V0 Canada
250-836-4493
Fax: 250-837-7170
sicamous@bdo.ca
Ken Davidson, Partner
Sioux Lookout
61 King St.
Sioux Lookout, ON P8T 1A5 Canada
807-737-1500
Fax: 807-737-4443
siouxlookout@bdo.ca
Slave Lake
PO Box 297
#303, Lakeland Centre
Slave Lake, AB T0G 2A0 Canada
780-849-3622
Fax: 780-849-3625
slavelake@bdo.ca
Ray McComb, Partner
Sorrento
PO Box 59
#2, 1266 Trans Canada Hwy.
Sorrento, BC V0E 2W0 Canada
250-675-3288
Fax: 250-832-2429
sorrento@bdo.ca
Squamish
PO Box 168
38143 - 2nd Ave.
Squamish, BC V0N 3G0 Canada
604-892-9424
Fax: 604-892-9356
squamish@bdo.ca
Theresa Walterhouse, Partner
St Pierre Jolys
Place Lavergne
#6, 467, rue Sabourin
St Pierre Jolys, MB R0A 1V0 Canada
204-433-7508
Fax: 204-433-7181
saintpierrejolys@bdo.ca
Mona Marcotte, Partner
St-Claude
76 First St.
St-Claude, MB R0G 1Z0 Canada
204-379-2332
800-268-3337
stclaude@bdo.ca
Henri Magne, Partner
Stratford
134 Waterloo St. South
Stratford, ON N5A 6S8 Canada
519-271-2491
Fax: 519-271-4013
stratford@bdo.ca
Montagu J. Smith, Managing Partner
Strathroy
28636 Centre Rd., RR#5
Strathroy, ON N7G 3H6 Canada
519-245-1913
Fax: 519-245-5987
strathroy@bdo.ca
Garry Harris, Partner
Sudbury
#202, 888 Regent St.
Sudbury, ON P3E 6C6 Canada
705-671-3336
Fax: 705-671-9552
877-820-0404
sudbury@bdo.ca
Ted Hargreaves, Partner
Summerland
c/o Bell Jacoe & Co.
13211 North Victoria Rd.
Summerland, BC V0H 1Z0 Canada
250-494-9255
Fax: 250-494-9755
summerland@bdo.ca
David Braumberger, Partner
Surrey
#200, 15225 - 104 Ave.
Surrey, BC V3R 6Y8 Canada
604-584-2121
Fax: 604-584-3823
surrey@bdo.ca
Larry C. Mueller, Partner

NON-DEPOSITORY INSTITUTIONS

BDO Dunwoody LLP (continued)

Thunder Bay
1095 Barton St.
Thunder Bay, ON P7B 5N3 Canada
807-625-4444
Fax: 807-623-8460
thunderbay@bdo.ca
John Aikin, Partner

Tiverton
84 Main St.
Tiverton, ON N0G 2T0 Canada
519-368-5331
tiverton@bdo.ca

Toronto
Royal Bank Plaza, 33rd Fl.
PO Box 32
Toronto, ON M5J 2J8 Canada
416-865-0200
Fax: 416-865-0887
toronto@bdo.ca
Keith Farlinger, Regional Managing Partner

Treherne
274 Railway Ave.
Treherne, MB R0G 2V0 Canada
204-723-2454
treherne@bdo.ca
Allan Nichol, Partner

Uxbridge
#1, 1 Brock St. East
Uxbridge, ON L9P 1P6 Canada
905-852-9714
Fax: 905-852-9898
uxbridge@bdo.ca
Randy Hickey, Partner

Vancouver
#600, 925 West Georgia St.
Vancouver, BC V6L 3L2 Canada
604-688-5421
Fax: 604-688-5132
vancouver@bdo.ca
Bill Cox, Partner

Vernon
3201 - 30th Ave.
Vernon, BC V1T 2C6 Canada
250-545-2136
Fax: 250-545-3364
vernon@bdo.ca
Brian Cockburn, Partner

Virden
PO Box 1900
255 Wellington St. West
Virden, MB R0M 2C0 Canada
204-748-1200
Fax: 204-748-1976
virden@bdo.ca
Bob Lawrence, Partner

Vulcan
112 - 3 Ave. North
Vulcan, AB TOL 2B0 Canada
403-485-2923
Fax: 403-485-6098
vulcan@bdo.ca

Walkerton
PO Box 760
121 Jackson St.
Walkerton, ON N0G 2V0 Canada
519-881-1211
Fax: 519-881-3530
walkerton@bdo.ca
Gary Munroe, Partner

Welland
37 Dorothy St.
Welland, ON L3B 3V6 Canada
905-735-6433
Fax: 905-735-6514
welland@bdo.ca
Dale Hajdu, Partner

Whistler
#104, 1080 Millar Creek Rd.
Whistler, BC V0N 1B1 Canada
604-932-3799
Fax: 604-932-3764
whistler@bdo.ca
Theresa Walterhouse, Partner

Whitehorse
#201, 3059 - 3rd Ave.
Whitehorse, YT Y1A 1E2 Canada
867-667-7907
Fax: 867-668-3087
whitehorse@bdo.ca
Ben Baartman, Partner

Wiarton
PO Box 249
663 Berford St.
Wiarton, ON N0H 2T0 Canada
519-534-1520
Fax: 519-534-3454
wiarton@bdo.ca
Forbes Simon, Partner

Windsor
3630 Rhodes Dr.
Windsor, ON N8W 5A4 Canada
519-944-6900
Fax: 519-944-6116
windsor@bdo.ca
Ted Herbert, Partner

Wingham
PO Box 1420
152 Josephine St.
Wingham, ON N0G 2W0 Canada
519-357-3231
Fax: 519-357-3230
wingham@bdo.ca
Allan Reed, Partner

Winkler
#2, 583 Main St.
Winkler, MB R6W 1A4 Canada
204-325-4787
Fax: 204-325-8040
winkler@bdo.ca
Frank Wiebe, Partner

Winnipeg
Wawanesa Bldg.
#700, 200 Graham Ave.
Winnipeg, MB R3C 4L5 Canada
204-956-7200
Fax: 204-926-7201
winnipeg@bdo.ca
David Anderson, Partner

Woodstock
PO Box 757
94 Graham St.
Woodstock, ON N4S 8A2 Canada
519-539-2081
Fax: 519-539-2571
woodstock@bdo.ca
Dwayne De Vries, Partner

Beallor & Partners LLP

Also listed under: *Accountants*
28 Overlea Blvd.
Toronto, ON M4H 1B6
416-423-0707
Fax: 416-423-7000
service@beallor.com
www.beallor.com
Ownership: Private
Year Founded: 1962
Number of Employees: 35
Executives:
Dennis Beallor, Partner; dbeallor@beallor.com
Morley Beallor, Partner; mbeallor@beallor.com
Allan Gutenberg, Partner; agutenberg@beallor.com
Rick Rooney, Partner; rrooney@beallor.com
Rob Wells, Partner; rwells@beallor.com
Ted White, Partner; twhite@beallor.com
Barry Flodder, Associate; bflodder@beallor.com

Branch & Associates Trustee Corporation

#318, 2099 Lougheed Hwy.
Port Coquitlam, BC V3B 1A8
604-944-0122
Fax: 604-944-9200
Year Founded: 1991
Executives:
Dudley W. Branch, President

Bresse & Associés

#220, 5350, boul Henri-Bourassa
Québec, QC J1H 6Y8
418-622-6767
Fax: 418-622-5154
syndic@bresse-associes.com
www.baisyndic.com
Ownership: Private
Year Founded: 1990
Number of Employees: 7
Executives:
Charles Bresse, Principal

Brian Raby & Associates Inc.

PO Box 683
166 Queen St.
Kingston, ON K7L 4X1
613-548-1816
Fax: 613-549-7156
brian.raby@bellnet.ca
Ownership: Private
Year Founded: 1988
Executives:
Brian Raby, President

Brief & Associates Limited

#408, 3854 Bathurst St.
Toronto, ON M3H 3N2
416-635-7337
Fax: 416-635-0462
800-372-7337
rbrief@brwc.com
www.brwc.com
Former Name: Harold Brief & Associates Limited
Number of Employees: 12
Profile: Full service insolvency firm.
Executives:
Harold Brief, Principal
Branches:

Brockville
#206, 43 King St.
Brockville, ON K6V 3P7 Canada
613-345-3860
Fax: 613-345-3896
800-372-7337

Kingston
353 Alfred St.
Kingston, ON K7L 1V8 Canada
613-549-5398
Fax: 613-544-8870
800-372-7337

Whitby
#200, 400 Dunsas St. West
Whitby, ON L1N 2M5 Canada
905-665-1240
Fax: 905-430-8207
800-372-7337

Burlingham Associates Inc.

Saskatoon Sq.
#400, 410 - 22nd St. East
Saskatoon, SK S7K 5T6
306-668-5599
Fax: 306-668-5650
800-820-0730
info@burlingham.ca
members.shaw.ca/burlingham
Ownership: Private
Profile: Specialists in personal bankruptcy issues, serving Saskatoon, Prince Albert, Lloydminster and North Battleford.
Executives:
Dean Burlingham

Burnside, Richard & Associates Ltd.

PO Box 504
100 - 10th St. West
Owen Sound, ON N4K 5P7
519-371-4333
Fax: 519-376-8078
burnside1@yahoo.com
Executives:
Richard Burnside, Principal

C. Topley & Company Ltd.

Also listed under: *Accountants*
#200, 260 West Esplanade
North Vancouver, BC V7M 3G7

604-987-8688
Fax: 604-904-8628
877-363-3437
info@bankruptcytrustee.ca
www.bankruptcytrustee.ca
Ownership: Private
Year Founded: 1998
Number of Employees: 10
Profile: The trustee in bankruptcy & accounting firm is also engaged in financial investigation.
Executives:
Colin W. Topley, CGA, CIRP, CFE, President; 604-982-1480; ctopley@topleyandcompany.com
Jennifer Rorison, CIRP, Vice-President; 604-982-1481; jrorison@topleyandcompany.com
Kelvin Tan, CA. CIRP, Vice-President; 604-982-1482; ktan@topleyandcompany.com
Marilyn E. Phelps, CFE, Sr. Manager; 604-982-1484; mphelps@topleyandcompany.com

Campbell, Saunders Ltd.
Also listed under: *Accountants*
#1000, 570 Granville St.
Vancouver, BC V6C 3P1
604-915-5550
Fax: 604-915-5560
info@csvan.com
www.csvan.com
Executives:
Harold Saunders, President
David Gray, Sr. Vice-President
Patty E. Wood, Vice-President
Branches:
Richmond
#5040, 8171 Ackroyd Rd.
Richmond, BC V6X 3K1 Canada
604-821-9882
Fax: 604-821-9870
info@csvan.com

Céline Chouinard & Associés Inc.
#201, 7100, rue St-Hubert
Montréal, QC H2S 2M9
514-272-1121
Fax: 514-271-7496
Ownership: Private
Year Founded: 1999
Executives:
Céline Chouinard, Présidente
Branches:
Laval
#310, 1545, boul de l'Avenir
Laval, QC H7S 2N5 Canada
450-687-6888
Céline Chouinard

Charles Wackett & Associates
#100, 1675 Bedford Row
Halifax, NS B3J 1T1
902-482-2000
Fax: 902-482-2005
800-561-3458
info@4debtrelief.com
www.4debtrelief.com
Former Name: Meretsky Wackett Inc.

The Clarke Henning Group
Also listed under: *Accountants*
#801, 10 Bay St.
Toronto, ON M5J 2R8
416-364-4421
Fax: 416-367-8032
888-422-1241
ch@clarkehenning.com
www.clarkehenning.com
Former Name: Clarke, Henning Inc.
Year Founded: 1915
Number of Employees: 40
Partners:
Liana Bell; lbell@clarkehenning.com
Dave Fry; dfry@clarkehenning.com
Donald M. Gellatly; dgellat@clarkehenning.com
Jim Henning; jhenning@clarkehenning.com
Darryl Hickman; dhickman@clarkehenning.com
Rollie Hill; rhill@clarkehenning.com
Gary MacGregor; garymac@clarkehenning.com
Vinay Raja; vraja@clarkehenning.com
Dennis Reid; dreid@clarkehenning.com
Bob Rose; brose@clarkehenning.com

Clarke Starke & Diegel(CSD)
Also listed under: *Accountants*
#202, 871 Victoria St. North
Kitchener, ON N2B 3S4
519-579-5520
Fax: 519-570-3611
www.csdca.com
Ownership: Private
Year Founded: 1972
Number of Employees: 22
Partners:
Allan Benson; albenson@csdca.com
Doug Burns; dburns@csdca.com
Scott Craig; scraig@csdca.com
Wayne Haves; wayne@csdca.com
Ellen Murphy; ellen@csdca.com
Stan Nahrgang; scnca@csdca.com

Collins Barrow Chartered Accountants - Orangeville
Also listed under: *Accountants*
Mono Plaza
RR#4
Orangeville, ON L9W 2Z1
519-941-5526
Fax: 519-941-8721
orangeville@collinsbarrow.com
Partners:
Grant Bartlett; gbartlett@collinsbarrow.com
Kerry Butler; kbutler@collinsbarrow.com

Collins Barrow Chartered Accountants - Cambridge
Also listed under: *Accountants*
#600, 73 Water St. North
Cambridge, ON N1R 7L6
519-623-3820
Fax: 519-622-3144
cbcambridge@collinsbarrow.com
Ownership: Private.
Profile: The firm's services include the following: assurance, business advisory, tax strategies & trustee in bankruptcy. It is affiliated with MRI (Moores Rowland International).
Partners:
William G. Mitchell, Principal; wmitchell@collinsbarrow.com
Vinod Arya; varya@collinsbarrow.com
Brian W. Hanna; bhanna@collinsbarrow.com
Frank J. Jaglowitz; fjaglowitz@collinsbarrow.com

Collins Barrow Chartered Accountants - Chatham
Also listed under: *Accountants*
PO Box 218
150 Richmond St.
Chatham, ON N7M 5K3
519-351-2024
Fax: 519-351-8831
chatham@collinsbarrow.com
Partners:
John D. Aitken, Principal; jaitken@collinsbarrow.com
Paul Cudmore; pcudmore@collinsbarrow.com
Jack Lambe; jlambe@collinsbarrow.com
William Loucks; wloucks@collinsbarrow.com
James Moir; jmoir@collinsbarrow.com
Tracey Myers; tmyers@collinsbarrow.com
Michael Pestowka; mpestowka@collinsbarrow.com
Jane Rivers; jrivers@collinsbarrow.com

Collins Barrow Chartered Accountants - Chelmsford
Also listed under: *Accountants*
PO Box 673
48 Main St. East
Chelmsford, ON P0M 1L0
705-855-9024
Fax: 705-855-3693
chelmsford@collinsbarrow.com
Partners:
Richard A. Schaak; rschaak@collinsbarrow.com

Collins Barrow Chartered Accountants - Elora
Also listed under: *Accountants*
PO Box 580
342, Gerrie Rd.
Elora, ON N0B 1S0
519-846-5315
Fax: 519-846-9120
info@collinsbarrow.com
Partners:
Anthony P. Campagnolo; acampagnolo@collinsbarrow.com
Todd Campbell; tcampbell@cbelora.com
Keith A. McIntosh; kmcintosh@collinsbarrow.com
Ed Mitukiewicz; emitukiewicz@collinsbarrow.com
Dennis D. Zinger; dzinger@collinsbarrow.com

Collins Barrow Chartered Accountants - Kapuskasing
Also listed under: *Accountants*
2 Ash St.
Kapuskasing, ON P5N 3H4
705-337-6411
Fax: 705-335-6563
kapuskasing@collinsbarrow.com
Partners:
Gilles R. Bisson; gbisson@collinsbarrow.com
Gérald Gagné; ggagne@collinsbarrow.com
Eric G. Gagnon; egagnon@collinsbarrow.com
Christiane Lapointe; clapointe@collinsbarrow.com

Collins Barrow Chartered Accountants - North Bay
Also listed under: *Accountants*
630 Cassells St.
North Bay, ON P1B 4A2
705-494-9336
Fax: 705-494-8783
northbay@collinsbarrow.com
Partners:
Daniel D. Longlade; dlonglade@collinsbarrow.com

Collins Barrow Chartered Accountants - Carleton Place
Also listed under: *Accountants*
143-A Bridge St.
Carleton Place, ON K7C 2V6
613-253-0014
Fax: 613-253-0129
carletonplace@collinsbarrow.com

Collins Barrow Chartered Accountants - Sarnia
Also listed under: *Accountants*
1350 L'Heritage Dr.
Sarnia, ON N7S 6H8
519-542-7725
Fax: 519-542-8321
sarnia@collinsbarrow.com
Partners:
David Coles; dcoles@collinsbarrow.com
Bruce W. Crerar; bcrerar@collinsbarrow.com
Larry H.A. Cross; lcross@collinsbarrow.com
Pat Filice; pfilice@collinsbarrow.com
Thomas Moore; tmoore@collinsbarrow.com

Collins Barrow Chartered Accountants - Sturgeon Falls
Also listed under: *Accountants*
PO Box 870
#A, 49 Queen St.
Sturgeon Falls, ON P2B 2C7
705-753-1830
Fax: 705-753-2496
sturgeonfalls@collinsbarrow.com
Partners:
Daniel Longlade; dlonglade@collinsbarrow.com

Collins Barrow Chartered Accountants - Sudbury
Also listed under: *Accountants*
1174 St. Jerome St.
Sudbury, ON P3A 2V9
705-560-5592
Fax: 705-560-8832
sudbury@collinsbarrow.com
Partners:
Robert Blais, Principal; roblais@collinsbarrow.com
Paul E. Arsenault
Marc A. Bertrand; mabertrand@collinsbarrow.com
Gary R. Crayen; gacrayen@collinsbarrow.com
Guy Desmarais; gudesmarais@collinsbarrow.com
Clément Y. Lafrenière
Gerald C.J. Lafrenière
Robert A. Mageau; romageau@collinsbarrow.com
Michel J. Paquette; mipaquette@collinsbarrow.com

Collins Barrow Chartered Accountants - Vaughan
Also listed under: *Accountants*
#600, 3300 Hwy. 7 West, 2nd Fl.
Vaughan, ON L4K 4M3
416-213-2600
Fax: 905-669-8705
info@collinsbarrowvaughan.com
Partners:
Gino F. Alberelli; galberelli@collinsbarrow.com
Joseph P. Colasanto; jcolasanto@collinsbarrow.com
Frank Fenos; ffenos@collinsbarrow.com
Richard N. Gargarella; rgargarella@collinsbarrow.com
Silvano Zamparo; szamparo@collinsbarrow.com

Collins Barrow Chartered Accountants - Waterloo
Also listed under: *Accountants*
554 Weber St. North
Waterloo, ON N2L 5C6
519-725-7700
Fax: 519-725-7708
cbwaterloo@collinsbarrow.com
Partners:
Faith E. Williamson, Principal
Tracey Denstedt
John H. Durland
David P. Webb

Collins Barrow Chartered Accountants - Banff
Also listed under: *Accountants*
Cascade Plaza
PO Box 1000
#370, 317 Banff Ave.
Banff, AB T1L 1H4
403-762-8383
Fax: 403-762-8384
cbbanff@cbrockies.com
Partners:
Darcy J. Allan
Mark Bohnet
Brian J. Mitchell

Collins Barrow Chartered Accountants - Canmore
Also listed under: *Accountants*
#1, 714 - 10th St.
Canmore, AB T1W 2A6
403-678-4444
Fax: 403-678-5163
canmore@collinsbarrow.com
Partners:
Darcy J. Allan; dallan@collinsbarrow.com
Mark Bohnet; mbohnet@collinsbarrow.com
Brian Mitchell; bmitchell@collinsbarrow.com

Collins Barrow Chartered Accountants - Drayton Valley
Also listed under: *Accountants*
PO Box 6927
5204 - 52nd Ave.
Drayton Valley, AB T7A 1S3
780-542-4468
Fax: 780-542-5275
888-542-4468
draytonvalley@collinsbarrow.com
Partners:
Barry Carlson; bcarlson@collinsbarrow.ca
Kenneth Roberts; kroberts@collinsbarrow.com

Collins Barrow Chartered Accountants - Red Deer
Also listed under: *Accountants*
#300, 5010 - 43 St.
Red Deer, AB T4N 6H2
403-342-5541
Fax: 403-347-3766
reddeer@collinsbarrow.com
www.collinsbarrowreddeer.ab.ca
Partners:
Bob Boser; bboser@collinsbarrow.com
Allan Collins; acollins@collinsbarrow.com
Robert A. Fischer; rfischer@collinsbarrow.com
Robin R. Kolton; rkolton@collinsbarrow.com
George R. Perry; gperry@collinsbarrow.com
Gary S. Pottage; gpottage@collinsbarrow.com
Marsha Smalley; msmalley@collinsbarrow.com
Grant Stange; gstange@collinsbarrow.com

Collins Barrow Chartered Accountants - Winnipeg
Also listed under: *Accountants*
Century Plaza
#401, 1 Wesley Ave.
Winnipeg, MB R3C 4C6
204-942-0221
Fax: 204-944-8371
winnipeg@collinsbarrow.com
Partners:
Gregory J. Bradshaw; gbradshaw@collinsbarrow.com
John A. Gray; jgray@collinsbarrow.com
Brian A. Hughes; bhughes@collinsbarrow.com
Robert A. McNamara; rmcnamara@collinsbarrow.com

Collins Barrow Chartered Accountants - Vancouver
Also listed under: *Accountants*
Burrard Bldg.
#800, 1030 West Georgia St.
Vancouver, BC V6E 3B9
604-685-0564
Fax: 604-685-2050
vancouver@collinsbarrow.com
Partners:
James R. Church; jchurch@collinsbarrow.com
Gordon C. Duff; cduff@collinsbarrow.com
Owen J. Manuel; omanuel@collinsbarrow.com
Harley Stanfield; hstanfield@collinsbarrow.com

Collins Barrow Chartered Accountants - Bobcaygeon
Also listed under: *Accountants*
PO Box 10
21 King St. West
Bobcaygeon, ON K0M 1A0
705-738-4166
Fax: 705-738-5787
bobcaygn@collinsbarrow.com

Collins Barrow Chartered Accountants - Lindsay
Also listed under: *Accountants*
237 Kent St. West
Lindsay, ON K9V 2Z3
705-324-5031
Fax: 705-328-3121
lindsay@collinsbarrow.com
Partners:
Erik J. Ellis; eellis@collinsbarrow.com
J. Hebert Gamble; hgamble@collinsbarrow.com
Mark Mooney; mmooney@collinsbarrow.com
Dennis W. Wright; dwright@collinsbarrow.com

Collins Barrow Chartered Accountants - Peterborough
Also listed under: *Accountants*
418 Sheridan St.
Peterborough, ON K9H 3J9
705-742-3418
Fax: 705-742-9775
peterborough@collinsbarrow.com
Partners:
Leah Curtis; lcurtis@collinsbarrow.com
Bob Fisher; bfisher@collinsbarrow.com
Steven Porter; sporter@collinsbarrow.com
Richard Steiginga; rsteiginga@collinsbarrow.com
J. Thomas Taylor; ttaylor@collinsbarrow.com

Collins Barrow Chartered Accountants - Ottawa
Also listed under: *Accountants*
#400, 301 Moodie Dr.
Ottawa, ON K2H 9C4
613-820-8010
Fax: 613-820-0465
ottawa@collinsbarrow.com
www.collinsbarrowottawa.com
Partners:
Bruce G. Brooks; bbrooks@collinsbarrow.com
David Brown; dbrown@collinsbarrow.com
T. Lynn Clapp
Dennis F. Medaglia; dmedaglia@collinsbarrow.com
Michael Merpaw; mmerpaw@collinsbarrow.com
David F. Muir; dmuir@collinsbarrow.com
Robert W. Rock; rrock@collinsbarrow.com
Kenneth Tammadge; ktammadge@collinsbarrow.com
D. Randy Tivy; rtivy@collinsbarrow.com
Joe Wattie; jwattie@collinsbarrow.com
Stewart A. Wilson; swilson@collinsbarrow.com

Collins Barrow Chartered Accountants - Kingston
Also listed under: *Accountants*
#301, 1471 Counter St.
Kingston, ON K7M 8S8
613-544-2903
Fax: 613-544-6151
kingston@collinsbarrow.com
Partners:
Brian Hogan; bhogan@collinsbarrow.com
Lennox Rowsell; lrowsell@collinsbarrow.com
Karen Sands; ksands@collinsbarrow.com
Brent Wilson; bwilson@collinsbarrow.com

Collins Barrow Chartered Accountants - Exeter
Also listed under: *Accountants*
PO Box 2405
412 Main St.
Exeter, ON N0M 1S7
519-235-0345
Fax: 519-235-3235
exeter@collinsbarrow.com
Partner:
Dan Daum; ddaum@collinsbarrow.com

Collins Barrow Chartered Accountants - London
Also listed under: *Accountants*
PO Box 5005
#700, 495 Richmond St.
London, ON N6A 5G4
519-679-8550
Fax: 519-679-1812
london@collinsbarrow.com
Partners:
Michael Bondy; mbondy@collinsbarrow.com
Jim Dunlop; jdunlop@collinsbarrow.com
Doug Greenhow; dgreenhow@collinsbarrow.com
Gerry Mills; gmills@collinsbarrow.com
Jason Timmermans; jtimmermans@collinsbarrow.com
David Wells; dwells@collinsbarrow.com

Collins Barrow Chartered Accountants - Waterloo National Office
Also listed under: *Accountants*
554 Weber St. North
Waterloo, ON N2L 5C6
519-725-7700
Fax: 519-725-7708
cbwaterloo@collinsbarrow.com
www.collinsbarrows.com
Partners:
Stephen Chris; sqchris@collinsbarrow.com
Todd MacDonald; tmacdonald@collinsbarrow.com
Ram Ramachandran; rramachandran@collinsbarrow.com

Collins Barrow Chartered Accountants - Stratford
Also listed under: *Accountants*
413 Hibernia St.
Stratford, ON N5A 5W2
519-272-0000
Fax: 519-272-0030
stratford@collinsbarrow.com
Partners:
Larry Batte; lbatte@collinsbarrow.com
Dan Daum; ddaum@collinsbarrow.com

Collins Barrow Windsor LLP
Also listed under: *Accountants*
441 Pellissier St.
Windsor, ON N9A 4L2
519-258-5800
Fax: 519-256-6152
windsor@collinsbarrow.com
www.collinsbarrow.com
Executives:
Doug David, Partner; ddavid@collinsbarrow.com
Mike Frenette, Partner; mwfrenette@collinsbarrow.com
David Gardner, Partner; dgardner@collinsbarrow.com
Brenda J. Griffith, Partner; bgriffith@collinsbarrow.com
Carl Hooper, Partner; cehooper@collinsbarrow.com
Denise Hrastovec, Partner; dhrastovec@collinsbarrow.com
Paul Kale, Partner; pkale@collinsbarrow.com
Donald Marsh, Partner; djmarsh@collinsbarrow.com
Gary J. Waghorn, Partner; gwaghorn@collinsbarrow.com

Connor & Associates Limited
#301, 295 George St.
Sydney, NS B1P 1J7

902-539-9850
Fax: 902-425-3777
888-666-5764
Year Founded: 1998

Cooper & Company Ltd.
***Also listed under:** Accountants*
#108, 1120 Finch Ave. West
Toronto, ON M3J 3H7
416-665-3383
Fax: 416-665-0897
info@cooperco.ca
www.cooperco.ca
Former Name: Rumanek & Cooper Ltd.
Number of Employees: 8
Executives:
Donna Cairns, Partner
Branches:
Brampton
#200, 36 Queen St. East
Brampton, ON L6V 1A2 Canada
905-454-4510
Fax: 905-454-4632
Toronto - Bloor St.
#3140, 3300 Bloor St. West, 11th Fl.
Toronto, ON M8X 2X3 Canada
416-252-3440
Fax: 416-665-0897
Toronto - Lawrence Ave.
#211, 1719 Lawrence Ave. East
Toronto, ON M1R 2X7 Canada
416-759-4664
Fax: 416-759-8294

Cyril Sapiro & Co. Ltd.
#302, 161 Eglinton Ave. East
Toronto, ON M4P 1J5
416-486-9660
Fax: 416-486-8024
Number of Employees: 10
Executives:
Cyril Sapiro

D&A MacLeod Company Ltd.
343 O'Connor St.
Ottawa, ON K2P 1V9
613-236-9111
Fax: 613-236-6766
admin@macleod.ca
www.macleod.ca
Year Founded: 1952
Number of Employees: 20
Profile: Act as trustees in bankruptcy, receivers, liquidators, agents for secured creditors and trustee under the Construction Lien Act.

Executives:
Allen W. MacLeod, Trustee
Donald A. MacLeod, Trustee
Peter Markham, Trustee

D. Manning & Associates Inc.
#520, 625 Howe St.
Vancouver, BC V6C 2T6
604-683-8030
Fax: 604-683-8327
info@manning-trustee.com
www.manning-trustee.com
Ownership: Private
Year Founded: 1995
Number of Employees: 12
Profile: Offers a full range of insolvency and consulting services to companies and individuals throughout British Columbia and Yukon Territory.

Executives:
Don Manning, President
William Choo, Sr. Vice-President
Ron B. Evans, Sr. Vice-President

David Sklar & Associates Inc.
#720, 245 Fairview Mall Dr.
Toronto, ON M2J 4T1
416-498-9200
Fax: 416-621-2359
dsklar@davidsklar.com
www.davidsklar.com
Year Founded: 1998
Profile: Services provided include bankruptcy counselling, proposals to creditors, credit counselling, and debt management. Serves the GTA area and South Western Ontario.

Executives:
David Sklar, President
Branches:
Toronto - Finch Ave. West
#411, 1280 Finch Ave. West
Toronto, ON M3J 3K6 Canada
Toronto - Four Seasons Pl.
#133, 21 Four Seasons Pl.
Toronto, ON M9B 6J8 Canada
Toronto - St. Clair Ave. West
845 St. Clair Ave. West, Main Fl.
Toronto, ON M6C 1C3 Canada

Davis Daignault Schick & Co.
#830, 840 - 7th Ave. SW
Calgary, AB T2P 3G2
403-262-3394
Fax: 403-269-3540
www.dds.ab.ca
Year Founded: 1970
Number of Employees: 4
Profile: Provides a wide array of services, including accounting and assurance, tax services, management advisory, information technology, and bookkeeping. Also assists individuals and businesses solve their financial problems.

Executives:
Chris Almond
Marie Kozlowski
Walter Reimer
Ken Stephens

Davis Martindale LLP
***Also listed under:** Financial Planning; Accounting & Law*
373 Commissioners Rd. West
London, ON N6J 1Y4
519-673-3141
Fax: 519-645-1646
info@davismartindale.com
www.davismartindale.com
Ownership: Private
Year Founded: 1967
Number of Employees: 28
Partners:
Bruce M. Barran
Mike D. Evans
William J.R. Gohn
Michael K. Koenig
L. Ron Martindale Sr.
Ron L. Martindale Jr.
Ian D. McIntosh
Paul R. Panabaker

de Billy - Tremblay & Associés Inc.
#1515, 1255, rue University
Montréal, QC H3B 3X2
514-875-1363
Fax: 514-875-1336
syndic@debilly-tremblay.com
www.debilly-tremblay.com
Ownership: Private
Year Founded: 1997
Number of Employees: 4
Profile: Provides a full range of personalized services in insolvency and reorganisation for individuals and corporations facing insolvency problems.

Executives:
Solange de Billy-Tremblay, President; solange@debilly-tremblay.com
Branches:
Montréal - Dorval
#207, 280, av Dorval
Montréal, QC H9S 3H4 Canada
514-875-1363
Fax: 514-875-1336
Montréal - Laval
#201, 4000, le Corbusier
Laval, QC H7L 5R2 Canada
450-686-6959
Montréal - Rosemont
#241, 3300, boul Rosemont
Montréal, QC H1X 1K2 Canada
514-875-1363
Fax: 514-875-1336
syndic@debilly-tremblay.com
Montréal - Verdun
4400, boul LaSalle
Montréal, QC H4G 2A8 Canada
514-875-1363
syndic@debilly-tremblay.com

Demers Beaulne, GPCA
#2010, 1100, boul René-Lévesque ouest
Montréal, QC H3B 4N4
514-878-9631
Fax: 514-874-0319
humanresources@demersbeaulne.com
www.demersbeaulne.com
Former Name: Stéphane Lachance & Associés Inc; Demers Beaulne Lachance Inc.
Ownership: Private
Profile: Provides the following services: audit, accounting, tax, forensic accounting, business vauation, human capital, corporate turnaround & insolvency, and corporate financing.

Executives:
Stéphane Lachance

Doyle Salewski Inc.
396 Bank St.
Ottawa, ON K2P 1Y5
613-237-5555
Fax: 613-237-5336
800-517-9926
la@doylegroup.ca
www.doylegroup.ca
Ownership: Private
Year Founded: 1996
Number of Employees: 10
Profile: Services provided include credit counselling, debt solutions, budget help, financial counselling, debt assistance & counselling, money management.

Executives:
Brian Doyle, President
Paul E. Salewski, Sr. Vice-President
Arthur Thornton, Vice-President
Branches:
Arnprior
c/o Douglas G. Legg, CA
75 Elgin St. West
Arnprior, ON K7S 3T9 Canada
613-623-2020
tm@doylegroup.ca
Barrys Bay
c/o Richard Robyn & Associates
9E Opeongo Dr.
Barrys Bay, ON K0J 1B0 Canada
613-756-7000
Richard Robyn
Brampton - Main St. North
c/o Dale Streiman & Kurz
480 Main St. North
Brampton, ON L6V 1P8 Canada
905-455-7300
streiman@dsklaw.com
Fred Streiman
Brampton - Mississauga Rd.
c/o McCarney Greenwood LLP
#100, 8501 Mississauga Rd.
Brampton, ON L6Y 5G8 Canada
905-451-4788
dthompson@mgca.com
Rory E. O'Neill
Brockville
c/o Henderson Johnston Fournier
61 King St. East
Brockville, ON K6V 5V4 Canada
613-345-3636
dt@doylegroup.ca
Paul J. Fournier
Burlington
c/o Total Investigation Services
3500 Main Way
Burlington, ON L7M 1A9 Canada
905-335-4313
billsimpson@totalinvestigations.ca
Bill Simpson
Carleton Place

NON-DEPOSITORY INSTITUTIONS

Doyle Salewski Inc. (continued)

c/o Partners Advantage, GMAC Real Estate
143 Bridge St.
Carleton Place, ON K2C 2V6 Canada
613-253-2227
dt@doylegroup.ca
Ralph Shaw

Cornwall
c/o Welch & Company
36 2nd St. E
Cornwall, ON K6J 3P5 Canada
613-932-7827
vg@doylegroup.ca
Bob Ogle

Gatineau
365, boul St-Joseph
Gatineau, QC J8Y 3Z6 Canada
819-766-7777
Fax: 819-766-6771
vl@doylegroup.ca

Hamilton
c/o Peter Smuk, CA
#10, 1405 Ottawa St. North
Hamilton, ON L8W 3Y4 Canada
905-318-1081
psmuk@vantageappraisals.com

London
c/o Kime, Mills, Dunlop
#700, 495 Richmond St.
London, ON N6A 5G4 Canada
519-679-8550
jdunlop@kmd.on.ca
Jim Dunlop

Pembroke
c/o Welch & Company LLP
270 Lake St.
Pembroke, ON K8A 6X9 Canada
613-635-4882
lm@doylegroup.ca
Richard Eustache

Perth
c/o Kelly Huibers McNeely
16 Gore St. West
Perth, ON K7H 2L6 Canada
613-264-0220
dt@doylegroup.ca
John Quigley

Renfrew
c/o Ferguson & Kubisheski
45 Renfrew Ave. East
Renfrew, ON K7V 4A3 Canada
613-432-2223
tm@doylegroup.ca
Stephen Kubisheski

Smiths Falls
c/o Rivington Management
7 Main St. West
Smiths Falls, ON K7A 0X0 Canada
613-283-5252
dt@doylegroup.ca
John Rivington

Sudbury
c/o Sostarich Ross Wright & Cecutti
487 Bouchard St.
Sudbury, ON P3E 2K8 Canada
705-522-2400
clilly@srwc.com
Chuck Lilly

Toronto - Bay St.
c/o McCarney Greenwood LLP
#900, 10 Bay St.
Toronto, ON M5J 2R8 Canada
416-362-6223
dgreenwood@mgca.com
David C. Greenwood

Toronto - Eglinton Ave. East
2425 Eglinton Ave. East
Toronto, ON M1K 5G8 Canada
416-755-4111
Fax: 416-755-4869
lb.doylegroup@bellnet.ca

Windsor
c/o Roth Mosey & Partners LLP
#300, 3100 Temple Dr.
Windsor, ON N8W 5J6 Canada
519-977-6410
proth@roth-mosey.com
Peter J. Roth

Elite Bailiff Services Ltd.

Also listed under: *Collection Agencies*
20473 Logan Ave.
Langley, BC V3A 4L8
604-539-9900
Fax: 604-539-5678
info@elitebailiff.com
www.elitebailiff.com
Ownership: Private
Year Founded: 1979
Profile: Specializes in commercial credit services.

Evancic Perrault Robertson

Also listed under: *Accountants*
PO Box 21148, Maple Ridge Square Stn. Maple Ridge Square
Maple Ridge, BC V2X 17P
604-476-2009
Fax: 604-467-1219
eprnat@epr.ca
www.epr.ca
Ownership: Private
Year Founded: 1979
Profile: Canada's largest & leading full services firm of Certified General Accountants, with member offices across the country, EPR has an international reach through its strong affiliations with NACPAF (US-based national association of CPA firms) & with Morison International (UK-based global accountancy & law office network). EPR has an integrated approach to auditing, accounting, taxation, & management consulting.

Executives:
Paul Walker, Chair
Malcolm Walker, Exec. Director
Verle Spindor, National Administrator

Branches:

Abbotsford
#201, 2669 Langdon St.
Abbotsford, BC V2T 3L3 Canada
604-853-1538
Fax: 604-853-7178
eprabby@mindlink.net
Henry Raap, Partner

Bathurst
1460, av St. Peter
Bathurst, NB E2A 4V1 Canada
506-548-1984
Fax: 506-548-0904
eprbath@eprbathurst.ca
André Doucet, Partner

Bradford
PO Box 753
27 John St. West
Bradford, ON L3Z 2B3 Canada
905-778-8964
Fax: 905-775-9550
800-246-5591
bbcm@bellnet.ca
Michael Falcone

Calgary
#300, 10655 Southport Rd. SW
Calgary, AB T2W 4Y1 Canada
403-278-5800
Fax: 403-253-9479
general@eprcal.com
Les Willms, Partner

Chatham
40 Centre Sq.
Centre St.
Chatham, ON N7M 5W3 Canada
519-436-0556
Fax: 519-436-1291
rieger@ciaccess.com
Lance Rieger, Partner

Coquitlam
566 Lougheed Hwy., 2nd Fl.
Coquitlam, BC V3K 3S3 Canada
604-936-4377
Fax: 604-936-8376
eprcoq@eprcoq.com
www.eprcoq.com
Ken Richardson, Partner

Fort Erie
PO Box 277
178 Central Ave.
Fort Erie, ON L2A 5M9 Canada
905-871-6620
Fax: 905-871-2544
eprfeo@eprnia.ca
Rick Forbes, Partner

Fredericton
#205, 206 Rookwood Ave.
Fredericton, NB E3B 2M2 Canada
506-458-8620
Fax: 506-450-8286
eprfred@nbnet.nb.ca
Larry Johnston, Partner

Grande Prairie
#215, 10006 - 101st Ave.
Grande Prairie, AB T8V 0Y1 Canada
780-539-3400
Fax: 780-538-1544
epgrand@telusplanet.net
Lyle Molyneaux, Partner

Hamilton
176 Rymal Rd. East
Hamilton, ON L9B 1C2 Canada
905-388-7453
Fax: 905-388-7397
eprhamilton@iprimus.ca
Andrew Barber, Partner

Langley
20688 - 56 Ave.
Langley, BC V3A 3Z1 Canada
604-534-1441
Fax: 604-534-1491
pwalker@erpcga.com
www.eprcga.com
Paul Walker, Partner

London
#804, 150 Dufferin Ave.
London, ON N6A 5N6 Canada
519-434-5847
Fax: 519-645-0727
Don DiCarlo, Partner

Maple Ridge
22377 Dewdney Trunk Rd.
Maple Ridge, BC V2X 3J4 Canada
604-467-5561
Fax: 604-467-1219
eprmr@eprcga.com
www.eprcga.com
Patrick Smith, Partner

Miramichi
Waterfront Place
1773 Water St.
Miramichi, NB E1N 1B2 Canada
506-773-6990
Fax: 506-773-3197
eprmira@nbnet.nb.ca
Vicky Malone, Partner

Moncton
770 Main St.
Moncton, NB E1C 1E7 Canada
506-857-3893
Fax: 506-859-4148
Paul Robichaud, Partner

Niagara Falls
#7, 3930 Montrose Rd.
Niagara Falls, ON L2H 3C9 Canada
905-358-5729
Fax: 905-358-7188
eprnfo@eprnia.ca
Rick Forbes, Partner

North Vancouver
#102, 1975 Lonsdale Ave.
North Vancouver, BC V7M 2K3 Canada
604-987-8101
Fax: 604-987-1794
cga@eprnv.ca
Bill Perrault, Partner

Saint-Hyacinthe
#1, 540, boul Casavant ouest
Saint-Hyacinthe, QC J2S 7S3 Canada
450-774-7165
Fax: 450-774-1589
eprsthyacinthe@cgaquebec.com
Rene Benoit, Partner

Saskatoon
259 Robin Cres.
Saskatoon, SK S7L 6M8 Canada
306-934-3944
Fax: 306-934-3409
eprstoon@sasktel.net
Nanette Neumann, Partner
Slave Lake
405 - 6th Ave. SW
Slave Lake, AB T0G 2A4 Canada
780-849-4949
Fax: 780-849-3401
eprslave@telusplanet.net
Gordon Ferguson, Partner
St-Jérôme
#200, 36, rue de Martigny ouest
Saint-Jérome, QC J7Y 2E9 Canada
450-569-2641
Fax: 450-569-2647
François Marchand, Partner
St. John's
74 O'Leary Ave.
St. John's, NL A1B 2C7 Canada
709-726-0000
Fax: 709-726-2200
eprstjohns@hotmail.com
Gerald Kirby, Partner
Stonewall
Westside Plaza Mall
PO Box 1038
Main St.
Stonewall, MB R0C 2Z0 Canada
204-467-5566
Fax: 204-467-9133
eprstonewall@shawcable.com
Ryan Smith, Partner
Terrebonne
3300, boul des Entreprises
Terrebonne, QC J6X 4J8 Canada
450-477-0377
Fax: 450-477-4023
Christian Pimpare, Partner
Tilbury
40 Queen Sq.
Tilbury, ON N0P 2L0 Canada
519-682-2300
Fax: 519-682-0705
reiger@ciaccess.com
White Rock
#104, 1656 Martin Dr.
White Rock, BC V4A 5E7 Canada
604-536-7778
Fax: 604-536-7745
Glenn Parks, Partner
Winnipeg
#1010, 1661 Portage Ave.
Winnipeg, MB R3J 3T7 Canada
204-954-9690
Fax: 204-786-1003
bemond@mts.net
Barry Edmond, Partner

Exelby & Partners Ltd.

#200, 10908 - 106 Ave.
Edmonton, AB T5J 0H8
780-425-7000
Fax: 780-425-7110
800-323-0097
exelby@telus.net
www.bankruptcyalberta.com/
Year Founded: 1995
Number of Employees: 20
Executives:
William A. Exelby, President
Branches:
Grande Prairie
Cooperators Square
#231, 9804 - 100 Ave.
Grande Prairie, AB T8V 0T8 Canada
780-513-6100
Fax: 780-513-6161
800-323-0097
Red Deer
#301, 4808 Ross St.
Red Deer, AB T4N 1X5 Canada
403-348-5880
800-323-0097

Faber & Company Inc.

10047 - 81 Ave.
Edmonton, AB T6E 1W7
780-448-4714
Fax: 780-436-0113
877-944-1177
dfaber@faber.ca
www.faber.ca
Executives:
David J. Turner, Trustee
Branches:
Cold Lake
#201, 4807 - 51 St.
Cold Lake, AB T9M 1P2 Canada
780-594-4441
Fax: 780-594-6608
Devon
35 Athabasca Ave.
Devon, AB T6E 1W7 Canada
780-987-2280
Fax: 780-987-2131
Edmonton - 156 St.
10158 - 156 St.
Edmonton, AB T5P 2P9 Canada
780-944-1177
Fax: 780-944-6979
Edmonton - 82 St.
12766 - 82 St.
Edmonton, AB T5E 2T1 Canada
780-944-1177
Fax: 780-944-6979
St. Albert
#201, 30 Green Grove Dr.
St Albert, AB T8N 5H6 Canada
780-418-3800
Fax: 780-418-5127
Stony Plain
#107, 4302 - 33 St.
Stony Plain, AB T7Z 2A9 Canada
780-963-9877
Fax: 780-963-9919

Fontaine & Associates Inc.

430 Westmount Ave.
Sudbury, ON P3A 5Z8
705-560-1212
Fax: 705-560-8076
www.bankruptcyontario.com
Profile: Services provided include bankruptcy, credit counselling, and debt settlement.

Executives:
Robert J. Fontaine, President
Branches:
Belleville
196 Front St.
Belleville, ON K8N 2Y7 Canada
613-961-1112
Fax: 613-745-2008
Elliot Lake
25 Columbia Walk
Elliot Lake, ON P5A 1Y6 Canada
705-461-1212
Fax: 705-560-8076
Kapuskasing
7 Cain St.
Kapuskasing, ON P5N 1S8 Canada
705-335-3333
Fax: 705-268-8277
Kingston
1379B Princess St.
Kingston, ON K7M 3E4 Canada
613-530-2511
Fax: 613-745-2008
New Liskeard
44 Armstrong St. North
New Liskeard, ON P0J 1P0 Canada
705-647-1212
Fax: 705-495-3142
North Bay
1306 Algonquin Ave.
North Bay, ON P1B 4Y2 Canada
705-495-1212
Fax: 705-495-3142
Ottawa - Montreal Rd.
#111, 150 Montreal Rd.
Ottawa, ON K1L 8H2 Canada
613-745-1212
Fax: 613-745-2008
Ottawa - Richmond Rd.
Richmond Square
#202, 1365 Richmond Rd
Ottawa, ON K2B 7Y4 Canada
613-820-1811
Fax: 613-820-9828
Pembroke
#3, 143 Pembroke St. West
Pembroke, ON K8A 3J7 Canada
613-635-7846
Fax: 613-820-9828
Sturgeon Falls
229 Main St.
Sturgeon Falls, ON P0H 2G0 Canada
705-753-3700
Fax: 705-495-3142
Timmins
194 Algonquin Blvd. East
Timmins, ON P4N 1A9 Canada
705-268-1212
Fax: 705-268-8277

François Huot & Associés Syndic Ltée.

#215, 2144, rue King ouest
Sherbrooke, QC J1J 2E8
819-821-3500
Fax: 819-821-3031
info@fhuotsyndic.com

Frank S. Kisluk Limited

307A Danforth Ave.
Toronto, ON M4K 1N7
416-463-9440
Fax: 416-778-6016
fkisluk@debtorconsulting.com
www.debtorconsulting.com
Number of Employees: 3
Executives:
Frank S. Kisluk, President

Fuller Landau Ltd.

151 Bloor St. West, 12th Fl.
Toronto, ON M5S 1S4
416-645-6500
Fax: 416-645-6501
info.tor@fullerlandau.com
www.fullerlandau.com
Number of Employees: 36
Profile: Mid-market, regional chartered accountant and consulting firm whose primary target market is privately held companies ranging from $10 million in revenues to complex organizations with annual revenues of $150 million.

Branches:
Montréal
Place du Canada
#200, 1010, de la Gauchetière ouest
Montréal, QC H3B 2N2 Canada
514-875-2865
Fax: 514-866-0247
info.mtl@fullerlandau.com

G. Slocombe & Associates Inc.

#13, 6421 Applecross Rd.
Nanaimo, BC V9V 1N1
250-390-5371
Fax: 250-390-5372
877-421-2288
info@slocombe-trustee.com
www.slocombe-trustee.com
Number of Employees: 5
Profile: Service by branches in Courtenay & Kootenay is by appointment only.

Executives:
Gareth F. Slocombe, President
Branches:
Courtenay
c/o Meyers Norris Penny
467 Cumberland Rd.
Courtenay, BC V9N 2C5 Canada

NON-DEPOSITORY INSTITUTIONS

G. Slocombe & Associates Inc. (continued)
250-338-6880
877-421-2288
Kootenay
c/o Kootenay Place Business Centre
801B Baker St.
Cranbrook, BC V1C 1A3 Canada
877-421-2288

Geary & Company Limited
#800, 1240 Bay St.
Toronto, ON M5R 2A7
416-927-7200
Fax: 416-927-7727
tim@gearyandcompany.com
www.gearyandcompany.com
Year Founded: 1989
Number of Employees: 3
Profile: Trustee in bankruptcy, consumer proposal, financial counselor.

Executives:
Tim Geary, Contact

Gene Drennan Ltd.
612 View St., 6th Fl.
Victoria, BC V8W 1J5
250-380-2407
Fax: 250-380-1004
800-639-4694
trustees@drennan.bc.ca
www.glover-drennan.com
Executives:
Gene Drennan, President

Ginsberg, Gingras & Associates Inc.
295 Richmond Rd.
Ottawa, ON K1Z 6X3
613-729-4391
Fax: 613-729-3929
800-565-8149
www.ginsberg-gingras.com
Ownership: Private
Year Founded: 1980
Number of Employees: 64
Executives:
Claude B. Gingras, Président
Richard Cadieux, Vice-président
Robert P. Racicot, Vice-président
Branches:
Gatineau - l'Hôpital
#200, 160, boul de l'Hôpital
Gatineau, QC J8T 8J1 Canada
819-243-1515
Fax: 819-243-8686
888-546-6767
Jean-Guy Chartrand, Manager
Gatineau - Portage
145, promenade du Portage
Gatineau, QC J8X 2K4 Canada
819-776-0283
Fax: 819-776-1254
800-567-1905
Claude B. Gingras, Manager
Montréal
#525, 1001, boul de Maisonneuve est
Montréal, QC H2L 4P9 Canada
514-878-4545
Fax: 514-878-4548
877-878-4545
Jacques Pesant, Manager
Québec
#460, 2795 boul Laurier
Québec, QC G1V 4M7 Canada
418-652-0585
Fax: 418-652-0595
800-652-0585
Laurier Richard, Manager
Rimouski
#103, 70, rue St-Germain est
Rimouski, QC G5L 7J9 Canada
418-724-9079
Fax: 418-724-9061
877-898-9079
Andrée E. Auclair, Manager
St-Jérôme
#100, 299, rue Labelle
Saint-Jérome, QC J7Y 5L2 Canada
450-432-3563
Fax: 450-432-6358
877-356-3563
Stephen V. Moyneur, Vice-President

Green Hunt Wedlake Inc.
Tower 1
#315, 7001 Mumford Rd.
Halifax, NS B3L 4N9
902-453-6600
Fax: 902-453-9257
800-265-0673
ghwi@ghjw.com
www.wedlakeinc.com
Former Name: Green, Haley Wedlake Incorporated; Green Jain Wedlake Inc.
Year Founded: 1987
Number of Employees: 11
Executives:
Peter D. Wedlake, President
Robert Hunt, Vice-President
Branches:
Sydney
#6A, 50 Dorchester St.
Sydney, NS Canada
800-265-0673
info@Wedlakeinc.com
Truro
Bank of Montreal Building
35 Commercial St.
Truro, NS B2N 3H9 Canada
902-897-2702
800-265-0673
info@Wedlakeinc.com

Groupe Thibault Van Houtte & Associés Ltée
#100, 70, rue Dalhousie
Québec, QC G1K 4B2
418-649-0767
Fax: 418-649-1518
800-461-0767
eric.villeneuve@gtvh.com
www.syndic-de-faillite.com
Former Name: Gérald Robitaille & Associés Ltée
Ownership: Private
Year Founded: 1988
Number of Employees: 40
Assets: $1-5 million
Revenues: $1-5 million
Profile: Specializes in personal and corporate bankruptcy.

Executives:
Pierre Delisle, President; pierre.delisle@gtvh.com
Patrice Van Houtte, Vice-President; 418-649-0767; patrice.van.houtte@gtvh.com
Brian Fiset, Trustee; 418-649-0767; brian.fiset@gtvh.com
André Thibault, Trustee; 514-847-0180; andre.thibault@gtvh.com

H.H. Davis & Associates Inc.
#400, 3333, boul Graham
Montréal, QC H3R 3L5
514-807-7151
Fax: 514-342-0589
Ownership: Private
Year Founded: 1994
Number of Employees: 10
Assets: $1-5 million
Revenues: $1-5 million
Executives:
Herbert H. Davis, CIP

Harold Frankel Trustees & Receivers Inc.
#310, 1110 Finch Ave. West
Toronto, ON M3J 2T2
416-665-7778
Fax: 416-665-4772
Ownership: Private
Year Founded: 1961
Executives:
Harold Frankel, Chartered Accountant

Harris & Partners Inc.
#300, 8920 Woodbine Ave.
Markham, ON L3R 9W9
905-477-0363
Fax: 905-477-3735
www.harrisandpartners.com
Profile: Offers financial services and professional advice to entrepreneurial business in Southern Ontario.

Executives:
Les Kirsch, Sr. Partner; leskirsh@harrisandpartners.com
Syd Muskrat, Sr. Partner; sydmuskat@harrisandpartners.com
Jack Hertzberg, Partner; jhertzberg@harrisandpartners.com
Ian Rothman, Sr. Manager; ianrothman@harrisandpartners.com

Hayes Stewart Little & Co.
823 Canada Ave.
Duncan, BC V9L 1V2
250-746-4406
Fax: 250-746-1950
hslco@hslco.com
www.hslco.com
Former Name: Hayes Debeck Stewart & Little
Executives:
Tara Benham
Chuck Chandler
Marty Eakins
Woody Hayes
Todd Humen
Dan Little
Nancy McMahon
David McNeill
Art Rotherham
Branches:
Nanaimo
#1, 256 Wallace St.
Nanaimo, BC V9R 5B3 Canada
250-754-9551
Fax: 250-754-1903
hslconan@hslco.com
Victoria
#900, 747 Fort St.
Victoria, BC V8W 3E9 Canada
250-383-8994
Fax: 250-383-8904
hslcovic@hslco.com

Herpers Chagani Gowling Inc.
***Also listed under:** Accountants*
#300, 4 Hughson St. South
Hamilton, ON L8N 3Z1
905-529-3328
Fax: 905-529-3980
888-735-9909
www.bankruptcyanswers.com
Former Name: Herpers Gowling Inc.
Also Known As: 310DEBT
Ownership: Private
Year Founded: 1996
Number of Employees: 33
Executives:
Alex Herpers, President
Mahmood Chagani, Vice-President
David Gowling, Vice-President
Branches:
Brampton
152 Queen St. East
Brampton, ON L6V 1B2 Canada
905-310-3328
Brantford
20B Borden St.
Brantford, ON N3R 2G8 Canada
519-310-3328
Burlington
#316, 2289 Fairview St.
Burlington, ON L7R 2E3 Canada
905-310-3328
Cambridge
19 Thorne St.
Cambridge, ON N1R 1S3 Canada
519-310-3328
Guelph
#202, 727 Woolwich St.
Guelph, ON N1H 3Z2 Canada
519-310-3328
Hamilton - Greenhill Ave.
#10, 625 Greenhill Ave.
Hamilton, ON L8K 5W9 Canada
905-529-3328
Hamilton - Upper Wentworth St.

836 Upper Wentworth St.
Hamilton, ON L9A 4W4 Canada
Kitchener
#706, 30 Duke St. West
Kitchener, ON N2H 3W5 Canada
London - Dundas St.
#5, 1700 Dundas St.
London, ON N5W 3C9 Canada
London - Wellington Rd. South
#209, 1069 Wellington Rd. South
London, ON N6E 2H6 Canada
Mississauga
#200, 33 City Centre Dr.
Mississauga, ON L5B 2N5 Canada
905-949-4555
Niagara Falls
4668 St. Clair Ave.
Niagara Falls, ON L2E 6X7 Canada
905-310-3328
Oakville
235 Lakeshore Rd.
Oakville, ON L6J 1H7 Canada
Simcoe
23 Argyle St.
Simcoe, ON N3Y 4N5 Canada
905-310-3328
St Catharines
#415, 80 King St.
St Catharines, ON L2R 7G1 Canada
905-310-3328
Stratford
100 Erie St.
Stratford, ON N5A 2M4 Canada
519-310-3328
Welland
32 East Main St.
Welland, ON L3G 3W3 Canada
905-310-3328

Hoyes, Michalos & Associates Inc.

#204, 607 King St. West
Kitchener, ON N2J 1C7
519-747-0660
Fax: 519-747-2418
866-747-0660
info@hoyes.com
www.hoyes.com
Former Name: Hoyes & Associates Inc.
Year Founded: 1997
Trustees:
John Douglas Hoyes
Rebecca Martyn
Benny Mendlowitz
Ted Michalos

Hudson & Company Insolvency Trustees Inc.

#300, 625 - 11th Ave. SW
Calgary, AB T2R 0E1
403-265-0340
Fax: 403-265-3142
info@hudsonca.ca
www.hudsonandco.com
Ownership: Private. Parent is Nexia International
Year Founded: 1973
Number of Employees: 65
Partners:
Doug Holland, CA
Bruce G. Hudson, CA CIRP
Paul Neilson, CA
Allan Payne, CA
Dave Pilkington, CA
Robert Price, CMA CIRP
Jim Scott, CA
Lorraine Walker, CA
Max Wiebe, CA CBV
Eric Wipf, CGA CFP
Branches:
Calgary - 36 St.
#231, 495 - 36th St. NE
Calgary, AB T2A 6K3 Canada
403-531-4357
Fax: 403-273-3308
Glory Jacklin
Calgary - MacLeod Trail
#600, 11012 MacLeod Trail SE
Calgary, AB T2J 6A5 Canada
403-571-4357
Fax: 403-234-8770
Okotoks
PO Box 1427
56 McRae St.
Okotoks, AB T1S 1B4 Canada
403-995-2425
Fax: 403-995-2420
Lorraine Walker

Ian P. Mackin & Associates Inc.

#405, 4901 - 48th St.
Red Deer, AB T4N 6M4
403-342-5380
Fax: 403-342-5388
Other Information: Toll Free: 1-800-372-9202 (Alta only)
ipmackin@telusplanet.net
www.albertabankruptcy.com
Ownership: Private
Number of Employees: 4
Executives:
Ian Patrick Mackin, President

Irving A. Burton Limited

#210, 1550 Kingston Rd.
Pickering, ON L1V 1C3
905-839-8981
Fax: 905-839-0084
Executives:
Irving A. Burton, Principal
Branches:
Oshawa
#207, 40 King St. West
Oshawa, ON L1N 1A4 Canada
905-438-0181
Fax: 905-839-0084
Peterborough
311 George St. North
Peterborough, ON K9J 3H3 Canada
705-742-7710
Whitby
107 Kent St.
Whitby, ON L1N 4Y1 Canada
905-666-1367

J. Lukca & associés inc

#390, 750, boul Marcel Laurin
Montréal, QC H4M 2M4
514-747-5181
Fax: 514-747-3493
Year Founded: 1997
Number of Employees: 7
Executives:
John Lukca
Branches:
Montréal - Décarie
5250, boul Décarie
Montréal, QC H3X 2H9 Canada
514-483-2841
Montréal - Newman
7655, boul Newman
Montréal, QC H8N 1X7 Canada
514-595-3116

J. Walter MacKinnon Ltd.

PO Box 729
Cornwall Village Sq.
Cornwall, PE C0A 1H0
902-892-2010
Fax: 902-892-2011
877-410-2010
jwm@jwaltermackinnon.pe.ca
www.jwaltermackinnon.pe.ca
Year Founded: 1997
Profile: Firm assists individuals and lenders with their financial difficulties.
Executives:
J. Walter McKinnon, President

J.G. Touchie & Associates Ltd.

#116 Weldon St.
Moncton, NB E1C 5W2
506-857-8222
Fax: 506-859-8898
800-387-8783
Branches:
Bathurst
1199 St. Peter Ave.
Bathurst, NB E2A 3A1 Canada
506-546-6226
Caraquet
259, boul St-Pierre ouest
Caraquet, NB E1W 1B9 Canada
506-727-4009
Charlottetown
129 Queen St.
Charlottetown, PE C1A 4A2 Canada
902-894-8783
Miramichi
13 Henderson St.
Miramichi, NB E1N 2P8 Canada
506-773-3553
Summerside
268 Water St.
Summerside, PE C1N 1B8 Canada
902-888-3553
800-387-8783

James B. Walker & Co. Ltd.

#202, 130 Dundas St. East
Mississauga, ON L5A 3V8
905-279-7000
Fax: 905-279-7900
jim@jamesbwalker.ca
www.jamesbwalker.ca
Executives:
James B. Walker, President

James Hunter & Associates Inc.

1351 Dundas St. West
Toronto, ON M6J 1Y3
416-534-2777
Fax: 416-534-5605
jameshunterassoc@on.aibn.com
www.ypca.com/jameshunterassociates
Year Founded: 1990
Number of Employees: 5
Executives:
James Hunter

Janes & Noseworthy Limited

Topsail Plaza
#201, 516 Topsail Rd.
St. John's, NL A1E 2C5
709-364-8148
Fax: 709-368-2146
800-563-9779
info@janesnoseworthy.ca
www.jnl.nf.ca
Ownership: Private
Year Founded: 1984
Assets: Under $1 million
Revenues: $1-5 million
Profile: Provides the following services: bankruptcy, consumer proposals, credit counselling, 3rd party settlements with creditors, and refinancing.
Executives:
Richard S. Janes
Branches:
Corner Brook
CIBC Bldg.
#302, 9 Main St.
Corner Brook, NL A2H 6J3 Canada
709-634-3631
Fax: 709-634-3638
877-934-4330
daisybennett@janesnoseworthy.ca
Grand Falls-Windsor
Town Square Mall
7 High St.
Grand Falls-Windsor, NL A2A 1C3 Canada
709-489-8219
Fax: 709-489-7550
866-489-8219
paulbutt@janesnoseworthy.ca
Marystown
228 Ville Marie Dr.
Marystown, NL A0E 2M0 Canada
709-279-3003
Fax: 709-279-0923
888-979-0923

Janes & Noseworthy Limited (continued)
jamiegair@janesnoseworthy.ca

Jean Fortin & associés syndic
#200, 2360, boul Marie-Victorin est
Longueuil, QC J4G 1B5
450-442-3260
Fax: 450-928-3477
www.endettement.com
Year Founded: 1985
Executives:
Michel Beauchamp
Robert Farmer
Jean Fortin
Pierre Fortin
Luc Latour
Guy Loslier
Jocelyn Marineau
André Nadeau
Denis Rémillard
André Thibodeau
Branches:
Beloeil
#200, 201, boul Laurier
Beloeil, QC J3G 4G8 Canada
450-442-3260
Brossard
#401, 6200, boul Taschereau
Brossard, QC J4W 3J8 Canada
450-442-3260
Châteauguay
168, rue Saint-Jean Baptiste
Châteauguay, QC J6K 3B5 Canada
450-699-3260
Drummondville
#450, 235, rue Hériot
Drummondville, QC J2C 1J9 Canada
819-477-0367
Gatineau - l'Hôpital
#11, 111, boul de l'Hôpital
Gatineau, QC J8T 7V1 Canada
819-561-3260
Gatineau - Principale
149, rue Principale
Gatineau, QC J9H 3M7 Canada
819-561-3260
Gatineau - St-Joseph
#101, 683, boul St-Joseph
Gatineau, QC J8Y 4B4 Canada
819-561-3260
Granby
100, rue Principale
Granby, QC J2G 2T4 Canada
450-375-7860
Joliette
264, rue de l'Industrie
Joliette, QC J6E 8V1 Canada
450-756-2776
La Tuque
58, rue Corbeil
La Tuque, QC G9X 4G6 Canada
877-797-2433
Laval
Place Laval
#162, 1, boul St-Martin ouest
Laval, QC H7N 1A1 Canada
450-667-6260
Fax: 450-629-3510
Mascouche
2942, rue Dupras
Mascouche, QC J7K 1T2 Canada
514-356-3260
Montréal - Crémazie ouest
#404, 50, Place Crémazie ouest
Montréal, QC H2P 2T1 Canada
514-382-3260
Fax: 514-382-3477

Montréal - Notre-Dame
#200, 3380, rue Notre-Dame ouest
Montréal, QC H8T 1W7 Canada
514-382-3260
Montréal - Sherbrooke est
#101, 7744, rue Sherbrooke est
Montréal, QC H1L 1A1 Canada
514-356-3260
Montréal - Wellington
#206, 4080, rue Wellington
Montréal, QC H4G 1V7 Canada
514-769-1818
Québec
#390-2, 1173, boul Charest ouest
Québec, QC G1N 2C9 Canada
418-683-5222
Repentigny
#301, 184, rue Notre-Dame
Repentigny, QC J6A 2P9 Canada
450-654-5777
Saint-Jean-sur-Richelieu
#218, 1050, du Séminaire
St-Jean-sur-Richelieu, QC J3A 1S7 Canada
450-348-2880
Saint-Jérôme
#100, 30, de Martigny ouest
Saint-Jérome, QC J7Z 2E9 Canada
450-432-0207
Saint-Sauveur
200B, Principale, 1er étage
Saint-Sauveur, QC J0R 1R0 Canada
800-465-3809
Sainte-Adèle
#210, 1520, boul Ste-Adèle
Sainte-Adèle, QC J8B 2N5 Canada
800-465-3809
Salaberry-de-Valleyfield
7, rue Bay
Salaberry-de-Valleyfield, QC J6S 1X3 Canada
450-373-5698
Fax: 450-373-7783
Shawinigan
500, ave Broadway, 2e étage
Shawinigan, QC G9N 1M3 Canada
819-536-3700
Sherbrooke
#103, 380, rue King ouest
Sherbrooke, QC J1H 1R4 Canada
819-822-4666
Sorel-Tracy
#220, 215, boul Fiset
Sorel-Tracy, QC J3P 3P3 Canada
450-742-2210
St-Eustache
159, rue St-Eustache
Saint-Eustache, QC J7R 2L5 Canada
514-382-3260
St-Hyacinthe
#109, 975, rue du Palais
Saint-Hyacinthe, QC J2S 5C6 Canada
450-771-0100
St-Nicolas
155, du Pont route, 2e étage
Saint-Nicolas, QC G7A 2T3 Canada
418-683-5222
Ste-Thérèse
#201, 269, boul Labelle
Sainte-Thérèse, QC J7E 2X8 Canada
450-433-8963
Terrebonne
692, boul des Seigneurs
Terrebonne, QC J6W 3W6 Canada
450-492-8309
Trois-Rivières - Forges
#202, 3910, boul des Forges
Trois-Rivières, QC G8Y 1V7 Canada
819-370-2020
Fax: 819-376-2751
Trois-Rivières - Thibeau
780, boul Thibeau
Trois-Rivières, QC G8T 7A6 Canada
819-370-2020
Vaudreuil-Dorion
202, 100, boul Hardwood
Vaudreuil-Dorion, QC J7V 1X9 Canada
450-424-3262

Victoriaville
333, boul des Bois-francs nord
Victoriaville, QC G6P 7B7 Canada
877-797-2433

Jeffrey Pinder & Associates Inc.
Eastwood Centre 1
#212, 3521 - 8th St. East
Saskatoon, SK S7H 0W5
306-653-1100
Fax: 306-653-1064
800-668-1234
pinderassociates@bankruptcysask.ca
www.bankruptcysask.ca
Ownership: Private
Executives:
Jeffrey W. Pinder

John D. McKeown Inc.
13 - 5th St. West
Cornwall, ON K6J 2T5
613-937-4576
jmckeown@on.aibn.com
Year Founded: 1998
Executives:
John David McKeown

John S. Beverley & Associates Inc.
1240 - 5th Ave.
Prince George, BC V2L 3L2
250-563-4396
Fax: 250-563-8600
800-708-4330
questions@jbeverley.com
www.jbeverley.com
Number of Employees: 6
Profile: Licensed trustee in bankruptcy serving clients throughout British Columbia.

Executives:
John S. Beverley, Trustee
Branches:
Kelowna
Spall Business Centre
#13, 1873 Spall Rd.
Kelowna, BC V1Y 4R2 Canada
250-861-5445
Fax: 250-563-8600
800-708-4330

Jolin, Turcotte & Associés
317, rue Racine
Granby, QC J2G 3B6
450-375-3702
Fax: 450-375-4407
nturcotte@jolinturcotte.ca
www.jolinturcotte.ca/index.html
Ownership: Private
Year Founded: 1981
Executives:
Normand J. Turcotte

Keith G. Collins Ltd.
#807, 386 Broadway
Winnipeg, MB R3C 3R6
204-944-0187
Fax: 204-947-3680
800-263-0070
kgcltd@mts.net
www.bankruptcy.mb.ca
Ownership: Private.
Executives:
Donna Collins, Contact
Douglas Collins

Ken Glover & Associates Inc.
612 View St., 6th Fl.
Victoria, BC V8W 1J5
250-380-2407
Fax: 250-380-1004
800-639-4694
trustees@glover.ca
www.glover-drennan.com
Ownership: Private
Year Founded: 1995
Number of Employees: 12
Executives:
Kenneth Glover, President; 250-995-4244

KPMG
Also listed under: *Accountants*

Box 31, Commerce Court Postal Station, Commerce Court West
199 Bay St.
Toronto, ON M5L 1B2
416-777-8500
Fax: 416-777-8818
webmaster@kpmg.ca
www.kpmg.ca
Ownership: Private
Year Founded: 1860
Number of Employees: 4,500
Assets: $500m-1 billion Year End: 20051001
Revenues: $500m-1 billion Year End: 20051001
Executives:
Bill Mackinnon, Chair/CEO
Peter Chiddy, Managing Partner, Advisory Services
Bruce Glexman, Managing Partner, Tax
Paul Weiss, Managing Partner, Audit
Bill Dillabough, Chief Marketing Officer
Mary Lou Hamher, CFO
Elizabeth Wilson, Chief HR Officer
Branches:
Abbotsford
32575 Simon Ave.
Abbotsford, BC V2T 4W6 Canada
604-854-2200
Fax: 604-853-2756
Burnaby
#2400, 4720 Kingsway
Burnaby, BC V5H 4N2 Canada
604-527-3600
Fax: 604-527-3636
Calgary
Bow Valley Square II
#1200, 205 - 5th Ave. SW
Calgary, AB T2P 4B9 Canada
403-691-8000
Fax: 403-691-8008
Jason Brown, Partner, Audit
Chilliwack
#200, 9123 Mary St.
Chilliwack, BC V2P 4H7 Canada
604-793-4700
Fax: 604-793-4747
Edmonton
Commerce Pl.
10125 - 102 St.
Edmonton, AB T5J 3V8 Canada
780-429-7300
Fax: 780-429-7379
Robert Borrelli, Partner, Audit
Fredericton
Frederick Sq., TD Tower
#700, 77 Westmorland St.
Fredericton, NB E3B 6Z3 Canada
506-452-8000
Fax: 506-450-0072
Todd MacIntosh, Partner, Tax
Halifax
Purdy's Wharf, Tower One
#1500, 1959 Upper Water St.
Halifax, NS B3J 3N2 Canada
902-429-6000
Fax: 902-423-1307
Gregory Simpson, Partner, Tax
Hamilton
Commerce Place
#700, 21 King St. West
Hamilton, ON L8P 4W7 Canada
905-523-8200
Fax: 905-523-2222
Kamloops
#200, 206 Seymour St.
Kamloops, BC V2C 6P5 Canada
250-372-5581
Fax: 250-828-2928
Kelowna
#300, 1674 Bertram St.
Kelowna, BC V1Y 9G4 Canada
250-763-5522
Fax: 250-763-0044
Kingston
#400, 863 Princess St.
Kingston, ON K7L 5N4 Canada
613-549-1550
Fax: 613-549-6349
Lethbridge
Lethbridge Centre Tower
#500, 400 - 4th Ave. South
Lethbridge, AB T1J 4E1 Canada
403-380-5700
Fax: 403-380-5760
London
#1400, 140 Fullarton St.
London, ON N6A 5P2 Canada
519-672-4880
Fax: 519-672-5684
Moncton
Place Marvin's
One Factory Lane
Moncton, NB E1C 9M3 Canada
506-856-4400
Fax: 506-856-4499
Montréal
#1900, 2000, av McGill College
Montréal, QC H3A 3H8 Canada
514-840-2100
Fax: 514-840-2187
Philippe Grubert, Partner, Audit
North Bay
PO Box 990
#300, 925 Stockdale Rd.
North Bay, ON P1B 8K3 Canada
705-472-5110
Fax: 705-472-1249
Ottawa
World Exchange Plaza
#1000, 45 O'Connor St.
Ottawa, ON K1P 1A4 Canada
613-212-5764
Fax: 613-212-2896
Andrew Newman, Partner, Audit
Penticton
498 Ellis St., 2nd Fl.
Penticton, BC V2A 4M2 Canada
250-492-8444
Fax: 250-492-8688
Prince George
#400, 177 Victoria St.
Prince George, BC V2L 5R8 Canada
250-563-7151
Fax: 250-563-5693
Regina
McCallum Hill Centre, Tower II
1881 Scarth St., 20th Fl.
Regina, SK S4P 4K9 Canada
306-791-1200
Fax: 306-757-4703
Saint John
Harbour Bldg.
PO Box 2388
#306, 133 Prince William St.
Saint John, NB E2L 3V6 Canada
506-634-1000
Fax: 506-633-8828
Saskatoon
#600, 128 - 4th Ave. South
Saskatoon, SK S7K 1M8 Canada
306-934-6200
Fax: 306-934-6233
Sault Ste Marie
#200, 111 Elgin St.
Sault Ste Marie, ON P6A 6L6 Canada
705-949-5811
Fax: 705-949-0911
St Catharines
#901, One Saint-Paul St.
St Catharines, ON L2R 7L2 Canada
905-685-4811
Fax: 905-682-2008
Sudbury
Claridge Executive Centre
144 Pine St.
Sudbury, ON P3C 1X3 Canada
705-675-8500
Fax: 705-675-7586
Laurie Bissonette, Partner, Audit
Sydney
Commerce Tower
15 Dorchester St., 5th Fl.
Sydney, NS B1P 5Y9 Canada
902-539-3900
Fax: 902-564-6062
Toronto
Yonge Corporate Centre
#200, 4100 Yonge St.
Toronto, ON M2P 2H3 Canada
416-228-7000
Fax: 416-228-7123
Vancouver
Pacific Centre
PO Box 10426
777 Dunsmuir St.
Vancouver, BC V7Y 1K3 Canada
604-691-3000
Fax: 604-691-3031
Jim Bennett, Partner, Audit
Vernon
Credit Union Bldg.
3205 - 32 St., 3rd Fl.
Vernon, BC V1T 9A2 Canada
250-503-5300
Fax: 250-545-6440
Waterloo
Marsland Centre
#300, 20 Erb St. West
Waterloo, ON N2L 1T2 Canada
519-747-8800
Fax: 519-747-8811
Shelley Wickenheiser, Partner, Tax
Windsor
Greenwood Centre
#618, 3200 Deziel Dr.
Windsor, ON N8W 5K8 Canada
519-251-3500
Fax: 519-251-3530
Winnipeg
#2000, One Lombard Place
Winnipeg, MB R3B 0X3 Canada
204-957-1770
Fax: 204-957-0808

L.C. Taylor & Co. Ltd.

Centennial Bldg.
#702, 310 Broadway
Winnipeg, MB R3C 0S6
204-925-6400
Fax: 204-956-2335
800-463-8371
lct@lctaylor.net
www.lctaylor.net
Ownership: Private
Year Founded: 1992
Profile: Services provided include consumer bankruptcies, consumer proposals, financial counselling, division 1 proposals, and receiverships.

Executives:
B. Hooley
L. Taylor
Offices:
Kenora
PO Box 2910
225 Main St. South, 2nd Fl.
Kenora, ON P2N 3X8 Canada
807-468-3406
B. Hooley, Trustee

Lazard & Associates Inc.

1208 Bank St.
Ottawa, ON K1S 3Y1
613-567-4357
Fax: 613-730-5259
866-560-4357
help@bankruptcy-advice.net
www.bankruptcy-advice.net
Former Name: Lazard, Zielski & Associates Inc.
Profile: Provides bankruptcy and financial services.

Executives:
Jean M. Lezard

Lazer Grant LLP Chartered Accountants & Business Advisors

***Also listed under:** Accountants*
#400, 309 McDermot Ave.
Winnipeg, MB R3A 1T3

Lazer Grant LLP Chartered Accountants & Business Advisors (continued)
204-942-0300
Fax: 204-957-5611
800-220-0005
LazerGrant@lazergrant.ca
www.lazergrant.ca
Year Founded: 1976
Number of Employees: 28
Profile: Services provided by chartered accountants & business advisors.

Partners:
Garry Chan, B.Sc., CA
David Glass, CA
Saul Greenberg, B.Comms., CA
Joel Lazer, CA, CIRP
Collin LeGall, CMA, CIRP, CFE
Martin H. Minuck, CA

Le Groupe Boudreau, Richard Inc.
33, rue St-Jacques, 5e étage
Montréal, QC H2Y 1K9
514-849-2100
Fax: 514-849-9292
rjboudreau@gbri.ca
www.gbri.ca
Ownership: Private
Year Founded: 1992
Number of Employees: 15
Assets: Under $1 million
Revenues: $1-5 million
Executives:
Réjean Boudreau
Branches:
St-Eustache
164, St-Laurent
Saint-Eustache, QC J7P 5G4 Canada
514-472-6100
Fax: 514-472-7099

Le Groupe Serpone Syndic de faillite inc.
#600, 7100, rue Jean-Talon est
Montréal, QC H1M 3S3
514-355-6553
Fax: 514-355-8423
johanne@groupeserpone.com
www.groupeserpone.com
Ownership: Private
Year Founded: 1995
Number of Employees: 12
Profile: Offers services in the field of corporate and personal bankruptcies and proposals, as well as in business reorganizations.

Executives:
Johanne Serpone, Contact
Branches:
Blainville
#201, 1340, boul. Curé Labelle
Blainville, QC J7C 2P2 Canada
450-420-3420
Montréal
#108, 1666, rue Thierry
Montréal, QC H8N 2K4 Canada
514-363-6565
Fax: 514-363-6565
St-Constant
191, rue St-Pierre
Saint-Constant, QC J5A 2G9 Canada
450-638-0682
Fax: 450-638-4278
St-Eustache
#3, 183, rue Saint-Eustache
Saint-Eustache, QC J7R 2L5 Canada
450-473-7898
Fax: 450-473-7898

Leblond et associés ltée
621, boul Charest est
Québec, QC G1K 3J5
418-525-4641
Fax: 418-525-4646
Former Name: Leblond, Buzzetti et Associés Ltée
Year Founded: 1995
Executives:
Stéphane Leblond

Litwin Boyadjian Inc.
#2720, 1, Place Ville Marie
Montréal, QC H3B 4G4
514-875-4000
Fax: 514-875-0598
Year Founded: 1975

M. Diamond Associates Inc.
#400, 345, av Victoria
Montréal, QC H3Z 2N2
514-483-2303
Fax: 514-483-2373
Former Name: H&M Diamond & Associates Inc.
Ownership: Private
Profile: Bankruptcy attorneys, bankruptcy services, and public accountants.

Executives:
Mayer Diamond
Michael Kovshoff
David Solomon

Mandelbaum Spergel Inc.
***Also listed under:* Accountants**
#200, 505 Consumers Rd.
Toronto, ON M2J 4V8
416-497-1660
Fax: 416-494-7199
800-563-8251
aspergel@trustee.com
www.trustee.com
Ownership: Private
Year Founded: 1979
Number of Employees: 35
Executives:
Alan Spergel, President
Carl Ritchie, Sr. Vice-President
Colin Boulton, Vice-President
Chris Galea, Vice-President
Directors:
Harold Mandelbaum
Carl Ritchie
Alan Spergel
Affiliated Companies:
Spergel & Associates Inc.
Branches:
Barrie
#102, 81 Maple Ave.
Barrie, ON L4N 1S1 Canada
705-722-5090
Fax: 705-722-7184
critchie@trustee.com
Carl Ritchie, Contact
Brampton - Nelson St.
#5, 14 Nelson St. West
Brampton, ON L6X 1B7 Canada
905-874-4905
Fax: 905-874-4789
cgalea@trustee.com
Brampton - Peel Centre Dr.
#201, 40 Peel Centre Dr.
Brampton, ON L6T 4B4 Canada
905-793-8377
cgalea@trustee.com
Chris Galea, Contact
Burlington
2108 Old Lakeshore Rd.
Burlington, ON L7R 1A3 Canada
905-319-8438
Fax: 905-527-6670
tpringle@trustee.com
Henry Lam Chi-leung, Branch Manager
Hamilton - King St. West
Commerce Place
PO Box 54
#803, 21 King St. West
Hamilton, ON L8P 4W7 Canada
905-527-2227
Fax: 905-527-6670
tpringle@trustee.com
Hamilton - Upper James St.
557 Upper James St.
Hamilton, ON L9C 2Y7 Canada
905-527-5468
Fax: 905-527-6670
tpringle@trustee.com
Lindsay
PO Box 997
11 Adelaide St. North
Lindsay, ON K9V 5N4 Canada
705-359-1618
cboulton@trustee.com
Colin Boulton, Contact
Mississauga
#204, 1425 Dundas St. East
Mississauga, ON L4X 2W4 Canada
905-602-4143
Fax: 905-602-8879
cgalea@trustee.com
Oshawa
#103, 187 King St. East
Oshawa, ON L1H 1C2 Canada
905-721-8251
Fax: 905-571-4682
800-563-8251
cboulton@trustee.com
Colin Boulton, Contact
Peterborough
209 Simcoe St.
Peterborough, ON K9H 2H6 Canada
705-748-3333
Fax: 705-748-6669
cboulton@trustee.com
Colin Boulton, Contact
Richmond Hill
10023 Yonge St., Upper Fl.
Richmond Hill, ON L4C 1T7 Canada
905-508-5400
critchie@trustee.com
Carl Ritchie, Contact
Toronto - Danforth Ave.
307A Danforth Ave.
Toronto, ON M4K 1N7 Canada
416-798-8813
Fax: 416-778-6016
nlivshitz@trustee.com
Joan Scullion, Contact
Toronto - Ellesmere Rd.
#211E, 2100 Ellesmere Rd.
Toronto, ON M1H 3B7 Canada
416-439-1251
Fax: 416-439-0537
critchie@trustee.com
Carl Ritchie, Contact
Toronto - Wilson Ave.
#201, 1013 Wilson Ave.
Toronto, ON M3K 1G1 Canada
416-633-1444
critchie@trustee.com
Carl Ritchie, Contact

Marchand syndics inc
10455, rue Laverdure
Montréal, QC H3L 2L5
514-381-7791
Fax: 514-381-7796
msimontreal@qc.aira.com
Number of Employees: 5
Executives:
Georges E. Marchand

McCuaig & Company Incorporated
Clayton Professional Centre
#108, 255 Lacewood Dr.
Halifax, NS B3M 4G2
902-423-3231
Fax: 902-446-3820
800-859-9336
info@mccuaig.ca
www.mccuaig.ca
Executives:
Robert McCuaig, President

McLennan & Company
289 Dufferin Ave.
London, ON N6B 1Z1
519-433-4728
Fax: 519-433-9100
bmclennan@mclennanandcompany.com
www.mclennanandcompany.com
Year Founded: 1995
Executives:

Bruce McLennan

Mendlowitz & Associates Inc.
Madison Centre
#1906, 4950 Yonge St.
Toronto, ON M2N 6K1
416-512-9200
Fax: 416-512-9800
benny@mendlowitz.com
www.mendlowitz.com
Year Founded: 1992
Number of Employees: 2
Profile: Specialized professional practice dealing exclusively in corporate recovery and insolvency matters, as well as personal bankruptcies and proposals.

Executives:
Benny Mendlowitz

Michel Verdier & Associés Inc.
723, rue Labelle
Saint-Jérôme, QC J7Z 5M2
450-438-3551
Fax: 450-436-5683
Executives:
Michel Verdier, Syndic

Murdoch David T., Receiver & Trustee Ltd.
6 Maple Ave.
Smiths Falls, ON K7A 1Z5
613-283-7323
Former Name: David Murdoch & Company Ltd.
Number of Employees: 1
Executives:
David T. Murdoch

Nexia Friedman
#500, 8000, boul Décarie
Montréal, QC H4P 2S4
514-731-7901
Fax: 514-731-2923
877-731-7901
info@nexiafriedman.ca
www.friedman.ca
Former Name: Friedman & Friedman Inc.
Year Founded: 1960
Profile: Provides ongoing counsel and guidance in a variety of areas including: assurance, taxation, financial, and consulting services.

Paddon+Yorke Inc.
95 Dundas St. East
Mississauga, ON L5A 1W7
905-272-3204
Fax: 905-272-3690
800-663-0779
mississauga@paddonyorke.com
www.paddonyorke.com
Year Founded: 1990
Number of Employees: 30
Profile: Provides financial counselling, proposals and bankruptcy services.

Executives:
Warren B. Paddon, President
Clyde E. Yorke, Exec. Vice-President
Branches:
Barrie
27 Clapperton St.
Barrie, ON L4M 3E6 Canada
705-722-9888
Fax: 705-722-9993
800-667-0779
Clyde E. Yorke, Exec. Vice-President
North Bay
#204, 222 McIntyre St. West
North Bay, ON P1B 2Y8 Canada
705-472-2640
Fax: 705-472-6241
800-461-9551

Orillia
525 West St. South
Orillia, ON L3V 5H2 Canada
705-327-2797
800-663-0779
Brenda Atkinson, Manager

Pat Robinson Inc.
#201, 15105 Yonge St.
Aurora, ON L4G 1M3
905-727-2577
Fax: 905-727-2067
pat@patrobinson.com
www.patrobinson.com
Ownership: Private
Profile: Bankruptcies, receiverships, proposals, debt management.

Executives:
Pat Robinson
Branches:
Richmond Hill
#401, 9555 Yonge St.
Richmond Hill, ON L4C 9M5 Canada
905-508-9493
Fax: 905-737-7691
Toronto
#800, 150 York St.
Toronto, ON M2H 3S5 Canada
416-410-6648
Fax: 905-727-2067

Paul J. Pickering Limited
#501, 495 Richmond St.
London, ON N6A 5A9
519-672-2494
Fax: 519-672-2532
paul@paulpickering.com
www.paulpickering.com
Year Founded: 1990
Number of Employees: 7
Profile: Offers credit counselling, arrangements with creditors, proposals, budgeting, reorganization, financial counselling, and personal & business bankruptcy services.

Executives:
Paul J. Pickering
Branches:
Clinton
PO Box 461
8 King St.
Clinton, ON N0M 1L0 Canada
519-482-8459
Fax: 519-482-8460
800-561-7451
Exeter
412 Main St. South
Exeter, ON N0M 1S0 Canada
519-235-4602
800-561-7451

Perry Krieger & Associates Inc.(PKA)
#300, 45 Vogell Rd.
Richmond Hill, ON L4B 3P6
905-508-0080
Fax: 905-508-0012
Other Information: Alternate Phone: 416/447-7200
www.perrykrieger.com
Year Founded: 1990
Number of Employees: 23
Executives:
Perry Krieger, President; perry@perrykrieger.com
Branches:
Ajax
#4-338, 700 Finley Ave.
Ajax, ON L1S 3Z2
905-686-0856
Fax: 905-426-2139
Brantford
148 Dalhousie St.
Brantford, ON N3T 2J4
519-751-7770
Burlington
Upper Canada Place
#208, 460 Brant St.
Burlington, ON L7R 4B6
905-333-3369
Fort Erie
#8, 450 Garrison Rd.
Fort Erie, ON L2A 1N2
905-354-5335
Hamilton - Centennial Pkwy.
211 Centennial Pkwy. North
Hamilton, ON L8E 1H8
985-573-2626
Fax: 985-573-2913

Hamilton - Concession St.
550 Concession St.
Hamilton, ON L8V 1A9
905-387-8886
Mississauga
#400, 918 Dundas St. East
Mississauga, ON L4Y 4H9
905-897-5500
Newmarket
#202, 390 Davis Dr.
Newmarket, ON L3Y 7T8
905-830-0441
Niagara Falls
4056 Dorchester Rd.
Niagara Falls, ON L2E 6M9
905-354-5335
St Catharines
154 James St.
St Catharines, ON L2R 5C5
905-984-8330
Thornhill
7620 Yonge St.
Thornhill, ON L4J 1V9
905-886-4121
Toronto - Bloor St. West
#200, 2200 Bloor St. West
Toronto, ON M6S 1N4
416-761-1989
Toronto - Kennedy Rd.
2223 Kennedy Rd.
Toronto, ON M1T 3G5
416-754-7544
Toronto - Wynford Dr.
#107, 40 Wynford Dr.
Toronto, ON M3C 1J5
Vaughan
#5, 3300 Steeles Ave. West
Vaughan, ON L4K 2Y4
905-660-7360

Petrie & Associates Inc.
#405, 2 Simcoe St. South
Oshawa, ON L1H 8C1
905-579-8636
Fax: 905-579-2533
800-504-9552
alison@alisonpetrie.com
www.alisonpetrie.com
Executives:
Alison Petrie

Pierre Roy et associés inc.
#202, 10, boul Grand
Ile-Perrot, QC J7V 7P8
514-453-9857
Fax: 514-453-2134
info@pierreroy.com
www.pierreroy.com
Year Founded: 1990
Executives:
Pierre Roy, President
Richard Lapointe
Branches:
Montréal
#802, 1290, rue St-Denis
Montréal, QC H2X 3J7 Canada
514-282-8667
Fax: 514-282-9667
Repentigny
#101, 579A, rue Notre-Dame
Repentigny, QC J6A 7L4 Canada
450-654-1441
Fax: 450-654-6280

Pollard & Associates Inc.
31 Wright St.
Richmond Hill, ON L4C 4A2
905-884-8191
Fax: 905-884-4310
akpollard@pollardandassoc.ca
Executives:
Angela Pollard

NON-DEPOSITORY INSTITUTIONS

Primeau Proulx & associés inc
#380, 101, boul Roland-Therrien
Longueuil, QC J4H 4B9
450-670-1040
Fax: 450-670-1542
syndic@primeauproulx.com
www.primeauproulx.com/
Former Name: Primeau Proulx Pigeon & Associés Inc.
Executives:
Richard Primeau

Quon & Associates Ltd.
Business Bldg.
#408, 23 Westmore Dr.
Toronto, ON M9V 3Y7
416-740-9180
Fax: 416-740-9325
Year Founded: 1980
Number of Employees: 1
Executives:
Edward Quon

R. West & Associates Inc.
#202, 7134 King George Hwy.
Surrey, BC V3W 5A3
604-591-7634
Fax: 604-591-9168
info@rwest.ca
www.rwest.ca
Ownership: Private
Branches:
Burnaby
9912 Lougheed Hwy.
Burnaby, BC V3J 1N3 Canada
604-420-6080
Fax: 604-591-9168

R.B. Hagen Associates Ltd.
PO Box 99
1185 McGillvray Ave.
Gabriola, BC V0R 1X0
250-247-8441
Fax: 250-247-8461
ralphhagen@rogers.com
Year Founded: 1990
Executives:
R.B. Hagen

R.D. Hamilton & Associates Inc.
1101 Henderson Hwy.
Winnipeg, MB R2G 1L4
204-947-2600
Fax: 204-947-2226
888-558-4442
rdh@rdhamilton.com
www.rdhamilton.com
Ownership: Private
Year Founded: 1997
Number of Employees: 2
Executives:
Richard D. Hamilton
Jennifer M. Hamilton, Administrator

Raymond Chabot Grant Thornton
Tour de la Banque Nationale
#1900, 600, rue de la Gauchetière ouest
Montréal, QC H3B 4L8
514-878-2691
Fax: 514-878-2127
www.rcgt.com
Former Name: Raymond, Chabot Inc.
Executives:
Pierre Monette, Partner
Branches:
Alma
535, rue Collard ouest
Alma, QC G8B 1N1 Canada
418-668-8351
Fax: 418-668-4913
Gratien Martel, Partner
Amos
66, 1re av ouest
Amos, QC J9T 1T8 Canada
819-732-3208
Fax: 819-732-0908
Gilles Plante, Partner
Amqui
#100, 20A, rue Desbiens
Amqui, QC G5J 3P1 Canada
418-629-2852
Fax: 418-629-4523
Yves Gauthier, Partner
Beauceville
668A, boul Renault
Beauceville, QC G5X 1M3 Canada
418-774-9833
Fax: 418-774-2183
Raymond Fortin, Partner
Bromont
#B202, 89, boul de Bromont
Bromont, QC J2L 1A9 Canada
450-534-3139
Fax: 450-534-2408
M. Marc Blanchette, Partner
Cabano
115, rue Commerciale
Cabano, QC G0L 1E0 Canada
418-854-2122
Fax: 418-854-0362
André Lang, Partner
Chandler
107, rue Commerciale ouest
Chandler, QC G0C 1K0 Canada
418-689-2683
Fax: 418-689-4674
Pierre Georges, Partner
Chicoutimi
#800, 255, rue Racine est
Chicoutimi, QC G7H 7L2 Canada
418-549-4142
Fax: 418-549-3961
Arthur Gobeil, Partner
Coaticook
79, rue Court
Coaticook, QC J1A 1L1 Canada
819-849-9171
Fax: 819-849-9175
Maurice DiStefano, Partner
Cowansville
104, rue Sud
Cowansville, QC J2K 2X2 Canada
450-263-2010
Fax: 450-263-9511
M. Luc Harbec, Partner
Disraéli
150A, rue Champoux
Disraéli, QC G0N 1E0 Canada
418-449-3875
Fax: 418-449-1626
François Gosselin, Partner
Dégelis
485, av Principale
Dégelis, QC G5T 1L7 Canada
418-853-2352
Fax: 418-853-3073
Denis Dionne, Partner
Edmundston
507, rue Victoria
Edmundston, NB E3V 2K9 Canada
506-739-1144
Fax: 506-739-1145
Paul Bérubé, Partner
Gaspé
#9, 1, rue Adams
Gaspé, QC G4X 1E5 Canada
418-368-5576
Fax: 418-368-6942
Richard Chrétien, Partner
Gatineau
#400, 15, rue Gamelin
Gatineau, QC J8Y 1V4 Canada
819-770-9833
Fax: 819-770-5398
Daniel Couture, Partner
Granby - Dufferin
35, rue Dufferin
Granby, QC J2G 4W5 Canada
450-375-4400
Fax: 450-375-0128
M. Marc Legendre, Partner
Granby - Lac
20, Place du Lac
Granby, QC J2G 9L9 Canada
450-378-2002
Fax: 450-378-0617
M. Jean-Guy Goyette, Partner
Hawkesbury
#102, 144, rue Main
Hawkesbury, ON K6A 1A3 Canada
613-632-0901
Fax: 613-632-5359
Diane Tittley, Partner
Jonquière
#203, 3750, boul du Royaume
Jonquière, QC G7X 9S4 Canada
418-695-4142
Fax: 418-695-4557
André Hébert, Partner
La Baie
#301, 105, boul de la Grande Baie nord
La Baie, QC G7B 3K1 Canada
418-544-6847
Fax: 418-544-7932
Éric Dufour, Partner
La Pocatière
400, 901, 5e rue
La Pocatière, QC G0R 1Z0 Canada
418-856-2547
Fax: 418-856-3687
Donald Boucher, Partner
La Sarre
286, rue Principale
La Sarre, QC J9Z 1Y8 Canada
819-333-5586
Fax: 819-333-5941
Mario Petitclerc, Partner
Lac-Mégantic
5320, rue Frontenac
Lac-Mégantic, QC G6B 1H3 Canada
819-583-0611
Fax: 819-583-5995
M. Guy Fauteux, Partner
Laval
#300, 2500, boul Daniel-Johnson
Laval, QC H7T 2P6 Canada
514-382-0270
Fax: 514-875-9797
Gaétan Desforges, Partner
Le Bic
172, rue Sainte-Cécile
Le Bic, QC G0L 1B0 Canada
418-736-4311
Fax: 418-736-8011
Claude Gauthier, Partner
Lebel-sur-Quévillon
PO Box 1179
81, place Quévillon
Lebel-sur-Quévillon, QC J0Y 1X0 Canada
819-755-4043
Fax: 819-755-4866
Alain Lemaire, Partner
Longueuil
#300, 370, ch de Chambly
Longueuil, QC J4H 3Z6 Canada
450-679-5110
Fax: 450-679-7596
800-267-2261
Bernard Grandmont, Partner
Lévis
#103, 5790, boul Étienne-Dallaire
Lévis, QC G6V 8V6 Canada
418-835-3965
Fax: 418-835-3975
Pierre Lapointe, Partner
Matane
PO Box 305
305, rue de la Gare
Matane, QC G4W 3N2 Canada
418-562-0203
Fax: 418-562-9411
Yves Gauthier, Partner
Montmagny
15, av Saint-Magloire
Montmagny, QC G5V 2W4 Canada
418-248-1303
Fax: 418-248-6187

Michel Proulx, Partner
Montréal
#390, 750, boul Marcel-Laurin
Montréal, QC H4M 2M4 Canada
514-747-2414
Fax: 514-747-3493
Yvon Girard, Partner
New Richmond
189, boul Perron ouest
New Richmond, QC G0C 2B0 Canada
418-392-5001
Fax: 418-392-5171
Michel Bernier, Partner
Ottawa
2505, boul Saint-Laurent
Ottawa, ON K1H 1E4 Canada
613-236-2211
Fax: 613-236-6104
Jean Schnob, Partner
Papineauville
221, rue Papineau
Papineauville, QC J0V 1R0 Canada
819-427-6241
Fax: 819-427-8393
Daniel Couture, Partner
Paspébiac
PO Box 235
104, boul Gérard-D.-Levesque ouest, 2e étage
Paspébiac, QC G0C 2K0 Canada
418-752-5606
Fax: 418-752-6382
Daniel Berthelot, Partner
Québec
#200, 140, Grande-Allée est
Québec, QC G1R 5P7 Canada
418-647-3151
Fax: 418-647-5939
Roger Demers, Partner
Richmond
139, rue Principale nord
Richmond, QC J0B 2H0 Canada
819-826-5559
Fax: 819-826-6616
M. Réjean Desrosiers, Partner
Rimouski
165, av Belzile, 2e étage
Rimouski, QC G5L 8Y2 Canada
418-722-4611
Fax: 418-722-4004
Claude Gauthier, Partner
Rivière-Bleue
37, rue de la Frontière est
Rivière-Bleue, QC G0L 2B0 Canada
418-893-5513
Fax: 418-893-2905
Denis Dionne, Partner
Rivière-du-Loup
300, boul de l'Hôtel-de-Ville
Rivière-du-Loup, QC G5R 5C6 Canada
418-862-6396
Fax: 418-862-3570
Jean Bernier, Partner
Roberval
775, boul Saint-Joseph
Roberval, QC G8H 2L4 Canada
418-275-4790
Fax: 418-275-2458
Marc Levesque, Partner
Rouyn-Noranda
158, rue Mgr. Tessier ouest
Rouyn-Noranda, QC J9X 2S6 Canada
819-762-1714
Fax: 819-762-3306
Jean-Claude Doré, Partner
Saint-Georges
#300, 11505, 1re av
Saint-Georges, QC G5Y 7X3 Canada
418-228-8969
Fax: 418-228-3612
Raymond Poulin, Partner
Saint-Hyacinthe
#2000, 1050, boul Casavant ouest
Saint-Hyacinthe, QC J2S 8B9 Canada
450-773-2424
Fax: 450-773-6363
800-363-5469
Jean Chagnon, Partner
Saint-Jean-Port-Joli
114, av de Gaspé est
Saint-Jean-Port-Joli, QC G0R 3G0 Canada
418-598-3331
Fax: 418-598-3332
Jocelyn Lavoie, Partner
Saint-Pascal
PO Box 576
506, rue Taché
Saint-Pascal, QC G0L 3Y0 Canada
418-492-9606
Fax: 418-492-9606
Jocelyn Lavoie, Partner
Saint-Éphrem
PO Box 2040
#300, 83, rte 108 est
Saint-Éphrem-de-Beauce, QC G0M 1R0 Canada
418-484-5690
Fax: 418-484-2910
Rémi Fortin, Partner
Sainte-Anne-des-Monts
32, rte du Parc
Sainte-Anne-des-Monts, QC G0E 2G0 Canada
418-763-7701
Fax: 418-763-5045
Jacques Gendron, Partner
Sainte-Marie
#216, 1017, boul Vachon nord
Sainte-Marie, QC G6E 1M3 Canada
418-387-3310
Fax: 418-387-7588
Claude Cliche, Partner
Senneterre
PO Box 848
771, 10e av
Senneterre, QC J0Y 2M0 Canada
819-737-2304
Fax: 819-737-2902
Alain Lemaire, Partner
Sherbrooke
#500, 455, rue King ouest
Sherbrooke, QC J1H 6G4 Canada
819-822-4000
Fax: 819-821-3640
M. Réal Y. Létourneau, Partner
Sorel-Tracy
13, rue George
Sorel-Tracy, QC J3P 1B7 Canada
450-742-3746
Fax: 450-742-9356
Serge Perreault, Partner
St-Félicien
#104, 1082, rue Saint-Christophe
St-Félicien, QC G8K 1Z2 Canada
418-679-9442
Fax: 418-679-3436
Marc Levesque, Partner
St-Jean-sur-Richelieu
357, boul du Séminaire nord
St-Jean-sur-Richelieu, QC J3B 8C5 Canada
450-348-6886
Fax: 450-348-3716
Denis Tougas, Partner
St-Joseph-de-Beauce
#201, 875, av du Palais
Saint-Joseph-de-Beauce, QC G0S 2V0 Canada
418-397-5217
Fax: 418-397-4277
Claude Cliche, Partner
Thetford Mines
257, rue Notre-Dame sud, 2e étage
Thetford Mines, QC G6G 1J7 Canada
418-335-7511
Fax: 418-335-2105
Richard Grenier, Partner
Val-d'Or
888, 3e av
Val-d'Or, QC J9P 5E6 Canada
819-825-6226
Fax: 819-825-1461
Mario Thouin, Partner
Waterloo
4796, rue Foster
Waterloo, QC J0E 2N0 Canada
450-539-0575
M. Steve Bernard, Partner
Weedon
241, 2e av
Weedon, QC J0B 3J0 Canada
819-877-2200
Fax: 819-877-3765
François Gosselin, Partner

Rémillard Moquin Nadeau Lebel Ltd. Inc.
#400, 5811, boul Taschereau
Brossard, QC J4Z 1A5
450-676-8585
Fax: 450-676-2202
www.rmnl.qc.ca
Profile: 12 other branches not entered

Executives:
Josée Bourgeois, CIRP
Éric Lebel, CA CIRP
Claude Trudeau, CA, CIRP
Robert Tull, CA, CIRP
Branches:
Boucherville
650, rue de Montbrun
Boucherville, QC J4B 5E4 Canada
450-449-2777
Fax: 514-875-6632
Éric Lebel
Chambly
175, rue Doody
Chambly, QC J3L 1K7 Canada
450-658-9784
Fax: 514-875-6632
Éric Lebel
Châteauguay
85B, boul St-Jean-Baptiste
Châteauguay, QC J6J 3H7 Canada
450-692-4998
Fax: 514-875-6632
Éric Lebel
Laval
300, 2500, boul Daniel-Johnson
Laval, QC H7T 2P6 Canada
450-669-7111
Fax: 450-663-9850
Réjean Bouchard, Contact
Longueuil
300, 370, ch de Chambly
Longueuil, QC J4H 3Z6 Canada
450-679-5510
Fax: 450-679-5511
Christan Bourque
Montréal - Henri-Bourassa
3650, Henri-Bourassa est
Montréal, QC H1H 1J6 Canada
514-325-4804
Fax: 514-875-6632
Robert Tull
Montréal - Marcel Laurin
#390, 750, boul Marcel Laurin
Montréal, QC H4M 2M4 Canada
514-748-6580
Fax: 514- 75-7
Éric Lebel
Montréal - Rachel
#105, 3925, rue Rachel est
Montréal, QC H1X 3G8 Canada
514-255-1003
Fax: 514-875-6632
Éric Lebel
Saint-Hyacinthe
#2001, 1050 boul Casavant ouest
Saint-Hyacinthe, QC J2S 8B9 Canada
450-774-4300
Fax: 450-771-0421
Louis Langevin
St-Jean-sur-Richelieu
357, boul du Séminaire nord
St-Jean-sur-Richelieu, QC J3B 8C5 Canada
450-348-1163
Fax: 450-348-3716
Claude Trudeau

NON-DEPOSITORY INSTITUTIONS

Richard Killen & Associates Ltd.
#402, 2130 Lawrence Ave. East
Toronto, ON M1R 3A6
416-285-9511
Fax: 416-285-9564
howard@rkillen.ca
www.rkillen.ca
Ownership: Private
Year Founded: 1992
Number of Employees: 15
Executives:
Richard Killen, President
Sean Killen, Manager, Systems Operations
Howard Landau, Trustee
Branches:
Brampton
#224, 284 Queen St. East
Brampton, ON L6V 1C2 Canada
905-456-3311
Fax: 905-456-0903
michele@rkillen.ca
Markham
#905, 3100 Steeles Ave. East
Markham, ON L3R 8T3 Canada
905-513-0699
Fax: 905-752-0310
trustee@rkillen.ca
Mississauga
#203, 2155 Leanne Blvd.
Mississauga, ON L5K 2K8 Canada
905-822-1151
Fax: 905-822-2264
sean@rkillen.ca
Toronto - Ellesmere
#113, 2100 Ellesmere Rd.
Toronto, ON M1H 3B7 Canada
416-644-1212
Fax: 416-640-0861
kathy@rkillen.ca

Richter, Allan & Taylor, LLC
#1410, 530 - 8th Ave. SW
Calgary, AB T2P 3S8
403-233-8462
Fax: 403-233-8688
Former Name: Allan & Taylor Inc.
Executives:
J. Stephens Allan, President

Risman Zysman Associates
#218, 1110 Finch Ave. West
Toronto, ON M3J 2T2
416-222-4600
Fax: 416-222-9682
Former Name: Frank Risman Associates (Canada) Ltd.
Executives:
Frank Risman

Robert Rusinek & Associates Inc.
#311, 2401 Eglinton Ave. East
Toronto, ON M1K 2M5
416-288-8048
Fax: 416-288-8429
Number of Employees: 8
Executives:
Robert Rusinek, President/Owner
Branches:
Brampton
#101, 180 Queen St. West
Brampton, ON L6X 1A8 Canada
905-453-4451
Mississauga
#204, 92 Lakeshore Rd. East
Mississauga, ON L5G 4S2 Canada
905-271-6488
Fax: 416-288-8429
Toronto
#215, 1920 Weston Rd.
Toronto, ON M9N 1W4 Canada
416-244-9130
Fax: 416-288-8429

RSM Richter
***Also listed under:** Accountants*
#1820, 2, Place Alexis Nihon
Montréal, QC H3Z 3C2
514-934-3400
Fax: 514-934-3408
mtlinfo@rsmrichter.com
www.richter.ca
Former Name: Richter Usher & Vineberg
Ownership: Private
Year Founded: 1926
Number of Employees: 120
Profile: Aboriginal advisory services, audit, corporate finance, financial reorganization, management consulting, professional search, risk management, tax, valuations & litigation support, and wealth management services are provided.
Principals:
Debbie Di Gregorio; ddigregorio@rsmrichter.com
Dimitra Glekas; dglekas@rsmrichter.com
Suzanne Grant; sgrant@rsmrichter.com
Leon Krantzberg; lkrantzberg@rsmrichter.com
Jeff Rowles; jrowles@rsmrichter.com
Barry Steinberg; bsteinberg@rsmrichter.com
Branches:
Calgary
#910, 736 - 8th Ave. SW
Calgary, AB T2P 1H4 Canada
403-206-0840
Fax: 403-206-0841
cgyinfo@rsmrichter.com
Toronto - King St.
#1100, 200 King St. West
Toronto, ON M5H 3T4 Canada
416-932-8000
Fax: 416-932-6200
torinfo@rsmrichter.com
John Swidler, Sr. Partner

St-Georges, Hébert Inc.
401, boul St-Joseph est
Montréal, QC H2J 1J6
514-844-1044
Fax: 514-844-5916
Executives:
Jean Guy St-Georges

Salyzyn & Associates Limited
#3, 833 Sackville Dr.
Lower Sackville, NS B4E 1S1
902-865-5444
Fax: 902-865-2228
877-216-5800
info@bankruptcyinfo.ca
www.bankruptcyinfo.ca
Number of Employees: 5
Executives:
Leanne Salyzyn
Michael A. Salyzyn
Branches:
Dartmouth
1038 Cole Harbour Rd.
Dartmouth, NS B2V 1E7 Canada
902-435-0338
Fax: 902-435-0817
Kentville
Cornwallis Inn
325 Main St.
Kentville, NS B4N 1K5 Canada
902-678-7900
Fax: 902-678-2228

Sam Lévy & associés inc
#926, 276, rue St-Jacques ouest
Montréal, QC H2Y 1N3
514-282-9999
Fax: 514-282-6607
Year Founded: 1994
Executives:
Samuel S. Lévy, President

Sands & Associates
#410, 1100 Melville St.
Vancouver, BC V6E 4A6
604-684-3030
Fax: 604-684-7277
Other Information: 1-800-661-3030 (Toll Free in BC)
trustee@sands-trustee.com
www.sands-trustee.com
Year Founded: 1990
Number of Employees: 20
Executives:
Gerard T. Foran, President, Trustee; gforan@sands-trustee.com
Bruce Gandossi, Trustee; bgandossi@sands-trustee.com
Tracey Lowe, Trustee; tlowe@sands-trustee.com
Cindy Wallas, Estate Manager; cwallas@sands-trustee.com
Branches:
Abbotsford
Clearbrook Shopping Centre
#316, 31935 South Fraser Way
Abbotsford, BC V2T 1V5 Canada
604-864-5799
Fax: 604-864-5797
Burnaby
#302, 5050 Kingsway
Burnaby, BC V5H 4H2 Canada
604-451-5799
Fax: 604-451-9636
Chilliwack
7105 Vedder Rd.
Chilliwack, BC V2R 4G3 Canada
604-824-5794
Fax: 604-824-5797
Langley
#205, 20651 - 56th Ave.
Langley, BC V3A 3Y9 Canada
604-539-0200
Fax: 604-539-0201
Surrey
#203, 10366 - 136A St.
Surrey, BC V3T 5R3 Canada
604-583-5499
Fax: 604-583-0797

Schonfeld Inc.
220 Bay St., 9th Fl.
Toronto, ON M5J 2W4
416-862-7785
Fax: 416-862-2136
info@schonfeldinc.com
www.schonfeldinc.com
Year Founded: 1999
Number of Employees: 2
Executives:
S. Harlan Schonfeld, Principal
Jim Merryweather, Principal

Schwartz Levitsky Feldman LLP(SLF)
***Also listed under:** Accountants*
1980, rue Sherbrooke ouest, 10e étage
Montréal, QC H3H 1E8
514-937-6392
Fax: 514-933-9710
www.slf.ca
Ownership: Private
Year Founded: 1960
Number of Employees: 142
Assets: $5-10 million
Revenues: $10-50 million
Profile: Provides a wide range of advisory services, including corporate finance, mergers & acquisitions, and management consulting.
Partners:
Hashim Ali, CA; 514-788-5634; hashim.ali@slf.ca
Luciano D'Ignazio, CA; 514-788-5613; luciano.dignazio@slf.ca
Harry H. Feldman, CA; 514-788-5604; harry.feldman@slf.ca
Peter H. Feldman, CA; 514-788-5609; peter.feldman@slf.ca
Bernard Jeanty; 514-788-5614; bernard.jeanty@slf.ca
Morty B. Lober, CA; 514-788-5603; morty.lober@slf.ca
Alain Mamane; 514-788-5619; alain.mamane@slf.ca
David Perlin, CA; 514-788-5607; david.perlin@slf.ca
Bill Reim; 514-788-5615; bill.reim@slf.ca
Leonard Sitcoff, CA; 514-788-5611; leonard.sitcoff@slf.ca
Sylvain Tellier; 514-788-5601; sylvain.tellier@slf.ca
Jason Yudcovitch; 514-788-5623; jason.yudcovitch@slf.ca
Offices:
Toronto
1167 Caledonia Rd.
Toronto, ON M6A 2X1 Canada
416-785-5353
Fax: 416-785-5663
Kai Chang

Scott & Pichelli Ltd.
***Also listed under:** Accountants*

#109, 3600 Billings Ct.
Burlington, ON L7N 3N6
905-632-5853
Fax: 905-632-6113
www.bankruptcy-trustees.ca/
Former Name: Scott, Pichelli & Graci Ltd., Scott, Pichelli & Arvanitis Ltd.
Ownership: Private
Year Founded: 1980

Segal & Partners Inc.
***Also listed under:** Accountants*
#500, 2005 Sheppard Ave. East
Toronto, ON M2J 5B4
416-391-1460
Fax: 416-391-2285
800-206-7307
info@segalpartners.com
www.segalbankruptcy.com
Ownership: Private
Branches:
Mississauga
#212, 1310 Dundas St. East
Mississauga, ON L4Y 2C1 Canada
Toronto - Bathurst St.
#318, 3768 Bathurst St.
Toronto, ON M3H 1M1 Canada
Toronto - Danforth Ave.
#301, 2179 Danforth Ave.
Toronto, ON M4C 1K4 Canada

Serge Morency et Associés Inc.
#100, 895, boul Charest ouest
Québec, QC G1N 2C9
418-650-2000
Fax: 418-650-2010
800-565-2050

Shimmerman Penn LLP
#400, 30 St. Clair Ave. West
Toronto, ON M4V 3A1
416-964-7200
Fax: 416-964-2025
info@spllp.com
www.spllp.com
Former Name: Shimmerman Penn Title & Associates Inc.
Ownership: Member of Nexia International
Year Founded: 1979
Executives:
Hy Penn, CFP, Managing Partner; hpenn@spllp.com
Irwin Choleva, CA, Partner, Assurance & Business Advisory; icholeva@spllp.com
Doug Hartkorn, CA, MBA, CFP, Partner, Taxation & Business Advisory; dhartkorn@spllp.com
Geoff Kritzinger, CA, Partner, Assurance & Business Advisory; gkritzinger@spllp.com
Sheldon Title, CA, CIRP, Partner, Corporate Recovery & Insolvency; stitle@spllp.com
Maj-Lis Vettoretti, CA, Partner, Assurance & Business Advisory; mvettoretti@spllp.com
Elaine Pantel, CGA, Principal, Assurance & Business Advisory; epantel@spllp.com

Shiner Kideckel Zweig Inc.
#4, 10 West Pearce St.
Richmond Hill, ON L4B 1B6
905-763-2436
Fax: 905-709-9952
800-641-8698
info@skz.ca
www.skz.ca
Ownership: Private
Year Founded: 1999
Number of Employees: 18
Revenues: $1-5 million
Executives:
Alan Shiner, President; 905-709-9950; ashiner@skz.ca

Smith Cageorge Bailey, Inc.
#700, 550 - 11 Ave. SW
Calgary, AB T2R 1M7
403-261-7779
Fax: 403-262-3917
877-806-2918
sbailey@bankruptcy.ab.ca
www.bankruptcy.ab.ca
Year Founded: 1998
Number of Employees: 4
Profile: The company assists individuals & businesses in Alberta. Services include debt counselling, creditor negotiations, consumer proposals, personal bankruptcy & corporate insolvencies.
Executives:
Senga Bailey, Managing Partner
Branches:
Banff
Wolf & Bear Mall
229 Bear St.
Banff, AB T0L 0C0 Canada
403-762-4488
Fax: 403-762-8581
877-762-8581
sbailey@bankruptcy.ab.ca
Canmore
#202, 502 Bow Valley Trail
Canmore, AB T1W 1N9 Canada
403-609-9213
Fax: 403-609-9214
877-806-2918
sbailey@bankruptcy.ab.ca
Drumheller
196 - 3 Ave. West
Drumheller, AB T0J 0Y0 Canada
403-823-1212
Fax: 403-823-1213
877-806-2918
sbailey@bankruptcy.ab.ca

Soberman LLP Chartered Accountants
***Also listed under:** Accountants*
#1100, 2 St. Clair Ave. East
Toronto, ON M4T 2T5
416-964-7633
Fax: 416-964-6454
info@soberman.com
www.soberman.com
Ownership: Private.
Year Founded: 1958
Number of Employees: 125+
Revenues: $10-50 million
Profile: The firm provides services in accounting, auditing, business valuation, corporate & personal bankruptcy, corporate finance, corporate workout & turnaround strategies, due diligence, ElderCare, estates & trusts, financial consulting, forensic investigation litigation support, management services, mergers & acquisitions, succession planning & tax (domestic & international), claims valuation & media services. Affiliates include Soberman Isenbaum Colomby Tessis Inc. & Soberman Due Diligence Inc.
Partners:
Eric Bornstein, Managing Partner; 416-963-7100
Martin Starr, Principal; 416-963-7119
Don Borts; 416-963-7101
Jerry Cukier; 416-963-7104
Rukshana Dinshaw; 416-963-7190
Daniel M. Edwards; 416-963-7221
Larry Goldstein; 416-963-7197
Dirk Joustra; 416-963-7110
Sam Kaner; 416-963-7111
Gary Kopstick; 416-963-7113
Des Levin; 416-963-7115
Karyn Lipman; 416-963-7159
Neil L. Maisel; 416-963-7116
Eli Palachi; 416-963-7123
Paul Rhodes; 416-963-7217
Adam Rubinoff; 416-963-7178
Karen Slezak; 416-963-7109
Deborah E. Stern; 416-963-7103
Ken Tessis; 416-963-7120
Alan Wainer; 416-963-7121
Sam Zuk; 416-963-7122

Soberman Tessis Inc.
#1000, 2 St. Clair Ave. East
Toronto, ON M4T 2T5
416-964-7633
Fax: 416-964-6454
info@soberman.com
www.soberman.com
Former Name: Silverman Tessis Inc
Executives:
Kenneth M. Tessis, President

Solange Chapuis & Associés
#2230, 2020, rue University
Montréal, QC H3A 2A5
514-842-8515
Fax: 514-842-8624
chapuis@total.net
www.syndics-chapuis.com
Ownership: Private
Year Founded: 1984
Executives:
Solange Chapuis

Stern Cohen Shier Inc.
#1400, 45 St. Clair Ave. West
Toronto, ON M4V 1L3
416-967-5100
Fax: 416-967-4372
contact@sterncohen.com
www.sterncohen.com
Former Name: Stern Cohen Shier Inc.; Alvin P. Rice Inc.
Ownership: Private
Partners:
Robert P. Baines
Harold Balderson
Paul Carroll
Marvin Cohen
Ann Galvin
James Horne
Lorne Lobow
Robert Masching
Michael McCleave
Keith Rosen
Robert Shier
Leonard Weinstein
Peter Weinstein
Graham Williams

Surgeson Carson Associates Inc.
***Also listed under:** Accountants*
#18, 99 Fifth Ave.
Ottawa, ON K1S 5K4
613-567-6434
Fax: 613-567-0752
questions@surgesoncarson.com
www.surgesoncarson.com
Number of Employees: 7
Executives:
Michael K. Carson, Trustee; mcarson@surgesoncarson.com
Kevin L. McCart, Trustee; kmccart@surgesoncarson.com
Richard Surgeson, Trustee; rsurgeson@surgesoncarson.com

T. Carleton & Co. Inc.
#1002, 74 Cedar Point Dr.
Barrie, ON L4N 5R7
705-734-1148
Fax: 705-734-2758
800-268-1847
Year Founded: 1983
Number of Employees: 4
Assets: $1-5 million
Revenues: Under $1 million
Executives:
T.J. Carleton, President
Branches:
Toronto - Lakeshore
#1, 2851 Lakeshore Blvd. West
Toronto, ON M8V 1H8 Canada
416-253-9966
Fax: 416-657-8507
800-268-1847
Toronto - St. Clair
#2, 1267A St. Clair Ave. West
Toronto, ON M6E 1B8 Canada
416-657-8866
Fax: 416-657-8507
Toronto - Town Centre
#700, 55 Town Centre Ct.
Toronto, ON M1P 4X4 Canada
416-296-8878

Taylor Leibow LLP, Accountants & Advisors
***Also listed under:** Accountants*
#700, 105 Main St. East
Hamilton, ON L8N 1G6

NON-DEPOSITORY INSTITUTIONS

Taylor Leibow LLP, Accountants & Advisors (continued)
905-523-0000
Fax: 905-523-4681
888-287-2525
info@taylorleibow.com
www.taylorleibow.com
Year Founded: 1947
Number of Employees: 60+
Executives:
Nigel Jacobs, CEO
Stephen Wiseman, Sr. Partner
Peter Cross, Partner
Branches:
Brantford
#403, 333 Colborne St.
Brantford, ON N3T 2H4 Canada
519-753-7361
Fax: 519-753-1711
Burlington
3410 South Service Rd., 1st Fl.
Burlington, ON L7N 3T2 Canada
905-637-9959
Fax: 905-637-3195
St Catharines
#604, 43 Church St.
St Catharines, ON L2R 7E1 Canada
905-680-4728
Fax: 905-523-2979

Tremblay & Cie Ltée Syndics et Gestionnaires
582, boul Saguenay est
Chicoutimi, QC G7H 1L2
418-549-5642
Fax: 418-549-5829
ftremblay@tremblaycie.com
www.tremblaycie.com
Ownership: Private
Year Founded: 1962
Number of Employees: 10
Executives:
Fabien Tremblay
Branches:
Alma
#102, 420, rue Collard ouest
Alma, QC G8B 1N2 Canada
418-662-5657
Fax: 418-668-7903
Roberval
#207, 755, boul St-Joseph
Roberval, QC G8H 2L4 Canada
418-275-5626
Fax: 418-275-6375

Vine & Williams Inc.
945 King St. East
Hamilton, ON L8M 1C1
905-549-8463
Fax: 905-549-6020
henryv@vine.on.ca
www.vineandwilliams.com
Year Founded: 1965
Profile: Services provided include funancial consulting, personal & corporate bankruptcies, consumer proposals, and receiverships.

Executives:
Henry Vine, Sr. Partner
Walter Williams, Sr. Partner
Leslie Mitchnick, Associate
Branches:
Burlington
#306, 720 Guelph Line
Burlington, ON L7R 4E2 Canada
905-332-4055
Hamilton
#222, 845 Upper James St.
Hamilton, ON L9C 3A3 Canada
905-383-5770
Stoney Creek
#208, 115 Hwy. #8
Stoney Creek, ON L8G 1C1 Canada
905-662-5936

Wasserman Limited
#2250, 5140 Yonge St.
Toronto, ON M2N 6L7
416-226-4631
Fax: 416-226-9562

Wasserman Stotland Bratt Grossbaum
#2010, 1155, boul René-Lévesque ouest
Montréal, QC H3B 2J8
514-861-9724
Fax: 514-861-9446
wsbg@wsbg.com
www.wsbg.com
Former Name: Wasserman Stotland Bratt Grossbaum & Pinsky Inc.
Ownership: Private
Year Founded: 1964
Number of Employees: 48
Executives:
Nathan Bratt, Contact
Louis Grossbaun, Contact
Bernard Stotland, Contact

Willis Associates
***Also listed under:** Financial Planning; Accounting & Law*
#100, 2903 - 35th Ave.
Vernon, BC V1T 2S7
250-549-2922
Fax: 250-542-8300
888-333-2922
www.willisassociates.ca
Profile: The following services are provided: accounting, assurance & taxation; insolvency; executor & trustee services; personal financial planning; fraud examination; as well as special engagements.

Executives:
David Patrick Willis, Chartered Accountant; Dave.Williams@willisassociates.ca

Wolrige Mahon Limited
#900, 400 Burrard St.
Vancouver, BC V6C 3B7
604-684-6212
Fax: 604-688-3497
email@wolrigemahon.com
www.wolrigemahon.com
Number of Employees: 60
Partners:
Mike Cheevers
Paul Gaster
Warren Gfeller
Armando Maglio
Alex McCready
Jes Raagner
Donald C. Selman
John Smiley
Gregg W. Smith
Paul Swinton

Young Parkyn McNab LLP(YPM)
***Also listed under:** Accountants*
#100, 530 - 8 St. South
Lethbridge, AB T1J 2J8
403-382-6800
Fax: 403-327-8990
800-665-5034
www.ypm.ca
Ownership: Private
Year Founded: 1933
Number of Employees: 75
Profile: Services include the following: agricultural; audit; bookkeeping & year-end; business advisory; business start-up; corporate finance; family-owned business; fraud prevention & forensic; information systems & technology; personal services; valuations & litigation.

Partners:
Harvey V. Labuhn; harvey.labuhn@ypm.ca
Ernie R. Lawson; ernie.lawson@ypm.ca
Thomas McNab; tom.mcnab@ypm.ca
Doug B. Mundell; doug.mundell@ypm.ca
Bob Rice; bob.rice@ypm.ca
George G. Virtue; george.virtue@ypm.ca
Branches:
Claresholm
4902 - 2nd St. West
Claresholm, AB T0L 0T0 Canada
403-625-4448
Fax: 403-625-4400
Fort MacLeod
PO Box 1780
2315 - 2 Ave.
Fort MacLeod, AB T0L 0Z0 Canada
403-553-3355
Fax: 403-553-2696
Jim S. Monteith, Partner
Milk River
125 Main St. NW
Milk River, AB T0K 1M0 Canada
403-647-3662
Fax: 403-647-3868
877-616-6064

Pincher Creek
710 Main St.
Pincher Creek, AB T0K 1W0 Canada
403-627-5510
Fax: 403-627-1440
Taber
5334 - 49th Ave.
Taber, AB T1G 1T8 Canada
403-223-0056
Fax: 403-223-0059
877-616-6064
bryce.bennett@ypm.ca
Bryce Bennett, Partner

Zwaig Consulting Inc.
***Also listed under:** Accountants*
#801, 20 Adelaide St. East
Toronto, ON M5X 2T6
416-863-0140
Fax: 416-863-0428
zwaigm@zwaig.com
www.zwaig.com
Ownership: Private.
Year Founded: 1998
Number of Employees: 20
Assets: $1-5 million Year End: 20060930
Revenues: $1-5 million Year End: 20060930
Profile: Financial restructuring & forensic accounting services are offered. The company is affiliated with Zwaig Associates, Inc.

Executives:
Melvin C. Zwaig, President/CEO; 416-863-5795; zwaigm@zwaig.com
Robert Cumming, Vice-President; cummingr@zwaig.com
Cameron A. McCaw, Vice-President; mccawc@zweig.com
John P. Curran, Counsel; curranj@zwaig.com

SECTION 3

Investment Management

Included in this section:

This section lists all those companies which use capital to invest in other firms or offer investment services or advice for a fee.

Financial Planning & Investment Management Companies include independent financial planners, financial corporations offering planning services to individual and corporate clients, retirement and estate planners, tax planners, and investment counsellors.

Holding & Other Investment Companies include firms whose function is to hold investments of other corporations. Also included are other investment companies, which invest in a portfolio of securities and other investments. Management of corporations is generally not their intention. This sub-section includes closed-end funds and trusts.

Investment Dealers include securities firms, which may also be a member of one or more of the country's stock exchanges. In addition to the address, communications and personnel information, membership on any of Canada's stock exchanges is also indicated.

Investment Fund Companies are organized alphabetically by firm name and listings contain the names of funds offered. The types of funds listed include mutual funds, pooled funds, and segregated funds. For many funds, information is provided regarding RRSP eligibility, inception date and fund managers.

Pension & Money Management Companies include pension fund managers and investment fund managers.

Stock Exchanges include details on Canada's exchanges (Canadian Trading & Quotation System, Inc., Canadian Unlisted Board, Montréal Exchange, Natural Gas Exchange Inc., NEX Board, Toronto Stock Exchange, TSX Venture Exchange, Winnipeg Commodity Exchange Inc.). The exchange member firms and participating organizations are listed alphabetically. Full listings of member firms are found in their respective sections in the directory.

Investment Management

Financial Planning

A.D. Vacca & Associates Financial Planning Group
333 Queenston Rd.
Hamilton, ON L8K 1H7
905-549-7526
Fax: 905-549-4274
866-406-7526
info@advacca.com
www.advacca.com
Ownership: Private
Number of Employees: 5
Assets: $5-10 million
Executives:
Armando Vacca, CFP, RFP, Owner
Dominic Agresta, Planner
Robert McCulloch, Planner
Lori Vacca, Planner, Manager

A.G. Leck Financial Consultants
156 MacLean St.
New Glasgow, NS B2H 5V5
902-752-2343
Fax: 902-755-2588
agleck@ns.sympatico.ca
www.leckfinancial.com
Executives:
Alan Leck

Abbott Financial Services Inc.
#201, 805 Notre Dame Dr.
Kamloops, BC V2C 5N8
250-372-3736
Fax: 250-372-7527
Executives:
Carl W. Abbott

ABN AMRO Asset Management Canada Limited
Toronto-Dominion Centre
PO Box 114, T-D Centre Stn. T-D Centre
#1500, 79 Wellington St. West
Toronto, ON M5K 2G8
416-365-6785
Fax: 416-365-2945
www.aaam.abnamro.ca
Year Founded: 1998
Profile: The company offers investment management capabilities to Canadian-based instiutional investors. Services for Canadian pension funds, First Nations trusts, charitable funds & other institutional investors include pooled funds & segregated mandates. Sub-advisory services are available to Canadian insurancecompanies closed-end funds, mutual fund companies & other providers of investment products.

Acker Finley Inc.
Also listed under: *Investment Fund Companies*
#1361, 181 University Ave.
Toronto, ON M5H 3M7
416-777-9005
Fax: 416-777-2096
success@ackerfinley.com
www.ackerfinley.com
Ownership: Private
Year Founded: 1992
Stock Exchange Membership: Toronto Stock Exchange
Executives:
Brian G. Acker, President/CEO; brian@ackerfinley.com
Joseph C. Finley, CFO & Managing Director; joseph@ackerfinley.com
Enrico Sgromo, Vice-President, Research; enrico@ackerfinley.com
Brenda Tilley, Vice-President, Private Clients; brenda@ackerfinley.com
Michelle Bain, FMA, Investment Advisor
Acker Finley:
QSA Select Canada Focus Fund
RRSP Eligible; Inception Year: 2004;
QSA Canada Focus Fund
RRSP Eligible; Inception Year: 2004;
QSA Select US Value 50 Fund
RRSP Eligible; Inception Year: 2003;

Acumen Capital Finance Partners Limited
Also listed under: *Investment Dealers*
#200, 513 - 8th Ave. SW
Calgary, AB T2P 1G3
403-571-0300
Fax: 403-571-0310
888-422-8636
info@acumencapital.com
www.acumencapital.com
Ownership: Private
Year Founded: 1995
Number of Employees: 27
Stock Exchange Membership: Toronto Stock Exchange, TSX Venture Exchange
Profile: Full service investment dealer.
Executives:
Brian D. Parker, CEO/President, Institutional Sales
Myja Miller, CFO, Chief Compliance Officer
C. Michael Stuart, Chair & Vice-President, Investment Banking
Douglas Gowland, Vice-President, Institutional Sales
Robert Laidlaw, Vice-President, Sr. Investment Advisor, Retail
Sheldon Le Lievre, Vice-President, Sr. Investment Advisor
Curtis Mayert, Vice-President, Sr. Investment Advisor
Brian D. Pow, Vice-President, Research
James A. Rothwell, Vice-President, Sr. Investment Advisor
Alfred Sailer, Vice-President, Investment Banking
James M.B. Welykocky, Vice-President, Oil & Gas

Adams Redding Wooley
Also listed under: *Pension & Money Management Companies; Accounting & Law*
824 - 1st St. South
Cranbrook, BC V1C 7H5
250-426-8277
Fax: 250-426-4109
mail@cgafirm.com
www.cgafirm.com
Former Name: Adams Redding & Co.; Adams, Brock, Redding & Co.
Ownership: Private
Year Founded: 1968
Number of Employees: 9
Executives:
David M. Adams, B.Sc., CGA, CFP
Brian F. Adams, FCGA
Alan Redding, B.Comm, CGA, CFP
James R. Wooley, BPE, CGA

AEGON Dealer Services Canada Inc.
Also listed under: *Pension & Money Management Companies*
5000 Yonge St.
Toronto, ON M2N 7J8
416-883-5744
Fax: 416-883-5737
800-561-3643
adsci-marketing@aegoncanada.ca
www.moneyconcepts.ca
Former Name: Money Concepts (Canada) Limited
Ownership: Private
Year Founded: 1984
Number of Employees: 40
Offices:
100 Mile House
385 S. Cedar Ave.
100 Mile House, BC V0K 2E0 Canada
250-395-2900
Fax: 250-395-2977
Judy Simkins, Contact
Barrie
35 Worsley St.
Barrie, ON L4M 1L7 Canada
705-722-3604
Fax: 705-727-7618
askdavid@financialplanning.on.ca
David H. Karas, President
Bedford
1356 Bedford Hwy.
Bedford, NS B4A 1E2 Canada
902-835-8822
Fax: 902-835-6632
Neal Gaudet
Brampton
3147 Mayfield Rd.
Brampton, ON L6Z 4PG Canada
905-584-4903
Fax: 905-584-4904
George Leoffler
Burnaby
3823 Henning Dr.
Burnaby, BC V5C 6P3 Canada
604-436-0088
Fax: 604-436-3630
Jeffrey P. Chin
Chilliwack
#106, 8645 Young St.
Chilliwack, BC V2P 4P3 Canada
604-795-4505
Fax: 604-795-4816
Paul Jackson
Cobourg
21 Buck St.
Cobourg, ON K9A 2L1 Canada
905-373-0300
Fax: 905-373-0302
Noel Milner
Coquitlam
#211, 3030 Lincoln Ave.
Coquitlam, BC V3B 6B4 Canada
604-945-7212
Fax: 604-941-4816
Maureen Cheung
Dartmouth
#204, 171 Main St.
Dartmouth, NS B2X 1S1 Canada
902-463-6063
Fax: 902-461-9172
mcbrice@ns.aliantzinc.ca
Brice Guerin
Fort St. John
10067 - 100 Ave.
Fort St John, BC V1J 1Y7 Canada
250-785-7566
Fax: 250-785-7546
Robert Leer
Fredericton
335 Queen St.
Fredericton, NB E3B 1B1 Canada
506-454-9135
Fax: 506-454-9137
Roland Porter, Contact
Gloucester
#3, 5330 Canotek Rd.
Gloucester, ON K1J 9C1 Canada
613-742-5471
Fax: 613-742-5466
Wally Morris
Grand Falls
#101, 166 Broadway
Grand Falls, NB E3Z 2J9 Canada
506-473-3838
Fax: 506-473-9898
moneycpt@nbnet.nb.ca
Martin Theriault
Guelph
320 Eramosa Rd.
Guelph, ON N1E 2M8 Canada
519-824-7554
Fax: 519-824-8837
dwilson@mc.ca
Pierre Brianceau, Contact
Kanata
101 Schneider Rd.
Kanata, ON K2K 1Y3 Canada

AEGON Dealer Services Canada Inc. (continued)

613-599-5477
Fax: 613-599-5478
info@mckanata.com
www.moneyconceptskanata.biz
Zul Devji, Executive Vice President

Kelowna
712 Bernard Ave.
Kelowna, BC V1Y 6P5 Canada
250-860-1733
Fax: 250-860-0177
888-860-1707
www.kelownamoney.com/
Bruce Adams

Langley
#202, 20316 - 56 Ave.
Langley, BC V3A 3Y7 Canada
604-533-7294
Fax: 604-533-7218
Rob Warren

London
118 Inverary Cresc.
London, ON N6G 3L8 Canada
519-473-7949
Fax: 519-473-7949
Ralph Kemme

Markham
#201, 7240 Woodbine Ave.
Markham, ON L3R 1A4 Canada
416-410-6669
Fax: 905-513-8176
866-868-6669
amarchao@adsci
Anthony S. Marchao

Miramichi
1808 Water St.
Miramichi, NB E1N 1B6 Canada
506-778-8446
Fax: 506-778-8459
Lowell Loveday

Mississauga
62 Queen St. South
Mississauga, ON L5M 1K4 Canada
905-286-1334
Fax: 905-286-1335
www.privatewealthmanagement.ca/
Rob Sylvester

Napanee
164 John St.
Napanee, ON K7R 1R5 Canada
613-354-2197
Fax: 613-354-6861
mconcept@ihorizons.net
Frank E. Streek

Nelson
#3, 373 Baker St.
Nelson, BC V1L 4H6 Canada
250-354-1822
Fax: 250-354-1788
dlehr@netidea.com
Duane Lehr, Contact

Nepean
39 Robertson Rd.
Nepean, ON K2H 8R2 Canada
613-828-4423
Fax: 613-828-4337
Tony Valle

Newcastle
37 King St. West
Newcastle, ON L1B 1H2 Canada
905-987-1631
Fax: 905-987-9809
John Bugelli

Oakville
112 Wilson St.
Oakville, ON L6K 3G6 Canada
905-844-3258
Fax: 905-844-4425
mcoakville@on.aibn.com
William L. Maynes

Orangeville
78 Broadway
Orangeville, ON L9W 1J9 Canada
519-942-2555
Fax: 519-942-1845
888-265-6669
Lisa Leblanc

Oshawa
158 Centre St. South
Oshawa, ON L1H 4A4 Canada
905-723-5745
Fax: 905-725-1060
John Hughes, Branch Manager

Ottawa - St. Laurent Blvd.
1725 St. Laurent Blvd.
Ottawa, ON K1G 3V4 Canada
613-834-3588
Fax: 613-834-8199
Mahmoud Visanji

Penticton
626 Martin St.
Penticton, BC V2A 5L6 Canada
250-490-8369
Fax: 250-490-9680
Laurie Sylvester

Peterborough - King St.
223 King St.
Peterborough, ON K9J 2R8 Canada
705-876-6086
Fax: 705-876-7882
Robert (Bob) MacLeod

Peterborough - Water St.
441 Water St., 2nd Fl.
Peterborough, ON K9H 3M2 Canada
705-740-0110
Fax: 705-740-9048
invest@moneyconceptspeterborough.com
Lloyd Spiers

Pickering
1410 Bayly St.
Pickering, ON L1W 3R3 Canada
905-421-9442
Fax: 905-421-9507
Timothy Kellar

Prescott
PO Box 2767
124 King St. West
Prescott, ON K0E 1T0 Canada
613-925-4626
Fax: 613-925-1063
dthroop@moneyconcepts.ca
Graham Cudlipp

Prince George
Penthouse
770 Brunswick St.
Prince George, BC V2L 2C2 Canada
250-563-0777
Fax: 250-564-9195
allanjohnson@moneyconcepts.ca
Allan Johnson

Prince George
#406, 550 Victoria St.
Prince George, BC V2L 2K1 Canada
250-564-7484
Fax: 250-564-7490
www.moneyconceptspg.bc.ca
Peter Tiani

Renfrew
274 Raglan St. South
Renfrew, ON K7V 1R4 Canada
613-432-5617
Fax: 613-432-2051
www.moneyconceptsov.com
John Wilson

Richmond
13451 Gilbert Rd.
Richmond, BC V7E 2H8 Canada
604-274-8822
Fax: 604-274-8881
www.peterlefeaux.com/
Peter Lefeaux

Richmond Hill
#204, 10825 Yonge St.
Richmond Hill, ON L4C 3E4 Canada
905-737-7777
Fax: 905-737-7348
Sharad N. Kothari

Richmond Hill - Yonge St.
#304, 9050 Yonge St.
Richmond Hill, ON L4C 9S6 Canada
905-731-7761
Fax: 905-886-5648
rpollock@moneyconcepts.ca
R.C. (Bob) Pollock

Russell
191 Castor St.
Russell, ON K4R 1E1 Canada
613-445-8624
Fax: 613-445-8626
www.moneyconceptsrv.com
Theresa Wever

Saint John
199 Westmorland Rd.
Saint John, NB E2J 2E9 Canada
506-633-5944
Fax: 506-634-6702
kkillamb@nbnet.nb.ca
Kim Killam Brown

St Catharines
5 Race St.
St Catharines, ON L2R 3M1 Canada
905-684-3332
Fax: 905-684-3352
Al Teeter

Summerside
Dominion Sq. Bldg.
250 Water St., 2nd Fl.
Summerside, PE C1N 1B6 Canada
902-436-4988
Brian Ramsay, Branch Manager

Toronto - Sheppard Ave. East
#304, 3410 Sheppard Ave. East
Toronto, ON M1T 3K4 Canada
416-293-4579
Fax: 416-293-4578
Devinder Sohi

Trail
1142 Cedar Ave.
Trail, BC V1R 4B7 Canada
250-364-0050
Wayne Miller, Branch Manager

Unionville
41 Main St. South
Unionville, ON L3R 2E5 Canada
905-940-4919
Fax: 905-940-0780
don@moneyconceptsunionville.com
Don Esber

Vancouver
#960, 1050 West Pender St.
Vancouver, BC V6E 3S7 Canada
604-801-6621
Fax: 604-801-6632
Al Ferguson

Vankleek Hill
116 Main St. East
Vankleek Hill, ON K0B 1R0 Canada
613-678-3861
Fax: 613-678-3669
www.moneyconceptsrv.com
Theresa Wever

Vernon
3200 - 27 St.
Vernon, BC V1T 4W7 Canada
250-542-7181
Fax: 250-542-7181
Les Fresorger

Victoria
1480 Fort St.
Victoria, BC V8S 1Z5 Canada
250-475-3698
Fax: 250-475-3697
mc.vic@moneyconcepts.ca
Tom McLean

Waterloo
#201, 30 Dupont St. East
Waterloo, ON N2J 2G9 Canada
519-886-7300
Fax: 519-886-7086
Michael Ellis

Whitby
#20, 10 Sunray St.
Whitby, ON L1N 9B5 Canada
905-430-4651
Fax: 905-430-3243

dmcculloch@moneyconcepts.ca
www.financialplanningontario.com/
Debbie McCulloch
Winnipeg
5204 Roblin Blvd.
Winnipeg, MB Canada
204-832-9148
Fax: 204-896-5907
www.money-mgmt.com/
Edward L. Thompson

Affinitas
#205, 660 Speedvale Ave. West
Guelph, ON N1K 1E5
519-837-2059
Fax: 519-837-0545
877-899-2194
info@affinitas.ca
www.affinitas.ca
Former Name: Robert J. Green & Associates
Year Founded: 1978
Profile: The risk management consulting firm provides the following services: retirement financial consultation, investment & strategic management planning, life & health insurance, & employee benefits.
Executives:
Sonia Spekkens, CSC, CPH, PFP, WMT, FMA, Manager, Retirement & Legacy Planner
Robert J. Green, CLU, CFP, Benefits Consultant, Financial Advisor
Fred Quinton, B.A., CEB, Consultant, Group Benefits
Allan Smofsky, Consultant
Branches:
Kitchener
25 Irvin St.
Kitchener, ON N2H 1K6
519-837-2059
Fax: 518-839-2194
877-899-2194
Mississauga
#303, 117 Lakeshore Rd. East
Mississauga, ON L5G 4T6
905-337-7416
Fax: 905-337-7418
877-899-2194

The Affolter Financial Group Inc.
1127 - 4th St.
Castlegar, BC V1N 2A8
250-365-2345
Fax: 250-365-3476
888-365-4888
info@affolterfinancial.com
www.affolterfinancial.com
Executives:
Tim Affolter, President
Debbie Pereversoff, Vice-President

AFT Trivest Management Inc.
2227 Folkestone Way
West Vancouver, BC V7S 2Y6
604-925-3041
Fax: 604-925-3045
trivest@nilsonco.com
www.nilsonco.com
Executives:
Don Nilson, Owner
Diane Lefeaux, Manager

AGF Private Investment Management Limited
***Also listed under:** Pension & Money Management Companies*
Toronto-Dominion Bank Tower
66 Wellington St. West, 31st Fl.
Toronto, ON M5K 1E9
416-865-4296
Fax: 416-367-4807
888-216-4424
www.agf.com
Also Known As: AGF PIM
Ownership: Public. Wholly owned subsidiary of AGF Management Ltd.
Executives:
Blake C. Goldring, Chair/CEO
Rob Badun, President
Lorne Steinberg, Chief Investment Officer
Peter Rawson, Vice-President & Portfolio Manager
Robert Bard, Managing Director
Lloyd Goldstein, Managing Director
David Andrews, Director, Investments
Mario Bourdon, Investment Counsellor
Natalie Circelli, Investment Counsellor
Affiliated Companies:
Cypress Capital Management Ltd.
Magna Vista Investment Management
P.J. Doherty & Associates Co. Ltd.

Ahsan Financial
354 Queen St. South
Mississauga, ON L5M 1M2
905-568-1274
Fax: 905-568-2452
atiya@rogers.com
ahsanfinancial.com
Year Founded: 1985
Executives:
Atiya Ahsan, Certified Financial Planner, Chartered Life Underwriter & Chartered Financial Consultant

Al G. Brown & Associates
#501, 970 Lawrence Ave. West
Toronto, ON M6A 3B6
416-787-6176
Fax: 416-787-0451
algbrown@algbrown.com
www.algbrown.com
Executives:
Al G. Brown
David Wm. Brown
Golda Brown
Cathy Marcoccia, Office Manager

Alan W. Strathdee
***Also listed under:** Pension & Money Management Companies*
35 Peachtree Path
Toronto, ON M9P 3S1
416-244-0085
Ownership: Private
Year Founded: 1990
Profile: Services include financial planning & investment advisory.
Executives:
Alan W. Strathdee, CFP, PFP, Owner

Alasco Services Inc.
#920, 10250 - 101 St.
Edmonton, AB T5J 3P4
780-424-0075
Fax: 780-429-3122
bpatterson@alasco.ab.ca
Ownership: Private
Year Founded: 1991

Alec G. Henley & Associates
PO Box 100
357 Duckworth St.
St. John's, NL A1C 5H5
709-753-7350
Fax: 709-753-1967
gendmin@alecghenleygroup.com
Executives:
Brian Henley, President
John Courtenay, Vice-President

Alexander Gluskin Investments Inc.
***Also listed under:** Pension & Money Management Companies*
120 Adelaide St. West
Toronto, ON M5H 1T1
416-777-6769
Fax: 416-777-6719
866-268-7795
agluskin@agluskin.com
Former Name: Gluskin Fagan, Inc.
Ownership: Private
Year Founded: 1991
Number of Employees: 6
Executives:
Alexander Gluskin, Ph.D., President/CEO, Chair

Alexis Inc.
100, crois de Callières
Laval, QC H7E 3N1
450-661-1653
Fax: 450-661-1745
1-800-660-1653
Other Information: 514-990-0650 (Alternative Phone)
info@assurancesalexis.com
www.assurancesalexis.com
Profile: Financial planning services & insurance products are offered.
Executives:
Frank DiGiandomenico, Financial Advisor

All-Sask Financial Services
#300, 806 Spadina Cres. East
Saskatoon, SK S7K 3H4
306-244-2424
Fax: 306-665-5576
877-954-2424
info@all-sask.com
www.all-sask.com
Year Founded: 1970
Number of Employees: 5
Executives:
Joe LaPointe, President
Lenard O. Cole, Brokerage Administrator

Allard Insurance Agencies
305 Ward St.
Nelson, BC V1L 1S5
250-352-5341
Fax: 250-352-2383
Year Founded: 1964
Number of Employees: 10
Executives:
Vic Coulter, General Manager

Allied Financial Services Limited
Allied House
210 Oxford St. East
London, ON N6A 1T6
519-673-1940
Fax: 519-673-0939
800-661-1956
info@alliedfinancial.ca
www.alliedgroup.ca

Alodium Financial Group Inc.
#204, 860 Main St.
Moncton, NB E1C 1G2
506-863-0580
Fax: 506-863-0599
800-994-5155
alodium@alodium.ca
www.alodium.ca
Executives:
Emily A. Murphy, CFP, CLU, Partner
John Patterson, Partner

Altamira Financial Services Limited
***Also listed under:** Investment Fund Companies*
The Exchange Tower
#900, 130 King St. West
Toronto, ON M5X 1K9
416-507-7050
Fax: 416-507-7111
800-263-2824
advice@altamira.com
www.altamira.com
Profile: With approximately $4.3 billion in assets under management, Altamira ranks as one of Canada's largest direct providers of mutual funds. It manages money for mutual funds, pension funds, corporations & other major institutions.
Executives:
Charles Guay, President/CEO, Investment Services
Nancy Cappadocia, CFO
James Whitman, Sr. Vice-President, Sales & Service
Altamira:
AltaFund Investment Corp. Fund
RRSP Eligible; Inception Year: 1986; Fund Managers: Natcan Investment Management Inc.
Asia Pacific Fund
RRSP Eligible; Inception Year: 1992; Fund Managers: Natcan Investment Management Inc.
Balanced Fund
RRSP Eligible; Inception Year: 1985; Fund Managers: Natcan Investment Management Inc.
Bond Fund
RRSP Eligible; Inception Year: 1987; Fund Managers: Natcan Investment Management Inc.

Altamira Financial Services Limited (continued)

Capital Growth Fund
RRSP Eligible; Inception Year: 1937; Fund Managers:
Natcan Investment Management Inc.
Dividend Fund
RRSP Eligible; Inception Year: 1985; Fund Managers:
Natcan Investment Management Inc.
Equity Fund
RRSP Eligible; Inception Year: 1987; Fund Managers:
Natcan Investment Management Inc.
European Equity Fund
RRSP Eligible; Inception Year: 1993; Fund Managers:
Natcan Investment Management Inc.
Global Bond Fund
RRSP Eligible; Inception Year: 1993; Fund Managers:
Natcan Investment Management Inc.
Global Discovery Fund
RRSP Eligible; Inception Year: 1994; Fund Managers:
Baillie Gifford Overseas
Global Diversified Fund
RRSP Eligible; Inception Year: 1985; Fund Managers:
Natcan Investment Management Inc.
Growth & Income Fund
RRSP Eligible; Inception Year: 1986; Fund Managers:
Natcan Investment Management Inc.
Income Fund
RRSP Eligible; Inception Year: 1970; Fund Managers:
Natcan Investment Management Inc.
Japanese Opportunity Fund
RRSP Eligible; Inception Year: 1994; Fund Managers:
Natcan Investment Management Inc.
Canadian Value Fund
RRSP Eligible; Inception Year: 1993; Fund Managers:
Natcan Investment Management Inc.
Precious & Strategic Metal Fund
RRSP Eligible; Inception Year: 1994; Fund Managers:
Natcan Investment Management Inc.
Select American Fund
RRSP Eligible; Inception Year: 1991; Fund Managers:
Natcan Investment Management Inc.
Short Term Global Income Fund
RRSP Eligible; Inception Year: 1991; Fund Managers:
Natcan Investment Management Inc.
Short Term Government Bond Fund
RRSP Eligible; Inception Year: 1994; Fund Managers:
Natcan Investment Management Inc.
Special Growth Fund
RRSP Eligible; Inception Year: 1985; Fund Managers:
Natcan Investment Management Inc.
US Larger Company Fund
RRSP Eligible; Inception Year: 1993; Fund Managers:
Natcan Investment Management Inc.
Science & Technology Fund
RRSP Eligible; Inception Year: 1995; Fund Managers:
Natcan Investment Management Inc.
Global Small Company Fund
RRSP Eligible; Inception Year: 1996; Fund Managers:
Natcan Investment Management Inc.
T-Bill Fund
RRSP Eligible; Inception Year: 1997; Fund Managers:
Natcan Investment Management Inc.
Short Term Canadian Income Fund
RRSP Eligible; Inception Year: 1997; Fund Managers:
Natcan Investment Management Inc.
Global Financial Services Fund
RRSP Eligible; Inception Year: 1999; Fund Managers:
Natcan Investment Management Inc.
Health Sciences Fund
RRSP Eligible; Inception Year: 1999; Fund Managers:
Natcan Investment Management Inc.
Biotechnology Fund
RRSP Eligible; Inception Year: 2000; Fund Managers:
Natcan Investment Management Inc.
e-business Fund
RRSP Eligible; Inception Year: 1998; Fund Managers:
Natcan Investment Management Inc.
Global 20 Fund
RRSP Eligible; Inception Year: 2000; Fund Managers:
Natcan Investment Management Inc.
Resource Fund
RRSP Eligible; Inception Year: 1989; Fund Managers:
Natcan Investment Management Inc.
High Yield Bond Fund
RRSP Eligible; Inception Year: 1995; Fund Managers:
Natcan Investment Management Inc.
Global Value Fund
RRSP Eligible; Inception Year: 2000; Fund Managers:
Natcan Investment Management Inc.
Monthly Income Fund
RRSP Eligible; Inception Year: 2004; Fund Managers:
Natcan Investment Management Inc.
Energy Fund
RRSP Eligible; Inception Year: 2004; Fund Managers:
Natcan Investment Management Inc.
Inflation-Adjusted Bond Fund
RRSP Eligible; Inception Year: 2005; Fund Managers:
Natcan Investment Management Inc.
High-Interest Cash Performer Fund
RRSP Eligible; Inception Year: 1990; Fund Managers:
Altamira Management Ltd.
Altamira Managed:
RSP Stable Income Portfolio FundInception Year: 1999; Fund Managers:
Natcan Investment Management Inc.
RSP Income Portfolio FundInception Year: 1999; Fund Managers:
Natcan Investment Management Inc.
RSP Income & Growth Portfolio FundInception Year: 1999; Fund Managers:
Natcan Investment Management Inc.
RSP Balanced Portfolio FundInception Year: 1999; Fund Managers:
Natcan Investment Management Inc.
RSP Growth & Income Portfolio FundInception Year: 1999; Fund Managers:
Natcan Investment Management Inc.
RSP Growth Portfolio FundInception Year: 1999; Fund Managers:
Natcan Investment Management Inc.
RSP Maximum Growth Portfolio FundInception Year: 1999; Fund Managers:
Natcan Investment Management Inc.
Stable Income Portfolio FundInception Year: 2003; Fund Managers:
Natcan Investment Management Inc.
Income Portfolio FundInception Year: 2003; Fund Managers:
Natcan Investment Management Inc.
Income & Growth Portfolio FundInception Year: 2003; Fund Managers:
Natcan Investment Management Inc.
Balanced Portfolio FundInception Year: 2003; Fund Managers:
Natcan Investment Management Inc.
Growth & Income Portfolio FundInception Year: 2003; Fund Managers:
Natcan Investment Management Inc.
Growth Portfolio FundInception Year: 1999; Fund Managers:
Natcan Investment Management Inc.
Maximum Growth Portfolio FundInception Year: 2003; Fund Managers:
Natcan Investment Management Inc.
RRIF Stable Income Portfolio FundInception Year: 2004; Fund Managers:
Natcan Investment Management Inc.
RRIF Income Portfolio FundInception Year: 2004; Fund Managers:
Natcan Investment Management Inc.
RRIF Income & Growth Portfolio FundInception Year: 2004; Fund Managers:
Natcan Investment Management Inc.
RRIF Balanced Portfolio FundInception Year: 2004; Fund Managers:
Natcan Investment Management Inc.
RRIF Growth Portfolio FundInception Year: 2004; Fund Managers:
Natcan Investment Management Inc.
Altamira Precision:
Canadian Index Fund
RRSP Eligible; Inception Year: 1998; Fund Managers:
Natcan Investment Management Inc.
European Index Fund
RRSP Eligible; Inception Year: 1999; Fund Managers:
Natcan Investment Management Inc.
European RSP Index Fund
RRSP Eligible; Inception Year: 1999; Fund Managers:
Natcan Investment Management Inc.
International RSP Index Fund
RRSP Eligible; Inception Year: 1998; Fund Managers:
Natcan Investment Management Inc.
US RSP Index Fund
RRSP Eligible; Inception Year: 1998; Fund Managers:
Natcan Investment Management Inc.
US Midcap Index Fund
RRSP Eligible; Inception Year: 1999; Fund Managers:
Natcan Investment Management Inc.
Dow 30 Index Fund
RRSP Eligible; Inception Year: 1999; Fund Managers:
Natcan Investment Management Inc.
Branches:
Calgary
Shell Centre
#117, 400 - 4th Ave. SW
Calgary, AB T2P 2H5 Canada
403-266-4941
Fax: 403-265-0831
800-263-284
Edmonton
Commerce Place
10150 Jasper Ave.
Edmonton, AB T5J 1W4 Canada
780-414-6001
Fax: 780-423-0183
800-263-2824
Halifax
1903 Barrington St.
Halifax, NS B3J 3L7 Canada
902-496-9600
Fax: 902-429-0656
London
620A Richmond St. #F
London, ON N6A 5J9 Canada
519-432-6440
Fax: 519-435-1722
877-612-2212
Montréal
#201, 2020, rue University
Montréal, QC H3A 2A5 Canada
514-499-1656
Fax: 514-499-9570
800-361-2354
Thornhill
#292, 505 Hwy. 7 East
Thornhill, ON L3T 7T1 Canada
905-882-0283
Fax: 905-882-8328
888-808-8277
Vancouver
Marine Bldg.
#M101, 355 Burrard St.
Vancouver, BC V6C 2G8 Canada
604-687-7926
Fax: 604-687-5932

Altimum Mutuals Inc.

Also listed under: *Investment Dealers*
94 Barbican Trail
St Catharines, ON L2T 4A8
905-680-8544
Fax: 905-680-8546
877-366-7343
www.altimum.ca
Ownership: Private.
Year Founded: 2003
Number of Employees: 11
Profile: Altimum Mutuals has investment advisors in the following locations: Stoney Creek, Grimsby, Niagara-on-the-Lake, St Catharines & Burlington.
Executives:
Donald Reid, CEO; 905-680-8544; don@altimum.ca
Edith Reid, President, Compliance Officer; 905-680-8544; edith@altimum.ca
Directors:
Don Reid
Edith Reid

The Amethyst Financial Group Ltd.

521 John St.
Thunder Bay, ON P7B 1Y3
807-345-3444
Fax: 807-345-1581
800-367-9813
admin@amethystfinancial.com
www.amethystfinancial.com
Number of Employees: 3

Executives:
Rick Kelly
Ian Hosegood

AMG Canada Corp.
Also listed under: *Pension & Money Management Companies*
North Tower, Royal Bank Plaza
#1840, 200 Bay St.
Toronto, ON M5J 2J4
416-920-1944
Fax: 416-920-1947
Former Name: First Asset Management Inc.
Ownership: Public. Foreign. Parent is Affiliated Managers Group Inc.
Year Founded: 1997
Number of Employees: 250
Stock Symbol: AMG
Executives:
Nathaniel Dalton, President
John Kingston, Director
Affiliated Companies:
First Asset Advisory Services Inc.

Amonson Wealth Management Inc.
15 MacKay Dr. SW
Calgary, AB T2V 2A3
403-231-1936
Fax: 403-215-0756
john@unbiasesadvice.com
Executives:
John Amonson, Chartered Financial Planner, Chartered Life Underwriter

AMT Financial Consulting
70 Lincrest Rd.
Winnipeg, MB R2V 2S7
204-334-6373
Fax: 204-334-6373
amtcfp@shaw.ca
Executives:
Alvin N. Toll, BSW, CFP

Andrew & Propp Estate Planning Corp.
#610, 717 - 7th Ave. SW
Calgary, AB T2P 0Z3
403-263-8070
Fax: 403-264-1027
Executives:
Richard D. Propp

Andy Lambe & Associates Inc.
20 Great George St.
Charlottetown, PE C1A 4J6
902-368-8320
877-433-8320
peilifequote.com
Executives:
Andy Lambe

Angeles & Associates Financial Services Inc.
246 Lindsay Cres.
Edmonton, AB T6R 2T2
780-988-2220
Fax: 780-988-2221

Anita MacLean Investments Inc.
2362 Whitehaven Cres.
Ottawa, ON K2B 5H4
613-721-9804
Fax: 613-820-2576
amaclean@magna.ca
Ownership: Private
Year Founded: 1992
Number of Employees: 1
Executives:
Anita MacLean, CFP, RFP, Owner

Anne Brandt Personal Financial Consulting
3108 Patullo Cres.
Coquitlam, BC V3E 2R2
604-552-1696
Fax: 604-942-0721
anne@annebrandtfinancial.com
www.annebrandtfinancial.com
Ownership: Private
Year Founded: 1994
Number of Employees: 1
Profile: The following fee only services are offered: financial planning, retirement planning, tax planning & preparation, severance & early retirement packages, pension analysis, investment management, risk management, will & estate planning & cash management.

Executives:
Anne Brandt, CFP, RFP, Financial Consultant

AQ Financial Group
1151 Portage Ave.
Winnipeg, MB R3G 0S9
204-985-6060
Fax: 204-943-6564
Ownership: Private
Number of Employees: 15
Executives:
Dennis Cale, President

ARCA Financial Group
237 Labrador Dr.
Waterloo, ON N2K 4M8
519-745-8500
Fax: 519-745-8283
877-745-8500
inquiries@arcafinancial.com
www.arcafinancial.com
Ownership: Private
Year Founded: 1999
Number of Employees: 27
Executives:
Christine Black, CFO, Tax & Estate Planning Consultant
Mark Leech, Principal, Financial Advisor
John Lunz, Principal, Financial Advisor
Doug McPhail, Principal, Financial Advisor
Kelly Strome, Principal, Financial Advisor
Bill Vollmer, Principal, Financial Advisor

Armstrong & Quaile Associates Inc.
5858 Rideau Valley Dr.
Manotick, ON K4M 1B3
613-692-0751
Fax: 613-692-0499
800-498-3911
kena@a-q.com
www.a-q.com
Ownership: Private.
Year Founded: 1991
Number of Employees: 190
Assets: $1-10 billion Year End: 20060831
Revenues: $10-100 billion Year End: 20060831
Profile: Armstrong & Quaile is licensed in all ten provinces.

Executives:
Kenneth Armstrong, President
John Armstrong, Vice-President
Heather Phillips, Vice-President
Sue Thompson, Office Manager
Affiliated Companies:
Brian Pike Financial Group
Cartile Financial Services/CFS
Cormier Financial
Janston Financial Group Inc.
META Financial Management Ltd.
Paula Meier Associates
RJS Private Wealth Management Inc.
Team O'Heron Investments
West Capital Wealth Management
Branches:
Carberry
PO Box 1109
40 Main St.
Carberry, MB R0K 0H0
204-834-3155
Fax: 204-834-3275
donfor@mts.net
Gatineau
#302, 194, rue Harold
Gatineau, QC J8P 4S4 Canada
819-663-6656
Fax: 819-663-6652
raydoucet@bellnet.ca
Raymond Doucet, Branch Manager
Halifax
3080 Agricola St.
Halifax, NS B3K 4G3 Canada
902-445-0669
Fax: 902-445-0670
pshea@allstream.net
Paul Shea, Branch Manager
Orleans
#204, 2451 St. Joseph Blvd.
Orleans, ON K1C 1E9 Canada
613-837-7117
Fax: 613-837-4224
potvin@bellnet.ca
Ray Doucet, Branch Manager
Red Deer
#102, 6470 Johnstone Dr.
Red Deer, AB T4P 3Y2
403-314-6586
Fax: 403-314-6583
norm.macdonald@shaw.ca
Thunder Bay
#17, 4A South Court St.
Thunder Bay, ON P7B 2W4 Canada
807-345-1850
Fax: 807-345-1855
david@davlor.ca
David Chow, Branch Manager
Vernon Bridge
RR#2
Vernon Bridge, PE C0A 2E0 Canada
902-651-2289
Fax: 902-651-2288
nobby.clarke@pei.aibn.com
John Michael (Nobby) Clarke, Branch Manager
Waterloo
#3, 279 Weber St., Lower Level
Waterloo, ON N2J 3H8 Canada
519-576-5766
Fax: 519-576-0192
johna@a-q.com
John Armstrong, Manager

Ascend Financial Planning Inc.
#203, 3027 Harvester Rd.
Burlington, ON L7N 3G7
905-634-4944
Fax: 905-634-6827
doug.lane@sympatico.ca
Ownership: Private
Year Founded: 1991
Number of Employees: 3
Assets: Under $1 million
Revenues: Under $1 million
Executives:
Douglas M. Lane, President
Branches:
Burlington
#1, 4145 White Birch Circle
Burlington, ON L7M 3T9 Canada
905-332-4833

Assante Wealth Management
#101, 33386 South Fraser Way
Abbotsford, BC V2S 2B5
604-852-1804
Fax: 604-852-0503
www.assante.com
Former Name: Assante Financial Management Ltd. - Reimer Financial Division
Ownership: CI Financial.
Year Founded: 1995
Stock Symbol: CIX
Executives:
Peter Gemmell, Advisor; pgemmell@assante.com

Atlantic Wealth Management Ltd.
#1220, 1801 Hollis St.
Halifax, NS B3J 3N4
902-429-4001
Fax: 902-429-3141
888-807-6804
Ownership: Private
Year Founded: 1991
Number of Employees: 6
Assets: Under $1 million
Revenues: Under $1 million
Executives:
Terence Thorne, President

INVESTMENT MANAGEMENT

INVESTMENT MANAGEMENT

Audentium Financial Corp.
Also listed under: *Investment Dealers*
191 University Ave. East
Cobourg, ON K9A 4X6
905-373-1234
Fax: 905-373-0645
joe@yalkezian.com
www.yalkezian.com
Executives:
Joe Yalkezian, CFP, CGA

Aurion Capital Management Inc.
Also listed under: *Pension & Money Management Companies*
#2205, 120 Adelaide St. West
Toronto, ON M5H 1T1
416-866-2422
Fax: 416-363-6206
866-828-7466
jclark@aurion.ca
www.aurion.ca
Year Founded: 1996
Number of Employees: 22
Assets: $1-10 billion Year End: 20060930
Revenues: $1-5 million Year End: 20060930
Profile: Investment services include portfolio management, pension fund management & alternative asset management.

Executives:
Neil Jacoby, President, Managing Partner
Bob Decker, CFA, MBA, Managing Partner, Canadian Equities
Paul Fahey, CFA, MBA, Managing Partner, Fixed Income
Janet Greenwood, BA, B.Admin., Managing Partner, Investment Solutions
Dennis Pellarin, CA, BBA, Chief Financial Officer
James Clark, CFA, CA, B.Sc., Vice-President, Business Development

Aurora Financial Management
19 Kennedy St. West
Aurora, ON L4G 2L3
905-841-3612
Fax: 905-841-3337
877-228-2658
www.aurorafinancial.com
Ownership: Private
Executives:
Jeffery M. White, President
John A. Gleeson, Vice-President

Avenue Investment Management Inc.
#300, 47 Colborne St.
Toronto, ON M5E 1P8
416-482-2004
Fax: 416-482-0007
www.avenueinvestment.com
Profile: The company is an independent investment counseling firm.

Executives:
Paul Gardner, Principal
Bill Harris, Principal
Paul A.M. Harris, Principal

Avis Lapham Financial Services
#200, 829 West 15th St.
North Vancouver, BC V7P 1M5
604-985-1000
Fax: 604-985-1063
avis_lapham@telus.net
Ownership: Private
Year Founded: 1994
Number of Employees: 1
Assets: Under $1 million
Revenues: Under $1 million
Profile: Avis Lapham specializes in retirement planning.

Executives:
Avis M. Lapham, CEO

Axiom Financial Inc.
#201, 120 Wellington St.
London, ON N6B 2K6
519-672-6060
Fax: 519-672-4750
tbuss@axiomfinancial.on.ca
Ownership: Private
Year Founded: 1994
Profile: Financial planning services, corporate seminars, & a range of personal financial services are provided.

Executives:
Tammy J. Buss, CFP, CLU, CHFC, President

Ayrton Financial Inc.
#1501, 1111 West Georgia St.
Vancouver, BC V6E 4M3
604-687-6808
Fax: 604-687-1554
888-811-6808
info@ayrtonfinancial.com
www.ayrtonfinancial.com
Executives:
W. Glenn Ayrton

Azotini MacLean Rounthwaite
478 Waterloo St.
London, ON N6B 2P6
519-673-0920
Fax: 519-434-8471
invest@amradvisors.com
www.amradvisors.com
Ownership: Private.
Profile: The company is affiliated with Retirement Planners of London.

Executives:
Ron Azotini, Contact
Jim MacLean, Contact
David Rounthwaite, Contact

B.L. Garbens Associates Inc.
39 Granlea Rd.
Toronto, ON M2N 2Z6
416-227-1543
Fax: 416-227-1547
bgarbens@pathcom.com
www.blgarbens.com
Former Name: B.L. Garbens & Associates
Ownership: Private
Year Founded: 1998
Number of Employees: 1
Assets: Under $1 million
Revenues: Under $1 million
Profile: B.L. Garbens Associates is a fee for service financial planning firm.

Executives:
Barbara Garbens, President

Baicorp Financial Inc.
1290 Cornwall Rd., Unit B
Oakville, ON L6J 7W5
905-844-8820
Fax: 905-844-8663
800-680-9709
pam@baicorp.ca
www.baicorp.ca
Ownership: Private
Executives:
Patrick Bailey, President
Steven M. Langdon, Vice-President, Group Sales & Marketing

Bairstow, Smart & Smith LLP
5 Douglas St.
Guelph, ON N1H 2S8
519-822-7670
Fax: 519-822-6997
bsh@bsh.on.ca
www.bsh.on.ca
Former Name: Bairstow, Smart & Hall LLP
Year Founded: 1967
Executives:
Ross E. Bairstow
D. Andrew Smart
Edward L. Smith

Bajus Financial Ltd.
#920, 1500 West Georgia St.
Vancouver, BC V2G 2Z6
604-331-2453
Fax: 604-669-2811
866-442-2587
www.bajusfinancial.com
Year Founded: 1971
Profile: Services include financial planning & insurance products.

Executives:
Paul Bajus, CFP, RHU, CLU, CH.F.C., Certified Financial Planner, Registered Health Underwriter; paul@bajusfinancial.com
Mark Bajus, CFP, CLU, CH.F.C., Certified Financial Planner, Chartered Financial Consultant
Cheron Calaway, Manager, Client Services

Banwell Financial Inc.
#203, 2 Lansing Sq.
Toronto, ON M2J 4P8
416-494-1099
Fax: 416-494-6675
info@banwellfinancial.com
www.banwellfinancial.com
Former Name: Banwell Financial Planning
Ownership: Private
Number of Employees: 5
Executives:
Frank Banwell, CFP, President
Michael Banwell, CFP, Vice-President

Barclays Global Investors Canada Limited(BGI)
Also listed under: *Investment Fund Companies*
PO Box 614
#2500, 161 Bay St.
Toronto, ON M5J 2S1
416-643-4000
Fax: 416-643-4049
866-275-2442
inquiriescanada@barclaysglobal.com
www.bglobal.com
Former Name: Wells Fargo NIKKO Investment Advisors Canada Limited
Also Known As: Barclays Canada
Ownership: Foreign. Indirect subsidiary of Barclays PLC. Part of BGI, a division of Barclays PLC.
Year Founded: 1992
Number of Employees: 65
Assets: $10-100 billion Year End: 20060900
Revenues: $10-50 million Year End: 20060900
Profile: The institutional investment manager is also the manager of index funds & ETFs. Barclays Canada's exchange traded fund (ETF) product line is iShares. It manages over $66 billion in Canadian assets & in other assets for Canadian clients.

Executives:
Rajiv Silgardo, CEO
Subhas Sen, CFO
Warren Collier, Counsel & Secretary
Howard Atkinson, Head, Public Funds
William F. Chinery, Head, Client Relationships
Heather Pelant, Head, Business Development, iShares
iUnits:
60 Canadian Equity Index Fund
RRSP Eligible; Inception Year: 1999; Fund Managers:
Ada Yin
Canadian Bonds Index Fund
RRSP Eligible; Inception Year: 2000; Fund Managers:
Freda Dong
LouPaolone
Composite Canadian Equity Capped Index Fund
RRSP Eligible; Inception Year: 2001; Fund Managers:
Ada Yin
Dividend Index Fund
RRSP Eligible; Inception Year: 2005;
Energy Sector Index Fund
RRSP Eligible; Inception Year: 2001; Fund Managers:
Ada Yin
Financial Sector Index Fund
RRSP Eligible; Inception Year: 2001; Fund Managers:
Ada Yin
Gold Sector Index Fund
RRSP Eligible; Inception Year: 2001; Fund Managers:
Ada Yin
Income Trust Sector Index Fund
RRSP Eligible; Inception Year: 2005;
International Equity C$ Index Fund
RRSP Eligible; Inception Year: 2001; Fund Managers:
Rob Bechard
RandallMalcolm
Amit Prakash
Materials Sector Index Fund
RRSP Eligible; Inception Year: 2005;

MidCap Canadian Equity Index Fund
RRSP Eligible; Inception Year: 2001; Fund Managers:
Ada Yin
Real Return Bond Index Fund
RRSP Eligible; Inception Year: 2005;
REIT Index Fund
RRSP Eligible; Inception Year: 2002; Fund Managers:
Ada Yin
S&P 500 C$ Index Fund
RRSP Eligible; Inception Year: 2001; Fund Managers:
Rob Bechard
RandallMalcolm
Amit Prakash
Short Bond Index Fund
RRSP Eligible; Inception Year: 2000; Fund Managers:
Freda Dong
LouPaolone
Technology Sector Index Fund
RRSP Eligible; Inception Year: 2001; Fund Managers:
Ada Yin
Branches:
Montréal
#1730, 1000, rue Sherbrooke ouest
Montréal, QC H3A 3G4 Canada
514-843-9595
Fax: 514-843-1082
Eric Leville, Manager

Barkman & Tanaka
Also listed under: *Accountants*
Lougheed Plaza
#225, 9600 Cameron St.
Burnaby, BC V3J 7N3
604-421-2591
Fax: 604-421-1171
dbarkman@barkman-tanaka.com
Executives:
Dale Barkman, Partner
Wayne Tanaka, Partner

Barrantagh Investment Management
#1700, 100 Yonge St.
Toronto, ON M5C 2W1
416-868-6295
Fax: 416-868-6593
888-778-0888
info@barrantagh.com
www.barrantagh.com
Former Name: McCutcheon Steinbach Comber Investment Management Inc.
Number of Employees: 8
Executives:
W. Peter Comber, Managing Director
Bruce R. Jackson, Managing Director
Wally Kusters, Managing Director
John O. McCutcheon, Managing Director

Barrington Wealth Partners Inc.
#244, 200 Waterfront Dr.
Bedford, NS B4A 4J4
902-832-9797
Fax: 902-832-9779
www.bwpartners.com
Year Founded: 2000
Executives:
Paul Brown, CLU, ChFC, President

Batirente
Also listed under: *Investment Fund Companies; Investment Management*
#203, 2175, boul de Maisonneuve
Montréal, QC H2K 4S3
514-525-5740
Fax: 514-525-2199
800-253-0131
info@batirente.qc.ca
www.batirente.qc.ca
Ownership: Private
Year Founded: 1987
Number of Employees: 6
Assets: $500m-1 billion Year End: 20051130
Executives:
Daniel Simard, General Coordinator; 514-525-5065; daniel.simard@batirente.qc.ca
Batirente:
Actions Internationales
RRSP Eligible; Inception Year: 1998; Fund Managers:
Hexavest Asset Management Inc.
Diversifié intrepide
RRSP Eligible; Inception Year: 1998; Fund Managers:
Hexavest Asset Management Inc.
Diversifié prévoyant
RRSP Eligible; Inception Year: 1988; Fund Managers:
Hexavest Asset Management Inc.
Actions Canadiennes
RRSP Eligible; Inception Year: 1988; Fund Managers:
Optimum Asset Management Inc.
Obligations
RRSP Eligible; Inception Year: 1988; Fund Managers:
Addenda Capital Inc.
Marché Monetaire
RRSP Eligible; Inception Year: 1988; Fund Managers:
Addenda Capital Inc.
Trésorerie
RRSP Eligible; Inception Year: 1998; Fund Managers:
Addenda Capital Inc.
Branches:
Québec
#500, 210, boul Charest est
Québec, QC G1K 3H1 Canada
418-522-9621
Martin Blais, Manager

BCO Wealth Management
#106, 4953 Dundas St.
Toronto, ON M9A 1B6
416-233-5303
Fax: 416-233-5155
888-357-7769
www.moneytalking.com
Profile: Assets under administration total $40 million.

Executives:
Paul D. Bar; paul@moneytalking.com
Lori Coverdale; lori@moneytalking.com
Ross O'Doherty; ross@moneytalking.com

Bedford & Associates Research Group
#1403, 75 Queen St. North
Hamilton, ON L8R 3J3
905-529-1439
800-351-1279
webmaster@baresearch.com
www.baresearch.com
Executives:
Terry Bedford, President
Joanne Harris, Manager, Marketing & Business Development

Belec & Company Ltd.
#201, 15023 - 123 Ave.
Edmonton, AB T5V 1J7
780-944-0666
Fax: 780-944-0683
877-232-5151
gerry@belecandcompany.com
www.belecandcompany.com
Executives:
Gerry Belec

Belmont Financial Group
3 Ralston Ave.
Dartmouth, NS B3B 1H5
902-465-5687
Fax: 902-464-4249
888-235-6169
belmail@belmontfinancial.com
www.belmontfinancial.com
Ownership: Private
Year Founded: 1995
Number of Employees: 18

Bencom fsgi
1060 Guelph St.
Kitchener, ON N2B 2E3
519-579-4730
Fax: 519-743-1631
888-664-5555
www.bencomfsgi.com
Executives:
Mark Beckham
Vivian MacLean
Nellie Mendes
Bob Ritzer
Silvia Weismann

Benefit Planners Inc.
#130, 6001 - 1A St. SW
Calgary, AB T2H 0G5
403-294-9077
Fax: 403-294-9079
Executives:
Robert A. McCullagh, RHU, CFP, CLU, CH.F.C., Financial Advisor

Bentall Investment Management
#300, 55 University Ave.
Toronto, ON M5J 2H7
416-681-3400
Fax: 416-681-3405
www.bentallcapital.com
Former Name: Penreal Capital Management
Executives:
Gary Whitelaw, President/CEO
Paul Zemla, CIO
Graham Senst, Exec. Vice-President
Dave Barry, Sr. Vice-President & Portfolio Manager
Chris Lawrence, Sr. Vice-President, Acquisitions
Christine Lundvall, Sr. Vice-President & Portfolio Manager
John McFadden, Sr. Vice-President & Portfolio Manager
Regional Offices:
Vancouver
Four Bentall Centre
#1800, 1055 Dunsmuir St.
Vancouver, BC V7X 1C4 Canada
604-646-2800
Fax: 604-246-2805
Malcolm Leitch, COO

Berg Naqvi Lehmann
507 Vernon St.
Nelson, BC V1L 4E9
250-352-3165
Fax: 250-352-7166
advice@bnl.ca
www.bnl.ca
Former Name: Berg, Naqvi & Co.
Number of Employees: 19
Executives:
Stefan Lehmann

Berglund Taylor Financial Services
#106, 3385 Harvester Rd.
Burlington, ON L7N 3N2
905-634-7785
Fax: 905-634-1138
glenda@berglundtaylor.com
Executives:
Kathy Berglund

Berkshire Investment Group Inc.
1375 Kerns Rd.
Burlington, ON L7R 4X8
800-991-2121
advisorservices@berkshire.ca
www.berkshire.ca
Year Founded: 1985
Profile: Financial planning is provided through 110 offices in Canada. It is also affiliated with Berkshire Insurance Services Inc.

Affiliated Companies:
Berkshire Securities Inc.

Best Advice Financial Services
#1111, 250 Consumers Rd.
Toronto, ON M2J 4V6
416-490-9866
Fax: 416-490-7921
bestadvice@sympatico.ca
Executives:
Abraham Jakarsezian

Beutel Goodman & Company Ltd.
Also listed under: *Pension & Money Management Companies*
PO Box 2005
#2000, 20 Eglinton Ave. West
Toronto, ON M4R 1K8
416-485-1010
Fax: 416-485-1799
800-461-4551
marketing@beutel-can.com

INVESTMENT MANAGEMENT

Beutel Goodman & Company Ltd. (continued)
www.beutelgoodman.com
Ownership: Private
Year Founded: 1967
Number of Employees: 53
Assets: $10-100 billion Year End: 20060930
Executives:
William W. Ashby, President
Greg Latremoille, President, Private Client Group
Bruce L. Cornell, COO/Sr. Vice-President, Fixed Income
James G. Edwards, Sr. Vice-President, Beutel Goodman Managed Funds
Mark D. Thomson, Sr. Vice-President, Director of Research, Canadian Equities
Steve Arpin, Vice-President, Canadian Equities
John Christie, Vice-President, Fixed Income
Stephen Clements, Vice-President, U.S. Equities, Private Client Group
David Gregoris, Vice-President, Fixed Income
Gavin Ivory, Vice-President, Global Equities
Sarah Khoo, Vice-President, Global Equities
Irene Lau, Vice-President, Canadian Equity Trader
Sue McNamara, Vice-President, Fixed Income
John Shuter, Vice-President
Steven Smith, Vice-President, Private Client Group
Andrew M. Sweeney, Vice-President, Canadian Equities
John Fuea, Asst. Vice-President, Fixed Income
Allison Morgan, Asst. Vice-President, International Equities
Glenn Fortin, Equity Analyst, U.S. Equities
Ehren Mendum, Equity Analyst, U.S. Equities, Private Client Group
William S. Otton, Equity Analyst, Canadian Equities
Pat Palozzi, Equity Analyst, Canadian Equitites
K.C. Parker, Equity Analyst, Global Equities
Craig Weisberg, Equity Trader, U.S. & Canadian Small Cap Equity Trader
Affiliated Companies:
Beutel Goodman Managed Funds Inc.

Beutel Goodman Managed Funds Inc.
***Also listed under:** Pension & Money Management Companies*
PO Box 2005
#2000, 20 Eglinton Ave. West
Toronto, ON M4R 1K8
416-932-6404
Fax: 416-485-8194
800-461-4551
marketing@beutelgoodman.com
www.beutelgoodman.com
Ownership: Private
Year Founded: 1991
Assets: $1-10 billion Year End: 20060930
Executives:
James Edwards, Sr. Vice-President

BGA Tax Specialists
157 Meadowbrook Dr.
Ancaster, ON L9G 4S9
905-304-9014
Fax: 905-304-0762
bryan@taxspecialists.ca
www.taxspecialists.ca
Former Name: Bryan G. Allendorf
Executives:
Bryan G. Allendorf, Principal

Bick Financial Security Corporation
***Also listed under:** Investment Dealers*
241 Wilson St. East
Ancaster, ON L9G 2B8
905-648-9559
Fax: 905-648-8185
888-777-2425
service@bickfinancial.com
www.bickfinancial.com
Executives:
Clarence Bick, President; cbick@bickfinancial.com
Leonard Bick, Managing Partner, Founder; lenbick@bickfinancial.com
Branches:
Grimsby
18 Ontario St.
Grimsby, ON L3M 3H1 Canada
905-309-6777
Fax: 905-309-4850
Sharon Rizzuto
Milton
142 Martin St.
Milton, ON L9T 2R2 Canada
905-875-1000
Fax: 905-875-6896
888-875-1008
Melissa DeBrouwer
St Catharines
40 Butler Cres.
St Catharines, ON L2M 7B4 Canada
905-937-6537
Fax: 905-937-8323
Stoney Creek
35 MacIntosh Dr.
Stoney Creek, ON L8E 4E4 Canada
905-662-1352
Fax: 905-662-1392

Bishop & Wallace Chartered Accountants
#433, 5811 Cooney Rd.
Richmond, BC V6X 3M1
604-273-1477
Fax: 604-273-0434
info@biswal.com
www.biswal.com
Executives:
Craig W. Wallace; cwallace@biswal.com
Bill Bishop

Blackmont Capital Inc.
***Also listed under:** Investment Dealers; Investment Management*
Bay Wellington Tower, BCE Place
PO Box 779
#900, 181 Bay St.
Toronto, ON M5J 2T3
416-864-3600
Fax: 416-864-9024
866-775-7704
info@blackmont.com
www.blackmont.com
Former Name: First Associates Investments Inc.; Yorkton Securities; Robert Caldwell Capital Corp.
Ownership: Wholly owned subsidiary of Rockwater Capital Corporation, Toronto, ON.
Stock Exchange Membership: Canadian Trading & Quotation System Inc, Toronto Stock Exchange, TSX Venture Exchange
Executives:
Stuart R. Raftus, President/COO
Gerald Throop, President, Capital Markets
Branches:
Calgary
#2200, 440 - 2 Ave. SW
Calgary, AB T2P 5E9 Canada
403-260-8400
Fax: 403-269-7870
800-661-1596
Edmonton
Manulife Place
#1375, 10180 - 101 St.
Edmonton, AB T5J 3S4 Canada
780-577-8150
Fax: 780-577-8170
800-661-1596
Guelph
193 Woolwich St.
Guelph, ON N1H 3V4 Canada
516-836-4440
Fax: 519-836-4067
866-811-4706
Halifax
Purdy's Wharf Tower II
#401, 1969 Upper Water St.
Halifax, NS B3J 3R7 Canada
902-422-2343
Fax: 902-422-5971
866-855-8760
Kelowna
#201, 1441 Ellis St.
Kelowna, BC V1Y 2A3 Canada
250-860-6990
Fax: 250-860-6929
800-820-1813
Montréal
#4215, 1250, boul René-Lévesque ouest
Montréal, QC H3B 4W8 Canada
514-937-3250
Fax: 514-937-4501
877-925-2850
Ottawa
Constitution Square I
#800, 360 Albert St.
Ottawa, ON K1R 7X7 Canada
613-569-7878
Fax: 613-569-4278
Toronto - Bay St. - Toronto Asset Management
BCE Place
PO Box 625
#4420, 161 Bay St.
Toronto, ON M5J 2S1 Canada
416-601-6888
Fax: 416-601-9744
866-601-6888
Toronto - Yonge St.
#503, 4100 Yonge St.
Toronto, ON M2P 2B5 Canada
416-221-5465
Fax: 416-221-1958
866-775-7704
Vancouver
#500, 550 Burrard St.
Vancouver, BC V6C 2B5 Canada
604-640-0400
Fax: 604-640-0300
866-640-0400
Victoria
St. Andrews Square II
#430, 730 View St.
Victoria, BC V8W 3V7 Canada
250-978-9393
Fax: 250-978-9395
Waterloo
#204, 460 Phillip St.
Waterloo, ON N2L 5J2 Canada
519-570-9900
Fax: 519-570-9910
800-461-4748

Bloom Investment Counsel, Inc.
National Bank Bldg.
#1710, 150 York St.
Toronto, ON M5H 3S5
416-861-9941
Ownership: Private
Profile: Bloom Investment Counsel is a money management firm & an investment counsellor.
Executives:
Paul Bloom, President

Bluestone Financial Corporation
***Also listed under:** Investment Dealers*
96 Queen St.
St Catharines, ON L2R 5H3
905-687-8222
Fax: 905-687-3325
bluestone@dundeewealth.com
www.bluestonefinancial.ca
Executives:
Terry Rempel, CFP, President
Patty Rempel, CFP, Manager, Business

Blundell Malabar Financial Group(BMFG)
#360, 2608 Granville St.
Vancouver, BC V6H 3V3
604-874-4377
Fax: 604-874-9799
866-874-4377
admin@bmgf.ca
www.bmfg.ca
Former Name: Blundell Malabar Financial Group; Blundell Malabar & Associates
Executives:
Brian Blundell, CFP, Sr. Partner; bblundell@bmfg.ca
Jeff Swanson, BBA, Certified Financial Planner; jswanson@bmfg.ca
Joleen Buchsbaum; jbuchsbaum@bmfg.ca
Keith Malabar; kmalabar@bmfg.ca

BMJ Financial Services
181 King St.
St Catharines, ON L2R 3J5

905-684-9989
Fax: 905-684-8410
Executives:
William Davidson

Bobb & VanderGaag
PO Box 2680
#200, 3848 - 3rd Ave.
Smithers, BC V0J 2N0
250-847-2257
Fax: 250-847-5102
888-499-2257
Executives:
John Bakker
Willy VanderGaag

Boyd Financial Services
PO Box 356
Carbon, AB T0M 0L0
403-947-2388
Fax: 403-947-2847
888-947-2693
boydfin@lincsat.com
www.boydfinancialservices.com
Year Founded: 1985
Executives:
Bob Boyd

Bradford Financial Services Inc.
774 Seymour St.
Kamloops, BC V2C 2H3
250-828-6767
Fax: 250-828-7941
Executives:
Allan Ross, Contact

Brady-Zavitz Financial Services
#2, 3250 Schmon Pkwy.
Thorold, ON L2V 4Y6
905-704-0070
Fax: 905-704-0074
800-444-5694
Ownership: Private
Number of Employees: 6
Executives:
Paul Scott, Partner
Mark Zavitz, Partner

Brian Bowes
49 Front St. East
Toronto, ON M5E 1B1
416-640-7770
www.brianbowes.ca
Executives:
Brian Bowes, CMA, CFP

Brian Mallard & Associates
#401, 123 - 2nd Ave. South
Saskatoon, SK S7K 7E6
306-934-6011
Fax: 306-934-6012
888-440-7787
info@brianmallard.com
www.brianmallard.com
Executives:
Brian Mallard, CFP, CLU, ChFC, President;
bmallard@brianmallard.com
Brenda Banbury, CFP; bbanbury@brianmallard.com
Roderick Baxter, BA, CFP, Financial Planner
Donald Bristow, B.Comm., CLU, Financial Planner
Frank Enns, M.Sc., CFP, CLU, Financial Planner
Timothy J. Leier, B.Comm., CFP, Financial Planner
Tanis Robertson, B.Comm., CFP, Financial Associate

Brian Pike Financial Group
1A Pinsent Dr.
Grand-Falls-Windsor, NL A2A 2S8
709-489-8943
Fax: 709-489-5892
brian.pike@nfld.net
Ownership: Private. Part of Armstrong & Quaile Associates Inc., Manotick, ON.
Executives:
Brian Pike, CFP, Manager

Bright & Associates
156 Brant Ave.
Brantford, ON N3T 3H7
519-751-2211
Fax: 519-751-2213
877-871-6108
info@brightandassociates.ca
www.brightandassociates.ca
Ownership: Private
Year Founded: 1988
Number of Employees: 5
Executives:
David Owen, President
Guy Boniferro, Manager, Client Services
Jeremy Voss, Advisor, Marketing
Branches:
Cambridge
#602, 73 Water St.
Cambridge, ON N1R 7L6 Canada
Paris
89 River St. North
Paris, ON N3L 2M3 Canada

Brophy Financial Planning
#106, 99 Holland Ave.
Ottawa, ON K1Y 0Y1
613-728-9573
Fax: 613-725-5642
www.brophyfinancial.com
Ownership: Private
Number of Employees: 4
Profile: Brophy Financial Planning specializes in retirement planning, designing severance packages, protecting income, shaping investment strategies & reducing income taxes.
Executives:
Charles Brophy, RFP, Owner; charlie@brophyfinancial.com
Joyce Owen; joyce@brophyfinancial.com

Brownstone Investment Planning Inc.
#203, 365 Evans Ave.
Toronto, ON M8Z 1K2
416-259-8222
Fax: 416-259-8202
877-676-6686
info@brownstone.ca
www.brownstone.ca
Former Name: Tranquility Financial Services Inc.
Branches:
Calgary
#210, 800 - 6th ave. SW
Calgary, AB T2P 3G3 Canada
403-266-1116
Fax: 403-266-1187
Calgary@brownstone.ca
Winnipeg
#1122, 444 St. Mary Ave.
Winnipeg, MB R3C 3T1 Canada
204-944-9911
Fax: 204-943-6741
866-287-8580

BRYLA Financial Services Ltd.
#1, 108 Allan St.
Oakville, ON L6J 3N1
905-842-1372
Fax: 905-842-6803
bobrizzuto@brylafinancial.com
Ownership: Private
Year Founded: 1994
Executives:
Robert L. Rizzuto, CLU, ChFC; bobrizzuto@brylafinancial.com

Bukovy Financial Services
905 Tungsten St.
Thunder Bay, ON P7B 5Z3
807-684-1820
Fax: 807-344-2117
info@bfinancial.com
www.bfinancial.com
Year Founded: 1997
Number of Employees: 7
Executives:
Ray Bukovy, CFP, President

Burchill Insurance & Financial Services Inc.
301 Front St. North
Sarnia, ON N7T 5S6
519-383-1030
Fax: 519-337-0615
800-386-6553
ken.burchill@clarica.com
Ownership: Private
Year Founded: 1990
Number of Employees: 2
Profile: Full financial & retirement services, insurance & investment fund (licence) are services offered.
Executives:
Ken Burchill, President

Burgeonvest Securities Limited
Also listed under: *Investment Dealers*
Commerce Place
PO Box 65
#1100, 21 King St. West
Hamilton, ON L8P 4W7
905-528-6505
Fax: 905-528-3540
800-209-8379
info@burgeonvest.com
www.burgeonvest.com
Ownership: Burgeonvest Financial Corporation
Year Founded: 1997
Number of Employees: 36
Stock Exchange Membership: Toronto Stock Exchange, TSX Venture Exchange
Executives:
Mario Frankovich, CEO
Morris Vaillancourt, CFO
John Cowman, Vice-President, Investment Advisor
David Ellerby, Vice-President, Compliance
Peter Long, Vice-President
Directors:
Mario Frankovich, Chair
David Ellerby
Peter Long
Morris Vaillancourt
Branches:
Burlington
#201, 1001 Champlain Ave.
Burlington, ON L7L 5Z4 Canada
905-336-9544
Peter Long, Vice-President & Branch Manager
Toronto
#704, 170 University Ave.
Toronto, ON M5H 3B3 Canada
416-246-8241
John De Goey, Branch Manager
Windsor
#200, 600 Ouellette Ave.
Windsor, ON N9A 6Z3 Canada
519-252-1336
866-331-3354
Tony Warden, Branch Manager

Butler Byers Insurance Ltd.
Also listed under: *Federal & Provincial*
301 - 4th Ave. North
Saskatoon, SK S7K 2L8
306-653-2233
Fax: 306-652-5335
office@butlerbyers.com
www.butlerbyers.com
Year Founded: 1907
Profile: The company provides personal & commercial insurance & associated financial services. Associated financial services include group or individual benefit plans, tax planning, RRSPs, & mutual fund investing.
Executives:
Drew Byers, President
Affiliated Companies:
Butler Byers Hail Insurance Ltd.
Branches:
Saskatoon - 8th St. East
#9, 3311 - 8th St. East
Saskatoon, SK S7H 4K1 Canada
306-934-8822
Fax: 306-955-2353
branchoffice@butlerbyers.com
www.butlerbyers.com

C.F.G. Heward Investment Management Ltd.
2115, rue de la Montagne
Montréal, QC H3G 1Z8
514-985-5757
Fax: 514-985-5755
800-567-5257
heward@heward.com
www.heward.com
Year Founded: 1981
Profile: The firm offers investment management & advisory services.

Executives:
Chilion F.G. Heward, Chair
James Heward, President
Willem Hanskamp, Sr. Vice-President
Renato Anzovino, Vice-President
Maurice Conti, Vice-President
C. Jamie Robertson, Vice-President

Campbell Graham Dundee Wealth Management
820 Development Dr.
Kingston, ON K7M 5V7
613-634-3191
Fax: 613-634-4465
800-683-2229
www.campbell-graham.com
Former Name: Campbell Graham, Financial Architects
Ownership: Private
Year Founded: 1990
Number of Employees: 10
Executives:
Michael A. Campbell, President

Canadian Financial Partners
21 MacDonald Rd.
Charlottetown, PE C1A 7H1
902-569-2625
Fax: 902-569-2577

Executives:
Barry Munn

Canadian Tire Financial Services Ltd.(CTAL)
***Also listed under:** Domestic Banks: Schedule I*
PO Box 2000
Welland, ON L3B 5S3
905-735-3131
Fax: 905-735-8962
800-464-9166
www.ctfs.com
Ownership: Wholly owned subsidiary of Canadian Tire Corporation Limited
Year Founded: 1966
Number of Employees: 1,300
Profile: Canadian Tire Financial Services offers a variety of financial products, primarily branded credit cards, that give Canadian Tire customers a choice of payment options, as well as increased loyalty rewards.

Executives:
Tom Gauld, President
Mary Turner, Vice-President, Customer Service & Operations

Canadian Wealth Management Ltd.
#400, 736 - 8th Ave. SW
Calgary, AB T2P 1H4
403-234-8191
Fax: 403-263-0812
cdnwlth@canadianwealth.com
www.canadianwealth.com
Ownership: Private. Owned by CWM Group.
Year Founded: 1983
Number of Employees: 9
Executives:
Robert Savin, Partner, Sr. Financial Advisor
Mark Shilling, Partner, Sr. Financial Advisor; mshilling@canadianwealth.com
Vic Bryant, Vice-President, Sr. Financial Advisor

Candor Financial Group Inc.
3581A Dundas St. West
Toronto, ON M6S 2S8
416-233-9282
Fax: 416-233-6167
general@candorgroup.com
www.candorgroup.com
Executives:
Glen Yuill, CEO; glen@yuillco.com
Michael Vumbaca, CGA, CFP, PFP, President; vumbacam@candorgroup.com

CanFin Financial Group Ltd.
#410, 2630 Skymark Ave.
Mississauga, ON L4W 5A4
905-282-0958
Fax: 905-282-0956
info@canfin.com
www.canfin.com

Canwa Financial & Insurance Services Inc.
#760, 5900 No.3 Rd.
Richmond, BC V6X 3P7
604-231-9980
Fax: 604-231-9670
simon_feng@telus.net
Ownership: Private.
Year Founded: 1998
Number of Employees: 5
Assets: Under $1 million Year End: 20051231
Revenues: Under $1 million Year End: 20051231
Executives:
Simon Feng, Contact
April Gao, Contact

Capital Concepts Group Inc.
#1030, 4720 Kingsway
Burnaby, BC V5H 4N2
604-432-7743
Fax: 604-439-7777
Executives:
Chad Ekren
Geoffrey Perrin

Capital Estate Planning Corporation
Greystone Pavilion
4222 - 97th St.
Edmonton, AB T6E 5Z9
780-463-6128
Fax: 780-462-7523
strategies@capital-planning.ca
www.capitalestateplanning.com
Ownership: Private
Year Founded: 1981
Number of Employees: 14
Executives:
Randy Olson, President
Branches:
Calgary
#100, 301 - 14th St.NW
Calgary, AB T2N 2A1 Canada
403-270-2165
Fax: 403-270-4235
877-330-7423
Shane O'Bryon, Manager

Capital Planning
***Also listed under:** Investment Dealers*
#A304, 555 Legget Dr.
Kanata, ON K2K 2X3
613-271-2108
Fax: 613-270-9540
carol@cpassfield.com
Ownership: Private
Year Founded: 1998
Number of Employees: 1
Assets: Under $1 million
Revenues: Under $1 million

Capri Intercity Financial Corp.
#204, 1835 Gordon Dr.
Kelowna, BC V1Y 3H5
250-860-2426
Fax: 250-860-1213
800-670-1877
receptionmain@capri.ca
www.capri.ca
Ownership: Private. Owned by Capri Group
Year Founded: 1993
Executives:
Robin Durrant, Manager; rdurrant@capri.ca
Doreen Rigby, Personal Lines Manager; drigby@capri.ca
Branches:
Kamloops - Tranquille Rd.
#39, 1800 Tranquille Rd.
Kamloops, BC V2B 3L9 Canada
250-376-2281
Fax: 250-376-0411
Laurie Slater, Manager
Kamloops South
Clock Tower Bldg., Tudor Village
#1, 1315 Summit Dr.
Kamloops, BC V2C 5R9 Canada
250-828-2135
Fax: 250-374-5557
Sue Clifford, Manager
Kelowna - Harvey Ave.
Orchard Park Mall
#1325, 2271 Harvey Ave.
Kelowna, BC V1Y 2H5 Canada
250-860-8741
Fax: 250-860-8749
Jan Lommer, Manager
Kelowna - Hwy. 97 North
Kelowna Crossing Shopping Centre
#125, 2463 Hwy. 97 North
Kelowna, BC V1X 4J2 Canada
250-860-2827
Fax: 250-860-5470
Jan Lommer, Manager
Penticton
396 Ellis St.
Penticton, BC V2A 4L7 Canada
250-492-5821
Fax: 250-492-6115
Teresa Ciardullo, Manager
Vernon - 48 Ave.
2702 - 48 Ave.
Vernon, BC V1T 3R4 Canada
250-542-0291
Fax: 250-260-3891
msundquist@capri.ca
Maria Sundquist, Manager
Vernon - Hwy. 6
Polson Place Mall
#255, 2306 Hwy. 6
Vernon, BC V1T 7E3 Canada
250-545-9135
Fax: 250-545-4464
gbaughen@capri.ca
Gordon Baughen, Manager
Westbank
#9, 2475 Dobbin Rd.
Westbank, BC V4T 2E9 Canada
250-768-3866
Fax: 250-768-1199
Judy Chase, Manager
Winfield
Winfield Shopping Centre
#15, 10051 Hwy. 97 North
Winfield, BC V4V 1P6 Canada
250-766-2929
Fax: 250-766-5014
fmacdonald@capri.ca
Faye MacDonald, Manager

Carels Financial Service
PO Box 338
100 Osborne St. North
Winnipeg, MB R3L 1Y5
204-946-8191
Fax: 204-946-8865
carels@mts.net
Profile: Carels Financial Services Inc. is an independent financial consulting business offering investment & insurance products & services such as Group Benefits, RRSP's, RIF's, Non-Registered Investments, Life, Critical Illness & Disability Insurance.

Executives:
Carleen Carels

Carleton Financial Services Ltd.
#2, 733 Main St.
Woodstock, NB E7M 2E6
506-328-8626
Fax: 506-328-8313
cfsfunds@nb.aibn.com
Year Founded: 1993
Number of Employees: 221

Cartile Financial Services(CFS)
#101, 900 Purdy Mills Rd.
Kingston, ON K7M 3M9
613-530-3560
Fax: 613-530-3847
info@cartilefinancial.com
www.cartilefinancial.com
Ownership: Private. Part of Armstrong & Quaile Associates Inc., Manotick, ON.
Year Founded: 1981
Executives:
Peter Cartile, President; pc@cartilefinancial.com

Castle Rock Financial
Also listed under: *Investment Dealers*
#209, 100, boul Alexis-Nihon
Montréal, QC H4M 2N7
514-748-8880
Fax: 514-748-1911

Catalyst Chartered Accountants & Consultants
Also listed under: *Accountants*
318 Centre St. South
High River, AB T1V 1N7
403-652-3032
Fax: 403-652-7051
inquire@catalystsolutions.ca
www.catalystsolutions.ca
Former Name: Coakwell Crawford Cairns LLP; Coakwell Moore

Ownership: Private
Partners:
Rodney L. Baceda, CA; rodb@catalystsolutions.ca
Brock D. Cairns, CA; brockc@catalystsolutions.ca
Gerald L. Coakwell, CA; gerryc@catalystsolutions.ca
Cam Crawford, FCA, CMC, CBV; camc@catalystsolutions.ca
Ted Finningley, TEP, CA; tedf@catalystsolutions.ca
Terri Mihaui, CA; terrim@catalystsolutions.ca
Donald C. Phillips, CA; donp@catalystsolutions.ca
Branches:
Calgary
#1620, Trimac House
Calgary, AB T2P 3T6 Canada
403-296-0082
Fax: 403-296-0415

Cedarpoint Investments Inc.
#900, 30 St. Clair Ave. West
Toronto, ON M4V 3A1
416-927-2000
Fax: 416-927-2013
dposluns@cedarpt.com
Ownership: Private
Year Founded: 1995
Number of Employees: 8
Executives:
David Posluns, Managing Director; 416-927-2007
Wilfred Posluns, Managing Director; 416-927-2011
Sydney Loftus; 416-927-2003
Lynn Posluns; 416-927-2002

Centre Financial Corp.
Also listed under: *Pension & Money Management Companies*
222 - 11 Ave. NW
Calgary, AB T2M 0B8
403-571-0000
Fax: 403-277-2289
mail@centrefinancial.com
Ownership: Private, JLK Holdings
Year Founded: 1994
Number of Employees: 7
Assets: $36,000
Revenues: $100,000
Executives:
John M. Knowles, President; 403-571-0002
Robert Stewart, CFP, Treasurer; 403-571-0000
Directors:
John M. Knowles
Robert Stewart

Champlain Consulting Associates Ltd.
Also listed under: *Financing & Loan Companies; Investment Management*
PO Box 103, H Stn. H
#5, 1254, rue MacKay
Montréal, QC H3G 2K5
514-931-9336
Fax: 514-371-1565
866-931-9336
ron@champlainconsulting.com
www.champlainconsulting.com
Ownership: Private
Year Founded: 1969
Profile: Acting as financial consultant &/or investment banker, the company provides strategic, creative business planning & innovative sourcing of financing for mid-sized companies, whose needs typically range from $1,000,000 - $50,000,000. Ranging from secured debt to venture capital, all industry sectors & stages of development are covered. Geographic experience includes the following: Canada, USA, Bahamas, Caribbean, Western Europe, & Israel.

Executives:
Ronald Raisman, President/CEO; ron@champlainconsulting.com

Chevalier Financial
50 Queen St. South
Tilbury, ON N0P 2L0
519-682-3632
Fax: 519-682-3991
Executives:
Randy R. Chevalier, Contact

Chevalier, Meunier et associés inc
#150, 1240, av Beaumont
Montréal, QC H3P 3E5
514-737-6446
Fax: 514-737-7038
866-737-6446
chevmeun@chevmeun.qc.ca
www.chevmeun.qc.ca
Year Founded: 1995
Executives:
Marie Chevalier, Présidente et co-fondatrice; mchevali@chevmeun.qc.ca
Pierre Meunier, Vice-président et co-fondateur; 514-737-6446; pmeunier@chevmeun.qc.ca
Jocelyne Renaud, Directrice générale; 514-737-6446; jrenaud@chevmeun.qc.ca

Chris Palmer & Associates
Sun Tower
#810, 1550 Bedford Hwy.
Bedford, NS B4A 1E6
902-832-9433
Fax: 902-832-9450
www.chrispalmer.com
Executives:
Chris Palmer, BBA, CMA, CFP

Christel Shuckburgh
4937 - 50th St.
Stettler, AB T0C 2L0
403-742-1423
Fax: 403-742-1424
888-898-1010
cshuckburgh@pipfs.com
Former Name: Gilbert Financial Services
Ownership: Private. Partners in Planning
Year Founded: 1995
Executives:
Christel Shuckburgh

CJS Financial Group
#200, 418 St Paul St.
Kamloops, BC V2C 2J6
250-314-6979
Fax: 250-314-6968
www.cjsfinancial.savetax.ca
Executives:
Mary-Anne Jensen; majensen@shaw.ca
Geoff Sharples; gsharp@mail.ocis.net

Clarke Financial Management
195 Dufferin Ave.
Brantford, ON N3T 4R4
519-758-5651
Fax: 519-758-0502
Executives:
Sean Clarke

Clements Financial Services Inc.
15447 Columbia Ave.
White Rock, BC V4B 1K3
604-535-6918
Fax: 604-535-6921
don@cfinancial.net
www.cfinancial.net
Executives:
Don Clements

Cole & Partners
Also listed under: *Accountants*
#2000, 80 Richmond St. West
Toronto, ON M5H 2A4
416-364-9700
Fax: 416-364-9707
www.coleandpartners.com
Year Founded: 1975
Profile: Advisory services are provided in mergers, acquisitions, divestitures & corporate finance, as well as litigation consulting & business valutation. Services include business & securities valuations & investigative & forensic accounting. North American clients range from medium sized private companies to large public companies.

Executives:
Stephen R. Cole, Advisor, Corporate Finance; scole@cole&partners.com
Larry Andrade, Associate
Enzo Carlucci, Associate

The Coles Group
Cogswell Tower
#900, 2000 Barrington St.
Halifax, NS B3J 3K1
902-421-1770
Fax: 902-425-8905
Service@ColesGroup.com
www.ColesGroup.com
Former Name: MacBurnie & Associates
Executives:
Keith R. Coles, CEO

Collins Barrow Chartered Accountants - Hearst
Also listed under: *Accountants*
PO Box 637
1021 George St.
Hearst, ON P0L 1N0
705-362-4261
Fax: 705-362-4641
hearst@collinsbarrow.com
Ownership: Private.
Year Founded: 1983
Number of Employees: 17
Assets: Under $1 million Year End: 20051130
Revenues: $1-5 million Year End: 20051130
Executives:
Noël Cantin, Partner; ncantin@collinsbarrow.com
Denis P. Hébert, Partner; dhebert@collinsbarrow.com

Comeau Financial
Also listed under: *Pension & Money Management Companies*
#300, 128 - 4th Ave. South
Saskatoon, SK S7K 1M8
306-652-7225
Fax: 306-665-0555
800-667-3929
jack@comeaufinancial.com
www.comeaufinancial.com
Ownership: Private
Year Founded: 1990
Number of Employees: 3
Executives:
Jack Comeau, CFP, RFP, ChFC, CLU, BSA, President

Community First Financial Planning
291 - 4th St.
Courtenay, BC V9N 1G7
250-703-4129
Fax: 250-703-4159
dougj@cvcu.com
Revenues: $10-50 million
Executives:
Doug Jefferson, BA, CFP

Community Futures Development Corporation of Alberni Clayoquot
Also listed under: *Financing & Loan Companies*

Community Futures Development Corporation of Alberni Clayoquot (continued)
4757 Tebo Ave.
Port Alberni, BC V9Y 8A9
250-724-1241
Fax: 250-724-1028
877-724-1241
info@cfdcac.ca
www.cfdcac.ca
Ownership: Non-profit
Number of Employees: 9

Complete Brokerage Services Inc.
#3000, 8171 Ackroyd Rd.
Richmond, BC V6X 3K1
604-270-2802
Fax: 604-270-2893
www.cbsinc.ca
Ownership: Private
Year Founded: 2000
Number of Employees: 6
Executives:
Gideon Leoganda, COO
Branches:
Burnaby
#214, 3823 Henning Dr.
Burnaby, BC V5C 6P3 Canada
Vancouver
Two Bentall Tower
#900, 555 Burrard St.
Vancouver, BC V6X 3K1 Canada
604-689-8805
Fax: 604-270-2893

Complete Financial Planning Inc.
6 Cumberland St.
Barrie, ON L4N 2P4
705-726-7526
Fax: 705-726-8371
aredmann@dundeewealth.com
Ownership: Private
Year Founded: 1996
Number of Employees: 11
Assets: Under $1 million
Revenues: $1-5 million
Executives:
Alfred Redmann, CFP, CDFA, CLU, Contact

Conder & Co. Financial Advisors
#212, 2628 Granville St.
Vancouver, BC V6H 4B4
604-734-9194
Fax: 604-734-8533
Former Name: Conder & Company Limited
Ownership: Private
Year Founded: 1991
Number of Employees: 1
Executives:
David Conder, CFP, RFP, President

Confident Financial Services (1969) Limited
Also listed under: *Pension & Money Management Companies*
#202, Apple Creek Blvd.
Markham, ON L3R 9X7
905-707-5900
Fax: 905-707-7476
confident@idirect.com
Ownership: Private
Year Founded: 1969
Profile: The company provides personal investment planning & wealth management.

Consultations Pierre St-Germain/ Pierre St-Germain Consulting
Also listed under: *Investment Dealers*
1958, rue de Cambrai
Saint-Bruno, QC J3V 3J3
450-441-2262
Fax: 450-653-6631
pstg@pstg.com
www.pstg.com
Executives:
Pierre St-Germain, Contact

Cooper Financial Services Group Inc.
Douglas Professional Centre
#550, 2950 Douglas St.
Victoria, BC V8T 4N4
250-475-0557
Fax: 250-475-0557
866-475-0552
cfg@cooperfinancial.ca
www.cooperfinancial.ca
Year Founded: 1986
Executives:
Carol Cooper, Owner & Operator

Cormier Financial
394 Ouellet St.
Shediac, NB E4P 2K7
506-532-2158
Fax: 506-532-8022
jeanc@nbnet.nb.ca
Ownership: Private.
Year Founded: 1986
Sue Thompson, Office Manager

Cornerstone Securities Canada Inc.
Also listed under: *Investment Dealers; Investment Management*
The Exchange Tower, 2 First Canadian Place
PO Box 427, First Canadian Pl. Stn. First Canadian Pl.
#1800, 130 King St. West
Toronto, ON M5X 1E3
416-862-8000
Fax: 416-862-8001
888-268-6735
counsel@cornerstonegroup.com
www.cornerstonegroup.com
Ownership: Private
Year Founded: 1978
Profile: The company offers the following services: financial & investment banking services; corporate & financial advisory services, including the placement of debt, equity & hybrid securities, tax-effective corporate finance & restructurings; advice on acquisitions & divestitures, mergers & consolidations, joint ventures & syndications, leveraged buyouts, internal expansions, & capital reorganizations, specialized financings & due diligence reviews, including legal, tax, valuation & pricing issues.

Executives:
Gerald Fields, LL.B., President/CEO

Corporate Concept Group
#903, 505 Consumers Rd.
Toronto, ON M2J 4V8
416-498-5550
Fax: 416-498-5188
www.corporateconceptgroup.com
Executives:
Scott Goddard; s.goddard@corporateconceptgroup.com
Russell Nagano; r.nagano@corporateconceptgroup.com

Corporate Planning Associates(CPA)
#1700, 320 Bay St.
Toronto, ON M5H 4A6
416-364-7898
Fax: 416-364-6438
jrooney@cpafin.com
www.cpafin.com
Ownership: Private
Year Founded: 1974
Profile: CPA provides financial services to Canadian corporate executives & high net-worth individuals. It is able to offer a range of products due to its alliance with Scotiabank. CPA has offices across Canada.

Executives:
P. Lee Fisher, President/CEO
Brigitte M. Murphy, Exec. Vice-President & CFO
David Vicic, Sr. Vice-President, Technical Services
John R. Ross, Chair
Branches:
Calgary
#3860, 855 - 2nd St. SW
Calgary, AB T2P 4J8 Canada
403-262-8130
Fax: 403-262-1473
John W. Davis, Sr. Vice-President, Consulting
Vancouver
#880, 666 Burrard St.
Vancouver, BC V6C 2X8 Canada
604-685-5550
Fax: 604-685-2262
Harris Abro, Sr. Vice-President

Corporation Financière Sommet
240, 46e rue ouest
Québec, QC G1H 5H9
514-623-2575
sommet@sympatico.ca
www3.sympatico.ca/sommet

Cougar Global Investments
Also listed under: *Pension & Money Management Companies*
#1001, 357 Bay St.
Toronto, ON M5H 2T7
416-368-5255
Fax: 416-368-7738
800-387-3779
info@cougarglobal.com
www.cougarglobal.com
Ownership: Private
Year Founded: 1993
Number of Employees: 11
Assets: $100-500 million Year End: 20061031
Revenues: $1-5 million Year End: 20061031
Executives:
James Breech, President/CEO; jbreech@cougarglobal.com
Art Hounsell, Sr. Vice-President, Operations; ahounsell@cougarglobal.com
Vicki Breech, Vice-President, Wealth Management Services; vbreech@cougarglobal.com
Directors:
Roy Bennett, Chair
Donald G. Baker
R. Peter McLaughlin

Cove Financial Planning Ltd.
4322 Gallant Ave.
North Vancouver, BC V7G 1K8
604-924-9152
Fax: 604-924-9153
888-783-5402
info@covefinancial.ca
www.covefinancial.ca
Profile: The firm incorporates a holistic financial planning program. It serves high income, high net worth individuals.

Executives:
Bernie Geiss, CFP, CLU, FMA, RHU, President
Alisen Brown, Contact, Business Operations
Katrina Stobbart, Contact, Insurance

Covenant Financial Inc.
20385 - 64th Ave.
Langley, BC V2Y 1N5
604-514-2105
Fax: 604-514-1994
service@covenant.ca
www.covenant.ca/covenant_financial.html
Former Name: Ronald Blue & Co. Canada
Ownership: The Covenant Group, Langley, BC.
Profile: Part of The Covenant Group, Covenant Financial is a registered mutual fund dealership.

Directors:
Henry Block
Ron Blue
Michael Gibney
Malcolm Seath
Kari Yli-Renko

Coventree Capital Group Inc.
390 Bay St., 18th Fl.
Toronto, ON M5H 2Y2
416-362-2125
Fax: 416-362-2124
admin@coventree.ca
www.coventree.ca
Profile: Coventree Capital is an investment bank which specializes in structured finance, by using securitization-based funding technology. Structuring & funding solutions are provided for issuing clients & innovative investment products are created for investing partners. An affiliated company is Nereus Financial Inc.

Cowan Benefits Consulting Limited
Also listed under: *Pension & Money Management Companies; Accounting & Law*
PO Box 1510
705 Fountain St. North
Cambridge, ON N1R 5T2

519-650-6361
Fax: 519-650-6367
800-609-5549
Other Information: 800-434-9606 (Toll Free, French)
infocbcl@cowangroup.ca
www.cowangroup.ca
Former Name: Cowan Wright Beauchamp Limited
Ownership: Wholly owned subsidiary of The Cowan Insurance Group, Cambridge, ON.
Year Founded: 1981
Number of Employees: 150
Revenues: $10-50 million
Profile: The advisory firm provides actuarial, consulting & administrative services in areas such as pensions, retirement & group benefits. The organization is affiliated with Cowan Insurance Brokers & Frank Cowan Company.

Executives:
Marcel Gingras, President
Karen Cooper, Vice-President, Finance
Branches:
Ottawa
641 Montreal Rd.
Ottawa, ON K1K 0T4 Canada
613-741-3313
Fax: 613-741-7771
888-509-7797
clients@cowangroup.ca
www.cowangroup.ca
Bob Proulx, Vice-President

CPP Investment Board

PO Box 101
#2600, One Queen St. East
Toronto, ON M5C 2W5
416-868-4075
Fax: 416-868-4760
866-557-9510
Other Information: TTY: 416/868-6035
csr@cppib.ca
www.cppib.ca
Also Known As: Canada Pension Plan Investment Board
Ownership: Crown corporation
Year Founded: 1997
Assets: $10-100 billion Year End: 20060930
Profile: The CPP Investment Board is a professional investment management organization. Its mandate, in accordance with legislation, is as follows: To invest in the best interests of CPP contributors & beneficiaries; to maximize long-term investment returns without undue risk; to provide cash management services to the Canada Pension Plan so that they can pay benefits. The Board is governed & managed independently of the Canada Pension Plan & at arm's length from federal & provincial governments. Stewards of the CPP are federal & provincial finance ministers. The Board is also accountable to Parliament & to approximately 16 million contributors & beneficiaries.

Executives:
David Denison, President/CEO
Myra Libenson, Chief Operations Officer
John H. Butler, Sr. Vice-President, General Counsel & Corporate Secretary
Ian Dale, Sr. Vice-President, Communications & Stakeholder Relations
Graeme Eadie, Sr. Vice-President, Real Estate Investments
John H. Ilkiw, Sr. Vice-President, Portfolio Design & Risk Management
Donald M. Raymond, Sr. Vice-President, Public Market Investments
David Wexler, Sr. Vice-President, Human Resources
Mark D. Wiseman, Sr. Vice-President, Private Investments
Graeme Bevans, Vice-President, Head of Infrastructure Investments
André Bourbonnais, Vice-President, Head of Principal Investing
John B. Breen, Vice-President & Head, Funds & Secondaries
Jennifer Thompson, Vice-President, Head of Information Technology
Directors:
Gail Cook-Bennett, Chair
Robert Astley
Germaine Gibara
Peter K. Hendrick
Jacob Levi
Philip MacDougall
Helen M. Meyer
Dale G. Parker
Mary C. Ritchie
Helen Sinclair
Ronald E. Smith
David Walker

Craig & Taylor Associates

#504, 1525 Carling Ave.
Ottawa, ON K1Z 8R9
613-725-3414
Fax: 613-725-9570
800-265-8244
askus@craigandtaylor.com
www.craigandtaylor.com
Ownership: Private.
Year Founded: 1984
Number of Employees: 19
Executives:
Jerry Taylor, CFP, RFP, CLU, CH.F.C., CSA, President; jtaylor@craigandtaylor.com
Jennifer A. Martin, CFP, CSA, Exec. Vice-President; jmartin@craigandtaylor.com
Stephen Cock, CFP, Vice-President, Director Technical Planning Division; scock@craigandtaylor.com
Todd Thompson, CFP, CSA, Vice-President; tthompson@craigandtaylor.com
Belle Severn, Branch Manager; bsevern@craigandtaylor.com
Vickie Snow, CFP, Sr. Planner; vsnow@craigandtaylor.com
David Cain, CFP, Financial Planner; dcain@craigandtaylor.com

Cranston, Gaskin, O'Reilly & Vernon Investment Counsel(CGO&V)

***Also listed under:** Pension & Money Management Companies*
35A Hazelton Ave.
Toronto, ON M5R 2E3
416-929-7145
Fax: 416-929-5281
don@cgovic.com
www.cgovic.com
Ownership: Private.
Year Founded: 1995
Number of Employees: 13
Assets: $500m-1 billion Year End: 20061231
Profile: bhe independent investment counselling firm manages approximately $1,000,000,000 on behalf of institutions, charitable organizations & high net worth invividuals.

Executives:
Mark Gaskin, Managing Partner; 416-929-8678; mark@cgovic.com
Don Cranston, Partner; 416-929-7236; don@cgovic.com
Jim Green, Partner; 416-847-8301; jimg@cgovic.com
Sheila Norman, Partner; 416-646-0192; sheila@cgovic.com
Gord O'Reilly, Partner; 416-929-9286; gord@cgovic.com
Ted Ecclestone, Chief Financial Officer, COO

Crawford, Graham & Associates

442 Winniett St.
Caledonia, ON N3W 1E4
905-765-9624
Fax: 905-765-9758
877-765-9624
www.crawfordgraham.com
Ownership: Private
Year Founded: 1988
Number of Employees: 4
Executives:
Bill Crawford
Branches:
Ancaster
28 Hackney Ct.
Ancaster, ON L9K 1M3 Canada
905-304-8341
Fax: 905-304-8342
888-304-7611
Carla Larochelle
Brantford
112 George St.
Brantford, ON N3T 2Y4 Canada
519-759-6160
Fax: 519-759-8106
877-301-6684
Rick Graham

Creative Planning Financial Group

#500, 1867 Yonge St.
Toronto, ON M4S 1Y5
416-487-5210
Fax: 416-487-7940
www.cpfg.com
Year Founded: 1971
Executives:
S. Sheldon Taerk, Chair
Melvin M. Gilbert

Credential Asset Management Inc.

#800, 1441 Creekside Dr.
Vancouver, BC V6J 4S7
604-714-3800
Fax: 604-714-3801
Executives:
Robert J. Mowbrey, President/CEO

Credential Financial Inc.

#800, 1111 West Georgia St.
Vancouver, BC V6E 4T6
Fax: 604-714-3801
877-384-4225
clientrelations@credential.com
www.credential.com
Former Name: Credential Group
Number of Employees: 4000
Executives:
Helen E. Blackburn, CA, Sr. Vice-President
Matt Edgar, Sr. Vice-President/CFO
Affiliated Companies:
Credential Asset Management Inc.
Credential Direct
Credential Insurance Services
Credential Securities Inc.
Credential Strategies
Offices:
Burlington
#200, 3430 South Service Rd.
Burlington, ON L7N 3T9 Canada
905-632-9200
Fax: 905-632-0032
Calgary
102A - 9705 Horton Rd. SW
Calgary, AB T2V 2X5 Canada
403-212-3936
Fax: 403-253-0056
Halifax
#329, 7071 Bayers Rd.
Halifax, NS B3L 2C2 Canada
902-454-6205
Fax: 902-453-6586
Regina
#200, 2500 - 13th Ave.
Regina, SK S4P 0W2 Canada
306-569-5500
Fax: 306-359-7575
Winnipeg
#760, 215 Garry St.
Winnipeg, MB R3C 3P3 Canada
204-927-7430
Fax: 204-927-7440
866-248-1421

Credit Counselling Services of Alberta Ltd.

***Also listed under:** Pension & Money Management Companies*
#225, 602 - 11 Ave. SW
Calgary, AB T2R 1J8
403-265-2201
Fax: 403-265-2240
800-294-0076
info@creditcounselling.com
www.creditcounselling.com
Ownership: Private. Community based limited not-for-profit.
Year Founded: 1997
Number of Employees: 35
Assets: $1-5 million
Revenues: $1-5 million
Profile: Credit Counselling Services of Alberta is a not-for-profit personal money management education & debt repayment services company. It offers counselling, workshops & programs in the following areas: basic money management, debt resolution & consumer education. There will be an office in Red Deer.

Executives:
Jim Thome, Executive Director; 403-234-6191; jthorne@creditcounselling.com

Credit Counselling Services of Alberta Ltd. (continued)
Tracy Watson, MCS, Manager, Communications; 403-234-6189; tracy@creditcounselling.com
Branches:
Edmonton
Sun Life Place
#440, 10123 - 99 St.
Edmonton, AB T5J 3H1 Canada
780-423-5265
Debbie Klein, Manager

Creststreet Asset Management Ltd.
Also listed under: *Investment Fund Companies*
#1450, 70 University Ave.
Toronto, ON M5J 2M4
416-864-6330
Fax: 416-862-8950
866-864-6330
info@creststreet.com
www.creststreet.com
Ownership: Public.
Year Founded: 2000
Stock Symbol: CRS.UN
Profile: Affiliated companies include the following: Creststreet Mutual Funds Limited, Creststreet Power & Income Fund LP, Creststreet Energy Hedge Fund LP, Creststreet 2004 Limited Partnership & Creststreet 2005 Limited Partnership.
Executives:
Eric McFadden, Managing Director
Erich Ossowski, Vice-President, Wind Power
Donna Shea, Vice-President, Finance
Sheryl J. Chiddenton, Manager, Investment Services
Aaron C.B. Maybin, Associate
Creststreet:
Resource Fund
RRSP Eligible; Inception Year: 2002; Fund Managers: Robert J. Toole
Managed Income Fund
RRSP Eligible; Inception Year: 2004; Fund Managers: Robert J. Toole
Managed Equity Index Fund
RRSP Eligible; Inception Year: 2004; Fund Managers: Robert J. Toole
Branches:
Calgary
#1040, 444 - 5th Ave. SW
Calgary, AB T2P 2T9 Canada
403-215-2265
Fax: 403-261- 443

Croissance Capital Inc.
Also listed under: *Investment Dealers*
#200, 714 rue King est
Sherbrooke, QC J1G 1C4
819-562-2877
Fax: 819-562-9294

Crown Capital Partners Inc.
#1900, 1874 Scarth St.
Regina, SK S4P 4B3
306-546-8000
Fax: 306-546-8010
www.crowncapital.ca/
Ownership: Private
Year Founded: 2000
Number of Employees: 15
Assets: $100-500 million
Profile: Crown Capital Partners manages over $150 million of Canadian venture capital, mezzanine and fixed income investments for Crown Life Insurance Company and the Saskatchewan Government Growth Fund.
Partners:
Christopher A. Johnson, Managing Partner, Chief Investment Officer
Christopher J. Anderson, Partner
Brent G. Hughes, Partner
Brian A. Johnson, Partner
Adam M. Rowe, Partner
Marble Point Energy Ltd.
Adeptron Technologies Corporation
Americ Disc Inc.
Rockford Corporation
Clothing for Modern Times Ltd.
Furniture Manufacturing Company
Software Company
Bioriginal Food and Science Corp.
Sherson Group
Elephant & Castle Group Inc.
Ranchgate Energy Inc.
Stegg Limited
Axia NetMedia Corporation
CrownAg International Inc.
Mid-Sask Terminal Ltd.
R Young Seeds Inc.
Richards Packaging Inc.
ETEC Environmental Technologies Equipment Corp.
Purcell Energy Ltd.
Harman Poultry Farm Ltd.
Saskcan Pulse Trading Inc.
Nu-Fab Burton LP
Tri-North Farms LP
Prairie Plant Systems Inc.
Quartus Energy Ltd.
Branches:
Toronto
#1316, 175 Bloor St. East
Toronto, ON M4W 3R8 Canada
416-927-1851
Fax: 416-927-0863

Crystal Wealth Management System Ltd.
#102, 5575 North Service Rd.
Burlington, ON L7L 6M1
905-332-4414
Fax: 905-332-6028
877-299-2854
info@crystalwealth.com
www.crystalwealth.com
Ownership: Wholly owned by its employees
Profile: For further information about Crystal Funds, contact Crystal Funds (www.iafunds.com).
Executives:
Clayton Smith, Managing Director
Gary Allen, Chief Market Strategist
Scott Whale, COO

Culliton Cerullo Financial Services
420 Weber St. West, #E
Waterloo, ON N2L 4E7
519-725-8311
Fax: 519-725-2998
www.cullitoncerullo.com
Executives:
Vince Cerullo, Contact

Cumberland Private Wealth Managment Inc.
Also listed under: *Investment Dealers; Investment Management*
#300, 99 Yorkville Ave.
Toronto, ON M5R 3K5
416-929-1090
Fax: 416-929-1172
800-929-8296
info@cpwm.ca
www.cpwm.ca
Former Name: Cumberland Asset Management Corp.
Ownership: Private. Owned by Cumberland Partners Ltd.
Year Founded: 1998
Number of Employees: 45
Profile: Discretionary investment management services are provided. Cumberland Private Wealth Management serves over 800 high net worth families, plus their related entities in Canada and other countries. Cumberland has approximately $1,800,000,000 assets under management..
Executives:
Gerald R. Connor, CEO
Gordon Cunningham, President
Peter Jackson, Vice-President
John Poulter, Vice-President, Chief Investment Officer
Directors:
Gerald R. Connor, Chair
Gordon Cunningham
Peter Jackson
John Poulter

Cumming & Cumming Wealth Managment Inc.
#202, 1540 Cornwall Rd.
Oakville, ON L6J 7W5
905-337-9984
Fax: 905-337-9985
Ownership: Private.
Executives:
Bruce Cumming, CFP, RFP, CLU, ChFC, CIM, TEP, RHU, Partner
Marie Cumming, MBA, Partner

Cunningham & Associates Financial Services
#202, 4303 Albert St.
Regina, SK S4S 3R6
306-585-3518
inquiries@cafin.com
www.cafin.com
Executives:
Karen M. Cunningham, CA, CFP, RFP, Chartered Accountant & Certified Financial Planner, Registered Financial Planner

Cypress Capital Management Ltd.
Also listed under: *Pension & Money Management Companies*
PO Box 11136
#1700, 1055 West Georgia St.
Vancouver, BC V6E 3P3
604-659-1850
Fax: 604-659-1899
877-659-1850
Ownership: AFG Private Investment Management, Toronto, ON.
Year Founded: 1998
Executives:
Carl Hoyt, CFA, Partner & Head, Research & Investment Management
Offices:
Calgary
Home Oil Tower
1155, 324 - 8th Ave. SW
Calgary, AB T2P 2Z2 Canada
403-663-6600
Fax: 403-451-9990

D.M. Johnston Financial Services
Owen Sound Professional Centre
#6B, 945 - 3rd Ave. East
Owen Sound, ON N4K 2K8
519-371-3273
Fax: 519-371-1269
dmj@bmts.com
Executives:
Donald M. Johnston

D.W. Robart Professional Corporation
Also listed under: *Accountants*
#1480, 540 - 5th Ave. SW
Calgary, AB T2P 0M2
403-266-2611
Fax: 403-265-8626
don@robart.ca
Ownership: Private
Executives:
D.W. Robart, RFP, President

Daryl Smith Estate & Financial Planning Inc.
#204, 6908 Roper Rd.
Edmonton, AB T6B 3H9
780-437-5070
Fax: 780-437-1575
877-301-5070
daryl@dsmithfinancial.com
www.dsmithfinancial.com
Ownership: Private
Year Founded: 1991
Number of Employees: 3
Assets: Under $1 million
Revenues: Under $1 million
Profile: Services include benefit & estate planning.
Executives:
Daryl Smith, President

Datile Securities
#208, 1 West Pearce St.
Richmond Hill, ON L4B 3K3
905-771-8500
Fax: 905-771-8501
Ownership: Private.
Number of Employees: 3
Executives:
Lewis Martin, President
Frank Bennett, Vice-President
Cathy Day, General Manager

Dave Dale Insurance Agencies Ltd.
PO Box 1480
386 Market Ave.
Grand Forks, BC V0H 1H0
250-442-2174
Fax: 250-442-8711
info@davedaleinsurance.com
www.davedaleinsurance.com
Executives:
Daniel P. McNamara, General Manager
Judy McNamara, Secretary
Robert Klassan, Certified Financial Planner

Dave P. Financial Corp.
Broadmead Office Park
#107, 4430 Chatterton Way
Victoria, BC V8X 5J2
250-727-7011
Fax: 250-388-5412
800-575-1237
davep@highspeedplus.com
www.mortgageinsurance.bc.ca
Former Name: Dave Pettenuzzo Financial Services
Year Founded: 1997
Number of Employees: 2
Revenues: $1-5 million
Profile: The company is also a broker for life, mortgage, disability & critical illness insurance, as well as corporate benefits.
Executives:
Dave E. Pettenuzzo, B. Comm., CFP, CLU, CH.F.C., RHU, Contact

David Ingram & Associates
Also listed under: *Accountants*
329 Waverly St.
Ottawa, ON K2P 0V9
613-234-8023
Fax: 613-234-8925
info@accessfp.com
Ownership: Private
Year Founded: 1981
Profile: The company is affiliated with Gro-net Financial Tax & Pension Planners.

David M. Voth
#7, 2366 Ave. C North
Saskatoon, SK S7L 5X5
306-242-3193
Fax: 306-931-8577
david@davidvoth.com
www.davidvoth.com
Ownership: Private
Executives:
David Voth, President

Davis Martindale LLP
Also listed under: *Trustees in Bankruptcy; Accounting & Law*
373 Commissioners Rd. West
London, ON N6J 1Y4
519-673-3141
Fax: 519-645-1646
info@davismartindale.com
www.davismartindale.com
Ownership: Private
Year Founded: 1967
Number of Employees: 28
Partners:
Bruce M. Barran
Mike D. Evans
William J.R. Gohn
Michael K. Koenig
L. Ron Martindale Sr.
Ron L. Martindale Jr.
Ian D. McIntosh
Paul R. Panabaker

Davis-Rea Ltd.
#1400, 95 St. Clair Ave. West
Toronto, ON M4V 1N6
416-961-2494
Fax: 416-925-1215
info@davisrea.com
www.davisrea.com
Ownership: Private
Year Founded: 1997
Number of Employees: 16
Assets: $100-500 million
Profile: The private investment counseling firm manages accounts for individuals, families, charities, foundations & private corporations.
Executives:
Douglas A.C. Davis, President, Secretary
James E. Houston, Sr. Vice-President; 416-961-2494; jh@davisrea.com
Joy M. Cunningham, Vice-President
Andrew E.M. Martyn, Vice-President, Portfolio Manager
P. Zachary Curry, Assistant Vice-President
Douglas A.R. Davis, Co-Manager, Business Development
Patrick Tryon, Co-Manager, Business Development
Directors:
David L. Rea, Chair
Donald Comish
Richard B. Lewis
Gary Van Nest

DD Humes Financial Services Inc.
#100, 589, av Marshall
Montréal, QC H9P 1E1
514-631-0725
Fax: 514-636-9365
dave@ddhumes.com
www.ddhumes.com
Executives:
David Dawson Humes

De Thomas Financial Corp.
#200, 7620 Yonge St.
Thornhill, ON L4J 1V9
905-731-9800
Fax: 905-731-9759
800-558-8519
info@dethomasfinancial.com
www.dethomasfinancial.com
Ownership: Private
Profile: De Thomas Financial is a full service mutual fund dealer. The organization provides advice regarding income needs, investment, taxation, retirement planning, employee & personal benefits, estate planning & insurance.
Executives:
Anthony De Thomasis, CFP, RFP, President
Stella Pearson, Advisor & Specialist, Estate & Insurance
Luisa Vivona, Coordinator, IT Systems
Cyndy De Thomasis, Contact, Financial Compliance
Michael J. Hill, Manager & Financial Advisor, Windsor Branch

Deichert Nesbitt Financial Strategies Inc.
165 Huron St.
Stratford, ON N5A 5S9
519-271-5279
Fax: 519-271-8244
info@deichertfinancial.ca
www.deichertfinancial.ca
Former Name: Deichert Financial Strategies Inc.
Executives:
Ron Deichert, CFP, CLU, Ch.F.C.
Ken Nesbitt, CFP, CLU, Ch.F.C.
Carolyn Debus

DIA Financial
#812, 10 Milner Business Ct.
Toronto, ON M1B 3C6
416-293-6666
Fax: 416-293-6206
diafinancial@on.aibn.com
Ownership: Private
Number of Employees: 3
Profile: Retirement financial planning, tax & investment planning & employee benefits analysis are offered.
Executives:
Rick Blake, CLU, CFP, President

Diamond Retirement Planning Ltd.
Also listed under: *Pension & Money Management Companies*
111 Pulford St.
Winnipeg, MB R3L 1X8
204-949-4749
866-949-7743
info@diamondretirement.com
www.diamondretirement.com
Ownership: Private
Year Founded: 1989
Number of Employees: 5
Executives:
Daryl Diamond, President/Co-owner
Karen Diamond, Co-Owner

Dias & Associates
295 Wolfe St.
London, ON N6B 2C4
519-434-1119
Fax: 519-434-1119
Former Name: Roy G. Dias
Executives:
Roy Dias

Dixon Davis & Company
1027 Pandora Ave.
Victoria, BC V8V 3P6
250-413-3230
Fax: 250-413-3231
lenore@dixondavis.com
www.dixondavis.com
Profile: Dixon Davis is a fee only financial planner.
Executives:
Lenore J. Davis, CFP, RFP; lenore@dixondavis.com
Howard Dixon, RFP, CFP; howard@dixondavis.com

Don Johnson & Associates Ltd.
8615 - 104th St.
Edmonton, AB T6E 4G6
780-430-6101
Fax: 780-430-7219
dja@telusplanet.net
Ownership: Private
Number of Employees: 6
Executives:
Don H. Johnson, Owner

Donaldson Niblett Financial Group
#101, 310 Main St. East
Milton, ON L9T 1P4
905-875-3366
Fax: 905-875-3574
info@donaldsonniblettfinancial.com
www.donaldsonniblettfinancial.com
Former Name: Donaldson Financial Group
Ownership: Private
Year Founded: 1978
Number of Employees: 5
Executives:
Helena Donaldson, CFP
Tim Niblett, CFP, CHFS

Donnelly & Co.
#100, 15023 - 123rd Ave.
Edmonton, AB T5V 1J7
780-488-7071
Fax: 780-488-4650
tim@donnellyco.ab.ca
www.donnellyco.ab.ca
Executives:
Timothy Donnelly
Pamela Sigvaldason

Donro Financial Corporation
Also listed under: *Pension & Money Management Companies*
#304, 63 Church St.
St Catharines, ON L2R 3C4
905-984-2100
Fax: 905-984-2102
donro@donro.on.ca
www.donro.on.ca
Ownership: Private
Profile: The full-service company provides the following services: professional financial planning; group benefits & pension consulting; mutual fund, annuity & life insurance brokerage; human resource management; & life style consulting services.
Executives:
Donald Robertson, President

Dore & Associates Ltd.
999 Lansdowne St. West
Peterborough, ON K9J 8N2
705-876-1565
Fax: 705-876-9073
dore@cgocable.net
Executives:

INVESTMENT MANAGEMENT

Dore & Associates Ltd. (continued)
Shane Dore

Douglas Dell Financial
#2, 215 Stafford St.
Winnipeg, MB R3M 2X1
204-987-2727
Fax: 204-987-2729
dougdell@escape.ca
Executives:
Chris Douglas

Drobot Financial Services Limited
PO Box 967
409 Main St.
Kindersley, SK S0L 1S0
306-463-6400
Fax: 306-463-3966
d.drobot@sasktel.net
www.drobotfinancial.com/
Ownership: Private
Executives:
Daniel Drobot, CFP, Co-Owner

Dundee Private Investors Inc.
Also listed under: *Investment Dealers*
1 Adelaide St. East, 27th Fl.
Toronto, ON M5C 2V9
416-350-3250
888-332-2661
inquiries@dundeewealth.com
www.dundeewealth.com
Former Name: Fortune Financial Corporation
Executives:
Ned Goodman, President/CEO & Chair, Dundee Wealth Management Inc.
Affiliated Companies:
Leadbeater Financial Services

Dundee Wealth Management Inc.
Also listed under: *Pension & Money Management Companies*
1 Adelaide St. East, 27th Fl.
Toronto, ON M5C 2V9
416-350-3250
888-332-2661
inquiries@dundeewealth.com
www.dundeewealth.com
Former Name: Goodman & Company Ltd.
Ownership: Public. Wholly owned subsidiary of Dundee Corporation
Executives:
Ned Goodman, CEO
Joanne Ferstman, CFO
Affiliated Companies:
Dynamic Mutual Funds/DMF
Dynamic Venture Opportunities Fund Ltd.

Dunphy-Molloy & Associates Ltd.
PO Box 7336
90 Barters Hill
St. John's, NL A1E 3Y5
709-579-2056
Fax: 709-579-3309
Executives:
Kevin Dunphy

Dusangh & Co.
#205, 12899 - 76 Ave.
Surrey, BC V3W 1E6
604-502-0509
Fax: 604-502-0549
jdusangh@sprint.ca
Former Name: Jessie Dusangh Ltd.
Ownership: Private
Year Founded: 1998
Executives:
Jessie Dusangh

ECC Group
#800, 90 Adelaide St. West
Toronto, ON M5H 3V9
416-364-0181
Fax: 416-364-5394
800-665-0181
info@eccgroup.ca
www.eccgroup.ca
Ownership: Private. Executive Compensation Consultants Ltd.
Year Founded: 1974
Number of Employees: 8
Assets: Under $1 million
Revenues: $1-5 million
Profile: ECC Group is a fee-based financial planning firm. Companies include ECC Capital Management, ECC Insurance Agency, Executive Compensation Consultants. Affiliated with IPC Network.
Executives:
J. Christopher Snyder, RFP, President

Eckler Ltd.
Also listed under: *Acturarial Consultants*
#900, 110 Sheppard Ave. East
Toronto, ON M2N 7A3
416-429-3330
Fax: 416-429-3794
www.eckler.ca
Former Name: Eckler Partners Ltd.
Ownership: Private.
Year Founded: 1927
Number of Employees: 230
Profile: Eckler Partners Ltd. changed its name to Eckler Ltd., effective January 1, 2007. The independent actuarial & consulting firm provides financial services, pension & employee benefits consulting, communications, investment management, pension administration, change management & technology. The Canadian-owned company has offices in Canada, Barbados, West Indies, Jamaica, & West Indies. The Milliman Global website is as follows: www.millimanglobal.com
Executives:
William T. Weiland, President; 416-696-3011; bweiland@eckler.ca
Steven A. Raiken, CAO, Secretary; 416-696-3001; sraiken@eckler.ca
Wafaa Babcock, Principal
Nicholas Bauer, Principal
Anthony Benjamin, Principal, Treasurer; 416-696-3027; abenjamin@eckler.ca
Richard Border, Principal
Gilles Bouchard, Principal
Sandra Dudley, Principal
Luc Farmer, Principal
Christine Finlay, Principal
Steve Gendron, Principal
Sylvain Goulet, Principal
David Grace, Principal
Stephen Haist, Principal
Paul Harrietha, Principal
Wendy Harrison, Principal
Peter Hayes, Principal
Charles Herbert, Principal
Cameron Hunter, Principal
Sean Keys, Principal
Richard Labelle, Principal
Greg Malone, Principal
Todd McLean, Principal
George Mitchell, Principal
Brian Pelly, Principal
Douglas Poapst, Principal
Cynthia Potts, Principal
André Racine, Principal
Pierre St-Onge, Principal
Jill M. Wagman, Principal
Thomas Weddell, Principal
Hugh White, Principal
Phillip Whittaker, Principal
Directors:
Anthony J. Benjamin; 416-696-3027
David Grace; 416-696-3072
Wendy Harrison; 604-682-1386
Charles Herbert; 246-228-0865
Todd McLean; 416-696-3059
William T. Weiland; 416-696-3011
Hugh White; 416-696-3030
Branches:
Halifax
#503, 1969 Upper Water St.
Halifax, NS B3J 3R7 Canada
902-492-2822
Fax: 902-454-9398
Peter Hayes, Partner
Montréal
#2200, 800, boul René-Lévesque ouest
Montréal, QC H3B 1X9 Canada
514-848-9077
Fax: 514-395-1188
Gilles Bouchard, Partner
Québec
#30, 3107, av des Hotels
Québec, QC G1W 4W5 Canada
418-780-1366
Fax: 418-780-1368
Richard Larouche, Contact
Vancouver
#980, 475 West Georgia St.
Vancouver, BC V6B 4M9 Canada
604-682-1381
Fax: 604-669-1510
Tom Weddel, Partner
Winnipeg
#1750, 1 Lombard Pl.
Winnipeg, MB R3B 0X3 Canada
204-988-1586
Fax: 204-988-1589
Doug Poapst, Partner

Ed Grainger Financial Services Inc.
PO Box 1395
#104, 320 Alexander St. NE
Salmon Arm, BC V1E 4P5
250-832-8090
Fax: 250-833-4898
edgrainger@telus.net
Executives:
E.H. Grainger

Edmond Financial Group Inc.(EFGI)
420 Academy Rd.
Winnipeg, MB R3N 0B9
204-478-8500
Fax: 204-488-6575
866-478-8500
efg@efgi.com
www.efgi.com
Ownership: Private.
Number of Employees: 10
Executives:
Paul Edmond, BA (Econ), CFP, President/Owner
Deana Laing, Manager, Business
Veronica Roth, AIAA, ACS, Manager, Administration
Howie Blatt, Sr. Financial Advisor
Doreen Sigurdson, B.Sc. (Math), CFP, RFP, CLU, Financial Advisor
D. Scott Spence, CFP, CIM, FCSI, Financial Advisor, Branch Manager

Eisenberg Financial
223 - 17th Ave. SE
Calgary, AB T2G 1H5
403-262-1600
Fax: 403-262-1635
eli@eisenbergfinancial.com
Former Name: E. Eisenberg & Associates
Ownership: Private
Number of Employees: 4
Executives:
Eli Eisenberg, Owner/President

Elliott & Associates
1216 - 8th St. East
Saskatoon, SK S7H 0S6
306-343-1671
Fax: 306-956-3944
info@elliottfinancial.ca
www.elliottfinancial.ca
Executives:
George P. Elliott

Elysium Wealth Management Inc.
#1220, One Lombard Place
Winnipeg, MB R3B 0X3
204-989-6200
Fax: 204-989-6209
ikalinowsky@elysiumwealth.com
www.elysiumwealth.com
Former Name: D.V. McQueen Ltd.
Ownership: Private
Number of Employees: 6
Executives:
R. Ian Kalinowsky, President

Branches:
Calgary
Sun Life Plaza
#2600, 144 - 4th Ave. SW
Calgary, AB T2P 3N4 Canada
403-269-1375
Fax: 403-716-3637
Ken Serbu, Vice-President

Emery Risk Management Inc.
#1401, 9803 - 24 St. SW
Calgary, AB T2V 1S5
403-282-1656

The Eminent Choice Financial Group
#1960, 777 Hornby St.
Vancouver, BC V6Z 1S4
604-681-7222
Fax: 604-681-7223
sunny_lam@eminentchoice.com
Ownership: Private
Number of Employees: 4
Executives:
Sunny Lam, RFP, President

Emondson Ball Davies LLP, Chartered Accountants
Also listed under: *Accountants*
#501, 10 Milner Business Ct.
Toronto, ON M1B 3C6
416-293-5560
Fax: 416-293-5377
www.ebdcas.com
Former Name: EBD Financial Planners Inc
Profile: The firm provides the following services to individuals & businesses: tax, financial planning, investment planning, estate planning & trust administration, documentation review & preparation, accounting & auditing, consulting, bookkeeping & preparation of business documentation.

Executives:
Roger E. Ball, Chartered Accountant
V.H. (Bert) Davies, Chartered Accountant
Joseph S. Macdonald, Chartered Accountant
Robert E. McLeod, Chartered Accountant
Branches:
Toronto - Lake Shore Blvd.
1840 Lake Shore Blvd. East
Toronto, ON M4L 6S8 Canada
416-988-7647
Fax: 416-293-5377

Empire Life Insurance Company
Also listed under: *Investment Fund Companies; Investment Management*
259 King St. East
Kingston, ON K7L 3A8
613-548-1881
Fax: 613-548-8096
800-561-1268
buildingempires@empire.ca
www.empire.ca
Also Known As: Empire Life
Ownership: Private. Subsidiary of E-L Financial Services Ltd., which is 81% owned by E-L Financial Corporation Limited.
Year Founded: 1923
Number of Employees: 600+
Assets: $1-10 billion Year End: 20051231
Revenues: $500m-1 billion Year End: 20051231
Profile: The company markets a full range of financial security & wealth management products & services for individuals & groups, including life, health & disability insurance plans, investments, retirement & estate planning, corporate services & employee benefits.

Executives:
Douglas G. Hogeboom, FSA, FCIA, President/CEO
Leslie C. Herr, MBA, CFP, CLU, CH.F.C., Sr. Vice-President, Individual Products
Michael C. Schneider, FSA, FCIA, Sr. Vice-President, Corporate

Anne Butler, Vice-President/Corporate Secretary & Director of Legal Services, Chief Compliance Officer & Chief Privacy Officer
Deborah K. Frame, MBA, CFA, Vice-President, Chief Investment Officer
J. Edward Gibson, FSA, FCIA, Vice-President & Actuary
Jake J. Hilberdink, FLMI, Vice-President, Employee Benefits
Timo Hytonen, MBA, FCIP, CHRP, CRM, Vice-President, Human Resources & Community Relations
Gary McCabe, CA, Vice-President & Controller
Wendy R.M. Merkley, Vice-President, Information Systems, Technology & Services
Steve S. Pong, BASc., Vice-President, Individual Marketing & Service
Shareholders' Directors:
Duncan N.R. Jackman, Chair
Graham W. Dumble
Robert G. Long
Roy Patrick, LL.B
Group Secretary, AEGON UK plc
Richard E. Rooney
Deanna Rosenswig
Clive P. Rowe
Partner, SLS Capital
Michael C. Schneider
Mark M. Taylor
Honorary Directors:
Henry N.R. Jackman, Honorary Chair
John N. Turner, PC, CC, QC
Partner, Miller Thomson LLP
Policyholders' Directors:
Mark J. Fuller, LLB
Ontario Pension Board
Douglas G. Hogeboom, FSA, FCIA
President/CEO, The Empire Life Insurance Group
James W. McCutcheon, QC
Counsel, McCarthy Tétrault
Douglas C. Townsend, FSA, FCIA
Manon R. Vennat, CM
Chair, Montréal, Spencer Stuart & Associates (Canada) Ltd.
Empire:
Asset Allocation Fund
RRSP Eligible; Inception Year: 1994;
Balanced Fund
RRSP Eligible; Inception Year: 1989;
Bond Fund
RRSP Eligible; Inception Year: 1986;
Dividend Growth Fund
RRSP Eligible; Inception Year: 1998;
Equity Growth Fund
RRSP Eligible; Inception Year: 1971;
International Equity Fund
RRSP Eligible; Inception Year: 1989;
Money Market Fund
RRSP Eligible; Inception Year: 1989;
Small Cap Equity Fund
RRSP Eligible; Inception Year: 1998;
U.S. Equity Index Fund
RRSP Eligible; Inception Year: 1998;
Premier Equity Fund
RRSP Eligible; Inception Year: 1964;
American Value Fund
RRSP Eligible; Inception Year: 2001;
Elite Equity Fund
RRSP Eligible; Inception Year: 1969;
Conservative Portfolio Fund
RRSP Eligible; Inception Year: 2004;
Balanced Portfolio Fund
RRSP Eligible; Inception Year: 2004;
Moderate Growth Portfolio Fund
RRSP Eligible; Inception Year: 2004;
Growth Portfolio Fund
RRSP Eligible; Inception Year: 2004;
Aggressive Growth Portfolio Fund
RRSP Eligible; Inception Year: 2004;
Global Balanced Fund
RRSP Eligible; Inception Year: 0;
Global Equity Fund
RRSP Eligible; Inception Year: 1989;
Canadian Equity Fund
RRSP Eligible; Inception Year: 2005;
Income Fund
RRSP Eligible; Inception Year: 2002;
Global Smaller Companies Fund
RRSP Eligible; Inception Year: 2005;
Group Sales & Marketing Offices:
Burlington
5500 North Service Rd., 4th Fl.
Burlington, ON L7L 6W6 Canada
905-335-6558
George Elliott, Sr. Group Representative
Calgary
#304, 1240 Kensington Rd. NW
Calgary, AB T2N 3P7 Canada
403-262-6386
Richard Dobing, Representative, Group Sales
Edmonton
Phipps-McKinnon Bldg.
#950, 10020 - 101A Ave.
Edmonton, AB T5J 3G2 Canada
780-482-4241
Shelly Robichaud, Representative, Group Sales
London
#404, 171 Queens Ave.
London, ON N6A 5J7 Canada
519-438-1751
Ken Nitska, Group Manager, Southwest & Northern Ontario
Montréal
#1600A, 600, boul de Maisonneuve ouest
Montréal, QC H3A 3J2 Canada
514-842-0003
Michel Tessier, Group Manager, Québec
Nepean
#236, 9 Antares Dr.
Nepean, ON K2E 7V5 Canada
613-225-1173
Wendi Stimson, Group Sales Representative, Eastern Ontario

Richmond
North Tower
#602, 5811 Cooney Rd.
Richmond, BC V6X 3M1 Canada
604-232-5558
Duncan Emslie, Group Manager
Toronto
#800, 2550 Victoria Park Ave.
Toronto, ON M2J 5A9 Canada
416-494-0900
Doug Cooper, National Director, Group Sales & Marketing
Waterloo
#250, 180 King St. South
Waterloo, ON N2J 1P8 Canada
519-569-7002
Christine Betts, Representative, Group Sales
Individual Sales & Marketing Office:
Burlington
5500 North Service Rd., 4th Fl.
Burlington, ON L7L 6W6 Canada
905-335-6558
Walter Kordiuk, Executive Account Manager, Wealth
Calgary
#305, 1240 Kensington Rd. NW
Calgary, AB T2N 3P7 Canada
403-269-1000
Stan Pappenfus, Executive Manager, Accounts
Edmonton
11810 Kingsway Ave.
Edmonton, AB T5G 0X5 Canada
780-482-4271
Ken Doll, Regional Manager, Accounts
London
#404, 171 Queens Ave.
London, ON N6A 5J7 Canada
519-438-2922
Doug Kennedy, Executive Manager, Accounts
Montréal
#1600, 600, boul de Maisonneuve ouest
Montréal, QC H3A 3J2 Canada
514-842-9151
Richard Charette, Director, Sales & Distribution
Nepean
#221, 9 Antares Dr.
Nepean, ON K2E 7V5 Canada
613-225-7530
George MacKenzie, Regional Manager, Accounts
Richmond
North Tower
#602, 5811 Cooney Rd.
Richmond, BC V6X 3M1 Canada
604-232-5557
Rick Forchuk, Director, Sales & Distribution
Saskatoon
#1000, 201 - 21st St. East
Saskatoon, SK S7K 0B8 Canada
306-934-3899
Steve Kook, Regional Manager, Investments
Toronto

Empire Life Insurance Company (continued)
#800, 2550 Victoria Park Ave.
Toronto, ON M2J 5A9 Canada
416-494-4890
Rick Forchuk, Director, Sales & Distribution
Waterloo
#250, 180 King St. South
Waterloo, ON N2J 1P8 Canada
518-569-7002
Donna Schultz, Manager, Regional Accounts
Winnipeg
#200, 5 Donald St.
Winnipeg, MB R3L 2T4 Canada
204-452-9138
Sandy Franczyk, Regional Investment Manager

Etherington's
#701, 170 University Ave.
Toronto, ON M5H 3B3
416-351-1464
Fax: 416-351-9535
reception@etheringtons.com
www.etheringtons.com
Executives:
Bruce W. Etherington

Ethical Funds Inc.(EFI)
***Also listed under:** Investment Fund Companies; Investment Management*
#800, 1111 West Georgia St.
Vancouver, BC V6E 4T6
604-714-3802
Fax: 604-714-3861
877-384-4225
clientrelations@ethicalfunds.com
www.ethicalfunds.com
Ownership: Private.
Year Founded: 1986
Number of Employees: 300
Assets: $1-10 billion Year End: 20060930
Profile: An affiliated company is Guardian Ethical Management Inc.

Executives:
Donald J. Rolfe, President/CEO; 604-714-3800
Ethical:
Growth Fund
RRSP Eligible; Inception Year: 1986; Fund Managers: Guardian Captial LP
Income Fund
RRSP Eligible; Inception Year: 1967; Fund Managers: Guardian Captial LP
Credential Money Market Fund
RRSP Eligible; Inception Year: 1980; Fund Managers: Central Financial
Special Equity Fund
RRSP Eligible; Inception Year: 1995; Fund Managers: QVGD Investors Inc.
Canadian Dividend Fund
RRSP Eligible; Inception Year: 2002; Fund Managers: Highstreet Asset Management Inc.
International Equity Fund
RRSP Eligible; Inception Year: 2002; Fund Managers: William Blair & Co. LLC
Canadian Index Fund
RRSP Eligible; Inception Year: 2004;
Balanced Fund
RRSP Eligible; Inception Year: 0; Fund Managers: Guardian Captial LP
Monthly Income Fund
RRSP Eligible; Inception Year: 0; Fund Managers: Guardian Captial LP
American Multi-Strategy FundInception Year: 0; Fund Managers: Manning & Napier Advisors Inc.

Excel Financial Growth Inc.
***Also listed under:** Investment Dealers*
#205, 80 Acadia Ave.
Markham, ON L3R 9V1
905-470-8222
Fax: 905-470-8306
www.excelfinancialgroup.ca
Profile: The licensed mutual fund dealer offers a range of professionally managed mutual funds. The company also offers the following financial planning services: retirement planning, estate planning, investment planning, education planning, taxation planning & tax return preparation.

Executives:
Marget Cheng, Contact, Investments
Pak Ming, Contact, Investments

ExcelPlan Financial
524 Locust St.
Burlington, ON L7S 1V2
905-639-8008
Fax: 905-639-2268
Ownership: Private
Year Founded: 1996
Number of Employees: 3

The Expatriate Group Inc.
#280, 926 - 5th Ave. SW
Calgary, AB T2P 0N7
403-232-8561
Fax: 403-294-1222
888-232-8561
expatriate@expat.ca
www.expat.ca
Ownership: Private
Year Founded: 1992
Number of Employees: 5
Profile: The Expatriate Group provides international personal tax/financial planning, global investment & offshore banking/currency exchange, estate planning & lifestyle-cultural & retirement strategies. Other services include Canadian/U.S. tax returns for U.S.A./Mexico \snowbirds\"".""

Executives:
Thomas Boleantu, President

F.W. Thompson Co. Ltd.
#1108, 1 St. Clair Ave. West
Toronto, ON M4V 1K6
416-515-9500
Fax: 416-515-9499
fwthomp@hotmail.com
Ownership: Private
Year Founded: 1963
Number of Employees: 3
Assets: $5-10 million
Revenues: Under $1 million
Executives:
Frederick W. Thompson, President

Falkenberg Agencies Limited
PO Box 459
Charlie Lake, BC V0C 1H0
250-787-7716
Fax: 250-787-7489
Executives:
Andreas D. Falkenberg, CFP

Family Financial Consultants
#220, 1982 Kensington Rd. NW
Calgary, AB T2N 3R5
403-242-7485
fayefa@shaw.ca
Ownership: Private
Number of Employees: 1
Profile: The company specializes in financial counselling.

Executives:
Faye Forbes-Anderson, CFP, President

Family First Financial Services Inc.
4901 - 48 St.
Red Deer, AB T4N 6M4
403-309-6300
Fax: 403-309-6301

Family Investment Planning Inc.
***Also listed under:** Investment Dealers*
#6, 195 Franklin Blvd.
Cambridge, ON N1R 8H3
519-740-1158
Fax: 519-740-9069
866-818-4798
info@fipi.ca
www.fipi.ca
Year Founded: 1998
Profile: Family Investment Planning is a mutual fund dealer. Financial planning services also include retirement, education & tax savings programs & life insurance.

Executives:
William (Bill) H. Maidment, CEO
Katherine A. Dooley, Vice-President, Administration, Chief Compliance Officer
Pauline Maidment, Coordinator, Group Benefits

Family Wealth Advisors Ltd.
***Also listed under:** Investment Dealers*
PO Box 126
22 Foster St.
Perth, ON K7H 3E3
613-267-1345
Fax: 613-267-3004
Profile: The company is an independent mutual fund dealership.

Branches:
Peterborough
PO Box K
270 George St. North, 2nd Fl.
Peterborough, ON K9H 3H1 Canada
705-742-2065
Fax: 705-742-0116
800-392-2224
www.bppeterborough.com
Philip Nuttall, Financial Advisor

Farm Mutual Financial Services Inc.
***Also listed under:** Investment Dealers*
PO Box 3637
1305 Bishop St. North
Cambridge, ON N3H 5C6
519-740-1194
Fax: 519-740-9272
866-777-6385
clientservices@fmfs.on.ca
www.fmfs.on.ca
Ownership: Private
Year Founded: 1996
Number of Employees: 15
Executives:
Don Howie, CEO
Betty Tomlinson, Manager, Compliance, Auditing & Training
Branches:
Ayr
1400 Northumberland St.
Ayr, ON N0B 1E0 Canada
519-632-9450
Fax: 519-632-9322
ayrfarm@golden.net
Dennis Charrette, Manager
Brockville
56 King St. East
Brockville, ON K6V 1B1 Canada
613-342-8911
Fax: 613-342-1551
800-654-1662
fmfsadmin@recorder.ca; gfs@ripnet.com
Heather Halladay, Manager
Caledonia
172 Argyle St. North
Caledonia, ON N3W 2J7 Canada
905-765-5000
Fax: 905-765-2220
interlake@sympatico.ca
Diane Sloat, Manager
Cambridge
12 Cambridge St.
Cambridge, ON N1R 3R7 Canada
519-623-3112
Fax: 519-623-4360
Colin Corner, Manager
Chatham
149 St. Clair St.
Chatham, ON N7L 3J4 Canada
519-355-0606
Fax: 519-355-0466
group1@ciaccess.com
Jamie Rainbird, Manager
Exeter
497 Main St. South
Exeter, ON N0M 1S1 Canada
519-235-4000
Fax: 519-235-4333
fmfs@execulink.com
John Manson, Manager
Newmarket

#11, 320 Harry Walker Pkwy. North
Newmarket, ON L3Y 7B3 Canada
905-895-0111
Fax: 905-895-4791
Richard Moore, Manager
Picton
13379 Loyalist Pkwy.
Picton, ON K0K 2T0 Canada
613-476-2223
Fax: 613-476-3160
fmfs.pic@sympatico.ca
Heather Halladay, Acting Manager
St Marys
PO Box 2758
293 Queen St. West
St Marys, ON N4X 1A5 Canada
519-284-4448
Fax: 519-284-4075
Jeff Swan, Manager
Strathroy
79 Caradoc St. North
Strathroy, ON N7G 2M5 Canada
519-245-5556
Fax: 519-245-3522
middwest@sympatico.ca
Lee Ann Jones, Manager

Faro Financial Group
Also listed under: *Investment Dealers*
315, boul Brunswick
Montréal, QC H9R 5M7
514-694-7606
Fax: 514-694-1630
Year Founded: 1998
Profile: Personal investment advice is offered related to financial planning. Mutual funds are among the products provided.

Executives:
Mike Purvis, President

Fauth Financial Group Ltd.
115 Sierra Morena Ct. SW
Calgary, AB T3H 2X8
403-237-9990
Fax: 403-263-5259
ffg@fauthfinancial.com
www.fauthfinancial.com
Ownership: Private
Number of Employees: 7
Executives:
Vern Fauth, CFP, CLU, President

FE Advisory Group
#1800, 10104 - 103 Ave.
Edmonton, AB T5J 4A7
780-423-2702
Fax: 780-429-7067
888-423-2702
www.feadvisory.com
Former Name: Fairley Erker Estate Planning
Ownership: Private
Number of Employees: 12
Executives:
Denis Erker, Partner; derker@feadvisory.com
W. Grant Fairley, Partner; gfairley@feadvisory.com
Michael Gaian; mgaian@feadvisory.com
John C. Goode; john@feadvisory.com
Peter E. Liden; pliden@feadvisory.com
David R. Sagan; dsagan@feadvisory.com
Doug K. Silverberg; doug@feadvisory.com
Branches:
Calgary
#300, 1400 - First St. SW
Calgary, AB T2R 0V8 Canada
403-509-4747
Fax: 403-509-4746
Kevin Erker

Feinberg Financial
Also listed under: *Investment Dealers*
#1507, 155 Carlton St.
Winnipeg, MB R3C 3H8
204-942-0904
Fax: 204-942-8329
866-942-0904
Ownership: Private
Year Founded: 1974
Number of Employees: 2
Assets: Under $1 million Year End: 20051010
Revenues: Under $1 million Year End: 20051010
Profile: Assets under administration total $20,000,000. Affiliated with IQON Financail Inc.

Executives:
Denzil Feinberg, CFP RFP, Proprietor; dfeinberg@aol.com
Randy Penner, Administrator; randypennerff@aol.com

Ferfolia Insurance & Investment Inc.
24 Darling St.
Brantford, ON N3T 2K2
519-756-0444
Fax: 519-756-0469
fii.ca
Executives:
John Ferfolia, President

Fernwood Consulting Group Inc.
288 Laird Dr.
Toronto, ON M4G 3X5
416-429-5705
Fax: 416-429-8219
lynn@fernwood.ca
www.fernwood.ca
Ownership: Private
Year Founded: 1999
Number of Employees: 2
Assets: Under $1 million Year End: 20041108
Revenues: Under $1 million Year End: 20041108
Profile: Fernwood is a fee-only financial consulting firm. Services provided include the design & delivery of seminars for employees of corporate clients as well as the development of training programs for financial advisors.

Executives:
Lynn Biscott, Partner
Peter Eberhardt, Partner

Fiduciary Trust Company of Canada
Also listed under: *Trust Companies*
#3100, 350 Seventh Ave. SW
Calgary, AB T2P 3N9
403-543-3950
Fax: 403-543-3955
800-574-3822
www.fiduciarytrust.ca
Former Name: Bissett & Associates Investment Management Ltd.
Year Founded: 1982
Profile: With regulatory approval, Fiduciary Trust Company of Canada was established in 2004.

Finactive
95 St. Clair Ave. West
Toronto, ON M4V 1N7
888-777-0700
advisor@dfs.com

Finance Matters Ltd.
69 Cavell Ave.
Toronto, ON M4J 1H5
416-469-2535
Ownership: Private
Year Founded: 1985
Number of Employees: 1
Executives:
Janet Freedman, RFP, President

Financial Architects Investments Inc.
Also listed under: *Investment Dealers; Investment Management*
#807, 505 Consumers Rd.
Toronto, ON M2J 4V8
416-285-7011
Fax: 416-285-7653
866-346-2724
www.fai.ca
Executives:
Chand Misir, Chair
Gaya Misir, President; gayamisir@fai.ca
Abbi Castro, Administrator, Operations

Financial Care Group
209 Hwy. 20 East, RR#1
Fonthill, ON L0S 1E6
905-892-1631
Fax: 905-892-3543
webmaster@financialcaregroup.com
www.financialcaregroup.ca
Executives:
Paul A. Lord

The Financial Centre of Collingwood
59 Hurontario St.
Collingwood, ON L9Y 2L7
705-445-5628
Fax: 705-445-8555
800-668-5628
admin@finctr.ca
www.finctr.ca
Executives:
J. Gregory Goldsworthy

Financial Decisions Inc.
1546 Bellevue Ave.
Sudbury, ON P3B 3G2
705-525-7526
Fax: 705-525-4632
plan@financialdecisions.ca
www.financialdecisions.ca
Former Name: Financial Education Services of Canada
Ownership: Private
Year Founded: 1994
Profile: Financial Decisions Inc. provides independent financial & investment advice in the areas of personal money management, tax, retirement, estate & divorce planning, sale of mutual funds, limited market dealer products & insurance products.

Executives:
Linda Cartier, CFP, RFP, Co-Owner
John Lindsay, Co-Owner

Financial Health Management
#603, 1088 - 6th Ave. SW
Calgary, AB T2P 5N3
403-216-1340
Fax: 403-216-1349
planners@fhminc.ab.ca
www.fhminc.ab.ca
Number of Employees: 3
Executives:
Diane Dekanic, CFP, RFP

The Financial Network Group
#12, 84 Charing Cross
Brantford, ON N3R 2H6
519-759-0415
Fax: 519-759-3687
marydawn@ipcbrantford.com

Financial Solutions
675 - 3 St. SE
Medicine Hat, AB T1A 0H4
403-526-1200
Fax: 403-526-9051
Executives:
Vern Hyde
Roger L. Larson

Fincor Financial Group
17709 - 103 Ave.
Edmonton, AB T5S 1N8
780-452-7296
Fax: 780-452-6491
888-452-7292
fincor@telusplanet.net
Ownership: Private.
Year Founded: 1975
Number of Employees: 14
Revenues: $1-5 million
Profile: Fincor is an investment management company that also offers employee benefit plans, life insurance & retirement income planning.

Executives:
Ronald Ewasiuk, CFP, RFP, Sr. Partner
Michael Smith, Sr. Partner
Branches:
Calgary
221 Hawkstone Dr. NW
Calgary, AB T3G 3R1 Canada

Fincor Financial Group (continued)
403-239-9211
Fax: 403-239-5370
Brent Lewis, Representative

Finestone Chan

#604, 5250, boul Décarie
Montréal, QC H3X 2H9
514-488-8800
Fax: 514-488-5788
www.finestonechan.com
Executives:
Shya M. Finestone; sfinest@decariecafirm.ca

First Affiliated Holdings Inc.

Also listed under: *Pension & Money Management Companies*
Plaza One, Meadowvale Corporate Center
#106, 2000 Argentia Rd.
Mississauga, ON L5N 1P7
905-812-2828
Fax: 905-812-8926
cclarke@firstaffiliated.on.ca
www.firstaffiliated.ca
Ownership: Private
Profile: The financial & investment planning organization is independent & fee-based. Wealth management services are provided by First Affilated Holdings Inc. / First Affiliated Secuities Inc. to affluent Canadians & family business owners.

Executives:
Christine Clarke, RFP, CA, President, Partner & Director
Karl Mortveit, CFO, COO & Partner
Barton Rowe, Investment Analyst & Partner
Karen McInnis, Manager, Client Service
Branches:
Collingwood
Arlington Bldg.
#302, 115 Hurontario St.
Collingwood, ON L9Y 2L9 Canada
705-455-7444
Fax: 705-455-0143
cclarke@firstaffiliated.on.ca

First Atlantic Financial

80 Elizabeth Ave.
St. John's, NL A1A 1W7
709-726-6005
Fax: 709-229-7668
800-563-7337
Executives:
Brendan Hunt, CIM, FSCI, CFP

First Capital Financial Planners

#1, 3009 - 43 Ave.
Vernon, BC V1T 3L4
250-558-4600
Fax: 250-260-3435
Executives:
Fred K. Soderberg

First Financial Consulting Group

#238 A14, 4261 Hwy. 7
Markham, ON L3R 9W6
416-726-2427
Fax: 905-415-1362
dzwicker@interlog.com
www.firstfinancialconsultinggroup.com, www.dhzwicker.com
Ownership: Private
Year Founded: 1999
Number of Employees: 3
Revenues: Under $1 million
Profile: First Financial Consulting Group is a wealth/risk management company.

Executives:
Daniel H. Zwicker, B.Sc.(Hons.), P.Eng., CFP, CH.F.C., C.F.S.B., Principal

First Prairie Financial Inc.

#1401, 10104 - 103rd Ave.
Edmonton, AB T5J 0H8
780-420-6633
Fax: 780-420-6655
877-920-6633
reception@fpfinancial.com
www.fpfinancial.com
Ownership: Private
Year Founded: 1999
Executives:
Kenneth P. Aberg, Managing General Agent
Joseph J. Ruddell, Managing Partner
Robert C. McNary, Associate General Agent, Calgary
Branches:
Calgary
#230, 1210 - 8th St. SW
Calgary, AB T2R 1L3 Canada
403-209-4010
Fax: 403-265-8720
866-680-4010

Fiscal Agents Financial Services Group

PO Box 5000
25 Lakeshore Rd. West
Oakville, ON L6J 5C7
905-844-7700
Fax: 905-844-8552
866-434-7225
mailroom@fiscalagents.com
www.fiscalagents.com
Ownership: Private
Year Founded: 1977

Fiscal Wellness Inc.

207 Huron St.
Stratford, ON N5A 5S9
519-271-4461
Fax: 519-271-0875
888-514-8881
info@fiscalwellness.com
www.fiscalwellness.com

Floyd Financial Services Ltd.

16 Lambert Dr.
Belleville, ON K8N 4K6
613-962-4524
Fax: 613-962-4951
brian@brianfloydfinancial.on.ca
www.brianfloydfinancial.on.ca
Executives:
Brian T. Floyd

Fonds des professionnels - Fonds d'investissement

Also listed under: *Investment Fund Companies*
Tour de l'Est
2, Complexe Desjardins, 31e étage
Montréal, QC H5B 1C2
514-350-5050
Fax: 514-350-5060
888-377-7337
fonds@groupefdp.com
www.groupefdp.com
Former Name: Fonds des Professionnels du Québec Inc.
Ownership: Private. Parent Fonds des Professionaels inc.
Year Founded: 1978
Number of Employees: 55
Assets: $1-10 billion Year End: 20041031
Revenues: $5-10 million Year End: 20041031
Directors:
Frédéric Bélanger
Pierre A. Boulianne
Martin Charland
Normand Doré
Jacques M. Gagnon
Roland Lefebvre
Jean-François Paris
Roger Perrault
Maurice Piette
Albert Plante
Michel Portelance
André Riopel
Québec Professionals:
Asian Equity Fund
RRSP Eligible; Inception Year: 1998; Fund Managers:
Robert Blais
MaxD'Alessandro
Balanced Fund
RRSP Eligible; Inception Year: 1982; Fund Managers:
Robert Blais
MaxD'Alessandro
Bond Fund
RRSP Eligible; Inception Year: 1978; Fund Managers:
Robert Blais
MaxD'Alessandro
Canadian Equity Fund
RRSP Eligible; Inception Year: 1987; Fund Managers:
Robert Blais
MaxD'Alessandro
European Equity Fund
RRSP Eligible; Inception Year: 1998; Fund Managers:
Robert Blais
MaxD'Alessandro
International Equity Fund
RRSP Eligible; Inception Year: 1993; Fund Managers:
Robert Blais
MaxD'Alessandro
Short Term Fund
RRSP Eligible; Inception Year: 1997; Fund Managers:
Robert Blais
MaxD'Alessandro
American Index Fund
RRSP Eligible; Inception Year: 0; Fund Managers:
Robert Blais
MaxD'Alessandro
Global Diversified Fund
RRSP Eligible; Inception Year: 0; Fund Managers:
Robert Blais
MaxD'Alessandro
Balanced Growth Fund
RRSP Eligible; Inception Year: 2001; Fund Managers:
Robert Blais
MaxD'Alessandro
Money Market Fund
RRSP Eligible; Inception Year: 0; Fund Managers:
Robert Blais
MaxD'Alessandro
Branches:
Montréal
#1425, 425, boul de Maisonneuve ouest
Montréal, QC H3A 3G5 Canada
Québec
2640, boul Laurier, 11e étage
Québec, QC G1V 5C2 Canada
Sherbrooke
1640, King ouest
Sherbrooke, QC J1J 2C3 Canada

Fortraco International Marketing Inc.

Also listed under: *Investment Dealers; Investment Management*
#260, 2113, Saint Regis
Montréal, QC H9B 2M9
514-421-3950
Fax: 514-683-6316
800-731-2438
info@wealthstarfs.com
www.tenstar.ca
Also Known As: Executive Financial Services
Ownership: Private
Year Founded: 1985
Number of Employees: 2
Assets: $10-50 million
Revenues: Under $1 million
Executives:
Ronald Greeley, President; 514-421-3430; rgreeley@wealthstarfs.com

Foster & Associates Financial Services Inc.

Also listed under: *Investment Dealers*
#506, 335 Bay St.
Toronto, ON M5H 2R3
416-369-1980
Fax: 416-369-1070
800-559-8853
tmanning@fostergroup.ca
www.fostergroup.ca
Ownership: Private.
Year Founded: 1994
Number of Employees: 15
Stock Exchange Membership: Toronto Stock Exchange, TSX Venture Exchange
Executives:
Briar Foster, President
Frank Florio, Vice-President
John Gallagher, Vice-President
Tony Manning, Vice-President
Directors:
Frank Florio
Briar Foster
John Gallagher
Tony Manning

Foyston, Gordon & Payne Inc.
#2600, 1 Adelaide St. East
Toronto, ON M5C 2V9
416-362-4725
Fax: 416-367-1183
877-795-4536
www.foyston.com
Executives:
James R. Martin, President, Canadian Equity Portfolio Manager
Stephen P. Copeland, Vice-President, Fixed Income Portfolio Manager
James W. Houston, Vice-President, Sub-Advisory Portfolio Manager
Murray J. Leiter, Vice-President, Private Client Portfolio Manager
Mark E. Thompson, Vice-President, Finance & Administration

Frank Russell Canada Limited
1 First Canadian Place
PO Box 476
#5900, 100 King St. West
Toronto, ON M5X 1E4
416-362-8411
Fax: 416-362-4494
888-509-1792
canada@russell.com
www.russell.com/ca
Also Known As: Russell Investment Group - Canada
Ownership: Wholly owned subsidiary of Frank Russell Company, Tacoma, WA, USA.
Year Founded: 1936
Profile: Russell's services include investment management, investment consulting, performance measurement, implementation services & investment strategy & research. The Toronto office opened in 1984.

Executives:
Irshaad Ahmad, President, Managing Director
Tim Hicks, Chief Investment Officer
David Bullock, Director, Private Client Programs
Bruce Curwood, Director, Research & Global Strategy
Jim Franks, Director, Consulting

The Fraser Financial Group Ltd.
3108 - 33rd St.
Vernon, BC V1T 9S7
250-545-5258
Fax: 250-545-6679
877-755-5757
www.fraserfinancial.com
Ownership: Private
Year Founded: 1993
Number of Employees: 20
Executives:
Rick Balfour, CFO
Branches:
Abbotsford
#301A, 32555 Simon Ave.
Abbotsford, BC V2T 4Y2 Canada
604-855-0034
Fax: 604-855-1734
888-549-1199
chuckw@fraserfinancial.com
George Sigaty
Kamloops
#207, 418 St. Paul St.
Kamloops, BC V2C 2J6 Canada
250-377-7664
Fax: 250-377-7668
888-414-0031
bobt@fraserfinancial.com
Bob Thomas
Kelowna
#704, 1708 Dolphin Ave.
Kelowna, BC V1Y 9S4 Canada
250-861-3200
Fax: 250-861-3202
888-611-3791
craigg@fraserfinancial.com
Craig Gronsdahl

Fraser Valley Credit Services Ltd.
#101, 6345 - 198 St.
Langley, BC V2Y 2E3
604-539-5001
Fax: 604-539-5002
877-356-3500
info@mydebtsolution.com
www.mydebtsolution.com
Year Founded: 1987
Profile: The debt pooling repayment company provides debt restructuring/managed repayment programs & debt settlement negotiations, an alternative to bankruptcy. Companies doing business include Fraser Valley Credit Counsellors & mydebtsolution.com.

Executives:
Laurier Bourassa, President
Blair Polischuk, Vice-President

Fred S. Gordon Financial Services Inc.
89 Bellroyal Cres.
Dartmouth, NS B2V 2B4
902-488-4456
Fax: 902-435-9385
fredgordon@eastlink.ca
Executives:
Fred S. Gordon, Contact

Frizell & Company
#108, 645 Fort St.
Victoria, BC V8R 1G2
250-383-5540
Fax: 250-383-5553
800-837-0457
Former Name: Garry Oak Financial Group Inc.
Year Founded: 1994
Executives:
Diana Frizell

frontierAlt Investment Management Corporation
42 Wellington St. East, 4th Fl.
Toronto, ON M5E 1C7
416-360-6226
Fax: 416-360-6202
866-745-5545
info@frontieralt.com
www.frontierAlt.com
Executives:
Asif Khan, Chair/CEO
Sunil Joseph, Chief Risk & Compliance Officer
Kurankye Sekyi-Otu, Exec. Vice-President
Affiliated Companies:
frontierAltOrbit Funds Management Limited

FundSoft Information Systems
6810 - 104 St.
Edmonton, AB T6H 2L6
780-466-6016
Fax: 780-432-5630
800-463-7638
info@fundsoft.com
www.fundsoft.com
Ownership: Private. Parent is Optrics Inc.
Year Founded: 1995
Number of Employees: 10
Revenues: Under $1 million
Profile: The company sells financial analysis software for private investors. Products include two technical-analysis software packages: MetaStock by Equis International & OmniTrader by Nirvana Systems.

Executives:
Bording Ostergaard, President

Fundtrade Financial Corp.
2829 Sherwood Heights Dr.
Oakville, ON L6J 7R7
905-829-5277
Fax: 905-829-5279
877-366-9787
info@fundtrade.ca
www.fundtrade.ca
Former Name: Inter-Equity Asset Management

Future Focus Financial Planners Ltd.
#902, 400 - 4th Ave. South
Lethbridge, AB T1J 4E1
403-380-2020
Fax: 403-380-2290
Year Founded: 1997
Executives:
Randy Trieber
John Warren

Future Values Estate & Financial Planning
#300, 906 - 12th Ave. SW
Calgary, AB T2R 1K7
403-750-2123
Fax: 403-750-2112
sterling@futurevalues.com
www.futurevalues.com
Executives:
Sterling Rempel

Futureworth Financial Planners Corp.
Also listed under: *Investment Dealers*
#500, 1130 West Pender St.
Vancouver, BC V6E 4A4
604-684-3372
Fax: 604-669-6978
www.futureworthfinancial.com
Ownership: Wholly owned by Western Pacific Trust Company, Vancouver, BC.
Year Founded: 1989
Profile: Products & services provided by the retail financial services company are related to investment & life insurance. Futureworth is a registered Mutual Fund Dealer.

G & F Financial Group
Also listed under: *Credit Unions/Caisses Populaires; Insurance Companies*
7375 Kingsway
Burnaby, BC V3N 3B5
604-517-5100
Fax: 604-659-4025
www.gffg.com
Former Name: Gulf & Fraser Fishermen's Credit Union
Year Founded: 1941
Number of Employees: 175
Assets: $500m-1 billion Year End: 20041231
Revenues: $1-5 million Year End: 20041231
Executives:
Richard Davies, CEO
Bill Kiss, CFO
Ken McBain, COO
Directors:
Ed MacIntosh, Chair
Vince Fiamango, 1st Vice-Chair
Aubrey Searle, 2nd Vice-Chair
Joe Boroevich
Lewis Bublé
Christine Dacre
Brian Hamaguchi
Jim Heeps
Howard Normann
Vila Nova Carvalho
Kevin Riley
Jayne Roberts
John Secord
Al Wagner
Gary Williamson
Mercedes Wong
Branches:
Burnaby - Kingsway (South)
7375 Kingsway
Burnaby, BC V3N 3B5 Canada
604-521-2315
Fax: 604-521-8759
Burnaby - Southpoint Dr.
Podium B
6911 Southpoint Dr.
Burnaby, BC V3N 4X8 Canada
604-528-8383
Fax: 604-528-8386
800-663-0248
New Westminster
760 - 6th St.
New Westminster, BC V3L 3C7 Canada
604-526-2122
Fax: 604-522-6614
Port Coquitlam
#400, 2748 Lougheed Hwy.
Port Coquitlam, BC V3B 6P2 Canada
604-941-8300
Fax: 604-941-8307
Richmond - Chatham St. (Steveston)
3471 Chatham St.
Richmond, BC V7E 2Y9 Canada
604-271-5911
Fax: 604-271-6033

INVESTMENT MANAGEMENT

G & F Financial Group (continued)
Richmond - Westminster Hwy. (Richmond Centre)
7971 Westminster Hwy.
Richmond, BC V6X 1A4 Canada
604-278-0220
Fax: 604-278-1572
Surrey - Fraser Hwy. (Fleetwood)
Fleetwood Park Village
#101, 15910 Fraser Hwy.
Surrey, BC V3S 2W4 Canada
604-599-6177
Fax: 604-599-6179
Surrey - Nordel Way
#101, 12020 Nordel Way
Surrey, BC V3W 1P6 Canada
604-507-8688
Fax: 604-507-8684
Vancouver - 41st Ave.
2735 East 41st Ave.
Vancouver, BC Canada
604-437-4774
Fax: 604-437-1174
Vancouver - Hastings St.
803 East Hastings St.
Vancouver, BC V6A 1R8 Canada
604-254-9811
Fax: 604-254-0215
Vancouver - Main St.
2949 Main St.
Vancouver, BC V5T 3G4 Canada
604-879-7131
Fax: 604-879-7397

G&B Allen Financial Corporation
PO Box 189
3 Main St.
Warkworth, ON K0K 3K0
705-924-2632
info@alleninsurance.ca
www.alleninsurance.ca
Executives:
Ruth Fleming
Branches:
Brighton
PO Box 1118
111 Main St.
Brighton, ON K0K 1H0 Canada
613-475-1172
Campbellford
PO Box 758
97 Front St.
Campbellford, ON K0L 1L0 Canada
705-653-1850
Fax: 705-653-0406
Cobourg
#2, 2 Strathy Rd.
Cobourg, ON K9A 5J7 Canada
905-372-4207
Havelock
PO Box 249
32 Ottawa St.
Havelock, ON K0L 1Z0 Canada
705-778-3338
Trenton
71 Division St.
Trenton, ON K8V 4W7 Canada
613-394-4888

G. Cook & Sons Financial Services Inc.
95 Gorham St.
Liverpool, NS B0T 1K0
902-354-5528
Fax: 902-354-2478
cood@ns.sympatico.ca
Executives:
George Cook

G.E. Noren & Partners
205 First Ave. NW
Moose Jaw, SK S6H 7Z2
306-693-0656
Fax: 306-692-3930
nortel@sasktel.net
Executives:
Keith Schick

G.F. MacKay
369 - 9th St.
Hanover, ON N4N 1L5
519-364-6400
Fax: 519-364-7678
mackay@whiteman.ca
Executives:
Gord MacKay

G.S. Hall Financial
16419 - 80th Ave. NW
Edmonton, AB T5R 3M8
780-481-2593
Profile: Services include independent financial planning.

Executives:
Gary Hall

G2 Financial Group Inc.
#1440, 333 - 11th Ave. SW
Calgary, AB T2R 1L9
403-262-1250
Fax: 403-262-3575
888-235-1547
lee@g2financial.ca
www.g2financial.ca
Ownership: Private
Year Founded: 1987
Number of Employees: 11
Executives:
Lee Raine, Vice-President

Galileo Equity Management Inc.
TD Canada Trust Tower, BCE Place
#4730, 161 Bay St.
Toronto, ON M5J 2S1
416-594-0606
Fax: 416-594-0991
mail@galileoequity.com
www.galileoequity.com
Profile: The investment firm specializes in growth oriented equities & royalty trust.

Executives:
Leighton McCarthy, Chair
Michael Waring, President
Peter Hanley, Vice-President
Colin Abbott, CFO

Gardhouse, Financial Counselling
Also listed under: *Financing & Loan Companies*
PO Box 399
41 Louisa St. West
Thornbury, ON N0H 2P0
519-599-6535
Fax: 519-599-6536
800-665-8250
gardhouse@on.aibn.com
Former Name: Gardhouse + Gardhouse, Financial Counselling Practice
Ownership: Private
Year Founded: 1986
Number of Employees: 3
Executives:
R. Larry Gardhouse, CFP, RFP
Bev Gardhouse, Office Administrator

Gardner Brown Consulting Inc.
#903, 2050 Nelson St.
Vancouver, BC V6G 1N6
604-608-0816
Fax: 604-608-2716
doreen@gardnerbrown.ca
www.gardnerbrown.ca
Year Founded: 1997
Executives:
Doreen Gardner Brown, President

Gary Bean Securities Ltd.
Also listed under: *Investment Dealers*
588 Main St. South
Exeter, ON N0M 1S1
519-235-4099
Fax: 519-235-4813
800-710-5216
www.garybean.on.ca
Ownership: Private
Year Founded: 1997
Profile: The independent securities firm provides investment management & integrated wealth management services. Products include bonds, income trusts, mutual funds, cash & GICs, speculative securities & common shares.

Executives:
Gary Bean, President
Suzanne Mathers, CA, Chief Financial Officer
Todd Robinson, Investment Advisor
Adam Skillen, Chartered Financial Analyst, Associate Portfolio Manager
Branches:
Erin
5328 9th Line, RR #2
Erin, ON N0B 1T0 Canada
519-833-2166
Fax: 519-833-7434
877-278-3666
Scott Keir, Investment Advisor
Hanover
192 - 10th St.
Hanover, ON N4N 1N7 Canada
519-364-4383
Fax: 519-364-3013
800-661-4960
Doug Williamson, Investment Advisor
London
#100, 256 Pall Mall St.
London, ON N6A 5P6 Canada
519-642-0626
Fax: 519-642-3880
800-276-0545
Paul Miller, Investment Advisor

Gary M. Renaud
#210, 1770 Woodward Dr.
Ottawa, ON K2C 0P8
613-228-7777
Fax: 613-238-4583
grenaud@lifespan.on.ca
Executives:
Gary M. Renaud

Gee, Lambert & Courneya
#401, 244 Pall Mall
London, ON N6A 5P6
519-673-1421
Fax: 519-679-8540
lgee@glc.on.ca
Executives:
Larry D. Gee

Generation Financial Corp.
Also listed under: *Investment Dealers*
Dominion Place
#240, 906 - 12th Ave. SW
Calgary, AB T2R 1K7
403-229-0501
Fax: 403-229-0573
tmcdonald@genfingroup.com
www.genfingroup.com/
Year Founded: 1998
Profile: The company is a privately owned mutual fund dealer. It has a network of 110 independent planning professionals, who are located in British Columbia, Alberta, Saskatchewan, Manitoba & the North West Territories.

Executives:
Dennis Albinati, CFP, President
Tammy McDonald, Administrative Manager

Genuity Capital Markets/ Marchés des capitaux Genuity
Also listed under: *Investment Dealers*
Scotia Plaza
PO Box 1007
#4900, 40 King St. West
Toronto, ON M5H 3Y2
416-603-6000
Fax: 416-603-3099
877-603-6001
investor.relations@genuitycm.com
www.genuitycm.com
Ownership: Private.
Stock Exchange Membership: Toronto Stock Exchange, TSX Venture Exchange
Profile: The independent firm offers the following services to its corporate clients: investment banking, equity research

resources, & institutional sales and trading. USA offices of Genuity Capital Markets USA Corp. are located in Boston, Massachusetts & New York, New York.

Executives:
David Kassie, Chair/CEO
Conrad Beyleveldt, Chief Financial Officer
Tom Briant, Chief Compliance Officer
Branches:
Calgary
Stock Exchange Tower
#1700, 300 - 5th Ave. SW
Calgary, AB T2P 3C4
403-266-3400
Fax: 403-266-1755
Montréal
#3000, 1800, av McGill College
Montréal, QC H3A 3J6
514-281-3250
Fax: 514-281-3022
Vancouver
Bentall Tower 5
PO Box 16
#1068, 550 Burrard St.
Vancouver, BC V6C 2B5
604-331-1444
Fax: 604-331-1446

Genus Capital Management Inc.
Also listed under: *Pension & Money Management Companies*
#1690, 999 West Hastings St.
Vancouver, BC V6C 2W2
604-683-4554
Fax: 604-683-7294
800-668-7366
www.genuscap.com
Year Founded: 1989
Profile: The independently owned investment counselling firm provides money management to individuals, families, foundations & institutions. In 2004, the firm acquired Maxima Investment Management.

Executives:
Wayne Wachell, CEO, Chief Investment Officer
Leslie Cliff, President & Director, Client Support
Rajan Dassan, Chief Information Officer
Brad Bondy, Director, Research
Chris Harrison, Controller
Robin Larsen, Manager, Communications
Branches:
Kelowna
#406, 1708 Dolphin Ave.
Kelowna, BC V1Y 9S4 Canada
250-712-2218
Fax: 250-862-9101
877-712-2217
quayle@genuscap.com
Dorothy Quayle, Portfolio Manager

George Abram Financial Services
2444 Beacon Ave.
Sidney, BC V8L 1X6
250-656-1154
abram@gulfislands.com, abramg@olympiatrust.com
Ownership: Private
Year Founded: 1988
Executives:
George Abram, Financial Planner, Employee Benefits Broker

The Gerald Flaherty Agency
111 Charles St.
Hamilton, ON L8P 3E4
905-525-4255
Fax: 905-525-4294
info@gfagency.com
gfagency.com
Year Founded: 1955
Executives:
Rick Nelson, President
Jessica Grasso, Vice-President
Sue Nelson, Office Manager

Gerard Matte Financial Inc.
100 Osborne St. North
Winnipeg, MB R3C 2H6
204-946-8212
Fax: 204-946-8840
gerry.matte@gwl.ca
www.mattefinancial.com
Former Name: Matte Agency Limited
Ownership: Private
Number of Employees: 4
Executives:
Gerard Matte, CFP, RFP, CLU, CH.F.C., Owner

Gestion de placements Eterna
Also listed under: *Pension & Money Management Companies*
#400, 1134, Grande allée ouest
Québec, QC G1S 1E5
418-692-9292
Fax: 418-266-1002
info@eterna.ca
www.eterna.ca
Former Name: Gestion de Placements Tardif Inc.; Trust Prêt et Revenu/Savings & Investment Trust
Ownership: Private. Parent is Trust Eterna.
Year Founded: 1998
Number of Employees: 28
Executives:
Paul Tardif, Chair/CEO & President
Robert Archer, Vice-President
Jean Duguay, Vice-President, Investments
Branches:
Montréal
#2140, 1155, rue Metcalfe
Montréal, QC H3B 2V6 Canada
514-908-6000
Fax: 514-908-6001
Jean Duguay, Vice-President, Investments

Gibbs Financial Group Ltd.
#1230, 1122 - 4th St. SW
Calgary, AB T2R 1M1
403-514-0080
Fax: 403-214-0380
info@gfgl.ca
www.gfgl.ca
Executives:
John Gibbs, CFP,CLU

GIC Financial Services
Golf Links Centre
#203, 34 Stone Church Rd. West
Ancaster, ON L9K 1P4
905-304-7574
Fax: 905-304-5198
877-368-0143
cindyd@gicfinancial.com
www.gicfinancial.com
Year Founded: 1979

GICdirect.com
#101, 1175 Cook St.
Victoria, BC V8V 4A1
250-592-7707
Fax: 250-592-7330
877-551-7283
info@gicdirect.com
www.gicdirect.com
Year Founded: 1999
Executives:
Michael J. Burden, CEO, Founder; michael@gicdirect.com
William A Ritchie, President, Founder; bill@gicdirect.com
Affiliated Companies:
LaPalm Insurance and Financial Solutions Inc.
Ottawa Asset Management Inc.
Vancea Financial Group
Branches:
Bradford
PO Box 490
129 Frederick St.
Bradford, ON L3Z 2B1 Canada
905-775-1102
Fax: 905-775-1104
financial.logic@sympatico.ca
Roch Beaulieu
Brantford
#406, 241 Dunsdon St.
Brantford, ON N3R 7C3 Canada
519-720-0936
Fax: 519-720-6904
888-497-8370
John Adkins
Burlington
3410 South Service Rd.
Burlington, ON L7N 3T2 Canada
905-333-6887
Fax: 905-333-6643
866-210-5552
ellisandassociates@bellnet.ca
Brian Ellis
Calgary
#320, 3115 - 12 St. NE
Calgary, AB T2E 7J2 Canada
403-215-3772
Fax: 413-215-3774
866-215-3711
bill.wealth@shawbiz.ca
Cambridge
#4, 48 Queen St. East
Cambridge, ON N3C 2A8 Canada
519-651-2572
Fax: 519-651-2571
frank.perri@aretefinancial.ca
Fort St. John
9519 - 100 Ave.
Fort St. John, BC V1J 1Y1 Canada
250-785-6285
Fax: 250-785-1677
888-322-6285
foster@ocol.com
Caroline Peters
Guelph
#5, 235 Starwood Dr.
Guelph, ON N1E 7M5
519-836-7989
Fax: 519-836-7397
info@cahillfinancial.ca
Kamloops
#500, 153 Seymour St.
Kamloops, BC V2C 2C7 Canada
250-372-9225
Fax: 250-372-9704
dougsmart@telus.net
Doug Smart
Kingston
#100, 785 Midpark Dr.
Kingston, ON K7M 7G3
Fax: 613-634-1667
866-454-9380
midpark@on.aibn.com
Langley
#119, 9440 - 202 St.
Langley, BC V1M 4A6 Canada
604-881-1200
Fax: 604-881-1299
gordflann@shawbiz.ca
Pat Chase
Lethbridge
#211, 1211 3rd Ave. South
Lethbridge, AB T1J 0J7
403-381-9195
Fax: 403-394-2195
rdale.butler@shaw.ca
London
690 Hale St.
London, ON N5W 1H4
519-453-5580
Fax: 519-453-0092
bestgicrates@yourfreedom.com
Nokomis
PO Box 418
Nokomis, SK S0B 3R0 Canada
306-528-2032
Fax: 306-528-4677
bill@riachfinancial.ca
Bill Riach
Ottawa - Preston St.
#200, 333 Preston St.
Ottawa, ON K1S 5N4 Canada
888-613-1234
Pembroke
870 Pembroke St. East
Pembroke, ON K8A 3M2 Canada
613-735-1500
Fax: 613-732-8885
theinsuranceman870@hotmail.com
Dave Gareau
Ponoka

INVESTMENT MANAGEMENT

GICdirect.com (continued)
5027 - 50th Ave
Ponoka, AB T4J 1C3 Canada
403-783-2233
Fax: 403-783-3359
service@diversifiedfinancial.ca
Port Perry
36 Water St.
Port Perry, ON L9L 1J2 Canada
866-311-4427
gic@powergate.com
Prince George
#103, 1268 - Fifth Ave.
Prince George, BC V2L 3L2 Canada
250-563-6666
Fax: 250-563-2671
bgale@balcom.ca
Richmond
#3180, 8788 McKim Way
Richmond, BC V6X 4E2
604-718-6699
Fax: 604-718-6698
connielam@inslinkfinancial.com
Sarnia
771 Esser Cres.
Sarnia, ON N7S 5W8 Canada
519-541-1702
cfc_financial@sympatico.ca
Simcoe
PO Box 99
36 Peel St.
Simcoe, ON N3Y 4K8 Canada
519-426-6932
Fax: 519-426-8053
866-426-6932
Smiths Falls
12 William St. West
Smiths Falls, ON K7A 1M9 Canada
613-283-5510
Fax: 613-283-4574
shawn@panko.ca
Shawn Panko
St Albert
28 Mission Ave.
St Albert, AB T8N 1H4 Canada
780-460-6460
Fax: 780-460-6461
877-460-6460
wanda@albertaplanner.com
Vancouver
610 West Broadway
Vancouver, BC V5Z 1G1 Canada
604-676-7777
Fax: 604-876-3308
ktwbrokers@shawcable.com
Victoria
#101, 1175 Cook St.
Victoria, BC V8V 4A1 Canada
250-592-7707
Fax: 250-592-7330
877-551-7283
info@gicdirect.com

Gillrie Financial
#106, 4246 - 97 St.
Edmonton, AB T6E 5Z9
780-485-6911
Fax: 780-466-6953
rgillrie@pipfs.com
www.pipfs.com/repLocator.html
Profile: Gillrie Financial is associated with Partners in Planning Financial Group Ltd.

Executives:
Rob Gillrie, CFP, CLU, CH.F.C., Chartered Financial Planner
Branches:
Tofield
#3, 5315 - 50 St.
Tofield, AB T0B 4J0 Canada
780-485-6911
Fax: 780-450-5634

Glavac Financial Planning Services
#3, 75 Lincoln St. West
Welland, ON L3C 5J3
905-788-1356
Fax: 905-788-3433
877-212-2680
info@glavacfinancial.com
www.glavacfinancial.com
Executives:
Andy Glavac, President

Global Benefit Plan Consultants Inc.
Also listed under: *Pension & Money Management Companies*
545 Wilson Ave.
Toronto, ON M3H 1V2
416-635-6000
Fax: 416-635-6464
Ownership: Private
Year Founded: 1961
Number of Employees: 87

Global Financial Services
#450, 800, boul René-Lévesque ouest
Montréal, QC H3B 1X9
514-399-9897
Fax: 514-399-1108
finance@globalmerchantbanker.ca
www.globalfinancialservices.ca
Year Founded: 1986

Global Securities Corporation
Also listed under: *Investment Dealers*
Three Bentall Centre
PO Box 49049
#1100, 595 Burrard St.
Vancouver, BC V7X 1C4
604-689-5400
Fax: 604-689-5401
800-455-5778
inquiries@globalsec.com
www.globalsec.com
Ownership: Private
Year Founded: 1987
Number of Employees: 130
Stock Exchange Membership: Canadian Trading & Quotation System Inc, Montreal Exchange, Toronto Stock Exchange, TSX Venture Exchange
Profile: The company is a full service brokerage firm which provides the following services: securities including all Canadian mutual funds, all types of fixed income & equities & options on all world exchanges, with research facilities; corporate finance; & mergers & acquisitions activities.

Executives:
Art M. Smolensky, Chair
Douglas Garrod, President
Duncan Boggs, CFO
Branches:
Delta
718 Tsawwassen Beach Rd.
Delta, BC V4M 4C7 Canada
604-943-0413
Fax: 604-943-0270
Nanaimo
253 Milton St.
Nanaimo, BC V9R 2K5 Canada
250-754-7723
Fax: 250-754-7757
North Vancouver
#430, 171 West Esplanade
North Vancouver, BC V7M 3J9 Canada
604-988-2088
Fax: 604-988-2082
Penticton
#101, 543 Ellis St.
Penticton, BC V2A 4M4 Canada
250-492-2585
Fax: 250-492-8458
Port Alberni
4994 Argyle St.
Port Alberni, BC V9Y 1V7 Canada
604-723-4970
Fax: 604-723-1151
Port Coquitlam
#6209, 2850 Shaughnessy St.
Port Coquitlam, BC V3C 6K5 Canada
604-552-9600
Fax: 604-552-3502
888-809-6541
Prince George
#401, 1777 Third Ave.
Prince George, BC V2L 3G7 Canada
250-614-0111
Fax: 250-614-0110
866-614-0111
Quesnel
#3, 334 Front St.
Quesnel, BC V2J 3K3 Canada
250-992-7448
Fax: 250-992-7458
Victoria - Boleskine St.
612 Boleskine St.
Victoria, BC V8Z 1E8 Canada
250-475-3088
Fax: 604-677-5788
Victoria - Douglas St.
#550, 2950 Douglas St.
Victoria, BC V8T 4N4 Canada
250-380-3801
Fax: 604-677-6096
West Vancouver
280 Hiawatha Dr.
West Vancouver, BC V7P 1E1 Canada
604-987-4774
Fax: 604-987-7273
Westbank
#2, 2413 Main St.
Westbank, BC V4T 2G3 Canada
250-768-1882
Fax: 250-768-2208
Williams Lake
#203, 197 - 2nd Ave. North
Williams Lake, BC V2G 1Z5 Canada
250-392-1012
Fax: 250-392-1090

GlobeInvest Capital Management Inc.
Also listed under: *Pension & Money Management Companies*
#3308, 20 Queen St. West
Toronto, ON M5H 3R3
416-591-7100
Fax: 416-591-7133
800-387-0784
info@globe-invest.com
www.globe-invest.com
Ownership: Private.
Year Founded: 1994
Number of Employees: 4
Assets: Under $1 million
Revenues: Under $1 million
Executives:
Peter A. Brieger, CFA, Chair/CEO
Wendy K. Sanita, CFP, Vice-President; wsanita@globe-invest.ca
Directors:
Peter A. Brieger, CFA

The Gogan Group Inc.
167 Carlton St.
Toronto, ON M5A 2K3
416-923-8585
info1@goganngroup.com
Executives:
Greg Gogan

Gold Key Financial
#1, 935 - 26th St.
Brandon, MB R7B 2B7
204-728-5909
Fax: 204-728-5967
Executives:
Sean F. McKiernan

Golden Capital Securities Limited
Also listed under: *Investment Dealers; Investment Management*
#168, 1177 West Hastings St.
Vancouver, BC V6E 2K3
604-688-1898
Fax: 604-682-8874
goldenfeedback@goldencapital.com
www.goldencapital.com
Ownership: Private
Year Founded: 1990

Stock Exchange Membership: Montreal Exchange, Toronto Stock Exchange, TSX Venture Exchange
Profile: Golden Capital serves both personal & corporate clients. Services include research, trading, corporate finance & money management servics.

Executives:
Peter Chu, President/CEO
Leo Wong, Chief Compliance Officer
Tony Chan, Exec. Vice-President
Jack Finkelstein, Vice-President
Daniel Siu, Vice-President

Goldring & Associates Financial Services Inc.
#100, 4145 North Service Rd.
Burlington, ON L7L 6A3
905-335-2291
Fax: 905-335-3104
888-588-0777
rgoldring@assante.com
Also Known As: Operating as Assante Financial Management Inc.
Ownership: Private
Year Founded: 1991
Number of Employees: 3
Executives:
Rick Goldring, CFP, RFP, President
Joan Cosby, Assistant

Gonzales Bay Financial Services
1157 Newport Ave., #C
Victoria, BC V8S 5E6
250-598-3863
Fax: 250-598-3354
Executives:
Dennis St. Arnault

Gooder Financial Management
3017 Tutt St.
Kelowna, BC V1Y 2H4
250-861-4481
Fax: 250-861-8944
info@gooderteam.com
www.gooderteam.com
Executives:
Stephen R. Gooder
Brenda Gooder, Office Administrator; brend@gooderteam.com

Goodreid Investment Cousel Corp.
Also listed under: *Investment Dealers*
#310, 145 Lakeshore Rd. East
Oakville, ON L6J 1H3
905-338-9090
Fax: 905-338-1660
Profile: Goodreid Investment serves the investing needs of private investors & small institutions. The organization manages US equities.

Executives:
Gordon Reid, President/CEO
Directors:
Tony Brebner, Chair

Gordon Stirrett & Associates
#1540, 1801 Hollis St.
Halifax, NS B3J 3N4
902-492-1119
Fax: 902-492-9494
info@gordonstirrett.com
www.gordonstirrett.com
Executives:
Gordon Stirrett

GP Capital Management Group Inc.
#120, 191 The West Mall
Toronto, ON M9C 5H8
416-622-9969
Fax: 416-622-5040
800-608-7707
info@gpcapital.com
www.gpcapital.com
Ownership: Private
Year Founded: 1988
Profile: GP Capital Management is an independent firm specializing in personal financial planning services & products.

Executives:
George Aguiar, President/CEO
Branches:
Cobourg
#102, 94 King St. West
Cobourg, ON K9A 2M3 Canada
905-372-6561
Hamilton
#3, 662 Fennel Ave. East
Hamilton, ON L8V 1V1 Canada
905-318-5222
Fax: 905-318-5019
Huntsville
#2, 23 Manominee St.
Huntsville, ON P1H 1K8 Canada
705-787-0080
Fax: 705-787-0081
800-215-3779
Markham
3A-91 Anderson Ave.
Markham, ON LE6 1A5 Canada
905-471-0098
Fax: 866-276-7131
Mississauga
#3, 2285 Dunwin Dr.
Mississauga, ON L5L 3S3 Canada
905-607-0120
Fax: 905-828-2856
Mississauga
2398 Haines Rd.
Mississauga, ON L4Y 1Y6 Canada
416-469-2626
Fax: 416-469-8466
Peterborough
270 George St. North
Peterborough, ON K9J 3H1 Canada
705-749-0953
Fax: 705-749-9336
Port Hope
#102, 25 Queen St.
Port Hope, ON L1A 2Y8 Canada
905-885-5996
Fax: 905-885-7719
Richmond Hill - Granton Dr.
#220, 111 Granton Dr.
Richmond Hill, ON L4B 1L5 Canada
905-882-5666
Fax: 905-882-5333
Richmond Hill - Hwy. 7
#212, 330 Hwy. 7 East
Richmond Hill, ON L4B 3P8 Canada
905-709-3989
Fax: 905-709-0389
St Catharines
30 Duke St.
St Catharines, ON L2R 5W5 Canada
905-327-7073
Toronto
#120, 191 The West Mall
Toronto, ON M9C 5K8 Canada
416-622-9969
Fax: 416-622-5040
800-608-7707
Whitby
173 Brock St. North
Whitby, ON L1N 4H3 Canada
905-668-2828
Fax: 905-668-2533

GP Financial Services Ltd.
2356 Scarth St.
Regina, SK S4P 2J7
306-584-2755
Fax: 306-586-7883
888-584-2755
gpfin@gpfinancial.ca
www.gpfinancial.ca
Number of Employees: 6
Executives:
Shelley Kelln-Trudelle, Owner

Grant King
174 Charlore Park Dr., RR#4
Omemee, ON K0L 2W0
705-799-7302
Former Name: Mutual Funds Plus
Ownership: Private
Year Founded: 1986
Executives:
Grant King, President

Granville West Group
#1425, 1075 West Georgia St.
Vancouver, BC V6E 3C9
604-687-5570
Fax: 604-688-3385
Ownership: Private
Year Founded: 1990
Number of Employees: 30

Green Financial Group Inc.
112 Springbank Ave. North
Woodstock, ON N4S 7P8
519-539-8212
Fax: 519-539-7415
800-539-8212
www.greenfinancialgroup.com
Ownership: Private
Number of Employees: 4
Executives:
Paul A. Green, CFP, President

Gregory P. Frost
#101, 30 Dupont St. East
Waterloo, ON N2J 2G9
519-741-8478
Fax: 519-741-0361
gfrost@dundeewealth.com
www.frostfinancial.com
Executives:
Gregory P. Frost

GrowthWorks Ltd.
Royal Centre
PO Box 11169
#2750, 1055 West Georgia St.
Vancouver, BC V6E 3R5
800-268-8244
client.services@growthworks.ca
www.growthworks.ca
Former Name: Canadian Science & Technology Growth Fund
Year Founded: 1996
Number of Employees: 80+
Assets: $500m-1 billion
Profile: GrowthWorks Ltd. is a venture capital company. Its affiliates manage several venture capital funds, including GrowthWorks Canadian Fund, GrowthWorks Commercialization Fund, GrowthWorks Atlantic Venture Fund, & the Working Opportunity Fund.

Executives:
David Levi, President/CEO
Affiliated Companies:
GrowthWorks Atlantic Venture Fund Ltd.
GrowthWorks Capital Ltd.
GrowthWorks WV Management Ltd.

Gryphon Investment Counsel Inc.
#1905, 20 Bay St.
Toronto, ON M5J 2N8
416-364-2299
Fax: 416-362-5552
mpears@gryphon.ca
www.gryphon.ca
Ownership: Private
Year Founded: 1981
Number of Employees: 37
Profile: Gryphon Investment Counsel Inc. specializes in pension & private investment management.

Executives:
George B. Kiddell, Chair
Terry Walsh, President & Managing Partner
Ronald E.F. Kaulbach, Managing Partner
Michael Pears, Managing Partner; mpears@gryphon.ca
Christopher M. Smith, Managing Partner
Alexander H. Becks, Principal
Lawrence V. McManus, Principal
Kathryn Collins, Investment Analyst
Stuart A. Carson, Director, Private Client Services
Branches:
Halifax
Purdy's Wharf Business Centre
#407, 1959 Upper Water St.
Halifax, NS B3J 3N2 Canada

INVESTMENT MANAGEMENT

Gryphon Investment Counsel Inc. (continued)
902-422-6356
Fax: 902-482-4797
Montréal
#1400, 1002, rue Sherbrooke ouest
Montréal, QC H3A 3L6 Canada
514-288-4122
Fax: 514-288-0461

Guardian Financial Planning Ltd.
#2, 105 Connell St.
Woodstock, NB E7M 1K7
506-325-2250
Fax: 506-325-2240
866-325-2250
www.guardianfinancial.ca
Executives:
Stephen LaPage, CFP, Contact; stephen@guardianfinancial.ca

Guidelite Financial Network Ltd.
#231, 1600 Steeles Ave. West
Concord, ON L4K 4M2
905-660-0776
Fax: 905-660-6343
guidelite@guidelitefinancial.com
Executives:
Ofer Rotman, Contact

GWL Realty Advisors
Stock Exchange Tower
#2990, 300 - 5 Ave. SW
Calgary, AB T2P 2Z1
403-777-0410
Fax: 403-269-3266
Year Founded: 1993
Executives:
Paul Finkbeiner, President
Ralf B. Dost, Exec. Vice-President, Portfolio Management & Finance
James Midwinter, Exec. Vice-President, Commercial Properties
William Briscoe, Sr. Vice-President, Commercial Investments
Don Harrison, Sr. Vice-President, Western Canada
Susan L. MacLaurin, Sr. Vice-President, Portfolio Management
Peter Accardo, Vice-President, Commercial Property Management
David House, Vice-President, Development
Paul Jussaume, Vice-President, Asset Management, Québec & Atlantic Canada
Evan Kirsh, Vice-President, Multi-Residential Asset Management
Mervin McCoubrey, Vice-President, Asset Management
Kevin Nicholson, Vice-President, Finance & Administration
Stephen Price, Vice-President, Multi-Residential
Tanyss Price, Vice-President, Account Management
Mike Snell, Vice-President, Asset Management
Tom Sullivan, Vice-President, Chief Account Manager
Scott Taylor, Vice-President, Asset Management, Priarie Region

Offices:
Montréal
Place London Life
#1820, 2001, rue University
Montréal, QC H3A 2A6 Canada
514-350-7940
Fax: 514-350-7954
Toronto
#830, 33 Yonge St.
Toronto, ON M5E 1G4 Canada
416-359-2929
Fax: 416-359-1199
Vancouver
PO Box 11505
#3000, 650 West Georgia St.
Vancouver, BC V6B 4N7 Canada
604-713-6450
Fax: 604-683-3264
Winnipeg
100 Osborne St. North, Fl. 2C
Winnipeg, MB R3C 3A5 Canada
204-946-7363
Fax: 204-946-8849

H&A Financial Advisors
1836 Angus St.
Regina, SK S4T 1Z4
306-584-2523
Fax: 306-584-8225
kelly@h-a-financial.ca
Year Founded: 1971
Executives:
Kelly Aikens, President
Ken G. Holliday, Contact

H.C. Lockhart Insurance & Financial Consulting Inc.
#202, 1726 Dolphin Ave.
Kelowna, BC V1Y 9R9
250-762-8711
Fax: 250-762-0883
hl@permanentfinancialsecurity.com
www.permanentfinancialsecurity.com
Executives:
Harley Lockhart, Owner

Hantke, Coffey, Redekop & Co.
27318 Fraser Hwy.
Aldergrove, BC V4W 3P8
604-856-5154
Fax: 604-857-0177
Executives:
Gary Hantke

Harris Chong & Crewe
#1202, 2025 Sheppard Ave. East
Toronto, ON M2J 5C2
416-499-3112
Fax: 416-499-7372
Executives:
Sonia Chong
Geoff Crewe

Harris Financial Services Inc.
9 Fifth Ave. North
Yorkton, SK S3N 0A1
306-783-3171
Executives:
Garry A. Harris

Hartwell Thayer Financial Services Group
#23, 2 Orchard Heights Blvd.
Aurora, ON L4G 3W3
905-713-9870
Fax: 905-727-5749
800-668-8976
doug.hartwell@hartwellthayer.com
www.hartwellthayer.com
Former Name: Tom Beck Insurance & Investments
Executives:
Barbara P. Hartwell, President; barb.hartwell@hartwellthayer.com
Tom Beck, Manager, Financial Services

Harvest Gold Financial
#18, 169 Dufferin St. South
Alliston, ON L9R 1E6
705-435-9778
Fax: 705-435-7233
bill@harvestgoldfinancial.com
Former Name: William Wray

Hatch & Muir
#202, 612 View St.
Victoria, BC V8W 1J5
250-953-6816
Fax: 250-953-6829
866-360-1020
info@hatchmuir.com
www.hatchmuir.com
Former Name: RWM Insurance & Financial Consulting
Executives:
Wayne Hatch, CLU, CFP
Robin W. Muir, CFP, CLU, CH.F.C.

Hatton Financial Inc.
Also listed under: *Pension & Money Management Companies*
#705, 10339 - 124th St.
Edmonton, AB T5N 3W1
780-482-2745
Fax: 780-488-1025
866-444-2745
klhatton@hatton.ca
www.hatton.ca
Former Name: Hatton Probe Financial Group Inc.
Ownership: Private
Year Founded: 1981
Number of Employees: 3
Assets: $5-10 million Year End: 20041029
Revenues: Under $1 million Year End: 20041029
Executives:
Keith Hatton, President

Heath Benefits Consulting
#500, 2025 West Broadway
Vancouver, BC V6J 1Z6
604-877-0488
Fax: 604-877-0325
www.heath.ca
Former Name: The Shasta Consulting Group; Heath Lambert Benefits Consulting
Ownership: Private
Number of Employees: 80
Revenues: $5-10 million
Profile: Health Benefits Consulting provides employee benefits.
Executives:
David Haber, President
Thomas Arnould, CFO
Heather Kisbee, Exec. Assistant
Branches:
Calgary
#460, 800 - 6th Ave. SW
Calgary, AB T2P 3G3 Canada
403-246-5228
Fax: 403-246-5257
877-432-8425
David Harstrom
Ottawa
#1203, 99 Metcalfe St.
Ottawa, ON K1P 6L7 Canada
613-238-4272
Fax: 613-238-3714
877-432-8468
Keith Morrallee
Toronto
#305, 191 The West Mall
Toronto, ON M9C 5K8 Canada
416-620-0779
Fax: 416-620-9416
877-432-8486
Keith Morrallee, Managing Director
Winnipeg
#105, 62 Hargrave St.
Winnipeg, MB R3C 1N1 Canada
204-487-1300
Fax: 204-487-0055
877-432-8494
Rob Poapst, Managing Consultant

Hein Financial Group
1421 - 100th St.
North Battleford, SK S9A 3K2
306-445-9455
Fax: 306-445-4966
888-436-4346
info@heinfinancial.com
www.heinfinancial.com
Ownership: Private
Number of Employees: 7
Profile: Hein Financial Group specializes in retirement & estate planning.
Executives:
Brian Hein, RFP, B.Com., CLU, CH.F.C., Registered Financial Planner, Chartered Life Underwriter & Chartered Financial Consultant; brian@heinfinancial.com
Greg Lightfoot, Manager; greg@heinfinancial.com
Karen Swanson, Assistant, Marketing
Branches:
Calgary
#204, 2210 - 10 Ave. SE
Calgary, AB T2G 0V9 Canada
403-231-8619
Fax: 403-231-8696
888-711-4346
Brian Hein, Associate

Henac Financial Ltd.
204 Peck Dr.
Riverview, NB E1B 1N1
506-856-7110
Fax: 506-856-7117
877-660-7110
henac@nb.aibn.com

Hendrickson Financial Inc.
#205, 8704 - 51st Ave.
Edmonton, AB T6E 5E8
780-466-2629
hfi@hendricksonfinancial.com
Executives:
Harland R. Hendrickson, Principal, Registered Deposit Broker

Hesselink & Associates
Also listed under: *Investment Dealers*
PO Box 69
11 Wellington St. South
Drayton, ON N0G 1P0
519-638-3328
Fax: 519-638-5070
admin@hesselink.ca
www.hesselink.ca
Former Name: C.A. Hesselink
Ownership: Private
Year Founded: 1989
Number of Employees: 5
Assets: $10-50 million Year End: 20051010
Revenues: Under $1 million Year End: 20051010
Executives:
Ab Hesselink, Chartered Financial Planner; ab@hesselink.ca
Jason Jack, Chartered Financial Planner; jason@hesselink.ca

Hibernian Capital Management Ltd.
PO Box 2009
#1001, 20 Eglinton Ave. West
Toronto, ON M4R 1K8
416-488-5800
Fax: 416-488-6150

Highland Financial & Insurance Services
5418 - 97th St.
Edmonton, AB T6E 5C1
780-448-1637
Fax: 780-436-9481
866-444-1637
postmaster@highlandfinancial.ca
www.highlandfinancial.ca
Executives:
Ed MacMillan, CFP

Hillier & Associates Financial Planners
15A Foster St.
Perth, ON K7H 1R5
613-264-1064
Fax: 613-264-0643
800-263-8074
shillier@on.aibn.com
Ownership: Private
Year Founded: 1994
Number of Employees: 4
Executives:
Stephen J. Hillier, CFP, RFP, Owner
Barbara Foster, Accountant

Hillsdale Investment Management Inc.
Also listed under: *Investment Fund Companies; Investment Management*
PO Box 228, TD Centre Stn. TD Centre
#2100, 100 Wellington St. West
Toronto, ON M5K 1J3
416-913-3900
Fax: 416-913-3901
website@hillsdaleinv.com
www.hillsdaleinv.com
Ownership: Private
Year Founded: 1996
Number of Employees: 12
Executives:
John Loeprich, Sr. Vice-President, Private Clients
John Motherwell, Vice-President, Institutional Marketing
Directors:
Gary Bryant
Ray Chantler
Arun Kaul
Hillsdale:
Canadian Aggressive Hedged A Fund
RRSP Eligible; Inception Year: 1999; Fund Managers:
Arun Kaul
ChrisGuthrie
Tony Batek
Canadian Aggressive Hedged I Fund
RRSP Eligible; Inception Year: 2001; Fund Managers:
Tony Batek
ChrisGuthrie
Arun Kaul
Canadian Market Neutral Equity A Fund
RRSP Eligible; Inception Year: 2000; Fund Managers:
Arun Kaul
TonyBatek
Chris Guthrie
Canadian Market Neutral Equity I Fund
RRSP Eligible; Inception Year: 2004; Fund Managers:
Chris Guthrie
ArunKaul
Tony Batek
Canadian Performance Equity A Fund
RRSP Eligible; Inception Year: 1996; Fund Managers:
Tony Batek
ChrisGuthrie
Arun Kaul
Canadian Performance Equity I Fund
RRSP Eligible; Inception Year: 2004; Fund Managers:
Arun Kaul
TonyBatek
Chris Guthrie
US Aggressive Hedged Equity A (US$) Fund
RRSP Eligible; Inception Year: 2000; Fund Managers:
Arun Kaul
ChrisGuthrie
US Performance Equity (US$) Fund
RRSP Eligible; Inception Year: 1996; Fund Managers:
Chris Guthrie
ArunKaul

Himmelman & Associates Financial Advisors Inc.
#1200, 1801 Hollis St.
Halifax, NS B3J 3N4
902-429-2422
Fax: 902-429-0807
info@himmelman.ca
www.himmelman.ca
Former Name: Himmelman Hinks Financial Advisors Inc.
Executives:
Brian Himmelman, B.Comm., CFP, Principal
Stephanie Holmes, Managing Partner

Hirji & Associates
#205, 13900 Maycrest Way
Richmond, BC V6V 3E2
604-279-0848
Fax: 604-273-9390
shah_hirji@telus.net
Executives:
Shah Hirji

Homeguard Funding Ltd.
Also listed under: *Financing & Loan Companies; Investment Management*
83 Dawson Manor Blvd.
Newmarket, ON L3X 2H5
905-895-1777
Fax: 905-895-9073
800-225-1777
homeguard@homeguardfunding.com
www.homeguardfunding.com
Ownership: Private
Year Founded: 1983
Number of Employees: 26
Revenues: $2,400,000
Profile: Homeguard provides mortgage services in York Region & its surrounding areas. The company specializes in helping first time home buyers. It has servied over 45,000 borrowers since its establishment.
Executives:
Wayne A. Sudsbury, President; waynesudsbury@homeguardfunding.com
William R. Eves, Exec. Vice-President; billeves@homeguardfunding.com
Sheilah A. Sudsbury, Sec.-Treas.
Ralph M. Larin, Manager, Area Sales
Branches:
Bancroft
Bancroft, ON K0L 1C0
613-332-5852
877-403-6639
Paul B. Cameron, Regional Manager, Kawartha Region
Cameron
Cameron Rd., General Delivery
Cameron, ON K0M 1G0 Canada
705-359-2066
888-887-1915
Paul B. Cameron, Regional Manager, Kawartha Region
Mississauga
5659 McAdam Rd.
Mississauga, ON L4Z 1N9 Canada
905-568-9255
Ron Butler, Regional Manager, Mississauga Region
Pefferlaw
3 Quinn Rd.
Pefferlaw, ON L0E 1N0 Canada
705-437-3293
Waterloo
78 King St. North
Waterloo, ON N2J 2X4 Canada
519-746-5547
Stephen Jennings, Regional Manager, Kitchener-Waterloo

HomeLife Cimerman Real Estate Ltd
28 Drewry Ave.
Toronto, ON M2M 1C8
416-226-9770
Fax: 416-226-0848
pdlfin@hotmail.com
www.homelife.ca/paullethbridge
Former Name: PDL Financial Consulting & Valuations Inc.
Profile: Activities include real estate appraisal & financial planning.
Executives:
Paul D. Lethbridge, CFP, CRES, MVA, Financial Planner, Broker

Howard Noble Insurance
PO Box 205
1 Hurontario St.
Collingwood, ON L9Y 3Z5
705-445-4738
Fax: 705-445-8100
insure@nobleins.on.ca
www.nobleins.on.ca
Executives:
Wayne J. Noble, Principal, President
Russell Poste, Principal, Sec.-Treas.
Laura Watson, General Manager
Branches:
Alliston
24 Victoria St. West
Alliston, ON L9R 1S8 Canada
705-435-5541
Fax: 705-435-7411
Barrie
#228, 80 Bradford St.
Barrie, ON L4N 6S7 Canada
705-737-0136
Fax: 705-737-2652
Elmvale
6 Queen St. East
Elmvale, ON L0L 1P0 Canada
705-322-2010
Fax: 705-322-0662

Howard, Barclay & Associates Ltd.
#302, 277 Lakeshore East
Oakville, ON L6J 1H9
905-337-2401
Fax: 905-337-2186
invest@howardbarclay.com
www.howardbarclay.com/

Howson Tattersall Investment Counsel Ltd.
Also listed under: *Pension & Money Management Companies*
PO Box 9
#1700, 151 Yonge St.
Toronto, ON M5C 2W7
416-227-1617
Fax: 416-979-7424
888-933-0335
www.htic.ca
Ownership: Private
Year Founded: 1962
Profile: Howson Tattersall Investment Counsel provides investment management service to a broad client base. The company also manages the Saxon Group of Funds. It currently manages over $7 billion in assets.

Howson Tattersall Investment Counsel Ltd. (continued)
Executives:
Allan W. Smith, CA, MBA, CFP, President/CEO
Richard Howson, Chief Investment Officer & Exec. Vice-President
Robert Leblanc, ASA, Vice-President, Investment Counsel
Brian M. Smith, CFA, Vice-President, Private Clients; brian.smith@htic.ca
Taras Klymenko, Manager, Institutional Service & Business Development
Affiliated Companies:
Saxon Mutual Funds
Branches:
Montréal
640-1000 de la Gauchetière ouest
Montréal, QC H3B 4W5 Canada
514-392-9151
Fax: 514-392-9222
866-361-9151
robert.leblanc@htic.ca
Robert Leblanc, Vice-President

HS Financial Services Inc.
PO Box 399
#3, 155 Edward St.
Aurora, ON L4G 3L5
905-727-7526
800-411-7979
Other Information: 800-411-7979 (Phone, Claims)
service@hsfinancial.ca
www.hsfinancial.ca
Profile: Services include personal, business & life insurance, mortgages & investments.

HSBC Investments (Canada) Limited
Also listed under: *Investment Fund Companies*
1066 West Georgia St., 19th Fl.
Vancouver, BC V6E 3X1
604-257-1000
Fax: 604-713-4308
800-830-8888
info@hsbc.ca
www.hsbc.ca
Ownership: Wholly owned by HSBC Bank Canada, which is in turn owned by HSBC Holdings plc.
Year Founded: 1991
Number of Employees: 75
Assets: $1-10 billion
Profile: Established in 1991, HSBC Investments (Canada) Limited is a mutual fund company based in British Columbia. A subsidiary of HSBC Bank Canada, it is the distributor of the HSBC Mutual Funds.

Executives:
Lindsay Gordon, President/CEO
Bob Anthony, Chief Credit Officer
Graham McIsaac, Chief Financial Officer
Sean O'Sullivan, Chief Operating Officer
Jeffrey Dowle, Exec. Vice-President
Sarah Morgan-Silvester, Exec. Vice-President
Francis Chartier, Vice-President, Institutional Investments
Sharee Ryan, Vice-President, Institutional Investments
Directors:
John Bond
Jacqueline Boutet
James Cleave
Peter Eng
Martin Glynn
Robert Martin
Samuel Minzberg
Gwyn Morgan
Youssef Nasr
Ross Smith
Keith Whitson
HSBC:
World Bond RSP Fund
RRSP Eligible; Inception Year: 1994; Fund Managers: HSBC Investments (Canada) Limited
European Fund
RRSP Eligible; Inception Year: 1994; Fund Managers: HSBC Investments (Canada) Limited
Canadian Balanced Fund
RRSP Eligible; Inception Year: 1989; Fund Managers: HSBC Investments (Canada) Limited
Canadian Bond Fund
RRSP Eligible; Inception Year: 1994; Fund Managers: HSBC Investments (Canada) Limited
Dividend Income Fund
RRSP Eligible; Inception Year: 1994; Fund Managers: HSBC Investments (Canada) Limited
Equity Fund
RRSP Eligible; Inception Year: 1989; Fund Managers: HSBC Investments (Canada) Limited
Canadian Money Market Fund
RRSP Eligible; Inception Year: 1989; Fund Managers: HSBC Investments (Canada) Limited
Mortgage Fund
RRSP Eligible; Inception Year: 1992; Fund Managers: HSBC Investments (Canada) Limited
Small Cap Growth Fund
RRSP Eligible; Inception Year: 1994; Fund Managers: HSBC Investments (Canada) Limited
US Equity Fund
RRSP Eligible; Inception Year: 1994; Fund Managers: HSBC Investments (Canada) Limited
US Dollar Money Market (US$) Fund
RRSP Eligible; Inception Year: 1998; Fund Managers: HSBC Investments (Canada) Limited
Global Technology Fund
RRSP Eligible; Inception Year: 2000; Fund Managers: HSBC Investments (Canada) Limited
AsiaPacific Fund
RRSP Eligible; Inception Year: 1993; Fund Managers: HSBC Investments (Canada) Limited
Emerging Markets Fund
RRSP Eligible; Inception Year: 1994; Fund Managers: HSBC Investments (Canada) Limited
Global Equity Fund
RRSP Eligible; Inception Year: 1998; Fund Managers: HSBC Investments (Canada) Limited
Chinese Equity Fund
RRSP Eligible; Inception Year: 2004; Fund Managers: HSBC Investments (Canada) Limited
LifeMap Conservative Portfolio Fund
RRSP Eligible; Inception Year: 2005; Fund Managers: HSBC Investments (Canada) Limited
LifeMap Moderate Conservative Portfolio Fund
RRSP Eligible; Inception Year: 2005; Fund Managers: HSBC Investments (Canada) Limited
LifeMap Balanced Portfolio Fund
RRSP Eligible; Inception Year: 2005; Fund Managers: HSBC Investments (Canada) Limited
LifeMap Growth Portfolio Fund
RRSP Eligible; Inception Year: 2005; Fund Managers: HSBC Investments (Canada) Limited
LifeMap Aggressive Growth Portfolio Fund
RRSP Eligible; Inception Year: 2005; Fund Managers: HSBC Investments (Canada) Limited
LifeMap MM Conservative Portfolio Fund
RRSP Eligible; Inception Year: 2005; Fund Managers: HSBC Investments (Canada) Limited
LifeMap MM Moderate Conservative Portfolio Fund
RRSP Eligible; Inception Year: 2005; Fund Managers: HSBC Investments (Canada) Limited
LifeMap MM Balanced Portfolio Fund
RRSP Eligible; Inception Year: 2005; Fund Managers: HSBC Investments (Canada) Limited
LifeMap MM Growth Portfolio Fund
RRSP Eligible; Inception Year: 2005; Fund Managers: HSBC Investments (Canada) Limited
LifeMap MM Aggressive Growth Portfolio Fund
RRSP Eligible; Inception Year: 2005; Fund Managers: HSBC Investments (Canada) Limited
Monthly Income Fund
RRSP Eligible; Inception Year: 2005; Fund Managers: HSBC Investments (Canada) Limited

Hub Financial Inc.
#1001 3700 Steeles Ave. West
Woodbridge, ON L4L 8M9
905-264-1634
Fax: 905-264-5463
800-561-2405
www.hubfinancial.com
Ownership: Subsidiary of Hub International Limited, Chicago, IL, USA
Profile: Hub Financial Inc. offers investment & risk management products & services. Employee benefits are also provided. The wealth management division is Hub Capital Inc.
Executives:
Terri DiFlorio, President
Jeff Botosan, Exec. Vice-President/COO
Jamie McGeachin, Vice-President, Operations
Kim Fernandes, Regional Vice-President
Bernard Applewhaite, Sr. Director, Marketing
Jason Fox, Director, Technology
Vera Pallova, Director, Finance
Shawn Redford, Director, Marketing
Lisa Brown, Regional Manager, Office
Brenda Alderson, Manager, Operations & Quality Assurance
Kim Moffatt, Manager, Contracting & Compensation
Affiliated Companies:
Hub Capital Inc.
Branches:
Calgary
#500, 1111 - 11th Ave. SW
Calgary, AB T2R 0G5 Canada
403-262-4466
Fax: 403-266-7541
800-661-9228
Judy Simpson, Regional Vice-President
Kelowna
#209, 1815 Kirschner Rd.
Kelowna, BC V1Y 4N7 Canada
250-861-3146
Fax: 250-717-5600
888-861-3146
Chris Brownrigg, Regional Director
London
#101, 557 Southdale Rd. East
London, ON N6E 1A2 Canada
519-641-3400
Fax: 519-641-3334
800-661-3400
Patricia Perger, Manager, Office
Montréal
110, boul Crémazie ouest, 7e étage
Montréal, QC H2P 1B9 Canada
514-374-3848
Fax: 514-382-9151
800-361-4052
Montse Klein, Regional Vice-President, Eastern & Maritime Region
New Westminster
#350, 628 - 6th Ave.
New Westminster, BC V3M 6Z1 Canada
604-526-4115
Fax: 604-526-4915
877-888-1222
Scott MacMillan, Director, Marketing
Vancouver
#800, 1185 West Georgia St.
Vancouver, BC V6E 4E6 Canada
604-684-0086
Fax: 604-684-9286
800-667-0310
Judy Simpson, Regional Vice-President
Victoria
#201, 755 Queens St.
Victoria, BC V8T 1M2 Canada
250-414-7272
Fax: 250-414-7270
800-661-7410
Tilly Enriquez, Managing Partner

Hunt Financial Services Inc.
311 Second St. West
Cornwall, ON K6J 1G8
613-933-2424
Fax: 613-938-1508
www.hunt-financial.com
Year Founded: 1956
Executives:
Edward A. Hunt, Founder
Brendon Hunt, President
Richard Mulligan, Vice-President, Sales
Branches:
Ingleside
Ingleside Shopping Centre
Ingleside, ON K0C 1M0 Canada
613-537-2241
Fax: 613-537-2810
888-537-4868

Hunter & Partners
#515, 20 Toronto St.
Toronto, ON M5C 2B8

416-304-0947
Fax: 416-304-1938
info@hunterpartners.on.ca
www.hunterpartners.on.ca
Ownership: Private
Profile: Financial counselling company.

Huntley O'Hagan Financial Planning
45 Allen St. West
Waterloo, ON N2L 1C9
519-570-3900
Fax: 519-570-1557
info@huntleyohagan.com
huntleyohagan.com
Executives:
Paul Huntley

Huss Consultants
148 Golf Links Dr.
Baden, ON N3A 3P1
519-634-9012
Fax: 519-634-9012
dennis@hussconsultants.com
www.hussconsultants.com
Profile: Management & financial consultation is provided.

Executives:
Dennis E. Huss, Certified Financial Planner

Hutton Investment Counsel Inc.
14 Knotty Pine Trail
Huntsville, ON P1H 1S9
705-787-0220
888-305-2698
Executives:
James A. Hutton, President

HW Annuity & Life Insurance Sales Ltd.
#375, 13220 St. Albert Trail NW
Edmonton, AB T5L 4W1
780-430-0499
Fax: 780-430-0629
advisorw@telus.net
Ownership: Private.
Year Founded: 1960
Number of Employees: 1
Revenues: Under $1 million
Profile: Financial planning, investments, segregated funds & life insurance sales are offered.

Executives:
Harry R. Williams, Certified Financial Planner, Chartered Life Underwriter & Chartered Financial Cons

I.A. Michael Investment Counsel Ltd.
#700, 8 King St. East
Toronto, ON M5C 1B5
416-365-9696
Fax: 416-365-9705
info@abcfunds.com
www.abcfunds.com
Also Known As: ABC Funds
Ownership: Private
Year Founded: 1988
Number of Employees: 5
Assets: Under $1 million
Executives:
Irwin A. Michael, President
ABC:
Fully-Managed Fund
RRSP Eligible; Inception Year: 1988;
Fundamental-Value Fund
RRSP Eligible; Inception Year: 1989;
American Value Fund
RRSP Eligible; Inception Year: 1996;

Ike Ahmed Financial Services & Insurance Ltd.
#1100, 120 King St. West
Hamilton, ON L8P 4V2
905-528-8691
Fax: 905-572-1144
ike.ahmed@clarica.com
Ownership: Private
Number of Employees: 3
Executives:
Ike Ahmed, CFP, CLU, President

Independent Agencies Ltd.
2 Broadway St. East
Yorkton, SK S3N 0K3
306-782-2275
Fax: 306-786-1870
barry.ind.agcy@sk.sympatico.ca
Executives:
Barry Marianchuk

Independent Financial Concepts Inc.
8309 - 34 Ave. NW
Calgary, AB T3B 1R1
403-571-0910
Fax: 403-571-0919
888-666-7166
ghunte@ifcmoney.com
Former Name: CBI Group Inc.
Ownership: Private
Year Founded: 1997
Number of Employees: 1
Assets: Under $1 million
Revenues: Under $1 million
Profile: Affiliated with Fundex Investments Inc.

Independent Financial Counsellors Inc.
51 Grady Bend Pl.
Winnipeg, MB R2V 4X2
204-786-8797
Fax: 204-788-0126
866-491-0032
ifcincorp.com
www.ifcincorp.com
Ownership: Private.
Number of Employees: 3
Profile: Tax preparations are also handled.

Executives:
Lyle Atkins, CFP, RFP, Investment Counsel
Grace Atkins, Contact

Independent Financial Services Limited
1001 - 3rd Ave. North
Saskatoon, SK S7K 2K5
306-244-7385
Fax: 306-664-1962
Ownership: Private
Year Founded: 1987
Number of Employees: 30
Profile: Independent Financial Services is a financial planning organization providing clients with multi-company access to a wide range of investment & insurance instruments.

Executives:
Mark Lord, RFP, Managing Director
George Clark, Sec.-Treas.
Rick Letts, Director
Branches:
Regina
4420 Albert St.
Regina, SK S4S 6B4 Canada
306-359-7705
Fax: 306-359-6693

Independent Planning Group Inc.
35 Antares Dr.
Ottawa, ON K2E 8B1
613-738-3388
Fax: 613-738-2904
800-565-9219
mail@joinipg.com
www.joinipg.com
Executives:
Vince Valenti, President; vvalenti@joinipg.com
Allan Bulloch, President, IPG Insurance; abulloch@joinipg.com

Info Financial Consulting Group Inc.
Also listed under: *Investment Dealers*
#PH8, 350 Hwy. 7 East
Richmond Hill, ON L4B 3N2
905-886-8811
Fax: 905-886-7532
inquiry@infofinancial.com
www.infofinancial.com
Ownership: Private.
Year Founded: 1992
Number of Employees: 6
Profile: The investment consultant is involved in investment banking. The group has 90 sales advisors.

Executives:
Gary Yung, President
Branches:
Mississauga
#38, 145 Traders Blvd.
Mississauga, ON L4Z 3L3 Canada
905-507-6018
Fax: 905-712-9536
Richmond Hill
Jubilee Square
#218, 300 West Beaver Creek Rd.
Richmond Hill, ON L4B 3B1 Canada
905-326-5428
Fax: 905-326-5405

Inhance Investment Management Inc.
#1200, 900 West Hastings St.
Vancouver, BC V6C 1E5
604-975-3300
Fax: 604-975-3319
866-646-5850
info@inhance.ca
www.inhance.ca
Former Name: Real Assets Investment Management Inc.
Ownership: Private
Year Founded: 2001
Number of Employees: 15
Assets: $50-100 million
Profile: Partners of the investment management company are VanCity and Renewal Partners.

Executives:
Kerry Ho, CEO
Steve MacInnes, Chief Investment Officer; stevemacinnes@inhance.ca
Lynn Shook, Sr. Vice-President, Operations & Human Resources; lynnshook@inhance.ca
Dermot Foley, Vice-President, Strategic Analysis; dermotfoley@inhance.ca

Integral Wealth Securities Limited
Also listed under: *Investment Dealers*
Waterpark Place
PO Box 18
#1305, 20 Bay St.
Toronto, ON M5J 2N8
416-203-2000
Fax: 416-203-5835
www.integralwealth.com
Ownership: Advisor-owned.
Stock Exchange Membership: Canadian Trading & Quotation System Inc, Toronto Stock Exchange, TSX Venture Exchange
Profile: Services include investment banking, portfolio investment management, fixed income & retail. Some financial products are stocks, income trusts, mutual funds, bonds, GICs, options, life insurance & annuities.

Executives:
David Cusson, Chief Compliance Officer

Integrated Benefit Consultants
Also listed under: *Pension & Money Management Companies*
#2, 4914 - 55th St.
Red Deer, AB T4N 2J4
403-340-3779
Ownership: Private
Executives:
John W. Ponto, CFP, President

Integrated Financial Services Inc.
#2, 4914 - 55th St.
Red Deer, AB T4N 2J4
403-346-3600
Fax: 403-340-3779
Ownership: Private
Number of Employees: 3
Executives:
Glen E. Pangle, President

Integrity Wealth Management
#215, 3385 Harvester Rd.
Burlington, ON L7N 3N2
Fax: 905-631-6345
866-325-6345
phil@cashcrisisprevention.com
www.cashcrisisprevention.com
Former Name: Halton Financial Group Ltd.
Ownership: Private.

INVESTMENT MANAGEMENT

Integrity Wealth Management (continued)
Year Founded: 2000
Number of Employees: 2
Assets: $10-50 million
Revenues: Under $1 million
Executives:
Philip Evenden, Contact

Interinvest Consulting Corporation of Canada Ltd.
Also listed under: *Pension & Money Management Companies*
Maison Interinvest
3655, rue Redpath
Montréal, QC H3G 2W8
514-393-3232
Fax: 514-393-3453
nminns@interinvest.com
www.interinvest.com
Ownership: Private
Year Founded: 1975
Profile: The corporation manages individual wealth & institutional assets, such as endowment & pension funds.

Executives:
Hans P. Black, President/CEO
Yves Séguin, Sr. Manager
Branches:
Toronto
250 Bloor St. East
Toronto, ON M4W 1E6 Canada

International Capital Management Inc.
Also listed under: *Investment Dealers*
#200, 940 The East Mall
Toronto, ON M9B 6J7
416-621-6299
Fax: 416-621-8013
877-341-8687
audrey@icm-canada.com
www.icm-canada.com
Former Name: Advanced Financial Concepts
Year Founded: 1990
Executives:
John Sanchez, Founder
Juan P. Sanchez, Founder

Invessa Services Financiers Inc.
Also listed under: *Investment Dealers*
#220, 2740, Pierre-Péladeau
Laval, QC H7T 3B3
450-781-6560
Fax: 450-781-4851
info@invessa.com
www.invessa.com
Executives:
Martin Rochon, Contact
Branches:
Boucherville
#311, 1550 rue Ampère
Boucherville, QC J4B 7L4 Canada
450-645-0400
Fax: 450-645-0350
cgr@invessa.com
Montréal - Fleury est
3739, rue Fleury est
Montréal, QC H1H 2S8 Canada
514-326-6020
Fax: 514-326-0850
senay@invessa.com
Montréal - Jean-Talon
#102, 4570, rue Jean-Talon est
Montréal, QC H1S 1K2 Canada
514-374-7580
Fax: 514-374-5998
ly@invessa.com
St-Jérôme
330, rue Saint-Georges
Saint-Jérome, QC J7Z 5A5 Canada
450-436-8989
Fax: 450-436-8402
filiatrault@invessa.com

Invest-A-Flex Financial Strategies Ltd.
#308, 938 Howe St.
Vancouver, BC V6Z 1N9
604-331-2520
Fax: 604-331-2540
888-496-3539
info@investaflex.com
www.investaflex.com
Ownership: Private.
Year Founded: 1995
Number of Employees: 7
Executives:
Malcolm Ross, President
Robert Radloff, Vice-President

InVested Interest
1276 Wellington St.
Ottawa, ON K1Y 3A7
613-798-2421
rick@invested-interest.ca
www.invested-interest.ca
Year Founded: 1986
Executives:
Rick Sutherland, RFP

The Investment Guild
Also listed under: *Pension & Money Management Companies*
#302, 345 Renfrew Dr.
Markham, ON L3R 9S9
905-470-9840
Fax: 905-470-6723
info@investmentguild.com
www.investmentguild.com
Ownership: Private
Year Founded: 1981
Number of Employees: 9
Assets: $1-5 million Year End: 20051130
Revenues: $1-5 million Year End: 20051130
Profile: The Guild also provides consulting on group insurance & employee benefits.

Executives:
J. Jeffrey Case, CLU, CFP, CH.F.C., President
W. Michael Thomas, CLU, CH.F.C., CFP, RFP, Vice-President

Investment House of Canada Inc.(IHOC)
Also listed under: *Investment Dealers*
#221, 1033 Bay St.
Toronto, ON M5S 3A5
416-926-9600
Fax: 416-926-9525
877-926-9600
www.ihoc.ca
Executives:
Vlad Trkulja, President/CEO
Sanjiv Sawh, CFO, Chief Compliance Officer
Darlene Gruwer, Managing Director

IOCT Financial
78 Spring Garden Ave.
Toronto, ON M2N 3G3
416-221-1564
Fax: 416-221-1032
info@astandofoaks.com
www.astandofoaks.com
Executives:
Michelle Bolhuis, President
Jeff Gebert, Partner
Jim Wilson, Vice-President, Operations

IQON Financial Inc.
2 Queen St. East, 19th Fl.
Toronto, ON M5C 3G7
Fax: 416-681-3244
1-877-236-0747
info@iqon.com
www.iqon.com
Executives:
Bruce Plaskett, Regl. Manager
Affiliated Companies:
Relegrity Financial Services Inc.

Irene McCardle
505 King George Hwy.
Miramichi, NB E1V 1M6
506-627-0288
Fax: 506-627-0154
irenemc@nbnet.nb.ca
Year Founded: 1992
Number of Employees: 3
Executives:
M. Irene McCardle, CMA, CFP

Ironshield Financial Planning
#310, 701 Evans Ave.
Toronto, ON M9C 1A3
416-626-6515
Fax: 416-626-2717
877-476-6744
info@ironshield.ca
www.ironshield.ca/index-2.html
Executives:
Scott E. Plaskett, CFP, CEO
Catherine L. Plaskett, CFP, President/CFO

J. Howard Lane, Chartered Accountant
15 Willow Grove Blvd.
Sharon, ON L0G 1V0
416-410-5488
howard.lane@sympatico.ca
www.howardlane.yp.ca
Executives:
J. Howard Lane, Chartered Accountant & Certified Financial Planner, Certified Public Accountant

J.L. Whiston Financial Services Limited
1951 County Rd. 27, RR#1
South Woodslee, ON N0R 1V0
519-975-1414
Fax: 519-975-1515
jlwltd@sympatico.ca
www.chambers.ca/jason_whiston
Executives:
Jason Whiston

James Dignan & Co. Independent Financial Planning Inc.
6509 Mississauga Rd., #D
Mississauga, ON L5N 1A6
905-302-1865
Fax: 905-858-3392
jpdignan@sympatico.ca
Former Name: Dignan & Co. Independent Financial Planning Inc.
Ownership: Private
Year Founded: 1997
Assets: Under $1 million
Revenues: Under $1 million
Executives:
James P. Dignan, President

Janice Charko
78 Mount Olive Dr.
Toronto, ON M9V 2C8
416-748-1822
Fax: 416-749-9532
charko1@rogers.com
Executives:
Janice Charko

Janice Paul & Company
#120, 19 River St.
Toronto, ON M5A 3P1
416-363-1515
Fax: 416-363-3845
balance@jpaulcga.com
Executives:
Janice Paul

Janston Financial Group
92 Norfolk St. South
Simcoe, ON N3Y 2W2
519-426-5683
Year Founded: 1999

Janston Financial Group Inc.
92 Norfolk St South
Simcoe, ON N3Y 2W2
519-426-3321
Fax: 519-426-0619
jkaminsky@janstonfinancial.com
Ownership: Private. Part of Armstrong & Quaile Associates Inc., Manotick, ON.
Year Founded: 1998
Executives:
Jane Kaminsky, President

Jardine Lloyd Thompson Canada
1111 West Georgia St., 16th Fl.
Vancouver, BC V6E 4G2

604-682-4211
Fax: 604-682-3520
800-708-1144
www.jltcanada.com
Former Name: Jardine Insurance Services Canada Inc.
Number of Employees: 150
Branches:
Calgary
#300, 112 - 4 Ave SW
Calgary, AB T2P 0H3 Canada
403-264-8600
Fax: 403-264-8608
800-461-5142
Paul Murphy, Regional Manager
Edmonton
#747, 10104 - 103rd Ave.
Edmonton, AB T5J 0H8 Canada
780-421-7188
Fax: 780-421-7717
877-666-2876
Montréal
#2720, 600, boul de Maisonneuve ouest
Montréal, QC H3A 3J2 Canada
514-908-1891
Fax: 514-908-1895
André Lebrun, Regional Manager
Surrey
#180, 10470 - 152nd St.
Surrey, BC V3R 0Y3 Canada
604-583-9800
Fax: 604-583-5777
888-290-9240
John Wright, Regional Manager
Toronto
#800, 55 University Ave.
Toronto, ON M5J 2H7 Canada
416-941-9551
Fax: 416-941-9022
800-268-9189
Peter Robinson, Regional Manager
Victoria
#350, 4396 West Saanich Rd.
Victoria, BC V8Z 3E9 Canada
250-388-4416
Fax: 250-388-9926
888-216-8018

Jenner Financial Services
Also listed under: *Pension & Money Management Companies; Investment Management*
#750, 926 - 5th Ave. SW
Calgary, AB T2P 0N7
403-777-4747
Fax: 403-777-4742
ajenner@telus.net
Former Name: Alison Jenner Financial Ltd.
Ownership: Private
Profile: An affiliated company is Peak Investment Services Inc.

Executives:
Alison Jenner, Contact

John S. Keenlyside & Company Ltd.
#622, 470 Granville St.
Vancouver, BC V6C 1V5
604-688-2378
Fax: 604-688-6455
www.keenlyside.ca
Ownership: Private
Year Founded: 1972
Executives:
John S. Keenlyside, President

Johnson & Robertson Financial Services
PO Box 3296
32 Sykes St. North
Meaford, ON N4L 1G1
519-538-9983
Fax: 519-538-5077
johnsonrobertson@rogers.com
Profile: Also provides mortgages services.

Executives:
Brian Johnson

Johnson Incorporated
95 Elizabeth Ave.
St. John's, NL A1B 1R7
709-737-1500
Fax: 709-737-1580
800-563-1650
headoffice@johnson.ca
www.johnson.ca
Year Founded: 1880
Executives:
C.C. Huang, President/CEO
Branches:
Ancaster
#308, 911 Golf Links Rd.
Ancaster, ON L9K 1H9 Canada
905-648-2298
Fax: 905-304-0911
888-609-4879
hamilton@johnson.ca
Calgary - 8th Ave.
#300, 736 - 8th Ave. SW
Calgary, AB T2P 1H4 Canada
403-263-6424
Fax: 403-262-3054
800-661-1233
clayrobinson@johnson.ca
Calgary - Johnson-Renfrew Insurance
#300, 736 - 8th Ave. SW
Calgary, AB T2P 1H4 Canada
403-298-8589
Fax: 403-262-3054
888-723-8332
Carbonear
PO Box 628
Trinity Conception Sq.
Carbonear, NL A1Y 1C1 Canada
709-596-5095
Fax: 709-596-1242
888-715-5095
carbonear@johnson.ca
Channel-Port-aux-Basques
PO Box 688
Grand Bay Mall
Channel-Port-aux-Basques, NL A0M 1C0 Canada
709-695-3663
Fax: 709-695-9344
888-892-3663
pabasques@johnson.ca
Charlottetown
200 Queen St.
Charlottetown, PE C1A 4B6 Canada
902-892-0108
Fax: 902-368-8941
888-388-5577
pei@johnson.ca
Clarenville
244A Memorial Dr.
Clarenville, NL A5A 1N9 Canada
709-466-6820
Fax: 709-466-6825
866-566-6820
clarenville@johnson.ca
Corner Brook
PO Box 69
Main St.
Corner Brook, NL A2H 6C3 Canada
709-634-5117
Fax: 709-634-7851
800-563-9333
cornerbrook@johnson.ca
Edmonton
West Chambers Bldg.
#301, 12220 Stony Plain Rd.
Edmonton, AB T5N 3Y4 Canada
780-413-6612
Fax: 780-420-6082
800-661-1973
edmonton@johnson.ca

Fredericton
PO Box 1176
650 Montgomery St.
Fredericton, NB E3B 5C8 Canada
506-458-1181
Fax: 506-453-9865
800-442-4428
fredericton@johnson.ca
Fredericton
336 Regent St.
Fredericton, NB E3B 3X4 Canada
506-460-1861
Fax: 506-453-9865
800-442-4428
fredericton@johnson.ca
Gander
The Gander Mall
132 Bennett Dr.
Gander, NL A1V 2H2 Canada
709-256-2341
Fax: 709-256-8206
888-308-7124
gander@johnson.ca
Gatineau
721, boul St-Joseph
Gatineau, QC J8Y 4B6 Canada
819-770-5200
Fax: 819-770-5378
Grand Falls-Windsor
PO Box 457
6 High St.
Grand Falls-Windsor, NL A2A 2J8 Canada
709-489-3859
Fax: 709-489-5362
800-929-5567
gfallswindsor@johnson.ca
Halifax
PO Box 9620
#400, 7 Maritime Pl.
Halifax, NS B3K 5S4 Canada
902-453-1010
Fax: 902-455-8229
800-588-3885
halifax@johnson.ca
Kingston - Foster Insurance
PO Box 9
408 Markland Rd.
Kingston, NS B0P 1R0 Canada
902-765-3374
Fax: 902-765-0403
800-387-2495
kingston@johnson.ca
Langley
Walnut Grove Commerce Center
#201, 9440 - 202nd St.
Langley, BC V1M 4A6 Canada
604-881-8820
Fax: 604-881-8828
888-412-8822
vancouver@johnson.ca
London
#230, 339 Wellington Rd. South
London, ON N6C 5Z9 Canada
519-668-1015
Fax: 519-668-6311
888-609-5529
london@johnson.ca
Marystown
Peninsula Mall
PO Box 1239
Columbia Dr.
Marystown, NL A0E 2M0 Canada
709-279-3447
Fax: 709-279-2330
800-922-1402
bjil@johnson.ca
Middleton - Balcom Insurance
PO Box 877
17 Commercial St.
Middleton, NS B0S 1P0 Canada
902-825-4857
Fax: 902-825-2252
800-203-0332
middleton@johnson.ca
Mississauga
#303, 350 Burnhamthorpe Rd. West
Mississauga, ON L5B 3J1 Canada
905-277-5496
Fax: 905-277-5449
888-321-1159
mississauga@johnson.ca
Moncton
1633 Mountain Rd.
Moncton, NB E1G 1A5 Canada

Johnson Incorporated (continued)
506-863-1155
Fax: 506-855-5861
888-428-9090
moncton@johnson.ca

Mount Pearl
Sobeys Square Mall
760 Topsail Rd.
Mount Pearl, NL A1N 3J5 Canada
709-737-1542
Fax: 709-737-1108
800-929-5866
sobeyssquare@johnson.ca
Orillia
40 Colbourne St. West
Orillia, ON L3V 2Y4 Canada
705-325-4489
Fax: 705-325-3828
800-461-8954
orillia@johnson.ca
Ottawa
#612, 1545 Carling Ave.
Ottawa, ON K1Z 8P9 Canada
613-728-6800
Fax: 613-728-2244
800-465-7240
ottawa@johnson.ca
Port Hawkesbury - Causeway Insurance
#2, 902 Reeves St.
Port Hawkesbury, NS B9A 2S3 Canada
902-625-2560
Fax: 902-625-2434
888-625-2560
hawkesbury@johnson.ca
Red Deer - Community Savings Insurance
#102B, 4901 - 48 St.
Red Deer, AB T4N 6M4 Canada
403-343-2091
Fax: 403-309-3626
877-343-2091
Richmond Hill
#600, 1595 - 16th Ave.
Richmond Hill, ON L4B 3S5 Canada
905-764-4884
Fax: 905-764-4163
800-461-4567
richmond@johnson.ca
St Catharines
#301, 63 Church St.
St Catharines, ON L2R 3C4 Canada
905-688-6611
Fax: 905-988-1299
888-321-1173
stcatharines@johnson.ca
St. John's
PO Box 12049
95 Elizabeth Ave.
St. John's, NL A1B 1R7 Canada
709-737-1654
Fax: 709-737-1118
888-737-6369
St. John's
PO Box 12049
68 Portugal Cove Rd.
St. John's, NL A1B 1R7 Canada
709-737-1689
Fax: 709-737-1012
888-737-1689
argyle@johnson.ca
St. John's
Memorial University of Newfoundland
PO Box 12049, A Sta. A
3016 Student Center, 3rd Fl.
St. John's, NL A1B 1R7 Canada
709-737-1669
Fax: 709-737-1110
888-737-6368
mun@johnson.ca
Stephenville
Stephenville Plaza
PO Box 254
Stephenville, NL A2N 2Z4 Canada
709-643-6760
Fax: 709-643-4554
866-643-6740
stephenville@johnson.ca
Sudbury
#10, 1895 Lasalle Blvd.
Sudbury, ON P3A 2A3 Canada
705-560-6715
Fax: 705-560-6518
888-321-1180
sudbury@johnson.ca
Sydney
Prince Street Plaza
325 Prince St.
Sydney, NS B1P 5K6 Canada
902-562-7566
Fax: 902-567-0301
866-226-3937
sydney@johnson.ca

Thunder Bay
521 Memorial Ave.
Thunder Bay, ON P7B 3Y6 Canada
807-766-2070
Fax: 807-766-2088
888-612-7873
thunderbay@johnson.ca
Toronto
18 Spadina Rd.
Toronto, ON M5R 2S7 Canada
416-920-4421
Fax: 416-920-1745
888-297-1127
toronto@johnson.ca
Waterloo
#102A, 151 Frobisher Dr.
Waterloo, ON N2V 2C9 Canada
519-883-6103
Fax: 519-883-6109
888-369-9903
waterloo@johnson.ca
Whitbourne
PO Box 39
Whitbourne, NL A0B 3K0 Canada
709-759-3000
Fax: 709-759-3001
888-759-0029
bjil@johnson.ca
Windsor
#510, 4510 Rhodes Dr.
Windsor, ON N8W 5K5 Canada
519-972-7454
Fax: 519-972-5523
888-372-2231
windsor@johnson.ca

JVK Life & Wealth Advisory Group
Also listed under: *Investment Dealers*
#206, 86 Ringwood Dr.
Stouffville, ON L4A 1C3
905-642-0654
Fax: 905-642-0786
800-767-5933
info@jvkgroup.com
www.jvkgroup.com
Profile: The independent financial planning company provides services to Ontario residents.

Executives:
John Niekraszewicz, President, Founder

K.J. Hill Financial Services
PO Box 646
12 Queen St. North
Tottenham, ON L0G 1W0
905-936-4242
Fax: 905-936-3675
kjhfinancialservices@on.aibn.com
Executives:
Ken Hill

Kanester Johal Chartered Accountants
Also listed under: *Accountants*
#208, 3993 Henning Dr.
Burnaby, BC V5C 6P7
604-451-8300
Fax: 604-451-8301
info@kjca.com
www.kjca.com
Ownership: Private.
Year Founded: 1992
Number of Employees: 15
Assets: Under $1 million
Revenues: $1-5 million
Executives:
Narinder Johal, Partner
Satpal S. Johl, Partner
Jeannie Wong, Contact

Kathken Group Inc.
290 George St.
Prescott, ON K0E 1T0
613-925-5984
Fax: 613-925-0790
Ownership: Private
Year Founded: 1995
Executives:
Kenneth J. Durand

KBSH Capital Management Inc.
Also listed under: *Pension & Money Management Companies*
#700, 1 Toronto St.
Toronto, ON M5C 2V6
416-863-1433
Fax: 416-868-1770
mail@kbsh.ca
www.kbsh.ca
Former Name: Knight, Bain, Seath & Holbrook
Ownership: Wholly owned subsidiary of Rockwater Capital Corporation, Toronto, ON.
Year Founded: 1980
Executives:
David Knight, Founding Partner
Peter Pennal, President/CEO
Geoffrey Hollands, Sr. Vice-President, Investments
Branches:
Halifax
Tower II, Purdy's Wharf
#1401A, 1969 Upper Water St.
Halifax, NS B3J 3R7 Canada
902-421-1564
Fax: 902-422-9755
Bob Rudderham, Vice-President, Marketing
Montréal
#2400, 1000, de la Gauchetière ouest
Montréal, QC H3B 4W5 Canada
514-499-5274
Fax: 514-499-0042
Tim Stinson, President, Private Client Group

Keith A. Jackson
125 Oshawa Blvd. South
Oshawa, ON L1H 5R4
905-576-7520
Fax: 905-725-9400
kjackson@durham.igs.net
Executives:
Keith A. Jackson

Ken Woods Certified Financial Planner
102 Fairway View NW
High River, AB T1V 1C9
403-652-5662
Executives:
Ken Woods

Keybase Financial Group
#600, 100 York Blvd.
Richmond Hill, ON L4B 1J8
905-709-7911
Fax: 905-709-7022
info@keybase.com
www.keybase.com
Ownership: Private
Number of Employees: 15
Executives:
Dax Sukhraj, President

Kimber & Company Financial Services Ltd.
509 Railway Ave.
Weyburn, SK S4H 0A8
306-842-6668
Fax: 306-842-1755
Ownership: Private
Number of Employees: 2
Executives:
Allan Kimber

Kime, Mills, Dunlop
PO Box 5005
#700, 495 Richmond St.
London, ON N6A 5G4
519-679-8550
Fax: 519-679-1812
Number of Employees: 27
Executives:
Michael Bondy, Partner
Dan Daum, Partner
Jim Dunlop, Partner
Doug Greenhow, Partner
Gerry Mills, Partner
David Wells, Partner
Branches:
Exeter
PO Box 2405
412 Main St.
Exeter, ON N0M 1S7 Canada
519-235-0345
Fax: 519-235-3235
Sebringville
PO Box 190
281 Huron Rd.
Sebringville, ON N0K 1X0 Canada
519-393-5030
Fax: 519-393-6035

KingsGate Wealth Management Services Limited
#300, 195 The West Mall
Toronto, ON M9C 5K1
416-626-9111
Fax: 416-626-9122
info@kingsgate.ca
www.kingsgate.ca
Ownership: Private.
Year Founded: 1999
Profile: Financial advisors offer financial planning, investment counseling, estate planning, tax planning, insurance planning, mortgages & securities.
Elizabeth Galoni, Manager
Affiliated Companies:
KingsGate Securities Limited
Branches:
Burlington
#101A, 3425 Harvester Rd.
Burlington, ON L7N 3N1
905-333-6694
Fax: 905-333-6694
Mississauga
#200, 176 Robert Speck Pkwy.
Mississauga, ON L4Z 3G1
905-272-8004
Fax: 905-272-8144
Oakville - Cornwall Rd.
1388 Cornwall Rd., #A
Oakville, ON L6J 7W5
905-338-8343
Fax: 905-330-5816
Oakville - Old Bridle Path
1312 The Old Bridle Path
Oakville, ON L6M 1A5
905-827-2853
Fax: 905-827-2853
St Catharines
156 Lake St.
St Catharines, ON L2R 5Y3
905-704-1595
Fax: 905-704-1969
Thorold
#14, 3350 Merrittville Hwy.
Thorold, ON L2V 4Y6
905-687-4111
Fax: 905-682-2221
Waterloo
#205, 370 University Ave. East
Waterloo, ON N2K 3N2
519-886-4755
Fax: 519-886-5580

Kingsway Financial Services Inc.
Also listed under: Federal & Provincial; Investment Management
#200, 5310 Explorer Dr.
Mississauga, ON L4W 5H8
905-629-7888
Fax: 905-629-5008
info@kingsway-financial.com
www.kingsway-financial.com
Ownership: Public
Year Founded: 1987
Number of Employees: 2,250
Assets: $1-10 billion Year End: 20041231
Stock Symbol: KFS
Profile: The company is a non-standard automobile, trucking, taxi & motorcycle insurer. Kingsway also offers a range of insurance services through its subsidiaries.
Executives:
William G. Star, President/CEO & Chair
W. Shaun Jackson, Exec. Vice-President/CFO
Frank Amodeo, Vice-President
Dennis Fielding, Vice-President
Shelly Gobin, Vice-President, Treasurer
Claude Smith, Vice-President, CIO
Dennis Cloutier, Chief Actuary
Directors:
William G. Star, Chair
David H. Atkins
John L. Beamish
Thomas A. Di Giacomo
Walter Farnam
Bernard Gluckstein
J. Brian Reeve
Jack Sullivan
F. Michael Walsh
Affiliated Companies:
JEVCO Insurance Company
Kingsway General Insurance Company
York Fire & Casualty Insurance Company

Kirschner Financial Services
#1260, 13401 - 108th Ave.
Surrey, BC V3T 5T3
604-930-3584
Fax: 604-930-3571
ken.kirschner@gwl.ca
www.kenkirschner.ca
Executives:
Ken A. Kirschner

Kopeck Financial Concepts Ltd.
#171, 4747 - 67 St.
Red Deer, AB T4N 6H3
403-340-2410
Fax: 403-342-6654
Ownership: Private
Year Founded: 1983
Number of Employees: 2
Assets: $1-5 million
Revenues: Under $1 million
Executives:
Garry Kopeck

Kroeger Financial Services
4838 - 49th St.
Camrose, AB T4V 1N2
780-672-6399
Fax: 780-679-4224
Executives:
Brandon Kroeger

L&A Financial Group Inc.
#200, 1030 Upper James St.
Hamilton, ON L9C 6X6
905-529-1210
Fax: 905-529-2812
email@la-financialgroup.on.ca
www.la-financialgroup.on.ca
Ownership: Private
Year Founded: 1985
Number of Employees: 7
Executives:
Pat Lynch
Dan Lynch

La Capitale Financial Management Inc./ La Capitale gestion financière inc.
625, rue Saint-Amable
Québec, QC G1R 2G5
418-644-4300
800-463-6742
www.lacapitale.com/groupe/gfi.jsp?lang=en
Ownership: Subsidiary of La Capital Financial Group Inc., Québec, QC.
Year Founded: 1985
Number of Employees: 35
Assets: $10-50 million
Revenues: $5-10 million
Executives:
Jacques Labrecque, President

La Capitale Insurance & Financial Services/ La Capitale assurances et gestion du patrimoine
Also listed under: Federal & Provincial
Édifice Le Delta II
#100, 2875, boul Laurier
Québec, QC G1V 2M2
418-644-4200
Fax: 418-644-5226
888-463-4856
collectif@lacapitale.com
www.lacapitale.com
Former Name: La Capitale Life Insurance Inc.
Ownership: Subsidiary of La Capitale Financial Group Inc., Québec, QC.
Year Founded: 1989
Profile: Group insurance products are provided for groups from the civil service & the private sector. Financial services include savings, loans & financial solutions for retired people.
Executives:
Robert St-Denis, President/COO
Francine Landry, Vice-President, Technology, Systems Development & E-Business
Branches:
Montréal
#820, 425, boul de Maisonneuve ouest
Montréal, QC H3A 3G5 Canada
514-873-2402
Fax: 514-873-8733
888 899-4959
Québec
Édifice Le Delta II
#100, 2875, boul Laurier
Québec, QC G1V 2M2 Canada
418-644-4200
Fax: 418-644-4352
800-363-9683

La Rochelle Financial Consultants, Inc.
33199 Huggard Rd.
Calgary, AB T3Z 2C4
403-685-4770
Fax: 403-249-6818
888-678-6680
lfci@pathcom.ca
www.denis.larochelle.savetax.ca
Ownership: Private
Year Founded: 1992
Revenues: Under $1 million
Executives:
Denis R. La Rochelle, President

Lake Huron Life
PO Box 365
84 Queen St.
Ripley, ON N0G 2R0
519-395-4508
Fax: 519-395-4760
lhlife@bmts.com
Executives:
Nancy McKinley

Laketon Investment Management Ltd.
#800, 130 Adelaide St. West
Toronto, ON M5H 3P5
416-864-0947
Fax: 416-868-1732
866-861-0947
info@laketon.com
www.laketon.com
Ownership: Private. Canada Life Assurance a shareholder.
Year Founded: 1979
Number of Employees: 45
Assets: $1-10 billion
Executives:
Alex Macdonald, President/Chief Compliance Officer

Laketon Investment Management Ltd. (continued)
Kevin Elliott, Sr. Vice-President, Director Equities Portfolio Manager
Gary Morris, Director, Fixed Income Portfolio Manager
Sean O'Hara, Director, Marketing & Business Development

Lanagan Lifestyles Ltd.
1820 - 33rd Ave. SW
Calgary, AB T2T 1Y9
403-238-2541
Fax: 403-238-5112
www.lanagan.com
Former Name: Lanagan Financial Services Limited
Ownership: Private
Year Founded: 1987
Profile: Offers a broad range of financial services including lifestyle planning.

Executives:
Lucette A. Simpson, CFP, RFP, Partner
Nick Simpson, Partner

LaPalm Insurance and Financial Solutions Inc.
#206, 329 Front St.
Belleville, ON K8N 2Z9
Fax: 613-962-0365
866-962-5586
admin@lapalmfinancial.com
www.lapalmfinancial.com
Year Founded: 1997

Lawrence Asset Management
#1500, 70 York St.
Toronto, ON M5J 1S9
416-362-4999
Fax: 416-362-0063
866-404-4999
info@lawvest.com
www.lawvest.com
Former Name: Lawrence & Co.
Executives:
Jack Lawrence, CEO
Ravi Sood, President/COO

Lawton Partners Financial Planning Services Limited
305 Broadway, 10th Fl.
Winnipeg, MB R3C 3J7
204-944-1144
Fax: 204-947-3512
888-944-1144
www.lawton.mb.ca
Ownership: Private
Year Founded: 1990
Number of Employees: 38
Profile: The company is affiliated with Lawton Partners Insurance & Estate Planning Ltd.

Executives:
James E. Lawton, President
Laurie Baird, Vice-President
Cameron Inglis, Vice-President
Dwaine P. King, Vice-President
Mark D. Mancini, Vice-President
Terry R. Snell, Vice-President
Susan Stobart, Vice-President
K. Wayne Townsend, Vice-President
Elden Wittmier, Secretary
DeWayne Osborn, General Manager

Lazard Canada Corporation
***Also listed under:** Investment Dealers*
#1610, 1501, av McGill College
Montréal, QC H3A 3M8
514-397-1016
Fax: 514-397-1317
www.lazard.com
Year Founded: 1848
Branches:
Toronto
PO Box 373, First Canadian Pl. Sta. First Canadian Pl.
#4610, 1 First Canadian Pl.
Toronto, ON M5X 1E2 Canada
416-216-5086
Fax: 416-216-5085

Leadbeater Financial Services
523 Elizabeth St.
Midland, ON L4R 2A2
705-527-1681
Fax: 705-527-7658
Year Founded: 1991
Executives:
Robert Leadbeater, Contact

LeadingEdge Financial Planning Inc.
332 - 11th Ave. SW
Calgary, AB T2R 0C5
403-237-7526
Fax: 403-265-5984
leadingedge@freedom55financial.com
www.leadingedgeplans.com
Executives:
Peter D.S. Jekill

Lee Nunn Financial Planner
410 Ogilvie St.
Whitehorse, YT Y1A 2S4
867-633-2301
Fax: 867-393-2200
leenunn@gmail.com
Former Name: The Prosperity Centre
Executives:
Lee Nunn

Leeland Financial Group
***Also listed under:** Pension & Money Management Companies*
#1088, 926 - 5 Ave. SW
Calgary, AB T2P 0N7
403-265-0235
Fax: 403-265-0311
800-341-1888
leeland@leeland.com
www.leeland.com
Ownership: Private
Year Founded: 1968
Number of Employees: 4
Assets: $10-50 million Year End: 20051201

Legacy Wealth Management Inc.
#300, 10655 Southport Rd. SW
Calgary, AB T2W 4Y1
403-203-0998
Fax: 403-203-0938
Ownership: Private
Year Founded: 1998
Number of Employees: 4
Assets: $1-5 million
Revenues: Under $1 million
Profile: The company provides personal & corporate financial planning services in areas such as wealth accumulation & transfer, retirement & estate planning, corporate buy-out & legacy protection, tax-efficient investment strategies as well as charitable giving concepts.

Executives:
Melanie D. Reidy, RFP, President
Randall J. Reidy, Exec. Vice-President

Legg Mason Canada Inc.
#1400, 320 Bay St.
Toronto, ON M5H 4A6
416-860-0616
Fax: 416-860-0628
800-565-6781
www.leggmasoncanada.com
Former Name: Perigee Investment Counsel Inc.
Ownership: Private. Parent is Legg Mason, Inc.
Year Founded: 1972
Number of Employees: 70
Executives:
Stephen J. Griggs, President/CEO
Louise Tymocko, Chief Operating Officer
Gia Steffensen, Exec. Vice-President, Chief Investment Officer
Dona Eull-Schultz, Sr. Vice-President, Marketing & Client Services
D. Walter McCormick, Sr. Vice-President & Portfolio Manager, Private Client
Branches:
Montréal
#1720, 2000, rue Mansfield
Montréal, QC H3A 3A6 Canada
514-286-6110
Fax: 514-286-2431
800-948-8599
Vancouver
#2001, 1188 West Georgia St.
Vancouver, BC V6E 4A2 Canada
604-688-7234
Fax: 604-684-6315
877-737-4433
Waterloo
Marsland Centre
20 Erb St. West, 6th Fl.
Waterloo, ON N2L 1T2 Canada
519-746-9633
Fax: 519-746-4950
800-565-6810

Leipert Financial Group
#200, 1514 - 11th St.
Regina, SK S4P 0H2
306-359-0776
Fax: 306-757-0776
info@leipertfinancial.com
www.leipertfinancial.com
Executives:
Brian L. Leipert
Branches:
Moose Jaw
#107, 111 Fairford St. East
Moose Jaw, SK S6H 7X5 Canada
info@leipertfinancial.com
Margaret Whiteley, Manager

Leith Wheeler Investment Counsel Ltd.
***Also listed under:** Investment Fund Companies; Investment Management*
#1500, 400 Burrard St.
Vancouver, BC V6C 3A6
604-683-3391
Fax: 604-683-0323
888-292-1122
info@leithwheeler.com
www.leithwheeler.com
Ownership: Private
Year Founded: 1982
Number of Employees: 26
Assets: $1-10 billion
Profile: The investment counsel provides portfolio management to non-profit organizations, pension plans & individual investors.

Executives:
William Wheeler, Chair
David Schaffner, President/CEO
Cecilia Wong, CFO
Bill Dye, Chief Investment Officer
David Ayriss, Vice-President
Gordon Gibbons, Vice-President, Client Services
Jonathon Palfrey, Vice-President & Portfolio Manager
Neil Watson, Vice-President
Directors:
Bruce Carlson
Leon Getz
David Schaffner
Leith Wheeler:
Money Market Fund
RRSP Eligible; Inception Year: 1994;
Balanced Fund
RRSP Eligible; Inception Year: 1987;
Canadian Equity Fund
RRSP Eligible; Inception Year: 1994;
Fixed Income Fund
RRSP Eligible; Inception Year: 1994;
US Equity Fund
RRSP Eligible; Inception Year: 1994;
International FundInception Year: 0; Fund Managers: Sprucegrove Investment Management Ltd.
Diversified Pooled FundInception Year: 2001;
Income Trust Fund
RRSP Eligible; Inception Year: 2005;

Lemoine Hyland Group LLP
***Also listed under:** Accountants*
#207, 2085 Hurontario St.
Mississauga, ON L5A 4G1
905-275-7794
Fax: 905-275-5677
877-544-7687
rlemoine@lhgroup.com
lhgroup.com
Former Name: Lemoine Hyland & Grover
Executives:

Doug Hyland
Richard Lemoine

Leo McCready Financial Services
34 Rivercrest Dr.
St Catharines, ON L2T 2P4
905-641-8781
Profile: Financial & life insurance services are offered.

Executives:
Leo McCready, President

Leon Frazer & Associates
#2001, 8 King St. East
Toronto, ON M5C 1B6
416-864-1120
Fax: 416-864-1491
800-418-7518
info@leonfrazer.com
www.leonfrazer.com
Former Name: The Glen Ardith-Frazer Corporation
Ownership: 83.5% owned by Jovian Asset Management Inc., a wholly owned subsidiary of Jovian Capital Corp.
Year Founded: 1939
Number of Employees: 28
Executives:
George Frazer, Chair; gfrazer@leonfrazer.com
William Tynkaluk, President; wtynkaluk@leonfrazer.com
Ed Osler, Sr. Vice-President, Compliance Officer; eosler@leonfazer.com
Directors:
George Frazer
William Tynkaluk
Bob Wong
Branches:
Vancouver
#780, 999 Canada Place
Vancouver, BC V6C 3E2 Canada
604-601-2088
Fax: 604-601-2089
866-266-4730
dhoover@leonfrazer.com
Doug Hoover, Vice-President, Marketing & Client Services

Leslie J. Dawson
3227 Roblin Blvd., #A
Winnipeg, MB R3C 0C6
204-832-2131
Fax: 204-896-9187
Year Founded: 1994
Number of Employees: 1
Executives:
Leslie Dawson

Liberty International Underwriters Canada
#1000, 181 Bay St.
Toronto, ON M5J 2T3
416-365-7587
Fax: 416-307-4372
www.libertyiu.com
Former Name: Liberty International Canada
Also Known As: LIU Canada
Year Founded: 1993
Number of Employees: 120
Profile: Multi-line commercial insurance products & services are supplied.

Executives:
Mike Molony, President
Donna Barclay, Sr. Vice-President
Betty Bingler, Sr. Vice-President, Strategic & Operational Initiatives
Ron Noblett, Sr. Vice-President
Darin Scanzano, Sr. Vice-President, Casualty, Specialty Casualty
Winston Chin, Vice-President, Energy & Property Services
David Michie, Vice-President
Rissa Revin, Vice-President
Mike Weiss, Vice-President

Lifestyle by Design, Financial Group
2363 McIntyre St.
Regina, SK S4P 2S3
306-757-6999
Fax: 306-352-1018
dfoster@fundsdirect.ca
Ownership: Private
Year Founded: 1994
Number of Employees: 9
Executives:
Doug A. Foster, RFP, President

The Lifestyle Protector Solution
#204, 830 Shamrock St.
Victoria, BC V8X 2V1
250-475-6682
Fax: 250-475-3098
888-475-6682
lifestyleprotector@shaw.ca
Ownership: Parent is London Life Insurance Company.
Year Founded: 1997
Number of Employees: 2
Assets: Under $1 million
Revenues: Under $1 million
Executives:
J. David Williams, Contact
Valerie J. Williams, Contact

Lifetime Financial Planning
#1235, 840 - 7 Ave. SW
Calgary, AB T2P 3G2
403-290-1211
Fax: 403-265-4384
Executives:
Stephen P. Murray

Lighthouse Wealth Management Ltd.
PO Box 730
141 Simpson St.
Brighton, ON K0K 1H0
613-475-5109
Fax: 613-475-1581
866-475-5109
sharp.ones@sympatico.ca
www.lighthousewealth.ca
Ownership: Private
Year Founded: 2000
Number of Employees: 3
Assets: Under $1 million
Revenues: Under $1 million
Executives:
David Sharp, President
Branches:
Campbellford
PO Box 1661
175 Front St. North
Campbellford, ON K0L 1L0 Canada
705-653-4681
Fax: 705-653-3431
sharp.ones@sympatico.ca

Lightyear Capital Inc.
Also listed under: *Investment Dealers; Non-Depository Institutions*
Bow Valley Square I
#660, 202 - 6 Ave. SW
Calgary, AB T2P 2R9
403-218-1400
Fax: 403-537-6512
info@lightyearcapital.com, investmentbanking@lightyearcapital.com
www.lightyearcapital.com
Stock Exchange Membership: Toronto Stock Exchange, TSX Venture Exchange
Profile: The company offers investment banking services. Clients include small-mid cap companies.

Executives:
Louise M. Duchesne, CA, Managing Director; louise.duchesne@lightyearcapital.com
Murray A. Weimer, CA, Managing Director; murray.weimer@lightyearcapital.com

Linear Grain Inc.
PO Box 219
67 Centre Ave. West
Carman, MB R0G 0J0
204-745-6747
Fax: 204-745-6573
800-514-1199
linear@lineargrain.com
www.lineargrain.com
Former Name: Linear Agra (Man.) Ltd.
Ownership: Private.
Year Founded: 1981
Profile: Linear Grain is an independent, licensed & bonded company.

Executives:
Ross McKnight, President

Liu Raymond C S Chartered Accountant
Also listed under: *Accountants*
#410, 10665 Jasper Ave.
Edmonton, AB T5J 3S9
780-429-1047
Ownership: Private
Year Founded: 1983
Number of Employees: 5
Revenues: Under $1 million
Profile: Personal financial planning & chartered accounting services are offered.

Executives:
Raymond Liu, RFP, Sr. Partner
George Eykelbosh, CA, Manager

LMS PROLINK Ltd.
#800, 480 University Ave.
Toronto, ON M5G 1V2
416-595-7484
Fax: 416-595-1649
800-663-6828
info@lms.ca
www.lms.ca
Ownership: Private. Parent is The PROLINK Insurance Group
Year Founded: 1982
Number of Employees: 200
Revenues: $100-500 million
Executives:
Joseph V. McCabe, President

M.A. Schneider Insurance Agencies Inc.
928 Pinesprings Rd.
Kamloops, BC V2B 8E8
250-579-8957
Fax: 250-579-8967
schneiderinsuranceinc@telus.net
www.schneiderinsuranceinc.com
Ownership: Private
Assets: $10-50 million
Revenues: $1-5 million
Executives:
Mark A. Schneider, President
Nancy L. Schneider, Secretary
Branches:
Kamloops
970 Laval Cres.
Kamloops, BC V2C 5P5 Canada
250-372-3224
Fax: 250-579-8967
Nancy L. Schneider, Manager

Macdonald Shymko & Company Ltd.
#950, 510 Burrard St.
Vancouver, BC V6C 3A8
604-687-7966
Fax: 604-687-1830
msc@msc-feeonly.com
www.macdonaldshymko.com
Ownership: Private
Year Founded: 1972
Number of Employees: 16
Profile: Services are provided to clients to develop & promote the accumulation & management of financial assets. The firm provides professional advice in all areas of personal financial planning & asset management, including retirement goals, investments, tax positions & deferral, & estate planning.

Executives:
Ian Black, RFP
Larry Jacobson, MBA, RFP
Douglas Macdonald, MBA, RFP
Gina Macdonald, RFP
Brinsley Saleken, RFP
David S. Shymko, MBA, RFP
Affiliated Companies:
MSC Financial Services Ltd.
Branches:
Kelowna
#406, 1708 Dolphin Ave.
Kelowna, BC V1Y 9S4 Canada

INVESTMENT MANAGEMENT

Macdonald Shymko & Company Ltd. (continued)
250-860-4700
Fax: 250-860-4799
dmoran@macdonaldshymko.com
Derek Moran

MacIntosh Financial Group Ltd.
Also listed under: *Investment Dealers*
1275 West 6th Ave., 3rd Fl.
Vancouver, BC V6H 1A6
604-737-8886
Fax: 604-737-8719
info@macintoshfinancial.com
www.macintoshfinancial.com
Former Name: Cameron MacIntosh & Co. Ltd.
Year Founded: 1985
Executives:
Peter MacIntosh, Sr. Financial Advisor
Justin Wee, Associate

MacKay-Robichaud Financial Consultants
196 Robinson St.
Moncton, NB E1C 5C4
506-857-2173
Fax: 506-383-8414
Executives:
Fernand H. Robichaud, CFP, CLU, CHFC

MacLean Hamilton Benefit Consulting
1331 Brenton St.
Halifax, NS B3J 2K5
902-423-2727
Fax: 902-423-8292
sandy.benefits@ns.sympatico.ca
Executives:
Alexander Hamilton

MacPherson Roche Smith & Associates
#200, 70 Kent St.
Charlottetown, PE C1A 1M9
902-566-2566
Fax: 902-368-3558
mrs@mrspei.ca
www.mrsn.pe.ca
Former Name: MacPherson Roche Smith & Noonan
Executives:
Stan H. MacPherson, Partner
Hal Roche, Partner
Andrew Smith, Partner

MacroPlan Wealth Strategies Inc.
#201, 1001 - 14th Ave. SW
Calgary, AB T2R 1L2
403-228-7997
Fax: 403-228-6794
kirkmar@telus.net
www.macroplanstrategies.com
Ownership: Private
Year Founded: 1988
Number of Employees: 2
Executives:
Russell L. Kirk, CA, CFP, RFP, Chartered Accountant, Financial Planner
Marlene Kirk, Corporate Coach/Trainer

Magna Vista Investment Management
Also listed under: *Pension & Money Management Companies*
#2000, 1200 McGill College av
Montréal, QC H3B 4G7
514-875-2625
Fax: 514-875-6945
888-310-1712
Ownership: AGF Private Investment Management Limited, Toronto, ON
Year Founded: 1992

Mahon Financial
291 Oxford St. East
London, ON N6A 1V3
519-433-2007
Fax: 519-433-6252
dmahon@on.aibn.com
Ownership: Private
Year Founded: 1996
Executives:
J. Douglas Mahon, RFP, Owner

Mallet & Assoc. Inc.
PO Box 822
Bathurst, NB E2A 4A5
506-546-4848
Fax: 506-546-5136
info@malletgroup.ca
www.malletgroup.ca
Former Name: Mallet & Associates
Year Founded: 1977
Number of Employees: 4
Executives:
Gabriel Mallet, CFP, CLU, ChFC, President; 506-546-5136

Manitou Investment Management Limited
Toronto Dominion Bank Tower
PO Box 342, TD Centre Stn. TD Centre
#2910, 66 Wellington St. West
Toronto, ON M5K 1K7
416-865-1867
Fax: 416-865-0525
877-336-3392
www.manitouinvestment.com
Principals:
R.B. (Biff) Matthews, President
Alan M. Dewling
Kevin Kuebler, CFA
Ming Lam, CFA
Deborah O'Reilly, CFO
Talia Rovinski
Stephen R. Scotchmer
Sean Yuile, CFA

Mann Financial Assurance Limited
PO Box 338
100 Osborne St. North
Winnipeg, MB R3C 2H6
204-946-8142
Fax: 204-946-8865
877-946-8142
david.mann@gwl.ca
www.mannfinancialassurance.com
Executives:
David C. Mann

Manulife Financial Individual Insurance
Also listed under: *Federal & Provincial*
PO Box 1669
500 King St. North
Waterloo, ON N2J 4Z6
888-626-8543
Valued_customer_centre@manulife.com
www.manulife.com
Ownership: Public
Year Founded: 1887
Number of Employees: 33,000
Assets: $60,067,000
Revenues: $14,152,000
Stock Symbol: MFC
Profile: Manulife Financial is a leading Canadian-based financial services company operating in 19 countries & territories worldwide. Through its extensive network of employees, agents & distribution partners, Manulife Financial offers clients a diverse range of financial protection products & wealth management services. The Corporation trades as MFC on the TSE, NYSE & PSE & under 9045 on the SEHK.
Executives:
Dominic D'Alessandro, President/CEO
Victor Apps, Exec. Vice-President & General Manager, Asia Operations
John DesPrez, Exec. Vice-President, US Operations
H. Bruce Gordon, Exec. Vice-President, Canadian Operations
Donald Guloien, Exec. Vice-President, Investment Operations, Chief Investment Officer
John Mather, Exec. Vice-President & Chief Information Officer
Trevor J. Matthews, Exec. Vice-President
Peter H. Rubenovitch, Exec. Vice-President/CFO
Diane Bean, Sr. Vice-President, Corporate Human Resources & Communications
Richard A. Lococo, Sr. Vice-President, Deputy General Counsel
Directors:
Arthur R. Sawchuk, Chair
Dominic D'Alessandro
Thomas P. d'Aquino
Kevin E. Benson
John M. Cassaday
Lino J. Celeste
Gail C.A. Cook-Bennett
Robert E. Dineen, Jr.
Pierre Y. Ducros
Allister P. Graham
Thomas E. Kierans
Lorna R. Marsden
Hugh W. Sloan, Jr.
Gordon G. Thiessen
Michael H. Wilson
Affiliated Companies:
First North American Insurance Company
Manufacturers Life Insurance Company
Manulife Bank of Canada
Manulife Capital
Manulife Securities International Ltd./MSIL

Maple Financial Group Inc.
Also listed under: *Financing & Loan Companies*
PO Box 328
#3500, 79 Wellington St. West
Toronto, ON M5K 1K7
416-350-8200
Fax: 416-350-8222
info@maplefinancial.com
www.maplefinancial.com
Ownership: Private
Year Founded: 1986
Number of Employees: 400
Assets: $19,000,000,000
Directors:
Bill Fung, Chair
Tom Higgins
Neil Petroff
Simon Ruddick
Jean Turmel
Affiliated Companies:
Maple Bank GmbH
Maple Securities Canada Ltd.
Maple Trade Finance Inc.

Marathon Financial Group Inc.
#301, 21 Allen St. West
Waterloo, ON N2L 1C7
519-578-9879
Fax: 519-578-1724
800-898-0643
Ownership: Private
Year Founded: 1995
Number of Employees: 3
Executives:
Brian L. Clegg, CFP, CLU, CH.F.C., President
Elizabeth Callon, CHU, CFP, CLU, Vice-President

Martell Insurance Services
3161 Antrobus Cres.
Victoria, BC V9B 5M6
250-391-9933
Fax: 250-391-9380
877-228-1501
admin@martellinsurance.com
www.martellinsurance.com
Executives:
Thomas D. Martell

Mary Beth Harris, Strategic & Financial Business Management
539, av Donegani
Montréal, QC H9R 2W8
514-426-0714
Fax: 514-426-4675
info@mbharris.ca
www.mbharris.ca
Year Founded: 1999
Profile: Financial planning/business advisory services.
Executives:
Mary Beth Harris, CA, CFP

Mary-Ellen Wiebe
322 West St.
Simcoe, ON N3Y 1T4
519-426-7773
Fax: 519-426-5347
mewiebe@kwic.com
www.mutualsolutions.ca/maryellen.php
Executives:
Mary-Ellen Wiebe

Maude, MacKay & Co. Ltd.

#304, 1682 West 7th Ave.
Vancouver, BC V6J 4S6
604-736-0181
Fax: 604-736-0314
acctdept@maudemackay.com
maudemackay.com
Ownership: Private
Year Founded: 1982
Number of Employees: 8
Profile: Offers investment, commercial & residential property services (investment, management & brokerage).

Executives:
Chris Maude, President & Co-Owner
Rod MacKay, Vice-President & Co-Owner; rodmac@maudemackay.com

Mawer Investment Management Ltd.

Also listed under: *Investment Fund Companies; Investment Management*
#900, 603 - 7th Ave. SW
Calgary, AB T2P 2T5
403-262-4673
Fax: 403-262-4099
800-889-6248
info@mawer.com
www.mawer.com
Ownership: Private
Year Founded: 1974
Number of Employees: 41
Profile: Mawer offers independent portfolio management to institutions & private clients, plus a family of pooled funds & eight no-load mutual funds.

Executives:
Paul Moroz, Director, Equity Analyst
Greg Peterson, Director & Manager, Sr. Private Client Portfolio; 403-267-1952
David Ragan, Director, Equity Analyst
W.R. David Stone, Director, Marketing & Sales; 403-267-1961
Diana Gabriel, Controller; 403-267-1993
Mawer:
Canadian Balanced Retirement Savings Fund
RRSP Eligible; Inception Year: 1988; Fund Managers:
Jane Depraitere
Canadian Diversified Investment Fund
RRSP Eligible; Inception Year: 1988; Fund Managers:
Craig D. Senyk
Canadian Equity Mid Large Cap Fund
RRSP Eligible; Inception Year: 1991; Fund Managers:
James C.E. Hall
Canadian Money Market Fund
RRSP Eligible; Inception Year: 1988; Fund Managers:
William R. MacLachlan
New Canada Fund
RRSP Eligible; Inception Year: 1988; Fund Managers:
Martin D. Ferguson
US Equity Fund
RRSP Eligible; Inception Year: 1992; Fund Managers:
Darrell A. Anderson
World Investment Fund
RRSP Eligible; Inception Year: 1987; Fund Managers:
Gerald A. Cooper-Key
Canadian Bond Fund
RRSP Eligible; Inception Year: 1991; Fund Managers:
Michael J. Crofts

MCAN Mortgage Corporation

Also listed under: *Financing & Loan Companies*
#400, 200 King St. West
Toronto, ON M5H 3T4
416-591-5214
Fax: 416-598-4142
800-387-4405
mcanexecutive@mcanmortgage.com
www.mcanmortgage.com
Former Name: MCAP Inc.; MTC Mortgage Investment Corporation
Ownership: Public.
Year Founded: 1991
Number of Employees: 12
Assets: $100-500 million Year End: 20051231
Revenues: $10-50 million Year End: 20051231
Stock Symbol: MKP
Profile: MCAN Mortgage is a mortgage investment corporation.

Executives:
Blaine Welch, President/CEO; 416-591-2726; bwelch@mcanmortgage.com
Michael Misener, Vice-President, Investments; 416-591-5205; mmisener@mcanmortgage.com
Tammy Oldenburg, Vice-President/CFO; 416-847-3542; toldenberg@mcanmortgage.com
Kevin Dwarte, Asst. Vice-President, Investments, Privacy Officer, Chief Anti-Money Laudering Officer, Business Contintuity/Disaster Recovery Coordinator; 416-591-2721; kdwarte@mcanmortgage.com
Derek Sutherland, Asst. Vice-President, Chief Compleance Officer, Risk Officer & Treasurer; 416-591-5535; dsutherland@mcanmortgage.com
John Tyas, Controller; 416-847-3489; jtyas@mcanmortgage.com
Sylvia Pinto, Corporate Secretary; 416-591-5214; spinto@mcanmortgage.com
Directors:
Ian Sutherland, Chair; 705-835-1542
David G. Broadhurst; 416-350-8228
Raymond Doré; 416-591-2713
Brian Johnson; 306-546-8008
David MacIntosh; 519-725-7537
Derek Norton; 416-591-2746
Jean Pinard; 450-538-3268
Robert A. Stuebing; 416-591-2712
Blaine Welch; 416-591-2726

McCurdy Financial Planning Inc.

#1925, 925 West Georgia St.
Vancouver, BC V6C 3L2
604-685-7928
Fax: 604-683-3011
diane@mccurdyfinancial.com
www.howmuchisenough.ca
Executives:
Diane L. McCurdy

McFaull Consulting Inc.

#999, 119 - 4th Ave. South
Saskatoon, SK S7K 5X2
306-665-0709
Fax: 306-665-0737
Executives:
John Thompson

McIntosh Financial Services & Associates Inc.

Also listed under: *Pension & Money Management Companies*
#106, 11 Bond St.
St Catharines, ON L2R 4Z4
905-684-2331
Fax: 905-684-0744
info@mcintoshfinancial.ca
www.mcintoshfinancial.ca
Former Name: Bob McIntosh Financial Services
Ownership: Private
Year Founded: 1975
Number of Employees: 3
Executives:
Bob McIntosh

McKay Financial Management

#1102, 330 Bay St.
Toronto, ON M5H 2S8
416-864-1674
Fax: 416-864-9483
Ownership: Private
Year Founded: 1989
Number of Employees: 4
Executives:
Stuart McKay, CA, CFP, President
Lorna L. McKay, CFP, RFP

McLean & Partners Wealth Management Ltd.

Also listed under: *Investment Dealers; Investment Management*
801 - 10 Ave. SW
Calgary, AB T2R 0B4
403-234-0005
Fax: 403-234-0606
888-665-0005
solutions@mcleanpartners.com
www.mcleanpartners.com
Former Name: McLean & Partners Private Capital Corporation
Ownership: Private.
Year Founded: 1999
Number of Employees: 25
Executives:
Brent McLean, President/CEO
Heather Gore-Hickman, Chief Financial Officer
Kevin Dehod, Vice-President
Anil Tahiliani, Head, Research

McLean Budden Ltd.

Also listed under: *Investment Fund Companies; Investment Management*
#2525, 145 King St. West
Toronto, ON M5H 1J8
416-862-9800
Fax: 416-862-0167
800-884-0436
Other Information: Mutual Fund Dept. Fax: 416/862-9624
www.mcleanbudden.com
Ownership: Private. Jointly owned by Sun Life Assurance Company of Canada
Year Founded: 1949
Profile: The company specializes in investment management.

Executives:
Douglas W. Mahaffy, President/CEO & Chair; dmahaffy@mcleanbudden.com
Heather Shannon, Sr. Vice-President; hshannon@mcleanbudden.com
MB:
Balanced Growth Fund
RRSP Eligible; Inception Year: 1996; Fund Managers:
Mary B. Hallward
AlanDaxner
Douglas Andrews
John Ackerl
Anthony Magri
Balanced Fund
RRSP Eligible; Inception Year: 1999; Fund Managers:
Alan Daxner
BenoitParadis
Colin Sinclare
Douglas Andrews
Hans van Monsjou
Roger J. Beauchemin
Susan Shuter
Edward E. Thompson
John Ackerl
Private Balanced Fund
RRSP Eligible; Inception Year: 1997; Fund Managers:
R. Bruce Murray
Mary B.Hallward
Robert V. Livingston
Edward Kwan
Susan Shuter
Edward E. Thompson
Anthony Magri
Canadian Equity Growth Fund
RRSP Eligible; Inception Year: 1980; Fund Managers:
William J. Giblin
R. BruceMurray
Mary B. Hallward
Douglas Andrews
John J Durfy
Miranda Hubbs
Canadian Equity Value Fund
RRSP Eligible; Inception Year: 1998; Fund Managers:
Alan Daxner
BrianDawson
Susan Shuter
Edward E. Thompson
John Tsagarelis
Canadian Equity Fund
RRSP Eligible; Inception Year: 1998; Fund Managers:
Alan Daxner
BenoitParadis
Douglas Andrews
Hans van Monsjou
Colin Sinclare
John Ackerl
Roger J. Beauchemin
Susan Shuter
Edward E. Thompson
Canadian Equity Plus Fund
RRSP Eligible; Inception Year: 1997; Fund Managers:
Alan Daxner
BenoitParadis
Colin Sinclare

INVESTMENT MANAGEMENT

McLean Budden Ltd. (continued)
Hans van Monsjou
John Ackerl
Roger J. Beauchemin
Susan Shuter
Edward E. Thompson
Global Equity Fund
RRSP Eligible; Inception Year: 1996; Fund Managers:
William J. Giblin
BrianDawson
R. Bruce Murray
Mary B. Hallward
Benoit Paradis
Bruce MacNabb
Fixed Income Fund
RRSP Eligible; Inception Year: 1981; Fund Managers:
Cort Conover
Peter P.Kotsopoulos
Anthony Magri
Paul Marcogliese
Cindy Nam
Fixed Income Plus Fund
RRSP Eligible; Inception Year: 1996; Fund Managers:
Cort Conover
AnthonyMagri
Peter P. Kotsopoulos
Cindy Nam
Long Term Fixed Income Fund
RRSP Eligible; Inception Year: 1998; Fund Managers:
Cort Conover
Peter P.Kotsopoulos
Anthony Magri
Paul Marcogliese
Cindy Nam
Money Market Fund
RRSP Eligible; Inception Year: 1995; Fund Managers:
Cort Conover
Peter P.Kotsopoulos
Anthony Magri
Paul Marcogliese
Cindy Nam
Balanced Growth Pension Fund
RRSP Eligible; Inception Year: 1993; Fund Managers:
Mary B. Hallward
AlanDaxner
Douglas Andrews
John Ackerl
Anthony Magri
American Equity Fund
RRSP Eligible; Inception Year: 1983; Fund Managers:
William J. Giblin
BrianDawson
R. Bruce Murray
Mary B. Hallward
Benoit Paradis
Bruce MacNabb
International Equity Fund
RRSP Eligible; Inception Year: 1999; Fund Managers:
Benoit Paradis
BrianDawson
R. Bruce Murray
Mary B. Hallward
Eleanor Wang
A. Monika Skiba
Select Balanced Fund
RRSP Eligible; Inception Year: 2000; Fund Managers:
Alan Daxner
Edward A.Harris
Edward Kwan
R. Bruce Murray
Mary B. Hallward
Edward E. Thompson
Anthony Magri
Select Canadian Equity Fund
RRSP Eligible; Inception Year: 2000; Fund Managers:
Alan Daxner
Edward A.Harris
Edward Kwan
Select Global Equity Fund
RRSP Eligible; Inception Year: 2000; Fund Managers:
Alan Daxner
Edward A.Harris
Edward Kwan
Select Fixed Income Fund
RRSP Eligible; Inception Year: 2000; Fund Managers:
Edward A. Harris
AnthonyMagri
Cort Conover
Balanced Value Fund
RRSP Eligible; Inception Year: 2001; Fund Managers:
Hans van Monsjou
JohnAckerl
Alan Daxner
Brian Dawson
A. Monika Skiba
Susan Shuter
Edward E. Thompson
Global Equity Growth Fund
RRSP Eligible; Inception Year: 2002; Fund Managers:
R. Bruce Murray
John JDurfy
Mary B. Hallward
Scott Connell
Michael Hakes
Global Equity Value Fund
RRSP Eligible; Inception Year: 2002; Fund Managers:
Brian Dawson
MaryMathers
Susan Shuter
Edward E. Thompson
A. Monika Skiba
LifePlan Income Fund
RRSP Eligible; Inception Year: 2002;
LifePlan Growth & Income Fund
RRSP Eligible; Inception Year: 2002;
LifePlan Growth Fund
RRSP Eligible; Inception Year: 2002;
Short Term Fixed Income Fund
RRSP Eligible; Inception Year: 2005; Fund Managers:
Cindy Nam
AdamGregg
Cort Conover
Paul Marcogliese
Peter P. Kotsopoulos
Anthony Magri
McLean Budden:
International Equity Fund
RRSP Eligible; Inception Year: 1998; Fund Managers:
Benoit Paradis
BrianDawson
R. Bruce Murray
Mary B. Hallward
Eleanor Wang
A. Monika Skiba
Money Market Fund
RRSP Eligible; Inception Year: 1989; Fund Managers:
Cort Conover
Peter P.Kotsopoulos
Anthony Magri
Paul Marcogliese
Cindy Nam
Canadian Equity Value Fund
RRSP Eligible; Inception Year: 1999; Fund Managers:
Alan Daxner
BrianDawson
John Tsagarelis
Susan Shuter
Edward E. Thompson
A. Monika Skiba
Fixed Income Fund
RRSP Eligible; Inception Year: 1989; Fund Managers:
Cort Conover
Peter P.Kotsopoulos
Anthony Magri
Paul Marcogliese
Cindy Nam
Balanced Growth Fund
RRSP Eligible; Inception Year: 1989; Fund Managers:
R. Bruce Murray
Mary B.Hallward
Lewis Jackson
Robert V. Livingston
Edward Kwan
Canadian Equity Growth Fund
RRSP Eligible; Inception Year: 1989; Fund Managers:
William J. Giblin
R. BruceMurray
Mary B. Hallward
Douglas Andrews
John J Durfy
Miranda Hubbs
Sheila E. Norman
Sue Eagleson
American Equity Fund
RRSP Eligible; Inception Year: 1989; Fund Managers:
William J. Giblin
BrianDawson
R. Bruce Murray
Mary B. Hallward
Benoit Paradis
Bruce MacNabb
Global Equity Fund
RRSP Eligible; Inception Year: 2001; Fund Managers:
Benoit Paradis
William J.Giblin
Brian Dawson
R. Bruce Murray
Mary B. Hallward
Bruce MacNabb
Balanced Value Fund
RRSP Eligible; Inception Year: 2003; Fund Managers:
Alan Daxner
BrianDawson
Craig S. Barnard
Peter P. Kotsopoulos
Paul Marcogliese
Susan Shuter
Edward E. Thompson
Anthony Magri
Canadian Equity Fund
RRSP Eligible; Inception Year: 2004; Fund Managers:
Alan Daxner
DouglasAndrews
John Ackerl
Susan Shuter
Edward E. Thompson
Branches:
Montréal
#2810, 1250, boul René-Lévesque ouest
Montréal, QC H3B 4W8 Canada
514-933-0033
Fax: 514-933-8163
Vancouver
Three Bentall Centre
PO Box 49105
#3043, 595 Burrard St.
Vancouver, BC V7X 1G4 Canada
604-623-3430
Fax: 604-623-3436

MDP Chartered Accountants(MDP LLP)
***Also listed under:** Accountants*
#200, 4230 Sherwoodtowne Blvd.
Mississauga, ON L4Z 2G6
905-279-7500
Fax: 905-279-9300
mdp@mdp.on.ca
www.mdp.on.ca
Also Known As: Martyn, Dooley & Partners LLP
Year Founded: 1992
Profile: MDP LLP's core business is professional accounting & tax services. Other financial services include financial reporting, income & commodity tax, business advisory, estates & trusts, & wealth management.

Menzies Financial Services Inc.
100 Osborne St. North
Winnipeg, MB R3C 1V3
204-946-4255
Ownership: Private
Year Founded: 1980
Executives:
Doug S. Menzies, President

Mercator Financial Inc.
#3, 250 Central Ave. North
Swift Current, SK S9H 0L2
306-778-6611
Fax: 306-778-7644
mercator@sasktel.net
www.mercatorfinancial.ca
Number of Employees: 11
Executives:
Larry L. Jensen

Merrill Lynch Canada Inc.

Also listed under: *Investment Dealers; Non-Depository Institutions*
Wellington Tower, BCE Place
181 Bay St., 4th & 5th Fl.
Toronto, ON M5J 2V8
416-369-7400
Fax: 416-369-7966
www.gmi.ml.com/canada
Ownership: Public. Part of Merrill Lynch & Co., Inc., New York, NY, USA.
Year Founded: 1990
Number of Employees: 300+
Stock Symbol: MLC
Stock Exchange Membership: Montreal Exchange, Toronto Stock Exchange, TSX Venture Exchange
Profile: Merrill Lynch is a full-service investment dealer that provides investment banking, equity & debt trading, & research products. Clients include institutions, government & corporations.

Executives:
Paul Allison, Managing Director, Exec. Vice-President & Co-Head, Canada Origination
M. Marianne Harris, Managing Director & President, Global Markets & Investment Banking
Daniel Mida, Managing Director, Exec. Vice-President & Co-Head, Canada Origination
Lynn Patterson, Managing Director & President, Global Markets Debt & Equity Sales & Trading
Robert Montesione, CFO, CAO
Mark Dickerson, Corporate Secretary
Offices:
Calgary
Bow Valley Square III
#2620, 255 - 5th Ave. SW
Calgary, AB T2P 3G6 Canada
403-231-7300
Fax: 403-237-7372
Montréal
#3715, 1250, boul René-Lévesque ouest
Montréal, QC H3B 4W8 Canada
514-846-1050
Fax: 514-846-3591
Guy Savard, Chair, Québec Operations
Vancouver
Cathedral Place
925 West Georgia St., 7th Fl.
Vancouver, BC V6C 3L2 Canada
604-691-7252
Fax: 604-691-7259

META Financial Management Ltd.

Also listed under: *Investment Dealers*
#229, 9030 Leslie St.
Richmond Hill, ON L4B 1G2
905-731-2251
Fax: 905-731-8626
service@metafinance.ca
www.metafinance.ca
Ownership: Private. Part of Armstrong & Quaile Associates Inc., Manotick, ON.
Year Founded: 1998
Number of Employees: 10+
Profile: META Financial, a branch of Armstrong & Quaile Associates Inc., operates as a mutual fund dealer.

Executives:
Ken Ng, Director; 905-731-2251
Len Seeto, Director; 905-731-2251

MGP Insurance Centre Ltd.(MGP)

1135 Lakewood Ct. North
Regina, SK S4X 3S3
306-924-2212
Fax: 306-924-2465
info@mgpfinancial.com
www.mgpfinancial.com
Year Founded: 1984
Profile: The company offers a range of insurance & investment services.

Executives:
Mark Glabus, Partner, CAIB
Doug Mortin, A.I.I.C., CIP, Partner
Rick Putz, CFP, CLU, CH.F.C., Partner

Midd-West Financial Services Inc.

85 Caradoc St. North
Strathroy, ON N7G 2M5
519-245-5556
Ownership: Subsidiary of Caradoc Delaware Mutual Fire Insurance Company, Mount Brydges, ON.
Executives:
Edgar Hooper, Contact

Middlefield Group

Also listed under: *Investment Fund Companies; Non-Depository Institutions*
#5855, First Canadian Place
PO Box 192, First Canadian Place Stn. First Canadian Place
Toronto, ON M5X 1A6
416-362-0714
Fax: 416-362-7925
888-890-1686
invest@middlefield.com
www.middlefield.com
Ownership: Private. Owned by employees.
Year Founded: 1979
Number of Employees: 85
Assets: $10-50 million Year End: 20060331
Revenues: $50-100 million Year End: 20060331
Profile: The group is the manager of financial assets on behalf of individual & institutional clients. Middlefield presently manages over $3.0 billion of assets, including resource funds, venture capital assets, real estate & mutual funds.

Executives:
Murray J. Brasseur, Managing Director
Douglas D. Sedore, President
J. Dennis Dunlop, Sr. Vice-President
Sylvia V. Stinson, Sr. Vice-President
Margaret Lok, Vice-President
Nancy Tham, Vice-President, Marketing
Directors:
Murray J. Brasseur; 416-857-5347
George S. Dembroski; 416-842-7504
H.R. Garland; 416-449-1750
W. Garth Jestley; 416-847-5346
Gordon Stollery
Charles B. Young
Affiliated Companies:
Middlefield Capital Corporation
Middlefield Income Funds:
Activenergy Income Fund
RRSP Eligible; Inception Year: 2004; Fund Managers:
Richard L. Faiella
W. GarthJestley
Dean Orrico
Guardian Capital LP
Compass Income Fund
RRSP Eligible; Inception Year: 2002; Fund Managers:
W. Garth Jestley
DeanOrrico
Richard L. Faiella
Core IncomePlus Fund
RRSP Eligible; Inception Year: 2005; Fund Managers:
Richard L. Faiella
DeanOrrico
W. Garth Jestley
Equal Sector Income FundInception Year: 2005; Fund Managers:
W. Garth Jestley
DeanOrrico
Indexplus Income Fund
RRSP Eligible; Inception Year: 2003; Fund Managers:
Richard L. Faiella
DeanOrrico
W. Garth Jestley
Indexplus 2 Income Fund
RRSP Eligible; Inception Year: 2003; Fund Managers:
Richard L. Faiella
DeanOrrico
W. Garth Jestley
Matrix Income Fund
RRSP Eligible; Inception Year: 2005; Fund Managers:
W. Garth Jestley
DeanOrrico
Maxin Income Fund
RRSP Eligible; Inception Year: 2003; Fund Managers:
Richard L. Faiella
W. GarthJestley
Dean Orrico
Guardian Capital LP
Mint Income Fund
RRSP Eligible; Inception Year: 1997; Fund Managers:
W. Garth Jestley
DeanOrrico
Pathfinder Income Fund
RRSP Eligible; Inception Year: 2002; Fund Managers:
Richard L. Faiella
W. GarthJestley
Dean Orrico
Stars Income Fund
RRSP Eligible; Inception Year: 2001; Fund Managers:
Richard L. Faiella
W. GarthJestley
Dean Orrico
Strata Income Fund
RRSP Eligible; Inception Year: 2004; Fund Managers:
Richard L. Faiella
W. GarthJestley
Dean Orrico
Yieldplus Income Fund
RRSP Eligible; Inception Year: 2004; Fund Managers:
Richard L. Faiella
W. GarthJestley
Dean Orrico
Middlefield Mutual Funds:
Money Market FundInception Year: 1996; Fund Managers:
Scott Roberts
Enhanced Yield Fund
RRSP Eligible; Inception Year: 1998; Fund Managers:
Robert Lauzon
W. GarthJestley
Canadian Balanced Class Fund
RRSP Eligible; Inception Year: 2001; Fund Managers:
Robert Lauzon
ScottRoberts
Equity Index Class Fund
RRSP Eligible; Inception Year: 2000; Fund Managers:
W. Garth Jestley
RobertLauzon
Growth Class Fund
RRSP Eligible; Inception Year: 1990; Fund Managers:
Robert Lauzon
DeanOrrico
Income & Growth Class FundInception Year: 2004; Fund Managers:
Dean Orrico
RobertLauzon
Income Plus Class Fund
RRSP Eligible; Inception Year: 2000; Fund Managers:
W. Garth Jestley
RobertLauzon
Index Income Class FundInception Year: 2003; Fund Managers:
Robert Lauzon
W. GarthJestley
Resource Class FundInception Year: 2002; Fund Managers:
James S. Parsons
Dennisda Silva
Short-Term Income Class FundInception Year: 2004; Fund Managers:
Robert Lauzon
ScottRoberts
US Equity Class Fund
RRSP Eligible; Inception Year: 2001; Fund Managers:
Dean Orrico
RobertLauzon
Middlefield Resource Funds:
Explorer III Resource Limited Partnership Fund
RRSP Eligible; Inception Year: 2005; Fund Managers:
James S. Parsons
Dennisda Silva
2005 Limited Partnership Fund
RRSP Eligible; Inception Year: 2005; Fund Managers:
Dennis da Silva
James S.Parsons
Explorer II Resource Limited Partnership Fund
RRSP Eligible; Inception Year: 2005; Fund Managers:
James S. Parsons
Dennisda Silva
2004 Limited Partnership Fund
RRSP Eligible; Inception Year: 2004; Fund Managers:
Dennis da Silva
James S.Parsons

INVESTMENT MANAGEMENT

Middlefield Group (continued)
Branches:
Calgary
#3063, 150 - 6th Ave. SW
Calgary, AB T2P 3Y7 Canada
403-538-5121
Fax: 403-538-5124
Dennis da Silva, Managing Director

Milestone Asset Management Ltd.
#207, 322 - 11th Ave. SW
Calgary, AB T2R 0C5
403-531-2444
Fax: 403-531-2449
mail@milestoneasset.ca
www.milestoneasset.ca
Former Name: Miles Financial Group Inc.
Executives:
Karen H. Miles, President/CEO
Stephen Booker, Vice-President & Managing Director

Milestone Investment Counsel Inc.
Berkley Castle
#309, 2 Berkeley St.
Toronto, ON M5A 2W3
416-365-3111
Fax: 416-365-7964
info@mstone.com
www.mstone.com
Year Founded: 1996
Executives:
Paul D. Mitchell, Partner
Donna L. Siler, Partner
Stephen J. Martin, Partner

Millennium Financial Services
2205 Des Grands Champs
Gloucester, ON K1W 1K2
613-830-0589
Fax: 613-830-4021
steve.arial@sympatico.ca
Ownership: Private
Year Founded: 1997
Number of Employees: 4
Assets: $10-50 million
Revenues: Under $1 million
Executives:
Steve Arial, President, Certified Financial Planner
Anne Arial, Office Manager

Mills Financial Services
1241 Garrison Rd.
Fort Erie, ON L2A 1P2
905-991-0587
Fax: 905-991-0588
wcmills@vaxxine.com
Executives:
Wayne Mills, Owner

Ming & Associates
21 Water St. West, 2nd Fl.
Cornwall, ON K6J 1A1
613-932-7526
Fax: 613-932-6555
888-826-5516
info@mingassociates.com
www.mingassociates.com
Former Name: Timothy Ming Financial Services
Year Founded: 1996
Executives:
Timothy Ming, Certified Financial Planner
Gilles Latour, Certified Sr. Advisor
Donna Villeneuve, Certified Financial Planner

Mirelis Investments Ltd.
#1010, 1134, rue Sainte-Catherine ouest
Montréal, QC H3B 1H4
514-861-9671
Fax: 514-866-4882
Year Founded: 1957
Profile: The company is a mortgage investment trust.

Mitchell Kelly Jones & Associates Inc.
Also listed under: *Accountants*
#1070, 340 - 12 Ave. SW
Calgary, AB T2R 1L5
403-265-8545
Fax: 403-265-8554
Former Name: Mitchell Jones Financial Services Inc.
Ownership: Private
Year Founded: 1996

Moncton - Louisbourg Investments Inc.
Also listed under: *Pension & Money Management Companies*
PO Box 160
770 Main St.
Moncton, NB E1C 8L1
506-853-5457
Ownership: Private. Montrusco Bolton Inc. & Assumption Life
Year Founded: 1991
Number of Employees: 10
Assets: $1-10 billion Year End: 20051200
Revenues: $1-5 million Year End: 20051200
Executives:
Martin Boudreau, Vice-President
Luc Gaudet, Vice President
Marc Lalonde, Vice-President
Mathieu Roy, Vice-President
Branches:
Halifax
#1602, 1791 Barrington St.
Halifax, NS B3J 3L1 Canada
902-421-1811
James S. Oland, Vice-President, Marketing & Client Servicing

Money Managers Inc.
249 Simcoe St.
Peterborough, ON K9H 2H9
705-743-7865
Fax: 705-743-6221
Ownership: Private
Profile: Money Managers Inc. is a financial planning firm specializing in estate planning & investment management.
Executives:
Franklin J. Konopaski, CFP, RFP, President

Money Minders Financial Services Inc.
2371 Silver Pl.
Kelowna, BC V1V 1M9
Ownership: Private
Year Founded: 1989
Profile: Services include financial planning software for financial planning professionals.
Executives:
Peter F. Baigent, RFP, Financial Planner & Consultant, Life Underwriter
Marie T. Baigent, RFP, Financial Planner & Consultant, Life Underwriter

Moneystrat Securities Inc.
Also listed under: *Investment Dealers*
13 Summerhill Ave.
Toronto, ON M4T 1A9
416-968-1444
Fax: 416-968-7808
800-810-1163
plan@moneystrat.com
www.moneystrat.com
Executives:
Earla Burke, President/CEO
Geordon Ferguson, Vice-President

MonyMap Financial
1515 - 56th St.
Delta, BC V4L 2A9
604-948-0944
Fax: 604-948-0947
ncmurphy@monymap.com
www.monymap.com
Profile: The life insurance & financial planning company offers a range of planning services, which include financial security, business, investment, retirement, tax & estate.
Executives:
Niall Murphy, CFP, CLU, CHFC, Financial Planner & Consultant, Chartered Life Underwriter

Morguard Investments Limited
Also listed under: *Pension & Money Management Companies*
#800, 55 City Centre Dr.
Mississauga, ON L5B 1M3
905-281-3800
Fax: 905-281-1800
headoffice@morguard.com
www.morguard.com
Ownership: Private. Subsidiary of Morguard Corporation (Stock Symbol MRC).
Year Founded: 1965
Number of Employees: 800
Assets: $1-10 billion Year End: 20050930
Revenues: $10-50 million Year End: 20050930
Profile: Morguard Investments also provides real estate advisory services.
Executives:
Stephen Taylor, President/COO; 905-281-5850; staylor@morguard.com
Andy Edmundson, Exec. Vice-President, Asset Managerment; 403-266-1695; aedmundson@morguard.com
W. Scott MacDonald, Exec. Vice-President, Asset Management; 905-281-5839; smacdonald@morguard.com
Pamela McLean, CFO & Sr. Vice-President, Finance; 905-281-5830; pmclean@morguard.com
Margaret Knowles, Sr. Vice-President, Development; 905-281-5817; mknowles@morguard.com
Gordon Vollmer, Sr. Vice-President; 905-281-3800; gvollmer@morguard.com
Suzanne Wiles, Sr. Vice-President, Strategic Advisory Services; 905-281-4806; swiles@morguard.com
Regional Offices:
Beloeil
544, boul Laurier
Beloeil, QC J3G 4H9 Canada
450-446-4004
Fax: 450-446-2863
montreal@morguard.com
A. Sirois, Vice-President, Retail Asset Management
Calgary
#200, 505 - 3rd St. SW
Calgary, AB T2P 3E6 Canada
403-266-1695
Fax: 403-265-9813
calgary@morguard.com
A. Edmundson, Sr. Vice-President, Office
Edmonton
Scotia Place
#1100, 10060 Jasper Ave.
Edmonton, AB T5J 3R8 Canada
780-421-8000
Fax: 780-424-7933
edmonton@morguard.com
G. Scheuerman, Manager, Operations
Ottawa
#402, 350 Sparks St.
Ottawa, ON K1R 7S8 Canada
613-237-6373
Fax: 613-237-0007
ottawa@morguard.com
A. Tallis, Vice-President
Toronto
#200, 200 Yorkland Blvd.
Toronto, ON M2J 5C1 Canada
416-496-2098
toronto@morguard.com
T. Capulli, Director, Property Management
Vancouver
#400, 333 Seymour St.
Vancouver, BC V6B 5A6 Canada
604-681-9474
Fax: 604-685-0161
vancouver@morguard.com
Tom Johnston, General Manager
Victoria
905 Gordon St.
Victoria, BC V8W 3P9 Canada
250-383-8093
Fax: 250-383-5097
victoria@morguard.com
Roberta Tower, Manager
Winnipeg
#1400, 363 Broadway
Winnipeg, MB R3C 3N9 Canada
204-632-9500
Fax: 204-632-1122
winnipeg@morguard.com
Karen Lund, General Manager

Morningstar Research Inc.
#301, 2221 Yonge St.
Toronto, ON M4S 2B4

416-489-6779
Fax: 416-489-7066
800-531-4725
info@morningstar.ca
www.morningstar.ca
Former Name: Morningstar Canada; Portfolio Analytics Limited
Ownership: Private. Owned by Morningstar Inc.
Year Founded: 1988
Number of Employees: 100
Profile: The investment research company creates & markets software for the analysis & selection of stocks, mutual funds & pooled funds. It also maintains databases of funds' holdings of securities & related issuer data & provides consulting services.

Executives:
Scott Mackenzie, President & CEO

MorPlan Financial Services Inc.
300 Prince Albert Rd.
Dartmouth, NS B2Y 4J2
902-464-0542
Fax: 902-466-1775
bmoore@morplanfinancial.com
www.morplanfinancial.com
Year Founded: 1997
Profile: The investment & retirement planning firm offers advice about financial planning, estate planning, retirement planning & intergenerational wealth transfer. Quadrus Investment Services is the company's mutual fund dealer.

Executives:
W.A. (Bill) Moore, CFP, CSA, Certified Financial Planner

MSC Financial Services Ltd.
#204, 1221 Lonsdale Ave.
North Vancouver, BC V7M 2H5
604-988-9876
Fax: 604-988-3444
tgreene@macdonaldshymko.com
Year Founded: 1993
Number of Employees: 2
Executives:
Terry Greene, RFP, Financial Planner

Multiplan Financial Group
#108, 4208 - 97 St.
Edmonton, AB T6E 5X9
780-465-4011
888-465-2320
dhunt@multiplan.ca
www.multiplan.ca
Ownership: Private
Year Founded: 1992
Number of Employees: 2
Assets: Under $1 million
Revenues: Under $1 million
Profile: Muliplan Financial Group specializes in retirement & estate planning.

Executives:
David Hunt, CFP, CLU, CH.F.C., President

Mutual Financial Solutions Inc.
18 Cambridge St.
Cambridge, ON N1R 3R7
519-623-3112
Fax: 519-623-4360
800-945-4090
info@mutualsolutions.ca
www.mutualsolutions.ca
Ownership: Brant Mutual Insurance, Dumfries Mutual Insurance, Oxford Mutual Insurance, North Blenheim Mutual Insurance & South Easthope Mutual Insurance
Profile: Brant-Dumfries Inc. & Tri-Mutual Financial Services amalgamated to create Mutual Financial Solutions Inc. The company offers investment services, insurance services, employee benefits, retirement, estate & succession planning, tax services & mortgage referral services.

Executives:
Colin Corner, B.A. (Econ), CFP, President, General Manager
R.L. (Don) Pancoe, CFP, Treasurer, Sr. Consultant

MWM Financial Group
181 Frederick St.
Kitchener, ON N2H 2M6
519-569-7800
Fax: 519-569-7264
800-665-0986
info@mwmgroup.com
www.mwmgroup.com
Former Name: Martin Wealth Management Ltd.
Executives:
Charles Martin, CFP, Founder & President

Mykytchuk Wyatt Financial Group
Also listed under: *Investment Dealers*
#300, 2184 - 12 Ave.
Regina, SK S4P 0M5
306-757-2735
Fax: 306-347-7710
800-584-4450
info@creatingpeaceofmind.com
Former Name: Mykytchuk, Wyatt Associates; Mykytchuk, Wyatt & Karst
Ownership: Private
Number of Employees: 5
Assets: $10-50 million Year End: 20061010
Revenues: $1-5 million Year End: 20061010
Executives:
John R. Mykytchuk, Partner
Cecile Wyatt, CFP, RFP, Partner

Nakonechny & Power Chartered Accountants Ltd.
Also listed under: *Accountants*
PO Box 880
31 Main St. South
Carman, MB R0G 0J0
204-745-2061
Fax: 204-745-6322
Executives:
Hellar Nakonechny, B.Sc., CA, CFP, Contact

NBF Turnkey Solutions Inc.
Also listed under: *Investment Fund Companies*
The Exchange Tower
#3030, 130 King St. West
Toronto, ON M5X 1J9
416-482-6787
Fax: 416-482-0200
877-296-7872
info@opus2financial.com
www.opus2financial.com
Former Name: Opus 2 Financial; Opus 2 Direct.com
Ownership: Private; subsidiary of National Bank Financial
Year Founded: 1999
Number of Employees: 6
Assets: $100-500 million Year End: 20051130
Revenues: $1-5 million Year End: 20051130
Executives:
Anthony L. Cox, COO; 416-869-8907
Directors:
Anthony L. Cox
Michel Falk
Gordon J. Gibson
Diplomat:
Balanced Portfolio Fund
RRSP Eligible; Inception Year: 1997;
Growth Portfolio Fund
RRSP Eligible; Inception Year: 1997;
Maximum Growth Portfolio Fund
RRSP Eligible; Inception Year: 1997;
Emissary:
Canadian Fixed Income Fund
RRSP Eligible; Inception Year: 2002; Fund Managers: Beutel Goodman & Company Ltd.
US Growth Fund
RRSP Eligible; Inception Year: 2002; Fund Managers: Northstar Capital Management
US Value Fund
RRSP Eligible; Inception Year: 2002; Fund Managers: Lord, Abbett & Co. LLC
Canadian Equity Fund
RRSP Eligible; Inception Year: 2002; Fund Managers: Bissett Investment Management
Global Equity RSP Fund
RRSP Eligible; Inception Year: 2002; Fund Managers: Toronto Dominion Quantitative Capital
International Equity EAFE Fund
RRSP Eligible; Inception Year: 2002; Fund Managers: Lazard Asset Management
US Small/Mid Cap Fund
RRSP Eligible; Inception Year: 2002; Fund Managers: AIM Private Asset Management Inc.

Neal, Pallett & Townsend LLP Chartered Accountants
Also listed under: *Accountants*
#300, 633 Colborne St.
London, ON N6B 2V3
519-432-5534
Fax: 519-432-6544
www.nptca.com
Ownership: Private
Year Founded: 1993
Number of Employees: 30
Assets: $1-5 million
Revenues: $1-5 million
Profile: Assists clients with accounting and strategic Canadian and US tax advice, best business practices and corporate financing.

Partners:
Glenn Hardman; ghardman@nptca.com
Barrie Neal; bneal@nptca.com
David Pallett; dpallett@nptca.com
Douglas E. Plummer; dplummer@nptca.com
John Prueter; jprueter@nptca.com
Piyush Shah; pshah@nptca.com
Jonathan Townsend; jtownsend@nptca.com
Sandy Wetstein; swetstein@nptca.com

Neale Insurance & Financial Brokers Inc.
#9, 700 Dundas St. East
Mississauga, ON L4Y 3Y5
905-848-3675
Fax: 905-848-3687

Networth Financial Corp.(NFC)
Also listed under: *Investment Dealers*
#208, 32450 Simon Ave.
Abbotsford, BC V2T 4V2
604-859-9992
Fax: 604-859-9994
admin@mynetworth.ca
www.networthfinancial.com
Year Founded: 1992
Profile: Networth Financial is a mutual fund dealer.

Executives:
Barry E. Jackson, President

New Diamond Financial Group Inc.
#128, 6061 No. 3 Rd.
Richmond, BC V6Y 2B2
604-279-0888
Fax: 604-279-0616
info@newdiamondfinancial.com, sales@newdiamondfinancial.com
www.newdiamondfinancial.com
Former Name: Ken Lam Insurance Agency Inc.
Year Founded: 1993
Profile: The company is engaged in risk management & money management. Planning services include financial, retirement, tax & estate.

Executives:
Ken Lam, President, Financial Planner

NewGrowth Corp.
Scotia Plaza
PO Box 4085, A Stn. A
40 King St. West, 26th Fl.
Toronto, ON M5W 2X6
416-862-3931
Fax: 416-863-7425
mc_newgrowth@scotiacapital.com
www.scotiamanagedcompanies.com
Ownership: Public. Managed by ScotiaMcLeod Inc.
Year Founded: 1992
Stock Symbol: NEW.A
Profile: The closed-end mutual fund company has the principal undertaking to invest in a portfolio of publicly listed common shares of selected Canadian chartered banks & utilities.

Executives:
Robert C. Williams, President/CEO
Michael K. Warman, CFO, Secretary
Directors:
Donald W. Paterson, Chair
Stanley M. Beck
David Mann
Brian D. McChesney
Michael K. Warman

NewGrowth Corp. (continued)
Robert C. Williams

Newton Financial Services Inc.
#31, 22374 Lougheed Hwy.
Maple Ridge, BC V2X 2T5
604-466-8369

Nexus Investment Management Inc.
#1010, 120 Adelaide St. West
Toronto, ON M5H 1T1
416-360-0580
Fax: 416-360-8289
888-756-9999
invest@nexusinvestments.com
www.nexusinvestments.com
Ownership: Private (owned by 4 Directors)
Year Founded: 1995
Number of Employees: 9
Assets: $100-500 million
Revenues: $1-5 million
Profile: Segregated & pooled portfolio management & financial counselling services are offered to private clients, including individuals, families & foundations.

Executives:
William W. Berghuis, President
Geoffrey J. Gouinlock, Vice-President
Fergus W. Gould, Vice-President
John C.A. Stevenson, Vice-President
Dianne E. White, Vice-President, Finance & Financial Counselling
Directors:
William W. Berghuis
Geoffrey J. Gouinlock
Fergus W. Gould
John C.A. Stevenson

Nicola Wealth Management
1508 West Broadway, 5th Fl.
Vancouver, BC V6J 1W8
604-739-6450
Fax: 604-739-6451
800-219-8032
www.nicolawealth.com
Former Name: John Nicola Financial Group Ltd.
Ownership: Private
Year Founded: 1995
Managing Partners:
Wayman Crosby
Jamie Duncan
Rob Edel
Karen Ikeda
John Nicola
Brian Sung
David Sung
Branches:
Kelowna
Landmark II
#520, 1632 Dickson Ave.
Kelowna, BC V1Y 7T2 Canada
250-763-9757
Fax: 250-763-9706

Noga & Associates Inc.
#406A, 250 Consumers Rd.
Toronto, ON M2J 4V6
416-498-6955
Fax: 416-498-6230
e.noga@on.aibn.com
Ownership: Private
Year Founded: 1990
Number of Employees: 2
Assets: Under $1 million
Revenues: Under $1 million
Executives:
Eugene A. Noga, RFP, President
G. Noga

The Norfolk International Group
#1100, 940 - 6th Ave. SW
Calgary, AB T2P 3T1
403-232-8545
Fax: 403-265-9425
800-672-6089
norfolk@norfolkgrp.com
www.norfolkgrp.com
Former Name: The Norfolk Financial Group
Ownership: Private
Year Founded: 1986
Number of Employees: 24
Executives:
Richard Albert, President
Branches:
Pickering
#13, 1845 Sandstone Manor
Pickering, ON L1W 3X9 Canada
905-420-5707
Fax: 905-420-7042
877-877-4969

NorMaxx Financial Group
#210, 180 Park Ave.
Thunder Bay, ON P7B 6J4
807-346-9700
Fax: 807-346-9772
877-667-6299
performance@normaxx.com
www.normaxx.com
Year Founded: 1998
Number of Employees: 12
Executives:
Glen Harris, President
Rod Nash, Vice-President
Roland Laframboise, Treasurer
Joe Johnson, Secretary

Norminton Financial Services Inc.
2225 Kingsway Dr.
Kitchener, ON N2C 1A2
519-579-5477
Fax: 519-744-5506
888-579-4466
lknorm@rogers.com
Former Name: L.K. Norminton Insurance & Investment Management
Ownership: Private
Executives:
Linda K. Norminton
John A. Norminton

Norstar Consulting
PO Box 1180
349 Main St.
Arborg, MB R0C 0A0
204-376-5474
Fax: 204-376-2440
Profile: The company is affiliated with Rice Financial, an independent financial solution provider.

North Growth Management Ltd.
***Also listed under:** Investment Fund Companies*
One Bentall Centre
PO Box 56
#830, 505 Burrard St.
Vancouver, BC V7X 1M4
604-688-5440
Fax: 604-688-5402
info@northgrowth.com
www.northgrowth.com
Year Founded: 1998
Executives:
Jamie Kozak, Portfolio Manager
North Growth:
Canadian Money Market Fund
RRSP Eligible; Inception Year: 1999;
US Equity Fund
RRSP Eligible; Inception Year: 1992; Fund Managers:
Rudy North
Rory E.North
Erica Lau
Cynthia Yen
Canadian Equity Fund
RRSP Eligible; Inception Year: 2000; Fund Managers:
Rory E. North
Currency Hedge Limited Partnership FundInception Year: 2003; Fund Managers:
NGM Currency Hedge GP Ltd.

Northern Credit Union
***Also listed under:** Credit Unions/Caisses Populaires*
681 Pine St.
Sault Ste Marie, ON P6B 3G2
705-253-9868
Fax: 705-949-1056
www.northerncu.com
Year Founded: 1957
Number of Employees: 208
Assets: $100-500 million Year End: 20041200
Executives:
Al Suraci, President/CEO; al.suraci@northerncu.com
Brent Chevis, CFO; brent.chevis@northerncu.com
Michael Evetts, Vice-President, Human Resources; michael.evetts@northerncu.com
Duane Fecteau, Vice-President, Sales & Service; duane.fecteau@northerncu.com
Dan O'Connor, Director, Commercial Credit; dan.oconnor@northerncu.com
Michael Imbeau, Area Director, Eastern Region; michael.imbeau@northerncu.com
Sina Kicz, Area Director, Central Region; sina.kicz@northerncu.com
Jeff Ringler, Area Director, North Region; jeff.ringler@northerncu.com
Mary Thillman, Area Director, Western Region; mary.thillman@northerncu.com
Fraser Carlyle, Manager, Marketing; fraser.carlyle@northerncu.com
Bill Smith, Manager, Consumer Credit; bill.smith@northerncu.com
Directors:
Geoff Shaw, Chair
Keir Kitchen, Vice-Chair
Tony Andreacchi
Paul Beaulieu
Jack Cleverdon
Rob deBortoli
John Fogarty
Dave Kilgour
John Mangone
David Porter
Billie Rheault
Ed Robb
Michael Walz
Branches:
Arnprior
PO Box 280
100 Madawaska Blvd.
Arnprior, ON K7S 1S7 Canada
613-623-3103
Fax: 613-623-5357
Wayne Lavallee, Branch Manager
Barrys Bay
PO Box 1028
19630 Opeongo Line
Barrys Bay, ON K0J 1B0 Canada
613-756-3097
Fax: 613-756-1902
Diane Prince, Branch Manager
Capreol
PO Box 668
10 Vaughan St.
Capreol, ON P0M 1H0 Canada
705-858-1711
Fax: 705-858-2162
George Lalonde, Branch Manager
Chapleau
PO Box 719
106 Birch St.
Chapleau, ON P0M 1K0 Canada
705-864-1841
Fax: 705-864-2747
Ingrid Doyon, Branch Manager
Coniston
PO Box 59
110 Second Ave.
Coniston, ON P0M 1M0 Canada
705-694-4741
Fax: 705-694-5868
Claudette Strom, Branch Manager
Deep River
Glendale Plaza
PO Box 306
Deep River, ON K0J 1P0 Canada
613-584-3355
Fax: 613-584-4440
Kevin Schilling, Branch Manager
Eganville

PO Box 10
237 John St.
Eganville, ON K0J 1T0 Canada
613-628-2244
Fax: 613-628-1628
Sylvie Hanniman, Branch Manager
Elliot Lake
289 Hillside Dr. South
Elliot Lake, ON P5A 1N7 Canada
705-848-7129
Fax: 705-848-5040
Robert Irving, Branch Manager
Englehart
PO Box 689
50 Fourth Ave.
Englehart, ON P0J 1H0 Canada
705-544-2248
Fax: 705-544-2542
Guy Boileau, Branch Manager
Garson
PO Box 359
3555 Falconbridge Hwy.
Garson, ON P3L 1S7 Canada
705-693-3411
Fax: 705-693-0788
Richard Campbell, Branch Manager
Hornepayne
PO Box 160
84 Front St.
Hornepayne, ON P0M 1Z0 Canada
807-868-2471
Fax: 807-868-2898
Albena Liebigt, Branch Manager
Kirkland Lake
PO Box 972
13 Government Rd. West
Kirkland Lake, ON P2N 3L1 Canada
705-567-3254
Fax: 705-567-5056
Neil Lloyd, Branch Manager
North Bay
525 Main St. East
North Bay, ON P1B 1B7 Canada
705-476-3500
Fax: 705-474-3674
Linda Blackall, Branch Manager
Pembroke
432 Boundary Rd. East
Pembroke, ON K8A 6L1 Canada
613-732-9967
Fax: 613-732-3474
Steve Hartmann, Branch Manager
Red Rock
65 Salls St.
Red Rock, ON P0T 2P0 Canada
807-886-2247
Fax: 807-886-2248
Jackie Brewer, Branch Manager
Richards Landing
PO Box 128
Richard St.
Richards Landing, ON P0R 1J0 Canada
705-246-3081
Fax: 705-246-3335
Tammy Ambeault, Branch Manager
Sault Ste Marie - 2nd Line
612 Second Line West
Sault Ste Marie, ON P6C 2K7 Canada
705-942-2333
Fax: 705-942-7355
Debbie Fabbro, Branch Manager
Sault Ste Marie - Bay St.
480 Bay St.
Sault Ste Marie, ON P6A 6Y9 Canada
705-942-2344
Fax: 705-942-7062
Betty Rusnell, Branch Manager
Sault Ste Marie - McNabb St.
PO Box 2200
264 McNabb St.
Sault Ste Marie, ON P6A 5N9 Canada
705-949-2644
Fax: 705-949-2988
Debbie Kempny, Branch Manager
Sudbury
532 Kathleen St.
Sudbury, ON P3C 2N2 Canada
705-674-9822
Fax: 705-674-5076
Hazel Turcotte, Branch Manager
Thessalon
186 Main St.
Thessalon, ON P0R 1L0 Canada
705-842-3916
Fax: 705-842-2685
Robin MacDonald, Branch Manager
Thunder Bay - Frederica St.
111 West Frederica St.
Thunder Bay, ON P7E 3V8 Canada
807-475-5817
Fax: 807-475-7103
Mary Thillman, Area Director
Thunder Bay - Red River Rd.
697 Red River Rd.
Thunder Bay, ON P7B 1J3 Canada
807-767-1300
Fax: 807-768-1898
Susan Olynick, Branch Manager
Timmins
70 Mountjoy St. North
Timmins, ON P4N 4V7 Canada
705-267-6846
Fax: 705-264-1742
Leo Morin, Branch Manager
Wawa
14 Mission Rd.
Wawa, ON P0S 1K0 Canada
705-856-2322
Fax: 705-856-2961
Bill Chapman, Branch Manager

Northern Savings Financial Services Ltd.

138 Third Ave. West
Prince Rupert, BC V8J 1K8
250-627-3612
800-330-9916
Ownership: Subsidiary of Northern Savings Credit Union, Prince Rupert, BC.
Branches:
Terrace
4702 Lazelle Ave.
Terrace, BC V8G 1T2
250-635-0515
877-213-0515

NORTIP Community Business Development Corporation

Also listed under: *Financing & Loan Companies*
PO Box 140
Plum Point, NL A0K 4A0
709-247-2040
Fax: 709-247-2630
gloria.toope@cbdc.ca
www.cbdc.ca
Ownership: Private
Year Founded: 1991
Executives:
Gloria Toope, Chair
Richard May, Executive Director; rmay@nortin.cbdc.ca

NPC Group S.A.

TD Tower
#1407, 10088 - 102 Ave.
Edmonton, AB T5J 2Z1
780-424-5700
Fax: 780-428-5100
info@npcgroup.ca
www.npcgroup.ca
Former Name: Newport Pacific Financial Group S.A.
Profile: The firm provides international financial & business services.

Olafson Financial Services

#209, 1433 St. Paul St.
Kelowna, BC V1Y 2E4
250-868-8866
Executives:
Wayne R. Olafson, Financial Planner, CFP, CLU, CH.F.C.

Olympian Financial Inc.

Also listed under: *Investment Dealers*
#802, 2300 Yonge St.
Toronto, ON M4P 1E4
416-544-9100
Fax: 416-544-9101
info@olympianfinancial.com
www.olympianfinancial.com
Year Founded: 1993
Executives:
Alexander Michael Mitonidis, Founder, Certified Financial Planner
Daniel Antonys Mitonides, Founder, Chartered Accountant

Optimum Group Inc.

Also listed under: *Holding & Other Investment Companies*
#1700, 425, boul de Maisonneuve ouest
Montréal, QC H3A 3G5
514-288-2010
Fax: 514-288-7692
webmaster@groupe-optimum.com
www.groupe-optimum.com
Year Founded: 1969
Number of Employees: 600
Assets: $100 billion +
Revenues: $500m-1 billion
Executives:
Gilles Blondeau, Chair/CEO
Jean-Claude Pagé, President/COO
Henri Joli-Coeur, Vice-Chair
Mario Georgiev, Sr. Vice-President
Alain Béland, Vice-President & Treasurer
Louis Fontaine, Vice-President & Secretary, Legal Affairs
Affiliated Companies:
Optimum Actuaires & Conseillers
Optimum Asset Management Inc.
Optimum Général inc
Optimum Placements Inc.
Optimum Reassurance Company

Orenda Corporate Finance

#4220, 161 Bay St.
Toronto, ON M5J 2S1
416-594-9020
Fax: 416-594-9026
orenda@orendacf.com
www.orendacf.com
Ownership: Private
Year Founded: 1990
Number of Employees: 17
Profile: Investment bankers.

Partners:
Wendy Bott
David B. Dunkin
Ross G. Fletcher
I. Scott Fowler
Michael Fricker
Jon Haick
John Jentz
Gilles Lamoureux
Dan Lioutas
David McAllister
Jeff Pocock
James Ro
Blair Roblin
David G. Ward
Jeff Wigle
Darrell Williams

Orr Insurance Brokers Inc.

50 Cobourg St.
Stratford, ON N5A 3E5
519-271-4340
Fax: 519-271-7626
800-876-4163
info@orrinsurance.net
www.orrinsurance.net
Year Founded: 1895
Profile: Orr Insurance offers the following financial products & services: life insurance, disability insurance, investment products, RRSPs, & employee benefits.

Executives:
Jeff Orr, Co-Owner
Rick Orr, CIP, Co-Owner
Jacques Laurin, Controller
Mike Daum, Manager, Marketing

INVESTMENT MANAGEMENT

Ottawa Asset Management Inc.
Also listed under: *Pension & Money Management Companies*
#201, 839 Shefford Rd.
Ottawa, ON K1J 9K8
613-748-7770
Fax: 613-748-9461
roger-c@sympatico.ca
www.gicdirect.com
Ownership: Part of GICdirect.com, Victoria, BC.

P.B. Fraser & Associates
1826 Woodward Dr.
Ottawa, ON K2C 0P7
613-727-0171
Fax: 613-727-0414
888-737-2737
info@pbfraser.com
www.pbfraser.com
Profile: Financial planning services include retirement, investment, estate, tax & insurance. Insurance products are provided through Dundee Insurance Agency Ltd.

Executives:
Peter B. Fraser, CFP, RFP, President, Investment Advisor
Chris L. Johnson, Investment Advisor
Robert W. Redman, CFP, CMA, Investment Advisor
Brent Vandermeer, Investment Advisor

P.J. Doherty & Associates Co. Ltd.
Also listed under: *Pension & Money Management Companies*
#700, 56 Sparks St.
Ottawa, ON K1P 5A9
613-238-6727
Fax: 613-238-3957
info@pjdoherty.com
www.pjdoherty.com
Also Known As: Doherty & Associates
Ownership: AGF Private Investment Management Limited, Toronto, ON.
Year Founded: 1979
Executives:
Peter Doherty, President
Douglas Cousins, Vice-President
Chris Stuart, Account Manager
John Doherty, Business Development Officer

Pacific Spirit Investment Management
Also listed under: *Pension & Money Management Companies*
#1100, 800 West Pender St.
Vancouver, BC V6C 2V6
604-687-0123
Fax: 604-687-0128
800-337-1388
pacificspirit@telus.net
www.pacificspirit.bc.ca
Year Founded: 1986
Executives:
John S. Clark, President

Page & Associates
Also listed under: *Pension & Money Management Companies*
9993 Yonge St.
Richmond Hill, ON L4C 1T9
905-508-8220
Fax: 905-884-3365
800-837-0134
www.askpage.com
Ownership: Private.
Year Founded: 1977
Number of Employees: 14
Profile: The company provides advice & guidance about financial management, including the following services: financial planning, retirement income analysis, insurance needs analysis, investment analysis, pensions & group benefits analysis, tax planning, GICs & mutual funds, RRSPs, RRIFs, LIFs & annuities, & group RSPs for businesses, estate planning, segregated funds & RESPs.

Executives:
John A. Page, CFP, RFP, President, Sr. Financial Planner
Frank Miemiec, Vice-President, Operations
Theresa Boyle, Manager, Fixed Income Deposits
Isaura Quinn, Manager, Accounts
Karissa Smith, Manager, Accounts
Jonathan G. Flawn, Sr. Financial Advisor
Don Page, Sr. Financial Advisor
Rick Page, Sr. Financial Advisor, Operations
Tony Porcheron, Contact

Pakeman Insurance
RR#1
Prescott, ON K0E 1T0
613-925-0731
Fax: 613-925-0732

PanFinancial
#401, 265 Yorkland Blvd.
Toronto, ON M2J 1S5
416-499-4222
Fax: 416-499-6540
888-472-6346
panfinancial@idirect.com
www.panfinancial.com
Executives:
Gordon Berger
Jack Pollock

Parkyn, Wermenlinger, Layton Capital Inc.(PWL)
Also listed under: *Investment Dealers*
#200, 215, av Redfern
Montréal, QC H3Z 3L5
514-875-7566
Fax: 514-875-9611
800-343-7566
capital@pwlcapital.com
www.pwlcapital.com
Also Known As: PWL Capital Inc.
Year Founded: 1995
Profile: PWL offers fee-based investment & planning advice.

Executives:
Hélène Gagné, Partner, Assistant Portfolio Manager & Security Advisor
Anthony S. Layton, MBA, Partner, Registered Financial Planner
James Parkyn, Partner, Registered Financial Planner
Laurent Wermenlinger, Partner, Canadian Investment Manager, Fellow Registered Financial Planner
Caroline Nalbantoglu, B.Adm., Certified Financial Planner
Branches:
Ottawa
#100, 265 Carling Ave.
Ottawa, ON K1S 2E1 Canada
613-237-5544
Fax: 613-237-5949
800-230-5544
ottawa@pwlcapital.com
Colin Cooke, Certified Financial Planner
Rivière-du-Loup
PO Box 397
494, rue Lafontaine
Rivière-du-Loup, QC G5R 3Y9 Canada
418-862-5643
Fax: 418-862-3585
800-774-7418
rdl@pwlcapital.com
André Morin, Contact
Toronto
#601, 3 Church St.
Toronto, ON M5E 1M2 Canada
416-203-0067
Fax: 416-203-0544
866-242-0203
toronto@pwlcapital.com
Jane Baker, Certified Financial Planner

Partners in Planning Financial Group Ltd.(PIP)
2330 - 15th Ave.
Regina, SK S4P 1A2
306-347-4450
Fax: 306-359-7442
877-967-4357
customerserviceteam@pipfs.com
www.partnersinplanning.com
Ownership: Private
Year Founded: 1986
Affiliated Companies:
Christel Shuckburgh
Pellegrini LeBlanc
Regional Offices:
Brandon - Manitoba
#1, 2430 Victoria Ave.
Brandon, MB R7B 0M5 Canada
204-571-3704
Fax: 204-727-7698
Emily Schuetz, Regional Manager
Burnaby - British Columbia
#410, 4400 Dominion St.
Burnaby, BC V5G 4G3 Canada
604-299-8683
Fax: 604-299-8503
Mike Hamilton, Regional Manager
Edmonton - Alberta
Greyston VII Bldg.
#108, 4208 - 97th St.
Edmonton, AB T5H 3B7 Canada
780-485-2151
Fax: 780-485-2185
Mike Couch, Regional Manager
Regina - Saskatchewan
2330 - 15th Ave.
Regina, SK S4P 1A2 Canada
306-347-4450
Fax: 306-359-7442
877-967-4357
Carol Krienke, Regional Manager
Richmond Hill - Ontario, Québec & Atlantic
#210, 1 West Pearce St.
Richmond Hill, ON L4B 3K3 Canada
905-762-0861
Fax: 905-762-1410
Ron Kearn, Regional Manager, Ontario, Québec & Atlantic Provinces

Paul Davies Financial Adviser
11 Front St. North
Thorold, ON L2V 1X3
905-680-4418
Fax: 905-680-4492
pgdavies@cogeco.net
Executives:
Paul Davies

Paula Meier Associates
Also listed under: *Investment Dealers*
23 Doxsee Ave. North
Campbellford, ON K0L 1L0
705-653-1606
Fax: 705-653-1643
paula@paulameier.com
Ownership: Private. Part of Armstrong & Quaile Associates Inc., Manotick, ON.
Executives:
Paula Meier, Contact

PEAK Financial Group
2000, rue Mansfield, 18e étage
Montréal, QC H3A 3A6
514-844-6000
Fax: 514-844-3739
info@peakgroup.com
www.peakgroup.com
Year Founded: 1990
Executives:
Robert Frances, President/CEO
Susan Monk, Director, Western Canada; 604-904-1303; smonk@peakgroup.com

Peckover Financial & Insurance Services Inc.
#1100, 390 Bay St.
Toronto, ON M5H 2Y2
416-594-1100
Fax: 416-594-1111
bruce@peckoverfinancial.com
www.peckoverfinancial.com
Ownership: Private
Year Founded: 1991
Executives:
Bruce D. Peckover

Peer Financial Ltd.
#207, 5809 Macleod Trail SW
Calgary, AB T2H 0J9
403-259-5035
Fax: 403-259-5001
800-414-4690
info@peerfinancial.com
www.peerfinancial.com
Ownership: Private
Year Founded: 1982
Profile: Tax, retirement & estate planning are offered.

Executives:
Ralph W. Burgess, Sr. Partner

Pellegrini LeBlanc
#2, 4914 - 55th St.
Red Deer, AB T4N 2J4
403-347-8833
Fax: 403-340-3779
info@pellegrinileblanc.com
www.pellegrinileblanc.com, www.pipfs.com
Former Name: LeBlanc Financial Advisors Ltd.
Executives:
Marcel LeBlanc, CFP, CLU,CH.F.C., Financial Planner; marcell@pellegrinileblanc.com
Perry Pellegrini, B.Comm., CFP, CLU, CH.F.C., Financial Planner; perryp@pellegrinileblanc.com
Branches:
Regina
2330 - 5 Ave.
Regina, SK S4P 1A2 Canada

Pension Optimum
1380, av Kingsley
Montréal, QC H9S 1G1
514-636-3883
Fax: 514-636-8200
info@pensionoptimum.com
www.pensionoptimum.com
Year Founded: 1990
Profile: The financial planning & investment advice company is independently owned & operated. Services include retirement planning, estate planning & tax planning.

Executives:
George Boucher, Founder
Charles Boucher, Office Manager

Perler Financial Group
Also listed under: *Pension & Money Management Companies*
#405, 2963 Glen Dr.
Coquitlam, BC V3B 2P7
604-468-0888
Fax: 604-468-0887
info@perlerfinancial.com
www.perlerfinancial.com
Executives:
Anita Perler, Sr. Partner
Harry Perler, Sr. Partner
Lavinra Joseph, Director, Administration

Pewter Financial Ltd.
Also listed under: *Investment Dealers*
43 Hollyburn Rd. SW
Calgary, AB T2V 3H2
403-255-1711
Fax: 403-259-2922
Profile: The company is a member of the Mutual Fund Dealers Association of Canada.

PFL Investments Canada Ltd.
Also listed under: *Investment Dealers*
Plaza V
#300, 2000 Argentia Rd.
Mississauga, ON L5N 2R7
905-812-2900
Fax: 905-813-5310

Philip Cook & Associates Insurance & Investments Inc.
PO Box 1117
43 Lincoln St.
Lunenburg, NS B0J 2C0
902-634-4494
Fax: 902-634-4158
pcookassoc@ns.sympatico.ca
Profile: The firm is associated with A.H. Bishop & Associates Inc.

Executives:
Philip Cook, Contact

Phillips, Hager & North Investment Management Ltd.

Also listed under: *Investment Fund Companies; Investment Management*
200 Burrard St., 20th Fl.
Vancouver, BC V6C 3N5
604-408-6100
Fax: 604-685-5712
800-661-6141
info@phn.com
www.phn.com
Also Known As: PH&N
Ownership: Private
Year Founded: 1964
Number of Employees: 294
Assets: $10-100 billion Year End: 20060930
Profile: Phillips, Hager & North offers a family of retail investment funds, as well as discretionary investment management. The firm manages over $50 billion in investments, on behalf of corporate & multi-employer pension plans, non-profit organizations & individuals across Canada. The company is affiliated with BonaVista Asset Management Ltd. & Sky Investment Counsel Inc.

Executives:
Scott M. Lamont, Lead Director
John S. Montalbano, President
Hanif Mamdani, Chief Investment Officer
Brian M. Walsh, Vice-President.CFO, Secretary
PH&N:
Balanced Fund
RRSP Eligible; Inception Year: 1991; Fund Managers: Sky Investment Counsel
Bond Fund
RRSP Eligible; Inception Year: 1970;
Canadian Equity Fund
RRSP Eligible; Inception Year: 1971;
Canadian Money Market Fund
RRSP Eligible; Inception Year: 1986;
Dividend Income Fund
RRSP Eligible; Inception Year: 1977;
Overseas Equity Pension Trust Fund
RRSP Eligible; Inception Year: 2000; Fund Managers: Sky Investment Counsel
US Growth Fund
RRSP Eligible; Inception Year: 1992;
Canadian Growth Fund
RRSP Eligible; Inception Year: 1987;
US Equity Fund
RRSP Eligible; Inception Year: 1964;
Short-Term Bond & Mortgage Fund
RRSP Eligible; Inception Year: 1993;
High Yield Bond Fund
RRSP Eligible; Inception Year: 2000;
Total Return Bond Fund
RRSP Eligible; Inception Year: 2000;
US Money Market Fund (US$)
RRSP Eligible; Inception Year: 1990;
Balanced Pension Trust Fund
RRSP Eligible; Inception Year: 2001;
Canadian Equity Plus Pension Trust Fund
RRSP Eligible; Inception Year: 1966;
Community Values Balanced Fund
RRSP Eligible; Inception Year: 2002; Fund Managers: Sky Investment Counsel
Community Values Bond Fund
RRSP Eligible; Inception Year: 2002;
Community Values Canadian Equity Fund
RRSP Eligible; Inception Year: 2002;
Community Values Global Equity Fund
RRSP Eligible; Inception Year: 2002; Fund Managers: Sky Investment Counsel
Global Equity Fund
RRSP Eligible; Inception Year: 2000; Fund Managers: Sky Investment Counsel
Overseas Equity Fund
RRSP Eligible; Inception Year: 2000; Fund Managers: Sky Investment Counsel
US Dividend Income Fund
RRSP Eligible; Inception Year: 2002;
Vintage Fund
RRSP Eligible; Inception Year: 1986;
Canadian Income Fund
RRSP Eligible; Inception Year: 2005;
Branches:
Calgary
West Tower, Bankers Hall
#4430, 888 - 3rd St. SW
Calgary, AB T2P 5C5 Canada
403-515-6825
Fax: 403-515-6849
Mark Williams, Vice-President
Montréal
#2821, 1 Place Ville Marie
Montréal, QC H3B 4R4 Canada
514-288-4966
Fax: 514-288-4876
Kathy Fazel, Vice-President
Toronto
One Financial Place
PO Box 207
#2320, 1 Adelaide St. East
Toronto, ON M5C 2V9 Canada
416-601-0027
Fax: 416-601-0109
A. Mark DeCelles, Vice-President
Victoria
St. Andrew's Square I
#312, 737 Yates St.
Victoria, BC V8W 1L6 Canada
250-405-7300
Fax: 250-405-7301
James Darke, Vice-President

PIMCO Canada
#2005, 120 Adelaide St. West
Toronto, ON M5H 1T1
416-368-3350
Fax: 416-368-3576
866-341-3350
www.pimco.com
Also Known As: Pacific Investment Management Company
Ownership: Pacific Investment Management Company LLC, Newport Beach, CA, USA.
Executives:
Margaret Isbey, President; 416-368-3350
Andrew Forsyth, Vice-President & Head, Business Development; 416-368-3349; andrew.forsyth@pimco.com

Pinch Group
Also listed under: *Investment Dealers*
#1000, 1175 Douglas St.
Victoria, BC V8W 2E1
250-405-2420
Fax: 250-405-2499
877-405-2400
pinchgroup@raymondjames.ca
www.pinchgroup.ca
Number of Employees: 5
Profile: The group offers investment management & financial planning. The website provides a resource on ethical, socially responsible or environmental/green investing. The financial/commercial institution is a member of the Social Investment Organization. Activities are conducted in British Columbia, Alberta, Ontario & the Northwest Territories..

Executives:
Brian Pinch, Investment Advisor
Frank Arnold, Investment Advisor
Michael Higgins, Investment Advisor
Branches:
Toronto
Scotia Plaza
PO Box 415
#5300, 40 King St. West
Toronto, ON M5H 3Y2 Canada
416-777-7000
Fax: 416-777-7020
877-363-1024
Vancouver
Cathedral Place
#800, 333 Seymour St.
Vancouver, BC V6B 5E2 Canada
604-654-1111
Fax: 604-654-0209
888-545-6624
Vancouver
Cathedral Place
#2100, 925 West Georgia St.
Vancouver, BC V6C 3L2 Canada
604-659-8000
Fax: 604-659-8099
888-545-6624

Plancorp Management Inc.
#300, 333 - 11 Ave. SW
Calgary, AB T2R 1L9
403-292-0707
Fax: 403-266-3377
jmalyk@pipfs.ab.ca
Also Known As: Partners in Planning Financial Services Ltd.
Year Founded: 1986

INVESTMENT MANAGEMENT

Plancorp Management Inc. (continued)
Number of Employees: 5
Executives:
John Malyk
Dennis Pianidin

Planifax inc.
444, ch de la Grande-Côte
Rosemère, QC J7A 1L1
450-621-1111
888-621-7111
info@planifax.net
www.planifax.net
Year Founded: 1988
Profile: The firm provides financial planning & private wealth management services, including retirement plans, annuities, insurance, RRSPs, LIRAs, RRIFs, & GICs. It is governed by Institut Québécois de Planification Financière (IQPF) as well as by the Ordre des Administrateurs Agréés du Québec (Adm. A).

Planification Copepco Inc.
Also listed under: *Investment Dealers*
858, rue du Haut-Bois sud
Sherbrooke, QC J1N 2J2
819-821-4378
Fax: 910-821-0193
Ownership: Private
Year Founded: 1990

Planmar Financial Corp.
Also listed under: *Investment Dealers*
#103, 400 York St.
London, ON N6B 3N2
519-673-3010
Fax: 519-673-6054
877-504-3010
info@planmar.net
www.planmar.com
Year Founded: 1987
Executives:
Tony Cuzzocrea, President

Planning Circle Financial Group Inc.
#220, 124 James St. South
Hamilton, ON L8P 2Z4
905-528-4853
Fax: 905-528-8840
800-483-7126
Profile: The financial planning organization is a memeber of the Mutual Fund Dealers Association of Canada.

Executives:
Adam Rosati, CFP, Financial Planner

The Planning Group NB Inc.
#201, 814 Main St.
Moncton, NB E1C 1E6
506-382-6111
Fax: 506-382-6100

Planwright Financial Ltd.
502 - 10th St.
Wainwright, AB T9W 1P4
780-842-1370
Fax: 780-842-3546
tdove@alberta-cu.com
www.PlanWright.com
Ownership: Wholly owned subsidiary of Wainwright Credit Union Ltd., Wainwright, AB.
Executives:
Tami H. Dove, Investment Specialist

Platinum Financial Partners Inc.
#10, 425 First St.
London, ON N5W 5K5
519-453-5580
Fax: 519-453-0092
888-419-0969
info@yourfreedom.com
www.yourfreedom.com
Former Name: Financial Tax Management Ltd
Year Founded: 1990
Profile: The firm offers the following services: insurance planning, personal financial planning, estate planning, mutual funds, & GICs.

Executives:
Rene Bouchard, CFP, Financial Planner, Tax Consultant; rene@yourfreedom.com
Michael Ede, Insurance Advisor; mede@yourfreedom.com

Branches:
Milton
#21, 781 Main St. East
Milton, ON L9T 5A9 Canada
905-864-4919
888-419-0969

Pollock Financial
Also listed under: *Pension & Money Management Companies*
172 Bellefair Ave.
Toronto, ON M4L 3T9
416-699-1292
Fax: 416-699-3119
aaap@idirect.com
Former Name: Aileen A.A. Pollock Chartered Financial Consultant
Ownership: Private
Year Founded: 1985
Number of Employees: 1
Revenues: Under $1 million
Executives:
Aileen A.A. Pollock, CFP, RFP, CH.F.C., CLU, Principal

Polson Bourbonnière Financial Planning Associates
#100, 7050 Woodbine Ave.
Markham, ON L3R 4G8
416-498-6181
Fax: 905-305-0885
800-263-0120
info@pbfinancial.com
www.worryfreeretirement.com
Ownership: Private
Year Founded: 1997
Executives:
Paul Bourbonnière, CFP, CLU, CH.F.C., Financial Planner; paul@pbfinancial.com
Kirk Polson, CFP, CLU, CH.F.C., Financial Planner; kirk@pbfinancial.com
Ruth Ashton, CFP, Financial Planner
Lydia Bzowej, CFP, EPC, Financial Planner
Allan Kalin, CFP, Financial Planner

Polygone Financial Services Inc./ Services Financiers Polygone
Also listed under: *Investment Dealers*
#1400, 1010, rue de la Gauchetière ouest
Montréal, QC H3B 2N2
514-866-7300
Fax: 514-866-4682
messages@polygone.net
www.polygone.net
Executives:
Guy Charron, President

Portfolio Strategies Corporation
Also listed under: *Investment Dealers*
#301B6, 2509 Dieppe Ave. SW
Calgary, AB T3E 7J9
403-252-5222
Fax: 403-252-1220
877-303-3233
info@portfoliostrategies.ca
www.portfoliostrategies.ca
Profile: The independent investment consulting firm provides financial planning & investment advice. It offers various investment products, such as mutual & segrgated funds, bonds & GICs, in addition to group RRSPs, DPSPs & pension plans.

Executives:
Mark S. Kent, President
Branches:
Calgary
1505 Macleod Trail SE
Calgary, AB T2G 2N6 Canada
403-705-5067
Fax: 403-262-0133
Kate Allard, Contact
Dawson Creek
#22, 1405 - 102 Ave.
Dawson Creek, BC V1G 2E1 Canada
250-782-7272
Fax: 250-782-7282
Howard Wyant, Contact
Lethbridge
Lethbridge Centre Tower
#902, 400- 4th Ave. South
Lethbridge, AB T1J 4E1 Canada
403-380-2020
Fax: 403-380-2290
Lisa Aucoin, Contact
Magrath
c/o Trading Company Office
86S - 1st St. West
Magrath, AB T0K 1J0 Canada
403-758-6631
Fax: 403-759-6878
Shannon Sabey, Contact
Markham
#211, 80 Acadia Ave.
Markham, ON L3R 9V1 Canada
905-940-2783
Fax: 905-940-8692
Frank Sui-Cheong Pa, Contact
Medicine Hat
#101, 623 - 4 St. SE
Medicine Hat, AB T1A 0L1 Canada
403-526-3283
Fax: 403-526-8082
Bob Olson, Contact
Red Deer
#207, 4921 - 49th St.
Red Deer, AB T4N 1V2 Canada
403-343-1181
Fax: 403-343-1182
Rick Baron, Contact
Regina
1836 Angus St.
Regina, SK S4T 1Z4 Canada
306-584-2523
Fax: 306-584-8225
Kelly Aikens, Contact
Richmond - #3 Rd.
#750, 5951 - #3 Rd.
Richmond, BC Canada
604-273-0232
Fax: 604-273-0232
Tina Ho, Contact
Richmond - #3 Rd.
#560, 5900 - #3 Rd.
Richmond, BC V6X 3P7 Canada
604-303-9700
Fax: 604-303-9705
Henry Liao, Contact
Richmond Hill
#14A, 30 Wertheim Ct.
Richmond Hill, ON L4B 1B9 Canada
905-695-1808
Fax: 905-695-1810
Elaine Kwan, Contact
Trail
#235, 8100 Rock Island Hwy.
Trail, BC V1R 4N7 Canada
250-368-9600
Fax: 250-364-3138
Frank DeFouw, Contact
Trochu
322 Arena Ave.
Trochu, AB T0M 2C0 Canada
403-442-2172
Fax: 403-442-2183
Barry Kletke, Contact
Vancouver
North Tower, Oakridge Centre
#555, 650 West 41st Ave.
Vancouver, BC V5Z 2M9 Canada
604-269-9888
Fax: 604-269-9588
Daniel Ng, Contact
White Rock - Russell Ave.
#235, 15233 Russell Ave.
White Rock, BC V4B 5C3 Canada
604-538-7643
Fax: 604-542-1025
Sam Esaw, Contact
White Rock - West Hastings St.
#1088, 999 West Hastings St.
Vancouver, BC V6C 2W2 Canada
604-605-1644
Fax: 604-605-1674

Sam Esaw, Contact
Winnipeg
#200, 1 Wesley Ave.
Winnipeg, MB R3C 4C8 Canada
204-940-5460
Fax: 204-940-5462
Margaret Koniuck, Contact

Pottruff & Smith Insurance Brokers Inc.

#300, 8001 Weston Rd.
Woodbridge, ON L4L 9C8
416-798-8001
Fax: 905-264-5165
888-768-8001
insurance@pottruffsmith.com
www.pottruffsmith.com
Ownership: Private. Parent company is Pottruff & Smith Investments Inc.
Year Founded: 1974
Number of Employees: 70
Revenues: $6,200,000 Year End: 20051200
Profile: Pottruff & Smith is a full service, national insurance brokerage which specializes in customized programs for professional associations, corporate clients & individuals. Classes of insurance offered include liability, life, property, automobile & personal accident & sickness. The insurance brokerage is also affiliated with Pottruff & Smith Travel Insurance Brokers Inc.

Executives:
Gary Pottruff, President/CEO; gpottruff@pottruffsmith.com
Cathy Baleck, Vice-President, Finance & Administration; cbaleck@potruffsmith.com
Michael Fitzgibbon, Vice-President, Commercial Lines, Partner; mfitzgibbon@pottruffsmith.com
Lynne Ray, Vice-President, Insurance Operations; lray@pottruffsmith.com
Marie Verschuuren, Vice-President, Marketing; mverschuuren@pottruffsmith.com

Powell River Credit Union Financial Group

Also listed under: *Credit Unions/Caisses Populaires*
4721 Joyce Ave.
Powell River, BC V8A 3B5
604-485-6206
Fax: 604-485-7112
800-393-6733
www.prcu.com
Year Founded: 1939
Number of Employees: 46
Assets: $100-500 million
Revenues: $5-10 million
Profile: Affiliates include Powell River Insurance Services Ltd. & Athena CUSO Management Ltd.

Executives:
David B. Craigen, CEO; 604-483-8680; dave-craigen@prcu.com

Shehzad Somji, CFO
Frank Oldale, Chief Technology Officer
Sandra Phillips, Manager, Sales, Marketing & Branch Operations
Directors:
Shawn Gullette, President
Patricia Salomi, Vice-President
Gail Curtis, Secretary
Ken Barton
Peter Dowding
Carl Floe
David Northrop
Carol Roberts
Sharon Sawyer
Branches:
Van Anda
1207 Marble Bay
Van Anda, BC V0N 3K0 Canada
604-486-7851
Fax: 604-486-7671
Jane Waterman, Manager

Premier Financial Planning

152 - 14th St.
Brandon, MB R7A 4T1
204-727-8204
Fax: 204-728-8276
premier@westman.wave.ca
Ownership: Private
Year Founded: 1991
Number of Employees: 5
Profile: The company is a full-service financial planning office, providing comprehensive financial plans. The member of FPSCC also provides a full range of products & services from mutual funds, banking, trust & insurance.

Executives:
David F. Janzen, President

Premier Financial Planning Services

373 Midland Ave.
Midland, ON L4R 3K8
705-527-6705
Fax: 705-527-1988
premier@premierfps.com
www.premierfps.com
Ownership: Private
Year Founded: 1993
Number of Employees: 3
Executives:
Jacqueline Skinner, CFP, Owner

Price Financial

#209, 5325 Cordova Bay Rd.
Victoria, BC V8Y 2L3
250-658-3515
Fax: 250-652-2408
800-920-2222
terry@terryprice.com
www.terryprice.com
Profile: The firm offers estate & retirement planning & business succession planning.

Executives:
Terry Price, Financial Planner

Prime Financial Group

#1005, 1661 Portage Ave.
Winnipeg, MB R3J 3T7
204-947-5691
Fax: 204-956-5986
info@pfgroup.com
www.pfgroup.com
Ownership: Private
Profile: The following services are provided by the Investment Planning Counsel company: portfolio management, retirement planning, tax planning, estate planning, risk management & cash & credit management.

Executives:
Mario Di Fonzo, CFP, CLU, CH.FC, Manager; mdifonzo@pfgroup.com

Professional Financial Planning

#602, 3200 Deziel Dr.
Windsor, ON N8W 5K8
519-944-9955
Fax: 519-944-9995
Ownership: Private
Year Founded: 1986

Professional Investment Services (Canada) Inc./Wolfe Financial

Also listed under: *Investment Dealers*
19 Oakdale Pl.
St Albert, AB T8N 6L7
780-458-4794
Fax: 780-418-7607
d.wolfe@shaw.ca
Former Name: Generation Financial Corp./Wolfe Financial
Year Founded: 2002
Number of Employees: 2
Assets: Under $1 million
Revenues: Under $1 million
Executives:
Debbie Wolfe, Contact

Professional Investments Inc.

1180 Clyde Ct.
Kingston, ON K7P 2E4
613-384-7511
Fax: 613-384-8919
ofisher@pro-invest.on.ca
www.pro-invest.on.ca
Ownership: Private
Year Founded: 1985
Number of Employees: 30
Revenues: $10-50 million
Executives:
Ossie Fisher, President
Paul Fisher, Vice-President
Lisa MacVicar
Branches:
Addison
8651 County Rd. 28, RR#2
Addison, ON K0E 1A0 Canada
613-926-0957
Tim Ross, Manager
Belleville - Front St.
183 Front St.
Belleville, ON K8N 2Y9 Canada
613-966-6446
Fax: 613-966-6513
Jason Cook, Manager
Cornwall
702 Second St. East
Cornwall, ON K6J 3R3 Canada
613-932-9847
Fax: 613-930-4891
Luke Bedard, Manager
Ottawa
1493 Merivale Rd.
Nepean, ON K2E 5P3 Canada
613-225-1500
Fax: 613-225-1800
John McRae, Manager

Progressive Financial Strategy

Also listed under: *Investment Dealers*
#203, 5170 Dixie Rd.
Mississauga, ON L4W 1E3
905-212-9149
Fax: 905-212-9201
pfs@pfs.ca
www.pfs.ca
Profile: The financial planning center is also an investment fund dealer & an independent insurance broker.

Puhl Employee Benefits Inc.

Also listed under: *Pension & Money Management Companies*
#309, 259 Midpark Way SE
Calgary, AB T2X 1M2
403-221-9300
Fax: 403-221-9309
888-508-0077
phsp@puhlemployeebenefits.com
www.puhlemployeebenefits.com
Ownership: Private
Year Founded: 1987
Executives:
David A. Puhl, CFP, President, Managing Partner
Lorna C. Phelps, CFP, Vice-President, Managing Partner

QFS Financial Services Ltd.

Also listed under: *Investment Dealers*
355 Plains Rd. East
Burlington, ON L7T 4H7
905-681-6555
Fax: 905-681-6755

Qualified Financial Services Inc.

#340, 3625 Dufferin St.
Toronto, ON M3K 1Z2
416-630-4000
Fax: 416-630-4022
800-263-4570
qfs@qfscanada.com
www.qfscanada.com
Executives:
Kevin Cott, President
Don Hart, Exec. Vice-President, Brokerage Development
Anna Boroni, Controller
Pat Armstrong, Coordinator, Broker Services
Dianna Sebastiao, Coordinator, Marketing

Queensbury Strategies Inc.

Also listed under: *Pension & Money Management Companies*
69 Yonge St., 2nd Fl.
Toronto, ON M5E 1K3
416-363-8500
webster@queensbury.com, rona@queensbury.com
www.queensbury.com
Ownership: Private. Part of Queensbury Group, Toronto, ON.
Year Founded: 1987

Queensbury Strategies Inc. (continued)
Profile: Part of the Queensbury Group, the firm is affiliated with Queensbury Securities Inc. & Queensbury Insurance Brokers. The following financial planning services are offered: needs assessment, tax planning, estate planning, retirement planning, & insurance analysis.
Executives:
John Webster, President
Branches:
Oakville
114 Forsythe St.
Oakville, ON L6K 3T3 Canada
905-845-1484
George Stephens, Vice-President

Quirion Financial Services
1085 Carrick St.
Thunder Bay, ON P7B 6L9
807-622-3700
Fax: 807-622-5001
800-785-2877
info@qfs.ca
www.qfs.ca
Profile: Services offered include personal financial planning, business planning, life, health & disability insurance, plus GICs & segregated funds.
Executives:
Roger Quirion, Manager, Financial Advisor
Kelly Kohanski, Assistant Manager
Pam Ossachuk, Manager, Client Service

Quorum Funding Corporation
Sun Life Tower
PO Box 5
#1505, 150 King St. West
Toronto, ON M5H 1J9
416-971-6998
Fax: 416-971-5955
mail@quorum.ca
www.quorum.ca
Ownership: Private
Year Founded: 1987
Number of Employees: 12
Assets: $1-5 million
Revenues: $1-5 million
Profile: Quorum is a venture capital investment manager. One branch is located in London, England, where Alex O'Cinneide is the Partner/CEO. A second branch is located in Hamilton, Bermuda. It is managed by Director, Bill Maycock.
Executives:
Wanda M. Dorosz, Managing Partner/CEO
Stephen Y.S. Li, Managing Partner, Canada
Richard Dole, Sr. Partner, Technology & Investment
Michael Goffin, Sr. Vice-President, Investments
Directors:
Richard Dole
Wanda M. Dorosz
Michael Goffin
Stephen Li

R&J Financial Services
393 Exmouth St.
Sarnia, ON N7T 5N8
519-344-0272
Profile: Services include financial planning & tax preparation. It is affiliated with Sterling Mutuals Inc.

R. Steinson & Co. Inc.
***Also listed under:** Accountants*
#301, 394 Duncan St.
Duncan, BC V9L 3W4
250-748-1426
Fax: 250-748-9724
Executives:
Rick Steinson, Accountant

R.B. Lachance & Associates Ltd.
#306, 125 Bell Farm Rd.
Barrie, ON L4M 6L2
705-721-7500
Fax: 705-728-5034
800-509-7526
beth@rblachance.com
www.rblachance.com
Executives:
Beth Lachance Hesson

R.J. White Financial Inc.
226 Beatrice St. West
Oshawa, ON L1G 7M9
905-571-1421
Fax: 905-571-6675

Rae & Lipskie Investment Counsel
***Also listed under:** Pension & Money Management Companies*
#201, 20 Erb St. West
Waterloo, ON N2L 1T2
519-578-6849
Fax: 519-578-7269
888-578-7542
rlic@raelipskie.com
www.raelipskie.com
Ownership: Private
Year Founded: 1989
Number of Employees: 18
Executives:
Ken E. Rae, CFA, Chair/CEO
Brian E. Lipskie, CFA, President/COO

Raimondo & Associates Ltd.
#329, 305 - 4625 Varsity Dr. NW
Calgary, AB T3A 0Z9
403-288-8561
Fax: 403-288-8705
800-786-0522
rose@raimondo-associates.com
www.raimondo-associates.com
Profile: The independent, fee-for-service financial education & counselling company is engaged in personal financial planning. Planning services are offered related to life transitions, such as loss of employment, divorce & death of a spouse. Seminars, especially on the topics of retirement planning & pensions, are delivered for employees.
Executives:
Rose Raimondo, B.B.A., CFP, R.F.P., PRP, Principal

Ramey Investments Incorporated
***Also listed under:** Investment Dealers*
72 Portland St.
Dartmouth, NS B2Y 1H6
902-466-7464
Fax: 902-461-4491
ramey@rameyinvestments.com
www.rameyinvestments.com
Year Founded: 1975
Profile: The independent firm provides financial & investment advice. Financial planning services include retirement, investment, tax, estate & education. Products include mutual funds & segregated funds.

Rapport Capital Formation Strategists Inc.
#703, 141 Adelaide St. West
Toronto, ON M5H 3L5
416-366-9264
Fax: 416-366-1855
rapport@rapport.ca
www.rapport.ca
Ownership: Private
Year Founded: 1974
Number of Employees: 7
Profile: The capital formation strategists & investor relations advisors service more than 400 Canadian entities.
Executives:
Edmond Eberts, President

Ratelle et Associés
8552, rue St-Denis
Montréal, QC H2P 2H2
514-385-5889
Fax: 514-385-3292
800-563-5637
contact@ratelle.ca
www.ratelle.ca

Raycroft Financial Planning Family Wealth Advisors Ltd.
PO Box A
#200, 270 George St. North
Peterborough, ON K9J 3H1
705-743-9650
Fax: 705-743-9651
service@raycroftfinancial.com
www.raycroftfinancial.com
Year Founded: 1983
Profile: The financial planning firm specializes in professional money management, retirement planning, investment planning, tax planning, estate planning, educational funding & life & disability insurance. Clients include individuals, employees & employers.
Executives:
William Raycroft, Registered Financial Planner, CFP, CLU; noreen@raycroftfinancial.com
Daniel Raycroft, CFP, Certified Financial Planner; dan@raycroftfinancial.com

Raymond James Ltd.
***Also listed under:** Investment Dealers*
Cathedral Place
#2200, 925 West Georgia St.
Vancouver, BC V6C 3L2
604-659-8000
Fax: 604-659-8099
888-545-6624
webcomments@raymondjames.ca
www.raymondjames.ca
Former Name: Goepel McDermid Securities Inc.
Ownership: Indirect wholly-owned subsidiary of Raymond James Financial, Inc., St. Petersburg, FL, USA.
Year Founded: 1962
Number of Employees: 689
Stock Exchange Membership: Montreal Exchange, Toronto Stock Exchange, TSX Venture Exchange
Profile: Raymond James is an independent, full service investment dealer & financial advising company. It offers professional investment services & products, including asset management, equity research, fixed income products, mutual funds, investment banking, institutional equity sales & trading, estate planning, financial planning, & insurance. Financial planning services are provided through Raymond James Financial Planning Ltd.
Executives:
Ken Shields, Chair
Peter Bailey, President/CEO
Lloyd Costley, Exec. Vice-President/CAO, Corporate Services
Jason Holtby, Sr. Managing Director, Investment Banking
Peter Kahnert, Sr. Vice-President, Corporate Communications & Marketing
George Karkoulas, Sr. Vice-President, Independent Financial Services
Kevin Whelly, Sr. Vice-President, Growth & Development
Terry Hetherington, Manager, National Sales
Branches:
Barrie - Caplan Ave.
#612, 92 Caplan Ave.
Barrie, ON L4N 0Z7
705-719-7967
Bromont
109, boul Bromont
Bromont, QC J2L 2K7
450-534-1900
Simon Bilodeau, Branch Manager
Burlington
1100 Walkers Line
Burlington, ON L7N 2G3
905-332-7861
Lynn Curtin Lange, Branch Manager
Calgary - 11th Ave. SW
#207, 322 - 11th Ave. SW
Calgary, AB T2R 0C5
403-531-2444
Calgary - 2nd St. SW
1409 2nd Street SW
Calgary, AB T2R 0W7
403-263-7999
Taylor Davison, Branch Manager
Calgary - 8th Ave. SW
#2500, 707 - 8th Ave. SW
Calgary, AB T2P 1H5
403-509-0500
Calgary - 8th Ave. SW
#2300, 707 8th Ave. SW
Calgary, AB T2P 1H5
403-221-0333
Mike Irwin, Branch Manager
Calgary - Varsity Dr. NW
#101, 4603 Varsity Dr. NW
Calgary, AB T3A 2V7
403-670-8871

Claresholm
4802 - 2nd St. West
Claresholm, AB T0L 0T0
403-625-1555
Cobourg - Division St.
#1, 438 Division St.
Cobourg, ON K9A 3R9
905-372-4333
Cobourg - Division St.
#2, 438 Division St.
Cobourg, ON K9A 3R9
905-372-1300
Courtenay
1255C Cliffe Ave.
Courtenay, BC V9N 2K3
250-334-9294
Delta - 12th Ave.
#102, 5405 - 12th Ave.
Delta, BC V4M 2B2
604-943-6360
Delta - 56th St.
#3, 1359 - 56th St.
Delta, BC V4L 2P3
604-943-5665
Duncan
351 Festubert St.
Duncan, BC V9L 3T1
250-715-0004
Edmonton
#2300, 10060 Jasper Ave.
10060 Jasper Ave, AB T5J 3R8
780-414-2500
Don Howden, Branch Manager
Elmvale
42 Queen St. West
Elmvale, ON L0L 1P0
705-322-2442
Brian Alger, Branch Manager
Essex
14 Victoria Ave.
Essex, ON N8M 1M3
519-776-7770
Fort McMurray
#101, 9816 Hardin St.
Fort McMurray, AB T9H 4K3
780-799-7820

Gatineau
#150, 160, boul de l'Hôpital
Gatineau, QC J8T 8J1
819-568-5025
Martin Boucher, Branch Manager
Halifax
TD Centre
#1030, 1791 Barrington St.
Halifax, NS B3J 3K9
902-444-9922
Kevin Van Amburg, Branch Manager
Hamilton
Commerce Place
#400, 1 King St. West
Hamilton, ON L8P 1A4
905-974-2900
Andrew Irwin, Branch Manager
High River
#2, 27 - 11th Ave. SE
High River, AB T1V 1Y1
403-652-2053
Cliff Squires, Branch Manager
Huntsville
39 King William St.
Huntsville, ON P1H 1G4
705-789-2100
Kamloops
#201, 242 Victoria St.
Kamloops, BC V2C 2A2
250-372-8117
Les Consenheim, Branch Manager
Kelowna
#500, 1726 Dolphin Ave.
Kelowna, BC V1Y 9R9
250-979-2700
Paul Johnson, Branch Manager
Kingston
#101, 1000 Gardiners Rd.
Kingston, ON K7P 3C4
613-634-4500
Paul Richardson, Branch Manager
London
#1510, 148 Fullarton St.
London, ON N6A 5P3
519-640-6894
Markham
#308, 7050 Woodbine Ave.
Markham, ON L3R 4G8
905-470-6222
Medicine Hat
#3, 202 - 5th Ave.
Medicine Hat, AB T1A 2P8
403-580-4375
Mississauga - Britannia Rd. East
256 Britannia Rd. East
Mississauga, ON L4Z 1S6
905-502-5537
Peter Daly, Branch Manager
Mississauga - Lakeshore Rd. West
305 Lakeshore Rd. West
Mississauga, ON L5H 1G5
905-891-5222
Mississauga - Robert Speck Pkwy.
#200, 176 Robert Speck Pkwy.
Mississauga, ON L4Z 3G1
905-281-5511
Nanaimo
Longwood Station
#1, 5767 Turner Rd.
Nanaimo, BC V9T 6L8
250-729-2830
New Minas
#2, 8903 Commercial St.
New Minas, NS B4N 3E1
902-679-2881
Newmarket
38 Prospect St.
Newmarket, ON L3Y 3S9
905-898-0489
Thane Fletcher, Branch Manager
North Vancouver - Chesterfield Pl.
15 Chesterfield Pl., #D
North Vancouver, BC V7M 3K3
604-981-2000

North Vancouver - West Esplanade
#480, 171 West Esplanade
North Vancouver, BC V7M 3J9
604-984-2235
Oakville
#2, 108 Allan St.
Oakville, ON L6J 3N1
905-815-8448
Matt Langsford, Branch Manager
Orangeville
24 First St.
Orangeville, ON L9W 2C7
519-938-8332
Gary Beck, Branch Manager
Ottawa - Gurdwara Rd.
#510, 2 Gurdwara Rd.
Ottawa, ON K2E 1A2
613-274-2662
Ottawa - Queen St.
#300, 100 Queen St.
Ottawa, ON K1P 1J9
613-788-2150
Mario Ruiz, Branch Manager
Penticton - Ellis St.
#100, 498 Ellis St.
Penticton, BC V2A 4M2
250-487-2000
Gerry Bate, Branch Manager
Penticton - Wade Ave. East
#104, 74 Wade Ave. East
Penticton, BC V2A 8M4
250-493-3711
Peterborough
999 Lansdowne St. West
Peterborough, ON K9J 8N2
705-743-1221
Dan Seabrooke, Branch Manager
Port Moody
2701 Clarke St.
Port Moody, BC V3H 1Z5
604-939-5800
Prince George - Central St. East
578 Central St. East
Prince George, BC V2M 3B7
250-564-2001
Gary Clarke, Branch Manager
Prince George - Third Ave.
#101, 1840 Third Ave.
Prince George, BC V2M 1G4
250-614-0888
Prince George - Victoria St.
#600, 550 Victoria St.
Prince George, BC V2L 2K1
250-564-2321
Qualicum Beach
#103, 193 West 2nd Ave.
Qualicum Beach, BC V9K 2N5
250-752-8184
Red Deer
#201, 4807 Gaetz Ave.
Red Deer, AB T4N 4A5
403-314-2600
Regina - 12th Ave.
#204, 2550 - 12th Ave.
Regina, BC S4P 3X1
306-791-1820
Kurt Daunheimer, Branch Manager
Regina - Smith St.
2237A Smith St.
Regina, SK S4P 2P5
306-757-1717
Doug Strand, Branch Manager
Saskatoon - 21st St. East
#700, 105 - 21st St. East
Saskatoon, SK S7K 0B3
306-651-4250
Susan Milburn, Branch Manager
Saskatoon - 25 St. East
#100, 333 - 25 St. East
Saskatoon, SK S7K 0L4
306-665-2133

Sudbury
265 Larch St.
Sudbury, ON P3B 1M2
705-523-2795
Toronto
Scotia Plaza
PO Box 415
#5300, 40 King St. West
Toronto, ON M5H 3Y2 Canada
416-777-7000
Fax: 416-777-7020
877-363-1024
Toronto - Bloor St. East
South Tower
#400, 175 Bloor St. East
Toronto, ON M4W 3R8
416-960-5781
Toronto - East Mall
#350, 300 The East Mall
Toronto, ON M9B 6B7
416-233-3072
Toronto - King St. West
Scotia Plaza
#5300, 40 King St. West
Toronto, ON M5H 3Y2
416-777-7000
John Donnelly, Branch Manager
Toronto - Yonge St.
#1900, 4950 Yonge St.
Toronto, ON M2N 6K1
416-222-7003
Nerio D'Ambrosi, Branch Manager
Vancouver - 10th Ave. West
3762 - 10th Ave. West
Vancouver, BC V6R 2G4
604-222-5484
Kevin Bogle, Branch Manager
Vancouver - West Georgia St.
#2100, 925 West Georgia St.
Vancouver, BC V6C 3L2

Raymond James Ltd. (continued)
604-659-8000
Vancouver - West Hastings St.
#1002, 1177 West Hastings St.
Vancouver, BC V6E 2K3
604-663-4200
Vaughan
#510, 7050 Weston Rd.
Vaughan, ON L4L 8G7
905-652-4625
Victoria
#1000, 1175 Douglas St.
Victoria, BC V8W 2E1
250-405-2400
Steve Werner, Branch Manager
Waterloo
#1001, 20 Erb Street West
Waterloo, ON N2L 1T2
519-883-6030
White Rock
15178 Buena Vista Ave.
White Rock, BC V4B 1Y3
604-531-3011
Williams Lake
#201, 366 Yorston St.
Williams Lake, BC V2G 4J5
250-398-2222
Windsor
2861 Temple Dr.
Windsor, ON N8W 5E5
519-251-0159
Yarmouth
Lovitt Plaza
#107, 368 Main St.
Yarmouth, NS B5A 1E9
902-742-8818
Stephen Bishop, Branch Manager
Executives:
Barrie - Bayfield St.
#300, 135 Bayfield St.
Barrie, ON L4M 3B3
705-734-6300
Brian Kennedy, Branch Manager
Mississauga - Sherwoodtowne Blvd.
#200, 4263 Sherwoodtowne Blvd.
Mississauga, ON L4Z 1Y5
905-272-3900
Saskatoon - 1st Ave. North
#400, 261 - 1st Ave. North
Saskatoon, SK S7K 1X2
306-657-5733

RBA Financial Group
51 Sykes St. North
Meaford, ON N4L 1X3
519-538-5254
800-567-1941
www.rbafinancial.com
Year Founded: 1980
Profile: Financial advisors offer the following services: investments, insurance, retirement planning, tax planning, estate planning & risk management.

Executives:
Todd Campbell, BBA, CMA, CFP, President; tcampbell@rbafinancial.com
Karen Campbell, BA, B Ed, General Manager; kcampbell@rbafinancial.com
Heather Acres, Branch Manager
Phyllis Vail, Controller
Gay Blacha, Life Administrator
Brian A. McMillan, Chartered Life Underwriter
Branches:
Collingwood
158 Hurontario St. North
Collingwood, ON L9Y 2M2
705-446-1900
866-992-9914

RBC Capital Markets
Also listed under: *Investment Dealers*
Royal Bank Plaza - South Tower
PO Box 50
200 Bay St.
Toronto, ON M5J 2W7
416-842-2000
Fax: 416-842-8044
marketing@rbccm.com
www.rbccm.com
Stock Exchange Membership: Toronto Stock Exchange, TSX Venture Exchange
Executives:
Charles M. Winograd, President/CEO
Anthony S. Fell, Chair
Andrew G. Scace, Vice-Chair
Bruce Rothney, Deputy Chair
John W. Burbridge, Managing Director/COO, Europe, Asia
Executives.:
Kirby Gavelin, Managing Director, Head, Equity Capital Markets
Mark Hughes, Managing Director, Head, Global Credit
Doug McGregor, Managing Director, Head, Global Investment Banking
Mark Standish, Managing Director, Head, Global Financial Products
Richard Tavoso, Managing Director, Head, Global Equity Derivatives
Affiliated Companies:
RBC Capital Partners
Branches:
Calgary
Banker's Hall
888 3rd St. SW
Calgary, AB T2T 5C5 Canada
403-299-7111
Vancouver
Park Place
#2100, 666 Burrard St.
Vancouver, BC V6C 3B1 Canada
604-257-7000

RBC Dexia Investor Services
Also listed under: *Investment Dealers; Investment Management*
North Tower
200 Bay St., 24th Fl.
Toronto, ON M5J 2J5
Fax: 416-955-2631
800-668-1320
benefpay@rbcdexia-is.com
www.rbcdexia-is.com
Ownership: A joint venture equally owned by Royal Bank of Canada & Dexia.
Year Founded: 2006
Profile: RBC Dexia Investor Services provides services to asset managers & distributors, pensions, financial institutions, & insurance companies.

Affiliated Companies:
RBC Dexia Investor Services Trust

RBM Financial Ltd.
#100, 67 Ward Dr.
Barrie, ON L4N 8A2
705-737-0016
Fax: 705-792-7892
888-307-0600
info@rbmfinancial.com
www.rbmfinancial.com
Executives:
R. Bruce Marshall, President

RealCap Holdings Limited
Also listed under: *Pension & Money Management Companies; Investment Management*
PO Box 2081
#1002, 20 Eglinton Ave. West
Toronto, ON M4R 1K8
416-486-7729
Fax: 416-486-9708
realgrowth@on.aibn.com
Ownership: Public. Major shareholders are D.S. Ades (69.67% interest) & R.M. Ades (29.65% interest)
Year Founded: 1962
Number of Employees: 3
Assets: $1,273,000 Year End: 20041231
Revenues: $424,000 Year End: 20041231
Stock Symbol: REAH.A
Profile: This is a financial services holding company which conducts activities as a registered investment counsel & portfolio manager. It is also involved in limited partnerships, oil & gas, & marketable securities. Affiliated companies include Realcap Inc. (USA), Realcap Funds Inc., (USA) & Realgrowth Resources (86) CP.

Executives:
David S. Ades, President; da_realgrowth@on.aibn.com
Ralph M. Ades, Exec. Vice-President, Sec.-Treas.; realgrowth@on.aibn.com
Directors:
David S. Ades
Ralph M. Ades
M. Guy Jones
Sigrid I. Welsch

Relegrity Financial Services Inc.
#502, 300 John St.
Thornhill, ON L3T 5W4
905-886-7929
Fax: 905-886-0024
don@relegrity.com
www.relegrity.com
Ownership: Private
Year Founded: 2002
Number of Employees: 2
Revenues: Under $1 million
Executives:
Don Macfarlane, CFP, President

Remy Richard Securities Inc.
Also listed under: *Investment Dealers*
Tower I
#104, 7001 Mumford Rd.
Halifax, NS B3L 4N9
902-455-4914
Fax: 902-455-4554
888-326-5257
rrsi@rrsi.ca
Ownership: Private
Year Founded: 1988
Profile: The firm is a registered mutual fund dealer in Nova Scotia.

Executives:
Remy Richard, CEO

Rice Financial Group Inc.
491 Portage Ave.
Winnipeg, MB R3B 2E4
204-788-4040
Fax: 204-783-3388
800-392-1388
info@ricefinancial.com
www.ricefinancial.com
Ownership: Private. Parent is Jovian Capital, Winnipeg, MB
Year Founded: 1968
Assets: $1-10 billion
Profile: Rice Financial Group Inc. commits to providing financial solutions to Canadians. The group works to meet their financial needs, including investments, insurance, wealth accumulation & management, retirement, tax & estate planning, as well as group benefits.

Executives:
Mal Anderson, President/CEO
Jack Murray, Sr. Vice-President
Branches:
Brandon
613 - 10th St.
Brandon, MB R7A 4G6 Canada
204-729-3400
Fax: 204-727-4568
Calgary
#102 - 1910 20th Ave. NW
Calgary, AB T2M 1H5 Canada
403-270-2108
Fax: 403-270-4235
Cornwall
132 - 2nd St East
Cornwall, ON K6H 1Y4
613-937-0118
Fax: 613-938-6718
Moose Jaw
PO Box 1627
24 Fairford St. West
Moose Jaw, SK S6H 7K7 Canada
306-693-6655
Fax: 306-693-3630
Olds

5016 - 50 Ave.
Olds, AB T4H 1S4 Canada
403-556-3271
Fax: 403-556-3255
Ottawa
1679 Carling Ave.
Ottawa, ON K2A 1C4
613-729-1455
Fax: 613-722-8992
Port Coquitlam
#306, 2540 Shaughnessy St.
Port Coquitlam, BC V3C 3W4 Canada
604-464-4000
Fax: 604-464-7633
Regina
PO Box 1187
1842 Scarth St.
Regina, SK S4P 2G3 Canada
306-525-2561
Fax: 306-757-5872
Saskatoon
330 - 20th St. East
Saskatoon, SK S7K 0A7 Canada
306-242-1188
Fax: 306-242-1220
Winnipeg - Portage Ave.
2525 Portage Ave.
Winnipeg, MB R3J 0P1 Canada
204-925-7390
Fax: 204-925-7396
Winnipeg - Portage Ave. - Main Branch
491 Portage Ave.
Winnipeg, MB R3B 2E4 Canada
204-788-4040
Fax: 204-783-3388
800-392-1388
Winnipeg - Reenders Dr.
#5A, 3 Reenders Dr.
Winnipeg, MB R2C 5K5 Canada
204-925-7420
Fax: 204-783-3388
Winnipeg - St. Mary's Rd.
1510 St. Mary's Rd.
Winnipeg, MB R2M 3V7 Canada
204-925-7423
Fax: 204-255-0682

Rich Graham Financial Services

6006 Atlas St.
Niagara Falls, ON L2J 1T1
905-357-5757
Fax: 905-357-6452
rgraham116@cogeco.ca
Profile: The financial planner is affiliated with Investia Financial Services Inc.

Executives:
Richard Graham, Certified Financial Planner

Richard P. Harvey & Associates Limited

BDC Place
#240, 119 Kent St.
Charlottetown, PE C1N 5S9
902-566-5883
Fax: 902-566-9263
800-461-6749
richard@richardpharvey.com
www.richardpharvey.com
Profile: The bilingual money management company serves mature Canadians. It is partnered with Manulife Financial & its subsidiary companies.

Executives:
Richard Harvey, CFP, CLU, CH.F.C., President; richard@richardpharvey.com
Anne Harvey, Associate Director; anne@richardpharvey.com

Richardson Partners Financial Limited(RPFL)

#1900, 1250, boul, René-Lévesque ouest
Montréal, QC H3B 4W8
514-932-7735
Fax: 514-989-4879
866-337-7735
www.rpfl.com
Ownership: Operating division of Richardson Financial Group
Year Founded: 2003
Profile: The independent family wealth management firm delivers advice & wealth management solutions. It is a member of the Canadian Investor Protection Fund. Richardson Partners is affiliated with James Richardson & Sons, Limited.

Executives:
Sue Dabarno, CEO
Bennett MacInnis, Chief Operating OFficer
Marc Lauzier, Regional Vice-President
C. Warren Reynolds, Sr. Vice-President, Western Canada
John Horwood, Member, Executive Management Committee
Directors:
Hartley T. Richardson, Honorary Chair
H. Sanford Riley, Chair
David Brown
Sue Dabarno
Jean-Guy Gourdeau
Jean-Pierre Janson
Susan Latremoille
Douglas F. Mair
Robert G. Puchniak
Royden R. Richardson
Winthrop H. Smith Jr.
Branches:
Calgary
#1000, 333 - 7th Ave. SW
Calgary, AB T2P 2Z1 Canada
403-355-7735
Fax: 403-355-6109
866-867-7735
Ron Cairns, Vice-President, Business Development, Central Canada
Edmonton
Manulife Place
#3360, 10180 - 101 St.
Edmonton, AB T5J 3S4 Canada
780-409-7735
Fax: 780-409-7777
866-205-3550
C. Warren Reynolds, Sr. Vice-President, Western Canada
Mississauga
#304, 350 Burnhamthorpe Rd. West
Mississauga, ON L5B 3J1 Canada
905-566-7735
Fax: 905-615-5653
866-205-3548
Jean-Pierre Janson, Regional Vice-President
Sherbrooke
#305, 455, rue King ouest
Sherbrooke, QC J1H 6E9 Canada
819-821-7035
Fax: 819-823-2140
Marc Lauzier, Regional Vice-President
Toronto
BCE Place
#3910, 181 Bay St.
Toronto, ON M5J 2T3 Canada
416-962-7735
Fax: 416-969-2950
866-205-3548
Jean-Pierre Janson, Regional Vice-President
Vancouver
Park Place
#1800, 666 Burrard St.
Vancouver, BC V6C 2X8 Canada
604-678-6566
Fax: 604-678-6640
866-364-7735
C. Warren Reynolds, Sr. Vice-President, Western Canada
Winnipeg
#1100, One Lombard Pl.
Winnipeg, MB R3B 0X3 Canada
204-957-7735
Fax: 204-946-0966
866-205-3549
Ron Cairns, Vice-President, Business Development, Central Canada

Rickert Financial Group Ltd.

#103, 375 University Ave. East
Waterloo, ON N2K 3M7
519-884-3360
Fax: 519-884-3361
888-477-9609
mail@rfgl.com
www.rfgl.com
Year Founded: 1978
Profile: The following services are provided: financial planning, tax planning, estate planning, life, disability & group insurance, mutual funds, GICs, RRSPsk, RRIFs & RESPs. Investment products are offered through Partners in Planning Financial Services Ltd.

Executives:
Andrew D. Rickert, BMath, CFP, Financial Planner
Anthony (Tony) E. Rickert, BA (Hons.), CFP, Financial Planner

Rissling Financial Corporation

Also listed under: *Investment Dealers*
4861 Prairie Lane
Grasswood, SK S7T 1A7
306-241-1576
Fax: 306-477-1882
Year Founded: 1995
Profile: The firm offers financial services mainly to the farming community. It is a member of the Mutual Fund Dealers Association of Canada.

The Rite Path

#325, 509 Commissioners Rd. West
London, ON N6J 3M8
519-858-7657
Fax: 519-657-9126
don@ritepath.on.ca
www.ritepath.ca
Profile: Investment advice & insurance services are provided. Mutual funds are provides through Worldsource Financial Management Inc.

Executives:
Don Gerrity, CFP, CLU, CHFC, CFSB, EPC, Financial Planner

RJS Private Wealth Management Inc.

#206, 5451 Hwy. 7
Woodbridge, ON
905-856-5999
Fax: 905-264-4021
info@rjsinvestments.com
www.rjsinvestments.com
Ownership: Private. Part of Armstrong & Quaile Associates Inc., Manotick, ON.
Profile: The consulting & investment advisory firm offers advice about alternative investments & wealth management.

Executives:
Tim Martins, President

Robbinex Inc.

80 Bancroft St.
Hamilton, ON L8E 2W5
905-523-7510
Fax: 905-523-4998
888-762-2463
robbinex@robbinex.com
www.robbinex.com
Former Name: Robbinex Capital Corporation
Ownership: Private.
Year Founded: 1974
Number of Employees: 20
Profile: Robbinex is a business intermediary which provides intermediary services, venture capital, syndication services & debt placement as well as general consulting services. Canadian affiliate offices are located in Windsor, Victoria & Vancouver. USA offices are in Buffalo, New York & Michagan. Offices of partners are situated in Maryland, Oregon, Northern & Southern California..

Executives:
Doug Robbins, President; dmr@robbinex.com
Heinz Schweinbenz, Chief Operating Officer; heinz@robbinex.com
Donald Forrest, Vice-President; don@robbinex.com
Bruce Johnstone, Contact; bruce@robbinex.com

Robert B. Roll

4333, rue Sainte-Catherine ouest
Montréal, QC H3Z 1P9
514-594-4774
Executives:
Robert B. Roll, Contact

Robert F. Fischer & Company Inc., C.G.A.

Also listed under: *Accountants*
#13, 327 Prideaux St.
Nanaimo, BC V9R 2N4

INVESTMENT MANAGEMENT

Robert F. Fischer & Company Inc., C.G.A. (continued)
250-753-7287
Fax: 250-753-7453

Robert K. Kowalski
#330, 21 Four Seasons Pl.
Toronto, ON M9B 6J8
416-626-6280
Fax: 416-626-0895
Former Name: Robert K. Kowalski Financial & Retirement Planning Services
Executives:
Robert K. Kowalski

Rogan Investment Management
Toronto Dominion Bank Tower
PO Box 166
#5402, 66 Wellington Ave. West
Toronto, ON M5K 1H6
416-366-4208
Fax: 416-367-2339
888-394-4421
invest@roganinvestment.com
Ownership: Private
Year Founded: 1979
Number of Employees: 5
Assets: $100-500 million Year End: 20050930
Executives:
William E. Rogan, President
David W. Rogan, Vice-President, Investments
Lindsay A. Rogan, Vice-President, Client Service
William C. Jephcott, Portfolio Manager

Ron Chan
9 Wedgeport Pl.
Toronto, ON M2N 4B3
416-733-2463
Executives:
Ron Chan, Financial Planner

Ron Graham and Associates Ltd.
#100, 10585 - 111 St.
Edmonton, AB T5H 3E8
780-429-6775
Fax: 780-424-0004
www.rgafinancial.com
Profile: The company offers both personal & corporate financial planning. Personal planning services include retirement, tax, investment, insurance, & estate planning. Education funding & debt management are also provided. Corporate services, such as seminars & counseling, are offerd to employees.
Executives:
Ron Graham, C.A., R.F.P., CFP, President

Ron Turley
KIIIG
#110, 27 Place D'Armes
Kingston, ON K7K 6Z6
613-544-8058
Fax: 613-152-2

Rose Lalonde
9 Broad St.
Brockville, ON K6V 6Z4
613-498-0777
Executives:
Rose Lalonde, Consultant, Financial Planning

Ross M. Durant Insurance Agency Limited
#508, 4950 Yonge St.
Toronto, ON M2N 6K1
416-222-2262
Fax: 416-222-2510
www.durant-financial.com
Executives:
Ross M. Durant, CLU, CH.F.C., CFP, Chair
C. Michele Wilson, CLU, CH.F.C., CFP, FMA, President; cmwilson@durant-financial.com
Lynn Hayes, Office Manager; lhayes@durant-financial.com

Ross Taylor Financial Corporation
Zellers Plaza
6851 Morrison St.
Niagara Falls, ON L2E 2G5
905-374-9550
Fax: 905-374-4780
877-325-7677
info@rtfc.ca
www.rtfc.ca
Executives:
Ross Taylor, President

Rothenberg Capital Management Inc.
Also listed under: *Investment Dealers*
4420, rue Sainte-Catherine ouest
Montréal, QC H3Z 1R2
514-934-0586
Fax: 514-934-3134
800-811-0527
corrigan@rothenberg.ca
www.rothenberg.ca
Ownership: Private. Part of The Rothenberg Group.
Year Founded: 1979
Profile: The company offers advice on a variety of investment opportunities. Services cover retirement planning, post-retirement, & estate planning.
Executives:
Robert Rothenberg, President
Helen Corrigan, Vice-President
Branches:
Calgary
1712 - 10th Ave. SW
Calgary, AB T2C 0J8 Canada
403-228-2378
Fax: 403-228-2426
800-456-0949
Cochrane
#7, 205 - 1 St. East
Cochrane, AB T4C 1X6
403-851-7777
Fax: 403-851-0793
866-456-0949
Montréal - Holiday
#150, 1, rue Holiday
Montréal, QC H9R 5N3
514-697-0035
Fax: 514-697-3351

Rowles Financial Planning
Park Place
#2338, 666 Burrard St.
Vancouver, BC V6C 2X8
604-684-8313
Fax: 604-684-8315
stuart@rowlesfinancial.com
www.rowlesfinancial.com
Profile: Personal financial advice is offered in areas such as insurance, group benefits, pension plans, investments, RRSPs, RRIFs, RESPs & annuities. Mutual funds are provided through Worldsource Financial Management Inc.
Executives:
Stuart Rowles, BA, CFP, CLU, ChFC, RHU, Financial Planner; stuart@rowlesfinancial.com

Roy Financial Services Inc.
16 Mission Ave.
St Albert, AB T8N 1H4
780-458-3500
Fax: 780-458-3505
800-463-0075
danroy@royfinancial.com
www.royfinancial.com
Ownership: Private
Year Founded: 1989
Number of Employees: 7
Profile: Roy Financial is a one-stop wealth management company serving small to large businesses & individual clients. The organization is licensed to sell mutual funds through IQON Financial Inc.
Executives:
Dan Roy, President

The Royal Trust Company
Also listed under: *Trust Companies*
Royal Bank
1, Place Ville-Marie, 6e étage sud
Montréal, QC H3B 2B2
514-874-7222
800-668-1990
Other Information: 866-553-5585 (Eastern Canada Toll Free); 888-299-5290 (Western Canada Toll Free); 866-474-4344 (Québec Toll Free); tradvmtl@rbc.com (Québec Email) tradvtor@rbc.com (East), tradvcal@rbc.com (West)
www.rbc.com
Ownership: Part of RBC Financial Group.
Year Founded: 1899
Profile: The trust company is engaged in securities custody & investment management. Clients include individuals, families & businesses. Its services are part of RBC Investments, Wealth Management Division & RBC Global Services.
Executives:
M. George Lewis, President

RPS Retirement Planning Specialists Inc.
#300, 110 - 21st St. East
Saskatoon, SK S7K 0B6
306-244-5911
Fax: 306-244-5966
877-444-6478
admin@rpsretire.com
www.rpsretire.com
Ownership: Private
Year Founded: 1995
Number of Employees: 18
Assets: $100-500 million
Revenues: $1-5 million
Executives:
Barry W. MacDonald
J.A. (Jerry) Meckelborg

Ryan Lamontagne Inc.
#304, 2249 Carling Ave.
Ottawa, ON K2B 7E9
613-596-3353
Fax: 613-596-2441
800-304-7180
info@ryanlamontagne.com
www.ryanlamontagne.com
Former Name: Ryan Lamontagne & Associates; Thomas Ryan & Associates
Ownership: Private
Profile: The fee-for-service financial planning & counselling firm specializes in wealth management strategies for high net worth individuals & families.
Executives:
Marc Lamontagne, CFP, R.F.P., FMA, Principal
Thomas Ryan, CFP, Principal

S&P Financial Services Inc.
3370 Smith Dr., RR#3
Armstrong, BC V0E 1B1
250-546-0244
Fax: 250-546-0266

Salmon Arm Financial Ltd.(SAF)
Also listed under: *Investment Dealers*
#308, 251 Trans Canada Hwy., NW
Salmon Arm, BC V1E 3B8
250-832-1088
Fax: 250-832-3912
info@salmonarmfinancial.com
www.salmonarmfinancial.com
Former Name: Hammer & Associates Financial Services Ltd.
Ownership: Private
Year Founded: 1998
Profile: The financial planning firm offers a variety of plans including education, retirement, pension, succession, & employee benefit. A range of products & services are provided such as insurance, annuities, RRSPs, RRIFs, RESPs, term deposits, & management & consolidation.
Executives:
Steven J. Hammer, President, Life Insurance Advisor; steve@salmonarmfinancial.com
Kevin Flynn, CFP, CLU, BComm, Specialist, Benefits

Sanderson Securities Ltd.
Also listed under: *Investment Dealers*
Princeton Towers
#410, 123 Second Ave. South
Saskatoon, SK S7K 7E6
306-242-5800
Fax: 306-244-0094
customerservice@sandersonsecurities.ca
www.sandersonsecurities.ca
Profile: Investment & financial planning services are provided.
Executives:
Wayne L. Sanderson, President

Sandra Gewirtz
123 Esther Cres.
Thornhill, ON L4J 3J8
905-709-0262
Ownership: Private
Year Founded: 1980
Executives:
Sandra Gewirtz, Contact

Sandra J. Crocker
PO Box 10046
108 Mile Ranch, BC V0K 2Z0
250-791-0029
sjcrocker@shaw.ca
Executives:
Sandra J. Crocker, CGA

Sandra Papsin Financial
#226, 1 Benvenuto Pl.
Toronto, ON M4V 2L1
416-964-6587
Ownership: Private
Executives:
Sandra Papsin, CFP, RFP, Financial Planner

Sceptre Investment Counsel Limited
Also listed under: *Investment Fund Companies*
#1200, 26 Wellington St. East
Toronto, ON M5E 1W4
416-601-9898
Fax: 416-367-8716
800-265-1888
mail@sceptre.ca
www.sceptre.ca
Ownership: Public
Year Founded: 1955
Number of Employees: 50
Assets: $10-50 million
Revenues: $10-50 million
Stock Symbol: SZ
Profile: Sceptre Investment Counsel Limited provides the following services: investment management to institutional clients; pension & savings plans to corporations, municipalities, universities, foundations & other organizations; & personal asset-management to individual investors.

Executives:
Richard Lee Knowles, President/CEO
Matthew Baillie, Managing Director
John J. Brophy, Managing Director
Glenn Inamoto, Managing Director
David B. Pennycook, Managing Director
Mario D. Richard, Managing Director
F. John Stittle, Managing Director
David R. Morris, Chief Financial Officer
Robert R. Lorimer, Vice-President
James A. Sutherland, Vice-President
Directors:
W. Ross Walker, Chair
Richard Lee Knowles
Patricia Meredith
Arthur R.A. Scace, QC
David R. Shaw
Robert Thomson
Sceptre:
Balanced Growth Fund
RRSP Eligible; Inception Year: 1985;
Bond Fund
RRSP Eligible; Inception Year: 1985; Fund Managers:
Thomas Czitron
Equity Growth Fund
RRSP Eligible; Inception Year: 1986; Fund Managers:
Allan Jacobs
Global Equity Fund
RRSP Eligible; Inception Year: 1986; Fund Managers:
Putnam Sub-Advisory Company Inc.
US Equity Fund
RRSP Eligible; Inception Year: 1998;
Canadian Equity Fund
RRSP Eligible; Inception Year: 1998;

Schroder Investment Management North America Limited - Canadian Representative Office
Also listed under: *Foreign Banks Representative Offices*
Canada Trust Tower, BCE Place
#4720, 161 Bay St.
Toronto, ON M5J 2S1
416-360-1200
Fax: 416-360-1202
www.schroders.com/ca
Former Name: Schroder Investment Management Canada Limited
Ownership: Office of Schroders plc, London, UK.
Profile: The Canadian office offers a wide range of investment products. Its global presence provides an integrated international research ability.

Schroeder Consulting
#212, 218 LaRonge Rd.
Saskatoon, SK S7K 8E5
306-931-7696
Profile: The organization is affiliated with Equitable Life Insurance Company of Canada.

Executives:
Darrell R. Schroeder, CFP, Financial Planner

Scotia Cassels Investment Counsel Limited
PO Box 85
#1200, 1 Queen St. East
Toronto, ON M5C 2W5
416-814-4000
Fax: 416-814-4455
Executives:
Jill Pepall, Chief Investment Officer

Seabrooke Financial
#9, 1600 Lansdowne St. West
Peterborough, ON K9J 7C7
705-743-1221
Fax: 705-743-4890

Seamark Asset Management Ltd.
#310, 1801 Hollis St.
Halifax, NS B3J 3N4
902-423-9367
Fax: 902-423-1518
information@seamark.ca
www.seamark.ca
Ownership: Public
Year Founded: 1982
Number of Employees: 35
Assets: $1-10 billion
Revenues: $5-10 million
Stock Symbol: SM
Profile: SEAMARK provides investment management services throughout Canada. It serves institutional clients, mutual fund companies, private clients & the managed portfolio advisory programs of Canadian investment dealers. It is listed on the Toronto Stock Exchange.

Executives:
Peter Marshall, Chair; marshall@seamark.ca
Robert McKim, President/CEO; mckim@seamark.ca
George Loughery, Vice-President, Research; loughery@seamark.ca
Tom MacLaren, Vice-President, Fixed Income; maclaren@seamark.ca
Branches:
Toronto
The Exchange Tower
#1800, 130 King St. West
Toronto, ON M5X 1E3 Canada
416-945-6645
Fax: 416-945-6646

Secord Kolo Wealth Management Group
#407, 638 - 11 Ave. SW
Calgary, AB T2R 0E2
403-292-0949
Fax: 403-292-0926
Executives:
Ian Secord, CFP, RFP, Financial Planner

Securcor Strategic Financial Solutions
Briarwood Business Park
#300, 420 North Service Rd.
Oakville, ON L6H 5R2
905-815-0526
Fax: 905-338-1560
info@securcor.com
www.securcor.com
Former Name: Securcor Financial Group
Profile: Customized securitization & structured financing services are provided to mid & large sized Canadian companies.

Executives:
Brian A. Rodd, President/CEO, Securcor Financial Group; barodd@securcor.com
Dara Coulter, Chief Financial Officer, Securcor Financial Group
Peter J. Freill, Managing Director
Jason Patterson, Managing Director
Lucy Smallbone, Director, Finance; lucys@securcor.com
Affiliated Companies:
Leasebank Capital Corporation

Securitel Canada
Also listed under: *Investment Dealers*
#100, 17, rue Valiquette
Trois-Rivières, QC G8T 3R4
819-371-1161
securitel@iforum.ca
Executives:
Louis G. Dumas, President

Security Financial Services & Investments Corp.
#406, 1 Yorkdale Rd.
Toronto, ON M6A 3A1
416-964-0440
Fax: 416-964-0091
888-988-0055
info@securityfinancial.ca
www.securityfinancial.ca
Year Founded: 1978
Profile: The independent financial planning firm provides the following planning services: tax, estate, retirement, investment, education, insurance & corporate. Mortgages, loans & lines of credit are offered through the company's alliances.

Cecilia Mendonca, Manager, Operations
Executives:
Leo Belmonte, BA, CFP, FMA, FCSI, CEO
Claire Xu, MBA, PFP, Associate Financial Advisor

Security Holdings Ltd.
#2, 8 Centennial Rd.
Hampton, NB E5N 6N2
506-832-1512
Fax: 506-832-1510
Profile: The firm is engaged in retirement & estate planning.

Select Financial Services Inc.
Also listed under: *Investment Dealers*
#200, 193 Pinebush Rd.
Cambridge, ON N1R 7H8
519-622-9613
Fax: 519-622-4612
Ownership: Private
Year Founded: 1985
Number of Employees: 8
Profile: The mutual fund dealer & financial planning firm offers estate planning, insurance services, RRSPs, group benefits, annuities, registered retirement income funds, GICs & mutual funds.

Branches:
London
#5, 650 Colborne St.
London, ON N6A 5A1 Canada
519-645-7163
Fax: 519-645-8536
Gary Alan Price, Financial Planner

Selectpath Benefits & Financial Inc
Plattswood Centre
#101, 219 Oxford St. West
London, ON N6H 1S5
519-675-1177
Fax: 519-675-1331
888-327-5777
info@selectpath.ca
www.selectpath.ca
Former Name: Select Benefit Services; Sabourin Financial Group
Year Founded: 1999
Profile: The following products & services are available: retirement & estate planning, registered & non-registered investment management, risk & wealth management, pension transfers, mortgages, banking services, RRSPs & RESPs, insurance & mutual funds. The company is allied with Manulife Securities International Ltd., a mutual fund dealer.

Selectpath Benefits & Financial Inc (continued)
Jamie Stiles, LLB, CGA, Manager, Business Operations

Sentinel Financial Management Corp.

#300, 128 - 4th Ave. South
Saskatoon, SK S7K 1M8
306-652-7225
Fax: 306-665-7754
800-667-3929
sentinel@sentinelgroup.ca
www.sentinel.sk.ca
Year Founded: 1994
Executives:
Merlin Chouinard, President
Branches:
Calgary
400-1109 - 17th Ave. SW
Calgary, AB T2T 5R9 Canada
403-531-1524
Fax: 403-531-1148
vincent@apexperformance.ca
Winnipeg
#520, 500 Portage Ave.
Winnipeg, MB R3C 3X1 Canada
204-944-8750
Fax: 204-942-5431
rblacker@sentinellife.com

Sentry Select Capital Corp.

Also listed under: *Investment Fund Companies*
The Exchange Tower
PO Box 104
#2850, 130 King St. West
Toronto, ON M5X 1A4
416-861-8729
Fax: 416-364-1330
888-246-6656
info@sentryselect.com
www.sentryselect.com
Ownership: Public.
Assets: $1-10 billion Year End: 20060000
Stock Symbol: SYI
Profile: Sentry Select Capital is a Canadian investment manager. Working in the income trust sector, the company provides administrative, investment & marketing services to the following: exchange-listed closed-end funds, principal-protected notes, flow-through limited partnerships & mutuals funds.

Executives:
John F. Driscoll, President/CEO
Al Canale, Sr. Vice-President, Corporate Development
Raniero Corsini, Sr. Vice-President, Global Structured Products
Michael Kovacs, Sr. Vice-President, Sales
David M. Schwartz, Sr. Vice-President
Gordon Thompson, Sr. Vice-President, Corporate Development
John Vooglaid, Sr. Vice-President/CFO
Wolfgang Kruning, Vice-President, International Dealer Relations
Brian J. McOstrich, Vice-President, Marketing
Don Perras, Vice-President, Business Development
Ara Nalbandian, Sr. Manager, Portfolio
Michael Simpson, CFA, Sr. Manager, Portfolio
John Sinkins, Sr. Manager, Portfolio
Laura Lau, Manager, Portfolio
Philip Yuzpe, Manager, Strategic Planning & Research
Ari Silverberg, Director, Real Estate Investments
CAPVEST Income Corp.:
Specialty Products Fund
RRSP Eligible; Inception Year: 2005;
Mortgage-Backed Securities Limited Partnership:
Adjustable Rate Income FundInception Year: 2004; Fund Managers:
Fixed Income Discount Advisory Company
Adjustable Rate Income II FundInception Year: 2005; Fund Managers:
Fixed Income Discount Advisory Company
Income Trust FundInception Year: 2003; Fund Managers:
Fixed Income Discount Advisory Company
NCE:
Diversified Flow-Through (05-02) Limited Partnership FundInception Year: 0; Fund Managers:
Kevin MacLean
GlennMacNeill
Pro-Vest:
Growth & Income FundInception Year: 2004; Fund Managers:
James Alexander (San McIntyre
Sentry:
Canadian Energy Growth Fund
RRSP Eligible; Inception Year: 1997; Fund Managers:
Glenn MacNeill
Canadian Resource Fund
RRSP Eligible; Inception Year: 2000; Fund Managers:
Glenn MacNeill
Precious Metals Growth Fund
RRSP Eligible; Inception Year: 1997; Fund Managers:
Kevin MacLean
Canadian Income Fund
RRSP Eligible; Inception Year: 2002; Fund Managers:
James Alexander (San McIntyre
REIT Fund
RRSP Eligible; Inception Year: 1997; Fund Managers:
James Alexander (San McIntyre
Focused 50 Income Fund
RRSP Eligible; Inception Year: 2003; Fund Managers:
James Alexander (San McIntyre
Money Market Fund
RRSP Eligible; Inception Year: 2003; Fund Managers:
James Alexander (San McIntyre
Diversified Total Return Fund
RRSP Eligible; Inception Year: 2005; Fund Managers:
Gordon R. Higgins
Small Cap Income Fund
RRSP Eligible; Inception Year: 2005; Fund Managers:
James Alexander (San McIntyre
Dividend Fund
RRSP Eligible; Inception Year: 2006; Fund Managers:
Gordon R. Higgins
Principal-Protected Blue Chip Notes Fund
RRSP Eligible; Inception Year: 2004;
Strategic Energy Fund
RRSP Eligible; Inception Year: 2002; Fund Managers:
Glenn MacNeill
Diversified Income Trust Portfolio FundInception Year: 1997; Fund Managers:
James Alexander (San McIntyre
Diversified Income Trust Portfolio II FundInception Year: 2002; Fund Managers:
James Alexander (San McIntyre
Premier Value Income Trust FundInception Year: 2005; Fund Managers:
James Alexander (San McIntyre
Focused Growth & Income Trust FundInception Year: 2002; Fund Managers:
James Alexander (San McIntyre
Commercial & Industrial Securities Income Trust FundInception Year: 2002; Fund Managers:
James Alexander (San McIntyre
Select 50 S-1 Income Trust FundInception Year: 2003; Fund Managers:
James Alexander (San McIntyre
Alliance Split Income Trust FundInception Year: 2004;
Multi Select Income Trust FundInception Year: 2004;
Select Commodities Income Trust FundInception Year: 2005; Fund Managers:
James Alexander (San McIntyre
Blue-Chip Income Trust Fund
RRSP Eligible; Inception Year: 2001;
Global Index Income Trust FundInception Year: 2001;
Diversified Preferred Share Trust FundInception Year: 2002;
Global DiSCS Trust 04-1 FundInception Year: 2004;
Oil Sands Split Trust FundInception Year: 2003;
Balanced Fund
RRSP Eligible; Inception Year: 2005; Fund Managers:
Gordon R. Higgins
Sentry FIDAC:
US Mortgage Trust FundInception Year: 2005; Fund Managers:
Fixed Income Discount Advisory Company
Sentry Rogers:
International Commodity Index Principal-Protected Notes Fund
RRSP Eligible; Inception Year: 2005; Fund Managers:
Diapason Commodities Management SA

SF Partnership, LLP

Also listed under: *Accountants*
The Madison Centre
#400, 4950 Yonge St.
Toronto, ON M2N 6K1
416-250-1212
Fax: 416-250-1225
info@sfgroup.ca
www.sfgroup.ca
Former Name: Solursh Feldman & Partners
Ownership: Private
Year Founded: 1997
Number of Employees: 96
Assets: $1-5 million Year End: 20051200
Revenues: $10-50 million Year End: 20051200
Profile: The full-service chartered accountancy firm has experience & expertise in the following service areas: audit & accounting, corporate & personal taxation, management advisory, insolvency, career transition & personal financial counselling, computer consulting, government grants & programs, forensic services, estate, & retirement & family planning.

Executives:
Stanley Rapkin, Managing Partner; 416-250-1212; srapkin@sfgroup.ca
Alex Mathews, Principal; amathews@sfgroup.ca
Ellis Orlan, Principal; eorlan@sfgroup.ca
Eugene Aceti, Partner; eaceti@sfgroup.ca
Gary Crystal, Partner; 416-250-1212; gcrystal@sfgroup.ca
Jason Crystal, Partner; jcrystal@sfgroup.ca
Irving Feldman, Partner; 416-250-1212; ifeldman@sfgroup.ca
Harold Franks, Partner; mfranks@sfgroup.ca
Michael Fromstein, Partner; 416-250-1212; mfromstein@sfgroup.ca
Paul Mandel, Partner; 416-250-1212; pmandel@sfgroup.ca
Saul Muskat, Partner; smuskat@sfgroup.ca
Phillip Spring, Partner; pspring@sfgroup.ca
Bradley Waese, Partner; 416-250-1212; bwaese@sfgroup.ca
Trustees:
Steven Goldberg; 416-250-1212; sgoldberg@sfgroup.ca

Shah Financial Planning Inc.(SFP)

Also listed under: *Investment Dealers*
#204, 3459 Sheppard Ave. East
Toronto, ON M1T 3K5
416-298-4900
Fax: 416-298-9759
info@shahfinancial.ca
www.shahfinancial.ca
Former Name: Shah Business Services
Year Founded: 1976
Profile: The firm offers planning in the following areas: financial, tax, estate & retirement. Other services include accounting, bookkkeeping, tax preparation, investments & life insurance.

Executives:
Narendra Shah, Financial Advisor
Ekta Chauhan, Financial Advisor
Dipa Shah, Tax Advisor

Sharp Edmonds Sharp LLP

#201, 111 Railside Rd.
Toronto, ON M3A 1B2
416-441-6357
Fax: 416-441-3156
johnsharp@sharpaccountants.com
www.sharpaccountants.com
Former Name: Sharp & Sharp
Year Founded: 1978
Executives:
John Sharp, President
Joe Edmonds, Partner
Don Sharp, Partner

Shirjorg Financial

PO Box 670
#4, 111 - 1st Ave.
Leader, SK S0N 1H0
306-628-3333
Fax: 306-628-4455
shirjorg@sk.sympatico.ca
www.sasktelwebsite.net/shirjorg
Profile: The firm offers financial planning, investments & insurance. Licensed in Saskatchewan & Alberta, the company's planning services include ranch & farm succession.

Executives:
Patricia Jorgenson, Certified Financial Planner
Watson Shircliff, Certified Financial Planner

Sidler & Company LLP

Also listed under: *Accountants*
#204, 6465 Millcreek Dr.
Mississauga, ON L5N 5R3
905-821-9215
Fax: 905-821-8212

info@sidler.ca
www.sidler.ca
Ownership: Private.
Year Founded: 1987
Number of Employees: 30
Assets: $1-5 million Year End: 20061013
Revenues: $1-5 million Year End: 20061013
Profile: Services include estate planning. An affiliated company is Sidler Clarke Inc.

Executives:
Richard Clarke, Partner
Curtis Link, Partner
Kalin L. McDonald, Partner
Jason O'Halloran, Partner
Annette Silva, Partner

Signet Financial Group Ltd.

#1002, 475 Howe St.
Vancouver, BC V6C 2B3
604-682-9505
Fax: 604-681-0059
info@signetfinancial.com
www.signetfinancial.com
Profile: Financial, retirement & estate planning services are available. Individual & group insurance is also offered.

Don D. Eyford, CFP, CLU, CHFC
Executives:
Alan Leader, CLU, RHU, CHFC
Fred Schneider, FLMI
Daniel Sember, B.Econ., CFP, CLU, CHFC, RHU

Sinden Financial Group(SFG)

307 Commissionners Rd. West
London, ON N6J 1Y4
519-471-9399
Fax: 519-474-2151
admin@sindenfinancial.com
www.sindenfinancial.com
Executives:
Robert Sinden, Financial Planner; robert@sindenfinancial.com
Kate Thompson, Contact; kate@sindenfinancial.com

Sionna Investment Managers

#1600, 8 King St. East
Toronto, ON M5C 1B5
416-203-8803
Fax: 416-203-8033
info@sionna.ca
www.sionna.ca
Assets: $1-10 billion
Profile: The firm manages Canadian equity portfolios.

Executives:
Maureen Farrow, Chair/COO
Kim Shannon, CFA, MBA, President/CIO
Lawrence Li, Vice-President, Systems & Portfolio Administration
Mary Lou McKeever, Vice-President, Operations

SISIP Financial Services/ Les Services financiers du RARM

National Defence Headquarters
234 Laurier Ave. West, Ground Fl.
Ottawa, ON K1A 0K2
613-233-2177
Fax: 613-233-5857
800-267-6681
www.sisip.ca
Profile: Provides financial products & services exclusively to the serving & retired military community.

Branches:
Alouette
CANEX Bldg. 147, 3 Wing Bagotville
PO Box 548
Alouette, QC G0V 1A0 Canada
418-677-1110
Borden
Bldg. 0-121, CANEX Plaza
PO Box 1
36 El Alamein Rd.
Borden, ON L0M 1C0 Canada
705-424-2262
Fax: 705-424-2262
Cold Lake
CANEX Mall, 4 Wing Cold Lake
PO Box 6320, Forces Sta. Forces
Cold Lake, AB T9M 2C5 Canada
780-594-4562
Fax: 780-594-4589
Courcelette
Valcartier Garrison
100, rue Dubé
Courcelette, QC G0A 1R1 Canada
418-844-0111
Fax: 418-844-0114
Greenwood
CANEX Mall, 14 Wing Greenwood
PO Box 1705
Ward Rd.
Greenwood, NS B0P 1N0 Canada
902-765-6714
Fax: 902-765-6455
Halifax
Bldg. S-21, A Block, Stradacona, CFB Halifax
PO Box 99000, Forces Sta. Forces
Halifax, NS B3K 5X5 Canada
902-425-6926
Kingston
CANEX Mall, CFB Kingston
PO Box 1749
29 Niagara Park Dr.
Kingston, ON K7L 5J6 Canada
613-547-1172
Lancaster Park
CANEX Bldg. 299, CFB Edmonton
PO Box 897
Falaise Ave.
Lancaster Park, AB T0A 2H0 Canada
780-973-3130
Fax: 780-973-3193
Lazo
CANEX Bldg. #1375, 19 Wing Comox
PO Box 400
Lazo, BC V0R 2K0 Canada
250-339-6597
Oromocto
Bldg. A-41, CFB Gagetown
Oromocto, NB E2V 4J5 Canada
506-357-3666
Fax: 506-357-3321
Petawawa
27 Festubert Blvd.
Petawawa, ON K8H 1N3 Canada
613-687-0025
Fax: 613-687-4108
Richelain
Jean-Victor Allard Bldg., St-Jean Garrison
PO Box 100
Richelain, QC J0J 1R0 Canada
Shilo
Bldg. L125, CANEX Mall, CFB Shilo
PO Box 99
Shilo, MB R0K 2A0 Canada
204-765-4675
Fax: 204-765-2317
St. John's
Bldg. 806, CFS St. John's
PO Box 2028
Churchill Ave.
St. John's, NL A1C 6B5 Canada
709-570-8481
Trenton
8 Wing Trenton
PO Box 1000, Forces Sta. Forces
Trenton, ON K0K 3W0 Canada
613-965-3258
Victoria
CANEX Bldg. 98 Naden, CFB Esquimalt
PO Box 410
#110, 174 Wilson St.
Victoria, BC V9A 7N7 Canada
250-360-0006
Fax: 360- 20-
Winnipeg
Bldg. 63, 17 Wing Winnipeg
PO Box 17000, Forces Sta. Forces
Winnipeg, MB R3J 3Y5 Canada
204-984-3222
Fax: 204-984-3343

Sloan Partners, LLP

Also listed under: *Pension & Money Management Companies; Accounting & Law*
#400, 7620 Yonge St.
Thornhill, ON L4J 1V9
905-886-7735
Fax: 905-764-6892
info@sloangroup.ca
www.sloangroup.ca
Former Name: Sloan Paskowitz Adelman
Ownership: Private
Year Founded: 1989
Profile: The firm is affiliated with Infologix Inc.

Executives:
Allen Sloan, Managing Partner
Dominic Kok, Partner
Jerry Paskowitz, Partner
Stan Swartz, Partner
Sam Metalin, Team Leader
Michael Spigelman, Associate

Solguard Financial Limited

#402, 645 Fort St.
Victoria, BC V8W 1G2
250-385-3636
Fax: 250-385-6361
877-500-3636
info@solguard.com
www.solguard.com
Ownership: Private
Number of Employees: 4
Executives:
W. Anthony Southwell, CFP, RFP, CIM; tsouthwell@solguard.com
J. Mark Gouws, CFP, CLU, CH.F.C.; mgouws@solguard.bc.ca
Branches:
Vancouver
#805, 675 West Hastings St.
Vancouver, BC V6B 1N2 Canada
604-688-9577
Fax: 604-688-7608
800-663-0644
info@solguard.com
John Gives

Solid Financial Options

#1529 - 20th Ave. NW
Calgary, AB T2M 1G7
403-233-2333
Fax: 403-266-3377
jfahie@pipfs.com
Ownership: Private
Number of Employees: 4
Revenues: Under $1 million
Executives:
Tyler Stanford, Investment Analyst; tstanford@pipfs.com

Soltermann Financial Inc.

968 Trillium Trail
Lakehurst, ON K0L 2J0
705-657-7700
Fax: 705-657-7156
www.soltermann.ca
Ownership: Private
Year Founded: 1990
Number of Employees: 5
Executives:
Mark Soltermann, RFP, President

Sound Financial Strategies Inc.

#215, 469 Bouchard St.
Sudbury, ON P3E 2K8
705-522-1422
Fax: 705-522-8335
800-837-1670
www.soundfs.ca
Ownership: Private
Profile: The independent financial planning firm provides services related to the areas of investment, retirement, tax, weatlh & estate planning.

Executives:
David T. Yurich, CFP, RFP, B.Comm., Managing Partner; dave@soundfs.ca
Susan Nardi, Hon.BA, CFP, Manager, Administration & Operations; susan@soundfs.ca

Southcott Davoli Professional Corporation
Also listed under: *Accountants*
PO Box 68
76 Main St. West
Grimsby, ON L3M 4G1
905-945-4942
Fax: 905-945-0306
contactus@southdav.com
Executives:
Delight Davoli
Mark Southcott

Southwest Financial Services Inc.
Also listed under: *Pension & Money Management Companies*
1070 Nashua Ave.
London, ON N6K 2C3
519-471-8292
Fax: 519-472-1493
dbradyca@rogers.com
Ownership: Private
Year Founded: 1991
Number of Employees: 5
Assets: Under $1 million
Revenues: Under $1 million
Executives:
David Brady, CA, CFP, President

Spectris Capital Finance Corporation
#1052, 1930 Yonge St.
Toronto, ON M4S 1Z4
416-491-7230
Ted.Danielson@SpectrisCapital.com
www.spectriscapital.com
Profile: The company is a corporate finance advisor to businesses.
Executives:
C.E. Ted Danielson, Managing Director
Stan Newman, Managing Director

Spergel & Associates Inc.
#201, 505 Consumers Rd.
Toronto, ON M2J 4V8
416-497-1660
Fax: 416-494-7199
877-776-7656
aspergel@trustee.com
www.trustee.com
Year Founded: 1989
Number of Employees: 10
Executives:
Alan Spergel, President
Directors:
Joe Albert
Harold Mandelbaum
Alan Spergel

Spire Sharwood Financial Inc.
Also listed under: *Financing & Loan Companies; Investment Management*
#100, 8 King St. East
Toronto, ON M5C 1B5
416-869-1598
Fax: 416-366-4892
info@sharwood.com
www.spiresharwood.com
Former Name: Sharwood Inc.; Sharwood & Company Limited; Sharwood Bioventures Inc.
Ownership: Private
Year Founded: 1976
Number of Employees: 10
Executives:
Timothy Gray, President/CEO
Gordon R. Sharwood, Chair
Michael Caven, Managing Director
Jeffrey Kahn, Managing Director
Jim McMinn, Managing Director
Stephen Sloan, Managing Director

SSQ Financial Group
Also listed under: *Federal & Provincial; Investment Management*
PO Box 10500, Sainte-Foy Stn. Sainte-Foy
2525, boul Laurier
Québec, QC G1V 4H6
418-651-7000
Fax: 418-688-7791
888-900-3457
communications@ssq.ca, mutuallife@ssq.ca
www.ssq.ca
Former Name: SSQ Vie Investissement et Retraite (Astra)
Ownership: Private
Year Founded: 1944
Number of Employees: 1,000
Assets: $1-10 billion
Revenues: $10-50 million
Profile: IP
Executives:
Yves Demers, Chair
Richard Bell, CEO, SSQ, Life Insurance Company Inc.
Marie-Josée Blanchette, CEO, SSQ, General Insurance Company Inc.
Jean Morency, CEO, SSQ, Realty Inc.
Affiliated Companies:
SSQ, Société d'assurance-vie inc

Staley, Okada & Partners, Chartered Accountants
#400, 889 West Pender St.
Vancouver, BC V6C 3B2
604-694-6070
Fax: 604-585-8377
info@staleyokada.com
www.staleyokada.com
Former Name: Staley, Okada, Chandler & Scott
Year Founded: 1959
Executives:
Larry Okada, CA, CPA, Managing Partner
Jitender Bhagirath, CA, Partner
Dean Larocque, CA, CFP, CPA, Partner, Standards
Ken Scott, CA, CPA, Partner
Gary Traher, CA, CPA, Partner, Personnel
Branches:
Surrey
10190 - 152A St., 3rd Fl.
Surrey, BC V3R 1J7 Canada
604-585-8300
Fax: 604-585-8377

Steven Brates
Also listed under: *Accountants*
#209, 5805 Whittle Rd.
Mississauga, ON L4Z 2J1
905-502-7505
Fax: 905-502-7662
Profile: Tax services are provided.
Executives:
Steven Brates, Principal

Stewart & Kett Financial Advisors Inc.
Also listed under: *Accountants*
#911, 123 Front St. West
Toronto, ON M5J 2M2
416-362-6322
Fax: 416-362-6302
www.stewartkett.com
Former Name: Stewart & Co. Financial Advisors Inc./Kett Financial Services
Ownership: Private
Year Founded: 1996
Number of Employees: 4
Profile: Stewart & Kett provides comprehensive, advice-only financial planning, accounting & tax services for business owners, senior executives, trusts & retirees. The following planning areas include: cash management, tax, investment, retirement, risk management & estate.
Executives:
Cynthia Kett, CA, CGA, RFP, CFP, Principal; ckett@stewartkett.com
David H. Stewart, MBA, RFP, CFP, Principal; dstewart@stewartkett.com

Stewart Financial Services
Also listed under: *Pension & Money Management Companies; Insurance Companies*
1282 Cornwall Rd., #B
Oakville, ON L6J 7W5
905-845-0990
Fax: 905-845-2882
888-845-0990
drew@stewartfinancial.ca
www.stewartfinancial.ca
Ownership: Private
Number of Employees: 8
Executives:
Drew L. Stewart, CFP, CLU, CH.F.C., Partner
Duncan Stewart, MBA, CIM, Director, Operations

Stonebridge Financial Corporation/ Stonebridge Financière
Also listed under: *Financing & Loan Companies*
#1201, Adelaide St. East
Toronto, ON Toronto
416-364-3001
Fax: 416-364-1557
info@stonebridge.ca
www.stonebridge.ca
Ownership: Canada Life Assurance Co., Manufacturers Life Insurance Co. & Industrial Alliance Insurance & Financial Services Inc., hold minority equity.
Year Founded: 1998
Profile: The company is engaged in structuring financings in the institutional market. The following financing services are provided: project finance, bulk lease finance, structured finance, advisory services & administrative services. A variety of domestic & international industries are served. Stonebridge specializes in the energy, infrastructure, environment & healthcare sectors.
Executives:
Denis Bourassa, MBA, Partner; dbourassa@stonebridge.ca
Robert M. Colliver, CFA, Partner; rcolliver@stonebridge.ca
Darrell Salter, Managing Director, Corporate & Portfolio Administration
John Estey, Director, Lease Financing
Jim Cahill, Vice-President, Structured & Project Financing
Rhea Dechaine, Manager, Lease Financing
Directors:
Richard Drouin, Chair
Denis Bourassa
Robert Colliver
Marc Dorion
Laurie Harding
Richard Legault
Branches:
Montréal
#2350, 1000, rue Sherbrooke ouest
Montréal, QC H3A 3G4
514-842-5001
Fax: 514-842-0557

StoneCreek Consulting Inc.
2245 Albert St.
Regina, SK S4P 2V5
306-525-7280
Fax: 306-525-7281
877-417-7280
info@stonecreek.biz
www.stonecreek.biz
Former Name: LifePlan Financial Consultants Inc.
Profile: The company offers business transition services to farmers, business owners, self-employed professionals & individuals. Issues such as taxation, succession planning, & retirement are covered.
Executives:
Abe E. Toews, CFP, CLU, CH.F.C, Chartered Financial Consultant
Tera Marr, Manager, Client Relationship
Greg Toews, Exec. Account Manager

Stoodley Financial Services Inc.
1 Main St.
Grand Bank, NL A0E 1W0
709-832-2459
Executives:
Allan M. Stoodley, CFP, CLU, CH.F.C., Contact

Strategic Analysis Corporation(SAC)
Also listed under: *Bond Rating Companies*
PO Box 2003
#1400, 20 Eglinton Ave. West
Toronto, ON M4R 1K8
416-489-3603
Fax: 416-489-8762
877-214-5641
info@strategicanalysis.ca
www.strategicanalysis.ca
Former Name: SAC The Solvency Analysis Corp.

Year Founded: 1979
Number of Employees: 9
Profile: SAC is a capital markets research firm with emphasis on the Dow Jones, S&P 500 & TSE 300 indices. The company publishes monthly valuation charts for each market, sector & individual stock for client use. SAC also provides a credit rating service covering the corporations on the TSE 300 index.

Executives:
C. Ross Healy, Chair/CEO

Strategic Financial Concepts Inc.

Also listed under: *Pension & Money Management Companies*
Capital Place
#406, 9707-110th St.
Edmonton, AB T5N 1R5
780-488-2644
Fax: 780-488-0844
800-463-1852
service@strategicfinancial.net
www.strategicfinancial.net
Former Name: Dataplan Consultants Limited
Ownership: Private
Year Founded: 1980
Number of Employees: 8
Assets: Under $1 million
Revenues: Under $1 million
Executives:
Darrell Starrie, RFP, CFP, PRP, CLU, CH.F.C., President
Branches:
Calgary
#301, 1100-8th Ave. SW
Calgary, AB T2R 0J6 Canada
780-488-2644
Fax: 780-488-0844
800-463-1852

Strategic Financial Services

Also listed under: *Pension & Money Management Companies*
#500, 2950 Douglas St.
Victoria, BC V8T 4N4
250-383-3634
Fax: 250-383-3027
800-663-7603
Ownership: Private
Year Founded: 1986
Number of Employees: 3
Profile: The financial planning company is an employee benefits & special risk consulting broker. Employee group benefits include group RRSP, group pension (RPP) & deferred profit sharing plan (DPSP), group dental & health, group disability insurance & executive life & disability insurance.

Strategic Wealth Planning Inc.

Quaker Landing
#150, 33 Ochterloney St.
Dartmouth, NS B2Y 4P5
902-481-0159
info@strategicwealth.ca
www.strategicwealth.ca
Year Founded: 1999
Profile: The independent firm provides comprehensive & directed financial planning to individuals. Advisory & consulting services are offered to financial planners & advisors. The following planning services are provided: education, retirement, estate, investment, cash management & budgeting, & risk management & insurance.

Executives:
Glen J. Furlong, CFP, CLU, CH.F.C., President
Matthew Furlong, B. Comm., Manager, Business Development

Strategy Institute

#401, 401 Richmond St. West
Toronto, ON M5V 3A8
416-944-9200
Fax: 416-944-0403
866-298-9343
info@strategyinstitute.com
www.strategyinstitute.com
Ownership: Private.
Year Founded: 1994
Profile: Changes & trends in business are communicated by the independent, research-based organization. Education, conferences, seminars & publications are provided to professionals & executives. The USA office is located at 230 Park Ave., 10th Fl., New York City, NY, 10169.

Executives:
David Laird, MBA, MSc, President

Stronach Financial Group

15 Manorpark Ct.
Toronto, ON M2J 1A1
416-497-3590
Fax: 416-495-9034
800-377-4761
daniel@stronach-financial.com
www.stronach-financial.com
Ownership: Private
Year Founded: 1993
Profile: Financial planning & management are provided to high net worth Canadians by the independent fee-only advisor firm.

Executives:
Daniel F. Stronach, BA, CFP, RFP, President

Summerhill Capital Management Inc.

Also listed under: *Pension & Money Management Companies*
#1108, 1 St. Clair Ave. West
Toronto, ON M4V 1K6
416-515-9429
Fax: 416-515-9499
info@sumcap.com
www.sumcap.com
Ownership: Private.
Year Founded: 2004
Assets: $100-500 million Year End: 20060930
Executives:
Mary Throop, President; 416-515-1492; mthroop@sumcap.com

Summit Financial Planners Inc.

#103, 2802 - 30th St.
Vernon, BC V1T 8G7
250-542-5500
Fax: 250-542-0044
866-888-8448
www.summitfinancial.bc.ca
Year Founded: 1988
Profile: Personal financial management is provided by the independent financial advisor firm. Planning services offered include the following: retirement, wealth, estate & succession & contingency.

Executives:
Calvin Hoy, Financial Advisor
Rob Irving, MSc., CFP, CLU, Certified Financial Planner, Chartered Life Underwriter
Greg Mussenden, R.F.P., CFP, Financial Planner
Branches:
Kelowna
#8, 2070 Harvey Ave.
Kelowna, BC V1Y 8P8
250-868-0555
Fax: 250-868-3777
Revelstoke
#6, 109 - 2nd St.
Revelstoke, BC V1Y 8P8
250-837-3555
dorothy@summitfinancial.bc.ca

Sun Life Financial Inc.

Also listed under: *Federal & Provincial*
150 King St. West
Toronto, ON M5H 1J9
416-979-9966
Fax: 416-979-4853
www.sunlife.com
Ownership: Public
Year Founded: 1865
Number of Employees: 16,500
Assets: $100 billion + Year End: 20051231
Revenues: $10-100 billion Year End: 20051231
Stock Symbol: SLF
Profile: IF

Executives:
Donald A. Stewart, CEO
Kevin P. Dougherty, President, Sun Life Financial Canada
Stephan Rajotte, President, Sun Life Financial Asia
Robert C. Salipante, President, Sun Life Financial US
David W. Davies, Chair, Sun Life Financial UK
James M.A. Anderson, Exec. Vice-President, Chief Investment Officer
Thomas A. Bogart, Exec. Vice-President/Chief Legal Officer
Dean A. Connor, Exec. Vice-President
Robert W. Mansbridge, Exec. Vice-President, CIO
Richard P. McKenney, Exec. Vice-President/CFO
Michael P. Stramaglia, Exec. Vice-President, Chief Asset & Liability Management Officer
Directors:
Ronald W. Osborne, FCA, Chair
James C. Baillie
George W. Carmany, III
John H. Clappison, FCA
William R. Fatt
David A. Ganong, CM
Germaine Gibara, CFA
Krystyna T. Hoeg, CA
David W. Kerr, CA
Idalene F. Kesner
Bertin F. Nadeau
Donald A. Stewart, FIA, FCIA
W. Vickery Stoughton
Affiliated Companies:
McLean Budden Ltd.
Sun Life Assurance Company of Canada
Sun Life Financial Trust Inc.
Waterloo
227 King St. South
Waterloo, ON N2J 4C5 Canada
519-888-3900

INVESTMENT MANAGEMENT

Sunshine Coast Credit Union

Also listed under: *Credit Unions/Caisses Populaires*
PO Box 799
985 Sunshine Coast Hwy.
Gibsons, BC V0N 1V0
604-886-2122
Fax: 604-886-0797
administration@sunshineccu.net
www.sunshineccu.com
Ownership: Member-owned
Year Founded: 1941
Number of Employees: 83
Assets: $100-500 million
Revenues: $100-500 million
Profile: A full-service community credit union. Affiliated with SunCu Financial Services Ltd.

Executives:
Dale Eichar, CEO
Rick Cooney, Manager, Operations & Development
Directors:
Brian Beecham, Chair
Karen Archer, 1st Vice-Chair
Bernard Bennett, 2nd Vice-Chair
Stan Anderson
Timothy Anderson
Harris Cole
Elfriede Hofmann
Robert Miller
Margaret Penney
Branches:
Gibsons
PO Box 715
985 Gibsons Coast Way
Gibsons, BC V0N 1V0 Canada
604-886-8121
Fax: 604-886-4831
gibsonsbranch@sunshineccu.com
Madeira Park
PO Box 28
12887 Madeira Park Rd.
Madeira Park, BC V0N 2H0 Canada
604-883-9531
Fax: 604-883-9475
penderbranch@sunshineccu.com
Sechelt
5655 Teredo St.
Sechelt, BC V0N 3A0 Canada
604-885-3255
Fax: 604-885-3278
secheltbranch@sunshineccu.com

Sutherland & Associates Financial Services

#4, 609 Baker St.
Nelson, BC V1L 4J3
250-352-3518
Fax: 250-352-3544
sutherg@netidea.com

Sutherland & Associates Financial Services (continued)
www.sutherlandfinancial.ca
Executives:
Glenn Sutherland, Contact

T.H.A. Bodnar & Company Investment Management Ltd.

Also listed under: *Pension & Money Management Companies*
#4, 69 Sydney St. South
Kitchener, ON N2G 3V1
519-576-1273
Fax: 519-576-2125
877-475-5517
terrybodnar@rogers.com
Ownership: Private
Year Founded: 1999
Number of Employees: 2
Revenues: Under $1 million Year End: 20041231
Profile: The total assets under management are $230,000,000.

Executives:
Terence H.A. Bodnar, President; terrybodnar@rogers.com
Judy Cameron, Vice-President, Canadian Equities; jacameron@sympatico.ca

Tasman Financial Services

#402, 1 Stafford Rd.
Nepean, ON K2H 1B9
613-820-0270
Fax: 613-820-2787
info@tasman.ca
www.tasman.ca
Ownership: Private
Year Founded: 1995
Profile: The following services are offered: retirement planning, estate planning, cash & debt management & investment planning.

Executives:
Scott Robertson, B.Eng, BComm, MBA, CFP, RFP, President

TaxVantage Financial Services

#101, 11 Evergreen Pl.
Winnipeg, MB R3L 2T9
204-992-1000
Fax: 204-477-1323
Ownership: Private
Executives:
Mike Daoust, Chartered Financial Planner, Chartered Life Underwriter
Leslie Daoust, Manager, Operations; ldaoust@taxvantage.ca

Taylor Financial Group Limited

10231 - 121st St.
Edmonton, AB T5N 1K6
780-451-3152
Fax: 780-451-3321
wayne@ethicaladvisor.com
www.ethicaladvisor.com
Ownership: Private
Year Founded: 1970
Number of Employees: 5
Profile: Taylor Financial Group is a fee & commission based financial planner. The company provides retirement lifestyle planning, investment advice & financial counselling.

Executives:
Wayne E. Taylor, PRP, President

TD Asset Management Inc.(TDAM)

Also listed under: *Investment Fund Companies; Investment Management*
77 Bloor St. West, 6th Fl.
Toronto, ON M5S 1M2
800-386-3757
td.mutualfunds@td.com
www.tdassetmanagement.com
Former Name: TD Quantitative Capital
Also Known As: TD Mutual Funds
Ownership: Public. Subsidiary of TD Bank Financial Group
Year Founded: 1987
Stock Symbol: TD
Profile: TDAM provides a diverse range of funds & portfolios. Funds are available at TD Canada Trust branches, through TD Investment Services Inc. representatives, TD Waterhouse Discount Brokerage, Financial Planning & Private Investment Advice, & also by investment dealers, independent brokers, advisors & financial planners.
Executives:
Tim Pinnington, President, TD Mutual Funds
Affiliated Companies:
TD Harbour Capital
GTD:
Managed Income & Moderate Growth Non-Registered Fund
RRSP Eligible; Inception Year: 1999;
US Blue Chip Equity Fund
RRSP Eligible; Inception Year: 1999; Fund Managers:
T. Rowe Price Associates Inc.
Balanced Growth Fund
RRSP Eligible; Inception Year: 1999; Fund Managers:
McLean Budden Limited
Health Sciences Fund
RRSP Eligible; Inception Year: 1999; Fund Managers:
T. Rowe Price Associates Inc.
Global Select Fund
RRSP Eligible; Inception Year: 1999; Fund Managers:
Oppenheimer Funds Inc.
Canadian Bond Fund
RRSP Eligible; Inception Year: 1999; Fund Managers:
Satish C. Rai
GeoffWilson
Canadian Equity Fund
RRSP Eligible; Inception Year: 1999; Fund Managers:
John Smolinski
ScottMargach
Canadian Value Fund
RRSP Eligible; Inception Year: 1999; Fund Managers:
Rachel Volynsky
DougWarwick
Managed Aggressive Growth Non-Registered Fund
RRSP Eligible; Inception Year: 1999;
Managed Aggressive Growth Registered Fund
RRSP Eligible; Inception Year: 1999;
Managed Balanced Growth Non-Registered Fund
RRSP Eligible; Inception Year: 1999;
Managed Balanced Growth Registered Fund
RRSP Eligible; Inception Year: 1999;
Managed Income & Moderate Growth Registered Fund
RRSP Eligible; Inception Year: 1999;
Managed Index Non-Registered Fund
RRSP Eligible; Inception Year: 1999;
Managed Index Registered Fund
RRSP Eligible; Inception Year: 1999;
Money Market Fund
RRSP Eligible; Inception Year: 1999; Fund Managers:
R.B. Kenneth Miner
TD:
Dividend Income Fund
RRSP Eligible; Inception Year: 1994; Fund Managers:
Doug Warwick
MichaelLough
US Equity Fund
RRSP Eligible; Inception Year: 1990; Fund Managers:
Rhonda Dalley
DavidSykes
High Yield Income Fund
RRSP Eligible; Inception Year: 1998; Fund Managers:
Gregory Kocik
NicholasLeach
Balanced Index Fund
RRSP Eligible; Inception Year: 1998; Fund Managers:
Craig Gaskin
Canadian Bond Fund
RRSP Eligible; Inception Year: 1988; Fund Managers:
Geoff Wilson
Satish C.Rai
Canadian Equity Fund
RRSP Eligible; Inception Year: 1998; Fund Managers:
Scott Margach
JohnSmolinski
Monthly Income Fund
RRSP Eligible; Inception Year: 1998; Fund Managers:
Gregory Kocik
DougWarwick
Michael Lough
Mortgage Fund
RRSP Eligible; Inception Year: 1979; Fund Managers:
David McCulla
GeoffWilson
NASDAQ RSP Index Fund
RRSP Eligible; Inception Year: 1999; Fund Managers:
Dino Bourdos
BruceGeddes
NASDAQ RSP Index e Fund
RRSP Eligible; Inception Year: 1999; Fund Managers:
Dino Bourdos
BruceGeddes
Precious Metals Fund
RRSP Eligible; Inception Year: 1994; Fund Managers:
Ari Levy
MargotNaudie
Real Return Bond Fund
RRSP Eligible; Inception Year: 1994; Fund Managers:
Satish C. Rai
GeoffWilson
Resource Fund
RRSP Eligible; Inception Year: 1993; Fund Managers:
Ari Levy
MargotNaudie
Science & Technology GIF II Fund
RRSP Eligible; Inception Year: 2000; Fund Managers:
T. Rowe Price Associates Inc.
US Index (US$) Fund
RRSP Eligible; Inception Year: 1986; Fund Managers:
Craig Gaskin
US Index (US$) e Fund
RRSP Eligible; Inception Year: 1999; Fund Managers:
Craig Gaskin
US Index Fund
RRSP Eligible; Inception Year: 1998; Fund Managers:
Craig Gaskin
US Index e Fund
RRSP Eligible; Inception Year: 1999; Fund Managers:
Craig Gaskin
US Mid-Cap Growth Fund
RRSP Eligible; Inception Year: 1993; Fund Managers:
T. Rowe Price Associates Inc.
US Money Market (US$) Fund
RRSP Eligible; Inception Year: 1988; Fund Managers:
R.B. Kenneth Miner
US RSP Index e Fund
RRSP Eligible; Inception Year: 1999; Fund Managers:
Dino Bourdos
BruceGeddes
US Small Cap Equity (US$) Fund
RRSP Eligible; Inception Year: 1999; Fund Managers:
T. Rowe Price Associates Inc.
US Small Cap Equity Fund
RRSP Eligible; Inception Year: 1997; Fund Managers:
T. Rowe Price Associates Inc.
US Blue Chip Equity GIF II Fund
RRSP Eligible; Inception Year: 2000; Fund Managers:
T. Rowe Price Associates Inc.
International RSP Index Fund
RRSP Eligible; Inception Year: 1998; Fund Managers:
Craig Gaskin
Japanese Growth Fund
RRSP Eligible; Inception Year: 1994; Fund Managers:
Charles Edwardes-Ker
BruceCooper
Japanese Index Fund
RRSP Eligible; Inception Year: 1998; Fund Managers:
Craig Gaskin
Health Sciences GIF II Fund
RRSP Eligible; Inception Year: 2000; Fund Managers:
T. Rowe Price Associates Inc.
International RSP Index e Fund
RRSP Eligible; Inception Year: 1999; Fund Managers:
Craig Gaskin
Japanese Index e Fund
RRSP Eligible; Inception Year: 1999; Fund Managers:
Craig Gaskin
Latin American Growth Fund
RRSP Eligible; Inception Year: 1994; Fund Managers:
Morgan Stanley Asset Management Inc.
Managed Aggressive Growth GIF II Fund
RRSP Eligible; Inception Year: 2000;
Canadian Money Market A Fund
RRSP Eligible; Inception Year: 2000; Fund Managers:
R.B. Kenneth Miner
Canadian Small Cap Equity Fund
RRSP Eligible; Inception Year: 1986; Fund Managers:
Connor, Clark & Lunn Investment Management
Canadian Index e Fund
RRSP Eligible; Inception Year: 1999; Fund Managers:
Craig Gaskin

Canadian Money Market GIF II Fund
RRSP Eligible; Inception Year: 2000; Fund Managers:
R.B. Kenneth Miner
Canadian T-Bill Fund
RRSP Eligible; Inception Year: 1992; Fund Managers:
R.B. Kenneth Miner
Canadian Index Fund
RRSP Eligible; Inception Year: 1985; Fund Managers:
Craig Gaskin
Dow Jones Industrial Average Index Fund
RRSP Eligible; Inception Year: 1998; Fund Managers:
Craig Gaskin
Dow Jones Industrial Average Index e Fund
RRSP Eligible; Inception Year: 1999; Fund Managers:
Craig Gaskin
Energy Fund
RRSP Eligible; Inception Year: 1994; Fund Managers:
Ari Levy
MargotNaudie
Entertainment & Communications GIF II Fund
RRSP Eligible; Inception Year: 2000; Fund Managers:
T. Rowe Price Associates Inc.
European Growth Fund
RRSP Eligible; Inception Year: 1994; Fund Managers:
Bruce Cooper
European Index Fund
RRSP Eligible; Inception Year: 1998; Fund Managers:
Craig Gaskin
European Index e Fund
RRSP Eligible; Inception Year: 1999; Fund Managers:
Craig Gaskin
Global RSP Bond Fund
RRSP Eligible; Inception Year: 1994; Fund Managers:
Geoff Wilson
DavidMcCulla
Global Select GIF II Fund
RRSP Eligible; Inception Year: 2000; Fund Managers:
Oppenheimer Funds Inc.
Asian Growth Fund
RRSP Eligible; Inception Year: 1994; Fund Managers:
Martin Currie Investment Inc
Balanced Growth A Fund
RRSP Eligible; Inception Year: 2000; Fund Managers:
McLean Budden Limited
Balanced Growth GIF II Fund
RRSP Eligible; Inception Year: 2000; Fund Managers:
McLean Budden Limited
Balanced Income Fund
RRSP Eligible; Inception Year: 1988; Fund Managers:
Jarislowsky Fraser Limited
Blue Chip Equity Fund
RRSP Eligible; Inception Year: 1987; Fund Managers:
Jarislowsky Fraser Limited
Canadian Bond GIF II Fund
RRSP Eligible; Inception Year: 2000; Fund Managers:
Satish C. Rai
GeoffWilson
Canadian Bond A Fund
RRSP Eligible; Inception Year: 2000; Fund Managers:
Satish C. Rai
GeoffWilson
Canadian Equity GIF II Fund
RRSP Eligible; Inception Year: 2000; Fund Managers:
John Smolinski
ScottMargach
Canadian Equity A Fund
RRSP Eligible; Inception Year: 2000; Fund Managers:
John Smolinski
ScottMargach
Managed Balanced Growth GIF II Fund
RRSP Eligible; Inception Year: 2000;
Managed Income & Moderate Growth GIF II Fund
RRSP Eligible; Inception Year: 2000;
Premium Money Market Fund
RRSP Eligible; Inception Year: 1997; Fund Managers:
R.B. Kenneth Miner
Canadian Money Market Fund
RRSP Eligible; Inception Year: 1988; Fund Managers:
R.B. Kenneth Miner
Managed Maximum Equity Growth Portfolio I Fund
RRSP Eligible; Inception Year: 1998;
Entertainment & Communications Fund
RRSP Eligible; Inception Year: 1997; Fund Managers:
T. Rowe Price Associates Inc.

Managed Index Aggressive Growth Portfolio I Fund
RRSP Eligible; Inception Year: 1998;
Managed Index Aggressive Growth Portfolio e Fund
RRSP Eligible; Inception Year: 2000;
Managed Balanced Growth Portfolio I Fund
RRSP Eligible; Inception Year: 1998;
Managed Index Balanced Growth Portfolio I Fund
RRSP Eligible; Inception Year: 1998;
Managed Balanced Growth RSP Portfolio I Fund
RRSP Eligible; Inception Year: 1998;
Canadian Value Fund
RRSP Eligible; Inception Year: 1993; Fund Managers:
Rachel Volynsky
DougWarwick
Global Asset Allocation Fund
RRSP Eligible; Inception Year: 1998; Fund Managers:
Geoff Wilson
DavidMcCulla
Balanced Fund
RRSP Eligible; Inception Year: 1987; Fund Managers:
Rachel Volynsky
GeoffWilson
Balanced Growth Fund
RRSP Eligible; Inception Year: 1987; Fund Managers:
McLean Budden Limited
Managed Aggressive Growth RSP Portfolio Fund
RRSP Eligible; Inception Year: 1998;
Managed Aggressive Growth Portfolio A Fund
RRSP Eligible; Inception Year: 2001;
AmeriGrowth RSP Fund
RRSP Eligible; Inception Year: 1993; Fund Managers:
Dino Bourdos
BruceGeddes
Canadian Value GIF II Fund
RRSP Eligible; Inception Year: 2000; Fund Managers:
Doug Warwick
RachelVolynsky
Canadian Value A Fund
RRSP Eligible; Inception Year: 2000; Fund Managers:
Doug Warwick
RachelVolynsky
Dividend Growth Fund
RRSP Eligible; Inception Year: 1987; Fund Managers:
Michael Lough
DougWarwick
Dividend Growth A Fund
RRSP Eligible; Inception Year: 2001; Fund Managers:
Michael Lough
DougWarwick
Canadian Bond Index Fund
RRSP Eligible; Inception Year: 1997; Fund Managers:
Bruce Geddes
Canadian Bond Index e Fund
RRSP Eligible; Inception Year: 2000; Fund Managers:
Bruce Geddes
Dow Jones Industrial Average Index (US$) Fund
RRSP Eligible; Inception Year: 1998; Fund Managers:
Craig Gaskin
Dow Jones Industrial Average Index (US$) e Fund
RRSP Eligible; Inception Year: 1999; Fund Managers:
Craig Gaskin
Entertainment & Communications A Fund
RRSP Eligible; Inception Year: 2000; Fund Managers:
T. Rowe Price Associates Inc.
Entertainment & Communications (US$) Fund
RRSP Eligible; Inception Year: 1999; Fund Managers:
T. Rowe Price Associates Inc.
Emerging Markets A Fund
RRSP Eligible; Inception Year: 2000; Fund Managers:
Morgan Stanley Asset Management Inc.
Global Select Fund
RRSP Eligible; Inception Year: 1994; Fund Managers:
Oppenheimer Funds Inc.
Health Sciences Fund
RRSP Eligible; Inception Year: 1996; Fund Managers:
T. Rowe Price Associates Inc.
Health Sciences (US$) Fund
RRSP Eligible; Inception Year: 1999; Fund Managers:
T. Rowe Price Associates Inc.
International Equity Fund
RRSP Eligible; Inception Year: 1987; Fund Managers:
UBS Global Asset Management (Canada) Co.
Latin American Growth (US$) Fund
RRSP Eligible; Inception Year: 1999; Fund Managers:
Morgan Stanley Asset Management Inc.

Real Return Bond A Fund
RRSP Eligible; Inception Year: 2001; Fund Managers:
Satish C. Rai
GeoffWilson
Science & Technology Fund
RRSP Eligible; Inception Year: 1993; Fund Managers:
T. Rowe Price Associates Inc.
Science & Technology (US$) Fund
RRSP Eligible; Inception Year: 1999; Fund Managers:
T. Rowe Price Associates Inc.
Science & Technology A Fund
RRSP Eligible; Inception Year: 2000; Fund Managers:
T. Rowe Price Associates Inc.
Short Term Bond Fund
RRSP Eligible; Inception Year: 1989; Fund Managers:
David McCulla
GeoffWilson
US Blue Chip Equity Fund
RRSP Eligible; Inception Year: 1996; Fund Managers:
T. Rowe Price Associates Inc.
US Blue Chip Equity (US$) Fund
RRSP Eligible; Inception Year: 1999; Fund Managers:
T. Rowe Price Associates Inc.
US Blue Chip Equity A Fund
RRSP Eligible; Inception Year: 2000; Fund Managers:
T. Rowe Price Associates Inc.
US Equity (US$) Fund
RRSP Eligible; Inception Year: 2000; Fund Managers:
Rhonda Dalley
DavidSykes
US Mid-Cap Growth A Fund
RRSP Eligible; Inception Year: 2000; Fund Managers:
T. Rowe Price Associates Inc.
US RSP Index Fund
RRSP Eligible; Inception Year: 1997; Fund Managers:
Dino Bourdos
BruceGeddes
Canadian Small Cap Equity A Fund
RRSP Eligible; Inception Year: 2002; Fund Managers:
Connor, Clark & Lunn Investment Management
Global Select A Fund
RRSP Eligible; Inception Year: 2000; Fund Managers:
Oppenheimer Funds Inc.
Health Sciences A Fund
RRSP Eligible; Inception Year: 2000; Fund Managers:
T. Rowe Price Associates Inc.
International Index Fund
RRSP Eligible; Inception Year: 1997; Fund Managers:
Craig Gaskin
High Yield Income A Fund
RRSP Eligible; Inception Year: 2002; Fund Managers:
Gregory Kocik
NicholasLeach
Managed Aggressive Growth Non-RSP GIF II Fund
RRSP Eligible; Inception Year: 2001;
Managed Aggressive Growth RSP Portfolio A Fund
RRSP Eligible; Inception Year: 2001;
Managed Aggressive Growth Portfolio I Fund
RRSP Eligible; Inception Year: 1998;
Managed Balanced Growth RSP Portfolio A Fund
RRSP Eligible; Inception Year: 2001;
Managed Index Balanced Growth Portfolio e Fund
RRSP Eligible; Inception Year: 2000;
Managed Index Income & Moderate Growth Portfolio e Fund
RRSP Eligible; Inception Year: 2000;
Managed Index Income Portfolio e Fund
RRSP Eligible; Inception Year: 2000;
Managed Index Income Portfolio I Fund
RRSP Eligible; Inception Year: 1998;
Managed Index Maximum Equity Growth Portfolio e Fund
RRSP Eligible; Inception Year: 2000;
Managed Income & Moderate Growth Portfolio I Fund
RRSP Eligible; Inception Year: 1998;
Managed Income & Moderate Growth RSP Portfolio A Fund
RRSP Eligible; Inception Year: 2001;
Managed Income & Moderate Growth RSP Portfolio I Fund
RRSP Eligible; Inception Year: 1998;
Managed Income RSP Portfolio I Fund
RRSP Eligible; Inception Year: 1998;
Managed Maximum Equity Growth Non-RSP GIF II Fund
RRSP Eligible; Inception Year: 2001;
Managed Maximum Equity Growth Portfolio A Fund
RRSP Eligible; Inception Year: 2001;
Managed Maximum Equity RSP Portfolio A Fund
RRSP Eligible; Inception Year: 2001;

TD Asset Management Inc.(TDAM) (continued)
Monthly Income A Fund
RRSP Eligible; Inception Year: 2002; Fund Managers:
Gregory Kocik
DougWarwick
Michael Lough
Resource A Fund
RRSP Eligible; Inception Year: 2002; Fund Managers:
Margot Naudie
AriLevy
US Large Cap Value A Fund
RRSP Eligible; Inception Year: 2002; Fund Managers:
Brian C. Rogers
Balanced Income A Fund
RRSP Eligible; Inception Year: 2002; Fund Managers:
Jarislowsky Fraser Limited
Canadian Blue Chip Equity A Fund
RRSP Eligible; Inception Year: 2002; Fund Managers:
Jarislowsky Fraser Limited
US Mid-Cap Growth (US$) Fund
RRSP Eligible; Inception Year: 1999; Fund Managers:
T. Rowe Price Associates Inc.
US Small Cap Equity A Fund
RRSP Eligible; Inception Year: 2002; Fund Managers:
T. Rowe Price Associates Inc.
Income Advantage Portfolio I Series Fund
RRSP Eligible; Inception Year: 2003;
US Large Cap Value Fund
RRSP Eligible; Inception Year: 2003; Fund Managers:
Brian C. Rogers
Global RSP Bond A Fund
RRSP Eligible; Inception Year: 2003; Fund Managers:
David McCulla
GeoffWilson
Income Advantage Portfolio A Fund
RRSP Eligible; Inception Year: 2003;
Short Term Bond A Fund
RRSP Eligible; Inception Year: 2003; Fund Managers:
David McCulla
GeoffWilson
Dividend Income A Fund
RRSP Eligible; Inception Year: 2003; Fund Managers:
Michael Lough
DougWarwick
International Equity A Fund
RRSP Eligible; Inception Year: 2003; Fund Managers:
UBS Global Asset Management (Canada) Co.
Canadian Bond Index F Fund
RRSP Eligible; Inception Year: 2000; Fund Managers:
Bruce Geddes
LoriMacKay
Managed Maximum Equity Growth RSP Fund
RRSP Eligible; Inception Year: 1998;
Canadian Money Market GIF II Class A Fund
RRSP Eligible; Inception Year: 2003; Fund Managers:
R.B. Kenneth Miner
Canadian Money Market GIF II Class B Fund
RRSP Eligible; Inception Year: 2003; Fund Managers:
R.B. Kenneth Miner
Canadian Bond GIF II Class A Fund
RRSP Eligible; Inception Year: 2003; Fund Managers:
Satish C. Rai
GeoffWilson
Canadian Bond GIF II Class B Fund
RRSP Eligible; Inception Year: 2003; Fund Managers:
Geoff Wilson
Satish C.Rai
Managed Balanced Growth GIF II Class A Fund
RRSP Eligible; Inception Year: 2003;
Managed Balanced Growth GIF II Class B Fund
RRSP Eligible; Inception Year: 2003;
Managed Income & Moderate Growth GIF II Class A Fund
RRSP Eligible; Inception Year: 2003;
Managed Income & Moderate Growth GIF II Class B Fund
RRSP Eligible; Inception Year: 2003;
Managed Aggressive Growth GIF II Class A Fund
RRSP Eligible; Inception Year: 2003;
Managed Aggressive Growth GIF II Class B Fund
RRSP Eligible; Inception Year: 2003;
Managed Maximum Equity Growth GIF II Fund
RRSP Eligible; Inception Year: 2000;
Managed Index Income & Moderate Growth Portfolio I Fund
RRSP Eligible; Inception Year: 1998;
Income Trust Capital Yield A Fund
RRSP Eligible; Inception Year: 2006; Fund Managers:
Doug Warwick
MichaelLough
Income Trust Capital Yield F Fund
RRSP Eligible; Inception Year: 2006; Fund Managers:
Michael Lough
DougWarwick
Income Trust Capital Yield I Fund
RRSP Eligible; Inception Year: 2006; Fund Managers:
Doug Warwick
MichaelLough
Income Advantage Portfolio H Fund
RRSP Eligible; Inception Year: 2006;
Income Advantage Portfolio S Fund
RRSP Eligible; Inception Year: 2006;
Income Advantage Portfolio T Fund
RRSP Eligible; Inception Year: 2006;
International Equity GIF II Fund
RRSP Eligible; Inception Year: 2000; Fund Managers:
UBS Global Asset Management (Canada) Co.
International Equity F Fund
RRSP Eligible; Inception Year: 2005; Fund Managers:
UBS Global Asset Management (Canada) Co.
International Index e Fund
RRSP Eligible; Inception Year: 2000; Fund Managers:
Craig Gaskin
Managed Maximum Equity Growth RSP P Fund
RRSP Eligible; Inception Year: 2005;
Managed Maximum Equity RSP Portfolio I Fund
RRSP Eligible; Inception Year: 1998;
Managed Income Portfolio P Fund
RRSP Eligible; Inception Year: 2005;
Managed Aggressive Growth RSP P Fund
RRSP Eligible; Inception Year: 2005;
Managed Balanced Growth RSP P Fund
RRSP Eligible; Inception Year: 2005;
Managed Maximum Equity Growth P Fund
RRSP Eligible; Inception Year: 2005;
Managed Aggressive Growth P Fund
RRSP Eligible; Inception Year: 2005;
Managed Balanced Growth P Fund
RRSP Eligible; Inception Year: 2005;
Managed Income & Moderate Growth Portfolio P Fund
RRSP Eligible; Inception Year: 2005;
Managed Income RSP Portfolio A Fund
RRSP Eligible; Inception Year: 2004;
Managed Income RSP Portfolio P Fund
RRSP Eligible; Inception Year: 2005;
Managed Income & Moderate Growth RSP P Fund
RRSP Eligible; Inception Year: 2005;
Monthly Income H Fund
RRSP Eligible; Inception Year: 2006; Fund Managers:
Doug Warwick
GregoryKocik
Monthly Income S Fund
RRSP Eligible; Inception Year: 2006; Fund Managers:
Gregory Kocik
DougWarwick
Monthly Income T Fund
RRSP Eligible; Inception Year: 2006; Fund Managers:
Gregory Kocik
DougWarwick
Pacific Rim I Fund
RRSP Eligible; Inception Year: 1993; Fund Managers:
Martin Currie Investment Inc
US Equity Advantage Portfolio A Fund
RRSP Eligible; Inception Year: 2004;
US Equity Advantage Portfolio I Fund
RRSP Eligible; Inception Year: 2004;
US Money Market (US$) P Fund
RRSP Eligible; Inception Year: 2004; Fund Managers:
R.B. Kenneth Miner
Emerging Markets Fund
RRSP Eligible; Inception Year: 1992; Fund Managers:
Morgan Stanley Asset Management Inc.
TD FundSmart:
Managed Aggressive Growth Portfolio I Fund
RRSP Eligible; Inception Year: 1998;
Managed Balanced Growth RSP Portfolio I Fund
RRSP Eligible; Inception Year: 1998;
Managed Balanced Growth Portfolio I Fund
RRSP Eligible; Inception Year: 1998;
Managed Aggressive RSP Portfolio I Fund
RRSP Eligible; Inception Year: 1998;
Managed Aggressive Growth Portfolio A Fund
RRSP Eligible; Inception Year: 2001;
Managed Aggressive RSP Portfolio A Fund
RRSP Eligible; Inception Year: 2001;
Managed Balanced Growth RSP Portfolio A Fund
RRSP Eligible; Inception Year: 2001;
Managed Income RSP Portfolio I Fund
RRSP Eligible; Inception Year: 1998;
Managed Income & Moderate Growth Portfolio I Fund
RRSP Eligible; Inception Year: 1998;
Managed Income & Moderate Growth RSP Portfolio A Fund
RRSP Eligible; Inception Year: 2001;
Managed Income & Moderate Growth RSP Portfolio I Fund
RRSP Eligible; Inception Year: 1998;
Managed Income Portfolio I Fund
RRSP Eligible; Inception Year: 1998;
Managed Maximum Equity Growth Portfolio A Fund
RRSP Eligible; Inception Year: 2001;
Managed Maximum Equity Growth Portfolio I Fund
RRSP Eligible; Inception Year: 1998;
Managed Maximum Equity RSP Portfolio A Fund
RRSP Eligible; Inception Year: 2001;
Managed Maximum Equity RSP Portfolio I Fund
RRSP Eligible; Inception Year: 1998;
Managed Aggressive Growth RSP Portfolio P Fund
RRSP Eligible; Inception Year: 2005;
Managed Balanced Growth RSP Portfolio P Fund
RRSP Eligible; Inception Year: 2005;
Managed Balanced Growth Portfolio P Fund
RRSP Eligible; Inception Year: 2005;
Managed Income & Moderate Growth Portfolio P Fund
RRSP Eligible; Inception Year: 2005;
Managed Income & Moderate Growth RSP Portfolio P Fund
RRSP Eligible; Inception Year: 2005;
Income RSP Portfolio A Fund
RRSP Eligible; Inception Year: 2004;
Managed Income Portfolio P Fund
RRSP Eligible; Inception Year: 2005;
Managed Income RSP Portfolio P Fund
RRSP Eligible; Inception Year: 2005;
Managed Maximum Equity Growth Portfolio P Fund
RRSP Eligible; Inception Year: 2005;
Managed Aggressive Growth Portfolio P Fund
RRSP Eligible; Inception Year: 2005;

TD Harbour Capital

BCE Place
161 Bay St., 34th Fl.
Toronto, ON M5J 2T2
416-308-9900
www.tdassetmanagement.com
Former Name: Harbour Capital Management Inc.
Ownership: Private
Year Founded: 1990

TD Waterhouse Canada Inc.

***Also listed under:** Investment Dealers*
Toronto Dominion Centre
55 King St. West, Concourse Level 1
Toronto, ON M5K 1A2
416-308-1600
Fax: 416-944-6750
800-465-5463
Other Information: 800-838-3223 (Toll Free, Cantonese/Mandarin); 866-966-6061 (TTY)
td.waterhouse@td.com
www.tdwaterhouse.ca
Stock Exchange Membership: Montreal Exchange, Toronto Stock Exchange
Profile: Investment advice, broker services, institutional sales & trading & retail services are offered.
Executives:
William H. Hatanaka, Chair/CEO
Richard LaFerrière, President, Financial Planning
Michael E. Reilly, President, Private Investment Advice
John See, President, Discount Brokerage, Financial Planning & Institutional Services
Gerard J. O'Mahoney, Exec. Vice-President/COO
Patricia Lovett-Reid, Sr. Vice-President, TD Waterhouse Canada
Branches:
Brossard
8330, boul Taschereau
Brossard, QC J4X 1C2
450-465-1121
866-900-1121
Calgary

505 - 2nd St. SW
Calgary, AB T2P 1N8 Canada
403-503-6578
Edmonton - 101st St. NW
#402, 10205 - 101st St. NW
Edmonton, AB T5J 4H5 Canada
780-448-8088
800-350-4832
Edmonton - 111 St. NW
2325 - 111 St. NW
Edmonton, AB T6J 5E5
780-448-8282
Halifax
PO Box 634
1785 Barrington St., 2nd Fl.
Halifax, NS B3J 2P6 Canada
902-420-2585
Hamilton
100 King St. West, Main Fl.
Hamilton, ON L8P 4W9 Canada
905-521-2120
Kanata
120 Earl Grey Dr.
Kanata, ON K2T 1B6 Canada
613-592-6563
Kelowna
#110, 1633 Ellis St.
Kelowna, BC V1Y 2A8 Canada
250-717-8129
866-717-8129
Kingston
94 Princess St.
Kingston, ON K7L 1A5 Canada
613-549-8525

Kitchener
381 King St. West, Main Fl.
Kitchener, ON N2G 1B8 Canada
519-571-7570
Laval
#150, 3080, boul le Carrefour
Laval, QC H7T 2R5 Canada
800-451-1647
London
275 Dundas St.
London, ON N6A 4S4 Canada
519-873-2099
Markham - Kennedy Rd.
#101, 7077 Kennedy Rd.
Markham, ON L3R 0N8 Canada
905-479-8008
877-479-8008
Markham - Steeles Ave. East
Tower 1, Liberty Centre
3500 Steeles Ave. East, 3rd Fl.
Markham, ON L3R 2Z1 Canada
416-904-5454
800-838-3223
Moncton
#101, 860 Main St.
Moncton, NB E1C 1G2 Canada
506-859-9530
866-816-6613
Montréal - Saint-Jean
#120, 755, boul Saint-Jean
Montréal, QC H9R 5M9 Canada
877-297-5559
Montréal - St. Jacques
500, rue St. Jacques, 6e étage
Montréal, QC H2Y 1S1 Canada
514-289-8439
800-361-2684
Montréal - Ste Catherine ouest
1101, rue Ste Catherine ouest
Montréal, QC H3B 1H8 Canada
514-289-8080
800-839-0888
Nanaimo
5777 Turner Rd., Upper Level
Nanaimo, BC V9T 6L8 Canada
250-390-5940
888-255-5522
Oakville
282 Lakeshore Rd. East
Oakville, ON L6J 5B2 Canada
905-337-3779
Ottawa - Coventry Rd.
525 Coventry Rd.
Ottawa, ON K1K 2C5 Canada
613-783-6322
800-267-8844
Ottawa - O'Connor St.
45 O'Connor St., 2nd Fl.
Ottawa, ON K1P 1A4 Canada
613-783-6379
Québec
#135, 2600, boul Laurier
Québec, QC G1V 4T3 Canada
418-654-0828
800-214-1345
Regina
1904 Hamilton St.
Regina, SK S4P 3N5 Canada
306-924-8902
800-667-9951
Richmond
5991 No. 3 Rd.
Richmond, BC V6X 3Y6 Canada
604-654-8863
877-596-3577
Richmond Hill
500 Hwy. 7 East
Richmond Hill, ON L4B 1J1 Canada
905-731-4436
866-658-4436
Saskatoon
170 - 2nd Ave. South
Saskatoon, SK S7K 1K5 Canada
306-975-7373
St. John's
TD Place
140 Water St., 2nd Fl.
St. John's, NL A1C 6H6 Canada
709-758-5098
Sudbury
43 Elm St., 2nd Fl.
Sudbury, ON P3E 4R7 Canada
705-670-8809
Toronto
77 Bloor St. West, Main Fl.
Toronto, ON M5S 1M2 Canada
416-542-0749
866-622-1022

Toronto - Bloor St. West
The Clarica Centre
#126, 3250 Bloor St. West
Toronto, ON M8X 2X9
416-239-3363
Toronto - Bremner Ave.
363 Bremner Ave.
Toronto, ON M5V 3V4
416-623-0158
Vancouver
#100, 888 Dunsmuir St.
Vancouver, BC V6C 3K4 Canada
604-654-3661
800-663-0480
Victoria
1070 Douglas St., Main Fl.
Victoria, BC V8W 2C4 Canada
250-356-4073
West Vancouver
1655 Marine Dr.
West Vancouver, BC V7V 1J2 Canada
604-981-4500
Whitby
404 Dundas St. West, 2nd Fl.
Whitby, ON L1N 2M7 Canada
905-668-1004
White Rock
Central Plaza Shopping Centre
15120 North Bluff Rd.
White Rock, BC V4B 3E5 Canada
604-541-2050
Windsor
#300, 586 Ouellette Ave.
Windsor, ON N9A 1B8 Canada
519-252-7022
Winnipeg
201 Portage Ave., Concourse Level
Winnipeg, MB R3C 2T2 Canada
204-988-2641

TE Financial Consultants Ltd.

#710, 26 Wellington St. East
Toronto, ON M5E 1S2
416-366-1451
Fax: 416-368-9801
info@tefinancial.com
www.tefinancial.com
Ownership: Private. Parent is Jovian Capital Corporation
Year Founded: 1972
Number of Employees: 100+
Assets: $1-10 billion Year End: 20050930
Stock Symbol: JVN.V
Executives:
Timothy Egan, Chair
Kostas Andrikopolous, President/CEO
Graeme Egan, Vice-President
Gayle Harris, Vice-President
Branches:
Calgary
Western Canadian Place
#2230, 700 - 99th Ave. SW
Calgary, AB T2P 3V4 Canada
403-233-8370
Fax: 403-233-8370
Gayle Harris, Vice-President & Regional Manager
Montréal
#2100, 2020, rue University
Montréal, QC H3A 2A5 Canada
514-845-3200
Fax: 514-845-9944
Diane Henry, Vice-President & Regional General Manager
Oakville
#11, 1155 North Service Rd. West
Oakville, ON L6M 3E3 Canada
905-523-7448
Fax: 905-469-0691
Ernie Coulson, Vice-President
Québec
#200, 710, rue Bouvier
Québec, QC G2J 1A7 Canada
418-627-9905
Fax: 418-622-2548
Gilles Rochette, Manager
Vancouver
#720, 475 West Georgia St.
Vancouver, BC V6B 4M9 Canada
604-684-2196
Fax: 604-684-2396
Graeme Egan, Vice-President & General Manager

Team O'Heron Investments

PO Box 245
2057 Victoria St. North
Breslau, ON N0B 1M0
519-648-2610
Fax: 519-648-3285
brian@oheron.com
Ownership: Private. Part of Armstrong & Quaile Associates Inc., Manotick, ON.

Ten Star Financial Services

95 Hamilton St. North
Waterdown, ON L0R 2H0
800-461-9501
info@tenstar.ca
www.tenstar.ca
Former Name: Ten Star Insurance & Financial
Ownership: Private
Profile: Ten Star Financial Services is the trading name of the following five integrated companies: Ten Star Life Insurance Brokers Inc., Ten Star Insurance Brokers Inc., Ten Star Financial Inc., Ten Star Group Benefit Specialists Inc., & Ten Star Actuarial Services Inc.

Executives:
David Baird, President
Affiliated Companies:
Fortraco International Marketing Inc.
Branches:
Barrie - Bryne Dr.
#1, 301 Bryne Dr.
Barrie, ON L4N 8V4 Canada

INVESTMENT MANAGEMENT

Ten Star Financial Services (continued)
705-722-0497
Fax: 705-792-0682
phunnef@tenstar.ca
Paul Hunnef, Branch Manager
Barrie - Fred Grant Sq.
8 Fred Grant Sq., 2nd Fl.
Barrie, ON L4M 1A2 Canada
Fax: 705-735-9543
888-427-8394
tenstarfinancial@rogers.com
Harvey Garraway, Branch Manager
Barrie - Mary St.
80 Mary St.
Barrie, ON L4N 1T1 Canada
705-733-9595
Fax: 705-733-9234
richgane@rogers.com
Richard Gane, Branch Manager
Burlington
#102A, 3425 Harvester Rd.
Burlington, ON L7N 3N1 Canada
905-634-8834
Fax: 905-634-8831
velma@vpfinancialgroup.com
www.tenstar.velmacarroll.com
Velma Carroll, Branch Manager
Calgary
#600, 2424 - 4th St. SW
Calgary, AB T2S 2T4 Canada
Fax: 403-229-2250
888-507-9599
mrtenstar@shaw.ca
www.tsfinancial.ca
Myles Rempel, Branch Manager
Carrying Place
2355 Rednersville Rd.
Carrying Place, ON K0K 1L0 Canada
613-966-2818
Fax: 613-962-3230
bill@weesefinancial.com
www.tenstar.weese-insurance.com
Bill Weese, Branch Manager
Cranbrook
6 - 10th Ave. South
Cranbrook, BC V1C 2M8 Canada
250-426-3651
Fax: 250-426-8939
edvien@shaw.ca
Edgar Vien, Branch Manager
Durham
131 Garafaxa St. South
Durham, ON N0G 1R0 Canada
Fax: 519-369-2640
877-369-3017
bparkin@secureinsurance.ca
www.tenstar.secure-financial-solutions.com
Brien Parkin, Branch Manager
Georgetown
21A Armstrong Ave.
Georgetown, ON L7G 4S1 Canada
905-873-9882
Fax: 905-873-9859
Graham Baker
Lindsay
316 Hwy. 36, RR#4
Lindsay, ON K9V 4R4 Canada
705-328-9130
Fax: 705-328-9136
866-328-9130
tenstar@cogeco.ca
www.tenstar.lindsayinsurancebrokers.com
Ken Greig, Branch Manager
London - Cranbrook Rd.
932 Cranbrook Rd.
London, ON N6K 4X8 Canada
519-432-4045
Fax: 519-432-7559
briansmith@legacywealthmgt.com
www.tenstar.legacylifeinsurance.com
Brian Smith, Branch Manager
London - Hamilton Rd.
369 Hamilton Rd.
London, ON N5Z 1R6 Canada
519-438-1959
Fax: 519-438-3019
Ron Van Rooyen, Branch Manager
Montréal - St. Regis
#260, 2113, rue Saint-Régis
Montréal, QC H9B 2M9 Canada
514-421-3950
Fax: 514-683-6316
info@wealthstarfs.com
Ron Greeley, Branch Manager
Oakville - Sixth Line
#18, 2520 Sixth Line
Oakville, ON L6H 6W5 Canada
905-257-6528
Fax: 905-257-4221
joliver@taxmanagementcentre.com
www.tenstar.taxmgmtcentre.com,
www.tenstar.taxmanagementcentre.com
June Oliver, Branch Manager
Oakville - Wilson St.
79 Wilson St.
Oakville, ON L6K 3G4 Canada
905-338-7689
Fax: 905-338-0831
brian@moneypeople.ca
www.mortgageplans.ca
Brian Poncelet, Branch Manager
Ottawa
#206, 1729 Bank St.
Ottawa, ON K1V 7Z5 Canada
613-247-9170
Fax: 613-247-1578
wane@tenstarfinancial.ca
Wane MacDow, Branch Manager
Regina
#321, 2505 - 11th Ave.
Regina, SK S4P 0K6 Canada
306-569-3120
Fax: 306-569-3384
tenstar@sasktel.net
Luis Simon, Branch Manager
Richmond Hill
29 Monaco Cres.
Richmond Hill, ON L4S 1X6 Canada
905-737-5256
Fax: 905-737-3042
Gloria Pasildo, Branch Manager
Toronto
#215, 885 Progress Ave.
Toronto, ON M1H 3G3 Canada
Fax: 416-282-7001
866-282-5383
jessdefrancia@rogers.com
www.tenstar.jdtoronto.com
Jesus De Francia, Branch Manager
Vancouver
#317, 1080 Mainland St.
Vancouver, BC V6B 2T4 Canada
604-682-7827
Fax: 604-682-7877
888-882-2822
ckwinter@tenstar.cc
www.tenstar.vancouverbranch.com
Candace Kwinter, Branch Manager
Winnipeg
#109, 161 Stafford St.
Winnipeg, MB R3M 2W9 Canada
204-885-6768
Fax: 204-885-6872
richard@icenter.net
Richard Desrochers, Branch Manager

Tera Capital Corp.
Also listed under: *Investment Fund Companies*
#337, 366 Adelaide St. East
Toronto, ON M5A 3X9
416-368-8372
Fax: 416-368-1427
anguelina@teracap.com
www.teracap.com
Year Founded: 1996
Executives:
Howard Sutton, President
Tera:
Capital Global Technology Fund
RRSP Eligible; Inception Year: 1998;
Public Venture Trust Fund
RRSP Eligible; Inception Year: 0;

Terrenex Acquisition Corporation
Guinness House
#1580, 727 Seventh Ave. SW
Calgary, AB T2P 0Z5
403-777-1185
Fax: 403-777-1578
terrenex@cia.com
Ownership: Public.
Year Founded: 1991
Assets: $10-50 million
Stock Symbol: TXA
Profile: The public investment company focuses on opportunities in domestic & international markets.

Executives:
Michael Binnion, President/CEO & CFO
Maria Rees, Controller
Directors:
Russell Hammond, Chair
Michael Binnion
Peder Paus
Maria Rees

Thierry Financial Planning
581 Eden Ave.
London, ON N6C 2Z5
519-686-6192
Fax: 519-686-8971
thierryfinancialplanning@sympatico.ca
Executives:
Donald L. Thierry, B.B.A., CFP, Certified Financial Planner

Thom & Associates Insurance Ltd.
#402, 580 Terry Fox Dr.
Kanata, ON K2L 4B9
613-592-2889
Fax: 613-592-1512
800-868-6692
g.thom@barinsurance.com
Former Name: Thom-Hall & Associates Financial Group Inc.
Executives:
Gary Thom, CFP, CLU, CH.F.C., RHU, Certified Financial Planner, Chartered Life Underwriter
Margo Thom, RHU, Registered Health Underwriter

Thomas O'Neill & Associates
Also listed under: *Pension & Money Management Companies*
Cathedral Place
#1918,925 West Georgia St.
Vancouver, BC V6C 3L2
604-484-4170
Fax: 604-608-6776
800-757-2799
ubfi@oneill-inc.com
Ownership: Private
Year Founded: 1985
Number of Employees: 7
Revenues: Under $1 million
Profile: Financial planning consultants.

Executives:
Thomas O'Neill, President

Time & Money Planners
#1, 219 Colonnade Rd. South
Nepean, ON K2E 7K3
613-225-4333
Fax: 613-225-2685
peter@timeandmoney.ca
www.timeandmoney.ca
Ownership: Private
Year Founded: 1998
Number of Employees: 5
Revenues: Under $1 million
Executives:
Peter Vogelsang, CFP, CLU, CH.F.C., President; 613-723-6663; peter@timeandmoney.ca
Michel J. Lemaire, CLU, CH.F.C., Vice-President; 613-224-8344; mitch.lemaire@timeandmoney.ca
Eric Roy, CFP, Treasurer; eric@timeandmoney.ca
Paul Virgin, CLU, Secretary; 613-224-9955; paul_virgin@hotmail.com
Directors:
Andy Lonie; 613-228-4014; andy@timeandmoney.ca

Shirley MacMillan; 613-722-0222; smacmillan@OmniInvestments.ca
Michael Roodman; mdrinsurance@rogers.com
Oral Rooke; oral.rooke@timeandmoney.ca
Eric Roy, CFP; 613-274-3076; eric@timeandmoney.ca

Timothy M. Shmigelsky
Canada Trust Tower
#600, 10104 - 103rd Ave.
Edmonton, AB T5J 0H8
780-917-7714
Fax: 780-429-2809
tim.shmigelsky@gwl.ca
Ownership: Private
Year Founded: 1981
Assets: $10-50 million
Revenues: Under $1 million
Executives:
Timothy M. Shmigelsky, Contact

Tipper Financial Services
#101, 340 Pinnacle St.
Belleville, ON K8N 3B4
613-771-1119
Fax: 613-771-9235
tip@bellnet.ca
Executives:
Roli Tipper

Todd & Associates Financial Knowledge Inc.
***Also listed under:** Pension & Money Management Companies*
#364, 305 - 4625 Varsity Dr. NW
Calgary, AB T3A 0Z9
403-547-0328
Fax: 403-547-7828
www.todd-associates.com
Ownership: Private
Year Founded: 1985
Number of Employees: 4
Assets: Under $1 million
Revenues: Under $1 million
Executives:
Russell Todd, RFP, CFP, Principal, Financial Planner

Tom Griffiths
1762 Queen St.
Alton, ON L7K 2N6
519-938-8046
mail@tomgriffiths.net, tgriff@the-wire.com
www.tomgriffiths.net/fp
Profile: Services provided include the following: Registered Retirement Savings Plans, Registered Education Savings Plans, estate planning, mutual funds, labour sponsored funds, debt reduction strategies, life & disability insurance, tax planning & wealth management.

Executives:
Tom Griffiths, Certified Financial Planner

Tony Copple
61 Highmont Ct.
Kanata, ON K2T 1B2
613-591-7639
Fax: 613-591-8943
888-291-7024
tony.copple@investorsgroup.com
www.ncf.ca/~aj624/finance.html
Executives:
Tony Copple, Financial Consultant

Torce Financial Group Inc.
***Also listed under:** Investment Dealers*
#200, 650 Hwy. 7 East
Richmond Hill, ON L4B 2N7
905-889-9139
Fax: 905-889-8927
www.torcefinancial.com
Profile: The organization offers wealth management concepts, insurance coverage, mutual funds, segregated funds, RRSPs, RRIFs, & RESPs.

Executives:
David Ho, CLU, CH.F.C., Principal
Najeeb Khan, CFP, CLU, CH.F.C., Consultant, Training
Katrina Lo, ACS, AIAA, Office Manager
Affiliated Companies:
Vance Financial Group Inc.

Tradex Management Inc./ Gestion Tradex Inc.
***Also listed under:** Investment Fund Companies*
#1120, 50 O'Connor St.
Ottawa, ON K1P 6L2
613-233-3394
Fax: 613-233-8191
800-567-3863
info@tradex.ca
www.tradex.ca
Ownership: Private
Year Founded: 1988
Number of Employees: 4
Assets: $100-500 million
Executives:
Robert C. White, President
John S. Rayner, Chair
Tradex:
Bond Fund
RRSP Eligible; Inception Year: 1989; Fund Managers:
TD Asset Management
Global Equity Fund
RRSP Eligible; Inception Year: 1999; Fund Managers:
City of London Investment Management Co. Ltd.
Equity Fund Limited
RRSP Eligible; Inception Year: 1960; Fund Managers:
Phillips, Hager & North Ltd.

Turner Financial Consultants Ltd.
9 Georgian Ct.
Toronto, ON M4P 2J7
416-486-8329
Fax: 416-486-4606
888-327-0171
terry@terryturner.com
www.terryturner.com
Ownership: Private
Year Founded: 1986
Profile: Financial planning services include the following: estate, tax, retirement, international, & investment. Mutual funds are offered through Keybase Financial Group. The organization also provides insurance & investments through Equinox Financial Group.

Executives:
Terry S. Turner, CFP, RFP, CIM, FCSI, President

Twerdun Financial
#400, 740 Rosser Ave.
Brandon, MB R7A 0K9
204-725-7220
Fax: 204-726-1746
btwerdun@mb.sympatico.ca
www.chambers.ca/barry_twerdun
Profile: The following financial services are provided: estate planning, retirement planning, business succession planning, employee benefit programs, insurance, investments, GICs, RRSPs & mutual funds.

Executives:
Barry F. Twerdun, CFP, CLU, CH.F.C., President

Tymchuk Financial Services Inc.
Oxford Tower
#1100, 10235 - 101st St.
Edmonton, AB T5J 3G1
780-424-6321
Fax: 780-421-7561
ttymchuk@planet.eon.net
Ownership: Private.
Executives:
Terry Tymchuk, CFP, President

UBS Bank (Canada)
***Also listed under:** Foreign Banks: Schedule II; Investment Management*
#800, 154 University Ave.
Toronto, ON M5H 3Z4
416-343-1800
Fax: 416-343-1900
800-268-9709
www.ubs.com/canada
Also Known As: UBS Canada
Ownership: Foreign. Public.
Year Founded: 1856
Number of Employees: 70,000
Assets: $100 billion + Year End: 20051231
Revenues: $10-100 billion Year End: 20051231
Stock Symbol: UBS
Profile: UBS Bank is a wealth management, financial planning & investment solutions services company.

Executives:
Grant Rasmussen, CEO & Managing Director
Sharon Ashton, Contact, Products Group
Anurag Deep, Contact, Finance
Balan Gunaratnam, Contact, Information Technology
Graeme Harris, Contact, Corporate Communications
Branches:
Calgary
#600, 326 - 11th Ave. SW
Calgary, AB T2R 0C5 Canada
403-532-2180
Beat Meier, Director
Montréal
#2710, 600, boul Maisonneuve ouest
Montréal, QC H3A 3J2 Canada
514-845-8828
Karel Nemel, Director
Vancouver
PO Box 24
#650, 999 West Hastings St.
Vancouver, BC V6C 2W2 Canada
604-669-5570
800-305-5181
Martine Cunliffe, Director

V Group Financial
15 Willowood Ct.
Toronto, ON M2J 2M2
416-491-1515
Fax: 416-490-0914
vgroup1@sympatico.ca
www.vgroup.to
Executives:
Ralph Vandervoort, Contact

Valern Investment Management Inc.
140 Trafalgar Rd.
Oakville, ON L6J 3G5
905-338-6608
Fax: 905-845-2121

Vance Financial Group Inc.
***Also listed under:** Investment Dealers*
South Tower
#201, 5811 Cooney Rd.
Richmond, BC V6X 3M1
604-233-0123
Fax: 604-271-4863
www.torcefinancial.com
Executives:
Paul Lui, Contact, Management Team
Michelle Leung, Administrator

Vancea Financial Group
216 Huron St.
Stratford, ON N5A 5S8
519-275-3333
Fax: 519-273-0154
866-282-6232
bestgic@rogers.com
www.vanceafinancial.com

Vancouver Financial Planning Consultants Inc.
#1600, 800 West Pender St.
Vancouver, BC V6C 2V6
604-685-1938
Fax: 604-685-9815
planning@vfpc.ca
www.vfpc.org
Ownership: Private
Year Founded: 1984
Executives:
Lawrence M. Winters, CFP, RFP, President
James B.F. Cripps, CFP, RFP
Wayne E. Gibson, CFP, RFP
Kenneth B. Labron, CFP, RFP
Robert A. Sawatzky, CFP, RFP
Les A. Trelenberg, CFP, RFP

VantageOne Financial Corporation
#219, 3205 - 32nd St.
Vernon, BC V1T 5M7
250-260-4513
www.vdcu.com/vantageone

VantageOne Financial Corporation (continued)
Ownership: Wholly-owned subsidiary of Vernon & District Credit Union, Vernon, BC.
Executives:
Clemence Bedard, CFP
Robert Irvine, CFP, CLU, CH.F.C.

Vestcap Investment Management Inc.
Commerce Court West
#2902, 199 Bay St.
Toronto, ON M5L 1G5
416-869-0991
Fax: 416-869-0666
800-237-0993
vestcap@vestcap.com
www.vestcap.com
Executives:
M. Nugent Schneider, President

Visionvest Financial Planning & Insurance Services Inc.
14441 - 19A Ave.
White Rock, BC V4A 6X3
604-542-2818
Fax: 604-542-2819
800-325-0872
dr.rrsp@telus.net
www3.telus.net/visionvest/
Executives:
Arnold Machel

Vistaplan Financial Group
#202, 10171 Saskatchewan Dr. NW
Edmonton, AB T6E 4R5
780-433-5055
Profile: Brokerage services for life insurance, equipment leases & accounts receivable financing are services offered.

W.A. Robinson & Associates Ltd.
Also listed under: *Financing & Loan Companies; Investment Management*
The Simonett Bldg.
PO Box 208
14216 Hwy. 38
Sharbot Lake, ON K0H 2P0
613-279-2116
Fax: 613-279-3130
877-279-2116
wayne.robinson@robinsonsgroup.com
www.robinsonsgroup.com
Ownership: Private
Year Founded: 1980
Number of Employees: 22
Assets: $1,000,000 Year End: 20041130
Revenues: $1-5 million Year End: 20041130
Profile: Services include business financing, mortgages, financial planning, corporate & transition planning & money management. Affiliated companies are Pillar Financial Services Inc. & Lake District Realty Corporation.

Executives:
Wayne A. Robinson, CFA, President, Financial Planner, Investment Counsel & Portfolio Man; wayne.robinson@robinsonsgroup.com
David Robinson, Controller
Karen Bertram, Portfolio Administrator
Alison Robinson, Broker, Lake District Realty Corporation

W.H. Stuart & Associates
16 Main St. South
Unionville, ON L3R 2E4
905-305-0880
Fax: 905-305-0878
800-668-1716
whs@whstuart.com
www.whstuart.com
Also Known As: Stuart & Partners
Year Founded: 1981
Number of Employees: 40
Profile: W.H. Stuart is a network of independent professionals marketing financial services across Canada.

Executives:
Howard Stuart, CEO/Owner
Dianne Stuart, Co-Owner

W.W. Smith Insurance Ltd.
208 Central Ave. North
Swift Current, SK S9H 0L2
306-773-1547
Fax: 306-773-0575
800-668-2242
insurance@wwsmith.ca
www.wwsmith.ca
Former Name: W.W. Smith Financial Ltd.
Year Founded: 1913
Number of Employees: 9
Profile: Insurance services are offered.

Executives:
Gord Smith, Principle Owner; gord@wwsmith.ca
Bob Armstrong, Partner
Dave Parenteau, Partner

Warrant Financial
#200, 1 Wesley Ave.
Winnipeg, MB R3C 4C6
204-336-7777
Fax: 204-925-1408
Profile: The firm is engaged in financial planning consultation.

Watson Aberant Chartered Accountants (L.L.P.)
Also listed under: *Accountants*
4212 - 98th St.
Edmonton, AB T6E 6A1
780-438-5969
Fax: 780-437-3918
info@watsonaberant.com
Ownership: Private
Year Founded: 1985
Number of Employees: 22
Assets: $1-5 million
Revenues: $1-5 million
Profile: The chartered accountant firm serves Edmonton & northern Alberta.

Executives:
Michael Aberant, Partner, Public Companies & Business Plans; mike@watsonaberant.com
Case Watson, Partner, Owner Managed Enterprises; case@watsonaberant.com

Wealth Creation & Preservation Inc.(WCP)
#203, 2249 Carling Ave.
Ottawa, ON K2B 7E9
613-596-3277
Fax: 613-596-2869
800-267-0653
info@mywcp.ca
www.mywcp.ca
Profile: Investments, insurance products & tax reduction strategies are services available from the financial planning company. For companies planning to go public, corporate financing is offered.

Executives:
Peter Nicholson, B.Comm, RHU, CFP, President
Sean Marsden, B.A., CIM, Sr. Partner
Allen Wong, BA, Sr. Partner
Irene Brown, Manager, Tax Reduction
Michelle Claude, Manager, Insurance

Wealth Strategies, Investment & Financial Planning
#209, 210 Centrum Blvd.
Orleans, ON K1E 3V7
613-841-8550
Fax: 613-830-0417
877-841-8550
info@wealthstrategies.com
www.wealthstrategies.com
Year Founded: 1996
Profile: The fee-based financial planning firm provides personalized financial advice & managed investments.

Executives:
Robert Abboud, CFP, PFP, President; rob@wealthstrategies.com
Diane Gaudet, Manager, Client Service; diane@wealthstrategies.com
Alain Secours, BA, Financial Advisor

Wealthco Financial Advisory Services Inc.
#301, 222 - 58th Ave. SW
Calgary, AB T2H 2S3
403-537-5853
Fax: 403-252-3020
www.wealthco.ca
Executives:
David Udy
Branches:
Saskatoon
1221B Idylwyld Dr. North
Saskatoon, SK S7L 1A1 Canada
306-975-1288
Fax: 306- 11-0

WealthMapping Inc.
PO Box 75111
20 Bloor St. East
Toronto, ON M4W 3T3
416-934-9826
Executives:
Carole Aronovitch, President

WealthWorks Financial Inc.
#16, 10815 Bathurst St.
Richmond Hill, ON L4C 9Y2
905-884-8898
Fax: 905-884-0028
service@wealthworks.com
www.wealthworks.com
Ownership: Private
Year Founded: 1990
Number of Employees: 1
Executives:
Jack DiNardo, President

Welch & Company LLP
Also listed under: *Accountants*
151 Slater St., 12th Fl.
Ottawa, ON K1P 5H3
613-236-9191
Fax: 613-236-8258
welch@welchandco.ca
www.welchandco.ca
Ownership: Private
Year Founded: 1918
Profile: The firm serves business, government & not-for-profit clients. Taxation, accounting, auditing, personal financial planning & wealth management services are provided.

Executives:
Mark Patry, CA, Principal; mpatry@welchandco.ca
Rick Reid, CA, Principal; rreid@welchandco.ca
Don Timmins, CA, Managing Partner, Ottawa; dtimmins@welchandco.ca
Branches:
Belleville
525 Dundas St. East
Belleville, ON K8N 1G4 Canada
613-966-2844
Fax: 613-966-2206
welchbvl@welch.on.ca
Glenn Collins, Partner
Campbellford
PO Box 1209
57 Bridge St. East
Campbellford, ON K0L 1L0 Canada
705-653-3194
Fax: 705-653-1703
mnorthey@welch.on.ca
Marie Northey, Partner
Cornwall
36 Second St. East
Cornwall, ON K6H 1Y3 Canada
613-932-4953
Fax: 613-932-1731
mail@welchcornwall.on.ca
Ron Mulligan, Partner
Gatineau
#201, 975, boul St-Joseph
Gatineau, QC J8Z 1W8 Canada
819-771-7381
Fax: 819-771-3089
lm@levesquemarchand.ca
Guy Coté, Partner
Napanee
58 Dundas St. East
Napanee, ON K7R 1H8 Canada
613-354-2169
Fax: 613-354-2160
datkinson@welch.on.ca
Dan Atkinson, Partner
Ottawa

151 Slater Street, 12th Fl.
Ottawa, ON K1P 5H3 Canada
613-236-9191
Fax: 613-236-8258
welch@welchandco.ca
Garth Steele, Partner
Pembroke
PO Box 757
270 Lake St.
Pembroke, ON K8A 6X9 Canada
613-735-1021
Fax: 613-735-2071
hward@welch-pembroke.com
Hal Ward, Partner
Picton
290 Main St.
Picton, ON K0K 2T0 Canada
613-476-3283
Fax: 613-476-1627
jrand@welch.on.ca
Judy Rand, Partner
Renfrew
101 Raglan St. North
Renfrew, ON K7V 1N7 Canada
613-432-8399
Fax: 613-432-9154
damyotte@welchandco.ca
Dan Amyotte, Partner
Trenton
#4, 290 Dundas St. West
Trenton, ON K8V 3S1 Canada
613-392-1287
Fax: 613-392-5456
jbailey@welch.on.ca
John Bailey, Partner
Tweed
PO Box 807
63 Victoria St. North
Tweed, ON K0K 3J0 Canada
613-478-5051
Fax: 613-478-3069
mnorthey@welch.on.ca
Marie Northey, Partner

Wellington West Aboriginal Investment Services

#400, 200 Waterfront Dr.
Winnipeg, MB R3B 3P1
204-925-2250
Fax: 204-942-6194
800-461-6314
www.wellingtonwestsecurities.com/wwais.html
Ownership: Division of Wellington West Capital Inc.
Year Founded: 1997
Profile: Advisors, researchers, & brokers provide investment advisory & trust investment management services. Clients are members of Canadian First Nations and Aboriginal communities and organizations.

Executives:
Doug Barrett, Managing Director & Vice-President, Investment Services
Ronni Silvari, Registered Representative
Branches:
Moose Jaw
#323, 310 Main St. North
Moose Jaw, SK S6H 3K1
306-691-6290
Fax: 306-691-6299
866-234-4418
David Black, Investment Advisor
Red Deer
#200, 4719 - 48th Ave.
Red Deer, AB T4N 3T1
403-348-2600
Fax: 403-348-0203
866-348-2633
Iain MacDougall, Investment Advisor
Regina
Tower 2, McCallum Hill Centre
#1770 - 1881 Scarth St., 17th Fl.
Regina, SK S4P 4K9
306-781-0500
Fax: 306-781-0505
866-488-0500
David Black, Investment Advisor
Saskatoon
Saskatoon Square
#1360, 410 - 22nd St. East
Saskatoon, SK S7K 5T6
306-934-8897
Fax: 306-244-9888
800-426-9105
Rick Wingate, Investment Advisor
Surrey
Windsor Square
1959 - 152nd St.
Surrey, BC V4A 9E3
604-542-2824
Fax: 604-542-2843
877-542-2843
Nancy Shewfelt, Vice-President
Swift Current
#301, 12 Cheadle St. West
Swift Current, SK S9H 0A9
306-778-4770
Fax: 306-778-4775
866-446-9444
Jerrod Schafer, Investment Advisor
Yorkton
132 Broadway St. West
Yorkton, SK S3N 0M4
306-782-6450
Fax: 306-782-6460
877-782-6450
Kris Sapara, Investment Advisor

Wellington West Financial Services Inc.(WWFS)

Also listed under: *Investment Dealers*
#300, 200 Waterfront Dr.
Winnipeg, MB R3B 3P1
204-925-2290
Fax: 204-956-1296
800-848-0580
wellingtonwest.com/about_wwfs.html
Ownership: Subsidiary of Wellington West Capital Inc.
Profile: Financial plans are developed for individuals, families & businesses.

Executives:
Wade Lawrence, B.Comm (Hons.), RHU, CLU, CH.F.C., CFP, RFP, TEP, President; 204-925-2071
Pierre L. Campeau, RHU, EPC, Vice-President
Rob White, CLU, CFP, Vice-President
Branches:
Calgary
Bow Valley Square 3
255 - 5th Ave. SW
Calgary, AB T2P 3G6 Canada
403-266-1410
Fax: 403-266-6121
800-242-4897
Debbie Ekkel, Financial Advisor
Headingley
5315 Portage Ave.
Headingley, MB R4H 1J9
204-989-7705
Fax: 204-987-7705
London
#802, 380 Wellington St.
London, ON N6A 5B5
Fax: 519-645-7392
800-643-8380
Roblin
PO Box 1440
Roblin, MB R0L 1P0 Canada
204-937-8897
Fax: 204-937-8897
866-937-4299
Vernon Brown, Financial Advisor
Saskatoon
Saskatoon Square
#1360, 410- 22nd St. East
Saskatoon, SK S7K 5T6
306-934-8897
Fax: 306-244-9888
800-426-9105
Ian DeCorby, Group & Pension Advisor
Ste Rose du Lac
PO Box 850
640 Central Ave.
Ste Rose du Lac, MB R0L 1S0 Canada
204-447-3034
Fax: 204-447-3442
Vancouver
#1488, 1333 West Broadway Ave.
Vancouver, BC V6H 4C1
Fax: 604-742-2141
866-738-5655
Victoria
1480 Fort St.
Victoria, BC V8S 1Z5
250-475-3698
Fax: 250-475-3697
888-661-7526
Scott Vanderwark, Financial Advisor

Wellington West Pro Ice Management

29 Ocean Ridge Dr.
Winnipeg, MB R3Y 1W7
204-284-9900
Fax: 204-488-8533
wellwest.ca/pro_ice.html
W. Grant Skinner, President; grants@wellwest.ca

Wellington West Total Wealth Management Inc.

#300, 200 Waterfront Dr.
Winnipeg, MB R3B 3P1
204-925-5156
Fax: 204-925-5148
www.wellingtonwest.com
Executives:
David Christianson, Sr. Advisor

Wentworth Financial Services Inc.

Also listed under: *Investment Dealers*
#605, 105 Main St. East
Hamilton, ON L8N 1G6
905-528-0193
Fax: 905-546-5039
Other Information: 1-800-463-5386
reception@wentworthfinancial.com
www.wentworthfinancial.com
Former Name: Allan H. Minaker CFP, CLU, CH.F.C.
Ownership: Private
Year Founded: 1981
Number of Employees: 15

West Capital Wealth Management

Also listed under: *Investment Dealers*
#400, 1306 Wellington St.
Ottawa, ON K1Y 3B2
613-722-1854
Fax: 613-722-6579
800-826-0877
info@westcap.ca
www.westcap.ca
Also Known As: WestCap
Ownership: Private. Part of Armstrong & Quaile Associates Inc., Manotick, ON.
Year Founded: 2000
Executives:
Terry Olsen, CFP, P.Eng., MAnager; tolsen@westcap.ca

Wiegers Financial & Insurance Planning Services Ltd.

901 - 3rd Ave. North
Saskatoon, SK S7K 2K4
306-244-0949
Fax: 306-244-4026
inquiries@wiegersfinancial.com
www.wiegersfinancial.com
Former Name: Wiegers Financial
Ownership: Private
Year Founded: 1991
Number of Employees: 10
Revenues: $1-5 million
Profile: Also Employee Benefit Consultants

Executives:
Clifford A. Wiegers, President
Vince S. Wiegers, Vice-President

Wilkinson & Company LLP

Also listed under: *Accountants*
PO Box 400
71 Dundas St. West
Trenton, ON K8V 5R6

INVESTMENT MANAGEMENT

Wilkinson & Company LLP (continued)
613-392-2592
Fax: 613-392-8512
888-713-7283
trenton@wilkinson.net
www.wilkinson.net
Year Founded: 1964
Profile: The firm specializes in accounting & tax planning & preparation. Specific services include audits, business advisory, financial planning, wealth management, succession planning, estate planning & retirement planning. It serves corporate, not-for-profit organization & personal clients.
Executives:
Rob Cory, CA, Partner
Jim L. Coward, CA, CFP, Partmer
Bob Robertson, CA, Partner
Stephen Thompson, CA, CFP, TEP, Partner
Robert Yager, CA, Partner
Branches:
Belleville
PO Box 757
139 Front St.
Belleville, ON K8N 5B5 Canada
613-966-5105
Fax: 613-962-7072
888-728-3890
belleville@wilkinson.net
R.G. (Rob) Deacon, Partner
Kingston
#201, 785 Midpark Dr.
Kingston, ON K7M 7G3 Canada
613-634-5581
Fax: 613-634-5585
866-692-0055
kingston@wilkinson.net
Jennifer Fisher, Partner

The William Douglas Group Inc.
1005 Skyview Dr.
Burlington, ON L7P 5B1
905-331-1442
Fax: 905-331-255
info@wdg.ca
www.wdg.ca
Ownership: Private
Executives:
William D. McElroy, CFP, President

Willis Associates
***Also listed under:** Trustees in Bankruptcy; Accounting & Law*
#100, 2903 - 35th Ave.
Vernon, BC V1T 2S7
250-549-2922
Fax: 250-542-8300
888-333-2922
www.willisassociates.ca
Profile: The following services are provided: accounting, assurance & taxation; insolvency; executor & trustee services; personal financial planning; fraud examination; as well as special engagements.
Executives:
David Patrick Willis, Chartered Accountant; Dave.Williams@willisassociates.ca

Windcroft Financial Counsel Ltd.
#1202, 67 Yonge St.
Toronto, ON M5E 1J8
416-947-1588
Fax: 416-864-0721
info@windcroft.com
www.windcroft.com
Ownership: Private
Year Founded: 1987
Executives:
Gordon Bruce, President, Treasurer
Mark Klinkow, Vice-President & Portfolio Manager

Woodstone Capital Inc.
***Also listed under:** Investment Dealers*
#310, 601 West Cordova St.
Vancouver, BC V6B 1G1
604-605-8300
Fax: 604-605-8310
888-388-3885
inquiries@woodstonecapital.com
www.woodstonecapital.com
Year Founded: 1997
Stock Exchange Membership: Montreal Exchange, Toronto Stock Exchange, TSX Venture Exchange
Profile: The indpendent firm offers investment products & services such as research, advice, retirement planning, estate planning, corporate finance expertise & trade execution.
Executives:
Mahmood S, Ahamed, President
Ginalee Holliday, Chief Financial Officer
Ben Hadala, Vice-President
Richard Roussel, Vice-President
Alexander Teh, B.Comm, Sr. Investment Advisor
Branches:
Calgary
#530, 510 - 5 St. SW
Calgary, AB T2P 3S2 Canada
403-777-3880
Canmore
139 Morris St.
Canmore, AB T1W 2W5 Canada
888-278-4282

World Financial Group, Inc., Canada(WFG)
#400, 3700 Steeles Ave. West
Vaughan, ON L4L 8M9
905-265-9005
www.wfg-online.ca, www.worldfinancialgroup.com
Former Name: World Marketing Alliance of Canada Inc.
Ownership: Part of World Financial Group, Inc., USA.
Profile: As a member of the AEGON family of companies, WFG offers the following services: insurance, mutual funds, segregated funds, college planning, retirement strategies & business client assistance. Offices are located across Canada.

Worldsource Financial Management Inc.
#700, 625 Cochrane Dr.
Markham, ON L3R 9R9
905-940-0044
Fax: 905-415-0184
800-287-4869
www.worldsourcewealth.com
Ownership: Division of Worldsource Wealth Management Inc.
Executives:
Andy Mitchell, President/COO; amitchell@worldsourcewealth.com

Worldsource Insurance Network(WIN)
Park Place
#2338, 666 Burrard St.
Vancouver, BC V6C 2X8
604-689-8289
Fax: 604-689-2801
888-338-9888
www.worldsourceinsurance.com
Ownership: Division of Worldsource Wealth Management Inc.
Year Founded: 1997
Profile: The managing general agency serves over 600 advisors throughout Canada through 12 insurance carriers. Banking & wealth management services are also available to clients.
Executives:
Robert Trowbridge, CLU, President/COO; btrowbridge@worldsourceinsurance.com
Bob Morden, CLU, ChFC, CFP, Exec. Vice-President; bmorden@worldsourceinsurance.com
Betsy Wan, FLMI, ACS, AIAA, Exec. Director, Agency Operations; bwan@worldsourceinsurance.com
Branches:
Markham
#700, 625 Cochrane Dr.
Markham, ON L3R 9R9
905-940-6091
Fax: 905-940-6092
866.853.1823
acarey@worldsourceinsurance.com
Anne Carey, Manager, Business

Worldsource Securities Inc.
***Also listed under:** Investment Dealers*
#700, 625 Cochrane Dr.
Markham, ON L3R 9R9
905-940-0094
Fax: 905-415-1812
866-740-7277
www.worldsourcesecurities.com
Ownership: Division of Worldsource Wealth Management Inc.
Profile: The investment dealer provides services regulated by the Investment Dealers Association of Canada (IDA). Financial advisory & wealth management services are also offered.
Executives:
John Hunt, President/COO

Worldsource Wealth Management Inc.
#700, 625 Cochrane Dr.
Markham, ON L3R 9R9
905-940-5500
Fax: 905-940-1410
888-323-8965
clientservices@worldsourcewealth.com
www.worldsourcewealth.com
Ownership: Member of the Guardian Capital Group.
Profile: The organization offers advice about wealth management planning. Planning services include education, insurance, retirement, estate, succession, high net worth & tax.
Executives:
Paul Brown, Managing Director
John Hunt, Managing Director
Robert E.L. Trowbridge, Managing Director
William (Bill) Donegan, Chief Compliance Officer
Alexandra (Alex) Vieira, Chief Financial Officer
Affiliated Companies:
Worldsource Financial Management Inc.
Worldsource Insurance Network/WIN
Worldsource Securities Inc.

The Wright Brothers Financial Services Inc.
#200, 755 Queens Ave.
Victoria, BC V8T 1M2
250-382-2366
Fax: 250-382-3545
866-382-2366
tracey@thewrightbrothers.com
thewrightbrothers.com
Ownership: Private
Executives:
Barry C. Wright, CH.F.C., CLU, CFP, Owner

Y.I.S. Financial Inc.
***Also listed under:** Investment Dealers*
215 Scott St.
St Catharines, ON L2N 1H5
905-937-3920
Fax: 905-646-0003
invest@yis.ca
Executives:
Rich Merrick, Advisor

York Financial Group
625 Davis Dr.
Newmarket, ON L3Y 2R2
905-853-6196
800-479-6576
admin@yorkfingroup.on.ca
www.yorkfingroup.on.ca
Year Founded: 1986
Profile: Financial planning services include investment, retirement, estate, pension plan, tax, & insurance.
Executives:
Tom Fodey, Partner; tfodey@yorkfingroup.on.ca
Linda Shaw, CFP, Financial Consultant; lshaw@yorkfingroup.on.ca

York Financial Services Inc.
#400, 494 Queen St.
Fredericton, NB E3B 1B6
506-443-7761
Fax: 506-458-1154
York.Financial@nb.aibn.com
Year Founded: 1995
Number of Employees: 22
Assets: $4,600,000 Year End: 20051031
Revenues: $2,800,000 Year End: 20051031
Profile: The independent firm offers finanacial advice.
Executives:
Alden Kaley, President

Yorkminster Insurance Brokers Ltd.
PO Box 234
105 Dorset St. West
Port Hope, ON L1A 1G4

905-885-4977
Fax: 905-885-2556
800-668-1751
sbhs@eagle.ca
www.yorkminster.ca
Profile: The following personal financial planning services are provided: personal protection planning, estate planning, investment planning, charitable gift planning, debt planning, retirement planning, education planning, job severance, & business succession planning

Executives:
Stephen B.H. Smith, BA, CEB, CFP, CSC, PRP, Financial Advisor

Young Financial Group
262 Queen St. South
Kitchener, ON N2G 1W3
519-885-5050
Fax: 519-885-6900
800-603-8171
Year Founded: 1982

Younker & Kelly Financial Advisors
119 Queen St.
Charlottetown, PE C1A 4B3
902-629-1112
Fax: 902-629-1113
Former Name: Younker & Kelly Inc.

yourCFO Wealth Management Inc.
Reimer Building
5500 North Service Rd., 3rd Fl.
Burlington, ON L7L 6W6
905-331-2885
Fax: 905-331-2886
888-539-5263
Profile: Financial planning services includes retirement, tax & estate planning. As an independent insurance agency, the firm also offers life insurance products.

Branches:
Burlington
#101, 5575 North Service Rd.
Burlington, ON L7L 6M1
905-335-5222
Fax: 905-335-5355
888-563-1231
Comox
#201, 1819 Beaufort Ave.
Comox, BC V9M 1R9
250-339-5776
Fax: 250-339-5778
Hamilton
#6A, 45 Goderich Dr.
Hamilton, ON L8E 4W8
905-560-8409
Fax: 905-560-2368
Kanata
68 Insmill Cres.
Kanata, ON K2T 1G4
613-599-8885
Fax: 613-592-5139
Mississauga
#4, 2285 Dunwin Dr.
Mississauga, ON L5L 3S3
905-607-1393
Fax: 905-607-1614
Nanaimo
#104, 6330 Dover Rd.
Nanaimo, BC V9V 1S4
250-390-0487
Fax: 250-390-4785
Ottawa
#309, 1755 Woodward Dr.
Ottawa, ON K2C 0P9
613-796-4817
Fax: 819-682-2358
Stoney Creek
4 Watercliff Pl.
Stoney Creek, ON L8E 6E5
905-592-1136
Fax: 905-643-8071
Victoria
760 Hillside Ave.
Victoria, BC V8T 1Z6
250-385-0099
Fax: 250-385-0078
877-385-0090

ZLC Financial Group
3711 Grange Rd.
Victoria, BC V8Z 4S9
250-727-3445
Fax: 250-479-9716
800-906-5666
Other Information: 250-744-2884 (Phone, Funds)
www.zlc.net
Former Name: Zlotnik, Lamb & Company
Year Founded: 1945
Profile: The company consists of the following divisions: Insurance & Retirement Solutions, Private Investment Management, Employee Benefits, & Structured Settlements.

Executives:
Garry Zlotnik, B.Comm., C.A., CFP, CLU, CH.F.C., President; gzlotnik@zlc.net
Peter G. Lamb, B.A., CLU, TEP, EPC, CSA, Founding Partner; plamb@zlc.net
Harold Zlotnik, CLU, Founding Partner; hzlotnik@zlc.net
Branches:
Vancouver
Park Place
#1200, 666 Burrard St.
Vancouver, BC V6C 2X8 Canada
604-688-7208
Fax: 604-688-7268
800-663-1499

Holding & Other Investment Companies

AEGON Canada Inc.
5000 Yonge St.
Toronto, ON M2N 7J8
416-883-5000
www.aegoncanada.com
Ownership: Private. Member of AEGON N.V., The Hague, The Netherlands.
Number of Employees: 750
Profile: AEGON Canada is also affiliated with Aegon Capital Management Inc. & Money Concepts (Canada) Limited. Through its subsidiary companies, AEGON provides insurance & investment solutions.

Executives:
Paul Reaburn, President/CEO
James Falle, Exec. Vice-President/CFO
Karen Gavan, Exec. Vice-President/COO
Iliana Arapis, Sr. Manager, Corporate Communications; iliana.arapis@aegoncanada.ca
Affiliated Companies:
AEGON Dealer Services Canada Inc.
AEGON Fund Management Inc.
Transamerica Life Canada

Allegiance Equity Corporation
79 Old Forest Hill Rd.
Toronto, ON M5P 2R6
416-489-6660
Fax: 416-482-2558
admin@allegiance-equity.com
www.allegiance-equity.com
Ownership: Public
Year Founded: 1974
Stock Symbol: ANQ
Profile: The company holds short & long-term investments, marketable securities & cash.

Executives:
David S. Solomon, Acting CEO
Marilyn H. Bloovol, Acting CFO

Almasa Capital Inc.
#300, 475, av Dumont
Montréal, QC H9S 5W2
514-631-2682
Fax: 514-631-1257
Ownership: Private
Year Founded: 1997
Assets: $28,000,000
Executives:
C.J. Winn, Vice-President, Finance

Amisk Inc.
Also listed under: *Financing & Loan Companies*
#101, 3633, rue Panet
Jonquière, QC G7X 8T7
418-546-1156
Fax: 418-546-0004
robert.taylor@amisk.qc.ca
www.amisk.qc.ca
Ownership: Public. Major shareholder Pan-O-Lac, 53.8% interest.
Year Founded: 1986
Number of Employees: 3
Assets: $10-50 million
Revenues: $1-5 million
Stock Symbol: AS.A
Profile: The investment company has principal investments in the following companies: Soccrent (8% interest), a venture capital firm which takes an equity position or makes loans to companies in the province of Québec; Panneaux MDF La Baie Inc. (12% interest), a medium density fibre panel producer in La Baie, Québec; Groupe Nova Inc. (13.125% interest), a hardwood flooring manufacturer in La Baie; & Scierie E. Tremblay (50% interest), a sawmill in Saint-Bruno d'Alma.

Executives:
Robert Taylor, General Manager
Directors:
Richard Harvey, President
Aimé Boudreau
Michel Dochesne; 418-669-9000
Pierre-Maurice Gagnon
Yvan Gagnon; 418-696-0666
Colette Gauthier
Germain Laroche
Jean-Robert Larouche
Normand Roy
Jean-Louis Vigneault; 418-542-5666

Aon Consulting/ Groupe-conseil Aon
Also listed under: *Acturarial Consultants*
#500, 145 Wellington St.
Toronto, ON M5J 1H8
416-542-5500
Fax: 416-542-5504
www.aon.com
Ownership: Public. Parent Aon Corporation
Year Founded: 1996
Number of Employees: 550
Stock Symbol: AOC
Profile: Aon Consulting is the consulting arm of Aon Corporation. It provides full integrated consulting services covering the wide spectrum of health & benefits, retirement, human resources, change management, compensation & workers' compensation requirements.

Executives:
Ashim Khemani, Chair/Chief Executive
Branches:
Calgary
Gulf Canada Square
#885, 401 - 9th Ave. SW
Calgary, AB T2P 3C5 Canada
403-261-6056
Fax: 403-262-2446
kaylynn.schroeder@aon.ca
Kaylynn Schroeder, Contact
Edmonton
#700, 10025 - 102A Ave.
Edmonton, AB T5J 2Z2 Canada
780-423-1010
Fax: 780-425-8295
kaylynn.schroeder@aon.ca
Kaylynn Schroeder, Contact
Halifax
Tower II, Purdy's Wharf
#1001, 1969 Upper Water St.
Halifax, NS B3J 3R7 Canada
902-423-8714
Fax: 902-423-8716
sherry.lee.gregory@aon.ca
Sherry Lee Gregory, Contact
London
One London Place
#1400, 255 Queens Ave.
London, ON N6A 5R8 Canada

Aon Consulting/ Groupe-conseil Aon (continued)

519-434-2114
Fax: 519-434-9950
888-337-3334
kaylynn.schroeder@aon.ca
Kaylynn Schroeder, Contact

Montréal
#1100, 1801, av McGill College
Montréal, QC H3A 3P4 Canada
514-845-6231
Fax: 514-845-0678
louis.p.gagnon@aon.ca
Louis P. Gagnon, Contact

Ottawa
#712, 1525 Carling Ave.
Ottawa, ON K1Z 8R9 Canada
613-728-5000
Fax: 513-728-5534
julie.joyal@aon.ca
Julie Joyal, Contact

Québec
Place de la Cité
PO Box 9850, Sainte-Foy Sta. Sainte-Foy
#750, 2600, boul Laurier
Québec, QC G1V 4C3 Canada
418-650-1119
Fax: 418-650-1440
france.bilodeau@aon.ca
France Bilodeau, Contact

Regina
#1000, 2103 - 11th Ave.
Regina, SK S4P 3Z8 Canada
306-569-6749
Fax: 306-359-0387
kaylynn.schroeder@aon.ca
Kaylynn Schroeder, Contact

Saskatoon
Canada Bldg.
105 - 21st St. East, 8th Fl.
Saskatoon, SK S7K 0B3 Canada
306-934-8680
Fax: 306-244-7597
kaylynn.schroeder@aon.ca
Kaylynn Schroeder, Contact

Vancouver
900 Howe St., 5th Fl.
Vancouver, BC V6B 3X8 Canada
604-688-8591
Fax: 604-684-9902
kaylynn.schroeder@aon.ca
Kaylynn Schroeder, Contact

Winnipeg
#1800, 1 Lombard Pl.
Winnipeg, MB R3B 2A3 Canada
204-954-5500
Fax: 204-954-5501
kaylynn.schroeder@aon.ca
Kaylynn Schroeder, Contact

ARC Energy Trust

#2100, 440 - 2nd Ave. SW
Calgary, AB T2P 5E9
403-503-8600
Fax: 403-503-8609
888-272-4900
ir@arcresources.com
www.arcresources.com
Ownership: Public. Subsidiary of ARC Resources
Year Founded: 1996
Number of Employees: 240
Assets: $1-10 billion
Revenues: $100-500 million
Stock Symbol: AET.UN
Profile: ARC Energy Trust is an actively managed royalty trust formed to provide investors with a tax efficient, indirect ownership of cash generating oil & gas assets, plus the liquidity of an equity investment. Unitholders receive distributable cash flow from the production & subsequent sale of crude oil & natural gas. Business risk is minimized through property & commodity diversification & the avoidance of higher risk exploration activities.

Executives:
John P. Dielwart, President/CEO
Steven Sinclair, CFO/Vice-President, Finance
Doug Bonner, Vice-President, Engineering
David P. Carey, Vice-President, Business Development
Susan D. Healy, Vice-President, Corporate Services
Myron M. Stadnyk, Vice-President, Operations & Land
Allan R. Twa, Corporate Secretary
Directors:
Walter De Boni, Chair
John Beddome
Fred Coles
John P. Dielwart
Fred Dyment
Michael Kanovsky
John Stewart
Mac Van Weilingen

Argus Corporation Limited

10 Toronto St.
Toronto, ON M5C 2B7
416-363-8721
800-387-0825
Also Known As: Argus
Ownership: Public. The Ravelston Corporation Limited owns 100% of common shares.
Year Founded: 1945
Stock Symbol: AR.PR.A, AR.PR.B, AR.PR.D
Profile: The holding company's major investment is a 62% interest in Hollinger Inc.

Executives:
F. David Radler, President
Monique Delorme, Chief Financial Officer
Peter Y. Atkinson, Exec. Vice-President
J.A. Boultbee, Exec. Vice-President
Peter G. White, Exec. Vice-President, Secretary
Directors:
Barbara Amiel Black
J.A. Boultbee
Jonathan Marler
Hollis T. McCurdy
F. David Radler
James A. (Jay) Richardson
Robert Emmett Tyrrell

Atlantis Systems Corp.

1 Kenview Blvd.
Brampton, ON L6T 5E6
905-792-1981
Fax: 905-792-7251
info@atlantissc.com
www.atlantissc.com
Former Name: Denbridge Capital Corporation
Ownership: Public.
Year Founded: 1978
Stock Symbol: AIQ
Profile: Atlantis is a global provider of integrated flight training & aircraft maintenance training to the military & commercial aviation sectors.

Executives:
Andrew Day, President/CEO
John F. Kalas, CA, CPA, Sr. Vice-President/CFO
Paul Maasland, Vice-President, Business Development
Douglas Donderi, Corporate Secretary
Directors:
Andrew Day
Julio DiGirolamo
Terence Donnelly
Donald Hathaway
David J. McFadden
Henry Pankratz
David Williams

Ausnoram Holdings Limited

#302, 277 Lakeshore Rd. East
Oakville, ON L6J 1H9
905-337-2643
Fax: 905-337-2186
Ownership: Public
Year Founded: 1965
Stock Symbol: ASNH.A
Executives:
Aubrey W. Baillie, President/CEO
Jeffrey Potwarka, Chief Financial Officer

Automodular Corporation

#420, 20 Toronto St.
Toronto, ON M5C 2B8
416-861-0662
Fax: 416-861-0063
invest@automodular.com
www.automodular.com
Former Name: Algonquin Mercantile Corporation
Year Founded: 1957
Stock Symbol: AM
Profile: The corporation is engaged in parts assembly for the automotive industry (Automotive Assemblies Inc.).

Executives:
Michael Blair, CEO
Christopher S. Nutt, Vice-President, Finance
Diane C. Erlinger, Corporate Secretary
Directors:
Russell Baranowski
Michael Blair
Andrew Brenton
Garth Davis
Henry Knowles
R. Peter McLaughlin
James Rodgers
Rae Wallin

AXA Canada Inc.

Also listed under: Federal & Provincial
#700, 2020, rue University
Montréal, QC H3A 2A5
514-282-1914
marketing.webmestre@axa-canada.com
www.axa.ca
Ownership: Member of the AXA Group, Paris, France.
Year Founded: 1985
Number of Employees: 2,300
Profile: The financial holding company offers a range of financial protection products & financial services through its network of subsidiaries in western Canada, Ontario, Québec, & the Atlantic provinces.

Executives:
Jean-François Blais, President/CEO
Iain Hume, Exec. Vice-President/CFO
Robert Landry, Exec. Vice-President, Life Insurance & Financial Services
Luci Martel, Vice-President, Human Resources
Suzie Pellerin, Manager, Communication; suzie.pellerin@axa-canada.com
Directors:
Jean-Denis Talon, Chair
Affiliated Companies:
AXA General Insurance Company
AXA Insurance (Canada)
AXA Pacific Insurance Company

BAM Investments Corp.

BCE Place
PO Box 762
#300, 181 Bay St.
Toronto, ON M5J 2T3
416-359-8620
Fax: 416-365-9642
Former Name: BNN Investments Ltd.; Consolidated Canadian Express Limited
Assets: $100-500 million
Stock Symbol: BNB
Profile: Listed on the Toronto Stock Exchange, the leveraged investment company's principal investment is in Brookfield Asset Management Inc. BAM Split Corp. is a subsidiary.

Executives:
Brian D. Lawson, President
Sachin G. Shah, Vice-President/CFO
Loretta M. Corso, Corporate Secretary
Directors:
Frank N.C. Lochan, Chair
James C. Bacon
Howard Driman
Brian D. Lawson
R. Frank Lewarne
Ralph J. Zarboni

Bancorp Financial Services Inc.

Also listed under: Financing & Loan Companies
#1420, 1090 West Georgia St.
Vancouver, BC V6E 3V7
604-608-2717
Fax: 604-609-7107
info@bancorpfinancial.com
www.bancorpfinancial.com
Year Founded: 1975

Profile: The company specializes in real estate lending & mortgage fund managing.

Branches:
Victoria
#101, 4420 Chatterton Way
Victoria, BC V8X 5J2
250-479-3999
Fax: 250-479-4494

Benvest New Look Income Fund
#3438, 1, Place Ville-Marie
Montréal, QC H3B 3N6
514-877-4295
Fax: 514-876-3956
benvest@benvest.com
www.benvest.com
Former Name: Benvest Capital Inc.
Ownership: Public
Year Founded: 2005
Assets: $10-100 billion Year End: 20050430
Stock Symbol: BCI-UN
Profile: An affilate of the income fund is New Look Eyewear Inc.

Trustees:
W. John Bennett, Chair; j.bennett@benvest.com
Richard Cherney
William Cleman
Paul S. Echenberg
William R. Ferguson
C. Emmett Pearson; e.pearson@benvest.com

Brascade Corporation
BCE Place
PO Box 762
#300, 181 Bay St.
Toronto, ON M5J 2T3
416-363-9491
Fax: 416-363-2856
Ownership: Public. Wholly owned subsidiary of Brookfield Asset Management Inc., Toronto, ON.
Stock Symbol: BCA.PR.B
Profile: Listed on the Toronto Stock Exchange, the investment company has investments in the forest products & real estate sectors. In 2007, it amalgamated with Diversified Canadian Financial II Corp. & Diversified Canadian Holdings Inc.

Executives:
Edward C. Kress, President
Lisa W. Chu, Vice-President, Controller
Alan V. Dean, Vice-President, Secretary
Sachin G. Shah, Vice-President/CFO
Directors:
Edward C. Kress, Chair
John P. Barratt
Alan V. Dean
James L. Kelly
Duncan A. McAlpine

British Controlled Oilfields Limited
#1720, 1080, côte du Beaver Hall
Montréal, QC H2Z 1S8
514-871-9571
Fax: 514-397-0816
Ownership: Public.
Year Founded: 1918
Stock Symbol: BCO
Profile: The holding company invests in stocks & bonds of publicly traded corporations. These corporations are situated mainly in the USA, UK, & Europe.

Executives:
Michael A. Salberg, President/CFO
David A. Johnson, Secretary
Directors:
Mario J. Choueiri
Anita M.G. Hecht
Michael A. Salberg
Robert Salberg

CAI Capital Corporation
Also listed under: *Financing & Loan Companies*
#200, 3429, rue Drummond
Montréal, QC H3G 1X6
514-849-1642
Fax: 514-849-1788
info@caifunds.com
www.caifunds.com
Year Founded: 1990
Stock Symbol: KCC
Profile: CAI is engaged in merchant banking activities.

Executives:
David M. Culver, Founding Partner
Mark P. Culver, Founding Partner
Leslie B. Daniels, Managing Partner
Peter M. Gottsegen, Managing Partner
Tracey L. McVicar, Managing Partner
Tim J. Patterson, Managing Partner
Mark B. Piotrowski, Managing Partner
Peter G. Restler, Managing Partner
Manfred W. Yu, Managing Partner
Craig A. Skolnick, CFO
Branches:
Toronto
Royal Bank Plaza, South Tower
#2320, 200 Bay St.
Toronto, ON M5J 2J1 Canada
416-306-9810
Fax: 416-306-9816
Vancouver
PO Box 11137, Royal Centre Sta. Royal Centre
#2028, 1155 West Georgia St.
Vancouver, BC V6E 3P3 Canada
604-694-2525
Fax: 604-694-2524

Canada Life Financial Corporation
330 University Ave.
Toronto, ON M5G 1R8
416-597-6981
888-252-1847
info@canadalife.com
www.canadalife.com
Year Founded: 1847
Stock Symbol: CL.PR.B

Canada Trust Income Investments(CTII)
c/o TD Asset Management Inc., TD Canada Trust Tower
161 Bay St., 35th Fl.
Toronto, ON M5J 2T2
416-982-6039
Fax: 416-983-1729
800-663-9097
tdetf@tdam.com
www.tdassetmanagement.com
Ownership: Public.
Year Founded: 1973
Stock Symbol: CNN.UN
Profile: Traded on the Toronto Stock Exchange, CTII is a closed-end income investment trust that distributes its net income monthly. Its manager is TD Asset Management Inc.

Executives:
Timothy Pinnington, President
Rudy Sankovic, Chief Financial Officer

Canadian Apartment Properties Real Estate Investment Trust
#401, 11 Church St.
Toronto, ON M5E 1W1
416-861-9404
Fax: 416-861-9209
ir@capreit.net
www.capreit.net
Ownership: Public
Year Founded: 1997
Number of Employees: 594
Assets: $1-10 billion Year End: 20051231
Revenues: $100-500 million Year End: 20051231
Stock Symbol: CAR.UN
Profile: CAP REIT is a real estate investment trust which specializes in multi-unit residential properties in the Greater Toronto Area & Ottawa, Ontario, Montréal, Québec, Halifax, Nova Scotia & Saskatoon, Saskatchewan.

Executives:
Thomas Schwartz, President/CEO
Michael Stein, Chair; 416-861-5788
Dino Chiesa, Vice-Chair
Yazdi Bharucha, CFO & Secretary
Maria Amaral, Vice-President, Finance
Mark Kenney, Vice-President, Operations
Trustees:
Catherine Barbaro
Robert Brown
Paul Harris
Edwin Hawken
Marvin Sadowski
Thomas Schwartz
Michael Stein
Stanley Swartzman
David M. Williams

Canadian Oil Sands Trust
First Canadian Centre
#2500, 350 - 7 Ave. SW
Calgary, AB T2P 3N9
403-218-6200
Fax: 403-218-6201
investor_relations@cos-trust.com
www.cos-trust.com
Ownership: Public
Year Founded: 1995
Stock Symbol: COS.UN
Profile: The open-ended investment trust generates income from its 21.74% working interest in the Syncrude Joint Venture. The Trust is managed by Canadian Oil Sands Investments Inc.

Executives:
Marcel R. Coutu, President/CEO
Directors:
C.E. Shultz, Chair
Marcel R. Coutu
E. Susan Evans, Q.C.
Wayne M. Newhouse
Walter B. O'Donoghue, Q.C.
Wesley Twiss
John B. Zaozirny

Canadian Real Estate Investment Trust
#1001, 130 Bloor St. West
Toronto, ON M5S 1N5
416-628-7771
Fax: 416-628-7777
info@creit.ca
www.creit.ca
Also Known As: CREIT
Ownership: Public
Year Founded: 1993
Stock Symbol: REF.UN
Profile: The equity real estate trust specializes in the acquisition & ownership of shopping centres, industrial & office properties in Canada.

Executives:
Stephen Johnson, President/CEO; 416-628-7878
Timothy McSorley, CFO & Vice-President
Trustees:
Robert Hewett
Stephen Johnson
W. Reay Mackay
John Marino
Lawrence Morassutti
James M. Tory
Robert Witterick

CanCap Preferred Corporation
CP 3400
#800, Place Victoria
Montréal, QC H4Z 1E9
514-397-4369
Fax: 514-397-7600
www.cancap.ca
Ownership: Public.
Year Founded: 1997
Assets: $500m-1 billion Year End: 20051231
Revenues: $10-50 million Year End: 20051231
Stock Symbol: CAC
Executives:
Caroline Beaudoin, President/CEO
Alain Fortin, Vice-President/CFO
Robert Y. Girard, Secretary
Directors:
Caroline Beaudoin
Claude Dalphond
Alain Fortin
Dany Gauthier
Robert Y. Girard
Normand Roy

Cantrell Capital Corp.
Also listed under: *Financing & Loan Companies*

Cantrell Capital Corp. (continued)
#201, 1682 West 7th Ave.
Vancouver, BC V6J 4S6
604-681-9100
Fax: 604-681-9101
Ownership: Public
Year Founded: 1986
Stock Symbol: CLJ
Directors:
Arthur Lyons, President
Louise E. Bastien
Russell Crum
Thomas H. Reissner

Central Fund of Canada Limited
#805, 1323 - 15th Ave. SW
Calgary, AB T3C 0X8
403-228-5861
Fax: 403-228-2222
info@centralfund.com
www.centralfund.com
Ownership: Major shareholder is P.M. Spicer & J.C.S. Spicer (49.97% interest)
Year Founded: 1961
Assets: $500m-1 billion Year End: 20041031
Revenues: Under $1 million Year End: 20041031
Stock Symbol: CEF.Nu.A, CEF.NV.U
Profile: Central Fund of Canada is a closed-end investment holding company. By its articles & policy, the company maintains the majority of its investments in gold & silver-related investments, primarily in the form of unencumbered, allocated & insured physical bullion. Central's shares qualify for inclusion in retirement accounts.

Executives:
J.C.S. Spicer, President/CEO
C.A. Spackman, CMA, Treasurer; cspackman@centralgroupalberta.com
Directors:
Philip M. Spicer, Chair
D.R. Spackman, QC, Co-Chair
John S. Elder, Q.C., Secretary
D.E. Heagle
I.M.T. McAvity
Michael A. Parente, CMA, CFP
R.R. Sale
J.C.S. Spicer
M.A. Taschereau
Branches:
Ancaster - Administrators Investor Enquires Office
PO Box 7319
Ancaster, ON L9G 3N6 Canada
905-648-7878
Fax: 905-648-4196

CITCO Growth Investments Ltd.
6952 Greenwood St.
Burnaby, BC V5A 1X8
604-420-4996
Fax: 604-420-2343
Ownership: Private. CITCO Holdings Ltd.
Year Founded: 1965
Number of Employees: 3
Profile: CITCO operates as an investment & real estate company.

Executives:
Donald J. Ropchan, President
G.G. Ropchan, Vice-President & Secretary
Directors:
P.G. Ropchan, Chair
Andrew Bury
Donald J. Ropchan
G.G. Ropchan
F.L. Terry

CML Global Capital Ltd.
Canadian Centre
#1200, 833 - 4 Ave. SW
Calgary, AB T2P 3T5
403-216-2660
Fax: 403-216-2661
www.cmlglobal.com
Former Name: Canadian Maple Leaf Financial Corporation
Ownership: Private.
Year Founded: 1992
Number of Employees: 5
Profile: Affiliated companies are ASPEN Properties Ltd. & Imperial Parking (Hong Kong) Ltd.

Executives:
Elizabeth Collet Funk, President/CEO
Scott Hutcheson, Chief Operating Officer
Veronica Bouvier, Vice-President, Corporate Secretary
Greg Guatto, Vice-President
Kelly Wildeman, Controller
Directors:
S.C. Funk, Chair
Veronica Bouvier
Elizabeth Collet Funk
Greg Guatto
R. Scott Hutcheson

Consolidated Firstfund Capital Corp.
***Also listed under:** Financing & Loan Companies*
#304, 837 West Hastings St.
Vancouver, BC V6C 3N6
604-683-6611
Fax: 604-662-8524
wngrant@telus.net
www.firstfund.ca
Ownership: Major shareholder William N. Grant (72.2% interest)
Year Founded: 1984
Number of Employees: 5
Assets: $1-5 million Year End: 20041231
Revenues: $1-5 million Year End: 20041231
Stock Symbol: FFP
Profile: The venture capital company is engaged in the tourism & hospitality industry. It is also engaged in financial consulting related to merchant banking & venture capital activities in Canada & the United States. Wholly owned subsidiaries are as follows: Costar Marketing Corp., Goldstar Resort Destinations, Inc.

Executives:
William N. Grant, President/CEO
Robert H. Grant, Vice-President
W. Douglas Grant, Vice-President/CFO
James W.F. Tutton, Vice-President, Real Estate, Secretary
Directors:
Robert H. McClelland, Chair
Robert H. Grant
William N. Grant
James W.F. Tutton

Consolidated Mercantile Inc.
106 Avenue Rd.
Toronto, ON M5R 2H3
416-920-0500
Fax: 416-920-7851
Year Founded: 1940
Assets: $100-500 million
Stock Symbol: CMC
Profile: The management holding company provides merchant banking. It invests in industries including packaging, swimming pool products, furniture & finance.

Executives:
Fred A. Litwin, President/CEO
Daniel S. Tamkin, Vice-President
Stan Abramowitz, Secretary
Directors:
Stan Abramowitz
Fred A. Litwin
Morton Litwin
Sol D. Nayman
Irwin Singer

Corporate Growth Assistance Limited
#420, 1 Benvenuto Pl.
Toronto, ON M4V 2L1
416-222-7772
Fax: 416-222-6091
millard@corporategrowth.ca
Ownership: Private
Year Founded: 1974
Number of Employees: 2
Assets: $1-5 million
Revenues: Under $1 million
Profile: The organization is a merchant investment bank with Private Equity Investments for SMEs.

Executives:
Dan Hill, Principal
Millard S. Roth, Principal

Davis & Henderson Income Fund
#201, 939 Eglinton Ave. East
Toronto, ON M4G 4H7
888-850-6656
investorrelations@dhif.com
www.dhif.com
Ownership: Public.
Year Founded: 1875
Number of Employees: 800+
Stock Symbol: DHF.UN
Profile: The company assists financial institutions with the operation of programs to their chequing & lending accounts.

Executives:
Robert J. Cronin, CEO
C. Sanford McFarlane, Exec. Vice-Chair
Catherine Martin, CFO
Chad Alderson, Vice-President & Chief Technology Officer
Yves Denommé, Vice-President, Operations
Suzanne Mandrozos, Vice-President, Human Resources
Serge Rivest, Vice-President, Sales, Marketing & Teleservices
Joanne Sisco, Vice-President, Corporate Data Services
Directors:
Robert J. Cronin
Paul Damp
Gordon J. Feeney
Allan Gotlieb
C. Sanford McFarlane
Brad Nullmeyer
Helen K. Sinclair

Desjardins Capital de risque/ Desjardins Venture Capital
***Also listed under:** Financing & Loan Companies*
CP 760, Desjardins Stn. Desjardins
#1717, 2, Complexe Desjardins
Montréal, QC H5B 1B8
514-281-7131
Fax: 514-281-7808
Other Information: Toll Free: 1-866-866-7000, poste 7131
www.dcrdesjardins.com
Former Name: Investissement Desjardins
Ownership: Private. Owned by Desjardins Cooperative Group
Year Founded: 1974
Number of Employees: 40
Executives:
Louis L. Roquet, President/CEO
Lucien Bergevin, Adjoint au président et Premier vice président, Ressources humaines, Administration et Réseau
Marie-Claude Boisvert, 1re vice-présidente, Chef de la direction financière
Sylvie Audet, Vice-présidente, Planification et communications
Roger Durand, Vice-président principal, Investissement régional
Ronald Gravel, Vice-président, Développement des affaires coopératives
Catherine Lenfant, Vice-présidente, Finances et évaluation du protefeuille
Fabrice Lucherini, Vice-président, Sciences de la vie, Technologie de l'information et Télécommunications
Claude Rhéaume, Vice-président, Gestion conseil
Gérald St-Aubin, Vice-président, Développement de marché

Desjardins Groupe d'assurances générales inc/ Desjardins General Insurance Group Inc.
***Also listed under:** Federal & Provincial*
6300, boul de la Rive-Sud
Lévis, QC G6V 6P9
888-277-8726
Former Name: Groupe Desjardins, Assurances générales
Ownership: Private. Parent company is Desjardins Group
Year Founded: 1989
Number of Employees: 431
Assets: $500m-1 billion Year End: 20041231
Revenues: $100-500 million Year End: 20041231
Executives:
Alban D'Amours, CEO
Jude Martineau, President/COO
Jean-François Chalifoux, Sr. Exec. Vice-President & General Manager, RoC Operations
Louis Chantal, Sr. Exec. Vice-President, Administration, Finances & Human Resources, Treasurer
Pierre Deschênes, Sr. Exec. Vice-President, Information Technology
Sylvie Paquette, Sr. Exec. Vice-President, Corporate Development

Pierre Rousseau, Sr. Exec. Vice-President, Legal Affairs, Corporate Secretary
Jean Vaillancourt, Sr. Exec. Vice-President & General Manager, Québec Operations
Directors:
Raymond Gagné, Chair
Jean-Robert Laporte, Vice-Chair
Yves Archambeault
Annie P. Bélanger
Jean J. Brossard
Stéphane Coudé
Roger Desrosiers
Jean-Louis Gauvin
Gabrielle Gosselin
Michel Lucas
Jude Martineau
Jocelyne Poulin
Clément Trottier
Yvon Vinet
Affiliated Companies:
Certas Direct Insurance Company
Desjardins assurances générales inc
The Personal General Insurance Inc.
The Personal Insurance Company
Branches:
Montréal
1, Complexe Desjardins, 17e étage, CP 2
Montréal, QC H5B 1B1 Canada
514-281-8101
866-350-8300
Hélène Lamontagne, Sr. Exec. Vice-President, Corporate Affairs

DGC Entertainment Ventures Corp.
Also listed under: *Investment Fund Companies*
EVC Management Inc.
#402, 111 Peter St.
Toronto, ON M5V 2H1
416-365-8053
Fax: 416-365-8037
800-382-1159
Number of Employees: 10
Executives:
Alan Goluboff, Chair
Robb W. Hindson, President
Pamela Brand, Secretary
DGC Entertainment Ventures Corp. Fund
RRSP Eligible; Inception Year: 1994; Fund Managers: EVC Management Inc.

Duncan Park Holdings Corporation
#406, 372 Bay St.
Toronto, ON M5H 2W9
416-203-0860
Fax: 416-203-3980
info@duncanpark.com
www.duncanpark.com
Ownership: Public.
Stock Symbol: DPH
Profile: Listed on the Toronto Stock Exchange's Venture Exchange, the intermediate gold company explores for gold and other precious metals in Nevada, USA.

Executives:
Leonard J. Taylor, President/CEO
Harold J. Doran, CA, Chief Financial Officer
Gregory L. Regional Manager, Chief Geologist
Directors:
Ronald Arnold
Larry Kornze
Ian McAvity
Eric P. Salsberg
Leonard J. Taylor

Dundee Corporation
Scotia Plaza
40 King St. West, 5th Fl.
Toronto, ON M5H 4A9
416-863-6990
Fax: 416-363-4536
lbeak@dundeebancorp.com
www.dundeebancorp.com
Former Name: Dundee Bancorp Inc.
Ownership: Major shareholder, Ned Goodman, directly & indirectly holds 68.84% voting interest.
Year Founded: 1984
Number of Employees: 74
Assets: $1-10 billion
Revenues: $100-500 million
Stock Symbol: DBC.A
Profile: Dundee Bancorp Inc. is primarily a holding company dedicated to wealth management & financial services. It is engaged in the provision of financial services domestically, through its 84% owned subsidiary Dundee Wealth Management Inc., & internationally from Bermuda & the Cayman Islands. The company also holds & manages its own investment & merchant banking portfolio directly & indirectly. Investments include the following companies: Black Hawk Mining Inc. (18% interest); Breakwater Resources Ltd. (27% interest); Dundee Realty Corporation (45% interest); Eurogas Corporation (50%+ interest); Iamgold (7% interest); and Zemex Corporation (39% interest).

Executives:
Ned Goodman, President/CEO
D.K. Charter, Exec. Vice-President
Joanne Ferstman, CFO & Exec. Vice-President
Daniella E. Dimitrov, Vice-President, General Counsel
Lucie Presot, Vice-President & Controller
Lori E. Beak, Secretary
Directors:
Harold P. Gordon, Chair
Garth A.C. MacRae, Vice-Chair
Normand Beauchamp
Paul A. Carroll
Jonathan Goodman
Ned Goodman
Frederick H. Lowy
Robert McLeish
K. Barry Sparks
Harry R. Steele
Affiliated Companies:
Dundee Bank of Canada/DBC
Dundee Wealth Management Inc.

Dynamic Venture Opportunities Fund Ltd.
1 Adelaide St. East, 29th Fl.
Toronto, ON M5C 2V9
416-365-5113
Fax: 416-365-4799
866-977-0477
invest@dynamic.ca
www.dynamic.ca
Former Name: Canadian Venture Opportunity Fund
Year Founded: 1993
Assets: $10-50 million
Profile: This is a labour sponsored venture capital fund. Dundee Wealth Management's investment management division is Goodman and Company Investment Counsel, which covers the Dynamic family of funds

Executives:
Ray Benzinger, BA, CA, CFA, President/CEO

E.D. Smith Income Fund
944 Hwy. 8
Winona, ON L8E 5S3
905-643-1211
800-263-9246
Year Founded: 1882
Stock Symbol: JAM.UN
Profile: The unincorporated, open-ended, limited purpose trust owns E.D. Smith & Sons, Limited & its subsidiaries.
Executives:
Michael G. Burrows, President/CEO
Mark Barr, Exec. Vice-President, Sales & Business Development
Bill Lewis, Exec. Vice-President, Operations
Bruce Smith, Exec. Vice-President/CFO
Alison Cross-Nicholls, Director, Human Resources
Maxwell Gotlieb, Corporate Secretary
Directors:
Michael F. Burrows
Edward S. Barr
John F. Dix
Michael M. Koerner
Robert J. Nobes
Jack H. Scott
Martin Thrasher

The Enerplus Group
The Dome Tower
#3000, 333 - 7th Ave. SW
Calgary, AB T2P 2Z1
403-298-2200
Fax: 403-298-2211
800-319-6462
www.enerplus.com
Year Founded: 1986
Stock Symbol: ERF.UN
Profile: The primary business of Enerplus is the design, creation, development & marketing of a range of energy investments as well as the management of oil & gas properties acquired.

Executives:
Gordon J. Kerr, President/CEO
Heather J. Culbert, Sr. Vice-President, Corporate Services
Garry A. Tanner, Sr. Vice-President & COO
Eric P. Tremblay, Sr. Vice-President, Capital Markets
Robert J. Waters, Sr. Vice-President/CFO
Jo-Anne M. Caza, Vice-President, Investor Relations
Darryl W. Cook, Vice-President, Operations
Larry Hammond, Vice-President, Opertations
Ian C. Dundas, Vice-President, Business Development
Rodney Gray, Vice-President, Finance
Daniel M. Stevens, Vice-President, Development Services
David A. McCoy, General Counsel & Corporate Secretary
Directors:
Douglas R. Martin, Chair
Edwin Dodge
Derek J.M. Fortune
Gordon J. Kerr
Robert L. Normand
Glen Roane
Mike Seth
Donald T. West
Harry B. Wheeler
Robert L. Zorich

ENSIS Growth Fund Inc.
#1120, 200 Graham Ave.
Winnipeg, MB R3C 4L5
204-949-3700
Fax: 204-949-0591
info@ensis.mb.ca
www.ensis.mb.ca
Former Name: ENSIS Management Inc.
Ownership: Public
Year Founded: 1997
Profile: The labour-sponsored venture capital fund is sponsored by the Association of Public Service Financial Administrators & managed by ENSIS Management Inc. The purpose of the Fund is to invest in small- & medium-sized eligible Manitoba businesses. Its objective is long-term capital appreciation.

Executives:
William E. Watchorn, President/CEO; 204-949-3710
Jenifer A. Bartman, CFO & Vice-President; 204-949-3716
O. Kenneth Bicknell, Vice-President; 204-949-3723
Harold Heide, Vice-President, Investments
Andrea E. Martens, Director, Marketing
Directors:
J. Robert Lavery, Chair
Andrew Bieber
Gary N. Coopland
Gene D. Dunn
James Ferguson
Merdon Hosking
Eugène L. Szabo
William E. Watchorn

Esstra Industries Inc.
Also listed under: *Financing & Loan Companies*
#218, 10458 Mayfield Rd.
Edmonton, AB T5P 4P4
780-484-3794
Fax: 780-484-4230
esstragroup@dsm.ca
Ownership: Public
Year Founded: 1996
Stock Symbol: ESS
Profile: Esstra owns 6 buildings with 122 luxury rental townhomes in Eagan, Minnesota. The wholly owned subsidiary is Waterford Apartments Corp.

Executives:
Peter G. Dickson, President/CEO/CFO
Sharon Lewis, Secretary
Directors:
Peter G. Dickson

Esstra Industries Inc. (continued)
Glenn Stogryn

Fairfax Financial Holdings Limited
#800, 95 Wellington St. West
Toronto, ON M5J 2N7
416-367-4941
Fax: 416-367-4946
www.fairfax.ca
Year Founded: 1951
Assets: $10-100 billion Year End: 20051231
Revenues: $1-10 billion Year End: 20051231
Stock Symbol: FFH.SV
Profile: The financial services holding company has the objective to achieve a high rate of return on invested capital. Some operating subsidiaries include Northbridge Financial Corporation, Crum & Forster, Falcon Insurance Company, First Capital & OdysseyRe. Shares are listed on the Toronto & New York Stock Exchanges.

Executives:
V. Prem Watsa, Chair/CEO
Greg Taylor, CFO & Vice-President
Trevor J. Ambridge, Vice-President
John Cassil, Vice-President
Francis Chou, Vice-President
Peter Clarke, Vice-President
Jean Cloutier, Vice-President, Chief Actuary
Hank Edmiston, Vice-President, Regulatory Affairs
Bradley P. Martin, Vice-President, Corporate Secretary
Paul Rivett, Vice-President
Eric P. Salsberg, Vice-President, Corporate Affairs
Ronald Schokking, Vice-President, Treasurer
M. Jane Williamson, Vice-President, Financial Reporting
Directors:
V. Prem Watsa, Chair
Frank B. Bennett
Anthony F. Griffiths
Robbert Hartog
Paul Murray
Brandon W. Sweitzer
Affiliated Companies:
Northbridge Financial Corporation

Fidelity Partnerships
c/o Fidelity Capital Funding Canada
#200, 483 Bay St.
Toronto, ON M5G 2N7
416-307-5300
Fax: 416-307-5535
www.fidelity.ca
Stock Symbol: FIP
Executives:
Robin Woolford, Sr. Vice-President, Finance, CFO

First Delta Securities Inc.
Also listed under: *Investment Dealers*
#202, 386 Wilson St. East
Ancaster, ON L9G 2C2
905-304-0250
Fax: 905-304-4183
rboychuk@firstdelta.com
www.firstdelta.com
Ownership: Private
Year Founded: 1995
Profile: Investment professionals provide services for a clientele which consists of institutions, hedge funds & high net worth individuals.

Executives:
Russell C. Boychuk, Managing Director, CFO & COO; 905-304-0250

The First Mercantile Currency Fund, Inc.
#250, 181 Bay St.
Toronto, ON M5J 2T3
416-364-1171
Fax: 416-364-0572
Ownership: Public.
Year Founded: 1985
Stock Symbol: FMF.UN
Profile: The closed-end investment trust distributes net income quarterly & net realized capital gain on at least an annual basis to unitholders. It is listed on the Toronto Stock Exchange.

Executives:
Herbert Alpert, President
Enrique Fenig, Sec.-Treas.
Directors:
Michael Harrison, Chair
Herbert Alpert
Enrique Fenig
Lloyd S.D. Fogler, Q.C
Albert D. Friedberg
Richard Sutin

First Premium Income Trust
c/o Mulvihill Capital Management Inc.
#2600, 121 King St. West
Toronto, ON M5H 3T9
416-681-3900
Fax: 416-681-3901
800-725-7172
hybrid@mulvihill.com
www.mulvihill.com
Also Known As: Mulvihill Premium Canadian
Year Founded: 1996
Stock Symbol: FPI.UN
Profile: The investment trust was established to hold a diversified portfolio of primarily common shares of major Canadian companies. It participates in covered call option writing on the securities within the portfolio. The trust is managed by Mulvihill Capital Management Inc.

Executives:
John P. Mulvihill, President/CEO, Chair
Don Biggs, Treasurer
Sheila Szela, CFO

Flagship Industries Inc.
375 Steelcase Rd. East
Markham, ON L3R 1G3
905-477-7689
Fax: 905-479-9870
Ownership: Public.
Year Founded: 1986
Stock Symbol: FII
Profile: Listed on the TSX Venture Exchange, the holding company holds investments in Canada.

Executives:
G. Michael Devine, CEO
Directors:
Cynthia J. Devine
G. Michael Devine
Joseph A. Devine
Sarah Langdon

Fortis Inc.
Fortis Bldg.
PO Box 8837
#1201, 139 Water St.
St. John's, NL A1B 3T2
709-737-2800
Fax: 709-737-5307
investorrelations@fortisinc.com
www.fortisinc.com
Year Founded: 1987
Assets: $1-10 billion
Revenues: $1-10 billion
Stock Symbol: FTS
Profile: The company is a diversified international distribution utility holding company. Fortis has holdings in electric distribution utilities, located in BC, AB, ON, PEI, NL, Belize, Grand Cayman & the Turks & Cayman Islands. Non-regualted generation operations are situated in BC, ON, NL, Belize, & New York. Through its wholly owned subsidiary, Fortis also holds investments in commercial real estate & hotels.

Executives:
H. Stanley Marshall, President/CEO
Barry V. Perry, Vice-President/CFO, Finance
Ronald W. McCabe, General Counsel & Secretary
Directors:
Bruce Chafe, Chair
Peter E. Case
Geoffrey F. Hyland
Linda L. Inkpen
H. Stanley Marshall
John S. McCallum
David G. Norris
Michael A. Pavey
Roy P. Rideout

Freehold Royalty Trust
#400, 144 - 4th Ave. SW
Calgary, AB T2P 3N4
403-221-0802
Fax: 403-221-0888
888-257-1873
ir@freeholdtrust.com
www.freeholdtrust.com
Ownership: Public. CN Pension Fund (20.55% interest)
Year Founded: 1996
Assets: $202,100,000 Year End: 20050930
Revenues: $58,600,000 Year End: 20050930
Stock Symbol: FRU.UN
Profile: The open-end investment trust receives & distributes royalty income from a diversified asset base of high quality oil & gas properties.

Executives:
David J. Sandmeyer, President/CEO
J. Frank George, Vice-President, Exploitation
Joseph N. Holowisky, Secretary/CFO & Vice-President, Finance & Administration
William O. Ingram, Vice-President, Production
Michael J. Okrusko, Vice-President, Land
Darren Gunderson, Controller
Directors:
William W. Siebens, Chair
D. Nolan Blades
Harry S. Campbell
Tullio Cedraschi
Peter T. Harrison
P. Michael Maher
David J. Sandmeyer

Garbell Holdings Limited
Standard Life Centre
PO Box 35
#1770, 121 King St. West
Toronto, ON M5H 3T9
416-947-1100
Fax: 416-947-0834
Year Founded: 1961
Number of Employees: 5
Assets: $50-100 million
Stock Symbol: GBH
Profile: Garbell Holdings is an investment company with interests in private companies, including $19,500,000 first preference shares of Gardiner Group Capital Limited & interests in Canadian & U.S. public securities.

Executives:
Edward A. Kukiel, President/COO
Muriel A. Simpson, Treasurer & Vice-President, Finance
Irena Vones, Secretary
Directors:
Arthur R.A. Scace, QC, Chair
Geoffrey A. Cumming, Vice-Chair
H. Anthony Arrell
Ralph M. Barford
David R. Beatty
Edward A. Kukiel

Gaz Métro inc
1717, rue du Havre
Montréal, QC H2K 2X3
514-598-3444
Fax: 514-598-3144
800-361-4005
affairespubliquesactivites@gazmetro.com
www.gazmetro.com
Number of Employees: 1,300
Stock Symbol: GZM.UN
Profile: Gaz Métro inc. acts as the general partner & financing vehicle for Gaz Métropolitain & Company, Limited Partnership, which operates an integrated system for the distribution, storage, & transportation of natural gas.

Executives:
Robert Tessier, President/CEO
Pierre Despars, Exec. Vice-President, Finance & Business Development
René Bédard, Vice-President, Legal Affairs, Corporate Secretary

Sophie Brochu, Vice-President, Québec Distribution
Jacques Charron, Vice-President, Operations
Luc Sicotte, President, Gaz Métro Plus
Directors:
Robert Parizeau
Jean Ariteboul
Pierre Anctil

Mel Belich
Jean-Guy Desjardins
Nicolle Forget
Ghislain Gantier
Louis P. Gignac
Emmanuel Hedde
Stephen J.J. Letwin
Pierre Michaud
Réal Sureau
Robert Parizeau
Robert Tessier

Gray Wolf Capital Corporation
#401, 15 Toronto St.
Toronto, ON M5C 2E3
416-360-3445
Fax: 416-360-5454
Former Name: Isomer Capital Corporation; Diversified Monthly Income Corporation
Ownership: Public.
Year Founded: 1994
Profile: The specialty finance & investment company's activities include establishing, managing & investing in a portfolio of private investment funds.

Executives:
Peter G.M. Dale, President, Sec.-Treas.; pdale@peterdale.com

The Great Eastern Corporation Limited
#2104, 1969 Upper Water St.
Halifax, NS B3J 3R7
902-423-8414
Fax: 902-422-7701
Ownership: Public.
Year Founded: 1941
Stock Symbol: GTN.PR.A; GTN.PR.B
Profile: Listed on the TSX Venture Exchange, the corporation is a holding company with a diversified investment portfolio. Its subsidiary is The North Eastern Corporation Limited.

Executives:
Fred S. Fountain, President
E.R. Richardson, Vice-President
J. Walter Thompson, Q.C., Secretary
Directors:
J.E. Brodie
F.S. Fountain
E. Richardson
F.T. Stanfield
J. Walter Thompson, Q.C.

Great Lakes Holdings Inc.
BCE Place
#300, 181 Bay St.
Toronto, ON M5J 2T3
416-369-8268
Fax: 416-363-2856
Former Name: GLP NT Corporation
Profile: In 2006, GLP NT Corporation amalgamated with Great Lakes Holdings Inc. & GLP Financial Limited.

Sachin G. Shah, Chief Financial Officer

Great-West Lifeco Inc.(GWO)
PO Box 6000
100 Osborne St. North
Winnipeg, MB R3C 3A5
204-946-1190
Fax: 204-946-4129
contactus@gwl.ca
www.greatwestlifeco.com
Ownership: Public. Major shareholder Power Financial Corp. holds a 70.6% interest
Year Founded: 1986
Assets: $10-100 billion Year End: 20051231
Revenues: $10-100 billion Year End: 20051231
Stock Symbol: GWO
Executives:
Raymond L. McFeetors, President/CEO
Mitchell T.G. Graye, Vice-President, Finance, United States
William W. Lovatt, Vice-President, Finance, Canada
Richard G. Schultz, Vice-President & Associate Counsel, USA
Sheila A. Wagar, Vice-President, Counsel & Secretary
Directors:
Robert Gratton, Chair
Gail S. Asper
Orest T. Dackow
André Desmarais
Paul Desmarais, Jr.
Michael Hepher
Daniel Johnson
Kevin P. Kavanagh
Peter Kruyt
Donald F. Mazankowski
William T. McCallum
Raymond L. McFeetors
Jerry E.A. Nickerson
David A. Nield
R. Jeffrey Orr
Michel Plessis-Bélair, FCA
Guy St-Germain, CM
Emöke Szathmáry
Murray Taylor
Gérard Veilleux, Q.C.
Affiliated Companies:
The Great-West Life Assurance Company/GWL

H&R Real Estate Investment Trust(H&R REIT)
#500, 3625 Dufferin St.
Toronto, ON M3K 1N4
416-635-7520
Fax: 416-398-0040
info@hr-reit.com
www.hr-reit.com
Ownership: Public.
Year Founded: 1996
Stock Symbol: HR.UN
Profile: The open-ended Real Estate Investment Trust has a portfolio of properties, which include office, single-tenant industrial & retail. The REIT also holds interests in development projects. All are situated mainly in the Greater Toronto Area.

Executives:
Thomas J. Hofstedter, President/CEO
Larry Froom, C.A., Chief Financial Officer
Nathan Uhr, Vice-President, Acquisitions
Trustees:
Sandor Hofstedter, Hon. Chair
Robert Dickson
Edward Gilbert
Thomas J. Hofstedter
Robert P. Kaplan
Laurence A. Lebovic
Mark S. Mandelbaum
Ronald C. Rutman

The Health Care & Biotechnology Venture Fund
c/o MDS Capital
100 International Blvd.
Toronto, ON M9W 6J6
416-675-7661
Fax: 416-213-4232
vc@mdscapital.com
www.mdscapital.com
Ownership: Public
Year Founded: 1992
Stock Symbol: HCB.UN
Profile: The closed end investment trust invests in a diversified portfolio of private & public venture capital investments in the health care & biotechnology industries.

Executives:
Peter van der Velden, President & Chair
Stephen Cummings, CFO
Greg D. Gubitz, COO
Eric Fredrickson, Director
Jacki Jenuth, Director, Business Intelligence
Don Qiu, Jr., Director, Asian Operations
Graysanne Bedell, Vice-President, Legal & Secretary
Michael Callaghan, Managing Director, Private Equity
Darrell Elliott, Managing Director, Private Equity
Richard Lockie, Managing Director, Private Equity
Brian Underdown, Managing Director, Technology Investing
Directors:
Jim Garner, Chair
Peter Brent
Michael Burns
Peter M. de Auer
Richard W. Johnston
James G. Oborne
R. Anthony Pullen
Peter van der Velden
Branches:
Montréal
#502, 1550 Metcalfe St.
Montréal, QC H3A 1X6 Canada
514-844-3637
Fax: 514-844-5607
Vancouver
#1120, 1095 West Pender St.
Vancouver, BC V6E 2M6 Canada
604-872-8464
Fax: 604-872-2977

Humboldt Capital Corporation
#1800, 633 - 6th Ave. SW
Calgary, AB T2P 2Y5
403-269-9889
Fax: 403-269-9890
info@humboldtcapital.com
www.humboldtcapital.com
Ownership: Public. Major shareholder is Robert W. Lamond
Year Founded: 1980
Number of Employees: 3
Assets: $50-100 million Year End: 20050630
Revenues: $5-10 million Year End: 20050630
Stock Symbol: HMB
Profile: An investment holding company, most of its asset base is invested in junior oil & gas companies.

Executives:
Robert W. Lamond, President/CEO
Charles A. Teare, Exec. Vice-President/CFO
D.K. Clark, Vice-President, Operations
C. Steven Cohen, Secretary
Directors:
Robert W. Lamond, Chair
Robert L. McPherson
Charles A. Teare
Allan R. Twa

IAT Air Cargo Facilities Income Fund
c/o IAT Management Inc.
#2000, 5000 Miller Rd.
Richmond, BC V7B 1K6
604-273-4611
Fax: 604-273-5624
www.iat-yvr.com
Stock Symbol: ACF.IR
Profile: The open-ended single-purpose trust was created to acquire all the notes & common shares of International Aviation Terminals Inc.

Executives:
Wayne A. Duzita, Sr. Vice-President
Denise E. Turner, Vice-President, Corporate Secretary
Directors:
W. John Dawson
Alvin G. Poettcker
Trustees:
Robert J. Mair, Q.C., Chair
Partner, Lawson Lundell Lawson & McIntosh
Thomas V. Milroy
Managing Director, Investment Banking, Nesbitt Burns

IBI Corporation
110 Ambleside Dr.
Port Perry, ON L9L 1B4
905-985-6510
Fax: 905-326-0232
g.fitchett@ibinvest.com
www.ibinvest.com
Ownership: Public
Year Founded: 1994
Number of Employees: 210
Assets: $1-5 million Year End: 20050930
Revenues: $1-5 million Year End: 20050930
Stock Symbol: IBI
Profile: The junior international mining & investment company, through its subsidiary, Canmin Resources Limited, mines & processes vermiculite from its project in Eastern Uganda. Through Canmin Gold Limited, IBI explores for gold.

Executives:
Gary A. Fitchett, CA, President/CEO
Adam Cegielski, Vice-President
Paul D. Mack, Corporate Secretary
David Duval, Director, Marketing & Sales
Dennis Mellersh, Contact, Investor Relations
Directors:
Gary A. Fitchett, CA, Chair
Leono Gouzoules

IBI Corporation (continued)
Paul D. Mack

IFL Investment Foundation (Canada) Limited(IFL)
#2000, 1010, rue de la Gauchetière ouest
Montréal, QC H3B 4J1
514-394-3454
Fax: 514-394-2678
Ownership: Public
Year Founded: 1977
Stock Symbol: IF
Profile: The closed-end investment corporation's activities include investment in marketable securities, predominantly common stock.

Executives:
A. Scott Fraser, President; 514-397-2780
Peter S. Martin, Vice-President
A. Keith Ham, Secretary
R. Michael McBean, Director

IGM Financial Inc.
One Canada Centre
447 Portage Ave.
Winnipeg, MB R3C 3B6
204-943-0361
Fax: 204-947-1659
www.igmfinancial.com
Stock Symbol: IGM; IGM.Pr.A
Profile: With over $83 billion in assets under management, the company serves the financial needs of Canadians through the following businesses: Investors Group Inc., Mackenzie Financial Corporation & Investment Planning Counsel. IGM is a member of the Power Financial Corporation group of companies.

Executives:
Charles R. Sims, Co-President/CEO
Murray J. Taylor, Co-President/CEO
Gregory D. Tretiak, Exec. Vice-President, Finance
W. Terrence Wright, Sr. Vice-President, General Counsel & Secretary
Directors:
Robert Gratton, Chair
James W. Burns
André Desmarais
Paul Desmarais, Jr.
Alan J. Dilworth
Daniel Johnson
Donald F. Mazankowski
John S. McCallum
Rayomond L. McFeetors
R. Jeffrey Orr
Roy W. Piper
Michel Plessis-Bélair
Susan Sherk
Charles R. Sims
Murrat J. Taylor
Gérard Veilleux
Affiliated Companies:
IPC Securities Corporation

Integrated Asset Management Corp.
***Also listed under:** Pension & Money Management Companies*
#2200, 130 Adelaide St. West
Toronto, ON M5H 3P5
416-360-7667
Fax: 416-360-7446
info@iamgroup.ca
www.iamgroup.ca
Former Name: Koloshuk Farrugia Corp.
Ownership: Public
Year Founded: 1998
Number of Employees: 250
Assets: $10-50 million
Revenues: $10-50 million
Stock Symbol: IAM
Profile: Services include asset management, private equity, private corporate debt, hedge funds, real estate & managed futures. The following are the company's subsidiaries: Integrated Private Debt Corp., Grenier-Pacaud Management Associates, Darton Property Advisors & Managers Inc., Integrated Partners, & BluMont Capital.

Executives:
Victor Koloshuk, President/CEO
David Mather, Exec. Vice-President
Stephen Johnson, Vice-President/CFO
Directors:
Victor Koloshuk, Chair
Tony Pacaud, Vice-Chair
David Atkins
George Elliott
George Engman
Veronika Hirsch
Stephen C. Johnson
Michel Lebel
Donald Lowe
David Mather
John Robertson
Affiliated Companies:
Blumont Capital Corporation
Integrated Private Debt Corp.

Inter-Asia Equities Inc.
1281 Alberni St.
Vancouver, BC V6E 4R4
604-609-2668
Fax: 604-609-2088
Year Founded: 1984
Assets: $1-5 million
Stock Symbol: IAE
Profile: Investment banking & acquisition of interests in venture companies make up the principal business. The company's subsidiary is BPR Holdings (Far East) Limited, & its wholly owned subsidiary is BPR Holdings B.C. Inc.

Executives:
Keow Y. Chan, President/CEO
Robert H. Trapp, CFO
Directors:
Keow Y. Chan
Robert H. Trapp
Simon C.K. Yau

Investors Group Inc.
***Also listed under:** Investment Fund Companies*
One Canada Centre
447 Portage Ave.
Winnipeg, MB R3C 3B6
204-943-3385
Fax: 204-956-7688
888-746-6344
Other Information: Toll Free, Quebec: 1-800-661-4578
feedback@investorsgroup.com
www.investorsgroup.com
Ownership: Major shareholder Power Financial Corporation
Year Founded: 1926
Number of Employees: 1,300
Stock Symbol: IGI
Profile: The holding company provides financial products & financial planning services to individuals & corporations, including the sale of mutual funds, investment certificates, insurance programs, education savings plans, pension plans, annuities & tax-sheltered plans. It also provides the following services: investment management & administrative services for its own mutual funds, company subsidiaries & various pension plans; tax preparation services; trust & management services; mortgage financing on residential, commercial & industrial property; investments in real estate.

Executives:
Murray Taylor, President/CEO
Gregory D. Tretiak, Exec. Vice-President & CFO
Gary Wilton, Exec. Vice-President, Client & Information Services

Alan Joudrey, Sr. Vice-President, Banking Products & Services
Murray D. Kilfoyle, Sr. Vice-President, Client Services
Kevin E. Regan, Sr. Vice-President, Marketing & Consulting Services
Donald W. Smith, Sr. Vice-President, Human Resources
John Wiltshire, Sr., Sr. Vice-President, Product & Financial Planning
W. Terrence Wright, Sr. Vice-President, General Counsel & Secretary
Directors:
James W. Burns
André Desmarais
Paul Desmarais, P.C., C.C.
Paul Desmarais, Jr.
Alan J. Dilworth
Wanda M. Dorosz
Robert Gratton
James L. Hunter
Daniel Johnson
Donald F. Mazankowski
John Stuart McCallum
Raymond L. McFeetors
R. Jeffrey Orr
Roy W. Piper
P. Michael Pitfield, P.C., Q.C.
Michel Plessis-Bélair
H. Sanford Riley
Susan Sherk
Gérard Veilleux
Affiliated Companies:
Tony Copple
Allegro:
Aggressive Portfolio C Fund
RRSP Eligible; Inception Year: 2001; Fund Managers: I.G. Investment Management
Aggressive Registered Portfolio C Fund
RRSP Eligible; Inception Year: 2001; Fund Managers: I.G. Investment Management
Conservative Portfolio C Fund
RRSP Eligible; Inception Year: 2001; Fund Managers: I.G. Investment Management
Moderate Aggressive Registered C Fund
RRSP Eligible; Inception Year: 2001; Fund Managers: I.G. Investment Management
Moderate Aggressive Portfolio C Fund
RRSP Eligible; Inception Year: 2001; Fund Managers: I.G. Investment Management
Moderate Conservative C Fund
RRSP Eligible; Inception Year: 2001; Fund Managers: I.G. Investment Management
Moderate Portfolio C Fund
RRSP Eligible; Inception Year: 2001; Fund Managers: I.G. Investment Management
Aggressive Registered Portfolio B Fund
RRSP Eligible; Inception Year: 2003; Fund Managers: I.G. Investment Management
Aggressive Portfolio A Fund
RRSP Eligible; Inception Year: 2003; Fund Managers: I.G. Investment Management
Aggressive Portfolio B Fund
RRSP Eligible; Inception Year: 2003; Fund Managers: I.G. Investment Management
Conservative Portfolio A Fund
RRSP Eligible; Inception Year: 2003; Fund Managers: I.G. Investment Management
Conservative Portfolio B Fund
RRSP Eligible; Inception Year: 2003; Fund Managers: I.G. Investment Management
Moderate Aggressive Registered A Fund
RRSP Eligible; Inception Year: 2003; Fund Managers: I.G. Investment Management
Moderate Aggressive Registered B Fund
RRSP Eligible; Inception Year: 2003; Fund Managers: I.G. Investment Management
Moderate Conservative A Fund
RRSP Eligible; Inception Year: 2003; Fund Managers: I.G. Investment Management
Moderate Conservative B Fund
RRSP Eligible; Inception Year: 2003; Fund Managers: I.G. Investment Management
Moderate Aggressive Portfolio A Fund
RRSP Eligible; Inception Year: 2003; Fund Managers: I.G. Investment Management
Moderate Aggressive Portfolio B Fund
RRSP Eligible; Inception Year: 2003; Fund Managers: I.G. Investment Management
Moderate Portfolio A Fund
RRSP Eligible; Inception Year: 2003; Fund Managers: I.G. Investment Management
Moderate Portfolio B Fund
RRSP Eligible; Inception Year: 2003; Fund Managers: I.G. Investment Management
Aggressive Registered Portfolio A Fund
RRSP Eligible; Inception Year: 2003; Fund Managers: I.G. Investment Management
Alto:
Aggressive Registered Portfolio A Fund
RRSP Eligible; Inception Year: 2003; Fund Managers: I.G. Investment Management
Aggressive Registered Portfolio B Fund
RRSP Eligible; Inception Year: 2003; Fund Managers: I.G. Investment Management
Aggressive Portfolio A Fund
RRSP Eligible; Inception Year: 2003; Fund Managers: I.G. Investment Management

Aggressive Portfolio B Fund
RRSP Eligible; Inception Year: 2003; Fund Managers:
I.G. Investment Management
Conservative Portfolio A Fund
RRSP Eligible; Inception Year: 2003; Fund Managers:
I.G. Investment Management
Conservative Portfolio B Fund
RRSP Eligible; Inception Year: 2003; Fund Managers:
I.G. Investment Management
Moderate Portfolio A Fund
RRSP Eligible; Inception Year: 2003; Fund Managers:
I.G. Investment Management
Moderate Portfolio B Fund
RRSP Eligible; Inception Year: 2003; Fund Managers:
I.G. Investment Management
Moderate Aggressive Portfolio A Fund
RRSP Eligible; Inception Year: 2003; Fund Managers:
I.G. Investment Management
Moderate Aggressive Portfolio B Fund
RRSP Eligible; Inception Year: 2003; Fund Managers:
I.G. Investment Management
Moderate Conservative Portfolio A Fund
RRSP Eligible; Inception Year: 2003; Fund Managers:
I.G. Investment Management
Moderate Conservative Portfolio B Fund
RRSP Eligible; Inception Year: 2003; Fund Managers:
I.G. Investment Management
Moderate Aggressive Registered Portfolio A Fund
RRSP Eligible; Inception Year: 2003; Fund Managers:
I.G. Investment Management
Moderate Aggressive Registered Portfolio B Fund
RRSP Eligible; Inception Year: 2003; Fund Managers:
I.G. Investment Management
Monthly Income Portfolio T-DSC Fund
RRSP Eligible; Inception Year: 2004; Fund Managers:
I.G. Investment Management
Monthly Income Portfolio T-NL Fund
RRSP Eligible; Inception Year: 2004; Fund Managers:
I.G. Investment Management
Monthly Income Portfolio A Fund
RRSP Eligible; Inception Year: 2004; Fund Managers:
I.G. Investment Management
Monthly Income Portfolio B Fund
RRSP Eligible; Inception Year: 2004; Fund Managers:
I.G. Investment Management
Monthly Income & Enhanced Growth Portfolio T-NL Fund
RRSP Eligible; Inception Year: 2004; Fund Managers:
I.G. Investment Management
Monthly Income & Enhanced Growth Portfolio T-DSC Fund
RRSP Eligible; Inception Year: 2004; Fund Managers:
I.G. Investment Management
Monthly Income & Enhanced Growth Portfolio A Fund
RRSP Eligible; Inception Year: 2004; Fund Managers:
I.G. Investment Management
Monthly Income & Enhanced Growth Portfolio B Fund
RRSP Eligible; Inception Year: 2004; Fund Managers:
I.G. Investment Management
Monthly Income & Growth Portfolio T-DSC Fund
RRSP Eligible; Inception Year: 2004; Fund Managers:
I.G. Investment Management
Monthly Income & Growth Portfolio T-NL Fund
RRSP Eligible; Inception Year: 2004; Fund Managers:
I.G. Investment Management
Monthly Income & Growth Portfolio A Fund
RRSP Eligible; Inception Year: 2004; Fund Managers:
I.G. Investment Management
Monthly Income & Growth Portfolio B Fund
RRSP Eligible; Inception Year: 2004; Fund Managers:
I.G. Investment Management
Aggressive Portfolio C Fund
RRSP Eligible; Inception Year: 2005; Fund Managers:
I.G. Investment Management
Conservative Portfolio C Fund
RRSP Eligible; Inception Year: 2005; Fund Managers:
I.G. Investment Management
Moderate Aggressive Portfolio C Fund
RRSP Eligible; Inception Year: 2005; Fund Managers:
I.G. Investment Management
Moderate Conservative Portfolio C Fund
RRSP Eligible; Inception Year: 2005; Fund Managers:
I.G. Investment Management
Moderate Portfolio C Fund
RRSP Eligible; Inception Year: 2005; Fund Managers:
I.G. Investment Management
Monthly Income Portfolio C Fund Fund
RRSP Eligible; Inception Year: 2005; Fund Managers:
I.G. Investment Management
Monthly Income Portfolio TC Fund Fund
RRSP Eligible; Inception Year: 2005; Fund Managers:
I.G. Investment Management
Monthly Income & Enhanced Growth Portfolio TC Fund
RRSP Eligible; Inception Year: 2005; Fund Managers:
I.G. Investment Management
Monthly Income & Enhanced Growth Portfolio C Fund
RRSP Eligible; Inception Year: 2005; Fund Managers:
I.G. Investment Management
Monthly Income & Growth Portfolio TC Fund
RRSP Eligible; Inception Year: 2005; Fund Managers:
I.G. Investment Management
Monthly Income & Growth Portfolio C Fund
RRSP Eligible; Inception Year: 2005; Fund Managers:
I.G. Investment Management

IG AGF:

Asian Growth C Fund
RRSP Eligible; Inception Year: 1999; Fund Managers:
AGF Funds
Canadian Growth C Fund
RRSP Eligible; Inception Year: 1996; Fund Managers:
AGF Funds
Canadian Diversified Growth C Fund
RRSP Eligible; Inception Year: 1999; Fund Managers:
AGF Funds
US Growth C Fund
RRSP Eligible; Inception Year: 1999; Fund Managers:
AGF Funds
Canadian Balanced C Fund
RRSP Eligible; Inception Year: 1996; Fund Managers:
AGF Funds
International Bond Fund
RRSP Eligible; Inception Year: 1996; Fund Managers:
Insight Investment Management
Asian Growth Class A Fund
RRSP Eligible; Inception Year: 2002; Fund Managers:
AGF Funds
Canadian Growth Class A Fund
RRSP Eligible; Inception Year: 2002;
Canadian Diversified Growth Class A Fund
RRSP Eligible; Inception Year: 2002;
US Growth Class A Fund
RRSP Eligible; Inception Year: 2002; Fund Managers:
AGF Funds
International Equity Class A Fund
RRSP Eligible; Inception Year: 2002;
Asian Growth A Fund
RRSP Eligible; Inception Year: 2003; Fund Managers:
AGF Funds
Asian Growth B Fund
RRSP Eligible; Inception Year: 2003; Fund Managers:
AGF Funds
Canadian Diversified Growth Class B Fund
RRSP Eligible; Inception Year: 2003;
Canadian Growth Class B Fund
RRSP Eligible; Inception Year: 2003;
Canadian Diversified Growth A Fund
RRSP Eligible; Inception Year: 2003; Fund Managers:
AGF Funds
Canadian Diversified Growth B Fund
RRSP Eligible; Inception Year: 2003; Fund Managers:
AGF Funds
Canadian Growth A Fund
RRSP Eligible; Inception Year: 2003; Fund Managers:
AGF Funds
Canadian Growth B Fund
RRSP Eligible; Inception Year: 2003; Fund Managers:
AGF Funds
Canadian Balanced A Fund
RRSP Eligible; Inception Year: 2003; Fund Managers:
AGF Funds
Canadian Balanced B Fund
RRSP Eligible; Inception Year: 2003; Fund Managers:
AGF Funds
International Equity Class B Fund
RRSP Eligible; Inception Year: 2003;
International Equity A Fund
RRSP Eligible; Inception Year: 2003; Fund Managers:
AGF Funds
International Equity B Fund
RRSP Eligible; Inception Year: 2003; Fund Managers:
AGF Funds
International Equity C Fund
RRSP Eligible; Inception Year: 1996; Fund Managers:
AGF Funds
US Growth A Fund
RRSP Eligible; Inception Year: 2003; Fund Managers:
AGF Funds
US Growth B Fund
RRSP Eligible; Inception Year: 2003; Fund Managers:
AGF Funds
US Growth Class B Fund
RRSP Eligible; Inception Year: 2003; Fund Managers:
AGF Funds
Canadian Equity Class B Fund
RRSP Eligible; Inception Year: 2003;
Asian Growth Class B Fund
RRSP Eligible; Inception Year: 2003; Fund Managers:
AGF Funds

IG Beutel Goodman:

Canadian Balanced C Fund
RRSP Eligible; Inception Year: 1996; Fund Managers:
Beutel Goodman
Canadian Equity C Fund
RRSP Eligible; Inception Year: 1996; Fund Managers:
Beutel Goodman
Canadian Small Cap C Fund
RRSP Eligible; Inception Year: 1996; Fund Managers:
Beutel Goodman
Canadian Equity Class A Fund
RRSP Eligible; Inception Year: 2002;
Canadian Balanced A Fund
RRSP Eligible; Inception Year: 2003; Fund Managers:
Beutel Goodman
Canadian Balanced B Fund
RRSP Eligible; Inception Year: 2003; Fund Managers:
Beutel Goodman
Canadian Equity A Fund
RRSP Eligible; Inception Year: 2003; Fund Managers:
Beutel Goodman
Canadian Equity B Fund
RRSP Eligible; Inception Year: 2003; Fund Managers:
Beutel Goodman
Canadian Equity Class B
RRSP Eligible; Inception Year: 2003;

IG Bissett:

Canadian Equity A Fund
RRSP Eligible; Inception Year: 2004; Fund Managers:
Bissett Investment Management
Canadian Equity B Fund
RRSP Eligible; Inception Year: 2004; Fund Managers:
Bissett Investment Management
Canadian Equity Class A Fund
RRSP Eligible; Inception Year: 2004; Fund Managers:
Bissett Investment Management
Canadian Equity Class B Fund
RRSP Eligible; Inception Year: 2004; Fund Managers:
Bissett Investment Management

IG FI:

Canadian Allocation C Fund
RRSP Eligible; Inception Year: 2000; Fund Managers:
Fidelity Investments
Global Equity C Fund
RRSP Eligible; Inception Year: 2000; Fund Managers:
Fidelity Investments
Global Equity Class A Fund
RRSP Eligible; Inception Year: 2002; Fund Managers:
Fidelity Investments
Canadian Equity C Fund
RRSP Eligible; Inception Year: 2000; Fund Managers:
Fidelity Investments
Canadian Equity Class A Fund
RRSP Eligible; Inception Year: 2002; Fund Managers:
Fidelity Investments
US Equity C Fund
RRSP Eligible; Inception Year: 2000; Fund Managers:
Fidelity Investments
US Equity Class A Fund
RRSP Eligible; Inception Year: 2002; Fund Managers:
Fidelity Investments
Canadian Equity Class B Fund
RRSP Eligible; Inception Year: 2003; Fund Managers:
Fidelity Investments
Canadian Equity A Fund
RRSP Eligible; Inception Year: 2003; Fund Managers:
Fidelity Investments

Investors Group Inc. (continued)

Canadian Equity B Fund
RRSP Eligible; Inception Year: 2003; Fund Managers: Fidelity Investments
Canadian Allocation A Fund
RRSP Eligible; Inception Year: 2003; Fund Managers: Fidelity Investments
Canadian Allocation B Fund
RRSP Eligible; Inception Year: 2003; Fund Managers: Fidelity Investments
Global Equity Class B Fund
RRSP Eligible; Inception Year: 2003; Fund Managers: Fidelity Investments
Global Equity A Fund
RRSP Eligible; Inception Year: 2003; Fund Managers: Fidelity Investments
Global Equity B Fund
RRSP Eligible; Inception Year: 2003; Fund Managers: Fidelity Investments
US Equity A Fund
RRSP Eligible; Inception Year: 2003; Fund Managers: Fidelity Investments
US Equity B Fund
RRSP Eligible; Inception Year: 2003; Fund Managers: Fidelity Investments
US Equity Class B Fund
RRSP Eligible; Inception Year: 2003; Fund Managers: Fidelity Investments

IG Goldman Sachs:

US Equity A Fund
RRSP Eligible; Inception Year: 2003; Fund Managers: Goldman Sachs Asset Management (New York)
US Equity B Fund
RRSP Eligible; Inception Year: 2003; Fund Managers: Goldman Sachs Asset Management (New York)
US Equity C Fund
RRSP Eligible; Inception Year: 2003; Fund Managers: Goldman Sachs Asset Management (New York)
US Equity Class A Fund
RRSP Eligible; Inception Year: 2003; Fund Managers: Goldman Sachs Asset Management (New York)
US Equity Class B Fund
RRSP Eligible; Inception Year: 2003; Fund Managers: Goldman Sachs Asset Management (New York)

IG Mackenzie:

Income Fund
RRSP Eligible; Inception Year: 1999; Fund Managers: Mackenzie Financial Corp.
Ivy European C Fund
RRSP Eligible; Inception Year: 1999; Fund Managers: Mackenzie Financial Corp.
Ivy European Class A Fund
RRSP Eligible; Inception Year: 2002;
Maxxum Dividend C Fund
RRSP Eligible; Inception Year: 1999; Fund Managers: Mackenzie Financial Corp.
Select Managers Canada C Fund
RRSP Eligible; Inception Year: 1999; Fund Managers: Mackenzie Financial Corp.
Select Managers Canada Class A Fund
RRSP Eligible; Inception Year: 2002;
Universal Emerging Market Class A Fund
RRSP Eligible; Inception Year: 2002;
Universal Global Future A Fund
RRSP Eligible; Inception Year: 2003; Fund Managers: Mackenzie Financial Corp.
Universal Global Future B Fund
RRSP Eligible; Inception Year: 2003; Fund Managers: Mackenzie Financial Corp.
Universal Global Future C Fund
RRSP Eligible; Inception Year: 2000; Fund Managers: Mackenzie Financial Corp.
Ivy European A Fund
RRSP Eligible; Inception Year: 2003; Fund Managers: Mackenzie Financial Corp.
Ivy European B Fund
RRSP Eligible; Inception Year: 2003; Fund Managers: Mackenzie Financial Corp.
Select Managers Canada A Fund
RRSP Eligible; Inception Year: 2003; Fund Managers: Mackenzie Financial Corp.
Select Managers Canada B Fund
RRSP Eligible; Inception Year: 2003; Fund Managers: Mackenzie Financial Corp.
Universal US Growth Leaders A Fund
RRSP Eligible; Inception Year: 2003; Fund Managers: Mackenzie Financial Corp.
Universal US Growth Leaders B Fund
RRSP Eligible; Inception Year: 2003; Fund Managers: Mackenzie Financial Corp.
Universal US Growth Leaders C Fund
RRSP Eligible; Inception Year: 2000; Fund Managers: Mackenzie Financial Corp.
Universal Emerging Market Class B Fund
RRSP Eligible; Inception Year: 2003;
Maxxum Dividend A Fund
RRSP Eligible; Inception Year: 2003; Fund Managers: Mackenzie Financial Corp.
Maxxum Dividend B Fund
RRSP Eligible; Inception Year: 2003; Fund Managers: Mackenzie Financial Corp.
Ivy European Class B Fund
RRSP Eligible; Inception Year: 2003; Fund Managers: Mackenzie Financial Corp.
Ivy Foreign Equity Class A Fund
RRSP Eligible; Inception Year: 2002; Fund Managers: Mackenzie Financial Corp.
Ivy Foreign Equity Class B Fund
RRSP Eligible; Inception Year: 2003; Fund Managers: Mackenzie Financial Corp.
Select Managers Canada Class B Fund
RRSP Eligible; Inception Year: 2003;
Universal US Growth Leaders Class A Fund
RRSP Eligible; Inception Year: 2002; Fund Managers: Mackenzie Financial Corp.
Universal US Growth Leaders Class B Fund
RRSP Eligible; Inception Year: 2003; Fund Managers: Mackenzie Financial Corp.
Universal Global Future Class A
RRSP Eligible; Inception Year: 2004; Fund Managers: Mackenzie Financial Corp.
Universal Global Future Class B
RRSP Eligible; Inception Year: 2004; Fund Managers: Mackenzie Financial Corp.

IG Templeton:

World Bond Fund
RRSP Eligible; Inception Year: 1996; Fund Managers: Franklin Templeton Investments
International Equity C Fund
RRSP Eligible; Inception Year: 1999; Fund Managers: Franklin Templeton Investments
World Allocation C Fund
RRSP Eligible; Inception Year: 1996; Fund Managers: Franklin Templeton Investments
International Equity Class A Fund
RRSP Eligible; Inception Year: 2002;
International Equity Class B Fund
RRSP Eligible; Inception Year: 2003;
International Equity A Fund
RRSP Eligible; Inception Year: 2003; Fund Managers: Franklin Templeton Investments
International Equity B Fund
RRSP Eligible; Inception Year: 2003; Fund Managers: Franklin Templeton Investments
World Allocation A Fund
RRSP Eligible; Inception Year: 2003; Fund Managers: Franklin Templeton Investments
World Allocation B Fund
RRSP Eligible; Inception Year: 2003; Fund Managers: Franklin Templeton Investments

IG/GWL:

Canadian Balanced Segregated Fund
RRSP Eligible; Inception Year: 1999; Fund Managers: I.G. Investment Management
Government Bond Segregated Fund
RRSP Eligible; Inception Year: 1999; Fund Managers: I.G. Investment Management
US Large Cap Value Segregated Fund
RRSP Eligible; Inception Year: 1999; Fund Managers: I.G. Investment Management
Money Market Segregated Fund
RRSP Eligible; Inception Year: 1999; Fund Managers: I.G. Investment Management
Summa Segregated Fund
RRSP Eligible; Inception Year: 1999; Fund Managers: I.G. Investment Management
Global Segregated Fund
RRSP Eligible; Inception Year: 0; Fund Managers: I.G. Investment Management
Dividend Segregated Fund
RRSP Eligible; Inception Year: 1999; Fund Managers: I.G. Investment Management
Canadian Equity Segregated Fund
RRSP Eligible; Inception Year: 1999; Fund Managers: I.G. Investment Management

Investors:

Tact Asset Allocation C Fund
RRSP Eligible; Inception Year: 1994; Fund Managers: I.G. Investment Management
Canadian Equity C Fund
RRSP Eligible; Inception Year: 1983; Fund Managers: I.G. Investment Management
Canadian Bond Fund
RRSP Eligible; Inception Year: 1994; Fund Managers: I.G. Investment Management
Dividend C Fund
RRSP Eligible; Inception Year: 1962; Fund Managers: I.G. Investment Management
Global Bond Fund
RRSP Eligible; Inception Year: 1992; Fund Managers: I.G. Investment Management
Global C Fund
RRSP Eligible; Inception Year: 1986; Fund Managers: I.G. Investment Management
Government Bond Fund
RRSP Eligible; Inception Year: 1979; Fund Managers: I.G. Investment Management
Growth Plus Portfolio C Fund
RRSP Eligible; Inception Year: 1989; Fund Managers: I.G. Investment Management
Growth Portfolio C Fund
RRSP Eligible; Inception Year: 1989; Fund Managers: I.G. Investment Management
Income Plus Portfolio C Fund
RRSP Eligible; Inception Year: 1989; Fund Managers: I.G. Investment Management
Income Portfolio Fund
RRSP Eligible; Inception Year: 1989; Fund Managers: I.G. Investment Management
Japanese Equity C Fund
RRSP Eligible; Inception Year: 1971; Fund Managers: I.G. Investment Management
Canadian Money Market Fund
RRSP Eligible; Inception Year: 1985; Fund Managers: I.G. Investment Management
Mortgage Fund
RRSP Eligible; Inception Year: 1973; Fund Managers: I.G. Investment Management
Mutual of Canada C Fund
RRSP Eligible; Inception Year: 1950; Fund Managers: I.G. Investment Management
North American Equity C Fund
RRSP Eligible; Inception Year: 1957; Fund Managers: I.G. Investment Management
Pacific International C Fund
RRSP Eligible; Inception Year: 1990; Fund Managers: I.G. Investment Management
Real Property C Fund
RRSP Eligible; Inception Year: 1984; Fund Managers: I.G. Investment Management
Retirement Growth Portfolio C Fund
RRSP Eligible; Inception Year: 1989; Fund Managers: I.G. Investment Management
Retirement Plus Portfolio C Fund
RRSP Eligible; Inception Year: 1989; Fund Managers: I.G. Investment Management
Summa C Fund
RRSP Eligible; Inception Year: 1987; Fund Managers: I.G. Investment Management
World Growth Portfolio C Fund
RRSP Eligible; Inception Year: 1993; Fund Managers: I.G. Investment Management
Canadian Natural Resource C Fund
RRSP Eligible; Inception Year: 1996; Fund Managers: I.G. Investment Management
Canadian Small Cap C Fund
RRSP Eligible; Inception Year: 1996; Fund Managers: I.G. Investment Management
US Opportunities C Fund
RRSP Eligible; Inception Year: 1996; Fund Managers: I.G. Investment Management
Québec Enterprise C Fund
RRSP Eligible; Inception Year: 1999; Fund Managers: I.G. Investment Management

Canadian Balanced C Fund
RRSP Eligible; Inception Year: 1998; Fund Managers:
I.G. Investment Management
Canadian High Yield Income Fund
RRSP Eligible; Inception Year: 1996; Fund Managers:
I.G. Investment Management
European Mid-Cap Growth C Fund
RRSP Eligible; Inception Year: 2000; Fund Managers:
I.G. Investment Management
Global Science & Technology C Fund
RRSP Eligible; Inception Year: 1998; Fund Managers:
I.G. Investment Management
Mergers & Acquisitions C Fund
RRSP Eligible; Inception Year: 2000; Fund Managers:
Camlin Asset Management
Retirement High Growth Portfolio C Fund
RRSP Eligible; Inception Year: 1999; Fund Managers:
I.G. Investment Management
US Large Cap Growth C Fund
RRSP Eligible; Inception Year: 1968; Fund Managers:
I.G. Investment Management
US Large Cap Value C Fund
RRSP Eligible; Inception Year: 1962; Fund Managers:
I.G. Investment Management
US Large Cap Value RSP C Fund
RRSP Eligible; Inception Year: 1999; Fund Managers:
I.G. Investment Management
Canadian Small Cap Growth C Fund
RRSP Eligible; Inception Year: 1998; Fund Managers:
I.G. Investment Management
Pan Asian Growth C Fund
RRSP Eligible; Inception Year: 2001; Fund Managers:
I.G. Investment Management
Global Financial Services C Fund
RRSP Eligible; Inception Year: 2001; Fund Managers:
I.G. Investment Management
Canadian Equity Class A Fund
RRSP Eligible; Inception Year: 2002; Fund Managers:
I.G. Investment Management
Canadian Small Cap Class A Fund
RRSP Eligible; Inception Year: 2002; Fund Managers:
I.G. Investment Management
Canadian High Yield Money Market Fund
RRSP Eligible; Inception Year: 2001; Fund Managers:
I.G. Investment Management
Canadian Large Cap Value C Fund
RRSP Eligible; Inception Year: 1972; Fund Managers:
I.G. Investment Management
Canadian Large Cap Value Class A Fund
RRSP Eligible; Inception Year: 2002; Fund Managers:
I.G. Investment Management
Canadian Small Cap Growth Class A Fund
RRSP Eligible; Inception Year: 2002; Fund Managers:
I.G. Investment Management
European Mid-Cap Growth Class A Fund
RRSP Eligible; Inception Year: 2002; Fund Managers:
I.G. Investment Management
European Equity C Fund
RRSP Eligible; Inception Year: 1990; Fund Managers:
I.G. Investment Management
Global Class A Fund
RRSP Eligible; Inception Year: 2002; Fund Managers:
I.G. Investment Management
Global Health Care Class A Fund
RRSP Eligible; Inception Year: 2002; Fund Managers:
I.G. Investment Management
European Equity Class A Fund
RRSP Eligible; Inception Year: 2002; Fund Managers:
I.G. Investment Management
Global Natural Resource Class A Fund
RRSP Eligible; Inception Year: 2002; Fund Managers:
I.G. Investment Management
Global Financial Services Class A Fund
RRSP Eligible; Inception Year: 2002; Fund Managers:
I.G. Investment Management
Global Infrastructure Class A Fund
RRSP Eligible; Inception Year: 2002; Fund Managers:
I.G. Investment Management
Global Science & Technology Class A Fund
RRSP Eligible; Inception Year: 2002; Fund Managers:
I.G. Investment Management
International Small Cap Class A Fund
RRSP Eligible; Inception Year: 2002; Fund Managers:
I.G. Investment Management

Japanese Equity Class A Fund
RRSP Eligible; Inception Year: 2002; Fund Managers:
I.G. Investment Management
Mergers & Acquisitions Class A Fund
RRSP Eligible; Inception Year: 2002; Fund Managers:
Camlin Asset Management
North American Equity Class A Fund
RRSP Eligible; Inception Year: 2002; Fund Managers:
I.G. Investment Management
Pacific International Class A Fund
RRSP Eligible; Inception Year: 2002; Fund Managers:
I.G. Investment Management
Pan Asian Growth Class A Fund
RRSP Eligible; Inception Year: 2002; Fund Managers:
I.G. Investment Management
Québec Enterprise Class A Fund
RRSP Eligible; Inception Year: 2002; Fund Managers:
I.G. Investment Management
Summa Class A Fund
RRSP Eligible; Inception Year: 2002; Fund Managers:
I.G. Investment Management
US Large Cap Growth Class A Fund
RRSP Eligible; Inception Year: 2002; Fund Managers:
I.G. Investment Management
US Large Cap Value Class A Fund
RRSP Eligible; Inception Year: 2002;
US Opportunities Class A Fund
RRSP Eligible; Inception Year: 2002; Fund Managers:
I.G. Investment Management
Managed Yield Class A Fund
RRSP Eligible; Inception Year: 2002; Fund Managers:
I.G. Investment Management
US Small Cap Class A Fund
RRSP Eligible; Inception Year: 2002; Fund Managers:
I.G. Investment Management
Tact Asset Allocation A Fund
RRSP Eligible; Inception Year: 2003; Fund Managers:
I.G. Investment Management
Tact Asset Allocation B Fund
RRSP Eligible; Inception Year: 2003; Fund Managers:
I.G. Investment Management
Canadian Small Cap Growth B Fund
RRSP Eligible; Inception Year: 2003; Fund Managers:
I.G. Investment Management
Canadian Balanced A Fund
RRSP Eligible; Inception Year: 2003; Fund Managers:
I.G. Investment Management
Canadian Balanced B Fund
RRSP Eligible; Inception Year: 2003; Fund Managers:
I.G. Investment Management
Canadian Equity Class B Fund
RRSP Eligible; Inception Year: 2003; Fund Managers:
I.G. Investment Management
Canadian Equity A Fund
RRSP Eligible; Inception Year: 2003; Fund Managers:
I.G. Investment Management
Canadian Equity B Fund
RRSP Eligible; Inception Year: 2003; Fund Managers:
I.G. Investment Management
Canadian Large Cap Value Class B Fund
RRSP Eligible; Inception Year: 2003; Fund Managers:
I.G. Investment Management
Canadian Large Cap Value A Fund
RRSP Eligible; Inception Year: 2003; Fund Managers:
I.G. Investment Management
Canadian Large Cap Value B Fund
RRSP Eligible; Inception Year: 2003; Fund Managers:
I.G. Investment Management
Canadian Natural Resource A Fund
RRSP Eligible; Inception Year: 2003; Fund Managers:
I.G. Investment Management
Canadian Natural Resource B Fund
RRSP Eligible; Inception Year: 2003; Fund Managers:
I.G. Investment Management
Canadian Small Cap Class B Fund
RRSP Eligible; Inception Year: 2003; Fund Managers:
I.G. Investment Management
Canadian Small Cap Growth A Fund
RRSP Eligible; Inception Year: 2003; Fund Managers:
I.G. Investment Management
Canadian Small Cap Growth Class B Fund
RRSP Eligible; Inception Year: 2003; Fund Managers:
I.G. Investment Management

Canadian Small Cap A Fund
RRSP Eligible; Inception Year: 2003; Fund Managers:
I.G. Investment Management
Canadian Small Cap B Fund
RRSP Eligible; Inception Year: 2003; Fund Managers:
I.G. Investment Management
Dividend A Fund
RRSP Eligible; Inception Year: 2003; Fund Managers:
I.G. Investment Management
Dividend B Fund
RRSP Eligible; Inception Year: 2003; Fund Managers:
I.G. Investment Management
European Equity Class B Fund
RRSP Eligible; Inception Year: 2003; Fund Managers:
I.G. Investment Management
European Mid-Cap Growth A Fund
RRSP Eligible; Inception Year: 2003; Fund Managers:
I.G. Investment Management
European Mid-Cap Growth B Fund
RRSP Eligible; Inception Year: 2003; Fund Managers:
I.G. Investment Management
European Mid-Cap Growth Class B Fund
RRSP Eligible; Inception Year: 2003; Fund Managers:
I.G. Investment Management
European Equity A Fund
RRSP Eligible; Inception Year: 2003; Fund Managers:
I.G. Investment Management
European Equity B Fund
RRSP Eligible; Inception Year: 2003; Fund Managers:
I.G. Investment Management
Global Cons Comp Class A Fund
RRSP Eligible; Inception Year: 2002; Fund Managers:
I.G. Investment Management
Global Cons Comp Class B Fund
RRSP Eligible; Inception Year: 2003; Fund Managers:
I.G. Investment Management
Global Infrasturcture Class B Fund
RRSP Eligible; Inception Year: 2003; Fund Managers:
I.G. Investment Management
Global Financial Services Class B Fund
RRSP Eligible; Inception Year: 2003; Fund Managers:
I.G. Investment Management
Global Health Care Class B Fund
RRSP Eligible; Inception Year: 2003; Fund Managers:
I.G. Investment Management
Global Natural Resource Class B Fund
RRSP Eligible; Inception Year: 2003; Fund Managers:
I.G. Investment Management
Global Science & Technology Class B Fund
RRSP Eligible; Inception Year: 2003; Fund Managers:
I.G. Investment Management
Global Financial Services A Fund
RRSP Eligible; Inception Year: 2003; Fund Managers:
I.G. Investment Management
Global Financial Services B Fund
RRSP Eligible; Inception Year: 2003; Fund Managers:
I.G. Investment Management
Global Science & Technology A Fund
RRSP Eligible; Inception Year: 2003; Fund Managers:
I.G. Investment Management
Global Science & Technology B Fund
RRSP Eligible; Inception Year: 2003; Fund Managers:
I.G. Investment Management
Global A Fund
RRSP Eligible; Inception Year: 2003; Fund Managers:
I.G. Investment Management
Global B Fund
RRSP Eligible; Inception Year: 2003; Fund Managers:
I.G. Investment Management
Growth Plus Portfolio A Fund
RRSP Eligible; Inception Year: 2003; Fund Managers:
I.G. Investment Management
Growth Plus Portfolio B Fund
RRSP Eligible; Inception Year: 2003; Fund Managers:
I.G. Investment Management
Growth Portfolio A Fund
RRSP Eligible; Inception Year: 2003; Fund Managers:
I.G. Investment Management
Growth Portfolio B Fund
RRSP Eligible; Inception Year: 2003; Fund Managers:
I.G. Investment Management
Income Plus Portfolio A Fund
RRSP Eligible; Inception Year: 2003; Fund Managers:
I.G. Investment Management

INVESTMENT MANAGEMENT

Investors Group Inc. (continued)
Income Plus Portfolio B Fund
RRSP Eligible; Inception Year: 2003; Fund Managers:
I.G. Investment Management
International Small Cap Class B Fund
RRSP Eligible; Inception Year: 2003; Fund Managers:
I.G. Investment Management
Japanese Equity Class B Fund
RRSP Eligible; Inception Year: 2003; Fund Managers:
I.G. Investment Management
Japanese Equity A Fund
RRSP Eligible; Inception Year: 2003; Fund Managers:
I.G. Investment Management
Japanese Equity B Fund
RRSP Eligible; Inception Year: 2003; Fund Managers:
I.G. Investment Management
Mergers & Acquisitions A Fund
RRSP Eligible; Inception Year: 2003; Fund Managers:
Camlin Asset Management
Mergers & Acquisitions B Fund
RRSP Eligible; Inception Year: 2003; Fund Managers:
Camlin Asset Management
Mergers & Acquisitions Class B Fund
RRSP Eligible; Inception Year: 2003; Fund Managers:
Camlin Asset Management
Managed Yield Class B Fund
RRSP Eligible; Inception Year: 2003; Fund Managers:
I.G. Investment Management
Mutual of Canada A Fund
RRSP Eligible; Inception Year: 2003; Fund Managers:
I.G. Investment Management
Mutual of Canada B Fund
RRSP Eligible; Inception Year: 2003; Fund Managers:
I.G. Investment Management
North American Equity Class B Fund
RRSP Eligible; Inception Year: 2003; Fund Managers:
I.G. Investment Management
North American Equity A Fund
RRSP Eligible; Inception Year: 2003; Fund Managers:
I.G. Investment Management
North American Equity B Fund
RRSP Eligible; Inception Year: 2003; Fund Managers:
I.G. Investment Management
Pacific International A Fund
RRSP Eligible; Inception Year: 2003; Fund Managers:
I.G. Investment Management
Pacific International Class B Fund
RRSP Eligible; Inception Year: 2003; Fund Managers:
I.G. Investment Management
Pacific International B Fund
RRSP Eligible; Inception Year: 2003; Fund Managers:
I.G. Investment Management
Pan Asian Growth A Fund
RRSP Eligible; Inception Year: 2003; Fund Managers:
I.G. Investment Management
Pan Asian Growth B Fund
RRSP Eligible; Inception Year: 2003; Fund Managers:
I.G. Investment Management
Pan Asian Growth Class B Fund
RRSP Eligible; Inception Year: 2003; Fund Managers:
I.G. Investment Management
Québec Enterprise Class B Fund
RRSP Eligible; Inception Year: 2003; Fund Managers:
I.G. Investment Management
Québec Enterprise A Fund
RRSP Eligible; Inception Year: 2003; Fund Managers:
I.G. Investment Management
Québec Enterprise B Fund
RRSP Eligible; Inception Year: 2003; Fund Managers:
I.G. Investment Management
Real Property A Fund
RRSP Eligible; Inception Year: 2003; Fund Managers:
I.G. Investment Management
Retirement High Growth Portfolio A Fund
RRSP Eligible; Inception Year: 2003; Fund Managers:
I.G. Investment Management
Retirement High Growth Portfolio B Fund
RRSP Eligible; Inception Year: 2003; Fund Managers:
I.G. Investment Management
Retirement Growth Portfolio A Fund
RRSP Eligible; Inception Year: 2003; Fund Managers:
I.G. Investment Management
Retirement Growth Portfolio B Fund
RRSP Eligible; Inception Year: 2003; Fund Managers:
I.G. Investment Management
Retirement Plus Portfolio A Fund
RRSP Eligible; Inception Year: 2003; Fund Managers:
I.G. Investment Management
Retirement Plus Portfolio B Fund
RRSP Eligible; Inception Year: 2003; Fund Managers:
I.G. Investment Management
Summa Class B Fund
RRSP Eligible; Inception Year: 2003; Fund Managers:
I.G. Investment Management
Summa A Fund
RRSP Eligible; Inception Year: 2003; Fund Managers:
I.G. Investment Management
Summa B Fund
RRSP Eligible; Inception Year: 2003; Fund Managers:
I.G. Investment Management
US Small Cap Class B Fund
RRSP Eligible; Inception Year: 2003; Fund Managers:
I.G. Investment Management
US Large Cap Growth Class B Fund
RRSP Eligible; Inception Year: 2003; Fund Managers:
I.G. Investment Management
US Large Cap Value Class B Fund
RRSP Eligible; Inception Year: 2003; Fund Managers:
I.G. Investment Management
US Large Cap Value RSP A Fund
RRSP Eligible; Inception Year: 2003; Fund Managers:
I.G. Investment Management
US Large Cap Value RSP B Fund
RRSP Eligible; Inception Year: 2003; Fund Managers:
I.G. Investment Management
US Large Cap Growth A Fund
RRSP Eligible; Inception Year: 2003; Fund Managers:
I.G. Investment Management
US Large Cap Growth B Fund
RRSP Eligible; Inception Year: 2003; Fund Managers:
I.G. Investment Management
US Large Cap Value A Fund
RRSP Eligible; Inception Year: 2003; Fund Managers:
I.G. Investment Management
US Large Cap Value B Fund
RRSP Eligible; Inception Year: 2003; Fund Managers:
I.G. Investment Management
US Opportunities Class B Fund
RRSP Eligible; Inception Year: 2003; Fund Managers:
I.G. Investment Management
US Opportunities A Fund
RRSP Eligible; Inception Year: 2003; Fund Managers:
I.G. Investment Management
US Opportunities B Fund
RRSP Eligible; Inception Year: 2003; Fund Managers:
I.G. Investment Management
World Growth Portfolio A Fund
RRSP Eligible; Inception Year: 2003; Fund Managers:
I.G. Investment Management
World Growth Portfolio B Fund
RRSP Eligible; Inception Year: 2003; Fund Managers:
I.G. Investment Management
Global Class B Fund
RRSP Eligible; Inception Year: 2003; Fund Managers:
I.G. Investment Management
Income Trust A Fund
RRSP Eligible; Inception Year: 2004; Fund Managers:
I.G. Investment Management
Income Trust B Fund
RRSP Eligible; Inception Year: 2004; Fund Managers:
I.G. Investment Management
Premium Money Market Fund
RRSP Eligible; Inception Year: 2001; Fund Managers:
I.G. Investment Management
Real Return Bond R Fund
RRSP Eligible; Inception Year: 2004; Fund Managers:
I.G. Investment Management
Short Term Capital Yield Class A Fund
RRSP Eligible; Inception Year: 2004; Fund Managers:
I.G. Investment Management
Short Term Capital Yield Class B Fund
RRSP Eligible; Inception Year: 2004; Fund Managers:
I.G. Investment Management
Cap Yield Class A Fund
RRSP Eligible; Inception Year: 2004; Fund Managers:
I.G. Investment Management
Cap Yield Class B Fund
RRSP Eligible; Inception Year: 2004; Fund Managers:
I.G. Investment Management
Global Dividend A Fund
RRSP Eligible; Inception Year: 2006;
Global Dividend B Fund
RRSP Eligible; Inception Year: 2006;
Global Dividend C Fund
RRSP Eligible; Inception Year: 2006;
Income Trust C Fund
RRSP Eligible; Inception Year: 2005; Fund Managers:
I.G. Investment Management
US Large Cap Value Class A Fund
RRSP Eligible; Inception Year: 2002; Fund Managers:
I.G. Investment Management
US Money Market ($US) Fund
RRSP Eligible; Inception Year: 1997; Fund Managers:
I.G. Investment Management

IPS Industrial Promotion Services Ltd.
***Also listed under:** Financing & Loan Companies*
#720, 60 Columbia Way
Markham, ON L3R 0C9
905-475-9400
Fax: 905-475-5003
info@ipscanada.com
www.ipscanada.com
Also Known As: IPS Canada
Ownership: Private. Foreign. IPS, Geneva, Switzerland.
Year Founded: 1979
Profile: Part of the Aga Khan Fund for Economic Development, IPS Canada is a venture capital & investment company. It is engaged in promoting, developing, supporting & managing industrial & related projects in North America.

Executives:
Nizar Alibhai, President

Kee West Financial Group Inc.
***Also listed under:** Financing & Loan Companies*
#502, 5920 MacLeod Trail South
Calgary, AB T2H 0K2
403-255-4643
Fax: 403-255-6892
www.keewestfinancial.com
Ownership: Private. Division of Kee West Financial Group Inc.
Year Founded: 1978
Number of Employees: 5
Profile: The mortgage banking company provides financing services in Canada, the United States & Mexico. It specializes in commercial real estate lending. Services also include private residential mortgage financing, mortgage transfers & refinances.

Executives:
Lorne Keetbaas, President

La Capitale Financial Group Inc.
625, rue Saint-Amable
Québec, QC G1R 2G5
418-643-3884
Fax: 418-646-0370
800-463-5549
Number of Employees: 1,800
Assets: $1-10 billion
Executives:
Jean-Yves Dupéré, Chair/CEO
Robert St-Denis, CEO, Personal Insurance Sector
John Strome, CEO, Insurance Sector
Monique L. Bégin, Vice-President, Communications & Public Relations
Hubert Auclair, Secretary
Affiliated Companies:
La Capitale Civil Service Insurer Inc.
La Capitale Financial Management Inc.
La Capitale General Insurance Inc.
La Capitale Insurance & Financial Services

Labrador Iron Ore Royalty Income Fund
Scotia Plaza
PO Box 4085, A Stn. A
40 King St. West, 26th Fl.
Toronto, ON M5W 2X6
416-863-7133
Fax: 416-863-7425
www.labradorironore.com
Ownership: Public
Year Founded: 1995
Assets: $500m-1 billion
Revenues: $10-50 million
Stock Symbol: LIF.UN

Profile: This is an unincorporated, limited purpose trust. Through its wholly-owned subsidiaries, Labrador Mining Company Ltd. & Hollinger-Hanna Ltd., it holds an equity interest in Iron Ore Company of Canada.

Executives:
Bruce C. Bone, Chair/CEO
James C. McCartney, Sec.-Treas.
Trustees:
Bruce C. Bone, Chair/CEO
William J. Corcoran, Vice-Chair
James C. McCartney
Paul H. Palmer
Alan R. Thomas
Donald J. Worth

Lombard Canada Ltd.

105 Adelaide St. West
Toronto, ON M5H 1P9
416-350-4400
Fax: 416-350-4417
www.lombard.ca
Ownership: Public
Year Founded: 1983
Number of Employees: 700
Assets: $1-5 million Year End: 20041100
Revenues: $500m-1 billion Year End: 20041100
Stock Symbol: NB
Executives:
Richard N. Patina, President/CEO
Peter B. Aumonier, President, Claims
Katharine M. Allan, Sr. Vice-President, Chief Underwriting Officer
Robert T. Coughlin, Sr. Vice-President, Claims
William J. Dunlop, Sr. Vice-President, Human Resources, General Counsel & Secretary
M. Jane Gardner, Sr. Vice-President/CFO
Kim H. Tan, Sr. Vice-President, Business & Corporate Development
Anne-Marie Vanier, Sr. Vice-President, Chief Actuary
Steven C. Cade, Vice-President, Western Region
Sandy Ewen, Vice-President, Developer Solutions
Peter Howling, Vice-President, Corporate Systems
Stan Keeping, Vice-President, Atlantic Region
Richard Lapierre, Vice-President, Québec Region
Mark L. Leblanc, Vice-President, Central Region
S. McManus, Vice-President, Finance, Asst. Treasurer
Dean Morrissey, Vice-President, Custom Marketing & Sales
Brian A.O. Moses, Vice-President, Information Services
Tony O'Brien, Vice-President, Risk Solutions
Robert G. Ryan, Vice-President, Special Operations
Peter Silk, Vice-President, Business Choice
Directors:
Robert T. Coughlin; 416-350-4405
William J. Dunlop; 416-350-4403
M. Jane Gardner; 416-350-4350
Robert J. Gunn; 416-350-4341
Richard N. Patina; 416-350-4401
Mark J. Ram; 416-350-4422
John C. Varnell; 416-550-4399
Affiliated Companies:
Lombard General Insurance Company of Canada
Lombard Insurance Company
Zenith Insurance Company
Branches:
Calgary
Northland Professional Centre
#301, 4600 Crowchild Trail NW
Calgary, AB T3A 2L6 Canada
403-289-2550
Fax: 403-288-3040
Cambridge - Agri-Business
#400, 1575 Bishop St.
Cambridge, ON N1R 7J4 Canada
519-740-8828
Fax: 519-740-6474
Robert G. Ryan, Vice-President, Special Operations
Halifax
Central Trust Bldg.
1801 Hollis St., 8th Fl.
Halifax, NS B3J 2L5 Canada
902-420-1221
Fax: 902-423-8640
Stan Keeping, Vice-President, Atlantic Region
Montréal - Québec Region
#1700, 2001, av University
Montréal, QC H3A 2A6 Canada
514-843-1111
Fax: 514-843-1103
Richard Lapierre, Vice-President, Québec Region
Québec
#2750, 2600, boul Laurier
Québec, QC G1V 4M6 Canada
418-659-6300
Fax: 418-659-2543
Richard Lapierre, Vice-President, Québec Region
Saskatoon - Crop & Hail
#201, 3301 Eighth St. West
Saskatoon, SK S7H 5K5 Canada
306-242-1415
Fax: 306-664-4492
J.C.(Clint) Holt, Vice-President
Thunder Bay
216 Camelot St.
Thunder Bay, ON P7A 4B1 Canada
807-344-1410
Fax: 807-345-6479
800-565-6931
Toronto - Central Region
105 Adelaide St. West
Toronto, ON M5H 1P9 Canada
416-350-4000
Fax: 416-350-4123
Mark LeBlanc, Vice-President
Vancouver
2 Bentall Centre
#600, 555 Burrard St.
Vancouver, BC V7X 1M8 Canada
604-683-0255
Fax: 604-631-6896
Steven Cade, Vice-President, Western Region

Mackenzie Ivy Enterprise Fund

c/o Mackenzie Financial Corporation
#M111, 150 Bloor St. West
Toronto, ON M5S 3B5
416-922-3217
Fax: 416-922-5660
800-387-0614
service@mackenziefinancial.com
www.mackenziefinancial.com/ivy
Profile: The Fund invests in a select group of smaller Canadian companies.

Executives:
Stephanie Griffiths, Fund Manager

Manulife Capital

200 Bloor St. East, 4th Fl.
Toronto, ON M4W 1E5
416-926-5727
Fax: 416-926-5737
www.manulife.com
Ownership: Private equite group of Manulife Financial Individual Insurance.
Year Founded: 1998
Executives:
Rajiv Bakshi, Assistant Vice-President
William Eeuwes, Vice-President
Vipon Ghai, Assistant Vice-President
Tom Vukota, Assistant Vice-President

McLean Watson Capital Inc.

PO Box 129
#2810, 1 First Canadian Place
Toronto, ON M5X 1A4
416-363-2000
Fax: 416-363-2010
information@mcleanwatson.com
www.mcleanwatson.com
Ownership: Private
Year Founded: 1993
Number of Employees: 10
Profile: Venture capital.

Partners:
P. Stanley Chan
John F. Eckert
Loudon McLean Owen
John R. Stewart
Emil Savov

Meloche Monnex Inc.

***Also listed under:** Federal & Provincial*
50, Place Crémazie, 12e étage
Montréal, QC H2P 1B6
514-382-6060
Fax: 514-385-2162
www.melochemonnex.com
Executives:
Alain Thibault, President/CEO
Jean R. Lachance, Exec. Chair, Affirmity Marketing Group
Chris D. Daniel, Chair, Affirmity Marketing Group
Daniel Demers, Exec. Vice-President
Richard Evans, Sr. Vice-President, Claims Service
François Faucher, Sr. Vice-President & CFO
Marilyn Flanagan, Sr. Vice-President, Client Services
Pierre Melançon, Sr. Vice-President, Marketing
Pierre Ménard, Sr. Vice-President, Change & Resources Management
Guy Vézina, Sr. Vice-President, Operations & Business Development
Raynald Lecavalier, Vice-President, Legal & Regulatory Affairs, Secretary
Antonietta DiGirolamo, Asst. Corporate Secretary
Directors:
Pierre Meloche, OC, Chair
Dianne Cunningham
Raymond A. Décarie
Daniel Demers
Bernard T. Dorval
Louis D. Hyndman
Sean Kilburn
C. Lajeunesse, OC
Damian J. McNamee
Dominic J. Mercuri
L. Robert Shaw
Alain Thibault
Fredric J. Tomczyk
Affiliated Companies:
Primmum Insurance Company
Security National Insurance Company
Branches:
Calgary
One Palliser Square
#1200, 125 - 9 Ave. SE
Calgary, AB T2G 0P6 Canada
403-269-1112
Fax: 403-298-2530
800-268-8955
Edmonton
#2300, 10025 - 102A Ave. NW
Edmonton, AB T5J 2Z2 Canada
780-429-1112
Fax: 780-420-2323
800-268-8955
Halifax
Founders Square
#104, 1701 Hollis St.
Halifax, NS B3J 3M8 Canada
902-420-1112
Fax: 902-424-1200
800-268-8955
Montréal
50, Place Crémazie, 12e étage
Montréal, QC H3P 1B6 Canada
514-384-1112
Fax: 514-385-2196
800-361-3821
Toronto
2161 Yonge St., 4th Fl.
Toronto, ON M4S 3A6 Canada
416-484-1112
Fax: 416-545-6125
800-268-8955

Mercantile Bancorp Limited

***Also listed under:** Financing & Loan Companies*
#1508, 999 West Hastings St.
Vancouver, BC V6C 2W2
604-685-5765
Fax: 604-685-2755
www.mercantilebancorp.com
Year Founded: 1989
Profile: The merchant investor invests in & assists in the management of industrial, service & consumer products companies in western Canada.

Mercantile Bancorp Limited (continued)
Executives:
Donald Steele, President
Bruno Kristensen, Manager

MICC Investments Limited
#1000, 33 Yonge St.
Toronto, ON M5E 1S9
416-591-5100
Fax: 416-591-5144
Ownership: Public.
Year Founded: 1963
Stock Symbol: MIVV
Profile: The investment holding company manages its investment portfolio & pursues investment opportunities.

Executives:
David A. Rattee, President/CEO
Bahir Manios, Controller
Angela Marier, Corporate Secretary
Directors:
Frank N.C. Lochan, Chair
Harold Corrigan
Brian D. Lawson
David A. Rattee
Robert M. Rennie

MPL Communications Inc.
#700, 133 Richmond St. West
Toronto, ON M5H 3M8
416-869-1177
Fax: 416-869-0616
800-804-8846
ir@mplcomm.com
www.adviceforinvestors.com
Ownership: Public. Major shareholder is Marpep Publishing Ltd. (76.9% of outstanding common shares).
Year Founded: 1988
Number of Employees: 49
Stock Symbol: MPZ
Profile: MPL publishes investment advisory periodical newsletters & other specialized publications for business professionals. Its wholly owned subsidiary is MPL Asset Management Inc.

Executives:
Barrie Martland, President
Mindy Tenenbaum, Vice-President, Marketing
Diana Yeo, Manager, Information Systems
Directors:
Stephen D. Pepper, Chair
Allie P. Ash, Jr.
Lynn Goth
Barrie Martland
William Scott

NAL Oil & Gas Trust
#600, 550 - 6 Ave. SW
Calgary, AB T2P 0S2
403-294-3600
Fax: 403-294-3601
888-223-8792
investor.relations@nal.ca
www.nal.ca
Ownership: Public
Year Founded: 1996
Number of Employees: 340
Assets: $500m-1 billion Year End: 20060930
Revenues: $100-500 million Year End: 20060930
Stock Symbol: NAE.UN
Profile: The open-end investment trust is engaged in the generation of distributions by acquiring, developing, producing & marketing oil, natural gas & natural gas liquids. Assets are owned by the trust in Ontario, Saskatchewan & Alberta. The units of the trust trade on the Toronto Stock Exchange.

Executives:
Andrew B. Wiswell, President/CEO
Jonathan A. Lexier, Chief Operating Officer
R. Ross Liland, CFO & Vice-President, Finance
Ben L. Bury, Vice-President, Marketing
Marlon McDougall, Vice-President, Operations
Directors:
J. Charles Caty, Chair
Dennis G. Flanagan
Irvine J. Koop
Gordon Lackenbauer
Barry D. Stewart
Warren A. Thomson
Andrew B. Wiswell

Newfoundland Capital Corporation Limited
745 Windmill Rd.
Dartmouth, NS B3B 1C2
902-468-7557
Fax: 902-468-7558
ncc@ncc.ca
www.ncc.ca
Ownership: Public
Year Founded: 1949
Number of Employees: 700
Assets: $100-500 million Year End: 20041231
Revenues: $50-100 million Year End: 20041231
Stock Symbol: NCC.SV.A, NCC.MV.A
Profile: The capital corporation operates 44 radio stations across Canada.

Executives:
Harry R. Steele, Chair
Robert G. Steele, President/CEO
Mack S. Maheu, Exec. Vice-President, COO
Scott G.M. Weatherby, CFO, Corporate Secretary
Directors:
Craig L. Dobbin
David I. Matheson
Robert G. Steele
Donald J. Warr

Northbridge Financial Corporation
105 Adelaide St. West
Toronto, ON M5H 1P9
416-350-4300
Fax: 416-350-4307
investorrelations@northbridgefinancial.com
www.northbridgefinancial.com
Ownership: Public.
Stock Symbol: NB
Executives:
Mark J. Ram, President/CEO
John Varnell, CFO, Corporate Secretary
Directors:
V. Prem Watsa, Chair
Jean Cloutier
Anthony F. Griffiths
Robert Gunn
Robbert Hartog
Bryan G. Smith
John Varnell
Affiliated Companies:
Federated Insurance Company of Canada
Lombard Canada Ltd.

Northfield Capital Corporation
#301, 141 Adelaide St. West
Toronto, ON M5H 3L5
416-628-5901
Fax: 416-628-5911
info@northfieldcapital.com
www.northfieldcapital.com
Ownership: Public.
Year Founded: 1981
Stock Symbol: NFD.A
Profile: The investment company has interests in the manufacturing, oil & gas, glass, & mining sectors. The company is listed on the TSX Venture Exchange.

Executives:
Robert D. Cudney, President/CEO
Brent J. Peters, Vice-President, Finance, Treasurer
Jay Goldman, Secretary
Directors:
William O. Ballard
Robert D. Cudney
Larry E. Kinden
John D. McBride
Thomas J. Pladsen

Northland Power Income Fund
c/o Iroquois Falls Power Management Inc.
30 St. Clair Ave. West, 17th Fl.
Toronto, ON M4V 3A2
416-962-6262
Fax: 416-962-6266
info@npifund.com
www.npifund.com
Ownership: Public
Year Founded: 1997
Number of Employees: 35
Assets: $100-500 million
Stock Symbol: NPI.UN
Profile: This is an unincorporated open-ended trust, which owns a cogeneration power plant in Iroquois Falls, ON, & a 25% interest in a cogeneration power plant located near Kingston, ON. The fund's wholly owned subsidiary is Iroquois Falls Power Corp. The fund is administered by Iroquois Falls Power Management Inc.

Executives:
John W. Brace, President/CEO
Anthony F. Anderson, CFO
Sam Mantenuto, COO

Novacap II, Limited Partnership
#210, 375, boul Roland-Therrien
Longueuil, QC J4H 4A6
450-651-5000
Fax: 450-651-7585
info@novacap.ca
www.novacap.ca
Former Name: Investissements Novacap Inc.
Year Founded: 2000
Number of Employees: 15
Assets: $100-500 million Year End: 20050101
Revenues: $100-500 million Year End: 20050101
Profile: A venture capital partnership, Novacap is a $250,000,000 fund specializing in high-technology & traditional industries. Novacap is actively investing in the telecommunications, medical & leisure sectors as well as in high value-added manufacturing operations.

Executives:
Jean-Pierre Chartrand, President, Novacap Industries; jpchartand@novacap.ca
Alain Belanger, Vice-President; abelanger@novacap.ca
François Chaurette, Vice-President; fchaurette@novacap.ca
Michel Coté, Vice-President; mcote@novacap.ca
Jacques Foisy, Vice-President, Finance; jfoisy@novacap.ca
Domenic Mancini, Vice-President; dmancini@novacap.ca
Pascal Tremblay, Vice-President; ptremblay@novacap.ca

Onex Corporation
BCE Place
PO Box 700
161 Bay St., 49th Fl.
Toronto, ON M5J 2S1
416-362-7711
Fax: 416-362-5765
info@onex.com
www.onex.com
Ownership: G.W. Schwartz beneficially holds all outstanding multiple voting shares & approximately 21% of outstanding subordinate voting shares
Year Founded: 1983
Number of Employees: 136,00
Assets: $10-50 million Year End: 20051231
Revenues: $10-50 million Year End: 20051231
Stock Symbol: OCX
Profile: Subsidiaries include Celestica Inc., ClientLogic Corporation, Spirit AeroSystems, Inc., Radian Communication Services Corp., Cineplex Entertainment LP, ResCare, Inc., Emergency Medical Services Corporation, Center for Diagnostic Imaging, Inc., Skilled Healthcare Group, Inc., Cosmetic Essence, Inc. & ONCAP.

Executives:
Gerald W. Schwartz, President/CEO
Timothy A.R. Duncanson, Managing Director
Ewout R. Heersink, Managing Director, CFO
Mark L. Hilson, Managing Director
Seth Mersky, Managing Director
Andrew J. Sheiner, Managing Director
Nigel S. Wright, Managing Director
Andrea E. Daly, Vice-President, General Counsel
Christopher A. Govan, Vice-President, Taxation
Donald W. Lewtas, Vice-President, Finance
John S. Elder, Q.C., Secretary
Directors:
Gerald W. Schwartz, Chair
Daniel C. Casey
Peter C. Godsoe
Serge Gouin
Brian M. King
John B. McCoy
J. Robert S. Prichard

Heather M. Reisman
Arni C. Thorsteinson

Optimum Group Inc.

Also listed under: *Financial Planning*
#1700, 425, boul de Maisonneuve ouest
Montréal, QC H3A 3G5
514-288-2010
Fax: 514-288-7692
webmaster@groupe-optimum.com
www.groupe-optimum.com
Year Founded: 1969
Number of Employees: 600
Assets: $100 billion +
Revenues: $500m-1 billion
Executives:
Gilles Blondeau, Chair/CEO
Jean-Claude Pagé, President/COO
Henri Joli-Coeur, Vice-Chair
Mario Georgiev, Sr. Vice-President
Alain Béland, Vice-President & Treasurer
Louis Fontaine, Vice-President & Secretary, Legal Affairs
Affiliated Companies:
Optimum Actuaires & Conseillers
Optimum Asset Management Inc.
Optimum Général inc
Optimum Placements Inc.
Optimum Reassurance Company

Parkland Income Fund

Riverside Office Plaza
#236, 4919 - 59th St.
Red Deer, AB T4N 6C9
403-357-6400
Fax: 403-346-3015
corpinfo@parkland.ca
www.parkland.ca
Ownership: Public
Year Founded: 1977
Number of Employees: 701
Assets: $100-500 million Year End: 20051231
Revenues: $500m-1 billion Year End: 20051231
Stock Symbol: PKI.UN
Profile: Parkland Income Fund operates retail & wholesale fuels & convenience store businesses, under it Fas Gas Plus, Fas Gas, Race Trac Fuels, & Short Stop Food Stores brands & through independent branded dealers. Fuel is transported through its Petrohaul division. With over 550 locations, Parkland has develped a strong market niche in western & northern Canadian non-urban markets. To maximize value for its unitholders, the Fund is focussed on the continuous refinement of its retail portfolio, increased revenue diversification through growth in non-fuel revenues, & active supply chain management. Parkland maintains ownership of the Bowden refinery, near Red Deer, Alberta, & is currently re-ctivating the site for production of drilling fluids.

Executives:
Michael W. Chorlton, President/CEO
Stewart MacPhail, Vice-President, Retail
John Schroeder, Vice-President/CFO
Bradley Williams, Vice-President, Supply, Wholesale & Distribution
Directors:
James Pantelidis, Chair
John Bechtold
Robert Brawn
Michael Chorlton
Jim Dinning
Alain Ferland
Kris Matthews
Ron Rogers
David Spencer

Pengrowth Energy Trust

East Tower, Petro-Canada Centre
#2900, 111 - 5th Ave. SW
Calgary, AB T2P 3Y6
403-233-0224
Fax: 403-265-6251
800-223-4122
pengrowth@pengrowth.com
www.pengrowth.com
Ownership: Public. Pengrowth Corporation.
Year Founded: 1988
Number of Employees: 289
Assets: $1-10 billion
Revenues: $500m-1 billion
Stock Symbol: PGF.B; PGF.A; PGH
Profile: The energy investment trust, through Pengrowth Corporation, acquires, holds & operates high quality, proven producing oil & natural gas properties in western Canada & offshore. 90% of all cashflow, net of management fees & expenses, is distributed monthly to unitholders. The trust is managed by Pengrowth Management Limited.

Executives:
James S. Kinnear, President/CEO; jimk@pengrowth.com
Christopher Webster, CFO; bobh@pengrowth.com
Gordon M. Anderson, Vice-President; gordona@pengrowth.com

Lynn Kis, Vice-President, Engineering; lynnk@pengrowth.com
Henry D. McKinnon, Vice-President, Operations
Charles V. Selby, Corporate Secretary
Lianne Bigham, Controller; lianneb@pengrowth.com
Directors:
James S. Kinnear, Chair
Thomas A. Cumming
Michael Parrett
William Stedman
Francis G. Vetsch
Stanley H. Wong
John B. Zaozirny
Branches:
Halifax
#407, 1959 Upper Water St.
Halifax, NS B3J 3N2 Canada
902-425-8778
Fax: 902-425-7887
Toronto
PO Box 72
#2315, 200 Bay St.
Toronto, ON M5J 2J2 Canada
416-362-1748
Fax: 416-362-8191
Sally Elliott, Contact, Investor Relations

Penn West Energy Trust

#2200, 425 - 1st St. SW
Calgary, AB T2P 3L8
403-777-2500
Fax: 403-777-2699
866-693-2707
investor_relations@pennwest.com
www.pennwest.com
Former Name: Petrofund Energy Trust; Penn West Petroleum Ltd.; Ultima Energy Trust; Maximum Energy Trust
Ownership: Public.
Year Founded: 1988
Stock Symbol: PWT.UN
Profile: In 2006, Petrofund Energy Trust merged with Penn West Energy Trust. The conventional oil and gas trust operates under the Penn West name. It operates in western Canada's sedimentary basin.

Executives:
William E. Andrew, President/CEO; bill.andrew@pennwest.com
David W. Middleton, Exec. Vice-President/COO
Thane A.E. Jensen, Sr. Vice-President, Exploration & Development
Todd Takeyasu, Sr. Vice-President/CFO
William Tang Kong, Sr. Vice-President, Corporate Development

Pinnacle Private Capital

Also listed under: *Financing & Loan Companies*
#410, 2431 - 37th Ave NE
Calgary, AB T2E 6Y7
403-250-3188
Fax: 403-735-9181
info@pinnacle-capital.com
www.pinnacle-capital.com
Former Name: Agilis Corporation
Ownership: Private.
Year Founded: 2001
Profile: The capital management organization provides venture capital & support for existing portfolio companies or beginning entrepreneurs.

Executives:
Kevin Starozik, CEO
Don Broadhead, Chief Financial Officer

Power Corporation of Canada

751, sq Victoria
Montréal, QC H2Y 2J3
514-286-7400
Fax: 514-286-7424
www.powercorp.com
Ownership: Major shareholder is Paul Desmarais & Associates (65.0% voting interest).
Year Founded: 1925
Number of Employees: 25,000
Stock Symbol: POW
Profile: A diversified management & holding company, Power Corporation of Canada has holdings in leading financial services, the communications sector, insurance, newspapers & Asian development ventures. Its wholly owned subsidiaries are Gesca Ltée & Power Technology Investment Corp. Through its European-based affiliate Pargesa group, Power Corporation holds significant positions in major media, energy, water, waste services, & specialty minerals companies. The company also has diversified interests in Asia.

Executives:
André Desmarais, President/Co-CEO
Paul Desmarais, Jr., Co-CEO
John A. Rae, Exec. Vice-President, Office of the Chair of the Executive Committee
Edward Johnson, Sr. Vice-President, Secretary & General Counsel
Arnaud Vial, Sr. Vice-President, Finance
Peter Kruyt, Vice-President
Denis Le Vasseur, Vice-President, Controller
Stephane Lemany, Vice-President, Asst. General Counsel
Gérard Veilleux, Vice-President
Pierre-Elliott Levasseur, Treasurer
Jeannine Robitaille, Asst. Secretary
Directors:
Paul Desmarais, Jr., Chair
Michel Plessis-Bélair, Vice-Chair
Pierre Beaudoin
Laurent Dassault
Amaury-Daniel De Seze
André Desmarais
Paul Desmarais, P.C., C.C.
Michel François-Poncet
Paul Frebourg
Anthony R. Graham
Robert Gratton
Donald F. Mazankowski
Jerry E.A. Nickerson
James R. Nininger
R. Jeffrey Orr
Robert Parizeau
Jean Peyrelevade
John A. Rae
Emöke Szathmáry
James W. Burns, Emeritus
P. Michael Pitfield, Emeritus
Affiliated Companies:
Power Financial Corporation
Branches:
Winnipeg
#2610, 1 Lombard Pl.
Winnipeg, MB R3B 0X5 Canada
204-925-5100
Fax: 204-925-5102

Power Financial Corporation

751, sq Victoria
Montréal, QC H2Y 2J3
514-286-7430
Fax: 514-286-7424
www.powerfinancial.com
Ownership: Public. Major shareholder Power Corporation of Canada holds a 67.1% interest
Year Founded: 1940
Number of Employees: 18,300
Stock Symbol: PWF
Executives:
R. Jeffrey Orr, President/CEO
Michel Plessis-Bélair, Exec. Vice-President/CFO
Edward Johnson, Sr. Vice-President, General Counsel & Secretary
Arnaud Vial, Sr. Vice-President, Finance
Denis Le Vasseur, Vice-President, Controller
Pierre-Elliott Levasseur, Treasurer
Jeannine Robitaille, Asst. Secretary
Directors:
Robert Gratton, Chair
André Desmarais, Deputy Chair

INVESTMENT MANAGEMENT

Power Financial Corporation (continued)
Paul Desmarais, P.C., C.C.
Paul Desmarais, Jr.
Gerald Frere
Anthony R. Graham
Donald F. Mazankowski
Jerry E.A. Nickerson
Michel Plessis-Bélair
Raymond Royer
Guy St-Germain, CM
Emöke Szathmáry
Affiliated Companies:
Great-West Lifeco Inc./GWO
Branches:
Winnipeg
#2600, 1 Lombard Pl.
Winnipeg, MB R3B 0X5 Canada
204-925-5100
Fax: 204-925-5102

Priszm Income Fund
101 Exchange Ave.
Vaughan, ON L4K 5R6
416-739-2900
866-774-7961
info@priszm.com, ir@priszm.com
www.priszm.com
Former Name: Priszm Canadian Income Fund
Stock Symbol: QSR.UN
Profile: The Priszm Income Fund looks for investment opportunities, including multi-brand select locations & new restaurants. The Fund has an interest in Priszm LP which owns & operates restaurants.

Executives:
John I. Bitove, Chair/CEO
Jeff O'Neill, President/COO
Peter Walkey, Chief Financial Officer
Directors:
John I Bitove
Lilly Di Massimo
Borden Rosiak
Glen M. Swire
Stanley A. Thomas

Retirement Residences Real Estate Investment Trust
55 Standish Ct., 8th Fl.
Mississauga, ON L5R 4B2
289-360-1200
Fax: 289-360-1201
888-549-5450
contactus@retirementreit.com
www.retirementreit.com
Year Founded: 2001
Number of Employees: 25,000
Assets: $1-5 million Year End: 20050630
Revenues: $900,000,000 Year End: 20050630
Stock Symbol: RRR.UN
Profile: The investment trust owns retirement, long-term care & subacute homes in Canada & the U.S. Home health care services operate under the trade names Central Health Services & Medisys Nursing Placement. The organization continues to upgrade its portfolio of homes by acquiring new developments.

Executives:
Derek Watchorn, President/CEO
David Beirnes, CFO
Alan Torrie, COO
C. William Dillane, Exec. Vice-President, Stratetic Initiatives
David Hamilton, Sr. Vice-President, Construction
Michael Chandler, Vice-President, Acquisitions & Finance
Michael Dennis
Trustees:
William G. Davis, P.C., C.C.,Q.C., Chair
John R. Evans
W. Darcy McKeough
Barry Reichmann
Paul Reichmann
Calvin Stiller
Derek J. Watchorn
Directors:
Douglas Bassett
Manfred Walt

Richco Investors Inc.
#900, 789 West Pender St.
Vancouver, BC V6C 1H2
604-689-4407
Fax: 604-408-8515
info@richcoinvestors.com
www.richcoinvestors.com
Year Founded: 1980
Assets: $1-5 million
Revenues: Under $1 million
Stock Symbol: RII.MV.A; RII.SV.B
Profile: The company's main business is the financing & developing of existing businesses. Securities are held in both public & private companies which conduct business in North America & offshore. On occasion, the company also acts as an investment banker. The company's subsidiaries are Richco Petroleum Ltd., Milco Petroleum Ltd., Richi Petroleum Corp., & Richco International Inc.

Executives:
Robert G. Smiley, President/ CEO
Directors:
Rauol N. Tsakok, Chair
A. Ken Kow, Secretary
Ernest K. Cheung
Robert G. Smiley
Sandra Tsakok

RioCan Real Estate Investment Trust
Exchange Tower
PO Box 378
#700, 130 King St. West
Toronto, ON M5X 1E2
416-866-3033
Fax: 416-866-3020
800-465-2733
inquires@riocan.com
www.riocan.com
Former Name: Counsel Real Estate Investment Trust
Also Known As: RioCan REIT
Ownership: Public
Year Founded: 1993
Number of Employees: 630
Assets: $1-10 billion Year End: 20051231
Revenues: $500m-1 billion Year End: 20051231
Stock Symbol: REI.UN
Profile: An unincorporated closed-end trust, it owns or has interests in a portfolio of 204 retail properties, including four under development, across Canada. Publicly traded on the Toronto Stock Exchange, its wholly owned subsidiary is RioCan Property Services Inc.

Executives:
Edward Sonshine, QC, President/CEO; 416-866-3018
Fred Waks, Sr. Vice-President/COO; 416-866-8445
John Ballantyne, Vice-President, Asset Management; 416-866-3097
Michael Connolly, Vice-President, Construction; 416-866-3045
Therese Cornelissen, Vice-President, Financial Reporting; 416-862-3667
Danny Kissoon, Vice-President, Operations; 416-866-8189
Donald MacKinnon, Vice-President, Real Estate Finance; 416-866-3047
Katy Ritcey, Vice-President, Investments; 416-866-8292
Jeff Ross, Vice-President, Leasing; 416-866-3044
Jordan Robins, Vice-President, Developments; 416-646-8330
Robert Wolf, Vice-President/CFO; 416-866-3198
Trustees:
Paul V. Godfrey, Chair; 416-597-4284
Clare R. Copeland
Raymond Gelgoot; 416-864-9700
Frank W. King; 403-247-7378
Dale H. Lastman; 416-979-2211
Ronald W. Osborne
Sharon Sallows; 416-920-5844
Edward Sonshine, QC; 416-866-3018
Michael Stephenson; 416-367-3811

Rockwater Capital Corporation
Bay Wellington Tower, BCE Place
PO Box 779
#900, 181 Bay St.
Toronto, ON M5J 2T3
416-865-4780
Fax: 416-865-4788
888-865-4780
info@rockwater.ca
www.rockwater.ca
Former Name: McCarvill Corporation
Ownership: Public.
Year Founded: 1996
Stock Symbol: RCC
Profile: Rockwater is an independent, diversified financial services company. Businesses include the capital markets, wealth management & asset management sectors.

Executives:
Robert Schultz, Chair
William D. Packham, President/CEO
Gordon Weir, Chief Financial Officer
Gerald Throop, Exec. Vice-President
Directors:
Robert Schultz, Chair
John A. Brough
Robert Buchan
John Crow
Edmund King
William Packham
Frank Potter
David Tuer
Robert Tweedy
Affiliated Companies:
Blackmont Capital Inc.
KBSH Capital Management Inc.

Royal Canadian Securities Limited
#800, 240 Graham Ave.
Winnipeg, MB R3C 0J7
204-947-2835
Fax: 204-947-0475
Year Founded: 1948
Executives:
Ashleigh Everett, President
Directors:
Richard Bracken, Chair

Sabina Silver Corporation
1124 Gainsborough Rd.
London, ON N6H 5N1
519-438-4555
Fax: 519-438-9666
info@sabinasilver.com
www.sabinasilver.com
Former Name: Sabina Resources Limited
Ownership: Public.
Year Founded: 1966
Assets: Under $1 million
Revenues: Under $1 million
Stock Symbol: SBB.V/TSX Venture; SBBFF/OTC
Profile: The Canadian public mineral exploration & development company has assets in the following areas: the Canadian Arctic, the Stewart-Eskay Creek Mining District & the Red Lake gold camp. In addition to be listed on stock exchanges in Canada & the USA, it is also listed on the Deutsche Bourse - Frankfurt, with the symbol, RXC.FR.

Executives:
William W. Cummins, BSc, CA, Chair/CEO
Abraham Drost, MSc, PGeo, President
Directors:
Duncan Caldwell, BASc, CGA, CFO, Secretary
Ewan Downie, Vice-President
John Whitton, BSc, PGeo, Manager, Exploration
William W. Cummins, Chair/CEO
Duncan J. Caldwell
Ewan Downie
Abraham Drost
Terry Eyton
Scott Hean
John Whitton
Roy Wilkes
Branches:
Thunder Bay
#401, 1113 Jade Ct.
Thunder Bay, ON P7B 6M7
807-766-1799
Fax: 807-345-0284

Scotia Investments Limited
3 Bedford Hills Rd.
Bedford, NS B4A 1J5
Ownership: Owned by Jodrey family, Hantsport, NS.
Year Founded: 1945
Profile: Scotia Investments is a private investment holding company. It has major interests in the following companies: CKF Inc., Minas Basin Pulp & Power Company Limited, Maritime Paper Products Limited, Annapolis Group Inc., Avon Valley

Greenhouses Limited, Crown Fibre Tube Inc., Envirosystems Inc., Scotia Recycling Limited plus other operating companies.

Executives:
George E. Bishop, CA, President
Robert Patzelt, QC, B.Comm. BA, LLM, FCIP, Vice-President, Risk Management, General Counsel

Scotiabank Private Equity Investments
Scotia Plaza
40 King St. West, 64th Fl.
Toronto, ON M5H 3Y2
416-945-4148
Fax: 416-945-4588
deal_flow@e-scotia.com
www.scotiabank.com/privateequity
Former Name: e-Scotia Acquisition Inc.
Ownership: Subsidiary of Scotiabank
Year Founded: 2000
Number of Employees: 7
Executives:
Gregory A. Milavsky, Managing Director & Group Head
Tony Cestra, Managing Director

Senvest Capital Inc.
#1180, 1140, boul de Maisonneuve ouest
Montréal, QC H3A 1M8
514-281-8082
Fax: 514-281-0166
800-603-8082
ir@senvest.com
www.senvest.com
Ownership: Major shareholder Victor Mashaal (30.62% interest)

Year Founded: 1968
Number of Employees: 6
Assets: $50-100 million
Revenues: $10-50 million
Stock Symbol: SEC
Profile: Senvest Capital is a holding company with interests in commercial printing, real estate, industrial electronic security products & systems. The company also has minority interests & investments in a number of businesses in Canada & the United States.

Executives:
Victor Mashaal, President
Richard Mashaal, Vice-President
George Malikotsis, CFO

Sheldon-Larder Mines Limited
#605, 80 Richmond St. West
Toronto, ON M5H 2S9
416-364-0042
Fax: 416-364-2630
Ownership: Public.
Year Founded: 1937
Stock Symbol: SLDM
Profile: The junior mining exploration company is engaged in the exploration of mineral properties. Sheldon-Larder retains the Magusi River property in northeastern Ontario, as well as a royalty interest in the McGarry Township property, which is also located in northeastern Ontario.

Executives:
Jeffrey J. Becker, President

Shiningbank Energy Income Fund
#1400, 111 - 5th Ave. SW
Calgary, AB T2P 3Y6
403-268-7477
Fax: 403-268-7499
866-268-7477
irinfo@shiningbank.com
www.shiningbank.com
Ownership: Public
Year Founded: 1996
Stock Symbol: SHN.UN
Profile: A publicly-traded Canadian conventional oil & gas trust, it purchases & develops producing oil & gas properties & pays tax-advantaged monthly distributions to unitholders.

Executives:
David M. Fitzpatrick, President/CEO
Bruce K. Gibson, Chief Financial Officer, Finance
Gregory D. Moore, Chief Operating Officer
Alan G. Glessing, Vice-President, Administration, Controller
J. Lance Petersen, Vice-President, Land
R. Bruce Thornhill, Vice-President, Geology
Murray J. Desrosiers, Corporate Sectretary, General Counsel
Directors:
Arne R. Nielsen, Chair
Edward W. Best
Richard W. Clark
David M. Fitzpatrick
D. Grant Gunderson
Robert B. Hodgins
Warren D. Steckley

Société générale de financement du Québec(SGF)
#1500, 600, rue de la Gauchetière ouest
Montréal, QC H3B 4L8
514-876-9290
Fax: 514-395-8055
info@sgfqc.com
www.sgfqc.com
Year Founded: 1962
Assets: $1-10 billion
Revenues: $500m-1 billion
Profile: The company is an industrial & financial holding company, which executes economic development projects, in cooperation with partners & in accordance with the economic development policy of the Government of Ontario. SGF targets projects in the following areas: agrifood; chemicals, petrochemicals, plastics, & energy; high technology; industrial logistics; machinery; transportation material; metals & minerals; forest products; recreotourism; & health.

Executives:
Pierre Shedleur, President, General Manager
Jean-Jacques Carrier, CFO, Vice-President
André Roy, Sr. Vice-President, Administration
André Archimbaud, Group Vice-President, Healthcare
Marc Filion, Group Vice-President, Mines, Metals & Industry
Alain Poirier, Group Vice-President, Technology
Luc Séguin, Group Vice-President, Chemicals & Petrochemicals

Chantal Malo, Director, Planning & Development
Directors:
Pierre Shedleur, Chair
Jean Bazin
Jean Bienvenue
Diane Lanctôt
John LeBoutillier
Jean-Pierre Montreux
Ashok K. Narang
Jean Pronovost
Richard J. Renaud
Stephen Rosenhek

Sonor Investments Limited
PO Box 68
#1010, 130 Adelaide St. West
Toronto, ON M5H 3P5
416-369-1499
Fax: 416-369-0280
Ownership: Major shareholder Michael R. Gardiner indirectly holds 21.8% voting interest & through Toodles Investment Corp. 6.8% voting interest
Year Founded: 1960
Assets: $102,171,000
Revenues: $7,682,000
Stock Symbol: SNI.A
Executives:
Michael R. Gardiner, President/CEO
Mike Gionas, CFO

StarPoint Energy Trust
Bow Valley Square II
#3900, 205 - 5th Ave. SW
Calgary, AB T2P 2V7
403-268-7800
Fax: 403-263-3388
800-838-9206
info@spnenergy.com
www.spnenergy.com
Ownership: Public
Year Founded: 2004
Stock Symbol: SPN.UN
Profile: StarPoint's focus is upon oil & natural gas. Its core areas are southern Saskatchewan, central Alberta & northeastern British Columbia. In 2005, APF Energy Trust & StarPoint Energy Trust merged.
Executives:
Paul Colborne, President/CEO
Brett Herman, CFO & Vice-President, Finance
Graham Kidd, Vice-President, Corporate Development
Murray Mason, Vice-President, Production
Eric Strachan, Vice-President, Production
Jeremy Wallis, Vice-President, Land
Directors:
Jim Bertram
Steven Cloutier
Fred Coles
Martin Hislop
Robert G. Peters
Jim Pasieka
Paul Starnino

Summit Real Estate Investment Trust
#200, 6285 Northam Dr.
Mississauga, ON L4V 1X5
866-756-6481
www.summitreit.com
Ownership: Public
Year Founded: 1984
Number of Employees: 17
Assets: $1,500,000,000
Revenues: $100-500 million
Stock Symbol: SMU.UN
Profile: Operating as an unincorporated closed-end trust, it provides investors with the opportunity to participate in a portfolio of income-producing real property investments located principally in Canada. Real estate investments consist of suburban shopping centres & industrial buildings.

Executives:
Louis Maroun, President/CEO
Paul Dykeman, CFO & Exec. Vice-President
Kathy Harder, Sr. Vice-President, Investments
Mark Hazell, Sr. Vice-President, Portfolio Management
Craig Newell, Vice-President, Finance
Jon Robbins, Vice-President, Analysis & Research
Trustees:
Allan Olson, Chair
Eugene Bodycott
Donald Carr
Daniel Fourier
Kenneth Mader
Louis Maroun
Judith Munro
Gary Patterson
Saul Shulman

Superior Plus Income Fund
#2820, 605 - 5 Ave. SW
Calgary, AB T2P 3H5
403-218-2952
Fax: 403-218-2973
866-490-7587
www.superiorplus.ca
Former Name: Superior Propane Income Fund
Ownership: Public
Year Founded: 1996
Number of Employees: 1,811
Assets: $1,274,800,000
Revenues: $650,000,000
Stock Symbol: SPF.UN
Profile: The diversified business trust holds 100% of Superior Plus LP. It has four Canadian operating divisions: Superior Propane; ERCO Worldwide; Winroc; and Superior Energy Management. The income fund's trust units trade on the Toronto Stock Exchange.

Executives:
Grant Billing, CEO
Geoffrey N. Mackey, President; gmackey@superiorplus.ca
Wayne M. Bingham, Exec. Vice-President/CFO
Trevor Bell, Vice-President, Tax; tbell@superiorplus.ca
Derren J. Newell, Vice-President, Business Process & Compliance; dnewell@superiorplus.ca
Teresia R. Reisch, Vice-President, Corporate Secretary; treisch@superiorplus.ca
Clint Warkentin, Vice-President, Treasurer
Directors:
Grant D. Billing, Exec. Chair
Peter A.W. Green, Lead Director
Robert J. Engbloom
Norman R. Gish
Allan G. Lennox
James S.A. MacDonald

INVESTMENT MANAGEMENT

Superior Plus Income Fund (continued)
Geoffrey N. Mackey
David P. Smith
Peter Valentine

Taylor NGL Limited Partnership

#2200, 800 - 5 Ave. SW
Calgary, AB T2P 3T6
403-781-8181
Fax: 403-777-1907
info@taylorngl.com
www.taylorngl.com
Former Name: Taylor Gas Liquids Fund
Ownership: Public
Year Founded: 1996
Stock Symbol: TAY.UN
Profile: Investors participate in the midstream sector of the energy business through Taylor's ownership of natural gas liquids extraction plants in northeastern British Columbia & central Alberta & natural gas processing assets in central & southeastern Alberta. Taylor is growing by developing business opportunities in its three core areas & through the acquisition of additional assets that meet Taylor's investment criteria. Growth will create value for unitholders by diversifying revenues & increasing distributions.

Executives:
Bob Pritchard, President/CEO
Brad Mattson, CFO & Secretary
David Schmunk, COO

TD Bank Financial Group

PO Box 1
55 King St. West
Toronto, ON M5K 1A2
416-982-8578
Fax: 416-982-5671
866-567-8888
Other Information: Shareholders Relations Dept.: 416/944-6367; 1-866-756-8936; tdshinfo@td.com
customer.service@td.com
www.td.com
Assets: $264,818,000,000
Profile: For more information about products & services, the following toll free numbers are also available: 1-866-233-2323 (French); 1-800-328-3698 (Cantonese & Mandarin); 1-800-361-1180 (Telephone device for the deaf)

Executives:
W. Edmund Clark, President/CEO
Robert E. Dorrance, Vice-Chair, TD Bank Financial Group
Bharat B. Masrani, Vice-Chair, Chief Risk Officer
Fedric J. Tomczyk, Vice-Chair, Corporate Operations
Bernard T. Dorval, Co-Chair, TD Canada Trust
Timothy D. Hockey, Co-Chair, TD Canada Trust
Theresa L. Currie, Exec. Vice-President, Oakville, Human Resources
Paul C. Douglas, Exec. Vice-President, Burlington, Commercial Banking
Brian J. Haier, Exec. Vice-President, Toronto, Retail Distribution
Colleen M. Johnston, Exec. Vice-President/CFO
Michael W. MacBain, Exec. Vice-President, TD Securities
Robert F. MacLellan, Exec. Vice-President, Chief Investment Officer
Daniel A. Marinangeli, Exec. Vice-President, Corporate Development
Christopher A. Montague, Exec. Vice-President, Oakville, General Counsel
John G. See, Exec. Vice-President, Oakville, Discount Brokerage & Financial Planning
Alain P. Thibault, Exec. Vice-President, Outremont, Property & Casualty Insurance
Riaz Ahmed, Sr. Vice-President, Oakville, Corporate Development
Sinan Akdeniz, Sr. Vice-President, Mississauga, Operations
Robert M. Aziz, Sr. Vice-President, Oakville, Legal
Cathy L. Beckett, Sr. Vice-President, Toronto, e.Bank
Joan D. Beckett, Sr. Vice-President, GTA, Suburban Area Retail Distribution
Warren W. Bell, Sr. Vice-President, Oakville, Human Resources
John A. Capozzolo, Sr. Vice-President, Toronto, Retail Sales & Service Retail Distribution
Mark R. Chauvin, Sr. Vice-President, Burlington, Credit Risk Management
Paul M. Clark, Sr. Vice-President, Toronto, Small Business Banking & Merchant Services
James E. Coccimiglio, Sr. Vice-President, Pickering, GTA Commercial Banking
John F. Coombs, Sr. Vice-President, Toronto, Credit Management
Barbara I. Cromb, Sr. Vice-President, Toronto, Corporate Development
Susan A. Cummings, Sr. Vice-President, Richmond Hill, Human Resources
John T. Davies, Sr. Vice-President, Mississauga, Enterprise Technology Solutions
Alan H. Desnoyers, Sr. Vice-President, Kirkland, Quebec District Commercial Banking
D. Suzanne Deuel, Sr. Vice-President, Toronto, Operational Risk & Insurance Management
Alexandra P. Dousmanis-Curtis, Sr. Vice-President, London, Ontario South, West Region Retail Distribution
Lisa A. Driscoll-Biggs, Sr. Vice-President, Bedford, Atlantic Region Retail Distribution
Donald E. Drummond, Sr. Vice-President, Toronto, TD Economics
Christopher D. Dyrda, Sr. Vice-President, Calgary, Western District Commercial Banking
William R. Fulton, Sr. Vice-President, Toronto, Private Client Services
William R. Gazzard, Sr. Vice-President, Toronto, Compliance
Phillip D. Ginn, Sr. Vice-President, Richmond Hill, Computing Services
Charles A. Hounsell, Sr. Vice-President, Oakville, Ontario Central Region Retail Distribution
Paul W. Huyer, Sr. Vice-President, Toronto, Finance
Martine M. Irman, Sr. Vice-President, Toronto, Global Foreign Exchange & Money Markets
Alan J. Jette, Sr. Vice-President, Toronto, Treasury & Balance Sheet Management
Sean E. Kilburn, Sr. Vice-President, Toronto, TD Life Group
Paul N. Langill, Sr. Vice-President, Toronto, Finance
Christine Marchildon, Sr. Vice-President, Pointe Claire, Québec Region Retail Distribution
Jason A. Marks, Sr. Vice-President, Toronto, Energy Trading & Int'l Proprietary Equity Tra
David W. McCaw, Sr. Vice-President, Oakville, Human Resources
Margo M. McConvey, Sr. Vice-President, Mississauga, Core Banking & Term Products
Ronald J. McInnis, Sr. Vice-President, Manotick, Ontario North & East Region Retail Distribut
Damian J. McNamee, Sr. Vice-President, Pickering, Finance
Nico Meijer, Sr. Vice-President, Toronto, Global Risk Management Strategy
Patrick B. Meneley, Sr. Vice-President, Toronto, Investment Banking
Dominic J. Mercuri, Sr. Vice-President, Burlington, Chief Marketing Officer
David I. Morton, Sr. Vice-President, Oakville, Sales & Service Commercial Banking
Dwight P. O'Neill, Sr. Vice-President, Toronto, Chief Risk Officer, Personal Banking
Barbara F. Palk, Sr. Vice-President, Toronto, TD Asset Management
Kerry A. Peacock, Sr. Vice-President, Toronto, Corporate & Public Affairs
John R. Pepperell, Sr. Vice-President, Toronto, TD Asset Management
David P. Pickett, Sr. Vice-President, Toronto, Practice Management
Timothy P. Pinnington, Sr. Vice-President, Toronto, TD Mutual Funds
Suzanne E. Poole, Sr. Vice-President, Vancouver, Pacific Region Retail Distribution
Robbie J. Pryde, Sr. Vice-President, Toronto, Institutional Equities
S. Kenneth Pustai, Sr. Vice-President, Ancaster, Human Resources
Satish C. Rai, Sr. Vice-President, Pickering, TD Asset Management
Lisa A. Reikman, Sr. Vice-President, Toronto, Commercial National Accounts
Heather D. Ross, Sr. Vice-President, Toronto, Retail Transformation
Rudy J. Sankovic, Sr. Vice-President, Pickering, Finance
Bruce M. Shirreff, Sr. Vice-President, Toronto, Real Estate Secured Lending & Credit Administ
J. David Sloan, Sr. Vice-President, Toronto, Audit
R. Iain Strump, Sr. Vice-President, Calgary, Prairie Region Retail Distribution
Ian B. Struthers, Sr. Vice-President, Toronto, Ontario District Commercial Banking
Steven L. Tennyson, Sr. Vice-President, Toronto, Chief Information Officer
Paul I. Verwymeren, Sr. Vice-President, Burlington, Commercial Credit Risk Management
Paul J. Vessey, Sr. Vice-President, Toronto, VISA & Unsecured Lending Products
Alan E. Wheable, Sr. Vice-President, Oakville, Taxation
Kevin J. Whyte, Sr. Vice-President, Oakville, Technology Solutions
M. Suellen Wiles, Sr. Vice-President, Mississauga, GTA Central Region Retail Distribution
David M. Fisher, Office of the Ombudsman
Directors:
John M. Thompson, Chair
William E. Bennett
Hugh J. Bolton
John L. Bragg
W. Edmund Clark
Marshall A. Cohen
Wendy K. Dobson
Darren Entwistle
Donna M. Hayes
Henry H. Ketcham
Pierre H. Lessard
Harold H. MacKay
Brian F. MacNeil
Irene R. Miller
Roger Phillips
Wilbur J. Prezzano
William R. Ryan
Helen K. Sinclair
John M. Thompson
Affiliated Companies:
TD Asset Management Inc./TDAM
TD General Insurance Company
TD Home & Auto Insurance Company
TD Life Insurance Company
TD Securities Inc.
TD Waterhouse Canada Inc.
The Toronto-Dominion Bank

Triax Diversified High-Yield Trust

#1400, 95 Wellington St.
Toronto, ON M5J 2N7
416-362-2929
Fax: 416-362-2199
800-407-0287
info@triaxcapital.com
www.triaxcapital.com
Year Founded: 1997
Assets: $100-500 million
Stock Symbol: TRH.UN

Urbana Corporation

#1702, 150 King St. West
Toronto, ON M5H 1J9
416-595-9106
Fax: 416-862-2498
investorrelations@urbanacorp.com
www.urbanacorp.com
Former Name: Macho River Gold Mines Limited
Ownership: Public.
Year Founded: 1947
Stock Symbol: URB
Profile: Common shares of the corporatiion are listed on The Toronto Stock Exchange & the Canadian Venture Exchange. An investment issuer, the company is considered a non-redeemable investment fund.

Executives:
Thomas S. Caldwell, President/CEO
John R. Campbell, Corporate Secretary
Directors:
Thomas S. Caldwell
John R. Campbell
Bethann Colle
Michael B.C. Gundy
Jean Ponter

UTS Energy Corporation

#1000, 350 - 7th Ave. SW
Calgary, AB T2P 3N9
403-538-7030
Fax: 403-538-7033
mail@uts.ca
www.uts.ca
Former Name: United Tri-Star Resources Limited

Ownership: Public
Year Founded: 1986
Number of Employees: 20
Assets: $262,000,000 Year End: 20040930
Revenues: $259,000 Year End: 20040930
Stock Symbol: UTS
Profile: A single-purpose corporation, its only asset is its investment in Fort Hills. The oil company focuses on growing & developing oil sands assets. Shares are listed on the TSE.
Executives:
Wayne Bobye, Vice-President/CFO; 403-538-7002; wbobye@uts.ca
Dennis A. Sharp, Exec. Chair
William Roach, President/CEO
Howard Lutley, Vice-President, Mining & Extraction; 403-538-7004; hlutley@uts.ca
Martin Sandell, Vice-President, Engineering; 403-538-7006; msandell@uts.ca
Daryl Wightman, Vice-President, Resource Development & Business Strategy; 403-538-7007; dwightman@uts.ca
Directors:
Douglas Baldwin
Campbell Deacon
Bruce Galloway
Marc Garneau
Douglas Mitchell
William Roach
Manfred Roth
Dennis Sharp
John D. Watson

Valdor Fibre Optics Inc.
#480, 789 West Pender St.
Vancouver, BC V6C 1H2
604-687-3775
Fax: 604-689-7654
bfindlay@valdor.com
www.valdor.com
Ownership: Foreign. Part of Valdor Fibre Optics Inc., Hayward, CA, USA.
Year Founded: 1985
Stock Symbol: VFO-V/Toronto Stock Exchange
Profile: A high technology company, it specializes in its fully patented Impact Mount & Heptoport technology, which is used to design & manufacture fiber optic connectors & other optical & optoelectronic components.
Executives:
Michel Y. Rondeau, President/CEO

Vancity Capital Corporation
#700, 815 West Hastings St.
Vancouver, BC V6C 1B4
604-877-6565
Fax: 604-871-5409
www.vancitycapital.com
Ownership: Private. Vancouver City Savings Credit Union
Year Founded: 1998
Number of Employees: 6
Profile: The investment, venture capital firm is BC-based.
Executives:
Lee Davis, President/CEO; lee_davis@vancity.com
Axel Christiansen, Investment Manager; 604-877-6582; axel_christiansen@vancity.com
Diane Friedman, Investment Manager; 604-877-6581; diane_friedman@vancity.com
Derek Gent, Investment Manager; 604-877-7657; derek_gent@vancity.com
Kristi Miller, Investment Manager; 604-877-7571; kristi_miller@vancity.com
Robert Napoli, Investment Manager; 604-877-8284; robert_napoli@vancity.com

Westerkirk Capital Inc.
Toronto-Dominion Centre
PO Box 29
#1410, 95 Wellington St. West
Toronto, ON M5J 2N7
416-927-2233
Fax: 416-923-2132
wwright@westerkirk.ca
www.westerkirkcapital.net
Ownership: Private.
Profile: The investment firm has holdings in the following sectors: real estate, custom manufacturing, education, aviation & hospitality.
Executives:
James Lawson, President/CEO
Douglas Bradley, Managing Director
David Nowak, Managing Director, Legal
Joanne Ranger, Managing Director, Finance
J. Peter Winters, Managing Director
David A. Brown, Member, Investment Advisory Committee
Stephen K. Gunn, Member, Investment Advisory Committee
Norman D. Inkster, Member, Investment Advisory Committee
Samuel Minzberg, Member, Investment Advisory Committee

Western America Capital Inc.
Also listed under: *Financing & Loan Companies*
#1500, 10025 - 102A Ave.
Edmonton, AB T5J 2Z2
780-498-9171
Fax: 780-496-9172
info@wacapital.com
www.wacapital.com
Ownership: Private
Year Founded: 1987
Number of Employees: 200
Profile: Acquisitions & venture capital.
Executives:
Richard D. Caron, CEO, Director
Don P. Caron, President, Director

Western Financial Group Inc.
Also listed under: *Federal & Provincial*
PO Box 5519
309 - 1st St. West
High River, AB T1V 1M6
403-652-2663
Fax: 403-652-2661
866-843-9378
info@westernfinancialgroup.net
www.westernfinancialgroup.net
Ownership: Public
Year Founded: 1994
Number of Employees: 580
Assets: $100-500 million Year End: 20041231
Revenues: $10-50 million Year End: 20041231
Stock Symbol: WES
Executives:
Scott A. Tannas, President/CEO
Thomas C. Dutton, Exec. Vice-President
Catherine A. Rogers, Corporate Secretary/CFO & Sr. Vice-President, Finance & Administration
R. William Rogers, Vice-President, Corporate Development
Directors:
Jim Dinning, Chair
Thomas C. Dutton
Gabor Jellinek
Robert G. Jennings
Catherine A. Rogers
J. Gregg Speirs
Jean-Denis Talon
Scott A. Tannas
Philip L. Webster
William Yuill
Affiliated Companies:
Bank West

Westshore Terminals Income Fund
#1800, 1067 West Cordova St.
Vancouver, BC V6E 1C7
604-488-5295
Fax: 604-687-2601
www.westshore.com
Year Founded: 1996
Stock Symbol: WTE.UN/Toronto Stock Exchange
Profile: The fund is an open-ended trust. It owns Westshore Terminals Ltd., which operates a coal export facility & a dry bulk transportation terminal in BC.
Executives:
William W. Stinson, CEO
Doug Souter, Chief Financial Officer
Trustees:
William W. Stinson, Chair
Jim G. Gardiner
Gordon Gibson
Michael J. Korenberg
Dallas H. Ross

Investment Dealers

Abria Financial Group
Also listed under: *Investment Fund Companies; Investment Management*
#300, 20 Adelaide St. East
Toronto, ON M5C 2T6
416-367-4777
Fax: 416-367-4555
877-512-2742
info@abriafunds.com
www.abriafunds.com
Former Name: Abria Financial Products Ltd.
Ownership: Private
Year Founded: 1999
Number of Employees: 20
Assets: $100-500 million Year End: 20041031
Revenues: $1-5 million Year End: 20041031
Executives:
Andrew Doman, COO; 416-367-9993; doman@abriafunds.com
Davee Gunn, Exec. Vice-President; 416-365-0224; gunn@abriafunds.com
Abria:
Diversified Arbitage Trust
RRSP Eligible; Inception Year: 2000; Fund Managers:
Dominic Staniscia
HenryKneis
Michael Doran
Michael Ding
Alternative Strategies Note
RRSP Eligible; Inception Year: 2004; Fund Managers:
Michael Ding
Diversified Arbitrage Trust (US$)
RRSP Eligible; Inception Year: 2000; Fund Managers:
Henry Kneis
DominicStaniscia
Michael Doran
Michael Ding
Guaranteed Alter Inc Nts Sr 1
RRSP Eligible; Inception Year: 2005; Fund Managers:
Henry Kneis
DominicStaniscia
Michael Doran
Michael Ding
Alter Combined Ret Nts Ser 1
RRSP Eligible; Inception Year: 2005; Fund Managers:
Henry Kneis
DominicStaniscia
Michael Doran
Michael Ding
Branches:
Calgary - Alberta Regional Office
Bow Valley Square IV
#1800, 250 - 6th Ave. SW
Calgary, AB T2T 6K8 Canada
403-685-7682
Fax: 403-685-4404
info@abriafunds.com

Vancouver - British Columbia Regional Office
#1500, 701 West Georgia St.
Vancouver, BC V7Y 1C6 Canada
604-609-0155
Fax: 604-801-5911
877460-0155
info@abriafunds.com

Acadian Securities Inc.
Barrington Place
#100, 1903 Barrington St., Pedway Level
Halifax, NS B3J 3L7
902-496-7580
Fax: 902-496-7599
800-565-8660
www.acadiansec.com
Stock Exchange Membership: TSX Venture Exchange
Executives:
David J. Hennigar, Chair
John Hanrahan, President/CEO
Lorne MacFarlane, CFO, Secretary
Branches:
Lunenburg
82 Duke St.
Lunenburg, NS B0J 2C0 Canada

Acadian Securities Inc. (continued)
Fax: 902-634-7227
866-655-0055
Sydney
81 Meech Ave.
Sydney, NS B2A 1R9 Canada
902-794-4393
Fax: 902-794-4933
Windsor
93 Garrish St.
Windsor, NS B0N 2T0 Canada
Fax: 902-798-0372
866-477-4177

Acumen Capital Finance Partners Limited
Also listed under: *Financial Planning*
#200, 513 - 8th Ave. SW
Calgary, AB T2P 1G3
403-571-0300
Fax: 403-571-0310
888-422-8636
info@acumencapital.com
www.acumencapital.com
Ownership: Private
Year Founded: 1995
Number of Employees: 27
Stock Exchange Membership: Toronto Stock Exchange, TSX Venture Exchange
Profile: Full service investment dealer.

Executives:
Brian D. Parker, CEO/President, Institutional Sales
Myja Miller, CFO, Chief Compliance Officer
C. Michael Stuart, Chair & Vice-President, Investment Banking
Douglas Gowland, Vice-President, Institutional Sales
Robert Laidlaw, Vice-President, Sr. Investment Advisor, Retail
Sheldon Le Lievre, Vice-President, Sr. Investment Advisor
Curtis Mayert, Vice-President, Sr. Investment Advisor
Brian D. Pow, Vice-President, Research
James A. Rothwell, Vice-President, Sr. Investment Advisor
Alfred Sailer, Vice-President, Investment Banking
James M.B. Welykocky, Vice-President, Oil & Gas

Aldersley Securities Inc.
491 - 10th St.
Hanover, ON N4N 1R2
519-364-6093
Fax: 519-364-6195
Year Founded: 1995

All-Canadian Management Inc.
Also listed under: *Investment Fund Companies; Investment Management*
#202, 386 Wilson St. East
Ancaster, ON L9G 2C2
905-648-2025
Fax: 905-648-5422
rboychuka@all-canadiansecurities.com
www.all-canadianfunds.com
Ownership: Private.
Year Founded: 1976
Number of Employees: 10
Assets: $1-5 million Year End: 20041031
Revenues: $1-5 million Year End: 20041031
Executives:
Russell C. Boychuk, Chair/CEO
Directors:
Russell C. Boychuk, Chair/CEO
All-Canadian Management:
All-Canadian Resources FundInception Year: 0; Fund Managers:
Harold A. Kent
All-Canadian Compound FundInception Year: 0; Fund Managers:
Harold A. Kent

Altimum Mutuals Inc.
Also listed under: *Financial Planning*
94 Barbican Trail
St Catharines, ON L2T 4A8
905-680-8544
Fax: 905-680-8546
877-366-7343
www.altimum.ca
Ownership: Private.
Year Founded: 2003
Number of Employees: 11
Profile: Altimum Mutuals has investment advisors in the following locations: Stoney Creek, Grimsby, Niagara-on-the-Lake, St Catharines & Burlington.

Executives:
Donald Reid, CEO; 905-680-8544; don@altimum.ca
Edith Reid, President, Compliance Officer; 905-680-8544; edith@altimum.ca
Directors:
Don Reid
Edith Reid

Altus Securities Inc.
#1100, 55 Yonge St.
Toronto, ON M5E 1J4
416-369-9211
Fax: 416-369-9268
altus@istar.ca
Ownership: Private
Stock Exchange Membership: Toronto Stock Exchange
Executives:
Ben. B. Kizemchuk, Chair/CEO
Gregg H. Blaha, Exec. Vice-President, Treasurer
Paul Jelec, Exec. Vice-President/CFO, Chief Compliance Officer

Elaine Knotek-Holmes, Exec. Vice-President/COO, Corporate Secretary

Aquilon Capital Corp.
135 King St. East
Toronto, ON M5C 1G6
416-363-3050
Fax: 416-368-4330
800-665-1757
info@aquilon.ca
www.aquilon.ca
Former Name: MMI Group Inc
Year Founded: 1990
Stock Exchange Membership: Toronto Stock Exchange
Executives:
Jeffrey D. Francoz, President
Scott Leckie, Sr. Vice-President

ARC Financial Group Ltd.
Also listed under: *Pension & Money Management Companies*
#4300, 400 - 3rd Ave. SW
Calgary, AB T2P 4H2
403-292-0680
Fax: 403-292-0693
genfeedback@arcfinancial.com
www.arcfinancial.com
Ownership: Private
Year Founded: 1989
Number of Employees: 55
Profile: The investment management & merchant banking company focuses on the energy sector in Canada.

Executives:
Kevin J. Brown, CEO
Lauchlan J. Currie, President
Tanya M. Causgrove, CFO, Finance & Administration
Nancy V. Lever, Sr. Vice-President, Energy Development & Services
William H. Slavin, Sr. Vice-President, Exploration & Production
Nancy L. Smith, Sr. Vice-President, Energy Development & Services
Paul J. Beitel, Vice-President, Exploration & Production
Brian P. Boulanger, Vice-President, Exploration & Production
Robert C. Cook, Vice-President, Exploration & Production
Andy L. Evans, Vice-President, Exploration & Production
Douglas C. Freel, Vice-President
Peter Tertzakian, Chief Energy Economist, Energy Research
Directors:
Philip C. Swift, Co-Chair
Mac Van Wielingen, Co-Chair
John M. Stewart, Vice-Chair

Argosy Securities Inc.
#600, 100 York Blvd.
Richmond Hill, ON L4B 1J8
905-709-7066
Fax: 905-709-7044
866-709-7066
info@argosynet.ca
www.argosysecurities.com
Ownership: Private.
Executives:
Dax Sukhraj, President
Ravinder Tulsiani, Chief Compliance Officer

Armstrong Financial Services Inc.
669 Wilson St.
Saint John, NB E2M 3V1
506-658-0156
Fax: 506-633-0435
kevinkirby@canada.com
www.armstrongfinancial.com
Profile: The independent organization offers financial advice regarding mutual funds, investments, savings plans, life insurance, loans & credit.

Executives:
H.R. Anstis, Compliance Officer
Kevin Kirby, Compliance Officer

ASL Direct Inc.
#203, 145 Front St. East
Toronto, ON M5A 1E3
416-306-9879
Fax: 416-306-9876
800-404-4891
info@asldirect.com
www.asldirect.com
Ownership: Private.
Profile: The mutual fund investing company is licensed to sell both Mutual Funds & Hedge Funds.

Audentium Financial Corp.
Also listed under: *Financial Planning*
191 University Ave. East
Cobourg, ON K9A 4X6
905-373-1234
Fax: 905-373-0645
joe@yalkezian.com
www.yalkezian.com
Executives:
Joe Yalkezian, CFP, CGA

Beacon Securities Limited
1707 Grafton St.
Halifax, NS B3J 2C6
902-423-1260
Fax: 902-425-5237
beacon@beaconsecurities.ns.ca
Ownership: Private
Year Founded: 1988
Number of Employees: 24
Profile: The company is a regional full-service dealer.

Executives:
Lonsdale Holland, President; 902-492-0469
Jane Smith, Vice-President/CFO
William D. Crowe, Vice-President
Graham Starrath, Vice-President
Branches:
Vancouver
1075 Marigold Pl.
North Vancouver, BC V7R 2E5 Canada
604-985-3479
William D. Crowe, Vice-President

Berkshire Securities Inc.
1375 Kearns Rd.
Burlington, ON L7R 4X8
905-331-9900
800-991-2121
advisorservices@berkshire.ca
www.berkshire.ca
Stock Exchange Membership: Toronto Stock Exchange, TSX Venture Exchange

Bick Financial Security Corporation
Also listed under: *Financial Planning*
241 Wilson St. East
Ancaster, ON L9G 2B8
905-648-9559
Fax: 905-648-8185
888-777-2425
service@bickfinancial.com
www.bickfinancial.com
Executives:
Clarence Bick, President; cbick@bickfinancial.com
Leonard Bick, Managing Partner, Founder; lenbick@bickfinancial.com
Branches:
Grimsby

18 Ontario St.
Grimsby, ON L3M 3H1 Canada
905-309-6777
Fax: 905-309-4850
Sharon Rizzuto
Milton
142 Martin St.
Milton, ON L9T 2R2 Canada
905-875-1000
Fax: 905-875-6896
888-875-1008
Melissa DeBrouwer
St Catharines
40 Butler Cres.
St Catharines, ON L2M 7B4 Canada
905-937-6537
Fax: 905-937-8323
Stoney Creek
35 MacIntosh Dr.
Stoney Creek, ON L8E 4E4 Canada
905-662-1352
Fax: 905-662-1392

Bieber Securities Inc.

#801, 400 St. Mary Ave.
Winnipeg, MB R3C 4K5
204-946-0297
Fax: 204-956-0747
800-205-9070
bieber@biebersecurities.com
www.biebersecurities.com
Ownership: Private.
Year Founded: 1995
Number of Employees: 35
Assets: $500m-1 billion
Revenues: $5-10 million
Stock Exchange Membership: TSX Venture Exchange
Profile: Bieber Securities' subsidiary is Bieber Financial Services Inc.

Executives:
Guy N. Bieber, President/CEO
Deborah Metcalfe, CFO & Investment Advisor
Claude M. Tetrault, Vice-President, Corporate Finance
Allan McLeod, Director
Offices:
Arborg
315 Main St.
Arborg, MB R0C 0A0 Canada
204-376-2673
800-205-9070
Brandon
1212 - 18th St., #B
Brandon, MB R7A 5C3 Canada
204-725-3933
866-894-6904
Dauphin
18 - 2nd Ave. NW
Dauphin, MB R7N 1H2 Canada
204-638-6446
866-638-6446

Portage La Prairie
190 River Rd., #E
Portage La Prairie, MB R1N 3V6 Canada
204-239-4987
888-239-4987

Blackmont Capital Inc.

Also listed under: *Financial Planning; Investment Management*

Bay Wellington Tower, BCE Place
PO Box 779
#900, 181 Bay St.
Toronto, ON M5J 2T3
416-864-3600
Fax: 416-864-9024
866-775-7704
info@blackmont.com
www.blackmont.com
Former Name: First Associates Investments Inc.; Yorkton Securities; Robert Caldwell Capital Corp.
Ownership: Wholly owned subsidiary of Rockwater Capital Corporation, Toronto, ON.
Stock Exchange Membership: Canadian Trading & Quotation System Inc, Toronto Stock Exchange, TSX Venture Exchange

Executives:
Stuart R. Raftus, President/COO
Gerald Throop, President, Capital Markets
Branches:
Calgary
#2200, 440 - 2 Ave. SW
Calgary, AB T2P 5E9 Canada
403-260-8400
Fax: 403-269-7870
800-661-1596
Edmonton
Manulife Place
#1375, 10180 - 101 St.
Edmonton, AB T5J 3S4 Canada
780-577-8150
Fax: 780-577-8170
800-661-1596
Guelph
193 Woolwich St.
Guelph, ON N1H 3V4 Canada
516-836-4440
Fax: 519-836-4067
866-811-4706
Halifax
Purdy's Wharf Tower II
#401, 1969 Upper Water St.
Halifax, NS B3J 3R7 Canada
902-422-2343
Fax: 902-422-5971
866-855-8760
Kelowna
#201, 1441 Ellis St.
Kelowna, BC V1Y 2A3 Canada
250-860-6990
Fax: 250-860-6929
800-820-1813
Montréal
#4215, 1250, boul René-Lévesque ouest
Montréal, QC H3B 4W8 Canada
514-937-3250
Fax: 514-937-4501
877-925-2850
Ottawa
Constitution Square I
#800, 360 Albert St.
Ottawa, ON K1R 7X7 Canada
613-569-7878
Fax: 613-569-4278
Toronto - Bay St. - Toronto Asset Management
BCE Place
PO Box 625
#4420, 161 Bay St.
Toronto, ON M5J 2S1 Canada
416-601-6888
Fax: 416-601-9744
866-601-6888
Toronto - Yonge St.
#503, 4100 Yonge St.
Toronto, ON M2P 2B5 Canada
416-221-5465
Fax: 416-221-1958
866-775-7704
Vancouver
#500, 550 Burrard St.
Vancouver, BC V6C 2B5 Canada
604-640-0400
Fax: 604-640-0300
866-640-0400
Victoria
St. Andrews Square II
#430, 730 View St.
Victoria, BC V8W 3V7 Canada
250-978-9393
Fax: 250-978-9395
Waterloo
#204, 460 Phillip St.
Waterloo, ON N2L 5J2 Canada
519-570-9900
Fax: 519-570-9910
800-461-4748

Blueprint Investment Corp.

#504, 1200 Eglinton Ave. East
Toronto, ON M3C 1H9
416-385-7500
Fax: 416-385-7501
mail@retirefit.ca
www.retirefit.ca
Ownership: Blueprint Wealth Management Group, Toronto, ON.

Profile: Affiliated with Blueprint Wealth Management Group, Blueprint Investment Corp. is a registered mutual funds dealer. Investment services are provided to both personal & business clients.

Bluestone Financial Corporation

Also listed under: *Financial Planning*
96 Queen St.
St Catharines, ON L2R 5H3
905-687-8222
Fax: 905-687-3325
bluestone@dundeewealth.com
www.bluestonefinancial.ca
Executives:
Terry Rempel, CFP, President
Patty Rempel, CFP, Manager, Business

Blumont Capital Corporation

PO Box 23
#1500, 220 Bay St.
Toronto, ON M5J 2W4
416-216-3566
Fax: 416-360-1102
866-473-7376
service@blumontcapital.com
www.blumontcapital.com
Former Name: Hirsch Asset Management Corporation; iPerformance Fund Corp.
Year Founded: 1997
Executives:
T. Stuart, President
Stephen Johnson, CFO
Donna Beasant, Vice-President, Operations; 416-360-1220
Directors:
Victor Koloshuk, Chair
Veronika Hirsch
Stephen Johnson

BMO InvestorLine Inc.

1 First Canadian Place, 20th Fl.
100 King St. West
Toronto, ON M5X 1A1
416-867-4000
888-776-6886
info@bmoinvestorline.com
www.bmoinvestorline.com
Offices:
Montréal
2015, rue Peel, 2e étage
Montréal, QC H3A 1T8 Canada
Toronto - King St.
First Canadian Place
100 King St. West, 20th Fl.
Toronto, ON M5X 1A1 Canada
Toronto - King St. - Storefront Centre
First Canadian Place, Concourse Level
100 King St. West
Toronto, ON M5X 1A1 Canada
fcp.store@bmoinvestorline.com

BMO Nesbitt Burns Inc.

1 First Canadian Place
PO Box 150
49th Fl.
Toronto, ON M5X 1H3
416-359-4000
Fax: 416-359-4311
contact@bmonb.com
www.nesbittburns.com
Ownership: BMO Financial Group
Year Founded: 1962
Stock Symbol: BMO
Stock Exchange Membership: Canadian Trading & Quotation System Inc, Montreal Exchange, Toronto Stock Exchange, TSX Venture Exchange, Winnepeg Commodities Exchange
Executives:
Yvan J.P. Bourdeau, CEO & Head, Investment Banking Group
Gilles G. Ouellette, Deputy Chair
Dean Manjuris, Vice-Chair
Glenn Sauntry, Vice-Chair, Investment Banking Group

BMO Nesbitt Burns Inc. (continued)
Thomas V. Milroy, Co-President
Eric C. Tripp, Co-President
Richard Mills, Exec. Vice-President & Manager, National Sales, Managing Director
Wendy A. Kelley, Managing Director, Associate General Counsel

Branches:

Abbotsford
#305, 2051 McCallum Rd.
Abbotsford, BC V2S 3N5 Canada
604-870-5550
Fax: 604-870-5560

Amherst
28 Church St.
Amherst, NS B4H 3A1 Canada
902-667-2005
Fax: 902-667-2044

Amos
101, 1e av ouest
Amos, QC J9T 1T8 Canada
819-732-7639
Fax: 819-732-7540

Ancaster
469 Wilson St. East
Ancaster, ON L9G 2B8 Canada
905-304-8030
Fax: 905-304-8316

Antigonish
155 Main St., 2nd Fl.
Antigonish, NS B2G 2B6 Canada
902-867-5620
Fax: 902-867-5622

Banff
107 Banff Ave.
Banff, AB T0L 0C0 Canada
403-762-5757
Fax: 403-762-5787

Barrie
#308, 190 Cundles Rd. East
Barrie, ON L4M 4S5 Canada
705-727-9741
Fax: 705-727-1343

Bedford
21 Dartmouth Rd.
Bedford, NS B4A 3X7 Canada
902-421-5095
Fax: 902-421-5099

Belleville
210 Front St.
Belleville, ON K8N 2Z2 Canada
613-967-2250
Fax: 613-967-6054

Brampton
1 Nelson St., 2nd Fl.
Brampton, ON L6X 3E4 Canada
905-455-5510
Fax: 905-455-5616

Brandon - Rosser Ave.
1000 Rosser Ave.
Brandon, MB R7A 0L6 Canada
204-726-2800
Fax: 204-726-2813

Brandon - Victoria Ave.
2412C Victoria Ave.
Brandon, MB R7B 0M5 Canada
204-571-9000
Fax: 204-571-9029

Brantford
45 Market St.
Brantford, ON N3T 2Z6 Canada
519-759-0059
Fax: 519-754-4172

Bridgewater
#300, 197 Dufferin St.
Bridgewater, NS B4V 2G9 Canada
902-543-7100
Fax: 902-543-5757

Brockville
1 Courthouse Sq.
Brockville, ON K6V 3X2 Canada
613-498-2228
Fax: 613-498-2946

Brossard
#400, 1850, rue Panama
Brossard, QC J4W 3C6 Canada
450-466-5500
Fax: 450-466-1224

Burlington
2119 Lakeshore Rd.
Burlington, ON L7R 1A4 Canada
905-681-2122
Fax: 905-681-2953

Burnaby
#268, 4820 Kingsway
Burnaby, BC V5H 4P1 Canada
604-654-1700
Fax: 604-654-1704

Calgary - 3rd St. SW
Bankers Hall West
#4100, 888 - 3rd St. SW
Calgary, AB T2P 5C5 Canada
403-260-9300
Fax: 403-260-9347

Calgary - 7th Ave. - Investment Banking
Canada Trust Tower
#1600, 421 - 7th Ave. SW
Calgary, AB T2P 4K9 Canada
403-515-1500
Fax: 403-515-1535

Calgary - 7th Ave. - Private Banking
First Canadian Centre
350 - 7th Ave. SW, 3rd Fl.
Calgary, AB T2P 3N9 Canada
403-296-1834
Fax: 403-262-0373

Calgary - 90th Ave
#201A, 1600 - 90th Ave. SW
Calgary, AB T2V 5A8 Canada
403-296-0700
Fax: 403-296-0701

Calgary - Crowfoot
101 Crowfoot Way
Calgary, AB T3G 2R2 Canada
403-261-9550
Fax: 403-296-1254

Calgary - First St. SW
Esso Plaza
#1600, 425 First St. SW
Calgary, AB T2P 3L8 Canada
403-261-9550
Fax: 403-261-9582

Cambridge - Hespler Rd.
600 Hespler Rd.
Cambridge, ON N1R 8H2 Canada
519-624-8939
Fax: 519-624-8720

Campbellville
PO Box 515
35 Crawford Cres., Unit DM9
Campbellville, ON L0P 1B0 Canada
905-854-4540
Fax: 905-854-4544

Camrose
4906 - 50 Ave.
Camrose, AB T4V 0S3 Canada
780-679-3130
Fax: 780-679-3133

Canmore - 8th St.
#203, Corner 802 - 8th St.
Canmore, AB T1W 2E7 Canada
403-678-9693
Fax: 403-609-6256

Canmore - McNeill
177 McNeill
Canmore, AB T1W 2R9 Canada
403-678-9457
Fax: 403-678-9463

Charlottetown
#300, 137 Queen St.
Charlottetown, PE C1A 4B3 Canada
902-628-6233
Fax: 902-628-6278

Chicoutimi
#440, 255, rue Racine est
Chicoutimi, QC G7H 7L2 Canada
450-545-8303
Fax: 450-545-9950

Cobourg
17 King St. East
Cobourg, ON K9A 1K6 Canada
905-373-1507
Fax: 905-373-9331

Collingwood
41 Hurontario St.
Collingwood, ON L9Y 2L7 Canada
705-446-2424
Fax: 705-446-0811

Comox
#204, 1771 Comox Ave.
Comox, BC V9M 3L9 Canada
250-339-1703
Fax: 250-339-1783

Coquitlam
#1, 1161 The High St.
Coquitlam, BC V3B 7W3 Canada
Fax: 604-927-1327
800-663-0242

Corner Brook
1 West St.
Corner Brook, NL A2H 6E2 Canada
709-637-6590
Fax: 709-637-6593

Cornwall
#100, 55 Water St. West
Cornwall, ON K6J 1A1 Canada
613-938-5646
Fax: 613-938-5645

Cranbrook
934 Baker St.
Cranbrook, BC V1C 1A5 Canada
250-417-3810
Fax: 250-417-3818

Drumheller
PO Box 1390
95 - 3rd Ave. West
Drumheller, AB T0J 0Y0 Canada
403-823-9583
Fax: 403-823-4165

Drummondville
108, rue Loring
Drummondville, QC J2C 4J8 Canada
450-478-7722
Fax: 450-478-5862

Dryden
26 Earl Ave.
Dryden, ON P8N 1X5 Canada
807-223-2600
Fax: 807-223-2690

Duncan
21 Station St.
Duncan, BC V9L 1M2 Canada
250-715-2352
Fax: 250-715-2356

Dundas
94 King St. West
Dundas, ON L9H 1T9 Canada
905-628-4166
Fax: 905-628-6614

Edmonton - 101 St. - BMO Small Business
10199 - 101 St.
Edmonton, AB T5J 3Y4 Canada
780-415-5024
Fax: 780-415-5026

Edmonton - 101st St.
Manulife Place
#800, 10180 - 101st St.
Edmonton, AB T5J 3S4 Canada
780-945-5200
Fax: 780-945-5292

Fredericton
Regency Park
PO Box 607
#200, 65 Regent St.
Fredericton, NB E3B 5A6 Canada
506-458-8570
Fax: 506-450-7193

Gatineau
#203, 224, rue Bellehumeur
Gatineau, QC J8T 8N6 Canada
819-243-8000
Fax: 819-243-8600

Gloucester
#200, 1400 Blair Pl.
Gloucester, ON K1J 9B8 Canada
613-742-7800
Fax: 613-742-6718
Granby
399, rue Principale
Granby, QC J2G 2W7 Canada
450-360-5016
Fax: 450-360-0548
Grande Prairie
Windsor Court
#500, 9835 - 101st. Ave.
Grande Prairie, AB T8V 5V4 Canada
780-831-1100
Fax: 780-831-1104
Guelph
#201, 98 Macdonell St.
Guelph, ON N1H 2Z6 Canada
519-823-1000
Fax: 519-823-1214
Halifax
Purdys Wharf Tower II
#1901, 1969 Upper Water St.
Halifax, NS B3J 3R7 Canada
902-429-3710
Fax: 902-423-7011
Hamilton
Hamilton City Centre
#301, 77 James St. North
Hamilton, ON L8R 2K3 Canada
905-570-8600
Fax: 905-570-8655
Hanover
293 - 10th St.
Hanover, ON N4N 1P1 Canada
519-364-4133
Fax: 519-364-5035
Huntsville
Brendale Square
PO Box 5499
Huntsville, ON P1H 2K8 Canada
705-789-9252
Fax: 705-789-9198
Ingersoll
104 Thames St.
Ingersoll, ON N5C 2T4 Canada
519-485-5968
Kamloops
#510, 175 Second Ave.
Kamloops, BC V2C 5W1 Canada
250-851-8200
Fax: 250-374-4847
Kanata
#121, 555 Legget Dr.
Kanata, ON K2K 2X3 Canada
613-599-1980
Fax: 613-599-1990
Kelowna
1484 Water St., 3rd Fl.
Kelowna, BC V1Y 1J5 Canada
250-717-2123
Fax: 250-762-2074
Kincardine
761 Queen St.
Kincardine, ON N2Z 2Y8 Canada
519-396-1260
Fax: 519-396-1259
Kingston
42 Bath Rd., 2nd Fl.
Kingston, ON K7L 1H5 Canada
613-547-5288
Fax: 613-547-9347
Laval - Carrefour - Sous-Succursale PVM
#800, 3080, boul Carrefour
Laval, QC H7T 2K9 Canada
450-681-7513
Fax: 450-681-6627
Laval - Carrefour
#800, 3080, boul Carrefour
Laval, QC H7T 2K9 Canada
450-978-6600
Fax: 450-978-6625
Lethbridge
600 - 5 Ave. South
Lethbridge, AB T1J 4G9 Canada
403-382-3495
Fax: 403-382-3497
Lindsay
17 Russell St. West
Lindsay, ON K9V 2W5 Canada
705-328-2600
Fax: 705-328-1313
London
One London Place
#1900, 255 Queens Ave.
London, ON N6A 5R8 Canada
519-672-8560
Fax: 519-679-8848
Markham
Market Village
4392 Steeles Ave. East
Markham, ON L3R 9V9 Canada
905-305-8000
Fax: 905-305-8008
Medicine Hat
101 Carry Dr. SE
Medicine Hat, AB T1B 3M6 Canada
403-528-1720
Fax: 403-528-6770
Merritt
PO Box 2280
#203, 1970 Quilchena Ave.
Merritt, BC V1K 1B8 Canada
250-378-6621
Fax: 250-378-8335
Mississauga
#210, 90 Burhamthorpe Rd. West
Mississauga, ON L5B 3C3 Canada
905-897-9200
Fax: 905-897-5229
Moncton
Moncton Place
#250, 633 Main St.
Moncton, NB E1C 9X9 Canada
506-858-5191
Fax: 506-855-3195
Montréal - Holiday
Tour ouest
#110, 1, rue Holiday
Montréal, QC H9R 5N3 Canada
514-428-2900
Fax: 514-428-2930
Montréal - Jean-Talon est
#704, 6455, rue Jean-Talon est
Montréal, QC H1S 3E8 Canada
514-251-7275
Fax: 514-251-7270
Montréal - McGill College
Tour McGill College
#3200, 1501, av McGill College
Montréal, QC H3A 3M8 Canada
514-286-7200
Fax: 514-286-7234
Montréal - McGill College - Saint-Jacques
Tour McGill College
#3000, 1501, av McGill College
Montréal, QC H3A 3M8 Canada
514-282-5810
Fax: 514-282-5883
Montréal - McGill College - Saint-Pierre
Tour McGill College
#3000, 1501, av McGill College
Montréal, QC H3A 3M8 Canada
514-282-5888
Fax: 514-282-8199
Nanaimo
#9, 6908 North Island Hwy.
Nanaimo, BC V9V 1P6 Canada
250-390-5600
Fax: 250-390-3613
Nelson
298 Baker St.
Nelson, BC V1L 4H3 Canada
250-354-1665
Fax: 250-354-1646
Newmarket
#11, 17310 Yonge St.
Newmarket, ON L3Y 7R9 Canada
905-830-4017
Fax: 905-830-9538
North Bay
154 Main St. East
North Bay, ON P1B 1A8 Canada
705-494-9850
Fax: 705-494-9033
North Vancouver
1505 Lonsdale Ave.
North Vancouver, BC V7M 2J4 Canada
604-981-4290
Fax: 604-981-4292
Oakville
132 Trafalgar Rd.
Oakville, ON L6J 3G5 Canada
905-337-2000
Fax: 905-337-2033
Olds
#1, 4602 - 49th Ave.
Olds, AB T4H 1C9 Canada
403-556-5120
Fax: 403-556-5126
Orillia
190 Memorial Ave., #A
Orillia, ON L3V 5X6 Canada
705-326-0891
Fax: 705-326-2218
Oshawa
Oshawa Centre
PO Box 30570
419 King St. West
Oshawa, ON L1J 2K5 Canada
905-404-8088
Fax: 905-404-0289
Ottawa - Carling Ave.
#700, 1600 Carling Ave.
Ottawa, ON K1Z 1B4 Canada
613-798-4200
Fax: 613-798-4240
Ottawa - Dalhousie St.
303 Dalhousie St.
Ottawa, ON K1N 7E8 Canada
613-562-6400
Fax: 613-562-6401
Ottawa - O'Connor St.
World Exchange Plaza
#1150, 45 O'Connor St.
Ottawa, ON K1P 1A4 Canada
613-567-6232
Fax: 613-237-7801
Owen Sound
#101, 887 - 3rd Ave. East
Owen Sound, ON N4K 2K6 Canada
519-379-4110
Fax: 519-376-2645
Parksville
#1, 220 West Island Hwy.
Parksville, BC V9P 2P3 Canada
250-248-2489
Fax: 250-248-2389
Pembroke
41 Pembroke St. West
Pembroke, ON K8A 5M5 Canada
613-735-3611
Penticton
Nanaimo Square
#101, 301 Main St.
Penticton, BC V2A 5B7 Canada
250-490-2900
Fax: 250-490-2901
Peterborough - Chemong Rd.
Portage Place
1154 Chemong Rd.
Peterborough, ON K9H 7J6 Canada
705-740-2066
Peterborough - George St.
PO Box 95
311 George St. North
Peterborough, ON K9J 6Y5 Canada
705-740-2363
Fax: 705-740-2374
Prince George

INVESTMENT MANAGEMENT

BMO Nesbitt Burns Inc. (continued)
#901, 299 Victoria St.
Prince George, BC V2L 5B8 Canada
250-614-4250
Fax: 250-614-4256
Québec - Grande-Allée
#720, 500, av Grande-Allée est
Québec, QC G1R 2J7 Canada
418-682-1644
Fax: 418-682-5235
Québec - René-Lévesque
#510, 900, boul René-Lévesque est
Québec, QC G1R 2B5 Canada
418-647-3124
Fax: 418-647-1775
Red Deer
#403, 4406 Gaetz Ave.
Red Deer, AB T4N 3Z6 Canada
403-340-4685
Fax: 403-340-4688
Regina - 11th Ave
#1171, 2103 - 11th Ave.
Regina, SK S4P 3Z8 Canada
306-780-9700
Fax: 306-870-9712
Regina - Central Ave.
213 Central Ave. North
Regina, SK S9H 0L3 Canada
306-778-5540
Fax: 306-778-5541
Regina - Gordon Rd.
#306, 2705 Gordon Rd.
Regina, SK S4S 6H7 Canada
306-780-9778
Fax: 306-780-9769
Richmond Hill
BMO Bank of Montreal Times Square Plaza
550 Hwy. 7 East
Richmond Hill, ON L4B 3Z4 Canada
905-886-6545
Fax: 905-886-3296
Rimouski
#110, 288, rue Pierre-Saindon
Rimouski, QC G5L 9A8 Canada
418-721-2260
Fax: 418-721-2263
Rivière-du-Loup
PO Box 70
428, rue Lafontaine
Rivière-du-Loup, QC G5R 3Y7 Canada
418-863-6769
Fax: 418-863-4158
Sackville
35 Salem St.
Sackville, NB E4L 4J5 Canada
506-536-2838
Fax: 506-536-3595
Saint John
Brunswick House
#1500, 44 Chipman Hill
Saint John, NB E2L 2A9 Canada
506-634-6880
Fax: 506-636-9079

Salt Spring Island
152A Fulford Ganges Rd.
Salt Spring Island, BC V8K 2T8 Canada
250-537-1654
Fax: 250-537-4896
Sarnia
#101, 10 Derby Lane
Sarnia, ON N7T 4S4 Canada
519-344-8821
Fax: 519-344-9651
Saskatoon
Princeton Tower, Scotia Centre Mall
#306, 123 - 2nd Ave. South
Saskatoon, SK S7K 7E6 Canada
306-653-8586
Fax: 306-653-7227
Sault Ste Marie
390 Bay St.
Sault Ste Marie, ON P6A 1X3 Canada
705-949-5000
Fax: 705-949-8081
Sept-×les
390, rue Brochu
Sept-×les, QC G4R 2W6 Canada
418-968-4600
Fax: 418-968-3311
Sherbrooke
#230, 65, rue Belvédère nord
Sherbrooke, QC J1H 4A7 Canada
819-820-7870
Fax: 819-821-9102
Sherwood Park
#300, 222 Baseline Rd.
Sherwood Park, AB T8H 1S8 Canada
780-417-8550
Fax: 780-417-8552
Sidney
#102, 9845 Resthaven Dr.
Sidney, BC V8L 3E9 Canada
250-655-2300
Fax: 250-655-4683
St Catharines
Corbloc Complex
#600, 800 King St.
St Catharines, ON L2R 7G1 Canada
905-685-6252
Fax: 905-685-6272
St Marys
PO Box 2950
136 Queen St. East
St Marys, ON N4X 1A6 Canada
519-284-4256
Fax: 519-284-4127
St. John's
Phase 1, Cabot Place
#390, 100 New Gower St.
St. John's, NL A1C 6K3 Canada
709-724-7320
Fax: 709-738-0325
Stratford
100 Erie St.
Stratford, ON N5A 2M4 Canada
519-273-0474
Fax: 519-273-7320
Sudbury
#301, 27 Cedar St.
Sudbury, ON P3E 1A1 Canada
705-675-8900
Fax: 705-675-8936
Summerside
268 Water St.
Summerside, PE C1N 1B6 Canada
902-888-4560
Fax: 902-888-4564
Sydney
180 Charlotte St.
Sydney, NS B1P 1C5 Canada
902-562-9540
Fax: 902-562-9541
Thetford Mines
257, rue Notre-Dame sud
Thetford Mines, QC G6G 1J7 Canada
418-338-4656
Fax: 418-338-4561
Thornhill - Hwy. 7 East
Commerce Gate Plaza
#318, 505 Hwy. 7 East
Thornhill, ON L3T 7T1 Canada
905-763-0378
Thornhill - Leslie St.
8500 Leslie St., Ground Fl.
Thornhill, ON L3T 7M8 Canada
905-763-0378
Fax: 905-763-7071
Thunder Bay
Woodgate Office Centre
#210, 1139 Alloy Dr.
Thunder Bay, ON P7B 6M8 Canada
807-343-1900
Fax: 807-345-6741
Toronto - Bay St.
302 Bay St.
Toronto, ON M5X 1A1 Canada
416-359-4392
Fax: 416-359-1788
Toronto - Bloor St. West
PO Box 408
#230, 55 Bloor St. West
Toronto, ON M4W 1A6 Canada
416-924-7702
Fax: 416-924-4406
Toronto - Bloor St. West
#650, 3300 Bloor St. West
Toronto, ON M8X 2X2 Canada
416-236-4010
Fax: 416-236-4080
Toronto - Consilium Pl.
Consilium Place
100 Consilium Pl., Ground Fl.
Toronto, ON M1H 3E3 Canada
416-296-0040
Fax: 416-296-0074
Toronto - First Canadian Pl.
First Canadian Place
PO Box 150, First Canadian Place Sta. First Canadian Place
Toronto, ON M5X 1H3 Canada
416-359-4000
Fax: 416-359-4311
Toronto - First Canadian Pl.
PO Box 150
1 First Canadian Pl., 48th Fl.
Toronto, ON M5X 1H3 Canada
416-359-7600
Fax: 416-359-1924
Toronto - First Canadian Pl.
PO Box 150
1 First Canadian Pl., 53rd Fl.
Toronto, ON M5X 1H3 Canada
416-359-5656
Fax: 416-359-4942
Toronto - First Canadian Pl.
PO Box 150
1 First Canadian Pl., 48th Fl.
Toronto, ON M5X 1H3 Canada
416-359-7600
Fax: 416-359-7240
Toronto - First Canadian Pl. - Dorfman Group
PO Box 150
1 First Canadian Place, 49th Fl.
Toronto, ON M5X 1H3 Canada
416-359-4440
Fax: 416-359-6225
Toronto - First Canadian Pl. - NB Securities Ltd.
PO Box 150
1 First Canadian Pl., 50th Fl.
Toronto, ON M5X 1H3 Canada
416-216-6912
Fax: 416-216-6916
Toronto - First Canadian Pl. - Newlands Group
PO Box 150
1 First Canadian Pl., 47th Fl.
Toronto, ON M5X 1H3 Canada
416-359-6524
Fax: 416-359-4941
Toronto - First Canadian Pl. - Private Banking
PO Box 150
1 First Canadian Pl.
Toronto, ON M5X 1H3 Canada
416-359-4392
Fax: 416-359-1788
Toronto - King St. West
Exchange Tower
PO Box 414
130 King St. West, 14th Fl.
Toronto, ON M5X 1J4 Canada
416-365-6000
Fax: 416-365-6007
Toronto - King St. West - J.H. Partners
Royal Trust Tower
PO Box 279
#4200, 77 King St. West
Toronto, ON M5K 1J5 Canada
416-359-5000
Fax: 416-359-5040
Toronto - Queen St. East
1815 Queen St. East
Toronto, ON M4L 3Z6 Canada
416-698-1525
Fax: 416-698-1522
Toronto - Sandhurst Circle

Woodside Square
1571 Sandhurst Circle
Toronto, ON M1V 1V2 Canada
416-292-8789
Fax: 416-292-8318
Toronto - Spadina Rd.
433 Spadina Rd., Ground Fl.
Toronto, ON M5P 2W3 Canada
416-481-2707
Fax: 416-481-3662
Toronto - St. Clair Ave. East
#1203, 22 St. Clair Ave. East
Toronto, ON M4T 2S7 Canada
416-928-3327
Fax: 416-928-1417
Toronto - Yonge St.
2444 Yonge St., 2nd Fl.
Toronto, ON M4P 2H4 Canada
416-487-2440
Fax: 416-487-2161
Toronto - Yonge St.
#2300, 5140 Yonge St.
Toronto, ON M2N 6L7 Canada
416-590-7600
Fax: 416-590-7601
Trail
#119, 1290 Esplanade
Trail, BC V1R 4T2 Canada
250-368-4500
Fax: 250-368-4507
Trois-Rivières
5885, boul Jean-XXIII
Trois-Rivières, QC G8Z 4N8 Canada
819-379-4266
Fax: 819-379-4873
Truro
#304, 35 Commercial St.
Truro, NS B2N 3H9 Canada
902-896-2031
Fax: 902-896-2036

Vancouver - Burrard St. - Private Banking
Three Bentall Centre
PO Box 49101
#933, 595 Burrard St.
Vancouver, BC V7X 1G4 Canada
604-665-7310
Fax: 604-669-4360
Vancouver - East Pender St. - Asian Banking Centre
168 East Pender St.
Vancouver, BC V6A 1T3 Canada
604-806-3100
Fax: 604-806-3111
Vancouver - West Georgia St.
Park Place
#1800, 885 West Georgia St.
Vancouver, BC V6C 3E8 Canada
604-669-7424
Fax: 604-631-2658
Vancouver - West Georgia St.
#1700, 885 West Georgia St.
Vancouver, BC V6C 3E8 Canada
604-685-5181
Fax: 604-443-1515
Vernon
#200, 3200 - 30th Ave.
Vernon, BC V1T 2C5 Canada
250-260-5750
Fax: 250-260-5774
Victoria - Douglas St. - Private Banking
1235 Douglas St., 2nd Fl.
Victoria, BC V8W E26 Canada
250-953-2360
Fax: 250-389-1790
Victoria - View St.
#1000, 730 View St.
Victoria, BC V8W 3E9 Canada
250-361-2400
Fax: 250-361-2430
Waterloo
Marsland Centre
20 Erb St. West
Waterloo, ON N2L 1T2 Canada
519-886-3100
Fax: 519-474-2236
White Rock
Windsor Square
#270, 1959 - 152nd St.
White Rock, BC V4A 9E3 Canada
604-535-4300
Fax: 604-535-4320
Windsor
#1100, 100 Ouellette Ave.
Windsor, ON N9A 6T3 Canada
519-977-6697
Fax: 519-256-3093
Winnipeg
Commodity Exchange Tower
#1300, 360 Main St.
Winnipeg, MB R3C 3Z3 Canada
204-949-2500
Fax: 204-947-2022
Wolfville
PO Box 130
270 Main St.
Wolfville, NS B0P 1X0 Canada
902-542-1818
Fax: 902-542-1919
Woodstock
12 Perry St.
Woodstock, ON N4S 3C2 Canada
519-421-3133
Fax: 519-421-2078
Yorkton
#5, 7 Broadway St. East
Yorkton, SK S3N 0K2 Canada
306-786-1811
Fax: 306-786-6944

BNP (Canada) Valeurs Mobilières Inc./ BNP (Canada) Securities Inc.

Also listed under: *Investment Fund Companies*
#500, 1981, av McGill College
Montréal, QC H3A 2W8
514-285-6000
Fax: 514-285-6278
Year Founded: 1991
Stock Exchange Membership: Montreal Exchange, Toronto Stock Exchange

Bolder Investment Partners Ltd.

#800, 1450 Creekside Dr.
Vancouver, BC V6J 5B3
604-714-2300
Fax: 604-714-2301
bwright@bolder.net
Stock Exchange Membership: Toronto Stock Exchange, TSX Venture Exchange
Executives:
C. Channing Buckland, Chair/CEO
David Chernoff, President
Jeana R. Traviss, CFO

Brant Securities Limited

#1400, 4 King St. West
Toronto, ON M5H 1B6
416-596-4545
Fax: 416-596-4546
888-544-9318
info@brantsec.com
www.brantsec.com
Year Founded: 1919
Stock Exchange Membership: Toronto Stock Exchange, TSX Venture Exchange
Executives:
Keith McMeekin, President

Brockhouse & Cooper Inc.

#4025, 1250, boul René-Lévesque ouest
Montréal, QC H3B 4W8
514-932-7171
Fax: 514-932-8288
pmcentyre@brockhousecooper.com
www.brockhousecooper.com
Ownership: Private
Stock Exchange Membership: Montreal Exchange, Toronto Stock Exchange, TSX Venture Exchange
Executives:
Ralph Loader, President/CEO
Richard L. Cooper, Chair, Secretary/Treasurer
Howard Messias, Vice-President, CFO, CCO
Patrick L. Belland, Director, Brokerage Sales

Burgeonvest Securities Limited

Also listed under: *Financial Planning*
Commerce Place
PO Box 65
#1100, 21 King St. West
Hamilton, ON L8P 4W7
905-528-6505
Fax: 905-528-3540
800-209-8379
info@burgeonvest.com
www.burgeonvest.com
Ownership: Burgeonvest Financial Corporation
Year Founded: 1997
Number of Employees: 36
Stock Exchange Membership: Toronto Stock Exchange, TSX Venture Exchange
Executives:
Mario Frankovich, CEO
Morris Vaillancourt, CFO
John Cowman, Vice-President, Investment Advisor
David Ellerby, Vice-President, Compliance
Peter Long, Vice-President
Directors:
Mario Frankovich, Chair
David Ellerby
Peter Long
Morris Vaillancourt
Branches:
Burlington
#201, 1001 Champlain Ave.
Burlington, ON L7L 5Z4 Canada
905-336-9544
Peter Long, Vice-President & Branch Manager
Toronto
#704, 170 University Ave.
Toronto, ON M5H 3B3 Canada
416-246-8241
John De Goey, Branch Manager
Windsor
#200, 600 Ouellette Ave.
Windsor, ON N9A 6Z3 Canada
519-252-1336
866-331-3354
Tony Warden, Branch Manager

Byron Securities Limited

#800, 357 Bay St.
Toronto, ON M5H 2T7
416-867-9800
Fax: 416-867-1020
Stock Exchange Membership: Canadian Trading & Quotation System Inc, Toronto Stock Exchange, TSX Venture Exchange
Executives:
Lorne Levy, President/CEO, Chief Financial Officer

Caldwell Securities Ltd.

PO Box 47
#1710, 150 King St. West
Toronto, ON M5H 1J9
416-862-7755
Fax: 416-862-2498
800-387-0859
info@caldwellsecurities.com
www.caldwellsecurities.com
Year Founded: 1981
Stock Exchange Membership: Toronto Stock Exchange, TSX Venture Exchange
Executives:
Brendan T.N. Caldwell, President/CEO
J. Dennis Freeman, Exec. Vice-President
Thomas S. Caldwell, Chair
Robert Caldwell, Vice-President
Sally Haldenby Haba, Vice-President, Secretary
Charles Hughson, Vice-President
Angela Stirpe, CFO
Branches:
London
#1080, 255 Queens Ave.
London, ON N6A 5R8 Canada
519-645-2400
Fax: 519-645-2445
887-499-7220
Charles B. Hughson, Contact
Niagara on the Lake

INVESTMENT MANAGEMENT

Caldwell Securities Ltd. (continued)
PO Box 701
9 Queen St., 2nd Fl.
Niagara on the Lake, ON L0S 1J0 Canada
905-468-0655
Fax: 905-468-1332
866-758-8804
James P. Caldwell, Contact
Whitby
515 Brock St. South
Whitby, ON L1N 4K8 Canada
905-665-1911
Fax: 905-665-1912
800-628-1959
Vincent L. John, Contact

Canaccord Capital Corporation
Pacific Centre
PO Box 10337
#2200, 609 Granville St.
Vancouver, BC V7Y 1H2
604-643-7300
Fax: 604-643-7606
800-663-1899
info@canaccord.com
www.canaccord.com
Ownership: Employee-owned
Year Founded: 1950
Number of Employees: 1,110
Assets: $1-10 billion
Revenues: $100-500 million
Stock Exchange Membership: Canadian Trading & Quotation System Inc, Montreal Exchange, Toronto Stock Exchange, TSX Venture Exchange
Profile: The independent full service investment dealer operates through its principal subsidiaries. It has capital markets operations in the USA and the UK. Canaccord is a publicly traded company. It is listed on both the Toronto Stock Exchange and AIM, which is a market operated by the London Stock Exchange.

Executives:
Peter M. Brown, Chair/CEO
Paul Reynolds, Vice-Chair
Michael G. Greenwood, President/COO
Paul A. Chalmers, Exec. Vice-President
Paul DiPasquale, Exec. Vice-President
Douglas A. Doiron, Exec. Vice-President, Private Client Eastern Canada
Matthew Gaasenbeek, Exec. Vice-President, Director, Institutional Sales & Trading
Robert M. Larose, Exec. Vice-President, Private Client Services
Mark Maybank, Exec. Vice-President, Managing Director, Deputy Head of Canaccord Adams
Peter Virvilis, Exec. Vice-President, Treasurer
Doug Gartland, Sr. Vice-President, Investment Advisor
Brad Kotush, Sr. Vice-President, CCO
Branches:
Abbotsford
#200, 32071 South Fraser Way
Abbotsford, BC V2T 1W3 Canada
604-504-1504
877-977-5677
Beloeil
275, rue Choquette
Beloeil, QC J3G 4V6 Canada
450-467-8294
Burlington
Burlington Mall
#206-207, 777 Guelph Line
Burlington, ON L7R 3N2 Canada
905-681-3675

Calgary
#2200, 450 - 1 St. SW
Calgary, AB T2P 5P8 Canada
403-508-3800
800-818-4119
Campbell River
#1, 1170 Shoppers Row
Campbell River, BC V9W 2C8 Canada
250-287-8807
800-347-0270
Christina Lake
3393 White Rd.
Christina Lake, BC V0H 1E1 Canada
250-447-2396
888-493-1155
Edmonton
Manulife Place
#2700, 10180 - 101st St.
Edmonton, AB T5J 3S4 Canada
780-408-1500
877-313-3035
Halifax
PO Box 338, CRO Sta. CRO
#1300, 1701 Hollis St.
Halifax, NS B3J 2N7 Canada
902-482-4487
866-371-2262
Kelowna
#602, 1708 Dolphin Ave
Kelowna, BC V1Y 9S4 Canada
250-712-1100
888-389-3331
Kingston
The Woolen Mill
#208, 4 Cataraqui St.
Kingston, ON K7K 1Z7 Canada
613-547-3997
Montréal
#1100, 1010, rue Sherbrooke ouest
Montréal, QC H3A 2R7 Canada
514-844-5443
800-361-4805
Nanaimo
75 Commercial St.
Nanaimo, BC V9R 5G3 Canada
250-754-1111
800-754-1907
Ottawa
World Exchange Plaza
#830, 45 O'Connor St.
Ottawa, ON K1P 1A4 Canada
613-233-3158
888-899-9994
Prince George
1520 - 3rd Ave.
Prince George, BC V2L 3G4 Canada
250-562-7255
800-667-3205
Québec
#2940, 2600, boul Laurier
Québec, QC G1V 4M6 Canada
418-658-2924
Saint-Lin-Laurentides
296, rue Salaberry
Saint-Lin-Laurentides, QC J0R 1C0 Canada
450-439-1842
Simcoe
49 Robinson St.
Simcoe, ON N3Y 1W5 Canada
519-428-7525
Toronto
PO Box 516
#3000, 161 Bay St.
Toronto, ON M5J 2S1 Canada
416-869-7368
800-896-1058
Vernon
3108 - 30 Ave.
Vernon, BC V1T 2C2 Canada
250-558-5431
800-665-2505
Victoria
#400, 737 Yates St.
Victoria, BC V8W 1L6 Canada
250-388-5354
877-666-2288
Waterloo
#101, 80 King St. South
Waterloo, ON N2J 1P5 Canada
519-886-1060
800-495-8071
White Rock
#305, 1688 - 152 St.
Surrey, BC V4A 4N2 Canada
604-538-8004
800-665-2001
Whitehorse
206D Jarvis St.
Whitehorse, YT Y1A 2H1 Canada
867-668-7111
800-661-0554

Canadian Derivatives Clearing Corporation(CDCC)
Tour de la Bourse
800, carré Victoria, 3e étage
Montréal, QC H4Z 1A9
514-871-3545
Fax: 514-871-3530
888-232-2457
operations@cdcc.ca
www.cdcc.ca
Former Name: Trans Canada Options Inc.
Ownership: Wholly-owned subsidiary of the Montréal Exchange

Year Founded: 1975
Number of Employees: 35
Stock Exchange Membership: Montreal Exchange
Directors:
Stephen J. Elgee, Chair
Branches:
Toronto
#700, 65 Queen St. West
Toronto, ON M5H 2M5 Canada
416-367-2463
Fax: 416-367-2473

Canadian General Investments, Limited
#1601, 110 Yonge St.
Toronto, ON M5C 1T4
416-366-2931
Fax: 416-366-2729
800-207-0067
cgifund@mmainvestments.com
www.mmainvestments.com
Ownership: Jonathan A. Morgan & Vanessa L. Morgan own or control 43.5% of the Company's common shares.
Year Founded: 1930
Assets: $100-500 million
Revenues: $5-10 million
Stock Symbol: CGI
Executives:
Jonathan A. Morgan, President/CEO
Colin D. Smith, Sec.-Treas.
Frank Fuernkranz, Asst. Treasurer
Directors:
Vanessa L. Morgan, Chair
Sec.-Treas., Denbridge Capital Corporation
James G. Cook
Jonathan A. Morgan
R. Neil Raymond
Michael A. Smedley
Richard O'C. Whittall

Canadian ShareOwner Investments Inc.
#806, 4 King St. West
Toronto, ON M5H 1B6
416-595-7200
Fax: 416-595-0400
866-644-6881
www.investments.shareowner.com

Canadian World Fund Limited
#1601, 110 Yonge St.
Toronto, ON M5C 1T4
416-366-2931
Fax: 416-366-2729
cwffund@mmainvestments.com
www.mmainvestments.com
Ownership: Jonathan A. Morgan & Vanessa L. Morgan own or control 56.27% of the company's common shares.
Year Founded: 1994
Assets: $10-50 million
Revenues: Under $1 million
Stock Symbol: CWF
Executives:
Jonathan Morgan, President/CEO
Colin D. Smith, Sec.-Treas.
Frank Fuernkranz, Asst. Treasurer
Directors:
Vanessa L. Morgan, Chair
James Cook
Jonathan Morgan
R.Neil Raymond

Michael A. Smedley
Richard O'C. Whittall

Capital Planning
Also listed under: *Financial Planning*
#A304, 555 Legget Dr.
Kanata, ON K2K 2X3
613-271-2108
Fax: 613-270-9540
carol@cpassfield.com
Ownership: Private
Year Founded: 1998
Number of Employees: 1
Assets: Under $1 million
Revenues: Under $1 million

Casgrain & Compagnie Limitée
1200, av McGill College, 21e étage
Montréal, QC H3B 4G7
514-871-8080
Fax: 514-871-1943
casgrain@casgrain.ca
Executives:
Guy Casgrain, President
Roger Casgrain, Exec. Vice-President
Martin Bellefeuille, Vice-President
Louis Claveau, Vice-President
Robert Kelsall, Vice-President
André Zanga, Vice-President & Comptroller
Pierre Casgrain, Secretary

Castle Rock Financial
Also listed under: *Financial Planning*
#209, 100, boul Alexis-Nihon
Montréal, QC H4M 2N7
514-748-8880
Fax: 514-748-1911

CIBC Investor Services Inc.
c/o Customer Satisfaction Department
800 Bay St., 2nd Fl.
Toronto, ON M5S 3A9
800-567-3343
feedback@cibc.com
www.investorsedge.cibc.com

CIBC Wood Gundy
BCE Place
PO Box 500
161 Bay St.
Toronto, ON M5J 2S8
416-594-7000
Fax: 416-594-7069
800-563-3193
client.relations@cibc.ca
www.woodgundy.com
Year Founded: 1905
Branches:

Abbotsford
#200, 32555 Simon Ave.
Abbotsford, BC V2T 4Y2 Canada
604-853-6668
Fax: 604-850-5391
800-853-2853

Ajax
Ajax Durham Centre
#4, 90 Kingston Rd. East
Ajax, ON L1Z 1G1 Canada
905-426-6685
Fax: 905-426-6779
800-367-5849

Barrie
#100, 126 Wellington St. West
Barrie, ON L4N 1K9 Canada
705-728-6215
Fax: 705-728-8733
800-461-5416

Belleville
Century Place
PO Box 783
#123, 199 Front St.
Belleville, ON K8N 9Z9 Canada
613-966-8888
Fax: 613-966-9260
800-267-2108

Bridgewater
37 Pleasant St.
Bridgewater, NS B4V 1M9 Canada
902-543-9882
Fax: 902-543-5396
800-242-0818

Burlington
Sims Square
#500, 390 Brant St.
Burlington, ON L7R 4J4 Canada
905-634-2200
Fax: 905-634-9666
866-841-8819

Calgary - 6th Ave.
Bow Valley Square 4
#2000, 250 - 6th Ave. SW
Calgary, AB T2P 3H7 Canada
403-508-3200
Fax: 403-264-1030
800-290-6643

Calgary - 8th Ave.
Western Gas Tower
#400, 530 - 8th Ave. SW
Calgary, AB T2P 3S8 Canada
403-260-0400
Fax: 403-260-0410

Charlottetown
#400, 119 Kent St.
Charlottetown, PE C1A 1N3 Canada
902-892-4231
Fax: 902-368-3964
800-207-0231

Cornwall
#401, 132 - 2nd St. East
Cornwall, ON K6H 1Y4 Canada
613-938-7777
Fax: 613-938-8486
800-661-4318

Cranbrook
#102, 117 Cranbrook St. North
Cranbrook, BC V1C 3P8 Canada
250-489-4745
Fax: 250-489-1494
800-665-2192

Duncan
#201, 55 Canada Ave.
Duncan, BC V9L 1T3 Canada
250-748-8138
Fax: 250-746-7293
800-667-2821

Edmonton
Manulife Place
#1780, 10180 - 101st St.
Edmonton, AB T5J 3S4 Canada
780-429-8900
Fax: 780-498-5050
800-232-7296

Fredericton
Frederick Square
77 Westmorland St.
Fredericton, NB E3B 6Z3 Canada
506-451-8830
Fax: 506-451-8838
800-268-8875

Granby
163, rue St-Jacques
Granby, QC J2G 9A7 Canada
450-776-1400
Fax: 450-776-1401
800-463-8454

Guelph
#201, 42 Wyndham St. North
Guelph, ON N1H 4E6 Canada
519-822-8830
Fax: 519-822-3061
800-265-4954

Halifax
Tower Two, Purdy's Wharf
PO Box 47
#1801, 1969 Upper Water St.
Halifax, NS B3J 3R7 Canada
902-425-6900
Fax: 902-429-8323
800-565-0601

Hamilton
#600, 21 King St. West
Hamilton, ON L8P 4W7 Canada
905-526-4700
Fax: 905-526-4716
800-263-2767

Kamloops
Continental Place
#400, 275 Landsdowne Rd.
Kamloops, BC V2C 1X8 Canada
250-314-3870
Fax: 250-314-3872
888-255-0015

Kanata
#1030, 555 Legget Dr.
Kanata, ON K2K 2X3 Canada
613-271-1511
Fax: 613-271-1509
888-801-3335

Kelowna
#1007, 1708 Dolphin Ave.
Kelowna, BC V1Y 9S4 Canada
250-717-2600
Fax: 250-762-2629
800-663-2206

Kentville
49 Cornwallis St.
Kentville, NS B4N 2E3 Canada
902-542-6410
Fax: 902-542-6411
888-542-6410

Kingston
#500, 366 King St. East
Kingston, ON K7K 6Y3 Canada
613-531-5522
Fax: 613-531-5523
800-267-0254

Kitchener
#1010, 305 King St. West
Kitchener, ON N2G 1B9 Canada
519-570-5620
Fax: 519-570-5617
800-265-2433

Laval
#800, 2540, boul Daniel-Johnson
Laval, QC H7T 2S3 Canada
450-688-1004
Fax: 450-688-5020
800-268-1004

London
One London Place
#2200, 255 Queens Ave.
London, ON N6A 5R8 Canada
519-663-5353
Fax: 519-663-5037
800-265-5982

Medicine Hat
Gaslight Plaza
#207, 579 - 3rd St. SE
Medicine Hat, AB T1A 0H2 Canada
403-527-1131
Fax: 403-526-6901
800-661-6341

Mississauga - Burnhamthorpe Rd.
East Tower, Sussex Centre
#601, 50 Burnhamthorpe Rd. West
Mississauga, ON L5B 3C2 Canada
905-897-3700
Fax: 905-897-2156
800-567-5859

Mississauga - Burnhamthorpe Rd.
#105, 90 Burnhamthorpe Rd. West
Mississauga, ON L5B 3C3 Canada
905-272-2200
Fax: 905-272-3733
800-469-2583

Moncton
Blue Cross Centre
#113, 644 Main St.
Moncton, NB E1C 1E2 Canada
506-857-8640
Fax: 506-857-1731
800-561-5559

Montréal - Cavendish
#100, 9000, boul Cavendish
Montréal, QC H4M 2V2 Canada

INVESTMENT MANAGEMENT

CIBC Wood Gundy (continued)
514-332-8224
Fax: 514-332-4908
800-577-8224
Montréal - Maisonneuve
#3050, 600, boul de Maisonneuve
Montréal, QC H3A 3J2 Canada
514-847-6300
Fax: 514-847-6397
888-847-6300

Montréal - Place Ville Marie
#4125, 1, Place Ville Marie
Montréal, QC H3B 3P9 Canada
514-392-7600
Fax: 514-392-7601
877-392-7600
Montréal - René-Lévesque ouest
#3100, 1250, boul René-Lévesque ouest
Montréal, QC H3B 4W8 Canada
514-846-3500
Fax: 514-846-3545
800-361-2773
Montréal - Sherbrooke
Le Ville Marie
#2020, 1000, rue Sherbrooke ouest
Montréal, QC H3A 3G4 Canada
514-282-6850
Fax: 514-282-6877
888-282-6850
Nanaimo
#1, 20 Townsite Rd.
Nanaimo, BC V9S 5T7 Canada
250-753-4366
Fax: 250-753-5486
800-563-8281
New Westminster
#409, 960 Quayside Dr.
New Westminster, BC V3M 6G2 Canada
604-525-0563
Fax: 604-525-7932
800-340-9909
North Bay
#501, 222 McIntyre St. West
North Bay, ON P1B 2Y8 Canada
705-476-1100
Fax: 705-476-1113
800-461-9545
Oakville
277 Lakeshore Rd. East
Oakville, ON L6J 1H9 Canada
905-842-6770
Fax: 905-842-7114
800-268-0621
Oshawa
1 Mary St. North
Oshawa, ON L1G 7W8 Canada
905-576-1726
Fax: 905-576-2919
800-661-0243
Ottawa
#800, 50 O'Connor St.
Ottawa, ON K1P 6L2 Canada
613-237-5775
Fax: 613-239-2917
800-267-9345
Owen Sound
#220, 945 - 3rd Ave. East
Owen Sound, ON N4K 2K8 Canada
519-371-4451
Fax: 519-371-1892
800-265-3128
Parksville
PO Box 909
109 West Hirst Ave.
Parksville, BC V9P 2G9 Canada
250-248-8774
Fax: 250-248-8770
Penticton
#105, 399 Main St.
Penticton, BC V2A 5B7 Canada
250-492-0212
Fax: 250-492-6022
800-694-0212
Peterborough
PO Box 1711
135 Charlotte St.
Peterborough, ON K9J 7X6 Canada
705-740-2447
Fax: 705-742-5239
800-711-7979
Prince George
#300, 177 Victoria St.
Prince George, BC V2L 5R8 Canada
250-563-0401
Fax: 250-563-7154
800-401-2447
Québec - Galeries
#500, 5500, boul des Galeries, 5e étage
Québec, QC G2K 2A2 Canada
418-627-9756
Fax: 418-627-9348
800-627-9756
Québec - Laurier
Place Iberville Quatre
#650, 2954, boul Laurier
Québec, QC G1V 4T2 Canada
418-652-8011
Fax: 418-654-1017
800-463-8317
Québec - St-Louis
Maison Cureux
86, rue St-Louis
Québec, QC G1R 3Z5 Canada
418-692-4200
Fax: 418-692-4274
800-263-4201
Regina
CIBC World Markets
#420, 1801 Hamilton St.
Regina, SK S4P 4B4 Canada
306-359-1577
Fax: 306-569-8616
800-667-3661
Richmond
Pacific Business Centre
#606, 5811 Cooney Rd.
Richmond, BC V6X 3M1 Canada
604-270-6457
Fax: 604-273-7684
800-341-9909
Saint John
#500, 44 Chipman Hill
Saint John, NB E2L 2A9 Canada
506-634-1220
Fax: 506-634-8214
800-266-9670
Salt Spring Island
118 Manson Rd.
Salt Spring Island, BC V8K 2T7 Canada
250-537-4771

Sarnia
The Nova Bldg.
#505, 201 Front St. North
Sarnia, ON N7T 7T9 Canada
519-332-1670
Fax: 519-332-1453
800-386-0025
Saskatoon
#500, 119 - 4th Ave. South
Saskatoon, SK S7K 5X2 Canada
306-975-3800
Fax: 306-975-3832
800-561-3800
Sault Ste Marie
#108, 477 Queen St. East
Sault Ste Marie, ON P6A 1Z5 Canada
705-949-5800
Fax: 705-949-5970
800-461-6000
Sherbrooke
#100, 3000, rue King ouest
Sherbrooke, QC J1L 1Y7 Canada
819-573-6000
Fax: 819-573-6001
800-561-3718
Sidney
#1, 2491 Bevan Ave.
Sidney, BC V8L 1W2 Canada
250-655-2200
Fax: 250-655-6750
888-246-6611
Simcoe
2 Talbot St. North
Simcoe, ON N3Y 3W4 Canada
519-428-2011
Fax: 519-428-5322
800-387-8529
St Catharines
1 St Paul St., Main Fl.
St Catharines, ON L2R 7L2 Canada
905-688-2013
Fax: 905-988-2970
800-263-7264
St Thomas
459 Talbot St.
St Thomas, ON N5P 1C1 Canada
519-631-1930
Fax: 519-631-6082
800-267-3267
St. John's
Atlantic Place
PO Box 77
215 Water St., 8th Fl.
St. John's, NL A1C 6C9 Canada
709-576-2700
Fax: 709-754-5469
800-563-0800
Sudbury
#601, 10 Elm St. East
Sudbury, ON P3C 1S8 Canada
705-675-3337
Fax: 705-675-6536
800-461-6369
Surrey
1688 - 152nd St., 4th Fl.
Surrey, BC V4A 4N2 Canada
604-535-3700
Fax: 604-535-8103
800-667-6132
Thornhill
#100, 123 Commerce Valley Dr. East
Thornhill, ON L3T 7W8 Canada
905-762-2300
Fax: 905-762-2301
800-668-3800
Thunder Bay
#101, 180 Park Ave.
Thunder Bay, ON P7B 6J4 Canada
807-345-5533
Fax: 807-343-7973
800-461-8909
Timmins
28 Pine St. South
Timmins, ON P4N 2J8 Canada
705-268-7500
Fax: 705-268-7798
800-461-0150
Toronto - Bay St.
BCE Place
PO Box 500
161 Bay St.
Toronto, ON M5J 2S8 Canada
416-594-7000
Fax: 416-594-7069
Toronto - Bay St.
BCE Place
#600, 181 Bay St.
Toronto, ON M5J 2V8 Canada
416-369-8100
Fax: 416-369-8987
800-387-1865
Toronto - King St. West
200 King St. West, 6th Fl.
Toronto, ON M5H 3Z8 Canada
416-594-8999
Fax: 416-594-8404
888-867-8175
Toronto - King St. West
200 King St. West, 8th Fl.
Toronto, ON M5H 3Z8 Canada
416-594-8600
Fax: 416-594-8842
888-867-8175

Toronto - King St. West - Gallery
200 King St. West, 18th Fl.
Toronto, ON M5H 3Z8 Canada
416-594-8680
Fax: 416-594-8500
888-806-4333
Toronto - King St. West - Private Clients Centre
PO Box 397
25 King St. West
Toronto, ON M5L 1E2 Canada
416-594-7897
Fax: 416-594-7880
Toronto - Simcoe St.
#200, 100 Simcoe St.
Toronto, ON M5H 3G2 Canada
416-594-7950
Fax: 416-594-7951
800-263-3803

Toronto - Yonge St.
Madison Centre
#2408, 4950 Yonge St.
Toronto, ON M2N 6K1 Canada
416-730-9882
Fax: 416-730-9892
866-866-4235
Toronto - Yonge St.
#600, 4110 Yonge St.
Toronto, ON M2P 2B7 Canada
416-229-5900
Fax: 416-229-5901
800-488-8688
Trail
1300 Cedar Ave.
Trail, BC V1R 4C2 Canada
250-364-2525
Fax: 250-364-1908
800-919-4344
Truro
Sun Professional Bldg.
PO Box 746
640 Prince St.
Truro, NS B2N 5E8 Canada
902-893-0300
Fax: 902-893-1134
800-782-1398
Vancouver - 41st Ave. West
#402, 2052 - 41st Ave. West
Vancouver, BC V6M 1Y8 Canada
604-267-7110
Fax: 604-267-7117
888-443-6643
Vancouver - Burrard St.
#3434, 666 Burrard St.
Vancouver, BC V6C 2X8 Canada
604-685-3434
Fax: 604-689-3434
800-661-9442
Vancouver - Dunsmuir St.
Four Bentall Centre
PO Box 49184
#2500, 1055 Dunsmuir St.
Vancouver, BC V7X 1K8 Canada
604-661-2300
Fax: 604-687-2120
877-331-5122
Vancouver - West Georgia St.
925 West Georgia St., 8th Fl.
Vancouver, BC V5C 3L2 Canada
604-806-5500
Fax: 604-661-7750
800-567-8014
Victoria - Douglas St.
International House
#102, 880 Douglas St.
Victoria, BC V8W 2B7 Canada
250-388-6411
Fax: 250-388-6963
800-665-9080
Victoria - View St.
730 View St., 9th Fl.
Victoria, BC V8W 1J8 Canada
250-388-5131
Fax: 250-385-5669
800-561-5864

Victoriaville
117, rue Notre-Dame est
Victoriaville, QC G6P 3Z9 Canada
819-751-0105
Fax: 819-751-0109
800-561-2568
Waterloo
#400, 255 King St. North
Waterloo, ON N2J 4V2 Canada
519-888-6688
Fax: 519-888-6887
800-265-2308
West Vancouver
#114, 100 Park Royal
West Vancouver, BC V7T 1A2 Canada
604-925-9210
Fax: 604-925-9235
800-772-9066
Windsor
#101, 2510 Ouellette Ave.
Windsor, ON N8X 1L4 Canada
519-972-0010
Fax: 519-972-3854
800-265-5832
Winnipeg
#1000, 1 Lombard Pl.
Winnipeg, MB R3B 3N9 Canada
204-942-0311
Fax: 204-943-2350
800-665-6789
Woodstock
412 Dundas St.
Woodstock, ON N4S 1B9 Canada
519-421-1197
Fax: 519-421-1334
800-451-5667

The CIBC World Markets Inc.

BCE Place
PO Box 500
161 Bay St.
Toronto, ON M5J 2S8
416-594-7000
Fax: 416-594-7618
info@cibc.com
www.cibcwm.com/wm
Former Name: CIBC Wood Gundy
Year Founded: 1982
Stock Exchange Membership: Montreal Exchange, Toronto Stock Exchange, TSX Venture Exchange, Winnepeg Commodities Exchange
Executives:
Brian Shaw, CEO, Chair
Richard E. Venn, Sr. Exec. Vice-President, Corporate Development, Deputy-Chair
Steven McGirr, Exec. Vice-President, Chief Risk Officer
David Clifford, Head, Merchant Banking, European Investment & Corporate Bank
David Leith, Head, Canadian Corporate & Investment Banking
Donald R. Lindsay, Managing Director
James R. McSherry, Managing Director & Exec. Vice-President, Commercial Banking
Gary Brown, Managing Director, Head, USA Region
Branches:
Calgary
Bankers Hall
855 - 2 St. SW, 9th Fl.
Calgary, AB T2P 4J7 Canada
403-260-0500
Montréal
#3050, 600, boul de Maisonneuve ouest
Montréal, QC H3A 3J2 Canada
514-847-6300
Ottawa
222 Queen St., 2nd Fl.
Ottawa, ON K1P 5V9 Canada
Vancouver
Commerce Place
400 Burrard St., 12th Fl.
Vancouver, BC V6C 3A6 Canada
604-891-6300

CIT Group Securities (Canada) Inc.

#700, 207 Queens Quay West
Toronto, ON M5J 1A7
416-507-2400
Fax: 416-507-5561
Executives:
J. Daryl MacLellan, President/COO, Director
Stephen M. Danner, Assistant Vice-President, Director

Citigroup Global Markets Canada Inc.

#1100, 123 Front St. West
Toronto, ON M5J 2M3
416-947-5344
Fax: 416-866-2311
www.citigroup.com
Stock Exchange Membership: Toronto Stock Exchange
Executives:
Robert J. Gemmell, President/CEO
Stanley H. Hartt, Chair

Clarus Securities Inc.

The Exchange Tower
#3640, 130 King St. West
Toronto, ON M5X 1A9
416-343-2777
Fax: 416-343-2799
info@clarussecurities.com
www.clarussecurities.com
Stock Exchange Membership: Toronto Stock Exchange, TSX Venture Exchange
Profile: The organization is engaged in research, institutional trading & sales & investment banking. Investment banking services in Toronto & Calgary are targeted at the following industries: industrial products & special situations, energy, technology & healthcare & income trusts.
Executives:
Alistair D. Maxwell, MBA, President/CEO
Tom Monahas, CA, CFO
Jim Christodoulis, B.Com., Managing Director, Institutional Equities
James E. Lorimer, MBA, Managing Director, Investment Banking

Brock Winterton, CFA, Managing Director, Research
Robert Catellier, CFA, Vice-President, Research Analyst
Richard Donohue, MBA, Vice-President, Institutional Equity Sales
Duncan McGregor, Vice-President, Institutional Equity Sales
Branches:
Calgary
First Canadian Centre
#3200, 350 - 7th Ave. SW
Calgary, AB T2P 3N9 Canada
403-269-5900
Fax: 403-269-8900
Vancouver
Cathedral Place
#1112, 925 West Georgia St.
Vancouver, BC V6C 3L2 Canada
604-605-5700
Fax: 604-605-5704

Commission Direct Inc.

PO Box 11
#1010, 121 King St. West
Toronto, ON M5H 3T9
416-842-4200
Fax: 416-842-4210
wayne.mcalpine@commissiondirect.com
www.commissiondirect.com
Ownership: Private
Year Founded: 1992
Number of Employees: 11
Stock Exchange Membership: Toronto Stock Exchange, TSX Venture Exchange

Commodity Management, Inc.

Plaza 124
#708, 10216 - 124 St.
Edmonton, AB T5N 4A3
780-488-3594
Fax: 780-488-6602
800-663-0294
cmi@cmifutures.com, cmi@compusmart.ab.ca
www.cmifutures.com
Year Founded: 1990
Executives:
Robert Haug, President/CEO
Alan Wigelsworth, Vice-President

Consultations Pierre St-Germain/ Pierre St-Germain Consulting

Also listed under: *Financial Planning*
1958, rue de Cambrai
Saint-Bruno, QC J3V 3J3
450-441-2262
Fax: 450-653-6631
pstg@pstg.com
www.pstg.com
Executives:
Pierre St-Germain, Contact

Cornerstone Securities Canada Inc.

Also listed under: *Financial Planning; Investment Management*

The Exchange Tower, 2 First Canadian Place
PO Box 427, First Canadian Pl. Stn. First Canadian Pl.
#1800, 130 King St. West
Toronto, ON M5X 1E3
416-862-8000
Fax: 416-862-8001
888-268-6735
counsel@cornerstonegroup.com
www.cornerstonegroup.com
Ownership: Private
Year Founded: 1978
Profile: The company offers the following services: financial & investment banking services; corporate & financial advisory services, including the placement of debt, equity & hybrid securities, tax-effective corporate finance & restructurings; advice on acquisitions & divestitures, mergers & consolidations, joint ventures & syndications, leveraged buyouts, internal expansions, & capital reorganizations, specialized financings & due diligence reviews, including legal, tax, valuation & pricing issues.

Executives:
Gerald Fields, LL.B., President/CEO

Credential Securities Inc.

#800, 111 West Georgia St.
Vancouver, BC V6E 4T6
604-714-3929
800-688-9933
clientrelations@credential.com
Ownership: Private
Number of Employees: 13
Branches:
Burlington
#200, 3430 South Service Rd.
Burlington, ON L7N 3T9 Canada
905-632-9200
Fax: 905-632-0032
Calgary
#102, 9705 Horton Rd. SW
Calgary, AB T2V 2X5 Canada
403-212-3936
Fax: 403-253-0056
Halifax
#329, 7071 Bayers Rd.
Halifax, NS B3L 2C2 Canada
902-454-6205
Fax: 902-453-6586
Regina
#200, 2500 - 13th Ave.
Regina, SK S4P 0W2 Canada
306-569-5500
Fax: 306-359-7575
Winnipeg
#760, 215 Garry St.
Winnipeg, MB R3C 3P3 Canada
204-927-7430
Fax: 204-927-7440

Credifinance Securities Limited

41A Avenue Rd.
Toronto, ON M5R 2G3
416-955-0159
Fax: 416-364-1522
info@credifinance.com
www.credifinance.com
Ownership: Private
Number of Employees: 15
Stock Exchange Membership: Montreal Exchange, Toronto Stock Exchange
Executives:
Georges Benarroch, President/CEO & Chair
M. Ann Glover, CFO & COO, Sec.-Treas.
William Magee, Vice-President
Stanley R. Smith, Vice-President

Croissance Capital Inc.

Also listed under: *Financial Planning*
#200, 714 rue King est
Sherbrooke, QC J1G 1C4
819-562-2877
Fax: 819-562-9294

Crosbie & Company Inc.

Also listed under: *Pension & Money Management Companies*
Sun Life Financial Tower
PO Box 95
150 King St. West, 15th Fl.
Toronto, ON M5H 1J9
416-362-7726
Fax: 416-362-3447
info@crosbieco.com
www.crosbieco.com
Ownership: Private
Year Founded: 1989
Number of Employees: 12
Profile: The company is a specialty investment banking firm. Investment banking services include the following: mergers, acquisitions & divestitures; debt & equity private placements; financial & corporate restructurings; management & employee buyouts; succession planning; shareholder liquidity alternatives; business & securities valuations; fairness opinions; investing as a principal & fund management.

Executives:
Allan H.T. Crosbie, Chair; 416-362-5138; acrosbie@crosbieco.com
Sharla Sigmund, Vice-President; 416-362-0684; ssigmund@crosbieco.com
Ed Giacomelli, Managing Director; 416-362-0020; egiacomelli@crosbieco.com
Ian K. MacDonell, Managing Director; 416-362-1953; imacdonell@crosbieco.com
Mel D. Margolese, Managing Director; 416-362-7805; mmargolese@crosbieco.com
Colin W. Walker, Managing Director; 416-362-7016; cwalker@crosbieco.com

CTI Capital Inc.

#1635, 1, Place Ville-Marie
Montréal, QC H3B 2B6
514-861-3500
Fax: 514-861-3230
rlacroix@cticap.com
www.cticap.com
Ownership: Private
Year Founded: 1987
Number of Employees: 22
Stock Exchange Membership: Toronto Stock Exchange, TSX Venture Exchange
Profile: CTI is a full-service investment dealer specializing in bond & stock market research & trading & corporate finance.

Executives:
Viêt Buu, President/CEO
Robert Lacroix, Sr. Vice-President; 514-861-4644
Pierre Colas, Vice-President, Finance
Affiliated Companies:
CTI Mutual Funds

Cumberland Private Wealth Managment Inc.

Also listed under: *Financial Planning; Investment Management*

#300, 99 Yorkville Ave.
Toronto, ON M5R 3K5
416-929-1090
Fax: 416-929-1172
800-929-8296
info@cpwm.ca
www.cpwm.ca
Former Name: Cumberland Asset Management Corp.
Ownership: Private. Owned by Cumberland Partners Ltd.
Year Founded: 1998
Number of Employees: 45
Profile: Discretionary investment management services are provided. Cumberland Private Wealth Management serves over 800 high net worth families, plus their related entities in Canada and other countries. Cumberland has approximately $1,800,000,000 assets under management..

Executives:
Gerald R. Connor, CEO
Gordon Cunningham, President
Peter Jackson, Vice-President
John Poulter, Vice-President, Chief Investment Officer
Directors:
Gerald R. Connor, Chair
Gordon Cunningham
Peter Jackson
John Poulter

Demers Conseil inc.

Also listed under: *Pension & Money Management Companies*
#1120, 615, boul René-Lévesque ouest
Montréal, QC H3B 1P5
514-879-1702
Fax: 514-879-5977
info@demersconseil.com
www.demersconseil.com
Ownership: Private
Year Founded: 1992
Stock Exchange Membership: Montreal Exchange

Denarius Financial Group

#101, 1179, rue de la Montagne
Montréal, QC H3G 1Z2
514-868-8888
Fax: 514-868-0492
888-336-2744
info@denarius.com
www.denarius.com
Ownership: Private
Year Founded: 1995
Number of Employees: 14
Profile: Denarius is a corporate foreign exchange brokerage firm specializing in hedging foreign exchange transactions on a spot or forward basis for corporate clients.

Executives:
Rocco Piccolo, President
Vincenzo Piccolo, Exec. Vice-President
Tonia Piccolo, Sec.-Treas.

Disnat

2020, rue University, 9e étage
Montréal, QC H3A 2A5
514-842-2685
Fax: 514-842-1430
800-268-8471
disnat@disnat.com, disnatclassic@disnat.com
www.disnat.com
Ownership: Divison of Desjardins Securities Inc.
Year Founded: 1982
Profile: Discount brokerage services are offered to investors.

Branches:
Québec
Place de la Cité
#130, 2600, boul Laurier
Québec, QC G1V 4T3 Canada
418-650-5898
Fax: 418-650-9196
800-463-1887
disnat@disnat.com, disnatclassic@disnat.com

DNL Money Management Ltd.

Also listed under: *Pension & Money Management Companies*
38 Colonnade Rd. North
Nepean, ON K2E 7J6
613-727-1020
Fax: 613-727-1410
888-530-9777
info@dnlgroup.com
www.dnlgroup.com
Ownership: DNL Group, Nepean, ON.
Year Founded: 1977
Executives:
Denis Emard, President, Owner

Dominick & Dominick Securities Inc.

#1714, 150 York St.
Toronto, ON M5H 3S5
416-363-0201
Fax: 416-366-8279
Stock Exchange Membership: Toronto Stock Exchange, TSX Venture Exchange
Executives:
Paul L. Morgante, President/CEO

Richard Cosburn, CFO
Peter Ruys De Perez, Vice-President, Trading
Richard S. Papazian, Vice-President, Trading
Peter Burns, Manager, Operations
Maggie Artkin, Compliance Officer

Dubeau Capital et cie ltée

#450530, 5600, boul des Galeries
Québec, QC G2K 2H6
418-628-5533
Fax: 418-628-7844
800-463-0005
bonjour@dubeaucapital.com
www.dubeaucapital.com
Executives:
Stéphane Dubeau, Founding Partner; s.dubeau@dubeaucapital.com
Eric Caouette, Partner; e.caouette@dubeaucapital.com
Hugues Dubeau, Partner; h.dubeau@dubeaucapital.com
Branches:
Montréal
#1528, 1 Place Ville-Marie
Montréal, QC H3B 2B5 Canada
514-875-0770
Fax: 514-875-9093
888-875-9093

Dundee Private Investors Inc.

Also listed under: *Financial Planning*
1 Adelaide St. East, 27th Fl.
Toronto, ON M5C 2V9
416-350-3250
888-332-2661
inquiries@dundeewealth.com
www.dundeewealth.com
Former Name: Fortune Financial Corporation
Executives:
Ned Goodman, President/CEO & Chair, Dundee Wealth Management Inc.
Affiliated Companies:
Leadbeater Financial Services

Dundee Securities Corp.

#400, 20 Queen St. West
Toronto, ON M5H 3R3
416-350-3489
Fax: 416-350-3252
800-301-6745
inquiries@dundeewealth.com
www.dundeewealth.com
Ownership: Employee-owned
Year Founded: 1995
Number of Employees: 130
Stock Exchange Membership: Montreal Exchange, Toronto Stock Exchange, TSX Venture Exchange
Executives:
Donald Charter, President/CEO & Chair
Robert Sellars, Exec. Vice-President/COO & CFO
Affiliated Companies:
Community First Financial Planning

E*TRADE Canada

#1200, 60 Yonge St.
Toronto, ON M5E 1H5
416-214-6457
888-872-3388
etca-service@etrade.ca
www.etrade.ca
Also Known As: E*Trade Canada Securities Corporation
Stock Exchange Membership: Montreal Exchange, Toronto Stock Exchange, TSX Venture Exchange

e3m Investments Inc.

#1503, 2 St. Clair Ave. West
Toronto, ON M4V 1L5
416-972-7490
Fax: 416-972-7518
Stock Exchange Membership: Canadian Trading & Quotation System Inc, Toronto Stock Exchange
Profile: The company is a full service investment dealer, offering equity trading, futures trading & retail.

Executives:
Robert Goldberg, President/CEO
William Oates, Chief Financial Officer
Armando Cassin, Vice-President, Sales

East Asia Securities Inc.

East Asia Center
#102-103, 350 Hwy. 7 East
Richmond Hill, ON L4B 3N2
905-882-8182
Fax: 905-882-5220
info@hkbea.ca
ca.hkbea.com/securities_inc.html
Ownership: Wholly-owned subsidiary of The Bank of East Asia (Canada), Richmond Hill, ON.
Profile: More than 300 funds are available from fund companies. Investment in mutual funds is offered by fund sales representatives.

Branches:
Markham
Pacific Mall
#88B, 4300 Steeles Ave. East
Markham, ON L3R 0Y5 Canada
905-940-2218
Fax: 905-940-3030
Mississauga
#GR05, 25 Watline Ave.
Mississauga, ON L4Z 2Z1 Canada
905-890-2388
Fax: 905-890-8800
Richmond
6740 - No. 3 Rd.
Richmond, ON V6Y 2C2 Canada
604-278-9668
Fax: 604-276-8606
Toronto
Dynasty Center
#38, 8 Glen Watford Dr.
Toronto, ON M1S 2B9 Canada
416-298-6883
Fax: 416-298-6880
Vancouver
3396 Cambie St.
Vancouver, BC V5Z 2W5 Canada
604-709-9668
Fax: 604-709-9660

Edgestone Capital Partners

The Exchange Tower
PO Box 187
#600, 130 King St. West
Toronto, ON M5X 1A6
416-860-3740
Fax: 416-860-9838
info@edgestone.com
www.edgestone.com
Executives:
Sam Duboc, President, Managing Partner; 416-860-3760; sduboc@edgestone.com
Gilbert S. Palter, COO, Managing Partner; 416-860-3789; gpalter@edgestone.com
Sandra Bosela, Vice-President, Equity Fund; 416-860-3792; sbosela@edgestone.com
Leslie Giller, Vice-President; 416-860-3772; lgiller@edgestone.com
Michael Hollend, Vice-President, Venture Fund; 416-860-3785; mhollend@edgestone.com
Romeo Leemrijse, Vice-President, Mezzanine Fund; 416-860-3782; rleemrijse@edgestone.com
Cynthia Wong, Vice-President, Finance; 416-860-3752; cwong@edgestone.com
Sandra Cowan, General Counsel; 416-860-3770; scowan@edgestone.com
Branches:
Montréal
#500, 1010, rue Sherbrooke ouest
Montréal, QC H3A 2R7 Canada
514-282-2100
Fax: 514-282-1944

Edward Jones

Sussex Centre
#902, 90 Burnhamthorpe Rd. West
Mississauga, ON L5B 3C3
905-306-8600
Fax: 905-306-8575
www.edwardjones.com
Ownership: Private. Subsidiary of Edward Jones, U.S.
Year Founded: 1922
Number of Employees: 25,000
Stock Exchange Membership: Toronto Stock Exchange
Profile: Through a network of over 500 investment representatives across Canada, Edward Jones services individual clients exclusively.

Executives:
Gary Reamey, Principal, Canada
Douglas B. Bennett, Director, Operations
Scott Bowmam, Director, Recruiting
Donald Burwell, Director, Compliance
Steve Seifert, Director, Products & Services

Emerging Equities Inc.

TD Canada Trust Tower
#3000, 421 - 7 Ave. SW
Calgary, AB T2P 4K9
403-216-8200
Fax: 403-216-8234
Stock Exchange Membership: TSX Venture Exchange
Executives:
James Hartwell, President
Kaan Camlioglu, Chief Financial Officer

Evangeline Securities Limited

PO Box 3058
1051 King St.
Windsor, NS B0N 2T0
902-792-1035
Fax: 902-792-1809
Ownership: Private. Parent company is ESL Financial Ltd.
Year Founded: 1994
Number of Employees: 12
Revenues: $100-500 million
Executives:
T.I. Hughes, President
G.B. Morrison, Vice-President
E.K. Reading, Vice-President
P.R. King, Treasurer
Directors:
T.I. Hughes
G.B. Morrison
E.K. Reading

Everest Securities/ Valeurs mobilières Everest

594, rue Victoria, 1e étage
Saint-Lambert, QC J4P 2J6
450-465-1393
Fax: 450-465-4137
877-656-5823
courrier@gfeverest.com
www.gfeverest.com
Ownership: Subsidiary of Everest Financial Group, Montréal, QC.
Profile: Investment products & services are offered.

Executives:
Jean-Pierre Duguay, President; jpduguay@gfeverest.com
Steve Goulet, Financial Advisor
Gérald Belley, Investment Advisor
Raymond Corbeil, Investment Advisor
Claude Cyrenne, Investment Advisor
Serge Lamarche, Investment Advisor
Sylvain Trottier, Investment Advisor
Branches:
Drummondville
115, rue Hériot
Drummondville, QC J2C 1J5 Canada
819-479-0761
Fax: 819-477-4148
lmagnan@gfeverest.com
Louis Magnan, Investment Advisor
Québec
#210, 2795, boul Laurier
Québec, QC G1V 4M7 Canada
418-651-0680
Fax: 418-651-3019
800-268-0680
courrier@gfeverest.com
Martin Lachance, Investment Advisor

Excel Financial Growth Inc.

Also listed under: *Financial Planning*
#205, 80 Acadia Ave.
Markham, ON L3R 9V1
905-470-8222
Fax: 905-470-8306
www.excelfinancialgroup.ca

INVESTMENT MANAGEMENT

Excel Financial Growth Inc. (continued)

Profile: The licensed mutual fund dealer offers a range of professionally managed mutual funds. The company also offers the following financial planning services: retirement planning, estate planning, investment planning, education planning, taxation planning & tax return preparation.

Executives:
Marget Cheng, Contact, Investments
Pak Ming, Contact, Investments

Family Investment Planning Inc.

Also listed under: *Financial Planning*
#6, 195 Franklin Blvd.
Cambridge, ON N1R 8H3
519-740-1158
Fax: 519-740-9069
866-818-4798
info@fipi.ca
www.fipi.ca
Year Founded: 1998
Profile: Family Investment Planning is a mutual fund dealer. Financial planning services also include retirement, education & tax savings programs & life insurance.

Executives:
William (Bill) H. Maidment, CEO
Katherine A. Dooley, Vice-President, Administration, Chief Compliance Officer
Pauline Maidment, Coordinator, Group Benefits

Family Wealth Advisors Ltd.

Also listed under: *Financial Planning*
PO Box 126
22 Foster St.
Perth, ON K7H 3E3
613-267-1345
Fax: 613-267-3004
Profile: The company is an independent mutual fund dealership.

Branches:
Peterborough
PO Box K
270 George St. North, 2nd Fl.
Peterborough, ON K9H 3H1 Canada
705-742-2065
Fax: 705-742-0116
800-392-2224
www.bppeterborough.com
Philip Nuttall, Financial Advisor

Farm Mutual Financial Services Inc.

Also listed under: *Financial Planning*
PO Box 3637
1305 Bishop St. North
Cambridge, ON N3H 5C6
519-740-1194
Fax: 519-740-9272
866-777-6385
clientservices@fmfs.on.ca
www.fmfs.on.ca
Ownership: Private
Year Founded: 1996
Number of Employees: 15
Executives:
Don Howie, CEO
Betty Tomlinson, Manager, Compliance, Auditing & Training
Branches:
Ayr
1400 Northumberland St.
Ayr, ON N0B 1E0 Canada
519-632-9450
Fax: 519-632-9322
ayrfarm@golden.net
Dennis Charrette, Manager
Brockville
56 King St. East
Brockville, ON K6V 1B1 Canada
613-342-8911
Fax: 613-342-1551
800-654-1662
fmfsadmin@recorder.ca; gfs@ripnet.com
Heather Halladay, Manager
Caledonia
172 Argyle St. North
Caledonia, ON N3W 2J7 Canada
905-765-5000
Fax: 905-765-2220
interlake@sympatico.ca
Diane Sloat, Manager
Cambridge
12 Cambridge St.
Cambridge, ON N1R 3R7 Canada
519-623-3112
Fax: 519-623-4360
Colin Corner, Manager
Chatham
149 St. Clair St.
Chatham, ON N7L 3J4 Canada
519-355-0606
Fax: 519-355-0466
group1@ciaccess.com
Jamie Rainbird, Manager
Exeter
497 Main St. South
Exeter, ON N0M 1S1 Canada
519-235-4000
Fax: 519-235-4333
fmfs@execulink.com
John Manson, Manager
Newmarket
#11, 320 Harry Walker Pkwy. North
Newmarket, ON L3Y 7B3 Canada
905-895-0111
Fax: 905-895-4791
Richard Moore, Manager
Picton
13379 Loyalist Pkwy.
Picton, ON K0K 2T0 Canada
613-476-2223
Fax: 613-476-3160
fmfs.pic@sympatico.ca
Heather Halladay, Acting Manager
St Marys
PO Box 2758
293 Queen St. West
St Marys, ON N4X 1A5 Canada
519-284-4448
Fax: 519-284-4075
Jeff Swan, Manager
Strathroy
79 Caradoc St. North
Strathroy, ON N7G 2M5 Canada
519-245-5556
Fax: 519-245-3522
middwest@sympatico.ca
Lee Ann Jones, Manager

Faro Financial Group

Also listed under: *Financial Planning*
315, boul Brunswick
Montréal, QC H9R 5M7
514-694-7606
Fax: 514-694-1630
Year Founded: 1998
Profile: Personal investment advice is offered related to financial planning. Mutual funds are among the products provided.

Executives:
Mike Purvis, President

Feinberg Financial

Also listed under: *Financial Planning*
#1507, 155 Carlton St.
Winnipeg, MB R3C 3H8
204-942-0904
Fax: 204-942-8329
866-942-0904
Ownership: Private
Year Founded: 1974
Number of Employees: 2
Assets: Under $1 million Year End: 20051010
Revenues: Under $1 million Year End: 20051010
Profile: Assets under administration total $20,000,000. Affiliated with IQON Financail Inc.

Executives:
Denzil Feinberg, CFP RFP, Proprietor; dfeinberg@aol.com
Randy Penner, Administrator; randypennerff@aol.com

FIMAT Canada Inc.

#1930, 1501, av McGill College
Montréal, QC H3A 3M8
514-841-6200
Fax: 514-841-6254
www.fimat.com
Former Name: FIMAT Produits Dérivés Canada Inc.
Ownership: Wholly owned by Société Générale.
Stock Exchange Membership: Montreal Exchange, Toronto Stock Exchange, TSX Venture Exchange, Winnepeg Commodities Exchange
Executives:
Jean-Pierre Gallardo, President/CEO
Mark Ashfield, Sr. Vice-President, Operations & Administration
Richard Audet, Sr. Vice-President, Marketing
Stan Casar, Sr. Vice-President, Manager, Winnipeg Office
Antoine Babule, Vice-President, Manager, Toronto Office
Benoit Carignan, Vice-President, Risk, Finances & Compliance

Claude Cyr, Vice-President, Electronic Trading
Jean-Pierre St-Cyr, Vice-President, Audit & Legal
Branches:
Toronto
#1000, 100 Yonge St.
Toronto, ON M5C 2W1 Canada
416-640-7400
Fax: 416-640-7499
Antoine Babule, Manager
Winnipeg
#515, 167 Lombard St
Winnipeg, MB R3B 0T6 Canada
204-943-4800
Fax: 204-956-7840
Stan Casar, Manager

Financial Architects Investments Inc.

Also listed under: *Financial Planning; Investment Management*

#807, 505 Consumers Rd.
Toronto, ON M2J 4V8
416-285-7011
Fax: 416-285-7653
866-346-2724
www.fai.ca
Executives:
Chand Misir, Chair
Gaya Misir, President; gayamisir@fai.ca
Abbi Castro, Administrator, Operations

First Asset Advisory Services Inc.

#810, 121 King St. West
Toronto, ON M5J 3T9
416-642-2967
Fax: 416-642-2968
Profile: The company specializes in creating custom, institutional-class investment solutions. Access to top-tier investment management firms is also offered.

Executives:
Lisa Langley, CEO

First Capital Financial

Also listed under: *Pension & Money Management Companies*
17B Manitoba St.
Bracebridge, ON P1L 1V3
705-646-0480
Fax: 705-646-0482
800-376-2293
martin@firstcapitalfinancial.ca
www.firstcapitalfinancial.ca
Profile: Services provided include wealth & risk management, and retirement & estate planning.

Executives:
Martin Weiler, President
Branches:
Gravenhurst
1st St. North
Gravenhurst, ON P1P 1H6 Canada
705-687-0630
Fax: 705-687-0671
greg@firstcapitalfinancial.ca
Greg Rasmussen, Investor Advisor Associate
Guelph
176 Woolwich St.
Guelph, ON N1H 3V5 Canada
519-829-1331
Fax: 519-829-3551
866-845-2751
martin@firstcapitalfinancial.ca

First Delta Securities Inc.
Also listed under: *Holding & Other Investment Companies*
#202, 386 Wilson St. East
Ancaster, ON L9G 2C2
905-304-0250
Fax: 905-304-4183
rboychuk@firstdelta.com
www.firstdelta.com
Ownership: Private
Year Founded: 1995
Profile: Investment professionals provide services for a clientele which consists of institutions, hedge funds & high net worth individuals.
Executives:
Russell C. Boychuk, Managing Director, CFO & COO; 905-304-0250

FirstEnergy Capital Corp.
#1100, 311 - 6th Ave. SW
Calgary, AB T2P 3H2
403-262-0600
Fax: 403-262-0633
webqueries@firstenergy.com
www.firstenergy.com
Ownership: Private
Year Founded: 1993
Number of Employees: 75
Stock Exchange Membership: Toronto Stock Exchange, TSX Venture Exchange
Executives:
James W. Davidson, CEO & Managing Director; 403-262-0672; jwdavidson@firstenergy.com
W. Brett Wilson, Chair & Managing Director; 403-262-0606; wbwilson@firstenergy.com
David G. Fenwick, Vice-President & Director, Institutional Trading; 403-262-0676; dgfenwick@firstenergy.com
Margaret Gal, Vice-President & Director, Finance; 403-262-0632; mhgal@firstenergy.com
Nicholas J. Johnson, Vice-President & Director, Corporate Finance; 403-262-0617; njjohnson@firstenergy.com
Ruby Wallis, Vice-President & Director, Compliance & Administration; 403-262-0631; rfwallis@firstenergy.com
M. Scott Bratt, Managing Director, Corporate Finance; 403-262-0645; msbratt@firstenergy.com
John Chambers, Managing Director, Corporate Finance; 403-262-0664; jschambers@firstenergy.com
Scott T. Inglis, Managing Director, Institutional Sales & Trading; 403-262-0621; stinglis@firstenergy.com
Martin P. Molyneaux, Managing Director, Institutional Research; 403-262-0629; mpmolyneaux@firstenergy.com
Kenneth W. Rowan, Managing Director, Institutional Sales; 403-262-0686; kwrowan@firstenergy.com
Rafi G. Tahmazian, Managing Director, Institutional Sales; 403-262-0684; rgtahmazian@firstenergy.com
Chandra A. Henry, Controller; 403-262-0623; cahenry@firstenergy.com

Fiscal Agents Ltd.
Also listed under: *Pension & Money Management Companies*
PO Box 5000
25 Lakeshore Rd. West
Oakville, ON L6K 5C7
905-844-7700
Fax: 905-844-8552
866-434-7225
mailroom@fiscalagents.com
www.fiscalagents.com
Year Founded: 1977
Profile: Investment advisory services are provided related to retirement planning, investment funds & life insurance.
Executives:
David Newman, Director, Information Services

Foresters Securities (Canada) Inc.
789 Don Mills Rd.
Toronto, ON M3C 1T9
416-429-3000
Fax: 416-429-4779
800-828-1540
service@foresters.biz
www.foresters.biz
Ownership: Wholly owned subsidiary of The Independent Order of Foresters, Toronto, ON.
Year Founded: 1874
Profile: Mutual & segregated funds, retirement & education planning & life insurance are some products & services offered. The financial services organization operates in Canada, USA & UK.
Executives:
George Mohacsi, President/CEO
Lynn Haight, CFO/COO
Nicholas J. DiRenzo, Sr. Vice-President, North American Sales
Suanne M. Nielsen, Sr. Vice-President, Human Resources & Communications
Paul M. Winokur, Sr. Vice-President, Chief Actuary
Sharon Giffen, Vice-President, Marketing
Gail Johnson Morris, Vice-President, Service Delivery Division
Katharine Rounthwaite, Vice-President, General Counsel
Directors:
W. Ross Walker, Chair
Bernard E. Bloom
James Daugherty
William B. Foster
Richard M. Freeborough
Patrick W. Kenny
Kash Manchuk
Louise L. McCormick
Barbara J. McDougall
Christopher H. McElvaine
John P. Meyerholz
E. Irene Miles
George Mohacsi
David E. Morrison
Branches:
Burlington
#402, 3027 Harvester Rd.
Burlington, ON L7N 3G7 Canada
905-333-2861
Burnaby
#120, 4401 Still Creek Dr.
Burnaby, BC V5C 6G9 Canada
604-320-3300
Calgary
#225, 10655 Southport Rd. SW
Calgary, AB T2W 4Y1 Canada
403-250-8666
Edmonton
Oxford Tower
#1311, 10235 - 101 St. NW
Edmonton, AB T5J 3G1 Canada
780-425-2948
London
#214, 395 Wellington Rd.
London, ON N6C 4P9 Canada
519-680-2257
Markham
#308, 3000 Steeles Ave. East
Markham, ON L3R 4T9 Canada
905-474-3665
Mississauga
Bldg. 11
#201, 5045 Orbitor Dr.
Mississauga, ON L4W 4Y4 Canada
905-238-2649
Waterloo
#103, 60 Bridgeport Rd. East
Waterloo, ON N2J 2J9 Canada
519-886-7114

Fortraco International Marketing Inc.
Also listed under: *Financial Planning; Investment Management*
#260, 2113, Saint Regis
Montréal, QC H9B 2M9
514-421-3950
Fax: 514-683-6316
800-731-2438
info@wealthstarfs.com
www.tenstar.ca
Also Known As: Executive Financial Services
Ownership: Private
Year Founded: 1985
Number of Employees: 2
Assets: $10-50 million
Revenues: Under $1 million
Executives:
Ronald Greeley, President; 514-421-3430; rgreeley@wealthstarfs.com

Foster & Associates Financial Services Inc.
Also listed under: *Financial Planning*
#506, 335 Bay St.
Toronto, ON M5H 2R3
416-369-1980
Fax: 416-369-1070
800-559-8853
tmanning@fostergroup.ca
www.fostergroup.ca
Ownership: Private.
Year Founded: 1994
Number of Employees: 15
Stock Exchange Membership: Toronto Stock Exchange, TSX Venture Exchange
Executives:
Briar Foster, President
Frank Florio, Vice-President
John Gallagher, Vice-President
Tony Manning, Vice-President
Directors:
Frank Florio
Briar Foster
John Gallagher
Tony Manning

Fraser Mackenzie Limited
#200, 83 Yonge St.
Toronto, ON M5C 1S8
416-955-4777
Fax: 416-955-0203
877-955-4777
info@frasermackenzie.com
www.frasermackenzie.com
Stock Exchange Membership: Toronto Stock Exchange, TSX Venture Exchange
Executives:
Geoff Plant-Richmond, Managing Director
Paul Bradley, COO & Director, Research
James Muir, Chief Compliance Officer
Mark Stableforth, Head, Trading

Friedberg Mercantile Group
Also listed under: *Investment Fund Companies*
BCE Place
PO Box 866
#250, 181 Bay St.
Toronto, ON M5J 2T3
416-364-2700
Fax: 416-364-5385
Ownership: Private
Year Founded: 1971
Number of Employees: 50
Stock Exchange Membership: Montreal Exchange, Toronto Stock Exchange, TSX Venture Exchange
Profile: The Group is one of Canada's largest futures & options discount broker.
Friedberg:
Currency Fund
RRSP Eligible; Inception Year: 1994; Fund Managers: Albert D. Friedberg
Diversified (US$) Fund
RRSP Eligible; Inception Year: 1996; Fund Managers: Albert D. Friedberg
Foreign Bond Fund
RRSP Eligible; Inception Year: 1996; Fund Managers: Albert D. Friedberg
Precious Metals Fund
RRSP Eligible; Inception Year: 1992; Fund Managers: Albert D. Friedberg
Futures (US$) Fund
RRSP Eligible; Inception Year: 1998; Fund Managers: Albert D. Friedberg
Equity Hedge (US$) Fund
RRSP Eligible; Inception Year: 1998; Fund Managers: Albert D. Friedberg
International Securities (US$) Fund
RRSP Eligible; Inception Year: 1998; Fund Managers: Albert D. Friedberg
Global-Macro Hedge (US$) Fund
RRSP Eligible; Inception Year: 2002; Fund Managers: Albert D. Friedberg
The First Mercantile Currency Fund
RRSP Eligible; Inception Year: 1985; Fund Managers: Albert D. Friedberg

Friedberg Mercantile Group (continued)
Niagara Comfort Class B Fund
RRSP Eligible; Inception Year: 1999; Fund Managers:
Albert D. Friedberg

FundEX Investments Inc.
#208, 25 Centurian Dr.
Markham, ON L3R 5N8
905-305-1651
Fax: 905-305-1698
800-324-6048
rcorbett@fundex.com
www.fundex.com
Ownership: Private.
Year Founded: 1995
Profile: The independent mutual fund dealership services financial planners throughout Canada.

Executives:
Michael Greer, President; mgreer@fundex.com
Christopher Enright, Exec. Vice-President; cenright@fundex.com
Robert Corbett, Vice-President, Sales
David Hawkins, Vice-President, Business Development; dhawkins@fundex.com

Futureworth Financial Planners Corp.
Also listed under: *Financial Planning*
#500, 1130 West Pender St.
Vancouver, BC V6E 4A4
604-684-3372
Fax: 604-669-6978
www.futureworthfinancial.com
Ownership: Wholly owned by Western Pacific Trust Company, Vancouver, BC.
Year Founded: 1989
Profile: Products & services provided by the retail financial services company are related to investment & life insurance. Futureworth is a registered Mutual Fund Dealer.

Gary Bean Securities Ltd.
Also listed under: *Financial Planning*
588 Main St. South
Exeter, ON N0M 1S1
519-235-4099
Fax: 519-235-4813
800-710-5216
www.garybean.on.ca
Ownership: Private
Year Founded: 1997
Profile: The independent securities firm provides investment management & integrated wealth management services. Products include bonds, income trusts, mutual funds, cash & GICs, speculative securities & common shares.

Executives:
Gary Bean, President
Suzanne Mathers, CA, Chief Financial Officer
Todd Robinson, Investment Advisor
Adam Skillen, Chartered Financial Analyst, Associate Portfolio Manager

Branches:
Erin
5328 9th Line, RR #2
Erin, ON N0B 1T0 Canada
519-833-2166
Fax: 519-833-7434
877-278-3666
Scott Keir, Investment Advisor

Hanover
192 - 10th St.
Hanover, ON N4N 1N7 Canada
519-364-4383
Fax: 519-364-3013
800-661-4960
Doug Williamson, Investment Advisor

London
#100, 256 Pall Mall St.
London, ON N6A 5P6 Canada
519-642-0626
Fax: 519-642-3880
800-276-0545
Paul Miller, Investment Advisor

Generation Financial Corp.
Also listed under: *Financial Planning*
Dominion Place
#240, 906 - 12th Ave. SW
Calgary, AB T2R 1K7
403-229-0501
Fax: 403-229-0573
tmcdonald@genfingroup.com
www.genfingroup.com/
Year Founded: 1998
Profile: The company is a privately owned mutual fund dealer. It has a network of 110 independent planning professionals, who are located in British Columbia, Alberta, Saskatchewan, Manitoba & the North West Territories.

Executives:
Dennis Albinati, CFP, President
Tammy McDonald, Administrative Manager

Genuity Capital Markets/ Marchés des capitaux Genuity
Also listed under: *Financial Planning*
Scotia Plaza
PO Box 1007
#4900, 40 King St. West
Toronto, ON M5H 3Y2
416-603-6000
Fax: 416-603-3099
877-603-6001
investor.relations@genuitycm.com
www.genuitycm.com
Ownership: Private.
Stock Exchange Membership: Toronto Stock Exchange, TSX Venture Exchange
Profile: The independent firm offers the following services to its corporate clients: investment banking, equity research resources, & institutional sales and trading. USA offices of Genuity Capital Markets USA Corp. are located in Boston, Massachusetts & New York, New York.

Executives:
David Kassie, Chair/CEO
Conrad Beyleveldt, Chief Financial Officer
Tom Briant, Chief Compliance Officer

Branches:
Calgary
Stock Exchange Tower
#1700, 300 - 5th Ave. SW
Calgary, AB T2P 3C4
403-266-3400
Fax: 403-266-1755

Montréal
#3000, 1800, av McGill College
Montréal, QC H3A 3J6
514-281-3250
Fax: 514-281-3022

Vancouver
Bentall Tower 5
PO Box 16
#1068, 550 Burrard St.
Vancouver, BC V6C 2B5
604-331-1444
Fax: 604-331-1446

Global Maxfin Investments Inc.
#800, 100 Allstate Pkwy.
Markham, ON L3R 6H3
416-741-1544
Fax: 416-847-0997
866-666-5266
www.globalmaxfin.ca
Profile: The mutual fund dealer is affiliated with the following companies: Global Insurance Solutions Inc., Global Educational Marketing Corporation & Global Maxfin Capital Inc.

Executives:
Bruce Day, Exec. Vice-President; dbday@globalfinancial.ca
Dagmar M. Mikkila, Chief Compliance Officer; dagmarm@globalfinancial.ca
Vije Kandiah, Sr. Manager, Operations; vijek@globalfinancial.ca
Glenn Moore, Regional Director, Sales
Eugene Park, Sr. Officer, Compliance; eugenep@globalfinancial.ca
Caroline Wheeler, Specialist, Advisor Services; carolinew@globalfinancial.ca

Branches:
Burnaby
#102, 4940 Canada Way
Burnaby, BC V5G 4K6 Canada
604-430-5475
Fax: 604-433-0711

Calgary
#136, 1935 - 32nd Ave. NE
Calgary, AB T2E 7C8 Canada
403-219-3131
Fax: 403-250-6779

Halifax
13 Kirk Rd.
Halifax, NS B3P 1A5 Canada
902-461-1313
Fax: 902-461-4728

Mississauga
2444 Hurontario St.
Mississauga, ON L5B 2V1 Canada
416-741-1544
Fax: 416-847-0997
866-666-5266

Montréal
#100, 555, boul Dr.-Frederik-Philips
Montréal, QC H4M 2X4 Canada
514-747-1222
Fax: 514-747-1236

Global Securities Corporation
Also listed under: *Financial Planning*
Three Bentall Centre
PO Box 49049
#1100, 595 Burrard St.
Vancouver, BC V7X 1C4
604-689-5400
Fax: 604-689-5401
800-455-5778
inquiries@globalsec.com
www.globalsec.com
Ownership: Private
Year Founded: 1987
Number of Employees: 130
Stock Exchange Membership: Canadian Trading & Quotation System Inc, Montreal Exchange, Toronto Stock Exchange, TSX Venture Exchange
Profile: The company is a full service brokerage firm which provides the following services: securities including all Canadian mutual funds, all types of fixed income & equities & options on all world exchanges, with research facilities; corporate finance; & mergers & acquisitions activities.

Executives:
Art M. Smolensky, Chair
Douglas Garrod, President
Duncan Boggs, CFO

Branches:
Delta
718 Tsawwassen Beach Rd.
Delta, BC V4M 4C7 Canada
604-943-0413
Fax: 604-943-0270

Nanaimo
253 Milton St.
Nanaimo, BC V9R 2K5 Canada
250-754-7723
Fax: 250-754-7757

North Vancouver
#430, 171 West Esplanade
North Vancouver, BC V7M 3J9 Canada
604-988-2088
Fax: 604-988-2082

Penticton
#101, 543 Ellis St.
Penticton, BC V2A 4M4 Canada
250-492-2585
Fax: 250-492-8458

Port Alberni
4994 Argyle St.
Port Alberni, BC V9Y 1V7 Canada
604-723-4970
Fax: 604-723-1151

Port Coquitlam
#6209, 2850 Shaughnessy St.
Port Coquitlam, BC V3C 6K5 Canada
604-552-9600
Fax: 604-552-3502
888-809-6541

Prince George
#401, 1777 Third Ave.
Prince George, BC V2L 3G7 Canada
250-614-0111
Fax: 250-614-0110
866-614-0111

Quesnel
#3, 334 Front St.
Quesnel, BC V2J 3K3 Canada
250-992-7448
Fax: 250-992-7458
Victoria - Boleskine St.
612 Boleskine St.
Victoria, BC V8Z 1E8 Canada
250-475-3088
Fax: 604-677-5788
Victoria - Douglas St.
#550, 2950 Douglas St.
Victoria, BC V8T 4N4 Canada
250-380-3801
Fax: 604-677-6096
West Vancouver
280 Hiawatha Dr.
West Vancouver, BC V7P 1E1 Canada
604-987-4774
Fax: 604-987-7273
Westbank
#2, 2413 Main St.
Westbank, BC V4T 2G3 Canada
250-768-1882
Fax: 250-768-2208
Williams Lake
#203, 197 - 2nd Ave. North
Williams Lake, BC V2G 1Z5 Canada
250-392-1012
Fax: 250-392-1090

GMP Securities L.P.

#1100, 145 King St. West
Toronto, ON M5H 1J8
416-367-8600
Fax: 416-367-8164
888-301-3244
www.gmponline.com
Former Name: Griffiths McBurney & Partners Ltd.
Ownership: GMP Capital Trust
Year Founded: 1995
Stock Exchange Membership: Canadian Trading & Quotation System Inc, Montreal Exchange, Toronto Stock Exchange, TSX Venture Exchange,
Executives:
Eugene C. McBurney, MA, LLB, Chair
Kevin M. Sullivan, BA, LLB CFA, CEO
Thomas A. Budd, MBA, CMA, President & Vice-Chair, Head, Investment Banking
J. Robert Fraser, MBA, Vice-Chair, Investment Banking
Paul Pew, CA CFA, Vice-Chair, Investment Banking
Dan Tsubouchi, MBA, Vice-Chair & Director, Research
Michael A. Wekerle, Vice-Chair, Institutional Trading
Leo Ciccone, Chief Compliance Officer, Managing Director
Christina Drake, CFO, Corporate Secretary
Branches:
Calgary
#1600, 500 - 4th Ave. SW
Calgary, AB T2P 2V6 Canada
403-543-3030
Fax: 403-543-3038
Montréal
#1900, 1002, rue Sherbrooke ouest
Montréal, QC H3A 3L6 Canada
514-288-7774
Fax: 514-288-1574

Golden Capital Securities Limited

Also listed under: *Financial Planning; Investment Management*

#168, 1177 West Hastings St.
Vancouver, BC V6E 2K3
604-688-1898
Fax: 604-682-8874
goldenfeedback@goldencapital.com
www.goldencapital.com
Ownership: Private
Year Founded: 1990
Stock Exchange Membership: Montreal Exchange, Toronto Stock Exchange, TSX Venture Exchange
Profile: Golden Capital serves both personal & corporate clients. Services include research, trading, corporate finance & money management servics.

Executives:
Peter Chu, President/CEO
Leo Wong, Chief Compliance Officer
Tony Chan, Exec. Vice-President
Jack Finkelstein, Vice-President
Daniel Siu, Vice-President

Goodreid Investment Cousel Corp.

Also listed under: *Financial Planning*
#310, 145 Lakeshore Rd. East
Oakville, ON L6J 1H3
905-338-9090
Fax: 905-338-1660
Profile: Goodreid Investment serves the investing needs of private investors & small institutions. The organization manages US equities.

Executives:
Gordon Reid, President/CEO
Directors:
Tony Brebner, Chair

Goodwood Inc.(GWD)

#201, 212 King St. West
Toronto, ON M5H 1K5
416-203-2022
Fax: 416-203-0734
866-681-4393
Other Information: 905-214-8150 (Phone, Dealer Services); 905-214-8100 (Fax, Dealer Services)
invest@goodwoodfunds.com
www.goodwoodfunds.com
Former Name: Rabin Puccetti & Partners Inc.
Year Founded: 1996
Executives:
Peter H. Puccetti, CFA, Chair, Chief Investment Officer
J. Cameron MacDonald, CFA, President/CEO
Curt Cumming, Partner, Trading
Robert Kittel, CA, CFA, Partner, Research Analyst

Guardian Capital Group Limited

Also listed under: *Pension & Money Management Companies; Investment Management*
PO Box 201
#3100, Commerce Ct. West
Toronto, ON M5L 1E8
416-364-8341
Fax: 416-947-0601
Former Name: a
Ownership: Public. Major shareholders: Minic Investments Ltd. (47.9 interest); Rosemary Short (11.8% interest) & Joseph Rotman (16.8% interest).
Year Founded: 1962
Number of Employees: 97
Assets: $100-500 million Year End: 20051231
Revenues: $50-100 million Year End: 20051231
Stock Symbol: GCG
Profile: The holding company is engaged, through subsidiaries & affiliates, in the following areas: the management of pension funds & private client portfolios; the provision of trust & corporate services; the sale & distribution of mutual funds & securities; the investment of its own assets in equity markets & private placement situations. The following companies are wholly owned subsidiaries: Alexandria Bancorp Limited, Guardian Capital Advisors LP, & Guardian Capital LP. Another investment is Worldsource Holdings Corp. (93.9% interest).

Executives:
John M. Christodoulou, CEO
Sam K. Greiss, Sr. Vice-President, Operations & Corporate Development
George Mavroudis, Sr. Vice-President, Strategic Planning & Development
C. Verner Christensen, Vice-President, Finance, Secretary
Michael Denuzzo, Controller
Directors:
John M. Christodoulou, Chair
James Anas
F.D. Barrett
James W. McCutcheon
Michel Sales
Peter Stormonth Darling

Hampton Securities Limited

#1800, 141 Adelaide St. West
Toronto, ON M5H 3L5
416-862-7800
Fax: 416-862-8650
877-225-0229
info@hamptonsecurities.com
www.hamptonsecurities.com
Number of Employees: 25
Stock Exchange Membership: Montreal Exchange, Toronto Stock Exchange, TSX Venture Exchange
Executives:
Michael Deeb, Chair
Peter Deeb, President/CEO
Manni Buttar, CFO
Michael Acerra, Sr. Vice-President, Trading
Robert Sherman, Sr. Vice-President, Private Client Group

Haywood Securities Inc.

#2000, 400 Burrard St.
Vancouver, BC V6C 3A6
604-697-7100
Fax: 604-697-7499
800-663-9499
needtoknow@haywood.com
www.haywood.com
Ownership: Employee-owned.
Year Founded: 1981
Number of Employees: 250+
Stock Exchange Membership: Canadian Trading & Quotation System Inc, Montreal Exchange, Toronto Stock Exchange, TSX Venture Exchange
Profile: The firm is associated with companies from the mining, oil & gas, biotechnology, telecommunication & technology sectors.

Executives:
John Tognetti, Chair; 604-697-7420
Rob Blanchard, President; 604-697-7170
Charles J. Dunlap, Chief Financial Officer; 604-697-7108
Aman Lidder, Vice-President, Operations; 604-697-7114
Bruce Thompson, Vice-President, Compliance; 604-697-6012
Elaine Anderson, Manager, Corporate Finance; 604-697-7140
Marilyn Dryhurst, Manager, Securities; 604-697-7161
Mark Maisonville, Manager, Compliance; 604-697-7105
Branches:
Calgary
#301, 808 First St. SW
Calgary, AB T2P 1M9 Canada
403-509-1900
Fax: 403-509-1999
877-604-0044
Tony Migliarese, Vice-President
Toronto
Bay Wellington Tower, BCE Place
#2910, 181 Bay St.
Toronto, ON M5J 2T3 Canada
416-507-2300
Fax: 416-507-2399
866-615-2225
Rick Paolone, Director, Institutional Sales

HDL Capital Corporation

#402, 116 Simcoe St.
Toronto, ON M5H 4E2
416-599-7330
Fax: 416-599-7957
bernie@hdlcapital.com
www.hdlcapital.com
Ownership: Private
Year Founded: 1993
Number of Employees: 3
Profile: Clients include both private & public corporations from a broad range of industries.

Executives:
Bernie Grybowski, President; bernie@hdlcapital.com
Tyler Lang, Vice-President; tyler@hdlcapital.com
Helen Simoulidis, Office Manager; helen@hdlcapital.com

Hesselink & Associates

Also listed under: *Financial Planning*
PO Box 69
11 Wellington St. South
Drayton, ON N0G 1P0
519-638-3328
Fax: 519-638-5070
admin@hesselink.ca
www.hesselink.ca
Former Name: C.A. Hesselink
Ownership: Private
Year Founded: 1989
Number of Employees: 5
Assets: $10-50 million Year End: 20051010

Hesselink & Associates (continued)
Revenues: Under $1 million Year End: 20051010
Executives:
Ab Hesselink, Chartered Financial Planner; ab@hesselink.ca
Jason Jack, Chartered Financial Planner; jason@hesselink.ca

HSBC Securities Canada Inc.

Royal York Hotel
#500, 70 York St.
Toronto, ON M5J 2S9
905-940-4722
Fax: 416-868-5484
888-310-4722
info@hsbc.com
www.hsbc.com
Ownership: Foreign. HSBC Holdings U.K.
Stock Exchange Membership: Montreal Exchange, TSX Venture Exchange
Executives:
Lindsay Gordon, President/CEO
Sean O'Sullivan, COO, North American Sales Director
Jeff Dowle, Exec. Vice-President & Head, Commercial Banking, Vanvoucer, National Director
Brad Meredith, Exec. Vice-President, Head, Corporate Investment Banking & Markets, Toronto, Sales Director; 416-868-5494
Geoff Hoy, Sr. Vice-President & Manager, Main Branch & Ontario Region
Branches:
Calgary
First Alberta Place
#2200, 777 - 8 Ave. SW
Calgary, AB T2P 3R5 Canada
403-218-3838
Fax: 403-237-6349
800-308-6671
Campbell River
1000 Shoppers Row
Campbell River, BC V9W 2C6 Canada
250-286-0011
Fax: 250-286-7466

Edmonton
Bell Tower
#205, 10104 - 103 Ave.
Edmonton, AB T5J 0H8 Canada
780-421-4455
Fax: 780-425-8692
800-267-5443
Kelowna
384 Bernard Ave.
Kelowna, BC V1Y 6N5 Canada
250-712-4900
Fax: 250-712-4909
800-709-8400
Langley
20045 Langley By-Pass
Langley, BC V3A 8R6 Canada
604-539-8888
Fax: 604-539-8899
877-512-4722
Mississauga
4550 Hurontario St.
Mississauga, ON L5R 4E4 Canada
905-568-8232
Fax: 905-568-7636
866-888-4722
Montréal
#300, 2001, av McGill College
Montréal, QC H3A 1G1 Canada
Fax: 514-339-6085
888-813-7171
Nanaimo
#101, 6551 Aulds Rd.
Nanaimo, BC V9T 6K2 Canada
250-390-8888
Fax: 250-390-8899
North Vancouver
1577 Lonsdale Ave.
North Vancouver, BC V7M 2J2 Canada
604-903-7091
Fax: 604-903-7099
866-847-4722
Ottawa
#300, 30 Metcalfe St.
Ottawa, ON K1P 5L4 Canada
613-238-5656
Fax: 613-238-2867
888-596-3333
Penticton
201 Main St.
Penticton, BC V2A 5B1 Canada
250-770-8000
Fax: 250-770-8008
866-854-4722
Port Coquitlam
Poco Place
#41, 2755 Lougheed Hwy.
Port Coquitlam, BC V3B 5Y9 Canada
604-949-8888
Fax: 604-949-8899
866-851-4722
Richmond
6168 No. 3 Rd., 2nd Fl.
Richmond, BC V6Y 2B3 Canada
604-658-8050
Fax: 604-658-8058
866-850-4722
Richmond Hill
#206, 330 Hwy. 7 East
Richmond Hill, ON L4B 3P8 Canada
905-731-5728
Fax: 905-731-0794
888-727-3238
Saskatoon
#202, 321A - 21st St. East
Saskatoon, SK S7K 0C1 Canada
306-249-6610
Fax: 306-249-6617
877-674-9440
Surrey
#410, 3099 - 152 St.
Surrey, BC V4P 3K1 Canada
604-949-8888
Fax: 604-949-8899
866-850-4722
Toronto - Victoria Park Ave.
3640 Victoria Park Ave.
Toronto, ON M2H 3B2 Canada
416-754-4016
Fax: 416-756-1282
888-463-5553
Toronto - York Mills Rd.
#100, 300 York Mills Rd.
Toronto, ON M2L 2Y5 Canada
416-864-2700
Fax: 416-447-2950
Toronto - York St.
70 York St., 9th Fl.
Toronto, ON M5J 1S9 Canada
416-868-4898
Fax: 416-864-2706
800-387-1883
Unionville
Peachtree Centre
#B5, 8390 Kennedy Rd.
Unionville, ON L3R 0W4 Canada
905-479-8076
Fax: 905-479-9811
Vancouver - Granville St.
5688 Granville St.
Vancouver, BC V6M 3C5 Canada
604-656-8180
Fax: 604-656-8199
Vancouver - Main St.
Wayfoong House
608 Main St., 5th Fl.
Vancouver, BC V6A 2V3 Canada
Fax: 604-717-8708
866-856-4722
Vancouver - West Georgia St.
885 West Georgia St., 6th Fl.
Vancouver, BC V6C 3E9 Canada
604-623-3284
Fax: 604-623-3212
866-858-4722

Vancouver - West Georgia St.
PO Box 1018
#1110, 885 West Georgia St.
Vancouver, BC V6C 3E8 Canada
604-685-6371
Fax: 604-685-0682
888-286-7833
Glenn Fung, Exec. Vice-President, Private Client Services, Western Canada
Vernon
3321 - 30th Ave.
Vernon, BC V1T 2C9 Canada
250-503-5888
Fax: 250-503-5899
866-853-4722
Victoria
#102, 771 Vernon Ave. 2nd Fl.
Victoria, BC V8X 5A7 Canada
250-953-5050
Fax: 250-953-5099
888-391-9311

Hub Capital Inc.

***Also listed under:** Pension & Money Management Companies*
#1001, 3700 Steeles Ave. West
Woodbridge, ON L4L 8M9
905-264-1634
Fax: 905-264-0864
800-561-2405
www.hubfinancial.com
Profile: Hub Capital is the wealth management division of Hub Financial Inc. The division is a mutual fund dealership.
Executives:
Terri DiFlorio, President; terri.diflorio@hubfinancial.com
Jeff Botosan, Exec. Vice-President, Chief Operations Officer; jeff.botosan@hubfinancial.com
John Lutrin, Exec. Vice-President, Chief Marketing Officer; john.lutrin@hubfinancial.com
Kim Fernandes, Vice-President; kim.fernandes@hubfinancial.com
Cheryl Hamilton, Vice-President, Chief Compliance Officer; cheryl.hamilton@hubfinancial.com
Branches:
Calgary
#300, 4723 - 1st St. SW
Calgary, AB T2G 4Y8 Canada
403-262-4466
Fax: 403-266-7541
800-661-9228
Judy Simpson, Vice-President
London
#101, 557 Southdale Rd. East
London, ON N6E 1A2 Canada
519-641-3400
Fax: 519-641-3334
800-661-3400
Paul Sincerbox, Director, Marketing, Wealth Management
Montréal
#625, 8000, boul Décarie
Montréal, QC H4P 2S4 Canada
514-374-3848
Fax: 514-382-9151
800-361-4052
Sylvain Decoste, Director, Marketing, Wealth Management
New Westminster
#550, 628 - 6th Ave.
New Westminster, BC V3M 6Z1 Canada
604-526-4115
Fax: 604-526-4915
877-888-1222
Gord Johnson, Marketing Director
Vancouver
#800, 1185 West Georgia St.
Vancouver, BC V6E 4E6 Canada
604-684-0086
Fax: 604-684-9286
800-667-0310
Christa Hewitt, Director, Marketing, Wealth Management
Victoria
#201, 755 Queens St.
Victoria, BC V8T 1M2 Canada
250-414-7272
Fax: 250-414-7270
800-661-7410
Heidi Zealand, Administrator, Marketing, Wealth Management

Independent Trading Group
#1212, 55 Yonge St.
Toronto, ON M5E 1J4
416-941-0046
Fax: 416-941-1556
Ownership: Private
Stock Exchange Membership: Toronto Stock Exchange
Profile: Services include pro trading, institutional trading, liability trading, jitneying & clearing.

Executives:
Matthew J. Taugher, President/CEO
Doug Christie, Vice-President/COO
Dave Houlding, Vice-President, Partner
Brian Jones, Vice President, Partner
Rob Russell, Vice-President, Partner
Jack Stevens, Vice President, Partner

Industrial Alliance Securities Inc./ L'Industrielle Alliance Valeurs mobilières inc.
CP 1907, Terminus Stn. Terminus
1080, Grande Allée ouest
Québec, QC GIK 7M3
418-684-5171
Fax: 418-684-5280
866-684-5171
www.inalco.com/english/individual/investment/securities/securities.jsp
Ownership: Wholly owned subsidiary of Industrial Alliance Insurance & Financial Services Inc.
Stock Exchange Membership: Montreal Exchange, Toronto Stock Exchange
Profile: The full-service brokerage firm provides a broad spectrum of financial products & services, including stocks, mutual funds, strip bonds, treasury bills, fixed-income securities, bank acceptances, guaranteed investment certificates, & options.

Executives:
Gaétan Plante, President
Lise Douville, Exec. Vice-President
Richard Roy, Sr. Vice-President
Walter Bobko, Vice-President
Pierre Demers, Vice-President
Hervé Pizem, Vice-President
Daniel Plante, Vice-President
Fred Roberts, Vice-President
Branches:
Halifax
#300, 5991 Spring Garden Rd.
Halifax, NS B3H 1Y6
902-420-1544
Fax: 902-425-8542
877-275-1544
Tom Lynch, Exec. Vice-President
Mississauga
#900, 350 Burnhamthorpe Rd. West
Mississauga, ON L5B 3J1
905-566-3500
Fax: 905-276-2907
Montréal
#350, 2200, av McGill College
Montréal, QC H3A 3P8 Canada
514-499-1066
Fax: 514-499-1071
800-361-7465

Info Financial Consulting Group Inc.
Also listed under: *Financial Planning*
#PH8, 350 Hwy. 7 East
Richmond Hill, ON L4B 3N2
905-886-8811
Fax: 905-886-7532
inquiry@infofinancial.com
www.infofinancial.com
Ownership: Private.
Year Founded: 1992
Number of Employees: 6
Profile: The investment consultant is involved in investment banking. The group has 90 sales advisors.

Executives:
Gary Yung, President
Branches:
Mississauga
#38, 145 Traders Blvd.
Mississauga, ON L4Z 3L3 Canada
905-507-6018
Fax: 905-712-9536
Richmond Hill
Jubilee Square
#218, 300 West Beaver Creek Rd.
Richmond Hill, ON L4B 3B1 Canada
905-326-5428
Fax: 905-326-5405

Instinet Canada Limited
The Exchange Tower
#2100, 130 King St. West
Toronto, ON M5X 1E3
416-368-2211
Fax: 416-368-2562
877-467-8463
Other Information: 888-819-3202 (Toll Free, Institutional Trading)

www.instinet.com
Ownership: Private. Part of Instinet, LLC, New York, NY, USA.
Year Founded: 1969
Stock Exchange Membership: Toronto Stock Exchange
Profile: The agency broker provides enhanced trading services.

Executives:
Mike Plunkett, President, North America

Integral Wealth Securities Limited
Also listed under: *Financial Planning*
Waterpark Place
PO Box 18
#1305, 20 Bay St.
Toronto, ON M5J 2N8
416-203-2000
Fax: 416-203-5835
www.integralwealth.com
Ownership: Advisor-owned.
Stock Exchange Membership: Canadian Trading & Quotation System Inc, Toronto Stock Exchange, TSX Venture Exchange
Profile: Services include investment banking, portfolio investment management, fixed income & retail. Some financial products are stocks, income trusts, mutual funds, bonds, GICs, options, life insurance & annuities.

Executives:
David Cusson, Chief Compliance Officer

Interactive Brokers Canada Inc.
#2106, 1800, av McGill College
Montréal, QC H3A 3J6
515-287-5900
Fax: 514-287-0152
877-745-4222
help@interactivebrokers.com
www.interactivebrokers.ca
Ownership: Private. Interactive Brokers Group LLC
Year Founded: 2002
Number of Employees: 500
Revenues: $10-50 million
Stock Exchange Membership: Toronto Stock Exchange
Executives:
Mark Bennett, Vice-President
Jean-Francois Bernier, Managing Director
Directors:
Mark Bennett
Jean-Francois Bernier
Paul J. Brody
Earl H. Nemser
Thomas Peterffy
Affiliated Companies:
Timber Hill Canada Company

International Capital Management Inc.
Also listed under: *Financial Planning*
#200, 940 The East Mall
Toronto, ON M9B 6J7
416-621-6299
Fax: 416-621-8013
877-341-8687
audrey@icm-canada.com
www.icm-canada.com
Former Name: Advanced Financial Concepts
Year Founded: 1990
Executives:
John Sanchez, Founder
Juan P. Sanchez, Founder

Invessa Services Financiers Inc.
Also listed under: *Financial Planning*
#220, 2740, Pierre-Péladeau
Laval, QC H7T 3B3
450-781-6560
Fax: 450-781-4851
info@invessa.com
www.invessa.com
Executives:
Martin Rochon, Contact
Branches:
Boucherville
#311, 1550 rue Ampère
Boucherville, QC J4B 7L4 Canada
450-645-0400
Fax: 450-645-0350
cgr@invessa.com
Montréal - Fleury est
3739, rue Fleury est
Montréal, QC H1H 2S8 Canada
514-326-6020
Fax: 514-326-0850
senay@invessa.com
Montréal - Jean-Talon
#102, 4570, rue Jean-Talon est
Montréal, QC H1S 1K2 Canada
514-374-7580
Fax: 514-374-5998
ly@invessa.com
St-Jérôme
330, rue Saint-Georges
Saint-Jérome, QC J7Z 5A5 Canada
450-436-8989
Fax: 450-436-8402
filiatrault@invessa.com

Investment House of Canada Inc.(IHOC)
Also listed under: *Financial Planning*
#221, 1033 Bay St.
Toronto, ON M5S 3A5
416-926-9600
Fax: 416-926-9525
877-926-9600
www.ihoc.ca
Executives:
Vlad Trkulja, President/CEO
Sanjiv Sawh, CFO, Chief Compliance Officer
Darlene Gruwer, Managing Director

Investors Group Securities Inc.
One Canada Centre
447 Portage Ave., 10th Fl.
Winnipeg, MB R3C 3B6
204-943-0361
Fax: 204-944-8985
888-746-6344
www.investorsgroup.com
Executives:
Renee S. DeMeyer Mesman, President
Daniel Stoller, CFO

Investpro Securities Inc.
#340, 800, boul René-Lévesque ouest
Montréal, QC H3B 1X9
514-875-5822
Fax: 514-875-6483
info@investpro.ca
www.investpro.ca
Stock Exchange Membership: TSX Venture Exchange
Executives:
Robert Laflamme, Chair
Denis Regimbald, President
Guy Dufresne, Sr. Vice-President
Jacques Y. Gadbois, Sr. Vice-President

IPC Securities Corporation
#100, 100 Simcoe St.
Toronto, ON M5H 3G2
416-360-0990
Fax: 416-360-0991
888-565-5503
www.ipcsecurities.com
Ownership: Private. Owned by Investment Planning Counsel Inc. Subsidiary of IGM Financial Inc., a public company.
Year Founded: 1998
Number of Employees: 100

IPC Securities Corporation (continued)
Assets: $1-10 billion Year End: 20051005
Revenues: $10-50 million Year End: 20051005
Stock Symbol: IPC-X
Stock Exchange Membership: Toronto Stock Exchange, TSX Venture Exchange
Executives:
Geoffrey K. McCord, President
Scott W. Franklin, Vice-President/CFO
Kelly Klatic, Vice-President, Equity Capital Markets
Directors:
Scott Franklin
Geoffrey K. McCord
John Novachis
Branches:
Montréal
#1485, 1981 av McGill College
Montréal, QC H3A 2Y1 Canada
514-871-8600
Oakville
#300, 1515 Rebecca St.
Oakville, ON L6L 5G8 Canada
905-469-8600
Fax: 905-469-0513

ITG Canada Corp.(ITG)
Exchange Tower
PO Box 83
#1040, 130 King St. West
Toronto, ON M5X 1B1
416-640-4484
Fax: 416-874-0690
877-640-4484
Other Information: 877-660-4484 (Phone, Sales & Trading)
itg@itgcan.com
www.itginc.com
Year Founded: 1987
Stock Exchange Membership: Toronto Stock Exchange, TSX Venture Exchange
Profile: The business is engaged in pre-trade analysis, order management, trade execution & post-trade evaluation.

Executives:
Nick Thadaney, CEO
Ian Camacho, President/COO
Gregory Davies, Chief Financial Officer, Secretary

J.C. Clark Ltd.
#3400, 130 Adelaide St. West
Toronto, ON M5H 3P5
416-361-6144
Fax: 416-361-0128
866-480-0002
swynn@jcclark.com
www.jcclark.com
Ownership: Private
Stock Exchange Membership: Toronto Stock Exchange, TSX Venture Exchange
Executives:
John Clark, President/CEO & Chair
Colin Stewart, Secretary

J.P. Morgan Securities Canada Inc.(JPMSC)
South Tower, Royal Bank Plaza
#1800, 200 Bay St.
Toronto, ON M5J 2J2
416-981-9200
Fax: 416-981-9133
www.jpmorgan.com
Ownership: Part of JPMorgan Worldwide Securities Services, a division of JPMorgan Chase Bank, N.A.
Stock Exchange Membership: Montreal Exchange, Toronto Stock Exchange, TSX Venture Exchange, Winnepeg Commodities Exchange
Profile: Services offered include investment banking, principal trading & institutional sales & trading.

Executives:
Adam Howard, President
Kenneth Knowles, Managing Director

Jennings Capital Inc.
#2600, 520 - 5 Ave. SW
Calgary, AB T2P 3R7
403-292-0970
Fax: 403-292-0979
888-292-0980
sales@jenningscapital.com
www.jenningscapital.com
Ownership: Private
Year Founded: 1993
Stock Exchange Membership: Toronto Stock Exchange, TSX Venture Exchange
Profile: Corporate institutional & private financial services are provided by the independent, full service, Canadian-owned investment dealer.

Executives:
Robert G. Jennings, Chair/CEO
Nancy L. Peck, CGA, CFO, COO
Robert Verhelst, BA, CFE, Chief Compliance Officer
Daryl Hodges, MSc, Sr. Managing Director, Investment Banking

Liam J. Balfour, CFA, Vice-President, Investment Banking
Ronald Coll, BSc., Vice-President & Sr. Analyst, Gold & Precious Minerals
Rich Morrow, BA, M.Div., MBA, Head of Research & Sr. Analyst, Industrial Products/Special Situations
Branches:
Calgary
#430, 520 - 5th Ave. SW
Calgary, AB T2P 3R7
403-292-9328
Fax: 403-292-9329
877-292-0970
James H. Ross, Sr. Managing Director
Toronto
#320, 33 Yonge St.
Toronto, ON M5E 1G4
416-214-0600
Fax: 416-214-0177
877-214-3303
G. Peter Taylor, President
Vancouver
Two Bentall Centre
PO Box 230
#1225, 555 Burrard St.
Vancouver, BC V7X 1M9
604-648-3250
Fax: 604-687-6678

Jitney Group Inc./ Le Groupe Jitney inc
360, rue St-Jacques ouest, 16e étage
Montréal, QC H2Y 1P5
514-985-8080
Fax: 514-985-8099
866-608-0099
Other Information: 514-985-8061 (Phone, Sales); 514-985-1121 (Phone, Clientele Services); 514-985-8063 (Risk Management)
info@jitneygroup.com, sales@jitneygroup.com
www.jitneyonline.com
Ownership: Private
Year Founded: 2001
Stock Exchange Membership: Montreal Exchange, Toronto Stock Exchange
Profile: The firm specializes in stocks, options & futures.

Executives:
Holly Morisson, Manager, Risk
Jean-Marc Bourgineau, Market Analyst
Paul Benwell, Advisor, Clientele Service
Stéphane Hermosilla, Market Strategist

Jones, Gable & Company Limited
#600, 110 Yonge St.
Toronto, ON M5C 1T6
416-365-8000
Fax: 416-365-8037
clientservices@jonesgable.com
www.jonesgable.com
Ownership: Private
Year Founded: 1965
Stock Exchange Membership: Canadian Trading & Quotation System Inc, Montreal Exchange, Toronto Stock Exchange, TSX Venture Exchange
Profile: The independent Canadian full service investment dealer offers financial investment products. It also assists companies to gain access to capital markets.

Executives:
Donald Ross, President
Todd J. Doige, Vice-President, Compliance
John Gunther, Vice-President
John Sharpe, Vice-President
Branches:
Aurora
Aurora, ON
905-726-9343
Fax: 905-726-9325
sforsey@jonesgable.com
Stephen Forsey, Investment Advisor
Collingwood
Collingwood, ON
705-444-5579
Fax: 705-444-0062
rcole@jonesgable.com
Richard Cole, Investment Advisor
London
London, ON
519-685-6283
Fax: 519-685-4758
pdegasperis@jonesgable.com
Peter Degasperis, Investment Advisor
Montréal
#230, 1178, Place Phillips
Montréal, QC H2B 3C8 Canada
514-288-2520
Fax: 514-288-7750
Jean Rainville, Director
Thunder Bay
Thunder Bay, ON
807-343-0103
Fax: 807-343-0103
Frank McLean, Investment Advisor
Vancouver
#324, 555 Burrard St.
Vancouver, BC V7X 1M7 Canada
604-685-1481
Fax: 604-684-3761
John R.E. Griffith, Branch Manager
Whitby
Whitby, ON Canada
905-430-2252
Fax: 905-430-8836
tmcgurk@jonesgable.com
Terry McGurk, Investment Advisor

Jory Capital Inc.
#2070, 360 Main St.
Winnipeg, MB R3C 3Z3
204-942-7711
Fax: 204-942-0047
800-545-4069
admin@jorycapital.com
www.jorycapital.com
Ownership: Private
Year Founded: 1999
Number of Employees: 16
Stock Exchange Membership: TSX Venture Exchange
Executives:
Patrick Cooney, Chair/CEO & President

JVK Life & Wealth Advisory Group
Also listed under: *Financial Planning*
#206, 86 Ringwood Dr.
Stouffville, ON L4A 1C3
905-642-0654
Fax: 905-642-0786
800-767-5933
info@jvkgroup.com
www.jvkgroup.com
Profile: The independent financial planning company provides services to Ontario residents.

Executives:
John Niekraszewicz, President, Founder

Kingsdale Capital Corporation
PO Box 156
#2950, 130 King St. West
Toronto, ON M5X 1C7
416-867-4550
Fax: 416-867-4566
877-373-6007
info@kingsdalecapital.com
www.kingsdalecapital.com
Ownership: Private
Stock Exchange Membership: Toronto Stock Exchange, TSX Venture Exchange
Profile: Assets under administration are between $100-500 million.
Executives:

David Carbonaro, Vice-Chair & Director, Legal Services
Peter Notidis, CFO

KingsGate Securities Limited
#300, 195 The West Mall
Toronto, ON M9C 5K1
416-626-9111
Fax: 416-626-9122
info@kingsgate.ca
www.kingsgate.ca
Ownership: Private. KingsGate Wealth Management Services Limited, Toronto, ON.
Executives:
Fred Roberts, CEO
Walter Bobko, President

Kingwest & Company
86 Avenue Rd.
Toronto, ON M5R 2H2
416-927-7740
Fax: 416-927-9264
info@kingwest.com
www.kingwest.com
Ownership: Private.
Stock Exchange Membership: Toronto Stock Exchange
Profile: The firm is engaged in portfolio investment management.

Executives:
Richard Fogler, Managing Director
Timothy Regan, Managing Director; tregan@kingwest.com
Valerie Ross, Chief Financial Officer

Laurentian Bank Securities Inc.
#100, 1981, av McGill College
Montréal, QC H3A 3K3
514-350-2800
Fax: 514-350-2899
888-350-8577
headoffice@blcvm.com
www.vmbl.ca
Former Name: BLC Securities Inc.
Year Founded: 1990
Number of Employees: 135
Assets: $10-100 billion
Revenues: $500m-1 billion
Stock Exchange Membership: Canadian Trading & Quotation System Inc, Montreal Exchange, Toronto Stock Exchange, TSX Venture Exchange
Executives:
Michel C. Trudeau, President/CEO
Yves Ruest, CFO, Vice-President
Pierre Godbout, Vice-President
Raymond Trudeau, Vice-President

Lazard Canada Corporation
Also listed under: *Financial Planning*
#1610, 1501, av McGill College
Montréal, QC H3A 3M8
514-397-1016
Fax: 514-397-1317
www.lazard.com
Year Founded: 1848
Branches:
Toronto
PO Box 373, First Canadian Pl. Sta. First Canadian Pl.
#4610, 1 First Canadian Pl.
Toronto, ON M5X 1E2 Canada
416-216-5086
Fax: 416-216-5085

Le Groupe Option Retraite inc.
1080, côte du Beaver Hall, 8e étage
Montréal, QC H2Z 1S8
514-861-0777
Fax: 514-861-1976
888-640-0777
marketing@option.ca
www.option.ca
Stock Exchange Membership: Montreal Exchange, Toronto Stock Exchange
Branches:
Chicoutimi
#10, 345, rue des Saguenéens
Chicoutimi, QC G7H 6K9 Canada
418-698-0777
Fax: 418-549-5333
888-451-7337
Gatineau
#420, 200, rue Montcalm
Gatineau, QC J8Y 3B5 Canada
819-770-0777
Fax: 819-770-1976
888-443-7337
Joliette
365, boul Manseau
Joliette, QC J6E 3C9
450-752-0787
Fax: 450-752-0767
866-661-7337
Laval
#104, 400, boul St-Martin ouest
Laval, QC H7M 3Y8 Canada
450-967-0777
Fax: 450-975-1976
800-421-7337
Longueuil
#140, 375, boul Roland Therrien
Longueuil, QC J4H 4A6 Canada
450-463-0777
Fax: 450-928-1976
888-297-7337
Montréal
6476, boul Jean-Talon est
Montréal, QC H1S 1M8 Canada
514-256-7767
Fax: 514-252-1976
888-460-7337
Québec
#105, 5550, boul des Galeries
Québec, QC G2K 2E2 Canada
418-627-5777
Fax: 418-627-5333
888-313-7337
Saint-Hyacinthe
#102, 2500, boul Casavant ouest
Saint-Hyacinthe, QC J2S 7R8 Canada
450-261-0777
Fax: 450-261-1976
888-710-7337
Saint-Sauveur
11, rue Robert
Saint-Sauveur, QC J0R 1R6
450-227-2777
Fax: 450-227-1976
888-499-7337
Sherbrooke
#20, 1650, rue Sherbrooke ouest
Sherbrooke, QC J1J 2C3
819-563-0777
Fax: 819-563-0601
888-294-7337
St-Jean-sur-Richelieu
#6, 1050, boul du Séminaire nord
St-Jean-sur-Richelieu, QC J3A 1S7 Canada
450-349-7777
Fax: 450-349-7770
866-678-7337
Toronto
998 Kingston Rd.
Toronto, ON M4E 1T2 Canada
416-485-0777
Fax: 416-485-1976
888-529-7337
Trois-Rivières
5185, boul des Forges
Trois-Rivières, QC G8Y 4Z3 Canada
819-376-0777
Fax: 819-376-9070
888-210-7337

Leduc & associés valeurs mobilières (Canada) ltée
#1065, 2020, rue University
Montréal, QC H3A 2A5
514-499-1170
Fax: 514-499-1063
a.nadon@leduc-associes.ca
Year Founded: 1986
Number of Employees: 40
Assets: $100-500 million
Revenues: $1-5 million
Executives:
Michel Leduc, President/CEO; mleduc@leduc-associes.ca
Marie-France Leduc, Vice-President; rroy@leduc-associes.ca

Leede Financial Markets Inc.
First Alberta Place
#2300, 777 - 8 Ave. SW
Calgary, AB T2P 3R5
403-531-6800
Fax: 403-531-6996
800-430-6999
reception@leedefinancial.com
www.leedefinancial.com
Former Name: Rogers & Partners Securities Inc
Ownership: Private
Year Founded: 1987
Stock Exchange Membership: Canadian Trading & Quotation System Inc, TSX Venture Exchange
Executives:
Robert Harrison, President/CEO
James Dale, CFO
Victor Taboika, Exec. Vice-President
Brian Bergen, Sr. Vice-President, Branch Manager
Judith Romanchuk, Sr. Vice-President, Private Equity
William Cummins, Vice-President, Corporate Finance
Shiraz Meghji, Vice-President
Directors:
Michael Zwack, Chair
Gordon Medland, Vice-Chair
Branches:
Vancouver
PO Box 2
#1800, 1140 West Pender St.
Vancouver, BC V6E 4G1 Canada
604-658-3000
Fax: 604-658-3099
888-878-6356
www.leedefinancial.com
Randy Butchard, Sr. Vice-President

Lightyear Capital Inc.
Also listed under: *Financial Planning; Non-Depository Institutions*
Bow Valley Square I
#660, 202 - 6 Ave. SW
Calgary, AB T2P 2R9
403-218-1400
Fax: 403-537-6512
info@lightyearcapital.com,
investmentbanking@lightyearcapital.com
www.lightyearcapital.com
Stock Exchange Membership: Toronto Stock Exchange, TSX Venture Exchange
Profile: The company offers investment banking services. Clients include small-mid cap companies.

Executives:
Louise M. Duchesne, CA, Managing Director;
louise.duchesne@lightyearcapital.com
Murray A. Weimer, CA, Managing Director;
murray.weimer@lightyearcapital.com

Loewen, Ondaatje, McCutcheon Limited(LOM)
East Tower, Hazelton Lanes
#2250, 55 Avenue Rd.
Toronto, ON M5R 3L2
416-964-4455
Fax: 416-964-4490
800-567-1566
contactus@lomltd.com
www.lomltd.com
Ownership: Subsidiary of LOM Bancorp Limited, a Canadian-controlled private corporation
Year Founded: 1970
Number of Employees: 36
Stock Exchange Membership: Montreal Exchange, Toronto Stock Exchange, TSX Venture Exchange
Profile: The company is engaged in institutional sales & trading of Canadian equities in Canada, the U.S.A. & Europe. Other activities include corporate finance, mergers, & acquisitions for North American corporate clients & retail brokerages in Western Canada.

Executives:
Garrett Herman, President/CEO; 416-964-4400

Loewen, Ondaatje, McCutcheon Limited(LOM) (continued)
Paul J. DesLauriers, Exec. Vice-President, Corporate Finance; 416-964-4432
Bernard Arokium, CFO; 416-964-4475; barokium@lomltd.com
Directors:
Garrett Herman, Chair
Paul J. DesLauriers
Patrick Gay
David Giacomodonato
Anthony Pullen
Botho von Bose
Branches:
Montréal
#1900, 1200, av McGill College
Montréal, QC H3B 4G7 Canada
514-393-4600
Fax: 514-879-9067
Garrett Herman, Manager

MacDougall, MacDougall & MacTier Inc.

Also listed under: *Pension & Money Management Companies; Investment Management*
Place du Canada
#2000, 1010, rue de la Gauchetière ouest
Montréal, QC H3B 4J1
514-394-3000
Fax: 514-871-1481
800-567-4465
macdougall@3macs.com
www.3macs.com
Ownership: Employee-owned.
Year Founded: 1858
Stock Exchange Membership: Canadian Trading & Quotation System Inc, Montreal Exchange, Toronto Stock Exchange, TSX Venture Exchange
Profile: Investment management advice & services are offered to private investors by the independent investment dealer. The firm's services include managed accounts, RRSPs, RESPs, RRIFs, life income funds, tax planning, estate planning, cash management, fixed income & record keeping.

Executives:
Timothy E. Price, President/CEO
William W. Black, CIM, Vice-President
Mark W. Gallop, MBA, FCSI, Vice-President
William L. Cowen, Branch Manager, Investment Advisor
Branches:
Kingston
208 Albert St.
Montréal, QC K7L 3V3 Canada
613-531-9746
866-588-3490
Bill Cowen, Contact
London
#202, 140 Fullarton St.
London, ON N6A 5P2 Canada
519-645-1110
Fax: 519-645-1096
800-267-0056
Robert C. Ketchabaw, Branch Manager
Québec
#800, 2875, boul Laurier
Québec, QC G1V 2M2 Canada
418-656-1212
Fax: 418-656-4222
888-462-3010
Michel G. Bergeron, Branch Manager
Toronto
PO Box 13
#2510, 150 King St. West
Toronto, ON M5H 1J9 Canada
416-977-0663
Fax: 416-596-7453
800-461-3485
Bart H. MacDougall, Chair

MacIntosh Financial Group Ltd.

Also listed under: *Financial Planning*
1275 West 6th Ave., 3rd Fl.
Vancouver, BC V6H 1A6
604-737-8886
Fax: 604-737-8719
info@macintoshfinancial.com
www.macintoshfinancial.com
Former Name: Cameron MacIntosh & Co. Ltd.
Year Founded: 1985
Executives:
Peter MacIntosh, Sr. Financial Advisor
Justin Wee, Associate

Maison Placements Canada Inc.

PO Box 99
#906, 130 Adelaide St. West
Toronto, ON M5H 3P5
416-947-6040
Fax: 416-947-6046
Ownership: Private
Year Founded: 1955
Stock Exchange Membership: Montreal Exchange, Toronto Stock Exchange, TSX Venture Exchange
Executives:
John R. Ing, President/CEO
Bill Dickson, Vice-President
Paul D. Aitkens, Sec.-Treas.

Man Financial Canada Co.

#1601, 123 Front St. West
Toronto, ON M5J 2M2
416-862-7000
Fax: 416-862-0576
800-268-9294
www.manfinancialcanada.ca
Former Name: Refco Futures (Canada) Limited
Ownership: Private
Year Founded: 1978
Stock Exchange Membership: Toronto Stock Exchange, TSX Venture Exchange, Winnepeg Commodities Exchange
Profile: In 2006, Man Financial, the futures & options brokerage division of Man Group plc, acquired Refco Canada Co. Refco is now known as Man Financial Canada Co.

Executives:
Pierre Gloutney, Chair
Branches:
Calgary - 5th Ave. SW
#2050, 300 - 5th Ave. SW
Calgary, AB T2P 3C4 Canada
403-264-8690
Fax: 403-262-5875
800-332-1408
Calgary - Thorncliffe Cres. NW
4 Thorncliffe Cres. NW
Calgary, AB T2K 3A9 Canada
403-216-2490
Fax: 403-275-4228
888-216-2490
Errol Anderson, Contact
Markham
#102, 50 Minthorn Blvd.
Markham, ON L3T 7X8 Canada
905-886-9899
Fax: 905-886-8992
888-773-8880

Montréal
#4110, 800, Place Victoria
Montréal, QC H4Z 1G8 Canada
514-866-1000
Fax: 514-866-4146
800-363-4693
Saskatoon
#200, 416 - 21 St. East
Saskatoon, SK S7K 0C2 Canada
306-249-9672
Fax: 306-249-5267
888-472-4648
Toronto
PO Box 270
100 King St. West, 37th Fl.
Toronto, ON M5X 1C9 Canada
416-777-2424
Fax: 416-777-1613
888-387-7463
Vancouver
#900, 650 West Georgia St.
Vancouver, BC V6B 6L7 Canada
604-687-1131
Fax: 604-687-3149
888-881-1162
Winnipeg
#310, 360 Main St.
Winnipeg, MB R3C 3Z3 Canada
204-988-9710
Fax: 204-956-7670
866-988-9710

Maple Securities Canada Ltd.

PO Box 328
#3500, 79 Wellington St. West
Toronto, ON M5K 1K7
416-350-8200
Fax: 416-350-8222
www.maplefinancial.com
Ownership: Part of Maple Financial Group
Stock Exchange Membership: Toronto Stock Exchange
Executives:
David E. Schnarr, CEO/COO
Bethany Curley, CFO

MCA Valeurs Mobilières Inc./ MCA Securities Inc.

#1405, 555, boul René-Lévesque ouest
Montréal, QC H2Z 1B1
514-877-4161
Fax: 514-877-3161
beauregardg@mca.qc.ca
www.mca.qc.ca
Former Name: M. Cousineau et Associés Inc.
Year Founded: 1992
Stock Exchange Membership: Toronto Stock Exchange, TSX Venture Exchange
Profile: MCA Securities is an independent full-service brokerage firm that offers investment & trading services. Clients are individual investors, businesses and institutions in Canada & abroad.

Executives:
Michel Cousineau, President/CEO
Gilles Beauregard, Acting CFO & Exec. Vice-President, Sales & Compliance
Alain Goyer, Vice President, Chief Compliance Officer & Branch Manager
Jean-Louis Tassé, Vice-President
Daniel Vaugeois, Vice-President, Institutional Fixed Income
Branches:
Lac-Beauport
14, ch des Pionniers
Lac-Beauport, QC G0A 2C0
418-561-3487
brownl@mca.qc.ca
Montréal - René-Lévesque ouest
#03RC, 55, boul René-Lévesque ouest
Montréal, QC H2Z 1B1
514-877-4170
Fax: 514-877-4174
beauregardg@mca.qc.ca
Montréal - University
#811, 1255, rue University
Montréal, QC H3B 3W3
514-876-4004
Fax: 514-876-1567
triheyk@mca.qc.ca

McElvaine Investment Management Ltd.

Also listed under: *Investment Fund Companies*
3 Bentall Centre
PO Box 49308
#463, 595 Burrard St.
Vancouver, BC V7X 1L3
604-601-8345
Fax: 604-601-8346
info@mcelvaine.com
www.mcelvaine.com
Ownership: Private
McElvaine:
Investment Trust Fund
RRSP Eligible; Inception Year: 1996;

McLean & Partners Wealth Management Ltd.

Also listed under: *Financial Planning; Investment Management*

801 - 10 Ave. SW
Calgary, AB T2R 0B4
403-234-0005
Fax: 403-234-0606
888-665-0005
solutions@mcleanpartners.com
www.mcleanpartners.com
Former Name: McLean & Partners Private Capital Corporation
Ownership: Private.

Year Founded: 1999
Number of Employees: 25
Executives:
Brent McLean, President/CEO
Heather Gore-Hickman, Chief Financial Officer
Kevin Dehod, Vice-President
Anil Tahiliani, Head, Research

MD Management Limited/ Gestion MD limitée

Also listed under: *Investment Fund Companies; Investment Management*
1870 Alta Vista Dr.
Ottawa, ON K1G 6R7
613-731-4552
Fax: 613-736-5368
800-663-7336
cmamsc@cma.ca
www.cma.ca; www.mdm.ca
Ownership: Private. Subsidiary of the Canadian Medical Association
Year Founded: 1969
Number of Employees: 1,100
Assets: $10-100 billion
Profile: The company provides professional, objective financial planning & price competitive, quality products & services to Canadian Medical Association physicians & their families. MD Management Limited is also affiliated with the following companies: CMA Holding Incorporated, MD Funds Management Inc., MD Private Trust Co., MD Life Insurance Co., Practice Solutions Ltd., MD Private Investment Management Inc.

Executives:
A.G. Bélanger, President/CEO
C.M. Allison, Chief Financial Officer
R.P. Bannerman, Vice-President & Secretary
C.K. Hamilton, Vice-President
T.R. Smith, Vice-President
R.S. Tanner, Vice-President
R. Thorpe, Vice-President
S.H. Wilson, Vice-President
J.M Arel, Asst. Vice-President
D. Hamilton, Asst. Vice-President
J.M. Klaas, Asst. Vice-President
D. Labonté, Asst. Vice-President
H. Miskelly, Asst. Vice-President
N. Thompson, Asst. Vice-President
Directors:
I. Warrack, Chair
R.P. Bannerman
A.G. Bélanger
B.F. Peters
T. Webb
S.H. Wilson
Affiliated Companies:
MD Life Insurance Company
MD:
Balanced Fund
RRSP Eligible; Inception Year: 1992; Fund Managers: MD Funds Management Inc.
Bond Fund
RRSP Eligible; Inception Year: 1988; Fund Managers: MD Funds Management Inc.
Bond & Mortgage Fund
RRSP Eligible; Inception Year: 1995; Fund Managers: MD Funds Management Inc.
Dividend Fund
RRSP Eligible; Inception Year: 1992; Fund Managers: MD Funds Management Inc.
Equity Fund
RRSP Eligible; Inception Year: 1966; Fund Managers: MD Funds Management Inc.
Growth Fund
RRSP Eligible; Inception Year: 1969; Fund Managers: MD Funds Management Inc.
Select Fund
RRSP Eligible; Inception Year: 1993; Fund Managers: MD Funds Management Inc.
International Growth Fund
RRSP Eligible; Inception Year: 2000; Fund Managers: MD Funds Management Inc.
US Small Cap Growth Fund
RRSP Eligible; Inception Year: 2000; Fund Managers: MD Funds Management Inc.
International Value Fund
RRSP Eligible; Inception Year: 2004; Fund Managers: MD Funds Management Inc.
Money Fund
RRSP Eligible; Inception Year: 1975; Fund Managers: MD Funds Management Inc.
US Large Cap Growth Fund
RRSP Eligible; Inception Year: 1992; Fund Managers: MD Funds Management Inc.
US Large Cap Value Fund
RRSP Eligible; Inception Year: 2000; Fund Managers: MD Funds Management Inc.
MDPIM:
Canadian Equity Pool Class A Fund
RRSP Eligible; Inception Year: 2000; Fund Managers: MD Funds Management Inc.
US Equity Pool Class A Fund
RRSP Eligible; Inception Year: 2000; Fund Managers: MD Funds Management Inc.
District Offices:
Abbotsford
#302, 33140 Mill Lake Rd.
Abbotsford, BC V2S 2A5 Canada
604-504-1666
Fax: 604-504-1663
888-326-9993
Barrie
#301, 125 Bell Farm Rd.
Barrie, ON L4M 6L2 Canada
705-721-0196
Fax: 705-721-0509
888-246-4996
Chicoutimi
#200, 345, rue des Saguenéens
Chicoutimi, QC G7H 6K9 Canada
418-543-4456
Fax: 418-543-1665
888-861-0131
Edmonton - 106th Ave.
#202, 12230 - 106th Ave. NW
Edmonton, AB T5N 3Z1 Canada
780-482-7045
Fax: 780-482-7047
800-282-6901
Edmonton - 112th St.
College Plaza
#1502, 8215 - 112th St.
Edmonton, AB T6G 2C8 Canada
780-436-1333
Fax: 780-436-3371
877-434-1333
Fredericton
#1, 176 York St.
Fredericton, NB E3B 3N7 Canada
506-452-2958
Fax: 506-452-2959
888-292-3131
Gatineau
#410, 200, Montcalm
Gatineau, QC J8Y 3B5 Canada
819-770-5101
Fax: 819-770-9525
888-246-5609
Hamilton
#1200, 1 King St. West
Hamilton, ON L8P 1A4 Canada
905-526-8999
Fax: 905-526-1198
800-883-6015
Kamloops
#108, 300 Columbia St.
Kamloops, BC V2C 6L1 Canada
250-377-0900
Fax: 250-377-0933
888-217-6888
Kelowna
#203, 3001 Tutt St.
Kelowna, BC V1Y 2H4 Canada
250-762-4261
Fax: 250-762-3142
800-249-1133
Kingston
#204, 275 Bagot St.
Kingston, ON K7L 3G4 Canada
613-548-8770
Fax: 613-548-3556
800-363-5527
Kitchener
#201, 525 Belmont Ave. West
Kitchener, ON N2M 5E2 Canada
519-744-1303
Fax: 519-744-7408
800-859-6715
Laval
#703, 3030, boul le Carrefour
Laval, QC H7T 2P5 Canada
450-682-2696
Fax: 450-682-5610
800-540-6211
Lethbridge
Lethbridge Centre Tower
#315, 400 - 4th Ave. South
Lethbridge, AB T1J 4E1 Canada
403-320-2992
Fax: 403-320-5885
888-320-3431
Longueuil
Tour est
#452, 111, rue St-Charles ouest
Longueuil, QC J4K 5G4 Canada
450-448-0611
Fax: 450-448-0939
888-627-3719
Mississauga
#601, 89 Queensway West
Mississauga, ON L5B 2V2 Canada
905-306-7788
Fax: 905-306-7824
800-321-0330
Moncton
#320, 1133 St. George Blvd.
Moncton, NB E1E 4E1 Canada
506-855-1994
Fax: 506-855-0220
800-664-2241
Montréal
#647, 1, rue Holiday
Montréal, QC H9R 5N3 Canada
514-630-7749
Fax: 514-630-8449
888-989-7749
Nanaimo
#202B, 1808 Bowen Rd.
Nanaimo, BC V9S 5W4 Canada
250-753-9800
Fax: 250-753-9828
888-326-9994
New Westminster
#420, 628 - 6th Ave.
New Westminster, BC V3M 6Z1 Canada
604-520-3315
Fax: 604-520-3301
800-498-1881
North Vancouver
#300, 1111 Lonsdale Ave.
North Vancouver, BC V7N 2H4 Canada
604-987-5553
Fax: 604-987-5583
877-987-5553
Oshawa
Oshawa Executive Centre
#306, 419 King St. West
Oshawa, ON L1J 2K5 Canada
905-579-1882
Fax: 905-579-6949
877-543-1201
Prince George
#320, 177 Victoria St.
Prince George, BC V2L 5R8 Canada
250-564-9600
Fax: 250-564-9660
888-326-9992
Regina
#375, 3303 Hillsdale St.
Regina, SK S4S 6W9 Canada
306-359-7200
Fax: 306-359-9900
888-880-6211
Richmond Hill
#206, 9050 Yonge St.
Richmond Hill, ON L4C 9S6 Canada

INVESTMENT MANAGEMENT

MD Management Limited/ Gestion MD limitée (continued)
905-889-2100
Fax: 905-889-2693
888-233-8858
Saint John
#101, 1 Magazine St.
Saint John, NB E2K 5S9 Canada
506-657-2020
Fax: 506-657-2002
888-292-3131
Sherbrooke
#520, 2665, rue King ouest
Sherbrooke, QC J1L 2G5 Canada
819-566-8240
Fax: 819-566-8291
800-584-9881
St Catharines
#105, 75 Corporate Park Dr.
St Catharines, ON L2S 3W2 Canada
905-641-0330
Fax: 905-641-0146
800-428-7184
St. John's
164 MacDonald Dr.
St. John's, NL A1A 4B3 Canada
709-729-2136
Fax: 709-726-2193
800-229-1798
Stratford
3 Myrtle St.
Stratford, PE C1B 1P4 Canada
902-892-2092
Fax: 902-892-2043
800-443-9711
Sudbury
#305, 27 Cedar St.
Sudbury, ON P3E 1A1 Canada
705-671-9746
Fax: 705-671-1254
800-547-8295
Sydney
Sydney Medical Arts Bldg.
#210, 336 Kings Rd.
Sydney, NS B1S 1A9 Canada
902-564-5700
Fax: 902-564-5727
888-356-3871
Thunder Bay
#203, 1205 Amber Dr.
Thunder Bay, ON P7B 6M4 Canada
807-346-2850
Fax: 807-346-2854
888-873-3320
Toronto - Milner Ave.
#1603, 325 Milner Ave.
Toronto, ON M1B 5N1 Canada
416-299-8841
Fax: 416-299-9787
800-846-0966
Toronto - Sheppard Ave.
#804, 45 Sheppard Ave. East
Toronto, ON M2N 5W9 Canada
416-224-9793
Fax: 416-224-9045
888-770-9223
Victoria
#100, 3550 Saanich Rd.
Victoria, BC V8X 1X2 Canada
250-480-5075
Fax: 250-480-5026
800-716-8498
Windsor
#350, 600 Tecumseh Rd. East
Windsor, ON N8X 4X9 Canada
519-254-2812
Fax: 519-254-5347
800-213-8472
Regional Offices:
Calgary
#300, 708 - 11th Ave. SW
Calgary, AB T2R 0E4 Canada
403-244-8000
Fax: 403-229-1146
800-661-4669
Halifax
Park Lane Terrace
PO Box 105
#704, 5657 Spring Garden Rd.
Halifax, NS B3J 3R4 Canada
902-425-4646
Fax: 902-422-2775
800-565-1771
London
#705, 380 Wellington St. North
London, ON N6A 5B5 Canada
519-432-0883
Fax: 519-432-0997
800-461-9587
Montréal
#650, 1000, rue de la Gauchetière ouest
Montréal, QC H3B 4W5 Canada
514-392-1434
Fax: 514-392-0387
800-361-5126
Ottawa
#200, 1565 Carling Ave.
Ottawa, ON K1Z 8R1 Canada
613-722-7688
Fax: 613-729-4735
800-387-4018
Québec
#2460, 2600, boul Laurier
Québec, QC G1V 4M6 Canada
418-657-6601
Fax: 418-652-7808
800-463-6288
Saskatoon
#900, CN Towers
Saskatoon, SK S7K 1J5 Canada
306-244-0077
Fax: 306-244-8685
800-667-0077
Toronto
#1100, 522 University Ave.
Toronto, ON M5G 1W7 Canada
416-598-1442
Fax: 416-340-1509
800-387-2646
Vancouver
#250, 1665 West Broadway
Vancouver, BC V6J 1X1 Canada
604-736-7778
Fax: 604-736-1202
800-663-7460
Winnipeg
#404, 1661 Portage Ave.
Winnipeg, MB R3J 3T7 Canada
204-783-2463
Fax: 204-772-1960
800-567-7526
winnipegregion@cma.ca

Merrill Lynch Canada Inc.

***Also listed under:** Financial Planning; Non-Depository Institutions*
Wellington Tower, BCE Place
181 Bay St., 4th & 5th Fl.
Toronto, ON M5J 2V8
416-369-7400
Fax: 416-369-7966
www.gmi.ml.com/canada
Ownership: Public. Part of Merrill Lynch & Co., Inc., New York, NY, USA.
Year Founded: 1990
Number of Employees: 300+
Stock Symbol: MLC
Stock Exchange Membership: Montreal Exchange, Toronto Stock Exchange, TSX Venture Exchange
Profile: Merrill Lynch is a full-service investment dealer that provides investment banking, equity & debt trading, & research products. Clients include institutions, government & corporations.

Executives:
Paul Allison, Managing Director, Exec. Vice-President & Co-Head, Canada Origination
M. Marianne Harris, Managing Director & President, Global Markets & Investment Banking
Daniel Mida, Managing Director, Exec. Vice-President & Co-Head, Canada Origination
Lynn Patterson, Managing Director & President, Global Markets Debt & Equity Sales & Trading
Robert Montesione, CFO, CAO
Mark Dickerson, Corporate Secretary
Offices:
Calgary
Bow Valley Square III
#2620, 255 - 5th Ave. SW
Calgary, AB T2P 3G6 Canada
403-231-7300
Fax: 403-237-7372
Montréal
#3715, 1250, boul René-Lévesque ouest
Montréal, QC H3B 4W8 Canada
514-846-1050
Fax: 514-846-3591
Guy Savard, Chair, Québec Operations
Vancouver
Cathedral Place
925 West Georgia St., 7th Fl.
Vancouver, BC V6C 3L2 Canada
604-691-7252
Fax: 604-691-7259

META Financial Management Ltd.

***Also listed under:** Financial Planning*
#229, 9030 Leslie St.
Richmond Hill, ON L4B 1G2
905-731-2251
Fax: 905-731-8626
service@metafinance.ca
www.metafinance.ca
Ownership: Private. Part of Armstrong & Quaile Associates Inc., Manotick, ON.
Year Founded: 1998
Number of Employees: 10+
Profile: META Financial, a branch of Armstrong & Quaile Associates Inc., operates as a mutual fund dealer.

Executives:
Ken Ng, Director; 905-731-2251
Len Seeto, Director; 905-731-2251

MGI Securities Inc.

#900, 26 Wellington St. East
Toronto, ON M5E 1S2
416-864-6477
Fax: 416-864-6485
866-269-7773
www.mgisecurities.com
Former Name: McFarlane Gordon Inc.
Ownership: Subsidiary of Jovian Capital Corporation.
Year Founded: 1999
Profile: The full-service investment firm is registered to carry client accounts in the following provinces: British Columbia, Alberta, Saskatchewan, Manitoba, Ontario, Quebec & Nova Scotia. Specialized services are provided for institutional investors. For individual investors, private wealth management solutions are offered.

Executives:
Derek Nelson, Chair
Mark L. Arthur, Vice-Chair
Lewis Reford, President/CEO
Crawford Gordon, Managing Director, Retail
Donald McFarlane, Managing Director, Retail
Scott Norris, Chief Compliance Officer
Sam Collins, Sr. Vice-President
Branches:
Calgary
Bankers Hall East, Hollingsworth Building
#610, 301 - 8th Ave. SW
Calgary, AB T2P 1C5
403-705-4970
Fax: 403-705-4971
866-614-4970
London
#1204, 140 Fullarton St.
London, ON N6A 5P2 Canada
519-963-8005
Fax: 519-963-8006
866-723-9297
Winnipeg
#500, 140 Bannatyne Ave.
Winnipeg, MB R3B 3C5 Canada

204-953-4400
Fax: 204-953-4411
866-768-6138

Middlefield Capital Corporation

First Canadian Place, 58th Fl.
PO Box 192
Toronto, ON M5X 1A6
416-362-0714
Fax: 416-362-7925
invest@middlefield.com
www.middlefield.com
Former Name: Middlefield Securities Limited
Ownership: Private
Year Founded: 1979
Number of Employees: 23
Assets: $10-50 million Year End: 20050331
Revenues: $5-10 million Year End: 20050331
Executives:
W. Garth Jestley, President/CEO
Dean Orrico, Exec. Vice-President
James S. Parsons, Exec. Vice-President
J. Dennis Dunlop, Sr. Vice-President
Fraser Kisel, Sr. Vice-President/CFO
Francis Z. Ramirez, Vice-President
Darren N. Cabral, Exec. Director, Research
Robert Lauzon, Exec. Director, Trading
Dennis DaSilva, Managing Director, Resource Group
Richard L. Farella, Managing Director, Corporate Finance
Scott A. Roberts, Director, Trading
Directors:
Murray J. Brasseur, Chair
W. Garth Jestley
Dean Orrice
James S. Parsons

Mirabaud Canada Inc./ Mirabaud Gestion inc

#2220, 1501, av McGill College
Montréal, QC H3A 3M8
514-393-1690
Fax: 514-875-8942
contact-us@mirabaud.com
www.mirabaud.com
Ownership: Wholly owned subsidiary of Mirabaud & Cie, Geneva, Switzerland.
Year Founded: 1985
Number of Employees: 24
Profile: Mirabaud Canada is an investment dealer, which offers clearing & execution services in foreign currencies, precious metals, bonds, stocks, money market instruments & various mutual & closed-end funds for private & institutional clients.
Executives:
George M. Paulez, Managing Director
David F. Kennedy, CFO
Olivier M. Rodrigues, Manager, Trading Desk
Directors:
Philip T. Nickels, Chair

Moneystrat Securities Inc.

Also listed under: *Financial Planning*
13 Summerhill Ave.
Toronto, ON M4T 1A9
416-968-1444
Fax: 416-968-7808
800-810-1163
plan@moneystrat.com
www.moneystrat.com
Executives:
Earla Burke, President/CEO
Geordon Ferguson, Vice-President

Morgan Stanley Canada Ltd.

BCE Place
#3700, 181 Bay St.
Toronto, ON M5J 2T3
416-943-8400
Fax: 416-943-8444
www.morganstanley.com
Ownership: Part of Morgan Stanley, New York, NY, USA.
Year Founded: 1935
Stock Exchange Membership: Montreal Exchange, Toronto Stock Exchange, TSX Venture Exchange
Profile: Investment banking, equity & derivatives trading, & research sales are provided to institutional clients.
Executives:
George Dell'Orletta, Exec. Director, CFO & CCO
Branches:
Calgary
#2900, 350 - 7th Ave. SW
Calgary, AB T2P 3N9 Canada
403-509-1022

Mykytchuk Wyatt Financial Group

Also listed under: *Financial Planning*
#300, 2184 - 12 Ave.
Regina, SK S4P 0M5
306-757-2735
Fax: 306-347-7710
800-584-4450
info@creatingpeaceofmind.com
Former Name: Mykytchuk, Wyatt Associates; Mykytchuk, Wyatt & Karst
Ownership: Private
Number of Employees: 5
Assets: $10-50 million Year End: 20061010
Revenues: $1-5 million Year End: 20061010
Executives:
John R. Mykytchuk, Partner
Cecile Wyatt, CFP, RFP, Partner

National Bank Direct Brokerage Inc./ Courtage direct Banque Nationale

1100, rue University, 7e étage
Montréal, QC H3B 2G7
514-866-6755
Fax: 514-394-6298
800-393-3511
web.trad@bnc.ca
w3.nbdb.ca
Former Name: National Bank Discount Brokerage Inc.
Ownership: Public
Year Founded: 1999
Number of Employees: 151
Assets: $100-500 million
Revenues: $10-50 million
Stock Exchange Membership: Montreal Exchange, Toronto Stock Exchange, TSX Venture Exchange
Executives:
Yves G. Breton, President

National Bank Financial Inc./ Financière Banque Nationale

1155, rue Metcalfe, 5e étage
Montréal, QC H3B 4S9
514-879-2222
Fax: 514-879-5321
800-361-8838
info@nbf.ca
info.nbf.ca
Ownership: Wholly owned by National Bank of Canada
Year Founded: 1902
Number of Employees: 3,000
Assets: $35,000,000,000
Revenues: $600,000,000
Stock Exchange Membership: Canadian Trading & Quotation System Inc, Montreal Exchange, Toronto Stock Exchange, TSX Venture Exchange
Executives:
Kym Anthony, President/CEO
Sam Reda, President/CEO, Natcan Investment Management
Jean Turmel, President, Financial Markets, Treasury, Investment Bank
Affiliated Companies:
NBF Turnkey Solutions Inc.
Services Financiers FBN
Branches:
Amqui
25, rue Ste-Ursule
Amqui, QC G5J 2Y2 Canada
418-629-5119
Fax: 418-629-5179
Baie-Comeau
337, boul Lasalle
Baie-Comeau, QC G4Z 2Z1 Canada
418-296-8838
Fax: 418-296-2246
Berthierville
779, rue Notre-Dame
Berthierville, QC J0K 1A0 Canada
450-836-2727
Fax: 450-836-3034
Burnaby
#206, 3815 Sunset St.
Burnaby, BC V5G 4W4 Canada
604-541-8500
Fax: 604-436-0392
Calgary
Trans Canada Pipelines Bldg.
#2800, 450 - 1st St.
Calgary, AB T2P 5H1 Canada
403-531-8400
Fax: 403-531-8413
Chatham
380 St. Clair St.
Chatham, ON N7L 3K2 Canada
519-351-7645
Fax: 519-351-5183
Chicoutimi
206, rue Racine est
Chicoutimi, QC G7H 1R9 Canada
418-549-8888
Fax: 418-549-6928
800-463-9830
Drumheller
356 Center St.
Drumheller, AB T0J 0Y0 Canada
403-823-6857
Fax: 403-823-6856
Drummondville
#401, 150, rue Marchand
Drummondville, QC J2C 4N1 Canada
819-477-5024
Fax: 819-474-7959
Edmonton
Manulife Place
#700, 10180 - 101st St.
Edmonton, AB T5J 3S4 Canada
780-412-6600
Fax: 780-424-5756
Gatineau
#100, 920, rue St-Joseph
Gatineau, QC J8Z 1S9 Canada
819-770-5337
Fax: 819-770-9329
Granby
#202, 150, rue St-Jacques
Granby, QC J2G 8V6 Canada
450-378-0442
Fax: 450-378-0572
Grand-Mère
602, 6e av
Grand-Mère, QC G9T 2H5 Canada
819-538-8628
Fax: 819-538-0283
Greenfield-Park
#150, 2120, rue Victoria
Greenfield-Park, QC J4V 1M9 Canada
450-923-8255
Fax: 450-923-8379
Halifax
Purdy's Wharf Tower 2
PO Box 668, M Sta. M
#1601, 1969 Upper Water St.
Halifax, NS B3J 2T3 Canada
902-496-7700
Fax: 902-496-7701
Joliette
#3500, 40, rue Gauthier sud
Joliette, QC J6E 4J4 Canada
450-760-9595
Fax: 450-760-9625
Kelowna
#500, 1632 Dickson Ave.
Kelowna, BC V1Y 7T2 Canada
250-717-5510
Fax: 250-717-5525
Kentville
PO Box 610
402 Main St.
Kentville, NS B4N 3X7 Canada
902-679-0077
Fax: 902-679-4858
La Pocatière
608 C, 4e av
La Pocatière, QC G0R 1Z0 Canada
418-856-4566
Fax: 418-856-9754

National Bank Financial Inc./ Financière Banque Nationale (continued)

Lac Mégantic
3621, rue Durand
Lac-Mégantic, QC G6B 3J5 Canada
819-583-6035
Fax: 819-583-0717

Laval - Daniel-Johnson
2504, boul Daniel-Johnson
Laval, QC H7T 2R3 Canada
450-686-1018
Fax: 450-686-8166

Laval - Place Laval
Édifice G.L.
#110, 1, Place Laval
Laval, QC H7N 1A1 Canada
450-629-3111
Fax: 450-629-7609

Lethbridge
404 - 6th St. South
Lethbridge, AB T1J 2C9 Canada
403-388-1900
Fax: 403-388-8204

London
333 Dufferin Ave.
London, ON N6B 1Z3 Canada
519-439-6228
Fax: 519-439-6016

Longueuil
Place Montérégie
#100, 101, boul Roland Therrien
Longueuil, QC J4H 4B9 Canada
450-646-9900
Fax: 450-646-9475

Matane
129, St-Pierre
Matane, QC G4W 2B6 Canada
418-562-0682
Fax: 418-562-0722

Mississauga
#603, 350 Burnhamthorpe Rd.
Mississauga, ON L5B 3J1 Canada
905-272-2799
Fax: 905-272-9478
888-640-9697

Moncton
#300, 735 Main St.
Moncton, NB E1C 1E5 Canada
506-857-9926
Fax: 506-857-0531

Mont St-Hilaire
279, boul Sir-Wilfrid-Laurier
Mont-Saint-Hilaire, QC J3H 3N8 Canada
450-467-4770
Fax: 450-467-8220

Mont-Laurier
726, rue de la Madone
Mont-Laurier, QC J9L 1S9 Canada
819-623-6002
Fax: 819-623-9468

Montréal - Gauchetiére
#2706, 600, de la Gauchetière
Montréal, QC H3B 4L2 Canada
514-879-2512
Fax: 514-861-9263

Montréal - Guertin
1460, rue Guertin
Montréal, QC H4L 4C2 Canada
514-748-8957

Montréal - Holiday
#145, 1, rue Holiday, Tour est
Montréal, QC H9R 5N3 Canada
514-426-2522
Fax: 514-426-2009

Montréal - Langlier
#402, 8000, Langelier
Montréal, QC H1P 3K2 Canada
514-328-3474
Fax: 514-328-9141

Montréal - Laurier ouest
#1, 1160, Laurier ouest
Montréal, QC H2V 2L5 Canada
514-276-3532
Fax: 514-276-9908

Montréal - Metcalfe
#14338, 1155, rue Metcalfe
Montréal, QC H3B 4S9 Canada
514-843-3088
Fax: 514-843-4447
866-843-3088

Montréal - Metcalfe
1155, rue Metcalfe 14e étage
Montréal, QC H3B 4S9 Canada
514-879-2511
Fax: 514-879-1015

Montréal - Place Ville-Marie
#1805, 1, Place Ville-Marie
Montréal, QC H3B 4A9 Canada
514-871-9000
Fax: 514-871-5031
Jean-François Lacroix

Montréal - Place Ville-Marie
1, Place Ville-Marie
Montréal, QC H3B 2B6 Canada
514-871-2991
Fax: 514-871-1059

North Bay
#101, 680 Cassells St.
North Bay, ON P1B 4A2 Canada
705-476-6360
Fax: 705-474-5950

Ottawa - Albert St.
Constitution Square Tower
#1020, 360 Albert St.
Ottawa, ON K1R 7X7 Canada
613-235-3303
Fax: 613-235-0956

Ottawa - O'Connor St.
#1602, 50 O'Connor St.
Ottawa, ON K1P 6L2 Canada
613-236-0103
Fax: 613-236-5916

Penticton
318 Main St.
Penticton, BC V2A 5C3 Canada
250-487-2600
Fax: 250-487-2649

Plessisville
1729, rue St-Calixte
Plessisville, QC G6L 1R2 Canada
819-362-6000
Fax: 819-758-5197

Québec - Laurier
Place de la Cité
#700, 2600, boul Laurier
Québec, QC G1V 4W2 Canada
418-654-2323
Fax: 418-654-2333
800-463-5659

Québec - René-Lévesque est
#640, 900, René-Lévesque est
Québec, QC G1R 2B5 Canada
418-649-2525
Fax: 418-649-2524
800-463-2635

Regina
#1240, 1801 Hamilton St.
Regina, SK S4P 4B4 Canada
306-525-0004
Fax: 306-525-8414

Repentigny
#201, 534, rue Notre-Dame
Repentigny, QC J6A 2T8 Canada
450-582-7001
Fax: 450-582-0264

Rimouski
#4, 180, rue des Gouverneurs
Rimouski, QC G5L 8G1 Canada
418-721-6767
Fax: 418-721-6777

Rivière-du-Loup
10, rue Beaubien
Rivière-du-Loup, QC G5R 1H7 Canada
418-867-7900
Fax: 418-862-3660

Rouyn-Noranda
74, av Principale
Rouyn-Noranda, QC J9X 4P2 Canada
819-762-4347
Fax: 819-762-9567

Saint-Bruno
1307, rue Roberval
Saint-Bruno, QC J3V 5J1 Canada
450-441-3300
Fax: 450-441-3322

Saint-Hyacinthe
#4100, 1355, rue Gauvin
Saint-Hyacinthe, QC J2S 8W7 Canada
450-774-5354
Fax: 450-774-8798
800-474-5354

Sainte-Agathe-des-Monts
#100, 31, rue Principale
Sainte-Agathe-des-Monts, QC J8C 1J5 Canada
819-326-6115
Fax: 819-326-3090

Sainte-Marie
PO Box Y458
#100, 249, rue du Collège
Sainte-Marie, QC G6E 3B7 Canada
418-387-8155
Fax: 418-387-7035

Salaberry-de-Valleyfield
47, rue Jacques-Cartier
Salaberry-de-Valleyfield, QC J6T 4P9 Canada
450-370-4656
Fax: 450-370-3590
866-254-4656

Saskatoon
#420, 410 - 22nd St. East
Saskatoon, SK S7K 5T6 Canada
306-683-1400
Fax: 306-933-4860

Sept-×les
#305, 1005, boul Laure
Sept-×les, QC G4R 4S6 Canada
418-962-9154
Fax: 418-962-8516

Sherbrooke
#600, 455, rue King ouest
Sherbrooke, QC J1H 6E9 Canada
819-566-7212
Fax: 819-566-5171

Sidney
#205, 2537 Beacon Ave.
Sidney, BC V8L 1Y3 Canada
250-657-2200
Fax: 250-654-0497

Sorel-Tracy
26, Place Charles-de-Montmagny
Sorel-Tracy, QC J3P 7E3 Canada
450-743-8474
Fax: 450-743-8949

St-Félicien
1120, boul Sacré-Coeur
St-Félicien, QC G8K 1P7 Canada
418-679-2684
Fax: 418-679-5473

St-Georges
#100, 11505, 1ère av est
St-Georges, QC G5Y 7X3 Canada
418-227-0121
Fax: 418-227-4671

St-Jean-sur-Richelieu
#400, 895, boul du Séminaire nord
St-Jean-sur-Richelieu, QC J3A 1J2 Canada
450-359-0555
Fax: 450-359-6999

St-Jérôme
#101, 55, rue Castonguay
Saint-Jérome, QC J7Y 2H9 Canada
450-569-8418
Fax: 450-569-0085

Sudbury
#501, 10 Elm St.
Sudbury, ON P3C 1S8 Canada
705-671-1160
Fax: 705-671-1161

Surrey
15119 - 16 Ave.
Surrey, BC V4A 6G3 Canada
604-541-4925
Fax: 604-541-4949

Thetford Mines

#107, 222, boul Frontenac ouest
Thetford Mines, QC G6G 6N7 Canada
418-338-6183
Fax: 418-338-2199
Toronto - King St. West
#3030, 130 King St. West
Toronto, ON M5X 1J9 Canada
416-869-8840
Fax: 416-869-1415
Toronto - King St. West
Exchange Tower
PO Box 21
#3200, 130 King St. West
Toronto, ON M5X 1J9 Canada
416-869-3707
Fax: 416-869-0089
Toronto - King St. West
#1700, 121 King St. West
Toronto, ON M5H 3T9 Canada
416-865-7400
Fax: 416-865-7604
Trois-Rivières - Forges
324, rue des Forges, 2e étage
Trois-Rivières, QC G9A 2G8 Canada
819-379-0000
Fax: 819-379-7639
Trois-Rivières - Jean-XXII
5495, boul Jean-XXII
Trois-Rivières, QC G8Z 4A8 Canada
819-376-9889
Fax: 819-376-2393
Val-d'Or
647, 3e av
Val-d'Or, QC J9P 1S7 Canada
819-824-3687
Fax: 819-824-3264
Vancouver - Burrard St
Two Bentall Centre
PO Box 270
#120, 555 Burrard St.
Vancouver, BC V7X 1M7 Canada
604-643-2774
Fax: 604-682-1026
800-665-6669
Vancouver - Burrard St.
Park Place
#1850, 666 Burrard St.
Vancouver, BC V6C 2X8 Canada
604-623-6777
Fax: 604-623-6780
Vancouver - Burrard St.
Park Place
#3300, 666 Burrard St.
Vancouver, BC V6C 2X8 Canada
604-623-6777
Fax: 604-681-7538
Vernon
#101, 3100 - 30th Ave.
Vernon, BC V1T 2C2 Canada
250-260-4580
Fax: 250-260-4599
Victoria
#700, 737 Yates St.
Victoria, BC V8W 1L6 Canada
250-953-8400
Fax: 250-953-8470
Victoriaville
#150, 650, rue Jutras est
Victoriaville, QC G6S 1E1 Canada
819-758-3191
Fax: 819-758-5197
800-567-7567
Waterloo
Allen Square Bldg.
#340, 180 King St. South
Waterloo, ON N2J 1P8 Canada
519-742-9991
Fax: 519-741-0781
Windsor
#600, 1 Riverside Dr. West
Windsor, ON N9A 5K3 Canada
519-258-5810
Fax: 519-258-5539
Winnipeg
#2100, 360 Main St.
Winnipeg, MB R3C 3Z3 Canada
204-949-8942
Fax: 204-942-1597

Networth Financial Corp.(NFC)

Also listed under: *Financial Planning*
#208, 32450 Simon Ave.
Abbotsford, BC V2T 4V2
604-859-9992
Fax: 604-859-9994
admin@mynetworth.ca
www.networthfinancial.com
Year Founded: 1992
Profile: Networth Financial is a mutual fund dealer.

Executives:
Barry E. Jackson, President

NM Rothschild & Sons Canada Ltd.

Canada Trust Tower, BCE Place
PO Box 206
#3150, 161 Bay St.
Toronto, ON M5J 2S1
416-369-9600
Fax: 416-864-1261
www.rothschild.com
Ownership: Private. Rothschilds Continuation Holdings AG.
Year Founded: 1990
Number of Employees: 16
Profile: The company offers the following services: investment banking, mergers & acquisitions, corporate finance, restructuring, & corporate strategy. The organization operates 40 offices in 30 countries & is affiliated with NM Rothchild & Sons Limited (London), Rothschild & Cie Banque (Paris) & Rothschild Inc. (New York).

Executives:
Daniel Labrecque, President/CEO
Directors:
Peter Teti
David Savard

Nomura Canada Inc.

#700, 2 Bloor St. West
Toronto, ON M4W 3R1
416-868-1683
Fax: 416-359-8956
www.nomura.com
Ownership: Foreign. Part of Nomura Securities International, Inc., New York, NY, USA.
Year Founded: 1927
Profile: Nomura Canada Inc. services Canadian institutional investors.

Norstar Securities International Inc./ Valeurs Mobilières Norstar International Inc.

First Toronto Tower
#107, 73 Richmond Street West
Toronto, ON M5H 4E8
416-619-2004
Fax: 416-619-2011
877-266-8179
www.norstar.ca
Stock Exchange Membership: Toronto Stock Exchange, TSX Venture Exchange
Executives:
Brenda Drisdelle, Officer & Director
Pauline Jarry, Officer & Director
Michael Sheridan, Officer & Director
Sean Sheridan, Officer & Director

Northern Securities Inc.

Also listed under: *Financing & Loan Companies*
PO Box 35
#1800, 150 York St.
Toronto, ON M5H 3S5
416-644-8100
Fax: 416-644-0270
info@northernsi.com
www.northernsi.com
Former Name: St. James Securities Inc.
Ownership: Private. Wholly owned subsidiary of Northern Financial Corporation
Stock Exchange Membership: Canadian Trading & Quotation System Inc, Toronto Stock Exchange, TSX Venture Exchange
Profile: The independent full service investment bank & brokerage firm provides the following services: retail & institutional distribution, equity research, online trading, online public offerings, online private placements, corporate finance, mergers & acquisitions, & financial restructuring. Clients are both retail & institutional, including small capitalization companies.

Executives:
Vic Alboini, President/CEO & Chair
Doug Chornoboy, Sr. Vice-President/CFO
Chris Shaule, Sr. Vice-President & Head, Private Client Group
Ann Krallisch, Director, Business Development
Richard Pinkerton, Managing Director, Investment Banking
Paul A. Thornton, Vice-President, Private Client Group
Frederick Vance, Vice-President, Chief Compliance Officer
Branches:
Bamfield
61 Scotts Lane
Bamfield, BC V0R 1B0
250-728-3494
Brandon
#5, 1711 Kirkcaldy Dr.
Brandon, MB R7A 0B9
204-728-7866
Fax: 204-728-9448
866-720-7866
Calgary
Standard Life Tower
#1940, 639 Fifth Ave. SW
Calgary, AB T2P 0M9
403-398-7390
Fax: 403-313-5642
866-966-1234
Edmonton
Manulife Place
#1150, 10180 - 101 St.
Edmonton, AB T5J 3S4
780-425-0080
Fax: 780-425-0088
866-485-0080
Kamloops
Kamloops, BC
250-377-6900
Fax: 250-377-6949
877-377-6901
Kelowna
#153, 3151 Lakeshore Rd.
Kelowna, BC V1W 3S9
Fax: 250-764-0379
888-764-4037
Lantzville
7810 Aats Rd.
Lantzville, BC V0R 2H0
250-714-6243
Fax: 250-390-3480
Montréal
Place Montréal
#2530, 1800, av McGill College
Montréal, QC H3A 3J6
514-288-4644
Fax: 514-288-5996
Ottawa
#600, 255 Albert St.
Ottawa, ON K1P 6A9
613-751-4447
Fax: 613-751-4467
Vancouver
One Bentall Centre
#2050, 505 Burrard St.
Vancouver, BC V7X 1M6
604-668-1800
Fax: 604-668-1816

Ocean Securities Inc.

310 Purcell's Cove Rd.
Halifax, NS B3P 1C6
902-423-1131
Fax: 902-423-1178
Ownership: Private
Year Founded: 1996
Profile: The investment dealer offers institutional sales & trading.

Executives:
Bruce R. Carroll, President/CEO
Robinson Manson, Vice-President

INVESTMENT MANAGEMENT

INVESTMENT MANAGEMENT

Octagon Capital Corporation
#400, 181 University Ave.
Toronto, ON M5H 3M7
416-368-3322
Fax: 416-368-3811
888-478-8888
info@octagoncap.com
www.octagoncap.com
Year Founded: 1993
Stock Exchange Membership: Canadian Trading & Quotation System Inc, Toronto Stock Exchange, TSX Venture Exchange
Profile: The full-service, independent investment dealer specializes in investment banking, institutional sales & trading, research & private client group services. Clients include institutional investors, issuing companies and retail.

Executives:
David J. McLeish, Chair
Peter Winnell, Vice-Chair
John P. Palumbo, President/CEO, Acting CFO
Jean Pierre Colin, Trading Officer
John Ponech, Trading Officer
Michael Sproule, Trading Officer
Branches:
Calgary
#1400, 606 - 4 St. SW
Calgary, AB T2P 1T1 Canada
403-750-0475
Fax: 403-750-0499
Montréal
#2500, 1155, boul René-Lévesque ouest
Montréal, QC H3B 2K4 Canada
514-875-9339

Odlum Brown Limited
#1100, 250 Howe St.
Vancouver, BC V6C 3S9
604-669-1600
Fax: 604-681-8310
888-886-3586
info@odlumbrown.com
www.odlumbrown.com
Ownership: Private
Year Founded: 1923
Number of Employees: 200
Stock Exchange Membership: Montreal Exchange, Toronto Stock Exchange, TSX Venture Exchange
Executives:
S. Ross Sherwood, President/CEO
Debra Hewson, Vice-President/COO
Peter Pacholko, Vice-President/CFO
Branches:
Campbell River
590A - 11th Ave.
Campbell River, BC V9W 4G5 Canada
250-286-3151
Fax: 250-703-0638
877-703-0637
Chilliwack
Cottonwood West Professional Bldg.
#103, 45425 Luckakuck Way
Chilliwack, BC V2R 2T7 Canada
604-858-2455
Fax: 604-824-4664
800-663-5251
Courtenay
#207, 501 - 4th St.
Courtenay, BC V9N 1H3 Canada
250-703-0637
Fax: 250-703-0638
877-703-0637
Kelowna
#4, 1890 Cooper Rd.
Kelowna, BC V1Y 8K5 Canada
250-861-5700
Fax: 250-861-7766
800-788-5677
Victoria
#710, 880 Douglas St.
Victoria, BC V8W 2B7 Canada
250-952-7777
Fax: 250-386-7782
888-293-0744

Olympian Financial Inc.
Also listed under: *Financial Planning*
#802, 2300 Yonge St.
Toronto, ON M4P 1E4
416-544-9100
Fax: 416-544-9101
info@olympianfinancial.com
www.olympianfinancial.com
Year Founded: 1993
Executives:
Alexander Michael Mitonidis, Founder, Certified Financial Planner
Daniel Antonys Mitonides, Founder, Chartered Accountant

Omni Capital Inc.
#2401, 1010, rue Sherbrooke ouest
Montréal, QC H3A 2R7
514-499-1577
Fax: 514-499-9315
info@omnicapital.com
www.omnicapital.com
Ownership: Part of Omni Capital, USA.
Year Founded: 1980
Profile: The securities dealer is fully-licensed in Quebec.

Executives:
Michael Weinberg, President

Orion Securities Inc.
BCE Place
PO Box 830
#3100, 181 Bay St.
Toronto, ON M5J 2T3
416-848-3500
Fax: 416-848-3162
concierge@orionsecurities.ca
www.orionsecurities.ca
Former Name: Yorkton Securities Inc.
Stock Exchange Membership: Montreal Exchange, Toronto Stock Exchange, TSX Venture Exchange
Executives:
John P.A. Budreski, President/CEO
Branches:
Calgary
Royal Bank Bldg.
#1210, 335 - 8th Ave. SW
Calgary, AB T2P 1C9 Canada
403-218-6650
Fax: 403-263-9794
Montréal
#3910, 1250, boul René-Lévesque
Montréal, QC H3B 4W8 Canada
514-925-2850
Fax: 514-925-2870
Vancouver
Three Bentall Centre
PO Box 49043
#2333, 595 Burrard St.
Vancouver, BC V7X 1C4 Canada
604-629-5575
Fax: 604-629-5578

Pacific International Securities Inc.
#1900, 666 Burrard St.
Vancouver, BC V6C 3N1
604-664-2900
Fax: 604-664-2666
info@pisecurities.com
www.pi-securities.com
Ownership: Private. 35% owned by National Bank of Canada
Year Founded: 1982
Number of Employees: 135
Assets: $100-500 million
Revenues: $10-50 million
Stock Exchange Membership: Canadian Trading & Quotation System Inc, Montreal Exchange, Toronto Stock Exchange, TSX Venture Exchange
Profile: Pacific International offers a full range of investment products & services.

Executives:
Max Meier, Chair/CEO; 604-664-2905
John T. Eymann, Vice-Chair, Director; 604-644-2907
Jean Paul Bachellerie, President/COO
David A. Murray, CFO
Alberto John Quattroiocchi, Exec. Vice-President, Director; 604-664-2925
Lawrence H. McQuid, Sr. Vice-President, Director; 604-664-2911
James Peter Defer, Vice-President, Corporate Finance, Director
Richard W. Thomas, Vice-President, Compliance, Corporate Secretary
Wendell M. Zerb, Vice-President, Institutional & Research
Directors:
Germain Carrière
Branches:
Calgary
#3440, 205 - 5 Ave. SW
Calgary, AB T2P 2V7 Canada
403-543-2900
Fax: 403-543-2800
Victoria
#210, 880 Douglas St.
Victoria, BC V8W 2B7 Canada
250-405-2900
Fax: 250-450-2911

Paradigm Capital Inc.
#2101, 95 Wellington St. West
Toronto, ON M5J 2N7
416-361-9892
Fax: 416-361-6050
toronto@paradigmcapinc.com
www.paradigmcap.com
Ownership: Employee-owned
Year Founded: 1999
Number of Employees: 55
Stock Exchange Membership: Toronto Stock Exchange, TSX Venture Exchange
Profile: Paradigm Capital is an independent institutional equity dealer which focuses upon Canadian equity markets. Over 150 companies are covered in the following sectors: resources, energy, energy services, technology, biotechnology, industrial products & entertainment. Paradigm provides equity research, sales, trading & investment banking coverage for over 200 institutional clients in Canada, the US, Europe & Australasia.

Executives:
David Roland, CEO
Michael Ward, Chief Financial Officer
John M. Warwick, Vice-President
Blair Abernathy, Manager, Research
Directors:
Peter J. Dey, Chair
Branches:
Calgary
Ford Tower
#630, 633 - 6th Ave. SW
Calgary, AB T2P 2Y5 Canada
Phil Moore, Partner, Energy Investment Banking

Parkyn, Wermenlinger, Layton Capital Inc.(PWL)
Also listed under: *Financial Planning*
#200, 215, av Redfern
Montréal, QC H3Z 3L5
514-875-7566
Fax: 514-875-9611
800-343-7566
capital@pwlcapital.com
www.pwlcapital.com
Also Known As: PWL Capital Inc.
Year Founded: 1995
Profile: PWL offers fee-based investment & planning advice.

Executives:
Hélène Gagné, Partner, Assistant Portfolio Manager & Security Advisor
Anthony S. Layton, MBA, Partner, Registered Financial Planner
James Parkyn, Partner, Registered Financial Planner
Laurent Wermenlinger, Partner, Canadian Investment Manager, Fellow Registered Financial Planner
Caroline Nalbantoglu, B.Adm., Certified Financial Planner
Branches:
Ottawa
#100, 265 Carling Ave.
Ottawa, ON K1S 2E1 Canada
613-237-5544
Fax: 613-237-5949
800-230-5544
ottawa@pwlcapital.com
Colin Cooke, Certified Financial Planner
Rivière-du-Loup
PO Box 397
494, rue Lafontaine
Rivière-du-Loup, QC G5R 3Y9 Canada

418-862-5643
Fax: 418-862-3585
800-774-7418
rdl@pwlcapital.com
André Morin, Contact
Toronto
#601, 3 Church St.
Toronto, ON M5E 1M2 Canada
416-203-0067
Fax: 416-203-0544
866-242-0203
toronto@pwlcapital.com
Jane Baker, Certified Financial Planner

Paula Meier Associates
Also listed under: *Financial Planning*
23 Doxsee Ave. North
Campbellford, ON K0L 1L0
705-653-1606
Fax: 705-653-1643
paula@paulameier.com
Ownership: Private. Part of Armstrong & Quaile Associates Inc., Manotick, ON.
Executives:
Paula Meier, Contact

Penson Financial Services Canada Inc.
360, rue St. Jacques ouest, 11 étage
Montréal, QC H2Y 1P5
514-841-9665
Fax: 514-841-9700
www.penson.ca
Former Name: ECE Electronic Clearing Inc.
Ownership: Wholly owned subsidiary of Penson Worldwide, Inc., Dallas, TX.
Year Founded: 1999
Number of Employees: 46
Stock Exchange Membership: Canadian Trading & Quotation System Inc, Montreal Exchange, Toronto Stock Exchange, TSX Venture Exchange
Profile: The company provides outsourcing services to the securities industry.
Executives:
Richard A. Ness, President/CEO
Raymond Désormeux, Chair
Terrence Bourne, Exec. Vice-President/COO
Liam Cheung, Exec. Vice-President
Ho Hirani, Exec. Vice-President, Chief Technology Officer
John Skain, Sr. Vice-President, Sales, Trading & Treasury Services
Laurie Ciotoli, Vice-President, Business Development
François Gervais, CFO
Branches:
Toronto
#711, 330 Bay St.
Toronto, ON M5H 2S8 Canada
416-943-4319
Fax: 416-943-9800

Peregrine Financial Group Canada, Inc.
#200, 1290 Central Pkwy West
Mississauga, ON L5C 4R3
905-896-8383
Fax: 905-896-8806
Profile: The investment dealer is engaged in commodities trading.

Perry Securities Ltd.
#102, 10135 - 101 Ave.
Grande Prairie, AB T8V 0Y4
780-532-7717
Fax: 780-538-0600
800-361-5562
kenperry@telusplanet.net
Executives:
Kenneth Perry, Manager

Peters & Co. Limited
Bankers Hall West
#3900, 888 - 3rd St. SW
Calgary, AB T2P 5C5
403-261-4850
Fax: 403-266-4116
info@petersco.com
www.petersco.com
Ownership: Private
Year Founded: 1972
Number of Employees: 70
Stock Exchange Membership: Toronto Stock Exchange, TSX Venture Exchange
Profile: The company's subsidiary is Peters & Co. Equities Inc.
Executives:
I. D. Bruce, President/CEO
M.J. Tims, Chair
W.A. Gobert, Vice-Chair
H.A. Benson, CFO & Vice-President, Finance
A.V. Boland, Managing Director, Research
C.S. Potter, Managing Director, Corporate Finance
R.C. Wigham, Managing Director, Capital Markets
M.D. Malloy, Director, Trading

Pewter Financial Ltd.
Also listed under: *Financial Planning*
43 Hollyburn Rd. SW
Calgary, AB T2V 3H2
403-255-1711
Fax: 403-259-2922
Profile: The company is a member of the Mutual Fund Dealers Association of Canada.

PFL Investments Canada Ltd.
Also listed under: *Financial Planning*
Plaza V
#300, 2000 Argentia Rd.
Mississauga, ON L5N 2R7
905-812-2900
Fax: 905-813-5310

PFSL Investments Canada Ltd.
Also listed under: *Investment Fund Companies*
Plaza V
#300, 2000 Argentia Rd.
Mississauga, ON L5N 2R7
905-812-2900
Fax: 905-813-5313
800-387-7876
www.primerica.com
Former Name: Primerica (PFSL) Invest Can Ltd.; PFS Canada
Ownership: Private. Wholly owned subsidiary of Primerica Financial Services (Canada) Ltd.
Year Founded: 1991
Number of Employees: 35
Assets: 20,074,113 Year End: 20051231
Revenues: $61,411,564 Year End: 20051231
Profile: The licensed mutual fund dealer is incorporated under the Canada Business Corporations Act. Other affiliated companies include Primerica Clients Services Inc., Primerica Financial Services Ltd., & Primerica Life Insurance Company of U.S.
Executives:
John Adams, CEO, Exec. Vice-President; 905-813-5345; johna.adams@primerica.com
Heather Koski, CFO & Vice-President, Finance
David Howarth, Sr. Vice-President, PFSL Operations; 905-813-5406; david.howarth@primerica.com
Guy Sauvé, Sr. Vice-President, Québec Marketing; 450-975-2400; guy.sauve@primerica.com
Elina C. DaSilva, Vice-President, Licensing & Agency Support; 905-813-5352; elina.dasilva@primerica.com
Waqas Rana, Vice-President, Chief Compliance Officer; 905-813-5327; waqas.rana@primerica.com
Directors:
John A. Adams; 905-813-5345
David Howarth; 905-813-5406
Heather Kaski; 905-813-5367
Affiliated Companies:
Primerica Life Insurance Company of Canada
Primerica:
Aggressive Growth Fund
RRSP Eligible; Inception Year: 0; Fund Managers: AGF Funds Inc.
Conservative Growth Fund
RRSP Eligible; Inception Year: 0; Fund Managers: AGF Funds Inc.
Moderate Growth Fund
RRSP Eligible; Inception Year: 0; Fund Managers: AGF Funds Inc.
Growth Fund
RRSP Eligible; Inception Year: 0; Fund Managers: AGF Funds Inc.
Income Fund
RRSP Eligible; Inception Year: 0; Fund Managers: AGF Funds Inc.
Canadian Money Market Fund
RRSP Eligible; Inception Year: 0; Fund Managers: AGF Funds Inc.

Pictet Canada LLP/ Pictet (Canada), société en commandite
#2900, 1800, av McGill College
Montréal, QC H3A 3J6
514-288-8161
Fax: 514-288-5472
www.pictet.com
Ownership: Foreign. Subsidiary of Pictet & Cie, Geneva, Switzerland.
Stock Exchange Membership: Montreal Exchange, Toronto Stock Exchange
Executives:
Jean-François Sauvé, President
Peter O'Reilly, Sr. Vice-President

Pinch Group
Also listed under: *Financial Planning*
#1000, 1175 Douglas St.
Victoria, BC V8W 2E1
250-405-2420
Fax: 250-405-2499
877-405-2400
pinchgroup@raymondjames.ca
www.pinchgroup.ca
Number of Employees: 5
Profile: The group offers investment management & financial planning. The website provides a resource on ethical, socially responsible or environmental/green investing. The financial/commercial institution is a member of the Social Investment Organization. Activities are conducted in British Columbia, Alberta, Ontario & the Northwest Territories..
Executives:
Brian Pinch, Investment Advisor
Frank Arnold, Investment Advisor
Michael Higgins, Investment Advisor
Branches:
Toronto
Scotia Plaza
PO Box 415
#5300, 40 King St. West
Toronto, ON M5H 3Y2 Canada
416-777-7000
Fax: 416-777-7020
877-363-1024
Vancouver
Cathedral Place
#800, 333 Seymour St.
Vancouver, BC V6B 5E2 Canada
604-654-1111
Fax: 604-654-0209
888-545-6624
Vancouver
Cathedral Place
#2100, 925 West Georgia St.
Vancouver, BC V6C 3L2 Canada
604-659-8000
Fax: 604-659-8099
888-545-6624

Planification Copepco Inc.
Also listed under: *Financial Planning*
858, rue du Haut-Bois sud
Sherbrooke, QC J1N 2J2
819-821-4378
Fax: 910-821-0193
Ownership: Private
Year Founded: 1990

Planmar Financial Corp.
Also listed under: *Financial Planning*
#103, 400 York St.
London, ON N6B 3N2
519-673-3010
Fax: 519-673-6054
877-504-3010
info@planmar.net
www.planmar.com
Year Founded: 1987
Executives:

INVESTMENT MANAGEMENT

Planmar Financial Corp. (continued)
Tony Cuzzocrea, President

Polar Securities Inc.
372 Bay St., 21st. Fl.
Toronto, ON M5H 2W9
416-367-4364
Fax: 416-367-0564
inquiries@polarsec.com
www.polarsec.com
Ownership: Employee-owned.
Year Founded: 1991
Stock Exchange Membership: Montreal Exchange, Toronto Stock Exchange, TSX Venture Exchange
Profile: The investment dealer is a hedge-fund manager.

Executives:
Paul Sabourin, MBA, Chair, Chief Investment Officer
Tom Sabourin, CA, CEO
Herman Gill, CA, Chief Financial Officer
Michael McNeil, MBA, CGA, CAIA, Vice-President, Marketing & Business Development
Robyn Schultz, CFA, Vice-President, Operations, Chief Compliance Officer
Peter Vanderploeg, CFA, Vice-President, Risk Management
Branches:
Calgary
#200, 333 - 5th Ave. SW
Calgary, AB T2P 3T6 Canada
403-705-7300
Fax: 403-705-7310

INVESTMENT MANAGEMENT

Pollitt & Co. Inc.
Commerce Court East
PO Box 94
#805, 21 Melinda St.
Toronto, ON M5L 1B9
416-365-3313
Fax: 416-368-0141
www.pollitt.com
Ownership: Employee-owned.
Stock Exchange Membership: Montreal Exchange, Toronto Stock Exchange, TSX Venture Exchange
Profile: The independent investment dealer serves institutional & private clients.

Executives:
Murray H. Pollitt, P.Eng., President
John T. Christie, Officer & Director
Robert MacNeil, Officer
Branches:
Montréal
#930, 625, boul René-Lévesque ouest
Montréal, QC H3B 1R2 Canada
514-395-8910
Fax: 514-395-8709

Polyfunds Investment Inc.
36 Yellow Birch Cres.
Richmond Hill, ON L4B 3R4
905-889-1838
Fax: 905-889-2938
polyfunds@sympatico.ca

Polygone Financial Services Inc./ Services Financiers Polygone
***Also listed under:** Financial Planning*
#1400, 1010, rue de la Gauchetière ouest
Montréal, QC H3B 2N2
514-866-7300
Fax: 514-866-4682
messages@polygone.net
www.polygone.net
Executives:
Guy Charron, President

Pope & Company
15 Duncan St.
Toronto, ON M5H 3P9
416-593-5535
Fax: 416-593-5099
www.popecompany.com
Ownership: Employee-owned.
Year Founded: 1934
Stock Exchange Membership: Toronto Stock Exchange, TSX Venture Exchange
Profile: Investment banking, capital markets & asset management services are provided by the independent brokerage firm. Clients include individuals & Canadian enterprises.

Executives:
Francis M. Pope, CEO
D'Arcy Mackenzie, Chief Financial Officer

Portfolio Strategies Corporation
***Also listed under:** Financial Planning*
#301B6, 2509 Dieppe Ave. SW
Calgary, AB T3E 7J9
403-252-5222
Fax: 403-252-1220
877-303-3233
info@portfoliostrategies.ca
www.portfoliostrategies.ca
Profile: The independent investment consulting firm provides financial planning & investment advice. It offers various investment products, such as mutual & segrgated funds, bonds & GICs, in addition to group RRSPs, DPSPs & pension plans.

Executives:
Mark S. Kent, President
Branches:
Calgary
1505 Macleod Trail SE
Calgary, AB T2G 2N6 Canada
403-705-5067
Fax: 403-262-0133
Kate Allard, Contact
Dawson Creek
#22, 1405 - 102 Ave.
Dawson Creek, BC V1G 2E1 Canada
250-782-7272
Fax: 250-782-7282
Howard Wyant, Contact
Lethbridge
Lethbridge Centre Tower
#902, 400- 4th Ave. South
Lethbridge, AB T1J 4E1 Canada
403-380-2020
Fax: 403-380-2290
Lisa Aucoin, Contact
Magrath
c/o Trading Company Office
86S - 1st St. West
Magrath, AB T0K 1J0 Canada
403-758-6631
Fax: 403-759-6878
Shannon Sabey, Contact
Markham
#211, 80 Acadia Ave.
Markham, ON L3R 9V1 Canada
905-940-2783
Fax: 905-940-8692
Frank Sui-Cheong Pa, Contact
Medicine Hat
#101, 623 - 4 St. SE
Medicine Hat, AB T1A 0L1 Canada
403-526-3283
Fax: 403-526-8082
Bob Olson, Contact
Red Deer
#207, 4921 - 49th St.
Red Deer, AB T4N 1V2 Canada
403-343-1181
Fax: 403-343-1182
Rick Baron, Contact
Regina
1836 Angus St.
Regina, SK S4T 1Z4 Canada
306-584-2523
Fax: 306-584-8225
Kelly Aikens, Contact
Richmond - #3 Rd.
#750, 5951 - #3 Rd.
Richmond, BC Canada
604-273-0232
Fax: 604-273-0232
Tina Ho, Contact
Richmond - #3 Rd.
#560, 5900 - #3 Rd.
Richmond, BC V6X 3P7 Canada
604-303-9700
Fax: 604-303-9705
Henry Liao, Contact
Richmond Hill
#14A, 30 Wertheim Ct.
Richmond Hill, ON L4B 1B9 Canada
905-695-1808
Fax: 905-695-1810
Elaine Kwan, Contact
Trail
#235, 8100 Rock Island Hwy.
Trail, BC V1R 4N7 Canada
250-368-9600
Fax: 250-364-3138
Frank DeFouw, Contact
Trochu
322 Arena Ave.
Trochu, AB T0M 2C0 Canada
403-442-2172
Fax: 403-442-2183
Barry Kletke, Contact
Vancouver
North Tower, Oakridge Centre
#555, 650 West 41st Ave.
Vancouver, BC V5Z 2M9 Canada
604-269-9888
Fax: 604-269-9588
Daniel Ng, Contact
White Rock - Russell Ave.
#235, 15233 Russell Ave.
White Rock, BC V4B 5C3 Canada
604-538-7643
Fax: 604-542-1025
Sam Esaw, Contact
White Rock - West Hastings St.
#1088, 999 West Hastings St.
Vancouver, BC V6C 2W2 Canada
604-605-1644
Fax: 604-605-1674
Sam Esaw, Contact
Winnipeg
#200, 1 Wesley Ave.
Winnipeg, MB R3C 4C8 Canada
204-940-5460
Fax: 204-940-5462
Margaret Koniuck, Contact

Prebon Canada Limited
#803, 1 Toronto St.
Toronto, ON M5C 2V6
416-941-0606
Fax: 416-941-0607
info@tullettprebon.com
www.tullettprebon.com
Former Name: Prebon Yamane (Canada) Limited; Tullett Liberty
Ownership: Part of Tullett Prebon Group Ltd., London, UK.
Year Founded: 1971
Profile: Tullett Prebon facilitates the trading activities of its clients. Clients include financial institutions & professional investors. Services include fixed income securities, treasury products, interest rate derivatives, equities, energy & information sales.

Executives:
Denis Marcotte, Managing Director
Bruce D. Meikle, Officer
Christopher Woolcock, Compliance Officer
Frank Klotz, Contact, Sales
Branches:
Calgary
#300, 615 3rd Ave. SW
Calgary, AB T2P 0G6
403-215-5500
Fax: 403-215-5570

Professional Investment Services (Canada) Inc./Wolfe Financial
***Also listed under:** Financial Planning*
19 Oakdale Pl.
St Albert, AB T8N 6L7
780-458-4794
Fax: 780-418-7607
d.wolfe@shaw.ca
Former Name: Generation Financial Corp./Wolfe Financial
Year Founded: 2002
Number of Employees: 2
Assets: Under $1 million
Revenues: Under $1 million
Executives:

Debbie Wolfe, Contact

Progressive Financial Strategy
Also listed under: *Financial Planning*
#203, 5170 Dixie Rd.
Mississauga, ON L4W 1E3
905-212-9149
Fax: 905-212-9201
pfs@pfs.ca
www.pfs.ca
Profile: The financial planning center is also an investment fund dealer & an independent insurance broker.

QFS Financial Services Ltd.
Also listed under: *Financial Planning*
355 Plains Rd. East
Burlington, ON L7T 4H7
905-681-6555
Fax: 905-681-6755

Qtrade Investor Inc.
One Bentall Centre
PO Box 85
#1920, 505 Burrard St.
Vancouver, BC V7X 1M6
604-605-4199
Fax: 604-484-2627
877-787-2330
info@qtrade.ca, techsupport@qtrade.ca, alliances@qtrade.ca
www.qtrade.ca/investor
Ownership: Part of Qtrade Financial Group, Vancouver, BC.
Profile: The independent brokerage offers services to Canadian financial institutions. Investment, trading, accounts & research are some of the services provided.

Executives:
Scott R. Gibner, CEO
Joseph E. Meehan, President
Bertila Espino, Vice-President, Compliance
Neil McCammon, Vice-President, Trading
Andrew Quinn, Vice-President, Trading

Quadrus Investment Services Ltd.
Also listed under: *Investment Fund Companies*
255 Dufferin Ave.
London, ON N6A 4K1
519-432-5281
Fax: 519-435-7679
888-532-3322
quadrusclientservices@quadrusinvestment.com
www.londonlife.com
Ownership: Wholly owned subsidiary of London Life Insurance Company, London, ON.
Profile: The mutual fund dealer has more than 3,400 registered investment representatives.

Executives:
Alf Goodall, Vice-President
Quadrus Group of Funds:
LLIM Canadian Diversified Equity Fund
RRSP Eligible; Inception Year: 1999; Fund Managers: London Life Investment Management Ltd.
LLIM Canadian Bond Fund
RRSP Eligible; Inception Year: 1999; Fund Managers: London Life Investment Management Ltd.
LLIM Income Plus Fund
RRSP Eligible; Inception Year: 1999; Fund Managers: London Life Investment Management Ltd.
Advanced Folio Fund
RRSP Eligible; Inception Year: 2001; Fund Managers: Mackenzie Financial Corporation
Aggressive Folio Fund
RRSP Eligible; Inception Year: 2001; Fund Managers: Mackenzie Financial Corporation
Balanced Folio Fund
RRSP Eligible; Inception Year: 2001; Fund Managers: Mackenzie Financial Corporation
Canadian Equity Folio Fund
RRSP Eligible; Inception Year: 2001; Fund Managers: Mackenzie Financial Corporation
Conservative Folio Fund
RRSP Eligible; Inception Year: 2001; Fund Managers: Mackenzie Financial Corporation
Fixed Income Folio Fund
RRSP Eligible; Inception Year: 2001; Fund Managers: Mackenzie Financial Corporation
Global Equity Folio Fund
RRSP Eligible; Inception Year: 2001; Fund Managers: Mackenzie Financial Corporation
GWLIM Canadian Growth Fund
RRSP Eligible; Inception Year: 2001; Fund Managers: GWL Investment Management Ltd.
GWLIM Canadian Mid Cap Fund
RRSP Eligible; Inception Year: 2001; Fund Managers: GWL Investment Management Ltd.
GWLIM Corporate Bond Fund
RRSP Eligible; Inception Year: 2001; Fund Managers: GWL Investment Management Ltd.
GWLIM Ethics Fund
RRSP Eligible; Inception Year: 2001; Fund Managers: GWL Investment Management Ltd.
GWLIM US Mid Cap Fund
RRSP Eligible; Inception Year: 2001; Fund Managers: GWL Investment Management Ltd.
LLIM US Equity Fund
RRSP Eligible; Inception Year: 2001; Fund Managers: London Life Investment Management Ltd.
LLIM US Growth Sectors Fund
RRSP Eligible; Inception Year: 2001; Fund Managers: London Life Investment Management Ltd.
Mackenzie Ivy European Capital Fund
RRSP Eligible; Inception Year: 2003; Fund Managers: Mackenzie Financial Corporation
Mackenzie Maxxum Canadian Balanced Fund
RRSP Eligible; Inception Year: 1988; Fund Managers: Mackenzie Financial Corporation
Mackenzie Maxxum Canadian Equity Growth Fund
RRSP Eligible; Inception Year: 1970; Fund Managers: Mackenzie Financial Corporation
Mackenzie Maxxum Dividend Fund
RRSP Eligible; Inception Year: 1986; Fund Managers: Mackenzie Financial Corporation
Mackenzie Maxxum Money Market Fund
RRSP Eligible; Inception Year: 1986; Fund Managers: Mackenzie Financial Corporation
Mackenzie Universal American Growth Capital Fund
RRSP Eligible; Inception Year: 2002; Fund Managers: Bluewater Investment Management Inc.
Mackenzie Universal Canadian Resource Fund
RRSP Eligible; Inception Year: 2002; Fund Managers: Mackenzie Financial Corporation
Mackenzie Universal Precious Metals Fund
RRSP Eligible; Inception Year: 2002; Fund Managers: Mackenzie Financial Corporation
Moderate Folio Fund
RRSP Eligible; Inception Year: 2001; Fund Managers: Mackenzie Financial Corporation
Quadrus Templeton Canadian Equity Fund
RRSP Eligible; Inception Year: 1999; Fund Managers: Franklin Templeton Investments
Quadrus Templeton International Equity Fund
RRSP Eligible; Inception Year: 1999; Fund Managers: Franklin Templeton Investments
Mackenzie Select Managers Canada Fund
RRSP Eligible; Inception Year: 2002; Fund Managers: Henderson Global Investors Ltd.
Quadrus Trimark Balanced Fund
RRSP Eligible; Inception Year: 2003; Fund Managers: AIM Trimark Investment Management
Mackenzie Universal Global Future Fund
RRSP Eligible; Inception Year: 1995; Fund Managers: Mackenzie Financial Corporation
Mackenzie Universal US Growth Leaders Fund
RRSP Eligible; Inception Year: 1995; Fund Managers: Waddell & Reed Inc.
Quadrus Trimark Global Equity Fund
RRSP Eligible; Inception Year: 2003; Fund Managers: AIM Trimark Investment Management
Mackenzie Select Managers Far East Capital Fund
RRSP Eligible; Inception Year: 2002; Fund Managers: Pacific Regional Group
Mackenzie Universal Emerging Markets Capital Fund
RRSP Eligible; Inception Year: 2002; Fund Managers: J.P. Morgan Fleming Asset Management
AIM Canadian Equity Growth Fund
RRSP Eligible; Inception Year: 2001; Fund Managers: AIM Trimark Investment Management
Cash Management Corporate Class Fund
RRSP Eligible; Inception Year: 2005;
Canadian Equity Corporate Class Fund
RRSP Eligible; Inception Year: 2005;
Canadian Specialty Corporate Class Fund
RRSP Eligible; Inception Year: 2005;
Fixed Income Corporate Class Fund
RRSP Eligible; Inception Year: 2005;
Laketon Fixed Income Series Q Fund
RRSP Eligible; Inception Year: 1974; Fund Managers: Laketon Investment Management
US & International Equity Corporate Class Fund
RRSP Eligible; Inception Year: 2005;
US & International Specialty Corporate Class Fund
RRSP Eligible; Inception Year: 2005;

Queensbury Securities Inc.
69 Yonge St., 2nd Fl.
Toronto, ON M5E 1K3
416-866-8600
webster@queensbury.com
www.queensbury.com
Ownership: Private. Part of Queensbury Group, Toronto, ON
Year Founded: 1987
Profile: The independent, full service firm services small & medium sized businesses. Debt & equity capital can be accessed by Queensbury. Part of the Queensbury Group, the firm is affiliated with Queensbury Insurance Brokers.

Executives:
Hugh McLelland, Chair/CEO
John Webster, President, Chief Compliance Officer
Bob Seal, Exec. Vice-President/CFO
Branches:
Oakville
114 Forsythe St.
Oakville, ON L6K 3T3
905-845-1484
drv@queensbury.com

Questrade, Inc.
#203, 5001 Yonge St.
Toronto, ON M2N 6P6
416-227-9876
Fax: 416-227-0078
888-783-7866
www.questrade.com
Former Name: Quest Capital Group Ltd.
Ownership: Private
Year Founded: 1999
Number of Employees: 6
Stock Exchange Membership: Toronto Stock Exchange
Executives:
Edward Kholodenko, President/CEO; 416-227-9876
Dean Percy, CFO; 416-227-9876
Gary Miskin, Vice-President, Business Development; 416-227-9876
Directors:
Edward Kholodenko
Inna Kholodenko
Gary Miskin
Dean Percy

Ramey Investments Incorporated
Also listed under: *Financial Planning*
72 Portland St.
Dartmouth, NS B2Y 1H6
902-466-7464
Fax: 902-461-4491
ramey@rameyinvestments.com
www.rameyinvestments.com
Year Founded: 1975
Profile: The independent firm provides financial & investment advice. Financial planning services include retirement, investment, tax, estate & education. Products include mutual funds & segregated funds.

Raymond James Ltd.
Also listed under: *Financial Planning*
Cathedral Place
#2200, 925 West Georgia St.
Vancouver, BC V6C 3L2
604-659-8000
Fax: 604-659-8099
888-545-6624
webcomments@raymondjames.ca
www.raymondjames.ca
Former Name: Goepel McDermid Securities Inc.
Ownership: Indirect wholly-owned subsidiary of Raymond James Financial, Inc., St. Petersburg, FL, USA.
Year Founded: 1962

Raymond James Ltd. (continued)
Number of Employees: 689
Stock Exchange Membership: Montreal Exchange, Toronto Stock Exchange, TSX Venture Exchange
Profile: Raymond James is an independent, full service investment dealer & financial advising company. It offers professional investment services & products, including asset management, equity research, fixed income products, mutual funds, investment banking, institutional equity sales & trading, estate planning, financial planning, & insurance. Financial planning services are provided through Raymond James Financial Planning Ltd.

Executives:
Ken Shields, Chair
Peter Bailey, President/CEO
Lloyd Costley, Exec. Vice-President/CAO, Corporate Services
Jason Holtby, Sr. Managing Director, Investment Banking
Peter Kahnert, Sr. Vice-President, Corporate Communications & Marketing
George Karkoulas, Sr. Vice-President, Independent Financial Services
Kevin Whelly, Sr. Vice-President, Growth & Development
Terry Hetherington, Manager, National Sales

Branches:
Barrie - Caplan Ave.
#612, 92 Caplan Ave.
Barrie, ON L4N 0Z7
705-719-7967
Bromont
109, boul Bromont
Bromont, QC J2L 2K7
450-534-1900
Simon Bilodeau, Branch Manager
Burlington
1100 Walkers Line
Burlington, ON L7N 2G3
905-332-7861
Lynn Curtin Lange, Branch Manager
Calgary - 11th Ave. SW
#207, 322 - 11th Ave. SW
Calgary, AB T2R 0C5
403-531-2444
Calgary - 2nd St. SW
1409 2nd Street SW
Calgary, AB T2R 0W7
403-263-7999
Taylor Davison, Branch Manager
Calgary - 8th Ave. SW
#2500, 707 - 8th Ave. SW
Calgary, AB T2P 1H5
403-509-0500
Calgary - 8th Ave. SW
#2300, 707 8th Ave. SW
Calgary, AB T2P 1H5
403-221-0333
Mike Irwin, Branch Manager
Calgary - Varsity Dr. NW
#101, 4603 Varsity Dr. NW
Calgary, AB T3A 2V7
403-670-8871
Claresholm
4802 - 2nd St. West
Claresholm, AB T0L 0T0
403-625-1555
Cobourg - Division St.
#1, 438 Division St.
Cobourg, ON K9A 3R9
905-372-4333
Cobourg - Division St.
#2, 438 Division St.
Cobourg, ON K9A 3R9
905-372-1300
Courtenay
1255C Cliffe Ave.
Courtenay, BC V9N 2K3
250-334-9294
Delta - 12th Ave.
#102, 5405 - 12th Ave.
Delta, BC V4M 2B2
604-943-6360
Delta - 56th St.
#3, 1359 - 56th St.
Delta, BC V4L 2P3
604-943-5665
Duncan
351 Festubert St.
Duncan, BC V9L 3T1
250-715-0004
Edmonton
#2300, 10060 Jasper Ave.
10060 Jasper Ave, AB T5J 3R8
780-414-2500
Don Howden, Branch Manager
Elmvale
42 Queen St. West
Elmvale, ON L0L 1P0
705-322-2442
Brian Alger, Branch Manager
Essex
14 Victoria Ave.
Essex, ON N8M 1M3
519-776-7770
Fort McMurray
#101, 9816 Hardin St.
Fort McMurray, AB T9H 4K3
780-799-7820
Gatineau
#150, 160, boul de l'Hôpital
Gatineau, QC J8T 8J1
819-568-5025
Martin Boucher, Branch Manager
Halifax
TD Centre
#1030, 1791 Barrington St.
Halifax, NS B3J 3K9
902-444-9922
Kevin Van Amburg, Branch Manager
Hamilton
Commerce Place
#400, 1 King St. West
Hamilton, ON L8P 1A4
905-974-2900
Andrew Irwin, Branch Manager
High River
#2, 27 - 11th Ave. SE
High River, AB T1V 1Y1
403-652-2053
Cliff Squires, Branch Manager
Huntsville
39 King William St.
Huntsville, ON P1H 1G4
705-789-2100
Kamloops
#201, 242 Victoria St.
Kamloops, BC V2C 2A2
250-372-8117
Les Consenheim, Branch Manager
Kelowna
#500, 1726 Dolphin Ave.
Kelowna, BC V1Y 9R9
250-979-2700
Paul Johnson, Branch Manager
Kingston
#101, 1000 Gardiners Rd.
Kingston, ON K7P 3C4
613-634-4500
Paul Richardson, Branch Manager
London
#1510, 148 Fullarton St.
London, ON N6A 5P3
519-640-6894
Markham
#308, 7050 Woodbine Ave.
Markham, ON L3R 4G8
905-470-6222
Medicine Hat
#3, 202 - 5th Ave.
Medicine Hat, AB T1A 2P8
403-580-4375
Mississauga - Britannia Rd. East
256 Britannia Rd. East
Mississauga, ON L4Z 1S6
905-502-5537
Peter Daly, Branch Manager
Mississauga - Lakeshore Rd. West
305 Lakeshore Rd. West
Mississauga, ON L5H 1G5
905-891-5222
Mississauga - Robert Speck Pkwy.
#200, 176 Robert Speck Pkwy.
Mississauga, ON L4Z 3G1
905-281-5511
Nanaimo
Longwood Station
#1, 5767 Turner Rd.
Nanaimo, BC V9T 6L8
250-729-2830
New Minas
#2, 8903 Commercial St.
New Minas, NS B4N 3E1
902-679-2881
Newmarket
38 Prospect St.
Newmarket, ON L3Y 3S9
905-898-0489
Thane Fletcher, Branch Manager
North Vancouver - Chesterfield Pl.
15 Chesterfield Pl., #D
North Vancouver, BC V7M 3K3
604-981-2000
North Vancouver - West Esplanade
#480, 171 West Esplanade
North Vancouver, BC V7M 3J9
604-984-2235
Oakville
#2, 108 Allan St.
Oakville, ON L6J 3N1
905-815-8448
Matt Langsford, Branch Manager
Orangeville
24 First St.
Orangeville, ON L9W 2C7
519-938-8332
Gary Beck, Branch Manager
Ottawa - Gurdwara Rd.
#510, 2 Gurdwara Rd.
Ottawa, ON K2E 1A2
613-274-2662
Ottawa - Queen St.
#300, 100 Queen St.
Ottawa, ON K1P 1J9
613-788-2150
Mario Ruiz, Branch Manager
Penticton - Ellis St.
#100, 498 Ellis St.
Penticton, BC V2A 4M2
250-487-2000
Gerry Bate, Branch Manager
Penticton - Wade Ave. East
#104, 74 Wade Ave. East
Penticton, BC V2A 8M4
250-493-3711
Peterborough
999 Lansdowne St. West
Peterborough, ON K9J 8N2
705-743-1221
Dan Seabrooke, Branch Manager
Port Moody
2701 Clarke St.
Port Moody, BC V3H 1Z5
604-939-5800
Prince George - Central St. East
578 Central St. East
Prince George, BC V2M 3B7
250-564-2001
Gary Clarke, Branch Manager
Prince George - Third Ave.
#101, 1840 Third Ave.
Prince George, BC V2M 1G4
250-614-0888
Prince George - Victoria St.
#600, 550 Victoria St.
Prince George, BC V2L 2K1
250-564-2321
Qualicum Beach
#103, 193 West 2nd Ave.
Qualicum Beach, BC V9K 2N5
250-752-8184
Red Deer
#201, 4807 Gaetz Ave.
Red Deer, AB T4N 4A5
403-314-2600
Regina - 12th Ave.

#204, 2550 - 12th Ave.
Regina, BC S4P 3X1
306-791-1820
Kurt Daunheimer, Branch Manager
Regina - Smith St.
2237A Smith St.
Regina, SK S4P 2P5
306-757-1717
Doug Strand, Branch Manager
Saskatoon - 21st St. East
#700, 105 - 21st St. East
Saskatoon, SK S7K 0B3
306-651-4250
Susan Milburn, Branch Manager
Saskatoon - 25 St. East
#100, 333 - 25 St. East
Saskatoon, SK S7K 0L4
306-665-2133
Sudbury
265 Larch St.
Sudbury, ON P3B 1M2
705-523-2795
Toronto
Scotia Plaza
PO Box 415
#5300, 40 King St. West
Toronto, ON M5H 3Y2 Canada
416-777-7000
Fax: 416-777-7020
877-363-1024
Toronto - Bloor St. East
South Tower
#400, 175 Bloor St. East
Toronto, ON M4W 3R8
416-960-5781
Toronto - East Mall
#350, 300 The East Mall
Toronto, ON M9B 6B7
416-233-3072
Toronto - King St. West
Scotia Plaza
#5300, 40 King St. West
Toronto, ON M5H 3Y2
416-777-7000
John Donnelly, Branch Manager
Toronto - Yonge St.
#1900, 4950 Yonge St.
Toronto, ON M2N 6K1
416-222-7003
Nerio D'Ambrosi, Branch Manager
Vancouver - 10th Ave. West
3762 - 10th Ave. West
Vancouver, BC V6R 2G4
604-222-5484
Kevin Bogle, Branch Manager
Vancouver - West Georgia St.
#2100, 925 West Georgia St.
Vancouver, BC V6C 3L2
604-659-8000
Vancouver - West Hastings St.
#1002, 1177 West Hastings St.
Vancouver, BC V6E 2K3
604-663-4200
Vaughan
#510, 7050 Weston Rd.
Vaughan, ON L4L 8G7
905-652-4625
Victoria
#1000, 1175 Douglas St.
Victoria, BC V8W 2E1
250-405-2400
Steve Werner, Branch Manager
Waterloo
#1001, 20 Erb Street West
Waterloo, ON N2L 1T2
519-883-6030
White Rock
15178 Buena Vista Ave.
White Rock, BC V4B 1Y3
604-531-3011
Williams Lake
#201, 366 Yorston St.
Williams Lake, BC V2G 4J5
250-398-2222
Windsor
2861 Temple Dr.
Windsor, ON N8W 5E5
519-251-0159
Yarmouth
Lovitt Plaza
#107, 368 Main St.
Yarmouth, NS B5A 1E9
902-742-8818
Stephen Bishop, Branch Manager
Executives:
Barrie - Bayfield St.
#300, 135 Bayfield St.
Barrie, ON L4M 3B3
705-734-6300
Brian Kennedy, Branch Manager
Mississauga - Sherwoodtowne Blvd.
#200, 4263 Sherwoodtowne Blvd.
Mississauga, ON L4Z 1Y5
905-272-3900
Saskatoon - 1st Ave. North
#400, 261 - 1st Ave. North
Saskatoon, SK S7K 1X2
306-657-5733

RBC Capital Markets

Also listed under: *Financial Planning*
Royal Bank Plaza - South Tower
PO Box 50
200 Bay St.
Toronto, ON M5J 2W7
416-842-2000
Fax: 416-842-8044
marketing@rbccm.com
www.rbccm.com
Stock Exchange Membership: Toronto Stock Exchange, TSX Venture Exchange
Executives:
Charles M. Winograd, President/CEO
Anthony S. Fell, Chair
Andrew G. Scace, Vice-Chair
Bruce Rothney, Deputy Chair
John W. Burbridge, Managing Director/COO, Europe, Asia
Executives.:
Kirby Gavelin, Managing Director, Head, Equity Capital Markets
Mark Hughes, Managing Director, Head, Global Credit
Doug McGregor, Managing Director, Head, Global Investment Banking
Mark Standish, Managing Director, Head, Global Financial Products
Richard Tavoso, Managing Director, Head, Global Equity Derivatives
Affiliated Companies:
RBC Capital Partners
Branches:
Calgary
Banker's Hall
888 3rd St. SW
Calgary, AB T2T 5C5 Canada
403-299-7111
Vancouver
Park Place
#2100, 666 Burrard St.
Vancouver, BC V6C 3B1 Canada
604-257-7000

RBC Capital Partners

Also listed under: *Pension & Money Management Companies; Investment Management*
North Tower, Royal Bank Plaza
200 Bay St., 4th Fl.
Toronto, ON M5J 2W7
416-842-4054
Fax: 416-842-4060
www.rbcap.com
Ownership: Private. Division of RBC Capital Markets
Year Founded: 2000
Number of Employees: 33
Assets: $500m-1 billion
Revenues: $50-100 million
Stock Symbol: RY
Executives:
Alan Hibben, CEO; alan.hibben@rbcap.com
Owen Trotter, Vice-President, Debt Instruments
Robert Bechard, Managing Partner, Equity
Wally Hunter, Managing Parnter, Equity
Barrie Laver, Managing Partner, Portfolio Management
Tony Manastersky, Managing Partner, Mezzanine Fund, Principal, Finance

RBC Dexia Investor Services

Also listed under: *Financial Planning; Investment Management*

North Tower
200 Bay St., 24th Fl.
Toronto, ON M5J 2J5
Fax: 416-955-2631
800-668-1320
benefpay@rbcdexia-is.com
www.rbcdexia-is.com
Ownership: A joint venture equally owned by Royal Bank of Canada & Dexia.
Year Founded: 2006
Profile: RBC Dexia Investor Services provides services to asset managers & distributors, pensions, financial institutions, & insurance companies.
Affiliated Companies:
RBC Dexia Investor Services Trust

RBC Direct Investing

Royal Bank Plaza, North Tower
PO Box 75
200 Bay St.
Toronto, ON M5J 2Z5
800-769-2560
www.actiondirect.com
Former Name: RBC Action Direct Inc.; Royal Bank Action Direct Inc.
Year Founded: 1992
Number of Employees: 940
Stock Symbol: RX

RBC Dominion Securities Inc.

PO Box 7500, A Stn. A
77 King St. West
Toronto, ON M5W 1P9
www.rbcinvestments.com/ds/
Year Founded: 1901
Stock Exchange Membership: Montreal Exchange, Winnepeg Commodities Exchange
Branches:
Abbotsford
#301, 2001 McCallum Rd., 3rd Fl.
Abbotsford, BC V2S 3N5 Canada
Aurora
15420 Bayview Ave.
Aurora, ON L4G 7J1 Canada
905-726-2120
Barrie
#100, 11 Victoria St.
Barrie, ON L4N 6T3 Canada
Belleville
10 South Front St., 3rd Fl.
Belleville, ON K8N 2Y3 Canada
Beloeil
#100, 203, boul Laurier
Beloeil, QC J3G 4G8 Canada
800-890-4003
Bracebridge
109 Kimberley Ave.
Bracebridge, ON P1L 1Z8 Canada
705-329-1224
Fax: 705-329-2245
Brampton
#300, 50 Queen St. West
Brampton, ON L6X 4H3 Canada
Brockville
82 King St. West
Brockville, ON K6V 3P9 Canada
Brossard
#260, 7250, boul Taschereau
Brossard, QC J4W 1M9 Canada
Burlington
#105, 3405 Harvester Rd.
Burlington, ON L7N 3N1 Canada
Calgary - 7th Ave.
#1400, 333 - 7th Ave. SW
Calgary, AB T2P 2Z1 Canada
Calgary - Shawville Blvd.
#144, 250 Shawville Blvd. SE
Calgary, AB T2Y 2Z7 Canada
Cambridge

INVESTMENT MANAGEMENT

RBC Dominion Securities Inc. (continued)

PO Box 1735
89 Main St.
Cambridge, ON N1R 7G8 Canada

Campbell River
1260 Shoppers Row, 2nd Fl.
Campbell River, BC V9W 2C8 Canada

Charlottetown
#602, 134 Kent St.
Charlottetown, PE C1A 8R8 Canada
902-566-5544
Fax: 902-566-1569
800-463-5544

Chatham
20 Emma St.
Chatham, ON N7M 5K1 Canada
519-337-3751
Fax: 519-337-3775
800-465-3374

Chicoutimi
#205, 114, rue Racine est
Chicoutimi, QC G7H 1R1 Canada

Cobourg
PO Box 296
204D Division St.
Cobourg, ON K9A 4K8 Canada

Collingwood
#401, 115 Hurontario St.
Collingwood, ON L9Y 2L9 Canada

Concord
3300 Hwy. 7 West, 2nd Fl.
Concord, ON L4K 4M3 Canada

Cornwall
10 - 3rd St. East
Cornwall, ON K6H 2C7 Canada

Courtenay
777A Fitzgerald Ave.
Courtenay, BC V9N 2R4 Canada

Cowansville
412, rue Sud
Cowansville, QC J2K 2X7 Canada

Cranbrook
925 Baker St.
Cranbrook, BC V1C 1A5 Canada

Duncan
395 Trunk Rd.
Duncan, BC V9L 2P4 Canada

Edmonton - 101 St.
10180 - 101 St.
Edmonton, AB T5J 3S4 Canada

Edmonton - 102 St.
#2300, 10155 - 102 St.
Edmonton, AB T5J 2P4 Canada

Edmonton - 103A Ave.
16909 - 103A Ave.
Edmonton, AB T5P 4Y5 Canada

Estevan
1129 - 4 St.
Estevan, SK S4A 0W6 Canada

Fort McMurray
8540 Manning Ave.
Fort McMurray, AB T9H 5G2 Canada

Fredericton
#100, 371 Queen St.
Fredericton, NB E3B 4Y9 Canada
506-458-9174
Fax: 506-459-2725
800-561-4920

Gatineau
#115, 975, boul St-Joseph
Gatineau, QC J8Z 1W8 Canada

Granby
35, rue Dufferin
Granby, QC J2G 4W5 Canada

Grand Bend
58 Ontario St.
Grand Bend, ON N0M 1T0 Canada

Grande Prairie
#106, 9856 - 97th Ave.
Grande Prairie, AB T8V 7K2 Canada

Guelph
42 Wyndham St. North, 3rd Fl.
Guelph, ON N1H 4E6 Canada

Halifax
Purdy's Wharf Tower 2
#1101, 1969 Upper Water St.
Halifax, NS B3J 3R7 Canada

Hamilton
#900, 100 King St. West
Hamilton, ON L8P 1A2 Canada
905-546-5650
800-461-0274

Kamloops
#402, 186 Victoria St.
Kamloops, BC V2C 5R3 Canada

Kelowna
#1100, 1708 Dolphin Ave.
Kelowna, BC V1Y 9S4 Canada
800-463-9315

Kingston
#210, 366 King St. East
Kingston, ON K7K 6Y3 Canada

Kitchener
#1001, 30 Duke St. West
Kitchener, ON N2H 3W5 Canada

Langley
19888 Willowbrook Dr.
Langley, BC V2Y 1K9 Canada

Laval
#330, 3100, boul le Carrefour
Laval, QC H7T 2K7 Canada
450-686-3478
800-567-7396

Lethbridge
204 - 1st Ave. South
Lethbridge, AB T1J 0A4 Canada

Lloydminster
4716 - 50 Ave.
Lloydminster, AB T9V 0W2 Canada
403-875-8787
Fax: 403-956-5218

London
#1900, 148 Fullarton St.
London, ON N6A 5P3 Canada

Maple Ridge
11855 - 224 St.
Maple Ridge, BC V2X 6B1 Canada

Medicine Hat
505 - 1st St. SE
Medicine Hat, AB T1A 0A9 Canada

Midland
512 Hugel Ave.
Midland, ON L4R 1V7 Canada
705-329-1224
Fax: 705-329-2245
800-430-8013

Mississauga
#210, 33 City Centre Dr., 2nd Fl.
Mississauga, ON L5B 2N5 Canada

Moncton
Blue Cross Centre
#603, 644 Main St.
Moncton, NB E1C 1E2 Canada

Montréal - Gauchetière
1000, boul de la Gauchetière ouest
Montréal, QC H3B 4W5 Canada

Montréal - McGill College
#2150, 1501, av McGill College
Montréal, QC H3A 3M8 Canada

Montréal - Place Ville-Marie
#300, 1, Place Ville-Marie
Montréal, QC H3B 4R8 Canada

Montréal - St-Jean
#500, 755, boul St-Jean
Montréal, QC H9R 5M9 Canada

Montréal - Westmount
#130, 4, carré Westmount
Montréal, QC H3Z 2S6 Canada

Moose Jaw
#102, 111 Fairford St. East
Moose Jaw, SK S6H 7X5 Canada

Nanaimo
#101, 5050 Uplands Dr.
Nanaimo, BC V9T 6N1 Canada

New Westminster
#201, 960 Quayside Dr.
New Westminster, BC V3M 6G2 Canada

Newmarket
#222, 16775 Yonge St.
Newmarket, ON L3Y 8J4 Canada
905-895-2377

Niagara Falls
4481 Queen St.
Niagara Falls, ON L2E 2L4 Canada

North Battleford
Royal Bank Tower
1101 - 101 St., 2nd Fl.
North Battleford, SK S9A 0Z5 Canada
306-937-5021
Fax: 306-956-5218
800-785-4722

North Bay
357 Ferguson St.
North Bay, ON P1B 8K3 Canada
705-523-3108
800-461-0120

North Vancouver
#300, 1789 Lonsdale Ave.
North Vancouver, BC V7M 2J6 Canada
Fax: 604-981-2305
800-380-7425

Oakville
239 Lakeshore Rd. East
Oakville, ON L6J 1H7 Canada
Fax: 905-815-8180
800-567-5615

Orangeville
#207, 210 Broadway Ave.
Orangeville, ON L9W 5G4 Canada
519-942-1811

Orillia
74 Mississauga St. East
Orillia, ON L3V 1V5 Canada
705-329-1224
Fax: 705-329-2245
800-430-8013

Oshawa
PO Box 705
111 Simcoe St. North
Oshawa, ON L1H 7M9 Canada
905-434-6010
800-267-1522

Ottawa - Blair Pl.
#801, 1420 Blair Pl.
Ottawa, ON K1J 9L8 Canada

Ottawa - Moodie Dr.
#5500, 303 Moodie Dr., 5th Fl.
Ottawa, ON K2H 9R4 Canada

Ottawa - O'Connor St.
World Exchange Plaza
#900, 45 O'Connor St.
Ottawa, ON K1P 1A4 Canada

Owen Sound
#2, 619 - 10th St. West
Owen Sound, ON N4K 3R8 Canada

Parksville
152 South Alberni Hwy.
Parksville, BC V9P 2G5 Canada

Penticton
#101, 100 Front St.
Penticton, BC V2A 1H1 Canada
800-463-9315

Peterborough
PO Box 575
#300, 360 George St. North
Peterborough, ON K9J 6Z6 Canada

Port Alberni
2925 - 3rd Ave.
Port Alberni, BC V9Y 2A6 Canada

Prince George
550 Victoria St.
Prince George, BC V2L 2K1 Canada
Fax: 250-960-4694
888-960-4692

Qualicum Beach
133 West Second Ave.
Qualicum Beach, BC V9K 1T1 Canada

Québec
#210, 801, ch St-Louis
Québec, QC G1S 1C1 Canada

Red Deer

#301, 4901 - 48th St.
Red Deer, AB T4N 6M4 Canada
Regina
2010 - 11th Ave., 4th Fl.
Regina, SK S4P 3M3 Canada
Richmond
Pacific Business Centre, South Tower
#401, 5811 Cooney Rd.
Richmond, BC V6X 3M1 Canada
Richmond Hill
260 East Beaver Creek, 3rd Fl.
Richmond Hill, ON L4B 3M3 Canada
905-764-6404
800-268-6959
Saint John
#800, 44 Chipman Hill St.
Saint John, NB E2L 2A9 Canada
Sarnia
340 North Front St.
Sarnia, ON N7T 5S7 Canada
Fax: 519-337-3775
800-465-3374
Saskatoon
PO Box 1908
#1070, 410 - 22nd St. East
Saskatoon, SK S7K 3S5 Canada
306-956-5201
Fax: 306-956-5218
800-785-4722
Sault Ste Marie
185 East St.
Sault Ste Marie, ON P6A 3C8 Canada
Fax: 705-759-0699
800-465-4691
Sechelt
#212, 5760 Teredo St.
Sechelt, BC V0N 3A0 Canada
Sherbrooke
#310, 455, rue King ouest
Sherbrooke, QC J1H 6E9 Canada
Sidney
#104, 9845 Resthaven Dr.
Sidney, BC V8L 3E7 Canada
250-356-4800
Fax: 250-356-3164
888-773-4477
Simcoe
61 Robinson St.
Simcoe, ON N3Y 1W5 Canada
800-461-0274
Smithers
1106 Main St.
Smithers, BC V0J 2N0 Canada
800-463-9315
St Catharines
#306, 63 Church St.
St Catharines, ON L2R 3C4 Canada
St-Georges
12095, 1ère av
St-Georges, QC G5Y 5C7 Canada
St. John's
#803, 10 Fort William Pl.
St. John's, NL A1C 5P9 Canada
709-576-4975
Fax: 709-576-4922
800-563-0935
Stratford
10 Downie St., 2nd Fl.
Stratford, ON N5A 7K4 Canada
519-271-4611
Fax: 519-271-7429
800-265-4596
Sudbury
1361 Paris St.
Sudbury, ON P3E 3B6 Canada
800-461-0120
Swift Current
137 - 1 Ave. NE
Swift Current, SK S9H 2B1 Canada

Thornhill
1136 Centre St.
Thornhill, ON L4J 3M8 Canada
800-268-6959
Thunder Bay
#301, 1159 Alloy Dr.
Thunder Bay, ON P7B 6M8 Canada
Fax: 807-345-3481
800-256-2798
Toronto - Bay St.
Wellington Tower
181 Bay St., 7th Fl.
Toronto, ON M5J 2T3 Canada
Toronto - Bay St.
Royal Bank Plaza
PO Box 88
#3900, 200 Bay St.
Toronto, ON M5J 2J2 Canada
Toronto - Bay St.
#600, 200 Bay St.
Toronto, ON M5J 2J1 Canada
Toronto - Bloor St. East
2 Bloor St. East, 3rd Fl.
Toronto, ON M4W 1A8 Canada
Toronto - Bloor St. West
East Tower
3250 Bloor St. West
Toronto, ON M8X 2X9 Canada
Toronto - Don Mills Rd.
1090 Don Mills Rd., 4th Fl.
Toronto, ON M3C 3R6 Canada
Toronto - Grangeway Ave.
111 Grangeway Ave., 2nd Fl.
Toronto, ON M1H 3E9 Canada
Toronto - Queen St.
#2, 2175 Queen St. East
Toronto, ON M4E 1E5 Canada
Toronto - Yonge St.
PO Box 28
#2120, 5140 Yonge St.
Toronto, ON M2N 6L7 Canada
Toronto - Yonge St.
2345 Yonge St., 10th Fl.
Toronto, ON M4P 2E5 Canada
Trois-Rivières
#100, 25, rue des Forges
Trois-Rivières, QC G9A 6A7 Canada
Vancouver - 41st Ave.
2052 - 41st Ave. West, 3rd Fl.
Vancouver, BC V6M 1Y8 Canada
Vancouver - Burrard St.
Vancouver Park Place
#2500, 666 Burrard St.
Vancouver, BC V6C 3B1 Canada
604-257-7200
Fax: 604-257-7391
800-427-7766
M.L. Cullen
Vernon
3129 - 30th Ave.
Vernon, BC V1T 2C4 Canada
Fax: 250-545-4139
800-663-6439
Victoria
#500, 730 View St., 5th Fl.
Victoria, BC V8W 3Y7 Canada
250-356-4800
Fax: 250-356-3164
Wallaceburg
302 James St.
Wallaceburg, ON N8A 2N5 Canada
West Vancouver - 15th St.
#201, 250 - 15th St.
West Vancouver, BC V7T 2X4 Canada
604-981-6600
Fax: 604-981-6601
800-375-0585
West Vancouver - Marine Dr.
1705 Marine Dr.
West Vancouver, BC V7V 1J5 Canada
800-375-0585
White Rock
1625 - 152nd St.
White Rock, BC V4A 4N3 Canada
604-535-3800
Whitehorse
#403, 3106 Third Ave.
Whitehorse, YT Y1A 5G1 Canada
Windsor
1922 Wyandotte St. East
Windsor, ON N8Y 1E4 Canada
Winnipeg
#800, One Lombard Place
Winnipeg, MB R3B 0Y2 Canada
Woodstock
26 Huron St.
Woodstock, ON N4S 6Z2 Canada

Remy Richard Securities Inc.

Also listed under: *Financial Planning*
Tower I
#104, 7001 Mumford Rd.
Halifax, NS B3L 4N9
902-455-4914
Fax: 902-455-4554
888-326-5257
rrsi@rrsi.ca
Ownership: Private
Year Founded: 1988
Profile: The firm is a registered mutual fund dealer in Nova Scotia.

Executives:
Remy Richard, CEO

Renaissance Capital Inc.(RCI)

#2110, 1800, av McGill College
Montréal, QC H3A 3J6
514-842-3666
Fax: 514-842-5666
info@rcican.com
www.rcican.com
Year Founded: 1998
Profile: Services provided by the investment dealer include the Immigrant Investor Program.

Executives:
Sylvain Payette, President/CEO
Sam Buffone, Vice-President, Marketing
Jacques Plante, CFO & Vice-President, Finance
Branches:
Vancouver
#1300, 1030 West Georgia St.
Vancouver, BC V6E 2Y3
604-689-0881
Fax: 604-689-3181
info@rcicapitalgroup.com
Tony Hu, Manager

Research Capital Corporation

Also listed under: *Financing & Loan Companies*
Commerce Court West
PO Box 368
#4500, 199 Bay St.
Toronto, ON M5L 1G2
416-860-7600
Fax: 416-860-7671
contact@researchcapital.com
www.researchcapital.com
Ownership: Employee-owned.
Year Founded: 1921
Number of Employees: 300
Stock Exchange Membership: Canadian Trading & Quotation System Inc, Montreal Exchange, Toronto Stock Exchange, TSX Venture Exchange
Profile: The integrated investment dealer includes investment banking services that focus upon small to mid-cap growth companies & growth investors. The full service firm's public venture capital group specializes in IPOs & small and micro-cap public company financings. Sales & trading professionals provide services to institutional investors. Research analysts offer coverage of growth companies. The private client division serves high-net worth investors.

Executives:
Ian G. Griffin, Honourary Chair; ian.griffin@researchcapital.com
Patrick G. Walsh, Chair/CEO;
patrick.walsh@researchcapital.com
Geoffrey G. Whitlam, President;
geoff.whitlam@researchcapital.com
Andrew Selbie, COO & Exec. Vice-President, Finance;
andrew.selbie@researchcapital.com
Greg Finkle, Exec. Vice-President, Managing Director
David Hetherington, Branch Manager;
david.hetherington@researchcapital.com
Branches:
Brantford

Research Capital Corporation (continued)
127 Charing Cross St.
Brantford, ON N3R 2J2 Canada
519-751-1311
Fax: 519-751-2629
800-516-9085
Caledonia
159 Haddington St.
Caledonia, ON N3W 1G1
905-765-0335
Fax: 905-765-0069
800-422-7032
Calgary
Sun Life Plaza II
#1330, 140 - 4 Ave. SW
Calgary, AB T2P 3N3 Canada
403-265-7400
Fax: 403-237-5951
Barb Richardson, Branch Manager
Delta
4337 River Rd. West
Delta, BC V4K 1R9
604-628-4463
866-300-2001
James H. Ross, Sr. Managing Director
Meaford
40 Gray Ave.
Meaford, ON N4L 1C4
519-538-3725
888-241-1103
Mississauga
2470 Oak Row Cres.
Mississauga, ON L5L 1P4
416-860-7628
Fax: 416-860-6798
Montréal
#100, 4, Place Ville-Marie
Montréal, QC H3B 2E7 Canada
514-399-1500
Fax: 514-399-1540
Donald Stevenson, Branch Manager
Pickering
560 Park Cres.
Pickering, ON L1W 2C9
905-839-8557
Fax: 905-839-2011
Regina
2400 College Ave., 5th Fl.
Regina, SK S4P 1C8
306-566-7550
Fax: 306-565-3718
Surrey
#412, 1787 - 154th St.
Surrey, BC V4A 4S1
604-662-1862
Fax: 604-662-1855
Terra Cotta
25589 Credit View Rd., RR#1
Terra Cotta, ON L7C 3G8
905-838-5070
Fax: 905-838-5069
Thornhill
44 Valleyview Rd.
Thornhill, ON L3T 6Y9
905-881-7980
Fax: 905-881-1759
800-282-8996
Toronto - Avoca Ave.
#903, 38 Avoca Ave.
Toronto, ON M4T 2B9
416-975-0262
Fax: 416-975-4042
Toronto - Douglas Cres.
35 Douglas Cres.
Toronto, ON M4W 2E6
416-323-6856
Fax: 416-923-8089
877-883-8885
Toronto - Lowther Ave.
#310, 4 Lowther Ave.
Toronto, ON M5R 1C6
416-920-9027
Fax: 416-920-4718
800-559-5537
Toronto - Minho Blvd.
24 Minho Blvd.
Toronto, ON M6G 4B3
416-537-7618
Fax: 416-537-9873
Toronto - Shaftesbury Ave.
42 Shaftesbury Ave.
Toronto, ON M4T 1A2
416-920-0684
Fax: 416-920-0685
888-211-0709
Toronto - Victoria Park Ave.
73 Victoria Park Ave.
Toronto, ON M4E 3S2
416-690-3732
Fax: 416-690-3729
866-860-4190
Toronto - Woodcrest Dr.
45 Woodcrest Dr.
Toronto, ON M9A 4J3
416-245-6128
Fax: 416-245-9867
888-866-1296
Vancouver
Four Bentall Centre
PO Box 49356
#564, 1055 Dunsmuir St.
Vancouver, BC V7X 1L4 Canada
604-662-1800
Fax: 604-662-1850
David Fawkes, Branch Manager
Victoria
4400 Meadowood Pl.
Victoria, BC V8X 4V7
250-658-8955
G. Peter Taylor, President
Whitby
62 Bluebell Cres.
Whitby, ON Whitby
416-860-7621
Fax: 905-665-7278
800-495-7749

Retire First Ltd.
#1, 4610 - 49th Ave.
Red Deer, AB T4N 6M5
403-314-5553
Fax: 403-314-5323
Douglas Allan, President

Rissling Financial Corporation
***Also listed under:** Financial Planning*
4861 Prairie Lane
Grasswood, SK S7T 1A7
306-241-1576
Fax: 306-477-1882
Year Founded: 1995
Profile: The firm offers financial services mainly to the farming community. It is a member of the Mutual Fund Dealers Association of Canada.

Rothenberg Capital Management Inc.
***Also listed under:** Financial Planning*
4420, rue Sainte-Catherine ouest
Montréal, QC H3Z 1R2
514-934-0586
Fax: 514-934-3134
800-811-0527
corrigan@rothenberg.ca
www.rothenberg.ca
Ownership: Private. Part of The Rothenberg Group.
Year Founded: 1979
Profile: The company offers advice on a variety of investment opportunities. Services cover retirement planning, post-retirement, & estate planning.

Executives:
Robert Rothenberg, President
Helen Corrigan, Vice-President
Branches:
Calgary
1712 - 10th Ave. SW
Calgary, AB T2C 0J8 Canada
403-228-2378
Fax: 403-228-2426
800-456-0949
Cochrane
#7, 205 - 1 St. East
Cochrane, AB T4C 1X6
403-851-7777
Fax: 403-851-0793
866-456-0949
Montréal - Holiday
#150, 1, rue Holiday
Montréal, QC H9R 5N3
514-697-0035
Fax: 514-697-3351

Russell Investments Canada Limited
***Also listed under:** Pension & Money Management Companies*
1 First Canadian Place
PO Box 476
#5900, 100 King St. West
Toronto, ON M5X 1E4
416-362-8411
888-509-1792
canada@russell.com
www.russell.com/ca
Ownership: Russell Investment Group
Year Founded: 1936
Profile: Russell offers investment products & investment planning services for individuals or for institutional investors & their employees. Russell Investments Canada also works with Frank Russell Company, a money management & pension fund consulting company, to offer investment solutions for company pension plans.

Executives:
Irshaad Ahmad, President, Managing Director
Susi McCord, Head, Marketing & Communications

Salman Partners Inc.
#2230, 885 West Georgia St.
Vancouver, BC V6C 3E8
604-685-2450
Fax: 604-685-2471
questions@salmanpartners.com
www.salmanpartners.com
Ownership: Private
Year Founded: 1994
Stock Exchange Membership: Toronto Stock Exchange, TSX Venture Exchange
Executives:
Terry K. Salman, President/CEO
Alan C. Herrington, Exec. Vice-President & Director
John Mitchell Todd, B.Com., CA, Vice-President/CFO
Branches:
Calgary
Gulf Canada Square
#835, 401 - 9th Ave. SW
Calgary, AB T2P 3C5 Canada
403-261-6065
Fax: 403-261-6069
Toronto
#802, 110 Yonge St.
Toronto, ON M5C 1T4 Canada
416-861-1270
Fax: 416-861-1935

Salmon Arm Financial Ltd.(SAF)
***Also listed under:** Financial Planning*
#308, 251 Trans Canada Hwy., NW
Salmon Arm, BC V1E 3B8
250-832-1088
Fax: 250-832-3912
info@salmonarmfinancial.com
www.salmonarmfinancial.com
Former Name: Hammer & Associates Financial Services Ltd.
Ownership: Private
Year Founded: 1998
Profile: The financial planning firm offers a variety of plans including education, retirement, pension, succession, & employee benefit. A range of products & services are provided such as insurance, annuities, RRSPs, RRIFs, RESPs, term deposits, & management & consolidation.

Executives:
Steven J. Hammer, President, Life Insurance Advisor; steve@salmonarmfinancial.com
Kevin Flynn, CFP, CLU, BComm, Specialist, Benefits

Salomon Smith Barney Canada Inc.
BCE Place
PO Box 631

#4600, 161 Bay St.
Toronto, ON M5J 2S8
416-866-2300
Fax: 416-866-7484
www.salomonsmithbarney.com
Ownership: Indirectly wholly owned by public foreign company, Citigroup Inc.
Year Founded: 1989
Number of Employees: 45
Profile: Investment banking services are provided to Canadian corporations & government clients. The firm maintains fixed-income sales & trading operations in Toronto. It also acts as a government distributor in the Canadian government bond market, further enhancing the service level provided to Canadian clients & reinforcing commitments to Canada.

Executives:
Robert J. Gemmell, President/CEO
Douglas Eberlee, Managing Director
Directors:
Stanley Hartt, Chair
Branches:
Montréal
#2450, 630, boul René-Lévesque ouest
Montréal, QC H3B 1S6 Canada
514-394-2586
Fax: 514-394-2588
Serge Gouin

Sanders Wealth Management

#2000, 10303 Jasper Ave.
Edmonton, AB T5J 3N6
780-424-1001
Fax: 780-425-4241
800-413-5923
www.sbsecurities.com
Former Name: Sanders & Beckingham Securities Limited
Executives:
Dave Sanders, President; 780-424-1001; dsanders@sbsecurities.com
Duncan Wade; 780-424-1001; dwade@sbsecurities.com
Branches:
Edmonton
4636 Calgary Trail South
Edmonton, AB T6H 6A1 Canada
780-424-6630
Fax: 780-432-2644
866-424-8784
info@teamporter.com
David Porter
St Albert
Grandin Park Plaza
#604, 22 Sir Winston Churchill Ave.
St Albert, AB T8N 1B4 Canada
780-460-6460
Fax: 780-460-6461
877-460-6460
Gordon Malic, Investment Advisor

Sanderson Securities Ltd.

Also listed under: *Financial Planning*
Princeton Towers
#410, 123 Second Ave. South
Saskatoon, SK S7K 7E6
306-242-5800
Fax: 306-244-0094
customerservice@sandersonsecurities.ca
www.sandersonsecurities.ca
Profile: Investment & financial planning services are provided.

Executives:
Wayne L. Sanderson, President

Scotia Capital Inc.

Scotia Plaza
PO Box 4085, A Stn. A
40 King St. West
Toronto, ON M5W 2X6
416-863-7411
Fax: 416-862-3052
www.scotiacapital.com
Also Known As: ScotiaMcLeod
Ownership: Wholly owned by The Bank of Nova Scotia
Year Founded: 1921
Number of Employees: 1,800
Stock Exchange Membership: Canadian Trading & Quotation System Inc, Montreal Exchange, Toronto Stock Exchange, TSX Venture Exchange, Winnepeg Commodities Exchange
Executives:
Stephen McDonald, Co-Chair & Co-CEO, Head, Global Corporate & Investment Banking
C. John Schumacher, Co-Chair & Co-CEO, Scotia Capital Inc., Head, Global Capital Markets
Kevin Ray, Vice-Chair & Deputy Head, US Corporate
Barry Wainstein, Vice-Chair & Head, Foreign Exchange & Precious Metals
Adam Waterous, Vice-Chair, President & Head, Scotia Waterous
Mike Durland, Managing Director, Capital Markets Group
Bob Finlay, Managing Director, Corporate Banking
Terry Fryett, Managing Director & CFO, Finance
Sarah Kananagh, Managing Director, Head, Canadian Relationship Management
Kathryn Kiplinger, Managing Director, Head, U.S. Corporate Risk Assessment & Execution
John F. Madden, Managing Director, Capital Markets Group
John McCartney, Managing Director, Co-Head, Institutional Equity
James McLeod, Managing Director, Head, Equity Research
Jim Mountain, Managing Director, Institutional Equity
James O'Sullivan, Managing Director, Canadian Relationship Management
Rod Reynolds, Managing Director, Head, Europe Corporate
John Ryan, Managing Director, Head, Loan Portfolio Management Group
Philip Smith, Managing Director, Head, Investment Banking
Mark Vader, Managing Director, Co-Head, Institutional Equity
Bob Williams, Managing Director, Equity Capital Markets
Cecilia Williams, Managing Director, Head, Compliance
Felipe de Yturbe, Managing Director, Head, Mexico Wholesale
Branches:
Calgary
Scotia Center
#2000, 700 - 2nd St. SW
Calgary, AB T2P 2W1 Canada
403-298-4096
Fax: 403-213-7773
Halifax
PO Box 2146
1709 Hollis St., 4th Fl.
Halifax, NS B3J 3B7 Canada
902-420-3700
Fax: 902-422-0664
Montréal
Tour Scotia
1002, rue Sherbrooke ouest, 9e étage
Montréal, QC H3A 3L6 Canada
514-287-3607
Fax: 514-499-8454
Vancouver
650 West Georgia St., 18th Floor
Vancouver, BC V6B 4N9 Canada
604-661-1478
Fax: 604-661-7496

Scotia Discount Brokerage Inc.

Scotia Plaza
40 King St. West, 5th Fl.
Toronto, ON M5H 1H1
416-866-2014
Fax: 416-866-2018
www.sdbi.com
Executives:
Andrew H. Scipio del Campo, President/CEO
Tom Kelly, Chief Compliance Officer
Bruce Dickson, Sr. Vice-President & National Sales Manager

Securitel Canada

Also listed under: *Financial Planning*
#100, 17, rue Valiquette
Trois-Rivières, QC G8T 3R4
819-371-1161
securitel@iforum.ca
Executives:
Louis G. Dumas, President

Select Financial Services Inc.

Also listed under: *Financial Planning*
#200, 193 Pinebush Rd.
Cambridge, ON N1R 7H8
519-622-9613
Fax: 519-622-4612
Ownership: Private
Year Founded: 1985
Number of Employees: 8
Profile: The mutual fund dealer & financial planning firm offers estate planning, insurance services, RRSPs, group benefits, annuities, registered retirement income funds, GICs & mutual funds.

Branches:
London
#5, 650 Colborne St.
London, ON N6A 5A1 Canada
519-645-7163
Fax: 519-645-8536
Gary Alan Price, Financial Planner

Shah Financial Planning Inc.(SFP)

Also listed under: *Financial Planning*
#204, 3459 Sheppard Ave. East
Toronto, ON M1T 3K5
416-298-4900
Fax: 416-298-9759
info@shahfinancial.ca
www.shahfinancial.ca
Former Name: Shah Business Services
Year Founded: 1976
Profile: The firm offers planning in the following areas: financial, tax, estate & retirement. Other services include accounting, bookkkeeping, tax preparation, investments & life insurance.

Executives:
Narendra Shah, Financial Advisor
Ekta Chauhan, Financial Advisor
Dipa Shah, Tax Advisor

Shorcan Brokers Limited

#1000, 20 Adelaide St. East
Toronto, ON M5C 2T6
416-360-2500
Fax: 416-360-2526
info@shorcan.com
www.shorcan.com
Ownership: Private
Year Founded: 1977
Profile: The firm is a Canadian inter-dealer broker.

Société Générale Securities Inc./ Société générale valeurs mobilières inc.

#1800, 1501, av McGill College
Montréal, QC H3A 3M8
514-841-6111
Fax: 514-841-6252
sgib.canada@socgen.com
www.socgen.com
Number of Employees: 156

Solium Capital Inc.

#200, 805 - 8th Ave.
Calgary, AB T2P 1H7
403-515-3910
Fax: 403-515-3919
877-380-7793
help@solium.com
www.solium.com
Former Name: Solium Capital Online Inc.
Year Founded: 1999
Executives:
Brian Craig, President/CEO
Marcos Lopez, President
Jeff English, Vice-President, Market Development
Ron Ratzlaff, Vice-President, Customer Operations
June Davenport, Chief Products Officer
Lynn Leong, CFO
Directors:
Russ Waterhouse, Exec. Chair
Mike Broadfoot
Brian Craig
Justin Ferrara
Tony Webb
Branches:
Montréal
#355, 1470, rue Peel
Montréal, QC H3A 1T1 Canada
514-499-8200
Fax: 514-499-8201
Toronto

INVESTMENT MANAGEMENT

Solium Capital Inc. (continued)
#1102, 20 Adelaide St. East
Toronto, ON M5C 2T6 Canada
416-365-7771
Fax: 416-365-9169

Sprott Securities Inc.
South Tower, Royal Bank Plaza
PO Box 63
#2750, 200 Bay St.
Toronto, ON M5J 2J2
416-362-7485
Fax: 416-943-6499
800-461-2275
info@sprott.ca
www.sprott.ca
Ownership: Employee-owned
Year Founded: 1981
Stock Exchange Membership: Montreal Exchange, Toronto Stock Exchange, TSX Venture Exchange
Profile: Sprott Securities Inc. is a full service, independent investment dealer focusing on small- to mid-capitalization companies. The employee-owned organization offers investment research on Canadian & US companies. A range of investment banking services is provided to corporate clients.

Executives:
Scott Lamacraft, CFA, CEO
Peter Grosskopf, CFA, President & Managing Director Investment Banking
Jeff Kennedy, CA, CFO
Peter Charton, Managing Director, Institutional Equity Sales, Director
Scott Connolly, Managing Director, Institutional Equity Trading, Director
Boris Novansky, Director, Mergers & Acquisitions
Ruan Shay, CA, CFA, Director, Institutional Equity Research, Oil & Gas
Affiliated Companies:
Sprott Asset Management Inc.
Branches:
Calgary
Stock Exchange Tower
#1800, 300 - 5th Ave. SW
Calgary, AB T2P 3C4 Canada
403-266-4240
Fax: 403-266-4250
800-461-9491
Montréal
#2104, 1800, av McGill College
Montréal, QC H3A 3J6 Canada
514-878-0009
Fax: 514-878-1514
800-699-5946

Standard Securities Capital Corporation
24 Hazelton Ave.
Toronto, ON M5R 2E2
416-515-0505
Fax: 416-515-0477
800-268-9095
info@standardsecurities.com
www.standardsecurities.com
Stock Exchange Membership: Toronto Stock Exchange, TSX Venture Exchange
Profile: The investment dealer offers investment services such as investment banking, wealth & portfolio management, & institutional & retail trading.

Executives:
Mark A. Marcello, President/CEO
Michael J. Bignell, Exec. Vice-President/COO
Elizabeth Videcak, Chief Financial Officer

State Street Global Markets Canada Inc.
State Street Financial Centre
#1100, 30 Adelaide St. East
Toronto, ON M5C 3G6
416-362-1100
Fax: 416-956-2525
888-287-8639
www.statestreet.ca
Ownership: Part of State Street Corporation
Year Founded: 1990
Number of Employees: 1,000+
Stock Exchange Membership: Toronto Stock Exchange
Profile: With over 15 percent of the world's tradable securities administered by State Street, the investment dealer offers unique global insight in institutional sales & trading services.

Executives:
John Walks, Managing Director

Stephen Avenue Securities Inc.
#608, 304 - 8th Ave. SW
Calgary, AB T2P 1C2
403-777-2442
Fax: 403-777-2469
Ownership: Private.
Year Founded: 1994
Profile: Services include principal trading, investment banking & retail.

Executives:
Terry Falkenberg, President/CEO

Stuart Investment Management Limited
PO Box 33
#910, 95 Wellington St. West
Toronto, ON M5J 2N7
416-363-8871
Fax: 416-368-6174
Ownership: Private.
Year Founded: 1987
Executives:
James E.D. Stuart, President
Myra K. Cameron, CFO, Treasurer
S. Grace Kumabe, Corporate Secretary

Swift Trade Inc.
55 St. Clair Ave. West
Toronto, ON M4V 2Y7
416-351-8118
Fax: 416-351-8118
info@swifttrade.com
www.swifttrade.com
Also Known As: Swift Trade Securities
Year Founded: 1997
Profile: The direct access electronic trading centre has offices in Canada, Europe, Asia and the Americas.

Executives:
Peter Beck, President
Charlie Kim, Vice-President
Branches:
Calgary
600 - 6th Ave. SW
Calgary, AB T2P 0S5
403-262-7748
info@calgary.swifttrade.com
Cambridge
260 Holiday Inn Dr.
Cambridge, ON N3C 1Z4 Canada
519-658-4500
Halifax
1660 Hollis St.
Halifax, NS B3J 1V7
902-405-3511
info@halifax.swifttrade.com
Kelowna
#102, 565 Bernard Ave.
Kelowna, BC V1Y 8R4 Canada
250-979-7000
info@kelowna.swifttrade.com
London
#510, 171 Queens Ave.
London, ON N6A 5J7 Canada
519-646-2929
info@london.swifttrade.com
Ottawa
#500, 85 Albert St.
Ottawa, ON K1P 6A4 Canada
613-233-0123
info@ottawa.swifttrade.com
Richmond Hill
#21, 30 Wertheim Crt.
Richmond Hill, ON L4B 1B9 Canada
905-764-1196
info@richmondhill.swifttrade.com
Saskatoon
610 - 2nd Ave. North
Saskatoon, SK S7K 2C8
306-975-0900
info@saskatoon.swifttrade.com
Victoria
#205, 3375 Whittier Ave.
Victoria, BC V8Z 3R1 Canada
250-380-9775
info@victoria.swifttrade.com
Whitby
#212, 114 Dundas St. East
Whitby, ON L1N 2H7 Canada
905-665-3376
info@whitby.swifttrade.com

TD Securities Inc.
TD Bank Tower
PO Box 1
66 Wellington St. West
Toronto, ON M5K 1A2
416-982-6160
Fax: 416-307-0338
contactus@tdsecurities.com
www.tdsecurities.com
Year Founded: 1987
Stock Exchange Membership: Montreal Exchange, Toronto Stock Exchange, TSX Venture Exchange
Executives:
Robert E. Dorrance, Chair/CEO
Michael W. MacBain, President
Branches:
Calgary
Home Oil Tower
#800, 324 - 8th Ave. SW
Calgary, AB T2P 2Z2 Canada
403-299-8572
Fax: 403-292-2772
Montréal
#2315, 1 Place Ville Marie
Montréal, QC H3B 3M5 Canada
514-289-1600
Fax: 514-289-1212
Vancouver
TD Tower
#1700, 700 Georgia St. West
Vancouver, BC V7Y 1B6 Canada
604-654-3332
Fax: 604-654-3671

TD Waterhouse Canada Inc.
***Also listed under:** Financial Planning*
Toronto Dominion Centre
55 King St. West, Concourse Level 1
Toronto, ON M5K 1A2
416-308-1600
Fax: 416-944-6750
800-465-5463
Other Information: 800-838-3223 (Toll Free, Cantonese/Mandarin); 866-966-6061 (TTY)
td.waterhouse@td.com
www.tdwaterhouse.ca
Stock Exchange Membership: Montreal Exchange, Toronto Stock Exchange
Profile: Investment advice, broker services, institutional sales & trading & retail services are offered.

Executives:
William H. Hatanaka, Chair/CEO
Richard LaFerrière, President, Financial Planning
Michael E. Reilly, President, Private Investment Advice
John See, President, Discount Brokerage, Financial Planning & Institutional Services
Gerard J. O'Mahoney, Exec. Vice-President/COO
Patricia Lovett-Reid, Sr. Vice-President, TD Waterhouse Canada
Branches:
Brossard
8330, boul Taschereau
Brossard, QC J4X 1C2
450-465-1121
866-900-1121
Calgary
505 - 2nd St. SW
Calgary, AB T2P 1N8 Canada
403-503-6578
Edmonton - 101st St. NW
#402, 10205 - 101st St. NW
Edmonton, AB T5J 4H5 Canada
780-448-8088
800-350-4832

Edmonton - 111 St. NW
2325 - 111 St. NW
Edmonton, AB T6J 5E5
780-448-8282
Halifax
PO Box 634
1785 Barrington St., 2nd Fl.
Halifax, NS B3J 2P6 Canada
902-420-2585
Hamilton
100 King St. West, Main Fl.
Hamilton, ON L8P 4W9 Canada
905-521-2120
Kanata
120 Earl Grey Dr.
Kanata, ON K2T 1B6 Canada
613-592-6563
Kelowna
#110, 1633 Ellis St.
Kelowna, BC V1Y 2A8 Canada
250-717-8129
866-717-8129
Kingston
94 Princess St.
Kingston, ON K7L 1A5 Canada
613-549-8525
Kitchener
381 King St. West, Main Fl.
Kitchener, ON N2G 1B8 Canada
519-571-7570
Laval
#150, 3080, boul le Carrefour
Laval, QC H7T 2R5 Canada
800-451-1647
London
275 Dundas St.
London, ON N6A 4S4 Canada
519-873-2099
Markham - Kennedy Rd.
#101, 7077 Kennedy Rd.
Markham, ON L3R 0N8 Canada
905-479-8008
877-479-8008
Markham - Steeles Ave. East
Tower 1, Liberty Centre
3500 Steeles Ave. East, 3rd Fl.
Markham, ON L3R 2Z1 Canada
416-904-5454
800-838-3223
Moncton
#101, 860 Main St.
Moncton, NB E1C 1G2 Canada
506-859-9530
866-816-6613
Montréal - Saint-Jean
#120, 755, boul Saint-Jean
Montréal, QC H9R 5M9 Canada
877-297-5559
Montréal - St. Jacques
500, rue St. Jacques, 6e étage
Montréal, QC H2Y 1S1 Canada
514-289-8439
800-361-2684
Montréal - Ste Catherine ouest
1101, rue Ste Catherine ouest
Montréal, QC H3B 1H8 Canada
514-289-8080
800-839-0888
Nanaimo
5777 Turner Rd., Upper Level
Nanaimo, BC V9T 6L8 Canada
250-390-5940
888-255-5522
Oakville
282 Lakeshore Rd. East
Oakville, ON L6J 5B2 Canada
905-337-3779
Ottawa - Coventry Rd.
525 Coventry Rd.
Ottawa, ON K1K 2C5 Canada
613-783-6322
800-267-8844
Ottawa - O'Connor St.
45 O'Connor St., 2nd Fl.
Ottawa, ON K1P 1A4 Canada
613-783-6379
Québec
#135, 2600, boul Laurier
Québec, QC G1V 4T3 Canada
418-654-0828
800-214-1345
Regina
1904 Hamilton St.
Regina, SK S4P 3N5 Canada
306-924-8902
800-667-9951
Richmond
5991 No. 3 Rd.
Richmond, BC V6X 3Y6 Canada
604-654-8863
877-596-3577
Richmond Hill
500 Hwy. 7 East
Richmond Hill, ON L4B 1J1 Canada
905-731-4436
866-658-4436
Saskatoon
170 - 2nd Ave. South
Saskatoon, SK S7K 1K5 Canada
306-975-7373
St. John's
TD Place
140 Water St., 2nd Fl.
St. John's, NL A1C 6H6 Canada
709-758-5098
Sudbury
43 Elm St., 2nd Fl.
Sudbury, ON P3E 4R7 Canada
705-670-8809
Toronto
77 Bloor St. West, Main Fl.
Toronto, ON M5S 1M2 Canada
416-542-0749
866-622-1022
Toronto - Bloor St. West
The Clarica Centre
#126, 3250 Bloor St. West
Toronto, ON M8X 2X9
416-239-3363
Toronto - Bremner Ave.
363 Bremner Ave.
Toronto, ON M5V 3V4
416-623-0158
Vancouver
#100, 888 Dunsmuir St.
Vancouver, BC V6C 3K4 Canada
604-654-3661
800-663-0480
Victoria
1070 Douglas St., Main Fl.
Victoria, BC V8W 2C4 Canada
250-356-4073
West Vancouver
1655 Marine Dr.
West Vancouver, BC V7V 1J2 Canada
604-981-4500
Whitby
404 Dundas St. West, 2nd Fl.
Whitby, ON L1N 2M7 Canada
905-668-1004
White Rock
Central Plaza Shopping Centre
15120 North Bluff Rd.
White Rock, BC V4B 3E5 Canada
604-541-2050
Windsor
#300, 586 Ouellette Ave.
Windsor, ON N9A 1B8 Canada
519-252-7022
Winnipeg
201 Portage Ave., Concourse Level
Winnipeg, MB R3C 2T2 Canada
204-988-2641

Timber Hill Canada Company

PO Box 2106
1800, av McGill College
Montréal, QC H3A 3J6
514-287-9035
Fax: 514-287-0152
www.interactivebrokers.ca
Ownership: Part of Interactive Brokers Group LLC.
Year Founded: 1998
Stock Exchange Membership: Montreal Exchange, Toronto Stock Exchange
Executives:
Jean-François Bernier, Vice-President
George W. Lennon, Vice-President
Directors:
Thomas Peterffy, Chair
Jean-François Bernier
Paul J. Brody
David W. Iles
George W. Lennon

Toll Cross Securities Inc.(TCS)

Royal Trust Tower
PO Box 138
#3120, 77 King St. West
Toronto, ON M5K 1H1
416-365-1960
Fax: 416-365-1962
infoo@tollcross.ca
www.tollcross.ca
Stock Exchange Membership: Toronto Stock Exchange, TSX Venture Exchange
Profile: Specializing in the areas of institutional equity sales & trading, equity research, & investment banking, the full service firm addresses the needs of small & mid-cap companies. It is registered in British Columbia, Alberta, Saskatchewan, Manitoba, Ontario, New Brunswick, Nova Scotia , PEI & Newfoundland.
Executives:
Marc Bouchard, Chair
Rodger Gray, President/CEO
Steve Somodi, Chief Financial Officer
Tom George, Manager, Trading
Branches:
Vancouver
#320, 1122 Mainland St.
Vancouver, BC V6B 5L1 Canada
604-677-4131
Fax: 604-687-4131

Torce Financial Group Inc.

Also listed under: *Financial Planning*
#200, 650 Hwy. 7 East
Richmond Hill, ON L4B 2N7
905-889-9139
Fax: 905-889-8927
www.torcefinancial.com
Profile: The organization offers wealth management concepts, insurance coverage, mutual funds, segregated funds, RRSPs, RRIFs, & RESPs.
Executives:
David Ho, CLU, CH.F.C., Principal
Najeeb Khan, CFP, CLU, CH.F.C., Consultant, Training
Katrina Lo, ACS, AIAA, Office Manager
Affiliated Companies:
Vance Financial Group Inc.

Trilon Securities Corporation

BCE Place
#300, 181 Bay St.
Toronto, ON M5J 2T3
416-956-5174
Fax: 416-365-9642
Year Founded: 1989
Executives:
Trevor D. Kerr, Vice-President, Chief Compliance Officer
Craig Noble, Acting Chief Financial Officer

Tristone Capital Inc.

#2020, 335 - 8th Ave. SW
Calgary, AB T2P 1C9
403-294-9541
Fax: 403-294-9543
info@tristonecapital.com
www.tristonecapital.com
Year Founded: 2000
Stock Exchange Membership: Toronto Stock Exchange, TSX Venture Exchange

INVESTMENT MANAGEMENT

Tristone Capital Inc. (continued)

Profile: The investment dealer is an energy advisory firm. Services include acquisitions & divestitures, global equity capital markets, & investment banking.

Executives:
George Gosbee, President/CEO & Chair
Michael Kehler, COO
Hinson Ng, Chief Compliance Officer
Andrew Abbott, Managing Director, Institutional Trading
Rob Colcleugh, Managing Director, Institutional Sales
Tom Ebbern, Managing Director, Institutional Sales
Brad Hurtubise, Managing Director, Investment Banking
Andrew Judson, Managing Director, Institutional Sales
Tom MacInnis, Managing Director, Investment Banking
Warren Robinson, Managing Director, Institutional Sales
David Street, Managing Director, Institutional Sales
Chris Theal, Managing Director, Institutional Research
David Vankka, Managing Director, Global Capital Markets
David Vetters, Managing Director, Investment Banking
Gurdeep Gill, Vice-President, Investment Banking
Kelly Grosky, Vice President & Director, Institutional Trading
Leslie Kende, Vice President & Director, Acquisitions & Divestitures
Cristina Lopez, Vice-President & Director, Institutional Research
Lane Mosby, Vice President & Director, Private Client Group
Don Rawson, Vice-President & Director, Institutional Research
Lynn Tsutsumi, Vice President, Finance

Tuscarora Capital Inc.

Also listed under: *Pension & Money Management Companies*
#400, 87 Front St. East
Toronto, ON M5E 1B8
416-364-0249
Fax: 416-364-8893
tuscapital@msn.com
Ownership: Private
Year Founded: 1996
Number of Employees: 5
Profile: Lines of business includes portfolio investment management, and principal trading.

Executives:
Gary Selke, President
Directors:
Norm Lamarche, Chair

UBS Securities Canada Inc.

BCE Place
PO Box 617
#4100, 161 Bay St.
Toronto, ON M5J 2S1
416-364-3293
Fax: 416-364-1976
www.ubs.com/investmentbank
Former Name: UBS Bunting Warburg Inc.
Ownership: Wholly owned subsidiary of Bunting Warburg Ltd.
Stock Exchange Membership: Montreal Exchange, Toronto Stock Exchange, TSX Venture Exchange
Profile: Services provided include mergers & acquisitions & securities trading.

Executives:
James Estey, President/CEO
Stephen Gerry, Financial Administrator
Branches:
Montréal
#2400, 1800, av McGill College
Montréal, QC H3A 3J6 Canada
514-842-8726
Fax: 514-842-8720
F. William Molson, Director

Union Securities Ltd.

#900, 700 West Geogia St.
Vancouver, BC V7Y 1H4
604-687-2201
Fax: 604-684-6307
www.union-securities.com
Ownership: Private
Year Founded: 1963
Number of Employees: 275
Stock Exchange Membership: Canadian Trading & Quotation System Inc, Montreal Exchange, Toronto Stock Exchange, TSX Venture Exchange
Executives:
Colin Browne, COO/Director
Branches:
Brampton
8 Main St. South
Brampton, ON L6W 2C3 Canada
905-451-2633
Fax: 905-451-6530
Calgary
#3260, 450 - 1st St. SW
Calgary, AB T2P 5H1 Canada
403-215-2180
Fax: 403-215-2189
Charlottetown
93 Pownal St.
Charlottetown, PE C1A 3W4 Canada
902-569-1583
Fax: 902-569-1504
Edmonton
Edmonton City Centre
#1000, 10025 - 102A Ave.
Edmonton, AB T5J 2Z2 Canada
780-413-3344
Fax: 780-413-1946
Fredericton
#230, 77 Westmorland St.
Fredericton, NB E3B 6Z3 Canada
506-457-1456
Fax: 506-472-9798
Halifax
Tower 2, Purdy's Wharf
#203, 1969 Upper Water St.
Halifax, NS B3J 3R7 Canada
902-422-9098
Fax: 902-425-4089
Kelowna
#320, 3275 Lakeshore Rd.
Kelowna, BC V1W 3S9 Canada
250-979-1750
Fax: 250-979-1779
Kitchener
#140, 50 Queen St. North
Kitchener, ON N2H 6P4 Canada
519-584-2600
Fax: 519-584-2611
Moncton
#104, 1133 St. George Blvd.
Moncton, NB E1E 4E1 Canada
506-855-9045
Fax: 506-854-1139
Oakville
Bronte Village Mall
2441 Lakeshore Rd. West
Oakville, ON L6L 1H6 Canada
905-827-6100
Fax: 905-827-2390
Regina
#102, 2022 Cornwall St.
Regina, SK S4P 2K5 Canada
306-525-7650
Fax: 306-525-7669
Saskatoon
1100 CN Tower
Saskatoon, SK S7K 1J5 Canada
306-244-2466
Fax: 306-244-2483
Thunder Bay
1204B Roland St.
Thunder Bay, ON P7B 5M4 Canada
807-626-5100
Fax: 807-626-5111
Timmins
#108, 85 Pine St. South
Timmins, ON P4N 2K1 Canada
705-360-4277
Fax: 705-360-4282
Toronto
#800, 69 Yonge St.
Toronto, ON M5E 1K3 Canada
416-777-0600
Fax: 416-777-1276
Whitby
#23A, 10 Sunray St.
Whitby, ON L1N 9B5 Canada
905-665-5473
Fax: 905-665-5717
White Rock
#300, 2099 - 152nd St.
White Rock, BC V4A 4N7 Canada
604-541-1378
Fax: 604-541-1648
Winnipeg
#500, 360 Main St.
Winnipeg, MB R3C 3Z3 Canada
204-987-7220
Fax: 204-987-7229

Valeurs mobilières Desjardins inc(VMD)/ Desjardins Securities Inc.

Tour de l'Est
CP 394, Desjardins Stn. Desjardins
2, Complexe Desjardins, 15e étage
Montréal, QC H5B 1J2
514-987-1749
Fax: 514-842-3137
800-361-4342
general@vmd.desjardins.com
www.vmd.ca
Ownership: Wholly owned subsidiary of Desjardins Laurentian Financial Corporation
Year Founded: 1982
Number of Employees: 476
Stock Exchange Membership: Canadian Trading & Quotation System Inc, Montreal Exchange, Toronto Stock Exchange, TSX Venture Exchange
Executives:
Jean-Pierre De Montigny, President/COO
Eric Bouchard, Sr. Vice-President
Pierre Charbonneau, Sr. Vice-President, Finance, Operations, Systems & Fixed Income
Richard Groome, Sr. Vice-President, Institutional Equity
Jacques Lemay, Sr. Vice-President, Corporate Finance
Yves Proteau, Sr. Vice-President, Private Clients
Brian L. Curry, Vice-President & Regional Manager, Ontario
Marc Jobin, Vice-President, Sales, Full Services Brokerage
J. Scott Tomenson, Vice-President
Affiliated Companies:
Disnat

Vance Financial Group Inc.

Also listed under: *Financial Planning*
South Tower
#201, 5811 Cooney Rd.
Richmond, BC V6X 3M1
604-233-0123
Fax: 604-271-4863
www.torcefinancial.com
Executives:
Paul Lui, Contact, Management Team
Michelle Leung, Administrator

Versant Partners Inc.

#1200, 1350, rue Sherbrooke ouest
Montréal, QC H3G 1J1
514-845-8111
Fax: 514-845-0200
800-465-5616
info@versantpartners.com
www.versantpartners.com
Former Name: Dlouhy Merchant Inc.; Dlouhy Investments Inc.
Ownership: Private
Number of Employees: 18
Stock Exchange Membership: Montreal Exchange, Toronto Stock Exchange, TSX Venture Exchange
Executives:
Michael Jams, President/CEO
Branches:
Toronto
#1030, 145 King St. West
Toronto, ON M5H 1S8 Canada
416-363-5757
Fax: 416-363-6609
866-442-4485

W.D. Latimer Co. Limited

PO Box 96, Toronto-Dominion Stn. Toronto-Dominion
#600, 100 Wellington St. West
Toronto, ON M5K 1G8
416-363-5631
Fax: 416-363-8022
courtb@pass.com

Stock Exchange Membership: Canadian Trading & Quotation System Inc, Montreal Exchange, Toronto Stock Exchange, TSX Venture Exchange
Executives:
C.M. Bracken
A.C. DeLuca
S. DeLuca
E.C. Featherstone
T.J.H. Miller

Watt Carmichael Inc.

PO Box 47
#610, 55 University Ave.
Toronto, ON M5J 2H7
416-864-1500
Fax: 416-864-0883
info@wattcar.com
www.wattcar.com
Number of Employees: 25
Executives:
Harry J. Carmichael, CEO

Wellington West Capital Inc.

Also listed under: *Pension & Money Management Companies*
#400, 200 Waterfront Dr.
Winnipeg, MB R3B 3P1
204-925-2250
Fax: 204-942-6194
800-461-6314
admin@wellwest.ca
www.wellingtonwest.com
Ownership: Private
Year Founded: 1993
Number of Employees: 400
Assets: $1-10 billion
Stock Exchange Membership: Toronto Stock Exchange, TSX Venture Exchange
Profile: Wellington West Capital Markets, Inc. is also an affiliated company.

Executives:
Charles D. Spiring, Chair/CEO
John Rothwell, President
Blaine Coates, CFO
Daniel McDonald, CCO
Directors:
Jerome Cohen
Gary Filmon
Kevin Hooke
Kevin Kelly
Nancy Shewfelt
Charles D. Spiring
Greg Thompson
Howard Young
Affiliated Companies:
Wellington West Aboriginal Investment Services
Wellington West Corporate Finance
Wellington West Financial Services Inc./WWFS
Wellington West Pro Ice Management
Wellington West Total Wealth Management Inc.
Branches:
Barrie
126 Collier St.
Barrie, ON L4M 1H4 Canada
705-719-1190
Fax: 705-719-1191
866-402-5940
Brenda Lennon, Branch Administrator
Brandon
3000 Victoria Ave., #E
Brandon, MB R7B 3Y3 Canada
204-571-3200
Fax: 204-571-3210
866-235-5914
Maria Boudehane, Branch Administrator
Calgary
Bow Valley Square 3
#1100, 255 - 5 Ave. SW
Calgary, AB T2P 3G6 Canada
403-215-2000
Fax: 403-261-4021
877-222-9378
Michelle Zimmerman, Contact
Charlottetown
BDC Tower
#310, 119 Kent St.
Charlottetown, PE C1A 1N3 Canada
902-569-8813
Fax: 902-569-8718
Cathy Shoemaker, Contact
Halifax - Brunswick St.
#120B, 1741 Brunswick St.
Halifax, NS B3J 3X8 Canada
902-425-2326
Fax: 902-425-0807
Tammy Hackett, Contact
Halifax - Spring Garden Rd.
5670 Spring Garden Rd.
Halifax, NS B3J 1H5 Canada
902-425-1283
Fax: 902-425-1835
866-243-1070
Sharon Whalen, Contact
London
City Centre
#802, 380 Wellington St.
London, ON N6A 5B5 Canada
519-645-4861
Fax: 519-645-0902
888-530-4786
Deanne Simpson, Branch Administrator
Moose Jaw
311A Main St. North
Moose Jaw, SK S6H 0W2 Canada
306-691-6292
Fax: 306-691-6299
866-234-4418
Monica White, Contact
Oakville
105 Robinson St., 2nd Fl.
Oakville, ON L6J 1G1 Canada
905-842-1925
Fax: 905-842-1172
888-778-3956
Noelle Tinus, Assistant Branch Manager
Red Deer
#200, 4719 - 48th Ave.
Red Deer, AB T4N 3T1 Canada
403-348-2600
Fax: 403-348-0203
866-248-2633
Diane Hughes, Branch Administrator
Regina
Tower 2, McCallum Hill Centre
1881 Scath St.
Regina, SK S4P 4BE Canada
306-781-0500
Fax: 306-781-0505
866-488-0500
Joyce Marbach, Branch Manager
Saskatoon
#1360, 410 - 22nd St. East
Saskatoon, SK S7K 5T6 Canada
306-657-4400
Fax: 360-657-4410
866-844-4400
Colleen Clavelle, Branch Administrator
Swift Current
#301, 12 Cheadle St. West
Swift Current, SK S9H 0A9 Canada
306-778-4770
Fax: 306-778-4775
866-446-9444
Michelle Schmeiss, Branch Administrator
Toronto - King St.
#700, 145 King St. West
Toronto, ON M5H 1J8 Canada
416-642-1900
Fax: 416-203-9901
Doug Haydock, Contact
Toronto - Yonge St.
Yonge Corporate Centre
#501, 4100 Yonge St.
Toronto, ON M2P 2B5 Canada
416-646-6901
Fax: 416-646-9650
800-438-3319
Tina Yeung, Branch Administrator
Vancouver
#1488, 1333 Broadway Ave. West
Vancouver, BC V6H 4C1 Canada
604-738-5655
Fax: 604-736-8155
877-588-9378
Cathy Foster, Branch Administrator
Victoria
#240, 730 View St.
Victoria, BC V8W 3Y7 Canada
250-418-8829
Tina Derix, Contact
White Rock
Windsor Square
#101, 1959 - 152 St.
White Rock, BC V4A 9E3 Canada
604-542-2824
Fax: 604-542-2843
888-866-8866
Roz Stefaniuk, Contact
Yorkton
132 Broadway St. West
Yorkton, SK S3N 0M3 Canada
306-782-6450
Fax: 306-782-6460
844-782-6450
Penny Sandercock, Contact

Wellington West Financial Services Inc.(WWFS)

Also listed under: *Financial Planning*
#300, 200 Waterfront Dr.
Winnipeg, MB R3B 3P1
204-925-2290
Fax: 204-956-1296
800-848-0580
wellingtonwest.com/about_wwfs.html
Ownership: Subsidiary of Wellington West Capital Inc.
Profile: Financial plans are developed for individuals, families & businesses.

Executives:
Wade Lawrence, B.Comm (Hons.), RHU, CLU, CH.F.C., CFP, RFP, TEP, President; 204-925-2071
Pierre L. Campeau, RHU, EPC, Vice-President
Rob White, CLU, CFP, Vice-President
Branches:
Calgary
Bow Valley Square 3
255 - 5th Ave. SW
Calgary, AB T2P 3G6 Canada
403-266-1410
Fax: 403-266-6121
800-242-4897
Debbie Ekkel, Financial Advisor
Headingley
5315 Portage Ave.
Headingley, MB R4H 1J9
204-989-7705
Fax: 204-987-7705
London
#802, 380 Wellington St.
London, ON N6A 5B5
Fax: 519-645-7392
800-643-8380
Roblin
PO Box 1440
Roblin, MB R0L 1P0 Canada
204-937-8897
Fax: 204-937-8897
866-937-4299
Vernon Brown, Financial Advisor
Saskatoon
Saskatoon Square
#1360, 410- 22nd St. East
Saskatoon, SK S7K 5T6
306-934-8897
Fax: 306-244-9888
800-426-9105
Ian DeCorby, Group & Pension Advisor
Ste Rose du Lac
PO Box 850
640 Central Ave.
Ste Rose du Lac, MB R0L 1S0 Canada
204-447-3034
Fax: 204-447-3442
Vancouver

Wellington West Financial Services Inc.(WWFS) (continued)
#1488, 1333 West Broadway Ave.
Vancouver, BC V6H 4C1
Fax: 604-742-2141
866-738-5655
Victoria
1480 Fort St.
Victoria, BC V8S 1Z5
250-475-3698
Fax: 250-475-3697
888-661-7526
Scott Vanderwark, Financial Advisor

Wentworth Financial Services Inc.
Also listed under: *Financial Planning*
#605, 105 Main St. East
Hamilton, ON L8N 1G6
905-528-0193
Fax: 905-546-5039
Other Information: 1-800-463-5386
reception@wentworthfinancial.com
www.wentworthfinancial.com
Former Name: Allan H. Minaker CFP, CLU, CH.F.C.
Ownership: Private
Year Founded: 1981
Number of Employees: 15

West Capital Wealth Management
Also listed under: *Financial Planning*
#400, 1306 Wellington St.
Ottawa, ON K1Y 3B2
613-722-1854
Fax: 613-722-6579
800-826-0877
info@westcap.ca
www.westcap.ca
Also Known As: WestCap
Ownership: Private. Part of Armstrong & Quaile Associates Inc., Manotick, ON.
Year Founded: 2000
Executives:
Terry Olsen, CFP, P.Eng., MAnager; tolsen@westcap.ca

Westwind Partners Inc.
70 York St., 10th Fl.
Toronto, ON M5J 1S9
416-815-0888
Fax: 416-815-1808
Other Information: 416-815-1621 (Fax, Equities)
www.westwindpartners.ca
Ownership: Private
Stock Exchange Membership: Toronto Stock Exchange, TSX Venture Exchange
Profile: Westwind Partners is an independent research & investment banking firm. Services include equity research on Canadian & US companies, equity trading capability & independent advice to corporations on M&A, financing & restructuring transactions. Westwind has offices in Toronto, Montreal, Calgary & London, UK. It is a member of the Canadian Investor Protection Fund & the Investment Dealers Association of Canada.

Executives:
Lionel Conacher, President/CEO
George Fowlie, Deputy Chair & Head, Investment Banking
Horst Hueniken, Deputy Chair
John Grandy, Managing Director & Head, Research
Sam Hardy, Managing Director & Head, Trading
Keith Harris, Managing Director, CFO
Branches:
Calgary
#500, 520 - 5th Ave. SW
Calgary, AB T2P 3R7
403-265-1939
Fax: 403-265-1935
Montréal
#1200, 1002, rue Sherbrooke ouest
Montréal, QC H3A 3L6
514-288-8388
Fax: 514-288-1886

Wolverton Securities Ltd.
PO Box 10115
777 Dunsmuir St., 17th Fl.
Vancouver, BC V7Y 1J5
604-622-1000
Fax: 604-662-5205
877-390-7771
info@wolverton.ca
www.wolverton.ca
Ownership: Private
Year Founded: 1910
Number of Employees: 145
Revenues: $5-10 million
Stock Exchange Membership: Canadian Trading & Quotation System Inc, Montreal Exchange, Toronto Stock Exchange, TSX Venture Exchange
Executives:
Brent N. Wolverton, President/CEO
K. Brian Ashton, Sr. Vice-President
Dan Smith, Sr. Vice-President
Nicole Stevens, Sr. Vice-President, Trading
Colman Wong, Sr. Vice-President, Sales
Ernest Crepnjak, Vice-President
Kellan Newsam, Vice-President & CIO
Blaine Parks, Vice-President
Ian Thomson, Vice-President, Research
K.C. Tsirigotis, Vice-President
Alexandra Williams, Vice-President
Ellen C. Paterson, CFO/Sec.-Treas.
Directors:
Ellen C. Paterson
Ian Thomson
Brent N. Wolverton
Mark F. Wolverton
Branches:
Calgary
PO Box 98
#2100, 335 - 8th Ave. SW
Calgary, AB T2P 1C9 Canada
403-263-8800
Fax: 403-269-8881
888-263-8808
Kelowna
#408, 1708 Dolphin Ave.
Kelowna, BC V1Y 9S4 Canada
250-763-2008
Fax: 250-979-7260
866-323-2232
Prince George
1839 - 1 Ave, 7th Fl.
Prince George, BC V2L 2Y8 Canada
250-562-0019
Fax: 250-562-0029
Red Deer
#100, 4922 - 53rd St.
Red Deer, AB T4N 2E9 Canada
403-346-7190
Fax: 403-342-1087
Saskatoon
1631 Forest Dr.
Saskatoon, SK S7N 3G7 Canada
306-249-1906
Fax: 306-249-1907

Woodstone Capital Inc.
Also listed under: *Financial Planning*
#310, 601 West Cordova St.
Vancouver, BC V6B 1G1
604-605-8300
Fax: 604-605-8310
888-388-3885
inquiries@woodstonecapital.com
www.woodstonecapital.com
Year Founded: 1997
Stock Exchange Membership: Montreal Exchange, Toronto Stock Exchange, TSX Venture Exchange
Profile: The indpendent firm offers investment products & services such as research, advice, retirement planning, estate planning, corporate finance expertise & trade execution.

Executives:
Mahmood S, Ahamed, President
Ginalee Holliday, Chief Financial Officer
Ben Hadala, Vice-President
Richard Roussel, Vice-President
Alexander Teh, B.Comm, Sr. Investment Advisor
Branches:
Calgary
#530, 510 - 5 St. SW
Calgary, AB T2P 3S2 Canada
403-777-3880
Canmore
139 Morris St.
Canmore, AB T1W 2W5 Canada
888-278-4282

Worldsource Securities Inc.
Also listed under: *Financial Planning*
#700, 625 Cochrane Dr.
Markham, ON L3R 9R9
905-940-0094
Fax: 905-415-1812
866-740-7277
www.worldsourcesecurities.com
Ownership: Division of Worldsource Wealth Management Inc.
Profile: The investment dealer provides services regulated by the Investment Dealers Association of Canada (IDA). Financial advisory & wealth management services are also offered.

Executives:
John Hunt, President/COO

Y.I.S. Financial Inc.
Also listed under: *Financial Planning*
215 Scott St.
St Catharines, ON L2N 1H5
905-937-3920
Fax: 905-646-0003
invest@yis.ca
Executives:
Rich Merrick, Advisor

YMG Capital Management Inc.
#2020, 1 Queen St. East
Toronto, ON M5C 2W5
416-364-3711
Fax: 416-955-4877
www.ymg.ca
Year Founded: 1983
Number of Employees: 46
Executives:
Eric A. Innes, President/CEO
Neil Nisker, President, YMG Private Wealth Management
Gerald Graham, Vice-President
Jim Craven, COO
Directors:
André D. Godbout, Chair
Stanley M. Beck, Q.C.
J. Anthony Boeckh
Tim A. Bowman
Eric A.T. Innes
Graeme E. Thom
Branches:
Montréal
Tour Scotia
#2240, 1002, rue Sherbrooke ouest
Montréal, QC H3A 3L6 Canada
514-842-8338
Fax: 514-842-3498

yourCFO Advisory Group Inc.
Reimer Building
5500 North Service Rd., 3rd Fl.
Burlington, ON L7L 6W6
905-331-2885
Fax: 905-331-2886
888-539-5263
inquiries@yourCFOinc.com
www.yourCFOinc.com
Former Name: Leyland, McLachlan Advisory Group Incorported
Ownership: Private.
Year Founded: 2000
Profile: The full-service, independent investment dealer offers products & services such as mutual funds, bonds, stocks, exchange trade funds, income trusts, retirement savings plans, & registered education savings plans.

Executives:
Douglas Leyland, Chair & President
Branches:
Burlington
#101, 5575 North Service Rd.
Burlington, ON L7L 6M1 Canada
905-335-5222
Fax: 905-335-5355
888-563-1231
E. Wendy Milne, Branch Manager
Comox

#201, 1819 Beaufort Ave.
Comox, BC V9M 1R9
250-339-5776
Fax: 250-339-5778

Hamilton
#6A, 45 Goderich Dr.
Hamilton, ON L8E 4W8
905-560-8409
Fax: 905-560-2368
Kanata
68 Insmill Cres.
Kanata, ON K2T 1G4
613-599-8885
Fax: 613-592-5139
Mississauga
#4, 2285 Dunwin Dr.
Mississauga, ON L5L 3S3 Canada
905-607-1393
Fax: 905-607-1614
Carol Ann Chyz, Branch Manager
Nanaimo
#104, 6330 Dover Rd.
Nanaimo, BC V9V 1S4
250-390-0487
Fax: 250-390-4785
Ottawa
#309, 1755 Woodward Dr.
Ottawa, ON K2C 0P9
613-796-4817
Fax: 819-682-2358
Stoney Creek
4 Watercliff Pl.
Stoney Creek, ON L8E 6E5
905-592-1136
Fax: 905-643-8071
Victoria
760 Hillside Ave.
Victoria, BC V8T 1Z6
250-385-0099
Fax: 250-385-0078
877-385-0090

Investment Fund Companies

Abria Financial Group
Also listed under: *Investment Dealers; Investment Management*
#300, 20 Adelaide St. East
Toronto, ON M5C 2T6
416-367-4777
Fax: 416-367-4555
877-512-2742
info@abriafunds.com
www.abriafunds.com
Former Name: Abria Financial Products Ltd.
Ownership: Private
Year Founded: 1999
Number of Employees: 20
Assets: $100-500 million Year End: 20041031
Revenues: $1-5 million Year End: 20041031
Executives:
Andrew Doman, COO; 416-367-9993; doman@abriafunds.com
Davee Gunn, Exec. Vice-President; 416-365-0224; gunn@abriafunds.com
Abria:
Diversified Arbitage Trust
RRSP Eligible; Inception Year: 2000; Fund Managers:
Dominic Staniscia
HenryKneis
Michael Doran
Michael Ding
Alternative Strategies Note
RRSP Eligible; Inception Year: 2004; Fund Managers:
Michael Ding
Diversified Arbitrage Trust (US$)
RRSP Eligible; Inception Year: 2000; Fund Managers:
Henry Kneis
DominicStaniscia
Michael Doran
Michael Ding
Guaranteed Alter Inc Nts Sr 1
RRSP Eligible; Inception Year: 2005; Fund Managers:
Henry Kneis
DominicStaniscia
Michael Doran
Michael Ding
Alter Combined Ret Nts Ser 1
RRSP Eligible; Inception Year: 2005; Fund Managers:
Henry Kneis
DominicStaniscia
Michael Doran
Michael Ding
Branches:
Calgary - Alberta Regional Office
Bow Valley Square IV
#1800, 250 - 6th Ave. SW
Calgary, AB T2T 6K8 Canada
403-685-7682
Fax: 403-685-4404
info@abriafunds.com
Vancouver - British Columbia Regional Office
#1500, 701 West Georgia St.
Vancouver, BC V7Y 1C6 Canada
604-609-0155
Fax: 604-801-5911
877460-0155
info@abriafunds.com

Acker Finley Inc.
Also listed under: *Financial Planning*
#1361, 181 University Ave.
Toronto, ON M5H 3M7
416-777-9005
Fax: 416-777-2096
success@ackerfinley.com
www.ackerfinley.com
Ownership: Private
Year Founded: 1992
Stock Exchange Membership: Toronto Stock Exchange
Executives:
Brian G. Acker, President/CEO; brian@ackerfinley.com
Joseph C. Finley, CFO & Managing Director; joseph@ackerfinley.com
Enrico Sgromo, Vice-President, Research; enrico@ackerfinley.com
Brenda Tilley, Vice-President, Private Clients; brenda@ackerfinley.com
Michelle Bain, FMA, Investment Advisor
Acker Finley:
QSA Select Canada Focus Fund
RRSP Eligible; Inception Year: 2004;
QSA Canada Focus Fund
RRSP Eligible; Inception Year: 2004;
QSA Select US Value 50 Fund
RRSP Eligible; Inception Year: 2003;

Acuity Investment Management Inc.
#1800, 65 Queen St. West
Toronto, ON M5H 2M5
416-366-9933
Fax: 416-366-2568
800-461-4570
mail@acuityfunds.com
www.acuityfunds.com
Ownership: Private
Year Founded: 1991
Number of Employees: 12
Acuity:
Canadian Balanced Fund
RRSP Eligible; Inception Year: 1998;
Canadian Equity Fund
RRSP Eligible; Inception Year: 1998;
High Income Fund
RRSP Eligible; Inception Year: 1991;
Money Market Fund
RRSP Eligible; Inception Year: 1998;
Global Equity Fund
RRSP Eligible; Inception Year: 1999;
All-Cap 30 Canadian Equity Fund
RRSP Eligible; Inception Year: 2000;
Fixed Income Fund
RRSP Eligible; Inception Year: 1998;
Income Trust Fund
RRSP Eligible; Inception Year: 2003;
Canadian Small Cap Fund
RRSP Eligible; Inception Year: 2005;
Conservative Asset Allocation Fund
RRSP Eligible; Inception Year: 2005;
Dividend Fund
RRSP Eligible; Inception Year: 2005; Fund Managers:
Ian O. Ihnatowycz
HughMcCaulay
Warren Fenton
David G. Stonehouse
Acuity Clean Environment:
Balanced Fund
RRSP Eligible; Inception Year: 1991;
Equity Fund
RRSP Eligible; Inception Year: 1991;
Global Equity Fund
RRSP Eligible; Inception Year: 1993;
Acuity Pooled:
Balanced Fund
RRSP Eligible; Inception Year: 1993;
Conservative Asset Allocation Fund
RRSP Eligible; Inception Year: 1993;
Income Trust Fund
RRSP Eligible; Inception Year: 2003;
Fixed Income Fund
RRSP Eligible; Inception Year: 1993;
Global Balanced Fund
RRSP Eligible; Inception Year: 1993;
Global Equity Fund
RRSP Eligible; Inception Year: 1993;
High Income Fund
RRSP Eligible; Inception Year: 1993;
Short Term Fund
RRSP Eligible; Inception Year: 1993;
Canadian Equity Fund
RRSP Eligible; Inception Year: 1993;
Canadian Small Cap Fund
RRSP Eligible; Inception Year: 2003;
Social Values Canadian Equity Fund
RRSP Eligible; Inception Year: 2003;
Environment, Science & Technology Fund
RRSP Eligible; Inception Year: 1993;
Growth & Income Fund
RRSP Eligible; Inception Year: 2003;
Pure Canadian Equity Fund
RRSP Eligible; Inception Year: 2002;
Acuity Social Values:
Canadian Equity Fund
RRSP Eligible; Inception Year: 2000;
Global Equity Fund
RRSP Eligible; Inception Year: 2000;

AEGON Fund Management Inc.
5000 Yonge St.
Toronto, ON M2N 7J8
Fax: 416-883-5520
866-462-9946
info@imaxxwealth.com
www.imaxxwealth.com
Executives:
Mark Jackson, President
imaxx:
Money Market Fund
RRSP Eligible; Inception Year: 2002; Fund Managers:
Barbara Berry
MarcGoldfried
Canadian Bond Fund
RRSP Eligible; Inception Year: 2002; Fund Managers:
Marc Goldfried
R.GregoryRoss
Canadian Fixed Pay Fund
RRSP Eligible; Inception Year: 2002; Fund Managers:
Glenn Paradis
Canadian Equity Growth Fund
RRSP Eligible; Inception Year: 2002; Fund Managers:
Glenn Paradis
Canadian Equity Value Fund
RRSP Eligible; Inception Year: 2002; Fund Managers:
Foyston, Gordon & Payne, Inc.
US Equity Growth Fund
RRSP Eligible; Inception Year: 2002; Fund Managers:
Transamerica Investment Management, LLC
US Equity Value Fund
RRSP Eligible; Inception Year: 2002; Fund Managers:
Bear Stearns Asset Management Ltd.
Global Equity Value Fund
RRSP Eligible; Inception Year: 2002; Fund Managers:
Foyston, Gordon & Payne, Inc.

INVESTMENT MANAGEMENT

AEGON Fund Management Inc. (continued)
Global Equity Growth Fund
RRSP Eligible; Inception Year: 2002; Fund Managers:
Walter Scott & Partners Ltd.
TOP Conservative Portfolio Fund
RRSP Eligible; Inception Year: 2002;
TOP Balanced Portfolio Fund
RRSP Eligible; Inception Year: 2002;
TOP RSP Balanced Portfolio Fund
RRSP Eligible; Inception Year: 2002;
TOP Growth Portfolio Fund
RRSP Eligible; Inception Year: 2002;
TOP RSP Growth Portfolio Fund
RRSP Eligible; Inception Year: 2002;
TOP Aggressive Growth Portfolio Fund
RRSP Eligible; Inception Year: 2002;

AGF Funds Inc.

Toronto-Dominion Bank Tower, 31st Fl.
PO Box 50, Toronto-Dominion Stn. Toronto-Dominion
Toronto, ON M5K 1E9
905-214-8203
Fax: 905-214-8243
800-268-8583
tiger@agf.com
www.agf.com
Ownership: Private
Number of Employees: 625
Executives:
C. Warren Goldring, Chair
Blake C. Goldring, President/CEO, AGF Management Limited
Randy Ambrosie, President
Robert Farquharson, CFA
Clive Coombs, Exec. Vice-President
Judy Goldring, Sr. Vice-President, Business Operations, General Counsel
Greg Henderson, Sr. Vice-President/CFO
Beatrice Ip, Sr. Vice-President, Corporate Secretary
AGF:
Aggressive Global Stock Fund
RRSP Eligible; Inception Year: 1996; Fund Managers:
Driehaus Capital Management Inc.
Aggressive Growth Fund
RRSP Eligible; Inception Year: 1993; Fund Managers:
Driehaus Capital Management Inc.
Emerging Markets Value Fund
RRSP Eligible; Inception Year: 1994; Fund Managers:
Patricia Perez-Coutts
American Growth Class Fund
RRSP Eligible; Inception Year: 1957; Fund Managers:
Tony Genua
Asian Growth Class Fund
RRSP Eligible; Inception Year: 1991; Fund Managers:
Eng Hock Ong
Canadian Bond Fund
RRSP Eligible; Inception Year: 1962; Fund Managers:
Scott Colbourne
Canadian Growth Equity Fund
RRSP Eligible; Inception Year: 1964; Fund Managers:
Bob Farquharson
CharlesOliver
Canadian Resources Fund
RRSP Eligible; Inception Year: 1960; Fund Managers:
Bob Farquharson
CharlesOliver
Germany Class Fund
RRSP Eligible; Inception Year: 1994; Fund Managers:
Deutsche Asset Management Group
Global Government Bond Fund
RRSP Eligible; Inception Year: 1986; Fund Managers:
Scott Colbourne
Aggressive Japan Class Fund
RRSP Eligible; Inception Year: 2000; Fund Managers:
Sumitomo Mitsui Asset Management Co. Ltd.
Special US Class Fund
RRSP Eligible; Inception Year: 1968; Fund Managers:
Tony Genua
Canada Class Fund
RRSP Eligible; Inception Year: 1997; Fund Managers:
Martin Hubbes
RSP Global Bond Fund
RRSP Eligible; Inception Year: 1993; Fund Managers:
Scott Colbourne
International Value Fund
RRSP Eligible; Inception Year: 1989; Fund Managers:
Harris Associates L.P.
Managed Futures Fund
RRSP Eligible; Inception Year: 1995; Fund Managers:
Zoran Vojvodic
Global Real Estate Equity Fund
RRSP Eligible; Inception Year: 1998; Fund Managers:
Stephen Way
International Stock Class Fund
RRSP Eligible; Inception Year: 1997; Fund Managers:
John Arnold
RoryFlynn
Canadian Stock Fund
RRSP Eligible; Inception Year: 1969; Fund Managers:
Martin Hubbes
World Balanced Fund
RRSP Eligible; Inception Year: 1987; Fund Managers:
Rory Flynn
JohnArnold
China Focus Class Fund
RRSP Eligible; Inception Year: 1994; Fund Managers:
Nomura Asset Management Co. Ltd.
Canadian Balanced Fund
RRSP Eligible; Inception Year: 1931; Fund Managers:
Christine Hughes
Global Financial Services Class Fund
RRSP Eligible; Inception Year: 2000; Fund Managers:
Rory Flynn
Global Health Sciences Class Fund
RRSP Eligible; Inception Year: 2000; Fund Managers:
Martin Hubbes
TonyGenua
Global Resources Class Fund
RRSP Eligible; Inception Year: 2000; Fund Managers:
Bob Farquharson
CharlesOliver
Japan Class Fund
RRSP Eligible; Inception Year: 1970; Fund Managers:
Nomura Asset Management Co. Ltd.
Canadian Small Cap Fund
RRSP Eligible; Inception Year: 1996; Fund Managers:
Charles Oliver
European Equity Class Fund
RRSP Eligible; Inception Year: 1994; Fund Managers:
John Arnold
RoryFlynn
Global Equity Class Fund
RRSP Eligible; Inception Year: 1995; Fund Managers:
Stephen Way
US Value Class Fund
RRSP Eligible; Inception Year: 2001; Fund Managers:
Rory Flynn
World Companies Fund
RRSP Eligible; Inception Year: 1994; Fund Managers:
Stephen Way
World Opportunities Fund
RRSP Eligible; Inception Year: 1997; Fund Managers:
Stephen Way
Precious Metals Fund
RRSP Eligible; Inception Year: 1993; Fund Managers:
Bob Farquharson
CharlesOliver
Canadian Money Market Account Fund
RRSP Eligible; Inception Year: 1975; Fund Managers:
Tristan Sones
Short-Term Income Class Fund
RRSP Eligible; Inception Year: 1975; Fund Managers:
Tristan Sones
US Dollar Money Market Account Fund
RRSP Eligible; Inception Year: 1988; Fund Managers:
Tristan Sones
Canadian Conservative Income Fund
RRSP Eligible; Inception Year: 1989; Fund Managers:
Tristan Sones
ScottColbourne
Canadian Real Value Fund
RRSP Eligible; Inception Year: 1992; Fund Managers:
Keith Graham
Global Technology Class Fund
RRSP Eligible; Inception Year: 2000; Fund Managers:
Tony Genua
CoulterWright
Canadian Large Cap Dividend Fund
RRSP Eligible; Inception Year: 1985; Fund Managers:
Connor, Clark & Lunn Investment Management Ltd.
Canadian Real Value Balanced Fund
RRSP Eligible; Inception Year: 1989; Fund Managers:
Keith Graham
International Value Class Fund
RRSP Eligible; Inception Year: 2002; Fund Managers:
Harris Associates L.P.
Canadian High Yield Bond Fund
RRSP Eligible; Inception Year: 1994; Fund Managers:
Scott Colbourne
TristanSones
Diversified Dividend Income Fund
RRSP Eligible; Inception Year: 2005; Fund Managers:
Cypress Capital Management
Dividend Income Fund
RRSP Eligible; Inception Year: 2003; Fund Managers:
ING Investment Management
Elements Balanced Portfolio
RRSP Eligible; Inception Year: 2005; Fund Managers:
Martin Hubbes
Elements Conservative Portfolio
RRSP Eligible; Inception Year: 2005; Fund Managers:
Martin Hubbes
Elements Global Portfolio
RRSP Eligible; Inception Year: 2005; Fund Managers:
Martin Hubbes
Elements Growth Portfolio
RRSP Eligible; Inception Year: 2005; Fund Managers:
Martin Hubbes
Elements Yield Portfolio
RRSP Eligible; Inception Year: 2005; Fund Managers:
Martin Hubbes
Global High Yield Bond
RRSP Eligible; Inception Year: 1994; Fund Managers:
Scott Colbourne
YvonneBrett
Global Perspective Class
RRSP Eligible; Inception Year: 2000; Fund Managers:
Rory Flynn
JohnArnold
Monthly High Income Fund
RRSP Eligible; Inception Year: 2005; Fund Managers:
Cypress Capital Management
US Risk Managed Class Fund
RRSP Eligible; Inception Year: 2005; Fund Managers:
Intech

AIC Group of Funds Ltd.

1375 Kerns Rd.
Burlington, ON L7R 4X8
905-331-4242
Fax: 905-331-1321
800-263-2144
info@aic.com
www.aic.com
Ownership: Private.
Year Founded: 1985
Assets: $1-10 billion
Executives:
David Whyte, Exec. Vice-President
Andrew Dorrington, Sr. Vice-President, Client Strategy
AIC:
Advantage Fund
RRSP Eligible; Inception Year: 1985; Fund Managers:
Michael Lee-Chin
RobertAlmeida
Chris Lowe
Greg Placidi
Value Fund
RRSP Eligible; Inception Year: 1990; Fund Managers:
Jonathan Wellum
PatNaccarato
Kevin J. Vandermeer
Anthony Hammill
World Equity Fund
RRSP Eligible; Inception Year: 1993; Fund Managers:
Anne-Mette de Place Filippini, MA
Bond Fund
RRSP Eligible; Inception Year: 1999; Fund Managers:
Randy LeClair, CFA
Global Bond Fund
RRSP Eligible; Inception Year: 1999; Fund Managers:
Randy LeClair, CFA
Global Diversified Fund
RRSP Eligible; Inception Year: 1999; Fund Managers:
Anne-Mette de Place Filippini, MA

Advantage Fund II
RRSP Eligible; Inception Year: 1996; Fund Managers:
Michael Lee-Chin
RobertAlmeida
Chris Lowe
Greg Placidi
Canadian Focused Fund
RRSP Eligible; Inception Year: 2000; Fund Managers:
James Cole, CFA
American Focused Fund
RRSP Eligible; Inception Year: 1999; Fund Managers:
James Cole, CFA
Global Advantage Fund
RRSP Eligible; Inception Year: 1998; Fund Managers:
Chris Lowe
GregPlacidi
Canadian Balanced Fund
RRSP Eligible; Inception Year: 1997; Fund Managers:
James Cole, CFA
RandyLeClair
Global Balanced Fund
RRSP Eligible; Inception Year: 2001; Fund Managers:
Anne-Mette de Place Filippini, MA
RandyLeClair
American Balanced Fund
RRSP Eligible; Inception Year: 1998; Fund Managers:
Randy LeClair, CFA
AnthonyHammill
Jonathan Wellum
Kevin J. Vandermeer
Pat Naccarato
Advantage II Corporate Class Fund
RRSP Eligible; Inception Year: 2001; Fund Managers:
Michael Lee-Chin
RobertAlmeida
Chris Lowe
Greg Placidi
Advantage II Segregated (100%) Fund
RRSP Eligible; Inception Year: 1999; Fund Managers:
Michael Lee-Chin
RobertAlmeida
Chris Lowe
Greg Placidi
Advantage II Segregated (75%) Fund
RRSP Eligible; Inception Year: 1999; Fund Managers:
Michael Lee-Chin
RobertAlmeida
Chris Lowe
Greg Placidi
American Balanced Segregated (100%) Fund
RRSP Eligible; Inception Year: 1999; Fund Managers:
Randy LeClair, CFA
AnthonyHammill
Jonathan Wellum
Pat Naccarato
Kevin J. Vandermeer
American Balanced Segregated (75%) Fund
RRSP Eligible; Inception Year: 1999; Fund Managers:
Randy LeClair, CFA
PatNaccarato
Kevin J. Vandermeer
Anthony Hammill
Jonathan Wellum
American Advantage Fund
RRSP Eligible; Inception Year: 1997; Fund Managers:
Jonathan Wellum
GregPlacidi
Chris Lowe
American Advantage Corporate Class Fund
RRSP Eligible; Inception Year: 2001; Fund Managers:
Jonathan Wellum
ChrisLowe
Greg Placidi
American Advantage Segregated (100%) Fund
RRSP Eligible; Inception Year: 1999; Fund Managers:
Jonathan Wellum
ChrisLowe
Greg Placidi
American Advantage Segregated (75%) Fund
RRSP Eligible; Inception Year: 1999; Fund Managers:
Jonathan Wellum
ChrisLowe
Greg Placidi
American Balanced Corporate Class Fund
RRSP Eligible; Inception Year: 2001; Fund Managers:
Randy LeClair, CFA
JonathanWellum
Kevin J. Vandermeer
Pat Naccarato
Anthony Hammill
American Focused Corporate Class Fund
RRSP Eligible; Inception Year: 2001; Fund Managers:
James Cole, CFA
American Focused Segregated (100%) Fund
RRSP Eligible; Inception Year: 2000; Fund Managers:
James Cole, CFA
American Focused Segregated (75%) Fund
RRSP Eligible; Inception Year: 2000; Fund Managers:
James Cole, CFA
Canadian Focused Corporate Class Fund
RRSP Eligible; Inception Year: 2001; Fund Managers:
James Cole, CFA
Canadian Balanced Corporate Class Fund
RRSP Eligible; Inception Year: 2001; Fund Managers:
Randy LeClair, CFA
JamesCole
Diversified Science & Technology Corporate Class Fund
RRSP Eligible; Inception Year: 2001; Fund Managers:
Kevin J. Vandermeer
Diversified Science & Technology Fund
RRSP Eligible; Inception Year: 2000; Fund Managers:
Kevin J. Vandermeer
Diversified Canada Fund
RRSP Eligible; Inception Year: 1995; Fund Managers:
Jonathan Wellum
Diversified Canada Corporate Class Fund
RRSP Eligible; Inception Year: 2001; Fund Managers:
Jonathan Wellum
Diversified Canada Segregated (100%) Fund
RRSP Eligible; Inception Year: 1999; Fund Managers:
Jonathan Wellum
Diversified Canada Segregated (75%) Fund
RRSP Eligible; Inception Year: 1999; Fund Managers:
Jonathan Wellum
Global Advantage Segregated (100%) Fund
RRSP Eligible; Inception Year: 2000; Fund Managers:
Chris Lowe
GregPlacidi
Global Advantage Segregated (75%) Fund
RRSP Eligible; Inception Year: 2000; Fund Managers:
Chris Lowe
GregPlacidi
Global Advantage Corporate Class Fund
RRSP Eligible; Inception Year: 2001; Fund Managers:
Chris Lowe
GregPlacidi
Global Diversified Corporate Class Fund
RRSP Eligible; Inception Year: 2001; Fund Managers:
Anne-Mette de Place Filippini, MA
Global Diversified Segregated (100%) Fund
RRSP Eligible; Inception Year: 2000; Fund Managers:
Anne-Mette de Place Filippini, MA
Global Diversified Segregated (75%) Fund
RRSP Eligible; Inception Year: 2000; Fund Managers:
Anne-Mette de Place Filippini, MA
Canadian Balanced Segregated (100%) Fund
RRSP Eligible; Inception Year: 1999; Fund Managers:
Randy LeClair, CFA
JamesCole
Canadian Balanced Segregated (75%) Fund
RRSP Eligible; Inception Year: 1999; Fund Managers:
Randy LeClair, CFA
JamesCole
Money Market Fund
RRSP Eligible; Inception Year: 1994; Fund Managers:
Randy LeClair, CFA
Money Market Corporate Class Fund
RRSP Eligible; Inception Year: 2001; Fund Managers:
Randy LeClair, CFA
Money Market Segregated (100%) Fund
RRSP Eligible; Inception Year: 1999; Fund Managers:
Randy LeClair, CFA
Money Market Segregated (75%) Fund
RRSP Eligible; Inception Year: 1999; Fund Managers:
Randy LeClair, CFA
Total Yield Corporate Class Fund
RRSP Eligible; Inception Year: 2002; Fund Managers:
Randy LeClair, CFA
US Money Market Fund
RRSP Eligible; Inception Year: 2001; Fund Managers:
Randy LeClair, CFA
Value Corporate Class Fund
RRSP Eligible; Inception Year: 2001; Fund Managers:
Jonathan Wellum
AnthonyHammill
Pat Naccarato
Kevin J. Vandermeer
Value Segregated (100%) Fund
RRSP Eligible; Inception Year: 1999; Fund Managers:
Jonathan Wellum
PatNaccarato
Kevin J. Vandermeer
Anthony Hammill
Value Segregated (75%) Fund
RRSP Eligible; Inception Year: 1999; Fund Managers:
Jonathan Wellum
PatNaccarato
Kevin J. Vandermeer
Anthony Hammill
World Equity Corporate Class Fund
RRSP Eligible; Inception Year: 2001; Fund Managers:
Anne-Mette de Place Filippini, MA
World Equity Segregated (100%) Fund
RRSP Eligible; Inception Year: 1999; Fund Managers:
Anne-Mette de Place Filippini, MA
World Equity Segregated (75%) Fund
RRSP Eligible; Inception Year: 1999; Fund Managers:
Anne-Mette de Place Filippini, MA
Dividend Income Fund
RRSP Eligible; Inception Year: 2004; Fund Managers:
James Cole, CFA
RobertAlmeida
Diversified Income Portfolio Fund
RRSP Eligible; Inception Year: 2004;
Balanced Income Portfolio Fund
RRSP Eligible; Inception Year: 2004;
Balanced Growth Portfolio Fund
RRSP Eligible; Inception Year: 2004;
Core Growth Portfolio Fund
RRSP Eligible; Inception Year: 2004;
American Focused Plus Fund
RRSP Eligible; Inception Year: 2001; Fund Managers:
James Cole, CFA
Global Focused Fund
RRSP Eligible; Inception Year: 2005; Fund Managers:
Third Avenue Management LLC
Global Focused Corporate Class Fund
RRSP Eligible; Inception Year: 2005; Fund Managers:
Third Avenue Management LLC
PPC Bond Pool Fund
RRSP Eligible; Inception Year: 2003;
PPC Canadian Pool Fund
RRSP Eligible; Inception Year: 2003;
PPC Global Pool Fund
RRSP Eligible; Inception Year: 2003;
PPC Income Pool Class T Units Fund
RRSP Eligible; Inception Year: 2003;
PPC Income Pool Units Fund
RRSP Eligible; Inception Year: 2003;

AIM Funds Management Inc.

#900, 5140 Yonge St.
Toronto, ON M2N 6X7
416-590-9855
Fax: 416-590-9868
800-874-6275
inquiries@aimtrimark.com
www.aimtrimark.com
Also Known As: AIM Trimark Investments
Ownership: Public. Parent is AMVESCAP PLC
Year Founded: 1994
Number of Employees: 982
Assets: $34,000,000,000
Stock Symbol: AVZ
Profile: AIM Trimark Investments is one of Canada's largest mutual fund companies with over $40.8 billion in assets under management. A subsidiary of U.K.-based AMVESCAP PLC, one of the world's largest independent investment managers, AIM Trimark employs more than 900 people in its Calgary, Montréal, Toronto & Vancouver offices.

Executives:
Philip Taylor, President/CEO
Patrick Farmer, Exec. Vice-President & Chief Investment Officer

AIM Funds Management Inc. (continued)
Drew Wallace, Exec. Vice-President, Sales
David C. Warren, Exec. Vice-President/CFO
Graham Anderson, Sr. Vice-President, Investment Operations & Analytics; 416-324-6598; Graham.Anderson@aimtrimark.com
Annie P. Chong, Sr. Vice-President, Corporate & Technology Services
Susan J. Han, Sr. Vice-President, General Counsel
William Henderson, Sr. Vice-President, Marketing; 416-324-6131; Bill.Henderson@aimtrimark.com
Peter Intraligi, Sr. Vice-President, Corporate Operations
Directors:
Patrick Farmer
William Henderson; 416-324-6131
Peter Intraligi; 416-324-6121
Philip Taylor
Drew Wallace; 416-324-6288
David Warren
AIM:
Indo-Pacific Fund
RRSP Eligible; Inception Year: 1994; Fund Managers:
INVESCO
Canadian Premier Class Fund
RRSP Eligible; Inception Year: 1994; Fund Managers:
AIM Capital Management Inc.
American Mid Cap Growth Class Fund
RRSP Eligible; Inception Year: 1994; Fund Managers:
AIM Capital Management Inc.
Short-Term Income Class Series A Fund
RRSP Eligible; Inception Year: 1995; Fund Managers:
AIM Capital Management Inc.
Canada Money Market Fund
RRSP Eligible; Inception Year: 1996; Fund Managers:
AIM Capital Management Inc.
Global Health Sciences Class Fund
RRSP Eligible; Inception Year: 1996; Fund Managers:
Heather Peirce
JimYoung
Global Theme Class Fund
RRSP Eligible; Inception Year: 1996; Fund Managers:
Eric Thaller
DuyNguyen
AIM Capital Management Inc.
Canadian Premier Fund
RRSP Eligible; Inception Year: 1990; Fund Managers:
AIM Capital Management Inc.
European Growth Fund
RRSP Eligible; Inception Year: 1992; Fund Managers:
AIM Capital Management Inc.
Global Technology Fund
RRSP Eligible; Inception Year: 1996; Fund Managers:
INVESCO
Canadian Balanced Fund
RRSP Eligible; Inception Year: 1992; Fund Managers:
Scott Johnson
BrendanGau
International Growth Class Fund
RRSP Eligible; Inception Year: 2000; Fund Managers:
Barrett K. Sides
AIM Capital Management Inc.
European Growth Class Fund
RRSP Eligible; Inception Year: 2000; Fund Managers:
AIM Capital Management Inc.
Global Technology Class Fund
RRSP Eligible; Inception Year: 2000; Fund Managers:
INVESCO
Global Health Sciences Fund
RRSP Eligible; Inception Year: 1992; Fund Managers:
Heather Peirce
JimYoung
American Growth Fund
RRSP Eligible; Inception Year: 1991; Fund Managers:
Heather Peirce
Short-Term Income Class Series B Fund
RRSP Eligible; Inception Year: 1995; Fund Managers:
AIM Capital Management Inc.
Canadian First Class Fund
RRSP Eligible; Inception Year: 1997; Fund Managers:
AIM Capital Management Inc.
AIM Trimark:
Core American Equity Class Fund
RRSP Eligible; Inception Year: 2001; Fund Managers:
Bruce Harrop
JimYoung
Heather Peirce
Core Canadian Balanced Class Fund
RRSP Eligible; Inception Year: 2001; Fund Managers:
Geoff MacDonald
ScottJohnson
Brendan Gau
AIM Capital Management Inc.
Core Canadian Equity Class Fund
RRSP Eligible; Inception Year: 2001; Fund Managers:
Ian Hardacre
AIM Capital Management Inc.
Core Global Equity Class Fund
RRSP Eligible; Inception Year: 2001; Fund Managers:
Tye Bousada
AIM Capital Management Inc.
Dialogue Growth Fund
RRSP Eligible; Inception Year: 2005; Fund Managers:
AIM Trimark
Dialogue Growth & Income Fund
RRSP Eligible; Inception Year: 2005; Fund Managers:
AIM Trimark
Dialogue Income & Growth Fund
RRSP Eligible; Inception Year: 2005; Fund Managers:
AIM Trimark
Dialogue Income Fund
RRSP Eligible; Inception Year: 2005; Fund Managers:
AIM Trimark
Dialogue Long-Term Growth Fund
RRSP Eligible; Inception Year: 2005; Fund Managers:
AIM Trimark
Trimark:
Canadian Bond Fund
RRSP Eligible; Inception Year: 1994; Fund Managers:
Rex Chong
AnthonyImbesi
Alfred Samson
Interest Series Fund
RRSP Eligible; Inception Year: 1987; Fund Managers:
Rex Chong
AnthonyImbesi
Alfred Samson
Canadian Endeavour Fund
RRSP Eligible; Inception Year: 1988; Fund Managers:
Geoff MacDonald
Select Balanced Segregated Fund
RRSP Eligible; Inception Year: 1998; Fund Managers:
Rex Chong
IanHardacre
Anthony Imbesi
Select Canadian Growth Fund
RRSP Eligible; Inception Year: 1992; Fund Managers:
Heather Hunter
Select Growth Fund
RRSP Eligible; Inception Year: 1989; Fund Managers:
Judith Adams
RichardJenkins
Discovery Fund
RRSP Eligible; Inception Year: 1996; Fund Managers:
Jim Young
BruceHarrop
International Companies Fund
RRSP Eligible; Inception Year: 1999; Fund Managers:
Judith Adams
DanaLove
Diversified Income Class Fund
RRSP Eligible; Inception Year: 1996; Fund Managers:
Roger Mortimer
RexChong
Don Simpson
Anthony Imbesi
Rory Ronan
Canadian Small Companies Fund
RRSP Eligible; Inception Year: 1998; Fund Managers:
Robert Mikalachki
Canadian Resources Fund
RRSP Eligible; Inception Year: 1998; Fund Managers:
Rory Ronan
Europlus Fund
RRSP Eligible; Inception Year: 1997; Fund Managers:
Judith Adams
DanaLove
Government Income Fund
RRSP Eligible; Inception Year: 1993; Fund Managers:
Rex Chong
AnthonyImbesi
Alfred Samson
Global High Yield Bond Fund
RRSP Eligible; Inception Year: 1999; Fund Managers:
Rex Chong
AnthonyImbesi
Alfred Samson
Income Growth Series A Fund
RRSP Eligible; Inception Year: 1999; Fund Managers:
Rex Chong
GeoffMacDonald
Anthony Imbesi
US Money Market Series SC Fund (US$)
RRSP Eligible; Inception Year: 2000; Fund Managers:
Rex Chong
AnthonyImbesi
Vince Hunt
Alfred Samson
Global Balanced Class Fund
RRSP Eligible; Inception Year: 2002; Fund Managers:
Rex Chong
RichardJenkins
Bruce Harrop
Anthony Imbesi
Global Balanced Fund
RRSP Eligible; Inception Year: 1999; Fund Managers:
Rex Chong
RichardJenkins
Bruce Harrop
Anthony Imbesi
Global Endeavour Class Fund
RRSP Eligible; Inception Year: 2002; Fund Managers:
Geoff MacDonald
JeffHyrich
Global Endeavour Fund
RRSP Eligible; Inception Year: 1993; Fund Managers:
Geoff MacDonald
Select Growth Class Fund
RRSP Eligible; Inception Year: 2001; Fund Managers:
Judith Adams
TyeBousada
Richard Jenkins
Bill Kanko
US Companies Class Fund
RRSP Eligible; Inception Year: 2001; Fund Managers:
Jim Young
US Small Companies Class Fund
RRSP Eligible; Inception Year: 2002; Fund Managers:
Robert Mikalachki
Advantage Bond Fund
RRSP Eligible; Inception Year: 1994; Fund Managers:
Rex Chong
AnthonyImbesi
Alfred Samson
Canadian Bond Segregated Fund
RRSP Eligible; Inception Year: 1998; Fund Managers:
Rex Chong
AnthonyImbesi
Alfred Samson
Income Growth Series SC Fund
RRSP Eligible; Inception Year: 1987; Fund Managers:
Rex Chong
GeoffMacDonald
Anthony Imbesi
Alfred Samson
Interest Segregated Fund
RRSP Eligible; Inception Year: 1998; Fund Managers:
Rex Chong
AnthonyImbesi
Alfred Samson
Select Canadian Growth Segregated Fund
RRSP Eligible; Inception Year: 1998; Fund Managers:
Heather Hunter
Select Growth Segregated Fund
RRSP Eligible; Inception Year: 1998; Fund Managers:
Judith Adams
RichardJenkins
Select Balanced Fund
RRSP Eligible; Inception Year: 1989; Fund Managers:
Rex Chong
IanHardacre
Anthony Imbesi
Trimark Series A Fund
RRSP Eligible; Inception Year: 1999; Fund Managers:
Tye Bousada
DanaLove

Trimark Series SC Fund
RRSP Eligible; Inception Year: 1981; Fund Managers:
Tye Bousada
DanaLove
Canadian Series A Fund
RRSP Eligible; Inception Year: 1999; Fund Managers:
Ian Hardacre
Canadian Series SC Fund
RRSP Eligible; Inception Year: 1981; Fund Managers:
Ian Hardacre
US Companies Fund
RRSP Eligible; Inception Year: 1999; Fund Managers:
Jim Young
Floating Rate Income Fund
RRSP Eligible; Inception Year: 2005; Fund Managers:
Anthony Imbesi
RexChong
Alfred Samson
Branches:
Calgary
Bankers Hall
#1930, 855 - 2nd St. SW
Calgary, AB T2P 4J7 Canada
403-543-7980
Fax: 403-543-7991
888-543-7980
Scott McLean, Manager
Montréal
McGill College Tower
#2110, 1501, av McGill College
Montréal, QC H3A 3M8 Canada
514-288-3647
Fax: 514-288-0890
800-567-7760
Denis Cloutier, Manager
Toronto
#700, 120 Bloor St. East
Toronto, ON M4W 1B7 Canada
416-225-5500
Fax: 416-590-7742
877-468-2468
Eric Cockshutt, Manager
Vancouver
HSBC Bldg.
#1600, 885 West Georgia St.
Vancouver, BC V6C 3E8 Canada
604-681-9393
Fax: 604-681-9355
800-667-8464
Doug Towill, Manager

All-Canadian Management Inc.

Also listed under: *Investment Dealers; Investment Management*
#202, 386 Wilson St. East
Ancaster, ON L9G 2C2
905-648-2025
Fax: 905-648-5422
rboychuka@all-canadiansecurities.com
www.all-canadianfunds.com
Ownership: Private.
Year Founded: 1976
Number of Employees: 10
Assets: $1-5 million Year End: 20041031
Revenues: $1-5 million Year End: 20041031
Executives:
Russell C. Boychuk, Chair/CEO
Directors:
Russell C. Boychuk, Chair/CEO
All-Canadian Management:
All-Canadian Resources FundInception Year: 0; Fund Managers:
Harold A. Kent
All-Canadian Compound FundInception Year: 0; Fund Managers:
Harold A. Kent

Altamira Financial Services Limited

Also listed under: *Financial Planning*
The Exchange Tower
#900, 130 King St. West
Toronto, ON M5X 1K9
416-507-7050
Fax: 416-507-7111
800-263-2824
advice@altamira.com
www.altamira.com
Profile: With approximately $4.3 billion in assets under management, Altamira ranks as one of Canada's largest direct providers of mutual funds. It manages money for mutual funds, pension funds, corporations & other major institutions.

Executives:
Charles Guay, President/CEO, Investment Services
Nancy Cappadocia, CFO
James Whitman, Sr. Vice-President, Sales & Service
Altamira:
AltaFund Investment Corp. Fund
RRSP Eligible; Inception Year: 1986; Fund Managers:
Natcan Investment Management Inc.
Asia Pacific Fund
RRSP Eligible; Inception Year: 1992; Fund Managers:
Natcan Investment Management Inc.
Balanced Fund
RRSP Eligible; Inception Year: 1985; Fund Managers:
Natcan Investment Management Inc.
Bond Fund
RRSP Eligible; Inception Year: 1987; Fund Managers:
Natcan Investment Management Inc.
Capital Growth Fund
RRSP Eligible; Inception Year: 1937; Fund Managers:
Natcan Investment Management Inc.
Dividend Fund
RRSP Eligible; Inception Year: 1985; Fund Managers:
Natcan Investment Management Inc.
Equity Fund
RRSP Eligible; Inception Year: 1987; Fund Managers:
Natcan Investment Management Inc.
European Equity Fund
RRSP Eligible; Inception Year: 1993; Fund Managers:
Natcan Investment Management Inc.
Global Bond Fund
RRSP Eligible; Inception Year: 1993; Fund Managers:
Natcan Investment Management Inc.
Global Discovery Fund
RRSP Eligible; Inception Year: 1994; Fund Managers:
Baillie Gifford Overseas
Global Diversified Fund
RRSP Eligible; Inception Year: 1985; Fund Managers:
Natcan Investment Management Inc.
Growth & Income Fund
RRSP Eligible; Inception Year: 1986; Fund Managers:
Natcan Investment Management Inc.
Income Fund
RRSP Eligible; Inception Year: 1970; Fund Managers:
Natcan Investment Management Inc.
Japanese Opportunity Fund
RRSP Eligible; Inception Year: 1994; Fund Managers:
Natcan Investment Management Inc.
Canadian Value Fund
RRSP Eligible; Inception Year: 1993; Fund Managers:
Natcan Investment Management Inc.
Precious & Strategic Metal Fund
RRSP Eligible; Inception Year: 1994; Fund Managers:
Natcan Investment Management Inc.
Select American Fund
RRSP Eligible; Inception Year: 1991; Fund Managers:
Natcan Investment Management Inc.
Short Term Global Income Fund
RRSP Eligible; Inception Year: 1991; Fund Managers:
Natcan Investment Management Inc.
Short Term Government Bond Fund
RRSP Eligible; Inception Year: 1994; Fund Managers:
Natcan Investment Management Inc.
Special Growth Fund
RRSP Eligible; Inception Year: 1985; Fund Managers:
Natcan Investment Management Inc.
US Larger Company Fund
RRSP Eligible; Inception Year: 1993; Fund Managers:
Natcan Investment Management Inc.
Science & Technology Fund
RRSP Eligible; Inception Year: 1995; Fund Managers:
Natcan Investment Management Inc.
Global Small Company Fund
RRSP Eligible; Inception Year: 1996; Fund Managers:
Natcan Investment Management Inc.
T-Bill Fund
RRSP Eligible; Inception Year: 1997; Fund Managers:
Natcan Investment Management Inc.
Short Term Canadian Income Fund
RRSP Eligible; Inception Year: 1997; Fund Managers:
Natcan Investment Management Inc.
Global Financial Services Fund
RRSP Eligible; Inception Year: 1999; Fund Managers:
Natcan Investment Management Inc.
Health Sciences Fund
RRSP Eligible; Inception Year: 1999; Fund Managers:
Natcan Investment Management Inc.
Biotechnology Fund
RRSP Eligible; Inception Year: 2000; Fund Managers:
Natcan Investment Management Inc.
e-business Fund
RRSP Eligible; Inception Year: 1998; Fund Managers:
Natcan Investment Management Inc.
Global 20 Fund
RRSP Eligible; Inception Year: 2000; Fund Managers:
Natcan Investment Management Inc.
Resource Fund
RRSP Eligible; Inception Year: 1989; Fund Managers:
Natcan Investment Management Inc.
High Yield Bond Fund
RRSP Eligible; Inception Year: 1995; Fund Managers:
Natcan Investment Management Inc.
Global Value Fund
RRSP Eligible; Inception Year: 2000; Fund Managers:
Natcan Investment Management Inc.
Monthly Income Fund
RRSP Eligible; Inception Year: 2004; Fund Managers:
Natcan Investment Management Inc.
Energy Fund
RRSP Eligible; Inception Year: 2004; Fund Managers:
Natcan Investment Management Inc.
Inflation-Adjusted Bond Fund
RRSP Eligible; Inception Year: 2005; Fund Managers:
Natcan Investment Management Inc.
High-Interest Cash Performer Fund
RRSP Eligible; Inception Year: 1990; Fund Managers:
Altamira Management Ltd.
Altamira Managed:
RSP Stable Income Portfolio FundInception Year: 1999; Fund Managers:
Natcan Investment Management Inc.
RSP Income Portfolio FundInception Year: 1999; Fund Managers:
Natcan Investment Management Inc.
RSP Income & Growth Portfolio FundInception Year: 1999; Fund Managers:
Natcan Investment Management Inc.
RSP Balanced Portfolio FundInception Year: 1999; Fund Managers:
Natcan Investment Management Inc.
RSP Growth & Income Portfolio FundInception Year: 1999; Fund Managers:
Natcan Investment Management Inc.
RSP Growth Portfolio FundInception Year: 1999; Fund Managers:
Natcan Investment Management Inc.
RSP Maximum Growth Portfolio FundInception Year: 1999; Fund Managers:
Natcan Investment Management Inc.
Stable Income Portfolio FundInception Year: 2003; Fund Managers:
Natcan Investment Management Inc.
Income Portfolio FundInception Year: 2003; Fund Managers:
Natcan Investment Management Inc.
Income & Growth Portfolio FundInception Year: 2003; Fund Managers:
Natcan Investment Management Inc.
Balanced Portfolio FundInception Year: 2003; Fund Managers:
Natcan Investment Management Inc.
Growth & Income Portfolio FundInception Year: 2003; Fund Managers:
Natcan Investment Management Inc.
Growth Portfolio FundInception Year: 1999; Fund Managers:
Natcan Investment Management Inc.
Maximum Growth Portfolio FundInception Year: 2003; Fund Managers:
Natcan Investment Management Inc.
RRIF Stable Income Portfolio FundInception Year: 2004; Fund Managers:
Natcan Investment Management Inc.
RRIF Income Portfolio FundInception Year: 2004; Fund Managers:
Natcan Investment Management Inc.
RRIF Income & Growth Portfolio FundInception Year: 2004; Fund Managers:
Natcan Investment Management Inc.

Altamira Financial Services Limited (continued)
RRIF Balanced Portfolio FundInception Year: 2004; Fund Managers:
Natcan Investment Management Inc.
RRIF Growth Portfolio FundInception Year: 2004; Fund Managers:
Natcan Investment Management Inc.
Altamira Precision:
Canadian Index Fund
RRSP Eligible; Inception Year: 1998; Fund Managers:
Natcan Investment Management Inc.
European Index Fund
RRSP Eligible; Inception Year: 1999; Fund Managers:
Natcan Investment Management Inc.
European RSP Index Fund
RRSP Eligible; Inception Year: 1999; Fund Managers:
Natcan Investment Management Inc.
International RSP Index Fund
RRSP Eligible; Inception Year: 1998; Fund Managers:
Natcan Investment Management Inc.
US RSP Index Fund
RRSP Eligible; Inception Year: 1998; Fund Managers:
Natcan Investment Management Inc.
US Midcap Index Fund
RRSP Eligible; Inception Year: 1999; Fund Managers:
Natcan Investment Management Inc.
Dow 30 Index Fund
RRSP Eligible; Inception Year: 1999; Fund Managers:
Natcan Investment Management Inc.
Branches:
Calgary
Shell Centre
#117, 400 - 4th Ave. SW
Calgary, AB T2P 2H5 Canada
403-266-4941
Fax: 403-265-0831
800-263-284
Edmonton
Commerce Place
10150 Jasper Ave.
Edmonton, AB T5J 1W4 Canada
780-414-6001
Fax: 780-423-0183
800-263-2824
Halifax
1903 Barrington St.
Halifax, NS B3J 3L7 Canada
902-496-9600
Fax: 902-429-0656
London
620A Richmond St. #F
London, ON N6A 5J9 Canada
519-432-6440
Fax: 519-435-1722
877-612-2212
Montréal
#201, 2020, rue University
Montréal, QC H3A 2A5 Canada
514-499-1656
Fax: 514-499-9570
800-361-2354
Thornhill
#292, 505 Hwy. 7 East
Thornhill, ON L3T 7T1 Canada
905-882-0283
Fax: 905-882-8328
888-808-8277
Vancouver
Marine Bldg.
#M101, 355 Burrard St.
Vancouver, BC V6C 2G8 Canada
604-687-7926
Fax: 604-687-5932

Arrow Hedge Partners Inc.

#750, 36 Toronto St.
Toronto, ON M5C 2C5
416-323-0477
Fax: 416-323-3199
877-327-6048
info@arrowhedge.com
www.arrowhedge.com
Ownership: Private
Year Founded: 1999
Number of Employees: 8
Assets: Under $1 million
Revenues: Under $1 million
Executives:
Fred Dalley, Managing Director, Portfolio Management; fdalley@arrowhedge.com
Robert Maxwell, Managing Director, Risk Management, CFO; rmaxwell@arrowhedge.com
Robert Parsons, Managing Director & COO; rparsons@arrowhedge.com
Keith Tomlinson, Director, Research
Arrow:
Clocktower Global Fund
RRSP Eligible; Inception Year: 2002; Fund Managers:
Clocktower Capital LLC
Goodwood Fund
RRSP Eligible; Inception Year: 2001; Fund Managers:
Goodwood Inc.
WF Asia Fund
RRSP Eligible; Inception Year: 2001; Fund Managers:
Ward Ferry Management
Elkhorn US Long/Short Fund
RRSP Eligible; Inception Year: 2002; Fund Managers:
Sanborn Kilcollin Partners Inc.
Global Long/Short Fund
RRSP Eligible; Inception Year: 2001;
Multi-Strategy Fund
RRSP Eligible; Inception Year: 2002;
Enso Global Fund
RRSP Eligible; Inception Year: 2002; Fund Managers:
Enso Capital Management LLC
Epic Capital Fund
RRSP Eligible; Inception Year: 2002; Fund Managers:
Epic Capital Management
High Yield Fund
RRSP Eligible; Inception Year: 2004; Fund Managers:
Marratt Asset Management Inc.
Distressed Securities Fund
RRSP Eligible; Inception Year: 2003; Fund Managers:
Schultze Asset Management
Elmwood Fund
RRSP Eligible; Inception Year: 2005;
Enhanced Income Fund
RRSP Eligible; Inception Year: 2005; Fund Managers:
James L. McGovern
MarkPurdy
Epic North American Diversified Fund
RRSP Eligible; Inception Year: 2003; Fund Managers:
Epic Capital Management
Focus Fund
RRSP Eligible; Inception Year: 2001;
Global Long/Short Equity Fund
RRSP Eligible; Inception Year: 2001;
Japan Long/Short Fund
RRSP Eligible; Inception Year: 2004;
PMC Global Long/Short Fund
RRSP Eligible; Inception Year: 2005; Fund Managers:
Matt Miller
PaulHolland
Branches:
Calgary - Prairie Provinces Region
#2700, 350 - 7 Ave. SW
Calgary, AB T2P 3N9 Canada
403-668-5546
Fax: 403-668-5520
888-861-6530
Robin Findlay, Managing Director, Sales, Alberta, Saskatchewan & Manitoba
Montréal - Eastern Provinces Region
#450, 800, boul René-Lévesque ouest
Montréal, QC H3B 1X9 Canada
514-395-0278
Fax: 514-871-1039
Alain Ostiguy, Managing Director, Sales, Quebec & Maritimes
Vancouver - British Columbia Region
#2300, 1066 West Hastings St.
Vancouver, BC V6E 3X2 Canada
604-601-8213
Fax: 604-408-8893
866-601-8213
Nigel Stewart, Managing Director, Sales, British Columbia

Assumption Life/ Assomption Compagnie Mutuelle d'Assurance-Vie

***Also listed under:** Federal & Provincial*
PO Box 160
770 Main St.
Moncton, NB E1C 8L1
506-853-6040
Fax: 506-853-5428
800-455-7337
financial.services@assumption.ca
www.assumption.ca
Ownership: Mutual
Year Founded: 1903
Number of Employees: 203
Profile: Classes of insurance offered also include group & critical illness & disability.
Executives:
Denis Losier, President/CEO
Larry Boudreau, Vice-President, Sales & Marketing
Patricia LeBlanc, Vice-President, Finance & Information Technologies
Kenneth Losier, Vice-President, Administration, Real Estate Holdings & Mortgage Loans
Raymond Martin, Vice-President, Actuarial Services
Odette Snow, Vice-President, Secretary & General Counsel
Directors:
Noël M. Després, Chair
Réjean Boudreau
Joël Drolet
Yves Gauvin
Louis LaBrie
Paul LeBlanc
Étienne LeBoeuf
Marc Robichaud
Ronnie Roussel
Derrick Smith
Assumption Life:
Balanced Fund
RRSP Eligible; Inception Year: 1995; Fund Managers:
Louisbourg Investments Inc.
Balanced B Fund
RRSP Eligible; Inception Year: 2002; Fund Managers:
Louisbourg Investments Inc.
Balanced C Fund
RRSP Eligible; Inception Year: 2002; Fund Managers:
Louisbourg Investments Inc.
Canadian Equity Fund
RRSP Eligible; Inception Year: 2002; Fund Managers:
Montrusco Bolton Inc.
Canadian Equity B Fund
RRSP Eligible; Inception Year: 2002; Fund Managers:
Montrusco Bolton Inc.
Canadian Equity C Fund
RRSP Eligible; Inception Year: 2002; Fund Managers:
Montrusco Bolton Inc.
Non-Taxable American Equity Fund
RRSP Eligible; Inception Year: 2002; Fund Managers:
Montrusco Bolton Inc.
Non-Taxable American Equity B Fund
RRSP Eligible; Inception Year: 2002; Fund Managers:
Montrusco Bolton Inc.
Non-Taxable American Equity C Fund
RRSP Eligible; Inception Year: 2002; Fund Managers:
Montrusco Bolton Inc.
Canadian Equity Plus Fund
RRSP Eligible; Inception Year: 1998; Fund Managers:
Louisbourg Investments Inc.
Canadian Equity Plus B Fund
RRSP Eligible; Inception Year: 2002; Fund Managers:
Louisbourg Investments Inc.
Canadian Equity Plus C Fund
RRSP Eligible; Inception Year: 2002; Fund Managers:
Louisbourg Investments Inc.
Assumption Life/CI:
Canadian Bond Fund
RRSP Eligible; Inception Year: 2002; Fund Managers:
CI Mutual Funds
Canadian Bond B Fund
RRSP Eligible; Inception Year: 2002; Fund Managers:
CI Mutual Funds
Canadian Bond C Fund
RRSP Eligible; Inception Year: 2002; Fund Managers:
CI Mutual Funds
Global Boomernomics Fund
RRSP Eligible; Inception Year: 2001; Fund Managers:
Trilogy Advisors LLC

Global Boomernomics B Fund
RRSP Eligible; Inception Year: 2002; Fund Managers:
Trilogy Advisors LLC
Global Boomernomics C Fund
RRSP Eligible; Inception Year: 2002; Fund Managers:
Trilogy Advisors LLC
Global Managers Fund
RRSP Eligible; Inception Year: 2001; Fund Managers:
Epoch Investment Partners
Global Managers B Fund
RRSP Eligible; Inception Year: 2002; Fund Managers:
Epoch Investment Partners
Global Managers C Fund
RRSP Eligible; Inception Year: 2002; Fund Managers:
Epoch Investment Partners
Harbour Growth & Income Fund
RRSP Eligible; Inception Year: 2002; Fund Managers:
CI Mutual Funds
Harbour Growth & Income B Fund
RRSP Eligible; Inception Year: 2002; Fund Managers:
CI Mutual Funds
Harbour Growth & Income C Fund
RRSP Eligible; Inception Year: 2002; Fund Managers:
CI Mutual Funds

Assumption Life/FDI:

Canadian Opportunities Fund
RRSP Eligible; Inception Year: 2001; Fund Managers:
Fidelity Investments Canada Ltd.
Canadian Opportunities B Fund
RRSP Eligible; Inception Year: 2002; Fund Managers:
Fidelity Investments Canada Ltd.
Canadian Opportunities C Fund
RRSP Eligible; Inception Year: 2002; Fund Managers:
Fidelity Investments Canada Ltd.
European Fund
RRSP Eligible; Inception Year: 2002; Fund Managers:
Fidelity Investments Canada Ltd.
European B Fund
RRSP Eligible; Inception Year: 2002; Fund Managers:
Fidelity Investments Canada Ltd.
European C Fund
RRSP Eligible; Inception Year: 2002; Fund Managers:
Fidelity Investments Canada Ltd.
Focus Healthcare Fund
RRSP Eligible; Inception Year: 2001; Fund Managers:
Fidelity Investments Canada Ltd.
Focus Healthcare B Fund
RRSP Eligible; Inception Year: 2002; Fund Managers:
Fidelity Investments Canada Ltd.
Focus Healthcare C Fund
RRSP Eligible; Inception Year: 2002; Fund Managers:
Fidelity Investments Canada Ltd.
Focus Technology Fund
RRSP Eligible; Inception Year: 2001; Fund Managers:
Fidelity Investments Canada Ltd.
Focus Technology B Fund
RRSP Eligible; Inception Year: 2002; Fund Managers:
Fidelity Investments Canada Ltd.
Focus Technology C Fund
RRSP Eligible; Inception Year: 2002; Fund Managers:
Fidelity Investments Canada Ltd.
True North Fund
RRSP Eligible; Inception Year: 2001; Fund Managers:
Fidelity Investments Canada Ltd.
True North B Fund
RRSP Eligible; Inception Year: 2002; Fund Managers:
Fidelity Investments Canada Ltd.
True North C Fund
RRSP Eligible; Inception Year: 2002; Fund Managers:
Fidelity Investments Canada Ltd.

Assumption Life/MB:

Canadian Small Cap Fund
RRSP Eligible; Inception Year: 1996; Fund Managers:
Montrusco Bolton Inc.
Canadian Small Cap B Fund
RRSP Eligible; Inception Year: 2002; Fund Managers:
Montrusco Bolton Inc.
Canadian Small Cap C Fund
RRSP Eligible; Inception Year: 2002; Fund Managers:
Montrusco Bolton Inc.
EAFE Equity Fund
RRSP Eligible; Inception Year: 1996; Fund Managers:
Montrusco Bolton Inc.
EAFE Equity B Fund
RRSP Eligible; Inception Year: 2002; Fund Managers:
Montrusco Bolton Inc.
EAFE Equity C Fund
RRSP Eligible; Inception Year: 2002; Fund Managers:
Montrusco Bolton Inc.
Fixed Income Fund
RRSP Eligible; Inception Year: 1996; Fund Managers:
Montrusco Bolton Inc.
Fixed Income B Fund
RRSP Eligible; Inception Year: 2002; Fund Managers:
Montrusco Bolton Inc.
Fixed Income C Fund
RRSP Eligible; Inception Year: 2002; Fund Managers:
Montrusco Bolton Inc.
Global Equity Fund
RRSP Eligible; Inception Year: 1998; Fund Managers:
Montrusco Bolton Inc.
Global Equity B Fund
RRSP Eligible; Inception Year: 2002; Fund Managers:
Montrusco Bolton Inc.
Global Equity C Fund
RRSP Eligible; Inception Year: 2002; Fund Managers:
Montrusco Bolton Inc.
T-Max Fund
RRSP Eligible; Inception Year: 1996; Fund Managers:
Montrusco Bolton Inc.
T-Max B Fund
RRSP Eligible; Inception Year: 2002; Fund Managers:
Montrusco Bolton Inc.
T-Max C Fund
RRSP Eligible; Inception Year: 2002; Fund Managers:
Montrusco Bolton Inc.
Taxable US Equity Fund
RRSP Eligible; Inception Year: 2001; Fund Managers:
Montrusco Bolton Inc.
Taxable US Equity B Fund
RRSP Eligible; Inception Year: 2002; Fund Managers:
Montrusco Bolton Inc.
Taxable US Equity C Fund
RRSP Eligible; Inception Year: 2002; Fund Managers:
Montrusco Bolton Inc.
TSX 100 Momentum Fund
RRSP Eligible; Inception Year: 2001; Fund Managers:
Montrusco Bolton Inc.
TSX 100 Momentum B Fund
RRSP Eligible; Inception Year: 2002; Fund Managers:
Montrusco Bolton Inc.
TSX 100 Momentum C Fund
RRSP Eligible; Inception Year: 2002; Fund Managers:
Montrusco Bolton Inc.

Assumption/CI:

Synergy American Fund
RRSP Eligible; Inception Year: 2005; Fund Managers:
Synergy Asset Management Inc.

Assumption/FDI:

Overseas Fund
RRSP Eligible; Inception Year: 2005; Fund Managers:
Fidelity Management & Research

Branches:

Bathurst
275 Main St.
Bathurst, NB E2A 1A9 Canada
506-548-2413
Yves Gauvin, Contact

Cap-aux-Meules
330, ch Arsenault
Cap-aux-Meules, QC G4T 1L8 Canada
418-968-4126
Jacques Boudreau, Manager

Edmundston
#200, 121, rue de l'Église
Edmundston, NB E3V 1J9 Canada
506-735-3322
Louis LaBrie, Contact

Shippagan
235 J.D. Gauthier Blvd.
Shippagan, NB E8S 1N2 Canada
506-336-4734
Yves Gauvin, Contact

Barclays Global Investors Canada Limited(BGI)

Also listed under: *Financial Planning*

PO Box 614
#2500, 161 Bay St.
Toronto, ON M5J 2S1
416-643-4000
Fax: 416-643-4049
866-275-2442
inquiriescanada@barclaysglobal.com
www.bglobal.com

Former Name: Wells Fargo NIKKO Investment Advisors Canada Limited
Also Known As: Barclays Canada
Ownership: Foreign. Indirect subsidiary of Barclays PLC. Part of BGI, a division of Barclays PLC.
Year Founded: 1992
Number of Employees: 65
Assets: $10-100 billion Year End: 20060900
Revenues: $10-50 million Year End: 20060900
Profile: The institutional investment manager is also the manager of index funds & ETFs. Barclays Canada's exchange traded fund (ETF) product line is iShares. It manages over $66 billion in Canadian assets & in other assets for Canadian clients.

INVESTMENT MANAGEMENT

Executives:
Rajiv Silgardo, CEO
Subhas Sen, CFO
Warren Collier, Counsel & Secretary
Howard Atkinson, Head, Public Funds
William F. Chinery, Head, Client Relationships
Heather Pelant, Head, Business Development, iShares

iUnits:

60 Canadian Equity Index Fund
RRSP Eligible; Inception Year: 1999; Fund Managers:
Ada Yin
Canadian Bonds Index Fund
RRSP Eligible; Inception Year: 2000; Fund Managers:
Freda Dong
LouPaolone
Composite Canadian Equity Capped Index Fund
RRSP Eligible; Inception Year: 2001; Fund Managers:
Ada Yin
Dividend Index Fund
RRSP Eligible; Inception Year: 2005;
Energy Sector Index Fund
RRSP Eligible; Inception Year: 2001; Fund Managers:
Ada Yin
Financial Sector Index Fund
RRSP Eligible; Inception Year: 2001; Fund Managers:
Ada Yin
Gold Sector Index Fund
RRSP Eligible; Inception Year: 2001; Fund Managers:
Ada Yin
Income Trust Sector Index Fund
RRSP Eligible; Inception Year: 2005;
International Equity C$ Index Fund
RRSP Eligible; Inception Year: 2001; Fund Managers:
Rob Bechard
RandallMalcolm
Amit Prakash
Materials Sector Index Fund
RRSP Eligible; Inception Year: 2005;
MidCap Canadian Equity Index Fund
RRSP Eligible; Inception Year: 2001; Fund Managers:
Ada Yin
Real Return Bond Index Fund
RRSP Eligible; Inception Year: 2005;
REIT Index Fund
RRSP Eligible; Inception Year: 2002; Fund Managers:
Ada Yin
S&P 500 C$ Index Fund
RRSP Eligible; Inception Year: 2001; Fund Managers:
Rob Bechard
RandallMalcolm
Amit Prakash
Short Bond Index Fund
RRSP Eligible; Inception Year: 2000; Fund Managers:
Freda Dong
LouPaolone
Technology Sector Index Fund
RRSP Eligible; Inception Year: 2001; Fund Managers:
Ada Yin

Branches:

Montréal
#1730, 1000, rue Sherbrooke ouest
Montréal, QC H3A 3G4 Canada

Barclays Global Investors Canada Limited(BGI) (continued)
514-843-9595
Fax: 514-843-1082
Eric Leville, Manager

Batirente

Also listed under: *Financial Planning; Investment Management*

#203, 2175, boul de Maisonneuve
Montréal, QC H2K 4S3
514-525-5740
Fax: 514-525-2199
800-253-0131
info@batirente.qc.ca
www.batirente.qc.ca
Ownership: Private
Year Founded: 1987
Number of Employees: 6
Assets: $500m-1 billion Year End: 20051130
Executives:
Daniel Simard, General Coordinator; 514-525-5065; daniel.simard@batirente.qc.ca
Batirente:
Actions Internationales
RRSP Eligible; Inception Year: 1998; Fund Managers:
Hexavest Asset Management Inc.
Diversifié intrepide
RRSP Eligible; Inception Year: 1998; Fund Managers:
Hexavest Asset Management Inc.
Diversifié prévoyant
RRSP Eligible; Inception Year: 1988; Fund Managers:
Hexavest Asset Management Inc.
Actions Canadiennes
RRSP Eligible; Inception Year: 1988; Fund Managers:
Optimum Asset Management Inc.
Obligations
RRSP Eligible; Inception Year: 1988; Fund Managers:
Addenda Capital Inc.
Marché Monetaire
RRSP Eligible; Inception Year: 1988; Fund Managers:
Addenda Capital Inc.
Trésorerie
RRSP Eligible; Inception Year: 1998; Fund Managers:
Addenda Capital Inc.
Branches:
Québec
#500, 210, boul Charest est
Québec, QC G1K 3H1 Canada
418-522-9621
Martin Blais, Manager

BEST Funds

#400, 20 Adelaide St. East
Toronto, ON M5C 2T6
416-203-7331
Fax: 416-203-6630
800-795-2378
info@bestfunds.ca
www.bestfunds.ca
Former Name: BEST Discoveries Fund
Executives:
Michael Israels, Partner
B.E.S.T.:
Discoveries Fund
RRSP Eligible; Inception Year: 1996; Fund Managers:
John Richardson
TomLunan
Discoveries II Fund
RRSP Eligible; Inception Year: 2002; Fund Managers:
John Richardson
TomLunan
Discoveries III Fund
RRSP Eligible; Inception Year: 2002; Fund Managers:
John Richardson
TomLunan
Total Return Fund
RRSP Eligible; Inception Year: 2003;

BMO Mutual Funds

BMO Investment Centre
55 Bloor St. West, 9th Fl.
Toronto, ON M4W 3N5
800-665-7700
www.bmo.com/mutualfunds/index.html
Former Name: BMO Investments Inc., Bank of Montreal Investment Management Ltd.
Profile: The company offers BMO mutual funds for a full range of investment opportunities which can be balanced to suit individual investment goals & risk tolerance. Mutual funds fall under four major categories determined by the investment of the fund.

Executives:
Edgar N. Legzdins, President
Robert Schauer, Treasurer & CFO
Louise Engelman, Secretary
BMO:
Bond Fund
RRSP Eligible; Inception Year: 1988; Fund Managers:
Jones Heward Investment Counsel Inc.
Dividend Fund
RRSP Eligible; Inception Year: 1994; Fund Managers:
Jones Heward Investment Counsel Inc.
Emerging Markets Fund
RRSP Eligible; Inception Year: 1994; Fund Managers:
Alliance Bernstein Investment Management
Equity Index Fund
RRSP Eligible; Inception Year: 1988; Fund Managers:
Jones Heward Investment Counsel Inc.
European Fund
RRSP Eligible; Inception Year: 1994; Fund Managers:
Alliance Capital Management
Equity Fund
RRSP Eligible; Inception Year: 1993; Fund Managers:
Jones Heward Investment Counsel Inc.
International Equity Fund
RRSP Eligible; Inception Year: 1992; Fund Managers:
Capital Guardian Trust Company
Japanese Fund
RRSP Eligible; Inception Year: 1994; Fund Managers:
Martin Currie Inc.
Money Market Fund
RRSP Eligible; Inception Year: 1988; Fund Managers:
Jones Heward Investment Counsel Inc.
Mortgage & Short-Term Fund
RRSP Eligible; Inception Year: 1974; Fund Managers:
Jones Heward Investment Counsel Inc.
NAFTA Advantage Fund
RRSP Eligible; Inception Year: 1994; Fund Managers:
State Street Global Advisors Limited
T-Bill Fund
RRSP Eligible; Inception Year: 1993; Fund Managers:
Jones Heward Investment Counsel Inc.
Premium Money Market Fund
RRSP Eligible; Inception Year: 1997; Fund Managers:
Jones Heward Investment Counsel Inc.
Asset Allocation Fund
RRSP Eligible; Inception Year: 1988; Fund Managers:
Jones Heward Investment Counsel Inc.
Resource Fund
RRSP Eligible; Inception Year: 1993; Fund Managers:
Jones Heward Investment Counsel Inc.
Global Science & Technology Fund
RRSP Eligible; Inception Year: 1997; Fund Managers:
Harris Investment Management Inc.
Monthly Income Fund
RRSP Eligible; Inception Year: 1999; Fund Managers:
Jones Heward Investment Counsel Inc.
Precious Metals Fund
RRSP Eligible; Inception Year: 1997; Fund Managers:
Jones Heward Investment Counsel Inc.
Special Equity Fund
RRSP Eligible; Inception Year: 1993; Fund Managers:
Jones Heward Investment Counsel Inc.
US Dollar Bond FundInception Year: 1998; Fund Managers:
Harris Investment Management Inc.
US Dollar Equity Index FundInception Year: 1998; Fund Managers:
Harris Investment Management Inc.
US Growth Fund
RRSP Eligible; Inception Year: 1993; Fund Managers:
Harris Investment Management Inc.
US Dollar Money Market Fund
RRSP Eligible; Inception Year: 1998;
US Special Equity Fund
RRSP Eligible; Inception Year: 1997; Fund Managers:
Harris Investment Management Inc.
International Index Fund
RRSP Eligible; Inception Year: 1999; Fund Managers:
State Street Global Advisors Limited
Air Miles Money Market FundInception Year: 2000; Fund Managers:
Jones Heward Investment Counsel Inc.
Short-Term Income Fund
RRSP Eligible; Inception Year: 2000; Fund Managers:
Jones Heward Investment Counsel Inc.
Global Bond Fund
RRSP Eligible; Inception Year: 2000; Fund Managers:
AGF Funds Inc.
Global Balanced Class Fund
RRSP Eligible; Inception Year: 2000; Fund Managers:
Insight Investment Management Limited
Global Equity Class Fund
RRSP Eligible; Inception Year: 2000; Fund Managers:
Insight Investment Management Limited
US Equity Index Fund
RRSP Eligible; Inception Year: 1997; Fund Managers:
Harris Investment Management Inc.
Global Monthly Income Fund
RRSP Eligible; Inception Year: 2004; Fund Managers:
UBS GLobal Asset Management (Canada) Co.
US Equity Class Fund
RRSP Eligible; Inception Year: 2004; Fund Managers:
UBS GLobal Asset Management (Canada) Co.
US Dollar Monthly Income FundInception Year: 2004; Fund Managers:
UBS GLobal Asset Management (Canada) Co.
Dividend Class Fund
RRSP Eligible; Inception Year: 2004; Fund Managers:
Jones Heward Investment Counsel Inc.
Canadian Equity Class Fund
RRSP Eligible; Inception Year: 2004; Fund Managers:
Jones Heward Investment Counsel Inc.
Greater China Class Fund
RRSP Eligible; Inception Year: 2004; Fund Managers:
Martin Currie Inc.
World Bond Fund
RRSP Eligible; Inception Year: 1993; Fund Managers:
Insight Investment Management Limited
Strategic Security Reg Portfolio Fund
RRSP Eligible; Inception Year: 1996;
Strategic Security NR Portfolio FundInception Year: 1996;
Strategic Growth Reg Portfolio Fund
RRSP Eligible; Inception Year: 1996;
Strategic Growth NR Portfolio Fund
RRSP Eligible; Inception Year: 1996;

BNP (Canada) Valeurs Mobilières Inc./ BNP (Canada) Securities Inc.

Also listed under: *Investment Dealers*
#500, 1981, av McGill College
Montréal, QC H3A 2W8
514-285-6000
Fax: 514-285-6278
Year Founded: 1991
Stock Exchange Membership: Montreal Exchange, Toronto Stock Exchange

Bullion Management Group Inc.

#280, 60 Renfrew Dr.
Markham, ON L3R 0E1
905-474-1001
Fax: 905-474-1091
888-474-1001
info@bmsinc.ca
www.bmsinc.ca
Former Name: Bullion Marketing Services Inc.
Also Known As: BMG Inc.
Ownership: Private.
Year Founded: 1998
Number of Employees: 10
Assets: $50-100 million Year End: 20061000
Revenues: Under $1 million Year End: 20061000
Profile: Affiliates include Bullion Marketing Services Inc., Bullion Management Services Inc. & Bullion Custodial Services Inc.

Executives:
Nick Barisheff, President/CEO
Glenn Cooper, Chief Financial Officer
Larry Gamble, Director
Millennium BullionFund:
Millenium Bullion Fund
RRSP Eligible; Inception Year: 2004; Fund Managers:
Bullion Management Services Inc.

Global Investors G Class Fund
RRSP Eligible; Inception Year: 0; Fund Managers: Bullion Management Services Inc.

Caldwell Investment Management Ltd.

#1710, 150 King St. West
Toronto, ON M5H 1J9
416-862-7755
Fax: 416-862-2498
800-387-0859
info@caldwellsecurities.com
www.caldwellmutualfunds.com
Ownership: Private
Executives:
Thomas Caldwell, Chair & Portfolio Manager
J. Dennis Freeman, President & Portfolio Manager
Brendan T.N. Caldwell, Vice-President & Portfolio Manager
Sally Haldenby Haba, Secretary
Affiliated Companies:
Caldwell Securities Ltd.
Caldwell:
America Fund
RRSP Eligible; Inception Year: 1997;
Balanced Fund
RRSP Eligible; Inception Year: 1990;
Canada Fund
RRSP Eligible; Inception Year: 1997;
Income Fund
RRSP Eligible; Inception Year: 1997;
Branches:
London
#1080, 255 Queens Ave.
London, ON N6A 5R8 Canada
519-645-2400
Fax: 519-645-2445
877-499-7220
Niagara on the Lake
PO Box 701
9 Queen St., 2nd Fl.
Niagara on the Lake, ON L0S 1J0 Canada
905-468-0655
Whitby
515 Brock St. South
Whitby, ON L1N 4K8 Canada
905-665-1911
Fax: 905-665-1912
800-628-1959

Canada Life Assurance Co. - Investment Division

Investment & Pension Operations
PO Box 86
438 University Ave.
Toronto, ON M5G 2K8
416-597-6981
888-252-1847
isp_customer_care@canadalife.com
www.canadalife.ca
Executives:
Dennis J. Davos, Exec. Vice-President, Individual Insurance & Investment Products
Canada Life:
Government Bond Fund (GWLIM)
RRSP Eligible; Inception Year: 1998; Fund Managers: GWL Investment Management Ltd.
Canadian Equity Fund (Bissett)
RRSP Eligible; Inception Year: 1997; Fund Managers: Bissett Investment Management
Harbour Canadian Fund (CI)
RRSP Eligible; Inception Year: 1998; Fund Managers: CI Funds Management Inc.
Harbour Growth & Income Fund (CI)
RRSP Eligible; Inception Year: 1998; Fund Managers: CI Funds Management Inc.
Indexed Balanced Fund (TDQC)
RRSP Eligible; Inception Year: 1998; Fund Managers: TD Asset Management Quantitative Capital
Indexed Canadian Bond Fund (TDQC)
RRSP Eligible; Inception Year: 1997; Fund Managers: TD Asset Management Quantitative Capital
Indexed Canadian Equity Fund (TDQC)
RRSP Eligible; Inception Year: 1997; Fund Managers: TD Asset Management Quantitative Capital
Indexed International Equity Fund (TDQC)
RRSP Eligible; Inception Year: 1997; Fund Managers: TD Asset Management Quantitative Capital
International Bond Fund (Laketon)
RRSP Eligible; Inception Year: 1994; Fund Managers: Laketon Investment Management
Dividend Fund (LLIM)
RRSP Eligible; Inception Year: 1998; Fund Managers: London Life Investment Management Ltd.
Enhanced Dividend Fund (Laketon)
RRSP Eligible; Inception Year: 1998; Fund Managers: Laketon Investment Management
Flex European Equity Fund (Setanta)
RRSP Eligible; Inception Year: 1995; Fund Managers: Laketon Investment Management
Flex Fixed Income Fund (Laketon)
RRSP Eligible; Inception Year: 1973; Fund Managers: Laketon Investment Management
North American Equity Fund (Ethical)
RRSP Eligible; Inception Year: 1999; Fund Managers: Ethical Funds Inc.
Small Cap Equity Fund (Bissett)
RRSP Eligible; Inception Year: 1997; Fund Managers: Bissett Investment Management
True North Fund (Fidelity)
RRSP Eligible; Inception Year: 1998; Fund Managers: Fidelity Investments Canada Ltd.
US Value Fund (LLIM)
RRSP Eligible; Inception Year: 1998; Fund Managers: London Life Investment Management Ltd.
World Equity Fund (AIC)
RRSP Eligible; Inception Year: 1998; Fund Managers: AIC Limited
Balanced Fund (Ethical)
RRSP Eligible; Inception Year: 1999; Fund Managers: Guardian Capital LP
Money Market Fund (Laketon)
RRSP Eligible; Inception Year: 1974; Fund Managers: Laketon Investment Management
Private Collection Euro Focus 20 (Setanta) Fund
RRSP Eligible; Inception Year: 2002; Fund Managers: Setanta Asset Management Ltd.
Flex Global Equity Fund (Setanta)
RRSP Eligible; Inception Year: 1984; Fund Managers: Setanta Asset Management Ltd.
Gens Managed Fund (Laketon)
RRSP Eligible; Inception Year: 1998; Fund Managers: Laketon Investment Management
American Growth Fund (AGF)
RRSP Eligible; Inception Year: 1999; Fund Managers: AGF Funds Inc.
Balanced Fund (Bissett)
RRSP Eligible; Inception Year: 1997; Fund Managers: Bissett Investment Management
Fixed Income Fund (Bissett)
RRSP Eligible; Inception Year: 1998; Fund Managers: Bissett Investment Management
Canadian Growth & Income Fund (AGF)
RRSP Eligible; Inception Year: 1999; Fund Managers: AGF Funds Inc.
Canadian Equity Fund (Templeton)
RRSP Eligible; Inception Year: 1994; Fund Managers: Franklin Templeton Investments
Growth Fund (Ethical)
RRSP Eligible; Inception Year: 1999; Fund Managers: Ethical Funds Inc.
International Portfolio Fund (Fidelity)
RRSP Eligible; Inception Year: 1998; Fund Managers: Fidelity Investments Canada Ltd.
Indexed US Equity Fund (TDQC)
RRSP Eligible; Inception Year: 1997; Fund Managers: TD Asset Management Quantitative Capital
No-Load Money Market Fund (Laketon)
RRSP Eligible; Inception Year: 1998; Fund Managers: Laketon Investment Management
Conservative Allocation Fund
RRSP Eligible; Inception Year: 2003;
Balanced Allocation Fund
RRSP Eligible; Inception Year: 2003;
Aggressive Allocation Fund
RRSP Eligible; Inception Year: 2003;
Advanced Allocation Fund
RRSP Eligible; Inception Year: 2003;
Moderate Allocation Fund
RRSP Eligible; Inception Year: 2003;
Canadian Asset Allocation Fund (Fidelity)
RRSP Eligible; Inception Year: 1998; Fund Managers: Fidelity Investments Canada Ltd.
Canadian Equity Value Fund (Laketon)
RRSP Eligible; Inception Year: 2003; Fund Managers: Laketon Investment Management
Canadian Equity Growth Fund (Mackenzie)
RRSP Eligible; Inception Year: 1997; Fund Managers: Mackenzie Financial Corporation
Canadian Resource Fund (Mackenzie)
RRSP Eligible; Inception Year: 2003; Fund Managers: Mackenzie Financial Corporation
Mid Cap Canada Fund (GWLIM)
RRSP Eligible; Inception Year: 2003; Fund Managers: GWL Investment Management Ltd.
Gens Canadian Equity Fund (LLIM)
RRSP Eligible; Inception Year: 2001; Fund Managers: London Life Investment Management Ltd.
US Growth Leaders Fund (Mackenzie)
RRSP Eligible; Inception Year: 2001; Fund Managers: Mackenzie Financial Corporation
American Disciplined Equity Fund (Fidelity)
RRSP Eligible; Inception Year: 2005; Fund Managers: Fidelity Investments Canada Ltd.
Canadian Equity Fund (LLIM)
RRSP Eligible; Inception Year: 2001; Fund Managers: London Life Investment Management Ltd.
Flex Managed Fund (Laketon)
RRSP Eligible; Inception Year: 1984; Fund Managers: Laketon Investment Management
Gens Balanced Fund (Trimark)
RRSP Eligible; Inception Year: 1998; Fund Managers: AIM Trimark Investments
Gens Canadian Equity Fund (Trimark)
RRSP Eligible; Inception Year: 1998; Fund Managers: AIM Trimark Investments
Canadian Growth Fund (AIM)
RRSP Eligible; Inception Year: 2001; Fund Managers: AIM Trimark Investments
Canadian Equity Fund (AGF)
RRSP Eligible; Inception Year: 1998; Fund Managers: AGF Funds Inc.
Canadian Equity Fund (Laketon)
RRSP Eligible; Inception Year: 1998; Fund Managers: Laketon Investment Management
Gens Fixed Income Fund
RRSP Eligible; Inception Year: 1998; Fund Managers: Laketon Investment Management
Far East Equity Fund (Mackenzie)
RRSP Eligible; Inception Year: 2001; Fund Managers: Mackenzie Financial Corporation
Global Future Fund (Mackenzie)
RRSP Eligible; Inception Year: 1998; Fund Managers: Mackenzie Financial Corporation
Gens Global Equity Fund (Setanta)
RRSP Eligible; Inception Year: 1998; Fund Managers: Setanta Asset Management Ltd.
Global Equity Fund (Trimark)
RRSP Eligible; Inception Year: 1998; Fund Managers: AIM Trimark Investments
Income Fund (Ethical)
RRSP Eligible; Inception Year: 1999; Fund Managers: Ethical Funds Inc.
International Equity Fund (Templeton)
RRSP Eligible; Inception Year: 1998; Fund Managers: Franklin Templeton Investments
Income Focus Fund
RRSP Eligible; Inception Year: 2005;
Income Growth Plus Fund
RRSP Eligible; Inception Year: 2005;
Income Growth Fund
RRSP Eligible; Inception Year: 2005;
Income Opportunity Fund (LLIM)
RRSP Eligible; Inception Year: 2005; Fund Managers: London Life Investment Management Ltd.
NorthStar Fund (Fidelity)
RRSP Eligible; Inception Year: 2005; Fund Managers: Fidelity Investments Canada Ltd.
Real Estate Fund (GWL)
RRSP Eligible; Inception Year: 2005; Fund Managers: GWL Investment Management Ltd.

Canadian Dental Service Plans Inc.

155 Lesmill Rd.
Toronto, ON M3B 2T8
416-296-9401
Fax: 416-296-8920
800-561-9401

INVESTMENT MANAGEMENT

Canadian Dental Service Plans Inc. (continued)
cdspi@cdspi.com
www.cdspi.com
Ownership: Private. Owned by the Canadian Dental Association
Year Founded: 1959
Number of Employees: 59
Assets: $100-500 million
Revenues: $5-10 million
Executives:
Kingsley D. Butler, President/CEO
Paul Harris, Vice-President, Marketing
Pierre Vezina, Vice-President, Investment Services
Ruby Zack, Vice-President, Finance & Internal Operations
CDA:
Aggressive Equity Fund
RRSP Eligible; Inception Year: 1994; Fund Managers:
Altamira Management
Balanced Fund
RRSP Eligible; Inception Year: 1978; Fund Managers:
Phillips, Hager & North
Bond & Mortgage Fund
RRSP Eligible; Inception Year: 1970; Fund Managers:
Fiera Capital
Canadian Equity Fund
RRSP Eligible; Inception Year: 1997; Fund Managers:
AIM Trimark Investments
Common Stock Fund
RRSP Eligible; Inception Year: 1958; Fund Managers:
Altamira Management
Emerging Markets Fund
RRSP Eligible; Inception Year: 1995; Fund Managers:
KBSH Capital Management Inc.
European Fund
RRSP Eligible; Inception Year: 1995; Fund Managers:
KBSH Capital Management Inc.
Fixed Income Fund
RRSP Eligible; Inception Year: 1998; Fund Managers:
McLean Budden Ltd.
Global Fund
RRSP Eligible; Inception Year: 1997; Fund Managers:
AIM Trimark Investments
Global Stock Fund
RRSP Eligible; Inception Year: 1998; Fund Managers:
Franklin Templeton Management Ltd.
International Equity Fund
RRSP Eligible; Inception Year: 1995; Fund Managers:
Connor, Clark & Lunn
S&P 500 Index Fund
RRSP Eligible; Inception Year: 1998; Fund Managers:
Barclays Global Investors Canada Ltd.
Special Equity Fund
RRSP Eligible; Inception Year: 1996; Fund Managers:
KBSH Capital Management Inc.
US Equity Fund
RRSP Eligible; Inception Year: 1996; Fund Managers:
KBSH Capital Management Inc.
Money Market Fund
RRSP Eligible; Inception Year: 1972; Fund Managers:
Fiera Capital
Pacific Basin Fund
RRSP Eligible; Inception Year: 1995; Fund Managers:
KBSH Capital Management Inc.
Balanced Value Fund
RRSP Eligible; Inception Year: 2002; Fund Managers:
McLean Budden Ltd.
GIC Funds
RRSP Eligible; Inception Year: 0; Fund Managers:
Sun Life Assurance Company of Canada
TSX Composite Index
RRSP Eligible; Inception Year: 2002; Fund Managers:
Barclays Global Investors Canada Ltd.
Dividend Fund
RRSP Eligible; Inception Year: 2005; Fund Managers:
Phillips, Hager & North

Capstone Consultants Limited

***Also listed under:** Pension & Money Management Companies*
#1601, 110 Yonge St.
Toronto, ON M5C 1T4
416-366-2931
Fax: 416-366-2729
866-443-6097
mma@mmainvestments.com
www.capstonefunds.com
Former Name: Capstone Consultants Limited.
Ownership: Private
Year Founded: 1984
Executives:
Vanessa L. Morgan, President; vmorgan@mmainvestments.com
Jonathan A. Morgan, Sr. Vice-President
Clive R. Robinson, Sr. Vice-President; crobinson@mmainvestments.com
Alex Sulzer, Vice-President; asulzer@mmainvestments.com
Capstone:
Jupiter Income
RRSP Eligible; Inception Year: 1987; Fund Managers:
Michael A. Smedley
D. GregEckel

Chou Associates Management Inc.

#710, 95 Wellington St. West
Toronto, ON M5J 2N7
416-214-0675
Fax: 416-214-1733
888-357-5070
admin@choufunds.com
www.choufunds.com
Chou:
Associates Fund
RRSP Eligible; Inception Year: 1986; Fund Managers:
Francis Chou
RRSP Fund
RRSP Eligible; Inception Year: 1986; Fund Managers:
Francis Chou
Asia Fund
RRSP Eligible; Inception Year: 2003; Fund Managers:
Francis Chou
Europe Fund
RRSP Eligible; Inception Year: 2003; Fund Managers:
Francis Chou
Bond Fund
RRSP Eligible; Inception Year: 2005; Fund Managers:
Francis Chou

CI Mutual Funds

151 Yonge St., 11th Fl.
Toronto, ON M5C 2W7
416-364-1145
Fax: 416-364-6299
800-563-5181
service@cifunds.com
www.cifunds.com
Also Known As: Canadian International Mutual Funds Inc.
Ownership: Major shareholder AIC Limited (20% interest) & G.R. Chang (15.5% interest)
Year Founded: 1994
Number of Employees: 500
Stock Symbol: CIX
Executives:
William T. Holland, Chair
Peter Anderson, President/CEO
Michael J. Killeen, Sr. Vice-President, Secretary & General Counsel
Directors:
Peter Anderson
William T. Holland
Michael J. Killeen
Stephen A. MacPhail
Altrinsic:
Opportunities Fund
RRSP Eligible; Inception Year: 2002; Fund Managers:
John Hock
BPI:
American Equity GIF Class A Fund
RRSP Eligible; Inception Year: 2000; Fund Managers:
Robert Beckwitt
American Equity GIF Class B Fund
RRSP Eligible; Inception Year: 2001; Fund Managers:
Robert Beckwitt
American Equity (US$) Fund
RRSP Eligible; Inception Year: 1989; Fund Managers:
Robert Beckwitt
AndréDesautels
C.I.:
American Equity Fund
RRSP Eligible; Inception Year: 1989; Fund Managers:
Robert Beckwitt
AndréDesautels
Canadian Bond Fund
RRSP Eligible; Inception Year: 1993; Fund Managers:
James Dutkiewicz
Emerging Markets Fund
RRSP Eligible; Inception Year: 1991; Fund Managers:
Pablo Salas
International Balanced Fund
RRSP Eligible; Inception Year: 1994; Fund Managers:
William Sterling
RobertBeckwitt
Greg Gigliotti
Pacific Fund
RRSP Eligible; Inception Year: 1981; Fund Managers:
William Priest
DanielGeber
Global Health Sciences Sector Fund
RRSP Eligible; Inception Year: 1996; Fund Managers:
Andrew Waight
Harbour Fund
RRSP Eligible; Inception Year: 1997; Fund Managers:
Gerald F. Coleman
StephenJenkins
Can-Am Small Cap Class Fund
RRSP Eligible; Inception Year: 1997; Fund Managers:
Peter Hodson
JoeJugovic
Leighton F. Pullen
Money Market Segregated Fund
RRSP Eligible; Inception Year: 1997;
Canadian Bond GIF Class A Fund
RRSP Eligible; Inception Year: 1999; Fund Managers:
James Dutkiewicz
Global GIF Class A Fund
RRSP Eligible; Inception Year: 1999; Fund Managers:
William Sterling
RobertBeckwitt
Global Segregated Fund
RRSP Eligible; Inception Year: 1997; Fund Managers:
William Sterling
GregGigliotti
Robert Beckwitt
Money Market Fund
RRSP Eligible; Inception Year: 1990;
European Fund
RRSP Eligible; Inception Year: 1991; Fund Managers:
Greg Gigliotti
Global Managers RSP Fund
RRSP Eligible; Inception Year: 2000; Fund Managers:
Robert Beckwitt
Global Value Segregated Fund
RRSP Eligible; Inception Year: 1997; Fund Managers:
William Sterling
Global Boomernomics GIF Class A Fund
RRSP Eligible; Inception Year: 1999; Fund Managers:
Robert Beckwitt
WilliamSterling
Harbour Sector Fund
RRSP Eligible; Inception Year: 1997; Fund Managers:
Gerald F. Coleman
Global Managers Sector Fund
RRSP Eligible; Inception Year: 2000; Fund Managers:
William Sterling
RobertBeckwitt
Greg Gigliotti
Global Value Sector Fund
RRSP Eligible; Inception Year: 1996; Fund Managers:
John Hock
Signature Dividend GIF Class A Fund
RRSP Eligible; Inception Year: 1999; Fund Managers:
Eric Bushell
Signature Dividend GIF Class B Fund
RRSP Eligible; Inception Year: 2001; Fund Managers:
Eric Bushell
Signature High Income GIF Class A Fund
RRSP Eligible; Inception Year: 2000; Fund Managers:
Eric Bushell
Signature High Income GIF Class B Fund
RRSP Eligible; Inception Year: 2001; Fund Managers:
Eric Bushell
Harbour GIF Class A Fund
RRSP Eligible; Inception Year: 1999; Fund Managers:
Gerald F. Coleman
Harbour GIF Class B Fund
RRSP Eligible; Inception Year: 2001; Fund Managers:
Gerald F. Coleman

Harbour Growth & Income GIF Class A Fund
RRSP Eligible; Inception Year: 1999; Fund Managers:
Gerald F. Coleman
Harbour Growth & Income GIF Class B Fund
RRSP Eligible; Inception Year: 2001; Fund Managers:
Gerald F. Coleman
Harbour Growth & Income Segregated Fund
RRSP Eligible; Inception Year: 1997; Fund Managers:
Gerald F. Coleman
StephenJenkins
Canadian Bond GIF Class B Fund
RRSP Eligible; Inception Year: 2001; Fund Managers:
James Dutkiewicz
Canadian Bond Segregated I Fund
RRSP Eligible; Inception Year: 1997; Fund Managers:
James Dutkiewicz
Canadian Bond Segregated II Fund
RRSP Eligible; Inception Year: 1999; Fund Managers:
James Dutkiewicz
American Managers RSP Fund
RRSP Eligible; Inception Year: 2000; Fund Managers:
John Hock
Global Value GIF Class A Fund
RRSP Eligible; Inception Year: 1999; Fund Managers:
John Hock
Global Value GIF Class B Fund
RRSP Eligible; Inception Year: 2001; Fund Managers:
John Hock
International Value Fund
RRSP Eligible; Inception Year: 1996; Fund Managers:
John Hock
Signature Canadian Balanced GIF Class A Fund
RRSP Eligible; Inception Year: 1999; Fund Managers:
Eric Bushell
Signature Canadian Balanced GIF Class B Fund
RRSP Eligible; Inception Year: 2001; Fund Managers:
Eric Bushell
Money Market GIF Class A Fund
RRSP Eligible; Inception Year: 1999;
Money Market Segregated I Fund
RRSP Eligible; Inception Year: 1998;
Money Market Segregated II Fund
RRSP Eligible; Inception Year: 1999;
Money Market GIF Class B Fund
RRSP Eligible; Inception Year: 2001;
Global Boomernomics GIF Class B Fund
RRSP Eligible; Inception Year: 2001; Fund Managers:
Robert Beckwitt
WilliamSterling
Global GIF Class B Fund
RRSP Eligible; Inception Year: 2001; Fund Managers:
William Sterling
RobertBeckwitt
International Balanced GIF Class A Fund
RRSP Eligible; Inception Year: 1999; Fund Managers:
William Sterling
RobertBeckwitt
International Balanced GIF Class B Fund
RRSP Eligible; Inception Year: 2001; Fund Managers:
William Sterling
RobertBeckwitt
Harbour Segregated Fund
RRSP Eligible; Inception Year: 1997; Fund Managers:
Gerald F. Coleman
American Equity Segregated II Fund
RRSP Eligible; Inception Year: 1999; Fund Managers:
Robert Beckwitt
Aggressive Growth GIF Portfolio Class A Fund
RRSP Eligible; Inception Year: 2001; Fund Managers:
Eric Bushell
JohnHock
William Sterling
William Priest
Andrew Waight
David Picton
Aggressive Growth GIF Portfolio Class B Fund
RRSP Eligible; Inception Year: 2001; Fund Managers:
Eric Bushell
JohnHock
William Sterling
William Priest
Andrew Waight
David Picton
Conservative GIF Portfolio Class A Fund
RRSP Eligible; Inception Year: 2001; Fund Managers:
Eric Bushell
JohnHock
William Sterling
David Picton
James Dutkiewicz
Richard Gluck
Conservative GIF Portfolio Class B Fund
RRSP Eligible; Inception Year: 2001; Fund Managers:
Eric Bushell
JohnHock
William Sterling
David Picton
James Dutkiewicz
Richard Gluck
Growth GIF Portfolio Class A Fund
RRSP Eligible; Inception Year: 2001; Fund Managers:
Eric Bushell
JohnHock
William Priest
William Sterling
Andrew Waight
David Picton
Richard Gluck
James Dutkiewicz
Growth GIF Portfolio Class B Fund
RRSP Eligible; Inception Year: 2001; Fund Managers:
Eric Bushell
JohnHock
William Priest
William Sterling
Andrew Waight
David Picton
Richard Gluck
James Dutkiewicz
Moderate GIF Portfolio A Fund
RRSP Eligible; Inception Year: 2001; Fund Managers:
Eric Bushell
WilliamSterling
James Dutkiewicz
Richard Gluck
David Picton
Moderate GIF Portfolio Class B Fund
RRSP Eligible; Inception Year: 2001; Fund Managers:
Eric Bushell
WilliamSterling
James Dutkiewicz
Richard Gluck
David Picton
American Managers Sector (US$) Fund
RRSP Eligible; Inception Year: 2000; Fund Managers:
William Priest
JohnHock
John Bichelmeyer
David Picton
American Small Companies Fund
RRSP Eligible; Inception Year: 1991; Fund Managers:
William Priest
American Small Companies (US$) Fund
RRSP Eligible; Inception Year: 1991; Fund Managers:
William Priest
American Value Fund
RRSP Eligible; Inception Year: 1957; Fund Managers:
William Priest
DavidPearl
American Value Sector (US$) Fund
RRSP Eligible; Inception Year: 2001; Fund Managers:
William Priest
DavidPearl
Canadian Asset Allocation Fund
RRSP Eligible; Inception Year: 1992; Fund Managers:
Kim Shannon
Canadian Balanced Portfolio Fund
RRSP Eligible; Inception Year: 1988; Fund Managers:
Eric Bushell
WilliamPriest
Kim Shannon
William Sterling
David Picton
James Dutkiewicz
Canadian Bond Sector Fund
RRSP Eligible; Inception Year: 2002; Fund Managers:
James Dutkiewicz
Canadian Conservative Portfolio Fund
RRSP Eligible; Inception Year: 1997; Fund Managers:
Robert Beckwitt
EricBushell
John Hock
David Pearl
William Priest
William Sterling
David Picton
James Dutkiewicz
Canadian Growth Portfolio Fund
RRSP Eligible; Inception Year: 1997; Fund Managers:
William Priest
KimShannon
William Sterling
André Desautels
James Dutkiewicz
David Picton
Canadian Income Portfolio Fund
RRSP Eligible; Inception Year: 1997; Fund Managers:
William Sterling
EricBushell
James Dutkiewicz
David Picton
André Desautels
Canadian Maximum Growth Portfolio Fund
RRSP Eligible; Inception Year: 1997; Fund Managers:
William Priest
KimShannon
David Picton
André Desautels
Emerging Markets (US$) Fund
RRSP Eligible; Inception Year: 1991; Fund Managers:
Pablo Salas
Emerging Markets Sector (US$) Fund
RRSP Eligible; Inception Year: 1992; Fund Managers:
Pablo Salas
European Sector (US$) Fund
RRSP Eligible; Inception Year: 1992; Fund Managers:
Greg Gigliotti
European Sector Fund
RRSP Eligible; Inception Year: 1992; Fund Managers:
Greg Gigliotti
Explorer Fund
RRSP Eligible; Inception Year: 1987; Fund Managers:
William Priest
Explorer Segregated II Fund
RRSP Eligible; Inception Year: 1999; Fund Managers:
William Priest
Explorer Segregated I Fund
RRSP Eligible; Inception Year: 1997; Fund Managers:
William Priest
Global Fund
RRSP Eligible; Inception Year: 1986; Fund Managers:
William Sterling
RobertBeckwitt
Greg Gigliotti
Global Small Companies Sector (US$) Fund
RRSP Eligible; Inception Year: 2000; Fund Managers:
William Priest
Global Small Companies Fund
RRSP Eligible; Inception Year: 1993; Fund Managers:
William Priest
Global Small Companies (US$) Fund
RRSP Eligible; Inception Year: 1993; Fund Managers:
William Priest
Global Small Companies Sector Fund
RRSP Eligible; Inception Year: 2000; Fund Managers:
William Priest
Global Science & Technology Sector (US$) Fund
RRSP Eligible; Inception Year: 1996; Fund Managers:
André Desautels
Global Value Sector (US$) Fund
RRSP Eligible; Inception Year: 1996; Fund Managers:
John Hock
International Value Sector Fund
RRSP Eligible; Inception Year: 1996; Fund Managers:
John Hock
International Fund
RRSP Eligible; Inception Year: 1999; Fund Managers:
William Sterling
RobertBeckwitt
Greg Gigliotti
Japanese Sector (US$) Fund
RRSP Eligible; Inception Year: 1998; Fund Managers:
Daniel Geber
WilliamPriest

INVESTMENT MANAGEMENT

CI Mutual Funds (continued)
Long-Term Bond Fund
RRSP Eligible; Inception Year: 1989; Fund Managers:
James Dutkiewicz
Pacific (US$) Fund
RRSP Eligible; Inception Year: 1981; Fund Managers:
William Priest
DanielGeber
Short-Term Bond Fund
RRSP Eligible; Inception Year: 1976; Fund Managers:
James Dutkiewicz
Short-Term Sector (US$) Fund
RRSP Eligible; Inception Year: 1987;
Global Balanced Portfolio Fund
RRSP Eligible; Inception Year: 2001; Fund Managers:
Eric Bushell
Gerald F.Coleman
John Hock
David Pearl
William Priest
William Sterling
David Picton
James Dutkiewicz
André Desautels
Global Balanced RSP Portfolio Fund
RRSP Eligible; Inception Year: 2001; Fund Managers:
James Dutkiewicz
Global Biotechnology Sector (US$) Fund
RRSP Eligible; Inception Year: 1999; Fund Managers:
Bradley Wilds
Global Bond Fund
RRSP Eligible; Inception Year: 1992; Fund Managers:
William Sterling
RichardGluck
Global Bond (US$) Fund
RRSP Eligible; Inception Year: 1992; Fund Managers:
William Sterling
RichardGluck
Global Boomernomics Sector (US$) Fund
RRSP Eligible; Inception Year: 1998; Fund Managers:
William Sterling
RobertBeckwitt
Greg Gigliotti
Global Conservative Portfolio (US$) Fund
RRSP Eligible; Inception Year: 2001; Fund Managers:
John Hock
Global Conservative Portfolio Fund
RRSP Eligible; Inception Year: 2001; Fund Managers:
Robert Beckwitt
EricBushell
Gerald F. Coleman
John Hock
David Pearl
William Priest
William Sterling
David Picton
James Dutkiewicz
Richard Gluck
André Desautels
Global Consumer Products Sector (US$) Fund
RRSP Eligible; Inception Year: 1997; Fund Managers:
John DeVita
JohnHock
Global Energy Sector (US$) Fund
RRSP Eligible; Inception Year: 1998; Fund Managers:
Eric Bushell
Global Finanical Services Sector (US$) Fund
RRSP Eligible; Inception Year: 1996; Fund Managers:
John Hock
Global Growth Portfolio Fund
RRSP Eligible; Inception Year: 2001; Fund Managers:
Robert Beckwitt
EricBushell
Gerald F. Coleman
John Hock
David Pearl
William Priest
William Sterling
David Picton
David Picton
James Dutkiewicz
Richard Gluck
Global Growth Portfolio (US$) Fund
RRSP Eligible; Inception Year: 2001; Fund Managers:
Robert Beckwitt

Global Maximum Growth Portfolio Fund
RRSP Eligible; Inception Year: 2001; Fund Managers:
Robert Beckwitt
EricBushell
Gerald F. Coleman
John Hock
David Pearl
William Priest
William Sterling
David Picton
André Desautels
Global Maximum Growth RSP Portfolio Fund
RRSP Eligible; Inception Year: 2001; Fund Managers:
Robert Beckwitt
EricBushell
Gerald F. Coleman
John Hock
David Pearl
William Priest
William Sterling
David Picton
Global Managers Sector (US$) Fund
RRSP Eligible; Inception Year: 2000; Fund Managers:
William Sterling
WilliamPriest
Nandu Narayanan
John Hock
Canadian Investment Sector (US$) Fund
RRSP Eligible; Inception Year: 2003; Fund Managers:
Kim Shannon
Global Bond RSP Fund
RRSP Eligible; Inception Year: 2002;
American Equity Segregated I Fund
RRSP Eligible; Inception Year: 1999; Fund Managers:
Robert Beckwitt
American Value Insight Fund
RRSP Eligible; Inception Year: 1993; Fund Managers:
David Pearl
Canadian Bond Insight Fund
RRSP Eligible; Inception Year: 2003; Fund Managers:
James Dutkiewicz
Canadian Investment Insight Fund
RRSP Eligible; Inception Year: 2003; Fund Managers:
Kim Shannon
Explorer Insight Fund
RRSP Eligible; Inception Year: 2000; Fund Managers:
William Priest
Global Bond Insight Fund
RRSP Eligible; Inception Year: 2003; Fund Managers:
William Sterling
Global Insight Fund
RRSP Eligible; Inception Year: 2003; Fund Managers:
William Sterling
International Insight Fund
RRSP Eligible; Inception Year: 2003; Fund Managers:
William Sterling
Global Small Companies Insight Fund
RRSP Eligible; Inception Year: 2003; Fund Managers:
William Priest
International Value Insight Fund
RRSP Eligible; Inception Year: 2003; Fund Managers:
John Hock
Money Market Insight Fund
RRSP Eligible; Inception Year: 2003;
Value Trust Insight Fund
RRSP Eligible; Inception Year: 2003; Fund Managers:
Bill Miller
Canadian Investment Fund
RRSP Eligible; Inception Year: 1932; Fund Managers:
Kim Shannon
CIBC:
High Yield Cash Fund
RRSP Eligible; Inception Year: 2000; Fund Managers:
CIBC Global Asset Management Inc.
Clarica MVP:
Asian-Pacific Non-RSP Equity Fund
RRSP Eligible; Inception Year: 1997; Fund Managers:
Daniel Geber
WilliamPriest
Asian-Pacific RSP Equity Fund
RRSP Eligible; Inception Year: 1996; Fund Managers:
Daniel Geber
WilliamPriest

Balanced Fund
RRSP Eligible; Inception Year: 1997; Fund Managers:
Eric Bushell
Bond Fund
RRSP Eligible; Inception Year: 1986; Fund Managers:
James Dutkiewicz
Equity Fund
RRSP Eligible; Inception Year: 1986; Fund Managers:
David Picton
Growth Fund
RRSP Eligible; Inception Year: 1992; Fund Managers:
Sun Life Assurance
Money Market Fund
RRSP Eligible; Inception Year: 1988;
US Equity Fund
RRSP Eligible; Inception Year: 1992; Fund Managers:
Bill Miller
European Growth Fund
RRSP Eligible; Inception Year: 1997; Fund Managers:
Greg Gigliotti
Small Cap American Fund
RRSP Eligible; Inception Year: 1997; Fund Managers:
William Priest
Dividend Fund
RRSP Eligible; Inception Year: 1998; Fund Managers:
Eric Bushell
Global Equity Fund
RRSP Eligible; Inception Year: 1996; Fund Managers:
William Sterling
Clarica SF Alpine:
Growth Equity Fund - Front End
RRSP Eligible; Inception Year: 1998; Fund Managers:
Ted Whitehead
Growth Equity Fund - DSC
RRSP Eligible; Inception Year: 1998; Fund Managers:
Ted Whitehead
Clarica SF CI:
Emerging Markets Fund - Front End
RRSP Eligible; Inception Year: 1998; Fund Managers:
Sun Life Assurance
Emerging Markets Fund - DSC
RRSP Eligible; Inception Year: 1998; Fund Managers:
Sun Life Assurance
Short-Term Bond Fund - Front End
RRSP Eligible; Inception Year: 2000; Fund Managers:
James Dutkiewicz
Short-Term Bond Fund - DSC
RRSP Eligible; Inception Year: 2000; Fund Managers:
James Dutkiewicz
European Fund - Front End
RRSP Eligible; Inception Year: 2000; Fund Managers:
Greg Gigliotti
European Fund - DSC
RRSP Eligible; Inception Year: 1998; Fund Managers:
Greg Gigliotti
Asian & Pacific Fund - DSC
RRSP Eligible; Inception Year: 2001; Fund Managers:
William Priest
DanielGeber
Asian & Pacific Fund - Front End
RRSP Eligible; Inception Year: 2001; Fund Managers:
William Priest
DanielGeber
Canadian Balanced Portfolio Fund
RRSP Eligible; Inception Year: 2003; Fund Managers:
Eric Bushell
WilliamPriest
Kim Shannon
William Sterling
James Dutkiewicz
David Picton
Nandu Narayanan
Canadian Conservative Portfolio Fund
RRSP Eligible; Inception Year: 2003; Fund Managers:
William Priest
KimShannon
William Sterling
Eric Bushell
James Dutkiewicz
David Picton
Canadian Income Portfolio Fund
RRSP Eligible; Inception Year: 2003; Fund Managers:
Eric Bushell
WilliamSterling

James Dutkiewicz
David Picton
Global Balanced Portfolio Fund
RRSP Eligible; Inception Year: 2003; Fund Managers:
Eric Bushell
DavidPearl
Gerald F. Coleman
John Hock
Robert Beckwitt
William Priest
William Sterling
David Picton
James Dutkiewicz
Richard Gluck
Global Conservative Portfolio Fund
RRSP Eligible; Inception Year: 2003; Fund Managers:
Eric Bushell
DavidPearl
Gerald F. Coleman
John Hock
Robert Beckwitt
William Priest
William Sterling
David Picton
James Dutkiewicz
Richard Gluck
Global Fund
RRSP Eligible; Inception Year: 2003; Fund Managers:
William Sterling
Global Growth Portfolio Fund
RRSP Eligible; Inception Year: 2003; Fund Managers:
David Pearl
EricBushell
Gerald F. Coleman
John Hock
Robert Beckwitt
William Priest
William Sterling
David Picton
James Dutkiewicz
Richard Gluck
Global Maximum Growth Portfolio Fund
RRSP Eligible; Inception Year: 2003; Fund Managers:
David Pearl
RobertBeckwitt
Eric Bushell
Gerald F. Coleman
John Hock
William Priest
William Sterling
David Picton
International Balanced Fund
RRSP Eligible; Inception Year: 2003; Fund Managers:
William Sterling
Money Market Fund
RRSP Eligible; Inception Year: 2003;
Pacific Fund - DSC
RRSP Eligible; Inception Year: 1998; Fund Managers:
William Priest
DanielGeber
Pacific Fund - Front End
RRSP Eligible; Inception Year: 1998; Fund Managers:
William Priest
DanielGeber
Signature Canadian Balanced Fund - DSC
RRSP Eligible; Inception Year: 1999; Fund Managers:
Eric Bushell
Signature Canadian Balanced Fund - Front End
RRSP Eligible; Inception Year: 1999; Fund Managers:
Eric Bushell
Clarica SF CI Signature:
Bond Fund
RRSP Eligible; Inception Year: 1999; Fund Managers:
AIM Funds Management Inc.
Clarica SF Signature:
Corporate Bond Fund - DSC
RRSP Eligible; Inception Year: 1999; Fund Managers:
James Dutkiewicz
Corporate Bond Fund - Front End
RRSP Eligible; Inception Year: 1999; Fund Managers:
James Dutkiewicz
Clarica SF Trimark:
Balanced Fund - Front End
RRSP Eligible; Inception Year: 1999; Fund Managers:
AIM Trimark Investments
Canadian Equity Fund - DSC
RRSP Eligible; Inception Year: 1999; Fund Managers:
AIM Trimark Investments
Discovery Fund - Front End
RRSP Eligible; Inception Year: 1999; Fund Managers:
AIM Trimark Investments
Global Equity Fund - Front End
RRSP Eligible; Inception Year: 1999; Fund Managers:
AIM Trimark Investments
Balanced Fund - DSC
RRSP Eligible; Inception Year: 2000; Fund Managers:
AIM Trimark Investments
Canadian Equity Fund - Front End
RRSP Eligible; Inception Year: 1999; Fund Managers:
AIM Trimark Investments
Discovery Fund - DSC
RRSP Eligible; Inception Year: 1999; Fund Managers:
AIM Trimark Investments
Global Equity Fund - DSC
RRSP Eligible; Inception Year: 1999; Fund Managers:
AIM Trimark Investments
DDJ:
Canadian High Yield Fund
RRSP Eligible; Inception Year: 1997; Fund Managers:
David Breazzano
US High Yield Fund
RRSP Eligible; Inception Year: 2003; Fund Managers:
David Breazzano
Harbour:
Growth & Income Fund
RRSP Eligible; Inception Year: 1997; Fund Managers:
Gerald F. Coleman
StephenJenkins
Growth & Income Class Z Fund
RRSP Eligible; Inception Year: 2003;
Foreign Growth & Income Sector (US$) Fund
RRSP Eligible; Inception Year: 2002; Fund Managers:
Gerald F. Coleman
StephenJenkins
Foreign Equity Sector (US$) Fund
RRSP Eligible; Inception Year: 2002; Fund Managers:
Stephen Jenkins
Gerald F.Coleman
Select:
Canadian Equity Managed Corporate Class Fund
RRSP Eligible; Inception Year: 2005; Fund Managers:
Synergy Asset Management
Income Managed Corporate Class Fund
RRSP Eligible; Inception Year: 2005; Fund Managers:
Eric Bushell
International Equity Managed Corporate Class Fund
RRSP Eligible; Inception Year: 2005; Fund Managers:
Trilogy Global Advisors
Staging Fund
RRSP Eligible; Inception Year: 2005;
US Equity Managed Corporate Class Fund
RRSP Eligible; Inception Year: 2005; Fund Managers:
Trilogy Global Advisors
Signature:
Dividend Income Class X Fund
RRSP Eligible; Inception Year: 2003; Fund Managers:
Eric Bushell
Canadian Resource Fund
RRSP Eligible; Inception Year: 1997; Fund Managers:
Robert Lyon
EricBushell
Dividend Fund
RRSP Eligible; Inception Year: 1996; Fund Managers:
Eric Bushell
Income & Growth Fund
RRSP Eligible; Inception Year: 2000; Fund Managers:
Eric Bushell
Select Canadian Fund
RRSP Eligible; Inception Year: 1998; Fund Managers:
Eric Bushell
High Income Fund
RRSP Eligible; Inception Year: 1996; Fund Managers:
Matt Shandro
EricBushell
Canadian Balanced Fund
RRSP Eligible; Inception Year: 1997; Fund Managers:
Eric Bushell
Canadian Resource Sector Fund
RRSP Eligible; Inception Year: 2001; Fund Managers:
Robert Lyon
Canadian Resource Sector (US$) Fund
RRSP Eligible; Inception Year: 2001; Fund Managers:
Robert Lyon
EricBushell
High Income Sector (US$) Fund
RRSP Eligible; Inception Year: 2002; Fund Managers:
Eric Bushell
Dividend Class Z Fund
RRSP Eligible; Inception Year: 2003; Fund Managers:
Eric Bushell
Corporate Bond Fund
RRSP Eligible; Inception Year: 2002; Fund Managers:
James Dutkiewicz
MattShandro
Corporate Bond Insight Fund
RRSP Eligible; Inception Year: 2003; Fund Managers:
James Dutkiewicz
Select Canadian Insight Fund
RRSP Eligible; Inception Year: 2003; Fund Managers:
Eric Bushell
Corporate Bond Corporate Class Fund
RRSP Eligible; Inception Year: 2003; Fund Managers:
James Dutkiewicz
MattShandro
Income & Growth Corporate Class Fund
RRSP Eligible; Inception Year: 2005; Fund Managers:
Eric Bushell
Select Canadian Corporate Class Fund
RRSP Eligible; Inception Year: 2001; Fund Managers:
Eric Bushell
SunWise Elite:
Aim Canadian First Class Fund
RRSP Eligible; Inception Year: 2005; Fund Managers:
AIM Trimark Investments
CI American Value Fund
RRSP Eligible; Inception Year: 2005; Fund Managers:
David Pearl
WilliamPriest
CI Canadian Asset Allocation Fund
RRSP Eligible; Inception Year: 2005; Fund Managers:
Kim Shannon
CI Canadian Balanced Fund
RRSP Eligible; Inception Year: 2005; Fund Managers:
Kim Shannon
WilliamSterling
William Priest
James Dutkiewicz
Eric Bushell
David Picton
CI Canadian Bond Fund
RRSP Eligible; Inception Year: 2005; Fund Managers:
James Dutkiewicz
CI Canadian Conservative Portfolio Fund
RRSP Eligible; Inception Year: 2005; Fund Managers:
Eric Bushell
JamesDutkiewicz
William Priest
David Pearl
David Picton
Kim Shannon
CI Canadian Income Portfolio Fund
RRSP Eligible; Inception Year: 2005; Fund Managers:
Eric Bushell
JamesDutkiewicz
William Priest
William Sterling
CI Canadian Investment Fund
RRSP Eligible; Inception Year: 2005; Fund Managers:
Kim Shannon
CI Global Balanced Portfolio Fund
RRSP Eligible; Inception Year: 2005; Fund Managers:
Eric Bushell
Gerald F.Coleman
James Dutkiewicz
Richard Gluck
Robert Beckwitt
John Hock
David Pearl
David Picton
William Priest
William Sterling
CI Global Bond Fund
RRSP Eligible; Inception Year: 2005; Fund Managers:
William Sterling
RichardGluck

INVESTMENT MANAGEMENT

CI Mutual Funds (continued)

CI Global Conservative Portfolio Fund
RRSP Eligible; Inception Year: 2005; Fund Managers:
Robert Beckwitt
EricBushell
Gerald F. Coleman
James Dutkiewicz
Richard Gluck
John Hock
David Pearl
David Picton
William Priest
William Sterling
CI Global Fund
RRSP Eligible; Inception Year: 2005; Fund Managers:
William Sterling
RobertBeckwitt
CI Global Growth Portfolio Fund
RRSP Eligible; Inception Year: 2005; Fund Managers:
Eric Bushell
Gerald F.Coleman
James Dutkiewicz
Robert Beckwitt
William Priest
Richard Gluck
John Hock
David Pearl
William Sterling
CI Global Maximum Growth Portfolio Fund
RRSP Eligible; Inception Year: 2005; Fund Managers:
Robert Beckwitt
EricBushell
Gerald F. Coleman
John Hock
David Pearl
David Picton
William Priest
William Sterling
CI Global Value Fund
RRSP Eligible; Inception Year: 2005; Fund Managers:
John Hock
CI Harbour Fund
RRSP Eligible; Inception Year: 2005; Fund Managers:
Gerald F. Coleman
CI Harbour Growth & Income Fund
RRSP Eligible; Inception Year: 2005; Fund Managers:
Gerald F. Coleman
CI International Balanced Fund
RRSP Eligible; Inception Year: 2005; Fund Managers:
Robert Beckwitt
WilliamSterling
CI International Value Fund
RRSP Eligible; Inception Year: 2005; Fund Managers:
John Hock
CI Money Market Fund
RRSP Eligible; Inception Year: 2005;
CI Signature Dividend Fund
RRSP Eligible; Inception Year: 2005; Fund Managers:
Eric Bushell
CI Signature High Income Fund
RRSP Eligible; Inception Year: 2005; Fund Managers:
Eric Bushell
CI Signature Income & Growth Fund
RRSP Eligible; Inception Year: 2005; Fund Managers:
Eric Bushell
CI Signature Select Canadian Fund
RRSP Eligible; Inception Year: 2005; Fund Managers:
Eric Bushell
CI Synergy American Fund
RRSP Eligible; Inception Year: 2005; Fund Managers:
David Picton
CI Synergy Canadian Fund
RRSP Eligible; Inception Year: 2005; Fund Managers:
David Picton
CI Synergy Global Corporate Fund
RRSP Eligible; Inception Year: 2005; Fund Managers:
David Picton
CI Value Trust Corporate Fund
RRSP Eligible; Inception Year: 2005; Fund Managers:
Bill Miller
Dynamic Power American Growth Fund
RRSP Eligible; Inception Year: 2005; Fund Managers:
Goodman & Company
Fidelity Canadian Asset Allocation Fund
RRSP Eligible; Inception Year: 2005; Fund Managers:
Fidelity Investments Canada Limited
Fidelity Global Asset Allocation Fund
RRSP Eligible; Inception Year: 2005; Fund Managers:
Fidelity Investments Canada Limited
Fidelity Growth America Fund
RRSP Eligible; Inception Year: 2005; Fund Managers:
Fidelity Investments Canada Limited
Fidelity NorthStar Fund
RRSP Eligible; Inception Year: 2005; Fund Managers:
Fidelity Investments Canada Limited
Fidelity True North Fund
RRSP Eligible; Inception Year: 2005; Fund Managers:
Fidelity Investments Canada Limited
Mackenzie Cundill Canadian Balanced Fund
RRSP Eligible; Inception Year: 2005; Fund Managers:
Peter Cundill & Associates
Mackenzie Cundill Canadian Security Fund
RRSP Eligible; Inception Year: 2005; Fund Managers:
Peter Cundill & Associates

SunWise Elite Trimark:

Global Balanced Fund
RRSP Eligible; Inception Year: 2005; Fund Managers:
AIM Trimark Investments
Select Growth Fund
RRSP Eligible; Inception Year: 2005; Fund Managers:
AIM Trimark Investments

SunWise Elite Trimmark:

Income Growth Fund
RRSP Eligible; Inception Year: 2005; Fund Managers:
AIM Trimark Investments

SunWise I:

Dynamic Power American Growth 75/75 Fund
RRSP Eligible; Inception Year: 1999; Fund Managers:
Goodman & Company
Dynamic Power American Growth 100/100 Fund
RRSP Eligible; Inception Year: 1999; Fund Managers:
Goodman & Company
Mackenzie Cundill Canadian Balanced 75/75 Fund
RRSP Eligible; Inception Year: 1999; Fund Managers:
Peter Cundill & Associates
Mackenzie Cundill Canadian Balanced 100/100 Fund
RRSP Eligible; Inception Year: 1999; Fund Managers:
Peter Cundill & Associates
Mackenzie Cundill Canadian Security 75/75 Fund
RRSP Eligible; Inception Year: 1999; Fund Managers:
Peter Cundill & Associates
Mackenzie Cundill Canadian Security 100/100 Fund
RRSP Eligible; Inception Year: 1999; Fund Managers:
Peter Cundill & Associates

SunWise I CI:

American Value Fund - Basic
RRSP Eligible; Inception Year: 1999; Fund Managers:
William Priest
DavidPearl
American Value Fund - Full
RRSP Eligible; Inception Year: 1999; Fund Managers:
David Pearl
Canadian Balanced Portfolio Fund - Basic
RRSP Eligible; Inception Year: 1999; Fund Managers:
Eric Bushell
WilliamPriest
Kim Shannon
Nandu Narayanan
William Sterling
James Dutkiewicz
David Picton
Canadian Balanced Portfolio Fund - Full
RRSP Eligible; Inception Year: 1999; Fund Managers:
Eric Bushell
WilliamPriest
Kim Shannon
Nandu Narayanan
William Sterling
James Dutkiewicz
David Picton
Canadian Bond Fund - Basic
RRSP Eligible; Inception Year: 1999; Fund Managers:
James Dutkiewicz
Canadian Bond Fund - Full
RRSP Eligible; Inception Year: 1999; Fund Managers:
James Dutkiewicz
Canadian Conservative Portfolio Fund - Basic
RRSP Eligible; Inception Year: 1999; Fund Managers:
David Pearl
EricBushell
William Priest
Kim Shannon
William Sterling
James Dutkiewicz
David Picton
Canadian Conservative Portfolio Fund - Full
RRSP Eligible; Inception Year: 1999; Fund Managers:
David Pearl
EricBushell
William Priest
Kim Shannon
William Sterling
James Dutkiewicz
David Picton
Canadian Equity Fund - Basic
RRSP Eligible; Inception Year: 1999; Fund Managers:
Kim Shannon
Canadian Equity Fund - Full
RRSP Eligible; Inception Year: 1999; Fund Managers:
Kim Shannon
Canadian Growth Portfolio Fund - Basic
RRSP Eligible; Inception Year: 1999; Fund Managers:
Nandu Narayanan
WilliamPriest
Kim Shannon
William Sterling
David Picton
Canadian Growth Portfolio Fund - Full
RRSP Eligible; Inception Year: 1999; Fund Managers:
Nandu Narayanan
WilliamPriest
Kim Shannon
William Sterling
James Dutkiewicz
David Picton
Canadian Income Portfolio Fund - Basic
RRSP Eligible; Inception Year: 1999; Fund Managers:
Eric Bushell
WilliamSterling
James Dutkiewicz
David Picton
Canadian Income Portfolio Fund - Full
RRSP Eligible; Inception Year: 1999; Fund Managers:
Eric Bushell
WilliamSterling
James Dutkiewicz
David Picton
Canadian Investment Fund - Basic
RRSP Eligible; Inception Year: 1999; Fund Managers:
Kim Shannon
Canadian Investment Fund - Full
RRSP Eligible; Inception Year: 1999; Fund Managers:
Kim Shannon
Canadian Maximum Growth Portfolio Fund - Basic
RRSP Eligible; Inception Year: 1999; Fund Managers:
Nandu Narayanan
WilliamPriest
Kim Shannon
David Picton
Canadian Maximum Growth Portfolio Fund - Full
RRSP Eligible; Inception Year: 1999; Fund Managers:
Nandu Narayanan
WilliamPriest
Kim Shannon
David Picton
Canadian Select Bond Fund - Basic
RRSP Eligible; Inception Year: 1999; Fund Managers:
James Dutkiewicz
Canadian Select Bond Fund - Full
RRSP Eligible; Inception Year: 1999; Fund Managers:
James Dutkiewicz
Canadian Special Bond Fund - Basic
RRSP Eligible; Inception Year: 1999; Fund Managers:
James Dutkiewicz
Canadian Special Bond Fund - Full
RRSP Eligible; Inception Year: 1999; Fund Managers:
James Dutkiewicz
Canadian Stock Fund - Basic
RRSP Eligible; Inception Year: 1999; Fund Managers:
Eric Bushell
Canadian Stock Fund - Full
RRSP Eligible; Inception Year: 1999; Fund Managers:
Eric Bushell
Dividend Fund - Basic
RRSP Eligible; Inception Year: 1999; Fund Managers:
Eric Bushell

Dividend Fund - Full
RRSP Eligible; Inception Year: 1999; Fund Managers:
Eric Bushell
Global Growth Portfolio Fund - Basic
RRSP Eligible; Inception Year: 1999; Fund Managers:
Robert Beckwitt
EricBushell
Gerald F. Coleman
John Hock
David Pearl
William Priest
William Sterling
James Dutkiewicz
David Picton
Richard Gluck
Global Growth Portfolio Fund - Full
RRSP Eligible; Inception Year: 1999; Fund Managers:
Robert Beckwitt
EricBushell
Gerald F. Coleman
John Hock
David Pearl
William Priest
William Sterling
James Dutkiewicz
David Picton
Richard Gluck
Harbour Growth & Income Fund - Basic
RRSP Eligible; Inception Year: 1999; Fund Managers:
Gerald F. Coleman
Harbour Growth & Income Fund - Full
RRSP Eligible; Inception Year: 1999; Fund Managers:
Gerald F. Coleman
Money Market Fund - Basic
RRSP Eligible; Inception Year: 1999;
Money Market Fund - Full
RRSP Eligible; Inception Year: 1999;
Signature Select Canadian Fund - Basic
RRSP Eligible; Inception Year: 1999; Fund Managers:
Eric Bushell
Signature Select Canadian Fund - Full
RRSP Eligible; Inception Year: 1999; Fund Managers:
Eric Bushell
US Equity Fund - Basic
RRSP Eligible; Inception Year: 1999; Fund Managers:
William Priest
US Equity Fund - Full
RRSP Eligible; Inception Year: 1999; Fund Managers:
William Priest
World Equity Fund - Basic
RRSP Eligible; Inception Year: 1999; Fund Managers:
John Hock
World Equity Fund - Full
RRSP Eligible; Inception Year: 1999; Fund Managers:
John Hock
SunWise I Fidelity:
Canadian Asset Allocation Fund - Full
RRSP Eligible; Inception Year: 1999; Fund Managers:
Fidelity Investments Canada Limited
Growth America Fund - Basic
RRSP Eligible; Inception Year: 1999; Fund Managers:
Fidelity Investments Canada Limited
Growth America Fund - Full
RRSP Eligible; Inception Year: 1999; Fund Managers:
Fidelity Investments Canada Limited
International Portfolio Fund - Basic
RRSP Eligible; Inception Year: 1999; Fund Managers:
Fidelity Investments Canada Limited
International Portfolio Fund - Full
RRSP Eligible; Inception Year: 1999; Fund Managers:
Fidelity Investments Canada Limited
True North Fund - Basic
RRSP Eligible; Inception Year: 1999; Fund Managers:
Fidelity Investments Canada Limited
True North Fund - Full
RRSP Eligible; Inception Year: 1999; Fund Managers:
Fidelity Investments Canada Limited
SunWise I Trimark:
Select Canadian Growth Fund - Basic
RRSP Eligible; Inception Year: 1999; Fund Managers:
AIM Trimark Investments
Select Canadian Growth Fund - Full
RRSP Eligible; Inception Year: 1999; Fund Managers:
AIM Trimark Investments
Select Growth Fund - Basic
RRSP Eligible; Inception Year: 1999; Fund Managers:
AIM Trimark Investments
Select Growth Fund - Full
RRSP Eligible; Inception Year: 1999; Fund Managers:
AIM Trimark Investments
SunWise II:
Dynamic Power American Growth Fund - Basic
RRSP Eligible; Inception Year: 2001; Fund Managers:
Goodman & Company
Dynamic Power American Growth Fund - Combined
RRSP Eligible; Inception Year: 2001; Fund Managers:
Goodman & Company
Dynamic Power American Growth Fund - Full
RRSP Eligible; Inception Year: 2001; Fund Managers:
Goodman & Company
Mackenzie Cundill Canadian Balanced Fund - Basic
RRSP Eligible; Inception Year: 2001; Fund Managers:
Peter Cundill & Associates
Mackenzie Cundill Canadian Balanced Fund - Combined
RRSP Eligible; Inception Year: 2001; Fund Managers:
Peter Cundill & Associates
Mackenzie Cundill Canadian Balanced Fund - Full
RRSP Eligible; Inception Year: 2001; Fund Managers:
Peter Cundill & Associates
Mackenzie Cundill Canadian Security Fund - Basic
RRSP Eligible; Inception Year: 2001; Fund Managers:
Peter Cundill & Associates
Mackenzie Cundill Canadian Security Fund - Combined
RRSP Eligible; Inception Year: 2001; Fund Managers:
Peter Cundill & Associates
Mackenzie Cundill Canadian Security Fund - Full
RRSP Eligible; Inception Year: 2001; Fund Managers:
Peter Cundill & Associates
Bond Index Fund - Basic
RRSP Eligible; Inception Year: 2001; Fund Managers:
TD Asset Management Inc.
Bond Index Fund - Combined
RRSP Eligible; Inception Year: 2001; Fund Managers:
TD Asset Management Inc.
Bond Index Fund - Full
RRSP Eligible; Inception Year: 2001; Fund Managers:
TD Asset Management Inc.
US Market Index Fund - Basic
RRSP Eligible; Inception Year: 2001; Fund Managers:
TD Asset Management Inc.
US Market Index Fund - Combined
RRSP Eligible; Inception Year: 2001; Fund Managers:
TD Asset Management Inc.
US Market Index Fund - Full
RRSP Eligible; Inception Year: 2001; Fund Managers:
TD Asset Management Inc.
SunWise II AIC:
American Focused Fund - Basic
RRSP Eligible; Inception Year: 2001; Fund Managers:
AIC Group of Funds
American Focused Fund - Combined
RRSP Eligible; Inception Year: 2001; Fund Managers:
AIC Group of Funds
American Focused Fund - Full
RRSP Eligible; Inception Year: 2001; Fund Managers:
AIC Group of Funds
Diversified Canada Fund - Basic
RRSP Eligible; Inception Year: 2001; Fund Managers:
AIC Group of Funds
Diversified Canada Fund - Combined
RRSP Eligible; Inception Year: 2001; Fund Managers:
AIC Group of Funds
Diversified Canada Fund - Full
RRSP Eligible; Inception Year: 2001; Fund Managers:
AIC Group of Funds
SunWise II AIM:
Canadian First Class Fund - Basic
RRSP Eligible; Inception Year: 2001; Fund Managers:
AIM Trimark Investments
Canadian First Class Fund - Combined
RRSP Eligible; Inception Year: 2001; Fund Managers:
AIM Trimark Investments
Canadian First Class Fund - Full
RRSP Eligible; Inception Year: 2001; Fund Managers:
AIM Trimark Investments
SunWise II CI:
American Growth Fund - Basic
RRSP Eligible; Inception Year: 2001; Fund Managers:
Bill Miller
American Growth Fund - Combined
RRSP Eligible; Inception Year: 2001; Fund Managers:
Bill Miller
American Growth Fund - Full
RRSP Eligible; Inception Year: 2001; Fund Managers:
Bill Miller
American Value Fund - Basic
RRSP Eligible; Inception Year: 2001; Fund Managers:
David Pearl
WilliamPriest
American Value Fund - Combined
RRSP Eligible; Inception Year: 2001; Fund Managers:
David Pearl
WilliamPriest
American Value Fund - Full
RRSP Eligible; Inception Year: 2001; Fund Managers:
David Pearl
WilliamPriest
Canadian Asset Allocation Fund - Basic
RRSP Eligible; Inception Year: 2001; Fund Managers:
Kim Shannon
Canadian Asset Allocation Fund - Combined
RRSP Eligible; Inception Year: 2001; Fund Managers:
Kim Shannon
Canadian Asset Allocation Fund - Full
RRSP Eligible; Inception Year: 2001; Fund Managers:
Kim Shannon
Canadian Balanced Portfolio Fund - Basic
RRSP Eligible; Inception Year: 2001; Fund Managers:
Eric Bushell
WilliamPriest
Kim Shannon
William Sterling
David Picton
James Dutkiewicz
Canadian Balanced Portfolio Fund - Combined
RRSP Eligible; Inception Year: 2001; Fund Managers:
Eric Bushell
NanduNarayanan
William Priest
Kim Shannon
William Sterling
David Picton
James Dutkiewicz
Canadian Balanced Portfolio Fund - Full
RRSP Eligible; Inception Year: 2001; Fund Managers:
Eric Bushell
NanduNarayanan
William Priest
Kim Shannon
William Sterling
David Picton
James Dutkiewicz
Canadian Bond Fund - Basic
RRSP Eligible; Inception Year: 2003; Fund Managers:
James Dutkiewicz
Canadian Bond Fund - Combined
RRSP Eligible; Inception Year: 2003; Fund Managers:
James Dutkiewicz
Canadian Bond Fund - Full
RRSP Eligible; Inception Year: 2003; Fund Managers:
James Dutkiewicz
Canadian Conservative Portfolio Fund - Basic
RRSP Eligible; Inception Year: 2001; Fund Managers:
Eric Bushell
KimShannon
David Pearl
William Priest
William Sterling
David Picton
James Dutkiewicz
Canadian Conservative Portfolio Fund - Combined
RRSP Eligible; Inception Year: 2001; Fund Managers:
Eric Bushell
DavidPearl
William Priest
Kim Shannon
William Sterling
David Picton
James Dutkiewicz
Canadian Conservative Portfolio Fund - Full
RRSP Eligible; Inception Year: 2001; Fund Managers:
Eric Bushell
DavidPearl
William Priest

INVESTMENT MANAGEMENT

CI Mutual Funds (continued)
Kim Shannon
William Sterling
David Picton
James Dutkiewicz
Canadian Growth Portfolio Fund - Basic
RRSP Eligible; Inception Year: 2001; Fund Managers:
Kim Shannon
WilliamSterling
William Priest
James Dutkiewicz
David Picton
Canadian Growth Portfolio Fund - Full
RRSP Eligible; Inception Year: 2001; Fund Managers:
Kim Shannon
WilliamSterling
Nandu Narayanan
William Priest
James Dutkiewicz
David Picton
Canadian Income Portfolio Fund - Basic
RRSP Eligible; Inception Year: 2001; Fund Managers:
Eric Bushell
WilliamSterling
James Dutkiewicz
David Picton
Canadian Income Portfolio Fund - Combined
RRSP Eligible; Inception Year: 2001; Fund Managers:
Eric Bushell
WilliamSterling
James Dutkiewicz
David Picton
Canadian Income Portfolio Fund - Full
RRSP Eligible; Inception Year: 2001; Fund Managers:
Eric Bushell
WilliamSterling
James Dutkiewicz
David Picton
Canadian Investment Fund - Basic
RRSP Eligible; Inception Year: 2001; Fund Managers:
Kim Shannon
Canadian Investment Fund - Combined
RRSP Eligible; Inception Year: 2001; Fund Managers:
Kim Shannon
Canadian Investment Fund - Full
RRSP Eligible; Inception Year: 2001; Fund Managers:
Kim Shannon
Canadian Maximum Growth Portfolio Fund - Basic
RRSP Eligible; Inception Year: 2001; Fund Managers:
Kim Shannon
NanduNarayanan
William Priest
David Picton
Canadian Maximum Growth Portfolio Fund - Combined
RRSP Eligible; Inception Year: 2001; Fund Managers:
Kim Shannon
NanduNarayanan
William Priest
David Picton
Canadian Maximum Growth Portfolio Fund - Full
RRSP Eligible; Inception Year: 2001; Fund Managers:
Kim Shannon
NanduNarayanan
William Priest
David Picton
Canadian Premier Bond Fund - Basic
RRSP Eligible; Inception Year: 2001; Fund Managers:
James Dutkiewicz
Canadian Premier Bond Fund - Combined
RRSP Eligible; Inception Year: 2001; Fund Managers:
James Dutkiewicz
Canadian Premier Bond Fund - Full
RRSP Eligible; Inception Year: 2001; Fund Managers:
James Dutkiewicz
Dividend Fund - Basic
RRSP Eligible; Inception Year: 2001; Fund Managers:
Eric Bushell
Dividend Fund - Combined
RRSP Eligible; Inception Year: 2001; Fund Managers:
Eric Bushell
Dividend Fund - Full
RRSP Eligible; Inception Year: 2001; Fund Managers:
Eric Bushell
Global Balanced Portfolio Fund - Basic
RRSP Eligible; Inception Year: 2003; Fund Managers:
Robert Beckwitt
EricBushell
Gerald F. Coleman
John Hock
David Pearl
William Priest
William Sterling
James Dutkiewicz
David Picton
Richard Gluck
Global Balanced Portfolio Fund - Combined
RRSP Eligible; Inception Year: 2003; Fund Managers:
Robert Beckwitt
EricBushell
Gerald F. Coleman
John Hock
David Pearl
William Priest
William Sterling
Andrew Waight
James Dutkiewicz
David Picton
Richard Gluck
Global Balanced Portfolio Fund - Full
RRSP Eligible; Inception Year: 2003; Fund Managers:
Robert Beckwitt
EricBushell
Gerald F. Coleman
John Hock
David Pearl
William Priest
William Sterling
Andrew Waight
James Dutkiewicz
David Picton
Richard Gluck
Global Bond Fund - Basic
RRSP Eligible; Inception Year: 2003; Fund Managers:
William Sterling
Global Bond Fund - Combined
RRSP Eligible; Inception Year: 2003; Fund Managers:
William Sterling
RichardGluck
Global Bond Fund - Full
RRSP Eligible; Inception Year: 2003; Fund Managers:
William Sterling
RichardGluck
Global Boomernomics Sector Fund - Basic
RRSP Eligible; Inception Year: 2001; Fund Managers:
William Sterling
RobertBeckwitt
Global Boomernomics Sector Fund - Combined
RRSP Eligible; Inception Year: 2001; Fund Managers:
William Sterling
RobertBeckwitt
Global Boomernomics Sector Fund - Full
RRSP Eligible; Inception Year: 2001; Fund Managers:
William Sterling
RobertBeckwitt
Global Conservative Portfolio Fund - Basic
RRSP Eligible; Inception Year: 2003; Fund Managers:
Robert Beckwitt
EricBushell
Gerald F. Coleman
John Hock
David Pearl
William Priest
William Sterling
Richard Gluck
James Dutkiewicz
David Picton
Global Conservative Portfolio Fund - Combined
RRSP Eligible; Inception Year: 2003; Fund Managers:
Robert Beckwitt
EricBushell
Gerald F. Coleman
John Hock
David Pearl
William Priest
William Sterling
Andrew Waight
Richard Gluck
James Dutkiewicz
David Picton
Global Conservative Portfolio Fund - Full
RRSP Eligible; Inception Year: 2003; Fund Managers:
Robert Beckwitt
EricBushell
Gerald F. Coleman
John Hock
David Pearl
William Priest
William Sterling
Andrew Waight
Richard Gluck
James Dutkiewicz
David Picton
Global Fund - Basic
RRSP Eligible; Inception Year: 2001; Fund Managers:
Robert Beckwitt
WilliamSterling
Global Fund - Combined
RRSP Eligible; Inception Year: 2001; Fund Managers:
Robert Beckwitt
WilliamSterling
Global Fund - Full
RRSP Eligible; Inception Year: 2001; Fund Managers:
Robert Beckwitt
WilliamSterling
Global Growth Portfolio Fund - Basic
RRSP Eligible; Inception Year: 2001; Fund Managers:
Robert Beckwitt
EricBushell
Gerald F. Coleman
John Hock
David Pearl
William Priest
William Sterling
Richard Gluck
James Dutkiewicz
David Picton
Global Growth Portfolio Fund - Combined
RRSP Eligible; Inception Year: 2001; Fund Managers:
Robert Beckwitt
EricBushell
Gerald F. Coleman
John Hock
David Pearl
William Priest
William Sterling
Andrew Waight
Richard Gluck
James Dutkiewicz
David Picton
Global Growth Portfolio Fund - Full
RRSP Eligible; Inception Year: 2001; Fund Managers:
Robert Beckwitt
EricBushell
Gerald F. Coleman
John Hock
David Pearl
William Priest
William Sterling
Andrew Waight
Richard Gluck
James Dutkiewicz
David Picton
Global Maximum Growth Portfolio Fund - Basic
RRSP Eligible; Inception Year: 2001; Fund Managers:
Robert Beckwitt
EricBushell
Gerald F. Coleman
John Hock
David Pearl
William Priest
William Sterling
David Picton
Global Maximum Growth Portfolio Fund - Combined
RRSP Eligible; Inception Year: 2001; Fund Managers:
Robert Beckwitt
EricBushell
Gerald F. Coleman
John Hock
David Pearl
William Priest
William Sterling
Andrew Waight
James Dutkiewicz
David Picton
Global Maximum Growth Portfolio Fund - Full
RRSP Eligible; Inception Year: 2001; Fund Managers:

Robert Beckwitt
EricBushell
Gerald F. Coleman
John Hock
David Pearl
William Priest
William Sterling
Andrew Waight
James Dutkiewicz
David Picton
Global Value Fund - Basic
RRSP Eligible; Inception Year: 2001; Fund Managers:
John Hock
Global Value Fund - Combined
RRSP Eligible; Inception Year: 2001; Fund Managers:
John Hock
Global Value Fund - Full
RRSP Eligible; Inception Year: 2001; Fund Managers:
John Hock
Harbour Fund - Basic
RRSP Eligible; Inception Year: 2001; Fund Managers:
Gerald F. Coleman
Harbour Fund - Combined
RRSP Eligible; Inception Year: 2001; Fund Managers:
Gerald F. Coleman
Harbour Fund - Full
RRSP Eligible; Inception Year: 2001; Fund Managers:
Gerald F. Coleman
Harbour Growth & Income Fund - Basic
RRSP Eligible; Inception Year: 2001; Fund Managers:
Gerald F. Coleman
Harbour Growth & Income Fund - Combined
RRSP Eligible; Inception Year: 2001; Fund Managers:
Gerald F. Coleman
Harbour Growth & Income Fund - Full
RRSP Eligible; Inception Year: 2001; Fund Managers:
Gerald F. Coleman
International Balanced Fund - Basic
RRSP Eligible; Inception Year: 2003; Fund Managers:
Robert Beckwitt
WilliamSterling
International Balanced Fund - Combined
RRSP Eligible; Inception Year: 2003; Fund Managers:
Robert Beckwitt
WilliamSterling
International Balanced Fund - Full
RRSP Eligible; Inception Year: 2003; Fund Managers:
Robert Beckwitt
WilliamSterling
International Fund - Basic
RRSP Eligible; Inception Year: 2003; Fund Managers:
Robert Beckwitt
WilliamSterling
International Fund - Combined
RRSP Eligible; Inception Year: 2003; Fund Managers:
Robert Beckwitt
WilliamSterling
International Fund - Full
RRSP Eligible; Inception Year: 2003; Fund Managers:
Robert Beckwitt
WilliamSterling
Money Market Fund - Basic
RRSP Eligible; Inception Year: 2001; Fund Managers:
Benedict Cheng
Money Market Fund - Combined
RRSP Eligible; Inception Year: 2001;
Money Market Fund - Full
RRSP Eligible; Inception Year: 2001; Fund Managers:
Benedict Cheng
Short-Term Bond Fund - Basic
RRSP Eligible; Inception Year: 2001; Fund Managers:
James Dutkiewicz
Short-Term Bond Fund - Combined
RRSP Eligible; Inception Year: 2001; Fund Managers:
James Dutkiewicz
Short-Term Bond Fund - Full
RRSP Eligible; Inception Year: 2001; Fund Managers:
James Dutkiewicz
Signature Canadian Balanced Fund - Basic
RRSP Eligible; Inception Year: 2001; Fund Managers:
Eric Bushell
Signature Canadian Balanced Fund - Combined
RRSP Eligible; Inception Year: 2001; Fund Managers:
Eric Bushell
Signature Canadian Balanced Fund - Full
RRSP Eligible; Inception Year: 2001; Fund Managers:
Eric Bushell
Signature Dividend Fund - Basic
RRSP Eligible; Inception Year: 2003; Fund Managers:
Eric Bushell
Signature Dividend Fund - Combined
RRSP Eligible; Inception Year: 2003; Fund Managers:
Eric Bushell
Signature Dividend Fund - Full
RRSP Eligible; Inception Year: 2001; Fund Managers:
Eric Bushell
Signature High Income Fund - Basic
RRSP Eligible; Inception Year: 2001; Fund Managers:
Eric Bushell
Signature High Income Fund - Combined
RRSP Eligible; Inception Year: 2001; Fund Managers:
Eric Bushell
Signature High Income Fund - Full
RRSP Eligible; Inception Year: 2001; Fund Managers:
Eric Bushell
Signature Select Canadian Fund - Basic
RRSP Eligible; Inception Year: 2001; Fund Managers:
Eric Bushell
Signature Select Canadian Fund - Combined
RRSP Eligible; Inception Year: 2001; Fund Managers:
Eric Bushell
Signature Select Canadian Fund - Full
RRSP Eligible; Inception Year: 2001; Fund Managers:
Eric Bushell
Value Trust Sector Fund - Basic
RRSP Eligible; Inception Year: 2001; Fund Managers:
Bill Miller
Value Trust Sector Fund - Combined
RRSP Eligible; Inception Year: 2001; Fund Managers:
Bill Miller
Value Trust Sector Fund - Full
RRSP Eligible; Inception Year: 2001; Fund Managers:
Bill Miller
World Equity Fund - Basic
RRSP Eligible; Inception Year: 2001; Fund Managers:
John Hock
World Equity Fund - Combined
RRSP Eligible; Inception Year: 2001; Fund Managers:
John Hock
World Equity Fund - Full
RRSP Eligible; Inception Year: 2001; Fund Managers:
John Hock
Canadian Equity Index Fund - Basic
RRSP Eligible; Inception Year: 2001; Fund Managers:
TD Asset Management Inc.
Canadian Equity Index Fund - Combined
RRSP Eligible; Inception Year: 2001; Fund Managers:
TD Asset Management Inc.
Canadian Equity Index Fund - Full
RRSP Eligible; Inception Year: 2001; Fund Managers:
TD Asset Management Inc.
International Value Fund - Combined
RRSP Eligible; Inception Year: 2001; Fund Managers:
John Hock
International Value Fund - Full
RRSP Eligible; Inception Year: 2001; Fund Managers:
John Hock
International Value Fund - Basic
RRSP Eligible; Inception Year: 2001; Fund Managers:
John Hock

SunWise II Fidelity:

Canadian Asset Allocation Fund - Basic
RRSP Eligible; Inception Year: 2001; Fund Managers:
Fidelity Investments Canada Limited
Canadian Asset Allocation Fund - Combined
RRSP Eligible; Inception Year: 2001; Fund Managers:
Fidelity Investments Canada Limited
Canadian Asset Allocation Fund - Full
RRSP Eligible; Inception Year: 2001; Fund Managers:
Fidelity Investments Canada Limited
Global Asset Allocation Fund - Basic
RRSP Eligible; Inception Year: 2001; Fund Managers:
Fidelity Investments Canada Limited
Global Asset Allocation Fund - Combined
RRSP Eligible; Inception Year: 2001; Fund Managers:
Fidelity Investments Canada Limited
Global Asset Allocation Fund - Full
RRSP Eligible; Inception Year: 2001; Fund Managers:
Fidelity Investments Canada Limited
Growth America Fund - Basic
RRSP Eligible; Inception Year: 2001; Fund Managers:
Fidelity Investments Canada Limited
Growth America Fund - Combined
RRSP Eligible; Inception Year: 2001; Fund Managers:
Fidelity Investments Canada Limited
Growth America Fund - Full
RRSP Eligible; Inception Year: 2001; Fund Managers:
Fidelity Investments Canada Limited
International Portfolio Fund - Basic
RRSP Eligible; Inception Year: 2001; Fund Managers:
Fidelity Investments Canada Limited
International Portfolio Fund - Combined
RRSP Eligible; Inception Year: 2001; Fund Managers:
Fidelity Investments Canada Limited
International Portfolio Fund - Full
RRSP Eligible; Inception Year: 2001; Fund Managers:
Fidelity Investments Canada Limited
True North Fund - Basic
RRSP Eligible; Inception Year: 2001; Fund Managers:
Fidelity Investments Canada Limited
True North Fund - Combined
RRSP Eligible; Inception Year: 2001; Fund Managers:
Fidelity Investments Canada Limited
True North Fund - Full
RRSP Eligible; Inception Year: 2001; Fund Managers:
Fidelity Investments Canada Limited

SunWise II Trimark:

Global Balanced Fund - Basic
RRSP Eligible; Inception Year: 2001; Fund Managers:
AIM Trimark Investments
Global Balanced Fund - Combined
RRSP Eligible; Inception Year: 2001; Fund Managers:
AIM Trimark Investments
Global Balanced Fund - Full
RRSP Eligible; Inception Year: 2001; Fund Managers:
AIM Trimark Investments
Income Growth Fund - Basic
RRSP Eligible; Inception Year: 2001; Fund Managers:
AIM Trimark Investments
Income Growth Fund - Combined
RRSP Eligible; Inception Year: 2001; Fund Managers:
AIM Trimark Investments
Income Growth Fund - Full
RRSP Eligible; Inception Year: 2001; Fund Managers:
AIM Trimark Investments
Select Growth Fund - Basic
RRSP Eligible; Inception Year: 2001; Fund Managers:
AIM Trimark Investments
Select Growth Fund - Combined
RRSP Eligible; Inception Year: 2001; Fund Managers:
AIM Trimark Investments
Select Growth Fund - Full
RRSP Eligible; Inception Year: 2001; Fund Managers:
AIM Trimark Investments
US Companies Fund - Basic
RRSP Eligible; Inception Year: 2001; Fund Managers:
AIM Trimark Investments
US Companies Fund - Combined
RRSP Eligible; Inception Year: 2001; Fund Managers:
AIM Trimark Investments
US Companies Fund - Full
RRSP Eligible; Inception Year: 2001; Fund Managers:
AIM Trimark Investments

Synergy:

Canadian Style Management Class Fund
RRSP Eligible; Inception Year: 1997; Fund Managers:
David Picton
KimShannon
Canadian Growth Class Fund
RRSP Eligible; Inception Year: 1997; Fund Managers:
Andrew McCreath
DavidPicton
Tactical Asset Allocation Fund
RRSP Eligible; Inception Year: 1998; Fund Managers:
David Picton
DavidPicton
Kim Shannon
Global Style Management RSP Fund
RRSP Eligible; Inception Year: 1999; Fund Managers:
Michael Mahoney
WilliamSterling
Bill Miller
Global Style Management Sector Fund
RRSP Eligible; Inception Year: 1998; Fund Managers:

CI Mutual Funds (continued)
Michael Mahoney
WilliamSterling
Bill Miller
Extreme Canadian Equity Fund
RRSP Eligible; Inception Year: 2000; Fund Managers:
David Picton
Extreme Global Equity Fund
RRSP Eligible; Inception Year: 2001; Fund Managers:
Michael Mahoney
Global Style Management Sector (US$) Fund
RRSP Eligible; Inception Year: 1998; Fund Managers:
Michael Mahoney
BillMiller
William Sterling
Canadian Corporate Class Insight Fund
RRSP Eligible; Inception Year: 2004; Fund Managers:
David Picton
American Corporate Class Fund
RRSP Eligible; Inception Year: 1992; Fund Managers:
David Picton
American Fund
RRSP Eligible; Inception Year: 1992; Fund Managers:
David Picton
Trident:
Global Opportunities Fund
RRSP Eligible; Inception Year: 2001; Fund Managers:
Nandu Narayanan
Global Opportunites (US$) Fund
RRSP Eligible; Inception Year: 2001; Fund Managers:
Nandu Narayanan
Branches:
Calgary
#1520, 555 - 4th Ave. SW
Calgary, AB T2P 3E7 Canada
403-205-4396
Fax: 403-205-4335
800-776-9027
Halifax
#1705, 1969 Upper Water St.
Halifax, NS B3J 3R7 Canada
902-422-2444
Fax: 902-420-0114
888-246-8887
Montréal
#1820, 630, boul René-Lévesque ouest
Montréal, QC H3B 1S6 Canada
514-875-0090
Fax: 514-875-6919
800-268-1602
Vancouver
#2420, 650 West Georgia St.
Vancouver, BC V6B 4N9 Canada
604-681-3346
Fax: 604-681-3367
800-665-6994

CIBC Asset Management Inc.
#800, 1500, rue University
Montréal, QC H3A 3S6
www.talvest.com
Profile: CM Investment Management & Talvest Fund Management integrated to form CIBC Asset Management.
Executives:
Sonia Baxendale, Chair
Tracy Chenier, Executive Director, Product Development & Management
Ginny Macdonald, Vice-President, Mutual Funds & Managed Solutions
Renaissance:
Canadian Bond Fund
RRSP Eligible; Inception Year: 1984; Fund Managers:
John Braive
Canadian Money Market Fund
RRSP Eligible; Inception Year: 1984; Fund Managers:
Steven Dubrovsky
Canadian T-Bill Fund
RRSP Eligible; Inception Year: 1987; Fund Managers:
Steven Dubrovsky
Canadian Balanced Value Fund
RRSP Eligible; Inception Year: 1999; Fund Managers:
Oppenheimer Asset Management Inc.
Canadian Core Value Fund
RRSP Eligible; Inception Year: 1994; Fund Managers:
Gaelan Morphet
NWQ Investment Management
Canadian Dividend Income Fund
RRSP Eligible; Inception Year: 2002; Fund Managers:
David Graham
GaelanMorphet
David Kunselman
Stephen Caldwell
Canadian Growth Fund
RRSP Eligible; Inception Year: 1985; Fund Managers:
McLean Budden Ltd
Canadian High Yield Bond Fund
RRSP Eligible; Inception Year: 1994; Fund Managers:
John Braive
MarkKanar
Canadian Income Trust Fund - II
RRSP Eligible; Inception Year: 2003; Fund Managers:
Gaelan Morphet
Canadian Income Trust Fund
RRSP Eligible; Inception Year: 1997; Fund Managers:
Gaelan Morphet
Canadian Small Cap Fund
RRSP Eligible; Inception Year: 1996; Fund Managers:
David Graham
Developing Cap Markets Fund
RRSP Eligible; Inception Year: 1996; Fund Managers:
Merrill Lynch Investment Managers, L.P.
Euro Fund
RRSP Eligible; Inception Year: 1993; Fund Managers:
Merrill Lynch Investment Managers, L.P.
Global Technology Fund
RRSP Eligible; Inception Year: 2000; Fund Managers:
Stephen Kahn
Global Growth Fund
RRSP Eligible; Inception Year: 1998; Fund Managers:
Walter Scott & Partners Ltd.
Global Opportunities Fund
RRSP Eligible; Inception Year: 1990; Fund Managers:
Global Value Investment Portfolio Management, PT
Global Sectors Fund
RRSP Eligible; Inception Year: 1999; Fund Managers:
Merrill Lynch Investment Managers, L.P.
International Growth Fund
RRSP Eligible; Inception Year: 1996; Fund Managers:
Walter Scott & Partners Ltd.
International Index Fund
RRSP Eligible; Inception Year: 1996; Fund Managers:
Karl Gauvin
Canadian Real Return Bond Fund
RRSP Eligible; Inception Year: 2003; Fund Managers:
Jacques Prévost
Tactical Allocation Fund
RRSP Eligible; Inception Year: 2000; Fund Managers:
Luc de la Durantaye
US Equity Value Fund
RRSP Eligible; Inception Year: 1998; Fund Managers:
UBS Global Asset Management (Canada) Co.
US Equity Growth Fund
RRSP Eligible; Inception Year: 1985; Fund Managers:
Merrill Lynch Investment Managers, L.P.
US Index Fund
RRSP Eligible; Inception Year: 1996; Fund Managers:
Karl Gauvin
US Money Market (US$) Fund
RRSP Eligible; Inception Year: 1987; Fund Managers:
Steven Dubrovsky
Renaissance Talvest:
China Plus Bond Fund
RRSP Eligible; Inception Year: 2005; Fund Managers:
Peter Chau
Global Health Care Fund
RRSP Eligible; Inception Year: 2005; Fund Managers:
Wellington Management Company
Millennium High Income Fund
RRSP Eligible; Inception Year: 2005; Fund Managers:
Morrison Williams Investment Management Limited
Sequence:
2010 Conservative Portfolio Fund
RRSP Eligible; Inception Year: 2005;
2010 Moderate Portfolio Fund
RRSP Eligible; Inception Year: 2005;
2020 Conservative Portfolio Fund
RRSP Eligible; Inception Year: 2005;
2020 Moderate Portfolio Fund
RRSP Eligible; Inception Year: 2005;
2030 Conservative Portfolio Fund
RRSP Eligible; Inception Year: 2005;
2030 Moderate Portfolio Fund
RRSP Eligible; Inception Year: 2005;
2040 Conservative Portofolio Fund
RRSP Eligible; Inception Year: 2005;
2040 Moderate Portfolio Fund
RRSP Eligible; Inception Year: 2005;
Income Portfolio Fund
RRSP Eligible; Inception Year: 2005;
Talvest:
Canadian Asset Allocation Class A Fund
RRSP Eligible; Inception Year: 1986; Fund Managers:
Gaelan Morphet
Bond Class A Fund
RRSP Eligible; Inception Year: 1973; Fund Managers:
John Braive
JefferyWaldman
High Yield Bond Class A Fund
RRSP Eligible; Inception Year: 1996; Fund Managers:
Mark Kanar
Income Class A Fund
RRSP Eligible; Inception Year: 1974; Fund Managers:
Jeffery Waldman
Money Market Class A Fund
RRSP Eligible; Inception Year: 1987; Fund Managers:
Steven Dubrovsky
Canadian Equity Growth Class A Fund
RRSP Eligible; Inception Year: 1997; Fund Managers:
Connor, Clark & Lunn Investment Management Ltd
Canadian Equity Value Class A Fund
RRSP Eligible; Inception Year: 1973; Fund Managers:
Gaelan Morphet
Canadian Multi Management Class A Fund
RRSP Eligible; Inception Year: 2000; Fund Managers:
David Graham
Dividend Class A Fund
RRSP Eligible; Inception Year: 1995; Fund Managers:
Gaelan Morphet
Millennium High Income Class A Fund
RRSP Eligible; Inception Year: 1997; Fund Managers:
Morrison Williams Investment Management Limited
Millennium Next Generation Class A Fund
RRSP Eligible; Inception Year: 1993; Fund Managers:
Morrison Williams Investment Management Limited
Small Cap Canadian Equity Class A Fund
RRSP Eligible; Inception Year: 1994; Fund Managers:
David Graham
Asian Fund
RRSP Eligible; Inception Year: 1990; Fund Managers:
Peter Chau
China Plus Class A Fund
RRSP Eligible; Inception Year: 1998; Fund Managers:
Peter Chau
European Class A Fund
RRSP Eligible; Inception Year: 1990; Fund Managers:
Shaun Hegarty
IanScullion
Global Asset Allocation Class A Fund
RRSP Eligible; Inception Year: 1987;
Global Bond Fund
RRSP Eligible; Inception Year: 1992; Fund Managers:
Jean Charbonneau
Global Equity Class A Fund
RRSP Eligible; Inception Year: 1998; Fund Managers:
NWQ Investment Management
Global Health Care Class A Fund
RRSP Eligible; Inception Year: 1996; Fund Managers:
Wellington Management Company
Global Markets Class A Fund
RRSP Eligible; Inception Year: 1993; Fund Managers:
Luc de la Durantaye
Global Multi Management Class A Fund
RRSP Eligible; Inception Year: 2000; Fund Managers:
Stephen Kahn
Global Resource Class A Fund
RRSP Eligible; Inception Year: 2002; Fund Managers:
KBSH Capital Management Inc.
Global Science & Technology Class A Fund
RRSP Eligible; Inception Year: 1996; Fund Managers:
Stephen Kahn
Global Science & Technology Class A (US$) Fund
RRSP Eligible; Inception Year: 1996; Fund Managers:
Stephen Kahn
Global Small Cap Class A Fund
RRSP Eligible; Inception Year: 1998; Fund Managers:
Wellington Management Company

International Equity Class A Fund
RRSP Eligible; Inception Year: 2001; Fund Managers:
GE Asset Management Ltd.
US Equity Fund
RRSP Eligible; Inception Year: 1991; Fund Managers:
UBS Global Asset Management (Canada) Co.
US Equity Class A (US$) Fund
RRSP Eligible; Inception Year: 1991; Fund Managers:
UBS Global Asset Management (Canada) Co.
Talvest AXIS:
Investment Series I Fund
RRSP Eligible; Inception Year: 2002;
Investment Series II Fund
RRSP Eligible; Inception Year: 2002;
Talvest CMDF:
Canadian Medical Discoveries II Fund
RRSP Eligible; Inception Year: 2002; Fund Managers:
Medical Discovery Management Corporation
Canadian Medical Discoveries Fund
RRSP Eligible; Inception Year: 1994; Fund Managers:
Medical Discovery Management Corporation
Talvest Renaissance:
Canadian Balanced Value Class A Fund
RRSP Eligible; Inception Year: 2005; Fund Managers:
Gaelan Morphet
JefferyWaldman
Canadian Real Return Bond Class A Fund
RRSP Eligible; Inception Year: 2005; Fund Managers:
Jacques Prévost
Canadian Core Value Class A Fund
RRSP Eligible; Inception Year: 2005; Fund Managers:
Gaelan Morphet
US Basic Value Fund
RRSP Eligible; Inception Year: 2005; Fund Managers:
UBS Global Asset Management (Canada) Co.
Branches:
Calgary - Prairies
East Tower, Bankers Hall
#740, 855 2nd St. SW
Calgary, AB T2P 4J7 Canada
Fax: 403-571-8024
Toronto - Ontario & Maritimes
#1402, 20 Bay St.
Toronto, ON M5J 2N8 Canada
Vancouver - British Columbia
Oceanic Plaza
#2600, 1066 West Hastings St.
Vancouver, BC V6E 3X1 Canada
Fax: 604-689-8306

CIBC Securities Inc.

800 Bay St., 5th Fl.
Toronto, ON M5S 3A9
416-980-3863
Fax: 416-351-4282
800-465-3863
www.cibc.com/ca/mutual-funds
Executives:
Ted Cadsby, President/CEO
CIBC:
Latin American Fund
RRSP Eligible; Inception Year: 1996; Fund Managers:
Boston Company Asset Management
Canadian Resources Fund
RRSP Eligible; Inception Year: 1995; Fund Managers:
Front Street Capital
Canadian T-Bill Fund
RRSP Eligible; Inception Year: 1990; Fund Managers:
CIBC Global Asset Management Inc.
Capital Appreciation Fund
RRSP Eligible; Inception Year: 1991; Fund Managers:
CIBC Global Asset Management Inc.
Emerging Economies Fund
RRSP Eligible; Inception Year: 1995; Fund Managers:
Boston Company Asset Management
Far East Prosperity Fund
RRSP Eligible; Inception Year: 1993; Fund Managers:
TAL CEF Global Asset Management Ltd.
Global Bond Fund
RRSP Eligible; Inception Year: 1994; Fund Managers:
CIBC Global Asset Management Inc.
Global Equity Fund
RRSP Eligible; Inception Year: 1988; Fund Managers:
CIBC Global Asset Management Inc.
Global Technology Fund
RRSP Eligible; Inception Year: 1995; Fund Managers:
CIBC Global Asset Management Inc.
Japanese Equity Fund
RRSP Eligible; Inception Year: 1995; Fund Managers:
TAL CEF Global Asset Management Ltd.
Money Market Fund
RRSP Eligible; Inception Year: 1988; Fund Managers:
CIBC Global Asset Management Inc.
Premium Canadian T-Bill Fund
RRSP Eligible; Inception Year: 1990; Fund Managers:
CIBC Global Asset Management Inc.
US Dollar Money Market Fund
RRSP Eligible; Inception Year: 1991; Fund Managers:
CIBC Global Asset Management Inc.
Canadian Short-Term Bond Index Fund
RRSP Eligible; Inception Year: 1993; Fund Managers:
CIBC Global Asset Management Inc.
Dividend Fund
RRSP Eligible; Inception Year: 1991; Fund Managers:
CIBC Global Asset Management Inc.
Canadian Index Fund
RRSP Eligible; Inception Year: 1996; Fund Managers:
CIBC Global Asset Management Inc.
US Index RRSP Fund
RRSP Eligible; Inception Year: 1996; Fund Managers:
CIBC Global Asset Management Inc.
International Index RRSP Fund
RRSP Eligible; Inception Year: 1996; Fund Managers:
CIBC Global Asset Management Inc.
North American Demographics Fund
RRSP Eligible; Inception Year: 1996; Fund Managers:
CIBC Global Asset Management Inc.
European Equity Fund
RRSP Eligible; Inception Year: 1995; Fund Managers:
CIBC Global Asset Management Inc.
Energy Fund
RRSP Eligible; Inception Year: 1996; Fund Managers:
Front Street Capital
Precious Metals Fund
RRSP Eligible; Inception Year: 1996; Fund Managers:
Front Street Capital
Financial Companies Fund
RRSP Eligible; Inception Year: 1997; Fund Managers:
CIBC Global Asset Management Inc.
Global Bond Index Fund
RRSP Eligible; Inception Year: 1998; Fund Managers:
CIBC Global Asset Management Inc.
Canadian Bond Index Fund
RRSP Eligible; Inception Year: 1997; Fund Managers:
CIBC Global Asset Management Inc.
Core Canadian Equity Fund
RRSP Eligible; Inception Year: 1988; Fund Managers:
CIBC Global Asset Management Inc.
International Index Fund
RRSP Eligible; Inception Year: 1998; Fund Managers:
CIBC Global Asset Management Inc.
Canadian Real Estate Fund
RRSP Eligible; Inception Year: 1997; Fund Managers:
Moreguard Financial Corp.
US Small Companies Fund
RRSP Eligible; Inception Year: 1995; Fund Managers:
Wellington Management Co.
International Small Companies Fund
RRSP Eligible; Inception Year: 1997; Fund Managers:
Pictet International Management
US Equity Index Fund
RRSP Eligible; Inception Year: 1991; Fund Managers:
CIBC Global Asset Management Inc.
Canadian Emerging Companies Fund
RRSP Eligible; Inception Year: 1997; Fund Managers:
Howson Tattersall Investment Counsel Ltd.
Canadian Imperial Equity Fund
RRSP Eligible; Inception Year: 1997; Fund Managers:
CIBC Global Asset Management Inc.
Japanese Index RRSP Fund
RRSP Eligible; Inception Year: 1999; Fund Managers:
CIBC Global Asset Management Inc.
Monthly Income Fund
RRSP Eligible; Inception Year: 1998; Fund Managers:
CIBC Global Asset Management Inc.
NASDAQ Index RRSP Fund
RRSP Eligible; Inception Year: 1999; Fund Managers:
CIBC Global Asset Management Inc.
Canadian Small Companies Fund
RRSP Eligible; Inception Year: 1997; Fund Managers:
CIBC Global Asset Management Inc.
European Index Fund
RRSP Eligible; Inception Year: 1998; Fund Managers:
CIBC Global Asset Management Inc.
European Index RRSP Fund
RRSP Eligible; Inception Year: 1999; Fund Managers:
CIBC Global Asset Management Inc.
Asia Pacific Index Fund
RRSP Eligible; Inception Year: 2000; Fund Managers:
CIBC Global Asset Management Inc.
Canadian Bond Fund
RRSP Eligible; Inception Year: 1987; Fund Managers:
CIBC Global Asset Management Inc.
Emerging Markets Index Fund
RRSP Eligible; Inception Year: 2000; Fund Managers:
CIBC Global Asset Management Inc.
NASDAQ Index Fund
RRSP Eligible; Inception Year: 2000; Fund Managers:
CIBC Global Asset Management Inc.
Balanced Fund
RRSP Eligible; Inception Year: 1987; Fund Managers:
CIBC Global Asset Management Inc.
Managed Aggressive Growth RRSP Portfolio Fund
RRSP Eligible; Inception Year: 2002; Fund Managers:
CIBC Global Asset Management Inc.
Managed Aggressive Growth Portfolio Fund
RRSP Eligible; Inception Year: 2002; Fund Managers:
CIBC Global Asset Management Inc.
Managed Balanced Growth Portfolio Fund
RRSP Eligible; Inception Year: 2002; Fund Managers:
CIBC Global Asset Management Inc.
Managed Balanced Growth RRSP Portfolio Fund
RRSP Eligible; Inception Year: 2002; Fund Managers:
CIBC Global Asset Management Inc.
Managed Growth Portfolio Fund
RRSP Eligible; Inception Year: 2002; Fund Managers:
CIBC Global Asset Management Inc.
Managed Growth RRSP Portfolio Fund
RRSP Eligible; Inception Year: 2002; Fund Managers:
CIBC Global Asset Management Inc.
Managed Income Plus Portfolio Fund
RRSP Eligible; Inception Year: 2002; Fund Managers:
CIBC Global Asset Management Inc.
Managed Income Portfolio Fund
RRSP Eligible; Inception Year: 2002; Fund Managers:
CIBC Global Asset Management Inc.
Global Technology (US$) Fund
RRSP Eligible; Inception Year: 2002; Fund Managers:
CIBC Global Asset Management Inc.
North American Demographics (US$) Fund
RRSP Eligible; Inception Year: 2002; Fund Managers:
CIBC Global Asset Management Inc.
NASDAQ Index (US$) Fund
RRSP Eligible; Inception Year: 2002; Fund Managers:
CIBC Global Asset Management Inc.
US Small Companies (US$) Fund
RRSP Eligible; Inception Year: 2002; Fund Managers:
Wellington Management Co.
US Equity Index (US$) Fund
RRSP Eligible; Inception Year: 2002; Fund Managers:
CIBC Global Asset Management Inc.
Managed Balanced Portfolio (US$)
RRSP Eligible; Inception Year: 2002; Fund Managers:
CIBC Global Asset Management Inc.
Managed Balanced Portfolio Fund
RRSP Eligible; Inception Year: 2002; Fund Managers:
CIBC Global Asset Management Inc.
Managed Growth Portfolio (US$)
RRSP Eligible; Inception Year: 2002; Fund Managers:
CIBC Global Asset Management Inc.
Managed Income Portfolio (US$)
RRSP Eligible; Inception Year: 2002; Fund Managers:
CIBC Global Asset Management Inc.
Mortgage & Short-Term Income Fund
RRSP Eligible; Inception Year: 1977; Fund Managers:
CIBC Global Asset Management Inc.
Diversified Income Fund
RRSP Eligible; Inception Year: 2005; Fund Managers:
CIBC Global Asset Management Inc.
Balanced Index Fund
RRSP Eligible; Inception Year: 1998; Fund Managers:
CIBC Global Asset Management Inc.

ClaringtonFunds Inc.

#1010, 181 University Ave.
Toronto, ON M5H 3M7
416-860-9880
Fax: 416-860-9884
888-860-9888
funds@clarington.ca
www.claringtonfunds.com
Also Known As: IA Clarington
Ownership: Wholly owned subsidiary of Clarington Corp. Indirect subsidiary of Industrial Alliance Insurance & Financial Services Inc., Québec
Year Founded: 1995
Assets: $1-10 billion
Revenues: $10-50 million
Profile: Clarington has offices located in Vancouver, Toronto, Ottawa & Montréal. Individual sales representatives are situated in the following cities: Calgary, Edmonton, Saskatoon, Winnipeg, Halifax & Saint John.

Executives:
Adrian Brouwers, President/CEO
Salvatore Tino, Exec. Vice-President/CFO
Mary Joyce Empensando, Vice-President, Operations & Compliance, Chief Compliance Officer
Gavin Foo, Vice-President, Finance
Eric Frape, Vice-President, Product Management
Suzanne Grimble, Vice-President, Corporate Development, Secretary
Directors:
Terence Stone, Chair
Adrian Brouwers
Michael J. Hayes
F. David D. Scott
Onofrio Sinopoli
Donald O. Wood
Clarington:
Canadian Balanced Fund
RRSP Eligible; Inception Year: 1996; Fund Managers: SEAMARK Asset Management Ltd.
Canadian Equity Fund
RRSP Eligible; Inception Year: 1996; Fund Managers: SEAMARK Asset Management Ltd.
Canadian Income Fund
RRSP Eligible; Inception Year: 1996; Fund Managers: SEAMARK Asset Management Ltd.
Money Market Fund
RRSP Eligible; Inception Year: 1996; Fund Managers: SEAMARK Asset Management Ltd.
Global Equity Fund
RRSP Eligible; Inception Year: 1998; Fund Managers: OppenheimerFunds, Inc.
Canadian Bond Fund Series B
RRSP Eligible; Inception Year: 1999; Fund Managers: SEAMARK Asset Management Ltd.
Canadian Dividend Fund
RRSP Eligible; Inception Year: 1999; Fund Managers: SEAMARK Asset Management Ltd.
Canadian Small Cap Fund
RRSP Eligible; Inception Year: 1997; Fund Managers: QVGD Investors Inc.
Global Small Cap Fund
RRSP Eligible; Inception Year: 1996; Fund Managers: Evergreen Investment Management Co., LLC
Navellier US All Cap (US$) Fund
RRSP Eligible; Inception Year: 2000; Fund Managers: Navellier & Associates, Inc.
Global Equity Class Fund
RRSP Eligible; Inception Year: 2000; Fund Managers: OppenheimerFunds, Inc.
Short-Term Income Class Fund
RRSP Eligible; Inception Year: 2000; Fund Managers: SEAMARK Asset Management Ltd.
Global Income Fund
RRSP Eligible; Inception Year: 2001; Fund Managers: SEAMARK Asset Management Ltd.
Core Portfolio Fund
RRSP Eligible; Inception Year: 2002; Fund Managers: QVGD Investors Inc.
Canadian Bond Fund Series A
RRSP Eligible; Inception Year: 2003; Fund Managers: SEAMARK Asset Management Ltd.
Canadian Income Fund II Series A-H
RRSP Eligible; Inception Year: 2002; Fund Managers: SEAMARK Asset Management Ltd.
Canadian Income Fund II Series A-L
RRSP Eligible; Inception Year: 2002; Fund Managers: SEAMARK Asset Management Ltd.
Diversified Income Fund
RRSP Eligible; Inception Year: 2003; Fund Managers: KBSH Capital Management Inc.
Income Trust Fund
RRSP Eligible; Inception Year: 2003; Fund Managers: KBSH Capital Management Inc.
Canadian Equity Class Fund
RRSP Eligible; Inception Year: 2000; Fund Managers: SEAMARK Asset Management Ltd.
Canadian Value Fund
RRSP Eligible; Inception Year: 2002; Fund Managers: Beutel, Goodman & Company Limited
Navellier US All Cap Fund
RRSP Eligible; Inception Year: 2000; Fund Managers: Navellier & Associates, Inc.
Global Income (US$) Fund
RRSP Eligible; Inception Year: 2001; Fund Managers: SEAMARK Asset Management Ltd.
Canadian Growth & Income A Fund
RRSP Eligible; Inception Year: 2004; Fund Managers: Jarislowsky, Fraser Limited
US Dividend Fund
RRSP Eligible; Inception Year: 2004; Fund Managers: TCW Investment Management Company
US Dividend (US$) Fund
RRSP Eligible; Inception Year: 2000; Fund Managers: TCW Investment Management Company
Global Equity (US$) Fund
RRSP Eligible; Inception Year: 1998; Fund Managers: OppenheimerFunds, Inc.
Canadian Resources Class Fund
RRSP Eligible; Inception Year: 2005; Fund Managers: KBSH Capital Management Inc.
Target Click 2010 Fund
RRSP Eligible; Inception Year: 2005; Fund Managers: ABN AMRO Asset Management Canada Limited
Target Click 2015 Fund
RRSP Eligible; Inception Year: 2005; Fund Managers: ABN AMRO Asset Management Canada Limited
Target Click 2020 Fund
RRSP Eligible; Inception Year: 2005; Fund Managers: ABN AMRO Asset Management Canada Limited
Target Click 2025 Fund
RRSP Eligible; Inception Year: 2005; Fund Managers: ABN AMRO Asset Management Canada Limited
Branches:
Toronto - Client & Dealer Services
c/o International Financial Data Services (Canada)
#1, 30 Adelaide St. East
Toronto, ON M5C 3G9 Canada
800-530-0204

Co-operators Life Insurance Company

Also listed under: *Federal & Provincial*
1920 College Ave.
Regina, SK S4P 1C4
306-347-6200
Fax: 306-347-6806
800-604-0050
www.cooperators.ca
Ownership: Public. The Cooperators Group Limited
Year Founded: 1945
Number of Employees: 880
Assets: $1-10 billion Year End: 20041231
Revenues: $500m-1 billion Year End: 20041231
Profile: Services also include wealth management & travel insurance. Other affiliated companies include the following: Co-operators Financial Services Limited, HB Group Insurance Management Limited, COSECO Insurance Company, Co-operators Investment Counselling Limited, Co-operators Development Corporation Limited, Federated Agencies Limited, L'Union canadienne Compagnie d'Assurances, Trent Health Insurance Company & TIC Travel Insurance Coordinators Ltd.

Executives:
Katherine Bardswick, President/CEO; 519-824-4400
Kevin Daniel, CFO, Treasurer
Dan Thornton, Chief Operating Officer; 306-347-6218
Randy Grimsrud, Vice-President, Group Insurance; 306-347-6458
David Hartman, Vice-President, Wealth Management; 519-767-3065
Garry Herback, Vice-President, Individual Insurance; 306-347-6270
Frank Lowery, Vice-President, General Counsel & Corporate Secretary; 519-824-4400
Terry MacDonald, Vice-President, Corporate Services; 306-347-6452
Bryan Sigurdson, Vice-President & Chief Actuary; 306-347-6650
Ruth Simons, Vice-President, Travel; 604-986-4292
Rein Tabur, Vice-President, Investments; 306-347-6221
Mary Turtle, Vice-President, Finance; 306-347-6578
Chuck Wilson, Vice-President & General Counsel; 306-347-6523
Linda Yeo, Vice-President, Information Systems; 306-347-6796
Directors:
Peter Podovinikoff, Chair; 604-501-4111
Johanna Bates; 403-282-7370
Karl Baumgardner; 306-843-8807
Christine Brodie; 604-816-9491
Bill Dobson; 780-745-2442
Connie Doucette; 902-569-2901
Ron Koppmann; 613-475-4221
John Lamb; 780-496-3732
Wayne Lee; 705-759-2958
Richard Lemoing; 204-874-2177
Sheena Lucas; 613-731-9059
Jim MacConnell; 902-485-8023
Wayne McLeod; 204-729-8852
Gilles Menard; 506-854-7902
Leonard Mortson; 705-487-2321
Terry Otto; 613-821-1428
Andre Perras; 306-424-2832
Donna Stewardson; 519-786-5469
Alexandra Wilson; 613-230-2201
Co-operators:
Balanced VA Fund
RRSP Eligible; Inception Year: 1992; Fund Managers: James F. MacDonald
Canadian Equity VP Fund
RRSP Eligible; Inception Year: 2003; Fund Managers: James M. Blake
Fixed Income VA Fund
RRSP Eligible; Inception Year: 1992; Fund Managers: Jim Lorimer
Money Market VA Fund
RRSP Eligible; Inception Year: 1997; Fund Managers: Jim Lorimer
US Diversified VA Fund
RRSP Eligible; Inception Year: 1997; Fund Managers: Bill Siddiqui
Conservative Balanced VA Fund
RRSP Eligible; Inception Year: 2000; Fund Managers: James F. MacDonald
US Growth VA Fund
RRSP Eligible; Inception Year: 2000; Fund Managers: Bill Siddiqui
Canadian Resource VA Fund
RRSP Eligible; Inception Year: 2003;
US Equity VA Fund
RRSP Eligible; Inception Year: 1994; Fund Managers: Bill Siddiqui
Aggressive Balanced VAII Fund
RRSP Eligible; Inception Year: 2000; Fund Managers: James F. MacDonald
Aggressive Balanced VA Fund
RRSP Eligible; Inception Year: 2000; Fund Managers: James F. MacDonald
Aggressive Balanced VP Fund
RRSP Eligible; Inception Year: 2003; Fund Managers: James F. MacDonald
Aggressive Balanced VPNL Fund
RRSP Eligible; Inception Year: 2004; Fund Managers: James F. MacDonald
Aggressive VA Portfolio Fund
RRSP Eligible; Inception Year: 2003; Fund Managers: Fidelity Investments Canada Ltd.
Aggressive VP Portfolio Fund
RRSP Eligible; Inception Year: 2003; Fund Managers: Fidelity Investments Canada Ltd.
Aggressive VAII Portfolio Fund
RRSP Eligible; Inception Year: 2003; Fund Managers: Fidelity Investments Canada Ltd.
Aggressive VPNL Portfolio Fund
RRSP Eligible; Inception Year: 2004; Fund Managers: Fidelity Investments Canada Ltd.

Balanced VAII Fund
RRSP Eligible; Inception Year: 1999; Fund Managers:
James F. MacDonald
Balanced VP Fund
RRSP Eligible; Inception Year: 2003; Fund Managers:
James F. MacDonald
Balanced VPNL Fund
RRSP Eligible; Inception Year: 2004; Fund Managers:
James F. MacDonald
Canadian Equity VPNL Fund
RRSP Eligible; Inception Year: 2004; Fund Managers:
James M. Blake
Canadian Equity VA Fund
RRSP Eligible; Inception Year: 1992; Fund Managers:
James M. Blake
Canadian Equity VAII Fund
RRSP Eligible; Inception Year: 1999; Fund Managers:
James M. Blake
Canadian Resource VAII Fund
RRSP Eligible; Inception Year: 2003;
Canadian Resource VP Fund
RRSP Eligible; Inception Year: 2003;
Canadian Resource VPNL Fund
RRSP Eligible; Inception Year: 2004;
Conservative Balanced VAII Fund
RRSP Eligible; Inception Year: 2000; Fund Managers:
James F. MacDonald
Conservative Balanced VP Fund
RRSP Eligible; Inception Year: 2003; Fund Managers:
James F. MacDonald
Conservative Balanced VPNL Fund
RRSP Eligible; Inception Year: 2004; Fund Managers:
James F. MacDonald
Conservative VA Portfolio Fund
RRSP Eligible; Inception Year: 2003; Fund Managers:
Fidelity Investments Canada Ltd.
Conservative VP Portfolio Fund
RRSP Eligible; Inception Year: 2003; Fund Managers:
Fidelity Investments Canada Ltd.
Conservative VAII Portfolio Fund
RRSP Eligible; Inception Year: 2003; Fund Managers:
Fidelity Investments Canada Ltd.
Conservative VPNL Portfolio Fund
RRSP Eligible; Inception Year: 2004; Fund Managers:
Fidelity Investments Canada Ltd.
Fixed Income VAII Fund
RRSP Eligible; Inception Year: 1999; Fund Managers:
Jim Lorimer
Fixed Income VP Fund
RRSP Eligible; Inception Year: 2003; Fund Managers:
Jim Lorimer
Fixed Income VPNL Fund
RRSP Eligible; Inception Year: 2004; Fund Managers:
Jim Lorimer
Moderate VA Portfolio Fund
RRSP Eligible; Inception Year: 2003; Fund Managers:
Fidelity Investments Canada Ltd.
Moderate VAII Portfolio Fund
RRSP Eligible; Inception Year: 2003; Fund Managers:
AIM Trimark Investment Management
Moderate VP Portfolio Fund
RRSP Eligible; Inception Year: 2003; Fund Managers:
Fidelity Investments Canada Ltd.
Moderate VPNL Portfolio Fund
RRSP Eligible; Inception Year: 2004; Fund Managers:
AIM Trimark Investment Management
Money Market VAII Fund
RRSP Eligible; Inception Year: 1999; Fund Managers:
Jim Lorimer
Money Market VP Fund
RRSP Eligible; Inception Year: 2003; Fund Managers:
Jim Lorimer
Money Market VPNL Fund
RRSP Eligible; Inception Year: 2004; Fund Managers:
Jim Lorimer
US Growth VAII Fund
RRSP Eligible; Inception Year: 2000; Fund Managers:
Bill Siddiqui
US Growth VP Fund
RRSP Eligible; Inception Year: 2003; Fund Managers:
Bill Siddiqui
US Growth VPNL Fund
RRSP Eligible; Inception Year: 2004; Fund Managers:
Bill Siddiqui
US Diversified VAII Fund
RRSP Eligible; Inception Year: 1999; Fund Managers:
Bill Siddiqui
US Diversified VP Fund
RRSP Eligible; Inception Year: 2003; Fund Managers:
Bill Siddiqui
US Diversified VPNL Fund
RRSP Eligible; Inception Year: 2004; Fund Managers:
Bill Siddiqui
US Equity VAII Fund
RRSP Eligible; Inception Year: 1999; Fund Managers:
Bill Siddiqui
US Equity VP Fund
RRSP Eligible; Inception Year: 2003; Fund Managers:
Bill Siddiqui
US Equity VPNL Fund
RRSP Eligible; Inception Year: 2004; Fund Managers:
Bill Siddiqui
Very Aggressive VA Portfolio Fund
RRSP Eligible; Inception Year: 2003; Fund Managers:
Fidelity Investments Canada Ltd.
Very Aggressive VP Portfolio Fund
RRSP Eligible; Inception Year: 2003; Fund Managers:
AIM Trimark Investment Management
Very Aggressive VPNL Portfolio Fund
RRSP Eligible; Inception Year: 2004; Fund Managers:
Fidelity Investments Canada Ltd.
Very Aggressive VAII Portfolio Fund
RRSP Eligible; Inception Year: 2003; Fund Managers:
AIM Trimark Investment Management
Very Conservative VAII Portfolio Fund
RRSP Eligible; Inception Year: 2003; Fund Managers:
Fidelity Investments Canada Ltd.
Very Conservative VA Portfolio Fund
RRSP Eligible; Inception Year: 2003; Fund Managers:
AIM Trimark Investment Management
Very Conservative VP Portfolio Fund
RRSP Eligible; Inception Year: 2003; Fund Managers:
Fidelity Investments Canada Ltd.
Very Conservative VPNL Portfolio Fund
RRSP Eligible; Inception Year: 2004; Fund Managers:
AIM Trimark Investment Management
Co-operators AIM:
Canadian First Class VA Fund
RRSP Eligible; Inception Year: 2003; Fund Managers:
AIM Capital Management
Canadian First Class VPNL Fund
RRSP Eligible; Inception Year: 2004; Fund Managers:
AIM Capital Management
Canadian First Class VP Fund
RRSP Eligible; Inception Year: 2003; Fund Managers:
AIM Capital Management
Co-operators Fidelity:
Canadian Bond A VA Fund
RRSP Eligible; Inception Year: 2003; Fund Managers:
Fidelity Investments Canada Ltd.
Canadian Bond A VAII Fund
RRSP Eligible; Inception Year: 2003; Fund Managers:
Fidelity Investments Canada Ltd.
Canadian Bond A VPNL Fund
RRSP Eligible; Inception Year: 2004; Fund Managers:
Fidelity Investments Canada Ltd.
Canadian Bond A VP Fund
RRSP Eligible; Inception Year: 2003; Fund Managers:
Fidelity Investments Canada Ltd.
International Portfolio VAII Fund
RRSP Eligible; Inception Year: 2003; Fund Managers:
Fidelity Investments Canada Ltd.
International Portfolio A VA Fund
RRSP Eligible; Inception Year: 2003; Fund Managers:
Fidelity Investments Canada Ltd.
International Portfolio A VP Fund
RRSP Eligible; Inception Year: 2003; Fund Managers:
Fidelity Investments Canada Ltd.
International Portfolio A VPNL Fund
RRSP Eligible; Inception Year: 2004; Fund Managers:
Fidelity Investments Canada Ltd.
True North A VA Fund
RRSP Eligible; Inception Year: 2003; Fund Managers:
Fidelity Investments Canada Ltd.
True North A VAII Fund
RRSP Eligible; Inception Year: 2003; Fund Managers:
Fidelity Investments Canada Ltd.
True North A VP Fund
RRSP Eligible; Inception Year: 2003; Fund Managers:
Fidelity Investments Canada Ltd.
True North A VPNL Fund
RRSP Eligible; Inception Year: 2004; Fund Managers:
Fidelity Investments Canada Ltd.
Co-operators Trimark:
Canadian Bond VPNL Fund
RRSP Eligible; Inception Year: 2004; Fund Managers:
AIM Trimark Investment Management
Canadian Bond VA Fund
RRSP Eligible; Inception Year: 2003; Fund Managers:
AIM Trimark Investment Management
Canadian Bond VP Fund
RRSP Eligible; Inception Year: 2003; Fund Managers:
AIM Trimark Investment Management
Canadian Bond VAII Fund
RRSP Eligible; Inception Year: 2003; Fund Managers:
AIM Trimark Investment Management
Government Income VPNL Fund
RRSP Eligible; Inception Year: 2004; Fund Managers:
AIM Trimark Investment Management
Government Income VA Fund
RRSP Eligible; Inception Year: 2003; Fund Managers:
AIM Trimark Investment Management
Government Income VP Fund
RRSP Eligible; Inception Year: 2003; Fund Managers:
AIM Trimark Investment Management
Government Income VAII Fund
RRSP Eligible; Inception Year: 2003; Fund Managers:
AIM Trimark Investment Management
Select Growth VPNL Fund
RRSP Eligible; Inception Year: 2004; Fund Managers:
AIM Trimark Investment Management
Select Growth VAII Fund
RRSP Eligible; Inception Year: 2003; Fund Managers:
AIM Trimark Investment Management
Select Growth VA Fund
RRSP Eligible; Inception Year: 2003; Fund Managers:
AIM Trimark Investment Management
Select Growth VP Fund
RRSP Eligible; Inception Year: 2003; Fund Managers:
AIM Trimark Investment Management
Co-opertors AIM:
Canadian First Class VAII Fund
RRSP Eligible; Inception Year: 2003; Fund Managers:
AIM Capital Management

Corporation Financière LaSalle inc

7676, rue Édouard
Montréal, QC H8P 1T4
514-365-8000
Fax: 514-365-8006
7676edouard@qc.aira.com
www.fondsplacementlasalle.com
Ownership: Private
Year Founded: 1988
Number of Employees: 3
Revenues: Under $1 million
Executives:
Pascale Houle, President; pascalehoule@qc.aira.com
LaSalle:
Balanced Fund
RRSP Eligible; Inception Year: 1988;
Equity Fund
RRSP Eligible; Inception Year: 0;

Cote 100 Inc.

561, rue Beaumont est
Saint-Bruno, QC J3V 2R2
450-461-2826
Fax: 450-461-2177
800-454-2683
cote100@cote100.com
www.cote100.com
Ownership: Private
Year Founded: 1988
Assets: $50-100 million
Revenues: $1-5 million
Profile: Specializes in portfolio management.

Cote 100:
Excel Fund
RRSP Eligible; Inception Year: 1998; Fund Managers:
Marc L'Ecuyer

INVESTMENT MANAGEMENT

Cote 100 Inc. (continued)
US Fund (US$)
RRSP Eligible; Inception Year: 1996; Fund Managers:
Philippe LeBlanc
GuyLeBlanc
VTA American Equity (US$) Fund
RRSP Eligible; Inception Year: 2000; Fund Managers:
Marc L'Ecuyer
VTA Canadian Equity Fund
RRSP Eligible; Inception Year: 2000; Fund Managers:
Marc L'Ecuyer
Income Fund
RRSP Eligible; Inception Year: 2000; Fund Managers:
Marc L'Ecuyer
Premier Fund
RRSP Eligible; Inception Year: 1992; Fund Managers:
Philippe LeBlanc
GuyLeBlanc
Actions-Crois PME (ACPME) Fund
RRSP Eligible; Inception Year: 1995; Fund Managers:
Guy LeBlanc
PhilippeLeBlanc

Counsel Wealth Management

#700, 2680 Skymark Ave.
Mississauga, ON L4W 5L6
905-625-9885
Fax: 905-625-6184
877-625-9885
info@counselwealth.com
www.counselwealth.com
Ownership: Private.
Year Founded: 1999
Executives:
John Croce, President/CEO
Rana Chauhan, Chief Investment Officer & Strategist
Richard L. Howard, CFO
Ron Belcot, Portfolio Manager
Counsel:
Managed Portfolio Fund
RRSP Eligible; Inception Year: 1999; Fund Managers:
Acuity Investment Management Inc.
Money Market Fund
RRSP Eligible; Inception Year: 2000; Fund Managers:
Cumberland Asset Management
All Equity Portfolio Fund
RRSP Eligible; Inception Year: 2002; Fund Managers:
Epoch Investment Partners
Balanced Portfolio Fund
RRSP Eligible; Inception Year: 2002; Fund Managers:
Marsico Capital Management LLC
Conservative Portfolio Fund
RRSP Eligible; Inception Year: 2002; Fund Managers:
Dreman Value Management, LLC
Growth Portfolio Fund
RRSP Eligible; Inception Year: 2002; Fund Managers:
Epoch Investment Partners
Select Canada Fund
RRSP Eligible; Inception Year: 2001; Fund Managers:
CI Synergy Asset Management
Fixed Income Fund
RRSP Eligible; Inception Year: 2001; Fund Managers:
Acuity Investment Management Inc.
Regular Pay Portfolio Fund
RRSP Eligible; Inception Year: 2004; Fund Managers:
Marsico Capital Management LLC
Select America Fund
RRSP Eligible; Inception Year: 2000; Fund Managers:
Dreman Value Management, LLC
Select International Fund
RRSP Eligible; Inception Year: 2001; Fund Managers:
Brandes Investment Partners
Select Small Cap Fund
RRSP Eligible; Inception Year: 2005; Fund Managers:
Epoch Investment Partners
Counsel Altus:
All Equity Portfolio Fund
RRSP Eligible; Inception Year: 2004; Fund Managers:
Epoch Investment Partners
Balanced Portfolio Fund
RRSP Eligible; Inception Year: 2004; Fund Managers:
Howson Tattersall Investment Counsel
Conservative Portfolio Fund
RRSP Eligible; Inception Year: 2004; Fund Managers:
Brandes Investment Partners
Regular Pay Portfolio Fund
RRSP Eligible; Inception Year: 2004; Fund Managers:
Marsico Capital Management LLC
Growth Portfolio Fund
RRSP Eligible; Inception Year: 2004; Fund Managers:
Epoch Investment Partners
Branches:
Toronto - Client Services
#M111, 150 Bloor St. West
Toronto, ON M5S 3B5 Canada
416-934-7002
Fax: 416-922-5660
877-216-4979

Covington Capital Corp.

PO Box 10
#3003, 200 Front St. West
Toronto, ON M5V 3K2
416-365-0060
Fax: 416-365-9822
info@covingtoncap.com
www.covingtoncap.com, www.triaxcovingtoncap.com
Year Founded: 1994
Profile: One of Canada's largest providers of venture capital investment funds.
Executives:
Lisa Low, CFO
Stephen Campbell, Chartered Accountant, Chartered Business Valuator
Covington:
Covington Fund II
RRSP Eligible; Inception Year: 1999; Fund Managers:
Chip Vallis
Scott D.Clark
Philip R. Reddon
Matthew Hall
Lily Lamb
William Jin
Jim Laird
Jeff G. Park
Strategic Capital Fund
RRSP Eligible; Inception Year: 2004; Fund Managers:
Chip Vallis
Scott D.Clark
Jeff G. Park
Philip R. Reddon
Matthew Hall
Lily Lamb
William Jin
Jim Laird
Financial Industry Opportunities Fund
RRSP Eligible; Inception Year: 2004; Fund Managers:
Scott D. Clark
Jeff G.Park
Philip R. Reddon
Lily Lamb
William Jin
Jim Laird
Matthew Hall
New Generation Biotech (Equity) Fund
RRSP Eligible; Inception Year: 2001; Fund Managers:
Genesys Capital Partners Inc.
Covington Fund I
RRSP Eligible; Inception Year: 1995; Fund Managers:
Chip Vallis
Scott D.Clark
Jeff G. Park
Philip R. Reddon
Matthew Hall
Lily Lamb
William Jin
Jim Laird
Covington Fund II:

RRSP Eligible; Inception Year: 1999;
Covington Venture:
Capital First Venture (Balanced) Fund
RRSP Eligible; Inception Year: 2004; Fund Managers:
Chip Vallis
Scott D.Clark
Jeff G. Park
Philip R. Reddon
Matthew Hall
Lily Lamb
William Jin
Jim Laird
Venture Partners (Balanced) Fund
RRSP Eligible; Inception Year: 2002; Fund Managers:
Chip Vallis
Scott D.Clark
Jeff G. Park
Philip R. Reddon
Matthew Hall
Lily Lamb
William Jin
Jim Laird
Venture Fund
RRSP Eligible; Inception Year: 2005; Fund Managers:
Chip Vallis
Scott D.Clark
Jeff G. Park
Philip R. Reddon
Matthew Hall
Lily Lamb
William Jin
Jim Laird
New Generation Biotech (Balanced) Fund
RRSP Eligible; Inception Year: 2001; Fund Managers:
Chip Vallis
Genesys Capital Partners Inc.
New Millennium Venture (Balanced) Fund
RRSP Eligible; Inception Year: 2000; Fund Managers:
Chip Vallis
JimLaird
Branches:
Toronto - Sales & Marketing
c/o Covington Group of Funds Inc.
#1400, 70 York St.
Toronto, ON M5J 1S9 Canada
416-365-9155
Fax: 416-362-2199
866-244-4714
Chris Guthrie, Contact

Creststreet Asset Management Ltd.

Also listed under: *Financial Planning*
#1450, 70 University Ave.
Toronto, ON M5J 2M4
416-864-6330
Fax: 416-862-8950
866-864-6330
info@creststreet.com
www.creststreet.com
Ownership: Public.
Year Founded: 2000
Stock Symbol: CRS.UN
Profile: Affiliated companies include the following: Creststreet Mutual Funds Limited, Creststreet Power & Income Fund LP, Creststreet Energy Hedge Fund LP, Creststreet 2004 Limited Partnership & Creststreet 2005 Limited Partnership.
Executives:
Eric McFadden, Managing Director
Erich Ossowski, Vice-President, Wind Power
Donna Shea, Vice-President, Finance
Sheryl J. Chiddenton, Manager, Investment Services
Aaron C.B. Maybin, Associate
Creststreet:
Resource Fund
RRSP Eligible; Inception Year: 2002; Fund Managers:
Robert J. Toole
Managed Income Fund
RRSP Eligible; Inception Year: 2004; Fund Managers:
Robert J. Toole
Managed Equity Index Fund
RRSP Eligible; Inception Year: 2004; Fund Managers:
Robert J. Toole
Branches:
Calgary
#1040, 444 - 5th Ave. SW
Calgary, AB T2P 2T9 Canada
403-215-2265
Fax: 403-261- 443

CTI Mutual Funds

#1635, 1, Place Ville-Marie
Montréal, QC H3B 2B6
514-861-3500
Fax: 514-861-3230
800-668-3500

cticapital@cticap.com
www.cticap.com
Profile: Part of CTI Capital, CTI Mutual Funds focuses on asset management. CTI stands for Concept Techniques institutionnelles.

Executives:
Viêt Buu, President/CEO
Robert Lacroix, Sr. Vice-President
Louis Pellerin, Contact, Mutual Funds, Conception & Implementation
CTI:
Canadian Equity Fund
RRSP Eligible; Inception Year: 1998;

Desjardins Financial Security/ Desjardins Sécurité financière

Also listed under: *Federal & Provincial*
200, av des Commandeurs
Lévis, QC G6V 6R2
418-838-7800
Fax: 418-838-7463
info@desjardinssecuritefinanciere.com
www.dsf-dfs.com
Former Name: Imperial Life Financial
Ownership: Private.
Assets: $10-100 billion Year End: 20061023
Revenues: $1-10 billion Year End: 20061023
Profile: Offers a broad spectrum of tailor-made life and health insurance and retirement savings products and services, through employees and partners committed to ensuring the satisfaction of its customers and caisse members.

Executives:
Richard Fortier, President/COO
Denis Berthiaume, Sr. Vice-President, Individual Insurance
Constance Lemieux, Sr. Vice-President, E-Business & Technology
Alain Thauvette, Sr. Vice-President, Group & Business Insurance
Monique Tremblay, Sr. Vice-President, Savings & Segregated Funds
Louise Turgeon, Sr. Vice-President, AssurFinance for Institutions, AssurDirect & Desjardins Relations
Gérard Guilbault, Chief Investment Officer
Directors:
Sylvie St-Pierre Babin, Chair
Serge Cloutier
Pierre Gingras
Serge Hamelin
Monique Lefebvre
Denis Levesque
Suzanne Maisonneuve-Benoit
Ursula Menke
Jocelyn Nadeau
Michel Rouleau
Michel Rouleau
Jacques Sylvestre
Affiliated Companies:
Gestion SFL inc.
Sigma Assistel Inc.
DFS Pooled:
Trimark Canadian Fund
RRSP Eligible; Inception Year: 1997; Fund Managers: AIM Trimark Investments
McLean Budden Balanced Growth Fund
RRSP Eligible; Inception Year: 1994; Fund Managers: McLean Budden Limited
McLean Budden Canadian Equity Growth Fund
RRSP Eligible; Inception Year: 1997; Fund Managers: McLean Budden Limited
McLean Budden Canadian Fixed Income Fund
RRSP Eligible; Inception Year: 1997; Fund Managers: McLean Budden Limited
Fiera Conservative Diversified Fund
RRSP Eligible; Inception Year: 1973; Fund Managers: Fiera Capital Management
Fiera Enhanced Mortgage Fund
RRSP Eligible; Inception Year: 1968; Fund Managers: Fiera Capital Management
Trimark Fund
RRSP Eligible; Inception Year: 1997; Fund Managers: AIM Trimark Investments
Fiera Canadian Equity GARP Fund
RRSP Eligible; Inception Year: 1961; Fund Managers: Fiera Capital Management
Fiera Global Balanced Fund
RRSP Eligible; Inception Year: 1999; Fund Managers: Fiera Capital Management
Trimark Income Growth Fund
RRSP Eligible; Inception Year: 1997; Fund Managers: AIM Trimark Investments
McLean Budden Global Equity Fund
RRSP Eligible; Inception Year: 1997; Fund Managers: McLean Budden Limited
Bissett Canadian Equity Fund
RRSP Eligible; Inception Year: 1999; Fund Managers: Bissett Investment Management
Fiera Money Market Fund
RRSP Eligible; Inception Year: 1981; Fund Managers: Fiera Capital Management
Fiera North American Small Company Fund
RRSP Eligible; Inception Year: 1999; Fund Managers: Fiera Capital Management
Bissett Small Cap Fund
RRSP Eligible; Inception Year: 1999; Fund Managers: Bissett Investment Management
Fiera Bond Fund
RRSP Eligible; Inception Year: 1961; Fund Managers: Fiera Capital Management
Fiera US Index Plus Fund
RRSP Eligible; Inception Year: 1997; Fund Managers: Fiera Capital Management
Aggressive Portfolio Fund
RRSP Eligible; Inception Year: 2002;
Balanced Portfolio Fund
RRSP Eligible; Inception Year: 2002;
Conservative Portfolio Fund
RRSP Eligible; Inception Year: 2002;
Dynamic Portfolio Fund
RRSP Eligible; Inception Year: 2002;
Energetic Portfolio Fund
RRSP Eligible; Inception Year: 2002;
Security Portfolio Fund
RRSP Eligible; Inception Year: 2002;
Jarislowsky Fraser Balanced Fund
RRSP Eligible; Inception Year: 2002; Fund Managers: Jarislowsky Fraser Ltd.
McLean Budden American Equity Fund
RRSP Eligible; Inception Year: 2002; Fund Managers: McLean Budden Limited
Templeton International Stock Fund
RRSP Eligible; Inception Year: 2002; Fund Managers: Franklin Templeton Investments
Mackenzie Cundill Canadian Security Portfolio Fund
RRSP Eligible; Inception Year: 1997; Fund Managers: Mackenzie Financial Corp.
Barclays Universe Bond Index Fund
RRSP Eligible; Inception Year: 2003; Fund Managers: Barclays Global Investors Canada Ltd.
Barclays EAFE Equity Index Fund
RRSP Eligible; Inception Year: 2004; Fund Managers: Barclays Global Investors Canada Ltd.
Barclays S&P/TSX Composite Index Fund
RRSP Eligible; Inception Year: 2003; Fund Managers: Barclays Global Investors Canada Ltd.
Barclays Active Canadian Equity Fund
RRSP Eligible; Inception Year: 2003; Fund Managers: Barclays Global Investors Canada Ltd.
New Star EAFE Fund
RRSP Eligible; Inception Year: 2004; Fund Managers: New Star Asset Management Limited
Addenda Canadian Bond Fund
RRSP Eligible; Inception Year: 2004; Fund Managers: Addenda Capital Inc.
GE Asset Management International Equity Fund
RRSP Eligible; Inception Year: 2004; Fund Managers: GE Asset Management
Jarislowsky Fraser Canadian Equity Fund
RRSP Eligible; Inception Year: 2003; Fund Managers: Jarislowsky Fraser Ltd.
Fiera Long Term Government Bond Fund
RRSP Eligible; Inception Year: 2003; Fund Managers: Fiera Capital Management
Fidelity Canadian Balanced Fund
RRSP Eligible; Inception Year: 2003;
Bernstein Canadian Value Equity Fund
RRSP Eligible; Inception Year: 2003; Fund Managers: Bernstein Management Inc.
Bernstein US Equity Value Fund
RRSP Eligible; Inception Year: 2003; Fund Managers: Bernstein Management Inc.
UBS Large Cap Equity Fund
RRSP Eligible; Inception Year: 2004; Fund Managers: UBS Global Asset Management (Canada) Co.
Fiera Canadian Equity Dividend Fund
RRSP Eligible; Inception Year: 2004; Fund Managers: Fiera Capital Management
Bernstein International Equity Fund
RRSP Eligible; Inception Year: 1996; Fund Managers: Bernstein Management Inc.
Canadian Growth Fund
RRSP Eligible; Inception Year: 2002; Fund Managers: McLean Budden Limited
Imperial Growth:
North American Equity Fund
RRSP Eligible; Inception Year: 1969; Fund Managers: Elantis
Canadian Equity Fund
RRSP Eligible; Inception Year: 1977; Fund Managers: Elantis
Diversified Fund
RRSP Eligible; Inception Year: 1988; Fund Managers: Elantis
Money Market Fund
RRSP Eligible; Inception Year: 1988; Fund Managers: Elantis
Millennia III:
Canadian Dividend 4 Fund
RRSP Eligible; Inception Year: 1998; Fund Managers: Fiera Capital Management
Income 1 Fund
RRSP Eligible; Inception Year: 1995; Fund Managers: Fiera Capital Management
Income 2 Fund
RRSP Eligible; Inception Year: 1995; Fund Managers: Fiera Capital Management
Income 3 Fund
RRSP Eligible; Inception Year: 1998; Fund Managers: Fiera Capital Management
Income 4 Fund
RRSP Eligible; Inception Year: 1998; Fund Managers: Fiera Capital Management
International Equity 1 Fund
RRSP Eligible; Inception Year: 1995; Fund Managers: Fiera Capital Management
International Equity 2 Fund
RRSP Eligible; Inception Year: 1995; Fund Managers: Fiera Capital Management
International Equity 3 Fund
RRSP Eligible; Inception Year: 1998; Fund Managers: Fiera Capital Management
International Equity 4 Fund
RRSP Eligible; Inception Year: 1998; Fund Managers: Fiera Capital Management
Money Market 1 Fund
RRSP Eligible; Inception Year: 1995; Fund Managers: Fiera Capital Management
Money Market 2 Fund
RRSP Eligible; Inception Year: 1995; Fund Managers: Fiera Capital Management
Money Market 3 Fund
RRSP Eligible; Inception Year: 1998; Fund Managers: Fiera Capital Management
Money Market 4 Fund
RRSP Eligible; Inception Year: 1998; Fund Managers: Fiera Capital Management
North American Small Company 1 Fund
RRSP Eligible; Inception Year: 1998; Fund Managers: Fiera Capital Management
North American Small Company 2 Fund
RRSP Eligible; Inception Year: 1998; Fund Managers: Fiera Capital Management
North American Small Company 3 Fund
RRSP Eligible; Inception Year: 1998; Fund Managers: Fiera Capital Management
North American Small Company 4 Fund
RRSP Eligible; Inception Year: 1998; Fund Managers: Fiera Capital Management
European Equity 3 Fund
RRSP Eligible; Inception Year: 1998; Fund Managers: Fiera Capital Management

Desjardins Financial Security/ Desjardins Sécurité financière (continued)

European Equity 4 Fund
RRSP Eligible; Inception Year: 1998; Fund Managers:
Fiera Capital Management
Canadian Equity 4 Fund
RRSP Eligible; Inception Year: 1998; Fund Managers:
Fiera Capital Management
Global Balanced 3 Fund
RRSP Eligible; Inception Year: 1998; Fund Managers:
Fiera Capital Management
Global Balanced 4 Fund
RRSP Eligible; Inception Year: 1998; Fund Managers:
Fiera Capital Management
Canadian Balanced 4 Fund
RRSP Eligible; Inception Year: 1998; Fund Managers:
Fiera Capital Management
Canadian Dividend 1 Fund
RRSP Eligible; Inception Year: 1998; Fund Managers:
Fiera Capital Management
Canadian Dividend 2 Fund
RRSP Eligible; Inception Year: 1998; Fund Managers:
Fiera Capital Management
Canadian Dividend 3 Fund
RRSP Eligible; Inception Year: 1998; Fund Managers:
Fiera Capital Management
Canadian Equity 1 Fund
RRSP Eligible; Inception Year: 1995; Fund Managers:
Fiera Capital Management
Canadian Equity 2 Fund
RRSP Eligible; Inception Year: 1995; Fund Managers:
Fiera Capital Management
Canadian Equity 3 Fund
RRSP Eligible; Inception Year: 1998; Fund Managers:
Fiera Capital Management
American Equity 1 Fund
RRSP Eligible; Inception Year: 1995; Fund Managers:
Fiera Capital Management
American Equity 3 Fund
RRSP Eligible; Inception Year: 1998; Fund Managers:
Fiera Capital Management
American Equity 4 Fund
RRSP Eligible; Inception Year: 1998; Fund Managers:
Fiera Capital Management
Canadian Balanced 1 Fund
RRSP Eligible; Inception Year: 1995; Fund Managers:
Fiera Capital Management
Canadian Balanced 2 Fund
RRSP Eligible; Inception Year: 1995; Fund Managers:
Fiera Capital Management
Canadian Balanced 3 Fund
RRSP Eligible; Inception Year: 1998; Fund Managers:
Fiera Capital Management
American Equity 2 Fund
RRSP Eligible; Inception Year: 1995; Fund Managers:
Fiera Capital Management
Bissett Canadian Equity 3 Fund
RRSP Eligible; Inception Year: 2000; Fund Managers:
Bissett Investment Management
Bissett Canadian Equity 4 Fund
RRSP Eligible; Inception Year: 2000; Fund Managers:
Bissett Investment Management
Bissett Dividend Income 3 Fund
RRSP Eligible; Inception Year: 2000; Fund Managers:
Bissett Investment Management
Bissett Dividend Income 4 Fund
RRSP Eligible; Inception Year: 2000; Fund Managers:
Bissett Investment Management
Bissett Small Cap 3 Fund
RRSP Eligible; Inception Year: 2000; Fund Managers:
Bissett Investment Management
Bissett Small Cap 4 Fund
RRSP Eligible; Inception Year: 2000; Fund Managers:
Bissett Investment Management
McLean Budden American Equity Growth 3 Fund
RRSP Eligible; Inception Year: 2000; Fund Managers:
McLean Budden Limited
McLean Budden American Equity Growth 4 Fund
RRSP Eligible; Inception Year: 2000; Fund Managers:
McLean Budden Limited
McLean Budden Balanced Growth 3 Fund
RRSP Eligible; Inception Year: 2000; Fund Managers:
McLean Budden Limited
McLean Budden Balanced Growth 4 Fund
RRSP Eligible; Inception Year: 2000; Fund Managers:
McLean Budden Limited
McLean Budden Canadian Equity Growth 3 Fund
RRSP Eligible; Inception Year: 2000; Fund Managers:
McLean Budden Limited
McLean Budden Canadian Equity Growth 4 Fund
RRSP Eligible; Inception Year: 2000; Fund Managers:
McLean Budden Limited
McLean Budden Canadian Equity Value 3 Fund
RRSP Eligible; Inception Year: 2000; Fund Managers:
McLean Budden Limited
McLean Budden Canadian Equity Value 4 Fund
RRSP Eligible; Inception Year: 2000; Fund Managers:
McLean Budden Limited
McLean Budden Fixed Income 3 Fund
RRSP Eligible; Inception Year: 2000; Fund Managers:
McLean Budden Limited
McLean Budden Fixed Income 4 Fund
RRSP Eligible; Inception Year: 2000; Fund Managers:
McLean Budden Limited
McLean Budden International Equity Growth 3 Fund
RRSP Eligible; Inception Year: 2000; Fund Managers:
McLean Budden Limited
McLean Budden International Equity Growth 4 Fund
RRSP Eligible; Inception Year: 2000; Fund Managers:
McLean Budden Limited
Talvest Global Asset Allocation RSP 3 Fund
RRSP Eligible; Inception Year: 2000; Fund Managers:
TAL Global Asset Management
Talvest Global Asset Allocation RSP 4 Fund
RRSP Eligible; Inception Year: 2000; Fund Managers:
TAL Global Asset Management
Talvest Balanced 3 Portfolio
RRSP Eligible; Inception Year: 2000; Fund Managers:
TAL Global Asset Management
Talvest Balanced 4 Portfolio
RRSP Eligible; Inception Year: 2000; Fund Managers:
TAL Global Asset Management
Talvest Conservative 3 Portfolio
RRSP Eligible; Inception Year: 2000; Fund Managers:
TAL Global Asset Management
Talvest Conservative 4 Portfolio
RRSP Eligible; Inception Year: 2000; Fund Managers:
TAL Global Asset Management
Talvest Global Bond RSP 3 Fund
RRSP Eligible; Inception Year: 2000; Fund Managers:
TAL Global Asset Management
Talvest Global Bond RSP 4 Fund
RRSP Eligible; Inception Year: 2000; Fund Managers:
TAL Global Asset Management
Talvest Global Equity 3 Fund
RRSP Eligible; Inception Year: 2000; Fund Managers:
TAL Global Asset Management
Talvest Global Equity 4 Fund
RRSP Eligible; Inception Year: 2000; Fund Managers:
TAL Global Asset Management
Talvest Growth 3 Portfolio
RRSP Eligible; Inception Year: 2000; Fund Managers:
TAL Global Asset Management
Talvest Growth 4 Portfolio
RRSP Eligible; Inception Year: 2000; Fund Managers:
TAL Global Asset Management
Bissett Multinational Growth 3 Fund
RRSP Eligible; Inception Year: 2003; Fund Managers:
Franklin Templeton Investments
Bissett Multinational Growth 4 Fund
RRSP Eligible; Inception Year: 2003; Fund Managers:
Franklin Templeton Investments
Trimark Canadian 3 Fund
RRSP Eligible; Inception Year: 2003; Fund Managers:
AIM Trimark Investments
Trimark Canadian 4 Fund
RRSP Eligible; Inception Year: 2003; Fund Managers:
AIM Trimark Investments
Jarislowsky Fraser Global Balanced 3 Fund
RRSP Eligible; Inception Year: 2003; Fund Managers:
Jarislowsky Fraser Ltd.
Jarislowsky Fraser Global Balanced 4 Fund
RRSP Eligible; Inception Year: 2003; Fund Managers:
Jarislowsky Fraser Ltd.
Mortgage 3 Fund
RRSP Eligible; Inception Year: 2003; Fund Managers:
Desjardins Global Asset Management
Mortgage 4 Fund
RRSP Eligible; Inception Year: 2003; Fund Managers:
Desjardins Global Asset Management
Fidelity International Portfolio 3 Fund
RRSP Eligible; Inception Year: 2003; Fund Managers:
Fidelity Investments Canada
Fidelity International Portfolio 4 Fund
RRSP Eligible; Inception Year: 2003; Fund Managers:
Fidelity Investments Canada
Northwest 3 Portfolio
RRSP Eligible; Inception Year: 2002; Fund Managers:
Northwest Mutual Funds
Northwest 4 Portfolio
RRSP Eligible; Inception Year: 2002; Fund Managers:
Northwest Mutual Funds
Northwest Quebec Growth 3 Fund
RRSP Eligible; Inception Year: 2003; Fund Managers:
Montrustco Bolton Inc.
Northwest Quebec Growth 4 Fund
RRSP Eligible; Inception Year: 2003; Fund Managers:
Montrustco Bolton Inc.
American Equity Value 3 Fund
RRSP Eligible; Inception Year: 2003; Fund Managers:
Bernstein Management Inc.
American Equity Value 4 Fund
RRSP Eligible; Inception Year: 2003; Fund Managers:
Bernstein Management Inc.
Ultimate Equity 3 Portfolio
RRSP Eligible; Inception Year: 2002; Fund Managers:
TAL Global Asset Management
Ultimate Equity 4 Portfolio
RRSP Eligible; Inception Year: 2002; Fund Managers:
TAL Global Asset Management
Bissett Canadian Balanced 3 Fund
RRSP Eligible; Inception Year: 2005; Fund Managers:
Bissett Investment Management
Bissett Canadian Balanced 4 Fund
RRSP Eligible; Inception Year: 2005; Fund Managers:
Bissett Investment Management
Bissett Bond 3 Fund
RRSP Eligible; Inception Year: 2000; Fund Managers:
Bissett Investment Management
Bissett Bond 4 Fund
RRSP Eligible; Inception Year: 2000; Fund Managers:
Bissett Investment Management
Jarislowsky Fraser Canadian Equity 3 Fund
RRSP Eligible; Inception Year: 2005; Fund Managers:
Jarislowsky Fraser Ltd.
Jarislowsky Fraser Canadian Equity 4 Fund
RRSP Eligible; Inception Year: 2005; Fund Managers:
Jarislowsky Fraser Ltd.

Offices:

Montréal
Tour Sud
1, Complexe Desjardins, 21e étage
Montréal, QC H5B 1E2 Canada
514-350-8700
877-750-8700

Québec
1150, rue de Claire-Fontaine
Québec, QC Canada
418-647-5000
888-893-1833

Toronto
#306, 95 St. Clair Ave. West
Toronto, ON M4V 1N7 Canada
416-926-2662
Fax: 416-926-2667
800-263-9641

Regional Offices:

Calgary
#560, 202 - 6th Ave. SW
Calgary, AB T2P 2R9 Canada
403-216-5800
Fax: 403-216-5807
800-661-8666

Dartmouth
#1400, 99 Wyse Rd.
Dartmouth, NS B3A 4S5 Canada
902-466-8881
Fax: 902-466-4074
800-567-8881

Lévis
Complexe Maurice-Tanguay
#203, 5790, boul Étienne-Dallaire
Lévis, QC G6V 8V6 Canada

418-838-7870
Fax: 418-833-6251
800-463-7870
Montréal
#2525, 2, Complexe Desjardins, Tour Est
Montréal, QC H5B 1E2 Canada
514-285-7880
Fax: 514-258-2442
800-363-3072
Ottawa
#120, 1102 Prince of Wales Dr.
Ottawa, ON K2C 3W7 Canada
613-224-3121
Fax: 613-224-6812
888-428-2485
Toronto
#306, 95 St. Clair Ave. West
Toronto, ON M4V 1N7 Canada
416-926-2662
Fax: 416-926-2667
800-263-9641
Vancouver
#1050, 401 West Georgia St.
Vancouver, BC V6B 5A1 Canada
604-718-4410
Fax: 604-718-4412
800-667-6267

Winnipeg
#1490, 363 Broadway
Winnipeg, MB R3C 3N9 Canada
204-989-4350
Fax: 204-989-7211
888-942-3383

DGC Entertainment Ventures Corp.

Also listed under: *Holding & Other Investment Companies*
EVC Management Inc.
#402, 111 Peter St.
Toronto, ON M5V 2H1
416-365-8053
Fax: 416-365-8037
800-382-1159
Number of Employees: 10
Executives:
Alan Goluboff, Chair
Robb W. Hindson, President
Pamela Brand, Secretary
DGC Entertainment Ventures Corp. Fund
RRSP Eligible; Inception Year: 1994; Fund Managers:
EVC Management Inc.

Dynamic Mutual Funds(DMF)/ Fonds d'investissement Dynamique

Scotia Plaza
40 King St. West, 55th Fl.
Toronto, ON M5H 4A9
416-365-5621
Fax: 416-363-5850
866-977-0477
invest@dynamic.ca
www.dynamic.ca
Profile: Offers comprehensive investment services that cover the entire spectrum of choice, including mutual funds, tax-advantaged products and customized high net worth programs.
Executives:
David J. Goodman, President/CEO
Kevin Hynes, Exec. Vice-President/COO
Simon Hitzig, Exec. Vice-President, Marketing
Annamaria Testani, Exec. Vice-President, Business Product Development
David A. Whyte, Exec. Vice-President, National Sales
Directors:
Ronald Singer, Chair
Dynamic:
Dollar-Cost Averaging Fund
RRSP Eligible; Inception Year: 1997; Fund Managers:
Goodman & Company
Dividend Value Fund
RRSP Eligible; Inception Year: 1985; Fund Managers:
Goodman & Company
Dividend Fund
RRSP Eligible; Inception Year: 1985; Fund Managers:
Goodman & Company
European Value Fund
RRSP Eligible; Inception Year: 1989; Fund Managers:
Sanderson Asset Management
Far East Value Fund
RRSP Eligible; Inception Year: 1994; Fund Managers:
Goodman & Company
Income Fund
RRSP Eligible; Inception Year: 1979; Fund Managers:
Goodman & Company
Money Market Fund
RRSP Eligible; Inception Year: 1992; Fund Managers:
Goodman & Company
Power American Growth Fund
RRSP Eligible; Inception Year: 1998; Fund Managers:
Goodman & Company
Power Balanced Fund
RRSP Eligible; Inception Year: 1998; Fund Managers:
Goodman & Company
Power Canadian Growth Fund
RRSP Eligible; Inception Year: 1985; Fund Managers:
Goodman & Company
RSP European Value Fund
RRSP Eligible; Inception Year: 1999; Fund Managers:
Sanderson Asset Management
RSP International Value Fund
RRSP Eligible; Inception Year: 1999; Fund Managers:
Sanderson Asset Management
Technology Fund
RRSP Eligible; Inception Year: 1997; Fund Managers:
Tera Capital
SAMI Fund
RRSP Eligible; Inception Year: 1999; Fund Managers:
Goodman & Company
QSSP Fund
RRSP Eligible; Inception Year: 1999; Fund Managers:
Goodman & Company
International Value Fund
RRSP Eligible; Inception Year: 2001; Fund Managers:
Goodman & Company
Canadian Value Class Fund
RRSP Eligible; Inception Year: 2001; Fund Managers:
Goodman & Company
Precious Metals Fund
RRSP Eligible; Inception Year: 1984; Fund Managers:
Goodman & Company
Value Fund of Canada
RRSP Eligible; Inception Year: 1957; Fund Managers:
Goodman & Company
Focus+ American Fund
RRSP Eligible; Inception Year: 1984; Fund Managers:
Goodman & Company
Focus+ Balanced Fund
RRSP Eligible; Inception Year: 1975; Fund Managers:
Goodman & Company
Focus+ Equity Fund
RRSP Eligible; Inception Year: 1987; Fund Managers:
Goodman & Company
Focus+ Diversified Income Trust Fund
RRSP Eligible; Inception Year: 2001; Fund Managers:
Goodman & Company
Focus+ Wealth Management Fund
RRSP Eligible; Inception Year: 1972; Fund Managers:
Goodman & Company
Money Market Class Fund
RRSP Eligible; Inception Year: 2001; Fund Managers:
Goodman & Company
Power American Growth Class Fund
RRSP Eligible; Inception Year: 2001; Fund Managers:
Goodman & Company
Power Canadian Growth Class Fund
RRSP Eligible; Inception Year: 2001; Fund Managers:
Goodman & Company
Dividend Income Fund
RRSP Eligible; Inception Year: 2003; Fund Managers:
Goodman & Company
International Value Fund Series T
RRSP Eligible; Inception Year: 1985; Fund Managers:
Sanderson Asset Management
American Value Fund
RRSP Eligible; Inception Year: 1979; Fund Managers:
Goodman & Company
Focus+ Resource Fund
RRSP Eligible; Inception Year: 1998; Fund Managers:
Goodman & Company
Focus+ Small Business Fund
RRSP Eligible; Inception Year: 1997; Fund Managers:
Goodman & Company
Focus+ Real Estate Fund
RRSP Eligible; Inception Year: 1996; Fund Managers:
Goodman & Company
Alpha Performance Fund
RRSP Eligible; Inception Year: 2002; Fund Managers:
Goodman & Company
Focus+ World Equity Fund
RRSP Eligible; Inception Year: 1996; Fund Managers:
Goodman & Company
Canadian Dividend Fund
RRSP Eligible; Inception Year: 1978; Fund Managers:
Goodman & Company
Canadian High Yield Bond Fund I
RRSP Eligible; Inception Year: 1995; Fund Managers:
Marret Asset Management Inc.
Canadian High Yield Bond Fund II
RRSP Eligible; Inception Year: 2003; Fund Managers:
Marret Asset Management Inc.
Focus+ Energy Income Trust Fund
RRSP Eligible; Inception Year: 2003; Fund Managers:
Goodman & Company
Focus+ Guaranteed American Fund
RRSP Eligible; Inception Year: 1998; Fund Managers:
Goodman & Company
Focus+ Guaranteed Balanced Fund
RRSP Eligible; Inception Year: 1998; Fund Managers:
Goodman & Company
Focus+ Guaranteed Canadian Fund
RRSP Eligible; Inception Year: 1998; Fund Managers:
Goodman & Company
Focus+ Guaranteed Wealth Management Fund
RRSP Eligible; Inception Year: 1998; Fund Managers:
Goodman & Company
Focus+ World Equity Fund I
RRSP Eligible; Inception Year: 1992; Fund Managers:
Goodman & Company
Power American Growth Fund (US$)
RRSP Eligible; Inception Year: 2002; Fund Managers:
Goodman & Company
Power Global Growth Class Fund
RRSP Eligible; Inception Year: 2001; Fund Managers:
Goodman & Company
Power Small Cap Fund
RRSP Eligible; Inception Year: 1995; Fund Managers:
Goodman & Company
World Convertible Debentures Fund
RRSP Eligible; Inception Year: 2000; Fund Managers:
Gamco Investor Inc.
Venture Opportunities Fund Series I
RRSP Eligible; Inception Year: 1993; Fund Managers:
Goodman & Company
American Value Fund (US$)
RRSP Eligible; Inception Year: 1979; Fund Managers:
Goodman & Company
International Value Fund (US$)
RRSP Eligible; Inception Year: 1999; Fund Managers:
Goodman & Company
Protected American Value Fund
RRSP Eligible; Inception Year: 1998; Fund Managers:
Goodman & Company
Protected Dividend Value Fund
RRSP Eligible; Inception Year: 1998; Fund Managers:
Goodman & Company
Protected International Value Fund
RRSP Eligible; Inception Year: 1998; Fund Managers:
Sanderson Asset Management
Value Balanced Fund
RRSP Eligible; Inception Year: 1992; Fund Managers:
Marret Asset Management Inc.
Power Hedge Fund
RRSP Eligible; Inception Year: 2002; Fund Managers:
Goodman & Company
Strategic Defensive Portfolio Fund
RRSP Eligible; Inception Year: 2004; Fund Managers:
Goodman & Company
Strategic Conservative Portfolio Fund
RRSP Eligible; Inception Year: 2004; Fund Managers:
Goodman & Company
Strategic Balanced Portfolio Fund
RRSP Eligible; Inception Year: 2004; Fund Managers:
Goodman & Company

Dynamic Mutual Funds(DMF)/ Fonds d'investissement Dynamique (continued)

Strategic Growth Portfolio Fund
RRSP Eligible; Inception Year: 1986; Fund Managers: Goodman & Company
Strategic High Growth Portfolio Fund
RRSP Eligible; Inception Year: 2004; Fund Managers: Goodman & Company
Strategic All Equity Portfolio Fund
RRSP Eligible; Inception Year: 2004; Fund Managers: Goodman & Company
Strategic All Income Portfolio Fund
RRSP Eligible; Inception Year: 2004; Fund Managers: Goodman & Company
Global Discovery Value Fund
RRSP Eligible; Inception Year: 2000; Fund Managers: Goodman & Company
Corporate Bond Fund
RRSP Eligible; Inception Year: 1998; Fund Managers: Goodman & Company
Dividend Fund Series C
RRSP Eligible; Inception Year: 2005; Fund Managers: Goodman & Company
Real Return Bond Fund
RRSP Eligible; Inception Year: 2004; Fund Managers: Goodman & Company
Global Value Class Fund
RRSP Eligible; Inception Year: 2001; Fund Managers: Goodman & Company
Dividend Value Fund Series T
RRSP Eligible; Inception Year: 2005; Fund Managers: Goodman & Company
International Value Fund Series T
RRSP Eligible; Inception Year: 1985; Fund Managers: Goodman & Company
Value Balanced Fund Series T
RRSP Eligible; Inception Year: 1992; Fund Managers: Marret Asset Management Inc.
Value Fund of Canada Series T
RRSP Eligible; Inception Year: 1957; Fund Managers: Goodman & Company
Focus+ Balanced Fund Series T
RRSP Eligible; Inception Year: 1975; Fund Managers: Goodman & Company
Power American Currency Neutral Fund
RRSP Eligible; Inception Year: 2005; Fund Managers: Goodman & Company
Power American Growth Fund Series T
RRSP Eligible; Inception Year: 1998; Fund Managers: Goodman & Company
Power Balanced Fund Series T
RRSP Eligible; Inception Year: 1998; Fund Managers: Goodman & Company
Power Canadian Growth Fund Series T
RRSP Eligible; Inception Year: 1985; Fund Managers: Goodman & Company
Diversified Real Asset Fund
RRSP Eligible; Inception Year: 2005; Fund Managers: Goodman & Company
Focus+ Global Financial Services Class Fund
RRSP Eligible; Inception Year: 2001;
Venture Opportunities Fund Series II
RRSP Eligible; Inception Year: 1993; Fund Managers: Goodman & Company

Dynamic Managed Portfolio:

Canadian Dividend Class Fund
RRSP Eligible; Inception Year: 2005; Fund Managers: Goodman & Company
Canadian Value Class Fund
RRSP Eligible; Inception Year: 2005; Fund Managers: Goodman & Company
Global Value Class Fund
RRSP Eligible; Inception Year: 2005; Fund Managers: Goodman & Company
Power Canadian Growth Class Fund
RRSP Eligible; Inception Year: 2005; Fund Managers: Goodman & Company
Power Growth Class Fund
RRSP Eligible; Inception Year: 2005; Fund Managers: Goodman & Company
Resource Class Fund
RRSP Eligible; Inception Year: 2005; Fund Managers: Goodman & Company

Marquis:

Diversified Conservative Portfolio Fund
RRSP Eligible; Inception Year: 2003; Fund Managers: Sanderson Asset Management
Diversified Balanced Portfolio Fund
RRSP Eligible; Inception Year: 2003; Fund Managers: Goodman & Company
Diversified Growth Portfolio Fund
RRSP Eligible; Inception Year: 2003; Fund Managers: Goodman & Company
Diversified All Equity Portfolio Fund
RRSP Eligible; Inception Year: 2003; Fund Managers: Standard Life Investments Inc.
Diversified Defensive Portfolio Fund
RRSP Eligible; Inception Year: 2004; Fund Managers: Goodman & Company
Diversified High Growth Portfolio Fund
RRSP Eligible; Inception Year: 2004; Fund Managers: Goodman & Company
Diversified All Income Portfolio Fund
RRSP Eligible; Inception Year: 2004; Fund Managers: Babson Capital Management LLC

Marquis Multipartners:

Equity Portfolio Fund
RRSP Eligible; Inception Year: 2002;
Growth Portfolio Fund
RRSP Eligible; Inception Year: 2002;
High Growth Portfolio Fund
RRSP Eligible; Inception Year: 1999;

Radiant:

All Equity Portfolio Fund
RRSP Eligible; Inception Year: 2004;
All Income Portfolio Fund
RRSP Eligible; Inception Year: 2004;
Balanced Portfolio Fund
RRSP Eligible; Inception Year: 2004;
Bond Portfolio Fund
RRSP Eligible; Inception Year: 2004;
Conservative Portfolio Fund
RRSP Eligible; Inception Year: 2004;
Defensive Portfolio Fund
RRSP Eligible; Inception Year: 2004;
Growth Portfolio Fund
RRSP Eligible; Inception Year: 2004;
High Growth Portfolio Fund
RRSP Eligible; Inception Year: 2004;

Branches:

Calgary
1st Canadian Center
#3250, 350 - 7th Ave. SW
Calgary, AB T2P 3N9 Canada
403-205-3996
Fax: 403-205-3388
877-205-3996

Halifax
#290, 1096 Queen St.
Halifax, NS B3H 2R9 Canada
902-425-8091
Fax: 902-429-6992

Montréal
#2300, 1200, av McGill College
Montréal, QC H3B 4G7 Canada
514-940-3510
Fax: 514-940-3511
877-681-0332

Vancouver
Bentall Centre
PO Box 49217
#3434, 1055 Dunsmuir St.
Vancouver, BC V7X 1K8 Canada
604-682-3622
Fax: 604-682-3623
800-565-3938

Empire Life Insurance Company

***Also listed under:** Financial Planning; Investment Management*

259 King St. East
Kingston, ON K7L 3A8
613-548-1881
Fax: 613-548-8096
800-561-1268
buildingempires@empire.ca
www.empire.ca

Also Known As: Empire Life
Ownership: Private. Subsidiary of E-L Financial Services Ltd., which is 81% owned by E-L Financial Corporation Limited.
Year Founded: 1923
Number of Employees: 600+
Assets: $1-10 billion Year End: 20051231
Revenues: $500m-1 billion Year End: 20051231
Profile: The company markets a full range of financial security & wealth management products & services for individuals & groups, including life, health & disability insurance plans, investments, retirement & estate planning, corporate services & employee benefits.

Executives:

Douglas G. Hogeboom, FSA, FCIA, President/CEO
Leslie C. Herr, MBA, CFP, CLU, CH.F.C., Sr. Vice-President, Individual Products
Michael C. Schneider, FSA, FCIA, Sr. Vice-President, Corporate

Anne Butler, Vice-President/Corporate Secretary & Director of Legal Services, Chief Compliance Officer & Chief Privacy Officer
Deborah K. Frame, MBA, CFA, Vice-President, Chief Investment Officer
J. Edward Gibson, FSA, FCIA, Vice-President & Actuary
Jake J. Hilberdink, FLMI, Vice-President, Employee Benefits
Timo Hytonen, MBA, FCIP, CHRP, CRM, Vice-President, Human Resources & Community Relations
Gary McCabe, CA, Vice-President & Controller
Wendy R.M. Merkley, Vice-President, Information Systems, Technology & Services
Steve S. Pong, BASc., Vice-President, Individual Marketing & Service

Shareholders' Directors:

Duncan N.R. Jackman, Chair
Graham W. Dumble
Robert G. Long
Roy Patrick, LL.B
Group Secretary, AEGON UK plc
Richard E. Rooney
Deanna Rosenswig
Clive P. Rowe
Partner, SLS Capital
Michael C. Schneider
Mark M. Taylor

Honorary Directors:

Henry N.R. Jackman, Honorary Chair
John N. Turner, PC, CC, QC
Partner, Miller Thomson LLP

Policyholders' Directors:

Mark J. Fuller, LLB
Ontario Pension Board
Douglas G. Hogeboom, FSA, FCIA
President/CEO, The Empire Life Insurance Group
James W. McCutcheon, QC
Counsel, McCarthy Tétrault
Douglas C. Townsend, FSA, FCIA
Manon R. Vennat, CM
Chair, Montréal, Spencer Stuart & Associates (Canada) Ltd.

Empire:

Asset Allocation Fund
RRSP Eligible; Inception Year: 1994;
Balanced Fund
RRSP Eligible; Inception Year: 1989;
Bond Fund
RRSP Eligible; Inception Year: 1986;
Dividend Growth Fund
RRSP Eligible; Inception Year: 1998;
Equity Growth Fund
RRSP Eligible; Inception Year: 1971;
International Equity Fund
RRSP Eligible; Inception Year: 1989;
Money Market Fund
RRSP Eligible; Inception Year: 1989;
Small Cap Equity Fund
RRSP Eligible; Inception Year: 1998;
U.S. Equity Index Fund
RRSP Eligible; Inception Year: 1998;
Premier Equity Fund
RRSP Eligible; Inception Year: 1964;
American Value Fund
RRSP Eligible; Inception Year: 2001;
Elite Equity Fund
RRSP Eligible; Inception Year: 1969;
Conservative Portfolio Fund
RRSP Eligible; Inception Year: 2004;
Balanced Portfolio Fund
RRSP Eligible; Inception Year: 2004;
Moderate Growth Portfolio Fund
RRSP Eligible; Inception Year: 2004;

Growth Portfolio Fund
RRSP Eligible; Inception Year: 2004;
Aggressive Growth Portfolio Fund
RRSP Eligible; Inception Year: 2004;
Global Balanced Fund
RRSP Eligible; Inception Year: 0;
Global Equity Fund
RRSP Eligible; Inception Year: 1989;
Canadian Equity Fund
RRSP Eligible; Inception Year: 2005;
Income Fund
RRSP Eligible; Inception Year: 2002;
Global Smaller Companies Fund
RRSP Eligible; Inception Year: 2005;

Group Sales & Marketing Offices:

Burlington
5500 North Service Rd., 4th Fl.
Burlington, ON L7L 6W6 Canada
905-335-6558
George Elliott, Sr. Group Representative

Calgary
#304, 1240 Kensington Rd. NW
Calgary, AB T2N 3P7 Canada
403-262-6386
Richard Dobing, Representative, Group Sales

Edmonton
Phipps-McKinnon Bldg.
#950, 10020 - 101A Ave.
Edmonton, AB T5J 3G2 Canada
780-482-4241
Shelly Robichaud, Representative, Group Sales

London
#404, 171 Queens Ave.
London, ON N6A 5J7 Canada
519-438-1751
Ken Nitska, Group Manager, Southwest & Northern Ontario

Montréal
#1600A, 600, boul de Maisonneuve ouest
Montréal, QC H3A 3J2 Canada
514-842-0003
Michel Tessier, Group Manager, Québec

Nepean
#236, 9 Antares Dr.
Nepean, ON K2E 7V5 Canada
613-225-1173
Wendi Stimson, Group Sales Representative, Eastern Ontario

Richmond
North Tower
#602, 5811 Cooney Rd.
Richmond, BC V6X 3M1 Canada
604-232-5558
Duncan Emslie, Group Manager

Toronto
#800, 2550 Victoria Park Ave.
Toronto, ON M2J 5A9 Canada
416-494-0900
Doug Cooper, National Director, Group Sales & Marketing

Waterloo
#250, 180 King St. South
Waterloo, ON N2J 1P8 Canada
519-569-7002
Christine Betts, Representative, Group Sales

Individual Sales & Marketing Office:

Burlington
5500 North Service Rd., 4th Fl.
Burlington, ON L7L 6W6 Canada
905-335-6558
Walter Kordiuk, Executive Account Manager, Wealth

Calgary
#305, 1240 Kensington Rd. NW
Calgary, AB T2N 3P7 Canada
403-269-1000
Stan Pappenfus, Executive Manager, Accounts

Edmonton
11810 Kingsway Ave.
Edmonton, AB T5G 0X5 Canada
780-482-4271
Ken Doll, Regional Manager, Accounts

London
#404, 171 Queens Ave.
London, ON N6A 5J7 Canada
519-438-2922
Doug Kennedy, Executive Manager, Accounts

Montréal
#1600, 600, boul de Maisonneuve ouest
Montréal, QC H3A 3J2 Canada
514-842-9151
Richard Charette, Director, Sales & Distribution

Nepean
#221, 9 Antares Dr.
Nepean, ON K2E 7V5 Canada
613-225-7530
George MacKenzie, Regional Manager, Accounts

Richmond
North Tower
#602, 5811 Cooney Rd.
Richmond, BC V6X 3M1 Canada
604-232-5557
Rick Forchuk, Director, Sales & Distribution

Saskatoon
#1000, 201 - 21st St. East
Saskatoon, SK S7K 0B8 Canada
306-934-3899
Steve Kook, Regional Manager, Investments

Toronto
#800, 2550 Victoria Park Ave.
Toronto, ON M2J 5A9 Canada
416-494-4890
Rick Forchuk, Director, Sales & Distribution

Waterloo
#250, 180 King St. South
Waterloo, ON N2J 1P8 Canada
518-569-7002
Donna Schultz, Manager, Regional Accounts

Winnipeg
#200, 5 Donald St.
Winnipeg, MB R3L 2T4 Canada
204-452-9138
Sandy Franczyk, Regional Investment Manager

The Equitable Life Insurance Company of Canada

Also listed under: *Federal & Provincial*
1 Westmount Rd. North
Waterloo, ON N2J 4C7
519-886-5110
Fax: 519-883-7400
800-265-8878
webmaster@equitable.ca
www.equitable.ca
Ownership: Policy-holders
Year Founded: 1920
Number of Employees: 500
Assets: $1-10 billion Year End: 20051231
Revenues: $100-500 million Year End: 20051231
Profile: Equitable Life is an independent mutual life insurance company that offers financial products, including life insurance, annuities, group life & health coverage, retirement savings, pension plans, residential & commercial mortgages, & segregated fund investments.

Executives:
Ronald E. Beettam, FSA, FCIA, President/CEO
Douglas W. Brooks, FSA, FCIA, Sr. Vice-President/CFO
W. (Willie) A.T. Young, FCSI, FCIB, Sr. Vice-President, Investments
Christopher Brown, Vice-President, Human Resources
Michael M. Dawe, Vice-President, Individual
Karen Mason, Vice-President, Group
Harley R. Rashleigh-Berry, LL.B., Vice-President, Chief Compliance Officer, Legal Counsel & Corporate Secretary
Ravinder Singh, P.Eng., Vice-President, Information Technology, Chief Information Officer

Directors:
Ronald D. Beettam, FSA, FCIA
Rita Burak, BA, CLF
Chair, Canadian General-Tower Ltd.
Douglas L. Derry, FCA
Douglas W. Dodds, FCAM
Chair/CEO, Schneider Corp.
Maureen Farrow, FCMC
President, Economap Inc.
Paul D. Mitchell, FCA, LL.D.
Chair, Ellis-Don Constructions Ltd.
Marc J. Somerville, Q.C.
Gowling, Strathy & Henderson
Donald Stevens
Chair/CEO, Gore Mutual Insurance Company
Lee Watchorn, BSc, FSA, FCIA
David S. Weinberg
President, Scott-Bathgate Ltd.

Equitable Life:
American Growth Fund
RRSP Eligible; Inception Year: 1999; Fund Managers: McLean Budden Ltd.
Asset Allocation Fund
RRSP Eligible; Inception Year: 1994; Fund Managers: McLean Budden Ltd.
Canadian Bond Fund
RRSP Eligible; Inception Year: 1992; Fund Managers: McLean Budden Ltd.
Canadian Stock Fund
RRSP Eligible; Inception Year: 1992; Fund Managers: McLean Budden Ltd.
Templeton Global Growth Fund
RRSP Eligible; Inception Year: 1999; Fund Managers: Franklin Templeton Investments
International Fund
RRSP Eligible; Inception Year: 1994; Fund Managers: Philip Pfeifer
TaraProper
Jeff Rabb
US Equity Fund
RRSP Eligible; Inception Year: 1999; Fund Managers: Philip Pfeifer
TaraProper
Jeff Rabb
Money Market Fund
RRSP Eligible; Inception Year: 1994; Fund Managers: Philip Pfeifer
European Equity Fund
RRSP Eligible; Inception Year: 1999; Fund Managers: Philip Pfeifer
TaraProper
Jeff Rabb
John Stilo
Segregated Common Stock Fund
RRSP Eligible; Inception Year: 1983; Fund Managers: McLean Budden Ltd.
Asian-Pacific Fund
RRSP Eligible; Inception Year: 1999; Fund Managers: Philip Pfeifer
TaraProper
Jeff Rabb
John Stilo
Segregated Accumulated Income Fund
RRSP Eligible; Inception Year: 1983; Fund Managers: McLean Budden Ltd.
Canadian Equity Value Fund
RRSP Eligible; Inception Year: 1999; Fund Managers: McLean Budden Ltd.
Templeton Global Bond Fund
RRSP Eligible; Inception Year: 1999; Fund Managers: Franklin Templeton Investments
AIM Canadian Premier Fund
RRSP Eligible; Inception Year: 2004; Fund Managers: AIM Trimark Investments
Trimark Europlus Fund
RRSP Eligible; Inception Year: 2004; Fund Managers: AIM Trimark Investments
Trimark Global Balanced Fund
RRSP Eligible; Inception Year: 2004; Fund Managers: AIM Trimark Investments
Bissett Dividend Income Fund
RRSP Eligible; Inception Year: 2004; Fund Managers: Bissett Investment Management
Franklin Templeton Balanced Growth Portfolio Fund
RRSP Eligible; Inception Year: 2005; Fund Managers: Franklin Templeton Investments
Franklin Templeton Balanced Income Portfolio Fund
RRSP Eligible; Inception Year: 2005; Fund Managers: Franklin Templeton Investments
Franklin Templeton Global Growth Portfolio Fund
RRSP Eligible; Inception Year: 2005; Fund Managers: Franklin Templeton Investments
Franklin Templeton Growth Portfolio Fund
RRSP Eligible; Inception Year: 2005; Fund Managers: Franklin Templeton Investments
Franklin Templeton Maximum Growth Portfolio Fund
RRSP Eligible; Inception Year: 2005; Fund Managers: Franklin Templeton Investments
Franklin Templeton Diversified Income Portfolio Fund
RRSP Eligible; Inception Year: 2005; Fund Managers: Franklin Templeton Investments

The Equitable Life Insurance Company of Canada (continued)
Mackenzie Universal US Emerging Growth Fund
RRSP Eligible; Inception Year: 2004; Fund Managers:
Mackenzie Financial
Regional Offices:
Calgary
MacLeod Place I
#500, 5920 MacLeod Trail South
Calgary, AB T2H 0K2 Canada
403-259-3392
Fax: 403-252-8998
888-888-8377
calgary@equitable.ca
Chris Presley, Manager, Group Marketing
Edmonton
#1668, 10303 Jasper Ave.
Edmonton, AB T5J 3N6 Canada
780-425-6622
Fax: 780-424-4496
888-999-0666
edmonton@equitable.ca
Jim Tetz, Manager, Group Marketing
Halifax
15 Bridgeview Dr.
Halifax, NS B3P 1E7 Canada
902-475-1629
Fax: 902-477-2863
866-662-6684
Greg Flack, Manager, Life Marketing
Hamilton
Village Atrium
#102, 10 George St.
Hamilton, ON L8P 1C8 Canada
905-540-9200
Fax: 905-540-9300
800-721-6887
hamilton@equitable.ca
Donna M. Plyley, Manager, Group Marketing
London
#301, 252 Pall Mall St.
London, ON N6A 5P6 Canada
519-433-0196
Fax: 519-642-7674
800-263-5559
london@equitable.ca
Doris Forbes, Manager, Group Marketing
Markham
#450, 11 Allstate Pkwy.
Markham, ON L3R 9T8 Canada
905-477-0063
Fax: 905-477-1525
800-565-6835
toronto-east@equitable.ca
Mary M. Caprio, Manager, Group Marketing
Ottawa
#312, 1545 Carling Ave.
Ottawa, ON K1Z 8P9 Canada
613-729-3174
Fax: 613-729-6448
800-704-9652
ottawa@equitable.ca
Phil DeLucia, Regional Director, Individual Sales & Distribution
Saskatoon
#208, 119 - 4th Ave. South
Saskatoon, SK S7K 5X2 Canada
306-664-9133
Fax: 306-664-9136
800-567-5389
prairie@equitable.ca
Adrian W. Boyko, Regional Director, Individual Sales & Distribution
Vancouver
2 Bentall Centre
PO Box 234
#1725, 555 Burrard St.
Vancouver, BC V7X 1M9 Canada
604-685-8364
Fax: 604-685-5974
800-260-3056
bc@equitable.ca
Glendine L. Skagen, Regional Director, Group Sales & Distribution
Waterloo
PO Box 1603, Waterloo Sta. Waterloo
1 Westmount Rd. North
Waterloo, ON N2J 4C7 Canada
519-746-5611
Fax: 519-746-5308
800-387-1704
k-w@equitable.ca
Lori Hederson, Manager, Group Marketing
Winnipeg
#104, 179 McDermitt Ave.
Winnipeg, MB R3B 0S1 Canada
Fax: 780-424-4496
888-999-0666
Jody Ford, Manager, Life Marketing

Ethical Funds Inc.(EFI)

***Also listed under:** Financial Planning; Investment Management*

#800, 1111 West Georgia St.
Vancouver, BC V6E 4T6
604-714-3802
Fax: 604-714-3861
877-384-4225
clientrelations@ethicalfunds.com
www.ethicalfunds.com
Ownership: Private.
Year Founded: 1986
Number of Employees: 300
Assets: $1-10 billion Year End: 20060930
Profile: An affiliated company is Guardian Ethical Management Inc.

Executives:
Donald J. Rolfe, President/CEO; 604-714-3800
Ethical:
Growth Fund
RRSP Eligible; Inception Year: 1986; Fund Managers:
Guardian Captial LP
Income Fund
RRSP Eligible; Inception Year: 1967; Fund Managers:
Guardian Captial LP
Credential Money Market Fund
RRSP Eligible; Inception Year: 1980; Fund Managers:
Central Financial
Special Equity Fund
RRSP Eligible; Inception Year: 1995; Fund Managers:
QVGD Investors Inc.
Canadian Dividend Fund
RRSP Eligible; Inception Year: 2002; Fund Managers:
Highstreet Asset Management Inc.
International Equity Fund
RRSP Eligible; Inception Year: 2002; Fund Managers:
William Blair & Co. LLC
Canadian Index Fund
RRSP Eligible; Inception Year: 2004;
Balanced Fund
RRSP Eligible; Inception Year: 0; Fund Managers:
Guardian Captial LP
Monthly Income Fund
RRSP Eligible; Inception Year: 0; Fund Managers:
Guardian Captial LP
American Multi-Strategy FundInception Year: 0; Fund Managers:
Manning & Napier Advisors Inc.

Excel Funds Management Inc.

Plaza 4
#280, 2000 Argentia Rd.
Mississauga, ON L5N 1W1
905-813-7111
Fax: 905-813-8884
888-813-9813
excel@excelfunds.com
www.excelfunds.com
Ownership: Private
Year Founded: 1996
Executives:
Bhim D. Asdhir, President/CEO
Excel:
India Fund
RRSP Eligible; Inception Year: 1998;
China Fund
RRSP Eligible; Inception Year: 2000;
India China Fund
RRSP Eligible; Inception Year: 1999;

Fidelity Investments Canada Ltd.

PO Box 90
#200, 483 Bay St.
Toronto, ON M5G 2N7
416-307-5200
Fax: 416-307-5523
800-263-4077
www.fidelity.ca
Ownership: Private. Wholly owned subsidiary of Fidelity Investment Management & Research, Boston
Year Founded: 1987
Number of Employees: 773
Executives:
Robert L. Strickland, President
Affiliated Companies:
Fidelity Partnerships

Fidelity:
Canadian Asset Allocation Fund
RRSP Eligible; Inception Year: 1994; Fund Managers:
Richard Habermann
AlanRadlo
Derek Young
David Prothro
Canadian Bond Fund
RRSP Eligible; Inception Year: 1988; Fund Managers:
David Prothro
Canadian Growth Company Fund
RRSP Eligible; Inception Year: 1994; Fund Managers:
Alan Radlo
Canadian Disciplined Equity Fund
RRSP Eligible; Inception Year: 1998; Fund Managers:
Robert Haber
Emerging Markets Fund
RRSP Eligible; Inception Year: 1994; Fund Managers:
Robert von Rekowsky
Far East Fund
RRSP Eligible; Inception Year: 1991; Fund Managers:
Joseph Tse
Latin America Fund
RRSP Eligible; Inception Year: 1994; Fund Managers:
Adam Kutas
BrentBottamini
Growth America Fund
RRSP Eligible; Inception Year: 1990; Fund Managers:
John Power
Small Cap America Fund
RRSP Eligible; Inception Year: 1994; Fund Managers:
Tom Hense
True North Fund
RRSP Eligible; Inception Year: 1996; Fund Managers:
Steve Binder
American High Yield Fund
RRSP Eligible; Inception Year: 1994; Fund Managers:
Matthew Conti
Canadian Balanced Fund
RRSP Eligible; Inception Year: 1998; Fund Managers:
Robert Haber
SteveBinder
Eric Mollenhauer
David Prothro
Canadian Money Market Fund
RRSP Eligible; Inception Year: 1991; Fund Managers:
Ken Anderson
Canadian Short Term Bond Fund
RRSP Eligible; Inception Year: 1995; Fund Managers:
David Prothro
Global Asset Allocation Fund
RRSP Eligible; Inception Year: 1993; Fund Managers:
Richard Habermann
AndyWeir
Derek Young
Robert Rowland
Anas Chakra
Joseph Tse
Keith Quinton
Overseas Fund
RRSP Eligible; Inception Year: 1999; Fund Managers:
Robert S. Feldman
LanceMcInerney
International Portfolio Fund
RRSP Eligible; Inception Year: 1987; Fund Managers:
Richard Habermann
RobertRowland
Joseph Tse

Michael Strong
James Rutherford
John Power
Japan Fund
RRSP Eligible; Inception Year: 1993; Fund Managers:
Robert Rowland
Canadian Opportunities Fund
RRSP Eligible; Inception Year: 2000; Fund Managers:
Maxime Lemieux
Canadian Large Cap Fund
RRSP Eligible; Inception Year: 1988; Fund Managers:
Doug Lober
American Opportunities Fund
RRSP Eligible; Inception Year: 2000; Fund Managers:
Robert Haber
Canadian Balanced Class Fund
RRSP Eligible; Inception Year: 2001; Fund Managers:
Robert Haber
SteveBinder
Eric Mollenhauer
Disciplined Equity Class Fund
RRSP Eligible; Inception Year: 2001;
Europe Fund
RRSP Eligible; Inception Year: 1992; Fund Managers:
Anas Chakra
Far East Class Fund
RRSP Eligible; Inception Year: 2001;
Growth America Class Fund
RRSP Eligible; Inception Year: 2001; Fund Managers:
Harry W. Lange
Small Cap America Class Fund
RRSP Eligible; Inception Year: 2001;
True North Class Fund
RRSP Eligible; Inception Year: 2001;
American Disciplined Equity Fund
RRSP Eligible; Inception Year: 2002; Fund Managers:
Bruce Dirks
American Value Fund
RRSP Eligible; Inception Year: 2002; Fund Managers:
Ciaran O'Neill
Global Disciplined Equity Fund
RRSP Eligible; Inception Year: 2002; Fund Managers:
Michael Strong
ChristopherGoudie
Global Opportunities Fund
RRSP Eligible; Inception Year: 2002; Fund Managers:
Harry W. Lange
MichaelJenkins
William Bower
NorthStar Fund
RRSP Eligible; Inception Year: 2002; Fund Managers:
Alan Radlo
JoelTilinghast
Monthly Income Fund
RRSP Eligible; Inception Year: 2003; Fund Managers:
Derek Young
MatthewConti
David Bagnani
Steve Binder
Cecilia Mo
David Prothro
US Money Market Fund
RRSP Eligible; Inception Year: 1994; Fund Managers:
Ken Anderson
American Disciplined Equity Class Fund
RRSP Eligible; Inception Year: 2002;
American Opportunities Class Fund
RRSP Eligible; Inception Year: 2001;
Canadian Growth Company Class Fund
RRSP Eligible; Inception Year: 2001;
Canadian Opportunities Class Fund
RRSP Eligible; Inception Year: 2004;
Europe Class Fund
RRSP Eligible; Inception Year: 2001;
Global Disciplined Equity Class Fund
RRSP Eligible; Inception Year: 2002;
International Portfolio Class Fund
RRSP Eligible; Inception Year: 2001;
Japan Class Fund
RRSP Eligible; Inception Year: 2001;
NorthStar Class Fund
RRSP Eligible; Inception Year: 2002;
Dividend Fund
RRSP Eligible; Inception Year: 2005; Fund Managers:
Steve Binder
CeciliaMo
David Prothro
Derek Young
Monthly High Income Fund
RRSP Eligible; Inception Year: 2005; Fund Managers:
Steve Binder
CeciliaMo
Matthew Conti
David Prothro
Derek Young
Income Trust Fund
RRSP Eligible; Inception Year: 2005; Fund Managers:
Cecilia Mo
Canadian Short Term Income Class Fund
RRSP Eligible; Inception Year: 2001;
Fidelity ClearPath:
Income Portfolio Fund
RRSP Eligible; Inception Year: 2005; Fund Managers:
Andrew Dierdorf
ChrisSharpe
2005 Portfolio Fund
RRSP Eligible; Inception Year: 2005; Fund Managers:
Andrew Dierdorf
ChrisSharpe
2010 Portfolio Fund
RRSP Eligible; Inception Year: 2005; Fund Managers:
Andrew Dierdorf
ChrisSharpe
2015 Portfolio Fund
RRSP Eligible; Inception Year: 2005; Fund Managers:
Andrew Dierdorf
ChrisSharpe
2020 Portfolio Fund
RRSP Eligible; Inception Year: 2005; Fund Managers:
Andrew Dierdorf
ChrisSharpe
2025 Portfolio Fund
RRSP Eligible; Inception Year: 2005; Fund Managers:
Andrew Dierdorf
ChrisSharpe
2030 Portfolio Fund
RRSP Eligible; Inception Year: 2005; Fund Managers:
Andrew Dierdorf
ChrisSharpe
2035 Portfolio Fund
RRSP Eligible; Inception Year: 2005; Fund Managers:
Andrew Dierdorf
ChrisSharpe
2040 Portfolio Fund
RRSP Eligible; Inception Year: 2005; Fund Managers:
Andrew Dierdorf
ChrisSharpe
2045 Portfolio Fund
RRSP Eligible; Inception Year: 2005; Fund Managers:
Andrew Dierdorf
ChrisSharpe
Fidelity Focus:
Health Care Fund
RRSP Eligible; Inception Year: 1997; Fund Managers:
Doug Nigen
Natural Resources Fund
RRSP Eligible; Inception Year: 1997; Fund Managers:
Jody Simes
ShawnBoire
Consumer Industries Fund
RRSP Eligible; Inception Year: 1997; Fund Managers:
Melissa Reilly
Financial Services Fund
RRSP Eligible; Inception Year: 1997; Fund Managers:
Pierre Sorel
Technology Fund
RRSP Eligible; Inception Year: 1997; Fund Managers:
Tetsuji Inoue
Telecommunications Fund
RRSP Eligible; Inception Year: 2000; Fund Managers:
Terra Chanpongsang
Health Care Class Fund
RRSP Eligible; Inception Year: 2001;
Technology Class Fund
RRSP Eligible; Inception Year: 2001;
Consumer Industries Class Fund
RRSP Eligible; Inception Year: 2001;
Financial Services Class Fund
RRSP Eligible; Inception Year: 2001;
Natural Resources Class Fund
RRSP Eligible; Inception Year: 2001;
Telecommunications Class Fund
RRSP Eligible; Inception Year: 2001;

Fiducie Desjardins/ Desjardins Trust

Also listed under: *Trust Companies*
CP 34, Desjardins Stn. Desjardins
1, Complexe Desjardins
Montréal, QC H5B 1E4
514-286-9441
Fax: 514-286-1131
800-361-6840
Other Information: 514-286-3225 (Business Centre Phone); 514-286-3100 (Asset Custody Service Phone); 514-499-8440 (Immigrant Investors Program Phone)
info@immigrantinvestor.com
www.fiduciedesjardins.com
Ownership: Part of the Desjardins Group.
Year Founded: 1963
Number of Employees: 850
Profile: Desjardins Trust offers the following services: trust services, asset custody services, Guaranteed Investment Certificates, & the Immigrant Investors Program. The trust company is responsible for the trust activities of the Desjardins caisses. Trust services are provided to both individuals & businesses. Business clientele includes pension funds, life insurance companies, full service brokers, portfolio managers, associations, plus private, public, parapublic & cooperative businesses. The company's activities also include the wholesale & distribution of mutual funds & private management services.

Executives:
Bertrand Laferrière, President
Marc Audet, Vice-President, Immigrant Investor Program
François Gagnon, Vice-President, Custody Services
Affiliated Companies:
Northwest Mutual Funds Inc.
Desjardins:
Québec Balanced Fund
RRSP Eligible; Inception Year: 1997; Fund Managers:
Fiera Capital
Canadian Balanced Fund
RRSP Eligible; Inception Year: 1986; Fund Managers:
Alliance Bernstein
Canadian Bond Fund
RRSP Eligible; Inception Year: 1959; Fund Managers:
Fiera Capital
Dividend Fund
RRSP Eligible; Inception Year: 1994; Fund Managers:
Fiera Capital
Environment Fund
RRSP Eligible; Inception Year: 1990; Fund Managers:
Fiera Capital
Canadian Small Cap Equity Fund
RRSP Eligible; Inception Year: 1994; Fund Managers:
Fiera Capital
Money Market Fund
RRSP Eligible; Inception Year: 1989; Fund Managers:
Desjardins Investment Management
Global Equity Value Fund
RRSP Eligible; Inception Year: 1959; Fund Managers:
Alliance Bernstein
Short Term Income Fund
RRSP Eligible; Inception Year: 1965; Fund Managers:
Fiera Capital
American Equity Value Fund
RRSP Eligible; Inception Year: 2004; Fund Managers:
Alliance Bernstein
Select Canadian Balanced Fund
RRSP Eligible; Inception Year: 1999; Fund Managers:
Northwest Mutual Funds
Select Canadian Equity Fund
RRSP Eligible; Inception Year: 1999; Fund Managers:
AIM Trimark
Ethical Canadian Balanced Fund
RRSP Eligible; Inception Year: 2000; Fund Managers:
Ethical Funds
Dividend T FundInception Year: 2002; Fund Managers:
Fiera Capital
Québec T FundInception Year: 2002; Fund Managers:
Fiera Capital
Canadian Equity Value FundInception Year: 2002; Fund Managers:
Alliance Bernstein

Fiducie Desjardins/ Desjardins Trust (continued)
Global Science & Technology FundInception Year: 2001; Fund Managers:
Alliance Bernstein
CI Canadian Investment Fund
RRSP Eligible; Inception Year: 2004; Fund Managers:
CI Mutual Funds
Fidelity True North Fund
RRSP Eligible; Inception Year: 2004; Fund Managers:
Fidelity Investment Canada
Fidelity Canadian Growth Company Fund
RRSP Eligible; Inception Year: 2004; Fund Managers:
Fidelity Investment Canada
Fidelity International Portfolio Fund
RRSP Eligible; Inception Year: 2004; Fund Managers:
Fidelity Investment Canada
Alternative Invesments Fund
RRSP Eligible; Inception Year: 2004; Fund Managers:
Montrusco Bolton
Global Equity Value T FundInception Year: 2004; Fund Managers:
Alliance Bernstein
Overseas Equity Value Fund
RRSP Eligible; Inception Year: 1998; Fund Managers:
Alliance Bernstein
Select Global Equity Fund
RRSP Eligible; Inception Year: 1999; Fund Managers:
Fidelity Investment Canada
Enhanced Bond Fund
RRSP Eligible; Inception Year: 2004; Fund Managers:
Alliance Bernstein
Select American Equity Fund
RRSP Eligible; Inception Year: 1999; Fund Managers:
AGF
CI Value Trust Corporate Class Fund
RRSP Eligible; Inception Year: 2004; Fund Managers:
CI Mutual Funds
Fidelity Small Cap America Fund
RRSP Eligible; Inception Year: 2004; Fund Managers:
Fidelity Investment Canada
Canadian Equity Fund
RRSP Eligible; Inception Year: 1959; Fund Managers:
Fiera Capital
Alternative Investment T FundInception Year: 2004; Fund Managers:
Montrusco Bolton
Branches:
Montréal
Tour est
PO Box 991, Desjardins Sta. Desjardins
2, complexe Desjardins, 22e étage
Montréal, QC H5B 1C1 Canada
514-286-3498
Fax: 514-286-3145
888-252-5332
Ottawa
#1650, 20 Laurier Ave. West
Ottawa, ON K1P 5Z9 Canada
613-567-2885
Fax: 613-567-4225
866-567-2885
Québec
#1100, 2875, boul Laurier
Québec, QC G1V 2M2 Canada
418-653-7922
Fax: 418-651-0371
800-653-7922

First Trust Portfolio

#1300, 330 Bay St.
Toronto, ON M5G 2S8
416-865-8065
Fax: 416-865-8058
877-622-5552
info@firsttrust.ca
www.firsttrust.ca
Executives:
Robert Carey, Chief Investment Officer
First Trust:
Pharmaceutical Trust 2001 Fund
RRSP Eligible; Inception Year: 2001;
Pharmaceutical Trust Fund
RRSP Eligible; Inception Year: 2002;
Dow 10 Strategy Fund
RRSP Eligible; Inception Year: 2002;
RBC Investment Focus List 2001 Fund
RRSP Eligible; Inception Year: 2001;
Highland Capital Floating Rate Income FundInception Year: 2005;
Highland Capital Floating Rate Income Fund IIInception Year: 2005;
ScotiaMcLeod:
Canadian Core Portfolio Fund
RRSP Eligible; Inception Year: 2003;
TD:
Canadian Quantitative Research Portfolio Fund
RRSP Eligible; Inception Year: 2006;

Fonds de solidarité des travailleurs du Québec(FTQ)

Also listed under: *Financing & Loan Companies*
#200, 545, boul Crémazie est
Montréal, QC H2M 2W4
514-383-8383
Fax: 514-850-4845
800-361-5017
www.fondsftq.com
Ownership: Public.
Year Founded: 1983
Number of Employees: 400
Assets: $1-10 billion
Revenues: $1-10 billion
Profile: The Fund finances primarily the growth of viable innovative companies that create permanent jobs. The Fund also makes investments directly or through its development fund network in the following types of projects: start-up, expansion, IPO, consolidation, mergers, acquisitions, & export.
Executives:
Henri Massé, Chair
Pierre Genest, CEO, Solidarity Fund QFL
Yvon Bolduc, Exec. Vice-President, Investments
Pierre Leblanc, Exec. Vice-President, Human Resources
Denis Leclerc, Sr. Vice-President, Shareholder Services & Development
Michel Pontbriand, Sr. Vice-President, Finance
Janie C. Béïque, Vice-President, Legal Affairs
René Roy, Secretary of the Board
QFL:
Québec Solidarity Fund
RRSP Eligible; Inception Year: 1984;
Fonds régionaux de solidarité:
Chibougamau
432B, 3e rue
Chibougamau, QC G8P 1N7 Canada
418-748-8180
Fax: 418-748-7121
888-748-8180
www.ndq.fondsreg.com
Raymond Grenier, Directeur régional
Gaspé
185, boul York est
Gaspé, QC G4X 2L1 Canada
418-368-7346
Fax: 418-368-4028
800-404-7429
mcayouette@gas.fondsreg.com
www.gas.fondsreg.com
Marc Cayouette, Directeur régional
Gatineau
#315, 259, boul St-Joseph
Gatineau, QC J8Y 6T1 Canada
819-778-2995
Fax: 819-778-2998
www.out.fondsreg.com
Michel Parent, Directeur régional
Joliette
284, rue Beaudry nord
Joliette, QC J6E 6A6 Canada
450-755-3992
Fax: 450-755-6560
888-755-3992
www.lan.fondsreg.com
Yves Landry, Directeur régional
Jonquière
#130, 2679, boul du Royaume
Jonquière, QC G7S 5T1 Canada
418-699-1485
Fax: 418-699-1187
888-699-1485
www.sls.fondsreg.com
Andrée Girard, Directrice régionale
Laval
#606, 3030, boul Le Carrefour
Laval, QC H7T 2P5 Canada
450-978-3344
Fax: 450-978-3313
info@lav.fondsreg.com
www.lav.fondsreg.com
Denis Bernier, Directeur régional
Lévis
#104B, 5790, boul Étienne-Dallaire
Lévis, QC G6V 8V6 Canada
418-837-1040
Fax: 418-837-3093
abelanger@cha.fondsreg.com
www.cha.fondsreg.com
Jean Roy, Directeur régional
Montréal
#610, 545, boul Crémazie est
Montréal, QC H2M 2V1 Canada
514-845-3233
Fax: 514-845-0625
dblanchard@mtl.fondsreg.com
www.mtl.fondsreg.com
Michel Parent, Directeur régional
Québec
#130, 5050, boul des Gradins
Québec, QC G2J 1P8 Canada
418-624-2773
Fax: 418-624-8975
www.que.fondsreg.com
Jean Roy, Directeur régional
Rimouski
#601, 2, rue Saint-Germain est
Rimouski, QC G5L 8T7 Canada
418-721-3565
Fax: 418-721-3564
888-456-3565
www.bsl.fondsreg.com
Marc Cayouette, Directeur régional
Rouyn-Noranda
#300, 75, boul Québec
Rouyn-Noranda, QC J9X 7A2 Canada
819-762-7422
Fax: 819-762-8335
www.abt.fondsreg.com
Raymond Grenier, Directeur régional
Sept-×les
#101, 818, boul Laure
Sept-×les, QC G4R 1Y8 Canada
418-968-3784
Fax: 418-962-2988
800-792-2488
www.cot.fondsreg.com
Marc Cayouette, Directeur régional
Sherbrooke
#140, 2100, rue King ouest
Sherbrooke, QC J1J 2E8 Canada
819-829-2220
Fax: 819-829-2263
www.est.fondsreg.com
Luc Pinard, Directeur régional
St-Jean-sur-Richeleau
#109, 923, boul du Séminaire nord
St-Jean-sur-Richelieu, QC J3A 1B6 Canada
450-359-3776
Fax: 450-359-3363
888-359-8939
www.mon.fondsreg.com
Luc Pinard, Directeur régional
St-Jérôme
333, rue Parent
Saint-Jérome, QC J7Z 2A2 Canada
450-569-6658
Fax: 450-569-6630
www.lau.fondsreg.com
Denis Bernier, Directeur régional
Trois-Rivières
#205, 7080, boul Marion
Trois-Rivières, QC G9A 6G4 Canada
819-370-3368
Fax: 819-370-1512
www.mcq.fondsreg.com
Yves Landry, Directeur régional

Fonds des professionnels - Fonds d'investissement

Also listed under: *Financial Planning*
Tour de l'Est
2, Complexe Desjardins, 31e étage
Montréal, QC H5B 1C2
514-350-5050
Fax: 514-350-5060
888-377-7337
fonds@groupefdp.com
www.groupefdp.com
Former Name: Fonds des Professionnels du Québec Inc.
Ownership: Private. Parent Fonds des Professionaels inc.
Year Founded: 1978
Number of Employees: 55
Assets: $1-10 billion Year End: 20041031
Revenues: $5-10 million Year End: 20041031
Directors:
Frédéric Bélanger
Pierre A. Boulianne
Martin Charland
Normand Doré
Jacques M. Gagnon
Roland Lefebvre
Jean-François Paris
Roger Perrault
Maurice Piette
Albert Plante
Michel Portelance
André Riopel
Québec Professionals:
Asian Equity Fund
RRSP Eligible; Inception Year: 1998; Fund Managers:
Robert Blais
MaxD'Alessandro
Balanced Fund
RRSP Eligible; Inception Year: 1982; Fund Managers:
Robert Blais
MaxD'Alessandro
Bond Fund
RRSP Eligible; Inception Year: 1978; Fund Managers:
Robert Blais
MaxD'Alessandro
Canadian Equity Fund
RRSP Eligible; Inception Year: 1987; Fund Managers:
Robert Blais
MaxD'Alessandro
European Equity Fund
RRSP Eligible; Inception Year: 1998; Fund Managers:
Robert Blais
MaxD'Alessandro
International Equity Fund
RRSP Eligible; Inception Year: 1993; Fund Managers:
Robert Blais
MaxD'Alessandro
Short Term Fund
RRSP Eligible; Inception Year: 1997; Fund Managers:
Robert Blais
MaxD'Alessandro
American Index Fund
RRSP Eligible; Inception Year: 0; Fund Managers:
Robert Blais
MaxD'Alessandro
Global Diversified Fund
RRSP Eligible; Inception Year: 0; Fund Managers:
Robert Blais
MaxD'Alessandro
Balanced Growth Fund
RRSP Eligible; Inception Year: 2001; Fund Managers:
Robert Blais
MaxD'Alessandro
Money Market Fund
RRSP Eligible; Inception Year: 0; Fund Managers:
Robert Blais
MaxD'Alessandro
Branches:
Montréal
#1425, 425, boul de Maisonneuve ouest
Montréal, QC H3A 3G5 Canada

Québec
2640, boul Laurier, 11e étage
Québec, QC G1V 5C2 Canada
Sherbrooke
1640, King ouest
Sherbrooke, QC J1J 2C3 Canada

Formula Growth Limited

#2300, 1010, rue Sherbrooke ouest
Montréal, QC H3A 2R7
514-288-5136
Fax: 514-844-4561
ari@formulagrowth.ca
www.formulagrowth.ca
Executives:
René Catafago, Exec. Vice-President
Formula Growth Fund
RRSP Eligible; Inception Year: 1960; Fund Managers:
Anthony Staples
Randall W.Kelly
Kimberley Holden
John Liddy
John W. Dobson

Franklin Templeton Investments Corp.

#2101, 1 Adelaide St. East
Toronto, ON M5C 3B8
416-364-4672
Fax: 416-364-1163
800-387-0830
service@franklintempleton.ca
www.franklintempleton.ca
Former Name: Templeton Management Ltd.
Ownership: Wholly owned by Franklin Resources Inc., California
Profile: The company provides global investment management, advisory & distribution services to individual, institutional & corporate clients worldwide.

Executives:
Martin L. Flanagan, President/Co-CEO
Gregory E. Johnson, President/Co-CEO
Murray L. Simpson, CFA, Exec. Vice-President & General Counsel
James R. Baio, Sr. Vice-President/CFO
Jennifer L. Bolt, Sr. Vice-President, Chief Counsel & Chief Informat
Leslie M. Kratter, Sr. Vice-President & Asst. Secretary
Penelope S. Alexander, Vice-President, Human Resource US
Holly E. Gibson, Vice-President, Corporate Communications
Donna Ikeda, Vice-President, Human Resources International
Kenneth A. Lewis, Vice-President & Treasurer
John M. Lusk, Vice-President
Bissett:
Bond A Fund
RRSP Eligible; Inception Year: 2000; Fund Managers:
Bissett Investments Management
Canadian Equity A Fund
RRSP Eligible; Inception Year: 2000; Fund Managers:
Bissett Investments Management
Dividend Income A Fund
RRSP Eligible; Inception Year: 2000; Fund Managers:
Bissett Investments Management
Multinational Growth A Fund
RRSP Eligible; Inception Year: 2000; Fund Managers:
Bissett Investments Management
Small Cap A Fund
RRSP Eligible; Inception Year: 2000; Fund Managers:
Bissett Investments Management
Income A Fund
RRSP Eligible; Inception Year: 2000; Fund Managers:
Bissett Investments Management
International Equity A Fund
RRSP Eligible; Inception Year: 2000; Fund Managers:
Bissett Investments Management
Microcap A Fund
RRSP Eligible; Inception Year: 2000; Fund Managers:
Bissett Investments Management
Large Cap A Fund
RRSP Eligible; Inception Year: 2000; Fund Managers:
Bissett Investments Management
Bond F Fund
RRSP Eligible; Inception Year: 1986; Fund Managers:
Bissett Investments Management
Canadian Balanced A Fund
RRSP Eligible; Inception Year: 2000; Fund Managers:
Bissett Investments Management
Canadian Balanced F Fund
RRSP Eligible; Inception Year: 1991; Fund Managers:
Bissett Investments Management
Canadian Equity Corporate Class Fund
RRSP Eligible; Inception Year: 2001; Fund Managers:
Bissett Investments Management
Canadian Equity F Fund
RRSP Eligible; Inception Year: 1983; Fund Managers:
Bissett Investments Management
Dividend Income F Fund
RRSP Eligible; Inception Year: 1988; Fund Managers:
Bissett Investments Management
Income F Fund
RRSP Eligible; Inception Year: 1996; Fund Managers:
Bissett Investments Management
International Equity F Fund
RRSP Eligible; Inception Year: 1994; Fund Managers:
Bissett Investments Management
Large Cap F Fund
RRSP Eligible; Inception Year: 1999; Fund Managers:
Bissett Investments Management
Microcap F Fund
RRSP Eligible; Inception Year: 1997; Fund Managers:
Bissett Investments Management
Multinational Growth Corporate Class Fund
RRSP Eligible; Inception Year: 2001; Fund Managers:
Bissett Investments Management
Multinational Growth F Fund
RRSP Eligible; Inception Year: 1995; Fund Managers:
Bissett Investments Management
Small Cap Corporate Class Fund
RRSP Eligible; Inception Year: 2001; Fund Managers:
Bissett Investments Management
Small Cap F Fund
RRSP Eligible; Inception Year: 1993; Fund Managers:
Bissett Investments Management
Canadian Short Term Bond A Fund
RRSP Eligible; Inception Year: 2003; Fund Managers:
Bissett Investments Management
Canadian Short Term Bond F Fund
RRSP Eligible; Inception Year: 2003; Fund Managers:
Bissett Investments Management
Income Trust & Dividend A Fund
RRSP Eligible; Inception Year: 2003; Fund Managers:
Bissett Investments Management
Income Trust & Dividend F Fund
RRSP Eligible; Inception Year: 2003; Fund Managers:
Bissett Investments Management
All Canadian Focus A Fund
RRSP Eligible; Inception Year: 2004; Fund Managers:
Bissett Investments Management
All Canadian Focus F Fund
RRSP Eligible; Inception Year: 2004; Fund Managers:
Bissett Investments Management
All Canadian Focus Corporate Class A Fund
RRSP Eligible; Inception Year: 2004; Fund Managers:
Bissett Investments Management
All Canadian Focus Corporate Class F Fund
RRSP Eligible; Inception Year: 2004; Fund Managers:
Bissett Investments Management
Franklin:
Japan Corporate Class Fund
RRSP Eligible; Inception Year: 2001; Fund Managers:
Franklin Advisers Inc.
Technology Corporate Class Fund
RRSP Eligible; Inception Year: 2000; Fund Managers:
Franklin Advisers Inc.
US Small-Mid Cap Growth Fund
RRSP Eligible; Inception Year: 1997; Fund Managers:
Franklin Advisers Inc.
US Small-Mid Cap Growth Corporate Class Fund
RRSP Eligible; Inception Year: 1997; Fund Managers:
Franklin Advisers Inc.
World Health Science & Biotech Corporate Class Fund
RRSP Eligible; Inception Year: 2001; Fund Managers:
Franklin Advisers Inc.
World Growth Corporate Class Fund
RRSP Eligible; Inception Year: 2001; Fund Managers:
Fiduciary International
World Health Science & Biotech Fund
RRSP Eligible; Inception Year: 2000; Fund Managers:
Franklin Advisers Inc.
High Income Fund
RRSP Eligible; Inception Year: 2003; Fund Managers:
Franklin Advisers Inc.
Strategic Income Fund
RRSP Eligible; Inception Year: 2003; Fund Managers:
Franklin Advisers Inc.
Flex Cap Growth Corporate Class (US$) Fund
RRSP Eligible; Inception Year: 2001; Fund Managers:
Franklin Advisers Inc.

Franklin Templeton Investments Corp. (continued)
Franklin Templeton:
Money Market A Fund
RRSP Eligible; Inception Year: 2000; Fund Managers: Bissett Investments Management
US Money Market Corporate Class Fund
RRSP Eligible; Inception Year: 2001; Fund Managers: Franklin Advisers Inc.
US Rising Dividend A Fund
RRSP Eligible; Inception Year: 2000; Fund Managers: Franklin Advisers Inc.
US Rising Dividend F Fund
RRSP Eligible; Inception Year: 1984; Fund Managers: Franklin Advisers Inc.
Money Market Corporate Class Fund
RRSP Eligible; Inception Year: 2001; Fund Managers: Bissett Investments Management
Money Market F Fund
RRSP Eligible; Inception Year: 1991; Fund Managers: Bissett Investments Management
Diversified Income Portfolio Fund
RRSP Eligible; Inception Year: 2003;
Balanced Growth Portfolio Fund
RRSP Eligible; Inception Year: 2002;
Balanced Income Portfolio Fund
RRSP Eligible; Inception Year: 2002;
Global Growth Portfolio Fund
RRSP Eligible; Inception Year: 2003;
Growth Portfolio Fund
RRSP Eligible; Inception Year: 2002;
Maximum Growth Portfolio Fund
RRSP Eligible; Inception Year: 2002;
Balanced Growth Corporate Class Portfolio Fund
RRSP Eligible; Inception Year: 2004;
Maximum Growth Corporate Class Portfolio Fund
RRSP Eligible; Inception Year: 2004;
Growth Corporate Class Portfolio Fund
RRSP Eligible; Inception Year: 2004;
Global Growth Corporate Class Fund
RRSP Eligible; Inception Year: 2004;
Diversified Income Corporate Class Fund
RRSP Eligible; Inception Year: 2004;
Canadian Growth Corporate Class Portfolio Fund
RRSP Eligible; Inception Year: 2004;
Canadian Growth Portfolio Fund
RRSP Eligible; Inception Year: 2004;
Balanced Income Corporate Class Fund
RRSP Eligible; Inception Year: 2002;
Mutual:
Beacon Fund
RRSP Eligible; Inception Year: 1997; Fund Managers: Franklin Mutual Advisors
Beacon Corporate Class Fund
RRSP Eligible; Inception Year: 2001; Fund Managers: Franklin Mutual Advisors
Discovery Fund
RRSP Eligible; Inception Year: 2003; Fund Managers: Franklin Mutual Advisors
Discovery Corporate Class Fund
RRSP Eligible; Inception Year: 2003; Fund Managers: Franklin Mutual Advisors
Templeton:
Balanced Fund
RRSP Eligible; Inception Year: 1990;
Canadian Asset Allocation Fund
RRSP Eligible; Inception Year: 1994;
Canadian Stock Fund
RRSP Eligible; Inception Year: 1989;
Emerging Markets Fund
RRSP Eligible; Inception Year: 1991; Fund Managers: Templeton Investment Management (Hong Kong) Ltd., Ph.D
Global Balanced Fund
RRSP Eligible; Inception Year: 1994;
Global Smaller Companies Fund
RRSP Eligible; Inception Year: 1989;
Growth Fund
RRSP Eligible; Inception Year: 1954;
International Stock Fund
RRSP Eligible; Inception Year: 1989;
Treasury Bill Fund
RRSP Eligible; Inception Year: 1988;
Canadian Stock Corporate Class Fund
RRSP Eligible; Inception Year: 2001;
Emerging Market Corporate Class Fund
RRSP Eligible; Inception Year: 2001; Fund Managers: Templeton Investment Management (Hong Kong) Ltd., Ph.D
European Corporate Class Fund
RRSP Eligible; Inception Year: 2001;
Growth Corporate Class Fund
RRSP Eligible; Inception Year: 2001;
International Stock Corporate Class Fund
RRSP Eligible; Inception Year: 2001;
Global Smaller Companies Corporate Class (US$) Fund
RRSP Eligible; Inception Year: 2001;
Global Bond Fund
RRSP Eligible; Inception Year: 1988;
BRIC Corporate Class Fund
RRSP Eligible; Inception Year: 2004;

Friedberg Mercantile Group
Also listed under: *Investment Dealers*
BCE Place
PO Box 866
#250, 181 Bay St.
Toronto, ON M5J 2T3
416-364-2700
Fax: 416-364-5385
Ownership: Private
Year Founded: 1971
Number of Employees: 50
Stock Exchange Membership: Montreal Exchange, Toronto Stock Exchange, TSX Venture Exchange
Profile: The Group is one of Canada's largest futures & options discount broker.
Friedberg:
Currency Fund
RRSP Eligible; Inception Year: 1994; Fund Managers: Albert D. Friedberg
Diversified (US$) Fund
RRSP Eligible; Inception Year: 1996; Fund Managers: Albert D. Friedberg
Foreign Bond Fund
RRSP Eligible; Inception Year: 1996; Fund Managers: Albert D. Friedberg
Precious Metals Fund
RRSP Eligible; Inception Year: 1992; Fund Managers: Albert D. Friedberg
Futures (US$) Fund
RRSP Eligible; Inception Year: 1998; Fund Managers: Albert D. Friedberg
Equity Hedge (US$) Fund
RRSP Eligible; Inception Year: 1998; Fund Managers: Albert D. Friedberg
International Securities (US$) Fund
RRSP Eligible; Inception Year: 1998; Fund Managers: Albert D. Friedberg
Global-Macro Hedge (US$) Fund
RRSP Eligible; Inception Year: 2002; Fund Managers: Albert D. Friedberg
The First Mercantile Currency Fund
RRSP Eligible; Inception Year: 1985; Fund Managers: Albert D. Friedberg
Niagara Comfort Class B Fund
RRSP Eligible; Inception Year: 1999; Fund Managers: Albert D. Friedberg

Front Street Capital
#400, 87 Front St. East
Toronto, ON M5E 1B8
416-364-1990
Fax: 416-364-8893
800-513-2832
advisorservice@frontstreetcapital.com
www.frontstreetcapital.com
Year Founded: 2001
Executives:
Norman Lamarche, Vice-President, Co-Chief Investment Officer
Frank Mersch, Vice-President, Co-Chief Investment Officer
Front Street:
Energy Growth Fund
RRSP Eligible; Inception Year: 2002;
Small Cap Canadian Fund
RRSP Eligible; Inception Year: 1985;
Canadian Hedge Fund
RRSP Eligible; Inception Year: 2003;
First Wave FundInception Year: 2000;
Energy & Power Offshore FundInception Year: 2003;
Performance Fund II
RRSP Eligible; Inception Year: 2004;
Mining Opportunities FundInception Year: 2005;
Performance Fund
RRSP Eligible; Inception Year: 2002;
Long/Short Income Fund
RRSP Eligible; Inception Year: 2005;
Resource Hedge FundInception Year: 2005;
Alternative Asset Fund
RRSP Eligible; Inception Year: 2005;
Flow Through 2004 FundInception Year: 2004;
Flow Through 2005 FundInception Year: 2005;
Flow Through 2006 FundInception Year: 2006;
Front Street Capital:
Special Opportunities Canadian Fund
RRSP Eligible; Inception Year: 1990;

frontierAltOrbit Funds Management Limited
#800, 1310, av Greene
Montréal, QC H3Z 2B2
514-932-3000
Fax: 514-989-2132
888-376-7815
info@orbitfunds.com
www.orbitfunds.com; www.frontieralt.com
Former Name: Orbit Mutual Fund Management Ltd.
Ownership: Private
Year Founded: 1988
Executives:
Feico Leemhuis, President
Orbit:
Canadian Equity Fund
RRSP Eligible; Inception Year: 1998; Fund Managers: AGF Magna Vista Investment Management
World Fund
RRSP Eligible; Inception Year: 1988; Fund Managers: Marvin & Palmer Associates, Inc.

GBC Asset Management Inc.
Also listed under: *Pension & Money Management Companies*
BCE Place, Canada Trust Tower
#4320, 161 Bay St.
Toronto, ON M5J 2S1
416-366-2550
Fax: 416-366-6833
800-668-7383
info@gbc.ca
www.gbc.ca
Ownership: Private
Year Founded: 1988
Number of Employees: 18
Assets: $500m-1 billion
Executives:
John Quinn, Partner
Russ Quinn, Partner & Manager, Administration
Jean-Paul Burlock, Contact, Sales
GBC:
Canadian Bond Fund
RRSP Eligible; Inception Year: 1984; Fund Managers: TDQC
Canadian Growth Fund
RRSP Eligible; Inception Year: 1988; Fund Managers: Pembroke Management Ltd.
International Growth Fund
RRSP Eligible; Inception Year: 1989; Fund Managers: William Blair & Co. LLC
Money Market Fund
RRSP Eligible; Inception Year: 1988; Fund Managers: TDQC
North American Growth US$ Fund
RRSP Eligible; Inception Year: 1997; Fund Managers: Pembroke Management Ltd.
North American Growth Fund
RRSP Eligible; Inception Year: 1977; Fund Managers: Pembroke Management Ltd.
Regional Offices:
Montréal
#1700, 1002, rue Sherbrooke ouest
Montréal, QC H3A 3S4 Canada
514-848-0716
Fax: 514-848-9620
800-667-0716
Daniel Thompson, Partner

Gestion Férique
Also listed under: *Pension & Money Management Companies*
#350, 1100 rue de la Gauchetière ouest
Montréal, QC H3B 2S2

514-840-9206
Fax: 514-840-9216
888-259-7969
info@ferique.com
www.ferique.com
Former Name: Ordre des Ingenieurs du Québec
Ownership: Non-profit
Year Founded: 1999
Number of Employees: 5
Assets: $500m-1 billion
Revenues: $5-10 million
Executives:
Michel Riverin, President
Claude R. Tremblay, Vice-President
Fabienne Lacoste, Exec. Director; 514-840-9206; fabienne.lacoste@ferique.com
Férique:
American Fund
RRSP Eligible; Inception Year: 1995; Fund Managers:
TAL Global Asset Management Inc.
Equity Fund
RRSP Eligible; Inception Year: 1975; Fund Managers:
Barclays Global Investors
International Equity Fund
RRSP Eligible; Inception Year: 1994; Fund Managers:
TAL Global Asset Management Inc.
Balanced Fund
RRSP Eligible; Inception Year: 1981; Fund Managers:
Foyston, Gordon & Payne
Short Term Income Fund
RRSP Eligible; Inception Year: 1975; Fund Managers:
TAL Global Asset Management Inc.
Europe Fund
RRSP Eligible; Inception Year: 2003; Fund Managers:
UBS
Asia Fund
RRSP Eligible; Inception Year: 2003; Fund Managers:
Normura Investment Management
Bond Fund
RRSP Eligible; Inception Year: 0; Fund Managers:
Addenda Capital

Golden Opportunities Fund Inc.

#1300, 410 - 22nd St. East
Saskatoon, SK S7K 5T6
306-652-5557
Fax: 306-652-8186
866-261-5686
info@goldenopportunities.ca
www.goldenopportunities.ca
Year Founded: 1999
Assets: $10-50 million Year End: 20041130
Stock Symbol: GOFS01
Directors:
Grant J. Kook, Chair
Douglas W. Banzet
Brian L. Barber
John W. Green
William McKnight
Marlene K. Moleski
Lorraine Sali
Golden Opportunities Fund Inc.
RRSP Eligible; Inception Year: 1999; Fund Managers:
Grant J. Kook
Douglas W.Banzet
Trevor S. Giles

The Great-West Life Assurance Company(GWL)/ Great-West, Compagnie d'Assurance Vie

Also listed under: *Federal & Provincial*
PO Box 6000
100 Osborne St. North
Winnipeg, MB R3C 3A5
204-946-1190
Fax: 204-946-4159
800-665-5758
www.greatwestlife.com
Ownership: Major shareholder Great-West Lifeco (100% interest)
Year Founded: 1891
Number of Employees: 5,740
Assets: $10-100 billion Year End: 20051231
Revenues: $10-100 billion Year End: 20051231
Stock Symbol: GWO
Profile: GWL is a leading Canadian insurer which operates a broad portfolio of financial security & benefit plan solutions for individuals, families, businesses & organizations. In addition to its domestic operations, the company is a supplier of reinsurance & specialty general insurance. A subsidiary is London Insurance Group Inc.
Executives:
Raymond L. McFeetors, President/CEO
Denis J. Devos, Chief Operating Officer
Dave Johnston, Exec. Vice-President, Group
Allen Loney, Exec. Vice-President & Chief Actuary, Capital Management
William W. Lovatt, Exec. Vice-President/CFO
Peter G. Munro, Exec. Vice-President & Chief Investment Officer

Ronald D. Saull, Sr. Vice-President & Chief Information Officer
Sheila A. Wagar, Sr. Vice-President, General Counsel & Secretary
Directors:
Robert Gratton, Chair
President/CEO, Power Financial Corporation
Gail S. Asper
Corporate Secretary, CanWest Global Communications Corp.
Orest T. Dackow
André Desmarais
President/Co-CEO, Power Corporation of Canada; Deputy Chair, Power Financial Cor
Paul Desmarais, Jr.
Chair/Co-CEO, Power Corporation of Canada; Chair, Power Financial Corporation
Michael Hepher
Daniel Johnson
Counsel to McCarthy Tétrault
Kevin P. Kavanagh, O.C.
Chancellor, University of Brandon
Peter Kruyt
Donald F. Mazankowski, O.C.
William T. McCallum
President/CEO, Great-West Life & Annuity Insurance Company; Co-President/CEO, Gr
Raymond L. McFeetors
President/CEO, The Great-West Assurance Co.; President/CEO, London Life Insuranc
Jerry E.A. Nickerson
Chair, H.B. Nickerson & Sons Limited
David Nield
R. Jeffrey Orr
President/CEO, Investors Group Inc.
Michel Plessis-Bélair, FCA
Vice-Chair/CFO, Power Corporation of Canada; Exec. Vice-President/CFO, Power Fin
Guy St-Germain, CM
President, Placements Laugerma inc.
Emöke Szathmáry
Murray Taylor
Gérard Veilleux, O.C.
President, Power Communications Inc.
Affiliated Companies:
Canada Life Financial Corporation
GWL Realty Advisors
London Life Insurance Company
GWL:
Advanced Portfolio DSC Fund
RRSP Eligible; Inception Year: 1996; Fund Managers:
GWL Investment Management Ltd.
Advanced Portfolio NL Fund
RRSP Eligible; Inception Year: 1996; Fund Managers:
GWL Investment Management Ltd.
Aggressive Portfolio DSC Fund
RRSP Eligible; Inception Year: 1996; Fund Managers:
GWL Investment Management Ltd.
Aggressive Portfolio NL Fund
RRSP Eligible; Inception Year: 1996; Fund Managers:
GWL Investment Management Ltd.
American Growth A-DSC Fund
RRSP Eligible; Inception Year: 1997; Fund Managers:
AGF Funds Inc.
American Growth A-NL Fund
RRSP Eligible; Inception Year: 1997; Fund Managers:
AGF Funds Inc.
Asian Growth A-DSC Fund
RRSP Eligible; Inception Year: 1997; Fund Managers:
AGF Funds Inc.
Asian Growth A-NL Fund
RRSP Eligible; Inception Year: 1997; Fund Managers:
AGF Funds Inc.
Balanced AT-DSC Fund
RRSP Eligible; Inception Year: 1996; Fund Managers:
Aim Trimark Investments
Balanced B-NL Fund
RRSP Eligible; Inception Year: 1996; Fund Managers:
Beutel Goodman & Co. Ltd.
Balanced B-DSC Fund
RRSP Eligible; Inception Year: 1996; Fund Managers:
Beutel Goodman & Co. Ltd.
Balanced AT-NL Fund
RRSP Eligible; Inception Year: 1996; Fund Managers:
Aim Trimark Investments
Balanced Portfolio NL Fund
RRSP Eligible; Inception Year: 1996; Fund Managers:
GWL Investment Management Ltd.
Balanced Portfolio DSC Fund
RRSP Eligible; Inception Year: 1996; Fund Managers:
GWL Investment Management Ltd.
Bond B-DSC Fund
RRSP Eligible; Inception Year: 1996; Fund Managers:
Beutel Goodman & Co. Ltd.
Bond B-NL Fund
RRSP Eligible; Inception Year: 1996; Fund Managers:
Beutel Goodman & Co. Ltd.
Bond L-DSC Fund
RRSP Eligible; Inception Year: 1996; Fund Managers:
London Life Investment Management Inc.
Bond L-NL Fund
RRSP Eligible; Inception Year: 1996; Fund Managers:
London Life Investment Management Inc.
Canadian Bond G-DSC Fund
RRSP Eligible; Inception Year: 1979; Fund Managers:
GWL Investment Management Ltd.
Canadian Bond G-NL Fund
RRSP Eligible; Inception Year: 1979; Fund Managers:
GWL Investment Management Ltd.
Canadian Equity G-DSC Fund
RRSP Eligible; Inception Year: 1987; Fund Managers:
GWL Investment Management Ltd.
Canadian Equity G-NL Fund
RRSP Eligible; Inception Year: 1987; Fund Managers:
GWL Investment Management Ltd.
Canadian Opportunity M-DSC Fund
RRSP Eligible; Inception Year: 1997; Fund Managers:
Mackenzie Financial Corp.
Canadian Opportunity M-NL Fund
RRSP Eligible; Inception Year: 1997; Fund Managers:
Mackenzie Financial Corp.
Canadian Resource A-DSC Fund
RRSP Eligible; Inception Year: 1996; Fund Managers:
AGF Funds Inc.
Canadian Resource A-NL Fund
RRSP Eligible; Inception Year: 1996; Fund Managers:
AGF Funds Inc.
Conservative Portfolio G-DSC Fund
RRSP Eligible; Inception Year: 1996; Fund Managers:
GWL Investment Management Ltd.
Conservative Portfolio G-NL Fund
RRSP Eligible; Inception Year: 1996; Fund Managers:
GWL Investment Management Ltd.
Diversified G-DSC Fund
RRSP Eligible; Inception Year: 1985; Fund Managers:
GWL Investment Management Ltd.
Diversified G-NL Fund
RRSP Eligible; Inception Year: 1988; Fund Managers:
GWL Investment Management Ltd.
Dividend G-NL Fund
RRSP Eligible; Inception Year: 1997; Fund Managers:
GWL Investment Management Ltd.
Dividend G-DSC Fund
RRSP Eligible; Inception Year: 1997; Fund Managers:
GWL Investment Management Ltd.
Equity M-DSC Fund
RRSP Eligible; Inception Year: 1996; Fund Managers:
Mackenzie Financial Corp.
Equity M-NL Fund
RRSP Eligible; Inception Year: 1996; Fund Managers:
Mackenzie Financial Corp.
Equity Index G-DSC Fund
RRSP Eligible; Inception Year: 1994; Fund Managers:
GWL Investment Management Ltd.
Equity Index G-NL Fund
RRSP Eligible; Inception Year: 1989; Fund Managers:
GWL Investment Management Ltd.

The Great-West Life Assurance Company(GWL)/ Great-West, Compagnie d'Assurance Vie (continued)

Equity/Bond G-DSC Fund
RRSP Eligible; Inception Year: 1994; Fund Managers:
GWL Investment Management Ltd.
Equity/Bond G-NL Fund
RRSP Eligible; Inception Year: 1988; Fund Managers:
GWL Investment Management Ltd.
European Equity S-DSC Fund
RRSP Eligible; Inception Year: 1997; Fund Managers:
Setanta Asset Management
European Equity S-NL Fund
RRSP Eligible; Inception Year: 1997; Fund Managers:
Setanta Asset Management
Global Income A-DSC Fund
RRSP Eligible; Inception Year: 1996; Fund Managers:
AGF Funds Inc.
Government Bond G-NL Fund
RRSP Eligible; Inception Year: 1994; Fund Managers:
GWL Investment Management Ltd.
Growth & Income A-DSC Fund
RRSP Eligible; Inception Year: 1996; Fund Managers:
AGF Funds Inc.
Growth & Income A-NL Fund
RRSP Eligible; Inception Year: 1996; Fund Managers:
AGF Funds Inc.
Growth & Income M-DSC Fund
RRSP Eligible; Inception Year: 1996; Fund Managers:
Mackenzie Financial Corp.
Growth & Income M-NL Fund
RRSP Eligible; Inception Year: 1996; Fund Managers:
Mackenzie Financial Corp.
Income M-DSC Fund
RRSP Eligible; Inception Year: 1996; Fund Managers:
Mackenzie Financial Corp.
Income M-NL Fund
RRSP Eligible; Inception Year: 1996; Fund Managers:
Mackenzie Financial Corp.
Growth Equity A-DSC Fund
RRSP Eligible; Inception Year: 1996; Fund Managers:
AGF Funds Inc.
Growth Equity A-NL Fund
RRSP Eligible; Inception Year: 1996; Fund Managers:
AGF Funds Inc.
Income G-NL Fund
RRSP Eligible; Inception Year: 1994; Fund Managers:
GWL Investment Management Ltd.
International Equity F-DSC Fund
RRSP Eligible; Inception Year: 1994;
International Equity F-NL Fund
RRSP Eligible; Inception Year: 1994;
International Opportunity F-NL Fund
RRSP Eligible; Inception Year: 1997; Fund Managers:
J.P. Morgan Fleming Asset Management
International Bond BW-DSC Fund
RRSP Eligible; Inception Year: 1994; Fund Managers:
Brandywine Asset Management
International Bond BW-NL Fund
RRSP Eligible; Inception Year: 1994; Fund Managers:
Brandywine Asset Management
Larger Company M-DSC Fund
RRSP Eligible; Inception Year: 1996; Fund Managers:
Mackenzie Financial Corp.
Larger Company M-NL Fund
RRSP Eligible; Inception Year: 1996; Fund Managers:
Mackenzie Financial Corp.
Mid Cap Canada G-DSC Fund
RRSP Eligible; Inception Year: 1997; Fund Managers:
GWL Investment Management Ltd.
Moderate Portfolio DSC Fund
RRSP Eligible; Inception Year: 1996; Fund Managers:
GWL Investment Management Ltd.
Moderate Portfolio NL Fund
RRSP Eligible; Inception Year: 1996; Fund Managers:
GWL Investment Management Ltd.
Money Market G-DSC Fund
RRSP Eligible; Inception Year: 1989; Fund Managers:
GWL Investment Management Ltd.
Money Market G-NL Fund
RRSP Eligible; Inception Year: 1989; Fund Managers:
GWL Investment Management Ltd.
Mortgage G-DSC Fund
RRSP Eligible; Inception Year: 1994; Fund Managers:
GWL Investment Management Ltd.
Mortgage G-NL Fund
RRSP Eligible; Inception Year: 1989; Fund Managers:
GWL Investment Management Ltd.

Government Bond G-DSC Fund
RRSP Eligible; Inception Year: 1994; Fund Managers:
GWL Investment Management Ltd.
Real Estate G-DSC Fund
RRSP Eligible; Inception Year: 1994; Fund Managers:
GWL Investment Management Ltd.
US Equity G-NL Fund
RRSP Eligible; Inception Year: 1994; Fund Managers:
GWL Investment Management Ltd.
US Equity G-DSC Fund
RRSP Eligible; Inception Year: 1994; Fund Managers:
GWL Investment Management Ltd.
Real Estate G-NL Fund
RRSP Eligible; Inception Year: 1989; Fund Managers:
GWL Investment Management Ltd.
Smaller Company M-DSC Fund
RRSP Eligible; Inception Year: 1996; Fund Managers:
Mackenzie Financial Corp.
Smaller Company M-NL Fund
RRSP Eligible; Inception Year: 1996; Fund Managers:
Mackenzie Financial Corp.
N.A. Equity B-DSC Fund
RRSP Eligible; Inception Year: 1996; Fund Managers:
Beutel Goodman & Co. Ltd.
N.A. Equity B-NL Fund
RRSP Eligible; Inception Year: 1996; Fund Managers:
Beutel Goodman & Co. Ltd.
Income G-DSC Fund
RRSP Eligible; Inception Year: 1994; Fund Managers:
GWL Investment Management Ltd.
International Opportunity F-DSC Fund
RRSP Eligible; Inception Year: 1997; Fund Managers:
J.P. Morgan Fleming Asset Management
Mid Cap Canada G-NL Fund
RRSP Eligible; Inception Year: 1997; Fund Managers:
GWL Investment Management Ltd.
Global Income A-NL Fund
RRSP Eligible; Inception Year: 1996; Fund Managers:
AGF Funds Inc.
Canadian Balanced M-DSC Fund
RRSP Eligible; Inception Year: 2000; Fund Managers:
Mackenzie Financial Corp.
Canadian Balanced M-NL Fund
RRSP Eligible; Inception Year: 2000; Fund Managers:
Mackenzie Financial Corp.
Canadian Equity Growth M-DSC Fund
RRSP Eligible; Inception Year: 2000; Fund Managers:
Mackenzie Financial Corp.
Canadian Equity Growth M-NL Fund
RRSP Eligible; Inception Year: 2000; Fund Managers:
Mackenzie Financial Corp.
Canadian Equity Portfolio G-DSC Fund
RRSP Eligible; Inception Year: 2000; Fund Managers:
GWL Investment Management Ltd.
Canadian Equity Portfolio G-NL Fund
RRSP Eligible; Inception Year: 2000; Fund Managers:
GWL Investment Management Ltd.
Canadian Science & Technology G-NL Fund
RRSP Eligible; Inception Year: 2000; Fund Managers:
GWL Investment Management Ltd.
Dividend M-DSC Fund
RRSP Eligible; Inception Year: 2000; Fund Managers:
Mackenzie Financial Corp.
Dividend M-NL Fund
RRSP Eligible; Inception Year: 2000; Fund Managers:
Mackenzie Financial Corp.
Emerging Markets M-DSC Fund
RRSP Eligible; Inception Year: 2000; Fund Managers:
Mackenzie Financial Corp.
Emerging Markets M-NL Fund
RRSP Eligible; Inception Year: 2000; Fund Managers:
Mackenzie Financial Corp.
Ethics G-DSC Fund
RRSP Eligible; Inception Year: 2000; Fund Managers:
GWL Investment Management Ltd.
Ethics G-NL Fund
RRSP Eligible; Inception Year: 2000; Fund Managers:
GWL Investment Management Ltd.
Fixed Income Portfolio G-DSC Fund
RRSP Eligible; Inception Year: 2000; Fund Managers:
GWL Investment Management Ltd.
Fixed Income Portfolio G-NL Fund
RRSP Eligible; Inception Year: 2000; Fund Managers:
GWL Investment Management Ltd.

Foreign Equity M-DSC Fund
RRSP Eligible; Inception Year: 2000; Fund Managers:
Mackenzie Financial Corp.
Foreign Equity M-NL Fund
RRSP Eligible; Inception Year: 2000; Fund Managers:
Mackenzie Financial Corp.
Global Equity Portfolio G-DSC Fund
RRSP Eligible; Inception Year: 2000; Fund Managers:
GWL Investment Management Ltd.
Global Equity Portfolio G-NL Fund
RRSP Eligible; Inception Year: 2000; Fund Managers:
GWL Investment Management Ltd.
Japan Equity M-NL Fund
RRSP Eligible; Inception Year: 2000; Fund Managers:
Mackenzie Financial Corp.
Japan Equity M-DSC Fund
RRSP Eligible; Inception Year: 2000; Fund Managers:
Mackenzie Financial Corp.
US Mid Cap G-DSC Fund
RRSP Eligible; Inception Year: 2000; Fund Managers:
GWL Investment Management Ltd.
US Mid Cap G-NL Fund
RRSP Eligible; Inception Year: 2000; Fund Managers:
GWL Investment Management Ltd.
Canadian Equity BT-DSC Fund
RRSP Eligible; Inception Year: 1996; Fund Managers:
Bissett Investment Management
Canadian Equity BT-NL Fund
RRSP Eligible; Inception Year: 1996; Fund Managers:
Bissett Investment Management
Canadian Value AT-DSC Fund
RRSP Eligible; Inception Year: 1997; Fund Managers:
Aim Trimark Investments
Canadian Value AT-NL Fund
RRSP Eligible; Inception Year: 1997; Fund Managers:
Aim Trimark Investments
International Equity U-DSC
RRSP Eligible; Inception Year: 1994; Fund Managers:
UBS Global Asset Management
International Equity U-NL
RRSP Eligible; Inception Year: 1994; Fund Managers:
UBS Global Asset Management
Science & Technology G-DSC Fund
RRSP Eligible; Inception Year: 2000; Fund Managers:
GWL Investment Management Ltd.

Group Sales Offices:

Calgary
Stock Exchange Tower
#1400, 300 - 5th Ave. SW
Calgary, AB T2P 3C4 Canada
403-515-5900
Fax: 403-234-0011
Scott France, Regional Director

Edmonton
Bell Tower
#1850, 10104 - 103rd Ave.
Edmonton, AB T5J 0H8 Canada
780-917-7800
Fax: 780-429-5088
Peter Doig, Regional Director

Halifax
#1900, 1801 Hollis St.
Halifax, NS B3J 3N4 Canada
902-429-8429
Fax: 902-429-0998
Barry Shea, Regional Director

Hamilton
#825, 1 King St. West
Hamilton, ON L8P 1A4 Canada
905-317-2650
Fax: 905-525-9070
Don Richardson, Regional Director

Kitchener
#800, 40 Weber St. East
Kitchener, ON N2H 6R3 Canada
519-744-7345
Fax: 519-744-3669
888-821-8626
Bob Hague, Regional Director

London
#2500, 255 Queens Ave.
London, ON N6A 5R8 Canada
519-432-6315
Fax: 519-432-4566
Bill Snoeks, Regional Director

Montréal
#1000, 2001, rue University
Montréal, QC H3A 1T9 Canada
514-350-7975
Fax: 514-350-4786
Jean Pierre Beaudet, Regional Director
Ottawa
Holland Cross
#410, 11 Holland Ave.
Ottawa, ON K1Y 4S1 Canada
613-761-3950
Fax: 613-728-2971
Peter Foley, Regional Director
Québec
Tour de la Cité
#800, 2600, boul Laurier, 8e étage
Québec, QC G1V 4W2 Canada
418-650-4200
Fax: 418-650-1561
Michael Henderson, Sr. Account Manager
Regina
Bank of Montréal Bldg.
#500, 2103 - 11th Ave.
Regina, SK S4P 3Z8 Canada
306-790-2330
Fax: 306-790-2340
Dave Cripps, Sr. Account Manager
Sudbury
#401, 144 Pine St.
Sudbury, ON P3C 1X3 Canada
705-699-2657
Fax: 705-675-0902
Wayne Toner, Sr. Account Manager
Toronto
#400, 330 University Ave.
Toronto, ON M5G 1R8 Canada
416-552-5050
Fax: 416-552-5450
David Henry, Managing Director
Vancouver
#1500, 1177 West Hastings St.
Vancouver, BC V6E 3Y9 Canada
604-331-2444
Fax: 604-688-9762
Ted Woodrow, Regional Director
Windsor
#200, 4520 Rhodes Dr.
Windsor, ON N8W 5C2 Canada
519-944-0686
Fax: 519-944-5104
800-808-6370
Kyle Baro, Sr. Account Manager
Winnipeg
#1C, 100 Osborne St. North
Winnipeg, MB R3C 1V3 Canada
204-946-7850
Fax: 204-946-8916
Day Woytko, Regional Director

Resource Centres:

Brossard
11, Place du Commerce
Brossard, QC J4W 2T9 Canada
450-466-6956
Fax: 450-466-1836
Michel Carrier, Manager
Calgary
Dominion Place
#300, 906 - 12th Ave. SW
Calgary, AB T2R 1K7 Canada
403-750-2100
Fax: 403-750-2150
Ralph Brust, Manager
Edmonton
Bell Tower
#600, 10104 - 103 Ave.
Edmonton, AB T5J 0H8 Canada
780-917-7700
Fax: 780-429-2809
John Liston, Manager
Grande Prairie - 97th Ave.
#203, 10134 - 97th Ave.
Grande Prairie, AB T8V 7X6 Canada
780-532-2818
Fax: 780-539-3455
Marc Lissoway, Manager
Grande Prairie - 97th Ave. - Northwest Territories & Yukon
Grand Central Station
#203, 10134 - 97th Ave.
Grande Prairie, AB T8V 7X6 Canada
780-532-2818
Fax: 780-539-3455
Marc Lissoway, Manager
Halifax
Purdy's Wharf Tower II
#407, 1959 Upper Water St.
Halifax, NS B3J 3N2 Canada
902-429-8653
Fax: 902-425-1968
800-461-3181
Mark Kenny, Manager
Hamilton
Stelco Tower
100 King St. West, 14th Fl.
Hamilton, ON L8P 1A2 Canada
905-525-5031
Fax: 905-521-2838
Rick Guiliani, Manager
Kelowna
Landmark IV
#400, 1628 Dickson Ave.
Kelowna, BC V1Y 7T2 Canada
250-712-7900
Fax: 250-762-0822
Matt Simpson, Manager
Kingston
#300, 1473 John Counter Blvd.
Kingston, ON K7M 8Z6 Canada
613-545-5670
Fax: 613-545-5972
Carolyn Wood, Manager
Kitchener
#900, 101 Frederick St.
Kitchener, ON N2H 6R2 Canada
519-746-1200
Fax: 519-746-1396
Don Mück, Manager
Laval
Les Tours Triomphes Phase I
#1004, 2500, boul Daniel-Johnson
Laval, QC H7T 2P6 Canada
450-681-1004
Fax: 450-681-1444
877-617-3000
Émile Arbour, Manager
London
140 Fullarton St., 10th Fl.
London, ON N6A 5P2 Canada
519-434-3268
Fax: 519-434-3280
Abbie MacMillan, Manager
Mississauga
#1206, 90 Burnhamthorpe Rd. West
Mississauga, ON L5B 3C3 Canada
905-270-6103
Fax: 905-270-1177
Todd Cloutier, Manager
Moncton
Heritage Court
#416, 95 Foundry St.
Moncton, NB E1C 5H7 Canada
506-859-4200
Fax: 506-859-9114
Blair Hayden, Manager
Montréal
#1300, 1800, av McGill College
Montréal, QC H3A 3J6 Canada
514-878-6111
Fax: 514-878-6172
Raymond Darveau, Manager
Oshawa
#400, 2 Simcoe St.
Oshawa, ON L1H 8C1 Canada
905-571-2676
Fax: 905-571-6168
Dan Hostick, Manager
Ottawa
#500, 515 Legget Dr.
Kanata, ON K2K 3G4 Canada
613-270-6844
Fax: 613-270-6801
Steven Chabot, Manager
Prince George
Bank of Nova Scotia Bldg.
#505, 1488 - 4 Ave.
Prince George, BC V2L 4Y2 Canada
250-614-7700
Fax: 250-563-1240
Marc Lissoway, Manager
Québec
Tour de la Cité
2600, boul Laurier, 8e étage
Québec, QC G1V 4W2 Canada
418-650-4200
Fax: 418-653-3037
Roger Gauthier, Manager
Regina
Royal Bank Bldg.
#600, 2010 - 11 Ave.
Regina, SK S4P 0J3 Canada
306-761-7500
Fax: 306-352-9474
Grant Laube, Manager
Saskatoon
Bank of Hong Kong Bldg.
#300, 321A - 21 St. East
Saskatoon, SK S7K 0C1 Canada
306-665-6244
Fax: 306-652-1919
Rick Kennedy, Manager
St. John's
Beothuck Bldg., 5th Fl.
Crosbie Pl.
St. John's, NL A1B 3Y8 Canada
709-754-2132
Fax: 709-754-0117
Ron Reid, Manager
Sudbury - Northern Ontario
#201, 144 Pine St.
Sudbury, ON P3C 1X3 Canada
705-675-2494
Fax: 705-675-6248
Craig MacTavish, Manager
Surrey
Station Tower, Gateway
#1260, 13401 - 108 Ave.
Surrey, BC V3T 5T3 Canada
604-930-3570
Fax: 604-930-3571
Craig Noren, Manager
Toronto
#600, 2005 Sheppard Ave. East
Toronto, ON M2J 5B4 Canada
416-492-4300
Fax: 416-492-1406
Mark Foris, Manager
Vancouver
#1200, 1177 West Hastings St.
Vancouver, BC V6E 3Y9 Canada
604-331-2430
Fax: 604-688-6588
Ray Fuller, Manager
Victoria
#610, 1675 Douglas St.
Victoria, BC V8W 2G5 Canada
250-953-1250
Fax: 250-383-0431
800-953-1250
Frank Goethals, Manager
Windsor
#200, 4520 Rhodes Dr.
Windsor, ON N8W 5C2 Canada
519-944-0686
Fax: 519-944-0630
Christy Bacik, Manager
Winnipeg
PO Box 338
100 Osborne St. North
Winnipeg, MB R3C 2H6 Canada
204-946-8100
Fax: 204-946-8865
Hugh Moncrieff, Manager

INVESTMENT MANAGEMENT

GrowthWorks Atlantic Venture Fund Ltd.

Purdy's Wharf Tower 1
#1401, 1959 Upper Water St.
Halifax, NS B3J 3N2
902-492-5164
Fax: 902-421-1808
800-251-5331
info@growthworks.ca
www.growthworks.ca

Executives:
Thomas J. Hayes, President/CEO

GrowthWorks:
Atlantic Balanced Fund
RRSP Eligible; Inception Year: 2005;
Atlantic Commercialization 405 Fund
RRSP Eligible; Inception Year: 2005;
Atlantic Commercialization 406 Fund
RRSP Eligible; Inception Year: 2005;

Branches:
Fredericton
#370, 777 Westmorland St.
Fredericton, NB E3B 6Z3 Canada
506-444-0091
800-456-0199
Halifax
Purdy's Wharf Tower 1
#1401, 1959 Upper Water St.
Halifax, NS B3J 3N2 Canada
902-492-5164
800-251-5331
St. John's
Highland Business Centre
239 Major's Path
St. John's, NL A1A 5A1 Canada
709- 69-8

GrowthWorks Capital Ltd.

Also listed under: *Financing & Loan Companies*
#2600, 1055 West Georgia St.
Vancouver, BC V6E 3R5
Fax: 604-688-9039
866-688-3430
info@growthworks.ca
www.growthworks.ca
Ownership: Private
Year Founded: 1999
Number of Employees: 90
Assets: $500m-1 billion
Profile: GrowthWorks means affiliates of GrowthWorks Ltd. It includes the manager of the Working Opportunity Fund (EVCC) Ltd., GrowthWorks WV Management Ltd., manager of GrowthWorks Canadian Fund Ltd. & GrowthWorks Commercialization Fund Ltd., & GrowthWorks Atlantic Ltd., manager of GrowthWorks Atlantic Venture Fund Ltd. GrowthWorks Capital Ltd., is a venture capital company. It manages the Working Opportunity Funds.

Executives:
David Levi, President/CEO
Craig Fookes, CFO & Vice-President, Finance
Donna Bridgeman, Sr. Vice-President, Corporate Affairs, Vice-President, Investments
Jim Charlton, Sr. Vice-President, Investments
Peter Fortin, Sr. Vice-President, Investments
Murray Munro, Sr. Vice-President, National Sales, Marketing & Government Relations
Carol Crow, Vice-President, Human Resources
Alex Irwin, Sr. Counsel

GrowthWorks:
Working Opportunity Commercialization 05 Fund
RRSP Eligible; Inception Year: 2005;
Working Opportunity Commercialization 06 Fund
RRSP Eligible; Inception Year: 2006;
Working Opportunity Balanced Series 1 Fund
RRSP Eligible; Inception Year: 1991;
Working Opportunity Balanced Series 2 Fund
RRSP Eligible; Inception Year: 2004;
Working Opportunity Diversified Fund
RRSP Eligible; Inception Year: 2006;
Working Opportunity Financial Fund
RRSP Eligible; Inception Year: 2006;
Working Opportunity Growth Series 1 Fund
RRSP Eligible; Inception Year: 2000;
Working Opportunity Growth Series 2 Fund
RRSP Eligible; Inception Year: 2004;
Working Opportunity Income Fund
RRSP Eligible; Inception Year: 2006;
Working Opportunity Resources Fund
RRSP Eligible; Inception Year: 2006;

Branches:
Halifax
Purdy's Wharf Tower 1
1959 Upper Water St., 14th Fl.
Halifax, NS B3J 3N2 Canada
902-492-5164
Fax: 902-421-1808
Saskatoon
#830, 410 - 22nd St. East
Saskatoon, SK S7K 5T6 Canada
306-242-1023
Fax: 306-242-9959
Brad Munro, Vice-President, Investments
Toronto
#3504, 20 Queen St.
Toronto, ON M5H 3R3 Canada
416-934-7777
Fax: 416-929-0901

GrowthWorks WV Management Ltd.

Also listed under: *Financing & Loan Companies*
#3504, 20 Queen St. West
Toronto, ON M5H 3R3
416-934-7777
Fax: 416-929-4390
800-463-1652
info@growthworks.ca
www.growthworks.ca
Former Name: Working Ventures Funds
Also Known As: GrowthWorks WV Funds
Year Founded: 1990
Assets: $500m-1 billion

Executives:
Les Lyall, Sr. Vice-President

GrowthWorks:
Canadian Fund
RRSP Eligible; Inception Year: 1990;
Canadian (CAVI) Fund
RRSP Eligible; Inception Year: 2005;
Canadian (CSTGF) Fund
RRSP Eligible; Inception Year: 2005;
Canadian Balanced I Fund
RRSP Eligible; Inception Year: 2003;
Canadian Balanced II Fund
RRSP Eligible; Inception Year: 2003;
Canadian Diversified I Fund
RRSP Eligible; Inception Year: 2003;
Canadian Diversified II Fund
RRSP Eligible; Inception Year: 2003;
Canadian Financial I Fund
RRSP Eligible; Inception Year: 2003;
Canadian Financial II Fund
RRSP Eligible; Inception Year: 2003;
Canadian Fund Ltd. (FOF Growth) Fund
RRSP Eligible; Inception Year: 2006;
Canadian Fund Ltd. (FOF Traditional) Fund
RRSP Eligible; Inception Year: 2006;
Canadian Growth I Fund
RRSP Eligible; Inception Year: 2003;
Canadian Growth II Fund
RRSP Eligible; Inception Year: 2003;
Canadian Income I Fund
RRSP Eligible; Inception Year: 2003;
Canadian Income II Fund
RRSP Eligible; Inception Year: 2003;
Canadian Resources I Fund
RRSP Eligible; Inception Year: 2003;
Canadian Resources II Fund
RRSP Eligible; Inception Year: 2003;
Commercialization 505 Fund
RRSP Eligible; Inception Year: 2005;
Commercialization 506 Fund
RRSP Eligible; Inception Year: 2005;

Branches:
Ottawa
#900, 275 Slater St.
Ottawa, ON K1P 5H9 Canada
613-567-3225
Saskatoon
#830, 410 - 22nd St. East
Saskatoon, SK S7K 5T6 Canada
306-242-1023
Toronto
#3504, 20 Queen St. West
Toronto, ON M5H 3R3 Canada
416-934-7777
800-463-1652

Hartford Investments Canada Corp.

#1103, 4 King St. West
Toronto, ON M5H 1B6
416-204-9916
Fax: 416-204-9952
Ownership: PUblic. Foreign. Owned by Hartford Financial Services Group.
Assets: $100 billion + Year End: 20061000
Stock Symbol: HIG

Executives:
Laurie Davis, President/CFO

Hartford:
Advisors Class B Fund
RRSP Eligible; Inception Year: 2000; Fund Managers: Greystone Managed Investments Inc.
Bond Class A Fund
RRSP Eligible; Inception Year: 2005; Fund Managers: Robert McHenry
Canadian Stock Class A Fund
RRSP Eligible; Inception Year: 2005; Fund Managers: Greystone Managed Investments Inc.
Global Leaders Class A Fund
RRSP Eligible; Inception Year: 2005; Fund Managers: Wellington Management Company, LLP
Money Market Class A Fund
RRSP Eligible; Inception Year: 2005; Fund Managers: Robert Crusha
US Capital Appreciation Class A Fund
RRSP Eligible; Inception Year: 2005; Fund Managers: Wellington Management Company, LLP
US Stock Class A Fund
RRSP Eligible; Inception Year: 2005; Fund Managers: Wellington Management Company, LLP
Advisors Class A Fund
RRSP Eligible; Inception Year: 2005; Fund Managers: Greystone Managed Investments Inc.
Canadian Stock Class B Fund
RRSP Eligible; Inception Year: 2000; Fund Managers: Greystone Managed Investments Inc.
Bond Class B Fund
RRSP Eligible; Inception Year: 2000; Fund Managers: Robert McHenry
Global Leaders Class B Fund
RRSP Eligible; Inception Year: 2000; Fund Managers: Wellington Management Company, LLP
Money Market Class B Fund
RRSP Eligible; Inception Year: 2000; Fund Managers: Robert Crusha
US Capital Appreciation Class B Fund
RRSP Eligible; Inception Year: 2000; Fund Managers: Wellington Management Company, LLP
US Stock Class B Fund
RRSP Eligible; Inception Year: 2000; Fund Managers: Wellington Management Company, LLP
Canadian Equity Income Class B Fund
RRSP Eligible; Inception Year: 2004; Fund Managers: Beutel, Goodman & Company Ltd.
Canadian Equity Income Class A Fund
RRSP Eligible; Inception Year: 2005; Fund Managers: Beutel, Goodman & Company Ltd.
Canadian Value Class A Fund
RRSP Eligible; Inception Year: 2005; Fund Managers: Beutel, Goodman & Company Ltd.
Canadian Value Class B Fund
RRSP Eligible; Inception Year: 2004; Fund Managers: Beutel, Goodman & Company Ltd.
US Capital Appreciation Class D Fund
RRSP Eligible; Inception Year: 2000; Fund Managers: Wellington Management Company, LLP
Global Leaders Class D Fund
RRSP Eligible; Inception Year: 2000; Fund Managers: Wellington Management Company, LLP
US Stock Class D Fund
RRSP Eligible; Inception Year: 2000; Fund Managers: Wellington Management Company, LLP
Canadian Stock Class D Fund
RRSP Eligible; Inception Year: 2000; Fund Managers: Greystone Managed Investments Inc.

Canadian Value Class D Fund
RRSP Eligible; Inception Year: 2004; Fund Managers:
Beutel, Goodman & Company Ltd.
Growth & Income Class A Fund
RRSP Eligible; Inception Year: 2005; Fund Managers:
Greystone Managed Investments Inc.
Growth & Income Class B Fund
RRSP Eligible; Inception Year: 2004; Fund Managers:
Greystone Managed Investments Inc.
Growth & Income Class D Fund
RRSP Eligible; Inception Year: 2004; Fund Managers:
Greystone Managed Investments Inc.
Canadian Equity Income Class D Fund
RRSP Eligible; Inception Year: 2004; Fund Managers:
Beutel, Goodman & Company Ltd.
Advisors Class D Fund
RRSP Eligible; Inception Year: 2000; Fund Managers:
Greystone Managed Investments Inc.
Bond Class D Fund
RRSP Eligible; Inception Year: 2000; Fund Managers:
Robert McHenry
Money Market Class D Fund
RRSP Eligible; Inception Year: 2000; Fund Managers:
Robert Crusha
US Growth & Income Class A FundInception Year: 0; Fund Managers:
Greystone Managed Investments Inc.
US Growth & Income Class B FundInception Year: 0; Fund Managers:
Greystone Managed Investments Inc.
US Growth & Income Class D FundInception Year: 0; Fund Managers:
Greystone Managed Investments Inc.

Hesperian Capital Management Ltd.

#175, 601 - 10th Ave. SW
Calgary, AB T2R 0B2
403-531-2650
Fax: 403-508-6120
877-431-1407
info@hesperiancapital.com
www.hesperiancapital.com
Former Name: Norrep Inc.
Year Founded: 1995
Executives:
William D.B. Koenig, Vice-President
Craig Millar, Vice-President
Norrep:
Norrep Fund
RRSP Eligible; Inception Year: 1997; Fund Managers:
Randy Oliver
AlexanderSasso
Norrep II Fund
RRSP Eligible; Inception Year: 2001; Fund Managers:
Randy Oliver
AlexanderSasso
Norrep Q Class Fund
RRSP Eligible; Inception Year: 2004; Fund Managers:
Alexander Sasso
KeithLeslie
Norrep Income Growth Class Fund
RRSP Eligible; Inception Year: 2005; Fund Managers:
Keith Leslie
AlexanderSasso
Norrep Global Small Cap LP FundInception Year: 2005; Fund Managers:
Alexander Sasso
CraigMillar
Norrep US Class Fund
RRSP Eligible; Inception Year: 2005; Fund Managers:
Alexander Sasso
CraigMillar

Highstreet Asset Management Inc.

Also listed under: *Pension & Money Management Companies*
#200, 244 Pall Mall St.
London, ON N6A 5P6
519-850-9500
Fax: 519-850-1214
877-850-9500
info@highstreet.ca
www.highstreet.ca
Ownership: Private
Year Founded: 1998
Number of Employees: 31
Assets: $1-10 billion Year End: 20051231
Revenues: $5-10 million Year End: 20051231
Executives:
Robert Badun, CEO
Paul Brisson, President
Jeffrey Brown, Chief Investment Officer
Dawn Butler, Chief Financial Officer
Douglas Crocker, Chief Risk Officer
Shaun Arnold, Vice-President
Lina Bowden, Vice-President
Rob Jackson, Vice-President
Peter Mastorakos, Vice-President
Grant McIntosh, Vice-President
Highstreet:
Balanced Fund
RRSP Eligible; Inception Year: 1998;
Canadian Bond Fund
RRSP Eligible; Inception Year: 1998;
Canadian Equity Fund
RRSP Eligible; Inception Year: 1998;
US Equity Fund
RRSP Eligible; Inception Year: 1998;
International Equity Fund
RRSP Eligible; Inception Year: 2002;
Money Market Fund
RRSP Eligible; Inception Year: 2002;
Growth Fund
RRSP Eligible; Inception Year: 0;
Small Cap Fund
RRSP Eligible; Inception Year: 0;

Hillsdale Investment Management Inc.

Also listed under: *Financial Planning; Investment Management*

PO Box 228, TD Centre Stn. TD Centre
#2100, 100 Wellington St. West
Toronto, ON M5K 1J3
416-913-3900
Fax: 416-913-3901
website@hillsdaleinv.com
www.hillsdaleinv.com
Ownership: Private
Year Founded: 1996
Number of Employees: 12
Executives:
John Loeprich, Sr. Vice-President, Private Clients
John Motherwell, Vice-President, Institutional Marketing
Directors:
Gary Bryant
Ray Chantler
Arun Kaul
Hillsdale:
Canadian Aggressive Hedged A Fund
RRSP Eligible; Inception Year: 1999; Fund Managers:
Arun Kaul
ChrisGuthrie
Tony Batek
Canadian Aggressive Hedged I Fund
RRSP Eligible; Inception Year: 2001; Fund Managers:
Tony Batek
ChrisGuthrie
Arun Kaul
Canadian Market Neutral Equity A Fund
RRSP Eligible; Inception Year: 2000; Fund Managers:
Arun Kaul
TonyBatek
Chris Guthrie
Canadian Market Neutral Equity I Fund
RRSP Eligible; Inception Year: 2004; Fund Managers:
Chris Guthrie
ArunKaul
Tony Batek
Canadian Performance Equity A Fund
RRSP Eligible; Inception Year: 1996; Fund Managers:
Tony Batek
ChrisGuthrie
Arun Kaul
Canadian Performance Equity I Fund
RRSP Eligible; Inception Year: 2004; Fund Managers:
Arun Kaul
TonyBatek
Chris Guthrie
US Aggressive Hedged Equity A (US$) Fund
RRSP Eligible; Inception Year: 2000; Fund Managers:
Arun Kaul
ChrisGuthrie
US Performance Equity (US$) Fund
RRSP Eligible; Inception Year: 1996; Fund Managers:
Chris Guthrie
ArunKaul

Horizons Funds Inc.

#206, 26 Wellington St. East
Toronto, ON M5E 1S2
416-601-2228
Fax: 416-601-1695
877-450-0722
marketing@horizonfunds.com
www.horizonsfunds.com
Former Name: First Horizon Captial Corp.
Ownership: Private
Year Founded: 1998
Executives:
Fred Purvis, Group CEO
Horizons:
Mondiale Hedge Fund
RRSP Eligible; Inception Year: 1997; Fund Managers:
First Horizon Management Inc.
Tactical Hedge Fund
RRSP Eligible; Inception Year: 2003; Fund Managers:
First Horizon Management Inc.
Mondiale Enhanced Fund
RRSP Eligible; Inception Year: 2004; Fund Managers:
First Horizon Management Inc.
Diversified Fund
RRSP Eligible; Inception Year: 2004; Fund Managers:
First Horizon Management Inc.
Branches:
Vancouver
#230, 375 Water St.
Vancouver, BC V6B 5C6 Canada
604-688-7333
800-665-1158
Graeme Allen

HSBC Investments (Canada) Limited

Also listed under: *Financial Planning*
1066 West Georgia St., 19th Fl.
Vancouver, BC V6E 3X1
604-257-1000
Fax: 604-713-4308
800-830-8888
info@hsbc.ca
www.hsbc.ca
Ownership: Wholly owned by HSBC Bank Canada, which is in turn owned by HSBC Holdings plc.
Year Founded: 1991
Number of Employees: 75
Assets: $1-10 billion
Profile: Established in 1991, HSBC Investments (Canada) Limited is a mutual fund company based in British Columbia. A subsidiary of HSBC Bank Canada, it is the distributor of the HSBC Mutual Funds.

Executives:
Lindsay Gordon, President/CEO
Bob Anthony, Chief Credit Officer
Graham McIsaac, Chief Financial Officer
Sean O'Sullivan, Chief Operating Officer
Jeffrey Dowle, Exec. Vice-President
Sarah Morgan-Silvester, Exec. Vice-President
Francis Chartier, Vice-President, Institutional Investments
Sharee Ryan, Vice-President, Institutional Investments
Directors:
John Bond
Jacqueline Boutet
James Cleave
Peter Eng
Martin Glynn
Robert Martin
Samuel Minzberg
Gwyn Morgan
Youssef Nasr
Ross Smith
Keith Whitson
HSBC:
World Bond RSP Fund
RRSP Eligible; Inception Year: 1994; Fund Managers:
HSBC Investments (Canada) Limited
European Fund
RRSP Eligible; Inception Year: 1994; Fund Managers:
HSBC Investments (Canada) Limited

HSBC Investments (Canada) Limited (continued)
Canadian Balanced Fund
RRSP Eligible; Inception Year: 1989; Fund Managers: HSBC Investments (Canada) Limited
Canadian Bond Fund
RRSP Eligible; Inception Year: 1994; Fund Managers: HSBC Investments (Canada) Limited
Dividend Income Fund
RRSP Eligible; Inception Year: 1994; Fund Managers: HSBC Investments (Canada) Limited
Equity Fund
RRSP Eligible; Inception Year: 1989; Fund Managers: HSBC Investments (Canada) Limited
Canadian Money Market Fund
RRSP Eligible; Inception Year: 1989; Fund Managers: HSBC Investments (Canada) Limited
Mortgage Fund
RRSP Eligible; Inception Year: 1992; Fund Managers: HSBC Investments (Canada) Limited
Small Cap Growth Fund
RRSP Eligible; Inception Year: 1994; Fund Managers: HSBC Investments (Canada) Limited
US Equity Fund
RRSP Eligible; Inception Year: 1994; Fund Managers: HSBC Investments (Canada) Limited
US Dollar Money Market (US$) Fund
RRSP Eligible; Inception Year: 1998; Fund Managers: HSBC Investments (Canada) Limited
Global Technology Fund
RRSP Eligible; Inception Year: 2000; Fund Managers: HSBC Investments (Canada) Limited
AsiaPacific Fund
RRSP Eligible; Inception Year: 1993; Fund Managers: HSBC Investments (Canada) Limited
Emerging Markets Fund
RRSP Eligible; Inception Year: 1994; Fund Managers: HSBC Investments (Canada) Limited
Global Equity Fund
RRSP Eligible; Inception Year: 1998; Fund Managers: HSBC Investments (Canada) Limited
Chinese Equity Fund
RRSP Eligible; Inception Year: 2004; Fund Managers: HSBC Investments (Canada) Limited
LifeMap Conservative Portfolio Fund
RRSP Eligible; Inception Year: 2005; Fund Managers: HSBC Investments (Canada) Limited
LifeMap Moderate Conservative Portfolio Fund
RRSP Eligible; Inception Year: 2005; Fund Managers: HSBC Investments (Canada) Limited
LifeMap Balanced Portfolio Fund
RRSP Eligible; Inception Year: 2005; Fund Managers: HSBC Investments (Canada) Limited
LifeMap Growth Portfolio Fund
RRSP Eligible; Inception Year: 2005; Fund Managers: HSBC Investments (Canada) Limited
LifeMap Aggressive Growth Portfolio Fund
RRSP Eligible; Inception Year: 2005; Fund Managers: HSBC Investments (Canada) Limited
LifeMap MM Conservative Portfolio Fund
RRSP Eligible; Inception Year: 2005; Fund Managers: HSBC Investments (Canada) Limited
LifeMap MM Moderate Conservative Portfolio Fund
RRSP Eligible; Inception Year: 2005; Fund Managers: HSBC Investments (Canada) Limited
LifeMap MM Balanced Portfolio Fund
RRSP Eligible; Inception Year: 2005; Fund Managers: HSBC Investments (Canada) Limited
LifeMap MM Growth Portfolio Fund
RRSP Eligible; Inception Year: 2005; Fund Managers: HSBC Investments (Canada) Limited
LifeMap MM Aggressive Growth Portfolio Fund
RRSP Eligible; Inception Year: 2005; Fund Managers: HSBC Investments (Canada) Limited
Monthly Income Fund
RRSP Eligible; Inception Year: 2005; Fund Managers: HSBC Investments (Canada) Limited

The Independent Order of Foresters

***Also listed under:** Federal & Provincial*
789 Don Mills Rd.
Toronto, ON M3C 1T9
416-429-3000
Fax: 416-467-2516
800-828-1540
service@foresters.biz
www.foresters.biz
Ownership: Private
Year Founded: 1874
Number of Employees: 1,700
Assets: $1-10 billion
Revenues: $50-100 million
Executives:
George Mohacsi, President/CEO
Lynn Haight, COO/CFO
Euan Allison, Sr. Vice-President & Group Managing Director, UK
Nicholas J. DiRenzo, Sr. Vice-President, North American Sales
Sharon Giffen, Sr. Vice-President, Chief Actuary
Gail Johnson Morris, Sr. Vice-President, Service Delivery Division
Suanne M. Nielsen, Sr. Vice-President, Human Resources & Communication
Christopher Pinkerton, Sr. Vice-President, Marketing
Directors:
W. Ross Walker, Chair
Bernard E. Bloom
James Daugherty
William Bentley Foster
Richard M. Freeborough
Patrick William Kenny
Kash Manchuk
Louise L. McCormick
Barbara J. McDougall
Christopher H. McElvaine
John P. Meyerholz
E. Irene Miles
David E. Morrison
Glenn K. Reid
Foresters:
Money Market Fund
RRSP Eligible; Inception Year: 1989;
Equity Fund
RRSP Eligible; Inception Year: 1989; Fund Managers: Jarislowsky Fraser Ltd.
Bond Fund
RRSP Eligible; Inception Year: 1989;
Balanced Fund
RRSP Eligible; Inception Year: 1989; Fund Managers: Jarislowsky Fraser Ltd.
American Index Fund
RRSP Eligible; Inception Year: 2000; Fund Managers: Barclays Global Investors Canada Ltd.
Canadian Index Fund
RRSP Eligible; Inception Year: 2000; Fund Managers: Barclays Global Investors Canada Ltd.
Eurasia Index Fund
RRSP Eligible; Inception Year: 2000; Fund Managers: Barclays Global Investors Canada Ltd.
Global Index Fund
RRSP Eligible; Inception Year: 2000; Fund Managers: Barclays Global Investors Canada Ltd.
Canadian Balanced Fund
RRSP Eligible; Inception Year: 2000; Fund Managers: Jarislowsky Fraser Ltd.
Canadian Bond Fund
RRSP Eligible; Inception Year: 2000;
Canadian Equity Fund
RRSP Eligible; Inception Year: 2000; Fund Managers: Jarislowsky Fraser Ltd.
Canadian Money Market Fund
RRSP Eligible; Inception Year: 2000;
Sales Offices:
Burlington
#402, 3027 Harvester Rd.
Burlington, ON L7N 3G7 Canada
905-333-2861
Burnaby
#120, 4401 Still Creek Dr.
Burnaby, BC V5C 6G9 Canada
604-320-3300
Calgary
#225, 10655 Southport Rd. SW
Calgary, AB T2W 4Y1 Canada
403-250-8666
Edmonton
Oxford Tower
#1311, 10235 - 101 St. NW
Edmonton, AB T5J 3G1 Canada
780-425-2948
London
#214, 395 Wellington Rd.
London, ON N6C 4P9 Canada
519-680-2257
Markham
#308, 3000 Steeles Ave. East
Markham, ON L3R 4T9 Canada
905-474-3665
Mississauga
Bldg. 11
#201, 5045 Orbitor Dr.
Mississauga, ON L4W 4Y4 Canada
905-238-2649
Waterloo
#103, 60 Bridgeport Rd. East
Waterloo, ON N2J 2J9 Canada
519-886-7114

Industrial Alliance Fund Management Inc.

522 University Ave., 7th Fl.
Toronto, ON M5G 1Y7
416-585-8816
Fax: 416-865-5738
877-876-6989
info@iafunds.com
www.iafunds.com
Former Name: Industrial Alliance Mutual Funds Inc.; Co-operators Mutual Funds Limited
Ownership: Public. Wholly owned subsidiary of Industrial Alliance Insurance & Financial Services Inc.
Year Founded: 2003
Assets: $100-500 million Year End: 20041130
Stock Symbol: IAG
Executives:
David Scandiffio, President; 519-767-3065
IA:
Canadian Conservative Equity Fund
RRSP Eligible; Inception Year: 2005;
Crystal Enhanced Index America Fund
RRSP Eligible; Inception Year: 1999;
Diversified Monthly Income Fund
RRSP Eligible; Inception Year: 2005;
Dividend Growth Fund
RRSP Eligible; Inception Year: 2005;
R Funds:
R Money Market Series A Fund
RRSP Eligible; Inception Year: 2000;
R Money Market Series B Fund
RRSP Eligible; Inception Year: 2002;
R Bond Fund
RRSP Eligible; Inception Year: 1987;
R High Yield Bond Fund
RRSP Eligible; Inception Year: 1994;
R Monthly Income Balanced Fund
RRSP Eligible; Inception Year: 1998;
R Balanced Fund
RRSP Eligible; Inception Year: 1972;
R Dividend Income Fund
RRSP Eligible; Inception Year: 2005;
R Canadian Leaders Fund
RRSP Eligible; Inception Year: 2001;
R Canadian Growth Fund
RRSP Eligible; Inception Year: 1956;
R Canadian Smaller Companies Fund
RRSP Eligible; Inception Year: 1998;
R American Fund
RRSP Eligible; Inception Year: 2000;
R Global Value Fund
RRSP Eligible; Inception Year: 2000;
R Global Growth Fund
RRSP Eligible; Inception Year: 1985;
R European Fund
RRSP Eligible; Inception Year: 2000;
R Asian Fund
RRSP Eligible; Inception Year: 2000;
R Life & Health Fund
RRSP Eligible; Inception Year: 2000;
Branches:
Québec
PO Box 1907, Terminus Sta. Terminus
1080, Saint-Louis Rd.
Québec, QC G1K 7M3 Canada

Industrial Alliance Pacific Life Insurance Company

***Also listed under:** Federal & Provincial*

PO Box 5900
2165 West Broadway
Vancouver, BC V6B 5H6
604-734-1667
Fax: 604-734-8221
800-665-4458
intouch@iaplife.com
www.iaplife.com
Former Name: The North West Life Assurance Company of Canada
Ownership: Private.
Year Founded: 1953
Number of Employees: 400
Assets: $1-10 billion Year End: 20041231
Revenues: $500m-1 billion Year End: 20041231
Profile: Industrial-Alliance Pacific Life Insurance Company is a federally incorporated Canadian life & health insurance company. It provides creditor's group life & disability insurance for the automotive industry & student accident insurance. Individual insurance & tailored risk coverage are offered for specialty groups.

Executives:
Gerald Bouwers, President/COO
Michael L. Stickney, Exec. Vice-President, USA Development
Paul R. Grimes, Sr. Vice-President, Sales
Mary Dinkel, Vice-President, USA Sales Development
Douglas A. Carrothers, Corporate Secretary, General Counsel
IAP:
APEX Balanced (AGF) Fund
RRSP Eligible; Inception Year: 1969;
APEX Canadian Growth (AGF) Fund
RRSP Eligible; Inception Year: 1971;
APEX Canadian Value (Dynamic) Fund
RRSP Eligible; Inception Year: 1998;
APEX Fixed Income Fund
RRSP Eligible; Inception Year: 1971;
APEX Growth & Income Fund
RRSP Eligible; Inception Year: 1996;
APEX Money Market Fund
RRSP Eligible; Inception Year: 1994;
Bonds Fund
RRSP Eligible; Inception Year: 1977;
Canadian Equity Index Fund
RRSP Eligible; Inception Year: 2001;
Mortgages Fund
RRSP Eligible; Inception Year: 1997;
Diversified Fund
RRSP Eligible; Inception Year: 1987;
Emerging Markets (Templeton) Fund
RRSP Eligible; Inception Year: 1997; Fund Managers:
Franklin Templeton Investments
Bissett Bonds Fund
RRSP Eligible; Inception Year: 1999; Fund Managers:
Bissett Investment Managment
US Equity Index Fund
RRSP Eligible; Inception Year: 1998; Fund Managers:
State Street Global Advisors (Boston)
European Equity (Rothschild) Fund
RRSP Eligible; Inception Year: 2005;
Global Equity (Templeton)Fund
RRSP Eligible; Inception Year: 2001; Fund Managers:
Franklin Templeton Investments
Money Market Fund
RRSP Eligible; Inception Year: 1994;
Asian Pacific (ABN AMRO) Fund
RRSP Eligible; Inception Year: 2000; Fund Managers:
ABM AMRO Asset Management
International Equity (Templeton) Fund
RRSP Eligible; Inception Year: 1996; Fund Managers:
Franklin Templeton Investments
Bonds-Series 2 Fund
RRSP Eligible; Inception Year: 1997;
Canadian Equity Growth Fund
RRSP Eligible; Inception Year: 2001;
Income Fund
RRSP Eligible; Inception Year: 1998;
Focus Balanced Fund
RRSP Eligible; Inception Year: 2002;
US DAQ Index Fund
RRSP Eligible; Inception Year: 1999; Fund Managers:
State Street Global Advisors (Boston)
APEX Canadian Stock Fund
RRSP Eligible; Inception Year: 1996;
Focus Prudent Fund
RRSP Eligible; Inception Year: 2002;
Focus Moderate Fund
RRSP Eligible; Inception Year: 2002;
Focus Growth Fund
RRSP Eligible; Inception Year: 2002;
Focus Aggressive Fund
RRSP Eligible; Inception Year: 2002;
Diversified Security Fund
RRSP Eligible; Inception Year: 1999;
Diversified Opportunity Fund
RRSP Eligible; Inception Year: 1999;
Fidelity Canadian Asset Allocation Fund
RRSP Eligible; Inception Year: 2001; Fund Managers:
Fidelity Investments
Diversified Income Fund
RRSP Eligible; Inception Year: 2003;
Dividend Income Fund
RRSP Eligible; Inception Year: 2005;
Dividend Growth Fund
RRSP Eligible; Inception Year: 2005;
Canadian Equity (Leon Frazer) Fund
RRSP Eligible; Inception Year: 2004; Fund Managers:
Leon Frazer & Associates
Select Canadian Fund
RRSP Eligible; Inception Year: 1998;
Canadian Equity Value Fund
RRSP Eligible; Inception Year: 1969;
Canadian Equity (Dynamic) Fund
RRSP Eligible; Inception Year: 2001; Fund Managers:
Dynamic Mutual Funds
Canadian Equity (Bissett) Fund
RRSP Eligible; Inception Year: 1999; Fund Managers:
Bissett Investment Managment
Fidelity True North Fund
RRSP Eligible; Inception Year: 1999; Fund Managers:
Fidelity Investments
Fidelity Canadian Growth Company Fund
RRSP Eligible; Inception Year: 1999; Fund Managers:
Fidelity Investments
Global Equity (New Star) Fund
RRSP Eligible; Inception Year: 2005; Fund Managers:
New Star Asset Management Limited
Fidelity NorthStar Fund
RRSP Eligible; Inception Year: 2005; Fund Managers:
Fidelity Investments
Boomernomics Fund
RRSP Eligible; Inception Year: 2001; Fund Managers:
CI Investments
International Equity Index Fund
RRSP Eligible; Inception Year: 1999; Fund Managers:
State Street Global Advisors (Boston)
Fidelity European Equity Fund
RRSP Eligible; Inception Year: 2005; Fund Managers:
Fidelity Investments
US Equity (McLean Budden) Fund
RRSP Eligible; Inception Year: 2005; Fund Managers:
McLean Budden
US Equity (Legg Mason) Fund
RRSP Eligible; Inception Year: 2001; Fund Managers:
Legg Mason Inc.
Global Financial Services (CI) Fund
RRSP Eligible; Inception Year: 2001; Fund Managers:
CI Investments
Global Health Care Fund
RRSP Eligible; Inception Year: 2001; Fund Managers:
Talvest Fund Management
Real Estate Income Fund
RRSP Eligible; Inception Year: 2003;
Global Technology (ABN AMRO) Fund
RRSP Eligible; Inception Year: 2001; Fund Managers:
ABM AMRO Asset Management
Multi-Management Diversified Aggressive Fund
RRSP Eligible; Inception Year: 2000;
Dividends Fund
RRSP Eligible; Inception Year: 1998;
Multi-Management Diversified Opportunity Fund
RRSP Eligible; Inception Year: 2000;
Canadian Equity Index (Small Cap) Fund
RRSP Eligible; Inception Year: 1998; Fund Managers:
State Street Global Advisors (Boston)
Global Equity (ABN AMRO) Fund
RRSP Eligible; Inception Year: 2000; Fund Managers:
ABM AMRO Asset Management
European Equity (ABN AMRO) Fund
RRSP Eligible; Inception Year: 2001; Fund Managers:
ABM AMRO Asset Management
US Equity (AGF) Fund
RRSP Eligible; Inception Year: 1997; Fund Managers:
AGF Funds Inc.
International Equity (McLean Budden) Fund
RRSP Eligible; Inception Year: 2001; Fund Managers:
McLean Budden
Regional Offices:
Brossard - Taschereau - SAL Group Québec Regional Office
#109B, 7900, boul Taschereau
Brossard, QC J4X 2T2 Canada
450-465-0603
Fax: 450-465-1663
Fax: saladmin@iaplif
Calgary - 8th Ave. SW - Special Markets Group Prairie Regional Office
#2050, 777 - 8th Ave. SW
Calgary, AB T2P 3R5 Canada
403-226-7582
Fax: 403-265-3346
800-661-1699
smgcgy@iaplife.com
Dartmouth - Brownlow Ave. - SAL Group Atlantic Provinces Regional Office
Park Place 2
#302, 283A Brownlow Ave.
Dartmouth, NS B3B 2B4 Canada
902-468-8698
Fax: 902-468-1559
saladmin@iaplife.com
Edmonton - Calgary Trail NW - SAL Group Alberta Regional Office
Terrace Plaza
#840, 4445 Calgary Trail NW
Edmonton, AB T6H 5R7
780-435-1833
Fax: 780-435-2185
888-435-1833
saladmin@iaplife.com
Langley - 202nd St. - SAL Group British Columbia Regional Office
#305, 9440 - 202nd St.
Langley, BC V1M 4A6
604-882-8220
Fax: 604-882-8210
877-882-8220
saladmin@iaplife.com
Montréal - Sherbrooke ouest - Special Markets Group Montréal Regional Office
PO Box 790, B Sta. B
#110, 680 rue Sherbrooke ouest
Montréal, QC H3B 3K6
514-499-3748
Fax: 514-499-3856
866-499-3748
Oakville - North Service Rd. West - SAL Ontario Regional Office
#6, 1155 North Service Rd. West
Oakville, ON L6M 3E3 Canada
905-847-7900
Fax: 905-847-7922
800-668-4702
saladmin@iaplife.com
Thunder Bay - Community Hall Rd. - SAL Group Thunder Bay Office
RR#12
Thunder Bay, ON P7B 5E3
807-626-8917
Fax: 807-768-9272
saladmin@iaplife.com
Toronto - Consumers Rd. - Special Markets Group Eastern Regional Office
#400, 515 Consumers Rd.
Toronto, ON M2J 4Z2 Canada
416-498-8319
Fax: 416-498-9892
800-611-6667
smgtor@iaplife.com
Vancouver - Broadway West - Special Markets Group
PO Box 5900
2165 Broadway West
Vancouver, BC V6B 5H6 Canada
800-266-5667
group@iaplife.com, student@iaplife.com
Vancouver - West Georgia St. - Mortgage Department
#1910, 1188 West Georgia St.
Vancouver, BC V6E 4A2

Industrial Alliance Pacific Life Insurance Company (continued)
604-688-8631
Fax: 604-734-7274
mortgages@iaplife.com
Vancouver - West Georgia St. - Special Markets Group British Columbia Regional Office
#1910, 1188 West Georgia St.
Vancouver, BC V6E 4A2 Canada
604-688-9641
Fax: 604-688-9482
888-725-2886
smgbc@iaplife.com
Winnipeg - Waverley St. - SAL Group Winnipeg Regional Office
#102 - 865 Waverley St.
Winnipeg, MB R3T 5P4
204-942-8907
Fax: 204-943-6952
saladmin@iaplife.com

Investors Group Inc.

Also listed under: *Holding & Other Investment Companies*
One Canada Centre
447 Portage Ave.
Winnipeg, MB R3C 3B6
204-943-3385
Fax: 204-956-7688
888-746-6344
Other Information: Toll Free, Quebec: 1-800-661-4578
feedback@investorsgroup.com
www.investorsgroup.com
Ownership: Major shareholder Power Financial Corporation
Year Founded: 1926
Number of Employees: 1,300
Stock Symbol: IGI
Profile: The holding company provides financial products & financial planning services to individuals & corporations, including the sale of mutual funds, investment certificates, insurance programs, education savings plans, pension plans, annuities & tax-sheltered plans. It also provides the following services: investment management & administrative services for its own mutual funds, company subsidiaries & various pension plans; tax preparation services; trust & management services; mortgage financing on residential, commercial & industrial property; investments in real estate.

Executives:
Murray Taylor, President/CEO
Gregory D. Tretiak, Exec. Vice-President & CFO
Gary Wilton, Exec. Vice-President, Client & Information Services

Alan Joudrey, Sr. Vice-President, Banking Products & Services
Murray D. Kilfoyle, Sr. Vice-President, Client Services
Kevin E. Regan, Sr. Vice-President, Marketing & Consulting Services
Donald W. Smith, Sr. Vice-President, Human Resources
John Wiltshire, Sr., Sr. Vice-President, Product & Financial Planning
W. Terrence Wright, Sr. Vice-President, General Counsel & Secretary

Directors:
James W. Burns
André Desmarais
Paul Desmarais, P.C., C.C.
Paul Desmarais, Jr.
Alan J. Dilworth
Wanda M. Dorosz
Robert Gratton
James L. Hunter
Daniel Johnson
Donald F. Mazankowski
John Stuart McCallum
Raymond L. McFeetors
R. Jeffrey Orr
Roy W. Piper
P. Michael Pitfield, P.C., Q.C.
Michel Plessis-Bélair
H. Sanford Riley
Susan Sherk
Gérard Veilleux

Affiliated Companies:
Tony Copple

Allegro:
Aggressive Portfolio C Fund
RRSP Eligible; Inception Year: 2001; Fund Managers:
I.G. Investment Management
Aggressive Registered Portfolio C Fund
RRSP Eligible; Inception Year: 2001; Fund Managers:
I.G. Investment Management
Conservative Portfolio C Fund
RRSP Eligible; Inception Year: 2001; Fund Managers:
I.G. Investment Management
Moderate Aggressive Registered C Fund
RRSP Eligible; Inception Year: 2001; Fund Managers:
I.G. Investment Management
Moderate Aggressive Portfolio C Fund
RRSP Eligible; Inception Year: 2001; Fund Managers:
I.G. Investment Management
Moderate Conservative C Fund
RRSP Eligible; Inception Year: 2001; Fund Managers:
I.G. Investment Management
Moderate Portfolio C Fund
RRSP Eligible; Inception Year: 2001; Fund Managers:
I.G. Investment Management
Aggressive Registered Portfolio B Fund
RRSP Eligible; Inception Year: 2003; Fund Managers:
I.G. Investment Management
Aggressive Portfolio A Fund
RRSP Eligible; Inception Year: 2003; Fund Managers:
I.G. Investment Management
Aggressive Portfolio B Fund
RRSP Eligible; Inception Year: 2003; Fund Managers:
I.G. Investment Management
Conservative Portfolio A Fund
RRSP Eligible; Inception Year: 2003; Fund Managers:
I.G. Investment Management
Conservative Portfolio B Fund
RRSP Eligible; Inception Year: 2003; Fund Managers:
I.G. Investment Management
Moderate Aggressive Registered A Fund
RRSP Eligible; Inception Year: 2003; Fund Managers:
I.G. Investment Management
Moderate Aggressive Registered B Fund
RRSP Eligible; Inception Year: 2003; Fund Managers:
I.G. Investment Management
Moderate Conservative A Fund
RRSP Eligible; Inception Year: 2003; Fund Managers:
I.G. Investment Management
Moderate Conservative B Fund
RRSP Eligible; Inception Year: 2003; Fund Managers:
I.G. Investment Management
Moderate Aggressive Portfolio A Fund
RRSP Eligible; Inception Year: 2003; Fund Managers:
I.G. Investment Management
Moderate Aggressive Portfolio B Fund
RRSP Eligible; Inception Year: 2003; Fund Managers:
I.G. Investment Management
Moderate Portfolio A Fund
RRSP Eligible; Inception Year: 2003; Fund Managers:
I.G. Investment Management
Moderate Portfolio B Fund
RRSP Eligible; Inception Year: 2003; Fund Managers:
I.G. Investment Management
Aggressive Registered Portfolio A Fund
RRSP Eligible; Inception Year: 2003; Fund Managers:
I.G. Investment Management

Alto:
Aggressive Registered Portfolio A Fund
RRSP Eligible; Inception Year: 2003; Fund Managers:
I.G. Investment Management
Aggressive Registered Portfolio B Fund
RRSP Eligible; Inception Year: 2003; Fund Managers:
I.G. Investment Management
Aggressive Portfolio A Fund
RRSP Eligible; Inception Year: 2003; Fund Managers:
I.G. Investment Management
Aggressive Portfolio B Fund
RRSP Eligible; Inception Year: 2003; Fund Managers:
I.G. Investment Management
Conservative Portfolio A Fund
RRSP Eligible; Inception Year: 2003; Fund Managers:
I.G. Investment Management
Conservative Portfolio B Fund
RRSP Eligible; Inception Year: 2003; Fund Managers:
I.G. Investment Management
Moderate Portfolio A Fund
RRSP Eligible; Inception Year: 2003; Fund Managers:
I.G. Investment Management
Moderate Portfolio B Fund
RRSP Eligible; Inception Year: 2003; Fund Managers:
I.G. Investment Management
Moderate Aggressive Portfolio A Fund
RRSP Eligible; Inception Year: 2003; Fund Managers:
I.G. Investment Management
Moderate Aggressive Portfolio B Fund
RRSP Eligible; Inception Year: 2003; Fund Managers:
I.G. Investment Management
Moderate Conservative Portfolio A Fund
RRSP Eligible; Inception Year: 2003; Fund Managers:
I.G. Investment Management
Moderate Conservative Portfolio B Fund
RRSP Eligible; Inception Year: 2003; Fund Managers:
I.G. Investment Management
Moderate Aggressive Registered Portfolio A Fund
RRSP Eligible; Inception Year: 2003; Fund Managers:
I.G. Investment Management
Moderate Aggressive Registered Portfolio B Fund
RRSP Eligible; Inception Year: 2003; Fund Managers:
I.G. Investment Management
Monthly Income Portfolio T-DSC Fund
RRSP Eligible; Inception Year: 2004; Fund Managers:
I.G. Investment Management
Monthly Income Portfolio T-NL Fund
RRSP Eligible; Inception Year: 2004; Fund Managers:
I.G. Investment Management
Monthly Income Portfolio A Fund
RRSP Eligible; Inception Year: 2004; Fund Managers:
I.G. Investment Management
Monthly Income Portfolio B Fund
RRSP Eligible; Inception Year: 2004; Fund Managers:
I.G. Investment Management
Monthly Income & Enhanced Growth Portfolio T-NL Fund
RRSP Eligible; Inception Year: 2004; Fund Managers:
I.G. Investment Management
Monthly Income & Enhanced Growth Portfolio T-DSC Fund
RRSP Eligible; Inception Year: 2004; Fund Managers:
I.G. Investment Management
Monthly Income & Enhanced Growth Portfolio A Fund
RRSP Eligible; Inception Year: 2004; Fund Managers:
I.G. Investment Management
Monthly Income & Enhanced Growth Portfolio B Fund
RRSP Eligible; Inception Year: 2004; Fund Managers:
I.G. Investment Management
Monthly Income & Growth Portfolio T-DSC Fund
RRSP Eligible; Inception Year: 2004; Fund Managers:
I.G. Investment Management
Monthly Income & Growth Portfolio T-NL Fund
RRSP Eligible; Inception Year: 2004; Fund Managers:
I.G. Investment Management
Monthly Income & Growth Portfolio A Fund
RRSP Eligible; Inception Year: 2004; Fund Managers:
I.G. Investment Management
Monthly Income & Growth Portfolio B Fund
RRSP Eligible; Inception Year: 2004; Fund Managers:
I.G. Investment Management
Aggressive Portfolio C Fund
RRSP Eligible; Inception Year: 2005; Fund Managers:
I.G. Investment Management
Conservative Portfolio C Fund
RRSP Eligible; Inception Year: 2005; Fund Managers:
I.G. Investment Management
Moderate Aggressive Portfolio C Fund
RRSP Eligible; Inception Year: 2005; Fund Managers:
I.G. Investment Management
Moderate Conservative Portfolio C Fund
RRSP Eligible; Inception Year: 2005; Fund Managers:
I.G. Investment Management
Moderate Portfolio C Fund
RRSP Eligible; Inception Year: 2005; Fund Managers:
I.G. Investment Management
Monthly Income Portfolio C Fund Fund
RRSP Eligible; Inception Year: 2005; Fund Managers:
I.G. Investment Management
Monthly Income Portfolio TC Fund Fund
RRSP Eligible; Inception Year: 2005; Fund Managers:
I.G. Investment Management
Monthly Income & Enhanced Growth Portfolio TC Fund
RRSP Eligible; Inception Year: 2005; Fund Managers:
I.G. Investment Management
Monthly Income & Enhanced Growth Portfolio C Fund
RRSP Eligible; Inception Year: 2005; Fund Managers:
I.G. Investment Management
Monthly Income & Growth Portfolio TC Fund
RRSP Eligible; Inception Year: 2005; Fund Managers:
I.G. Investment Management

Monthly Income & Growth Portfolio C Fund
RRSP Eligible; Inception Year: 2005; Fund Managers: I.G. Investment Management
IG AGF:
Asian Growth C Fund
RRSP Eligible; Inception Year: 1999; Fund Managers: AGF Funds
Canadian Growth C Fund
RRSP Eligible; Inception Year: 1996; Fund Managers: AGF Funds
Canadian Diversified Growth C Fund
RRSP Eligible; Inception Year: 1999; Fund Managers: AGF Funds
US Growth C Fund
RRSP Eligible; Inception Year: 1999; Fund Managers: AGF Funds
Canadian Balanced C Fund
RRSP Eligible; Inception Year: 1996; Fund Managers: AGF Funds
International Bond Fund
RRSP Eligible; Inception Year: 1996; Fund Managers: Insight Investment Management
Asian Growth Class A Fund
RRSP Eligible; Inception Year: 2002; Fund Managers: AGF Funds
Canadian Growth Class A Fund
RRSP Eligible; Inception Year: 2002;
Canadian Diversified Growth Class A Fund
RRSP Eligible; Inception Year: 2002;
US Growth Class A Fund
RRSP Eligible; Inception Year: 2002; Fund Managers: AGF Funds
International Equity Class A Fund
RRSP Eligible; Inception Year: 2002;
Asian Growth A Fund
RRSP Eligible; Inception Year: 2003; Fund Managers: AGF Funds
Asian Growth B Fund
RRSP Eligible; Inception Year: 2003; Fund Managers: AGF Funds
Canadian Diversified Growth Class B Fund
RRSP Eligible; Inception Year: 2003;
Canadian Growth Class B Fund
RRSP Eligible; Inception Year: 2003;
Canadian Diversified Growth A Fund
RRSP Eligible; Inception Year: 2003; Fund Managers: AGF Funds
Canadian Diversified Growth B Fund
RRSP Eligible; Inception Year: 2003; Fund Managers: AGF Funds
Canadian Growth A Fund
RRSP Eligible; Inception Year: 2003; Fund Managers: AGF Funds
Canadian Growth B Fund
RRSP Eligible; Inception Year: 2003; Fund Managers: AGF Funds
Canadian Balanced A Fund
RRSP Eligible; Inception Year: 2003; Fund Managers: AGF Funds
Canadian Balanced B Fund
RRSP Eligible; Inception Year: 2003; Fund Managers: AGF Funds
International Equity Class B Fund
RRSP Eligible; Inception Year: 2003;
International Equity A Fund
RRSP Eligible; Inception Year: 2003; Fund Managers: AGF Funds
International Equity B Fund
RRSP Eligible; Inception Year: 2003; Fund Managers: AGF Funds
International Equity C Fund
RRSP Eligible; Inception Year: 1996; Fund Managers: AGF Funds
US Growth A Fund
RRSP Eligible; Inception Year: 2003; Fund Managers: AGF Funds
US Growth B Fund
RRSP Eligible; Inception Year: 2003; Fund Managers: AGF Funds
US Growth Class B Fund
RRSP Eligible; Inception Year: 2003; Fund Managers: AGF Funds
Canadian Equity Class B Fund
RRSP Eligible; Inception Year: 2003;
Asian Growth Class B Fund
RRSP Eligible; Inception Year: 2003; Fund Managers: AGF Funds
IG Beutel Goodman:
Canadian Balanced C Fund
RRSP Eligible; Inception Year: 1996; Fund Managers: Beutel Goodman
Canadian Equity C Fund
RRSP Eligible; Inception Year: 1996; Fund Managers: Beutel Goodman
Canadian Small Cap C Fund
RRSP Eligible; Inception Year: 1996; Fund Managers: Beutel Goodman
Canadian Equity Class A Fund
RRSP Eligible; Inception Year: 2002;
Canadian Balanced A Fund
RRSP Eligible; Inception Year: 2003; Fund Managers: Beutel Goodman
Canadian Balanced B Fund
RRSP Eligible; Inception Year: 2003; Fund Managers: Beutel Goodman
Canadian Equity A Fund
RRSP Eligible; Inception Year: 2003; Fund Managers: Beutel Goodman
Canadian Equity B Fund
RRSP Eligible; Inception Year: 2003; Fund Managers: Beutel Goodman
Canadian Equity Class B
RRSP Eligible; Inception Year: 2003;
IG Bissett:
Canadian Equity A Fund
RRSP Eligible; Inception Year: 2004; Fund Managers: Bissett Investment Management
Canadian Equity B Fund
RRSP Eligible; Inception Year: 2004; Fund Managers: Bissett Investment Management
Canadian Equity Class A Fund
RRSP Eligible; Inception Year: 2004; Fund Managers: Bissett Investment Management
Canadian Equity Class B Fund
RRSP Eligible; Inception Year: 2004; Fund Managers: Bissett Investment Management
IG FI:
Canadian Allocation C Fund
RRSP Eligible; Inception Year: 2000; Fund Managers: Fidelity Investments
Global Equity C Fund
RRSP Eligible; Inception Year: 2000; Fund Managers: Fidelity Investments
Global Equity Class A Fund
RRSP Eligible; Inception Year: 2002; Fund Managers: Fidelity Investments
Canadian Equity C Fund
RRSP Eligible; Inception Year: 2000; Fund Managers: Fidelity Investments
Canadian Equity Class A Fund
RRSP Eligible; Inception Year: 2002; Fund Managers: Fidelity Investments
US Equity C Fund
RRSP Eligible; Inception Year: 2000; Fund Managers: Fidelity Investments
US Equity Class A Fund
RRSP Eligible; Inception Year: 2002; Fund Managers: Fidelity Investments
Canadian Equity Class B Fund
RRSP Eligible; Inception Year: 2003; Fund Managers: Fidelity Investments
Canadian Equity A Fund
RRSP Eligible; Inception Year: 2003; Fund Managers: Fidelity Investments
Canadian Equity B Fund
RRSP Eligible; Inception Year: 2003; Fund Managers: Fidelity Investments
Canadian Allocation A Fund
RRSP Eligible; Inception Year: 2003; Fund Managers: Fidelity Investments
Canadian Allocation B Fund
RRSP Eligible; Inception Year: 2003; Fund Managers: Fidelity Investments
Global Equity Class B Fund
RRSP Eligible; Inception Year: 2003; Fund Managers: Fidelity Investments
Global Equity A Fund
RRSP Eligible; Inception Year: 2003; Fund Managers: Fidelity Investments
Global Equity B Fund
RRSP Eligible; Inception Year: 2003; Fund Managers: Fidelity Investments
US Equity A Fund
RRSP Eligible; Inception Year: 2003; Fund Managers: Fidelity Investments
US Equity B Fund
RRSP Eligible; Inception Year: 2003; Fund Managers: Fidelity Investments
US Equity Class B Fund
RRSP Eligible; Inception Year: 2003; Fund Managers: Fidelity Investments
IG Goldman Sachs:
US Equity A Fund
RRSP Eligible; Inception Year: 2003; Fund Managers: Goldman Sachs Asset Management (New York)
US Equity B Fund
RRSP Eligible; Inception Year: 2003; Fund Managers: Goldman Sachs Asset Management (New York)
US Equity C Fund
RRSP Eligible; Inception Year: 2003; Fund Managers: Goldman Sachs Asset Management (New York)
US Equity Class A Fund
RRSP Eligible; Inception Year: 2003; Fund Managers: Goldman Sachs Asset Management (New York)
US Equity Class B Fund
RRSP Eligible; Inception Year: 2003; Fund Managers: Goldman Sachs Asset Management (New York)
IG Mackenzie:
Income Fund
RRSP Eligible; Inception Year: 1999; Fund Managers: Mackenzie Financial Corp.
Ivy European C Fund
RRSP Eligible; Inception Year: 1999; Fund Managers: Mackenzie Financial Corp.
Ivy European Class A Fund
RRSP Eligible; Inception Year: 2002;
Maxxum Dividend C Fund
RRSP Eligible; Inception Year: 1999; Fund Managers: Mackenzie Financial Corp.
Select Managers Canada C Fund
RRSP Eligible; Inception Year: 1999; Fund Managers: Mackenzie Financial Corp.
Select Managers Canada Class A Fund
RRSP Eligible; Inception Year: 2002;
Universal Emerging Market Class A Fund
RRSP Eligible; Inception Year: 2002;
Universal Global Future A Fund
RRSP Eligible; Inception Year: 2003; Fund Managers: Mackenzie Financial Corp.
Universal Global Future B Fund
RRSP Eligible; Inception Year: 2003; Fund Managers: Mackenzie Financial Corp.
Universal Global Future C Fund
RRSP Eligible; Inception Year: 2000; Fund Managers: Mackenzie Financial Corp.
Ivy European A Fund
RRSP Eligible; Inception Year: 2003; Fund Managers: Mackenzie Financial Corp.
Ivy European B Fund
RRSP Eligible; Inception Year: 2003; Fund Managers: Mackenzie Financial Corp.
Select Managers Canada A Fund
RRSP Eligible; Inception Year: 2003; Fund Managers: Mackenzie Financial Corp.
Select Managers Canada B Fund
RRSP Eligible; Inception Year: 2003; Fund Managers: Mackenzie Financial Corp.
Universal US Growth Leaders A Fund
RRSP Eligible; Inception Year: 2003; Fund Managers: Mackenzie Financial Corp.
Universal US Growth Leaders B Fund
RRSP Eligible; Inception Year: 2003; Fund Managers: Mackenzie Financial Corp.
Universal US Growth Leaders C Fund
RRSP Eligible; Inception Year: 2000; Fund Managers: Mackenzie Financial Corp.
Universal Emerging Market Class B Fund
RRSP Eligible; Inception Year: 2003;
Maxxum Dividend A Fund
RRSP Eligible; Inception Year: 2003; Fund Managers: Mackenzie Financial Corp.
Maxxum Dividend B Fund
RRSP Eligible; Inception Year: 2003; Fund Managers: Mackenzie Financial Corp.

Investors Group Inc. (continued)

Ivy European Class B Fund
RRSP Eligible; Inception Year: 2003; Fund Managers:
Mackenzie Financial Corp.
Ivy Foreign Equity Class A Fund
RRSP Eligible; Inception Year: 2002; Fund Managers:
Mackenzie Financial Corp.
Ivy Foreign Equity Class B Fund
RRSP Eligible; Inception Year: 2003; Fund Managers:
Mackenzie Financial Corp.
Select Managers Canada Class B Fund
RRSP Eligible; Inception Year: 2003;
Universal US Growth Leaders Class A Fund
RRSP Eligible; Inception Year: 2002; Fund Managers:
Mackenzie Financial Corp.
Universal US Growth Leaders Class B Fund
RRSP Eligible; Inception Year: 2003; Fund Managers:
Mackenzie Financial Corp.
Universal Global Future Class A
RRSP Eligible; Inception Year: 2004; Fund Managers:
Mackenzie Financial Corp.
Universal Global Future Class B
RRSP Eligible; Inception Year: 2004; Fund Managers:
Mackenzie Financial Corp.

IG Templeton:

World Bond Fund
RRSP Eligible; Inception Year: 1996; Fund Managers:
Franklin Templeton Investments
International Equity C Fund
RRSP Eligible; Inception Year: 1999; Fund Managers:
Franklin Templeton Investments
World Allocation C Fund
RRSP Eligible; Inception Year: 1996; Fund Managers:
Franklin Templeton Investments
International Equity Class A Fund
RRSP Eligible; Inception Year: 2002;
International Equity Class B Fund
RRSP Eligible; Inception Year: 2003;
International Equity A Fund
RRSP Eligible; Inception Year: 2003; Fund Managers:
Franklin Templeton Investments
International Equity B Fund
RRSP Eligible; Inception Year: 2003; Fund Managers:
Franklin Templeton Investments
World Allocation A Fund
RRSP Eligible; Inception Year: 2003; Fund Managers:
Franklin Templeton Investments
World Allocation B Fund
RRSP Eligible; Inception Year: 2003; Fund Managers:
Franklin Templeton Investments

IG/GWL:

Canadian Balanced Segregated Fund
RRSP Eligible; Inception Year: 1999; Fund Managers:
I.G. Investment Management
Government Bond Segregated Fund
RRSP Eligible; Inception Year: 1999; Fund Managers:
I.G. Investment Management
US Large Cap Value Segregated Fund
RRSP Eligible; Inception Year: 1999; Fund Managers:
I.G. Investment Management
Money Market Segregated Fund
RRSP Eligible; Inception Year: 1999; Fund Managers:
I.G. Investment Management
Summa Segregated Fund
RRSP Eligible; Inception Year: 1999; Fund Managers:
I.G. Investment Management
Global Segregated Fund
RRSP Eligible; Inception Year: 0; Fund Managers:
I.G. Investment Management
Dividend Segregated Fund
RRSP Eligible; Inception Year: 1999; Fund Managers:
I.G. Investment Management
Canadian Equity Segregated Fund
RRSP Eligible; Inception Year: 1999; Fund Managers:
I.G. Investment Management

Investors:

Tact Asset Allocation C Fund
RRSP Eligible; Inception Year: 1994; Fund Managers:
I.G. Investment Management
Canadian Equity C Fund
RRSP Eligible; Inception Year: 1983; Fund Managers:
I.G. Investment Management
Canadian Bond Fund
RRSP Eligible; Inception Year: 1994; Fund Managers:
I.G. Investment Management
Dividend C Fund
RRSP Eligible; Inception Year: 1962; Fund Managers:
I.G. Investment Management
Global Bond Fund
RRSP Eligible; Inception Year: 1992; Fund Managers:
I.G. Investment Management
Global C Fund
RRSP Eligible; Inception Year: 1986; Fund Managers:
I.G. Investment Management
Government Bond Fund
RRSP Eligible; Inception Year: 1979; Fund Managers:
I.G. Investment Management
Growth Plus Portfolio C Fund
RRSP Eligible; Inception Year: 1989; Fund Managers:
I.G. Investment Management
Growth Portfolio C Fund
RRSP Eligible; Inception Year: 1989; Fund Managers:
I.G. Investment Management
Income Plus Portfolio C Fund
RRSP Eligible; Inception Year: 1989; Fund Managers:
I.G. Investment Management
Income Portfolio Fund
RRSP Eligible; Inception Year: 1989; Fund Managers:
I.G. Investment Management
Japanese Equity C Fund
RRSP Eligible; Inception Year: 1971; Fund Managers:
I.G. Investment Management
Canadian Money Market Fund
RRSP Eligible; Inception Year: 1985; Fund Managers:
I.G. Investment Management
Mortgage Fund
RRSP Eligible; Inception Year: 1973; Fund Managers:
I.G. Investment Management
Mutual of Canada C Fund
RRSP Eligible; Inception Year: 1950; Fund Managers:
I.G. Investment Management
North American Equity C Fund
RRSP Eligible; Inception Year: 1957; Fund Managers:
I.G. Investment Management
Pacific International C Fund
RRSP Eligible; Inception Year: 1990; Fund Managers:
I.G. Investment Management
Real Property C Fund
RRSP Eligible; Inception Year: 1984; Fund Managers:
I.G. Investment Management
Retirement Growth Portfolio C Fund
RRSP Eligible; Inception Year: 1989; Fund Managers:
I.G. Investment Management
Retirement Plus Portfolio C Fund
RRSP Eligible; Inception Year: 1989; Fund Managers:
I.G. Investment Management
Summa C Fund
RRSP Eligible; Inception Year: 1987; Fund Managers:
I.G. Investment Management
World Growth Portfolio C Fund
RRSP Eligible; Inception Year: 1993; Fund Managers:
I.G. Investment Management
Canadian Natural Resource C Fund
RRSP Eligible; Inception Year: 1996; Fund Managers:
I.G. Investment Management
Canadian Small Cap C Fund
RRSP Eligible; Inception Year: 1996; Fund Managers:
I.G. Investment Management
US Opportunities C Fund
RRSP Eligible; Inception Year: 1996; Fund Managers:
I.G. Investment Management
Québec Enterprise C Fund
RRSP Eligible; Inception Year: 1999; Fund Managers:
I.G. Investment Management
Canadian Balanced C Fund
RRSP Eligible; Inception Year: 1998; Fund Managers:
I.G. Investment Management
Canadian High Yield Income Fund
RRSP Eligible; Inception Year: 1996; Fund Managers:
I.G. Investment Management
European Mid-Cap Growth C Fund
RRSP Eligible; Inception Year: 2000; Fund Managers:
I.G. Investment Management
Global Science & Technology C Fund
RRSP Eligible; Inception Year: 1998; Fund Managers:
I.G. Investment Management
Mergers & Acquisitions C Fund
RRSP Eligible; Inception Year: 2000; Fund Managers:
Camlin Asset Management
Retirement High Growth Portfolio C Fund
RRSP Eligible; Inception Year: 1999; Fund Managers:
I.G. Investment Management
US Large Cap Growth C Fund
RRSP Eligible; Inception Year: 1968; Fund Managers:
I.G. Investment Management
US Large Cap Value C Fund
RRSP Eligible; Inception Year: 1962; Fund Managers:
I.G. Investment Management
US Large Cap Value RSP C Fund
RRSP Eligible; Inception Year: 1999; Fund Managers:
I.G. Investment Management
Canadian Small Cap Growth C Fund
RRSP Eligible; Inception Year: 1998; Fund Managers:
I.G. Investment Management
Pan Asian Growth C Fund
RRSP Eligible; Inception Year: 2001; Fund Managers:
I.G. Investment Management
Global Financial Services C Fund
RRSP Eligible; Inception Year: 2001; Fund Managers:
I.G. Investment Management
Canadian Equity Class A Fund
RRSP Eligible; Inception Year: 2002; Fund Managers:
I.G. Investment Management
Canadian Small Cap Class A Fund
RRSP Eligible; Inception Year: 2002; Fund Managers:
I.G. Investment Management
Canadian High Yield Money Market Fund
RRSP Eligible; Inception Year: 2001; Fund Managers:
I.G. Investment Management
Canadian Large Cap Value C Fund
RRSP Eligible; Inception Year: 1972; Fund Managers:
I.G. Investment Management
Canadian Large Cap Value Class A Fund
RRSP Eligible; Inception Year: 2002; Fund Managers:
I.G. Investment Management
Canadian Small Cap Growth Class A Fund
RRSP Eligible; Inception Year: 2002; Fund Managers:
I.G. Investment Management
European Mid-Cap Growth Class A Fund
RRSP Eligible; Inception Year: 2002; Fund Managers:
I.G. Investment Management
European Equity C Fund
RRSP Eligible; Inception Year: 1990; Fund Managers:
I.G. Investment Management
Global Class A Fund
RRSP Eligible; Inception Year: 2002; Fund Managers:
I.G. Investment Management
Global Health Care Class A Fund
RRSP Eligible; Inception Year: 2002; Fund Managers:
I.G. Investment Management
European Equity Class A Fund
RRSP Eligible; Inception Year: 2002; Fund Managers:
I.G. Investment Management
Global Natural Resource Class A Fund
RRSP Eligible; Inception Year: 2002; Fund Managers:
I.G. Investment Management
Global Financial Services Class A Fund
RRSP Eligible; Inception Year: 2002; Fund Managers:
I.G. Investment Management
Global Infrastructure Class A Fund
RRSP Eligible; Inception Year: 2002; Fund Managers:
I.G. Investment Management
Global Science & Technology Class A Fund
RRSP Eligible; Inception Year: 2002; Fund Managers:
I.G. Investment Management
International Small Cap Class A Fund
RRSP Eligible; Inception Year: 2002; Fund Managers:
I.G. Investment Management
Japanese Equity Class A Fund
RRSP Eligible; Inception Year: 2002; Fund Managers:
I.G. Investment Management
Mergers & Acquisitions Class A Fund
RRSP Eligible; Inception Year: 2002; Fund Managers:
Camlin Asset Management
North American Equity Class A Fund
RRSP Eligible; Inception Year: 2002; Fund Managers:
I.G. Investment Management
Pacific International Class A Fund
RRSP Eligible; Inception Year: 2002; Fund Managers:
I.G. Investment Management
Pan Asian Growth Class A Fund
RRSP Eligible; Inception Year: 2002; Fund Managers:
I.G. Investment Management

Québec Enterprise Class A Fund
RRSP Eligible; Inception Year: 2002; Fund Managers:
I.G. Investment Management
Summa Class A Fund
RRSP Eligible; Inception Year: 2002; Fund Managers:
I.G. Investment Management
US Large Cap Growth Class A Fund
RRSP Eligible; Inception Year: 2002; Fund Managers:
I.G. Investment Management
US Large Cap Value Class A Fund
RRSP Eligible; Inception Year: 2002;
US Opportunities Class A Fund
RRSP Eligible; Inception Year: 2002; Fund Managers:
I.G. Investment Management
Managed Yield Class A Fund
RRSP Eligible; Inception Year: 2002; Fund Managers:
I.G. Investment Management
US Small Cap Class A Fund
RRSP Eligible; Inception Year: 2002; Fund Managers:
I.G. Investment Management
Tact Asset Allocation A Fund
RRSP Eligible; Inception Year: 2003; Fund Managers:
I.G. Investment Management
Tact Asset Allocation B Fund
RRSP Eligible; Inception Year: 2003; Fund Managers:
I.G. Investment Management
Canadian Small Cap Growth B Fund
RRSP Eligible; Inception Year: 2003; Fund Managers:
I.G. Investment Management
Canadian Balanced A Fund
RRSP Eligible; Inception Year: 2003; Fund Managers:
I.G. Investment Management
Canadian Balanced B Fund
RRSP Eligible; Inception Year: 2003; Fund Managers:
I.G. Investment Management
Canadian Equity Class B Fund
RRSP Eligible; Inception Year: 2003; Fund Managers:
I.G. Investment Management
Canadian Equity A Fund
RRSP Eligible; Inception Year: 2003; Fund Managers:
I.G. Investment Management
Canadian Equity B Fund
RRSP Eligible; Inception Year: 2003; Fund Managers:
I.G. Investment Management
Canadian Large Cap Value Class B Fund
RRSP Eligible; Inception Year: 2003; Fund Managers:
I.G. Investment Management
Canadian Large Cap Value A Fund
RRSP Eligible; Inception Year: 2003; Fund Managers:
I.G. Investment Management
Canadian Large Cap Value B Fund
RRSP Eligible; Inception Year: 2003; Fund Managers:
I.G. Investment Management
Canadian Natural Resource A Fund
RRSP Eligible; Inception Year: 2003; Fund Managers:
I.G. Investment Management
Canadian Natural Resource B Fund
RRSP Eligible; Inception Year: 2003; Fund Managers:
I.G. Investment Management
Canadian Small Cap Class B Fund
RRSP Eligible; Inception Year: 2003; Fund Managers:
I.G. Investment Management
Canadian Small Cap Growth A Fund
RRSP Eligible; Inception Year: 2003; Fund Managers:
I.G. Investment Management
Canadian Small Cap Growth Class B Fund
RRSP Eligible; Inception Year: 2003; Fund Managers:
I.G. Investment Management
Canadian Small Cap A Fund
RRSP Eligible; Inception Year: 2003; Fund Managers:
I.G. Investment Management
Canadian Small Cap B Fund
RRSP Eligible; Inception Year: 2003; Fund Managers:
I.G. Investment Management
Dividend A Fund
RRSP Eligible; Inception Year: 2003; Fund Managers:
I.G. Investment Management
Dividend B Fund
RRSP Eligible; Inception Year: 2003; Fund Managers:
I.G. Investment Management
European Equity Class B Fund
RRSP Eligible; Inception Year: 2003; Fund Managers:
I.G. Investment Management
European Mid-Cap Growth A Fund
RRSP Eligible; Inception Year: 2003; Fund Managers:
I.G. Investment Management
European Mid-Cap Growth B Fund
RRSP Eligible; Inception Year: 2003; Fund Managers:
I.G. Investment Management
European Mid-Cap Growth Class B Fund
RRSP Eligible; Inception Year: 2003; Fund Managers:
I.G. Investment Management
European Equity A Fund
RRSP Eligible; Inception Year: 2003; Fund Managers:
I.G. Investment Management
European Equity B Fund
RRSP Eligible; Inception Year: 2003; Fund Managers:
I.G. Investment Management
Global Cons Comp Class A Fund
RRSP Eligible; Inception Year: 2002; Fund Managers:
I.G. Investment Management
Global Cons Comp Class B Fund
RRSP Eligible; Inception Year: 2003; Fund Managers:
I.G. Investment Management
Global Infrasturcture Class B Fund
RRSP Eligible; Inception Year: 2003; Fund Managers:
I.G. Investment Management
Global Financial Services Class B Fund
RRSP Eligible; Inception Year: 2003; Fund Managers:
I.G. Investment Management
Global Health Care Class B Fund
RRSP Eligible; Inception Year: 2003; Fund Managers:
I.G. Investment Management
Global Natural Resource Class B Fund
RRSP Eligible; Inception Year: 2003; Fund Managers:
I.G. Investment Management
Global Science & Technology Class B Fund
RRSP Eligible; Inception Year: 2003; Fund Managers:
I.G. Investment Management
Global Financial Services A Fund
RRSP Eligible; Inception Year: 2003; Fund Managers:
I.G. Investment Management
Global Financial Services B Fund
RRSP Eligible; Inception Year: 2003; Fund Managers:
I.G. Investment Management
Global Science & Technology A Fund
RRSP Eligible; Inception Year: 2003; Fund Managers:
I.G. Investment Management
Global Science & Technology B Fund
RRSP Eligible; Inception Year: 2003; Fund Managers:
I.G. Investment Management
Global A Fund
RRSP Eligible; Inception Year: 2003; Fund Managers:
I.G. Investment Management
Global B Fund
RRSP Eligible; Inception Year: 2003; Fund Managers:
I.G. Investment Management
Growth Plus Portfolio A Fund
RRSP Eligible; Inception Year: 2003; Fund Managers:
I.G. Investment Management
Growth Plus Portfolio B Fund
RRSP Eligible; Inception Year: 2003; Fund Managers:
I.G. Investment Management
Growth Portfolio A Fund
RRSP Eligible; Inception Year: 2003; Fund Managers:
I.G. Investment Management
Growth Portfolio B Fund
RRSP Eligible; Inception Year: 2003; Fund Managers:
I.G. Investment Management
Income Plus Portfolio A Fund
RRSP Eligible; Inception Year: 2003; Fund Managers:
I.G. Investment Management
Income Plus Portfolio B Fund
RRSP Eligible; Inception Year: 2003; Fund Managers:
I.G. Investment Management
International Small Cap Class B Fund
RRSP Eligible; Inception Year: 2003; Fund Managers:
I.G. Investment Management
Japanese Equity Class B Fund
RRSP Eligible; Inception Year: 2003; Fund Managers:
I.G. Investment Management
Japanese Equity A Fund
RRSP Eligible; Inception Year: 2003; Fund Managers:
I.G. Investment Management
Japanese Equity B Fund
RRSP Eligible; Inception Year: 2003; Fund Managers:
I.G. Investment Management
Mergers & Acquisitions A Fund
RRSP Eligible; Inception Year: 2003; Fund Managers:
Camlin Asset Management
Mergers & Acquisitions B Fund
RRSP Eligible; Inception Year: 2003; Fund Managers:
Camlin Asset Management
Mergers & Acquisitions Class B Fund
RRSP Eligible; Inception Year: 2003; Fund Managers:
Camlin Asset Management
Managed Yield Class B Fund
RRSP Eligible; Inception Year: 2003; Fund Managers:
I.G. Investment Management
Mutual of Canada A Fund
RRSP Eligible; Inception Year: 2003; Fund Managers:
I.G. Investment Management
Mutual of Canada B Fund
RRSP Eligible; Inception Year: 2003; Fund Managers:
I.G. Investment Management
North American Equity Class B Fund
RRSP Eligible; Inception Year: 2003; Fund Managers:
I.G. Investment Management
North American Equity A Fund
RRSP Eligible; Inception Year: 2003; Fund Managers:
I.G. Investment Management
North American Equity B Fund
RRSP Eligible; Inception Year: 2003; Fund Managers:
I.G. Investment Management
Pacific International A Fund
RRSP Eligible; Inception Year: 2003; Fund Managers:
I.G. Investment Management
Pacific International Class B Fund
RRSP Eligible; Inception Year: 2003; Fund Managers:
I.G. Investment Management
Pacific International B Fund
RRSP Eligible; Inception Year: 2003; Fund Managers:
I.G. Investment Management
Pan Asian Growth A Fund
RRSP Eligible; Inception Year: 2003; Fund Managers:
I.G. Investment Management
Pan Asian Growth B Fund
RRSP Eligible; Inception Year: 2003; Fund Managers:
I.G. Investment Management
Pan Asian Growth Class B Fund
RRSP Eligible; Inception Year: 2003; Fund Managers:
I.G. Investment Management
Québec Enterprise Class B Fund
RRSP Eligible; Inception Year: 2003; Fund Managers:
I.G. Investment Management
Québec Enterprise A Fund
RRSP Eligible; Inception Year: 2003; Fund Managers:
I.G. Investment Management
Québec Enterprise B Fund
RRSP Eligible; Inception Year: 2003; Fund Managers:
I.G. Investment Management
Real Property A Fund
RRSP Eligible; Inception Year: 2003; Fund Managers:
I.G. Investment Management
Retirement High Growth Portfolio A Fund
RRSP Eligible; Inception Year: 2003; Fund Managers:
I.G. Investment Management
Retirement High Growth Portfolio B Fund
RRSP Eligible; Inception Year: 2003; Fund Managers:
I.G. Investment Management
Retirement Growth Portfolio A Fund
RRSP Eligible; Inception Year: 2003; Fund Managers:
I.G. Investment Management
Retirement Growth Portfolio B Fund
RRSP Eligible; Inception Year: 2003; Fund Managers:
I.G. Investment Management
Retirement Plus Portfolio A Fund
RRSP Eligible; Inception Year: 2003; Fund Managers:
I.G. Investment Management
Retirement Plus Portfolio B Fund
RRSP Eligible; Inception Year: 2003; Fund Managers:
I.G. Investment Management
Summa Class B Fund
RRSP Eligible; Inception Year: 2003; Fund Managers:
I.G. Investment Management
Summa A Fund
RRSP Eligible; Inception Year: 2003; Fund Managers:
I.G. Investment Management
Summa B Fund
RRSP Eligible; Inception Year: 2003; Fund Managers:
I.G. Investment Management

Investors Group Inc. (continued)
US Small Cap Class B Fund
RRSP Eligible; Inception Year: 2003; Fund Managers:
I.G. Investment Management
US Large Cap Growth Class B Fund
RRSP Eligible; Inception Year: 2003; Fund Managers:
I.G. Investment Management
US Large Cap Value Class B Fund
RRSP Eligible; Inception Year: 2003; Fund Managers:
I.G. Investment Management
US Large Cap Value RSP A Fund
RRSP Eligible; Inception Year: 2003; Fund Managers:
I.G. Investment Management
US Large Cap Value RSP B Fund
RRSP Eligible; Inception Year: 2003; Fund Managers:
I.G. Investment Management
US Large Cap Growth A Fund
RRSP Eligible; Inception Year: 2003; Fund Managers:
I.G. Investment Management
US Large Cap Growth B Fund
RRSP Eligible; Inception Year: 2003; Fund Managers:
I.G. Investment Management
US Large Cap Value A Fund
RRSP Eligible; Inception Year: 2003; Fund Managers:
I.G. Investment Management
US Large Cap Value B Fund
RRSP Eligible; Inception Year: 2003; Fund Managers:
I.G. Investment Management
US Opportunities Class B Fund
RRSP Eligible; Inception Year: 2003; Fund Managers:
I.G. Investment Management
US Opportunities A Fund
RRSP Eligible; Inception Year: 2003; Fund Managers:
I.G. Investment Management
US Opportunities B Fund
RRSP Eligible; Inception Year: 2003; Fund Managers:
I.G. Investment Management
World Growth Portfolio A Fund
RRSP Eligible; Inception Year: 2003; Fund Managers:
I.G. Investment Management
World Growth Portfolio B Fund
RRSP Eligible; Inception Year: 2003; Fund Managers:
I.G. Investment Management
Global Class B Fund
RRSP Eligible; Inception Year: 2003; Fund Managers:
I.G. Investment Management
Income Trust A Fund
RRSP Eligible; Inception Year: 2004; Fund Managers:
I.G. Investment Management
Income Trust B Fund
RRSP Eligible; Inception Year: 2004; Fund Managers:
I.G. Investment Management
Premium Money Market Fund
RRSP Eligible; Inception Year: 2001; Fund Managers:
I.G. Investment Management
Real Return Bond R Fund
RRSP Eligible; Inception Year: 2004; Fund Managers:
I.G. Investment Management
Short Term Capital Yield Class A Fund
RRSP Eligible; Inception Year: 2004; Fund Managers:
I.G. Investment Management
Short Term Capital Yield Class B Fund
RRSP Eligible; Inception Year: 2004; Fund Managers:
I.G. Investment Management
Cap Yield Class A Fund
RRSP Eligible; Inception Year: 2004; Fund Managers:
I.G. Investment Management
Cap Yield Class B Fund
RRSP Eligible; Inception Year: 2004; Fund Managers:
I.G. Investment Management
Global Dividend A Fund
RRSP Eligible; Inception Year: 2006;
Global Dividend B Fund
RRSP Eligible; Inception Year: 2006;
Global Dividend C Fund
RRSP Eligible; Inception Year: 2006;
Income Trust C Fund
RRSP Eligible; Inception Year: 2005; Fund Managers:
I.G. Investment Management
US Large Cap Value Class A Fund
RRSP Eligible; Inception Year: 2002; Fund Managers:
I.G. Investment Management
US Money Market ($US) Fund
RRSP Eligible; Inception Year: 1997; Fund Managers:
I.G. Investment Management

Leith Wheeler Investment Counsel Ltd.
Also listed under: *Financial Planning; Investment Management*

#1500, 400 Burrard St.
Vancouver, BC V6C 3A6
604-683-3391
Fax: 604-683-0323
888-292-1122
info@leithwheeler.com
www.leithwheeler.com
Ownership: Private
Year Founded: 1982
Number of Employees: 26
Assets: $1-10 billion
Profile: The investment counsel provides portfolio management to non-profit organizations, pension plans & individual investors.

Executives:
William Wheeler, Chair
David Schaffner, President/CEO
Cecilia Wong, CFO
Bill Dye, Chief Investment Officer
David Ayriss, Vice-President
Gordon Gibbons, Vice-President, Client Services
Jonathon Palfrey, Vice-President & Portfolio Manager
Neil Watson, Vice-President
Directors:
Bruce Carlson
Leon Getz
David Schaffner
Leith Wheeler:
Money Market Fund
RRSP Eligible; Inception Year: 1994;
Balanced Fund
RRSP Eligible; Inception Year: 1987;
Canadian Equity Fund
RRSP Eligible; Inception Year: 1994;
Fixed Income Fund
RRSP Eligible; Inception Year: 1994;
US Equity Fund
RRSP Eligible; Inception Year: 1994;
International FundInception Year: 0; Fund Managers:
Sprucegrove Investment Management Ltd.
Diversified Pooled FundInception Year: 2001;
Income Trust Fund
RRSP Eligible; Inception Year: 2005;

Les Fonds d'investissement FMOQ inc
#1111, 1440, rue Ste-Catherine ouest
Montréal, QC H3G 1R8
514-868-2081
Fax: 514-868-2088
info@fondsfmoq.com
www.fondsfmoq.com
Ownership: Private
Year Founded: 1997
Number of Employees: 11
Executives:
Jean-Pierre Tremblay, Vice-président exécutif
FMOQ:
Canadian Equity Fund
RRSP Eligible; Inception Year: 1994; Fund Managers:
Barclays Global Investment
International Equity Fund
RRSP Eligible; Inception Year: 1994; Fund Managers:
CIBC Global Asset Management Inc.
Money Market Fund
RRSP Eligible; Inception Year: 1989; Fund Managers:
Natcan Investment Management
Omnibus Fund
RRSP Eligible; Inception Year: 1979; Fund Managers:
CIBC Global Asset Management Inc.
Canadian Bond Fund
RRSP Eligible; Inception Year: 2001; Fund Managers:
Tal Global Asset Management
Investment Fund
RRSP Eligible; Inception Year: 1983; Fund Managers:
Natcan Investment Management
Branches:
Québec
Place Iberville III
#40, 2960, boul Laurier
Québec, QC G1V 4S1 Canada
418-657-5777
Fax: 418-657-7418
877-323-5777
Claude Parent

Les Fonds FISQ
142 rue Heriot
Drummondville, QC J2C 1J8
514-393-1555
Fax: 514-393-1777
877-393-1555
info@fisq.ca
www.fisq.ca
Also Known As: Les Fonds d'Investissements Spécialisés du Québec Inc.
Executives:
Jacques Desbiens, President/CEO & Chair
FISQ:
Fonds Municipal - profil Québec
RRSP Eligible; Inception Year: 1999; Fund Managers:
Gestion Sodagep Inc.
Fonds Zéro coupon - profil Québec
RRSP Eligible; Inception Year: 1999; Fund Managers:
Gestion Sodagep Inc.
Canadian Foreign Currency Bond Fund
RRSP Eligible; Inception Year: 2004; Fund Managers:
Gestion Sodagep Inc.
Real Return Bond Fund
RRSP Eligible; Inception Year: 2004; Fund Managers:
Gestion Sodagep Inc.

Lincluden Management Limited
Also listed under: *Pension & Money Management Companies*
#607, 1275 North Service Rd. West
Oakville, ON L6M 3G4
905-825-9000
Fax: 905-825-9525
800-532-7071
lynn.eplett@lincluden.com
www.lincluden.com
Ownership: Wholly-owned affiliate of Old Mutual Asset Management
Year Founded: 1982
Number of Employees: 14
Assets: $1-10 billion Year End: 20041231
Profile: Lincluden specializes in pension fund management.

Executives:
George M. Youssef, Chair
Phil Evans, President/CEO
Peter Chin, Vice-President
C. Lynn Eplett, Vice-President, Client Services
James Lampard, Vice-President
Marc Noble, Vice-President, Business Development
John Richardson, Vice-President
Bob Sanderson, Vice-President
Richard Wong, Vice-President
Lincluden:
Balanced Fund
RRSP Eligible; Inception Year: 2000;

Mackenzie Financial Corporation
Also listed under: *Pension & Money Management Companies*
#111M, 150 Bloor St. West
Toronto, ON M5S 3B5
416-922-5322
Fax: 416-922-5660
800-387-0780
service@mackenziefinancial.com
www.mackenziefinancial.com
Ownership: Public
Year Founded: 1967
Number of Employees: 516
Stock Symbol: MKF
Profile: Mackenzie manages a family of mutual funds on behalf of almost one million Canadian investors. In addition, through subsidiary companies, Mackenzie provides investment advisory services to private client accounts, & operates a trust company.

Executives:
Jim Hunter, President/CEO
Ed Merchand, CFO
W. Sian B. Brown, Sr. Vice-President, General Counsel & Secretary
Peter Dawkins, Exec. Vice-President, Chief Investment Strategist
Laurie J. Munro, Exec. Vice-President, Strategic & Business Planning
Andrew Dalglish, President/CEO, MRS Group
David Feather, President, Mackenzie Financial Services Inc.

Directors:
Philip F. Cunningham, Chair
Affiliated Companies:
M.R.S. Trust Company
Cundill:
Canadian Balanced Series C Fund
RRSP Eligible; Inception Year: 1998; Fund Managers:
Peter Cundill & Associates (Bermuda) Ltd.
Canadian Security Fund
RRSP Eligible; Inception Year: 1980; Fund Managers:
Peter Cundill & Associates (Bermuda) Ltd.
Canadian Security Series B Fund
RRSP Eligible; Inception Year: 1997; Fund Managers:
Peter Cundill & Associates (Bermuda) Ltd.
Canadian Security Series C Fund
RRSP Eligible; Inception Year: 1998; Fund Managers:
Peter Cundill & Associates (Bermuda) Ltd.
Global Balanced Series C Fund
RRSP Eligible; Inception Year: 1999; Fund Managers:
Peter Cundill & Associates (Bermuda) Ltd.
Recovery Series C Fund
RRSP Eligible; Inception Year: 1998; Fund Managers:
Peter Cundill & Associates (Bermuda) Ltd.
Value Fund
RRSP Eligible; Inception Year: 1974; Fund Managers:
Peter Cundill & Associates (Bermuda) Ltd.
Value Series B Fund
RRSP Eligible; Inception Year: 1997; Fund Managers:
Peter Cundill & Associates (Bermuda) Ltd.
Value Series C Fund
RRSP Eligible; Inception Year: 1998; Fund Managers:
Peter Cundill & Associates (Bermuda) Ltd.
Value Capital Class Fund
RRSP Eligible; Inception Year: 2000; Fund Managers:
Peter Cundill & Associates (Bermuda) Ltd.
Canadian Balanced Segregated Fund
RRSP Eligible; Inception Year: 1999; Fund Managers:
Peter Cundill & Associates (Bermuda) Ltd.
Canadian Balanced Series T Fund
RRSP Eligible; Inception Year: 2002; Fund Managers:
Peter Cundill & Associates (Bermuda) Ltd.
Canadian Security Capital Class Fund
RRSP Eligible; Inception Year: 2003; Fund Managers:
Peter Cundill & Associates (Bermuda) Ltd.
Global Balanced Series T Fund
RRSP Eligible; Inception Year: 2002; Fund Managers:
Peter Cundill & Associates (Bermuda) Ltd.
Value Segregated Fund
RRSP Eligible; Inception Year: 1999; Fund Managers:
Peter Cundill & Associates (Bermuda) Ltd.
American Capital Class Fund
RRSP Eligible; Inception Year: 2003; Fund Managers:
Peter Cundill & Associates (Bermuda) Ltd.
Canadian Security Segregated Fund
RRSP Eligible; Inception Year: 1999; Fund Managers:
Peter Cundill & Associates (Bermuda) Ltd.
Ivy:
Enterprise Fund
RRSP Eligible; Inception Year: 1994; Fund Managers:
Stephanie Griffiths
Growth & Income Fund
RRSP Eligible; Inception Year: 1992; Fund Managers:
Jerry Javasky
Canadian Fund
RRSP Eligible; Inception Year: 1992; Fund Managers:
Jerry Javasky
Foreign Equity Fund
RRSP Eligible; Inception Year: 1992; Fund Managers:
Jerry Javasky
PaulMusson
Canadian Capital Class Fund
RRSP Eligible; Inception Year: 2000; Fund Managers:
Jerry Javasky
Enterprise Capital Class Fund
RRSP Eligible; Inception Year: 2000; Fund Managers:
Stephanie Griffiths
Foreign Equity Capital Class Fund
RRSP Eligible; Inception Year: 2000; Fund Managers:
Jerry Javasky
Canadian Segregated Fund
RRSP Eligible; Inception Year: 1999; Fund Managers:
Jerry Javasky
Enterprise Segregated Fund
RRSP Eligible; Inception Year: 1999; Fund Managers:
Stephanie Griffiths

Foreign Equity Segregated Fund
RRSP Eligible; Inception Year: 1999; Fund Managers:
Jerry Javasky
Global Balanced Fund
RRSP Eligible; Inception Year: 1993; Fund Managers:
Jerry Javasky
PaulMusson
Global Balanced Series T Fund
RRSP Eligible; Inception Year: 2002; Fund Managers:
Jerry Javasky
PaulMusson
Growth & Income Series T Fund
RRSP Eligible; Inception Year: 2002; Fund Managers:
Jerry Javasky
European Capital Class Fund
RRSP Eligible; Inception Year: 2002; Fund Managers:
Jerry Javasky
PaulMusson
Global Balanced Segregated Fund
RRSP Eligible; Inception Year: 1999; Fund Managers:
Jerry Javasky
PaulMusson
Growth & Income Segregated Fund
RRSP Eligible; Inception Year: 1999; Fund Managers:
Jerry Javasky
Keystone:
Investment Balanced Growth & Income Fund
RRSP Eligible; Inception Year: 1998;
Investment Conservative Income & Growth Fund
RRSP Eligible; Inception Year: 1998;
Investment Long-Term Growth Fund
RRSP Eligible; Inception Year: 1998;
Investment Maximum Equity Growth Fund
RRSP Eligible; Inception Year: 1998;
Investment Maximum Long-Term Growth Fund
RRSP Eligible; Inception Year: 1998;
Balanced Growth & Income Fund
RRSP Eligible; Inception Year: 1998;
Conservative Income & Growth Fund
RRSP Eligible; Inception Year: 1998;
Long-Term Growth Fund
RRSP Eligible; Inception Year: 1998;
Maximum Equity Growth Fund
RRSP Eligible; Inception Year: 1998;
Maximum Long-Term Growth Fund
RRSP Eligible; Inception Year: 1998;
Balanced Growth Portfolio Fund
RRSP Eligible; Inception Year: 2003; Fund Managers:
Waddell & Reed Inc.
Balanced Portfolio Fund
RRSP Eligible; Inception Year: 2003; Fund Managers:
MFC Global Investment Management
Conservative Portfolio Fund
RRSP Eligible; Inception Year: 2003; Fund Managers:
MFC Global Investment Management
Growth Portfolio Fund
RRSP Eligible; Inception Year: 2003; Fund Managers:
Waddell & Reed Inc.
Maximum Growth Portfolio Fund
RRSP Eligible; Inception Year: 2004; Fund Managers:
MFC Global Investment Management
Balanced Growth Portfolio Segregated Fund
RRSP Eligible; Inception Year: 1999;
Balanced Portfolio Segregated Fund
RRSP Eligible; Inception Year: 1999;
Conservative Portfolio Segregated Fund
RRSP Eligible; Inception Year: 1999;
Growth Portfolio Segregated Fund
RRSP Eligible; Inception Year: 1999;
Maximum Growth Portfolio Segregated Fund
RRSP Eligible; Inception Year: 1999;
Dynamic Power Small-Cap Capital Class Fund
RRSP Eligible; Inception Year: 2005; Fund Managers:
Goodman & Company Investment Counsel
Balanced Growth Portfolio Series T Fund
RRSP Eligible; Inception Year: 2004; Fund Managers:
Franklin Templeton Investments
Balanced Portfolio Series T Fund
RRSP Eligible; Inception Year: 2004; Fund Managers:
MFC Global Investment Management
Conservative Portfolio Series T Fund
RRSP Eligible; Inception Year: 2005; Fund Managers:
MFC Global Investment Management

Diversified Income Portfolio Fund
RRSP Eligible; Inception Year: 2005; Fund Managers:
MFC Global Investment Management
Diversified Income Portfolio Series T Fund
RRSP Eligible; Inception Year: 2005; Fund Managers:
MFC Global Investment Management
Keystone AGF:
Equity Fund
RRSP Eligible; Inception Year: 1998; Fund Managers:
AGF Fund Management
Keystone AIM/Trimark:
Canadian Equity Fund
RRSP Eligible; Inception Year: 1998; Fund Managers:
AIM Funds Management Inc.
Global Equity Fund
RRSP Eligible; Inception Year: 1998; Fund Managers:
AIM Funds Management Inc.
US Companies Fund
RRSP Eligible; Inception Year: 1998; Fund Managers:
AIM Funds Management Inc.
Keystone Beutel Goodman:
Bond Fund
RRSP Eligible; Inception Year: 1998; Fund Managers:
Beutel Goodman
Keystone Bissett:
Canadian Equity Fund
RRSP Eligible; Inception Year: 1998; Fund Managers:
Bissett & Co.
Keystone Elliott & Page:
High Income Fund
RRSP Eligible; Inception Year: 1998; Fund Managers:
MFC Global Investment Management
Keystone Saxon:
Smaller Companies Fund
RRSP Eligible; Inception Year: 1998; Fund Managers:
Saxon
Keystone Templeton:
International Stock Capital Class Fund
RRSP Eligible; Inception Year: 2003;
Mackenzie:
Growth Fund
RRSP Eligible; Inception Year: 1967; Fund Managers:
Fred Sturm
BenoitGervais
Shechar Dworski
Alternative Strategies Fund
RRSP Eligible; Inception Year: 2001; Fund Managers:
Tremont Capital Management Corp.
Balanced Series T Fund
RRSP Eligible; Inception Year: 2002; Fund Managers:
FairLane Asset Management
Balanced Segregated Fund
RRSP Eligible; Inception Year: 1999; Fund Managers:
FairLane Asset Management
Balanced Fund
RRSP Eligible; Inception Year: 1991; Fund Managers:
FairLane Asset Management
Maxxum:
Canadian Balanced Fund
RRSP Eligible; Inception Year: 1988; Fund Managers:
Chris Kresic
ChuckRoth
Canadian Balanced Series T Fund
RRSP Eligible; Inception Year: 2003; Fund Managers:
Chris Kresic
ChuckRoth
Canadian Equity Growth Fund
RRSP Eligible; Inception Year: 1970; Fund Managers:
Chuck Roth
Canadian Value Capital Class Fund
RRSP Eligible; Inception Year: 2000; Fund Managers:
Bill Procter
AndrewKnezy
James Leung
Joe Mastrolonardo
Michele Calpin
Dividend Fund
RRSP Eligible; Inception Year: 1986; Fund Managers:
Bill Procter
JoeMastrolonardo
Michele Calpin
Andrew Knezy
James Leung
Dividend Growth Fund
RRSP Eligible; Inception Year: 1975; Fund Managers:

Mackenzie Financial Corporation (continued)
Bill Procter
AndrewKnezy
Joe Mastrolonardo
Michele Calpin
James Leung
Money Market FundInception Year: 1986; Fund Managers:
Chris Kresic
Monthly Income Fund
RRSP Eligible; Inception Year: 1971; Fund Managers:
Bill Procter
JoeMastrolonardo
Michele Calpin
Andrew Knezy
James Leung
Monthly Income Series T Fund
RRSP Eligible; Inception Year: 2002; Fund Managers:
Bill Procter
AndrewKnezy
Joe Mastrolonardo
Michele Calpin
James Leung
Dividend Capital Class Fund
RRSP Eligible; Inception Year: 2003; Fund Managers:
Bill Procter
AndrewKnezy
Joe Mastrolonardo
Michele Calpin
James Leung
Monthly Income Segregated Fund
RRSP Eligible; Inception Year: 1999; Fund Managers:
Bill Procter
AndrewKnezy
James Leung
Joe Mastrolonardo
Michele Calpin
Canadian Equity Growth Capital Class Fund
RRSP Eligible; Inception Year: 2003; Fund Managers:
Chuck Roth
Canadian Value Fund
RRSP Eligible; Inception Year: 1987; Fund Managers:
Bill Procter
AndrewKnezy
Joe Mastrolonardo
Michele Calpin
James Leung
Dividend Growth Segregated Fund
RRSP Eligible; Inception Year: 1999; Fund Managers:
Bill Procter
AndrewKnezy
James Leung
Joe Mastrolonardo
Michele Calpin
Global Explorer Capital Class Fund
RRSP Eligible; Inception Year: 2000; Fund Managers:
Alan Pasnik
STAR:
Canadian Balanced Growth & Income Fund
RRSP Eligible; Inception Year: 1996;
Canadian Conservative Income & Growth Fund
RRSP Eligible; Inception Year: 1996;
Canadian Long-Term Growth Fund
RRSP Eligible; Inception Year: 1996;
Canadian Maximum Equity Growth Fund
RRSP Eligible; Inception Year: 1996;
Canadian Maximum Long-Term Growth Fund
RRSP Eligible; Inception Year: 1996;
Foreign Balanced Growth & Income Fund
RRSP Eligible; Inception Year: 1995;
Foreign Maximum Long-Term Growth Fund
RRSP Eligible; Inception Year: 1995;
Foreign Maximum Equity Growth Fund
RRSP Eligible; Inception Year: 1995;
Investment Balanced Growth & Income Fund
RRSP Eligible; Inception Year: 1995;
Investment Conservative Income & Growth Fund
RRSP Eligible; Inception Year: 1995;
Investment Long-Term Growth Fund
RRSP Eligible; Inception Year: 1995;
Investment Maximum Long-Term Growth Fund
RRSP Eligible; Inception Year: 1995;
Balanced Growth & Income Fund
RRSP Eligible; Inception Year: 1995;
Conservative Income & Growth Fund
RRSP Eligible; Inception Year: 1995;

Long-Term Growth Fund
RRSP Eligible; Inception Year: 1995;
Maximum Equity Growth Fund
RRSP Eligible; Inception Year: 1995;
Maximum Long-Term Growth Fund
RRSP Eligible; Inception Year: 1995;
Select Managers:
Far East Capital Class Fund
RRSP Eligible; Inception Year: 2002; Fund Managers:
Allianz Dresdner Asset Management
International Capital Class Fund
RRSP Eligible; Inception Year: 2000; Fund Managers:
Jerry Javasky
PaulMusson
Henderson Global Investors
Japan Capital Class Fund
RRSP Eligible; Inception Year: 2002; Fund Managers:
Henderson Global Investors
Canada Capital Class Fund
RRSP Eligible; Inception Year: 2000; Fund Managers:
Ian Ainsworth
BillProcter
Jerry Javasky
Michele Calpin
Bluewater Investment Management
Select Managers Fund
RRSP Eligible; Inception Year: 1998; Fund Managers:
Henderson Global Investors
Capital Class Fund
RRSP Eligible; Inception Year: 2000; Fund Managers:
Henderson Global Investors
USA Capital Class Fund
RRSP Eligible; Inception Year: 2002; Fund Managers:
Credit Suisse Asset Management
Canada Fund
RRSP Eligible; Inception Year: 2002; Fund Managers:
Bill Procter
JerryJavasky
Ian Ainsworth
Michele Calpin
Peter Cundill & Associates (Bermuda) Ltd.
Segregated Fund
RRSP Eligible; Inception Year: 1999; Fund Managers:
Henderson Global Investors
Canada Segregated Fund
RRSP Eligible; Inception Year: 2001;
Sentinel:
Bond Fund
RRSP Eligible; Inception Year: 1989; Fund Managers:
Chris Kresic
Cash Management Fund
RRSP Eligible; Inception Year: 1984;
Short Term Bond Fund
RRSP Eligible; Inception Year: 1999; Fund Managers:
Chris Kresic
Canadian Managed Yield Capital Class Fund
RRSP Eligible; Inception Year: 2000;
US Managed Yield Capital Class FundInception Year: 2000;
Bond Segregated Fund
RRSP Eligible; Inception Year: 1999; Fund Managers:
Chris Kresic
Cash Management Segregated Fund
RRSP Eligible; Inception Year: 1999;
Income Segregated Fund
RRSP Eligible; Inception Year: 1999; Fund Managers:
Bill Procter
ChrisKresic
Money Market Fund
RRSP Eligible; Inception Year: 1991;
Money Market Series B Fund
RRSP Eligible; Inception Year: 2001;
Managed Return Capital Class Fund
RRSP Eligible; Inception Year: 2002; Fund Managers:
Chris Kresic
Mortgage Fund
RRSP Eligible; Inception Year: 1994;
Income Fund
RRSP Eligible; Inception Year: 1974; Fund Managers:
Bill Procter
ChrisKresic
Income Series B Fund
RRSP Eligible; Inception Year: 1998; Fund Managers:
Bill Procter
ChrisKresic

Corporate Bond Fund
RRSP Eligible; Inception Year: 1999; Fund Managers:
Chris Kresic
DanBastasic
Waddell & Reed Inc.
High Income Fund
RRSP Eligible; Inception Year: 2003; Fund Managers:
Chris Kresic
BillProcter
Dan Bastasic
James Leung
Real Return Bond Fund
RRSP Eligible; Inception Year: 2003; Fund Managers:
Chris Kresic
RRSP Global Bond Fund
RRSP Eligible; Inception Year: 1975; Fund Managers:
Waddell & Reed Inc.
Tactical Global Bond Fund
RRSP Eligible; Inception Year: 1994; Fund Managers:
Alliance Capital Management
Corporate Bond Segregated Fund
RRSP Eligible; Inception Year: 2001;
Money Market Segregated Fund
RRSP Eligible; Inception Year: 1999;
Income Series C Fund
RRSP Eligible; Inception Year: 2004; Fund Managers:
Bill Procter
ChrisKresic
Symmetry:
Canadian Stock Capital Class Fund
RRSP Eligible; Inception Year: 2004; Fund Managers:
Ian Ainsworth
Peter Cundill & Associates (Bermuda) Ltd.
EAFE Stock Capital Class Fund
RRSP Eligible; Inception Year: 2004; Fund Managers:
Ian Ainsworth
Franklin Templeton Investments
Managed Return Capital Class Fund
RRSP Eligible; Inception Year: 2004; Fund Managers:
Chris Kresic
Waddell & Reed Inc.
Registered Fixed Income Pool Fund
RRSP Eligible; Inception Year: 2004; Fund Managers:
Chris Kresic
Waddell & Reed Inc.
Specialty Stock Capital Class Fund
RRSP Eligible; Inception Year: 2004; Fund Managers:
Stephanie Griffiths
Peter Cundill & Associates (Bermuda) Ltd.
US Stock Capital Class Fund
RRSP Eligible; Inception Year: 2004; Fund Managers:
Dreman Value Management L.L.C.
Universal:
Canadian Growth Fund
RRSP Eligible; Inception Year: 1995; Fund Managers:
Bluewater Investment Management
Canadian Resource Fund
RRSP Eligible; Inception Year: 1978; Fund Managers:
Fred Sturm
BenoitGervais
European Opportunities Fund
RRSP Eligible; Inception Year: 1994; Fund Managers:
Henderson Global Investors
Future Fund
RRSP Eligible; Inception Year: 1987; Fund Managers:
Ian Ainsworth
MarkGrammer
Wendy Chua
World Growth RRSP Fund
RRSP Eligible; Inception Year: 1994; Fund Managers:
Karen Bleasby
Canadian Balanced Fund
RRSP Eligible; Inception Year: 1996; Fund Managers:
Bluewater Investment Management
International Stock Fund
RRSP Eligible; Inception Year: 1985; Fund Managers:
Henderson Global Investors
Precious Metals Fund
RRSP Eligible; Inception Year: 1994; Fund Managers:
Fred Sturm
BenoitGervais
European Opportunities Capital Class Fund
RRSP Eligible; Inception Year: 2000; Fund Managers:
Henderson Global Investors

Future Capital Class Fund
RRSP Eligible; Inception Year: 2000; Fund Managers:
Ian Ainsworth
MarkGrammer
Wendy Chua
Global Future Capital Class Fund
RRSP Eligible; Inception Year: 2000; Fund Managers:
Ian Ainsworth
MarkGrammer
Wendy Chua
Health Sciences Capital Class Fund
RRSP Eligible; Inception Year: 2000; Fund Managers:
Ian Ainsworth
WendyChua
World Resource Capital Class Fund
RRSP Eligible; Inception Year: 2000; Fund Managers:
Fred Sturm
BenoitGervais
World Science & Technology Capital Class Fund
RRSP Eligible; Inception Year: 2002; Fund Managers:
Polar Capital Partners Ltd.
Canadian Growth Capital Class Fund
RRSP Eligible; Inception Year: 2000; Fund Managers:
Bluewater Investment Management
Global Future Fund
RRSP Eligible; Inception Year: 1995; Fund Managers:
Ian Ainsworth
MarkGrammer
Wendy Chua
World Precious Metals Capital Class Fund
RRSP Eligible; Inception Year: 2000; Fund Managers:
Fred Sturm
BenoitGervais
US Blue Chip Capital Class Fund
RRSP Eligible; Inception Year: 2000; Fund Managers:
Waddell & Reed Inc.
US Emerging Growth Capital Class Fund
RRSP Eligible; Inception Year: 2000; Fund Managers:
Waddell & Reed Inc.
Canadian Growth Segregated Fund
RRSP Eligible; Inception Year: 1999; Fund Managers:
Bluewater Investment Management
Canadian Balanced Series T Fund
RRSP Eligible; Inception Year: 2002; Fund Managers:
Bluewater Investment Management
European Opportunities Segregated Fund
RRSP Eligible; Inception Year: 1999; Fund Managers:
Henderson Global Investors
Future Segregated Fund
RRSP Eligible; Inception Year: 1999; Fund Managers:
Ian Ainsworth
WendyChua
Mark Grammer
Growth Trends Capital Class Fund
RRSP Eligible; Inception Year: 2002; Fund Managers:
Alliance Capital Management
International Stock Capital Class Fund
RRSP Eligible; Inception Year: 2000; Fund Managers:
Henderson Global Investors
Emerging Technologies Capital Class Fund
RRSP Eligible; Inception Year: 2002; Fund Managers:
Ian Ainsworth
MarkGrammer
Wendy Chua
American Growth Capital Class Fund
RRSP Eligible; Inception Year: 2002; Fund Managers:
Bluewater Investment Management
Sustainable Opportunities Capital Class Fund
RRSP Eligible; Inception Year: 2002; Fund Managers:
Aberdeen Asset Management
US Growth Leaders Capital Class Fund
RRSP Eligible; Inception Year: 2003; Fund Managers:
Waddell & Reed Inc.
US Growth Leaders Fund
RRSP Eligible; Inception Year: 1995; Fund Managers:
Waddell & Reed Inc.
Canadian Balanced Segregated Fund
RRSP Eligible; Inception Year: 1999; Fund Managers:
Bluewater Investment Management
Emerging Markets Capital Class Fund
RRSP Eligible; Inception Year: 2002; Fund Managers:
JP Morgan Fleming
World Real Estate Capital Class Fund
RRSP Eligible; Inception Year: 2002; Fund Managers:
ABN AMRO Asset Management

Manulife Securities International Ltd.(MSIL)

500 King St. North
Waterloo, ON N2J 4C6
519-747-7000
Fax: 519-747-6968
msil.marketing@manulife.com
www.manulife.ca
Ownership: Wholly owned subsidiary of Manufacturers Life Insurance Company
Year Founded: 1994
Executives:
Krysia Bates, CFO
Mark Wendland, Asst. Vice-President, Marketing & Product Development
Directors:
Bruce Gordon, Chair
J. Roman Fedchyshyn
Gordon M. Hill
Phil Walton
MIX:
AIM Canadian First Class Fund
RRSP Eligible; Inception Year: 2002; Fund Managers:
MFC Global Investment Management
Canadian Equity Value Class Fund
RRSP Eligible; Inception Year: 2002; Fund Managers:
MFC Global Investment Management
Canadian Large Cap Core Class Fund
RRSP Eligible; Inception Year: 2002; Fund Managers:
MFC Global Investment Management
Canadian Large Cap Growth Class Fund
RRSP Eligible; Inception Year: 2002; Fund Managers:
MFC Global Investment Management
Canadian Large Cap Value Class Fund
RRSP Eligible; Inception Year: 2002; Fund Managers:
MFC Global Investment Management
China Opportunities Class Fund
RRSP Eligible; Inception Year: 2004; Fund Managers:
MFC Global Investment Management
Elliott & Page Growth Opportunities Class Fund
RRSP Eligible; Inception Year: 2002; Fund Managers:
MFC Global Investment Management
Elliott & Page US Mid Cap Class Fund
RRSP Eligible; Inception Year: 2002; Fund Managers:
MFC Global Investment Management
F.I. Canadian Disciplined Equity Class Fund
RRSP Eligible; Inception Year: 2002; Fund Managers:
MFC Global Investment Management
F.I. Growth America Class Fund
RRSP Eligible; Inception Year: 2002; Fund Managers:
MFC Global Investment Management
F.I. International Portfolio Class Fund
RRSP Eligible; Inception Year: 2002; Fund Managers:
MFC Global Investment Management
Global Equity Class Fund
RRSP Eligible; Inception Year: 2002; Fund Managers:
MFC Global Investment Management
Global Value Class Fund
RRSP Eligible; Inception Year: 2002; Fund Managers:
MFC Global Investment Management
International Growth Class Fund
RRSP Eligible; Inception Year: 2002; Fund Managers:
MFC Global Investment Management
International Value Class Fund
RRSP Eligible; Inception Year: 2002; Fund Managers:
MFC Global Investment Management
Japanese Class Fund
RRSP Eligible; Inception Year: 2002; Fund Managers:
MFC Global Investment Management
SEAMARK Total Canadian Equity Class Fund
RRSP Eligible; Inception Year: 2002; Fund Managers:
SEAMARK Asset Management Limited
SEAMARK Total Global Equity Class Fund
RRSP Eligible; Inception Year: 2002; Fund Managers:
SEAMARK Asset Management Limited
SEAMARK Total US Equity Class Fund
RRSP Eligible; Inception Year: 2002; Fund Managers:
SEAMARK Asset Management Limited
Short Term Yield Class Fund
RRSP Eligible; Inception Year: 2002; Fund Managers:
MFC Global Investment Management
Structured Bond Class Fund
RRSP Eligible; Inception Year: 2003; Fund Managers:
MFC Global Investment Management
Trimark Global Class Fund
RRSP Eligible; Inception Year: 2002; Fund Managers:
MFC Global Investment Management
Trimark Select Canadian Class Fund
RRSP Eligible; Inception Year: 2002; Fund Managers:
MFC Global Investment Management
US Large Cap Core Class Fund
RRSP Eligible; Inception Year: 2002; Fund Managers:
MFC Global Investment Management
US Large Cap Growth Class Fund
RRSP Eligible; Inception Year: 2002; Fund Managers:
MFC Global Investment Management
US Large Cap Value Class Fund
RRSP Eligible; Inception Year: 2002; Fund Managers:
MFC Global Investment Management
US Mid Cap Value Class Fund
RRSP Eligible; Inception Year: 2002; Fund Managers:
MFC Global Investment Management
MLI:
CI Global Guaranteed Investment Fund
RRSP Eligible; Inception Year: 1986; Fund Managers:
CI Investments
Elliott & Page Sector Rotation Guaranteed Investment Fund
RRSP Eligible; Inception Year: 1998; Fund Managers:
MFC Global Investment Management
Elliott & Page Value Equity Guaranteed Investment Fund
RRSP Eligible; Inception Year: 1997; Fund Managers:
MFC Global Investment Management
Fidelity Canadian Bond Guaranteed Investment Fund
RRSP Eligible; Inception Year: 1998; Fund Managers:
Fidelity Investments Canada Limited
Fidelity Growth America Guaranteed Investment Fund
RRSP Eligible; Inception Year: 1990; Fund Managers:
Fidelity Investments Canada Limited
Fidelity International Portfolio Guaranteed Investment Fund
RRSP Eligible; Inception Year: 1987; Fund Managers:
Fidelity Investments Canada Limited
Fidelity True North Guaranteed Investment Fund
RRSP Eligible; Inception Year: 1996; Fund Managers:
Fidelity Investments Canada Limited
CI Harbour Guaranteed Investment Fund
RRSP Eligible; Inception Year: 1997; Fund Managers:
CI Investments
CI Harbour Growth & Income Guaranteed Investment Fund
RRSP Eligible; Inception Year: 1997; Fund Managers:
CI Investments
Talvest Canadian Asset Allocation Guaranteed Investment Fund
RRSP Eligible; Inception Year: 1986; Fund Managers:
CIBC Global Asset Management
Talvest Income Guaranteed Investment Fund
RRSP Eligible; Inception Year: 1974; Fund Managers:
CIBC Global Asset Management
Trimark Select Balanced Guaranteed Investment Fund
RRSP Eligible; Inception Year: 1989; Fund Managers:
AIM Trimark Investments
Trimark Select Canadian Growth Guaranteed Investment Fund
RRSP Eligible; Inception Year: 1992; Fund Managers:
AIM Trimark Investments
Trimark Select Growth Guaranteed Investment Fund
RRSP Eligible; Inception Year: 1989; Fund Managers:
AIM Trimark Investments
Canadian Equity Index Guaranteed Investment Fund
RRSP Eligible; Inception Year: 1998; Fund Managers:
MFC Global Investment Management
Fidelity Canadian Asset Allocation Guaranteed Investment Fund
RRSP Eligible; Inception Year: 1994; Fund Managers:
Fidelity Investments Canada Limited
Fidelity Canadian Large Cap Guaranteed Investment Fund
RRSP Eligible; Inception Year: 1988; Fund Managers:
Fidelity Investments Canada Limited
AIC Advantage II Guaranteed Investment Fund
RRSP Eligible; Inception Year: 1996; Fund Managers:
AIC Limited
AIC American Focused Guaranteed Investment Fund
RRSP Eligible; Inception Year: 1999; Fund Managers:
AIC Limited
AIM Canadian Balanced Guaranteed Investment Fund
RRSP Eligible; Inception Year: 1992; Fund Managers:
AIM Trimark Investments
AIM Canadian First Class Guaranteed Investment Fund
RRSP Eligible; Inception Year: 1997; Fund Managers:
AIM Trimark Investments
AIM Canadian Premier Class Guaranteed Investment Fund
RRSP Eligible; Inception Year: 1990; Fund Managers:
AIM Trimark Investments

INVESTMENT MANAGEMENT

Manulife Securities International Ltd.(MSIL) (continued)
American Equity Index Guaranteed Investment Fund
RRSP Eligible; Inception Year: 1998; Fund Managers:
MFC Global Investment Management
Balanced Ethics (McLean Budden) Guaranteed Investment Fund
RRSP Eligible; Inception Year: 2000; Fund Managers:
McLean Budden Limited
BPI Global Equity Guaranteed Investment Fund
RRSP Eligible; Inception Year: 1985; Fund Managers:
CI Investments
Canadian Balanced (SEAMARK) Guaranteed Investment Fund
RRSP Eligible; Inception Year: 1997; Fund Managers:
SEAMARK Asset Management Limited
Canadian Small Cap Equity (Howson Tattersall) Guaranteed Investm
RRSP Eligible; Inception Year: 1999; Fund Managers:
Howson Tattersall Investment Counsel Ltd.
CI International Balanced Guaranteed Investment Fund
RRSP Eligible; Inception Year: 1997; Fund Managers:
CI Investments
Dollar-Cost Averaging Advantage Guaranteed Investment Fund
RRSP Eligible; Inception Year: 2003;
Elliott & Page Corporate Bond Guaranteed Investment Fund
RRSP Eligible; Inception Year: 2003; Fund Managers:
MFC Global Investment Management
Elliott & Page Generation Wave Guaranteed Investment Fund
RRSP Eligible; Inception Year: 1998; Fund Managers:
MFC Global Investment Management
Elliott & Page Growth Opportunities Guaranteed Investment Fund
RRSP Eligible; Inception Year: 1998; Fund Managers:
MFC Global Investment Management
Elliott & Page Money Guaranteed Investment Fund
RRSP Eligible; Inception Year: 1984; Fund Managers:
MFC Global Investment Management
Elliott & Page Monthly High Income Guaranteed Investment Fund
RRSP Eligible; Inception Year: 1997; Fund Managers:
MFC Global Investment Management
Elliott & Page US Mid Cap Guaranteed Investment Fund
RRSP Eligible; Inception Year: 1997; Fund Managers:
MFC Global Investment Management
Elliott & Page Canadian Equity Guaranteed Investment Fund
RRSP Eligible; Inception Year: 1994; Fund Managers:
MFC Global Investment Management
Elliott & Page Dividend Guaranteed Investment Fund
RRSP Eligible; Inception Year: 2003; Fund Managers:
MFC Global Investment Management
Fidelity Europe Guaranteed Investment Fund
RRSP Eligible; Inception Year: 1992; Fund Managers:
Fidelity Investments Canada Limited
Fidelity NorthStar Guaranteed Investment Fund
RRSP Eligible; Inception Year: 2002; Fund Managers:
Fidelity Investments Canada Limited
Fidelity RSP International Portfolio Guaranteed Investment Fund
RRSP Eligible; Inception Year: 1987; Fund Managers:
Fidelity Investments Canada Limited
Global Bond (Oechsle) Guaranteed Investment Fund
RRSP Eligible; Inception Year: 1999; Fund Managers:
Oechsle International
International Equity (Templeton) Guaranteed Investment Fund
RRSP Eligible; Inception Year: 1999; Fund Managers:
Franklin Templeton Investments Management Corpor
Ivy Foreign Equity (Mackenzie) Guaranteed Investment Fund
RRSP Eligible; Inception Year: 2005; Fund Managers:
Mackenzie Financial Corporation
MIX Canadian Large Cap Value Guaranteed Investment Fund
RRSP Eligible; Inception Year: 2002; Fund Managers:
MFC Global Investment Management
Renaissance Canadian Balanced Guaranteed Investment Fund
RRSP Eligible; Inception Year: 1984; Fund Managers:
CIBC Global Asset Management
Renaissance Canadian Core Value Guaranteed Investment Fund
RRSP Eligible; Inception Year: 1994; Fund Managers:
CIBC Global Asset Management
Renaissance US Basic Value Guaranteed Investment Fund
RRSP Eligible; Inception Year: 1998; Fund Managers:
CIBC Global Asset Management
Sentinel Income (Mackenzie) Guaranteed Investment Fund
RRSP Eligible; Inception Year: 2005; Fund Managers:
Mackenzie Financial Corporation
Talvest Canadian Equity Growth Guaranteed Investment Fund
RRSP Eligible; Inception Year: 1997; Fund Managers:
CIBC Global Asset Management
Trimark Advantage Bond Guaranteed Investment Fund
RRSP Eligible; Inception Year: 1994; Fund Managers:
AIM Trimark Investments
US Equity (SEAMARK) Guaranteed Investment Fund
RRSP Eligible; Inception Year: 1997; Fund Managers:
SEAMARK Asset Management Limited
MIX Global Equity Class Guaranteed Investment Fund
RRSP Eligible; Inception Year: 2002; Fund Managers:
MFC Global Investment Management
MIX Global Value Class Guaranteed Investment Fund
RRSP Eligible; Inception Year: 2002; Fund Managers:
MFC Global Investment Management
MIX SEAMARK Total Global Equity Class Guaranteed Investment Fund
RRSP Eligible; Inception Year: 2002; Fund Managers:
SEAMARK Asset Management Limited
MIX US Large Cap Growth Guaranteed Investment Fund
RRSP Eligible; Inception Year: 2002; Fund Managers:
MFC Global Investment Management
MIX US Large Cap Value Class Guaranteed Investment Fund
RRSP Eligible; Inception Year: 2002; Fund Managers:
MFC Global Investment Management
Elliott & Page Tax Managed Growth Guaranteed Investment Fund
RRSP Eligible; Inception Year: 2001; Fund Managers:
MFC Global Investment Management
Maxxum Dividend Growth Guaranteed Investment Fund
RRSP Eligible; Inception Year: 2005; Fund Managers:
Mackenzie Financial Corporation
Simplicity Aggressive Portfolio Guaranteed Investment Fund
RRSP Eligible; Inception Year: 1999; Fund Managers:
MFC Global Investment Management
Simplicity Balanced Portfolio Guaranteed Investment Fund
RRSP Eligible; Inception Year: 1999; Fund Managers:
MFC Global Investment Management
Simplicity Conservative Portfolio Guaranteed Investment Fund
RRSP Eligible; Inception Year: 1999; Fund Managers:
MFC Global Investment Management
Simplicity Growth Portfolio Guaranteed Investment Fund
RRSP Eligible; Inception Year: 1999; Fund Managers:
MFC Global Investment Management
Simplicity Income Portfolio Guaranteed Investment Fund
RRSP Eligible; Inception Year: 1999; Fund Managers:
MFC Global Investment Management
Simplicity Moderate Portfolio Guaranteed Investment Fund
RRSP Eligible; Inception Year: 1999; Fund Managers:
MFC Global Investment Management

Maritime Life:
Aggressive Equity Fund
RRSP Eligible; Inception Year: 1996; Fund Managers:
Altamira Management Ltd.
American Growth & Income Fund
RRSP Eligible; Inception Year: 1994; Fund Managers:
John F. Snyder
Balanced Fund
RRSP Eligible; Inception Year: 1986; Fund Managers:
John Montgomery
WayneWachell
Len Racioppo
Peter Harrison
Jeffrey M. Waldman
Greystone Management Investment Inc.
Bond Fund
RRSP Eligible; Inception Year: 1989; Fund Managers:
TAL Global Asset Management Inc.
Canadian Growth R Fund
RRSP Eligible; Inception Year: 1994; Fund Managers:
Royal & SunAlliance Investment Management
Canadian Equity Fund
RRSP Eligible; Inception Year: 1995; Fund Managers:
Martin E. Downie
Stephen C.A.Harris
Discovery Fund
RRSP Eligible; Inception Year: 1996; Fund Managers:
Jamie Rome
Dividend Income Fund
RRSP Eligible; Inception Year: 1995; Fund Managers:
Peter A. Stuart, CFA
AlfredSamson
Alan Wicks
Fidelity Europe Segregated Fund
RRSP Eligible; Inception Year: 1992; Fund Managers:
Fidelity Investments Canada Limited
Fidelity International Portfolio Segregated Fund
RRSP Eligible; Inception Year: 1987; Fund Managers:
Fidelity Investments Canada Limited
Fidelity True North Segregated Fund
RRSP Eligible; Inception Year: 1996; Fund Managers:
Fidelity Investments Canada Limited
Growth Fund
RRSP Eligible; Inception Year: 1968; Fund Managers:
Wayne Wachell
PeterHarrison
Greystone Management Investment Inc.
Talvest Canadian Asset Allocation Segregated Fund
RRSP Eligible; Inception Year: 1986; Fund Managers:
CIBC Global Asset Management
Talvest Global Bond RSP Segregated Fund
RRSP Eligible; Inception Year: 1993; Fund Managers:
CIBC Global Asset Management
Talvest Global RSP Segregated Fund
RRSP Eligible; Inception Year: 1993; Fund Managers:
CIBC Global Asset Management
Trimark Advantage Bond Series R Segregated Fund
RRSP Eligible; Inception Year: 1994; Fund Managers:
AIM Trimark Investments
Trimark Discovery Series R Segregated Fund
RRSP Eligible; Inception Year: 1996; Fund Managers:
AIM Trimark Investments
Trimark Europlus Series R Segregated Fund
RRSP Eligible; Inception Year: 1997; Fund Managers:
AIM Trimark Investments
US Equity II Series R Fund
RRSP Eligible; Inception Year: 2002;
US Equity Series R Fund
RRSP Eligible; Inception Year: 1995; Fund Managers:
SEAMARK Asset Management Limited
Balanced Pooled Fund
RRSP Eligible; Inception Year: 2003; Fund Managers:
McLean Budden Limited
Canadian Dividend R Fund
RRSP Eligible; Inception Year: 1998; Fund Managers:
Alan Wicks
Canadian Equity Pooled Fund
RRSP Eligible; Inception Year: 2003; Fund Managers:
Marc Trottier
Canadian Income Pooled Fund
RRSP Eligible; Inception Year: 2003; Fund Managers:
Addenda Capital Inc.
Canadian Small Cap Fund
RRSP Eligible; Inception Year: 2002; Fund Managers:
Ted Whitehead
Fidelity Canadian Asset Allocation Segregated Fund
RRSP Eligible; Inception Year: 1994; Fund Managers:
Fidelity Investments Canada Limited
Small Cap Canadian Pooled Fund
RRSP Eligible; Inception Year: 2003; Fund Managers:
Peter Harrison
Talvest Canadian Asset Allocation B Segregated Fund
RRSP Eligible; Inception Year: 1986; Fund Managers:
TAL Global Asset Management Inc.
Talvest Canadian Equity Growth Segregated Fund
RRSP Eligible; Inception Year: 1997; Fund Managers:
Connor, Clarke & Lunn Investment Management
Talvest Millennium High Income Segregated Fund
RRSP Eligible; Inception Year: 1997; Fund Managers:
CIBC Global Asset Management
US Equity Fund
RRSP Eligible; Inception Year: 2002; Fund Managers:
SEAMARK Asset Management Limited
US Special Equity Pool H Fund
RRSP Eligible; Inception Year: 2003; Fund Managers:
John F. Snyder
American Equity Index Fund
RRSP Eligible; Inception Year: 1998; Fund Managers:
MFC Global Investment Management
American Equity Pooled Fund
RRSP Eligible; Inception Year: 2002; Fund Managers:
SEAMARK Asset Management Limited
Canadian Equity Index Fund
RRSP Eligible; Inception Year: 1998; Fund Managers:
MFC Global Investment Management
Canadian Equity Index Series R Fund
RRSP Eligible; Inception Year: 1998; Fund Managers:
MFC Global Investment Management
CI International Balanced Segregated Fund
RRSP Eligible; Inception Year: 1994; Fund Managers:
CI Investments

Elliott & Page Canadian Equity Segregated Fund
RRSP Eligible; Inception Year: 1994; Fund Managers:
MFC Global Investment Management
Elliott & Page Corporate Bond Segregated Fund
RRSP Eligible; Inception Year: 2003; Fund Managers:
MFC Global Investment Management
Elliott & Page Corporate Bond Series R Segregated Fund
RRSP Eligible; Inception Year: 2003; Fund Managers:
MFC Global Investment Management
Elliott & Page Money Segregated Fund
RRSP Eligible; Inception Year: 1984; Fund Managers:
MFC Global Investment Management
Elliott & Page Money Series R Segregated Fund
RRSP Eligible; Inception Year: 1984; Fund Managers:
MFC Global Investment Management
Elliott & Page Monthly High Income Segregated Fund
RRSP Eligible; Inception Year: 1997; Fund Managers:
MFC Global Investment Management
Elliott & Page US Mid-Cap Segregated Fund
RRSP Eligible; Inception Year: 1997; Fund Managers:
MFC Global Investment Management
Elliott & Page Value Equity Segregated Fund
RRSP Eligible; Inception Year: 1997; Fund Managers:
MFC Global Investment Management
Global Bond (Oechsle) Fund
RRSP Eligible; Inception Year: 1999; Fund Managers:
Oechsle International
Sentinel Income (Mackenzie) Fund
RRSP Eligible; Inception Year: 2005; Fund Managers:
Mackenzie Financial Corporation
Trimark Select Growth Segregated Fund
RRSP Eligible; Inception Year: 1989; Fund Managers:
AIM Trimark Investments
Trimark Europlus Segregated Fund
RRSP Eligible; Inception Year: 1997; Fund Managers:
AIM Trimark Investments
Trimark Select Balanced Segregated Fund
RRSP Eligible; Inception Year: 1989; Fund Managers:
AIM Trimark Investments
Trimark Select Canadian Growth Series R Segregated Fund
RRSP Eligible; Inception Year: 1992; Fund Managers:
AIM Trimark Investments
American Equity Index Series R Fund
RRSP Eligible; Inception Year: 1998; Fund Managers:
MFC Global Investment Management
Dollar-Cost Adveraging Advantage Fund
RRSP Eligible; Inception Year: 1984; Fund Managers:
MFC Global Investment Management

NAL:

Canadian Diversified Fund
RRSP Eligible; Inception Year: 1987; Fund Managers:
Elliott & Page
Canadian Equity Fund
RRSP Eligible; Inception Year: 1987; Fund Managers:
Elliott & Page
Canadian Money Market Fund
RRSP Eligible; Inception Year: 1989; Fund Managers:
Elliott & Page

Synchrony:

Conservative RRSP Portfolio Fund
RRSP Eligible; Inception Year: 1998; Fund Managers:
Karl Gauvin
Lucde la Durantaye
Conservative Portfolio Fund
RRSP Eligible; Inception Year: 1998; Fund Managers:
Karl Gauvin
Lucde la Durantaye
Income & Growth Portfolio Fund
RRSP Eligible; Inception Year: 1998; Fund Managers:
Karl Gauvin
Lucde la Durantaye
Performance RRSP Portfolio Fund
RRSP Eligible; Inception Year: 1998; Fund Managers:
Karl Gauvin
Lucde la Durantaye
Performance Portfolio Fund
RRSP Eligible; Inception Year: 1998; Fund Managers:
Karl Gauvin
Lucde la Durantaye

Synchrony (TM):

Conservative B Portfolio Fund
RRSP Eligible; Inception Year: 1998; Fund Managers:
Luc de la Durantaye
Conservative RRSP B Portfolio Fund
RRSP Eligible; Inception Year: 1998; Fund Managers:
Luc de la Durantaye
Income & Growth B Portfolio Fund
RRSP Eligible; Inception Year: 1998; Fund Managers:
Luc de la Durantaye
Performance RRSP B Portfolio Fund
RRSP Eligible; Inception Year: 1998; Fund Managers:
Luc de la Durantaye
Performance B Portfolio Fund
RRSP Eligible; Inception Year: 1998; Fund Managers:
Luc de la Durantaye

Mavrix Fund Management Inc.

Also listed under: *Pension & Money Management Companies*
#600, 36 Lombard St.
Toronto, ON M5C 2X3
416-362-3077
Fax: 416-362-7191
888-964-3533
clientservices@mavrixfunds.com
www.mavrixfunds.com
Year Founded: 1983
Number of Employees: 72
Assets: $10-100 billion
Stock Symbol: YMG

Executives:

Malvin C. Spooner, President/CEO
Mario Arra, Sr. Vice-President, National Sales
William Shaw, Sr. Vice-President & Sec.-Treas.
Raymond M. Steele, Sr. Vice-President/CFO
David Balsdon, Vice-President, Operations & Administration
Roger Dent, Vice-President, Research
Sergio Di Vito, Vice-President, Trading
Alex Nayyar, Vice-President, External Sales

Mavrix:

Dividend & Income Fund
RRSP Eligible; Inception Year: 1985;
Growth Fund
RRSP Eligible; Inception Year: 1985;
Money Market Fund
RRSP Eligible; Inception Year: 1987;
Strategic Bond Fund
RRSP Eligible; Inception Year: 1998;
Enterprise Fund
RRSP Eligible; Inception Year: 1998;
Canada Fund
RRSP Eligible; Inception Year: 1998;
Diversified Fund
RRSP Eligible; Inception Year: 1981;
Explorer Fund
RRSP Eligible; Inception Year: 2002;
Sierra Equity Fund
RRSP Eligible; Inception Year: 1999;
Global Fund
RRSP Eligible; Inception Year: 2002; Fund Managers:
Pictet International Management
American Growth Fund
RRSP Eligible; Inception Year: 1998;
Canadian Income Trust Fund
RRSP Eligible; Inception Year: 2003;
Strategic Small Cap Fund
RRSP Eligible; Inception Year: 1996;
Multi-Series Canadian Equity Fund
RRSP Eligible; Inception Year: 2004;
Multi-Series Explorer Fund
RRSP Eligible; Inception Year: 2004;
Multi-Series Income Fund
RRSP Eligible; Inception Year: 2004;
Multi-Series Short Term Income Fund
RRSP Eligible; Inception Year: 2004;
Small Companies Fund
RRSP Eligible; Inception Year: 2004;
Lawrence Enterprise Fund
RRSP Eligible; Inception Year: 2001; Fund Managers:
Lawrence Asset Management Inc.
Balanced Income & Growth Trust Fund
RRSP Eligible; Inception Year: 2004;
Resource Fund 2004 LP
RRSP Eligible; Inception Year: 2004;
Resource Fund 2004 II LP
RRSP Eligible; Inception Year: 2004;
Resource Fund 2005 II LP
RRSP Eligible; Inception Year: 2005;
Resource Fund 2005 LP
RRSP Eligible; Inception Year: 2005;

Mawer Investment Management Ltd.

Also listed under: *Financial Planning; Investment Management*

#900, 603 - 7th Ave. SW
Calgary, AB T2P 2T5
403-262-4673
Fax: 403-262-4099
800-889-6248
info@mawer.com
www.mawer.com
Ownership: Private
Year Founded: 1974
Number of Employees: 41
Profile: Mawer offers independent portfolio management to institutions & private clients, plus a family of pooled funds & eight no-load mutual funds.

Executives:

Paul Moroz, Director, Equity Analyst
Greg Peterson, Director & Manager, Sr. Private Client Portfolio; 403-267-1952
David Ragan, Director, Equity Analyst
W.R. David Stone, Director, Marketing & Sales; 403-267-1961
Diana Gabriel, Controller; 403-267-1993

Mawer:

Canadian Balanced Retirement Savings Fund
RRSP Eligible; Inception Year: 1988; Fund Managers:
Jane Depraitere
Canadian Diversified Investment Fund
RRSP Eligible; Inception Year: 1988; Fund Managers:
Craig D. Senyk
Canadian Equity Mid Large Cap Fund
RRSP Eligible; Inception Year: 1991; Fund Managers:
James C.E. Hall
Canadian Money Market Fund
RRSP Eligible; Inception Year: 1988; Fund Managers:
William R. MacLachlan
New Canada Fund
RRSP Eligible; Inception Year: 1988; Fund Managers:
Martin D. Ferguson
US Equity Fund
RRSP Eligible; Inception Year: 1992; Fund Managers:
Darrell A. Anderson
World Investment Fund
RRSP Eligible; Inception Year: 1987; Fund Managers:
Gerald A. Cooper-Key
Canadian Bond Fund
RRSP Eligible; Inception Year: 1991; Fund Managers:
Michael J. Crofts

McElvaine Investment Management Ltd.

Also listed under: *Investment Dealers*
3 Bentall Centre
PO Box 49308
#463, 595 Burrard St.
Vancouver, BC V7X 1L3
604-601-8345
Fax: 604-601-8346
info@mcelvaine.com
www.mcelvaine.com
Ownership: Private

McElvaine:

Investment Trust Fund
RRSP Eligible; Inception Year: 1996;

McLean Budden Ltd.

Also listed under: *Financial Planning; Investment Management*

#2525, 145 King St. West
Toronto, ON M5H 1J8
416-862-9800
Fax: 416-862-0167
800-884-0436
Other Information: Mutual Fund Dept. Fax: 416/862-9624
www.mcleanbudden.com
Ownership: Private. Jointly owned by Sun Life Assurance Company of Canada
Year Founded: 1949
Profile: The company specializes in investment management.

Executives:

Douglas W. Mahaffy, President/CEO & Chair; dmahaffy@mcleanbudden.com

INVESTMENT MANAGEMENT

McLean Budden Ltd. (continued)
Heather Shannon, Sr. Vice-President;
hshannon@mcleanbudden.com
MB:
Balanced Growth Fund
RRSP Eligible; Inception Year: 1996; Fund Managers:
Mary B. Hallward
AlanDaxner
Douglas Andrews
John Ackerl
Anthony Magri
Balanced Fund
RRSP Eligible; Inception Year: 1999; Fund Managers:
Alan Daxner
BenoitParadis
Colin Sinclare
Douglas Andrews
Hans van Monsjou
Roger J. Beauchemin
Susan Shuter
Edward E. Thompson
John Ackerl
Private Balanced Fund
RRSP Eligible; Inception Year: 1997; Fund Managers:
R. Bruce Murray
Mary B.Hallward
Robert V. Livingston
Edward Kwan
Susan Shuter
Edward E. Thompson
Anthony Magri
Canadian Equity Growth Fund
RRSP Eligible; Inception Year: 1980; Fund Managers:
William J. Giblin
R. BruceMurray
Mary B. Hallward
Douglas Andrews
John J Durfy
Miranda Hubbs
Canadian Equity Value Fund
RRSP Eligible; Inception Year: 1998; Fund Managers:
Alan Daxner
BrianDawson
Susan Shuter
Edward E. Thompson
John Tsagarelis
Canadian Equity Fund
RRSP Eligible; Inception Year: 1998; Fund Managers:
Alan Daxner
BenoitParadis
Douglas Andrews
Hans van Monsjou
Colin Sinclare
John Ackerl
Roger J. Beauchemin
Susan Shuter
Edward E. Thompson
Canadian Equity Plus Fund
RRSP Eligible; Inception Year: 1997; Fund Managers:
Alan Daxner
BenoitParadis
Colin Sinclare
Hans van Monsjou
John Ackerl
Roger J. Beauchemin
Susan Shuter
Edward E. Thompson
Global Equity Fund
RRSP Eligible; Inception Year: 1996; Fund Managers:
William J. Giblin
BrianDawson
R. Bruce Murray
Mary B. Hallward
Benoit Paradis
Bruce MacNabb
Fixed Income Fund
RRSP Eligible; Inception Year: 1981; Fund Managers:
Cort Conover
Peter P.Kotsopoulos
Anthony Magri
Paul Marcogliese
Cindy Nam
Fixed Income Plus Fund
RRSP Eligible; Inception Year: 1996; Fund Managers:
Cort Conover
AnthonyMagri
Peter P. Kotsopoulos
Cindy Nam
Long Term Fixed Income Fund
RRSP Eligible; Inception Year: 1998; Fund Managers:
Cort Conover
Peter P.Kotsopoulos
Anthony Magri
Paul Marcogliese
Cindy Nam
Money Market Fund
RRSP Eligible; Inception Year: 1995; Fund Managers:
Cort Conover
Peter P.Kotsopoulos
Anthony Magri
Paul Marcogliese
Cindy Nam
Balanced Growth Pension Fund
RRSP Eligible; Inception Year: 1993; Fund Managers:
Mary B. Hallward
AlanDaxner
Douglas Andrews
John Ackerl
Anthony Magri
American Equity Fund
RRSP Eligible; Inception Year: 1983; Fund Managers:
William J. Giblin
BrianDawson
R. Bruce Murray
Mary B. Hallward
Benoit Paradis
Bruce MacNabb
International Equity Fund
RRSP Eligible; Inception Year: 1999; Fund Managers:
Benoit Paradis
BrianDawson
R. Bruce Murray
Mary B. Hallward
Eleanor Wang
A. Monika Skiba
Select Balanced Fund
RRSP Eligible; Inception Year: 2000; Fund Managers:
Alan Daxner
Edward A.Harris
Edward Kwan
R. Bruce Murray
Mary B. Hallward
Edward E. Thompson
Anthony Magri
Select Canadian Equity Fund
RRSP Eligible; Inception Year: 2000; Fund Managers:
Alan Daxner
Edward A.Harris
Edward Kwan
Select Global Equity Fund
RRSP Eligible; Inception Year: 2000; Fund Managers:
Alan Daxner
Edward A.Harris
Edward Kwan
Select Fixed Income Fund
RRSP Eligible; Inception Year: 2000; Fund Managers:
Edward A. Harris
AnthonyMagri
Cort Conover
Balanced Value Fund
RRSP Eligible; Inception Year: 2001; Fund Managers:
Hans van Monsjou
JohnAckerl
Alan Daxner
Brian Dawson
A. Monika Skiba
Susan Shuter
Edward E. Thompson
Global Equity Growth Fund
RRSP Eligible; Inception Year: 2002; Fund Managers:
R. Bruce Murray
John JDurfy
Mary B. Hallward
Scott Connell
Michael Hakes
Global Equity Value Fund
RRSP Eligible; Inception Year: 2002; Fund Managers:
Brian Dawson
MaryMathers
Susan Shuter
Edward E. Thompson
A. Monika Skiba
LifePlan Income Fund
RRSP Eligible; Inception Year: 2002;
LifePlan Growth & Income Fund
RRSP Eligible; Inception Year: 2002;
LifePlan Growth Fund
RRSP Eligible; Inception Year: 2002;
Short Term Fixed Income Fund
RRSP Eligible; Inception Year: 2005; Fund Managers:
Cindy Nam
AdamGregg
Cort Conover
Paul Marcogliese
Peter P. Kotsopoulos
Anthony Magri
McLean Budden:
International Equity Fund
RRSP Eligible; Inception Year: 1998; Fund Managers:
Benoit Paradis
BrianDawson
R. Bruce Murray
Mary B. Hallward
Eleanor Wang
A. Monika Skiba
Money Market Fund
RRSP Eligible; Inception Year: 1989; Fund Managers:
Cort Conover
Peter P.Kotsopoulos
Anthony Magri
Paul Marcogliese
Cindy Nam
Canadian Equity Value Fund
RRSP Eligible; Inception Year: 1999; Fund Managers:
Alan Daxner
BrianDawson
John Tsagarelis
Susan Shuter
Edward E. Thompson
A. Monika Skiba
Fixed Income Fund
RRSP Eligible; Inception Year: 1989; Fund Managers:
Cort Conover
Peter P.Kotsopoulos
Anthony Magri
Paul Marcogliese
Cindy Nam
Balanced Growth Fund
RRSP Eligible; Inception Year: 1989; Fund Managers:
R. Bruce Murray
Mary B.Hallward
Lewis Jackson
Robert V. Livingston
Edward Kwan
Canadian Equity Growth Fund
RRSP Eligible; Inception Year: 1989; Fund Managers:
William J. Giblin
R. BruceMurray
Mary B. Hallward
Douglas Andrews
John J Durfy
Miranda Hubbs
Sheila E. Norman
Sue Eagleson
American Equity Fund
RRSP Eligible; Inception Year: 1989; Fund Managers:
William J. Giblin
BrianDawson
R. Bruce Murray
Mary B. Hallward
Benoit Paradis
Bruce MacNabb
Global Equity Fund
RRSP Eligible; Inception Year: 2001; Fund Managers:
Benoit Paradis
William J.Giblin
Brian Dawson
R. Bruce Murray
Mary B. Hallward
Bruce MacNabb
Balanced Value Fund
RRSP Eligible; Inception Year: 2003; Fund Managers:
Alan Daxner
BrianDawson
Craig S. Barnard

Peter P. Kotsopoulos
Paul Marcogliese
Susan Shuter
Edward E. Thompson
Anthony Magri
Canadian Equity Fund
RRSP Eligible; Inception Year: 2004; Fund Managers:
Alan Daxner
DouglasAndrews
John Ackerl
Susan Shuter
Edward E. Thompson
Branches:
Montréal
#2810, 1250, boul René-Lévesque ouest
Montréal, QC H3B 4W8 Canada
514-933-0033
Fax: 514-933-8163
Vancouver
Three Bentall Centre
PO Box 49105
#3043, 595 Burrard St.
Vancouver, BC V7X 1G4 Canada
604-623-3430
Fax: 604-623-3436

MD Management Limited/ Gestion MD limitée

Also listed under: *Investment Dealers; Investment Management*
1870 Alta Vista Dr.
Ottawa, ON K1G 6R7
613-731-4552
Fax: 613-736-5368
800-663-7336
cmamsc@cma.ca
www.cma.ca; www.mdm.ca
Ownership: Private. Subsidiary of the Canadian Medical Association
Year Founded: 1969
Number of Employees: 1,100
Assets: $10-100 billion
Profile: The company provides professional, objective financial planning & price competitive, quality products & services to Canadian Medical Association physicians & their families. MD Management Limited is also affiliated with the following companies: CMA Holding Incorporated, MD Funds Management Inc., MD Private Trust Co., MD Life Insurance Co., Practice Solutions Ltd., MD Private Investment Management Inc.

Executives:
A.G. Bélanger, President/CEO
C.M. Allison, Chief Financial Officer
R.P. Bannerman, Vice-President & Secretary
C.K. Hamilton, Vice-President
T.R. Smith, Vice-President
R.S. Tanner, Vice-President
R. Thorpe, Vice-President
S.H. Wilson, Vice-President
J.M Arel, Asst. Vice-President
D. Hamilton, Asst. Vice-President
J.M. Klaas, Asst. Vice-President
D. Labonté, Asst. Vice-President
H. Miskelly, Asst. Vice-President
N. Thompson, Asst. Vice-President
Directors:
I. Warrack, Chair
R.P. Bannerman
A.G. Bélanger
B.F. Peters
T. Webb
S.H. Wilson
Affiliated Companies:
MD Life Insurance Company
MD:
Balanced Fund
RRSP Eligible; Inception Year: 1992; Fund Managers:
MD Funds Management Inc.
Bond Fund
RRSP Eligible; Inception Year: 1988; Fund Managers:
MD Funds Management Inc.
Bond & Mortgage Fund
RRSP Eligible; Inception Year: 1995; Fund Managers:
MD Funds Management Inc.
Dividend Fund
RRSP Eligible; Inception Year: 1992; Fund Managers:
MD Funds Management Inc.
Equity Fund
RRSP Eligible; Inception Year: 1966; Fund Managers:
MD Funds Management Inc.
Growth Fund
RRSP Eligible; Inception Year: 1969; Fund Managers:
MD Funds Management Inc.
Select Fund
RRSP Eligible; Inception Year: 1993; Fund Managers:
MD Funds Management Inc.
International Growth Fund
RRSP Eligible; Inception Year: 2000; Fund Managers:
MD Funds Management Inc.
US Small Cap Growth Fund
RRSP Eligible; Inception Year: 2000; Fund Managers:
MD Funds Management Inc.
International Value Fund
RRSP Eligible; Inception Year: 2004; Fund Managers:
MD Funds Management Inc.
Money Fund
RRSP Eligible; Inception Year: 1975; Fund Managers:
MD Funds Management Inc.
US Large Cap Growth Fund
RRSP Eligible; Inception Year: 1992; Fund Managers:
MD Funds Management Inc.
US Large Cap Value Fund
RRSP Eligible; Inception Year: 2000; Fund Managers:
MD Funds Management Inc.
MDPIM:
Canadian Equity Pool Class A Fund
RRSP Eligible; Inception Year: 2000; Fund Managers:
MD Funds Management Inc.
US Equity Pool Class A Fund
RRSP Eligible; Inception Year: 2000; Fund Managers:
MD Funds Management Inc.
District Offices:
Abbotsford
#302, 33140 Mill Lake Rd.
Abbotsford, BC V2S 2A5 Canada
604-504-1666
Fax: 604-504-1663
888-326-9993
Barrie
#301, 125 Bell Farm Rd.
Barrie, ON L4M 6L2 Canada
705-721-0196
Fax: 705-721-0509
888-246-4996
Chicoutimi
#200, 345, rue des Saguenéens
Chicoutimi, QC G7H 6K9 Canada
418-543-4456
Fax: 418-543-1665
888-861-0131
Edmonton - 106th Ave.
#202, 12230 - 106th Ave. NW
Edmonton, AB T5N 3Z1 Canada
780-482-7045
Fax: 780-482-7047
800-282-6901
Edmonton - 112th St.
College Plaza
#1502, 8215 - 112th St.
Edmonton, AB T6G 2C8 Canada
780-436-1333
Fax: 780-436-3371
877-434-1333
Fredericton
#1, 176 York St.
Fredericton, NB E3B 3N7 Canada
506-452-2958
Fax: 506-452-2959
888-292-3131
Gatineau
#410, 200, Montcalm
Gatineau, QC J8Y 3B5 Canada
819-770-5101
Fax: 819-770-9525
888-246-5609
Hamilton
#1200, 1 King St. West
Hamilton, ON L8P 1A4 Canada
905-526-8999
Fax: 905-526-1198
800-883-6015
Kamloops
#108, 300 Columbia St.
Kamloops, BC V2C 6L1 Canada
250-377-0900
Fax: 250-377-0933
888-217-6888
Kelowna
#203, 3001 Tutt St.
Kelowna, BC V1Y 2H4 Canada
250-762-4261
Fax: 250-762-3142
800-249-1133
Kingston
#204, 275 Bagot St.
Kingston, ON K7L 3G4 Canada
613-548-8770
Fax: 613-548-3556
800-363-5527
Kitchener
#201, 525 Belmont Ave. West
Kitchener, ON N2M 5E2 Canada
519-744-1303
Fax: 519-744-7408
800-859-6715
Laval
#703, 3030, boul le Carrefour
Laval, QC H7T 2P5 Canada
450-682-2696
Fax: 450-682-5610
800-540-6211
Lethbridge
Lethbridge Centre Tower
#315, 400 - 4th Ave. South
Lethbridge, AB T1J 4E1 Canada
403-320-2992
Fax: 403-320-5885
888-320-3431
Longueuil
Tour est
#452, 111, rue St-Charles ouest
Longueuil, QC J4K 5G4 Canada
450-448-0611
Fax: 450-448-0939
888-627-3719
Mississauga
#601, 89 Queensway West
Mississauga, ON L5B 2V2 Canada
905-306-7788
Fax: 905-306-7824
800-321-0330
Moncton
#320, 1133 St. George Blvd.
Moncton, NB E1E 4E1 Canada
506-855-1994
Fax: 506-855-0220
800-664-2241
Montréal
#647, 1, rue Holiday
Montréal, QC H9R 5N3 Canada
514-630-7749
Fax: 514-630-8449
888-989-7749
Nanaimo
#202B, 1808 Bowen Rd.
Nanaimo, BC V9S 5W4 Canada
250-753-9800
Fax: 250-753-9828
888-326-9994
New Westminster
#420, 628 - 6th Ave.
New Westminster, BC V3M 6Z1 Canada
604-520-3315
Fax: 604-520-3301
800-498-1881
North Vancouver
#300, 1111 Lonsdale Ave.
North Vancouver, BC V7N 2H4 Canada
604-987-5553
Fax: 604-987-5583
877-987-5553
Oshawa
Oshawa Executive Centre
#306, 419 King St. West
Oshawa, ON L1J 2K5 Canada
905-579-1882
Fax: 905-579-6949

MD Management Limited/ Gestion MD limitée (continued)
877-543-1201

Prince George
#320, 177 Victoria St.
Prince George, BC V2L 5R8 Canada
250-564-9600
Fax: 250-564-9660
888-326-9992
Regina
#375, 3303 Hillsdale St.
Regina, SK S4S 6W9 Canada
306-359-7200
Fax: 306-359-9900
888-880-6211
Richmond Hill
#206, 9050 Yonge St.
Richmond Hill, ON L4C 9S6 Canada
905-889-2100
Fax: 905-889-2693
888-233-8858
Saint John
#101, 1 Magazine St.
Saint John, NB E2K 5S9 Canada
506-657-2020
Fax: 506-657-2002
888-292-3131
Sherbrooke
#520, 2665, rue King ouest
Sherbrooke, QC J1L 2G5 Canada
819-566-8240
Fax: 819-566-8291
800-584-9881
St Catharines
#105, 75 Corporate Park Dr.
St Catharines, ON L2S 3W2 Canada
905-641-0330
Fax: 905-641-0146
800-428-7184
St. John's
164 MacDonald Dr.
St. John's, NL A1A 4B3 Canada
709-729-2136
Fax: 709-726-2193
800-229-1798
Stratford
3 Myrtle St.
Stratford, PE C1B 1P4 Canada
902-892-2092
Fax: 902-892-2043
800-443-9711
Sudbury
#305, 27 Cedar St.
Sudbury, ON P3E 1A1 Canada
705-671-9746
Fax: 705-671-1254
800-547-8295
Sydney
Sydney Medical Arts Bldg.
#210, 336 Kings Rd.
Sydney, NS B1S 1A9 Canada
902-564-5700
Fax: 902-564-5727
888-356-3871
Thunder Bay
#203, 1205 Amber Dr.
Thunder Bay, ON P7B 6M4 Canada
807-346-2850
Fax: 807-346-2854
888-873-3320
Toronto - Milner Ave.
#1603, 325 Milner Ave.
Toronto, ON M1B 5N1 Canada
416-299-8841
Fax: 416-299-9787
800-846-0966
Toronto - Sheppard Ave.
#804, 45 Sheppard Ave. East
Toronto, ON M2N 5W9 Canada
416-224-9793
Fax: 416-224-9045
888-770-9223
Victoria
#100, 3550 Saanich Rd.
Victoria, BC V8X 1X2 Canada
250-480-5075
Fax: 250-480-5026
800-716-8498
Windsor
#350, 600 Tecumseh Rd. East
Windsor, ON N8X 4X9 Canada
519-254-2812
Fax: 519-254-5347
800-213-8472

Regional Offices:
Calgary
#300, 708 - 11th Ave. SW
Calgary, AB T2R 0E4 Canada
403-244-8000
Fax: 403-229-1146
800-661-4669
Halifax
Park Lane Terrace
PO Box 105
#704, 5657 Spring Garden Rd.
Halifax, NS B3J 3R4 Canada
902-425-4646
Fax: 902-422-2775
800-565-1771
London
#705, 380 Wellington St. North
London, ON N6A 5B5 Canada
519-432-0883
Fax: 519-432-0997
800-461-9587
Montréal
#650, 1000, rue de la Gauchetière ouest
Montréal, QC H3B 4W5 Canada
514-392-1434
Fax: 514-392-0387
800-361-5126
Ottawa
#200, 1565 Carling Ave.
Ottawa, ON K1Z 8R1 Canada
613-722-7688
Fax: 613-729-4735
800-387-4018
Québec
#2460, 2600, boul Laurier
Québec, QC G1V 4M6 Canada
418-657-6601
Fax: 418-652-7808
800-463-6288

Saskatoon
#900, CN Towers
Saskatoon, SK S7K 1J5 Canada
306-244-0077
Fax: 306-244-8685
800-667-0077
Toronto
#1100, 522 University Ave.
Toronto, ON M5G 1W7 Canada
416-598-1442
Fax: 416-340-1509
800-387-2646
Vancouver
#250, 1665 West Broadway
Vancouver, BC V6J 1X1 Canada
604-736-7778
Fax: 604-736-1202
800-663-7460
Winnipeg
#404, 1661 Portage Ave.
Winnipeg, MB R3J 3T7 Canada
204-783-2463
Fax: 204-772-1960
800-567-7526
winnipegregion@cma.ca

Middlefield Group

***Also listed under:** Financial Planning; Non-Depository Institutions*
#5855, First Canadian Place
PO Box 192, First Canadian Place Stn. First Canadian Place
Toronto, ON M5X 1A6
416-362-0714
Fax: 416-362-7925
888-890-1686
invest@middlefield.com
www.middlefield.com
Ownership: Private. Owned by employees.
Year Founded: 1979
Number of Employees: 85
Assets: $10-50 million Year End: 20060331
Revenues: $50-100 million Year End: 20060331
Profile: The group is the manager of financial assets on behalf of individual & institutional clients. Middlefield presently manages over $3.0 billion of assets, including resource funds, venture capital assets, real estate & mutual funds.

Executives:
Murray J. Brasseur, Managing Director
Douglas D. Sedore, President
J. Dennis Dunlop, Sr. Vice-President
Sylvia V. Stinson, Sr. Vice-President
Margaret Lok, Vice-President
Nancy Tham, Vice-President, Marketing
Directors:
Murray J. Brasseur; 416-857-5347
George S. Dembroski; 416-842-7504
H.R. Garland; 416-449-1750
W. Garth Jestley; 416-847-5346
Gordon Stollery
Charles B. Young
Affiliated Companies:
Middlefield Capital Corporation
Middlefield Income Funds:
Activenergy Income Fund
RRSP Eligible; Inception Year: 2004; Fund Managers:
Richard L. Faiella
W. GarthJestley
Dean Orrico
Guardian Capital LP
Compass Income Fund
RRSP Eligible; Inception Year: 2002; Fund Managers:
W. Garth Jestley
DeanOrrico
Richard L. Faiella
Core IncomePlus Fund
RRSP Eligible; Inception Year: 2005; Fund Managers:
Richard L. Faiella
DeanOrrico
W. Garth Jestley
Equal Sector Income FundInception Year: 2005; Fund Managers:
W. Garth Jestley
DeanOrrico
Indexplus Income Fund
RRSP Eligible; Inception Year: 2003; Fund Managers:
Richard L. Faiella
DeanOrrico
W. Garth Jestley
Indexplus 2 Income Fund
RRSP Eligible; Inception Year: 2003; Fund Managers:
Richard L. Faiella
DeanOrrico
W. Garth Jestley
Matrix Income Fund
RRSP Eligible; Inception Year: 2005; Fund Managers:
W. Garth Jestley
DeanOrrico
Maxin Income Fund
RRSP Eligible; Inception Year: 2003; Fund Managers:
Richard L. Faiella
W. GarthJestley
Dean Orrico
Guardian Capital LP
Mint Income Fund
RRSP Eligible; Inception Year: 1997; Fund Managers:
W. Garth Jestley
DeanOrrico
Pathfinder Income Fund
RRSP Eligible; Inception Year: 2002; Fund Managers:
Richard L. Faiella
W. GarthJestley
Dean Orrico
Stars Income Fund
RRSP Eligible; Inception Year: 2001; Fund Managers:
Richard L. Faiella
W. GarthJestley
Dean Orrico
Strata Income Fund
RRSP Eligible; Inception Year: 2004; Fund Managers:
Richard L. Faiella

W. GarthJestley
Dean Orrico
Yieldplus Income Fund
RRSP Eligible; Inception Year: 2004; Fund Managers:
Richard L. Faiella
W. GarthJestley
Dean Orrico
Middlefield Mutual Funds:
Money Market FundInception Year: 1996; Fund Managers:
Scott Roberts
Enhanced Yield Fund
RRSP Eligible; Inception Year: 1998; Fund Managers:
Robert Lauzon
W. GarthJestley
Canadian Balanced Class Fund
RRSP Eligible; Inception Year: 2001; Fund Managers:
Robert Lauzon
ScottRoberts
Equity Index Class Fund
RRSP Eligible; Inception Year: 2000; Fund Managers:
W. Garth Jestley
RobertLauzon
Growth Class Fund
RRSP Eligible; Inception Year: 1990; Fund Managers:
Robert Lauzon
DeanOrrico
Income & Growth Class FundInception Year: 2004; Fund Managers:
Dean Orrico
RobertLauzon
Income Plus Class Fund
RRSP Eligible; Inception Year: 2000; Fund Managers:
W. Garth Jestley
RobertLauzon
Index Income Class FundInception Year: 2003; Fund Managers:
Robert Lauzon
W. GarthJestley
Resource Class FundInception Year: 2002; Fund Managers:
James S. Parsons
Dennisda Silva
Short-Term Income Class FundInception Year: 2004; Fund Managers:
Robert Lauzon
ScottRoberts
US Equity Class Fund
RRSP Eligible; Inception Year: 2001; Fund Managers:
Dean Orrico
RobertLauzon
Middlefield Resource Funds:
Explorer III Resource Limited Partnership Fund
RRSP Eligible; Inception Year: 2005; Fund Managers:
James S. Parsons
Dennisda Silva
2005 Limited Partnership Fund
RRSP Eligible; Inception Year: 2005; Fund Managers:
Dennis da Silva
James S.Parsons
Explorer II Resource Limited Partnership Fund
RRSP Eligible; Inception Year: 2005; Fund Managers:
James S. Parsons
Dennisda Silva
2004 Limited Partnership Fund
RRSP Eligible; Inception Year: 2004; Fund Managers:
Dennis da Silva
James S.Parsons
Branches:
Calgary
#3063, 150 - 6th Ave. SW
Calgary, AB T2P 3Y7 Canada
403-538-5121
Fax: 403-538-5124
Dennis da Silva, Managing Director

Montrusco Bolton Inc.

***Also listed under:** Pension & Money Management Companies*
#4600, 1250, boul René-Lévesque ouest
Montréal, QC H3B 5J5
514-842-6464
Fax: 514-282-2550
marketing@montruscobolton.com
www.montruscobolton.com
Year Founded: 1984
Executives:
Sylvain Boulé, President/CEO
Richard Guay, Sr. Vice-President
Jean Mathieu, Sr. Vice-President & Chief Investment Officer, Private Wealth Management
Normande Boucher, Vice-President, Private Investment Management
Colette Bournival, Vice-President, Private Investment Management
Yves Filion, Vice-President, Private Wealth Management
Jean Meloche, Vice-President
Affiliated Companies:
Moncton - Louisbourg Investments Inc.
Montrusco Bolton:
Balanced Plus Fund
RRSP Eligible; Inception Year: 1993; Fund Managers:
Érik Giasson
Canadian Small Cap B Fund
RRSP Eligible; Inception Year: 1999; Fund Managers:
Peter Harrison
Canadian Equity B Fund
RRSP Eligible; Inception Year: 1999; Fund Managers:
Peter Harrison
Fixed Income B Fund
RRSP Eligible; Inception Year: 1999; Fund Managers:
François Lagarde
US Equity B Fund (US$)
RRSP Eligible; Inception Year: 1999; Fund Managers:
Nadim Rizk
Balanced B Fund
RRSP Eligible; Inception Year: 1999; Fund Managers:
Érik Giasson
Global Equity B Fund
RRSP Eligible; Inception Year: 1999; Fund Managers:
Nadim Rizk
E.A.F.E. Equity B Fund
RRSP Eligible; Inception Year: 1999; Fund Managers:
Jean-Sébastien Garant
Enterprise Fund
RRSP Eligible; Inception Year: 1987; Fund Managers:
Peter Harrison
International Equity Fund (US$)
RRSP Eligible; Inception Year: 1987; Fund Managers:
Jean-Sébastien Garant
T-Max Fund
RRSP Eligible; Inception Year: 1995; Fund Managers:
François Lagarde
Taxable US Equity Fund (US$)
RRSP Eligible; Inception Year: 1987; Fund Managers:
Nadim Rizk
Income Trust Fund
RRSP Eligible; Inception Year: 2002; Fund Managers:
Peter Harrison
Canadian Equity Plus Fund
RRSP Eligible; Inception Year: 1998; Fund Managers:
Marc Lalonde
Bond Total Return Fund
RRSP Eligible; Inception Year: 1996; Fund Managers:
Érik Lacombe
Montrusco Bolton Focus:
Absolute Return Global FundInception Year: 0; Fund Managers:
Érik Giasson
Focus Investment Group
Branches:
Calgary
Bow Valley Square III
#3190, 255 - 5th Ave. SW
Calgary, AB T2P 3G6 Canada
403-234-0373
Kenneth W. Stout, Vice-President
Halifax - Louisbourg Investments Inc.
#1602, 1791 Barrington St.
Halifax, NS B3J 3L1 Canada
902-421-1811
Fax: 902-420-1780
James Oland, Vice-President, Marketing & Client Servicing
Québec
Tour de la Cité
#860, 2600, boul Laurier
Québec, QC G1V 4W2 Canada
418-650-4420
Normand Lessard, Exec. Vice-President
Saint-Hyacinthe
1365, rue Gauvin
Saint-Hyacinthe, QC J2S 8W7 Canada
450-774-8131
André Benoit, Portfolio Manager
Toronto
North Tower, Royal Bank Plaza
#1840, 200 Bay St.
Toronto, ON M5J 2J1 Canada
416-860-1257
Timothy J. Russell, Vice-President

National Bank Securities Inc./ Placements banque nationale inc.

1100, rue Université, 10e étage
Montréal, QC H3B 2G7
514-871-2082
Fax: 514-394-8804
888-270-3941
funds@nbc.ca
www.nbc.ca
Ownership: Private
Year Founded: 1987
Number of Employees: 23
Assets: $1-10 billion
Revenues: $50-100 million
Executives:
Charles Guay, President/CEO
Marc Knuepp, CFO
Renée Piette, Chief Compliance Officer
Martin Lavigne, Sr. Vice-President, Products & Sales
Michel Tremblay, Sr. Vice-President
Jean Blouin, Vice-President, Product Management; 514-394-6185
John Shephard Kennedy, Provincial Compliance Officer
Brigitte Roby, Section Manager, Registration
Sophie Clermont, Asst. Secretary
Directors:
Michel Tremblay, Chair
Gilles Corriveau
Pierre Desbiens
Denis Gauthier
Charles Guay
Françoise E. Lyon
National Bank:
Canadian Equity Fund
RRSP Eligible; Inception Year: 1988; Fund Managers:
Natcan Investment Management Inc.
Corporate Cash Management Fund
RRSP Eligible; Inception Year: 1995; Fund Managers:
Natcan Investment Management Inc.
Dividend Fund
RRSP Eligible; Inception Year: 1992; Fund Managers:
Natcan Investment Management Inc.
European Equity Fund
RRSP Eligible; Inception Year: 1992; Fund Managers:
Natcan Investment Management Inc.
Money Market Fund
RRSP Eligible; Inception Year: 1990; Fund Managers:
Natcan Investment Management Inc.
Mortgage Fund
RRSP Eligible; Inception Year: 1991; Fund Managers:
Natcan Investment Management Inc.
Retirement Balanced Fund
RRSP Eligible; Inception Year: 1988; Fund Managers:
Natcan Investment Management Inc.
Treasury Bill Plus Fund
RRSP Eligible; Inception Year: 1990; Fund Managers:
Natcan Investment Management Inc.
US Money Market Fund
RRSP Eligible; Inception Year: 1991; Fund Managers:
Natcan Investment Management Inc.
Bond Fund
RRSP Eligible; Inception Year: 1966; Fund Managers:
Natcan Investment Management Inc.
Treasury Management Fund
RRSP Eligible; Inception Year: 1997; Fund Managers:
Natcan Investment Management Inc.
American Index Plus Fund
RRSP Eligible; Inception Year: 1997; Fund Managers:
Natcan Investment Management Inc.
Protected Canadian Bond Fund
RRSP Eligible; Inception Year: 1998; Fund Managers:
Natcan Investment Management Inc.
Protected Retirement Balanced Fund
RRSP Eligible; Inception Year: 1998; Fund Managers:
Natcan Investment Management Inc.
Protected Growth Balanced Fund
RRSP Eligible; Inception Year: 1998; Fund Managers:
Natcan Investment Management Inc.

National Bank Securities Inc./ Placements banque nationale inc. (continued)

Protected Canadian Equity Fund
RRSP Eligible; Inception Year: 1998; Fund Managers:
Natcan Investment Management Inc.
Balanced Diversified Fund
RRSP Eligible; Inception Year: 1986; Fund Managers:
Natcan Investment Management Inc.
American Index Fund
RRSP Eligible; Inception Year: 1999; Fund Managers:
Natcan Investment Management Inc.
Canadian Index Fund
RRSP Eligible; Inception Year: 1999; Fund Managers:
Natcan Investment Management Inc.
Conservative Diversified Fund
RRSP Eligible; Inception Year: 1998; Fund Managers:
Natcan Investment Management Inc.
Emerging Markets Fund
RRSP Eligible; Inception Year: 2000; Fund Managers:
Baillie Gifford & Co.
European Small Capitalization Fund
RRSP Eligible; Inception Year: 2000; Fund Managers:
Natcan Investment Management Inc.
Future Economy Fund
RRSP Eligible; Inception Year: 1999; Fund Managers:
Natcan Investment Management Inc.
Global Equity Fund
RRSP Eligible; Inception Year: 2000; Fund Managers:
Natcan Investment Management Inc.
Global Bond Fund
RRSP Eligible; Inception Year: 1995; Fund Managers:
Natcan Investment Management Inc.
Global Technologies Fund
RRSP Eligible; Inception Year: 1999; Fund Managers:
Natcan Investment Management Inc.
International Index Fund
RRSP Eligible; Inception Year: 1998; Fund Managers:
Natcan Investment Management Inc.
Moderate Diversified Fund
RRSP Eligible; Inception Year: 1998; Fund Managers:
Natcan Investment Management Inc.
Natural Resources Fund
RRSP Eligible; Inception Year: 1999; Fund Managers:
Natcan Investment Management Inc.
Protected Global Fund
RRSP Eligible; Inception Year: 1998; Fund Managers:
Natcan Investment Management Inc.
Québec Growth Fund
RRSP Eligible; Inception Year: 1999; Fund Managers:
Natcan Investment Management Inc.
Secure Diversified Fund
RRSP Eligible; Inception Year: 1998; Fund Managers:
Natcan Investment Management Inc.
Small Capitalization Fund
RRSP Eligible; Inception Year: 1988; Fund Managers:
Natcan Investment Management Inc.
Asia-Pacific Fund
RRSP Eligible; Inception Year: 1994; Fund Managers:
Natcan Investment Management Inc.
American Index Plus Fund (US$)
RRSP Eligible; Inception Year: 1997; Fund Managers:
Natcan Investment Management Inc.
American Index Fund (US$)
RRSP Eligible; Inception Year: 1999; Fund Managers:
Natcan Investment Management Inc.
Canadian Opportunities Fund
RRSP Eligible; Inception Year: 1999; Fund Managers:
Natcan Investment Management Inc.
Growth Diversified Fund
RRSP Eligible; Inception Year: 1998; Fund Managers:
Natcan Investment Management Inc.
Canadian Index Plus Fund
RRSP Eligible; Inception Year: 1997; Fund Managers:
Natcan Investment Management Inc.
Balanced RSP Strategic Portfolio Fund
RRSP Eligible; Inception Year: 2001; Fund Managers:
Fidelity Investments
Balanced Strategic Portfolio Fund
RRSP Eligible; Inception Year: 2001; Fund Managers:
Fidelity Investments
Conservative Strategic Portfolio Fund
RRSP Eligible; Inception Year: 2001; Fund Managers:
Fidelity Investments
Conservative RSP Strategic Portfolio Fund
RRSP Eligible; Inception Year: 2001; Fund Managers:
Fidelity Investments
High Yield Bond Fund
RRSP Eligible; Inception Year: 2001; Fund Managers:
Natcan Investment Management Inc.
Equity Strategic Portfolio Fund
RRSP Eligible; Inception Year: 2001; Fund Managers:
Fidelity Investments
Moderate Strategic Portfolio Fund
RRSP Eligible; Inception Year: 2001; Fund Managers:
Fidelity Investments
Secure Strategic Portfolio Fund
RRSP Eligible; Inception Year: 2001; Fund Managers:
Natcan Investment Management Inc.
Strategic Yield Class Institutional Series FundInception Year: 2002; Fund Managers:
Natcan Investment Management Inc.
Strategic Yield Class M Series FundInception Year: 2002; Fund Managers:
Natcan Investment Management Inc.
Strategic Yield Class FundInception Year: 2002; Fund Managers:
Natcan Investment Management Inc.
Monthly Income Fund
RRSP Eligible; Inception Year: 2003; Fund Managers:
Natcan Investment Management Inc.
Growth Strategic Portfolio Fund
RRSP Eligible; Inception Year: 2001; Fund Managers:
Fidelity Investments
National Bank/Fidelity:
Canadian Asset Allocation Fund
RRSP Eligible; Inception Year: 2000; Fund Managers:
Fidelity Investments
International Portfolio Fund
RRSP Eligible; Inception Year: 2000; Fund Managers:
Fidelity Investments
True North Fund
RRSP Eligible; Inception Year: 2001; Fund Managers:
Fidelity Investments

NBF Turnkey Solutions Inc.

Also listed under: *Financial Planning*
The Exchange Tower
#3030, 130 King St. West
Toronto, ON M5X 1J9
416-482-6787
Fax: 416-482-0200
877-296-7872
info@opus2financial.com
www.opus2financial.com
Former Name: Opus 2 Financial; Opus 2 Direct.com
Ownership: Private; subsidiary of National Bank Financial
Year Founded: 1999
Number of Employees: 6
Assets: $100-500 million Year End: 20051130
Revenues: $1-5 million Year End: 20051130
Executives:
Anthony L. Cox, COO; 416-869-8907
Directors:
Anthony L. Cox
Michel Falk
Gordon J. Gibson
Diplomat:
Balanced Portfolio Fund
RRSP Eligible; Inception Year: 1997;
Growth Portfolio Fund
RRSP Eligible; Inception Year: 1997;
Maximum Growth Portfolio Fund
RRSP Eligible; Inception Year: 1997;
Emissary:
Canadian Fixed Income Fund
RRSP Eligible; Inception Year: 2002; Fund Managers:
Beutel Goodman & Company Ltd.
US Growth Fund
RRSP Eligible; Inception Year: 2002; Fund Managers:
Northstar Capital Management
US Value Fund
RRSP Eligible; Inception Year: 2002; Fund Managers:
Lord, Abbett & Co. LLC
Canadian Equity Fund
RRSP Eligible; Inception Year: 2002; Fund Managers:
Bissett Investment Management
Global Equity RSP Fund
RRSP Eligible; Inception Year: 2002; Fund Managers:
Toronto Dominion Quantitative Capital
International Equity EAFE Fund
RRSP Eligible; Inception Year: 2002; Fund Managers:
Lazard Asset Management
US Small/Mid Cap Fund
RRSP Eligible; Inception Year: 2002; Fund Managers:
AIM Private Asset Management Inc.

North Growth Management Ltd.

Also listed under: *Financial Planning*
One Bentall Centre
PO Box 56
#830, 505 Burrard St.
Vancouver, BC V7X 1M4
604-688-5440
Fax: 604-688-5402
info@northgrowth.com
www.northgrowth.com
Year Founded: 1998
Executives:
Jamie Kozak, Portfolio Manager
North Growth:
Canadian Money Market Fund
RRSP Eligible; Inception Year: 1999;
US Equity Fund
RRSP Eligible; Inception Year: 1992; Fund Managers:
Rudy North
Rory E.North
Erica Lau
Cynthia Yen
Canadian Equity Fund
RRSP Eligible; Inception Year: 2000; Fund Managers:
Rory E. North
Currency Hedge Limited Partnership FundInception Year: 2003; Fund Managers:
NGM Currency Hedge GP Ltd.

Northwest Mutual Funds Inc.

#715, 55 University Ave.
Toronto, ON M5J 2H7
416-594-6633
Fax: 416-594-3370
888-809-3333
clientservices@northwestfunds.com
www.northwestfunds.com
Year Founded: 1997
Number of Employees: 40
Assets: $1-10 billion
Profile: Northwest has over $2 billion in assets under administration and operates as a subsidiary of Desjardins Trust.
Executives:
Michael Butler, President/COO
Northwest:
Growth & Income Fund
RRSP Eligible; Inception Year: 1995; Fund Managers:
Kingwest & Company
Canadian Equity Fund
RRSP Eligible; Inception Year: 1992; Fund Managers:
Kingwest & Company
Foreign Equity Fund
RRSP Eligible; Inception Year: 1995; Fund Managers:
Foyston, Gordon & Payne
Money Market Fund
RRSP Eligible; Inception Year: 1992; Fund Managers:
Desjardins Global Asset Management Inc.
Specialty Equity Fund
RRSP Eligible; Inception Year: 1986; Fund Managers:
Montrusco Bolton Investments Inc.
Specialty High Yield Bond Fund
RRSP Eligible; Inception Year: 1992; Fund Managers:
AmerUs Capital Management
Specialty Innovations Fund
RRSP Eligible; Inception Year: 2000; Fund Managers:
Selective Asset Management
Canadian Bond Fund
RRSP Eligible; Inception Year: 0; Fund Managers:
Addenda Capital Inc.
Canadian Dividend Fund
RRSP Eligible; Inception Year: 0; Fund Managers:
Beutel, Goodman & Company Ltd.
Foreign EAFE Fund
RRSP Eligible; Inception Year: 0; Fund Managers:
Foyston, Gordon & Payne
Specialty Growth Fund Inc.
RRSP Eligible; Inception Year: 0; Fund Managers:
Montrusco Bolton Investments Inc.

US Equity Fund
RRSP Eligible; Inception Year: 0; Fund Managers: Kingwest & Company
Global High Yield Bond Fund
RRSP Eligible; Inception Year: 2005; Fund Managers: AmerUs Capital Management
Monthly Income Portfolio Fund
RRSP Eligible; Inception Year: 2005; Fund Managers: Northwest Asset Management Inc.
Northwest Quadrant:
All Equity Portfolio Fund
RRSP Eligible; Inception Year: 2005; Fund Managers: Northwest Asset Management Inc.
Growth & Income Portfolio Fund
RRSP Eligible; Inception Year: 2005; Fund Managers: Northwest Asset Management Inc.
Conservative Portfolio Fund
RRSP Eligible; Inception Year: 2005; Fund Managers: Northwest Asset Management Inc.
Branches:
Montréal
#1100, 615, boul René-Lévesque ouest
Montréal, QC H3B 1P5 Canada
514-286-3292
Fax: 514-286-3489
877-906-3332
Martin Hemcoui, Vice-President, National Sales, QCard, Eastern Canada
Vancouver
#570, 999 West Hastings St.
Vancouver, BC V6C 2W2 Canada
604-633-0615
Fax: 604-633-0619
866-888-0615
Lisa Stewart, Vice-President, National Sales, BC & AB

Optimum Placements Inc./ Optimum Investments Inc.

#30, 425, boul Maisonneuve ouest
Montréal, QC H3A 3G5
514-288-1600
Fax: 514-288-1567
888-678-4686
opi@groupe-optimum.com
www.fondsoptimum.com
Year Founded: 1986
Optimum:
Fonds Actions
RRSP Eligible; Inception Year: 1994; Fund Managers: Optimum Asset Management Inc.
Fonds Croissance et Revenus
RRSP Eligible; Inception Year: 1998; Fund Managers: Optimum Asset Management Inc.
Fonds Épargne
RRSP Eligible; Inception Year: 1986; Fund Managers: Optimum Asset Management Inc.
Fonds Équilibré
RRSP Eligible; Inception Year: 1986; Fund Managers: Optimum Asset Management Inc.
Fonds International
RRSP Eligible; Inception Year: 1994; Fund Managers: Optimum Asset Management Inc.
Fonds Obligations
RRSP Eligible; Inception Year: 1986; Fund Managers: Optimum Asset Management Inc.

OTG Financial Inc.

57 Mobile Dr.
Toronto, ON M4A 1H5
416-752-9410
Fax: 416-752-6649
800-263-9541
www.otgfinancial.com
Former Name: Ontario Teachers' Group
Year Founded: 1975
Executives:
Bob Dameron, President/CEO; bobd@otgfinancial.com
Marie Blanchet, Manager, Client Advisory Services
Georgiana Wan, Manager, Mortgage Services
OTG:
Balanced Fund
RRSP Eligible; Inception Year: 1984; Fund Managers: AEGON Capital Management Inc.
Diversified Fund
RRSP Eligible; Inception Year: 1975; Fund Managers: AEGON Capital Management Inc.
Growth Fund
RRSP Eligible; Inception Year: 1975; Fund Managers: Jones Heward Investment Counsel Inc.
Mortgage & Income Fund
RRSP Eligible; Inception Year: 1975; Fund Managers: HSBC Investments (Canada) Limited
Global Fund
RRSP Eligible; Inception Year: 1990; Fund Managers: HSBC Investments (Canada) Limited
Dividend Fund
RRSP Eligible; Inception Year: 2000; Fund Managers: Jones Heward Investment Counsel Inc.
Money Market Fund
RRSP Eligible; Inception Year: 1975; Fund Managers: AEGON Capital Management Inc.

PFSL Investments Canada Ltd.

Also listed under: *Investment Dealers*
Plaza V
#300, 2000 Argentia Rd.
Mississauga, ON L5N 2R7
905-812-2900
Fax: 905-813-5313
800-387-7876
www.primerica.com
Former Name: Primerica (PFSL) Invest Can Ltd.; PFS Canada
Ownership: Private. Wholly owned subsidiary of Primerica Financial Services (Canada) Ltd.
Year Founded: 1991
Number of Employees: 35
Assets: 20,074,113 Year End: 20051231
Revenues: $61,411,564 Year End: 20051231
Profile: The licensed mutual fund dealer is incorporated under the Canada Business Corporations Act. Other affiliated companies include Primerica Clients Services Inc., Primerica Financial Services Ltd., & Primerica Life Insurance Company of U.S.

Executives:
John Adams, CEO, Exec. Vice-President; 905-813-5345; johna.adams@primerica.com
Heather Koski, CFO & Vice-President, Finance
David Howarth, Sr. Vice-President, PFSL Operations; 905-813-5406; david.howarth@primerica.com
Guy Sauvé, Sr. Vice-President, Québec Marketing; 450-975-2400; guy.sauve@primerica.com
Elina C. DaSilva, Vice-President, Licensing & Agency Support; 905-813-5352; elina.dasilva@primerica.com
Waqas Rana, Vice-President, Chief Compliance Officer; 905-813-5327; waqas.rana@primerica.com
Directors:
John A. Adams; 905-813-5345
David Howarth; 905-813-5406
Heather Kaski; 905-813-5367
Affiliated Companies:
Primerica Life Insurance Company of Canada
Primerica:
Aggressive Growth Fund
RRSP Eligible; Inception Year: 0; Fund Managers: AGF Funds Inc.
Conservative Growth Fund
RRSP Eligible; Inception Year: 0; Fund Managers: AGF Funds Inc.
Moderate Growth Fund
RRSP Eligible; Inception Year: 0; Fund Managers: AGF Funds Inc.
Growth Fund
RRSP Eligible; Inception Year: 0; Fund Managers: AGF Funds Inc.
Income Fund
RRSP Eligible; Inception Year: 0; Fund Managers: AGF Funds Inc.
Canadian Money Market Fund
RRSP Eligible; Inception Year: 0; Fund Managers: AGF Funds Inc.

Phillips, Hager & North Investment Management Ltd.

Also listed under: *Financial Planning; Investment Management*

200 Burrard St., 20th Fl.
Vancouver, BC V6C 3N5
604-408-6100
Fax: 604-685-5712
800-661-6141
info@phn.com
www.phn.com
Also Known As: PH&N
Ownership: Private
Year Founded: 1964
Number of Employees: 294
Assets: $10-100 billion Year End: 20060930
Profile: Phillips, Hager & North offers a family of retail investment funds, as well as discretionary investment management. The firm manages over $50 billion in investments, on behalf of corporate & multi-employer pension plans, non-profit organizations & individuals across Canada. The company is affiliated with BonaVista Asset Management Ltd. & Sky Investment Counsel Inc.

Executives:
Scott M. Lamont, Lead Director
John S. Montalbano, President
Hanif Mamdani, Chief Investment Officer
Brian M. Walsh, Vice-President.CFO, Secretary
PH&N:
Balanced Fund
RRSP Eligible; Inception Year: 1991; Fund Managers: Sky Investment Counsel
Bond Fund
RRSP Eligible; Inception Year: 1970;
Canadian Equity Fund
RRSP Eligible; Inception Year: 1971;
Canadian Money Market Fund
RRSP Eligible; Inception Year: 1986;
Dividend Income Fund
RRSP Eligible; Inception Year: 1977;
Overseas Equity Pension Trust Fund
RRSP Eligible; Inception Year: 2000; Fund Managers: Sky Investment Counsel
US Growth Fund
RRSP Eligible; Inception Year: 1992;
Canadian Growth Fund
RRSP Eligible; Inception Year: 1987;
US Equity Fund
RRSP Eligible; Inception Year: 1964;
Short-Term Bond & Mortgage Fund
RRSP Eligible; Inception Year: 1993;
High Yield Bond Fund
RRSP Eligible; Inception Year: 2000;
Total Return Bond Fund
RRSP Eligible; Inception Year: 2000;
US Money Market Fund (US$)
RRSP Eligible; Inception Year: 1990;
Balanced Pension Trust Fund
RRSP Eligible; Inception Year: 2001;
Canadian Equity Plus Pension Trust Fund
RRSP Eligible; Inception Year: 1966;
Community Values Balanced Fund
RRSP Eligible; Inception Year: 2002; Fund Managers: Sky Investment Counsel
Community Values Bond Fund
RRSP Eligible; Inception Year: 2002;
Community Values Canadian Equity Fund
RRSP Eligible; Inception Year: 2002;
Community Values Global Equity Fund
RRSP Eligible; Inception Year: 2002; Fund Managers: Sky Investment Counsel
Global Equity Fund
RRSP Eligible; Inception Year: 2000; Fund Managers: Sky Investment Counsel
Overseas Equity Fund
RRSP Eligible; Inception Year: 2000; Fund Managers: Sky Investment Counsel
US Dividend Income Fund
RRSP Eligible; Inception Year: 2002;
Vintage Fund
RRSP Eligible; Inception Year: 1986;
Canadian Income Fund
RRSP Eligible; Inception Year: 2005;
Branches:
Calgary
West Tower, Bankers Hall
#4430, 888 - 3rd St. SW
Calgary, AB T2P 5C5 Canada
403-515-6825
Fax: 403-515-6849
Mark Williams, Vice-President
Montréal
#2821, 1 Place Ville Marie
Montréal, QC H3B 4R4 Canada

Phillips, Hager & North Investment Management Ltd. (continued)
514-288-4966
Fax: 514-288-4876
Kathy Fazel, Vice-President
Toronto
One Financial Place
PO Box 207
#2320, 1 Adelaide St. East
Toronto, ON M5C 2V9 Canada
416-601-0027
Fax: 416-601-0109
A. Mark DeCelles, Vice-President
Victoria
St. Andrew's Square I
#312, 737 Yates St.
Victoria, BC V8W 1L6 Canada
250-405-7300
Fax: 250-405-7301
James Darke, Vice-President

Quadrus Investment Services Ltd.

Also listed under: *Investment Dealers*
255 Dufferin Ave.
London, ON N6A 4K1
519-432-5281
Fax: 519-435-7679
888-532-3322
quadrusclientservices@quadrusinvestment.com
www.londonlife.com
Ownership: Wholly owned subsidiary of London Life Insurance Company, London, ON.
Profile: The mutual fund dealer has more than 3,400 registered investment representatives.
Executives:
Alf Goodall, Vice-President
Quadrus Group of Funds:
LLIM Canadian Diversified Equity Fund
RRSP Eligible; Inception Year: 1999; Fund Managers: London Life Investment Management Ltd.
LLIM Canadian Bond Fund
RRSP Eligible; Inception Year: 1999; Fund Managers: London Life Investment Management Ltd.
LLIM Income Plus Fund
RRSP Eligible; Inception Year: 1999; Fund Managers: London Life Investment Management Ltd.
Advanced Folio Fund
RRSP Eligible; Inception Year: 2001; Fund Managers: Mackenzie Financial Corporation
Aggressive Folio Fund
RRSP Eligible; Inception Year: 2001; Fund Managers: Mackenzie Financial Corporation
Balanced Folio Fund
RRSP Eligible; Inception Year: 2001; Fund Managers: Mackenzie Financial Corporation
Canadian Equity Folio Fund
RRSP Eligible; Inception Year: 2001; Fund Managers: Mackenzie Financial Corporation
Conservative Folio Fund
RRSP Eligible; Inception Year: 2001; Fund Managers: Mackenzie Financial Corporation
Fixed Income Folio Fund
RRSP Eligible; Inception Year: 2001; Fund Managers: Mackenzie Financial Corporation
Global Equity Folio Fund
RRSP Eligible; Inception Year: 2001; Fund Managers: Mackenzie Financial Corporation
GWLIM Canadian Growth Fund
RRSP Eligible; Inception Year: 2001; Fund Managers: GWL Investment Management Ltd.
GWLIM Canadian Mid Cap Fund
RRSP Eligible; Inception Year: 2001; Fund Managers: GWL Investment Management Ltd.
GWLIM Corporate Bond Fund
RRSP Eligible; Inception Year: 2001; Fund Managers: GWL Investment Management Ltd.
GWLIM Ethics Fund
RRSP Eligible; Inception Year: 2001; Fund Managers: GWL Investment Management Ltd.
GWLIM US Mid Cap Fund
RRSP Eligible; Inception Year: 2001; Fund Managers: GWL Investment Management Ltd.
LLIM US Equity Fund
RRSP Eligible; Inception Year: 2001; Fund Managers: London Life Investment Management Ltd.
LLIM US Growth Sectors Fund
RRSP Eligible; Inception Year: 2001; Fund Managers: London Life Investment Management Ltd.
Mackenzie Ivy European Capital Fund
RRSP Eligible; Inception Year: 2003; Fund Managers: Mackenzie Financial Corporation
Mackenzie Maxxum Canadian Balanced Fund
RRSP Eligible; Inception Year: 1988; Fund Managers: Mackenzie Financial Corporation
Mackenzie Maxxum Canadian Equity Growth Fund
RRSP Eligible; Inception Year: 1970; Fund Managers: Mackenzie Financial Corporation
Mackenzie Maxxum Dividend Fund
RRSP Eligible; Inception Year: 1986; Fund Managers: Mackenzie Financial Corporation
Mackenzie Maxxum Money Market Fund
RRSP Eligible; Inception Year: 1986; Fund Managers: Mackenzie Financial Corporation
Mackenzie Universal American Growth Capital Fund
RRSP Eligible; Inception Year: 2002; Fund Managers: Bluewater Investment Management Inc.
Mackenzie Universal Canadian Resource Fund
RRSP Eligible; Inception Year: 2002; Fund Managers: Mackenzie Financial Corporation
Mackenzie Universal Precious Metals Fund
RRSP Eligible; Inception Year: 2002; Fund Managers: Mackenzie Financial Corporation
Moderate Folio Fund
RRSP Eligible; Inception Year: 2001; Fund Managers: Mackenzie Financial Corporation
Quadrus Templeton Canadian Equity Fund
RRSP Eligible; Inception Year: 1999; Fund Managers: Franklin Templeton Investments
Quadrus Templeton International Equity Fund
RRSP Eligible; Inception Year: 1999; Fund Managers: Franklin Templeton Investments
Mackenzie Select Managers Canada Fund
RRSP Eligible; Inception Year: 2002; Fund Managers: Henderson Global Investors Ltd.
Quadrus Trimark Balanced Fund
RRSP Eligible; Inception Year: 2003; Fund Managers: AIM Trimark Investment Management
Mackenzie Universal Global Future Fund
RRSP Eligible; Inception Year: 1995; Fund Managers: Mackenzie Financial Corporation
Mackenzie Universal US Growth Leaders Fund
RRSP Eligible; Inception Year: 1995; Fund Managers: Waddell & Reed Inc.
Quadrus Trimark Global Equity Fund
RRSP Eligible; Inception Year: 2003; Fund Managers: AIM Trimark Investment Management
Mackenzie Select Managers Far East Capital Fund
RRSP Eligible; Inception Year: 2002; Fund Managers: Pacific Regional Group
Mackenzie Universal Emerging Markets Capital Fund
RRSP Eligible; Inception Year: 2002; Fund Managers: J.P. Morgan Fleming Asset Management
AIM Canadian Equity Growth Fund
RRSP Eligible; Inception Year: 2001; Fund Managers: AIM Trimark Investment Management
Cash Management Corporate Class Fund
RRSP Eligible; Inception Year: 2005;
Canadian Equity Corporate Class Fund
RRSP Eligible; Inception Year: 2005;
Canadian Specialty Corporate Class Fund
RRSP Eligible; Inception Year: 2005;
Fixed Income Corporate Class Fund
RRSP Eligible; Inception Year: 2005;
Laketon Fixed Income Series Q Fund
RRSP Eligible; Inception Year: 1974; Fund Managers: Laketon Investment Management
US & International Equity Corporate Class Fund
RRSP Eligible; Inception Year: 2005;
US & International Specialty Corporate Class Fund
RRSP Eligible; Inception Year: 2005;

R.A. Floyd Capital Management Inc.

1649 Birchwood Dr.
Mississauga, ON L5J 1T5
905-823-2500
Fax: 905-823-4288
877-734-2500
Ownership: Private
Year Founded: 1999
Number of Employees: 2
Assets: $1-5 million Year End: 20051105
Revenues: Under $1 million Year End: 20051105
Executives:
Judith Socha, Manager, Marketing & Administration; 905-823-2500; j_socha@rafloydcapital.com
Floyd:
Growth Fund
RRSP Eligible; Inception Year: 2000; Fund Managers: Robert Floyd

RBC Asset Management Inc. - RBC Funds

TD Centre, Royal Trust Tower
PO Box 7500, A Stn. A
Toronto, ON M5W 1P9
800-769-2599
funds@rbc.com
www.rbcfunds.com
Former Name: Royal Mutual Funds Inc.
Executives:
George Lewis, CEO
Brenda Vince, President; 955-223-
Dan Chornous, Chief Investment Officer
RBC:
Asian Equity Fund
RRSP Eligible; Inception Year: 1993; Fund Managers: RBC Investment Management (Asia) Ltd.
Balanced Fund
RRSP Eligible; Inception Year: 1987;
Canadian Growth Fund
RRSP Eligible; Inception Year: 1993; Fund Managers: Warner Sulz
Energy Fund
RRSP Eligible; Inception Year: 1980; Fund Managers: Gordon P. Zive
European Equity Fund
RRSP Eligible; Inception Year: 1987; Fund Managers: RBC Asset Management (UK) Ltd.
International Equity Fund
RRSP Eligible; Inception Year: 1993; Fund Managers: RBC Investment Management (Asia) Ltd.
Life Science & Technology Fund
RRSP Eligible; Inception Year: 1995; Fund Managers: Raymond Mawhinney
VincentFernandez
Precious Metals Fund
RRSP Eligible; Inception Year: 1988; Fund Managers: Chris Beer
US Equity Fund
RRSP Eligible; Inception Year: 1966; Fund Managers: Raymond Mawhinney
Global Bond Fund
RRSP Eligible; Inception Year: 1991;
Money Market Fund (US$)
RRSP Eligible; Inception Year: 1990; Fund Managers: Walter Posiewko
Canadian Equity Fund
RRSP Eligible; Inception Year: 1967; Fund Managers: John Varao
WarnerSulz
Canadian Money Market Fund
RRSP Eligible; Inception Year: 1986; Fund Managers: Walter Posiewko
Dividend Fund
RRSP Eligible; Inception Year: 1993; Fund Managers: John Varao
ShaneJones
Doug Raymond
Monthly Income Fund
RRSP Eligible; Inception Year: 1997; Fund Managers: John Varao
Balanced Growth Fund
RRSP Eligible; Inception Year: 1998; Fund Managers: Warner Sulz
MartinPaleczny
Canadian Index Fund
RRSP Eligible; Inception Year: 1998; Fund Managers: State Street Global Advisors
US RSP Index Fund
RRSP Eligible; Inception Year: 1998; Fund Managers: State Street Global Advisors
Premium Money Market Fund
RRSP Eligible; Inception Year: 1997; Fund Managers: Walter Posiewko

US Index Fund
RRSP Eligible; Inception Year: 1998; Fund Managers:
State Street Global Advisors
International RSP Index Fund
RRSP Eligible; Inception Year: 1998; Fund Managers:
State Street Global Advisors
Canadian T-Bill Fund
RRSP Eligible; Inception Year: 1991; Fund Managers:
Walter Posiewko
Canadian Bond Index Fund
RRSP Eligible; Inception Year: 2000; Fund Managers:
Suzanne Gaynor
Select Choices Aggressive Growth Portfolio Fund
RRSP Eligible; Inception Year: 2000; Fund Managers:
John Varao
Select Choices Balanced Portfolio Fund
RRSP Eligible; Inception Year: 2000; Fund Managers:
John Varao
Select Choices Growth Portfolio Fund
RRSP Eligible; Inception Year: 2000; Fund Managers:
John Varao
Select Choices Conservative Portfolio Fund
RRSP Eligible; Inception Year: 2000; Fund Managers:
John Varao
O'Shaughnessy Canadian Equity Fund
RRSP Eligible; Inception Year: 1997; Fund Managers:
Bear Stearns Asset Management Inc.
O'Shaughnessy US Value Fund
RRSP Eligible; Inception Year: 1997; Fund Managers:
Bear Stearns Asset Management Inc.
O'Shaughnessy US Growth Fund
RRSP Eligible; Inception Year: 1997; Fund Managers:
Bear Stearns Asset Management Inc.
Global Balanced Fund
RRSP Eligible; Inception Year: 1995; Fund Managers:
Sarah Khoo
Global Communications & Media Sector Fund
RRSP Eligible; Inception Year: 2000; Fund Managers:
Raymond Mawhinney
PatrickLau
Global Consumer Trends Sector Fund
RRSP Eligible; Inception Year: 2000; Fund Managers:
Paul Johnson
Global Financial Services Sector Fund
RRSP Eligible; Inception Year: 2000; Fund Managers:
Vincent Fernandez
Global Health Sciences Sector Fund
RRSP Eligible; Inception Year: 2000; Fund Managers:
Vincent Fernandez
RaymondMawhinney
Global Industrials Sector Fund
RRSP Eligible; Inception Year: 2000; Fund Managers:
Paul Johnson
Global Resources Sector Fund
RRSP Eligible; Inception Year: 2000; Fund Managers:
Chris Beer
Global Technology Sector Fund
RRSP Eligible; Inception Year: 2000; Fund Managers:
Raymond Mawhinney
Global Titans Fund
RRSP Eligible; Inception Year: 2000; Fund Managers:
Sarah Khoo
Select Balanced Portfolio Fund
RRSP Eligible; Inception Year: 1986; Fund Managers:
John Varao
Select Growth Portfolio Fund
RRSP Eligible; Inception Year: 1986; Fund Managers:
John Varao
US Equity (US$) Fund
RRSP Eligible; Inception Year: 1972; Fund Managers:
Raymond Mawhinney
US Mid-Cap Equity Fund
RRSP Eligible; Inception Year: 1992; Fund Managers:
Raymond Mawhinney
US Mid-Cap Equity (US$) Fund
RRSP Eligible; Inception Year: 1992; Fund Managers:
Raymond Mawhinney
Canadian Value Fund
RRSP Eligible; Inception Year: 1998; Fund Managers:
Stuart Kedwell
DougRaymond
Global Education Fund
RRSP Eligible; Inception Year: 1998; Fund Managers:
Raymond Mawhinney
Tax Managed Return Fund
RRSP Eligible; Inception Year: 2002; Fund Managers:
John Varao
Canadian Short-Term Income Fund
RRSP Eligible; Inception Year: 1992; Fund Managers:
Walter Posiewko
Bond Fund
RRSP Eligible; Inception Year: 1972;
Global High Yield Fund
RRSP Eligible; Inception Year: 2001; Fund Managers:
Jane Lesslie
FrankGambino
Global Corporate Bond Fund
RRSP Eligible; Inception Year: 2004; Fund Managers:
Frank Gambino
Cash Flow Portfolio Fund
RRSP Eligible; Inception Year: 2004; Fund Managers:
John Varao
Enhanced Cash Flow Portfolio Fund
RRSP Eligible; Inception Year: 2004; Fund Managers:
John Varao
Select Conservative Portfolio Fund
RRSP Eligible; Inception Year: 1986; Fund Managers:
John Varao
Target 2010 Education Fund
RRSP Eligible; Inception Year: 2004; Fund Managers:
John Varao
Target 2015 Education Fund
RRSP Eligible; Inception Year: 2004; Fund Managers:
John Varao
Target 2020 Education Fund
RRSP Eligible; Inception Year: 2004; Fund Managers:
John Varao
O'Shaughnessy Equity Fund
RRSP Eligible; Inception Year: 2005; Fund Managers:
Bear Stearns Asset Management Inc.
Advisor Canadian Bond Fund
RRSP Eligible; Inception Year: 1999; Fund Managers:
Suzanne Gaynor
Income (US$) Fund
RRSP Eligible; Inception Year: 2005; Fund Managers:
Raymond Mawhinney
StuartKedwell
Frank Gambino
Doug Raymond
Blue Chip Canadian Equity Fund
RRSP Eligible; Inception Year: 2001; Fund Managers:
Shane Jones
JohnVarao
Doug Raymond
US Equity Currency Neutral Fund
RRSP Eligible; Inception Year: 2006; Fund Managers:
Raymond Mawhinney
US Mid-Cap Equity Currency Neutral Fund
RRSP Eligible; Inception Year: 2006; Fund Managers:
Raymond Mawhinney
DS Aggressive Growth Global Portfolio Fund
RRSP Eligible; Inception Year: 2005;
DS Balanced Global Portfolio Fund
RRSP Eligible; Inception Year: 2005;
DS Canadian Focus Fund
RRSP Eligible; Inception Year: 2004;
DS Growth Global Portfolio Fund
RRSP Eligible; Inception Year: 2005;
DS North American Focus Fund
RRSP Eligible; Inception Year: 2003;

Retrocom Growth Fund Inc.

#400, 135 Queens Plate Dr.
Toronto, ON M9W 6V1
416-745-5775
Fax: 416-745-5766
888-743-5627
info@retro.ca
www.rgfjobs.com
Ownership: Public
Year Founded: 1995
Profile: Retrocom is a labour-sponsored investment fund corporation. The Fund presently has assets invested in a portfolio of investments in the following sectors: commercial & residential construction, resort condominium, sports entertainment, facilities management & tourism.

Executives:
Walter Davies, Interim CEO, Retrocom Mid-Market Real Estate Investment Trust
David Fiume, CFO & Vice-President, Finance
Paul McKenna, Contact, Investor Relations; PMckenna@retrocom.ca
Directors:
Patrick Lavelle, Chair
Retrocom:
Growth Fund
RRSP Eligible; Inception Year: 1995; Fund Managers:
Dean Wilkinson
RogerKeane
Growth C Fund
RRSP Eligible; Inception Year: 1995; Fund Managers:
Roger Keane
DeanWilkinson
Growth V Fund
RRSP Eligible; Inception Year: 2005; Fund Managers:
Roger Keane
Growth V Fund
RRSP Eligible; Inception Year: 2005; Fund Managers:
Dean Wilkinson
Branches:
Bedford
#404, 80 Waterfront Dr.
Bedford, NS B4A 4E4 Canada
902-832-0821
Fax: 902-832-9724
jcoulos@eastlink.ca
Mississauga
2920 Matheson Blvd. East
Mississauga, ON L4W 5J4 Canada
905-214-8155
Fax: 905-214-8100
866-249-8819

Saxon Mutual Funds

PO Box 9
#1700, 151 Yonge St.
Toronto, ON M5C 2W7
416-979-1818
Fax: 416-979-7424
888-287-2966
service@saxonfunds.com
www.saxonfunds.com
Ownership: Private
Year Founded: 1985
Profile: Total assets under management exceed $300 million. Funds carry no sales charge, redemption fees, set up costs, no RSP & RIF fees, & no switching fees. The minimum investment per fund is $5,000.

Saxon:
Balanced Fund
RRSP Eligible; Inception Year: 1986; Fund Managers:
Howson Tatersall Investment Counsel Ltd.
High Income Fund
RRSP Eligible; Inception Year: 1997; Fund Managers:
Howson Tatersall Investment Counsel Ltd.
Small Cap Fund
RRSP Eligible; Inception Year: 1986; Fund Managers:
Howson Tatersall Investment Counsel Ltd.
Stock Fund
RRSP Eligible; Inception Year: 1986; Fund Managers:
Howson Tatersall Investment Counsel Ltd.
World Growth Fund
RRSP Eligible; Inception Year: 1986; Fund Managers:
Howson Tatersall Investment Counsel Ltd.
Money Market Fund
RRSP Eligible; Inception Year: 2004; Fund Managers:
Howson Tatersall Investment Counsel Ltd.
Bond Fund
RRSP Eligible; Inception Year: 2004; Fund Managers:
Howson Tatersall Investment Counsel Ltd.
US Equity Fund
RRSP Eligible; Inception Year: 2005; Fund Managers:
Howson Tatersall Investment Counsel Ltd.
International Equity Fund
RRSP Eligible; Inception Year: 2005; Fund Managers:
Howson Tatersall Investment Counsel Ltd.

Sceptre Investment Counsel Limited

Also listed under:* *Financial Planning
#1200, 26 Wellington St. East
Toronto, ON M5E 1W4

INVESTMENT MANAGEMENT

Sceptre Investment Counsel Limited (continued)
416-601-9898
Fax: 416-367-8716
800-265-1888
mail@sceptre.ca
www.sceptre.ca
Ownership: Public
Year Founded: 1955
Number of Employees: 50
Assets: $10-50 million
Revenues: $10-50 million
Stock Symbol: SZ
Profile: Sceptre Investment Counsel Limited provides the following services: investment management to institutional clients; pension & savings plans to corporations, municipalities, universities, foundations & other organizations; & personal asset-management to individual investors.

Executives:
Richard Lee Knowles, President/CEO
Matthew Baillie, Managing Director
John J. Brophy, Managing Director
Glenn Inamoto, Managing Director
David B. Pennycook, Managing Director
Mario D. Richard, Managing Director
F. John Stittle, Managing Director
David R. Morris, Chief Financial Officer
Robert R. Lorimer, Vice-President
James A. Sutherland, Vice-President
Directors:
W. Ross Walker, Chair
Richard Lee Knowles
Patricia Meredith
Arthur R.A. Scace, QC
David R. Shaw
Robert Thomson
Sceptre:
Balanced Growth Fund
RRSP Eligible; Inception Year: 1985;
Bond Fund
RRSP Eligible; Inception Year: 1985; Fund Managers:
Thomas Czitron
Equity Growth Fund
RRSP Eligible; Inception Year: 1986; Fund Managers:
Allan Jacobs
Global Equity Fund
RRSP Eligible; Inception Year: 1986; Fund Managers:
Putnam Sub-Advisory Company Inc.
US Equity Fund
RRSP Eligible; Inception Year: 1998;
Canadian Equity Fund
RRSP Eligible; Inception Year: 1998;

Scotia Securities Inc.

Scotia Plaza
40 King St. West, 16th Fl.
Toronto, ON M5H 1H1
416-750-3863
Fax: 416-288-4455
800-268-9269
email@scotiabank.ca
www.scotiabank.ca
Ownership: Wholly owned subsidiary of the Bank of Nova Scotia
Year Founded: 1986
Stock Symbol: BNS
Profile: Mutual funds are distributed across Canada.

Executives:
Karen J. Fisher, President/CEO; 416-866-2021
Scotia:
Canadian Balanced Fund
RRSP Eligible; Inception Year: 1990; Fund Managers:
Scotia Cassels Investment Counsel Ltd.
Canadian Blue Chip Fund
RRSP Eligible; Inception Year: 1986; Fund Managers:
Scotia Cassels Investment Counsel Ltd.
Canadian Growth Fund
RRSP Eligible; Inception Year: 1961; Fund Managers:
Scotia Cassels Investment Counsel Ltd.
T-Bill Fund
RRSP Eligible; Inception Year: 1991; Fund Managers:
Scotia Cassels Investment Counsel Ltd.
Latin American Growth Fund
RRSP Eligible; Inception Year: 1994; Fund Managers:
TCW Investment Management Co.
Money Market Fund
RRSP Eligible; Inception Year: 1990; Fund Managers:
Scotia Cassels Investment Counsel Ltd.
Mortgage Income Fund
RRSP Eligible; Inception Year: 1992; Fund Managers:
Scotia Cassels Investment Counsel Ltd.
Pacific Rim Growth Fund
RRSP Eligible; Inception Year: 1994; Fund Managers:
TCW Investment Management Co.
Premium T-Bill Fund
RRSP Eligible; Inception Year: 1992; Fund Managers:
Scotia Cassels Investment Counsel Ltd.
Total Return Fund
RRSP Eligible; Inception Year: 1989; Fund Managers:
Connor, Clark & Lunn Investment Management
European Growth Fund
RRSP Eligible; Inception Year: 1996; Fund Managers:
Alliance Capital Management Canada, Inc.
Canadian Income Fund
RRSP Eligible; Inception Year: 1957; Fund Managers:
Scotia Cassels Investment Counsel Ltd.
CanGlobal Income Fund
RRSP Eligible; Inception Year: 1994; Fund Managers:
Scotia Cassels Investment Counsel Ltd.
Canadian Stock Index Fund
RRSP Eligible; Inception Year: 1996; Fund Managers:
State Street Global Advisors Ltd.
American Growth Fund
RRSP Eligible; Inception Year: 1986; Fund Managers:
Scotia Cassels Investment Counsel Ltd.
Canadian Small Cap Fund
RRSP Eligible; Inception Year: 1992; Fund Managers:
Scotia Cassels Investment Counsel Ltd.
International Stock Index Fund
RRSP Eligible; Inception Year: 1999; Fund Managers:
State Street Global Advisors Ltd.
Canadian Bond Index Fund
RRSP Eligible; Inception Year: 1999; Fund Managers:
State Street Global Advisors Ltd.
Canadian Dividend Fund
RRSP Eligible; Inception Year: 1992; Fund Managers:
Scotia Cassels Investment Counsel Ltd.
Global Growth Fund
RRSP Eligible; Inception Year: 1961; Fund Managers:
Capital International Asset Management (Canada)
NASDAQ Index Fund
RRSP Eligible; Inception Year: 2000; Fund Managers:
Scotia Cassels Investment Counsel Ltd.
Premium T-Bill ($250-$1MM) Fund
RRSP Eligible; Inception Year: 1999; Fund Managers:
Scotia Cassels Investment Counsel Ltd.
Premium T-Bill ($1MM) Fund
RRSP Eligible; Inception Year: 1999; Fund Managers:
Scotia Cassels Investment Counsel Ltd.
Resource Fund
RRSP Eligible; Inception Year: 1993; Fund Managers:
Scotia Cassels Investment Counsel Ltd.
Young Investors Fund
RRSP Eligible; Inception Year: 2000; Fund Managers:
Scotia Cassels Investment Counsel Ltd.
Capital Global Discovery Fund
RRSP Eligible; Inception Year: 2000; Fund Managers:
Capital International Asset Management (Canada)
Capital Global Small Companies Fund
RRSP Eligible; Inception Year: 2000; Fund Managers:
Capital International Asset Management (Canada)
Capital International Large Companies Fund
RRSP Eligible; Inception Year: 2000; Fund Managers:
Capital International Asset Management (Canada)
Capital US Large Companies Fund
RRSP Eligible; Inception Year: 2000; Fund Managers:
Capital International Asset Management (Canada)
Capital US Small Companies Fund
RRSP Eligible; Inception Year: 2000; Fund Managers:
Capital International Asset Management (Canada)
American Stock Index Fund
RRSP Eligible; Inception Year: 1996; Fund Managers:
State Street Global Advisors Ltd.
Diversified Monthly Income Fund
RRSP Eligible; Inception Year: 2005; Fund Managers:
Scotia Cassels Investment Counsel Ltd.
Scotia CanAm:
Stock Index Fund
RRSP Eligible; Inception Year: 1993; Fund Managers:
Scotia Cassels Investment Counsel Ltd.
US Income (US$) Fund
RRSP Eligible; Inception Year: 1992;
US Money Market (US$) Fund
RRSP Eligible; Inception Year: 1996; Fund Managers:
Scotia Cassels Investment Counsel Ltd.
Scotia Partners:
Income & Modest Growth Portfolio Fund
RRSP Eligible; Inception Year: 2002; Fund Managers:
Scotia Capital Inc.
Balanced Income & Growth Portfolio Fund
RRSP Eligible; Inception Year: 2002; Fund Managers:
Scotia Capital Inc.
Conservative Growth Portfolio Fund
RRSP Eligible; Inception Year: 2002; Fund Managers:
Scotia Capital Inc.
Aggressive Growth Portfolio Fund
RRSP Eligible; Inception Year: 2002; Fund Managers:
Scotia Capital Inc.
Scotia Selected:
Income & Modest Growth Fund
RRSP Eligible; Inception Year: 2003; Fund Managers:
Scotia Capital Inc.
Balanced Income & Growth Fund
RRSP Eligible; Inception Year: 2003; Fund Managers:
Scotia Capital Inc.
Conservative Growth Fund
RRSP Eligible; Inception Year: 2003; Fund Managers:
Scotia Capital Inc.
Aggressive Growth Fund
RRSP Eligible; Inception Year: 2003; Fund Managers:
Scotia Capital Inc.
Scotia Vision:
Conservative 2010 Fund
RRSP Eligible; Inception Year: 2005; Fund Managers:
Scotia Capital Inc.
Aggressive 2010 Fund
RRSP Eligible; Inception Year: 2005; Fund Managers:
Scotia Capital Inc.
Conservative 2015 Fund
RRSP Eligible; Inception Year: 2005; Fund Managers:
Scotia Capital Inc.
Aggressive 2015 Fund
RRSP Eligible; Inception Year: 2005; Fund Managers:
Scotia Capital Inc.
Conservative 2020 Fund
RRSP Eligible; Inception Year: 2005; Fund Managers:
Scotia Capital Inc.
Aggressive 2020 Fund
RRSP Eligible; Inception Year: 2005; Fund Managers:
Scotia Capital Inc.
Conservative 2030 Fund
RRSP Eligible; Inception Year: 2005; Fund Managers:
Scotia Capital Inc.
Aggressive 2030 Fund
RRSP Eligible; Inception Year: 2005; Fund Managers:
Scotia Capital Inc.

Sentry Select Capital Corp.

Also listed under: *Financial Planning*
The Exchange Tower
PO Box 104
#2850, 130 King St. West
Toronto, ON M5X 1A4
416-861-8729
Fax: 416-364-1330
888-246-6656
info@sentryselect.com
www.sentryselect.com
Ownership: Public.
Assets: $1-10 billion Year End: 20060000
Stock Symbol: SYI
Profile: Sentry Select Capital is a Canadian investment manager. Working in the income trust sector, the company provides administrative, investment & marketing services to the following: exchange-listed closed-end funds, principal-protected notes, flow-through limited partnerships & mutuals funds.

Executives:
John F. Driscoll, President/CEO
Al Canale, Sr. Vice-President, Corporate Development
Raniero Corsini, Sr. Vice-President, Global Structured Products
Michael Kovacs, Sr. Vice-President, Sales
David M. Schwartz, Sr. Vice-President
Gordon Thompson, Sr. Vice-President, Corporate Development
John Vooglaid, Sr. Vice-President/CFO

Wolfgang Kruning, Vice-President, International Dealer Relations
Brian J. McOstrich, Vice-President, Marketing
Don Perras, Vice-President, Business Development
Ara Nalbandian, Sr. Manager, Portfolio
Michael Simpson, CFA, Sr. Manager, Portfolio
John Sinkins, Sr. Manager, Portfolio
Laura Lau, Manager, Portfolio
Philip Yuzpe, Manager, Strategic Planning & Research
Ari Silverberg, Director, Real Estate Investments
CAPVEST Income Corp.:
Specialty Products Fund
RRSP Eligible; Inception Year: 2005;
Mortgage-Backed Securities Limited Partnership:
Adjustable Rate Income FundInception Year: 2004; Fund Managers:
Fixed Income Discount Advisory Company
Adjustable Rate Income II FundInception Year: 2005; Fund Managers:
Fixed Income Discount Advisory Company
Income Trust FundInception Year: 2003; Fund Managers:
Fixed Income Discount Advisory Company
NCE:
Diversified Flow-Through (05-02) Limited Partnership FundInception Year: 0; Fund Managers:
Kevin MacLean
GlennMacNeill
Pro-Vest:
Growth & Income FundInception Year: 2004; Fund Managers:
James Alexander (San McIntyre
Sentry:
Canadian Energy Growth Fund
RRSP Eligible; Inception Year: 1997; Fund Managers:
Glenn MacNeill
Canadian Resource Fund
RRSP Eligible; Inception Year: 2000; Fund Managers:
Glenn MacNeill
Precious Metals Growth Fund
RRSP Eligible; Inception Year: 1997; Fund Managers:
Kevin MacLean
Canadian Income Fund
RRSP Eligible; Inception Year: 2002; Fund Managers:
James Alexander (San McIntyre
REIT Fund
RRSP Eligible; Inception Year: 1997; Fund Managers:
James Alexander (San McIntyre
Focused 50 Income Fund
RRSP Eligible; Inception Year: 2003; Fund Managers:
James Alexander (San McIntyre
Money Market Fund
RRSP Eligible; Inception Year: 2003; Fund Managers:
James Alexander (San McIntyre
Diversified Total Return Fund
RRSP Eligible; Inception Year: 2005; Fund Managers:
Gordon R. Higgins
Small Cap Income Fund
RRSP Eligible; Inception Year: 2005; Fund Managers:
James Alexander (San McIntyre
Dividend Fund
RRSP Eligible; Inception Year: 2006; Fund Managers:
Gordon R. Higgins
Principal-Protected Blue Chip Notes Fund
RRSP Eligible; Inception Year: 2004;
Strategic Energy Fund
RRSP Eligible; Inception Year: 2002; Fund Managers:
Glenn MacNeill
Diversified Income Trust Portfolio FundInception Year: 1997; Fund Managers:
James Alexander (San McIntyre
Diversified Income Trust Portfolio II FundInception Year: 2002; Fund Managers:
James Alexander (San McIntyre
Premier Value Income Trust FundInception Year: 2005; Fund Managers:
James Alexander (San McIntyre
Focused Growth & Income Trust FundInception Year: 2002; Fund Managers:
James Alexander (San McIntyre
Commercial & Industrial Securities Income Trust FundInception Year: 2002; Fund Managers:
James Alexander (San McIntyre
Select 50 S-1 Income Trust FundInception Year: 2003; Fund Managers:
James Alexander (San McIntyre
Alliance Split Income Trust FundInception Year: 2004;
Multi Select Income Trust FundInception Year: 2004;
Select Commodities Income Trust FundInception Year: 2005; Fund Managers:
James Alexander (San McIntyre
Blue-Chip Income Trust Fund
RRSP Eligible; Inception Year: 2001;
Global Index Income Trust FundInception Year: 2001;
Diversified Preferred Share Trust FundInception Year: 2002;
Global DiSCS Trust 04-1 FundInception Year: 2004;
Oil Sands Split Trust FundInception Year: 2003;
Balanced Fund
RRSP Eligible; Inception Year: 2005; Fund Managers:
Gordon R. Higgins
Sentry FIDAC:
US Mortgage Trust FundInception Year: 2005; Fund Managers:
Fixed Income Discount Advisory Company
Sentry Rogers:
International Commodity Index Principal-Protected Notes Fund
RRSP Eligible; Inception Year: 2005; Fund Managers:
Diapason Commodities Management SA

Skylon Advisors Inc.

CI Place
151 Yonge St., 10th Fl.
Toronto, ON M5C 2W7
416-681-8894
Fax: 416-364-2969
800-822-0245
info@skylonadvisor.com
www.skyloncapital.com
Former Name: Skylon Capital Corp.; VentureLink Capital Corp.
Ownership: Wholly-owned subsidiary of CI Financial.
Year Founded: 2000
Assets: $1-10 billion
Executives:
David R. MacBain, President & CEO
Douglas J. Jamieson, Chief Financial Officer
Michael J. Killeen, Corporate Secretary & Director
DDJ:
High Yield FundInception Year: 1997; Fund Managers:
David J. Breazzano
US High Yield FundInception Year: 2003; Fund Managers:
David J. Breazzano
Signature:
Diversified Value Trust FundInception Year: 0; Fund Managers:
CI Investments Inc., Signature Funds Group
Skylon:
Capital Yield Trust Fund
RRSP Eligible; Inception Year: 2002; Fund Managers:
Marret Asset Management Inc.
International Advantage Yield Trust Series A Fund
RRSP Eligible; Inception Year: 0; Fund Managers:
Pacific Investment Management Company LLC (PIMCO
International Advantage Yield Trust Series B (US$) Fund
RRSP Eligible; Inception Year: 0; Fund Managers:
Pacific Investment Management Company LLC (PIMCO
Convertible & Yield Advantage Trust Fund
RRSP Eligible; Inception Year: 2003; Fund Managers:
MFC Global Investment Management
High Yield & Mortgage Plus Trust FundInception Year: 2003; Fund Managers:
Marret Asset Management Inc.
Growth & Income Trust FundInception Year: 2004; Fund Managers:
CI Investments Inc., Signature Funds Group
Global Resource Split Corp. Mutual FundInception Year: 2004; Fund Managers:
CI Investments Inc., Signature Funds Group
All Asset Trust Fund
RRSP Eligible; Inception Year: 2004; Fund Managers:
Tremont Capital Management
Yield Advantage Income TrustInception Year: 2005; Fund Managers:
CI Investments Inc., Signature Funds Group
Global Capital Yield Trust Fund
RRSP Eligible; Inception Year: 2002; Fund Managers:
Pacific Investment Management Company LLC (PIMCO
Global Capital Yield Trust II Fund
RRSP Eligible; Inception Year: 2003; Fund Managers:
Pacific Investment Management Company LLC (PIMCO
Tremont:
Capital Opportunity Trust Fund
RRSP Eligible; Inception Year: 0; Fund Managers:
Tremont Capital Management

Sprott Asset Management Inc.

South Tower, Royal Bank Plaza
PO Box 27
#2700, 200 Bay St.
Toronto, ON M5J 2J1
416-943-6707
Fax: 416-362-4928
866-299-9906
invest@sprott.ca
www.sprott.com
Ownership: Private. Investment management division of Sprott Securities Inc. Owned by its employees.
Year Founded: 2000
Assets: $1-10 billion
Executives:
Neal Nenadovic, CA, CFA, CFO, Chief Compliance Officer
James Fox, MBA, Vice-President, Sales & Marketing
Peter J. Hodson, Investment Strategist
Sprott:
Canadian Equity Fund
RRSP Eligible; Inception Year: 1997; Fund Managers:
Eric Sprott, CA
Anne L.Spork
Jean-François Tardif
Gold & Precious Minerals Fund
RRSP Eligible; Inception Year: 2001; Fund Managers:
John Embry
Hedge LP FundInception Year: 2000; Fund Managers:
Eric Sprott, CA
Anne L.Spork
Jean-François Tardif
Bull/Bear RSP Fund
RRSP Eligible; Inception Year: 2002; Fund Managers:
Eric Sprott, CA
Anne L.Spork
Jean-François Tardif
Hedge Fund LP IIInception Year: 2002; Fund Managers:
Eric Sprott, CA
Anne L.Spork
Jean-François Tardif
Energy Fund
RRSP Eligible; Inception Year: 2004; Fund Managers:
Eric Sprott, CA
Whitley Energy Capital Partners L.P.
Growth Fund
RRSP Eligible; Inception Year: 2006;
Opportunities Hedge Fund LPInception Year: 2004; Fund Managers:
Jean-François Tardif
Opportunities RSP Fund
RRSP Eligible; Inception Year: 2005; Fund Managers:
Jean-François Tardif
Offshore FundInception Year: 0;
Capital Fund LPInception Year: 0;
Strategic Offshore Gold FundInception Year: 0;
Strategic Gold Fund LPInception Year: 0;
Canadian Equity Class F Fund
RRSP Eligible; Inception Year: 2004; Fund Managers:
Eric Sprott, CA
Anne L.Spork
Jean-François Tardif

SSQ Financial Group Investment and Retirement/ SSQ Groupe financier Investissement et retraite

#460, 1200, av Papineau
Montréal, QC H2K 4R5
514-521-7365
Fax: 514-521-1106
800-361-8100
invest.ret-serv@ssq.ca
investissement.ssq.ca
Profile: ASTRA Funds are a line of segregated funds. They cover all asset categories.

Executives:
Johanne Goulet, Sr. Vice-President
Astra:
110 Fund
RRSP Eligible; Inception Year: 1997; Fund Managers:
Natcan Investment Management Inc.
110-Series II Fund
RRSP Eligible; Inception Year: 1998; Fund Managers:
Natcan Investment Management Inc.
125 Fund
RRSP Eligible; Inception Year: 1998; Fund Managers:
Natcan Investment Management Inc.

SSQ Financial Group Investment and Retirement/ SSQ Groupe financier Investissement et retraite (continued)

Greystone Canadian Growth Equity Fund
RRSP Eligible; Inception Year: 2001; Fund Managers:
Greystone Managed Investments Inc.
Canadian Small Cap Equity Fund
RRSP Eligible; Inception Year: 2001; Fund Managers:
Natcan Investment Management Inc.
Dividend Fund
RRSP Eligible; Inception Year: 1997; Fund Managers:
Natcan Investment Management Inc.
Addenda Bond Fund
RRSP Eligible; Inception Year: 1998; Fund Managers:
Addenda Capital
Jarislowsky Fraser Ltd. US Value Equity Fund
RRSP Eligible; Inception Year: 2001; Fund Managers:
Jarislowsky Fraser Limited
Jarislowsky Fraser Ltd. Canadian Value Equity Fund
RRSP Eligible; Inception Year: 2001; Fund Managers:
Jarislowsky Fraser Limited
Balanced Strategy Fund
RRSP Eligible; Inception Year: 1997; Fund Managers:
Jarislowsky Fraser Limited
Conservative Strategy Fund
RRSP Eligible; Inception Year: 1998; Fund Managers:
McLean Budden Limited
Growth Strategy Fund
RRSP Eligible; Inception Year: 1998; Fund Managers:
Jarislowsky Fraser Limited
Ivy Diversified Growth & Income Fund
RRSP Eligible; Inception Year: 2001; Fund Managers:
Mackenzie Financial Corporation
Jarislowsky Fraser Ltd. International Value Equity Fund
RRSP Eligible; Inception Year: 2003; Fund Managers:
Jarislowsky Fraser Limited
McLean Budden US Equity Fund
RRSP Eligible; Inception Year: 1997; Fund Managers:
McLean Budden Limited
McLean Budden Diversified Growth Fund
RRSP Eligible; Inception Year: 2001; Fund Managers:
McLean Budden Limited
Natcan Bond Fund
RRSP Eligible; Inception Year: 1997; Fund Managers:
Natcan Investment Management Inc.
Natcan Canadian Equity Fund
RRSP Eligible; Inception Year: 1997; Fund Managers:
Natcan Investment Management Inc.
Talvest Global Health Care Fund
RRSP Eligible; Inception Year: 2001; Fund Managers:
Talvest Fund Management
Money Market Fund
RRSP Eligible; Inception Year: 1997; Fund Managers:
Natcan Investment Management Inc.
Aggressive Strategy Fund
RRSP Eligible; Inception Year: 2005; Fund Managers:
Natcan Investment Management Inc.
McLean Budden Canadian Equity Fund
RRSP Eligible; Inception Year: 2001; Fund Managers:
McLean Budden Limited
Optimum Asset Management Inc. Canadian Equity Fund
RRSP Eligible; Inception Year: 1998; Fund Managers:
Optimum Asset Management Inc.
International Equity Fund
RRSP Eligible; Inception Year: 1997; Fund Managers:
Hexavest Asset Management
Global Equity Fund
RRSP Eligible; Inception Year: 2001; Fund Managers:
McLean Budden Limited
Howson Tatersall Global Equity Fund
RRSP Eligible; Inception Year: 2005; Fund Managers:
Howson Tatersall Investment Counsel Ltd.
Demographic Trends Fund
RRSP Eligible; Inception Year: 1997; Fund Managers:
Natcan Investment Management Inc.
Bond Index Fund
RRSP Eligible; Inception Year: 2005; Fund Managers:
Barclays Global Investors Canada Ltd.
Canadian Index Fund
RRSP Eligible; Inception Year: 1998; Fund Managers:
Barclays Global Investors Canada Ltd.
US Index Fund
RRSP Eligible; Inception Year: 1998; Fund Managers:
Barclays Global Investors Canada Ltd.
International Index Fund
RRSP Eligible; Inception Year: 2005; Fund Managers:
Barclays Global Investors Canada Ltd.

Branches:
Québec
PO Box 10510
#210, 1245, ch Sainte-Foy
Québec, QC G1V 4H5 Canada
Fax: 418-688-7791
888-391-9299

Standard Life Investments Inc.(SLI)

Also listed under: *Pension & Money Management Companies*
#700, 1001, boul de Maisonneuve ouest
Montréal, QC H3A 3C8
514-499-6844
Fax: 514-499-4340
888-841-6633
information@sli.ca
www.sli.ca
Former Name: Standard Life Portfolio Management Limited
Ownership: Private. Subsidiary of Standard Life Investments Limited, Edinburgh, Scotland.
Year Founded: 1973
Assets: $10-100 billion
Executives:
Keith Skeoch, CEO, Standard Life Investments Limited, Chair, Standard Life Investments Inc.
Roger Renaud, President, Director
Norman Raschkowan, Chief Investment Officer, Director
Charles Jenkins, Sr. Vice-President, Director
Antonio Maturo, Sr. Vice-President, Portfolio Management, Director
Michel Pelletier, Sr. Vice-President, Fixed Income, Director
Roger A. Renaud, Sr. Vice-President Designate, Director; roger.renaud@standardlife.ca
Claude Turcot, Sr. Vice-President, Quantitative Management, Director
Standard Life:
Bond Fund
RRSP Eligible; Inception Year: 1989;
Canadian Equity Fund
RRSP Eligible; Inception Year: 1995;
Canadian Small Cap Equity Fund
RRSP Eligible; Inception Year: 1996;
International Equity Fund
RRSP Eligible; Inception Year: 1995;
Money Market Fund
RRSP Eligible; Inception Year: 1975;
US Equity Fund
RRSP Eligible; Inception Year: 1985;
Mortgage Fund
RRSP Eligible; Inception Year: 1969;
Diversified Fund
RRSP Eligible; Inception Year: 1987;
Capped Canadian Equity Fund
RRSP Eligible; Inception Year: 2000;
Core Canadian Equity Fund
RRSP Eligible; Inception Year: 1966;
Real Estate Fund
RRSP Eligible; Inception Year: 1983;
Canadian Bond Index Fund
RRSP Eligible; Inception Year: 1998;
Canadian Equity Capped Index Fund
RRSP Eligible; Inception Year: 2001;
Canadian Equity Index Fund
RRSP Eligible; Inception Year: 1998;
US Equity Index Fund
RRSP Eligible; Inception Year: 1998;
Synthetic US Equity Index Fund
RRSP Eligible; Inception Year: 1999;
Canadian Dividend Fund
RRSP Eligible; Inception Year: 1998;
Canadian Value Equity Fund
RRSP Eligible; Inception Year: 2003;
Long Term Bond Fund
RRSP Eligible; Inception Year: 2003;
Real Return Bond Fund
RRSP Eligible; Inception Year: 2003;
Corporate Bond FundInception Year: 0;
Branches:
Calgary
The Standard Life Bldg.
#1500, 639 - 5th Ave. SW
Calgary, AB T2P 0M9 Canada
R.A. Milner, Vice-President, Western Canada
Toronto
#840, 121 King St. West
Toronto, ON M5H 3T9 Canada
A. Jay Waters, Vice-President, Central Canada

Stone & Co. Limited

#710, 36 Toronto St.
Toronto, ON M5C 2C5
416-364-9188
Fax: 416-364-8456
800-336-9528
clientservices@stoneco.com
www.stoneco.com
Ownership: Private
Year Founded: 1994
Profile: The company is a Canadian mutual fund management & distribution organization.
Executives:
Richard G. Stone, President/CEO
Stone & Co.:
Flagship Stock Fund - A
RRSP Eligible; Inception Year: 1995; Fund Managers:
Stone Asset Management Limited
Flagship Growth & Income Fund - A
RRSP Eligible; Inception Year: 1996; Fund Managers:
Marret Asset Management Inc.
Flagship Money Market Fund - A
RRSP Eligible; Inception Year: 1996; Fund Managers:
Stone Asset Management Limited
Flagship Global Growth Fund - A
RRSP Eligible; Inception Year: 1999; Fund Managers:
Gryphon International Investment Corporation
Flagship Growth Industries Fund - A
RRSP Eligible; Inception Year: 2002; Fund Managers:
Stone Asset Management Limited
Dividend Growth Fund - A
RRSP Eligible; Inception Year: 2002; Fund Managers:
Stone Asset Management Limited
Dividend Growth Fund - B
RRSP Eligible; Inception Year: 2002; Fund Managers:
Stone Asset Management Limited
Dividend Growth Fund - C
RRSP Eligible; Inception Year: 2003; Fund Managers:
Stone Asset Management Limited
Dividend Growth Fund - F
RRSP Eligible; Inception Year: 2003; Fund Managers:
Stone Asset Management Limited
Flagship Global Growth Fund - B
RRSP Eligible; Inception Year: 1999; Fund Managers:
Gryphon International Investment Corporation
Flagship Global Growth Fund - C
RRSP Eligible; Inception Year: 2003; Fund Managers:
Gryphon International Investment Corporation
Flagship Global Growth Fund - F
RRSP Eligible; Inception Year: 2003; Fund Managers:
Gryphon International Investment Corporation
Flagship Growth & Income Fund - B
RRSP Eligible; Inception Year: 1996; Fund Managers:
Marret Asset Management Inc.
Flagship Growth & Income Fund - C
RRSP Eligible; Inception Year: 2003; Fund Managers:
Marret Asset Management Inc.
Flagship Growth & Income Fund - F
RRSP Eligible; Inception Year: 2003; Fund Managers:
Marret Asset Management Inc.
Flagship Growth Industries Fund - B
RRSP Eligible; Inception Year: 2002; Fund Managers:
Stone Asset Management Limited
Flagship Growth Industries Fund - C
RRSP Eligible; Inception Year: 2003; Fund Managers:
Stone Asset Management Limited
Flagship Growth Industries Fund - F
RRSP Eligible; Inception Year: 2003; Fund Managers:
Stone Asset Management Limited
Flagship Money Market Fund - B
RRSP Eligible; Inception Year: 1996; Fund Managers:
Stone Asset Management Limited
Flagship Money Market Fund - C
RRSP Eligible; Inception Year: 2003; Fund Managers:
Stone Asset Management Limited
Flagship Stock Fund - B
RRSP Eligible; Inception Year: 1995; Fund Managers:
Stone Asset Management Limited
Flagship Stock Fund - C
RRSP Eligible; Inception Year: 2003; Fund Managers:
Stone Asset Management Limited

INVESTMENT MANAGEMENT

Flagship Stock Fund - F
RRSP Eligible; Inception Year: 2001; Fund Managers:
Stone Asset Management Limited
Longevity Fund - B
RRSP Eligible; Inception Year: 2005; Fund Managers:
Stone Asset Management Limited
Longevity Fund - C
RRSP Eligible; Inception Year: 2005; Fund Managers:
Stone Asset Management Limited
Longevity Fund - A
RRSP Eligible; Inception Year: 2005; Fund Managers:
Stone Asset Management Limited
Stone Flow-Through Limited Partnership:
Resource Plus Class Fund - A
RRSP Eligible; Inception Year: 2005; Fund Managers:
Stone Asset Management Limited
Resource Plus Class Fund - B
RRSP Eligible; Inception Year: 2005; Fund Managers:
Stone Asset Management Limited
Resource Plus Class Fund - C
RRSP Eligible; Inception Year: 2005; Fund Managers:
Stone Asset Management Limited

TD Asset Management Inc.(TDAM)

***Also listed under:** Financial Planning; Investment Management*

77 Bloor St. West, 6th Fl.
Toronto, ON M5S 1M2
800-386-3757
td.mutualfunds@td.com
www.tdassetmanagement.com
Former Name: TD Quantitative Capital
Also Known As: TD Mutual Funds
Ownership: Public. Subsidiary of TD Bank Financial Group
Year Founded: 1987
Stock Symbol: TD
Profile: TDAM provides a diverse range of funds & portfolios. Funds are available at TD Canada Trust branches, through TD Investment Services Inc. representatives, TD Waterhouse Discount Brokerage, Financial Planning & Private Investment Advice, & also by investment dealers, independent brokers, advisors & financial planners.

Executives:
Tim Pinnington, President, TD Mutual Funds
Affiliated Companies:
TD Harbour Capital
GTD:
Managed Income & Moderate Growth Non-Registered Fund
RRSP Eligible; Inception Year: 1999;
US Blue Chip Equity Fund
RRSP Eligible; Inception Year: 1999; Fund Managers:
T. Rowe Price Associates Inc.
Balanced Growth Fund
RRSP Eligible; Inception Year: 1999; Fund Managers:
McLean Budden Limited
Health Sciences Fund
RRSP Eligible; Inception Year: 1999; Fund Managers:
T. Rowe Price Associates Inc.
Global Select Fund
RRSP Eligible; Inception Year: 1999; Fund Managers:
Oppenheimer Funds Inc.
Canadian Bond Fund
RRSP Eligible; Inception Year: 1999; Fund Managers:
Satish C. Rai
GeoffWilson
Canadian Equity Fund
RRSP Eligible; Inception Year: 1999; Fund Managers:
John Smolinski
ScottMargach
Canadian Value Fund
RRSP Eligible; Inception Year: 1999; Fund Managers:
Rachel Volynsky
DougWarwick
Managed Aggressive Growth Non-Registered Fund
RRSP Eligible; Inception Year: 1999;
Managed Aggressive Growth Registered Fund
RRSP Eligible; Inception Year: 1999;
Managed Balanced Growth Non-Registered Fund
RRSP Eligible; Inception Year: 1999;
Managed Balanced Growth Registered Fund
RRSP Eligible; Inception Year: 1999;
Managed Income & Moderate Growth Registered Fund
RRSP Eligible; Inception Year: 1999;
Managed Index Non-Registered Fund
RRSP Eligible; Inception Year: 1999;
Managed Index Registered Fund
RRSP Eligible; Inception Year: 1999;
Money Market Fund
RRSP Eligible; Inception Year: 1999; Fund Managers:
R.B. Kenneth Miner
TD:
Dividend Income Fund
RRSP Eligible; Inception Year: 1994; Fund Managers:
Doug Warwick
MichaelLough
US Equity Fund
RRSP Eligible; Inception Year: 1990; Fund Managers:
Rhonda Dalley
DavidSykes
High Yield Income Fund
RRSP Eligible; Inception Year: 1998; Fund Managers:
Gregory Kocik
NicholasLeach
Balanced Index Fund
RRSP Eligible; Inception Year: 1998; Fund Managers:
Craig Gaskin
Canadian Bond Fund
RRSP Eligible; Inception Year: 1988; Fund Managers:
Geoff Wilson
Satish C.Rai
Canadian Equity Fund
RRSP Eligible; Inception Year: 1998; Fund Managers:
Scott Margach
JohnSmolinski
Monthly Income Fund
RRSP Eligible; Inception Year: 1998; Fund Managers:
Gregory Kocik
DougWarwick
Michael Lough
Mortgage Fund
RRSP Eligible; Inception Year: 1979; Fund Managers:
David McCulla
GeoffWilson
NASDAQ RSP Index Fund
RRSP Eligible; Inception Year: 1999; Fund Managers:
Dino Bourdos
BruceGeddes
NASDAQ RSP Index e Fund
RRSP Eligible; Inception Year: 1999; Fund Managers:
Dino Bourdos
BruceGeddes
Precious Metals Fund
RRSP Eligible; Inception Year: 1994; Fund Managers:
Ari Levy
MargotNaudie
Real Return Bond Fund
RRSP Eligible; Inception Year: 1994; Fund Managers:
Satish C. Rai
GeoffWilson
Resource Fund
RRSP Eligible; Inception Year: 1993; Fund Managers:
Ari Levy
MargotNaudie
Science & Technology GIF II Fund
RRSP Eligible; Inception Year: 2000; Fund Managers:
T. Rowe Price Associates Inc.
US Index (US$) Fund
RRSP Eligible; Inception Year: 1986; Fund Managers:
Craig Gaskin
US Index (US$) e Fund
RRSP Eligible; Inception Year: 1999; Fund Managers:
Craig Gaskin
US Index Fund
RRSP Eligible; Inception Year: 1998; Fund Managers:
Craig Gaskin
US Index e Fund
RRSP Eligible; Inception Year: 1999; Fund Managers:
Craig Gaskin
US Mid-Cap Growth Fund
RRSP Eligible; Inception Year: 1993; Fund Managers:
T. Rowe Price Associates Inc.
US Money Market (US$) Fund
RRSP Eligible; Inception Year: 1988; Fund Managers:
R.B. Kenneth Miner
US RSP Index e Fund
RRSP Eligible; Inception Year: 1999; Fund Managers:
Dino Bourdos
BruceGeddes
US Small Cap Equity (US$) Fund
RRSP Eligible; Inception Year: 1999; Fund Managers:
T. Rowe Price Associates Inc.
US Small Cap Equity Fund
RRSP Eligible; Inception Year: 1997; Fund Managers:
T. Rowe Price Associates Inc.
US Blue Chip Equity GIF II Fund
RRSP Eligible; Inception Year: 2000; Fund Managers:
T. Rowe Price Associates Inc.
International RSP Index Fund
RRSP Eligible; Inception Year: 1998; Fund Managers:
Craig Gaskin
Japanese Growth Fund
RRSP Eligible; Inception Year: 1994; Fund Managers:
Charles Edwardes-Ker
BruceCooper
Japanese Index Fund
RRSP Eligible; Inception Year: 1998; Fund Managers:
Craig Gaskin
Health Sciences GIF II Fund
RRSP Eligible; Inception Year: 2000; Fund Managers:
T. Rowe Price Associates Inc.
International RSP Index e Fund
RRSP Eligible; Inception Year: 1999; Fund Managers:
Craig Gaskin
Japanese Index e Fund
RRSP Eligible; Inception Year: 1999; Fund Managers:
Craig Gaskin
Latin American Growth Fund
RRSP Eligible; Inception Year: 1994; Fund Managers:
Morgan Stanley Asset Management Inc.
Managed Aggressive Growth GIF II Fund
RRSP Eligible; Inception Year: 2000;
Canadian Money Market A Fund
RRSP Eligible; Inception Year: 2000; Fund Managers:
R.B. Kenneth Miner
Canadian Small Cap Equity Fund
RRSP Eligible; Inception Year: 1986; Fund Managers:
Connor, Clark & Lunn Investment Management
Canadian Index e Fund
RRSP Eligible; Inception Year: 1999; Fund Managers:
Craig Gaskin
Canadian Money Market GIF II Fund
RRSP Eligible; Inception Year: 2000; Fund Managers:
R.B. Kenneth Miner
Canadian T-Bill Fund
RRSP Eligible; Inception Year: 1992; Fund Managers:
R.B. Kenneth Miner
Canadian Index Fund
RRSP Eligible; Inception Year: 1985; Fund Managers:
Craig Gaskin
Dow Jones Industrial Average Index Fund
RRSP Eligible; Inception Year: 1998; Fund Managers:
Craig Gaskin
Dow Jones Industrial Average Index e Fund
RRSP Eligible; Inception Year: 1999; Fund Managers:
Craig Gaskin
Energy Fund
RRSP Eligible; Inception Year: 1994; Fund Managers:
Ari Levy
MargotNaudie
Entertainment & Communications GIF II Fund
RRSP Eligible; Inception Year: 2000; Fund Managers:
T. Rowe Price Associates Inc.
European Growth Fund
RRSP Eligible; Inception Year: 1994; Fund Managers:
Bruce Cooper
European Index Fund
RRSP Eligible; Inception Year: 1998; Fund Managers:
Craig Gaskin
European Index e Fund
RRSP Eligible; Inception Year: 1999; Fund Managers:
Craig Gaskin
Global RSP Bond Fund
RRSP Eligible; Inception Year: 1994; Fund Managers:
Geoff Wilson
DavidMcCulla
Global Select GIF II Fund
RRSP Eligible; Inception Year: 2000; Fund Managers:
Oppenheimer Funds Inc.
Asian Growth Fund
RRSP Eligible; Inception Year: 1994; Fund Managers:
Martin Currie Investment Inc

TD Asset Management Inc.(TDAM) (continued)
Balanced Growth A Fund
RRSP Eligible; Inception Year: 2000; Fund Managers:
McLean Budden Limited
Balanced Growth GIF II Fund
RRSP Eligible; Inception Year: 2000; Fund Managers:
McLean Budden Limited
Balanced Income Fund
RRSP Eligible; Inception Year: 1988; Fund Managers:
Jarislowsky Fraser Limited
Blue Chip Equity Fund
RRSP Eligible; Inception Year: 1987; Fund Managers:
Jarislowsky Fraser Limited
Canadian Bond GIF II Fund
RRSP Eligible; Inception Year: 2000; Fund Managers:
Satish C. Rai
GeoffWilson
Canadian Bond A Fund
RRSP Eligible; Inception Year: 2000; Fund Managers:
Satish C. Rai
GeoffWilson
Canadian Equity GIF II Fund
RRSP Eligible; Inception Year: 2000; Fund Managers:
John Smolinski
ScottMargach
Canadian Equity A Fund
RRSP Eligible; Inception Year: 2000; Fund Managers:
John Smolinski
ScottMargach
Managed Balanced Growth GIF II Fund
RRSP Eligible; Inception Year: 2000;
Managed Income & Moderate Growth GIF II Fund
RRSP Eligible; Inception Year: 2000;
Premium Money Market Fund
RRSP Eligible; Inception Year: 1997; Fund Managers:
R.B. Kenneth Miner
Canadian Money Market Fund
RRSP Eligible; Inception Year: 1988; Fund Managers:
R.B. Kenneth Miner
Managed Maximum Equity Growth Portfolio I Fund
RRSP Eligible; Inception Year: 1998;
Entertainment & Communications Fund
RRSP Eligible; Inception Year: 1997; Fund Managers:
T. Rowe Price Associates Inc.
Managed Index Aggressive Growth Portfolio I Fund
RRSP Eligible; Inception Year: 1998;
Managed Index Aggressive Growth Portfolio e Fund
RRSP Eligible; Inception Year: 2000;
Managed Balanced Growth Portfolio I Fund
RRSP Eligible; Inception Year: 1998;
Managed Index Balanced Growth Portfolio I Fund
RRSP Eligible; Inception Year: 1998;
Managed Balanced Growth RSP Portfolio I Fund
RRSP Eligible; Inception Year: 1998;
Canadian Value Fund
RRSP Eligible; Inception Year: 1993; Fund Managers:
Rachel Volynsky
DougWarwick
Global Asset Allocation Fund
RRSP Eligible; Inception Year: 1998; Fund Managers:
Geoff Wilson
DavidMcCulla
Balanced Fund
RRSP Eligible; Inception Year: 1987; Fund Managers:
Rachel Volynsky
GeoffWilson
Balanced Growth Fund
RRSP Eligible; Inception Year: 1987; Fund Managers:
McLean Budden Limited
Managed Aggressive Growth RSP Portfolio Fund
RRSP Eligible; Inception Year: 1998;
Managed Aggressive Growth Portfolio A Fund
RRSP Eligible; Inception Year: 2001;
AmeriGrowth RSP Fund
RRSP Eligible; Inception Year: 1993; Fund Managers:
Dino Bourdos
BruceGeddes
Canadian Value GIF II Fund
RRSP Eligible; Inception Year: 2000; Fund Managers:
Doug Warwick
RachelVolynsky
Canadian Value A Fund
RRSP Eligible; Inception Year: 2000; Fund Managers:
Doug Warwick
RachelVolynsky

Dividend Growth Fund
RRSP Eligible; Inception Year: 1987; Fund Managers:
Michael Lough
DougWarwick
Dividend Growth A Fund
RRSP Eligible; Inception Year: 2001; Fund Managers:
Michael Lough
DougWarwick
Canadian Bond Index Fund
RRSP Eligible; Inception Year: 1997; Fund Managers:
Bruce Geddes
Canadian Bond Index e Fund
RRSP Eligible; Inception Year: 2000; Fund Managers:
Bruce Geddes
Dow Jones Industrial Average Index (US$) Fund
RRSP Eligible; Inception Year: 1998; Fund Managers:
Craig Gaskin
Dow Jones Industrial Average Index (US$) e Fund
RRSP Eligible; Inception Year: 1999; Fund Managers:
Craig Gaskin
Entertainment & Communications A Fund
RRSP Eligible; Inception Year: 2000; Fund Managers:
T. Rowe Price Associates Inc.
Entertainment & Communications (US$) Fund
RRSP Eligible; Inception Year: 1999; Fund Managers:
T. Rowe Price Associates Inc.
Emerging Markets A Fund
RRSP Eligible; Inception Year: 2000; Fund Managers:
Morgan Stanley Asset Management Inc.
Global Select Fund
RRSP Eligible; Inception Year: 1994; Fund Managers:
Oppenheimer Funds Inc.
Health Sciences Fund
RRSP Eligible; Inception Year: 1996; Fund Managers:
T. Rowe Price Associates Inc.
Health Sciences (US$) Fund
RRSP Eligible; Inception Year: 1999; Fund Managers:
T. Rowe Price Associates Inc.
International Equity Fund
RRSP Eligible; Inception Year: 1987; Fund Managers:
UBS Global Asset Management (Canada) Co.
Latin American Growth (US$) Fund
RRSP Eligible; Inception Year: 1999; Fund Managers:
Morgan Stanley Asset Management Inc.
Real Return Bond A Fund
RRSP Eligible; Inception Year: 2001; Fund Managers:
Satish C. Rai
GeoffWilson
Science & Technology Fund
RRSP Eligible; Inception Year: 1993; Fund Managers:
T. Rowe Price Associates Inc.
Science & Technology (US$) Fund
RRSP Eligible; Inception Year: 1999; Fund Managers:
T. Rowe Price Associates Inc.
Science & Technology A Fund
RRSP Eligible; Inception Year: 2000; Fund Managers:
T. Rowe Price Associates Inc.
Short Term Bond Fund
RRSP Eligible; Inception Year: 1989; Fund Managers:
David McCulla
GeoffWilson
US Blue Chip Equity Fund
RRSP Eligible; Inception Year: 1996; Fund Managers:
T. Rowe Price Associates Inc.
US Blue Chip Equity (US$) Fund
RRSP Eligible; Inception Year: 1999; Fund Managers:
T. Rowe Price Associates Inc.
US Blue Chip Equity A Fund
RRSP Eligible; Inception Year: 2000; Fund Managers:
T. Rowe Price Associates Inc.
US Equity (US$) Fund
RRSP Eligible; Inception Year: 2000; Fund Managers:
Rhonda Dalley
DavidSykes
US Mid-Cap Growth A Fund
RRSP Eligible; Inception Year: 2000; Fund Managers:
T. Rowe Price Associates Inc.
US RSP Index Fund
RRSP Eligible; Inception Year: 1997; Fund Managers:
Dino Bourdos
BruceGeddes
Canadian Small Cap Equity A Fund
RRSP Eligible; Inception Year: 2002; Fund Managers:
Connor, Clark & Lunn Investment Management

Global Select A Fund
RRSP Eligible; Inception Year: 2000; Fund Managers:
Oppenheimer Funds Inc.
Health Sciences A Fund
RRSP Eligible; Inception Year: 2000; Fund Managers:
T. Rowe Price Associates Inc.
International Index Fund
RRSP Eligible; Inception Year: 1997; Fund Managers:
Craig Gaskin
High Yield Income A Fund
RRSP Eligible; Inception Year: 2002; Fund Managers:
Gregory Kocik
NicholasLeach
Managed Aggressive Growth Non-RSP GIF II Fund
RRSP Eligible; Inception Year: 2001;
Managed Aggressive Growth RSP Portfolio A Fund
RRSP Eligible; Inception Year: 2001;
Managed Aggressive Growth Portfolio I Fund
RRSP Eligible; Inception Year: 1998;
Managed Balanced Growth RSP Portfolio A Fund
RRSP Eligible; Inception Year: 2001;
Managed Index Balanced Growth Portfolio e Fund
RRSP Eligible; Inception Year: 2000;
Managed Index Income & Moderate Growth Portfolio e Fund
RRSP Eligible; Inception Year: 2000;
Managed Index Income Portfolio e Fund
RRSP Eligible; Inception Year: 2000;
Managed Index Income Portfolio I Fund
RRSP Eligible; Inception Year: 1998;
Managed Index Maximum Equity Growth Portfolio e Fund
RRSP Eligible; Inception Year: 2000;
Managed Income & Moderate Growth Portfolio I Fund
RRSP Eligible; Inception Year: 1998;
Managed Income & Moderate Growth RSP Portfolio A Fund
RRSP Eligible; Inception Year: 2001;
Managed Income & Moderate Growth RSP Portfolio I Fund
RRSP Eligible; Inception Year: 1998;
Managed Income RSP Portfolio I Fund
RRSP Eligible; Inception Year: 1998;
Managed Maximum Equity Growth Non-RSP GIF II Fund
RRSP Eligible; Inception Year: 2001;
Managed Maximum Equity Growth Portfolio A Fund
RRSP Eligible; Inception Year: 2001;
Managed Maximum Equity RSP Portfolio A Fund
RRSP Eligible; Inception Year: 2001;
Monthly Income A Fund
RRSP Eligible; Inception Year: 2002; Fund Managers:
Gregory Kocik
DougWarwick
Michael Lough
Resource A Fund
RRSP Eligible; Inception Year: 2002; Fund Managers:
Margot Naudie
AriLevy
US Large Cap Value A Fund
RRSP Eligible; Inception Year: 2002; Fund Managers:
Brian C. Rogers
Balanced Income A Fund
RRSP Eligible; Inception Year: 2002; Fund Managers:
Jarislowsky Fraser Limited
Canadian Blue Chip Equity A Fund
RRSP Eligible; Inception Year: 2002; Fund Managers:
Jarislowsky Fraser Limited
US Mid-Cap Growth (US$) Fund
RRSP Eligible; Inception Year: 1999; Fund Managers:
T. Rowe Price Associates Inc.
US Small Cap Equity A Fund
RRSP Eligible; Inception Year: 2002; Fund Managers:
T. Rowe Price Associates Inc.
Income Advantage Portfolio I Series Fund
RRSP Eligible; Inception Year: 2003;
US Large Cap Value Fund
RRSP Eligible; Inception Year: 2003; Fund Managers:
Brian C. Rogers
Global RSP Bond A Fund
RRSP Eligible; Inception Year: 2003; Fund Managers:
David McCulla
GeoffWilson
Income Advantage Portfolio A Fund
RRSP Eligible; Inception Year: 2003;
Short Term Bond A Fund
RRSP Eligible; Inception Year: 2003; Fund Managers:
David McCulla
GeoffWilson

Dividend Income A Fund
RRSP Eligible; Inception Year: 2003; Fund Managers:
Michael Lough
DougWarwick
International Equity A Fund
RRSP Eligible; Inception Year: 2003; Fund Managers:
UBS Global Asset Management (Canada) Co.
Canadian Bond Index F Fund
RRSP Eligible; Inception Year: 2000; Fund Managers:
Bruce Geddes
LoriMacKay
Managed Maximum Equity Growth RSP Fund
RRSP Eligible; Inception Year: 1998;
Canadian Money Market GIF II Class A Fund
RRSP Eligible; Inception Year: 2003; Fund Managers:
R.B. Kenneth Miner
Canadian Money Market GIF II Class B Fund
RRSP Eligible; Inception Year: 2003; Fund Managers:
R.B. Kenneth Miner
Canadian Bond GIF II Class A Fund
RRSP Eligible; Inception Year: 2003; Fund Managers:
Satish C. Rai
GeoffWilson
Canadian Bond GIF II Class B Fund
RRSP Eligible; Inception Year: 2003; Fund Managers:
Geoff Wilson
Satish C.Rai
Managed Balanced Growth GIF II Class A Fund
RRSP Eligible; Inception Year: 2003;
Managed Balanced Growth GIF II Class B Fund
RRSP Eligible; Inception Year: 2003;
Managed Income & Moderate Growth GIF II Class A Fund
RRSP Eligible; Inception Year: 2003;
Managed Income & Moderate Growth GIF II Class B Fund
RRSP Eligible; Inception Year: 2003;
Managed Aggressive Growth GIF II Class A Fund
RRSP Eligible; Inception Year: 2003;
Managed Aggressive Growth GIF II Class B Fund
RRSP Eligible; Inception Year: 2003;
Managed Maximum Equity Growth GIF II Fund
RRSP Eligible; Inception Year: 2000;
Managed Index Income & Moderate Growth Portfolio I Fund
RRSP Eligible; Inception Year: 1998;
Income Trust Capital Yield A Fund
RRSP Eligible; Inception Year: 2006; Fund Managers:
Doug Warwick
MichaelLough
Income Trust Capital Yield F Fund
RRSP Eligible; Inception Year: 2006; Fund Managers:
Michael Lough
DougWarwick
Income Trust Capital Yield I Fund
RRSP Eligible; Inception Year: 2006; Fund Managers:
Doug Warwick
MichaelLough
Income Advantage Portfolio H Fund
RRSP Eligible; Inception Year: 2006;
Income Advantage Portfolio S Fund
RRSP Eligible; Inception Year: 2006;
Income Advantage Portfolio T Fund
RRSP Eligible; Inception Year: 2006;
International Equity GIF II Fund
RRSP Eligible; Inception Year: 2000; Fund Managers:
UBS Global Asset Management (Canada) Co.
International Equity F Fund
RRSP Eligible; Inception Year: 2005; Fund Managers:
UBS Global Asset Management (Canada) Co.
International Index e Fund
RRSP Eligible; Inception Year: 2000; Fund Managers:
Craig Gaskin
Managed Maximum Equity Growth RSP P Fund
RRSP Eligible; Inception Year: 2005;
Managed Maximum Equity RSP Portfolio I Fund
RRSP Eligible; Inception Year: 1998;
Managed Income Portfolio P Fund
RRSP Eligible; Inception Year: 2005;
Managed Aggressive Growth RSP P Fund
RRSP Eligible; Inception Year: 2005;
Managed Balanced Growth RSP P Fund
RRSP Eligible; Inception Year: 2005;
Managed Maximum Equity Growth P Fund
RRSP Eligible; Inception Year: 2005;
Managed Aggressive Growth P Fund
RRSP Eligible; Inception Year: 2005;

Managed Balanced Growth P Fund
RRSP Eligible; Inception Year: 2005;
Managed Income & Moderate Growth Portfolio P Fund
RRSP Eligible; Inception Year: 2005;
Managed Income RSP Portfolio A Fund
RRSP Eligible; Inception Year: 2004;
Managed Income RSP Portfolio P Fund
RRSP Eligible; Inception Year: 2005;
Managed Income & Moderate Growth RSP P Fund
RRSP Eligible; Inception Year: 2005;
Monthly Income H Fund
RRSP Eligible; Inception Year: 2006; Fund Managers:
Doug Warwick
GregoryKocik
Monthly Income S Fund
RRSP Eligible; Inception Year: 2006; Fund Managers:
Gregory Kocik
DougWarwick
Monthly Income T Fund
RRSP Eligible; Inception Year: 2006; Fund Managers:
Gregory Kocik
DougWarwick
Pacific Rim I Fund
RRSP Eligible; Inception Year: 1993; Fund Managers:
Martin Currie Investment Inc
US Equity Advantage Portfolio A Fund
RRSP Eligible; Inception Year: 2004;
US Equity Advantage Portfolio I Fund
RRSP Eligible; Inception Year: 2004;
US Money Market (US$) P Fund
RRSP Eligible; Inception Year: 2004; Fund Managers:
R.B. Kenneth Miner
Emerging Markets Fund
RRSP Eligible; Inception Year: 1992; Fund Managers:
Morgan Stanley Asset Management Inc.
TD FundSmart:
Managed Aggressive Growth Portfolio I Fund
RRSP Eligible; Inception Year: 1998;
Managed Balanced Growth RSP Portfolio I Fund
RRSP Eligible; Inception Year: 1998;
Managed Balanced Growth Portfolio I Fund
RRSP Eligible; Inception Year: 1998;
Managed Aggressive RSP Portfolio I Fund
RRSP Eligible; Inception Year: 1998;
Managed Aggressive Growth Portfolio A Fund
RRSP Eligible; Inception Year: 2001;
Managed Aggressive RSP Portfolio A Fund
RRSP Eligible; Inception Year: 2001;
Managed Balanced Growth RSP Portfolio A Fund
RRSP Eligible; Inception Year: 2001;
Managed Income RSP Portfolio I Fund
RRSP Eligible; Inception Year: 1998;
Managed Income & Moderate Growth Portfolio I Fund
RRSP Eligible; Inception Year: 1998;
Managed Income & Moderate Growth RSP Portfolio A Fund
RRSP Eligible; Inception Year: 2001;
Managed Income & Moderate Growth RSP Portfolio I Fund
RRSP Eligible; Inception Year: 1998;
Managed Income Portfolio I Fund
RRSP Eligible; Inception Year: 1998;
Managed Maximum Equity Growth Portfolio A Fund
RRSP Eligible; Inception Year: 2001;
Managed Maximum Equity Growth Portfolio I Fund
RRSP Eligible; Inception Year: 1998;
Managed Maximum Equity RSP Portfolio A Fund
RRSP Eligible; Inception Year: 2001;
Managed Maximum Equity RSP Portfolio I Fund
RRSP Eligible; Inception Year: 1998;
Managed Aggressive Growth RSP Portfolio P Fund
RRSP Eligible; Inception Year: 2005;
Managed Balanced Growth RSP Portfolio P Fund
RRSP Eligible; Inception Year: 2005;
Managed Balanced Growth Portfolio P Fund
RRSP Eligible; Inception Year: 2005;
Managed Income & Moderate Growth Portfolio P Fund
RRSP Eligible; Inception Year: 2005;
Managed Income & Moderate Growth RSP Portfolio P Fund
RRSP Eligible; Inception Year: 2005;
Income RSP Portfolio A Fund
RRSP Eligible; Inception Year: 2004;
Managed Income Portfolio P Fund
RRSP Eligible; Inception Year: 2005;
Managed Income RSP Portfolio P Fund
RRSP Eligible; Inception Year: 2005;

Managed Maximum Equity Growth Portfolio P Fund
RRSP Eligible; Inception Year: 2005;
Managed Aggressive Growth Portfolio P Fund
RRSP Eligible; Inception Year: 2005;

Tera Capital Corp.

Also listed under: *Financial Planning*
#337, 366 Adelaide St. East
Toronto, ON M5A 3X9
416-368-8372
Fax: 416-368-1427
anguelina@teracap.com
www.teracap.com
Year Founded: 1996
Executives:
Howard Sutton, President
Tera:
Capital Global Technology Fund
RRSP Eligible; Inception Year: 1998;
Public Venture Trust Fund
RRSP Eligible; Inception Year: 0;

Thornmark Asset Management Inc.

Also listed under: *Pension & Money Management Companies*
#701, 119 Spadina Ave.
Toronto, ON M5V 2L1
416-204-6620
Fax: 416-204-6229
info@thornmark.com
www.thornmark.com
Ownership: Private
Year Founded: 1998
Number of Employees: 7
Assets: $100-500 million Year End: 20051018
Executives:
Daniel L. Bain, Chair, Chief Investment Officer; dbain@thornmark.com
Neil Jamieson, President
James F. Allan, Vice-President; jallan@thornmark.com
Geoffrey Spidle, Vice-President, Business Development; 416-204-6225
Thornmark:
Dividend & Income Fund
RRSP Eligible; Inception Year: 1998;
Enhanced EquityInception Year: 1998;

Tradex Management Inc./ Gestion Tradex Inc.

Also listed under: *Financial Planning*
#1120, 50 O'Connor St.
Ottawa, ON K1P 6L2
613-233-3394
Fax: 613-233-8191
800-567-3863
info@tradex.ca
www.tradex.ca
Ownership: Private
Year Founded: 1988
Number of Employees: 4
Assets: $100-500 million
Executives:
Robert C. White, President
John S. Rayner, Chair
Tradex:
Bond Fund
RRSP Eligible; Inception Year: 1989; Fund Managers:
TD Asset Management
Global Equity Fund
RRSP Eligible; Inception Year: 1999; Fund Managers:
City of London Investment Management Co. Ltd.
Equity Fund Limited
RRSP Eligible; Inception Year: 1960; Fund Managers:
Phillips, Hager & North Ltd.

Twenty-First Century Funds Inc.

Also listed under: *Pension & Money Management Companies*
#2315, 401 Bay St.
Toronto, ON M5H 2Y4
416-364-9993
Fax: 416-364-1218
888-299-2121
invest21@invest21.com
Ownership: Private. Owned by Twenty-First Century Investments Inc.
Year Founded: 1996
Number of Employees: 8
Assets: $50-100 million

INVESTMENT MANAGEMENT

Twenty-First Century Funds Inc. (continued)
Revenues: $1-5 million
Executives:
Robert B. Stewart, President
Denis C. Decle, Exec. Vice-President; denis@invest21.com
Frank H. Nettleton, Vice-President
Directors:
Denis C. Decle
Andre Gervais
Craig Graham
David Platt
Brian Smith
Robert B. Stewart
Twenty-First Century:
American Equity Fund
RRSP Eligible; Inception Year: 1997; Fund Managers:
The Boston Company Asset Management
Canadian Bond Fund
RRSP Eligible; Inception Year: 1997; Fund Managers:
Aurion Capital Management Inc.
Canadian Equity Fund
RRSP Eligible; Inception Year: 1997; Fund Managers:
Hillsdale Investment Management Inc.
International Equity Fund
RRSP Eligible; Inception Year: 1997; Fund Managers:
Pinnacle Associates, Ltd.

United Financial Corp.

Also listed under: *Pension & Money Management Companies*
#1900, 360 Main St.
Winnipeg, MB R3C 3Z3
204-957-1730
Fax: 204-947-2103
800-267-1730
access@assante.com
www.assante.com/canada
Former Name: Assante Asset Management Ltd.; Loring Ward Investment Counsel
Ownership: Assante Corp.
Year Founded: 1988
Executives:
Joseph C. Canavan, Chair/CEO
Steven J. Donald, President/COO
Robert J. Dorrell, Sr. Vice-President, Distribution Services
James E. Ross, Sr. Vice-President, Risk Management
Stephen Clarke, Vice-President, Marketing
Brent Wagner, Vice-President, National Sales
Artisan:
Moderate Portfolio Fund
RRSP Eligible; Inception Year: 1998;
Conservative Portfolio Fund
RRSP Eligible; Inception Year: 1998;
Growth Portfolio Fund
RRSP Eligible; Inception Year: 1998;
Maximum Growth Portfolio Fund
RRSP Eligible; Inception Year: 1998;
High Growth Portfolio Fund
RRSP Eligible; Inception Year: 1998;
New Economy Portfolio Fund
RRSP Eligible; Inception Year: 2000;
Most Conservative Portfolio Fund
RRSP Eligible; Inception Year: 1998;
Canadian T-Bill Portfolio Fund
RRSP Eligible; Inception Year: 1998;
United:
Canadian Equity Diversified Pooled Fund
RRSP Eligible; Inception Year: 2000; Fund Managers:
Trimark
Canadian Fixed Income Pooled Fund
RRSP Eligible; Inception Year: 1993; Fund Managers:
CI Investment Funds
Global Fixed Income Pooled Fund
RRSP Eligible; Inception Year: 1994; Fund Managers:
Trilogy Advisors
International Equity Diversified Pooled Fund
RRSP Eligible; Inception Year: 1994; Fund Managers:
Alliance Capital Management
Real Estate Investment Pooled Fund
RRSP Eligible; Inception Year: 1996; Fund Managers:
Cohen & Steers Capital Management
US Equity Diversified Pooled Fund
RRSP Eligible; Inception Year: 2000; Fund Managers:
CI Investment Funds
Canadian Equity Growth Pooled Fund
RRSP Eligible; Inception Year: 2000; Fund Managers:
Connor, Clark & Lunn
Canadian Equity Small Cap Pooled Fund
RRSP Eligible; Inception Year: 2000; Fund Managers:
Dimensional Fund Advisors
Canadian Equity Value Pooled Fund
RRSP Eligible; Inception Year: 1993; Fund Managers:
Tetrem Capital Partners
International Equity Growth Pooled Fund
RRSP Eligible; Inception Year: 2000; Fund Managers:
Alliance Capital Management
International Equity Value Pooled Fund
RRSP Eligible; Inception Year: 2000; Fund Managers:
AGF Funds
US Equity Growth Pooled Fund
RRSP Eligible; Inception Year: 2000; Fund Managers:
AGF Funds
US Equity Value Pooled Fund
RRSP Eligible; Inception Year: 1994; Fund Managers:
Deutshe Investment Management Americas
Branches:
Toronto - Queen St. East
2 Queen St East, 19th Fl.
Toronto, ON M5C 3G7 Canada
416-644-5650
Fax: 416-644-5693
866-644-5650
Toronto - Yonge St.
151 Yonge St., 9th Fl.
Toronto, ON M5C 2W7 Canada
416-645-4000
Fax: 0-645-4005
800-467-5762

Value Contrarian Asset Management Inc.

Bank of Commerce Centre
#2500, 1155, boul René Levesque ouest
Montréal, QC H3B 2K4
514-398-0808
Fax: 514-398-9602
benh@valuecontrarian.com
www.valuecontrarian.com
Value Contrarian:
Canadian Equity Fund
RRSP Eligible; Inception Year: 1997; Fund Managers:
Benjamin Horwood

VenGrowth Capital Management

Also listed under: *Financing & Loan Companies*
#200, 145 Wellington St. West
Toronto, ON M5J 1H8
416-971-6656
Fax: 416-971-6519
800-382-7720
info@vengrowth.com
www.vengrowth.com
Ownership: Public
Year Founded: 1994
Profile: Labour-sponsored investment fund.

Executives:
Michael S. Cohen, Managing General Partner
Douglas Michael, General Partner, CFO
Peter Carrescia, General Partner
Jay Heller, General Partner
Mark Janoska, General Partner
Graham Matthews, General Partner
Peter Seeligsohn, General Partner
VenGrowth:
Investment II Fund
RRSP Eligible; Inception Year: 2000; Fund Managers:
Allen Lupyrypa
R. EarlStorie
Patrick DiPietro
David Ferguson
Luc Margengère
Graham McBride
Advanced Life Sciences Fund
RRSP Eligible; Inception Year: 2002; Fund Managers:
Luc Margengère
JeffCourtney
Investment I Fund
RRSP Eligible; Inception Year: 1995; Fund Managers:
Allen Lupyrypa
R. EarlStorie
Patrick DiPietro
David Ferguson
Luc Margengère
Graham McBride
Traditional Industries Fund
RRSP Eligible; Inception Year: 2003; Fund Managers:
Graham McBride
AllenLupyrypa
R. Earl Storie
Michael Wolfe
Gavin Muranake
Vengrowth:
Investment III Diversified Fund
RRSP Eligible; Inception Year: 2004; Fund Managers:
Allen Lupyrypa
R. EarlStorie
Patrick DiPietro
David Ferguson
Luc Margengère
Graham McBride
Cash Management Fund
RRSP Eligible; Inception Year: 2006; Fund Managers:
TD Asset Management

Vertex One Asset Management Inc.

#1920, 1177 West Hastings St.
Vancouver, BC V6E 2K3
604-681-5787
Fax: 604-681-5146
866-681-5787
invest@vertexone.com
www.vertexone.com
Year Founded: 1997
Executives:
Jeff McCord, Managing Director
Vertex:
Balanced Fund
RRSP Eligible; Inception Year: 1998;
Vertex Fund
RRSP Eligible; Inception Year: 1998;

Workers Investment Fund Inc.

#202, 1133 Regent St.
Fredericton, NB E3B 3Z2
506-444-0091
Fax: 506-444-0816
thefund@nbnet.nb.ca
www.workersinvestmentfund.com
Ownership: Public
Year Founded: 1996
Number of Employees: 6
Assets: $10-50 million Year End: 20040930
Revenues: $1-5 million Year End: 20040930
Stock Symbol: WKF
Profile: Labour sponsored venture capital fund.

Executives:
Larry Simpson, President/CEO
Joan Chandra, Financial Officer
Directors:
Thomas Steep, Chair
Terry Carter, Vice-Chair
Sandy Beckingham, Corporate Treasurer
John Murphy, Corporate Secretary
Mac Burns
Blair Doucet
Harry Evans
John Gagnon
Denis Losier
Maureen Michaud
Max Michaud
Larry Simpson
Workers:
Investment Fund
RRSP Eligible; Inception Year: 1997;

Pension & Money Management Companies

Adams Redding Wooley

Also listed under: *Financial Planning; Accounting & Law*
824 - 1st St. South
Cranbrook, BC V1C 7H5
250-426-8277
Fax: 250-426-4109
mail@cgafirm.com
www.cgafirm.com
Former Name: Adams Redding & Co.; Adams, Brock, Redding & Co.

Ownership: Private
Year Founded: 1968
Number of Employees: 9
Executives:
David M. Adams, B.Sc., CGA, CFP
Brian F. Adams, FCGA
Alan Redding, B.Comm, CGA, CFP
James R. Wooley, BPE, CGA

AEGON Dealer Services Canada Inc.

Also listed under: *Financial Planning*
5000 Yonge St.
Toronto, ON M2N 7J8
416-883-5744
Fax: 416-883-5737
800-561-3643
adsci-marketing@aegoncanada.ca
www.moneyconcepts.ca
Former Name: Money Concepts (Canada) Limited
Ownership: Private
Year Founded: 1984
Number of Employees: 40
Offices:
100 Mile House
385 S. Cedar Ave.
100 Mile House, BC V0K 2E0 Canada
250-395-2900
Fax: 250-395-2977
Judy Simkins, Contact
Barrie
35 Worsley St.
Barrie, ON L4M 1L7 Canada
705-722-3604
Fax: 705-727-7618
askdavid@financialplanning.on.ca
David H. Karas, President
Bedford
1356 Bedford Hwy.
Bedford, NS B4A 1E2 Canada
902-835-8822
Fax: 902-835-6632
Neal Gaudet
Brampton
3147 Mayfield Rd.
Brampton, ON L6Z 4PG Canada
905-584-4903
Fax: 905-584-4904
George Leoffler
Burnaby
3823 Henning Dr.
Burnaby, BC V5C 6P3 Canada
604-436-0088
Fax: 604-436-3630
Jeffrey P. Chin
Chilliwack
#106, 8645 Young St.
Chilliwack, BC V2P 4P3 Canada
604-795-4505
Fax: 604-795-4816
Paul Jackson
Cobourg
21 Buck St.
Cobourg, ON K9A 2L1 Canada
905-373-0300
Fax: 905-373-0302
Noel Milner
Coquitlam
#211, 3030 Lincoln Ave.
Coquitlam, BC V3B 6B4 Canada
604-945-7212
Fax: 604-941-4816
Maureen Cheung
Dartmouth
#204, 171 Main St.
Dartmouth, NS B2X 1S1 Canada
902-463-6063
Fax: 902-461-9172
mcbrice@ns.aliantzinc.ca
Brice Guerin
Fort St. John
10067 - 100 Ave.
Fort St John, BC V1J 1Y7 Canada
250-785-7566
Fax: 250-785-7546
Robert Leer
Fredericton
335 Queen St.
Fredericton, NB E3B 1B1 Canada
506-454-9135
Fax: 506-454-9137
Roland Porter, Contact
Gloucester
#3, 5330 Canotek Rd.
Gloucester, ON K1J 9C1 Canada
613-742-5471
Fax: 613-742-5466
Wally Morris
Grand Falls
#101, 166 Broadway
Grand Falls, NB E3Z 2J9 Canada
506-473-3838
Fax: 506-473-9898
moneycpt@nbnet.nb.ca
Martin Theriault
Guelph
320 Eramosa Rd.
Guelph, ON N1E 2M8 Canada
519-824-7554
Fax: 519-824-8837
dwilson@mc.ca
Pierre Brianceau, Contact
Kanata
101 Schneider Rd.
Kanata, ON K2K 1Y3 Canada
613-599-5477
Fax: 613-599-5478
info@mckanata.com
www.moneyconceptskanata.biz
Zul Devji, Executive Vice President
Kelowna
712 Bernard Ave.
Kelowna, BC V1Y 6P5 Canada
250-860-1733
Fax: 250-860-0177
888-860-1707
www.kelownamoney.com/
Bruce Adams
Langley
#202, 20316 - 56 Ave.
Langley, BC V3A 3Y7 Canada
604-533-7294
Fax: 604-533-7218
Rob Warren
London
118 Inverary Cresc.
London, ON N6G 3L8 Canada
519-473-7949
Fax: 519-473-7949
Ralph Kemme
Markham
#201, 7240 Woodbine Ave.
Markham, ON L3R 1A4 Canada
416-410-6669
Fax: 905-513-8176
866-868-6669
amarchao@adsci
Anthony S. Marchao
Miramichi
1808 Water St.
Miramichi, NB E1N 1B6 Canada
506-778-8446
Fax: 506-778-8459
Lowell Loveday
Mississauga
62 Queen St. South
Mississauga, ON L5M 1K4 Canada
905-286-1334
Fax: 905-286-1335
www.privatewealthmanagement.ca/
Rob Sylvester
Napanee
164 John St.
Napanee, ON K7R 1R5 Canada
613-354-2197
Fax: 613-354-6861
mconcept@ihorizons.net
Frank E. Streek
Nelson
#3, 373 Baker St.
Nelson, BC V1L 4H6 Canada
250-354-1822
Fax: 250-354-1788
dlehr@netidea.com
Duane Lehr, Contact
Nepean
39 Robertson Rd.
Nepean, ON K2H 8R2 Canada
613-828-4423
Fax: 613-828-4337
Tony Valle
Newcastle
37 King St. West
Newcastle, ON L1B 1H2 Canada
905-987-1631
Fax: 905-987-9809
John Bugelli
Oakville
112 Wilson St.
Oakville, ON L6K 3G6 Canada
905-844-3258
Fax: 905-844-4425
mcoakville@on.aibn.com
William L. Maynes
Orangeville
78 Broadway
Orangeville, ON L9W 1J9 Canada
519-942-2555
Fax: 519-942-1845
888-265-6669
Lisa Leblanc
Oshawa
158 Centre St. South
Oshawa, ON L1H 4A4 Canada
905-723-5745
Fax: 905-725-1060
John Hughes, Branch Manager
Ottawa - St. Laurent Blvd.
1725 St. Laurent Blvd.
Ottawa, ON K1G 3V4 Canada
613-834-3588
Fax: 613-834-8199
Mahmoud Visanji
Penticton
626 Martin St.
Penticton, BC V2A 5L6 Canada
250-490-8369
Fax: 250-490-9680
Laurie Sylvester
Peterborough - King St.
223 King St.
Peterborough, ON K9J 2R8 Canada
705-876-6086
Fax: 705-876-7882
Robert (Bob) MacLeod
Peterborough - Water St.
441 Water St., 2nd Fl.
Peterborough, ON K9H 3M2 Canada
705-740-0110
Fax: 705-740-9048
invest@moneyconceptspeterborough.com
Lloyd Spiers
Pickering
1410 Bayly St.
Pickering, ON L1W 3R3 Canada
905-421-9442
Fax: 905-421-9507
Timothy Kellar
Prescott
PO Box 2767
124 King St. West
Prescott, ON K0E 1T0 Canada
613-925-4626
Fax: 613-925-1063
dthroop@moneyconcepts.ca
Graham Cudlipp
Prince George
Penthouse
770 Brunswick St.
Prince George, BC V2L 2C2 Canada
250-563-0777
Fax: 250-564-9195
allanjohnson@moneyconcepts.ca
Allan Johnson
Prince George

AEGON Dealer Services Canada Inc. (continued)
#406, 550 Victoria St.
Prince George, BC V2L 2K1 Canada
250-564-7484
Fax: 250-564-7490
www.moneyconceptspg.bc.ca
Peter Tiani
Renfrew
274 Raglan St. South
Renfrew, ON K7V 1R4 Canada
613-432-5617
Fax: 613-432-2051
www.moneyconceptsov.com
John Wilson
Richmond
13451 Gilbert Rd.
Richmond, BC V7E 2H8 Canada
604-274-8822
Fax: 604-274-8881
www.peterlefeaux.com/
Peter Lefeaux
Richmond Hill
#204, 10825 Yonge St.
Richmond Hill, ON L4C 3E4 Canada
905-737-7777
Fax: 905-737-7348
Sharad N. Kothari
Richmond Hill - Yonge St.
#304, 9050 Yonge St.
Richmond Hill, ON L4C 9S6 Canada
905-731-7761
Fax: 905-886-5648
rpollock@moneyconcepts.ca
R.C. (Bob) Pollock
Russell
191 Castor St.
Russell, ON K4R 1E1 Canada
613-445-8624
Fax: 613-445-8626
www.moneyconceptsrv.com
Theresa Wever
Saint John
199 Westmorland Rd.
Saint John, NB E2J 2E9 Canada
506-633-5944
Fax: 506-634-6702
kkillamb@nbnet.nb.ca
Kim Killam Brown
St Catharines
5 Race St.
St Catharines, ON L2R 3M1 Canada
905-684-3332
Fax: 905-684-3352
Al Teeter
Summerside
Dominion Sq. Bldg.
250 Water St., 2nd Fl.
Summerside, PE C1N 1B6 Canada
902-436-4988
Brian Ramsay, Branch Manager
Toronto - Sheppard Ave. East
#304, 3410 Sheppard Ave. East
Toronto, ON M1T 3K4 Canada
416-293-4579
Fax: 416-293-4578
Devinder Sohi
Trail
1142 Cedar Ave.
Trail, BC V1R 4B7 Canada
250-364-0050
Wayne Miller, Branch Manager
Unionville
41 Main St. South
Unionville, ON L3R 2E5 Canada
905-940-4919
Fax: 905-940-0780
don@moneyconceptsunionville.com
Don Esber
Vancouver
#960, 1050 West Pender St.
Vancouver, BC V6E 3S7 Canada
604-801-6621
Fax: 604-801-6632
Al Ferguson
Vankleek Hill
116 Main St. East
Vankleek Hill, ON K0B 1R0 Canada
613-678-3861
Fax: 613-678-3669
www.moneyconceptsrv.com
Theresa Wever
Vernon
3200 - 27 St.
Vernon, BC V1T 4W7 Canada
250-542-7181
Fax: 250-542-7181
Les Fresorger
Victoria
1480 Fort St.
Victoria, BC V8S 1Z5 Canada
250-475-3698
Fax: 250-475-3697
mc.vic@moneyconcepts.ca
Tom McLean
Waterloo
#201, 30 Dupont St. East
Waterloo, ON N2J 2G9 Canada
519-886-7300
Fax: 519-886-7086
Michael Ellis
Whitby
#20, 10 Sunray St.
Whitby, ON L1N 9B5 Canada
905-430-4651
Fax: 905-430-3243
dmcculloch@moneyconcepts.ca
www.financialplanningontario.com/
Debbie McCulloch
Winnipeg
5204 Roblin Blvd.
Winnipeg, MB Canada
204-832-9148
Fax: 204-896-5907
www.money-mgmt.com/
Edward L. Thompson

AGF Management Limited

Toronto-Dominion Bank Tower
66 Wellington St. West, 31st Fl.
Toronto, ON M5K 1E9
905-214-8202
Fax: 905-214-8243
800-520-0620
tiger@agf.com
www.agf.com
Year Founded: 1957
Number of Employees: 627
Assets: $100-500 million
Revenues: $100-500 million
Stock Symbol: AGF.NV
Profile: AGF promotes & manages mutual funds & provides investment management services to pension funds, corporations & individuals. The company also offers administrative services for group RRSPs, RESPs & other pension management. Trust services are provided to individual & institutional investors in Canada. AFR offices are located throughout Canada, & subsideiaries are around the world.

Executives:
Blake C. Goldring, Chair/CEO; 416-865-4242
Greg Henderson, Sr. Vice-President/CFO
C. Warren Goldring, Honorary Chair
Stuart E. Eagles, Director
Walter A. Keyser, Director, Terra Cotta, Ontario
David King, Director, Islington, Ontario
Milan M. Nastich, Director, Toronto, Ontario
Claudette MacKay-Lassonde, Director
Clive H. J. Coombs, Sr. Vice-President
Affiliated Companies:
AGF Funds Inc.
AGF Private Investment Management Limited
AGF Trust Company

AGF Private Investment Management Limited

***Also listed under:** Financial Planning*
Toronto-Dominion Bank Tower
66 Wellington St. West, 31st Fl.
Toronto, ON M5K 1E9
416-865-4296
Fax: 416-367-4807
888-216-4424
www.agf.com
Also Known As: AGF PIM
Ownership: Public. Wholly owned subsidiary of AGF Management Ltd.
Executives:
Blake C. Goldring, Chair/CEO
Rob Badun, President
Lorne Steinberg, Chief Investment Officer
Peter Rawson, Vice-President & Portfolio Manager
Robert Bard, Managing Director
Lloyd Goldstein, Managing Director
David Andrews, Director, Investments
Mario Bourdon, Investment Counsellor
Natalie Circelli, Investment Counsellor
Affiliated Companies:
Cypress Capital Management Ltd.
Magna Vista Investment Management
P.J. Doherty & Associates Co. Ltd.

Alan W. Strathdee

***Also listed under:** Financial Planning*
35 Peachtree Path
Toronto, ON M9P 3S1
416-244-0085
Ownership: Private
Year Founded: 1990
Profile: Services include financial planning & investment advisory.

Executives:
Alan W. Strathdee, CFP, PFP, Owner

Alexander Gluskin Investments Inc.

***Also listed under:** Financial Planning*
120 Adelaide St. West
Toronto, ON M5H 1T1
416-777-6769
Fax: 416-777-6719
866-268-7795
agluskin@agluskin.com
Former Name: Gluskin Fagan, Inc.
Ownership: Private
Year Founded: 1991
Number of Employees: 6
Executives:
Alexander Gluskin, Ph.D., President/CEO, Chair

AMG Canada Corp.

***Also listed under:** Financial Planning*
North Tower, Royal Bank Plaza
#1840, 200 Bay St.
Toronto, ON M5J 2J4
416-920-1944
Fax: 416-920-1947
Former Name: First Asset Management Inc.
Ownership: Public. Foreign. Parent is Affiliated Managers Group Inc.
Year Founded: 1997
Number of Employees: 250
Stock Symbol: AMG
Executives:
Nathaniel Dalton, President
John Kingston, Director
Affiliated Companies:
First Asset Advisory Services Inc.

AMI Partners Inc.

#800, 26 Wellington St. East
Toronto, ON M5E 1S2
416-865-0731
Fax: 416-865-9241
clabbett@amipartners.com
www.amipartners.com
Ownership: Private
Year Founded: 1959
Number of Employees: 34
Assets: $1-10 billion
Profile: The investment counsel firm offers a broad spectrum of investment services to institutional investors.

Executives:
Robert H. Gibson, CFA, President/CEO
Robert J. Ritchie, CA, Chief Operating Officer
Craig Labbett, Vice-President, Marketing
Regional Offices:
Montréal

#1830, 1002, rue Sherbrooke ouest
Montréal, QC H3A 3L6 Canada
514-286-4500
Fax: 514-286-9370
Joanne Skalos, Manager, Portfolio Administration
Vancouver
#840, 1100 Melville St.
Vancouver, BC V6E 4A6 Canada
604-687-1393
Fax: 604-683-1921
Larry E. Avant, Managing Partner

ARC Financial Group Ltd.

Also listed under: *Investment Dealers*
#4300, 400 - 3rd Ave. SW
Calgary, AB T2P 4H2
403-292-0680
Fax: 403-292-0693
genfeedback@arcfinancial.com
www.arcfinancial.com
Ownership: Private
Year Founded: 1989
Number of Employees: 55
Profile: The investment management & merchant banking company focuses on the energy sector in Canada.

Executives:
Kevin J. Brown, CEO
Lauchlan J. Currie, President
Tanya M. Causgrove, CFO, Finance & Administration
Nancy V. Lever, Sr. Vice-President, Energy Development & Services
William H. Slavin, Sr. Vice-President, Exploration & Production
Nancy L. Smith, Sr. Vice-President, Energy Development & Services
Paul J. Beitel, Vice-President, Exploration & Production
Brian P. Boulanger, Vice-President, Exploration & Production
Robert C. Cook, Vice-President, Exploration & Production
Andy L. Evans, Vice-President, Exploration & Production
Douglas C. Freel, Vice-President
Peter Tertzakian, Chief Energy Economist, Energy Research
Directors:
Philip C. Swift, Co-Chair
Mac Van Wielingen, Co-Chair
John M. Stewart, Vice-Chair

Argosy Partners - The Shotgun Fund & The Succession Fund

Also listed under: *Financing & Loan Companies; Investment Management*
#760, 141 Adelaide St. West
Toronto, ON M5H 3L5
416-367-3617
Fax: 416-367-3895
info@shotgunfund.com
www.shotgunfund.com, www.successionfund.com
Ownership: Private
Year Founded: 1999
Number of Employees: 6
Assets: $50-100 million Year End: 20060930
Profile: Argosy Partners manages several private equity limited partnerships. The Shotgun Fund will buy equity positions in private companies from departing shareholders during shareholder disputes. The fund will move quickly when a shotgun clause is activated. The Succession Fund provides equity financing for family business ownership change, management buyouts, & entrepreneurs who want to take \Chips off the Table\"". The Fund will take secondary equity positions in profitable private companies. Argosy Partners is also affiliated with The Bridge Fund.""

Executives:
Larry Klar, Partner
Jim Ambrose, Partner
Richard Reid, Partner
Directors:
Robert Cross
Pierre Gagnon
Craig Graham
Donald Jackson
John Kettlewell
Warren Kettlewell
Robert Rubinoff

Assuris

#1600, One Queen St. East
Toronto, ON M5C 2X9
416-359-2001
Fax: 416-955-9688
866-878-1225
info@assuris.ca
www.assuris.ca
Former Name: CompCorp
Also Known As: Canadian Life & Health Insurance Compensation Corporat
Ownership: Not-for-profit; no share capital owned by members.
Year Founded: 1990
Profile: Assuris' mission is to mitigate the impact on Canadian policyholders of the financial failure of a life insurance company. The not for profit corporation works in partnership with regulators on any necessary interventions, seeking to both minimize long-term costs & preserve consumer perceptions of industry strength.

Executives:
Gordon M. Dunning, President/CEO; gdunning@assuris.ca
Michael A. Hale, Exec. Vice-President; mhale@assuris.ca
Helen Delyannis, Vice-President, Finance & Administration
Directors:
Michael Beck, Chair
David Baird
G. Douglas Carr
Jacques Dumont
Gordon M. Dunning
Donald R. Glover
Fred Gorbet
Louise Ménard
Rob Smithen

Aurion Capital Management Inc.

Also listed under: *Financial Planning*
#2205, 120 Adelaide St. West
Toronto, ON M5H 1T1
416-866-2422
Fax: 416-363-6206
866-828-7466
jclark@aurion.ca
www.aurion.ca
Year Founded: 1996
Number of Employees: 22
Assets: $1-10 billion Year End: 20060930
Revenues: $1-5 million Year End: 20060930
Profile: Investment services include portfolio management, pension fund management & alternative asset management.

Executives:
Neil Jacoby, President, Managing Partner
Bob Decker, CFA, MBA, Managing Partner, Canadian Equities
Paul Fahey, CFA, MBA, Managing Partner, Fixed Income
Janet Greenwood, BA, B.Admin., Managing Partner, Investment Solutions
Dennis Pellarin, CA, BBA, Chief Financial Officer
James Clark, CFA, CA, B.Sc., Vice-President, Business Development

Baskin Financial Services Inc.

#900, 95 St. Clair Ave. West
Toronto, ON M4V 1N6
416-969-9540
Fax: 416-969-9225
877-227-5468
davidbaskin@baskinfinancial.com
www.baskinfinancial.com
Ownership: Private
Year Founded: 1992
Number of Employees: 7
Profile: Registered investment counselling firm.

Executives:
David Baskin, President
Barry Schwartz, Vice-President; bschwartz@baskinfinancial.com

Toby Harrison, Executive Assistant; tharrison@baskinfinancial.com

Beutel Goodman & Company Ltd.

Also listed under: *Financial Planning*
PO Box 2005
#2000, 20 Eglinton Ave. West
Toronto, ON M4R 1K8
416-485-1010
Fax: 416-485-1799
800-461-4551
marketing@beutel-can.com
www.beutelgoodman.com
Ownership: Private
Year Founded: 1967
Number of Employees: 53
Assets: $10-100 billion Year End: 20060930
Executives:
William W. Ashby, President
Greg Latremoille, President, Private Client Group
Bruce L. Cornell, COO/Sr. Vice-President, Fixed Income
James G. Edwards, Sr. Vice-President, Beutel Goodman Managed Funds
Mark D. Thomson, Sr. Vice-President, Director of Research, Canadian Equities
Steve Arpin, Vice-President, Canadian Equities
John Christie, Vice-President, Fixed Income
Stephen Clements, Vice-President, U.S. Equities, Private Client Group
David Gregoris, Vice-President, Fixed Income
Gavin Ivory, Vice-President, Global Equities
Sarah Khoo, Vice-President, Global Equities
Irene Lau, Vice-President, Canadian Equity Trader
Sue McNamara, Vice-President, Fixed Income
John Shuter, Vice-President
Steven Smith, Vice-President, Private Client Group
Andrew M. Sweeney, Vice-President, Canadian Equities
John Fuea, Asst. Vice-President, Fixed Income
Allison Morgan, Asst. Vice-President, International Equities
Glenn Fortin, Equity Analyst, U.S. Equities
Ehren Mendum, Equity Analyst, U.S. Equities, Private Client Group
William S. Otton, Equity Analyst, Canadian Equities
Pat Palozzi, Equity Analyst, Canadian Equitites
K.C. Parker, Equity Analyst, Global Equities
Craig Weisberg, Equity Trader, U.S. & Canadian Small Cap Equity Trader
Affiliated Companies:
Beutel Goodman Managed Funds Inc.

Beutel Goodman Managed Funds Inc.

Also listed under: *Financial Planning*
PO Box 2005
#2000, 20 Eglinton Ave. West
Toronto, ON M4R 1K8
416-932-6404
Fax: 416-485-8194
800-461-4551
marketing@beutelgoodman.com
www.beutelgoodman.com
Ownership: Private
Year Founded: 1991
Assets: $1-10 billion Year End: 20060930
Executives:
James Edwards, Sr. Vice-President

Bluewater Investment Management Inc.

PO Box 63
#1502, 150 King St. West
Toronto, ON M5H 1J9
416-599-5300
Fax: 416-599-7333
Ownership: Private
Year Founded: 1994
Number of Employees: 6
Assets: $1-10 billion
Executives:
Dina DeGeer, Principal
Dennis Starritt, Principal
Phil Taller, Principal

Burgundy Asset Management Ltd.

Bay Wellington Tower, BCE Place
PO Box 778
#4510, 181 Bay St.
Toronto, ON M5J 2T3
416-869-3222
Fax: 416-869-9036
888-480-1790
info@burgundyasset.com
www.burgundy-asset.com
Ownership: Private
Year Founded: 1991
Number of Employees: 25
Profile: Discretionary investment management to private individuals, charitable foundations, & select institutional investors is offered by Burgundy. .

Executives:
H. Anthony Arrell, Chair/CEO; tarrell@burgundyasset.com

INVESTMENT MANAGEMENT

Burgundy Asset Management Ltd. (continued)
Richard E. Rooney, President; rrooney@burgundyasset.com
Brad Badeau, Sr. Vice-President & CFO; bbadeau@burgundyasset.com
Lloyd G. Barbara, Sr. Vice-President, US Client Group; lbarbara@burgundyasset.com
Allan MacDonald, Sr. Vice-President; amacdonald@burgundyasset.com
Stephen G. Mitchell, Sr. Vice-President; stmitchell@burgundyasset.com
Craig Pho, Sr. Vice-President; cpho@burgundyasset.com
Joel H. Raby, Sr. Vice-President; jraby@burgundyasset.com
David Vanderwood, Sr. Vice-President; dvanderwood@burgundyasset.com
Kelly Battle, Vice-President, US Client Group; kbattle@burgundyasset.com
Claude Bédard, Vice-President
Jonathan Bloomberg, Vice-President; jbloomberg@burgundyasset.com
Kenneth A. Broekaert, Vice-President
Franca DeBartolo, Vice-President, US Client Group; fdebartolo@burgundyasset.com
Jennifer Dunsdon, Vice-President
Mark Gallien, Vice-President; mgallien@burgundyasset.com
Curtis Gazdewich, Vice-President; cgazdewich@burgundyasset.com
Eric Goldstrand, Vice-President, Canadian Client Group; egoldstrand@burgundyasset.com
Vincent E. Hunt, Vice-President; vhunt@burgundyasset.com
Darren P. McKiernan, Vice-President; dmckiernan@burgundyasset.com
James Meadows, Vice-President, Administration Team; jmeadows@burgundyasset.com
Jennifer Luong, Controller

C.A. Delaney Capital Management Ltd.

Canada Trust Tower, BCE Place
#3130, 161 Bay St.
Toronto, ON M5J 2S1
416-361-0688
Fax: 416-361-0089
800-268-2733
info@delaneycapital.com
www.delaneycapital.com
Year Founded: 1992
Profile: Over $1 billion in assets is managed, including equity & balanced portfolios.

Executives:
Catherine Delaney, President
Nancy McKellar, Exec. Vice-President
Lynn Miller, Partner/Portfolio Manager
Julia Robertson, Partner & Investment Analyst
Linda Lee, Partner & Sr. Trader
Gregory Bent, Partner & Investment Analyst
Grant Parson, Vice President, Compliance & Financial Reporting

Caisse de dépôt et placement du Québec

1000, Place Jean-Paul-Riopelle
Montréal, QC H2Z 2B3
514-842-3261
Fax: 514-847-2498
866-330-3936
info@lacaisse.com
www.lacaisse.com
Former Name: CDP Capital
Ownership: Public.
Year Founded: 1965
Number of Employees: 824
Assets: $100 billion + Year End: 20051231
Profile: The organization manages funds for public & private pension & insurance funds. The following are the company's main depositors: the Régime de retraite des employés du gouvernement et des organismes publics; the Régie des rentes du Québec; the Fonds d'amortissement des régimes de retraite; the Commission de la santé et de la sécurité du travail; the Commission de la construction du Québec; the Société de l'assurance automobile du Québec; & the Régime de retraite du personnel d'encadrement. The company strives to obtain an optimal financial return for its depositors. The leading institutional fund manager in Canada, with close to $130 billion of assets under management, the caisse invests in the main liquid markets, as well as in private equity & real estate. Subsidiaries include Société immobiliè Trans-Québec (SITQ), Ivanhoe Cambridge & Cadim Inc.

Executives:
Henri-Paul Rousseau, President/CEO
Fernand Perreault, President, Real Estate Group
Robert Desnoyers, Exec. Vice-President, Human Resources & Organizational Development
François Grenier, Exec. Vice-President, Equity Markets
Richard Guay, Exec. Vice-President, Chief Investment Officer
Susan Kudzman, Exec. Vice-President, Risk Management & Depositors' Accounts Management
Michel Malo, Exec. Vice-President, Hedge Funds
Suzanne Masson, Exec. Vice-President, Corporate Affairs, Secretary
Ghislain Parent, Exec. Vice-President, Finance, Treasury & Strategic Initiatives
Christian Pestre, Exec. Vice-President, Chief Strategist
V.P. Pham, Exec. Vice-President, Information Technology & Investment Administration
Normand Provost, Exec. Vice-President, Private Equity

Directors:
Pierre Brunet, Chair
Yvan Allaire
Claudette Carbonneau
President, Confédération des syndicats nationaux
Louise Charette
Steven Cummings
Alban D'Amours
Silvie Dillard
Partner, Biron, Lapierre & Associés
Claude Garcia
A. Michel Lavigne
Henri Massé
Pierre Prémont
Duc Vu
President, Fédération des travailleurs et travailleuses du Québec
John T. Wall

Affiliated Companies:
CDP Capital - Mortgages
CDP Capital - Technology Ventures

Canadian Corporate Funding Limited(CCFL)

Also listed under: *Financing & Loan Companies*
#2140, Canadian Pacific Tower
PO Box 86, T-D Centre Stn. T-D Centre
Toronto, ON M5K 1G8
416-977-1450
Fax: 416-977-6764
info@ccfl.com
www.ccfl.com
Ownership: Private
Year Founded: 1979
Number of Employees: 26
Profile: Affiliated companies are CCFL Advisory Services & CCFL Mezzanine Partners.

Executives:
Richard Kinlough, Co-President, CCFL Mezzanine Partners; rkinlough@ccfl.com
Robert Olsen, Co-President, CCFL Mezzanine Partners; rolsen@ccfl.com
Philip J. Mauchel, Sr. Vice-President, CCFL Mezzanine Partners; pmauchel@ccfl.com
Nagib Premji, Vice-President, CCFL Mezzanine Partners; npremji@ccfl.com
Patrick Trainor, Sr. Manager, CCFL Mezzanine Partners; ptrainor@ccfl.com

Directors:
Paul Lowenstein, Chair; plowenstein@ccfl.com

Branches:
Montréal
#2210, 1010, rue Sherbrooke ouest
Montréal, QC H3A 2R7 Canada
514-287-9884
Fax: 514-287-9030

The Canadian Depository for Securities Limited(CDS)/ La Caisse canadienne de dépôt de valeurs limitée

85 Richmond St. West
Toronto, ON M5H 2C9
416-365-8400
Fax: 416-365-0842
cdswebmaster@cds.ca
www.cds.ca
Ownership: Private
Year Founded: 1970
Number of Employees: 400
Profile: Canada's national securities depository is an information provider for capital markets. CDS provides securities-related services in domestic & international markets.

Executives:
Allan R. Cooper, President/CEO
Ian Gilhooley, Chief Operating Officer
Brian Gill, Chief Information Officer
David Stanton, Chief Risk Officer
Keith Evans, Sr. Vice-President, Operations
Raymond E. Mitchell, Sr. Vice-President/CFO
Bruce Butterill, Vice-President, Products
Allan Cheung, Vice-President & Chief Auditor
Ansley Currie, Vice-President, e-Regulation
Toomas Marley, Vice-President & Corporate Secretary
Wendy Nunn, Vice-President, Human Resources
Lindsay A. Wallace, Vice-President, Strategy Development
Mark S. Weseluck, Vice-President & Chief Risk Officer
Lynne Litzenberger, Regional Vice-President, Western Region

Directors:
Charles R. Moses, Chair
Allan R. Cooper
Charles Freedman
Charyl Galpin
Norman K. J. Graham
Raymond Lafontaine
Yvan Naud
Gerard J. O'Mahoney
Robert M. Phillips
Barbara G. Stymiest
Peter Virvilis
J. Kenton Warren
W. David Wood

Branches:
Calgary
#630, 300 - 5th Ave. SW
Calgary, AB T2P 3C4 Canada
403-265-7577
Fax: 403-269-2474
Halifax
Barrington Tower
1894 Barrington St., 3rd Fl.
Halifax, NS B3J 2A8 Canada
902-425-0929
Fax: 902-425-0769
Montréal
#210, 600, boul de Maisonneuve ouest
Montréal, QC H3A 3J2 Canada
514-848-1010
Fax: 514-848-9745

Vancouver
Canaccord Tower
PO Box 10324
609 Granville St., 8th Fl.
Vancouver, BC V7Y 1J8 Canada
604-631-6000
Fax: 604-631-6066

Capstone Consultants Limited

Also listed under: *Investment Fund Companies*
#1601, 110 Yonge St.
Toronto, ON M5C 1T4
416-366-2931
Fax: 416-366-2729
866-443-6097
mma@mmainvestments.com
www.capstonefunds.com
Former Name: Capstone Consultants Limited.
Ownership: Private
Year Founded: 1984

Executives:
Vanessa L. Morgan, President; vmorgan@mmainvestments.com

Jonathan A. Morgan, Sr. Vice-President
Clive R. Robinson, Sr. Vice-President; crobinson@mmainvestments.com
Alex Sulzer, Vice-President; asulzer@mmainvestments.com

Capstone:
Jupiter Income
RRSP Eligible; Inception Year: 1987; Fund Managers:
Michael A. Smedley
D. GregEckel

Cardinal Capital Management Inc.
#506, 1780 Wellington Ave.
Winnipeg, MB R3H 1B3
204-783-0716
Fax: 204-783-0725
800-310-4664
enquiries@cardinal.ca
www.cardinal.ca
Ownership: Private
Year Founded: 1992
Number of Employees: 14
Assets: $500m-1 billion Year End: 20050930
Revenues: $1-5 million Year End: 20050930
Profile: The employee-owned, registered investment counselling firm provides conservative investment management services to both individuals & institutions, including pension funds & foundations. The firm offers extensive expertise in the management of equity, balanced & fixed-income accounts. Assets managed include Canadian, U.S., & international stocks & bonds. The company has clients residing in Ontario, Manitoba, Saskatchewan, Alberta & British Columbia. The firm has no formal affiliation with any other financial institution.

Executives:
Timothy E. Burt, Principal, President; teburt@cardinal.ca
Daniel R. Stoller, Vice-President, Chief Financial Officer; dstoller@cardinal.ca
Steven London, Vice-President, Chief Compliance Officer; E-mail: slondon@cardinal.ca

CDP Capital - Mortgages
Centre CDP Capital
1001, square Victoria
Montréal, QC H2Z 2A8
514-842-3261
Fax: 514-847-2494
realestategroup@lacaisse.com
www.cdpcapital.com
Executives:
Fernand Perreault, Exec. Vice-President
Guy Charette, Vice-President, Real Estate Financing
Karen Laflamme, Vice-President, Real Estate Portfolio
Geneviève B. Beaulieu, Corporate Secretary

CDP Capital - Technology Ventures
Also listed under: *Financing & Loan Companies*
1000, place Jean-Paul-Riopelle
Montréal, QC H2Z 2B3
514-842-3261
Fax: 514-847-2628
technologyventures@cdpcapital.com
Former Name: Capital Technologies CDPQ Inc.
Ownership: Subsidiary of Caisse de dépôt et placement du Québec
Year Founded: 1995
Number of Employees: 32

Celtic House Venture Partners
#530, Tower B
555 Legget Dr.
Kanata, ON K2K 2X3
613-271-2020
Fax: 613-271-2025
info@celtic-house.com
www.celtic-house.com
Former Name: Celtic House International
Ownership: Private
Year Founded: 1994
Number of Employees: 13
Assets: $100-500 million
Profile: Private venture capital fund.

Executives:
Andrew Waitman, Managing Partner
Roger Maggs, Partner & Founder
David Adderley, Partner & COO
Brian Antonen, Partner
Ron Dizy, Partner
Tomas Valis, Partner
Branches:
Ottawa
Tower B
#530, 555 Legget Dr.
Ottawa, ON K2K 2X3 Canada
613-271-2020
Fax: 613- 22-6
info@celtic-house.com

Toronto
#301, 165 Avenue Rd.
Toronto, ON M5R 3S4 Canada
416-924-7000
Fax: 416-924-7090
info@celtic-house.com

Centerfire Capital Management Ltd.
1392 Hurontario St.
Mississauga, ON L5G 3H4
416-777-0707
Fax: 416-777-0706
888-777-2949
www.centerfirecapital.com
Year Founded: 1996
Number of Employees: 3
Assets: $10-50 million
Profile: Main focus is to develop strategic relationships with niche market investment specialists whose products have performed above average for at least 10 years, and to invest in stable high quality low risk securities.

Executives:
Stanley Archdekin, President/CEO; sarchdekin@centerfirecapital.com
Karen A. Hickling, Vice-President; khickling@centrefirecapital.com
Centerfire Pooled:
Balanced Fuund
RRSP Eligible; Inception Year: 0;
International FundInception Year: 0;
Global FundInception Year: 0;

Centre Financial Corp.
Also listed under: *Financial Planning*
222 - 11 Ave. NW
Calgary, AB T2M 0B8
403-571-0000
Fax: 403-277-2289
mail@centrefinancial.com
Ownership: Private, JLK Holdings
Year Founded: 1994
Number of Employees: 7
Assets: $36,000
Revenues: $100,000
Executives:
John M. Knowles, President; 403-571-0002
Robert Stewart, CFP, Treasurer; 403-571-0000
Directors:
John M. Knowles
Robert Stewart

Co-operative Superannuation Society Pension Plan
PO Box 1850
Saskatoon, SK S7K 3S2
306-244-1539
Fax: 306-244-1088
www.csspen.com
Year Founded: 1939
Profile: One of Canada's major registered pension plans, it was established as a defined contribution pension plan to serve co-operatives & credit unions, & now serves more than 500 member organizations & their employees. The CSS Pension Plan provides pension & retirement services to more than 30,000 non-retired employee members. It also provides monthly retirement income directly to more than 5,600 retired co-operative & credit union employees.

Executives:
Peter Zakreski, Sr. Vice-President

Co-operators Investment Counselling Limited
130 MacDonell St.
Guelph, ON N1H 6P8
519-767-3901
Fax: 519-824-7040
800-265-2612
www.cooperatorsinvestment.ca/
Ownership: Wholly owned subsidiary of The Co-operators Group.
Year Founded: 1985
Number of Employees: 36
Assets: $1-10 billion
Executives:
Michael White, President
Jim MacDonald, Chief Operating Officer
Nancy Collins, Vice-President, Canadian Equities
Gregory J. Dweyer, Vice-President, Mortgages
Judith Lowes, Vice-President, Investment Services
Ian A. McKinnon, Vice-President, Fixed Income
Lorraine Mickler, Vice-President, Insurance Fixed Income
Bill Siddiqui, Vice-President, U.S. Equities
Rein Tabur, Vice-President, Life Investments

Coleford Investment Management Ltd.
#1701, 44 Victoria St.
Toronto, ON M5C 1Y2
416-864-1233
Fax: 416-867-9706
877-813-8883
hill@coleford.net; agostini@coleford.net
www.coleford.net
Ownership: Private
Year Founded: 1989
Number of Employees: 8
Assets: $100-500 million
Profile: Coleford Investment Management Ltd. provides discretionary investment management services to private wealth clients & charitable foundations. Coleford is primarily a balanced-fund manager investing in North American securities.

Executives:
Alain Agostini, CFA, Managing Director
Todd Edgar, BA, Managing Director
William Fillmore, CFA, Managing Director
Robert J. Hill, CFA, Managing Director
Craig Middaugh, CFA, Managing Director
Laura M. Wallace, CFA, Managing Director
Roger Wilson, CFA, Managing Director

Comeau Financial
Also listed under: *Financial Planning*
#300, 128 - 4th Ave. South
Saskatoon, SK S7K 1M8
306-652-7225
Fax: 306-665-0555
800-667-3929
jack@comeaufinancial.com
www.comeaufinancial.com
Ownership: Private
Year Founded: 1990
Number of Employees: 3
Executives:
Jack Comeau, CFP, RFP, ChFC, CLU, BSA, President

Confident Financial Services (1969) Limited
Also listed under: *Financial Planning*
#202, Apple Creek Blvd.
Markham, ON L3R 9X7
905-707-5900
Fax: 905-707-7476
confident@idirect.com
Ownership: Private
Year Founded: 1969
Profile: The company provides personal investment planning & wealth management.

Continental Corporation(CBOC)
Also listed under: *Financing & Loan Companies*
#402, 4 King St. West
Toronto, ON M5H 1B6
416-867-9079
Fax: 416-867-1961
Former Name: Prairie Capital Inc; ATI Corporation
Ownership: Public. Major shareholder is The Coastal Group (48.1% interest directly & indirectly held)
Year Founded: 1962
Number of Employees: 3
Stock Symbol: CTL
Profile: The company holds a portfolio of medium- to long-term investments, participates in privately placed debt & equity issues, & provides cash management services & short-term financing facilities.

Executives:
Gordon Flatt, President
Lori Tange, Vice-President, Finance, Corporate Secretary
Directors:
J. Ian Flatt, Chair
Roy E. Collins
Gordon Flatt

Cougar Global Investments
Also listed under: *Financial Planning*
#1001, 357 Bay St.
Toronto, ON M5H 2T7

INVESTMENT MANAGEMENT

Cougar Global Investments (continued)
416-368-5255
Fax: 416-368-7738
800-387-3779
info@cougarglobal.com
www.cougarglobal.com
Ownership: Private
Year Founded: 1993
Number of Employees: 11
Assets: $100-500 million Year End: 20061031
Revenues: $1-5 million Year End: 20061031
Executives:
James Breech, President/CEO; jbreech@cougarglobal.com
Art Hounsell, Sr. Vice-President, Operations; ahounsell@cougarglobal.com
Vicki Breech, Vice-President, Wealth Management Services; vbreech@cougarglobal.com
Directors:
Roy Bennett, Chair
Donald G. Baker
R. Peter McLaughlin

Cowan Benefits Consulting Limited
Also listed under: *Financial Planning; Accounting & Law*
PO Box 1510
705 Fountain St. North
Cambridge, ON N1R 5T2
519-650-6361
Fax: 519-650-6367
800-609-5549
Other Information: 800-434-9606 (Toll Free, French)
infocbcl@cowangroup.ca
www.cowangroup.ca
Former Name: Cowan Wright Beauchamp Limited
Ownership: Wholly owned subsidiary of The Cowan Insurance Group, Cambridge, ON.
Year Founded: 1981
Number of Employees: 150
Revenues: $10-50 million
Profile: The advisory firm provides actuarial, consulting & administrative services in areas such as pensions, retirement & group benefits. The organization is affiliated with Cowan Insurance Brokers & Frank Cowan Company.

Executives:
Marcel Gingras, President
Karen Cooper, Vice-President, Finance
Branches:
Ottawa
641 Montreal Rd.
Ottawa, ON K1K 0T4 Canada
613-741-3313
Fax: 613-741-7771
888-509-7797
clients@cowangroup.ca
www.cowangroup.ca
Bob Proulx, Vice-President

Cranston, Gaskin, O'Reilly & Vernon Investment Counsel(CGO&V)
Also listed under: *Financial Planning*
35A Hazelton Ave.
Toronto, ON M5R 2E3
416-929-7145
Fax: 416-929-5281
don@cgovic.com
www.cgovic.com
Ownership: Private.
Year Founded: 1995
Number of Employees: 13
Assets: $500m-1 billion Year End: 20061231
Profile: bhe independent investment counselling firm manages approximately $1,000,000,000 on behalf of institutions, charitable organizations & high net worth invividuals.

Executives:
Mark Gaskin, Managing Partner; 416-929-8678; mark@cgovic.com
Don Cranston, Partner; 416-929-7236; don@cgovic.com
Jim Green, Partner; 416-847-8301; jimg@cgovic.com
Sheila Norman, Partner; 416-646-0192; sheila@cgovic.com
Gord O'Reilly, Partner; 416-929-9286; gord@cgovic.com
Ted Ecclestone, Chief Financial Officer, COO

Credit Counselling Services of Alberta Ltd.
Also listed under: *Financial Planning*
#225, 602 - 11 Ave. SW
Calgary, AB T2R 1J8
403-265-2201
Fax: 403-265-2240
800-294-0076
info@creditcounselling.com
www.creditcounselling.com
Ownership: Private. Community based limited not-for-profit.
Year Founded: 1997
Number of Employees: 35
Assets: $1-5 million
Revenues: $1-5 million
Profile: Credit Counselling Services of Alberta is a not-for-profit personal money management education & debt repayment services company. It offers counselling, workshops & programs in the following areas: basic money management, debt resolution & consumer education. There will be an office in Red Deer.

Executives:
Jim Thorne, Executive Director; 403-234-6191; jthorne@creditcounselling.com
Tracy Watson, MCS, Manager, Communications; 403-234-6189; tracy@creditcounselling.com
Branches:
Edmonton
Sun Life Place
#440, 10123 - 99 St.
Edmonton, AB T5J 3H1 Canada
780-423-5265
Debbie Klein, Manager

Crosbie & Company Inc.
Also listed under: *Investment Dealers*
Sun Life Financial Tower
PO Box 95
150 King St. West, 15th Fl.
Toronto, ON M5H 1J9
416-362-7726
Fax: 416-362-3447
info@crosbieco.com
www.crosbieco.com
Ownership: Private
Year Founded: 1989
Number of Employees: 12
Profile: The company is a specialty investment banking firm. Investment banking services include the following: mergers, acquisitions & divestitures; debt & equity private placements; financial & corporate restructurings; management & employee buyouts; succession planning; shareholder liquidity alternatives; business & securities valuations; fairness opinions; investing as a principal & fund management.

Executives:
Allan H.T. Crosbie, Chair; 416-362-5138; acrosbie@crosbieco.com
Sharla Sigmund, Vice-President; 416-362-0684; ssigmund@crosbieco.com
Ed Giacomelli, Managing Director; 416-362-0020; egiacomelli@crosbieco.com
Ian K. MacDonell, Managing Director; 416-362-1953; imacdonell@crosbieco.com
Mel D. Margolese, Managing Director; 416-362-7805; mmargolese@crosbieco.com
Colin W. Walker, Managing Director; 416-362-7016; cwalker@crosbieco.com

Cundill Investment Research Ltd.
Sun Life Plaza
#200, 1100 Melville St.
Vancouver, BC V6E 4A6
604-601-8300
Fax: 604-601-8301
invest@cundill.com
www.cundill.com
Former Name: Peter Cundill & Associates Ltd.
Ownership: Private
Year Founded: 1974
Number of Employees: 18
Assets: $1-10 billion
Executives:
Lisa Pankratz, President

Cypress Capital Management Ltd.
Also listed under: *Financial Planning*
PO Box 11136
#1700, 1055 West Georgia St.
Vancouver, BC V6E 3P3
604-659-1850
Fax: 604-659-1899
877-659-1850
Ownership: AFG Private Investment Management, Toronto, ON.
Year Founded: 1998
Executives:
Carl Hoyt, CFA, Partner & Head, Research & Investment Management
Offices:
Calgary
Home Oil Tower
1155, 324 - 8th Ave. SW
Calgary, AB T2P 2Z2 Canada
403-663-6600
Fax: 403-451-9990

D&H Group
Also listed under: *Accountants*
1333 West Broadway St., 10th Fl.
Vancouver, BC V6H 4C1
604-731-5881
Fax: 604-731-9923
info@dhgroup.ca
www.dhgroup.ca
Former Name: Dyke & Howard
Ownership: Private
Year Founded: 1952
Number of Employees: 50
Executives:
Larry Bisaro, Sr. Partner; lbisaro@dhgroup.ca
Arthur Azana; aazana@dhgroup.ca
Craig Cox; ccox@@dhgroup.ca
Gordon Cummings; gcummings@dhgroup.ca
Brant Grondin; bgrondin@dhgroup.ca
Tom Hamar; thamar@dhgroup.ca
Dennis Louie; dlouie@dhgroup.ca
Michael Louie; mlouie@dhgroup.ca
Bruce MacFarlane; bmacfarlane@dhgroup.ca
Michael Nakanishi; mnakanishi@dhgroup.ca
Michael Wong; mwong@dhgroup.ca

Deans Knight Capital Management Ltd.
#730, 999 Hastings St. West
Vancouver, BC V6C 2W2
604-669-0212
Fax: 604-669-0238
Ownership: Private
Year Founded: 1992
Number of Employees: 8
Assets: $500m-1 billion
Profile: The investment company focuses on Canadian small-cap equity & high yield bond management.

Executives:
Wayne Deans
Douglas Knight
Michael Simonetta

Demers Conseil inc.
Also listed under: *Investment Dealers*
#1120, 615, boul René-Lévesque ouest
Montréal, QC H3B 1P5
514-879-1702
Fax: 514-879-5977
info@demersconseil.com
www.demersconseil.com
Ownership: Private
Year Founded: 1992
Stock Exchange Membership: Montreal Exchange

Diamond Retirement Planning Ltd.
Also listed under: *Financial Planning*
111 Pulford St.
Winnipeg, MB R3L 1X8
204-949-4749
866-949-7743
info@diamondretirement.com
www.diamondretirement.com
Ownership: Private
Year Founded: 1989
Number of Employees: 5
Executives:
Daryl Diamond, President/Co-owner
Karen Diamond, Co-Owner

DNL Money Management Ltd.
Also listed under: *Investment Dealers*
38 Colonnade Rd. North
Nepean, ON K2E 7J6
613-727-1020
Fax: 613-727-1410
888-530-9777
info@dnlgroup.com
www.dnlgroup.com
Ownership: DNL Group, Nepean, ON.
Year Founded: 1977
Executives:
Denis Emard, President, Owner

Donro Financial Corporation
Also listed under: *Financial Planning*
#304, 63 Church St.
St Catharines, ON L2R 3C4
905-984-2100
Fax: 905-984-2102
donro@donro.on.ca
www.donro.on.ca
Ownership: Private
Profile: The full-service company provides the following services: professional financial planning; group benefits & pension consulting; mutual fund, annuity & life insurance brokerage; human resource management; & life style consulting services.

Executives:
Donald Robertson, President

Dundee Wealth Management Inc.
Also listed under: *Financial Planning*
1 Adelaide St. East, 27th Fl.
Toronto, ON M5C 2V9
416-350-3250
888-332-2661
inquiries@dundeewealth.com
www.dundeewealth.com
Former Name: Goodman & Company Ltd.
Ownership: Public. Wholly owned subsidiary of Dundee Corporation
Executives:
Ned Goodman, CEO
Joanne Ferstman, CFO
Affiliated Companies:
Dynamic Mutual Funds/DMF
Dynamic Venture Opportunities Fund Ltd.

Envoy Capital Management
#740, 404 - 6th Ave. SW
Calgary, AB T2P 0R9
403-233-9370
Fax: 403-265-9334
info@envoycapital.com
www.envoycapital.com
Ownership: Private
Year Founded: 2000
Profile: Venture capital firm focused exclusively on commercializing energy and industrial technologies.

Executives:
Warren Dowd, President/CEO
Linda Machaalany

First Affiliated Holdings Inc.
Also listed under: *Financial Planning*
Plaza One, Meadowvale Corporate Center
#106, 2000 Argentia Rd.
Mississauga, ON L5N 1P7
905-812-2828
Fax: 905-812-8926
cclarke@firstaffiliated.on.ca
www.firstaffiliated.ca
Ownership: Private
Profile: The financial & investment planning organization is independent & fee-based. Wealth management services are provided by First Affilated Holdings Inc. / First Affiliated Secuities Inc. to affluent Canadians & family business owners.

Executives:
Christine Clarke, RFP, CA, President, Partner & Director
Karl Mortveit, CFO, COO & Partner
Barton Rowe, Investment Analyst & Partner
Karen McInnis, Manager, Client Service
Branches:
Collingwood
Arlington Bldg.
#302, 115 Hurontario St.
Collingwood, ON L9Y 2L9 Canada
705-455-7444
Fax: 705-455-0143
cclarke@firstaffiliated.on.ca

First Capital Financial
Also listed under: *Investment Dealers*
17B Manitoba St.
Bracebridge, ON P1L 1V3
705-646-0480
Fax: 705-646-0482
800-376-2293
martin@firstcapitalfinancial.ca
www.firstcapitalfinancial.ca
Profile: Services provided include wealth & risk management, and retirement & estate planning.

Executives:
Martin Weiler, President
Branches:
Gravenhurst
1st St. North
Gravenhurst, ON P1P 1H6 Canada
705-687-0630
Fax: 705-687-0671
greg@firstcapitalfinancial.ca
Greg Rasmussen, Investor Advisor Associate
Guelph
176 Woolwich St.
Guelph, ON N1H 3V5 Canada
519-829-1331
Fax: 519-829-3551
866-845-2751
martin@firstcapitalfinancial.ca

First National Financial Corporation
North Tower
#700, 100 University Ave
Toronto, ON M5J 1V6
416-593-1100
Fax: 416-593-1900
customer@firstnational.ca
www.firstnational.ca
Ownership: Private
Year Founded: 1988
Number of Employees: 200
Assets: $1-10 billion
Revenues: $50-100 million
Profile: Services include mortgage banking & administration.

Regional Offices:
Calgary
#801, 550 - 11th Ave. SW
Calgary, AB T2R 1M7 Canada
403-509-0900
Fax: 403-509-0909
888-923-9194
Halifax
25 Main St.
Bedford, NS B4A 2M8 Canada
902-452-0776
Fax: 902-835-2157
Montréal
#307, 630, rue Sherbrooke ouest
Montréal, QC H3A 1E4 Canada
514-499-8900
Fax: 514-499-8902
Vancouver
#1606, 1166 Alberni St.
Vancouver, BC V6E 3Z3 Canada
605-681-5300
Fax: 604-681-7200

Fiscal Agents Ltd.
Also listed under: *Investment Dealers*
PO Box 5000
25 Lakeshore Rd. West
Oakville, ON L6K 5C7
905-844-7700
Fax: 905-844-8552
866-434-7225
mailroom@fiscalagents.com
www.fiscalagents.com
Year Founded: 1977
Profile: Investment advisory services are provided related to retirement planning, investment funds & life insurance.

Executives:
David Newman, Director, Information Services

Friedberg Commodity Management Inc.(FCMI)
BCE Place
PO Box 866
#250, 181 Bay St
Toronto, ON M5J 2T3
416-364-1171
Fax: 416-364-0572
800-346-7761
friedberg@friedberg.ca
www.friedberg.com
Ownership: Private
Number of Employees: 42
Profile: FCMI is the Friedberg Group's commodity trading advisor and portfolio manager.

Executives:
Albert D. Friedberg, President/Chair
Henry Fenig, Exec. Vice-President & Treasurer
Herbert S. Alpert, Secretary
Directors:
Herbert S. Alpert
Henry Fenig
Lloyd S.D. Fogler
Albert D. Friedberg
Albert Gnat
S. Jeffrey Hertz

GBC Asset Management Inc.
Also listed under: *Investment Fund Companies*
BCE Place, Canada Trust Tower
#4320, 161 Bay St.
Toronto, ON M5J 2S1
416-366-2550
Fax: 416-366-6833
800-668-7383
info@gbc.ca
www.gbc.ca
Ownership: Private
Year Founded: 1988
Number of Employees: 18
Assets: $500m-1 billion
Executives:
John Quinn, Partner
Russ Quinn, Partner & Manager, Administration
Jean-Paul Burlock, Contact, Sales
GBC:
Canadian Bond Fund
RRSP Eligible; Inception Year: 1984; Fund Managers: TDQC
Canadian Growth Fund
RRSP Eligible; Inception Year: 1988; Fund Managers: Pembroke Management Ltd.
International Growth Fund
RRSP Eligible; Inception Year: 1989; Fund Managers: William Blair & Co. LLC
Money Market Fund
RRSP Eligible; Inception Year: 1988; Fund Managers: TDQC
North American Growth US$ Fund
RRSP Eligible; Inception Year: 1997; Fund Managers: Pembroke Management Ltd.
North American Growth Fund
RRSP Eligible; Inception Year: 1977; Fund Managers: Pembroke Management Ltd.
Regional Offices:
Montréal
#1700, 1002, rue Sherbrooke ouest
Montréal, QC H3A 3S4 Canada
514-848-0716
Fax: 514-848-9620
800-667-0716
Daniel Thompson, Partner

Genus Capital Management Inc.
Also listed under: *Financial Planning*
#1690, 999 West Hastings St.
Vancouver, BC V6C 2W2
604-683-4554
Fax: 604-683-7294
800-668-7366

Genus Capital Management Inc. (continued)
www.genuscap.com
Year Founded: 1989
Profile: The independently owned investment counselling firm provides money management to individuals, families, foundations & institutions. In 2004, the firm acquired Maxima Investment Management.
Executives:
Wayne Wachell, CEO, Chief Investment Officer
Leslie Cliff, President & Director, Client Support
Rajan Dassan, Chief Information Officer
Brad Bondy, Director, Research
Chris Harrison, Controller
Robin Larsen, Manager, Communications
Branches:
Kelowna
#406, 1708 Dolphin Ave.
Kelowna, BC V1Y 9S4 Canada
250-712-2218
Fax: 250-862-9101
877-712-2217
quayle@genuscap.com
Dorothy Quayle, Portfolio Manager

Gestion de placements Eterna

***Also listed under:** Financial Planning*
#400, 1134, Grande allée ouest
Québec, QC G1S 1E5
418-692-9292
Fax: 418-266-1002
info@eterna.ca
www.eterna.ca
Former Name: Gestion de Placements Tardif Inc.; Trust Prêt et Revenu/Savings & Investment Trust
Ownership: Private. Parent is Trust Eterna.
Year Founded: 1998
Number of Employees: 28
Executives:
Paul Tardif, Chair/CEO & President
Robert Archer, Vice-President
Jean Duguay, Vice-President, Investments
Branches:
Montréal
#2140, 1155, rue Metcalfe
Montréal, QC H3B 2V6 Canada
514-908-6000
Fax: 514-908-6001
Jean Duguay, Vice-President, Investments

Gestion Férique

***Also listed under:** Investment Fund Companies*
#350, 1100 rue de la Gauchetière ouest
Montréal, QC H3B 2S2
514-840-9206
Fax: 514-840-9216
888-259-7969
info@ferique.com
www.ferique.com
Former Name: Ordre des Ingenieurs du Québec
Ownership: Non-profit
Year Founded: 1999
Number of Employees: 5
Assets: $500m-1 billion
Revenues: $5-10 million
Executives:
Michel Riverin, President
Claude R. Tremblay, Vice-President
Fabienne Lacoste, Exec. Director; 514-840-9206; fabienne.lacoste@ferique.com
Férique:
American Fund
RRSP Eligible; Inception Year: 1995; Fund Managers: TAL Global Asset Management Inc.
Equity Fund
RRSP Eligible; Inception Year: 1975; Fund Managers: Barclays Global Investors
International Equity Fund
RRSP Eligible; Inception Year: 1994; Fund Managers: TAL Global Asset Management Inc.
Balanced Fund
RRSP Eligible; Inception Year: 1981; Fund Managers: Foyston, Gordon & Payne
Short Term Income Fund
RRSP Eligible; Inception Year: 1975; Fund Managers: TAL Global Asset Management Inc.
Europe Fund
RRSP Eligible; Inception Year: 2003; Fund Managers: UBS
Asia Fund
RRSP Eligible; Inception Year: 2003; Fund Managers: Normura Investment Management
Bond Fund
RRSP Eligible; Inception Year: 0; Fund Managers: Addenda Capital

Gestion Fiera Capital

#900, 1501, Ave McGill College
Montréal, QC H3A 3M8
514-954-3300
Fax: 514-395-8752
info@fieracapital.com
www.fieracapital.ca
Former Name: Elantis Investment Management Inc.; Canagex Inc.
Ownership: Division of Desjardins Asset Management
Year Founded: 2003
Number of Employees: 50
Assets: $1-10 billion
Executives:
Jean-Guy Desjardins, MBA,CFA, CEO & Chief Investment Officer, Chair
Sylvain Brosseau, M.Sc., President/COO
Luc Sarrazin, CGA, Vice-President/CFO
Charles Desmeules, Vice-President, Client Service
Pierre Payeur, Vice-President, Investment Funds
André Sirard, Vice-President, Private Wealth Management
Sylvain Roy, M.SC.,CFA, Sr. Portfolio Manager, Quantitative Strategy & Derivative Products
Branches:
Richmond Hill
#710, 225 East Beaver Creek Rd.
Richmond Hill, ON L4B 3P4 Canada
905-771-9050
Fax: 905-771-8672

Global Benefit Plan Consultants Inc.

***Also listed under:** Financial Planning*
545 Wilson Ave.
Toronto, ON M3H 1V2
416-635-6000
Fax: 416-635-6464
Ownership: Private
Year Founded: 1961
Number of Employees: 87

GlobeInvest Capital Management Inc.

***Also listed under:** Financial Planning*
#3308, 20 Queen St. West
Toronto, ON M5H 3R3
416-591-7100
Fax: 416-591-7133
800-387-0784
info@globe-invest.com
www.globe-invest.com
Ownership: Private.
Year Founded: 1994
Number of Employees: 4
Assets: Under $1 million
Revenues: Under $1 million
Executives:
Peter A. Brieger, CFA, Chair/CEO
Wendy K. Sanita, CFP, Vice-President; wsanita@globe-invest.ca
Directors:
Peter A. Brieger, CFA

Gluskin Sheff + Associates Inc.

BCE Place
PO Box 774
#4600, 181 Bay St.
Toronto, ON M5J 2T3
416-681-6000
Fax: 416-681-6060
www.gluskinsheff.com
Ownership: Private
Year Founded: 1984
Number of Employees: 40
Assets: $500m-1 billion
Revenues: $10-50 million
Stock Symbol: GS
Profile: Gluskin Sheff + Associates Inc. is a wealth management firm. Its sole business is managing equity portfolios for high net worth individuals & institutional investors. Subordinate voting shares are listed on the Toronto Stock Exchange.
Executives:
Gerald Sheff, Chair/CEO
Ira Gluskin, President, Chief Investment Officer
Valerie Barker, CFO, Secretary
Jeremy Freedman, Chief Operating Officer
Ron Lloyd, Vice-President, Client Service

GTI Capital

***Also listed under:** Financing & Loan Companies*
#200, 255, rue St. Jacques
Montréal, QC H2Y 1M6
514-845-3800
Fax: 514-845-3810
info@gticapital.com
www.gticapital.com
Ownership: Private
Year Founded: 1992
Number of Employees: 12
Assets: $100-500 million
Profile: Venture capital.
Executives:
Bernard Hamel, Chair & Sr. General Partner
Roger Jenkins, Sr. General Partner
Jean-Francois Couturier, General Partner
Jean Desjardins, Partner
François Veilleux, CFO
Joanne Bessette, Controller

Guardian Capital Group Limited

***Also listed under:** Investment Dealers; Investment Management*
PO Box 201
#3100, Commerce Ct. West
Toronto, ON M5L 1E8
416-364-8341
Fax: 416-947-0601
Former Name: a
Ownership: Public. Major shareholders: Minic Investments Ltd. (47.9 interest); Rosemary Short (11.8% interest) & Joseph Rotman (16.8% interest).
Year Founded: 1962
Number of Employees: 97
Assets: $100-500 million Year End: 20051231
Revenues: $50-100 million Year End: 20051231
Stock Symbol: GCG
Profile: The holding company is engaged, through subsidiaries & affiliates, in the following areas: the management of pension funds & private client portfolios; the provision of trust & corporate services; the sale & distribution of mutual funds & securities; the investment of its own assets in equity markets & private placement situations. The following companies are wholly owned subsidiaries: Alexandria Bancorp Limited, Guardian Capital Advisors LP, & Guardian Capital LP. Another investment is Worldsource Holdings Corp. (93.9% interest).
Executives:
John M. Christodoulou, CEO
Sam K. Greiss, Sr. Vice-President, Operations & Corporate Development
George Mavroudis, Sr. Vice-President, Strategic Planning & Development
C. Verner Christensen, Vice-President, Finance, Secretary
Michael Denuzzo, Controller
Directors:
John M. Christodoulou, Chair
James Anas
F.D. Barrett
James W. McCutcheon
Michel Sales
Peter Stormonth Darling

Hatton Financial Inc.

***Also listed under:** Financial Planning*
#705, 10339 - 124th St.
Edmonton, AB T5N 3W1
780-482-2745
Fax: 780-488-1025
866-444-2745
klhatton@hatton.ca
www.hatton.ca
Former Name: Hatton Probe Financial Group Inc.
Ownership: Private

Year Founded: 1981
Number of Employees: 3
Assets: $5-10 million Year End: 20041029
Revenues: Under $1 million Year End: 20041029
Executives:
Keith Hatton, President

Hemisphere Capital Management
#2000, 444 - 5th Ave. SW
Calgary, AB T2P 2T8
403-205-3533
Fax: 403-205-3588
800-471-7853
info@hemisphere.ca
www.hemisphere.ca
Ownership: Private
Year Founded: 1993
Number of Employees: 5
Assets: $100-500 million Year End: 20040930
Revenues: $1-5 million Year End: 20040930
Executives:
Jim Aronitz, President
Tom Loucks, Vice-President
Rick M. Riffel, Vice-President

Highstreet Asset Management Inc.
Also listed under: *Investment Fund Companies*
#200, 244 Pall Mall St.
London, ON N6A 5P6
519-850-9500
Fax: 519-850-1214
877-850-9500
info@highstreet.ca
www.highstreet.ca
Ownership: Private
Year Founded: 1998
Number of Employees: 31
Assets: $1-10 billion Year End: 20051231
Revenues: $5-10 million Year End: 20051231
Executives:
Robert Badun, CEO
Paul Brisson, President
Jeffrey Brown, Chief Investment Officer
Dawn Butler, Chief Financial Officer
Douglas Crocker, Chief Risk Officer
Shaun Arnold, Vice-President
Lina Bowden, Vice-President
Rob Jackson, Vice-President
Peter Mastorakos, Vice-President
Grant McIntosh, Vice-President
Highstreet:
Balanced Fund
RRSP Eligible; Inception Year: 1998;
Canadian Bond Fund
RRSP Eligible; Inception Year: 1998;
Canadian Equity Fund
RRSP Eligible; Inception Year: 1998;
US Equity Fund
RRSP Eligible; Inception Year: 1998;
International Equity Fund
RRSP Eligible; Inception Year: 2002;
Money Market Fund
RRSP Eligible; Inception Year: 2002;
Growth Fund
RRSP Eligible; Inception Year: 0;
Small Cap Fund
RRSP Eligible; Inception Year: 0;

Hospitals of Ontario Pension Plan(HOOPP)
#1400, 1 Toronto St.
Toronto, ON M5C 3B2
416-369-9212
Fax: 416-369-0225
888-333-3659
clientservices@hoopp.com
www.hoopp.com
Year Founded: 1960
Profile: HOOPP is a multi-employer pension plan.

Executives:
John Crocker, President/CEO
Douglas Carr, CFO & Sr. Vice-President, Finance
George Buse, Sr. Vice-President, Plan Operations
Victoria Hubbell, Sr. Vice-President, Strategic Planning & Employee Services
Josephine E. Marks, Sr. Vice-President, Investment Management, Chief Investment Officer
David L. Miller, General Counsel & Sr. Vice-President, Governance
Directors:
Kelly Butt, Chair
Dan Anderson, Vice-Chair
David Alexander
Lesley Bell
Warren Chant
Helen Fetterly
Marcia Gillespie
Marcelle Goldenberg
Susan Lewis
Deborah Menzies
Ronald Meredith-Jones
Louis Rodrigues
James Sanders
Greg Shaw
Deepak Shukla

Howson Tattersall Investment Counsel Ltd.
Also listed under: *Financial Planning*
PO Box 9
#1700, 151 Yonge St.
Toronto, ON M5C 2W7
416-227-1617
Fax: 416-979-7424
888-933-0335
www.htic.ca
Ownership: Private
Year Founded: 1962
Profile: Howson Tattersall Investment Counsel provides investment management service to a broad client base. The company also manages the Saxon Group of Funds. It currently manages over $7 billion in assets.

Executives:
Allan W. Smith, CA, MBA, CFP, President/CEO
Richard Howson, Chief Investment Officer & Exec. Vice-President
Robert Leblanc, ASA, Vice-President, Investment Counsel
Brian M. Smith, CFA, Vice-President, Private Clients; brian.smith@htic.ca
Taras Klymenko, Manager, Institutional Service & Business Development
Affiliated Companies:
Saxon Mutual Funds
Branches:
Montréal
640-1000 de la Gauchetière ouest
Montréal, QC H3B 4W5 Canada
514-392-9151
Fax: 514-392-9222
866-361-9151
robert.leblanc@htic.ca
Robert Leblanc, Vice-President

Hub Capital Inc.
Also listed under: *Investment Dealers*
#1001, 3700 Steeles Ave. West
Woodbridge, ON L4L 8M9
905-264-1634
Fax: 905-264-0864
800-561-2405
www.hubfinancial.com
Profile: Hub Capital is the wealth management division of Hub Financial Inc. The division is a mutual fund dealership.

Executives:
Terri DiFlorio, President; terri.diflorio@hubfinancial.com
Jeff Botosan, Exec. Vice-President, Chief Operations Officer; jeff.botosan@hubfinancial.com
John Lutrin, Exec. Vice-President, Chief Marketing Officer; john.lutrin@hubfinancial.com
Kim Fernandes, Vice-President; kim.fernandes@hubfinancial.com
Cheryl Hamilton, Vice-President, Chief Compliance Officer; cheryl.hamilton@hubfinancial.com
Branches:
Calgary
#300, 4723 - 1st St. SW
Calgary, AB T2G 4Y8 Canada
403-262-4466
Fax: 403-266-7541
800-661-9228
Judy Simpson, Vice-President
London
#101, 557 Southdale Rd. East
London, ON N6E 1A2 Canada
519-641-3400
Fax: 519-641-3334
800-661-3400
Paul Sincerbox, Director, Marketing, Wealth Management
Montréal
#625, 8000, boul Décarie
Montréal, QC H4P 2S4 Canada
514-374-3848
Fax: 514-382-9151
800-361-4052
Sylvain Decoste, Director, Marketing, Wealth Management
New Westminster
#550, 628 - 6th Ave.
New Westminster, BC V3M 6Z1 Canada
604-526-4115
Fax: 604-526-4915
877-888-1222
Gord Johnson, Marketing Director
Vancouver
#800, 1185 West Georgia St.
Vancouver, BC V6E 4E6 Canada
604-684-0086
Fax: 604-684-9286
800-667-0310
Christa Hewitt, Director, Marketing, Wealth Management
Victoria
#201, 755 Queens St.
Victoria, BC V8T 1M2 Canada
250-414-7272
Fax: 250-414-7270
800-661-7410
Heidi Zealand, Administrator, Marketing, Wealth Management

IDC Financial
260 Brunel Rd.
Mississauga, ON L4Z 1T5
905-366-3866
Fax: 905-366-3877
877-742-5432
info@idcfinancial.com
www.idcfinancial.com
Executives:
Andy Gellatly, Principal
Ron Madzia, Principal
Jocelyn Florendo, Partner, National Operations
Greg Osmak, Partner, Business Development Executive
Eric Wachtel, Manager, Mutual Fund Branch

Integrated Asset Management Corp.
Also listed under: *Holding & Other Investment Companies*
#2200, 130 Adelaide St. West
Toronto, ON M5H 3P5
416-360-7667
Fax: 416-360-7446
info@iamgroup.ca
www.iamgroup.ca
Former Name: Koloshuk Farrugia Corp.
Ownership: Public
Year Founded: 1998
Number of Employees: 250
Assets: $10-50 million
Revenues: $10-50 million
Stock Symbol: IAM
Profile: Services include asset management, private equity, private corporate debt, hedge funds, real estate & managed futures. The following are the company's subsidiaries: Integrated Private Debt Corp., Grenier-Pacaud Management Associates, Darton Property Advisors & Managers Inc., Integrated Partners, & BluMont Capital.

Executives:
Victor Koloshuk, President/CEO
David Mather, Exec. Vice-President
Stephen Johnson, Vice-President/CFO
Directors:
Victor Koloshuk, Chair
Tony Pacaud, Vice-Chair
David Atkins
George Elliott
George Engman
Veronika Hirsch
Stephen C. Johnson
Michel Lebel

Integrated Asset Management Corp. (continued)
Donald Lowe
David Mather
John Robertson
Affiliated Companies:
Blumont Capital Corporation
Integrated Private Debt Corp.

Integrated Benefit Consultants
Also listed under: *Financial Planning*
#2, 4914 - 55th St.
Red Deer, AB T4N 2J4
403-340-3779
Ownership: Private
Executives:
John W. Ponto, CFP, President

Integrated Private Debt Corp.
Also listed under: *Financing & Loan Companies*
#2200, 130 Adelaide St. West
Toronto, ON M5H 3P5
416-367-2044
Fax: 416-367-2594
probson@iamgroup.ca
www.iamgroup.com
Former Name: First Treasury Corporation
Ownership: Public. Subsidiary of Integrated Asset Management
Year Founded: 1987
Number of Employees: 15
Assets: $500m-1 billion Year End: 20041201
Stock Symbol: IAM-X
Executives:
John F.K. Robertson, President
Ben Bacigalupi, Managing Director
Donald Bangay, Managing Director
B. Frank Duffy, Managing Director
Michael LeClair, Managing Director
Philip S. Robson, Managing Director
Doug Zinkiewich, Managing Director
Nushi Kazemian, Associate Director
Vanessa B.Z. Luce, Controller
Directors:
Stephen Johnson
Victor Koloshuk
John F.K. Robertson
Branches:
Calgary
3116 - 4th St NW
Calgary, AB T2M 3A4 Canada
403-283-0152
Fax: 403-283-0165

Interinvest Consulting Corporation of Canada Ltd.
Also listed under: *Financial Planning*
Maison Interinvest
3655, rue Redpath
Montréal, QC H3G 2W8
514-393-3232
Fax: 514-393-3453
nminns@interinvest.com
www.interinvest.com
Ownership: Private
Year Founded: 1975
Profile: The corporation manages individual wealth & institutional assets, such as endowment & pension funds.
Executives:
Hans P. Black, President/CEO
Yves Séguin, Sr. Manager
Branches:
Toronto
250 Bloor St. East
Toronto, ON M4W 1E6 Canada

The Investment Guild
Also listed under: *Financial Planning*
#302, 345 Renfrew Dr.
Markham, ON L3R 9S9
905-470-9840
Fax: 905-470-6723
info@investmentguild.com
www.investmentguild.com
Ownership: Private
Year Founded: 1981
Number of Employees: 9
Assets: $1-5 million Year End: 20051130
Revenues: $1-5 million Year End: 20051130
Profile: The Guild also provides consulting on group insurance & employee benefits.
Executives:
J. Jeffrey Case, CLU, CFP, CH.F.C., President
W. Michael Thomas, CLU, CH.F.C., CFP, RFP, Vice-President

Jarislowsky, Fraser Limited
#2005, 1010, rue Sherbrooke ouest
Montréal, QC H3A 2R7
514-842-2727
Fax: 514-842-1882
dmazzarello@jfl.ca
www.jfl.ca
Ownership: Private
Year Founded: 1955
Number of Employees: 100
Profile: Registered investment counseling firm, managing pension funds, pooled funds, endowment funds and corporate and private portfolios for clients in North America and Europe.
Executives:
M. Stephen Jarislowsky, Chair/CEO
Pierre Lapointe, Exec. Vice-President
Branches:
Calgary
#1640, 140 - 4th St. SW
Calgary, AB T2P 3N3 Canada
403-233-9117
Fax: 403-233-9144
jmorton@jfl.ca
Robert J. Tilden
Toronto
#3100, 20 Queen St. West
Toronto, ON M5H 3R3 Canada
416-363-7417
Fax: 416-363-8079
mritchie@jfl.ca
James Morton
Vancouver
PO Box 12129
#2080 - 555 West Hastings St.
Vancouver, BC V6B 4N6 Canada
604-676-3612
Fax: 604-676-3616
bhowes@jfl.ca

Jenner Financial Services
Also listed under: *Financial Planning; Investment Management*
#750, 926 - 5th Ave. SW
Calgary, AB T2P 0N7
403-777-4747
Fax: 403-777-4742
ajenner@telus.net
Former Name: Alison Jenner Financial Ltd.
Ownership: Private
Profile: An affiliated company is Peak Investment Services Inc.
Executives:
Alison Jenner, Contact

Jones Heward Investment Counsel Inc.
#4200, 77 King St. West
Toronto, ON M5K 1J5
416-359-5000
Fax: 416-359-5950
www.jonesheward.com
Ownership: Public
Number of Employees: 90
Profile: Canadian institutional money manager with over $32 billion in total assets under management. Clients include pensions, endowments, trusts, insurance company reserves, corporate surpluses and mutual funds.
Executives:
Michael Stanley, Chief Investment Officer

KBSH Capital Management Inc.
Also listed under: *Financial Planning*
#700, 1 Toronto St.
Toronto, ON M5C 2V6
416-863-1433
Fax: 416-868-1770
mail@kbsh.ca
www.kbsh.ca
Former Name: Knight, Bain, Seath & Holbrook
Ownership: Wholly owned subsidiary of Rockwater Capital Corporation, Toronto, ON.
Year Founded: 1980
Executives:
David Knight, Founding Partner
Peter Pennal, President/CEO
Geoffrey Hollands, Sr. Vice-President, Investments
Branches:
Halifax
Tower II, Purdy's Wharf
#1401A, 1969 Upper Water St.
Halifax, NS B3J 3R7 Canada
902-421-1564
Fax: 902-422-9755
Bob Rudderham, Vice-President, Marketing
Montréal
#2400, 1000, de la Gauchetière ouest
Montréal, QC H3B 4W5 Canada
514-499-5274
Fax: 514-499-0042
Tim Stinson, President, Private Client Group

Leeland Financial Group
Also listed under: *Financial Planning*
#1088, 926 - 5 Ave. SW
Calgary, AB T2P 0N7
403-265-0235
Fax: 403-265-0311
800-341-1888
leeland@leeland.com
www.leeland.com
Ownership: Private
Year Founded: 1968
Number of Employees: 4
Assets: $10-50 million Year End: 20051201

Lincluden Management Limited
Also listed under: *Investment Fund Companies*
#607, 1275 North Service Rd. West
Oakville, ON L6M 3G4
905-825-9000
Fax: 905-825-9525
800-532-7071
lynn.eplett@lincluden.com
www.lincluden.com
Ownership: Wholly-owned affiliate of Old Mutual Asset Management
Year Founded: 1982
Number of Employees: 14
Assets: $1-10 billion Year End: 20041231
Profile: Lincluden specializes in pension fund management.
Executives:
George M. Youssef, Chair
Phil Evans, President/CEO
Peter Chin, Vice-President
C. Lynn Eplett, Vice-President, Client Services
James Lampard, Vice-President
Marc Noble, Vice-President, Business Development
John Richardson, Vice-President
Bob Sanderson, Vice-President
Richard Wong, Vice-President
Lincluden:
Balanced Fund
RRSP Eligible; Inception Year: 2000;

MacDougall, MacDougall & MacTier Inc.
Also listed under: *Investment Dealers; Investment Management*
Place du Canada
#2000, 1010, rue de la Gauchetière ouest
Montréal, QC H3B 4J1
514-394-3000
Fax: 514-871-1481
800-567-4465
macdougall@3macs.com
www.3macs.com
Ownership: Employee-owned.
Year Founded: 1858
Stock Exchange Membership: Canadian Trading & Quotation System Inc, Montreal Exchange, Toronto Stock Exchange, TSX Venture Exchange
Profile: Investment management advice & services are offered to private investors by the independent investment dealer. The firm's services include managed accounts, RRSPs, RESPs, RRIFs, life income funds, tax planning, estate planning, cash management, fixed income & record keeping.
Executives:

Timothy E. Price, President/CEO
William W. Black, CIM, Vice-President
Mark W. Gallop, MBA, FCSI, Vice-President
William L. Cowen, Branch Manager, Investment Advisor
Branches:
Kingston
208 Albert St.
Montréal, QC K7L 3V3 Canada
613-531-9746
866-588-3490
Bill Cowen, Contact
London
#202, 140 Fullarton St.
London, ON N6A 5P2 Canada
519-645-1110
Fax: 519-645-1096
800-267-0056
Robert C. Ketchabaw, Branch Manager
Québec
#800, 2875, boul Laurier
Québec, QC G1V 2M2 Canada
418-656-1212
Fax: 418-656-4222
888-462-3010
Michel G. Bergeron, Branch Manager
Toronto
PO Box 13
#2510, 150 King St. West
Toronto, ON M5H 1J9 Canada
416-977-0663
Fax: 416-596-7453
800-461-3485
Bart H. MacDougall, Chair

Mackenzie Financial Corporation

Also listed under: *Investment Fund Companies*
#111M, 150 Bloor St. West
Toronto, ON M5S 3B5
416-922-5322
Fax: 416-922-5660
800-387-0780
service@mackenziefinancial.com
www.mackenziefinancial.com
Ownership: Public
Year Founded: 1967
Number of Employees: 516
Stock Symbol: MKF
Profile: Mackenzie manages a family of mutual funds on behalf of almost one million Canadian investors. In addition, through subsidiary companies, Mackenzie provides investment advisory services to private client accounts, & operates a trust company.

Executives:
Jim Hunter, President/CEO
Ed Merchand, CFO
W. Sian B. Brown, Sr. Vice-President, General Counsel & Secretary
Peter Dawkins, Exec. Vice-President, Chief Investment Strategist
Laurie J. Munro, Exec. Vice-President, Strategic & Business Planning
Andrew Dalglish, President/CEO, MRS Group
David Feather, President, Mackenzie Financial Services Inc.
Directors:
Philip F. Cunningham, Chair
Affiliated Companies:
M.R.S. Trust Company
Cundill:
Canadian Balanced Series C Fund
RRSP Eligible; Inception Year: 1998; Fund Managers:
Peter Cundill & Associates (Bermuda) Ltd.
Canadian Security Fund
RRSP Eligible; Inception Year: 1980; Fund Managers:
Peter Cundill & Associates (Bermuda) Ltd.
Canadian Security Series B Fund
RRSP Eligible; Inception Year: 1997; Fund Managers:
Peter Cundill & Associates (Bermuda) Ltd.
Canadian Security Series C Fund
RRSP Eligible; Inception Year: 1998; Fund Managers:
Peter Cundill & Associates (Bermuda) Ltd.
Global Balanced Series C Fund
RRSP Eligible; Inception Year: 1999; Fund Managers:
Peter Cundill & Associates (Bermuda) Ltd.
Recovery Series C Fund
RRSP Eligible; Inception Year: 1998; Fund Managers:
Peter Cundill & Associates (Bermuda) Ltd.
Value Fund
RRSP Eligible; Inception Year: 1974; Fund Managers:
Peter Cundill & Associates (Bermuda) Ltd.
Value Series B Fund
RRSP Eligible; Inception Year: 1997; Fund Managers:
Peter Cundill & Associates (Bermuda) Ltd.
Value Series C Fund
RRSP Eligible; Inception Year: 1998; Fund Managers:
Peter Cundill & Associates (Bermuda) Ltd.
Value Capital Class Fund
RRSP Eligible; Inception Year: 2000; Fund Managers:
Peter Cundill & Associates (Bermuda) Ltd.
Canadian Balanced Segregated Fund
RRSP Eligible; Inception Year: 1999; Fund Managers:
Peter Cundill & Associates (Bermuda) Ltd.
Canadian Balanced Series T Fund
RRSP Eligible; Inception Year: 2002; Fund Managers:
Peter Cundill & Associates (Bermuda) Ltd.
Canadian Security Capital Class Fund
RRSP Eligible; Inception Year: 2003; Fund Managers:
Peter Cundill & Associates (Bermuda) Ltd.
Global Balanced Series T Fund
RRSP Eligible; Inception Year: 2002; Fund Managers:
Peter Cundill & Associates (Bermuda) Ltd.
Value Segregated Fund
RRSP Eligible; Inception Year: 1999; Fund Managers:
Peter Cundill & Associates (Bermuda) Ltd.
American Capital Class Fund
RRSP Eligible; Inception Year: 2003; Fund Managers:
Peter Cundill & Associates (Bermuda) Ltd.
Canadian Security Segregated Fund
RRSP Eligible; Inception Year: 1999; Fund Managers:
Peter Cundill & Associates (Bermuda) Ltd.
Ivy:
Enterprise Fund
RRSP Eligible; Inception Year: 1994; Fund Managers:
Stephanie Griffiths
Growth & Income Fund
RRSP Eligible; Inception Year: 1992; Fund Managers:
Jerry Javasky
Canadian Fund
RRSP Eligible; Inception Year: 1992; Fund Managers:
Jerry Javasky
Foreign Equity Fund
RRSP Eligible; Inception Year: 1992; Fund Managers:
Jerry Javasky
PaulMusson
Canadian Capital Class Fund
RRSP Eligible; Inception Year: 2000; Fund Managers:
Jerry Javasky
Enterprise Capital Class Fund
RRSP Eligible; Inception Year: 2000; Fund Managers:
Stephanie Griffiths
Foreign Equity Capital Class Fund
RRSP Eligible; Inception Year: 2000; Fund Managers:
Jerry Javasky
Canadian Segregated Fund
RRSP Eligible; Inception Year: 1999; Fund Managers:
Jerry Javasky
Enterprise Segregated Fund
RRSP Eligible; Inception Year: 1999; Fund Managers:
Stephanie Griffiths
Foreign Equity Segregated Fund
RRSP Eligible; Inception Year: 1999; Fund Managers:
Jerry Javasky
Global Balanced Fund
RRSP Eligible; Inception Year: 1993; Fund Managers:
Jerry Javasky
PaulMusson
Global Balanced Series T Fund
RRSP Eligible; Inception Year: 2002; Fund Managers:
Jerry Javasky
PaulMusson
Growth & Income Series T Fund
RRSP Eligible; Inception Year: 2002; Fund Managers:
Jerry Javasky
European Capital Class Fund
RRSP Eligible; Inception Year: 2002; Fund Managers:
Jerry Javasky
PaulMusson
Global Balanced Segregated Fund
RRSP Eligible; Inception Year: 1999; Fund Managers:
Jerry Javasky
PaulMusson
Growth & Income Segregated Fund
RRSP Eligible; Inception Year: 1999; Fund Managers:
Jerry Javasky
Keystone:
Investment Balanced Growth & Income Fund
RRSP Eligible; Inception Year: 1998;
Investment Conservative Income & Growth Fund
RRSP Eligible; Inception Year: 1998;
Investment Long-Term Growth Fund
RRSP Eligible; Inception Year: 1998;
Investment Maximum Equity Growth Fund
RRSP Eligible; Inception Year: 1998;
Investment Maximum Long-Term Growth Fund
RRSP Eligible; Inception Year: 1998;
Balanced Growth & Income Fund
RRSP Eligible; Inception Year: 1998;
Conservative Income & Growth Fund
RRSP Eligible; Inception Year: 1998;
Long-Term Growth Fund
RRSP Eligible; Inception Year: 1998;
Maximum Equity Growth Fund
RRSP Eligible; Inception Year: 1998;
Maximum Long-Term Growth Fund
RRSP Eligible; Inception Year: 1998;
Balanced Growth Portfolio Fund
RRSP Eligible; Inception Year: 2003; Fund Managers:
Waddell & Reed Inc.
Balanced Portfolio Fund
RRSP Eligible; Inception Year: 2003; Fund Managers:
MFC Global Investment Management
Conservative Portfolio Fund
RRSP Eligible; Inception Year: 2003; Fund Managers:
MFC Global Investment Management
Growth Portfolio Fund
RRSP Eligible; Inception Year: 2003; Fund Managers:
Waddell & Reed Inc.
Maximum Growth Portfolio Fund
RRSP Eligible; Inception Year: 2004; Fund Managers:
MFC Global Investment Management
Balanced Growth Portfolio Segregated Fund
RRSP Eligible; Inception Year: 1999;
Balanced Portfolio Segregated Fund
RRSP Eligible; Inception Year: 1999;
Conservative Portfolio Segregated Fund
RRSP Eligible; Inception Year: 1999;
Growth Portfolio Segregated Fund
RRSP Eligible; Inception Year: 1999;
Maximum Growth Portfolio Segregated Fund
RRSP Eligible; Inception Year: 1999;
Dynamic Power Small-Cap Capital Class Fund
RRSP Eligible; Inception Year: 2005; Fund Managers:
Goodman & Company Investment Counsel
Balanced Growth Portfolio Series T Fund
RRSP Eligible; Inception Year: 2004; Fund Managers:
Franklin Templeton Investments
Balanced Portfolio Series T Fund
RRSP Eligible; Inception Year: 2004; Fund Managers:
MFC Global Investment Management
Conservative Portfolio Series T Fund
RRSP Eligible; Inception Year: 2005; Fund Managers:
MFC Global Investment Management
Diversified Income Portfolio Fund
RRSP Eligible; Inception Year: 2005; Fund Managers:
MFC Global Investment Management
Diversified Income Portfolio Series T Fund
RRSP Eligible; Inception Year: 2005; Fund Managers:
MFC Global Investment Management
Keystone AGF:
Equity Fund
RRSP Eligible; Inception Year: 1998; Fund Managers:
AGF Fund Management
Keystone AIM/Trimark:
Canadian Equity Fund
RRSP Eligible; Inception Year: 1998; Fund Managers:
AIM Funds Management Inc.
Global Equity Fund
RRSP Eligible; Inception Year: 1998; Fund Managers:
AIM Funds Management Inc.
US Companies Fund
RRSP Eligible; Inception Year: 1998; Fund Managers:
AIM Funds Management Inc.
Keystone Beutel Goodman:
Bond Fund
RRSP Eligible; Inception Year: 1998; Fund Managers:
Beutel Goodman

Mackenzie Financial Corporation (continued)

Keystone Bissett:
Canadian Equity Fund
RRSP Eligible; Inception Year: 1998; Fund Managers:
Bissett & Co.
Keystone Elliott & Page:
High Income Fund
RRSP Eligible; Inception Year: 1998; Fund Managers:
MFC Global Investment Management
Keystone Saxon:
Smaller Companies Fund
RRSP Eligible; Inception Year: 1998; Fund Managers:
Saxon
Keystone Templeton:
International Stock Capital Class Fund
RRSP Eligible; Inception Year: 2003;
Mackenzie:
Growth Fund
RRSP Eligible; Inception Year: 1967; Fund Managers:
Fred Sturm
BenoitGervais
Shechar Dworski
Alternative Strategies Fund
RRSP Eligible; Inception Year: 2001; Fund Managers:
Tremont Capital Management Corp.
Balanced Series T Fund
RRSP Eligible; Inception Year: 2002; Fund Managers:
FairLane Asset Management
Balanced Segregated Fund
RRSP Eligible; Inception Year: 1999; Fund Managers:
FairLane Asset Management
Balanced Fund
RRSP Eligible; Inception Year: 1991; Fund Managers:
FairLane Asset Management
Maxxum:
Canadian Balanced Fund
RRSP Eligible; Inception Year: 1988; Fund Managers:
Chris Kresic
ChuckRoth
Canadian Balanced Series T Fund
RRSP Eligible; Inception Year: 2003; Fund Managers:
Chris Kresic
ChuckRoth
Canadian Equity Growth Fund
RRSP Eligible; Inception Year: 1970; Fund Managers:
Chuck Roth
Canadian Value Capital Class Fund
RRSP Eligible; Inception Year: 2000; Fund Managers:
Bill Procter
AndrewKnezy
James Leung
Joe Mastrolonardo
Michele Calpin
Dividend Fund
RRSP Eligible; Inception Year: 1986; Fund Managers:
Bill Procter
JoeMastrolonardo
Michele Calpin
Andrew Knezy
James Leung
Dividend Growth Fund
RRSP Eligible; Inception Year: 1975; Fund Managers:
Bill Procter
AndrewKnezy
Joe Mastrolonardo
Michele Calpin
James Leung
Money Market FundInception Year: 1986; Fund Managers:
Chris Kresic
Monthly Income Fund
RRSP Eligible; Inception Year: 1971; Fund Managers:
Bill Procter
JoeMastrolonardo
Michele Calpin
Andrew Knezy
James Leung
Monthly Income Series T Fund
RRSP Eligible; Inception Year: 2002; Fund Managers:
Bill Procter
AndrewKnezy
Joe Mastrolonardo
Michele Calpin
James Leung
Dividend Capital Class Fund
RRSP Eligible; Inception Year: 2003; Fund Managers:
Bill Procter
AndrewKnezy
Joe Mastrolonardo
Michele Calpin
James Leung
Monthly Income Segregated Fund
RRSP Eligible; Inception Year: 1999; Fund Managers:
Bill Procter
AndrewKnezy
James Leung
Joe Mastrolonardo
Michele Calpin
Canadian Equity Growth Capital Class Fund
RRSP Eligible; Inception Year: 2003; Fund Managers:
Chuck Roth
Canadian Value Fund
RRSP Eligible; Inception Year: 1987; Fund Managers:
Bill Procter
AndrewKnezy
Joe Mastrolonardo
Michele Calpin
James Leung
Dividend Growth Segregated Fund
RRSP Eligible; Inception Year: 1999; Fund Managers:
Bill Procter
AndrewKnezy
James Leung
Joe Mastrolonardo
Michele Calpin
Global Explorer Capital Class Fund
RRSP Eligible; Inception Year: 2000; Fund Managers:
Alan Pasnik
STAR:
Canadian Balanced Growth & Income Fund
RRSP Eligible; Inception Year: 1996;
Canadian Conservative Income & Growth Fund
RRSP Eligible; Inception Year: 1996;
Canadian Long-Term Growth Fund
RRSP Eligible; Inception Year: 1996;
Canadian Maximum Equity Growth Fund
RRSP Eligible; Inception Year: 1996;
Canadian Maximum Long-Term Growth Fund
RRSP Eligible; Inception Year: 1996;
Foreign Balanced Growth & Income Fund
RRSP Eligible; Inception Year: 1995;
Foreign Maximum Long-Term Growth Fund
RRSP Eligible; Inception Year: 1995;
Foreign Maximum Equity Growth Fund
RRSP Eligible; Inception Year: 1995;
Investment Balanced Growth & Income Fund
RRSP Eligible; Inception Year: 1995;
Investment Conservative Income & Growth Fund
RRSP Eligible; Inception Year: 1995;
Investment Long-Term Growth Fund
RRSP Eligible; Inception Year: 1995;
Investment Maximum Long-Term Growth Fund
RRSP Eligible; Inception Year: 1995;
Balanced Growth & Income Fund
RRSP Eligible; Inception Year: 1995;
Conservative Income & Growth Fund
RRSP Eligible; Inception Year: 1995;
Long-Term Growth Fund
RRSP Eligible; Inception Year: 1995;
Maximum Equity Growth Fund
RRSP Eligible; Inception Year: 1995;
Maximum Long-Term Growth Fund
RRSP Eligible; Inception Year: 1995;
Select Managers:
Far East Capital Class Fund
RRSP Eligible; Inception Year: 2002; Fund Managers:
Allianz Dresdner Asset Management
International Capital Class Fund
RRSP Eligible; Inception Year: 2000; Fund Managers:
Jerry Javasky
PaulMusson
Henderson Global Investors
Japan Capital Class Fund
RRSP Eligible; Inception Year: 2002; Fund Managers:
Henderson Global Investors
Canada Capital Class Fund
RRSP Eligible; Inception Year: 2000; Fund Managers:
Ian Ainsworth
BillProcter
Jerry Javasky
Michele Calpin
Bluewater Investment Management
Select Managers Fund
RRSP Eligible; Inception Year: 1998; Fund Managers:
Henderson Global Investors
Capital Class Fund
RRSP Eligible; Inception Year: 2000; Fund Managers:
Henderson Global Investors
USA Capital Class Fund
RRSP Eligible; Inception Year: 2002; Fund Managers:
Credit Suisse Asset Management
Canada Fund
RRSP Eligible; Inception Year: 2002; Fund Managers:
Bill Procter
JerryJavasky
Ian Ainsworth
Michele Calpin
Peter Cundill & Associates (Bermuda) Ltd.
Segregated Fund
RRSP Eligible; Inception Year: 1999; Fund Managers:
Henderson Global Investors
Canada Segregated Fund
RRSP Eligible; Inception Year: 2001;
Sentinel:
Bond Fund
RRSP Eligible; Inception Year: 1989; Fund Managers:
Chris Kresic
Cash Management Fund
RRSP Eligible; Inception Year: 1984;
Short Term Bond Fund
RRSP Eligible; Inception Year: 1999; Fund Managers:
Chris Kresic
Canadian Managed Yield Capital Class Fund
RRSP Eligible; Inception Year: 2000;
US Managed Yield Capital Class FundInception Year: 2000;
Bond Segregated Fund
RRSP Eligible; Inception Year: 1999; Fund Managers:
Chris Kresic
Cash Management Segregated Fund
RRSP Eligible; Inception Year: 1999;
Income Segregated Fund
RRSP Eligible; Inception Year: 1999; Fund Managers:
Bill Procter
ChrisKresic
Money Market Fund
RRSP Eligible; Inception Year: 1991;
Money Market Series B Fund
RRSP Eligible; Inception Year: 2001;
Managed Return Capital Class Fund
RRSP Eligible; Inception Year: 2002; Fund Managers:
Chris Kresic
Mortgage Fund
RRSP Eligible; Inception Year: 1994;
Income Fund
RRSP Eligible; Inception Year: 1974; Fund Managers:
Bill Procter
ChrisKresic
Income Series B Fund
RRSP Eligible; Inception Year: 1998; Fund Managers:
Bill Procter
ChrisKresic
Corporate Bond Fund
RRSP Eligible; Inception Year: 1999; Fund Managers:
Chris Kresic
DanBastasic
Waddell & Reed Inc.
High Income Fund
RRSP Eligible; Inception Year: 2003; Fund Managers:
Chris Kresic
BillProcter
Dan Bastasic
James Leung
Real Return Bond Fund
RRSP Eligible; Inception Year: 2003; Fund Managers:
Chris Kresic
RRSP Global Bond Fund
RRSP Eligible; Inception Year: 1975; Fund Managers:
Waddell & Reed Inc.
Tactical Global Bond Fund
RRSP Eligible; Inception Year: 1994; Fund Managers:
Alliance Capital Management
Corporate Bond Segregated Fund
RRSP Eligible; Inception Year: 2001;
Money Market Segregated Fund
RRSP Eligible; Inception Year: 1999;
Income Series C Fund
RRSP Eligible; Inception Year: 2004; Fund Managers:

Bill Procter
ChrisKresic
Symmetry:
Canadian Stock Capital Class Fund
RRSP Eligible; Inception Year: 2004; Fund Managers:
Ian Ainsworth
Peter Cundill & Associates (Bermuda) Ltd.
EAFE Stock Capital Class Fund
RRSP Eligible; Inception Year: 2004; Fund Managers:
Ian Ainsworth
Franklin Templeton Investments
Managed Return Capital Class Fund
RRSP Eligible; Inception Year: 2004; Fund Managers:
Chris Kresic
Waddell & Reed Inc.
Registered Fixed Income Pool Fund
RRSP Eligible; Inception Year: 2004; Fund Managers:
Chris Kresic
Waddell & Reed Inc.
Specialty Stock Capital Class Fund
RRSP Eligible; Inception Year: 2004; Fund Managers:
Stephanie Griffiths
Peter Cundill & Associates (Bermuda) Ltd.
US Stock Capital Class Fund
RRSP Eligible; Inception Year: 2004; Fund Managers:
Dreman Value Management L.L.C.
Universal:
Canadian Growth Fund
RRSP Eligible; Inception Year: 1995; Fund Managers:
Bluewater Investment Management
Canadian Resource Fund
RRSP Eligible; Inception Year: 1978; Fund Managers:
Fred Sturm
BenoitGervais
European Opportunities Fund
RRSP Eligible; Inception Year: 1994; Fund Managers:
Henderson Global Investors
Future Fund
RRSP Eligible; Inception Year: 1987; Fund Managers:
Ian Ainsworth
MarkGrammer
Wendy Chua
World Growth RRSP Fund
RRSP Eligible; Inception Year: 1994; Fund Managers:
Karen Bleasby
Canadian Balanced Fund
RRSP Eligible; Inception Year: 1996; Fund Managers:
Bluewater Investment Management
International Stock Fund
RRSP Eligible; Inception Year: 1985; Fund Managers:
Henderson Global Investors
Precious Metals Fund
RRSP Eligible; Inception Year: 1994; Fund Managers:
Fred Sturm
BenoitGervais
European Opportunities Capital Class Fund
RRSP Eligible; Inception Year: 2000; Fund Managers:
Henderson Global Investors
Future Capital Class Fund
RRSP Eligible; Inception Year: 2000; Fund Managers:
Ian Ainsworth
MarkGrammer
Wendy Chua
Global Future Capital Class Fund
RRSP Eligible; Inception Year: 2000; Fund Managers:
Ian Ainsworth
MarkGrammer
Wendy Chua
Health Sciences Capital Class Fund
RRSP Eligible; Inception Year: 2000; Fund Managers:
Ian Ainsworth
WendyChua
World Resource Capital Class Fund
RRSP Eligible; Inception Year: 2000; Fund Managers:
Fred Sturm
BenoitGervais
World Science & Technology Capital Class Fund
RRSP Eligible; Inception Year: 2002; Fund Managers:
Polar Capital Partners Ltd.
Canadian Growth Capital Class Fund
RRSP Eligible; Inception Year: 2000; Fund Managers:
Bluewater Investment Management
Global Future Fund
RRSP Eligible; Inception Year: 1995; Fund Managers:
Ian Ainsworth
MarkGrammer
Wendy Chua
World Precious Metals Capital Class Fund
RRSP Eligible; Inception Year: 2000; Fund Managers:
Fred Sturm
BenoitGervais
US Blue Chip Capital Class Fund
RRSP Eligible; Inception Year: 2000; Fund Managers:
Waddell & Reed Inc.
US Emerging Growth Capital Class Fund
RRSP Eligible; Inception Year: 2000; Fund Managers:
Waddell & Reed Inc.
Canadian Growth Segregated Fund
RRSP Eligible; Inception Year: 1999; Fund Managers:
Bluewater Investment Management
Canadian Balanced Series T Fund
RRSP Eligible; Inception Year: 2002; Fund Managers:
Bluewater Investment Management
European Opportunities Segregated Fund
RRSP Eligible; Inception Year: 1999; Fund Managers:
Henderson Global Investors
Future Segregated Fund
RRSP Eligible; Inception Year: 1999; Fund Managers:
Ian Ainsworth
WendyChua
Mark Grammer
Growth Trends Capital Class Fund
RRSP Eligible; Inception Year: 2002; Fund Managers:
Alliance Capital Management
International Stock Capital Class Fund
RRSP Eligible; Inception Year: 2000; Fund Managers:
Henderson Global Investors
Emerging Technologies Capital Class Fund
RRSP Eligible; Inception Year: 2002; Fund Managers:
Ian Ainsworth
MarkGrammer
Wendy Chua
American Growth Capital Class Fund
RRSP Eligible; Inception Year: 2002; Fund Managers:
Bluewater Investment Management
Sustainable Opportunities Capital Class Fund
RRSP Eligible; Inception Year: 2002; Fund Managers:
Aberdeen Asset Management
US Growth Leaders Capital Class Fund
RRSP Eligible; Inception Year: 2003; Fund Managers:
Waddell & Reed Inc.
US Growth Leaders Fund
RRSP Eligible; Inception Year: 1995; Fund Managers:
Waddell & Reed Inc.
Canadian Balanced Segregated Fund
RRSP Eligible; Inception Year: 1999; Fund Managers:
Bluewater Investment Management
Emerging Markets Capital Class Fund
RRSP Eligible; Inception Year: 2002; Fund Managers:
JP Morgan Fleming
World Real Estate Capital Class Fund
RRSP Eligible; Inception Year: 2002; Fund Managers:
ABN AMRO Asset Management

Magna Vista Investment Management

Also listed under: *Financial Planning*
#2000, 1200 McGill College av
Montréal, QC H3B 4G7
514-875-2625
Fax: 514-875-6945
888-310-1712
Ownership: AGF Private Investment Management Limited, Toronto, ON
Year Founded: 1992

Mavrix Fund Management Inc.

Also listed under: *Investment Fund Companies*
#600, 36 Lombard St.
Toronto, ON M5C 2X3
416-362-3077
Fax: 416-362-7191
888-964-3533
clientservices@mavrixfunds.com
www.mavrixfunds.com
Year Founded: 1983
Number of Employees: 72
Assets: $10-100 billion
Stock Symbol: YMG
Executives:
Malvin C. Spooner, President/CEO
Mario Arra, Sr. Vice-President, National Sales
William Shaw, Sr. Vice-President & Sec.-Treas.
Raymond M. Steele, Sr. Vice-President/CFO
David Balsdon, Vice-President, Operations & Administration
Roger Dent, Vice-President, Research
Sergio Di Vito, Vice-President, Trading
Alex Nayyar, Vice-President, External Sales
Mavrix:
Dividend & Income Fund
RRSP Eligible; Inception Year: 1985;
Growth Fund
RRSP Eligible; Inception Year: 1985;
Money Market Fund
RRSP Eligible; Inception Year: 1987;
Strategic Bond Fund
RRSP Eligible; Inception Year: 1998;
Enterprise Fund
RRSP Eligible; Inception Year: 1998;
Canada Fund
RRSP Eligible; Inception Year: 1998;
Diversified Fund
RRSP Eligible; Inception Year: 1981;
Explorer Fund
RRSP Eligible; Inception Year: 2002;
Sierra Equity Fund
RRSP Eligible; Inception Year: 1999;
Global Fund
RRSP Eligible; Inception Year: 2002; Fund Managers:
Pictet International Management
American Growth Fund
RRSP Eligible; Inception Year: 1998;
Canadian Income Trust Fund
RRSP Eligible; Inception Year: 2003;
Strategic Small Cap Fund
RRSP Eligible; Inception Year: 1996;
Multi-Series Canadian Equity Fund
RRSP Eligible; Inception Year: 2004;
Multi-Series Explorer Fund
RRSP Eligible; Inception Year: 2004;
Multi-Series Income Fund
RRSP Eligible; Inception Year: 2004;
Multi-Series Short Term Income Fund
RRSP Eligible; Inception Year: 2004;
Small Companies Fund
RRSP Eligible; Inception Year: 2004;
Lawrence Enterprise Fund
RRSP Eligible; Inception Year: 2001; Fund Managers:
Lawrence Asset Management Inc.
Balanced Income & Growth Trust Fund
RRSP Eligible; Inception Year: 2004;
Resource Fund 2004 LP
RRSP Eligible; Inception Year: 2004;
Resource Fund 2004 II LP
RRSP Eligible; Inception Year: 2004;
Resource Fund 2005 II LP
RRSP Eligible; Inception Year: 2005;
Resource Fund 2005 LP
RRSP Eligible; Inception Year: 2005;

McIntosh Financial Services & Associates Inc.

Also listed under: *Financial Planning*
#106, 11 Bond St.
St Catharines, ON L2R 4Z4
905-684-2331
Fax: 905-684-0744
info@mcintoshfinancial.ca
www.mcintoshfinancial.ca
Former Name: Bob McIntosh Financial Services
Ownership: Private
Year Founded: 1975
Number of Employees: 3
Executives:
Bob McIntosh

McKenna Gale Capital Inc.

Also listed under: *Financing & Loan Companies*
#1220, 145 King St. West
Toronto, ON M5H 1J8
416-364-8884
Fax: 416-364-8444
info@mckennagale.com
www.mckennagale.com
Executives:
Robert Gale, Managing Director; bgale@mckennagale.com
Kevin McKenna, Managing Director; kmckenna@mckennagale.com

INVESTMENT MANAGEMENT

McKenna Gale Capital Inc. (continued)
Stephen Stewart, Managing Director; sstewart@mckennagale.com
Gary Wade, Managing Director
T. Craig Ferguson, Principal; cferguson@mckennagale.com
Jeffrey A. Sujitno, Principal; jsujitno@mckennagale.com
Mark A. Shulgan, Vice-President; mshulgan@mckennagale.com

MDS Capital Corporation(MDSCC)

Also listed under: *Financing & Loan Companies*
100 International Blvd.
Toronto, ON M9W 6J6
416-675-7661
Fax: 416-213-4232
info@mdscapital.com
www.mdscapital.com
Ownership: Private.
Year Founded: 1988
Number of Employees: 25
Assets: $100-500 million
Revenues: $10-50 million
Profile: The venture capital company supplies development capital for emerging health & life sciences companies with innovative technologies. In addition to its Canadian locations, MDS Capital has two branches in the USA. The Boston/Cambridge office is situated at Suite 1800, 245 First St., Cambridge MA, 02142. The second American office is located at Suite 315, 435 Tasso St., Palo Alto, CA, 94301-1552.

Executives:
Peter van der Velden, CEO
Stephen L. Cummings, Chief Financial Officer
Michael Callaghan, Managing Director
Richard Lockie, Managing Director
Brian Underdown, Managing Director
Directors:
Jim Garner, Chair
Peter M. de Auer
Peter Brent
Richard W. Johnston
James G. Oborne
R. Anthony Pullen
Peter van der Velden
Branches:
Montréal
#502, 1550 rue Metcalfe
Montréal, QC H3A 1X6 Canada
514-844-3637
Fax: 514-844-5607
Daniel Hetu, Manager
Toronto
#343, 20 Bay St., 11th Fl.
Toronto, ON M5J 2N8 Canada
647-435-9376
Peter van der Velden, CEO

Moncton - Louisbourg Investments Inc.

Also listed under: *Financial Planning*
PO Box 160
770 Main St.
Moncton, NB E1C 8L1
506-853-5457
Ownership: Private. Montrusco Bolton Inc. & Assumption Life
Year Founded: 1991
Number of Employees: 10
Assets: $1-10 billion Year End: 20051200
Revenues: $1-5 million Year End: 20051200
Executives:
Martin Boudreau, Vice-President
Luc Gaudet, Vice President
Marc Lalonde, Vice-President
Mathieu Roy, Vice-President
Branches:
Halifax
#1602, 1791 Barrington St.
Halifax, NS B3J 3L1 Canada
902-421-1811
James S. Oland, Vice-President, Marketing & Client Servicing

Montrusco Bolton Inc.

Also listed under: *Investment Fund Companies*
#4600, 1250, boul René-Lévesque ouest
Montréal, QC H3B 5J5
514-842-6464
Fax: 514-282-2550
marketing@montruscobolton.com
www.montruscobolton.com
Year Founded: 1984
Executives:
Sylvain Boulé, President/CEO
Richard Guay, Sr. Vice-President
Jean Mathieu, Sr. Vice-President & Chief Investment Officer, Private Wealth Management
Normande Boucher, Vice-President, Private Investment Management
Colette Bournival, Vice-President, Private Investment Management
Yves Filion, Vice-President, Private Wealth Management
Jean Meloche, Vice-President
Affiliated Companies:
Moncton - Louisbourg Investments Inc.
Montrusco Bolton:
Balanced Plus Fund
RRSP Eligible; Inception Year: 1993; Fund Managers:
Érik Giasson
Canadian Small Cap B Fund
RRSP Eligible; Inception Year: 1999; Fund Managers:
Peter Harrison
Canadian Equity B Fund
RRSP Eligible; Inception Year: 1999; Fund Managers:
Peter Harrison
Fixed Income B Fund
RRSP Eligible; Inception Year: 1999; Fund Managers:
François Lagarde
US Equity B Fund (US$)
RRSP Eligible; Inception Year: 1999; Fund Managers:
Nadim Rizk
Balanced B Fund
RRSP Eligible; Inception Year: 1999; Fund Managers:
Érik Giasson
Global Equity B Fund
RRSP Eligible; Inception Year: 1999; Fund Managers:
Nadim Rizk
E.A.F.E. Equity B Fund
RRSP Eligible; Inception Year: 1999; Fund Managers:
Jean-Sébastien Garant
Enterprise Fund
RRSP Eligible; Inception Year: 1987; Fund Managers:
Peter Harrison
International Equity Fund (US$)
RRSP Eligible; Inception Year: 1987; Fund Managers:
Jean-Sébastien Garant
T-Max Fund
RRSP Eligible; Inception Year: 1995; Fund Managers:
François Lagarde
Taxable US Equity Fund (US$)
RRSP Eligible; Inception Year: 1987; Fund Managers:
Nadim Rizk
Income Trust Fund
RRSP Eligible; Inception Year: 2002; Fund Managers:
Peter Harrison
Canadian Equity Plus Fund
RRSP Eligible; Inception Year: 1998; Fund Managers:
Marc Lalonde
Bond Total Return Fund
RRSP Eligible; Inception Year: 1996; Fund Managers:
Érik Lacombe
Montrusco Bolton Focus:
Absolute Return Global FundInception Year: 0; Fund Managers:
Érik Giasson
Focus Investment Group
Branches:
Calgary
Bow Valley Square III
#3190, 255 - 5th Ave. SW
Calgary, AB T2P 3G6 Canada
403-234-0373
Kenneth W. Stout, Vice-President
Halifax - Louisbourg Investments Inc.
#1602, 1791 Barrington St.
Halifax, NS B3J 3L1 Canada
902-421-1811
Fax: 902-420-1780
James Oland, Vice-President, Marketing & Client Servicing
Québec
Tour de la Cité
#860, 2600, boul Laurier
Québec, QC G1V 4W2 Canada
418-650-4420
Normand Lessard, Exec. Vice-President
Saint-Hyacinthe
1365, rue Gauvin
Saint-Hyacinthe, QC J2S 8W7 Canada
450-774-8131
André Benoit, Portfolio Manager
Toronto
North Tower, Royal Bank Plaza
#1840, 200 Bay St.
Toronto, ON M5J 2J1 Canada
416-860-1257
Timothy J. Russell, Vice-President

Morguard Investments Limited

Also listed under: *Financial Planning*
#800, 55 City Centre Dr.
Mississauga, ON L5B 1M3
905-281-3800
Fax: 905-281-1800
headoffice@morguard.com
www.morguard.com
Ownership: Private. Subsidiary of Morguard Corporation (Stock Symbol MRC).
Year Founded: 1965
Number of Employees: 800
Assets: $1-10 billion Year End: 20050930
Revenues: $10-50 million Year End: 20050930
Profile: Morguard Investments also provides real estate advisory services.

Executives:
Stephen Taylor, President/COO; 905-281-5850; staylor@morguard.com
Andy Edmundson, Exec. Vice-President, Asset Managerment; 403-266-1695; aedmundson@morguard.com
W. Scott MacDonald, Exec. Vice-President, Asset Management; 905-281-5839; smacdonald@morguard.com
Pamela McLean, CFO & Sr. Vice-President, Finance; 905-281-5830; pmclean@morguard.com
Margaret Knowles, Sr. Vice-President, Development; 905-281-5817; mknowles@morguard.com
Gordon Vollmer, Sr. Vice-President; 905-281-3800; gvollmer@morguard.com
Suzanne Wiles, Sr. Vice-President, Strategic Advisory Services; 905-281-4806; swiles@morguard.com
Regional Offices:
Beloeil
544, boul Laurier
Beloeil, QC J3G 4H9 Canada
450-446-4004
Fax: 450-446-2863
montreal@morguard.com
A. Sirois, Vice-President, Retail Asset Management
Calgary
#200, 505 - 3rd St. SW
Calgary, AB T2P 3E6 Canada
403-266-1695
Fax: 403-265-9813
calgary@morguard.com
A. Edmundson, Sr. Vice-President, Office
Edmonton
Scotia Place
#1100, 10060 Jasper Ave.
Edmonton, AB T5J 3R8 Canada
780-421-8000
Fax: 780-424-7933
edmonton@morguard.com
G. Scheuerman, Manager, Operations
Ottawa
#402, 350 Sparks St.
Ottawa, ON K1R 7S8 Canada
613-237-6373
Fax: 613-237-0007
ottawa@morguard.com
A. Tallis, Vice-President
Toronto
#200, 200 Yorkland Blvd.
Toronto, ON M2J 5C1 Canada
416-496-2098
toronto@morguard.com
T. Capulli, Director, Property Management
Vancouver
#400, 333 Seymour St.
Vancouver, BC V6B 5A6 Canada
604-681-9474
Fax: 604-685-0161
vancouver@morguard.com
Tom Johnston, General Manager

Victoria
905 Gordon St.
Victoria, BC V8W 3P9 Canada
250-383-8093
Fax: 250-383-5097
victoria@morguard.com
Roberta Tower, Manager
Winnipeg
#1400, 363 Broadway
Winnipeg, MB R3C 3N9 Canada
204-632-9500
Fax: 204-632-1122
winnipeg@morguard.com
Karen Lund, General Manager

Morneau Sobeco
***Also listed under:** Acturarial Consultants*
1 Morneau Sobeco Centre
#700, 895 Don Mills Rd.
Toronto, ON M3C 1W3
416-445-2700
Fax: 416-445-7989
www.morneausobeco.com
Ownership: Public. Parent is Morneau Sobeco Income Fund.
Year Founded: 1966
Number of Employees: 1,018
Assets: $100-500 million Year End: 20051231
Revenues: $100-500 million Year End: 20051231
Stock Symbol: MSI.UN
Profile: Morneau Sobeco provides actuarial consultancy & pension & benefits administration. Affiliates include Morneau Sobeco Ltd., Morneau Sobeco Limited Partnership, Morneau Sobeco Corporation, Morneau Sobeco Group Limited Partnership, Morneau Sobeco GP Inc., & Morneau Sobeco Income Trust.

Executives:
William F. Morneau Jr., President/CEO; 416-383-6451; bmorneau@morneausobeco.com
Nancy Reid, Chief Financial Officer; 416-383-6488; nreid@morneausobeco.com
Pierre Sobeco, Chief Operating Officer
Branches:
Calgary
#1110, 940 - 6th Ave. SW
Calgary, AB T2P 3T1 Canada
403-246-5228
Fax: 403-246-5257
Doug Sample, Sr. Consultant
Edmonton
Scotia Place 2
#1601, 10060 Jasper Ave.
Edmonton, AB T5J 3R8 Canada
780-424-3756
Fax: 780-428-4819
Joyce Melnyk, Benefit Consultant
Fredericton
Carleton Place
#850, 520 King St.
Fredericton, NB E3B 6G3 Canada
506-458-9081
Fax: 506-458-9548
Conrad Ferguson, Partner
Halifax
CIBC Building
#701, 1809 Barrington St.
Halifax, NS B3J 3K8 Canada
902-429-8013
Fax: 902-420-1932
Greg Forbes, Partner
London
#700, 255 Queens Ave.
London, ON N6A 5R8 Canada
519-438-0193
Fax: 519-438-0196
Ramona Robinson, Principal
Montréal - René-Lévesque ouest
#1100, 500, boul René-Lévesque ouest
Montréal, QC H2Z 1W7 Canada
514-878-9090
Fax: 514-875-2673
Raymond Gaudet, Exec. Vice-President
Montréal - University
1060, rue University, 9e étage
Montréal, QC H3B 4V3 Canada
514-878-9090
Fax: 514-395-8773
Pierre Chamberland, Exec. Vice-President
Ottawa
#1203, 99 Metcalfe St.
Ottawa, ON K1P 6L7 Canada
613-238-4272
Fax: 613-238-3714
Denis Dupont, Principal
Québec
#100, 79, boul René-Lévesque est
Québec, QC G1R 5N5 Canada
418-529-4536
Fax: 418-529-6447
Pierre Courcy, Partner
St. John's
Fortis Bldg.
#602, 139 Water St.
St. John's, NL A1C 1B2 Canada
709-753-4500
Fax: 709-753-3207
Linda Evans, Principal
Vancouver
One Bentall Centre
#1580, 505 Burrard St.
Vancouver, BC V7X 1M5 Canada
604-642-5200
Fax: 604-632-9930
David Haber, Principal
Winnipeg
#105, 62 Hargrave St.
Winnipeg, MB R3C 1N1 Canada
204-487-1300
Fax: 204-487-0055
Bill Chapman, Contact

Morrison Williams Investment Management Ltd.
#405, 1 Toronto St.
Toronto, ON M5C 2V6
416-777-2922
Fax: 416-777-0954
Ownership: Private
Year Founded: 1992
Number of Employees: 9
Assets: $1-10 billion
Executives:
Barry A. Morrison, Principal
K. Leslie Williams, Principal
Karen A. Fenton, Sr. Vice-President
Cynthia M. McNabb, Sr. Vice-President
Denis Ryan, Sr. Vice-President, Marketing; 416-474-5190
Joe Vickers, Sr. Vice-President, Marketing; 416-777-2922

Mulvihill Capital Management Inc.
Standard Life Centre
#2600, 121 King St. West
Toronto, ON M5H 3T9
416-681-3900
Fax: 416-681-3901
800-725-7172
info@mulvihill.com
www.mulvihill.com
Ownership: Private
Year Founded: 1995
Number of Employees: 46
Profile: Through segregated & pooled funds, MCM manages over $3 billion for pension funds, corporations, insurance companies, endowments, foundations & mutual & closed-end funds, under a wide variety of investment mandates.

Executives:
John Mulvihill, Chair/CEO
John Simpson, CFA, President, Wealth Management & Product Distribution
Don Biggs, Sr. Vice-President, Structured Products
Mark J. Carpani, CFA, Vice-President, Bonds & Marketing
Paul W. Meyer, CFA, Vice-President, Equities
Peggy Shiu, CFA, Vice-President
Jack Way, CFA, Vice-President, Equities
Mulvihill:
Pro-Ams U.S. FundInception Year: 0;
Pro-Ams RSP FundInception Year: 0;
Pro-Ams 100 Plus Fund (Cdn $)Inception Year: 0;
Pro-Ams 100 Plus Fund (US$)Inception Year: 0;
Premium Canadian FundInception Year: 0;
Premium U.S. FundInception Year: 0;
Premium Oil & Gas FundInception Year: 0;
Premium 60 Plus FundInception Year: 0;
Premium Global Plus FundInception Year: 0;
Premium Canadian Bank FundInception Year: 0;
Premium Split Share FundInception Year: 0;
Premium Global Telecom FundInception Year: 0;
Summit Digital World FundInception Year: 0;

Northern Trust Global Advisors
BCE Place
PO Box 526
#4540, 161 Bay St.
Toronto, ON M5J 2S1
416-366-2020
Fax: 416-366-2033
Ownership: Owned by Northern Trust
Number of Employees: 12
Executives:
Michael Gallimore, CEO
Robert D. Furnari, Exec. Vice-President, Director, Client Services

Northwater Capital Management Inc.
BCE Place
PO Box 794
#4700, 181 Bay St.
Toronto, ON M5J 2T3
416-360-5435
Fax: 416-360-0671
800-422-1867
mpt@northwatercapital.com
www.northwatercapital.com
Former Name: Newcastle Capital Management; NewQuant Capital
Ownership: Private
Year Founded: 1989
Number of Employees: 89
Profile: Northwater manages over $US 9 billion in assets, applying innovative investment strategies & sophisticated proprietary software in assisting major institutions to build optimal portfolios. Northwater clients include over 50 pension plans of major corporations, governments, & universities in Canada, the United States, & Europe.

Executives:
David Patterson, Chair/CEO
Paul W. Robson, President
Dennis Cook, Exec. Vice-President
Daniel C. Mills, Managing Director
Benita M. Warmbold, Managing Director

Northwood Stephens Private Counsel Inc.
#200, 3650 Victoria Park Ave.
Toronto, ON M2H 3P7
416-502-9393
Fax: 416-502-9394
nsc@nigel.com
www.nigel.com
Former Name: Nigel Stephens Counsel Inc.
Ownership: Private
Year Founded: 1988
Assets: $100-500 million
Profile: Offers comprehensive net worth management to wealthy families and foundations.

Executives:
J. Ian Dalrymple, Chairman, Chief Investment Officer; idalrymple@northwoodstephens.com
Tom McCullough, President, Chief Executive Officer; tmccullough@northwoodstephens.com
Scott Hayman, Exec. Vice-President; shayman@northwoodstephens.com
Roger Coe, Senior Vice-President; rcoe@northwoodstephens.com

Ontario Municipal Employees Retirement System(OMERS)
#700, 1 University Ave.
Toronto, ON M5J 2P1
416-369-2400
Fax: 416-360-0217
800-387-0813
client@omers.com
www.omers.com
Year Founded: 1962
Assets: $10-100 billion
Profile: The pension plan provides retirement benefits to approximately 365,000 active & retired members. It works on

INVESTMENT MANAGEMENT

Ontario Municipal Employees Retirement System(OMERS) (continued)

behalf of 900 local government employers in Ontario. OMERS Capital Partners invests & manages OMERS private equity investments.

Executives:
Paul G. Haggis, President/CEO
Paul G. Renaud, President/CEO, OMERS Capital Partners
Jennifer Brown, Sr. Vice-President, Pension Division
Selma M. Lussenburg, Sr. Vice-President, General Counsel & Corporate Se
Debbie Oakley, Sr. Vice-President, Corporate Affairs
Paul Pugh, Sr. Vice-President, Public Investments
Paul G. Renaud, Sr. Vice-President/CFO
John Liu, Vice-President, Chief Internal Auditor
Flo Paladino, Vice-President, Human Resources
Directors:
David Kingston, Chair
Frederick Biro
David Carrington
Richard Faber, Employee Representative, Retired Members
Marianne Love
Rick Miller
Ann Mulvale
David S. O'Brien
Michael Power
Peter Routliff
John Sabo
Gerard Sequeira
John Weatherup
Cam Weldon, Employer Representative

Ontario Teachers' Pension Plan Board
5650 Yonge St.
Toronto, ON M2M 4H5
416-228-5900
Fax: 416-730-5349
877-812-7989
communications@otpp.com
www.otpp.com
Ownership: Semi-private pension fund
Year Founded: 1990
Number of Employees: 550
Assets: $73,000,000 Year End: 20051031
Revenues: $7,000,000 Year End: 20051031
Profile: The pension plan is responsible for administering the retirement income of approximately 264,000 current & retired elementary & secondary school teachers. The Ontario Teachers' Pension Plan is sponsored by a partnership between the Ontario government & plan members, who are represented by the Ontario Teachers' Federation.

Executives:
Claude Lamoureux, President/CEO
Robert Bertram, Exec. Vice-President, Investments
Brian Gibson, Sr. Vice-President, Public Equities
James William Leech, Sr. Vice-President, Private Capital
Morgan McCague, Sr. Vice-President, Asset Mix & Risk
Rosemarie McClean, Sr. Vice-President, Member Services
Neil Petroff, Sr. Vice-President, Tactical Asset Allocation & Alternative Investments
Sean Rogister, Sr. Vice-President, Fixed Income
Roger Barton, Vice-President, General Counsel & Secretary
John Brennan, Vice-President, Human Resources & Public Affairs
Russ Bruch, Vice-President, Investment Operations, CFO
Zev Frishman, Vice-President, Structured Portfolios & External Managers
Dan Houle, Vice-President, Business Solutions
Wayne Kozun, Vice-President, Tactical Asset Allocation
Ron Lepin, Vice-President, Infrastructure
Peter Maher, Vice-President, Audit Services; 416-730-7662
David McGraw, Vice-President & CFO
Dean Metcalf, Vice-President, Canada
Ron Mock, Vice-President, Alternative Investments
Phil Nichols, Vice-President, IT Member Services
Lee Sienna, Vice-President, U.S.
Erol Uzumeri, Vice-President, International, Teachers' Private Capital
Rosemary Zigrossi, Vice-President, Venture Capital
Directors:
Robert W. Korthals, Chair
Jill Denham
J. Douglas Grant
Helen M. Kearns
Raymond Koskie
Guy Matte
Eileen Mercier
Thomas O'Neill
Gary Porter
Carol Stephenson

Ottawa Asset Management Inc.
Also listed under: *Financial Planning*
#201, 839 Shefford Rd.
Ottawa, ON K1J 9K8
613-748-7770
Fax: 613-748-9461
roger-c@sympatico.ca
www.gicdirect.com
Ownership: Part of GICdirect.com, Victoria, BC.

P.J. Doherty & Associates Co. Ltd.
Also listed under: *Financial Planning*
#700, 56 Sparks St.
Ottawa, ON K1P 5A9
613-238-6727
Fax: 613-238-3957
info@pjdoherty.com
www.pjdoherty.com
Also Known As: Doherty & Associates
Ownership: AGF Private Investment Management Limited, Toronto, ON.
Year Founded: 1979
Executives:
Peter Doherty, President
Douglas Cousins, Vice-President
Chris Stuart, Account Manager
John Doherty, Business Development Officer

Pacific Spirit Investment Management
Also listed under: *Financial Planning*
#1100, 800 West Pender St.
Vancouver, BC V6C 2V6
604-687-0123
Fax: 604-687-0128
800-337-1388
pacificspirit@telus.net
www.pacificspirit.bc.ca
Year Founded: 1986
Executives:
John S. Clark, President

Page & Associates
Also listed under: *Financial Planning*
9993 Yonge St.
Richmond Hill, ON L4C 1T9
905-508-8220
Fax: 905-884-3365
800-837-0134
www.askpage.com
Ownership: Private.
Year Founded: 1977
Number of Employees: 14
Profile: The company provides advice & guidance about financial management, including the following services: financial planning, retirement income analysis, insurance needs analysis, investment analysis, pensions & group benefits analysis, tax planning, GICs & mutual funds, RRSPs, RRIFs, LIFs & annuities, & group RSPs for businesses, estate planning, segregated funds & RESPs.

Executives:
John A. Page, CFP, RFP, President, Sr. Financial Planner
Frank Miemiec, Vice-President, Operations
Theresa Boyle, Manager, Fixed Income Deposits
Isaura Quinn, Manager, Accounts
Karissa Smith, Manager, Accounts
Jonathan G. Flawn, Sr. Financial Advisor
Don Page, Sr. Financial Advisor
Rick Page, Sr. Financial Advisor, Operations
Tony Porcheron, Contact

Pembroke Management Ltd.
#1700, 1002, rue Sherbrooke ouest
Montréal, QC H3A 3S4
514-848-1991
Fax: 514-848-1725
866-848-1991
tlindsay@pml.ca
www.pml.ca
Also Known As: Gestion Pembroke Limitée
Ownership: Private
Year Founded: 1968
Number of Employees: 16
Profile: Pembroke Management is an independent investment management company that manages U.S. & Canadian institutional equity portfolios & GBC asset management funds. Special emphasis is placed on the identification & analysis of small- to medium-sized growth companies.

Executives:
A. Scott Taylor, Chair
Ian A. Soutar, Vice-Chair
A. Ian Aitken, Managing Partner
Nicolas G. Chevalier, Partner
Mike P. McLaughlin, Partner/CFO
Michael C. Shannon, Partner
Jeffrey S.D. Tory, Partner
Affiliated Companies:
GBC Asset Management Inc.

Penfund Partners, Inc.
Also listed under: *Financing & Loan Companies*
#1720, 390 Bay St.
Toronto, ON M5H 2Y2
416-865-0707
Fax: 416-364-4149
www.penfund.com
Also Known As: Penfund
Year Founded: 1979
Profile: Assets under management are $200 million..

Executives:
John Bradlow, Contact
Richard Bradlow, Contact
Adam Breslin, Contact
Barry Yontef, Contact

Perler Financial Group
Also listed under: *Financial Planning*
#405, 2963 Glen Dr.
Coquitlam, BC V3B 2P7
604-468-0888
Fax: 604-468-0887
info@perlerfinancial.com
www.perlerfinancial.com
Executives:
Anita Perler, Sr. Partner
Harry Perler, Sr. Partner
Lavinra Joseph, Director, Administration

Pollock Financial
Also listed under: *Financial Planning*
172 Bellefair Ave.
Toronto, ON M4L 3T9
416-699-1292
Fax: 416-699-3119
aaap@idirect.com
Former Name: Aileen A.A. Pollock Chartered Financial Consultant
Ownership: Private
Year Founded: 1985
Number of Employees: 1
Revenues: Under $1 million
Executives:
Aileen A.A. Pollock, CFP, RFP, CH.F.C., CLU, Principal

Priority Capital Management Inc.
#402, 4145 North Service Rd.
Burlington, ON L7R 6A3
905-333-4915
Ownership: Private
Year Founded: 1988
Number of Employees: 3
Assets: $10-50 million
Executives:
Fred Marconi, President
Norman W. Stefnitz, Chair
Affiliated Companies:
Rae & Lipskie Investment Counsel

Priveq Capital Funds
Also listed under: *Financing & Loan Companies; Investment Management*
#711, 1500 Don Mills Rd.
Toronto, ON M3B 3K4
416-447-3330
Fax: 416-447-3331
www.priveq.ca
Also Known As: Priveq
Ownership: Private
Year Founded: 1994

Number of Employees: 8
Assets: $37,000,000
Profile: Priveq provides tailor-made $3-$7 million of equity to growing companies. As an equity partner, it provides capital, strategic direction & business financial assistance to entrepreneurs & business owners to further enhance their company's value & provide superior returns for all stakeholders.

Executives:
Bradley W. Ashley, Managing Partner
Kevin B. Melnyk, Partner

Puhl Employee Benefits Inc.
Also listed under: *Financial Planning*
#309, 259 Midpark Way SE
Calgary, AB T2X 1M2
403-221-9300
Fax: 403-221-9309
888-508-0077
phsp@puhlemployeebenefits.com
www.puhlemployeebenefits.com
Ownership: Private
Year Founded: 1987
Executives:
David A. Puhl, CFP, President, Managing Partner
Lorna C. Phelps, CFP, Vice-President, Managing Partner

Quant Investment Strategies Inc.
1 First Canadian Place
PO Box 23
#2400, 120 Adelaide St. West
Toronto, ON M5H 1T1
416-815-9000
Fax: 416-815-0129
info@quantinvestment.com
www.quantinvestment.com
Ownership: Private. SciVest Canadian Holdings Inc. holds a significant interest.
Year Founded: 1998
Profile: The company specializes in developing quantitative investment strategies & providing financial advisory services

Executives:
Craig Lee, President/CEO

Queensbury Strategies Inc.
Also listed under: *Financial Planning*
69 Yonge St., 2nd Fl.
Toronto, ON M5E 1K3
416-363-8500
webster@queensbury.com, rona@queensbury.com
www.queensbury.com
Ownership: Private. Part of Queensbury Group, Toronto, ON.
Year Founded: 1987
Profile: Part of the Queensbury Group, the firm is affiliated with Queensbury Securities Inc. & Queensbury Insurance Brokers. The following financial planning services are offered: needs assessment, tax planning, estate planning, retirement planning, & insurance analysis.

Executives:
John Webster, President
Branches:
Oakville
114 Forsythe St.
Oakville, ON L6K 3T3 Canada
905-845-1484
George Stephens, Vice-President

Rae & Lipskie Investment Counsel
Also listed under: *Financial Planning*
#201, 20 Erb St. West
Waterloo, ON N2L 1T2
519-578-6849
Fax: 519-578-7269
888-578-7542
rlic@raelipskie.com
www.raelipskie.com
Ownership: Private
Year Founded: 1989
Number of Employees: 18
Executives:
Ken E. Rae, CFA, Chair/CEO
Brian E. Lipskie, CFA, President/COO

RBC Capital Partners
Also listed under: *Investment Dealers; Investment Management*
North Tower, Royal Bank Plaza
200 Bay St., 4th Fl.
Toronto, ON M5J 2W7
416-842-4054
Fax: 416-842-4060
www.rbcap.com
Ownership: Private. Division of RBC Capital Markets
Year Founded: 2000
Number of Employees: 33
Assets: $500m-1 billion
Revenues: $50-100 million
Stock Symbol: RY
Executives:
Alan Hibben, CEO; alan.hibben@rbcap.com
Owen Trotter, Vice-President, Debt Instruments
Robert Bechard, Managing Partner, Equity
Wally Hunter, Managing Parnter, Equity
Barrie Laver, Managing Partner, Portfolio Management
Tony Manastersky, Managing Partner, Mezzanine Fund, Principal, Finance

RealCap Holdings Limited
Also listed under: *Financial Planning; Investment Management*

PO Box 2081
#1002, 20 Eglinton Ave. West
Toronto, ON M4R 1K8
416-486-7729
Fax: 416-486-9708
realgrowth@on.aibn.com
Ownership: Public. Major shareholders are D.S. Ades (69.67% interest) & R.M. Ades (29.65% interest)
Year Founded: 1962
Number of Employees: 3
Assets: $1,273,000 Year End: 20041231
Revenues: $424,000 Year End: 20041231
Stock Symbol: REAH.A
Profile: This is a financial services holding company which conducts activities as a registered investment counsel & portfolio manager. It is also involved in limited partnerships, oil & gas, & marketable securities. Affiliated companies include Realcap Inc. (USA), Realcap Funds Inc., (USA) & Realgrowth Resources (86) CP.

Executives:
David S. Ades, President; da_realgrowth@on.aibn.com
Ralph M. Ades, Exec. Vice-President, Sec.-Treas.; realgrowth@on.aibn.com
Directors:
David S. Ades
Ralph M. Ades
M. Guy Jones
Sigrid I. Welsch

Russell Investments Canada Limited
Also listed under: *Investment Dealers*
1 First Canadian Place
PO Box 476
#5900, 100 King St. West
Toronto, ON M5X 1E4
416-362-8411
888-509-1792
canada@russell.com
www.russell.com/ca
Ownership: Russell Investment Group
Year Founded: 1936
Profile: Russell offers investment products & investment planning services for individuals or for institutional investors & their employees. Russell Investments Canada also works with Frank Russell Company, a money management & pension fund consulting company, to offer investment solutions for company pension plans.

Executives:
Irshaad Ahmad, President, Managing Director
Susi McCord, Head, Marketing & Communications

Schroders & Associates Canada Inc.
#3000, 1800, av McGill College
Montréal, QC H3A 3J6
514-397-0700
Fax: 514-861-2495
schroders.associates@schroders.ca
www.schroders.ca
Ownership: Private
Year Founded: 1987
Number of Employees: 8
Profile: Schroders & Associates Canada Inc. provides advisory services to three Canadian buy-out funds totalling $360 million raised mainly from institutional investors.

Executives:
Paul S. Echenberg, President/CEO
Michel Auclair, Vice-President
Cecile Ducharme, Vice-President
Mathieu Gauvin, Vice-President
Jean E. Douville, Special Advisor

SEI Investments
#1600, 70 York St.
Toronto, ON M5J 1S9
416-777-9700
Fax: 416-777-9093
tli@seic.com
www.seic.ca
Former Name: Primus Capital Advisors Co.
Also Known As: SEI
Ownership: Public
Year Founded: 1968
Number of Employees: 45
Assets: $6,000,000,000 Year End: 20050630
Stock Symbol: SEIC
Profile: SEI is an affiliate of SEI Capital, with 2,000 employees globally. The global revenue for 2004 was $692,000,000 (US). Global assets were $160,000,000,000 (Canadian) as of June 30, 2005.

Executives:
Patrick Walsh, President
George Butcher, Sr. Vice-President
Murray McLean, Chief Investment Officer
Directors:
Christopher Bardsley
Edward Loughin
Hartland McKeown
Patrick Walsh
SEI:
Canadian Equity Fund
RRSP Eligible; Inception Year: 1996;
Canadian Fixed Income Fund
RRSP Eligible; Inception Year: 1996;
Money Market Fund
RRSP Eligible; Inception Year: 1997;
E.A.F.E. Equity Fund
RRSP Eligible; Inception Year: 1997;
Emerging Market Equity Fund
RRSP Eligible; Inception Year: 1997;
Enhanced Global Bond Fund
RRSP Eligible; Inception Year: 1998;
International Synthetic Fund
RRSP Eligible; Inception Year: 1996;
U.S. Large Company Equity Fund
RRSP Eligible; Inception Year: 1999;
U.S. Small Company Equity Fund
RRSP Eligible; Inception Year: 1999;
Canadian Small Company Equity Fund
RRSP Eligible; Inception Year: 0;
Long Duration Bonds Fund
RRSP Eligible; Inception Year: 0;
U.S. Large Cap Synthetic Fund
RRSP Eligible; Inception Year: 0;
U.S. MidCap Synthetic Fund
RRSP Eligible; Inception Year: 0;
Canadian Index Fund
RRSP Eligible; Inception Year: 0;
Canadian Large Cap Index Fund
RRSP Eligible; Inception Year: 0;
Futures Index FundInception Year: 0;
3XL Futures Index FundInception Year: 0;
Managed Futures Fund
RRSP Eligible; Inception Year: 0;
Balanced Income Fund
RRSP Eligible; Inception Year: 0;
Core Balanced Fund
RRSP Eligible; Inception Year: 0;
Balanced Growth Fund
RRSP Eligible; Inception Year: 0;
Balanced Growth Plus Fund
RRSP Eligible; Inception Year: 0;
Diversified Equity Fund
RRSP Eligible; Inception Year: 0;
Currency Overlay Fund
RRSP Eligible; Inception Year: 0;

SEI Investments (continued)

Branches:

Calgary

#2145, 300 - 5th Ave. SW
Calgary, AB T2P 3C4 Canada
403-538-5487
Fax: 403-444-1175
Tracy Zimac, Regional Director

Halifax

#1800, 1959 Upper Water St.
Halifax, NS B3J 3N2 Canada
902-425-0269
Fax: 902-429-8060
Michael O'Connor, Regional Director

Montréal

#2650, 1002, rue Sherbrooke ouest
Montréal, QC H3A 3L6 Canada
514-844-3038
Fax: 514-844-9471
Paul Boisvert, Portfolio Manager

Vancouver

#1030, 1040 West Georgia St.
Vancouver, BC V6E 4H1 Canada
604-685-1220
Fax: 604-685-5375
Cheryl Perreault, Office Manager

Sloan Partners, LLP

***Also listed under:** Financial Planning; Accounting & Law*
#400, 7620 Yonge St.
Thornhill, ON L4J 1V9
905-886-7735
Fax: 905-764-6892
info@sloangroup.ca
www.sloangroup.ca
Former Name: Sloan Paskowitz Adelman
Ownership: Private
Year Founded: 1989
Profile: The firm is affiliated with Infologix Inc.

Executives:
Allen Sloan, Managing Partner
Dominic Kok, Partner
Jerry Paskowitz, Partner
Stan Swartz, Partner
Sam Metalin, Team Leader
Michael Spigelman, Associate

Société d'Investissements en Participations inc(SIPAR)

#2500, 1155, boul René-Lévesque ouest
Montréal, QC H3B 2K4
514-861-9252
Fax: 514-871-1269
sipar@sipar.ca
www.sipar.ca
Former Name: Serge Leclerc & Associés Inc.
Ownership: Private
Year Founded: 1991
Number of Employees: 7
Assets: $100-500 million
Revenues: $1-5 million
Executives:
Serge Leclerc, President
Richard Morrison, Vice-President

Southwest Financial Services Inc.

***Also listed under:** Financial Planning*
1070 Nashua Ave.
London, ON N6K 2C3
519-471-8292
Fax: 519-472-1493
dbradyca@rogers.com
Ownership: Private
Year Founded: 1991
Number of Employees: 5
Assets: Under $1 million
Revenues: Under $1 million
Executives:
David Brady, CA, CFP, President

Standard Life Investments Inc.(SLI)

***Also listed under:** Investment Fund Companies*
#700, 1001, boul de Maisonneuve ouest
Montréal, QC H3A 3C8
514-499-6844
Fax: 514-499-4340
888-841-6633
information@sli.ca
www.sli.ca
Former Name: Standard Life Portfolio Management Limited
Ownership: Private. Subsidiary of Standard Life Investments Limited, Edinburgh, Scotland.
Year Founded: 1973
Assets: $10-100 billion
Executives:
Keith Skeoch, CEO, Standard Life Investments Limited, Chair, Standard Life Investments Inc.
Roger Renaud, President, Director
Norman Raschkowan, Chief Investment Officer, Director
Charles Jenkins, Sr. Vice-President, Director
Antonio Maturo, Sr. Vice-President, Portfolio Management, Director
Michel Pelletier, Sr. Vice-President, Fixed Income, Director
Roger A. Renaud, Sr. Vice-President Designate, Director; roger.renaud@standardlife.ca
Claude Turcot, Sr. Vice-President, Quantitative Management, Director

Standard Life:
Bond Fund
RRSP Eligible; Inception Year: 1989;
Canadian Equity Fund
RRSP Eligible; Inception Year: 1995;
Canadian Small Cap Equity Fund
RRSP Eligible; Inception Year: 1996;
International Equity Fund
RRSP Eligible; Inception Year: 1995;
Money Market Fund
RRSP Eligible; Inception Year: 1975;
US Equity Fund
RRSP Eligible; Inception Year: 1985;
Mortgage Fund
RRSP Eligible; Inception Year: 1969;
Diversified Fund
RRSP Eligible; Inception Year: 1987;
Capped Canadian Equity Fund
RRSP Eligible; Inception Year: 2000;
Core Canadian Equity Fund
RRSP Eligible; Inception Year: 1966;
Real Estate Fund
RRSP Eligible; Inception Year: 1983;
Canadian Bond Index Fund
RRSP Eligible; Inception Year: 1998;
Canadian Equity Capped Index Fund
RRSP Eligible; Inception Year: 2001;
Canadian Equity Index Fund
RRSP Eligible; Inception Year: 1998;
US Equity Index Fund
RRSP Eligible; Inception Year: 1998;
Synthetic US Equity Index Fund
RRSP Eligible; Inception Year: 1999;
Canadian Dividend Fund
RRSP Eligible; Inception Year: 1998;
Canadian Value Equity Fund
RRSP Eligible; Inception Year: 2003;
Long Term Bond Fund
RRSP Eligible; Inception Year: 2003;
Real Return Bond Fund
RRSP Eligible; Inception Year: 2003;
Corporate Bond FundInception Year: 0;

Branches:

Calgary

The Standard Life Bldg.
#1500, 639 - 5th Ave. SW
Calgary, AB T2P 0M9 Canada
R.A. Milner, Vice-President, Western Canada

Toronto

#840, 121 King St. West
Toronto, ON M5H 3T9 Canada
A. Jay Waters, Vice-President, Central Canada

State Street Global Advisors Ltd. (Canada)

#1100, 770, rue Sherbrooke ouest
Montréal, QC H3A 1G1
514-282-2400
Fax: 514-282-2439
www.ssga.com/canada/
Year Founded: 1991
Executives:
Carl S. Bang, Managing Director, Canada
Gregory Chrispin, Chief Information Officer
Violaine Des Rochers, Director, Legal Affairs & Compliance
Marilina Mastronardi, Director, Operations
Robert Watson, National Director, Marketing

Branches:

Toronto

PO Box 65
#6910, 100 King St. West
Toronto, ON M5X 1B1 Canada
416-956-2474
Fax: 416-956-2464

Vancouver

#500, 666 Burrard St.
Vancouver, BC V6C 3P6 Canada
604-602-9122
Fax: 604-639-3132

Stewart Financial Services

***Also listed under:** Financial Planning; Insurance Companies*
1282 Cornwall Rd., #B
Oakville, ON L6J 7W5
905-845-0990
Fax: 905-845-2882
888-845-0990
drew@stewartfinancial.ca
www.stewartfinancial.ca
Ownership: Private
Number of Employees: 8
Executives:
Drew L. Stewart, CFP, CLU, CH.F.C., Partner
Duncan Stewart, MBA, CIM, Director, Operations

Strategic Financial Concepts Inc.

***Also listed under:** Financial Planning*
Capital Place
#406, 9707-110th St.
Edmonton, AB T5N 1R5
780-488-2644
Fax: 780-488-0844
800-463-1852
service@strategicfinancial.net
www.strategicfinancial.net
Former Name: Dataplan Consultants Limited
Ownership: Private
Year Founded: 1980
Number of Employees: 8
Assets: Under $1 million
Revenues: Under $1 million
Executives:
Darrell Starrie, RFP, CFP, PRP, CLU, CH.F.C., President

Branches:

Calgary

#301, 1100-8th Ave. SW
Calgary, AB T2R 0J6 Canada
780-488-2644
Fax: 780-488-0844
800-463-1852

Strategic Financial Services

***Also listed under:** Financial Planning*
#500, 2950 Douglas St.
Victoria, BC V8T 4N4
250-383-3634
Fax: 250-383-3027
800-663-7603
Ownership: Private
Year Founded: 1986
Number of Employees: 3
Profile: The financial planning company is an employee benefits & special risk consulting broker. Employee group benefits include group RRSP, group pension (RPP) & deferred profit sharing plan (DPSP), group dental & health, group disability insurance & executive life & disability insurance.

Summerhill Capital Management Inc.

***Also listed under:** Financial Planning*
#1108, 1 St. Clair Ave. West
Toronto, ON M4V 1K6
416-515-9429
Fax: 416-515-9499
info@sumcap.com
www.sumcap.com
Ownership: Private.
Year Founded: 2004
Assets: $100-500 million Year End: 20060930
Executives:
Mary Throop, President; 416-515-1492; mthroop@sumcap.com

INVESTMENT MANAGEMENT

T.H.A. Bodnar & Company Investment Management Ltd.
Also listed under: *Financial Planning*
#4, 69 Sydney St. South
Kitchener, ON N2G 3V1
519-576-1273
Fax: 519-576-2125
877-475-5517
terrybodnar@rogers.com
Ownership: Private
Year Founded: 1999
Number of Employees: 2
Revenues: Under $1 million Year End: 20041231
Profile: The total assets under management are $230,000,000.

Executives:
Terence H.A. Bodnar, President; terrybodnar@rogers.com
Judy Cameron, Vice-President, Canadian Equities; jacameron@sympatico.ca

Thomas O'Neill & Associates
Also listed under: *Financial Planning*
Cathedral Place
#1918,925 West Georgia St.
Vancouver, BC V6C 3L2
604-484-4170
Fax: 604-608-6776
800-757-2799
ubfi@oneill-inc.com
Ownership: Private
Year Founded: 1985
Number of Employees: 7
Revenues: Under $1 million
Profile: Financial planning consultants.

Executives:
Thomas O'Neill, President

Thornmark Asset Management Inc.
Also listed under: *Investment Fund Companies*
#701, 119 Spadina Ave.
Toronto, ON M5V 2L1
416-204-6620
Fax: 416-204-6229
info@thornmark.com
www.thornmark.com
Ownership: Private
Year Founded: 1998
Number of Employees: 7
Assets: $100-500 million Year End: 20051018
Executives:
Daniel L. Bain, Chair, Chief Investment Officer; dbain@thornmark.com
Neil Jamieson, President
James F. Allan, Vice-President; jallan@thornmark.com
Geoffrey Spidle, Vice-President, Business Development; 416-204-6225
Thornmark:
Dividend & Income Fund
RRSP Eligible; Inception Year: 1998;
Enhanced EquityInception Year: 1998;

Todd & Associates Financial Knowledge Inc.
Also listed under: *Financial Planning*
#364, 305 - 4625 Varsity Dr. NW
Calgary, AB T3A 0Z9
403-547-0328
Fax: 403-547-7828
www.todd-associates.com
Ownership: Private
Year Founded: 1985
Number of Employees: 4
Assets: Under $1 million
Revenues: Under $1 million
Executives:
Russell Todd, RFP, CFP, Principal, Financial Planner

Toron Capital Markets
#200, 590 King St. West
Toronto, ON M5V 1M3
416-977-6767
Fax: 416-977-7650
800-463-7475
www.toron.com
Executives:
Peter Sacks, Managing Partner
Nicola Bishop, Partner
David Driscoll, Partner
Arthur Heinmaa, Partner
Bing Monahan, Partner
Barbara Ross, Partner
Terry Vaughan, Partner
John A. Welch, Partner
Branches:
Vancouver
#1640, 1177 West Hastings
Vancouver, BC V6E 2K3 Canada
604-642-6768
Fax: 604-642-6769
866-642-6768

Tulett, Matthews & Associates Inc.
#703, 3535, boul St. Charles
Montréal, QC H9H 5B9
514-695-0096
Fax: 514-695-9340
don@TMA-invest.com
www.tma-invest.com
Former Name: Tulett Financial Services Inc.
Ownership: Private
Year Founded: 1995
Number of Employees: 5
Assets: $10-50 million
Revenues: Under $1 million
Executives:
Donald P. Tulett, President
Hugh Campbell, Vice-President; hugh@tma-invest.com
Keith Matthews, Vice-President

Tuscarora Capital Inc.
Also listed under: *Investment Dealers*
#400, 87 Front St. East
Toronto, ON M5E 1B8
416-364-0249
Fax: 416-364-8893
tuscapital@msn.com
Ownership: Private
Year Founded: 1996
Number of Employees: 5
Profile: Lines of business includes portfolio investment management, and principal trading.

Executives:
Gary Selke, President
Directors:
Norm Lamarche, Chair

Twenty-First Century Funds Inc.
Also listed under: *Investment Fund Companies*
#2315, 401 Bay St.
Toronto, ON M5H 2Y4
416-364-9993
Fax: 416-364-1218
888-299-2121
invest21@invest21.com
Ownership: Private. Owned by Twenty-First Century Investments Inc.
Year Founded: 1996
Number of Employees: 8
Assets: $50-100 million
Revenues: $1-5 million
Executives:
Robert B. Stewart, President
Denis C. Decle, Exec. Vice-President; denis@invest21.com
Frank H. Nettleton, Vice-President
Directors:
Denis C. Decle
Andre Gervais
Craig Graham
David Platt
Brian Smith
Robert B. Stewart
Twenty-First Century:
American Equity Fund
RRSP Eligible; Inception Year: 1997; Fund Managers: The Boston Company Asset Management
Canadian Bond Fund
RRSP Eligible; Inception Year: 1997; Fund Managers: Aurion Capital Management Inc.
Canadian Equity Fund
RRSP Eligible; Inception Year: 1997; Fund Managers: Hillsdale Investment Management Inc.
International Equity Fund
RRSP Eligible; Inception Year: 1997; Fund Managers: Pinnacle Associates, Ltd.

UBS Global Asset Management (Canada) Co.
#3900, 161 Bay St.
Toronto, ON M5J 2S1
416-681-5200
Fax: 416-681-5100
www.ubs.com
Former Name: Brinson Canada Co.
Ownership: Foreign. Wholly owned subsidiary of UBS AG
Year Founded: 1981
Number of Employees: 110
Stock Symbol: UBS
Profile: The institutional fund manager has over $400 billion in discretionary assets managed for pension funds, corporations, insurance firms, central banks & charities.

Executives:
Peter Clarke, Exec. Director
Branches:
Montréal
600, boul de Maisonneuve ouest
Montréal, QC H3A 3J2 Canada
514-840-8987
Fax: 514-870-0401
Vancouver
Park Place
#3220, 666 Burrard St.
Vancouver, BC V6C 2X8 Canada
604-482-5250
Fax: 604-685-6722

United Financial Corp.
Also listed under: *Investment Fund Companies*
#1900, 360 Main St.
Winnipeg, MB R3C 3Z3
204-957-1730
Fax: 204-947-2103
800-267-1730
access@assante.com
www.assante.com/canada
Former Name: Assante Asset Management Ltd.; Loring Ward Investment Counsel
Ownership: Assante Corp.
Year Founded: 1988
Executives:
Joseph C. Canavan, Chair/CEO
Steven J. Donald, President/COO
Robert J. Dorrell, Sr. Vice-President, Distribution Services
James E. Ross, Sr. Vice-President, Risk Management
Stephen Clarke, Vice-President, Marketing
Brent Wagner, Vice-President, National Sales
Artisan:
Moderate Portfolio Fund
RRSP Eligible; Inception Year: 1998;
Conservative Portfolio Fund
RRSP Eligible; Inception Year: 1998;
Growth Portfolio Fund
RRSP Eligible; Inception Year: 1998;
Maximum Growth Portfolio Fund
RRSP Eligible; Inception Year: 1998;
High Growth Portfolio Fund
RRSP Eligible; Inception Year: 1998;
New Economy Portfolio Fund
RRSP Eligible; Inception Year: 2000;
Most Conservative Portfolio Fund
RRSP Eligible; Inception Year: 1998;
Canadian T-Bill Portfolio Fund
RRSP Eligible; Inception Year: 1998;
United:
Canadian Equity Diversified Pooled Fund
RRSP Eligible; Inception Year: 2000; Fund Managers: Trimark
Canadian Fixed Income Pooled Fund
RRSP Eligible; Inception Year: 1993; Fund Managers: CI Investment Funds
Global Fixed Income Pooled Fund
RRSP Eligible; Inception Year: 1994; Fund Managers: Trilogy Advisors
International Equity Diversified Pooled Fund
RRSP Eligible; Inception Year: 1994; Fund Managers: Alliance Capital Management

United Financial Corp. (continued)
Real Estate Investment Pooled Fund
RRSP Eligible; Inception Year: 1996; Fund Managers:
Cohen & Steers Capital Management
US Equity Diversified Pooled Fund
RRSP Eligible; Inception Year: 2000; Fund Managers:
CI Investment Funds
Canadian Equity Growth Pooled Fund
RRSP Eligible; Inception Year: 2000; Fund Managers:
Connor, Clark & Lunn
Canadian Equity Small Cap Pooled Fund
RRSP Eligible; Inception Year: 2000; Fund Managers:
Dimensional Fund Advisors
Canadian Equity Value Pooled Fund
RRSP Eligible; Inception Year: 1993; Fund Managers:
Tetrem Capital Partners
International Equity Growth Pooled Fund
RRSP Eligible; Inception Year: 2000; Fund Managers:
Alliance Capital Management
International Equity Value Pooled Fund
RRSP Eligible; Inception Year: 2000; Fund Managers:
AGF Funds
US Equity Growth Pooled Fund
RRSP Eligible; Inception Year: 2000; Fund Managers:
AGF Funds
US Equity Value Pooled Fund
RRSP Eligible; Inception Year: 1994; Fund Managers:
Deutshe Investment Management Americas
Branches:
Toronto - Queen St. East
2 Queen St East, 19th Fl.
Toronto, ON M5C 3G7 Canada
416-644-5650
Fax: 416-644-5693
866-644-5650
Toronto - Yonge St.
151 Yonge St., 9th Fl.
Toronto, ON M5C 2W7 Canada
416-645-4000
Fax: 0-645-4005
800-467-5762

INVESTMENT MANAGEMENT

Wellington West Capital Inc.
Also listed under: *Investment Dealers*
#400, 200 Waterfront Dr.
Winnipeg, MB R3B 3P1
204-925-2250
Fax: 204-942-6194
800-461-6314
admin@wellwest.ca
www.wellingtonwest.com
Ownership: Private
Year Founded: 1993
Number of Employees: 400
Assets: $1-10 billion
Stock Exchange Membership: Toronto Stock Exchange, TSX Venture Exchange
Profile: Wellington West Capital Markets, Inc. is also an affiliated company.

Executives:
Charles D. Spiring, Chair/CEO
John Rothwell, President
Blaine Coates, CFO
Daniel McDonald, CCO
Directors:
Jerome Cohen
Gary Filmon
Kevin Hooke
Kevin Kelly
Nancy Shewfelt
Charles D. Spiring
Greg Thompson
Howard Young
Affiliated Companies:
Wellington West Aboriginal Investment Services
Wellington West Corporate Finance
Wellington West Financial Services Inc./WWFS
Wellington West Pro Ice Management
Wellington West Total Wealth Management Inc.
Branches:
Barrie
126 Collier St.
Barrie, ON L4M 1H4 Canada
705-719-1190
Fax: 705-719-1191
866-402-5940
Brenda Lennon, Branch Administrator
Brandon
3000 Victoria Ave., #E
Brandon, MB R7B 3Y3 Canada
204-571-3200
Fax: 204-571-3210
866-235-5914
Maria Boudehane, Branch Administrator
Calgary
Bow Valley Square 3
#1100, 255 - 5 Ave. SW
Calgary, AB T2P 3G6 Canada
403-215-2000
Fax: 403-261-4021
877-222-9378
Michelle Zimmerman, Contact
Charlottetown
BDC Tower
#310, 119 Kent St.
Charlottetown, PE C1A 1N3 Canada
902-569-8813
Fax: 902-569-8718
Cathy Shoemaker, Contact
Halifax - Brunswick St.
#120B, 1741 Brunswick St.
Halifax, NS B3J 3X8 Canada
902-425-2326
Fax: 902-425-0807
Tammy Hackett, Contact
Halifax - Spring Garden Rd.
5670 Spring Garden Rd.
Halifax, NS B3J 1H5 Canada
902-425-1283
Fax: 902-425-1835
866-243-1070
Sharon Whalen, Contact
London
City Centre
#802, 380 Wellington St.
London, ON N6A 5B5 Canada
519-645-4861
Fax: 519-645-0902
888-530-4786
Deanne Simpson, Branch Administrator
Moose Jaw
311A Main St. North
Moose Jaw, SK S6H 0W2 Canada
306-691-6292
Fax: 306-691-6299
866-234-4418
Monica White, Contact
Oakville
105 Robinson St., 2nd Fl.
Oakville, ON L6J 1G1 Canada
905-842-1925
Fax: 905-842-1172
888-778-3956
Noelle Tinus, Assistant Branch Manager
Red Deer
#200, 4719 - 48th Ave.
Red Deer, AB T4N 3T1 Canada
403-348-2600
Fax: 403-348-0203
866-248-2633
Diane Hughes, Branch Administrator
Regina
Tower 2, McCallum Hill Centre
1881 Scath St.
Regina, SK S4P 4BE Canada
306-781-0500
Fax: 306-781-0505
866-488-0500
Joyce Marbach, Branch Manager
Saskatoon
#1360, 410 - 22nd St. East
Saskatoon, SK S7K 5T6 Canada
306-657-4400
Fax: 360-657-4410
866-844-4400
Colleen Clavelle, Branch Administrator
Swift Current
#301, 12 Cheadle St. West
Swift Current, SK S9H 0A9 Canada
306-778-4770
Fax: 306-778-4775
866-446-9444
Michelle Schmeiss, Branch Administrator
Toronto - King St.
#700, 145 King St. West
Toronto, ON M5H 1J8 Canada
416-642-1900
Fax: 416-203-9901
Doug Haydock, Contact
Toronto - Yonge St.
Yonge Corporate Centre
#501, 4100 Yonge St.
Toronto, ON M2P 2B5 Canada
416-646-6901
Fax: 416-646-9650
800-438-3319
Tina Yeung, Branch Administrator
Vancouver
#1488, 1333 Broadway Ave. West
Vancouver, BC V6H 4C1 Canada
604-738-5655
Fax: 604-736-8155
877-588-9378
Cathy Foster, Branch Administrator
Victoria
#240, 730 View St.
Victoria, BC V8W 3Y7 Canada
250-418-8829
Tina Derix, Contact
White Rock
Windsor Square
#101, 1959 - 152 St.
White Rock, BC V4A 9E3 Canada
604-542-2824
Fax: 604-542-2843
888-866-8866
Roz Stefaniuk, Contact
Yorkton
132 Broadway St. West
Yorkton, SK S3N 0M3 Canada
306-782-6450
Fax: 306-782-6460
844-782-6450
Penny Sandercock, Contact

Wirth Associates Inc.
#302, 3300 Yonge St.
Toronto, ON M4N 2L6
416-482-5337
Fax: 416-483-0963
agfw@bloomberg.net
www.wirthassociates.ca
Ownership: Private
Year Founded: 1992
Number of Employees: 8
Assets: $100-500 million
Revenues: $1-5 million
Executives:
A.G. Wirth, President
Shirley Hom, Treasurer
Tom Starkey, Associate
Michael Blower, Sr. Analyst

Stock Exchanges

Canadian Trading & Quotation System Inc.
Canada Trust Tower, BCE Place
PO Box 207
#3850, 161 Bay St.
Toronto, ON M5J 2S1
416-572-2000
Fax: 416-572-4160
www.cnq.ca
Also Known As: CNQ
Ownership: Private.
Year Founded: 2003
Number of Employees: 15
Stock Exchange Membership: Canadian Trading & Quotation System Inc
Profile: Recognized by the Ontario Securities Commission in 2004, Canada's newest stock exchange addresses the needs of emerging companies, their investors & investment dealers.
Executives:

Ian Bandeen, CEO
Robert Cook, President; Robert.Cook@cnq.ca
Bob Medland, Chief Financial Officer
Richard Carleton, Vice-President, Corporate Development
Mark Faulkner, Director, Listings & Regulation
Timothy Baikie, Corporate Secretary, General Counsel
David Timpany, Manager, Trading System
Directors:
John MacNaughton, Chair
Ian Bandeen, Vice-Chair
Bill Braithwaite
Gordon Cheesbrough
Adam Conyers
Robert Cook
Roy Hill
Tom Lunan
Jeffrey MacIntosh
Steven Small
Member Firms & Participating Orgs.:
Blackmont Capital Inc.
BMO Nesbitt Burns Inc.
Byron Securities Limited
Canaccord Capital Corporation
Canadian Trading & Quotation System Inc.
e3m Investments Inc.
Global Securities Corporation
GMP Securities L.P.
Haywood Securities Inc.
Integral Wealth Securities Limited
Jones, Gable & Company Limited
Laurentain Bank Securities Inc.
Leede Financial Markets Inc.
James H. Ross, Sr. Managing Director
MacDougall MacDougall & MacTier Inc.
National Bank Financial Inc.
G. Peter Taylor, President
Northern Securities Inc.
Octagon Capital Corporation
Pacific International Securities Inc.
Penson Financial Services Canada Inc.
Research Capital Corporation
Scotia Capital Inc.
Union Securities Ltd.
Valeurs mobilières Desjardins inc
W.D. Latimer Co. Limited
Wolverton Securities Ltd.
Offices:
Vancouver
#630, 1188 West Georgia St.
Vancouver, BC V6C 4A2 Canada
604-331-1213
Fax: 604-687-1188
Don Gordon, Sr. Advisor

Canadian Unlisted Board Inc.

The Exchange Tower, Trading Services, Toronto Stock Exchange
130 King St. West
Toronto, ON M5X 1J2
416-947-4705
Fax: 416-947-4280
cubadmin@cub.ca
www.cub.ca
Also Known As: CUB
Year Founded: 2000
Profile: Replacing the TSE/CATS reporting mechanism, CUB offers an internet web-based system for dealers to report trades in unlisted & unquoted equity securities.

Montréal Exchange(MX)/ Bourse de Montréal Inc.

Tour de la Bourse
CP 61
800, square Victoria
Montréal, QC H4Z 1A9
514-871-2424
Fax: 514-871-3514
800-361-5353
www.m-x.ca
Ownership: Private
Year Founded: 1874
Stock Exchange Membership: Montreal Exchange
Profile: Canada's financial derivatives exchange offers trading in Canadian interst rate, index & equity derivatives. In addition to financial derivatives markets, areas of expertise also include information technology solutions & clearing services.
Executives:
Luc Bertrand, President/CEO
Louise Laflamme, Exec. Vice-President/CFO
Philippe Loumeau, Sr. Exec. Vice-President/COO
Directors:
Jean Turmel, Chair
Carmand Normand, Vice-Chair
Luc Bertrand
Denyse Chicoyne
Stephen J. Elgee
Wayne Finch
Marie Giguère
William W. Moriarty
Richard Schaeffer
Louis Vachon
Laurent Verreault
Affiliated Companies:
Canadian Derivatives Clearing Corporation/CDCC
Approved Participants:
BMO Nesbitt Burns Inc.
BNP (Canada) Valeurs Mobilieres Inc.
Brockhouse & Cooper Ltd.
Canaccord Capital Corporation
Canadian Derivatives Clearing Corporation
Credifinance Securities Limited
Demers Conseil Inc.
Dundee Securities Corporation
E*TRADE Canada
FIMAT Canada Inc.
Friedberg Mercantile Group
Global Securities Corporation
GMP Securities L.P.
Golden Capital Securities Limited
Hampton Securities Limited
Haywood Securities Inc.
HSBC Securities Canada Inc.
Industrial Alliance Securities Inc.
J.P. Morgan Securities Canada Inc.
Jitney Group Inc.
Jones, Gable & Company Limited
Laurentian Bank Securities Inc.
Le Groupe Option Retraite Inc.
Loewen, Ondaatje, McCutcheon Limited
MacDougall, MacDougall & MacTier Inc.
Maison Placements Canada Inc.
Merrill Lynch Canada Inc.
Montréal Exchange
Morgan Stanley Canada Ltd.
National Bank Direct Brokerage Inc.
National Bank Financial Inc.
Odlum Brown Limited
Orion Securities Ltd.
Pacific International Securities Ltd.
Penson Financial Services Canada Inc.
Pictet Canada LLP
Polar Securities Inc.
Pollitt & Co. Inc.
Raymond James Ltd.
RBC Dominion Securities Inc.
Research Capital Corporation
Research Capital Corporation
Scotia Capital Inc.
Sprott Securities Ltd.
TD Securities Inc.
TD Waterhouse Canada Inc.
The CIBC World Markets Inc.
Timber Hall Canada Company
UBS Securities Canada Inc.
Union Securities Ltd.
Valeurs mobiliéres Desjardins inc
Versant Partners Inc.
W.D. Latimer Co. Limited
Wolverton Securities Ltd.
Woodstone Capital Inc.
Branches:
Toronto
#700, 65 Queen St. West
Toronto, ON M5H 2M5
416-367-2467

Natural Gas Exchange Inc.(NGX)

#2330, 140 - 4 St. SW
Calgary, AB T2P 3N3
403-974-1700
Fax: 403-974-1719
ngx@ngx.com
www.ngx.com
Also Known As: NGX
Ownership: Wholly owned by TSX Group Inc., Toronto, ON.
Year Founded: 1994
Profile: The Natural Gas Exchange is an energy exchange for electronic trading and central counterparty clearing natural gas and electricity contracts. Based in Calgary, there is also an office in Houston, Texas.
Executives:
Peter Krenkel, President; Peter.Krenkel@ngx.com
Cheryl Graden, Chief Legal Counsel; Cheryl.Graden@ngx.com
Stephen Butler, Vice-President, Corporate Development; Stephen.Butler@ngx.com
Gary Gault, Vice-President, Sales & Marketing; Gary.Gault@ngx.com
Myles Marshall, Vice-President, Information Technology; Myles.Marshall@ngx.com
Simon Ward, Vice-President, Finance & Administration; Simon.Ward@ngx.com
Dan Zastawny, Vice-President, Clearing & Compliance; Dan.Zastawny@ngx.com

NEX Board

PO Box 11633
#2700, 650 West Georgia St.
Vancouver, BC V6B 4N9
604-689-3334
Fax: 604-844-7502
866-344-5639
nex@tsxventure.com
www.tse.com/en/nex
Also Known As: NEX
Year Founded: 2003
Profile: A separate board of TSX Venture Exchange, NEX provides a trading forum for companies that have fallen below TSX Venture's ongoing listing requirements. Companies with low levels of business activity, or that have ceased to carry on active business, trade on the NEX board.
Executives:
Ungad Chadda, Director, NEX & Ontario Listed Issuer Services; 416-365-2206; ungad.chadda@tsxventure.com
Gary Lee, Corporate Analyst; 604-488-3126; gary.lee@tsxventure.com

The Toronto Stock Exchange(TSX)

The Exchange Tower
PO Box 450
130 King St. West , 3rd Fl.
Toronto, ON M5X 1J2
416-947-4670
Fax: 416-947-4662
888-873-8392
Other Information: marketregs@tsx.com (Email, Investor Services)
info@tsx.com
www.tsx.com
Year Founded: 1878
Stock Exchange Membership: Toronto Stock Exchange
Executives:
Kevan Cowan, Sr. Vice-President, Business Development
Richard Nadeau, Sr. Vice-President
Member Firms & Participating Orgs.:
Acker Finley Inc.
Acumen Capital Finance Partners Limited
Altus Securities Inc.
Aquilon Capital Corp.
Berkshire Securities Inc.
Blackmont Capital Inc.
BMO Nesbitt Burns Inc.
BNP (Canada) Valeurs Mobilièrs Inc.
Bolder Investment Partners Ltd.
Brant Securities Limited
Brockhouse & Cooper Inc.
Burgeonvest Securities Limited
Byron Securities Limited
Caldwell Securities Ltd.
Canaccord Capital Corporation
Citigroup Global Markets Canada Inc.
Clarus Securities Inc.
Commission Direct Inc.
Credifinance Securities Limited
CTI Capital Inc.
Dominick & Dominick Securities Inc.
Dundee Securities Corp.

The Toronto Stock Exchange(TSX) (continued)
E*TRADE Canada
e3m Investments Inc.
Edward Jones
FIMAT Canada Inc.
FirstEnergy Capital Corp
Foster & Associates Financial Services Inc.
Fraser Mackenzie Limited
Friedberg Mercantile Group
Genuity Capital Markets
Global Securities Corporation
GMP Securities L.P.
Golden Capital Securities Limited
Hampton Securities Limited
Haywood Securities Inc.
Independent Trading Group
Industrial Alliance Securities Inc.
Instinet Canada Limited
Integral Wealth Securities Limited
Interactive Brokers Canada Inc.
IPC Securities Corporation
ITG Canada Corp.
J.C. Clark Ltd.
J.P. Morgan Securities Canada Inc.
Jennings Capital Inc.
Jitney Group Inc.
Jones, Gable & Company Limited
Kingsdale Capital Corporation
Kingwest & Company
Laurentian Bank Securities Inc.
Le Groupe Option Retraite inc
Lightyear Capital Inc.
Loewen, Ondaatje, McCutcheon Limited
MacDougall MacDougall & MacTier Inc.
Maison Placements Canada Inc.
Man Financial Canada Co.
Maple Securities Canada Ltd.
MCA Valeurs Mobiliès Inc.
Merrill Lynch Canada Inc.
Morgan Stanley Canada Ltd.
National Bank Direct Brokerage Inc.
National Bank Financial Inc.
Norstar Securities International Inc.
Northern Securities Inc.
Octagon Capital Corporation
Odlum Brown Limited
Orion Securities Inc.
Pacific International Securities Inc.
Paradigm Capital Inc.
Penson Financial Services Canada Inc.
Peters & Co. Limited
Pictet Canada LLP
Polar Securities Inc.
Pollitt & Co. Inc.
Pope & Company
Questrade, Inc.
Raymond James Ltd.
RBC Capital Markets
Research Capital Corporation
Salman Partners Inc.
Scotia Capital Inc.
Sprott Securities Inc.
Standard Securities Capital Corporation
State Street Global Markets Canada Inc.
TD Securities Inc.
TD Waterhouse Canada Inc.
The CIBC World Markets Inc.
Timber Hill Canada Company
Toll Cross Securities Inc.
Tristone Capital Inc.
UBS Securities Canada Inc.
Union Securities Ltd.
Valeurs mobiliès Desjardins inc
Versant Partners Inc.
W.D. Latimer Co. Limited
Wellington West Capital Inc.
Westwind Partners Inc.
Wolverton Securities Ltd.
Woodstone Capital Inc.

TSX Group Inc.
PO Box 450
130 King St. West, 3rd Fl.
Toronto, ON M5X 1J2
416-947-4670
Fax: 416-947-4662
888-873-8392
info@tsx.com
www.tsx.com
Profile: TSX Group operates the Toronto Stock Exchange, the TSX Venture Exchange, as well as the Natural Gas Exchange (NGX). The Group also includes TSX Markets, TSX Technologies & TSX Datalinx.

Executives:
Richard Nesbitt, CEO
John Cieslak, Chief Information & Administration Officer, Exec. Vice-President
Michael Ptasznik, Chief Financial Officer
Rik Parkhill, Exec. Vice-President
James Magee, Sr. Vice-President, Fixed Income
Sharon Pel, Sr. Vice-President, Legal & Business Affairs
Directors:
Wayne C. Fox, Chair
Tullio Cedraschi
Raymond Chan
Raymond Garneau
John A Hagg
Harry A. Jaako
J. Spencer Lanthier
Jean Martel
Owen McCreery
Doug McGregor
John P. Mulvihill
Richard W. Nesbitt
Kathleen M. O'Neill
Geraldine B. Sinclair
Affiliated Companies:
Natural Gas Exchange Inc./NGX
TSX Venture Exchange
The Toronto Stock Exchange/TSX
Offices:
Montréal
 #1100, 1000, rue Sherbrooke ouest
 Montréal, QC H3A 3G4
 514-788-2451
 Fax: 514-788-2421
 877-590-7555
 K. Nanhu, Pavilion Money Manager

TSX Venture Exchange
PO Box 450
130 King St. West, 3rd Fl.
Toronto, ON M5X 1J2
416-365-2200
Fax: 416-365-2224
877-421-2369
information@tsxventure.com
www.tsxventure.com
Former Name: Canadian Venture Exchange
Stock Exchange Membership: TSX Venture Exchange
Profile: TSX Venture Exchange serves the public venture equity market. It gives access to capital for companies at the early stages of their growth.

Executives:
Linda Hohol, President
Kevan Cowan, Sr. Vice-President
Member Firms & Participating Orgs.:
Acadian Securities Inc., Halifax
Acumen Capital Finance Partners Limited, Calgary
Berkshire Securities Inc., Burlington
Bieber Securities Inc., Burlington
Blackmont Capital Inc., Toronto
BMO Nesbitt Burns INc., Toronto
Bolder Investment Partners Ltd., Vancouver
Brant Securities Limited
Brant Securities Limited, Toronto
Brockhouse & Cooper Inc., Montreal
Burgeonvest Securities Limited, Hamilton
Byron Securities Inc., Toronto
Caldwell Securities Ltd., Toronto
Canaccord Capital Corporation, Vancouver
Clarus Securities Inc., Toronto
Commission Direct Inc., Toronto
CTI Capital Inc., Montreal
Dominick & Dominick Securities Inc., Toronto
Dundee Securities Corp., Toronto
E*TRADE Canada, Toronto
Emerging Equities Inc., Calgary
FIMAT Canada Inc., Montreal
FirstEnergy Capital Corp., Calgary
Foster & Associates Financial Services Inc., Toronto
Fraser Mackenzie Limited, Toronto
Friedberg Mercantile Group, Toronto
Genuity Capital Markets, Toronto
Global Securities Corporation, Vancouver
GMP Securities L.P., Toronto
Golden Capital Securities Limited, Vancouver-D.Y.H. Siu
Hampton Securities Limtied, Toronto
Haywood Securities Inc., Vancouver
HSBC Securities Canada Inc.
Integral Wealth Securities Limited, Toronto
Investpro Securities Inc., Montreal
IPC Securities Corporation, Toronto
ITG Canada Corp., Toronto
J.C. Clark Ltd., Toronto
J.P. Morgan Securities Canada Inc., Toronto
Jennings Capital Inc., Calgary
Jones, Gable & Company Limited, Toronto
Jory Capital Inc., Winnipeg
Kingsdale Capital Corporation, Toronto
Laurentian Bank Securities Inc., Montreal
Leede Financial Markets Inc., Calgary
Lightyear Capital Inc., Calgary
Loewwen, Ondaatje, McCutcheon Limited, Toronto
MacDougall MacDougall & MacTier Inc., Montreal
Madison Placements Canada Inc., Toronto
Man Financial Canada Co., Toronto
MCA Valeurs Mobilieres Inc., Montreal
Merrill Lynch Canada Inc., Toronto
Morgan Stanley Canada Ltd., Toronto
National Bank Direct Brokerage Inc., Montreal
National Bank Financial Inc., Montreal
Norstar Securities International Inc., Toronto
Northern Securities Inc., Toronto
Octagon Capital Canada Corporation, Toronto
Odlum Brown Limited, Vancouver
Orion Securities Inc., Toronto
Pacific International Securities Inc., Vancouver
Paradigm Capital Inc., Toronto
Penson Financial Services Canada Inc., Montreal
Peters & Co. Limited, Calgary
Polar Securities Inc., Toronto
Pollitt & Co. Inc., Toronto
Pope & Company, Toronto
Raymond James Ltd., Vancouver
RBC Capital Markets, Toronto
Research Capital Corporation, Toronto
Salman Partners Inc., Vancouver
Scotia Capital Inc., Toronto
Sprott Securities Inc., Toronto
Standard Securities Capital Corporation, Toronto
TD Securities Inc., Toronto
The CIBC World Markets Inc., Toronto
Toll Cross Investments, Toronto
Tristone Capital Inc., Calgary
TSX Vebtyre Exchange
UBS Securities Canada Inc., Toronto
Union Securities Ltd., Vancouver
Valeurs mobilieres Desjardins Inc, Montreal
Versant Partners Inc., Montreal
W.D. Latimer Co. Limited, Toronto
Wellington West Capital Inc., Winnipeg
Westwind Partners Inc., Toronto
Wolverton Securities Ltd., Vancouver
Woodstone Capital Inc., Vancouver
Offices:
Calgary
 300 - 5 Ave. SW, 10th Fl.
 Calgary, AB T2P 3C4 Canada
 403-218-2800
 Fax: 403-237-0450
 877-884-2369
Montréal
 #1100, 1000, rue Sherbrooke ouest
 Montréal, QC H3A 3G4 Canada
 514-788-2423
 Fax: 514-788-2421
 866-881-2369

Vancouver
 PO Box 11633
 #2700, 650 West Georgia St.
 Vancouver, ON V6B 4N9 Canada

604-689-3334
Fax: 604-688-6051
877-421-2369
Winnipeg
#600, 1 Lombard Pl.
Winnipeg, MB R3B 0X3 Canada
204-927-2369
Fax: 204-927-2368

Winnipeg Commodity Exchange Inc.

Commodity Exchange Tower
#400, 360 Main St.
Winnipeg, MB R3C 3Z4
204-925-5000
Fax: 204-943-5448
contact@wce.ca
www.wce.ca
Stock Exchange Membership: Winnepeg Commodities Exchange
Profile: The Winnipeg Commodity Exchange is Canada's only agricultural futures & options exchange. Situated in the heart of the Canadian Prairies, the historic centre of North America's grain trade, WCE operates under a mission to provide a public marketplace for responsive price discovery & risk transfer of commodities with efficiency & integrity.

Executives:
Mike Gagné, President/CEO
Will Hill, Sr. Vice-President
Doug Betz, Vice-President, Information Technology
Linda Cox Vincent, Vice-President, Market Regulation, General Counsel
Clearing Participants:
BMO Nesbitt Burns Inc.
FIMAT Canada Inc.
J.P. Morgan Securities Canada Inc.
RBC Dominion Securities Inc.
Scotia Capital Inc.
The CIBC World Markets Inc.
Winnipeg Commodity Exchange Inc.

SECTION 4

Insurance Companies

Included in this section are federally & provincially incorporated insurance companies, reinsurance companies, mutual benefit companies, fraternal benefit societies & reciprocal exchanges, with the classes of insurance they offer.

Insurance companies are registered to conduct business under the federal *Insurance Companies Act* and/or corresponding provincial legislation. Life insurance companies are registered to underwrite life insurance, accident and sickness insurance and annuity business. Property and casualty insurance companies are registered to underwrite insurance other than life insurance.

Insurance Companies

ACA Assurance
3050, boul St-Jean
Trois-Rivières, QC G9A 5E1
819-377-1777
Fax: 819-377-3587
1-800-830-3436
infocan@aca-assurance.org
www.aca-assurance.org
Also Known As: Association Canado-Américaine
Year Founded: 1896
Classes of Insurance: Accident, Life
Incorporation: Federally Incorporated Insurance Company
Profile: The Franco-American fraternal benefit society offers life insurance, travel insurance, accidental death & dismemberment protection, travel insurance plus annuities.

Executives:
Serge J. Beaudoin, President
Jean-Maurice Bergeron, Vice-President, Canada
Normand Morneault, Vice-President, USA
André Bellemare, Secretary
Normand Stevenson, Treasurer
Directors:
Paul H. LaFlamme
Daniel LaPointe
Jean-René Lussier
Adrien Longchamps
Robert E. Raiche
Christiane Vallée

Acadia Life/ Acadie Vie
CP 5554
295, boul St-Pierre ouest
Caraquet, NB E1W 1B7
506-726-4202
Fax: 506-726-8204
888-822-2343
acadievie@acadie.net
www.acadie.com
Former Name: La Société d'assurance des Caisses populaires acadiennes
Classes of Insurance: Personal Accident & Sickness, Life
Incorporation: Provincially Incorporated Insurance Company
Executives:
Yves Duguay, Directeur, Planification financière, support & coordination
Offices:
Toronto
c/o Blake, Cassels & Graydon LLP
PO Box 35, Commerce Court West Sta. Commerce Court West
199 Bay St.
Toronto, ON M5L 1A9
416-863-3863
Fax: 416-863-2653
Ernest McNee, Chief Agent

ACE INA Insurance
130 King St. West, 12th Fl.
Toronto, ON M5X 1A6
416-368-2911
Fax: 416-594-2600
www.ace-ina-canada.com
Ownership: Owned by ACE INA Overseas Insurance Company
Year Founded: 1999
Number of Employees: 154
Assets: $500m-1 billion
Revenues: $100-500 million
Classes of Insurance: Accident, Aircraft, Auto, Liability, Boiler & Machinery, Credit, Marine, Fidelity, Property, Fire, Surety, Hail & Crop
Incorporation: Federally Incorporated Insurance Company
Profile: This federally registered company was incorporated in 1977 & is licensed to transact in all provinces & territories. An agency writer, it is a stock company ultimately owned by ACE Limited. It is affiliated in Canada with & ACE INA Life Insurance. Classes of insurance also include energy & directors & officers.

Executives:
Daniel P. Courtemanche, President/CEO
John Lupica, President/CEO, ACE USA
Karen L. Barkley, Chief Operations Officer
Paul Primiani, Chief Underwriting Officer
Cynthia T. Santiago, Exec. Vice-President/CFO, Secretary
Terri Mitchell, Sr. Vice-President, Accident & Health
Carlo Petosa, Sr. Vice-President, ACE Global Energy
Shawn Doherty, Vice-President, Actuarial
David MacDonald, Vice-President, Capital Risk Group
Tony Rivera, Vice-President, Claims
Norma E. Ross, Director, Human Resources & Administration
Directors:
John Lupica, Chair
James W. Blaney
Jess C. Bush
Daniel P. Courtemanche; 416-594-2561
Richard Freeborough
Norma E. Ross; 416-594-3037
Cynthia T. Santiago; 416-594-3035
Affiliated Companies:
ACE INA Life Insurance
Branches:
Vancouver
#1445, 885 West Georgia St.
Vancouver, BC V6C 3E8 Canada
604-681-7581
Debra Agostino, Business Development Manager

ACE INA Life Insurance/ Assurance-vie ACE INA
The Exchange Tower
130 King St. West, 12th Fl.
Toronto, ON M5X 1A6
416-594-2561
Fax: 416-594-3000
Classes of Insurance: Personal Accident & Sickness, Liability
Incorporation: Federally Incorporated Insurance Company
Profile: Another class of insurance offered by the company is loss of employment.

Executives:
Daniel P. Courtemanche, President/CEO

ACTRA Fraternal Benefit Society(AFBS)
1000 Yonge St.
Toronto, ON M4W 2K2
416-967-6600
Fax: 416-967-4744
800-387-8897
benefits@actrafrat.com
www.actrafrat.com
Ownership: Member-owned
Year Founded: 1975
Classes of Insurance: Personal Accident & Sickness, Life
Incorporation: Federally Incorporated Insurance Company
Profile: The not-for-profit insurance company offers services to its members who are mainly from ACTRA & The Writers Guild of Canada.

Executives:
Robert M. Underwood, President/CEO
Directors:
Thor Bishopric, Chair
David H. Atkins, Vice-Chair
Tecca Crosby
Ferne Downey
David Ferry
Guy Gauthier
Peggy Mahon
Guy Mayson
Sean Mulcahy
Marie-P (Charette) Poulin
Pierre Racicot
William Samples
Sugith Varughese
Branches:
Vancouver
#301, 856 Homer St.
Vancouver, BC V6B 2W5 Canada
604-801-6550
Fax: 604-801-6580
866-801-6550
afbswest@actrafrat.com

Aetna Life Insurance Company of Canada
#2, 1145 Nicholson Rd.
Newmarket, ON L3Y 9C3
905-853-0858
Fax: 905-853-0183
Classes of Insurance: Personal Accident & Sickness, Life
Incorporation: Federally Incorporated Insurance Company
Profile: This is a foreign life insurance company regulated by the Office of the Superintendent of Financial Institutions Canada.

Executives:
Colleen Anne Sexsmith, Chief Agent

Affiliated FM Insurance Company
#500, 165 Commerce Valley Dr. West
Thornhill, ON L3T 7V8
905-763-5555
Fax: 905-763-5556
www.fmglobal.com
Ownership: Factory Mutual Insurance Company, USA
Year Founded: 1949
Number of Employees: 25
Assets: $100-500 million Year End: 20041231
Revenues: $50-100 million Year End: 20041231
Classes of Insurance: Liability, Boiler & Machinery, Fidelity, Property, Fire, Surety
Incorporation: Federally Incorporated Insurance Company
Profile: The company specializes in commercial property insurance, including crime & fidelity.

Executives:
Shivan S. Subramaniam, President/CEO
Ruud H. Bosman, Exec. Vice-President
Brian J. Hurley, Exec. Vice-President
Perry R. Brazeau, Sr. Vice-President & Chief Agent
Directors:
Walter J. Galvin
George J. Harad
John A. Luke, Jr.
Robert J. O'Toole
James W. Owens
David Pulman
William C. Stivers
Elisabeth Struckwell
Shivan S. Subramaniam
James C. Thyen
Alfred J. Verrecchia
Branches:
Montréal
#1400, 600, rue de la Gauchetière ouest
Montréal, QC H3B 4W5 Canada
514-866-9955
Fax: 514-866-3202
Gervais Landry, Vice-President, Operations
Thornhill
#500, 165 Commerce Valley Dr. West
Thornhill, ON L3T 7V8 Canada
905-763-5555
Perry R. Brazeau, Sr. Vice-President/Manager, Canadian Operations

Agriculture Financial Services Corporation(AFSC)
***Also listed under:** Financing & Loan Companies*
5718 - 56 Ave.
Lacombe, AB T4J 1R5
403-782-3000
Fax: 403-782-4226
www.afsc.ca
Ownership: Crown corporation
Year Founded: 1972
Number of Employees: 700
Assets: $1-10 billion Year End: 20060331
Revenues: $500m-1 billion Year End: 20060331
Classes of Insurance: Hail & Crop

INSURANCE COMPANIES

Agriculture Financial Services Corporation(AFSC) (continued)

Incorporation: Provincially Incorporated Insurance Company

Profile: Provincial crown corporation with a private sector Board of Directors that provides farmers, agribusinesses and other small businesses loans, crop insurance and farm income disaster assistance.

Executives:

Brad Klak, President & Managing Director; 403-782-8309; brad.klak@afsc.ca

Richard Bell, Vice-President, Lending; 403-782-8335; richard.bell@afsc.ca

Merle Jacobson, Vice-President, Insurance Operations; 403-782-8229; merle.jacobson@afsc.ca

Krish Krishnaswamy, Vice-President, Finance; 403-782-8284; krish.krishnaswamy@afsc.ca

Directors:

Lynn Dechant
Gene Dextrase
Harry Haney
Barry Holmes
Brad Klak
Joe Makowecki
Barry Mehr
Gerard Oosterhuis
Wayne Wagner
Gail Surkan

Insurance & Lending Offices:

Airdrie
909 Irricana Rd.
Airdrie, AB T4A 2G6 Canada
403-948-8543
Fax: 403-948-1418

Athabasca
Provincial Bldg.
#100, 4903 - 50th St.
Athabasca, AB T9S 1E2 Canada
780-675-4007
Fax: 780-675-3827

Barrhead
Provincial Bldg.
6203 - 49 St., Main Fl.
Barrhead, AB T7N 1A4 Canada
780-674-8282
Fax: 780-674-8362

Brooks
Provincial Bldg.
220 - 4 Ave. West
Brooks, AB T1R 0B1 Canada
403-362-1262
Fax: 403-362-8078

Calgary - 8th St. NE - District Office
Deerfoot Atrium Bldg. North
#150, 6815 - 8th St. NE
Calgary, AB T2E 7H7 Canada
403-297-6261
Fax: 403-297-8461

Camrose - 52 St. - Regional Office
PO Box 5000, M Sta. M
4910 - 52 St.
Camrose, AB T4V 4E8 Canada
780-679-1340
Fax: 780-679-1323

Cardston
Provincial Bldg.
PO Box 1228
576 Main St.
Cardston, AB T0K 0K0 Canada
403-653-5154
Fax: 403-653-5156

Claresholm
Provincial Bldg.
109 - 46 Ave. West
Claresholm, AB T0L 0T0 Canada
403-625-3534
Fax: 403-625-2862

Drumheller
PO Box 2319
#100, 515 Hwy. 10 East
Drumheller, AB T0J 0Y0 Canada
403-823-1684
Fax: 403-823-5083

Fairview - 109 St. - Regional Office
Provincial Bldg.
PO Box 1188
10209 - 109 St., 2nd Fl.
Fairview, AB T0H 1L0 Canada
780-835-4975
Fax: 780-835-5834

Falher
M.D. Bldg.
Main St.
Falher, AB T0H 1M0 Canada
780-837-2521
Fax: 780-837-8223

Fort Vermilion
Agriculture Canada Experimental Farm
Fort Vermilion, AB T0H 1N0 Canada
780-927-4209
Fax: 780-927-3838

Grande Prairie - 99 St.
Provincial Bldg.
10320 - 99 St.
Grande Prairie, AB T8V 6J4 Canada
780-538-5220
Fax: 780-532-2560

Grimshaw
5306 - 50th St.
Grimshaw, AB T0H 1W0 Canada
780-332-4494
Fax: 780-332-1044

Hanna
Provincial Bldg.
401 Centre St.
Hanna, AB T0J 1P0 Canada
403-854-5525
Fax: 403-854-2590

Lamont
5014 - 50 Ave.
Lamont, AB T0B 2R0 Canada
780-895-2266
Fax: 780-895-7755

Leduc - Sparrow Dr.
6547 Sparrow Dr.
Leduc, AB T9E 7C7 Canada
780-986-4088
Fax: 780-986-1085

Lethbridge
County of Lethbridge Bldg.
#200, 905 - 4th Ave. South
Lethbridge, AB T1J 0P4 Canada
403-381-5474
Fax: 403-382-4527

Medicine Hat
Provincial Bldg.
#107, 346 - 3rd St. SE
Medicine Hat, AB T1A 0G7 Canada
403-529-3600
Fax: 403-528-5264

Olds
Provincial Bldg.
#101, 5030 - 50th St.
Olds, AB T4H 1S1 Canada
403-556-4334
Fax: 403-556-4255

Ponoka
PO Box 4426
5110 - 49 Ave.
Ponoka, AB T4J 1R5 Canada
403-783-7071
Fax: 403-783-7079

Red Deer - 51st St. - Regional Office
Provincial Bldg.
#302, 4920 - 51st St.
Red Deer, AB T4N 6K8 Canada
403-340-5326
Fax: 403-340-7004

Rimbey
Provincial Bldg.
5025 - 55 St.
Rimbey, AB T0C 2J0 Canada
403-843-4516
Fax: 403-843-4516

Smoky Lake
Provincial Bldg.
108 Wheatland Ave.
Smoky Lake, AB T0A 3C0 Canada
780-656-3644
Fax: 780-656-3669

Spirit River
Provincial Bldg.
4602 - 50 St., 1st Fl.
Spirit River, AB T0H 3G0 Canada
780-864-3896
Fax: 780-864-2529

Stettler
Provincial Bldg.
4705 - 49 Ave.
Stettler, AB T0C 2L0 Canada
403-742-7536
Fax: 403-742-7911

Stony Plain
Provincial Bldg.
4709 - 44 Ave.
Stony Plain, AB T7Z 1N4 Canada
780-963-0600
Fax: 780-963-1251

Strathmore
325 - 3 Ave.
Strathmore, AB T1P 1B4 Canada
403-934-3616
Fax: 403-934-5018

Taber
Provincial Bldg.
5011 - 49 Ave.
Taber, AB T1G 1V9 Canada
403-223-7900
Fax: 403-223-7985

Three Hills
Provincial Bldg.
160 - 3 Ave. South
Three Hills, AB T0M 2A0 Canada
403-443-8515
Fax: 403-443-7519

Vegreville
Vinet's Village Mall
#138, 4925 - 50th Ave.
Vegreville, AB T9C 1S6 Canada
780-632-5431
Fax: 780-632-3385

Vermilion
Provincial Bldg.
4701 - 52 St.
Vermilion, AB T9X 1J9 Canada
780-853-8266
Fax: 780-853-1982

Vulcan
101 - 1 St. South
Vulcan, AB T0L 2B0 Canada
403-485-2766
Fax: 403-485-2947

Wainwright
Provincial Bldg.
810 - 14th Ave.
Wainwright, AB T9W 1R2 Canada
780-842-7547
Fax: 780-842-4948

Westlock
Provincial Bldg. #2
10003 - 100th St.
Westlock, AB T9P 2E8 Canada
780-349-4544
Fax: 780-349-2484

Offices:

Calgary - 8th St. NE
Deerfoot Atrium Bldg. North
#170, 6815 - 8th St. NE
Calgary, AB T2E 7H7 Canada
Fax: 403-297-4136

Castor
PO Box 719
4902 - 50th Ave.
Castor, AB T0C 0X0 Canada
403-882-3770
Fax: 403-882-2746

Edmonton
JG O'Donoghue Bldg.
10209 - 113 St.
Edmonton, AB T6H 5T6 Canada
780-427-2140
Fax: 780-422-9738

Edson

PO Box 7110
4924 - 1 Ave.
Edson, AB T7E 1V4 Canada
780-723-8233
Fax: 780-723-8575
Fairview
PO Box 159
Fairview, AB T0H 1L0 Canada
Foremost
218 Main St.
Foremost, AB T0K 0X0 Canada
403-867-3666
Fax: 403-867-2038
Fort McMurray
#102, 9816 Hardin St.
Fort McMurray, AB T9H 4K3 Canada
780-791-5875
Fax: 780-791-7257

Grande Prairie - 102 St.
Provincial Bldg.
#1128, 9909 - 102 St.
Grande Prairie, AB T8V 6J4 Canada
780-538-5220
Fax: 780-532-5531
High Prairie
PO Box 1259
High Prairie, AB T0G 1E0 Canada
780-523-6529
High Prairie - 53 Ave.
Provincial Bldg.
5226 - 53 Ave.
High Prairie, AB T0G 1E0 Canada
780-523-6507
Fax: 780-523-6569
High River
129 - 4 Ave. SW
High River, AB T1V 1M4 Canada
403-652-8313
Fax: 403-652-8306
Lacombe - 56 Ave. - District Office
5718 - 56 Ave.
Lacombe, AB T4L 1B1 Canada
403-782-6800
Fax: 403-782-6753
Leduc - 50 St.
4301 - 50 St.
Leduc, AB T9E 7H3 Canada
Manning
116 - 4 Ave. SW
Manning, AB T0H 2M0 Canada
780-836-3573
Fax: 780-836-2844
Oyen
212 Main St.
Oyen, AB T0J 2J0 Canada
403-664-3677
Fax: 403-664-2687
Peace River
PO Box 900
#23, 9809 - 98th Ave.
Peace River, AB T8S 1J5 Canada
780-624-6387
Fax: 780-624-6493
Provost
Provincial Bldg.
5419 - 44 St.
Provost, AB T0B 3S0 Canada
780-753-2150
Fax: 780-753-2876
Sedgewick
Flagstaff County Bldg.
4902 - 50 St.
Sedgewick, AB T0B 4C0 Canada
780-384-3880
Fax: 780-384-2156
St Paul
Provincial Bldg.
5025 - 49 Ave.
St Paul, AB T0A 3A4 Canada
780-645-6221
Fax: 780-645-2848
Thorhild
County Administration Bldg.
PO Box 400
801 - 1 St.
Thorhild, AB T0A 3J0 Canada
780-398-3933
Fax: 780-398-2087
Valleyview
Provincial Bldg.
5112 - 50 Ave.
Valleyview, AB T0H 3N0 Canada
780-524-3838
Fax: 780-524-4565

AIG Assurance Canada

60 Yonge St.
Toronto, ON M5E 1H5
416-362-2961
Fax: 416-362-6845
800-387-9855
Other Information: 800-387-9554 (French Toll Free)
directissue@aig.com
www.aigassurance.ca
Ownership: Member company of American International Group Inc. (AIG), USA.
Year Founded: 1967
Classes of Insurance: Personal Accident & Sickness, Life
Incorporation: Federally Incorporated Insurance Company
Profile: The company also offers travel insurance.

AIG Life Insurance Company of Canada

60 Yonge St.
Toronto, ON M5E 1H5
416-596-3900
Fax: 416-596-4143
877-742-5244
Other Information: Claims: 416/350-3932
aiglifecainfo@aig.com
www.aiglife.ca
Former Name: American International Assurance Life Company Ltd.
Ownership: Private. Subsidiary of American International Group, Inc.
Number of Employees: 160
Classes of Insurance: Personal Accident & Sickness, Life
Incorporation: Federally Incorporated Insurance Company
Executives:
David Blodgett, Contact, Ontario & Western Canada
Sales Offices:
Calgary
#505, 11012 Macleod Trail South
Calgary, AB T2J 6A5 Canada
403-265-7016
877-847-8160
Montréal
#840, 2000, av McGill College
Montréal, QC H3A 3H3 Canada
514-987-2904
Fax: 514-987-2929
800-361-7211
Paul Lalond, Contact, Québec-Atlantic Region
Toronto - Lansing Sq.
#601, 2 Lansing Sq.
Toronto, ON M2J 4P8 Canada
416-756-3640
Fax: 416-756-2908
800-608-7303
Toronto - Yonge St.
60 Yonge St.
Toronto, ON M5E 1H5 Canada
416-596-2937
Fax: 416-596-7732
888-250-5743
group.manager@aig.com
Vancouver
#1001, 543 Granville St.
Vancouver, BC V6C 1X8 Canada
604-682-4157
Fax: 604-682-4626
877-877-1272

AIG United Guaranty Mortgage Insurance Company Canada

#909, 123 Front Street West
Toronto, ON M5J 2M2
416-640-8924
Fax: 416-640-8948
866-414-9109
Other Information: 1-877-244-8422 (Toll Free underwriting related inquiries)
info@aigug.ca
www.aigug.ca
Ownership: Subsidiary of AIG United Guaranty Corporation, Greensboro, NC, USA.
Incorporation: Federally Incorporated Insurance Company
Profile: This insurance company is licensed for mortages. It is part of American International Group, Inc.

Executives:
Andrew Charles, President/CEO
John Gaines, Chief Operating Officer
Mario Vachon, Chief Risk Officer
Brian Bell, Vice-President, Corporate Development
Maria Pimenta, Vice-President, Sales
Darren Kirk, Director of Sales, Western Canada; 403-473-8482
Mary Putnam, Director of Sales, Ontario & Eastern Canada; 416-640-8936
Geoff Scott, Director, Underwriting
BlazePhotoonics
Bookham Technology
ITF Optical Technologies
Cavendish Kinetics
Diablo Technologies
Extreme Packet Devices
Fresco Microchip
MEMSIC
RedMere Technology
SiRiFIC
SkyStone Systems
Synad Technologies
Virtensys
VIXS Systems
Avalere
Avesta Technologies
Camilion Solutions
FastLane Technologies
Got Corp.
iMagicTV
MODASolutions
NCipher
noHold
OLAP@Work
Orchestream
Third Brigade
TrialStat
Ubiquity Software
Abatis Systems
BlueArc
Cambrian Systems
DragonWave
Northchurch Communications
NOVX Systems
OctigaBay Systems
PixStream
Sandvine
Tropic Networks

Alberta Blue Cross

Blue Cross Place
10009 - 108th St. NW
Edmonton, AB T5J 3C5
780-498-8000
Fax: 780-425-4627
800-661-6995
Other Information: Travel Coverage: 780/498-8550; Individual Health & Dental Plans: 780/498-8008; Group Sales: 780/498-8500
www.ab.bluecross.ca
Ownership: Not-for-profit. Member of Canadian Association of Blue Cross Plans, Toronto, ON.
Year Founded: 1948
Number of Employees: 700+
Classes of Insurance: Personal Accident & Sickness
Incorporation: Provincially Incorporated Insurance Company
Profile: The organization provides supplementary health & dental benefit programs for individuals, families, seniors, & employers in Alberta. Health programs are also administered for provincial, territorial & federal governments.

Executives:
Ron W. Malin, President/CEO
Susan K. Adam, Vice-President, Human Resources
Nicholas O. Arscott, Vice-President, Benefit Services
Laraine T. Barby, Vice-President, Application Development & Support

Alberta Blue Cross (continued)
Graham D. Ferguson, Vice-President, Government
Richard L. Martin, Vice-President/CFO
David W. Miller, Vice-President & Chief Information Officer
Ray R. Pisani, Vice-President, Group & Individual
David F. Andrews, Sr. Manager, Group Underwriting & Administration
Branches:
Calgary
715 - 5 Ave. SW
Calgary, AB T2P 2X6 Canada
403-234-9666
Fax: 403-266-5644
Fort McMurray
Plaza II Mall
#619, 8600 Franklin Ave.
Fort McMurray, AB T9H 4G8 Canada
780-790-3390
Fax: 780-791-6999

Grande Prairie
#101A, 10712 - 100th St.
Grande Prairie, AB T8V 3X8 Canada
780-532-3505
Fax: 780-539-0455
Lethbridge
Chancery Court
#470, 220 - 4th St.
Lethbridge, AB T1J 4J7 Canada
403-328-1785
Fax: 403-327-9823
Medicine Hat
Chinook Place
#203, 623 - 4th St. SE
Medicine Hat, AB T1A 0L1 Canada
403-529-5553
Fax: 403-527-3798
Red Deer
Riverside Office Plaza
#152, 4919 - 59th St.
Red Deer, AB T4N 6C9 Canada
403-343-7009
Fax: 403-340-1098

Alberta Motor Association Insurance Co.
PO Box 8180, South Stn. South
Edmonton, AB T6H 5X9
780-430-5555
800-615-5897
Other Information: Membership Inquiries Toll Free: 800-222-6400
www.ama.ab.ca
Ownership: Fully owned subsidiary of the Alberta Motor Association.
Year Founded: 1974
Classes of Insurance: Personal Accident & Sickness, Auto, Life, Property, Fire
Incorporation: Provincially Incorporated Insurance Company
Service Centres:
Calgary - 17 Ave. SW - Main
4700 - 17 Ave. SW
Calgary, AB T3E 0E3 Canada
403-240-5333
Calgary - 20 Ave. NE - Sunridge
3650 - 20 Ave. NE
Calgary, AB T1Y 6E8 Canada
403-571-4120
Calgary - 8 Ave. SW
#100, 530 - 8 Ave. SW
Calgary, AB T2P 3S8 Canada
403-517-4262
Calgary - Crowfoot Cres. NW
Crowfoot Centre
220 Crowfoot Cres. NW
Calgary, AB T3G 3N5 Canada
403-517-4262
Calgary - MacLeod Trail SE
Willowpark Village
#532, 10816 MacLeod Trail SE
Calgary, AB T2J 5N8 Canada
403-571-8500
Calgary - Shawville Blvd. SE
#600, 85 Shawville Blvd. SE
Calgary, AB T2Y 3W5 Canada
403-254-6777
Camrose
6702 - 48 Ave.
Camrose, AB T4V 4S3 Canada
780-679-5060
Edmonton - 109 St. NW
11220 - 109 St. NW
Edmonton, AB T5G 2T6 Canada
780-471-3550
Edmonton - 170 St. NW
9938 - 170 St. NW
Edmonton, AB T5T 6G7 Canada
780-471-3550
Edmonton - G.A. MacDonald Ave. NW
10310 G.A. MacDonald (39A) Ave.
Edmonton, AB T6J 6R7 Canada
780-471-3550
Edmonton - Manning Dr. NW
5040 Manning Dr. NW
Edmonton, AB T5A 5B4 Canada
780-471-3550
Fort McMurray
4 Hospital St.
Fort McMurray, AB T9H 5E4 Canada
780-743-2653
Grande Prairie
11401 - 99 St.
Grande Prairie, AB T8V 2H6 Canada
780-538-2733

Lethbridge
120 Scenic Dr. South
Lethbridge, AB T1J 4R4 Canada
403-328-1333
Medicine Hat
2710 - 13 Ave. SE
Medicine Hat, AB T1A 3P8 Canada
403-527-1183
Red Deer - 50 Ave.
Southpointe Common
#141, 2004 - 50 Ave.
Red Deer, AB T4R 3A2
403-342-6632
Red Deer - Bremner Ave.
2965 Bremner Ave.
Red Deer, AB T4R 1S2 Canada
403-342-6632
Sherwood Park
#236, 22 Baseline Rd.
Sherwood Park, AB T8H 1S8
780-467-8520

Alberta School Boards Insurance Exchange(ASBIE)

www.asbie.com
Classes of Insurance: Liability, Fidelity, Property
Incorporation: Provincially Incorporated Insurance Company
Profile: The ASBIE insurance program is sponsored & managed by the Alberta School Board Association (ASBA). Member school boards of ASBA may join the ASBIE programs.

Executives:
Janice Boiko, Program Director, Risk Manager; 780-930-3827; jboiko@lloydadd.com

Algoma Mutual Insurance Company
131 Main St.
Thessalon, ON P0R 1L0
705-842-3345
Fax: 705-842-3500
800-461-7260
www.amico.on.ca
Year Founded: 1899
Classes of Insurance: Auto, Property
Incorporation: Provincially Incorporated Insurance Company
Profile: The property & casualty insurance company offers coverage for home, farm, commercial & automobile risks.

Executives:
Cameron Ross, Chief Executive Officer

Allianz Life Insurance Company of North America
#700, 2005 Sheppard Ave. East
Toronto, ON M2J 5B4
Fax: 416-502-2555
Classes of Insurance: Personal Accident & Sickness, Life
Incorporation: Federally Incorporated Insurance Company
Executives:
Bruce Elliott, Chief Agent; 905-502-2500

Allstate Insurance Company of Canada/ Allstate du Canada, Compagnie d'assurance
#100, 27 Allstate Pkwy.
Markham, ON L3R 5P8
905-477-6900
Fax: 905-415-4831
800-255-7828
Other Information: Claims Toll Free Numbers: 800-387-0462 (AB, BC, MB, ON, SK); 800-463-2813 (QC); 800-561-7222 (NS, NB, PE, NL)
1800allstateM@allstate.ca, 1800allstateM@allstate.ca
www.allstate.ca
Ownership: Private. Subsidiary of Allstate Corporation, Northbrook, IL.
Year Founded: 1953
Number of Employees: 1,450
Classes of Insurance: Personal Accident & Sickness, Legal Expense, Auto, Liability, Boiler & Machinery, Fidelity, Property, Surety
Incorporation: Federally Incorporated Insurance Company
Executives:
Michael J. Donoghue, President/CEO
Affiliated Companies:
Pembridge Insurance Company
Branches:
Montréal
#120, 7100, rue Jean-Talon est
Montréal, QC H1M 3S3
Fax: 514-351-6312
800-255-7828
1800allstateQC@allstate.ca

American Bankers Life Insurance Company of Florida/ American Bankers Compagnie d'Assurances-Vie de la Floride
#500, 5160 Yonge St.
Toronto, ON M2N 7C7
416-733-3360
Ownership: Foreign. Branch of American Bankers Life Insurance Company of Florida, Miami, FL, USA.
Year Founded: 1947
Classes of Insurance: Accident, Personal Accident & Sickness, Life
Incorporation: Federally Incorporated Insurance Company
Executives:
Steven K. Phillips, Chief Agent

American Health & Life Insurance Company
201 Queens Ave.
London, ON N6A 1J1
519-672-1070
Fax: 519-660-2625
Former Name: Associates Financial Life Insurance Company
Ownership: Foreign. Canadian branch of USA company.
Year Founded: 1954
Assets: $100-500 million Year End: 20041231
Revenues: $10-50 million Year End: 20041231
Classes of Insurance: Life
Incorporation: Federally Incorporated Insurance Company
Profile: The firm is managed by its sister company.

Executives:
Darrell Gambero, CEO
Anthony W. Miles, Chief Agent, Canada
Dava Carson, Chief Financial Officer
Richard C. Agnello, Exec. Vice-President
Henryka Anderson, Vice-President
Directors:
Darrell Gambero, Chair
Peter B. Dahlberg, Vice-Chair

American Home Assurance Company
145 Wellington St. West
Toronto, ON M5J 1H8
416-596-3000
AHAC@aig.com
www.aigamericanhome.com
Ownership: Member company of American International Group, Inc. (AIG), USA.
Classes of Insurance: Personal Accident & Sickness, Aircraft, Auto, Liability, Boiler & Machinery, Credit, Fidelity, Property, Surety, Hail & Crop
Incorporation: Federally Incorporated Insurance Company
Executives:
Gary Arthur McMillan, Chief Agent

INSURANCE COMPANIES

American Income Life Insurance Company
c/o McLean & Kerr
#2800, 130 Adelaide St. West
Toronto, ON M5H 3P5
416-364-5371
Fax: 416-366-8571
Ownership: Foreign. Owned by Torchmark.
Year Founded: 1954
Assets: $74,661,000
Revenues: $31,462,000
Classes of Insurance: Personal Accident & Sickness, Life
Incorporation: Federally Incorporated Insurance Company

American International Underwriters, Canada
145 Wellington St. West
Toronto, ON M5J 2T4
416-596-3000
www.aig.com
Ownership: Member company of American International Group, Inc. (AIG), USA.
Year Founded: 1969
Classes of Insurance: Property
Incorporation: Federally Incorporated Insurance Company

American Re-Insurance Company
Munich Re Centre
390 Bay St., 22 Fl.
Toronto, ON M5H 2Y2
416-591-8668
Ownership: Member of Munich Re Group
Assets: $100-500 million
Classes of Insurance: Accident, Personal Accident & Sickness, Auto, Liability, Boiler & Machinery, Credit, Marine, Fidelity, Property, Surety, Hail & Crop, Reinsurance
Incorporation: Federally Incorporated Insurance Company

The American Road Insurance Company
#2, 1145 Nicholson Rd.
Newmarket, ON L3Y 9C3
905-853-0858
Classes of Insurance: Auto, Liability, Boiler & Machinery, Credit, Property, Surety
Incorporation: Federally Incorporated Insurance Company
Executives:
Colleen Sexsmith, Chief Agent

AMEX Assurance Company/ AMEX Compagnie d'Assurance
c/o Focus Group Inc.
#500, 36 King St. East
Toronto, ON M5C 1E5
416-361-1728
Fax: 416-361-6113
Classes of Insurance: Personal Accident & Sickness, Life
Incorporation: Federally Incorporated Insurance Company

Amherst Island Mutual Insurance Company
RR#1
Stella, ON K0H 2S0
613-389-2012
Fax: 613-389-9986
Former Name: Amherst Island Mutual Fire Insurance Company
Year Founded: 1894
Classes of Insurance: Personal Accident & Sickness, Liability, Property
Incorporation: Provincially Incorporated Insurance Company
Executives:
W. Bruce Caughey, Secretary-Manager

Antigonish Farmers' Mutual Insurance Company
188 Main St.
Antigonish, NS B2G 2B9
902-863-3544
Fax: 902-863-0664
Other Information: Toll Free (Maritimes only): 1-800-565-3544
wjc@antigonish-mutual.com
www.antigonish-mutual.com
Former Name: Antigonish Farmers' Mutual Fire Insurance Company
Ownership: Policy-holders
Year Founded: 1910
Number of Employees: 9
Assets: $10-50 million Year End: 20041231
Revenues: $1-5 million Year End: 20041231
Classes of Insurance: Marine, Property, Fire
Incorporation: Federally Incorporated Insurance Company
Executives:
C. Van de Sande, President
George Baxter, Vice-President
W.J. Chisholm, General Manager, Sec.-Treas.
Directors:
Mary Bekkers
Duncan MacInnis
Charlie Mackenzie
Al Masters
Ted Mattie
Sid Taylor
Joanne Van der Linden

Ascentus Insurance Ltd.
10 Wellington St. East
Toronto, ON M5E 1L5
800-871-5743
Other Information: Claims: 1-877-275-3698
Incorporation: Federally Incorporated Insurance Company

Assumption Life/ Assomption Compagnie Mutuelle d'Assurance-Vie
Also listed under: *Investment Fund Companies*
PO Box 160
770 Main St.
Moncton, NB E1C 8L1
506-853-6040
Fax: 506-853-5428
800-455-7337
financial.services@assumption.ca
www.assumption.ca
Ownership: Mutual
Year Founded: 1903
Number of Employees: 203
Classes of Insurance: Accident, Personal Accident & Sickness, Life
Incorporation: Provincially Incorporated Insurance Company
Profile: Classes of insurance offered also include group & critical illness & disability.

Executives:
Denis Losier, President/CEO
Larry Boudreau, Vice-President, Sales & Marketing
Patricia LeBlanc, Vice-President, Finance & Information Technologies
Kenneth Losier, Vice-President, Administration, Real Estate Holdings & Mortgage Loans
Raymond Martin, Vice-President, Actuarial Services
Odette Snow, Vice-President, Secretary & General Counsel
Directors:
Noël M. Després, Chair
Réjean Boudreau
Joël Drolet
Yves Gauvin
Louis LaBrie
Paul LeBlanc
Étienne LeBoeuf
Marc Robichaud
Ronnie Roussel
Derrick Smith
Assumption Life:
Balanced Fund
RRSP Eligible; Inception Year: 1995; Fund Managers: Louisbourg Investments Inc.
Balanced B Fund
RRSP Eligible; Inception Year: 2002; Fund Managers: Louisbourg Investments Inc.
Balanced C Fund
RRSP Eligible; Inception Year: 2002; Fund Managers: Louisbourg Investments Inc.
Canadian Equity Fund
RRSP Eligible; Inception Year: 2002; Fund Managers: Montrusco Bolton Inc.
Canadian Equity B Fund
RRSP Eligible; Inception Year: 2002; Fund Managers: Montrusco Bolton Inc.
Canadian Equity C Fund
RRSP Eligible; Inception Year: 2002; Fund Managers: Montrusco Bolton Inc.
Non-Taxable American Equity Fund
RRSP Eligible; Inception Year: 2002; Fund Managers: Montrusco Bolton Inc.
Non-Taxable American Equity B Fund
RRSP Eligible; Inception Year: 2002; Fund Managers: Montrusco Bolton Inc.
Non-Taxable American Equity C Fund
RRSP Eligible; Inception Year: 2002; Fund Managers: Montrusco Bolton Inc.
Canadian Equity Plus Fund
RRSP Eligible; Inception Year: 1998; Fund Managers: Louisbourg Investments Inc.
Canadian Equity Plus B Fund
RRSP Eligible; Inception Year: 2002; Fund Managers: Louisbourg Investments Inc.
Canadian Equity Plus C Fund
RRSP Eligible; Inception Year: 2002; Fund Managers: Louisbourg Investments Inc.
Assumption Life/CI:
Canadian Bond Fund
RRSP Eligible; Inception Year: 2002; Fund Managers: CI Mutual Funds
Canadian Bond B Fund
RRSP Eligible; Inception Year: 2002; Fund Managers: CI Mutual Funds
Canadian Bond C Fund
RRSP Eligible; Inception Year: 2002; Fund Managers: CI Mutual Funds
Global Boomernomics Fund
RRSP Eligible; Inception Year: 2001; Fund Managers: Trilogy Advisors LLC
Global Boomernomics B Fund
RRSP Eligible; Inception Year: 2002; Fund Managers: Trilogy Advisors LLC
Global Boomernomics C Fund
RRSP Eligible; Inception Year: 2002; Fund Managers: Trilogy Advisors LLC
Global Managers Fund
RRSP Eligible; Inception Year: 2001; Fund Managers: Epoch Investment Partners
Global Managers B Fund
RRSP Eligible; Inception Year: 2002; Fund Managers: Epoch Investment Partners
Global Managers C Fund
RRSP Eligible; Inception Year: 2002; Fund Managers: Epoch Investment Partners
Harbour Growth & Income Fund
RRSP Eligible; Inception Year: 2002; Fund Managers: CI Mutual Funds
Harbour Growth & Income B Fund
RRSP Eligible; Inception Year: 2002; Fund Managers: CI Mutual Funds
Harbour Growth & Income C Fund
RRSP Eligible; Inception Year: 2002; Fund Managers: CI Mutual Funds
Assumption Life/FDI:
Canadian Opportunities Fund
RRSP Eligible; Inception Year: 2001; Fund Managers: Fidelity Investments Canada Ltd.
Canadian Opportunities B Fund
RRSP Eligible; Inception Year: 2002; Fund Managers: Fidelity Investments Canada Ltd.
Canadian Opportunities C Fund
RRSP Eligible; Inception Year: 2002; Fund Managers: Fidelity Investments Canada Ltd.
European Fund
RRSP Eligible; Inception Year: 2002; Fund Managers: Fidelity Investments Canada Ltd.
European B Fund
RRSP Eligible; Inception Year: 2002; Fund Managers: Fidelity Investments Canada Ltd.
European C Fund
RRSP Eligible; Inception Year: 2002; Fund Managers: Fidelity Investments Canada Ltd.
Focus Healthcare Fund
RRSP Eligible; Inception Year: 2001; Fund Managers: Fidelity Investments Canada Ltd.
Focus Healthcare B Fund
RRSP Eligible; Inception Year: 2002; Fund Managers: Fidelity Investments Canada Ltd.
Focus Healthcare C Fund
RRSP Eligible; Inception Year: 2002; Fund Managers: Fidelity Investments Canada Ltd.
Focus Technology Fund
RRSP Eligible; Inception Year: 2001; Fund Managers: Fidelity Investments Canada Ltd.
Focus Technology B Fund
RRSP Eligible; Inception Year: 2002; Fund Managers: Fidelity Investments Canada Ltd.

INSURANCE COMPANIES

Assumption Life/ Assomption Compagnie Mutuelle d'Assurance-Vie (continued)

Focus Technology C Fund
RRSP Eligible; Inception Year: 2002; Fund Managers: Fidelity Investments Canada Ltd.
True North Fund
RRSP Eligible; Inception Year: 2001; Fund Managers: Fidelity Investments Canada Ltd.
True North B Fund
RRSP Eligible; Inception Year: 2002; Fund Managers: Fidelity Investments Canada Ltd.
True North C Fund
RRSP Eligible; Inception Year: 2002; Fund Managers: Fidelity Investments Canada Ltd.

Assumption Life/MB:
Canadian Small Cap Fund
RRSP Eligible; Inception Year: 1996; Fund Managers: Montrusco Bolton Inc.
Canadian Small Cap B Fund
RRSP Eligible; Inception Year: 2002; Fund Managers: Montrusco Bolton Inc.
Canadian Small Cap C Fund
RRSP Eligible; Inception Year: 2002; Fund Managers: Montrusco Bolton Inc.
EAFE Equity Fund
RRSP Eligible; Inception Year: 1996; Fund Managers: Montrusco Bolton Inc.
EAFE Equity B Fund
RRSP Eligible; Inception Year: 2002; Fund Managers: Montrusco Bolton Inc.
EAFE Equity C Fund
RRSP Eligible; Inception Year: 2002; Fund Managers: Montrusco Bolton Inc.
Fixed Income Fund
RRSP Eligible; Inception Year: 1996; Fund Managers: Montrusco Bolton Inc.
Fixed Income B Fund
RRSP Eligible; Inception Year: 2002; Fund Managers: Montrusco Bolton Inc.
Fixed Income C Fund
RRSP Eligible; Inception Year: 2002; Fund Managers: Montrusco Bolton Inc.
Global Equity Fund
RRSP Eligible; Inception Year: 1998; Fund Managers: Montrusco Bolton Inc.
Global Equity B Fund
RRSP Eligible; Inception Year: 2002; Fund Managers: Montrusco Bolton Inc.
Global Equity C Fund
RRSP Eligible; Inception Year: 2002; Fund Managers: Montrusco Bolton Inc.
T-Max Fund
RRSP Eligible; Inception Year: 1996; Fund Managers: Montrusco Bolton Inc.
T-Max B Fund
RRSP Eligible; Inception Year: 2002; Fund Managers: Montrusco Bolton Inc.
T-Max C Fund
RRSP Eligible; Inception Year: 2002; Fund Managers: Montrusco Bolton Inc.
Taxable US Equity Fund
RRSP Eligible; Inception Year: 2001; Fund Managers: Montrusco Bolton Inc.
Taxable US Equity B Fund
RRSP Eligible; Inception Year: 2002; Fund Managers: Montrusco Bolton Inc.
Taxable US Equity C Fund
RRSP Eligible; Inception Year: 2002; Fund Managers: Montrusco Bolton Inc.
TSX 100 Momentum Fund
RRSP Eligible; Inception Year: 2001; Fund Managers: Montrusco Bolton Inc.
TSX 100 Momentum B Fund
RRSP Eligible; Inception Year: 2002; Fund Managers: Montrusco Bolton Inc.
TSX 100 Momentum C Fund
RRSP Eligible; Inception Year: 2002; Fund Managers: Montrusco Bolton Inc.

Assumption/CI:
Synergy American Fund
RRSP Eligible; Inception Year: 2005; Fund Managers: Synergy Asset Management Inc.

Assumption/FDI:
Overseas Fund
RRSP Eligible; Inception Year: 2005; Fund Managers: Fidelity Management & Research

Branches:
Bathurst
275 Main St.
Bathurst, NB E2A 1A9 Canada
506-548-2413
Yves Gauvin, Contact
Cap-aux-Meules
330, ch Arsenault
Cap-aux-Meules, QC G4T 1L8 Canada
418-968-4126
Jacques Boudreau, Manager
Edmundston
#200, 121, rue de l'Église
Edmundston, NB E3V 1J9 Canada
506-735-3322
Louis LaBrie, Contact
Shippagan
235 J.D. Gauthier Blvd.
Shippagan, NB E8S 1N2 Canada
506-336-4734
Yves Gauvin, Contact

Assurance-Vie Banque Nationale/ National Bank Life Insurance Company

1100, rue University, 11e étage
Montréal, QC H3B 2G7
514-871-7500
Fax: 514-394-6604
877-871-7500
assurances@nbc.ca
www.nbc.ca
Ownership: Public. Wholly-owned subsidiary of National Bank of Canada.
Year Founded: 1995
Assets: $100-500 million
Revenues: $100-500 million
Classes of Insurance: Personal Accident & Sickness, Life, Credit
Incorporation: Provincially Incorporated Insurance Company
Executives:
Alain Brunet, President; 514-871-7173; alain.brunet@bnc.ca
Georges A. Ferland, Exec. Vice-President; 514-394-6945; georges.ferland@avbn.bnc.ca
Richard Hebert, Vice-President; 514-394-6371; richard.hebert@bnc.ca
Directors:
Helene Bergeron; 514-394-6429
Manon Dansereau; 514-871-7133
Linda Desjardins; 514-394-6432
L. Doyon; 514-394-8624
Thelma Pia Martinez; 514-394-5000
Johanne Paquette; 514-394-8624

Assurant Solutions Canada

#500, 5160 Yonge St.
Toronto, ON M2N 7C7
416-733-3360
Fax: 416-733-7826
800-561-3232
shari.doherty@assurant.com
www.assurantsolutions.ca
Ownership: Parent is Assurant, Inc., New York, NY, USA
Year Founded: 1968
Classes of Insurance: Credit
Incorporation: Federally Incorporated Insurance Company
Profile: Assurant Solutions Canada provides creditor insurance & warranty insurance for financial institutions, retailers, manufacturers & automobile & recreational vehicle dealers.
Executives:
Kathy Burke, Vice-President, Customer Services
Steven K. Phillips, Managing Director
Branches:
Kingston
1287 Gardiners Rd.
Kingston, ON K7P 3J6 Canada
800-550-2827

Atlantic Insurance Company Limited

64 Commonwealth Ave.
Mount Pearl, NL A1N 1W8
709-364-5209
Fax: 709-364-5262
Year Founded: 1976
Classes of Insurance: Auto, Liability, Boiler & Machinery, Fidelity, Property, Surety
Incorporation: Provincially Incorporated Insurance Company

Avemco Insurance Company

#401, 133 Richmond St. West
Toronto, ON M5H 2L3
416-363-6103
Fax: 416-363-7454
Classes of Insurance: Personal Accident & Sickness, Aircraft, Marine
Incorporation: Federally Incorporated Insurance Company
Profile: The foreign property & casualty insurance company is limited to the servicing of existing policies.
Executives:
Donald G. Smith, Chief Agent

Aviation & General Insurance Company Limited

#201, 3650 Victoria Park Ave.
Toronto, ON M2H 3P7
416-496-1148
Fax: 416-496-1089
Classes of Insurance: Aircraft, Liability
Incorporation: Federally Incorporated Insurance Company
Profile: The foreign property & casualty insurance company is limited to the servicing of existing policies.

Aviva Canada Inc./ Aviva, Compagnie d'Assurance du Canada

2206 Eglinton Ave. East
Toronto, ON M1L 4S8
416-288-1800
Fax: 416-288-5888
800-387-4518
www.avivacanada.com
Former Name: Canadian General Insurance Group Limited; CGU Group Canada Ltd.
Also Known As: Aviva Insurance Company of Canada
Ownership: Wholly owned subsidiary of Aviva plc, UK.
Year Founded: 1912
Number of Employees: 3,100+
Assets: $1-10 billion
Classes of Insurance: Personal Accident & Sickness, Aircraft, Legal Expense, Auto, Liability, Boiler & Machinery, Marine, Fidelity, Property, Surety, Hail & Crop
Incorporation: Federally Incorporated Insurance Company
Profile: Aviva Canada is a property & casualty insurance group. The group of companies comprises 40 locations & works with over 3,000 independent broker partners across Canada.
Executives:
Igal Mayer, President/CEO
Andrea Bodnar, Exec. Vice-President, Business Services
Gillian Platt, Exec. Vice-President, Human Resources & Communications
Robin Spencer, Exec. Vice-President/CFO, Treasurer
Affiliated Companies:
Elite Insurance Company
Pilot Insurance Company
Scottish & York Insurance Co. Limited
Traders General Insurance Company
Branches:
Calgary - 4th Ave. SW
#2400, 140 - 4th Ave. SW
Calgary, AB T2P 3W4 Canada
403-750-0600
Fax: 403-263-5105
Calgary - 4th Ave. SW - Mid-Western P/L Service & Billing Centre
#530, 140 - 4th Ave. SW
Calgary, AB T2P 3W4 Canada
403-303-4350
Fax: 403-265-9246
Dartmouth
#1600, 99 Wyse Rd.
Dartmouth, NS B3A 4S5 Canada
902-460-3100
Fax: 902-463-2293
Edmonton
#1700, 10250 - 101st St.
Edmonton, AB T5J 3P4 Canada
780-428-1822
Fax: 780-426-0707
Hamilton
Commerce Place
#600, 1 King St. West
Hamilton, ON L8B 1A4 Canada
905-527-4407
Fax: 905-527-4707
London

1 London Place
#1500, 255 Queen's Ave.
London, ON N6A 5R8 Canada
519-438-2981
Fax: 519-438-8220
Montréal - René-Lévesque ouest - Commercial Lines Branch
#900, 630, boul René-Lévesque ouest
Montréal, QC H3B 1S6 Canada
514-399-1200
Fax: 514-395-0771
Montréal - René-Lévesque ouest - Personal Lines Branch
#700, 630, boul René-Lévesque ouest
Montréal, QC H3B 1S6 Canada
514-399-1200
Fax: 514-395-0771
Montréal - René-Lévesque ouest - Regional Office
#900, 630, boul René-Lévesque ouest
Montréal, QC H3B 1S6 Canada
514-399-1200
Fax: 514-399-1452
Nepean
#250, 161 Greenbank Rd.
Nepean, ON K2H 5V6 Canada
613-235-6775
Fax: 613-235-2096
Québec - LeBourgneuf - Eastern Québec Commercial Lines Branch
#207, 1305, boul LeBourgneuf
Québec, QC G2K 2E4 Canada
418-621-9393
Fax: 418-621-9333
Québec - LeBourgneuf - Eastern Québec Personal Lines Branch
#207, 1305, boul LeBourgneuf
Québec, QC G2K 2E4
418-621-9393
Fax: 418-621-9333
Saint John
#201, 85 Charlotte St.
Saint John, NB E2L 2J2 Canada
506-634-1111
Fax: 506-634-1403
St. John's
Bally Rou Place
#130, 280 Torbay Rd.
St. John's, NL A1W 4A4 Canada
709-753-7772
Fax: 709-753-8313
Toronto - King St. West - B.O.N.U.S. Branch
Standard Life Centre
PO Box 116
#1400, 121 King St. West
Toronto, ON M5H 3T9 Canada
416-363-9363
Fax: 416-363-9397
Toronto - King St. West - Corporate Risk Services
Standard Life Centre
PO Box 116
#1400, 121 King St. West
Toronto, ON M5H 3T9 Canada
416-363-9363
Fax: 416-868-7154
Toronto - King St. West - Plans & Programs Branch
Standard Life Centre
PO Box 116
#1400, 121 King St. West
Toronto, ON M5H 3T9 Canada
416-363-9363
Fax: 416-307-4888
Vancouver
#1100, 1125 Howe St.
Vancouver, BC V6Z 2Y6 Canada
604-669-3212
Fax: 604-684-2339
Winnipeg
T-D Centre
#900, 201 Portage Ave.
Winnipeg, MB R3B 3K6
204-942-0424
Fax: 204-943-1334

AXA Canada Inc.

Also listed under: *Holding & Other Investment Companies*
#700, 2020, rue University
Montréal, QC H3A 2A5
514-282-1914
marketing.webmestre@axa-canada.com
www.axa.ca
Ownership: Member of the AXA Group, Paris, France.
Year Founded: 1985
Number of Employees: 2,300
Profile: The financial holding company offers a range of financial protection products & financial services through its network of subsidiaries in western Canada, Ontario, Québec, & the Atlantic provinces.

Executives:
Jean-François Blais, President/CEO
Iain Hume, Exec. Vice-President/CFO
Robert Landry, Exec. Vice-President, Life Insurance & Financial Services
Luci Martel, Vice-President, Human Resources
Suzie Pellerin, Manager, Communication; suzie.pellerin@axa-canada.com
Directors:
Jean-Denis Talon, Chair
Affiliated Companies:
AXA General Insurance Company
AXA Insurance (Canada)
AXA Pacific Insurance Company

AXA Corporate Solutions Assurance

#600, 2020, rue University
Montréal, QC H3A 2A5
514-392-6033
Fax: 514-392-7392
www.axa-corporatesolutions.com
Ownership: Foreign. Part of AXA Corporate Solutions Assurance, Paris, France.
Classes of Insurance: Personal Accident & Sickness, Aircraft, Legal Expense, Auto, Liability, Boiler & Machinery, Credit, Fidelity, Property, Surety, Hail & Crop
Incorporation: Federally Incorporated Insurance Company
Profile: AXA Corporate Solutions provides financial protection especially for multinational companies.

Executives:
Patrick Lemoine, Chief Agent
Iain Hume, Exec. Vice-President/CFO
Branches:
Toronto
c/o AXA Insurance (Canada)
#1400, 5700 Yonge St.
Toronto, ON M2M 4K2 Canada
416-250-1992
Fax: 416-218-4175
Joseph K. Fung, Agent

AXA Equitable Life Insurance Company/ AXA Equitable assurance-vie

PO Box 14
#606, 55 Town Centre Ct.
Toronto, ON M1P 4X4
416-290-6666
Fax: 416-290-0732
www.axa-equitable.com
Former Name: The Equitable Life Assurance Society of the United States
Ownership: Foreign. Part of AXA Financial, Inc., New York, NY.

Assets: $10-50 million
Revenues: $10-50 million
Classes of Insurance: Personal Accident & Sickness, Life
Incorporation: Federally Incorporated Insurance Company
Executives:
M. Eman Hassan, Chief Agent
Branches:
Calgary
c/o Bennett Jones Vercheres
4500 Bankers Hall East
Calgary, AB T2P 0X9
Vancouver
c/o Davis & Company Barristers & Solicitors, Park Place
#2800, 666 Burrard St.
Vancouver, BC V6C 2Z7

AXA General Insurance Company/ AXA Assurances générales

Triton Bldg.
#600, 2020, rue University
Montréal, QC H3A 2A5
877-292-4968
www.axa.ca
Former Name: Insurance Corporation of Newfoundland Ltd.; Anglo Canada General Insurance Company
Ownership: Wholly owned subsidiary of AXA Assurances Inc., which is wholly owned by AXA Canada Inc., Montréal, QC.
Year Founded: 1960
Classes of Insurance: Personal Accident & Sickness, Aircraft, Legal Expense, Auto, Liability, Boiler & Machinery, Fidelity, Property, Surety, Hail & Crop
Incorporation: Federally Incorporated Insurance Company
Profile: In 2007, AXA General Insurance and Insurance Corporation of Newfoundland Limited were amalgamated & continued as one company under the name AXA General Insurance. Another class of insurance offered is loss of employment. Classes accident & sickness, boiler & machinery, fidelity, hail, legal expenses and surety are limited to the reinsurance of risks.

Executives:
Jean-François Blais, President/CEO
Branches:
Grand Falls-Windsor
12 Pinsent Dr.
Grand Falls-Windsor, NL A2A 2R6
709-489-3211
St. John's
Triton Bldg.
PO Box 8485
35 Blackmarsh Rd., 2nd Fl.
St. John's, NL A1B 3N9
709-758-5650
Fax: 709-579-4500
Toronto
#1400, 5700 Yonge St.
Toronto, ON M2M 4K2
Fax: 416-218-4175
Mathieu Lamy, Chief Agent

AXA Insurance (Canada)/ AXA Assurances (Canada)

#600, 2020, rue University
Montréal, QC H3A 2A5
800-565-4550
av.operations@axa-assurances.ca
www.axa-insurance.ca
Ownership: Part of the AXA Canada, Montréal, QC.
Classes of Insurance: Personal Accident & Sickness, Aircraft, Legal Expense, Auto, Liability, Boiler & Machinery, Fidelity, Property, Surety, Hail & Crop
Incorporation: Federally Incorporated Insurance Company
Profile: A wide range of insurance products is offered through the AXA broker network across Canada. Another class of insurance offered is loss of employment. The classes of aircraft & loss of employment are limited to reinsurance based on risks undertaken by The Citadel General Assurance Company.

Executives:
Jean-François Blais, President/CEO
Branches:
Calgary
#2310, 801 - 6th Ave. SW
Calgary, AB T2P 3W2 Canada
403-269-9900
Edmonton
Oxford Tower
#1200, 10235 - 101st St. NW.
Edmonton, AB T5J 3G1 Canada
780-428-7510
Kelowna
#605, 1708 Dolphin Ave.
Kelowna, BC V1Y 9S4 Canada
250-762-4880
London - York St. - Ontario Head Office
#200, 250 York St.
London, ON N6A 5P9 Canada
877-292-4968
Montréal
1100, boul René-Lévesque ouest, 16e étage
Montréal, QC H3B 4P4 Canada
514-392-6000
Prince George - Quebec St. - Regional Office
Fane Building
#204, 411 Quebec St.
Prince George, BC V2L 1W5 Canada
250-562-6695
Québec - Laurier - Québec Regional Office

AXA Insurance (Canada)/ AXA Assurances (Canada) (continued)
2640, boul Laurier
Québec, QC G1V 5C2 Canada
418-654-3400
Saint John
Place 400
#2046, 400 Main St.
Saint John, NB E2K 4N5 Canada
506-634-7690
St. John's - Blackmarsh Rd. - Atlantic Provinces Head Office
Robert Charles Anthony Building
PO Box 8485
35 Blackmarsh Rd.
St. John's, NL A1B 3N9 Canada
709-758-5650
Toronto - Yonge St.
#1400, 5700 Yonge St.
Toronto, ON M2M 4K2 Canada
416-250-1992
Fax: 416-218-4175
877-292-4968
Mathieu Lamy, Chief Agent
Toronto - Yonge St. - Surety Regional Office
#1400, 5700 Yonge St.
Toronto, ON M2M 4K2 Canada
416-250-1992
Fax: 416-250-7386
Vancouver - West Hastings St. - Western Canada Head Office
AXA Place
PO Box 22
999 West Hastings St.
Vancouver, BC V6C 2W2 Canada
604-669-0595
Victoria
1007 Fort St., 2nd Fl.
Victoria, BC V8V 3K5 Canada
250-381-1535
Winnipeg
#620, 1 Lombard Pl.
Winnipeg, MB R3B 0X3 Canada
204-942-6611

AXA Pacific Insurance Company/ AXA Pacifique Compagnie d'Assurance

#600, 2020 rue University
Montréal, ON H3A 2A5
877-292-4175
www.axa-pacific.ca
Ownership: Member of the AXA Group, Montréal, QC.
Year Founded: 1992
Classes of Insurance: Personal Accident & Sickness, Aircraft, Legal Expense, Auto, Liability, Boiler & Machinery, Credit, Fidelity, Property, Surety, Hail & Crop
Incorporation: Federally Incorporated Insurance Company
Profile: A broad range of insurance products & financial services is offered across Canada by the Canadian property & casualty insurance company. The class of loss of employment is limited to reinsurance based on risks undertaken by The Citadel General Assurance Company.

Executives:
Jean-François Blais, President/CEO
Branches:
Calgary
#2310, 801 - 6 Ave. SW, 23rd Fl.
Calgary, AB T2P 3W2 Canada
403-269-9900
Fax: 403-265-8752
Daniel Munroe, Attorney
Edmonton
Allstream Canada Tower
#1200, 10235 - 101 St. NW
Edmonton, AB T5J 3G1 Canada
780-428-7510
Kelowna
#605, 1708 Dolphin Ave.
Kelowna, BC V1Y 9S4 Canada
250-762-4880
Fax: 250-862-2922
Prince George
#204, 411 Quebec St.
Prince George, BC V2L 1W5 Canada
250-562-6695
Toronto
#1400, 5700 Yonge St.
Toronto, ON M2M 4K2 Canada
Fax: 416-218-4175
877-292-4968
Vancouver
PO Box 22
999 West Hastings St., 3rd Fl.
Vancouver, BC V6C 2W2 Canada
Victoria
1007 Fort St.
Victoria, BC V8V 3K5
250-381-1535
Winnipeg
#620, 1 Lombard Pl.
Winnipeg, MB R3B 0X3 Canada
204-942-6611

AXA RE

Place Montréal Trust
#2000, 1800, av McGill College
Montréal, QC H3A 3J6
514-842-9262
www.axa-re.com
Ownership: Foreign. Wholly owned subsidiary of the AXA Group, Paris, France.
Classes of Insurance: Personal Accident & Sickness, Aircraft, Auto, Liability, Boiler & Machinery, Life, Marine, Fidelity, Property, Surety, Hail & Crop
Incorporation: Federally Incorporated Insurance Company
Executives:
Carol Desbiens, Chief Agent
Branches:
Toronto
c/o AXA Insurance (Canada)
#1400, 5700 Yonge St.
Toronto, ON M2M 4K2
416-250-1992
Fax: 416-250-5833
Joseph K. Fung, Chief Agent

Bay of Quinte Mutual Insurance Co.

PO Box 1460
13379 Loyalist Pkwy.
Picton, ON K0K 2T0
613-476-2145
800-267-2126
info@bayofquintemutual.com
www.bayofquintemutual.com
Ownership: Policy-holders
Year Founded: 1874
Classes of Insurance: Personal Accident & Sickness, Auto, Liability, Boiler & Machinery, Fidelity, Property
Incorporation: Provincially Incorporated Insurance Company
Profile: Commercial insurance products are available for churches, retail stores, offices, apartment building owners & contractors.

Executives:
Jeffery D. Howell, General Manager
David Crawford, Manager, Policy Service Department
Susanne Lyons, Manager, Claims
Cathy Miles, Manager, Commercial Department
Muriel Wager, Manager, Policy Administration
Patti Welsh, Manager, Finance & Technology
Directors:
Dalton Arthur
Mark Henry
Grant Ketcheson
Donald Martin
Steve Raymond
Harry Scanlan
George Taylor
Art Wiersma
Richard (Dick) Williams

Belair Insurance Company Inc./ La Compagnie d'Assurance Belair Inc.

#300, 7101, rue Jean-Talon est
Montréal, QC H1M 3T6
514-270-9111
888-270-9111
Other Information: 888-280-8549, 888-270-9732 (Toll Free, Auto & Home); 1-877-874-5433 (Toll Free, Travel Insurance); 877-270-9124 (Toll Free, Claims Emergency)
belairdirect@belairdirect.com,
belairdirect.ontario@belairdirect.com
www.belairdirect.com
Also Known As: belairdirect
Ownership: Part of ING Canada.
Year Founded: 1955
Classes of Insurance: Personal Accident & Sickness, Legal Expense, Auto, Liability, Boiler & Machinery, Marine, Fidelity, Property, Surety
Incorporation: Provincially Incorporated Insurance Company
Profile: The company also provides travel insurance. CAA-Québec is the official insurer.
Executives:
Peter DaSilva, Chief Agent
Branches:
Alma
721, ch du Pont-Taché nord
Alma, QC G8B 5B7 Canada
418-668-3308
Chicoutimi
Place du Royaume
1401, boul Talbot
Chicoutimi, QC G7H 5N6 Canada
418-543-7704
Joliette
Galeries Joliette
1075, boul Firestone
Joliette, QC J6E 6X6 Canada
450-759-3022
Montréal
#300, 7101, rue Jean-Talon est
Montréal, QC H1M 3T6 Canada
514-270-9111
888-270-9111
Ottawa
#301, 1111 Prince of Wales Dr.
Ottawa, ON K2C 3T2 Canada
613-228-6400
888-280-9111
belairdirect.ontario@belairdirect.com
Québec
#500, 5400, boul des Galeries
Québec, QC G2K 2B4 Canada
418-627-7222
888-270-9111
Rouyn-Noranda
76, av Principale
Rouyn-Noranda, QC J9X 4P2 Canada
819-797-4955
Sept-×les
Édifice Le Concorde
350, rue Smith
Sept-×les, QC G4R 3X2 Canada
418-968-1414
Sherbrooke
2655, rue King ouest
Sherbrooke, QC J1L 2G4 Canada
819-565-9202
Sorel-Tracy
367, boul Fiset
Sorel-Tracy, QC J3P 3R3 Canada
450-742-4508
St-Jérôme
Centre commercial Les Galeries Laurentides
500, boul Des Laurentides
St-Jérôme, QC J7Z 4M2 Canada
450-432-5220
Toronto
#1100, 700 University Ave.
Toronto, ON M2M 0A2 Canada
416-250-6363
888-280-9111
belairdirect.ontario@belairdirect.com
Trois-Rivières
4085, boul Des Récollets
Trois-Rivières, QC G9A 6M1 Canada
819-379-6431
Val-d'Or
1651, 3e av
Val-d'Or, QC J9P 1V9 Canada
819-825-8551

Berkley Insurance Company

#201, 3650 Victoria Park Ave.
Toronto, ON M2H 3P7
416-496-1148
Fax: 416-496-1089

Classes of Insurance: Personal Accident & Sickness, Aircraft, Legal Expense, Auto, Liability, Boiler & Machinery, Credit, Fidelity, Property, Surety, Hail & Crop
Incorporation: Federally Incorporated Insurance Company

Bertie & Clinton Mutual Insurance Co.

1789 Merrittville Hwy., RR#2
Welland, ON L3B 5N5
905-892-0606
Fax: 905-892-0365
800-263-0494
info@bertieandclinton.com
www.bertieandclinton.com
Ownership: Policy-holders.
Year Founded: 1880
Classes of Insurance: Personal Accident & Sickness, Auto, Liability, Boiler & Machinery, Fidelity, Property
Incorporation: Provincially Incorporated Insurance Company
Profile: Bertie & Clinton is known for the provision of farm insurance in the Niagara region. Other insurance services offered include commercial insurance, & directors & officers liability for non-profit organizations. Packages are available for homeowners, boatowners, tenants & condominiums, & churches. Other financial services are provided through the affiliate company, Farm Mutual Financial Services Inc.

Executives:
Keith Hallborg, Secretary-Manager
Directors:
Lubert Doornekamp, President
David Wiley, Vice-President
Carrie Aiello
Howard Augustine
David Gill
Keith Hallborg
Brian Heaslip
Larry Hipple
Domenic Ioannoni
Phillip Lambert

BMO Life Insurance Company

55 Bloor St. West, 15th Fl.
Toronto, ON M4W 3N5
416-927-6344
Fax: 416-927-3740
Classes of Insurance: Personal Accident & Sickness, Life
Incorporation: Federally Incorporated Insurance Company
Profile: Another class of insurance offered by the Canadian life insurance company is loss of employment.

The Boiler Inspection & Insurance Company of Canada(BI&I)

18 King St. East
Toronto, ON M5C 1C4
416-363-5491
Fax: 416-363-0538
corporate@biico.com
www.biico.com
Also Known As: BI&I
Ownership: Hartford Steam Boiler
Year Founded: 1875
Classes of Insurance: Liability, Boiler & Machinery, Property
Incorporation: Federally Incorporated Insurance Company
Profile: BI&I insures boilers, machinery & electrical equipment. In addition, the company also offers engineering & consulting services for institutions, businesses & industries.

Executives:
Hans A. Schols, President/CEO
Rod W. Hampson, Sr. Vice-President/CFO
Tom Howe, Sr. Vice-President, Underwriting
John Mulvihill, Sr. Vice-President/COO
Gary Young, Sr. Vice-President, Field Operations
Brenda Crookshank, Vice-President, Controller
Dave Picot, Vice-President, Corporate Secretary
Don Cox, Assistant Vice-President
Jean Dubois, Assistant Vice-President
Brian Storey, Assistant Vice-President
Jacques Trudel, Assistant Vice-President
Rob West, Assistant Vice-President
Branches:
Calgary
#400, 808 - 4th Ave. SW
Calgary, AB T2P 0K4 Canada
403-265-2813
Fax: 403-264-9024
calgary@biico.com
Hugh Blauveldt, Manager
Halifax
Purdy's Wharf
PO Box 10
#1611, 1969 Upper Water St.
Halifax, NS B3J 3R7 Canada
902-423-6276
Fax: 902-422-6942
halifax@biico.com
Thom Hori, Manager
Hamilton
#1700, 25 Main St. West
Hamilton, ON L8P 1H1 Canada
905-528-8751
Fax: 905-528-3636
hamilton@biico.com
Patricia Sagl, Manager
Montréal
#1735, 800, boul René-Lévesque ouest
Montréal, QC H3B 1X9 Canada
514-861-8261
Fax: 514-861-6922
montreal@biico.com
Jacques Trudel, Manager
Québec
#316, 1245, ch Sainte-Foy
Québec, QC G1S 4P2 Canada
418-681-7857
Fax: 418-681-6099
quebec@biico.com
Louise Paquet, Representative, Marketing
Toronto
18 King St. East, 2nd Fl.
Toronto, ON M5C 1C4 Canada
416-362-1203
Fax: 416-362-6601
toronto@biico.com
Jean Dubois, Manager
Vancouver
#814, 470 Granville St.
Vancouver, BC V6C 1V5 Canada
604-683-0341
Fax: 604-683-1799
vancouver@biico.com
Harvey Kenworthy, Manager

Brant Mutual Insurance Company

207 Greenwich St.
Brantford, ON N3S 2X7
519-752-0088
Fax: 519-752-7917
insurance@brantmutual.com
www.brantmutual.com
Ownership: Policy-holders.
Year Founded: 1861
Classes of Insurance: Personal Accident & Sickness, Auto, Liability, Boiler & Machinery, Fidelity, Property, Hail & Crop
Incorporation: Provincially Incorporated Insurance Company
Profile: The company is licensed to write property & casualty insurance in Ontario.

Executives:
Ken Pettit, CEO

British Columbia Automobile Association Insurance Agency

4567 Canada Way
Burnaby, BC V5G 4T1
604-268-5000
Fax: 604-268-5569
800-719-2224
Other Information: Claims: 604-268-5260; Toll Free, TeleCentre: 1-877-325-8888; Toll Free, BCAA Advantage Home Policy: 310-2345; Customer Contact Centre: 604 268-5555
www.bcaa.com
Also Known As: BCAA Insurance Agency
Ownership: Wholly owned by the British Columbia Automobile Association, Burnaby, BC.
Year Founded: 1969
Classes of Insurance: Personal Accident & Sickness, Auto, Life, Property, Fire
Incorporation: Provincially Incorporated Insurance Company
Profile: The BCAA Insurance Agencies sell insurance. It is underwritten by various underwriters.

Executives:
William G. Bullis, President/CEO
Rod D. Dewar, Sr. Vice-President/COO
Colin G. MacKinnon, Sr. Vice-President/CFO
Dennis A. Côté, Vice-President, Product Development & Support
John A. Evans, Vice-President, Human Resources & Corporate Communications
Scott P. McBride, Vice-President, Sales & Service Delivery
Daniel Mirkovic, Vice-President, Insurance
Ken Ontko, Vice-President, Information Services, Chief Information Officer
Gavin T. Toy, Vice-President, Finance & Corporate Development
Directors:
Howard W. Lailey, Chair
Douglas W. Potentier, Vice-Chair
William G. Bullis
Keith M. Dunn
Craig M. East
Imelda (Meldy) L. Harris
Brian E. Minter
Saida Rasul
Vernard G. Slaney
Bob Smith
V. Daniel (Dan) Smithson
John H.D. Sturgess
Leonard Zirnhelt
John R. (Jack) Whittaker
Branches:
Abbotsford
33310 South Fraser Way
Abbotsford, BC V2S 2B4
604-870-3850
Fax: 604-870-3899
Burnaby
4567 Canada Way
Burnaby, BC V5G 4T1
604-268-5500
Fax: 604-268-5562
877-325-8888
Chilliwack
#190, 45428 Luckakuck Way
Chilliwack, BC V2R 3X9
604-824-2720
Fax: 604-824-2749
Coquitlam
#50, 2773 Barnet Hwy.
Coquitlam, BC V3B 1C2
604-268-5750
Fax: 604-268-5799
Courtenay
#17, 1599 Cliffe Ave.
Courtenay, BC V9N 2K6
250-703-2328
Fax: 250-703-2329
Delta
Scott 72 Centre
7343 - 120th St.
Delta, BC V4C 6P5
604-268-5900
Fax: 604-268-5949
Kamloops
#400, 500 Notre Dame Dr.
Kamloops, BC V2C 6T6
250-852-4600
Fax: 250-852-4637
Kelowna
#18, 1470 Harvey Ave.
Kelowna, BC V1Y 9K8
250-870-4900
Fax: 250-870-4937
Langley
#10, 20190 Langley Bypass
Langley, BC V3A 9J9
604-268-5950
Fax: 604-268-5999
Maple Ridge
#500, 20395 Lougheed Hwy.
Maple Ridge, BC V2X 2P9
604-205-1200
Fax: 604-205-1249
Nanaimo
Metral Place
#400, 6581 Aulds Rd.
Nanaimo, BC V9T 6J6

British Columbia Automobile Association Insurance Agency (continued)
250-390-7700
Fax: 250-390-7739
Nelson
596 Baker St.
Nelson, BC V1L 4H9
250-505-1720
Fax: 250-505-1749
New Westminster
501 Sixth St.
New Westminster, BC V3L 3B9
604-268-5700
Fax: 604-268-5749
North Vancouver
333 Brooksbank Ave.
North Vancouver, BC V7J 3S8
604-205-1050
Fax: 604-990-1547
Penticton
#100, 2100 Main St.
Penticton, BC V2A 5H7
250-487-2450
Fax: 250-487-2479
Prince George
492 Victoria St.
Prince George, BC V2L 2J7
250-649-2399
Fax: 250-649-2397
Richmond
#180, 5951 No. 3 Rd.
Richmond, BC V6X 2E3
604-268-5850
Fax: 604-268-5899
Surrey - 101 Ave.
#4C, 15285 - 101 Ave.
Surrey, BC V3R 9V8
604-205-1000
Fax: 604-205-1049
Surrey - King George Hwy.
#130, 2655 King George Hwy.
Surrey, BC V4P 1H7
604-205-1150
Fax: 604-205-1199
Vancouver - West 41st Ave.
2347 West 41st Ave.
Vancouver, BC V6M 2A3
604-268-5800
Fax: 604-268-5848
Vancouver - West Broadway
999 West Broadway
Vancouver, BC V5Z 1K5
604-268-5600
Fax: 604-268-5649
Vernon
Vernon Square
#520, 4400 - 32nd St.
Vernon, BC V1T 9H2
250-550-2400
Fax: 250-550-2429
Victoria - Millstream Rd.
#169, 2401C Millstream Rd.
Victoria, BC V9B 3R5
250-391-3250
Fax: 250-391-3299
Victoria - Quadra St.
1262 Quadra St.
Victoria, BC V8W 2K7
250-414-8320
Fax: 250-414-8369
Victoria - Royal Oak Dr.
#120, 777 Royal Oak Dr.
Victoria, BC V8X 4V1
250-704-1750
Fax: 250-704-1789
West Vancouver
608 Park Royal North
West Vancouver, BC V7T 1H9
604-268-5650
Fax: 604-268-5699
Westbank
#301, 3550 Carrington Rd.
Westbank, BC V4T 2Z1
250-707-4800
Fax: 250-707-4849

British Columbia Life & Casualty Company

PO Box 7000
Vancouver, BC V6B 4E1
604-419-2000
Fax: 604-419-2990
888-275-4672
www.pac.bluecross.ca
Ownership: Private. Wholly owned subsidiary of PBC Health Benefits Society.
Assets: $10-50 million Year End: 20041231
Revenues: $50-100 million Year End: 20041231
Classes of Insurance: Personal Accident & Sickness, Life
Incorporation: Provincially Incorporated Insurance Company
Executives:
Kenneth G. Martin, President/CEO; 604-419-2099
Catherine Boivie, Sr. Vice-President, Information Systems; 604-419-2003
John D. Crawford, Sr. Vice-President, Financial Services; 604-419-2002
Anne Kinvig, Sr. Vice-President, HR & Employee Wellness; 604-419-2012
Leza Muir, Sr. Vice-President, Business Services; 604-419-2006

Morris Nord, Sr. Vice-President, Client Development; 604-419-2005
Directors:
Marilyn Clark
J.W. Elwick
John Fitzpatrick
John Hope
Kenneth G. Martin
K.R. Mitchell
E.Y. Mitterndorfer
L.F. Molgat

Butler Byers Hail Insurance Ltd.

301 - 4th Ave. North
Saskatoon, SK S7K 2L8
306-653-2233
Fax: 306-652-5335
800-997-4245
Year Founded: 1907
Classes of Insurance: Hail & Crop
Incorporation: Provincially Incorporated Insurance Company
Executives:
Drew Byers, President
Scott Byers, Vice-President & General Manager
Barry Slowski, Controller
Branches:
Brandon - Manitoba Division
305D - 18th St. North
Brandon, MB R7A 6Z2 Canada
204-726-1012
Fax: 204-726-8993
877-587-7703
Lito Aytona, Contact

Butler Byers Insurance Ltd.

***Also listed under:** Financial Planning*
301 - 4th Ave. North
Saskatoon, SK S7K 2L8
306-653-2233
Fax: 306-652-5335
office@butlerbyers.com
www.butlerbyers.com
Year Founded: 1907
Classes of Insurance: Personal Accident & Sickness, Auto, Life, Marine, Property
Incorporation: Provincially Incorporated Insurance Company
Profile: The company provides personal & commercial insurance & associated financial services. Associated financial services include group or individual benefit plans, tax planning, RRSPs, & mutual fund investing.

Executives:
Drew Byers, President
Affiliated Companies:
Butler Byers Hail Insurance Ltd.
Branches:
Saskatoon - 8th St. East
#9, 3311 - 8th St. East
Saskatoon, SK S7H 4K1 Canada
306-934-8822
Fax: 306-955-2353
branchoffice@butlerbyers.com
www.butlerbyers.com

CAA Insurance Company (Ontario)

60 Commerce Valley Dr. East
Thornhill, ON L3T 7P9
905-771-3000
Fax: 905-771-3101
800-268-3750
Other Information: 877-222-3939 (Auto & Property); 800-387-2656 (Claims); 866-999-4222 (Health & Dental); 877-942-4222 (Group Life)
info@caasco.ca
www.caasco.on.ca/insurance
Classes of Insurance: Personal Accident & Sickness, Legal Expense, Auto, Liability, Life, Marine, Property, Surety
Incorporation: Provincially Incorporated Insurance Company
Profile: The company also offers travel insurance.

Executives:
Nicholas J. Parks, President/CEO
Branches:
Barrie
Springwater Market Place
411 Bayfield St.
Barrie, ON L4M 6E5
705-726-1803
Fax: 705-726-4193
barrie@caasco.ca
Cambridge
#2B, 600 Hespeler Rd.
Cambridge, ON N1R 8H2
519-624-2582
Fax: 519-622-2799
cambridge@caasco.ca
Georgetown
#1-2, 374 Guelph St.
Georgetown, ON L7G 4B7
905-702-1139
Fax: 905-702-9019
georgetown@caasco.ca
Guelph
#6, 170 Silvercreek Pkwy. North
Guelph, ON N1H 7P7
519-823-2582
Fax: 519-821-9942
guelph@caasco.ca
Hamilton
990 Upper Wentworth St.
Hamilton, ON L9A 5E9
905-385-8500
Fax: 905-385-0220
mountain@caasco.ca
Kingston
2300 Princess St.
Kingston, ON K7M 3G4
613-546-2596
Fax: 613-546-1875
kingston@caasco.ca
Kitchener
655 Fairway Rd. South
Kitchener, ON N2C 1X2
519-893-9604
Fax: 519-741-1841
kitchener@caasco.ca
London
#1A, 841 Wellington Rd. South
London, ON N6E 3R5
519-685-2582
Fax: 519-685-3170
wellington@caasco.ca
Markham
#5-6, 8355 Woodbine Ave.
Markham, ON L3R 2P4
905-305-7644
Fax: 905-305-0710
thornhill@caasco.ca
Newmarket
Newmarket Plaza
#2, 130 Davis Dr.
Newmarket, ON L3Y 2N1
905-836-5171
Fax: 905-836-8231
newmarket@caasco.ca
Oakville
#8B-9B, 360 Dundas St. East
Oakville, ON L6H 6Z9
905-845-9680
Fax: 905-845-0138

oakville@caasco.ca
Orangeville
78 First St.
Orangeville, ON L9W 2E4
519-941-8360
Fax: 519-941-2833
orangeville@caasco.ca
Orillia
Orillia Square Mall
PO Box 46
RR#4
Orillia, ON L3V 6H4
705-325-7211
Fax: 705-325-1960
orillia@caasco.ca
Oshawa
Plaza Ten Fifty
1050 Simcoe St. North
Oshawa, ON L1G 4W5
905-723-5203
Fax: 905-723-4570
oshawa@caasco.ca
Peterborough
680 The Queensway
Peterborough, ON K9J 7X7
705-743-4343
Fax: 705-743-9740
peterborough@caasco.ca
Sarnia
1095 London Rd.
Sarnia, ON N7S 1P2
519-344-8686
Fax: 519-344-9191
sarnia@caasco.ca
Toronto - Lawrence Ave. East
Cedarbrae Mall
3563 Lawrence Ave. East
Toronto, ON M1H 1B3
416-439-6371
Fax: 416-439-3688
scarborough@caasco.ca
Toronto - The East Mall
225 The East Mall
Toronto, ON M9B 6J1
416-231-4438
Fax: 416-231-1103
eastmall@caasco.ca

Caisse Centrale de Réassurance

#1900, 1080, côte de Beaver Hall
Montréal, QC H2Z 1S8
514-878-2600
Fax: 514-878-9309
Ownership: Foreign
Number of Employees: 6
Assets: $50-100 million
Revenues: $10-50 million
Classes of Insurance: Accident, Aircraft, Legal Expense, Auto, Liability, Boiler & Machinery, Fidelity, Property, Fire, Surety
Incorporation: Federally Incorporated Insurance Company
Executives:
Jacques Mailloux, Chief Agent; jmailloux@jdl.ca
André Fredette, Sr. Vice-President, General Manager
Branches:
Toronto
#2110, 181 University Ave.
Toronto, ON M5H 3M7
416-644-0821
Fax: 416-644-0822

Canadian Direct Insurance Incorporated

#600, 750 Cambie St.
Vancouver, BC V6B 0A2
604-699-3838
Fax: 604-699-3860
888-225-5234
Other Information: 888-261-8888 (Toll Free, Claims)
insurancegeneral@canadiandirect.com
www.canadiandirect.com
Former Name: HSBC Canadian Direct Insurance Incorporated
Ownership: Wholly owned subsidiary of Canadian Western Bank.
Year Founded: 1996
Classes of Insurance: Personal Accident & Sickness, Liability, Property
Incorporation: Federally Incorporated Insurance Company
Profile: Home insurance is offered, including tenants & condominiums. Travel insurance is provided through Travel Underwriters of Richmond, BC.

Executives:
Brian Young, President/CEO
Colin Brown, Chief Operating Officer
Michael Martino, Chief Financial Officer
Susannah Bach, Vice-President, Corporate & Strategic Operations
Vince Muto, Vice-President, Claims
Branches:
Edmonton
10250 - 101st St., 11th Fl.
Edmonton, AB T5J 3P4
780-413-5933
Fax: 780-413-5932
888-225-5234
insurancegeneral@canadiandirect.com
Toronto
c/o Fraser Milner Casgrain LLP, 1 First Canadian Place
100 King St. West
Toronto, ON M5X 1B2
416-863-4732
Sander Grieve, Agent

Canadian Farm Insurance Corporation(CFIC)

#208, 62 Hargrave St.
Winnipeg, MB R3C 1N1
866-346-3276
Other Information: 1-877-909-3276 (Toll Free livestock claims assistance)
www.cdnfarmins.com
Classes of Insurance: Personal Accident & Sickness, Liability, Boiler & Machinery, Fidelity, Property, Surety
Incorporation: Provincially Incorporated Insurance Company
Profile: The insurance company's jurisdiction of incorporation is Manitoba.

Signature Advisors
Harbour Advisors
Tetrem Capital Partners Inc.
Epoch Investment Partners Inc.
Legg Mason Capital Management
Trilogy Global Advisors LLC
Synergy Asset Management
Altrinsic Global Advisors LLC
QVGD Investors Inc.
Trident Investment Management LLC
Branches:
Calgary
135 Ranch View Mews
Calgary, AB T3G 1M6
403-374-1041
Fax: 403-374-1055
Edmonton
#375, 13220 St. Albert Trail
Edmonton, AB T5L 4W1
780-447-3276
Fax: 780-732-3607
877-909-3276
Robert Anderson, Attorney, Alberta
Fenwick
28 Cherry Ridge Blvd.
Fenwick, ON L0S 1C0
905-984-1069
Kelowna
525 South Crest Dr.
Kelowna, BC V1W 4W8
250-764-5450
Fax: 250-764-5462
Prince George
1033 - 3rd Ave.
Prince George, BC V2L 3E3
Toronto
c/o MacDonald Porter Drees, Barristers & Solicitors
#1700, 65 Queen St. West
Toronto, ON M5H 2M5
416-366-1700
Fax: 416-367-2502
Lawrence K. Porter, Chief Agent

Canadian Lawyers Insurance Association/ L'Association d'Assurance des Juristes Canadiens

#306, 20 Queen St. West
Toronto, ON M5H 3R3
416-408-3721
800-268-9484
info@clia.ca
www.clia.ca
Year Founded: 1988
Incorporation: Provincially Incorporated Insurance Company
Executives:
Patrick Mahoney, General Manager; 416-408-5393
Norma Ibbetson, Assistant General Manager; 416-408-5294

Canadian Lawyers Liability Assurance Society(CLLAS)

c/o Torys LLP
#3000, 79 Wellington St. West
Toronto, ON M5K 1N2
416-865-7337
Fax: 416-865-7380
Ownership: Private.
Classes of Insurance: Liability
Incorporation: Provincially Incorporated Insurance Company
Profile: The society provides professional liability insurance to thirteen major Canadian law firms.

Executives:
Michael G. Thorley, Chair, Attorney-In-Fact

Canadian Northern Shield Insurance Company(CNS)

#1900, 555 Hastings St. West
Vancouver, BC V6B 4N6
604-662-2911
Fax: 604-662-5698
corporate_service@cns.ca
www.cns.ca
Ownership: Fully autonomous subsidiary of CUMIS Group, Burlington, ON.
Year Founded: 1985
Number of Employees: 150
Revenues: $165,000,000
Classes of Insurance: Auto, Liability, Property
Incorporation: Federally Incorporated Insurance Company
Profile: CNS insures homes, private automobiles & businesses in British Columbia.

Executives:
Carol Jardine, President/COO
Ryan Gabert, Vice-President, Operations
Branches:
Kelowna
#400, 1633 Ellis St.
Kelowna, BC V1Y 2A8 Canada
800-667-1211
Dan O'Fee, Branch Manager
Nanaimo
#502, 495 Dunsmuir St.
Nanaimo, BC V9R 6B9 Canada
800-661-2127
Chuck Rogerson, Branch Manager
Vancouver
#1900, 555 West Hastings St.
Vancouver, BC V6B 4N6
604-662-2911
K. Duffield, Branch Manager
Victoria
#510, 1675 Douglas St.
Victoria, BC V8W 2G5 Canada
800-663-6104
Chuck Rogerson, Branch Manager

Canadian Petroleum Insurance Exchange Ltd.(CPIX)

#500, 717 - 7th Ave. SW
Calgary, AB T2P 0Z3
403-261-6061
Fax: 403-261-6068
insurance@cpix.com
www.cpix.com
Also Known As: CPIX Ltd.
Ownership: Private.
Year Founded: 1988
Classes of Insurance: Auto, Liability, Property, Theft
Incorporation: Provincially Incorporated Insurance Company
Profile: CPIX offers energy companies insurance & risk services. It acts as the Attorney-in-Fact for Energy Insurance Reciprocal (EIR).

Executives:
Ross Collett, Attorney

INSURANCE COMPANIES

Canadian Premier Life Insurance Company

80 Tiverton Ct., 5th Fl.
Markham, ON L3R 0G4
905-479-7500
Fax: 905-479-3224
800-598-6918
www.canadianpremier.ca
Ownership: Private. Part of AEGON Group.
Year Founded: 1955
Classes of Insurance: Personal Accident & Sickness, Life, Credit
Incorporation: Federally Incorporated Insurance Company
Profile: Another class of insurance offered by the Canadian life insurance company is loss of employment.

Executives:
Isaac Sananes, President/CEO

Canadian Professional Sales Association(CPSA)

#800, 310 Front St. West
Toronto, ON M5V 3B5
416-408-2685
Fax: 416-408-2684
888-267-2772
www.cpsa.com
Ownership: Member-owned.
Year Founded: 1874
Classes of Insurance: Accident, Personal Accident & Sickness, Auto, Life, Property
Incorporation: Federally Incorporated Insurance Company
Profile: CPSA partners with Reliable Life Insurance Company, Manulife Financial, & Pottruff & Smith to offer insurance products & services to its members.

Executives:
Harvey Copeman, President/CEO
Directors:
Valerie Payn, Chair
Arnie Josephson, Vice-Chair
Bruce Andrew
Debora Bloom
Sophie Chauvin
Harvey Copeman
Bill Hanson
Rory Lesperance
Craig Lindsay
Wendy Sue Lyttle
Gary McKeown
Don McWilliam
Dave Sclanders
Glenn Walker
Alfred Whiffen
Rhordon Wikkramatileke

Canadian Slovak League

#6, 259 Traders Blvd. East
Mississauga, ON L4Z 2E5
905-735-5624
Classes of Insurance: Life
Incorporation: Federally Incorporated Insurance Company
Executives:
Branislav Galap, Secretary

Canadian Universities Reciprocal Insurance Exchange

5500 North Service Rd., 9th Fl.
Burlington, ON L7L 6W6
905-336-3366
Fax: 905-336-3373
888-462-8743
inquiry@curie.org
www.curie.org
Year Founded: 1988
Classes of Insurance: Aircraft, Liability, Marine, Property
Incorporation: Provincially Incorporated Insurance Company
Executives:
Keith Shakespeare, Chief Operating Officer, Attorney-in-Fact; kshakespeare@curie.org
John Breen, Manager, Risk Reduction & Loss Control
Carrie Green, Manager, Finance & Administration
Stewart Roberts, Manager, Claims

Canassurance Insurance Company

c/o Ontario Blue Cross
#600, 185 The West Mall
Toronto, ON M9C 5P1
416-626-1688
Fax: 416-626-0134
Former Name: Canassurance Life Insurance Company
Year Founded: 1942
Classes of Insurance: Personal Accident & Sickness, Liability, Life, Property
Incorporation: Provincially Incorporated Insurance Company
Executives:
Incoronata Greco, Chief Agent

Caradoc Delaware Mutual Fire Insurance Company

PO Box 460
22508 Adelaine Rd.
Mount Brydges, ON N0L 1W0
519-264-2298
Fax: 519-264-9101
877-707-2298
info@cdmins.com
www.cdmins.com
Ownership: Policy-holders.
Year Founded: 1884
Classes of Insurance: Personal Accident & Sickness, Auto, Liability, Boiler & Machinery, Property
Incorporation: Provincially Incorporated Insurance Company
Profile: The company serves homeowners, farmers & small businesses in the Middlesex County area of Ontario.

Executives:
Richard Kilborne, President
Dave McNamara, B.Sc., CIP, Manager
Affiliated Companies:
Midd-West Financial Services Inc.

Carleton Mutual Insurance Company

301 Main St.
Florenceville, NB E7L 3G5
506-392-6041
Fax: 506-392-8243
800-561-1550
cmi@nb.aibn.com
www.carletonmutual.com
Former Name: Carleton Mutual Fire Insurance Company
Ownership: Policy-holders.
Classes of Insurance: Auto, Property, Fire
Incorporation: Provincially Incorporated Insurance Company
Profile: The company offers home, farm & automobile insurance.

Executives:
Elaine Hunter, Manager

Cavell Insurance Company Limited

c/o D.M. Williams & Associates Ltd.
#201, 3650 Victoria Park Ave.
Toronto, ON M2H 3P7
416-496-1148
Fax: 416-496-1089
Former Name: NW Reinsurance Corporation Limited
Classes of Insurance: Personal Accident & Sickness, Auto, Liability, Boiler & Machinery, Marine, Fidelity, Property, Surety, Hail & Crop
Incorporation: Federally Incorporated Insurance Company
Executives:
V. Lorraine Williams, Chief Agent; Lorraine.Williams@dmwilliams.com

Certas Direct Insurance Company/ Certas Direct, compagnie d'assurances

PO Box 3500
6300, boul de la Rive-Sud
Lévis, QC G6V 6P9
905-306-3900
Fax: 418-835-5599
800-565-6020
www.certas.ca
Former Name: The Personal Direct Insurance Company of Canada
Ownership: Private.
Year Founded: 2001
Number of Employees: 61
Assets: $100-500 million Year End: 20041231
Revenues: $100-500 million Year End: 20041231
Classes of Insurance: Auto, Liability, Property, Surety
Incorporation: Federally Incorporated Insurance Company
Executives:
Jude Martineau, President/CEO
Jean-François Chalifoux, Sr. Exec. Vice-President & General Manager, RoC Operations
Louis Chantal, Sr. Exec. Vice-President, Administration, Finance & Human Resources, Treasurer
Pierre Deschênes, Sr. Exec. Vice-President, Information Technology
Sylvie Paquette, Sr. Exec. Vice-President, Corporate Development
Pierre Rousseau, Sr. Exec. Vice-President, Legal Affairs, Corporate Secretary
Directors:
Raymond Gagné, Chair
Jean-Robert Laporte, Vice-Chair
Yves Archambault
Annie P. Bélanger
Jean J. Brossard
Stéphane Coudé
Roger Desrosiers
Jean-Louis Gauvin
Gabrielle Gosselin
Michel Lucas
Jude Martineau
Jocelyne Poulin
Clément Trottier
Yvon Vinet
Branches:
Mississauga
3 Robert Speck Pkwy.
Mississauga, ON L4Z 3Z9 Canada
905-306-3900
800-565-6020

Chicago Title Insurance Company Canada

2700 Argentia Rd.
Mississauga, ON L5N 5V4
905-816-4485
Fax: 902-816-4988
888-868-4853
info@chicagotitle.ca
www.ctic.ca
Ownership: Owned by Fidelity National Financial Inc.
Stock Symbol: FNF
Incorporation: Federally Incorporated Insurance Company
Profile: CTIC has been licensed to provide title insurance in Canada for more than 30 years.

Executives:
Pat Harrison, Manager Commercial Services; pharrison@fnf.ca

Chubb Insurance Company of Canada/ Chubb du Canada Compagnie d'Assurance

One Financial Place
1 Adelaide St. East
Toronto, ON M5C 2V9
416-863-0550
Fax: 416-863-5010
www.chubb.com/international/canada
Ownership: Private. Part of the Chubb Group of Insurance Companies, New Jersey.
Year Founded: 1981
Classes of Insurance: Personal Accident & Sickness, Aircraft, Auto, Liability, Boiler & Machinery, Marine, Fidelity, Property, Surety
Incorporation: Federally Incorporated Insurance Company
Executives:
Ellen J. Moore, President/CEO
Geoffrey Shields, CA, Sr. Vice-President/CFO
James V. Newman, Sr. Vice-President, Human Resources
Paul Morrissette, Manager, Personal Insurance
Affiliated Companies:
Federal Insurance Company
Branches:
Calgary
#2100, 333 - 7th Ave. SW
Calgary, AB T2P 2Z1 Canada
403-261-3881
Fax: 403-269-2907
Montréal
1250, boul René-Lévesque ouest, 27e étage
Montréal, QC H3B 4W8 Canada
514-938-4000
Fax: 514-938-2288
Vancouver
#910, 250 Howe St.
Vancouver, BC V6C 3R8 Canada
604-685-2113
Fax: 604-685-3811

CIBC Life Insurance Company Limited/ Compagnie d'Assurance-Vie CIBC Limitée

#900, 3 Robert Speck Pkwy.
Mississauga, ON L4Z 2G5
905-306-4904
Fax: 905-306-4957
Classes of Insurance: Personal Accident & Sickness, Life
Incorporation: Federally Incorporated Insurance Company
Executives:
Rick W. Lancaster, President/CEO

CIGNA Life Insurance Company of Canada

PO Box 14
#606, 55 Town Centre Ct.
Toronto, ON M1P 4X4
416-290-6666
Fax: 416-290-0732
www.cigna.com
Ownership: Private. Foreign. Parent is Connecticut General Corporation
Year Founded: 1978
Number of Employees: 8
Assets: $50-100 million Year End: 20051231
Revenues: $10-50 million Year End: 20051231
Stock Symbol: CI
Classes of Insurance: Accident, Personal Accident & Sickness, Life, Credit
Incorporation: Federally Incorporated Insurance Company
Profile: CIGNA Life Insurance Co. is affiliated with Life Insurance Company of North America & Connecticut General Life Insurance Co. It also offers long-term disability insurance & expatriate benefits.

Executives:
M. Eman Hassan, President/CEO
Marlene Clementson, Manager, Claims
Anna Liu, Controller
Directors:
David Atkins
James W. Blaney
Richard A. Brownmiller
Jess C. Bush
Marlene Clementson
M. Eman Hassan
David Scheibe
Crawford W. Spratt

The Citadel General Assurance Company

#1200, 1075 Bay St.
Toronto, ON M5S 2W5
416-928-8500
Fax: 416-928-1553
cit-web-info@citadel.ca
www.citadel.ca
Also Known As: The Citadel
Ownership: Private. Foreign. Part of the Winterthur Swiss Insurance Group.
Year Founded: 1919
Assets: $500m-1 billion Year End: 20041231
Revenues: $100-500 million Year End: 20041231
Classes of Insurance: Accident, Personal Accident & Sickness, Auto, Liability, Fidelity, Property, Fire, Surety, Theft
Incorporation: Federally Incorporated Insurance Company
Profile: The Citadel is part of the Winterthur Swiss Insurance Group (WSI), the insurance arm of Credit Suisse Group. It is one of the world's largest financial services groups, with assets of approximately $1,274 billion (Cdn.). Headquartered in Winterthur, Switzerland, for over 100 years, WSI has a record of financial stability & an A- (excellent) rating by A.M. Best. Credit Suisse Group, founded in 1856, is headquartered in Zurich & listed on the Swiss Stock Exchange as well as the exchanges of London, Frankfurt, Tokyo & New York. These international industry leaders support The Citadel. The Citadel provides property, casualty & special risks products & services, through a network of independent agents & brokers. Classes of insurance include group accident & sickness.

Executives:
William T. Breckles, President/CEO
Malcolm R. Scott, Exec. Vice-President, Corporate Services, CFO
Michael A. Finnegan, Vice-President, Head Office Underwriting, Accident & Sickness
Philip W. Jeffery, FCAS, FCIA, Vice-President, Actuarial Services & Personal Lines
Roger J. Keightley, AIIC, Vice-President, Head Office Underwriting, Commercial Lines & Reinsuran
Tara McMahon, CHRP, Vice-President, Human Resources
John J. O'Hoski, BA, LL.B., Vice-President, Head Office Claims, General Counsel & Corporate Secretary
Brian H. Skuffham, CFA, Vice-President, Investments
Directors:
Nadia Boruch, M.D.
William T. Breckles
F. Stuart Lang
Paul E. Renaud, M.D.
Richard J. Roberts, Q.C.
Gabor G.S. Takach
Honorary Directors:
Frederick A. Lang
Branches:
Dartmouth
Burnside Park
#220, 111 Ilsley Ave.
Dartmouth, NS B3B 1S8 Canada
902-420-1464
Fax: 902-429-9892
Edmonton
#720, 10055 - 106 St.
Edmonton, AB T5J 2Y2 Canada
780-414-1734
Fax: 780-429-7475
London
#208, 1071 Wellington Rd.
London, ON N6E 1W4 Canada
519-668-5327
Fax: 519-668-6330
Québec
#408, 5600, boul des Galeries
Québec, QC G2K 2H6 Canada
905-885-4882
Fax: 905-885-5319
Vancouver
#1350, 1090 West Georgia St.
Vancouver, BC V6E 3V7 Canada
604-684-6381
Fax: 604-684-9195
Winnipeg
PO Box 35001, RPO Henderson
Winnipeg, MB R2K 4J9 Canada
204-988-9290
Fax: 204-988-9292
Regional Offices:
Calgary - Western
#1400, 645 - 7th Ave. SW
Calgary, AB T2P 4G8 Canada
403-261-3100
Fax: 403-261-3141
Montréal - Eastern
#1850, 2001, rue University
Montréal, QC H3A 2L8 Canada
514-842-2121
Fax: 514-842-1700
Saint John - Atlantic
Place 400
#2094, 400 Main St.
Saint John, NB E2K 4N5 Canada
506-633-3700
Fax: 506-632-3480
Toronto - Central
1075 Bay St., 11th Fl.
Toronto, ON M5S 2W5 Canada
416-928-8619
Fax: 416-928-7471

Clare Mutual Insurance Company

3300 Hwy. 1
Belliveau Cove, NS B0W 1J0
902-837-4597
Fax: 902-837-7745
877-818-0887
claremutual@sympatico.ns.ca
www.claremutual.com
Ownership: Policyholders.
Year Founded: 1937
Classes of Insurance: Property, Fire, Hail & Crop
Incorporation: Federally Incorporated Insurance Company
Profile: Insurance is provided for homes, farms & businesses in southwest Nova Scotia.

Executives:
Diane M. Belliveau, General Manager; dianebelliveau@rushcomm.com
Directors:
Henry J. Thibodeau, President

Co-operative Hail Insurance Company Ltd.

PO Box 777
2709 - 13th Ave.
Regina, SK S4P 3A8
306-522-8891
Fax: 306-352-9130
info@coophail.com
www.coophail.com
Ownership: Member-owned
Year Founded: 1947
Number of Employees: 7
Assets: $40,311,000
Revenues: $25,242,000
Classes of Insurance: Hail & Crop
Incorporation: Provincially Incorporated Insurance Company
Executives:
W. Bruce Lutz, President
Denis D. Stumph, CEO
Nick Gayton, Asst. Executive Officer
Bob Milton, Corporate Treasurer
Directors:
W.J. Barry Bromley
W. Bruce Lutz
Dennis Lynch
William G. Mayer
Waind MacDonald
Blaine R. Mitchell
Brian Nast
Grattan O'Grady
R. Terry Quinn
Alan Raiton
Tate Sakundiak
Samuel Sinclair

Co-operators General Insurance Company

Priory Sq., 7th Fl.
Guelph, ON N1H 6P8
519-824-4400
Fax: 519-824-0599
877-795-7272
service@cooperators.ca
www.cooperators.ca
Ownership: Members/owners are 34 cooperatives, credit unions & similar organizations
Year Founded: 1945
Number of Employees: 2,857
Revenues: $2,044,000,000
Stock Symbol: CCS
Classes of Insurance: Personal Accident & Sickness, Aircraft, Auto, Boiler & Machinery, Life, Fidelity, Property, Fire, Surety, Hail & Crop, Theft
Incorporation: Federally Incorporated Insurance Company
Profile: The general insurance company offers home, farm, commercial & automobile insurance throughout Canada. The company also distributes both travel & life insurance.

Executives:
Katherine Bardswick, President/CEO
Rick McCombie, Sr. Vice-President, Distribution
Martin-Éric Tremblay, Sr. Vice-President, General Insurance
Affiliated Companies:
COSECO Insurance Company
Co-operators Investment Counselling Limited
Co-operators Life Insurance Company
L'Union Canadienne Compagnie d'Assurances

Co-operators Life Insurance Company

***Also listed under:** Investment Fund Companies*
1920 College Ave.
Regina, SK S4P 1C4
306-347-6200
Fax: 306-347-6806
800-604-0050
www.cooperators.ca
Ownership: Public. The Cooperators Group Limited
Year Founded: 1945
Number of Employees: 880
Assets: $1-10 billion Year End: 20041231
Revenues: $500m-1 billion Year End: 20041231
Classes of Insurance: Personal Accident & Sickness, Life
Incorporation: Federally Incorporated Insurance Company
Profile: Services also include wealth management & travel insurance. Other affiliated companies include the following: Co-operators Financial Services Limited, HB Group Insurance

INSURANCE COMPANIES

Co-operators Life Insurance Company (continued)
Management Limited, COSECO Insurance Company, Co-operators Investment Counselling Limited, Co-operators Development Corporation Limited, Federated Agencies Limited, L'Union canadienne Compagnie d'Assurances, Trent Health Insurance Company & TIC Travel Insurance Coordinators Ltd.

Executives:
Katherine Bardswick, President/CEO; 519-824-4400
Kevin Daniel, CFO, Treasurer
Dan Thornton, Chief Operating Officer; 306-347-6218
Randy Grimsrud, Vice-President, Group Insurance; 306-347-6458
David Hartman, Vice-President, Wealth Management; 519-767-3065
Garry Herback, Vice-President, Individual Insurance; 306-347-6270
Frank Lowery, Vice-President, General Counsel & Corporate Secretary; 519-824-4400
Terry MacDonald, Vice-President, Corporate Services; 306-347-6452
Bryan Sigurdson, Vice-President & Chief Actuary; 306-347-6650

Ruth Simons, Vice-President, Travel; 604-986-4292
Rein Tabur, Vice-President, Investments; 306-347-6221
Mary Turtle, Vice-President, Finance; 306-347-6578
Chuck Wilson, Vice-President & General Counsel; 306-347-6523
Linda Yeo, Vice-President, Information Systems; 306-347-6796

Directors:
Peter Podovinikoff, Chair; 604-501-4111
Johanna Bates; 403-282-7370
Karl Baumgardner; 306-843-8807
Christine Brodie; 604-816-9491
Bill Dobson; 780-745-2442
Connie Doucette; 902-569-2901
Ron Koppmann; 613-475-4221
John Lamb; 780-496-3732
Wayne Lee; 705-759-2958
Richard Lemoing; 204-874-2177
Sheena Lucas; 613-731-9059
Jim MacConnell; 902-485-8023
Wayne McLeod; 204-729-8852
Gilles Menard; 506-854-7902
Leonard Mortson; 705-487-2321
Terry Otto; 613-821-1428
Andre Perras; 306-424-2832
Donna Stewardson; 519-786-5469
Alexandra Wilson; 613-230-2201

Co-operators:
Balanced VA Fund
RRSP Eligible; Inception Year: 1992; Fund Managers: James F. MacDonald
Canadian Equity VP Fund
RRSP Eligible; Inception Year: 2003; Fund Managers: James M. Blake
Fixed Income VA Fund
RRSP Eligible; Inception Year: 1992; Fund Managers: Jim Lorimer
Money Market VA Fund
RRSP Eligible; Inception Year: 1997; Fund Managers: Jim Lorimer
US Diversified VA Fund
RRSP Eligible; Inception Year: 1997; Fund Managers: Bill Siddiqui
Conservative Balanced VA Fund
RRSP Eligible; Inception Year: 2000; Fund Managers: James F. MacDonald
US Growth VA Fund
RRSP Eligible; Inception Year: 2000; Fund Managers: Bill Siddiqui
Canadian Resource VA Fund
RRSP Eligible; Inception Year: 2003;
US Equity VA Fund
RRSP Eligible; Inception Year: 1994; Fund Managers: Bill Siddiqui
Aggressive Balanced VAII Fund
RRSP Eligible; Inception Year: 2000; Fund Managers: James F. MacDonald
Aggressive Balanced VA Fund
RRSP Eligible; Inception Year: 2000; Fund Managers: James F. MacDonald
Aggressive Balanced VP Fund
RRSP Eligible; Inception Year: 2003; Fund Managers: James F. MacDonald
Aggressive Balanced VPNL Fund
RRSP Eligible; Inception Year: 2004; Fund Managers: James F. MacDonald
Aggressive VA Portfolio Fund
RRSP Eligible; Inception Year: 2003; Fund Managers: Fidelity Investments Canada Ltd.
Aggressive VP Portfolio Fund
RRSP Eligible; Inception Year: 2003; Fund Managers: Fidelity Investments Canada Ltd.
Aggressive VAII Portfolio Fund
RRSP Eligible; Inception Year: 2003; Fund Managers: Fidelity Investments Canada Ltd.
Aggressive VPNL Portfolio Fund
RRSP Eligible; Inception Year: 2004; Fund Managers: Fidelity Investments Canada Ltd.
Balanced VAII Fund
RRSP Eligible; Inception Year: 1999; Fund Managers: James F. MacDonald
Balanced VP Fund
RRSP Eligible; Inception Year: 2003; Fund Managers: James F. MacDonald
Balanced VPNL Fund
RRSP Eligible; Inception Year: 2004; Fund Managers: James F. MacDonald
Canadian Equity VPNL Fund
RRSP Eligible; Inception Year: 2004; Fund Managers: James M. Blake
Canadian Equity VA Fund
RRSP Eligible; Inception Year: 1992; Fund Managers: James M. Blake
Canadian Equity VAII Fund
RRSP Eligible; Inception Year: 1999; Fund Managers: James M. Blake
Canadian Resource VAII Fund
RRSP Eligible; Inception Year: 2003;
Canadian Resource VP Fund
RRSP Eligible; Inception Year: 2003;
Canadian Resource VPNL Fund
RRSP Eligible; Inception Year: 2004;
Conservative Balanced VAII Fund
RRSP Eligible; Inception Year: 2000; Fund Managers: James F. MacDonald
Conservative Balanced VP Fund
RRSP Eligible; Inception Year: 2003; Fund Managers: James F. MacDonald
Conservative Balanced VPNL Fund
RRSP Eligible; Inception Year: 2004; Fund Managers: James F. MacDonald
Conservative VA Portfolio Fund
RRSP Eligible; Inception Year: 2003; Fund Managers: Fidelity Investments Canada Ltd.
Conservative VP Portfolio Fund
RRSP Eligible; Inception Year: 2003; Fund Managers: Fidelity Investments Canada Ltd.
Conservative VAII Portfolio Fund
RRSP Eligible; Inception Year: 2003; Fund Managers: Fidelity Investments Canada Ltd.
Conservative VPNL Portfolio Fund
RRSP Eligible; Inception Year: 2004; Fund Managers: Fidelity Investments Canada Ltd.
Fixed Income VAII Fund
RRSP Eligible; Inception Year: 1999; Fund Managers: Jim Lorimer
Fixed Income VP Fund
RRSP Eligible; Inception Year: 2003; Fund Managers: Jim Lorimer
Fixed Income VPNL Fund
RRSP Eligible; Inception Year: 2004; Fund Managers: Jim Lorimer
Moderate VA Portfolio Fund
RRSP Eligible; Inception Year: 2003; Fund Managers: Fidelity Investments Canada Ltd.
Moderate VAII Portfolio Fund
RRSP Eligible; Inception Year: 2003; Fund Managers: AIM Trimark Investment Management
Moderate VP Portfolio Fund
RRSP Eligible; Inception Year: 2003; Fund Managers: Fidelity Investments Canada Ltd.
Moderate VPNL Portfolio Fund
RRSP Eligible; Inception Year: 2004; Fund Managers: AIM Trimark Investment Management
Money Market VAII Fund
RRSP Eligible; Inception Year: 1999; Fund Managers: Jim Lorimer
Money Market VP Fund
RRSP Eligible; Inception Year: 2003; Fund Managers: Jim Lorimer
Money Market VPNL Fund
RRSP Eligible; Inception Year: 2004; Fund Managers: Jim Lorimer
US Growth VAII Fund
RRSP Eligible; Inception Year: 2000; Fund Managers: Bill Siddiqui
US Growth VP Fund
RRSP Eligible; Inception Year: 2003; Fund Managers: Bill Siddiqui
US Growth VPNL Fund
RRSP Eligible; Inception Year: 2004; Fund Managers: Bill Siddiqui
US Diversified VAII Fund
RRSP Eligible; Inception Year: 1999; Fund Managers: Bill Siddiqui
US Diversified VP Fund
RRSP Eligible; Inception Year: 2003; Fund Managers: Bill Siddiqui
US Diversified VPNL Fund
RRSP Eligible; Inception Year: 2004; Fund Managers: Bill Siddiqui
US Equity VAII Fund
RRSP Eligible; Inception Year: 1999; Fund Managers: Bill Siddiqui
US Equity VP Fund
RRSP Eligible; Inception Year: 2003; Fund Managers: Bill Siddiqui
US Equity VPNL Fund
RRSP Eligible; Inception Year: 2004; Fund Managers: Bill Siddiqui
Very Aggressive VA Portfolio Fund
RRSP Eligible; Inception Year: 2003; Fund Managers: Fidelity Investments Canada Ltd.
Very Aggressive VP Portfolio Fund
RRSP Eligible; Inception Year: 2003; Fund Managers: AIM Trimark Investment Management
Very Aggressive VPNL Portfolio Fund
RRSP Eligible; Inception Year: 2004; Fund Managers: Fidelity Investments Canada Ltd.
Very Aggressive VAII Portfolio Fund
RRSP Eligible; Inception Year: 2003; Fund Managers: AIM Trimark Investment Management
Very Conservative VAII Portfolio Fund
RRSP Eligible; Inception Year: 2003; Fund Managers: Fidelity Investments Canada Ltd.
Very Conservative VA Portfolio Fund
RRSP Eligible; Inception Year: 2003; Fund Managers: AIM Trimark Investment Management
Very Conservative VP Portfolio Fund
RRSP Eligible; Inception Year: 2003; Fund Managers: Fidelity Investments Canada Ltd.
Very Conservative VPNL Portfolio Fund
RRSP Eligible; Inception Year: 2004; Fund Managers: AIM Trimark Investment Management

Co-operators AIM:
Canadian First Class VA Fund
RRSP Eligible; Inception Year: 2003; Fund Managers: AIM Capital Management
Canadian First Class VPNL Fund
RRSP Eligible; Inception Year: 2004; Fund Managers: AIM Capital Management
Canadian First Class VP Fund
RRSP Eligible; Inception Year: 2003; Fund Managers: AIM Capital Management

Co-operators Fidelity:
Canadian Bond A VA Fund
RRSP Eligible; Inception Year: 2003; Fund Managers: Fidelity Investments Canada Ltd.
Canadian Bond A VAII Fund
RRSP Eligible; Inception Year: 2003; Fund Managers: Fidelity Investments Canada Ltd.
Canadian Bond A VPNL Fund
RRSP Eligible; Inception Year: 2004; Fund Managers: Fidelity Investments Canada Ltd.
Canadian Bond A VP Fund
RRSP Eligible; Inception Year: 2003; Fund Managers: Fidelity Investments Canada Ltd.
International Portfolio VAII Fund
RRSP Eligible; Inception Year: 2003; Fund Managers: Fidelity Investments Canada Ltd.

INSURANCE COMPANIES

International Portfolio A VA Fund
RRSP Eligible; Inception Year: 2003; Fund Managers: Fidelity Investments Canada Ltd.
International Portfolio A VP Fund
RRSP Eligible; Inception Year: 2003; Fund Managers: Fidelity Investments Canada Ltd.
International Portfolio A VPNL Fund
RRSP Eligible; Inception Year: 2004; Fund Managers: Fidelity Investments Canada Ltd.
True North A VA Fund
RRSP Eligible; Inception Year: 2003; Fund Managers: Fidelity Investments Canada Ltd.
True North A VAII Fund
RRSP Eligible; Inception Year: 2003; Fund Managers: Fidelity Investments Canada Ltd.
True North A VP Fund
RRSP Eligible; Inception Year: 2003; Fund Managers: Fidelity Investments Canada Ltd.
True North A VPNL Fund
RRSP Eligible; Inception Year: 2004; Fund Managers: Fidelity Investments Canada Ltd.
Co-operators Trimark:
Canadian Bond VPNL Fund
RRSP Eligible; Inception Year: 2004; Fund Managers: AIM Trimark Investment Management
Canadian Bond VA Fund
RRSP Eligible; Inception Year: 2003; Fund Managers: AIM Trimark Investment Management
Canadian Bond VP Fund
RRSP Eligible; Inception Year: 2003; Fund Managers: AIM Trimark Investment Management
Canadian Bond VAII Fund
RRSP Eligible; Inception Year: 2003; Fund Managers: AIM Trimark Investment Management
Government Income VPNL Fund
RRSP Eligible; Inception Year: 2004; Fund Managers: AIM Trimark Investment Management
Government Income VA Fund
RRSP Eligible; Inception Year: 2003; Fund Managers: AIM Trimark Investment Management
Government Income VP Fund
RRSP Eligible; Inception Year: 2003; Fund Managers: AIM Trimark Investment Management
Government Income VAII Fund
RRSP Eligible; Inception Year: 2003; Fund Managers: AIM Trimark Investment Management
Select Growth VPNL Fund
RRSP Eligible; Inception Year: 2004; Fund Managers: AIM Trimark Investment Management
Select Growth VAII Fund
RRSP Eligible; Inception Year: 2003; Fund Managers: AIM Trimark Investment Management
Select Growth VA Fund
RRSP Eligible; Inception Year: 2003; Fund Managers: AIM Trimark Investment Management
Select Growth VP Fund
RRSP Eligible; Inception Year: 2003; Fund Managers: AIM Trimark Investment Management
Co-opertors AIM:
Canadian First Class VAII Fund
RRSP Eligible; Inception Year: 2003; Fund Managers: AIM Capital Management

Coachman Insurance Company

802 The Queensway
Toronto, ON M8Z 1N5
416-255-3417
Fax: 416-255-3347
800-361-2622
Year Founded: 1979
Assets: $100-500 million Year End: 20051231
Classes of Insurance: Auto
Incorporation: Provincially Incorporated Insurance Company
Executives:
Jon Schubert, President

Coast Underwriters Limited

#1610, 200 Granville St.
Vancouver, BC V6C 1S4
604-683-5631
Fax: 604-683-8561
Incorporation: Federally Incorporated Insurance Company

Combined Insurance Company of America/ Compagnie d'assurance Combined d'Amérique

7300 Warden Ave., 3rd. Fl.
Markham, ON L3R 0X3
905-305-1922
Fax: 905-305-8600
888-234-4466
Other Information: Mailing Address: PO Box 3720, MIP, Markham, ON, L3R 0X5
www.combined.ca
Ownership: Foreign. Subsidiary of Aon Corporation, Chicago, IL, USA.
Classes of Insurance: Personal Accident & Sickness, Life
Incorporation: Federally Incorporated Insurance Company
Profile: Another class of insurance offered by the foreign life insurance company is loss of employment.

Executives:
Dan C. Evans, Chief Agent
Branches:
Boucherville
#200, 1570, rue Ampère
Boucherville, QC J4B 7L4
450-645-9030
Fax: 450-645-9000
Burlington
#400, 1100 Burloak Dr.
Burlington, ON L7L 6B2
905-332-8322
Fax: 905-332-8663
Calgary
#242S, 3030 - 3rd Ave. NE
Calgary, AB T2A 6T7
403-569-7981
Fax: 403-207-1544
Dartmouth
Metropolitan Place
#450, 99 Wyse Rd.
Dartmouth, NS B3A 4S5
902-464-0409
Fax: 902-464-9335

Connecticut General Life Insurance Co.(CGLIC)

c/o CIGNA Life Insurance Company of Canada
55 Town Centre Ct.
Toronto, ON M1P 4X4
416-290-6666
Fax: 416-290-0732
800-668-7029
www.cigna.com
Ownership: Private. Parent is CIGNA Corp., Philadelphia, PA., USA.
Year Founded: 1946
Assets: $50-100 million Year End: 20051231
Revenues: $10-50 million Year End: 20051231
Classes of Insurance: Accident, Personal Accident & Sickness, Life
Incorporation: Federally Incorporated Insurance Company
Profile: Connecticut General Life Insurance is affiliated with CIGNA Life Insurance Company of Canada & Life Insurance Company of North America.

Executives:
M. Eman Hassan, Chief Agent

Constitution Insurance Company of Canada

#202, 1232C Lawrence Ave. East
Toronto, ON M3A 1B9
416-585-9876
Fax: 416-595-5302
Year Founded: 1964
Classes of Insurance: Accident, Legal Expense, Auto, Liability, Fidelity, Property, Surety
Incorporation: Federally Incorporated Insurance Company
Profile: The Canadian property & casualty insurance company is limited to the servicing of existing policies.

Executives:
Frank DiTomasso, President/CEO & Chair

Continental Casualty Company

#1500, 250 Yonge St.
Toronto, ON M5B 2L7
416-542-7300
Fax: 416-542-7310
800-268-9399
www.cnacanada.ca/portal/
Ownership: Foreign. CNA Financial Corporation, Chicago, Illinois
Year Founded: 1897
Classes of Insurance: Accident, Personal Accident & Sickness, Aircraft, Auto, Liability, Boiler & Machinery, Credit, Fidelity, Property, Surety, Hail & Crop
Incorporation: Federally Incorporated Insurance Company
Executives:
Denis Dei Cont, Vice-President Underwriting, Ontario Region
Howard Potter, Vice-President & Marine Manager for Canada

COSECO Insurance Company

5600 Cancross Ct.
Mississauga, ON L5R 3E9
905-507-6156
Fax: 905-507-8661
service@cooperators.ca.
www.cooperators.ca
Ownership: Private. Wholly owned subsidiary of Co-operators Group Limited.
Year Founded: 1979
Assets: $100-500 million
Classes of Insurance: Auto, Property
Incorporation: Federally Incorporated Insurance Company
Executives:
Katherine A. Bardswick, President/CEO
Kevin Daniel, Sr. Vice-President, Finance, CFO
Martin-Eric Tremblay, Sr. Vice-President, Insurance Operations
Directors:
Peter Podovinikoff, Chair

Cowan Insurance Group

PO Box 96
#270, 100 Regina St. South
Waterloo, ON N2J 3Z6
519-886-1690
800-609-5549
Other Information: Toll Free French: 1-800-434-9606
info@cowaninsurancegroup.com
www.cowaninsurancegroup.com
Year Founded: 1927
Incorporation: Provincially Incorporated Insurance Company
Profile: Insurance products & actuarial services are offered through Cowan Insurance Group's operating companies. Frank Cowan Company, Cowan Insurance Brokers & Cowan Wright Beauchamp are part of the family of companies.

Executives:
Janet Passmore, President/CEO
Affiliated Companies:
Cowan Benefits Consulting Limited
Frank Cowan Company Limited

Croatian Fraternal Union of America

c/o Deloitte & Touche
#1400, 181 Bay St.
Toronto, ON M5J 2V1
416-601-6150
Fax: 416-601-6590
www.croatianfraternalunion.org
Ownership: Foreign. Part of Croatian Fraternal Union, Pittsburgh, PA, USA.
Year Founded: 1895
Classes of Insurance: Personal Accident & Sickness, Life
Incorporation: Federally Incorporated Insurance Company
Executives:
Douglas H. Gray, Chief Agent

Culross Mutual Insurance Company(CMI)

PO Box 173
28 Clinton St.
Teeswater, ON N0G 2S0
519-392-6260
Fax: 519-392-8177
888-800-8666
ken@culrossmutual.com
www.culrossmutual.com
Year Founded: 1872
Incorporation: Provincially Incorporated Insurance Company
Executives:
Ken Hawkins, Manager
Donald Murray, Consumer Complaint Officer

CUMIS General Insurance Company

PO Box 5065
151 North Service Rd.
Burlington, ON L7R 4C2

CUMIS General Insurance Company (continued)
905-632-1221
Fax: 905-632-9412
800-263-9120
www.cumis.com
Ownership: Private, joint stock company. Forms part of The CUMIS Group Ltd.
Year Founded: 1980
Classes of Insurance: Auto, Boiler & Machinery, Fidelity, Property, Fire, Theft
Incorporation: Federally Incorporated Insurance Company
Executives:
T. Michael Porter, President/CEO
D'Arcy Delamere, Sr. Vice-President, Sales & Marketing
Shirley Knight, Chief Strategic Officer
Branches:
Burlington
PO Box 5065
151 North Service Rd.
Burlington, ON L7R 4C2 Canada
905-632-1221
Fax: 905-632-9412
Calgary
Heritage Square
#2105, 8500 MacLeod Trail SE
Calgary, AB T2H 2N1 Canada
403-253-6600
Fax: 403-253-0056
Halifax
#331, 7071 Bayers Rd.
Halifax, NS B3K 2C2 Canada
902-453-0931
Fax: 902-454-9802
Regina
#300, 1900 Albert St.
Regina, SK S4P 4K8 Canada
306-525-1833
Fax: 306-522-8780
Saskatoon
333 - 3rd Ave. North
Saskatoon, SK S7K 2M2 Canada
306-652-6677
Fax: 0-653-4482
Vancouver
555 West Hastings St., 18th Fl.
Vancouver, BC V6B 4N5 Canada
604-662-5620
Fax: 604-662-5642
Winnipeg
#740, 215 Garry St.
Winnipeg, MB R3C 3P3 Canada
204-942-0721

The CUMIS Group Limited
PO Box 5065
151 North Service Rd.
Burlington, ON L7R 4C2
905-632-1221
Fax: 905-632-9412
800-263-9120
customer.service@cumis.com
www.cumis.com
Ownership: Private. CUNA Mutual Group (US)
Year Founded: 1937
Classes of Insurance: Personal Accident & Sickness, Auto, Life, Property
Incorporation: Federally Incorporated Insurance Company
Executives:
Kenneth W. Lalonde, President/CEO
David Wade, Sr. Vice-President, CFO
D'Arcy Delamere, Sr. Vice-President, Sales & Marketing
Carol Jardine, Sr. Vice-President
Ken Kawall, Sr. Vice-President, Customer Services & Information Technology
David L. Schurman, Vice-President, Sales & Relationship Management
Shirley Knight, Chief Strategic Officer
Jim Barr, Corporate Secretary
Stephen Mitchell, Regional Manager, Sales & Relationship Management, BC Region
Steve Richard, Regional Manager, Atlantic Canada
Tony Saad, Regional Manager, Sales & Relationship Management, MB Region
Directors:
Chris Catliff, Chair
Gilles Lepage, Vice-Chair
Fay Booker
Jim Bryan
Marcel J. Chorel
Gilles Colbert
Robert A. Effa
Russ Fast
Scott Kennedy
John Lahey
William Mills
T. Michael Porter
Affiliated Companies:
CUMIS General Insurance Company
CUMIS Life Insurance Company
Canadian Northern Shield Insurance Company/CNS

CUMIS Life Insurance Company
PO Box 5065
151 North Service Rd.
Burlington, ON L7R 4C2
905-632-1221
Fax: 905-632-9412
800-263-9120
customer.service@cumis.com
www.cumis.com
Ownership: Private.
Year Founded: 1977
Number of Employees: 550
Assets: $500m-1 billion Year End: 20041231
Revenues: $100-500 million Year End: 20041231
Classes of Insurance: Accident, Personal Accident & Sickness, Auto, Life, Credit, Fidelity, Property, Fire, Theft
Incorporation: Federally Incorporated Insurance Company
Executives:
T. Michael Porter, President/CEO; 905-632-1221; mike.porter@cumis.com
Ken Kawall, Chief Information Officer; 905-632-1221; ken.kawall@cumis.com
David Wade, Chief Financial Officer; 905-632-1221; david.wade@cumis.com
D'Arcy Delamere, Sr. Vice-President, Sales & Marketing; 905-632-1221; darcy.delamare@cumis.com
Shirley Knight, Sr. Vice-President, Strategy & Business Lines; 905-632-1221; shirley.knight@cumis.com
Craig Marshall, Corporate Secretary; 905-632-1221; craig.marshall@cumis.com
Branches:
Halifax
6074 Lady Hammond Rd.
Halifax, NS B3K 2R7 Canada
902-453-0931
Steve Richard, Regional Manager
Regina
#300, 1900 Albert St.
Regina, SK S4P 4K8 Canada
306-525-1833
800-667-3559
Stephen Mitchell, Regional Manager
Vancouver
555 West Hastings St., 18th Fl.
Vancouver, BC V6B 5G3 Canada
604-662-5620
Fax: 604-662-5680
800-667-3559
Winnipeg
#740, 215 Garry St.
Winnipeg, MB R3C 3P3 Canada
204-940-2730
Geoff Gibson, Regional Manager

DaimlerChrysler Insurance Company(DCIC)
1 Riverside Dr. West, 12th Fl.
Windsor, ON N9A 7E3
800-837-6667
www.insurance.daimlerchrysler.com
Former Name: Chrysler Insurance Company
Ownership: Part of DaimlerChrysler Insurance Company, Farmington Hills, MI, USA.
Year Founded: 1964
Classes of Insurance: Auto, Liability, Property, Surety
Incorporation: Federally Incorporated Insurance Company
Profile: The foreign property & casualty insurance company provides protection for dealerships, their employees & customers.
Executives:
Richard Wong, CEO
William Charman, Vice-President; wac@daimlerchrysler.com
Branches:
Mississauga
#300, 2425 Matheson Blvd. East
Mississauga, ON L4W 5N7
905-629-6064
Fax: 905-629-6067
800-837-6667

Desjardins assurances générales inc/ Desjardins General Insurance Inc.
PO Box 3500
6300, boul de la Rive-Sud
Lévis, QC G6V 6P9
418-835-4850
Fax: 418-835-5599
800-277-8726
www.desjardinsassurancesgenerales.com
Former Name: Assurances générales des caisses Desjardins inc.
Ownership: Private; Subsidiary of Desjardins General Insurance Group
Year Founded: 1987
Number of Employees: 1,614
Assets: $500m-1 billion Year End: 20041231
Revenues: $500m-1 billion Year End: 20041231
Classes of Insurance: Auto, Liability, Boiler & Machinery, Property, Surety
Incorporation: Provincially Incorporated Insurance Company
Executives:
Jude Martineau, President/CEO
Louis Chantal, Sr. Exec. Vice-President, Administration, Finance & Human Resources, Treasurer
Pierre Deschênes, Sr. Exec. Vice-President, Information Technology
Sylvie Paquette, Sr. Exec. Vice-President, Corporate Development
Pierre Rousseau, Sr. Exec. Vice-President, Legal Affairs, Corporate Secretary
Jean Vaillancourt, Sr. Exec. Vice-President & General Manager, Québec Operations
Directors:
Raymond Gagné, Chair
Jean-Robert Laporte, Vice-Chair
Yves Archambault
Annie P. Bélanger
Jean J. Brossard
Stéphane Coudé
Roger Desrosiers
Jean-Louis Gauvin
Gabrielle Gosselin
Michel Lucas
Jude Martineau
Jocelyne Poulin
Clément Trottier
Yvon Vinet
Branches:
Montréal
Tour sud
PO Box 2, Pl-Desjardins Sta. Pl-Desjardins
1, Complexe Desjardins, 10e étage
Montréal, QC H5B 1B1 Canada
514-350-8484
866-350-8484

Desjardins Financial Security/ Desjardins Sécurité financière
***Also listed under:** Investment Fund Companies*
200, av des Commandeurs
Lévis, QC G6V 6R2
418-838-7800
Fax: 418-838-7463
info@desjardinssecuritefinanciere.com
www.dsf-dfs.com
Former Name: Imperial Life Financial
Ownership: Private.
Assets: $10-100 billion Year End: 20061023
Revenues: $1-10 billion Year End: 20061023
Classes of Insurance: Life
Profile: Offers a broad spectrum of tailor-made life and health insurance and retirement savings products and services, through employees and partners committed to ensuring the satisfaction of its customers and caisse members.
Executives:
Richard Fortier, President/COO

INSURANCE COMPANIES

Denis Berthiaume, Sr. Vice-President, Individual Insurance
Constance Lemieux, Sr. Vice-President, E-Business & Technology
Alain Thauvette, Sr. Vice-President, Group & Business Insurance
Monique Tremblay, Sr. Vice-President, Savings & Segregated Funds
Louise Turgeon, Sr. Vice-President, AssurFinance for Institutions, AssurDirect & Desjardins Relations
Gérard Guilbault, Chief Investment Officer
Directors:
Sylvie St-Pierre Babin, Chair
Serge Cloutier
Pierre Gingras
Serge Hamelin
Monique Lefebvre
Denis Levesque
Suzanne Maisonneuve-Benoit
Ursula Menke
Jocelyn Nadeau
Michel Rouleau
Michel Rouleau
Jacques Sylvestre
Affiliated Companies:
Gestion SFL inc.
Sigma Assistel Inc.
DFS Pooled:
Trimark Canadian Fund
RRSP Eligible; Inception Year: 1997; Fund Managers:
AIM Trimark Investments
McLean Budden Balanced Growth Fund
RRSP Eligible; Inception Year: 1994; Fund Managers:
McLean Budden Limited
McLean Budden Canadian Equity Growth Fund
RRSP Eligible; Inception Year: 1997; Fund Managers:
McLean Budden Limited
McLean Budden Canadian Fixed Income Fund
RRSP Eligible; Inception Year: 1997; Fund Managers:
McLean Budden Limited
Fiera Conservative Diversified Fund
RRSP Eligible; Inception Year: 1973; Fund Managers:
Fiera Capital Management
Fiera Enhanced Mortgage Fund
RRSP Eligible; Inception Year: 1968; Fund Managers:
Fiera Capital Management
Trimark Fund
RRSP Eligible; Inception Year: 1997; Fund Managers:
AIM Trimark Investments
Fiera Canadian Equity GARP Fund
RRSP Eligible; Inception Year: 1961; Fund Managers:
Fiera Capital Management
Fiera Global Balanced Fund
RRSP Eligible; Inception Year: 1999; Fund Managers:
Fiera Capital Management
Trimark Income Growth Fund
RRSP Eligible; Inception Year: 1997; Fund Managers:
AIM Trimark Investments
McLean Budden Global Equity Fund
RRSP Eligible; Inception Year: 1997; Fund Managers:
McLean Budden Limited
Bissett Canadian Equity Fund
RRSP Eligible; Inception Year: 1999; Fund Managers:
Bissett Investment Management
Fiera Money Market Fund
RRSP Eligible; Inception Year: 1981; Fund Managers:
Fiera Capital Management
Fiera North American Small Company Fund
RRSP Eligible; Inception Year: 1999; Fund Managers:
Fiera Capital Management
Bissett Small Cap Fund
RRSP Eligible; Inception Year: 1999; Fund Managers:
Bissett Investment Management
Fiera Bond Fund
RRSP Eligible; Inception Year: 1961; Fund Managers:
Fiera Capital Management
Fiera US Index Plus Fund
RRSP Eligible; Inception Year: 1997; Fund Managers:
Fiera Capital Management
Aggressive Portfolio Fund
RRSP Eligible; Inception Year: 2002;
Balanced Portfolio Fund
RRSP Eligible; Inception Year: 2002;
Conservative Portfolio Fund
RRSP Eligible; Inception Year: 2002;
Dynamic Portfolio Fund
RRSP Eligible; Inception Year: 2002;
Energetic Portfolio Fund
RRSP Eligible; Inception Year: 2002;
Security Portfolio Fund
RRSP Eligible; Inception Year: 2002;
Jarislowsky Fraser Balanced Fund
RRSP Eligible; Inception Year: 2002; Fund Managers:
Jarislowsky Fraser Ltd.
McLean Budden American Equity Fund
RRSP Eligible; Inception Year: 2002; Fund Managers:
McLean Budden Limited
Templeton International Stock Fund
RRSP Eligible; Inception Year: 2002; Fund Managers:
Franklin Templeton Investments
Mackenzie Cundill Canadian Security Portfolio Fund
RRSP Eligible; Inception Year: 1997; Fund Managers:
Mackenzie Financial Corp.
Barclays Universe Bond Index Fund
RRSP Eligible; Inception Year: 2003; Fund Managers:
Barclays Global Investors Canada Ltd.
Barclays EAFE Equity Index Fund
RRSP Eligible; Inception Year: 2004; Fund Managers:
Barclays Global Investors Canada Ltd.
Barclays S&P/TSX Composite Index Fund
RRSP Eligible; Inception Year: 2003; Fund Managers:
Barclays Global Investors Canada Ltd.
Barclays Active Canadian Equity Fund
RRSP Eligible; Inception Year: 2003; Fund Managers:
Barclays Global Investors Canada Ltd.
New Star EAFE Fund
RRSP Eligible; Inception Year: 2004; Fund Managers:
New Star Asset Management Limited
Addenda Canadian Bond Fund
RRSP Eligible; Inception Year: 2004; Fund Managers:
Addenda Capital Inc.
GE Asset Management International Equity Fund
RRSP Eligible; Inception Year: 2004; Fund Managers:
GE Asset Management
Jarislowsky Fraser Canadian Equity Fund
RRSP Eligible; Inception Year: 2003; Fund Managers:
Jarislowsky Fraser Ltd.
Fiera Long Term Government Bond Fund
RRSP Eligible; Inception Year: 2003; Fund Managers:
Fiera Capital Management
Fidelity Canadian Balanced Fund
RRSP Eligible; Inception Year: 2003;
Bernstein Canadian Value Equity Fund
RRSP Eligible; Inception Year: 2003; Fund Managers:
Bernstein Management Inc.
Bernstein US Equity Value Fund
RRSP Eligible; Inception Year: 2003; Fund Managers:
Bernstein Management Inc.
UBS Large Cap Equity Fund
RRSP Eligible; Inception Year: 2004; Fund Managers:
UBS Global Asset Management (Canada) Co.
Fiera Canadian Equity Dividend Fund
RRSP Eligible; Inception Year: 2004; Fund Managers:
Fiera Capital Management
Bernstein International Equity Fund
RRSP Eligible; Inception Year: 1996; Fund Managers:
Bernstein Management Inc.
Canadian Growth Fund
RRSP Eligible; Inception Year: 2002; Fund Managers:
McLean Budden Limited
Imperial Growth:
North American Equity Fund
RRSP Eligible; Inception Year: 1969; Fund Managers:
Elantis
Canadian Equity Fund
RRSP Eligible; Inception Year: 1977; Fund Managers:
Elantis
Diversified Fund
RRSP Eligible; Inception Year: 1988; Fund Managers:
Elantis
Money Market Fund
RRSP Eligible; Inception Year: 1988; Fund Managers:
Elantis
Millennia III:
Canadian Dividend 4 Fund
RRSP Eligible; Inception Year: 1998; Fund Managers:
Fiera Capital Management
Income 1 Fund
RRSP Eligible; Inception Year: 1995; Fund Managers:
Fiera Capital Management
Income 2 Fund
RRSP Eligible; Inception Year: 1995; Fund Managers:
Fiera Capital Management
Income 3 Fund
RRSP Eligible; Inception Year: 1998; Fund Managers:
Fiera Capital Management
Income 4 Fund
RRSP Eligible; Inception Year: 1998; Fund Managers:
Fiera Capital Management
International Equity 1 Fund
RRSP Eligible; Inception Year: 1995; Fund Managers:
Fiera Capital Management
International Equity 2 Fund
RRSP Eligible; Inception Year: 1995; Fund Managers:
Fiera Capital Management
International Equity 3 Fund
RRSP Eligible; Inception Year: 1998; Fund Managers:
Fiera Capital Management
International Equity 4 Fund
RRSP Eligible; Inception Year: 1998; Fund Managers:
Fiera Capital Management
Money Market 1 Fund
RRSP Eligible; Inception Year: 1995; Fund Managers:
Fiera Capital Management
Money Market 2 Fund
RRSP Eligible; Inception Year: 1995; Fund Managers:
Fiera Capital Management
Money Market 3 Fund
RRSP Eligible; Inception Year: 1998; Fund Managers:
Fiera Capital Management
Money Market 4 Fund
RRSP Eligible; Inception Year: 1998; Fund Managers:
Fiera Capital Management
North American Small Company 1 Fund
RRSP Eligible; Inception Year: 1998; Fund Managers:
Fiera Capital Management
North American Small Company 2 Fund
RRSP Eligible; Inception Year: 1998; Fund Managers:
Fiera Capital Management
North American Small Company 3 Fund
RRSP Eligible; Inception Year: 1998; Fund Managers:
Fiera Capital Management
North American Small Company 4 Fund
RRSP Eligible; Inception Year: 1998; Fund Managers:
Fiera Capital Management
European Equity 3 Fund
RRSP Eligible; Inception Year: 1998; Fund Managers:
Fiera Capital Management
European Equity 4 Fund
RRSP Eligible; Inception Year: 1998; Fund Managers:
Fiera Capital Management
Canadian Equity 4 Fund
RRSP Eligible; Inception Year: 1998; Fund Managers:
Fiera Capital Management
Global Balanced 3 Fund
RRSP Eligible; Inception Year: 1998; Fund Managers:
Fiera Capital Management
Global Balanced 4 Fund
RRSP Eligible; Inception Year: 1998; Fund Managers:
Fiera Capital Management
Canadian Balanced 4 Fund
RRSP Eligible; Inception Year: 1998; Fund Managers:
Fiera Capital Management
Canadian Dividend 1 Fund
RRSP Eligible; Inception Year: 1998; Fund Managers:
Fiera Capital Management
Canadian Dividend 2 Fund
RRSP Eligible; Inception Year: 1998; Fund Managers:
Fiera Capital Management
Canadian Dividend 3 Fund
RRSP Eligible; Inception Year: 1998; Fund Managers:
Fiera Capital Management
Canadian Equity 1 Fund
RRSP Eligible; Inception Year: 1995; Fund Managers:
Fiera Capital Management
Canadian Equity 2 Fund
RRSP Eligible; Inception Year: 1995; Fund Managers:
Fiera Capital Management
Canadian Equity 3 Fund
RRSP Eligible; Inception Year: 1998; Fund Managers:
Fiera Capital Management
American Equity 1 Fund
RRSP Eligible; Inception Year: 1995; Fund Managers:
Fiera Capital Management

Desjardins Financial Security/ Desjardins Sécurité financière (continued)

American Equity 3 Fund
RRSP Eligible; Inception Year: 1998; Fund Managers:
Fiera Capital Management
American Equity 4 Fund
RRSP Eligible; Inception Year: 1998; Fund Managers:
Fiera Capital Management
Canadian Balanced 1 Fund
RRSP Eligible; Inception Year: 1995; Fund Managers:
Fiera Capital Management
Canadian Balanced 2 Fund
RRSP Eligible; Inception Year: 1995; Fund Managers:
Fiera Capital Management
Canadian Balanced 3 Fund
RRSP Eligible; Inception Year: 1998; Fund Managers:
Fiera Capital Management
American Equity 2 Fund
RRSP Eligible; Inception Year: 1995; Fund Managers:
Fiera Capital Management
Bissett Canadian Equity 3 Fund
RRSP Eligible; Inception Year: 2000; Fund Managers:
Bissett Investment Management
Bissett Canadian Equity 4 Fund
RRSP Eligible; Inception Year: 2000; Fund Managers:
Bissett Investment Management
Bissett Dividend Income 3 Fund
RRSP Eligible; Inception Year: 2000; Fund Managers:
Bissett Investment Management
Bissett Dividend Income 4 Fund
RRSP Eligible; Inception Year: 2000; Fund Managers:
Bissett Investment Management
Bissett Small Cap 3 Fund
RRSP Eligible; Inception Year: 2000; Fund Managers:
Bissett Investment Management
Bissett Small Cap 4 Fund
RRSP Eligible; Inception Year: 2000; Fund Managers:
Bissett Investment Management
McLean Budden American Equity Growth 3 Fund
RRSP Eligible; Inception Year: 2000; Fund Managers:
McLean Budden Limited
McLean Budden American Equity Growth 4 Fund
RRSP Eligible; Inception Year: 2000; Fund Managers:
McLean Budden Limited
McLean Budden Balanced Growth 3 Fund
RRSP Eligible; Inception Year: 2000; Fund Managers:
McLean Budden Limited
McLean Budden Balanced Growth 4 Fund
RRSP Eligible; Inception Year: 2000; Fund Managers:
McLean Budden Limited
McLean Budden Canadian Equity Growth 3 Fund
RRSP Eligible; Inception Year: 2000; Fund Managers:
McLean Budden Limited
McLean Budden Canadian Equity Growth 4 Fund
RRSP Eligible; Inception Year: 2000; Fund Managers:
McLean Budden Limited
McLean Budden Canadian Equity Value 3 Fund
RRSP Eligible; Inception Year: 2000; Fund Managers:
McLean Budden Limited
McLean Budden Canadian Equity Value 4 Fund
RRSP Eligible; Inception Year: 2000; Fund Managers:
McLean Budden Limited
McLean Budden Fixed Income 3 Fund
RRSP Eligible; Inception Year: 2000; Fund Managers:
McLean Budden Limited
McLean Budden Fixed Income 4 Fund
RRSP Eligible; Inception Year: 2000; Fund Managers:
McLean Budden Limited
McLean Budden International Equity Growth 3 Fund
RRSP Eligible; Inception Year: 2000; Fund Managers:
McLean Budden Limited
McLean Budden International Equity Growth 4 Fund
RRSP Eligible; Inception Year: 2000; Fund Managers:
McLean Budden Limited
Talvest Global Asset Allocation RSP 3 Fund
RRSP Eligible; Inception Year: 2000; Fund Managers:
TAL Global Asset Management
Talvest Global Asset Allocation RSP 4 Fund
RRSP Eligible; Inception Year: 2000; Fund Managers:
TAL Global Asset Management
Talvest Balanced 3 Portfolio
RRSP Eligible; Inception Year: 2000; Fund Managers:
TAL Global Asset Management
Talvest Balanced 4 Portfolio
RRSP Eligible; Inception Year: 2000; Fund Managers:
TAL Global Asset Management
Talvest Conservative 3 Portfolio
RRSP Eligible; Inception Year: 2000; Fund Managers:
TAL Global Asset Management
Talvest Conservative 4 Portfolio
RRSP Eligible; Inception Year: 2000; Fund Managers:
TAL Global Asset Management
Talvest Global Bond RSP 3 Fund
RRSP Eligible; Inception Year: 2000; Fund Managers:
TAL Global Asset Management
Talvest Global Bond RSP 4 Fund
RRSP Eligible; Inception Year: 2000; Fund Managers:
TAL Global Asset Management
Talvest Global Equity 3 Fund
RRSP Eligible; Inception Year: 2000; Fund Managers:
TAL Global Asset Management
Talvest Global Equity 4 Fund
RRSP Eligible; Inception Year: 2000; Fund Managers:
TAL Global Asset Management
Talvest Growth 3 Portfolio
RRSP Eligible; Inception Year: 2000; Fund Managers:
TAL Global Asset Management
Talvest Growth 4 Portfolio
RRSP Eligible; Inception Year: 2000; Fund Managers:
TAL Global Asset Management
Bissett Multinational Growth 3 Fund
RRSP Eligible; Inception Year: 2003; Fund Managers:
Franklin Templeton Investments
Bissett Multinational Growth 4 Fund
RRSP Eligible; Inception Year: 2003; Fund Managers:
Franklin Templeton Investments
Trimark Canadian 3 Fund
RRSP Eligible; Inception Year: 2003; Fund Managers:
AIM Trimark Investments
Trimark Canadian 4 Fund
RRSP Eligible; Inception Year: 2003; Fund Managers:
AIM Trimark Investments
Jarislowsky Fraser Global Balanced 3 Fund
RRSP Eligible; Inception Year: 2003; Fund Managers:
Jarislowsky Fraser Ltd.
Jarislowsky Fraser Global Balanced 4 Fund
RRSP Eligible; Inception Year: 2003; Fund Managers:
Jarislowsky Fraser Ltd.
Mortgage 3 Fund
RRSP Eligible; Inception Year: 2003; Fund Managers:
Desjardins Global Asset Management
Mortgage 4 Fund
RRSP Eligible; Inception Year: 2003; Fund Managers:
Desjardins Global Asset Management
Fidelity International Portfolio 3 Fund
RRSP Eligible; Inception Year: 2003; Fund Managers:
Fidelity Investments Canada
Fidelity International Portfolio 4 Fund
RRSP Eligible; Inception Year: 2003; Fund Managers:
Fidelity Investments Canada
Northwest 3 Portfolio
RRSP Eligible; Inception Year: 2002; Fund Managers:
Northwest Mutual Funds
Northwest 4 Portfolio
RRSP Eligible; Inception Year: 2002; Fund Managers:
Northwest Mutual Funds
Northwest Quebec Growth 3 Fund
RRSP Eligible; Inception Year: 2003; Fund Managers:
Montrustco Bolton Inc.
Northwest Quebec Growth 4 Fund
RRSP Eligible; Inception Year: 2003; Fund Managers:
Montrustco Bolton Inc.
American Equity Value 3 Fund
RRSP Eligible; Inception Year: 2003; Fund Managers:
Bernstein Management Inc.
American Equity Value 4 Fund
RRSP Eligible; Inception Year: 2003; Fund Managers:
Bernstein Management Inc.
Ultimate Equity 3 Portfolio
RRSP Eligible; Inception Year: 2002; Fund Managers:
TAL Global Asset Management
Ultimate Equity 4 Portfolio
RRSP Eligible; Inception Year: 2002; Fund Managers:
TAL Global Asset Management
Bissett Canadian Balanced 3 Fund
RRSP Eligible; Inception Year: 2005; Fund Managers:
Bissett Investment Management
Bissett Canadian Balanced 4 Fund
RRSP Eligible; Inception Year: 2005; Fund Managers:
Bissett Investment Management
Bissett Bond 3 Fund
RRSP Eligible; Inception Year: 2000; Fund Managers:
Bissett Investment Management
Bissett Bond 4 Fund
RRSP Eligible; Inception Year: 2000; Fund Managers:
Bissett Investment Management
Jarislowsky Fraser Canadian Equity 3 Fund
RRSP Eligible; Inception Year: 2005; Fund Managers:
Jarislowsky Fraser Ltd.
Jarislowsky Fraser Canadian Equity 4 Fund
RRSP Eligible; Inception Year: 2005; Fund Managers:
Jarislowsky Fraser Ltd.

Offices:

Montréal
Tour Sud
1, Complexe Desjardins, 21e étage
Montréal, QC H5B 1E2 Canada
514-350-8700
877-750-8700

Québec
1150, rue de Claire-Fontaine
Québec, QC Canada
418-647-5000
888-893-1833

Toronto
#306, 95 St. Clair Ave. West
Toronto, ON M4V 1N7 Canada
416-926-2662
Fax: 416-926-2667
800-263-9641

Regional Offices:

Calgary
#560, 202 - 6th Ave. SW
Calgary, AB T2P 2R9 Canada
403-216-5800
Fax: 403-216-5807
800-661-8666

Dartmouth
#1400, 99 Wyse Rd.
Dartmouth, NS B3A 4S5 Canada
902-466-8881
Fax: 902-466-4074
800-567-8881

Lévis
Complexe Maurice-Tanguay
#203, 5790, boul Étienne-Dallaire
Lévis, QC G6V 8V6 Canada
418-838-7870
Fax: 418-833-6251
800-463-7870

Montréal
#2525, 2, Complexe Desjardins, Tour Est
Montréal, QC H5B 1E2 Canada
514-285-7880
Fax: 514-258-2442
800-363-3072

Ottawa
#120, 1102 Prince of Wales Dr.
Ottawa, ON K2C 3W7 Canada
613-224-3121
Fax: 613-224-6812
888-428-2485

Toronto
#306, 95 St. Clair Ave. West
Toronto, ON M4V 1N7 Canada
416-926-2662
Fax: 416-926-2667
800-263-9641

Vancouver
#1050, 401 West Georgia St.
Vancouver, BC V6B 5A1 Canada
604-718-4410
Fax: 604-718-4412
800-667-6267

Winnipeg
#1490, 363 Broadway
Winnipeg, MB R3C 3N9 Canada
204-989-4350
Fax: 204-989-7211
888-942-3383

Desjardins Groupe d'assurances générales inc/ Desjardins General Insurance Group Inc.

***Also listed under:* Holding & Other Investment Companies**

6300, boul de la Rive-Sud
Lévis, QC G6V 6P9
888-277-8726
Former Name: Groupe Desjardins, Assurances générales
Ownership: Private. Parent company is Desjardins Group
Year Founded: 1989
Number of Employees: 431
Assets: $500m-1 billion Year End: 20041231
Revenues: $100-500 million Year End: 20041231
Incorporation: Provincially Incorporated Insurance Company
Executives:
Alban D'Amours, CEO
Jude Martineau, President/COO
Jean-François Chalifoux, Sr. Exec. Vice-President & General Manager, RoC Operations
Louis Chantal, Sr. Exec. Vice-President, Administration, Finances & Human Resources, Treasurer
Pierre Deschênes, Sr. Exec. Vice-President, Information Technology
Sylvie Paquette, Sr. Exec. Vice-President, Corporate Development
Pierre Rousseau, Sr. Exec. Vice-President, Legal Affairs, Corporate Secretary
Jean Vaillancourt, Sr. Exec. Vice-President & General Manager, Québec Operations
Directors:
Raymond Gagné, Chair
Jean-Robert Laporte, Vice-Chair
Yves Archambeault
Annie P. Bélanger
Jean J. Brossard
Stéphane Coudé
Roger Desrosiers
Jean-Louis Gauvin
Gabrielle Gosselin
Michel Lucas
Jude Martineau
Jocelyne Poulin
Clément Trottier
Yvon Vinet
Affiliated Companies:
Certas Direct Insurance Company
Desjardins assurances générales inc
The Personal General Insurance Inc.
The Personal Insurance Company
Branches:
Montréal
1, Complexe Desjardins, 17e étage, CP 2
Montréal, QC H5B 1B1 Canada
514-281-8101
866-350-8300
Hélène Lamontagne, Sr. Exec. Vice-President, Corporate Affairs

The Dominion of Canada General Insurance Company/ Compagnie d'assurance générale dominion du Canada

165 University Ave.
Toronto, ON M5H 3B9
416-362-7231
Fax: 416-362-9918
800-268-8447
www.thedominion.ca
Ownership: Public. Wholly owned by E-L Financial Corporation Limited
Year Founded: 1887
Number of Employees: 912
Assets: $4,731,000,000
Revenues: $1,380,000,000
Classes of Insurance: Auto, Liability, Property, Fire, Surety, Theft
Incorporation: Federally Incorporated Insurance Company
Executives:
George L. Cooke, President/CEO; 416-947-2556
Janet E. Babcock, Vice-President/CIO; 416-947-2540
Nathalie Bégin, Vice-President & Chief Actuary; 416-947-2565
Vivian N. Bercovici, Vice-President, Legal & Public Affairs, Corporate Secretary; 416-947-2551
Jerry Dalla Corte, Vice-President, Claims; 416-350-3717
Alan J. Hanks, Vice-President, Field Operations; 416-350-3703
R. Doug Hogan, Vice-President/CFO; 416-947-2528
Lorne D. McCubbin, Vice-President, Special Claims; 416-947-2559
Shelly A. Rae, Vice-President, Human Resources; 416-947-2530
Steven Whitelaw, Vice-President, Business Process, Delivery & Information; 416-350-3759
Directors:
Duncan N.R. Jackman, Chair
P. Cantor
George L. Cooke
William J. Corcoran
Mark J. Fuller
R.G. Long
J.W. McCutcheon, Q.C.
Richard E. Rooney
D. Rosenweig
Clive P. Rowe
M.M. Taylor
D.C. Townsend
M. Vennat
Branches:
Calgary - Western Regional Centre
#1700, 777 - 8th Ave. SW
Calgary, AB T2P 3R5 Canada
403-231-6600
Fax: 403-263-8193
800-363-1075
Charlottetown
4 Harbourside Access Rd.
Charlottetown, PE C1A 8R4 Canada
902-892-2008
Fax: 902-566-1245
800-308-2008
Halifax - Atlantic Regional Centre
Purdy's Wharf, Tower II
#601, 1969 Upper Water St.
Halifax, NS B3J 3R7 Canada
902-429-6813
Fax: 902-423-6812
800-268-4543
London - Western Ontario Regional Centre
#510, 285 King St.
London, ON N6B 3M6 Canada
519-433-7201
Fax: 519-433-2193
800-265-4768
Oakville - Metro West Regional Centre
1275 North Service Rd. West
Oakville, ON L6M 3M3 Canada
905-825-6400
Fax: 905-825-5029
800-561-3501
Ottawa - Regional Centre
#300, 155 Queen St.
Ottawa, ON K1P 6L1 Canada
613-233-1363
Fax: 613-233-9667
800-268-4172
Toronto - Metro East Regional Centre
#300, 300 Consilium Place
Toronto, ON M1H 3G2 Canada
416-296-1555
Fax: 416-296-0098
800-265-4408
Vancouver - Pacific Regional Centre
Royal Centre
PO Box 11114
#2400, 1055 West Georgia St.
Vancouver, BC V6E 3P3 Canada
604-684-5811
Fax: 604-688-0053
800-663-9319

Dufferin Mutual Insurance Company

712 Main St. East
Shelburne, ON L0N 1S0
519-925-2026
Fax: 519-925-3357
800-265-9115
info@dufferinmutual.com
www.dufferinmutual.com
Year Founded: 1895
Classes of Insurance: Personal Accident & Sickness, Auto, Liability, Boiler & Machinery, Fidelity, Property
Incorporation: Provincially Incorporated Insurance Company
Profile: The mutual insurance company provides farm, home, business & automobile insurance. Insurance is offered through independent brokers in south-central Ontario.
Executives:
Ronald Wettlaufer, Secretary-Manager

Dumfries Mutual Insurance Company

12 Cambridge St.
Cambridge, ON
519-621-4660
Fax: 519-740-8732
info@dumfriesmutual.com
www.dumfriesmutual.com
Ownership: Policy-holders.
Year Founded: 1856
Classes of Insurance: Auto, Liability, Boiler & Machinery, Property, Hail & Crop
Incorporation: Provincially Incorporated Insurance Company
Profile: Dumfries Mutual Insurance is an Ontario farm mutual insurance company.
Executives:
Shelley Sutton, Secretary-Manager, Privacy Officer
Jim Howarth, Treasurer
Directors:
John Borda
Bruce Dickieson
Harold Hamilton
John Innes
Anne Jones
William Masters
Gordon Taylor
Bruce Telfer
Ted Westbrook

Eagle Star Insurance Company Ltd.

c/o Focus Group Inc.
#500, 36 King St. East
Toronto, ON M5C 1E5
416-361-1728
Fax: 416-361-6113
www.eaglestar.ie
Ownership: Foreign. Part of Eagle Star, Dublin, Ireland.
Year Founded: 1872
Classes of Insurance: Personal Accident & Sickness, Aircraft, Auto, Liability, Boiler & Machinery, Fidelity, Property, Surety
Incorporation: Federally Incorporated Insurance Company
Executives:
Philip H. Cook, Chief Agent

Ecclesiastical Insurance Office plc/ Société des Assurances écclésiastiques

PO Box 2004
#2200, 20 Eglinton Ave. West
Toronto, ON M4R 1K8
416-484-4555
Fax: 416-484-6352
info@eccles-ins.com
www.eigcanada.com, www.ecclesiastical.co.uk
Ownership: Member of Ecclesiastical Insurance Group, UK.
Year Founded: 1972
Classes of Insurance: Auto, Liability, Boiler & Machinery, Marine, Fidelity, Property
Incorporation: Federally Incorporated Insurance Company
Profile: The foreign property & casualty insurance company provides faith insurance, as well as a customized Retirement Community Living product. Profits are returned to the owner, a charitable trust.
Executives:
Stephanie Jacinta Whyte, General Manager, Chief Agent
Steve Lovisek, Chief Financial Officer
Debbie Hastings, Manager, Claims
Lorna McIntosh, Manager, Human Resources
Stuart Rowley, Manager, Underwriting & Operations
Cynthia Oudin, Manager, Central Region
Branches:
Calgary
Bow Valley Square 1
PO Box 20
#630, 202 - 6th Ave. SW
Calgary, AB T2P 2R9 Canada
403-538-0175
Fax: 403-538-0182
Betty Dietz, Manager, Western Region
Halifax
Tower 2, Purdy's Wharf
#2106, 1969 Upper Water St.
Halifax, NS B3J 3R7 Canada

INSURANCE COMPANIES

Ecclesiastical Insurance Office plc/ Société des Assurances écclésiastiques (continued)

902-492-4548
Fax: 902-492-4484
Beth Durkee, Manager, Atlantic Region
Vancouver
Two Bentall Centre
PO Box 239
#1795, 555 Burrard St.
Vancouver, BC V7X 1M9 Canada
604-605-1111
Fax: 604-605-1140
Elissa Mak, Manager, British Columbia

Echelon General Insurance Company

#310, 1550 Enterprise Rd.
Mississauga, ON L4W 4P4
905-564-9215
Fax: 905-565-7992
800-324-3566
www.echelon-insurance.ca
Former Name: John Deere Insurance Company of Canada
Ownership: Public. Parent is EGI Financial Holdings Inc.
Year Founded: 1998
Number of Employees: 100
Assets: $100-500 million Year End: 20051231
Revenues: $100-500 million Year End: 20051231
Stock Symbol: EFH
Classes of Insurance: Accident, Personal Accident & Sickness, Legal Expense, Auto, Liability, Fidelity, Property, Fire, Surety
Incorporation: Federally Incorporated Insurance Company
Profile: EGI Financial Holdings Inc.'s website is www.egi.ca.

Executives:
Douglas McIntyre, CEO; 905-565-7961; dmcintyre@egi.ca
George Kalopsis, President/COO; 905-565-7962; gkalopsis@egi.ca
Mark Sylvia, Exec. Vice-President, Niche Products Division; 905-565-7954; msylvia@egi.ca
Hemraj Singh, Chief Financial Officer; 905-565-7999; hsingh@egi.ca
John Czerwinski, Vice-President, Business Development & Sales; 905-565-7994; jczerwinski@egi.ca
Bob Fuller, Vice-President, Claims; 905-565-7970; bfuller@egi.ca
Steve Steele, Vice-President, Underwriting; 905-565-7967; ssteele@egi.ca
Directors:
Paul Little, Chair
Peter Crawford; 519-886-9358
Kevin Daniel; 519-831-0115
Angus Ross; 416-266-2025
Branches:
Laval
#300, 500, boul St-Martin ouest
Laval, QC H7M 3Y2 Canada
450-662-0222
Fax: 450-662-6290
Reginald Roy, Manager

The Economical Insurance Group

PO Box 2000
111 Westmount St. South
Waterloo, ON N2J 4S4
519-570-8200
Fax: 519-570-8389
www.economicalinsurance.com
Year Founded: 1871
Number of Employees: 2,100
Assets: $3,294,061,000 Year End: 20041231
Revenues: $1,696,880,000 Year End: 20041231
Profile: The large Canadian-owned & operated property & casualty insurer services customers through offices across the country.

Executives:
Noel G. Walpole, President/CEO
Linda Goss, Chief Actuary
John Martin, Chief Information Officer
Jorge Arruda, Sr. Vice-President, Operations
Sandeep Uppal, Sr. Vice-President/CFO
Yvan Aubin, Vice-President, Controller
Dean Bulloch, Vice-President, Human Resources
Catherine Coulson, H.B.Sc., MBA, AIIC, Vice-President, Personal Insurance
David Crozier, BA, CIP, CRM, Vice-President, Commercial Insurance
Louis Durocher, Vice-President, Actuarial Services
David M. Fitzpatrick, CHRP, Vice-President, Corporate Services
Katherine Kipper, Vice-President, Sales & Marketing
Rocco Neglia, Vice-President, Claims
Michael O'Neill, Vice-President, Investments
William Stinson, Vice-President, Information Technology
Directors:
Gerald A. Hooper, Chair
Mary N. Bales
A. Scott Carson
David A. MacIntosh
Charles M.W. Ormston
Terry J. Reidel
Brian J. Ruby
Harold E. Seegmiller
Honourary Directors:
John S. Acheson
Douglas W. Brown
Ralph A. Forbes
John M. Harper
Gordan A. Mackay
William D. McGregor
John H. Panabaker
Peter Sims
John A. Vila
Affiliated Companies:
Economical Mutual Insurance Company
Federation Insurance Company of Canada
La Compagnie d'Assurance Missisquoi
Perth Insurance Company
Waterloo Insurance Company

Economical Mutual Insurance Company

PO Box 2000
111 Westmount Rd. South
Waterloo, ON N2J 4S4
519-570-8200
Fax: 519-570-8389
800-607-2424
www.economicalinsurance.com
Ownership: Mutual company. Part of The Economical Insurance Group.
Year Founded: 1871
Number of Employees: 1,550
Classes of Insurance: Auto, Boiler & Machinery, Property, Surety
Incorporation: Federally Incorporated Insurance Company
Executives:
Noel G. Walpole, President/CEO
Jorge Arruda, Sr. Vice-President, Operations
Linda Goss, Sr. Vice-President, Chief Actuary
John Martin, Sr. Vice-President, Chief Information Officer
Sandeep Uppal, Sr. Vice-President/CFO
Dean Bulloch, Vice-President, Human Resources
Catherine Coulson, Vice-President, Sales & Marketing
Louis Durocher, Vice-President, Actuarial Services
David M. Fitzpatrick, CHRP, Vice-President, Corporate Services
Bill Lowe, Vice-President, Commercial Insurance
Rocco Nerlia, Vice-President, Claims
Michael O'Neill, Vice-President, Investments
William Stinson, Vice-President, Information Technology Operation & Subsidiaries
Directors:
Gerald A. Hooper, Chair
Mary N. Bales
A. Scott Carson
David A. Macintosh
Charles M.W. Ormston
Terry J. Reidel
Brian J. Ruby
Harold E. Seegmiller
Noel G. Walpole, FIIC
Branches:
Calgary
#2700, 801 - 6th Ave. SW
Calgary, AB T2P 3W2 Canada
403-265-8590
Fax: 403-264-2591
Debbie Archambault, Regional Vice-President, Western Region
Edmonton
#1600, 10250 - 101 St.
Edmonton, AB T5J 3P4 Canada
780-426-5925
Fax: 780-428-6166
Robert MacKay, Branch Manager
Halifax
#300, 200 Waterfront Dr.
Halifax, NS B4A 4J4 Canada
902-835-6214
Fax: 902-835-8503
Dan Spears, Regional Vice-President, Atlantic Region
Hamilton
#750, 120 King St. West
Hamilton, ON L8P 4V2 Canada
905-522-4984
Fax: 905-577-1145
Giuliano Manazzone, Branch Manager
Kitchener
590 Riverbend Dr.
Kitchener, ON N2K 3S2 Canada
519-570-8335
Fax: 519-570-8312
Terry Denomme, Branch Manager
London
Talbot Centre
#1200, 148 Fullarton St.
London, ON N6A 4Z4 Canada
519-673-5990
Fax: 519-661-0085
Linda Ewing, Branch Manager
Moncton
#200, 1600 Main St.
Moncton, NB E1E 1G5 Canada
506-857-8830
Fax: 506-853-8214
G. Fox, Branch Manager
Ottawa
#400, 333 Preston St.
Ottawa, ON K1S 5N4 Canada
613-567-7060
Fax: 613-567-6981
G. Burton, Branch Manager
Toronto - Yonge St.
#1600, 5700 Yonge St.
Toronto, ON M2M 4K2 Canada
416-590-9040
Fax: 416-590-9575
Larry Nickel, Acting Branch Manager
Toronto - York Mills Rd.
#500, 20 York Mills Rd.
Toronto, ON M2P 2C2 Canada
416-733-1777
Fax: 416-733-1463
Vern Van Dussen, Manager
Vancouver
#1900, 1055 West Georgia St
Vancouver, BC V6E 3P3 Canada
604-684-1194
Fax: 604-684-1197
Gary Harger, Branch Manager
Woodstock - Western General Farm Division
PO Box 37
#200, 959 Dundas St.
Woodstock, ON N4S 1H2 Canada
519-539-9883
Fax: 519-539-0957
800-607-2424
Ruth Zapfe, Division General Manager

Elite Insurance Company

2205 Eglinton Ave. East
Toronto, ON M1L 4S8
416-288-1800
Fax: 416-288-5888
Other Information: 800-590-5003 (Toll Free, After Hours Emergency Service, Atlantic Canada); 800-561-9899 (Toll Free, NB, 8am-5pm); 800-565-7153 (Toll Free, NS, PE, NL)
www.avivacanada.com
Ownership: Member company of Aviva Canada Inc.
Year Founded: 1954
Classes of Insurance: Personal Accident & Sickness, Aircraft, Auto, Liability, Boiler & Machinery, Marine, Fidelity, Property, Surety
Incorporation: Federally Incorporated Insurance Company
Profile: The insurer of specialty personal insurance products covers mobile homes, recreational vehicles, pleasure crafts & antique & custom cars.

Executives:
Igal Mayer, President/CEO
Branches:
Drummondville

#100, 578, rue Lindsay
Drummondville, QC J2B 1H5
819-477-3879
Fax: 819-477-0884
Vancouver
#1100, 1125 Howe St.
Vancouver, BC V6Z 2Y6 Canada
604-669-2626
Fax: 604-669-9754

Employers Insurance Company of Wausau/ Société d'assurance mutuelle des employeurs de Wau

BCE Place
#1000, 181 Bay St.
Toronto, ON M5J 2T3
416-307-4353
Fax: 416-365-7281
Former Name: Employers Insurance of Wausau - a Mutual Company
Classes of Insurance: Personal Accident & Sickness, Aircraft, Auto, Liability, Boiler & Machinery, Fidelity, Property, Surety
Incorporation: Federally Incorporated Insurance Company
Executives:
Mike Molony, Chief Agent; mike.molony@libertyiu.com

Employers Reassurance Corporation

#300, 1 University Ave.
Toronto, ON M5J 2P1
416-217-5500
Fax: 416-217-5505
800-850-8891
Classes of Insurance: Personal Accident & Sickness, Life
Incorporation: Federally Incorporated Insurance Company
Profile: The foreign life insurance company is limited to the business of reinsurance.

Executives:
Marsha Ethel Walker, Chief Agent
Alan Ryder, Sr. Vice-President

Employers Reinsurance Corporation

PO Box 50
#2200, 150 King St. West
Toronto, ON M5H 1J9
416-217-5555
Fax: 416-217-5566
www.swissre.com
Ownership: Foreign. Member of Swiss Re Group.
Classes of Insurance: Personal Accident & Sickness, Aircraft, Auto, Liability, Boiler & Machinery, Credit, Fidelity, Property, Surety, Hail & Crop
Incorporation: Federally Incorporated Insurance Company
Executives:
Peter Borst, Chief Agent

The Equitable Life Insurance Company of Canada

Also listed under: *Investment Fund Companies*
1 Westmount Rd. North
Waterloo, ON N2J 4C7
519-886-5110
Fax: 519-883-7400
800-265-8878
webmaster@equitable.ca
www.equitable.ca
Ownership: Policy-holders
Year Founded: 1920
Number of Employees: 500
Assets: $1-10 billion Year End: 20051231
Revenues: $100-500 million Year End: 20051231
Classes of Insurance: Life
Incorporation: Federally Incorporated Insurance Company
Profile: Equitable Life is an independent mutual life insurance company that offers financial products, including life insurance, annuities, group life & health coverage, retirement savings, pension plans, residential & commercial mortgages, & segregated fund investments.

Executives:
Ronald E. Beettam, FSA, FCIA, President/CEO
Douglas W. Brooks, FSA, FCIA, Sr. Vice-President/CFO
W. (Willie) A.T. Young, FCSI, FCIB, Sr. Vice-President, Investments
Christopher Brown, Vice-President, Human Resources
Michael M. Dawe, Vice-President, Individual
Karen Mason, Vice-President, Group
Harley R. Rashleigh-Berry, LL.B., Vice-President, Chief Compliance Officer, Legal Counsel & Corporate Secretary
Ravinder Singh, P.Eng., Vice-President, Information Technology, Chief Information Officer
Directors:
Ronald D. Beettam, FSA, FCIA
Rita Burak, BA, CLF
Chair, Canadian General-Tower Ltd.
Douglas L. Derry, FCA
Douglas W. Dodds, FCAM
Chair/CEO, Schneider Corp.
Maureen Farrow, FCMC
President, Economap Inc.
Paul D. Mitchell, FCA, LL.D.
Chair, Ellis-Don Constructions Ltd.
Marc J. Somerville, Q.C.
Gowling, Strathy & Henderson
Donald Stevens
Chair/CEO, Gore Mutual Insurance Company
Lee Watchorn, BSc, FSA, FCIA
David S. Weinberg
President, Scott-Bathgate Ltd.
Equitable Life:
American Growth Fund
RRSP Eligible; Inception Year: 1999; Fund Managers: McLean Budden Ltd.
Asset Allocation Fund
RRSP Eligible; Inception Year: 1994; Fund Managers: McLean Budden Ltd.
Canadian Bond Fund
RRSP Eligible; Inception Year: 1992; Fund Managers: McLean Budden Ltd.
Canadian Stock Fund
RRSP Eligible; Inception Year: 1992; Fund Managers: McLean Budden Ltd.
Templeton Global Growth Fund
RRSP Eligible; Inception Year: 1999; Fund Managers: Franklin Templeton Investments
International Fund
RRSP Eligible; Inception Year: 1994; Fund Managers: Philip Pfeifer
TaraProper
Jeff Rabb
US Equity Fund
RRSP Eligible; Inception Year: 1999; Fund Managers: Philip Pfeifer
TaraProper
Jeff Rabb
Money Market Fund
RRSP Eligible; Inception Year: 1994; Fund Managers: Philip Pfeifer
European Equity Fund
RRSP Eligible; Inception Year: 1999; Fund Managers: Philip Pfeifer
TaraProper
Jeff Rabb
John Stilo
Segregated Common Stock Fund
RRSP Eligible; Inception Year: 1983; Fund Managers: McLean Budden Ltd.
Asian-Pacific Fund
RRSP Eligible; Inception Year: 1999; Fund Managers: Philip Pfeifer
TaraProper
Jeff Rabb
John Stilo
Segregated Accumulated Income Fund
RRSP Eligible; Inception Year: 1983; Fund Managers: McLean Budden Ltd.
Canadian Equity Value Fund
RRSP Eligible; Inception Year: 1999; Fund Managers: McLean Budden Ltd.
Templeton Global Bond Fund
RRSP Eligible; Inception Year: 1999; Fund Managers: Franklin Templeton Investments
AIM Canadian Premier Fund
RRSP Eligible; Inception Year: 2004; Fund Managers: AIM Trimark Investments
Trimark Europlus Fund
RRSP Eligible; Inception Year: 2004; Fund Managers: AIM Trimark Investments
Trimark Global Balanced Fund
RRSP Eligible; Inception Year: 2004; Fund Managers: AIM Trimark Investments
Bissett Dividend Income Fund
RRSP Eligible; Inception Year: 2004; Fund Managers: Bissett Investment Management
Franklin Templeton Balanced Growth Portfolio Fund
RRSP Eligible; Inception Year: 2005; Fund Managers: Franklin Templeton Investments
Franklin Templeton Balanced Income Portfolio Fund
RRSP Eligible; Inception Year: 2005; Fund Managers: Franklin Templeton Investments
Franklin Templeton Global Growth Portfolio Fund
RRSP Eligible; Inception Year: 2005; Fund Managers: Franklin Templeton Investments
Franklin Templeton Growth Portfolio Fund
RRSP Eligible; Inception Year: 2005; Fund Managers: Franklin Templeton Investments
Franklin Templeton Maximum Growth Portfolio Fund
RRSP Eligible; Inception Year: 2005; Fund Managers: Franklin Templeton Investments
Franklin Templeton Diversified Income Portfolio Fund
RRSP Eligible; Inception Year: 2005; Fund Managers: Franklin Templeton Investments
Mackenzie Universal US Emerging Growth Fund
RRSP Eligible; Inception Year: 2004; Fund Managers: Mackenzie Financial
Regional Offices:
Calgary
MacLeod Place I
#500, 5920 MacLeod Trail South
Calgary, AB T2H 0K2 Canada
403-259-3392
Fax: 403-252-8998
888-888-8377
calgary@equitable.ca
Chris Presley, Manager, Group Marketing
Edmonton
#1668, 10303 Jasper Ave.
Edmonton, AB T5J 3N6 Canada
780-425-6622
Fax: 780-424-4496
888-999-0666
edmonton@equitable.ca
Jim Tetz, Manager, Group Marketing
Halifax
15 Bridgeview Dr.
Halifax, NS B3P 1E7 Canada
902-475-1629
Fax: 902-477-2863
866-662-6684
Greg Flack, Manager, Life Marketing
Hamilton
Village Atrium
#102, 10 George St.
Hamilton, ON L8P 1C8 Canada
905-540-9200
Fax: 905-540-9300
800-721-6887
hamilton@equitable.ca
Donna M. Plyley, Manager, Group Marketing
London
#301, 252 Pall Mall St.
London, ON N6A 5P6 Canada
519-433-0196
Fax: 519-642-7674
800-263-5559
london@equitable.ca
Doris Forbes, Manager, Group Marketing
Markham
#450, 11 Allstate Pkwy.
Markham, ON L3R 9T8 Canada
905-477-0063
Fax: 905-477-1525
800-565-6835
toronto-east@equitable.ca
Mary M. Caprio, Manager, Group Marketing
Ottawa
#312, 1545 Carling Ave.
Ottawa, ON K1Z 8P9 Canada
613-729-3174
Fax: 613-729-6448
800-704-9652
ottawa@equitable.ca
Phil DeLucia, Regional Director, Individual Sales & Distribution
Saskatoon
#208, 119 - 4th Ave. South
Saskatoon, SK S7K 5X2 Canada

The Equitable Life Insurance Company of Canada (continued)
306-664-9133
Fax: 306-664-9136
800-567-5389
prairie@equitable.ca
Adrian W. Boyko, Regional Director, Individual Sales & Distribution
Vancouver
2 Bentall Centre
PO Box 234
#1725, 555 Burrard St.
Vancouver, BC V7X 1M9 Canada
604-685-8364
Fax: 604-685-5974
800-260-3056
bc@equitable.ca
Glendine L. Skagen, Regional Director, Group Sales & Distribution
Waterloo
PO Box 1603, Waterloo Sta. Waterloo
1 Westmount Rd. North
Waterloo, ON N2J 4C7 Canada
519-746-5611
Fax: 519-746-5308
800-387-1704
k-w@equitable.ca
Lori Hederson, Manager, Group Marketing
Winnipeg
#104, 179 McDermitt Ave.
Winnipeg, MB R3B 0S1 Canada
Fax: 780-424-4496
888-999-0666
Jody Ford, Manager, Life Marketing

Erie Mutual Fire Insurance Co.

711 Main St. East
Dunnville, ON N1A 2W5
905-774-8566
Fax: 905-774-6468
800-263-6484
www.eriemutual.com
Ownership: Policyholders.
Year Founded: 1871
Classes of Insurance: Personal Accident & Sickness, Auto, Liability, Boiler & Machinery, Fidelity, Property
Incorporation: Provincially Incorporated Insurance Company
Profile: Insurance products are offered for homes, farms, condominiums, greenhouses, & tenants.

Executives:
William Holmes, President
Isaac Fry, Vice-President
J.W. Holmes, Sec.-Treas.
Directors:
Valentine Dohn
Daniel Hoover
Jacob Mehlenbacher
Solomon Moyer
Daniel Rose
Joseph Ross

Euler Hermes Canada

#1702, 1155, boul René-Lévesque ouest
Montréal, QC H3B 3Z7
514-876-9656
Fax: 514-876-9658
877-509-3224
canada.info@eulerhermes.com
www.eulerhermes.com/canada
Ownership: Public. Foreign. Owned by Euler Hermes Group
Year Founded: 1893
Number of Employees: 40
Assets: $10-50 million Year End: 20051231
Revenues: $50-100 million Year End: 20051231
Classes of Insurance: Credit
Incorporation: Federally Incorporated Insurance Company
Profile: The company specializes in credit insurance.

Executives:
Robert Labelle, Sr. Vice-President & Chief Agent, Canada; 514-876-7039; bob.labelle@eulerhermes.com
Branches:
Calgary
PO Box 28011, Cranstom RPO Sta. Cranstom RPO
Calgary, AB T3M 1K4 Canada
403-554-5437
Fax: 403-697-3773
877-511-3224
Mississauga
#507, 2085 Hurontario St.
Mississauga, ON L5A 4G1 Canada
905-615-9030
Fax: 905-615-9123
877-509-3224
St-Augustin-de-Desmaures
392, ch Plage St Laurent
Saint-Augustin-de-Desmaures, QC G3Z 2X6 Canada
418-659-5672
Fax: 659- 28-5
877-509-3224
Vancouver
#404, 999 Canada Place
Vancouver, BC V6C 3L2 Canada
604-687-6703
Fax: 604-689-8491
877-509-3224

Everest Insurance Company of Canada/ La Compagnie d'assurance Everest du Canada

The Exchange Tower
PO Box 431
#2520, 130 King St. West
Toronto, ON M5X 1E3
416-862-1228
Fax: 416-366-5899
Classes of Insurance: Aircraft, Auto, Liability, Boiler & Machinery, Credit, Marine, Property, Surety, Hail & Crop
Incorporation: Federally Incorporated Insurance Company
Executives:
William G. Jonas, President/CEO

Everest Reinsurance Company

The Exchange Tower
PO Box 431
#2520, 130 King St. West
Toronto, ON M5X 1E3
416-862-1228
Fax: 416-366-5899
www.everestre.com
Former Name: Prudential Reinsurance Company (of America)
Ownership: Part of Everest Re Group, Ltd., Liberty Corner, NJ, USA.
Year Founded: 1978
Classes of Insurance: Personal Accident & Sickness, Aircraft, Auto, Liability, Boiler & Machinery, Credit, Fidelity, Property, Surety, Hail & Crop
Incorporation: Federally Incorporated Insurance Company
Profile: The foreign property & casualty insurance company is limited to the business of reinsurance.
Executives:
William G. Jonas, Chief Agent; bill.jonas@everestre.com

Farmers' Mutual Insurance Company (Lindsay)

PO Box 28
336 Angeline St. South
Lindsay, ON K9V 4R8
705-324-2146
Fax: 705-324-2356
800-461-0310
www.farmerslindsay.com
Year Founded: 1895
Classes of Insurance: Personal Accident & Sickness, Auto, Liability, Boiler & Machinery, Marine, Fidelity, Property
Incorporation: Provincially Incorporated Insurance Company
Profile: The company also provides commercial insurance.

Directors:
Tim Shauf, CEO
Robert Lightbody, President
Wayne Strachan, Vice-President
Mike Whittamore, 2nd Vice-President
Steve Carruthers
Rick Carter
Terry Malcolm
Fred McIntyre
Murray Moore
Hugh Snoddon

Federal Insurance Company

One Financial Place
1 Adelaide St. East
Toronto, ON M5C 2V9
416-863-0550
Fax: 416-863-5010
gdamiano@chubb.com
www.chubb.com/international/canada
Year Founded: 1901
Classes of Insurance: Personal Accident & Sickness, Auto, Liability, Boiler & Machinery, Marine, Fidelity, Property, Surety
Incorporation: Federally Incorporated Insurance Company
Executives:
Ellen J. Moore, Chief Agent

Federated Insurance Company of Canada

PO Box 5800
717 Portage Ave.
Winnipeg, MB R3C 3C9
204-786-6431
Fax: 204-784-6755
800-665-1934
webmaster@federated.ca
www.federated.ca
Ownership: Private. Wholly owned by Northbridge Financial Corporation.
Year Founded: 1987
Number of Employees: 321
Assets: $389,000,000 Year End: 20051231
Revenues: $132,000,000 Year End: 20051231
Classes of Insurance: Accident, Auto, Liability, Boiler & Machinery, Fidelity, Property, Fire, Surety, Theft
Incorporation: Federally Incorporated Insurance Company
Branches:
Calgary
2443 Pegasus Rd. NE
Calgary, AB T2E 8C3 Canada
403-254-8500
Fax: 403-254-8806
800-342-9157
Edmonton
#730, 5555 Calgary Trail NW
Edmonton, AB T6H 5N9 Canada
780-435-3064
Fax: 780-435-3992
800-661-8617

Laval
#660, 3100, boul Le Carrefour
Laval, QC H7T 2K7 Canada
450-687-8650
Fax: 450-687-6663
800-361-0790
London
#200, 735 Wonderland Rd. North
London, ON N6H 4L1 Canada
519-473-5610
Fax: 519-473-5815
800-461-3117
Mississauga
#710, 5770 Hurontario St.
Mississauga, ON L5R 3G5 Canada
905-507-2777
Fax: 905-507-2788
800-361-0790
New Westminster
#201, 604 Columbia St.
New Westminster, BC V3M 1A5 Canada
604-540-8645
Fax: 604-540-9521
800-939-7788
Saskatoon
#31, 1736 Quebec Ave.
Saskatoon, SK S7K 1V9 Canada
306-244-4131
Fax: 306-664-6400
866-291-0523

Federation Insurance Company of Canada/ La Fédération Compagnie d'Assurances du Canada

#500, 1000, de la Gauchetière ouest
Montréal, QC H3B 4W5
514-875-5790
Fax: 514-875-9769
800-361-7573
admin@federation.ca
www.federation.ca
Ownership: Private. Owned by Economical Mutual Insurance Company
Year Founded: 1947
Number of Employees: 340
Assets: $100-500 million Year End: 20041231
Revenues: $100-500 million Year End: 20041231

Classes of Insurance: Accident, Legal Expense, Auto, Liability, Boiler & Machinery, Fidelity, Property, Fire, Surety, Hail & Crop
Incorporation: Federally Incorporated Insurance Company
Executives:
Noel G. Walpole, President/CEO
Ron Pavelack, Exec. Vice-President/COO
Michel Bédard, Vice-President, Underwriting
M. Chevalier, Vice-President, Business Development
G. Langlois, CA, Vice-President, Finance
Ian C. Wismer, Corporate Secretary
P.H. Sims, Chair
Branches:
Montréal
#500, 1000, de la Gauchetière ouest
Montréal, QC H3B 4W5 Canada
514-875-5790
Fax: 514-875-9769
G. Pelletier, Manager
Ottawa
#1000, 427 Laurier Ave. West
Ottawa, ON K1R 7Y2 Canada
613-236-7234
Fax: 613-236-8912
800-267-9588
Gary Burton, Manager
Tillsonburg
PO Box 187
38 Brock St. East
Tillsonburg, ON N4G 1Z5 Canada
519-688-3344
Fax: 519-842-6072
800-265-6040
Don Courtney, Manager
Toronto
5700 Yonge St., 16th Fl.
Toronto, ON M2M 4K2 Canada
416-218-6906
Fax: 416-590-0656
800-847-8062
Mirella Sood, Manager
Vancouver
Royal Centre
#1900, 1055 West Georgia St.
Vancouver, BC V6E 3P3 Canada
604-681-2048
Fax: 604-681-2058
800-801-2048
Gary Norga, Manager

First Canadian Title
2235 Sheridan Garden Dr.
Oakville, ON L6J 7Y5
905-287-1000
Fax: 905-287-2400
800-307-0370
www.firstcanadiantitle.com
Ownership: Foreign. Owned by First American Title Insurance Company
Year Founded: 1991
Number of Employees: 500+
Incorporation: Federally Incorporated Insurance Company
Profile: The company offers title insurance for both residential & commercial transactions.
Executives:
Thomas H. Grifferty, CEO
Patrick J. Chetcuti, President/COO
Mark Harmsworth, Sr. Vice-President/CFO
Michael LeBlanc, Sr. Vice-President
David Wybrow, Sr. Vice-President
Gary Ford, Vice-President, Sales & Marketing
Susan Leslie, Vice-President, Claims & Underwriting
Barbara Locke-Geier, Vice-President, Legal
John Rider, Vice-President, Commercial Division
Eric Haslett, Asst. Vice-President, Commercial Division
Howard Turk, Asst. Vice-President, Businesss Development
Branches:
Calgary - Western Region
#1120, 639 Fifth Ave. SW
Calgary, AB T2P 0M9 Canada
403-265-4088
Fax: 403-232-1411
800-771-4313
Lisha Dodsworth, Regional Sales Manager, Prairies
Dartmouth - Atlantic Region
#530, 33 Alderney Dr.
Dartmouth, NS B2Y 2N4 Canada
902-464-0024
Fax: 902-469-0986
888-418-1010
Debra Shepherd, Regional Sales Manager, Atlantic Canada
Montréal - Québec Region
#500, 6505 TransCanada Hwy.
Montréal, QC H4T 1S3 Canada
514-744-1509
Fax: 514-744-2881
800-735-8771
Line Robillard, Regional Sales Manager, QC

First North American Insurance Company
#1600, 5650 Yonge St.
Toronto, ON M2M 4G4
800-668-0195
am_service@manulife.com
www.manulife.ca
Ownership: Wholly owned subsidiary of Manulife Financial
Classes of Insurance: Personal Accident & Sickness, Auto, Property
Incorporation: Federally Incorporated Insurance Company
Executives:
Steve M. Dobronyi, President/CEO

FM Global
#500, 165 Commerce Valley Dr. West
Thornhill, ON L3T 7V8
905-763-5555
Fax: 905-763-5556
www.fmglobal.com
Former Name: Allendale Mutual Insurance Company
Also Known As: FM Global
Ownership: Foreign. Factory Mutual Insurance Company
Year Founded: 1835
Number of Employees: 200
Assets: $500m-1 billion Year End: 20041231
Revenues: $100-500 million Year End: 20041231
Classes of Insurance: Boiler & Machinery, Property
Incorporation: Federally Incorporated Insurance Company
Profile: Global provides property insurance & loss control management to companies within the manufacturing & service industries.
Executives:
Shivan S. Subramaniam, President/CEO
Ruud H. Bosman, Exec. Vice-President
Brian J. Hurley, Exec. Vice-President
Perry R. Brazeau, Sr. Vice-President, Manager, Canadian Operations
Directors:
Walter J. Galvin
Mary L. Howell
John A. Luke, Jr.
Gracie C. Martore
Robert J. O'Toole
James W. Owens
David Pulman
Elisabeth Struckwell
Shivan S. Subramaniam
James C. Thyen
Alfred J. Verrecchia
Affiliated Companies:
Affiliated FM Insurance Company
Branches:
Montréal
600, rue de la Gauchetière ouest, 14e étage
Montréal, QC H3B 4L8 Canada
514-876-7400
Fax: 514-876-7497
Benoit Charbonneau, Vice-President & Manager, Operations
Thornhill
#500, 165 Commerce Valley Dr.
Thornhill, ON L3T 7V8 Canada
905-763-5555
Fax: 905-763-5556
David M. Thompson, Vice-President & Manager, Operations
Vancouver
Bentall 5
#1028, 550 Burrard St.
Vancouver, BC V6C 2B5 Canada
604-688-8581
Fax: 604-688-6446
Marc Ragazzi, Manager

FNF Canada
2700 Argentia Rd.
Mississauga, ON L5N 5V4
905-821-2262
Fax: 905-821-7918
877-526-3232
info@fnf.ca
www.fnf.ca
Incorporation: Federally Incorporated Insurance Company
Profile: Title insurance is offered.
Executives:
Gary Patrick Mooney, President/CEO

Folksamerica Reinsurance Company
#1202, 80 Bloor St. West
Toronto, ON M5S 2V1
416-961-0400
Fax: 416-961-5797
marketing@folksamerica.com
www.folksamerica.com
Former Name: Christiana General Insurance Corporation
Ownership: Subsidiary of White Mountains Re Group, Ltd., USA
Year Founded: 1980
Classes of Insurance: Auto, Liability, Fidelity, Property, Surety, Hail & Crop
Incorporation: Federally Incorporated Insurance Company
Executives:
John Game, Sr. Vice-President, Chief Agent;
John_Game@folksamerica.com
Gina Ferris, Vice-President, Underwriting

Fonds d'assurance responsabilité professionnelle de la Chambre des notaires du Québec
#1500, 1200, av McGill College
Montréal, QC H3B 4G7
514-871-4999
Fax: 514-879-1781
www.cdnq.org
Year Founded: 1991
Incorporation: Federally Incorporated Insurance Company
Executives:
Marlène Ouellet, President
André Auclair, Vice-President
Paulette Legauld, General Director

Fonds d'assurance responsabilité professionnelle du Barreau du Québec
#550, 445, boul Saint-Laurent
Montréal, QC H2Y 3T8
514-954-3452
Fax: 514-954-3454
Other Information: Toll Free: 1-800-361-8495, poste 3280
info@assurance-barreau.com
www.assurance-barreau.com
Former Name: Barreau du Québec
Year Founded: 1988
Incorporation: Provincially Incorporated Insurance Company
Executives:
René Langlois, Directeur général

Frank Cowan Company Limited
4 Cowan St. East
Princeton, ON N0J 1V0
519-458-4331
Fax: 519-458-4366
800-265-4000
mail@frankcowan.com
www.frankcowan.com
Ownership: Wholly owned subsidiary of The Cowan Insurance Group, Waterloo, ON.
Year Founded: 1927
Classes of Insurance: Liability
Incorporation: Provincially Incorporated Insurance Company
Executives:
Derek Sarluis, Vice-President, Claims

Fundy Mutual Insurance Company
1022 Main St.
Sussex, NB E4E 2M3
506-432-1535
Fax: 506-433-6788
800-222-9550
info@fundymutual.com
www.fundymutual.com

Fundy Mutual Insurance Company (continued)
Year Founded: 1940
Classes of Insurance: Auto, Liability, Boiler & Machinery, Property
Incorporation: Provincially Incorporated Insurance Company
Profile: The company offers the following types of insurance: residential & tenant, automobile, commercial & farm.

Executives:
Jim Wilson, General Manager; Jim.Wilson@fundymutual.com
David Ehrhardt, Manager, Underwriting; David.Ehrhardt@fundymutual.com
Branches:
Grand Bay-Westfield
201 River Valley Dr.
Grand Bay-Westfield, NB E5K 1A3 Canada
506-738-8500
David Beckett, Agent
Hampton
#1, 8 Centennial Dr.
Hampton, NB E5N 6N2 Canada
506-832-5925
Sheryl Moore, Agent
Rothesay
53C Clark Rd.
Rothesay, NB E2E 2K8
506-849-3833
Edgar Young, Agent

GAN Assurances Vie Compagnie française d'assurances vie mixte

#1470, 1155, rue Metcalfe
Montréal, QC H3B 2V6
514-286-9007
eclark@bellnet.ca
Former Name: GAN VIE, Compagnie Française d'Assurance sur la Vie
Ownership: Foreign
Classes of Insurance: Life
Incorporation: Federally Incorporated Insurance Company
Profile: The company is limited to servicing existing policies.

Executives:
Eric L. Clark, Chief Agent

GCAN Insurance Company(GCAN)/ GCAN compagnie d'assurances

#1000, 181 University Ave.
Toronto, ON M5H 3M7
416-682-5300
Fax: 416-682-9213
head.office@gcan.ca
www.gcan.ca
Former Name: Gerling Canada Insurance Company
Ownership: Teachers' Private Capital (investment arm of the Ontario Teachers' Pension Plan).
Year Founded: 1955
Classes of Insurance: Personal Accident & Sickness, Aircraft, Auto, Liability, Boiler & Machinery, Credit, Marine, Fidelity, Property, Surety, Hail & Crop
Incorporation: Provincially Incorporated Insurance Company
Profile: The insurance company offers a range of commercial insurance coverages. Both monoline policies & combined business policies are provided. Protection is provided to commercial & industrial companies.

Executives:
David Huebel, President/CEO
Branches:
Calgary - Western Regional Office
Petro-Canada Centre
#3640, 150 - 6th Ave. SW
Calgary, AB T2P 3Y7 Canada
403-265-9161
Fax: 403-233-7217
western.office@gcan.ca
Montréal - Québec Regional Office
#1011, 1001, rue du Square-Dorchester
Montréal, QC H3B 1N1 Canada
514-286-9333
Fax: 514-286-1141
quebec.office@gcan.ca
Toronto - Central Regional Office
#1000, 181 University Ave.
Toronto, ON M5H 3M7 Canada
416-682-5300
Fax: 416-682-9213
central.office@gcan.ca
Vancouver - Pacific Regional Office
#1101, 750 West Pender St.
Vancouver, BC V6C 2T8 Canada
604-687-8700
Fax: 604-684-9609
pacific.office@gcan.ca

General American Life Insurance Company(GALIC)

c/o RGA Life Reinsurance Company of Canada
#1000, 1255, rue Peel
Montréal, QC H3B 2T9
514-985-5260
Fax: 514-985-3066
800-985-4326
mail@rgare.ca
Ownership: Foreign branch of General America Life Insurance Company, USA.
Assets: $1-10 billion Year End: 20051231
Revenues: $100-500 million Year End: 20051231
Classes of Insurance: Life, Reinsurance
Incorporation: Federally Incorporated Insurance Company
Profile: The company services individuals & groups of employers with life & health insurance as well as retirement & related financial services. GALIC provides reinsurance & investment services to other insurance companies. Life reinsurance represents 99% of business.

Executives:
André St-Amour, Chairman
Alain Neemeh, President/CEO

General Reinsurance Corporation

PO Box 471
#5705, 1 First Canadian Pl.
Toronto, ON M5X 1E4
416-869-0490
Fax: 416-360-2020
AskGenRe@genre.com
www.genre.com
Also Known As: Gen Re
Ownership: General Re Corporation, Stamford, CT, USA.
Classes of Insurance: Personal Accident & Sickness, Aircraft, Auto, Liability, Boiler & Machinery, Credit, Fidelity, Property, Surety, Hail & Crop
Incorporation: Federally Incorporated Insurance Company
Executives:
Matthew Spensieri, Chief Agent, Canada
Kathy A. MacDonald, Vice-President
Gavin C. Rowatt, Vice-President, Manager
Valerie J. Sheehy, Vice-President, Manager
J. David Smith, Vice-President
Kacy Crumb, Second Vice-President
Murray McCutcheon, Second Vice-President
Christopher E. Walton, Second Vice-President
Mary M. Williams, Second Vice-President
Branches:
Montréal
#2000, 1002, rue Sherbrooke ouest
Montréal, QC H3A 3L6 Canada
514-288-9667
Fax: 514-288-6751
Claudine Gendron, Vice-President

Genworth Financial Mortgage Insurance Company Canada

#300, 2060 Winston Park Drive
Oakville, ON L6HL5N 5P9
800-511-8888
mortgage.info@genworth.com
www.gemortgage.ca
Former Name: GE Capital Mortgage Insurance Company (Canada)
Also Known As: Genworth Financial Canada
Year Founded: 1995
Incorporation: Federally Incorporated Insurance Company
Profile: The company offers mortgage default insurance products for the purchase, renovation or refinancing of homes.

Executives:
Peter M. Vukanovich, CEO, Corporate Officer

Gerber Life Insurance Company

PO Box 986, F Stn. F
50 Charles St. East
Toronto, ON M4Y 2T2
800-518-8884
Classes of Insurance: Life
Incorporation: Federally Incorporated Insurance Company

Germania Farmers' Mutual Fire Insurance Company

PO Box 30
610 Alfred St.
Ayton, ON N0G 1C0
519-665-7715
Fax: 519-665-7558
800-265-3433
info@germaniamutual.com
www.germaniamutual.com
Ownership: Policyholders.
Year Founded: 1878
Classes of Insurance: Personal Accident & Sickness, Auto, Liability, Boiler & Machinery, Fidelity, Property
Incorporation: Provincially Incorporated Insurance Company
Executives:
Dan Hill, CIP, General Manager, Sec.-Treas.
Directors:
Carol Leibold, President
Lawrie Weppler, Vice-President
John Cummings
John Flanagan
Mary Golem
Wayne Lytle
Dale Pallister
Bev Schenk

Germania Mutual Insurance Company

PO Box 57
423 Kaiser William Ave.
Langenburg, SK S0A 2A0
306-743-5363
Fax: 306-743-2250
germania@sasktel.net
Year Founded: 1909
Number of Employees: 4
Revenues: Under $1 million Year End: 20041130
Classes of Insurance: Liability, Property, Fire, Theft
Incorporation: Provincially Incorporated Insurance Company
Executives:
Don Layh, President
Ernest Mitterhuber, Vice-President
Ron Buchberger, Sec.-Manager
Directors:
Jason Remus
M. Roden
Harold Yeske
Michelle Yeske

Glengarry Farmers' Mutual Fire Insurance Co.

PO Box 159
57 Main St. North
Alexandria, ON K0C 1A0
613-525-2557
Fax: 613-525-5162
800-263-7684
glenins@glenins.ca
www.glenins.ca
Ownership: Policy-holders
Year Founded: 1895
Number of Employees: 10
Assets: $5-10 million
Revenues: $5-10 million
Classes of Insurance: Personal Accident & Sickness, Legal Expense, Auto, Liability, Boiler & Machinery, Fidelity, Property, Fire, Theft
Incorporation: Provincially Incorporated Insurance Company
Executives:
Brian Fisher, Manager
Directors:
Richard Allinotte
Allan Barton
Gary Bradley
Jean Dewar
John Hope
Murray Howes
Michel Lalonde
Harold MacLeod
Finlay McDonnell
Alex McNaughton
Denis Pommainville
Jacques Tranchemontagne

Global Aerospace Underwriting Managers (Canada) Limited

#200, 100 Renfrew Dr.
Markham, ON L3R 9R6

905-479-2244
Fax: 905-479-0751
Jzigrossi@global-aero.com
www.global-aero.co.uk
Former Name: British Aviation Insurance Group; Associated Aviation Underwriters
Ownership: Foreign. Owned by Global Aerospace Underwriting Managers, London, UK.
Year Founded: 1930
Classes of Insurance: Personal Accident & Sickness, Aircraft, Liability, Property
Incorporation: Federally Incorporated Insurance Company
Profile: The aviation insurance group was formed with the merger of British Aviation Insurance Group & Associated Aviation Underwriters.

Executives:
Joseph Zigrossi, President/CEO, Chief Agent; jzigrossi@global-aero.ca

Gore Mutual Insurance Company
PO Box 70, Galt Stn. Galt
262 Dundas St.
Cambridge, ON N1R 5T3
519-623-1910
800-265-8600
webserver@goremutual.ca
www.goremutual.ca
Ownership: Mutual company
Year Founded: 1839
Number of Employees: 215
Assets: $100-500 million
Revenues: $100-500 million
Classes of Insurance: Personal Accident & Sickness, Auto, Liability, Property, Fire, Theft
Incorporation: Federally Incorporated Insurance Company
Profile: Gore Mutual offers property & casualty insurance, primarily to individuals & to small & medium-sized businesses. Marketing is through independent brokers.

Executives:
William E. Hetherington, Chair
Kevin W. McNeil, President/CEO
Lorne Motton, BBA, CA, CFO & Secretary
Barry M. Kennedy, CIP, Vice-President, Marketing & Regional Operations
Jamie McDougall, Vice-President, Claims
Ross McMaster, Vice-President, Human Resources
Richard Meertens, MBA, PMP, CMC, Vice-President, Information Technology
Heidi Sevcik, FCIP, Vice-President, Underwriting
Directors:
Charles A. Cipolla
Joan S. Fisk
Peter A.W. Green
C. Thomas LeBrun
Lorna R. Marsden, Ph.D.
Ross A. Morrison
Regional Offices:
Vancouver - British Columbia
One Bentall Centre
#1780, 505 Burrard St.
Vancouver, BC V7X 1M6 Canada
604-682-0998
Fax: 604-682-8798
800-663-9437
Terri Johnson, Vice-President & General Manager, B.C. Region

Grain Insurance & Guarantee Company
#1240, One Lombard Place
Winnipeg, MB R3B 0V9
204-943-0721
Fax: 204-943-6419
800-665-3351
fewilliams@graininsurance.com
www.graininsurance.com
Ownership: Private
Year Founded: 1919
Number of Employees: 60
Assets: $50-100 million Year End: 20041231
Revenues: $52,000,000 Year End: 20041231
Classes of Insurance: Liability, Boiler & Machinery, Fidelity, Property, Fire, Surety, Theft
Incorporation: Federally Incorporated Insurance Company
Executives:
Ralph N. Jackson, President/General Manager
G.W. Dyson, Vice-President, Marketing
C.L. Madden, Vice-President, Underwriting
F.E. Williams, Vice-President, Finance & Secretary
Directors:
C.R. Vossen, Chair
Ralph N. Jackson
S. Mielitz
W.S. Parrish
A.B. Paterson
L. Penner
L.O. Pollard
F.E. Williams
J.W. Zacharias
Branches:
Halifax
#1209, 1505 Barrington St.
Halifax, NS B3J 3K5 Canada
902-425-9228
Fax: 902-425-9291
K. Weeks, Manager
London
1750 Ernest Ave., 2nd Fl.
London, ON N6E 3H3 Canada
519-433-9991
Fax: 519-433-7666
J. Demarais, Manager
Regina
2150 Scarth St.
Regina, SK S4P 2H7 Canada
306-757-1691
Fax: 306-359-6440
N. McGregor, Manager

The Grand Orange Lodge of British America Beneficent Fund
94 Sheppard Ave. West
Toronto, ON M2N 1M5
416-223-1690
Fax: 416-223-1324
800-565-6248
info@grandorangelodge.ca
www.grandorangelodge.ca
Also Known As: Orange Insurance
Ownership: Private
Year Founded: 1881
Classes of Insurance: Life
Incorporation: Federally Incorporated Insurance Company
Executives:
James Bell, CEO
William Johnston, President

Granite Insurance Company
#200, 2 Eva Rd.
Toronto, ON M9C 2A8
416-622-0660
Fax: 416-622-8809
800-342-5243
dsymons@gorancapital.com
Ownership: Public
Year Founded: 1964
Number of Employees: 9
Classes of Insurance: Accident, Personal Accident & Sickness, Auto, Liability, Boiler & Machinery, Credit, Fidelity, Property, Fire, Surety, Hail & Crop, Theft
Incorporation: Federally Incorporated Insurance Company
Executives:
Douglas H. Symons, CEO

Great American Insurance Company
c/o Cassels, Brock & Blackwell, Scotia Plaza
#2100, 40 King St. West
Toronto, ON M5H 3C2
416-869-5300
Fax: 416-360-8877
Ownership: Foreign. Part of Great American Insurance Group, Cincinnati, OH, USA.
Classes of Insurance: Personal Accident & Sickness, Aircraft, Auto, Liability, Boiler & Machinery, Marine, Fidelity, Property, Surety, Hail & Crop
Incorporation: Federally Incorporated Insurance Company

Executives:
J. Brian Reeve, Chief Agent

The Great-West Life Assurance Company(GWL)/ Great-West, Compagnie d'Assurance Vie
Also listed under: *Investment Fund Companies*
PO Box 6000
100 Osborne St. North
Winnipeg, MB R3C 3A5
204-946-1190
Fax: 204-946-4159
800-665-5758
www.greatwestlife.com
Ownership: Major shareholder Great-West Lifeco (100% interest)
Year Founded: 1891
Number of Employees: 5,740
Assets: $10-100 billion Year End: 20051231
Revenues: $10-100 billion Year End: 20051231
Stock Symbol: GWO
Classes of Insurance: Personal Accident & Sickness, Life
Profile: GWL is a leading Canadian insurer which operates a broad portfolio of financial security & benefit plan solutions for individuals, families, businesses & organizations. In addition to its domestic operations, the company is a supplier of reinsurance & specialty general insurance. A subsidiary is London Insurance Group Inc.

Executives:
Raymond L. McFeetors, President/CEO
Denis J. Devos, Chief Operating Officer
Dave Johnston, Exec. Vice-President, Group
Allen Loney, Exec. Vice-President & Chief Actuary, Capital Management
William W. Lovatt, Exec. Vice-President/CFO
Peter G. Munro, Exec. Vice-President & Chief Investment Officer

Ronald D. Saull, Sr. Vice-President & Chief Information Officer
Sheila A. Wagar, Sr. Vice-President, General Counsel & Secretary
Directors:
Robert Gratton, Chair
President/CEO, Power Financial Corporation
Gail S. Asper
Corporate Secretary, CanWest Global Communications Corp.
Orest T. Dackow
André Desmarais
President/Co-CEO, Power Corporation of Canada; Deputy Chair, Power Financial Cor
Paul Desmarais, Jr.
Chair/Co-CEO, Power Corporation of Canada; Chair, Power Financial Corporation
Michael Hepher
Daniel Johnson
Counsel to McCarthy Tétrault
Kevin P. Kavanagh, O.C.
Chancellor, University of Brandon
Peter Kruyt
Donald F. Mazankowski, O.C.
William T. McCallum
President/CEO, Great-West Life & Annuity Insurance Company; Co-President/CEO, Gr
Raymond L. McFeetors
President/CEO, The Great-West Assurance Co.; President/CEO, London Life Insuranc
Jerry E.A. Nickerson
Chair, H.B. Nickerson & Sons Limited
David Nield
R. Jeffrey Orr
President/CEO, Investors Group Inc.
Michel Plessis-Bélair, FCA
Vice-Chair/CFO, Power Corporation of Canada; Exec. Vice-President/CFO, Power Fin
Guy St-Germain, CM
President, Placements Laugerma inc.
Emőke Szathmáry
Murray Taylor
Gérard Veilleux, O.C.
President, Power Communications Inc.
Affiliated Companies:
Canada Life Financial Corporation
GWL Realty Advisors
London Life Insurance Company
GWL:
Advanced Portfolio DSC Fund
RRSP Eligible; Inception Year: 1996; Fund Managers: GWL Investment Management Ltd.

INSURANCE COMPANIES

The Great-West Life Assurance Company(GWL)/ Great-West, Compagnie d'Assurance Vie (continued)

Advanced Portfolio NL Fund
RRSP Eligible; Inception Year: 1996; Fund Managers:
GWL Investment Management Ltd.
Aggressive Portfolio DSC Fund
RRSP Eligible; Inception Year: 1996; Fund Managers:
GWL Investment Management Ltd.
Aggressive Portfolio NL Fund
RRSP Eligible; Inception Year: 1996; Fund Managers:
GWL Investment Management Ltd.
American Growth A-DSC Fund
RRSP Eligible; Inception Year: 1997; Fund Managers:
AGF Funds Inc.
American Growth A-NL Fund
RRSP Eligible; Inception Year: 1997; Fund Managers:
AGF Funds Inc.
Asian Growth A-DSC Fund
RRSP Eligible; Inception Year: 1997; Fund Managers:
AGF Funds Inc.
Asian Growth A-NL Fund
RRSP Eligible; Inception Year: 1997; Fund Managers:
AGF Funds Inc.
Balanced AT-DSC Fund
RRSP Eligible; Inception Year: 1996; Fund Managers:
Aim Trimark Investments
Balanced B-NL Fund
RRSP Eligible; Inception Year: 1996; Fund Managers:
Beutel Goodman & Co. Ltd.
Balanced B-DSC Fund
RRSP Eligible; Inception Year: 1996; Fund Managers:
Beutel Goodman & Co. Ltd.
Balanced AT-NL Fund
RRSP Eligible; Inception Year: 1996; Fund Managers:
Aim Trimark Investments
Balanced Portfolio NL Fund
RRSP Eligible; Inception Year: 1996; Fund Managers:
GWL Investment Management Ltd.
Balanced Portfolio DSC Fund
RRSP Eligible; Inception Year: 1996; Fund Managers:
GWL Investment Management Ltd.
Bond B-DSC Fund
RRSP Eligible; Inception Year: 1996; Fund Managers:
Beutel Goodman & Co. Ltd.
Bond B-NL Fund
RRSP Eligible; Inception Year: 1996; Fund Managers:
Beutel Goodman & Co. Ltd.
Bond L-DSC Fund
RRSP Eligible; Inception Year: 1996; Fund Managers:
London Life Investment Management Inc.
Bond L-NL Fund
RRSP Eligible; Inception Year: 1996; Fund Managers:
London Life Investment Management Inc.
Canadian Bond G-DSC Fund
RRSP Eligible; Inception Year: 1979; Fund Managers:
GWL Investment Management Ltd.
Canadian Bond G-NL Fund
RRSP Eligible; Inception Year: 1979; Fund Managers:
GWL Investment Management Ltd.
Canadian Equity G-DSC Fund
RRSP Eligible; Inception Year: 1987; Fund Managers:
GWL Investment Management Ltd.
Canadian Equity G-NL Fund
RRSP Eligible; Inception Year: 1987; Fund Managers:
GWL Investment Management Ltd.
Canadian Opportunity M-DSC Fund
RRSP Eligible; Inception Year: 1997; Fund Managers:
Mackenzie Financial Corp.
Canadian Opportunity M-NL Fund
RRSP Eligible; Inception Year: 1997; Fund Managers:
Mackenzie Financial Corp.
Canadian Resource A-DSC Fund
RRSP Eligible; Inception Year: 1996; Fund Managers:
AGF Funds Inc.
Canadian Resource A-NL Fund
RRSP Eligible; Inception Year: 1996; Fund Managers:
AGF Funds Inc.
Conservative Portfolio G-DSC Fund
RRSP Eligible; Inception Year: 1996; Fund Managers:
GWL Investment Management Ltd.
Conservative Portfolio G-NL Fund
RRSP Eligible; Inception Year: 1996; Fund Managers:
GWL Investment Management Ltd.
Diversified G-DSC Fund
RRSP Eligible; Inception Year: 1985; Fund Managers:
GWL Investment Management Ltd.
Diversified G-NL Fund
RRSP Eligible; Inception Year: 1988; Fund Managers:
GWL Investment Management Ltd.
Dividend G-NL Fund
RRSP Eligible; Inception Year: 1997; Fund Managers:
GWL Investment Management Ltd.
Dividend G-DSC Fund
RRSP Eligible; Inception Year: 1997; Fund Managers:
GWL Investment Management Ltd.
Equity M-DSC Fund
RRSP Eligible; Inception Year: 1996; Fund Managers:
Mackenzie Financial Corp.
Equity M-NL Fund
RRSP Eligible; Inception Year: 1996; Fund Managers:
Mackenzie Financial Corp.
Equity Index G-DSC Fund
RRSP Eligible; Inception Year: 1994; Fund Managers:
GWL Investment Management Ltd.
Equity Index G-NL Fund
RRSP Eligible; Inception Year: 1989; Fund Managers:
GWL Investment Management Ltd.
Equity/Bond G-DSC Fund
RRSP Eligible; Inception Year: 1994; Fund Managers:
GWL Investment Management Ltd.
Equity/Bond G-NL Fund
RRSP Eligible; Inception Year: 1988; Fund Managers:
GWL Investment Management Ltd.
European Equity S-DSC Fund
RRSP Eligible; Inception Year: 1997; Fund Managers:
Setanta Asset Management
European Equity S-NL Fund
RRSP Eligible; Inception Year: 1997; Fund Managers:
Setanta Asset Management
Global Income A-DSC Fund
RRSP Eligible; Inception Year: 1996; Fund Managers:
AGF Funds Inc.
Government Bond G-NL Fund
RRSP Eligible; Inception Year: 1994; Fund Managers:
GWL Investment Management Ltd.
Growth & Income A-DSC Fund
RRSP Eligible; Inception Year: 1996; Fund Managers:
AGF Funds Inc.
Growth & Income A-NL Fund
RRSP Eligible; Inception Year: 1996; Fund Managers:
AGF Funds Inc.
Growth & Income M-DSC Fund
RRSP Eligible; Inception Year: 1996; Fund Managers:
Mackenzie Financial Corp.
Growth & Income M-NL Fund
RRSP Eligible; Inception Year: 1996; Fund Managers:
Mackenzie Financial Corp.
Income M-DSC Fund
RRSP Eligible; Inception Year: 1996; Fund Managers:
Mackenzie Financial Corp.
Income M-NL Fund
RRSP Eligible; Inception Year: 1996; Fund Managers:
Mackenzie Financial Corp.
Growth Equity A-DSC Fund
RRSP Eligible; Inception Year: 1996; Fund Managers:
AGF Funds Inc.
Growth Equity A-NL Fund
RRSP Eligible; Inception Year: 1996; Fund Managers:
AGF Funds Inc.
Income G-NL Fund
RRSP Eligible; Inception Year: 1994; Fund Managers:
GWL Investment Management Ltd.
International Equity F-DSC Fund
RRSP Eligible; Inception Year: 1994;
International Equity F-NL Fund
RRSP Eligible; Inception Year: 1994;
International Opportunity F-NL Fund
RRSP Eligible; Inception Year: 1997; Fund Managers:
J.P. Morgan Fleming Asset Management
International Bond BW-DSC Fund
RRSP Eligible; Inception Year: 1994; Fund Managers:
Brandywine Asset Management
International Bond BW-NL Fund
RRSP Eligible; Inception Year: 1994; Fund Managers:
Brandywine Asset Management
Larger Company M-DSC Fund
RRSP Eligible; Inception Year: 1996; Fund Managers:
Mackenzie Financial Corp.
Larger Company M-NL Fund
RRSP Eligible; Inception Year: 1996; Fund Managers:
Mackenzie Financial Corp.
Mid Cap Canada G-DSC Fund
RRSP Eligible; Inception Year: 1997; Fund Managers:
GWL Investment Management Ltd.
Moderate Portfolio DSC Fund
RRSP Eligible; Inception Year: 1996; Fund Managers:
GWL Investment Management Ltd.
Moderate Portfolio NL Fund
RRSP Eligible; Inception Year: 1996; Fund Managers:
GWL Investment Management Ltd.
Money Market G-DSC Fund
RRSP Eligible; Inception Year: 1989; Fund Managers:
GWL Investment Management Ltd.
Money Market G-NL Fund
RRSP Eligible; Inception Year: 1989; Fund Managers:
GWL Investment Management Ltd.
Mortgage G-DSC Fund
RRSP Eligible; Inception Year: 1994; Fund Managers:
GWL Investment Management Ltd.
Mortgage G-NL Fund
RRSP Eligible; Inception Year: 1989; Fund Managers:
GWL Investment Management Ltd.
Government Bond G-DSC Fund
RRSP Eligible; Inception Year: 1994; Fund Managers:
GWL Investment Management Ltd.
Real Estate G-DSC Fund
RRSP Eligible; Inception Year: 1994; Fund Managers:
GWL Investment Management Ltd.
US Equity G-NL Fund
RRSP Eligible; Inception Year: 1994; Fund Managers:
GWL Investment Management Ltd.
US Equity G-DSC Fund
RRSP Eligible; Inception Year: 1994; Fund Managers:
GWL Investment Management Ltd.
Real Estate G-NL Fund
RRSP Eligible; Inception Year: 1989; Fund Managers:
GWL Investment Management Ltd.
Smaller Company M-DSC Fund
RRSP Eligible; Inception Year: 1996; Fund Managers:
Mackenzie Financial Corp.
Smaller Company M-NL Fund
RRSP Eligible; Inception Year: 1996; Fund Managers:
Mackenzie Financial Corp.
N.A. Equity B-DSC Fund
RRSP Eligible; Inception Year: 1996; Fund Managers:
Beutel Goodman & Co. Ltd.
N.A. Equity B-NL Fund
RRSP Eligible; Inception Year: 1996; Fund Managers:
Beutel Goodman & Co. Ltd.
Income G-DSC Fund
RRSP Eligible; Inception Year: 1994; Fund Managers:
GWL Investment Management Ltd.
International Opportunity F-DSC Fund
RRSP Eligible; Inception Year: 1997; Fund Managers:
J.P. Morgan Fleming Asset Management
Mid Cap Canada G-NL Fund
RRSP Eligible; Inception Year: 1997; Fund Managers:
GWL Investment Management Ltd.
Global Income A-NL Fund
RRSP Eligible; Inception Year: 1996; Fund Managers:
AGF Funds Inc.
Canadian Balanced M-DSC Fund
RRSP Eligible; Inception Year: 2000; Fund Managers:
Mackenzie Financial Corp.
Canadian Balanced M-NL Fund
RRSP Eligible; Inception Year: 2000; Fund Managers:
Mackenzie Financial Corp.
Canadian Equity Growth M-DSC Fund
RRSP Eligible; Inception Year: 2000; Fund Managers:
Mackenzie Financial Corp.
Canadian Equity Growth M-NL Fund
RRSP Eligible; Inception Year: 2000; Fund Managers:
Mackenzie Financial Corp.
Canadian Equity Portfolio G-DSC Fund
RRSP Eligible; Inception Year: 2000; Fund Managers:
GWL Investment Management Ltd.
Canadian Equity Portfolio G-NL Fund
RRSP Eligible; Inception Year: 2000; Fund Managers:
GWL Investment Management Ltd.
Canadian Science & Technology G-NL Fund
RRSP Eligible; Inception Year: 2000; Fund Managers:
GWL Investment Management Ltd.
Dividend M-DSC Fund
RRSP Eligible; Inception Year: 2000; Fund Managers:
Mackenzie Financial Corp.

Dividend M-NL Fund
RRSP Eligible; Inception Year: 2000; Fund Managers:
Mackenzie Financial Corp.
Emerging Markets M-DSC Fund
RRSP Eligible; Inception Year: 2000; Fund Managers:
Mackenzie Financial Corp.
Emerging Markets M-NL Fund
RRSP Eligible; Inception Year: 2000; Fund Managers:
Mackenzie Financial Corp.
Ethics G-DSC Fund
RRSP Eligible; Inception Year: 2000; Fund Managers:
GWL Investment Management Ltd.
Ethics G-NL Fund
RRSP Eligible; Inception Year: 2000; Fund Managers:
GWL Investment Management Ltd.
Fixed Income Portfolio G-DSC Fund
RRSP Eligible; Inception Year: 2000; Fund Managers:
GWL Investment Management Ltd.
Fixed Income Portfolio G-NL Fund
RRSP Eligible; Inception Year: 2000; Fund Managers:
GWL Investment Management Ltd.
Foreign Equity M-DSC Fund
RRSP Eligible; Inception Year: 2000; Fund Managers:
Mackenzie Financial Corp.
Foreign Equity M-NL Fund
RRSP Eligible; Inception Year: 2000; Fund Managers:
Mackenzie Financial Corp.
Global Equity Portfolio G-DSC Fund
RRSP Eligible; Inception Year: 2000; Fund Managers:
GWL Investment Management Ltd.
Global Equity Portfolio G-NL Fund
RRSP Eligible; Inception Year: 2000; Fund Managers:
GWL Investment Management Ltd.
Japan Equity M-NL Fund
RRSP Eligible; Inception Year: 2000; Fund Managers:
Mackenzie Financial Corp.
Japan Equity M-DSC Fund
RRSP Eligible; Inception Year: 2000; Fund Managers:
Mackenzie Financial Corp.
US Mid Cap G-DSC Fund
RRSP Eligible; Inception Year: 2000; Fund Managers:
GWL Investment Management Ltd.
US Mid Cap G-NL Fund
RRSP Eligible; Inception Year: 2000; Fund Managers:
GWL Investment Management Ltd.
Canadian Equity BT-DSC Fund
RRSP Eligible; Inception Year: 1996; Fund Managers:
Bissett Investment Management
Canadian Equity BT-NL Fund
RRSP Eligible; Inception Year: 1996; Fund Managers:
Bissett Investment Management
Canadian Value AT-DSC Fund
RRSP Eligible; Inception Year: 1997; Fund Managers:
Aim Trimark Investments
Canadian Value AT-NL Fund
RRSP Eligible; Inception Year: 1997; Fund Managers:
Aim Trimark Investments
International Equity U-DSC
RRSP Eligible; Inception Year: 1994; Fund Managers:
UBS Global Asset Management
International Equity U-NL
RRSP Eligible; Inception Year: 1994; Fund Managers:
UBS Global Asset Management
Science & Technology G-DSC Fund
RRSP Eligible; Inception Year: 2000; Fund Managers:
GWL Investment Management Ltd.

Group Sales Offices:

Calgary
Stock Exchange Tower
#1400, 300 - 5th Ave. SW
Calgary, AB T2P 3C4 Canada
403-515-5900
Fax: 403-234-0011
Scott France, Regional Director

Edmonton
Bell Tower
#1850, 10104 - 103rd Ave.
Edmonton, AB T5J 0H8 Canada
780-917-7800
Fax: 780-429-5088
Peter Doig, Regional Director

Halifax
#1900, 1801 Hollis St.
Halifax, NS B3J 3N4 Canada
902-429-8429
Fax: 902-429-0998
Barry Shea, Regional Director

Hamilton
#825, 1 King St. West
Hamilton, ON L8P 1A4 Canada
905-317-2650
Fax: 905-525-9070
Don Richardson, Regional Director

Kitchener
#800, 40 Weber St. East
Kitchener, ON N2H 6R3 Canada
519-744-7345
Fax: 519-744-3669
888-821-8626
Bob Hague, Regional Director

London
#2500, 255 Queens Ave.
London, ON N6A 5R8 Canada
519-432-6315
Fax: 519-432-4566
Bill Snoeks, Regional Director

Montréal
#1000, 2001, rue University
Montréal, QC H3A 1T9 Canada
514-350-7975
Fax: 514-350-4786
Jean Pierre Beaudet, Regional Director

Ottawa
Holland Cross
#410, 11 Holland Ave.
Ottawa, ON K1Y 4S1 Canada
613-761-3950
Fax: 613-728-2971
Peter Foley, Regional Director

Québec
Tour de la Cité
#800, 2600, boul Laurier, 8e étage
Québec, QC G1V 4W2 Canada
418-650-4200
Fax: 418-650-1561
Michael Henderson, Sr. Account Manager

Regina
Bank of Montréal Bldg.
#500, 2103 - 11th Ave.
Regina, SK S4P 3Z8 Canada
306-790-2330
Fax: 306-790-2340
Dave Cripps, Sr. Account Manager

Sudbury
#401, 144 Pine St.
Sudbury, ON P3C 1X3 Canada
705-699-2657
Fax: 705-675-0902
Wayne Toner, Sr. Account Manager

Toronto
#400, 330 University Ave.
Toronto, ON M5G 1R8 Canada
416-552-5050
Fax: 416-552-5450
David Henry, Managing Director

Vancouver
#1500, 1177 West Hastings St.
Vancouver, BC V6E 3Y9 Canada
604-331-2444
Fax: 604-688-9762
Ted Woodrow, Regional Director

Windsor
#200, 4520 Rhodes Dr.
Windsor, ON N8W 5C2 Canada
519-944-0686
Fax: 519-944-5104
800-808-6370
Kyle Baro, Sr. Account Manager

Winnipeg
#1C, 100 Osborne St. North
Winnipeg, MB R3C 1V3 Canada
204-946-7850
Fax: 204-946-8916
Day Woytko, Regional Director

Resource Centres:

Brossard
11, Place du Commerce
Brossard, QC J4W 2T9 Canada
450-466-6956
Fax: 450-466-1836
Michel Carrier, Manager

Calgary
Dominion Place
#300, 906 - 12th Ave. SW
Calgary, AB T2R 1K7 Canada
403-750-2100
Fax: 403-750-2150
Ralph Brust, Manager

Edmonton
Bell Tower
#600, 10104 - 103 Ave.
Edmonton, AB T5J 0H8 Canada
780-917-7700
Fax: 780-429-2809
John Liston, Manager

Grande Prairie - 97th Ave.
#203, 10134 - 97th Ave.
Grande Prairie, AB T8V 7X6 Canada
780-532-2818
Fax: 780-539-3455
Marc Lissoway, Manager

Grande Prairie - 97th Ave. - Northwest Territories & Yukon
Grand Central Station
#203, 10134 - 97th Ave.
Grande Prairie, AB T8V 7X6 Canada
780-532-2818
Fax: 780-539-3455
Marc Lissoway, Manager

Halifax
Purdy's Wharf Tower II
#407, 1959 Upper Water St.
Halifax, NS B3J 3N2 Canada
902-429-8653
Fax: 902-425-1968
800-461-3181
Mark Kenny, Manager

Hamilton
Stelco Tower
100 King St. West, 14th Fl.
Hamilton, ON L8P 1A2 Canada
905-525-5031
Fax: 905-521-2838
Rick Guiliani, Manager

Kelowna
Landmark IV
#400, 1628 Dickson Ave.
Kelowna, BC V1Y 7T2 Canada
250-712-7900
Fax: 250-762-0822
Matt Simpson, Manager

Kingston
#300, 1473 John Counter Blvd.
Kingston, ON K7M 8Z6 Canada
613-545-5670
Fax: 613-545-5972
Carolyn Wood, Manager

Kitchener
#900, 101 Frederick St.
Kitchener, ON N2H 6R2 Canada
519-746-1200
Fax: 519-746-1396
Don Mück, Manager

Laval
Les Tours Triomphes Phase I
#1004, 2500, boul Daniel-Johnson
Laval, QC H7T 2P6 Canada
450-681-1004
Fax: 450-681-1444
877-617-3000
Émile Arbour, Manager

London
140 Fullarton St., 10th Fl.
London, ON N6A 5P2 Canada
519-434-3268
Fax: 519-434-3280
Abbie MacMillan, Manager

Mississauga
#1206, 90 Burnhamthorpe Rd. West
Mississauga, ON L5B 3C3 Canada
905-270-6103
Fax: 905-270-1177
Todd Cloutier, Manager

Moncton

The Great-West Life Assurance Company(GWL)/ Great-West, Compagnie d'Assurance Vie (continued)

Heritage Court
#416, 95 Foundry St.
Moncton, NB E1C 5H7 Canada
506-859-4200
Fax: 506-859-9114
Blair Hayden, Manager
Montréal
#1300, 1800, av McGill College
Montréal, QC H3A 3J6 Canada
514-878-6111
Fax: 514-878-6172
Raymond Darveau, Manager
Oshawa
#400, 2 Simcoe St.
Oshawa, ON L1H 8C1 Canada
905-571-2676
Fax: 905-571-6168
Dan Hostick, Manager
Ottawa
#500, 515 Legget Dr.
Kanata, ON K2K 3G4 Canada
613-270-6844
Fax: 613-270-6801
Steven Chabot, Manager
Prince George
Bank of Nova Scotia Bldg.
#505, 1488 - 4 Ave.
Prince George, BC V2L 4Y2 Canada
250-614-7700
Fax: 250-563-1240
Marc Lissoway, Manager
Québec
Tour de la Cité
2600, boul Laurier, 8e étage
Québec, QC G1V 4W2 Canada
418-650-4200
Fax: 418-653-3037
Roger Gauthier, Manager
Regina
Royal Bank Bldg.
#600, 2010 - 11 Ave.
Regina, SK S4P 0J3 Canada
306-761-7500
Fax: 306-352-9474
Grant Laube, Manager
Saskatoon
Bank of Hong Kong Bldg.
#300, 321A - 21 St. East
Saskatoon, SK S7K 0C1 Canada
306-665-6244
Fax: 306-652-1919
Rick Kennedy, Manager
St. John's
Beothuck Bldg., 5th Fl.
Crosbie Pl.
St. John's, NL A1B 3Y8 Canada
709-754-2132
Fax: 709-754-0117
Ron Reid, Manager
Sudbury - Northern Ontario
#201, 144 Pine St.
Sudbury, ON P3C 1X3 Canada
705-675-2494
Fax: 705-675-6248
Craig MacTavish, Manager
Surrey
Station Tower, Gateway
#1260, 13401 - 108 Ave.
Surrey, BC V3T 5T3 Canada
604-930-3570
Fax: 604-930-3571
Craig Noren, Manager
Toronto
#600, 2005 Sheppard Ave. East
Toronto, ON M2J 5B4 Canada
416-492-4300
Fax: 416-492-1406
Mark Foris, Manager
Vancouver
#1200, 1177 West Hastings St.
Vancouver, BC V6E 3Y9 Canada
604-331-2430
Fax: 604-688-6588
Ray Fuller, Manager
Victoria
#610, 1675 Douglas St.
Victoria, BC V8W 2G5 Canada
250-953-1250
Fax: 250-383-0431
800-953-1250
Frank Goethals, Manager
Windsor
#200, 4520 Rhodes Dr.
Windsor, ON N8W 5C2 Canada
519-944-0686
Fax: 519-944-0630
Christy Bacik, Manager
Winnipeg
PO Box 338
100 Osborne St. North
Winnipeg, MB R3C 2H6 Canada
204-946-8100
Fax: 204-946-8865
Hugh Moncrieff, Manager

Green Shield Canada

#1600, 5001 Yonge St.
Toronto, ON M2N 6P6
416-221-7001
Fax: 416-733-1955
800-268-6613
www.greenshield.ca
Ownership: Not-for-profit health carrier.
Year Founded: 1957
Number of Employees: 420
Assets: $100-500 million Year End: 20051231
Revenues: $500m-1 billion Year End: 20051231
Classes of Insurance: Personal Accident & Sickness
Incorporation: Federally Incorporated Insurance Company
Profile: The individual & group health & dental benefits specialist offers the following: PharmALERT - Canada's first quality-managed, cost-effective drug care program & network; DentALERT - Canada's first intelligent dental system; & HealthALERT - a broad range of high-quality, cost-effective programs, including extended health care, vision, hospital, travel, nursing & home care products. Branches are located in Windsor, London, Toronto, Ottawa, & Vancouver.

Executives:
J. David Garner, President
Steve Bradie, Exec. Vice-President/COO; 519-739-1133
Ken A. MacTavish, CFO & Vice-President, Finance; 416-221-7001
T. Catherwood, Vice-President, Human Resources
Ray Gollmer, Vice-President, Information Technology
Steve Moffatt, Vice-President, Sales & Marketing
Wendy Murkar, Vice-President, Claims & Administration
Jim Bates, Director, Sales & Marketing; 416-221-7001
Mike Brown, Director, Strategic Alliances; 519-739-1133
Erwin Daichendt, Director, Systems Group, Health Solutions Group
Charles Rosen, Director, Business Relations, Health Solutions Group
Dave Bedard, Manager, Customer Application Support
Sal Cimino, Manager, Pharmacy & Provider Issues
Jim Mastronardi, Manager, Technical Services & Operations
Tony Pether, Manager, Benefits Administration
Stan Poulson, Manager, Rate & Economic Analysis
Cathy Morrison, Controller
Directors:
Robert J. Myers, Chair
Vernon K. Chiles, Vice-Chair; 519-542-9833

Grenville Mutual Insurance Co.

PO Box 10
3005 County Rd. 21
Spencerville, ON K0E 1X0
613-658-2013
Fax: 613-658-3374
800-267-4400
www.grenvillemutual.com
Year Founded: 1892
Classes of Insurance: Personal Accident & Sickness, Auto, Liability, Boiler & Machinery, Fidelity, Property
Incorporation: Provincially Incorporated Insurance Company
Profile: Services include commercial, agri-business, residential, automobile, home & farm insurance.

Executives:
Ron Greaves, President
Heather Bellinger, Manager, Business Operations
Diane Carriere, Corporate Secretary
Directors:
James Locke, Chair
Ian Wade, Vice-Chair
Diane Carriere, Corporate Secretary
Greg Beach
Hubert Ferguson
Ron Greaves
Glenn Pemberton
Ivan Peterson
George Robinson
Gordon Smith

Grey & Bruce Mutual Insurance Co.

517 - 10th St.
Hanover, ON N4N 1R4
519-364-2250
Fax: 519-364-6067
Year Founded: 1878
Classes of Insurance: Personal Accident & Sickness, Auto, Liability, Boiler & Machinery, Property
Incorporation: Provincially Incorporated Insurance Company
Executives:
Albert D. McArthur, Manager, Sec.-Treas.

Groupe Promutuel, Fédération de sociétés mutuelles d'assurance générale

1091, ch Saint-Louis
Québec, QC G1S 4Y7
866-999-2433
federation@promutuel.ca
www.promutuel.ca
Ownership: Member-owned
Year Founded: 1852
Number of Employees: 1,500
Assets: $500m-1 billion
Revenues: $100-500 million
Incorporation: Provincially Incorporated Insurance Company
Profile: The following services are provided: financial security, financial services & damage insurance.

Executives:
Adrien Viens, Président
Claude Robitaille, Directeur général
Affiliated Companies:
Promutuel Réassurance
Promutuel Vie inc
Mutual Insurance Members:
Hébertville - Promutuel du Lac au Fjord
11, rue Commerciale
Hébertville, QC G8N 1N3 Canada
418-344-1565
Fax: 418-344-4500
800-463-9646
dulacaufjord@promutuel.ca
Promutuel Appalaches - St-François
525, rte de l'Église
Saint-Pierre-Baptiste, QC G0P 1K0 Canada
418-453-2166
Fax: 418-453-2955
800-461-2166
appalaches@promutuel.ca
Promutuel Bagot
PO Box 60
1840, rang Saint-Édouard
Saint-Liboire, QC J0H 1R0 Canada
450-793-4471
Fax: 450-793-4470
800-361-0087
bagot@promutuel.ca
Promutuel Beauce
650, boul Renault
Beauceville, QC G5X 3P2 Canada
418-774-3621
Fax: 418-774-3623
800-463-1651
beauce@promutuel.ca
Promutuel Bellechasse
340, rue Principale
Saint-Gervais, QC G0R 3C0 Canada
418-887-6511
Fax: 418-887-6186
800-463-1911
bellechasse@promutuel.ca
Promutuel Bois-Francs
30, rue Hôtel-de-Ville
Warwick, QC J1A 1M0 Canada

819-358-4000
Fax: 819-358-4040
800-463-3829
boisfrancs@promutuel.ca
Raymond Beaudet, Directeur général

Promutuel Charlevoix-Montmorency
951, boul Mgr-de-Laval
Baie-Saint-Paul, QC G3Z 2W3 Canada
418-435-2793
Fax: 418-435-6062
800-363-0119
charlevoix@promutuel.ca

Promutuel Coaticook-Sherbrooke
102, rue Child
Coaticook, QC J1A 2B3 Canada
819-849-9891
Fax: 819-849-6855
coaticook@promutuel.ca

Promutuel de l'Est
149, rue Saint-Germain est
Rimouski, QC G5L 1A9 Canada
418-724-4354
Fax: 418-722-4025
800-463-0854
delest@promutuel.ca

Promutuel Deux-Montagnes
9036, rue Saint-Étienne
Mirabel, QC J7N 2P6 Canada
450-476-9263
Fax: 450-258-4981
866-476-9263
deuxmontagnes@promutuel.ca

Promutuel Dorchester
78, boul Bégin
Sainte-Claire, QC G0R 2V0 Canada
418-883-2251
Fax: 418-883-2434
800-463-8846
dorchester@promutuel.ca

Promutuel Drummond
1500, boul Lemire
Drummondville, QC J2C 5A4 Canada
819-477-8844
Fax: 819-477-3341
877-799-8844
drummond@promutuel.ca

Promutuel Gaspésie-les-Iles
6, rue Saint-Jacques Nord
Causapscal, QC G0J 1J0 Canada
418-756-3456
Fax: 418-756-6108
800-463-0705
gaspesielesiles@promutuel.ca

Promutuel Haut St-Laurent
#104, 869, boul St-Jean-Baptiste
Mercier, QC J6R 2L3 Canada
450-699-6666
Fax: 450-699-7777
800-363-5133
hautstlaurent@promutuel.ca

Promutuel Kamouraska - Côte-Nord
PO Box 159
267, rue Rochette
Saint-Pascal, QC G0L 3Y0 Canada
418-492-2014
Fax: 418-492-2144
800-561-4623
kamcotenord@promutuel.ca

Promutuel L'Abitibienne
282, 1e av est
Amos, QC J9T 1H3 Canada
819-732-1531
Fax: 819-732-4293
800-848-1531
abitibienne@promutuel.ca

Promutuel L'Islet
600, rte de l'Église
Saint-Jean-Port-Joli, QC G0R 3G0 Canada
418-598-3018
Fax: 418-598-3010
800-955-3018
lislet@promutuel.ca

Promutuel L'Outaouais
629, rte 321
Saint-André-Avellin, QC J0V 1W0 Canada
819-983-6141
Fax: 819-983-6147
800-567-1129
outaouais@promutuel.ca

Promutuel La Vallée
PO Box 179
34, rue Victoria
Shawville, QC J0X 2Y0 Canada
819-647-2953
Fax: 819-647-2817
888-292-2953
lavallee@promutuel.ca

Promutuel Lac St-Pierre - Les Forges
PO Box 70
300, rte Marie Victorin
Baie-du-Febvre, QC J0G 1A0 Canada
450-783-6455
Fax: 450-783-6302
888-783-6455
lacstpierre@promutuel.ca

Promutuel Lanaudière
249, rue Principale
Saint-Alexis-de-Montcalm, QC J0K 1T0 Canada
450-839-7233
Fax: 450-839-2229
800-363-1760
lanaudiere@promutuel.ca

Promutuel Les Prairies
48, boul Taschereau
La Prairie, QC J5R 6C1 Canada
450-444-0988
Fax: 450-444-7229
800-492-0988
lesprairies@promutuel.ca

Promutuel Lotbinière
175, boul Laurier
Laurier-Station, QC G0S 1N0 Canada
418-728-4110
Fax: 418-728-3977
800-561-4110
lotbiniere@promutuel.ca

Promutuel Lévisienne-Orléans
671, 4e av
Saint-Romuald, QC G6W 5M6 Canada
418-839-1341
Fax: 418-839-1935
800-441-1341
levisienne@promutuel.ca

Promutuel Montmagny
PO Box 355
124, boul Taché ouest
Montmagny, QC G5V 3S7 Canada
418-248-7940
Fax: 418-248-1713
888-265-7940
montmagny@promutuel.ca

Promutuel Monts et Rives
5240, boul des Vétérans
Lac-Mégantic, QC G6B 2G5 Canada
819-583-4555
Fax: 819-583-0627
800-267-4555
montsetrives@promutuel.ca

Promutuel Portneuf-Champlain
257, boul Centenaire
Saint-Basile, QC G0A 3G0 Canada
418-329-3330
Fax: 418-329-3328
800-463-6133
portneufchamplain@promutuel.ca

Promutuel Rivière-du-Loup (L'Isle-Verte)
PO Box 98
135, rue Saint-Jean-Baptiste
L'Isle-Verte, QC G0L 1K0 Canada
418-898-2311
Fax: 418-898-2043
800-267-2311
riviereduloup@promutuel.ca

Promutuel Rivière-du-Loup (Montréal)
#150, 1555, boul Jean-Paul-Vincent
Longueuil, QC J4N 1L6 Canada
450-679-9950
888-679-9950

Promutuel Rouyn-Noranda - Témiscamingue
31B, rue des Oblats nord
Ville-Marie, QC J9V 1H9 Canada
819-622-0024
Fax: 819-622-0717
800-201-1283
rouyntemis@promutuel.ca

Promutuel Soulanges
245, rte 338
Les Côteaux, QC J7X 1A2 Canada
450-267-9297
Fax: 450-267-0914
800-363-5391
soulanges@promutuel.ca

Promutuel Témiscouata
195, 7e rue est
Dégelis, QC G5T 2K3 Canada
418-853-3524
Fax: 418-853-3563
800-363-3155
temiscouata@promutuel.ca

Promutuel Valmont
PO Box 1460
4733, rue Foster
Waterloo, QC J0E 2N0 Canada
450-539-0384
Fax: 450-539-4370
800-361-7408
valmont@promutuel.ca

Promutuel Vaudreuil
64, rue Saint-Viateur
Rigaud, QC J0P 1P0 Canada
450-451-5389
Fax: 450-451-0087
800-667-2958
vaudreuil@promutuel.ca

Promutuel Verchères
97, rue Verchères
Saint-Marc-sur-Richelieu, QC J0L 2E0 Canada
450-584-2211
Fax: 450-584-3460
800-363-5059
vercheres@promutuel.ca

The Guarantee Company of North America/ La Garantie, Compagnie d'Assurance de l'Amérique d

Madison Centre
#1400, 4950 Yonge St.
Toronto, ON M2N 6K1
416-223-9580
Fax: 416-223-6577
800-260-6617
www.gcna.com

Ownership: Public
Year Founded: 1872
Number of Employees: 286
Assets: $500m-1 billion Year End: 20041231
Revenues: $100-500 million Year End: 20041231
Classes of Insurance: Accident, Personal Accident & Sickness, Legal Expense, Auto, Liability, Boiler & Machinery, Credit, Fidelity, Property, Fire, Surety, Hail & Crop, Theft
Incorporation: Federally Incorporated Insurance Company
Profile: The company provides bonding & insurance coverage. It specializes in credit, surety bonding, corporate risk insurance, property & casualty insurance & automobile insurance. An affiliated company is The Guarantee Company of North America USA.

Executives:
Jules R. Quenneville, CA, President/CEO
Robert A. Dempsey, Exec. Vice-President & Regional General Manager, Central & Atlantic Region
Chris Campbell, National Vice-President, Corporate Risk
John R. Emory, National Vice-President, Personal Lines, Vice-President & Regional General Manager, Québec
Robert Smith, National Vice-President, Surety
Guy Bonin, Vice-President, Personal Lines, Québec
Ron Burns, Vice-President, Personal Lines, Central Region
Alex Campbell, Vice-President, Regional General Manager, Western Region
Patrick Cowan, Vice-President, Finance, CFO
Bob Gallimore, Vice-President, Prairies Region
Richard Longland, Vice-President, Surety Bonding, Central & Atlantic Region
Randall L. Musselman, Vice-President, Risk Management & Government Regulation, Corporate Secretary

The Guarantee Company of North America/ La Garantie, Compagnie d'Assurance de l'Amérique d (continued)

Norman Nemetz, Vice-President, Reinsurance & Business Analysis
Gérard Philippon, Vice-President, Credit Insurance
Richard Pouliot, Vice-President, Claims
Douglas R. Smith, Vice-President, Investments
Pierre Surprenant, Vice-President, Surety Underwriting Standards, Québec

Directors:
Bruno Desjardins, Q.C., Chair
André Bureau
Pierre Côté, CM
Maureen Cowan
Robert H. Cowan
Louis Hollander
Robert G. Hunter
Thomas C. MacMillan
Robert L. Munro
Jules R. Quenneville, CA
John Quinlan
Norman R. Roth
Richard N. Waterous

Branches:

Edmonton
Scotia Place
#750, 10060 Jasper Ave.
Edmonton, AB T5J 3R8 Canada
780-424-2266
Fax: 780-424-3310
Bob Gallimore, Vice-President, Prairies Region

Halifax
Tower II, Purdy's Wharf
#1707, 1969 Upper Water St.
Halifax, NS B3J 3R7 Canada
902-425-4700
Fax: 902-425-4702
Dan Fletcher, Manager, Surety

Montréal
Place du Canada
#1560, 1010, rue de la Gauchetière ouest
Montréal, QC H3B 2R4 Canada
514-866-6351
Fax: 514-866-0157
John Emory, National Vice-President, Personal Lines

Québec
Tour Belle Cour
#2770, 2600, boul Laurier
Québec, QC G1V 4M6 Canada
418-652-1676
Fax: 418-652-9626
Guy Bonin, Vice-President, Personal Lines, Québec

Toronto
Madison Centre
#1400, 4950 Yonge St.
Toronto, ON M2M 6K1 Canada
416-223-9580
Fax: 416-223-6577
Robert A. Dempsey, Exec. Vice-President

Vancouver
#810, 400 Burrard St.
Vancouver, BC V6C 3A6 Canada
604-687-7688
Fax: 604-687-8861
Alex Campbell, Vice-President

Woodstock
PO Box 668
954 Dundas St. East
Woodstock, ON N4S 7Z9 Canada
519-539-9868
Fax: 519-539-2569
Ron Burns, Vice-President, Personal Lines, Central Region

Halwell Mutual Insurance Company

PO Box 60
812 Woolwich St.
Guelph, ON N1H 6J6
519-836-2860
Fax: 519-836-2831
800-267-5706
reception@halwellmutual.com
www.halwellmutual.com
Former Name: Halton Union Farmers Mutual; Puslinch Mutual; Eramosa Mutual
Year Founded: 1858
Number of Employees: 14
Assets: $10-50 million
Classes of Insurance: Auto, Liability, Boiler & Machinery, Fidelity, Property
Incorporation: Provincially Incorporated Insurance Company

Executives:
John Glasgow, President
Allan Miller, Vice-President
Katherine Wilson, Treasurer, Controller
Doug Winer, General Manager, Secretary
Patti Henderson, Manager, Underwriting
Lorraine Wigood, Manager, Claims

Directors:
George Bird
Lois Howlett
Barry Lee
Alex McNabb
Alan Orr
Annette Winter

Hamilton Township Mutual Insurance Company

PO Box 201
1176 Division St.
Cobourg, ON K9A 4K5
905-372-0186
Fax: 905-372-1364
800-263-3935
hamtwpmu@eagle.ca
Former Name: Hamilton Township Farmers Mutual Fire Insurance Company
Ownership: Private
Year Founded: 1898
Number of Employees: 18
Assets: $10-50 million
Revenues: $10-50 million
Classes of Insurance: Marine, Fire
Incorporation: Provincially Incorporated Insurance Company

Executives:
R. Murray Mills, General Manager/CEO
Howard Sheppard, President
Eugene Brahaney, 1st Vice-President
Ron Ireland, 2nd Vice-President
Terrye Calnan, Sec.-Treas., Manager, Financial & Technology Services
Walter Banit, Manager, Loss Control Services
Steve O'Connell, Manager, Claims Services
Robert Williams, Manager, Underwriting Services

Directors:
Gerald Brown
Jack Dorland
MacKenzie Haig
William O'Grady
Scott Robinson
Earle Windrem

Hannover Rückversicherungs AG

#201, 3650 Victoria Park Ave.
Toronto, ON M2H 3P7
416-496-1148
Fax: 416-496-1089
www.hannover-rueck.de
Also Known As: US Reinsurance Trust
Ownership: Foreign. Branch of Hannover Rückversicherung AG, Hannover, Germany.
Classes of Insurance: Personal Accident & Sickness, Aircraft, Auto, Liability, Boiler & Machinery, Fidelity, Property, Surety, Hail & Crop
Incorporation: Federally Incorporated Insurance Company
Profile: The foreign property & casualty insurance company is limited to the business of reinsurance.

Executives:
Laurel E. Grant, Chief Agent

Hartford Fire Insurance Company

PO Box 600
#504, 36 York Mills Rd.
Toronto, ON M2P 2E9
416-733-9265
Fax: 416-733-0510
888-898-8334
Ownership: Public. Foreign. Parent is Hartford Financial Services Group.
Year Founded: 1836
Number of Employees: 19
Assets: $100-500 million Year End: 20051231
Revenues: $10-50 million Year End: 20051231
Stock Symbol: HIG
Classes of Insurance: Personal Accident & Sickness, Aircraft, Auto, Liability, Boiler & Machinery, Fidelity, Property, Fire, Surety, Hail & Crop, Theft
Incorporation: Federally Incorporated Insurance Company

Executives:
Illona V. Kirsh, Chief Agent, Canada

Hay Mutual Insurance Company

PO Box 130
43 Main St.
Zurich, ON N0M 2T0
519-236-4381
Fax: 519-236-7681
staff@haymutual.on.ca
www.haymutual.on.ca
Year Founded: 1875
Classes of Insurance: Auto, Liability, Property, Hail & Crop
Incorporation: Provincially Incorporated Insurance Company

Executives:
John R. Consitt, Secretary-Manager

Henderson Insurance Inc.

339 Main St. North
Moose Jaw, SK S6H 0W2
306-694-5959
Fax: 306-693-0117
888-661-5959
hii@hendersoninsurance.ca
www.hendersoninsurance.ca
Former Name: Western Agricultural Insurance Corp.
Ownership: Private
Classes of Insurance: Aircraft, Auto, Liability, Marine, Property, Hail & Crop
Incorporation: Provincially Incorporated Insurance Company
Profile: Automobile, residential, farm & commercial insurance are offered.

Executives:
David Reidy, President/CEO
Dennis Reidy, Partner
Greg Reidy, Partner
Rick Smith, Partner

Howard Mutual Insurance Co.

PO Box 398
20 Ebenezer St. West
Ridgetown, ON N0P 2C0
519-674-5434
Fax: 519-674-2029
Former Name: Howard Mutual Fire Insurance Company
Classes of Insurance: Personal Accident & Sickness, Auto, Liability, Fidelity, Property, Hail & Crop
Incorporation: Provincially Incorporated Insurance Company

Executives:
Stephen L. Benishek, General Manager

Howick Mutual Insurance Company

PO Box 30
1091 Centre St.
Wroxeter, ON N0G 2X0
519-335-3561
Fax: 519-335-6416
800-265-3033
howick@howickmutual.com
www.howickmutual.com
Ownership: Policyholders.
Year Founded: 1873
Number of Employees: 14
Classes of Insurance: Personal Accident & Sickness, Auto, Liability, Boiler & Machinery, Fidelity, Property, Hail & Crop
Incorporation: Provincially Incorporated Insurance Company

Executives:
John Crispin, President
Sandra Edgar, Manager

Directors:
John Crispin
Dennis Dosman
Don Eadie
Niel Edgar
Lloyd Michie
Bill Quipp

The Independent Order of Foresters

Also listed under: Investment Fund Companies
789 Don Mills Rd.
Toronto, ON M3C 1T9

416-429-3000
Fax: 416-467-2516
800-828-1540
service@foresters.biz
www.foresters.biz
Ownership: Private
Year Founded: 1874
Number of Employees: 1,700
Assets: $1-10 billion
Revenues: $50-100 million
Classes of Insurance: Personal Accident & Sickness, Life
Executives:
George Mohacsi, President/CEO
Lynn Haight, COO/CFO
Euan Allison, Sr. Vice-President & Group Managing Director, UK

Nicholas J. DiRenzo, Sr. Vice-President, North American Sales
Sharon Giffen, Sr. Vice-President, Chief Actuary
Gail Johnson Morris, Sr. Vice-President, Service Delivery Division
Suanne M. Nielsen, Sr. Vice-President, Human Resources & Communication
Christopher Pinkerton, Sr. Vice-President, Marketing
Directors:
W. Ross Walker, Chair
Bernard E. Bloom
James Daugherty
William Bentley Foster
Richard M. Freeborough
Patrick William Kenny
Kash Manchuk
Louise L. McCormick
Barbara J. McDougall
Christopher H. McElvaine
John P. Meyerholz
E. Irene Miles
David E. Morrison
Glenn K. Reid
Foresters:
Money Market Fund
RRSP Eligible; Inception Year: 1989;
Equity Fund
RRSP Eligible; Inception Year: 1989; Fund Managers: Jarislowsky Fraser Ltd.
Bond Fund
RRSP Eligible; Inception Year: 1989;
Balanced Fund
RRSP Eligible; Inception Year: 1989; Fund Managers: Jarislowsky Fraser Ltd.
American Index Fund
RRSP Eligible; Inception Year: 2000; Fund Managers: Barclays Global Investors Canada Ltd.
Canadian Index Fund
RRSP Eligible; Inception Year: 2000; Fund Managers: Barclays Global Investors Canada Ltd.
Eurasia Index Fund
RRSP Eligible; Inception Year: 2000; Fund Managers: Barclays Global Investors Canada Ltd.
Global Index Fund
RRSP Eligible; Inception Year: 2000; Fund Managers: Barclays Global Investors Canada Ltd.
Canadian Balanced Fund
RRSP Eligible; Inception Year: 2000; Fund Managers: Jarislowsky Fraser Ltd.
Canadian Bond Fund
RRSP Eligible; Inception Year: 2000;
Canadian Equity Fund
RRSP Eligible; Inception Year: 2000; Fund Managers: Jarislowsky Fraser Ltd.
Canadian Money Market Fund
RRSP Eligible; Inception Year: 2000;
Sales Offices:
Burlington
#402, 3027 Harvester Rd.
Burlington, ON L7N 3G7 Canada
905-333-2861
Burnaby
#120, 4401 Still Creek Dr.
Burnaby, BC V5C 6G9 Canada
604-320-3300
Calgary
#225, 10655 Southport Rd. SW
Calgary, AB T2W 4Y1 Canada
403-250-8666
Edmonton
Oxford Tower
#1311, 10235 - 101 St. NW
Edmonton, AB T5J 3G1 Canada
780-425-2948
London
#214, 395 Wellington Rd.
London, ON N6C 4P9 Canada
519-680-2257
Markham
#308, 3000 Steeles Ave. East
Markham, ON L3R 4T9 Canada
905-474-3665
Mississauga
Bldg. 11
#201, 5045 Orbitor Dr.
Mississauga, ON L4W 4Y4 Canada
905-238-2649
Waterloo
#103, 60 Bridgeport Rd. East
Waterloo, ON N2J 2J9 Canada
519-886-7114

Industrial Alliance Insurance & Financial Services Inc./ Industrielle Alliance Assurance et Services Financ

CP 1907, Terminus Stn. Terminus
1080, ch Saint-Louis
Québec, QC G1K 7M3
418-684-5000
800-463-6236
info@inalco.com, customers@inalco.com
www.inalco.com
Former Name: L'Industrielle-Alliance, Compagnie d'Assurance sur la Vie/Industrial-Alliance Life Insurance Company
Also Known As: Industrial Alliance
Ownership: Public.
Year Founded: 1892
Number of Employees: 2,400+
Assets: $10-100 billion
Stock Symbol: IAG
Classes of Insurance: Personal Accident & Sickness, Auto, Life
Incorporation: Provincially Incorporated Insurance Company
Executives:
Yvon Charest, President/CEO
Michel Laurin, President/COO, Auto & Home Insurance
Normand Pépin, Exec. Vice-President, Life Subsidiaries, Individual Insurance & Annuities
René Chabot, Sr. Vice-President, Group Pensions
Denis Ricard, Sr. Vice-President, Chief Actuary
Raymond Bertrand, Vice-President, Sales, Careers Section
Jean-François Boulet, Vice-President, Human Resources
Jacques Carrière, Vice-President, Investor Relations
Yvon Côté, Vice-President & General Manager, Finance & Investments
Réjean Devin, Vice-President, Information Systems
Michel Gauthier, Vice-President & General Manager, Administration, Individual Insurance & Annuities
Maurice Germain, Vice-President, Internal Audit
Jocelyne Guay, Vice-President, Operations, Auto & Home Insurance
Richard Legault, Vice-President, Investments, General Funds
Bruno Michaud, Vice-President, Sales, General Agents, Québec & Atlantic Provinces
Jean-Pierre Paradis, Vice-President, Mortgage Loans
Jacques Parent, Vice-President, Sales & Underwriting, Group Insurance
Yvon Sauvageau, Vice-President, Development, Financial Services
Georges Smith, Vice-President & General Manager, Corporate Affairs, Secretary
Claude Tessier, Vice-President, Real Estate Investment
Directors:
Raymond Garneau, Chair
Gilles Laroche, Vice-Chair
Georges Smith, Secretary
Jennifer Dibblee, Asst. Secretary
Mary C. Arnold
Francesco Bellini
Louis Bernard
Pierre Brodeur
Yvon Charest
Anne Dutil
Michel Gervais
Lise Lachapelle
John LeBoutillier
Francis McGuire
Jim Pantelidis
David Peterson
Guy Savard
Affiliated Companies:
ClaringtonFunds Inc.
Industrial Alliance Fund Management Inc.
Industrial Alliance Pacific Life Insurance Company
Industrial Alliance Securities Inc.
Industrial Alliance Trust Inc.
Branches:
Calgary
#2050, 777 - 8th Ave. SW
Calgary, AB T2P 3R5 Canada
403-532-1500
Fax: 403-532-1510
888-532-1505
Dartmouth
#320, 238 Brownlow Ave.
Dartmouth, NS B3B 1Y2 Canada
902-422-6479
Fax: 902-422-1183
800-255-2116
Montréal
PO Box 790, B Sta. B
680, rue Sherbrooke ouest, 9e étage
Montréal, QC H3A 3K6 Canada
514-499-3750
Fax: 514-499-6698
877-499-3750
Québec - Campanile
#107, 3700, rue du Campanile
Québec, QC G1X 4G6 Canada
418-650-1821
Fax: 418-650-1824
800-463-7274
Québec - Saint-Louis
#340, 925, ch Saint-Louis
Québec, QC G1S 1C1 Canada
418-650-4600
Fax: 418-650-4612
877-650-4612
Toronto - Eglinton Ave. East
160 Eglinton Ave. East, 7th Fl.
Toronto, ON M4P 3B5 Canada
416-487-0242
800-268-8882
oro@inalco.com
Toronto - University Ave.
522 University Ave.
Toronto, ON M5G 1Y7 Canada
416-585-8921
Fax: 416-598-5131
877-422-6487
groupinsurance@inalco.com

Vancouver
#1130, 1055 West Hastings St.
Vancouver, BC V6E 2E9 Canada
604-689-0388
Fax: 604-689-0537
800-557-2515

Industrial Alliance Pacific Life Insurance Company

Also listed under: *Investment Fund Companies*
PO Box 5900
2165 West Broadway
Vancouver, BC V6B 5H6
604-734-1667
Fax: 604-734-8221
800-665-4458
intouch@iaplife.com
www.iaplife.com
Former Name: The North West Life Assurance Company of Canada
Ownership: Private.
Year Founded: 1953
Number of Employees: 400
Assets: $1-10 billion Year End: 20041231
Revenues: $500m-1 billion Year End: 20041231
Classes of Insurance: Personal Accident & Sickness, Life
Incorporation: Federally Incorporated Insurance Company
Profile: Industrial-Alliance Pacific Life Insurance Company is a federally incorporated Canadian life & health insurance

Industrial Alliance Pacific Life Insurance Company (continued)

company. It provides creditor's group life & disability insurance for the automotive industry & student accident insurance. Individual insurance & tailored risk coverage are offered for specialty groups.

Executives:
Gerald Bouwers, President/COO
Michael L. Stickney, Exec. Vice-President, USA Development
Paul R. Grimes, Sr. Vice-President, Sales
Mary Dinkel, Vice-President, USA Sales Development
Douglas A. Carrothers, Corporate Secretary, General Counsel

IAP:
APEX Balanced (AGF) Fund
RRSP Eligible; Inception Year: 1969;
APEX Canadian Growth (AGF) Fund
RRSP Eligible; Inception Year: 1971;
APEX Canadian Value (Dynamic) Fund
RRSP Eligible; Inception Year: 1998;
APEX Fixed Income Fund
RRSP Eligible; Inception Year: 1971;
APEX Growth & Income Fund
RRSP Eligible; Inception Year: 1996;
APEX Money Market Fund
RRSP Eligible; Inception Year: 1994;
Bonds Fund
RRSP Eligible; Inception Year: 1977;
Canadian Equity Index Fund
RRSP Eligible; Inception Year: 2001;
Mortgages Fund
RRSP Eligible; Inception Year: 1997;
Diversified Fund
RRSP Eligible; Inception Year: 1987;
Emerging Markets (Templeton) Fund
RRSP Eligible; Inception Year: 1997; Fund Managers:
Franklin Templeton Investments
Bissett Bonds Fund
RRSP Eligible; Inception Year: 1999; Fund Managers:
Bissett Investment Managment
US Equity Index Fund
RRSP Eligible; Inception Year: 1998; Fund Managers:
State Street Global Advisors (Boston)
European Equity (Rothschild) Fund
RRSP Eligible; Inception Year: 2005;
Global Equity (Templeton)Fund
RRSP Eligible; Inception Year: 2001; Fund Managers:
Franklin Templeton Investments
Money Market Fund
RRSP Eligible; Inception Year: 1994;
Asian Pacific (ABN AMRO) Fund
RRSP Eligible; Inception Year: 2000; Fund Managers:
ABM AMRO Asset Management
International Equity (Templeton) Fund
RRSP Eligible; Inception Year: 1996; Fund Managers:
Franklin Templeton Investments
Bonds-Series 2 Fund
RRSP Eligible; Inception Year: 1997;
Canadian Equity Growth Fund
RRSP Eligible; Inception Year: 2001;
Income Fund
RRSP Eligible; Inception Year: 1998;
Focus Balanced Fund
RRSP Eligible; Inception Year: 2002;
US DAQ Index Fund
RRSP Eligible; Inception Year: 1999; Fund Managers:
State Street Global Advisors (Boston)
APEX Canadian Stock Fund
RRSP Eligible; Inception Year: 1996;
Focus Prudent Fund
RRSP Eligible; Inception Year: 2002;
Focus Moderate Fund
RRSP Eligible; Inception Year: 2002;
Focus Growth Fund
RRSP Eligible; Inception Year: 2002;
Focus Aggressive Fund
RRSP Eligible; Inception Year: 2002;
Diversified Security Fund
RRSP Eligible; Inception Year: 1999;
Diversified Opportunity Fund
RRSP Eligible; Inception Year: 1999;
Fidelity Canadian Asset Allocation Fund
RRSP Eligible; Inception Year: 2001; Fund Managers:
Fidelity Investments
Diversified Income Fund
RRSP Eligible; Inception Year: 2003;
Dividend Income Fund
RRSP Eligible; Inception Year: 2005;
Dividend Growth Fund
RRSP Eligible; Inception Year: 2005;
Canadian Equity (Leon Frazer) Fund
RRSP Eligible; Inception Year: 2004; Fund Managers:
Leon Frazer & Associates
Select Canadian Fund
RRSP Eligible; Inception Year: 1998;
Canadian Equity Value Fund
RRSP Eligible; Inception Year: 1969;
Canadian Equity (Dynamic) Fund
RRSP Eligible; Inception Year: 2001; Fund Managers:
Dynamic Mutual Funds
Canadian Equity (Bissett) Fund
RRSP Eligible; Inception Year: 1999; Fund Managers:
Bissett Investment Managment
Fidelity True North Fund
RRSP Eligible; Inception Year: 1999; Fund Managers:
Fidelity Investments
Fidelity Canadian Growth Company Fund
RRSP Eligible; Inception Year: 1999; Fund Managers:
Fidelity Investments
Global Equity (New Star) Fund
RRSP Eligible; Inception Year: 2005; Fund Managers:
New Star Asset Management Limited
Fidelity NorthStar Fund
RRSP Eligible; Inception Year: 2005; Fund Managers:
Fidelity Investments
Boomernomics Fund
RRSP Eligible; Inception Year: 2001; Fund Managers:
CI Investments
International Equity Index Fund
RRSP Eligible; Inception Year: 1999; Fund Managers:
State Street Global Advisors (Boston)
Fidelity European Equity Fund
RRSP Eligible; Inception Year: 2005; Fund Managers:
Fidelity Investments
US Equity (McLean Budden) Fund
RRSP Eligible; Inception Year: 2005; Fund Managers:
McLean Budden
US Equity (Legg Mason) Fund
RRSP Eligible; Inception Year: 2001; Fund Managers:
Legg Mason Inc.
Global Financial Services (CI) Fund
RRSP Eligible; Inception Year: 2001; Fund Managers:
CI Investments
Global Health Care Fund
RRSP Eligible; Inception Year: 2001; Fund Managers:
Talvest Fund Management
Real Estate Income Fund
RRSP Eligible; Inception Year: 2003;
Global Technology (ABN AMRO) Fund
RRSP Eligible; Inception Year: 2001; Fund Managers:
ABM AMRO Asset Management
Multi-Management Diversified Aggressive Fund
RRSP Eligible; Inception Year: 2000;
Dividends Fund
RRSP Eligible; Inception Year: 1998;
Multi-Management Diversified Opportunity Fund
RRSP Eligible; Inception Year: 2000;
Canadian Equity Index (Small Cap) Fund
RRSP Eligible; Inception Year: 1998; Fund Managers:
State Street Global Advisors (Boston)
Global Equity (ABN AMRO) Fund
RRSP Eligible; Inception Year: 2000; Fund Managers:
ABM AMRO Asset Management
European Equity (ABN AMRO) Fund
RRSP Eligible; Inception Year: 2001; Fund Managers:
ABM AMRO Asset Management
US Equity (AGF) Fund
RRSP Eligible; Inception Year: 1997; Fund Managers:
AGF Funds Inc.
International Equity (McLean Budden) Fund
RRSP Eligible; Inception Year: 2001; Fund Managers:
McLean Budden

Regional Offices:

Brossard - Taschereau - SAL Group Québec Regional Office
#109B, 7900, boul Taschereau
Brossard, QC J4X 2T2 Canada
450-465-0603
Fax: 450-465-1663
Fax: saladmin@iaplif

Calgary - 8th Ave. SW - Special Markets Group Prairie Regional Office
#2050, 777 - 8th Ave. SW
Calgary, AB T2P 3R5 Canada
403-226-7582
Fax: 403-265-3346
800-661-1699
smgcgy@iaplife.com

Dartmouth - Brownlow Ave. - SAL Group Atlantic Provinces Regional Office
Park Place 2
#302, 283A Brownlow Ave.
Dartmouth, NS B3B 2B4 Canada
902-468-8698
Fax: 902-468-1559
saladmin@iaplife.com

Edmonton - Calgary Trail NW - SAL Group Alberta Regional Office
Terrace Plaza
#840, 4445 Calgary Trail NW
Edmonton, AB T6H 5R7
780-435-1833
Fax: 780-435-2185
888-435-1833
saladmin@iaplife.com

Langley - 202nd St. - SAL Group British Columbia Regional Office
#305, 9440 - 202nd St.
Langley, BC V1M 4A6
604-882-8220
Fax: 604-882-8210
877-882-8220
saladmin@iaplife.com

Montréal - Sherbrooke ouest - Special Markets Group Montréal Regional Office
PO Box 790, B Sta. B
#110, 680 rue Sherbrooke ouest
Montréal, QC H3B 3K6
514-499-3748
Fax: 514-499-3856
866-499-3748

Oakville - North Service Rd. West - SAL Ontario Regional Office
#6, 1155 North Service Rd. West
Oakville, ON L6M 3E3 Canada
905-847-7900
Fax: 905-847-7922
800-668-4702
saladmin@iaplife.com

Thunder Bay - Community Hall Rd. - SAL Group Thunder Bay Office
RR#12
Thunder Bay, ON P7B 5E3
807-626-8917
Fax: 807-768-9272
saladmin@iaplife.com

Toronto - Consumers Rd. - Special Markets Group Eastern Regional Office
#400, 515 Consumers Rd.
Toronto, ON M2J 4Z2 Canada
416-498-8319
Fax: 416-498-9892
800-611-6667
smgtor@iaplife.com

Vancouver - Broadway West - Special Markets Group
PO Box 5900
2165 Broadway West
Vancouver, BC V6B 5H6 Canada
800-266-5667
group@iaplife.com, student@iaplife.com

Vancouver - West Georgia St. - Mortgage Department
#1910, 1188 West Georgia St.
Vancouver, BC V6E 4A2
604-688-8631
Fax: 604-734-7274
mortgages@iaplife.com

Vancouver - West Georgia St. - Special Markets Group British Columbia Regional Office
#1910, 1188 West Georgia St.
Vancouver, BC V6E 4A2 Canada
604-688-9641
Fax: 604-688-9482
888-725-2886
smgbc@iaplife.com

Winnipeg - Waverley St. - SAL Group Winnipeg Regional Office
#102 - 865 Waverley St.
Winnipeg, MB R3T 5P4
204-942-8907
Fax: 204-943-6952
saladmin@iaplife.com

ING Insurance Company of Canada - Corporate Office (Specialty Lines)
ING Tower
181 University Ave., 9th Fl.
Toronto, ON M5H 3M7
416-941-5221
800-557-7232
Other Information: Marine Toll Free: 1-888-773-2228
Classes of Insurance: Marine, Surety
Incorporation: Federally Incorporated Insurance Company
Profile: Niche, surety & marine lines are offered.

Regional Offices:
Calgary - Surety (Southern Alberta)
#1300, 321 - 6th Ave. SW
Calgary, AB T2P 4W7 Canada
403-269-7961
Fax: 403-265-7754
800-668-8384
Halifax - Surety
#100, 5657 Spring Garden Rd.
Halifax, NS B3J 3H6 Canada
902-420-1732
Fax: 902-423-6756
Montréal - Niche Products
1611, boul Crémazie boul est
Montréal, QC H2M 2R9 Canada
514-388-5466
Fax: 514-288-7853
Ottawa - Surety
#300, 1400 St. Laurent Blvd.
Ottawa, ON K1K 4H4 Canada
613-748-3000
Fax: 613-748-0376

Vancouver - Niche Products & Surety
#400, 2955 Virtual Way
Vancouver, BC V5M 4X6 Canada
604-891-5400
Fax: 604-689-0535
800-663-9468

ING Insurance Company of Canada - Corporate Office (Québec Region)
2450, rue Girouard ouest
Saint-Hyacinthe, QC J2S 3B3
450-773-9701
Fax: 450-773-3515
800-363-5401
Incorporation: Federally Incorporated Insurance Company
Regional Offices:
Montréal
1611, boul Crémazie est
Montréal, QC H2M 2R9 Canada
514-388-5466
Fax: 514-288-7853
Québec
#100, 1305, boul Lebourgneuf
Québec, QC G2K 2E4 Canada
418-626-9555
Fax: 418-626-2753

ING Insurance Company of Canada - Corporate Office (Central & Atlantic Region)
75 Eglinton Ave. East
Toronto, ON M4P 3A4
416-440-1000
Fax: 416-440-4129
800-387-8823
infoING@ingcanada.com
www.ingcanada.com
Former Name: The Halifax Insurance Company
Ownership: Parent is ING Canada Inc.
Year Founded: 1809
Number of Employees: 5,000
Assets: $5,000,000,000
Revenues: $3,100,000,000
Classes of Insurance: Personal Accident & Sickness, Auto, Property
Incorporation: Federally Incorporated Insurance Company
Profile: In 2002, The Commerce Group Insurance Company, ING Insurance Company of Canada & ING Wellington Insurance Company amalgamated into ING Insurance Company of Canada.

Executives:
Derek Iles, Exec. Vice-President, ING Canada
Sharon Bridge, Vice-President, Commercial Lines
Steve Cohen, Vice-President, Actuarial
Larry Lythgoe, Vice-President, Integrated Financial Services
Ronald French, Vice-President, Finance
Benoit Morrissette, Vice-President, Personal Lines
John McArel, Vice-President, Marketing & Communications
Ed Nolan, Vice-President, Claims
Lorraine O'Connor, Vice-President, Human Resources
Debbie Coull-Chcchini, COO, Ontario Region
Regional Offices:
Ajax - Durham
59 Westney Rd.
Ajax, ON L1S 2C9 Canada
905-686-0200
Fax: 905-686-8780
Tracy Laughlin, Regional Vice-President
Halifax
#100, 5657 Spring Garden Rd.
Halifax, NS B3J 3H6 Canada
902-420-1732
Fax: 902-423-6756
800-565-4040
Alan Blair, President, Atlantic Division
Kitchener
#302, 10 Duke St.
Kitchener, ON N2H 3W4 Canada
519-571-1757
Fax: 519-571-0810
London
255 Queens Ave., 8th Fl.
London, ON N6A 5R8 Canada
519-432-6721
Fax: 519-432-0818
Stephen Greig, Regional Vice-President
Mississauga
6733 Mississauga Rd., 4th Fl.
Mississauga, ON L5N 6J5 Canada
905-858-1070
Fax: 905-858-2772
Paul Meyer, Regional Vice-President
Moncton
869 Main St.
Moncton, NB E1C 1G5 Canada
506-854-7281
Fax: 506-382-5441
Ottawa
#300, 1400 St. Laurent Blvd.
Ottawa, ON KIK 4H4 Canada
613-748-3000
Fax: 613-748-0376
800-267-1836
Joe D'Annunzio, Regional Vice-President
Saint John
40 Wellington Row, 3rd Fl.
Saint John, NB E2L 3H3 Canada
506-636-9955
Fax: 506-648-0787
Thunder Bay
#207, 1205 Amber Dr.
Thunder Bay, ON P7B 6M4 Canada
807-346-7677
Fax: 807-346-7684
Toronto
1 Eglinton Ave. East
Toronto, ON M4P 3A4 Canada
416-440-8500
Fax: 416-440-4129
Mack Rooney, Regional Vice-President
Winnipeg
#805, 386 Broadway Ave.
Winnipeg, MB R3C 3R6 Canada
204-942-8402
Fax: 204-957-5483
Kevin Briscoe, Regional Vice-President

ING Insurance Company of Canada - Corporate Office (Western Region)
#1200, 321 - 6 Ave. SW
Calgary, AB T2P 4W7
403-269-7961
Fax: 403-265-7754
800-668-8384
infoING@ingcanada.com
www.ingcanada.com
Former Name: ING Western Union Insurance Company; Western Union Insurance Company
Ownership: ING Group. Parent is ING Canada P&C Inc.
Year Founded: 1940
Number of Employees: 1,000
Assets: $500m-1 billion
Revenues: $100-500 million
Classes of Insurance: Accident, Personal Accident & Sickness, Legal Expense, Auto, Boiler & Machinery, Credit, Fidelity, Property, Fire, Surety, Theft
Incorporation: Federally Incorporated Insurance Company
Profile: The company specializes in providing diversified insurance products including property & casualty.

Executives:
Jetse F. de Vries, Chief Operating Officer
Hein Bleeksma, Vice-President, Technology Services
Luisa Currie, Vice-President, Marketing
Darren Godfrey, Vice-President, Claims
Todd Klapak, Vice-President, Personal Insurance
Chris Sayer, Vice-President, Commercial Insurance
Derrek Wong, Vice-President, Finance
Branches:
Calgary
#1200, 321 - 6 Ave. SW
Calgary, AB T2P 4W7 Canada
403-269-7961
Rick Howe, Regional Vice-President, Southern Alberta
Edmonton
#800, 10130 - 103 St.
Edmonton, AB T5T 3N9 Canada
780-428-7544
Keith Jerke, Regional Vice-President, Northern Alberta
Vancouver
#400, 2955 Virtual Way
Vancouver, BC V5M 4X6 Canada
604-682-2636
Carla Smith, Regional Vice-President, BC Mainland
Victoria
#201, 780 Tolmie Ave.
Victoria, BC V8X 3W4 Canada
250-385-0866
Phil Wynne, Regional Vice-President, Vancouver Island

ING Novex Insurance Company of Canada/ ING Novex Compagnie d'Assurance du Canada
#1500A, 700 University Ave.
Toronto, ON M5G 0A1
416-341-1464
Fax: 416-941-0006
800-387-8823
infonov@ingnovex.com
www.ingnovex.com
Former Name: ING Novex Insurance Co. of Canada; Canadian Group Underwriters Insurance Company
Ownership: Part of ING Canada.
Year Founded: 1988
Classes of Insurance: Personal Accident & Sickness, Legal Expense, Auto, Liability, Boiler & Machinery, Credit, Fidelity, Property, Surety
Incorporation: Federally Incorporated Insurance Company
Profile: Both personal & commercial group insurance coverage are offered by the Canadian property & casualty insurance company.

Executives:
Claude Dussault, President/CEO
Branches:
Calgary
#1300, 321 - 6th Ave. SW
Calgary, AB T2P 4W7 Canada
403-269-7961
Fax: 403-269-8802
800-668-8384
Jetsi deVries, Attorney
Montréal
1611, boul Crémazie est
Montréal, QC H2M 2R9 Canada
514-388-5466
Fax: 514-842-2942
888-654-5466

Insurance Company of Prince Edward Island
48 Grafton St.
Charlottetown, PE C1A 1K5
902-368-3675
Fax: 902-566-4662

Insurance Company of Prince Edward Island (continued)
www.cooke.ca/peiinsurance.html
Year Founded: 1975
Assets: $10-50 million Year End: 20051231
Classes of Insurance: Auto, Life, Property
Incorporation: Provincially Incorporated Insurance Company
Executives:
Charlie Cooke, President; ccooke@icpei.ca

Insurance Corporation of British Columbia(ICBC)
151 West Esplanade
North Vancouver, BC V7M 3H9
604-661-2800
Fax: 604-646-7400
800-663-3051
www.icbc.com
Ownership: Crown. Owned by the Province of British Columbia.

Year Founded: 1973
Classes of Insurance: Auto
Incorporation: Provincially Incorporated Insurance Company
Profile: ICBC provides universal auto insurance to BC motorists. The Corporation is also responsible for driver licensing, vehicle registration & licensing.

Executives:
Paul Taylor, President/CEO
Bill Goble, COO
Geri Prior, CFO
Donnie Wing, Sr. Vice-President, Insurance
John V. Madden, Vice-President, Human Resources & Corporate Law
Keith Stewart, Vice-President, Information Services
Directors:
T. Richard Turner, Chair
Neil de Gelder
Alice Downing
Diane Fulton
Kenneth G. Martin
Susan I. Paish
Lisa Pankratz
Bob Quart
Terry Squire
Branches:
Surrey - Customer Service Centre
#405, 10470 - 152nd St.
Surrey, BC V3R 0Y4 Canada
604-587-3419
800-667-7740
Surrey - Ongoing Claims Service Centre
#500, 10470 - 152nd St.
Surrey, BC V3R 0Y3 Canada
604-592-8800
800-667-7740

JEVCO Insurance Company/ La Compagnie d'Assurances JEVCO
#100, 5250, boul Décarie
Montréal, QC H3X 2H9
514-284-9350
Fax: 514-289-9257
800-361-8500
Other Information: 514-284-4823 (Commercial); 514-284-3805 (Claims); 514-284-3390 (Motoplan)
communications@jevco.ca
www.jevco.ca
Ownership: Subsidiary of Kingsway Financial Services Inc., Mississauga, ON.
Year Founded: 1980
Classes of Insurance: Auto, Property
Incorporation: Federally Incorporated Insurance Company
Profile: JEVCO is licensed to write all classes of insurance, except life, in every Canadian province & territory.

Executives:
William G. Star, President/CEO
W. Shaun Jackson, Exec. Vice-President
Ralph Golberg, Vice-President
Serge Lavoie, Vice-President, General Manager
Jean-Guy Leclerc, Vice-President/CFO
Directors:
David H. Atkins
Mike Cascio
Thomas A. Di Giacomo
W. Shaun Jackson
Jean Lariviere
J. Brian Reeve
William G. Star

Kent & Essex Mutual Insurance Company
PO Box 356
250 St. Clair St.
Chatham, ON N7M 5K4
519-352-3190
Fax: 519-352-5344
800-265-5206
www.kentessexmutual.com
Ownership: Policyholders
Year Founded: 1888
Classes of Insurance: Personal Accident & Sickness, Auto, Liability, Boiler & Machinery, Fidelity, Property
Incorporation: Provincially Incorporated Insurance Company
Profile: Farm, home & automobile insurance are provided.

Executives:
Bernard Macneil, General Manager

The Kings Mutual Insurance Company
PO Box 10
220 Commercial St.
Berwick, NS B0P 1G0
902-538-3187
Fax: 902-538-7271
800-565-7220
kings.mutual@ns.sympatico.ca
www.kingsmutual.ns.ca
Year Founded: 1904
Classes of Insurance: Liability, Property, Fire
Incorporation: Federally Incorporated Insurance Company
Profile: Farm & home insurance are available from the company which serves all counties in Nova Scotia.

Executives:
Barry Phillip Maxner, Chief Executive Officer

Kingsway Financial Services Inc.
***Also listed under:** Financial Planning; Investment Management*

#200, 5310 Explorer Dr.
Mississauga, ON L4W 5H8
905-629-7888
Fax: 905-629-5008
info@kingsway-financial.com
www.kingsway-financial.com
Ownership: Public
Year Founded: 1987
Number of Employees: 2,250
Assets: $1-10 billion Year End: 20041231
Stock Symbol: KFS
Classes of Insurance: Auto, Property, Reinsurance
Profile: The company is a non-standard automobile, trucking, taxi & motorcycle insurer. Kingsway also offers a range of insurance services through its subsidiaries.

Executives:
William G. Star, President/CEO & Chair
W. Shaun Jackson, Exec. Vice-President/CFO
Frank Amodeo, Vice-President
Dennis Fielding, Vice-President
Shelly Gobin, Vice-President, Treasurer
Claude Smith, Vice-President, CIO
Dennis Cloutier, Chief Actuary
Directors:
William G. Star, Chair
David H. Atkins
John L. Beamish
Thomas A. Di Giacomo
Walter Farnam
Bernard Gluckstein
J. Brian Reeve
Jack Sullivan
F. Michael Walsh
Affiliated Companies:
JEVCO Insurance Company
Kingsway General Insurance Company
York Fire & Casualty Insurance Company

Kingsway General Insurance Company
#200, 5310 Explorer Dr.
Mississauga, ON L4W 5H8
905-629-7888
Fax: 905-629-5008
800-265-5458
kgmarketing@kingsway-general.com
www.kingsway-general.com
Ownership: Subsidiary of Kingsway Financial Services Inc., Mississauga, ON.
Year Founded: 1986
Classes of Insurance: Auto, Liability, Property, Surety
Incorporation: Provincially Incorporated Insurance Company
Executives:
John L. McGlynn, President/CEO
Azmin Daya, Vice-President/CFO, Sec-Treas.
Ralph Golberg, Vice-President
W. Shaun Jackson, Vice-President
Tom Mallozzi, Vice-President
Linda Paccanaro, Vice-President
Lili Pacevicius, Vice-President
Shelly Gobin, Asst. Sec.-Treas.
Directors:
David H. Atkins
John L. Beamish
Paul Iacono
W. Shaun Jackson
William G. Star

Knights of Columbus
25 Campbell St.
Belleville, ON K8N 1S6
613-962-5347
Fax: 613-968-7359
kjs@sodenco.com
Ownership: Branch of US corporation, Knights of Columbus
Year Founded: 1882
Classes of Insurance: Life
Incorporation: Federally Incorporated Insurance Company
Profile: Also insures Long-Term Care.

Executives:
Kerry J. Soden, CA, Chief Agent

Koch B&Y Insurance Services Ltd.
1944 Como Lake Ave.
Coquitlam, BC V3J 3R3
604-937-3601
Fax: 604-937-5062
www.kbyinsurance.com
Former Name: B & Y Agencies Ltd.
Number of Employees: 75
Classes of Insurance: Aircraft, Auto, Life, Marine, Surety
Incorporation: Provincially Incorporated Insurance Company
Executives:
Lorne Middler, President
Judy Fisher, Manager, Accounting
Doreen Scott, Manager, Personal Lines
Lynn Woodcock, Manager, Commercial Lines
Branches:
Abbotsford Office
#101, 2975 Gladwin Rd.
Abbotsford, BC V2T 5T4 Canada
604-853-7111
Fax: 604-852-6756
Tracy Dance, Manager, Office
Burnaby Office
#39, 4567 Lougheed Hwy.
Burnaby, BC V5C 3Z6 Canada
604-299-0651
Fax: 604-299-4526
Ron Bakker, Manager, Office
Chilliwack Office
Vedder Crossing Plaza
#2, 6014 Vedder Rd.
Chilliwack, BC V2R 5M4 Canada
604-824-4849
Fax: 604-824-4840
Rob Vissers, Manager, Office
Maple Ridge Office
11924 - 207 St.
Maple Ridge, BC V2X 1X7 Canada
604-467-5111
Fax: 604-467-1102
Gail Holland, Manager, Office
North Vancouver Office
#540, 333 Brooksbank Ave.
North Vancouver, BC V7J 3S8 Canada
604-980-7298
Fax: 604-980-5889
Jahan Famili, Manager, Office
White Rock Office
11457A Johnston Rd.
White Rock, BC V4B 2Z4 Canada
604-538-8833
Fax: 604-531-4832

Dorothy Juda, Manager, Office

L'ALPHA, compagnie d'assurances inc.

#119, 430, rue Saint-Georges
Drummondville, QC J2C 4H4
819-474-7958
Fax: 819-477-6139
drummond@assurance-alpha.com
www.assurance-alpha.com/alpha.php
Ownership: Private.
Year Founded: 1906
Classes of Insurance: Auto, Property, Surety
Incorporation: Provincially Incorporated Insurance Company
Executives:
Geneviève Verrier, Directrice, Opérations
Branches:
Plessisville
1787, rue Saint-Calixte
Plessisville, QC G6L 1R4
Fax: 819-362-8972
888-525-7428
plessis@assurance-alpha.com
Québec
#210, 455, rue Marais
Québec, QC G1M 3A2
Fax: 418-692-4995
888-525-7428
quebec@assurance-alpha.com
Saint-Hyacinthe
720, boul. Casavant ouest
Saint-Hyacinthe, QC J2S 7S3
Fax: 450-773-3604
888-525-7428
sthyacinthe@assurance-alpha.com
Sherbrooke
Place Jacques-Cartier
#30, 1650, rue King ouest
Sherbrooke, QC J1J 2C3
Fax: 819-563-5619
888-525-7428
sherbrooke@assurance-alpha.com
Trois-Rivières
5515, boul. des Forges
Trois-Rivières, QC G8Y 5L5
Fax: 819-693-8570
888-525-7428
troisrivieres@assurance-alpha.com
Victoriaville
36, rue Perreault
Victoriaville, QC G6P 5C8
Fax: 819-758-4292
888-525-7428
victo@assurance-alpha.com

L'Assurance Mutuelle des Fabriques de Montréal

1071, rue de la Cathédrale
Montréal, QC H3B 2V4
514-395-4969
Fax: 514-861-8921
800-567-6586
info.general@amf-mtl.com
Ownership: Member-owned
Year Founded: 1853
Number of Employees: 10
Assets: $10-50 million Year End: 20041231
Revenues: $5-10 million Year End: 20041231
Classes of Insurance: Liability, Boiler & Machinery, Property, Fire, Theft
Incorporation: Provincially Incorporated Insurance Company
Profile: The mutual insurance company specializes in insuring church & religious institutions.

Executives:
René Ferland, President; 450-753-7596
André Charbonneau, Vice-President; 450-446-1825
Serge Léonard, General Manager; 450-622-6290
Maurice Lemay, Administrator; 450-373-8122

L'Entraide assurance, compagnie mutuelle/ L'Entraide Assurance Mutual Company

CP 2324
520, boul Charest est, 1er étage
Québec, QC G1K 7P5
418-658-0663
Fax: 418-658-5065
800-536-8724
service@lentraide.com
www.lentraide.com
Former Name: L'Entraide assurance-vie, compagnie mutuelle
Ownership: Public
Year Founded: 1967
Number of Employees: 25
Assets: $10-50 million Year End: 20051231
Revenues: $10-50 million Year End: 20051231
Classes of Insurance: Accident, Personal Accident & Sickness, Life
Incorporation: Provincially Incorporated Insurance Company
Profile: The company also offers creditors' insurance.

Executives:
Gaëtan Gagné, Président du conseil, Chef de la direction
Richard Bureau, Vice-président, Développement et affaires générales
Noël Verville, Vice-président, Finances et exploitation
Omer Gagnon, Directeur médical
Pierrette Lapointe, Directrice, Centre des services à la clientèle
Directors:
Gaëtan Gagné, Président
Richard Beaudry
Philippe Borel
Michel Giguère
Marcel Jobin
Nabil T. Khoury
Réal Moffet
Louis Têtu

L'Excellence, Compagnie d'assurance-vVie

#202, 5055, boul Métropolitain est
Montréal, QC H1R 1Z7
514-327-0020
800-465-5818
service@excellence.qc.ca
www.excellence.qc.ca
Ownership: Private
Year Founded: 1962
Classes of Insurance: Personal Accident & Sickness, Life
Incorporation: Provincially Incorporated Insurance Company
Executives:
Antoine Ponce, FSA, FICA, CFA, Président

L'Internationale, compagnie d'assurance-vie/ The International Life Insurance Company

CP 696
143, rue Hériot
Montréal, QC J2B 6W9
514-478-1315
Fax: 819-474-1990
800-310-2166
courrier@linternationale.qc.ca
www.linternationale.qc.ca
Ownership: Private
Year Founded: 1957
Number of Employees: 26
Assets: 12,000,000
Revenues: 16,000,000
Classes of Insurance: Personal Accident & Sickness, Life
Incorporation: Provincially Incorporated Insurance Company
Executives:
Jacques Desbiens, Président du conseil d'administration, Directeur général

L'Union Canadienne Compagnie d'Assurances

2475, boul Laurier
Québec, QC G1T 1C4
418-651-3551
800-463-3382
www.unioncanadienne.com
Ownership: Part of The Co-operators Group Limited.
Year Founded: 1943
Number of Employees: 350
Classes of Insurance: Auto, Property
Incorporation: Provincially Incorporated Insurance Company
Executives:
Katherine Bardswick, President/CEO
Branches:
Montréal
#700, 2000, av McGill College
Montréal, QC H3A 3H3 Canada
514-847-8000
Fax: 514-847-8021
800-363-6442

L'Union-Vie, compagnie mutuelle d'assurance/ The Union Life, Mutual Assurance Company

CP 696
142, rue Hériot
Drummondville, QC J2B 6W9
819-478-1315
Fax: 819-474-1990
800-567-0988
direction@union-vie.qc.ca
www.union-vie.qc.ca
Ownership: Member-owned
Year Founded: 1889
Number of Employees: 65
Assets: $100-500 million Year End: 20051231
Revenues: $50-100 million Year End: 20051231
Classes of Insurance: Personal Accident & Sickness, Life, Reinsurance
Incorporation: Provincially Incorporated Insurance Company
Profile: L'Union-Vie is also affiliated with Les fonds d'investissements spécialisés du Québec & La financière l'union-vie inc.

Executives:
Jacques Desbiens, FSA, FCIA, President
Jean Audet, Vice-President, Technology
Michel Parizeau, Vice-President, Sales & Marketing
Luc Pellerin, Vice-President, Actuary
Carl Têtu, Vice-President, Finance
Affiliated Companies:
L'Internationale, compagnie d'assurance-vie

La Capitale Civil Service Insurer Inc.

625, rue Saint-Amable
Québec, QC G1R 2G5
418-643-3884
Fax: 418-528-0457
800-463-5549
www.lacapitale.com
Ownership: Subsidiary of La Capitale Financial Group Inc., Québec, QC.
Year Founded: 1941
Number of Employees: 331
Assets: $1-10 billion
Revenues: $100-500 million
Classes of Insurance: Life
Incorporation: Provincially Incorporated Insurance Company
Profile: Exclusively serves Québec employees in the public & para-public sector; other services include life insurance, health & salary insurance, annuities & savings plans, financial planning.

Executives:
Jean-Yves Dupéré, CEO
Robert St-Denis, President/COO
Steven Ross, Exec. Vice-President, Individual Insurance
Marcel Bilodeau, Vice-President, Group Insurance
Pierre Dansereau, Vice-President, Marketing & Communications

Pierre Grenier, Vice-President, Finance & Administration, Treasurer
Francine Landry, Vice-President, Technology
Michel Lévesque, Vice-President, Investment, Appointed Actuary
Alain Roch, Vice-President, Legal Affairs
Hubert Auclair, Secretary
Directors:
Jean-Yves Dupéré, Chair
Jacquelin Bergeron, Vice-Chair
Jean-Paul Beaulieu
Louise Potvin
René Rouleau
Branches:
Brossard
#204, 5855, boul Taschereau
Brossard, QC J4Z 1A5 Canada
514-864-4189
Christian Breton
Chicoutimi - Saguenay
305, rue Hôtel-de-Ville
Chicoutimi, QC G7H 4W8 Canada
418-698-3675
Yves Lavoie
Laval
#520, 3080, boul Le Carrefeur
Laval, QC H7T 2R5 Canada
514-873-9364
Benoit Goulet

INSURANCE COMPANIES

La Capitale Civil Service Insurer Inc. (continued)

Québec
#30, 2875, boul Laurier
Québec, QC G1V 2M2 Canada
418-643-3990
Lorne Brennan

Sherbrooke
#130A, 2100, rue King ouest
Sherbrooke, QC J1J 2E8 Canada
819-820-3585
Sandrate Larouche

La Capitale General Insurance Inc./ La Capitale assurances générales inc.

Édifice Hector-Fabre
CP 17100
525, boul René-Lévesque est
Québec, QC G1K 9E2
418-266-1700
Fax: 418-646-5425
800-463-4432
Other Information: Phone, Claims: 418-266-9760; Fax, Claims: 418-266-3454; Toll Free, Claims: 800-461-0770
www.lacapitale.com
Ownership: Subsidiary of La Capitale Financial Group Inc., Québec, QC.
Year Founded: 1976
Classes of Insurance: Auto, Property
Incorporation: Provincially Incorporated Insurance Company
Profile: The insurance company services the Québec Civil Service. Classes of insurance offered also include legal access insurance & business & self-employed workers insurance.
Executives:
John Strome, President/CEO
Sylvain Simard, Vice-President, Sales & Development
Branches:

Baie-Comeau
#203, 337, boul Lasalle
Baie-Comeau, QC G4Z 2Z1 Canada
418-294-6300
Fax: 418-294-8624
800-463-8554

Blainville
#001, 28, côte Saint-Louis ouest
Blainville, QC J7C 1B8 Canada
514-906-1700
Fax: 450-433-6460
800-361-0646

Boucherville
#100, 204, boul De Montarville
Boucherville, QC J4B 6S2 Canada
514-906-1700
Fax: 450-449-2671
800-361-0646

Brossard
#170, 7005, boul Taschereau
Brossard, QC J4Z 1A7 Canada
514-906-1700
Fax: 450-462-6850
800-361-0646

Chicoutimi
#200, 305, rue de l'Hôtel-de-Ville
Chicoutimi, QC G7H 4W8 Canada
418-698-5900
Fax: 418-698-3733
800-463-9918

Drummondville
121, rue Hériot
Drummondville, QC J2C 1J5 Canada
819-475-1799
Fax: 819-475-8798
800-567-0965

Gatineau
#201, 290, boul Saint-Joseph
Gatineau, QC J8Y 3Y3 Canada
819-420-1700
Fax: 819-772-3979
800-567-9673

Granby
151, rue Saint-Jacques
Granby, QC J2G 9A7 Canada
450-777-1750
Fax: 450-777-2880
800-465-3200

Jonquière
#102, 2106, rue Sainte-Famille
Jonquière, QC G7X 4X1 Canada
418-547-4597
Fax: 418-547-2007
800-463-9918

La Sarre
65A, 5e av est
La Sarre, QC J9Z 1L1 Canada
819-333-6140
Fax: 819-339-7565
800-567-6495

Laval
#101, 3030, boul Le Carrefour
Laval, QC H7T 2P5 Canada
514-906-1700
Fax: 450-680-7074
800-361-0646

Montréal - Maisonneuve ouest
#500, 425, boul de Maisonneuve ouest
Montréal, QC H3A 3G5 Canada
514-906-1700
Fax: 514-904-4225
800-361-0646

Montréal - Roseraies
#200, 7333, Place des Roseraies
Montréal, QC H1M 2X6 Canada
514-906-1700
Fax: 514-353-6832
800-361-0646

Montréal - Saint-Jean
#140, 755, boul Saint-Jean
Montréal, QC H9R 5M9 Canada
514-906-1700
Fax: 514-695-5328
800-361-0646

Rimouski
#21, 92 - 2e rue ouest
Rimouski, QC G5L 8B3 Canada
418-724-0777
Fax: 418-727-3831
800-463-9074

Rouyn-Noranda
170, av Principale
Rouyn-Noranda, QC J9X 4P7 Canada
819-764-2700
Fax: 819-763-3387
800-567-6495

Sept-×les
421, av Arnaud
Sept-×les, QC G4R 3B3 Canada
418-968-0044
Fax: 418-964-8322
800-463-1760

Sherbrooke
#250, 2100, rue King ouest
Sherbrooke, QC J1J 2E8 Canada
819-822-0060
Fax: 819-564-1837
800-567-6060

Sorel-Tracy
16200, ch Saint-Roch
Sorel-Tracy, QC J3P 5N3 Canada
450-561-1529
Fax: 450-742-5216
800-361-0646

St-Georges
9012, boul Lacroix
St-Georges, QC G5Y 5P4 Canada
418-227-5461
Fax: 418-226-3236
800-463-1669

Trois-Rivières
Édifice Le Trifluvien
#200, 4450, boul des Forges
Trois-Rivières, QC G8Y 1W5 Canada
819-374-3050
Fax: 819-371-6661
800-567-8527

La Capitale Insurance & Financial Services/ La Capitale assurances et gestion du patrimoine

Also listed under: *Financial Planning*
Édifice Le Delta II
#100, 2875, boul Laurier
Québec, QC G1V 2M2
418-644-4200
Fax: 418-644-5226
888-463-4856
collectif@lacapitale.com
www.lacapitale.com
Former Name: La Capitale Life Insurance Inc.
Ownership: Subsidiary of La Capitale Financial Group Inc., Québec, QC.
Year Founded: 1989
Classes of Insurance: Personal Accident & Sickness, Life
Incorporation: Provincially Incorporated Insurance Company
Profile: Group insurance products are provided for groups from the civil service & the private sector. Financial services include savings, loans & financial solutions for retired people.
Executives:
Robert St-Denis, President/COO
Francine Landry, Vice-President, Technology, Systems Development & E-Business
Branches:

Montréal
#820, 425, boul de Maisonneuve ouest
Montréal, QC H3A 3G5 Canada
514-873-2402
Fax: 514-873-8733
888 899-4959

Québec
Édifice Le Delta II
#100, 2875, boul Laurier
Québec, QC G1V 2M2 Canada
418-644-4200
Fax: 418-644-4352
800-363-9683

La Compagnie d'Assurance Missisquoi/ The Missisquoi Insurance Company

#500, 1000, de la Gauchetière ouest
Montréal, QC H3B 4W5
514-875-5790
Fax: 514-875-9769
800-361-7573
Ownership: Subsidiary of Economical Insurance Company
Year Founded: 1835
Number of Employees: 200
Assets: $100-500 million Year End: 20041231
Revenues: $100-500 million Year End: 20041231
Classes of Insurance: Legal Expense, Auto, Liability, Boiler & Machinery, Fidelity, Property, Fire, Surety, Theft
Incorporation: Provincially Incorporated Insurance Company
Executives:
M. Pavelack, COO/Exec. Vice-President; 514-954-4230
M. Bédard, Vice-President, Underwriting; 514-954-5469
M. Chevalier, Vice-President, Business Development; 514-954-5418
Gilles Langlois, CA, Vice-President, Finance; 514-954-4229
Branches:

Frelighsburg
50, rue Principale
Frelighsburg, QC J0J 1C0 Canada
450-298-5251
Fax: 450-298-5410
Ginette Clermont, Manager

Montréal
#500, 1000, de la Gauchetière ouest
Montréal, QC H3B 4W5 Canada
514-875-5790
Fax: 514-875-9769
L.G. Pelletier, Manager

Québec
Place Iberville
#30, 11, 1175, rue Lavigerie
Québec, QC G1V 4P1 Canada
418-652-2333
Fax: 418-652-7409
Therese Bergeron, Manager

La Mutuelle d'Église de l'Inter-ouest

180, boul Mont-Bleu
Gatineau, QC J8Z 3J5
819-595-0708
Fax: 819-595-2678
Incorporation: Provincially Incorporated Insurance Company
Executives:
Réal Fournelle, Président

La Survivance, compagnie mutuelle d'assurance vie
CP 10 000
1555, rue Girouard ouest
Saint-Hyacinthe, QC J2S 7C8
450-773-6051
Fax: 450-773-6470
800-773-8404
info@lasurvivance.com
Ownership: Mutual.
Year Founded: 1938
Number of Employees: 91
Assets: $100-500 million
Revenues: $50-100 million
Classes of Insurance: Personal Accident & Sickness, Life
Incorporation: Provincially Incorporated Insurance Company
Executives:
Richard Gagnon, Président, Chef de la direction
Luc Bergeron, FSA, FICA, Vice-président, Actuariat
Marc Bourduas, Vice-président, Finances et administration
Tony Di Stavolo, FLMI, FALU, ACS, Vice-président, Opérations d'assurances
Stéphane Rochon, B.Com., AVA, RHU, Vice-président, Marketing et ventes, Assurance individuelle
Marc Thomassin, Vice-président, Développement, Assurance collective
Gilles Valiquette, Directeur, Technologies, Survitech
Gisèle Boivin, Conseillère au président, Ressources humaines

Lambton Mutual Insurance Company
PO Box 520
7873 Confederation Line
Watford, ON N0M 2S0
519-876-2304
Fax: 519-876-3940
800-561-4136
info@lambtonmutual.com
www.lambtonmutual.com
Year Founded: 1875
Classes of Insurance: Personal Accident & Sickness, Auto, Liability, Boiler & Machinery, Fidelity, Property, Hail & Crop
Incorporation: Provincially Incorporated Insurance Company
Profile: Insurance products include the following: residential, agribusiness, automobile & commercial.
Executives:
Ronald Perry, Secretary-Manager
Directors:
Ross L. Smith, President
Clare Moffatt, Vice-President

Lanark Mutual Insurance Company
96 South St., Scotch Line Rd.
Perth, ON K7H 0A2
613-267-5554
Fax: 613-267-6793
800-267-7908
lmadmin@LanarkMutual.com
www.lanarkmutual.com
Ownership: Policyholders
Year Founded: 1896
Classes of Insurance: Auto, Liability, Boiler & Machinery, Property, Hail & Crop, Theft
Incorporation: Provincially Incorporated Insurance Company

Lawyers' Professional Indemnity Company(LAWPRO)
PO Box 75
#2200, 1 Dundas St W.
Toronto, ON M5G 1Z3
416-598-5800
Fax: 416-599-8341
800-410-1013
service@LAWPRO.ca
www.lawpro.ca
Also Known As: LawPro
Year Founded: 1995
Classes of Insurance: Liability
Incorporation: Federally Incorporated Insurance Company
Profile: LawPro is licensed to provide professional liability insurance & title insurance in numerous jurisdictions across Canada. The company's malpractice insurance service insures lawyers & offers them risk & practice management programs. TitlePLUS title insurance gives protection to buyers & lenders.
Executives:
Michelle Strom, President/CEO
Craig Allen, Vice-President, Actuary
Duncan Gosnell, Vice-President, Underwriting
Akhil J. Wagh, Vice-President, Finance, Treasurer
Kathleen Waters, Vice-President, TitlePLUS
Caron Wishart, Vice-President, Claims
Directors:
Kim A. Carpenter-Gunn, Chair
Ian D. Croft, Vice-Chair
George D. Anderson
Constance Backhouse
Abdul A. Chahbar
Douglas F. Cutbush
Lawrence A. Eustace
Frederick W. Gorbet
Malcolm L. Heins
Rita Hoff
William G. Holbrook
Vern Krishna
Laurie H. Pawlitza
Michelle Strom
Gerald A. Swaye

Le Groupe Estrie-Richelieu, compagnie d'assurance(GER)
770, rue Principale
Granby, QC J2G 2Y7
450-378-0101
Fax: 450-378-5189
info@ger.qc.ca
www.ger.qc.ca
Year Founded: 1986
Number of Employees: 53
Assets: $50-100 million
Revenues: $10-50 million
Classes of Insurance: Auto, Liability, Boiler & Machinery, Property, Fire
Incorporation: Provincially Incorporated Insurance Company
Executives:
Michel Prévost, Président/Chef de la direction, Chef des opérations
Johanne Ménard, Secrétaire
François Savaria, Trésorier, Controleur
Directors:
François Beaudry
Paul Bellefroid
Branches:
Granby
770, rue Principale
Granby, QC J2Y 2Y7 Canada
450-378-0101
Fax: 450-378-5189

Legacy General Insurance Company/ Compagnie d'Assurances Générales Legacy
80 Tiverton Ct., 5th Fl.
Markham, ON L3R 0G4
905-479-7500
Fax: 905-479-3224
www.canadianpremier.ca
Ownership: Private. Subsidiary of Canadian Premier Holdings Ltd. Parent is Vereniging Aegon Netherlands Membership Association.
Year Founded: 1994
Assets: $10-50 million
Revenues: $10-50 million
Classes of Insurance: Personal Accident & Sickness, Liability, Property
Incorporation: Federally Incorporated Insurance Company
Profile: In 2006, all assets and liabilities of Heritage General Insurance Company were transferred to Legacy General Insurance Company. Another class of insurance offered is loss of employment.
Executives:
Isaac Sananes, President/CEO
T. Daniel McGahey, Exec. Vice-President
Denise Compton, Vice-President
David Lipps, Vice-President
Joe Noone, Vice-President
Tamesh Paraboo, Asst. Vice-President, Asst. Controller
Michael Eubanks, Secretary
Michael L. Wilson, Controller
Directors:
Marilyn Carp, Chair
J.C. Chartrand
Jay Huckle
Gordon Johnson
Robert McDowell
T. Daniel McGahey
Issac Sananes

Lennox & Addington Fire Mutual Insurance Company
PO Box 174
32 Mill St.
Napanee, ON K7R 3M3
613-354-4810
Fax: 613-354-7112
800-267-7812
www.l-amutual.com
Also Known As: L&A Mutual Insurance Company
Year Founded: 1876
Classes of Insurance: Personal Accident & Sickness, Auto, Liability, Marine, Property
Incorporation: Provincially Incorporated Insurance Company
Profile: The mutual company offers services for farms, homes, businesses, automobiles & watercraft.
Executives:
Rick Walters, Manager; rwalters@l-amutual.com
Barb Delaney, Accountant
Directors:
Paul Burns
Cameron Craven
Duncan Hough
Reginald Keech
Clarence Kennedy
Roy Pierse

Liberty Mutual Insurance Company/ La Compagnie d'Assurance Liberté Mutuelle
#1000, 181 Bay St.
Toronto, ON M5J 2T3
416-307-4353
Fax: 416-365-7281
www.libertymutual.com
Ownership: Foreign. Part of Liberty Mutual Group, Inc., Boston, MA, USA.
Classes of Insurance: Personal Accident & Sickness, Aircraft, Auto, Liability, Boiler & Machinery, Fidelity, Property, Surety
Incorporation: Federally Incorporated Insurance Company
Executives:
Michael L. Molony, Chief Agent

Life Insurance Company of North America(LINA)
#606, 55 Town Centre Ct.
Toronto, ON M1P 4X4
416-290-6666
Fax: 416-290-0726
www.cigna.com
Ownership: Private. Parent is CIGNA Corporation, Philadelphia, PA, USA.
Year Founded: 1963
Assets: $50-100 million Year End: 20051231
Revenues: $1-5 million Year End: 20051231
Classes of Insurance: Accident, Personal Accident & Sickness, Life
Incorporation: Federally Incorporated Insurance Company
Profile: LINA is affiliated with CIGNA Life Insurance Company of Canada & Connecticut General Life Insurance Co.
Executives:
M. Eman Hassan, Chief Agent

Lloyd's Underwriters
#1540, 1155, rue Metcalfe
Montréal, QC H3B 2V6
514-861-8361
Fax: 514-861-0470
877-455-6937
info@lloyds.ca
www.lloyds.com
Former Name: Lloyd's Canada Inc.
Ownership: Foreign
Year Founded: 1688
Classes of Insurance: Personal Accident & Sickness, Aircraft, Legal Expense, Auto, Liability, Boiler & Machinery, Fidelity, Property, Fire, Surety, Reinsurance
Incorporation: Federally Incorporated Insurance Company
Executives:
Nicholas Smith, Attorney-in-Fact

Lombard General Insurance Company of Canada
105 Adelaide St. West
Toronto, ON M5H 1P9

Lombard General Insurance Company of Canada (continued)
416-350-4400
Fax: 416-350-4412
Ownership: Private.
Year Founded: 1994
Classes of Insurance: Personal Accident & Sickness, Aircraft, Legal Expense, Auto, Liability, Boiler & Machinery, Credit, Fidelity, Property, Surety, Hail & Crop, Theft
Incorporation: Federally Incorporated Insurance Company
Executives:
Richard N. Patina, President/CEO
M. Jane Gardner, Sr. Vice-President/CFO
Katharine M. Allan, Sr. Vice-President, Chief Underwriting Officer
Robert T. Coughlin, Sr. Vice-President, Claims
William J. Dunlop, Sr. Vice-President, Human Resources, General Counsel
Kim H. Tan, Sr. Vice-President, Corporate & Business Development
Anne-Marie Vanier, Sr. Vice-President, Chief Actuary
Peter Howling, Vice-President, Corporate Systems
Stephen F. McManus, Vice-President, Finance
Richard Lapierre, Regional Vice-President, Québec Region
Steven Cade, Regional Vice-President, Western Region
Stan Keeping, Regional Vice-President, Atlantic, Commercial Lines
Brent Dodge, Director, Internal Audit
Josée Lambert, Director, Actuarial Services
Peter Aumonier, Asst. Vice-President, Claims
Directors:
Byron G. Messier, Chair
Frank B. Bennett
Winslow W. Bennett
Robert J. Gunn
Richard Patina
Bryan S. Smith
D. Gregory Taylor
John C. Varnell
Branches:
Cambridge - Farm/Agriculture
#400, 1575 Bishop St.
Cambridge, ON N1R 7J4 Canada
519-740-8828
Fax: 516-740-6474
877-740-8828
Halifax - Atlantic Region
PO Box 6
1801 Hollis St., 8th Fl.
Halifax, NS B3J 2L5 Canada
902-422-1221
Fax: 902-423-8640
Montréal
#1700, 2001, av University
Montréal, QC H3A 2A6 Canada
514-843-1111
Fax: 514-843-1103
Québec
Tour Belle Cour
#2750, 2600, boul Laurier
Québec, QC G1V 4M6 Canada
418-659-6300
Fax: 418-659-2543
Saskatoon - Canadian Hail Agencies
#201, 3301 - 8 St. East
Saskatoon, SK S7H 5K5 Canada
306-242-1415
Fax: 306-664-4492
Thunder Bay
216 Camelot St.
Thunder Bay, ON P7A 4B1 Canada
807-344-1410
Fax: 807-345-6079
800-465-6931
Toronto
105 Adelaide St. West
Toronto, ON M5H 1P9 Canada
416-350-4000
Fax: 416-350-4412
Vancouver
Two Bentall Centre
#600, 555 Burrard St.
Vancouver, BC V7X 1M8 Canada
604-631-0255
Fax: 604-631-6896

Lombard Insurance Company
105 Adelaide St. West
Toronto, ON M5H 1P9
416-350-4400
Fax: 416-350-4412
www.lombard.ca
Ownership: Private. Owned by Lombard Canada Ltd., a wholly owned subsidiary of Northbridge Financial Corporation
Year Founded: 1994
Classes of Insurance: Personal Accident & Sickness, Aircraft, Legal Expense, Auto, Liability, Boiler & Machinery, Credit, Marine, Fidelity, Property, Fire, Surety, Hail & Crop, Theft
Incorporation: Federally Incorporated Insurance Company
Executives:
Richard N. Patina, President/CEO
Katherine M. Allan, Sr. Vice-President, Chief Underwriting Officer
Robert T. Coughlin, Sr. Vice-President, Claims
William J. Dunlop, Sr. Vice-President, Gen. Counsel & Human Resources
M. Jane Gardner, Sr. Vice-President & CFO
Kim H. Tan, Sr. Vice-President, Corporate & Business Development
Anne-Marie Vanier, Sr. Vice-President, Chief Actuary
Peter Howling, Vice-President, Corporate Systems
Steven Cade, Regional Vice-President, Western Region
Stan Keeping, Regional Vice-President, Atlantic Region
Richard Lapierre, Regional Vice-President, Québec Region
Mark LeBlanc, Regional Vice-President, Central Region
Branches:
Cambridge
#400, 1575 Bishop St.
Cambridge, ON N1R 7J4 Canada
519-740-8828
Fax: 519-740-6474
877-740-8828
Halifax - Atlantic Region
Central Trust Bldg.
1801 Hollis St., 8th Fl.
Halifax, NS B3J 2L5 Canada
902-422-1221
Fax: 902-423-8640
Montréal
#1700, 2001, av University
Montréal, QC H3A 2A6 Canada
514-843-1111
Fax: 514-843-1103
Québec
#2750, 2600, boul Laurier
Québec, QC G1V 4M6 Canada
418-659-6300
Fax: 418-659-2543
Saskatoon - Canadian Hail Agencies
#201, 3301 - 8th St. East
Saskatoon, SK S7H 5K5 Canada
306-242-1415
Fax: 306-664-4492
Thunder Bay
216 Camelot St.
Thunder Bay, ON P7A 4B1 Canada
807-344-1410
Fax: 807-345-6479
Toronto - Central Region
105 Adelaide St. West
Toronto, ON M5H 1P9 Canada
416-350-4000
Fax: 416-350-4123
Vancouver - Western Region
Two Bentall Centre
#600, 555 Burrard St.
Vancouver, BC V7X 1M8 Canada
604-683-0255
Fax: 604-631-6896

London & Midland General Insurance Company
201 Queens Ave.
London, ON N6A 1J1
519-672-1070
Fax: 519-660-2625
800-285-8623
Year Founded: 1947
Number of Employees: 20
Assets: $100-500 million Year End: 20041231
Revenues: $50-100 million Year End: 20041231
Classes of Insurance: Accident, Personal Accident & Sickness, Auto, Boiler & Machinery, Life, Fidelity, Property, Fire, Surety, Theft
Incorporation: Federally Incorporated Insurance Company
Executives:
A.W. Miles, Sr. Vice-President & General Manager; 519-660-2611
H. Anderson, Vice-President/CFO; 519-660-2602

London Life Insurance Company/ London Life, Compagnie d'Assurance-Vie
255 Dufferin Ave.
London, ON N6A 4K1
519-432-5281
corporate.information@londonlife.com
www.londonlife.com
Ownership: Wholly owned by London Insurance Group, a publicly traded company which is 100% held by The Great West Life Assurance Company.
Year Founded: 1874
Assets: $10-100 billion Year End: 20060930
Revenues: $10-100 billion Year End: 20060930
Classes of Insurance: Personal Accident & Sickness, Life, Reinsurance
Incorporation: Federally Incorporated Insurance Company
Executives:
Raymond L. McFeetors, President/CEO
William L. Acton, President/COO, Europe
Denis J. Devos, President/COO, Canada
D. Allen Loney, Exec. Vice-President & Chief Actuary, Capital Management
William W. Lovatt, Exec. Vice-President/CFO
Peter G. Munro, Exec. Vice-President, Chief Investment Officer
Elwood C. Haas, Sr. Vice-President, Chief Internal Audior
Sheila A. Wagar, Sr. Vice-President, General Counsel & Secretary
Directors:
Robert Gratton, Chair
President/CEO, Power Financial Corporation
Gail S. Asper
General Counsel & Corporate Secretary, CanWest Global Communications Corp.
Orest T. Dackow, O.C.
André Desmarais, O.C.
President/Co-CEO, Power Corporation of Canada; Deputy Chair, Power Financial Cor
Paul Desmarais, Jr., O.C.
Chair, Executive Committee, Power Corporation of Canada
Michael L. Hepher
Daniel Johnson
Counsel, McCarthy Tétrault
Kevin P. Kavanagh, O.C.
Chancellor, University of Brandon
Peter Kruyt
Donald F. Mazankowski, P.C., O.C.
William T. McCallum
Co-President/CEO, Great-West Lifeco
Raymond L. McFeetors
President/CEO, The Great-West Life Assurance Co.; Co-President/CEO, Great-West L
Jerry E.A. Nickerson
Chair, H.B. Nickerson & Sons Limited
David A. Nield
R. Jeffrey Orr
President/CEO, Investors Group Inc.
Michel Plessis-Bélair, FCA
Exec. Vice-President & CFO & Vice-Chair, Power Corporation of Canada
Guy St-Germain, CM
President, Placements Laugerma inc.
Emőke J.E. Szathmáry, C.M.
Murray J. Taylor
Gérard Veilleux
Vice-President, Power Communications Inc.
Affiliated Companies:
Quadrus Investment Services Ltd.
The Lifestyle Protector Solution

The Loyalist Insurance Company
#106, 911 Golf Links Rd.
Ancaster, ON L9K 1H9
905-648-6767
Fax: 905-648-7220
dfcoons@loyalistinsurance.com
www.loyalistinsurance.com
Ownership: Public. Loyalist Insurance Group Ltd.

Year Founded: 1981
Stock Symbol: LOY
Incorporation: Provincially Incorporated Insurance Company
Executives:
Donald W. Coons, CEO/CFO, Secretary/Treasurer
Directors:
James D. Coons, Chair

Lumbermen's Underwriting Alliance

#300, 455, boul Fénélon
Montréal, QC H9S 5T8
514-631-2710
Fax: 514-631-9788
www.lumbermensunderwriting.com
Year Founded: 1905
Classes of Insurance: Boiler & Machinery, Property
Incorporation: Federally Incorporated Insurance Company
Profile: The organization insures property primarily in the forest products industry in Canada & USA.

Executives:
Jacques Gagnon, Vice-President
Maurice Vialette, Chief Agent
Branches:
Québec
#100, 979, av Bourgogne
Québec, QC G1W 2L4 Canada
418-622-1580
Fax: 418-622-0523

Surrey
#2005, 7445 - 132 St.
Surrey, BC V3W 1J8 Canada
604-596-2771
Fax: 604-596-2778
Toronto - North York
#203, 155 Gordon Baker Rd.
Toronto, ON M2H 3N7 Canada
416-492-4810
Fax: 416-492-5263

Manitoba Agricultural Services Corporation - Insurance Corporate Office(MASC)

Also listed under: *Financing & Loan Companies*
#400, 50 - 24th St. NW
Portage La Prairie, MB R1N 3V9
204-239-3499
Fax: 204-239-3401
mailbox@masc.mb.ca
www.masc.mb.ca
Former Name: Manitoba Crop Insurance Corporation; Manitoba Agricultural Credit Corporation
Ownership: Crown corporation.
Year Founded: 1960
Number of Employees: 0
Classes of Insurance: Hail & Crop
Incorporation: Provincially Incorporated Insurance Company
Profile: In 2005, the Manitoba Agricultural Credit Corporation & the Manitoba Crop Insurance Corporation merged to create the Manitoba Agricultural Services Corporation. The corporation offers the following insurance programs: production, forage, hail, fall frost, wildlife damage compensation, & young farmer crop plan credit.

Executives:
Neil Hamilton, President/CEO
Directors:
John Plohman, Chair
Walter Kolisnyk, Vice-Chair
Frieda Krpan, Vice-Chair
Anders Bruun
Frank Fiarchuk
Wilfred Harder
Carol Masse
Harry Sotas
Sandy Yanick
Branches:
Altona
PO Box 1209
67 - 2nd St. NE
Altona, MB R0G 0B0 Canada
204-324-2800
Fax: 204-324-2803
altona.insurance@masc.mb.ca
Beausejour
Provincial Government Building
PO Box 50
Beausejour, MB R0E 0C0 Canada
204-268-6001
Fax: 204-268-6060
beausejour.insurance@masc.mb.ca
Birtle
PO Box 39
726 Main St.
Birtle, MB R0M 0C0 Canada
204-842-7700
Fax: 204-824-7705
birtle.insurance@masc.mb.ca
Carman
PO Box 490
65 - 3rd Ave. NE
Carman, MB R0G 0J0 Canada
204-745-5600
Fax: 204-745-5605
carman.insurance@masc.mb.ca
Dauphin
Provincial Government Building
27 - 2nd Ave. SW
Dauphin, MB R7N 3E5 Canada
204-622-2017
Fax: 204-622-2076
dauphin.insurance@masc.mb.ca
Deloraine
PO Box 529
101 Finlay Ave. East
Deloraine, MB R0M 0M0 Canada
204-747-2050
Fax: 204-747-2889
deloraine.insurance@masc.mb.ca
Fisher Branch
PO Box 359
Fisher Branch, MB R0C 0Z0 Canada
204-372-6619
Fax: 204-372-6554
fisher.insurance@masc.mb.ca
Glenboro
PO Box 250
103 Broadway St.
Glenboro, MB R0K 0X0 Canada
204-827-8870
Fax: 204-827-8875
glenboro.insurance@masc.mb.ca
Grandview
PO Box 236
221 Roland Ave.
Grandview, MB R0L 0Y0 Canada
204-546-5010
Fax: 204-546-5015
grandview.insurance@masc.mb.ca
Hamiota
PO Box 50
221 Elm St.
Hamiota, MB R0M 0T0 Canada
204-764-3000
Fax: 204-764-3014
hamiota.insurance@masc.mb.ca
Neepawa
PO Box 1179
41 Main St. East
Neepawa, MB R0J 1H0 Canada
204-476-7050
Fax: 204-476-7094
neepawa.insurance@masc.mb.ca
Portage La Prairie
#200, 50 - 24th St. NW
Portage La Prairie, MB R1N 3V7 Canada
204-239-3499
Fax: 204-239-3401
portage.insurance@masc.mb.ca
Sanford
PO Box 7
8 Main St.
Sanford, MB R0G 2J0 Canada
204-736-5010
Fax: 204-736-5015
sanford.insurance@masc.mb.ca
Somerset
PO Box 190
279 Carlton St.
Somerset, MB R0G 2L0 Canada
204-744-4062
Fax: 204-744-4060
somerset.insurance@mascmb.ca
Souris
PO Box 610
95 - 1st St. North
Souris, MB R0K 2C0 Canada
204-483-5060
Fax: 204-483-5065
souris.insurance@masc.mb.ca
St Pierre Jolys
PO Box 249
466 Sabourin St. South
St Pierre Jolys, MB R0A 1V0 Canada
204-433-7298
Fax: 204-433-3282
stpierre.insurance@masc.mb.ca
Stonewall
PO Box 277
383 Main St.
Stonewall, MB R0C 2Z0 Canada
204-467-4710
Fax: 204-467-4715
stonewall.insurance@masc.mb.ca
Swan River
PO Box 1108
120 - 6th Ave. North
Swan River, MB R0L 1Z0 Canada
204-734-9326
Fax: 204-734-2685
swan.insurance@masc.mb.ca
Virden
PO Box 1570
247 Wellington St. West
Virden, MB R0M 2C0 Canada
204-748-4280
Fax: 204-748-4284
virden.insurance@masc.mb.ca

Manitoba Blue Cross

Polo Park Shopping Centre
PO Box 1046
#100A, 1485 Portage Ave.
Winnipeg, MB R3C 2X7
204-775-0151
Fax: 204-786-5965
888-873-2583
www.mb.bluecross.ca
Ownership: Not-for-profit. Member of Canadian Association of Blue Cross Plans, Toronto, ON.
Year Founded: 1974
Classes of Insurance: Personal Accident & Sickness, Life
Incorporation: Provincially Incorporated Insurance Company
Profile: The organization also offers group life, weekly indemnity, long term disability insurance, as well as life insurance for individuals in Manitoba.

Manitoba Public Insurance

PO Box 6300
Winnipeg, MB R3C 4A4
204-985-7000
800-665-2410
Other Information: TTY/TDD: 204-985-8832
www.mpi.mb.ca
Ownership: Crown corporation
Year Founded: 1970
Number of Employees: 1,600+
Classes of Insurance: Auto
Incorporation: Provincially Incorporated Insurance Company
Profile: The non-profit corporation provides basic automobile coverage. Operations also include driver & vehicle licensing. The Crown corporation is governed by The Manitoba Public Insurance Corporation Act & The Drivers & Vehicles Act.

Executives:
Marilyn McLaren, President/CEO
Barry Galenzoski, CFO & Vice-President, Corporate Finance, CAO
Wilf Bedard, Vice-President, Corporate Claims
Clarke Campbell, Vice-President, Corporate Information Technology, CIO
John Douglas, Vice-President, Corporate Public Affairs
Dan Guimond, Vice-President, Corporate Insurance Operations
Kevin McCulloch, Vice-President, Corporate Legal, General Counsel & Corporate Secretary
Charles Rogers, Vice-President, Corporate Resources

Manitoba Public Insurance (continued)

Directors:
Shari Decter Hirst, Chair
Kerry Bittner, Vice-Chair
Ed Arndt
Andrew Clarke
Mary Johnson
Annette Maloney
Marilyn McLaren
Manisha Pandya
Dale Paterson
Daryl Reid

Administration Offices:
Brandon - 1st St.
731 - 1st St.
Brandon, MB R7A 6C3 Canada
204-729-9400

Claims Office:
Arborg
PO Box 418
323 Sunset Blvd.
Arborg, MB R0C 0A0 Canada
204-376-6633

Beausejour
PO Box 100A
848 Park Ave.
Beausejour, MB R0E 0C0 Canada
204-268-6400

Brandon
731 - 1st St.
Brandon, MB R7A 6C3 Canada
204-729-9555
800-852-2743

Dauphin
PO Box 3000
217 Industrial Rd.
Dauphin, MB R7N 2V5 Canada
204-622-2750

Flin Flon
PO Box 250
8 Timber Lane
Flin Flon, MB R8A 1M9 Canada
204-681-2200

Portage La Prairie
PO Box 1150
2007 Saskatchewan Ave. West
Portage La Prairie, MB R1N 3J9 Canada
204-856-2600

Selkirk
630 Sophia St.
Selkirk, MB R1A 2K1 Canada
204-482-1400

Steinbach
PO Box 2139
91 North Front Dr.
Steinbach, MB R5G 1N7 Canada
204-326-4453

Swan River
PO Box 1959
125 - 4th Ave. North
Swan River, MB R0L 1Z0 Canada
204-734-4574

The Pas
PO Box 9100
424 Fischer Ave.
The Pas, MB R9A 1R5 Canada
204-627-2200

Thompson
PO Box 760
53 Commercial Pl.
Thompson, MB R8N 1N5 Canada
204-677-1400

Winkler
PO Box 1990
355 Boundary Trail
Winkler, MB R6W 4B7 Canada
204-325-9538

Winnipeg - Bodily Injury
PO Box 6300
Winnipeg, MB R3C 4A4 Canada
204-985-7000

Winnipeg - Casualty & Rehabilitation
PO Box 6300
Winnipeg, MB R3C 4A4 Canada
204-985-7200

Winnipeg - King Edward St. East
125 King Edward St. East
Winnipeg, MB R3H 0V9 Canada
Fax: 204-783-0374

Winnipeg - King St.
445 King St.
Winnipeg, MB R2W 5H2 Canada
Fax: 204-942-8317

Winnipeg - Pacific Ave.
1103 Pacific Ave.
Winnipeg, MB R3E 1G7 Canada
Fax: 204-783-2764

Winnipeg - Pembina Hwy.
420 Pembina Hwy.
Winnipeg, MB R3L 2E9 Canada
Fax: 204-284-7675

Winnipeg - Plessis Rd. - Physical Damage Centre
1981 Plessis Rd., PO Box 45064, RPO Regent.
Winnipeg, MB R2C 5C7 Canada
204-985-7771

Winnipeg - Rehabilitative Case Management
PO Box 6300
Winnipeg, MB R3C 4A4 Canada
204-985-7200

Winnipeg - St. Mary's Rd.
930 St. Mary's Rd.
Winnipeg, MB R2M 4A8 Canada
Fax: 204-254-0308

Driver & Vehicle Licencing Centres:
Brandon
602 - 1st St.
Brandon, MB R7A 6K5 Canada
204-729-9487

Dauphin
Provincial Bldg.
27 - 2nd Ave. SW
Dauphin, MB R7N 3E5 Canada
204-622-2783

Portage La Prairie
Provincial Bldg.
25 Tupper St. North
Portage La Prairie, MB R1N 3K1 Canada
204-856-2624

Thompson
Provincial Bldg.
#105, 59 Elizabeth Dr.
Thompson, MB R8N 1X4 Canada
204-677-1421

Winnipeg - Corydon Ave.
2020 Corydon Ave.
Winnipeg, MB R3P 0N2 Canada
204-985-8992

Winnipeg - McPhillips St.
2188 McPhillips St.
Winnipeg, MB R2V 3C8 Canada
204-985-8984

Winnipeg - Nairn Ave.
1006 Nairn Ave.
Winnipeg, MB R2L 0Y2 Canada
204-985-8043

Winnipeg - Portage Ave.
1075 Portage Ave.
Winnipeg, MB R3G 0S1 Canada
204-985-1100

Winnipeg - Portage Ave.
3137 Portage Ave.
Winnipeg, MB R3K 0W4 Canada
204-985-1100

Winnipeg - St. Mary's Rd.
1504 St. Mary's Rd.
Winnipeg, MB R2M 3V7 Canada
204-985-1100

Manufacturers Life Insurance Company/ La Compagnie d'Assurance-Vie Manufacturers

200 Bloor St. East
Toronto, ON M4W 1E5
888-626-8543
www.manulife.ca
Also Known As: Manulife Financial
Ownership: Wholly owned subsidiary of Manulife Financial Corporation.
Year Founded: 1887
Classes of Insurance: Personal Accident & Sickness, Life
Incorporation: Federally Incorporated Insurance Company

Executives:
Dominic D'Alessandro, President/CEO

Affiliated Companies:
Manulife Canada Ltd.

Branches:
Toronto - Affinity Market
2 Queen St. East
Toronto, ON M5C 3G7 Canada
800-668-0195
am_service@manulife.com

Waterloo - Individual Insurance
PO Box 1669
500 King St. North
Toronto, ON N2J 4Z6 Canada
888-626-8543
valued_customer_centre@manulife.com

Manulife Canada Ltd./ Manuvie Canada Ltée

PO Box 1669
500 King St. North
Waterloo, ON N2J 4Z6
888-626-8543
Valued_customer_centre@manulife.com
www.manulife.ca
Former Name: Zurich Life Insurance Company of Canada
Ownership: Subsidiary of Manufacturers Life Insurance Company
Classes of Insurance: Life
Incorporation: Federally Incorporated Insurance Company

Manulife Financial Individual Insurance

Also listed under: *Financial Planning*
PO Box 1669
500 King St. North
Waterloo, ON N2J 4Z6
888-626-8543
Valued_customer_centre@manulife.com
www.manulife.com
Ownership: Public
Year Founded: 1887
Number of Employees: 33,000
Assets: $60,067,000
Revenues: $14,152,000
Stock Symbol: MFC
Classes of Insurance: Life
Incorporation: Federally Incorporated Insurance Company
Profile: Manulife Financial is a leading Canadian-based financial services company operating in 19 countries & territories worldwide. Through its extensive network of employees, agents & distribution partners, Manulife Financial offers clients a diverse range of financial protection products & wealth management services. The Corporation trades as MFC on the TSE, NYSE & PSE & under 9045 on the SEHK.

Executives:
Dominic D'Alessandro, President/CEO
Victor Apps, Exec. Vice-President & General Manager, Asia Operations
John DesPrez, Exec. Vice-President, US Operations
H. Bruce Gordon, Exec. Vice-President, Canadian Operations
Donald Guloien, Exec. Vice-President, Investment Operations, Chief Investment Officer
John Mather, Exec. Vice-President & Chief Information Officer
Trevor J. Matthews, Exec. Vice-President
Peter H. Rubenovitch, Exec. Vice-President/CFO
Diane Bean, Sr. Vice-President, Corporate Human Resources & Communications
Richard A. Lococo, Sr. Vice-President, Deputy General Counsel

Directors:
Arthur R. Sawchuk, Chair
Dominic D'Alessandro
Thomas P. d'Aquino
Kevin E. Benson
John M. Cassaday
Lino J. Celeste
Gail C.A. Cook-Bennett
Robert E. Dineen, Jr.
Pierre Y. Ducros
Allister P. Graham
Thomas E. Kierans
Lorna R. Marsden
Hugh W. Sloan, Jr.
Gordon G. Thiessen
Michael H. Wilson

Affiliated Companies:
First North American Insurance Company
Manufacturers Life Insurance Company
Manulife Bank of Canada
Manulife Capital
Manulife Securities International Ltd./MSIL

Markel Insurance Company of Canada

55 University Ave.
Toronto, ON M5J 2H7
416-364-7800
Fax: 416-364-5655
888-627-5351
letstalk@markel.ca
www.markel.ca
Ownership: Owned by Fairfax Financial Holdings Ltd.
Year Founded: 1951
Stock Symbol: FFH
Classes of Insurance: Auto
Incorporation: Federally Incorporated Insurance Company
Profile: Markel is a trucking insurer. The company serves single operators to large fleets.

Executives:
Silvy Wright, President/CEO
Branches:
Edmonton
#1250, 10130 - 103rd St. NW
Edmonton, AB T5J 3N9 Canada
780-421-7890
Fax: 780-421-4744
800-661-7351
contact_edmonton@markel.ca
Al Sibilo, Manager
Montréal
9310, boul des Sciences
Montréal, QC H1J 3A9 Canada
514-284-3124
Fax: 514-284-9253
André Paradis, Manager

Massachusetts Mutual Life Insurance Company

c/o Cassels Brock & Blackwell LLP, Scotia Plaza
#2100, 40 King St. West
Toronto, ON M5H 3C2
416-869-5745
Fax: 416-350-6955
www.massmutual.com
Also Known As: MassMutual
Ownership: Foreign. Part of MassMutual Financial Group, Springfield, MA, USA.
Classes of Insurance: Personal Accident & Sickness, Life
Incorporation: Federally Incorporated Insurance Company
Executives:
J. Brian Reeve, Chief Agent

McKillop Mutual Insurance Company

PO Box 819
91 Main St. South
Seaforth, ON N0K 1W0
519-527-0400
Fax: 519-527-2777
800-463-9204
mckillo@tcc.on.ca
www.mckillopmutual.com
Ownership: Policyholders.
Year Founded: 1876
Classes of Insurance: Personal Accident & Sickness, Auto, Liability, Boiler & Machinery, Fidelity, Property
Incorporation: Provincially Incorporated Insurance Company
Executives:
Ken Jone, Manager, Sec.-Treas.

MD Life Insurance Company

1870 Alta Vista Dr.
Ottawa, ON K1G 6R7
Classes of Insurance: Life
Incorporation: Federally Incorporated Insurance Company
Executives:
Sanders Wilson, President/CEO

Medavie Blue Cross

PO Box 220
644 Main St.
Moncton, NB E1C 8L3
506-853-1811
Fax: 506-867-4651
800-667-4511
Other Information: Group Benefits, Atlantic Provinces & Ontario: 1-888-227-3400; Group Benefits, Québec: 1-888-588-1212
www.medavie.bluecross.ca
Former Name: Atlantic Blue Cross Care
Ownership: Member of Canadian Association of Blue Cross Plans, Toronto, ON.
Year Founded: 1943
Number of Employees: 1,450
Assets: $100-500 million
Revenues: $500m-1 billion
Classes of Insurance: Personal Accident & Sickness, Life
Incorporation: Provincially Incorporated Insurance Company
Profile: Medavie Blue Cross is the name adopted by Blue Cross in 2005 for the Atlantic Provinces, as well as for Group Benefits in Ontario & Québec. The insurance company offers individual & group health, travel, life & disability benefits.

Executives:
Pierre-Yves Julien, FCIA, FSA, President/CEO
Paul Dowie, CGA, Chief Operating Officer
Lorne G. Blanche, BA, Vice-President, Information Services
John P. Diamond, CA, Vice-President, Finance
Gilles Drapeau, FCIA, FSA, Vice-President, Québec Operations & Actuarial Services
Laurier S. Fecteau, B.Com., Vice-President, Marketing
Martin G. Haynes, CA, Vice-President, Corporate Services
Carolyn Johnson, BA, MPA, CHE, Vice-President, Government Programs
Daniel Marcil, B.Com., MBA, Vice-President, Customer Services

Ruth Rappini, MBA, Vice-President, Human Resources
Stephen M. Stewart, B.Com., Vice-President, Sales
Directors:
R. Doug Winsor, Chair
Yves Doucet
Eric B. Howatt
Pierre-Yves Julien
Gilles Lepage
H. Wade MacLauchlan
John McGarry
Steve Parker
Jean-Pierre Provencher
Joseph P. Shannon
Carol K. Snider
John R. Sobey
William H. Steeves
Eileen M. Young
Dartmouth
7 Spectacle Lake Dr.
Dartmouth, NS B3J 3C6 Canada
800-667-4511
Montréal
550, rue Sherbrooke ouest
Montréal, QC H3A 1B9 Canada
888-588-1212
Toronto
PO Box 2000
#1200, 185 The West Mall
Toronto, ON M9C 5P1 Canada
800-355-9133
Branches:
Bathurst
St. Anne Street Plaza
#4, 930 St. Anne St.
Bathurst, NB E2A 6X2 Canada
800-667-4511
Charlottetown
#120, 90 University Ave.
Charlottetown, PE C1A 4K9 Canada
800-667-4511
Fredericton
#2, 1055 Prospect St.
Fredericton, NB E3B 5B9 Canada
800-667-4511
Halifax
Barrington Tower, Scotia Square
1894 Barrington St.
Halifax, NS B3J 2A8 Canada
800-667-4511
Moncton
PO Box 220
664 Main St.
Moncton, NB E1C 8L3 Canada
800-667-4511
Saint John
47A Consumers Dr.
Saint John, NB E2J 4Z7 Canada
800-667-4511
St. John's
Board of Trade Bldg.
#102, 66 Kenmount Rd.
St. John's, NL A1B 3V7 Canada
800-667-4511

Meloche Monnex Inc.

***Also listed under:** Holding & Other Investment Companies*
50, Place Crémazie, 12e étage
Montréal, QC H2P 1B6
514-382-6060
Fax: 514-385-2162
www.melochemonnex.com
Incorporation: Federally Incorporated Insurance Company
Executives:
Alain Thibault, President/CEO
Jean R. Lachance, Exec. Chair, Affirmity Marketing Group
Chris D. Daniel, Chair, Affirmity Marketing Group
Daniel Demers, Exec. Vice-President
Richard Evans, Sr. Vice-President, Claims Service
François Faucher, Sr. Vice-President & CFO
Marilyn Flanagan, Sr. Vice-President, Client Services
Pierre Melançon, Sr. Vice-President, Marketing
Pierre Ménard, Sr. Vice-President, Change & Resources Management
Guy Vézina, Sr. Vice-President, Operations & Business Development
Raynald Lecavalier, Vice-President, Legal & Regulatory Affairs, Secretary
Antonietta DiGirolamo, Asst. Corporate Secretary
Directors:
Pierre Meloche, OC, Chair
Dianne Cunningham
Raymond A. Décarie
Daniel Demers
Bernard T. Dorval
Louis D. Hyndman
Sean Kilburn
C. Lajeunesse, OC
Damian J. McNamee
Dominic J. Mercuri
L. Robert Shaw
Alain Thibault
Fredric J. Tomczyk
Affiliated Companies:
Primmum Insurance Company
Security National Insurance Company
Branches:
Calgary
One Palliser Square
#1200, 125 - 9 Ave. SE
Calgary, AB T2G 0P6 Canada
403-269-1112
Fax: 403-298-2530
800-268-8955
Edmonton
#2300, 10025 - 102A Ave. NW
Edmonton, AB T5J 2Z2 Canada
780-429-1112
Fax: 780-420-2323
800-268-8955
Halifax
Founders Square
#104, 1701 Hollis St.
Halifax, NS B3J 3M8 Canada
902-420-1112
Fax: 902-424-1200
800-268-8955
Montréal
50, Place Crémazie, 12e étage
Montréal, QC H3P 1B6 Canada
514-384-1112
Fax: 514-385-2196
800-361-3821
Toronto
2161 Yonge St., 4th Fl.
Toronto, ON M4S 3A6 Canada
416-484-1112
Fax: 416-545-6125
800-268-8955

INSURANCE COMPANIES

Mennonite Mutual Fire Insurance Company
PO Box 190
Waldheim, SK S0K 4R0
306-945-2239
Fax: 306-945-4666
mmfi@sasktel.net
www.mmfi.com
Ownership: Policy-holders
Year Founded: 1894
Number of Employees: 24
Assets: $12,151,483 Year End: 20041231
Revenues: $9,014,400 Year End: 20041231
Classes of Insurance: Boiler & Machinery, Property, Fire, Theft
Incorporation: Provincially Incorporated Insurance Company
Executives:
Earl W. Harder, CEO

Mennonite Mutual Insurance Co. (Alberta) Ltd.(MMI)
#300, 2946 - 32nd St. NE
Calgary, AB T1Y 6J7
403-275-6996
Fax: 403-291-6733
866-222-6996
office@mmiab.ca
Ownership: Private
Year Founded: 1960
Number of Employees: 8
Assets: $5-10 million Year End: 20041231
Revenues: $1-5 million Year End: 20041231
Classes of Insurance: Auto, Liability, Property, Fire
Incorporation: Provincially Incorporated Insurance Company
Executives:
Sheryl D. Janzen, General Manager; 403-275-6996; sheryl@mmiab.ca

Metro General Insurance Corp. Limited
T.D. Place
PO Box 548
#700, 140 Water St.
St. John's, NL A1C 5K9
709-726-1922
Fax: 709-726-5207
Year Founded: 1972
Classes of Insurance: Auto, Liability, Property
Incorporation: Provincially Incorporated Insurance Company
Executives:
Kevin Hutchings, President, Sec.-Treas.

Metropolitan Life Insurance Company, Canadian Branch
Constitution Square
#1750, 360 Albert St.
Ottawa, ON K1R 7X7
613-237-7171
Fax: 613-237-7585
ldumas@metlife.com
www.metlife.com
Ownership: Public. Ultimate shareholder is Metlife Inc. USA
Year Founded: 1872
Assets: $1-10 billion
Revenues: $50-100 million
Classes of Insurance: Personal Accident & Sickness, Life
Incorporation: Federally Incorporated Insurance Company
Executives:
Karen C. Sauvé, Managing Director & Chief Agent for Canada; 613-237-6205; ksauve@metlife.com
P. James Anderson, CFO, Canadian Operations; 613-237-7171; janderson@metlife.com

Minnesota Life Insurance Company/ Compagnie d'Assurance-vie Minnesota
c/o McLean & Kerr LLP
#2800, 130 Adelaide St. West
Toronto, ON M5H 3P5
416-364-5371
Fax: 416-366-8571
www.minnesotamutual.com
Ownership: Foreign. Part of Minnesota Life, St. Paul, MN, USA.

Classes of Insurance: Life
Incorporation: Federally Incorporated Insurance Company
Executives:
Robin B. Cumine, Chief Agent

Mitsui Sumitomo Insurance Co., Limited.
Chubb Insurance Company of Canada, One Financial Place
#1500A, 1 Adelaide St. East
Toronto, ON M5C 2V9
416-863-0550
Fax: 416-863-3144
www.ms-ins.com/english/index.html
Former Name: The Sumitomo Marine & Fire Insurance Co. Ltd.; Mitsui Marine & Fire Insurance Company, Ltd.
Ownership: Foreign. Part of Mitsui Sumitomo Insurance Co., Limited, Tokyo, Japan.
Year Founded: 1985
Classes of Insurance: Personal Accident & Sickness, Aircraft, Auto, Liability, Boiler & Machinery, Fidelity, Property, Surety
Incorporation: Federally Incorporated Insurance Company
Executives:
Ellen Jane Moore, Chief Agent

Motors Insurance Corporation
#400, 8500 Leslie St.
Thornhill, ON L3T 7M8
905-882-3900
Fax: 905-882-3955
Ownership: Foreign. Parent is GMAC Insurance Holdings
Year Founded: 1956
Number of Employees: 106
Assets: $500m-1 billion Year End: 20051231
Revenues: $100-500 million Year End: 20051231
Classes of Insurance: Auto, Liability, Boiler & Machinery
Incorporation: Federally Incorporated Insurance Company
Executives:
C.W. Hastings, Chief Agent

Munich Reinsurance Company - Canada Life
Munich Re Centre
390 Bay St., 26th Fl.
Toronto, ON M5H 2Y2
416-359-2200
Fax: 416-361-0305
generalenquiries@munichre.ca
www.munichre.ca
Also Known As: Munich Re
Ownership: Foreign. Part of Munich Re Group, Germany.
Year Founded: 1959
Number of Employees: 120+
Classes of Insurance: Personal Accident & Sickness, Life, Reinsurance
Incorporation: Federally Incorporated Insurance Company
Profile: Munich Re Group was established in 1880 in Germany. The reinsurance company has more than 5,000 clients in 150 countries. In Canada, Munich Re provides reinsurance solutions to clients throughout Canada & the Caribbean. Services include individual life, disability, critical illness, long term care, & group life & health insurance.

Executives:
James A. Brierley, President, Munich Life Management Corporation, Life & Health Insurance Operations, Munich Re, Canada & the Caribbean
Lloyd Steinke, Leader, Global Strategy Project
Mary Forrest, Exec. Vice-President, Individual Life, Group & Living Benefits
Richard Letarte, Vice-President, Quebec & Caribbean
Lloyd Milani, Vice-President, Individual Life
Bernard Naumann, Vice-President, Actuarial Services
Branches:
Montréal
630, boul René-Lévesque ouest, 26e étage
Montréal, QC H3B 1S6 Canada
514-866-6825
Fax: 514-875-7389

Munich Reinsurance Company of Canada
390 Bay St., 22nd Fl.
Toronto, ON M5H 2Y2
416-366-9206
Fax: 416-366-4330
800-444-5321
www.mroc.com
Also Known As: Munich Re
Ownership: Foreign. Part of Munich Re Group, Germany.
Year Founded: 1960
Number of Employees: 135
Classes of Insurance: Auto, Liability, Property, Theft
Incorporation: Federally Incorporated Insurance Company
Executives:
Kenneth B. Irvin, President/CEO
John Martin, Exec. Vice-President, Secretary
Linda Wahrer, Exec. Vice-President
Peter Walker, Sr. Vice-President
Regional Offices:
Montréal
#2630, 630, boul René-Lévesque est
Montréal, QC H3B 1S6 Canada
514-866-1841
Fax: 514-875-7389
800-363-2685
Daniel Muzzin, Vice-President, Marketing
Toronto
390 Bay St., 21st Fl.
Toronto, ON M5H 2Y2 Canada
416-366-6245
Fax: 416-366-5302
800-268-9705
Wayne Dawe, Asst. Vice-President & Manager, Casualty
Vancouver
#1110, 1040 West Georgia St.
Vancouver, BC V6E 4H1 Canada
604-681-7445
Fax: 604-681-7530
Mark Kuhlmann, Vice-President, Marketing

Municipal Insurance Association of British Columbia(MIA)
#390, 1050 Homer St.
Vancouver, BC V6E 2W9
604-683-6266
Fax: 604-683-6244
www.miabc.org
Year Founded: 1987
Classes of Insurance: Liability
Incorporation: Provincially Incorporated Insurance Company
Executives:
Tom Barnes, Executive Director
Mitchell Kenyon, Deputy Executive Director
Sherman Chow, Manager, Claims
Keith Gibson, Manager, Risk

MUNIX Reciprocal(MUNIX)
10507 Saskatchewan Dr.
Edmonton, AB T6E 4S1
780-433-4431
Fax: 780-409-4314
800-272-8848
Also Known As: Alberta Municipal Insurance Exchange
Year Founded: 2002
Classes of Insurance: Liability, Property
Incorporation: Provincially Incorporated Insurance Company
Profile: MUNIX Reciprocal involves a group of municipalities which pool their resources to finance recovery from accidental losses.

The Mutual Fire Insurance Company of British Columbia
#201, 9366 - 200A St.
Langley, BC V1M 4B3
604-881-1250
Fax: 604-881-1440
www.mutualfirebc.com
Year Founded: 1902
Classes of Insurance: Property, Fire
Incorporation: Provincially Incorporated Insurance Company
Directors:
Jake Bredenhof, President
Len Bouwman, Vice-President
Daryl Cherry, Treasurer
Doug Bose, Past President
Warren Nottingham
Joe Taylor
Ralph Terpstra
Rick Thiessen

New India Assurance Company, Limited
30 Wellington St. East
Toronto, ON M5R 1A3
www.newindia.co.in
Classes of Insurance: Personal Accident & Sickness, Auto, Boiler & Machinery, Life, Property, Fire, Hail & Crop
Incorporation: Federally Incorporated Insurance Company
Profile: All classes of insurance are limited to servicing existing policies.

Executives:
Fermao Ferreira, Chief Agent

NIPPONKOA Insurance Company, Limited
c/o St. Paul Fire & Marine Insurance Company
PO Box 93
#1200, 121 King St. West
Toronto, ON M5H 3T9
416-601-2543
Fax: 416-601-4432
www.nipponkoa.co.jp/english
Former Name: Nippon Fire & Marine Insurance Co, Ltd.; The Koa Fire & Marine Insurance Co., Ltd.
Ownership: Foreign. Part of NIPPONKOA Insurance Co., Ltd., Tokyo, Japan.
Year Founded: 2001
Classes of Insurance: Personal Accident & Sickness, Aircraft, Auto, Liability, Boiler & Machinery, Marine, Fidelity, Property, Surety
Incorporation: Federally Incorporated Insurance Company
Executives:
Robert J. Fellows, Chief Agent

The Nordic Insurance Company of Canada
181 University Ave., 7th Fl.
Toronto, ON M5H 3M7
416-941-5151
Fax: 416-941-5322
Ownership: Parent company is ING Canada Inc.
Classes of Insurance: Accident, Legal Expense, Auto, Liability, Boiler & Machinery, Fidelity, Property, Surety
Incorporation: Federally Incorporated Insurance Company
Executives:
Claude Dussault, CEO

Norfolk Mutual Insurance Company
PO Box 515
33 Park Rd.
Simcoe, ON N3Y 4L5
519-426-1294
Fax: 519-426-7594
www.norfolkmutualinsco.on.ca
Former Name: Norfolk Mutual Fire Insurance Company
Year Founded: 1881
Classes of Insurance: Auto, Property, Fire
Incorporation: Provincially Incorporated Insurance Company
Executives:
Carrol E. Lambert, CEO Manager

North Bleinheim Mutual Insurance Co.
11 Baird St. North
Bright, ON N0J 1B0
519-454-8661
Fax: 519-454-8785
800-665-6888
north.blenheim@sympatico.ca
www.northblenheim.omia.com
Year Founded: 1861
Number of Employees: 11
Classes of Insurance: Auto, Liability, Property
Incorporation: Provincially Incorporated Insurance Company

North Kent Mutual Fire Insurance Company
PO Box 478
Dresden, ON N0P 1M0
519-683-4484
Fax: 519-683-4509
888-736-4705
nkm@nkmutual.com
www.nkmutual.com
Ownership: Mutual
Year Founded: 1910
Number of Employees: 8
Assets: $10-50 million Year End: 20060930
Revenues: $5-10 million Year End: 20060930
Classes of Insurance: Auto, Liability, Property, Fire, Hail & Crop, Theft
Incorporation: Provincially Incorporated Insurance Company
Executives:
John W. Leeson, Manager

The North Waterloo Farmers Mutual Insurance Company
100 Erb St. East
Waterloo, ON N2J 1L9
519-886-4530
Fax: 519-746-0222
800-265-8813
insurance@nwfm.com
www.nwfm.com
Ownership: Mutual.
Year Founded: 1874
Number of Employees: 49
Assets: $50-100 million Year End: 20051231
Revenues: $10-50 million Year End: 20051231
Classes of Insurance: Auto, Liability, Boiler & Machinery, Fidelity, Property, Fire, Hail & Crop
Incorporation: Federally Incorporated Insurance Company

Executives:
Carlos A. Rodrigues, President/CEO
John W. King, CFO & Vice-President, Finance
Neil M. Bishop, Vice-President, Underwriting
Leslie H. Card, Vice-President, Information Technology
James H. Zyta, Vice-President, Claims
Directors:
Ronald D. Hare, Chair

The North West Commercial Travellers' Association of Canada(NWC)
PO Box 336
28 Queen Elizabeth Way
Winnipeg, MB R3C 2H6
204-284-8900
Fax: 204-284-8909
800-665-6928
nwcta@nwcta.com
www.nwcta.com
Ownership: Membership-based association
Year Founded: 1949
Classes of Insurance: Life
Incorporation: Federally Incorporated Insurance Company
Profile: The association offers group insurance in the following areas: air travel accident, business & pleasure accident, critical choice care, extended health & dental care, term life insurance & long term disability.

Executives:
Terry D. Carruthers, CEO, General Manager
Gordon Dmytriw, Manager, Sales & Marketing
Gayle Gifford, Manager, Insurance Services
Diane McDonald, Manager, Member Services
Lois Payette, Controller

Odyssey America Reinsurance Corp., Canadian Branch
#1600, 55 University Ave.
Toronto, ON M5J 2H7
416-862-0162
Fax: 416-367-3248
www.odysseyre.com
Former Name: Odyssey Reinsurance Company of Canada
Ownership: Foreign. Branch of Odyssey America Reinsurance Corporation, USA.
Assets: $100-500 million Year End: 20051231
Revenues: $50-100 million Year End: 20051231
Classes of Insurance: Accident, Aircraft, Auto, Liability, Boiler & Machinery, Property, Fire, Surety, Hail & Crop, Reinsurance
Incorporation: Federally Incorporated Insurance Company
Profile: OdysseyRe is an underwriter of property & casulty reinsurance.

Executives:
W. Fransen, Chief Agent

Old Republic Insurance Company of Canada/ L'Ancienne République, Compagnie d'Assurance du Ca
PO Box 557
100 King St. West
Hamilton, ON L8N 3K9
905-523-5936
Fax: 905-528-4685
Ownership: Foreign. Subsidiary of Old Republic International Corporation.
Year Founded: 1994
Classes of Insurance: Accident, Aircraft, Auto, Liability, Property, Reinsurance
Incorporation: Federally Incorporated Insurance Company
Executives:
Paul M. Field, Chief Executive Officer, Chief Financial Officer
Tat L. Wong, Asst. Vice-President, Underwriting
Affiliated Companies:
Reliable Life Insurance Company

Ontario Blue Cross
PO Box 2000
#600, 185 The West Mall
Toronto, ON M9C 5P1
416-626-1447
Fax: 416-626-0997
800-873-2583
bco.indhealth@ont.bluecross.ca
www.useblue.com
Ownership: Member of Canadian Association of Blue Cross Plans, Toronto, ON.
Classes of Insurance: Personal Accident & Sickness
Incorporation: Provincially Incorporated Insurance Company
Profile: Individual health & travel insurance is provided to residents of Ontario.

Ontario Mutual Insurance Association
PO Box 3187
1305 Bishop St. North
Cambridge, ON N3H 4S6
519-622-9220
Fax: 519-622-9227
information@omia.com
www.omia.com
Year Founded: 1882
Classes of Insurance: Personal Accident & Sickness, Auto, Property
Incorporation: Provincially Incorporated Insurance Company

Ontario School Boards' Insurance Exchange(OSBIE)
91 Westmount Rd.
Guelph, ON N1H 5J2
519-767-2182
Fax: 519-767-0281
800-668-6724
info@osbie.on.ca
www.osbie.on.ca
Ownership: 106 members
Year Founded: 1987
Number of Employees: 21
Assets: $150,000,000 Year End: 20051200
Revenues: $25,000,000 Year End: 20051200
Classes of Insurance: Auto, Liability, Boiler & Machinery, Property, Fire
Incorporation: Provincially Incorporated Insurance Company
Profile: The primary goals of the Exchange are to insure subscribers against losses & to promote solid risk management practices.

Executives:
Jim Sami, General Manager
Dave Beal, Manager, Risk
Teresa Hepburn, Manager, Claims
Sandra Taylor, Manager, Accounting
Directors:
Penny Allen
Bob Allison
François Bertrand
Dean Carrie
Diane Cayen-Arnold
Brian Greene
Gordon Greffe
Edward Hodgins
Teresa Larson
Helen Mitchell
Cathy Modesto
David Niven
Michel Paulin
Barry Peterson
Branches:
Toronto - Legal Dept.
#1101, 111 Richmond St. West.
Toronto, ON M5H 2G4 Canada
416-867-1581
Fax: 416-867-1023
Zenon Fedorowycz, Legal Counsel

Optimum Assurance Agricole inc/ Optimum Farm Insurance Inc.
#250, 1500, rue Royale
Trois-Rivières, QC G9A 6E6
819-373-2040
Fax: 819-373-2801
www.optimum-general.com
Ownership: Subsidiary of Optimum Général Inc.
Year Founded: 1897

Optimum Assurance Agricole inc/ Optimum Farm Insurance Inc. (continued)

Number of Employees: 12
Classes of Insurance: Auto, Property, Fire
Incorporation: Provincially Incorporated Insurance Company
Executives:
Jean-Claude Pagé, President/CEO
Mario Dumas, Sr. Vice-President, Operations; mdumas@oaa.qc.ca
Louis P. Pontbriand, Sr. Vice-President/CFO
Louis Fontaine, Vice-President, Legal Affairs, Secretary
Directors:
Gilles Blondeau, Chair
Henri Joli-Coeur, Vice-Chair
Jean-Caude Pagé, Vice-Chair
Ronald Blondeau
Jean-Marc Fortier
Marcel Marcoux
Pierre Martin
Gaston Paradis
Jacques Proulx

Optimum Général inc/ Optimum General Inc.

#1500, 425, boul de Maisonneuve ouest
Montréal, QC H3A 3G5
514-288-8725
Fax: 514-288-0760
www.optimum-general.com
Ownership: Public. Subsidiary of Optimum Group Inc.
Number of Employees: 250
Stock Symbol: OGI.SV.A
Classes of Insurance: Auto, Liability, Property
Incorporation: Federally Incorporated Insurance Company
Executives:
Jean-Claude Pagé, President/CEO
Martin Carrier, Sr. Vice-President, Insurance Operations, Vice-President, Commercial Lines
André Nadon, Sr. Vice-President, Appointed Actuary
Louis P. Pontbriand, Sr. Vice-President/CFO
Clifford P. Quesnel, Sr. Vice-President, Branch Operations
Noella Anthony, Vice-President, Claims
Louis Fontaine, Vice-President, Legal Affairs, Secretary
J.-Sébastien Lagarde, Vice-President, Business Development
Paul Tremblay, Vice-President, Actuarial Services
Jean-Marie Villemure, Vice-President, Information Technology
Directors:
Gilles Blondeau, Chair
Henri Joli-Coeur, Vice-Chair
Jean-Claude Pagé, Vice-Chair
Gilles Demers
Claude Fontaine
Yvon Fontaine
Jacques M. Gagnon
Raymond Lafontaine
Gaston Paradis
Ronald T. Riley
Affiliated Companies:
Optimum Assurance Agricole inc
Optimum Société d'Assurance inc/OSA

Optimum Reassurance Company

#1200, 425, boul de Maisonneuve ouest
Montréal, QC H3A 3G5
514-288-1900
Fax: 514-288-8099
andre.gaudreault@optimumre.ca
www.optimumre.ca
Ownership: Private. Optimum Group
Year Founded: 1957
Number of Employees: 50
Assets: $100-500 million Year End: 20051231
Revenues: $100-500 million Year End: 20051231
Classes of Insurance: Accident, Personal Accident & Sickness, Life, Reinsurance
Incorporation: Provincially Incorporated Insurance Company
Executives:
Mario Georgiev, President
Claude Lamonde, Exec. Vice-President
Alain Béland, Sr. Vice-President, Finance
André Gaudreault, Sr. Vice-President, Development
Serge Goulet, Sr. Vice-President, Administration & Underwriting
Richard Houde, Sr. Vice-President, Risk Management, Chief Actuary
Jacques Ross, Sr. Vice-President, Reinsurance Development
Diane Brûlé, First Vice-President, Systems
Laurent Lessard, First Vice-President, International Development
Robert Desgroseilliers, Vice-President, Quality Assurance & Special Projects
Odette Gauvreau, Vice-President, Underwriting
Gary Mooney, Vice-President, Business Development
Pierre Saddik, Vice-President, Travel Insurance Development
François Sestier, Vice-President, Medical Director
Cathy Shum-Adams, Vice-President, Individual Development
Michel Simard, Vice-President, Group Development
Harvey Campbell, Appointed Actuary
Directors:
Gilles Blondeau, Chair
Charles Belzil, Vice-Chair
Henri Joli-Coeur, Vice-Chair
Ronald Blondeau
Pierre Bourgie
Yves Dugré
Jacques M. Gagnon
Mario Georgiev
Jean-Luc Landry
Mark J. Oppenheim
Jean-Claude Pagé
Gaston Paradis

Optimum Société d'Assurance inc(OSA)/ Optimum Insurance Company Inc.

#1500, 425, boul de Maisonneuve ouest
Montréal, QC H3A 3G5
514-288-8711
Fax: 514-288-8269
Former Name: Société Nationale d'Assurance Inc.
Ownership: Subsidiary of Optimum Général Inc.
Year Founded: 1940
Number of Employees: 50
Classes of Insurance: Auto, Liability, Property
Incorporation: Provincially Incorporated Insurance Company
Executives:
Jean-Claude Pagé, President/CEO
Martin Carrier, Sr. Vice-President, Insurance Operations, Vice-President, Commercial Lines
Louis P. Pontbriand, Sr. Vice-President/CFO, Treasurer
Raymond Dubé, Regional Vice-President, Montreal; rdube@opsa.qc.ca
Directors:
Gilles Blondeau, Chair
Henri Joli-Coeur, Vice-Chair
Jean-Claude Pagé, Vice-Chair
Ronald Blondeau
Jean-Marc Fortier
Marcel Marcoux
Pierre Martin
Gaston Paradis
Jacques Proulx
Branches:
Québec
#102, 250, av Grand-Allée ouest
Québec, QC G1R 2H4 Canada
418-522-4757
Fax: 418-522-6494
Linda Gosselin, Regional Vice-President, Québec

The Order of United Commercial Travelers of America(UCT)

#300, 901 Centre St. North
Calgary, AB T2E 2P6
403-277-0745
Fax: 403-277-6662
www.uct.org
Ownership: Foreign. Part of United Commercial Travelers of America, USA.
Year Founded: 1888
Classes of Insurance: Personal Accident & Sickness, Life
Incorporation: Federally Incorporated Insurance Company
Executives:
Lindsay B. Maxwell, Chief Agent; lmaxwell@uct.org
Joyce Pierre, Contact; jpierre@uct.org

Ordre des Architectes du Québec

1825, boul René-Lévesque ouest
Montréal, QC H3H 1R4
514-937-6168
Fax: 514-933-0242
800-599-6168
info@oaq.com
www.oaq.com
Incorporation: Provincially Incorporated Insurance Company

Ordre des dentistes du Québec

625, boul René-Lévesque ouest, 15e étage
Montréal, QC H3B 1R2
514-875-8511
Fax: 514-393-9248
800-361-4887
com@odq.ac.ca
www.odq.qc.ca
Incorporation: Provincially Incorporated Insurance Company
Executives:
Claude Lamarche, DMD, Président

Oxford Mutual Insurance Co.

PO Box 430
RR#4
Thamesford, ON N0M 2M0
519-285-2916
Fax: 519-285-3099
800-461-6933
mail@oxfordmutual.com
www.oxfordmutual.com
Ownership: Policyholders.
Year Founded: 1878
Classes of Insurance: Personal Accident & Sickness, Aircraft, Auto, Liability, Boiler & Machinery, Fidelity, Property, Hail & Crop
Incorporation: Provincially Incorporated Insurance Company
Profile: Products include automobile, residential, agricultural & commercial insurance.
Executives:
Betty Semeniuk, President
Clark Riddle, Vice-President
Bill Jellous, CIP, Secretary-Manager
Deborah Squire, Treasurer

Pacific Blue Cross

PO Box 7000
4250 Canada Way
Vancouver, BC V6B 4E1
604-419-2000
Fax: 604-419-2990
800-487-3228
www.pac.bluecross.ca
Year Founded: 1940
Number of Employees: 650
Assets: $100-500 million Year End: 20051231
Revenues: $500m-1 billion Year End: 20051231
Classes of Insurance: Accident, Personal Accident & Sickness, Life
Incorporation: Provincially Incorporated Insurance Company
Executives:
Kenneth G. Martin, President/CEO
Catherine Boivie, Sr. Vice-President, Information Technology
John Crawford, Sr. Vice-President, Financial Services
Anne Kinvig, Sr. Vice-President, Human Resources
Wren Long, Sr. Vice-President, Client Development
Leza Muir, Sr. Vice-President, Client Services
Cindy Bratkowski, Vice-President, Client Services

Pacific Coast Fishermen's Mutual Marine Insurance Company

3757 Canada Way
Burnaby, BC V5G 1G5
604-438-4240
Fax: 604-438-5756
Other Information: Toll Free (BC only): 1-888-438-4242
info@mutualmarine.bc.ca
www.mutualmarine.bc.ca
Ownership: Member-owned
Year Founded: 1945
Number of Employees: 7
Assets: $10-50 million
Revenues: $5-10 million
Classes of Insurance: Marine
Incorporation: Provincially Incorporated Insurance Company
Profile: Commercial fishing vessels are insured.

Executives:
Vince Fiamengo, President; 604-433-9577
Anton Mijacika, Vice-President; 604-433-8638
Tony Thompson, General Manager & Secretary
Lee Varseveld, Asst. General Manager & Treasurer
Directors:
Lee Anderson
Lawrence Atchison
Lewis Bublé
Lenard Carr

INSURANCE COMPANIES

Mark DeCorte
Vince Fiamengo
Bill Forbes
Ronald Fowler
Donald Haines
Glen Hanson
Ronald Haugan
Ross Holkestad
Anton Mijacika
Kenneth Murray
Peter Sakich
John Secord
Richard Shaw
James Sloman
Leslie Soleway
Robert Strom
Wayne R. Watson

Palliser Insurance Company Limited

#103, 3502 Taylor St. East
Saskatoon, SK S7H 5H9
306-955-4814
Fax: 306-955-1317
info@palliserinsurance.com
www.palliserinsurance.com
Number of Employees: 1
Classes of Insurance: Hail & Crop
Incorporation: Provincially Incorporated Insurance Company
Executives:
Rennie N. McQueen, Officer

PartnerRe SA

PO Box 166
#2300, 130 King St. West
Toronto, ON M5X 1C7
416-861-0033
Fax: 416-861-0200
800-363-6800
www.partnerre.com
Former Name: SAFR PartnerRe
Ownership: Foreign. Branch of PartnerRe SA, France
Assets: $100-500 million Year End: 20041231
Revenues: $100-500 million Year End: 20041231
Classes of Insurance: Personal Accident & Sickness, Auto, Life, Property
Incorporation: Federally Incorporated Insurance Company
Executives:
Pierre Michel, Chief Agent

PC Financial Insurance Agency

2202 Eglinton Ave. East
Toronto, ON M1L 4S8
866-660-9035
Other Information: 1-866-472-2683 (Claims)
talktous@homeauto.pcinsurance.ca
www.pcinsurance.ca
Also Known As: PC Financial Insurance
Classes of Insurance: Auto, Property
Incorporation: Federally Incorporated Insurance Company
Branches:
Winnipeg - PC Financial Pet Insurance
777 Portage Ave.
Winnipeg, MB R3G 0N3 Canada
877-723-7387

Peace Hills General Insurance Company

#300, 10709 Jasper Ave., 3rd Fl.
Edmonton, AB T5J 3N3
780-424-3986
Fax: 780-424-0396
800-272-5614
phi@peacehillsinsurance.com
www.peacehillsinsurance.com
Ownership: Private. Parent is Samson Management Limited.
Year Founded: 1982
Number of Employees: 100+
Assets: $182,422,105 Year End: 20041231
Revenues: $110,895,241 Year End: 20041231
Classes of Insurance: Accident, Aircraft, Auto, Liability, Boiler & Machinery, Credit, Marine, Fidelity, Property, Fire, Surety, Theft
Incorporation: Provincially Incorporated Insurance Company
Profile: Mortgage insurance is also offered.

Executives:
Diane Brickner, CIP, President/CEO
Robert Doiron, CIP, Vice-President, Claims
Jamie Hotte, FCIP, Vice-President, Marketing & Underwriting
John Morgan, CMA, Vice-President, Finance & Administration
Directors:
Marvin Yellowbird, Chair
Diane Brickner, President/CEO
Pat Buffalo, Exec. Vice-President
Trevor Swampy, Sec.-Treas.
Victor Bruno
Victor Buffalo
John Crier
Leiha Crier
Williams Kordyback
Julian Koziak
Gabe Lee
Dennis Leonard
Walter Lighting
Lawrence Saddleback
John Szumlas
Branches:
Calgary
Encor Place
645 - 7th Ave. SW
Calgary, AB T2P 4G8 Canada
403-262-7600
Fax: 403-237-5593
800-372-9295
Fergus Kavanagh, Vice-President & Manager, Southern Alberta
Edmonton
#300, 10709 Jasper Ave.
Edmonton, AB T5J 3N3 Canada
780-424-3986
Fax: 780-424-0396
800-272-5614
Sheldon Bos, Branch Manager
Vancouver
#2000, 1066 West Hastings St.
Vancouver, BC V6E 3X2 Canada
604-408-4708
Fax: 604-408-4718
877-408-4708
Daryl Kochan, Regional Manager, British Columbia

Peel Maryborough Mutual Insurance Company

PO Box 190
103 Wellington St.
Drayton, ON N0G 1P0
519-638-3304
Fax: 519-638-3521
800-265-2473
pmmutual@pmmutual.on.ca
www.pmmutual.on.ca
Ownership: Policyholders.
Year Founded: 1887
Incorporation: Provincially Incorporated Insurance Company
Profile: Farm, residential, commercial & church services are offered by brokers.

Executives:
Alan Simpson, CIP, General Manager
Sonny D'Agostino, Manager, Claims
Teresa Hilpert, CIP, Manager, Underwriting
Ruth Donkersgoed, CIP, Assistant Manager
Directors:
Harry Hiddema, President
George Mitchell, First Vice-President
Robert Brenner
Jan Dadson
Carl Hall
Bert Moore
Elbert Walter
Bruce Whale
Richard Wright

Peel Mutual Insurance Co.

103 Queen St. West
Brampton, ON L6Y 1M3
905-451-2386
info@peelmutual.com
www.peelmutual.com
Ownership: Policyholders
Year Founded: 1876
Classes of Insurance: Auto, Liability, Boiler & Machinery, Fidelity, Property
Incorporation: Provincially Incorporated Insurance Company
Executives:
Philip H. Haynes, General Manager

Pembridge Insurance Company

#100, 27 Allstate Pkwy.
Markham, ON L3R 5P8
905-513-4012
Fax: 905-513-4020
877-736-2743
www.pembridge.com
Classes of Insurance: Accident, Marine, Property
Incorporation: Federally Incorporated Insurance Company
Executives:
Bob Tisdale, President/CEO
John Greb, Vice-President, Claims

Penncorp Life Insurance Company

55 Superior Blvd.
Mississauga, ON L5T 2X9
Fax: 905-795-2316
800.268.2835
cs@penncorp.ca
www.penncorp.ca
Classes of Insurance: Personal Accident & Sickness, Life
Incorporation: Federally Incorporated Insurance Company
Profile: Penncorp is a specialty disability insurance company. It focuses on the self employed, the skilled trades & blue collar occupations, & small business owners.

Executives:
Lynn Grenier-Lew, Exec. Vice-President/CFO
Scott Hunt, Vice-President, Underwriting & New Business
Eli Pichelli, Vice-President, Sales and Marketing
Branches:
Barrie
#2, 431 Huronia Rd.
Barrie, ON L4N 9B3
705-728-5580
Fax: 705-728-9613
800-268-5168
kgibbons@penncorp.ca
Bedford
Sunnyside Place
#209, 1600 Bedford Hwy.
Burford, ON B4A 1E8 Canada
902-835-9203
Fax: 902-835-1353
swarman@penncorp.ca
Calgary
#A16B, 6120 - 2nd St. SE
Calgary, AB T2H 2L8 Canada
403-252-7757
Fax: 403-252-6766
calgary@penncorp.ca
Edmonton
#240, 9743 - 51 Ave.
Edmonton, AB T6E 4W8 Canada
780-438-2420
Fax: 780-436-8871
rbreunesse@penncorp.ca
London
#129, 4026 Meadowbrooke Dr.
London, ON N6L 1A4
519-652-0250
Manotick
PO Box 334
1165 Beaverwood
Manotick, ON K4M 1A5
613-692-3590
Fax: 613-692-6307
thickey@penncorp.ca
Montréal
#140, 4949, boul Métropolitain est
Montréal, QC H1R 1Z6
514-735-2058
Fax: 514-323-5940
bjean@Penncorp.ca
Lena Graves, Branch Manager
Québec
#1030, 1265, boul Charest
Québec, QC G1N 2C9
418-687-2058
Fax: 418-687-5880
hhoule@Penncorp.ca
Saskatoon
#5, 2345 Ave. C North
Saskatoon, SK S7L 5Z5

Penncorp Life Insurance Company (continued)

306-955-3000
Fax: 306-374-1110
jmann@penncorp.ca
Surrey
#203B, 10190 - 152A St.
Surrey, ON V3R 1J7 BC
604-589-1381
Fax: 604-589-1382
brubin@penncorp.ca
Thunder Bay
#301, 1265 East Arthur St.
Thunder Bay, ON P7E 5H7
807-473-0005
Fax: 807-473-0006
thunderbay@penncorp.ca
Winnipeg
#16, 1313 Border St.
Winnipeg, MB R3H 0X4 Canada
204-985-1580
Fax: 204-697-0823
ecrozier@penncorp.ca

The Personal General Insurance Inc./ La Personnelle, assurances générales inc.

PO Box 3500
6300, boul de la Rive-Sud
Lévis, QC G6V 6P9
418-835-9040
Fax: 418-835-5599
800-463-6416
info@lapersonnelle.com
www.lapersonnelle.com
Former Name: La Securité, assurances générales
Also Known As: The Personal/La Personnelle
Ownership: Private
Year Founded: 1981
Number of Employees: 266
Assets: $100-500 million Year End: 20041231
Revenues: $100-500 million Year End: 20041231
Classes of Insurance: Auto, Liability, Boiler & Machinery, Property, Surety
Incorporation: Provincially Incorporated Insurance Company
Executives:
Jude Martineau, President/CEO
Louis Chantal, Sr. Exec. Vice-President, Administration, Finance & Human Resources, Treasurer
Pierre Deschênes, Sr. Exec. Vice-President, Information Technology
Sylvie Paquette, Sr. Exec. Vice-President, Corporate Development
Pierre Rousseau, Sr. Exec. Vice-President, Legal Affairs, Corporate Secretary
Jean Vaillancourt, Sr. Exec. Vice-President & General Manager, Québec Operations
Directors:
Raymond Gagné, Chair
Jean-Robert Laporte, Vice-Chair
Yves Archambault
Annie P. Bélanger
Jean J. Brossard
Stéphane Coudé
Roger Desrosiers
Jean-Louis Gauvin
Gabrielle Gosselin
Michel Lucas
Jude Martineau
Jocelyne Poulin
Clément Trottier
Yvon Vinet
Branches:
Montréal
PO Box 2, Pl-Desjardins Sta. Pl-Desjardins
1, Complexe Desjardins, 10e étage
Montréal, QC H5B 1B1 Canada
514-281-8121
800-363-6344

The Personal Insurance Company/ La Personnelle, compagnie d'assurances

PO Box 3500
6300, boul de la Rive-Sud
Lévis, QC G6V 6P9
905-306-3350
Fax: 418-835-5599
800-268-2620
www.thepersonal.com
Ownership: Private
Year Founded: 1973
Number of Employees: 863
Assets: $500m-1 billion Year End: 20041231
Revenues: $100-500 million Year End: 20041231
Classes of Insurance: Personal Accident & Sickness, Aircraft, Auto, Liability, Boiler & Machinery, Fidelity, Property, Surety
Incorporation: Federally Incorporated Insurance Company
Executives:
Jude Martineau, President/CEO
Jean-François Chalifoux, Sr. Exec. Vice-President & General Manager, RoC Operations
Louis Chantal, Sr. Exec. Vice-President, Administration, Finance & Human Resources, Treasurer
Pierre Deschênes, Sr. Exec. Vice-President, Information Technology
Sylvie Paquette, Sr. Exec. Vice-President, Corporate Development
Pierre Rousseau, Sr. Exec. Vice-President, Legal Affairs, Corporate Secretary
Directors:
Raymond Gagné, Chair
Jean-Robert Laporte, Vice-Chair
Yves Archambault
Annie P. Bélanger
Jean J. Brossard
Stéphane Coudé
Roger Desrosiers
Jean-Louis Gauvin
Gabrille Gosselin
Michel Lucas
Jude Martineau
Jocelyne Poulin
Clément Trottier
Yvon Vinet
Branches:
Mississauga
3 Robert Speck Pkwy.
Mississauga, ON L4Z 3Z9 Canada

Perth Insurance Company

#1600, 5700 Yonge St.
Toronto, ON M2M 4K2
416-590-0171
www.economicalinsurance.com
Ownership: Private. Subsidiary of The Economical Insurance Group
Classes of Insurance: Auto, Property
Incorporation: Federally Incorporated Insurance Company
Executives:
Noel G. Walpole, FPIC, President/CEO
Sandeep Uppal, HBA, MBA, CA, CFO
John Martin, B.Sc, Chief Information Officer
Jorge Arruda, B.Comm, Vice-President, Claims
Dean Bulloch, Vice-President, Human Resources
Catherine Coulson, BA, FCIP, Vice-President, Sales & Marketing
Louis Durocher, Vice-President, Actuarial Services
David M. Fitzpatrick, CHRP, Vice-President, Field Operations
Bill Lowe, BA, CIP, Vice-President, Commerical Insurance
Michael O'Neill, BA, MBA, CIP, Vice-President, Investments
Tom Reikman, H.B.Sc., MBA, AIIC, Vice-President, Personal Insurance
Bill Stinson, B.Math., FLMI, Vice-President, Information Technology
Linda Goss, FCIA, FCAS, FSA, Chief Actuary
Walt Leszkowicz, Manager, Operations
Directors:
P.H. Sims, Chair
M.N. Bales
David A. MacIntosh, CA
Charles M.W. Ormston
John H. Panabaker
J.A. Rogers
Brian J. Ruby
Harold E. Seegmiller
Noel G. Walpole, FIIC

Pictou County Farmers' Mutual Fire Insurance Company

PO Box 130
50 Front St.
Pictou, NS B0K 1H0
902-485-4542
Fax: 902-485-5136
888-485-4542
www.pictoumutual.com
Year Founded: 1904
Classes of Insurance: Liability, Property
Incorporation: Federally Incorporated Insurance Company
Profile: The Canadian property & casualty insurance company's activities are restricted to Nova Scotia. Policies are offered for farm & residential properties, churches & church halls.
Executives:
Reg Holman, President
Harry Redmond, Vice-President
Ruth Campbell, Manager, Sec.-Treas.
Don McInnes, Sr. Financial Advisor

Pilot Insurance Company

90 Eglinton Ave. West
Toronto, ON M4R 2E4
416-487-5141
Fax: 416-487-6905
800-268-7306
ehelpdesk@pilot.ca
www.pilot.ca
Ownership: Private
Year Founded: 1927
Number of Employees: 420
Classes of Insurance: Auto, Property
Incorporation: Provincially Incorporated Insurance Company
Profile: Pilot Insurance has 23 claims service offices & partners with over 290 independent insurance brokers.
Executives:
Maurice Tulloch, President
Claims Office:
Barrie
#22, 15 Cedarpoint Dr.
Barrie, ON L4N 5R7 Canada
705-726-2310
Mark King, Manager
Belleville
#102, 135 Victoria Ave.
Belleville, ON K8N 2B1 Canada
613-962-3476
Steve Gurnsey, Manager
Brampton
#345, 2 County Court Blvd.
Brampton, ON L6W 3W8 Canada
905-451-3672
Marie Barbosa, Manager
Chatham
#1, 84 Dover St.
Chatham, ON N7L 1T1 Canada
519-352-1714
Alan Livesey, Manager
Guelph
#107, 450 Speedvale Ave. West
Guelph, ON N1H 7Y6 Canada
519-824-1800
Charles Stewart, Manager
Hamilton
#402, 883 Upper Wentworth St.
Hamilton, ON L9A 4Y6 Canada
905-387-9336
Judy Avery, Manager
Hanover
428 - 10th St.
Hanover, ON N4N 1P9 Canada
519-364-1810
Bill Fowler, Manager
Kingston
#104, 920 Princess St.
Kingston, ON K7L 1H1 Canada
613-549-2251
Dave Halliday, Manager
Kitchener - Waterloo
Unit A, 55 Bridgeport Rd. East
Kitchener, ON N2J 2J7 Canada
519-746-5240
Paul Mazzocca, Manager
London
#100, 252 Pall Mall St.
London, ON N6A 5P6 Canada
519-672-2880
Bill Hamilton, Manager
Markham
Ashgrove Medical Centre
#209, 6633 Hwy. #7
Markham, ON L3P 7P2 Canada

905-294-2340
Clare Nichol, Manager
Mississauga
#3, 2160 Dunwin Dr.
Mississauga, ON L5L 1C7 Canada
905-828-2444
Wayne Carpenter, Manager
Morrisburg
73 Pilot Way
Morrisburg, ON K0C 1X0 Canada
613-543-2904
Jason Hess, Manager
Newmarket
The Yonge & Mulock Centre
#1-10, 16775 Yonge St.
Newmarket, ON L3Y 8J4 Canada
905-952-0124
Bill Perkins, Manager
North Bay
#5, 1495 Seymour St.
North Bay, ON P1B 8G4 Canada
705-474-4603
John Couch, Manager
Oshawa
#11, 191 Bloor St. East
Oshawa, ON L1H 3M3 Canada
905-723-1103
Karen Preuten, Manager
Ottawa
#200, 161 Greenbank Rd.
Nepean, ON K2H 5V6 Canada
613-828-6169
Richard McCall, Manager
Peterborough
#15, 1840 Landsdowne St. West
Peterborough, ON K9K 2M9 Canada
705-748-3433
Steve Carter, Manager
Smiths Falls
270 Brockville St.
Smiths Falls, ON K7A 5L4 Canada
613-283-2000
Mark Conlin, Manager
St Catharines
#3D, 211 Martindale Rd.
St Catharines, ON L2S 3V7 Canada
905-685-8463
Gary Washuta, Manager
Toronto - Milner Ave.
#107, 325 Milner Ave.
Toronto, ON M1B 5N1 Canada
416-265-8474
Wade Russell, Manager
Toronto - Yorkdale Rd.
#408, 1 Yorkdale Rd.
Toronto, ON M6A 3A1 Canada
416-787-1731
Anthony Low, Manager
Woodstock
408 Dundas St.
Woodstock, ON N4S 1B9 Canada
519-537-2101
Scott Garraway, Manager

Pool Insurance Company

#1301, 220 Portage Ave.
Winnipeg, MB R3C 0A5
204-942-0658
Fax: 204-989-2235
800-361-6669
slivingston@canpool.com
Ownership: Owned by Saskatchewan Wheat Pool & Agricore United.
Classes of Insurance: Property
Incorporation: Federally Incorporated Insurance Company
Profile: The company is a property insurer for owners & their affiliates.

Executives:
Peter Cox, President/CEO
Branches:
Daysland
PO Box 147
Daysland, AB T0B 1A0 Canada
780-374-2104
Fax: 780-374-2137
Allan Mueller, Contact
Grenfell
PO Box 787
Grenfell, SK S0G 2B0 Canada
306-697-3392
Fax: 306-697-2953
Ron Kraushaar, Contact
Lethbridge
123 Chippewa Cres.
Lethbridge, AB T1K 5B4 Canada
403-381-2645
Fax: 403-381-1401
Tim Johnson, Contact
Rosetown
PO Box 1045
Rosetown, SK S9V 1Z3 Canada
306-882-3988
Fax: 306-882-4307
Bradley Hauser, Contact
Winkler
147 Scotia Dr.
Winkler, MB R6W 2Z4 Canada
204-325-4292
Fax: 204-325-6453
Peter Neufeld, Contact

The Portage La Prairie Mutual Insurance Company

PO Box 340
749 Saskatchewan Ave. East
Portage La Prairie, MB R1N 3B8
204-857-3415
Fax: 204-239-6655
www.portagemutual.com
Also Known As: Portage Mutual Insurance
Ownership: Mutual
Year Founded: 1884
Number of Employees: 175
Assets: $100-500 million
Revenues: $100-500 million
Classes of Insurance: Legal Expense, Auto, Liability, Property
Incorporation: Federally Incorporated Insurance Company
Profile: The mutual insurance company operates across Canada through some 500 independent agents & brokers.

Executives:
Thomas W. McCartney, President/CEO
Randy L. Clark, Vice-President/Asst. General Manager
Douglas G. Pedden, Treasurer, Chief Financial Officer
Greg R. Kirk, Manager, Corporate Marketing
John G. Mitchell, Manager, Corporate Business Strategies
Michael R. Tarr, Manager, Corporate Claims
Kevin L. Wallis, Manager, Corporate Claims
Directors:
Donald L. Blight, Chair
Barrie E. Braden
Thomas W. McCartney
James R. Moorhouse
Hugh G. Owens
Henry F. Riendeau
Douglas G. Simpson
Dennis W. Thompson
J. Tobe Trimble
Branches:
Edmonton
First Edmonton Place
#1340, 10665 Jasper Ave.
Edmonton, AB T5J 3S9 Canada
780-423-3102
Fax: 780-429-0630
C. Wayne Wyborn, Regional Manager
Halifax
#502, 1695 Bedford Hwy.
Bedford, NS B4A 3Y4 Canada
902-835-1054
Fax: 902-835-7975
D. Gary Coolen, Manager, Atlantic
St Catharines
PO Box 2518, B Sta. B
320 Vine St., 3rd Fl.
St Catharines, ON L2M 7M8 Canada
905-937-0100
Fax: 905-937-0083
E. J. Forbes, Manager, Ontario
Offices:
Brandon
20 - 18 St.
Brandon, MB R7A 5A3 Canada
204-832-1351
Fax: 204-888-8717
M. Edgar, Representative, Marketing
Calgary
#101, 1717 - 10th St. NW
Calgary, AB T2M 4S2 Canada
403-264-0420
Fax: 403-263-6452
C.A. Henderson, Representative, Marketing
Dauphin
19 Memorial Blvd.
Dauphin, MB R7N 2A5 Canada
204-638-5108
Fax: 204-638-5211
C.S. Halliday, Representative, Claims
Saskatoon
#301, 3301 - 8th St. East
Saskatoon, SK S7H 5K5 Canada
306-249-3838
Fax: 306-249-0282
L.D. Todd, Representative, Marketing
Winnipeg
2147 Portage Ave.
Winnipeg, MB R3J 0L4 Canada
R.J. Owens, Representative, Marketing

Primerica Life Insurance Company of Canada

Plaza V
#300, 2000 Argentia Rd.
Mississauga, ON L5N 2R7
905-812-2900
Fax: 905-813-5310
800-387-7876
www.primerica.com
Ownership: Private. Subsidiary of Citigroup.
Classes of Insurance: Personal Accident & Sickness, Life
Incorporation: Federally Incorporated Insurance Company
Executives:
John A. Adams, CEO, Exec. Vice-President

Primmum Insurance Company/ Primmum compagnie d'assurance

999, boul de Maisonneuve ouest, 3e étage
Montréal, QC H3A 3L4
514-954-2463
Fax: 514-874-0463
866-454-8911
www.primmum.com
Former Name: Canada Life Casualty Insurance Company
Classes of Insurance: Auto, Property
Incorporation: Federally Incorporated Insurance Company
Branches:
Calgary
One Palliser Square
125-9th Ave. SE, 12th Fl.
Calgary, AB T2G 0P6 Canada
403-233-2467
Fax: 403-640-0252
866-454-8911
Edmonton
#2300, 10025 102-A Ave. NW
Edmonton, AB T5J 2Z2 Canada
403-233-2467
Fax: 403- 89-
866-454-8911
Halifax
Founders Square
170 Hollis St.
Halifax, NS B3J 3M8N4 Canada
902-425-2439
Fax: 902-424-1200
866-454-8911
Lois Burton, Director, Regional Operations
Toronto
The Valhalla Executive Centre
304 The East Mall, 6th Fl.
Toronto, ON M9B 6E2 Canada
416-233-7590
Fax: 416-233-9171
866-454-8911

Prince Edward Island Mutual Insurance Company

201 Water St.
Summerside, PE C1N 1B4

Prince Edward Island Mutual Insurance Company (continued)
902-436-2185
Fax: 902-436-0148
800-565-5441
protect@peimutual.com
www.peimutual.com
Ownership: Private
Year Founded: 1885
Number of Employees: 41
Assets: $10-50 million Year End: 20041231
Revenues: $10-50 million Year End: 20041231
Classes of Insurance: Liability, Property, Fire, Theft
Incorporation: Provincially Incorporated Insurance Company
Executives:
Brian MacKinley, President
Terrance Shea, CEO
Peggy Affleck, Vice-President
Blair Campbell, Secretary
Rudy Smith, Treasurer
Directors:
Percy Affleck
Claude Dorgan
John Furness
Allison Johnson
Brian MacKinley
Stewart MacRae
George Matheson
Gordon Vessey
Blair Wood

Principal Life Insurance Company/ Compagnie d'assurance-vie Principal
c/o John Milnes & Associates
1300 Bay St., 4th Fl.
Toronto, ON M5R 3K8
416-964-0067
Fax: 416-964-3338
www.principal.com
Former Name: Principal Mutual Life Insurance Company
Ownership: Part of Principal Financial Group, Des Moines, IA, USA.
Classes of Insurance: Personal Accident & Sickness, Life
Incorporation: Federally Incorporated Insurance Company
Executives:
John R. Milnes, Chief Agent

Progressive Casualty Insurance Company
#1500-28, 5650 Yonge St.
Toronto, ON M2M 4G3
416-499-6599
Fax: 416-499-7478
www.progressive.com
Ownership: Foreign. Part of The Progressive Corporation, Mayfield Village, OH, USA.
Year Founded: 1990
Classes of Insurance: Auto, Liability, Property, Surety
Incorporation: Federally Incorporated Insurance Company
Profile: The foreign property & casualty insurance company is limited to servicing existing policies.

Executives:
Subram Suriyan, Chief Agent

Promutuel Réassurance
1091, Grande Allée ouest
Québec, QC G1S 1Y7
418-683-1212
Fax: 418-683-2559
800-463-4888
sylvain.fauchon@promutuel.ca
www.promutuel.ca
Ownership: Private. Subsidary of Groupe Promutuel Fédération de sociétés mutuelles d'assurance générale
Year Founded: 1976
Number of Employees: 30
Assets: $100-500 million Year End: 20051231
Revenues: $100-500 million Year End: 20051231
Classes of Insurance: Accident, Liability, Boiler & Machinery, Property, Fire, Surety, Theft, Reinsurance
Incorporation: Provincially Incorporated Insurance Company
Executives:
Claude Robitaille, CEO
Sylvain Fauchon, First Vice-President, Insurance
Michel Gosselin, First Vice-President, Finance & Treasury
Gaétan Goulet, First Vice-President, Information Systems
Serge Roy, First Vice-President, Marketing & Business Development
Directors:
Fernand Timmons, President
Adrien Viens, Vice-President
Roger Brouard
Marc Couillard
Jacques Éthier
Gaétan Ménard
Jean Mottard

Promutuel Vie inc
1091, Grande Allée ouest
Québec, QC G1S 4Y7
418-683-1212
Fax: 418-683-2559
federation@promutuel.ca
www.promutuel.ca
Year Founded: 1988
Number of Employees: 7
Assets: $5-10 million
Revenues: $5-10 million
Classes of Insurance: Accident, Personal Accident & Sickness, Life
Incorporation: Provincially Incorporated Insurance Company
Executives:
Adrien Viens, Président du Conseil d'administration
Claude Robitaille, Chef de la direction
Gaétan Goulet, Premier Vice-président, Systèmes d'information
Carl Cleary, Vice-président, Finance et trésorie
Sylvain Fauchon, Premier vice-président, Assurances
Normand Morin, Vice-président, Vérification et inspection

Protective Insurance Company
John Milnes & Associates
1300 Bay St., 4th Fl.
Toronto, ON M5R 3K8
416-964-0067
Fax: 416-964-3338
www.protective.com
Ownership: Foreign. Part of Protective Life Corporation, Birmingham, AL, USA.
Classes of Insurance: Personal Accident & Sickness, Auto, Liability, Property
Incorporation: Federally Incorporated Insurance Company
Executives:
John R. Milnes, Chief Agent

Providence Washington Insurance Company
#2, 1145 Nicholson Rd.
Newmarket, ON L3Y 9C3
905-853-0858
Classes of Insurance: Marine, Property
Incorporation: Federally Incorporated Insurance Company
Executives:
Colleen Sexsmith, Chief Agent

Québec Blue Cross/ Croix Bleue du Québec
#9B, 550, rue Sherbrooke ouest
Montréal, QC H3C 3S3
514-286-8403
Fax: 514-286-8358
877-909-7686
info@qc.bluecross.ca, info@qc.croixbleue.ca
www.qc.bluecross.ca, www.qc.croixbleue.ca
Ownership: Parent company is Canasuurance Hospital Service Association. Member of Canadian Association of Blue Cross Plans, Toronto, ON.
Year Founded: 1942
Number of Employees: 275
Assets: $100-500 million
Revenues: $100-500 million
Classes of Insurance: Accident, Personal Accident & Sickness, Auto, Liability, Life
Incorporation: Provincially Incorporated Insurance Company
Profile: Individual health & travel insurance is offered.

Executives:
Claude Boivin, President/CEO
Louis Gosselin, Sr. Vice-President
Richard Lachance, Vice-President
Marc Lamirande, Vice-President
Branches:
Toronto
185 The West Mall
Toronto, ON M9C 5L5 Canada
416-626-1688

RBC General Insurance Company/ Compagnie d'assurance generale RBC
6880 Financial Dr.
Mississauga, ON L5N 7Y5
905-816-2452
Fax: 905-816-2450
800-769-2526
www.rbcinsurance.com
Ownership: RBC Insurance, Mississauga, ON.
Classes of Insurance: Personal Accident & Sickness, Auto, Liability, Property, Fire, Theft
Incorporation: Federally Incorporated Insurance Company
Profile: Residence insurance includes homeowners, condominium unit owners' & renters' insurance. Automobile insurance includes motocycle, camper/trailer & all terrain vehicle insurance.

Executives:
Stanley W. Seggie, President/CEO
Branches:
Calgary
#600, 10655 Southport Rd. SW
Calgary, AB T2W 4Y1 Canada
866-715-3757
Edmonton
#2050, 10303 Jasper Ave.
Edmonton, AB T5J 3N6 Canada
866-715-3757
Montréal
#1300, 1, Place Ville Marie
Montréal, QC H3C 2S1 Canada
Fax: 514-384-5088
800-769-2526
Toronto
#406, 111 Grangeway Ave.
Toronto, ON M1H 3E9
Fax: 905-813-4791
888-269-2515

RBC Insurance
Tower 1
6880 Financial Dr.
Mississauga, ON L5N 7Y5
905-949-3663
Fax: 905-813-4853
877-749-7224
www.rbcinsurance.com
Former Name: RBC Insurance Services Inc.
Ownership: Member of RBC Financial Group
Classes of Insurance: Personal Accident & Sickness, Auto, Life, Property
Incorporation: Federally Incorporated Insurance Company
Profile: Services also include loan, mortgage & credit card balance protection. In addition, the company offers RBC Insurance Guaranteed Investment Funds.

Executives:
Neil Skelding, President/CEO
David Black, Head, USA Insurance
Diane Churilla, Head, Finance
Tom Dalinda, Head, Investments
Karen Leggett, Head, Insurance Operations
Louise Mitchell, Head, Bank Distributed Products
Kathy Pryden, Head, Reinsurance & International Markets
Stan Seggie, Head, Property & Casualty Insurance
John Young, Head, Life & Health Insurance
Affiliated Companies:
RBC General Insurance Company
RBC Life Insurance Company
RBC Travel Insurance Company
Branches:
Brossard
Place Portobello
7250, boul Taschereau
Brossard, QC J4W 1M9
450-932-5122
Fax: 450-923-5121
Halifax
#110, 287 Lacewood Dr.
Halifax, NS B3M 3Y7
902-421-5518
Fax: 902-421-7937
Hamilton
Centre Mall
1227 Barton St. East
Hamilton, ON L8H 2V4

905-548-5790
Fax: 905-548-5401
Kingston
#2, 65 Princess St.
Kingston, ON K7L 1A6
613-549-7300
Fax: 613-549-7655
Mississauga - Financial Dr.
6880 Financial Dr.
Mississauga, ON L5N 7Y5
905-286-5099
Fax: 905-286-1187
Mississauga - Hurontario St.
#3B, 4557 Hurontario St.
Mississauga, ON L4M 3M2
905-712-3236
Fax: 905-712-8959
Montréal - St. Charles
Place Grilli
3535, boul St. Charles
Montréal, QC H9H 5B9
514-630-1908
Fax: 514-630-5001
Montréal - Ville Marie
#11325, 1, Place Ville Marie
Montréal, QC H3B 3Y1
514-874-2282
Fax: 514-874-2141
Toronto - Bloor St. East
2 Bloor St. East, Lower Concourse
Toronto, ON M4W 1A8
416-974-2760
Fax: 416-974-2878
Toronto - Queen St. East
2175 Queen St. East, 2nd Fl.
Toronto, ON M4E 1E5
416-699-3877
Toronto - Queen's Quay West
#121, 207 Queen's Quay West
Toronto, ON M5J 1A7
416-955-2550
Fax: 416-955-2588
Toronto - Sandhurst Circle
1571 Sandhurst Circle
Toronto, ON M1V 1V2
416-292-6466
Fax: 416-292-6490
Toronto - Warden Ave.
2175 Queen St. East, 2nd Fl.
Toronto, ON M4E 1E5
416-699-3977

RBC Life Insurance Company

West Tower
6880 Financial Dr.
Mississauga, ON L5N 7Y5
905-606-1785
Fax: 905-813-4850
877-519-9501
Other Information: 866-223-7113 (Toll Free, New Life Insurance Inquiries); 800-461-1413 (Toll Free, Existing Life Insurance Inquiries)
www.rbcinsurance.com
Ownership: RBC Insurance, Mississauga, ON
Classes of Insurance: Personal Accident & Sickness, Life
Incorporation: Federally Incorporated Insurance Company
Profile: The Canadian life insurance company offers term life insurance, permanent life insurance, universal life insurance, & personal accident insurance. The company serves clients in both Canada & the USA.
Executives:
John Young, President/CEO
Branches:
Burlington
1122 International Blvd.
Burlington, ON L7R 4C1 Canada
905-319-9501
Fax: 905-319-9490

Calgary
#600, 10655 Southport Rd. SW
Calgary, AB T2W 4Y1 Canada
403-264-8686
Fax: 403-263-5591
Edmonton
#610, 10117 Jasper Ave.
Edmonton, AB T5J 1W8 Canada
780-423-0066
Fax: 780-428-1925
Halifax
5161 George St., 12th Fl.
Halifax, NS B3J 1M7 Canada
902-492-3444
Fax: 902-492-2171
Kitchener
30 Duke St. West, 8th Fl.
Kitchener, ON N2H 3W5 Canada
519-579-4770
Fax: 519-579-4787
London
#205, 380 Wellington St.
London, ON N6A 5B5 Canada
519-679-9590
Fax: 519-945-4383
Montréal
#710, 1100, boul René-Lévesque ouest
Montréal, QC H3B 4N4 Canada
514-954-1205
Fax: 514-954-1206
Ottawa
90 Sparks St., 2nd Fl.
Ottawa, ON K1P 5T6 Canada
613-564-2040
Fax: 613-564-2017
Québec
#470, 1000, rte de L'Église
Québec, QC G1V 3V9 Canada
418-623-7285
Fax: 418-623-9608
Saskatoon
#201, 135 - 21 St. East
Saskatoon, SK S7K 0B4 Canada
306-933-3222
Fax: 306-665-1106
Toronto
#600, 30 Adelaide St.
Toronto, ON M5C 3G8 Canada
416-594-3700
Fax: 416-861-0897
Vancouver
#900, 1055 West Georgia St.
Vancouver, BC V6E 3P3 Canada
604-689-1783
Fax: 604-683-3320
Windsor
245 Ouellette Ave.
Windsor, ON N9A 7J2 Canada
519-781-9042
Fax: 519-945-4383
Winnipeg
#1206, 220 Portage Ave.
Winnipeg, MB R3B 0A5 Canada
204-985-9497
Fax: 204-944-8855

RBC Travel Insurance Company

West Tower
6880 Financial Dr., 5th Fl.
Mississauga, ON L5N 7Y5
905-816-2452
Fax: 905-813-4850
Other Information: Toll Free, Trip Cancellation Insurance Claim: 800-387-2487; Mail Address, Trip Cancellation Insurance Claim: PO Box 97, Stn. A, Mississauga, L5A 2Y9
www.rbcinsurance.com/travel
Former Name: Voyageur Insurance Company
Ownership: RBC Insurance, Mississauga, ON.
Classes of Insurance: Personal Accident & Sickness, Life
Incorporation: Federally Incorporated Insurance Company
Profile: A range of products & services are available, such as trip cancellation, interruption & emergency assistance. Clients are in both Canada & the United States. RBC travel insurance can also be purchased at certain travel agencies & from insurance brokers across Canada.
Executives:
Stanley W. Seggie, President/CEO
Branches:
Calgary
#600, 10655 Southport Rd. SW
Calgary, AB T2W 4Y1 Canada
403-271-0504
Fax: 403-271-8168

Montréal
1, Place Ville Marie, 13e étage
Montréal, QC H3C 3A9 Canada
514-748-1457
Fax: 514-748-2588
Vancouver
#300, 2985 Virtual Way
Vancouver, BC V5M 4X7 Canada
604-718-6700
Fax: 604-718-6752

Real Estate Insurance Exchange(REIX)

#205, 4954 Richard Rd. SW
Calgary, AB T3E 6L1
403-228-2667
Fax: 403-229-3466
877-462-7349
info@reix.ca
www.reix.ca
Also Known As: Alberta Real Estate Insurance Exchange
Year Founded: 1991
Classes of Insurance: Liability
Incorporation: Provincially Incorporated Insurance Company
Profile: REIX administers a program of errors & omissions insurance.
Executives:
Harvey Gamble, Executive Director
Directors:
Dale Russell, Chair

Red River Valley Mutual Insurance Company

PO Box 940
245 Centre Ave. East
Altona, MB R0G 0B0
204-324-6434
Fax: 204-324-1316
800-370-2888
info@redrivermutual.com
Ownership: Policy-holders
Year Founded: 1875
Number of Employees: 42
Assets: $50-100 million Year End: 20041231
Revenues: $10-50 million Year End: 20041231
Classes of Insurance: Liability, Boiler & Machinery, Fidelity, Property, Fire, Surety, Theft
Incorporation: Provincially Incorporated Insurance Company
Profile: Specializes in residential, farm & commercial lines in the Provinces of Manitoba & Saskatchewan.
Executives:
Harvey G. Heinrichs, President/CEO
Alvin Ginter, Vice-President
Lyndon Friesen, Manager, Claims
Robert Pranys, Comptroller
Directors:
Hans P. Werner, Chair
Ray Loewen, Vice-Chair
Brian Esau, Secretary
Paul Brandt
Frank Friesen
Cornelius A. Janzen
Abe J. Riediger
W.J. Siemens
Wes Unger

Reliable Life Insurance Company

PO Box 557
100 King St. West
Hamilton, ON L8N 3K9
905-523-5587
Fax: 905-522-7211
800-465-0661
service@reliablelifeinsurance.com
www.reliablelifeinsurance.com
Ownership: Foreign. Parent is Old Republic International Corporation (Stock Symbol ORI). Reliable is part of Old Republic Insurance Group.
Year Founded: 1887
Number of Employees: 103
Assets: $10-50 million Year End: 20051231
Revenues: $10-50 million Year End: 20051231
Classes of Insurance: Personal Accident & Sickness, Life
Incorporation: Federally Incorporated Insurance Company

Reliable Life Insurance Company (continued)

Executives:
Paul M. Field, CEO, CFO
Joseph J. Henderson, President
Barry Gagnon, Vice-President, Marketing
Sharon Bros, Asst. Vice-President, Claims
Directors:
R. Scott Rager, Chair
J. Brian Reeve, Secretary
Thomas A. Hickey
Spencer A. LeRoy
Gary E. Lewis
David Rattee
J.W. Nevil Thomas
Richard J. Wilson
Aldo C. Zucaro

ReliaStar Life Insurance Company/ Compagnie d'Assurance-Vie ReliaStar

c/o D.M. Williams & Assoc. Ltd.
#201, 3650 Victoria Park Ave.
Toronto, ON M2H 3P7
416-496-1148
www.ing.com/us/reliastar
Former Name: Northwestern National Life Insurance Company
Ownership: Affiliate of ING North America Insurance Corporation.
Classes of Insurance: Personal Accident & Sickness, Life
Incorporation: Federally Incorporated Insurance Company
Executives:
V. Lorraine Williams, Chief Agent

Revios Reinsurance

#1600, 480 University Ave.
Toronto, ON M5G 1V6
416-598-4688
Fax: 416-598-9244
Former Name: Gerling Global Reinsurance Company
Ownership: Private-foreign. Operated by Revios North America
Year Founded: 1957
Classes of Insurance: Aircraft, Auto, Liability, Boiler & Machinery, Credit, Marine, Fidelity, Property, Fire, Surety, Hail & Crop
Incorporation: Provincially Incorporated Insurance Company
Executives:
Eugene M. Woodward, President/CEO; 416-542-1730

RGA Life Reinsurance Company of Canada/ RGA Compagnie de réassurance-vie du Canada

#1100, 55 University Ave.
Toronto, ON M5J 2H7
416-682-0000
Fax: 416-777-9526
800-433-4326
www.rgare.com/global/canada.asp
Ownership: Private. Subsidiary of Reinsurance Group of America Incorporated.
Year Founded: 1992
Assets: $1-10 billion Year End: 20041231
Revenues: $100-500 million Year End: 20041231
Classes of Insurance: Reinsurance
Incorporation: Federally Incorporated Insurance Company
Executives:
Alain Neemeh, CA, President/CEO
Jackie DeForest, Vice-President, Underwriting
Brian Louth, Vice-President, Development
Gary Walters, Vice-President, Group Reinsurance
Directors:
Charles Galloway
John Gardner
Claude Genest
Douglas Hicks
Cameron Leamy
André St-Amour
Branches:
Montréal
#1000, 1255, rue Peel
Montréal, QC H3B 2T9 Canada
514-985-5260
Fax: 514-985-3066
800-985-4326
Alain Neemeh, Exec. Vice-President, Operations

Royal & SunAlliance Insurance Company of Canada

10 Wellington St. East
Toronto, ON M5E 1L5
416-366-7511
Fax: 416-367-9869
800-268-8406
www.royalsunalliance.ca/royalsun/
Former Name: Royal Insurance Company of Canada
Ownership: Parent is Royal & SunAlliance Insurance Group plc.

Year Founded: 1845
Number of Employees: 2,400
Classes of Insurance: Property
Incorporation: Federally Incorporated Insurance Company
Profile: Casualty insurance is also offered.

Executives:
Rowan Saunders, President/CEO
C.C. Huang, President/CEO, Johnson Corporation
Ed Sikorski, President, Noraxis Capital Corporation
Irene Bianchi, Vice-President, Claims & Corporate Services
Shawn DeSantis, Vice-President, Personal Insurance
Joy Flowers, Vice-President, Human Resources
Michael Jakeman, Vice-President, Commercial Insurance
Steve Knoch, Vice-President, Information Services & Change Management
Winsome Leong, Vice-President, Actuarial
Mike Wallace, Vice-President, Risk, Underwriting & Reinsurance

Directors:
Marcel J. Bundock, Chair
George Anderson
Guy G. Dufresne
George Harvey
Simon Lee
Derek Oland
Rowan Saunders
Affiliated Companies:
Ascentus Insurance Ltd.
Coast Underwriters Limited
Western Assurance Company
Branches:
Calgary - 11 Ave. SW - Western Regional Centre
PO Box 2507, M Sta. M
#300, 326 - 11 Ave. SW
Calgary, AB T2P 3Z3 Canada
403-233-6000
Fax: 403-233-6900
Western_Region@royalsunalliance.ca
Dartmouth - Garland Ave. - Atlantic Regional Centre
50 Garland Ave.
Dartmouth, NS B3B 0A3 Canada
902-493-1500
Fax: 902-468-7472
800-565-7651
Atlantic_Region@royalsunalliance.ca
Mississauga - Erin Mills Pkwy. - Ontario Regional Centre
Sheridan Insurance Centre
#1000, 2225 Erin Mills Pkwy.
Mississauga, ON L5K 2S9 Canada
905-403-2333
Fax: 905-403-3324

Montréal - de Maisonneuve ouest - Québec Office
#1400, 1001, boul de Maisonneuve ouest
Montréal, QC H3A 3C8 Canada
514-844-1116
Fax: 514-844-0726
Quebec_Region@royalsunalliance.ca
Toronto - Wellington St. East - Specialized Products & Services Group
10 Wellington St. East, 7th Fl.
Toronto, ON M5E 1L5 Canada
416-366-7511
Fax: 416-366-0930
800-268-8406
Toronto - Yonge St. - Technical Resource Group
#630, 48 Yonge St.
Toronto, ON M5E 1G6 Canada
416-363-0814
Fax: 416-363-0459
Vancouver
#440, 580 Hormby St.
Vancouver, BC V6C 3B6 Canada
604-684-8111
Fax: 604-662-3599
800-663-1272

St. Paul Fire & Marine Insurance Company/ La Compagnie d'Assurance Saint Paul

PO Box 93
#1200, 121 King St. West
Toronto, ON M5H 3T9
416-366-8301
Fax: 416-366-0846
800-268-8481
askcanada@stpaul.com
Also Known As: The St. Paul
Ownership: St Paul Companies Inc., USA.
Year Founded: 1928
Assets: $10-100 billion
Revenues: $1,072,249,000
Classes of Insurance: Aircraft, Auto, Liability, Boiler & Machinery, Marine, Fidelity, Property, Fire, Surety, Reinsurance
Incorporation: Federally Incorporated Insurance Company
Profile: Brand name is St. Paul Travelers.

Executives:
Jay Steven Fisherman, President
Robert Fellows, Chief Agent
Directors:
Jay Benet
Charles Clarke
Douglas Elliot
William Heyman
Brian MacLean
Timothy Michael Miller
Kent Douglas Urness
Branches:
Calgary
Manulife House
#525, 603 - 7th Ave. SW
Calgary, AB T2P 2T2 Canada
403-265-6252
Fax: 403-264-0971
Joseph (Joe) Lundrigan, Manager, Prairie Region
Edmonton
#600, 10025 - 102A Ave. NW
Edmonton, AB T5J 2Z3 Canada
780-435-5921
Fax: 780-435-5961
Kathryn (Kathy) Maksymec, Specialist, Sr. Underwriting
Montréal
#1100, 1010, rue de la Gauchetière ouest
Montréal, QC H3B 2N2 Canada
514-871-3363
Fax: 514-875-2155
Richard Lavoie, Asst. Vice-President
Vancouver
#2500, 650 West Georgia St.
Vancouver, BC V6B 4N7 Canada
604-696-8523
Fax: 604-684-5172
Mo Kaur, Manager, Pacific Region

St. Paul Guarantee Insurance Company

PO Box 284
77 King St. West, 34th Fl.
Toronto, ON M5K 1K2
416-360-8183
Fax: 416-360-8267
Other Information: Toll Free: 1-800-387-1581, 1-800-330-5033
www.stpaulguarantee.com
Former Name: London Gurantee Insurance Company; Northern Indemnity Inc.
Year Founded: 2003
Classes of Insurance: Surety
Incorporation: Federally Incorporated Insurance Company
Profile: The company is a surety bond & specialty insurance provider. Products include contract surety, commercial surety, developer surety, home warranty in BC, title insurance & risk solutions.

Executives:
George Petropoulos, President/CEO
Robert A. Burns, Sr. Vice-President, Credit/Underwriting
Shirley Lewis, Assistant Vice-President, Marketing
Branches:
Montréal
#1100, 1010, rue de la Gauchetière ouest
Montréal, QC H3B 2N2 Canada
514-875-0600
Fax: 514-875-0666
800-361-9427

Luc Gauvin, Vice-President & Branch Manager
Vancouver
PO Box 11542
#2500, 650 West Georgia St.
Vancouver, BC V6B 4N7 Canada
604-682-2663
Fax: 604-682-2664
800-555-9431
Darryll McDonald, Vice-President & Branch Manager

Saskatchewan Auto Fund
2260 - 11th Ave.
Regina, SK S4P 0J9
306-751-1200
Fax: 306-565-8666
www.sgi.sk.ca
Ownership: Crown. Wholly owned by the Government of Saskatchewan
Year Founded: 1984
Assets: $1-10 billion Year End: 20051231
Revenues: $500m-1 billion Year End: 20051231
Classes of Insurance: Auto
Incorporation: Provincially Incorporated Insurance Company
Executives:
Jon Schubert, President
Cheryl Barber, Vice-President, Human Resources
Earl Cameron, Vice-President, Claims & Salvage
John Dobie, Vice-President, Canadian Operations
Randy Heise, Vice-President, Underwriting
Don Thompson, Vice-President, Finance & Administration
Dwain Wells, Vice-President, Systems
Sherry Wolf, Vice-President, Auto Fund
Directors:
Nancy E. Hopkins, Chair
J. Walter Bardua, Vice-Chair
Dale Bloom, Corporate Secretary, Crown Investments Corp.
Joan F.D. Baldwin
Joan D. Bellegarde
Kendra Chesney
Merin Coutts
Robert Fenwick
William J.A. Heidt
Wayne Hovdebo
Arleen Hynd
Jim Mills
Ron Osika

Saskatchewan Blue Cross
PO Box 4030
516 - 2nd Ave. North
Saskatoon, SK S7K 3T2
306-244-2662
Fax: 306-652-5751
800-667-6853
www.sk.bluecross.ca
Former Name: Medical Services Incorporated
Ownership: Not-for-profit. Member of Canadian Association of Blue Cross Plans, Toronto, ON.
Year Founded: 1946
Classes of Insurance: Personal Accident & Sickness, Life
Incorporation: Provincially Incorporated Insurance Company
Profile: Health benefits, including prescription drug benefits, vision & dental care, travel coverage, life insurance & income replacement coverage, are provided to individuals & employers in Saskatchewan.
Branches:
Regina
#100, 1870 Albert St.
Regina, SK S4P 4B7 Canada
306-525-5025
Fax: 306-525-2124
800-873-2583

Saskatchewan Crop Insurance Corporation
PO Box 3000
484 Prince William Dr.
Melville, SK S0A 2P0
306-728-7200
Fax: 306-728-7268
888-935-0000
customer.service@scic.gov.sk.ca
www.saskcropinsurance.com
Ownership: Provincial crown corporation
Year Founded: 1973
Classes of Insurance: Hail & Crop
Incorporation: Provincially Incorporated Insurance Company
Executives:
Stan Benjamin, Acting General Manager
Donna Bellamy, Exec. Manager, Field Operations
Mike Cooper, Exec. Manager, Audits
Bill Cudmore, Exec. Manager, Human Resources
Terry Dingle, Exec. Manager, Information Technology
Keith Hayward, Exec. Manager, Research & Development
Terri Kentel-Weinheimer, Exec. Manager, Communications
Lorne Warnes, Exec. Manager, Finance & Administration

Saskatchewan Motor Club Insurance Company Ltd.
200 Albert St. North
Regina, SK S4R 5E2
306-791-4321
Fax: 306-949-4461
www.caasask.sk.ca
Ownership: Private. Subsidiary of Saskatchewan Motor Club Inc.
Assets: $1-5 million
Revenues: Under $1 million
Classes of Insurance: Accident
Incorporation: Provincially Incorporated Insurance Company
Executives:
Fred Titanich, President/CEO
Dave Roszell, Director, Finance
Directors:
Terry Brodziek; 306-773-0900
William S. Elliott; 306-522-5671
Dave Harding; 306-338-2336
Garth Knakoske; 306-773-7285
Tom Phillipson; 306-693-5862
Vic H. Pizzey; 306-975-0407
Fred Titanich; 306-791-4331

Saskatchewan Municipal Hail Insurance Association
2100 Cornwall St.
Regina, SK S4P 2K7
306-569-1852
Fax: 306-522-3717
877-414-7644
smhi@smhi.ca
www.smhi.ca
Ownership: Non-profit association
Year Founded: 1917
Number of Employees: 100
Assets: $100-500 million Year End: 20041101
Revenues: $50-100 million Year End: 20041101
Classes of Insurance: Hail & Crop
Incorporation: Provincially Incorporated Insurance Company
Executives:
Murray Otterson, CEO
Rodney Schoettler, COO
Directors:
Wayne Black, President
Arnold Boyko, Vice-President
Murray Purcelli, Exec. Member

Saskatchewan Mutual Insurance Company(SMI)
279 - 3 Ave. North
Saskatoon, SK S7K 2H8
306-653-4232
Fax: 306-653-3260
800-667-3067
headoffice@saskmutual.com
www.saskmutual.com
Ownership: Policy-holders.
Year Founded: 1908
Number of Employees: 50
Assets: $10-50 million Year End: 20051231
Revenues: $10-50 million Year End: 20051231
Classes of Insurance: Auto, Liability, Boiler & Machinery, Fidelity, Property
Incorporation: Federally Incorporated Insurance Company
Profile: The company writes insurance in the provinces of Saskatchewan, Manitoba & Alberta.
Executives:
R.W. Trost, President/CEO
L.M. Wiebe, Exec. Vice-President
K.L. Heuchert, Vice-President, Technology
D.M. Thiessen, Vice-President, Underwriting & Marketing
S.L. Willick, Vice-President, Finance & Administration
R.J. Wotherspoon, Vice-President, Claims
Directors:
A.G. Ayers, Chair
D.R. Arnold, Vice-Chair
T.G. Davis
B.A. Latrace-Henderson
P.L. Salisbury
R.F. Simmer
R.W. Trost
M.E. Van Impe
L.M. Wiebe
Branches:
Regina
2505 - 11th Ave.
Regina, SK S4P 0K6 Canada
306-545-2855
Fax: 306-545-3082
Winnipeg
2151 Portage Ave., #J
Winnipeg, MB R3J 0L4 Canada
204-256-2078
Fax: 204-256-2642

SCOR Canada Reinsurance Company/ SCOR Canada Compagnie de Réassurance
TD Canada Trust Tower, BCE Place
PO Box 615
#5000, 161 Bay St.
Toronto, ON M5J 2S1
416-869-3670
Fax: 416-365-9393
800-268-8207
ca@scor.com
www.scor.com
Ownership: Foreign. SCOR, France.
Classes of Insurance: Reinsurance
Incorporation: Federally Incorporated Insurance Company
Executives:
Henry Klecan, President/CEO, SCOR Canada & SCOR US
Affiliated Companies:
SCOR Vie - Succursale du Canada
Branches:
Montréal
#4512, 1250, boul René-Lévesque ouest
Montréal, QC H3B 4W8 Canada
514-939-1937
Fax: 514-393-3599

SCOR Vie - Succursale du Canada/ SCOR Life - Canada Branch
TD Canada Trust Tower, BCE Place
#5000, 161 Bay St.
Toronto, ON M5J 2S1
416-304-6536
Fax: 416-304-6574
ca@scor.com
www.scor.com
Ownership: Foreign. SCOR, France
Classes of Insurance: Personal Accident & Sickness, Life
Incorporation: Federally Incorporated Insurance Company
Executives:
Marc Archambault, Chief Agent, Exec. Vice-President
William Hazelwood, Manager, Marketing
Branches:
Montréal
#4510, 1250, boul René-Lévesque ouest
Montréal, QC H3B 4W8 Canada
514-933-6994
Fax: 514-933-6435
ca@scor.com

Scotia Life Insurance Company/ Scotia-Vie Compagnie d'Assurance
#400, 100 Yonge St.
Toronto, ON M5H 1H1
416-866-5412
Fax: 416-866-5810
800-387-9844
www.scotiabank.com
Also Known As: ScotiaLife
Classes of Insurance: Personal Accident & Sickness, Life
Incorporation: Federally Incorporated Insurance Company
Executives:
Oscar Zimmerman, President/CEO

Scottish & York Insurance Co. Limited
c/o Aviva Canada Inc.
2206 Eglinton Ave. East
Toronto, ON M1L 4S8

INSURANCE COMPANIES

Scottish & York Insurance Co. Limited (continued)
416-288-1800
Fax: 416-288-5888
800-387-4518
info@avivacanada.com
www.avivacanada.com
Ownership: Parent is Aviva Canada Inc., Toronto, ON.
Classes of Insurance: Legal Expense, Auto, Liability, Boiler & Machinery, Fidelity, Property, Surety
Incorporation: Provincially Incorporated Insurance Company
Executives:
Igal Mayer, President/CEO

Security National Insurance Company/ Sécurité Nationale compagnie d'assurance

50, Place Crémazie, 12e étage
Montréal, QC H2P 1B6
514-382-6060
Fax: 514-385-2162
800-361-3821
www.melochemonnex.com
Ownership: Subsidiary of Meloche Monnex Inc., Montréal, QC.
Year Founded: 1934
Classes of Insurance: Personal Accident & Sickness, Auto, Property, Fire
Incorporation: Federally Incorporated Insurance Company
Executives:
Alain Thibault, President/CEO
Daniel Demers, Exec. Vice-President
Richard Evans, Sr. Vice-President, Claims Services
François Faucher, Sr. Vice-President & CFO
Guy Vézina, Sr. Vice-President, Operations & Business Development
Antonietta DiGirolamo, Asst. Corporate Secretary
Directors:
Dianne Cunningham
Raymond A. Décarie
Daniel Demers
Bernard T. Dorval
Louis D. Hyndman
Sean Kilburn
C. Lajeunesse, O.C.
J. David Livingston
Damian J. McNamee
Dominic J. Mercuri
L. Robert Shaw
Alain Thibault
Fredric J. Tomczyk

SGI CANADA Consolidated

2260 - 11th Ave.
Regina, SK S4P 0J9
306-751-1200
Fax: 306-565-8666
www.sgi.sk.ca
Ownership: Crown. Wholly owned by the Government of Saskatchewan
Year Founded: 1944
Number of Employees: 1,637
Assets: $500m-1 billion Year End: 20051231
Classes of Insurance: Accident, Aircraft, Auto, Liability, Boiler & Machinery, Fidelity, Property, Surety, Reinsurance
Incorporation: Provincially Incorporated Insurance Company
Profile: The company conducts a property/casualty insurance business in the province of Saskatchewan. It is affiliated with SGI Canada Insurance Services Ltd.

Executives:
Jon Schubert, President; 306-751-1717
Dwain Wells, Vice-President, Systems
Cheryl Barber, Vice-President, Human Resources & Corporate Services
Earl Cameron, Vice-President, Claims & Salvage
Sherry Wolf, Vice-President, Auto Fund
John Dobie, Vice-President, Canadian Operations
Randy Heise, Vice-President, Underwriting
Don Thompson, Vice-President, Finance & Administration
Directors:
Nancy E. Hopkins, Q.C., Chair
J. Walter Bardua, Vice-Chair
Joan F.D. Baldwin
Joan D. Bellegarde
Dale Bloom, Corporate Secretary, Crown Investments Corp.
Kendra Chesney
Merin Coutts
Robert Fenwick
W.J.A. (Bill) Heidt
Arleen Hynd
Affiliated Companies:
Coachman Insurance Company
Insurance Company of Prince Edward Island
Saskatchewan Auto Fund
Branches:
Estevan - Claims Centre
1009 - 5th St.
Estevan, SK S4A 2L8 Canada
Ron Grobbink, Manager
Kindersley - Claims Centre
821 - 9th St. West
Kindersley, SK S0L 1S0 Canada
Brad Relland, Manager
Lloydminster - Claims Centre
4805 - 50th St.
Lloydminster, SK S9V 0M8 Canada
Connie Rissling, Manager
Meadow Lake - Claims Centre
313 - 3rd St. East
Meadow Lake, SK S0M 1V0 Canada
Connie Rissling, Manager
Moose Jaw - Claims Centre
105 - 4th Ave. NW
Moose Jaw, SK S6H 4N9 Canada
Walter Reihl, Manager
North Battleford - Claims Centre
1002 - 103rd St.
North Battleford, SK S9A 1K4 Canada
Roxanne Greyeyes, Manager
Prince Albert
501 - 15th St. East
Prince Albert, SK S6B 1G3 Canada
Robert Smisko, Manager
Regina - Fleet St. - Claims Technical Services
450 Fleet St.
Regina, SK S4N 6M2 Canada
John Schick, Manager
Regina - Fleet St. - Commercial Claims Centre
440 Fleet St.
Regina, SK S4N 6M2 Canada
Gerry Lareau, Manager
Regina - Henderson Dr. - General Claims
435 Henderson Dr.
Regina, SK S4N 4Y1 Canada
Joe Scarfe, Manager
Regina - McCarthy Blvd. North - Northwest Claims Centre
1121 McCarthy Blvd. North
Regina, SK S4X 3T6 Canada
Doug Sargent, Manager
Regina - Pasqua St. - South Claims Centre
3825 Pasqua St.
Regina, SK S4P 3J1 Canada
Arlene Franko, Manager, Injury South
Regina - Victoria Ave. East - East Claims Centre
2110 Victoria Ave. East
Regina, SK S4P 3C2 Canada
Doug Sargent, Manager
Saskatoon - 2nd Ave. North - Central Claims Centre
523 - 2nd Ave. North
Saskatoon, SK S7K 0H3 Canada
Gary Kading, Manager
Saskatoon - Fairmont Dr. - West Claims Centre
345 Fairmont Dr.
Saskatoon, SK S7M 5N5 Canada
Ernie Karolat, Manager
Saskatoon - Taylor St. East - East Claims Centre
4045 Taylor St. East
Saskatoon, SK S7H 5P2 Canada
Ernie Karolat, Manager
Swift Current - Claims Centre
110 - 3rd Ave. NS
Swift Current, SK S9H 0R8 Canada
Frank Urquhart, Manager
Tisdale - Claims Centre
819 - 100th St.
Tisdale, SK S0E 1T0 Canada
Dave Forster, Manager
Weyburn - Claims Centre
1738 - 1st Ave. NE
Weyburn, SK S4H 3E8 Canada
Ron Grobbink, Manager
Yorkton - Claims Centre
245 York Rd. East
Yorkton, SK S3N 3N7 Canada
Jeff Estabrooks, Manager

Société de l'assurance automobile du Québec

CP 19600, Terminus Stn. Terminus
333, boul Jean-Lesage
Québec, QC G1K 8J6
418-643-7620
800-361-7620
Other Information: Montréal: 514/873-7620
www.saaq.gouv.qc.ca
Ownership: Crown. Government of Québec.
Assets: $1-10 billion Year End: 20051231
Revenues: $500m-1 billion Year End: 20051231
Classes of Insurance: Accident, Auto
Incorporation: Provincially Incorporated Insurance Company
Executives:
Jean-François Brouard, Directeur général, Contrôle routier Québec
John Harbour, Président/Directeur général
Martin Breton, Vice-président, Affaires Institutionnelles
Claude Hallé, Vice-président, Services à la clientele
André Legault, Vice-président, Administration et finances
Johanne St-Cyr, Vice-présidente, Sécurité routière
Nathalie Tremblay, Vice-présidente, Opérations du Fonds d'Assurance Automobile

Sons of Scotland Benevolent Association

#202, 40 Eglinton Ave. East
Toronto, ON M4P 3A2
416-482-1250
Fax: 416-482-9576
800-387-3382
info@sonsofscotland.com
www.sonsofscotland.com
Year Founded: 1876
Number of Employees: 4
Assets: $10-50 million
Revenues: $1-5 million
Classes of Insurance: Life
Incorporation: Federally Incorporated Insurance Company
Profile: Each member is entitled to group insurance coverage.

Executives:
Robert Stewart, Sec.-Treas.
Directors:
Jim Bain
Robert Brown
May Cook
Keith Feir
Gordon Gardiner
Effie MacFie

South Easthope Mutual Insurance Co.

PO Box 33
62 Woodstock St.
Tavistock, ON N0B 2R0
519-655-2011
Fax: 519-655-2021
seins@seins.on.ca
www.seins.on.ca
Ownership: Policyholders
Year Founded: 1871
Number of Employees: 14
Classes of Insurance: Accident, Auto, Boiler & Machinery, Property
Incorporation: Provincially Incorporated Insurance Company
Executives:
Frank A. Rider, Secretary/Manager, Chief Privacy Officer & Consumer Complaints Officer
Steven M. Howell, Treasurer
Directors:
Lawrence G. Diamond, President
C. Jack Wettlaufer, 1st Vice-President
Wayne J. Tebbutt, 2nd Vice-President
Lloyd G. Debus
Gordon L. Gross
Donald S. Henry
Murray R. McGonigle
Murray H. Schlotzhauer
Douglas C. Wettlaufer

Southeastern Mutual Insurance Company

378 Coverdale Rd.
Riverview, NB E1B 3J7
506-386-9002
Fax: 506-386-3325
800-561-7223

ray.white@semutual.nb.ca
www.semutual.nb.ca
Former Name: Southeastern Mutual Fire Insurance Company
Ownership: Mutual Insurance Company.
Year Founded: 1938
Number of Employees: 7
Assets: $5-10 million Year End: 20041231
Revenues: $1-5 million Year End: 20041231
Classes of Insurance: Liability, Boiler & Machinery, Property, Fire
Incorporation: Provincially Incorporated Insurance Company
Executives:
D. Bruce Williams, Chair; 506-372-9147
Donald E. Howe, Vice-Chair; 506-387-8733
Ray W. White, FCIP, President; 506-384-5300
Directors:
Leslie Cail; 506-785-2345
Leon Gaudet; 506-758-9087
Winston Johnson; 506-576-6816
Jim Stark; 506-756-2296
George Trueman; 506-536-2769

SSQ Financial Group

***Also listed under:** Financial Planning; Investment Management*

PO Box 10500, Sainte-Foy Stn. Sainte-Foy
2525, boul Laurier
Québec, QC G1V 4H6
418-651-7000
Fax: 418-688-7791
888-900-3457
communications@ssq.ca, mutuallife@ssq.ca
www.ssq.ca
Former Name: SSQ Vie Investissement et Retraite (Astra)
Ownership: Private
Year Founded: 1944
Number of Employees: 1,000
Assets: $1-10 billion
Revenues: $10-50 million
Classes of Insurance: Personal Accident & Sickness, Auto, Life, Theft
Profile: IP

Executives:
Yves Demers, Chair
Richard Bell, CEO, SSQ, Life Insurance Company Inc.
Marie-Josée Blanchette, CEO, SSQ, General Insurance Company Inc.
Jean Morency, CEO, SSQ, Realty Inc.
Affiliated Companies:
SSQ, Société d'assurance-vie inc

SSQ, Société d'assurance-vie inc/ SSQ, Life Insurance Company Inc.

CP 10500
2525, boul Laurier
Québec, QC G1V 4H6
418-651-7000
Fax: 418-652-2739
www.ssq.ca
Ownership: Private. Part of SSQ Financial Group
Year Founded: 1946
Number of Employees: 1250
Assets: $1-10 billion Year End: 20041231
Classes of Insurance: Accident, Personal Accident & Sickness, Auto, Liability, Life, Property, Fire
Incorporation: Provincially Incorporated Insurance Company
Executives:
Richard Bell, FSA, FCIA, CEO
Serge Boiteau, Sr. Vice-President, Investments, Corporate Actuary
Johanne Goulet, Sr. Vice-President, Investments & Retirement
René Hamel, B.Sc.Act., ASA, Sr. Vice-President, Group Insurance
Denis Légaré, Sr. Vice-President, Human Resources
Gilles Mourette, Sr. Vice-President, Information Technology
Hélène Plante, Corporate Secretary
Affiliated Companies:
SSQ Financial Group Investment and Retirement
SSQ, Société d'assurances générales inc.

SSQ, Société d'assurances générales inc./ SSQ General Insurance Company Inc.

Édifice Le Delta 2
CP 10530
#500, 2875, boul Laurier
Québec, QC G1V 4H5
418-683-0554
Fax: 418-683-5603
800-463-2343
email@ssqgenerale.com
www.ssqgenerale.com
Ownership: Private
Year Founded: 1986
Number of Employees: 300
Assets: $100-500 million Year End: 20041231
Revenues: $50-100 million Year End: 20041231
Classes of Insurance: Accident, Auto, Liability, Property, Fire, Theft
Incorporation: Provincially Incorporated Insurance Company
Executives:
Marie-Josée Blanchette, Présidente/Directrice générale

The Standard Life Assurance Company of Canada

1245, rue Sherbrooke ouest
Montréal, QC H3G 1G3
514-499-8855
Fax: 514-499-4908
888-841-6633
information@standardlife.ca
www.standardlife.ca
Ownership: Public. Foreign.
Number of Employees: 2170
Assets: $10-100 billion Year End: 20051231
Revenues: $1-10 billion Year End: 20051231
Stock Symbol: SL
Classes of Insurance: Personal Accident & Sickness, Life
Incorporation: Federally Incorporated Insurance Company
Profile: The Standard Life Assurance Company of Canada & its affiliated companies in Canada have $40.5 billion in assets under management as of December 31, 2005. They offer a wide range of financial products & services to over 1.28 million individuals, including group insurance & pension plan members. Products & services include group savings & retirement, group insurance, individual life insurance, savings & retirement, mutual funds & portfolio management. Total premium income & deposits reached $5.2 billion in 2005.

Executives:
Joseph Iannicelli, President/CEO; 514-499-7999; Joseph.Iannecelli@standardlife.ca
Anthony Cardone, Sr. Vice-President, Group Savings & Retirement; 514-499-7999; Anthony.Cardone@standardlife.ca
Jean Guay, Sr. Vice-President, Group Insurance; 514-499-7999; Jean.Guay@standardlife.ca
Perla Kessous, Sr. Vice-President, Human Resources & Corporate Service; 514-499-7999; Perla.Kessous@standardlife.ca
Christian Martineau, Sr. Vice-President, Finance & Information Technology; 514-499-7999; Christian.Martineau@standardlife.ca
Penny J. Westman, Sr. Vice-President, Legal & Compliance; 514-499-7999; Penny.Westman@standardlife.ca
Vincenzo Ciampi, Vice-President, Strategy & Corporate Development; 514-499-7999; Vincenzo.Ciampi@standardlife.ca
Sylvie Des Roches, Vice-President, Compliance; 514-499-7999; Sylvie.Desroches@standardlife.ca
Michèle Parent, Vice-President, External Communications & Corporate Affairs; 514-499-7999; Michele.Parent@standardlife.ca
Directors:
Jocelyn Proteau, Chair
William A. Black
Sandy Crombie
Maurice Forget
Joseph Iannicelli
Christian Martineau
Jeffrey J. McCaig
Dale E. Richmond
Affiliated Companies:
Standard Life Investments Inc./SLI
Standard Life Trust Company
Group Life & Health Offices:
Calgary
Standard Life Bldg.
#1000, 639 - 5th Ave. SW
Calgary, AB T2P 0M9 Canada
403-531-1100
Fax: 403-531-1147
800-805-1631
westerncanada.groupinsurance@standardlife.ca
Edmonton
Standard Life Centre
#550, 10405 Jasper Ave.
Edmonton, AB T5J 3N4 Canada
780-944-0660
Fax: 780-425-8810
888-944-0600
westerncanada.groupinsurance@standardlife.ca
London
#1280, 255 Queens Ave.
London, ON N6A 5R8 Canada
519-672-6063
Fax: 519-672-3148
800-268-9714
ontariocanada.groupinsurance@standardlife.ca
Montréal
#880, 1001, boul de Maisonneuve ouest
Montréal, QC H3A 3C8 Canada
514-841-6642
Fax: 514-841-6672
800-363-4360
easterncanada.groupinsurance@standardlife.ca
Ottawa
#450, 1145 Hunt Club Rd.
Ottawa, ON K1V 0Y3 Canada
613-737-6860
Fax: 613-237-5365
800-263-3219
easterncanada.groupinsurance@standardlife.ca
Québec
#250, 1220, boul Lebourgneuf
Québec, QC G2K 2G4 Canada
418-684-2400
Fax: 418-681-7164
800-503-2358
easterncanada.groupinsurance@standardlife.ca
Toronto
#1158, 100 Sheppard Ave. East
Toronto, ON M2N 6N5 Canada
416-224-3200
Fax: 416-224-3433
800-465-2581
ontariocanada.groupinsurance@standardlife.ca
Vancouver
#900, 625 Howe St.
Vancouver, BC V6C 2T6 Canada
604-664-8030
Fax: 604-664-8033
800-663-1673
westerncanada.groupinsurance@standardlife.ca
Winnipeg
#1640, 155 Carlton St.
Winnipeg, MB R3C 3H8 Canada
204-949-4241
Fax: 204-956-2530
800-663-7372
westerncanada.groupinsurance@standardlife.ca
Group Savings & Retirement Offices:
Calgary
Standard Life Bldg.
#1130, 639 - 5th Ave. SW
Calgary, AB T2P 0M9 Canada
403-531-1100
Fax: 403-531-1149
888-434-5433
westerncanada.grouppension@standardlife.ca
Edmonton
Standard Life Centre
#559, 10405 Jasper Ave.
Edmonton, AB T5J 3N4 Canada
780-944-0660
Fax: 780-425-8810
888-944-0600
westerncanada.grouppension@standardlife.ca
Halifax
#1010, 1791 Barrington St.
Halifax, NS B3J 3L1 Canada
902-423-8888
Fax: 905-423-7083
maritimescanada.groupinsurance@standardlife.ca
London
#1280, 255 Queens Ave.
London, ON N6A 5R8 Canada

INSURANCE COMPANIES

The Standard Life Assurance Company of Canada (continued)
519-672-6063
Fax: 519-672-3148
800-268-9714
ontariocanada.grouppension@standardlife.ca
Montréal
#800, 1001, boul de Maisonneuve ouest
Montréal, QC H3A 3C8 Canada
514-841-6699
Fax: 514-841-6673
800-363-4360
easterncanada.grouppension@standardlife.ca
Ottawa
#450, 1145 Hunt Club Rd.
Ottawa, ON K1V 0Y3 Canada
613-737-6860
Fax: 613-237-5365
800-263-3219
easterncanada@grouppension@standardlife.ca
Québec
#250, 1220, boul Lebourneuf
418-684-2400
Fax: 418-681-7164
eastercanada.grouppension@standardlife.ca
Toronto
100 Sheppard Ave. East
Toronto, ON M2N 6N5 Canada
416-224-3535
Fax: 416-224-3434
800-827-5747
ontariocanada.grouppension@standardlife.ca
Vancouver
Standard Life Bldg.
#900, 625 Howe St.
Vancouver, BC V6C 2T6 Canada
604-664-8030
Fax: 604-664-8033
westerncanada.grouppension@standardlife.ca
Winnipeg
#1640, 155 Carlton St.
Winnipeg, MB R3C 3H8 Canada
204-949-4241
Fax: 204-956-2530
800-663-7372
westerncanada.grouppension@standardlife.ca
Individual Sales & Marketing Office:
Montréal
1245 rue Sherbrooke ouest
Montréal, QC H3G 1G3 Canada

Stanley Mutual Insurance Company
32 Irishtown Rd.
Stanley, NB E6B 1B6
506-367-2273
Fax: 506-367-3076
800-442-9714
info@StanleyMutual.com
www.stanleymutual.com
Year Founded: 1937
Classes of Insurance: Auto, Liability, Boiler & Machinery, Property
Incorporation: Provincially Incorporated Insurance Company
Profile: Insurance offered includes home, commercial, farm, automobile & trailer/camper insurance.

Executives:
James F. Pinnock, President; jpinnock@nbnet.nb.ca
Directors:
Arthur Wilson, Chair
J. William Smith, Vice-Chair

State Farm Fire & Casualty Company
333 First Commerce Dr.
Aurora, ON L4G 8A4
905-750-4204
Fax: 905-750-4719
www.statefarm.ca
Ownership: Foreign. Part of State Farm Group, USA.
Year Founded: 1935
Classes of Insurance: Aircraft, Auto, Liability, Boiler & Machinery, Fidelity, Property, Fire, Surety
Incorporation: Federally Incorporated Insurance Company
Executives:
Robert J. Cooke, Chief Agent

State Farm Life Insurance Company
333 First Commerce Dr.
Aurora, ON L4G 8A4
905-750-4204
Fax: 905-750-4719
info@statefarm.com
www.statefarm.ca
Ownership: Foreign. Part of State Farm Group, USA
Year Founded: 1929
Classes of Insurance: Life
Incorporation: Federally Incorporated Insurance Company
Executives:
Robert J. Cooke, Chief Agent

State Farm Mutual Automobile Insurance Company
333 First Commerce Dr.
Aurora, ON L4G 8A4
905-750-4204
Fax: 905-750-4719
info@statefarm.com
www.statefarm.ca
Ownership: Foreign. Part of State Farm Group, USA.
Year Founded: 1922
Classes of Insurance: Personal Accident & Sickness, Auto
Incorporation: Federally Incorporated Insurance Company
Executives:
Robert J. Cooke, Chief Agent

Stewart Title Guaranty Company
North Tower, Royal Bank Plaza
#2200, 200 Bay St.
Toronto, ON M5J 2J2
416-307-3300
Fax: 416-307-3305
888-667-5151
inquirycda@stewart.com
www.stewart.ca
Ownership: Stewart Information Services Corporation, USA.
Year Founded: 1893
Incorporation: Federally Incorporated Insurance Company
Profile: The company protects property owners & lenders against the title risks in residential & commercial real estate transactions.

Executives:
Steven M. Lessack, President, Canadian Division
Reta E. Coburn, Vice-President, Canadian Division, Operations Manager
Wayne C. Lipton, Vice-President, Sr. Counsel
Marco Polsinelli, Vice-President, Claims
David Tye, Vice-President, Finance
Branches:
Barrie - Northern Ontario Region
158 Dunlop St. East
Barrie, ON L4M 1B1 Canada
705-792-0725
Fax: 705-722-7785
888-292-1588
Homer Frank, Counsel
Calgary - Western Canada Region
#2340, 700 Second St. SW
Calgary, AB T2P 2W2 Canada
403-538-5125
Fax: 403-538-5126
866-515-8401
Tony McGrath, Director, Western Canada Operations
Halifax - Atlantic Region
Duke Tower
#1201, 5251 Duke St.
Halifax, NS B3J 1P3 Canada
902-420-0802
Fax: 902-420-0804
888-757-0078
Denise Avery, Office Coordinator, Atlantic Region
Laval - Québec Region
#304, 3090, boul Le Carréfour
Laval, QC H7T 2K9 Canada
450-973-4446
Fax: 450-973-4447
866-235-9152
June Levesque, Vice President & Director, Québec Operations
London - Western Ontario Region
380 Wellington St.
London, ON N6A 5B5 Canada
519-453-9221
Fax: 519-679-8432
866-818-1194
Kevin Rogers, Counsel
Ottawa - Eastern Ontario Region
#900, 275 Slater St.
Ottawa, ON K1P 5H9 Canada
613-236-8318
Fax: 613-236-7807
888-795-1577
David Leith, Counsel
Vancouver - Pacific Region
The Marine Bldg.
#1000, 355 Burrard St.
Vancouver, BC V6C 2G8 Canada
604-678-9363
Fax: 604-608-6163
800-280-1659
William D. Todd, Officer, Business Development

Suecia Reinsurance Company
763 Pape Ave.
Toronto, ON M4K 3T2
416-361-0056
Former Name: Trygg-Hansa Reinsurance Company of Canada
Ownership: Private. Suecia Holding Corporation
Year Founded: 1977
Number of Employees: 1
Classes of Insurance: Personal Accident & Sickness, Auto, Liability, Fidelity, Property, Hail & Crop, Reinsurance
Incorporation: Federally Incorporated Insurance Company

Sun Life Assurance Company of Canada
Corporate Office
150 King St. West
Toronto, ON M5H 1J9
416-979-9966
Fax: 416-979-4853
corp_website@sunlife.com
www.sunlife.ca
Ownership: Public. Wholly owned subsidiary of Sun Life Financial Inc.
Year Founded: 1871
Stock Symbol: SLF
Classes of Insurance: Personal Accident & Sickness, Life
Incorporation: Federally Incorporated Insurance Company
Executives:
Donald A. Stewart, CEO
Ronald W. Osborne, FCA, Chairman
Branches:
Montréal
1155, rue Metcalfe
Montréal, QC H3B 2V9 Canada
514-866-6411
800-786-5433
Ottawa
99 Bank St.
Ottawa, ON K19 5A3 Canada
613-560-7888
Toronto
225 King St. West
Toronto, ON M5V 3C5 Canada
800-786-5433
Waterloo
PO Box 1601, Waterloo Sta. Waterloo
227 King St. South
Waterloo, ON N2J 4C5 Canada
519-888-2290

Sun Life Financial Inc.
Also listed under: *Financial Planning*
150 King St. West
Toronto, ON M5H 1J9
416-979-9966
Fax: 416-979-4853
www.sunlife.com
Ownership: Public
Year Founded: 1865
Number of Employees: 16,500
Assets: $100 billion + Year End: 20051231
Revenues: $10-100 billion Year End: 20051231
Stock Symbol: SLF
Classes of Insurance: Life
Incorporation: Federally Incorporated Insurance Company
Profile: IF
Executives:
Donald A. Stewart, CEO
Kevin P. Dougherty, President, Sun Life Financial Canada
Stephan Rajotte, President, Sun Life Financial Asia
Robert C. Salipante, President, Sun Life Financial US

David W. Davies, Chair, Sun Life Financial UK
James M.A. Anderson, Exec. Vice-President, Chief Investment Officer
Thomas A. Bogart, Exec. Vice-President/Chief Legal Officer
Dean A. Connor, Exec. Vice-President
Robert W. Mansbridge, Exec. Vice-President, CIO
Richard P. McKenney, Exec. Vice-President/CFO
Michael P. Stramaglia, Exec. Vice-President, Chief Asset & Liability Management Officer
Directors:
Ronald W. Osborne, FCA, Chair
James C. Baillie
George W. Carmany, III
John H. Clappison, FCA
William R. Fatt
David A. Ganong, CM
Germaine Gibara, CFA
Krystyna T. Hoeg, CA
David W. Kerr, CA
Idalene F. Kesner
Bertin F. Nadeau
Donald A. Stewart, FIA, FCIA
W. Vickery Stoughton
Affiliated Companies:
McLean Budden Ltd.
Sun Life Assurance Company of Canada
Sun Life Financial Trust Inc.
Waterloo
227 King St. South
Waterloo, ON N2J 4C5 Canada
519-888-3900

Supreme Council of the Royal Arcanum
PO Box 990
#400, 21 King St. West
Hamilton, ON L8N 3R1
905-528-8411
888-272-2686
www.royalarcanum.com
Ownership: Foreign. Supreme Council of Royal Arcanum, Boston, MA, USA.
Number of Employees: 1
Classes of Insurance: Personal Accident & Sickness, Life
Incorporation: Federally Incorporated Insurance Company
Executives:
J.Benjamin Simpson, QC, Chief Agent

Swiss Re Frankona Rückversicherungs-Aktiengesellschaft
#1000, 150 King St. West
Toronto, ON M5H 1J9
416-814-2272
Fax: 416-364-7308
Former Name: ERC Frankona Rückversicherungs-AG
Ownership: Foreign.
Classes of Insurance: Personal Accident & Sickness, Life
Incorporation: Federally Incorporated Insurance Company

Swiss Reinsurance Company Canada
PO Box 50
#2200, 150 King St. West
Toronto, ON M5H 1J9
416-408-0272
Fax: 416-408-4222
800-268-7116
www.swissre.com
Also Known As: Swiss Re
Ownership: Swiss Re, Switzerland
Year Founded: 1953
Number of Employees: 75+
Classes of Insurance: Marine, Fidelity, Property, Surety, Reinsurance
Incorporation: Federally Incorporated Insurance Company
Executives:
Brian Gray, President/CEO
Susan Armstrong, Sr. Vice-President
William Lacourt, Sr. Vice-President
Gerard Martins, Sr. Vice-President
Sean Russell, Sr. Vice-President
Branches:
Montréal
#930, 1010, rue Sherbrooke ouest
Montréal, QC H3A 2R7 Canada
514-288-3134
Fax: 514-288-8588

TD General Insurance Company
c/o Meloche Monnex Inc.
50, Place Crémazie, 12e étage
Montréal, QC H2P 1B6
www.tdcanadatrust.com/tdinsurance
Former Name: CT Direct Insurance Inc.
Ownership: Member of TD Bank Financial Group.
Classes of Insurance: Personal Accident & Sickness, Aircraft, Auto, Liability, Boiler & Machinery, Fidelity, Property, Surety
Incorporation: Federally Incorporated Insurance Company
Executives:
Alain Thibault, President/CEO
Branches:
Toronto
c/o Meloche Monnex Financial Services Inc.
2161 Yonge St., 4th Fl.
Toronto, ON M4S 3A6
416-484-1112
Fax: 416-545-6130

TD Home & Auto Insurance Company/ Compagnie d'Assurance Habitation et Auto TD
2161 Yonge St., 4th Fl.
Toronto, ON M4S 3A6
800-338-0218
Other Information: 866-955-5558 (Toll Free, Quotes); 866-322-5854 (Toll Free, Client Services); 866-482-1919 (Toll Free, Claims)
www.tdcanadatrust.com/tdinsurance, www.mytdigroup.com
Ownership: Member of TD Bank Financial Group, Toronto, ON.

Classes of Insurance: Auto, Liability, Property
Incorporation: Federally Incorporated Insurance Company
Profile: Property insurance is offered to those with a house, a condominium, or a rental unit. The automobile insurance program is not available in British Columbia, Saskatchewan, & Manitoba, because of provincial legislation. Automobile insurance is underwritten by TD General Insurance Company in Ontario. In all other provinces & territories, automobile insurance is underwritten by Primmum Insurance Company and TD Home and Auto Insurance Company.

Executives:
Alain Thibault, President/CEO
Richard M. Evans, Vice-President
Branches:
Toronto
3650 Victoria Park Ave., 9th Fl.
Toronto, ON M2H 3M6 Canada
416-774-3794

TD Life Insurance Company/ TD, Compagnie d'assurance-vie
120 Adelaide St. West, 2nd Fl.
Toronto, ON M5H 1T1
416-982-3006
Fax: 416-944-5859
877-397-4187
TD.InsuranceLifeAndHealth@td.com
www.tdcanadatrust.com/tdinsurance/life
Former Name: Toronto Dominion General Insurance Company; Toronto Dominion Life Insurance Company
Also Known As: TD Life
Ownership: Affiliate of TD Bank Financial Group.
Classes of Insurance: Personal Accident & Sickness, Life
Incorporation: Federally Incorporated Insurance Company
Executives:
Sean E. Kilburn, President/CEO & Vice-Chair

The Toa Reinsurance Company of America
PO Box 17
#2420, 401 Bay St.
Toronto, ON M5H 2Y4
416-366-5888
Fax: 416-366-7444
info@toare.com
www.toare.com
Also Known As: Toa Re America
Ownership: Foreign. Wholly owned subsidiary of Toa Tokyo; Toronto office is branch of The Toa Reinsurance Company of America, Morristown, NJ.
Year Founded: 1982
Classes of Insurance: Reinsurance
Incorporation: Federally Incorporated Insurance Company
Profile: Toa Re provides treaty, program & facultative products largely through reinsurance intermediaries.

Executives:
David Wilmot, Sr. Vice-President & Chief Agent, Canada; dwilmot@toare.com
Caroline Kane, Vice-President, Marketing/Underwriting
Peter K. Harding, Manager, Underwriting

The Tokio Marine & Nichido Fire Insurance Co., Ltd.
c/o Lombard Canada Ltd.
105 Adelaide St. West
Toronto, ON M5H 1P9
416-350-4400
Fax: 416-350-4412
Ownership: The Tokio Marine & Fire Insurance Co., Ltd., Japan

Year Founded: 1944
Classes of Insurance: Auto, Marine, Property, Fire
Incorporation: Federally Incorporated Insurance Company
Profile: Lombard Canada Ltd. provides insurance management services for the Tokio Marine & Fire Insurance Company Ltd.

Town & Country Mutual Insurance Company
79 Caradoc St. North
Strathroy, ON N7G 2M5
519-246-1132
Fax: 519-246-1115
888-868-5064
info@town-country-ins.ca
www.town-country-ins.ca
Former Name: East Williams Mutual Fire Insurance Co.
Ownership: Policyholders
Year Founded: 1875
Classes of Insurance: Personal Accident & Sickness, Auto, Liability, Boiler & Machinery, Fidelity, Property, Hail & Crop
Incorporation: Provincially Incorporated Insurance Company
Profile: Services are offered for home, farms, home-based businesses, retail stores, churches, offices, contractors, apartment buildings & automobiles. Financial products are offered through the company's subsidiary, Midd-West Financial.

Executives:
Robert G. Pearson, General Manager

Townsend Farmers' Mutual Fire Insurance Company
Waterford Place Plaza
PO Box 1030
Waterford, ON N0E 1Y0
519-443-7231
Fax: 519-443-5198
888-302-6052
www.townsendfarmers.com
Also Known As: Townsend Mutual
Ownership: Member owned.
Year Founded: 1879
Classes of Insurance: Personal Accident & Sickness, Auto, Liability, Boiler & Machinery, Property, Hail & Crop
Incorporation: Provincially Incorporated Insurance Company
Profile: Services provided include farm, commercial, home & automobile insurance. Other financial services are offered through its affiliated company, Farm Mutual Financial Services' Inc.

Executives:
Mike Kekes, Agent; mkekes@townsendfarmers.com
Kevin Reimer, Agent; kreimer@townsendfarmers.com
Bryan (Fred) Thompson, Agent; bthompson@townsendfarmers.com
Larry Wilson, Agent; lwilson@townsendfarmers.com

Traders General Insurance Company/ Compagnie d'Assurance Traders Générale
c/o Aviva Canada Inc.
2206 Eglinton Ave. East
Toronto, ON M1L 4S8
416-288-1800
800-387-4518
info@avivacanada.com
www.avivacanada.com
Ownership: Parent is Aviva Canada Inc.
Classes of Insurance: Auto, Property
Incorporation: Federally Incorporated Insurance Company
Executives:
Igal Mayer, President/CEO, Aviva Canada Inc.
Cindy Jeffrey, Manager, Atlantic Region
Chris Lockhart, Manager, Western Region
Jean Roy, Manager, Québec Region
Victor Wiwchau, Manager, Ontario Region

Tradition Mutual Insurance Company
PO Box 10
264 Huron Rd.
Sebringville, ON N0K 1X0
519-393-6402
Fax: 519-393-5185
800-263-1961
www.traditionmutual.com
Former Name: Downie Mutual Insurance Company; Blanshard Mutual Insurance Company
Ownership: Policyholders.
Number of Employees: 14
Classes of Insurance: Accident, Auto, Liability, Boiler & Machinery, Fidelity, Property, Hail & Crop
Incorporation: Provincially Incorporated Insurance Company
Profile: The property & casualty insurance company operates in Perth County and the surrounding area. The following types of insurance are provided: automobile, home, farm, tenant, & commercial.

Executives:
B. Alec Harmer, Manager; alec@traditionmutual.com
Directors:
Doug Ahrens
Larry Barker
Doug Brown
Don Brubacher
Glen Coulthard
John Hudson
Jim McCutcheon
Joan Schmidt
Jim Watt

Trans Global Insurance Company(TGI)
c/o Fraser Milner Cosgrain LLP, First Canadian Place
100 King St. West, 42nd Fl.
Toronto, ON T5X 1B2
416-862-3418
Fax: 416-863-4592
Ownership: Subsidiary of Trans Global Warranty Corp.
Classes of Insurance: Personal Accident & Sickness, Liability, Property
Incorporation: Provincially Incorporated Insurance Company
Profile: Another class of insurance is loss of employment.

Executives:
John P. Rhude, Chief Agent
Branches:
Edmonton
#275, 16930 - 114 Ave.
Edmonton, AB T5M 3S2
888-226-7876
Vancouver
c/o Godman Phillips & Vineburg, Barristers & Solicitors
#1900, 355 Burrard St.
Vancouver, BC V6C 2G8

Trans Global Life Insurance Company(TGLI)
c/o Fraser Milner Cosgrain LLP, First Canadian Place
100 King St. West, 42nd Fl.
Toronto, ON M5X 1B2
416-862-3418
Fax: 416-863-4592
Ownership: Subsidiary of Trans Global Warranty Corp.
Classes of Insurance: Personal Accident & Sickness, Life
Incorporation: Provincially Incorporated Insurance Company
Executives:
John P. Rhude, Chief Agent
Branches:
Edmonton
#275, 16930 - 114 Ave.
Edmonton, AB T5M 3S2
888-226-7876
Vancouver
c/o Godman Phillips & Vineburg, Barristers & Solicitors
#1900, 355 Burrard St.
Vancouver, BC V6C 2G8

Transamerica Life Canada
5000 Yonge St.
Toronto, ON M2N 7J8
416-883-5000
Fax: 416-883-5012
webmaster.canada@aegoncanada.ca
www.transamerica.ca
Ownership: Wholly owned subsidiary of Aegon N.V., The Netherlands.
Year Founded: 1927
Number of Employees: 688
Classes of Insurance: Personal Accident & Sickness, Life
Incorporation: Federally Incorporated Insurance Company

Executives:
Paul Reaburn, President/CEO
James Falle, Exec. Vice-President/CFO
Scott D. Sinclair, Sr. Vice-President

Transatlantic Reinsurance Company
145 Wellington St. West
Toronto, ON M5J 1H8
416-596-3960
Fax: 416-971-8782
www.transre.com
Ownership: Subsidiary of Transatlantic Holdings Inc., USA
Year Founded: 1980
Classes of Insurance: Personal Accident & Sickness, Credit, Property, Surety, Reinsurance
Incorporation: Federally Incorporated Insurance Company
Profile: The federally registered company offers reinsurance products on both a treaty & facultative basis.

Executives:
Cameron MacDonald, Vice-President, Branch Manager
Rob Barclay, Regional Asst. Vice-President, Manager, Facultative Property
Lyn Croydon, Regional Asst. Vice-President, Manager, Facultative Casualty
Graz Perizzolo, Regional Asst. Vice-President, Treaty Operations
Christine Cheung, Manager, Accounting

Trillium Mutual Insurance Company
10 John St.
Formosa, ON N0G 2W0
519-367-5600
Fax: 519-367-5681
admin@trilliummutual.com
www.trilliummutual.com
Former Name: Formosa Mutual; Elma Mutual
Ownership: Policyholders.
Classes of Insurance: Accident, Auto, Liability, Boiler & Machinery, Marine, Fidelity, Property, Hail & Crop
Incorporation: Provincially Incorporated Insurance Company
Profile: Farm, residential, commercial, automobile & pleasure craft insurance is offered.

Executives:
Joesph Dietrich, CEO, General Manager; jdietrich@trilliummutual.com
Kevin Inglis, Manager, Claims; kinglis@trilliummutual.com
Ron Lipsett, Manager, Marketing & Broker Relations; rlipsett@trilliummutual.com
Ron Wilson, Manager, Finance; rwilson@trilliummutual.com
Bruce Wallis, Assistant General Manager; bwallis@trilliummutual.com
Directors:
John Clancey, President
Frank Coulter
Stan Eby
Karen Galbraith
Gordon Jack
Len Metcalfe
Allan Royce
Murray Scholl
Ross Stone
Branches:
Atwood
130 John St.
Atwood, ON N0G 1B0 Canada
519-356-2582
Fax: 519-356-2654
admin@trilliummutual.com

Ukrainian Fraternal Association of America(UFA)
c/o Burns Hubley
#406, 2800 - 14 Ave.
Markham, ON L3R 0E4
416-495-1755
Fax: 416-495-1838
Ownership: Foreign. Part of Ukrainian Fraternal Association, Scranton, PA, USA.
Classes of Insurance: Life
Incorporation: Federally Incorporated Insurance Company
Executives:
Robert F. Burns, Chief Agent

Ukrainian Fraternal Society of Canada
235 McGregor St.
Winnipeg, MB R2W 4W5
204-586-4482
Fax: 204-589-6411
800-988-8372
Ownership: Private
Year Founded: 1921
Number of Employees: 1
Assets: $5-10 million Year End: 20051011
Revenues: Under $1 million Year End: 20051011
Classes of Insurance: Life
Incorporation: Federally Incorporated Insurance Company
Executives:
Boris Salamon, President
Michael Lasko, Vice-President

Ukrainian Mutual Benefit Association of Saint Nicholas of Canada
804 Selkirk Ave.
Winnipeg, MB R2W 2N6
204-582-4882
Fax: 204-586-2095
866-582-4882
umbaofsn@mts.net
www.ukrainianmutual.com
Also Known As: St. Nicholas Mutual
Year Founded: 1905
Classes of Insurance: Personal Accident & Sickness, Life
Incorporation: Federally Incorporated Insurance Company
Profile: The Canadian fraternal benefit society offers benefits to people of Ukrainian descent & their extended families who reside in Canada.

Executives:
John Petryshyn, President
Jean Motkaluk, Treasurer
Branches:
Markham
4986 - 19th Ave.
Markham, ON L6C 1M2
905-887-1712
Fax: 905-887-4964
John Rybuck, Chief Agent

Ukrainian National Association(UNA)
c/o Burns Hubley LLP
#406, 2800 - 14 Ave.
Markham, ON L3R 0E4
416-495-1755
Fax: 416-495-1838
www.unamember.com
Ownership: Foreign. Part of Ukrainian National Association, Inc., Parsippany, NJ.
Year Founded: 1894
Classes of Insurance: Personal Accident & Sickness, Life
Incorporation: Federally Incorporated Insurance Company
Profile: The foreign fraternal benefit society offers insurance services & mortgages.

Executives:
Robert F. Burns, Chief Agent

Union of Canada Life Insurance
PO Box 717, A Stn. A
325 Dalhousie St.
Ottawa, ON K1P 5P8
613-241-3660
Fax: 613-241-7880
877-966-6676
union@on.aira.com
www.ucav.ca
Year Founded: 1863
Number of Employees: 85
Assets: $100-500 million Year End: 20051231
Revenues: $10-50 million Year End: 20051231
Classes of Insurance: Accident, Life
Incorporation: Provincially Incorporated Insurance Company
Profile: Union of Canada Life Insurance is a provincially incorporated mutual insurance company. An affiliated organization is Union of Canada, Employees' Pension Fund Society.
Executives:
Gerard Desjardins, President/CEO
Jean Cloutier, COO & Vice-President, Finance

Marc A. Parent, Secretary & Vice-President, Legal
Marcel Campeau, Director, Sales Operations
B. Yassine, Director, Sales Development
Directors:
René Bergeron
Raymond Burke
Gerard Desjardins
Jean-Pierre Desjardins
Jean-Pierre Gascon
Claude Racette
Branches:
Chicoutimi
#250, 345, rue des Saguenéens
Chicoutimi, QC G7H 6K9 Canada
418-696-4909
Fax: 418-696-1484
udc.chicoutimi@ucav.ca
Jean Beaulieu, Directeur, ventes
Joliette
457, rue de Lanaudière
Joliette, QC J6E 3M3 Canada
450-752-4000
Fax: 450-752-4002
udc.joliette@ucav.ca
Montréal
6830, rue Jarry est
Montréal, QC H1P 1W3 Canada
514-321-3143
Fax: 450-321-2930
udc.montreal@ucav.ca
Ottawa
Union of Canada Bldg.
325 Dalhousie St.
Ottawa, ON K1N 7G2 Canada
613-241-3660
Fax: 613-241-7880
Marcel Campeau, Director, Sales
Québec
Immeuble Commercial
#200, 4715, av des Replats
Québec, QC G2J 1B8 Canada
418-628-0678
Fax: 416-628-0881
udc.quebec@ucav.ca
Yvan Mainguy, Branch Manager
Rimouski
166, rue St-Germain ouest
Rimouski, QC G5L 4B7 Canada
418-724-4787
Fax: 418-724-8068
udc.rimouski@ucav.ca
Pierre Tremblay, Directeur, ventes
Sherbrooke
151, boul Jacques-Cartier sud
Sherbrooke, QC J1J 2Z4 Canada
819-566-5226
Fax: 819-566-5919
Louis-Denis Coté, Directeur, ventes

United American Insurance Company(UA)
c/o McLean & Kerr LLP
#2800, 130 Adelaide St. West
Toronto, ON M5H 3P5
416-369-6624
Fax: 416-366-8571
www.unitedamerican.com
Ownership: Private. Part of United American Insurance Company, Texas, USA.
Year Founded: 1947
Classes of Insurance: Personal Accident & Sickness, Life
Incorporation: Federally Incorporated Insurance Company
Executives:
Robin B. Cumine, Chief Agent

United General Insurance Corporation
860 Prospect St.
Fredericton, NB E3B 2T8
506-459-5120
don.dougherty@ugic.nb.ca
Ownership: Private
Year Founded: 1993
Classes of Insurance: Auto
Incorporation: Provincially Incorporated Insurance Company
Executives:
Rick Embleton, Manager; rick.embleton@ugic.nb.ca

Unity Life of Canada
#400, 100 Milverton Dr.
Mississauga, ON L5RL4W 5S8
905-219-8000
Fax: 905-219-8121
800-267-8777
info@unitylife.ca
www.unitylife.ca
Former Name: Toronto Mutual Life Insurance Company; The Western Life Assurance Company
Ownership: Private
Year Founded: 1898
Classes of Insurance: Personal Accident & Sickness, Life
Incorporation: Federally Incorporated Insurance Company
Executives:
Anthony W. Poole, President
Hendrik Verdurmen, Vice-President & CEO
Mervyn P. Gillson, Vice-President & Chief Underwriter
Carol Moellers, FSA,FCIA, Assistant Vice-President & Pricing Actuary
Branches:
Toronto
#910, 191 The West Mall
Toronto, ON M9C 5K8 Canada
905-219-8000
Fax: 905-219-8121
800-267-8777

Usborne & Hibbert Mutual Fire Insurance Co.
507 Main St. South
Exeter, ON N0M 1S1
519-235-0350
Fax: 519-235-3623
usborne@on.aibn.com
Year Founded: 1876
Incorporation: Provincially Incorporated Insurance Company
Executives:
Sharon Doxtator, Secretary-Manager

Virginia Surety Company, Inc.(VCS)/ Compagnie de Sûreté Virginia Inc.
#201, 3650 Victoria Park Ave.
Toronto, ON M2H 3P7
www.thewarrantygroup.com
Ownership: Foreign. The Warranty Group, Chicago, IL, USA.
Year Founded: 1927
Classes of Insurance: Auto, Liability, Boiler & Machinery, Property
Incorporation: Federally Incorporated Insurance Company
Executives:
V. Lorraine Williams, Chief Agent

Wabisa Mutual Insurance Company
PO Box 621
35 Talbot St. East
Jarvis, ON N0A 1J0
519-587-4454
Fax: 519-587-5470
www.wabisa.omia.com
Year Founded: 1867
Classes of Insurance: Personal Accident & Sickness, Auto, Liability, Fidelity, Property
Incorporation: Provincially Incorporated Insurance Company
Profile: Automobile, home, farm & commercial insurance are available.

Executives:
Pat Payne, Secretary-Manager

Waterloo Insurance Company
590 Riverbend Dr.
Kitchener, ON N2K 3S2
519-570-8322
Fax: 519-570-8693
www.economicalinsurance.com
Ownership: Private. Subsidiary of Economical Mutual Insurance Company
Year Founded: 1995
Number of Employees: 28
Classes of Insurance: Auto, Property
Incorporation: Federally Incorporated Insurance Company
Executives:
Noel G. Walpole, FIIC, President/CEO
Sandy Uppal, B.A. (Hon.), CA, MBA, CFO
Jorge Arruda, B.Comm., Vice-President, Claims
Dean Bulloch, Vice-President, Human Resources
David Fitzpatrick, CHRP, Vice-President, Field Operations
Linda Goss, FCIA, FCAS, FSA, Vice-President, Actuarial Services
Bill Lowe, BA, CIP, Vice-President, Commercial Insurance
John Martin, B.Sc., Vice-President, Business Solutions
Michael O'Neill, CFA, Vice-President, Investments
Tom Reikman, H.B.Sc., MBA, AIIC, Vice-President, Personal Insurance
Bill Stinson, B.Math., FLMI, Vice-President, Information Services

Wendy DaSilva, Manager, Group Operations; 519-570-8539
Cindy Graham, Manager, Marketing Communications; 519-570-8627; cindy.graham@economicalinsurance.cm
Directors:
P.H. Sims, Chair
M.N. Bales
A.S. Carson
Charles M.W. Ormston
J.A. Rogers
Brian J. Ruby
Harold E. Seegmiller
Noel G. Walpole, FIIC

The Wawanesa Life Insurance Company
#200, 191 Broadway
Winnipeg, MB R3C 3P1
204-985-3940
Fax: 204-985-3872
800-263-6785
life@wawanesa.com
www.wawanesalife.com
Ownership: Subsidiary of the Wawanesa Mutual Insurance Company
Year Founded: 1896
Number of Employees: 100
Assets: $100-500 million
Revenues: $50-100 million
Classes of Insurance: Personal Accident & Sickness, Life
Incorporation: Federally Incorporated Insurance Company
Executives:
Gregg Hanson, FCA, FCIP, FLMI, President/CEO
Mary K. Nemeth, CA, FLMI, Vice President/COO
George Bass, Vice-President, General Counsel & Secretary
Ian R. Macdonald, Vice-President & Actuary
Directors:
Barry W. Harrison, Chair
R.R. Bracken
D.C.W. Crewson
G.J. Hanson
D.M. Jessiman
John S. McCallum
M.E. Northey
A.B. Ransom
D.G. Unruh
S.M. Van De Velde
Branches:
Brandon - Western Manitoba Region
#411, 1011 Rosser Ave.
Brandon, MB R7A 0L5 Canada
Fax: 204-571-3125
877-660-6662
Calgary
#600, 708 - 11 Ave. SW
Calgary, AB T2R 0E4 Canada
403-260-9286
Fax: 403-262-1588
Edmonton
#100, 8657 - 51st Ave.
Edmonton, AB T6E 6A8 Canada
Fax: 780-469-5515
800-625-7891
Moncton - Atlantic Region
1010 St. George Blvd.
Moncton, NB E1C 8M9 Canada
Fax: 506-862-7070
877-862-7073
Regina
#205, 2631 - 28th Ave.
Regina, SK S4S 6X3 Canada
Fax: 306-585-0022
866-751-8363
Toronto - Ontario Region
#100, 4110 Yonge St.
Toronto, ON M2P 2B7 Canada
416-228-7855
Fax: 416-888-7931

The Wawanesa Life Insurance Company (continued)
Vancouver - British Columbia Region
#310, 1985 West Broadway
Vancouver, BC V6J 4Y3 Canada
604-629-8205
Fax: 604-739-5413
800-665-2778
Winnipeg
#701, 200 Main St.
Winnipeg, MB R3C 1A8 Canada
204-985-3905
Fax: 204-985-5781
800-665-7076

The Wawanesa Mutual Insurance Company

191 Broadway
Winnipeg, MB R3C 3P1
204-985-3811
Fax: 204-942-7724
www.wawanesa.com
Ownership: 1.6m policyholders
Year Founded: 1896
Number of Employees: 2,000
Assets: $1-10 billion Year End: 20041030
Revenues: $1-10 billion Year End: 20041030
Classes of Insurance: Auto, Liability, Boiler & Machinery, Property, Fire, Surety, Theft
Incorporation: Federally Incorporated Insurance Company
Profile: The mutual insurer is represented across Canada by approximately 1,300 brokers.

Executives:
G.J. Hanson, FCA, FCIP, FLMI, President/CEO
K.E. McCrea, CA, FLMI, Vice-President/CFO
David J. McFarlane, Vice-President/COO
G.N. Bass, Q.C., Vice-President, General Counsel & Secretary
M.J. Bjornson, FCIP, FLMI, Vice-President, Marketing & Property Underwriting
P.R. Goodman, CA, Vice-President & Comptroller
S.J. Goy, ACAS, Vice-President, Corporate Automobile Underwriting
R.G. LaPage, FCIP, Vice-President, Claims
C.B. Luby, FCIP, CRM, Vice-President, Branch Operations
B.A. MacKinnon, FCAS, FCIA, MAAA, Vice-President & Chief Actuary
Tracy Nelson, FLMI, CHRP, Vice-President, Human Resources
Paul A. Thorimbert, FLMI, Vice-President, Information Systems
P.R. Mulaire, B.Comm, CMA, FCIP, CIA, Manager, Internal Audit
Directors:
Barry W. Harrison, Chair
Richard R. Bracken
D.C.W. Crewson
G.J. Hanson, FCA, FCIP, FLMI
D.M. Jessiman
John S. McCallum
M.E. Northey
A.B. Ransom
D.G. Unruh
S.M. Van De Velde
Affiliated Companies:
The Wawanesa Life Insurance Company
Branches:
Calgary - Southern Alberta
#600, 708 - 11 Ave. SW
Calgary, AB T2R 0E4 Canada
J.A. Breau, Vice-President, Southern Alberta Region
Edmonton - Northern Alberta
#100, 8657 - 51st Ave.
Edmonton, AB T6E 6A8 Canada
N.D. Miller, Vice-President, Northern Alberta Region
Moncton - Atlantic
1010 St. George Blvd.
Moncton, NB E1E 4R5 Canada
S.M. Gates, Vice-President, Maritime Region
Montréal - Québec
8585, boul Décarie
Montréal, QC H4P 2J4 Canada
C. Auclair, Vice-President, Québec Region
Toronto - Ontario
#100, 4110 Yonge St
Toronto, ON M2P 2B7 Canada
T.R. Greer, Vice-President, Ontario Region
Vancouver - British Columbia
#400, 1985 West Broadway
Vancouver, BC V6J 4Y3 Canada
K.L. Coates, Vice-President, British Columbia Region
Wawanesa - Prairies
Wawanesa, MB R0K 2G0 Canada
W.G. McGregor, Vice-President, Prairie Region
Winnipeg
191 Broadway
Winnipeg, MB R3C 3P1 Canada
E. Rossong, Vice-President

Wedgwood Insurance Ltd.

PO Box 13370, A Stn. A
85 Thorburn Rd.
St. John's, NL A1B 4B7
709-753-3210
Fax: 709-753-8238
800-706-2676
www.wedgwoodinsurance.com
Ownership: Private
Year Founded: 1978
Classes of Insurance: Aircraft, Auto, Life, Marine, Property
Incorporation: Provincially Incorporated Insurance Company
Profile: The insurance company provides services to individuals & corporations.

Executives:
Geoff Wedgwood, President/CEO; gwedgwood@wedgwood.nf.net
Tom Hickey, Exec. Vice-President, Administration; thickey@wedgwood.nf.net
Wayne Clarke, Vice-President, Commercial Lines; wclarke@wedgwood.nf.net
Darlene Haley, Vice-President, Personal Lines; dhaley@wedgwood.nf.net
Steve Wedgwood, Director, Business Development; swedgwood@wedgwood.nf.net
Chris Skinner, Comptroller; cskinner@wedgwood.nf.net
John Penney, Manager, Sales, Commercial Lines; jpenney@wedgwood.nf.net
Branches:
Clarenville
76 Manitoba Dr., #B
Clarenville, NL A5A 1K6 Canada
709-466-6000
Fax: 709-466-1679
Cheryl Stringer, Account Manager, Personal Lines
Corner Brook
55 Park St.
Corner Brook, NL A2H 2X1 Canada
709-634-1555
Fax: 709-634-4146
Gloria Russell, Account Executive, Personal Lines

West Elgin Mutual Insurance Company

PO Box 130
274 Currie Rd.
Dutton, ON N0L 1J0
519-762-3530
Fax: 519-762-3801
800-265-7635
info@westelgin.com
www.westelgin.com
Former Name: Dunwich Farmers' Mutual Fire Insurance Company
Ownership: Policyholders
Year Founded: 1880
Classes of Insurance: Personal Accident & Sickness, Auto, Liability, Fidelity, Property, Hail & Crop
Incorporation: Provincially Incorporated Insurance Company
Profile: The mutual insurance company is an amalgamation of Dunwich Farmers' Mutual Fire Insurance Company & Southwold Farmers' Mutual Fire Insurance Company. Home, farm, commercial & automobile insurance are offered.

Executives:
Brian Downie, General Manager; bdownie@westelgin.com

West Wawanosh Mutual Insurance Company

PO Box 130
81 Southampton St., RR#1
Dungannon, ON N0M 1R0
519-529-7922
Fax: 519-529-3211
800-265-5595
wawains@wwmic.com
www.wwmic.com
Ownership: Policyholders.
Year Founded: 1879
Classes of Insurance: Personal Accident & Sickness, Auto, Liability, Boiler & Machinery, Fidelity, Property
Incorporation: Provincially Incorporated Insurance Company
Profile: Insurance services include farm, residential, commercial & automobile.

Executives:
Cathie Simpson, General Manager; Cathie.Simpson@wwmic.com
Joanne Johnston, Manager, Claims; Joanne.Johnston@wwmic.com
Steve Wright, Manager, Underwriting; Steve.Wright@wwmic.com

Western Assurance Company

Sheridan Insurance Centre
#1000, 2225 Erin Mills Pkwy.
Mississauga, ON L5K 2S9
905-686-8326
www.royalsunalliance.ca/royalsun
Ownership: Private. Parent company is Roins Financial Services Limited. Part of Royal & Sun Alliance Group plc Canadian group of companies.
Year Founded: 1982
Assets: $500m-1 billion Year End: 20051231
Revenues: $100-500 million Year End: 20051231
Classes of Insurance: Personal Accident & Sickness, Aircraft, Auto, Liability, Boiler & Machinery, Marine, Fidelity, Property, Surety
Incorporation: Federally Incorporated Insurance Company
Executives:
Rowan Saunders, President/CEO
Irene Bianchi, Vice-President, Claims, Strategic Sourcing & Corporate Services
Shawn DeSantis, Vice-President, Personal Insurance
Joy Flowers, Vice-President, Human Resources
Mike Jakeman, Vice-President, Commercial Insurance
Steve Knoch, Vice-President, Information Services & Change Management
Winsome Leong, Vice-President, Actuary
Ed Sikorski, Vice-President, Marketing & Distribution
Mike Wallace, Vice-President, Risk, Underwriting & Reinsurance

Robin G. Richardson, Secretary
Directors:
Marcel Bundock, Chair
George Anderson
Guy Dufresne
George Harvey
Simon Lee
Robert McFarlane
Shelley Miller
Derek Oland
Rowan Saunders

Western Financial Group Inc.

***Also listed under:** Holding & Other Investment Companies*
PO Box 5519
309 - 1st St. West
High River, AB T1V 1M6
403-652-2663
Fax: 403-652-2661
866-843-9378
info@westernfinancialgroup.net
www.westernfinancialgroup.net
Ownership: Public
Year Founded: 1994
Number of Employees: 580
Assets: $100-500 million Year End: 20041231
Revenues: $10-50 million Year End: 20041231
Stock Symbol: WES
Classes of Insurance: Accident, Personal Accident & Sickness, Auto, Liability, Boiler & Machinery, Life, Fidelity, Property, Fire, Surety, Hail & Crop, Theft
Incorporation: Provincially Incorporated Insurance Company
Executives:
Scott A. Tannas, President/CEO
Thomas C. Dutton, Exec. Vice-President
Catherine A. Rogers, Corporate Secretary/CFO & Sr. Vice-President, Finance & Administration
R. William Rogers, Vice-President, Corporate Development
Directors:
Jim Dinning, Chair
Thomas C. Dutton
Gabor Jellinek
Robert G. Jennings

Catherine A. Rogers
J. Gregg Speirs
Jean-Denis Talon
Scott A. Tannas
Philip L. Webster
William Yuill
Affiliated Companies:
Bank West

Western Life Assurance Company
717 Portage Ave., 4th Fl.
Winnipeg, MB R3G OM8
204-784-6900
Fax: 204-783-6913
888-647-5433
Other Information: Mailling Address: PO Box 3300, Winnipeg, MB R3C 5S2
info@westernlife.com
www.westernlifeassurance.net
Former Name: Federated Life Insurance Company of Canada
Also Known As: Western Life
Ownership: Ssubsidiary of Western Financial Group, High River, AB
Classes of Insurance: Personal Accident & Sickness, Life
Incorporation: Federally Incorporated Insurance Company
Profile: Federated Life Insurance Company of Canada now operates as Western Life, after its acquisition by Western Financial Group. Another class of insurance is loss of employment.

Executives:
Bruce Ratzlaff, CEO
Branches:
High River
1010 - 24 St. SE
High River, AB T1V 2A7
403-652-2663

Kitchener
#903, 30 Duke St. West
Kitchener, ON N2H 3W5 Canada
519-489-4225
Fax: 519-749-8872

Western Surety Company
PO Box 527
#2000, 1874 Scarth St.
Regina, SK S4P 4B3
306-791-3735
Fax: 306-359-0929
800-475-4454
wscinfo@westernsurety.ca
www.westernsurety.ca
Former Name: Saskatchewan Guarantee & Fidelity Company Ltd.
Ownership: Private. Part of The Hill Companies.
Year Founded: 1909
Classes of Insurance: Fidelity, Surety
Incorporation: Federally Incorporated Insurance Company
Profile: The Canadian property & casualty insurance company is licensed in all provinces & territories. It writes surety bonds for the construction industry. A full line of commercial surety bonds is also available.

Executives:
David Dykes, FCIP, President/CEO; ddykes@westernsurety.ca
Neil Penner, General Manager; npenner@westernsurety.ca
Branches:
Halifax
1559 Brunswick St.
Halifax, NS B3J 2G1 Canada
902-425-6985
Fax: 902-425-7021
866-615-4547
Stephen Myrer, Manager, Atlantic Region Branch

Woman's Life Insurance Society
PO Box 234
1455 Lakeshore Rd.
Sarnia, ON N7S 2M4
519-542-2826
Fax: 810-985-6970
800-521-9292
www.womanslifeins.com
Ownership: Foreign. Part of Woman's Life Insurance Society, Port Huron, MI, USA.
Classes of Insurance: Life
Incorporation: Federally Incorporated Insurance Company
Profile: The foreign fraternal benefit society provides life insurance & fraternal benefits to its members & their families.

Executives:
Joseph Haselmayer, Chief Agent

XL Insurance Company Limited(XL)
#1802, 100 Yonge St.
Toronto, ON M5C 2W1
416-928-5586
Fax: 416-928-8858
www.xlinsurance.com
Ownership: XL Capital Ltd., Hamilton, Bermuda.
Year Founded: 1986
Classes of Insurance: Personal Accident & Sickness, Auto, Liability, Boiler & Machinery, Property, Surety
Incorporation: Federally Incorporated Insurance Company
Profile: XL Insurance is a foreign property & casualty insurance company.

Executives:
Robert Alexander, Chief Agent
Branches:
Toronto
48 Yonge St., 4th Fl.
Toronto, ON M5E 1G6
416-363-2933
Fax: 416-363-4517

XL Reinsurance America Inc.
Scotia Plaza
#1702, 100 Yonge St.
Toronto, ON M5C 2W1
416-598-1084
Fax: 416-598-1980
www.xlre.com
Former Name: NAC Reinsurance Corporation
Also Known As: XL Re Europe
Ownership: XL Capital Ltd., Hamilton, Bermuda.
Classes of Insurance: Personal Accident & Sickness, Aircraft, Auto, Liability, Boiler & Machinery, Fidelity, Property, Surety, Hail & Crop
Incorporation: Federally Incorporated Insurance Company
Profile: This is a foreign property & casualty insurance company.

Executives:
Chris Colle, Chief Agent

Yarmouth Mutual Fire Insurance Company
1229 Talbot St. East
St Thomas, ON N5P 1G9
519-631-1572
Fax: 519-631-6058
office@yarmouth-ins.com
www.yarmouth-ins.com
Ownership: Policyholders.
Year Founded: 1881
Classes of Insurance: Auto, Liability, Property, Hail & Crop
Incorporation: Provincially Incorporated Insurance Company
Profile: Insurance is offered for homes, farms, commercial properties & automobiles.

Executives:
Iris Brown, Manager

York Fire & Casualty Insurance Company
#201, 5310 Explorer Dr.
Mississauga, ON L4W 5H9
905-629-8444
Fax: 905-629-5008
yfmarketing@york-fire.com
www.york-fire.com
Ownership: Public. Subsidiary of Kingsway Financial Services Inc., Mississauga, ON.
Year Founded: 1955
Number of Employees: 130
Assets: $286,703,118 Year End: 20041231
Revenues: $173,855,200 Year End: 20041231
Stock Symbol: KFS
Classes of Insurance: Auto, Liability, Property
Incorporation: Provincially Incorporated Insurance Company
Executives:
William G. Star, President/CEO; wstar@kingsway-financial.com
Katherine Evans, Vice-President/CFO; kevans@york-fire.com
Shaun Jackson, Vice-President; sjackson@kingsway-financial.com
Colin Simpson, Vice-President/COO; csimpson@york-fire.com
Tom Walton, Asst. Vice-President, Marketing
Directors:
William G. Star, Chair
John L. Beamish
Bernard Gluckstein
Paul Iacono
Shaun Jackson

Zenith Insurance Company/ Compagnie d'Assurance Zenith
c/o Lombard Canada Ltd.
105 Adelaide St. West, 3rd Fl.
Toronto, ON M5H 1P9
416-350-4400
Fax: 416-350-4417
888-440-4876
inquiries@zenithinsurance.ca
www.zenithinsurance.ca
Ownership: Holding company is Lombard Canada Ltd., Toronto, ON.
Year Founded: 1997
Classes of Insurance: Personal Accident & Sickness, Auto, Liability, Property
Incorporation: Federally Incorporated Insurance Company
Profile: The Canadian property & casualty insurance company focuses upon customers over the age of 50.

Executives:
Richard N. Patina, President/CEO

Zurich Canada
400 University Ave., 25th Fl.
Toronto, ON M5G 1S7
416-586-3000
Fax: 416-586-2525
800-387-5454
zurich.information@zurich.com
www.zurichcanada.com
Former Name: Zurich North America Canada; Zurich Insurance Company
Ownership: Public. Foreign. Canadian branch of Zurich Insurance Company, Zurich, Switzerland.
Year Founded: 1923
Number of Employees: 500+
Assets: $1-10 billion Year End: 20060930
Revenues: $1-10 billion Year End: 20060930
Classes of Insurance: Accident, Personal Accident & Sickness, Auto, Liability, Boiler & Machinery, Credit, Marine, Fidelity, Property, Fire, Surety, Theft
Incorporation: Federally Incorporated Insurance Company
Executives:
Robert Landry, CEO, Chief Agent
Nigel Ayers, Chief Financial Officer
Gordon Thompson, Exec. Vice-President, Legal, General Counsel
Douglas Jamieson, Vice-President, Operations
Offices:
Edmonton
Manulife Place
#2240, 10180 - 101 St.
Edmonton, AB T5J 3S4 Canada
780-425-0872
Fax: 780-429-6640
800-232-1910
Montréal
#710, 2000, rue Peel
Montréal, QC H3A 2W5 Canada
514-393-7222
Fax: 514-393-6104
800-363-4707
Toronto
400 University Ave.
Toronto, ON M5G 1S7 Canada
416-813-3800
Fax: 416-813-3941
800-268-9168
Vancouver
One Bentall Centre
#1640, 505 Burrard St.
Vancouver, BC V7X 1M6 Canada
604-685-9241
Fax: 604-844-3466
800-663-9975

SECTION 5

Accounting & Law

Included in this section:

Accountants are organized alphabetically by the name of the accounting firm. Senior accountants listed within each firm may include Chartered Accountants, Certified General Accountants and Certified Management Accountants.

Actuarial Consultants incorporate organizations which provide actuarial advice.

Law Firms complete this section. Only those lawyers who practice in the many areas of financial law are listed. Where provided, a Head of Financial Law is included. To assist in gauging the size of a firm, each firm profile contains the total number of lawyers practicing within the firm.

Study Shows Business Performance Consistently Benefits from CA Advantage

TORONTO, February 5, 2007 - A recent study by the Canadian Institute of Chartered Accountants (CICA) shows that companies with a Chief Executive Officer or President who is a Chartered Accountant consistently outperform companies led by non-CAs.

Each year the CICA reviews the positions of Chairman, CEO, president, CFO, COO and corporate secretary at companies listed in the Globe and Mail's Report on Business(tm) (ROB) magazine's Top 1000 Companies to determine how many senior positions are held by CAs. The CICA report also reviews the financial performance of this group of 1000 largest publicly-traded Canadian corporations to assess the relative performance of companies with CFOs who are CAs.

"Once again, this year's study shows that companies with CAs in leadership positions are rewarded with better corporate performance, a correlation that has been consistent since we began conducting this analysis in 1998," said CICA President & CEO Kevin J. Dancey, FCA. "We are also encouraged to see that since the year 2000, the percentage of Chairman who are CAs in the Top 1000 companies has more than doubled."

The CICA study found that companies having a CA in the CFO position achieved a 5-year average return on capital of 2.8%, while companies with a non-CA in that position averaged minus 1.9 per cent.

Companies with a CA as top officer (President or CEO) also consistently performed better than companies headed by non-CAs on several key indicators:

Key Indicator	CEO or President is a CA	CEO or President is not a CA
5 Year Average ROE	3.8%	-2.1%
5 Year Average ROC	2.5%	0.6%
1 Year Average ROA	5.0%	0.7%

The study also showed that in 2006, 23% of the top officers in the ROB 1000 were CAs. Looking more broadly at leadership positions, 61% of ROB 1000 companies had a CA in at least one of their top 6 positions (Chair, CEO, president, CFO, COO and/or corporate secretary).

In terms of actual numbers, CAs held 57.9% of CFO positions in the 2006 ROB's Top 1000 Companies. This compares to 58.1% last year, 56.8% in 2004, 55.1% in 2003, 54.5% in 2002, and 53% in 2001.

The percentage of ROB's Top 1000 company Chairs who are CAs has more than doubled since that position was first included in the analysis in 2000. In total, 13.9% of the Chairs on the list were CAs, as were 9.8% of the CEOs, 9.6% of the Presidents, 17.5% of the corporate secretaries, and 8% of the COOs.

"Canada's Chartered Accountants are consistently chosen for influential leadership positions because of the financial expertise, business insight and strategic thinking they contribute to management teams," said Dancey. "The results of this study clearly show the positive impact their contribution can have on a company's bottom line."

The Canadian Institute of Chartered Accountants (CICA), together with the provincial, territorial and Bermuda Institutes/Ordre of Chartered Accountants, represents a membership of approximately 71,000 CAs and 9,500 students in Canada and Bermuda. The CICA conducts research into current business issues and supports the setting of accounting, auditing and assurance standards for business, not-for-profit organizations and government. It issues guidance on control and governance, publishes professional literature, develops continuing education programs and represents the CA profession nationally and internationally

The Canadian Institute of Chartered Accountants
277 Wellington Street West
Toronto, ON M5V 3H2 Canada
Tel: (416) 977-3222
Fax: (416) 977-8585
www.cica.ca

L'Institut Canadien Des Comptables Agréés
277, rue Wellington Ouest
Toronto, ON M5V 3H2 Canada
Tel: (416) 977-3222
Fax: (416) 977-8585
www.icca.ca

ACCOUNTING & LAW

Accounting & Law

Accountants

A.L. Schellenberg, Chartered Accountant
474 Panet Rd.
Winnipeg, MB R2C 3B9
204-669-5143
Fax: 204-669-5145
leon@mts.net
Executives:
Leon Schellenberg

Accountatax Inc.
147 Spring Garden Rd.
Montréal, QC H9B 2T7
514-685-7394
Fax: 514-685-7411
877-685-7394
www.accountatax.ca
Profile: Provides a wide range of tax, accounting and business advisory services.

Executives:
Patrick Kébreau, Chief Executive Officer

Albert L. Stal
#301, 1370 Don Mills Rd.
Toronto, ON M3B 3N7
416-449-0130
Fax: 416-444-7363
albertstal@bondexec.com
Ownership: Private
Year Founded: 1986
Number of Employees: 4
Executives:
Albert L. Stal, CA, CFP, Proprietor

Allen, Paquet & Arseneau LLP
PO Box 519
207 Roseberry St.
Campbellton, NB E3N 3G9
506-789-0820
Fax: 506-759-7514
apada@apa-ca.com
www.apa-ca.com
Year Founded: 1979
Profile: Provides a full range of services including accounting, auditing, corporate and personal income tax, financial planning, estate and business planning, business plan preparation and business forecasts.

Executives:
David L. Allen, CA, Administrative Partner; apada@apa-ca.com
Yves Arseneau, CA, Partner; apaya@apa-ca.com
Branches:
Bathurst
PO Box 482
270 Douglas Ave.
Bathurst, NB E2A 3Z4 Canada
506-546-1460
Fax: 506-546-9950
apabath@apa-ca.com

Aubry, Hijazi, CA - s.e.n.c.r.l.
#215, 1331, ave. Green
Montréal, QC H3Z 2A5
514-935-7787
Fax: 514-935-5865
info@aubryhijazi.com
www.aubryhijazi.com
Profile: Offers a variety of services including assurance (Audit, Review Engagement, and Notice to Reader), taxation, consulting, computerized accounting, business law, and international taxation.

Avery Cooper & Co.
Laurentian Building
PO Box 1620
Yellowknife, NT X1A 2P2
867-873-3441
Fax: 867-873-2353
800-661-0787
avery@averyco.nt.ca
www.averyco.nt.ca
Ownership: Private
Year Founded: 1969
Number of Employees: 25
Profile: The largest accounting firm in the Northwest Territories has offices located in Yellowknife. It is affiliated with Avery Cooper Financial Corp.

Executives:
Gerald F. Avery, FCGA, Managing Partner; avery@averyco.nt.ca
Douglas E. Cooper, CGA, Partner, Audit; dcooper@averyco.nt.ca
Cathy Cudmore, Partner; cathey@averyco.nt.ca
Kent D. Ferguson, CFE, FCGA, Partner; kent@averyco.nt.ca
W. Brent Hinchey, CGA, Partner, Tax; brent@averyco.nt.ca

Barkman & Tanaka
Also listed under: *Financial Planning*
Lougheed Plaza
#225, 9600 Cameron St.
Burnaby, BC V3J 7N3
604-421-2591
Fax: 604-421-1171
dbarkman@barkman-tanaka.com
Executives:
Dale Barkman, Partner
Wayne Tanaka, Partner

Bass & Murphy Chartered Accountants LLP
885 Progress Ave., #LPH1
Toronto, ON M1H 3G3
416-431-3030
Fax: 416-431-3340
tina@bassmurphy.com
www.bassmurphy.com
Year Founded: 1988
Executives:
David Bass, Contact; dave@bassmurphy.com
Branches:
Uxbridge
11 Brock St. East
Uxbridge, ON L9P 1M4 Canada
905-852-1066
Fax: 416-431-3340
Tom Murphy, Resident Partner

Bateman MacKay
PO Box 5015
4200 South Service Rd.
Burlington, ON L7R 3Y8
905-632-6400
Fax: 905-639-2285
866-787-1117
info@batemanmackay.com
www.batemanmackay.com
Ownership: Private
Year Founded: 1982
Number of Employees: 9
Revenues: $1-5 million
Executives:
Gary L. Bateman, P.Eng., MBA, CA, Partner; bateman@batemanmackay.com

BC&C Professional Corporation
6700 Morrison St.
Niagara Falls, ON L2E 6Z8
905-371-2300
Fax: 905-371-2344
corfield@vaxxine.com
www.vaxxine.com/corfield
Executives:
John Corfield; johnc@corfield.com

BCCA LLP Chartered Accountants
#1505, 444 St Mary Ave.
Winnipeg, MB R3C 3T1
204-957-7000
Fax: 204-949-1191
mail@bccallp.com
www.bccallp.com
Number of Employees: 25
Profile: Range of services includes audit, accounting, taxation, financial consulting, litigation support, computer consulting, management consulting, human resources, forensic accounting and business valuations.

Executives:
James J. Smith, FCA, CA-IFA; 204-953-7990; jsmith@bccallp.com
Michael Averbach, CA, CFP; 204-953-7999; maverbach@bccallp.com
Larry Gander, CA, CMA; 204-953-7989; lgander@bccallp.com

BDO Dunwoody LLP
Also listed under: *Trustees in Bankruptcy*
Royal Bank Plaza, South Tower
200 Bay St., 30th Fl.
Toronto, ON M5J 2J8
416-865-0111
Fax: 416-367-3912
national@bdo.ca
www.bdo.ca
Ownership: Private
Year Founded: 1921
Number of Employees: 1,965
Revenues: $214,000,000
Profile: Canada's sixth-largest accounting firm concentrates on the special needs of independent business & community-based organizations. The firm provides a full range of comprehensive business advisory services.

Executives:
Gilles Chaput, CEO
R.J. Berry, COO
Directors:
Dianne McMullen, Chair, Policy Board
Walter Flasza, Member, Policy Board
Kenneth Grower, Member, Policy Board
Anne McArel, Member, Policy Board
Kurt Oelschlagel, Member, Policy Board
Offices:
Abbotsford
#100, 2890 Garden St.
Abbotsford, BC V2T 4W7 Canada
604-853-6677
Fax: 604-853-4876
abbotsford@bdo.ca
Ben Baartman, Partner
Alexandria
55 Anik St.
Alexandria, ON K0C 1A0 Canada
613-525-1585
Fax: 613-525-1436
alexandria@bdo.ca
Pierre Vaillancourt, Partner
Alfred
PO Box 539
497 St-Philippe St.
Alfred, ON K0B 1A0 Canada
613-679-1332
Fax: 613-679-1801
alfred@bdo.ca
Alliston
#13, 169 Dufferin St. South
Alliston, ON L9R 1E6 Canada
705-435-5585
Fax: 705-435-5587
alliston@bdo.ca
Doug Holmes, Partner
Altona
26 Centre Ave. East
Altona, MB R0G 0B0 Canada
204-324-8653
Fax: 204-324-1629
altona@bdo.ca
Robert Martins, Partner
Barrie

BDO Dunwoody LLP (continued)

#300, 300 Lakeshore Dr.
Barrie, ON L4N 0B4 Canada
705-726-6331
Fax: 705-722-6588
barrie@bdo.ca
Joe Hilton, Manager

Boissevain
372 South Railway St.
Boissevain, MB R0K 0E0 Canada
204-534-6935
boissevain@bdo.ca
Tony DeVligere, Partner & Trustee

Bracebridge
#239, 1 Manitoba St.
Bracebridge, ON P1L 1S2 Canada
705-645-5215
Fax: 705-645-8125
bracebridge@bdo.ca
Murray Maw, Managing Partner

Brandon
117 - 10th St.
Brandon, MB R7A 4E7 Canada
204-727-0671
Fax: 204-726-4580
brandon@bdo.ca
Tony DeVliegere, Partner & Trustee

Brantford
#110B, 325 West St.
Brantford, ON N3R 3V6 Canada
519-759-8320
Fax: 519-759-8421
brantford@bdo.ca
Bill H. Kavelman, Partner

Calgary
#1900, 801 - 6 Ave. SW
Calgary, AB T2P 3W2 Canada
403-266-5608
Fax: 403-233-7833
calgary@bdo.ca
Richard Edwards, Partner/Sr. Vice-President

Cambridge
764 King St. East
Cambridge, ON N3H 3N9
519-653-7126
Fax: 519-653-8218
cambridge@bdo.ca
Don Laird, Chartered Accountant

Cardston
259 Main St.
Cardston, AB T0K OKO Canada
403-653-4137
cardson@bdo.ca

Charlottetown
PO Box 2158
91 Water St.
Charlottetown, PE C1A 8B9 Canada
902-892-5365
Fax: 902-892-0383

Chatham
375 St. Clair St.
Chatham, ON N7L 3K3 Canada
519-354-1560
Fax: 519-354-9346
chatham@bdo.ca
Rick Elliott, Partner

Cobourg
PO Box 627
204 Division St.
Cobourg, ON K9A 4L3 Canada
905-372-6863
Fax: 905-372-6650
cobourg@bdo.ca
Michael Machon, Partner

Collingwood
#202, 186 Hurontario St.
Collingwood, ON L9Y 3Z5 Canada
705-445-4421
Fax: 705-445-6691
collingwood@bdo.ca
Pierre Vaillancourt, Partner

Cornwall
PO Box 644
113 Second St. East
Cornwall, ON K6H 5T3 Canada
613-932-8691
Fax: 613-932-7591
cornwall@bdo.ca
Pierre Vaillancourt, Partner

Cranbrook
#200, 35 - 10 Ave. South
Cranbrook, BC V1C 2M9 Canada
250-426-4285
Fax: 250-426-8886
cranbrook@bdo.ca
Harley Lee, Partner

Dryden
37 King St.
Dryden, ON P8N 3G3 Canada
807-223-5321
Fax: 807-223-2978
dryden@bdo.ca
Doug Hannah, Partner

Edmonton
First Edmonton Pl.
#1000, 10665 Jasper Ave. NW
Edmonton, AB T5J 3S9 Canada
780-423-4353
Fax: 780-424-2110
edmonton@bdo.ca
Orest Bilous, Partner

Embrun
PO Box 128
991 Limoges Rd.
Embrun, ON K0A 1W0 Canada
613-443-5201
Fax: 613-443-2538
embrun@bdo.ca
Pierre Bourgon, Partner

Essex
180 Talbot St. South
Essex, ON N8M 1B6 Canada
519-776-6488
Fax: 519-776-6090
essex@bdo.ca
Mike McCreight, Partner

Fort Frances
375 Scott St.
Fort Frances, ON P9A 1H1 Canada
807-274-9848
Fax: 807-274-5142
fortfrances@bdo.ca
Marie Allan, Partner

Golden
PO Box 1709
#205, 421 - 9th Ave. North
Golden, BC V0A 1H0 Canada
250-344-5845
Fax: 250-344-7131
golden@bdo.ca
John Wilkey, Partner

Grande Prairie
Grande Prairie Place
9909 - 102 St., 5th Fl.
Grande Prairie, AB T8V 2V4 Canada
780-539-7075
Fax: 780-538-1890
grandeprairie@bdo.ca
Don Blonke, Partner

Guelph
#201, 660 Speedvale Ave. West
Guelph, ON N1K 1E5 Canada
519-824-5410
Fax: 519-824-5497
877-236-4835
Dan Cremasco, Partner

Hamilton
#2, 505 York Blvd.
Hamilton, ON L8R 3K4 Canada
905-525-6800
Fax: 905-525-6566
888-236-2383
hamilton@bdo.ca
Rino H. Bellavia, Partner

Hanover
485 - 10th St.
Hanover, ON N4N 1R2 Canada
519-364-3790
Fax: 519-364-5334
hanover@bdo.ca
John Hunt, Partner

Huntsville
PO Box 5484
2 Elm St.
Huntsville, ON P1H 2K8 Canada
705-789-4469
Fax: 705-789-1079
huntsville@bdo.ca
Bill McDonnell

Kamloops
#300, 272 Victoria St.
Kamloops, BC V2C 1Z6 Canada
250-372-9505
Fax: 250-374-6323
kamloops@bdo.ca
Bill Callandar, Partner

Kelowna
Landmark Technology Centre
#300, 1632 Dickson Ave.
Kelowna, BC V1Y 7T2 Canada
250-763-6700
Fax: 250-763-4457
kelowna@bdo.ca
Kevin Berry, Partner

Kenora
#300, 301 First Ave. South
Kenora, ON P9N 4E9 Canada
807-468-5531
Fax: 807-468-9774
kenora@bdo.ca
Jim Corbett, Partner

Kincardine
970 Queen St.
Kincardine, ON N2Z 2Y2 Canada
519-396-3425
Fax: 519-396-9829
kincardine@bdo.ca
Steven Watson, Partner

Kitchener
#401, 305 King St. West
Kitchener, ON N2G 1B9 Canada
519-576-5220
Fax: 519-576-5471
kitchenerwaterloo@bdo.ca
Dean Elliott, Partner

Langley
#220, 19916 - 64th Ave.
Langley, BC V2Y 1A2 Canada
604-534-8691
Fax: 604-534-8900
langley@bdo.ca
Ken Baker, Partner

Lethbridge
Southland Terrace
#200, 220 - 3rd Ave. South
Lethbridge, AB T1J 0G9 Canada
403-328-5292
Fax: 403-328-9534
lethbridge@bdo.ca
Jim Berezan, Partner

Lindsay
PO Box 358
165 Kent St. West
Lindsay, ON K9V 4S3 Canada
705-324-3579
Fax: 705-324-0774
lindsay@bdo.ca
Paul Allen, Partner

London
Station Park
#201, 252 Pall Mall St.
London, ON N6A 5P6 Canada
519-672-8940
Fax: 519-672-5562
london@bdo.ca
Ed Ramsay, Partner

MacGregor
78 Hampton St.
MacGregor, MB R0H 0R0 Canada
204-685-2323
Fax: 204-685-2341
macgregor@bdo.ca
Bernard Lapchuk, Partner

Manitou

330 Main St.
Manitou, MB R0G 1G0 Canada
204-242-2637
manitou@bdo.ca
Ron Westfall, Partner
Markham
#400, 60 Columbia Way
Markham, ON L3R 0C9 Canada
905-946-1066
Fax: 905-946-9524
markham@bdo.ca
Mohammad Ashraf, Partner
Minnedosa
39 Main St. South
Minnedosa, MB R0J 1E0 Canada
204-867-2957
minnedosa@bdo.ca
Jeanne Mills, Partner
Mississauga
4255 Sherwoodtowne Blvd.
Mississauga, ON L4Z 1Y5 Canada
905-270-7700
Fax: 905-671-7915
mississauga@bdo.ca
Glenn Agro, Partner
Mitchell
PO Box 792
11 Victoria St.
Mitchell, ON N0K 1N0 Canada
519-348-8412
Fax: 519-348-4300
mitchell@bdo.ca
Coralee J. Foster, Partner
Montréal
Westmount Premier
#600, 4150, rue Ste-Catherine ouest
Montréal, QC H3Z 2Y5 Canada
514-931-0841
Fax: 514-931-9491
montreal@bdo.ca
Pierre Lussier, Regional Managing Partner
Morden
133 - 7th St.
Morden, MB R6M 1S3 Canada
204-822-5486
Fax: 204-822-4828
morden@bdo.ca
Sam Andrew, Partner
Mount Forest
PO Box 418
191 Main St. South
Mount Forest, ON N0G 2L0 Canada
519-323-2351
Fax: 519-323-3661
mountforest@bco.ca
Kevin Drier, Partner
Nakusp
PO Box 1078
220 Broadway St.
Nakusp, BC V0G 1R0 Canada
250-265-4750
Fax: 250-837-7170
nakusp@bdo.ca
Ken Davidson, Partner
Newmarket
Gates of York Plaza
#2, 17310 Yonge St.
Newmarket, ON L3Y 7R8 Canada
905-898-1221
Fax: 905-898-0028
866-275-8836
newmarket@bdo.ca
Michael Jones, Partner
North Bay
PO Box 20001
142 Main St. West
North Bay, ON P1B 9N1 Canada
705-495-2000
Fax: 705-495-2001
800-461-6324
northbay@bdo.ca
Jack Campbell, Partner
Oakville
151 Randall St.
Oakville, ON L6J 1P5 Canada
905-844-3206
Fax: 905-844-7513
oakville@bdo.ca
Jim Booth, Partner
Orangeville
77 Broadway Ave., 2nd Fl.
Orangeville, ON L9W 1K1 Canada
519-941-0681
Fax: 519-941-8272
orangeville@bdo.ca
James Blackwell, Partner
Orillia
PO Box 670
19 Front St. North
Orillia, ON L3V 6K5 Canada
705-325-1386
Fax: 705-325-6649
orillia@bdo.ca
Ross Mitchell, Regional Managing Partner
Oshawa
Oshawa Executive Centre
#502, 419 King St. West
Oshawa, ON L1J 2K5 Canada
905-576-3430
Fax: 905-436-9138
oshawa@bdo.ca
Nigel Allen, Partner
Ottawa
#204, 260 Centrum Blvd
Ottawa, ON K1E 3P4 Canada
613-837-3300
Fax: 613-837-7733
800-754-1579
ottawa@bdo.ca
Daniel Suprenant, Partner
Owen Sound
PO Box 397
1717 - 2nd Ave. East
Owen Sound, ON N4K 5P7 Canada
519-376-6110
Fax: 519-376-4741
owensound@bdo.ca
Steve Lowe, Partner
Penticton
#102, 100 Front St.
Penticton, BC V2A 1H1 Canada
250-492-6020
Fax: 250-492-8110
penticton@bdo.ca
Michael Bovin, Partner
Peterborough
PO Box 1018
#202, 201 George St. North
Peterborough, ON K9J 7A5 Canada
705-742-4271
Fax: 705-742-3420
888-369-6600
peterborough@bdo.ca
Bill Gordanier, Partner
Petrolia
PO Box 869
4495 Petrolia Line
Petrolia, ON N0N 1R0 Canada
519-882-3333
Fax: 519-882-2703
petrolia@bdo.ca
Doug Johnston, Partner
Picture Butte
339 Highway Ave.
Picture Butte, AB T0K 1V0 Canada
403-732-4469
Fax: 403-732-5701
picturebutte@bdo.ca
Phillip Wever, Sr. Manager
Port Elgin
PO Box 1390
625 Mill St.
Port Elgin, ON N0H 2C0 Canada
519-832-2049
Fax: 519-832-5659
portelgin@bdo.ca
Mike Bolton, Partner
Portage La Prairie
480 Saskatchewan Ave. West
Portage La Prairie, MB R1N 0M4 Canada
204-857-2856
Fax: 204-239-1664
portagelaprairie@bdo.ca
John Chapman, Partner
Red Deer
4719 - 48 Ave., 3rd Fl.
Red Deer, AB T4N 3T1 Canada
403-346-1566
Fax: 403-343-3070
reddeer@bdo.ca
James Scott, Partner
Red Lake
PO Box 234
207 Discovery Centre
Red Lake, ON P0V 2M0 Canada
807-727-3227
Fax: 807-727-1172
redlake@bdo.ca
Revelstoke
PO Box 2100
#202, 103 - 1st St. East
Revelstoke, BC V0E 2S0 Canada
250-837-5225
Fax: 250-837-7170
revelstoke@bdo.ca
Ken Davidson, Partner
Ridgetown
211 Main St. East
Ridgetown, ON N0P 2C0 Canada
519-674-5418
Fax: 519-674-5410
ridgetown@bdo.ca
Rick Elliott, Partner
Rockland
#5, 2784 Laurier St.
Rockland, ON K4K 1A2 Canada
613-446-6497
Fax: 613-446-7117
rockland@bdo.ca
Judith Gratton, Partner
Salmon Arm
#201, 571 - 6th St. NE
Salmon Arm, BC V1E 1R6 Canada
250-832-7171
Fax: 250-832-2429
salmonarm@bdo.ca
Doug Adams, Partner
Sarnia
PO Box 730
250 Christina St. North
Sarnia, ON N7T 7V3 Canada
519-336-9900
Fax: 519-332-4828
sarnia@bdo.ca
Don Dafoe, Partner
Sault Ste Marie
PO Box 1109
747 Queen St. East
Sault Ste Marie, ON P6A 5N7 Canada
705-945-0990
Fax: 705-942-7979
ssm@bdo.ca
Thom Ambeault, Partner
Selkirk
378 Main St.
Selkirk, MB R1A 1T8 Canada
204-482-5626
Fax: 204-482-4969
selkirk@bdo.ca
Bill Findlater, Partner
Sicamous
PO Box 392
314 Finlayson St.
Sicamous, BC V0E 2V0 Canada
250-836-4493
Fax: 250-837-7170
sicamous@bdo.ca
Ken Davidson, Partner
Sioux Lookout
61 King St.
Sioux Lookout, ON P8T 1A5 Canada
807-737-1500
Fax: 807-737-4443
siouxlookout@bdo.ca
Slave Lake

BDO Dunwoody LLP (continued)

PO Box 297
#303, Lakeland Centre
Slave Lake, AB T0G 2A0 Canada
780-849-3622
Fax: 780-849-3625
slavelake@bdo.ca
Ray McComb, Partner

Sorrento
PO Box 59
#2, 1266 Trans Canada Hwy.
Sorrento, BC V0E 2W0 Canada
250-675-3288
Fax: 250-832-2429
sorrento@bdo.ca

Squamish
PO Box 168
38143 - 2nd Ave.
Squamish, BC V0N 3G0 Canada
604-892-9424
Fax: 604-892-9356
squamish@bdo.ca
Theresa Walterhouse, Partner

St Pierre Jolys
Place Lavergne
#6, 467, rue Sabourin
St Pierre Jolys, MB R0A 1V0 Canada
204-433-7508
Fax: 204-433-7181
saintpierrejolys@bdo.ca
Mona Marcotte, Partner

St-Claude
76 First St.
St-Claude, MB R0G 1Z0 Canada
204-379-2332
800-268-3337
stclaude@bdo.ca
Henri Magne, Partner

Stratford
134 Waterloo St. South
Stratford, ON N5A 6S8 Canada
519-271-2491
Fax: 519-271-4013
stratford@bdo.ca
Montagu J. Smith, Managing Partner

Strathroy
28636 Centre Rd., RR#5
Strathroy, ON N7G 3H6 Canada
519-245-1913
Fax: 519-245-5987
strathroy@bdo.ca
Garry Harris, Partner

Sudbury
#202, 888 Regent St.
Sudbury, ON P3E 6C6 Canada
705-671-3336
Fax: 705-671-9552
877-820-0404
sudbury@bdo.ca
Ted Hargreaves, Partner

Summerland
c/o Bell Jacoe & Co.
13211 North Victoria Rd.
Summerland, BC V0H 1Z0 Canada
250-494-9255
Fax: 250-494-9755
summerland@bdo.ca
David Braumberger, Partner

Surrey
#200, 15225 - 104 Ave.
Surrey, BC V3R 6Y8 Canada
604-584-2121
Fax: 604-584-3823
surrey@bdo.ca
Larry C. Mueller, Partner

Thunder Bay
1095 Barton St.
Thunder Bay, ON P7B 5N3 Canada
807-625-4444
Fax: 807-623-8460
thunderbay@bdo.ca
John Aikin, Partner

Tiverton
84 Main St.
Tiverton, ON N0G 2T0 Canada
519-368-5331
tiverton@bdo.ca

Toronto
Royal Bank Plaza, 33rd Fl.
PO Box 32
Toronto, ON M5J 2J8 Canada
416-865-0200
Fax: 416-865-0887
toronto@bdo.ca
Keith Farlinger, Regional Managing Partner

Treherne
274 Railway Ave.
Treherne, MB R0G 2V0 Canada
204-723-2454
treherne@bdo.ca
Allan Nichol, Partner

Uxbridge
#1, 1 Brock St. East
Uxbridge, ON L9P 1P6 Canada
905-852-9714
Fax: 905-852-9898
uxbridge@bdo.ca
Randy Hickey, Partner

Vancouver
#600, 925 West Georgia St.
Vancouver, BC V6L 3L2 Canada
604-688-5421
Fax: 604-688-5132
vancouver@bdo.ca
Bill Cox, Partner

Vernon
3201 - 30th Ave.
Vernon, BC V1T 2C6 Canada
250-545-2136
Fax: 250-545-3364
vernon@bdo.ca
Brian Cockburn, Partner

Virden
PO Box 1900
255 Wellington St. West
Virden, MB R0M 2C0 Canada
204-748-1200
Fax: 204-748-1976
virden@bdo.ca
Bob Lawrence, Partner

Vulcan
112 - 3 Ave. North
Vulcan, AB TOL 2B0 Canada
403-485-2923
Fax: 403-485-6098
vulcan@bdo.ca

Walkerton
PO Box 760
121 Jackson St.
Walkerton, ON N0G 2V0 Canada
519-881-1211
Fax: 519-881-3530
walkerton@bdo.ca
Gary Munroe, Partner

Welland
37 Dorothy St.
Welland, ON L3B 3V6 Canada
905-735-6433
Fax: 905-735-6514
welland@bdo.ca
Dale Hajdu, Partner

Whistler
#104, 1080 Millar Creek Rd.
Whistler, BC V0N 1B1 Canada
604-932-3799
Fax: 604-932-3764
whistler@bdo.ca
Theresa Walterhouse, Partner

Whitehorse
#201, 3059 - 3rd Ave.
Whitehorse, YT Y1A 1E2 Canada
867-667-7907
Fax: 867-668-3087
whitehorse@bdo.ca
Ben Baartman, Partner

Wiarton
PO Box 249
663 Berford St.
Wiarton, ON N0H 2T0 Canada
519-534-1520
Fax: 519-534-3454
wiarton@bdo.ca
Forbes Simon, Partner

Windsor
3630 Rhodes Dr.
Windsor, ON N8W 5A4 Canada
519-944-6900
Fax: 519-944-6116
windsor@bdo.ca
Ted Herbert, Partner

Wingham
PO Box 1420
152 Josephine St.
Wingham, ON N0G 2W0 Canada
519-357-3231
Fax: 519-357-3230
wingham@bdo.ca
Allan Reed, Partner

Winkler
#2, 583 Main St.
Winkler, MB R6W 1A4 Canada
204-325-4787
Fax: 204-325-8040
winkler@bdo.ca
Frank Wiebe, Partner

Winnipeg
Wawanesa Bldg.
#700, 200 Graham Ave.
Winnipeg, MB R3C 4L5 Canada
204-956-7200
Fax: 204-926-7201
winnipeg@bdo.ca
David Anderson, Partner

Woodstock
PO Box 757
94 Graham St.
Woodstock, ON N4S 8A2 Canada
519-539-2081
Fax: 519-539-2571
woodstock@bdo.ca
Dwayne De Vries, Partner

Beallor & Partners LLP

Also listed under: *Trustees in Bankruptcy*
28 Overlea Blvd.
Toronto, ON M4H 1B6
416-423-0707
Fax: 416-423-7000
service@beallor.com
www.beallor.com
Ownership: Private
Year Founded: 1962
Number of Employees: 35
Executives:
Dennis Beallor, Partner; dbeallor@beallor.com
Morley Beallor, Partner; mbeallor@beallor.com
Allan Gutenberg, Partner; agutenberg@beallor.com
Rick Rooney, Partner; rrooney@beallor.com
Rob Wells, Partner; rwells@beallor.com
Ted White, Partner; twhite@beallor.com
Barry Flodder, Associate; bflodder@beallor.com

Beauchemin Trépanier Comptables agréés inc.

#1102, 4200, boul. St-Laurent
Montréal, QC H2W 2R2
514-847-0182
Fax: 514-849-9082
bt@btca.qc.ca
www.btca.qc.ca
Profile: Full-service accounting firm which provides accounting, taxation, and financial planning services.

Executives:
Paul Beauchemin, CA, Partner
Sophie Trépanier, CA, Partner

Beers Neal LLP

#301, 53 King St.
Saint John, NB E2L 1G5
506-632-9020
Fax: 506-632-9030
gbeers@beersneal.ca
www.beersneal.ca
Profile: Firm focuses in the areas of manufacturing, hospitality, aquaculture, retail and not-for-profit industries.

Executives:

Glenn Beers, CA, Partner; 506-632-9023; gbeers@beersneal.ca

Christopher Neal, CA, Partner; 506-632-9022; cneal@beersneal.ca

Belanger Clarke
PO Box 8505
108 Lemarchant Rd.
St John's, NL A1B 3N9
709-579-2161
Fax: 709-738-2391
Former Name: Walter P. Miller Co.
Year Founded: 1965
Profile: Professional services currently provided by the firm include audit and accounting, forensic investigative services, personal and corporate income tax consulting, accounting system design, management consulting and in-house computerized accounting.

Executives:
Steve Belanger, FCA, Partner; steve@belangerclarke.ca
Boyde Clarke, FCA, Partner; boyde@belangerclarke.ca
William A. McGettigan, CA, Partner; bill@belangerclarke.ca

Belliveau Veinotte Inc.
PO Box 29
11 Dominion St.
Bridgewater, NS B4V 2W6
902-543-4278
Fax: 902-543-1818
office@bvca.ca
Year Founded: 1998
Profile: Full-service accounting firm serving Southwest Nova Scotia.

Executives:
Paul Belliveau, CA, Partner
Robert Veinotte, CA, Partner
Branches:
Barrington Passage
#2, 3588 Hwy. 3
Barrington Passage, NS B0W 1G0 Canada
902-637-1637
Fax: 902-637-1638
866-457-5450
bvsh@ns.sympatico.ca
Shelburne
PO Box 189
157 Water St.
Shelburne, NS B0T 1W0 Canada
902-875-1051
Fax: 902-875-1052
bvsh@ns.sympatico.ca

Bennett Gold Chartered Accountants
#302, 1 Concorde Gate
Toronto, ON M3C 3N6
416-449-2249
Fax: 416-449-4133
rygold@bennettgold.ca
www.bennettgold.ca
Year Founded: 1979
Executives:
Robert Gold, MBA, CA, Managing Partner
Donald Bennett, B.Sc.(Econ), CA, Partner

Bergeron Lavigne SENC
1390, O'neil
Québec, QC G1P 2G9
418-872-5115
Fax: 418-872-1664
bergeronlavigne@videotron.ca
www.guideformationquickbooks.com
Executives:
Michel Bergeron, CA; michelbergeronca@videotron.ca
Claude Lavigne, CA; bergeronlavigne@videotron.ca

Bernard Martens Professional Corp.
#217, 5809 Macleod Trail South
Calgary, AB T2H 0J9
403-255-1262
Fax: 403-640-4652
b.martens@home.com
www.eca.ca/sites/bernardmartens
Ownership: Private
Year Founded: 1979
Number of Employees: 2
Executives:
Bernard Martens, President

Bernhard Brinkmann Chartered Accountant
#200, 3205 - 97 St. NW
Edmonton, AB T6N 1B7
780-434-2756
Fax: 780-463-7605
bhbrinkmann@brinkmann.ca
www.brinkmann.ca
Ownership: Private
Year Founded: 1993
Executives:
Bernhard Brinkmann, CA, B.Com., Chartered Accountant

Bessner Gallay Kreisman
#300, 215, av Redfern
Montréal, QC H3Z 3L5
514-908-3600
Fax: 514-908-3630
admin@bgk.com
www.bgsk.com
Former Name: Bessner Gallay Schapira Kreisman
Year Founded: 1950
Number of Employees: 57
Business Advisors:
Morton Benjamin, CA; mbenjamin@bgsk.ca
Sydney H. Berger, CA; sberger@bgsk.ca
Samuel Bernard, CA, TEP; sbernard@bgsk.ca
Mark Bindman; mbindman@bgsk.ca
Ronald E. Gallay, FCA; rgallay@bgsk.ca
Harold S. Greenspon, CA; hgreenspon@bgsk.ca
Martin M. Isaif, MBA, CA; misaif@bgsk.ca
Irving Kaplan, CA; ikaplan@bgsk.ca
Abraham Kreisman, CFE, CA; akreisman@bgsk.com
Brian Kreisman; briank@bgk.ca
David Lesser, CA; dlesser@bgsk.ca
Philip C. Levi, CMC, CFE, FCA, CPA; philevi@bgsk.ca
Louis Ruta, CA; lruta@bgsk.ca
Derek Silverman; dsilverman@bgk.ca

Bing C. Wong & Associates Ltd.
124 East Pender St., 3rd Fl.
Vancouver, BC V6A 1T3
604-682-7561
Fax: 604-682-7665
Ownership: Private
Year Founded: 1950
Number of Employees: 14
Revenues: Under $1 million
Profile: Accounting, tax planning & bookkeeping services are provided. Consulting services include financial, business & immigration.

Executives:
Bing C. Wong, President
Janis Ho, Manager, Information Systems
Glen J. Wong, Manager, Office

Bishop & Company Chartered Accountants Inc.
189 Dykeland St.
Wolfville, NS B4P 1A3
902-542-7665
Fax: 902-542-4554
rbishop@bcica.ca
Year Founded: 1982
Number of Employees: 14
Profile: Provides services in the areas of audit, accounting, taxation, business information technology, assurance, succession and estate planning, business planning and risk management.

Executives:
Raymond F. Bishop, CA, Partner; rbishop@bcica.ca
Todd Jones, CA, Partner; tjones@bcica.ca
Loretta Kalkman, CA, Partner; lkalkman@bcica.ca
Greg Miller, CA, Partner; gmiller@bcica.ca

Blair Crosson Voyer Chartered Accountants
Commerce Pl.
#1650, 400, Burrard St.
Vancouver, BC V6C 3A6
604-684-3371
Fax: 604-684-9832
bcv@taxsolve.com
Partners:
Alan Bennett
Vern Blair
Richard Crosson
Marilyn de Rooy
Ronald Hooge
Grace Lau
Ron Patrickson
Ron Voyer; voyer@taxsolve.com

Blouin, Julien, Potvin Comptables agréés, S.E.N.C.
#300, 2795, boul Laurier
Québec, QC G1V 4M7
418-651-0405
Fax: 418-651-0285
groupe@boulinjulienpotvin.qc.ca

Boisjoli Sabbag Chartered Accountants LLP
3424, rue Drummond
Montréal, QC H3G 1Y1
514-287-0833
Fax: 514-287-0778
info@boisjoli.com
www.boisjoli.com
Profile: Services provided includes assurance, taxation, commodity taxes, accounting, financing & government assistance, mergers & acquisitions, management consulting, and business insolvency & turnaround.

Booke & Partners
#500, 5 Donald St.
Winnipeg, MB R3L 2T4
204-284-7060
Fax: 204-284-7105
booke@bookeandpartners.ca
www.bookeandpartners.ca
Year Founded: 1993
Number of Employees: 30
Profile: Offers a full range of auditing, accounting, tax planning and management consulting services.

Executives:
Larry Booke, CA, Partner

Brassard Carrier, Comptables Agréés
#200, 1651, chemin Ste-Foy
Québec, QC G1S 2P1
418-682-2929
Fax: 418-682-0282
info@groupebca.com
www.groupebca.com
Executives:
Bruno Brassard, CA
Richard Carrier, CA

Brief Rotfarb Wynberg Cappe
#402, 3854 Bathurst St.
Toronto, ON M3H 3N2
416-635-9080
Fax: 416-635-0462
lcappe@brwc.com
www.brwc.com
Executives:
Harold Brief
Leonard Cappe
Brian Gillispie
Maurice Rotfarb
Leo Wynberg

Bringloe Feeney
#401, 212 Queen St.
Fredericton, NB E3B 1A8
506-458-8326
Fax: 506-458-9293
www.acgca.ca/fredericton.htm
Former Name: Bourque & Bringloe
Year Founded: 1976
Number of Employees: 9
Partners:
Wilson L.G. Donovan; wilson.donovan@bringloefeeney.ca
E. Shawn Bringloe, CA; shawn.bringloe@bringloefeeney.ca
John E. Feeney, CA; john.feeney@bringloefeeney.ca

Bringloe Feeney LLP
#401, 212 Queen St.
Fredericton, NB E3B 1A8
506-458-8326
Fax: 506-458-9293
shawn.bringloe@bringloefeeney.ca
www.bringloefeeney.ca
Year Founded: 1976
Number of Employees: 9

Bringloe Feeney LLP (continued)
Profile: Services include accounting, taxation, computer, business valuation, audit, business advisory and strategic planning.
Executives:
Shawn Bringloe, CA, Partner; 506-458-0740; shawn.bringloe@bringloefeeney.ca
Wilson Donovan, CA, Partner; 506-458-8326; wilson.donovan@bringloefeeney.ca
John Feenry, CA, Partner; 506-458-0744; john.feeney@bringloefeeney.ca

Brownlow & Associates
259 Wilson St. East
Ancaster, ON L9G 2B8
905-648-0404
Fax: 905-648-0403
888-648-0404
info@brownlowcas.com
www.brownlowcas.com
Partners:
Barry Brownlow
Dave Brownlow
John DeVries

Buchanan Barry LLP
#800, 840 - 6th Ave. SW
Calgary, AB T2P 3E5
403-262-2116
Fax: 403-265-0845
mailbox@buchananbarry.ca
www.buchananbarry.ca
Ownership: Private
Year Founded: 1960
Number of Employees: 35
Partners:
W. Martin Barry, CA; marty.barry@buchananbarry.ca
Gray S. Graves, CA; gray.graves@buchananbarry.ca
John O. Taylor, CA; john.taylor@buchananbarry.ca
Julie A. Swanson, CA; julie.swanson@buchananbarry.ca
Vern F. Varga, CA; vern.varga@buchananbarry.ca

Buttar & Associates Inc.
#11, 499 Ray Lawson Blvd.
Brampton, ON
905-866-6543
Fax: 905-866-6761
delta@buttarbuttar.com
www.buttar.ca
Executives:
Kanwal Buttar, President; pbuttar@buttarbuttar.com

C. Topley & Company Ltd.
Also listed under: *Trustees in Bankruptcy*
#200, 260 West Esplanade
North Vancouver, BC V7M 3G7
604-987-8688
Fax: 604-904-8628
877-363-3437
info@bankruptcytrustee.ca
www.bankruptcytrustee.ca
Ownership: Private
Year Founded: 1998
Number of Employees: 10
Profile: The trustee in bankruptcy & accounting firm is also engaged in financial investigation.
Executives:
Colin W. Topley, CGA, CIRP, CFE, President; 604-982-1480; ctopley@topleyandcompany.com
Jennifer Rorison, CIRP, Vice-President; 604-982-1481; jrorison@topleyandcompany.com
Kelvin Tan, CA. CIRP, Vice-President; 604-982-1482; ktan@topleyandcompany.com
Marilyn E. Phelps, CFE, Sr. Manager; 604-982-1484; mphelps@topleyandcompany.com

C.R. Barclay, CA, CMA, MBA
10 Woods Hollow
Gravenhurst, ON P1P 1Y7
705-684-8115
Fax: 705-684-8227
877-644-4838
cbarclay1@cogeco.ca
Ownership: Private. Sole proprietorship
Year Founded: 1991
Number of Employees: 1
Executives:
Colin Barclay, RFP, CFP, Sole Practitioner

Campbell, Saunders Ltd.
Also listed under: *Trustees in Bankruptcy*
#1000, 570 Granville St.
Vancouver, BC V6C 3P1
604-915-5550
Fax: 604-915-5560
info@csvan.com
www.csvan.com
Executives:
Harold Saunders, President
David Gray, Sr. Vice-President
Patty E. Wood, Vice-President
Branches:
Richmond
#5040, 8171 Ackroyd Rd.
Richmond, BC V6X 3K1 Canada
604-821-9882
Fax: 604-821-9870
info@csvan.com

Carmichael, Toews, Irving Inc.
247 Baker St.
Nelson, BC V1L 4H4
250-354-4451
Fax: 250-354-4427
admin@cti-cga.com
www.cti-cga.com
Former Name: Exner, Wickland, Carmichael Inc.
Executives:
Bryan Carmichael
Gladene Toews
Brent Irving, CGA

Catalyst Chartered Accountants & Consultants
Also listed under: *Financial Planning*
318 Centre St. South
High River, AB T1V 1N7
403-652-3032
Fax: 403-652-7051
inquire@catalystsolutions.ca
www.catalystsolutions.ca
Former Name: Coakwell Crawford Cairns LLP; Coakwell Moore

Ownership: Private
Partners:
Rodney L. Baceda, CA; rodb@catalystsolutions.ca
Brock D. Cairns, CA; brockc@catalystsolutions.ca
Gerald L. Coakwell, CA; gerryc@catalystsolutions.ca
Cam Crawford, FCA, CMC, CBV; camc@catalystsolutions.ca
Ted Finningley, TEP, CA; tedf@catalystsolutions.ca
Terri Mihaui, CA; terrim@catalystsolutions.ca
Donald C. Phillips, CA; donp@catalystsolutions.ca
Branches:
Calgary
#1620, Trimac House
Calgary, AB T2P 3T6 Canada
403-296-0082
Fax: 403-296-0415

Cauchon Turcotte Thériault Latouche
Place Iberville Un
#310, 1195, av Lavigerie
Québec, QC G1V 4N3
418-658-8808
Fax: 418-658-3136
www.cttlca.com
Number of Employees: 20
Executives:
Rodrigue Cauchon, CA
Bruno Latouche, CA
Marc Thériault, CA
Yves Turcotte, CA

Cawley & Associates
1622 - 7th Ave. West, 3rd Fl.
Vancouver, BC V6J 1S5
604-731-1191
Fax: 604-731-3511
info@cawley-assoc.com
www.cawley-assoc.com
Ownership: Private
Executives:
Brian Cawley, CA
Grant Curran

Chartered Accountants For You, LLP
5917 - 1A St. SW
Calgary, AB T2H 0G4
403-209-2248
Fax: 403-539-2248
calgaryhelp@ca4u.ca
www.ca4u.ca
Former Name: Nagy Rubin Financial Services
Ownership: Private
Year Founded: 1998
Number of Employees: 15
Executives:
Peggy Churchward, CFP, RFP

Choquette & Company Accounting Group
10662 - 240A St.
Maple Ridge, BC V2W 2B1
604-463-8202
Fax: 604-463-8210
800-667-9254
info@choquetteco.com
www.choquetteco.com

Choquette Corriveau, Chartered Accountants
Place Iberville I
#300, 1195, av Lavigerie
Québec, QC G1V 4N3
418-658-5555
Fax: 418-658-1010
courrier@choquettecorriveau.com
choquettecorriveau.com
Profile: Offers services in three fields of expertise: taxation, assurance & business advisory services, corporate financial advice.

Church Pickard & Co.
#301, 17 Church St.
Nanaimo, BC V9R 5H5
250-754-6396
Fax: 250-754-8177
866-754-6396
mail@churchpickard.com
www.churchpickard.com
Partners:
John Annesley, BA, CA; johnannesley@churchpickard.com
Fred Downs, CA; freddowns@churchpickard.com
Lorana Laporte, B.Comm., CFP, CA; loranalaporte@churchpickard.com
Grant McDonald, B.Sc., CA; grantmcdonald@churchpickard.com

The Clarke Henning Group
Also listed under: *Trustees in Bankruptcy*
#801, 10 Bay St.
Toronto, ON M5J 2R8
416-364-4421
Fax: 416-367-8032
888-422-1241
ch@clarkehenning.com
www.clarkehenning.com
Former Name: Clarke, Henning Inc.
Year Founded: 1915
Number of Employees: 40
Partners:
Liana Bell; lbell@clarkehenning.com
Dave Fry; dfry@clarkehenning.com
Donald M. Gellatly; dgellat@clarkehenning.com
Jim Henning; jhenning@clarkehenning.com
Darryl Hickman; dhickman@clarkehenning.com
Rollie Hill; rhill@clarkehenning.com
Gary MacGregor; garymac@clarkehenning.com
Vinay Raja; vraja@clarkehenning.com
Dennis Reid; dreid@clarkehenning.com
Bob Rose; brose@clarkehenning.com

Clarke Starke & Diegel(CSD)
Also listed under: *Trustees in Bankruptcy*
#202, 871 Victoria St. North
Kitchener, ON N2B 3S4
519-579-5520
Fax: 519-570-3611
www.csdca.com
Ownership: Private
Year Founded: 1972
Number of Employees: 22
Partners:
Allan Benson; albenson@csdca.com

Doug Burns; dburns@csdca.com
Scott Craig; scraig@csdca.com
Wayne Haves; wayne@csdca.com
Ellen Murphy; ellen@csdca.com
Stan Nahrgang; scnca@csdca.com

Clarkson Rouble LLP
5190 Shuttle Dr.
Mississauga, ON L4W 4J8
905-629-4047
Fax: 905-629-3070
office@clarksonrouble.on.ca
clarksonrouble.on.ca/
Ownership: Partnership
Year Founded: 1965
Number of Employees: 24
Profile: The regional full-service chartered accounting firm has 11 chartered accountants dealing with a wide variety of owner-managed businesses.

Executives:
Larry L. Cook
Tom Rouble
Jim Scullion

Clewes & Associates Life Insurance Consultancy Inc.
#803, 251 Queen St. South
Mississauga, ON L5M 1L7
416-493-5586
Fax: 416-493-5061
clewesb@sympatico.ca
www.clewesconsult.com
Year Founded: 1983
Executives:
Brian D. Clewes

Cole & Partners
Also listed under: *Financial Planning*
#2000, 80 Richmond St. West
Toronto, ON M5H 2A4
416-364-9700
Fax: 416-364-9707
www.coleandpartners.com
Year Founded: 1975
Profile: Advisory services are provided in mergers, acquisitions, divestitures & corporate finance, as well as litigation consulting & business valutation. Services include business & securities valuations & investigative & forensic accounting. North American clients range from medium sized private companies to large public companies.

Executives:
Stephen R. Cole, Advisor, Corporate Finance; scole@cole&partners.com
Larry Andrade, Associate
Enzo Carlucci, Associate

Collins Barrow Chartered Accountants - Orangeville
Also listed under: *Trustees in Bankruptcy*
Mono Plaza
RR#4
Orangeville, ON L9W 2Z1
519-941-5526
Fax: 519-941-8721
orangeville@collinsbarrow.com
Partners:
Grant Bartlett; gbartlett@collinsbarrow.com
Kerry Butler; kbutler@collinsbarrow.com

Collins Barrow Chartered Accountants - Cambridge
Also listed under: *Trustees in Bankruptcy*
#600, 73 Water St. North
Cambridge, ON N1R 7L6
519-623-3820
Fax: 519-622-3144
cbcambridge@collinsbarrow.com
Ownership: Private.
Profile: The firm's services include the following: assurance, business advisory, tax strategies & trustee in bankruptcy. It is affiliated with MRI (Moores Rowland International).

Partners:
William G. Mitchell, Principal; wmitchell@collinsbarrow.com
Vinod Arya; varya@collinsbarrow.com
Brian W. Hanna; bhanna@collinsbarrow.com
Frank J. Jaglowitz; fjaglowitz@collinsbarrow.com

Collins Barrow Chartered Accountants - Chatham
Also listed under: *Trustees in Bankruptcy*
PO Box 218
150 Richmond St.
Chatham, ON N7M 5K3
519-351-2024
Fax: 519-351-8831
chatham@collinsbarrow.com
Partners:
John D. Aitken, Principal; jaitken@collinsbarrow.com
Paul Cudmore; pcudmore@collinsbarrow.com
Jack Lambe; jlambe@collinsbarrow.com
William Loucks; wloucks@collinsbarrow.com
James Moir; jmoir@collinsbarrow.com
Tracey Myers; tmyers@collinsbarrow.com
Michael Pestowka; mpestowka@collinsbarrow.com
Jane Rivers; jrivers@collinsbarrow.com

Collins Barrow Chartered Accountants - Chelmsford

Also listed under: *Trustees in Bankruptcy*
PO Box 673
48 Main St. East
Chelmsford, ON P0M 1L0
705-855-9024
Fax: 705-855-3693
chelmsford@collinsbarrow.com
Partners:
Richard A. Schaak; rschaak@collinsbarrow.com

Collins Barrow Chartered Accountants - Elora
Also listed under: *Trustees in Bankruptcy*
PO Box 580
342, Gerrie Rd.
Elora, ON N0B 1S0
519-846-5315
Fax: 519-846-9120
info@collinsbarrow.com
Partners:
Anthony P. Campagnolo; acampagnolo@collinsbarrow.com
Todd Campbell; tcampbell@cbelora.com
Keith A. McIntosh; kmcintosh@collinsbarrow.com
Ed Mitukiewicz; emitukiewicz@collinsbarrow.com
Dennis D. Zinger; dzinger@collinsbarrow.com

Collins Barrow Chartered Accountants - Hearst
Also listed under: *Financial Planning*
PO Box 637
1021 George St.
Hearst, ON P0L 1N0
705-362-4261
Fax: 705-362-4641
hearst@collinsbarrow.com
Ownership: Private.
Year Founded: 1983
Number of Employees: 17
Assets: Under $1 million Year End: 20051130
Revenues: $1-5 million Year End: 20051130
Executives:
Noël Cantin, Partner; ncantin@collinsbarrow.com
Denis P. Hébert, Partner; dhebert@collinsbarrow.com

Collins Barrow Chartered Accountants - Kapuskasing
Also listed under: *Trustees in Bankruptcy*
2 Ash St.
Kapuskasing, ON P5N 3H4
705-337-6411
Fax: 705-335-6563
kapuskasing@collinsbarrow.com
Partners:
Gilles R. Bisson; gbisson@collinsbarrow.com
Gérald Gagné; ggagne@collinsbarrow.com
Eric G. Gagnon; egagnon@collinsbarrow.com
Christiane Lapointe; clapointe@collinsbarrow.com

Collins Barrow Chartered Accountants - North Bay
Also listed under: *Trustees in Bankruptcy*
630 Cassells St.
North Bay, ON P1B 4A2
705-494-9336
Fax: 705-494-8783
northbay@collinsbarrow.com
Partners:
Daniel D. Longlade; dlonglade@collinsbarrow.com

Collins Barrow Chartered Accountants - Carleton Place
Also listed under: *Trustees in Bankruptcy*
143-A Bridge St.
Carleton Place, ON K7C 2V6
613-253-0014
Fax: 613-253-0129
carletonplace@collinsbarrow.com

Collins Barrow Chartered Accountants - Sarnia
Also listed under: *Trustees in Bankruptcy*
1350 L'Heritage Dr.
Sarnia, ON N7S 6H8
519-542-7725
Fax: 519-542-8321
sarnia@collinsbarrow.com
Partners:
David Coles; dcoles@collinsbarrow.com
Bruce W. Crerar; bcrerar@collinsbarrow.com
Larry H.A. Cross; lcross@collinsbarrow.com
Pat Filice; pfilice@collinsbarrow.com
Thomas Moore; tmoore@collinsbarrow.com

Collins Barrow Chartered Accountants - Sturgeon Falls
Also listed under: *Trustees in Bankruptcy*
PO Box 870
#A, 49 Queen St.
Sturgeon Falls, ON P2B 2C7
705-753-1830
Fax: 705-753-2496
sturgeonfalls@collinsbarrow.com
Partners:
Daniel Longlade; dlonglade@collinsbarrow.com

Collins Barrow Chartered Accountants - Sudbury
Also listed under: *Trustees in Bankruptcy*
1174 St. Jerome St.
Sudbury, ON P3A 2V9
705-560-5592
Fax: 705-560-8832
sudbury@collinsbarrow.com
Partners:
Robert Blais, Principal; roblais@collinsbarrow.com
Paul E. Arsenault
Marc A. Bertrand; mabertrand@collinsbarrow.com
Gary R. Crayen; gacrayen@collinsbarrow.com
Guy Desmarais; gudesmarais@collinsbarrow.com
Clément Y. Lafrenière
Gerald C.J. Lafrenière
Robert A. Mageau; romageau@collinsbarrow.com
Michel J. Paquette; mipaquette@collinsbarrow.com

Collins Barrow Chartered Accountants - Vaughan
Also listed under: *Trustees in Bankruptcy*
#600, 3300 Hwy. 7 West, 2nd Fl.
Vaughan, ON L4K 4M3
416-213-2600
Fax: 905-669-8705
info@collinsbarrowvaughan.com
Partners:
Gino F. Alberelli; galberelli@collinsbarrow.com
Joseph P. Colasanto; jcolasanto@collinsbarrow.com
Frank Fenos; ffenos@collinsbarrow.com
Richard N. Gargarella; rgargarella@collinsbarrow.com
Silvano Zamparo; szamparo@collinsbarrow.com

Collins Barrow Chartered Accountants - Waterloo
Also listed under: *Trustees in Bankruptcy*
554 Weber St. North
Waterloo, ON N2L 5C6
519-725-7700
Fax: 519-725-7708
cbwaterloo@collinsbarrow.com
Partners:
Faith E. Williamson, Principal
Tracey Denstedt
John H. Durland
David P. Webb

Collins Barrow Chartered Accountants - Banff
Also listed under: *Trustees in Bankruptcy*
Cascade Plaza
PO Box 1000
#370, 317 Banff Ave.
Banff, AB T1L 1H4

ACCOUNTING & LAW

Collins Barrow Chartered Accountants - Banff (continued)
403-762-8383
Fax: 403-762-8384
cbbanff@cbrockies.com
Partners:
Darcy J. Allan
Mark Bohnet
Brian J. Mitchell

Collins Barrow Chartered Accountants - Canmore
Also listed under: *Trustees in Bankruptcy*
#1, 714 - 10th St.
Canmore, AB T1W 2A6
403-678-4444
Fax: 403-678-5163
canmore@collinsbarrow.com
Partners:
Darcy J. Allan; dallan@collinsbarrow.com
Mark Bohnet; mbohnet@collinsbarrow.com
Brian Mitchell; bmitchell@collinsbarrow.com

Collins Barrow Chartered Accountants - Drayton Valley
Also listed under: *Trustees in Bankruptcy*
PO Box 6927
5204 - 52nd Ave.
Drayton Valley, AB T7A 1S3
780-542-4468
Fax: 780-542-5275
888-542-4468
draytonvalley@collinsbarrow.com
Partners:
Barry Carlson; bcarlson@collinsbarrow.ca
Kenneth Roberts; kroberts@collinsbarrow.com

Collins Barrow Chartered Accountants - Edmonton
Allstream Tower
#1550, 10250 - 101 St.
Edmonton, AB T5J 3P4
780-428-1522
Fax: 780-425-8189
edmonton@collinsbarrow.com
Ownership: Private
Year Founded: 1950
Number of Employees: 20
Assets: Under $1 million
Revenues: $1-5 million
Profile: The organization provides accounting & taxation services.

Partners:
Douglas G. Kroetsch; ext-234-; dkroetsch@collinsbarrow.com
Joseph Man; ext-232-; jman@collinsbarrow.com
Samuel C. Young; ext-228-; syoung@collinsbarrow.com

Collins Barrow Chartered Accountants - Red Deer
Also listed under: *Trustees in Bankruptcy*
#300, 5010 - 43 St.
Red Deer, AB T4N 6H2
403-342-5541
Fax: 403-347-3766
reddeer@collinsbarrow.com
www.collinsbarrowreddeer.ab.ca
Partners:
Bob Boser; bboser@collinsbarrow.com
Allan Collins; acollins@collinsbarrow.com
Robert A. Fischer; rfischer@collinsbarrow.com
Robin R. Kolton; rkolton@collinsbarrow.com
George R. Perry; gperry@collinsbarrow.com
Gary S. Pottage; gpottage@collinsbarrow.com
Marsha Smalley; msmalley@collinsbarrow.com
Grant Stange; gstange@collinsbarrow.com

Collins Barrow Chartered Accountants - Winnipeg
Also listed under: *Trustees in Bankruptcy*
Century Plaza
#401, 1 Wesley Ave.
Winnipeg, MB R3C 4C6
204-942-0221
Fax: 204-944-8371
winnipeg@collinsbarrow.com
Partners:
Gregory J. Bradshaw; gbradshaw@collinsbarrow.com
John A. Gray; jgray@collinsbarrow.com
Brian A. Hughes; bhughes@collinsbarrow.com
Robert A. McNamara; rmcnamara@collinsbarrow.com

Collins Barrow Chartered Accountants - Vancouver
Also listed under: *Trustees in Bankruptcy*
Burrard Bldg.
#800, 1030 West Georgia St.
Vancouver, BC V6E 3B9
604-685-0564
Fax: 604-685-2050
vancouver@collinsbarrow.com
Partners:
James R. Church; jchurch@collinsbarrow.com
Gordon C. Duff; cduff@collinsbarrow.com
Owen J. Manuel; omanuel@collinsbarrow.com
Harley Stanfield; hstanfield@collinsbarrow.com

Collins Barrow Chartered Accountants - Bobcaygeon
Also listed under: *Trustees in Bankruptcy*
PO Box 10
21 King St. West
Bobcaygeon, ON K0M 1A0
705-738-4166
Fax: 705-738-5787
bobcaygn@collinsbarrow.com

Collins Barrow Chartered Accountants - Lindsay
Also listed under: *Trustees in Bankruptcy*
237 Kent St. West
Lindsay, ON K9V 2Z3
705-324-5031
Fax: 705-328-3121
lindsay@collinsbarrow.com
Partners:
Erik J. Ellis; eellis@collinsbarrow.com
J. Hebert Gamble; hgamble@collinsbarrow.com
Mark Mooney; mmooney@collinsbarrow.com
Dennis W. Wright; dwright@collinsbarrow.com

Collins Barrow Chartered Accountants - Peterborough
Also listed under: *Trustees in Bankruptcy*
418 Sheridan St.
Peterborough, ON K9H 3J9
705-742-3418
Fax: 705-742-9775
peterborough@collinsbarrow.com
Partners:
Leah Curtis; lcurtis@collinsbarrow.com
Bob Fisher; bfisher@collinsbarrow.com
Steven Porter; sporter@collinsbarrow.com
Richard Steiginga; rsteiginga@collinsbarrow.com
J. Thomas Taylor; ttaylor@collinsbarrow.com

Collins Barrow Chartered Accountants - Ottawa
Also listed under: *Trustees in Bankruptcy*
#400, 301 Moodie Dr.
Ottawa, ON K2H 9C4
613-820-8010
Fax: 613-820-0465
ottawa@collinsbarrow.com
www.collinsbarrowottawa.com
Partners:
Bruce G. Brooks; bbrooks@collinsbarrow.com
David Brown; dbrown@collinsbarrow.com
T. Lynn Clapp
Dennis F. Medaglia; dmedaglia@collinsbarrow.com
Michael Merpaw; mmerpaw@collinsbarrow.com
David F. Muir; dmuir@collinsbarrow.com
Robert W. Rock; rrock@collinsbarrow.com
Kenneth Tammadge; ktammadge@collinsbarrow.com
D. Randy Tivy; rtivy@collinsbarrow.com
Joe Wattie; jwattie@collinsbarrow.com
Stewart A. Wilson; swilson@collinsbarrow.com

Collins Barrow Chartered Accountants - Manotick
PO Box 291
1136 Clapp Lane
Manotick, ON K4M 1A3
613-692-2553
Fax: 613-692-2995
manotick@collinsbarrow.com
www.collinsbarrow.com
Ownership: Private
Partners:
R. Jeffrey Sullivan

Collins Barrow Chartered Accountants - Kingston
Also listed under: *Trustees in Bankruptcy*
#301, 1471 Counter St.
Kingston, ON K7M 8S8
613-544-2903
Fax: 613-544-6151
kingston@collinsbarrow.com
Partners:
Brian Hogan; bhogan@collinsbarrow.com
Lennox Rowsell; lrowsell@collinsbarrow.com
Karen Sands; ksands@collinsbarrow.com
Brent Wilson; bwilson@collinsbarrow.com

Collins Barrow Chartered Accountants - Exeter
Also listed under: *Trustees in Bankruptcy*
PO Box 2405
412 Main St.
Exeter, ON N0M 1S7
519-235-0345
Fax: 519-235-3235
exeter@collinsbarrow.com
Partner:
Dan Daum; ddaum@collinsbarrow.com

Collins Barrow Chartered Accountants - London
Also listed under: *Trustees in Bankruptcy*
PO Box 5005
#700, 495 Richmond St.
London, ON N6A 5G4
519-679-8550
Fax: 519-679-1812
london@collinsbarrow.com
Partners:
Michael Bondy; mbondy@collinsbarrow.com
Jim Dunlop; jdunlop@collinsbarrow.com
Doug Greenhow; dgreenhow@collinsbarrow.com
Gerry Mills; gmills@collinsbarrow.com
Jason Timmermans; jtimmermans@collinsbarrow.com
David Wells; dwells@collinsbarrow.com

Collins Barrow Chartered Accountants - Waterloo National Office
Also listed under: *Trustees in Bankruptcy*
554 Weber St. North
Waterloo, ON N2L 5C6
519-725-7700
Fax: 519-725-7708
cbwaterloo@collinsbarrow.com
www.collinsbarrows.com
Partners:
Stephen Chris; sqchris@collinsbarrow.com
Todd MacDonald; tmacdonald@collinsbarrow.com
Ram Ramachandran; rramachandran@collinsbarrow.com

Collins Barrow Chartered Accountants - Stratford
Also listed under: *Trustees in Bankruptcy*
413 Hibernia St.
Stratford, ON N5A 5W2
519-272-0000
Fax: 519-272-0030
stratford@collinsbarrow.com
Partners:
Larry Batte; lbatte@collinsbarrow.com
Dan Daum; ddaum@collinsbarrow.com

Collins Barrow Leamington LLP
92 Talbot St. East
Leamington, ON N8H 1L3
519-326-2666
Fax: 519-326-7008
general@cbleamington.com
Former Name: Collins Barrow Enns Derksen LLP; Collins Barrow Chartered Accountants - Leamington
Assets: Under $1 million
Revenues: $1-5 million
Partners:
David H. Cornies
Jeff Kelly
Melchior Pace
Victor Penner; vicpenner@cbleamington.com
Ron Vandervecht

Collins Barrow Windsor LLP
Also listed under: *Trustees in Bankruptcy*
441 Pellissier St.
Windsor, ON N9A 4L2
519-258-5800
Fax: 519-256-6152
windsor@collinsbarrow.com
www.collinsbarrow.com
Executives:

Doug David, Partner; ddavid@collinsbarrow.com
Mike Frenette, Partner; mwfrenette@collinsbarrow.com
David Gardner, Partner; dgardner@collinsbarrow.com
Brenda J. Griffith, Partner; bgriffith@collinsbarrow.com
Carl Hooper, Partner; cehooper@collinsbarrow.com
Denise Hrastovec, Partner; dhrastovec@collinsbarrow.com
Paul Kale, Partner; pkale@collinsbarrow.com
Donald Marsh, Partner; djmarsh@collinsbarrow.com
Gary J. Waghorn, Partner; gwaghorn@collinsbarrow.com

Cookson Kooyman Chartered Accountants
#220, 5001 - 52nd St.
Lacombe, AB T4L 2A6
403-782-3361
Fax: 403-782-3070
lacombe@ckca.net

Cooper & Company Ltd.
Also listed under: *Trustees in Bankruptcy*
#108, 1120 Finch Ave. West
Toronto, ON M3J 3H7
416-665-3383
Fax: 416-665-0897
info@cooperco.ca
www.cooperco.ca
Former Name: Rumanek & Cooper Ltd.
Number of Employees: 8
Executives:
Donna Cairns, Partner
Branches:
Brampton
#200, 36 Queen St. East
Brampton, ON L6V 1A2 Canada
905-454-4510
Fax: 905-454-4632
Toronto - Bloor St.
#3140, 3300 Bloor St. West, 11th Fl.
Toronto, ON M8X 2X3 Canada
416-252-3440
Fax: 416-665-0897
Toronto - Lawrence Ave.
#211, 1719 Lawrence Ave. East
Toronto, ON M1R 2X7 Canada
416-759-4664
Fax: 416-759-8294

Craig & Ross Chartered Accountants
#1515, 1 Lombard Place
Winnipeg, MB R3B 0X3
204-956-9400
Fax: 204-956-9424
info@craigross.com
www.craigross.com
Profile: Provides a range of financial and technology solutions on a personal, consultative basis, with a focus on owner-managed companies and a depth of experience in the not-for-profit segment.

Executives:
John Craig, CA, Partner; 204-956-9401; jcraig@craigross.com
Hugh Ross, CA, Partner; 204-956-9404; hross@craigross.com

Curry & Betts
Admiral Beatty Building
PO Box 6789, A Stn. A
72 Charlotte St.
Saint John, NB E2L 4S2
506-635-8181
Fax: 506-633-5943
888-635-8181
curbetts@nbnet.nb.ca
www.curry-betts.ca
Profile: Provides a number of services including accounting, assurance and tax.

Executives:
Becky L. Betts, CA, Partner; 506-637-9922; bbetts@curry-betts.ca
Edward J. Betts, CA, Partner; 506-637-9921; ebetts@curry-betts.ca
Christopher J. Curry, CA, Partner; 506-637-9926; ccurry@curry-betts.ca

D&H Group
Also listed under: *Pension & Money Management Companies*
1333 West Broadway St., 10th Fl.
Vancouver, BC V6H 4C1
604-731-5881
Fax: 604-731-9923
info@dhgroup.ca
www.dhgroup.ca
Former Name: Dyke & Howard
Ownership: Private
Year Founded: 1952
Number of Employees: 50
Executives:
Larry Bisaro, Sr. Partner; lbisaro@dhgroup.ca
Arthur Azana; aazana@dhgroup.ca
Craig Cox; ccox@@dhgroup.ca
Gordon Cummings; gcummings@dhgroup.ca
Brant Grondin; bgrondin@dhgroup.ca
Tom Hamar; thamar@dhgroup.ca
Dennis Louie; dlouie@dhgroup.ca
Michael Louie; mlouie@dhgroup.ca
Bruce MacFarlane; bmacfarlane@dhgroup.ca
Michael Nakanishi; mnakanishi@dhgroup.ca
Michael Wong; mwong@dhgroup.ca

D.W. Robart Professional Corporation
Also listed under: *Financial Planning*
#1480, 540 - 5th Ave. SW
Calgary, AB T2P 0M2
403-266-2611
Fax: 403-265-8626
don@robart.ca
Ownership: Private
Executives:
D.W. Robart, RFP, President

Dallaire Forest Kirouac
#580, 1175, ave. Lavigne
Québec, QC
418-650-2266
Fax: 418-650-2529
877-650-2266
comptable@dfk.qc.ca
www.dfk.qc.ca
Year Founded: 1982
Number of Employees: 42

David Ingram & Associates
Also listed under: *Financial Planning*
329 Waverly St.
Ottawa, ON K2P 0V9
613-234-8023
Fax: 613-234-8925
info@accessfp.com
Ownership: Private
Year Founded: 1981
Profile: The company is affiliated with Gro-net Financial Tax & Pension Planners.

Davidson & Co.
Stock Exchange Tower
PO Box 10372
#1200, 609 Granville St.
Vancouver, BC V7Y 1G6
604-687-0947
Fax: 604-687-6172
davidson@davidson-co.com
www.davidson-co.com
Year Founded: 1984
Number of Employees: 40
Profile: The full service Chartered Accountancy firm is centrally located in downtown Vancouver. It offers accounting, audit, taxation, business consulting & computer expertise to individuals & to a wide variety of businesses in Canada & abroad.

Partners:
Brad Allen
Clark Anderson
Lise Bendrodt
Grant Block
Bill Davidson
Cyrus Driver
Dave Harris
Peter Maloff
Lori Oliver
Glenn Parchomchuk
Bob Poole
Guy Thomas

Deloitte & Touche LLP
PO Box 8
#1200, 2 Queen St. East
Toronto, ON M5C 3G7
416-874-3875
Fax: 416-874-3888
www.deloitte.ca
Ownership: Private partnership
Year Founded: 1861
Number of Employees: 5,568
Revenues: $500m-1 billion
Partners:
David Laidley, Chair
Alan MacGibbon, Managing Partner & CEO
Branches:
Alma
Complexe Jacques Gagnon
#110, 100, rue St-Joseph sud
Alma, QC G8B 7A6 Canada
418-669-6969
Fax: 418-668-2966
Amos
#200, 101, av 1re est
Amos, QC J9T 1H4 Canada
819-732-8273
Fax: 819-732-9143
Baie-Comeau
1191, boul Laflèche, 2e étage
Baie-Comeau, QC G5C 1E1 Canada
418-589-5761
Fax: 418-589-5764
Calgary
Scotia Centre
#3000, 700 - 2nd St. SW
Calgary, AB T2P 0S7 Canada
403-267-1700
Fax: 403-264-2871
Chicoutimi
#400, 901, boul Talbot
Chicoutimi, QC G7H 0A1 Canada
418-549-6650
Fax: 418-549-4694
Dolbeau-Mistassini
110, 8e av
Dolbeau-Mistassini, QC G8L 1Y9 Canada
418-276-0133
Fax: 418-276-8559
Edmonton
Manulife Place
#2000, 10180 - 101st St.
Edmonton, AB T5J 4E4 Canada
780-421-3611
Fax: 780-421-3782
Farnham
149, rue Desjardins est
Farnham, QC J2N 2W6 Canada
450-293-5327
Fax: 450-293-2817
Granby
PO Box 356
74, rue Court
Granby, QC J2G 4Y5 Canada
450-372-3347
Fax: 450-372-8643

Grand-Mère
PO Box 280
1671, 6e av
Grand-Mère, QC G9T 5K8 Canada
819-538-1721
Fax: 819-538-1882
Halifax
Purdy's Wharf Tower II
#1500, 1569 Upper Water St.
Halifax, NS B3J 3R7 Canada
902-422-8541
Fax: 902-423-5820
Hamilton
#202, 1005 Skyview Dr.
Hamilton, ON L7P 5B1 Canada
905-315-6770
Fax: 905-315-6700
866-836-6770
Hawkesbury

Deloitte & Touche LLP (continued)

300, rue McGill
Hawkesbury, ON K6A 1P8 Canada
613-632-4178
Fax: 613-632-7703

Jonquière
Complexe A E Fortin
2266, boul René Lévesque
Jonquière, QC G7S 6C5 Canada
418-542-9523
Fax: 418-542-8814

Kitchener
4210 King St. East
Kitchener, ON N2P 2G5 Canada
519-650-7600
Fax: 519-650-7601

La Baie
365, rue Victoria
La Baie, QC G7B 3M5 Canada
418-544-7313
Fax: 418-544-0275

La Sarre
226, 2e rue est
La Sarre, QC J9Z 2G9 Canada
819-339-5764
Fax: 819-333-2517

Langley
#225, 20316 - 56th Ave.
Langley, BC V3A 3Y7 Canada
604-534-7477
Fax: 604-534-4220

Laval
Les Tours Triomphe
#300, 2450, boul Daniel-Johnson
Laval, QC H7T 2S3 Canada
514-978-3500
Fax: 514-382-4984

London
One London Place
255 Queen's Ave., 7th Fl.
London, ON N6A 5R8 Canada
519-679-1880
Fax: 519-640-4625

Longueuil
Tour Est
#550, 1111, rue St-Charles ouest
Longueuil, QC J4K 5G4 Canada
450-670-4270
Fax: 450-670-6420

Magog
#203, 101, rue du Moulin
Magog, QC J1X 4A1 Canada
819-843-6596
Fax: 819-843-6931

Markham
#400, 15 Allstate Pkwy.
Markham, ON L3R 5B4 Canada
905-948-6200
Fax: 905-948-6250

Matane
750, rue de Phare ouest
Matane, QC G42 3N2 Canada
418-566-2637
Fax: 418-566-2830

Mississauga - Britannia Rd. East
#132, 425 Britannia Rd. East
Mississauga, ON L4Z 3E7 Canada
416-601-6150
Fax: 416-601-6151

Mississauga - City Centre Dr.
#1100, 1 City Centre Dr.
Mississauga, ON L5B 1M2 Canada
905-601-6150
Fax: 905-803-5101

Montréal
#3000, 1, Place Ville-Marie
Montréal, QC H3B 4T9 Canada
514-393-7115
Fax: 514-390-4100

Ottawa
#800, 100 Queen St.
Ottawa, ON K1P 5T8 Canada
613-236-2442
Fax: 613-236-2195

Prince Albert
#5, 77 - 15 St. East
Prince Albert, SK S6V 1E9 Canada
306-763-7411
Fax: 306-763-0191

Prince George
#500, 299 Victoria St.
Prince George, BC V2L 5B8 Canada
250-564-1111
Fax: 250-562-4950

Québec
#400, 925, ch Saint-Louis
Québec, QC G1S 4Z4 Canada
418-624-3333
Fax: 418-624-0414

Regina
Bank of Montreal Bldg.
#900, 2103 - 11th Ave.
Regina, SK S4P 3Z8 Canada
306-525-1600
Fax: 306-525-2244

Rimouski
#503, 320, rue St-Germain est
Rimouski, QC G5L 1C2 Canada
418-724-4136
Fax: 418-724-3807

Roberval
713, boul St-Joseph
Roberval, QC G8H 2L3 Canada
418-275-2111
Fax: 418-275-6398

Rouyn-Noranda
155, av Dallaire
Rouyn-Noranda, QC J9X 4T3 Canada
819-762-5764
Fax: 819-797-1471

Saint John
Brunswick House
PO Box 6549
44 Chipman Hill, 7th Fl.
Saint John, NB E2L 4R9 Canada
506-632-1080
Fax: 506-632-1210

Saint-Hyacinthe
2200, av Léon-Pratte
Saint-Hyacinthe, QC J2S 4B6 Canada
450-774-4000
Fax: 450-774-1709

Saskatoon
PCS Tower
#300, 122 - 1st Ave.
Saskatoon, SK S7K 7E5 Canada
306-343-4400
Fax: 306-343-4480

Sept-×les
#200, 421, av Arnaud
Sept-×les, QC G4R 3B3 Canada
418-962-2513
Fax: 418-968-6422

Sherbrooke
#300, 2727, rue King ouest
Sherbrooke, QC J1L 1C2 Canada
819-823-1616
Fax: 819-564-8078

St Catharines
75 Corporate Park Dr., 4th Fl.
St Catharines, ON L2S 3W2 Canada
905-323-6000
Fax: 905-323-6001

St-Félicien
1133, rue Notre-Dame
St-Félicien, QC G8K 1Z7 Canada
418-679-4711
Fax: 418-679-8723

St. John's
Fort William Bldg.
10 Factory Lane
St. John's, NL A1C 6H5 Canada
709-576-8480
Fax: 709-576-8460

Toronto - Bay St.
BCE Place, Bay Wellington Tower
#1400, 181 Bay St.
Toronto, ON M5J 2V1 Canada
416-601-6150
Fax: 416-601-6151

Toronto - King St.
#300, 121 King St.
Toronto, ON M5H 3T9 Canada
416-601-6150
Fax: 416-601-5901

Toronto - Yonge St.
North York City Centre
#1700, 5140 Yonge St.
Toronto, ON M2N 6L7 Canada
416-601-6150
Fax: 416-229-2524

Trois-Pistoles
3121, rue Notre-Dame, 2e étage
Trois-Pistoles, QC G0L 4K0 Canada
418-851-2232
Fax: 418-851-4244

Trois-Rivières
PO Box 1600
1660, rue Royale
Trois-Rivières, QC G9A 5L9 Canada
819-691-1212
Fax: 819-691-1127

Val-d'Or
#240, 450 - 3e av
Val-d'Or, QC J9P 1S2 Canada
819-825-4101
Fax: 819-825-1155

Vancouver
4 Bentall Centre
#2800, 1055 Dunsmuir St.
Vancouver, BC V7X 1P4 Canada
604-669-4466
Fax: 604-685-0395

Windsor
#200, 150 Ouellette Place
Windsor, ON N8Y 1L9 Canada
519-967-0388
Fax: 519-967-0324

Winnipeg
#2300, 360 Main St.
Winnipeg, MB R3C 3Z3 Canada
204-942-0051
Fax: 204-947-9390

Den Harder & McNames

174 Sydenham St. East
Aylmer, ON N5H 1L7
519-773-5348
Fax: 519-773-7409
den.mc@amtelecom.net

Desjardins & Company

PO Box 1600
4440 - 50 Ave.
St Paul, AB T0A 3A0
780-645-5516
Fax: 780-645-6010
office@desjardins-co.com
www.desjardins-co.com
Ownership: Private
Year Founded: 1979
Executives:
Donna Desjardins, Office Manager
Ray Desjardins

DFK Canada Inc.

1923 - 151 Ave.
Edmonton, AB T5Y 1W1
780-472-4334
Fax: 780-472-4334
lvarga@dfk.ca
www.dfk.ca

Dick Cook Whyte Schulli Chartered Accountants

#555, 999 - 8th St. SW
Calgary, AB T3K 2L2
403-245-1717
Fax: 403-244-9306
Former Name: Dick Cook Schulli Chartered Accountants
Executives:
Michael M. Shackleton

Dockrill Horwich Rossiter

#205, 362 Lacewood Dr.
Halifax, NS B3S 1M7
902-835-0232
Fax: 902-835-0060
dhr@dhrgroup.ca
Profile: Provides a wide range of public accounting, tax and business consulting services.

Executives:
Michael Dockrill, CA, Partner; MikeD@dhrgroup.ca
Jim Horwich, CA, Partner; JimH@dhrgroup.ca
Philip Rossiter, CA, Partner; PhilR@dhrgroup.ca

Dubé & Tétreault, CA

#200, 3065, chemin de Chambly
Longueil, QC J4L 1N3
450-442-0944
Fax: 450-442-2166
richard@dube-tetreault.com
www.dube-tetreault.com
Year Founded: 1988
Number of Employees: 10
Profile: Services provided include accounting, taxation, forensic accounting, financial services, administrative organization, financial management, training on accounting software and when needed, the purchase or sale of a business.

Executives:
Richard Dubé, CA, Partner; richard@dube-tetreault.com
Jacques Tétreault, CA, Partner; jacques@dube-tetreault.com

Duffy, Allain & Rutten LLP

908 The East Mall
Toronto, ON M9B 6K2
416-620-7740

Eidsvik & Co.

#303, 1100 Island Hwy.
Campbell River, BC V9W 8C6
250-286-6629
Fax: 250-286-6779
manager@eidsvik.com
www.eidsvik.com
Executives:
Chris Eidsvik; chris@eidsvik.com

Emondson Ball Davies LLP, Chartered Accountants

Also listed under: *Financial Planning*
#501, 10 Milner Business Ct.
Toronto, ON M1B 3C6
416-293-5560
Fax: 416-293-5377
www.ebdcas.com
Former Name: EBD Financial Planners Inc
Profile: The firm provides the following services to individuals & businesses: tax, financial planning, investment planning, estate planning & trust administration, documentation review & preparation, accounting & auditing, consulting, bookkeeping & preparation of business documentation.

Executives:
Roger E. Ball, Chartered Accountant
V.H. (Bert) Davies, Chartered Accountant
Joseph S. Macdonald, Chartered Accountant
Robert E. McLeod, Chartered Accountant
Branches:
Toronto - Lake Shore Blvd.
1840 Lake Shore Blvd. East
Toronto, ON M4L 6S8 Canada
416-988-7647
Fax: 416-293-5377

Ernst & Young LLP

Ernst & Young Tower, Toronto-Dominion Centre
PO Box 251
222 Bay St.
Toronto, ON M5K 1J7
416-864-1234
Fax: 416-864-1174
www.ey.com
Ownership: Private
Year Founded: 1864
Number of Employees: 2,907
Profile: The following services are offered: assurance & advisory business services; corporate finance; tax; & other services. It is affiliated with Ernst & Young Orenda Corporate Finance/EGAN LLP.

Executives:
Louis P. Pagnutti, Chair/CEO
Irene David
Guy Fréchette
Murray McDonald
Fiona Macfarlane
Paul Roberts

Evancic Perrault Robertson

Also listed under: *Trustees in Bankruptcy*
PO Box 21148, Maple Ridge Square Stn. Maple Ridge Square
Maple Ridge, BC V2X 17P
604-476-2009
Fax: 604-467-1219
eprnat@epr.ca
www.epr.ca
Ownership: Private
Year Founded: 1979
Profile: Canada's largest & leading full services firm of Certified General Accountants, with member offices across the country, EPR has an international reach through its strong affiliations with NACPAF (US-based national association of CPA firms) & with Morison International (UK-based global accountancy & law office network). EPR has an integrated approach to auditing, accounting, taxation, & management consulting.

Executives:
Paul Walker, Chair
Malcolm Walker, Exec. Director
Verle Spindor, National Administrator
Branches:
Abbotsford
#201, 2669 Langdon St.
Abbotsford, BC V2T 3L3 Canada
604-853-1538
Fax: 604-853-7178
eprabby@mindlink.net
Henry Raap, Partner
Bathurst
1460, av St. Peter
Bathurst, NB E2A 4V1 Canada
506-548-1984
Fax: 506-548-0904
eprbath@eprbathurst.ca
André Doucet, Partner
Bradford
PO Box 753
27 John St. West
Bradford, ON L3Z 2B3 Canada
905-778-8964
Fax: 905-775-9550
800-246-5591
bbcm@bellnet.ca
Michael Falcone
Calgary
#300, 10655 Southport Rd. SW
Calgary, AB T2W 4Y1 Canada
403-278-5800
Fax: 403-253-9479
general@eprcal.com
Les Willms, Partner
Chatham
40 Centre Sq.
Centre St.
Chatham, ON N7M 5W3 Canada
519-436-0556
Fax: 519-436-1291
rieger@ciaccess.com
Lance Rieger, Partner
Coquitlam
566 Lougheed Hwy., 2nd Fl.
Coquitlam, BC V3K 3S3 Canada
604-936-4377
Fax: 604-936-8376
eprcoq@eprcoq.com
www.eprcoq.com
Ken Richardson, Partner
Fort Erie
PO Box 277
178 Central Ave.
Fort Erie, ON L2A 5M9 Canada
905-871-6620
Fax: 905-871-2544
eprfeo@eprnia.ca
Rick Forbes, Partner
Fredericton
#205, 206 Rookwood Ave.
Fredericton, NB E3B 2M2 Canada
506-458-8620
Fax: 506-450-8286
eprfred@nbnet.nb.ca
Larry Johnston, Partner
Grande Prairie
#215, 10006 - 101st Ave.
Grande Prairie, AB T8V 0Y1 Canada
780-539-3400
Fax: 780-538-1544
epgrand@telusplanet.net
Lyle Molyneaux, Partner
Hamilton
176 Rymal Rd. East
Hamilton, ON L9B 1C2 Canada
905-388-7453
Fax: 905-388-7397
eprhamilton@iprimus.ca
Andrew Barber, Partner
Langley
20688 - 56 Ave.
Langley, BC V3A 3Z1 Canada
604-534-1441
Fax: 604-534-1491
pwalker@eprcga.com
www.eprcga.com
Paul Walker, Partner
London
#804, 150 Dufferin Ave.
London, ON N6A 5N6 Canada
519-434-5847
Fax: 519-645-0727
Don DiCarlo, Partner
Maple Ridge
22377 Dewdney Trunk Rd.
Maple Ridge, BC V2X 3J4 Canada
604-467-5561
Fax: 604-467-1219
eprmr@eprcga.com
www.eprcga.com
Patrick Smith, Partner
Miramichi
Waterfront Place
1773 Water St.
Miramichi, NB E1N 1B2 Canada
506-773-6990
Fax: 506-773-3197
eprmira@nbnet.nb.ca
Vicky Malone, Partner
Moncton
770 Main St.
Moncton, NB E1C 1E7 Canada
506-857-3893
Fax: 506-859-4148
Paul Robichaud, Partner
Niagara Falls
#7, 3930 Montrose Rd.
Niagara Falls, ON L2H 3C9 Canada
905-358-5729
Fax: 905-358-7188
eprnfo@eprnia.ca
Rick Forbes, Partner
North Vancouver
#102, 1975 Lonsdale Ave.
North Vancouver, BC V7M 2K3 Canada
604-987-8101
Fax: 604-987-1794
cga@eprnv.ca
Bill Perrault, Partner
Saint-Hyacinthe
#1, 540, boul Casavant ouest
Saint-Hyacinthe, QC J2S 7S3 Canada
450-774-7165
Fax: 450-774-1589
eprsthyacinthe@cgaquebec.com
Rene Benoit, Partner
Saskatoon
259 Robin Cres.
Saskatoon, SK S7L 6M8 Canada
306-934-3944
Fax: 306-934-3409
eprstoon@sasktel.net
Nanette Neumann, Partner
Slave Lake

ACCOUNTING & LAW

Evancic Perrault Robertson (continued)

405 - 6th Ave. SW
Slave Lake, AB T0G 2A4 Canada
780-849-4949
Fax: 780-849-3401
eprslave@telusplanet.net
Gordon Ferguson, Partner

St-Jérôme
#200, 36, rue de Martigny ouest
Saint-Jérome, QC J7Y 2E9 Canada
450-569-2641
Fax: 450-569-2647
François Marchand, Partner

St. John's
74 O'Leary Ave.
St. John's, NL A1B 2C7 Canada
709-726-0000
Fax: 709-726-2200
eprstjohns@hotmail.com
Gerald Kirby, Partner

Stonewall
Westside Plaza Mall
PO Box 1038
Main St.
Stonewall, MB R0C 2Z0 Canada
204-467-5566
Fax: 204-467-9133
eprstonewall@shawcable.com
Ryan Smith, Partner

Terrebonne
3300, boul des Entreprises
Terrebonne, QC J6X 4J8 Canada
450-477-0377
Fax: 450-477-4023
Christian Pimpare, Partner

Tilbury
40 Queen Sq.
Tilbury, ON N0P 2L0 Canada
519-682-2300
Fax: 519-682-0705
reiger@ciaccess.com

White Rock
#104, 1656 Martin Dr.
White Rock, BC V4A 5E7 Canada
604-536-7778
Fax: 604-536-7745
Glenn Parks, Partner

Winnipeg
#1010, 1661 Portage Ave.
Winnipeg, MB R3J 3T7 Canada
204-954-9690
Fax: 204-786-1003
bemond@mts.net
Barry Edmond, Partner

The Exchange LLP, Chartered Accountants

#100, 123 Bannatyne Ave.
Winnipeg, MB R3B 0R3
204-943-4584
Fax: 204-957-5195
info@exg.ca
www.exg.ca
Year Founded: 1962
Profile: Services provided include assurance, consulting, eBusiness, tax, supply chain security, & retail solutions.

Fine et associés/ Fine & Associates

5101, rue Buchan
Montréal, QC H4P 1S4
514-731-0761
Fax: 514-731-4639
Former Name: Fine Schwartz Uman Goldstein
Ownership: Partnership
Year Founded: 1950
Number of Employees: 15
Assets: Under $1 million
Revenues: $1-5 million
Partners:
Edward Fine
Allan Goldstein
Morris Katz
Eli Uman

Flood & Associates Consulting Ltd.

#410, 840 - 6 Ave. SW
Calgary, AB T2P 3E5
403-263-1523
Fax: 403-263-1524
flood_co@telusplanet.net
Former Name: Flood & Company
Ownership: Private
Year Founded: 1975
Number of Employees: 10
Executives:
Donald W. Flood, Partner
Glen S. Flood, Partner
Louisa K. Mung, Partner
William A. Shackleton, Partner
R. Bryan Whitby, Partner
James W. White, Partner

Fukushima Enstrom LLP

577 Eleventh Ave.
Thunder Bay, ON P7B 2R5
807-345-1393
Fax: 807-345-4630
mail@fe-llp.com
Year Founded: 1980
Number of Employees: 7
Assets: Under $1 million
Revenues: Under $1 million
Executives:
Douglas J. Enstrom
S. Gordon Fukushima

Gagnon, Moisan, Comptables agréés

#227, 945, av Newton
Québec, QC G1P 4M3
418-871-6262
Fax: 418-871-9526
www.fortune1000.ca/gagnon-moisan/
Profile: Offers accounting services to small businesses in the Quebec region.

Executives:
Jean-Paul Gagnon, CA
Sylvain Moisan, CA

Gagnon, Roy, Brunet & associés

#105, 3925, rue Rachel est
Montréal, QC H1X 3G8
514-255-1001
Also Known As: GRB & Associés
Ownership: Private
Year Founded: 1993
Number of Employees: 15
Executives:
Pierre St-Louis, Director
Rhéal Brunet, CA, Partner
Luc Dubé, CA, Partner
Donal Mailly, CA, Partner
Gratien Roy, CA, Partner

Galano, Enzo & Associates

#400, 20 Hughson St. South
Hamilton, ON L8N 2A1
905-528-0144
Fax: 905-528-0144
enzo@netinc.ca
Ownership: Private
Profile: The company provides consulting & management services, preparation of financial statements, tax preparation & filing for individuals & corporations. The fax is the same as the phone number.

Executives:
Enzo Galano, Proprietor

Gardner Zuk Dessen, Chartered Accountants

#205, 265 Rimrock Rd.
Toronto, ON M3J 3C6
416-631-9800
Fax: 416-631-9183
info@gzd.ca
www.gzd.ca
Executives:
Harvey Gardner, Partner
Sergio Urbano, Partner
Leonard Zuk, Partner

Gariépy, Gravel, Larouche comptables agréés S.E.N.C.

601, av du Cénacle
Beauport, QC G1E 6W4
418-666-3704
Fax: 418-666-6913
www.gglca.qc.ca
Executives:
Réjean Gariépy, CA; rejean.gariepy@gglca.qc.ca
Serge Gravel, CA; serge.gravel@gglca.qc.ca
Martin Larouche, CA; martin.larouche@gglca.qc.ca

Gaviller & Company LLP

PO Box 460
#201, 945 - 3rd Ave. East
Owen Sound, ON N4K 5P7
519-376-5850
Fax: 519-376-5532
800-567-7234
owensound@gaviller.on.ca
www.gaviller.on.ca
Ownership: Private
Year Founded: 1950
Number of Employees: 50
Partners:
James H. Kearns, B.Sc., CA
Karen L. Marcell, B.Math, CA, CFP
David J. Todd, B.Comm., CA, CFP
Robert J. Turbitt, BBA, CA, CFP
Branches:

Collingwood
115 Hurontario St.
Collingwood, ON L9Y 3Z4 Canada
705-445-2020
Fax: 705-444-5833
collingwood@gaviller.on.ca
Ian D. McAllister

Meaford
98 Sykes St. North
Meaford, ON N4L 1N8 Canada
519-538-1690
Fax: 519-538-5832
meaford@gaviller.on.ca
James H. Kearns

Walkerton
PO Box 129
7 Victoria St. South
Walkerton, ON N0G 2V0 Canada
519-881-2100
Fax: 519-881-2602
800-263-4088
walkerton@gaviller.on.ca
Joseph O. Heisz

Gestion Tellier St-Germain

PO Box 324, P.A.T. Stn. P.A.T.
11536 Lagauchetière
Montréal, QC H1B 5J5
514-640-8922
Fax: 514-640-4801
ghislaine@gestionrg.qc.ca
www.gestionrg.qc.ca
Year Founded: 1992
Profile: Full-service accounting firm which provides the following services: accounting, bookkeeping, financial & tax planning, GST & QST reports, source deductions reports, computerized payroll systems, financial statements, and incorporation applications.

Gitzel Krejci Dand Peterson

PO Box 460
4912 - 51 St.
Stettler, AB T0C 2L0
403-742-4431
Fax: 403-742-1266
877-742-4431
rdand@gkdpca.com
www.gkdpca.com
Ownership: Private
Year Founded: 1956
Number of Employees: 20
Assets: Under $1 million
Revenues: $1-5 million
Executives:
Rodney Dand, Contact

Goldsmith Hersh s.e.n.c.r.l.

#200, 1411, rue Fort
Montréal, QC H3H 2N6

514-933-8611
Fax: 514-933-1142
info@ghmca.com
www.gmhca.com
Number of Employees: 25
Profile: Medium-sized firm which provides services in accounting, auditing, forensic & valuations, information systems, taxation, estates & trusts, and non-profit organizations.

Executives:
Martin Goldsmith, CA, Partner; mgoldsmith@gmhca.com
Donald Hersh, CA, Partner; dhersh@gmhca.com
Jack Rosenthal, CA, Partner; jrosenthal@gmhca.com
Watson Woo, CA, Partner; wwoo@gmhca.com
Michael Yuck, CA, Partner; myuck@gmhca.com

Grant Thornton LLP

50 Bay St., 12th Fl.
Toronto, ON M5J 2Z8
416-366-4420
Fax: 416-360-4944
800-366-0100
national@grantthornton.ca
www.grantthornton.ca
Ownership: Private
Year Founded: 1939
Number of Employees: 1,172
Revenues: $100-500 million
Executives:
Alex MacBeath, CEO & Exec. Partner; amacbeath@grantthornton.ca
John Garritsen, Partner, Administration; jgarritsen@grantthornton.ca
John Holdstock, Partner, Client & Services; jholdstock@grantthornton.ca
Phil Noble, Chief Operating Officer; pnoble@grantthornton.ca
Donna Carmichael, Director, Marketing & Business Development; donnacarmichael@grantthornton.ca
Sharon Healy, Director, Human Resources; shealy@grantthornton.ca
Anita Ferrari, Regional Managing Partner; aferrari@grantthornton.ca
Kevin Ladner, Regional Managing Partner; kladner@grantthornton.ca
Rick Mudie, Regional Managing Partner; rmudie@grantthornton.ca
Glenn Williams, Regional Managing Partner; gwilliams@grantthornton.ca
Branches:

Antigonish
PO Box 1480
257 Main St.
Antigonish, NS B2G 2L7 Canada
902-863-4587
Fax: 902-863-0917
B.M. Cullen, Partner

Barrie
#205, 85 Bayfield St.
Barrie, ON L4M 3A7 Canada
705-730-6574
Fax: 705-730-6575
R.D. Woodman, Partner

Bathurst
Harbourview Pl.
PO Box 220
#500, 275 Main St.
Bathurst, NB E2A 3Z2 Canada
506-546-6616
Fax: 506-548-5622

Bridgewater
PO Box 220
166 North St.
Bridgewater, NS B4V 2V6 Canada
902-543-8115
Fax: 902-543-7707
R.W. Oakley, Partner

Calgary
#1000, 112 - 4th Ave. SW
Calgary, AB T3P 0H3 Canada
403-260-2500
Fax: 403-260-2571
G.G. McFarlane, Partner

Charlottetown
PO Box 187
#501, 199 Grafton St.
Charlottetown, PE C1A 7K4 Canada
902-892-6547
Fax: 902-566-5358
J.K. Ladner, Partner

Corner Brook
PO Box 356
#49, 51 Park St.
Corner Brook, NL A2H 6E3 Canada
709-634-4382
Fax: 709-634-9158
R.G. Flynn, Partner

Dartmouth
#301, 238A Brownlow Ave
Dartmouth, NS B3B 2B4 Canada
902-463-4900
Fax: 902-492-2860
R.S. Jamieson, Partner

Digby
Basin Place
PO Box 848
68 Water St.
Digby, NS B0V 1A0 Canada
902-245-2553
Fax: 902-245-6161
Digby@GrantThornton.ca
M. Rutherford, Partner

Edmonton
Scotia Place 2
#1401, 10060 Jasper Ave. NW
Edmonton, AB T5J 3R8 Canada
780-422-7114
Fax: 780-426-3208
G.G. McFarlane, Partner

Fredericton
PO Box 1054
#400, 570 Queen St.
Fredericton, NB E3B 5C2 Canada
506-458-8200
Fax: 506-453-7029
Bruce Lewis, Partner

Grand Falls - Windsor
PO Box 83
9 High St.
Grand Falls-Windsor, NL A2A 2J3 Canada
709-489-6622
Fax: 709-489-6625
K. Simms, Principal

Halifax
Cogswell Tower
#1100, 2000 Barrington St.
Halifax, NS B3J 3K1 Canada
902-421-1734
Fax: 902-420-1068
Michele Williams, Partner

Hamilton
Standard Life Centre
#1040, 120 King St. West
Hamilton, ON L8P 4V2 Canada
905-525-1930
Fax: 905-527-4413
D.A. MacLean, Partner

Kelowna
200 Ellis St.
Kelowna, BC V1Y 2A8 Canada
250-712-6800
Fax: 250-661-3416
J.P. Mills, Partner

Kentville
PO Box 68
15 Webster St.
Kentville, NS B4N 3V9 Canada
902-678-7307
Fax: 902-679-1870
G.B. Caldwell, Partner

Langley
#200, 20033 - 64th Ave.
Langley, BC V2Y 1M9 Canada
604-532-3761
Fax: 604-532-8130
T.G. Davies, Partner

London
#902, 150 Dufferin Ave.
London, ON N6A 5N6 Canada
519-672-2930
Fax: 519-672-6455
P.R. Coleman, Partner

Markham
#200, 15 Allstate Pkwy.
Markham, ON L3R 5B4 Canada
905-475-1100
Fax: 905-475-8906
A.R. Byrne, Partner

Marystown
PO Box 518
2 Queen St.
Marystown, NL A0E 2M0 Canada
709-279-2300
Fax: 709-279-2340
Marystown@GrantThornton.ca

Miramichi
135 Henry St.
Miramichi, NB E1V 2N5 Canada
506-622-0637
Fax: 506-622-5174
H.K. Raper, Partner

Mississauga
#401, 350 Burnhamthorpe Rd. West
Mississauga, ON L5R 3J1 Canada
905-804-0905
Fax: 905-804-0509
G.R. Popp, Partner

Moncton
PO Box 1005
#500, 633 Main St.
Moncton, NB E1C 8P2 Canada
506-857-0100
Fax: 506-857-0105
Jean Marc Delaney, Partner

Montague
PO Box 70
1 Bailey Dr.
Montague, PE C0A 1R0 Canada
902-838-4121
Fax: 902-838-4802
C. Chapman, Partner

New Glasgow
PO Box 427
610 East River Rd.
New Glasgow, NS B2H 5E5 Canada
902-752-8393
Fax: 902-752-4009
B.L. Wilson, Partner

New Liskeard
PO Box 2170
17 Wellington St.
New Liskeard, ON P0J 1P0 Canada
705-647-8100
Fax: 705-647-7026
R.R. Hacquard, Partner

New Westminster
628 - 6th Ave., 6th Fl.
New Westminster, BC V3M 6Z1 Canada
604-521-3761
Fax: 604-521-8170
R.W. Mudie, Partner

North Bay
#200, 222 McIntyre St. West
North Bay, ON P1B 2Y8 Canada
705-472-6500
Fax: 705-472-7760
G.G. Weckwerth, Partner

Orillia
279 Coldwater Rd. West
Orillia, ON L3V 3M1 Canada
705-326-7605
Fax: 705-326-0837
R.D. Woodman, Partner

Port Colborne
PO Box 336
222 Catharine St, #B
Port Colborne, ON L3K 5W1 Canada
905-834-3651
Fax: 905-834-5095
J. Brennan, Principal

Saint John
Brunswick House
44 Chipman Hill, 4th Fl.
Saint John, NB E2L 2A9 Canada
506-634-2900
Fax: 506-634-4569
G. Dewar, Partner

ACCOUNTING & LAW

Grant Thornton LLP (continued)
Sault Ste Marie
421 Bay St., 5th Fl.
Sault Ste Marie, ON P6A 1X3 Canada
705-945-9700
Fax: 705-945-9705
B.C. Magill, Partner
St Catharines
PO Box 2011
#304, 55 King St. West
St Catharines, ON L2R 3H5 Canada
905-688-4822
Fax: 905-688-4837
L. MacKenzie, Partner
St. John's
PO Box 8037
187 Kenmount Rd.
St. John's, NL A1B 3P9 Canada
709-722-5960
Fax: 709-722-7892
Jeff Pardy, Partner
Summerside
Royal Bank Bldg.
PO Box 1660
220 Water St.
Summerside, PE C1N 2V5 Canada
902-436-9155
Fax: 902-436-6913
L.B. Murray, Partner
Sydney
George Place
#200, 500 George St.
Sydney, NS B1P 1K6 Canada
902-562-5581
Fax: 902-562-0073
J. MacNeil, Partner
Thunder Bay
#300, 979 Alloy Dr.
Thunder Bay, ON P7B 5Z8 Canada
807-345-6571
Fax: 807-345-0032
D. Vanderwey, Partner
Truro
PO Box 725
#400, 35 Commercial St.
Truro, NS B2N 5E8 Canada
902-893-1150
Fax: 902-893-9757
G.D. Hutchings, Partner
Vancouver
#1600, 333 Seymour St.
Vancouver, BC V6B 0A4 Canada
604-687-2711
Fax: 604-685-6569
Vancouver@GrantThornton.ca
P.B. Noble, Partner
Victoria
888 Fort St., 3rd Fl.
Victoria, BC V8W 1H8 Canada
250-383-4191
Fax: 250-381-4623
S. Mehinagic, Partner
Wetaskiwin
5108 - 51st Ave.
Wetaskiwin, AB T9A 0V2 Canada
780-352-1679
Fax: 780-352-2451
T.R. Bolivar, Partner
Winnipeg
#900, 1 Lombard Pl.
Winnipeg, MB R3B 0X3 Canada
204-944-0100
Fax: 204-957-5442
D.H. Anthony, Partner
Yarmouth
PO Box 297
328 Main St.
Yarmouth, NS B5A 4B2 Canada
902-742-7842
Fax: 902-742-0224
M. Rutherford, Partner

Hamilton & Rosenthal Chartered Accountants
1034 - 8th Ave. SW
Calgary, AB T2P 1J2
403-266-2175
Fax: 403-514-2211
www.hamrose.com
Ownership: Private
Year Founded: 1988
Number of Employees: 5
Partners:
Debbie Bosomworth; 403-514-2224; bosomworth@hamrose.com
David Hamilton; 403-514-2216; hamilton@hamrose.com
Cathy Madley; 403-226-2176; madley@hamrose.com
Susan Mayfield; 403-514-2222; mayfield@hamrose.com
Jayda Rosenthal; 403-514-2200; rosenthal@hamrose.com

Harel Drouin - PKF
#1200, 215, rue Saint-Jacques
Montréal, QC H2Y 1M6
514-845-9253
Fax: 514-845-3859
info@hd-pkf.ca
Profile: Provides services in general assurance & accounting, taxation, scientific research & experimental development, financing, and forensic accounting.

Executives:
Gilles Drouin, CA, Partner; gdrouin@hd-pkf.ca
G. André Harel, CA, Partner; aharel@hd-pkf.ca

Harendorf, Lebane, Moss LLP
#200, 8500 Leslie St.
Thornhill, ON L3T 7M8
905-886-8812
Fax: 905-886-6034
888-337-9222
hlm@hlmca.com
www.hlmca.com
Year Founded: 1967
Partners:
Jeff S. Ambrose; jeff@hsmca.ca
Irvin W. Harendorf; irv@hsmca.ca
Maurice A. Moss; maurice@hsmca.ca
Sandy Shessel; sandy@hsmca.ca

Hawkings Epp Dumont Chartered Accountants
#101, 17107 - 107 Ave.
Edmonton, AB T5S 1G3
780-489-9606
Fax: 780-484-9689
www.hawkings.com
Ownership: Private
Year Founded: 1962
Number of Employees: 25
Executives:
Wayne Dumont, Partner
Michael Epp, Partner
E.A. Hawkings, Partner
Branches:
Stony Plain
#101, 5300 - 50th St.
Stony Plain, AB T7Z 1T8 Canada
780-963-2727
Fax: 780-963-1294

Hébert, Turgeon, CGA
#250, 3930, montée Saint-Hubert
Saint-Hubert, QC J3Y 7K1
450-676-0624
Fax: 450-676-7677
info@htcga.qc.ca
www.htcga.qc.ca
Year Founded: 1983
Profile: Services provided include taxation, accounting, finance & management, and starting businesses.

Executives:
Micheline Hébert, CGA
Robert Turgeon, CGA

Herpers Chagani Gowling Inc.
***Also listed under:** Trustees in Bankruptcy*
#300, 4 Hughson St. South
Hamilton, ON L8N 3Z1
905-529-3328
Fax: 905-529-3980
888-735-9909
www.bankruptcyanswers.com
Former Name: Herpers Gowling Inc.
Also Known As: 310DEBT
Ownership: Private
Year Founded: 1996
Number of Employees: 33
Executives:
Alex Herpers, President
Mahmood Chagani, Vice-President
David Gowling, Vice-President
Branches:
Brampton
152 Queen St. East
Brampton, ON L6V 1B2 Canada
905-310-3328
Brantford
20B Borden St.
Brantford, ON N3R 2G8 Canada
519-310-3328
Burlington
#316, 2289 Fairview St.
Burlington, ON L7R 2E3 Canada
905-310-3328
Cambridge
19 Thorne St.
Cambridge, ON N1R 1S3 Canada
519-310-3328
Guelph
#202, 727 Woolwich St.
Guelph, ON N1H 3Z2 Canada
519-310-3328
Hamilton - Greenhill Ave.
#10, 625 Greenhill Ave.
Hamilton, ON L8K 5W9 Canada
905-529-3328
Hamilton - Upper Wentworth St.
836 Upper Wentworth St.
Hamilton, ON L9A 4W4 Canada
Kitchener
#706, 30 Duke St. West
Kitchener, ON N2H 3W5 Canada
London - Dundas St.
#5, 1700 Dundas St.
London, ON N5W 3C9 Canada
London - Wellington Rd. South
#209, 1069 Wellington Rd. South
London, ON N6E 2H6 Canada
Mississauga
#200, 33 City Centre Dr.
Mississauga, ON L5B 2N5 Canada
905-949-4555
Niagara Falls
4668 St. Clair Ave.
Niagara Falls, ON L2E 6X7 Canada
905-310-3328
Oakville
235 Lakeshore Rd.
Oakville, ON L6J 1H7 Canada
Simcoe
23 Argyle St.
Simcoe, ON N3Y 4N5 Canada
905-310-3328
St Catharines
#415, 80 King St.
St Catharines, ON L2R 7G1 Canada
905-310-3328
Stratford
100 Erie St.
Stratford, ON N5A 2M4 Canada
519-310-3328
Welland
32 East Main St.
Welland, ON L3G 3W3 Canada
905-310-3328

Hillson & Co. LLP
#8, 350 Speedvale Ave. West
Guelph, ON N1H 7M7
519-821-3011
Fax: 519-821-3240
www.hillson.ca
Partners:
David L. Bell; dbell@hillson.ca
Arlene Campbell; acampbell@hillson.ca
H. Kevin Embree; kembree@hillson.ca
Joanne F. Pucchio; jpucchio@hillson.ca
Peter M. Tonin; pmt@hillson.ca

Branches:
Cambridge
76 George St. North
Cambridge, ON N1S 2N2 Canada
519-621-5660

Hounjet Tastad
#2, 2220 Northridge Dr.
Saskatoon, SK S7L 6X8
306-653-5100
Fax: 306-653-5141
hounjet@sk.sympatico.ca
Former Name: Hounjet & Company
Ownership: Private
Year Founded: 1995
Number of Employees: 8
Executives:
Roseline Hounjet, Partner; roseline@hounjettastad.ca
Allyn Tastad, Partner; allyn@hounjettastad.ca

Hunter Belgrave Adamson
Cambridge 1
#200, 202 Brownlow Ave.
Dartmouth, NS B3B 1T5
902-468-1949
Fax: 902-468-4865
service@achba.ca
Year Founded: 1991
Profile: Full service CA firm offering tax, estate and financial planning services as well as tax compliance, financial statements and financial projections. Also advises owner-managed businesses on financing, computer systems and related matters.

Executives:
Boyd Hunter, CA, CFP, Partner; boyd@achba.ca
Rosemary Belgrave, CA, Partner; rosemary@achba.ca
Tracy Adamson, CA, CFP, Partner; tracy@achba.ca

Info Comptabilité Plus
#201, 2035, Côte de Liesse
Montréal, QC H4N 2M5
514-337-2677
Fax: 514-337-1594
info@infocplus.com
www.infocplus.com
Executives:
Bassam Yared, Director

J. Kromida, Chartered Accountant
#550, 100, Alexis Nihon
Montréal, QC H4M 2P1
514-747-3413
Fax: 514-747-0799
jamesk@kromida.com
www.kromida.com
Year Founded: 1984
Profile: Provides a wide range of accounting, tax and consulting services to both corporations and individuals.

Executives:
James Kromida, CA; jamesk@kromida.com

J. Pike & Company
PO Box 1031
Corner Brook, NL A2H 6J3
709-639-7774
Fax: 709-639-7775
ajpca@roadrunner.nf.net

Jacques Davis Lefaivre & Associés
#1900, 1080, côte du Beaver Hall
Montréal, QC H2Z 1S8
514-878-2600
Fax: 514-878-2600
800-363-6800
jdl@jdl.ca
Ownership: Private
Year Founded: 1958
Number of Employees: 40
Executives:
Robert Gratton, CA, Associé
Pierre Guertin, CA, Associé
Jacques Mailloux, CGA
Luc Massé, Avocat
Louise Papin, CA, Associée
Pierre Poirier, CA, Associé
Lucette Poliquin, CA, Associée

Affiliated Companies:
Lefaivre Labrèche Gagné, sencrl
Martin, Boulard & Associés, sencrl

Jean J. Drouin, CGA
#201, 6455, rue Christophe-Colomb
Montréal, QC H2S 2G5
514-274-6831
Fax: 514-274-8128
info@drouin-cga.com
http://drouin-cga.com
Profile: Services provided include accounting, taxation, financial statements, bookkeeping, and payroll.

Executives:
Jean J. Drouin, CGA

Jody Murphy, Chartered Accountant
PO Box 508
437 Creston Blvd.
Creston, NL A0E 1K0
709-279-1888
Fax: 709-279-1895
jmurphyca@nf.sympatico.ca
Executives:
Jody Murphy, CA, CFP

John Van Dyk, Professional Corporation
#801B, 3 Ave. South
Lethbridge, AB T1J 2B9
403-317-4500
Fax: 403-317-4501
justin.vandyk@telus.net
Executives:
John Van Dyk, CA

Kanester Johal Chartered Accountants
***Also listed under:** Financial Planning*
#208, 3993 Henning Dr.
Burnaby, BC V5C 6P7
604-451-8300
Fax: 604-451-8301
info@kjca.com
www.kjca.com
Ownership: Private.
Year Founded: 1992
Number of Employees: 15
Assets: Under $1 million
Revenues: $1-5 million
Executives:
Narinder Johal, Partner
Satpal S. Johl, Partner
Jeannie Wong, Contact

Kendall Wall Pandya, Chartered Accountants
118 Cree Rd.
Thompson, MB R8N 0C1
204-778-7312
Fax: 204-778-7919
Executives:
Robert Wall

Kenneth Michalak
1576 Bloor St. West
Toronto, ON M6P 1A4
416-588-2808
Fax: 416-588-3634
866-258-4788
kenmicha@look.ca
kenmichalakcga.com
Ownership: Private
Year Founded: 1986
Number of Employees: 6
Executives:
Kenneth Michalak, Contact

Kentner, Kelly & Wilson
15 Barrie Blvd.
St Thomas, ON N5P 4B9
519-631-6360
Fax: 519-631-2198
www.kkw.on.ca
Ownership: Private
Number of Employees: 9
Partners:
Jim Kee
Wayne Kentner
Don Wilson

Kenway Mack Slusarchuk Stewart LLP
#220, 333 - 11 Ave. SW
Calgary, AB T2R 1L9
403-233-7750
Fax: 403-266-5267
info@kmss.ca
www.kmss.ca
Ownership: Private
Year Founded: 1986
Number of Employees: 50
Partners:
Roland Bishop; rbishop@kmss.ca
Carol A. Chester, CA,MBA; cchester@kmss.ca
Bryce P. Eidsness; beidsness@kmss.ca
Gary L. Gray; ggray@kmss.ca
Bruce J. Kenway; bkenway@kmss.ca
Raymond P. Mack; rmack@kmss.ca
Kirby Rogers; krogers@kmss.ca
Barry J. Slusarchuk; bslusarchuk@kmss.ca
David Somerville; dsomerville@kmss.ca
N. Calvin Stewart; cstewart@kmss.ca
Scott Timson; stimson@kmss.ca
John Tobin; jtobin@kmss.ca
Branches:
Banff
PO Box 930
201 Bear St.
Banff, AB T1L 1A9 Canada
403-762-2271
Fax: 403-762-8817

Kestenberg, Rabinowicz & Partners
2797 John St.
Markham, ON L3R 2Y8
905-946-1300
Fax: 905-946-9797
enquiries@krp.ca
www.krp.ca
Ownership: Private
Year Founded: 1973
Number of Employees: 25
Assets: $1-5 million
Revenues: $1-5 million
Executives:
Hartley Cohen
Marshall Egelnick
George Grigano
Vazken Izakel
Harvey Kestenberg
Harris Kligman
Ralph Rabinowicz
Larry Stockhamer

King & Company
#1201, Energy Sq.
10109 - 106 St.
Edmonton, AB T5J 3L7
780-423-2437
Fax: 780-426-5861
Executives:
Edward King
Kenneth E. King
Gary G. Kleebaum
Richard S. Pirnak
Hector R. Therrien
Michael G. Troke

Kingston Ross Pasnak LLP Chartered Accountants
#2900 Bell Tower
10104 - 103rd Ave.
Edmonton, AB T5J 0H8
780-424-3000
Fax: 780-429-4817
info@krpgroup.com
www.krpgroup.com
Ownership: Private
Year Founded: 1990
Number of Employees: 70
Partners:
Robert Wilson, CA, CEO; manderson@krpgroup.com
Barth W. Bradley, CA; bbradley@krpgroup.com
Neil Cockburn, CA; ncockburn@krpgroup.com
Robert M. Heron, CA. CFP; rheron@krpgroup.com
Harold M. Kingston, CA, CFP, TEP; hkingston@krpgroup.com
Deanna Muise, CA, TEP; dmuise@krpgroup.com
Kenneth M. Pasnak, CA; kpasnak@krpgroup.com

Kingston Ross Pasnak LLP Chartered Accountants (continued)
Randy Popik, B.Comm., CA, CBV, ASA; rpopik@krpgroup.com
Brian D. Rosser, CMA., CA; brosser@krpgroup.com

Knowles Warkentin & Bridges, Chartered Accountants

#800, 125 Garry St.
Winnipeg, MB R3C 3P2
204-982-3878
Fax: 204-982-3888
connor@kwb.ca
www.kwb.ca
Profile: Provides acccounting services to Manitoba farmers.

Executives:
Connor Bridges, CA, Partner
Branches:
Gimli
72 Centre St.
Gimli, MB R0C 1B0 Canada
204-642-5020
Fax: 204-642-5121
ray@kwb.ca
Niperville
Main St.
Niperville, MB R0A 1E0 Canada
204-388-6303
connor@kwb.ca

Koehli Wickenberg Chartered Accountants

#105, 4990 - 92nd Ave.
Edmonton, AB T6B 2V4
780-466-6204
Fax: 780-466-6262
Info@partnershipaccounting.ca
www.partnershipaccounting.ca/

Koster, Spinks & Koster LLP(KSK)

4 Glengrove Ave. West
Toronto, ON M4R 1N4
416-489-8100
Fax: 416-489-9194
info@ksk.ca
www.ksk.ca
Ownership: Private partnership
Year Founded: 1978
Number of Employees: 40
Profile: Services include financial, tax & strategic planning.

Partners:
Jeffrey D. Spinks, CA, Managing Partner
Graeme R. Duff, CA
Mark Humphrey
Blair Kennedy, CA
Michael Koster, CA
Paul Koster, CA
Gyan P. Sharma, CA

KPMG

Also listed under: *Trustees in Bankruptcy*
Box 31, Commerce Court Postal Station, Commerce Court West
199 Bay St.
Toronto, ON M5L 1B2
416-777-8500
Fax: 416-777-8818
webmaster@kpmg.ca
www.kpmg.ca
Ownership: Private
Year Founded: 1860
Number of Employees: 4,500
Assets: $500m-1 billion Year End: 20051001
Revenues: $500m-1 billion Year End: 20051001
Executives:
Bill Mackinnon, Chair/CEO
Peter Chiddy, Managing Partner, Advisory Services
Bruce Glexman, Managing Partner, Tax
Paul Weiss, Managing Partner, Audit
Bill Dillabough, Chief Marketing Officer
Mary Lou Hamher, CFO
Elizabeth Wilson, Chief HR Officer
Branches:
Abbotsford
32575 Simon Ave.
Abbotsford, BC V2T 4W6 Canada
604-854-2200
Fax: 604-853-2756
Burnaby
#2400, 4720 Kingsway
Burnaby, BC V5H 4N2 Canada
604-527-3600
Fax: 604-527-3636
Calgary
Bow Valley Square II
#1200, 205 - 5th Ave. SW
Calgary, AB T2P 4B9 Canada
403-691-8000
Fax: 403-691-8008
Jason Brown, Partner, Audit
Chilliwack
#200, 9123 Mary St.
Chilliwack, BC V2P 4H7 Canada
604-793-4700
Fax: 604-793-4747
Edmonton
Commerce Pl.
10125 - 102 St.
Edmonton, AB T5J 3V8 Canada
780-429-7300
Fax: 780-429-7379
Robert Borrelli, Partner, Audit
Fredericton
Frederick Sq., TD Tower
#700, 77 Westmorland St.
Fredericton, NB E3B 6Z3 Canada
506-452-8000
Fax: 506-450-0072
Todd MacIntosh, Partner, Tax
Halifax
Purdy's Wharf, Tower One
#1500, 1959 Upper Water St.
Halifax, NS B3J 3N2 Canada
902-429-6000
Fax: 902-423-1307
Gregory Simpson, Partner, Tax
Hamilton
Commerce Place
#700, 21 King St. West
Hamilton, ON L8P 4W7 Canada
905-523-8200
Fax: 905-523-2222
Kamloops
#200, 206 Seymour St.
Kamloops, BC V2C 6P5 Canada
250-372-5581
Fax: 250-828-2928

Kelowna
#300, 1674 Bertram St.
Kelowna, BC V1Y 9G4 Canada
250-763-5522
Fax: 250-763-0044
Kingston
#400, 863 Princess St.
Kingston, ON K7L 5N4 Canada
613-549-1550
Fax: 613-549-6349
Lethbridge
Lethbridge Centre Tower
#500, 400 - 4th Ave. South
Lethbridge, AB T1J 4E1 Canada
403-380-5700
Fax: 403-380-5760
London
#1400, 140 Fullarton St.
London, ON N6A 5P2 Canada
519-672-4880
Fax: 519-672-5684
Moncton
Place Marvin's
One Factory Lane
Moncton, NB E1C 9M3 Canada
506-856-4400
Fax: 506-856-4499
Montréal
#1900, 2000, av McGill College
Montréal, QC H3A 3H8 Canada
514-840-2100
Fax: 514-840-2187
Philippe Grubert, Partner, Audit
North Bay
PO Box 990
#300, 925 Stockdale Rd.
North Bay, ON P1B 8K3 Canada
705-472-5110
Fax: 705-472-1249
Ottawa
World Exchange Plaza
#1000, 45 O'Connor St.
Ottawa, ON K1P 1A4 Canada
613-212-5764
Fax: 613-212-2896
Andrew Newman, Partner, Audit
Penticton
498 Ellis St., 2nd Fl.
Penticton, BC V2A 4M2 Canada
250-492-8444
Fax: 250-492-8688
Prince George
#400, 177 Victoria St.
Prince George, BC V2L 5R8 Canada
250-563-7151
Fax: 250-563-5693
Regina
McCallum Hill Centre, Tower II
1881 Scarth St., 20th Fl.
Regina, SK S4P 4K9 Canada
306-791-1200
Fax: 306-757-4703
Saint John
Harbour Bldg.
PO Box 2388
#306, 133 Prince William St.
Saint John, NB E2L 3V6 Canada
506-634-1000
Fax: 506-633-8828
Saskatoon
#600, 128 - 4th Ave. South
Saskatoon, SK S7K 1M8 Canada
306-934-6200
Fax: 306-934-6233
Sault Ste Marie
#200, 111 Elgin St.
Sault Ste Marie, ON P6A 6L6 Canada
705-949-5811
Fax: 705-949-0911
St Catharines
#901, One Saint-Paul St.
St Catharines, ON L2R 7L2 Canada
905-685-4811
Fax: 905-682-2008
Sudbury
Claridge Executive Centre
144 Pine St.
Sudbury, ON P3C 1X3 Canada
705-675-8500
Fax: 705-675-7586
Laurie Bissonette, Partner, Audit
Sydney
Commerce Tower
15 Dorchester St., 5th Fl.
Sydney, NS B1P 5Y9 Canada
902-539-3900
Fax: 902-564-6062
Toronto
Yonge Corporate Centre
#200, 4100 Yonge St.
Toronto, ON M2P 2H3 Canada
416-228-7000
Fax: 416-228-7123
Vancouver
Pacific Centre
PO Box 10426
777 Dunsmuir St.
Vancouver, BC V7Y 1K3 Canada
604-691-3000
Fax: 604-691-3031
Jim Bennett, Partner, Audit
Vernon
Credit Union Bldg.
3205 - 32 St., 3rd Fl.
Vernon, BC V1T 9A2 Canada
250-503-5300
Fax: 250-545-6440
Waterloo
Marsland Centre
#300, 20 Erb St. West
Waterloo, ON N2L 1T2 Canada

519-747-8800
Fax: 519-747-8811
Shelley Wickenheiser, Partner, Tax
Windsor
Greenwood Centre
#618, 3200 Deziel Dr.
Windsor, ON N8W 5K8 Canada
519-251-3500
Fax: 519-251-3530
Winnipeg
#2000, One Lombard Place
Winnipeg, MB R3B 0X3 Canada
204-957-1770
Fax: 204-957-0808

L K Toombs Chartered Accountants
#207, 73 Milltown Blvd.
St. Stephen, NB E3L 1G5
506-466-3291
Fax: 506-466-9825
lktpc@nb.aibn.com
Year Founded: 2000
Profile: Focuses on meeting the accounting, tax, assurance and business advisory needs of small businesses in a wide variety of industries, non-profit organizations, and individuals.

Executives:
Lori K. Toombs, CA, Partner; lori.toombs@lktoombs.ca
Alana MacLeod, CA; alana.macleod@lktoombs.ca
Susan McGillicuddy, CA; susan.mcgillicuddy@lktoombs.ca

Laberge Lafleur
#1060, 2590, boul Laurier
Québec, QC G1V 4M6
418-659-7265
Fax: 418-659-5937
mbegin@laberge-lafleur.qc.ca
Ownership: Private
Year Founded: 1984
Number of Employees: 20
Executives:
Maurice Bégin
Jean Brown
Jean Laberge
Roméo Lafleur

Lalani & Co.
#101, 4707 - 1 St. SW
Calgary, AB T2G 0A1
403-693-3310
Fax: 403-214-7869
Ownership: Private
Year Founded: 1979
Number of Employees: 5
Assets: Under $1 million
Revenues: Under $1 million
Executives:
Kabirdin Lalani

Lazer Grant LLP Chartered Accountants & Business Advisors
Also listed under: *Trustees in Bankruptcy*
#400, 309 McDermot Ave.
Winnipeg, MB R3A 1T3
204-942-0300
Fax: 204-957-5611
800-220-0005
LazerGrant@lazergrant.ca
www.lazergrant.ca
Year Founded: 1976
Number of Employees: 28
Profile: Services provided by chartered accountants & business advisors.

Partners:
Garry Chan, B.Sc., CA
David Glass, CA
Saul Greenberg, B.Comms., CA
Joel Lazer, CA, CIRP
Collin LeGall, CMA, CIRP, CFE
Martin H. Minuck, CA

Le Groupe Belzile Tremblay
655, boul. Crémazie est
Montréal, QC H2M 2K9
514-384-3620
Fax: 514-384-3710
bt@belziletremblay.ca
www.belziletremblay.ca
Former Name: Tremblay, Chevalier, Rosso; Belzile, Saint-Jean, Branchaud
Year Founded: 1991
Number of Employees: 37
Profile: Offers a wide range of accoting and related services: audited and non-audited financial statements, management consulting, company and personal taxation, personal financing planning, fiscal planning, successions, accounting executive recruitment, and computer system evaluation and implementation.

Leblanc Nadeau Bujold
11 Englehart St.
Dieppe, NB E1A 7Y7
506-853-3097
Fax: 506-859-7190
dieppe@lnb.ca
http://lnb.ca/
Number of Employees: 70
Profile: Offers a wide range of services including assurance, taxation and business consulting.

Executives:
Daniel LeBlanc, CA, Partner; daniel.leblanc@lnb.ca
Marc LeBlanc, CA, Partner; marc.leblanc@lnb.ca
Branches:
Edmundston
25, rue Carrier
Edmundston, NB E3V 4A3 Canada
506-735-1820
Fax: 506-735-1821
edmundston@lnb.ca
Grand Falls
796, boul Éverard H. Daigle
Grand Falls, NB E3Z 3C8 Canada
506-473-4240
Fax: 506-473-9450
grand-falls@lnb.ca

Lemoine Hyland Group LLP
Also listed under: *Financial Planning*
#207, 2085 Hurontario St.
Mississauga, ON L5A 4G1
905-275-7794
Fax: 905-275-5677
877-544-7687
rlemoine@lhgroup.com
lhgroup.com
Former Name: Lemoine Hyland & Grover
Executives:
Doug Hyland
Richard Lemoine

Lifestyle Financial Planning & Management Services Ltd.
190 Division St.
Welland, ON L3B 4A2
905-732-1640
Fax: 905-732-1397
stalosi@lifestylefinancial.com
Ownership: Private
Year Founded: 2000
Number of Employees: 2
Profile: Deposit brokers offer bookkeeping & income tax services.

Executives:
Steve Talosi

Liu Raymond C S Chartered Accountant
Also listed under: *Financial Planning*
#410, 10665 Jasper Ave.
Edmonton, AB T5J 3S9
780-429-1047
Ownership: Private
Year Founded: 1983
Number of Employees: 5
Revenues: Under $1 million
Profile: Personal financial planning & chartered accounting services are offered.

Executives:
Raymond Liu, RFP, Sr. Partner
George Eykelbosh, CA, Manager

Lizée Gauthier Certified General Accountants
473 - 2nd Ave. North
Saskatoon, SK S7K 2C1
306-653-4444
Fax: 306-665-5662
lizee@sasktel.net
Former Name: Lizee & Company
Ownership: Private.
Year Founded: 1980
Number of Employees: 7
Executives:
Mike Gauthier, Contact

Lyle Tilley Davidson
#720, 1718 Argyle St.
Halifax, NS B3J 3N6
902-423-7225
Fax: 902-422-3649
info@ltdca.com; ward@ltdca.com
www.ltdca.com
Ownership: Private
Year Founded: 1978
Number of Employees: 26
Executives:
Hugh Davidson, Partner; hugh@ltdca.com
Brian J. Horner, Partner; brian@tldca.com
Mark Stewart, Partner; mark@ltdca.com
Graham Sweett, Partner; graham@ltdca.com
Boyd Tilley, Partner; boyd@ltdca.com

M. Schwab Accounting Services Ltd.
#606, 94 Cumberland St.
Toronto, ON M5R 1A3
416-324-9933
Fax: 416-324-8733
Executives:
Michael Schwab, President

MacDonald Ng & Co.
Mosquito Creek Marina
PO Box 3
415 West Esplanade
Vancouver, BC V7M 1A6
604-669-2265
taxmatters@taxmatters.ca
www.taxmatters.ca
Executives:
W. Murray MacDonald, CGA, CFP

MacGillivray Partners, LLP
33 Main St. East
Hamilton, ON L8N 4K5
905-523-7732
Fax: 905-572-9333
hamilton@macgillivray.com
www.macgillivray.com
Year Founded: 1933
Number of Employees: 70
Partners:
Luigi V. Celli
John C. Dow
Paul Gibel
Branches:
Brampton
#301, 8501 Mississauga Rd.
Brampton, ON L6Y 5G8 Canada
905-453-3232
Fax: 905-453-3522
Brian L. Braun
St Catharines
PO Box 848
#1001, 1 St. Paul St.
St Catharines, ON L2R 6Z6 Canada
905-682-8363
Fax: 905-682-2191
Brian R. St. Hilaire

MacIsaac Younker Roche Soloman
16 Garfield St.
Charlottetown, PE C1A 6A5
902-368-2643
Fax: 902-566-5633
office@myrs.pe.ca
Ownership: Private
Year Founded: 1981
Number of Employees: 25
Profile: Services include the following: accounting, auditing, bookkeeping, personal & corporate tax services, management consulting, computer training, & assistance in the development of business plans.

ACCOUNTING & LAW

MacIsaac Younker Roche Soloman (continued)

Executives:
Shaun MacIsaac, CA, Partner
Everett Roche, CA, Partner
Terry Soloman, CA, Partner
Colin Younker, Partner
Michelle Burge, Contact
Jennifer Dunn, Contact
Jannifer Fitzpatrick, Contact
Neil Handrahan, Contact

MacKay LLP

#1100, 1177 West Hastings St.
Vancouver, BC V6E 4T5
604-687-4511
Fax: 780-425-8780
800-351-0426
Other Information: Fax: 604/687-5805
HughLivingstone@Van.MacKayLLP.ca
www.mackayllp.ca
Ownership: Private
Year Founded: 1969
Number of Employees: 150
Profile: Services provided include bookkeeping, audit and accounting, taxation, corporate financing, executive financial planning, microcomputer support, management consulting, business investigation, valuation and litigation support, solvency & restructuring, and international affiliations.

Executives:
S.H. (Steve) Barnes, Partner
Peter Busch, Partner
Sean Gilbert, Partner
Russell D. Law, Partner
Hugh G. Livingstone, Partner
Iain R.V. MacKay, Partner
Matthew So, Partner
York Wong, Partner
Hugh Livingstone, Manager

Branches:

Calgary - 7 Avenue
Iveagh House
#1110, 707 7 Ave. SW
Calgary, AB T2P 3H6 Canada
403-294-9292
Fax: 403-294-9262
garrycook@cal.mackayllp.ca

Calgary - Macleod Trail
Southcentre Executive Tower
#400, 11012 MacLeod Trail SE
Calgary, AB T2J 6A5 Canada
403-640-2227
Fax: 403-640-2505
lornehenrickson@cal.MackayLLP.ca
Lorne E.R. Henrickson, General Manager

Edmonton
Highfield Place
#705, 10010 - 106th St.
Edmonton, AB T5J 3L8 Canada
780-420-0626
Fax: 780-425-8780
800-622-5293
donsmith@edm.MackayLLP.ca
Don Smith, General Manager

Kelowna
#500, 1620 Dickson Ave.
Kelowna, BC V1Y 9Y2 Canada
250-763-5021
Fax: 250-763-3600
866-763-5021
DonTurri@Kel.MacKayLLP.ca
Don Turri, General Manager

Surrey
#112, 7565 - 132nd St.
Surrey, BC V3W 1K5 Canada
604-591-6181
Fax: 604-591-5676
KeithGagnon@van.mackayllp.ca
Keith Gagnon, Manager

Whitehorse
#200, 303 Strickland St.
Whitehorse, YT Y1A 2J8 Canada
867-667-7651
Fax: 867-668-3797
markp@mackayandpartners.ca
Norman McIntyre

Yellowknife
PO Box 727
4910 - 50th St.
Yellowknife, NT X1A 2N5 Canada
867-920-4404
Fax: 867-920-4135
866-920-4404
johnlaratta@yel.MackayLLP.ca
John Laratta

MacNeill Edmundson

82 Wellington St.
London, ON N6B 2K3
519-660-6060
Fax: 519-672-6416
info@meb.on.ca
www.meb.on.ca
Partners:
James B. MacNeill, CA; jim@meb.on.ca
Robert F. Edmundson, CA; bob@meb.on.ca

Magnus & Buffie Chartered Accountants

#1810, 444 St. Mary Ave.
Winnipeg, MB R3C 3T1
204-942-4441
Fax: 204-944-0400
Executives:
Blair Magnus
Brent Magnus

Malenfant Dallaire Comptables Agréés

Place de la Cité
#872, 2600, boul Laurier
Québec, QC G1V 4W2
418-654-0636
Fax: 418-654-0639
maldal@malenfantdallaire.com
www.malenfantdallaire.com
Year Founded: 1982
Profile: Provides public accounting and consulting services to companies operating throughout Quebec, and in most lines of business.

Executives:
Yves Dallaire, CA
Georges Malenfant, CA

Mandelbaum Spergel Inc.

Also listed under: *Trustees in Bankruptcy*
#200, 505 Consumers Rd.
Toronto, ON M2J 4V8
416-497-1660
Fax: 416-494-7199
800-563-8251
aspergel@trustee.com
www.trustee.com
Ownership: Private
Year Founded: 1979
Number of Employees: 35
Executives:
Alan Spergel, President
Carl Ritchie, Sr. Vice-President
Colin Boulton, Vice-President
Chris Galea, Vice-President
Directors:
Harold Mandelbaum
Carl Ritchie
Alan Spergel
Affiliated Companies:
Spergel & Associates Inc.
Branches:

Barrie
#102, 81 Maple Ave.
Barrie, ON L4N 1S1 Canada
705-722-5090
Fax: 705-722-7184
critchie@trustee.com
Carl Ritchie, Contact

Brampton - Nelson St.
#5, 14 Nelson St. West
Brampton, ON L6X 1B7 Canada
905-874-4905
Fax: 905-874-4789
cgalea@trustee.com

Brampton - Peel Centre Dr.
#201, 40 Peel Centre Dr.
Brampton, ON L6T 4B4 Canada
905-793-8377
cgalea@trustee.com
Chris Galea, Contact

Burlington
2108 Old Lakeshore Rd.
Burlington, ON L7R 1A3 Canada
905-319-8438
Fax: 905-527-6670
tpringle@trustee.com
Henry Lam Chi-leung, Branch Manager

Hamilton - King St. West
Commerce Place
PO Box 54
#803, 21 King St. West
Hamilton, ON L8P 4W7 Canada
905-527-2227
Fax: 905-527-6670
tpringle@trustee.com

Hamilton - Upper James St.
557 Upper James St.
Hamilton, ON L9C 2Y7 Canada
905-527-5468
Fax: 905-527-6670
tpringle@trustee.com

Lindsay
PO Box 997
11 Adelaide St. North
Lindsay, ON K9V 5N4 Canada
705-359-1618
cboulton@trustee.com
Colin Boulton, Contact

Mississauga
#204, 1425 Dundas St. East
Mississauga, ON L4X 2W4 Canada
905-602-4143
Fax: 905-602-8879
cgalea@trustee.com

Oshawa
#103, 187 King St. East
Oshawa, ON L1H 1C2 Canada
905-721-8251
Fax: 905-571-4682
800-563-8251
cboulton@trustee.com
Colin Boulton, Contact

Peterborough
209 Simcoe St.
Peterborough, ON K9H 2H6 Canada
705-748-3333
Fax: 705-748-6669
cboulton@trustee.com
Colin Boulton, Contact

Richmond Hill
10023 Yonge St., Upper Fl.
Richmond Hill, ON L4C 1T7 Canada
905-508-5400
critchie@trustee.com
Carl Ritchie, Contact

Toronto - Danforth Ave.
307A Danforth Ave.
Toronto, ON M4K 1N7 Canada
416-798-8813
Fax: 416-778-6016
nlivshitz@trustee.com
Joan Scullion, Contact

Toronto - Ellesmere Rd.
#211E, 2100 Ellesmere Rd.
Toronto, ON M1H 3B7 Canada
416-439-1251
Fax: 416-439-0537
critchie@trustee.com
Carl Ritchie, Contact

Toronto - Wilson Ave.
#201, 1013 Wilson Ave.
Toronto, ON M3K 1G1 Canada
416-633-1444
critchie@trustee.com
Carl Ritchie, Contact

Manning Elliott

1050 West Pender, 11th Fl.
Vancouver, BC V6J 3S7
604-714-3600
Fax: 604-714-3669
info@manningelliott.com
www.manningelliott.com

Former Name: Manning Jamison Ltd.
Partners:
Barrie L. Anderson
Alden A. Aumann
Michael Bedford
Tony Chang
Bruce G. Charlish
Michael J. Corney
Fernando Costa
A. Blair East
Keith S. Elliott
Robin A.W. Elliott
Bernie Frambach
Terry Gunderson
Lisa M. Humer
Don M. Prest
Jim Purewal
Steven R. Reed
Howard Reich
Branches:
Abbotsford
#201, 2001 McCallum Rd.
Abbotsford, BC V2S 3N5 Canada
604-857-9509
Fax: 604-850-7399
info@manningelliott.com
Rick G. Gendemann
Surrey
Station Tower Gateway
#1405, 13401 - 108 Ave.
Surrey, BC V3T 5T3 Canada
604-588-4491
Fax: 604-585-6255
info@manningelliott.com
Jeffrey E. Richards

Marek Chartered Accountants
710 Corydon Ave.
Winnipeg, MB R3M 0X9
204-992-7200
Fax: 204-947-3333
sean@markca.com
www.marekca.com
Profile: Full-service accounting firm which provides services in accounting, tax planning & preparation, consulting, accounting software selection & implementation, audits, reviews & compilations, computer consulting, and cash flow & budgeting analysis.

Executives:
Sean Marek, CA; 204-992-7201; sean@marekca.com

Martel Desjardins
Édifice de la Banque Nationale de Paris
#1440, 1981, av McGill College
Montréal, QC H3A 2Y1
514-849-2793
Fax: 514-849-7104
md@marteldesjardins.com
www.marteldesjardins.com
Year Founded: 1983
Partners:
Régent-Yves Desjardins
Alain Robichaud

Martin & Cie
#207, 655, 32e ave.
Montréal, QC H8T 3G6
514-637-7887
Fax: 514-637-3566
l.martin@martin-cie.com
www2.martin-cie.com:81
Number of Employees: 14
Executives:
Louis Martin, CA

McCain & Company Chartered Accountants
PO Box 437
393 Main St.
Florenceville, NB E7L 1Y9
506-392-5517
Fax: 506-392-5341
fhmccain@mccainandco.com
www.mccainandco.com
Profile: Provides the following services: accounting, audits, reviews & compilations, tax, bookeeping & consulting.

Executives:
David McCain, CA, Partner; dmccain@mccainandco.com
Fred H. McCain, CA, Partner; fhmccain@mccainandco.com
Branches:
Woodstock
#1, 105 Connell St.
Woodstock, NB E7M 1K7 Canada
506-325-3309
Fax: 506-328-4449
dmccain@mccainandco.com

McDonald & Co.
#301, 2955 Gladwin Rd.
Abbotsford, BC V2T 5T4
604-853-5225
Ownership: Private
Year Founded: 1992
Number of Employees: 1
Executives:
Donald L. McDonald, CGA, CFP, Owner

McGovern, Hurley, Cunningham LLP
#300, 2005 Sheppard Ave. East
Toronto, ON M2J 5B4
416-496-1234
Fax: 416-496-0125
info@mhc-ca.com
www.mhc-ca.com
Year Founded: 1984
Number of Employees: 20

McKinnon & Co., Chartered Accountants
740, 10655 Southport Rd. SW
Calgary, AB T2W 4Y1
403-262-9260

McLarty & Co.
#200, 900 Morrison Dr.
Ottawa, ON K2H 8K7
613-726-1010
Fax: 613-726-9009
www.mclartyco.ca
Former Name: McIntyre & McLarty, LLP, Chartered Accountants
Ownership: Private
Year Founded: 1981
Number of Employees: 35
Profile: The provision of accounting services includes the following: audits, reviews & compilations; tax planning & preparation services; retirement & severance package planning; business planning, budgeting & forecasting; computerized accounting; business valuations; business process renewal; internal control evaluation; litigation support; forensic accounting & special investigations; new business assessment & financing; business advisory services related to corporate reorganizations, divestitures, mergers, acquisitions & turnarounds.

Executives:
J. Douglas McLarty, Managing Director

MDP Chartered Accountants(MDP LLP)
Also listed under: *Financial Planning*
#200, 4230 Sherwoodtowne Blvd.
Mississauga, ON L4Z 2G6
905-279-7500
Fax: 905-279-9300
mdp@mdp.on.ca
www.mdp.on.ca
Also Known As: Martyn, Dooley & Partners LLP
Year Founded: 1992
Profile: MDP LLP's core business is professional accounting & tax services. Other financial services include financial reporting, income & commodity tax, business advisory, estates & trusts, & wealth management.

Meyers Norris Penny(MNP)
Also listed under: *Financing & Loan Companies*
715 - 5th Ave. SW, 7th Fl.
Calgary, AB T2P 2X6
403-444-0150
Fax: 403-444-0199
www.mnp.ca
Year Founded: 1945
Number of Employees: 1300
Revenues: $100-500 million
Profile: MNP is a leading Western Canadian chartered accountancy & business advisory firm. In addition to traditional accounting services like taxation & assurance, MNP offers business services including corporate financing, human resource consulting, business & strategic planning, succession planning, valuations support, information technology consulting, self-employment training & agricultural advisory services.

Executives:
Daryl Ritchie, CA, CEO; 403-444-0190; daryl.ritchie@mnp.ca
Kelly Bernakevitch, Exec. Vice-President, Operations; 306-978-6302; kelly.bernakevitch@mnp.ca
Ted Poppitt, Exec. Vice-President, Practice Development; 403-444-0192; ted.poppitt@mnp.ca
Laurel Wood, CA, Exec. Vice-President, Advisory Services; 403-444-0177; laurel.wood@mnp.ca
Cheryl Lemieux, Vice-President, Finance & Administration; 403-444-0164; cheryl.lemieux@mnp.ca
Jeff Llewellyn, Vice-President, Taxation Services; 403-444-0176; jeff.llewellyn@mnp.ca
Randy Mowat, Vice-President, Marketing & Practice Development; 403-537-7669; randy.mowat@mnp.ca
Phil O'Brien-Moran, Vice-President, Information Technology; 204-571-7658; phil.obrienmoran@mnp.ca
Bob Twerdun, Vice-President, Human Capital; 403-444-0162; bob.twerdun@mnp.ca
Affiliated Companies:
Tamarack Capital Advisors Inc.
Full Time Offices:
Abbotsford
#300, 2975 Gladwin Rd.
Abbotsford, BC V2T 5T4 Canada
604-853-9471
Fax: 604-850-3672
Darrell P. Tracey, Contact
Arborg
349 Main St.
Arborg, MB R0C 0A0 Canada
204-376-2479
Jim Dangerfield
Baldur
211 Elizabeth St. West
Baldur, MB R0K 0B0 Canada
204-535-2205
Fax: 204-523-4538
Ron Schultz
Big River
PO Box 280
Big River, SK S0J 0E0 Canada
306-665-6766
Fax: 306-665-9910
Tom Plishka
Boissevain
PO Box 837
400 South Railway St.
Boissevain, MB R0K 0E0 Canada
204-534-2270
Fax: 204-534-2388
Julee Galvin
Bow Island
#6, 604 Centre St.
Bow Island, AB T0K 0G0 Canada
403-545-6309
Fax: 403-320-5066
Harry Gross
Brandon
1401 Princess Ave.
Brandon, MB R7A 7L7 Canada
204-727-0661
Fax: 204-726-1543
800-446-0890
Jeff Cristall
Brooks
247 - 1st St. West
Brooks, AB T1R 1C1 Canada
403-362-8909
Fax: 403-362-6869
877-500-5696
Randy Dykin
Calgary
#600, 808 - 4th Ave. SW
Calgary, AB T2P 3E8 Canada
403-263-3385
Fax: 403-269-8450
Durell Wiley
Campbell River
#201, 990 Cedar St.
Campbell River, BC V9W 7Z8 Canada

Meyers Norris Penny(MNP) (continued)
250-287-2131
Fax: 250-287-2134
800-450-9977
Carberry
46 Main St.
Carberry, MB R0K 0H0 Canada
204-834-2125
Fax: 204-834-3340
Tim Dekker
Carlyle
204 Main St.
Carlyle, SK S0C 0R0 Canada
306-453-6121
Fax: 306-453-6007
Heather Farfard
Caroline
PO Box 550
Caroline, AB T0M 0M0 Canada
403-722-3059
Fax: 403-722-2359
Gary Porter
Chilliwack
#1, 45780 Yale Rd.
Chilliwack, BC V2P 2N4 Canada
604-792-1915
Fax: 604-795-6526
800-444-4070
Darrell P. Tracey
Coleman
8509 - 19th Ave.
Coleman, AB T0K 0M0 Canada
800-207-8584
Kris Holbeck
Courtenay
467 Cumberland Rd.
Courtenay, BC V9N 2C5 Canada
250-338-5464
Fax: 250-338-0609
800-445-9988
info@huxham.com
Ben Vanderhorst
Dauphin
PO Box 6000
32 - 2nd Ave. SW
Dauphin, MB R7N 2V5 Canada
204-638-6767
Fax: 204-638-8634
877-500-0790
Gerry Musey
Deloraine
207 North Railway West
Deloraine, MB R0M 0M0 Canada
204-747-3111
Fax: 204-747-2989
Julee Galvin
Drumheller
365 - 2nd St. East
Drumheller, AB T0J 0Y0 Canada
403-823-7800
Fax: 403-823-8914
877-932-3387
Jeff Hall
Edmonton
West Tower
#500, 14310 - 111 Ave.
Edmonton, AB T5M 3Z7 Canada
780-451-4406
Fax: 780-454-1908
800-661-7778
Gordon Reid
Estevan
Wicklow Centre
#306, 1133 - 4th St.
Estevan, SK S4A 0W6 Canada
306-634-8447
Fax: 306-634-8448
Brian Drayton
Fairview
R&R Insurance Bldg.
Main St.
Fairview, AB T0H 1C0 Canada
780-835-3363
Rick Bisson
Foremost
102 - 2 Ave. West
Foremost, AB T0K 0X0 Canada
403-382-3688
Fax: 403-320-5066
Ed Stromsmoe
Fort McMurray
9707 Main St.
Fort McMurray, AB T9H 1T5 Canada
780-791-9000
Fax: 780-791-9047
Pat Olivier
Gladstone
24 Dennis St. West
Gladstone, MB R0J 0T0 Canada
204-385-0660
David Henlisia
Glenboro
604 Railway Ave.
Glenboro, MB R0K 0X0 Canada
204-827-2009
Fax: 204-523-4538
877-500-0760
Ron Schultz
Grande Prairie
214 Place
9909 - 102 St., 7th Fl.
Grande Prairie, AB T8V 2V4 Canada
780-831-1700
Fax: 780-539-9600
888-831-2870
Bridget Henniger
Hope
PO Box 1689
388 Wallace St.
Hope, BC V0X 1L0 Canada
604-869-9599
Fax: 604-869-3044
800-969-6060
Keith Britz, Contact
Hudson Bay
103 Churchill St.
Hudson Bay, SK S0E 0Y0 Canada
306-865-3783
Fax: 306-865-3319
Rhonda Lovell
Humboldt
701 - 9th St.
Humboldt, SK S0K 2A0 Canada
306-682-2673
Fax: 306-682-5910
877-500-0789
Larry Rode
Innisfail
4923 - 5th St.
Innisfail, AB T4G 1S7 Canada
403-227-3763
Fax: 403-227-2388
Sandra Steele
Kenora
101 Chipman St.
Kenora, ON P9N 1V7 Canada
807-468-3338
Fax: 807-468-1418
Joseph Fregeau
Killarney
501 Broadway Ave.
Killarney, MB R0K 1G0 Canada
204-523-4633
Fax: 204-523-4538
877-500-0760
Carla Beaudry
La Ronge
PO Box 1079
1309 La Ronge Ave.
La Ronge, SK S0J 1L0 Canada
306-425-2215
Fax: 306-425-3882
Gordon John
Lacombe
#5, 5265 - 45th St.
Lacombe, AB T4L 2A2 Canada
403-782-7790
Fax: 403-782-7703
Gerald Wasylyshen
Leduc
#200, 5019 - 49th Ave.
Leduc, AB T9E 6T5 Canada
780-986-2626
Fax: 780-986-2621
Deborah A. Sarnecki
Lethbridge
3425 - 2nd Ave. South
Lethbridge, AB T1J 4V1 Canada
403-329-1552
Fax: 403-329-1540
Gordon Tait
Lloydminster
103 Resource Centre
5704 - 44th St.
Lloydminster, AB T9V 2A1 Canada
780-875-9855
Fax: 780-875-9640
Ralph Cormack
Maple Creek
42 Pacific Ave.
Maple Creek, SK S0N 1N0 Canada
306-662-3127
Dena Weiss
Medicine Hat
666 - 4 St. SE
Medicine Hat, AB T1A 7G5 Canada
403-527-4441
Fax: 403-526-6218
877-500-0786
Michael Keck, Managing Partner
Melfort
609 Main St.
Melfort, SK S0E 1A0 Canada
306-752-5800
Fax: 306-752-5933
877-500-0787
John Harder
Melita
133 Main St. South
Melita, MB R0M 1L0 Canada
204-522-3333
Murray Gray
Milk River
PO Box 119
Milk River, AB T0K 1M0 Canada
403-647-3882
Fax: 403-320-5066
Don Hornford
Minnedosa
32 Main St. South
Minnedosa, MB R0J 1E0 Canada
204-867-2048
Marvin Beaumont
Moosomin
PO Box 670
715 Main St.
Moosomin, SK S0G 3N0 Canada
306-435-3347
Fax: 306-435-2494
877-500-0784
Layne McFarlane
Naicam
304 - 2nd Ave. North
Naicam, SK S0K 2Z0 Canada
306-874-2045
Bruce Ramstead
Nanaimo
PO Box 514
96 Wallace St.
Nanaimo, BC V9R 5L5 Canada
250-753-8251
Fax: 250-754-3999
877-340-3330
Lucie Gosselin
Neepawa
251 Davidson St.
Neepawa, MB R0J 1H0 Canada
204-476-2326
Fax: 204-476-3663
877-500-0795
Marvin Beaumont
Oyen
215B Main St.
Oyen, AB T0J 2J0 Canada

403-527-4441
Fax: 403-526-6218
Ronald Anderson
Peace River
PO Box 6030
10012 - 101st St.
Peace River, AB T8S 1S1 Canada
780-624-3252
Fax: 780-624-8758
Bill Hirtle
Pincher Creek
PO Box 1060
697 Main St.
Pincher Creek, AB T0K 1W0 Canada
403-627-3313
Fax: 403-627-5259
800-207-8584
Rita Kilkenny
Portage La Prairie
14 Tupper St. South
Portage La Prairie, MB R1N 1W6 Canada
204-239-6117
Fax: 204-857-3972
ronaldk@mnp.ca
Jerry Lupkowski
Preeceville
17 - 1st Ave. NW
Preeceville, SK S0A 3B0 Canada
306-547-3357
Fax: 306-865-3319
Rhonda Lovell
Prince Albert
25 - 11th St. East
Prince Albert, SK S6V 0Z8 Canada
306-764-6873
Fax: 306-763-0766
reidg@mnp.ca
Garth Busch
Radville
210 Main St.
Radville, SK S0C 2G0 Canada
306-869-4140
Fax: 306-869-4149
Blair Kotz
Red Deer
#102, 4922 - 53 St.
Red Deer, AB T4N 2E9 Canada
403-346-8878
Fax: 403-341-5599
877-500-0779
Tim Dekker
Redvers
PO Box 337
15 Broadway St.
Redvers, SK S0C 2H0 Canada
306-452-3382
Fax: 306-452-6458
Roy Olsen
Regina
#900, 2010 - 11th Ave.
Regina, SK S4P 0J3 Canada
306-790-7900
Fax: 306-790-7990
877-500-0780
Don Stewart
Rimbey
PO Box 317
4714A - 50th Ave.
Rimbey, AB T0C 2J0 Canada
403-843-4666
Fax: 403-843-4616
Chris Simpson
Roblin
PO Box 878
206 Main St.
Roblin, MB R0L 1P0 Canada
204-937-8019
Fax: 204-937-8067
Kelly Brook, Contact
Rocky Mountain House
PO Box 2138
5004 - 50th St.
Rocky Mountain House, AB T4T 1B6 Canada
403-845-2422
Fax: 403-845-3794
Gary Porter
Russell
227 Main St. North
Russell, MB R0J 1W0 Canada
204-773-2225
Fax: 204-773-3950
John Orisko
Saskatoon
366 - 3rd Ave. South
Saskatoon, SK S7K 1M5 Canada
306-665-6766
Fax: 306-665-9910
877-500-0778
David Kunaman
Ste Rose du Lac
635 Central Ave.
Ste Rose du Lac, MB R0L 1S0 Canada
204-447-2177
Fax: 204-447-3135
Tere Stykalo
Steinbach
316A Main St.
Steinbach, MB R5G 1Z1 Canada
204-326-9816
Fax: 204-326-9586
Alyson Kennedy
Swift Current
140 - 2nd Ave. NW
Swift Current, SK S9H 0P2 Canada
306-773-8375
Fax: 306-773-7735
877-500-0762
Al Lightfoot
Virden
233 Queen St. West
Virden, MB R0M 2C0 Canada
204-748-1340
Fax: 204-748-3294
Tom Kirkup
Wainwright
711 - 10 St.
Wainwright, AB T9W 1P3 Canada
780-842-4171
Fax: 780-842-4169
877-500-0763
Don Isaman
Wawota
111 Main St.
Wawota, SK S0G 5A0 Canada
306-739-2757
David Ablass
Weyburn
8 - 4th St. NE
Weyburn, SK S4H 0X7 Canada
306-842-8915
Fax: 306-842-1966
Sean Wallace
Winnipeg
#500, 1661 Portage Ave.
Winnipeg, MB R3J 3T7 Canada
204-775-4531
Fax: 204-783-8329
877-500-0795
Wayne McWhirter

Michael Argue, Chartered Accountant, Professional Corporation

#206, 1210 Sheppard Ave. East
Toronto, ON M2K 1E3
416-490-8544
Fax: 416-490-8096
michaelargue@bellnet.ca
www.argueca.com
Profile: The following services are provided: tax, accounting, auditing, information systems, business valuation & finance, plus management advisory services.

Executives:
Michael Argue, Chartered Accountant

Millard Rouse & Rosebrugh

PO Box 367
96 Nelson St.
Brantford, ON N3T 5N3
519-759-3511
Fax: 519-759-7961
mail@millards.com
www.millards.com
Ownership: Private
Year Founded: 1920
Number of Employees: 80
Revenues: $5-10 million
Profile: The following services are provided: auditing, accounting, personal & corporate taxation, computer consulting & business valuation services.

Partners:
T.A. Bateson, CA
J.O. Carr, CA
D.J. Christilaw, CA
K.M. Cloet, CA
M.J. Dixon, CA
B.S. Gillespie, CA
S.E. Goodwin, CA
R.E. Hooton, CA
W.A. Hyde, CA, CFP
H.C. Johnston, CA
T.J. Leyzer, CA
M.M. McGraw, CA
J.C. Regan, CA
J.F. Rolland, CA
R.D. Sciannella, CA
A.S. Tarantello, CA
M.E. Terdik, CA
R.D. White, CA, CFP
B.L. Wright, CA
Offices:
Delhi
148 Church St. West
Delhi, ON N4B 1W1 Canada
519-582-3110
Fax: 519-582-1140
Hagersville
91 Main St. South
Hagersville, ON N0A 1H0 Canada
905-768-3121
Fax: 905-768-5843
Norwich
1 Stover St. North
Norwich, ON N0J 1P0 Canada
519-863-3554
Fax: 519-863-3557
Simcoe
85 Robinson St.
Simcoe, ON N3Y 1W7 Canada
519-426-1606
Fax: 519-426-5070
Tillsonburg
24 Harvey St.
Tillsonburg, ON N4G 3J8 Canada
519-688-9991
Fax: 519-688-2576

Mintz & Partners LLP

#200, 1 Concorde Gate
Toronto, ON M3C 4G4
416-391-2900
Fax: 416-391-2748
info@mintzca.com
www.mintzca.com
Ownership: Private partnership
Year Founded: 1949
Number of Employees: 120
Assets: $10-50 million
Revenues: $20,000,000
Profile: Services are provided in the following areas: arbitration & mediation, auditing & accounting, corporate finance, corporate recovery & insolvency, forensic accounting, health-care & professional practice services, hospitality consulting, information technology, litigation support, management consulting, mergers & acquisitions, real-estate consulting, small-business consulting & taxation & valuations. An affiliated company is Mintz & Partners Financial Services.

Executives:
Lyle Strachan, CEO
Bryan A. Tannenbaum, Managing Partner
Penny Arena, Manager, Office
M. Mazengia, Manager, Information Technology
Nancy Stallone, Manager, Human Resources
Partners:
Dan Amadori, Mergers & Acquisitions
Syd Bojarski, Advisory & Assurance

Mintz & Partners LLP (continued)
Steve Callan, Advisory & Assurance
Allan Cheskes, Advisory & Assurance
Steve Dolman, Advisory & Assurance
Mario Fallico, Advisory & Assurance
Douglas Gough, Corporate Finance
Phil Iorio, Advisory & Assurance
Elliot Jacobson, Advisory & Assurance
Lorn Kutner, Tax
Phil Lev, Advisory & Assurance
Harley Mintz, Tax
Eddie Pal, Advisory & Assurance
Carey Singer, U.S. Tax
Stan Spencer, Advisory & Assurance
Tom Strezos, Litigation
Erwin Stuart, Advisory & Assurance
Bryan Tannenbaum, Corporate Recovery & Insolvency
Daniel Weisz, Corporate Recovery & Insolvency
Andy Yap, Tax

Mitchell Kelly Jones & Associates Inc.
Also listed under: *Financial Planning*
#1070, 340 - 12 Ave. SW
Calgary, AB T2R 1L5
403-265-8545
Fax: 403-265-8554
Former Name: Mitchell Jones Financial Services Inc.
Ownership: Private
Year Founded: 1996

Mortfield & Orvitz
#300, 8500 Leslie St.
Thornhill, ON L3T 7M8
905-889-1549
Fax: 905-889-2054
mortfieldandorvitz@on.aibn.com
www.interlog.com/~mortorvi
Ownership: Private
Year Founded: 1979
Number of Employees: 3
Profile: Provides services to the owner-managed business.

Executives:
Ralph Orvitz, Partner

Nakonechny & Power Chartered Accountants Ltd.
Also listed under: *Financial Planning*
PO Box 880
31 Main St. South
Carman, MB R0G 0J0
204-745-2061
Fax: 204-745-6322
Executives:
Hellar Nakonechny, B.Sc., CA, CFP, Contact

Neal, Pallett & Townsend LLP Chartered Accountants
Also listed under: *Financial Planning*
#300, 633 Colborne St.
London, ON N6B 2V3
519-432-5534
Fax: 519-432-6544
www.nptca.com
Ownership: Private
Year Founded: 1993
Number of Employees: 30
Assets: $1-5 million
Revenues: $1-5 million
Profile: Assists clients with accounting and strategic Canadian and US tax advice, best business practices and corporate financing.

Partners:
Glenn Hardman; ghardman@nptca.com
Barrie Neal; bneal@nptca.com
David Pallett; dpallett@nptca.com
Douglas E. Plummer; dplummer@nptca.com
John Prueter; jprueter@nptca.com
Piyush Shah; pshah@nptca.com
Jonathan Townsend; jtownsend@nptca.com
Sandy Wetstein; swetstein@nptca.com

Newton & Co.
#1205, 150 Isabella St.
Ottawa, ON K1S 1V7
613-236-2939
Fax: 613-236-1220
nco@newtonco.com
www.newtonco.com
Ownership: Private
Year Founded: 1975
Number of Employees: 19
Assets: Under $1 million
Revenues: Under $1 million
Profile: Public accounting firm with a 25 year history of providing tax, accounting and financial advice to individuals and corporations in the Ottawa area.

Executives:
David L. Brown, Partner
Phil Byrne, Partner
Jane Francis, Partner
Andrew Misener
Branches:
Manotick
PO Box 978
5494 Main St., 2nd Fl.
Manotick, ON K4M 1A8 Canada
613-692-3501
Fax: 613-692-2874

Pacak Kowal Hardie & Company, Chartered Accountants
PO Box 1660
#100, 4th Avenue North
Swan River, MB R0L 1Z0
204-734-9331
Fax: 204-734-4785
800-743-8447
pkhl@mts.net
www.pacakkowalhardie.com
Profile: Provides services in the areas of auditing, accounting and income tax.

Executives:
Bruce Hardie, CA, Partner
Dennis Kowal, CA, Partner
Stan Pacak, CA, Partner

Perreault Wolman Grzywacz & Co.
#814, 5250, rue Ferrier
Montréal, QC H4P 2N7
514-731-7987
Fax: 514-731-8782
www.pwgca.com
Ownership: Private
Year Founded: 1945
Number of Employees: 37
Assets: $1-5 million
Revenues: $5-10 million
Profile: Services offered include the following: financial business advice, personal services, tax services, mergers & acquisitions, financing, estate planning insurance, investment advice & USA tax services.

Partners:
Harold Golfman
Arthur P. Greenberg
Willie Grzywacz
David Hart
Eddy Perreault
George Retek
Samuel Rudski
Martin Segal
Philip Shait
Barry Silverman
Shlomo Solomon
Mark Strohl
Edward Wolkove
Dov Wolman
Leonard M. Wolman

Petrie Raymond Inc.
#1000, 255, boul Crémazie Est
Montréal, QC H2M 1M2
514-342-4740
Fax: 514-737-4049
info@petrieraymond.qc.ca
www.petrieraymond.qc.ca/
Profile: The following services are provided: corporate reorganization & restructuring, mergers & acquisitions.

PKBW Group, Chartered Accountants & Business Advisors Inc.
219 Fort St.
Winnipeg, MB R3C 1E2
204-942-0861
Fax: 204-947-6834
admin@pkbwgroup.ca
www.pkbwgroup.ca
Number of Employees: 16
Profile: Provides assurance, taxation, advisory, and information technology services.

Executives:
Gary Burdey, CA, Director; burdey@pkbwgroup.ca
Richard Senez, CA, Director; senez@pkbwgroup.ca
Bob Walker, CA, Director; bob.walker@pkbwgroup.ca
Tim B. Walker, CA, Director; tim.walker@pkbwgroup.ca
Mary A. Wladyka, FCA, Director; wladyka@pkbwgroup.ca

PKF Hill LLP
#200, 41 Valleybrook Dr.
Toronto, ON M3B 2S6
416-449-9171
Fax: 416-449-7401
info@pkfhill.com
www.pkfhill.com
Year Founded: 1968
Number of Employees: 50+
Partners:
John Adams
Steve Aprile
John Fiorino
Peter Fullerton
Donald Hill
Phil Holt
Ian Hulbert
Ron Kretchman
Wendy MacDonald
Vicki McKinnon
Dale Varney
Deryck Williams

Pope & Brookes, DFK LLP, Chartered Accountants
#300, 530 Kenaston Blvd.
Winnipeg, MB R3N 1Z4
204-487-7957
Fax: 204-487-1243
advice@pb-dfk.com
www.pb-dfk.com
Year Founded: 1984
Profile: Services include taxation, business advice, business valuations assessment, auditing, accounting, management consulting, personal financial planning, and computer systems support for accounting packages.

Executives:
Richard D. Pope, CA, Managing Partner, Chief Executive Officer; rpope@pb-dfk.com
Geoffrey A. Brookes, CA, Partner; gbrookes@pb-dfk.com
Branches:
Altona
PO Box 1026
Altona, MB R0G 0B0 Canada
204-324-8994
Fax: 204-324-8994
leiler@mts.net

Powell, Jones
121 Anne St. South
Barrie, ON L4N 7B6
705-728-7461
Fax: 705-728-8317
info@powelljones.ca
www.powelljones.ca
Ownership: Private
Number of Employees: 30
Profile: The firm has extensive experience in all areas of financial reporting, tax compliance and planning for individuals, corporations and Trusts, estate planning and business advisory services.

Partners:
Don Edward, CA
Greg Ferguson, CA
Larry Jones, CA
Scott A. Mackay, CA
Alan Priest, CA, CFP
Scott Wilson, CA, CFE

PPW Chartered Accountants LLP
#209, 1661 Portage Ave.
Winnipeg, MB R3J 3T7

204-772-4936
Fax: 204-774-4462
solutions@ppw.ca
www.ppw.ca
Year Founded: 2004
Number of Employees: 10
Profile: Full-service accounting firm whose services include accounting, business finance, taxation, estate planning and business valuation.

Executives:
Gerald I. Peterson, CA, Partner; gerald@ppw.ca
Alex M. Watt, CA, Partner; alex@ppw.ca

Prapavessis Jasek
3410 South Service Rd., Lower Fl.
Burlington, ON L7N 3T2
905-634-8999
Fax: 905-634-5057
jim@pj.on.ca
Ownership: Private
Year Founded: 1992
Number of Employees: 4
Executives:
Frank Jasek, CA, Partner; frank@pj.on.ca
Jim Prapavessis, CA, Partner; jim@pj.on.ca

PSB
#400, 3333, boul Graham
Montréal, QC H3R 3L5
514-341-5511
Fax: 514-342-0589
877-341-5058
info@psb.ca
www.psb.ca
Ownership: Private
Year Founded: 1966
Number of Employees: 65
Assets: $5-10 million
Revenues: $10-50 million
Executives:
Marc Elman, CA, CBV, Managing Partner
Ellis Basevitz, CA, Partner
Herbert H. Davis, CIRP, Partner
Tony Ferracane, CA, Partner
Michael Fogel, CA, Partner
Patrick Grosjean, CA, CBV, Partner
Andrée Guy, CA, F.Adm.A, Partner
Steve Moses, CA, Partner
Howard M. Oksenberg, Partner; oksenberg@psb.ca
Sam Spatari, CA, Partner

R. Steinson & Co. Inc.
Also listed under: *Financial Planning*
#301, 394 Duncan St.
Duncan, BC V9L 3W4
250-748-1426
Fax: 250-748-9724
Executives:
Rick Steinson, Accountant

Ralph H. Green & Associates
#200, 53 King St.
Saint John, NB E2L 1G5
506-632-3000
Fax: 506-632-1007
igreen@rhgreenassociates.ca
www.rhgreenassociates.ca
Profile: Offers a wide variety of professional services including taxation, accounting and auditing.

Executives:
Ralph Green, CA; 506-632-3000; rhgreen@rhgreenassociates.ca

Rashid & Quinney Chartered Accountants
#401, 216 Chrislea Rd.
Woodbridge, ON L4L 8S5
905-856-2677
Fax: 905-856-2679
rick@randg.ca
Former Name: Quinney & Associates Ltd.
Ownership: Private
Year Founded: 1998
Number of Employees: 3
Assets: Under $1 million
Revenues: Under $1 million
Profile: Accounting, Tax Preparation, Bookkeeping and Payroll Services.

Executives:
Richard Quinney

RDK Chartered Accountant Ltd.
5 Whitkirk Place
Winnipeg, MB R3R 2A2
204-885-5280
Fax: 204-831-6670
admin@rdkcharteredaccountant.com
www.rdkcharteredaccountant.com
Profile: Provides accounting, income tax, and management consulting services.

Executives:
Randy G. Neufeld, CA

Reimer & Company Inc.
PO Box 146
1000 Main St.
Swan River, MB R0L 1Z0
204-734-2599
Fax: 204-734-3184
info@reimerco.ca
www.reimerco.ca
Year Founded: 2000
Number of Employees: 10
Profile: Offers assurance, accounting, taxation, business advisory, and estate & financial planning services.

Executives:
Chris Reimer, CA, CFP

Robert F. Fischer & Company Inc., C.G.A.
Also listed under: *Financial Planning*
#13, 327 Prideaux St.
Nanaimo, BC V9R 2N4
250-753-7287
Fax: 250-753-7453

Robinson & Company LLP
512 Woolwich St.
Guelph, ON N1H 3X7
519-837-3113
Fax: 519-837-9883
800-598-6400
info@robinson.ca
www.robinson.ca
Ownership: Private. Partnership
Year Founded: 1986
Number of Employees: 24
Executives:
Sharon D. Brown, B.Math., CA, Partner; sharon@robinson.ca
Kristine A. Doyle-Sanders, CA, CBV, CFP, Partner; kristine@robinson.ca
Jason P. Evans, CA, Partner; jason@robinson.ca
Emmie Hull, CA, Partner; emmie@robinson.ca
Jean Pritchard, CA, CFP, Partner; jean@robinson.ca
Grant C. Robinson, FCA, CFP, Partner; grant@robinson.ca
Branches:
Toronto
185 Claireport Cres.
Toronto, ON M8W 6P7 Canada
905-858-1786
Fax: 519-837-9883
800-598-6400

Robinson, Lott & Brohman LLP
15 Lewis Rd.
Guelph, ON N1H 1E9
519-822-9933
Fax: 519-822-9212
866-822-9992
guelph_inquiries@rlb.ca
www.rlb.ca
Ownership: Private
Year Founded: 1951
Number of Employees: 50
Profile: The firm offers auditing, accounting, taxation, computer, & special financial services. Services are provided to over 2,000 corporate & individual clients involved in commercial, industrial, financial, professional, farm, & municipal activities.

Partners:
Gord Barr, CA; gord@rlb.ca
Peter Cuttini, CA, CPA; peterc@rlb.ca
Tom Gaskell, CA; tom@rlb.ca
Bill Koornstra, CA; billk@rlb.ca
Michael A. Manera, CA, CFP, CMC; mike@rlb.ca
William A. Martin; bmartin@rlb.ca
Dave McEllistrum, CA; dave@rlb.ca
M. Bruce Robinson, CA; bruce@rlb.ca
Wynne Wright, CA, CMA; wynne@rlb.ca

Romanovsky & Associates Chartered Accountants
10260 - 112 St.
Edmonton, AB T5K 1M4
780-447-5830
Fax: 780-451-6291
800-861-5830
www.romanovsky.com
Ownership: Private
Year Founded: 1980
Number of Employees: 25
Assets: Under $1 million
Revenues: $1-5 million
Profile: Services provided include personal tax, corporate tax, business plans, business financing, bookkeeping, review and audits.

Partners:
Selwyn Romanovsky, CA; ram@romanovsky.com
Keith Anderson, CA; keith.anderson@romanovsky.com
Yvonne Anderson, CA; yvonne.anderson@romanovsky.com
Neil Bronsch, CA, CFP; neil.bronsch@romanovsky.com
Alan Jacobson, CA; alan.jacobson@romanovsky.com

Rosenthal Consulting Group
13 Balmoral Ave.
Toronto, ON M4V 1J5
416-617-9966
Fax: 416-964-2371
hsrosenthal@alumni.uwaterloo.ca
Former Name: Rosenthal, Howard, C.A.
Year Founded: 1997
Profile: Consulting, training, & financial services are provided.

Executives:
Howard Rosenthal, C.A., President

Roth Mosey & Partners
#300, 3100 Temple
Windsor, ON N8W 5J6
519-977-6410
Fax: 519-977-7083
info@roth-mosey.com
www.roth-mosey.com
Ownership: Private
Year Founded: 1983
Number of Employees: 23
Partners:
Tom Baker; tbaker@roth-mosey.com
Michael Marchand; mmarchand@roth-mosey.com
Greg Mosey; gmosey@roth-mosey.com
Peter Roth; proth@roth-mosey.com
Claire Wales; cwales@roth-mosey.com
Beth Yeh; byeh@roth-mosey.com

Roy, Labrecque, Busque, Comptables Agréés
#160, 5055, boul Hamel ouest
Québec, QC G2E 2G6
418-871-0013
Fax: 418-871-0162
rlb@roylabrecquebusque.com
www.roylabrecquebusque.com
Executives:
Gilles Busque, CA; busque@roylabrecquebusque.com
Jacques Labrecque, CA; labrec@roylabrecquebusque.com
Réjean Roy, CA; roy@roylabrecquebusque.com

RSM Richter
Also listed under: *Trustees in Bankruptcy*
#1820, 2, Place Alexis Nihon
Montréal, QC H3Z 3C2
514-934-3400
Fax: 514-934-3408
mtlinfo@rsmrichter.com
www.richter.ca
Former Name: Richter Usher & Vineberg
Ownership: Private
Year Founded: 1926
Number of Employees: 120
Profile: Aboriginal advisory services, audit, corporate finance, financial reorganization, management consulting, professional

RSM Richter (continued)
search, risk management, tax, valuations & litigation support, and wealth management services are provided.

Principals:
Debbie Di Gregorio; ddigregorio@rsmrichter.com
Dimitra Glekas; dglekas@rsmrichter.com
Suzanne Grant; sgrant@rsmrichter.com
Leon Krantzberg; lkrantzberg@rsmrichter.com
Jeff Rowles; jrowles@rsmrichter.com
Barry Steinberg; bsteinberg@rsmrichter.com
Branches:
Calgary
#910, 736 - 8th Ave. SW
Calgary, AB T2P 1H4 Canada
403-206-0840
Fax: 403-206-0841
cgyinfo@rsmrichter.com
Toronto - King St.
#1100, 200 King St. West
Toronto, ON M5H 3T4 Canada
416-932-8000
Fax: 416-932-6200
torinfo@rsmrichter.com
John Swidler, Sr. Partner

Ruby Stein Wagner S.E.N.C. Chartered Accountants
Place du Parc
#1900, 300, rue Léo-Pariseau
Montréal, QC H2X 4B5
514-842-3911
Fax: 514-849-3447
866-842-3911
info@rswca.com
www.rswca.com
Profile: Full-service accounting firm that offers accounting, bookkeeping, audit, forensic accounting, business development consulting, personal financial planning, estate planning, taxation, and real estate management services.

SBLR LLP Chartered Accountants
#300, 2345 Yonge St.
Toronto, ON M4P 2E5
416-488-2345
Fax: 416-488-3765
www.sblr.ca
Former Name: Granatstein Baker Lerner
Partners:
Joel Baker
Howard Lerner; hlerner@sblr.ca
Shawn Rosenzweig; srosenzweig@sblr.ca
Cary Selby; cselby@sblr.ca
Mitch Silverstein; msilverstein@sblr.ca

Scarrow & Donald
#100, 5 Donald St.
Winnipeg, MB R3L 2T4
204-982-9800
Fax: 204-474-2886
sd@scarrowdonald.mb.ca
www.scarrowdonald.mb.ca
Ownership: Private
Year Founded: 1985
Number of Employees: 18
Profile: Provides a full range of services to small public companies, owner-managed companies, associations and not-for-profit organizations.

Partners:
Peter J. Donald
Keith G. Findlay
Tom Frain
John F. Kelly
Douglas J. Smith

Schlesinger Newman Goldman
#1100, 625, boul René-Lévesque ouest
Montréal, QC H3B 1R2
514-866-8553
Fax: 514-866-8469
info@sng.ca
www.sng.ca
Ownership: Private
Year Founded: 1975
Number of Employees: 55
Profile: Audit and assurance, accounting, business advisory, business reorganizations and turnarounds, business valuations, corporate financing, corporate tax planning, estates & trusts, family business succession, government financial assistance, initial public offerings, litigation support, mergers & acquisitions, personal tax planning, real estate, & wealth management services are provided.

Partners:
Howard Berish; howard.berish@sng.ca
Antoinette Coloni; antoinette.coloni@sng.ca
Lionel Goldman; lionel.goldman@sng.ca
Jeffrey Greenberg; jeffrey.greenberg@sng.ca
Tyna Jallet; tyna.jallet@sng.ca
Stuart Ladd; stuart.ladd@sng.ca
Sonia Medvescek; sonia.medvescek@sng.ca
Lorne Richter; lorne.richter@sng.ca
Joseph Schlesinger; joe.schlesinger@sng.ca
Abe Zylberlicht; abe.zylberlicht@sng.ca

Schurman Sudsbury & Associates Ltd.
189 Water St.
Summerside, PE C1N 1B2
902-436-2171
Fax: 902-436-0960
schurman-sudsbury@isn.net
Ownership: Private
Year Founded: 1974
Number of Employees: 12
Profile: Accounting, computer consulting, income tax, & management consulting services are offered by the firm.

Partners:
Derek Huestis
James T. Schurman
Clair Sudsbury

Schwartz Levitsky Feldman LLP(SLF)
Also listed under: *Trustees in Bankruptcy*
1980, rue Sherbrooke ouest, 10e étage
Montréal, QC H3H 1E8
514-937-6392
Fax: 514-933-9710
www.slf.ca
Ownership: Private
Year Founded: 1960
Number of Employees: 142
Assets: $5-10 million
Revenues: $10-50 million
Profile: Provides a wide range of advisory services, including corporate finance, mergers & acquisitions, and management consulting.

Partners:
Hashim Ali, CA; 514-788-5634; hashim.ali@slf.ca
Luciano D'Ignazio, CA; 514-788-5613; luciano.dignazio@slf.ca
Harry H. Feldman, CA; 514-788-5604; harry.feldman@slf.ca
Peter H. Feldman, CA; 514-788-5609; peter.feldman@slf.ca
Bernard Jeanty; 514-788-5614; bernard.jeanty@slf.ca
Morty B. Lober, CA; 514-788-5603; morty.lober@slf.ca
Alain Mamane; 514-788-5619; alain.mamane@slf.ca
David Perlin, CA; 514-788-5607; david.perlin@slf.ca
Bill Reim; 514-788-5615; bill.reim@slf.ca
Leonard Sitcoff, CA; 514-788-5611; leonard.sitcoff@slf.ca
Sylvain Tellier; 514-788-5601; sylvain.tellier@slf.ca
Jason Yudcovitch; 514-788-5623; jason.yudcovitch@slf.ca
Offices:
Toronto
1167 Caledonia Rd.
Toronto, ON M6A 2X1 Canada
416-785-5353
Fax: 416-785-5663
Kai Chang

Scott & Pichelli Ltd.
Also listed under: *Trustees in Bankruptcy*
#109, 3600 Billings Ct.
Burlington, ON L7N 3N6
905-632-5853
Fax: 905-632-6113
www.bankruptcy-trustees.ca/
Former Name: Scott, Pichelli & Graci Ltd., Scott, Pichelli & Arvanitis Ltd.
Ownership: Private
Year Founded: 1980

Scott Rankin Gordon & Gardiner Chartered Accountants
#207, 2650 Queensview Dr.
Ottawa, ON K2B 8H6
613-596-2767
Fax: 613-596-2775
info@srgg.com
www.srgg.com
Partners:
Lynda J.B. Carter; lcarter@srgg.com
K. Lyman Gardiner; lgardiner@srgg.com
Douglas A.S. Rankin; drankin@srgg.com
J. Brian Scott; bscott@srgg.com

Segal & Partners Inc.
Also listed under: *Trustees in Bankruptcy*
#500, 2005 Sheppard Ave. East
Toronto, ON M2J 5B4
416-391-1460
Fax: 416-391-2285
800-206-7307
info@segalpartners.com
www.segalbankruptcy.com
Ownership: Private
Branches:
Mississauga
#212, 1310 Dundas St. East
Mississauga, ON L4Y 2C1 Canada
Toronto - Bathurst St.
#318, 3768 Bathurst St.
Toronto, ON M3H 1M1 Canada
Toronto - Danforth Ave.
#301, 2179 Danforth Ave.
Toronto, ON M4C 1K4 Canada

SF Partnership, LLP
Also listed under: *Financial Planning*
The Madison Centre
#400, 4950 Yonge St.
Toronto, ON M2N 6K1
416-250-1212
Fax: 416-250-1225
info@sfgroup.ca
www.sfgroup.ca
Former Name: Solursh Feldman & Partners
Ownership: Private
Year Founded: 1997
Number of Employees: 96
Assets: $1-5 million Year End: 20051200
Revenues: $10-50 million Year End: 20051200
Profile: The full-service chartered accountancy firm has experience & expertise in the following service areas: audit & accounting, corporate & personal taxation, management advisory, insolvency, career transition & personal financial counselling, computer consulting, government grants & programs, forensic services, estate, & retirement & family planning.

Executives:
Stanley Rapkin, Managing Partner; 416-250-1212; srapkin@sfgroup.ca
Alex Mathews, Principal; amathews@sfgroup.ca
Ellis Orlan, Principal; eorlan@sfgroup.ca
Eugene Aceti, Partner; eaceti@sfgroup.ca
Gary Crystal, Partner; 416-250-1212; gcrystal@sfgroup.ca
Jason Crystal, Partner; jcrystal@sfgroup.ca
Irving Feldman, Partner; 416-250-1212; ifeldman@sfgroup.ca
Harold Franks, Partner; mfranks@sfgroup.ca
Michael Fromstein, Partner; 416-250-1212; mfromstein@sfgroup.ca
Paul Mandel, Partner; 416-250-1212; pmandel@sfgroup.ca
Saul Muskat, Partner; smuskat@sfgroup.ca
Phillip Spring, Partner; pspring@sfgroup.ca
Bradley Waese, Partner; 416-250-1212; bwaese@sfgroup.ca
Trustees:
Steven Goldberg; 416-250-1212; sgoldberg@sfgroup.ca

Sidler & Company LLP
Also listed under: *Financial Planning*
#204, 6465 Millcreek Dr.
Mississauga, ON L5N 5R3
905-821-9215
Fax: 905-821-8212
info@sidler.ca
www.sidler.ca
Ownership: Private.
Year Founded: 1987
Number of Employees: 30
Assets: $1-5 million Year End: 20061013
Revenues: $1-5 million Year End: 20061013
Profile: Services include estate planning. An affiliated company is Sidler Clarke Inc.

Executives:
Richard Clarke, Partner
Curtis Link, Partner
Kalin L. McDonald, Partner
Jason O'Halloran, Partner
Annette Silva, Partner

Signature comptable Mc Nicoll CA inc.
#210, 1220, boul Lebourgneuf
Québec, QC G2K 2G4
418-622-6666
Fax: 418-622-3904
mcnicollp@signaturecomptable.ca
www.signaturecomptable.ca
Executives:
Paule McNicoll, CA, President

sj mcisaac Chartered Accountants
PO Box 217
Amherst, NS B4H 3Z2
902-661-1027
Fax: 902-667-0884
877-282-6632
contact@sjmcisaac.ca
www.sjmcisaac.ca
Profile: Full-service accounting firm, providing planning and advisory services in addition to traditional tax and accounting work to a variety of industries and non-profit organizations.

Executives:
Susan J. McIsaac, CA, Partner; susan.mcisaac@sjmcisaac.ca
Vicki Darragh, CA, Partner; vicki.darragh@sjmcisaac.ca

SMCA Professional Corporation
#201, 197 County Court Blvd.
Brampton, ON L6W 4P6
905-451-4034
Fax: 905-451-7158
888-524-4844
www.smca.ca
Former Name: Savage & Moles Chartered Accountants
Number of Employees: 12

Soberman LLP Chartered Accountants
Also listed under: *Trustees in Bankruptcy*
#1100, 2 St. Clair Ave. East
Toronto, ON M4T 2T5
416-964-7633
Fax: 416-964-6454
info@soberman.com
www.soberman.com
Ownership: Private.
Year Founded: 1958
Number of Employees: 125+
Revenues: $10-50 million
Profile: The firm provides services in accounting, auditing, business valuation, corporate & personal bankruptcy, corporate finance, corporate workout & turnaround strategies, due diligence, ElderCare, estates & trusts, financial consulting, forensic investigation litigation support, management services, mergers & acquisitions, succession planning & tax (domestic & international), claims valuation & media services. Affiliates include Soberman Isenbaum Colomby Tessis Inc. & Soberman Due Diligence Inc.

Partners:
Eric Bornstein, Managing Partner; 416-963-7100
Martin Starr, Principal; 416-963-7119
Don Borts; 416-963-7101
Jerry Cukier; 416-963-7104
Rukshana Dinshaw; 416-963-7190
Daniel M. Edwards; 416-963-7221
Larry Goldstein; 416-963-7197
Dirk Joustra; 416-963-7110
Sam Kaner; 416-963-7111
Gary Kopstick; 416-963-7113
Des Levin; 416-963-7115
Karyn Lipman; 416-963-7159
Neil L. Maisel; 416-963-7116
Eli Palachi; 416-963-7123
Paul Rhodes; 416-963-7217
Adam Rubinoff; 416-963-7178
Karen Slezak; 416-963-7109
Deborah E. Stern; 416-963-7103
Ken Tessis; 416-963-7120
Alan Wainer; 416-963-7121
Sam Zuk; 416-963-7122

Soden & Co.
25 Campbell St.
Belleville, ON K8N 1S6
613-968-3495
Fax: 613-968-7359
Year Founded: 1971
Number of Employees: 12
Executives:
Kenneth Soden, CA, Partner
Kerry Soden, CA, Partner

Sone & Rovet
#512, 1200 Sheppard Ave. East
Toronto, ON M2K 2S5
416-498-7200
Fax: 416-498-6877
www.sonerovet.com
Year Founded: 1990
Number of Employees: 10
Profile: Provides services in accounting & auditing, taxation, financial planning, business consulting, and record keeping.

Executives:
Monica Alimchandani, Manager; monica@sonerovet.com
Randy M. Rovet, Partner; randy@sonerovet.com
Howard Sone, Partner; howard@sonerovet.com

Southcott Davoli Professional Corporation
Also listed under: *Financial Planning*
PO Box 68
76 Main St. West
Grimsby, ON L3M 4G1
905-945-4942
Fax: 905-945-0306
contactus@southdav.com
Executives:
Delight Davoli
Mark Southcott

Stanley Kwan & Company
#1400, 4950 Yonge St.
Toronto, ON M2N 6K1
416-226-6668
Fax: 416-226-6862
stankwan@skco.ca
Ownership: Private
Year Founded: 1993
Number of Employees: 15
Partners:
Stanley Kwan, CA, MBA
Michelle Ha, CA
Anne Law, CA

Starkman Salsberg & Feldberg
#316, 1600 Steeles Ave. West
Concord, ON L4K 4M2
905-669-9900
Fax: 905-669-9901

Steven Brates
Also listed under: *Financial Planning*
#209, 5805 Whittle Rd.
Mississauga, ON L4Z 2J1
905-502-7505
Fax: 905-502-7662
Profile: Tax services are provided.

Executives:
Steven Brates, Principal

Stevenson & Lehocki
310 Plains Rd. East
Burlington, ON L7T 4J2
905-632-0640
Fax: 905-632-0645
joe@stevensonlehocki.com
www.stevensonlehocki.com
Ownership: Private
Year Founded: 1981
Number of Employees: 11
Revenues: $1-5 million
Profile: The firm provides accounting, auditing, financing & taxation services. It also installs computerized accounting systems for small & medium-sized businesses.

Executives:
Joe Lehocki, Partner; joe@stevensonlehocki.com
Ron Lehocki, Partner; ron@stevensonlehocki.com
Bob Stevenson, Partner; bob@stevensonlehocki.com

Stevenson & Partners LLP
567 Coverdale Rd.
Riverview, NB E1B 3K7
506-387-4044
Fax: 506-387-7270
sp@PARTNERSNB.COM
Year Founded: 1982
Profile: Provides public accounting services to clients throughout the Moncton area.

Executives:
David W. Stevenson, CA, Partner; dave.stevenson@PARTNERSNB.com
David P. Lund, CA, Partner; david.lund@PARTNERSNB.com
W. Alex Mattice, CA, Partner; alex.mattice@PARTNERSNB.com

Douglas W. Seeglitz, CA, Partner; doug.seeglitz@PARTNERSNB.com

Stewart & Kett Financial Advisors Inc.
Also listed under: *Financial Planning*
#911, 123 Front St. West
Toronto, ON M5J 2M2
416-362-6322
Fax: 416-362-6302
www.stewartkett.com
Former Name: Stewart & Co. Financial Advisors Inc./Kett Financial Services
Ownership: Private
Year Founded: 1996
Number of Employees: 4
Profile: Stewart & Kett provides comprehensive, advice-only financial planning, accounting & tax services for business owners, senior executives, trusts & retirees. The following planning areas include: cash management, tax, investment, retirement, risk management & estate.

Executives:
Cynthia Kett, CA, CGA, RFP, CFP, Principal; ckett@stewartkett.com
David H. Stewart, MBA, RFP, CFP, Principal; dstewart@stewartkett.com

Surgeson Carson Associates Inc.
Also listed under: *Trustees in Bankruptcy*
#18, 99 Fifth Ave.
Ottawa, ON K1S 5K4
613-567-6434
Fax: 613-567-0752
questions@surgesoncarson.com
www.surgesoncarson.com
Number of Employees: 7
Executives:
Michael K. Carson, Trustee; mcarson@surgesoncarson.com
Kevin L. McCart, Trustee; kmccart@surgesoncarson.com
Richard Surgeson, Trustee; rsurgeson@surgesoncarson.com

SVS Group LLP
#100, 17010 - 103 Ave.
Edmonton, AB T5S 1K7
780-486-3357
Fax: 780-486-3320
info@svsgroup.ca
www.svsgroup.ca
Former Name: Slamko Visser Severin & Company LLP; Slamko Visser Chartered Accountants
Ownership: Private
Year Founded: 1983
Number of Employees: 20
Profile: An affiliated company is Advanex Consulting Group.

Partners:
Nancy L. Beauchemin
Burt Krull
Rod Robertson
Brad Severein
Gerry Slamko
Dennis Visser
David A. Williams

Taylor Leibow LLP, Accountants & Advisors
Also listed under: *Trustees in Bankruptcy*
#700, 105 Main St. East
Hamilton, ON L8N 1G6
905-523-0000
Fax: 905-523-4681
888-287-2525
info@taylorleibow.com

ACCOUNTING & LAW

Taylor Leibow LLP, Accountants & Advisors (continued)
www.taylorleibow.com
Year Founded: 1947
Number of Employees: 60+
Executives:
Nigel Jacobs, CEO
Stephen Wiseman, Sr. Partner
Peter Cross, Partner
Branches:
Brantford
#403, 333 Colborne St.
Brantford, ON N3T 2H4 Canada
519-753-7361
Fax: 519-753-1711
Burlington
3410 South Service Rd., 1st Fl.
Burlington, ON L7N 3T2 Canada
905-637-9959
Fax: 905-637-3195
St Catharines
#604, 43 Church St.
St Catharines, ON L2R 7E1 Canada
905-680-4728
Fax: 905-523-2979

Terlesky Braithwaite Janzen, Certified General Accountants
#300, 180 Victoria St.
Prince George, BC V2L 2J2
250-564-2014
Fax: 250-564-5613
888-564-2014
tbjpg@tbjcga.com
www.tbjcga.com
Former Name: Curtis, Terlesky & Company; R.B. Terlesky & Company; Terlesky Braithwaite & Co.
Year Founded: 1978
Number of Employees: 20
Profile: McNeill & Co. & Rob Robson, Chartered Accountant were purchased by TBJ to form the present firm. Services include accounting & auditing, taxation, goods & services tax, management consulting & estates & trusts.

Executives:
Jeff A. Janzen, Partner
Ian H. McInnes, Partner
Dan McNeill, Associate
Branches:
Mackenzie
PO Box 311
577 Skeena Dr.
Mackenzie, BC V0J 2C0 Canada
250-997-6611
Fax: 250-997-3499
888-997-6611
tbjmk@tbjcga.com
Murray F. Braithwaite, Partner

Transport Financial Services Ltd.
***Also listed under:** Financing & Loan Companies*
105 Bauer Pl.
Waterloo, ON N2L 6B5
519-886-8070
Fax: 519-886-5214
800-461-5970
www.tfsgroup.com/tfs
Ownership: Private
Year Founded: 1974
Offices:
Oshawa
PO Box 264
#27, 1300 King St. East
Oshawa, ON L1H 8J4 Canada
905-432-8070
Fax: 905-432-8071
frang@tfsgroup.com
Fran Graham, Manager

Truster Zweig LLP
#200, 66 West Beaver Creek Rd.
Richmond Hill, ON L4B 1G5
416-222-5555
Fax: 905-707-1322
perry@trusterzweig.com
Ownership: Private
Year Founded: 1993
Number of Employees: 30
Profile: Provides accounting, tax preparation, bookkeeping and payroll services.

Partners:
Brian Lusthaus
Mario Marrelli
Mark Pelchovitz
Steven Pelchovitz
Monty Shelson
Perry Truster, FCA, TEP

V.B. Sharma Professional Corporation, Chartered Accountants
#200, 3390 Midland Ave.
Toronto, ON M1V 5K3
416-292-4431
Fax: 416-292-7247
vbsharma@vbsharma.ca
www.vbsharma.ca
Year Founded: 1974
Number of Employees: 12
Profile: The firm provides auditing, review, compilation, taxation & consulting services. It has international contacts for collaborations & tax planning.

Executives:
V.B. Sharma, CA, CPA, B.Com., FCA, Owner, Chartered Accountant

Valerie L. Burrell Chartered Accountant
#201, 101 - 6 St. SW
Sundre, AB T0M 1X0
403-638-3116
Fax: 403-638-9166
valb@telusplanet.net
www.sundre-cornerbrook.com/Accountant/
Ownership: Private
Year Founded: 1999
Number of Employees: 2
Executives:
Valerie Burrell, Owner

Verrier Paquin Hébert SENCRL
212, rue Heriot
Drummondville, QC J2C 1J8
819-477-6311
Fax: 819-477-9572
drville@verrier.com
www.verrier.com

Vertefeuille Kassam Chartered Accountants
#401, 304 - 8 Ave. SW
Calgary, AB T2P 1C2
403-294-0733
Fax: 403-294-0734
www.vertkassam.com
Ownership: Private
Year Founded: 1999
Number of Employees: 8
Profile: The firm provides accounting, assurance, financial advisory, tax planning & consulting services to an extensive variety of clients across a broad range of industries.

Partners:
Kevin Vertefeuille, CMA, CA
Minaz Kassam, CA

Wade & Partners LLP, Chartered Accountants
#102, 5096 South Service Rd.
Burlington, ON L7L 5H4
905-333-9888
Fax: 905-333-9583
ca@wadegroup.ca
www.wadegroup.ca
Ownership: Private
Year Founded: 1968
Number of Employees: 20
Partners:
James E. Chagnon
Mark J. Matson
William E. Sloper
Lawrence E. Wade

Waked
#2825, 500, Place d'Armes
Montréal, QC H2Y 2W2
514-875-6400
Fax: 514-861-6301
waked@wakedcma.com
www.wakedcma.com
Profile: Provides accounting, assurance, financial & management consulting, and tax services.

Executives:
Tony Waked, CMA; waked@wakedcma.com

Walters Hoffe
30 Roe Av.
Gander, NL A1V 1X5
709-651-4100
Ownership: Private
Year Founded: 1970
Number of Employees: 20
Revenues: $1-5 million
Profile: Chartered accountants provide a full range of accounting, auditing, taxation & consulting services.

Branches:
Clarenville
PO Box 716
1 Manitoba Dr.
Clarenville, NL A0E 1J0 Canada
709-466-2658
Fax: 709-466-3928
Gander
PO Box 31
30 Roe Ave.
Gander, NL A1V 1X5 Canada
709-651-4100
Fax: 709-256-2950
Happy Valley - Goose Bay
PO Box 1029, B Sta. B
167 Hamilton River Rd.
Happy Valley-Goose Bay, NL A0P 1E0 Canada
709-896-2961
Fax: 709-896-9160

Watson Aberant Chartered Accountants (L.L.P.)
***Also listed under:** Financial Planning*
4212 - 98th St.
Edmonton, AB T6E 6A1
780-438-5969
Fax: 780-437-3918
info@watsonaberant.com
Ownership: Private
Year Founded: 1985
Number of Employees: 22
Assets: $1-5 million
Revenues: $1-5 million
Profile: The chartered accountant firm serves Edmonton & northern Alberta.

Executives:
Michael Aberant, Partner, Public Companies & Business Plans; mike@watsonaberant.com
Case Watson, Partner, Owner Managed Enterprises; case@watsonaberant.com

WBLI Chartered Accountants
26 Union St.
Bedford, NS B4A 2B5
902-835-7333
Fax: 902-835-5297
www.wbli.ca
Profile: The firm provides audits, review and compilation engagements, special purpose audits, financial investigations, systems analysis, operational reviews, projections and pro forma reporting, accounting systems/software selection and training, CRA remittances and compliance advice, payroll administration, and bookkeeping services.

Partners:
R. Brian Burgess; bburgess@wbli.ca
Kirk D. Higgins; khiggins@wbli.ca
Brad J. Langille; blangille@wbli.ca
Stephanie O'Connor; soconnor@wbli.ca
Gerald J. White
Branches:
Truro
PO Box 1435
#301, 640 Prince St.
Truro, NS B2N 5V2 Canada
902-897-9291
Fax: 902-897-9293

Weiler & Company
#3, 512 Woolwich St.
Guelph, ON N1H 3X7

519-837-3111
Fax: 519-837-1049
888-239-3111
weiler@weiler.ca
www.weiler.ca
Ownership: Private
Year Founded: 1986
Number of Employees: 20
Assets: $1-5 million
Revenues: $1-5 million
Profile: Accounting & computer consulting services are provided.

Partners:
Lori Halliday, CA
Michael Kerr, CA
Fred Neil, CA
Dan Waterson, CA
Dennis Weiler, CA
Martha Zettle, CA

Welch & Company LLP

Also listed under: *Financial Planning*
151 Slater St., 12th Fl.
Ottawa, ON K1P 5H3
613-236-9191
Fax: 613-236-8258
welch@welchandco.ca
www.welchandco.ca
Ownership: Private
Year Founded: 1918
Profile: The firm serves business, government & not-for-profit clients. Taxation, accounting, auditing, personal financial planning & wealth management services are provided.

Executives:
Mark Patry, CA, Principal; mpatry@welchandco.ca
Rick Reid, CA, Principal; rreid@welchandco.ca
Don Timmins, CA, Managing Partner, Ottawa; dtimmins@welchandco.ca
Branches:
Belleville
525 Dundas St. East
Belleville, ON K8N 1G4 Canada
613-966-2844
Fax: 613-966-2206
welchbvl@welch.on.ca
Glenn Collins, Partner
Campbellford
PO Box 1209
57 Bridge St. East
Campbellford, ON K0L 1L0 Canada
705-653-3194
Fax: 705-653-1703
mnorthey@welch.on.ca
Marie Northey, Partner
Cornwall
36 Second St. East
Cornwall, ON K6H 1Y3 Canada
613-932-4953
Fax: 613-932-1731
mail@welchcornwall.on.ca
Ron Mulligan, Partner
Gatineau
#201, 975, boul St-Joseph
Gatineau, QC J8Z 1W8 Canada
819-771-7381
Fax: 819-771-3089
lm@levesquemarchand.ca
Guy Coté, Partner
Napanee
58 Dundas St. East
Napanee, ON K7R 1H8 Canada
613-354-2169
Fax: 613-354-2160
datkinson@welch.on.ca
Dan Atkinson, Partner
Ottawa
151 Slater Street, 12th Fl.
Ottawa, ON K1P 5H3 Canada
613-236-9191
Fax: 613-236-8258
welch@welchandco.ca
Garth Steele, Partner
Pembroke
PO Box 757
270 Lake St.
Pembroke, ON K8A 6X9 Canada
613-735-1021
Fax: 613-735-2071
hward@welch-pembroke.com
Hal Ward, Partner
Picton
290 Main St.
Picton, ON K0K 2T0 Canada
613-476-3283
Fax: 613-476-1627
jrand@welch.on.ca
Judy Rand, Partner
Renfrew
101 Raglan St. North
Renfrew, ON K7V 1N7 Canada
613-432-8399
Fax: 613-432-9154
damyotte@welchandco.ca
Dan Amyotte, Partner
Trenton
#4, 290 Dundas St. West
Trenton, ON K8V 3S1 Canada
613-392-1287
Fax: 613-392-5456
jbailey@welch.on.ca
John Bailey, Partner
Tweed
PO Box 807
63 Victoria St. North
Tweed, ON K0K 3J0 Canada
613-478-5051
Fax: 613-478-3069
mnorthey@welch.on.ca
Marie Northey, Partner

Wilkinson & Company LLP

Also listed under: *Financial Planning*
PO Box 400
71 Dundas St. West
Trenton, ON K8V 5R6
613-392-2592
Fax: 613-392-8512
888-713-7283
trenton@wilkinson.net
www.wilkinson.net
Year Founded: 1964
Profile: The firm specializes in accounting & tax planning & preparation. Specific services include audits, business advisory, financial planning, wealth management, succession planning, estate planning & retirement planning. It serves corporate, not-for-profit organization & personal clients.

Executives:
Rob Cory, CA, Partner
Jim L. Coward, CA, CFP, Partner
Bob Robertson, CA, Partner
Stephen Thompson, CA, CFP, TEP, Partner
Robert Yager, CA, Partner
Branches:
Belleville
PO Box 757
139 Front St.
Belleville, ON K8N 5B5 Canada
613-966-5105
Fax: 613-962-7072
888-728-3890
belleville@wilkinson.net
R.G. (Rob) Deacon, Partner
Kingston
#201, 785 Midpark Dr.
Kingston, ON K7M 7G3 Canada
613-634-5581
Fax: 613-634-5585
866-692-0055
kingston@wilkinson.net
Jennifer Fisher, Partner

Williams Rawding MacDonald

400 East River Rd.
New Glasgow, NS B2H 3P7
902-752-0463
Fax: 902-755-2823
admin@wrmca.ca
http://www.wrmca.ca
Former Name: Steele Williams & Rawding
Number of Employees: 14
Profile: Full-service accounting firm which provides services throughout North East Nova Scotia, but particularly in Pictou County.

Executives:
Kent Williams, CA, Partner; fkw@wrmca.ca
John C. Rawding, CA, Partner; john@wrmca.ca
Kevin MacDonald, CA, Partner; Kevin@wrmca.ca

Young Parkyn McNab LLP(YPM)

Also listed under: *Trustees in Bankruptcy*
#100, 530 - 8 St. South
Lethbridge, AB T1J 2J8
403-382-6800
Fax: 403-327-8990
800-665-5034
www.ypm.ca
Ownership: Private
Year Founded: 1933
Number of Employees: 75
Profile: Services include the following: agricultural; audit; bookkeeping & year-end; business advisory; business start-up; corporate finance; family-owned business; fraud prevention & forensic; information systems & technology; personal services; valuations & litigation.

Partners:
Harvey V. Labuhn; harvey.labuhn@ypm.ca
Ernie R. Lawson; ernie.lawson@ypm.ca
Thomas McNab; tom.mcnab@ypm.ca
Doug B. Mundell; doug.mundell@ypm.ca
Bob Rice; bob.rice@ypm.ca
George G. Virtue; george.virtue@ypm.ca
Branches:
Claresholm
4902 - 2nd St. West
Claresholm, AB T0L 0T0 Canada
403-625-4448
Fax: 403-625-4400
Fort MacLeod
PO Box 1780
2315 - 2 Ave.
Fort MacLeod, AB T0L 0Z0 Canada
403-553-3355
Fax: 403-553-2696
Jim S. Monteith, Partner
Milk River
125 Main St. NW
Milk River, AB T0K 1M0 Canada
403-647-3662
Fax: 403-647-3868
877-616-6064
Pincher Creek
710 Main St.
Pincher Creek, AB T0K 1W0 Canada
403-627-5510
Fax: 403-627-1440
Taber
5334 - 49th Ave.
Taber, AB T1G 1T8 Canada
403-223-0056
Fax: 403-223-0059
877-616-6064
bryce.bennett@ypm.ca
Bryce Bennett, Partner

Zeifman & Company

201 Bridgeland Ave.
Toronto, ON M6A 1Y7
416-256-4000
Fax: 416-256-4001
info@zeifman.ca
www.zeifman.ca
Ownership: Private
Year Founded: 1959
Number of Employees: 55
Profile: Services include the following: auditing & accounting, taxation, mergers & acquisitions, corporate finance & management, international diversification & acquisition consulting, corporate recovery & insolvency, and corporate turnaround management.

Partners:
Robert J. Benmergui, Principal
Edward M. Kalkstein, CA

Zeifman & Company (continued)
Brian T. McGee, CA
Steven I. Roth, CA
Allan A. Rutman, CA
Ronald C. Rutman, CA
Israel S. Schon, CA
C. Meyer Zeifman, CA, Counsel
Jeffrey Zeifman, BAS, Principal
Laurence W. Zeifman, CA

Zwaig Consulting Inc.
Also listed under: *Trustees in Bankruptcy*
#801, 20 Adelaide St. East
Toronto, ON M5X 2T6
416-863-0140
Fax: 416-863-0428
zwaigm@zwaig.com
www.zwaig.com
Ownership: Private.
Year Founded: 1998
Number of Employees: 20
Assets: $1-5 million Year End: 20060930
Revenues: $1-5 million Year End: 20060930
Profile: Financial restructuring & forensic accounting services are offered. The company is affiliated with Zwaig Associates, Inc.
Executives:
Melvin C. Zwaig, President/CEO; 416-863-5795; zwaigm@zwaig.com
Robert Cumming, Vice-President; cummingr@zwaig.com
Cameron A. McCaw, Vice-President; mccawc@zweig.com
John P. Curran, Counsel; curranj@zwaig.com

Actuarial Consultants

ACS HR Solutions
#1500, 95 Wellington St. West
Toronto, ON M5J 2N7
416-865-0060
Fax: 416-865-1301
infocanada@acs-hro.com
www.buckconsultants.com; www.acs-inc.com
Former Name: Buck Consultants
Ownership: Public
Year Founded: 1998
Number of Employees: 53,000
Stock Symbol: ACS
Profile: The following services are offered: pension, benefits, insurance consulting, compensation consulting, actuarial, administration, HR consulting & benefits outsourcing.
Executives:
Jan Grude, President/CEO, Canada; jan.grude@acs-hro.com
Greg Fayarchuk, Sr. Vice-President, Business Development; greg.fayarchuk@acs-hro.com
Jacquie Walker, Sr. Vice-President, Client Relationship Management; jacquie.walker@acs-hro.com
Jo-Anne Billinger, Sr. Vice-President, Client Relationship Management; jo-anne.billinger@acs-hro.com
Branches:
Montréal
#1750, 999, boul de Maisonneuve ouest
Montréal, QC H3A 3L4 Canada
514-987-1510
Fax: 514-987-6422
Normand Gendron, Office Manager
Ottawa
Dow's Lake Court
#440, 875 Carling Ave.
Ottawa, ON K1S 5P1 Canada
613-798-2825
Fax: 613-798-7142
Richard Laberge, Office Manager

Actuarial Experts Consulting Ltd.
#264, 1096 Queen St.
Halifax, NS B3H 2R9
902-425-5008
Fax: 902-425-6246
acturay@ns.sympatico.ca
Executives:
Paul Conrad, Actuary

Aon Consulting/ Groupe-conseil Aon
Also listed under: *Holding & Other Investment Companies*
#500, 145 Wellington St.
Toronto, ON M5J 1H8
416-542-5500
Fax: 416-542-5504
www.aon.com
Ownership: Public. Parent Aon Corporation
Year Founded: 1996
Number of Employees: 550
Stock Symbol: AOC
Profile: Aon Consulting is the consulting arm of Aon Corporation. It provides full integrated consulting services covering the wide spectrum of health & benefits, retirement, human resources, change management, compensation & workers' compensation requirements.
Executives:
Ashim Khemani, Chair/Chief Executive
Branches:
Calgary
Gulf Canada Square
#885, 401 - 9th Ave. SW
Calgary, AB T2P 3C5 Canada
403-261-6056
Fax: 403-262-2446
kaylynn.schroeder@aon.ca
Kaylynn Schroeder, Contact
Edmonton
#700, 10025 - 102A Ave.
Edmonton, AB T5J 2Z2 Canada
780-423-1010
Fax: 780-425-8295
kaylynn.schroeder@aon.ca
Kaylynn Schroeder, Contact
Halifax
Tower II, Purdy's Wharf
#1001, 1969 Upper Water St.
Halifax, NS B3J 3R7 Canada
902-423-8714
Fax: 902-423-8716
sherry.lee.gregory@aon.ca
Sherry Lee Gregory, Contact
London
One London Place
#1400, 255 Queens Ave.
London, ON N6A 5R8 Canada
519-434-2114
Fax: 519-434-9950
888-337-3334
kaylynn.schroeder@aon.ca
Kaylynn Schroeder, Contact
Montréal
#1100, 1801, av McGill College
Montréal, QC H3A 3P4 Canada
514-845-6231
Fax: 514-845-0678
louis.p.gagnon@aon.ca
Louis P. Gagnon, Contact
Ottawa
#712, 1525 Carling Ave.
Ottawa, ON K1Z 8R9 Canada
613-728-5000
Fax: 513-728-5534
julie.joyal@aon.ca
Julie Joyal, Contact
Québec
Place de la Cité
PO Box 9850, Sainte-Foy Sta. Sainte-Foy
#750, 2600, boul Laurier
Québec, QC G1V 4C3 Canada
418-650-1119
Fax: 418-650-1440
france.bilodeau@aon.ca
France Bilodeau, Contact
Regina
#1000, 2103 - 11th Ave.
Regina, SK S4P 3Z8 Canada
306-569-6749
Fax: 306-359-0387
kaylynn.schroeder@aon.ca
Kaylynn Schroeder, Contact
Saskatoon
Canada Bldg.
105 - 21st St. East, 8th Fl.
Saskatoon, SK S7K 0B3 Canada
306-934-8680
Fax: 306-244-7597
kaylynn.schroeder@aon.ca
Kaylynn Schroeder, Contact
Vancouver
900 Howe St., 5th Fl.
Vancouver, BC V6B 3X8 Canada
604-688-8591
Fax: 604-684-9902
kaylynn.schroeder@aon.ca
Kaylynn Schroeder, Contact
Winnipeg
#1800, 1 Lombard Pl.
Winnipeg, MB R3B 2A3 Canada
204-954-5500
Fax: 204-954-5501
kaylynn.schroeder@aon.ca
Kaylynn Schroeder, Contact

Baron Insurance Services Inc.
#205, 206 Laird Dr.
Toronto, ON M4G 3W4
416-486-0093
Fax: 416-486-6300
www.baronactuaries.com
Year Founded: 1998
Profile: Actuaries & consultants.
Executives:
Barb Addie, Principal; 416-486-0093; barb@baronactuaries.com
Ron Miller, Principal; 416-486-0097; ron@baronactuaries.com

BCM Actuarial Consulting Ltd.
939 Ferndale Cres.
Newmarket, ON L3Y 6B6
905-898-3843
Fax: 905-898-3849
bruce@consultbcm.com
Profile: Pension administration & actuarial consulting are offered.
Bruce Michael; bruce@consultbcm.com

Burnell Actuarial Consulting Inc.
#2200, 1969 Upper Water St.
Halifax, NS B3J 3R7
902-491-4278
Fax: 902-429-0971
bburnell@purdyswharf.com
www.burnellactuarial.ns.ca
Profile: Actuarial services are offered in the following areas: wrongful dismissal, pension value, personal injury & fatal injury.
Executives:
Brian L. Burnell, President

Capital G Consulting Inc.
#210, 1 Balmoral Ave.
Toronto, ON M4V 3B9
416-513-1400
Fax: 416-920-7060
inquiries@capitalgconsulting.com
www.capitalgconsulting.com
Profile: Actuarial advice & retirement education are among services provided.
Executives:
Brian FitzGerald, Consulting Actuary

Christie Consulting Inc.
6849 Adera St.
Vancouver, BC V6P 5C2
604-269-0827
Fax: 604-269-0826
john-christie@shaw.ca
Executives:
John Christie, Contact

Crozier Consultants
BCE Place
#4200, 181 Bay St.
Toronto, ON M5J 2T3
416-361-0695
Executives:
A. Crozier, Actuary

Demner Consulting Services Ltd.
#280, 2025 West 42nd Ave.
Vancouver, BC V6M 2B5
604-266-2445
Fax: 604-266-1530
dcs@demner.com
www.demner.com

Profile: DCS offers actuarial & financial services.

Executives:
Michael Demner, Actuary
Elizabeth Demner, Administrator, Benefits
Rose Wong, Administrator, Pension & Savings Plans
Sindy Martinez, Manager, Marketing
David Demner, Systems Analyst

Dilkes, Jeffery & Associates Inc.
#217, 379 Dundas St.
London, ON
519-673-6680
Fax: 519-663-9833
j2.jeffery@sympatico.ca
James Jeffery; j2.jeffery@sympatico.ca

Dion, Durrell & Associates Inc.
#306, 20 Queen St. West
Toronto, ON M5H 3R3
416-408-2626
Fax: 416-408-3721
www.dion-durrell.com
Profile: The actuarial & insurance consultants create & implement strategies which encompass risk financing, insurance management & insurance distribution.

Branches:
Montréal
#2940, 630, boul René-Lévesque ouest
Montréal, QC H3B 1S6 Canada
514-395-9991
Fax: 514-395-8174
866-395-9991

Donaldson Vincent Associates Limited
#1, 26 Lesmill Rd.
Toronto, ON M3B 2T5
416-447-7900
Fax: 416-445-4504
dva@dvassociates.com
www.dvassociates.com
Former Name: Donaldson Associates; B.J. Vincent Company Limited
Ownership: Private.
Year Founded: 1997
Number of Employees: 5
Assets: Under $1 million
Revenues: Under $1 million
Profile: DV Associates provides actuarial, employee benefit & investment consulting.

Executives:
Donald Armstrong, Principal

DSW Actuarial Services Inc.
#236-35B, 10520 Yonge St.
Richmond Hill, ON L4C 3C7
905-770-7300
Fax: 905-780-5756
information@dswactuarial.com
www.dswactuarial.com
Year Founded: 2002
Profile: One area of actuarial service offered is pension consulting to both organizations & individuals.

Executives:
David Wolgelerenter, Actuary

Eckler Ltd.
***Also listed under:** Financial Planning*
#900, 110 Sheppard Ave. East
Toronto, ON M2N 7A3
416-429-3330
Fax: 416-429-3794
www.eckler.ca
Former Name: Eckler Partners Ltd.
Ownership: Private.
Year Founded: 1927
Number of Employees: 230
Profile: Eckler Partners Ltd. changed its name to Eckler Ltd., effective January 1, 2007. The independent actuarial & consulting firm provides financial services, pension & employee benefits consulting, communications, investment management, pension administration, change management & technology. The Canadian-owned company has offices in Canada, Barbados, West Indies, Jamaica, & West Indies. The Milliman Global website is as follows: www.millimanglobal.com

Executives:
William T. Weiland, President; 416-696-3011; bweiland@eckler.ca
Steven A. Raiken, CAO, Secretary; 416-696-3001; sraiken@eckler.ca
Wafaa Babcock, Principal
Nicholas Bauer, Principal
Anthony Benjamin, Principal, Treasurer; 416-696-3027; abenjamin@eckler.ca
Richard Border, Principal
Gilles Bouchard, Principal
Sandra Dudley, Principal
Luc Farmer, Principal
Christine Finlay, Principal
Steve Gendron, Principal
Sylvain Goulet, Principal
David Grace, Principal
Stephen Haist, Principal
Paul Harrietha, Principal
Wendy Harrison, Principal
Peter Hayes, Principal
Charles Herbert, Principal
Cameron Hunter, Principal
Sean Keys, Principal
Richard Labelle, Principal
Greg Malone, Principal
Todd McLean, Principal
George Mitchell, Principal
Brian Pelly, Principal
Douglas Poapst, Principal
Cynthia Potts, Principal
André Racine, Principal
Pierre St-Onge, Principal
Jill M. Wagman, Principal
Thomas Weddell, Principal
Hugh White, Principal
Phillip Whittaker, Principal
Directors:
Anthony J. Benjamin; 416-696-3027
David Grace; 416-696-3072
Wendy Harrison; 604-682-1386
Charles Herbert; 246-228-0865
Todd McLean; 416-696-3059
William T. Weiland; 416-696-3011
Hugh White; 416-696-3030
Branches:
Halifax
#503, 1969 Upper Water St.
Halifax, NS B3J 3R7 Canada
902-492-2822
Fax: 902-454-9398
Peter Hayes, Partner
Montréal
#2200, 800, boul René-Lévesque ouest
Montréal, QC H3B 1X9 Canada
514-848-9077
Fax: 514-395-1188
Gilles Bouchard, Partner
Québec
#30, 3107, av des Hotels
Québec, QC G1W 4W5 Canada
418-780-1366
Fax: 418-780-1368
Richard Larouche, Contact
Vancouver
#980, 475 West Georgia St.
Vancouver, BC V6B 4M9 Canada
604-682-1381
Fax: 604-669-1510
Tom Weddel, Partner
Winnipeg
#1750, 1 Lombard Pl.
Winnipeg, MB R3B 0X3 Canada
204-988-1586
Fax: 204-988-1589
Doug Poapst, Partner

Gmeiner Actuarial Services Inc.
Clayton Professional Centre
#214, 255 Lacewood Dr.
Halifax, NS B3M 4G2
902-457-2553
Fax: 902-443-0739
jessie@gmact.ca
www.gmact.ca
Year Founded: 1993
Profile: Specializes in providing actuarial reports and consulting services for law firms. Their expertise lies in the quantification of future financial losses and the division of property on marriage breakdown.

Executives:
Jessie Shaw Gmeiner, Actuary

Gooden & Kerr Actuaries & Retirement Plan Consultants
#250, 505 - 3 St. SW
Calgary, AB T2P 3E6
403-263-5027
Fax: 403-264-4872
info@goodenandkerr.com
www.goodenandkerr.com
Profile: The actuarial consulting firm focuses upon retirement benefits.

Executives:
W.J. (Bill) Gooden, Principal
J. Robert Kerr, Principal

Gordon B. Lang & Associates Inc., Actuaries & Financial Consultants
#260, 1209 - 59th Ave. SE
Calgary, AB T2H 2P6
403-249-1820
Fax: 403-246-2431
877-249-2999
info@glinc.ca, admin@gblinc.ca, support@gblinc.ca
www.gblinc.ca
Year Founded: 1995
Profile: GBL Inc. offers actuarial & tax consulting services to incorporated businesses.

Executives:
Gordon B. Lang, President/CEO; gordon.lang@gblinc.ca
Andrew Holden, Sr. Vice-President, Alberta & Saskatchewan
Jeff UnRuh, Vice-President, Southern Alberta
Branches:
Surrey
1441 King George Hwy.
Surrey, BC V4A 9R3 Canada
604-538-0723
Fax: 604-538-0725
info@gblinc.ca
Martin Horsburgh, Sr. Vice-President, British Columbia
Toronto
#1001, 100 Adelaide St. West
Toronto, ON M5H 1S3 Canada
416-941-9829
Fax: 416-941-9840
888-941-9829
info@gblinc.ca
Trevor R. Parry, Exec. Vice-President, Sales & Marketing

Hart Actuarial Consulting Ltd.
2851 Rainbow Cres.
Mississauga, ON L5L 2H7
905-820-4810
Fax: 905-820-5520
dhart@an-actual-actuary.com
www.an-actual-actuary.com
Ownership: Private
Year Founded: 1993
Number of Employees: 1
Assets: Under $1 million
Revenues: Under $1 million
Profile: Actuarial consultant.

Executives:
David C. Hart, FSA, FCIA, Consulting Actuary; 905-820-4810; dhart@an-actual-actuary.com
Directors:
David C. Hart, FSA, FCIA
Shirley M. Hart

The IAO Actuarial Consultants Services
#430, 90 Allstate Pkwy.
Markham, ON L3R 6H3
905-474-7428
Fax: 905-474-5123
800-268-8080
asif.sardar at iao.ca
www.iao.ca
Number of Employees: 5

The IAO Actuarial Consultants Services (continued)
Profile: Provider of risk information, loss prevention & control services, commercial inspections, actuarial & other specialized risk management & insurance consulting services.

Executives:
Kevin A. Lee, Vice-President

Karp Actuarial Services Ltd. (1985)
#209, 3540 West 41st Ave.
Vancouver, BC V6N 3E6
604-266-0936
Fax: 604-266-3340
ian@karpactuarial.com
www.karpactuarial.com
Year Founded: 1985
Profile: Specializes in work for B.C. lawyers in litigation cases, in the following areas: personal injury & fatal accident cases, pension matrimonial, wrongful dismissal cases, criminal rate of interest calculations, estate calculations, and other matters involving present value calculations, or pension plan issues.

Executives:
Ian M. Karp, Consulting Actuary

Mercer Investment Consulting, Inc.
#800, 1981, av McGill College, 8e étage
Montréal, QC H3A 3T5
514-285-1802
Fax: 514-285-8831
www.merceric.ca
Ownership: Marsh & McLennan Companies, New York, USA.
Year Founded: 1945
Profile: Mercer Investment Consulting is part of Mercer Human Resource Consulting, which is part of Mercer Inc. Mercer Inc. is a wholly owned subsidiary of Marsh & McLennan Companies. The investment consulting company assists with institutional investing, including ongoing portfolio management.

Executives:
Peter Muldowney, Principal, Mercer Investment Consulting, Canada
Sylvie St-Onge, Principal, Human Capital Advisory Services
Branches:
Calgary
Sun Life Tower II
#2800, 140 Fourth Ave SW
Calgary, AB T2P 3N3 Canada
403-269-4945
Fax: 403-261-6938
Edmonton
#2260, 10180 - 101st St.
Edmonton, AB T5J 3S4 Canada
780-483-5288
Fax: 780-483-5850
Halifax
#1300, 1801 Hollis St.
Halifax, NS B3J 3N4 Canada
902-429-7050
Fax: 902-423-1060
London
One London Place
#2400, 255 Queens Ave.
London, ON N6A 5R8 Canada
519-672-9310
Fax: 519-672-3472
Ottawa
Constitution Square I
#701, 360 Albert St.
Ottawa, ON K1R 7X7 Canada
613-230-9348
Fax: 613-230-9357
Québec
#400, 2954, boul Laurier
Québec, QC G1V 4T2 Canada
418-658-3435
Fax: 418-658-1768
Saskatoon
PCS Tower
#301, 122 - 1st Ave. South
Saskatoon, SK S7K 7E5 Canada
306-683-6950
Fax: 306-653-5090
St. John's
#900, 100 New Gower St.
St. John's, NL A1C 6K3 Canada
709-576-7146
Fax: 709-576-7098
Toronto - Bay St.
BCE Place
PO Box 501
161 Bay St.
Toronto, ON M5J 2S5 Canada
416-868-2000
Fax: 416-868-7671
Toronto - King St.
Sun Life Centre
#1802, 150 King St. West
Toronto, ON M5H 1J9 Canada
416-868-2000
Fax: 416-868-7900
Toronto - University Ave.
PO Box 5
70 University Ave.
Toronto, ON M5J 2M4 Canada
416-868-2000
Fax: 416-868-7671
Vancouver
#900, 550 Burrard St.
Vancouver, BC V6C 3S8 Canada
604-683-6761
Fax: 604-683-4639
Winnipeg
#1410, 1 Lombard Pl.
Winnipeg, MB R3B 0X5 Canada
204-947-0055
Fax: 204-943-8442

Morneau Sobeco
***Also listed under:** Pension & Money Management Companies*
1 Morneau Sobeco Centre
#700, 895 Don Mills Rd.
Toronto, ON M3C 1W3
416-445-2700
Fax: 416-445-7989
www.morneausobeco.com
Ownership: Public. Parent is Morneau Sobeco Income Fund.
Year Founded: 1966
Number of Employees: 1,018
Assets: $100-500 million Year End: 20051231
Revenues: $100-500 million Year End: 20051231
Stock Symbol: MSI.UN
Profile: Morneau Sobeco provides actuarial consultancy & pension & benefits administration. Affiliates include Morneau Sobeco Ltd., Morneau Sobeco Limited Partnership, Morneau Sobeco Corporation, Morneau Sobeco Group Limited Partnership, Morneau Sobeco GP Inc., & Morneau Sobeco Income Trust.

Executives:
William F. Morneau Jr., President/CEO; 416-383-6451; bmorneau@morneausobeco.com
Nancy Reid, Chief Financial Officer; 416-383-6488; nreid@morneausobeco.com
Pierre Sobeco, Chief Operating Officer
Branches:
Calgary
#1110, 940 - 6th Ave. SW
Calgary, AB T2P 3T1 Canada
403-246-5228
Fax: 403-246-5257
Doug Sample, Sr. Consultant
Edmonton
Scotia Place 2
#1601, 10060 Jasper Ave.
Edmonton, AB T5J 3R8 Canada
780-424-3756
Fax: 780-428-4819
Joyce Melnyk, Benefit Consultant
Fredericton
Carleton Place
#850, 520 King St.
Fredericton, NB E3B 6G3 Canada
506-458-9081
Fax: 506-458-9548
Conrad Ferguson, Partner
Halifax
CIBC Building
#701, 1809 Barrington St.
Halifax, NS B3J 3K8 Canada
902-429-8013
Fax: 902-420-1932
Greg Forbes, Partner
London
#700, 255 Queens Ave.
London, ON N6A 5R8 Canada
519-438-0193
Fax: 519-438-0196
Ramona Robinson, Principal
Montréal - René-Lévesque ouest
#1100, 500, boul René-Lévesque ouest
Montréal, QC H2Z 1W7 Canada
514-878-9090
Fax: 514-875-2673
Raymond Gaudet, Exec. Vice-President
Montréal - University
1060, rue University, 9e étage
Montréal, QC H3B 4V3 Canada
514-878-9090
Fax: 514-395-8773
Pierre Chamberland, Exec. Vice-President
Ottawa
#1203, 99 Metcalfe St.
Ottawa, ON K1P 6L7 Canada
613-238-4272
Fax: 613-238-3714
Denis Dupont, Principal
Québec
#100, 79, boul René-Lévesque est
Québec, QC G1R 5N5 Canada
418-529-4536
Fax: 418-529-6447
Pierre Courcy, Partner
St. John's
Fortis Bldg.
#602, 139 Water St.
St. John's, NL A1C 1B2 Canada
709-753-4500
Fax: 709-753-3207
Linda Evans, Principal
Vancouver
One Bentall Centre
#1580, 505 Burrard St.
Vancouver, BC V7X 1M5 Canada
604-642-5200
Fax: 604-632-9930
David Haber, Principal
Winnipeg
#105, 62 Hargrave St.
Winnipeg, MB R3C 1N1 Canada
204-487-1300
Fax: 204-487-0055
Bill Chapman, Contact

Satanove & Flood Consulting Ltd.
849 West 63rd Ave.
Vancouver, BC V6P 2H3
604-323-9363
Fax: 604-648-8410
info@satanoveflood.com
www.satanoveflood.com
Year Founded: 1999
Profile: Investment & pension consulting & communication services are provided to Western & Northern Canadian clients.

Executives:
Harry Satanove, Actuary & Consultant, Investments
Elspeth Flood, Consultant, Business Communications

Scott, Go Associates Inc.
#2200, 4950 Yonge St.
Toronto, ON M2N 6K1
416-585-2878
Fax: 416-585-9351
sga@ScottGo.ca
www.scottgo.ca
Profile: Actuarial consultation related to pensions are among services provided by the firm.

Executives:
Tian-Teck Go, Consulting Actuary

The Segal Company Ltd.
45 St. Clair Ave. West
Toronto, ON M4V 1K9
416-969-3960
Fax: 416-961-2101
www.segalco.ca
Branches:
Calgary

ACCOUNTING & LAW

#303, 6707 Elbow Dr. SW
Calgary, AB T2V 0E5 Canada
403-692-2264

Thompson Tomev Actuarial
87 Wolverleigh Blvd.
Toronto, ON M4J 1R8
416-466-3782
Fax: 416-406-4484
anne@thompson-actuarial.com
www.thompson-actuarial.com, www.personalpension.ca
Former Name: Thompson Actuarial Limited
Profile: The actuarial consulting firm provides solutions to small & medium-sized employers.

Executives:
Frederick J. Thompson, FSA, FCIA, President; 416-406-3037; fred@thompson-actuarial.com
Chris Tomev, FSA, FCIA, Partner; 416-466-3782; chris@thompson-actuarial.com
Scott Parkinson, FSA, FCIA, CFA, Actuary; 514-249-1533; scott@thompson-actuarial.com

Towers Perrin
South Tower
#1501, 175 Bloor St. East
Toronto, ON M4W 3T6
416-960-2700
Fax: 416-960-2819
www.towersperrin.com
Profile: The professional services firm helps financial services industries & reinsurance intermediary services in the following areas: human resource consulting, management & acutuarial consulting.

Executives:
Bruce Near, Managing Director
Wendy Poirier, Managing Principal, Health & Welfare, HR Services
Marc R. Ullman, Leader, Executive Compensation & Rewards
Pierre Geoffrion, Sr. Consultant, Exec. Compensation & Rewards
John Hammond, Sr. Consultant, Executive Compensation & Rewards
Jane Petruniak, Western Canada Leader, Health & Welfare
Branches:
Calgary
#1600, 111 - 5th Ave. SW
Calgary, AB T2P 3Y6 Canada
403-261-1400
Fax: 403-237-6733
Montréal
#2200, 1800, av McGill College
Montréal, QC H3A 3J6 Canada
514-982-9411
Fax: 514-982-9269
Michel Tougas, Managing Principal
Vancouver
#1600, 1100 Melville St.
Vancouver, BC V6E 4A6 Canada
604-691-1000
Fax: 604-691-1062

Townsend & Kavanagh, Actuarial Consultants
870 Pembridge Cres.
Kingston, ON K7M 6A4
613-384-0884
Fax: 613-384-3302
Executives:
Douglas Townsend, Actuary
Branches:
Kingston - Wellington St.
#503, 350 Wellington St.
Kingston, ON K7K 7J7 Canada
613-549-6264
Fax: 613-531-3938
Michael Kavanagh, Actuary

Watson Wyatt Worldwide
#1100, 1 Queen St. East
Toronto, ON M5C 2Y4
416-862-0393
Fax: 416-366-9691
866-206-5723
infocanada@watsonwyatt.com
www.watsonwyatt.com
Former Name: Watson Wyatt & Company
Ownership: Public
Revenues: $500m-1 billion
Stock Symbol: WW
Profile: The global human capital & financial management consulting firm specializes in the following areas: employee benefits, human capital strategies, technology solutions, insurance & financial services.

Executives:
Michel Guay, Managing Director, Canada
Dave Novak, Managing Consultant, Central Canada
Bob Crawford, Director, Client Development, Central Canada
Branches:
Calgary
#2700, Scotia Centre
350 - 7th Ave. SW
Calgary, AB T2P 3N9 Canada
403-237-7373
Fax: 403-237-7862
Montréal
#2400, 600, boul de Maisonneuve ouest
Montréal, QC H3A 3J2 Canada
514-284-1055
Fax: 514-844-4570
Vancouver
Four Bentall Centre
PO Box 49120
#764, 1055 Dunsmuir St.
Vancouver, BC V7X 1G4 Canada
604-688-6211
Fax: 604-685-5213
Waterloo
#916, 22 Frederick St.
Kitchener, ON N2H 6M6 Canada
519-742-5650
Fax: 519-742-3929

Welton Parent Inc.
#210, 5310 Canotek Rd.
Ottawa, ON K1J 9N5
613-842-4220
Fax: 613-741-8542
sparent@wpi.ca
www.wpi.ca
Profile: Actuarial & retirement planning consultation services are provided. Welton Parent's subsidiary company is the Retirement Planning Institute (www.rpi-ipr.com), which is located at the same address.

Westcoast Actuaries Inc.
#113, 3855 Henning Dr.
Burnaby, BC V5C 6N3
604-730-1898
Fax: 604-730-1886
888-888-1668
queries@westcoast-actuaries.com
www.westcoast-actuaries.com
Former Name: Baker Actuarial Services & Stejoe Consultants Inc.
Profile: The actuarial consulting firm provides actuarial & pension administration services.

Executives:
Ian Baker, Principal, Consulting Actuary
Stephen Cheng, Principal, Consulting Actuary
Peggy Chang, Manager, Actuarial & Pension Administration
Lana Hall, Manager, Corporate Administration
Ross McCully, Manager, New IPPs (Individual Pension Plans)
Justin Zhang, Manager, Systems

Woods & Associates
18 Lismer Cres.
Ottawa, ON K2K 1A2
613-591-8150
Fax: 613-592-3735
woods.actuary@on.aibn.com
Profile: Services include consultation related to employee benefits.

Executives:
Wayne H. Woods, President

Law Firms

Aikins, MacAulay & Thorvaldson LLP
Commodity Exchange Tower
360 Main St., 30th Fl.
Winnipeg, MB R3C 4G1
204-957-0050
Fax: 204-957-0840
amt@aikins.com
www.aikins.com
Founded: 1879
Number of Lawyers: 93
Profile: All aspects of the financial services business sector, including commercial & real estate lending, consumer lending, agricultural lending, construction financing, inventory financing by suppliers, lending to aboriginal groups, security documentation & registrations, mortgage foreclosure, debt & loan restructuring & work outs, loan recovery & enforcement

Finance Lawyers:
Christopher M. Ateah, Corporate & Commercial; Securities
204-957-4828 e-mail: cma@aikins.com
Richmond J. Bayes, Securities
204-957-4884 e-mail: rjb@aikins.com
Judith M. Blair, Family
204-957-4648 e-mail: jmb@aikins.com
Theodor E. Bock, Insurance Law
204-957-4673 e-mail: reb@aikins.com
Harley C. Boles, Commercial & Real Estate Financing; Financial Services
204-957-4637 e-mail: hcb@aikins.com
Kevin R. Bolt, Corporate & Commercial; Financial Services; Commercial Real Estate
204-957-4693 e-mail: krb@aikins.com
Krista L. Boryskavich, Corporate & Commercial; Municipal
204-957-4285 e-mail: klb@aikins.com
Aaron J. Bowler, Corporate & Commercial; Commercial Real Estate
204-957-4892 e-mail: ajb@aikins.com
John R. Braun, Financial Services; Commercial Real Estate; Corporate & Commercial
204-957-4672 e-mail: jrb@aikins.com
Shandra N. Bresoline, Labour & Employment
204-957-4878 e-mail: snb@aikins.com
Jennifer J.B. Burnell, Insurance Law
204-957-4663 e-mail: jjbb@aikins.com
G. Todd Campbell, Insurance Law
204-957-4644 e-mail: gtc@aikins.com
Florence I. Carey, Corporate & Commercial; Taxation
204-957-4891 e-mail: flc@aikins.com
David M. Carrick, Corporate & Commercial
204-957-4649 e-mail: dmc@aikins.com
Charles L. Chappell, Commercial Real Estate
204-957-4638 e-mail: clc@aikins.com
J. Milton Christiansen, Labour & Employment
204-957-4645 e-mail: jmc@aiken.com
Larry R. Crane, Corporate & Commercial
204-957-4625 e-mail: lrc@aikins.com
Nicole Cyr Hiebert, Securities & Finances
204-957-4621 e-mail: nch@aikins.com
Thomas P. Dooley, Corporate & Commercial
204-957-4628 e-mail: tpd@aikins.com
Peter F. Drazic, Corporate & Commercial
204-957-4619 e-mail: pfd@aikins.com
William K.A. Emslie, Insurance Law
204-957-4674 e-mail: wkac@aikins.com
Keith J. Ferbers, Insurance Law
204-957-4691 e-mail: kjf@aikins.com
James A. Ferguson, Corporate & Commercial; Securities
204-957-4696 e-mail: jaf@aikins.com
David C. Filmon, Corporate & Commercial; Securities
204-957-4677 e-mail: dcf@aikins.com
Gregory M. Fleetwood, Insurance Law
204-957-4690 e-mail: gmf@aikins.com
Robert T. Gabor, Corporate & Commercial
204-957-4642 e-mail: rtg@aikins.com
Kristin L. Gibson, Administrative Law; Labour & Employment
204-957-4692 e-mail: klg@aikins.com
Jason A. Goldberg, Taxation
204-957-4684 e-mail: jeg@aikins.com
Shelley L. Haner, Business & Securities
204-957-4620 e-mail: slh@aikins.com
Roger J. Hansell, Corporate & Commercial
204-957-4606 e-mail: rjh@aikins.com

Aikins, MacAulay & Thorvaldson LLP (continued)
Thor J. Hansell, Securities; Insurance Law
204-957-4694 e-mail: tjh@aikins.com
Betty A. Johnstone, Construction Law; Civil Litigation; Arbitration/Mediation Law
204-957-4650 e-mail: baj@aikins.com
J. Guy Joubert, Corporate & Commercial
204-957-4680 e-mail: jgj@aikins.com
Allison L. Kindle, Civil Litigation
204-957-4888 e-mail: alk@aikins.com
Bryan D. Klein, Corporate & Commercial; Taxation
204-957-4617 e-mail: bdk@aikins.com
Tyler J. Kochanski, Insurance Law
204-957-4633 e-mail: tlk@aikins.com
Steven J. Kohn, Corporate & Commercial; Taxation
204-957-4607 e-mail: sjk@aikins.com
Cyril G. Labman, Insurance Law
204-957-4624 e-mail: cgl@aikins.com
Robert C. Lee, Corporate & Commercial; Taxation
204-957-4683 e-mail: rlc@aikins.com
Brian D. Lerner, Financial Services; Commercial Real Estate
204-957-4603 e-mail: bdl@aikins.com
Adam L. Levene, Corporate & Commercial; Taxation
204-957-4632 e-mail: all@aikins.com
Marla S. Levene, Financial Services; Commercial Real Estate
204-957-4602 e-mail: msl@aikins.com
Colin R. MacArthur, Civil Litigation; Fiancial Services; Municipal Law; Construction Law
204-957-4627 e-mail: crm@aikins.com
Barbara S. MacDonald, Civil Litigation; Wills & Trusts
204-957-4689 e-mail: bsm@aikins.com
John B. Martens, Civil & Commercial Litigation
204-957-4856 e-mail: jbm@aikins.com
Paul A. McDonald, Labour & Employment Law
204-957-4869 e-mail: pam@aikins.com
A.J. (Telly) Mercury, Corporate & Commercial; Insurance Law
204-957-4610 e-mail: ajm@aikins.com
Michael J. Mercury, Corporate & Commercial
204-957-4609 e-mail: mjm@aikins.com
James A. Mercury, Litigation; Municipal Assessment & Taxation; Administrative Law
204-957-4896 e-mail: jam@aikins.com
Martin S. Minuk, Specialty & Civil Litigation; Tax Litigation; Criminal Law; Constitutional Law; Aboriginal Law; Immigration
204-957-4697 e-mail: msm@aikins.com
David P. Negus, Labour Law; Civil Litigation; Employment Law; Administrative Law
204-957-4604 e-mail: dpn@aikins.com
Don K. O'Hara, Corporate & Commercial; Commercial Real Estate
204-957-4859 e-mail: dko@aikins.com
R. Reis Pagtakhan, Corporate & Commercial
204-957-4640 e-mail: rrp@aikins.com
Gerald D. Parkinson, Municipal & Human Resource Law
902-957-4636 e-mail: gdp@aikins.com
E. Wells Peever, Financial Services; Commercial Real Estate
204-957-4667 e-mail: ewp@aikins.com
Carmele N. Peter, Corporate & Commercial; Taxation
204-957-4611 e-mail: cnp@aikins.com
Herbert J. Peters, Financial Services
204-957-4634 e-mail: hjp@aikins.com
Curtis M. Peters, Corporate & Commercial
204-957-4868 e-mail: cmp@aikins.com
Kerry-Krista Pinkowski, Corporate & Commercial
204-957-4641 e-mail: kknp@aikins.com
Michelle R. Redekopp, Corporate & Commercial; Financial Services; Securities
204-957-4698 e-mail: mrr@aikins.com
Maria C. Reimer, Commercial Real Estate; Financial Real Estate
204-957-4867 e-mail: mar@aikins.com
Pearl J. Reimer, Administrative; Labour & Employment; Civil Litigation
204-957-4829 e-mail: pjr@aikins.com
Daryl J. Rosin, Insurance Law
204-957-4665 e-mail: djr@aikins.com
Brent E. Ross, Civil & Commercial Litigation; Administrative Law
204-957-4681 e-mail: ber@aikins.com
J. Timothy Samson, Corporate & Commercial
204-957-4623 e-mail: jts@aikins.com
Michael A. Selchen, Taxation
204-957-4614 e-mail: mas@aikins.com
Mary J. Shariff, Construction Law; Commercial; Civil Litigation
204-957-4851 e-mail: mjs@aikins.com
Barbara M. Shields, Taxation
204-957-4615 e-mail: bms@aikins.com
J. Douglas Sigurdson, Financial Services; Commercial Real Estate
204-957-4654 e-mail: jds@aikins.com
Robert G. Sly, Corporate & Commercial; Taxation
204-957-4652 e-mail: rgs@aikins.com
Rod E. Stephenson, Insurance Law
204-957-4635 e-mail: res@aikins.com
W. Douglas Stewart, Corporate & Commercial; Securities
204-957-4890 e-mail: wds@aikins.com
Lucia M. Stuhldreier, Transportation Litigation
204-957-4676 e-mail: lms@aikins.com
Todd W. Thomson, Securities; Corporate & Commercial; Intellectual Property; Trade-Marks
204-957-4653 e-mail: twt@aikins.com
Robert L. Tyler, Financial Services; Commercial Real Estate
204-957-4630 e-mail: rlt@aikins.com
Curtis M. Unfried, Civil & Commercial Litigation; Criminal Law
204-957-4686 e-mail: cmu@aikins.com
Helga D. Van Iderstine, Civil Litigation; Administrative Law
204-957-4679 e-mail: hdv@aikins.com
Edward L. Warkentin, Corporate & Commercial; Commercial Real Estate
204-957-4662 e-mail: elw@aikins.com
Nicole M. Watson, Administrative Law; Civil Litigation; Professional Liability Litigation
902-957-4695 e-mail: nmw@aikins.com
Joel A. Weinstein, Corporate & Commercial; Taxation
204-957-4631 e-mail: jaw@aikins.com
Erin M. Wilcott, Litigation
204-957-4843 e-mail: emw@aikins.com
David M. Wright, Insurance Law
204-957-4618 e-mail: dmw@aikins.com
Richard L. Yaffe, Corporate & Commercial; Securities
204-957-4670 e-mail: rly@aikins.com
Stuart A Zacharias, Insurance Litigation
204-957-4889 e-mail: saz@aikins.com

Alexander Holburn Beaudin & Lang LLP

#2700
PO Box 10057
700 West Georgia St.
Vancouver, BC V7Y 1B8
604-484-1700
Fax: 604-484-9700
877-688-1351
info@ahbl.ca
www.ahbl.ca
Founded: 1973
Number of Lawyers: 66

Finance Lawyers:
Roger M. Bourbonnais, Banking & Lending
604-484-1701 e-mail: rbourbonnais@ahbl.ca
Patrick S. Cleary, Banking & Lending; Corporate Commercial
Todd R. Davies, Insurance
Bruno De Vita, Insurance
Barbara L. Devlin, Insurance
John W. Elwick, Commercial Litigation; Insurance
604-643-2105 e-mail: jelwick@ahbl.ca
D. Christopher Fong, Insurance
David A. Garner, Commercial Lending; Commercial Litigation; Insolvency & Restructuring; Insurance
Michel E. Giasson, Corporate Commercial
604-643-2134 e-mail: mgiasson@ahbl.ca
D. John Goundrey, Real Estate
604-484-1710 e-mail: jgoundrey@ahbl.ca
Lawrance J. Gwozd, Corporate Commercial; Commercial Lending; Insolvency & Restructuring
604-643-2123 e-mail: lgwozd@ahbl.ca
Christopher E. Hirst, Insurance
William M. Holburn, Insurance
604-484-1717 e-mail: wholburn@ahbl.ca
Dianna S. Hwang, Insurance; Wealth Preservation & Estate Litigation
Judith P. Kennedy, Insurance
Ingrid M. Kolodziej, Corporate Commercial
604-643-2229 e-mail: ikolodziej@ahbl.ca
Jason D. Lattanzio, Insurance
Darcie A. Laurient, Insurance
Mark D. Lavitt, Insurance
Andrew S. MacKay, Wealth Preservation & Estate Litigation
604-484-1715 e-mail: amackay@ahbl.ca
Derek M. Mah, Insurance
David T. McKnight, Insolvency & Restructuring; Insurance
Kevin J. McLaren, Insurance
Robert M. McLennan, Commercial Litigation; Insurance
Gary M. Nijman, Insurance; Reinsurance; Excess Insurance; General Litigation
604-643-2428 e-mail: gnijman@ahbl.ca
Darryl G. Pankratz, Insurance
Jeremy M. Poole, Insurance
Michael P. Ragona, Insurance
Michael V. Roche, Corporate Commercial
604-484-1724 e-mail: mroche@ahbl.ca
Alan M. Ross, Insurance
Judith A. Rost, Commercial Litigation; Franchise Law; Insolvency & Restructuring; Insurance
Susan Sangha, Insurance
Ross Shamenski, Insurance
Peter V. Snell, Franchise Law
604-484-1730 e-mail: psnell@ahbl.ca
Hillary S. Stephenson, Commercial Litigation
J. Dale Stewart, Insurance
Emily A. Stock, Financial Services
Sharon M. Urquhart, Insolvency & Restructuring
604-484-1757 e-mail: surquhart@ahbl.ca
Eileen E. Vanderburgh, Insurance
Terry C. Vos, Insurance
David B. Wende, Financial Professional Services
604-484-1795 e-mail: dwende@ahbl.ca
Mary-Helen Wright, Commercial Litigation; Insurance; Wealth Preservation & Estate Litigation
Christine M. York, Insurance
Karen R. Zimmer, Commercial Litigation; Insolvency & Restructuring; Wealth Preservation & Estate Litigation

Amy, Appleby & Brennan

372 Erb St. West
Waterloo, ON N2L 1W6
519-884-7330
Fax: 519-884-7390
aab-lawoffice@rogers.com
Founded: 1971
Number of Lawyers: 3

Finance Lawyers:
David G. Amy, General Finance
William R. Appleby, General Finance

Andriessen & Associates

#900
701 Evans Ave.
Toronto, ON M9C 1A3
416-620-7020
Fax: 416-620-1398
info@andriessen.ca
www.andriessen.ca
Founded: 1993
Number of Lawyers: 3
Profile: Corporate & Commercial Litigation

Finance Lawyers:
Inga B. Andriessen, Corporate & Commercial Litigation
e-mail: iandriessen@andriessen.ca
Fred W. Sheldon, Wills & Estates; Real Estate; Corporate/Commercial Transactions
e-mail: fsheldon@andriessen.ca
Paul H. Voorn, Corporate & Commercial Litigation
e-mail: pvoorn@andriessen.ca

Antymniuk & Antymniuk

#11
1500 Dakota St.
Winnipeg, MB R2N 3Y7
204-254-3511
Fax: 204-257-5139
Number of Lawyers: 3

Finance Lawyers:
Ross A. Antymniuk

Aster & Aster

#410
345, av Victoria
Westmount, QC H3Z 2N2
514-483-2445
Fax: 514-483-0009
asterma@asterlaw.com
www.asterlaw.com
Founded: 1972
Number of Lawyers: 2

Finance Lawyers:
Martin A. Aster, Administrative Law; Appeals from Workman's Compensations Decisions; Bankruptcy Law, Civil Responsibility; General Law
514-483-2445 e-mail: asterma@asterlaw.com
Margaret A. Aster, Estates & Successions; Tax Matters; Corporate/Commercial; Contracts

Austring, Fendrick, Fairman & Parkkari

The Drury Bldg.
3081 - 3rd Ave.
Whitehorse, YT Y1A 4Z7
867-668-4405
Fax: 867-668-3710
800-661-0533
info@lawyukon.com
Founded: 1961
Number of Lawyers: 8
Profile: Secured Transactions; Purchase & Sale of Business; Securities; Wills & Estates

Finance Lawyers:
Gregory A. Fekete, Corporate Commercial
e-mail: gf@lawyukon.com
Keith D. Parkkari, Corporate Commercial
e-mail: kparkkari@lawyukon.com
Jessica E. Sisk Roehle, Corporate Commercial
e-mail: jsroehle@lawyukon.com

Aylesworth LLP

Ernst & Young Tower, TD Centre
PO Box 124
222 Bay St., 18th Fl.
Toronto, ON M5K 1H1
416-777-0101
Fax: 416-865-1398
ekay@aylaw.com
www.aylesworth.com
Founded: 1861
Number of Lawyers: 36
Profile: "Aylesworth - Client Focused - Since 1861" is a highly reputable & experienced business law firm; we are in our third century of service to businesses in the Greater Toronto Area, throughtout Ontario, across Canada & around the World; we are a proud member of Lawyers Associated Worldwide (www.lawyersworldwide.com) linking over 70 independent commercial law firms located in the Americas, Europe, the Middle East, & Asia & the Pacific; while work with major financial institutions continues to be the foundation of our reputation & gives us the opportunity to handle complex transactions & litigation, our practice continues to grow in the area of serving mid-sized enterprises; we serve them by providing proactive advice, acting on transactions & resolving disputes through alternative dispute resolution or litigation, all in a practical, timely & cost-effective manner; our commitment to quality is demonstrated by our registration to ISO 9001:2000 & our Client Stewardship Program which provi

Finance Lawyers:
Harry Andrew, Corporate/Commercial; Estates & Trusts; Tax
416-777-4009 e-mail: handrew@aylaw.com
Paul Bain, Corporate/Commercial
416-646-8364 e-mail: pbain@aylaw.com
Ismail Barmania, Estates & Trusts; Tax
416-777-4016 e-mail: ibarmania@aylaw.com
Leonard Bosschart, Estate Planning & Estate Law
416-777-4035 e-mail: lbosschart@aylaw.com
John D. Brunt, Corporate/Commercial
Justin Connidis, Business
416-565-1253 e-mail: jconnidis@aylaw.com
Lynsey Connors, Commercial Litigation
416-646-4605 e-mail: lconnors@aylaw.com
Sam De Caprio, Insolvency
Julia Dublin, Corporate Securities
Dan Giantsopoulos, Corporate/Commercial; Financial Services; Estates & Trusts; Taxes
416-777-4026 e-mail: dgiantsopoulos@aylaw.com
David J. Gray, Franchising; Corporate/Commercial
416-777-4047 e-mail: dgray@aylaw.com
Steven J. Gray, Corporate/Commerical; Real Estate
416-777-4032 e-mail: sgray@aylaw.com
Douglas A. Hendler, Corporate/Commercial; Real Estate
416-777-4024 e-mail: dhendler@aylaw.com
Paul E. Heney, Corporate/Commercial; Securities
416-777-4005 e-mail: pheney@aylaw.com
Eric Kay, Commericial Litigation
416-777-4011 e-mail: ekay@aylaw.com
James P. Kelleher, Corporate/Commercial; International Trade
416-777-4005 e-mail: jkelleher@aylaw.com
H. Kari Kim, Corporate/Commercial; Financial Services
416-777-4004 e-mail: kkim@aylaw.com
James G. Klein, Lending; Real Estate
416-777-4001 e-mail: jklein@aylaw.com
Marc A. Lean, Corporate/Commercial
416-777-4015 e-mail: mlean@aylaw.com
Corey Levin, Franchising & Licensing
416-646-8366 e-mail: clevin@aylaw.com
James G. McPherson, Corporate/Commercial
416-777-4006 e-mail: jmcpherson@aylaw.com
Michael B. Miller, Commercial Litigation
416-777-4007 e-mail: mmiller@aylaw.com
Michael D.R. O'Brien, Mediation
416-777-4036 e-mail: mobrien@aylaw.com
Andrew J. Skinner, Financial Services; Corporate/Commercial; Insolvency
416-777-4033 e-mail: askinner@aylaw.com
James W. Spence, Corporate/Commercial; Securities
416-777-4000 e-mail: jspence@aylaw.com
Andrea J. Taylor, Commercial Litigation
416-777-4022 e-mail: ataylor@aylaw.com
Peter R. Welsh, Insolvency; Financial Services
905-337-3121 e-mail: pwelsh@aylaw.com
Trevor Whiffen, Commercial Litigation
416-777-2399 e-mail: twhiffen@aylaw.com
Sean Zaboroski, Securities; Corporate/Commercial
416-777-4037 e-mail: szaboroski@aylaw.com

Aylward, Chislett & Whitten

PO Box 5835, C Sta.
261 Duckworth St.
St. John's, NL A1C 5X3
709-722-6000
Fax: 709-726-1225
Founded: 1990
Number of Lawyers: 3
Profile: Corporate/Commercial; Insurance; Estates

Finance Lawyers:
Geoffrey Aylward

Baker & McKenzie LLP

#2100
PO Box 874
181 Bay St.
Toronto, ON M5J 2T3
416-863-1221
Fax: 416-863-6275
www.bakernet.com
Founded: 1959
Number of Lawyers: 47
Profile: Global legal capability defined by Canadian expertise; Baker & McKenzie's Canadian Financial Services & Securities Group is a multidisciplinary team bringing together a broad range of local, national & international experience in all aspects of banking, lending, securities, real estate, equipment financing & restructuring matters; we apply the vast knowledge base of our global network to sophisticated cross-border & domestic transactions, & our thorough familiarity with the Canadian market to exceed the unique expectations of our strong domestic client base; our team approach, coupled with our use of leading edge technology enables us to effectively & consistently deliver the highest quality of legal services

Finance Lawyers:
Nurhan Aycan, Mergers & Acquisitions; Venture Capital; Securities; Financial Restructuring
416-865-6971 e-mail: nurhan.aycan@bakernet.com
Adam Balinsky, Securities; Venture Capital; Mergers & Acquisitions
416-865-6962 e-mail: adam.balinsky@bakernet.com
Salvador M. Borraccia, Tax
416-865-6904 e-mail: salvador.m.borraccia@bakernet.com
Michael Brady, Financial Restructuring; Real Estate
416-865-6937 e-mail: mike.brady@bakernet.com
Paul D. Burns, Taxes; Commodity Tax
416-865-6912 e-mail: paul.d.burns@bakernet.com
Victoria Coombs, Mergers & Acquisitions; Corporate
416-865-2324 e-mail: victoria.coombs@bakernet.com
Lisa M. Douglas, Commercial
416-865-6972 e-mail: lisa.douglas@bakernet.com
Matthew Grant, Corporate; Securities
416-865-2315 e-mail: matthew.grant@bakernet.com
Yoon Han, Financial Services; E-Finance; Corporate; Structured Finance; Creditors Rights
416-865-6968 e-mail: yoon.han@bakernet.com
S. Janice McAuley, Mergers & Acquisitions; Corporate
416-865-6905 e-mail: s.janice.mcauley@bakernet.com
Linda Misetich, Corporate; Securities
416-865-2323 e-mail: linda.misetich@bakernet.com
Jeffrey Rosekat, Financial Restructuring; Creditors Rights
416-865-2310 e-mail: jeffrey.rosekat@bakernet.com
Randall Schwartz, Taxes; Commodity Tax
416-865-2306 e-mail: randy.schwartz@bakernet.com
Leneo E. Sdao, Loans & Credit; Real Estate
416-865-2334 e-mail: leneo.e.sdao@bakernet.com
Brian D. Segal, Tax; International Private Banking
416-865-6920 e-mail: brian.d.segal@bakernet.com
James Sennema, Tax
416-865-6950 e-mail: james.r.sennema@bakernet.com

Balfour Moss

#600
123 - 2nd Ave. South
Saskatoon, SK S7K 7E6
306-665-7844
Fax: 306-652-1586
balfourmoss.saskatoon@balfourmoss.com
www.balfourmoss.com
Founded: 1895
Number of Lawyers: 4
Profile: Balfour Moss acts for several of Canada's leading financial institutions & provides a full range of legal services to both lenders & borrowers from offices in Saskatoon & Regina

Finance Lawyers:
David G. Gerecke, Banking; Debt Recovery
e-mail: david.gerecke@balfourmoss.com
Brian J. Scherman
e-mail: brian.scherman@balfourmoss.ca

Balfour Moss

#700
2103 - 11th Ave.
Regina, SK S4P 4G1
306-347-8300
Fax: 306-347-8350
balfourmoss.regina@balfourmoss.com
www.balfourmoss.com
Founded: 1895
Number of Lawyers: 19

Finance Lawyers:
A. John Beke, Corporate; Commercial; Securities; Reorganizations
Stewart Berringer, Corporate; Securities; Banking; Reorganizations; Secured Transactions; Real Estate
Jeff N. Grubb, Insurance; Bankruptcy & Insolvency
Fred McBeth, Corporate; Commercial; Real Estate; Securities; Secured Transactions; Banking
George E. Nystrom, Corporate; Wills & Estates; Trusts; Real Estate; Debt Recovery; Taxation
Garret J. Oledzki, Corporate; Commercial; Real Estate
Yens Pedersen, Bankruptcy; Debt Recovery; Taxation; Wills & Trusts
Kathleen A. Peterson, Debt Recovery

Barry Spalding

Royal Bank Bldg.
PO Box 6010, A Sta.
85 Charlotte St.
Saint John, NB E2L 4R5
506-633-4226
Fax: 506-633-4206
888-743-4226
info@barryspalding.com
www.barryspalding.com
Number of Lawyers: 17

Finance Lawyers:
David G. Barry, Corporate & Business Law
e-mail: dgb@law-bsr.com
Jack M. Blackier, Corporate & Business Law
e-mail: jmb@law-bsr.com
Duane M. McAfee, Corporate & Business Law
e-mail: dmm@law-bsr.com
Serena R. Newman, Corporate & Business Law
e-mail: sm@law-bsr.com
Brenda G. Noble, Wills, Estates & Trusts
David G. O'Brien, Wills, Estates & Trusts

Barry Spalding (continued)
Peter T. Zed, Corporate & Business Law
e-mail: ptz@law-bsr.com

Barry Spalding
#100
PO Box 1066, Main Sta.
1077 St. George Blvd.
Moncton, NB E1C 8P2
506-859-1244
Fax: 506-859-1249
info@barryspalding.com
www.barry-oneil.com
Number of Lawyers: 6

Finance Lawyers:
Hélène L. Beaulieu, Corporate & Business Law
e-mail: hlb@law-bsr.com
Richard E. DeBow, Corporate & Business Law; Wills, Estates & Trusts
e-mail: red@law-bsr.com
Cyril W. Johnston, Corporate & Business Law; Wills, Estates & Trusts
e-mail: cwj@law-bsr.com
William B. White, Wills, Estates & Trusts

Basman, Smith
#1400
111 Richmond St. West
Toronto, ON M5H 2G4
416-365-0300
Fax: 416-365-9276
877-262-0001
Telex: 06-980391hello@basmansmith.com
www.basmansmith.com
Founded: 1960
Number of Lawyers: 16

Finance Lawyers:
Lloyd W. Ament, Business Law
Michael Armstrong, Business Law
Marvin Barkin, Business Law; Tax Law; Wills, Trusts & Estate Planning
Muni Basman, General Finance
Robert H. Saunders, General Finance
Mary Wahbi, General Finance; Wills, Trusts & Estate Planning

Batcher, Wasserman & Associates
#500
718 Wilson Ave.
Toronto, ON M3K 1E2
416-635-6300
Fax: 416-635-6376
877-813-0820
Founded: 1986
Number of Lawyers: 4
Profile: Corporate, Commercial & Mortgage Financing; Litigation; Real Estate

Finance Lawyers:
Mark E. Joseph, Litigation
416-635-6300 e-mail: markjosephlaw@hotmail.com
Leonard Naymark, Real Estate
416-635-6300 e-mail: lnaymark@aol.com
Melvin Wasserman, Real Estate; Corporate; Commercial
416-635-6300 e-mail: melwasserman@yahoo.com

BCF LLP
1100, boul René-Lévesque ouest, 25e étage
Montréal, QC H3B 5C9
514-397-8500
Fax: 514-397-8515
chc@bcf.ca
www.bcf.ca
Number of Lawyers: 66

Finance Lawyers:
Pierre Allard, Corporate Reorganizations; Life Insurance; Taxation of Financial Products
Jocelyn Auger, Venture Capital Financing
Annie Claude Beauchemin, Bankruptcy & Insolvency
François Brabant, Institutional Investors; Mutual Funds
Mario Charpentier, Corporate Reorganizations; Institutional Investors
Jacques Des Marais, Corporate Reorganizations
Julie Doré, Corporate Reorganizations
Pierre Dozois, Financial Institutions; Corporate Reorganizations; Institutional Investors
Guy Dubé, Corporate Reorganizations; Taxation of Financial Products
Richard Epstein, Institutional Investors
Jean-Marc Fortier, Financial Institutions; Mutual Funds
Jean-Yves Fortin, Bankruptcy & Insolvency
Pascal Fréchette, Bankruptcy & Insolvency
Nathalie Gagnon, Institutional Investors
Maria Isabel Garcia, Bankruptcy & Insolvency
Bertrand Giroux, Bankruptcy & Insolvency
Jean-Pierre Huard, Mutual Funds
Jean-François Hudon, Financial Institutions; Institutional Investors
Martin Jannelle, Asset Based Lending; Banking & Finance
Robert Korne, Mergers & Acquisitions; Taxation & Financial Products
Catherine Lapointe, Institutional Investors
Julie Lavigne, Taxation
Serge LeBel, Financial Institutions
François Lefebvre, Corporate Reorganizations
Melanie Martel, Bankruptcy & Insolvency
Nicolas Mateesco Matte, Institutional Investors
André Morrissette, Corporate Reorganizations; Life Insurance; Taxation of Financial Products
Keyvan Nassiry, Financial Institutions; Institutional Investors
Brigitte Nepveu, Corporate Finance
Eric Orlup, Bankruptcy & Insolvency
Eric Ouimet, Wealth Management
Marc Philibert, Corporate Finance
Patrice Picard, Financial Institutions
Christian Racicot, Corporate Reorganizations
Jean Rodrigue, Corporate Reorganizations
Élise Rouillard, Corporate Finance
André Ryan, Bankruptcy & Insolvency
Pierre D. Saint-Aubin, Taxation
Hubert Sibre, Financial Institutions
Martin Sills, Financial Institutions; Institutional Investors
Pierre-Philippe Taché, Mergers & Acquisitions
Bernard Tremblay, Financial Institutions; Institutional Investors
Vicky Trépanier, Corporate Finance
Jules Turcotte, Financial Institutions; Corporate Reorganizations; Life Insurance; Mutual Funds
Laurent Vanier-Levac, Corporate Finance
Geneviève Vigneault, Corporate Reorganizations
Cathy Villeneuve, Corporate Finance
Pascal de Guise, Corporate Reorganizations; Institutional Investors

Beach, Hepburn
#1000
36 Toronto St.
Toronto, ON M5C 2C5
416-350-3500
Fax: 416-350-3510
gpiper@beachlaw.com
www.beachlaw.com
Founded: 1985
Number of Lawyers: 4
Profile: Securities; Corporate; Commercial Real Estate

Finance Lawyers:
Wayne G. Beach, Partner, Corporate
416-350-3511 e-mail: wbeach@beachlaw.com
Lyle R. Hepburn, Partner, Corporate Commercial
416-350-3525 e-mail: hepburn@beachlaw.com
Andrej F. Markes, Partner, Real Estate
416-350-3655 e-mail: markes@beachlaw.com
Mark F. Wheeler, Partner, Securities
416-350-3501 e-mail: wheeler@beachlaw.com

Beard, Winter
#701
130 Adelaide St. West
Toronto, ON M5H 2K4
416-593-5555
Fax: 416-593-7760
www.beardwinter.com
Number of Lawyers: 47

Finance Lawyers:
Rick Aucoin, Insurance
416-306-1787 e-mail: raucoin@beardwinter.com
Debra Backstein, Insurance
416-306-1783 e-mail: dbackstein@beardwinter.com
Kenneth J. Bialkowski, Insurance
416-306-1770 e-mail: kbialkow@beardwinter.com
Christopher Bialkowski, Insurance
416-306-1722 e-mail: cbialkowski@beardwinter.com
Saloni Bowry, Insurance
416-306-1731 e-mail: sbowry@beardwinter.ca
Michael P. Canning, Insurance
416-306-1725 e-mail: mcannning@beardwinter.com
Frederick W. Chenoweth, Insurance
416-306-1750 e-mail: cheno@beardwinter.com
George D. Crossman, Corporate/Commercial; Restructuring
416-306-1700 e-mail: crossman@beardwinter.com
Alexander Curry, Insurance
416-306-1803 e-mail: acurry@beardwinter.com
John D. Dean, Insurance
416-306-1720 e-mail: jddean@beardwinter.com
Penny Debora-Worth, Insurance
416-306-1789 e-mail: pworth@beardwinter.com
David A. Decker, Corporate/Commercial; Insurance
416-306-1775 e-mail: ddecker@beardwinter.com
David Delagran, Commercial; Estates; Insurance
416-306-1710 e-mail: ddelagran@beardwinter.com
Frank S.M. Devito, Insurance
416-306-1781 e-mail: fdevito@beardwinter.com
Julian L. Doyle, Corporate/Commercial
416-306-1771 e-mail: jdoyle@beardwinter.com
Mark L.J. Edwards, Insurance
416-306-1808 e-mail: medwards@beardwinter.com
Erik J. Fish, Business; Commercial; Securities
416-306-1777 e-mail: efish@beardwinter.com
Penny Georgoudis, Insurance
416-306-1745 e-mail: pgeorgoudis@beardwinter.com
Robert Gray, Insurance
416-306-1724 e-mail: rgray@beardwinter.com
Stephen E. Haller, Corporate/Commercial
416-306-1780 e-mail: shaller@beardwinter.com
Robert C. Harason, Financial Services
416-306-1707 e-mail: rharason@beardwinter.com
Melanie C. Hoad, Commercial
416-306-1739 e-mail: mhoad@beardwinter.com
Paul Iacono, Insurance
416-306-1810 e-mail: piacono@beardwinter.com
David A. Jarvis, Family
416-306-1733 e-mail: djarvis@beardwinter.com
Melissa Kehrer, Commercial
416-306-1763 e-mail: mkehrer@beardwinter.com
Edmund Kent, Insurance
416-306-1735 e-mail: ekent@beardwinter.com
June Kim, Insurance
416-306-1793 e-mail: jkim@beardwinter.com
Seth Kornblum, Insurance
416-306-1790 e-mail: skornblum@beardwinter.com
James Leone, Insurance
416-306-1744 e-mail: jleone@beardwinter.com
Stanley Letofsky, Corporate/Commercial; Sales & Acquisitions
416-306-1703 e-mail: letofsky@beardwinter.com
Monika Liberek, Insurance
416-306-1764 e-mail: mliberek@beardwinter.com
Darrell March, Insurance
416-306-1711 e-mail: dmarch@beardwinter.com
Tricia McAvoy, Insurance
416-306-1794 e-mail: tmcavoy@beardwinter.com
Sherree Mosoff, Insurance
416-306-1740 e-mail: smosoff@beardwinter.com
Aaron Murray, Insurance
416-306-1715 e-mail: amurray@beardwinter.ca
John A. Olah, Commercial; Insurance
416-306-1818 e-mail: jolah@beardwinter.com
Richard H. Parker, Dispute Resolution Services
416-306-1775 e-mail: rparker@beardwinter.com
Aldo Picchetti, Insurance
416-306-1741 e-mail: apicchetti@beardwinter.com
David R. Rothwell, Commercial; Insolvency; Financial Services
416-306-1718 e-mail: drothwell@beardwinter.com
N. Peter Silverberg, Corporate/Commercial; Mergers & Acquisitions; Restructuring
416-306-1737 e-mail: psilverberg@beardwinter.com
Shmuel Stern, Family
416-306-1706 e-mail: sstern@beardwinter.com
John Syrtash, Family
416-306-1733 e-mail: jsyrtash@beardwinter.com
David J. Wilson, Corporate/Commercial; Mergers & Acquisitions
416-306-1796 e-mail: dwilson@beardwinter.com
Richard I.R. Winter, Corporate; Wills & Trusts
416-306-1800 e-mail: rwinter@beardwinter.com
Victoria Winter, Corporate; Wills; Estates
416-306-1713 e-mail: vwinter@beardwinter.com

Mary Ann Winterhalt, Insurance
416-306-1743 e-mail: mwinterhalt@beardwinter.ca
John W. Wright, Corporate/Commercial; Mergers & Acquisitions
416-306-1717 e-mail: jwright@beardwinter.com

Jean L. Beauchamp
405, rue Santerre
Laval, QC H7H 2X6
450-628-6230
Fax: 450-628-6389
Number of Lawyers: 1

Finance Lawyers:
Jean L. Beauchamp, Commercial Law

Beaudry, Bertrand s.e.n.c.
Maison du Citoyen #400
25, rue Laurier
Gatineau, QC J8X 4C8
819-770-4880
Fax: 819-595-4979
avocats@beaudry-bertrand.com
Founded: 1929
Number of Lawyers: 14

Finance Lawyers:
Guy Bélanger, Insurance Law
Joan Cournoyer-Archer, Insurance Law
Pierre McMartin, Corporate Litigation

Beauvais, Truchon Avocats
#200
79, boul René-Lévesque est
Québec, QC G1R 5N5
418-692-4180
Fax: 418-692-1599
www.beauvaistruchon.com
Number of Lawyers: 28

Finance Lawyers:
Mark Fortier
e-mail: mfortier@avbt.com

Beechie, Madison, Sawchuk LLP
439 Waterloo St.
London, ON N6B 2P1
519-673-1070
Fax: 519-439-4363
Founded: 1952
Number of Lawyers: 3

Finance Lawyers:
T.J. Madison

Bell, Jacoe & Company
PO Box 520
13211 Victoria Rd. North
Summerland, BC V0H 1Z0
250-494-6621
Fax: 250-494-8055
800-663-0392
belljacoe@shaw.ca
Founded: 1994
Number of Lawyers: 3
Profile: Mortgages

Finance Lawyers:
Patrick A. Bell
Joseph P. Jacoe

Belowus Easton English
100 Ouellette Ave., 7th Fl.
Windsor, ON N9A 6T3
519-973-1900
Fax: 519-973-0225
Number of Lawyers: 3

Finance Lawyers:
R.B. Easton, Taxation; Business Law; Commercial & Property Litigation
e-mail: easton@winlaw.ca

Bennett & Company
#101
116 Simcoe St.
Toronto, ON M5H 4E2
416-363-8688
Fax: 416-363-8083
bennett@ican.net
www.bennettonbankruptcy.com
Founded: 1993
Number of Lawyers: 2
Profile: Bankruptcy; Insolvency; Creditor & Debtor; Receivership

Finance Lawyers:
Frank Bennett, Bankruptcy & Insolvency Law
Russell Bennett, Bankruptcy & Insolvency Law

Bennett Best Burn LLP
#1700
150 York St.
Toronto, ON M5H 3S5
416-362-3400
Fax: 416-362-2211
info@bbburn.com
www.bbburn.com
Founded: 1992
Number of Lawyers: 10
Profile: Mergers & acquisitions & financing for medium sized enterprises

Finance Lawyers:
David W. Burn, General Finance
e-mail: davidburn@bbburn.com
Robyn Lachine, Real Estate & Commercial Law
e-mail: rlachine@bbburn.com
Paul Mahaffy, General Finance
e-mail: pmahaffy@bbburn.com

Bennett Jones LLP
Bankers Hall East Tower #4500
855 - 2nd St. SW
Calgary, AB T2P 4K7
403-298-3100
Fax: 403-265-7219
Telex: 038-24524firmwatch@bennettjones.ca
www.bennettjones.ca
Founded: 1922
Number of Lawyers: 159
Profile: Bennett Jones' Financial Services & Banking Practice Group has broad experience in all types of Canadian debt financing transactions; in addition this group has had frequent involvement in cross-border debt financings; our lawyers are used to working with sophisticated finance executives from many of Canada's largest corporations as well as finance professionals from North America's leading banks & investment dealers; Bennett Jones has extensive expertise in all aspects of financing for companies involved in the oil & gas, power & telecommunications industries; our group's services include: syndicated bank lending transactions; subordinated debt transactions; public & private debt offerings; cross-border public & private debt offerings; leasing & other asset-based structured financings; project finance; hedging agreements; debt restructuring; insolvency & litigation

Finance Lawyers:
Farouk S. Adatia, Leasing; Banking; Secured Transactions
403-298-3342 e-mail: adatiaf@bennettjones.ca
Zahra O. Allu, Corporate & Commercial Law
Shaheen K. Amirali, Financing Transactions
403-298-8139 e-mail: amiralis@bennettjones.ca
Donald G. Anderson, Corporate Commercial; Financial Services; Project Finance
403-298-3110 e-mail: andersond@bennettjones.ca
Ronald M. Barron, Real Estate Transactions & Financings
403-298-3491 e-mail: barronr@bennettjones.ca
Joan Bilsland, Corporate Law
Scott Bodie, Tax; Acquisitions & Divestitures
Patrick J. Brennan, Leasing; Financing
403-298-3433 e-mail: brennanp@bennettjones.ca
Denise D. Bright, Financial Transactions & Securities
403-298-4468 e-mail: brightd@bennettjones.ca
W.E. Brett Code, Corporate Commercial Disputes
Murray G. Coleman, Commercial Transactions; Secured Transactions; Banking
403-298-3336 e-mail: colemanm@bennettjones.ca
Frank R. Dearlove, Commercial Litigation; Insolvency & Restructuring
403-298-3202 e-mail: dearlovef@bennettjones.ca
Paul M. Farion, Mergers & Acquisitions; Corporate
403-298-3610 e-mail: farionp@bennettjones.ca
Heather I. Forester, Corporate Governance
403-298-3240 e-mail: foresterh@bennettjones.ca
J. Douglas Foster, Mergers & Acquisitions
403-298-3213 e-mail: fosterd@bennettjones.ca
Tiffany A. Franklin, Securities Litigation
Bryan C.G. Haynes, Commercial Transactions; Mergers & Acquisitions
403-298-3162 e-mail: haynesb@bennettjones.ca
Timothy D. Kerrigan, Bank Financing; Commercial Real Estate
403-298-3346 e-mail: kerrigant@bennettjones.ca
John H. Kousinioris, Securities; Mergers & Acquisitions
403-298-4469 e-mail: kousinioris@bennettjones.ca
Margaret G. Lemay, Project Finance
403-298-3122 e-mail: lemaym@bennettjones.ca
David M. Lennox, Asset/Equipment Finance & Leasing
403-298-3124 e-mail: lennoxd@bennettjones.ca
Kenneth T. Lenz, Commercial Litigation; Insolvency & Restructuring
403-298-3317 e-mail: lenzk@bennettjones.ca
Terry M. Livermore
403-298-3069 e-mail: livermoret@bennettjones.ca
Andrew Lloyd, Banking; Mergers & Acquisitions
John D. MacNeil, Mergers & Acquisitions
403-298-3394 e-mail: macneilj@bennettjones.ca
David J. Macaulay, Investments
403-298-3479 e-mail: macaulayd@bennettjones.ca
Patrick T. Maguire, Commercial Transactions
403-298-3184 e-mail: maguirep@bennettjones.ca
Tara S. Mah, Corporate Commercial
403-298-3278 e-mail: maht@bennettjones.ca
David J. Mercier, Corporate Tax
R. Vance Milligan
403-298-3242 e-mail: milliganv@bennettjones.ca
Angus B. Mitchell, International Share & Asset Acquisitions
403-298-3023 e-mail: mitchella@bennettjones.ca
Darcy D. Moch, Corporate Tax Planning
403-298-3390 e-mail: mochd@bennettjones.ca
Mark S. Powell, Corporate Commercial; Securities
403-298-3365 e-mail: powellm@bennettjones.ca
Renée M. Ratke, Mergers & Acquisitions; Corporate Reorganizations
403-298-3615 e-mail: ratker@bennettjones.ca
Christopher D. Simard, Restructuring & Bankruptcy
403-298-4485 e-mail: simardc@bennettjones.ca
Christopher R. Skelton, Corporate & Commercial
403-298-3309 e-mail: skeltonc@bennettjones.ca
James G. Smeltzer, Corporate/Commercial
403-298-3168 e-mail: smeltzerj@bennettjones.ca
C. Perry Spitznagel, Corporate/Commercial; Securities; Mergers & Acquisitions
403-298-3153 e-mail: spitznagelp@bennettjones.ca
Jon C. Truswell, Securities; Mergers & Acquisitions
403-298-3097 e-mail: truswellj@bennettjones.ca
Joanne M. Vandale, Corporate Tax; Mergers & Acquisitions
Vivek T.A. Warrier, Corporate & Commercial
403-298-3040 e-mail: warrierv@bennettjones.ca
D. Mitchell Williams, Banks & Other Financial Institutions; Commercial Contracting
403-298-3151 e-mail: williamsm@bennettjones.ca

Bennett Jones LLP
ATCO Centre #1000
10035 - 105th St. NW
Edmonton, AB T5J 3T2
780-421-8133
Fax: 780-421-7951
firmwatch@bennettjones.ca
www.bennettjones.ca
Number of Lawyers: 23

Finance Lawyers:
Enzo J. Barichello
780-917-4269 e-mail: barichelloe@bennettjones.ca
Donald R. Cranston
780-917-4267 e-mail: cranstond@bennettjones.ca
David Finlay
James J. Heelan
780-917-4275 e-mail: heelanj@bennettjones.ca
Mark P. Kortbeek
780-917-4273 e-mail: kortbeekm@bennettjones.ca

Bennett Jones LLP
One First Canadian Place #3400
PO Box 130
Toronto, ON M5X 1A4
416-863-1200
Fax: 416-863-1716
info@bennettjones.ca
www.bennettjones.ca
Number of Lawyers: 96

Bennett Jones LLP (continued)

Finance Lawyers:
Juliana J. Abdo
416-777-4801 e-mail: abdoj@bennettjones.ca
Hugo M. Alves
416-777-5735 e-mail: alvesh@bennettjones.ca
Mark W.S. Bain
416-777-4845 e-mail: bainm@bennettjones.ca
Alan Bell, Securities
416-777-5770 e-mail: bella@bennettjones.ca
Douglas Benson
Peter B. Birkness
Paul D. Blundy, Corporate/Commercial; Project Finance
416-777-4854 e-mail: blundyp@bennettjones.ca
Stephen W. Bowman, Corporate & Personal Tax Planning
416-777-4624 e-mail: bowmans@bennettjones.ca
Duncan C. Card, Corporate; Commercial
416-777-6446 e-mail: cardd@bennettjones.ca
Simon P. Crawford
416-777-4815 e-mail: crawfords@bennettjones.ca
Gavin H. Finlayson
416-777-5762 e-mail: finlaysong@bennettjones.ca
Cosimo Fiorenza, Tax
Justin R.G. Fogarty
416-777-4859 e-mail: fogartyj@bennettjones.ca
Daniel A. Ford
416-777-4860 e-mail: fordd@bennettjones.ca
J. Kyle Genga
416-777-4832 e-mail: gengak@bennettjones.ca
Grant R.M. Haynen, Corporate & Commercial
Lindsey A. Hutton
416-777-4850 e-mail: huttonl@bennettjones.ca
Jeffrey Kerbel, Mergers & Acquisitions; Securities
416-777-5772 e-mail: kerbelj@bennettjones.ca
Steven J. Lutz
416-777-5732 e-mail: lutzs@bennettjones.ca
Hugh L. MacKinnon
416-777-4810 e-mail: mackinnonh@bennettjones.ca
Tara A. Mackay
416-777-4869 e-mail: mackayt@bennettjones.ca
S. Paul Mantini
416-777-4837 e-mail: mantinisp@bennettjones.ca
Bernard Morris, Tax
John R. Owen, Corporate & Personal Tax Planning
416-777-4622 e-mail: owenj@bennettjones.ca
Donna Parish, Corporate/Commercial
416-777-4640 e-mail: parishd@bennettjones.ca
Ruth E. Promislow
416-777-4688 e-mail: promislowr@bennettjones.ca
William B. Vass, Corporate; Commercial
Kevin J. Zych
416-777-5738 e-mail: zychk@bennettjones.ca
John van Gent

Benson Myles
Atlantic Place #900
PO Box 1538
215 Water St.
St. John's, NL A1C 5N8
709-579-2081
Fax: 709-579-2647
info@bensonmyles.com
www.bensonmyles.com
Number of Lawyers: 21

Finance Lawyers:
Jeffrey P. Benson, General Corporate & Commercial Law; Secured Financing & Bankruptcy
Bernadette A. Cole, General Corporate & Commercial Law
Jason A. Edwards, General Corporate & Commercial Law; Secured Financing & Bankruptcy
Francis P. Fowler, General Corporate & Commercial Law
Brian R. Gosse, General Corporate & Commercial Law
Benjamin J. Kavanagh, General Corporate & Commercial Law
709-570-7252 e-mail: bkavanagh@bensonmyles.com
Susan E. Marsh, General Corporate & Commercial Law; Secured Financing & Bankruptcy
Robert M. Matthews, General Corporate & Commercial Law
R. Wayne Myles, General Corporate & Commercial Law; Secured Financing & Bankruptcy
709-570-7232 e-mail: wmyles@bensonmyles.com
Joan F. Myles, Secured Financing & Bankruptcy
Jay Neville, General Corporate & Commercial Law
Philip J. Osborne, General Corporate & Commercial Law
Garry F. Peddle, General Corporate & Commercial Law; Secured Financing & Bankruptcy
Geoffrey L. Spencer, Secured Financing & Bankruptcy
709-570-7263 e-mail: gspencer@bensonmyles.com

Bernard, Brassard, s.e.n.c. avocats
#200
101, boul Roland-Therrien
Longueuil, QC J4H 4B9
450-670-7900
Fax: 450-670-0673
888-670-7900
commitment@bernard-brassard.com
www.bernard-brassard.com
Number of Lawyers: 12

Finance Lawyers:
Catherine Cloutier, Banking; Commercial Litigation
e-mail: ccloutier@bernard-brassard.com
Louis-Denis Laberge, Banking; Bankruptcy & Insolvency; Commercial Litigation
Renaud Lanthier, Corporate/Commercial; Mergers & Acquisitions
Frédéric Lévesque, Bankruptcy & Insolvency; Mergers & Acquisitions
e-mail: flevesque@bernard-brassard.com
Pierre-Marc Mallette, Banking; Bankruptcy & Insolvency; Commercial Litigation
e-mail: pmmallette@bernard-brassard.com
François Normand, Corporate/Commercial; Mergers & Acquisitions
e-mail: fnormand@bernard-brassard.com
Catherine Rioux, Corporate/Commercial; Mergers & Acquisitions

Judy Sab, Banking; Bankruptcy & Insolvency
e-mail: jsab@bernard-brassard.com

Bishop & Company
#206
347 Leon Ave.
Kelowna, BC V1Y 8C7
250-861-4022
Fax: 250-862-3937
bishopco@shaw.ca
Number of Lawyers: 3

Finance Lawyers:
Howard F. Peet, General Finance

Bitner & Associates Law Offices
6932 Roper Rd. NW
Edmonton, AB T6B 3H9
780-461-6633
Fax: 780-461-9239
Founded: 1993
Number of Lawyers: 1
Profile: Corporate/Commercial

Finance Lawyers:
Head of Financial Law: Laura A. Bitner

Bjornsson & Wight Law Office
#3
PO Box 1769
314 Edwards Ave.
The Pas, MB R9A 1L5
204-627-1200
Fax: 204-627-1210
dblwlaw@cancom.net
Founded: 1998
Number of Lawyers: 2

Finance Lawyers:
Donald G. Bjornsson, Corporate & Commercial; Real Estate
Laurel F. Wight, Real Estate; Estates; Wills

Roger Blais avocat inc
215, rue Lindsay
Drummondville, QC J2C 1N8
819-477-2235
Fax: 819-477-8674
blaisavocats@9bit.com
Founded: 1970
Number of Lawyers: 2
Profile: General collection & mortgage security; contract & execution of contract & insurance law

Finance Lawyers:
Francis Léger, Commercial Law
819-477-2235 e-mail: blaisavocats@9bit.com

Blake, Cassels & Graydon LLP
Commerce Court West #2800
199 Bay St.
Toronto, ON M5L 1A9
416-863-2400
Fax: 416-863-2653
Telex: 06-219687toronto@blakes.com
www.blakes.com
Founded: 1856
Number of Lawyers: 299
Profile: Financial Services; Mergers & Acquisitions; Structured Finance; Securities; Business; Commodity Tax & Trade; Corporate Governance; E-commerce; Restructuring & Insolvency; Taxation; Pension & Employee Benefits

Finance Lawyers:
Jennifer Allen, Business
416-863-2426 e-mail: jennifer.allen@blakes.com
Frank P. Arnone, Securities; Business, Corporate Governance
416-863-4295 e-mail: frank.arnone@blakes.com
Stephen R. Ashbourne, Structured Finance; Securities
416-863-3086 e-mail: stephen.ashbourne@blakes.com
Alan Aucoin, E-Commerce
416-863-2635 e-mail: jaa@blakes.com
Barbara J. Austin, Pension & Employee Benefits; Taxation
416-863-3893 e-mail: barbara.austin@blakes.com
Bryan C. Bailey, Taxation; Business; Commodity Tax & Trade
416-863-2297 e-mail: bryan.bailey@blakes.com
Randy V. Bauslaugh, Pension & Employee Benefits
416-863-2960 e-mail: randy.bauslaugh@blakes.com
Christina Beaudoin, Business; Mergers & Acquisitions; Securities
416-863-2252 e-mail: christina.beaudoin@blakes.com
Paul Belanger, Financial Services; Mergers & Acquisitions; Insurance
416-863-4284 e-mail: paul.belanger@blakes.com
Ted Betts, Business; Mergers & Acquisitions
416-863-4198 e-mail: ted.betts@blakes.com
Ian J. Binnie, Financial Services
416-863-3250 e-mail: ian.binnie@blakes.com
Bob A. Bondy, Business; Securities
416-863-2530 e-mail: rab@blakes.com
Elizabeth H. Boyd, Pension & Employee Benefits; Taxation
416-863-4172 e-mail: elizabeth.boyd@blakes.com
Alan F. Brown, Business; Securities
416-863-2674 e-mail: alan.brown@blakes.com
Michael Bunn, Securities; Mergers & Acquisitions; Business
416-863-3168 e-mail: michael.bunn@blakes.com
Michael E. Burke, Financial Services; Structured Finance; Business
416-863-3866 e-mail: michael.burke@blakes.com
Sheldon Burshtein, E-Commerce; Franchising
416-863-2934 e-mail: sb@blakes.com
Kathryn M. Bush, Taxation; Pension & Employee Benefits
416-863-2633 e-mail: kathryn.bush@blakes.com
Catherine Campbell, Taxation
416-863-2387 e-mail: catherine.campbell@blakes.com
Nathan Cheifetz, Business; Financial Services
416-863-2969 e-mail: nathan.cheifetz@blakes.com
Milly Chow, Restructuring & Insolvency; Financial Services
416-863-2594 e-mail: milly.chow@blakes.com
Rob Collins, Mergers & Acquisitions; Business; Real Estate
416-863-2519 e-mail: rob.collins@blakes.com
Richard Corley, Business
416-863-2183 e-mail: richard.corley@blakes.com
Silvana M. D'Alimonte, Restructuring & Insolvency
416-863-3860 e-mail: smda@blakes.com
John D. DeSipio, Estates & Trusts
416-863-2538 e-mail: john.desipio@blakes.com
Paul Dimitriadis, Pensions & Employee Benefits
416-863-2744 e-mail: paul.dimitriadis@blakes.com
Anoop Dogra, Securities; Business; Mergers & Acquisitions
416-863-3052 e-mail: anoop.dogra@blakes.com
Jim P. Dube, Restructuring & Insolvency
416-863-2532 e-mail: jim.dube@blakes.com
Sharissa Ellyn, Financial Services
416-863-4167 e-mail: sharissa.ellyn@blakes.com
Michael Fabbri, Business; Mergers & Acquisitions
416-863-3054 e-mail: michael.fabbri@blakes.com
Shlomi Feiner, Business; Mergers & Acquisitions; Securities
416-863-2393 e-mail: shlomi.feiner@blakes.com
Simon A. Finch, Financial Services
416-863-2159 e-mail: simon.finch@blakes.com

Martin Fingerhut, Structured Finance; Financial Services; Business; E-commerce
416-863-2638 e-mail: martin.fingerhut@blakes.com
Jeremy J. Forgie, Pension & Employee Benefits; Taxation
416-863-3888 e-mail: jeremy.forgie@blakes.com
Greg. Frenette, Business; Mergers & Acquisitions; Insurance
416-863-2693 e-mail: greg.frenette@blakes.com
Andrea M. Freund, Business
416-863-3090 e-mail: andrea.freund@blakes.com
Beth M. Gearing, Business; Mergers & Acquisitions; E-commerce
416-863-2597 e-mail: beth.gearing@blakes.com
Allan J. Gelkopf, Commodity Tax & Trade; E-commerce
416-863-2634 e-mail: allan.gelkopf@blakes.com
Jake Gilbert, Business
416-863-5831 e-mail: jake.gilbert@blakes.com
Peter W. Gilchrist, Mergers & Acquisitions
416-863-2160 e-mail: peter.gilchrist@blakes.com
Jeff L. Glass, Securities; Business; Corporate Governance
416-863-4162 e-mail: jeff.glass@blakes.com
Ian Goldberg, Business; Securities
416-863-4302 e-mail: ian.goldberg@blakes.com
Calvin S. Goldman, Competition & Trade
416-863-2288 e-mail: cal.goldman@blakes.com
Andrew Gordon, Securities
416-863-2398 e-mail: andrew.gordon@blakes.com
Robert M. Granatstein, Business; Mergers & Acquisitions
416-863-2748 e-mail: robert.granatstein@blakes.com
Leena Grover, Corporate Governance; Securities
416-863-3284
Susan M. Grundy, Restructuring & Insolvency; Financial Services, Business
416-863-2572 e-mail: susan.grundy@blakes.com
Frank D. Guarascio, Business; Mergers & Acquisitions; Securities
416-863-3296 e-mail: frank.guarascio@blakes.com
Christopher C. Hale, E-commerce; Franchising
416-863-2798 e-mail: chris.hale@blakes.com
Kim Harle, Business
416-863-4294 e-mail: kim.harle@blakes.com
Michael R. Harquail, Financial Services; Business
416-863-2929 e-mail: michael.harquail@blakes.com
Ian R. Hay, E-commerce
416-863-3289 e-mail: ian.hay@blakes.com
Caroline L. Helbronner, Pension & Employee Benefits; Taxation
416-863-2968 e-mail: caroline.helbronner@blakes.com
Martin Herman, Financial Services; Business; Structured Finance
416-863-2654 e-mail: martin.herman@blakes.com
Chris Hewat, Securities; Business; Corporate Governance
416-863-2761 e-mail: chris.hewat@blakes.com
Jim Hilton, Real Estate; Financial Services
416-863-2714 e-mail: jim.hilton@blakes.com
Peter Hogg, Estates & Trusts
416-863-3194 e-mail: peter.hogg@blakes.com
Chris Huband, Business; Real Estate
416-863-2758 e-mail: cah@blakes.com
Pamela Huff, Restructuring & Insolvency
416-863-2958 e-mail: pamela.huff@blakes.com
Pamela Hughes, Securities; Business, Corporate Governance
416-863-2226 e-mail: pamela.hughes@blakes.com
John Hutmacher, Business; Real Estate
416-863-2219 e-mail: john.hutmacher@blakes.com
Christine G. Ing, E-commerce
416-863-2667 e-mail: christine.ing@blakes.com
David Jackson, Business; Securities; Mergers & Acquisitions; E-commerce, Corporate Governance
416-863-2636 e-mail: david.jackson@blakes.com
Chris J. Javornik, Securities; Mergers & Acquisitions; Business
416-863-2245 e-mail: chris.javornik@blakes.com
Dawn Jetten, Financial Services; Insurance
416-863-2956 e-mail: dawn.jetten@blakes.com
Mark Johnson, Business; Mergers & Acquisitions
416-863-3318 e-mail: mark.johnson@blakes.com
Navin Joneja, Commodity Tax & Trade
416-863-2352 e-mail: navin.joneja@blakes.com
Christopher Jones, Securities
416-863-2704 e-mail: christopher.jones@blakes.com
Greg Kanargelidis, Commodity Tax & Trade
416-863-4306 e-mail: greg.kanargelidis@blakes.com
Joan C. Kennedy, Business
416-863-2587 e-mail: joan.kennedy@blakes.com
John A. Kolada, Business, Mergers & Acquisitions, Corporate Governance
416-863-4171 e-mail: john.kolada@blakes.com

Robert Kreklewich, Commodity Tax & Trade
416-863-3278 e-mail: robert.kreklewich@blakes.com
David Kruse, Business; Mergers & Acquisitions; Securities
416-863-2467 e-mail: david.kruse@blakes.com
Manfred Lam, Financial Services; Structured Finance
416-863-3173 e-mail: manfred.lam@blakes.com
Michelle Laniel, Financial Services
416-863-2443 e-mail: michelle.laniel@blakes.com
Alexis Levine, Financial Services; Securities; Structured Finance; Mergers & Acquisitions
416-863-2749 e-mail: alexis.levine@blakes.com
Gail D. Lilley, Mergers & Acquisitions; Business
416-863-2647 e-mail: gail.lilley@blakes.com
Jeffrey R. Lloyd, Securities, Mergers & Acquisitions, Business, Corporate Governance
416-863-5848 e-mail: jeff.lloyd@blakes.com
Peter S. MacGowan, Financial Services; Business
416-863-2278 e-mail: peter.macgowan@blakes.com
David MacLachlan, Financial Services; Business
416-863-5830 e-mail: david.maclachlan@blakes.com
Anna I. MacMillan, Business; Mergers & Acquisitions
416-863-3022 e-mail: aim@blakes.com
Janice McCart, Taxation
416-863-2669 e-mail: janice.mccart@blakes.com
Kate McGilvray, Business, Mergers & Acquisitions
416-863-2243 e-mail: kate.mcgilvray@blakes.com
Michael McGraw, Restructuring & Insolvency
416-863-4247 e-mail: michael.mcgraw@blakes.com
Ric C. McIvor, Financial Services; Restructuring & Insolvency; Business
416-863-2658 e-mail: rcm@blakes.com
Ross McKee, Securities; Business; Mergers & Acquisitions; Corporate Governance
416-863-3277 e-mail: ross.mckee@blakes.com
Tom A. McKee, Business; Mergers & Acquisitions; Securities
416-863-2747 e-mail: tom.mckee@blakes.com
Stacy McLean, Business; Securities
416-863-4325 e-mail: stacy.mclean@blakes.com
Elizabeth L. McNaughton, E-commerce
416-863-2556 e-mail: elizabeth.mcnaughton@blakes.com
Ernest D. McNee, Securities; Mergers & Acquisitions; Corporate Governance
416-863-3863 e-mail: ernest.mcnee@blakes.com
Matthew Merkley, Mergers & Acquisitions; Securities
416-863-3328 e-mail: matthew.merkley@blakes.com
Eric Moncik, Securities; Business; Mergers & Acquisitions
416-863-2536 e-mail: eric.moncik@blakes.com
Leslie J. Morgan, Taxation
416-863-2696 e-mail: leslie.morgan@blakes.com
William D. Mugford, Business; Mergers & Acquisitions
416-863-2980 e-mail: william.mugford@blakes.com
Sheila A. Murray, Business; Securities; Corporate Governance
416-863-2985 e-mail: sheila.murray@blakes.com
Mario Nigro, Business
416-863-2537 e-mail: mario.nigro@blakes.com
Karen Park, Restructuring & Insolvency
416-863-3320 e-mail: karen.park@blakes.com
R. Kenneth S. Pearce, Business; Securities; Mergers & Acquisitions
416-863-3286 e-mail: kenneth.pearce@blakes.com
Kathleen V. Penny, Taxation
416-863-3898 e-mail: kathleen.penny@blakes.com
André B. Perey, Business; Mergers & Acquisitions; E-Commerce
416-863-2291 e-mail: andre.perey@blakes.com
Edward M. Perlmutter, Business
416-863-2973 e-mail: ted.perlmutter@blakes.com
Mark Platteel, Business; Mergers & Acquisitions
416-863-2358 e-mail: mark.platteel@blakes.com
Beth Posno, Restructuring & Insolvency
416-863-2605 e-mail: beth.posno@blakes.com
J.A. Prestage, Pension & Employee Benefits
416-863-2955 e-mail: ja.prestage@blakes.com
Sam C. Principi, Structured Finance; Financial Services
416-863-2608 e-mail: sam.principi@blakes.com
Brendan D. Reay, Securities; Business
416-863-5273 e-mail: brendan.reay@blakes.com
Ron Richler, Taxation
416-863-3854 e-mail: ron.richler@blakes.com
Colin Ritchie, Business; Mergers & Acquisitions
416-863-3155 e-mail: colin.ritchie@blakes.com
Maurizio Romano, Business; Mergers & Acquisitions
416-863-2384 e-mail: maruizio.romano@blakes.com
Parna Sabet, E-commerce
416-863-4320 e-mail: parna.sabet@blakes.com

Elizabeth Sale, Business
416-863-2602 e-mail: elizabeth.sale@blakes.com
Farha Salim, Estates & Trusts
416-863-5260 e-mail: farha.salim@blakes.com
Cynthia Sargeant, Securities
416-863-2401 e-mail: cynthia.sargeant@blakes.com
Kurt Sarno, Business; Mergers & Acquisitions
416-863-2681 e-mail: kurt.sarno@blakes.com
Cheryl Satin, Business; Mergers & Acquisitions
416-863-2575 e-mail: cheryl.satin@blakes.com
John Sawicki, Taxation
416-863-3281 e-mail: john.sawicki@blakes.com
Michelle Schwartzberg, Financial Services; Structured Finance
416-863-5801 e-mail: michelle.schwartzberg@blakes.com
Gregory Segal, E-commerce
416-863-4195 e-mail: greg.segal@blakes.com
Mark J. Selick, Financial Services; Business; Structured Finance
416-863-2924 e-mail: mark.selick@blakes.com
Joel Shafer, Taxation; Structured Finance
416-863-2944 e-mail: joel.shafer@blakes.com
James J. Shanks, Business; Financial Services
416-863-3845 e-mail: james.shanks@blakes.com
Michael W. Sharp, Securities; Mergers & Acquisitions; Business
416-863-2777 e-mail: michael.sharp@blakes.com
David Shaw, Business; Franchising; Mergers & Acquisitions
416-863-4196 e-mail: david.shaw@blakes.com
Gary R. Shiff, Business; Mergers & Acquisitions
416-863-2170 e-mail: gary.shiff@blakes.com
Jacqueline D. Shinfield, Financial Services; Restructuring & Insolvency; Mergers & Acquisitions
416-863-3290 e-mail: jacqueline.shinfield@blakes.com
Paul Singh, Business
416-863-2385 e-mail: paul.singh@blakes.com
Susan E. Slattery, Business; Estates & Trusts
416-863-4308 e-mail: susan.slattery@blakes.com
Graham Smith, Business; Mergers & Acquisitions; Structured Finance
416-863-2558 e-mail: graham.smith@blakes.com
Marianne Smith, Business
416-863-3156 e-mail: marianne.smith@blakes.com
Kenneth Snider, Taxation
416-863-5844 e-mail: kenneth.snider@blakes.com
John M. Solursh, Pension & Employee Benefits; Taxation; Estates & Trusts
416-863-2550 e-mail: john.solursh@blakes.com
Jeffrey P. Sommers, Pension & Employee Benefits; Taxation
416-863-2534 e-mail: jeffrey.sommers@blakes.com
Eric Spindler, Business; Mergers & Acquisitions; Securities; Corporate Governance
416-863-2374 e-mail: eric.spindler@blakes.com
David Spiro, Taxation
416-863-2755 e-mail: david.spiro@blakes.com
Paul Stepak, Taxation
416-863-2457 e-mail: paul.stepak@blakes.com
Catherine A. Stephen, Securities; Business
416-863-4253 e-mail: catherine.stephen@blakes.com
Michael Stevenson, Business
416-863-2458 e-mail: michael.stevenson@blakes.com
John Stewart, Estates & Trusts
416-863-2524 e-mail: john.stewart@blakes.com
Bryson A. Stokes, Business
416-863-2179 e-mail: bryson.stokes@blakes.com
Jillian M. Swartz, Business; Mergers & Acquisitions
416-863-3280 e-mail: jillian.swartz@blakes.com
Paul K. Tamaki, Taxation; Structured Finance
416-863-2697 e-mail: paul.tamaki@blakes.com
John W. Teolis, Financial Services; Business; E-commerce
416-863-2548 e-mail: john.teolis@blakes.com
Craig C. Thorburn, Business; Mergers & Acquisitions
416-863-2965 e-mail: craig.thorburn@blakes.com
David J. Toswell, Securities; Mergers & Acquisitions; Corporate Governance
416-863-4246 e-mail: david.toswell@blakes.com
Jeffrey C. Trossman, Taxation
416-863-4290 e-mail: jeffrey.trossman@blakes.com
John M. Tuzyk, Business; Securities; Corporate Governance; Mergers & Acquisitions
416-863-2918 e-mail: john.tuzyk@blakes.com
Andrea D. Vabalis, Structured Finance; Business; Mergers & Acquisitions
416-863-2166 e-mail: adv@blakes.com
David D. Valentine, Business; Securities
416-863-2933 e-mail: david.valentine@blakes.com
Chris Van Loan, Taxation
416-863-2687 e-mail: chris.vanloan@blakes.com

Blake, Cassels & Graydon LLP (continued)

Sheldon Vanderkooy, Taxation
416-863-2461 e-mail: sheldon.vanderkooy@blakes.com
Markus Viirland, Business; Securities
416-863-3097 e-mail: markus.viirland@blakes.com
Peter M. Viitre, Franchising; Mergers & Acquisitions
416-863-2225 e-mail: peter.viitre@blakes.com
Dorothy Wahl, Financial Services; Business
416-863-2610 e-mail: dorothy.wahl@blakes.com
Matthew Watson, Business; Mergers & Acquisition
416-863-3253 e-mail: matthew.watson@blakes.com
Steven J. Weisz, Restructuring & Insolvency
416-863-2616 e-mail: steven.weisz@blakes.com
Brian C. Westlake, Business; Mergers & Acquisitions
416-863-2544 e-mail: brian.westlake@blakes.com
Bliss A. White, Mergers & Acquisitions; Business
416-863-4286 e-mail: bliss.white@blakes.com
John Wilkin, Securities; Mergers & Acquisitions; Business
416-863-2785 e-mail: john.wilkin@blakes.com
Robert Willetts, Financial Services
416-863-2417 e-mail: robert.willetts@blakes.com
Julie Wilson, Business
416-863-2492 e-mail: julie.wilson@blakes.com
Leslie Wong, Securities; Mergers & Acquisitions
416-863-4323 e-mail: leslie.wong@blakes.com
Jennifer Woo, Securities; Business
416-863-2609 e-mail: jennifer.woo@blakes.com
Micah Wood, Business
416-863-4164 e-mail: micah.wood@blakes.com
Sean Zhang, E-commerce
416-863-5839 e-mail: sean.zhang@blakes.com
Thomas von Hahn, Business; Financial Services
416-863-4333 e-mail: thomas.vanhahn@blakes.com

Blake, Cassels & Graydon LLP

Bankers Hall East Tower #3500
855 - 2nd St. SW
Calgary, AB T2P 4J8
403-260-9600
Fax: 403-260-9700
calgary@blakes.com
www.blakes.com
Founded: 1856
Number of Lawyers: 84
Profile: Blakes Calgary was the first office to open outside Toronto & signified the Firm's status as a player in Western Canadian transactions; Calgary is the focal point of the Firm's oil & gas practice, which runs the gamut from finance through joint ventures & acquisitions to advice on environmental matters; Blakes Calgary has a broad financial services practice & has been involved in many of the most sophisticated real estate transations in the province

Finance Lawyers:
Robert Anderson, Restructuring & Insolvency; Business
403-260-9624 e-mail: raa@blakes.com
Garth Anderson, Structured Finance
403-260-9778 e-mail: garth.anderson@blakes.com
Ross A. Bentley, Securities; Business; Mergers & Acquisitions
403-260-9720 e-mail: ross.bentley@blakes.com
Rayla Boyd, Restructuring & Insolvency
403-260-9738 e-mail: rayla.boyd@blakes.com
Chris A. Christopher, Business
403-260-9662 e-mail: chr@blakes.com
Scott W. Clarke, Business; Securities
403-260-9712 e-mail: scott.clarke@blakes.com
Scott Cochlan, Securities; Business; Corporate Governance; Mergers & Acquisitions
403-260-9684 e-mail: src@blakes.com
Ronald A. Deyholos, Business
403-260-9718 e-mail: ronald.deyholos@blakes.com
Dallas L. Droppo, Securities; Corporate Governance
403-260-9612 e-mail: dld@blakes.com
John Eamon, Business; Securities; Mergers & Acquisitions
403-260-9724 e-mail: john.eamon@blakes.com
Pat C. Finnerty, Securities; Mergers & Acquisitions; Corporate Governance
403-260-9608 e-mail: pcf@blakes.com
Kevin A. Fougere, Financial Services; Structured Finance; Business
403-260-9646 e-mail: kevin.fougere@blakes.com
Brock W. Gibson, Securities; Business; Corporate Governance; Mergers & Acquisitions
403-260-9610 e-mail: brock.gibson@blakes.com
Edmund Gill, Business; Taxation
403-260-9772 e-mail: edmond.gill@blakes.com
Mungo Hardwicke-Brown, Financial Services; Mergers & Acquisitions
403-260-9674 e-mail: mhb@blakes.com
Evan Hillman, Securities
403-260-9796 e-mail: evan.hillman@blakes.com
Jason Holowachuk, Restructuring & Insolvency
403-260-9776 e-mail: jason.holowachuk@blakes.com
Sophie Hsia, Business
403-260-9773 e-mail: sophie.hsia@blakes.com
Jason Husack, Business; Mergers & Acquisitions
403-260-9730 e-mail: jason.husack@blakes.com
Lindsay Keele, Business; Real Estate
403-260-9748 e-mail: lindsay.keele@blakes.com
Cheryl Kelly, Business
406-260-9791 e-mail: cheryl.kelly@blakes.com
Michael Kicis, Securities; Business; Mergers & Acquisitions
403-260-9739 e-mail: michael.kicis@blakes.com
David Kobylnyk, Restructuring & Insolvency
403-260-9725 e-mail: david.kobylnyk@blakes.com
Michael Laffin, Mergers & Acquisitions
403-260-9692 e-mail: michael.laffin@blakes.com
Selina Lee-Andersen, Business
403-260-9793 e-mail: selina.lee-andersen@blakes.com
Cassandra Malfair, Restructuring & Insolvency
403-260-9744 e-mail: cassandra.malfair@blakes.com
Ronald W. Mar, Taxation
403-260-9704 e-mail: ron.mar@blakes.com
Jodi Mason, Restructuring & Insolvency
403-260-9694 e-mail: jodi.mason@blakes.com
Dalton W. McGrath, Business
403-260-9654 e-mail: dalton.mcgrath@blakes.com
Daniel McLeod, Securities; Business; Mergers & Acquisitions
403-260-9629 e-mail: daniel.mcleod@blakes.com
Christa L. Nicholson, Restructuring & Insolvency
403-260-9746 e-mail: christa.nicholson@blakes.com
Warren B. Nishimura, Business; Financial Services
403-260-9664 e-mail: warren.nishimura@blakes.com
Janan Paskaran, Business; Securities
403-260-9695 e-mail: janan.paskaran@blakes.com
Cameron Proctor, Business; Securities; Mergers & Acquisitions
403-260-9715 e-mail: cameron.proctor@blakes.com
Doris Reimer, Business; Securities
403-260-9797 e-mail: doris.reimer@blakes.com
Douglas Richardson, Taxation, Mergers & Acquisitions
403-260-9708 e-mail: doug.richardson@blakes.com
Ben Rogers, Business; Mergers & Acquisitions
403-260-9702 e-mail: ben.rogers@blakes.com
Edward Rowe, Taxation
403-260-9798 e-mail: edward.rowe@blakes.com
Wanda Rumball, Taxation
403-260-9794 e-mail: wanda.rumball@blakes.com
Chad C. Schneider, Securities; Business; Mergers & Acquisitions
403-260-9660 e-mail: chad.schneider@blakes.com
Monica Sharma, Business
403-260-9782 e-mail: monica.sharman@blakes.com
Wallace Y. Shaw, Taxation
403-260-9766 e-mail: wally.shaw@blakes.com
Sabeen Sheikh, Business
403-260-9707 e-mail: sabeen.sheikh@blakes.com
Craig Spurn, Mergers & Acquisitions
403-260-9750 e-mail: craig.spurn@blakes.com
Chastine Taerum, Taxation
403-260-9607 e-mail: chastine.taerum@blakes.com
Ted Thiessen, Taxation
403-260-9779 e-mail: ted.thiessen@blakes.com
Nick Tropak, Financial Services
403-260-9777 e-mail: nick.tropak@blakes.com
Jonathan Troyer, Financial Services
David Tupper, Securities
403-260-9722 e-mail: david.tupper@blakes.com
Anca Turta, Restructuring & Insolvency
403-260-9640 e-mail: anca.turta@blakes.com
Rosa Twyman, Business
403-260-9714 e-mail: rosa.twyman@blakes.com

Blake, Cassels & Graydon LLP

Tour KPMG #2000
600, boul de Maisonneuve ouest
Montréal, QC H3A 3J2
514-982-4000
Fax: 514-982-4099
montreal@blakes.com
www.blakes.com
Founded: 1856
Number of Lawyers: 42
Profile: Corporate/commercial law with emphasis on banking, financial services, securities, mergers & acquisitions, restructuring, real estate & project finance

Finance Lawyers:
Michael Bantey, Business; Securities; Corporate Governance; Mergers & Acquisitions
514-982-4003 e-mail: michael.bantey@blakes.com
Yannick Beaudoin, Financial Services; Structured Finance; Restructuring & Insolvency
514-982-4025 e-mail: yannick.beaudoin@blakes.com
Nadine Bellefleur, Business
514-982-5027 e-mail: nadine.bellefleur@blakes.com
Bernard Boucher, Restructuring & Insolvency
514-982-4006 e-mail: bernard.boucher@blakes.com
Denis Boudreault, Securities; Financial Services; Corporate Governance; Mergers & Acquisitions
514-982-4004 e-mail: denis.boudreault@blakes.com
Alfred Buggé, Business; Securities; Mergers & Acquisitions
514-982-4021 e-mail: alfred.bugge@blakes.com
Natalie Bussière, Pension & Employee Benefits
514-982-4080 e-mail: natalie.bussiere@blakes.com
Marise Chabot, Real Estate; Financial Services
514-982-5037 e-mail: marise.chabot@blakes.com
Mélanie Charbonneau, Financial Services; Business; Mergers & Acquisitions
514-982-4061 e-mail: melanie.charbonneau@blakes.com
Marie-Hélène Constantin, Business
514-982-4031 e-mail: marie-helene.constantin@blakes.com
Annick Demers, Business; Financial Services; Mergers & Acquisitions
514-982-4017 e-mail: annick.demers@blakes.com
Philippe Décary, Business; Securities; Mergers & Acquisitions
514-982-4074 e-mail: philippe.decary@blakes.com
Daniel Ferreira, Business; Financial Services
514-982-4017 e-mail: daniel.ferreira@blakes.com
Jean Gagnon, Taxation
514-982-5025 e-mail: jean.gagnon@blakes.com
Katherine Girard, Business
514-982-5028 e-mail: katherine.girard@blakes.com
Stephanie Grondin, Financial Services
514-982-4042 e-mail: stephanie.grondin@blakes.com
Sébastien Guy, Restructuring & Insovlency
514-982-4020 e-mail: sebastien.guy@blakes.com
Viorelia Guzun, Business
514-982-4087 e-mail: viorella.guzun@blakes.com
Sunny Handa, Mergers & Acquisitions
514-982-4008 e-mail: sunny.handa@blakes.com
Tricia Kuhl, Business
514-982-5020 e-mail: tricia.kuhl@blakes.com
Marc-Antoine La Rochelle, Business; Financial Services; Mergers & Acquisitions
514-982-4026 e-mail: marc-antoine.larochelle@blakes.com
Annie Lagacé, Business
514-982-4077 e-mail: annie.lagace@blakes.com
Corinne Lemire, Business; Financial Services
514-982-4070 e-mail: corinne.lemire@blakes.com
John Leopardi, Taxation; Mergers & Acquisitions
514-982-5030 e-mail: john.leopardi@blakes.com
Angelo Noce, Business; Securities; Mergers & Acquisitions
514-982-4062 e-mail: angelo.noce@blakes.com
James Papadimitriou, Business; Financial Services; Real Estate
514-982-4002 e-mail: james.papadimitriou@blakes.com
Eric Poole, Business; Securities
514-982-4019 e-mail: eric.poole@blakes.com
Marie Sabourin, Business
514-982-4072 e-mail: marie.sabourin@blakes.com
Robert Torralbo, Securities
514-982-4014 e-mail: robert.torralbo@blakes.com

Blake, Cassels & Graydon LLP

World Exchange Plaza #2000
45 O'Connor St.
Ottawa, ON K1P 1A4
613-788-2200
Fax: 613-788-2247
ottawa@blakes.com
www.blakes.com
Founded: 1856
Number of Lawyers: 13
Profile: Corporate/Commercial; Securities; Restructuring & Insolvency; Banking & Administrative Law

Finance Lawyers:
Alan T. Blackwell, Business; Mergers & Acquisitions
613-788-2210 e-mail: alan.blackwell@blakes.com

Gary O. Jessop, Business Law; Securities
613-788-2224 e-mail: gary.jessop@blakes.com
David Kidd, Mergers & Acquisitions
613-788-2203 e-mail: david.kidd@blakes.com
Randy Proulx, Business; Securities
613-788-2204 e-mail: randy.proulx@blakes.com

Blake, Cassels & Graydon LLP
Three Bentall Centre #2600
PO Box 49314
595 Burrard St.
Vancouver, BC V7X 1L3
604-631-3300
Fax: 604-631-3309
vancouver@blakes.com
www.blakes.com
Founded: 1856
Number of Lawyers: 64
Profile: Blakes Vancouver has broad-based & experienced financial services & real estate groups who have advised on the most complex & sophisticated transactions; our lawyers are experienced in all areas of counsel work, including corporate/commercial litigation, securities law matters, & restructuring & insolvency matters

Finance Lawyers:
Michael Adams, Business; Mergers & Acquisitions; Private Equity & Venture Capital
604-631-4253 e-mail: michael.adams@blakes.com
Dori C. Assaly, Business; Securities
604-631-3384 e-mail: dori.assaly@blakes.com
Michelle Audet, Securities; Business
604-631-4236 e-mail: michelle.audet@blakes.com
Angela D. Austman, Business; Securities
604-631-3326 e-mail: angela.austman@blakes.com
Farhad Bayati, Business; Securities
604-631-3341 e-mail: farhad.bayati@blakes.com
John-Paul Bodgen, Business; Mergers & Acquisitions
604-631-3375 e-mail: johnpaul.bogden@blakes.com
Teresa Budd, Securities; Business
604-631-4258 e-mail: teresa.budd@blakes.com
Francis Chang, Business; Mergers & Acquisitions
604-631-3332 e-mail: francis.chang@blakes.com
Karla Everatt, Securities
604-631-3337 e-mail: karla.everatt@blakes.com
Caroline Findlay, Business
604-631-3333 e-mail: caroline.findlay@blakes.com
Delaney Fisher, Business; Securities
604-631-3381 e-mail: delaney.fisher@blakes.com
Jonathan Goheen, Corporate Governance
604-631-3308 e-mail: jonathan.goheen@blakes.com
David Gruber, Restructuring & Insolvency
604-631-3376 e-mail: david.gruber@blakes.com
Bahar Hafzi, Financial Services
604-631-3388 e-mail: bahar.hafzi@blakes.com
Gayle G. Hunter, Business
604-631-3352 e-mail: gh@blakes.com
Peter C. Kalbfleisch, Business; Securities; Corporate Governance
604-631-3377 e-mail: peter.kalbfleisch@blakes.com
William C. Kaplan, Restructuring; Insolvency
604-631-3304 e-mail: bill.kaplan@blakes.com
Jocelyn M. Kelley, Business; Mergers & Acquisitions
604-631-3370 e-mail: jmk@blakes.com
Ian N. MacIntosh, Business; Securities; Corporate Governance; Mergers & Acquisitions
604-631-3373 e-mail: ian.macintosh@blakes.com
Richard McDerby, Business; Mergers & Acquisitions; Private Equity & Venture Capital
604-631-3319 e-mail: richard.mcderby@blakes.com
Grace McDonald, Business; Securities
604-631-3389 e-mail: grace.mcdonald@blakes.com
Andrew J. McLeod, Business; Securities
604-631-3399 e-mail: andrew.mcleod@blakes.com
Jeffrey Merrick, Business; Mergers & Acquisitions
604-631-3386 e-mail: jeff.merrick@blakes.com
Maria A. Morellato, Commodity Tax & Trade
604-631-3324 e-mail: maria.morellato@blakes.com
Wendy S. Morrison, Business; Securities; Mergers & Acquisitions
604-631-3380 e-mail: wm@blakes.com
Peter J. O'Callaghan, Securities; Mergers & Acquisitions; Corporate Governance
604-631-3345 e-mail: peter.ocallaghan@blakes.com
Samantha Richer, Financial Services
604-631-4159 e-mail: samantha.richer@blakes.com
Trisha Robertson, Securities; Business
604-631-3320 e-mail: trisha.robertson@blakes.com
Peter L. Rubin, Restructuring & Insovlency
604-631-3315 e-mail: peter.rubin@blakes.com
Tanya Sadlo, Business
604-631-3393 e-mail: tanya.sadlo@blakes.com
Wei Shao, Business
604-631-3349 e-mail: wei.shao@blakes.com
Mark Smith, Financial Services
604-631-3391 e-mail: mark.smith@blakes.com
Anne M. Stewart, Business; Financial Services; Mergers & Acquisitions
604-631-3313 e-mail: anne.stewart@blakes.com
Greg W. Umbach, Business
604-631-3378 e-mail: greg.umbach@blakes.com
Neal B. Wang, Business; Financial Services
604-631-3328 e-mail: neal.wang@blakes.com
Jennifer Williams, Real Estate
604-631-3367 e-mail: jennifer.williams@blakes.com
Bob J. Wooder, Business; Securities
604-631-3330 e-mail: bob.wooder@blakes.com
Kevin P. Zimka, Business; Taxation
604-631-3363 e-mail: kevin.zimka@blakes.com

Blaney McMurtry LLP
#1500
2 Queen St. East
Toronto, ON M5C 3G5
416-593-1221
Fax: 416-593-5437
Telex: 06-22326info@blaney.com
www.blaney.com
Founded: 1954
Number of Lawyers: 108

Finance Lawyers:
Michael J. Bennett, Securities; Corporate Insurance; Corporate/Commercial; Corporate Finance & Securities
416-593-3905 e-mail: mbennett@blaney.com
James W. Blaney, Corporate Insurance; Corporate/Commercial
416-593-3906 e-mail: jblaney@blaney.com
Lou Brzezinski, Business Reorganization & Insolvency
Renato Chiaradia, Corporate/Commercial
416-593-3982 e-mail: rchiaradia@blaney.com
Robert Cohen, Commercial Real Estate
416-593-3908 e-mail: bcohen@blaney.com
Patrick J. Cummins, Corporate/Commercial; Corporate Finance & Securities
416-593-3928 e-mail: pcummins@blaney.com
Jack Ditkofsky, Corporate/Commercial
416-593-3913 e-mail: jditkofsky@blaney.com
Colin Empke, Commercial Insurance
Reeva M. Finkel, Business Reorganization & Insolvency
Joan H. Garson, Corporate Commercial; Corporate Finance; Business Reorganization & Insolvency
416-593-3925 e-mail: jgarson@blaney.com
Eric Golden, Business Reorganization & Insolvency
Barry T. Grant, Real Estate; Corporate/Commercial
416-593-3929 e-mail: bgrant@blaney.com
H. Todd Greenbloom, Corporate/Commercial
416-593-3931 e-mail: tgreenbloom@blaney.com
Deborah S. Grieve, Corporate & Debt Restructuring; Bankruptcy & Receivership; Cross Border Transactions
416-593-2951 e-mail: dgrieve@blaney.com
Andrew J. Heal, Business Reorganization & Insolvency
416-593-3934 e-mail: aheal@blaney.com
Faithlyn Hemmings, Corporate/Commercial
416-593-2990 e-mail: fhemmings@blaney.com
Steven P. Jeffery, Corporate/Commercial
416-593-3939 e-mail: sjeffery@blaney.com
Regina Ko, Corporate/Commercial
416-593-3933 e-mail: rko@blaney.com
Stanley Kugelmass, Corporate Insurance; Corporate/Commercial
416-593-3943 e-mail: skugelmass@blaney.com
Ivan Lavrence, Business Reorganization & Insolvency
James Leech, Corporate/Commercial
416-596-2893 e-mail: jleech@blaney.com
Domenico Magisano, Business Reorganization & Insolvency
Jill E. McCutcheon, Corporate Insurance
416-593-2956 e-mail: jmccutcheon@blaney.com
Maureen E. Merrill, Corporate/Commercial; Commercial Leasing
416-593-3945 e-mail: mmerrill@blaney.com
Alexander A. Mesbur, Corporate/Commercial; Commercial Leasing
416-593-3949 e-mail: amesbur@blaney.com
Robert Muir, Business Reorganization & Insolvency
416-593-3951 e-mail: rmuir@blaney.com
Lea Nebel, Business Reorganization & Insolvency
John C. Papadakis, Corporate/Commercial
416-593-3998 e-mail: jpapadakis@blaney.com
Bradley Phillips, Business Reorganization & Insolvency
John Polyzogopoulos, Business Reorganization & Insolvency
Steve S. Popoff, Corporate Insurance; Corporate/Commercial; Corporate Finance & Securities
416-593-3972 e-mail: spopoff@blaney.com
Eric Schjerning, Insurance
Paul Schnier, Tax Law
416-593-3956 e-mail: pschnier@blaney.com
Bruno P. Soucy, Corporate/Commercial
416-593-2950 e-mail: bsoucy@blaney.com
Crawford W. Spratt, Corporate Insurance; Corporate/Commercial
416-593-3965 e-mail: cspratt@blaney.com
Mona R. Taylor, Tax Law
416-593-3967 e-mail: mtaylor@blaney.com
Nadim Wakeam, Corporate/Commercial
416-593-2980 e-mail: nwakeam@blaney.com

Blois, Nickerson & Bryson
#500
PO Box 2147
1568 Hollis St.
Halifax, NS B3J 3B7
902-425-6000
Fax: 902-429-7347
info@bloisnickerson.com
www.bloisnickerson.com
Founded: 1993
Number of Lawyers: 17

Finance Lawyers:
Roberta J. Clarke, Estate; Wills; Trusts
e-mail: rclarke@bloisnickerson.com
Franklyn W. Cordon, Commercial; Corporate; Tax Law
e-mail: fcordon@bloisnickerson.com
Elias A. Metlej, Corporate/Commercial; Leasing

Blumberg Segal LLP
#1202
390 Bay St.
Toronto, ON M5H 2Y2
416-361-1982
Fax: 416-363-8451
info@blumbergs.ca
www.blumbergs.ca
Number of Lawyers: 6
Profile: Corporate/Commercial Litigation

Finance Lawyers:
Henry G. Blumberg, Litigation
e-mail: henry@blumbergs.ca
Mark A. Blumberg, Corporate/Commercial
e-mail: mark@blumbergs.ca
Ronald S. Segal, Corporate/Commercial
e-mail: rsegal@blumbergs.ca
Darren J. Smith, Litigation
e-mail: darren@blumberts.ca
Lize-Mari Swanepoel, Corporate/Commercial
e-mail: lize-mari@blumbergs.ca

Bondy, Riley, Koski
#310
176 University Ave. West
Windsor, ON N9A 5P1
519-258-1641
Fax: 519-258-1725
info@bondyriley.com
Founded: 1964
Number of Lawyers: 2
Profile: Corporate & Commercial Law

Finance Lawyers:
Gerald W. Koski, Corporate/Commercial; Business Law; Real Estate, Commercial & Residential

Borden Ladner Gervais LLP
Canterra Tower #1000
400 - 3rd Ave. SW
Calgary, AB T2P 4H2

Borden Ladner Gervais LLP (continued)
403-232-9500
Fax: 403-266-1395
info@blgcanada.com
www.blgcanada.com
Number of Lawyers: 100
Profile: Our Financial Services Group, in conjunction with our other Practice Groups, provides comprehensive & specialized advice & legal services in all aspects of financial services law; our group is a large multidisciplinary team with expertise in all areas of financial services law, including banking, lending, structured finance, project finance, securitizations, regulatory matters, bankruptcy, insolvency, restructuring, & related disciplines; our multidisciplinary approach reflects the reality of financial services both domestically & internationally where traditional financial sectors have become integrated & traditional activities require special expertise; our Financial Services Group provides a wide range of services to major Canadian & foreign banks, financial institutions, trust companies, credit unions, insurance companies & investment dealers; the Group also represents numerous corporate borrowers & lessees in diverse sectors of the economy; we make it our business to know & understand the financial services marketplace & to respond practically & efficiently to our client's needs

Finance Lawyers:
Randall W. Block, Regional Leader, Directors' & Officers' Liability Group
403-232-9572 e-mail: rblock@blgcanada.com
Ross D. Freeman, Regional Leader, Tax Group
403-232-9457 e-mail: rfreeman@blgcanada.com
Nancy L. Golding, Regional Leader, Wealth Management Group
403-232-9485 e-mail: ngolding@blgcanada.com
John L. Ircandia, Regional Leader, Banking Litigation Group
403-232-9406 e-mail: jircandia@blgcanada.com
D. George Kelly, Regional Leader, Mergers & Acquisitions Group
403-232-9508 e-mail: gkelly@blgcanada.com
Daniel G. Kolibar, Regional Leader, Corporate Finance Group
403-232-9559 e-mail: dkolibar@blgcanada.com
Terence Lidster, Regional Leader, Financial Services Group
403-232-9573 e-mail: tlidster@blgcanada.com
Patrick T. McCarthy, National Leader, Insolvency & Restructuring Group
403-232-9441 e-mail: pmccarthy@blgcanada.com
Allan D. Nielsen, Regional Leader, Structured Finance & Leasing Group; Corporate Commercial Group
403-232-9487 e-mail: anielsen@blgcanada.com
Brad J. Pierce, Regional Leader, Venture Capital Group
403-232-9421 e-mail: bpierce@blgcanada.com
James A.W. Williams, Regional Leader, Corporate Tax Group
403-232-9701 e-mail: jwilliams@blgcanada.com

Borden Ladner Gervais LLP
#900
1000, rue de La Gauchetière ouest
Montréal, QC H3B 5H4
514-879-1212
Fax: 514-954-1905
info@blgcanada.com
www.blgcanada.com
Number of Lawyers: 117
Profile: Our Financial Services Group, in conjunction with our other Practice Groups, provides comprehensive & specialized advice & legal services in all aspects of financial services law; our group is a large multidisciplinary team with expertise in all areas of financial services law, including banking, lending, structured finance, project finance, securitizations, regulatory matters, bankruptcy, insolvency, restructuring, & related disciplines; our multidisciplinary approach reflects the reality of financial services both domestically & internationally where traditional financial sectors have become integrated & traditional activities require special expertise; our Financial Services Group provides a wide range of services to major Canadian & foreign banks, financial institutions, trust companies, credit unions, insurance companies & investment dealers; the Group also represents numerous corporate borrowers & lessees in diverse sectors of the economy; we make it our business to know & unders

Finance Lawyers:
Virginia Chan, Regional Leader, Corporate Tax Group
514-954-3160 e-mail: vchan@blgcanada.com
Robert E. Charbonneau, Regional Leader, Directors' & Officers' Liability Group
514-954-2518 e-mail: rcharbonneau@blgcanada.com
Pierre B. Côté, Regional Leader, Structured Finance & Leasing Group; Financial Services Group
514-954-3111 e-mail: pcote@blgcanada.com
Marc Duchesne, Regional Leader, Banking Litigation Group; Insolvency & Restructuring Group
514-954-3102 e-mail: mduchesne@blgcanada.com
André Dufour, Regional Leader, Venture Capital Group
514-954-2526 e-mail: adufour@blgcanada.com
Fred Enns, Regional Leader, Securities & Capital Markets Group
514-954-2536 e-mail: fenns@blgcanada.com
H. John Godber, Regional Leader, Corporate Commercial Group; Mergers & Acquisitions Group
514-954-3165 e-mail: jgodber@blgcanada.com
Paul R. Marchand, Regional Leader, Wealth Management Group
514-954-3172 e-mail: pmarchand@blgcanada.com
Beno(140t Provost, National Leader, Commercial Lending Group
514-954-3107 e-mail: bprovost@blgcanada.com
Brian M. Schneiderman, Regional Leader, Tax Group
514-954-3120 e-mail: bschneiderman@blgcanada.com
Richard W. Shannon, Regional Leader, Corporate Finance Group
514-954-3103 e-mail: rshannon@blgcanada.com
Ian Taylor, National Leader, Commercial Leasing Group
514-954-2559 e-mail: itaylor@blgcanada.com

Borden Ladner Gervais LLP
World Exchange Plaza #1100
100 Queen St.
Ottawa, ON K1P 1J9
613-237-5160
Fax: 613-230-8842
info@blgcanada.com
www.blgcanada.com
Number of Lawyers: 89
Profile: Our Financial Services Group, in conjunction with our other Practice Groups, provides comprehensive & specialized advice & legal services in all aspects of financial services law; our group is a large multidisciplinary team with expertise in all areas of financial services law, including banking, lending, structured finance, project finance, securitizations, regulatory matters, bankruptcy, insolvency, restructuring, & related disciplines; our multidisciplinary approach reflects the reality of financial services both domestically & internationally where traditional financial sectors have become integrated & traditional activities require special expertise; our Financial Services Group provides a wide range of services to major Canadian & foreign banks, financial institutions, trust companies, credit unions, insurance companies & investment dealers; the Group also represents numerous corporate borrowers & lessees in diverse sectors of the economy; we make it our business to know & unders

Finance Lawyers:
Head of Financial Law: Yvan G. Morin, Lending; Insolvency & Restructuring; Commercial
613-787-3526 e-mail: ymorin@blgcanada.com
Rocco D'Angelo, Lending; Corporate; Commercial
613-787-3549 e-mail: rdangelo@blgcanada.com
Sybil Johnson-Abbott, Lending; Corporate; Commercial
613-787-3725 e-mail: sjohnsonabbott@blgcanada.com
Marc Jolicoeur, Commercial; Lending; Insolvency & Restructuring
613-787-3515 e-mail: mjolicoeur@blgcanada.com
Yves J. Ménard, Commercial; Lending
613-787-3518 e-mail: ymenard@blgcanada.com
Josee Virgo, Lending; Corporate
613-787-3742 e-mail: jvirgo@blgcanada.com

Borden Ladner Gervais LLP
Scotia Plaza
40 King St. West
Toronto, ON M5H 3Y4
416-367-6000
Fax: 416-367-6749
Telex: 0622687 Betorinfo@blgcanada.com
www.blgcanada.com
Founded: 1936
Number of Lawyers: 249
Profile: Our Financial Services Group, in conjunction with our other Practice Groups, provides comprehensive & specialized advice & legal services in all aspects of financial services law; our group is a large multidisciplinary team with expertise in all areas of financial services law, including banking, lending, structured finance, project finance, securitizations, regulatory matters, bankruptcy, insolvency, restructuring, & related disciplines; our multidisciplinary approach reflects the reality of financial services both domestically & internationally where traditional financial sectors have become integrated & traditional activities require special expertise; our Financial Services Group provides a wide range of services to major Canadian & foreign banks, financial institutions, trust companies, credit unions, insurance companies & investment dealers; the Group represents numerous corporate borrowers & lessees in diverse sectors of the economy; we make it our business to know & understand

Finance Lawyers:
Francis R. Allen, Mergers & Acquisitions
Kenneth S. Atlas, Financial Services
Linda L. Bertoldi, Corporate Commercial
416-367-6647 e-mail: lbertoldi@blgcanada.com
Meaghan D. Bethune, Corporate Commercial
416-367-6033 e-mail: mbethune@blgcanada.com
Neda Bizzotto, Mergers & Acquisitions
Frank S. Callaghan, Corporate Commercial
416-367-6014 e-mail: fcallaghan@blgcanada.com
Eva Chan, Corporate Commercial
416-367-6722 e-mail: evachan@blgcanada.com
Tracy D. Chin, Corporate Commercial
Anne C. Corbett, Corporate Commercial
416-367-6013 e-mail: acorbett@blgcanada.com
William C. Cortis, Lending; General Business
416-367-6043 e-mail: wcortis@blgcanada.com
Amanda Darrach, Financial Services
Heather Douglas, Public Finance
416-361-6177 e-mail: hdouglas@blgcanada.com
Jonathan F. Dyck, Lending; Insolvency
416-367-6124 e-mail: jdyck@blgcanada.com
James R. Elder, Corporate Commercial
416-367-6188 e-mail: jelder@blgcanada.com
Adam F. Fanaki, Corporate Commercial
416-367-6107 e-mail: afanaki@blgcanada.com
David J. Faye, Corporate Commercial
Joanne E. Foot, Lending
416-367-6193 e-mail: jfoot@blgcanada.com
Bruce E. Fowler, Lending
416-367-6194 e-mail: bfowler@blgcanada.com
Shane Freitag, Corporate Commercial
416-367-6137 e-mail: sfreitag@blgcanada.com
Elissa M. Goodman, Banking Litigation
Jeffrey S. Graham, Financial Services
Stefan Guttensohn, Mergers & Acquisitions
Andrew G. Harrison, Regulatory; Pensions
416-367-6046 e-mail: aharrison@blgcanada.com
Craig J. Hill, Insolvency & Restructuring
416-367-6156 e-mail: chill@blgcanada.com
Roger Jaipargas, Insolvency & Restructuring
416-367-6266 e-mail: rjaipargas@blgcanada.com
Gus Karantzoulis, Lending
416-367-6336 e-mail: gkarantzoulis@blgcanada.com
Ziad J. Katul, Corporate Commercial
416-367-6713 e-mail: zkatul@blgcanada.com
C. Graham W. King, Corporate Commercial
416-367-6051 e-mail: gking@blgcanada.com
Carlyn D. Klebuc, Lending
416-367-6540 e-mail: cklebuc@blgcanada.com
Tanya M. Kozak, Insolvency & Restructuring
416-367-6145 e-mail: tkozak@blgcanada.com
Reid Lester, Banking Litigation
Christine E. Long, Corporate Commercial
416-367-6683 e-mail: clong@blgcanada.com
Terence Lui, Lending
416-367-6229 e-mail: tlui@blgcanada.com
Robert B. MacLellan, Lending; Insolvency
416-367-6050 e-mail: rmaclellan@blgcanada.com
Michael J. MacNaughton, Insolvency & Restructuring
416-367-6646 e-mail: mmacnaughton@blgcanada.com
Sonia T. Mak, Corporate Commercial
416-367-6171 e-mail: smak@blgcanada.com
John D. Marshall, Banking Litigation
James W. Mathers, Lending; Insolvency
416-367-6035 e-mail: jmathers@blgcanada.com
Kevin A. McGrath, Lending
416-367-6057 e-mail: kmcgrath@blgcanada.com
William R. McLean, Corporate Commercial
416-367-6021 e-mail: wmclean@blgcanada.com
Daniel McNamara, Financial Services
Brent W. Mescall, Banking Litigation

Karin E. Millar, Corporate Commercial
416-367-6736
Richard J. Morelli, Corporate Commercial
416-367-6197 e-mail: rmorelli@blgcanada.com
Rosalind Morrow, Mergers & Acquisitions
Anna C. Naud, Corporate Commercial
Ira Nishisato, Banking Litigation
416-367-6349 e-mail: inishisato@blgcanada.com
Thomas W. Ouchterlony, Corporate Commercial
416-367-6100 e-mail: touchterlony@blgcanada.com
Lisa M. Pagano, Corporate Commercial
William T. Pashby, Corporate Commercial
416-367-6249 e-mail: bpashby@blgcanada.com
Shane B. Pearlman, Lending; Insolvency
416-367-6693 e-mail: spearlman@blgcanada.com
Joanne M. Poljanowski, Lending
416-367-6254 e-mail: jpoljanowski@blgcanada.com
Laura Pottie, Banking Litigation
Andrew D. Powers, Mergers & Acquisitions
Victoria Prince, Corporate Commercial
416-367-6648 e-mail: vprince@blgcanada.com
Gordon G. Raman, Financial Services
Stephen J. Redican, Lending; Regulatory
416-367-6134 e-mail: sredican@blgcanada.com
John M. Risk, Corporate Commercial
J. Mark Rodger, Corporate Commercial
416-367-6190 e-mail: mrodger@blgcanada.com
Martin Sclisizzi, Banking Litigation
Simon B. Scott, Lending
416-367-6261 e-mail: sscott@blgcanada.com
Michael D. Shadbolt, Corporate Commercial
416-367-6172 e-mail: mshadbolt@blgcanada.com
James C. Sidlofsky, Corporate Commercial
416-367-6277 e-mail: jsidlofsky@blgcanada.com
Howard S. Silverman, Lending
416-367-6119 e-mail: hsilverman@blgcanada.com
Alexandria Sjöman, Mergers & Acquisitions
Colleen Spring Zimmerman, Corporate Commercial
416-367-6710 e-mail: cpspringzimmerman@blgcanada.com
Philippe Tardif
Will W. Wallace, Corporate Commercial
John F.T. Warren, Corporate Commercial
Sean Weir, Pension
416-367-6040 e-mail: sweir@blgcanada.com
George E. Whyte, Corporate Commercial
416-367-6588 e-mail: gwhyte@blgcanada.com
Kelly A. Zalec, Corporate Commercial
Gordon J. Zimmerman, Corporate Commercial
416-367-6282 e-mail: gzimmerman@blgcanada.com
H. Alexander Zimmerman, Financial Services

Borden Ladner Gervais LLP

Waterfront Centre #1200
PO Box 48600
200 Burrard St.
Vancouver, BC V7X 1T2
604-687-5744
Fax: 604-687-1415
info@blgcanada.com
www.blgcanada.com
Founded: 1911
Number of Lawyers: 117
Profile: Our Financial Services Group, in conjunction with our other Practice Groups, provides comprehensive & specialized advice & legal services in all aspects of financial services law; our group is a large multidisciplinary team with expertise in all areas of financial services law, including banking, lending, structured finance, project finance, securitizations, regulatory matters, bankruptcy, insolvency, restructuring, & related disciplines; our multidisciplinary approach reflects the reality of financial services both domestically & internationally where traditional financial sectors have become integrated & traditional activities require special expertise; our Financial Services Group provides a wide range of services to major Canadian & foreign banks, financial institutions, trust companies, credit unions, insurance companies & investment dealers; the Group also represents numerous corporate borrowers & lessees in diverse sectors of the economy; we make it our business to know & unders

Finance Lawyers:
Clive S. Bird, Regional Leader, Insolvency & Restructuring Group
604-640-4103 e-mail: cbird@blgcanada.com
Donald G. Bird, Regional Leader, Commercial Lending Group; Structured Finance & Leasing Group
604-640-4175 e-mail: dbird@blgcanada.com
Nigel P. Cave, Securities & Capital Markets Group
604-640-4161 e-mail: ncave@blgcanada.com
D. Ross McGowan, Regional Leader, Banking Litigation Group
604-640-4173 e-mail: rmcgowan@blgcanada.com
Christopher J. O'Connor, Regional Leader, Directors' & Officers' Liability Group
604-640-4125 e-mail: coconnor@blgcanada.com
Deborah H. Overholt, Regional Leader, Corporate Commercial Group
604-640-4164 e-mail: doverholt@blgcanada.com
Fred R. Pletcher, Regional Leader, Venture Capital Group
604-640-4245 e-mail: fpletcher@blgcanada.com
Bruce R. Sinclair, National Leader, Tax Group
604-640-4228 e-mail: bsinclair@blgcanada.com
Carolynn Vivian, Regional Leader, Commercial Leasing Group
604-640-4131 e-mail: cvivian@blgcanada.com
Gary J. Wilson, National Leader, Wealth Management Group
604-640-4155 e-mail: gwilson@blgcanada.com

Boughton Law Corporation

Three Bentall Centre #1000
PO Box 49290
595 Dunsmuir St.
Vancouver, BC V7X 1S8
604-687-6789
Fax: 604-683-5317
lawyers@boughton.ca
www.boughton.ca
Number of Lawyers: 41

Finance Lawyers:
Merle C. Alexander, Corporate & Business
604-647-4145 e-mail: malexander@boughton.ca
Gordon V. Anderson, Corporate Recovery
Peter J. Anderson, Corporate & Business
604-647-4138 e-mail: panderson@boughton.ca
James D. Baird, Corporate & Business
604-647-4140 e-mail: jbaird@boughton.ca
Alan H. Brown, Corporate Recovery & Realization
604-647-6426 e-mail: abrown@boughton.ca
George E.H. Cadman, Bankruptcy, Insolvency; Securities
604-647-4123 e-mail: gehcqc@boughton.ca
Hugh H. Claxton, Banking & Financing; Corporate & Business
James M. Coady, Securities
604-647-4105 e-mail: jcoady@boughton.ca
William H. Cooper, Taxation, Wills & Estates
604-647-4137 e-mail: wcooper@boughton.ca
Heather Craig, Securities
604-647-4121 e-mail: hcraig@boughton.ca
Janet Derbawka, Banking & Financing
604-647-4179 e-mail: jderbawka@boughton.ca
Mark P. Eikland, Corporate & Business
604-647-4168 e-mail: meikland@boughton.ca
Stella D. Frame, Banking; Insolvency
604-647-4111 e-mail: sframe@boughton.ca
Gordon A. Fulton, Taxation, Wills & Estates
604-647-4104 e-mail: gfulton@boughton.ca
Jeffrey S. Glasner, Taxation, Wills & Estates
604-647-5527 e-mail: jglasner@boughton.ca
Rory S. Godinho, Securities
604-647-5525 e-mail: rgodinho@boughton.ca
Ernest A. Hee, Corporate & Business
604-647-6424 e-mail: ehee@boughton.ca
Douglas H. Hopkins, Banking & Financing; Corporate & Business
Daryn R. Leas, Corporate & Business
867-393-3356 e-mail: dleas@boughton.ca
Claudia Losie, Corporate & Business
604-647-4149 e-mail: closie@boughton.ca
Scott M. MacKenzie, Securities
604-647-4116 e-mail: smackenzie@boughton.ca
Gary J. Matson, Corporate & Business
604-647-4139 e-mail: gmatson@boughton.ca
Paul R. Miller, Securities
604-647-4102 e-mail: pmiller@boughton.ca
John Mostowich, Corporate Recovery & Realization
604-647-4113 e-mail: jmostowich@boughton.ca
Leslie R. Peterson, Corporate & Business
604-647-4156 e-mail: lpeterson@boughton.ca
Gregg E. Rafter, Corporate Recovery & Realization
604-647-4108 e-mail: grafter@boughton.ca
Martin Sennott, Banking; Real Estate; Commercial
604-647-4106 e-mail: msennott@boughton.ca
Jay Shin, Banking & Financing
604-647-4173 e-mail: jshin@boughton.ca
Kathy H. Tang, Corporate & Business
604-647-4117 e-mail: ktang@boughton.ca
R. David Toyoda, Corporate & Business
604-647-6424 e-mail: rtoyoda@boughton.ca
Richard K. Uhrle, Banking & Financing
604-647-4126 e-mail: ruhrle@boughton.ca
Peter A. Wong, Taxation & Trusts

Boyne Clarke

Belmont House #700
PO Box 876
33 Alderney Dr.
Dartmouth, NS B2Y 3Z5
902-469-9500
Fax: 902-463-7500
800-207-6589
admin@boyneclarke.ns.ca
www.boyneclarke.ns.ca
Founded: 1972
Number of Lawyers: 39
Profile: The lawyers in our Corporate/Commercial Group provide specialized counsel & assistance to business clients, they are committed to helping companies, banks, trust companies & other financial institutions; we provide full service legal advice with respect to all aspects of corporate/commercial & securities law including: organizing & structuring of corporations, partnerships, joint ventures & other types of corporate entities; amalgamations & reorganizations; acquisitions & sale of companies; bank & institutional financing; provincial & regional share offerings; commercial leasing; franchising & licensing

Finance Lawyers:
Patricia A. Davis, Securities
902-460-3415 e-mail: pdavis@boyneclarke.ns.ca
Peter J. Driscoll, Pensions & Benefits
902-460-3414 e-mail: pdriscoll@boyneclarke.ns.ca
Christene H. Hirschfeld, Entertainment/Film Financing
902-460-3413 e-mail: chirschfel@boyneclarke.ns.ca
Bryce W. Morrison, PPSA; Taxation
902-460-3433 e-mail: bmorrison@boyneclarke.ns.ca
Kelly J. Powell
902-460-3458 e-mail: kpowell@boyneclarke.ns.ca
David A. Thompson, Securities
902-460-3421 e-mail: dthompson@boyneclarke.ns.ca
Leah D. Tinkham
902-460-3459 e-mail: ltinkham@boyneclarke.ns.ca
John A. Young
902-460-3406 e-mail: jyoung@boyneclarke.ns.ca

Bratty & Partners LLP

#200
7501 Keele St.
Vaughan, ON L4K 1Y2
905-760-2600
Fax: 905-760-2900
www.bratty.com
Number of Lawyers: 14
Profile: The corporate/commercial department regularly acts on asset & share transactions, shareholder agreements, corporate financing & reorganizations, commercial transactions, succession planning, estate freezes & tax implementation

Finance Lawyers:
Paola F. Baldassarra
Daniel Botelho
Rudolph P. Bratty
Joseph De Tomasso
Stephen J. Marano
Paul Merrick
Larry Trifon
Nickolas Vlitas
Michael C. Volpatti
Herbert L. Wisebrod

Brazeau Seller LLP

#750
55 Metcalfe St.
Ottawa, ON K1P 6L5
613-237-4000
Fax: 613-237-4001
mail@brazeauseller.com
www.brazeauseller.com
Founded: 1989

ACCOUNTING & LAW

Brazeau Seller LLP (continued)
Number of Lawyers: 16
Profile: Corporate & Commercial; E-Business; Real Estate; Tax & Estate Planning

Finance Lawyers:
Donald H. Brazeau, Wills & Estate, Corporate
613-237-4000 e-mail: dbrazeau@brazeauseller.com
Frederick Cogan, Counsel, Commercial Law
613-237-4000 e-mail: fcogan@brazeauseller.com
Harold J. Feder, Corporate; Wills; Estates; Taxation
613-237-4000 e-mail: hfeder@brazeauseller.com
Trina K. Fraser, Litigation; Gaming Laws, Corporate, Commercial
613-237-4000 e-mail: tfraser@brazeauseller.com
Marcia Green, Litigation
e-mail: mgreen@brazeauseller.com
Melanie McDonald, Wills & Estates
613-237-4000 e-mail: mmcdonald@brazeauseller.com
Ronald Prehogan, Corporate Commercial
613-237-4000 e-mail: rprehogan@brazeauseller.com
Najma Rashid, Litigation
613-237-4000 e-mail: nrashid@braseauseller.com
Fred E. Seller, Litigation; Gaming Laws, Corporate, Commercial
613-237-4000 e-mail: fseller@brazeauseller.com
Steve Sheppard, Real Estate
613-237-4000 e-mail: ssheppard@brazeauseller.com
Jamie Wyllie, Corporate, Patents
e-mail: jwylie@brazeauseller.com
Howard Yegendorf, Litigation, Gaming Laws
613-237-4000 e-mail: hyegendorf@brazeauseller.com

Bull, Housser & Tupper LLP

Royal Centre #3000
PO Box 11130
1055 West Georgia St.
Vancouver, BC V6E 3R3
604-687-6575
Fax: 604-641-4949
888-687-6575
Telex: 04-53395mailbox@bht.com
www.bht.com
Founded: 1890
Number of Lawyers: 86

Finance Lawyers:
David R. Bain, Banking
604-641-4812 e-mail: drb@bht.com
R. John Kearns, Insolvency
604-641-4816 e-mail: rjk@bht.com
Margaret H. Mason, Wills/Estates
604-641-4405 e-mail: mhm@bht.com
R. Eric P. Maurice, Banking
604-641-4808 e-mail: rem@bht.com
E. Jane Milton, Insolvency
604-641-4823 e-mail: ejm@bht.com
Alan N. Robertson, Tax
604-641-4828 e-mail: anr@bht.com
Richard Sarabando, Banking
604-641-4924 e-mail: ris@bht.com
Christopher G. Speakman, Tax
604-641-4835 e-mail: cgs@bht.com
James E. Sutcliffe, Banking
604-641-4909 e-mail: jes@bht.com
Carmen S. Thériault, Wills & Estates
604-641-4937 e-mail: cst@bht.com
Philip B. Webber, Tax
604-641-4833 e-mail: pbw@bht.com
Michael Welters, Tax
604-641-4954 e-mail: mjw@bht.com

Burchell Hayman Parish

#1800
1801 Hollis St.
Halifax, NS B3J 3N4
902-423-6361
Fax: 902-420-9326
firm@burchells.ca
www.burchells.ca
Founded: 1912
Number of Lawyers: 23

Finance Lawyers:
Jane Anderson, Corporate/Commercial
902-423-8363 e-mail: janderson@burchells.ca
Brian Awad, Securities
902-442-8375 e-mail: bawad@burchells.ca
Thomas J. Burchell, Corporate/Commercial
902-423-6361 e-mail: tburchell@burchells.ca
David A. Cameron, Business Litigation
902-428-8390 e-mail: dcameron@burchells.ca
Cheryl A. Canning, Commercial
902-442-8372 e-mail: ccanning@burchells.ca
D. Bruce Clarke, Corporate/Commercial; Bankruptcy & Insolvency
902-423-6361 e-mail: bclarke@burchells.ca
Brian Curry, Corporate/Commercial
902-442-8319 e-mail: bcurry@burchells.ca
Kelly L. Greenwood, Corporate/Commercial
902-428-8391 e-mail: kgreenwood@burchells.ca
Alan G. Hayman, Corporate/Commercial; Real Estate
902-442-8311 e-mail: ahayman@burchells.ca
Wayne F. Howatt, Corporate/Commercial
902-442-8329 e-mail: whowatt@burchells.ca
David G. Hutt, Banking & Insolvency; Business
902-442-8373 e-mail: dhutt@burchells.ca
David Lewis, Commercial
902-428-5301 e-mail: dlewis@burchells.ca
Anastasia Makrigiannis, Corporate/Commercial
902-442-8336 e-mail: amakrigiannis@burchells.ca
Alan V. Parish, Banking & Insolvency; Business; Securities
902-442-8366 e-mail: aparish@burchells.ca
Kevin Quigley, Banking & Insolvency
902-442-8368 e-mail: kquigley@burchells.ca
Andrew Rankin, Business
902-442-8370 e-mail: arankin@burchells.ca
Jennifer Ross, Business Litigation
902-442-8322 e-mail: jross@burchells.ca
Cory J. Withrow, Corporate/Commercial; Banking & Insolvency; Business
902-442-8386 e-mail: cwithrow@burchells.ca

Burnet, Duckworth & Palmer LLP

First Canadian Centre #1400
350 - 7th Ave. SW
Calgary, AB T2P 3N9
403-260-0100
Fax: 403-260-0332
counsel@bdplaw.com
www.bdplaw.com
Founded: 1915
Number of Lawyers: 118
Profile: Corporate; Commercial; Taxation; Real Estate; Securities

Finance Lawyers:
Allford, Securities
403-260-0247 e-mail: rba@bdplaw.com
Robert D. Betteridge, Banking; Project Finance
403-260-0188 e-mail: rdb@bdplaw.com
Brian W. Borich, Securities
403-260-0346 e-mail: bwb@bdplaw.com
Michel H. Bourque, Tax Litigation
403-260-0191 e-mail: mhb@bdplaw.com
John A. Brussa, Tax
403-260-0131 e-mail: jab@bdplaw.com
Gary Bugeaud, Securities
403-260-0155 e-mail: grb@bdplaw.com
Stephen J. Chetner, Securities
403-260-0265 e-mail: sjc@bdplaw.com
C. Steven Cohen, Securities
403-260-0103 e-mail: csc@bdplaw.com
Barry R. Crump, Realizations & Insolvencies
403-260-0352 e-mail: brc@bdplaw.com
Frederick D. Davidson, Securities
403-260-5718 e-mail: fdd@bdplaw.com
Patricia M. Fehr, Corporate Banking
403-260-0201 e-mail: pmf@bdplaw.com
Corrine Fiesel, Securities
403-260-0199 e-mail: cnf@bdplaw.com
Michael J. Flatters, Tax
403-260-0107 e-mail: mjf@bdplaw.com
Daryl S. Fridhandler, Securities
403-260-0113 e-mail: dsf@bdplaw.com
Shannon M. Gangl, Securities
403-260-0279 e-mail: smg@bdplaw.com
Cheryl Gottselig, Counsel, Commercial Real Estate
403-260-0202 e-mail: ccg@bdplaw.com
Keith A. Greenfield, Securities
403-260-0309 e-mail: kag@bdplaw.com
David A. Grout, Banking
403-260-9469 e-mail: dag@bdplaw.com
Brent T. Herman, Securities
403-260-0321 e-mail: bth@bdplaw.com
Craig R. Hill, Real Estate & Financing
403-260-0187 e-mail: crh@bdplaw.com
Scott D. Kearl, Securities
403-260-0395 e-mail: sdk@bdplaw.com
James L. Kidd, Securities
403-260-0181 e-mail: jlk@bdplaw.com
David S. Kolesar, Banking
403-260-0213 e-mail: dsk@bdplaw.com
Annette Lambert, Commercial Real Estate
403-260-0371 e-mail: ajl@bdplaw.com
Margot D. Langdon, Banking; Real Estate
403-260-0205 e-mail: mdl@bdplaw.com
Jeff G. Lawson, Securities
403-260-0267 e-mail: jgl@bdplaw.com
Michael G. Martin, Commercial Transactions; Private Mergers & Acquisitions
403-260-5738 e-mail: mgm@bdplaw.com
William S. Maslechko, Securities
403-260-0377 e-mail: wsm@bdplaw.com
Daniel J. McDonald, Securities Litigation
403-260-5724 e-mail: djm@bdplaw.com
Douglas A. McGillivray, Securities Litigation
403-260-0349 e-mail: dam@bdplaw.com
Denise W. McMullen, Tax
403-260-0361 e-mail: ddm@bdplaw.com
Tom M. Mix, Securities
403-260-0358 e-mail: tmm@bdplaw.com
Carla A. Murray, Realizations & Insolvencies
403-260-0326 e-mail: cam@bdplaw.com
Doug Nishimura, Realizations; Insolvency
403-260-0269 e-mail: dsn@bdplaw.com
Brian P. O'Leary, Realizations; Insolvency
403-260-0373 e-mail: bpo@bdplaw.com
Jeff T. Oke, Securities
403-260-0116 e-mail: jto@bdplaw.com
Arnold Olyan, Corporate Commercial; Major Projects
403-260-0249 e-mail: aho@bdplaw.com
James S. Palmer, Tax
e-mail: jsp@bdplaw.com
John Peters, Corporate Commercial; Securities; Real Estate
403-260-5748 e-mail: jap@bdplaw.com
Kathy L. Pybus, Corporate Banking
403-260-0196 e-mail: klp@bdplaw.com
Patricia Quinton-Campbell, Realizations & Insolvency
403-260-0308 e-mail: pqc@bdplaw.com
Jay P. Reid, Securities
403-260-0340 e-mail: jpr@bdplaw.com
David W. Ross, Tax
403-260-0296 e-mail: dwr@bdplaw.com
Michael D. Sandrelli, Securities
403-260-0115 e-mail: mds@bdplaw.com
Ken G. Stewart, Real Estate
403-260-0307 e-mail: kgs@bdplaw.com
Carla J. Tait, Securities
403-260-0207 e-mail: cjt@bdplaw.com
Allan R. Twa, Mergers & Acquisitions
403-260-0221 e-mail: art@bdplaw.com
Beth Vogel, Commercial Real Estate
403-260-0301 e-mail: bzv@bdplaw.com
John A. Wilmot, Corporate Banking & Lending; Project Finance
403-260-0117 e-mail: jaw@bdplaw.com
W.H. Winters, Project Finance; Commercial Transactions
403-260-0248 e-mail: whw@bdplaw.com
Grant A. Zawalsky, Securities
403-260-0376 e-mail: gaz@bdplaw.com
Chris C. von Vegesack, Securities
403-260-0121 e-mail: cvv@bdplaw.com

Burns, Fitzpatrick, Rogers & Schwartz

#1400
510 Burrard St.
Vancouver, BC V6C 3A8
604-685-0121
Fax: 604-685-2104
bfrs@bfrs.ca
www.bfrs.ca
Number of Lawyers: 8

Finance Lawyers:
Head of Financial Law: Stephen Z. Schwartz, Securities
604-685-2104 e-mail: sschwartz@bfrs.ca
J. Christopher Chan, Corporate & Commercial; Banking
Dennis K. Fitzpatrick, Banking; Bankruptcy & Insolvency

Tim Wong, Bankruptcy & Insolvency

Buset & Partners LLP
1121 Barton St.
Thunder Bay, ON P7B 5N3
807-623-2500
Fax: 807-622-7808
law@buset-partners.com
www.buset-partners.com
Founded: 1991
Number of Lawyers: 12

Finance Lawyers:
G.R. Birston, Insurance & Litigation
e-mail: gbirston@buset-partners.com
Chantal M. Brochu, Insurance & Litigation
e-mail: cbrochu@buset-partners.com
Kristi L. Burns, Real Estate; Wills & Estates, Corporate & Commercial
e-mail: kburns@buset-partners.com
T. Michael Strickland, Corporate & Commercial; Tax; Litigation
e-mail: mstrickland@buset-partners.com

Cain Lamarre Casgrain Wells
#202
855, 3e ave
Val-d'Or, QC J9P 1T2
819-825-4153
Fax: 819-825-9769
robert.dufresne@clcw.qc.ca
Founded: 1991
Number of Lawyers: 7

Finance Lawyers:
Stephan Ferron, Insurance & Liability; Corporate; Banking
e-mail: stephan.ferron@clcw.qc.ca
Sophie Gareau, Insurance & Liability; Business; Commercial/Corporate; Banking
e-mail: sophie.gareau@clcw.qc.ca

Cain Lamarre Casgrain Wells
889, boul St-Joseph
Roberval, QC G8H 2L8
418-275-2472
Fax: 418-275-6878
Number of Lawyers: 3

Finance Lawyers:
Beno(140t Amyot, Business; Commercial/Corporate; Banking
e-mail: benoit.amyot@clcw.qc.ca
Marie-Noe@#l Gagnon, Business; Corporate & Commercial
e-mail: marie.noel.gagnon@clcw.qc.ca
Normand Gilbert, Business; Corporate & Commercial

Cain Lamarre Casgrain Wells
1124, rue Notre-Dame
Saint-Félicien, QC G8K 1Z5
418-679-1331
Fax: 418-679-9344
Number of Lawyers: 2

Finance Lawyers:
Martin Dallaire, Tax Law; Bankruptcy & Restructuring; Insurance & Liability; Business; Commercial/Corporate; Banking
e-mail: martin.dallire@clcw.qc.ca
Daniel-François Tremblay, Insurance & Liability
e-mail: daniel.francois.tremblay@clcw.qc.ca

Cain Lamarre Casgrain Wells
#350
11535, 1re av
Saint-Georges, QC G5Y 7H5
418-228-2074
Fax: 418-228-6016
Number of Lawyers: 3

Finance Lawyers:
Frank D'Amours, Banking & Insolvency
e-mail: frank.damours@clcw.qc.ca

Cain Lamarre Casgrain Wells
1, Place Mignan
Sept-Iles, QC G4R 4L8
418-962-6572
Fax: 418-968-8576
Number of Lawyers: 8

Finance Lawyers:
Marc Brouillette, Commercial
e-mail: marc.brouillette@clcw.qc.ca
Michel Claveau, Insurance & Liability; Business; Commercial/Corporate; Banking
e-mail: michel.claveau@clcw.qc.ca
André Gauthier, Bankruptcy & Restructuring; Business; Commercial/Corporate; Banking
e-mail: andre.gauthier@clcw.qc.ca
Nancy Jourdain, Insurance & Liability; Business; Commercial/Corporate; Banking
e-mail: nancy.jourdain@clcw.qc.ca
Geneviève Laforest, Business; Corporate & Commercial
Julie Lapointe, Insurance & Liability; Business; Commercial/Corporate; Banking
e-mail: julie.lapointe@clcw.qc.ca

Cain Lamarre Casgrain Wells
Complexe Jacques-Gagnon #3
100, St-Joseph sud
Alma, QC G8B 7A6
418-669-4580
Fax: 418-669-0088
Number of Lawyers: 4

Finance Lawyers:
Nancy Gervais, Business; Commercial/Corporate; Banking
e-mail: nancy.gervais@clcw.qc.ca
Paul Pomerleau, Business; Corporate & Commercial
Jacques J. Villeneuve, Business; Commercial/Corporate; Banking
e-mail: jacquesj.villeneuve@clcw.qc.ca

Cain Lamarre Casgrain Wells
20, rue Desbiens
Amqui, QC G5J 3P1
418-629-3302
Fax: 418-629-3333
Number of Lawyers: 1

Finance Lawyers:
Jean-Michel Delaunais, Business; Commercial/Corporate; Banking
e-mail: jean.michel.delaunais@clcw.qc.ca

Cain Lamarre Casgrain Wells
#600
PO Box 5420
255, rue Racine est
Chicoutimi, QC G7H 6J6
418-545-4580
Fax: 418-549-9590
info@clcw.qc.ca
www.clcw.qc.ca
Founded: 1928
Number of Lawyers: 28

Finance Lawyers:
Richard Bergeron, Insurance & Liability; Business; Commercial/Corporate; Banking
e-mail: richard.bergeron@clcw.qc.ca
Michael H. Cain, Insurance & Liability; Business; Commercial/Corporate; Banking
e-mail: michaelh.cain@clcw.qc.ca
Louis Coulombe, Bankruptcy & Restructuring; Insurance & Liability; Business; Commercial/Corporate; Banking
e-mail: louis.coulombe@clcw.qc.ca
Jean Dauphinais, Tax Law; Bankruptcy & Restructuring; Business; Commercial/Corporate; Banking
e-mail: jean.dauphinais@clcw.qc.ca
Gina Doucet, Trusts; Bankruptcy & Restructuring; Business; Commercial/Corporate; Banking
e-mail: gina.doucet@clcw.qc.ca
Chantal Durand, Business; Commercial/Corporate; Banking
e-mail: chantal.durand@clcw.qc.ca
Vassilis Fasfalis, Commercial; Business; Commercial/Corporate; Banking
e-mail: vassilis.fasfalis@clcw.qc.ca
Nancy Fillion, Business; Commercial/Corporate; Banking
e-mail: nancy.fillion@clcw.qc.ca
Chantal Lavallée, Insurance & Liability
e-mail: chantal.lavallee@clcw.qc.ca
Isabelle Racine, Insurance & Liability
e-mail: isabelle.racine@clcw.qc.ca
Jean-Jacques Rancourt, Bankruptcy & Restructuring; Insurance & Liability; Business; Commercial/Corporate; Banking
e-mail: jean.jacques.rancourt@clcw.qc.ca
Rita Vaillancourt, Insurance & Liability
e-mail: rita.vaillancourt@clcw.qc.ca

Cain Lamarre Casgrain Wells
#201
3750, boul du Royaume
Jonquière, QC G7X 0A4
418-695-4580
Fax: 418-547-9590
Number of Lawyers: 6

Finance Lawyers:
Sonia Bérubé, Business; Commercial/Corporate; Banking
Julie St-Onge, Business; Corporate & Commercial

Cain Lamarre Casgrain Wells
#2780
630, boul René-Lévesque ouest
Montréal, QC H3B 1S6
514-393-4580
Fax: 514-393-9590
info@clcw.qc.ca
www.clcw.qc.ca
Founded: 1877
Number of Lawyers: 20

Finance Lawyers:
Irène Chrisantopoulos, Commercial Litigation; Corporate
e-mail: irene.chrisantopoulos@clcw.qc.ca
Denis Cloutier, Bankruptcy & Restructuring; Insurance & Liability; Commercial Litigation
e-mail: denis.cloutier@clcw.qc.ca
Josée Davidson, Commercial Litigation
e-mail: josee.davidson@clcw.qc.ca
Pierre F. Delorme, Mergers & Acquisitions; Financing; Business; Commercial/Corporate; Banking
e-mail: pierref.delorme@clcw.qc.ca
Suzanne-Hélène Desaulniers, Tax Law
e-mail: suzanneh.desaulniers@clcw.qc.ca
Marie-Claude Drouin, Insurance & Liability; Commercial Litigation
e-mail: marie.claude.drouin@clcw.qc.ca
Stéphane Gauthier, Insurance & Liability; Commercial Litigation
e-mail: stephane.gauthier@clcw.qc.ca
André Gauthier, Business Law; Commercial/Corporate; Banking; Banktruptcy & Restructuring
e-mail: andre.gauthier@clcw.qc.ca
Pierre Gauthier, Professional Law; Expropriation
e-mail: pierre.gauthier@clcw.qc.ca
Benoit Groleau, Commercial Corporate
e-mail: benoit.groleau@clcw.qc.ca
François Lamarre, Franchising; Insurance & Liability
e-mail: francois.lamarre@clcw.qc.ca
Jean-François Lépine, Insurance; Liability; Commercial Litigation; Bankruptcy & Insolvency
e-mail: jean.francois.lepine@clcw.qc.ca
Alain Létourneau, Insurance & Liability; Commercial Litigation, Arbitration
e-mail: alain.letourneau@clcw.qc.ca
Claude Mageau, Commercial Litigation
e-mail: claude.mageau@clcw.qc.ca
Alain Ménard, Tax Law; Commercial Corporate
e-mail: alain.menard@clcw.qc.ca
J. Lucien Perron, Business; Commercial Corporate; Banking
e-mail: lucien.perron@clcw.qc.ca
Katia Sebastiani, Tax Law; Commercial/Corporate
e-mail: katia.sebastiani@clcw.qc.ca

Cain Lamarre Casgrain Wells
#440
580, Grande Allée est
Québec, QC G1R 2K2
418-522-4580
Fax: 418-529-9590
Number of Lawyers: 28

Finance Lawyers:
Pierre Caouette, International Business Law
e-mail: pierre.caouette@clcw.qc.ca
Hélène Carrier, Insurance & Liability
e-mail: helene.carrier@clcw.qc.ca

ACCOUNTING & LAW

Cain Lamarre Casgrain Wells (continued)

Stéphane Cliche, Tax Law; Bankruptcy & Restructuring; Business; Commercial/Corporate; Banking
e-mail: stephane.cliche@clcw.qc.ca
Jean Cote, Insurance & Liability; Business; Commercial/Corporate; Banking
e-mail: jean.cote@clcw.qc.ca
Guy Dussault, International Business Law
Marie-Douce Huard, Insurance & Liability
e-mail: marie.douce.huard@clcw.qc.ca
Isabelle Leblond, Business Law; Corporate & Commercial
Sylvain Lepage, Insurance & Liability; Business; Commercial/Corporate; Banking
e-mail: sylvain.lepage@clcw.qc.ca
Pierre Martin, Bankruptcy & Restructuring
e-mail: pierre.martin@clcw.qc.ca
Stéphane Martin, Bankruptcy & Restructuring; Insurance & Liability; Business; Commercial/Corporate; Banking
e-mail: stephane.martin@clcw.qc.ca
Françoise Mercure, Retirement Plans; Bankruptcy & Restructuring; Business; Commercial/Corporate; Banking
e-mail: francoise.mercure@clcw.qc.ca
Chantal Ouellet, Bankruptcy & Restructuring; Insurance & Liability
e-mail: chantal.ouellet@clcw.qc.ca
Martin St-Amant, Business; Commercial/Corporate; Banking
e-mail: martin.st.amant@clcw.qc.ca
Julie St-Onge, Banking & Insolvency Law
Myriam Trudel, Insurance & Liability
e-mail: myriam.trudel@clcw.qc.ca

Campbell Lea

PO Box 429
15 Queen St.
Charlottetown, PE C1A 7K7
902-566-3400
Fax: 902-566-9266
office@campbelllea.com
www.campbelllea.com
Number of Lawyers: 9

Finance Lawyers:
Kenneth L. Godfrey, Insurance
e-mail: klgodfrey@campbelllea.com
Karolyn M. Godfrey, Insurance; Business
e-mail: kmgodfrey@campbelllea.com
Alexander P. Godfrey
Mitchell T. Macleod
Paul D. Michael, Corporate/Commercial; Securities; Insurance
e-mail: pmichael@campbelllea.com
Laura A. Nicholson, Corporate & Commercial Transactions; Wills, Estates & Probate; Insurance
e-mail: lnicholson@campbelllea.com
M. Jane Ralling, Estates; Corporate/Commercial
e-mail: jralling@campbelllea.com
Robert Tocchet, Insurance
e-mail: rtocchet@campbelllea.com

Campbell Marr

10 Donald St.
Winnipeg, MB R3C 1L5
204-942-3311
Fax: 204-943-7997
dimarr@campbellmarr.com
www.campbellmarr.com
Founded: 1990
Number of Lawyers: 13

Finance Lawyers:
Anders Bruun, Corporate/Commercial; Wills, Estates & Trusts
204-942-3311 e-mail: abruun@campbellmarr.com
Kenton Fast, Corporate/Commercial; Wills, Estates & Trusts
204-942-3311 e-mail: klfast@campbellmarr.com
G. Thomas Hodgson, Corporate/Commercial; Wills, Estates & Trusts
204-942-3311 e-mail: thodgson@campbellmarr.com
Gregory Juliano, Wills, Estates & Trusts
204-942-3311 e-mail: gjuliano@campbellmarr.com
Megan A. Kelly, Corporate/Commercial; Wills, Estates & Trusts
204-942-3311 e-mail: makelly@campbellmarr.com
David I. Marr, Insurance
204-942-3311 e-mail: dimarr@campbellmarr.com
Joseph A. Pollock, Insurance
204-942-3311 e-mail: jpollock@campbellmarr.com
Garth P. Reimer, Corporate/Commercial; Wills, Estates & Trusts
204-942-3311 e-mail: greimer@campbellmarr.com
Orlando Santos, Business Law; Real Estate, Wills & Estates
204-942-3311 e-mail: osantos@campbellmarr.com
James H. Saper, Wills, Estates & Trusts; Corporate/Commercial
204-942-3311 e-mail: jsaper@campbellmarr.com
J. Graeme E. Young, Commercial Litigation; Insurance
204-942-3311 e-mail: gyoung@campbellmarr.com

Cardinal Law

736 Broughton St.
Victoria, BC V8W 1E1
250-386-8707
Fax: 250-386-3265
800-459-9499
info@cardlaw.com
www.cardlaw.com
Founded: 1977
Number of Lawyers: 7

Finance Lawyers:
Max D. Durando, Insurance Law
Carlos R. MacDonald, Business Law & Financing
Harold J. Rusk, Business Law & Financing; Insurance

Caron, Garneau, Bellavance

268, boul Bois Francs nord
Victoriaville, QC G6P 1G5
819-758-8251
Fax: 819-752-4520
avocatscg@bellnet.ca
Founded: 1950
Number of Lawyers: 3

Finance Lawyers:
Claude Caron, General Finance

Carr & Company

#900
10020 - 101A Ave. NW
Edmonton, AB T5J 3G2
780-425-5959
Fax: 780-423-4728
mail@carrlaw.com
www.carrlaw.com
Founded: 1982
Number of Lawyers: 3
Profile: Business & Personal Financial Strategies

Finance Lawyers:
Linda Svob

Carrel+Partners LLP

1136 Alloy Dr.
Thunder Bay, ON P7B 6M9
807-346-3000
Fax: 807-346-3600
800-263-0578
info@carrel.com
www.carrel.com
Number of Lawyers: 15
Profile: Full service provider of financial security services, experience in private & public financings, secured lending, tax advice & insolvency issues

Finance Lawyers:
Cynthia Cline, Corporate; Commercial; Public Financing
807-346-3014 e-mail: clinec@carrel.com
Rodi-Lynn Rusnick-Kinisky, Corporate, Commercial
807-346-3019 e-mail: rusnickr@carrel.com

Cassels Brock & Blackwell LLP

Scotia Plaza #2100
40 King St. West
Toronto, ON M5H 3C2
416-869-5300
Fax: 416-360-8877
888-869-5344
Telex: 06-23415postmaster@casselsbrock.com
www.casselsbrock.com
Founded: 1888
Number of Lawyers: 184
Profile: Provides legal advice with respect to: valuation of property &/or business in respect of insolvency, long-term corporate strategies, due diligence, officers' & directors' liability

Finance Lawyers:
Jason Arbuck
416-860-6889 e-mail: jarbuck@casselsbrock.com
Bruce C. Bell
416-869-5737 e-mail: bbell@casselsbrock.com
Joseph J. Bellissimo
416-860-6572 e-mail: jbellissimo@casselsbrock.com
Christopher W. Besant
416-869-5739 e-mail: cbesant@casselsbrock.com
John N. Birch
416-860-5225 e-mail: jbirch@casselsbrock.com
Daniel Bourque
416-869-5777 e-mail: dbourgque@casselsbrock.com
David Budd
416-869-5392 e-mail: dbudd@casselsbrock.com
William J. Burden
416-869-5963 e-mail: bburden@casselsbrock.com
Candace Chan
416-867-5767 e-mail: cchan@casselsbrock.com
Erin Finlay
416-869-5749 e-mail: efinlay@casselsbrock.com
Jonathan Fleisher
416-860-6596 e-mail: jfleisher@casselsbrock.com
Gordon Goodman
416-869-5712 e-mail: ggoodman@casselsbrock.com
Donald G. Gray
416-869-5998 e-mail: dgray@casselsbrock.com
Tilly Gray
416-869-5408 e-mail: tgray@casselsbrock.com
Terence D. Hall, Financial Services
416-860-2992 e-mail: thall@casselsbrock.com
Renate Herbst
416-860-6617 e-mail: rherbst@casselsbrock.com
Jim Janetos
416-869-5994 e-mail: jjanetos@casselsbrock.com
Linda I. Knol
416-860-6614 e-mail: lknol@casselsbrock.com
E. Bruce Leonard
416-869-5757 e-mail: bleonard@casselsbrock.com
Alison R. Manzer
416-869-5469 e-mail: amanzer@casselsbrock.com
Bruce T. McNeely
416-869-5399 e-mail: bmcneely@casselsbrock.com
R. Marc Mercier
416-869-5770 e-mail: mmercier@casselsbrock.com
Charles Newman
416-860-6603 e-mail: cnewman@casselsbrock.com
Damian Rogers
416-869-5792 e-mail: drogers@casseslbrock.com
James Rossiter
416-869-5464 e-mail: jrossiter@casselsbrock.com
Lydia Salvi
416-869-5409 e-mail: lsalvi@casselsbrock.com
Frank Spizzirri
416-869-5798 e-mail: fspizzirri@casselsbrock.com
Marcel Théroux
416-860-6725 e-mail: mtheroux@casselsbrock.com
Carlo Vairo
416-860-6880 e-mail: cvairo@casselsbrock.com
David S. Ward
416-869-5960 e-mail: dward@casselsbrock.com
Amy Wilson
416-860-6571 e-mail: awilson@casselsbrock.com

Cawkell Brodie Glaister LLP

#1260
1188 Georgia St. West
Vancouver, BC V6E 4A2
604-684-3323
Fax: 604-684-3350
info@cawkell.org
www.cawkell.com
Number of Lawyers: 4

Finance Lawyers:
J. Scott Brodie, Commercial Real Estate; Estate Planning & Wealth Preservation; Corporate & Commercial Transactions
Kenneth A. Cawkell, Corporate Securities & Finance; Corporate & Commercial Transactions
Nancy E. Glaister, Corporate Securities & Finance; Corporate & Commercial Transactions
Scott Homenick, Corporate Securities & Finance; Franchising

Chaitons LLP

185 Sheppard Ave. West
Toronto, ON M2N 1M9
416-222-8888
Fax: 416-222-8402
info@chaitons.com
www.chaiton.com
Number of Lawyers: 24

Finance Lawyers:
George Benchetrit, Bankruptcy & Insolvency; Litigation
David Chaiton, Bankruptcy & Insolvency; Corporate & Commercial
Harvey Chaiton, Bankruptcy & Insolvency; Litigation
Karine De Champlain, Bankruptcy & Insolvency; Litigation
Gary Feldman, Bankruptcy & Insolvency; Business Banking
Benjamin Frydenberg, Bankruptcy & Insolvency; Litigation
Harvey Garman, Bankruptcy & Insolvency; Business Banking
Mark Hartman, Litigation; Mortgage Enforcement
Katharine Ho, Corporate & Commercial
Marlin Horst, Corporate & Commercial; Real Estate
Edmund Huang, Litigation
Emma Kenley, Litigation
Mark Klar, Bankruptcy & Insolvency; Business Banking
Aran Kwinta, Corporate & Commercial
Eva Lake, Mortgage Enforcement
Seth Mandell, Bankruptcy & Insolvency; Corporate & Commercial
Robert Miller, Real Estate
Jason Moyse, Litigation
Stephen Schwartz, Bankruptcy & Insolvency; Litigation
Craig Segal, Bankruptcy & Insolvency; Business Banking
Christopher Staples, Bankruptcy & Insolvency; Litigation
Harvey Tanzer, Corporate & Commercial
Philip Taylor, Bankruptcy & Insolvency; Corporate & Commercial; Real Estate

Chojnacki, Ford, O'Neail
#601
6733 Mississauga Rd.
Mississauga, ON L5N 6J5
905-821-3644
Fax: 905-821-8355
Number of Lawyers: 3

Finance Lawyers:
Richard C. Chojnacki, General Finance
905-821-3644 e-mail: rclawfirm@bellnet.ca

Christies
Confederation Sq. #301
20 Richmond St. East
Toronto, ON M5C 2R9
416-367-0680
Fax: 416-367-0429
Number of Lawyers: 8

Finance Lawyers:
Michael R. Raycraft, General Finance
Victor M. Saccucci, General Finance

Clark Wilson LLP
HSBC Bldg. #800
885 Georgia St. West
Vancouver, BC V6C 3H1
604-687-5700
Fax: 604-687-6314
contact@cwilson.com
www.cwilson.com
Number of Lawyers: 71

Finance Lawyers:
Jonathan L.S. Hodes, Insurance Defence & Coverage; Commercial Litigation
604-643-3168 e-mail: jlh@cwilson.com
Roy A. Nieuwenburg
604-643-3112 e-mail: ran@cwilson.com
Aaron B. Singer
604-643-3108 e-mail: abs@cwilson.com
Hannelie G. Stockenstrom
604-643-3145 e-mail: hgs@cwilson.com

Cleall Barristers Solicitors
Commerce Place #2500
10155 - 102nd St.
Edmonton, AB T5J 4G8
780-425-2500
Fax: 780-425-1222
main@cleall.ca
www.cleall.ca
Founded: 1973
Number of Lawyers: 12

Finance Lawyers:
Kenneth F. Cleall, Securities; Corporate/Commercial; Real Estate
780-917-8600 e-mail: kenc@cleall.ca
Paul K. Lachambre, Securities; Corporate/Commercial; Real Estate
780-917-8608 e-mail: pkl@cleall.ca
Aran Veylan, Litigation; Real Estate
780-917-8614 e-mail: aveylan@cleall.ca

Cleveland & Doan
1321 Johnston Rd.
White Rock, BC V4B 3Z3
604-536-5002
Fax: 604-536-7002
lawyers@cleveland-doan.com
www.cleveland-doan.com
Founded: 1995
Number of Lawyers: 3
Profile: Business; Corporate & Commercial Law

Finance Lawyers:
Richard A. Cleveland, Finance Litigation

Cobb & Jones LLP
PO Box 548
23 Argyle St.
Simcoe, ON N3Y 4N5
519-428-0170
Fax: 519-428-3105
cobblaw@cobbjones.ca
www.cobbjones.ca
Founded: 1974
Number of Lawyers: 8

Finance Lawyers:
M.E. Cobb, Corporate; Commercial; Real Estate
K.M. Jones, Corporate; Commercial; Real Estate

Cole Sawler
PO Box 400
7 Bridge St.
Middleton, NS B0S 1P0
902-825-6288
Fax: 902-825-4340
csawler@istar.ca
Founded: 1984
Number of Lawyers: 2
Profile: Corporate/Commercial; Real Estate

Finance Lawyers:
Stephen I. Cole, Real Estate; Commercial
Craig G. Sawler, Real Estate; Wills & Estates

Conroy Trebb Scott Hurtubise LLP
164 Elm St.
Sudbury, ON P3C 1T7
705-674-6441
Fax: 705-673-9567
800-627-1825
gahurtubise@sudburylegal.com
www.sudburylegal.com
Number of Lawyers: 6
Profile: Bankruptcy & Insolvency; Corporate/Commercial; Contract Law

Finance Lawyers:
Leighton T. Roslyn, Bankruptcy, Insolvency, Corporate, Commercial
e-mail: ltroslyn@sudburylegal.com
Murray A. Scott, Corporate/Commercial
e-mail: mascott@sudburylegal.com

Cook Roberts LLP
1175 Douglas St., 7th Fl.
Victoria, BC V8W 2E1
250-385-1411
Fax: 250-413-3300
lawmark@cookroberts.bc.ca
www.cookroberts.bc.ca
Founded: 1970
Number of Lawyers: 22
Profile: Negotiation & preparation of security documentation including mortgages & general security agreements, realizations, foreclosures & bankruptcy matters

Finance Lawyers:
Ralston S. Alexander, General Finance; Corporate; Commercial
e-mail: ralexander@cookroberts.bc.ca
Ronald Carson Cook, Associate Counsel, Corporate; Commercial
e-mail: rcook@cookroberts.bc.ca
Peter C.M. Freeman, General Finance
e-mail: pfreeman@cookroberts.bc.ca
Michael S. Greene, General Finance; Corporate; Commercial
e-mail: mgreene@cookroberts.bc.ca
Robert S. Sheffman, General Finance
e-mail: rsheffman@cookroberts.bc.ca
John T. Van Cuylenborg, Corporate, Commercial
e-mail: johnvc@cookroberts.bc.ca

Coutts, Crane, Ingram
#700
480 University Ave.
Toronto, ON M5G 1V2
416-977-0956
Fax: 416-977-5331
info@couttscrane.com
www.couttscrane.com
Founded: 1950
Number of Lawyers: 9

Finance Lawyers:
Elgin E. Coutts
Michele D. Guy
e-mail: mguy@couttscrance.com
Michael B. Ingram
e-mail: mingram@couttscrance.com
Harry Polizos
e-mail: hpolizos@couttscrane.com

Couzin Taylor LLP
PO Box 4550, B Sta.
Montréal, QC H3B 5J3
514-879-6600
Fax: 514-879-2666
marcel.guilbault@ca.ey.com
Number of Lawyers: 3

Finance Lawyers:
Jean-Hugues Chabot
Marcel Guilbault
Angelo Nikolakakis

Couzin Taylor LLP
#1600
100 Queen St.
Ottawa, ON K1P 1K1
613-598-4800
Fax: 613-598-4888
Number of Lawyers: 1

Finance Lawyers:
Roger Tylor

Couzin Taylor LLP
Ernst & Young Tower
PO Box 143
222 Bay St.
Toronto, ON M5K 1H1
416-943-2600
Fax: 416-943-2700
Number of Lawyers: 6
Profile: Tax Lawyers

Finance Lawyers:
Reya Ali-Dabydeen
Robert Couzin
Heather Kerr
Konstantina Korovilas
Pearl Schusheim
Paul Vienneau

Cox Hanson O'Reilly Matheson
Phoenix Sq. #400
PO Box 310
371 Queen St.
Fredericton, NB E3B 4Y9
506-453-7771
Fax: 506-453-9600
fredericton@coxhanson.ca
www.coxhanson.ca
Number of Lawyers: 23

Finance Lawyers:

Cox Hanson O'Reilly Matheson (continued)
Catherine M. Bowlen, Insurance
506-453-9641 e-mail: cbowlen@coxhanson.ca
Michael E. Bowlin, Insurance
506-453-9675 e-mail: mbowlin@coxhanson.ca
Christopher R. DeLong, Insurance
506-453-9640 e-mail: cdelong@coxhanson.ca
Julian A.G. Dickson, Estates & Wills; Insurance
506-453-9677 e-mail: jdickson@coxhanson.ca
Amanda J. Frenette, Insurance
506-453-9642 e-mail: afrenette@coxhanson.ca
John M. Hanson, Corporate/Commercial; Bankruptcy & Corporate Restructuring
506-453-9673 e-mail: jhanson@coxhanson.ca
David T. Hashey, Insurance
506-453-9672 e-mail: dhashey@coxhanson.ca
Bruce D. Hatfield, Corporate & Commercial; Estates & Trusts
Stephen Hill, Banking & Financial Institutions
506-444-9202 e-mail: shill@coxhanson.ca
Michael L. Hynes, Insurance
506-444-9288 e-mail: hynesm@coxhanson.ca
John D. Larlee, Corporate/Commercial; Estates & Trusts; Bankruptcy & Corporate Restructuring
506-453-9643 e-mail: jlarlee@coxhanson.ca
Derek S.J. McKinnon
Gary A. Miller
Terrence J. Morrison, Corporate/Commercial; Estates & Trusts; Insurance; Bankruptcy & Corporate Restructuring
506-453-9604 e-mail: tmorrison@coxhanson.ca
David M. Norman, Tax
506-453-9678
Deborah M. Power, Corporate/Commercial
506-453-9645 e-mail: dmpower@coxhanson.ca
Lucie Richard, Insurance
506-453-9606 e-mail: lrichard@coxhanson.ca
J. Marc Richard, Insurance
506-453-9659 e-mail: mrichard@coxhanson.ca
Jade A. Spalding, Insurance
506-453-9657 e-mail: jspalding@coxhanson.ca
Paul J. White, Corporate/Commercial; Insurance
506-453-7771 e-mail: pwhite@coxhanson.ca
Monika M.L. Zauhar, Insurance
506-453-9644 e-mail: mzauhar@coxhanson.ca

Cox Hanson O'Reilly Matheson
#202
119 Queen St.
Charlottetown, PE C1A 4B3
902-894-7051
Fax: 902-368-3762
charlottetown@coxhanson.ca
www.coxhanson.ca
Number of Lawyers: 9

Finance Lawyers:
Gary G. Demeulenaere, Banking & Financial Institutions; Corporate & Commercial
902-368-7828 e-mail: gdemeulenaere@coxhanson.ca
Sophie MacDonald, Insurance
902-368-7823 e-mail: smacdonald@coxhanson.ca
M. Lynn Murray, Insurance
902-368-7821 e-mail: lmurray@coxhanson.ca
Kerri Seward, Banking & Financial Institutions; Bankruptcy & Corporate Restructuring; Corporate & Commercial
902-368-7826 e-mail: kseward@coxhanson.ca

Cox Hanson O'Reilly Matheson
Purdy's Wharf Tower #1100
PO Box 2380
1959 Upper Water St.
Halifax, NS B3J 3E5
902-421-6262
Fax: 902-421-3130
halifax@coxhanson.ca
www.coxhanson.ca
Founded: 1854
Number of Lawyers: 47
Profile: Cox Hanson O'Reilly Matheson is a full-service Atlantic Canadian law firm, providing legal solutions for clients throughout the region & beyond

Finance Lawyers:
Robin K. Aitken, Corporate/Commercial
902-491-4228 e-mail: raitken@coxhanson.ca
Sandra O. Arab Clarke, Insurance
902-491-4203 e-mail: sarabclarke@coxhanson.ca
P. Robert Arkin, Corporate/Commercial; Tax Law
902-491-4101 e-mail: rarkin@coxhanson.ca
John Arnold, Estates & Trusts
902-491-4122 e-mail: jarnold@coxhanson.ca
Ian B. Bilek, Corporate/Commercial
902-491-4127 e-mail: ibilek@coxhanson.ca
D. Kevin Burke, Insurance; Litigation
902-491-4202 e-mail: kburke@coxhanson.ca
Daniel M. Campbell, Corporate/Commercial; Litigation
902-491-4105 e-mail: dmcampbell@coxhanson.ca
Jocelyn M. Campbell, Insurance; Litigation
902-491-4210 e-mail: jmcampbell@coxhanson.ca
Robert W. Carmichael, Corporate/Commercial; Oil & Gas
902-491-4102 e-mail: rcarmichael@coxhanson.ca
Colin J. Clarke, Litigation
e-mail: cclarke@coxhanson.ca
Michael E. Dunphy, Insurance
902-491-4205 e-mail: mdunphy@coxhanson.ca
Patrick G.E. Fitzgerald, Corporate/Commercial; Intellectual Property
902-491-4117 e-mail: pfitzgerald@coxhanson.ca
Wayne Francis, Insurance
902-491-4136 e-mail: wfrancis@coxhanson.ca
Jonathan R. Gale, Corporate/Commercial; Bankruptcy & Corporate Restructuring
902-491-4119 e-mail: jgale@coxhanson.ca
Daniel F. Gallivan, Corporate/Commercial; Securities
902-491-4126 e-mail: dgallivan@coxhanson.ca
W. Glenn Hodge, Insurance
902-491-4222 e-mail: ghodge@coxhanson.ca
Jeffrey A. Hoyt, Corporate/Commercial; Securities; Bankruptcy & Corporate Restructuring
902-491-4107 e-mail: jhoyt@coxhanson.ca
Daniel W. Ingersoll, Insurance
902-491-4211 e-mail: ingersoll@coxhanson.ca
John A. Keith, Bankruptcy & Corporate Restructuring; Litigation
902-491-4217 e-mail: jkeith@coxhanson.ca
Michelle M. Kelly, Insurance
902-491-4465 e-mail: mkelly@coxhanson.ca
D. Kevin Latimer, Insurance; Litigation
902-491-4212 e-mail: klatimer@coxhanson.ca
Gavin D.F. MacDonald, Corporate/Commercial
902-491-4464 e-mail: gmacdonald@coxhanson.ca
Michael J. Messenger, Insurance; Litigation
902-491-4227 e-mail: mmessenger@coxhanson.ca
Lara E. Morrison, Business Immigration; Corporate/Commercial
902-491-4229 e-mail: lmorrison@coxhanson.ca
A. James Musgrave, Corporate/Commercial; Securities; Bankruptcy & Corporate Restructuring
902-491-4118 e-mail: jmusgrave@coxhanson.ca
Richard S. Niedermeyer, Corporate/Commercial; Estates & Trusts; Tax Law
902-491-4207 e-mail: rniedermayer@coxhanson.ca
Joey D. Palov, Insurance; Litigation
902-491-4201 e-mail: jpalov@coxhanson.ca
Jennifer E. Parsons, Corporate/Commercial; Tax Law; Securities
902-491-4113 e-mail: jparsons@coxhanson.ca
David A. Reid, Corporate/Commercial; Oil & Gas
902-491-4131 e-mail: dreid@coxhanson.ca
Suzanne I. Rix, Business Immigration; Corporate/Commercial
902-491-4124 e-mail: srix@coxhanson.ca
Michael S. Ryan, Corporate/Commercial; Litigation
902-491-4221 e-mail: mryan@coxhanson.ca
Michael Schweiger, Corporate/Commercial; Business Immigration
902-491-4231 e-mail: mschweiger@coxhanson.ca
Alexa Steponaitis, Insurance
902-491-4208 e-mail: asteponaitis@coxhanson.ca
Brian A. Tabor, Corporate/Commercial; Real Estate
902-491-4108 e-mail: btabor@coxhanson.ca
Loretta M. Taylor, Insurance
902-491-4125 e-mail: ltaylor@coxhanson.ca
Harry W. Thurlow, Insurance
902-491-4232 e-mail: hthurlow@coxhanson.ca

Cox Hanson O'Reilly Matheson
Scotia Centre #401
235 Water St.
St. John's, NL A1C 1B6
709-726-3321
Fax: 709-726-2992
stjohns@coxhanson.ca
www.coxhanson.ca
Number of Lawyers: 21

Finance Lawyers:
Reginald H. Brown, Insurance
709-570-5323 e-mail: rbrown@coxhanson.ca
Sandra R. Chaytor, Estates & Trusts; Insurance
709-570-5329 e-mail: schaytor@coxhanson.ca
Lisa M. Daly, Banking & Financial Institutions; Corporate & Commercial
709-570-5332 e-mail: ldaly@coxhanson.ca
Denis J. Fleming, Insurance
709-570-5321 e-mail: dfleming@coxhanson.ca
F. Richard Gosse, General Finance
709-570-5330 e-mail: fgosse@coxhanson.ca
John Hogan, Insurance
709-570-5340 e-mail: jhogan@coxhanson.ca
Paul M. McDonald, Estates & Trusts; Insurance
709-570-5328 e-mail: pmcdonald@coxhanson.ca
Jeffery W. Miller, Corporate/Commercial; Banking & Financial Institutions
709-570-5341 e-mail: jmiller@coxhanson.ca
Kathleen M. O'Neill, Insurance
709-570-5333 e-mail: koneill@coxhanson.ca
Thomas J. O'Reilly, Estates & Trusts; Insurance
709-570-5320 e-mail: toreilly@coxhanson.ca
Christopher J. Peddigrew, Banking & Financial Institutions
709-570-5338 e-mail: cpeddigrew@coxhanson.ca
Christopher Quigley, Banking & Financial Institutions
709-570-5339 e-mail: crquigley@coxhanson.ca
D. Richard Robbins, Corporate/Commercial; Estates & Trusts
709-570-5325 e-mail: rrobbins@coxhanson.ca
Griffith D. Roberts, Corporate/Commercial; Tax Law; Securities; Bankruptcy & Corporate Restructuring
709-570-5336 e-mail: groberts@coxhanson.ca
Jorge P. Segovia, Insurance
709-726-3321 e-mail: jsegovia@coxhanson.ca
Peter D. Shea, Insurance
709-570-5334 e-mail: pshea@coxhanson.ca
Randall W. Smith, Corporate/Commercial; Bankruptcy & Corporate Restructuring
709-570-5326 e-mail: rsmith@coxhanson.ca
Roland C. Snelgrove, Banking & Financial Institutions
709-570-5324 e-mail: rsnelgrove@coxhanson.ca
William E. Wells, Corporate/Commercial; Insurance; Labour & Employment
709-570-5337 e-mail: bwells@coxhanson.ca
Michelle A. Willette, Bankruptcy & Corporate Restructuring
709-570-5335 e-mail: mwillette@coxhanson.ca

Crease, Harman & Company
#800
PO Box 997
1070 Douglas St.
Victoria, BC V8W 2S8
250-388-5421
Fax: 250-388-4294
creaseharman@creaseharman.com
www.creaseharman.com
Founded: 1885
Number of Lawyers: 12

Finance Lawyers:
Head of Financial Law: R.L. Spooner, Loan Security Creation & Realization
e-mail: rlspooner@creaseharman.com

Paul J. Crowe
#2200
4950 Yonge St.
Toronto, ON M2N 6K1
416-733-0255
Fax: 416-221-9965
877-649-9999
pauljcrowe@hotmail.com
Founded: 1986
Number of Lawyers: 1
Profile: Provides mortgage services

Finance Lawyers:
P. Crowe, Real Estate; Wills; Estates; Incorporations

Cunningham, Swan, Carty, Little & Bonham LLP
City Place II #201
1473 John Counter Blvd.
Kingston, ON K7M 8Z6
613-544-0211
Fax: 613-542-9814

ACCOUNTING & LAW

pmcleod@cswan.com
www.cswan.com
Founded: 1988
Number of Lawyers: 18
Profile: Real Estate; Wills & Estates; Business Law

Finance Lawyers:
D.H. Bonham, General Finance; Wills & Estates
613-546-8062 e-mail: dbonham@cswan.com
A.D. Bonham, Business
613-546-8076 e-mail: abonham@cswan.com
Roy B. Conacher, Real Estate
613-544-7030 e-mail: rconacher@cswan.com
R.P. Tchegus, Real Estate
613-546-8073 e-mail: rtchegus@cswan.com
Peter J. Trousdale, Real Estate
613-546-2231 e-mail: ptrousdale@cswan.com

D'Arcy & Deacon LLP
330 St. Mary Ave., 12th Fl.
Winnipeg, MB R3C 4E1
204-942-2271
Fax: 204-943-4242
inquiries@darcydeacon.com
www.darcydeacon.com
Founded: 1860
Number of Lawyers: 34
Profile: Our firm prides itself in providing competent, timely & effective business & commercial services primarily to small & medium sized businesses; we provide advice to these clients in a variety of areas, including, purchases of assets & shares, sales of assets & shares, financing (with banks, credit unions & other lenders), contracts, leases, franchises, mortgages, loan agreements, construction agreements & development agreements, to name but a few areas

Finance Lawyers:
Jeff Brown, Business, Commercial, Will & Estate, Real Estate
204-925-5364 e-mail: jbrown@darcydeacon.com
John E. Deacon, Wills & Estate, Business & Commercial, Administrative & Regulatory
204-925-5352 e-mail: jdeacon@darcydeacon.com
Kenneth A. Filkow, Business & Commercial; Lotteries & Gaming
204-925-5351 e-mail: kfilkow@darcydeacon.com
Michael G. Finlayson, Insurance
204-925-5363 e-mail: mfinlayson@darcydeacon.com
Jonathan L. Goldenberg, Business & Commercial; Real Estate
204-925-5371 e-mail: jgoldenberg@darcydeacon.com
Roger D. Gripp, Business & Commercial
204-925-5369 e-mail: rgripp@darcydeacon.com
James G. Harley, Business & Commecial, Real Estate, Wills & Estates
204-925-5354 e-mail: jharley@darcydeacon.com
Gwen B. Hatch, Real Estate
204-925-5362 e-mail: ghatch@darcydeacon.com
Harold K. Irving, Wills & Estates
204-925-5356 e-mail: hirving@darcydeacon.com
Greg A. Johnson, Business & Commercial
204-925-5374 e-mail: gjohnson@darcydeacon.com
Brenda A. Johnston, Business & Commercial
204-925-5395 e-mail: bjohnson@darcydeacon.com
David Morry, Business & Commercial, Real Estate, Wills & Estates
204-925-5385 e-mail: dmorry@darcydeacon.com
Kenneth J. Muys, Insurance
204-925-5379 e-mail: kmuys@darcydeacon.com
Bradley D. Regehr, Business & Commercial
204-925-5388 e-mail: bregehr@darcydeacon.com
Richard M. Rice, Business & Commerical
204-925-5358 e-mail: rrice@darcydeacon.com
Erin K. Romeo, Insurance
204-925-5390 e-mail: eromeo@darcydeacon.com
Paul G. Saranchuk, Business & Commercial
204-925-5357 e-mail: psaranchuk@darcydeacon.com
Diane M. Stasiuk, Business & Commericial
204-925-5386 e-mail: dstasiuk@darcydeacon.com
Grant A. Stefanson, Insurance
204-925-5376 e-mail: gstefanson@darcydeacon.com
John C. Stewart, Business & Commercial; Real Estate
204-925-5368 e-mail: jstewart@darcydeacon.com
Walter Thiessen, Business & Commercial; Wills & Estates; Real Estate
204-925-5375 e-mail: wthiessen@darcydeacon.com
Michael Willcock, Municipal, Business & Commercial, Intellectual Property
204-925-5361 e-mail: mwillcock@darcydeacon.com

Daniel & Partners LLP
Dominion Bldg.
PO Box 24022
39 Queen St.
St Catharines, ON L2R 7P7
905-688-9411
Fax: 905-688-5747
800-263-3650
lawyers@niagaralaw.ca
Founded: 1922
Number of Lawyers: 9
Profile: Mortgage; Power of Sale; Foreclosure; Bankruptcy & Insolvency; Insurance

Finance Lawyers:
Donald C. DeLorenzo, Corporate/Commercial Litigation
e-mail: delorenzod@niagaralaw.ca

Davies Ward Phillips & Vineberg LLP
#4400
1 First Canadian Place
Toronto, ON M5X 1B1
416-863-0900
Fax: 416-863-0871
info@dwpv.com
www.dwpv.com
Founded: 1961
Number of Lawyers: 147
Profile: Business transactions & business operations including acquisitions, divestitures, financing, securities, real estate & land development

Finance Lawyers:
William M. Ainley, Corporate Finance & Securities; Mergers & Acquisitions
416-863-5509 e-mail: wainley@dwpv.com
Christopher Anderson, Tax
416-367-7448 e-mail: canderson@dwpv.com
Neal H. Armstrong, Tax
416-863-5543 e-mail: narmstrong@dwpv.com
Donna Aronson, Corporate Finance; Securities; Mergers & Acquisitions
416-367-7430 e-mail: daronson@dwpv.com
Tim Baron, Structured Finance
416-863-5539 e-mail: tbaron@dwpv.com
Patrick G. Barry, Corporate Finance & Securities; Mergers & Acquisitions
416-367-6917 e-mail: pbarry@dwpv.com
Sarbjit S. Basra, Corporate Finance & Securities; Mergers & Acquisitions
416-367-6926 e-mail: sbasra@dwpv.com
Sonny Bhalla, Corporate Finance & Securities; Mergers & Acquisitions
416-863-5599 e-mail: sbhalla@dwpv.com
Paul Budovitch, Corporate
416-367-7465 e-mail: pbudovitch@dwpv.com
Brendan Cahill, Corporate Finance & Securities
416-367-6928 e-mail: bcahill@dwpv.com
R. Brian Calalang, Corporate Finance & Securities; Mergers & Acquisitions
416-863-5553 e-mail: bcalalang@dwpv.com
Colin Campbell, Tax
416-863-5529 e-mail: ccampbell@dwpv.com
Michael W. Clifford, Corporate Finance & Securities; Mergers & Acquisitions
416-863-5501 e-mail: mclifford@dwpv.com
Mark Q. Connelly, Corporate Finance & Securities; Mergers & Acquisitions
416-863-5526 e-mail: mconnelly@dwpv.com
R. Ian Crosbie, Tax
416-367-6958 e-mail: icrosbie@dwpv.com
Lisa C. Damiani, Corporate Finance & Securities; Mergers & Acquisitions
416-367-6905 e-mail: ldamiani@dwpv.com
Michael Disney, Corporate Finance & Securities; Mergers & Acquisitions
416-863-5540 e-mail: mdisney@dwpv.com
Conrad Druzeta, Corporate Finance & Securities
416-367-7442 e-mail: cdruzeta@dwpv.com
Robert J. Druzeta, Corporate Finance & Securities
416-367-7476 e-mail: rdruzeta@dwpv.com
Mitchell P. Finkelstein, Corporate Finance & Securities; Mergers & Acquisitions
416-367-6939 e-mail: mfinkelstein@dwpv.com
Richard Fridman, Mergers & Acquisitions; Corporate Finance & Securities
416-367-7483 e-mail: rfridman@dwpv.com
Christian P. Gauthier, Mergers & Acquisitions; Corporate Finance & Securities
416-367-7437 e-mail: cgauthier@dwpv.com
Chrissy Giannoulias, Corporate, Corporate Finance & Securities
416-367-466 e-mail: cgiannoulias@dwpv.com
Mindy B. Gilbert, Corporate Finance & Securities; Mergers & Acquisitions
416-367-6907 e-mail: mgilbert@dwpv.com
A. Gerold Goldlist, Corporate Finance & Securities; Mergers & Acquisitions
416-863-5507 e-mail: ggoldlist@dwpv.com
Ivana Gotzeva, Corporate Finance; Securities; Mergers & Acquisitions
416-367-7475 e-mail: igotzeva@dwpv.com
Kathleen Grandy, Corporate, Corporate Finance & Securities
416-367-7467 e-mail: kgrandy@dwpv.com
Ryan Grist, Corporate
416-367-7468 e-mail: rgrist@dwpv.com
Jennifer Grossklaus, Mergers & Acquisitions; Corporate Finance & Securities
416-367-7438 e-mail: jgrossklaus@dwpv.com
William N. Gula, Mergers & Acquistisions, Corporate Finance, Securities
416-863-5511 e-mail: bgula@dwpv.com
Edward Hannah, Structured Finance; Securitization; Venture Capital
416-863-5536 e-mail: ehannah@dwpv.com
Carol Hansell, Corporate Finance & Securities; Mergers & Acquisitions
416-863-5592 e-mail: chansell@dwpv.com
Greg Harnish, Corporate Finance & Securities
416-367-7480 e-mail: gharnish@dwpv.com
Steven M. Harris, Corporate Finance & Securities; Mergers & Acquisitions
416-367-6936 e-mail: sharris@dwpv.com
Peter Hong, Mergers & Acquisitions; Corporate Finance & Securities
416-863-5557 e-mail: phong@dwpv.com
Scott R. Hyman, Banking & Project Finance; Corporate Finance; Securities; Mergers & Acquisitions
416-863-5581 e-mail: shyman@dwpv.com
Brooke Jamison, Mergers & Acquisitions; Corporate Finance & Securities
416-367-7477 e-mail: bjamison@dwpv.com
Andrea Jeffrey, Corporate Finance & Securities
416-367-6954 e-mail: ajeffrey@dwpv.com
Raj Juneja, Tax
416-863-5508 e-mail: rjuneja@dwpv.com
Claire M.C. Kennedy, Tax
416-367-6977 e-mail: ckennedy@dwpv.com
Kenneth G. Klassen, Corporate Finance & Securities
416-863-5568 e-mail: kklassen@dwpv.com
Joshua Kuretzky, Corporate, Corporate Finance & Securities
416-367-7469 e-mail: jkuretzky@dwpv.com
Paul Lamarre, Finance; Securities; Mergers & Acquisitions
416-367-7439 e-mail: plamarre@dwpv.com
Nicholas J. Leblovic, Banking & Project Finance; Corporate Finance & Securities; Mergers & Acquisitions
416-863-5514 e-mail: nleblovic@dwpv.com
Jennifer Longhurst, Corporate Finance & Securities
416-367-7453 e-mail: jlonghurst@dwpv.com
Carl D. MacArthur, Tax
416-367-7441 e-mail: cmacarthur@dwpv.com
Natasha MacParland, Corporate Finance & Securities
416-863-5567 e-mail: nmacparland@dwpv.com
Jennifer Mao, Corporate
416-367-7470 e-mail: jmao@dwpv.com
Ian R. McBride, Banking & Project Finance; Corporate Finance & Securities; Mergers & Acquisitions
416-863-5530 e-mail: imcbride@dwpv.com
D. Shawn McReynolds, Corporate Finance & Securities; Mergers & Acquisitions
416-863-5538 e-mail: smcreynolds@dwpv.com
Vincent A. Mercier, Corporate Finance & Securities; Mergers & Acquisitions
416-863-5579 e-mail: vmercier@dwpv.com
K.A. Siobhan Monaghan, Tax
416-863-5558 e-mail: smonaghan@dwpv.com
J. Alexander Moore, Corporate Finance & Securities
416-863-5570 e-mail: amoore@dwpv.com
Patrick E. Moyer, Corporate Finance & Securities; Mergers & Acquisitions
416-367-6967 e-mail: pmoyer@dwpv.com

Davies Ward Phillips & Vineberg LLP (continued)

Robert S. Murphy, Corporate Finance & Securities; Mergers & Acquisitions
416-863-5537 e-mail: rmurphy@dwpv.com
I. Berl Nadler, Banking & Project Finance; Corporate Finance & Securities; Financial Restructuring & Insolvency; Mergers & Acquisitions
416-863-5512 e-mail: bnadler@dwpv.com
Rosemary A. Newman, Corporate Finance & Securities; Mergers & Acquisitions
416-367-6970 e-mail: rnewman@dwpv.com
Jim Nikopoulos, Mergers & Acquisitions; Corporate Finance & Securities
416-367-7478 e-mail: jnikopoulos@dwpv.com
William M. O'Reilly, Corporate Finance & Securities; Mergers & Acquisitions
416-863-5573 e-mail: woreilly@dwpv.com
Kerry O'Reilly, Mergers & Acquisitions; Corporate Finance & Securities
416-367-7479 e-mail: koreilly@dwpv.com
Patricia L. Olasker, Corporate Finance & Securities; Mergers & Acquisitions
416-863-5551 e-mail: polasker@dwpv.com
Dale J. Osadchuk, Corporate Finance; Securities; Mergers & Acquisitions
416-367-7451 e-mail: dosadchuk@dwpv.com
Duncan G. Osborne, Tax
416-863-5560 e-mail: dosborne@dwpv.com
Jennifer E. Pankratz, Corporate Finance, Securities
416-367-7481 e-mail: jpankratz@dwpv.com
Carol D. Pennycook, Banking & Project Finance; Corporate Finance & Securities; Mergers & Acquisitions
416-863-5546 e-mail: cpennycook@dwpv.com
James R. Reid, Corporate Finance & Securities; Mergers & Acquisitions
416-367-6974 e-mail: jreid@dwpv.com
Elie Roth, Tax
416-863-5587 e-mail: eroth@dwpv.com
Philippe C. Rousseau, Corporate Finance & Securities; Mergers & Acquisitions
416-863-5589 e-mail: prousseau@dwpv.com
Stephen S. Ruby, Tax
416-863-5515 e-mail: sruby@dwpv.com
James G. Rumball, Project Finance & Securitization
416-863-5524 e-mail: jrumball@dwpv.com
Cameron M. Rusaw, Corporate Finance & Securities; Mergers & Acquisitions
416-863-5555 e-mail: crusaw@dwpv.com
Jason Saltzman, Corporate Finance & Securities
416-863-5518 e-mail: jsaltzman@dwpv.com
Arthur S. Shiff, Corporate Finance & Securities; Mergers & Acquisitions
416-863-5513 e-mail: ashiff@dwpv.com
Melanie A. Shishler, Corporate Finance & Securities; Mergers & Acquisitions
416-863-5510 e-mail: mshishler@dwpv.com
David W. Smith, Tax
416-863-5542 e-mail: dsmith@dwpv.com
Erinn E. Somerville, Corporate Finance & Securities; Mergers & Acquisitions
416-863-5545 e-mail: esomerville@dwpv.com
Gillian R. Stacey, Mergers & Acquisitions; Corporate Finance & Securities
416-367-6934 e-mail: gstacey@dwpv.com
Lori K. Sullivan, Corporate Finance & Securities; Mergers & Acquisitions
416-863-5556 e-mail: lsullivan@dwpv.com
Jay A. Swartz, Banking & Project Finance; Corporate Finance & Securities; Financial Restructuring/Insolvency; Mergers/Acquisitions
416-863-5520 e-mail: jswartz@dwpv.com
Kevin J. Thomson, Corporate Finance & Securities; Mergers & Acquisitions
416-863-5590 e-mail: kthomson@dwpv.com
Kamal Toor, Corporate, Corporate Finance & Securities
416-367-7482 e-mail: ktoor@dwpv.com
Geoffrey S. Turner, Tax
416-367-6914 e-mail: gturner@dwpv.com
John M. Ulmer, Tax
416-863-5505 e-mail: julmer@dwpv.com
Banu Unal, Corporate Finance & Securities
416-863-5577 e-mail: bunal@dwpv.com
Robin Upshall, Corporate Finance & Securities
416-367-6981 e-mail: rupshall@dwpv.com
Derek R.G. Vesey, Banking & Project Finance; Corporate Finance & Securities; Mergers & Acquisitions
416-367-6921 e-mail: dvesey@dwpv.com
David A. Ward, Tax
416-863-5504 e-mail: dward@dwpv.com
Kevin West, Corporate Finance & Securities
416-863-5561 e-mail: kwest@dwpv.com
Peter G. Westcott, Corporate Finance & Securities; Mergers & Acquisitions
416-863-5594 e-mail: pwestcott@dwpv.com
David M.R. White, Corporate Finance & Securities; Mergers & Acquisitions
416-863-5586 e-mail: dwhite@dwpv.com
Tarne P. Whiteley, Corporate Finance & Securities; Mergers & Acquisitions
416-367-6980 e-mail: twhiteley@dwpv.com
Ronald S. Wilson, Tax
416-863-5584 e-mail: rwilson@dwpv.com
David Wilson, Corporate Finance & Securities
416-863-5517 e-mail: dwildon@dwpv.com
James Wilson, Corporate, Corporate Finance & Securities
416-367-7484 e-mail: jwilson@dwpv.com
Timothy G. Youdan, Tax
416-367-6904 e-mail: tyoudan@dwpv.com
John A. Zinn, Tax
416-863-5528 e-mail: jzinn@dwpv.com

Davies Ward Phillips & Vineberg S.E.N.C.R.L., s.r.l.

1501, av McGill College, 26e étage
Montréal, QC H3A 3N9
514-841-6400
Fax: 514-841-6499
888-841-6400
dwpv@dwpv.com
www.dwpv.com
Founded: 1895
Number of Lawyers: 81

Finance Lawyers:
Maryse Bertrand
514-841-6460 e-mail: mbertrans@dwpv.com

Davis & Company LLP

#2800 Park Place
666 Burrard St.
Vancouver, BC V6C 2Z7
604-687-9444
Fax: 604-687-1612
www.davis.ca
Founded: 1892
Number of Lawyers: 97
Profile: Davis & Company provides a comprehensive range of legal services to clients around the world; it is the only national Canadian law firm based in Vancouver & the only Canadian law firm with an office in Japan; Davis & Company's areas of financial practice include the following: Banking & Finance; Bankruptcy & Insolvency; Insurance; International Business Transactions & Trade Law; Litigation & Dispute Resolution; Mergers & Aquisitions; Pensions & Benefits Trusts; Securities & Corporate Finance; Taxation; Wills, Trusts & Estates

Finance Lawyers:
Scott R. Anderson, Financial Institutions; Insolvency
604-643-6411 e-mail: sra@davis.ca
Kate N. Bake-Paterson, Financial Institutions
604-643-6375 e-mail: kbakepaterson@davis.ca
Robert T. Banno, Corporate Commercial
604-643-2903 e-mail: robert_banno@davis.ca
Donald R.M. Bell, Financial Institutions
604-643-2949 e-mail: don_bell@davis.ca
Colin D. Brousson, Financial Institutions; Insolvency
604-643-6309 e-mail: cbrousson@davis.ca
Andrew J.G. Burton, Securities & Corporate Finance
604-643-2962 e-mail: aburton@davis.ca
Michael P. Carroll
604-643-2910 e-mail: mpcarroll@davis.ca
Ruby M.B. Chan, Securities & Corporate Finance
604-643-6462 e-mail: rubychan@davis.ca
Brian L. Child, Financial Institutions; Insolvency
604-643-6331 e-mail: bchild@davis.ca
Donald R. Collie, Securities & Corporate Finance
604-643-6472 e-mail: dcollie@davis.ca
Warren H. Downs, General Finance
604-643-2916 e-mail: whdowns@davis.ca
Megan A. Filmer, Financial Institutions; Commercial Lending & Project Finance
604-643-6441 e-mail: mafilmer@davis.ca
Shelley C. Fitzpatrick, Financial Institutions; Insolvency
604-643-6329 e-mail: sfitzpatrick@davis.ca
Patrick J. Furlong, Securities & Corporate Finance
604-643-2923 e-mail: pjfurlong@davis.ca
Catherine Gibson, Financial Institutions
604-643-6468 e-mail: cgibson@davis.ca
Robert T. Groves, Financial Institutions; Insolvency
604-643-2927 e-mail: rtgroves@davis.ca
Shawn Hatch, Corporate Commercial
604-643-2969
Brian F. Hiebert, Corporate Commercial
604-643-2917 e-mail: brian_hiebert@davis.ca
Lloyd Hong, Financial Institutions
604-643-6313 e-mail: lhong@davis.ca
Albert J. Hudec, Securities & Corporate Finance
604-643-6463 e-mail: ajhudec@davis.ca
Suzanne M. Kennedy, Corporate Commercial
604-643-6470 e-mail: suzanne_kennedy@davis.ca
Yukiko Kojima, Securities & Corporate Finance
604-643-2908 e-mail: ykojima@davis.ca
Peter C. Lee, Insolvency
604-643-2936 e-mail: pclee@davis.ca
Roger D. Lee, Insolvency
604-643-2981 e-mail: rdlee@davis.ca
Richard J. Lord, Corporate Commercial
Brian D. MacKay, Corporate Commercial
604-643-6402 e-mail: brian_mackay@davis.ca
J. Brent MacLean, Insolvency
Robert E. Marriott, General Finance
604-643-2944 e-mail: remarriott@davis.ca
John I. McLean, Insolvency
604-643-2939 e-mail: jimclean@davis.ca
Alan L. Monk, Securities & Corporate Finance
604-643-2976 e-mail: amonk@davis.ca
Stuart B. Morrow, Securities & Corporate Finance
604-643-2948 e-mail: sbmorrow@davis.ca
Craig Natsuhara, Corporate Commercial
604-643-6498
Linda I. Parsons, Financial Institutions; Debt Financing Lenders/Borrowers
604-643-6445 e-mail: linda_parsons@davis.ca
David R. Reid, Securities & Corporate Finance
604-643-6428 e-mail: drreid@davis.ca
A.C. Robertson, Corporate Commercial
604-643-6431 e-mail: arobertson@davis.ca
Mary L. Ruhl, Securities & Corporate Finance
604-643-2909 e-mail: mary_ruhl@davis.ca
Dale G. Sanderson, Insolvency
604-643-6330 e-mail: dsanderson@davis.ca
Doug G. Shields, Securities & Corporate Finance
604-643-2998 e-mail: doug_shields@davis.ca
Robert B.D. Swift, Financial Institutions; Personal Property Security, Automotive Retail & Wholesale Floor Plan Financing; Aircraft Leasing & Financing
604-643-2974 e-mail: rbswift@davis.ca
Michael J. Todd, Financial Institutions; Insolvency
604-643-2976 e-mail: michael_todd@davis.ca
Franco E. Trasolini, Corporate Commercial
604-643-2964 e-mail: franco_trasolini@davis.ca
Rosanna Wong, Securities & Corporate Finance
604-643-6320 e-mail: rosanna_wong@davis.ca

Davis & Company LLP

Shell Centre #3000
400 - 4th Ave. SW
Calgary, AB T2P 0J4
403-296-4470
Fax: 403-296-4474
www.davis.ca
Number of Lawyers: 15

Finance Lawyers:
Derrick Auch, Securities & Corporate Finance
403-296-5346 e-mail: dauch@davis.ca
James G.M. Bell, Securities & Corporate Finance; Financial Insitutions
403-296-4472 e-mail: james.bell@davis.ca
Timothy P. Chick, Insolvency
403-296-5404 e-mail: tchick@davis.ca
Roy Hudson, Securities & Corporate Finance
403-296-5345 e-mail: rhusdon@davis.ca

Catherine A. S. Kay, Securities & Corporate Finance
403-296-5405 e-mail: ckay@davis.ca
Dan Kenney, Securities & Corporate Finance; Financial Institutions
403-296-4473 e-mail: dkenney@davis.ca
Denise Nawata, Securites & Corporate Finance
403-296-5344 e-mail: dnawata@davis.ca
Gwen Randall, Insolvency
403-296-5402 e-mail: grandall@davis.ca
Trevor Wong-Chor, Securities & Corporate Finance
403-296-5333 e-mail: twong-chor@davis.ca

Davis & Company LLP
Scotia Tower 2 #1201
10060 Jasper Ave.
Edmonton, AB T5J 4E5
780-426-5330
Fax: 780-428-1066
800-567-7174
dstratton@davis.ca
www.davis.ca
Founded: 1892
Number of Lawyers: 22

Finance Lawyers:
Douglas A. Bodner, Financial Institutions; Insolvency
780-429-6822 e-mail: dbodner@davis.ca
Deborah L. Dresen
780-429-6820 e-mail: ddresen@davis.ca
Gordon V. Garside, Financial Institutions
780-429-6819 e-mail: ggarside@davis.ca
Rachel J. Hamilton, Securities & Corporate Finance
780-429-6633 e-mail: rhamilton@davis.ca
Aman S. Randhawa, Securities & Corporate Finance
780-429-6837 e-mail: arandhawa@davis.ca
Douglas H. Shell, Financial Institutions; Insolvency
780-429-6811 e-mail: dshell@davis.ca
Donald J. Wilson, Insolvency
780-429-6817 e-mail: dwilson@davis.ca

Davis & Company LLP
#1400
1501, av McGill College
Montréal, QC H3A 3M8
514-392-1991
Fax: 514-392-1999
haram@davis.ca
www.davis.ca
Number of Lawyers: 8

Finance Lawyers:
Pablo Guzman, Insolvency
514-392-1991 e-mail: gusmanp@davis.ca
David W. Rothschild, Insolvency
514-392-1991 e-mail: rothchildd@davis.ca
Ian R. Rudnikoff, Financial Institutions; Insolvency
514-392-1991 e-mail: rudnikoff@davis.ca

Davis & Company LLP
1 First Canadian Place #5600
PO Box 367
100 King St. West
Toronto, ON M5X 1E2
416-365-6188
Fax: 416-365-7886
www.davis.ca
Number of Lawyers: 26

Finance Lawyers:
M. Sandra Appel, Financial Institutions; Insolvency
416-365-3524 e-mail: sandra_appel@davis.ca
Douglas B. Buchanan, Securities & Corporate Finance; Financial Institutions
416-365-3507 e-mail: dbuchanan@davis.ca
Jonathan M. Davis-Sydor, Insolvency
416-941-5397 e-mail: jdavissydor@davis.ca
David W. Foulds, Insolvency
416-941-5392 e-mail: dfoulds@davis.ca
Susan E. Friedman, Insolvency
416-365-3503 e-mail: sfriedman@davis.ca
John S. Grant, Securities & Corporate Finance
419-941-7812 e-mail: jgrant@davis.ca
Nicole S. Kapos, Securities & Corporate Finance
416-941-5418 e-mail: nkapos@davis.ca
Ted Maduri, Securities & Corporate Finance
416-941-5412 e-mail: tmaduri@davis.ca
Mitchell Mostyn, Securities & Corporate Finance
416-941-7813 e-mail: mmostyn@davis.ca
Richard Neville, Insolvency
416-365-3526 e-mail: rneville@davis.ca
Kate E. Watson, Securities & Corporate Finance
416-941-5408 e-mail: kwatson@davis.ca

Davis & Company LLP
#200
304 Jarvis St.
Whitehorse, YT Y1A 2H2
867-393-5100
Fax: 867-667-2669
www.davis.ca
Founded: 1892
Number of Lawyers: 2

Finance Lawyers:
Sean M. Kelly, Insolvency; Financial Institutions
867-393-5115 e-mail: skelly@davis.ca
Rodney A. Snow, Financial Institutions
867-393-5105 e-mail: rod_snow@davis.ca

De Grandpré Chait SENCRL-LLP
#2900
1000, rue de la Gauchetière ouest
Montréal, QC H3B 4W5
514-878-4311
Fax: 514-878-4333
info@dgclex.com
www.dgclex.com
Founded: 1928
Number of Lawyers: 68

Finance Lawyers:
André P. Asselin, General Finance
514-878-3220 e-mail: aasselin@dgclex.com
François Beauchamp, Insurance
514-878-3280 e-mail: fbeauchamp@dgclex.com
Marc Beauchemin, Insurance
514-878-3219 e-mail: mbeauchemin@dgclex.com
Michel G. Beaudin, Business Law
514-878-3224 e-mail: mbeaudin@dgclex.com
Martin Bergeron, Insolvency
514-878-3269 e-mail: mbergeron@dgclex.com
Denis Boudrias, Insurance
514-878-3270 e-mail: dboudrias@dgclex.com
Julie Bourduas, Business Law
514-878-3222 e-mail: jbourduas@dgclex.com
Jacques Bourque, Business Law
514-878-3245 e-mail: jbourque@dgclex.com
Arthur I. Bronstein, Business Law
514-878-3200 e-mail: abronstein@dgclex.com
Jules Brossard, Corporate Tax
514-878-3260 e-mail: jbrossard@dgclex.com
Jean-Didier Bussières, Business Law
514-878-3233 e-mail: jdbussieres@dgclex.com
Fred Carsley, Commercial Real Estate Law
514-878-3262 e-mail: fcarsley@dgclex.com
Martin Castonguay, Insolvency
514-878-3268 e-mail: mcastonguay@dgclex.com
Sylvain Choinière, Insolvency
514-878-3291 e-mail: schoiniere@dgclex.com
J. Brian Cornish, Business Law
514-878-3253 e-mail: bcornish@dgclex.com
Daniel Courteau, Business Law
514-878-3249 e-mail: dcourteau@dgclex.com
Michel De Broux, Business Law
514-878-3256 e-mail: mdebroux@dgclex.com
Louis Demers, Business Law
514-878-3205 e-mail: ldemers@dgclex.com
Jo-Anne Durand, Real Estate
514-878-3278 e-mail: jdurand@dgclex.com
Claude Désy, Business Law
514-878-3207 e-mail: cdesy@dgclex.com
Les Erdle, Commercial Litigation
514-878-3225 e-mail: lberdle@dgclex.com
Gilles Fafard, Real Estate
514-878-3240 e-mail: gfafard@dgclex.com
Renée Gagnon, Real Estate
e-mail: rgagnon@dgclex.com
Geoffrey J. Gelber, Business Law
514-878-3244 e-mail: ggelber@dgclex.com
Marie-Claude Gendron, Real Estate
e-mail: mcgendron@dgclex.com
Guy Gilain, Real Estate
514-878-3221 e-mail: ggilain@dgclex.com
Julie Guérette, Insurance
514-878-3264 e-mail: jguerette@dgclex.com
Mylène Henrie, Business Law
514-878-3248 e-mail: mhenrie@dgclex.com
Yves Hébert, Business Law
514-878-3236 e-mail: yhebert@dgclex.com
Frederica Jacobs, Insurance
514-878-3246 e-mail: fjacobs@dgclex.com
David H. Kauffman, Business Law
514-878-3217 e-mail: dkauffman@dgclex.com
Gabriel Kordovi, General Finance
514-878-3250 e-mail: gkordovi@dgclex.com
Stéphanie La Rocque, Real Estate
514-878-3276 e-mail: slarocque@dgclex.com
Pierre Labelle, Insurance
514-878-3290 e-mail: plabelle@dgclex.com
Eric Lalanne, Business Law
514-878-3258 e-mail: elalanne@dgclex.com
Virginia Lam, Business Law
514-878-3273 e-mail: vlam@dgclex.com
Gilles Lareau, Business Law
514-878-3209 e-mail: glareau@dgclex.com
Marie Laure Leclercq, Business Law
514-878-3204 e-mail: mlleclercq@dgclex.com
Ronald H. Levy, Business Law
514-878-3251 e-mail: rlevy@dgclex.com
C. Ralph Lipper, Business Law
514-878-3285 e-mail: rlipper@dgclex.com
François Marchand, Insurance
514-878-3228 e-mail: fmarchand@dgclex.com
Daniel J. Martin, Real Estate
514-878-3238 e-mail: dmartin@dgclex.com
Steve McInnes, Real Estate
514-878-3227 e-mail: smcinnes@dgclex.com
Audrey Mulholland, Business Law
514-878-3266 e-mail: amulholland@dgclex.com
Etienne Panet-Raymond, Business Law
514-878-3243 e-mail: epenetraymond@dgclex.com
Benoit Pelchat, Insolvency
514-878-3234 e-mail: bpelchat@dgclex.com
Pierre-Paul Persico, Business Law
514-878-3288 e-mail: pppersico@dgclex.com
Vincent Piazza, Business Law
514-878-3229 e-mail: vpiazza@dgclex.com
Yves Poirier, Real Estate
514-878-3275 e-mail: ypoirier@dgclex.com
Martin Raymond, Business Law
514-878-3267 e-mail: mraymond@dgclex.com
Alain Robichaud, General Finance; Banking
514-878-3255 e-mail: arobichaud@dgclex.com
Marc J. Rubin, Business Law
514-878-3252 e-mail: mrubin@dgclex.com
Louis Samuel, Business Law
514-878-3283 e-mail: lsamuel@dgclex.com
Ari Y. Sorek, Insurance
Ronald L. Stein, Real Estate
514-878-3254 e-mail: rstein@dgclex.com
Christian M. Tremblay, Business Law
514-878-3211 e-mail: ctremblay@dgclex.com
Martin Tétreault, Business Law
514-878-3272 e-mail: mtetreault@dgclex.com
Serge Vaillancourt, Real Estate
Alyssa Yufe, Real Estate
514-878-3279 e-mail: ayufe@dgclex.com
Philippe de Grandmont, Business Law
514-878-3294 e-mail: pdegrandmont@dgclex.com

Deacon Taws
PO Box 247
476 Elizabeth St.
Midland, ON L4R 4K8
705-526-3791
Fax: 705-526-2688
admin@deacontaws.com
www.deacontaws.com
Founded: 1900
Number of Lawyers: 2
Profile: Corporate/Commercial; Estate Planning; Commercial Litigation; Commercial Leases & Lease Remedies

Finance Lawyers:
Peter R. Deacon, Estate Planning
e-mail: pdeacon@deacontaws.com

ACCOUNTING & LAW

Deacon Taws (continued)
William P. Taws, Mortgages
e-mail: wtaws@deacontaws.com

Deckert Allen Cymbaluk Genest
#301
PO Box 6060
5201 - 51st Ave.
Wetaskiwin, AB T9A 2E8
780-352-3301
Fax: 780-352-5976
Number of Lawyers: 4

Finance Lawyers:
A.H. Deckert, General Finance

Demiantschuk, Milley, Burke & Hoffinger
#1200
1015 - 4th St. SW
Calgary, AB T2R 1J4
403-252-9937
Fax: 403-263-8529
assistance@legalsolutions.ca
www.legalsolutions.ca
Founded: 1995
Number of Lawyers: 7

Finance Lawyers:
J.D. Burke, Financial Litigation & Foreclosure
e-mail: judy.burke@legalsolutions.ca
N. Demiantschuk, General Finance; Real Estate & Commercial Transactions
e-mail: nick.demiantschuk@legalsolutions.ca
M. Hoffinger, General Finance & Commercial Transactions
e-mail: mark.hoffinger@legalsolutions.ca
T.E. Milley, General Finance & Corporate Securities
e-mail: tom.milley@legalsolutions.ca

Desjardins Ducharme, S.E.N.C.R.L.
Tour de la Banque Nationale #2400
600, rue de la Gauchetière ouest
Montréal, QC H3B 4L8
514-878-9411
Fax: 514-878-4800
800-670-0102
www.desjardinsducharme.ca
Founded: 1928
Number of Lawyers: 87
Profile: DDSM has a team of specialists in private financing, representing lenders & borrowers & offers legal advice to both businesses & financial institutions; DDSM negotiates the legal aspects of all forms of financing, including lines of credit, bridge financing, term loads, project financing, leasing agreements & financial leases; negotiates the legal aspects of venture capital financing & drafts the required documentation; represents Canadian & foreign financial institutions in connection with the financing of activities both in Quebec & abroad; provides clients with fast & efficient legal counsel & assistance in matters ranging from corporate debt restructuring to the design of complex financing structures, such as financing of aircraft & hydroelectric power projects, as well as financing involving national or foreign banking syndicates

Finance Lawyers:
Head of Financial Law: Gérard Coulombe, Financial Institutions
514-878-5526 e-mail: gerard.coulombe@ddsm.ca
Dominique Bélisle, Financial Institutions; Bank Financing; Financing: Immigrant Investors Program
514-878-5506 e-mail: dominique.belisle@ddsm.ca
Lyne Duhaime, Pension
Jacques Paquin, Bank Financing; Public Financing
514-878-5579 e-mail: jacques.paquin@ddsm.ca
Louis Payette, Bank Financing
514-878-5581 e-mail: louis.payette@ddsm.ca
Carl Ravinsky
François Renaud, Bank Financing
514-878-5586 e-mail: francois.renaud@ddsm.ca
Marc Rochefort, Public Financing
514-878-5587 e-mail: marc.rochefort@ddsm.ca
Martin Rolland, Bank Financing
514-878-5532 e-mail: martin.rolland@ddsm.ca
Gilles Seguin
514-878-5517 e-mail: gilles.seguin@ddsm.ca
Jean-Paul Zigby, Financial Institutions
e-mail: jean-paul.zigby@ddsm.ca

Desjardins Ducharme, S.E.N.C.R.L.
#300
70, rue Dalhousie
Québec, QC G1K 4B2
418-529-6531
Fax: 418-523-5391
avocat@ddsm.ca
www.ddsm.ca
Founded: 1871
Number of Lawyers: 52

Finance Lawyers:
Jean Brunet, Bank Financing
e-mail: brunjea@ddsm.ca
Michel Demers, Bank Financing
e-mail: dememic@ddsm.ca
Charles G. Gagnon, Bank Financing
e-mail: gagncha@ddsm.ca
Paule Gauthier, Financial Institutions; Public Financing
e-mail: gautpau@ddsm.ca
Claude Girard, Bank Financing; Public Financing
e-mail: giracla@ddsm.ca
Odette St-Laurent, Public Financing
e-mail: stlaode@ddsm.ca

Desjardins, Lapointe, Mousseau, Bélanger
#2185
600, rue de la Gauchetière ouest
Montréal, QC H3B 4L8
514-875-5404
Fax: 514-875-5647
sbelanger@notarius.net
Founded: 1961
Number of Lawyers: 9

Finance Lawyers:
Serge Bélanger, General Finance
Yvan Desjardins, General Finance
Louis Dumont, General Finance
Pierre Lapointe, General Finance
Jean Mousseau, General Finance
Alain Rivard, General Finance

Dickson MacGregor Appell LLP
#306
10 Alcorn Ave.
Toronto, ON M4V 3A9
416-927-0891
Fax: 416-927-0385
ellis@dicksonlawyers.com
Founded: 1983
Number of Lawyers: 10

Finance Lawyers:
Mary MacGregor, Wills; Estates; Financial Planning; Estate Mediation
e-mail: macgregor@dicksonlawyers.com
Jennifer A. Pfuetzner
e-mail: pfuetzner@dicksonlawyers.com
Wenda Yenson
e-mail: yenson@dicksonlawyers.com

Doak Shirreff LLP
Chancery Place #200
537 Leon Ave.
Kelowna, BC V1Y 2A9
250-763-4323
Fax: 250-763-4780
800-661-4959
thefirm@doakshirreff.com
www.doakshirreff.com
Founded: 1968
Number of Lawyers: 12

Finance Lawyers:
Grant E. Shirreff, Commercial Real Estate
e-mail: gshirreff@doakshirreff.com
Roy H. Sommerey, Commercial Real Estate
e-mail: rsommerey@doakshirreff.com

Doyle & Prendergast
10 Sydenham St. East
Aylmer, ON N5H 1L2
519-773-3105
Fax: 519-765-1728
Number of Lawyers: 2

Finance Lawyers:
Michael Doyle
Donald J. Prendergast

DuMoulin, Boskovich
Pacific Landmark #1800 Box: 52
1095 Pender St. West
Vancouver, BC V6E 2M6
604-669-5500
Fax: 604-688-8491
800-288-9893
info@dubo.com
Founded: 1972
Number of Lawyers: 21

Finance Lawyers:
Anthony B.P. DuMoulin

Duncan & Craig LLP
Scotia Place #2800
10060 Jasper Ave.
Edmonton, AB T5J 3V9
780-428-6036
Fax: 780-428-9683
800-782-9409
duncancraig@dcllp.com
www.dcllp.com
Founded: 1894
Number of Lawyers: 51
Profile: Bankruptcy/Receivership Law; Commercial Litigation; Commercial Real Estate; Corporate/Commercial Transactions; Real Property Tax

Finance Lawyers:
Darren R. Bieganek, Debt Recovery
780-441-4386 e-mail: dbieganek@dcllp.com
Jessie A. Davies, Financial Services & Banking
780-441-4357 e-mail: jdavies@dcllp.com
Peter J. Dobbie, Taxation
780-632-2877 e-mail: pdobbie@dcllp.com
Robert C. Dunseith, Taxation
780-441-4395 e-mail: rdunseith@dcllp.com
Ronald W. Dutchak, Corporate & Commercial
780-441-4336 e-mail: rdutchak@dcllp.com
Blair Falconer, Debt Recovery
780-441-4306 e-mail: rswanson@dcllp.com
Edward R. Feehan, Insolvency, Receivership & Bankruptcy
780-441-4314 e-mail: erfeehan@dcllp.com
Jeff Fixsen, Corporate & Commercial
780-409-2658 e-mail: jfixsen@dcllp.com
Douglas P. Gahn, Financial Services & Banking
780-441-4304 e-mail: dpgahn@dcllp.com
Brewster H. Kwan, Corporate & Commercial
780-441-4367 e-mail: bhkwan@dcllp.com
Roberto Noce, Corporate & Commercial
780-441-4368 e-mail: rnoce@dcllp.com
Helen Park, Corporate & Commercial
780-409-2652 e-mail: hpark@dcllp.com
Russell A. Rimer, Debt Recovery
780-441-4368 e-mail: rrimer@dcllp.com
Solomon J. Rolingher, Corporate & Commercial
780-441-4310 e-mail: srolingher@dcllp.com
Tanya Smith, Insolvency, Receivership & Bankruptcy
780-409-2659 e-mail: tsmith@dcllp.com
Ross W.D. Swanson, Corporate & Commercial
780-441-4360 e-mail: rswanson@dcllp.com

Duncan & Craig LLP
PO Box 700
4925 - 50 St.
Vegreville, AB T9C 1R7
780-632-2877
Fax: 780-632-2898
duncanandcraig@dcllp.com
Number of Lawyers: 1

Finance Lawyers:
Peter .J. Dobbie, Tax Law

Duncan & Craig LLP
#103
4725 - 56 St.
Wetaskiwin, AB T9A 1V6
780-352-1662
Fax: 780-352-2970
duncancraig@dcllp.com

ACCOUNTING & LAW

Number of Lawyers: 1

Finance Lawyers:
Robert C, Dunseith, Corporate & Commercial; Taxation

Dunphy Best Blocksom LLP

#2100
777 - 8th Ave. SW
Calgary, AB T2P 3R5
403-265-7777
Fax: 403-269-8911
mail@dbb.com
www.dbblaw.com
Founded: 1979
Number of Lawyers: 18
Profile: Corporate/Commercial

Finance Lawyers:
Fulvio M. Durante, General Finance
403-750-1156 e-mail: durante@dbblaw.com
John F. Minchin, General Finance
403-750-1113 e-mail: minchin@dbblaw.com
Rick Wilson, Corporate; Commercial & Securities
403-750-1124 e-mail: wilson@dbblaw.com

Elkind, Lipton & Jacobs LLP

#1900
1 Queen St. East
Toronto, ON M5C 2W6
416-367-0871
Fax: 416-367-9388
info@elkindlipton.com
www.eljlaw.com
Number of Lawyers: 11

Finance Lawyers:
Jordan M. Cohen, General Finance
Saul D. Paton, Corporate/Commercial
Elliot Y. Rand, General Finance
Tariq Taherbhai, Corporate/Commercial; Mergers & Acquisitions

Emery Jamieson LLP

Oxford Tower #1700
10235 - 101st St.
Edmonton, AB T5J 3G1
780-426-5220
Fax: 780-420-6277
866-212-5220
general@emeryjamieson.com
www.emeryjamieson.com
Founded: 1893
Number of Lawyers: 25
Profile: Secured Financial Transactions; Commercial Transactions; Commercial & Residential Mortgages; Secured & Unsecured Recovery; Foreclosures; Bankruptcy & Insolvency

Finance Lawyers:
Sydney A. Bercov, General Finance
e-mail: sabercov@emeryjamieson.com
Scott H. Chen
e-mail: schen@emeryjamieson.com
Kate L. Hurlburt
e-mail: khurlburt@emeryjamieson.com
Valerie D. Meier
e-mail: vmeier@emeryjamison.com
Rex M. Nielsen, General Finance
e-mail: rnielsen@emeryjamieson.com
Michael J. Penny
e-mail: mpenny@emeryjamison.com
Frederica L. Schutz
e-mail: fschutz@emeryjamieson.com
Natalie D. Tymchuk
e-mail: ntymchuk@emeryjamieson.com
James R. Vaage
e-mail: jvaage@emeryjamieson.com
Stuart J. Weatherill, General Finance
e-mail: sweatherill@emeryjamieson.com
Wendy A. Young
e-mail: wyoung@emeryjamieson.com

Evans, Philp

PO Box 930, A Sta.
Hamilton, ON L8N 3P9
905-525-1200
Fax: 905-525-7897
info@evansphilp.com
www.evansphilp.com
Founded: 1919
Number of Lawyers: 22

Finance Lawyers:
Cara L. Boddy, Insurance
e-mail: cboddy@evansphilp.com
Larry G. Culver, Insurance
e-mail: lculver@evansphilp.com
Kieran C. Dickson, Insurance
e-mail: kdickson@evansphilp.com
Kimberly Farrington, Insurance
e-mail: kfarrington@evansphilp.com
Mark R. Giavedoni, Commercial Transactions; Mortgages
e-mail: mgiavedoni@evansphilp.com
W. Ian Gordon, Wills, Trusts & Estates; Mortgages; Commercial Transactions
e-mail: igordon@evansphilp.com
Kevin Griffiths, Insurance
e-mail: kgriffiths@evansphilp.com
Antonio Maddalena, Mortgages, Commercial Transactions
e-mail: amaddalena@evansphilp.com
Linda M. O'Brien, Insurance
e-mail: lobrien@evansphilp.com
Paul H. Philp, Insurance
e-mail: philp@evansphilp.com
Pamela J. Quesnel, Insurance
e-mail: pquesnel@evansphilp.com
Kathleen Robb, Insurance
e-mail: krobb@evansphilp.com
Robert H. Rogers, Insurance
e-mail: rrogers@evansphilp.com
Carolynne J. Wahlman, Insurance
e-mail: cwahlman@evansphilp.com

Farris, Vaughan, Wills & Murphy LLP

Pacific Centre South #2500
PO Box 10026
700 West Georgia St.
Vancouver, BC V7Y 1B3
604-684-9151
Fax: 604-661-9349
Telex: 04-507819info@farris.com
www.farris.com
Founded: 1903
Number of Lawyers: 71
Profile: The firm has extensive experience in the areas of acquisitions, reorganizations, mergers, joint ventures, public securities issues, private placements & banking transactions; also European & U.S./Canada financings; counsel in many real estate financing for both borrower & lender; acquisitions financings & privatization transactions

Finance Lawyers:
Brian R. Canfield, Corporate Commercial; Securities
604-661-9362 e-mail: bcanfield@farris.com
R. Hector MacKay-Dunn, Corporate Commercial; Securities
604-661-9307 e-mail: hmackay-dunn@farris.com
Brock R. Rowland, Real Estate Law
604-661-9327 e-mail: browland@farris.com

Fasken Martineau DuMoulin LLP

Tour Stock Exchange #3400
PO Box 242
800, Place Victoria
Montréal, QC H4Z 1E9
514-397-7400
Fax: 514-397-7600
800-361-6266
info@mtl.fasken.com
www.fasken.com
Founded: 1907
Number of Lawyers: 201

Finance Lawyers:
Claudette Allard, Securities; Mergers & Acquisitions
Claude Auger, Taxation
Lévy Bazinet, Corporate & Commercial; Securities; Mergers & Acquisitions
Diane Bertrand, Corporate & Commercial; Securities; Mergers & Acquisitions
Frédéric Boucher, Securities; Mergers & Acquisitions
Luc Bourbonnais, Corporate & Commercial; Securities; Mergers & Acquisitions
Sylvie Bourdeau, Corporate & Commercial; Securities; Mergers & Acquisitions
Luc Béliveau, Insolvency & Restructuring
Gilles Carli, Wealth Management; Taxation
Gabriel Castiglio, Securities; Mergers & Acquisitions
Stéphane Caïdi, Corporate & Commercial; Securities; Mergers & Acquisitions
Jean-Pierre Chamberland, Corporate & Commercial; Securities; Mergers & Acquisitions
Pierre-Yves Châtillon, Corporate & Commercial; Securities; Mergers & Acquisitions
Verna E. Cuthbert, Corporate & Commercial
Isabelle Deschamps, Insolvency & Restructuring
Isabelle Dongier, Corporate & Commercial
R. Andrew Ford, Securities; Mergers & Acquisitions
Maurice A. Forget, Securities; Mergers & Acquisitions
Francis Fox, Corporate & Commercial
Étienne Gadbois, Taxation
Patricia Gagnon, Corporate & Commercial; Securities; Mergers & Acquisitions
Sébastien Ghantous, Insolvency & Restructuring
Frédéric Gilbert, Insolvency & Restructuring
Robert Y. Girard, Corporate & Commercial; Securities; Mergers & Acquisitions
Gae@#l C. Gravenor, Securities; Mergers & Acquisitions
514-397-7524 e-mail: ggravenor@mtl.fasken.com
Félix Gutierrez, Banking & Finance
Serge F. Guérette, Insolvency & Restructuring
Louis-François Hogue, Securities; Mergers & Acquisitions
Teri Hoppenheim, Corporate & Commercial; Securities; Mergers & Acquisitions
Sébastien Hébert, Corporate & Commercial; Securities; Mergers & Acquisitions
Catherine Isabelle, Securities; Mergers & Acquisitions
Claude Jodoin, Taxation
514-797-7489 e-mail: cjodoin@mtl.fasken.com
Andrew Klug, Banking & Finance
Jocelyn Lafond, Securities; Mergers & Acquisitions
Stéphane Lalande, Banking & Finance
Stéphanie Lapierre, Insolvency & Restructuring; Securities; Mergers & Acquisitions
Jean-Michel Lapierre, Corporate & Commercial; Securities; Mergers & Acquisitions
Gilles Leclerc, Securities; Mergers & Acquisitions
David Lemieux, Banking & Finance; Insolvency & Restructuring
Peter R.D. MacKell, Counsel, Securities; Mergers & Acquisitions

Paul Marcotte, Corporate & Commercial
Paul Martel, Corporate & Commercial
Yvon Martineau, Corporate & Commercial; Securities; Mergers & Acquisitions
Xeno C. Martis, Banking & Finance; Insolvency & Restructuring
Jean M. Masson, Securities; Mergers & Acquisitions
Luc Morin, Insolvency & Restructuring
Éric Ménard, Insolvency & Restructuring
Marie-Josée Neveu, Securities; Mergers & Acquisitions
Marc Novello, Banking & Finance
Angela Onesi, Banking & Finance
Robert Paré, Securities; Mergers & Acquisitions
Hugo Patenaude, Wealth Management; Taxation
Jean-François Perreault, Taxation
Daniel Picotte, Corporate; Securities; Mergers & Acquisitions
514-397-7527 e-mail: dpicotte@mtl.fasken.com
Jan-Fryderyk Pleszczynski, Corporate & Commercial; Securities; Mergers & Acquisitions
Martin Racicot, Banking & Finance
Alain Ranger, Taxation
Alain Riendeau, Insolvency & Restructuring
Lucie Rivest, Corporate & Commercial; Securities; Mergers & Acquisitions
Pierre-Etienne Simard, Corporate & Commercial; Securities; Mergers & Acquisitions
Robert J. Stocks, Securities; Mergers & Acquisitions
Louis H. Séguin, Securities; Mergers & Acquisitions
Louis Tassé, Wealth Management; Taxation
J. Lambert Toupin, Counsel, Securities; Mergers & Acquisitions
Mireille Tremblay, Securities; Mergers & Acquisitions
Marie Vanasse, Corporate & Commercial
Peter Villani, Securities; Mergers & Acquisitions
Gilda Villaran, Corporate & Commercial
Marie-Josée Vincelli, Corporate & Commercial; Securities; Mergers & Acquisitions
Lawrence P. Yelin, Banking & Finance; Corporate & Commercial

Daniel Yelin, Securities; Mergers & Acquisitions
Eleni Yiannakis, Insolvency & Restructuring

Fasken Martineau DuMoulin LLP
#800
140, Grande Allée est
Québec, QC G1R 5M8
418-640-2000
Fax: 418-647-2455
800-463-2827
info@qc.fasken.com
www.fasken.com
Founded: 1983
Number of Lawyers: 37

Finance Lawyers:
Yves Chassé, Real Estate
Mathieu Comeau, Business Law
Jacques Croteau, Financial Institutions
418-640-2080 e-mail: jcroteau@qc.fasken.com
Yves Lacroix, Corporate Finance
418-640-2072 e-mail: ylacroix@qc.fasken.com
Yves Letarte, Real Estate
Gary Makila, Banking
Jean G. Morency, Financial Institutions
418-640-2002 e-mail: jmorency@qc.fasken.com
René Roy, Tax

Fasken Martineau DuMoulin LLP
TD Centre #4200
PO Box 20
66 Wellington St. West
Toronto, ON M5K 1N6
416-366-8381
Fax: 416-364-7813
800-268-8424
info@tor.fasken.com
www.fasken.com
Founded: 1863
Number of Lawyers: 227
Profile: Fasken Marineau provides legal services to the full array of participants in the financial services industry; our clients include leading Canadian & foreign banks, life & property & casualty insurance companies, loan & trust companies, cooperatives & credit unions, finance companies, insurance agents & brokers & other financial services providers; we pride ourselves on knowing each client's business & the current issues & trends affecting them; we work closely with our clients across the breadth of their transactional investment & other activities & in their relations with Canadian regulators; our group regularly provides advice regarding mergers & acquisitions, financings, restructurings, the establishment of financial services businesses, the development & distribution of financial services products & all manner of regulatory issues with both federal & provincial regulators

Finance Lawyers:
Anil Aggarwal, Corporate & Commercial; Securities; Mergers & Acquisitions
Andrew C. Alleyne, Corporate & Commercial; Insolvency & Restructuring
Alfred Apps, Corporate & Commercial
e-mail: aapps@tor.fasken.com
Jennifer I. Armstrong, Securities; Mergers & Acquisitions
Peter Ascherl, Corporate & Commercial; Insolvency & Restructuring
Aaron Atkinson, Corporate & Commercial; Insolvency & Restructuring
David E. Baird, Insolvency & Restructuring
Tony Baldanza, Corporate & Commercial
A. Wojtek Baraniak, Corporate & Commercial; Financial Institutions & Services
Daniel Batista, Corporate & Commercial
Allan Beach, Corporate & Commercial
John P. Beardwood, Corporate & Commercial
William J. Bies, Taxation
S. Bruce Blain, Corporate & Commercial; Insolvency & Restructuring
James A. Bradshaw, Counsel, Corporate & Commercial
Stuart Brotman, Insolvency & Restructuring
Howard M. Carr, Wealth Management
Paul Casuccio, Taxation
Koker K. Christensen, Corporate & Commercial; Financial Institutions & Services
416-868-3495 e-mail: kchristensen@tor.fasken.com
Geoffrey Clarke, Corporate & Commercial; Insolvency & Restructuring
416-868-3524 e-mail: gclarke@tor.fasken.com
Kevin Clinton, Corporate & Commercial; Insolvency & Restructuring
Scott Conover, Corporate & Commercial
Bozidar Crnatovic, Insolvency & Restructuring
Angela Di Padova, Corporate & Commercial
David M. Doubilet, Corporate & Commercial
Georges Dubé, Insolvency & Restructuring
Janne Duncan, Corporate & Commercial; Insolvency & Restructuring
Nancy Eastman, Securities; Mergers & Acquisitions
Dugan R. Edmison, Corporate & Commercial
Robert E. Elliott, Financial Institutions & Services
416-865-4382 e-mail: relliott@tor.fasken.com
Garfield H. Emerson, Corporate & Commercial; Insolvency & Restructuring
416-865-4350 e-mail: gemerson@tor.fasken.com
Stephen Erlichman, Insolvency & Restructuring
Daniel Fabiano, Corporate & Commercial
David H. Ferris, Banking & Finance
Amanda A. Field, Corporate & Commercial; Insolvency & Restructuring
Gary S. Fogler, Corporate & Commercial; Insolvency & Restructuring
416-868-3543 e-mail: gfogler@tor.fasken.com
Garth J. Foster, Insolvency & Restructuring
David Fox, Taxation
Catherine K. Fraser, Corporate & Commercial
Brad A. Freelan, Corporate & Commercial; Insolvency & Restructuring
Ralph Glass, Corporate & Commercial; Insolvency & Restructuring
Michael T. Gleeson, Corporate & Commercial; Insolvency & Restructuring
George C. Glover, Insolvency & Restructuring
Lynne Golding, Corporate & Commercial
Kathleen Hanly, Taxation
e-mail: khanly@tor.fasken.com
David Harley, Corporate & Commercial
David A. Hausman, Insolvency & Restructuring
Cynthia L. Heinz, Corporate & Commercial
Charles Higgings, Corporate & Commercial
Gregory Ho Yuen, Insolvency & Restructuring
Elena Hoffstein, Wealth Management
Jon J. Holmstrom, Banking & Finance; Insolvency & Restructuring
416-865-5125 e-mail: jholmstrom@tor.fasken.com
Tracy Hooey, Corporate & Commercial; Insolvency & Restructuring
John H. Hough, Counsel, Corporate & Commercial
Carole Hunter, Insolvency & Restructuring
Anita M. Huntley, Corporate & Commercial
Janice J. Javier, Corporate & Commercial
David Johnson, Banking & Finance
416-868-3368 e-mail: djohnson@tor.fasken.com
Richard E. Johnston, Insolvency & Restructuring
Daye Kaba, Securities; Mergers & Acquisitions
Aubrey E. Kauffman, Insolvency & Restructuring
Jason J. Kee, Corporate & Commercial
Stephen B. Kerr, Corporate & Commercial; Financial Institutions & Services
416-865-5141 e-mail: skerr@tor.fasken.com
Arthur R. Kitamura, Corporate & Commercial
Karoline A. Kralka, Corporate & Commercial; Insolvency & Restructuring
John Kruk, Securities; Mergers & Acquisitions
Andrew B. Laidlaw, Corporate & Commercial; Insolvency & Restructuring
416-865-4491 e-mail: alaidlaw@tor.fasken.com
Edmond F.B. Lamek, Insolvency & Restructuring
416-865-4506 e-mail: elamek@tor.fasken.com
Jonathan A. Levin, Banking & Finance; Insolvency & Restructuring; Securities; Mergers & Acquisitions
416-865-4401 e-mail: jlevin@tor.fasken.com
Ian MacGregor, Corporate & Commercial
Lisa Marcuzzi, Corporate & Commercial
Robert Mason, Corporate & Commercial
Roxanne E. McCormick, Corporate & Commercial
Thomas M. Meagher, Corporate & Commercial; Banking & Finance
416-865-5473 e-mail: tmeagher@tor.fasken.com
Barbara Miller, Corporate & Commercial
416-865-4410 e-mail: bmiller@tor.fasken.com
Donald E. Milner, Insolvency & Restructuring
416-865-4411 e-mail: dmilner@tor.fasken.com
C. Scott Mitchell, Corporate & Commercial; Financial Institutions & Services
416-865-4516 e-mail: csmitchell@tor.fasken.com
Sean Morley, Corporate & Commercial
Kenneth C. Morlock, Corporate & Commercial
Douglas C. New, Corporate & Commercial
Ronald Nobrega, Taxation
Andrew S. Nunes, Corporate & Commercial
William Orr, Corporate & Commercial
Walter J. Palmer, Corporate & Commercial
416-868-3432 e-mail: walter_palmer@fasken.com
Jamie C. Pennell, Corporate & Commercial
R. Graham Phoenix, Insolvency & Restructuring
David Robertson, Taxation
Leslie H. Rose, Corporate & Commercial
e-mail: lrose@tor.fasken.com
John Sabetti, Corporate & Commercial
David W. Salomon, Corporate & Commercial
416-865-4430 e-mail: dsalomon@tor.fasken.com
Munier Saloojee, Corporate & Commercial
Alan M. Schwartz, Taxation
Douglas R. Scott, Corporate & Commercial
Robert L. Shirriff, Corporate & Commercial
e-mail: rshiriff@tor.fasken.com
Lisa Simone, Wealth Management
Don. Steadman, Counsel, Corporate & Commercial
Aaron Stefan, Corporate & Commercial
Sean S. Stevens, Corporate & Commercial
J. Mark Stinson, Corporate & Commercial
Stacey I. Stoneham, Corporate & Commercial
Robert M. Sutherland, Corporate & Commercial
Mitchell L. Thaw, Taxation
John W. Torrey, Banking & Finance
416-865-4394 e-mail: jtorrey@tor.fasken.com
Krisztian Toth, Corporate & Commercial
David Turgeon, Corporate & Commercial
Liana L. Turrin, Corporate & Commercial; Insolvency & Restructuring
416-868-3401 e-mail: lturrin@tor.fasken.com
Peter W. Vair, Taxation
Corina Weigl, Wealth Management
Laura E. West, Wealth Management
Roger D. Wilson, Corporate & Commercial
Brian G. Wright, Banking & Finance
416-865-5488 e-mail: bwright@tor.fasken.com
Kathleen E. Yoa, Corporate & Commercial; Financial Institutions & Services
416-865-5451 e-mail: kyoa@tor.fasken.com

Fasken Martineau DuMoulin LLP
#2100
1075 West Georgia St.
Vancouver, BC V6E 3G2
604-631-3131
Fax: 604-631-3232
866-635-3131
info@van.fasken.com
www.fasken.com
Founded: 1889
Number of Lawyers: 136

Finance Lawyers:
Lata Casciano, Securities; Mergers & Acquisitions; Corporate Finance; Investment Funds
604-631-4746 e-mail: lcasciano@van.fasken.com
Donald M. Dalik, Corporate Commercial; Communications; Financial Institutions; Banking & Finance; Property Financing
604-631-4739 e-mail: ddalik@van.fasken.com
George W. Hungerford, Corporate Commercial; Property Financing
604-631-4833 e-mail: ghungerford@van.fasken.com
Andrew Jackson, Banking; Private Debt Financing & Securitization; Corporate Commercial
604-631-3124 e-mail: ajackson@van.fasken.com
Brent J. Lewis, Banking; Private Debt Financing & Securitization
604-631-4889 e-mail: blewis@van.fasken.com
Edmond C. Luke, Corporate Commercial; Property Financing & Development
604-631-4829 e-mail: eluke@van.fasken.com
KC Miu, Banking & Finance, Corporate/Commercial, Litigation & Dispute Resolution
604-631-4980 e-mail: kmiu@van-fasken.com
Michael D. Parrish, Commercial Litigation; International Dispute Resolution
604-631-4863 e-mail: mparrish@van.fasken.com

James D. Piers, Property Financing
604-631-4769 e-mail: jpiers@van.fasken.com
Robert W. Quon, Financial Institutions & Services; Trust, Wills & Estates; Charities
604-631-4962 e-mail: rquon@van.fasken.com

Jon M. Feldman
#1500
1 Westmount Sq.
Montréal, QC H3Z 2P9
514-935-6222
Fax: 514- -
jfeldman@jlaw.ca
Number of Lawyers: 1

Finance Lawyers:
J.M. Feldman, Corporate/Commercial

Felesky Flynn
Petro Canada Centre #5000
150 - 6th Ave. SW
Calgary, AB T2P 3Y7
403-260-3300
Fax: 403-263-9649
felesky@felesky.com
www.felesky.com
Founded: 1978
Number of Lawyers: 18
Profile: Provides legal advice & representation in the complex areas of tax law

Finance Lawyers:
D. Brett Anderson, Tax
403-260-5637 e-mail: banderson@felesky.com
Donald K. Biberdorf, Tax
403-260-5404 e-mail: dbiberdoft@felesky.com
Flavia Boll, Tax
403-260-5407 e-mail: fboll@felesky.com
John C. Burghardt, Tax
403-260-6672 e-mail: jburghardt@felesky.com
Mark Coleman, Tax
403-260-6673 e-mail: mcoleman@felesky.com
Brian A. Felesky, Tax
403-260-3301 e-mail: bfelesky@felesky.com
Siobhan A. Goguen, Tax
403-260-3313 e-mail: sgoguen@felesky.com
Sandra E. Jack, Tax
403-260-3308 e-mail: sjack@felesky.com
Craig M. Jones, Tax
403-260-6676 e-mail: cjones@felesky.com
Greg Lindsey, Tax
403-260-3311 e-mail: glindsey@felesky.com
Kim Lynch, Tax
403-260-5638 e-mail: klynch@felesky.com
H. George McKenzie, Tax
403-260-3303 e-mail: gmckenzie@felesky.com
Blair Nixon, Tax
403-260-3307 e-mail: bnixon@felesky.com
Ken Skingle, Tax
403-260-3309 e-mail: kskingle@felesky.com
Jason Stephan, Tax
403-260-5639 e-mail: jstephan@felesky.com
Anthony Strawson, Tax
403-260-5634 e-mail: astrawson@felesky.com
Joe Struck, Tax
406-260-3302 e-mail: jstruck@felesky.com

Felesky Flynn
Canada Trust Tower #2250
10104 - 103 Ave.
Edmonton, AB T5J 0H8
780-428-8310
Fax: 780-421-8820
felesky@telusplanet.net
Number of Lawyers: 13

Finance Lawyers:
Donald N. Cherniawsky, Tax
780-643-3060 e-mail: dcherniawsky@felesky.com
Laura Durrance, Tax
780-643-3058 e-mail: ldurrance@felesky.com
Douglas J. Forer, Tax
780-643-3065 e-mail: dforer@felesky.com
Gregory J. Gartner, Tax
780-643-3070 e-mail: ggartner@felesky.com
F. Patrick Kirby, Tax
780-643-3055 e-mail: pkirby@felesky.com
Timothy Kirby, Tax
780-643-3062 e-mail: tkirby@felesky.com
Richard Kirby, Tax
780-643-3063 e-mail: rkirby@felesky.com
John McClure, Tax
780-643-3059 e-mail: jmcclure@felesky.com
James C. Yaskowich, Tax
780-643-3064 e-mail: jyaskowich@felesky.com

Field LLP
First Canadian Centre #1900
350 - 7th Ave. SW
Calgary, AB T2P 3N9
403-260-8500
Fax: 403-264-7084
lawyers@fieldlaw.com
www.fieldlaw.com
Number of Lawyers: 36

Finance Lawyers:
Meenu Ahluwalia Barr
Nancy Bains
Barbara Boeckx, Insurance
Roy D. Boettger, Wills, Trusts & Estates; Transactional & Corporate
403-260-8507 e-mail: rboettger@fieldlaw.com
Michael F. Casey, Insurance
403-260-8505 e-mail: mcasey@fieldlaw.com
Faralee A. Chanin, Taxation Law
403-260-8514 e-mail: fchanin@fieldlaw.com
Justin Denis
403-260-8585 e-mail: jdenis@fieldlaw.com
Dan Downe, Insurance
403-232-1754 e-mail: ddowne@fieldlaw.com
Jim Doyle
403-260-8578 e-mail: jdoyle@fieldlaw.com
Trisha Gizen
Todd W. Kathol, Insurance
403-260-8581 e-mail: tkathol@fieldlaw.com
Wayne Logan
A.M. Lydia Lytwyn, Transactional & Corporate
403-232-1757 e-mail: llytwyn@fieldlaw.com
Doreen M. Saunderson, Insurance
403-260-8539 e-mail: dsaunderson@fieldlaw.com
Nancy-Lynn Stevenson, Wills, Trusts & Estates
403-260-8518 e-mail: nstevenson@fieldlaw.com
Anne Wallis
Ray Wong
Jean C. van der Lee, Insurance
403-260-8520 e-mail: jvanderlee@fieldlaw.com

Field LLP
Scotia Centre #203
5102 - 50th Ave.
Yellowknife, NT X1A 3S8
867-920-4542
Fax: 867-873-4790
lawyers@fieldlaw.com
www.fieldlaw.com
Founded: 2000
Number of Lawyers: 2

Finance Lawyers:
William M. Rouse, Corporate/Commercial; Business Law
867-920-4542 e-mail: wrouse@fieldlaw.com
Jack R. Williams, Transactional & Corporate; Insurance
867-920-4542 e-mail: jwilliams@fieldlaw.com

Joseph Y. Fisch
419 College St.
Toronto, ON M5T 1T1
416-920-6312
Fax: 416-920-1780
josephyfisch@hotmail.com
Founded: 1969
Number of Lawyers: 2
Profile: Commercial & Corporate Law; Real Estate Law

Finance Lawyers:
J.Y. Fisch, Real Estate
e-mail: josephyfisch@hotmail.com
Aliza Fisch, Real Estate

Fitzsimmons & Company Professional Corporation
#1510
5140 Yonge St.
Toronto, ON M2N 6L7
416-224-8044
Fax: 416-250-7008
fitzsimmons@fitzlaw.ca
www.fitzlaw.ca
Number of Lawyers: 4
Profile: Tax Litigation; Estate Planning

Finance Lawyers:
Peter V. Aprile, Tax Litigation; Corporate Law; Estate Planning
Richard G. Fitzsimmons, Tax Litigation; Corporate Law; Estate Planning
Joseph LoPresti, Tax Litigation; Corporate Law; Estate Planning
Leigh Somerville Taylor, Tax Litigation; Corporate Law; Estate Planning

Fogler, Rubinoff LLP
Toronto-Dominion Centre #1200
95 Wellington St. West
Toronto, ON M5J 2Z9
416-864-9700
Fax: 416-941-8852
thefirm@foglerubinoff.com
www.foglerubinoff.com
Founded: 1982
Number of Lawyers: 66

Finance Lawyers:
Bruce S. Batist, General Finance
Stephen A. Bernofsky, General Finance
J. Anthony Caldwell, General Finance
S. Dale Denis, General Finance
Michael Donsky, General Finance
Gary C. Grierson, General Finance
Martin R. Kaplan, General Finance
Charles W. Skipper, General Finance

Fraser & Company
#1200
999 Hastings St. West
Vancouver, BC V6C 2W2
604-669-5244
Fax: 604-669-5791
securities@fraserlaw.com
Number of Lawyers: 9

Finance Lawyers:
David K. Fraser
Richard D. Rabson
David W. Smalley
Barbara G. Wohl

Fraser Milner Casgrain LLP
1 First Canadian Place
PO Box 100
#4200, 100 King St. West
Toronto, ON M5X 1B2
416-863-4511
Fax: 416-863-4592
webmaster@fmc-law.com
www.fmc-law.com
Founded: 1839
Number of Lawyers: 160
Profile: Our Financial Services Group, one of the largest at any major Canadian law firm, is recognized as a leader in the financial services sector; the group provides specialized legal advice in banking, financing, regulatory & insolvency matters to meet the changing needs & demands of our financial institution clients; in addition to advising on traditional bank lending, acting for either lenders or corporate borrowers, we have considerable experience in equipment leasing, finance transactions, synthetic leases, asset-based securitizations & financial instruments transactions; key service areas include advising domestic & international clients on the regulation of banks & other financial institutions in Canada; assistance to establish financial service businesses in Canada & incorporating Canadian domestic banking subsidiaries; structuring, negotiating & documenting credit transactions of all types including loans, syndications, trade finance, factoring, financial leasing, project financing

Finance Lawyers:
Abbas Ali Khan, Corporate/Commercial; Securities; Mergers & Acquisitions
E. James Arnett, Corporate/Commercial
Paul F. Baston, Tax Law
e-mail: paul.baston@fmc-law.com
Michael G. Beairsto, Corporate/Commercial
Doug Benson, Privatization; Commercial Real Estate

Fraser Milner Casgrain LLP (continued)

R. Brendan Bissell, Insurance; Corporate/Commercial; Insolvency
e-mail: brendan.bissell@fmc-law.com
Frank Bowman, Insurance
e-mail: frank.bowman@fmc-law.com
Patrick J. Boyle, Tax Law
e-mail: patrick.boyle@fmc-law.com
Maggie A. Brady, Corporate/Commercial; Financial Services; Commercial Real Estate
416-862-3457 e-mail: maggie.brady@fmc-law.com
Nicole D. Brown, Corporate/Commercial
Nicole A. Brown, Corporate/Commercial; Securities
Scott Burke, Commercial Real Estate
e-mail: scott.burke@fmc-law.com
Brian R. Carr, Tax Law
416-863-4366 e-mail: brian.carr@fmc-law.com
Andrea Centa, Commercial Real Estate
e-mail: andrea.centa@fmc-law.com
Lori Lyn Chanda, Financial Services
e-mail: lori.chanda@fmc-law.com
Chia-yi Chua, Tax Law
James Clare, Corporate/Commercial; Securities; Mergers & Acquisitions
Heidi E. Clark, Financial Services; Corporate/Commercial; E-Commerce
416-863-4626 e-mail: heidi.clark@fmc-law.com
Barbara A. Conway, Corporate/Commercial
Frank L. Davis, Securities; Mergers & Acquisitions
416-862-3440 e-mail: frank.davis@fmc-law.com
Joseph Debono, Commercial Real Estate
416-361-2338 e-mail: joseph.debono@fmc-law.com
Jane Dietrich, Financial Services
Dan R. Dowdall, Financial Services; Insolvency
416-863-4700 e-mail: dan.dowdall@fmc-law.com
James A.S. Dunbar, Insurance
e-mail: james.dunbar@fmc-law.com
John S. Elder, Securities; Mergers & Acquisitions; Corporate/Commercial
416-863-4652 e-mail: john.elder@fmc-law.com
Norman J. Emblem, Securities; Insurance; Insolvency
e-mail: norman.emblem@fmc-law.com
Martin Emmons, Commercial Real Estate
416-367-6800 e-mail: marty.emmons@fmc-law.com
Andrea L. Feltham, Corporate/Commercial
Gennady Ferenbok, Corporate/Commercial; Securities
David G. Fuller, Wills & Estates; Tax Law
e-mail: david.fuller@fmc-law.com
Netta Genua, Insurance
e-mail: ninetta.genua@fmc-law.com
Paul P. Ginou, Commercial Real Estate; Privatization
416-863-4706 e-mail: paul.ginou@fmc-law.com
Ronald A. Goldenberg, Commercial Real Estate; Privatization
416-863-4724 e-mail: ronald.goldenberg@fmc-law.com
David Gossen, Corporate/Commercial; Securities; Mergers & Acquisitions
416-862-3424 e-mail: david.gossen@fmc-law.com
Sander A.J.R. Grieve, Securities; Corporate/Commercial; Privatization
416-863-4732 e-mail: sander.grieve@fmc-law.com
Barbara L. Grossman, Commercial Real Estate; Insolvency
Colin W. Ground, Corporate/Commercial; Private Equity; Mergers & Acquisitions
Aron Halpern, Corporate/Commercial; Securities; Mergers & Acquisitions
Christopher Hluchan, Insurance
416-367-6824 e-mail: christopher.hluchan@fmc-law.com
Sonja K. Homenuck, Commerical Real Estate
Randal T. Hughes, Mergers & Aquisitions
e-mail: randy.hughes@fmc-law.com
Victor Hum, Securities; Mergers & Acquisitions; Corporate/Commercial
e-mail: victor.hum@fmc-law.com
Thomas J. Hunter, Financial Services; Insolvency; Corporate/Commercial
416-863-4555 e-mail: tom.hunter@fmc-law.com
D. Chad Hutchison, Corporate/Commercial; Securities; Mergers & Acquisitions
Alex A. Ilchenko, Insolvency; Litigation & Advocacy; Financial Services
416-863-4748 e-mail: alex.ilchenko@fmc-law.com
William I. Innes, Tax Law; Wills & Estates
e-mail: william.innes@fmc-law.com
James J. Janetos, Mergers & Acquisitions; Financial Services; Securities; Corporate/Commercial; Private Equity; Privatization
416-863-4415 e-mail: jim.janetos@fmc-law.com
Andrew Jeanrie, Commercial Real Estate
416-863-4793 e-mail: andrew.jeanrie@fmc-law.com
Mike Kaplan, Mergers & Acquisitions; Corporate/Commercial
e-mail: mike.kaplan@fmc-law.com
Meenu Khindri, Corporate/Commercial; Securities; Mergers & Acquisitions
Russel Z. Kowalyk, Financial Services
416-862-3478 e-mail: russel.kowalyk@fmc-law.com
Shayne R. Kukulowicz, Insolvency; Litigation & Advocacy; Corporate/Commercial; Financial Services
416-863-4740 e-mail: shayne.kukulowicz@fmc-law.com
John M. Langs, Securities; Mergers & Acquisitions; Corporate/Commercial
e-mail: john.langs@fmc-law.com
Jules L. Lewy, Tax Law; Wills & Estates; Corporate/Commercial
e-mail: jules.lewy@fmc-law.com
Donald F. Luck, Corporate/Commercial
Don Macintosh, Mergers & Acquisitions; Corporate/Commercial; Securities
416-361-2330 e-mail: don.macintosh@fmc-law.com
Joseph O. Marin, Financial Services; Insolvency
416-863-4730 e-mail: joseph.marin@fmc-law.com
Ronald J. Matheson, Financial Services; Commercial Real Estate; Insolvency
416-863-4692 e-mail: ron.matheson@fmc-law.com
John Lorn McDougall, Insolvency
416-863-4624 e-mail: john.lorn.mcdougall@fmc-law.com
Michael Melanson, Mergers & Acquisitions; Securities; Corporate/Commercial
416-863-4382 e-mail: michael.melanson@fmc-law.com
Duane R. Milot, Tax Law
David J.T. Mungovan, Insurance; Insolvency
e-mail: david.mungovan@fmc-law.com
Peter E. Murphy, Financial Services; Insolvency; Regulatory; Corporate/Commercial
416-863-4503 e-mail: peter.murphy@fmc-law.com
Ali Naushahi, Corporate/Commercial; Securities; Mergers & Acquisitions
Le D.T. Nguyen, Financial Services; Corporate/Commercial; Insolvency; Commercial Real Estate
Zahra Nurmohamed, Tax Law
e-mail: zahra.nurmohamed@fmc-law.com
Tracey Patel, Corporate/Commercial
e-mail: tracey.patel@fmc-law.com
Roger J. Pead, Commercial Real Estate
Catherine Pham, Corporate/Commercial
Christopher Pinnington, Commercial Real Estate
John P. Rhude, Corporate/Commercial; Insurance; Commercial Real Estate; Securities; Mergers & Acquisitions
416-862-3418 e-mail: john.rhude@fmc-law.com
Charles Rich, Financial Services; Bankruptcy & Insolvency
416-863-4606 e-mail: charles.rich@fmc-law.com
Alex C. Roberts, Corporate/Commercial' Securities
John D. Russo, Financial Services; Insolvency
416-863-4648 e-mail: john.russo@fmc-law.com
John Sabine, Securities; Mergers & Acquisitions; Corporate/Commercial
416-863-4374 e-mail: john.sabine@fmc-law.com
Andrew E. Salem, Commercial Real Estate
Michael Schafler, Corporate/Commercial
Tony Schweitzer, Tax Law
e-mail: tony.schweitzer@fmc-law.com
Richard A. Scott, Securities; Mergers & Acquisitions; Corporate/Commercial
416-863-4370 e-mail: richard.scott@fmc-law.com
Doug H. Scott, Mergers & Acquisitions; Corporate/Commercial; Privatization; Securities
416-367-6767 e-mail: doug.scott@fmc-law.com
Paul D. Shantz, Commercial Real Estate
416-863-4768 e-mail: paul.shantz@fmc-law.com
Ralph Shay, Securities Law
Peter A. Shiroky, Tax Law
e-mail: peter.shiroky@fmc-law.com
Jillian E. Shortt, Commercial Real Estate
Ted Shoub, Corporate/Commercial
David P. Smith, Commercial Real Estate
Jeffrey Smolkin, Financial Services
Christopher J. Steeves, Tax Law; Mergers & Acquisitions; Corporate/Commercial
e-mail: christopher.steeves@fmc-law.com
Winxie Tse, Tax Law
e-mail: winxie.tse@fmc-law.com
Chris Turney, Securities; Mergers & Acquisitions; Corporate/Commercial
e-mail: chris.turney@fmc-law.com
Lara Vos Smith, Corporate/Commercial; Securities; Mergers & Acquisitions
Ross W. Walker, Insolvency; Financial Services
416-863-4742 e-mail: ross.walker@fmc-law.com
Dennis R. Wiebe, Financial Services
416-863-4475 e-mail: dennis.wiebe@fmc-law.com
Pat J. Williams, Wills & Estates
e-mail: pat.williams@fmc-law.com
Natasha Wong, Financial Services; Insolvency
Christopher D. Woodbury, Corporate/Commercial; Insolvency
Michael J. Wunder, Financial Services
416-863-4715 e-mail: michael.wunder@fmc-law.com
Joshua Yarmus, Corporate/Commercial
Scott Yelle, Corporate/Commercial
Doug J.S. Younger, Corporate/Commercial; Private Equity; Privatization: Mergers & Acquisitions
Corina Zatreanu, Corporate/Commercial; Securities; Mergers & Acquisitions

Fraser Milner Casgrain LLP

Fifth Avenue Place
237 - 4 Ave. SW, 30th Fl.
Calgary, AB T2P 4X7
403-268-7000
Fax: 403-268-3100
quincy.smith@fmc-law.com
www.fmc-law.com
Number of Lawyers: 115
Profile: Our Financial Services Group, one of the largest at any major Canadian law firm, is recognized as a leader in the financial services sector; the group provides sophisticated legal advice in banking, financing, regulatory & insolvency matters to meet the changing needs & demands of our financial institution clients; in addition to advising on traditional bank lending, where we act for either the lender or the borrower, we have considerable experience in equipment leasing & finance transactions, synthetic leases, asset-based securitizations, & financial instruments transactions; key service areas include advising domestic & international clients on the regulation of banks & other financial institutions in Canada; assistance to establish financial service businesses in Canada & incorporating Canadian domestic banking subsidiaries; structuring, negotiating & documenting credit transactions of all types including loans, syndications, trade finance, factoring, financial leasing, project fina

Finance Lawyers:
Thoburn (Toby) B. Allan, Corporate/Commercial
Vasiliki Antoniou, Mergers & Acquisitions
George Antonopoulos, Mergers & Acquisitions
Douglas J. Black, Corporate/Commercial; Mergers & Acquisitions
e-mail: doug.black@fmc-law.com
Anne Calverley, Tax
Stephanie A. Campbell, Financial Services; Commercial Real Estate
403-268-7186 e-mail: stephanie.campbell@fmc-law.com
Raymond A. Coad, Insurance
e-mail: raymond.coad@fmc-law.com
Gary J. Cochrane, Commercial Real Estate; Financial Services; Insolvency; Corporate/Commercial
403-268-7134 e-mail: gary.cochrane@fmc-law.com
Dorothy A. Dawe, Securities; Mergers & Acquisitions
e-mail: dorothy.dawe@fmc-law.com
William DeJong, Securities; Corporate Finance
Brent Epp, Corporate/Commercial
D. Brian Foster, Insurance
e-mail: brian.foster@fmc-law.com
Roxanne Gallon, Insurance
William G. Gilliland, Financial Services; Securities; Mergers & Acquisitions
e-mail: william.gilliland@fmc-law.com
Heather Greenberg, Securities; Corporate Finance
Donald T. Hatch, Wills & Estates
e-mail: don.hatch@fmc-law.com
Jehad Haymour, Tax Law
e-mail: jehad.haymour@fmc-law.com
Kent J. Hehr, Insurance
Neil Herle, Mergers & Acquisitions
403-268-7313 e-mail: neil.herle@fmc-law.com
Alex Himour, Corporate/Commercial
Keith Inman, Securities; Corporate Finance

William K. Jenkins, Financial Services; Securities; Mergers & Acquisitions; Corporate Governance; Corporate/Commercial
403-268-6835 e-mail: bill.jenkins@fmc-law.com
Nick Kangles, Corporate/Commercial
e-mail: nick.kangles@fmc-law.com
Michael Kariya, Mergers & Acquisitions
Dave B. Kitchen, Insurance
Don G. Kowalenko, Commercial Real Estate; Corporate/Governance; Financial Services
403-268-7078 e-mail: don.kowalenko@fmc-law.com
Barbara A. Krahn, Wills & Estates
e-mail: barbara.krahn@fmc-law.com
Phillip J. LaFlair, Insurance
David LeGeyt, Insolvency; Financial Services
e-mail: david.legeyt@fmc-law.com
Matthew R. Lindsay, Litigation; Advocacy; Financial Services
403-268-3037 e-mail: matt.lindsay@fmc-law.com
H. Derek Lloyd, Insurance
e-mail: derek.lloyd@fmc-law.com
David G. Loader, Commercial Real Estate
e-mail: david.loader@fmc-law.com
Joseph P. Lougheed, Securities; Mergers & Acquisitions
e-mail: joseph.lougheed@fmc-law.com
Irene T. Ludwig, Financial Services; Securities
e-mail: irene.ludwig@fmc-law.com
Geoffrey L. MacLeod, Corporate/Commercial
403-268-6310 e-mail: geoffrey.macleod@fmc-law.com
Karim H. Mahmud, Corporate/Commercial
David W. Mann, Insolvency; Financial Services; Corporate/Commercial
403-268-7097 e-mail: david.mann@fmc-law.com
Robert D. Maxwell, Insurance; Wills & Estates
e-mail: robert.maxwell@fmc-law.com
Erin A. McAlister, Insurance
G. Neil McDermid, Insurance
e-mail: neil.mcdermid@fmc-law.com
Robert J. McKinnon, Financial Services; Commercial Real Estate
403-268-7191 e-mail: robert.mckinnon@fmc-law.com
Trevor S.P. McLeod, Corporate/Commercial
403-268-3116 e-mail: trevor.mcleod@fmc-law.com
M. Jenny McMordie, Insurance
Robb McNaughton, Corporate/Commercial
Trevor Q. Morawski, Financial Services; Corporate/Commercial
403-268-7019 e-mail: trevor.morawski@fmc-law.com
Lindsay A. Mullen, Insurance
e-mail: lindsay.mullen@fmc-law.com
Chima Nkemdirim, Securities
e-mail: chimi.nkemdirim@fmc-law.com
Natalie Nowiski, Insurance
Thomas P. O'Leary, Insurance; Litigation; Advocacy; Financial Services
403-268-7303 e-mail: tom.oleary@fmc-law.com
Jerry J. Patterson, Insurance
e-mail: jerry.patterson@fmc-law.com
G. Cameron Peacock, Insurance
Thomas F. Pepevnak, Financial Services; Corporate/Commercial; Insolvency
403-268-7198 e-mail: tom.pepevnak@fmc-law.com
Joe Pfaefflin, Mergers & Acquisitions
Miles F. Pittman, Corporate/Commercial
John T. Prowse, Insolvency
John E.P. Reynolds, Corporate/Commercial
Laura M. Safran, Mergers & Acquisitions
e-mail: laura.safran@fmc-law.com
Scott W. Sangster, Financial Services
403-268-7286 e-mail: scott.sangster@fmc-law.com
Phillip J. Scheibel, Insurance
e-mail: phil.scheibel@fmc-law.com
B.A.R. Smith, Insolvency; Bankruptcy
e-mail: quincy.smith@fmc-law.com
Mylene D. Tiessen, Insurance
e-mail: mylene.tiessen@fmc-law.com
Zul Verjee, Corporate/Commercial
David J. Wachowich, Insurance
e-mail: davide.wachowich@fmc-law.com
Melissa S. Young, Corporate/Commercial
Laura J. Zurowski, Financial Services; Corporate/Commercial
403-268-7048 e-mail: laura.zurowski@fmc-law.com

Fraser Milner Casgrain LLP
Manulife Pl. #2900
10180 - 101 St.
Edmonton, AB T5J 3V5
780-423-7100
Fax: 780-423-7276
www.fmc-law.com
Number of Lawyers: 79
Profile: Our Financial Services Group, one of the largest at any major Canadian law firm, is recognized as a leader in the financial services sector; the group provides specialized legal advice in banking, financing, regulatory & insolvency matters to meet the changing needs & demands of our financial institution clients; in addition to advising on traditional bank lending, acting for either lenders or corporate borrowers, we have considerable experience in equipment leasing, finance transactions, synthetic leases, asset-based securitizations & financial instruments transactions; key service areas include advising domestic & international clients on the regulation of banks & other financial institutions in Canada; assistance to establish financial service businesses in Canada & incorporating Canadian domestic banking subsidiaries; structuring, negotiating & documenting credit transactions of all types including loans, syndications, trade finance, factoring, financial leasing, project financing

Finance Lawyers:
Heather Barnhouse, Corporate/Commercial
780-423-7215 e-mail: heather.barnhouse@fmc-law.com
Gary Biasini, Tax Law; Wills & Estates
780-423-7216 e-mail: gary.biasini@fmc-law.com
Dana Bissoondatt, Corporate/Commercial; Securities
780-423-7184 e-mail: dana.bissoondatt@fmc-law.com
Dwight I. Bliss, Corporate/Commercial
780-423-7262 e-mail: dwight.bliss@fmc-law.com
Lyle Brookes, Insolvency
780-423-7164 e-mail: lyle.brookes@fmc-law.com
Colleen Cebuliak, Securities
780-423-7136 e-mail: colleen.cebuliak@fmc-law.com
William Connauton, Financial Services; Commercial Real Estate
780-970-5280 e-mail: william.connauton@fmc-law.com
Richard J. Cotter, Insolvency; Commercial Foreclosure; Corporate/Commercial; Financial Services; Commercial Real Estate
780-423-7316 e-mail: richard.cotter@fmc-law.com
Richard Cruickshank, Tax Law; Wills & Estates; Securities; Mergers & Acquisitions
780-970-5255 e-mail: rick.cruickshank@fmc-law.com
John R. Day, Real Estate
780-423-7318 e-mail: john.day@fmc-law.com
Gary Draper, Commercial & Insurance Litigation
780-423-7308 e-mail: gary.draper@fmc-law.com
David Eigenseher, Litigation
780-423-7244 e-mail: david.eigenseher@fmc-law.com
Benjamin C. Evans, Taxation
780-423-7178 e-mail: benjamin.evans@fmc-law.com
Kevin Feehan, Litigation
780-423-7330 e-mail: kevin.feehan@fmc-law.com
Robert M. Fulton, Strategic Transactional Advice
780-423-7234 e-mail: robert.fulton@fmc-law.com
Cheryl A. Gibson, Tax Law
780-970-5237 e-mail: cheryl.gibson@fmc-law.com
Ward Hanson, Insurance Defense; Litigation
780-423-7134 e-mail: ward.hanson@fmc-law.com
Lorena Harris, Litigation
780-423-7315 e-mail: lorena.harris@fmc-law.com
John T. Henderson, Litigation
780-423-7320 e-mail: john.henderson@fmc-law.com
Percy L. Herring, Insurance
780-423-7202 e-mail: percy.herring@fmc-law.com
Jon Hillson, Litigation
780-423-7194 e-mail: jon.hillson@fmc-law.com
Mercedes Hitesman, Litigation & Insurance Defense
780-423-7307 e-mail: mercedes.hitesman@fmc-law.com
Andrew J. Hladyshevsky, Corporate/Commercial
780-970-5234 e-mail: andrew.hladyshevsky@fmc-law.com
Peter Jasper, Ligitation
780-970-5217 e-mail: peter.jasper@fmc-law.com
John D. Karvellas, Financial Services; Securities
780-970-5269 e-mail: john.karvellas@fmc-law.com
Anna Loparco, Securities
780-423-7137 e-mail: anna.loparco@fmc-law.com
Lloyd D. Lutic, Commercial Real Estate
780-423-7122 e-mail: lloyd.lutic@fmc-law.com
Debra Marr
780-423-7132 e-mail: debra.marr@fmc-law.com
Tom Mayson, Corporate/Commercial
780-423-7210 e-mail: tom.mayson@fmc-law.com
Craig McDougall, Securities
780-423-7398 e-mail: craig.mcdougall@fmc-law.com
Carman McNary, Tax Law
780-423-7236 e-mail: carman.mcnary@fmc-law.com
Richard A. Miller, Financial Services; Corporate/Commercial; Mergers & Acquisitions
780-423-7242 e-mail: rich.miller@fmc-law.com
Shauna Miller, Professional Liability; Insurance
780-423-7338 e-mail: shauna.miller@fmc-law.com
Shelley Miller, Professional Liability; Commercial Litigation; Insurance
780-970-5286 e-mail: shelley.miller@fmc-law.com
Ken Neilsen, Professional Liability; Construction; Mediation & Arbitration; Insurance Litigation
780-423-7340 e-mail: ken.neilsen@fmc-law.com
Michael D. Obert, Corporate/Commercial; Financial Services
780-423-7238 e-mail: michael.obert@fmc-law.com
Eugene H.J. Phoa, Commercial Real Estate; Financial Services
780-423-7130 e-mail: eugene.phoa@fmc-law.com
Dennis Picco, Insurance Defense; Intellectual Property; Litigation
780-423-7322 e-mail: dennis.picco@@fmc-law.com
Gordon Plewes, Commercial Real Estate
780-423-7200 e-mail: gordon.plewes@fmc-law.com
Joe Rosselli, Litigation; Intellectual Property; Alternative Dispute Resolution
780-423-7142 e-mail: joe.rosselli@fmc-law.com
Robert R. Roth, Mergers & Acquisitions; Securities; Corporate & Commercial Law
780-423-7228 e-mail: robert.roth@fmc-law.com
Ray C. Rutman, Creditors' Remedies; Insolvency; Commercial Real Estate; Financial Services
780-423-7246 e-mail: ray.rutman@fmc-law.com
Gordon A. Salembier, Corporate/Commercial
780-423-7232 e-mail: gordon.salembien@fmc-law.com
Dennis Schmidt, Litigation
780-970-5248 e-mail: dennis.schmidt@fmc-law.com
Darlene W. Scott, Corporate/Commercial; Commercial Real Estate
780-970-5203 e-mail: darlene.scott@fmc-law.com
Tom A. Sides, Securities
780-423-7138 e-mail: tom.sides@fmc-law.com
Don R. Sommerfeldt, Tax Law
780-970-5260 e-mail: don.sommerfeldt@fmc-law.com
Bill Sowa, Litigation
780-423-7304 e-mail: william.sowa@fmc-law.com
Lynette Stanley-Maddocks, Corporate & Commercial; Mergers & Acquisitons; Competition & Anti-Trust
780-423-7139 e-mail:
lynette.stanley-maddocks@fmc-law.com
John C. Stavropoulos, Tax Law
780-970-5298 e-mail: john.stavropoulos@fmc-law.com
Brian W. Summers, Financial Services; Insolvency; Commercial Real Estate; Litigation & Advocacy
780-423-7102 e-mail: brian.summers@fmc-law.com
Philip Tinkler, Litigation
780-423-7102 e-mail: philip.tinkler@fmc-law.com
Leah M. Tolton, Corporate/Commercial
780-423-7192 e-mail: leah.tolton@fmc-law.com
Robert J. Turner, Finance
780-423-7192 e-mail: robert.turner@fmc-law.com
Grant Vogel, Financial Services; Commercial Real Estate; Mergers & Acquisitions
780-970-5283 e-mail: grant.vogel@fmc-law.com
Shawna K. Vogel, Mergers & Acquisitions
780-970-5263 e-mail: shawna.vogel@fmc-law.com
Kimberley D. Wakefield, Litigation; Intellectual Property
780-423-7302 e-mail: kim.wakefield@fmc-law.com
Thomas W. Wakeling, Arbitration
780-423-7342 e-mail: tom.wakeling@fmc-law.com
Cristina R.C. Wendel, Insolvency
780-423-7353 e-mail: cristina.desousa@fmc-law.com
P. Daryl Wilson, Litigation
780-970-5261 e-mail: daryl.wilson@fmc-law.com
Mark Woltersdorf, Tax Law
780-423-7250 e-mail: mark.woltersdorf@fmc-law.com
Gordon J. Yakemchuk, Commercial Real Estate
780-970-5241 e-mail: gordon.yakemchuk@fmc-law.com
Barry Zalmanowitz, Competition; Litigation
780-423-7344 e-mail: barry.zalmanowitz@fmc-law.com
Herbert R. Zechel, Financial Services
780-423-7230 e-mail: herb.zechel@fmc-law.com

Fraser Milner Casgrain LLP
#3900
1, Place Ville-Marie
Montréal, QC H3B 4M7

ACCOUNTING & LAW

Fraser Milner Casgrain LLP (continued)
514-878-8800
Fax: 514-866-2241
Telex: 05-24195www.fmc-law.com
Number of Lawyers: 100
Profile: Our Financial Services Group, one of the largest at any major Canadian law firm, is recognized as a leader in the financial services sector; the group provides specialized legal advice in banking, financing, regulatory & insolvency matters to meet the changing needs & demands of our financial institution clients; in addition to advising on traditional bank lending, acting for either lenders or corporate borrowers, we have considerable experience in equipment leasing, finance transactions, synthetic leases, asset-based securitizations & financial instruments transactions; key service areas include advising domestic & international clients on the regulation of banks & other financial institutions in Canada; assistance to establish financial service businesses in Canada & incorporating Canadian domestic banking subsidiaries; structuring, negotiating & documenting credit transactions of all types including loans, syndications, trade finance, factoring, financial leasing, project financing

Finance Lawyers:
Ronald Audette, Insolvency; Financial Services
514-878-8830 e-mail: ronald.audette@fmc-law.com
Jean-Claude Bachand, Securities; Financial Services
514-878-8853 e-mail: j-c.bachand@fmc-law.com
Jean Bazin, Business Strategy
514-878-8804 e-mail: jean.bazin@fmc-law.com
Yan Besner, Commercial Real Estate, Business Strategy, Financial Services
514-878-5824 e-mail: yan.besner@fmc-law.com
Alexandre Boileau, Insolvency
514-878-5836 e-mail: alexandre.boileau@fmc-law.com
Marc Bourgeois, Wills; Estates; Trusts
514-878-8822 e-mail: marc.bourgeois@fmc-law.com
François Brais, Securities, Business Strategy
514-878-5845 e-mail: francois.brais@fmc-law.com
Michel A. Brunet, Securities, Financial Services
514-878-8832 e-mail: michel.brunet@fmc-law.com
Robert Béland, Commercial Real Estate
514-878-8867 e-mail: robert.beland@fmc-law.com
Adrien Bélanger, Business Strategy
514-878-5856 e-mail: adrien.belanger@fmc-law.com
Jean Olier Caron, Securities
514-878-5819 e-mail: oiler.caron@fmc-law.com
Mathilde Carrière, Business Strategy, Financial Services
514-878-5823 e-mail: mathilde.carriere@fmc-law.com
Maxime Cloutier, Financial Services
514-878-8861 e-mail: maxime.cloutier@fmc-law.com
Louis Clément, Financial Services
514-878-8845 e-mail: louis.clement@fmc-law.com
Alexia Colson-Duparchy, Financial Services
514-878-5848 e-mail: a.colson-duparchy@fmc-law.com
Stéphane Dansereau, Insolvency; Workout; Real Estate
514-878-8854 e-mail: stephane.dansereau@fmc-law.com
Julie Desrochers, Commercial Real Estate
514-878-8831 e-mail: julie.desrochers@fmc-law.com
Paul F. Dingle, Securities; Competition Law
514-878-8803 e-mail: paul.dingle@fmc-law.com
Pascale Dionne-Bourassa, Competition Law; Insurance
514-878-5844 e-mail: p.dionne-bourassa@fmc-law.com
Mara Karina Do Santos, Financial Services
514-878-5837 e-mail: mara.dosantos@fmc-law.com
Marie-Hélène Dufour, Insurance
514-878-5876 e-mail: m-h.dufour@fmc-law.com
Gérard Dugré, Banking Litigation
514-878-8827 e-mail: gerard.dugre@fmc-law.com
Louis Dumont, Insolvency; Workout; Litigation
514-878-8828 e-mail: louis.dumont@fmc-law.com
Jean-Pierre Dépelteau, Insurance, Financial Services
514-878-8814 e-mail: j-p.depelteau@fmc-law.com
Barbara Farina, Insolvency; Banking; Financial Services
514-878-8819 e-mail: barbara.farina@fmc-law.com
Virginie Fortin, Commercial Real Estate
514-878-5889 e-mail: virginie.fortin@fmc-law.com
Nicolas Frenette, Securities; Financial Services
514-878-5868 e-mail: nicolas.frenette@fmc-law.com
Richard Gauthier, Taxation; Wills, Estates, Trusts
514-878-8840 e-mail: richard.gauthier@fmc-law.com
Luc Giroux, Real Estate
514-878-8855 e-mail: luc.giroux@fmc-law.com
Aude Godfroy, Financial Services; Banking
514-878-5865 e-mail: aude.godfroy@fmc-law.com
Jean Groleau, Taxation
514-878-8851 e-mail: jean.groleau@fmc-law.com
Jonathan Halwagi, Securities; Financial Services
514-878-5843 e-mail: jonathan.halwagi@fmc-law.com
Sacha Haque, Competition Law; Financial Services
514-878-8817 e-mail: sache.haque@fmc-law.com
John Hurley, Commercial Real Estate
514-878-8826 e-mail: john.hurley@fmc-law.com
Claude Imbeau, Securities; Business Strategy; Financial Services
514-878-8844 e-mail: claude.imbeau@fmc-law.com
Mélanie Jacques, Insurance
514-878-5869 e-mail: melanie.jacques@fmc-law.com
Gentiane Joyal, Banking; Financial Services
514-878-5826 e-mail: gentiane.joyal@fmc-law.com
Paulina Kallas, Taxation; Wills, Estates, Trusts
514-878-5818 e-mail: paulina.kallas@fmc-law.com
Neil Katz, Banking; Financial Services; Competition Law; Commercial Real Estate
514-878-8883 e-mail: neil.katz@fmc-law.com
Morgan Kendall, Financial Services
514-878-5887 e-mail: morgan.kendall@fmc-law.com
Constantine Kyres, Taxation; Wills, Estates, Trusts, Business Strategy
514-878-8834 e-mail: constantine.kyres@fmc-law.com
Claude E. Leduc, Business Strategy
514-878-8805 e-mail: claude.leduc@fmc-law.com
E. Paul Legault, Competition Law
514-879-1124 e-mail: paul.legaul@fmc-law.com
Stephen Lloyd, Commercial Real Estate; Business Strategy; Municipal
514-878-5831 e-mail: stephen.lloyd@fmc-law.com
Christopher Main, Securities, Financial Services
514-878-8887 e-mail: christopher.main@fmc-law.com
Joseph Mastrogiuseppe, Banking; Financial Services; Insolvency
514-878-5817 e-mail: joey.mastrogiuseppe@fmc-law.com
Claude Morency, Insurance
514-878-8870 e-mail: claude.morency@fmc-law.com
Laurent Nahmiash, Insurance
514-878-8818 e-mail: laurent.nahmiash@fmc-law.com
Philipp Park, Financial Services
514-878-8872 e-mail: philipp.park@fmc-law.com
Jacques Plante, Taxation
514-878-5864 e-mail: jacques.plante@fmc-law.com
Martin Poulin, Insurance
514-878-5882 e-mail: martin.poulin@fmc-law.com
Jenny Ross, Commercial Real Estate
514-878-5870 e-mail: jenny.ross@fmc-law.com
Nicolas Roy, Securities
514-878-5861 e-mail: nicolas.roy@fmc-law.com
Vitale A. Santoro, Securities, Business Strategy, Financial Services
514-878-8810 e-mail: vitale.santoro@fmc-law.com
Pierre Setlakwe, Commercial Real Estate
514-878-8866 e-mail: pierre.setlakwe@fmc-law.com
Roger P. Simard, Insolvency
514-878-5834 e-mail: roger.simard@fmc-law.com
Charles R. Spector, Securities, Financial Services
514-878-8847 e-mail: charles.spector@fmc-law.com
Véronique Théorêt, Commercial Real Estate
514-878-8874 e-mail: veronique.theoret@fmc-law.com
Sébastien Tisserand, Insurance
514-878-8894 e-mail: sebastien.tisserand@fmc-law.com
Francis Trifiro, Banking; Financial Services
514-878-8858 e-mail: francis.trifiro@fmc-law.com
Sebastien Vilder, Banking; Financial Services
514-878-5846 e-mail: sebastien.vilder@fmc-law.com
Margaret Weltrowska, Insurance
514-878-5841 e-mail: margaret.weltrowska@fmc-law.com
Kerry Williams, Financial Services; Banking
514-878-5867 e-mail: kerry.williams@fmc-law.com

Fraser Milner Casgrain LLP
#1420
99 Bank St.
Ottawa, ON K1P 1H4
613-783-9600
Fax: 613-783-9690
Telex: 06-219825 FRASBeric.shaver@fmc-law.com
www.fmc-law.com
Number of Lawyers: 28
Profile: Our Financial Services Group, one of the largest at any major Canadian law firm, is recognized as a leader in the financial services sector; the group provides specialized legal advice in banking, financing, regulatory & insolvency matters to meet the changing needs & demands of our financial institution clients; in addition to advising on traditional bank lending, acting for either lenders or corporate borrowers, we have considerable experience in equipment leasing, finance transactions, synthetic leases, asset-based securitizations & financial instruments transactions; key service areas include advising domestic & international clients on the regulation of banks & other financial institutions in Canada; assistance to establish financial service businesses in Canada & incorporating Canadian domestic banking subsidiaries; structuring, negotiating & documenting credit transactions of all types including loans, syndications, trade finance, factoring, financial leasing, project financing

Finance Lawyers:
Susan H. Brown, Financial Services; Commercial Real Estate; Corporate/Commercial; Insolvency; Litigation & Advocacy
613-783-9658 e-mail: susan.brown@fmc-law.com
Catherine Coulter, Litigation & Advocacy; Financial Services
613-783-9660 e-mail: catherine.coulter@fmc-law.com
Thomas Houston, Securities; Mergers & Acquisitions
e-mail: tom.houston@fmc-law.com
Andrea Johnson, Securities
e-mail: andrea.johnson@fmc-law.com
Monique Lacasse, Corporate/Commercial
John F. Lee, E-commerce
David P. Little, Securities
e-mail: david.little@fmc-law.com
Shannon Miller, Financial Services; Commercial Real Estate
e-mail: shannon.miller@fmc-law.com
Tom Reaume, Mergers & Acquisitions
e-mail: tom.reaume@fmc-law.com
Philip Rimer, Insolvency; Financial Services; Commercial Real Estate
613-783-9634 e-mail: philip.rimer@fmc-law.com
Karen L. Shaver, Securities; Mergers & Acquisitions
e-mail: karen.shaver@fmc-law.com
Eric Smith, Mergers & Acquisitions
e-mail: eric.shaver@fmc-law.com

Fraser Milner Casgrain LLP
Grosvenor Bldg.
1040 West Georgia St., 15th Fl.
Vancouver, BC V6E 4H8
604-687-4460
Fax: 604-683-5214
Telex: 04-55593www.fmc-law.com
Founded: 1980
Number of Lawyers: 50
Profile: Our Financial Services Group, one of the largest at any major Canadian law firm, is recognized as a leader in the financial services sector; the group provides specialized legal advice in banking, financing, regulatory & insolvency matters to meet the changing needs & demands of our financial institution clients; in addition to advising on traditional bank lending, acting for either lenders or corporate borrowers, we have considerable experience in equipment leasing, finance transactions, synthetic leases, asset-based securitizations & financial instruments transactions; key service areas include advising domestic & international clients on the regulation of banks & other financial institutions in Canada; assistance to establish financial service businesses in Canada & incorporating Canadian domestic banking subsidiaries; structuring, negotiating & documenting credit transactions of all types including loans, syndications, trade finance, factoring, financial leasing, project financing

Finance Lawyers:
Michael R. Axford, Financial Services
604-443-7137 e-mail: michael.axford@fmc-law.com
Tibor T. Bezeredi, Financial Services
604-443-7124 e-mail: tim.bezeredi@fmc-law.com
Mary I.A. Buttery, Insolvency
604-443-7144 e-mail: mary.buttery@fmc-law.com
Jennifer D.S. Dezell, Financial Services
604-443-7133 e-mail: jen.dezell@fmc-law.com
Sherryl A. Dubo, Insolvency
604-622-5157 e-mail: sherryl.dubo@fmc-law.com
Gordon W. Esau, Financial Services
604-443-7105 e-mail: gordon.esau@fmc-law.com
Robert A. Goodrich, Corporate/Commercial
604-443-7108 e-mail: robert.goodrich@fmc-law.com
Benjamin J. Ingram, Insolvency
604-443-7123 e-mail: ben.ingram@fmc-law.com
Douglas I. Knowles, Insolvency
604-443-7104 e-mail: doug.knowles@fmc-law.com
Christine N. Matthews
604-622-5152 e-mail: christine.matthews@fmc-law.com
Christopher J. Ramsay, Insolvency
604-622-5151 e-mail: chris.ramsay@fmc-law.com

John R. Sandrelli, Insolvency
604-443-7132 e-mail: john.sandrelli@fmc-law.com
Juliet D.W. Smith, Financial Services
604-443-7135 e-mail: juliet.smith@fmc-law.com

Gordon J. Fretwell Law Corp.

#1780
400 Burrard St.
Vancouver, BC V6C 3A6
604-689-1280
Fax: 604-689-1288
gord@fretwell.ca
Number of Lawyers: 1

Finance Lawyers:
Gordon J. Fretwell, Securities

David G. Fysh

520 Springbank Dr.
London, ON N6J 1G8
519-472-3974
Fax: 519-472-3756
david@davidfysh.com
www.davidfysh.com
Founded: 1994
Number of Lawyers: 1

Finance Lawyers:
David G. Fysh, Small Business Law

Gaertner Tobin LLP

#400
144 Front St. West
Toronto, ON M5J 2L7
416-599-7700
Fax: 416-599-7800
mkent@gtllp.com
www.gtllp.com
Number of Lawyers: 6

Finance Lawyers:
Bruce Baron
Arie Gaertner
Peter H. Math
Dennis J. Tobin
Alexander P. Torgov

Gagné Letarte

#400
79, boul René-Lévesque est
Québec, QC G1R 5N5
418-522-7900
Fax: 418-523-7900
www.gagneletarte.qc.ca
Number of Lawyers: 11
Profile: Bankruptcy & Insolvency Law; Mergers & Acquisitions; Cooperatives; Non-profit Corporations; Banking Law; Financing; Venture Capital; Joint Venture; Partnerships; Franchising; Securities; Tax; Reorganizations; Trusts

Finance Lawyers:
Jacques Beaudet, Business Law
Lina Beaulieu, Business Law
Daniel Cantin, Business Law
J. Michel Doyon, Business Law
Nadia El-Ghandouri, Business Law
Pierre-Philip Garneau, Business Law
Marie Houde, Business Law
Lina Lalancette, Business Law
Jean Pelletier, Business Law
Louis Trudelle, Business Law
Marc Watters, Business Law

Garfin Zeidenberg LLP

Yonge Norton Centre #800
5255 Yonge St.
Toronto, ON M2N 6P4
416-512-8000
Fax: 416-512-9992
877-529-9910
smc@gzlegal.com
www.gzlegal.com
Number of Lawyers: 10

Finance Lawyers:
Stephen M. Cohen, Corporate; Commercial

Gasee, Cohen & Youngman, Barrister & Solicitor

#200
65 Queen St. West
Toronto, ON M5H 2M5
416-363-3351
Fax: 416-363-0252
youngman@gcylaw.com
www.gcylaw.com
Number of Lawyers: 6
Profile: Civil litigation, debt collection

Finance Lawyers:
Mark Youngman

Getz Prince Wells LLP

#1810
1111 West Georgia St.
Vancouver, BC V6E 4M3
604-685-6367
Fax: 604-685-9798
admin@getzpw.com
www.getzpw.com
Number of Lawyers: 8

Finance Lawyers:
Gerald A. Cuttler, Corporate/Commercial/Securities Litigation
604-665-4297 e-mail: gerry@getzpw.com
Leon Getz, Corporate Finance; Mergers & Acquisitions
604-665-4290 e-mail: leon@getzpw.com
D. Jeff Larkins, Corporate Finance; Mergers & Acquisitions
604-665-4293 e-mail: jeff@getzpw.com
Dana H. Prince, Corporate/Commercial/Securities Litigation
604-665-4291 e-mail: dana@getzpw.com
Zahra H. Ramji, Corporate Finance; Mergers & Acquisitions
604-665-4295 e-mail: zahra@getzpw.com
Sunny Rothschild, Corporate/Commercial
604-665-4296 e-mail: sunny@getzpw.com
Chris Theodoropoulos, Corporate Finance; Mergers & Acquisitions; Corporate Restructuring
604-685-4298 e-mail: chris@getzpw.com
Drew B. Wells, Corporate Finance; Mergers & Acquisitions
604-665-4292 e-mail: drew@getzpw.com

Gilbert's LLP

49 Wellington St. East
Toronto, ON M5E 1C9
416-703-1100
Fax: 416-703-7422
tim@gilbertslaw.ca
Number of Lawyers: 4

Finance Lawyers:
Jeffrey Johnstone

Gilbert, McGloan, Gillis

PO Box 7174
22 King St.
Saint John, NB E2L 4S6
506-634-3600
Fax: 506-634-3612
888-246-4529
gmg@gmglaw.com
www.gmglaw.com
Founded: 1976
Number of Lawyers: 12

Finance Lawyers:
John E. Bujold, Property; Corporate
Catherine A. Fawcett, Insurance; Corporate/Commercial
A.G. Warwick Gilbert, Insurance
Rodney J. Gillis, Corporate/Commercial; Bankruptcy & Insolvency
John C. Gillis, Corporate/Commercial; Banking & Financial
Anne F. MacNeill, Wills & Estates
Nancy J. Martel, Corporate/Commercial
Tricia L. Osborne, Corporate/Commercial; Tax
Claire B.N. Porter, Wills & Estates
David N. Rogers, Insurance
J. Danie Roy, Insurance

Gilbertson Davis Emerson LLP

#2020
20 Queen St. West
Toronto, ON M5H 3R3
416-979-2020
Fax: 416-979-1285
office@gilbertsondavis.com
www.gilbertsondavis.com
Founded: 1982
Number of Lawyers: 8

Finance Lawyers:
James E. Adamson
e-mail: jadamson@gilbertsondavis.com

Goldberg Stroud LLP

486 Gladstone Ave.
Ottawa, ON K2P 0P7
613-237-4922
Fax: 613-237-2920
info@gsklaw.com
www.gsklaw.com
Founded: 1959
Number of Lawyers: 5
Profile: Commercial Law; Condominium Law; Real Estate; Wills & Estates; Civil Litigation; Leasing

Finance Lawyers:
Arnell Goldberg, Real Estate; Commercial Law
613-237-4922 e-mail: agoldberg@gsklaw.com
David W. Hollingsworth, Litigation
613-237-4922 e-mail: dhollingsworth@gsklaw.com
C. Warren Stroud, Real Estate
613-237-4922 e-mail: wstroud@gsklaw.com
Charles Wiseman, Estate Planning; Corporate Commercial
613-237-4922 e-mail: cwiseman@gsklaw.com

Goodman and Carr LLP

#2300
200 King St. West
Toronto, ON M5H 3W5
416-595-2300
Fax: 416-595-0567
800-890-7319
mail@goodmancarr.com
www.goodmancarr.com
Founded: 1965
Number of Lawyers: 104
Profile: Goodman & Carr's financial services group represents Canadian & international lenders, investors & borrowers, including chartered & foreign banks, bank holding companies, government, institutional, individual & financial intermediary borrowers

Finance Lawyers:
Anna Balinsky, Business Law
Kenneth Beallor, Leasing
Diane Brooks, Business Law
416-595-2366 e-mail: dbrooks@goodmancarr.com
David W. Chodikoff, Tax Litigation
Michael Herman, Corporate Finance
416-595-2422 e-mail: mherman@goodmancarr.com
Steve Watson, Corporate & Commercial
416-595-2379 e-mail: swatson@goodmancarr.com

Goodmans LLP

#2400
250 Yonge St.
Toronto, ON M5B 2M6
416-979-2211
Fax: 416-979-1234
info@goodmans.ca
www.goodmans.ca
Founded: 1917
Number of Lawyers: 185
Profile: Goodmans is a leading Canadian law firm, well-recognized across Canada & internationally for its excellence & market leadership in large-scale corporate transactions; Goodmans is a full-service business law firm that offers clients a wide range of services & expertise in all of the major business law areas, including: Broadcasting, Telecommunications & New Media; Commercial Real Estate; Corporate & Commercial; Corporate Restructuring; Corporate Finance & Securities; Litigation; Mergers & Acquisitions; Municipal, Planning & Property Tax; Pensions; Trusts & Estates & Tax; with over 175 lawyers, Goodmans provides a complete spectrum of legal advice & representation to domestic & foreign business clients ranging from emerging technology companies to financial institutions & conglomerates from offices in Toronto & Vancouver

Finance Lawyers:
Gesta A. Abols, Corporate Finance; Securities
416-597-4186 e-mail: gabols@goodmans.ca

Goodmans LLP (continued)
Christina Alaimo, Corporate; Finance; Securities
416-597-4169 e-mail: calaimo@goodmans.ca
William V. Alcamo, Corporate & Commercial
416-597-4100 e-mail: walcamo@goodmans.ca
Jean Anderson, Financial Services
416-597-4297 e-mail: janderson@goodmans.ca
Greg Aronson, Banking & Financial Services
Justin Beber, Competition; Corporate & Commercial; Corporate Finance & Securities; Mergers & Acquisitions; REITs & Income Funds
416-597-4252 e-mail: jbeber@goodmans.ca
Scott Bell, Corporate & Commercial; Corporate Finance & Securities; Mergers & Acquisitions
416-597-4253 e-mail: sbell@goodmans.ca
Paolo Berard, Mergers & Acquisitions
David Bish, Corporate Restructuring
416-597-6276 e-mail: dbish@goodmans.ca
Derek Bulas, Corporate Restructuring
461-597-5914 e-mail: dbulas@goodmans.ca
Jay A. Carfagnini, Banking & Finance Law
416-597-4107 e-mail: jcarfagnini@goodmans.ca
Robert J. Chadwick, Banking & Finance Law
416-597-4285 e-mail: rchadwick@goodmans.ca
Lawrence Chernin, Corporate Finance; Securities
416-597-5903 e-mail: lchernin@goodmans.ca
Jeff Citron, Banking; Finance; Corporate; Securities
416-597-4256 e-mail: jcitron@goodmans.ca
Krista Coburn, Corporate; Finance; Securities
416-597-5144 e-mail: kcoburn@goodmans.ca
John Connon, Corporate; Finance; Securities
416-597-5499 e-mail: jconnon@goodmans.ca
Caroline Cook, Corporate; Finance; Securities
416-597-5926 e-mail: ccook@goodmans.ca
Caterina Costa, Corporate Restructuring
416-597-6273 e-mail: ccosta@goodmans.ca
Mario Di Fiore, Banking & Finance Law; Corporate & Commercial
416-597-4158 e-mail: mdifiore@goodmans.ca
Sarah Diamond, Mergers & Acquisitions
Brian F. Empey, Banking & Finance Law
416-597-4194 e-mail: bempey@goodmans.ca
Jay Feldman, Banking & Finance Law; Corporate & Commercial
416-597-4151 e-mail: jfeldman@goodmans.ca
Jonathan Feldman, Mergers & Acquisitions
Sheldon Freeman, Corporate Finance; Securities
416-597-6273 e-mail: sfreeman@goodmans.ca
Susan A. Garvie, Corporate Finance & Securities; Financial Services; Mergers & Acquisitions; Corporate & Commercial
416-597-4141 e-mail: sgarvie@goodmans.ca
Allan Goodman, Corporate Finance; Securities
416-597-4243 e-mail: agoodman@goodmans.ca
William (Bill) Gorman, Corporate Finance; Securities
416-597-4118 e-mail: wgorman@goodmans.ca
Brenda Gosselin, Corporate & Commercial
416-597-4254 e-mail: bgosselin@goodmans.ca
Avi Greenspoon, Corporate Finance; Securities
416-597-4236 e-mail: agreenspoon@goodmans.ca
Stephen H. Halperin, Corporate; Finance; Securities
416-597-4115 e-mail: shalperin@goodmans.ca
Peter Hawkins, Mergers & Acquisitions
Tim Heeney, Corporate Finance; Securities
416-597-4195 e-mail: theeney@goodmans.ca
Gail Jaffe, Mergers & Acquisitions
Karen Karvat, Corporate; Finance; Securities
416-597-4264 e-mail: kkarvat@goodmans.ca
Jonathan Lampe, Corporate; Finance; Securities
416-597-4128 e-mail: jlampe@goodmans.ca
Dale H. Lastman, Corporate; Finance; Securities
416-597-4129 e-mail: dlastman@goodmans.ca
Victor Liu, Corporate; Finance; Securities
416-597-5141 e-mail: vliu@goodmans.ca
Pollyanna Lord, Corporate Finance; Securities
416-597-4291 e-mail: plord@goodmans.ca
Scott MacIntosh, Mergers & Acquisitions
Kari MacKay, Corporate Finance; Securities
416-597-6282 e-mail: kmackay@goodmans.ca
Lisa Mantello, Banking & Finance Law
416-849-6013 e-mail: lmantello@goodmans.ca
David J. Matlow, Corporate; Finance; Securities
416-597-4147 e-mail: dmatlow@goodmans.ca
Neill May, Corporate; Finance; Securities
416-597-4187 e-mail: nmay@goodmans.ca
Grant McGlaughlin, Corporate; Finance; Securities
416-597-4199 e-mail: gmcglaughlin@goodmans.ca
Shevaun McGrath, Corporate; Finance; Securities
416-597-4217 e-mail: smcgrath@goodmans.ca
Juli Morrow, Banking & Finance Law
416-597-4135 e-mail: jmorrow@goodmans.ca
Frederick L. Myers, Corporate Restructuring
416-597-5923 e-mail: fmyers@goodmans.ca
David Nadler, Banking & Finance Law
416-597-4246 e-mail: dnadler@goodmans.ca
David Nathanson, Corporate Finance; Securities
416-849-6890 e-mail: dnathanson@goodmans.ca
Brendan O'Neill, Corporate Restructuring
416-849-6017 e-mail: boneill@goodmans.ca
Karen Paguandas, Banking & Financial Services
Michael Partridge, Corporate; Finance; Securities
416-597-5498 e-mail: mpartridge@goodmans.ca
Joseph Pasquariello, Financial Services; Corporate Restructuring
416-597-4216 e-mail: jpasquariello@goodmans.ca
Christa Rambert, Corporate Finance; Securities
416-849-6022 e-mail: crambert@goodmans.ca
Kirk Rauliuk, Corporate Finance; Securities
416-849-6018 e-mail: krauliuk@goodmans.ca
Celia K. Rhea, Financial Services; Corporate & Commercial; Mergers & Acquisitions
416-597-4178 e-mail: crhea@goodmans.ca
James A. Riley, Banking & Financial Services
Eric Robb, Corporate Restructuring
416-597-5909 e-mail: erobb@goodmans.ca
Patricia A. Robinson, Estates; Trusts
416-597-4144 e-mail: probinson@goodmans.ca
William P. Rosenfeld, Corporate Finance; Securities
416-597-4145 e-mail: wrosenfeld@goodmans.ca
Brad Ross, Corporate; Finance; Securities
416-849-6010 e-mail: bross@goodmans.ca
Meredith Roth, Corporate; Finance; Securities
416-597-6260 e-mail: meroth@goodmans.ca
Michelle Roth, Corporate Finance; Securities
416-597-6261 e-mail: miroth@goodmans.ca
Susan Rowland, Corporate Restructuring
416-597-4277 e-mail: srowland@goodmans.ca
Gale Rubenstein, Financial Services; Corporate Restructuring
416-597-4148 e-mail: grubenstein@goodmans.ca
Rosella Santilli, Banking; Finance
416-597-5490 e-mail: rsantilli@goodmans.ca
Joel S. Schachter, Banking; Corporate; Finance; Securities
416-597-4152 e-mail: jschachter@goodmans.ca
Candy S. Schaffel, Corporate Restructuring
416-597-4153 e-mail: cschaffel@goodmans.ca
Jaclyn Seidman, Mergers & Acquisitions
Jennifer Sernaker, Corporate; Finance; Securities
416-597-5161 e-mail: jsernaker@goodmans.ca
Mona Shah, Corporate Restructuring
416-849-6024 e-mail: mshah@goodmans.ca
Neil M. Sheehy, Corporate Finance; Securities
416-597-4229 e-mail: nsheehy@goodmans.ca
Mariana Silva, Pensions; Trusts & Estates
416-597-5148 e-mail: msilva@goodmans.ca
Mark Spiro, Corporate; Finance; Securities
416-597-5140 e-mail: mspiro@goodmans.ca
Jana Steele, Pensions, Trusts & Estates
416-597-6274 e-mail: jsteele@goodmans.ca
Mark A. Surchin, Financial Services; Corporate & Commercial; Mergers & Acquisitions
416-597-4165 e-mail: msurchin@goodmans.ca
Ryan Szainwald, Corporate Finance; Securities
416-849-6892 e-mail: rszainwald@goodmans.ca
Samantha Traub, Corporate; Finance; Securities
416-597-5493 e-mail: straub@goodmans.ca
Robert Vaux, Corporate Finance; Securities
416-597-6265 e-mail: rvaux@goodmans.ca
Melaney Wagner, Corporate Restructuring
416-597-4258 e-mail: mwagner@goodmans.ca
Caroline Wang, Mergers & Acquisitions
Kenneth R. Wiener, Corporate Finance; Securities
416-597-4106 e-mail: kwiener@goodmans.ca
Kevin Wilson, Corporate Finance; Securities
416-849-6019 e-mail: kwilson@goodmans.ca
Brian Wise, Banking; Finance
416-849-6012 e-mail: bwise@goodmans.ca
David Wiseman, Banking & Finance Law
416-597-6266 e-mail: dwiseman@goodmans.ca
Vanessa Yeung, Banking & Financial Services
Catherine Youdan, Corporate; Finance; Securities
416-597-6283 e-mail: cyoudan@goodmans.ca
Susan C. Zimmerman, Corporate & Restructuring
416-597-4171 e-mail: szimmerman@goodmans.ca

Goodmans LLP
#1900
355 Burrard St.
Vancouver, BC V6C 2G8
604-682-7737
Fax: 604-682-7131
Founded: 1996
Number of Lawyers: 9
Profile: Business law firm specializing in corporate finance, mergers & acquisitions, securities & commercial law

Finance Lawyers:
Karlena Bowker, Corporate Finance; Securities
604-608-4555 e-mail: kbowker@goodmans.ca
Paul Goldman, Corporate Finance; Securities
604-608-4550 e-mail: pgoldman@goodmans.ca
Jonathan O'Connor, Corporate Finance; Securities
604-608-4580 e-mail: joconnor@goodmans.ca
David L. Redford, Corporate Finance; Securities
604-608-4560 e-mail: dredford@goodmans.ca
Steven G. Robertson, Corporate Finance; Securities
604-608-4552 e-mail: srobertson@goodmans.ca
Bruce M. Wright, Corporate Finance; Securities
604-608-4551 e-mail: bwright@goodmans.ca

Goodwin & Mark
#217
713 Columbia St.
New Westminster, BC V3M 1B2
604-522-9884
Fax: 604-526-8044
gm@goodmark.ca
Founded: 1953
Number of Lawyers: 5
Profile: Corporate/Commercial; Wills; Trusts; Estates

Finance Lawyers:
Virginia Hayes, Wills; Trust; Estates

Goulin & Patrick
500 Windsor Ave.
Windsor, ON N9A 6Y5
519-258-8073
Fax: 519-977-0694
goulinpa@wincom.net
Founded: 1997
Number of Lawyers: 2

Finance Lawyers:
Bonnie G. Patrick, Corporate Commercial Law; Estate Planning; Real Estate

Gowling Lafleur Henderson LLP
Scotia Centre #1400
700 - 2nd St. SW
Calgary, AB T2P 4V5
403-298-1000
Fax: 403-263-9193
info@gowlings.com
www.gowlings.com
Founded: 1972
Number of Lawyers: 100
Profile: Gowlings is a leading Canadian law firm with 700 professionals & offices across Canada & in Moscow, an acknowledged leader in intellectual property law. Provides services in business law & advocacy across a broad range of industries & in virtually every area of law.

Finance Lawyers:
Eli D. Abergel, Business Law
403-298-1874 e-mail: ali.abergel@gowlings.com
Tina M. Antony, Corporate Finance
403-298-1075 e-mail: tina.antony@gowlings.com
John Ballem, Business Law
403-292-9801 e-mail: john.ballem@gowlings.com
Gail P. Black, Tax; Estates & Trusts
403-298-1856 e-mail: gail.black@gowlings.com
David J. Brett, Business Law
403-298-1804 e-mail: david.brett@gowlings.com
Jeff W. Bright, Business Law
403-292-9802 e-mail: jeff.bright@gowlings.com
Jo-Anne M. Bund, Business Law
403-298-1809 e-mail: jo-anne.bund@gowlings.com
Lisa Buriak, Corporate Commercial
403-298-1855 e-mail: lisa.buriak@gowlings.com

John S. Burns, Business Law
403-298-9818 e-mail: john.burns@gowlings.com
Melanie Choch, Business Law
403-298-1039 e-mail: melanie.choch@gowlings.com
Richard W. Clark, Business Law
403-298-1990 e-mail: richard.clark@gowlings.com
Thomas S. Cumming, Lending; Insolvency, Restructuring & Creditors' Rights
403-298-1938 e-mail: tom.cumming@gowlings.com
Syliva E. De Angelis, Business Law
403-292-9876 e-mail: sylvia.deangelis@gowlings.com
Jimmi Duce, Business Law
403-298-1956 e-mail: jimmi.duce@gowlings.com
Jeffrey E. Dyck, Corporate Commercial; Corporate Finance & Securities
403-298-1052 e-mail: jeffrey.dyck@gowlings.com
Eugene Friess, Business Law
403-298-1818 e-mail: eugene.freiss@gowlings.com
Richard J.C. Grant, Business Law
403-298-1062 e-mail: richard.grant@gowlings.com
Robert R. Hagerman, Corporate Commercial; Tax; Estates & Trusts
403-298-1080 e-mail: robert.hagerman@gowlings.com
H. Ronald Hansford, Business Law
403-298-9862 e-mail: ronald.hansford@gowlings.com
Brian J. Hughson, Corporate Commercial
403-292-9814 e-mail: brian.hughson@gowlings.com
John N. Iredale, Corporate Commercial; Corporate Finance & Securities
403-298-1850 e-mail: john.iredale@gowlings.com
Alan Jochelson, Business Law
403-298-1837 e-mail: alan.jochelson@gowlings.com
Peter S. Jull, Insolvency, Restructuring & Creditors' Rights
403-292-9807 e-mail: peter.jull@gowlings.com
Kevin W. Keyes, Corporate Commercial; Real Estate
403-298-1920 e-mail: kevin.keyes@gowlings.com
Kurtis T. Kulman, Corporate Commercial; Corporate Finance & Securities
403-298-1830 e-mail: kurtis.kulman@gowlings.com
Erin Lee, Business Law
403-298-1819 e-mail: erin.lee@gowlings.com
Evan D. Low, Business Law
403-298-1958 e-mail: evan.low@gowlings.com
Michael J. Major, Business Law
403-292-9871 e-mail: mj.major@gowlings.com
Shashi B. Malik, Corporate Commercial; Tax
403-298-1822 e-mail: shashi.malik@gowlings.com
Donald F. Mazankowski, Business Law
403-298-1060 e-mail: don.mazankowski@gowlings.com
Jason McCormick, Business Law
403-298-1872 e-mail: jason.mccormick@gowlings.com
Robert D. McCue, Tax
403-298-1070 e-mail: robert.mccue@gowlings.com
Richard W. Myers, Corporate Commercial; Lending
403-298-1068 e-mail: richard.myers@gowlings.com
Forbes Newman, Business Law
403-292-9809 e-mail: forbes.newman@gowlings.com
H. Vincent O'Connor, Business Law
403-298-1827 e-mail: vincent.oconnor@gowlings.com
Katherine M. O'Connor, Business Law
403-298-1086 e-mail: katherine.o'connor@gowlings.com
Lorne R. O'Reilly, Business Law
403-298-1907 e-mail: lorne.oreilly@gowlings.com
Andrew L. Oppenheim, Corporate Commercial; Lending; Real Estate
403-298-1064 e-mail: andrew.oppenheim@gowlings.com
Gregory E. Peterson, Corporate Commercial
403-292-9812 e-mail: gregory.peterson@gowlings.com
L. Alan Rautenberg, Tax
403-298-1857 e-mail: alan.rautenberg@gowlings.com
Nick F. Salaysay, Corporate Commercial
403-298-1041 e-mail: nick.salaysay@gowlings.com
Clark Schow, Business Law
403-298-1809 e-mail: clark.schow@gowlings.com
Eric L. Semmens, Corporate Commercial; Real Estate
403-298-1040 e-mail: eric.semmens@gowlings.com
John R. Sherman, Business Law
403-292-9821 e-mail: john.sherman@gowlings.com
Patricia Steele, Business Law
403-298-1908 e-mail: patricia.steele@gowlings.com
Darren J. Taylor, Business Law
403-298-1091 e-mail: darren.taylor@gowlings.com
Scott D. Whitby, Business Law
403-298-1085 e-mail: scott.whitby@gowlings.com
Bennett K. Wong, Business Law
403-298-1925 e-mail: bennett.wong@gowlings.com
Brian A. Yaworski, Business Law
403-298-1992 e-mail: brian.yaworski@gowlings.com

Gowling Lafleur Henderson LLP
One Main St. West
Hamilton, ON L8P 4Z5
905-540-8208
Fax: 905-528-5833
www.gowlings.com
Number of Lawyers: 28

Finance Lawyers:
Lawrence Bremner, Business Law
905-540-3265 e-mail: larry.bremner@gowlings.com
Victor Buza, Corporate Commercial
905-540-3263 e-mail: victor.buza@gowlings.com
Louis A. Frapporti, Business Law
905-540-3262 e-mail: louis.frapporti@gowlings.com
Terry Moffatt, Business Law
905-540-3297 e-mail: terrance.moffatt@gowlings.com
Rina Patel, Business Law
905-540-3243 e-mail: rina.patel@gowlings.com
Alex Spyridakis, Business Law
905-540-7103 e-mail: alex.spyridakis@gowlings.com
Mark Tamminga, Business Law
William J. Walker, Insolvency, Restructuring & Creditors' Rights; Recovery
905-540-3250 e-mail: bill.walker@gowlings.com
Roderick Wilkinson, Banking & Restructuring
905-540-7111 e-mail: rod.wilkinson@gowlings.com

Gowling Lafleur Henderson LLP
#1020
50 Queen St. North
Kitchener, ON N2H 6M2
519-576-6910
Fax: 519-576-6030
info@gowlings.com
Number of Lawyers: 33

Finance Lawyers:
Sharon A. Bennett, Tax
519-569-4563 e-mail: sharon.bennett@gowlings.com
Bruce S. Dawe, Commercial Litigation; Insurance & Product Liability; Insolvency, Restructuring & Creditors' Rights
519-575-7524 e-mail: bruce.dawe@gowlings.com
Viona M. Duncan, Business Law
519-575-7516 e-mail: viona.duncan@gowlings.com
F. John Durdan, Business Law
519-575-7535 e-mail: john.durdan@gowlings.com
V. Sean Gomes, Business Law
519-575-7541 e-mail: sean.gomes@gowlings.com
John M. Harper, Counsel, Business Law
519-575-7504 e-mail: jack.harper@gowlings.com
John D. Hiscock, Business Law
519-575-7543 e-mail: john.hiscock@gowlings.com
Thomas K. Hunter, Corporate Commercial
519-575-7503 e-mail: tom.hunter@gowlings.com
Rose M. Johnson, Business Law
519-575-7546 e-mail: rose.johnson@gowlings.com
Peter M. Koch, Corporate Commercial; Corporate Finance & Securities
519-575-7540 e-mail: peter.koch@gowlings.com
Bryce A. Kraeker, Corporate Finance
519-575-7545 e-mail: bryce.kraeker@gowlings.com
C. Thomas Lebrun, Business Law
519-575-7510 e-mail: tom.lebrun@gowlings.com
Rosa Lupo, Business Law
519-575-7511 e-mail: rosa.lupo@gowlings.com
Gordon A. Mackay, Sr., Corporate Commercial
519-575-7508 e-mail: gordon.mackay@gowlings.com
Manuel A. Martins, Corporate Commercial; Real Estate
519-575-7542 e-mail: manuel.martins@gowlings.com
W. David Petras, Corporate Commercial
519-575-7506 e-mail: david.petras@gowlings.com
Terrence R. Williston, Corporate Commercial; Tax
519-575-7536 e-mail: terry.williston@gowlings.com

Gowling Lafleur Henderson LLP
1, Place Ville Marie, 37e étage
Montréal, QC H3B 3P4
514-878-9641
Fax: 514-878-1450
www.gowlings.com
Founded: 1887
Number of Lawyers: 78
Profile: Securities; Corporate; Mergers & Acquisitions; Structured Finance; Commercial Lending & Secured Financings

Finance Lawyers:
Nai@#m Alexandre Antaki, Business Law
Marie-France Béland, Business Law
Martin Cauchon, Business Law
Ariane Champoux-Cadoche, Business Law
Douglas W. Clarke, Business Law
Robert Dorion, Business Law
Beno(140t Gascon, Corporate Commercial; Corporate Finance & Securities
514-392-9535 e-mail: benoit.gascon@gowlings.com
Martine Guimond, Commercial Corporate; Corporate Finance & Securities
514-392-9583 e-mail: martine.guimond@gowlings.com
Pierre-André Hamel, Business Law
514-392-9523 e-mail: pah@lafleurbrown.ca
David B. Kierans, Business Law
514-392-9551 e-mail: dbk@lafleurbrown.ca
Simon Labrecque, Business Law
Marc Laflèche, Corporate Commercial; Corporate Finance & Securities
514-392-9546 e-mail: marc.lafleche@gowlings.com
Alain Lalonde, Business Law
514-392-9547 e-mail: al@lafleurbrown.ca
Henri Lanctôt, Corporate Commercial; Corporate Finance & Securities
514-392-9566 e-mail: henri.lanctot@gowlings.com
Jean-François LeMay, Business Law
514-392-9561 e-mail: jfl@lafleurbrown.ca
Luc Lissoir, Corporate Commercial; Corporate Finance & Securities
514-392-9571 e-mail: luc.lissoir@gowlings.com
Pierre Lissoir, Corporate Commercial; Corporate Finance & Securities
514-392-9543 e-mail: pierre.lissoir@gowlings.com
Claude J. Melançon, Corporate Commercial; Real Estate
514-392-9542 e-mail: claude.melancon@gowlings.com
Alain Morin, Business Law
Sophie Morin, Business Law
Yves Ouellette, Tax
514-392-9521 e-mail: yves.ouellette@gowlings.com
John A. Penhale, Corporate Commercial; Real Estate; Lending
514-392-9548 e-mail: john.penhale@gowlings.com
Jean-Philippe Riverin, Business Law
Charles-Antoine Robitaille, Corporate Commercial; Corporate Finance & Securities
514-392-9584 e-mail: charlesantoine.robitaille@gowlings.com
Elyse Rosen, Commercial Litigation; Insolvency, Restructuring & Creditors' Rights
514-392-9585 e-mail: elyse.rosen@gowlings.com
Richard J. Roy, Corporate Commercial
514-392-9554 e-mail: richard.roy@gowlings.com
Leonard Serafini, Corporate Commercial; Corporate Finance & Securities
514-392-9534 e-mail: leonard.serafini@gowlings.com
Gilles Séguin, Tax; Estates & Trusts
514-392-9559 e-mail: gilles.seguin@gowlings.com

Gowling Lafleur Henderson LLP
#2600
160 Elgin St.
Ottawa, ON K1P 1C3
613-233-1781
Fax: 613-563-9869
info@gowlings.com
www.gowlings.com
Founded: 1887
Number of Lawyers: 163
Profile: Comprised of two national practice groups, Financial Regulatory & Financial Services, the Financial Institutions Industry Group offers legal expertise in all relevant areas; our clients include government departments & industry associations as well as domestic & international financial institutions such as Schedule I & II banks, credit unions & insurance companies; the combination of regulatory & transactional expertise gives this group a depth of knowledge & breadth of experience that is unsurpassed; playing a pivotal role in the development & drafting of federal regulations affecting the financial sector, our professionals offer first-hand understanding of current regulatory matters & expert insight into future trends

Finance Lawyers:

Gowling Lafleur Henderson LLP (continued)

Martin Aquilina, Corporate Finance; Securities; Public Mergers & Acquisitions
613-786-0170 e-mail: martin.aquilina@gowlings.com
Louis R. Benoit, Business Law; Corporate Commercial
613-786-0160 e-mail: louis.benoit@gowlings.com
Michael Boehm, Corporate Finance & Securities; Mergers & Acquisitions; Venture Capital; Private Equity
613-783-8843 e-mail: michael.boehm@gowlings.com
Hy Calof, Business Law; Financial Regulatory Law; Corporate Commercial
613-786-0193 e-mail: hy.calof@gowlings.com
Carole Chouinard, Tax
613-786-8668 e-mail: carole.chouinard@gowlings.com
Michael R. Clancy, Business Law; Franchise Law; Corporate Commercial
613-786-0214 e-mail: michael.clancy@gowlings.com
Hugh R. Cowan, Corporate Commercial, Lending, Financial Regulatory Law, Secured Financing, Export Finance, International Lending
613-786-0118 e-mail: hugh.cowan@gowlings.com
Stephen Cross, Business Law
613-786-8661 e-mail: stephen.cross@gowlings.com
Anne M.K. Curtis, Financial Services, Real Estate, Secured Financing
613-786-0146 e-mail: anne.curtis@gowlings.com
Keith T. Desjardins, Business Law; Corporate Commercial
613-786-0249 e-mail: keith.desjardins@gowlings.com
Cynthia L. Elderkin, Corporate Commercial, Lending, Secured Financing, Licence Agreements
613-786-0179 e-mail: cynthia.elderkin@gowlings.com
Michael M.K. Fitzpatrick, Business Law; Estates & Trusts
613-786-0201 e-mail: michael.fitzpatrick@gowlings.com
J. Scott Fletcher, Corporate Commercial, Corporate Finance, Securities, Mergers & Acquisitions, Privatizations
613-786-0167 e-mail: scott.fletcher@gowlings.com
Andrew A. Foti, Corporate Commercial, Corporate Finance, Securities
613-786-0198 e-mail: andrew.foti@gowlings.com
Christopher A. Fournier, Lending, Insolvency, Restructuring & Creditors' Rights, Real Estate, Banking, Joint Ventures
613-786-0113 e-mail: christopher.fournier@gowlings.com
Ronald G. Gravelle, Tax, Estate Planning
613-786-0120 e-mail: ronald.gravelle@gowlings.com
Jamal Hejazi, Tax; Transfer Pricing
613-786-8660 e-mail: yamal.hejazi@gowlings.com
Dale Hill, Tax Services; Transfer Pricing
613-786-0102 e-mail: dale.hill@gowlings.com
W. Anderson Joyce, Corporate Commercial, Lending, Insovency, Joint Venture Agreements
613-786-0121 e-mail: w.anderson.joyce@gowlings.com
Wayne A. Kerrick, Financial Services, Real Estate, Secured Lending, Mortgage Enforcement
613-786-0184 e-mail: wayne.kerrick@gowlings.com
Mark Kirkey, Tax; Transfer Pricing
613-786-8688 e-mail: mark.kirkey@gowlings.com
Monte MacGregor, Corporate Commercial, Corporate Finance, Securities, Secured Lending
613-786-0109 e-mail: monte.macgregor@gowlings.com
Sean Moore, Financial Regulatory Law
613-786-0216 e-mail: sean.moore@gowlings.com
Michael S. Polowin, Business Law; Commercial; Financing
613-786-0158 e-mail: michael.polowin@gowlings.com
E. Michael Power, Corporate Commercial, Security, Privacy
613-786-8685 e-mail: michael.power@gowlings.com
Lewis Retik, Business Law; Corporate Commercial & Regulatory Law
613-783-8849 e-mail: lewis.retik@gowlings.com
Julian C. Robertson, Business Law; Corporate Finance; Securities; Public Mergers & Acquisitions; Venture Capital; Private Equity
613-786-8696 e-mail: julian.robertson@gowlings.com
Laurie J. Sanderson, Business Law
613-786-0169 e-mail: laurie.sanderson@gowlings.com
Lorne W. Segal, Corporate Commercial; Lending; Insolvency, Restructuring & Creditors' Rights
613-786-0141 e-mail: lorne.segal@gowlings.com
Mark L. Siegel, Corporate Commercial; Tax
613-786-0136 e-mail: mark.siegel@gowlings.com
Ned A. Steinman, Business Law; Franchise
613-786-8676 e-mail: ned.steinman@gowlings.com
P. Thomas Taggart, Corporate Commercial; Real Estate; Securities; Mergers & Acquisitions; Shareholder Rights
613-786-0129 e-mail: tom.taggart@gowlings.com
Joel B. Taller, Business Law
613-786-0163 e-mail: joel.taller@gowlings.com
Wayne B. Warren, Corporate Commercial; Corporate Finance; Securities; Mergers & Acquisitions
613-786-0191 e-mail: wayne.warren@gowlings.com
Benjamin Westelman, Corporate Commerical; Mergers & Acquisitions
613-783-8829 e-mail: benjamin.westelman@gowlings.com

Gowling Lafleur Henderson LLP

1 First Canadian Place #1600
100 King St. West
Toronto, ON M5X 1G5
416-862-7525
Fax: 416-862-7661
www.gowlings.com
Number of Lawyers: 163

Finance Lawyers:

Kevin R. Aalto, Banking Litigation
416-862-4307 e-mail: kevin.aalto@gowlings.com
Neil S. Abbott, Insolvency, Restructuring & Creditors' Rights; Recovery
416-862-4376 e-mail: neil.abbott@gowlings.com
Christopher Alam, Business Law
416-369-4590 e-mail: christopher.alam@gowlings.com
Michael J. Anderson, Business Law
416-369-7235 e-mail: michael.anderson@gowlings.com
Paul R. Basso, Insolvency, Restructuring & Creditors' Rights
416-862-5749 e-mail: paul.basso@gowlings.com
Ellen J. Bessner, Banking Litigation
416-862-4306 e-mail: ellen.bessner@gowlings.com
Rob Blackstein, Business Law
416-862-4613 e-mail: rob.blackstein@gowlings.com
Karyn Bradley, Business Law
416-862-5430 e-mail: karyn.bradley@gowlings.com
Leila Burden, Banking & Restructuring
416-862-4402 e-mail: leila.burden@gowlings.com
Michael Bussmann, Business Law
416-369-4663 e-mail: michael.bussmann@gowlings.com
Harold D. Chataway, Corporate Finance
416-862-4495 e-mail: harold.chataway@gowlings.com
Susan D. Clarke, Lending; Insolvency, Restructuring & Creditors' Rights
416-862-4381 e-mail: susan.clarke@gowlings.com
Stephen R. Clarke, Business Law
416-862-5706 e-mail: stephen.clarke@gowlings.com
Graeme A. Coffin, Business Law
416-862-4684 e-mail: graeme.coffin@gowlings.com
Rachel C. Conway, Corporate Finance
416-862-4434 e-mail: rachel.conway@gowlings.com
Robert Dechert, Business Law
416-862-3521 e-mail: robert.dechert@gowlings.com
Nicholas E.J. Dietrich, Business Law
416-369-7288 e-mail: nicholas.dietrich@gowlings.com
D'Arcy Doherty, Business Law
416-369-6185 e-mail: darcy.doherty@gowlings.com
Richard Dusome, Corporate Finance
416-862-5423 e-mail: richard.dusome@gowlings.com
Myron B. Dzulynsky, Business Law
416-369-7370 e-mail: myron.dzulynsky
Chris J. Eustace, Business Law
416-862-4467 e-mail: chris.eustace@gowlings.com
Cameron Ferris, Business Law
416-862-5726 e-mail: cameron.ferris@gowlings.com
Robert D. Finlayson, Business Law
416-369-7294 e-mail: robert.finlayson@gowlings.com
John R. Finley, Business Law
416-369-7214 e-mail: john.finley@gowlings.com
Filomena Frisina, Business Law
416-862-5754 e-mail: filomena.frisina@gowlings.com
Gloria J. Geddes, Business Law
416-369-4583 e-mail: gloria.geddes@gowlings.com
Dom Glavota, Banking & Restructuring
416-862-3607 e-mail: dom.glavota@gowlings.com
Leslie Gord, Business Law
416-369-7309 e-mail: leslie.gord@gowlings.com
Bruce M. Graham, Business Law
416-369-7302 e-mail: bruce.graham@gowlings.com
Gary D. Graham, Business Law
905-540-3255 e-mail: gary.graham@gowlings.com
Elaine M. Gray, Insolvency, Restructuring & Creditors' Rights
416-862-5727 e-mail: elaine.gray@gowlings.com
Eric Gross, Business Law
416-862-5409 e-mail: eric.gross@gowlings.com
Ash Gupta, Business Law
416-369-7366 e-mail: ash.gupta@gowlings.com
David R.B. Hamilton, Banking & Restructuring
416-862-4305 e-mail: david.hamilton@gowlings.com
Paul H. Harricks, Business Law
416-369-7296 e-mail: paul.harricks@gowlings.com
Henry A. Harris, Corporate Finance
416-862-4393 e-mail: henry.harris@gowlings.com
Daniel R. Hayhurst, Business Law
416-369-4635 e-mail: daniel.hayhurst@gowlings.com
Robert G.S. Hull, Business Law
416-369-7313 e-mail: robert.hull@gowlings.com
Vince F. Imerti, Business Law
416-369-6645 e-mail: vince.imerti@gowlings.com
Alan James, Business Law
416-369-6186 e-mail: alan.james@gowlings.com
Stephen P. Johnston, Lending; Insolvency, Restructuring & Creditors' Rights
416-862-5705 e-mail: steve.johnston@gowlings.com
Edward Johnston, Business Law
416-369-6176 e-mail: edward.johnston@gowlings.com
Sam Johnston, Business Law
416-369-4587 e-mail: sam.johnston@gowlings.com
Gregory P. King, Banking & Restructuring
416-862-3618 e-mail: gregory.king@gowlings.com
N. Kluge, Banking Litigation
416-369-4610 e-mail: nicholas.kluge@gowlings.com
Katerina Kouretas, Business Law
416-862-4342 e-mail: katerina.kouretas@gowlings.com
Pamela Krauss Bamford, Business Law
416-369-4665 e-mail: pamela.kraussbamford@gowlings.com
Michèle Legault, Banking & Restructuring
416-862-4695 e-mail: michele.legault@gowlings.com
Edward Levitt, Business Law
416-862-3628 e-mail: edward.levitt@gowlings.com
Lisa R. Lifshitz, Business Law
416-369-4632 e-mail: lisa.lifshitz@gowlings.com
Bradley Limpert, Business Law
416-862-4447 e-mail: bradley.limpert@gowlings.com
Ian Macdonald, Business Law
416-369-4602 e-mail: ian.macdonald@gowlings.com
Frances Macklin, Banking & Restructuring
416-862-3617 e-mail: frances.macklin@gowlings.com
P.E. Manderville, Banking Litigation
416-369-4580 e-mail: peter.manderville@gowlings.com
Donald C. Matheson, Business Law
416-862-3595 e-mail: don.matheson@gowlings.com
Charles McCarragher, Business Law
416-369-4670 e-mail: charles.mccarragher@gowlings.com
Don McCutchan, Business Law
416-862-3513 e-mail: don.mccutchan@gowlings.com
David J. McFadden, Business Law
416-369-7243 e-mail: david.mcfadden@gowlings.com
Stephen D. McKersie, Corporate Finance
416-862-4461 e-mail: Corporate Finance
Terence A. McNally, Business Law
416-369-6189 e-mail: terence.mcnally@gowlings.com
Farida Merali, Business Law
416-369-4643 e-mail: farida.merali@gowlings.com
Robert E. Milnes, Business Law
416-369-7236 e-mail: robert.milnes@gowlings.com
Rudy Morrone, Business Law
416-862-5424 e-mail: rudy.morrone@gowlings.com
Peter Murphy, Business Law
416-369-4674 e-mail: peter.murphy@gowlings.com
Eric G. Nazzer, Corporate Finance
416-862-3553 e-mail: eric.nazzer@gowlings.com
Letitia Ng, Business Law
416-369-6683 e-mail: letitia.ng@gowlings.com
Angela Nikolakakos, Corporate Finance
416-862-5704 e-mail: angela.nikolakakos@gowlings.com
Stevan Novoselac, Business Law
416-862-3630 e-mail: stevan.novoselac@gowlings.com
David W. Pamenter, Business Law
416-862-3611 e-mail: david.pamenter@gowlings.com
Catherine A. Pawluch, Business Law
416-862-4371 e-mail: catherine.pawluch@gowlings.com
Stephen A. Pike, Business Law
416-369-7349 e-mail: stephen.pike@gowlings.com
Kathleen M. Ritchie, Business Law
416-369-4579 e-mail: kathleen.ritchie@gowlings.com
Iain A. Robb, Corporate Finance
416-862-5748 e-mail: iain.robb@gowlings.com
Susan D. Rosen, Corporate Finance; Real Estate
416-862-3519 e-mail: susan.rosen@gowlings.com
John L. Ross, Corporate Finance
416-862-5736 e-mail: john.ross@gowlings.com

Marie C. Rounding, Business Law
e-mail: marie.rounding@gowlings.com
David Rubin, Business Law
416-862-3520 e-mail: david.rubin@gowlings.com
Kristen Rudzitis, Business Law
416-369-6187 e-mail: kristen.rudzitis@gowlings.com
Jason A. Saltzman, Corporate Finance
416-862-4479 e-mail: jason.saltzman@gowlings.com
Dean Saul, Business Law
416-862-4330 e-mail: dean.saul@gowlings.com
Lorne W. Segal, Business Law
416-862-4635 e-mail: lorne.segal@gowlings.com
Ariane Siegel, Business Law
416-369-7228 e-mail: ariane.siegel@gowlings.com
R. Bruce Smith, Banking Litigation
416-369-4616 e-mail: bruce.smith@gowlings.com
Brian R.D. Smith, Business Law
416-369-7371 e-mail: brian.smith@gowlings.com
John D. Stevenson, Business Law
416-369-7207 e-mail: john.stevenson@gowlings.com
Wendy J. Thompson, Business Law
416-862-4470 e-mail: wendy.thompson@gowlings.com
Carl A. Turner, Business Law
416-862-5412 e-mail: carl.turner@gowlings.com
Harry R. VanderLugt, Banking & Restructuring
416-862-5723 e-mail: harry.vanderlugt@gowlings.com
Timothy S. Wach, Business Law
416-369-4645 e-mail: timothy.wach@gowlings.com
Danielle Waldman, Business Law
416-369-6182 e-mail: danielle.waldman@gowlings.com
Robin Walker, Insolvency, Restructuring & Creditors' Rights
416-862-4401 e-mail: robin.walker@gowlings.com
Shoshanah Webber, Business Law
416-862-5703 e-mail: shoshanah.webber@gowlings.com
Alan N. West, Corporate Commercial; Insurance Product & Liability
416-862-4308 e-mail: alan.west@gowlings.com
Alan West, Business Law
416-862-4308 e-mail: alan.west@gowlings.com
Ben Westelman, Business Law
416-369-6168 e-mail: benjamin.westelman@gowlings.com
Heath P.L. Whiteley, Commercial Litigation; Insolvency, Restructuring & Creditors' Rights; Recovery; Banking Litigation
416-862-4400 e-mail: heath.whiteley@gowlings.com
John M. Whyte, Lending; Insolvency, Restructuring & Creditors' Rights
416-862-5702 e-mail: john.whyte@gowlings.com
George A. Wilson, Business Law
416-862-5710 e-mail: george.wilson@gowlings.com
Lilly A. Wong, Business Law
416-369-4630 e-mail: lilly.wong@gowlings.com

Gowling Lafleur Henderson LLP

Bentall IV #2300
PO Box 49122
1055 Dunsmuir St.
Vancouver, BC V7X 1J1
604-683-6498
Fax: 604-683-3558
www.gowlings.com
Number of Lawyers: 36

Finance Lawyers:
Daniel Allen, Corporate Commercial; Corporate Finance & Securitites
604-891-2710 e-mail: daniel.allen@gowlings.com
Andrew Bury, Insolvency, Restructuring & Creditors' Rights; Recovery Services
604-443-7615 e-mail: andrew.bury@gowlings.com
G. Henry Ellis, Corporate Commercial; Lending
604-891-2250 e-mail: henry.ellis@gowlings.com
Brett A. Kagetsu, Corporate Commercial
604-683-6498 e-mail: brett.kagetsu@gowlings.com
Cyndi D. Laval, Corporate Commercial; Corporate Finance & Securities
604-891-2712 e-mail: cyndi.laval@gowlings.com
Louis Montpellier, Corporate Commercial; Corporate Finance & Securities;
604-891-2737 e-mail: louis.montpellier@gowlings.com
Irene M. Stewart, Corporate Commercial; Corporate Finance & Securities; Lending; Real Estate
604-891-2270 e-mail: irene.stewart@gowlings.com
David J. Sutherland, Corporate Commercial
604-443-7600 e-mail: david.sutherland@gowlings.com

Groia & Company Professional Corporation

Sterling Tower #1000
372 Bay St.
Toronto, ON M5H 2W9
416-203-2115
Fax: 416-203-9231
postmaster@groiaco.com
www.groiaco.com
Founded: 2000
Number of Lawyers: 9
Profile: Concentrates on corporate commercial & securities litigation

Finance Lawyers:
Jennifer Badley, Securities
416-203-4492 e-mail: jbadley@groiaco.com
Robert Brush, Securities
416-203-4476 e-mail: rbrush@groiaco.com
Karen Danielson, Securities
416-203-4474 e-mail: kdanielson@groiaco.com
Joseph P. Groia, Securities
416-203-4472 e-mail: jgroia@groiaco.com
Cullen Price, Securities
416-203-4473 e-mail: cprice@groiaco.com
Kevin Richard, Securities
416-203-4485 e-mail: krichard@groiaco.com
Abbas Sabur, Securities
416-203-4482 e-mail: asabur@groiaco.com
Kellie Seaman, Securities
416-203-4471 e-mail: kseaman@groiaco.com
Gavin Smyth, Securities
416-203-4475 e-mail: gsmyth@groiaco.com

Grondin, Poudrier, Bernier

#900
500, Grande Allée est
Québec, QC G1R 2J7
418-683-3000
Fax: 418-683-8784
800-463-5172
gpb@grondinpoudrier.com
www.grondinpoudrier.com
Founded: 1948
Number of Lawyers: 40

Finance Lawyers:
Jean-Paul Bernier, Droit des assurances
e-mail: jpbernier@grondinpoudrier.com
Jacqueline Bissonnette, Droit des assurances
e-mail: jbissonnette@grondinpoudrier.com
Pierre Bolduc, Droit commercial
e-mail: pbolduc@grondinpoudrier.com
Sylvie Boucher, Droit des assurances
e-mail: sboucher@grondinpoudier.com
Philippe Bouvier, Droit des assurances
e-mail: pbouvier@grondinpoudrier.com
Marianne Bureau, Droit des assurances collectives
e-mail: mbureau@grondinpoudrier.com
François-P. Cloutier, Droit commercial et corporatif
e-mail: fpcloutier@grondinpoudrier.com
Daniel Des Aulniers, Droit commercial; droit de la faillite et de l'insolvabilité
e-mail: ddesaulniers@grondinpoudrier.com
Marie-Christine Dufour, Droit des assurances collectives
e-mail: mcdufour@grondinpoudrier.com
Vincent Fortier, Droit des assurances
e-mail: vfortier@grondinpoudrier.com
Jean Gagnon, Droit commercial; droit de la faillite et d'insolvabilité
e-mail: jgagnon@grondinpoudrier.com
Michel Gilbert, Droit des assurances collectives
e-mail: mgilbert@grondinpoudrier.com
Denis Houle, Droit des assurances
e-mail: dhoule@grondinpoudrier.com
Pierre Ouellet, Droit des assurances
e-mail: pouellet@grondinpoudrier.com
Gilles Reny, Droit des affaires
e-mail: greny@grondinpoudrier.com

Bernard Gropper

#300
261 Davenport Rd.
Toronto, ON M5R 1K3
416-962-3000
Fax: 416-487-3002
bgropper@gropperlaw.com
Founded: 1996
Number of Lawyers: 1

Finance Lawyers:
Bernard Gropper, Business Law
e-mail: bgropper@groppergreenwood.com

Gurevitch Headon & Associates

9931 - 106 Ave.
Grande Prairie, AB T8V 1J4
780-539-3710
Fax: 780-532-2788
gplaw@telusplanet.net
www.grandeprairielaw.ca
Founded: 1980
Number of Lawyers: 2
Profile: Banking & Security Preparation & Enforcement; Corporate & Commercial; Wills & Estates

Finance Lawyers:
Clifford M. Headon, Commercial Litigation
e-mail: cliff@grandeprairielaw.ca

Peter F. Haber

325 Mutual St.
Toronto, ON M4Y 1X6
416-961-0265
Fax: 416-961-1860
888-841-1104
peterhaber@rogers.com
Founded: 1989
Number of Lawyers: 1
Profile: Lawyer: General Practice; Chartered Accountant

Finance Lawyers:
Peter F. Haber

Hacker Gignac Rice

518 Yonge St.
Midland, ON L4R 2C5
705-526-2231
Fax: 705-526-0313
800-205-4052
hgr@hgr.ca
www.hgr.ca
Founded: 1981
Number of Lawyers: 14
Profile: Corporate; Commercial & Real Estate Law

Finance Lawyers:
John Barzo, Insurance
705-327-6655
Ron Crane, Commercial
John Gignac, Real Estate & Wills
e-mail: john@hgr.ca
Frederick W. Hacker, Commercial
e-mail: fred@hgr.ca
Rob Maciver, Real Estate; Business Law
705-526-2231 e-mail: rob@hgr.ca
Andrew Mae, Corporate/Commercial
Christine Manners, Real Estate; Wills; Corporate
705-327-6655 e-mail: christine@hgr.ca
Greg Rice, Estate Planning
e-mail: greg@hgr.ca
Tracey Rynard, Wills; Estate Planning
Ted Symons, Real Estate; Wills
Bruce Waite, Business Planning; Commercial; Finance; Franchises
705-327-6655

Hallgren & Faulkner

PO Box 939
6595 Sooke Rd.
Sooke, BC V0S 1N0
250-642-5271
Fax: 250-642-6006
800-358-5271
hallgrenfaulkner@shaw.ca
Founded: 1980
Number of Lawyers: 2

Finance Lawyers:
Peter G.V. Faulkner, Real Estate & Mortgages; Corporate & Business; Wills, Estates, Trusts
e-mail: pgvfaulkner@shaw.ca
Marvin W. Hallgren, Real Estate & Mortgages; Corporate & Business; Wills, Estates, Trusts
e-mail: mwhallgren@shaw.ca

Hamilton Duncan Armstrong & Stewart LLP, Barristers & Solicitors
#1450
13401 - 108th Ave.
Surrey, BC V3T 5T3
604-581-4677
Fax: 604-581-5947
info@hdas.com
www.hdas.com
Number of Lawyers: 14

Finance Lawyers:
J.M. Borkowski, Corporate & Commercial; Mergers & Acquisitions; Real Estate; Securities
e-mail: jmb@hdas.com
T.R. Britnell, Commercial Litigation; Estates; Securities
e-mail: trb@hdas.com
B.C. Duncan, Mergers & Acquisitions; Debtor/Creditor
e-mail: bcd@hdas.com
D.M. Kamachi, Corporate & Commercial
H.S. Mundi, Business & Corporate Law; Financial
e-mail: hsm@hdas.com
S.L. Nicoll, Corporate & Commercial
e-mail: sln@hdas.com
J.B. Stewart, Corporate & Commercial; Estates, Wills & Trusts
e-mail: jbs@hdas.com
G.B. Stickland, Corporate & Commercial; Banking; Mergers & Acquisitions; Real Estate
e-mail: gbs@hdas.com

Haney, Haney & Kendall
PO Box 185
41 Erb St. East
Waterloo, ON N2J 3Z9
519-747-1010
Fax: 519-747-9323
hhk@haneylaw.com
Number of Lawyers: 5

Finance Lawyers:
Reginald A. Haney, General Finance
Mary Anne Haney, General Finance
John J. Kendall, General Finance

Hans & Hans
17 Wembley Rd.
Toronto, ON M6C 2E8
416-960-5445
Fax: 416-924-7541
hansoff10@rogers.com
Number of Lawyers: 1

Finance Lawyers:
Judith Z. Hans, General Finance

Zakaul Haque
#205
1058A Albion Rd.
Toronto, ON M9V 1A7
416-743-6302
Fax: 416-743-4783
Founded: 1975
Number of Lawyers: 1

Finance Lawyers:
Zakaul Haque, Real Estate; Mortgages; Leases

Harper Grey LLP
Vancouver Centre #3200
650 West Georgia St.
Vancouver, BC V6B 4P7
604-687-0411
Fax: 604-669-9385
info@harpergrey.com
www.harpergrey.com
Number of Lawyers: 53

Finance Lawyers:
Richard P. Attisha, Commercial Litigation; Bankruptcy & Insolvency
604-895-2811 e-mail: rattisha@harpergrey.com
Bryan G. Baynham, Insurance Law; Commercial Litigation
Salman Y. Bhura, Commercial Litigation; Business Law; Bankruptcy & Insolvency
Rebeka Breder, Commercial Litigation
Guy P. Brown, Insurance Law
Alison W. Bruneau, Commercial Litigation
Bernard S. Buettner, Insurance Law
G. Bruce Butler, Commercial Litigation
604-895-2806 e-mail: bbutler@harpergrey.com
William S. Clark, Insurance Law
Shanti M. Davies, Insurance Law
Suzannah Denholm, Commercial Litigation
David A. Gagnon, Bankruptcy & Insolvency; Business Law; Commercial Litigation
Mandeep K. Gill, Commercial Litigation
Christopher E. Hinkson, Commercial Litigation
604-895-2822 e-mail: chinkson@harpergrey.com
Kimberly J. Jakeman, Commercial Litigation
Larry H. Koo, Bankruptcy & Insolvency; Commercial Litigation; Business Law
James M. Lepp, Commercial Litigation
Maryam Lindsay, Insurance Law
Maureen L.A. Lundell, Insurance Law
William D. MacRae, Business Law
L. Neil Matheson, Insurance Law
Jonathan Meadows, Insurance Law
George D. Mucalov, Business Law
Barbara J. Norell, Insurance Law
Ron Pelletier
David W. Pilley, Insurance Law
Susanne K. Raab, Commercial Litigation
Robert J. Rose, Business Law
Christoper M. Rusnak, Insurance Law
604-895-2838 e-mail: crusnak@harpergrey.com
Raj Samtani, Insurance Law; Commercial Litigation
Bena W. Stock, Insurance Law
John P. Sullivan, Bankruptcy & Insolvency; Commercial Litigation
W. Sean Taylor, Insurance Law
Michael G. Thomas, Insurance Law
Nigel L. Trevethan, Insurance Law
Abigail C.F. Turner, Insurance Law
Steve M. Vorbrodt, Insurance Law
Katherine Wellburn, Commercial Litigation
Henning Wiebach, Commercial Litigation
Peter M. Willcock, Insurance Law; Commercial Litigation
Jonathan M.S. Woolley, Commercial Litigation
Jennifer Woznesensky, Insurance Law
Roselle Wu, Commercial Litigation

Harris & Harris LLP
#300
2355 Skymark Ave.
Mississauga, ON L4W 4Y6
905-629-7800
Fax: 905-629-4350
info@harrisandharris.com
www.harrisandharris.com
Number of Lawyers: 9

Finance Lawyers:
Gregory H. Harris, General Finance
Mark L. Swartz, General Finance

Harrison Pensa LLP
PO Box 3237
450 Talbot St.
London, ON N6A 4K3
519-679-9660
Fax: 519-667-3362
lawyers@harrisonpensa.com
www.harrisonpensa.com
Founded: 1938
Number of Lawyers: 51
Profile: Multi-disciplined Business & Financial Services group delivers a comprehensive range of services to small businesses, corporations, government agencies & financial institutions; provides proactive legal advice, from corporate reorganizations & municipal planning to E-business & protection of intellectual properties, based on the unique needs of every client

Finance Lawyers:
James R. Adams, Insurance Defence
519-661-6761 e-mail: jadams@harrisonpensa.com
Tammie Ashton, Corporate Commercial; Estates
519-675-4102 e-mail: tashton@harrisonpensa.com
Steven J. Atkinson, Commercial
519-661-6763 e-mail: satkinson@harrisonpensa.com
Arthur J. Campbell, Commercial Litigation
519-661-6764 e-mail: acampbell@harrisonpensa.com
David R. Canton, Electronic Commerce
519-661-6776 e-mail: dcanton@harrisonpensa.com
Janet A. Clark, Wills; Estates
519-661-6704 e-mail: jclark@harrisonpensa.ca
J. Robert Cowan, Commercial; Real Estate; Corporate; Estate
519-661-6714 e-mail: bcowan@harrisonpensa.com
Louis J. Crowley, Commercial; Insurance
519-661-6767 e-mail: lcrowley@harrisonpensa.ca
Ronald Dickie, Real Estate; Commercial Law
519-672-9500 e-mail: rdickie@harrisonpensa.ca
Susan M.H. Fincher-Stoll, Taxation; Wills; Estates
519-661-6737 e-mail: sfincherstoll@harrisonpensa.com
Christian J. Hamber, Corporate Commercial; Real Estate
519-661-6742 e-mail: chamber@harrisonpensa.com
Timothy C. Hogan, Commercial Litigation; Bankruptcy; Insolvency
519-661-6743 e-mail: thogan@harrisonpensa.ca
Hillary A. Houston, Estate Litigation
519-661-6710 e-mail: hhouston@harrisonpensa.com
Ryan Huggett, Insolvency; Commercial Litigation
519-661-6736 e-mail: rhuggett@harrisonpensa.com
Robert J. Israel, Corporate Commercial; Financial
519-661-6715 e-mail: bisrael@harrisonpensa.com
Paul D. Kiteley, Real Estate; Corporate Commercial; Wills & Estates
519-661-6772 e-mail: pkiteley@harrisonpensa.ca
Tracy L. Leckie, Insurance Defence
519-661-6773 e-mail: tleckie@harrisonpensa.ca
L. Michele Mannering, Corporate Financial
519-661-6721 e-mail: mmannering@harrisonpensa.com
Timothy T. McCullough, Corporate Financial
519-661-6718 e-mail: tmccullough@harrisonpensa.com
Maurice M. Pellarin, Real Estate; Commercial
519-661-6724 e-mail: mpellarin@harrisonpensa.ca
Claude M. Pensa, Commercial
519-661-6778 e-mail: cpensa@harrisonpensa.ca
Lorraine J. Por, Commercial
519-661-6723 e-mail: lpor@harrisonpensa.com
K. Daniel Reason, Bankruptcy; Insolvency; Commercial
519-661-6725 e-mail: dreason@harrisonpensa.com
Thomas S. Robson, Insolvency; Commercial; Bankruptcy
519-661-6766 e-mail: trobson@harrisonpensa.ca
Peter H.E. Schwartz, Corporate/Commercial; Mergers & Acquisitions; Financial; Estate
519-661-6716 e-mail: pschwartz@harrisonpensa.com
J. Douglas Scott, Real Estate; Corporate; Commercial
519-661-6727 e-mail: dscott@harrisonpensa.ca
Paul Siskind, Mortgage Financing & Recovery
519-661-6745 e-mail: psiskind@harrisonpensa.com
J. Douglas Skinner, Commercial; Estate; Insurance
519-661-6702 e-mail: dskinner@harrisonpensa.ca
Peter Spence, Corporate Commercial; Mergers & Acquisitions; Financial
519-675-4101 e-mail: pspence@harrisonpensa.com
Scott T. Spindler, Corporate Commercial; Securities
519-661-6734 e-mail: sspindler@harrisonpensa.com
David S. Swift, Commercial; Bankruptcy
519-661-6735 e-mail: dswift@harrisonpensa.ca
Gerard T. Tillmann, Insurance Defence; Commercial Litigation; Estate
519-661-6781 e-mail: gtillmann@harrisonpensa.ca
Harry F. Van Bavel, Bankruptcy; Insolvency; Banking; Creditors Rights
519-661-6726 e-mail: hvanbavel@harrisonpensa.com
Ian C. Wallace, Bankruptcy; Insolvency; Banking; Creditors Rights
519-661-6729 e-mail: iwallace@harrisonpensa.com
David B. Williams, Insurance; Commercial
519-661-6782 e-mail: dwilliams@harrisonpensa.ca

Beatrice A. Havlovic
1459 Brenton St.
Halifax, NS B3J 3S7
902-423-8100
Fax: 902-423-6011
bhavlovic@linguanet.ca
Number of Lawyers: 1
Profile: Property & Corporate Commercial

Finance Lawyers:
Beatrice A. Havlovic

Heenan Blaikie SENCRL-SRL/LLP
#2500
1250, boul René-Lévesque ouest
Montréal, QC H3B 4Y1

514-846-1212
Fax: 514-846-3427
www.heenanblaikie.com
Founded: 1973
Number of Lawyers: 137
Profile: Heenan Blaikie LLP business law practitioners provide a full range of services to some of Canada's largest corporations & financial institutions, as well as to many smaller, growth-oriented companies in all types of transactions & corporate governance issues: mergers & acquisitions, international & domestic joint ventures, reorganizations, regulatory matters, venture capital investment, financing arrangements with commercial & private lenders, directors' & officers' liabilities, trademark & copyright matters; software licensing & outsourcing contracts

Finance Lawyers:
Ryan Allen, General Corporate
514-846-7057 e-mail: rallen@heenan.ca
Rosanna Anobile, Corporate Governance
514-846-7238 e-mail: ranobile@heenan.ca
Poupak Bahamin, Corporate & Commercial
514-846-2377 e-mail: pbahamin@heenan.ca
Sébastien Bellefleur, Corporate Governance
514-846-2351 e-mail: sbellefleur@heenan.ca
Claudette Bellemare, Mergers & Acquisitions; Shareholders Agreements; Business & Commercial Contracts; Commercial Transactions; Corporate Reorganizations
514-846-2248 e-mail: cbellemar@heenan.ca
Karen Bengualid Payne, General Corporate
514-846-2336 e-mail: kbengualid@heenan.ca
Yasser Bouhid, Corporate Governance
514-846-2227 e-mail: ybouhid@heenan.ca
Carl Bélanger, Secured Transactions; Commercial Transactions; General Corporate/Commercial
514-846-2212 e-mail: cbelanger@heenan.ca
Joel Cabelli, Mergers & Acquisitions
514-846-7245 e-mail: jcabelli@heenan.ca
Jason Caron, Partnership & Joint Ventures
514-846-2370 e-mail: jcaron@heenan.ca
Andrew M. Cohen, Mergers & Acquisitions; Business & Commercial Contracts; Commercial Transactions; Corporate Reorganizations; Foreign Investments
514-846-2338 e-mail: acohen@heenan.ca
Melanie De Souza, Corporate Finance
514-846-2254
Terry Didus, Banking & Financing
514-846-2341 e-mail: tdidus@heenan.ca
Karine Fleury, Banking & Financing
514-846-2334 e-mail: kfleury@heenan.ca
Brian Casey Forget, General Corporate
514-846-7213 e-mail: bforget@heenan.ca
Joel Goldberg, Mergers & Acquisitions; Real Estate
514-846-2310 e-mail: jgoldberg@heenan.ca
Stephen D. Hart, General Corporate
514-846-7225 e-mail: shart@heenan.ca
Donald J. Johnston, Corporate Governance
514-846-2280 e-mail: djohnston@heenan.ca
Manon Jolicoeur, Real Estate; Leasing
514-846-2220 e-mail: mjolicoeur@heenan.ca
Bernard Jolin, Banking; Bankruptcy
Antoine Leduc, Lending & Restructuring; Corporate Commercial
514-846-6881 e-mail: aleduc@heenan.ca
Thomas Lellouche
Bobby Lemieux, General Corporate
514-846-2361 e-mail: blemieux@heenan.ca
Eric M. Levy, Securities; Corporate; Commercial Transactions
514-846-2256 e-mail: elevy@heenan.ca
Mariella Lo Papa, Corporate & Commercial; Real Estate
514-846-2309 e-mail: mlopapa@heenan.ca
Stavroula Makris, Corporate & Commercial; Reorganizations; Mergers & Acquisitions; Financing
514-846-2240
Eric Maldoff, Partnership & Joint Ventures; Commercial Transactions; Corporate Governance; Mergers & Acquisitions; Shareholders Agreements
514-846-2249 e-mail: emaldoff@heenan.ca
Auguste Masson, Mergers & Acquisitions; Corporate Reorganizations; Licensing; Business & Commercial Contracts; International Business; Shareholder Agreements
514-846-2206 e-mail: amasson@heenan.ca
Bruce McNiven, Mergers & Acquisitions; Business & Commercial Contracts; Commercial Transactions; International Business; Licensing; Shareholder Agreements
514-846-2244 e-mail: bmcniven@heenan.ca
Monica Montanaro, Mergers & Acquisitions
514-846-6882 e-mail: mmontanaro@heenan.ca
Lise Morissette, Mergers & Acquisitions; Real Estate; Banking & Financing; Business & Commercial Contracts; Commercial Transactions; Corporate & Commercial
514-846-2258 e-mail: lmorisset@heenan.ca
Suzanne Owen, General Corporate
514-846-2286 e-mail: sowen@heenan.ca
Antonella Penta, Corporate Governance
514-846-2365 e-mail: apenta@heenan.ca
Nicolas Plourde, Bankruptcy; Insolvency
Normand Quesnel, Real Estate; Secured Transactions; Leasing
514-846-2217 e-mail: nquesnel@heenan.ca
François A. Raymond, Licensing; Commercial Transactions; Corporate Reorganizations; General Corporate/Commercial; International Business; Mergers & Acquisitions
514-846-2225 e-mail: fraymond@heenan.ca
Douglas C. Robertson, Business Law
514-846-6892 e-mail: drobertson@heenan.ca
Michel Saint-Pierre, General Corporate; Tax; Mergers & Acquisitions; Bankruptcy & Insolvency
e-mail: msaintpierre@heenan.ca
Alan Sarhan, General Corporate
514-846-7233 e-mail: asarhan@heenan.ca
Chantal Sylvestre, Corporate & Commercial; Real Estate
514-846-2344 e-mail: csylvestr@heenan.ca
Michel E. Taillefer, Bankruptcy & Insolvency; Shareholders Recourses
514-846-7229 e-mail: mtaillefer@heenan.ca
Marie-Andrée Thibault, General Corporate
514-846-1212 e-mail: mthibault@heenan.ca
Jean Trudel, Mergers & Acquisitions; Shareholders Agreements; Venture Capital; Business & Commercial Contracts; Commercial Transactions; Corporate Governance; Corporate Reor
514-846-2236 e-mail: jtrudel@heenan.ca
Patrice Vachon, Mergers & Acquisitions; Corporate Reorganizations; Partnership & Joint Ventures; Arbitration; Shareholders Dispute & Resolution; Venture Capital; Licensing; Est
514-846-2247 e-mail: pvachon@heenan.ca
Neil Wiener, Corporate Finance
514-846-2208 e-mail: nwiener@heenan.ca

Heenan Blaikie SENCRL-SRL/LLP
425 - 1 St. SW, 12th Fl.
Calgary, AB T2P 3L8
403-232-8223
Fax: 403-234-7987
www.heenanblaikie.com
Number of Lawyers: 23
Profile: Corporate, commercial, energy, litigation law

Finance Lawyers:
Brian Bidyk, Corporate & Commercial
403-781-3389 e-mail: bbidyk@heenan.ca
Michael J. Black, Corporate & Commercial
403-261-3467 e-mail: mblack@heenan.ca
Felicia B. Bortolussi, Corporate & Commercial; Securities & Corporate Finance
403-261-3470 e-mail: fbortolussi@heenan.ca
Thomas N. Cotter, Securities; Corporate & Commercial
403-261-3451 e-mail: tcotter@heenan.ca
David Elder, Securities & Corporate Finance; Corporate & Commercial
403-261-3464 e-mail: delder@heenan.ca
Mark Franko, Securities & Corporate Finance
403-781-3390 e-mail: mfranko@heenan.ca
James Pasieka, Securities & Corporate Finance; Corporate & Commercial
403-781-3382 e-mail: jpasieka@heenan.ca
Mitchell E. Shier, Corporate & Commercial
403-781-3394 e-mail: mshier@heenan.ca
Peter Soby, Corporate & Commercial
403-261-3460 e-mail: psoby@heenan.ca
Lloyd Symons, Securities & Corporate Finance; Corporate & Commercial
403-234-3125 e-mail: lsymons@heenan.ca
Edward Wooldridge, Banking; Corporate Finance
403-261-3454 e-mail: ewooldridge@heena.ca
Peter Yates, Securities & Corporate Financing; Corporate & Commercial

Heenan Blaikie SENCRL-SRL/LLP
#300
55 Metcalfe St.
Ottawa, ON K1P 6L5
613-236-1668
Fax: 613-236-9632
www.heenanblaikie.com
Number of Lawyers: 15

Finance Lawyers:
Paul Franco, Securities; Mergers & Acquisitions; Corporate Reorganizations; General Corporate/Commercial; Commercial Transactions
613-236-4469 e-mail: pfranco@heenan.ca
Peter Mantas, International Business
613-237-1733 e-mail: pmantas@heenan.ca

Heenan Blaikie SENCRL-SRL/LLP
#600
900, boul René-Lévesque est
Québec, QC G1R 2B5
418-524-5131
Fax: 418-524-1717
www.heenanblaikie.com
Founded: 1973
Number of Lawyers: 25
Profile: Droit des affairs, droit du travail et de l'emploi, fiscalite, litige, divertissement, propriété intellectuelle

Finance Lawyers:
Éric Amyot, Venture Capital; Securities; Corporate/Commercial
418-649-5463 e-mail: eamyot@heenan.ca
Marcel Aubut, Mergers & Acquisitions
Marie-Eve Auclair, Mergers & Acquisitions
Pierre Beaulieu, Bankruptcy & Insolvency
Jean-François Bienjonetti, Insurance
David F. Blair, Mergers & Acquisitions
Louis Carrière, Bankruptcy & Insolvency
Annie-Claude Labrecque, Insurance
Pierre Picard, International Business; Banking & Financing; Bankruptcy & Insolvency
418-649-5466 e-mail: ppicard@heenan.ca
Guy Plante, Tax/Taxation Law; Business & Commercial Contracts; Corporate Reorganizations; Mergers & Acquisitions; Partnership & Joint Ventures
418-649-5460 e-mail: gplante@heenan.ca
Gilles Warren, Real Estate; Commercial Transactions; Estate Planning; Banking & Financing; Lending; Mergers & Acquisitions; Secured Transactions
418-649-5462 e-mail: gwarren@heenan.ca

Heenan Blaikie SENCRL-SRL/LLP
#210
455, rue King ouest
Sherbrooke, QC J1H 6E9
819-346-5058
Fax: 819-346-5007
www.heenanblaikie.com
Founded: 1973
Number of Lawyers: 23

Finance Lawyers:
Luc R. Borduas, Bankruptcy & Insolvency
Astrid Bourassa, Insurance
Christian Dumoulin, Mergers & Acquisitions; Insurance
Alain Heyne, Bankruptcy & Insolvency
Marcel Lacroix, Mergers & Acquisitions
Isabelle Mercure, Mergers & Acquisitions
Sylvain Provencher, Bankruptcy & Insolvency
Hubert Pépin, Mergers & Acquisitions
Yanick Vlasak, Bankruptcy & Insolvency

Heenan Blaikie SENCRL-SRL/LLP
South Tower, Royal Bank Plaza #2600
PO Box 185, Royal Bank Sta.
200 Bay St.
Toronto, ON M5J 2J4
416-360-6336
Fax: 416-360-8425
www.heenanblaikie.com
Founded: 1973
Number of Lawyers: 118

Finance Lawyers:
Maneli Badii, Corporate & Commercial
416-643-6849 e-mail: mbadii@heenan.ca
Jeff Barnes, Mergers & Acquisitions; Corporate Finance; Project Finance; Corporate Governance; Securities
Catherine Bate, Business Law
416-643-6875 e-mail: cbate@heenan.ca

Heenan Blaikie SENCRL-SRL/LLP (continued)

Vivian Bercovici, Business Law
416-643-6869 e-mail: vbercovici@heenan.ca
Henry Bertossi, Mergers & Acquisitions
416-643-6862 e-mail: hbertossi@heenan.ca
Malcolm W. Boyd, Banking & Financing; Mergers & Acquisitions; Corporate Governance
416-643-6843 e-mail: mboyd@heenan.ca
Andrew Brunton, Business Law
416-360-3570 e-mail: abrunton@heenan.ca
Christina Buchli, Corporate & Commercial
416-643-6808 e-mail: cbuchli@heenan.ca
Mary Anne Bueschkens, Tax Law
416-643-6802 e-mail: mabueschkens@heenan.ca
David Carbonaro, Mergers & Acquisitions
416-643-6836 e-mail: dcarbonaro@heenan.ca
Lori Charnetski, Corporate & Commercial
416-643-6814 e-mail: lcharnetski@heenan.ca
Simon Chester, Business Law
416-643-6905 e-mail: schester@heenan.ca
Jeffrey Citron, Business Law
416-360-2290 e-mail: jcitron@heenan.ca
Peter L. Clark, Tax Law
416-360-3543 e-mail: pclark@heenan.ca
W. Kip Daechsel, Securities; Banking & Financing; Mergers & Acquisitions; Business & Commercial Contracts; Commercial Transactions
416-360-3531 e-mail: kdaechsel@heenan.ca
Ilia N. Danef, Business Law
416-643-6904 e-mail: idanef@heenan.ca
Wendy Del Mul, Mergers & Acquisitions
416-360-6336 e-mail: wdelmul@heenan.ca
Ken Dhaliwal, Corporate & Commercial
416-360-3523 e-mail: kdhaliwal@heenan.ca
Jay Duffield, Private Equity; Venture Capital
Joanna Fine, Business Law
416-360-3599 e-mail: jfine@heenan.ca
Stanley Freedman, Mergers & Acquisitions; Commercial Transactions; International Business
416-643-6886 e-mail: sfreedman@heenan.ca
John Fuke, Tax Law
416-360-3532 e-mail: jfuke@heenan.ca
Allen H. Garson, Mergers & Acquisitions
416-360-3533 e-mail: agarson@heenan.ca
Noam Goodman, Corporate & Commercial
416-643-6817 e-mail: ngoodman@heenan.ca
Michael Henriques, Business Law
416-643-6891 e-mail: mhenriques@heenan.ca
Mark Jadd, Tax Law
416-360-3549 e-mail: mjadd@heenan.ca
Adam Kardash, Securities; Mergers & Acquisitions; Commercial Transactions; Corporate Governance; General Corporate/Commercial
416-360-3559 e-mail: akardash@heenan.ca
Nita Kemp, Tax Law
e-mail: nkemp@heenan.ca
Kenneth Kraft, Bankruptcy & Insolvency; Lending; Banking & Financing; Secured Transactions; Security Enforcement
416-643-6822 e-mail: kkraft@heenan.ca
Paul Lalonde, Corporate & Commercial
416-643-6828 e-mail: plalonde@heenan.ca
Michael F. Ledgett, Corporate & Commercial; Mergers & Acquisitions
416-643-6840 e-mail: mledgett@heenan.ca
Richard Lewin, Business Law
416-360-3545 e-mail: rlewin@heenan.ca
Corey MacKinnon, Mergers & Acquisitions
416-643-6850 e-mail: cmackinnon@heenan.ca
James McDermott, Real Estate; Business & Commercial Contracts; Partnership & Joint Ventures
416-360-3540 e-mail: jmcdermott@heenan.ca
John Place, Corporate; Commercial; Gaming
Wendy S. Reed, Business Law
Kevin Rooney, Securities; Corporate Finance
416-643-6899 e-mail: krooney@heenan.ca
Andrea Rush, Business Law
416-360-3541 e-mail: arush@heenan.ca
Jim Russell, Corporate & Commercial; Lending
416-360-3561 e-mail: jrussell@heenan.ca
Andrea Safer, Commercial Transactions
416-643-6801 e-mail: asafer@heenan.ca
Neil Saxe, Business Law
416-643-6912 e-mail: nsaxe@heenan.ca
Brett Seifred, Corporate Finance; Securities
Rajeev Sharma, Business Law
416-643-6864 e-mail: rsharma@heenan.ca
Samuel Slutsky, Tax Law
416-643-6807 e-mail: sslutsky@heenan.ca
David Steinberg, Corporate & Commercial
416-360-3552 e-mail: dsteinber@heenan.ca
Bob Tarantino, Corporate & Commercial
416-643-6815 e-mail: btarantino@heenan.ca
Stephanie Thompson, Corporate Finance
Cyndee Todgham Cherniak, Tax
Andrea L. White, Real Estate
416-643-6819 e-mail: awhite@heenan.ca
Sonia Yung, Securities & Finance
416-643-6872 e-mail: syung@heenan.ca
Stephen G. Zolf, Business Law
416-643-6811 e-mail: szolf@heenan.ca

Heenan Blaikie SENCRL-SRL/LLP

#360
1500, rue Royale
Trois-Rivières, QC G9A 6E6
819-373-7000
Fax: 819-373-0943
Founded: 1992
Number of Lawyers: 7

Finance Lawyers:
François Daigle, Insolvency & Restructuring; Tax; Structured Finance; Securities
819-373-7343 e-mail: fdaigle@heenan.ca
Mélisa McMahon Mathieu, Insolvency & Restructuring; Commercial Litigation; General Corporate; Bankruptcy & Insolvency
819-373-5497 e-mail: mmcmahon@heenan.ca
Yves Rocheleau, Lending; Restructuring; Venture Capital; Commercial Agreements; Mergers & Acquisitions; Securities
819-373-6948 e-mail: yrocheleau@heenan.ca

Heenan Blaikie SENCRL-SRL/LLP

#2200
1055 West Hastings St.
Vancouver, BC V6E 2E9
604-669-0011
Fax: 604-669-5101
Number of Lawyers: 29

Finance Lawyers:
Anjili Bahadoorsingh, Banking & Financing; Lending; Secured Transactions; Business & Commercial Contracts; Commercial Transactions; Financing
604-891-1180 e-mail: abahadoor@heenan.ca
Rod Kirkham, Securities; Mergers & Acquisitions; Corporate Governance; Security Inforcement; Business & Commercial Contracts
604-891-1159 e-mail: rkirkham@heenan.ca
Tobin Robbins, Business Law
William Skelly, Bankruptcy & Insolvency; Commercial Transactions; Banking & Financing; Lending; Secured Transactions; Business & Commerce
604-891-1177 e-mail: wskelly@heenan.ca

Hendrickson Gower Massing & Olivieri LLP

Scotia 1 #2250
10060 Jasper Ave.
Edmonton, AB T5J 3R8
780-421-8816
Fax: 780-424-5864
800-421-8816
www.hgmolaw.com
Number of Lawyers: 8

Finance Lawyers:
L. Neil Gower, Corporate & Commercial; Estates, Wills & Trusts; Mergers & Acquisitions; Real Estate
Leonard W. Hendrickson, Corporate & Commercial; Bankruptcy/Insolvency; Banking; Debtor/Creditor

John Hicks Law Office

#7
541 Brant St.
Burlington, ON L7R 2G6
905-681-3131
Fax: 905-333-6688
john.hicks@bellnet.ca
Founded: 1986
Number of Lawyers: 1
Profile: Business; Corporate/Commercial; Real Estate

Finance Lawyers:
Russell John Thomas Beare Hicks

Hobbs Hargrave

301 Franklyn St.
Nanaimo, BC V9R 2X5
250-753-3477
Fax: 250-753-7927
bhobbs@hobbslaw.com
www.hobbslaw.com
Number of Lawyers: 2

Finance Lawyers:
Rederick Naknakim, Corporate
e-mail: rodn@connected.ca

Holmes & Company

#1880
1066 Hastings St. West
Vancouver, BC V6E 3X1
604-688-7861
Fax: 604-688-0426
sdh@holmescompany.com
Founded: 2005
Number of Lawyers: 2
Profile: Tax; Off-Shore Trusts; Companies; Financings; Stock Exchanges

Finance Lawyers:
Alina Nikolaeva, Tax
e-mail: alina@holmescompany.com

Hook, Seller & Lundin

Bannister Centre #204
301 - 1 Ave. South
Kenora, ON P9N 1W2
807-468-9831
Fax: 807-468-8384
jthook@hsllawyers.com
www.hsllawyers.com
Number of Lawyers: 4

Finance Lawyers:
E. James T. Hook, General Finance
e-mail: jthook@hsllawyers.com
Stephen R. Lundin, General Finance
e-mail: slundin@hsllawyers.com
W. Randall F. Seller, General Finance
e-mail: wrseller@hsllawyers.com
Cheryl C.M. Siran, General Finance
e-mail: csiran@hsllawyers.com

Hope Heinrich

1598 - 6 Ave.
Prince George, BC V2L 5G7
250-563-0681
Fax: 250-562-3761
800-663-8230
lawyers@hh.bc.ca
www.hh.bc.ca
Founded: 1966
Number of Lawyers: 9

Finance Lawyers:
Gerald C. Coole, Wills & Estates; Corporate & Commercial
e-mail: gcc@hh.bc.ca
David E. Jones, Wills & Estates; Corporate & Commercial
e-mail: dej@hh.bc.ca

Huestis Ritch

CIBC Bldg. #1200
1809 Barrington St.
Halifax, NS B3J 3K8
902-429-3400
Fax: 902-422-4713
info@hrlaw.net
www.hrlaw.net
Number of Lawyers: 13

Finance Lawyers:
Philip M. Chapman, Insurance
e-mail: pmc@hrlaw.net
Margot Ferguson, Insurance
e-mail: mf@hrlaw.net
Elissa Hoverd, Insurance
e-mail: eh@hrlaw.net
Jean McKenna, Insurance
e-mail: jmck@hrlaw.net

W. Mark Penfound, Wills, Estates & Trusts
e-mail: wmp@hrlaw.net
Lisa Richards, Insurance; Corporate
e-mail: lr@hrlaw.net
W. Augustus Richardson, Insurance
e-mail: war@hrlaw.net
Murray J. Ritch, Insurance
e-mail: mjr@hrlaw.net
Roger T. Shepard, Insurance
e-mail: rts@hrlaw.net
Matthew G. Williams, Insurance; Commercial
e-mail: mgw@hrlaw.net

Hunter Voith
#2100
1040 Georgia St. West
Vancouver, BC V6E 4H1
604-891-2400
Fax: 604-647-4554
www.litigationcounsel.ca
Number of Lawyers: 12
Profile: Corporate & Commercial Litigation

Finance Lawyers:
John J. Hunter
604-891-2401 e-mail: jhunter@litigationcounsel.ca
Peter G. Voith
604-891-2402 e-mail: pvoith@litigationcounsel.ca

Frederick Innis
8 Ruskin Row
Winnipeg, MB R3M 2R6
204-231-9600
Fax: 204- -
innis@shaw.ca
Number of Lawyers: 1

Finance Lawyers:
Frederick Innis, Offshore Trusts

Alex Irwin Law Corp.
4750 Caulfield Dr., 2nd Fl.
West Vancouver, BC V7W 1G5
604-925-4419
Fax: 604-925-4407
alex@iwjlaw.com
Number of Lawyers: 1

Finance Lawyers:
Alexander H. Irwin, General Finance

Jaskula, Sherk
#915
25 Main St. West
Hamilton, ON L8P 1H1
905-577-1040
Fax: 905-577-7775
csherk@jaskulasherk.com
Number of Lawyers: 2

Finance Lawyers:
Catherine E. Newell, Corporate, Commercial, Real Estate
905-577-1040
Christopher B. Sherk, General Finance, Corporate, Commercial, Real Estate
905-577-1040 e-mail: csherk@jaskulasherk.com

Jasman & Evans
PO Box 2530
985 East Ave.
Pincher Creek, AB T0K 1W0
403-627-2877
Fax: 403-627-4495
Number of Lawyers: 2
Profile: Real Estate; Mortgages

Finance Lawyers:
D.J. Evans, General Finance
G.L. Jasman, General Finance

Jomha, Skrobot LLP
#2260
10123 - 99th St. NW
Edmonton, AB T5J 3H1
780-424-0688
Fax: 780-424-0695
jomhalaw@telusplanet.net
Founded: 1990
Number of Lawyers: 3

Finance Lawyers:
A.M. Jomha

Jutras et associés
449, rue Hériot
Drummondville, QC J2B 1B4
819-477-6321
Fax: 819-474-5691
info@jutras.qc.ca
www.jutras.qc.ca
Number of Lawyers: 5

Finance Lawyers:
Germain Jutras, General Finance
Christine Jutras, General Finance

E. Kahlke
#101
5019 - 49th Ave.
Leduc, AB T9E 6T5
780-986-8427
Fax: 780-986-3108
Number of Lawyers: 1

Finance Lawyers:
Eric Kahlke

Kahn Zack Ehrlich Lithwick
#270
10711 Cambie Rd.
Richmond, BC V6X 3G5
604-270-9571
Fax: 604-270-8282
888-529-6368
general@kzellaw.com
www.kzellaw.com
Founded: 1980
Number of Lawyers: 11
Profile: Business & Commercial Law, Real Estate

Finance Lawyers:
Perry S. Ehrlich, Business Law; Wills; Estates
Jessica Sisk Roehle, Business Law
e-mail: jsiskroehle@kzellaw.com

Kane, Shannon & Weiler
#220
7565 - 132nd St.
Surrey, BC V3W 1K5
604-591-7321
Fax: 604-591-7149
info@ksw.bc.ca
www.ksw.bc.ca
Number of Lawyers: 16

Finance Lawyers:
Heather W. Blatchford, Corporate Franchise
R. Christopher Boulton, Corporate/Commercial
Larry J. Hagan, Tax; Corporate Law
Brendan D. Home, Corporate
Peter J. McCrank, Tax; Business Law
Sean P. O'Neill, Business; Finance; Franchise

Kanuka Thuringer LLP
#1400
2500 Victoria Ave.
Regina, SK S4P 3X2
306-525-7200
Fax: 306-359-0590
firm@kanukathuringer.com
www.kanukathuringer.com
Founded: 1952
Number of Lawyers: 27

Finance Lawyers:
Randall J. Baker, General Finance
306-525-7228 e-mail: rbaker@kanukathuringer.com
Paul R. McIntyre, Insurance
Ronald M. Warsaba, General Finance
306-525-7207 e-mail: rwarsaba@kanukathuringer.com
Laurance J. Yakimowski, General Finance
306-525-7214 e-mail: lyakimowski@kanukathuringer.com

Harvey Katz Professional Corporation
14 Hess St. South
Hamilton, ON L8P 3M8
905-523-1442
Fax: 905-525-3817
harvey@hjklaw.on.ca
www.hjklaw.on.ca
Founded: 1979
Number of Lawyers: 2
Profile: Firm provides wills & estate planning; D. Schell, also of the New York Bar

Finance Lawyers:
David Schell, Commercial Litigation

Kitchen Kitchen Simeson McFarlane
PO Box 428
86 Simcoe St. South
Oshawa, ON L1H 7L5
905-579-5302
Fax: 905-579-6073
888-669-6446
mail@kksm.com
www.kksm.com
Founded: 1978
Number of Lawyers: 7
Profile: Corporate; Commercial; Bankruptcy

Finance Lawyers:
Jason D.D. Hunt, Debt Collection
905-579-5302 e-mail: jhunt@kksm.com
Ronald J. Kitchen, Corporate/Commercial; Wills & Estates
905-579-5302 e-mail: rkitchen@kksm.com
Kevin P. Mara, Corporate/Commercial; Wills & Estates
905-579-5302 e-mail: kmara@kksm.com

Klaiman, Edmonds
#1000
60 Yonge St.
Toronto, ON M5E 1H5
416-867-9600
Fax: 416-867-9783
edmonds@klaimanedmonds.com
www.klaimanedmonds.com
Number of Lawyers: 2
Profile: Commercial Litigation; Securities Litigation; Shareholders Disputes; Estate Litigation; Mediation; Arbitration

Finance Lawyers:
Diana M. Edmonds
e-mail: edmonds@klaimanedmonds.com
Mark A. Klaiman
e-mail: klaiman@klaimanedmonds.com

Koffman Kalef LLP
885 West Georgia St., 19th Fl.
Vancouver, BC V6C 3H4
604-891-3688
Fax: 604-891-3788
ls@kkbl.com, info@kkbl.com
www.kkbl.com
Founded: 1993
Number of Lawyers: 25
Profile: Act for investors & developers as well as major financial institutions in the borrowing & lending of loans & mortgages

Finance Lawyers:
Morley Koffman, Corporate/Commercial Law
604-891-3688 e-mail: mk@kkbl.com
David S. Pedlow, Tax Law
604-891-3617 e-mail: dsp@kkbl.com
Bernard A. Poznanski, Securities Law
604-891-3606 e-mail: pb@kkbl.com

Kornfeld Mackoff Silber LLP
Bentall Centre, Box 11 #1100
505 Burrard St.
Vancouver, BC V7X 1M5
604-331-8300
Fax: 604-683-0570
866-331-8999
general@kmslawyers.com
www.kmslawyers.com
Number of Lawyers: 13
Profile: Our Corporate Commercial practice group represents clients in a wide range of traditional & emerging industries; from manufacturing, distribution & sales to real estate & hospitality, our client base is a testament to the firm's broad scope of business expertise & first-rate service; the lawyers in our Insolvency & Corporate Restructuring Group have a thorough understanding of the legal issues that arise & are able to provide

Kornfeld Mackoff Silber LLP (continued)
advice in foreclosures, realizations, bankruptcies & corporate restructuring

Finance Lawyers:
Shafik Bhalloo, Corporate Commercial Litigation
604-331-8308 e-mail: sbhalloo@kmslawyers.com
Catherine Craw, Insolvency; Restructuring; Creditors' Remedies; Banking Litigation
604-331-5315 e-mail: ccraw@kmslawyers.com
Donald Haslam, Commercial Real Estate Practice
604-331-8317 e-mail: dhaslam@kmslawyers.com
Lisa Hobman, Corporate, Commercial & Real Estate Law
604-331-8304 e-mail: lhobman@kmslawyers.com
Douglas Hyndman, Insolvency, Foreclosure & Loan Enforcement
604-331-8303 e-mail: dhyndman@kmslawyers.com
Carol Kerfoot, Business; Real Estate
604-331-8302 e-mail: ckerfoot@kmslawyers.com
Neil Kornfeld, Real Property Law; Bankruptcy & Insolvency
604-331-8301 e-mail: nkornfeld@kmslawyers.com
Lana Li, Commercial Litigation
604-331-8309 e-mail: lli@kmslawyers.com
James McRae, Real Estate; Corporate Commercial Law
604-331-8319 e-mail: jmcrae@kmslawyers.com
Joshua D. Sadovnick, Corporate Commercial Law
604-331-8323 e-mail: jsadovnick@kmslawyers.com
Herbert Silber, Estate Litigation
604-331-8313 e-mail: hsilber@kmslawyers.com
Veronica Singer, Corporate Law; Commercial Law; Real Estate Law
604-331-8322 e-mail: vsinger@kmslawyers.com

Kugler Kandestin

#2101
1, Place Ville-Marie
Montréal, QC H3B 2C6
514-878-2861
Fax: 514-875-8424
info@kugler-kandestin.com
www.kugler-kandestin.com
Number of Lawyers: 7

Finance Lawyers:
Jean-François Carpentier, Financing Transactions; Insolvency & Business Restructuring
Michael Gaon, Business; Financing Transactions
Gerald F. Kandestin, Business; Financing Transactions; Insolvency & Business Restructuring
Robert J. Kandestin, Business; Financing Transactions
Robert Kugler, Insolvency & Business Restructuring
Gordon Levine, Business; Insolvency & Business Restructuring
Arthur J. Wechsler, Business

Lacroix, Forest LLP/s.r.l.

Place Balmoral
36 Elgin St.
Sudbury, ON P3C 5B4
705-674-1976
Fax: 705-674-6978
office@sudburylaw.com
www.sudburylaw.com
Founded: 1957
Number of Lawyers: 10
Profile: Financing of small & medium size businesses

Finance Lawyers:
Andre Lacroix, Real Estate
e-mail: alacroix@sudburylaw.com
A.M. Lacroix, Real Estate
e-mail: amlacroix@sudburylaw.com
Alesia Sostarich, Litigation
e-mail: asostarich@sudburylaw.com

Lancaster, Brooks & Welch LLP

PO Box 790
80 King St.
St Catharines, ON L2R 6Z1
905-641-1551
Fax: 905-641-1830
www.lbwlawyers.com
Founded: 1886
Number of Lawyers: 17
Profile: Corporate/Commercial

Finance Lawyers:
Gary L. Black, Corporate/Commercial
e-mail: gblack@lbwlawyers.com
David L. Edwards, Corporate/Commercial
e-mail: dedwards@lbwlawyers.com
Rodger A. Gordon, Corporate/Commercial
e-mail: rgordon@lbwlawyers.com
Michael A. Mann, Corporate/Commercial
R. Bruce Smith, Corporate/Commercial

Lang Michener LLP

BCE Place #2500
PO Box 747
181 Bay St.
Toronto, ON M5J 2T7
416-360-8600
Fax: 416-365-1719
info@langmichener.ca
www.langmichener.ca
Founded: 1992
Number of Lawyers: 88
Profile: As one of Canada's leading business law firms, Lang Michener couonsels a full array of financial & financial service institutions; our lawyers regularly advice commercial & investment banks, mortgage lenders insurers, investment dealers & investment funds on their transactional, operational & regulatory needs; members of our team have held positions with regulatory agencies, served in executive positions with financial industry clients, have been trained as Certified Public Accountants, & hold leadership positions in numerous financial industry organizations & associations; we speak the language of our financial clients, & provide practical solutions to meet their legal & business needs

Finance Lawyers:
David H. Atkins, Banking & Restructuring; Insurance
416-307-4041 e-mail: datkinds@langmichener.ca
Bronwyn Atkinson, Financial Institutions
416-307-4136 e-mail: batkinson@langmichener.ca
Gerald Badali, Financial Institutions
416-307-4064 e-mail: gbadali@langmichner.ca
David Burstein, Financial Institutions
416-307-4145 e-mail: dburstein@langmichener.ca
Ron Carinci, Real Estate; Tax
416-307-4125 e-mail: dcarinci@langmichener.ca
Paul Collins, Securities
416-307-4050 e-mail: pcollins@langmichner.ca
Behn E. Conroy, Financial Institutions; Banking & Restructuring
416-307-4177 e-mail: bconroy@langmichener.ca
John S. Contini, Financial Institutions
416-307-4148 e-mail: jcontini@langmichener.ca
John Conway, Securities
416-307-4222 e-mail: jconway@langmichener.ca
Robert R. Cranston, General Finance
416-307-4038 e-mail: rcranston@langmichener.ca
Joseph C. D'Angelo, Financial Institutions
416-307-4088 e-mail: jdangelo@langmichener.ca
Adam Davis, Securities
416-307-4231 e-mail: adavis@langmichener.ca
Carl A. De Vuono, General Finance
416-307-4055 e-mail: cdevuono@langmichener.ca
John L. Dillman, General Finance
416-307-4034 e-mail: jdillman@langmichener.ca
Howard M. Drabinsky, General Finance
416-307-4033 e-mail: hdrabinsky@langmichener.ca
Dunia El-Jawhari, Securities
416-307-4180 e-mail: deljawhari@langmichener.ca
Arnold Englander, Tax
416-307-4057 e-mail: aenglander@langmichener.ca
Eric Friedman, Financial Institutions
416-307-4030 e-mail: efriedman@langmichener.ca
Christopher Garrah, Financial Institutions
416-307-4211 e-mail: cgarrah@langmichener.ca
Matthew German, Financial Institutions
416-307-4146 e-mail: mgerman@langmichener.ca
Peter Giddens, Financial Institutions
416-307-4042 e-mail: pgiddens@langmichener.ca
Robert E. Glass, General Finance
416-307-4108 e-mail: rglass@langmichener.ca
David Hager, Financial Institutions
416-307-4074 e-mail: dhager@langmichener.ca
Peter Hayden, Business Law
416-307-4054 e-mail: phayden@langmichener.ca
Alison Hayman, Financial Institutions
416-307-4155 e-mail: ahayman@langmichener.ca
Jeff Heinbuch, Banking & Restructuring
416-307-4152 e-mail: jheinbuch@langmichener.ca
Emilie Kydd, Insurance
416-307-4191 e-mail: ekydd@langmichener.ca
Howard A. Levitt, Financial Institutions
416-307-4059 e-mail: hlevitt@langmichener.ca
Carol Virginia Lyons, Financial Institutions
416-307-4106 e-mail: clyons@langmichener.ca
Craig Manuel, Securities
416-307-4170 e-mail: cmanuel@langmichener.ca
Robert M. McDerment, General Finance
416-307-4058 e-mail: rmcderment@langmichener.ca
Bruce A. McKenna, Real Estate
416-307-4112
Richard Meagher, Insurance
416-307-4025 e-mail: rmeagher@langmichener.ca
Michael Mulroy, Financial Institutions
416-307-4076 e-mail: mmulroy@langmichener.ca
Geofrey Myers, Corporate Finance/Securities
416-307-4040 e-mail: gmyers@langmichener.ca
Frank Palmay, Financial Institutions
416-307-4037 e-mail: fpalmay@langmichener.ca
John Payne, Financial Institutions
416-307-4218 e-mail: jpayne@langmichener.ca
Patrick J. Phelan, General Finance
416-307-4068 e-mail: pphelan@langmichener.ca
Donald N. Plumley, Financial Institutions
416-307-4046 e-mail: dplumley@langmichener.ca
Martin D. Rabinovitch, General Finance
416-307-4115 e-mail: mrabinovitch@langmichener.ca
J. Mark Richardson, General Finance
416-307-4142 e-mail: mrichardson@langmichener.ca
Nika Robinson, Financial Institutions
416-307-4244 e-mail: nrobinson@langmichener.ca
William A. Rowlands, General Finance
416-307-4065 e-mail: wrowlands@langmichener.ca
William J.V. Sheridan, Securities
416-307-4060 e-mail: wsheridan@langmichener.ca
Jeffrey B. Simpson, Financial Institutions; Insurance
416-307-4011 e-mail: jsimpson@langmichener.ca
Hellen L. Siwanowicz, Securities
416-307-4032 e-mail: hsiwanowicz@langmichener.ca
Kalle Soomer, Tax
416-307-4117 e-mail: ksoomer@langmichener.ca
Timothy Squire, Financial Institutions
416-307-4113 e-mail: tsquire@langmichener.ca
James Stranges, Financial Institutions
416-307-4183 e-mail: jstranges@langmichener.ca
George Waggott, Financial Institutions
416-307-4221 e-mail: gwaggott@langmichener.ca
R. Nairn Waterman, Financial Institutions
416-307-4024 e-mail: waterman@toronto.langmichener.ca
Patrick Westaway, Tax
416-307-4160 e-mail: pwestaway@langmichener.ca
Marni M.K. Whitaker, Tax
416-307-4161 e-mail: mwhitaker@langmichener.ca
Leslie A. Wittlin, Financial Institutions; Banking & Restructuring
416-307-4087 e-mail: lwittlin@langmichener.ca
David N.W. Young, Insurance
416-307-4118 e-mail: dyoung@langmichener.ca

Lang Michener LLP

#300
50 O'Connor St.
Ottawa, ON K1P 6L2
613-232-7171
Fax: 613-231-3191
emulhall@langmichener.ca
www.langmichener.ca
Number of Lawyers: 35

Finance Lawyers:
Norman M. Fera, Financial Institutions
613-232-7171 e-mail: nfera@langmichener.ca
John G.M. Hooper, Tax & Estates
613-232-7171 e-mail: jhooper@langmichener.ca
Geoffrey C. Kubrick, Real Estate
613-232-7171
Emanuel Montenegrino, Banking & Project Finance
e-mail: emontenegrino@langmichener.ca
P.K. Pal, Securities
613-232-7171
Terry W. Peterman, Corporate Finance/Securities
613-232-7171 e-mail: tpeterman@langmichener.ca
Ronald S. Petersen, Tax & Estates
e-mail: rpetersen@langmichener.ca
Michael S. Rankin, Banking & Restructuring
613-232-7171 e-mail: mrankin@langmichener.ca

Pierre de Neuville Richard, Business Law
613-232-7171 e-mail: prichard@langmichener.ca
Charles Saikaley, Banking & Project Finance
e-mail: csaikaley@langmichener.ca
Barbara J. Sinclair, Tax & Estates
e-mail: bsinclair@langmichener.ca
Marc Smith, Insurance
e-mail: msmith@langmichener.ca
Michael Switzer, Insurance
e-mail: mswitzer@langmichener.ca
Martin Thompson, Insurance
613-232-7171 e-mail: mthompson@langmichener.ca
Jennifer A. Ward, Tax & Estates
e-mail: jward@langmichener.ca

Lang Michener LLP

Royal Centre #1500
PO Box 11117
1055 West Georgia
Vancouver, BC V6E 4N7
604-689-9111
Fax: 604-685-7084
www.langmichener.ca
Founded: 1926
Number of Lawyers: 61

Finance Lawyers:
Candice Alderson, Corporate Finance/Securities
e-mail: calderson@lmls.com
Desmond Balakrishnan, Corporate Finance/Securities
e-mail: dbalakrishnan@lmls.com
Edward A. Bence, Corporate Finance/Securities
e-mail: ebence@lmls.com
Richard James Bennett, Mergers & Acquisitions
e-mail: rbennett@lmls.com
James M. Bond, Franchise & Distribution
e-mail: jbond@lmls.com
Peter Botz, Mergers & Acquisitions
e-mail: pbotz@lmls.com
Barbara Collins, Corporate Finance/Securities
e-mail: bcollins@lmls.com
David J. Cowan, Mergers & Acquisitions
e-mail: dcowan@lmls.com
Tom Deutsch, Corporate Finance/Securities
e-mail: tdeutsch@lmls.com
G. Barry Finlayson, Corporate Finance/Securities
e-mail: bfinlayson@lmls.com
Tracey P. Gibb, Corporate Finance/Securities
e-mail: tgibb@lmls.com
Stacey J. Handley, Banking & Project Finance
e-mail: shandley@lmls.com
Linda J. Hogg, Corporate Finance/Securities
e-mail: lhogg@lmls.com
Zaichi Hu, Corporate Finance/Securities
e-mail: zhu@lmls.com
Larry S. Hughes, Mergers & Acquisitions
e-mail: lhughes@lmls.com
Rubina Jamal, Corporate Finance/Securities
e-mail: rjamal@lmls.com
Cory H. Kent, Corporate Finance/Securities
e-mail: ckent@lmls.com
Sandra M. Knowler, Mergers & Acquisitions
e-mail: sknowler@lmls.com
Christopher Lee, Corporate Finance/Securities
e-mail: clee@lmls.com
Steve Mathiesen, Corporate Finance/Securities
e-mail: smathiesen@lmls.com
Graham Matthews, Banking & Project Finance
e-mail: gmatthews@lmls.com
Christine Mingie, Business Law
e-mail: cmingie@lmls.com
Charlotte A. Morganti, Corporate Finance/Securities
e-mail: cmorganti@lmls.com
John D. Morrison, Banking Law; Business Law
e-mail: jmorrison@lmls.com
James Munro, Corporate Finance/Securities
e-mail: jmunro@lmls.com
Herb Ono, Corporate Finance/Securities
e-mail: hono@lmls.com
Douglas H. Pedlow, Banking & Project Finance
e-mail: dpedlow@lmls.com
Laurel Petryk, Corporate Finance/Securities
e-mail: lpetryk@lmls.com
Leo Raffin, Corporate Finance/Securities
e-mail: lraffin@lmls.com
David J. Ross, Mergers & Acquisitions
e-mail: dross@lmls.com
Amandeep Sandhu, Corporate Finance/Securities
e-mail: asandhu@lmls.com
Evie Sheppard, Corporate Finance/Securities
e-mail: esheppard@lmls.com
Jeffrey Sheremeta, Corporate Finance/Securities
e-mail: jsheremeta@lmls.com
Robert Standerwick, Corporate Finance/Securities
e-mail: rstanderwick@lmls.com
George Stevens, Corporate Finance/Securities
e-mail: gstevens@lmls.com
Michael H. Taylor, Corporate Finance/Securities
e-mail: mtaylor@lmls.com
Tom Theodorakis, Corporate Finance/Securities
e-mail: ttheodorakis@lmls.com
François E.J. Tougas, Mergers & Acquisitions
e-mail: ftougas@lmls.com
Sharon Wong, Corporate Finance/Securities
e-mail: swong@lmls.com
Stephen D. Wortley, Corporate Finance/Securities
e-mail: swortley@lmls.com
Bernhard Zinkhofer, Corporate Finance/Securities
e-mail: bzinkhofer@lmls.com

Langevin Morris LLP

190 O'Connor St., 9th Fl.
Ottawa, ON K2P 2R3
613-230-5787
Fax: 613-230-8563
general@langevinmorris.com
www.langevinmorris.com
Number of Lawyers: 14
Profile: Tax Law & Corporate Law

Finance Lawyers:
Jeffrey Langevin, Real Estate

Lapointe Rosenstein

#1400
1250, boul René-Lévesque ouest
Montréal, QC H3B 5E9
514-925-6300
Fax: 514-925-9001
general@lapointerosenstein.com
www.lapointerosenstein.com
Founded: 1966
Number of Lawyers: 52
Profile: Built on the successful practice of business & commercial law, we have developed our expertise to address the highly specialized needs of the corporate finance & securities, venture capital, life sciences, licences & technology, energy, franchising & real estate sectors

Finance Lawyers:
Pierre Barnard, Corporate & Securities; Venture Capital; Mergers & Acquisitions
514-925-6376 e-mail: pierre.barnard@lapointerosenstein.com

Claude Bergeron, Corporate & Securities; Venture Capital; Mergers & Acquisitions
514-925-6303 e-mail:
claude.bergeron@lapointerosenstein.com
Annie Buzzanga, Venture Capital; Mergers & Acquisitions
514-925-6377 e-mail:
annie.buzzanga@lapointerosenstein.com
Alexandre Béchard, Commercial
514-925-6308 e-mail:
alexandre.bechard@lapointerosenstein.com
Joyce Carestia, Corporate; Securities; Mergers; Acquisitions
514-925-6339 e-mail: joyce.carestia@lapointerosenstein.com

Steven Chaimberg, Corporate & Securities
514-925-6342 e-mail:
steven.chaimberg@lapointerosenstein.com
Denis Chaurette, Corporate & Securities; Venture Capital; Mergers & Acquisitions; Real Estate
514-925-6378 e-mail:
denis.chaurette@lapointerosenstein.com
Karine Chênevert, Commercial Litigation
514-925-6391 e-mail:
karine.chenevert@lapointerosenstein.com
Alexandre Ciocilteu, Corporate & Securities
514-925-6302 e-mail:
alexandre.ciocilteu@lapointerosenstein.c
Martine Comeau, Corporate & Securities; Mergers & Acquisitions; Tax; Real Estate
514-925-6379 e-mail:
martine.comeau@lapointerosenstein.com
Lara Daniel, Franchising
514-925-6374 e-mail: lara.daniel@lapointerosenstein.com
Howard W. Dermer, Commercial
514-925-6307 e-mail:
howard.dermer@lapointerosenstein.com
Jean-Sébastien Dugas, Corporate & Securities; Venture Capital; Mergers & Acquisitions
514-925-6380 e-mail:
jean-sebastien.dugas@lapointerosenstein.
Sébastien Dyotte, Commercial; Bankruptcy & Insolvency
514-925-6381 e-mail:
sebastien.dyotte@lapointerosenstein.com
Bruno Floriani, Corporate & Securities; Mergers & Acquisitions
514-925-6310 e-mail: bruno.floriani@lapointerosenstein.com
Jeanne Fortin, Corporate & Securities; Mergers & Acquisitions
514-925-6311 e-mail: jeanne.fortin@lapointerosenstein.com
Brahm M. Gelfand, Mergers & Acquisitions
514-925-6313 e-mail:
brahm.gelfand@lapointerosenstein.com
Bernard Gravel, Commercial Bankruptcy & Bankruptcy
514-925-6382 e-mail:
bernard.gravel@lapointerosenstein.com
Seti K. Hamalian, Venture Capital; Mergers & Acquisitions
514-925-6363 e-mail: seti.hamalian@lapointerosenstein.com
Paul Hardy, Corporate & Securities; Mergers & Acquisitions; Real Estate
514-925-6383 e-mail: paul.hardy@lapointerosenstein.com
Jean-Charles Hare, Venture Capital; Tax
514-925-6306 e-mail:
jean-charles.hare@lapointerosenstein.com
Luc Huppé, Commercial
514-925-6385 e-mail: luc.huppe@lapointerosenstein.com
Allen D. Israel, Intellectual Property
514-925-6365 e-mail: allen.israel@lapointerosenstein.com
Norman Issley, Mergers & Acquisitions
514-925-6317 e-mail: norman.issley@lapointerosenstein.com

Michael Kaylor, Tax
514-925-6337 e-mail:
michael.kaylor@lapointerosenstein.com
Perry Kliot, Venture Capital; Mergers & Acquisitions
514-925-6318 e-mail: perry.kliot@lapointerosenstein.com
Alexander S. Konigsberg, Business Law
514-925-6319 e-mail:
alex.konigsberg@lapointerosenstein.com
Ian MacPhee, Intellectual Property
514-925-6323 e-mail: ian.macphee@lapointerosenstein.com
Angela Markakis, Commercial
514-925-6314 e-mail:
angela.markakis@lapointerosenstein.com
Antonietta Melchiorre, Commercial; Corporate & Securities
514-925-6355 e-mail:
antonietta.melchiorre@lapointerosenstein
Patrick Menda, Mergers, Acquisitions, Licensing, Technology
514-925-6321 e-mail: patrick.menda@lapointerosenstein.com

Michel Ménard, Commercial; Corporate & Securities
514-925-6328 e-mail:
michel.menard@lapointerosenstein.com
Elizabeth Pedzik, Venture Capital; Mergers & Acquisitions
514-925-6347 e-mail:
elizabeth.pedzik@lapointerosenstein.com
Eric Potvin, Commercial
514-925-6371 e-mail: eric.potvin@lapointerosenstein.com
Norman Rishikof, Venture Capital; Mergers & Acquisitions
514-925-6333 e-mail:
norman.rishikof@lapointerosenstein.com
Melissa Rivest, Commercial
514-925-6387 e-mail: melissa.rivest@lapointerosenstein.com

Mark M. Rosenstein, Corporate & Securities; Mergers & Acquisitions
514-925-6335 e-mail:
mark.rosenstein@lapointerosenstein.com
Jacques Rossignol, Commercial
514-925-6336 e-mail:
jacques.rossignol@lapointerosenstein.com
André Rousseau, Commercial; Insolvency & Bankruptcy
514-925-6389 e-mail:
andre.rousseau@lapointerosenstein.com
Stéphane Roy, Commercial
514-925-6349 e-mail: stephane.roy@lapointerosenstein.com

Lapointe Rosenstein (continued)
Alexandre Sirois-Trahan, Taxation & Estate Planning
514-925-6375 e-mail:
alexandre.siroistrahan@lapointerosenstei
Carole Turcotte, Corporate & Securities
514-925-6334 e-mail:
carole.turcotte@lapointerosenstein.com

Wayne S. Laski
#1800
4950 Yonge St.
Toronto, ON M2N 6K1
416-224-0200
Fax: 416-224-0758
wlaski@wlaski.com
Number of Lawyers: 1

Finance Lawyers:
Wayne S. Laski, Corporate/Commercial

Laven & Co.
#900
700 - 4th Ave. SW
Calgary, AB T2P 3J4
403-263-2444
Fax: 403-265-1792
contact@lavenco.com
www.lavenco.com
Founded: 1952
Number of Lawyers: 3

Finance Lawyers:
Shel J. Laven, Wills & Estates; Real Estate; Small Business

Lavery, de Billy
#4000
1, Place Ville-Marie
Montréal, QC H3B 4M4
514-871-1522
Fax: 514-871-8977
info@lavery.qc.ca
www.laverydebilly.com
Founded: 1913
Number of Lawyers: 116

Finance Lawyers:
Head of Financial Law: Serge Bourque, Business Transactions
Philippe Asselin, Business Transaction
Josianne Beaudry, Securities
Pascale Blanchet, Business Transactions
Michel Blouin, Securities
Valérie Boucher, Business Transactions
Patrick Bourbeau, Business Transactions
René Branchaud, Securities
Patrick Buchholz, Business Transactions
Richard Burgos, Business Transactions
Pierre Cadotte, Business Transactions
André Champagne, Business Transactions
Daniel Alain Dagenais, Business Transactions
Pierre Denis, Business Transactions
Pierre Denis
Francis Desmarais
Richard F. Dolan, Business Transactions
Georges Dubé, Securities
David M. Eramian, Business Transactions
Marie-Andrée Gravel, Business Transactions
Benjamin David Gross
Roxanne Hurtubise, Financial Services
Isabelle Lamarre
André Laurin, Business Transactions
André Laurin
Nicolas Leblanc, Business Transactions
Simon Lemay, Business Transactions
Benoit Mallette
Larry Markowitz, Business Transactions
Jean Martel
Nicole Messier, Business Transactions
Philip Nolan, Business Transactions
André Paquette, Business Transactions
Luc Pariseau
Jacques Paul-Hus, Business Transactions
David Pineault
Michel Servant, Securities
Marc Talbot, Business Transactions
Sandrine Tremblay
Patrice André Vaillancourt, Business Transactions
Sébastien Vézina, Securities

Lavery, de Billy
#500
925, ch St-Louis
Québec, QC G1S 1C1
418-688-5000
Fax: 418-688-3458
800-463-4002
info@lavery.qc.ca
www.laverydebilly.com
Founded: 1913
Number of Lawyers: 24

Finance Lawyers:
Michel C. Bernier, Business Transactions
Martin J. Edwards, Business Transactions
Olga Farman, Business Transactions
Jacques R. Gingras, Business Transactions
Stéphane Harvey, Business Transactions
Claude Lacroix, Business Transactions
Jean-Philippe Riverin, Business Transactions
Louis Rochette, Business Transactions

Lawson Lundell LLP
Cathedral Place #1600
925 West Georgia St.
Vancouver, BC V6C 3L2
604-685-3456
Fax: 604-669-1620
genmail@lawsonlundell.com
www.lawsonlundell.com
Founded: 1910
Number of Lawyers: 100
Profile: Our range of practice mirrors our clients' needs: corporate finance, mergers & acquisitions, general business & commercial matters, pensions, tax, labour & employment, real estate & the resolution of disputes through negotiations, mediation arbitration or litigation

Finance Lawyers:
Khaled S. Abdel-Barr, Corporate & Commercial, Mergers & Acquisitions
604-631-9233 e-mail: kabdel-barr@lawsonlundell.com
David A. Allard, Corporate & Commercial, Corporate Finance & Securities, Megers & Acquistions
604-631-9108 e-mail: dallard@lawsonlundell.com
Deborah D. Anderson, Banking & Insolvency
604-631-9143 e-mail: danderson@lawsonlundell.com
Rita C. Andreone, Corporate & Commercial
604-631-9205 e-mail: randreone@lawsonlundell.com
Monica T. Balaski, Corporate & Commercial, Banking & Insolvency
403-218-7508 e-mail: mbalaski@lawsonlundell.com
Chris G. Baldwin, Corporate & Commercial, Mergers & Acquisitions
604-631-9151 e-mail: cbaldwin@lawsonlundell.com
Andrew P. Bedford, Banking & Insolvency, Real Estate
403-218-7522 e-mail: abedford@lawsonlundell.com
Marjorie Brown, Corporate & Commercial; Tax Law
604-631-6717 e-mail: mbrown@lawsonlundell.com
Joanna Cameron, Corporate Finance & Securities, Corporate & Commercial
604-631-9159 e-mail: mjcameron@lawsonlundell.com
Amy J. Carruthers, Corporate & Commercial, Mergers & Acquistions
604-631-6711 e-mail: acarruthers@lawsonlundell.com
Gordon R. Chambers, Corporate & Commercial, Corporate Finance & Securities, Mergers & Acquistions
604-631-9191 e-mail: grchambers@lawsonlundell.com
Randall Chatwin, Corporate & Commercial; Corporate Finance & Securities
604-631-6799 e-mail: rchatwin@lawsonlundell.com
John T.C. Christian, Corporate & Commercial, Corporate Finance & Securities, Mergers & Acquisitions
604-631-9243 e-mail: john.christian@lawsonlundell.com
Gordon M. Craig, Corporate & Commercial, Mergers & Acquisitions
604-631-9155 e-mail: gcraig@lawsonlundell.com
Nathan G.A. Daniels, Corporate & Commercial, Mergers & Acquisitions, Corporate Finance & Securities
604-631-6736 e-mail: ndaniels@lawsonlundell.com
Guy Davis, Corporate & Commercial
604-631-9279 e-mail: gdavis@lawsonlundell.com
Mandeep Dhaliwal, Banking & Insolvency
604-631-6742 e-mail: mdhaliwal@lawsonlundell.com
William F. Dickson, Corporate & Commercial, Corporate Finance & Sercurities, Mergers & Acquisitions
604-631-9169 e-mail: wfdickson@lawsonlundell.com
Heather M. Ferris, Banking & Insolvency
604-631-9145 e-mail: hferris@lawsonlundell.com
Johanna Fipke, Corporate & Commercial; Mergers & Acquisitions
604-631-6709 e-mail: jfipke@lawsonlundell.com
Ken Flowers, Corporate & Commercial, Banking & Insolvency, Mergers & Acquisitions
403-218-7524 e-mail: kflowers@lawsonlundell.com
Brian D. Fulton, Corporate & Commercial, Mergers & Acquisitions
604-631-9185 e-mail: bfulton@lawsonlundell.com
Linda Garvey, Corporate & Commercial, Real Estate, Banking & Insolvency
403-218-7510 e-mail: lgarvey@lawsonlundell.com
Bryan C. Gibbons, Banking & Insolvency
604-631-9152 e-mail: bgibbons@lawsonlundell.com
Leonard Glass, Tax Law
604-631-9140 e-mail: lglass@lawsonlundell.com
Chris J. Hoeschen, Corporate Finance & Securities, Corporate & Commercial
604-631-9238 e-mail: choeschen@lawsonlundell.com
Greg Hollingsworth, Corporate & Commercial; Tax Law
604-631-9240 e-mail: ghollingsworth@lawsonlundell.com
John Houghton, Corporate & Commercial
403-781-9465 e-mail: jhoughton@lawsonlundell.com
Chery Hsu, Corporate & Commercial
604-631-9141 e-mail: chsu@lawsonlundell.com
Reinhold G. Krahn, Tax Law
604-631-9147 e-mail: rgkrahn@lawsonlundell.com
Irving D. Laskin, Banking & Insolvency
604-631-9235 e-mail: ilaskin@lawsonlundell.com
Michael L. Lee, Corporate & Commercial, Corporate Finance & Securities, Mergers & Acquisitions
604-631-9139 e-mail: mlee@lawsonlundell.com
Bonita Lewis-Hand, Banking & Insolvency
604-631-9157 e-mail: blewis-hand@lawsonlundell.com
Michael J. Low, Banking & Insolvency
604-631-9137 e-mail: mlow@lawsonlundell.com
Salman Manki, Corporate & Commercial, Corporate Finance & Securities
604-631-9113 e-mail: smanki@lawsonlundell.com
Valerie C. Mann, Corporate & Commercial, Mergers & Acquisitions, Corporate Finance & Securities
604-631-9173 e-mail: vcmann@lawsonlundell.com
L. Neil Marshall, Corporate & Commercial, Mergers & Acquisitions
604-631-9162 e-mail: nmarshall@lawsonlundell.com
Stephen McCullough, Banking & Insolvency, Real Estate
604-631-9118 e-mail: smccullough@lawsonlundell.com
Michael B. Morgan, Banking & Insolvency, Litigation
604-631-9227 e-mail: mmorgan@lawsonlundell.com
H. Jane Murdoch, Corporate & Commercial, Corporate Finance & Securities
604-631-9198 e-mail: hjmurdoch@lawsonlundell.com
Peter J. Roberts, Banking & Insolvency, Litigation, Products Liablity, Insurance
604-631-9158 e-mail: proberts@lawsonlundell.com
William L. Roberts, Banking & Insolvency
604-631-9163 e-mail: wroberts@lawsonlundell.com
Jerry Schramm, Corporate & Commercial; Corporate Finance & Securities; Mergers & Acquisitions
604-631-9131 e-mail: jschramm@lawsonlundell.com
Jag Shergill, Corporate & Commercial
604-631-6793 e-mail: jshergill@lawsonlundell.com
Lana M. Shipley, Corporate & Commercial
604-631-6756 e-mail: lshipley@lawsonlundell.com
John Smith, Wealth Preservation; Mergers & Acquisitions; Corporate Finance & Securities, Corporate & Commercial
604-631-9120 e-mail: jsmith@lawsonlundell.com
Chandra Snow, Corporate & Commercial; Real Estate
604-631-6737 e-mail: csnow@lawsonlundell.com
Geoffrey Wiest, Corporate & Commercial, Corporate Finance & Securities, Real Estate
867-669-5544 e-mail: gwiest@lawsonlundell.com
Edward L. Wilson, Corporate & Commercial; Real Estate, Insurance Law
604-631-9148 e-mail: ewilson@lawsonlundell.com
Suzanne J. Woolley, Corporate & Commercial
604-631-9280 e-mail: swoolley@lawsonlundell.com
Karen de Ridder, Banking & Insolvency, Real Estate
604-631-9199 e-mail: kderidder@lawsonlundell.com

Lawson Lundell LLP
Bow Valley Sq. 2 #3700
205 - 5th Ave. SW
Calgary, AB T2P 2V7
403-269-6900
Fax: 403-269-9494
skoehler@lawsonlundell.com
www.lawsonlundell.com
Founded: 1998
Number of Lawyers: 10

Finance Lawyers:
Andrew P. Bedford, Banking & Insolvency
403-218-7522 e-mail: abedford@lawsonlundell.com
Ken B. Flowers, Banking & Insolvency
403-218-7524 e-mail: kflowers@lawsonlundell.com
Linda Garvey, Corporate & Commercial
403-218-7510 e-mail: lgarvey@lawsonlundell.com
John Houghton, Corporate Commercial
403-781-9465 e-mail: jhoughton@lawsonlundell.com
Jerrold W. Schramm, Corporate & Commercial
403-781-9475 e-mail: jschramm@lawsonlundell.com

Lawson Lundell LLP
PO Box 818
4908 - 49 St.
Yellowknife, NT X1A 2N6
867-669-5500
Fax: 867-920-2206
888-465-7608
genmail@lawsonlundell.com
www.lawsonlundell.com
Founded: 1910
Number of Lawyers: 6

Finance Lawyers:
Kerry Penney, Corporate & Commercial
867-669-5525 e-mail: kpenney@lawsonlundell.com
Geoffrey P. Wiest, Corporate & Commercial
867-669-5544 e-mail: gwiest@lawsonlundell.com

Lax, O'Sullivan, Scott LLP
#1920
145 King St. West
Toronto, ON M5H 1J8
416-598-1744
Fax: 416-598-3730
Number of Lawyers: 11

Finance Lawyers:
Amy Block
416-360-8481 e-mail: ablock@counsel-toronto.com
Nathaniel Carnegie
416-598-8051 e-mail: ncarnegie@counsel-toronto.com
Rocco DiPucchio
416-598-2268 e-mail: rdipucchio@counsel-toronto.com
Noah Klar
416-598-8648 e-mail: nklar@counsel-toronto.com
Ashley Lattal
416-598-2870 e-mail: alattal@counsel-toronto.com
Clifford Lax
416-598-0988 e-mail: clax@counsel-toronto.com
Paul Michell
416-644-5359 e-mail: pmichell@counsel-toronto.com
Terrence J. O'Sullivan
416-598-3556 e-mail: tosullivan@counsel-toronto.com
Charles Scott
416-646-7997 e-mail: cscott@counsel-toronto.com
Brooke Shulman
416-598-7873 e-mail: bshulman@counsel-toronto.com
Tracy Wynne
416-598-7835 e-mail: twynne@counsel-toronto.com

LeBlanc Boudreau Maillet
#200
735 Main St.
Moncton, NB E1C 1E5
506-858-5666
Fax: 506-858-5570
leblord@nbnet.nb.ca
Number of Lawyers: 6

Finance Lawyers:
Pierre A. Boudreau, Corporate & Commercial Law
Ronald J. LeBlanc, Corporate & Commercial Law

J. Robert LeBlanc
125 Durham St., 2nd Fl.
Sudbury, ON P3E 3M9
705-674-5858
Fax: 705-674-9137
887-674-5858
bleblanc@cyberbeach.net
Founded: 1975
Number of Lawyers: 1

Finance Lawyers:
J. Robert LeBlanc, Bankruptcy & Insolvency
e-mail: bleblanc@cyberbeach.net

Lerners LLP
PO Box 2335
80 Dufferin Ave.
London, ON N6A 4G4
519-672-4131
Fax: 519-672-2044
lerner.london@lerners.ca
www.lerners.ca
Founded: 1929
Number of Lawyers: 64
Profile: Lerners LLP advises individuals, large & small businesses & financial institutions on a wide range of business issues including financing of commercial & residential real estate projects, mergers & acquisitions, secured transactions, debtor/creditor matters, bankruptcy & insolvency, banking law matters & commercial litigation

Finance Lawyers:
Jeffrey A. Ablett, Business Law
519-640-6361 e-mail: jablett@lerners.ca
Bradley D. Bain, Mortgages & Refinancing, Residential & Commercial Real Estate, Commercial Leasing, Purchase & Sale of Business
519-640-6354 e-mail: bbain@lerners.ca
Barbara L. Blew, Business Law, Franchises, Contracts & Leases, Acquisition & Sale of Business, Financing
519-640-6352 e-mail: bblew@lerners.ca
Ottavio Colosimo, General Finance, Business Law, Bank Financing, Real Estate
519-640-6308 e-mail: ocolosimo@lerners.ca
Thomas M. Conway, General Finance, Banking Law, Creditor Remedies, Business Law
519-640-6326 e-mail: tconway@lerners.ca
Ronald C. Delanghe, Acquistions, planning, financing, development of residential & commercial properties; Commercial & Retail Leases
519-640-6350 e-mail: rdelanghe@lerners.ca
James W. Dunlop, General Finance, Business Law
519-640-6347 e-mail: jdunlop@lerners.ca
R. Gregory Hatt, Mergers & Acquisitions, Debt & Equity Financing, Business Law
519-640-6390 e-mail: ghatt@lerners.ca
Peter C. Johnson, Mergers & Acquisitions, Financing, Governance, Corporate Restructurings including CCAA, Business Law
519-640-6390 e-mail: pjohnson@lerners.ca
Anne M. Reinhart
519-640-6304 e-mail: areinhart@lerners.ca
Ian D. Shewan, General Finance, Corporate Financing, Business Law
519-640-6334 e-mail: ishewan@lerners.ca
David G. Waites, General Finance, Debtor/Creditor Rights, Bankruptcy & Insolvency
519-640-6391 e-mail: dwaites@lerners.ca
David M. Woodward, General Finance, Sales, Leases, Financing, Commercial Lending, Business Law
519-640-6341 e-mail: dwoodward@lerners.ca

Lerners LLP
#2400
130 Adelaide St. West
Toronto, ON M5H 3P5
416-867-3076
Fax: 416-867-9192
lerner.toronto@lerners.ca
www.lerners.ca
Number of Lawyers: 47

Finance Lawyers:
Jasmine T. Akbarali, Commercial Litigation & Dispute Resolution
416-601-2380 e-mail: jakbarali@lerners.ca
Rebecca Case, Commercial Litigation & Dispute Resolution
416-601-4186 e-mail: rcase@lerners.ca
Earl A. Cherniak, Commercial Litigation & Dispute Resolution
416-601-2350 e-mail: echerniak@lerners.ca
George S. Glezos, Commercial Litigation & Dispute Resolution
416-601-2371 e-mail: gglezos@lerners.ca
Clifford M. Goldlist, Tax; Corporate/Commercial; Estate Planning Law; Business Law
416-601-4117 e-mail: cgoldlist@lerners.ca
Elizabeth K.P. Grace, Commercial Litigation & Dispute Resolution
416-601-2378 e-mail: egrace@lerners.ca
Gillian T. Hnatiw, Commercial Litigation & Dispute Resolution
416-601-2354 e-mail: ghnatiw@lerners.ca
Don H. Jack, Commercial
416-601-4121 e-mail: djack@lerneres.ca
Peter R. Jervis, Commercial Litigation & Dispute Resolution
416-601-2356 e-mail: pjervis@lerners.ca
Karen Kiang, Commercial Litigation & Dispute Resolution
416-601-2659 e-mail: kkiang@lerners.ca
Michael W. Kortes, Commercial Litigation & Dispute Resolution
416-601-2382 e-mail: mkortes@lerners.ca
Cynthia B. Kuehl, Commercial Litigation & Dispute Resolution
416-601-2363 e-mail: ckuehl@lerners.ca
Jennifer C. Mathers, Commercial Litigation & Dispute Resolution, Tax Law, Employment Law
416-601-2657 e-mail: jmathers@lerners.ca
Robert J. Morris, Commercial Litigation & Dispute Resolution
416-601-2352 e-mail: rmorris@lerners.ca
Lisa C. Munro, Commercial Litigation & Dispute Resolution
416-601-2360 e-mail: lmunro@lerners.ca
David C. Nathanson, Tax; Commercial Litigation & Dispute Resolution
416-601-4130 e-mail: dnathanson@lerners.ca
Brian N. Radnoff, Commercial Litigation & Dispute Resolution
416-601-2387 e-mail: bradnoff@lerners.ca
Christine P. Snow, Commercial Litigation & Dispute Resolution
416-601-4128 e-mail: jsouthren@lerners.ca
John Sorensen, Tax Law, Commercial Litigation & Dispute Resolution
416-601-2389 e-mail: jsorensen@lerners.ca
Anne E. Spafford, Commercial Litigation & Dispute Resolution
416-601-2388 e-mail: aspafford@lerners.ca
Roy E. Stephenson, Commercial Litigation & Dispute Resolution
416-601-2397 e-mail: rstephenson@lerners.ca
Kirk F. Stevens, Commercial Litigation & Dispute Resolution
416-601-2358 e-mail: kstevens@lerners.ca
David R. Street, Commercial Transactions; Start-up & Expansion of Entrepreneurial Businesses; Mergers & Acquisitions; Complex Commercial
416-601-4141 e-mail: dstreet@lerners.ca
Adrienne K. Woodyard, Taxation & Business Law
416-601-4146 e-mail: awoodyard@lerners.ca
Susan B. Wortzman, Commercial Litigation & Dispute Resolution
416-601-2365 e-mail: swortzman@lerners.ca

P. Yoel Lichtblau
499 Wilson Heights Blvd.
Toronto, ON M3H 2V7
416-633-2465
Fax: 416-398-3369
ylichtblau@rogers.com
Number of Lawyers: 1

Finance Lawyers:
P. Yoel Lichtblau, Corporate; Commercial; Real Estate; Intellectual Property

Lindgren, Blais, Frank & Illingworth
PO Box 940
1301 - 101 St.
North Battleford, SK S9A 2Z3
306-445-2422
Fax: 306-445-2313
mlbfh@sasktel.net
Founded: 1969
Number of Lawyers: 4

Finance Lawyers:
Ray J. Blais, General Finance
Ivan S. Frank, General Finance
Brent Illingworth
Eldon B. Lindgren

Lindsay Kenney
#1800
401 West Georgia St.
Vancouver, BC V6B 5A1
604-687-1323
Fax: 604-687-2347
866-687-1323
info@lklaw.ca
www.lklaw.ca
Founded: 1980
Number of Lawyers: 40

Finance Lawyers:
Christopher K. Haines, Banking; Secured Lending
e-mail: chaines@lklaw.ca
Maria Holman, Intellectual Property
e-mail: mholman@lklaw.ca
Philip J. Jones, Corporate/Commercial
e-mail: pjones@lklaw.ca
Julian T.W. Kenney, Corporate/Commercial
e-mail: jkenney@lklaw.ca
Christopher D. Martin, Tax; Pensions; Estates; Banking; Secured Lending & Realizations
e-mail: cmartin@lklaw.ca
James D. Noel, Corporate/Commercial
e-mail: jnoel@lklaw.ca
Dennis B. Peterson, Wills, Estates
e-mail: dpeterson@lklaw.ca
Frank G. Potts, Banking; Secured Lending & Realizations
e-mail: fpotts@lklaw.ca
James T. Rust, Real Estate
e-mail: jrust@lklaw.ca
James G. Shatford, Insolvency & Foreclosure
e-mail: jshatford@lklaw.ca
Kelvin R. Stephens, Corporate/Commercial
e-mail: kstephens@lklaw.ca
Angela E. Thiele, Tax, Pension, Estates, Wealth Preservation
e-mail: athiele@lklaw.ca
Shawn Tryon, Corporate/Commercial
e-mail: stryon@lklaw.ca

Lindsay Kenney
#400
20033 - 64th Ave.
Langley, BC V2Y 1M9
604-534-5114
Fax: 604-534-5927
866-687-1323
info@lklaw.ca
www.lklaw.ca
Number of Lawyers: 13

Finance Lawyers:
Don G. Burrell, Real Estate, Corporate
e-mail: dburrell@lklaw.ca
Darlene M. Dort, Mortgages, Lending
e-mail: ddort@lklaw.ca
Trevor S. Fowler, Insolvency/Foreclosure
e-mail: tfowler@lklaw.ca
Joel R. Hagyard, Insolvency/Foreclosure; Corporate/Commercial
e-mail: jhagyard@lklaw.ca
Duncan Magnus, Corporate/Commercial
e-mail: dmagnus@lklaw.ca
D. Kirk Poje, Corporate/Commercial

John Lo Faso
#600
3700 Steeles Ave. West
Woodbridge, ON L4L 8K8
905-856-3700
Fax: 905-850-9969
johnlofaso@westonlaw.ca
Number of Lawyers: 1

Finance Lawyers:
John Lo Faso

Lockyer Spence LLP
#600
465 Richmond St.
London, ON N6A 5P4
519-675-1058
Fax: 519-675-1086
Number of Lawyers: 1

Finance Lawyers:
T.L. Ashton, Banking; Mergers & Acquisitions; Estates, Wills & Trusts; Corporate & Commercial Law

Lawrence M. Lychowyd
236A Bain Ave.
Toronto, ON M4K 1G3
416-466-8063
Fax: 416-466-9589
larrythelawyer@sympatico.ca
Founded: 1988
Number of Lawyers: 1

Finance Lawyers:
Lawrence M. Lychowyd, Real Estate; Estates; Corporate

MacDermid Lamarsh
#320
728 Spadina Cres. East
Saskatoon, SK S7K 3H2
306-652-9422
Fax: 306-242-1554
macmarsh@macmarsh.com
www.macdermidlamarsh.com
Founded: 1903
Number of Lawyers: 13

Finance Lawyers:
R.B. Emigh, Corporate; Commercial
e-mail: emigh@macmarsh.com

Macdonald & Company
#200
204 Lambert St.
Whitehorse, YT Y1A 3T2
867-667-7885
Fax: 867-667-7600
gmacdonald@anton.yk.ca
Founded: 1949
Number of Lawyers: 3

Finance Lawyers:
Gareth C. Howells, Corporate & Commercial
e-mail: ghowells@anton.yk.ca

Machida Mack Shewchuk Meagher LLP
#1300
707 - 7 Ave. SW
Calgary, AB T2P 3H6
403-221-8333
Fax: 403-221-8339
machidam@mmsbarristers.ab.ca
Founded: 1989
Number of Lawyers: 6

Finance Lawyers:
P.R. Mack, Bankruptcy

MacKenzie Fujisawa LLP
#1600
1095 West Pender St.
Vancouver, BC V6E 2M6
604-689-3281
Fax: 604-685-6494
lawyers@maclaw.bc.ca
www.mackenziefujisawa.com
Founded: 1963
Number of Lawyers: 18
Profile: Banking & Finance Practice Group have significant expertise advising clients with respect to commercial loans, mortgages, other credit granting instruments & all other collateral security; negotiates & drafts project financial agreements for a large range of real estate developments & assists in arranging & documenting the necessary financial instruments for other project acquisition facilities; where required, acts for clients in securing loan transactions under Personal Property Security legislation

Finance Lawyers:
J. Ewen Cameron, Wills & Estates; Banking & Finance; Corporate/Commercial
604-443-1201
Patrick M. Holmes, Corporate/Commercial; Wills & Estates
604-443-1215
Brian J. Konst, Corporate/Commercial
604-443-1207
Kenneth V. Krohman, Banking & Finance; Corporate/Commercial
604-443-1208 e-mail: kkrohman@maclaw.bc.ca
Graham C. MacKenzie, Wills & Estates; Corporate/Commercial
Daniel B. McIntyre, Banking & Finance; Corporate/Commercial
604-688-1418 e-mail: dmcintyre@maclaw.bc.ca
Michael D. Murphy, Wills & Estates
604-443-1210
Judy G. Williams, Corporate/Commercial
604-443-1214 e-mail: jwilliams@maclaw.bc.ca

Macleod Dixon LLP
Canterra Tower #3700
400 Third Ave. SW
Calgary, AB T2P 4H2
403-267-8222
Fax: 403-264-5973
www.macleoddixon.com

Finance Lawyers:
Caroline Abougoush, Real Estate
403-267-8214 e-mail: caroline.abougoush@macleoddixon.com
Marcus W. Archer, Finance
403-267-9547 e-mail: marcus.archer@macleoddixon.com
Kevin E. Barr, Insolvency & Restructuring
403-267-8142 e-mail: kevin.barr@macleoddixon.com
D.L. Baxter, Securities; Aircraft Finance
403-267-8320 e-mail: dan.baxter@macleoddixon.com
C.W. Berard, Securities
403-267-8389 e-mail: charlie.berard@macleoddixon.com
W.H. Bonney, Banking & Private Capital
403-267-8332 e-mail: william.bonney@macleoddixon.com
R.P. Borden, Banking & Private Capital
403-267-8362 e-mail: rick.borden@macleoddixon.com
John P. Carleton, Project Development & Finance
403-267-9406 e-mail: john.carleton@macleoddixon.com
Tricia A. Chrzanowski, Corporate/Commercial
403-267-8133 e-mail: tricia.chrzanowski@macleoddixon.com
J.H. Coleman, Banking & Private Capital; Securities
403-267-8373 e-mail: jim.coleman@macleoddixon.com
Stephen Cooper, Securities
403-267-8384 e-mail: stephen.cooper@macleoddixon.com
Kathleen Cowick, Securities
403-267-8372 e-mail: kathleen.cowick@macleoddixon.com
David Craddock, Corporate/Commercial; Project Development & Finance
403-267-9558 e-mail: david.craddock@macleoddixon.com
David Cuschieri, Corporate/Commercial
403-267-8139 e-mail: david.cuschieri@macleoddixon.com
Deidre Derworiz, Corporate/Commercial
403-267-8328 e-mail: deidre.derworiz@macleoddixon.com
Ryan Doig, Corporate/Commercial
403-267-9469 e-mail: ryan.doig@macleoddixon.com
S.F. Durante, Corporate/Commercial
403-267-8243 e-mail: samuel.durante@macleoddixon.com
Robert J. Engbloom, Securities
403-267-9405 e-mail: robert.engbloom@macleoddixon.com
W.W. Fedun, Banking & Private Capital
403-267-9414 e-mail: wayne.fedun@macleoddixon.com
Justin E. Ferrara, Corporate/Commercial; Securities
403-267-8393 e-mail: justin.ferrara@macleoddixon.com
J.D. Fitzgerald, Securities
403-267-9599 e-mail: john.fitzgerald@macleoddixon.com
Michael Flach, Corporate/Commercial
403-267-9415 e-mail: michael.flach@macleoddixon.com
Joel S. Friley, Project Development & Finance; Banking
e-mail: joel.friley@macleoddixon.com
Jamie L. Gagner, Securities
403-267-9563 e-mail: jamie.gagner@macleoddixon.com
Crae Garrett, Corporate/Commercial
403-267-8254 e-mail: crae.garrett@macleoddixon.com
Mark R. Gerlitz, Corporate/Commercial
403-267-8325 e-mail: mark.gerlitz@macleoddixon.com
H.A. Gorman, Insolvency & Restructuring
403-267-8144 e-mail: howard.gorman@macleoddixon.com
T. Gruchalla-Wesierski, Securities; Finance; Banking
e-mail: tad.gruchalla-wesierski@macleoddixon.com
D.A. Guichon Jr., Project Development & Finance
403-267-9511 e-mail: dave.guichon@macleoddixon.com
Sanjay Gupta, Securities
403-267-8137 e-mail: sanjay.gupta@macleoddixon.com
B.J. Hayden, Corporate/Commercial
403-267-8360 e-mail: brad.hayden@macleoddixon.com

ACCOUNTING & LAW

D.P. Hays, Senator, Corporate/Commercial
403-267-8338 e-mail: dan.hays@macleoddixon.com
Candace Herman, Securities
403-267-9499 e-mail: candace.herman@macleoddixon.com
T.E. Hirst, Banking & Private Capital
403-267-8211 e-mail: tom.hirst@macleoddixon.com
R.C. Hoskins, Securities; Mergers & Acquisitions
267-820-4 e-mail: craig.hoskins@macleoddixon.com
Robert T. Housman, Real Estate
403-267-8118 e-mail: robert.housman@macleoddixon.com
Darren B. Hribar, Securities
403-267-9416 e-mail: darren.hribar@macleoddixon.com
Darren D. Hueppelsheuser, Tax
403-267-8242 e-mail:
darren.hueppelsheuser@macleoddixon.com
H.A. Jacques, Tax
403-267-8357 e-mail: harold.jacques@macleoddixon.com
Salimah Janmohamed, Insolvency & Restructuring; Banking
403-267-8229 e-mail:
salimah.janmohamed@macleoddixon.com
K.E. Johnson, Securities
403-267-8250 e-mail: kevin.johnson@macleoddixon.com
Ricki T. Johnston, Insolvency & Restructuring
403-267-8182 e-mail: ricki.johnston@macleoddixon.com
Neville Jugnauth, Securities; Mergers & Acquisitions
403-267-8257 e-mail: neville.jugnauth@macleoddixon.com
Ryan W. Keays, Corporate/Commercial
403-267-9523 e-mail: ryan.keays@macleoddixon.com
J.K. Kennedy, Securities
403-267-8188 e-mail: jennifer.kennedy@macleoddixon.com
Kathy L. Krug, Securities
403-267-9528 e-mail: kathy.krug@macleoddixon.com
Kent D. Kufeldt, Securities
403-267-9410 e-mail: kent.kufeldt@macleoddixon.com
Dion J. Legge, Tax; Wealth Preservation; Trusts
403-267-9438 e-mail: dion.legge@macleoddixon.com
Steven H. Leitl, Insolvency & Restructuring
403-267-8140 e-mail: steven.leitl@macleoddixon.com
K.-L.G. Litton, Corporate/Commercial
403-267-8192 e-mail: kaylynn.litton@macleoddixon.com
KayLynn G. Litton, Corporate/Commercial
403-267-8192 e-mail: kaylynn.litton@macleoddixon.com
Kirk A. Litvenenko, Securities
267-941-9 e-mail: kirk.litvenenko@macleoddixon.com
K.J. Logan, Banking & Private Capital
403-267-8340 e-mail: kerrie.logan@macleoddixon.com
A.G. Love, Securities
403-267-8366 e-mail: andrew.love@macleoddixon.com
John W. Love, Real Estate
403-267-8318 e-mail: john.love@macleoddixon.com
Harry J. Ludwig, Project Development & Finance
403-267-8235 e-mail: harry.ludwig@macleoddixon.com
Jack MacGillivray, Corporate/Commercial; Securities; Banking
403-267-9407 e-mail: jack.macgillivray@macleoddixon.com
H.E. MacKichan, Banking & Private Capital; Finance
403-267-8388 e-mail:
howard.mackichan@macleoddixon.com
D.S. MacKimmie, Banking & Private Capital; Real Estate
403-267-9403 e-mail:
donald.mackimmie@macleoddixon.com
Ian E. MacRae, Corporate/Commercial; Banking; Real Estate; Finance
403-267-8153 e-mail: ian.macrae@macleoddixon.com
Craig Maurice, Tax
403-267-8294 e-mail: craig.maurice@macleoddixon.com
Daniel G. McElroy, Securities
403-267-8396 e-mail: daniel.mcelroy@macleoddixon.com
S.M. Negraiff, Securities
403-267-8175 e-mail: scott.negraiff@macleoddixon.com
Rujuta Patel, Corporate/Commercial
403-267-9422 e-mail: rujuta.patel@macleoddixon.com
Chrysten E. Perry, Project Development & Finance
403-267-8170 e-mail: chrysten.perry@macleoddixon.com
K.B. Potter, Securities; Banking
403-267-8184 e-mail: brandon.potter@macleoddixon.com
Kenneth Potter, Securities; Banking
403-267-8299 e-mail: ken.potter@macleoddixon.com
Katherine Prusinkiewicz, Securities
403-267-8313 e-mail:
katherine.prusinkiewicz@macleoddixon.com
S.G. Raby, Real Estate
403-267-8226 e-mail: steve.raby@macleoddixon.com
Ryan J. Rovere, Corporate/Commercial; Banking
403-267-8176 e-mail: ryan.rovere@macleoddixon.com
Stacey Scott, Securities; Corporate/Commercial; Finance
403-267-8352 e-mail: stacey.scott@macleoddixon.com
Rashi Sengar, Corporate/Commercial; Project Development & Finance
403-267-8350 e-mail: rashi.sengar@macleoddixon.com
B.D. Sherman, Real Estate
403-267-8216 e-mail: brian.sherman@macleoddixon.com
D.R. Skeith, Securities
403-267-8165 e-mail: rick.skeith@macleoddixon.com
Kirsten T. Sklar, Securities; Banking; Corporate/Commercial
403-267-9574 e-mail: kirsty.sklar@macleoddixon.com
Marlene G. Stewart, Securities; Project Development & Finance
403-267-9418 e-mail: marlene.stewart@macleoddixon.com
S.C. Stimpson, Corporate/Commercial; Finance; Banking
403-267-9549 e-mail:
stephanie.stimpson@macleoddixon.com
D. Tse, Securities
403-267-8249 e-mail: don.tse@macleoddixon.com
W.H. Tuer, Banking & Private Capital
403-267-8385 e-mail: bill.tuer@macleoddixon.com
Karen Uehara, Securities; Corporate/Commercial
403-267-8392 e-mail: karen.uehara@macleoddixon.com
R.S. Van de Mosselaer, Insolvency & Restructuring
403-267-8196 e-mail: vandemr@macleoddixon.com
Paul Varga, Corporate/Commercial
403-267-8219 e-mail: paul.varga@macleoddixon.com
Christopher M. Wolfenberg, Securities
403-267-8317 e-mail: chris.wolfenberg@macleoddixon.com
Michael I. Wylie, Banking & Private Capital
403-267-9467 e-mail: michael.wylie@macleoddixon.com

Macnutt & Dumont

PO Box 965
57 Water St.
Charlottetown, PE C1A 7M4
902-894-5003
Fax: 902-368-3782
info@macnuttdumont.ca
Number of Lawyers: 4

Finance Lawyers:
Daphne E. Dumont, Real Estate; Wills & Estates
e-mail: ddumont@macnuttdumont.ca
Paula M. MacFadyen, Wills
e-mail: pmacfadyen@macnuttdumont.ca
James W. Macnutt, Litigation; Commercial; Real Estate; Wills
e-mail: info@macnuttdumont.ca
Trevor W. Nicholson, Real Estate, Wills
e-mail: tnicholson@macnuttdumont.ca

MacPherson Leslie & Tyerman LLP

Hill Centre I #1500
1874 Scarth St.
Regina, SK S4P 4E9
306-347-8000
Fax: 306-352-5250
www.mlt.com
Founded: 1920
Number of Lawyers: 34
Profile: Client-centered & business-oriented law firm; our experience extends from the more traditional practice areas of business law (such as corporate finance, mergers & acquisitions, tax, insolvency, commercial litigation) to other rapidly developing areas

Finance Lawyers:
Head of Financial Law: Harold H. MacKay, Corporate & Commercial
e-mail: hmackay@mlt.com
Douglas A. Ballou, Securities
Brian A. Barrington-Foote
Randy U. Brunet, Business Law
James D. Camplin, Banking & Corporate Finance
John A. Dipple, Banking & Corporate Finance
306-347-8414 e-mail: jdipple@mlt.com
Conrad D. Hadubiak, Insolvency
Deron A. Kuski, Insolvency
Lisette LeBlanc, Insolvency & Restructuring
Stathy G. Markatos, Business Law
Michael J. Phillips, Insolvency & Restructuring
Aaron D. Runge, Banking & Corporate Finance; Securities
Bradley N. Vance, Business Law
Donald K. Wilson, Banking & Corporate Finance; Securities

MacPherson Leslie & Tyerman LLP

Canterra Tower #4505
400 - 3rd Ave. SW
Calgary, AB T2P 4H2
403-693-4300
Fax: 403-263-4302
866-693-0999
jkerby@mlt.com
www.mlt.com
Founded: 1920
Number of Lawyers: 14
Profile: Business law firm providing services in the areas of corporate/commercial law & insolvency law

Finance Lawyers:
Richard Billington, Insolvency & Restructuring
Michael J. Clark, Banking & Corporate Finance; Securities
403-693-4303 e-mail: mclark@mlt.com
Scott A. Exner, Banking & Corporate Finance; Securities
403-693-4301 e-mail: exner@mlt.com
Janine Lavoie, Insolvency & Restructuring
Kelly Nicholson, Insolvency
Michael Wright, Business Law

MacPherson Leslie & Tyerman LLP

TD Tower #2105
10088 - 102nd Ave.
Edmonton, AB T5J 2Z1
780-969-3500
Fax: 780-969-3549
Number of Lawyers: 3

Finance Lawyers:
Gordon Beck
Garnet Matsuba

MacPherson Leslie & Tyerman LLP

#1500
410 - 22nd St. East
Saskatoon, SK S7K 5T6
306-975-7100
Fax: 306-975-7145
www.mlt.com
Number of Lawyers: 35

Finance Lawyers:
Kim Bodnarchuk, Business Law
Carol L. Carlson, Insolvency
Kelly Caruk, Business Law
Alain J. Gaucher, Taxation & Estate Planning
Lynn E. Hnatick, Insolvency; Securities
Robert Kasian, Corporate Commercial
Jeffrey M. Lee, Insolvency
R. Neil MacKay, Banking & Corporate Finance; Insolvency
W. Thomas Molloy, Business Law
Vanessa L. Monar-Enweani, Insurance; Insolvency
Douglas L. Osborn, Banking & Corporate Finance
Todd M. Rosenberg, Taxation & Estate Planning; Banking & Corporate Finance
Crystal L. Taylor, Taxation & Estate Planning
Linda Widdup, Business Law
Kurt G. Wintermute, Taxation & Estate Planning
Chris A. Woodland, Business Law

MacPherson MacNeil Macdonald

#5-Feb
188 Main St.
Antigonish, NS B2G 2B9
902-863-2925
Fax: 902-863-2925
mthree@eastlink.com
Founded: 1950
Number of Lawyers: 2
Profile: Work on behalf of financial institutions & clients in preparing mortgages; work also in probating estates

Finance Lawyers:
C. MacNeil Macdonald, Corporate Finance
Donald L. Macdonald, Corporate Finance

MacPherson Mitchell

67 Alma St.
Moncton, NB E1C 4Y3
506-853-1105
Fax: 506-853-9348
judith.macpherson@nb.aibn.com
Founded: 1980
Number of Lawyers: 2

MacPherson Mitchell (continued)
Profile: Financing documents including mortgages, personal property security, purchase & sale of real estate, mechanics liens, debt collections including judgment recovery, examination - debtors

Finance Lawyers:
Judith F. MacPherson, General Finance
e-mail: judith.macpherson@nb.aibn.com
Peter S.A. Mitchell, General Finance
e-mail: peter.mitchell@nb.aibn.com

Maitland & Company
Standard Life Bldg. #700
625 Howe St.
Vancouver, BC V6C 2T6
604-681-7474
Fax: 604-681-3896
maitco@maitland.com
www.maitland.com
Founded: 1976
Number of Lawyers: 5

Finance Lawyers:
Jeffrey B. Lightfoot, Securities
Ronald G. Paton, Securities; Business Law
Michael L. Seifert, Securities
e-mail: seifert@maitland.com

Manning & Kirkhope
430 Wentworth St.
Nanaimo, BC V9R 3E1
250-753-6766
Fax: 250-753-0080
877-753-6766
office@mannkirk.com
www.mannkirk.com
Founded: 1994
Number of Lawyers: 2
Profile: Corporate/Commercial; Real Estate

Finance Lawyers:
Brian Kirkhope, Commercial Litigation; Foreclosures

Marchand, Melançon, Forget
#1900
1, Place Ville-Marie
Montréal, QC H3B 2C3
514-393-1155
Fax: 514-861-0727
800-270-3881
info@mmflegal.com
www.mmflegal.com
Founded: 1950
Number of Lawyers: 36

Finance Lawyers:
Fabienne Beauvais, Insurance
514-393-0087 e-mail: fbeauvais@mmflegal.com
Marc-André Blain, Litigation; Commercial
514-908-3581 e-mail: mablain@mmflegal.com
Frédéric Blanchette, Insurance
514-393-4582 e-mail: fblanchette@mmflegal.com
Jean-Roch Boivin, Taxation; Business Law
514-393-4178 e-mail: jrboivin@mmflegal.com
Serge Boucher, Financing; Business Law
514-393-1437 e-mail: sboucher@mmflegal.com
Jonathan Brochu, Financing; Business Law
514-908-3576 e-mail: jbrochu@mmflegal.com
Jacquelin Caron, Securities; Business Law
514-393-1446 e-mail: jcaron@mmflegal.com
Jean-Pierre Desmarais, Business Law
514-393-1913 e-mail: jpdesmarais@mmflegal.com
Nicolas Dufresne, Business Law
514-908-3580 e-mail: ndufresne@mmflegal.com
Alain Falardeau, Financing; Securities; Business Law
514-908-3579 e-mail: afalardeau@mmflegal.com
Pierre Gonthier, Taxation, Business Law
514-393-0092 e-mail: pgonthier@mmflegal.com
François Haché, Insurance
514-908-3575 e-mail: fhache@mmflegal.com
Guillaume Hébert, Securities; Business Law
514-908-3577 e-mail: ghebert@mmflegal.com
Anne Jacob, Insurance
514-908-3574 e-mail: ajacob@mmflegal.com
Nader Khalil, Taxation; Business Law
514-393-6227 e-mail: nkhalil@mmflegal.com
Valerie Korozs, Litigation; Insurance
514-393-6228 e-mail: vkorozs@mmflegal.com
Marie-Claude Leber, Litigation; Insurance
514-908-3582 e-mail: mcleber@mmflegal.com
Pierre Lessard, Taxation; Business Law
514-393-4201 e-mail: plessard@mmflegal.com
Michel Marchand, Financing; Business Law
514-393-1916 e-mail: mmarchand@mmflegal.com
Francis C. Meagher, Financing; Securities; Business Law; Insurance
514-393-1918 e-mail: fcmeagher@mmflegal.com
Paul A. Melançon, Insurance
514-393-1912 e-mail: pamelancon@mmflegal.com
Antoine Melançon, Insurance
514-393-1920 e-mail: amelancon@mmflegal.com
Eric Messier, Business Law, Commercial
514-393-6260 e-mail: emessier@mmflegal.com
Bertrand Paiment, Insurance
514-393-1917 e-mail: bpaiement@mmflegal.com
Catherine Rayle-Doiron, Insurance
514-940-8469 e-mail: crayle-doiron@mmflegal.com
Mathilde Rompré, Securities; Business Law
514-393-6249 e-mail: mrompre@mmflegal.com
Michel Savonitto, Litigation
514-393-1439 e-mail: nsavonitto@mmflegal.com
Philippe Senécal, Insurance
514-393-4215 e-mail: psenecal@mmflegal.com
Gabriel Senécal, Tax Law; Business Law
514-393-6226 e-mail: gsenecal@mmflegal.com
Michel Tourangeau, Financing; Securities; Business Law
514-393-0227 e-mail: mtourangeau@mmflegal.com
Catherine Tremblay, Taxation; Business Law
514-393-4156 e-mail: catremblay@mmflegal.com
Ann Tremblay, Litigation; Insurance; Commercial
514-393-0852 e-mail: atremblay@mmflegal.com
Martine Trudeau, Commercial Litigation
514-393-1438 e-mail: mtrudeau@mmflegal.com
Ruth Veilleux, Insurance
514-908-3573 e-mail: rveilleux@mmflegal.com

Marchi, Bellemare
#500
266, rue Notre-Dame ouest
Montréal, QC H2Y 1T6
514-288-5753
Fax: 514-284-6606
Number of Lawyers: 5

Finance Lawyers:
Claire Bellemare
Nadine Marchi

Marshall & Lamperson
PO Box 879
710 Memorial Ave.
Qualicum Beach, BC V9K 1T2
250-752-5615
Fax: 250-752-2055
lawfirm@bcsupernet.com
Founded: 1996
Number of Lawyers: 3
Profile: Act for institutional & private lenders to secure commercial & residential transactions; enforce commercial & residential security

Finance Lawyers:
Ronald G. Lamperson, Enforcement of Security

Martin Sheppard Fraser LLP
4701 St. Clair Ave., 2nd Fl.
Niagara Falls, ON L2E 6V7
905-354-1611
Fax: 905-354-5540
800-263-2502
lawyers@martinshep.com
www.martinshep.com
Founded: 1887
Number of Lawyers: 12
Profile: Corporate & Commercial Law; Tax Law

Finance Lawyers:
Raymond L. Steele
e-mail: steele@martinshep.com

Martin, Martin, Evans, Husband
#700
4 Hughson St. South
Hamilton, ON L8N 3Z1
905-525-8873
Fax: 905-525-7737
inquire@martinslaw.ca
www.martinslaw.ca
Founded: 1855
Number of Lawyers: 7
Profile: General Corporate & Commercial Law; Estates; Tax Law

Finance Lawyers:
Martin Luxton

Matheson & Company LLP
10410 - 81 Ave.
Edmonton, AB T6E 1X5
780-433-5881
Fax: 780-432-9453
general@mathesonlaw.com
Number of Lawyers: 6

Finance Lawyers:
Lawrence Ewanchuk, General Finance
e-mail: l.ewanchuk@mathesonlaw.com

Matthews McCrea Elliott
197 Main St.
Fredericton, NB E3A 1E1
506-458-5959
Fax: 506-460-5934
office@matthewsmccreaelliott.com
www.matthewsmccreaelliott.com
Number of Lawyers: 6

Finance Lawyers:
William J. Matthews
e-mail: bill@matthewsmccreaelliott.com

McBride Wallace Laurent & Cord LLP
#200
5464 Dundas St. West
Toronto, ON M9B 1B4
416-231-6555
Fax: 416-231-6630
Number of Lawyers: 8
Profile: Mortgages; Real Estate; Estates & Wills

Finance Lawyers:
MaryLou Ambrosi, Litigation
416-231-6555
Marion E. Howard, Income Tax; Corporate Law
905-878-2989
Paul R. Laurent, Estates & Wills; General Finance
416-231-6555 e-mail: plaurent@mwlc.ca
Joseph M. McBride, Estates & Wills; General Finance
416-231-6555 e-mail: jmcbride@mwlc.ca
Michael C.J. McBride, Estates & Wills; General Finance
416-231-6555 e-mail: mmcbride@mwlc.ca
Gregory M. Uhrynuk, Estates, Wills & Secured Finance
416-231-6555

McCarthy Tétrault LLP
Toronto-Dominion Bank Tower #4700
PO Box 48, TD Tower Sta.
Toronto, ON M5K 1E6
416-362-1812
Fax: 416-868-0673
toronto@mccarthy.ca
www.mccarthy.ca
Founded: 1855
Number of Lawyers: 311
Profile: One of our largest practice areas is in corporate finance, where we represent public issuers & underwriters in corporate finance matters involving the preparation of prospectuses & other offering documents for public & private offerings; we have extensive experience in dealing with mergers & acquisitions & corporate reorganizations; our practice has involved us in many significant takeovers, as well as the development & implementation of defensive strategies in hostile bid situations to improve shareholder values

Finance Lawyers:
Thomas Akin, Tax
416-601-7934 e-mail: takin@mccarthy.ca
Ian Arellano, Mergers & Acquisitions; Secured Transactions; Project Finance; PPSA; Banking; Corporate Finance; Corporate Reorganizatio
416-601-7520 e-mail: iarellan@mccarthy.ca

Gordon Baird, Secured Transactions; PPSA; Corporate Finance; Corporate Reorganizations; Foreign Investments; Mergers & Acquisitions
416-601-7892 e-mail: gbaird@mccarthy.ca
Oliver Borgers, International Transactions; Competitions & Anti-trust; Corporate Finance; Corporate Reorganizations; Foreign Investment
416-601-7654 e-mail: oborgers@mccarthy.ca
Douglas Cannon, Tax
416-601-7815 e-mail: dcannon@mccarthy.ca
Nancy Carroll, Corporate Reorganization; Mergers & Acquisitions; Corporate Finance; Insurance; Banking; Foreign Investment; Privatizati
416-601-7733 e-mail: ncarroll@mccarthy.ca
Stephen Clark, Capital Markets; Secured Transactions; Securitization; Project Finance; PPSA; International Transactions; Trade Finance
416-601-7755 e-mail: sdaclark@mccarthy.ca
Bernadette Dietrich, Trusts & Estates
416-601-7618 e-mail: bdietric@mccarthy.ca
James M. Farley, Senior Counsel
Stephen Furlan, Banking
416-601-7708 e-mail: sfurlan@mccarthy.ca
James Gage, Bankruptcy
416-601-7539 e-mail: jgage@mccarthy.ca
Garth Girvan, Corporate Finance; Directors' & Officers' Liability; Mergers & Acquisitions; Securities
416-601-7574 e-mail: ggirvan@mccarthy.ca
Graham Gow, Corporate Finance; Mergers & Acquisitions; Securities
416-601-7677 e-mail: ggow@mccarthy.ca
Christopher Hunter, E-Commerce
416-601-7875 e-mail: chunter@mccarthy.ca
David Judson, Capital Markets; Corporate Finance; Corporate Reorganizations; Mergers & Acquisitions; Securities; Acquisitions & Financ
416-601-7882 e-mail: djudson@mccarthy.ca
Edward Kerwin, International Transactions; Corporate Finance; Corporate Reorganizations; Directors' & Officers' Liability; Foreign Investments
416-601-7997 e-mail: ekerwin@mccarthy.ca
David Lever, Public-Private Partnership; Secured Transactions; Banking; Corporate Finance; Corporate Reorganizations; Mergers & Acquisitions
416-601-7655 e-mail: dlever@mccarthy.ca
Glen MacArthur, Banking; Competition & Anti-trust; Corporate Finance; Corporate Reorganizations; Directors' & Officers' Liability
416-601-7888 e-mail: gmacarth@mccarthy.ca
Marc MacMullin, Asset Securitization; Corporate Finance; Mutual Funds; Mergers & Acquisitions; Securities
416-601-7558 e-mail: mmacmull@mccarthy.ca
Daryl McLean, Corporate Finance; Corporate Reorganizations; Mergers & Acquisitions
416-601-7700 e-mail: dmclean@mccarthy.ca
Richard Miner, Project Finance; Corporate Finance; Corporate Reorganizations; Franchising; Mergers & Acquisitions; Privatizations; Secu
416-601-7910 e-mail: rminer@mccarthy.ca
Philip Moore, Joint Ventures; Project Finance; International Transactions; Corporate Finance; Corporate Reorganizations
416-601-7916 e-mail: pmoore@mccarthy.ca
Michael Nicholas, Securities; Licensing; Market Regulation; Investment Funds; Mutual Funds; Corporate Finance; Mergers & Acquisitions
416-601-8147 e-mail: mnichola@mccarthy.ca
Linda Pieterson, Banking
416-601-7587 e-mail: lpieters@mccarthy.ca
Steven Rapkin, Secured Financing; Equipment Financing; Lease or Loan Securitizations; Corporate Finance; Mergers & Acquisitions
416-601-7922 e-mail: srapkin@mccarthy.ca
Gabrielle M.R. Richards, Tax
416-601-7766 e-mail: grichards@mccarthy.ca
Sean Sadler, Mutual Funds; Securities; Corporate Finance; Corporate Reorganizations; Directors' & Officers' Liability; Asset Securitization
416-601-7511 e-mail: ssadler@mccarthy.ca
Ronald Schwass, Investment Funds; Mutual Funds; Corporate Finance; Securities
416-601-7684 e-mail: rschwass@mccarthy.ca
Joel Scoler, Banking
416-601-7864 e-mail: jscoler@mccarthy.ca
Rene Sorell, Securities; Capital Markets; Mergers & Acquisitions; Joint Ventures; Investment Funds; International Transactions
416-601-7947 e-mail: rsorell@mccarthy.ca
David Tennant, Corporate Finance; Mergers & Acquisitions
416-601-7777 e-mail: dtennant@mccarthy.ca
Michael Weizman, Corporate Finance; Corporate Reorganizations; Insolvency; Bankruptcy & Financial Restructuring; Mergers & Acquisitions
416-601-7793 e-mail: mweizman@mccarthy.ca
Henry Wiercinski, Public-Private Partnership; Receivership; Secured Transactions; Securitizations; PPSA; Trade Finance; Banking
416-601-7842 e-mail: hwiercin@mccarthy.ca
David Woollcombe, Corporate Finance; Securities; Mergers & Acquisitions; Corporate Reorganizations
416-601-7555 e-mail: dwoollc@mccarthy.ca

McCarthy Tétrault LLP

#3300
421 - 7th Ave. SW
Calgary, AB T2P 4K9
403-260-3500
Fax: 403-260-3501
calgary@mccarthy.ca
www.mccarthy.ca
Number of Lawyers: 49

Finance Lawyers:
Marc Adler, Financial Services
403-260-3665 e-mail: madler@mccarthy.ca
Crispin J. Arthur, Securities; Corporate & Commercial
403-260-3713 e-mail: carthur@mccarthy.ca
Michael J. Bennett, Securities
403-260-3532 e-mail: mbennett@mccarthy.ca
Michael A. Birch, Business Law
403-260-3594 e-mail: mbirch@mccarthy.ca
Keith Byblow, Business Law
403-260-3738 e-mail: kbyblow@mccarthy.ca
Ira Cooper, Corporate & Commercial
403-260-3580 e-mail: icooper@mccarthy.ca
George Craven, Corporate, Commercial, Tax Law
406-260-3687 e-mail: gcraven@mccarthy.ca
Terence Dalgleish, Corporate, Commercial
403-260-3516 e-mail: tdalgleish@mccarthy.ca
Don Davies, Oil & Gas
Robert N. DePoe, Corporate, Commercial
403-260-3702 e-mail: rdepoe@mccarthy.ca
Mark G. Eade, Corporate & Commercial; Securities
403-260-3524 e-mail: meade@mccarthy.ca
Douglas S. Ewens, Corporate & Commercial; Tax Law
403-260-3616 e-mail: dewens@mccarthy.ca
Derek S. Flaman, Corporate; Commercial
403-206-5559 e-mail: dflaman@mccarthy.ca
Juliamai Giffen, Business Law
403-260-3592 e-mail: jgiffen@mccarthy.ca
Sanjib Gill, Corporate & Commercial
403-206-5529 e-mail: sgill@mccarthy.ca
Andrew D. Grasby, Corporate & Commercial; Securities
403-260-3530 e-mail: agrasby@mccarthy.ca
Andrea M. Hatzinikolas, Corporate, Commercial
403-260-3632 e-mail: ahatzinikolas@mccarthy.ca
Autumn D. Howell, Corporate; Commercial
403-260-3593 e-mail: ahowell@mccarthy.ca
David H. Izett, Corporate & Commercial
403-260-3705 e-mail: dizett@mccarthy.ca
T.J. Kang, Corporate; Commercial; Tax Law
403-260-3520 e-mail: tkang@mccarthy.ca
Barclay A. Laughland, Corporate & Commercial; Securities
403-260-3701 e-mail: blaughland@mccarthy.ca
Nicole Lougheed, Corporate, Commercial
e-mail: nlougheed@mccarthy.ca
Bruce L. MacPhail, Corporate & Commercial; Securities
403-260-3657 e-mail: bmacphail@mccarthy.ca
Donald J. McLeod, Corporate & Commercial
403-260-3748 e-mail: dmcleod@mccarthy.ca
Reena B. Modha, Corporate & Commercial; Securities
403-260-3688 e-mail: rmodha@mccarthy.ca
Robert Nearing, Tax
403-260-3678 e-mail: rnearing@mccarthy.ca
Rick W. Pawluk, Corporate & Commercial; Securities
403-206-5522 e-mail: rpawluk@mccarthy.ca
David F. Phillips, Corporate & Commercial; Securities
403-260-3646 e-mail: dfphillips@mccarthy.ca
Cathy Samuel, Business Law
403-206-5528 e-mail: csamuel@mccarthy.ca
Cameron F. Schepp, Corporate & Commercial
403-260-3731 e-mail: cschepp@mccarthy.ca
Dan Sears, Corporate Finance
403-260-3589 e-mail: dsears@mccarthy.ca
Richard A. Shaw, Corporate & Commercial; Bankruptcy & Insolvency; Banking; Securities
403-260-3636 e-mail: rshaw@mccarthy.ca
William H. Smith, Corporate & Commercial; Securities
403-260-3653 e-mail: wsmith@mccarthy.ca
Nicole D. Springer, Corporate; Commercial
403-260-3639 e-mail: nspringer@mccarthy.ca
David J. Stanford, Corporate & Commercial
403-260-3650 e-mail: dstanford@mccarthy.ca
Gregory G. Turnbull, Corporate & Commercial
403-206-5555 e-mail: gturnbull@mccarthy.ca
Annie C. Tétrault, Corporate & Commercial; Securities
403-260-3715 e-mail: atetrault@mccarthy.ca
Lori Wheeler, Business Law
403-260-3711 e-mail: lwheeler@mccarthy.ca
John B. Zaozirny, Corporate & Commercial
403-260-3613 e-mail: jbzaozir@mccarthy.ca

McCarthy Tétrault LLP

One London Place #2000
255 Queens Ave.
London, ON N6A 5R8
519-660-3587
Fax: 519-660-3599
800-460-6619
dhamer@mccarthy.ca
www.mccarthy.ca
Number of Lawyers: 19

Finance Lawyers:
Gordon B. Carmichael, Secured Transactions; Banking; Corporate Finance; Corporate Reorganizations; Directors' & Officers' Liability; Securitie
A. Duncan Grace, Bankruptcy & Restructuring
R. Gregory Hatt, Corporate Finance
519-660-7236 e-mail: ghatt@mccarthy.ca
F. Glenn Jones, Joint Ventures; Banking; Corporate Finance; Corporate Reorganizations; Directors' & Officers' Liability; Foreign Investm
519-660-7211 e-mail: gjones@mccarthy.ca
Alissa K. Mitchell, Bankruptcy & Restructuring
Kristina M. Shaw, Corporate Finance
Ryan T. Sills, Bankruptcy & Restructuring
519-660-7223 e-mail: rsills@mccarthy.ca
Anthony J.G. Van Klink, Bankruptcy & Restructuring

McCarthy Tétrault LLP

The Chambers #1400
40 Elgin St.
Ottawa, ON K1P 5K6
613-238-2000
Fax: 613-563-9386
ottawa@mccarthy.ca
www.mccarthy.ca
Number of Lawyers: 14
Profile: Business Law; Corporate Finance; Taxation; Bankruptcy & Restructuring; Competition; Electronic Commerce

Finance Lawyers:
Colin S. Baxter, Bankruptcy & Restructuring; Business; Realization of Security
613-238-2121 e-mail: cbaxter@mccarthy.ca
Thomas G. Conway, Arbitration & Mediation; Bankruptcy & Restructuring; Business Disputes; Commercial Litigation; Financial Restructuring
613-238-2102 e-mail: tconway@mccarthy.ca
Barbara A. McIsaac, Business Disputes; Commercial Litigation
613-238-2105 e-mail: bmcisaac@mccarthy.ca
Virginia K. Schweitzer, Corporate Finance; Securities; Mergers & Acquisitions
613-238-2174 e-mail: vschweit@mccarthy.ca
Anna M. Tosto, Capital Markets; Secured Transactions; Securitization; International Transactions; Corporate Finance; Mergers & Acquisitions
613-238-2167 e-mail: atosto@mccarthy.ca

McCarthy Tétrault LLP

Le Complexe St-Amable
1150, rue de Claire-Fontaine, 7e étage
Québec, QC G1R 5G4
418-521-3000
Fax: 418-521-3099

McCarthy Tétrault LLP (continued)
quebec@mccarthy.ca
www.mccarthy.ca
Number of Lawyers: 32

Finance Lawyers:
François Amyot, Joint Ventures; Corporate Finance; Corporate Reorganizations; Franchising; Mergers & Acquisitions; Privatizations; Securities
418-521-3001 e-mail: famyot@mccarthy.ca
Pierre Boivin, Acquisitions & Financing; Business; Joint Ventures; Project Finance
418-521-3012 e-mail: piboivin@mccarthy.ca
Jean-Philippe Buteau, Acquisitions & Financing; Corporate Finance; Mergers & Acquisitions; Transactions
Anastassia Chtaneva, Acquisitions & Financing; Contracts; Corporate Finance; Mergers & Acquisitions; Transactions
Doris Dion, Business; Corporate Reorganizations; Mergers & Acquisitions
418-521-3005 e-mail: ddion@mccarthy.ca
Marc N. Dorion, Joint Ventures; Public-Private Partnerships; Project Finance; PPSA; Banking; Corporate Finance; Corporate Reorganization
418-521-3007 e-mail: mdorion@mccarthy.ca
Danielle Drolet, Acquisitions & Financing; Commercial Leasing
Marie-Paule Gagnon, Bankruptcy & Restructuring; Commercial Litigation; Debtor & Creditor; Financial Services; Secured Transactions
Louise Gauthier, Business; Corporate Finance
418-521-3028 e-mail: lgauthier@mccarthy.ca
Marc Germain, Receivership; Secured Transactions; Banking; Corporate Finance; Corporate Reorganizations; Insolvency; Bankruptcy & Reststructuring
418-521-3009 e-mail: mgermain@mccarthy.ca
Isabelle Germain, Business Disputes; Commercial Litigation
Pierre Jolin, Commercial Litigation
Stéphanie Julien, Commercial Litigation
Mathieu Laflamme, Acquisitions & Financing; Corporate Finance; Mergers & Acquisitions; Transactions
Simon Marchand-Fortier, Corporate Finance
Nathalie Marcoux, Business Disputes; Commercial Litigation; Insurance
Jean-François Routhier, Acquisitions & Financing; Business; E-commerce; Transactions
Kim Thomassin, Acquisitions & Financing; Mergers & Acquisitions; Project Finance; Transactions
Sophie Vézina, Community Litigation

McCarthy Tétrault LLP
Pacific Centre #1300
PO Box 10424
777 Dunsmuir St.
Vancouver, BC V7Y 1K2
604-643-7100
Fax: 604-643-7900
vancouver@mccarthy.ca
www.mccarthy.ca
Number of Lawyers: 106

Finance Lawyers:
Richard J. Balfour, Capital Markets; Competition & Anti-Trust; Corporate Finance; Directors' & Officers' Liability; Mergers & Acquisitions
Trevor Bell
Russell G. Benson
Linda G. Brown, Capital Markets; Corporate Finance; Corporate Reorganizations; Directors' & Officers' Liability; Mergers & Acquisitions
Donna J. Cooke
Cappone D'Angelo
Peter D. Fairey, Pensions & Retirement Income Planning; Corporate Finance; Foreign Investments; Mergers & Acquisitions; Joint Ventures
Christopher T. Falk
Joseph A. Garcia
Ashley F. Hilliard, Counsel
George W. Holloway, Corporate Finance; Corporate Reorganizations; Mergers & Acquisitions; Securities
A. Brent Kerr
D. Anthony Knox, Corporate Finance; Corporate Reorganizations; Directors' & Officers' Liability; Mergers & Acquisitions; Corporate & Commercial
Ted I. Koffman, Corporate Finance; Corporate Reorganizations; Directors' & Officers' Liability; Foreign Investment; Mergers & Acquisitions
Ed G. Kroft
Joyce Lee
Tim P. McCafferty, Corporate Finance; Mergers & Acquisitions; Corporate Reorganizations; Securities; Acquisitions & Financing; Capital Mark
Sven Milelli, Corporate Finance
Peter A. Pagnan
John W. Pearson, Business Law
Jill R. Pereira
Matthew D. Peters
Robert J. Sewell, Corporate Litigation
Robin M. Sirett, Corporate Finance
Scott D. Smythe
Daniel E. Steiner
Roger Taplin
Michael G. Urbani, Capital Markets; Corporate Finance; Mergers & Acquisitions; Securities
Brian E. Vick, Corporate Finance; Corporate Reorganizations; Mergers & Acquisitions; Securities
Rosemarie Wertschek, Tax
Derek T. Winnett
Kevin Wright, Secured Transactions; PPSA; Banking; Corporate Finance; Equipment Financing; Acquisitions & Financing
Naomi M. Youngson, Acquisitions & Financing; Transactions; Corporate Reorganizations; Mergers & Acquisitions

McCarthy Tétrault S.E.N.C.R.L., s.r.l.
#2500
1000, rue de la Gauchetière ouest
Montréal, QC H3B 0A2
514-397-4100
Fax: 514-875-6246
877-397-4100
www.mccarthy.ca
Founded: 1855
Number of Lawyers: 164
Profile: Provides advice to Canadian chartered banks & foreign banks, investment institutions, insurance companies & borrowers on matters concerning banking & financial services law, as well as regulation in Canada; practitioners advise on a broad range of issues, including financial institutions regulation, payments systems, personal property security, electronic securities, foreign exchange clearing & settlement systems, domestic & international capital funding programs, lending activities & major commercial projects & financings; assists in domestic & foreign banking groups & syndicates in significant Canadian project financings & aquisitions, as well as corporate loan workouts

Finance Lawyers:
Michel Bergeron, Corporate Finance
514-397-4193 e-mail: mbergeron@mccarthy.ca
Jean-Pierre Bertrand, Bankryptcy & Restructuring
514-397-4222 e-mail: jpbertrand@mccarthy.ca
Jean-François Boisvenu, Corporate Finance
514-397-4189 e-mail: jfboisvenu@mccarthy.ca
Martin Boodman, Competition & Antitrust
514-397-4117 e-mail: mboodman@mccarthy.ca
Patrick Boucher, Corporate Finance; Income Tax; Securities; Acquisitions & Financing
514-397-4237 e-mail: pboucher@mccarthy.ca
Philippe Bourassa, Corporate Finance
514-397-7805 e-mail: pbourassa@mccarthy.ca
Miguel Bourbonnais, Bankruptcy & Restructuring
Mélanie Béland, Bankruptcy & Restructuring
Philippe H. Bélanger, Bankruptcy & Restructuring
514-397-4203 e-mail: pbelanger@mccarthy.ca
Daniel Bénay, Banking; Corporate Finance; Corporate Reorganizations; Mergers & Acquisitions; Securities
514-397-4168 e-mail: dbenay@mccarthy.ca
Yves Bériault, Competition & Antitrust
514-397-4120 e-mail: yberiault@mccarthy.ca
Andrée-Claude Bérubé, Financial Services
514-397-5476 e-mail: acberube@mccarthy.ca
Yves Comtois, Competition & Antitrust
614-397-4282 e-mail: ycomtois@mccarthy.ca
Frèdèric Cotnoir, Corporate Finance
514-397-4407 e-mail: fcotnoir@mccarthy.ca
Thomas R.M. Davis, Corporate Finance; Corporate Reorganizations; Foreign Investment; Insurance; Mergers & Acquisitions; Acquisitions & Financings
514-397-4126 e-mail: trmdavis@mccarthy.ca
Michael Dennis, Mergers & Acquisitions; Corporate Restructuring & Financings
514-397-4122 e-mail: mdennis@mccarthy.ca
Claude P. Desaulniers, Financial Services
514-397-4269 e-mail: cdesaulniers@mccarthy.ca
J. Michel Deschamps, Banking; Corporate Finance; Corporate Reorganizations; Insolvency; Bankruptcy; Financial Restructuring
514-397-4138 e-mail: jmdeschamps@mccarthy.ca
J. Robert Doyle, Corporate Finance
514-397-4169 e-mail: jrdoyle@mccarthy.ca
François Dupuis, Capital Management; Corporate Finance
514-397-7837 e-mail: fdupuis@mccarthy.ca
Mireille Fontaine, Corporate Finance
514-397-4129 e-mail: mfontaine@mccarthy.ca
Nathalie Forcier, Corporate Finance
514-397-5462 e-mail: nforcier@mccarthy.ca
Philippe Fortier, Corporate Finance
514-397-4176 e-mail: pfortier@mccarthy.ca
Jean-François Fortin, Corporate Finance
514-397-7820 e-mail: jffortrin@mccarthy.ca
Marie-France Gagnon, Corporate Finance
514-397-5454 e-mail: mfgagnon@mccarthy.ca
Guy A. Gagnon, Tax
514-397-5660 e-mail: gaganon@mccarthy.ca
Jean-René Gauthier, Corporate Finance
514-397-4299 e-mail: jrgauthier@mccarthy.ca
Warren M. Goodman, Financial Services
514-397-4153 e-mail: wgoodman@mccarthy.ca
Eric Gosselin, Corporate Finance
514-397-4271 e-mail: egosselin@mccarthy.ca
Yves Jobin, Corporate Finance
514-397-4133 e-mail: yjobin@mccarthy.ca
Martine Kaigle, Corporate Finance; Corporate Reorganizations; Directors' & Officers' Liability; Mergers & Acquisitions; Privatization
514-397-4119 e-mail: mkaigle@mccarthy.ca
Pierre Laflamme, Mergers, Acquisitions & Reorganizations
514-397-5696 e-mail: plaflamme@mccarthy.ca
Marc Lemieux, Financial Services
514-397-4208 e-mail: mlemieux@mccarthy.ca
Valérie Lemieux, E-commerce
514-397-5461 e-mail: vlemieux@mccarthy.ca
Pierre-Denis Leroux, Bankruptcy & Restructuring
514-397-4121 e-mail: pdleroux@mccarthy.ca
Clemens Mayr, Business Law
George Maziotis, Commercial; Securities; Venture Law
Robert P. Metcalfe, Banking; Secured Transactions; International Transactions; Trade Finance; Corporate Finance; Mergers & Acquisitions; Lea
514-397-4164 e-mail: rmetcalfe@mccarthy.ca
Richard O'Doherty, Financial Services
514-397-5467 e-mail: rodoherty@mccarthy.ca
Neil A. Peden, Bankruptcy & Restructuring
Mary Jeanne Phelan, Commercial Lending; Derivative & Credit Transactions
Mason Poplaw, Bankruptcy & Restructuring
514-397-4155 e-mail: mpoplaw@mccarthy.ca
Simon V. Potter, Tax
514-397-4268 e-mail: spotter@mccarthy.ca
Madeleine Renaud, Competition & Antitrust
514-397-4252 e-mail: mrenaud@mccarthy.ca
Matthieu Rheault, Corporate Finance
514-397-4452 e-mail: mrheault@mccarthy.ca
Benjamin H. Silver, Banking; Corporate Finance; Corporate Reorganizations; Mergers & Acquisitions; Securities
514-397-4154 e-mail: bhsilver@mccarthy.ca
Sonia Struthers, Mergers & Acquisitions; Corporate Finance; Corporate Reorganizations; Securities; Investment Funds; Mutual Funds
514-397-4232 e-mail: sstruthers@mccarthy.ca
Karl Tabbakh, Corporate Finance
514-397-5479 e-mail: ktabbakh@mccarthy.ca
Alain N. Tardif, Bankruptcy & Restructuring
514-397-4274 e-mail: atardif@mccarthy.ca
Lorna J. Telfer, Corporate Finance; Corporate Reorganizations; Securities; Mergers & Acquisitions; Privatizations; Mutual Funds; Investme
514-397-4184 e-mail: ljtelfer@mccarthy.ca
Sylvain A. Vauclair, Bankruptcy & Restructuring
514-397-4102 e-mail: savauclair@mccarthy.ca

McCrank Stewart Johnson
#208
2208 Scarth St.
Regina, SK S4P 2J6
306-525-2191
Fax: 306-757-8138
vrm@sasktel.net
Number of Lawyers: 9

Finance Lawyers:
Robert D. McCrank, General Finance

McCullough O'Connor Irwin
#1100
888 Dunsmuir St.
Vancouver, BC V6C 3K4
604-687-7077
Fax: 604-687-7099
moimail@moisolicitors.com
www.moisolicitors.com
Founded: 1994
Number of Lawyers: 11
Profile: This firm's practice is restricted to corporate & securities law matters; the firm's pricipal clients are investment dealers & financial institutions

Finance Lawyers:
Mia Bacic
Gillian Case, Securities; Corporate
604-646-3313 e-mail: gcase@moisolicitors.com
David Gunasekera
G.W. Douglas Irwin, Securities; Corporate
604-646-3305 e-mail: dirwin@moisolicitors.com
Jonathan McCullough, Securities; Corporate
604-646-3306 e-mail: jmccullough@moisolicitors.com
Kristin Novak

McDougall Gauley
1500 - 1881 Scarth St.
Regina, SK S4P 4K9
306-757-1641
Fax: 306-359-0785
www.mcdougallgauley.com
Founded: 2001
Number of Lawyers: 31

Finance Lawyers:
Wayne L. Bernakevitch, Business Law/Commercial Law; Corporate Law & Governance
Megan D. Dolo, Business Law/Commercial Law; Corporate Law & Governance
Terence G. Graf, Business Law/Commercial Law
Erin M.S. Kleisinger, Banking & Financial Institutions; Bankruptcy, Insolvency, Receivership & Debt Recovery; Business Law/Commercial Law; Corporate Law & Governance
Gordon J. Kuski, Corporate Law & Governance
Ryan J. Laidlaw, Banking & Financial Institutions; Bankruptcy, Insolvency, Receivership & Debt Recovery; Corporate Law & Governance
Kevin A. Lang, Business Law/Commercial Law; Corporate Law & Governance
E. Craig Lothian, Business Law/Commercial Law; Corporate Finance & Securities
Michael W. Milani, Banking & Financial Institutions; Bankruptcy, Insolvency, Receivership & Debt Recovery; Business Law/Commercial Law; Cor
Robert N. Millar, Business Law/Commercial Law; Corporate Law & Governance; Corporate Finance & Securities; Tax
Amanda M. Quayle, Bankruptcy, Insolvency, Receivership & Debt Recovery
James F. Rybchuk, Business Law/Commercial Law; Corporate Law & Governance; Corporate Finance & Securities
Murray R. Sawatzky, Bankruptcy, Insolvency, Receivership & Debt Recovery
306-565-5141 e-mail: msawatzky@mcdougallgauley.com
Lynn A. Smith, Banking & Financial Institutions; Business Law/Commercial Law
Paul G. Wagner, Banking & Financial Institutions; Bankruptcy, Insolvency, Receivership & Debt Recovery; Business Law/Commercial Law; Cor
Foster J. Weisgerber, Business Law/Commercial Law; Corporate Law & Governance
Christopher S. Weitzel, Corporate Law & Governance
Stuart J. Wicijowski, Banking & Financial Institutions; Business Law/Commercial Law; Corporate Law & Governance

McDougall Gauley
Wicklow Centre #300
1133 - 4th St.
Estevan, SK S4A 0W6
306-634-6334
Fax: 306-634-3852
bbridges@mcdougallgauley.com
Number of Lawyers: 1

Finance Lawyers:
Barry D. Bridges, Business Law/Commercial Law; Corporate Law & Governance; Corporate Finance & Securities

McDougall Gauley
PO Box 638
701 Broadway Ave.
Saskatoon, SK S7K 3L7
306-653-1212
Fax: 306-652-1323
sstrueby@mcdougallgauley.com
www.mcdougallgauley.com
Number of Lawyers: 32

Finance Lawyers:
Brent Barilla, Bankruptcy, Insolvency, Receivership & Debt Recovery
Christopher Boychuk, Banking & Financial Institutions; Bankruptcy, Insolvency, Receivership & Debt Recovery; Tax
Neal Caldwell, Banking & Financial Institutions; Business Law/Commercial Law; Corporate Law & Governance; Corporate Finance & Securities
Richard Danyliuk, Bankruptcy, Insolvency, Receivership & Debt Recovery
Joseph Dierker, Banking & Financial Institutions; Corporate Law & Governance; Corporate Finance & Securities
e-mail: jdierfer@mcdougallgauley.com
Chad Haaf, Bankruptcy, Insolvency, Receivership & Debt Recovery; Business Law/Commercial Law; Corporate Law & Governance; Tax
Jenny Hoffman, Business Law/Commercial Law; Corporate Law & Governance
Nancy Hopkins, Business Law/Commercial Law; Corporate Law & Governance; Tax
Christine Johnston, Business Law/Commercial Law; Corporate Law & Governance
Dale Linn, Business Law/Commercial Law; Corporate Law & Governance
David McKeague, Banking & Financial Institutions; Business Law/Commercial Law; Corporate Law & Governance; Corporate Finance & Securitie
Ronald Miller, Banking & Financial Institutions; Corporate Law & Governance
William Nickel, Banking & Financial Institutions; Business Law/Commercial Law; Corporate Law & Governance; Corporate Finance & Securitie
Randall Rooke, Banking & Financial Institutions; Bankruptcy, Insolvency, Receivership & Debt Recovery; Corporate Law & Governance
William Shaw, Banking & Financial Institutions; Corporate Law & Governance
Ian Sutherland, Banking & Financial Institutions; Bankruptcy, Insolvency, Receivership & Debt Recovery; Business Law/Commercial Law; Cor
Scott Waters, Corporate Law & Governance; Tax
Raymond Wiebe, Business Law/Commercial Law; Tax

McGee Richard
Weber Centre #1155
5555 Calgary Trail NW
Edmonton, AB T6H 5P9
780-437-2240
Fax: 780-438-5788
trichard@mcgeerichard.com
Founded: 1988
Number of Lawyers: 3
Profile: Business Law

Finance Lawyers:
John E. McGee, Corporate; Commercial; Development; Commercial Real Estate

McInnes Cooper
BDC Pl. #620
119 Kent St.
Charlottetown, PE C1A 1N3
902-368-8473
Fax: 902-368-8346
mcctn@mcinnescooper.com
www.mcinnescooper.com
Founded: 1859
Number of Lawyers: 8

Finance Lawyers:
Head of Financial Law: Horace B. Carver, Estates, Trusts & Wealth Planning; Corporate/Commercial
902-892-1224 e-mail: horace.carver@mcinnescooper.com
Susan M. Connolly, Wills; Corporate/Commercial
902-629-6274 e-mail: susan.connolly@mcinnescooper.com
Michael G. Drake, Banking & Financial Institutions; Estates; Trusts; Wealth Planning
902-629-6267 e-mail: michael.drake@mcinnescooper.com
Kevin J. Kiley, Insurance; Banking & Financial Institutions
902-629-6262 e-mail: kevin.kiley@mcinnescooper.com
Roger B. Langille, Insurance; Litigation
902-629-6254 e-mail: roger.langille@mcinnescooper.com
Robert I.S. MacGregor, Corporate/Commercial; Banking & Financial Institutions
902-629-6271 e-mail: robert.macgregor@mcinnescooper.com
Murray L. Murphy, Corporate/Commercial
902-629-6253 e-mail: murray.murphy@mcinnescooper.com

McInnes Cooper
Barker House #600
PO Box 610, A Sta.
570 Queen St.
Fredericton, NB E3B 5A6
506-458-8572
Fax: 506-458-9903
mcfton@mcinnescooper.com
www.mcinnescooper.com
Number of Lawyers: 11

Finance Lawyers:
Heather A. Black, Corporate, Commercial
506-458-1541 e-mail: heather.black@mcinnescooper.com
Steven D. Christie, Estates, Trusts & Wealth Planning; Corporate/Commercial
506-458-1521 e-mail: steven.christie@mcinnescooper.com
Jaime O. Connolly, Corporate/Commercial
506-458-1544 e-mail: jaime.connolly@mcinnescooper.com
Leonard T. Hoyt, Banking & Financial Institutions; Corporate/Commercial
506-458-1622 e-mail: len.hoyt@mcinnescooper.com
Ann Marie McDonald, Insurance
506-458-1546 e-mail: ann_marie.mcdonald@mcinnescooper.com
Alan T. Rockwell, Corporate/Commercial
506-458-1547 e-mail: alan.rockwell@mcinnescooper.com
Patrick V. Windle, Banking & Financial Institutions
506-458-1628 e-mail: patrick.windle@mcinnescooper.com
David Duncan Young, Corporate/Commercial; Banking & Financial Institutions
506-458-1623 e-mail: david.young@mcinnescooper.com

McInnes Cooper
Summit Place
PO Box 730
1601 Lower Water St.
Halifax, NS B3J 2V1
902-425-6500
Fax: 902-425-6350
mchfx@mcinnescooper.com
www.mcinnescooper.com
Number of Lawyers: 62

Finance Lawyers:
Michelle C. Awad, Insurance, Corporate/Commercial
902-444-8509 e-mail: michelle.awad@mcinnescooper.com
Tracy Bastow, Insurance
902-424-1311 e-mail: tracy.bastow@mcinnescooper.com
Robert G. Belliveau, Insurance, Corporate/Commercial
902-424-1344 e-mail: robert.belliveau@mcinnescooper.com
David Demirkan, Insurance
902-424-1388 e-mail: david.demirkan@mcinnescooper.com
Michael Deturbide, Corporate, Commercial
902-425-6500 e-mail: michael.deturbide@mcinnescooper.com
Lawrence A. Freeman, Corporate/Commercial; Banking & Financial Institutions
902-444-8536 e-mail: lawrence.freeman@mcinnescooper.com
Kevin D. Gibson, Insurance
902-424-1337 e-mail: kevin.gibson@mcinnescooper.com
David A. Graves, Insurance
902-424-1330 e-mail: david.graves@mcinnescooper.com
W.Lindsay Hawker, Corporate/Commercial
902-428-1412 e-mail: lindsay.hawker@mcinnescooper.com

ACCOUNTING & LAW

McInnes Cooper (continued)

Lawrence J. Hayes, Estates, Trusts & Wealth Planning; Corporate/Commercial
902-424-1307 e-mail: lawrence.hayes@mcinnescooper.com
Andrew Inch, Corporate/Commercial
902-428-1415 e-mail: andrew.inch@mcinnescooper.com
John Kulik, Insurance
902-424-1339 e-mail: john.kulik@mcinnescooper.com
Douglas Lutz, Insurance
902-424-1352 e-mail: doug.lutz@mcinnescooper.com
George W. MacDonald, Insurance; Corporate/Commercial
902-424-1365 e-mail: george.macdonald@mcinnescooper.com
Janet J. MacNeil, Corporate/Commercial
Christopher C. Robinson, Insurance
902-424-1325 e-mail: chris.robinson@mcinnescooper.com
Alan J. Stern, Estates, Trusts & Wealth Planning; Corporate/Commercial
902-424-1314 e-mail: alan.stern@mcinnescooper.com
Harry E. Wrathall, Insurance
902-424-1327 e-mail: harry.wrathall@mcinnescooper.com
Hugh Wright, Insurance; Banking & Financial Institutions
902-424-1360 e-mail: hugh.wright@mcinnescooper.com

McInnes Cooper

Moncton Place
PO Box 1368
655 Main St.
Moncton, NB E1C 8T6
506-857-8970
Fax: 506-857-4095
mcmctn@mcinnescooper.com
www.mcinnescooper.com
Number of Lawyers: 13

Finance Lawyers:
Rémy Boudreau, Corporate, Commercial
506-877-0849 e-mail: remy.boudreau@mcinnescooper.com
Christa A. Bourque, Insurance
506-877-0838 e-mail: christa.bourque@mcinnescooper.com
Marc-Antoine Chiasson, Insurance
506-861-1920 e-mail: marc.chiasson@mcinnescooper.com
Monique Imbeault, Corporate/Commercial
506-877-0872 e-mail: monique.imbeault@mcinnescooper.com
Denise A. LeBlanc, Insurance
506-877-0862 e-mail: denise.leblanc@mcinnescooper.com
Eric LeDrew, Insurance
506-877-0836 e-mail: eric.ledrew@mcinnescooper.com
Donna L. MacEwen, Insurance
506-877-0874 e-mail: donna.macewen@mcinnescooper.com
Bernard F. Miller, Estates, Trusts & Wealth Planning; Corporate/Commercial; Banking & Financial Institutions
506-877-0837 e-mail: bernard.miller@mcinnescooper.com
Brent E. Sabean, Corporate/Commercial
506-877-0870
Allan D. White, Corporate/Commercial; Real Estate
506-877-0835

McInnes Cooper

Brunswick House
PO Box 6370, A Sta.
44 Chipman Hill, 6th Fl.
Saint John, NB E2L 4R8
506-643-6500
Fax: 506-643-6505
mcsjn@mcinnescooper.com
www.mcinnescooper.com
Number of Lawyers: 8

Finance Lawyers:
Marco R. Cloutier, Banking & Financial Institutions, Insurance
506-635-2238 e-mail: marco.clouthier@mcinnescooper.com
Richard B. Costello, Insurance
506-643-6507 e-mail: richard.costello@mcinnescooper.com
M. Shane Dugas, Corporate/Commercial; Banking & Financial Institutions
506-643-6510 e-mail: shane.dugas@mcinnescooper.com
Matthew T. Hayes, Insurance
506-643-6509 e-mail: matt.hayes@mcinnescooper.com
Mark D. McElman, Corporate/Commercial
506-635-2230 e-mail: mark.mcelman@mcinnescooper.com
Thomas G. O'Neil, Insurance
506-643-6506 e-mail: tom.oneil@mcinnescooper.com
Guy C. Spavold, Tax Law; Banking & Financial Institutions; Corporate/Commercial
506-643-6508 e-mail: guy.spavold@mcinnescooper.com

McInnes Cooper

PO Box 5939
10 Fort William Place, 5th Fl.
St. John's, NL A1C 5X4
709-722-8735
Fax: 709-722-1763
mcsjs@mcinnescooper.com
www.mcinnescooper.com
Founded: 1859
Number of Lawyers: 21

Finance Lawyers:
James R. Chalker, Corporate/Commercial
709-724-8255 e-mail: james.chalker@mcinnescooper.com
Dennis N. Clarke, Corporate/Commercial
709-724-8282 e-mail: dennis.clarke@mcinnescooper.com
Matthew J. Clarke, Insurance
Michael J. Crosbie, Insurance
709-724-8242 e-mail: michael.crosbie@mcinnescooper.com
Susan M. Day, Insurance
709-724-8224 e-mail: susan.day@mcinnescooper.com
J. David B. Eaton, Banking & Financial Institutions
709-724-8262 e-mail: david.eaton@mcinnescooper.com
Sandra A. Gogal, Corporate/Commercial
709-724-8264 e-mail: sandra.gogal@mcinnescooper.com
Deborah L.J. Hutchings, Corporate/Commercial; Banking & Financial Institutions
709-724-8254 e-mail: deborah.hutchings@mcinnescooper.com
Thomas R. Kendell, Tax Law; Estates, Trusts & Wealth Planning; Corporate/Commercial; Banking & Financial Institutions
709-724-8278 e-mail: thomas.kendell@mcinnescooper.com
Barry C. Lake, Corporate/Commercial
709-724-8280 e-mail: barry.lake@mcinnescooper.com
John V. O'Dea, Corporate/Commercial; Banking & Financial Institutions
709-724-8261 e-mail: john.odea@mcinnescooper.com
Caroline C. Watton, Corporate/Commercial
709-724-8251 e-mail: caroline.watton@mcinnescooper.com

McKercher McKercher & Whitmore LLP

#1100
1801 Hamilton St.
Regina, SK S4P 4B4
306-352-7661
Fax: 306-781-7113
info@mckercher.ca
www.mckercher.ca
Number of Lawyers: 8

Finance Lawyers:
Nicholas M. Cann, Insurance
e-mail: n.cann@mckercher.ca
Brad D. Hunter, Insurance
e-mail: b.hunter@mckercher.ca
Kara-Dawn Jordan, Insurance
e-mail: k.jordan@mckercher.ca
Daniel P. Kwochka, Insurance
e-mail: d.kwochka@mckercher.ca
David J. McCashin, Insurance
e-mail: d.mccashin@mckercher.ca
David E. Thera, Insurance
e-mail: d.thera@mckercher.ca
Peter A. Whitmore, Corporate & Commercial; Securities; Wills & Estates
e-mail: p.whitmore@mckercher.ca

McKercher McKercher & Whitmore LLP

374 Third Ave. South
Saskatoon, SK S7K 1M5
306-653-2000
Fax: 306-653-2669
info@mckercher.ca
www.mckercher.ca
Founded: 1926
Number of Lawyers: 39
Profile: Our firm offers a complete range of legal services, focusing on banking, securities, corporate & commercial, insurance, real property, taxation, estate planning & wealth management

Finance Lawyers:
L.J. Dick Batten, Corporate Governance & Finance; Taxation
e-mail: d.batten@mckercher.ca
John R. Beckman, Taxation
e-mail: j.beckman@mckercher.ca
Thomas G.(Casey) Davis, Corporate Governance & Finance; Taxation; Securities
e-mail: c.davis@mckercher.ca
Kaylea M. Dunn, Insurance Law
e-mail: k.dunn@mckercher.ca
Xiaoling Fan, International Business Transactions
e-mail: x.fan@mckercher.ca
Peter Fenton, Corporate & Commercial; Insurance
e-mail: p.fenton@mckercher.ca
James P. Gorkoff, Corporate/Commercial
306-664-1343 e-mail: j.gorkoff@mckercher.ca
Paul D. Grant, Securities; Real Estate Development; Corporate; Commercial
e-mail: p.grant@mckercher.ca
George Green, Debt Recovery; Small Business; Real Estate
e-mail: g.green@mckercher.ca
Donald S. McKercher, Commercial; Wills & Estates
e-mail: d.mckercher@mckercher.ca
Violet M. Paradis, Corporate & Commercial
e-mail: v.paradis@mckercher.ca
Michael T. Petrescue, Corporate Commercial
e-mail: m.petrescue@mckercher.ca
John H. Pringle, Corporate & Commercial
306-664-1352 e-mail: j.pringle@mckercher.ca
Douglas B. Richardson, Corporate; Commercial & Financial Issues
e-mail: d.richardson@mckercher.ca
Nicole A. Rudachyk, Corporate & Commercial; Estates & Estate Planning
306-664-1299 e-mail: n.rudachyk@mckercher.ca
James T. Sproule, Corporate & Commercial; Securities
e-mail: j.sproule@mckercher.ca
David M. Stack, Corporate & Commercial Law
e-mail: d.stack@mckercher.ca
Marie K. Stack, Corporate & Commercial
e-mail: m.stack@mckercher.ca
Gregory A. Thompson, Insurance
e-mail: g.thompson@mckercher.ca
Gordon S. Wyant, Banking Law; Insolvency; Corporate & Commercial
e-mail: g.wyant@mckercher.ca

McLean & Kerr LLP

#2800
130 Adelaide St. West
Toronto, ON M5H 3P5
416-364-5371
Fax: 416-366-8571
mail@mcleankerr.com
www.mcleankerr.com
Number of Lawyers: 23
Profile: Commercial Real Estate & Leasing; Corporate & Commercial; Finance; Insurance; Securities & Corporate Finance

Finance Lawyers:
Elaine M. Gray, Bankruptcy & Insolvency; Commercial
Jon J. Venutti, Commercial Law

McLennan Ross LLP

West Chambers #600
12220 Stony Plain Rd.
Edmonton, AB T5N 3Y4
780-482-9200
Fax: 780-482-9100
800-567-9200
info@mross.com
www.mross.com
Number of Lawyers: 46
Profile: Insurance; Corporate; Commercial; Securities; Banking & Insolvency; Commercial Litigation

Finance Lawyers:
Darren B. Becker, Corporate Commercial; Securities
780-482-9206 e-mail: dbecker@mross.com
Daniel R. Bokenfohr, Labour & Employment; Occupational Health & Safety
780-482-9118 e-mail: dbokenfohr@mross.com
Douglas J. Boyer, Insurance; Commercial Litigation
780-482-9282 e-mail: dboyer@mross.com
Chad J. Brown, Commercial Litigation; Banking; Insolvency; Insurance
780-482-9209 e-mail: cbrown@mross.com

Leo E. Caffaro, Corporate Commercial Securities; Banking; Insolvency
780-482-9214 e-mail: lcaffaro@mross.com
Stuart W. Chambers, Commercial Litigation; Professional Liability
780-482-9113 e-mail: schambers@mross.com
Michelle G. Crighton, Commercial Litigation
780-482-9228 e-mail: mcrighton@mross.com
Corbin D. Devlin, Commercial Litigation
780-482-9261 e-mail: cdevlin@mross.com
Doug I. Evanchuk, Corporate Commercial; Securities
780-482-9106 e-mail: devanchuk@mross.com
Kenneth W. Fitz, Commercial Litigation; Insurance; Professional Liability
780-482-9231 e-mail: kfitz@mross.com
Vicki Giannacopoulos, Commercial Litigation
780-482-9237 e-mail: vgiannacopoulos@mross.com
Victoria L. Giles, Commercial Litigation
780-482-9123 e-mail: vgiles@mross.com
Teresa R. Haykowsky, Labour & Employment
780-482-9247 e-mail: thaykowsky@mross.com
Scott Hipfner, Corporate Commercial; Securities
780-482-9112 e-mail: shipfner@mross.com
Raymond D. Hupfer, Corporate Commercial; Securities; Wills & Estates
780-482-9249 e-mail: rhupfer@mross.com
Christopher J. Lane, Commercial Litigation
780-482-9238 e-mail: clane@mross.com
Stephen J. Livingstone, Banking; Insolvency; Insurance; Commercial Litigation
780-482-9242 e-mail: slivingstone@mross.com
James Mallet, Commercial Litigation
780-482-9211 e-mail: jmallet@mross.com
Donald J. McGarvey, Insurance; Commercial Litigation
780-482-9241 e-mail: dmcgarvey@mross.com
Roderick A. McLennan, Commercial Litigation; Professional Liability
780-482-9201 e-mail: rmclennan@mross.com
R. Graham McLennan, Commercial Litigation; Professional Liability; Construction; Media
780-482-9221 e-mail: gmclennan@mross.com
Alexis N. Moulton, Wills & Estate Planning; Insurance; Commercial Litigation; Professional Liability
780-482-9239 e-mail: amoulton@mross.com
David Myrol, Occupational Health & Safety; Labour & Employment; Energy, Environmental & Regulatory
780-482-9290 e-mail: dmyrol@mross.com
Kevin R. Ozubko, Corporate Commercial; Securities
780-482-9232 e-mail: kozubko@mross.com
Karen A. Platten, Wills & Estates
780-482-9278 e-mail: kplatten@mross.com
Milovan Prelevic, Corporate; Commerical; Securities
780-482-9273 e-mail: mprelevic@mross.com
Denise Prokopiuk, Banking & Insolvenvy; Corporate; Commercial; Securities; Construction
780-482-9205 e-mail: dprokopiuk@mross.com
David D. Risling, Insurance; Commercial Litigation
780-482-9114 e-mail: drisling@mross.com
Jonathan P. Rossall, Insurance; Commercial Litigation, Municipal
780-482-9216 e-mail: jrossall@mross.com
William S. Rosser, Corporate Commercial; Securities
780-482-9222 e-mail: brosser@mross.com
Gerhard J. Seifner, Commercial Litigation; Construction
780-482-9230 e-mail: gseifner@mross.com
Lisa K. Semenchuk, Commercial Litigation; Energy, Environmental & Regulatory; Insurance
780-482-9110 e-mail: lsemenchuk@mross.com
Christopher W. Spasoff, Banking; Insolvency; Commercial Litigation; Insurance
780-482-9236 e-mail: cspasoff@mross.com
Peter P. Taschuk, Commercial Litigation
780-482-9203 e-mail: ptaschuk@mross.com
Christina Tchir, Commercial Litigation; Insurance; Wills, Estates
780-482-9246 e-mail: ctchir@mross.com
Yolanda S. Van Wachem, Wills & Estates
780-482-9225 e-mail: yvanwachem@mross.com
Scott A. Watson, Corporate Commercial; Securities; Banking; Insolvency
780-482-9292 e-mail: swatson@mross.com
Sandra J. Weber, Insurance
780-482-9244 e-mail: sweber@mross.com

McLennan Ross LLP

Precambrian Bldg. #802
4920 - 52 St.
Yellowknife, NT X1A 3T1
867-766-7677
Fax: 867-766-7678
888-836-6684
info@mross.com
www.mross.com
Number of Lawyers: 3
Profile: Provides clients with a full range of corporate & commercial legal services

Finance Lawyers:
Edward Gullberg, Banking; Insolvency; Commercial Litigation; Corporate Commercial; Securities
867-766-7680 e-mail: egullberg@mross.com

E. Michael McMahon

#204
2408 Haywood Ave.
West Vancouver, BC V7V 1Y1
604-926-1076
Fax: 604-926-1023
Number of Lawyers: 1

Finance Lawyers:
E. Michael McMahon, Tax Litigation

McMillan Binch Mendelsohn

BCE Place, Bay Wellington Tower #4400
181 Bay St.
Toronto, ON M5J 2T3
416-865-7000
Fax: 416-865-7048
888-622-4624
info@mcmbm.com
www.mcmbm.com
Founded: 1903
Number of Lawyers: 145

Finance Lawyers:
Michael Burns, Financial Services
416-865-7261 e-mail: michael.burns@mcmbm.com
Michael Campbell, Financial Services
416-865-7114 e-mail: michael.campbell@mcmbm.com
Bruce Chapple, Financial Services
416-865-7024 e-mail: bruce.chapple@mcmbm.com
John W. Craig, Business Law
416-865-7128 e-mail: john.craig@mcmbm.com
Bindu Cudjoe, Banking; Finance
e-mail: bindu.cudjoe@mcmbm.com
Carmen Diges, Banking; Finance
416-865-7925 e-mail: carmen.diges@mcmbm.com
Stephanie Donaher, Banking; Finance
416-865-7892 e-mail: stephanie.donaher@mcmbm.com
David Dunlop, Banking & Finance; Insolvency
416-865-7175 e-mail: david.dunlop@mcmbm.com
Sean Farrell, Financial Services
416-865-7910 e-mail: sean.farrell@mcmbm.com
Mary Flynn-Guglietti, Commercial Real Estate
416-865-7256 e-mail: mary.flynn@mcmbm.com
Pat Forgione, Financial Services
416-865-7798 e-mail: pat.forgione@mcmbm.com
Nicole Frew, Financial Services Group
416-865-7904 e-mail: nicole.frew@mcmbm.com
Chris N. Germanakos, Financial Services
416-865-7865 e-mail: chris.germanakos@mcmbm.com
Richard T. Higa, Financial Services
416-865-7864 e-mail: richard.higa@mcmbm.com
Michael Hollinger, Banking; Finance
416-865-7926 e-mail: michael.hollinger@mcmbm.com
David Hudson, Banking; Finance
e-mail: david.hudson@mcmbm.com
Vern Kakoschke, Corporate/Commercial
416-865-7830 e-mail: vern.kakoschke@mcmbm.com
Andrew J.F. Kent, Banking & Finance; Insolvency
416-865-7160 e-mail: andrew.kent@mcmbm.com
Lisa H. Kerbel-Caplan, Banking; Finance
416-865-7803 e-mail: lisa.kerbel.caplan@mcmbm.com
Alex L. MacFarlane, Banking; Finance; Insolvency; Corporate Restructuring
416-865-7879 e-mail: alex.macfarlane@mcmbm.com
Luigi Macchione, Commercial Real Estate
416-865-7116 e-mail: luigi.macchione@mcmbm.com
Adam Maerov, Banking; Finance
416-865-7285 e-mail: adam.maerov@mcmbm.com
Kathy Martin, Banking; Finance
416-865-7889 e-mail: kathy.martin@mcmbm.com
David I. Matheson, Corporate Commercial
416-865-7219 e-mail: david.matheson@mcmbm.com
Robert K. McDermott, Securities; Financial Services
416-865-7085 e-mail: robert.mcdermott@mcmbm.com
Andrew McFarlane, Banking; Finance
416-865-7110 e-mail: andrew.mcfarlane@mcmbm.com
Margaret C. McNee, Banking & Finance; Securities
416-865-7284 e-mail: margaret.mcnee@mcmbm.com
Shahen Mirakian, Banking; Finance
416-865-7238 e-mail: shahen.mirakian@mcmbm.com
Gary K. Ostoich, Banking & Finance
416-865-7802 e-mail: gary.ostoich@mcmbm.com
George K.S. Payne, Commercial Real Estate
416-865-7053 e-mail: george.payne@mcmbm.com
Kimberly J. Poster, Banking; Finance
416-865-7890 e-mail: kimberly.poster@mcmbm.com
Ed Ra, Financial Services
416-865-7294 e-mail: ed.ra@mcmbm.com
Stephen C.E. Rigby, Banking; Finance, Corporate Commercial
416-865-7793 e-mail: stephen.rigby@mcmbm.com
Stephanie M. Robinson, Banking; Finance
416-865-7204 e-mail: stephanie.robinson@mcmbm.com
Jeff Rogers, Banking & Finance
416-865-7818 e-mail: jeff.rogers@mcmbm.com
David N. Ross, Commercial Real Estate
416-865-7015 e-mail: david.ross@mcmbm.com
Wael Rostom, Banking; Finance
416-865-7790 e-mail: wael.rostom@mcmbm.com
Jim Sahdra, Banking; Finance
e-mail: jim.sahdra@mcmbm.com
Robert M. Scavone, Banking & Finance
416-865-7901 e-mail: rob.scavone@mcmbm.com
Thomas E. (Ted) Scott, Banking & Finance
416-865-7183 e-mail: ted.scott@mcmbm.com
Cheryl Stacey, Banking & Finance; Asset Based Lending
416-865-7243 e-mail: cheryl.stacey@mcmbm.com
Greg Walters, Banking; Finance
e-mail: greg.walters@mcmbm.com
Cindy Wan, Banking, Finance
416-865-7190 e-mail: cindy.wan@mcmbm.com
Michael C. Ward, Financial Services
416-865-7176 e-mail: michael.ward@mcmbm.com
Don M.E. Waters, Banking; Finance
416-865-7920 e-mail: don.waters@mcmbm.com
Tushara Weerasooriya, Banking; Finance
e-mail: tushara.weerasooriya@mcmbm.com
Ted E.K. Weir, Banking; Finance
416-865-7050 e-mail: ted.weir@mcmbm.com
Jamie M. Wilks, Tax
416-865-7804 e-mail: jamie.wilks@mcmbm.com
Peter A. Willis, Banking; Finance
416-865-7210 e-mail: peter.willis@mcmbm.com
William Woloshyn, Banking & Finance; Insolvency
416-865-7063 e-mail: bill.woloshyn@mcmbm.com
Vickie S. Wong, Banking & Finance
416-865-7846 e-mail: vickie.wong@mcmbm.com

McMillan Binch Mendelsohn

1000, rue Sherbrooke ouest, 27e étage
Montréal, QC H3A 3G4
514-987-5000
Fax: 514-987-1213
info@mcmbm.com
www.mcmbm.com
Founded: 1951
Number of Lawyers: 47
Profile: The Financial Services Law Group has considerable involvement in the structuring of loan transactions, drafting of loan & intercreditor agreements & the development of security documentation; it has expertise in factoring & asset-based lending

Finance Lawyers:
Jessica Abdulezer, Banking & Financial Transactions
514-987-5059 e-mail: jessica.abdulezer@mcmbm.com
Michael L. Blumenstein, Securities
514-987-5050 e-mail: michael.blumstein@mcmbm.com
Marc Cantin, Securities; Corporate & Commercial
514-987-5034 e-mail: marc.cantin@mcmbm.com
Earl S. Cohen, Real Estate; Environmental Law
514-987-5045 e-mail: earl.cohen@mcmbm.com

ACCOUNTING & LAW

McMillan Binch Mendelsohn (continued)
Louis-Frédérick Côté, Tax
514-987-5016 e-mail: louis-frederick.cote@mcmbm.com
Marie-Christine Demers
514-987-5001 e-mail: marie-christine.demers@mcmbm.com
Philipp Duffy, Corporate & Commercial, Real Estate
514-987-5079 e-mail: philipp.duffy@mcmbm.com
Andrew Etcovitch, Tax Law; Estates, Wills & Trusts
514-987-5064 e-mail: andrew.etcovitch@mcmbm.com
Michael Garonce, Corporate & Commercial Real Estate
514-987-5033 e-mail: michael.garonce@mcmbm.com
Arthur A. Garvis, Insolvency & Restructuring
514-987-5011 e-mail: arthur.garvis@cmbm.com
Eloi@#se Gratton, Corporate & Commercial
514-987-5093 e-mail: elise.gratton@mcmbm.com
Kiriakoula Hatzikiriakos, Banking & Financing Transactions
514-987-5025 e-mail: kirikoula.hatzikiriakos@mcmbm.com
Judie K. Jokinen, Banking & Financing Transactions; Reorganizations & Insolvency
514-987-5026 e-mail: judie.jokinen@mcmbm.com
Anne-Marie Laberge, Corporate & Commercial
514-987-5071 e-mail: anne-marie.laberge@mcmbm.com
Josée Massicotte, Tax Law
514-987-5095 e-mail: josee.massicotte@mcmbm.com
Max Mendelsohn, Reorganizations & Insolvency; Banking & Financing Transactions
514-987-5042 e-mail: max.mendelsohn@mcmbm.com
Marc-André Morin, Reorganizations & Insolvency; Banking & Financing Transactions
514-987-5082 e-mail: marc-andre.morin@mcmbm.com
Voula Neofotistos, Real Estate
514-987-5022 e-mail: voula.neofotistos@mcmbm.com
Julie Normand, Banking & Financial Transactions, Insolvency & Restructuring
514-987-5012 e-mail: julie.normand@mcmbm.com
Élise S. Paul-Hus, Securities; Corporate & Commercial
514-987-5040 e-mail: elise.paul-hus@mcmbm.com
Jean-Francois Pelland, Business Law
514-987-5081 e-mail: jean-francois.pelland@mcmbm.com
Illana Perez, Real Estate, Banking & Financing Transactions
514-987-5090 e-mail: illana.perez@mcmbm.com
Marco P. Rodrigues, Banking & Financing Transactions
514-987-5063 e-mail: marco.rodrigues@mcmbm.com
Leo Rosentzveig, Real Estate
514-987-5021 e-mail: leo.rosentzveig@mcmbm.com
David L. Rosentzveig, Business Law, Corporate & Commercial Real Estate
514-987-5038 e-mail: david.rosentzveig@mcmbm.com
Emmanuelle Saucier, Reorganizations & Insolvency
514-987-5053 e-mail: emmanuelle.saucier@mcmbm.com
Nicholas Scheib, Real Estate, Reorganizations & Insolvency
514-987-5091 e-mail: nicholas.scheib@mcmbm.com
Manuel Shacter, Corporate & Commercial; Wills, Estates & Trusts
514-987-5023 e-mail: manuel.shacter@mcmbm.com
Céline Tessier, Insolvency & Restructuring
514-987-5032 e-mail: celine.tessier@mcmbm.com
Eric Vallières, Corporate & Commercial; Reorganizations & Insolvency; Banking & Financing Transactions
514-987-5068 e-mail: eric.vallieres@mcmbm.com
Beatrice van Rutten, Banking & Financing Transactions
514-987-5061 e-mail: beatrice.vanrutten@mcmbm.com

Medjuck & Medjuck
PO Box 1074
1601 Lower Water St.
Halifax, NS B3J 2X1
902-429-4061
Fax: 902-422-7639
medjuck@ns.sympatico.ca
Number of Lawyers: 1
Profile: Commercial/Corporate, Real Estate

Finance Lawyers:
Franklyn D. Medjuck, Corporate Finance

Merchant Law Group
First Nations Bank Bldg. #501
224 Fourth Ave. South
Saskatoon, SK S7K 5M5
306-653-7777
Fax: 306-975-1983
866-653-7777
Number of Lawyers: 11

Finance Lawyers:
Timothy E. Turple
e-mail: tturple@merchantlaw.com

Yves Messier
1922, boul de Portland
Sherbrooke, QC J1J 1T6
819-563-0798
Fax: 819-563-0953
yavocat@videotron.ca
www.quebeclegal.com
Founded: 1968
Number of Lawyers: 1

Finance Lawyers:
Yves Messier, Overdue Debt Collection
e-mail: yvavocat@videotron.ca

Miles, Davison LLP
Bow Valley Sq. II #1600
205 - 5th Ave. SW
Calgary, AB T2P 2V7
403-298-0333
Fax: 403-263-6840
thefirm@milesdavison.com
www.milesdavison.com
Number of Lawyers: 23

Finance Lawyers:
Donald J. Kelly
Susan L. Robinson Burns
William L. Severson

Millar Kreklewetz LLP
BCE Place
PO Box 745
181 Bay St., 28th Fl.
Toronto, ON M5J 2T3
416-864-6200
Fax: 416-864-6201
mkmail@taxandtradelaw.com
www.taxandtradelaw.com
Number of Lawyers: 6

Finance Lawyers:
Wendy A. Brousseau, Taxation
e-mail: wab@taxandtradelaw.com
Robert G. Kreklewetz, Taxation
e-mail: rgk@taxandtradelaw.com
W. Jack Millar, Taxation
e-mail: wjm@mwktaxlawyers.com
Vern Vipul, Taxation
e-mail: vv@taxandtradelaw.com

Miller & Miller
1577 Bloor St. West
Toronto, ON M6P 1A6
416-536-1159
Fax: 416-536-3618
Number of Lawyers: 2

Finance Lawyers:
Albert Miller

Miller Canfield Paddock & Stone LLP
#300
PO Box 1390
443 Ouellette Ave.
Windsor, ON N9A 6R4
519-977-1555
Fax: 519-977-1566
www.millercanfield.com
Number of Lawyers: 21

Finance Lawyers:
Bob Baksi, Corporate & Securities; Capital Markets Lending; Real Estate; Franchise & Distribution
519-561-7436
Gerard P. Charette, Corporate & Securities
519-561-7402
Carl S. Cohen, Corporate & Securities; Real Estate
519-561-7403
Angela D'Alessandro, Bankruptcy
519-561-7447
Julie R. Daniel, Corporate & Securities
519-561-7405
Jerry L. Goldberg, Real Estate
519-561-7408
John M. Jedlinski, Corporate & Securities
519-561-7411
Mary-Ann Keefner, Corporate & Securities
519-561-7409
Jack Ramieri, Real Estate
519-561-7420
Jennifer L. Shilson, Corporate & Securities

Miller Thomson LLP
Scotia Plaza #5800
40 King St. West
Toronto, ON M5H 3S1
416-595-8500
Fax: 416-595-8695
888-762-5559
toronto@millerthomson.com
www.millerthomson.com
Founded: 1957
Number of Lawyers: 129
Profile: Bankruptcy; Corporate Commercial; E-Commerce; Estates/Pensions; Financial Services; Franchising; Insolvency & Insurance; Mergers & Acquisitions; Securities; Tax Law

Finance Lawyers:
E. Peter Auvinen, Banking; Commercial Litigation; Insurance
416-595-8162 e-mail: pauvinen@millerthomson.com
Jennifer E. Babe, Commercial Law; Insolvency
416-595-8555 e-mail: jbabe@millerthomson.com
Douglas F. Best, Commercial Litigation
416-595-8588 e-mail: dbest@millerthomson.com
Anthony K. Crossley, Corporate Commercial Law; Banking; Franchising; Trade & Competition Law
416-595-8689 e-mail: acrossley@millerthomson.com
Maurice V.R. Fleming, Corporate Commercial; Banking; Financial Services; Insolvency; Restructuring
416-595-8686 e-mail: mfleming@millerthomson.com
James D.M. Fraser, Commercial Real Estate; Leasing; Lending; Insolvency; Franchising
416-595-8527 e-mail: jfraser@millerthomson.com
Jennifer Hewitt, Corporate Commercial Law
416-595-2972 e-mail: jhewitt@millerthomson.com
Elizabeth A. Hutchison, Corporate Commercial Law
416-595-8190 e-mail: ehutchison@millerthomson.com
Richard D. Leblanc, Corporate Law; Banking Law; Financial Institutions Law; Secured Transactions; Franchising
416-595-8657 e-mail: rleblanc@millerthomson.com
F. Max E. Maréchaux, Real Estate; Commercial Law; Leasing; Lending
416-595-8522 e-mail: mmarechaux@millerthomson.com
James A. Proskurniak, Corporate Law; Commercial Law; Business Law; Mergers & Acquisitions; Banking; Financial Services
416-595-8598 e-mail: jproskurniak@millerthomson.com
Robert J. Shipcott, Corporate Law; Commercial Law; Mergers & Acquisitions; Securities
416-595-8628 e-mail: rshipcott@millerthomson.com
Tom Tower, Corporate Commercial; Insolvency & Restructuring
416-595-8674 e-mail: ttower@millerthomson.com

Miller Thomson LLP
#3000
700 - 9th Ave. SW
Calgary, AB T2P 3V4
403-298-2400
Fax: 403-262-0007
888-298-2400
calgary@millerthomson.com
www.millerthomson.com
Founded: 1957
Number of Lawyers: 34
Profile: Miller Thompson's Financial Services Law group consists of a multi-disciplinary team of lawyers with specific expertise in lending & real estate transactions, securities & insurance law, trusts & taxation as well as other specialty areas of law including international business, communications & environmental law; we have extensive experience in the regulation of financial institutions & maintain long-standing working relationships with regulators at both federal & provincial levels; our client base includes major Canadian & foreign banks, trust & insurance companies, pension funds, credit unions, finance companies, government loan agencies & governments, & numerous corporate borrowers from diverse sectors of the economy

Finance Lawyers:

Richard L.G. Gushue, Energy Financing; Oil & Gas; International; Mergers & Acquisitions
403-298-2444 e-mail: rgushue@millerthomson.com
David L. Sevalrud, Oil & Gas; Corporate Commercial; Financial Services; Securities; Intellectual Property
403-298-2440 e-mail: dsevalrud@millerthomson.com
Robert C. Stemp, Insolvency & Restructuring; Financial Services; Commercial Real Estate; Corporate Foreclosures
403-298-2485 e-mail: rstemp@millerthomson.com
Nicole T. Taylor-Smith, Insolvency & Restructuring; Financial Services; Commercial Debt Recovery; Construction
403-298-2453 e-mail: ntaylorsmith@millerthomson.com

Miller Thomson LLP

2700 Commerce Place
10155 - 102nd St.
Edmonton, AB T5J 4G8
780-429-1751
Fax: 780-424-5866
800-215-1016
edmonton@millerthomson.com
www.millerthomson.com
Founded: 1957
Number of Lawyers: 40
Profile: Miller Thompson's Financial Services Law group consists of a multi-disciplinary team of lawyers with specific expertise in lending & real estate transactions, securities & insurance law, trusts & taxation as well as other specialty areas of law including international business, communications & environmental law; we have extensive experience in the regulation of financial institutions & maintain long-standing working relationships with regulators at both federal & provincial levels; our client base includes Canadian & foreign banks, trust & insurance companies, pension funds, credit unions, finance companies, government loan agencies & governments, & numerous corporate borrowers from diverse sectors of the economy

Finance Lawyers:
Edwin S. Cook, Banking Law; Bankruptcy; Insolvency
780-429-9746 e-mail: ecook@millerthomson.com
Geoffrey N.W. Edgar, Insolvency, Banking
780-429-9760 e-mail: gedgar@millerthomson.com
Richard T.G. Reeson, Insolvency; Banking
780-429-9719 e-mail: rreeson@millerthomson.com
Kevin D. Trumpour, Corporate Law; Commercial Law; Banking Law
780-429-9707 e-mail: ktrumpour@millerthomson.com
Terrence M. Warner, Corporate Litigation; Commercial Litigation; Bankruptcy; Insolvency
780-429-9727 e-mail: twarner@millerthomson.com
Barrett K. Westerlund, Collections; Foreclosures; Residential Bankruptcy; Insolvency
780-429-9705 e-mail: bwesterlund@millerthomson.com

Miller Thomson LLP

#600
60 Columbia Way
Markham, ON L3R 0C9
905-415-6700
Fax: 905-415-6777
866-348-2432
markham@millerthomson.com
www.millerthomson.com
Founded: 1957
Number of Lawyers: 14

Finance Lawyers:
Head of Financial Law: Judson D. Whiteside, Commercial Law; Business Law
905-415-6701 e-mail: jwhiteside@millerthomson.com

Miller Thomson LLP

Robson Ct. #1000
840 Howe St.
Vancouver, BC V6Z 2M1
604-687-2242
Fax: 604-643-1200
vancouver@millerthomson.com
www.millerthomson.com
Founded: 1957
Number of Lawyers: 63
Profile: Bankruptcy; Corporate; Real Estate; Securities; Taxation

Finance Lawyers:
John P. Ferber, Corporate Law; Commercial Law; Mergers, Acquisitions & Divestitures; Reorganizations; Banking; Secured Transactions
604-643-1241 e-mail: jferber@millerthomson.com
Gordon G. Plottel, Commercial Litigation; Insolvency; Franchise Law
604-643-1245 e-mail: gplottel@millerthomson.com
Thomas J. Potter, Bankruptcy & Insolvency Litigation; Estate Law; Commercial Litigation
604-643-1259 e-mail: tpotter@millerthomson.com
Stephen R. Ross, Bankruptcy & Insolvency Law; Corporate & Commercial Litigation; Creditor
604-643-1205 e-mail: sross@millerthomson.com

Miller Thomson Pouliot SENCRL

1155, boul René-Lévesque ouest, 31e étage
Montréal, QC H3B 3S6
514-875-5210
Fax: 514-875-4308
www.millerthomson.com
Founded: 1953
Number of Lawyers: 51

Finance Lawyers:
Alexandre Ajami, Business
514-871-5484 e-mail: aajami@millerthomsonpouliot.com
Ronald M. Auclair, Bankruptcy; Insolvency; Taxation
514-871-5477 e-mail: rauclair@millerthomsonpouliot.com
Gilles Bertrand, Corporate/Commercial
514-871-5473 e-mail: gbertrand@millerthomsonpouliot.com
Yvon Brizard, Financing
514-871-5470 e-mail: ybrizard@millerthomsonpouliot.com
Gilles Brunelle, Estates & Trusts
514-871-5444 e-mail: gbrunelle@millerthomsonpouliot.com
Pascale Cloutier, Bankruptcy & Insolvency
514-871-5486 e-mail: pcloutier@millerthomsonpouliot.com
Louis Coallier, Bankruptcy & Insolvency
514-871-5488 e-mail: lcoallier@millerthomsonpouliot.com
Serge Desrochers, Acquisitions, Sales & Mergers; Financing
514-871-5404 e-mail: sdesrochers@millerthomsonpouliot.com
José P. Dorais, Corporate/Business
514-871-5412 e-mail: jpdorais@millerthomsonpouliot.com
André Dugas, Corporate/Commercial
514-871-5410 e-mail: adugas@millerthomsonpouliot.com
Richard Fontaine, Estates & Trusts
514-871-5496 e-mail: rfontaine@millerthomsonpouliot.com
Daniel Gagné, Acquisitions, Sales & Mergers; Financing
514-871-5422 e-mail: dgagne@millerthomsonpouliot.com
François Garneau, Commercial
514-871-5415 e-mail: fgarneau@millerthomsonpouliot.com
Anne-Marie Gauthier, Corporate/Commercial
514-871-5402 e-mail: amgauthier@millerthomsonpouliot.com
Marie-Hélène Gay, Banking & Insolvency; Commercial Litigation
514-871-5485 e-mail: mhgay@millerthomsonpouliot.com
Stéphane Hébert, Bankruptcy & Insolvency
514-871-5466 e-mail: shebert@millerthomsonpouliot.com
David Johnston, Acquisitions, Sales & Mergers; Financing
514-871-5471 e-mail: djohnston@millerthomsonpouliot.com
Chantal Joubert, Acquisitions, Sales & Mergers
514-841-5481 e-mail: cjoubert@millerthomsonpouliot.com
Fernand Lalonde, Corporate; Business
514-871-5495 e-mail: flalonde@millerthomsonpouliot.com
Pierre Marquis, Financing; Acquisitions, Sales & Mergers
514-871-5425 e-mail: pmarquis@millerthomsonpouliot.com
François Martel, Financing
514-871-5491 e-mail: fmartel@millerthomsonpouliot.com
J. Brent Muir, Estates & Trusts
514-871-5478 e-mail: bmuir@millerthomsonpouliot.com
Alain Nadon, Acquisitions, Sales & Mergers; Securities
514-871-5407 e-mail: anadon@millerthomsonpouliot.com
Pierre Paquet, Estates & Trusts
514-871-5427 e-mail: ppaquet@millerthomsonpouliot.com
Steven Parienté, Corporate; Mergers & Acquisitions; Reorganizations & Financing
514-871-5441 e-mail: spariente@millerthomsonpouliot.com
Micheline Perrault, Bankruptcy & Insolvency
514-871-5497 e-mail: mperrault@millerthomsonpouliot.com
Georges A. Pouliot, Estates & Trusts; Acquisitions, Sales & Mergers
514-871-5401 e-mail: gpouliot@millerthomsonpouliot.com
Maxime B. Rhéaume, Financing; Acquisitions, Sales & Mergers
514-871-5461 e-mail: mrheaume@millerthomsonpouliot.com
Normand Royal, Estates & Trusts; Acquisitions, Sales & Mergers
514-871-5453 e-mail: nroyal@millerthomsonpouliot.com
Stéphane Teasdale, Bankruptcy & Insolvency
514-871-5465 e-mail: steasdale@millerthomsonpouliot.com
Robert Tessier, Bankruptcy & Insolvency
514-871-5474 e-mail: rtessier@millerthomsonpouliot.com
Louise Tremblay, Commercial Litigation
514-871-5476 e-mail: ltremblay@millerthomsonpouliot.com
Louis-Michel Tremblay, Estates & Trusts
514-871-5421 e-mail: lmtremblay@millerthomson.com

Minden Gross Grafstein & Greenstein LLP

#700
111 Richmond St. West
Toronto, ON M5H 2H5
416-362-3711
Fax: 416-864-9223
dcarty@mindengross.com
www.mindengross.com
Number of Lawyers: 50

Finance Lawyers:
Robert W. Beattie, Corporate/Commercial
416-369-4119 e-mail: rbeattie@mindengross.com
Jules N. Berman, Insolvency
416-369-4122 e-mail: jberman@mindengross.com
Phillip G. Bevans, Corporate/Commercial
416-369-4102
Howard S. Black, Wills
416-369-4332 e-mail: hblack@mindengross.com
Mordecai Bobrowsky, Commercial Leasing
416-369-4129
Geoffrey D. Brown, Corporate/Commercial
416-369-4319 e-mail: gbrown@mindengross.com
Timothy Royston Dunn, Insolvency
416-369-4335 e-mail: tdunn@mindengross.com
Catherine Francis, Insolvency
416-369-4137 e-mail: cfrancis@mindengross.com
Marco A. Gammone, Commercial Leasing
416-369-4126
Michael A. Goldberg, Tax Law
416-369-4317 e-mail: mgoldberg@mindengross.com
Jerry S. Grafstein, Counsel, Corporate/Commercial
416-369-4108 e-mail: jgrafstein@mindengross.com
Aaron S. Grubner, Corporate/Commercial
416-369-4318 e-mail: agrubner@mindengross.com
Michael S. Horowitz, Commercial Leasing
416-369-4121
Joan E. Jung, Tax Law
416-369-4306 e-mail: jjung@mindengross.com
Kenneth L. Kallish, Insolvency
416-369-4124 e-mail: kkallish@mindengross.com
C. Robyn Kestenberg, Commercial Leasing
416-369-4313
Christina Kobi, Commercial Leasing
416-369-4154
Glen O. Lewis, Insolvency
416-369-4133
Alan D. Litwack, Corporate/Commercial
416-369-4146 e-mail: alitwack@mindengross.com
David Louis, Tax Law
416-369-4111 e-mail: dlouis@mindengross.com
Stephen J. Messinger, Commercial Leasing
416-369-4147
Hartley R. Nathan, Corporate/Commercial
416-369-4109 e-mail: hnathan@mindengross.com
Adam L. Perzow, Commercial Leasing
416-369-4132
J. Stephen Posen, Commercial Leasing
416-369-4103
Samantha A. Prasad, Tax Law
416-369-4155 e-mail: sprasad@mindengross.com
Daniel A. Rothberg, Corporate/Commercial
416-369-4112 e-mail: drothberg@mindengross.com
Daniel Sandler, Tax Law
416-369-4308 e-mail: dsandler@mindengross.com
Jack B. Tannerya, Corporate/Commercial
416-369-4145 e-mail: jtannerya@mindengross.com
David T. Ullmann, Insolvency
416-369-4148
Stephen N. Witten, Corporate/Commercial
416-369-4118 e-mail: switten@mindengross.com

Morel Law Office

#777
505 - 3rd St. SW
Calgary, AB T2P 3E6

ACCOUNTING & LAW

Morel Law Office (continued)
403-261-8858
Fax: 403-264-7189
Number of Lawyers: 1

Finance Lawyers:
Cas H. Morel

Ronald F. Mossman
#300
34 Village Centre Pl.
Mississauga, ON L4Z 1V9
905-848-4020
Fax: 905-848-4026
ronmossman@rmossman.com
Number of Lawyers: 1
Profile: Finance for small business; secured transactions & equity investment

Finance Lawyers:
Ronald F. Mossman, Corporate Finance

Murray & Thomson
PO Box 1060
912 - 2 Ave. West
Owen Sound, ON N4K 6K6
519-376-6350
Fax: 519-376-0835
message@mtlaw.ca
www.mtlaw.ca
Founded: 1982
Number of Lawyers: 1
Profile: All aspects including estate planning; corporate amalgamations; litigation/insurance settlements; leases

Finance Lawyers:
Ross H. Thomson
e-mail: ththomson@mtlaw.ca

Narvey, Green
#1770
770, rue Sherbrooke ouest
Montréal, QC H3A 1G1
514-282-9144
Fax: 514-844-7290
Number of Lawyers: 2

Finance Lawyers:
Irving Narvey, Commercial/Corporate

Nathanson, Schachter & Thompson LLP
#750
900 Howe St.
Vancouver, BC V6Z 2M4
604-662-8840
Fax: 604-684-1598
info@nst.bc.ca
www.nst.bc.ca
Founded: 1987
Number of Lawyers: 8
Profile: Specializing in corporate & business litigation; we represent clients in complex commercial disputes such as: shareholders' disputes, hostile take-over bids & derivative actions, securities matters, class & representative proceedings, pension litigation, actions for professional negligence, administrative proceedings

Finance Lawyers:
Irwin G. Nathanson
Stephen R. Schachter
Ardella A. Thompson

Nelligan O'Brien Payne
#1900
66 Slater St.
Ottawa, ON K1P 5H1
613-238-8080
Fax: 613-238-2098
info@nplaw.com
www.nplaw.com
Number of Lawyers: 42

Finance Lawyers:
Head of Financial Law: Mark Geddes, General Finance
611- - e-mail: mark.geddes@nplaw.com
Gordon Archibald, General Finance
Deborah A. Bellinger, General Finance
Ronald F. Caza, General Finance
David Charles, General Finance
Peter J.E. Cronyn, General Finance
Gregory Hiscock, General Finance
John E. Johnson, General Finance
Jennifer McLean, General Finance
Lisa Nickerson, General Finance
Richard O'Reilly, General Finance
Janice B. Payne, General Finance
Denis J. Power, General Finance
David A. Stout, General Finance

Nimegeers, Schuck, Wormsbecker & Bobbitt
PO Box 8
319 Souris Ave. NE
Weyburn, SK S4H 2J8
306-842-4654
Fax: 306-842-0522
law@nswb.com
www.nswb.com
Founded: 1968
Number of Lawyers: 3
Profile: We act for most financial institutions in our city in mortgage, personal property, foreclosures & collections

Finance Lawyers:
Ronald J. Wormsbecker, Collections
e-mail: rwormsbecker@nswb.com

Northwest Law Group
#1880
1055 West Georgia St.
Vancouver, BC V6E 3P3
604-687-5792
Fax: 604-687-6650
Founded: 1991
Number of Lawyers: 6
Profile: Representation of emerging issuers listed on the TSX-Venture Exchange, TSE & U.S. markets

Finance Lawyers:
Stephen F.X. O'Neill, General Finance; Securities
e-mail: son@stockslaw.com
Michael F. Provenzano, General Finance; Securities
e-mail: mfprovenzano@telus.net

Mark T. Nowak
370 Frederick St.
Kitchener, ON N2H 2P3
519-746-8340
Fax: 519-746-8144
marknowak@bellnet.ca
Founded: 1977
Number of Lawyers: 1

Finance Lawyers:
Mark T. Nowak

O'Connor MacLeod Hanna LLP
700 Kerr St.
Oakville, ON L6K 3W5
905-842-8030
Fax: 905-842-2460
info@omh.ca
www.omh.ca
Founded: 1991
Number of Lawyers: 16

Finance Lawyers:
Jeffrey S. Burkett, Corporate & Commercial
e-mail: burkett@omh.ca
Christine A.M. Fisher
e-mail: fisher@omh.ca
Larry S. Gangbar, Wills, Trusts, Estates
e-mail: gangbar@omh.ca
Brian J. Hanna, Real Estate
e-mail: hanna@omh.ca
Thomas C. Hays, Real Estate
e-mail: hays@omh.ca
Andrew C. Knox, Real Estate
e-mail: knox@omh.ca
Robert Krizman, Corporate & Commercial
e-mail: krizman@omh.ca
Tanya A. Leedale, Corporate & Commercial
e-mail: leedale@omh.ca
Jarvis G. Sheridan, Corporate & Commercial
e-mail: sheridan@omh.ca

Ogilvie LLP
#1400
10303 Jasper Ave.
Edmonton, AB T5J 3N6
780-421-1818
Fax: 780-429-4453
bpodgurny@ogilvielaw.com
www.ogilvielaw.com
Founded: 1920
Number of Lawyers: 26
Profile: Legal services covering all aspects of corporate, commercial & financing for businesses

Finance Lawyers:
Robert P. Assaly
780-429-6243 e-mail: rassaly@ogilvielaw.com
Michael C. Elias
780-429-6225 e-mail: melias@ogilvielaw.com
Jerry J. Flaman, Business Transactions; Banking; Financing & Commercial Real Estate
780-429-6238 e-mail: jflaman@ogilvielaw.com
Craig J. Grubisich
780-429-6215 e-mail: cgrubisich@ogilvielaw.com
David J. Hiebert
780-429-6216 e-mail: dhiebert@ogilvielaw.com
Barbara K. Komisar
780-429-6281 e-mail: bkomisar@ogilvielaw.com
Robert V. Lloyd
780-429-6266 e-mail: rlloyd@ogilvielaw.com
Michelle D. Millard
780-429-6284 e-mail: mmillard@ogilvielaw.com
Paul H. Nothof
780-429-6244 e-mail: pnothof@ogilvielaw.com
Ronald W. Odynski
780-429-6259 e-mail: rodynski@ogilvielaw.com
William J. Page
780-429-6276 e-mail: wpage@ogilvielaw.com
Trevor J. Reddekopp
780-429-6217 e-mail: treddekopp@ogilvielaw.com
Mark A. Saxton
780-429-6269 e-mail: msaxton@ogilvielaw.com
Arun Shourie
780-429-6273 e-mail: ashourie@ogilvielaw.com

Ogilvy Renault LLP/S.E.N.C.R.L., s.r.l.
#1100
1981, av McGill College
Montréal, QC H3A 3C1
514-847-4747
Fax: 514-286-5474
info@ogilvyrenault.com
www.ogilvyrenault.com
Founded: 1879
Number of Lawyers: 176
Profile: Asset-based Lending; Banking & Financial Products; Corporate & Commercial Law; Insolvency & Restructuring; Mergers & Acquisitions; Projects & Project Finance; Securities; Tax

Finance Lawyers:
Jules Charette, Key Contact, Tax
514-847-4450 e-mail: jcharette@ogilvyrenault.com
Arnold Cohen, Key Contact, Asset-based Lending; Banking & Financial Products; Insolvency & Restructuring
514-847-6082 e-mail: acohen@ogilvyrenault.com
Louis J. Gouin, Key Contact, Insolvency & Restructuring; Banking & Financial Products
514-847-4425 e-mail: lgouin@ogilvyrenault.com
Francis R. Legault, Key Contact, Securities; Mergers & Acquisitions; Corporate & Commercial Law
514-847-4495 e-mail: flegault@ogilvyrenault.com

Ogilvy Renault LLP/S.E.N.C.R.L., s.r.l.
Royal Bank Plaza South Tower #3800
PO Box 84
200 Bay St.
Toronto, ON M5J 2Z4
416-216-4000
Fax: 416-216-3930
toronto@ogilvyrenault.com
www.ogilvyrenault.com
Number of Lawyers: 131
Profile: Asset-based Lending; Banking & Financial Products; Corporate & Commercial Law; Insolvency & Restructuring; Mergers & Acquisitions; Projects & Project Finance; Securities; Tax

Finance Lawyers:

David M.A. Amato, Asset-based Lending; Banking & Financial Products; Projects & Project Finance
416-216-1861 e-mail: damato@ogilvyrenault.com
James R. Cade, Corporate & Commercial Law; Mergers & Acquisitions
416-216-4840 e-mail: jcade@ogilvyrenault.com
Jacques Demers, Banking & Financial Products; Corporate & Commercial Law; Projects & Project Finance
416-216-4804 e-mail: jdemers@ogilvyrenault.com
Brian C. Kelsall, Projects & Project Finance; Banking & Financial Products
416-216-4789 e-mail: bkelsall@ogilvyrenault.com
Michael J. Lang, Securities; Mergers & Acquisitions; Corporate & Commercial Law
416-216-3939 e-mail: mlang@ogilvyrenault.com
Kevin J. Morley, Asset-based Lending; Banking & Financial Products
416-216-2300 e-mail: kmorley@ogilvyrenault.com
Adrienne F. Oliver, Tax
416-216-1854 e-mail: aoliver@ogilvyrenault.com
Derrick C. Tay, Insolvency & Restructuring
416-216-4832 e-mail: tday@ogilvyrenault.com

Oligny & Jacques

#107, 1394, du Mont-Royal est
Montréal, QC H2J 1Y7
514-871-2240
Fax: 514-871-0874
oligny@generation.net
Number of Lawyers: 2

Finance Lawyers:
Fernand Oligny, General Finance

Olson Lemons LLP

744 - 4 Ave. SW
Calgary, AB T2P 3T4
403-974-3400
Fax: 403-974-3427
www.olsonlemons.com
Founded: 1992
Number of Lawyers: 6

Finance Lawyers:
T.H. Olson, Corporate; Commercial; Tax Law
J.K. Reid, Corporate; Commercial; Tax Law

Orle, Davidson, Giesbrecht, Bargen

280 Stradbrook Ave.
Winnipeg, MB R3L 0J6
204-989-2760
Fax: 204-989-2774
general@odgb.mb.ca
www.odgb.mb.ca
Number of Lawyers: 10

Finance Lawyers:
John Davidson, Corporate Finance, Mergers, Acquisitions

Osler, Hoskin & Harcourt LLP

PO Box 50
One First Canadian Place
Toronto, ON M5X 1B8
416-362-2111
Fax: 416-862-6666
counsel@osler.com
www.osler.com
Number of Lawyers: 292
Profile: Advises many of Canada's corporate leaders as well as U.S. & international parties with extensive interests in Canada; third-party research confirms the firm's preeminent position in the marketplace; with over 400 lawyers based in Toronto, Montréal, Ottawa, Calgary & New York, our critical mass of experience with the largest domestic & cross-border business combinations enables us to exercise acknowledged strengths in mergers & acquisitions, tax, competition & litigation, & leverage our specialty expertise in fields like commercial property & infrastructure projects, IP & IT, among many others

Finance Lawyers:
Andrew W. Aziz, Corporate; Commercial
416-862-6840 e-mail: aaziz@osler.com
Joyce Bernasek, Corporate; Commercial
416-862-4283 e-mail: jbernasek@osler.com
Richard M. Borins, Corporate; Commercial
416-862-6731 e-mail: rborins@osler.com
Rupert H. Chartrand, Insolvency; Restructuring
416-862-6575 e-mail: rchartrand@osler.com
Linda G. Currie, Corporate; Commercial
416-862-6600 e-mail: lcurrie@osler.com
Rod Davidge, Corporate; Commercial
416-862-4934 e-mail: rdavidge@osler.com
Michael J. Davies, Corporate; Commercial
416-862-6556 e-mail: mdavies@osler.com
Deepesh Daya
416-652-4275 e-mail: ddaya@osler.com
Michael De Lellis, Insolvency, Restructuring
416-862-5997 e-mail: mdelellis@osler.com
Danna Donald, Corporate; Commercial
416-862-4214 e-mail: ddonald@osler.com
Tara Elliott
416-862-4606 e-mail: telliott@osler.com
Richard Fullerton, Corporate; Commercial
416-862-4604 e-mail: rfullerton@osler.com
Victoria Graham, Business Law
416-862-4856 e-mail: vgraham@osler.com
Michael S. Hart, Corporate; Commercial
416-862-6740 e-mail: mhart@osler.com
Adrian P. Hartog, Business Law
416-862-6543 e-mail: ahartog@osler.ca
Scott Horner, Corporate; Commercial
416-862-6596 e-mail: shorner@osler.com
John Jason, Business Law
416-862-4702 e-mail: jjason@osler.com
Keith Lau, Financial Services
416-862-6772 e-mail: klau@osler.com
Janet Lee, Commercial Property
416-862-5983 e-mail: jklee@osler.com
Jolie Lin, Corporate; Commercial
416-862-4277 e-mail: jlin@osler.com
Stephen W. Luff, Business Law
416-862-6552 e-mail: sluff@osler.com
Michael Matheson, Corporate; Commercial
416-862-5955 e-mail: mmatheson@osler.com
Heather R. McKean, Corporate; Commercial
416-862-6612 e-mail: hmckean@osler.com
Peter Milligan, Corporate; Commercial
416-862-6634 e-mail: pmilligan@osler.com
Andrew Moshoian, Corporate; Commercial
416-862-5969 e-mail: amoshoian@osler.com
Eden M. Oliver, Corporate; Commercial
416-862-6606 e-mail: eoliver@osler.com
Christopher Portner, Corporate; Commercial
416-862-6412 e-mail: cportner@osler.com
Randall W. Pratt, Corporate; Commercial
416-862-5908 e-mail: rpratt@osler.com
Richard Pratt, Corporate; Commercial
416-862-4720 e-mail: ripratt@osler.com
Mark Rasile
446-862-5970 e-mail: mrasile@osler.com
Robin B. Schwill, Insolvency, Restructuring
416-862-4208 e-mail: rschwill@osler.com
Edward A. Sellers, Corporate; Commercial
416-862-5959 e-mail: esellers@osler.com
Dale Seymour, Business Law
416-862-4916 e-mail: dseymour@osler.com
Laurie Shieff, Business Law
416-862-4602 e-mail: lshieff@osler.com
Steven W. Smith, Corporate
416-862-6547 e-mail: ssmith@osler.com
Terrence J. Tone, Corporate; Commercial
416-862-4225 e-mail: ttone@osler.com
George M. Valentini, Corporate; Commercial
416-862-6649 e-mail: gvalentini@osler.com
Julie Walsh, Corporate; Commercial
416-862-4855 e-mail: jawalsh@osler.com
Marc Wasserman, Insolvency, Restructuring
416-862-4908 e-mail: mwaserman@osler.com
Simon Wormwell
416-862-4912 e-mail: swormwell@osler.com
Charles Zienius, Corporate; Commercial
416-862-4222 e-mail: czienius@osler.com

Osler, Hoskin & Harcourt LLP

TransCanada Tower #2500
450 - 1st St. S
Calgary, AB T2P 5H1
403-260-7000
Fax: 403-260-7024
counsel@osler.com
www.osler.com
Number of Lawyers: 48

Finance Lawyers:
Amy Arthur, Corporate
Sherri L. Fountain, Corporate; Commercial
403-260-7039 e-mail: sfountain@osler.com
Craig Harkness, Real Estate
403-260-7016 e-mail: charkness@osler.com

Osler, Hoskin & Harcourt LLP

#2100
1000, de la Gauchetière ouest
Montréal, QC H3B 4W5
514-904-8100
Fax: 514-904-8101
Telex: 055-61368 GDT Mcounsel@osler.com
www.osler.com
Number of Lawyers: 64
Profile: Advises many of Canada's corporate leaders as well as U.S. & international parties with extensive interests in Canada; third-party research confirms the firm's preeminent position in the marketplace; with over 400 lawyers based in Toronto, Montréal, Ottawa, Calgary & New York, our critical mass of experience with the largest domestic & cross-border business combinations enables us to exercise acknowledged strengths in mergers & acquisitions, tax, competition & litigation, & leverage our specialty expertise in fields like commercial property & infrastructure projects, IP & IT, among many others

Finance Lawyers:
Natalie Gosselin, Financial Services
514-904-5633 e-mail: sgosselin@osler.com
Etienne Massicotte, Financial Services
514-904-5778 e-mail: emassicotte@osler.com
Constantine Troulis, Corporate & Commercial
514-904-8105 e-mail: ctroulis@osler.com

Pallett Valo LLP

#1600
90 Burnhamthorpe Rd. West
Mississauga, ON L5B 3C3
905-273-3300
Fax: 905-273-6920
800-323-3781
administrator@pallettvalo.com
www.pallettvalo.com
Founded: 1948
Number of Lawyers: 26

Finance Lawyers:
Murray Box, Business
905-273-3300 e-mail: mbox@pallettvalo.com
David Contant, Business; Litigation
905-273-3022 e-mail: dcontant@pallettvalo.com
Karen Groulx, Business; Litigation
905-273-3022 e-mail: kgroulx@pallettvalo.com
Priscilla Healy, Insolvency & Corporate Restructuring
905-273-3300 e-mail: phealy@pallettvalo.com
Anne Kennedy, Business; Litigation
905-273-3300 e-mail: akennedy@pallettvalo.com
Maureen McKay, Business
905-273-3022 e-mail: mmkay@pallettvalo.com
Michael Nowina, Insolvency & Corporate Restructuring
905-273-3000 e-mail: mnowina@pallettvalo.com
Brian Reiss, Business
905-273-3300 e-mail: breiss@pallettvalo.com
Craig Ross, Wills, Estates & Trust Services
905-273-3300 e-mail: cross@pallettvalo.com
John Russo, Insolvency & Corporate Restructuring; Litigation
905-273-3300 e-mail: jrusso@pallettvalo.com
Bobby Sachdeva, Lending & Insolvency; Litigation
905-273-3300 e-mail: sachdeva@pallettvalo.com
Alex Tarantino, Business
905-273-3022 e-mail: atarantino@pallettvalo.com
John R. Varley, Lending & Insolvency
905-273-3300 e-mail: jvarley@pallettvalo.com
Bonnie Yagar, Wills, Estates & Trust Services
905-273-3300 e-mail: byagar@pallettvalo.com

Patterson Law

Bank of Montreal Tower #1600
PO Box 247
5151 George St.
Halifax, NS B3J 2N9
902-444-8414
Fax: 902-484-5339
888-699-7746

Patterson Law (continued)
pgrogers@pattersonpalmer.ca
www.pattersonpalmer.ca
Founded: 1928
Number of Lawyers: 5

Finance Lawyers:
Robert L. Mellish, Corporate/Commercial
902-444-8486 e-mail: rmellish@pattersonlaw.ca
Adriana Meloni, Insurance, Litigation
902-405-8123 e-mail: ameloni@pattersonlaw.ca
Robert M. Purdy, Insurance, Litigation
902-405-8130 e-mail: rpurdy@pattersonlaw.ca
M. Gerard Tompkins, Corporate, Commercial
902-444-8490 e-mail: gtompkins@pattersonlaw.ca
Wyman W. Webb, Taxation
902-444-8420 e-mail: wwebb@pattersonlaw.ca

Patterson Palmer
Scotia Centre #1000
PO Box 610
235 Water St.
St. John's, NL A1C 5L3
709-726-6124
Fax: 709-722-0483
888-699-7746
nfld@pattersonpalmer.ca
www.pattersonpalmer.ca
Founded: 1952
Number of Lawyers: 25

Finance Lawyers:
Steve Barnes, Business; Corporate Commercial Law
709-570-5546 e-mail: sbarnes@pattersonpalmer.ca
Angela Blagdon, Insurance
709-570-5504 e-mail: ablagdon@pattersonpalmer.ca
Greg Connors, Business; Corporate Commercial Law
709-570-5502 e-mail: gconnors@pattersonpalmer.ca
Frederick Constantine, Insurance
709-570-5518 e-mail: fconstantine@pattersonpalmer.ca
Anna M. Cook, Business; Corporate/Commercial
709-570-5565 e-mail: acook@pattersonpalmer.ca
John C. Crosbie, Business; Corporate/Commercial; Competition; Public Private Partnering
e-mail: jcrosbie@pattersonpalmer.ca
Nancy Furlong, Business; Corporate Commercial Law
709-570-5510 e-mail: nfurlong@pattersonpalmer.ca
Brenda B. Grimes, Insurance
709-570-5542 e-mail: bgrimes@pattersonpalmer.ca
Barrie Heywood, Business; Corporate Commercial Law
709-570-5538 e-mail: bheywood@pattersonpalmer.ca
Stephanie S. Hickman, Financial Services
709-570-5536 e-mail: shickman@pattersonpalmer.ca
Kimberly J. Mackay, Insurance
709-520-5521 e-mail: kmackay@pattersonpalmer.ca
Carey Majid, Insurance
709-570-5503 e-mail: cmajid@pattersonpalmer.ca
M. John Mate, Financial Services
709-570-5530 e-mail: jmate@pattersonpalmer.ca
Stephen J. May, Insurance
709-570-5528 e-mail: smay@pattersonpalmer.ca
Glen L.C. Noel, Insurance
709-570-5534 e-mail: gnoel@pattersonpalmer.ca
Leanne M. O'Leary, Insurance
709-570-5516 e-mail: loleary@pattersonpalmer.ca
Robert M. Sinclair, Insurance
709-570-5508 e-mail: rsinclair@pattersonpalmer.ca
Raylene Stokes, Financial Services
709-570-5564 e-mail: rstokes@pattersonpalmer.ca
Andrew Wadden, Insurance
709-570-5525 e-mail: awadden@pattersonpalmer.ca
Douglas Wright, Business; Corporate/Commercial; Securities; Taxation
709-520-5544 e-mail: dwright@pattersonpalmer.ca

Patterson Palmer
Landing Place
PO Box 486
20 Great George St.
Charlottetown, PE C1A 7L1
902-628-1033
Fax: 902-566-2639
888-699-7746
dwells@pattersonpalmer.ca
www.pattersonpalmer.ca
Number of Lawyers: 10

Finance Lawyers:
Gregory A. Cann, Insurance
David W. Hooley, Tax Law; Financial Services
Mary-Lynn Kane, Insurance
Wendy E. Reid, Financial Services
Pamela J. Williams, Securities; Insurance; Financial Services

Patterson Palmer
Blue Cross Centre #502
644 Main St.
Moncton, NB E1C 1E2
506-856-9800
Fax: 506-856-8150
888-699-7746
www.pattersonpalmer.ca
Number of Lawyers: 12

Finance Lawyers:
Aaron J. Bourque, Insurance
Blair C. Fraser
Steven P. Gallagher, Insurance
Brian M. Hunt, Banking; Business; Corporate/Commercial
Christian E. Michaud
Isabelle C. Moreau, Business; Corporate/Commercial
Rick F.T. Nesbitt, Insurance
April L. Parker
Bruno G. Roy, Insurance
Kathryn Stratton, Financial Services
Tracy L. Wong, Business; Corporate/Commercial; Commercial Real Estate; Wills
Peter M. Wright, Business; Corporate; Commercial; Corporate; Finance

Patterson Palmer
#1500
PO Box 1324
One Brunswick Sq.
Saint John, NB E2L 4H8
506-632-8900
Fax: 506-632-8809
gpoirier@pattersonpalmer.ca
Number of Lawyers: 21

Finance Lawyers:
Arthur T. Doyle, Business; Corporate/Commercial; Corporate Finance
R.Gary Faloon, Financial Services
Raymond T. French, Bankruptcy/Insolvency; Business; Corporate/Commercial Law
Michael A. Gillis, Business; Corporate/Commercial
Raymond F. Glennie, Securities; Financial Services
Edward W. Keyes, Financial Services
John D. Laidlaw, Financial Services
Rodney E. Larsen, Insurance
Franklin O. Leger, Business; Corporate/Commercial; Corporate Finance; Wills, Trusts, Estates
Cortney M. Luscombe, Insurance
Joshua J.B. McElman, Banking; Bankruptcy/Insolvency
Gerald W. O'Brien, Securities
James K. O'Connell, Insurance
William F. O'Connell, Insurance
Anne B. Sedgwick, Commercial Real Estate; Business/Corporate; Commercial Law
A. David Seely, Business; Corporate/Commercial; Wills, Trusts, Estates
William H. Teed, Financial Services
Charles D. Whelly, Banking; Bankruptcy/Insolvency
J. Ian M. Whitcomb, Securities
Craig Wilson
M. Douglas Young

Patterson Palmer
PO Box 1068
10 Church St.
Truro, NS B2N 5G9
902-897-2000
Fax: 902-893-3071
dshice@pattersonlaw.ca
www.pattersonlaw.ca
Number of Lawyers: 17

Finance Lawyers:
Logan E. Barnhill, Property
e-mail: lbarnhill@pattersonlaw.com
Clarence A. Beckett, Litigation/Insurance
905-896-6128 e-mail: cbeckett@pattersonlaw.ca
Lloyd I. Berliner, Litigation
e-mail: lberliner@pattersonlaw.ca
Ryan P. Brennan, Property
902-896-6114
Douglas A. Caldwell, Litigation
e-mail: dcaldwell@pattersonla.ca
Sarah M. Campbell, Corporate/Commercial
e-mail: scampbell@pattersonlaw.ca
J. Ronald Creighton, Property
e-mail: rcreighton@pattersonlaw.ca
Jeffrey R. Hunt, Litigation
902-896-6185 e-mail: jhunt@pattersonlaw.ca
Dennis J. James, Litigation
902-896-6149 e-mail: djames@pattersonlaw.com
M. Ann Levangie, Litigation
e-mail: alevangie@pattesonlaw.ca
Alan C. MacLean, Wills & Estates
e-mail: amaclean@pattersonlaw.ca
John E. McKim, Litigation, Insurance
902-896-6164 e-mail: jmckim@pattersonlaw.ca
Paul E. Morris, Litigation
902-896-6122 e-mail: pmorris@pattersonlaw.ca
S. Raymond Morse, Litigation
e-mail: rmorse@pattersonlaw.com
Martina Munden, Corporate/Commercial
e-mail: mmunden@pattersonlaw.ca
Robert H. Pineo, Litigation
902-896-6177 e-mail: rpineo@pattersonlaw.ca
George L. White, Corporate/Commercial
e-mail: gwhite@pattersonlaw.ca

Pavey, Law & Wannop LLP
PO Box 1707, Galt Sta.
19 Cambridge St.
Cambridge, ON N1R 7G8
519-621-7260
Fax: 519-621-1304
info@paveylaw.com
www.paveylaw.com
Founded: 1922
Number of Lawyers: 7

Finance Lawyers:
Brian R. Law, Commercial Litigation
519-621-7260 e-mail: law@paveylaw.com
Donovan W. Pavey, Corporate Law
519-621-7260 e-mail: pavey@paveylaw.com
Stephen F. Witteveen, Corporate Law
519-621-7260 e-mail: witteveen@paveylaw.com

Perks & Hanson
#901
130 Adelaide St. West
Toronto, ON M5H 3P5
416-362-3366
Fax: 416-362-3174
perks@perksandhanson.com
Number of Lawyers: 2

Finance Lawyers:
S.I.R. Hanson, Tax
W.T. Perks, Tax

Perley-Robertson, Hill & McDougall LLP
#400
90 Sparks St.
Ottawa, ON K1P 1E2
613-238-2022
Fax: 613-238-8775
800-268-8292
lawyers@perlaw.ca
www.perlaw.ca
Founded: 1971
Number of Lawyers: 36
Profile: Our firm provides legal & business guidance to a range of clients within the software design, hardware manufacture, bio-technology, photonics & e-commerce world; our involvement ranges from helping startups secure capital to taking them public; we specialize in corporate governance, strategic planning, venture capital & securities

Finance Lawyers:
Dirk Bouwer, Business
613-566-2850 e-mail: dbouwer@perlaw.ca

Paul G. Bregman, Real Estate & Wills; Estate Planning; Business Law; Corporate Finance & Technical Venture Capital
613-566-2812 e-mail: pbregman@perlaw.ca
Sean D. Caulfeild, Business Law
613-566-2821 e-mail: scaulfeild@perlaw.ca
Denno M. Chen, Business Law
613-566-2819 e-mail: dchen@perlaw.ca
Meagan A. Cornell, Business Law
613-566-2838 e-mail: mcornell@perlaw.ca
Michael A. Gerrior, Business; Securities; Corporate Law; Corporate Finance; Mergers & Acquisitions
613-566-2813 e-mail: mgerrior@perlaw.ca
David H. Hill, Business Law; Estate Planning
613-566-2800 e-mail: dhill@perlaw.ca
Jay C. Humphrey, Tax
613-566-2810 e-mail: jhumphrey@perlaw.ca
Stanley J. Kershman, Business Law
613-566-2862 e-mail: skershman@perlaw.ca
Robert P. Kinghan, Business Law
613-566-2848 e-mail: rkinghan@perlaw.ca
David J. Lowdon, Business Law
613-566-2809 e-mail: djlowdon@perlaw.ca
Shawn W. Minnis, Business Law
613-566-2843 e-mail: sminnis@perlaw.ca
Joshua P. Moon, Commercial Real Estate; Business Law
613-566-2801 e-mail: jmoon@perlaw.ca
Robin A. Ritchie, Mergers & Acquisitions; International Transactions; Insolvency
613-566-2811 e-mail: rritchie@perlaw.ca
Paul A. Salvatore, Business Law
613-566-2814 e-mail: psalvatore@perlaw.ca
Timothy J. Thomas, Real Estate; Business Law
613-566-2805 e-mail: tthomas@perlaw.ca

Perras Mongenais

10B Circle St.
Kapuskasing, ON P5N 1T3
705-335-3939
Fax: 705-335-3960
Founded: 1993
Number of Lawyers: 2

Finance Lawyers:
Pierre Perras, Corporate Finance; Taxes

Perry & Company

PO Box 790
1081 Main St.
Smithers, BC V0J 2N0
250-847-4341
Fax: 250-847-5634
mail@perryco.ca
www.perryco.ca
Founded: 1952
Number of Lawyers: 4

Finance Lawyers:
Dale E. Perry

Petrone Hornak Garofalo Mauro

76 Algoma St. North
Thunder Bay, ON P7A 4Z4
807-344-9191
Fax: 807-345-8391
800-465-3988
Number of Lawyers: 7
Profile: Mortgage Securities & Enforcement; Personal Property Securities & Enforcement

Finance Lawyers:
James P. Garofalo, General Finance
e-mail: james@petronelaw.on.ca

Pettitt, Schwarz

#403
73 Water St. North
Cambridge, ON N1R 7L6
519-621-2450
Fax: 519-621-5750
bob@pettittschwarz.com
Founded: 1970
Number of Lawyers: 2

Finance Lawyers:
Robert C. Pettitt, Wills & Estates; Real Property
e-mail: bob@pettittschwarz.com

R.G. Phelps

#8
1638 Pandosy St.
Kelowna, BC V1Y 1P8
250-762-2345
Fax: 250-861-3664
Number of Lawyers: 1

Finance Lawyers:
R.G. Phelps, Mortgages; Sales of Business

Phillips, Friedman, Kotler

Place du Canada #900
1010, rue de la Gauchetière ouest
Montréal, QC H3B 2P8
514-878-3371
Fax: 514-878-3691
info@pfklaw.com
www.pfklaw.com/
Number of Lawyers: 18
Profile: The firm acts for a broad range of lenders in relation to financing transactions of all kinds, primarily involving medium-sized borrowers

Finance Lawyers:
Geracimos J. Analytis, General Finance
e-mail: janalytis@pfklaw.com
Ezra Beinhaker, General Finance
e-mail: ebeinhaker@pfklaw.com
Wolfe M. Friedman, General Finance, Tax & Corporate
e-mail: wfriedman@pfklaw.com
W. Robert Golfman, General Finance
e-mail: bgolfman@pfklaw.com
Julian Kotler, General Finance, Corporate & Leasing
e-mail: jkotler@pfklaw.com
Nathalie Markatos, Corporate
Robert Pancer, Commercial
Angeliki Papadimitropoulos, Commercial
Melvin S. Schiff, General Finance & Leasing
e-mail: mschiff@pfklaw.com
Norton H. Segal, General Finance & Immigration
e-mail: nsegal@pfklaw.com
Irving Shapiro, General Finance
e-mail: ishapiro@pfklaw.com
Benard Stern, General Finance
e-mail: bstern@pfklaw.com

Pitblado LLP

Commodity Exchange Tower #2500
360 Main St.
Winnipeg, MB R3C 4H6
204-956-0560
Fax: 204-957-0227
firm@pitblado.com
www.pitblado.com
Founded: 1882
Number of Lawyers: 57

Finance Lawyers:
Joseph D. Barnsley, Business; Insurance
204-956-3522
Brian T.D. Bowman, E-commerce; Corporate/Commercial
Edward D. Brown, Banks; Business; Commercial; Finance
Richard Buchwald, Trusts; Taxation; Commercial Law
Allan P. Cantor, Corporate/Commercial
Dennis M. Foerster, Commercial Litigation
Robert B. Giesbrecht, Financial Law; Wills
Randall M. Gray, Corporate Finance; Acquisitions & Divestitures; Insolvency & Restructuring
Yude M. Henteleff, Corporate/Commercial
Adam R. Herstein, Corporate/Commercial
Catherine E. Howden, Commercial Litigation; Debtor & Creditor
Bruce H. King, Business; Corporate
204-956-3541
Thomas J.D. Kormylo
Jack R. London, Counsel, Taxation
204-956-3500
John T. McGoey, Corporate & Commercial
Howard L. Morry, Taxation
Howard P. Nerman, Business & Corporate; Finance
204-956-3530 e-mail: nerman@pba-law.com
Andrew D.M. Ogaranko, Business & Commercial; Franchises; Financing & Securities
Judith R.A. Payne, Contracts; Business Law
Norm Promislow, Taxation; Corporate/Commercial
David B.N. Ramsay, Commercial Law; Insolvency
204-956-3529
E. Scott Ransom, Corporate/Commercial
Carol Lynn Schafer, Corporate Law
Rodney E. Shannon, Insurance
Philip M. Sheps, Business Law
John R. Toone, Corporate/Commercial
Douglas G. Ward, Insolvency & Restructuring
204-956-3534 e-mail: ward@pba-law.com
Roger W. Wight, Business Law

Poole Althouse

Western Trust Bldg.
PO Box 812
49 - 51 Park St.
Corner Brook, NL A2H 6H7
709-634-3136
Fax: 709-634-8247
info@pa-law.ca
Founded: 1955
Number of Lawyers: 9

Finance Lawyers:
J. Annette Bennett
709-637-6431 e-mail: abennett@pa-law.ca

Pouliot L'Ecuyer

Tour des Laurentides
2525, boul Laurier, 10e étage
Québec, QC G1V 2L2
418-658-1080
Fax: 418-658-1414
Telex: 051-3786avocat@droit.com
www.droit.com
Founded: 1963
Number of Lawyers: 26

Finance Lawyers:
Lisa Barabé, Corporate
Daniel St-Pierre, Banking
e-mail: dst-pierre@droit.com

Pullan Kammerloch Frohlinger

#300
240 Kennedy St.
Winnipeg, MB R3C 1T1
204-956-0490
Fax: 204-947-3747
firm@pkf-law.com
Number of Lawyers: 10

Finance Lawyers:
Herbert H. Rempel
204-956-0490 e-mail: hrempel@pkf-law.com

Ramsay Lampman Rhodes

111 Wallace St.
Nanaimo, BC V9R 5B2
250-754-3321
Fax: 250-754-1148
info@rlr-law.com
www.rlr-law.com
Number of Lawyers: 14

Finance Lawyers:
David Covey, Business
John Horn, Commercial Litigation
Derek Jonson, Commercial Litigation
Jonathan W. Lampman, Business; Commercial Financing; Commercial Negotiation
e-mail: jlampman@rlr-law.com
J. Parker MacCarthy, Corporate & Commercial; Wills, Trusts & Estate Planning
Stephen McPhee, Commercial Litigation
D. Peter Ramsay, Estates
Richard N. Rhodes, Estates; Commercial Law
Michael Wasserman, Collections; Estates; Corporate Commercial Transactions

Rancourt, Legault & St-Onge

175, rue Salaberry ouest
Salaberry-de-Valleyfield, QC J6T 2J1
450-371-2221
Fax: 450-371-2094
courrier@rancourtlegault.com
www.rancourtlegault.com
Number of Lawyers: 7

ACCOUNTING & LAW

Rancourt, Legault & St-Onge (continued)

Finance Lawyers:
Marie Legault, Insurance
e-mail: m.legault@rancourtlegault.com

Reynolds, Mirth, Richards & Farmer LLP
Manulife Pl. #3200
10180 - 101 St.
Edmonton, AB T5J 3W8
780-425-9510
Fax: 780-429-3044
800-661-7673
mail@rmrf.com
www.rmrf.com
Founded: 1915
Number of Lawyers: 36
Profile: Serving the financial services industry is one of RMRF's primary practice areas; we act for a variety of financial institutions including banks, insurance companies, credit unions & other institutional lenders; the depth of knowledge of our bankruptcy & insolvency lawyers is significant; our Commercial Real Estate Group have extensive experience in all types of commercial real estate & finance transactions

Finance Lawyers:
D.C. Alguire
K.L. Becker Brookes
Doris. Bonora
780-497-3370 e-mail: dbonora@rmrf.com
Shelly Chamaschuk
780-497-3364 e-mail: schamasc@rmrf.com
Rick Ewasiuk
780-497-3384 e-mail: rewasiuk@rmrf.com
Allan Farmer
780-497-3360 e-mail: afarmer@rmrf.com
R.I. Giardino
John Paul Janssens
Cherisse Killick-Dzenick
780-497-3372 e-mail: ckillick@rmrf.com
N.L. Kortbeek
Frederick Kozak
780-497-3358 e-mail: fkozak@rmrf.com
V.L. Lirette
M.J. McCabe
Randall McCreary
780-497-3348 e-mail: rmccreary@rmrf.com
Sonny Mirth
780-497-3346
Margaret Mrazek
780-497-3356 e-mail: mmrazek@rmrf.com
A. Omkar
W.M. Pedruski
F.C.R. Price
T.A. Shipley
D.R. Stollery
D.N. Tkachuk

Richards Buell Sutton
#700
401 West Georgia St.
Vancouver, BC V6B 5A1
604-682-3664
Fax: 604-688-3830
info@rbs.ca
www.rbs.ca
Number of Lawyers: 26

Finance Lawyers:
Mark Baron, Commercial Litigation
Tim H.R. Brown, Business Law
Mark R. Davies, Commercial Litigation
Silvana M. Facchin, Wealth Preservation; Business Law
David W. Hay, Commercial Litigation
D. Scott Lamb, Business Law
Michael Leroux, Business Law
Peter Lightbody, Commercial Litigation
Jeffrey J. Lowe, Business Law
H. Scott MacDonald, Commercial Litigation
C. Nicole Mangan, Commercial Litigation
A. Steve Michoulas, Business Law
Colin A. Millar, Commercial Litigation
Patrick Montens, Business Law
Jay M. Munsie, Business Law
J. Raymond Pollard, Commercial Litigation
Georg D. Reuter, Business Law
Sharon E. White, Business Law
Sze-Mei Yeung, Business Law

Rick Associates
#6
591 March Rd.
Kanata, ON K2K 2M5
613-592-0088
Fax: 613-592-3322
jrick@rickassociates.com
Founded: 1993
Number of Lawyers: 1

Finance Lawyers:
W. John Rick

Rigobon, Carli
#401
3700 Steeles Ave. West
Woodbridge, ON L4L 8K8
905-850-5060
Fax: 905-850-5066
michael@rigoboncarli.com
www.rigoboncarli.com
Number of Lawyers: 3

Finance Lawyers:
Walter J. Rigobon

Robertson Stromberg Pedersen LLP
Bank of Canada #500
PO Box 1037
2220 - 12 Ave.
Regina, SK S4P 3B2
306-569-9000
Fax: 306-565-6565
rs.regina@thinkrsplaw.com
www.thinkrsplaw.com
Number of Lawyers: 19

Finance Lawyers:
David J. Bishop, Corporate & Commercial
Gerald Naylen, Corporate & Commercial
Patricia Warsaba, Corporate & Commercial

Robinson Sheppard Shapiro
Tour Stock Exchange #4600
PO Box 322
800, Place Victoria
Montréal, QC H4Z 1H6
514-878-2631
Fax: 514-878-1865
Telex: 05-27343info@rsslex.com
www.rsslex.com
Founded: 1920
Number of Lawyers: 61
Profile: Commercial & Real Estate Transactions; Mergers & Acquisitions; Corporate Organization, Reorganization & Restructuring; Income Tax Interpretation & Planning; Advice on Goods & Service Tax; Enforcement of Creditor Rights; Financial Restructuring; Financing Contracts; Banking Contracts; Collection & Insolvency; Bankruptcy; Banking Litigation; Franchising & Distributing; Joint Ventures; Leases; Licenses; Partnerships; Shareholder Rights; Estate Planning; Wills & Trusts; Mediation & Arbitration in Civil & Commercial Matters

Finance Lawyers:
Louise Baillargeon, Corporate & Commercial
Jean-François Bilodeau, Commercial
Eric Boulva, Commercial, Banking & Insolvency
Charles E. Flam, General Finance
Luc Fleurant, Banking & Commercial
Genevieve Goulet, Commercial
Andrey Hollinger, Commercial; Real Estate; Banking
Normand Laurendeau, Commercial & Corporate
Martin Lord, Tax
Rhuna Luger, Commercial
Jonathan Robinson, Commercial
Barry H. Shapiro, General Finance & Commercial
C.A. Sheppard, Commercial Litigation
Jean Pierre Sheppard, Commercial Litigation

Robson, O'Connor
PO Box 1890
22 High St.
Ladysmith, BC V9G 1B4
250-245-7141
Fax: 250-245-2921
800-641-1311
robcon@shawcable.com
Founded: 1987
Number of Lawyers: 2

Finance Lawyers:
Douglas B. Robson, General Finance

D.A. Roper
334 West 15th St.
North Vancouver, BC V7M 1S5
604-986-0488
Fax: 604-984-3463
roperlaw@shawbiz.ca
Founded: 1980
Number of Lawyers: 1
Profile: Corporate & Commercial

Finance Lawyers:
D.A. Roper

Roy Elliott Kim O'Connor LLP
#1400
10 Bay St.
Toronto, ON M5J 2R8
416-362-1989
Fax: 416-362-6204
info@reko.ca
www.reko.ca
Number of Lawyers: 11
Profile: Has a dynamic commercial litigation practice representing a diverse clientele; whether pursuing claims for aggrieved individuals or defending the interests of some of the world's major corporations, our firm can assist you with any commercial dispute; areas of expertise include securities litigation, injunctions, oppression remedies, shareholders disputes, contractual disputes and debt collection

Finance Lawyers:
R. Douglas Elliott, Commercial; Insurance
Won J. Kim, Securities
Patricia A. LeFebour, Estate Planning & Litigation
Megan B. McPhee, Commercial
R. Trent Morris, Commercial
Victoria Paris, Securities; Commercial

Salley Bowes Harwardt LLP
#1750
1185 Georgia St. West
Vancouver, BC V6E 4E6
604-688-0788
Fax: 604-688-0778
sbh@sbh.bc.ca
www.sbh.bc.ca
Founded: 1995
Number of Lawyers: 4
Profile: Corporate Finance; Securities

Finance Lawyers:
Paul A. Bowes
Victor P. Harwardt
Hugh McNicoll
Louis P. Salley

Schnell Hardy Jones LLP
#504
4909 - 49th St.
Red Deer, AB T4N 1V1
403-342-7400
Fax: 403-340-0520
800-342-7405
lawyers@schnell-law.com
www.schnell-law.com
Founded: 1958
Number of Lawyers: 9
Profile: Advising financial institutions; drafting, filing & enforcing securities; representing financial institutions in collections & enforcement litigation

Finance Lawyers:
David L. Hardy, Financial Services; Real Estate; Corporate/Commercial
e-mail: david@schnell-law.com
S. Marty Jones, Collections & Enforcement Litigation
e-mail: marty@schnell-law.com

Seon Gutstadt Lash LLP
#1800
4950 Yonge St.
Toronto, ON M2N 6K1
416-224-0224
Fax: 416-224-0758
boblash@torlaw.com
Number of Lawyers: 6

Finance Lawyers:
Eli Gutstadt
Stephen D. Seon

Shandro Dixon Edgson
#400
999 Hastings St. West
Vancouver, BC V6C 2W2
604-689-0400
Fax: 604-685-2009
law@sdelawyers.com
www.sdelawyers.com
Number of Lawyers: 6
Profile: We specialize in the area of insolvency & bankruptcy litigation; we also have expertise in dealing with general corporate/commercial matters, including mergers & acquisitions, real estate transactions & corporate litigation

Finance Lawyers:
J. Joseph D. Bateman, Banking Litigation; Bankruptcy & Insolvency.
Larry S. Blaschuk, Corporate/Commercial/Real Estate Law; Insolvency
James F. Dixon, Bankruptcy; Insolvency; Receivership; Foreclosure; Bank Security
Arthur L. Edgson, Foreclosure; Bank Security
Robert B. Rogers, Commercial & Insolvency Law
Frederick W. Shandro, Bankruptcy; Insolvency; Receivership & Foreclosure

Stephen L. Shanfield
#333
880 Ouellette Ave.
Windsor, ON N9A 1C7
519-258-3338
Fax: 519-258-3335
ssh@mnsi.net
www.shanfieldlaw.com
Founded: 1977
Number of Lawyers: 1

Finance Lawyers:
Stephen L. Shanfield

Shea Nerland Calnan
#2800
715 - 5th Ave. SW
Calgary, AB T2P 2X6
403-299-9600
Fax: 403-299-9601
snc@snclaw.com
Founded: 1990
Number of Lawyers: 10
Profile: Corporate/Commercial Law; Commercial Litigtaion; Estates Law; Securities; Tax Law; Wills

Finance Lawyers:
David M. Calnan, Securities
403-299-9606 e-mail: dmc@snclaw.com
Dennis L. Nerland, Tax
403-299-9605 e-mail: snc@snclaw.com
James G. Shea, Commercial Litigation
403-299-9604 e-mail: jgs@snclaw.com

Shook, Wickham, Bishop & Field
906 Island Hwy.
Campbell River, BC V9W 2C3
250-287-8355
Fax: 250-287-8112
info@crlawyers.ca
www.crlawyers.ca
Founded: 1975
Number of Lawyers: 8

Finance Lawyers:
Jay Kirkland, Business Law
Daniel A.J. Wickham, Business Law

Silbernagel & Company
#700
595 Howe St.
Vancouver, BC V6C 2T5
604-687-9621
Fax: 604-687-5960
stephen@silbernagellaw.com
Founded: 1975
Number of Lawyers: 2
Profile: Financing & security for banks

Finance Lawyers:
Andrew Davis, Tax

Alan G. Silverstein
#318
1600 Steeles Ave. West
Concord, ON L4K 4M2
905-761-1600
Fax: 905-761-0948
alan.silverstein@rogers.com
Founded: 1977
Number of Lawyers: 1
Profile: Extensive experience in residential mortgage transactions, including enforcement work; has also written books & articles on mortgage financing in Canada

Finance Lawyers:
A.G. Silverstein, Real Estate

Simpson, Wigle LLP
Sims Square Bldg. #501
390 Brant St.
Burlington, ON L7R 4J4
905-639-1052
Fax: 905-333-3960
matthewsl@simpsonwigle.com
www.simpsonwigle.com
Founded: 1990
Number of Lawyers: 6
Profile: Corporate Reorganizations; Secured Lending; Enforcement of Security; Insolvency & Receivership

Finance Lawyers:
Michael G. Emery, Commercial Litigation
e-mail: emerym@simpsonwigle.com
Rosemary Fisher, Commercial Litigation; Estate Litigation; Insolvency; Debtor-Creditor Litigation
e-mail: fisherr@sipsonwigle.com
Stuart Law, Commercial Litigation
e-mail: laws@simpsonwigle.com

Simpson, Wigle LLP
#400
PO Box 990
21 King St. West
Hamilton, ON L8N 3R1
905-528-8411
Fax: 905-528-9008
800-464-4414
postmaster@simpsonwigle.com
www.simpsonwigle.com
Founded: 1986
Number of Lawyers: 25
Profile: Commercial Law; Franchising & Licensing; Bank Financing; Business Law, Commercial Real Estate/Secured Transactions; Commercial Leasing; Construction Law & Commercial Litigation; Commercial Tenancy; Insolvency & Creditor's Rights & Priorities

Finance Lawyers:
James C. Brown, Finance
905-528-8411 e-mail: brownj@simpsonwigle.com
Rosemary Fisher, General Finance
905-528-8411 e-mail: fisherr@simpsonwigle.com
David J.H. Jackson, General Finance
905-528-8411 e-mail: jacksond@simpsonwigle.com
John H. Loukidelis, General Finance
905- -
L.W. Matthews, General Finance
905-639-1052 e-mail: matthewsl@simpsonwigle.com
Joseph C. Monaco, Finance
905-528-8411 e-mail: monacoj@simpsonwigle.com
Kathryn L. Osborne, General Finance
905-528-8411 e-mail: osbornek@simpsonwigle.com
Derek A. Schmuck, Finance
e-mail: schmuck@simpsonwigle.com

Sims & Company
PO Box 460
76 Main St. South
Minnedosa, MB R0J 1E0
204-867-2717
Fax: 204-867-2434
minnedosa@simsco.mb.ca
www.simsco.mb.ca
Founded: 1983
Number of Lawyers: 2
Profile: We provide advice to local banks & credit unions on all aspects of loan financing, including residential & commercial mortgages & farm lending; in addition, we also assist in realizing on loans for area financial institutions

Finance Lawyers:
Norman H. Sims, General Finance
e-mail: nsims@simsco.mb.ca

Jennifer L. Sims
#201
303 Bagot St.
Kingston, ON K7K 5W7
613-530-2230
Fax: 613-530-2231
Founded: 1992
Number of Lawyers: 1
Profile: Residential & commercial financings on real & personal property

Finance Lawyers:
Jennifer L. Sims, Corporate/Commercial

Singleton Urquhart LLP
#1200
925 Georgia St. West
Vancouver, BC V6C 3L2
604-682-7474
Fax: 604-682-1283
su@singleton.com
www.singleton.com
Founded: 1986
Number of Lawyers: 24

Finance Lawyers:
John R. Singleton, Insurance
e-mail: jrs@singleton.com

Siskind, Cromarty, Ivey & Dowler LLP
PO Box 2520
680 Waterloo St.
London, ON N6A 3V8
519-672-2121
Fax: 519-672-6065
877-672-2121
info@siskinds.com
www.siskinds.com
Founded: 1933
Number of Lawyers: 65
Profile: Bankruptcy & Insolvency Law; Business Law; Commercial Litigation; Creditors Rights; Financial Institutions; Franchise Law; Insurance Law

Finance Lawyers:
Henry Berg, Business Law
519-672-2121 e-mail: henry.berg@siskinds.com
Fausto Boniferro, General Finance
519-672-2121 e-mail: fausto.boniferro@siskinds.com
Stacey Bothwell, Commercial Litigation
519-672-2121 e-mail: stacey.bothwell@siskinds.com
David Broad, Commercial Litigation
519-672-2121 e-mail: david.broad@siskinds.com
Catherine Bruni, Insurance
519-672-2121 e-mail: catherine.bruni@siskinds.com
Douglas Bryce, Business
519-672-2121 e-mail: doug.bryce@siskinds.com
James R. Caskey, Insurance
519-672-2121 e-mail: jim.caskey@siskinds.com
Craig Clarke, General Finance
519-672-2121 e-mail: craig.clarke@siskinds.com
Barry Cleaver, Business
519-672-2121 e-mail: barry.cleaver@siskinds.com
Chris Collins, Insurance
519-672-2121 e-mail: chris.collins@siskinds.com
Peter Dillon, Business, Franchise
519-672-2121 e-mail: peter.dillon@siskinds.com
Nick Fursman, Insurance
519-672-2121 e-mail: nick.fursman@siskinds.com

Siskind, Cromarty, Ivey & Dowler LLP (continued)
Rene Gasparotto, Commercial Litigation
519-672-2121 e-mail: renato.gasparotto@siskinds.com
R.K. Wayne Goldstein, Creditors' Rights
519-671-2121 e-mail: wayne.goldstein@siskinds.com
Shawn Graham, Commercial Litigation
519-672-2121 e-mail: shawn.graham@siskinds.com
John Kennedy, Business Law
519-672-221 e-mail: john.kennedy@siskinds.com
Raymond Leach, Commercial Litigation
519-672-2121 e-mail: ray.leach@siskinds.com
Richard Lockwood, Commercial Litigation
519-672-2121 e-mail: dick.lockwood@siskinds.com
Dan MacKeigan, Commercial Litigation
519-672-2121 e-mail: dan.mackeigan@siskinds.com
James Mays, Insurance Law
519-672-2121 e-mail: jim.mays@siskinds.com
Fred Rose, Commercial Litigation
519-672-2121 e-mail: fred.rose@siskinds.com
Stephanie Ross, Commercial Litigation
519-672-2121
Paul Scott, Insurance Law
519-672-2121 e-mail: paul.scott@siskinds.com
Graeme Sperryn, Business Law
519-672-2121 e-mail: graeme.sperryn@siskinds.com
Paul Strickland, Commercial Litigation
519-672-2121 e-mail: paul.strickland@siskinds.com
David S. Thompson, Litigation
519-672-2121 e-mail: david.thompson@siskinds.com
Barbara Van Bunderen, Bankruptcy; Insolvency
519-672-2121 e-mail: barbara.vanbunderen@siskinds.com
James Virtue, Insurance Law
519-672-2121 e-mail: jim.virtue@siskinds.com
Taimi Williamson, Business Franchise
519-682-2121 e-mail: taimi.williamson@siskinds.com

Skadden, Arps, Slate, Meagher & Flom LLP

#1750
PO Box 258, Toronto Do Sta.
222 Bay St.
Toronto, ON M5K 1J5
416-777-4700
Fax: 416-777-4747
Number of Lawyers: 9
Profile: The Toronto office of Skadden, Arps advises a variety of clients on U.S. legal matters, principally relating to cross-border debt & equity offerings & mergers & acquisitions; we also represent Canadian clients in various other areas, including international trade, litigation, tax, banking, restructuring and bankruptcy reorganization; our attorneys are registered as foreign legal consultants & do not advise on Canadian law

Finance Lawyers:
David P. Armstrong, Corporate
Ryan J. Dzierniejko, Corporate
Riccardo A. Leofanti, Corporate
Christopher W. Morgan, Corporate; Securities
Karen Papadopoulos, Corporate
Jason M. Saltzman, Corporate
Eric Spindel, Corporate
Sally D. Whitehead, Corporate
Raziel Zisman, Corporate

Snyder & Associates LLP

#2500
10123 - 99 St.
Edmonton, AB T5J 3H1
780-426-4133
Fax: 780-424-1588
www.snyder.ca
Number of Lawyers: 12

Finance Lawyers:
Edwin A. Bridges
e-mail: ebridges@snyder.ca
Russell A. Flint
e-mail: rflint@snyder.ca
Colin P. Neufeldt
e-mail: cneufeldt@snyder.ca
Michael D. Roberts
e-mail: mroberts@snyder.ca
Stephen C. Snyder
e-mail: ssnyder@snyder.ca
Howard L. Starkman
e-mail: hstarkman@snyder.ca
Bryan W. Westerman
e-mail: bwesterman@snyder.ca

Solomon, Grosberg LLP

#1704
55 University Ave.
Toronto, ON M5J 2H7
416-366-7828
Fax: 416-366-3513
lawyers@solgro.com
Number of Lawyers: 6

Finance Lawyers:
G.R. Solomon

Soloway, Wright LLP

#900
427 Laurier Ave. West
Ottawa, ON K1R 7Y2
613-236-0111
Fax: 613-238-8507
800-207-5880
info@solowaywright.com
www.solowaywright.com
Founded: 1946
Number of Lawyers: 21
Profile: Commercial Law

Finance Lawyers:
Dan Coderre, Business Law
613-544-7334 e-mail: acoderre@solowaywright.com
Richard McNevin, Securities & Real Estate
613-544-7334 e-mail: mcnevinr@solowaywright.com
John E. Moss, Business & Commercial
613-544-7334 e-mail: mossj@solowaywright.com
Lawrence J. Soloway, Business & Insolvency
613-782-3203 e-mail: lsoloway@solowaywright.com
Sanjay Srivastava, Corporate, Commercial & Real Estate
613-782-3207 e-mail: srivastava@solowaywright.com
Kenneth J. Webb, Estates
613-782-3200 e-mail: kenwebb@solowaywright.com

Speigel Nichols Fox

#400
44 Peel Centre Dr.
Brampton, ON L6T 4B5
905-791-6262
Fax: 905-791-6446
snf1@ontlaw.com
www.ontlaw.com
Number of Lawyers: 7
Profile: Commercial; Business; Tax Law

Finance Lawyers:
Susan Balpataky, Commercial Litigation
Ian Latimer, Commercial Litigation
Robert McIntyre, Business Law; Wills & Estates
Jonathan Speigel, Commercial Litigation

Spry Hawkins Micner

#440
5900 No. 3 Rd.
Richmond, BC V6X 3P7
604-233-7001
Fax: 604-233-7017
jack@willpowerlaw.com
www.willpowerlaw.com
Number of Lawyers: 1

Finance Lawyers:
Jack Micner, Collections; Foreclosures; Wills & Estates
e-mail: jackm@shmlaw.ca

Stewart McKelvey Stirling Scales

Purdy's Wharf Tower One #900
PO Box 997, Central Sta.
1959 Upper Water St.
Halifax, NS B3J 2X2
902-420-3200
Fax: 902-420-1417
halifax@smss.com
www.smss.com
Founded: 1867
Number of Lawyers: 91

Finance Lawyers:
Tricia L. Avery, Insurance
902-420-3350 e-mail: tavery@smss.com
T. Arthur Barry, Insurance
902-420-3364 e-mail: abarry@smss.com
Daniela F. Bassan, Insurance
902-420-3354 e-mail: dbassan@smss.com
Marc J. Belliveau, Securities/Corporate Finance; Corporate/Commercial
902-420-3343 e-mail: mbelliveau@smss.com
Karen N. Bennett-Clayton, Insurance
902-420-3377 e-mail: kbennettclayton@smss.com
Clare E. Bilek, Insurance
902-420-3351 e-mail: cbilek@smss.com
J. Corinne Boudreau, Corporate/Commercial
902-420-3380 e-mail: cboudreau@smss.com
Lydia S. Bugden, Corporate/Commercial
902-420-3372 e-mail: lbugden@smss.com
Kimberly Bungay, Corporate/Commercial
Andrew V. Burke, Securities/Corporate Finance; Corporate/Commercial
902-420-3359 e-mail: jburke@smss.com
Mark S. Bursey, Tax Law: Corporate/Commercial
902-420-3371 e-mail: mbursey@smss.com
George A. Caines, Corporate/Commercial
902-420-3307 e-mail: gcaines@smss.com
Tyana R. Caplan, Insurance
902-420-3356 e-mail: tcaplan@smss.com
James L. Chipman, Insurance
902-420-3368 e-mail: jchipman@smss.com
Warren B. Chornoby, Securities/Corporate Finance; Corporate/Commercial
902-420-3339 e-mail: wchornoby@smss.com
Sheree L. Conlon, Insurance
902-420-3375 e-mail: sconlon@smss.com
Dawn Cottreau, Corporate/Commercial
James S. Cowan, Corporate/Commercial
902-420-3311 e-mail: jcowan@smss.com
James K. Cruickshank, Tax Law; Corporate/Commercial
902-420-3394 e-mail: jcruickshank@smss.com
Robert P. Dexter, Corporate/Commercial
902-420-3324 e-mail: rdexter@maritimemarlin.ca
Kendrick H. Douglas, Insurance
David P.S. Farrar, Insurance; Financial Services
902-420-3362 e-mail: dfarrar@smss.com
Paul W. Festeryga, Tax Law
902-420-3302 e-mail: pfesteryga@smss.com
Robert G. Grant, Insurance
902-420-3328 e-mail: rgrant@smss.com
Christa M. Hellstrom, Insurance
902-420-3331 e-mail: chellstrom@smss.com
Richard A. Hirsch, Financial Services; Corporate/Commercial
902-420-3348 e-mail: rhirsch@smss.com
Richard K. Jones, Securities/Corporate Finance; Corporate/Commercial
902-420-3317 e-mail: rjones@smss.com
D. Fraser MacFadyen, Securities/Corporate Finance; Corporate/Commercial
902-450-3365 e-mail: fmacfadyen@smss.com
Deanne MacLeod, Securities/Corporate Finance; Corporate/Commercial
902-420-3313 e-mail: dmacleod@smss.com
J. Thomas MacQuarrie, Financial Services; Corporate/Commercial
902-420-3305 e-mail: tmacquarrie@smss.com
D. Geoffrey Machum, Insurance
902-420-3338 e-mail: gmachum@smss.com
Douglas J. Mathews, Corporate/Commercial
902-420-3320 e-mail: dmathews@smss.com
Timothy C. Matthews, Financial Services; Corporate/Commercial
902-420-3325 e-mail: tmatthews@smss.com
Carman G. McCormick, Insurance
John S. McFarlane, Financial Services; Corporate/Commercial
902-420-3315 e-mail: jmcfarlane@smss.com
Andrew J. McFarlane, Corporate/Commercial
David A. Miller, Insurance
902-420-3319 e-mail: dmiller@smss.com
John D. Moore, Corporate/Commercial
902-420-3303 e-mail: jdm@auracom.com
Nancy I. Murray, Insurance
902-420-3334 e-mail: nmurray@smss.com
Scott C. Norton, Insurance
902-420-3349 e-mail: snorton@smss.com
Colin D. Piercey, Insurance
902-420-3345 e-mail: cpiercey@smss.com
Charles S. Reagh, Securities/Corporate Finance; Corporate/Commercial
902-420-3335 e-mail: csr@smss.com

John M. Rogers, Insurance
902-420-3340 e-mail: jrogers@smss.com
Roderick H. Rogers, Insurance
902-420-3369 e-mail: rrogers@smss.com
Nancy G. Rubin, Insurance
902-420-3337 e-mail: nrubin@smss.com
William L. Ryan, Insurance
Richard F. Southcott, Insurance
902-420-3304 e-mail: rsouthcott@smss.com
David A. Stewart, Tax Law; Corporate/Commercial
902-420-3306 e-mail: dstewart@smss.com
Lawrence J. Stordy, Securities/Corporate Finance; Corporate/Commercial
902-420-3347 e-mail: lstordy@smss.com
Ian A. Sutherland, Corporate/Commercial
Candace L. Thomas, Corporate/Commercial
902-420-3373 e-mail: cthomas@smss.com
Brent D. Timmons, Corporate/Commercial
902-420-3385 e-mail: btimmons@smss.com
Shelley A. Wood, Insurance
902-420-3353 e-mail: swood@smss.com

Stewart McKelvey Stirling Scales
PO Box 2140, Central Sta.
65 Grafton St.
Charlottetown, PE C1A 8B9
902-629-4549
Fax: 902-566-5283
charlottetown@smss.com
www.smss.com
Number of Lawyers: 22

Finance Lawyers:
Keith M. Boswell, Securities/Corporate Finance; Insurance; Corporate/Commercial
902-629-4511 e-mail: kboswell@smss.com
D. Spencer Campbell, Insurance
902-629-4549 e-mail: scampbell@smss.com
Janet M.R. Clark, Insurance
902-629-4562 e-mail: jclark@smss.com
Tracey L. Clements, Insurance
902-629-4538 e-mail: tclements@smss.com
Geoffrey D. Connolly, Corporate/Commercial
902-629-4515 e-mail: gdconnolly@smss.com
Keya Desgupta, Corporate/Commercial
James W. Gormley, Corporate/Commercial
902-629-4513 e-mail: jgormley@smss.com
Thomas P. Laughlin, Insurance; Corporate/Commercial
902-629-4554 e-mail: tlaughlin@smss.com
J. Scott MacKenzie, Financial Services; Corporate/Commercial
902-629-4507 e-mail: smackenzie@smss.com
Jennifer S. MacPherson, Corporate/Commercial; Insurance
Chris S. Montigny, Corporate/Commercial
Eugene P. Rossiter, Insurance
902-629-4502 e-mail: erossiter@smss.com
Alan K. Scales, Insurance
902-629-4500 e-mail: ascales@smss.com
Barbara E. Smith, Financial Services; Corporate/Commercial
902-629-4514 e-mail: bsmith@smss.com
Curtis A. Toombs, Corporate/Commercial
James C. Travers, Securities/Corporate Finance; Financial Services; Corporate/Commercial
902-629-4504 e-mail: jtravers@smss.com

Stewart McKelvey Stirling Scales
#600
PO Box 730
77 Westmorland St.
Fredericton, NB E3B 5B4
506-458-1970
Fax: 506-444-8974
fredericton@smss.com
Number of Lawyers: 14

Finance Lawyers:
Hugh J. Cameron, Insurance; Corporate/Commercial
506-443-0120 e-mail: hcameron@smss.com
J.E. Britt Dysart, Financial Services; Corporate/Commercial
506-443-0153 e-mail: bdysart@smss.com
Allison J. McCarthy, Tax Law; Insurance; Corporate/Commercial
506-444-8977 e-mail: amccarthy@smss.com
Frederick C. McElman, Insurance; Corporate/Commercial
506-444-8979 e-mail: fmcelman@smss.com
Aaron M. Savage, Tax Law; Financial Services; Corporate/Commercial
506-443-0157 e-mail: asavage@smss.com
Kimberly A. Wylde, Corporate/Commercial
506-443-0129 e-mail: kwylde@smss.com

Stewart McKelvey Stirling Scales
Blue Cross Centre #601
PO Box 28051
644 Main St.
Moncton, NB E1C 9N4
506-853-1970
Fax: 506-858-8454
moncton@smss.com
www.smss.com
Number of Lawyers: 15

Finance Lawyers:
Marie-Claude Bélanger-Richard, Insurance, Litigation
506-853-1972 e-mail: mcbelanger@smss.com
Melanie L. Cassidy, Litigation, Insurance
506-853-1959 e-mail: mcassidy@smss.com
Levi E. Clain, Litigation
506-383-2229 e-mail: lclain@smss.com
Tracey K. Deware, Insurance, Litigation
506-853-1971 e-mail: tdeware@smss.com
Denise Doiron-Bourgeois, Corporate, Commercial, Litigation, Property & Real Estate Management
506-383-2221 e-mail: ddoiron@smss.com
Robert M. Dysart, Insurance, Litigation - Corporate, Commercial
506-383-2230 e-mail: rdysart@smss.com
Luc J. Elslinger, Insurance; Corporate/Commercial
506-383-2232 e-mail: lelsliger@smss.com
Charles A. LeBlond, Litigation, Insurance, Litigation - Commercial
506-853-1976 e-mail: cleblond@smss.com
Stéphanie Luce, Litigation, Insurance
506-383-2234 e-mail: sluce@ssms.com
Allison S. MacLean, Insurance, Litigation
506-853-1966 e-mail: asmaclean@smss.com
Sasha D. Morisset, Insurance, Litigation - Corporate, Commercial
506-853-1960 e-mail: smorisset@smss.com
John Eric Pollabauer, Financial Services; Corporate/Commercial, Property & RealEstate, Corporate Restructuring & Insolvency
506-853-1960 e-mail: jep@smss.com
André G. Richard, Insurance; Litigation - Corporate, Commercial
506-853-1962 e-mail: arichard@smss.com
Joléne M. Richard, Insurance; Litigation
e-mail: jrichard@smss.com

Stewart McKelvey Stirling Scales
Brunswick House #1000
PO Box 7289, A Sta.
44 Chipman Hill
Saint John, NB E2L 4S6
506-632-1970
Fax: 506-652-1989
saint-john@smss.com
Number of Lawyers: 33

Finance Lawyers:
D. Hayward Aiton, Corporate/Commercial; Property & Real Estate Development; Media & Entertainment; Asset Securitization
506-632-2765 e-mail: haiton@smss.com
Steven F. Bainbridge, Corporate/Commercial
506-632-8533 e-mail: sbainbridge@smss.com
Lee C. Bell-Smith, Financial Services; Corporate/Commercial; Owner-Manager Business; Corporate Restructuring & Insolvency; Asset Based Lend
506-632-2793 e-mail: lbellsmith@smss.com
Cynthia J. Benson, Insurance; Litigation
506-632-8301 e-mail: cbenson@smss.com
Scott A. Brittain, Litigation
506-632-8786 e-mail: sbrittain@smss.com
Lynne M. Burnham, Tax Law; Corporate/Commercial; Directors & Officers Liability; Estate Planning & Litigation; Mergers & Acquisitions; Pro
506-632-2767 e-mail: lburnham@smss.com
Chantal N. Daigle, Insurance; Litigation; Family
506-632-2761 e-mail: cdaigle@smss.com
Jill DeWitt, Litigation; Construction Law
506-632-4232 e-mail: jdewitt@smss.com
Sarah M. Dever, Litigation; Insurance
506-632-2764 e-mail: sdever@smss.com
William B. Goss, Labour & Employment; Occupational Health & Safety; Labour Relations; Pensions & Employee Benefits
506-632-4515 e-mail: wgoss@smss.com
Rodney D. Gould, Tax Law; Financial Services; Corporate/Commercial; Personal Securities
506-632-2762 e-mail: rgould@smss.com
Gregory S. Harding, Corporate/Commercial; Energy & Natural Resources; Construction Law; Environmental; Technology & Intellectual Property
506-634-6417 e-mail: gharding@smss.com
J. Paul M. Harquail, Tax Law; Insurance; Litigation; Marine; Life & Disability; Shipping & Maritime Law; Corporate
506-632-8313 e-mail: pharquail@smss.com
Stephen J. Hutchison, Litigation - Insurance, Corporate, Commercial; Life & Disability; Corporate Restructuring; Insolvency; Product Liability
506-632-2784 e-mail: shutchison@smss.com
Peter M. Klohn, Securities/Corporate Finance; Corporate/Commercial; Technology & Intellectual Property; Public-Private Partnership; Owner-Manager Business
506-632-2788 e-mail: pklohn@smss.com
Catherine A. Lahey, Insurance; Litigation; Labour & Employment; Environmental; Corporate Restructuring & Insolvency
506-632-8307 e-mail: clahey@smss.com
James F. LeMesurier, Employment & Labour Law; Labour Relations; Occupational Health & Safety; Pensions & Employee Benefits; Workers' Compensation; Workplace Human Rights
506-632-2776
Neal L.D. Leard, Financial Services; Corporate/Commercial; Property & Real Estate; Development, Technology & Intellectual Property; Owner-Manager Business
506-634-6416 e-mail: nleard@smss.com
Kenneth B. McCullogh, Securities/Corporate Finance; Insurance; Litigation; Construction Law; Marine
506-632-2781 e-mail: kmccullogh@smss.com
Gerald S. McMackin, Financial Services; Corporate/Commercial; Owner-Manager Business; Energy & Natural Resources; Health; Personal Services
506-632-2768 e-mail: gmcmackin@smss.com
James D. Murphy, Financial Services; Corporate/Commercial; Property & Real Estate Development; Media & Entertainment
506-632-8312 e-mail: jdmurphy@smss.com
Jeffrey R. Parker, Litigation; Commercial Insurance
506-632-2779 e-mail: jparker@smss.com
Gregory S. Sinclair, Insurance Litigation; Securities Litigation; Personal Injury; Workers' Compensation
506-632-2782 e-mail: gsinclair@smssc.om
C. Paul W. Smith, Securities/Corporate Finance; Corporate/Commercial; Technology & Intellectual Property
506-632-2787 e-mail: psmith@smss.com
Darrell J. Stephenson, Financial Services; Corporate/Commercial; Owner-Manager Business; Marine; Technology & Intellectual Property; Corporate Restructuring & Insolvency
506-632-2790 e-mail: dstephenson@smss.com
Janet Thompson Price, Insurance Litigation; Environmental; Immigration Law
506-637-9230 e-mail: jthompsonprice@smss.com
John D. Wallace, Corporate/Commercial; Environmental Marine; Energy & Natural Resources
506-637-9221 e-mail: jwallace@smss.com
Michael D. Wennberg, Financial Services; Corporate/Commercial; Technology & Intellectual Property; Energy & Natural Resources; Construction Law; Franchising Law
506-632-2771 e-mail: mwennberg@smss.com

Stewart McKelvey Stirling Scales
Cabot Place #1100
PO Box 5038
100 New Gower St.
St. John's, NL A1C 5V3
709-722-4270
Fax: 709-722-4565
st-johns@smss.com
www.smss.com
Number of Lawyers: 36

Finance Lawyers:
Lewis B. Andrews, Securities/Corporate Finance; Insurance
709-570-8822 e-mail: landrews@smss.com
Janet M. Henley Andrews, Insurance
709-570-8843 e-mail: jhenleyandrews@smss.com

ACCOUNTING & LAW

Stewart McKelvey Stirling Scales (continued)

Daniel M. Boone, Insurance
709-570-8879 e-mail: dboone@smss.com
R. Wayne Bruce, Insurance
709-570-8897 e-mail: rbruce@smss.com
Janie L. Bussey, Insurance; Corporate/Commercial
709-570-8891 e-mail: jbussey@smss.com
John L.D. Cook, Insurance; Financial Services; Corporate/Commercial
709-570-8827 e-mail: jcook@smss.com
Paul L. Coxworthy, Insurance; Corporate/Commercial
709-570-8830 e-mail: pcoxworthy@smss.com
Robert J. Dillon, Insurance
709-570-8894 e-mail: rdillon@smss.com
Gerry R. Fleming, Insurance; Corporate/Commercial
709-570-8836 e-mail: gfleming@smss.com
Margaret M. Gillies, Insurance; Financial Services; Corporate/Commercial
709-570-8840 e-mail: mgillies@smss.com
William H. Goodridge, Insurance
709-570-8823 e-mail: wgoodridge@smss.com
Bruce C. Grant, Financial Services; Corporate/Commercial
709-570-8882 e-mail: bgrant@smss.com
Michael F. Harrington, Insurance
709-570-8848 e-mail: mharrington@smss.com
Neil L. Jacobs, Financial Services; Corporate/Commercial
709-570-8888 e-mail: njacobs@smss.com
Susan E. Norman, Corporate/Commercial; Insurance
Stephen F. Penney, Insurance
709-570-8881 e-mail: spenney@smss.com
Tammy L. Pike Farrell, Tax Law; Financial Services; Corporate/Commercial
709-570-8832 e-mail: tpike_farrell@smss.com
Ernest G. Reid, Financial Services
709-570-8825 e-mail: ereid@smss.com
Twila Reid, Insurance; Corporate/Commercial
709-570-8828 e-mail: treid@smss.com
Dennis J. Ryan, Securities/Corporate Finance; Financial Services; Corporate/Commercial
709-570-8824 e-mail: dryan@smss.com
Maureen E. Ryan, Financial Services; Corporate/Commercial
709-570-8880 e-mail: mryan@smss.com
Colm St. Roch Seviour, Insurance; Corporate/Commercial
709-570-8847 e-mail: cseviour@smss.com
Harold M. Smith, Corporate/Commercial
Cecily Y. Strickland, Insurance
709-570-8826 e-mail: cstrickland@smss.com
Kenneth A. Templeton, Insurance
709-570-8893 e-mail: ktempleton@smss.com
Ian C. Wallace, Corporate/Commercial
709-570-8839 e-mail: iwallace@smss.com
Kimberly Walsh, Corporate/Commercial; Insurance
709-570-8834 e-mail: kwalsh@smss.com
Rodney J. Zdebiak, Securities/Corporate Finance; Insurance; Corporate/Commercial
709-570-8841 e-mail: rzdebiak@smss.com

Stikeman Elliott LLP

Commerce Court West #5300
199 Bay St.
Toronto, ON M5L 1B9
416-869-5500
Fax: 416-947-0866
Telex: 06-22536info@stikeman.com
www.stikeman.com
Founded: 1952
Number of Lawyers: 200
Profile: As a full-service business law firm, we advise on a wide range of matters including securities, structured financial products, investment activity, mergers & acquisitions, joint ventures, public-private partnerships & government advisory mandates; our particular strength lies in developing innovative, workable solutions to complex legal concerns; our success in building an international profile is reflected in our consistent inclusion in international "league tables" in such areas as project finance, privatizations & international securities transactions

Finance Lawyers:
Sumbul Ali, Taxation
416-869-5278 e-mail: sali@stikeman.com
Andrea L. Alliston, Corporate
416-869-5694 e-mail: aalliston@stikeman.com
Jennifer Armstrong, Corporate
416-869-5650 e-mail: jarmstrong@stikeman.com
Robert Assal, Corporate
416-869-5223 e-mail: rassal@stikeman.com
Aaron E. Atcheson, Corporate Finance; Mergers & Acquisitions
416-869-5588 e-mail: aatcheson@stikeman.com
Alethea Au, Corporate
416-869-5514 e-mail: aau@stikeman.com
Rhoda Aylward, Corporate & Commercial Law
416-869-5292 e-mail: raylward@stikeman.com
Timothy Banks, Litigation
416-869-5216 e-mail: tbanks@stikeman.com
Roderick F. Barrett, Mergers & Acquisitions
416-869-5524 e-mail: rbarrett@stikeman.com
Donald Belovich, Corporate
416-869-5606 e-mail: dbelovich@stikeman.com
Karie Ann Benham, Employment & Labour Law
416-869-5677 e-mail: kbenham@stikeman.com
Ritu Bhasin
416-869-5203 e-mail: rbhasin@stikeman.com
Ricco Bhasin, Corporate & Commercial Law
416-869-5677 e-mail: arbhasin@skikeman.com
Alan Biecher, Corporate & Commercial Law
416-869-5220 e-mail: abiecher@stikeman.com
Joel Binder, Corporate Finance & Transactional; Income Funds & Investment Income Trusts; Mergers & Acquisitions; Public Offerings
416-869-5233 e-mail: jbinder@stikeman.com
Joanna Bliss, Corporate
416-869-5126 e-mail: jbliss@stikeman.com
Andrea Boctor, Pension/Employment Law
416-869-5245 e-mail: aboctor@stikeman.com
William J. Braithwaite, Securities
416-869-5654 e-mail: wbraithwaite@stikeman.com
Elizabeth Breen, Corporate Finance; Commercial Law
416-869-5267 e-mail: ebreen@stikeman.com
Doug Bryce, Corporate
416-869-5513 e-mail: dbryce@stikeman.com
Michael Burkett, Corporate
416-869-5675 e-mail: mburkett@stikeman.com
David Byers, Litigation
416-869-5697 e-mail: dbyers@stikeman.com
Thomas Caldwell, Corporate & Commercial Law
416-869-5640 e-mail: tcaldwell@stikeman.com
Roberta Carano, Corporate
416-869-5670 e-mail: rcarano@stikeman.com
Michael R. Carman, Asset Securitization
416-869-5547 e-mail: mcarman@stikeman.com
Eric Carmona, Real Estate
416-869-5597 e-mail: ecarmona@stikeman.com
Stuart S. Carruthers, Mergers & Acquisitions
416-869-5600 e-mail: scarruthers@stikeman.com
Kathryn Chalmers, Litigation
416-869-5544 e-mail: kchalmers@stikeman.com
Gwen Cheung, Corporate
416-869-5699 e-mail: gcheung@stikeman.com
Timothy Chubb, Corporate
416-869-5206 e-mail: tchubb@stikeman.com
John Ciardullo, Corporate
416-869-5235 e-mail: jciardullo@stikeman.com
Richard E. Clark, Mergers & Acquisitions
416-869-5546 e-mail: rclark@stikeman.com
Larry Cobb, Real Estate
416-869-5618 e-mail: lcobb@stikeman.com
Paul Collins, Competition
416-869-5577 e-mail: pcollins@stikeman.com
Andrea Crum-Ewing, Corporate; Securities
416-869-5214 e-mail: acrumewing@stikeman.com
Curtis A. Cusinato, Securities
416-869-5221 e-mail: ccusinato@stikeman.com
Alan D'Silva, Corporate/Commercial Disputes; Insurance; Banking; Pension; Shareholder/Oppression
416-869-5204 e-mail: adsilva@stikeman.com
James C. Davis, Corporate Finance
416-869-5539 e-mail: jdavis@stikeman.com
Bradley Davis, Litigation
416-869-5594 e-mail: bdavis@stikeman.com
Lisa De Piante, Employment/Labour Law
416-869-5673 e-mail: ldepiante@stikeman.com
Ross DeBoni, Corporate & Commercial Law
416-869-5620 e-mail: rdeboni@stikeman.com
Rocco M. Delfino, Corporate
416-869-5512 e-mail: rdelfino@stikeman.com
John R. Dow, Real Property
416-869-5615 e-mail: jdow@stikeman.com
Patrick Duffy, Litigation
416-869-5257 e-mail: pduffy@stikeman.com
Sean F. Dunphy, Litigation
416-869-5662 e-mail: sdunphy@stikeman.com
Ronald K. Durand, Taxation
416-869-5542 e-mail: rdurand@stikeman.com
David Ehrlich, Corporate Law; Real Estate; Securities & Structured Finance
416-869-5225 e-mail: dehrlich@stikeman.com
Jeffrey R. Elliott, Securities; Mergers & Acquisitions; Corporate/Commercial
416-869-5655 e-mail: jelliott@stikeman.com
Andrew Elliott, Real Estate
416-869-5255 e-mail: aelliott@stikeman.com
Jennifer Estrela, Securities; Public & Private Mergers & Acquisitions; Corporate Finance
416-869-5273 e-mail: jestrela@stikeman.com
Manizeh Fancy, Litigation
416-869-5629 e-mail: mfancy@stikeman.com
Mark Fedorowycz, Corporate
416-869-5592 e-mail: mfedorowycz@stikeman.com
David N. Finkelstein, Taxation
416-869-5536 e-mail: dfinkelstein@stikeman.com
Aaron Fransen, Corporate
416-869-5231 e-mail: afransen@stikeman.com
Robert Galea, Corporate & Commercial Law
416-869-5279 e-mail: rgalea@stikeman.com
Marie Garneau, Corporate
416-869-5696 e-mail: mgarneau@stikeman.com
Matthew Getzier, Taxation Law
416-869-5527 e-mail: mgetzier@stikeman.com
Himesh Ghai, Corporate & Commercial Law
416-869-5280 e-mail: hgai@stikeman.com
Angelo Giannetta, Real Estate
416-869-5207 e-mail: agiannetta@stikeman.com
Lynn Gluckman, Corporate
416-869-5516 e-mail: lgluckman@stikeman.com
Ivan Grbesic, Corporate
416-869-5229 e-mail: igrbesic@stikeman.com
Ramandeep Grewal
416-869-5265 e-mail: rgrewal@stikeman.com
Andrew Grossman, Corporate
416-869-5595 e-mail: agrossman@stikeman.com
Margaret E. Grottenthaler, Derivative Products
416-869-5686 e-mail: mgrottenthaler@stikeman.com
Neil Guthrie
416-869-5230 e-mail: nguthrie@stikeman.com
Douglas Harrison, Litigation
416-869-5693 e-mail: dharrison@stikeman.com
Nevinne Hassan, Corporate
416-869-5681 e-mail: nhassan@stikeman.com
Brenda Hebert, Real Property
416-869-5578 e-mail: bhebert@stikeman.com
Leela Hemmings, Tax
416-869-5248 e-mail: lhemmings@stikeman.com
Phil Henderson, Corporate
416-869-5691 e-mail: phenderson@stikeman.com
L. Milton Hess, Real Property
416-869-5548 e-mail: mhess@stikeman.com
Stacey Hoisak, Corporate
416-869-5269 e-mail: shoisak@stikeman.com
Ruth A.C. Horn, Real Property
416-869-5584 e-mail: rhorn@stikeman.com
Samantha G. Horn, Corporate
416-869-5636 e-mail: shorn@stikeman.com
Samanen Hosseini, Civil Litigation
416-869-5522 e-mail: shosseini@stikeman.com
Peter Howard, Litigation
416-869-5613 e-mail: phoward@stikeman.com
Jill Inkin, Corporate
416-869-5501 e-mail: jinkin@stikeman.com
Karen E. Jackson, Mergers & Acquisitions
416-869-5601 e-mail: kjackson@stikeman.com
Stephen Johnson, Corporate & Commercial Law
416-869-5639 e-mail: sjohnson@stikeman.com
John Judge, Litigation
416-869-5503 e-mail: jjudge@stikeman.com
Diana Juricevic, Litigation
416-869-5224 e-mail: djuricevic@stikeman.com
Zoe Kalmanson, Real Estate
416-869-5275 e-mail: zkalmanson@stikeman.com
Abas Kanu, Corporate
416-869-5253 e-mail: akanu@stikeman.com
Katherine Kay, Litigation
416-869-5507 e-mail: kkay@stikeman.com
Jay C. Kellerman, Securities
416-869-5201 e-mail: jkellerman@stikeman.com
Kevin B. Kelly, Taxation
416-869-5605 e-mail: kkelly@stikeman.com

Alan Keningsberg, Tax
416-869-5266 e-mail: akeningsberg@stikeman.com
Michael Kilby, Competition Law
416-869-5282 e-mail: mkilby@stikeman.com
Doug Klaassen, Real Estate
416-869-5271 e-mail: dklaassen@stikeman.com
Adam Kline, Corporate
416-869-5607 e-mail: akline@stikeman.com
Eliot Kolers, Litigation
416-869-5637 e-mail: ekolers@stikeman.com
Savvas Kotsopoulos, Real Estate
416-869-5644 e-mail: skotsopoulos@stikeman.com
Dean P. Koumanakos, Corporate
416-869-5661 e-mail: dkoumanakos@stikeman.com
Dean Kraus, Taxation
416-869-5215 e-mail: dkraus@stikeman.com
P. Jason Kroft, Corporate
416-869-5534 e-mail: jkroft@stikeman.com
Peter Laflamme, Corporate
416-869-5621 e-mail: plaflamme@stikeman.com
Adrian Lang, Litigation
416-869-5653 e-mail: alang@stikeman.com
Martin R. Langlois, Corporate
416-869-5672 e-mail: mlanglois@stikeman.com
Jill Lankin, Corporate & Commercial Law
416-869-5501 e-mail: jlankin@stikeman.com
Jennifer Legge, Banking
416-869-5660 e-mail: jlegge@stikeman.com
Vivian Leung, Corporate
416-869-5624 e-mail: vleung@stikeman.com
Amanda Linett, Corporate/Commercial; Securities; Mergers & Acquisitions; Corporate Finance
416-869-5217 e-mail: alinett@stikeman.com
Rosemarie Lipman, Tax
416-869-5540 e-mail: rlipman@stikeman.com
John G. Lorito, Taxation
416-869-5272 e-mail: jlorito@stikeman.com
Shanin Lott
416-869-5625 e-mail: slott@stikeman.com
Jacky Luk, Corporate
416-869-5241 e-mail: jluk@stikeman.com
Mairi MacGillivray, Corporate
416-869-5291 e-mail: mmacgillivray@stikeman.com
Daphne J. MacKenzie, Banking
416-869-5695 e-mail: dmackenzie@stikeman.com
Kathy Mah, Litigation
416-869-5652 e-mail: kmay@stikeman.com
Maninder Malli, Corporate & Commercial Law
416-869-5580 e-mail: mmalli@stikeman.com
Quentin Markin, Corporate
416-869-5213 e-mail: gmarkin@stikeman.com
David R. McCarthy, Mergers & Acquisitions
416-869-5627 e-mail: dmccarthy@stikeman.com
Anne C. McConville, Litigation
416-869-5234 e-mail: amcconville@stikeman.com
Timothy McCormick, Corporate & Commercial Law
416-869-5674 e-mail: tmccormick@stikeman.com
Raymond A. McDougall, Corporate
416-869-5227 e-mail: rmcdougall@stikeman.com
Mark E. McElheran, Corporate
416-869-5679 e-mail: mmcelheran@stikeman.com
Trevor McGowan, Tax Law
416-869-5630 e-mail: tmcgowan@stikeman.com
Kate Menear, Litigation
416-869-5209 e-mail: kmenear@stikeman.com
Nathalie L. Mercure, Corporate
416-869-5658 e-mail: nmercure@stikeman.com
Leslie Middaugh, Litigation
416-869-5538 e-mail: lmiddaugh@stikeman.com
E. Lianne Miller, Taxation
416-869-5589 e-mail: lmiller@stikeman.com
Craig Mitchell, Corporate
416-869-5509 e-mail: cmitchell@stikeman.com
Jonathan Moncrieff, Corporate & Commercial Law
416-869-5239 e-mail: jmoncrieff@stikeman.com
David Muha, Tax
416-869-5244 e-mail: dmuha@stikeman.com
Daniel Murdoch, Civil Litigation
416-869-5529 e-mail: dmurdock@stikeman.com
Gary Nachshen, Taxation
416-869-5250 e-mail: gnachshen@stikeman.com
Ignatius Navascues, Real Estate
416-869-5590 e-mail: inavascues@stikeman.com
Shawn Neylan, Competition
416-869-5545 e-mail: sneylan@stikeman.com
Wesley Ng, Corporate
416-869-5218 e-mail: wng@stikeman.com
Robert W.A. Nicholls, Securities
416-869-5582 e-mail: rnicholls@stikeman.com
Kelly Niebergall, Corporate
416-869-5505 e-mail: kniebergall@stikeman.com
D'Arcy Nordick, Corporate
416-869-5508 e-mail: dnordick@stikeman.com
Jennifer Northcote, Securities
416-869-5642 e-mail: jnorthcote@stikeman.com
Patrick O'Kelly, Litigation
416-869-5633 e-mail: pokelly@stikeman.com
Meaghan Obee Tower, Corporate & Commercial Law
416-869-5274 e-mail: mobeetower@stikeman.com
Tanya Padberg, Corporate
416-869-5208 e-mail: tpadberg@stikeman.com
Marie Isabelle Palacios-Hardy, Civil Litigation
416-869-5659 e-mail: mpalacioshardy@stikeman.com
Justin Parappally, Corporate
416-869-5591 e-mail: jparappally@stikeman.com
Sheel Parekh, Corporate
416-869-5634 e-mail: sparekh@stikeman.com
C. Mario Paura, Corporate Finance
416-869-5638 e-mail: mpaura@stikeman.com
Jessica Penley, Real Estate
416-869-5500 e-mail: jpenley@stikeman.com
David Pickwoad, Corporate
416-869-5698 e-mail: dpickwoad@stikeman.com
Elizabeth Pillon, Litigation
416-869-5623 e-mail: epillon@stikeman.com
Katy Pitch, Taxation Law
416-869-5535 e-mail: kpitch@stikeman.com
Aaron Platt, Real Estate
416-869-5643 e-mail: aplatt@stikeman.com
Ken Pogrin, Corporate
416-869-5562 e-mail: kpogrin@stikeman.com
Sharon C. Polan, Banking
416-869-5645 e-mail: spolan@stikeman.com
Bruce Pollock, Litigation
416-869-5566 e-mail: bpollock@stikeman.com
Dana S. Porter, Real Property
416-869-5533 e-mail: dporter@stikeman.com
Corrine Pruzanski, Real Estate
416-869-6800 e-mail: cpruzanski@stikeman.com
Brian M. Pukier, Securities
416-869-5567 e-mail: bpukier@stikeman.com
Ian Putnam, Corporate
416-869-5506 e-mail: iputnam@stikeman.com
Dee Rajpal, Securities
416-869-5576 e-mail: drajpal@stikeman.com
Nancy Ramalho, Employment/Labour Law
416-869-5683 e-mail: nramalho@stikeman.com
Sarah Rancier, Corporate
416-869-5558 e-mail: srancier@stikeman.com
Cliff Rand, Tax
416-869-5242 e-mail: crand@stikeman.com
Kenton Rein, Corporate
416-869-5614 e-mail: krein@stikeman.com
Darin R. Renton, Corporate
416-869-5685 e-mail: drenton@stikeman.com
Anne L. Ristic, Corporate
416-869-5682 e-mail: aristic@stikeman.com
Simon A. Romano, Securities
416-869-5596 e-mail: sromano@stikeman.com
W. Brian Rose, Mergers & Acquisitions
416-869-5685 e-mail: brose@stikeman.com
Alexander Rose, Litigation
416-869-5261 e-mail: arose@stikeman.com
Danielle Royal, Litigation
416-869-5254 e-mail: droyal@stikeman.com
Michael D. Rumball, Corporate
416-869-5671 e-mail: mrumball@stikeman.com
Debbie Salzberger, International Trade
416-869-5667 e-mail: dsalzberger@stikeman.com
Melissa Schyven, Real Estate
416-869-5232 e-mail: mschyven@stikeman.com
William A. Scott, Corporate
416-869-5521 e-mail: wscott@stikeman.com
Wayne E. Shaw, Mergers & Acquisitions
416-869-5520 e-mail: wshaw@stikeman.com
Danielle Shields, Corporate
416-869-5676 e-mail: dshields@stikeman.com
Jeffrey Singer, Corporate; Mergers & Acquisitions; Structured Finance; Private Equity
416-869-5656 e-mail: jsinger@stikeman.com
Litza K. Smirnakis, Corporate
416-869-5563 e-mail: lsmirnakis@stikeman.com
Lewis T. Smith, Banking
416-869-5210 e-mail: lsmith@stikeman.com
Emily Smith, Litigation
416-869-5293 e-mail: esmith@stikeman.com
Danielle Smith, Civil Litigation
416-869-5285 e-mail: dsmith@stikeman.com
Ellen Snow, Civil Litigation
416-869-5286 e-mail: esnow@stikeman.com
Sandra Sorenson, Corporate
416-869-5556 e-mail: ssorenson@stikeman.com
Stewart Sutcliffe, Corporate
416-869-5511 e-mail: ssutcliffe@stikeman.com
Katrina Svihran, Corporate & Commercial Law
416-869-5288 e-mail: ksvihran@stikeman.com
Maurice J. Swan, Corporate Finance
416-869-5517 e-mail: mswan@stikeman.com
Ashley Taylor, Litigation
416-869-5236 e-mail: ataylor@stikeman.com
Susan Thomson, Tax
416-869-5251 e-mail: sthomson@stikeman.com
Sean Vanderpol, Securities
416-869-5523 e-mail: avanderpol@stikeman.com
Mihkel E. Voore, Securities
416-869-5646 e-mail: mvoore@stikeman.com
Edward J. Waitzer, Corporate Finance
416-869-5587 e-mail: ewaitzer@stikeman.com
Sandra Walker, Competition
416-869-5593 e-mail: swalker@stikeman.com
Mark Walli, Civil Litigation
416-869-5277 e-mail: mwalli@stikeman.com
Kathleen G. Ward, Securities
416-869-5617 e-mail: kward@stikeman.com
David Weinberger, Corporate Finance; Private Equity Transactions; Public & Private Mergers & Acquisitions
416-869-5515 e-mail: dweinberger@stikeman.com
Jonathan Weisstub, Corporate & Civil Litigation
416-869-5649 e-mail: jweisstub@stikeman.com
Charles Whitburn, Corporate & Commercial Law
416-869-5565 e-mail: cwhitburn@stikeman.com
Cheryl Wiles-Pooran, Employment & Labour Law
416-869-5289 e-mail: cwiles-pooran@stikeman.com
Marvin Yontef, Mergers & Acquisitions
416-869-5530 e-mail: myontef@stikeman.com
Alison J. Youngman, Mergers & Acquisitions
416-869-5684 e-mail: ayoungman@stikeman.com
Wendy Yu, Corporate
416-869-5574 e-mail: wyu@stikeman.com
Glenn Zacher, Litigation
416-869-5688 e-mail: gzacher@stikeman.com
Erin Zipes, Corporate
416-869-5585 e-mail: ezipes@skikeman.com

Stikeman Elliott LLP
Bankers Hall West #4300
888 - 3rd St. SW
Calgary, AB T2P 5C5
403-266-9000
Fax: 403-266-9034
www.stikeman.com
Founded: 1992
Number of Lawyers: 42

Finance Lawyers:
Kathryn Blair, Corporate
403-266-9005 e-mail: kblair@stikeman.com
James T. Bruvall, Corporate Finance
403-266-9010 e-mail: jbruvall@stikeman.com
Glenn Cameron, Financial Institutions
403-266-9011 e-mail: gcameron@stikeman.com
Keith R. Chatwin, Corporate Finance
403-266-9088 e-mail: kchatwin@stikeman.com
Gordon L. Chmilar, Corporate Finance
403-266-9093 e-mail: gchmilar@stikeman.com
Mark A. Christensen, Corporate
403-266-9087 e-mail: mchristensen@stikeman.com
Leland P. Corbett, Corporate Finance
403-266-9046 e-mail: lcorbett@stikeman.com
Michael L. Dyck, Corporate
403-266-9030 e-mail: mdyck@stikeman.com
Alyson F. Goldman, Corporate Finance
403-266-9015 e-mail: agoldman@stikeman.com
Lisa M. Grams, Corporate, Securities
403-266-9071 e-mail: lgrams@stikeman.com

Stikeman Elliott LLP (continued)
Kerri L. Howard, Corporate
403-266-9094 e-mail: khoward@stikeman.com
Nick J. Kangles, Corporate
403-266-9004 e-mail: nkangles@stikeman.com
Charles R. Kraus, Corporate Finance
403-266-9095 e-mail: ckraus@stikeman.com
David R.J. Lefebvre, Corporate; Securities
403-266-9052 e-mail: dlefebvre@stikeman.com
Christopher W. Nixon, Corporate Finance
403-266-9017 e-mail: cnixon@stikeman.com
Stuart M. Olley, Corporate Finance, Securities
403-266-9057 e-mail: solley@stikeman.com
Ryan G. Smith, Corporate Finance
403-266-9074 e-mail: rsmith@stikeman.com
Craig A. Story, Corporate Finance
403-266-9098 e-mail: cstory@stikeman.com
David Taniguchi, Corporate Finance; Securities
403-266-9084 e-mail: dtaniguchi@stikeman.com

Stikeman Elliott LLP
#4000
1155, boul René-Lévesque ouest
Montréal, QC H3B 3V2
514-397-3000
Fax: 514-397-3222
Telex: 05-267316www.stikeman.com
Founded: 1952
Number of Lawyers: 154
Profile: The firm acts for corporations & lending institutions such as mergers & acquisitions, public offerings, financing & privatization; also advises in cases of liability of directors & officers

Finance Lawyers:
David W. Angus, Corporate
514-397-3127 e-mail: dangus@stikeman.com
Marc Barbeau, Corporate - Sociétés et affaires
514-397-3212 e-mail: mbarbeau@stikeman.com
Bruno Barrette, Corporate
514-397-3297 e-mail: bbarrette@stikeman.com
Luc Bernier, Fiscalité
514-397-3672 e-mail: lbernier@stikeman.com
Nicolas J. Beugnot, Corporate - Sociétés et affaires
514-397-3319 e-mail: nbeugnot@stikeman.com
Caroline Boutin, Corporate - Sociétés et affaires
514-397-3665 e-mail: cboutin@stikeman.com
Frédéric Brassard, Corporate
514-397-2407 e-mail: fbrassard@stikeman.com
Roanne Bratz, Fiscalité/Tax
514-397-3296 e-mail: rbratz@stikeman.com
Don Bunker, Corporate
514-397-3389 e-mail: dbunker@stikeman.com
France Margaret Bélanger, Corporate - Sociétés et affaires
514-397-3158 e-mail: fmbelanger@stikeman.com
Marc-André Bélanger, Tax
514-397-2443 e-mail: mabelanger@stikeman.com
Robert Carelli, Corporate - Sociétés et affaires
514-397-2408 e-mail: rcarelli@stikeman.com
Jean Carrier, Environment; Natural resources; Mining; Corporate - Sociétés et affaires
514-397-3101 e-mail: jcarrier@stikeman.com
Peter Castiel, Corporate - Sociétés et affaires
514-397-3272 e-mail: pcastiel@stikeman.com
Viateur Chénard, Corporate - Sociétés et affaires
514-397-3386 e-mail: vchenard@stikeman.com
Edward B. Claxton, Corporate - Sociétés et affaires
514-397-3364 e-mail: eclaxton@stikeman.com
Stuart H. (Kip) Cobbett, Corporate - Sociétés et affaires
514-397-3266 e-mail: scobbett@stikeman.com
Glenn A. Cranker, Fiscalité/Tax
514-397-3084 e-mail: gcranker@stikeman.com
Sterling Dietze, Corporate - Sociétés et affaires
514-397-3076 e-mail: sdietze@stikeman.com
Beno(140t C. Dubord, Corporate - Sociétés et affaires
514-397-3655 e-mail: bdubord@stikeman.com
Jean Farley, Corporate - Sociétés et affaires
514-397-3041 e-mail: jfarley@stikeman.com
Myriam Fortin, Corporate
514-397-3270 e-mail: mfortin@stikeman.com
Franco Gadoury, Tax
514-397-3189 e-mail: fgadoury@stikeman.com
Charles C. Gagnon, Tax
514-397-3384 e-mail: cgagnon@stikeman.com
James A. Grant, Hon., Corporate - Sociétés et affaires
514-397-3004 e-mail: tgrant@stikeman.com
Michel Gélinas, Corporate - Sociétés et affaires
514-397-3050 e-mail: mgelinas@stikeman.com
Stacey Herman, Corporate
514-397-3128 e-mail: sherman@stikeman.com
Robert Hogan, Fiscalité/Tax
514-397-3238 e-mail: rhogan@stikeman.com
Sidney M. Horn, Corporate - Sociétés et affaires
514-397-3342 e-mail: shorn@stikeman.com
Jean-Marc Huot, Corporate - Sociétés et affaires
514-397-3276 e-mail: jmhuot@stikeman.com
Catherine Jenner, Corporate - Sociétés et affaires
514-397-3356 e-mail: cjenner@stikeman.com
Kevin Kyte, Corporate - Sociétés et affaires
514-397-3346 e-mail: kkyte@stikeman.com
Hubert T. Lacroix, Corporate
514-397-3390 e-mail: Corporate
Sophie Lamonde, Corporate
514-397-2410
Jean G. Lamothe, Corporate - Sociétés et affaires
514-397-3326 e-mail: jlamothe@stikeman.com
Pierre-Yves Leduc, Corporate
514-397-3696 e-mail: pyleduc@stikeman.com
Michel Legendre, Fiscalité/Tax
514-397-3309 e-mail: mlegendre@stikeman.com
John W. Leopold, Corporate - Sociétés et affaires
514-397-3111 e-mail: jleopold@stikeman.com
Daniel Levinson, Corporate - Sociétés et affaires
514-397-3008 e-mail: dlevinson@stikeman.com
Valérie Mac-Seing, Corporate - Sociétés et affaires
514-397-2425 e-mail: vmacseing@stikeman.com
Pierre Martel, Fiscalité/Tax
514-397-3045 e-mail: pmartel@stikeman.com
R. Guy Masson, Fiscalité/Tax
514-397-3039 e-mail: rmasson@stikeman.com
David Massé, Corporate
514-397-3685 e-mail: dmasse@stikeman.com
Frank Mathieu, Tax
514-397-2442 e-mail: fmathieu@stikeman.com
Christian Meighen, Fiscalité/Tax
514-397-3028 e-mail: cmeighen@stikeman.com
Bertrand Ménard, Corporate - Sociétés et affaires
514-397-3147 e-mail: bmenard@stikeman.com
Gayle Noble, Corporate - Sociétés et affaires
514-397-3205 e-mail: gnoble@stikeman.com
François H. Ouimet, Corporate - Sociétés et affaires
514-397-3057 e-mail: fouimet@stikeman.com
John Anthony Penhale, Corporate - Sociétés et affaires
514-397-2403 e-mail: apenhale@stikeman.com
Richard W. Pound, Fiscalité/Tax
514-397-3037 e-mail: rpound@stikeman.com
Pierre A. Raymond, Corporate - Sociétés et affaires
514-397-3061 e-mail: praymond@stikeman.com
Michael L. Richards, Corporate - Sociétés et affaires
514-397-3010 e-mail: mrichards@stikeman.com
Erik Richer La Flèche, Corporate - Sociétés et affaires
514-397-3109 e-mail: ericherlafleche@stikeman.com
Steve Robitaille, Corporate - Sociétés et affaires
514-397-3024 e-mail: srobitaille@stikeman.com
Anna C. Romano, Corporate - Sociétés et affaires
514-397-3244 e-mail: aromano@stikeman.com
William Rosenberg, Corporate - Sociétés et affaires
514-397-3333 e-mail: wrosenberg@stikeman.com
Howard J. Rosenoff, Corporate - Sociétés et affaires
514-397-3253 e-mail: hrosenoff@stikeman.com
Franziska Ruf, Corporate - Sociétés et affaires
514-397-3670 e-mail: fruf@stikeman.com
Maurice A. Régnier, Fiscalité/Tax
514-397-3047 e-mail: mregnier@stikeman.com
Jean-Guillaume Shooner, Fiscalité/Tax
514-397-3680 e-mail: lgshooner@stikeman.com
Warren Silversmith, Corporate
514-397-3181 e-mail: wsilversmith@stikeman.com
Jason Streicher, Corporate - Sociétés et affaires
514-397-2420 e-mail: jstreicher@stikeman.com
Antoine Stébenne, Tax
514-397-3363 e-mail: astebenne@stikeman.com
Michael Szlamkowicz, Corporate
514-397-2434 e-mail: mszlamkowica@stikeman.com
Johanne Tanguay, Corporate Litigation
511-379-3367 e-mail: jtanguay@stikeman.com
Serge Tousignant, Corporate - Sociétés et affaires
514-397-3121 e-mail: stousignant@stikeman.com
Maxime Turcotte, Corporate
514-397-2421 e-mail: mturcotte@stikeman.com
Nicolas Vanasse, Corporate
514-397-2418 e-mail: nvanasse@stikeman.com
Claire Zikovsky, Corporate - Sociétés et affaires
514-397-3340 e-mail: szikovsky@stikeman.com
Alix d'Anglejan-Chatillon, Corporate
514-397-3240 e-mail: adanglejan@stikeman.com

Stikeman Elliott LLP
#1600
50 O'Connor St.
Ottawa, ON K1P 6L2
613-234-4555
Fax: 613-230-8877
www.stikeman.com
Number of Lawyers: 18
Profile: 01/04: Added Goldenberg from G&M -sy

Finance Lawyers:
Kim Alexander-Cook
D. Jeffrey Brown
e-mail: jebrown@stikeman.com
Nicholas P. McHaffie

Stikeman Elliott LLP
Park Pl. #1700
666 Burrard St.
Vancouver, BC V6C 2X8
604-631-1300
Fax: 604-681-1825
866-631-1300
info@stikeman.com
www.stikeman.com
Founded: 1988
Number of Lawyers: 34
Profile: Corporate Commercial Law; Corporate Finance; Mergers & Acquisitions; Commercial Litigation; Banking; Commercial Real Property

Finance Lawyers:
Amyn M. Abdula, Corporate; Securities
604-631-1322 e-mail: aabdula@stikeman.com
Valerie Aberdeen, Corporate/Commercial
604-631-1381 e-mail: vaberdeen@stikeman.com
John F. Anderson, Corporate/Commercial; Securities; Mergers & Acquisitions
604-631-1307 e-mail: janderson@stikeman.com
Kimberly E. Burns, Corporate/Commercial
604-631-1391 e-mail: kburns@stikeman.com
Jonathan S. Drance, Corporate/Commercial; Securities; Mergers & Acquisitions
604-631-1361 e-mail: jdrance@stikeman.com
Annette E.F. Dueck, Corporate, Financing, Regulatory
604-631-1315 e-mail: adueck@stikeman.com
David E. Gillanders, Real Property
604-631-1321 e-mail: dgillanders@stikeman.com
Philip G. Griffin, Mergers & Acquisitions; Corporate; Commercial
604-631-1325 e-mail: pgriffin@stikeman.com
Rachel V. Hutton, Real Property
604-631-1342 e-mail: rhutton@stikeman.com
Richard J. Jackson, Real Property; Corporate
604-631-1357 e-mail: rjackson@stikeman.com
Argiro M. Kotsalis, Corporate; Mergers & Acquisitions; Securities
604-631-1317 e-mail: akotsalis@stikeman.com
Eugene H. Kwan, Corporate
604-631-1386 e-mail: ekwan@stikeman.com
Beayne C. Louie, Corporate/Commercial
604-631-1363 e-mail: blouie@stikeman.com
John Lundell, Corporate
604-631-1348 e-mail: jlundell@stikeman.com
Ralph J. Lutes, Corporate
604-631-1340 e-mail: rlutes@stikeman.com
Ross A. MacDonald, Real Estate; Corporate/Commercial
604-631-1367 e-mail: rmacdonald@stikeman.com
Jennifer MacGregor-Greer, Corporate, Commercial
604-631-1397 e-mail: jmacgregor-greer@stikeman.com
Neville J. McClure, Securities
604-631-1324 e-mail: nmcclure@stikeman.com
Jonathan M. McLean, Commercial Litigation
604-631-1347 e-mail: jmclean@stikeman.com
Scott L. Perrin, Corporate; Banking
604-631-1310 e-mail: sperrin@stikeman.com
C. Inge Poulus, Securities; Corporate
604-631-1371 e-mail: ipoulus@stikeman.com
John E. Stark, Corporate/Commercial
604-631-1395 e-mail: jstark@stikeman.com
Thomas Wachowski, Corporate
604-631-1300 e-mail: twachowski@stikeman.com

Virginia Wigmore, Real Property
604-631-1375 e-mail: vwigmore@stikeman.com
Paul Yeung, Real Estate
604-631-1360 e-mail: pyeung@stikeman.com

Stikeman, Graham, Keeley & Spiegel LLP

220 Bay St., 7th Fl.
Toronto, ON M5J 2W4
416-367-1930
Fax: 416-365-1813
Founded: 1985
Number of Lawyers: 4
Profile: Corporate & Securities Law

Finance Lawyers:
Head of Financial Law: H. Robert H. Stikeman, Securities Law
e-mail: bob@stikeman.to
James A. Graham, Litigation
e-mail: graham@stikeman.to
Helen E. Keeley, Estate Law
e-mail: hkeeley@stikeman.to
Michael W. Pasternack, Securities Law; Corporate & Commercial Law
e-mail: pasternack@stikeman.to
Robert N. Spiegel, Securities Law
e-mail: spiegel@stikeman.to

Stockwoods LLP

#2512
150 King St. West
Toronto, ON M5H 1J9
416-593-2488
Fax: 416-593-9345
Number of Lawyers: 2

Finance Lawyers:
David T. Stockwood, Corporate/Commercial
e-mail: davids@stockwoods.ca

Stringam Denecky

PO Box 757
314 - 3 St. South
Lethbridge, AB T1J 3Z6
403-328-5576
Fax: 403-327-1141
results@stringam.ca
www.stringam.ca
Founded: 1913
Number of Lawyers: 8

Finance Lawyers:
Paul G. Pharo
e-mail: pgpharo@stringam.ca

Sullivan, Mahoney LLP

PO Box 1360
40 Queen St.
St Catharines, ON L2R 6Z2
905-688-6655
Fax: 905-688-5814
lawyers@sullivan-mahoney.com
www.sullivan-mahoney.com
Founded: 1953
Number of Lawyers: 27

Finance Lawyers:
J.R. Bush, General Finance
e-mail: jrbush@sullivan-mahoney.com
R.B. Culliton, General Finance
e-mail: rculliton@sullivan-mahoney.com
Carmelina D'Angelo, Banking
Douglas A. Goslin, Corporate/Commercial
Marvin D. Kriluck, General Finance
e-mail: mdkriluck@sullivan-mahoney.com
G.W. McCann, General Finance
e-mail: gwmccann@sullivan-mahoney.com
Thomas Wall, Banking

Sutts, Strosberg LLP

Westcourt Place #600
251 Goyeau St.
Windsor, ON N9A 6V4
519-258-9333
Fax: 519-186-6613
www.strosbergco.com
Founded: 1958
Number of Lawyers: 20
Profile: Sutts Strosberg LLP represents closely-held borrowers & issuers primarily doing business in the automotive sector, & their private & institutional lenders in connection with conventional financing, capital markets/venture capital/private placement transactions; export financing; & banking group & debtor-in-possession superpriority financing; Sutts Strosberg LLP is also adept at arranging documenting & implementing provincial & national class action funding for lead & line counsel

Finance Lawyers:
Werner H. Keller, Corporate; Commercial
519-561-6233 e-mail: werner_h_keller@strosbergco.com

Talmage, Stratton & DiFiore

PO Box 97
221 Division St.
Welland, ON L3B 5P2
905-732-4477
Fax: 905-732-4718
talstradi@iaw.on.ca
Founded: 1955
Number of Lawyers: 3

Finance Lawyers:
C. Allan Talmage, Commercial Law & Associated Financing

Taylor McCaffrey LLP

400 St. Mary Ave., 9th Fl.
Winnipeg, MB R3C 4K5
204-949-1312
Fax: 204-957-0945
www.tmlawyers.com
Number of Lawyers: 62

Finance Lawyers:
Gerald Arron, Corporate & Business Law
Ronald L. Coke, Corporate & Business Law
Remo De Sordi, Corporate & Business Law
Douglas E. Finkbeiner, Corporate & Finance
e-mail: definkbeiner@tmlawyers.com
Paul B. Forsyth, Insolvency & Realization
e-mail: pforsyth@tmlawyers.com
David R.M. Jackson, Financial Services
David C. King, Corporate & Business Law
Fred R. Klein, Corporate & Business Law
e-mail: fklein@tmlawyers.com
Timothy A. Kurbis, Corporate & Business Law
Alain L.J. Laurencelle, Corporate & Business Law
e-mail: alaurencelle@tmlawyers.com
Frank Lavitt, Corporate & Business Law; Taxation
Eric G. Lister, Corporate & Business Law
e-mail: elister@tmlawyers.com
Len J. Lucas, Corporate & Business Law
Ken G. Mandzuik, Financial Services
Marc E. Marion, Corporate & Business Law; Taxation
A. David Marshall, Corporate & Business Law
Nicole D.S. Merrick, Corporate & Business Law
Kevin C. Nenka, Corporate & Business Law
Melviille Neuman, Corporate & Business Law
Donn A.J. Pirie, Corporate & Business Law
Paul J.M. Prendergast, Corporate & Business Law; Securities; Taxation
G. Patrick S. Riley, Financial Services
Bruce H. Rutherford, Financial Services
Brian D. Sexton, Corporate & Business Law; Taxation
David J. Skinner, Corporate & Business Law
Norman K. Snyder, Corporate & Business Law
Herbert E. Suderman, Corporate & Business Law
J.F. Reeh Taylor, Senior Counsel, Corporate & Business Law
Kevin T. Williams, Insurance
Kristen Wittman, Corporate & Business Law; Securities

Tedford Delehanty Rinzler

#201
PO Box 1083
272 George St.
Moncton, NB E1C 8P6
506-857-3030
Fax: 506-857-0085
mail@tedford-delehanty.nb.ca
www.tedford-delehanty.nb.ca
Number of Lawyers: 3

Finance Lawyers:
Edmund E. Tedford, General Finance

Teed & Teed

PO Box 6639, A Sta.
127 Prince William St.
Saint John, NB E2L 4S1
506-634-7320
Fax: 506-634-7423
info@teedandteed.com
Founded: 1918
Number of Lawyers: 3
Profile: Provides services in Income Tax, Real Estate, Wills & Estates

Finance Lawyers:
Peter E.L. Teed

Tees Kiddle Spencer

#200
1260 Shoppers Row
Campbell River, BC V9W 2C8
250-287-7755
Fax: 250-287-3999
800-224-7755
tks@tkslaw.com
www.tkslaw.com
Number of Lawyers: 5

Finance Lawyers:
Michael C.A. Clare, General Finance
Brook G. Kiddle, General Finance
Bruce Murdoch, General Finance

Templeman Menninga LLP

#200
PO Box 234
205 Dundas St. East
Belleville, ON K8N 5A2
613-966-2620
Fax: 613-966-2866
info@templemanmenninga.com
www.templemanmenninga.com
Founded: 1985
Number of Lawyers: 9

Finance Lawyers:
David W. DeMille, Litigation
613-966-2620 e-mail: dwd@tmlegal.ca
Jamie Thomas Fraser, Business
e-mail: jtf@tmlegal.ca
Rolf M. Renz
613-966-2620 e-mail: rmr@tmlegal.ca
Ian B. Sullivan, Wills & Estate Planning
e-mail: ibs@tmlegal.ca

Thompson Dorfman Sweatman LLP

CanWest Global Place #2200
201 Portage Ave.
Winnipeg, MB R3B 3L3
204-957-1930
Fax: 204-934-0570
tds@tdslaw.com
www.tdslaw.com
Founded: 1887
Number of Lawyers: 68

Finance Lawyers:
Richard H.G. Adams, Commercial Real Estate; Banking; Leases
204-934-2439 e-mail: rhga@tdslaw.com
Glen W. Agar, Securities
204-934-2590 e-mail: gwa@tdslaw.com
Dinh N. Bo-Maguire, Acquisitions; Financing
204-934-2379 e-mail: dbm@tsdlaw.com
G.V. Brickman, Banking; Crown Corporations; Securities
204-934-2428 e-mail: gvb@tdslaw.com
William J. Burnett, Equipment Leasing
204-934-2487 e-mail: wjb@tdslaw.com
Michael A. Choiselat, Banking; Debentures; Leasing
204-934-2557 e-mail: mac@tdslaw.com
Donald G. Douglas, Banking; Debentures; Insolvency
204-934-2466 e-mail: dgd@tdslaw.com
Douglas J. Forbes, Banking
204-934-2426 e-mail: djf@tdslaw.com
Peter J. Glowacki, Wills & Estates; Real Estate
204-934-2572 e-mail: pjg@tdslaw.com
Elmer J. Gomes, Banking; Financing; Equipment Leasing
204-934-2353 e-mail: ejg@tdslaw.com
Antoine F. Hacault, Banking; Real Estate
204-934-2513 e-mail: afh@tdslaw.com

ACCOUNTING & LAW

Thompson Dorfman Sweatman LLP (continued)
Jeffrey B. Hirsch, Banking; Litigation/Insolvency
204-934-2336 e-mail: jbh@tdslaw.com
Karen Jarema Cornejo, Banking
204-934-2345 e-mail: kjc@tdslaw.com
Leilani J. Kagan, Mergers & Acquisitions; Corporate Restructuring
204-934-2363 e-mail: ljk@tdslaw.com
D. Sean Kells, Real Estate
204-934-2556 e-mail: dsk@tdslaw.com
Jeffrey A. Kowall, Securities; Real Estate
204-934-2521 e-mail: ajk@tdslaw.com
Barry N. MacTavish, Banking; Securities
204-934-2338 e-mail: bnm@tdslaw.com
Albina P. Moran, Banking; Real Estate
204-934-2503 e-mail: apm@tdslaw.com
Ross A.L. Nugent, Commercial Real Estate
204-934-2431 e-mail: raln@tdslaw.com
Chrys Pappas, Banking; Debentures; Equipment Leasing
204-934-2452 e-mail: cp@tdslaw.com
Sergio Pustogorodsky, Tax
204-934-2444 e-mail: sp@tdslaw.com
James A. Ripley, Banking; Debentures; Equipment Leasing
204-934-2430 e-mail: jar@tdslaw.com
Arthur J. Stacey, Banking
204-934-2537 e-mail: ajs@tdslaw.com
Lisa J. Stiver, Venture Capital; Acquisition Financing
204-934-2375 e-mail: ljs@tdslaw.com
Alan Sweatman, Banking; Corporate; Public Utilities; Securities
204-934-2401 e-mail: as@tdslaw.com
B. Douglas Tait, Real Estate
204-934-2440 e-mail: bdt@tdslaw.com
Gregory J. Tallon, Banking; Debentures; Leasing
204-934-2478 e-mail: gjt@tdslaw.com
Bruce S. Thompson, Securities
204-934-2453 e-mail: bst@tdslaw.com
Silvia V. de Sousa, Commercial Real Estate
204-934-2592 e-mail: svd@tdslaw.com

Thompson, MacColl & Stacy
#5
1020 Matheson Blvd. East
Mississauga, ON L4W 4J9
905-625-5591
Fax: 905-238-3313
Founded: 1986
Number of Lawyers: 9

Finance Lawyers:
Charles R. MacColl, General Finance
e-mail: cmaccoll@tmslaw.com
James E. Stacy, General Finance
e-mail: jstacy@tmslaw.com

ThorntonGroutFinnigan
Canadian Pacific Tower, TD Centre #3200
PO Box 329
100 Wellington St. West
Toronto, ON M5K 1K7
416-304-1616
Fax: 416-304-1313
info@tgf.ca
www.tgf.ca
Number of Lawyers: 14
Profile: Insolvency, litigation, boutique

Finance Lawyers:
Gregory R. Azeff, Insolvency
416-304-0778 e-mail: gazeff@tgf.ca
John L. Finnigan, Commercial Litigation
416-304-0558 e-mail: jfinnigan@tgf.ca
James H. Grout, Insolvency
416-304-0557 e-mail: jgrout@tgf.ca
Leanne M. Hoyles, Insolvency
416-304-0060 e-mail: lhoyles@tgf.ca
Kyla E.M Mahar, Insolvency
416-304-0594 e-mail: kmahar@tgf.ca
D.J. Miller, Insolvency
416-304-0559 e-mail: djmiller@tgf.ca
Grant B. Moffat, Insolvency
416-304-0599 e-mail: gmoffat@tgf.ca
Freya M. Painting, Commercial Litigation
416-304-0597 e-mail: fpainting@tgf.ca
Deborah E. Palter, Commercial Litigation
416-304-0148 e-mail: dpalter@tgf.ca
Ray Thapar, Commercial Litigation
416-304-0595 e-mail: rthapar@tgf.ca
Robert I. Thornton, Insolvency
416-304-0560 e-mail: rthornton@tgf.ca

Thorsteinssons LLP Tax Lawyers
BCE Place
PO Box 786
181 Bay St., 33rd Fl.
Toronto, ON M5J 2T3
416-864-0829
Fax: 416-864-1106
888-666-9998
managingpartner@thor.ca
www.thor.ca
Founded: 1964
Number of Lawyers: 15

Finance Lawyers:
Thomas A. Bauer, Corporate & Personal Tax Planning; Representation & Tax Litigation
David R. Baxter, Corporate & Personal Tax Planning; International Tax Planning; Cross-Border Structures
David Christian, Canadian Tax Planning; Representation & Litigation
Michael W. Colborne, Corporate & International Tax Planning; Tax Representation & Litigation
David Davies, Tax Litigation & Representation
Paul J. Gibney, Corporate Tax; International Tax; Tax Representation & Litigation; Estate Planning
Robert Madden, Personal & Corporate Tax Planning; Tax Representation & Civil Tax Litigation
Douglas Mathew, Taxpayer Representation; Corporate & Personal Tax Planning
Thomas E. McDonnell, Domestic & International Law
Warren Mitchell, Civil Tax Litigation
James Murdoch, Corporate, Personal Tax & Estate Planning; International Tax; Tax Representation
Michael O'Keefe, Corporate Tax Planning; International Tax Planning; Dispute Resolution
Colin S. Smith, Personal & Corporate Tax Planning
Kristina Soutar, Personal & Corporate Tax Planning; Tax Representaion & Civil Tax Litigation
Matthew G. Williams, Personal & Corporate Tax Planning; Tax Representation & Civil Tax Litigation

Timms & McCombs
16 Hackney Ct.
Ancaster, ON L9K 1M3
905-945-7873
Fax: 905- -
ouhm@deere.com
Number of Lawyers: 2

Finance Lawyers:
David G. Timms, General Finance

TingleMerrett LLP
#1250
639 - 5th Ave. SW
Calgary, AB T2P 0M9
403-571-8000
Fax: 403-571-8008
Number of Lawyers: 11

Finance Lawyers:
Paul A. Bolger
Christopher D. Croteau
Jeffrey A. Helper
Scott M. Reeves
R.D. Tingle
Bryce Tingle

Torys LLP
Toronto-Dominion Centre #3000
PO Box 270
79 Wellington St. West
Toronto, ON M5K 1N2
416-865-0040
Fax: 416-865-7380
info@torys.com
www.torys.com
Number of Lawyers: 202
Profile: An international business law firm with more than 330 lawyers in its Toronto & New York offices; the firm acts for all types of financial institutions, including banks, life insurance companies, property & casualty insurance companies, trust & loan companies & securities dealers; we act as corporate counsel to a number of Canada's largest life insurance companies; our banking involvement includes work for Canada's five largest banks, as well as for numerous foreign banks; we are frequently retained to act on special projects, regulatory matters, merchant banking, secured transactions, institutional lending, & investment funds & management matters; Torys has also acted for a number of major foreign banks that have invested in Canadian entities & established Canadian banking subsidiaries, branches & other business vehicles in Canada

Finance Lawyers:
Rose T. Bailey
416-865-8206
James C. Baillie, General Finance
416-865-7395 e-mail: jbaillie@torys.com
Richard J. Balfour, Financial Institutions
416-865-7339 e-mail: rbalfour@torys.com
Philip J. Brown, General Finance
416-865-8238 e-mail: pbrown@torys.com
Corrado Cardarelli, Tax
416-865-7386
Matthew W. Cockburn, Corporate
416-865-7662 e-mail: mcockburn@torys.com
Tony DeMarinis, Restructuring & Insolvency
416-865-8162 e-mail: tdemarinis@torys.com
Adam E. Delean, Secured Transactions
416-865-8232
John E. Emanoilidis, General Finance
416-865-8145 e-mail: jemanoilidis@torys.com
Michael K. Feldman, Secured Transactions
416-865-7513
Patrick D. Flaherty, Litigation
416-865-8113 e-mail: pflaherty@torys.com
Sharon C. Geraghty, Mergers & Acquisitions
416-865-8138
Paul M. Kennedy, Real Estate
416-865-8156 e-mail: pkennedy@torys.com
Patricia A. Koval, General Finance
416-865-7356 e-mail: pkoval@torys.com
Alison Lacy, Project Finance
416-865-7503
Conor D.M. McCourt, Intellecual Property
416-865-8181 e-mail: emccourt@torys.com
Eileen M. McMahon, Intellectual Property
416-865-8181 e-mail: emccourt@torys.com
Linda M. Plumpton, Litigation
416-865-8193 e-mail: lplumpton@torys.com
Donald B. Roger, Secured Transactions
416-865-7347
Michael B. Rotsztain, Restructuring & Insolvency
416-865-7508
James D. Scarlett, General Finance
416-865-8199 e-mail: jscarlett@torys.com
John J. Tobin, Tax Law
416-865-7999
John Unger, Tax
416-865-7312 e-mail: junger@torys.com
Jonathan B. Weisz, Project Finance
416-865-8157
James W. Welkoff, Tax
416-865-7326 e-mail: jwelkoff@torys.com

Traub Moldaver
#1801
4 King St. West
Toronto, ON M5H 1B6
416-214-6500
Fax: 416-214-7275
877-727-6500
Founded: 1990
Number of Lawyers: 5

Finance Lawyers:
Elaine Harris, General Finance

Turkstra Mazza Associates
15 Bold St.
Hamilton, ON L8P 1T3
905-529-3476
Fax: 905-529-3663
pauldmazza@hotmail.com
Founded: 1977
Number of Lawyers: 15
Profile: Refinancing; Power of Sale; Collection

Finance Lawyers:
James Oliver

Howard Ungerman
37 Maitland St.
Toronto, ON M4Y 1C8
416-924-4111
Fax: 416-924-4112
Founded: 1995
Number of Lawyers: 1

Finance Lawyers:
Howard Ungerman, Corporate; Commercial

Vector Corporate Finance Lawyers
#1040
999 West Hastings St.
Vancouver, BC V6C 2W2
604-683-1102
Fax: 604-683-2643
www.vectorlaw.com
Number of Lawyers: 2

Finance Lawyers:
Stewart L. Lockwood, Securities
e-mail: slockwood@vectorlaw.com
Graham H. Scott, Securities
e-mail: gscott@vectorlaw.com

Vining, Senini
PO Box 190, Main Sta.
30 Front St.
Nanaimo, BC V9R 5K9
250-754-1234
Fax: 250-754-8080
Number of Lawyers: 6

Finance Lawyers:
Doug Torrie

Waechter, Magwood, Van De Vyvere & Thompson
#8280
215 Durham St.
Walkerton, ON N0G 2V0
519-881-3230
Fax: 519-881-3595
wmvt@bmts.com
Founded: 1957
Number of Lawyers: 4

Finance Lawyers:
B.J. Van de Vyvere

Walker, Head
Corporate Centre #200
1305 Pickering Pkwy.
Pickering, ON L1V 3P2
905-839-4484
Fax: 905-420-1073
wlkhd@walkerhead.com
www.walkerhead.com
Number of Lawyers: 8
Profile: Wide range of legal services including corporate & commercial law, business banking law, wills & estates

Finance Lawyers:
Victor A. Sgro, Corporate/Commercial Law

Waterbury Newton
PO Box 98
469 Main St.
Kentville, NS B4N 3V9
902-678-3257
Fax: 902-678-7727
mail@waterburynewton.ns.ca
www.nslawyers.com
Founded: 1949
Number of Lawyers: 13
Profile: A full-service law firm, including services in the areas of corporate & commercial; wills, estates & trusts; general finance & foreclosures

Finance Lawyers:
Randall P.H. Balcome, General Finance
902-678-3257 e-mail: rbalcome@nslawyers.com
Siobhan E. Doyle, Wills, Estates & Trusts
e-mail: sdoyle@nslawyers.com
David R. Greener, Wills, Estates & Trusts
e-mail: dgreener@nslawyers.com
Randall L. Prime, General Finance; Foreclosures
e-mail: rprime@nslawyers.com

Waterous, Holden, Amey, Hitchon LLP
PO Box 1510
20 Wellington St.
Brantford, ON N3T 5V6
519-759-6220
Fax: 519-759-8360
law@waterousholden.com
www.waterousholden.com
Founded: 1921
Number of Lawyers: 20

Finance Lawyers:
David H. Clement, Corporate & Commercial; Mergers & Acquisitions; Debtor & Creditor
e-mail: dclement@waterousholden.com
Brian G. Finnigan, Corporate & Commercial Law; Taxation
e-mail: bfinnigan@waterousholden.com
James A. Hitchon, Corporate & Commercial; Insolvency & Bankruptcy; Mergers & Acquisitions
e-mail: jhitchon@waterousholden.com
H. Clark Holden, Corporate & Commercial; Taxation
e-mail: cholden@waterousholden.com
Leah A. Noe@#l, Corporate; Business Law
Lorne E. Parkhill, Corporate & Commercial; Debtor & Creditor Law
e-mail: lparkhill@waterousholden.com
Steven P. Portelli, Corporate; Business Law
Timothy R. Sheldon, Corporate & Commercial
e-mail: tsheldon@waterousholden.com
Richard N. Waterous, Corporate & Commercial; Taxation; Mergers & Acquisitions
e-mail: rwaterous@waterousholden.com
Carol L. Woodcock, Corporate & Commercial; Taxation; Mergers & Acquisitions
e-mail: cwoodcock@waterousholden.com

Weaver, Simmons LLP
PO Box 158
Sudbury, ON P3E 4N5
705-674-6421
Fax: 705-674-9948
thefirm@weaversimmons.com
www.weaversimmons.com
Founded: 1931
Number of Lawyers: 30

Finance Lawyers:
Peter Archambault, Insurance
705-671-3292 e-mail: pjarchambault@weaversimmons.com
R. Martin Bayer, Commercial
705-671-3286 e-mail: rmbayer@weaversimmons.com
Harold P. Beaudry, Counsel, Commercial Law & Litigation
705-671-3270 e-mail: hpbeaudry@weaversimmons.com
Peter P. Diavolitis, Commercial Litigation
705-671-3282 e-mail: ppdiavolitsis@weaversimmons.com
Boris J. Fesyk, Estates, Trusts & Wills; Corporate & Commercial
705-671-3294 e-mail: bjfesyk@weaversimmons.com
Charles T. Fouriezos, Counsel, Estates, Trusts & Wills; Corporate & Commercial
705-671-3280 e-mail: ctfourienzos@weaversimmons.com
Stevens D. Horton, Counsel, Real Estate; Estates, Trusts & Wills; Corporate & Commercial
705-671-3277 e-mail: sdhorton@weaversimmons.com
Marc A.J. Huneault, Commercial Litigation
705-671-3262 e-mail: majhuneault@weaversimmons.com
Paul A. Lefebvre, Tax Law
705-671-3289 e-mail: palefebvre@weaversimmons.com
R.W. Howard Lightle, Insurance Coverage; Subrogation
705-671-3285 e-mail: howlightle@weaversimmons.com
Andrew M. Little, Estates, Trusts & Wills
705-671-3291 e-mail: amlittle@weaversimmons.com
Douglas J. Los, Litigation
705-671-3297 e-mail: djlos@weaversimmons.com
Gerard McAndrew, Counsel, Corporate & Commercial
705-671-3276 e-mail: gemcandrew@weaversimmons.com
Steve S. Moutsatsos, Estates, Trusts & Wills; Corporate & Commercial
705-671-3290 e-mail: ssmoutsatsos@weaversimmons.com
Bill T. Rolston, Counsel, Estates, Trusts & Wills; Corporate & Commercial
705-671-3279 e-mail: btrolston@weaversimmons.com

WeirFoulds LLP
Exchange Tower #1600
PO Box 480
130 King St. West
Toronto, ON M5X 1J5
416-365-1110
Fax: 416-365-1876
firm@weirfoulds.com
www.weirfoulds.com
Founded: 1860
Number of Lawyers: 78
Profile: Excels in planning & experience with complex & sophisticated legal problems; focus is on commercial litigation; corporate/securities; commercial real estate

Finance Lawyers:
D.S. Brown, Corporate & Commercial Law; Banking Law; Intellectual Property (Trade Marks)
416-943-5046 e-mail: dbrown@weirfoulds.com
D.P. Ferguson, Corporate & Commercial Law; Banking Law
416-947-5029 e-mail: ferguson@weirfoulds.com
J.D. McKellar, Corporate & Commercial Law; Banking Law
416-947-5018 e-mail: jmckellar@weirfoulds.com
J.L. Pandell, Corporate & Commercial Law; Banking Law
416-947-5034 e-mail: jpandell@weirfoulds.com
A.S. Wakim, Corporate & Commercial Law; Raising Capital
416-943-5050 e-mail: swakim@weirfoulds.com
J.B.A. Wilkinson, Corporate & Commercial Law; Intellectual Property Law (Trade Marks)
416-947-5010 e-mail: jwilkinson@weirfoulds.com

White, Ottenheimer & Baker
Baine Johnson Centre
PO Box 5457
10 Fort William Pl.
St. John's, NL A1C 5W4
709-722-7584
Fax: 709-722-9210
wob@wob.nf.ca
www.wob.nf.ca
Founded: 1972
Number of Lawyers: 20
Profile: Banking Law; Commercial Finance; Corporate Reorganization; Bankruptcy & Insolvency

Finance Lawyers:
Robert B. Andrews, General Finance
709-570-7331 e-mail: rba@wob.nf.ca
William C. Boyd, General Finance
709-570-7306 e-mail: wboyd@wob.nf.ca
Gregory W. Dickie, Bankruptcy & Insolvency; General Finance
709-570-7307 e-mail: gdickie@wob.nf.ca
Rosalie E. McGrath, General Finance
709-570-7344
Neil F. Pittman, General Finance
709-570-7358
Wayne F. Spracklin, Commercial Finance
709-570-7321
Charles W. White, Commercial Finance
709-570-7308
Sheri H. Wicks, General Finance
709-570-7360

Wickwire Holm
#2100
PO Box 1054
1801 Hollis St.
Halifax, NS B3J 2X6
902-429-4111
Fax: 902-429-8215
866-429-4111
wh@wickwireholm.com
www.wickwireholm.com
Number of Lawyers: 22
Profile: Legal services for all types of financing, insolvency & receivership

Finance Lawyers:
Pamela J. Clarke, Partner
902-482-7019 e-mail: pclarke@wickwireholm.com
Alanna Robinson, Associate
902-482-7012 e-mail: arobinson@wickwireholm.com
Geoffrey Saunders, Managing Partner
902-482-7005 e-mail: gsaunders@wickwireholm.com

Wildeboer Dellelce LLP
#B-2
72 Victoria St. South
Kitchener, ON N2G 4Y9
519-741-8708
Fax: 519-741-9576

ACCOUNTING & LAW

Wildeboer Dellelce LLP (continued)
Number of Lawyers: 3

Finance Lawyers:
David Fedy, Corporate & Commercial; Banking
Carolyn Musselman, Corporate & Commercial; Banking

Wildeboer Dellelce LLP
365 Bay St., 8th Fl.
Toronto, ON M5H 2V1
416-361-3121
Fax: 416-361-1790
webmaster@wildlaw.ca
www.wildlaw.ca
Founded: 1993
Number of Lawyers: 21

Finance Lawyers:
James Brown, Securities; Corporate & Commercial
416-361-2934 e-mail: jbrown@wildlaw.ca
J. Rory Cattanach, Securities; Banking; Corporate & Commercial
416-361-4766 e-mail: rory@wildlaw.ca
Lisa Cunningham, Banking, Securities, Corporate & Commercial
416-361-4778 e-mail: lcunningham@wildlaw.ca
Perry N. Dellelce, Securities; Corporate & Commercial
416-361-5899 e-mail: perry@wildlaw.ca
Andrew Elbaz, Corporate & Commercial
416-361-4789 e-mail: aelbaz@wildlaw.ca
Diana Escobar, Securites, Corporate, Commercial
416-361-5898 e-mail: descobar@wildlaw.ca
Robert Fonn, Securities; Corporate & Commercial
416-361-4787 e-mail: rfonn@wildlaw.ca
Ashleigh Frankel, Corporate & Commercial, Securities
416-361-4761 e-mail: afrankel@wildlaw.ca
Kevin Fritz, Tax
416-361-2933 e-mail: kfritz@wildlaw.ca
Vaughn R. MacLellan, Securities; Corporate & Commercial
416-361-2932 e-mail: vaughan@wildlaw.ca
Charles S. Malone, Securities; Corporate & Commercial
416-361-1267 e-mail: cmalone@wildlaw.ca
Susan L. Mitchell, Securities; Corporate & Commercial
416-361-4768 e-mail: smitchell@wildlaw.ca
George Nehme, Tax
416-361-4788 e-mail: gnehme@wildlaw.ca
Chris Partridge, Banking; Finance
416-361-0359 e-mail: cpartridge@wildlaw.ca
Sanjeev V. Patel, Securities, Corporate & Commercial
416-361-4779 e-mail: spatel@wildlaw.ca
R. Troy Pocaluyko, Securities; Corporate & Commercial
416-361-5802 e-mail: troy@wildlaw.ca
Derek M. Sigel, Securities; Corporate & Commercial
416-361-4775 e-mail: dsigel@wildlaw.ca
Al Wiens, Securities; Corporate & Commercial
416-361-4791 e-mail: awiens@wildlaw.ca
Randy Williamson, Corporate & Commercial, Banking
416-361-4784 e-mail: rwilliamson@wildlaw.ca
Mark Wilson, Corporate & Commercial
416-361-4763 e-mail: mwilson@wildlaw.ca
Robert D. Wortzman, Securities; Corporate & Commercial
416-361-2930 e-mail: rwortzman@wildlaw.ca

Wilson, Vukelich LLP
#710
60 Columbia Way
Markham, ON L3R 0C9
905-940-8700
Fax: 905-940-8785
866-508-8700
information@wilsonvukelich.com
www.wilsonvukelich.com
Founded: 1990
Number of Lawyers: 13

Finance Lawyers:
Andy Ayotte, Commercial Litigation, Employment
Gwen Benjamin, Tax & Estates
Dan Condon, Commercial Litigation, Employment
Jordan Dolgin, Corporate Commercial
Jeff Goldenthal, Financial Services
Douglas D. Langley, Insolvency; Commercial, Litigation
Robin MacKnight, Tax & Estates
R. John Moore, Corporate Commercial
Ivka Starcevic, Banking
Heather Whitten, Corporate Commercial
Sonja Williams, Commercial Litigation
Brian Wilson, Tax & Estates

Stephen K. Winter Law Corp.
#1010
1030 West Georgia St.
Vancouver, BC V6E 2Y3
604-682-3733
Fax: 604-688-5590
swinters@uniserve.com
Number of Lawyers: 1

Finance Lawyers:
Stephen K. Winters

Woods & Partners
#1700
2000, rue McGill College
Montréal, QC H3A 3H3
514-982-4545
Fax: 514-284-2046
general@woods.qc.ca
www.litigationboutique.com
Number of Lawyers: 16

Finance Lawyers:
Babak Barin

Zenith Hookenson LLP
Mayfair Place #218
6707 Elbow Dr. SW
Calgary, AB T2V 0E4
403-259-5041
Fax: 403-258-0719
zenithco@telusplanet.net
Founded: 1979
Number of Lawyers: 3

Finance Lawyers:
Leonard M. Zenith, General Finance

SECTION 6

Major Canadian Companies

Included in this section:

Listings typically include:

- name of company
- address
- phone, fax, toll free numbers, email address, URL
- type of company (Public, Private, Crown Corporation)
- financial contact person
- company activity or type of business

Listings are organized under the following categories:

Recent Trends in Corporate Finance

Recent Trends in Corporate Finance

*By A. Tomas**

Introduction

Over much of the last decade, corporations have been posting record profits. Meanwhile, business fixed capital investment has been relatively sluggish in recent years. These two factors combined have led to a significant shift in the corporate sector's net lending/ borrowing position – from one of a chronic deficit position to one of sustained surplus. After having run deficits for almost 30 years, corporations have emerged with significant surplus positions in the last decade.

In conjunction with this, there have been major structural shifts in the economy, in terms of the net lending/ borrowing positions of other sectors. Traditional surplus sectors in the Canadian economy – households and non-residents – have moved into deficit positions, while traditional deficit sectors (corporations and governments) have generated surplus positions. This has placed the corporate sector in a new role – that of increasingly supplying funds to the rest of the economy.

This note will look at the corporate surplus phenomenon from a few angles, focusing on non-financial corporations. First, the note will examine the generation of net lending and its principal components: saving and non-financial investment. It will also explore the uses of the corporate surplus, along with the shift in the composition of corporate financing. Lastly, it will underline the restructuring of corporate balance sheets.

Generation of corporate surplus

Corporations posted a record net lending position of $80.6 billion in 2005. This trend began from 1993 to 1996, when the sector had four straight surpluses after generating only one in the previous 29 years. Following a brief slide to a deficit position in 1997-1999, the sector rebounded to accumulate impressive surpluses over the past six years.

Today's surplus positions are far removed from the situation just a decade and a half ago. Traditionally, corporations have run deficits, with non-financial capital acquisition exceeding internally-generated funds.

The sector experienced a record deficit position of $22.8 billion in 1981. The deep recession of 1981-82 marked by historically high nominal interest rates was the harbinger of a steep decline in corporate

* This article is adapted from the publication 13-604-MIE2006050, Income and expenditure accounts division (613) 951-9277.

Tendances récentes du financement des sociétés

*par A. Tomas**

Introduction

Au cours d'une bonne partie de la dernière décennie, les sociétés ont réalisé des bénéfices records. Cependant, leurs investissements en capital fixe ont été relativement léthargiques ces dernières années. L'effet conjugué de ces deux facteurs a inversé la position de prêt net/d'emprunt net du secteur des sociétés, laquelle est passée d'un déficit chronique à un excédent soutenu. Au terme de près de 30 années de déficit, les sociétés dégagent d'importantes positions excédentaires depuis 10 ans.

Dans un même temps, l'économie a subi d'importantes mutations structurelles sous l'aspect des positions de prêt net/d'emprunt net des autres secteurs. Les secteurs des ménages et non-résidents qui, du point de vue historique, étaient en situation excédentaire, sont passés en situation déficitaire, tandis que les secteurs qui ont le plus souvent été en déficit – sociétés et administrations publiques – dégagent maintenant des excédents. La situation a conféré un nouveau rôle au secteur des sociétés, qui accorde de plus en plus de financement aux autres secteurs de l'économie.

La présente étude examine le phénomène de l'excédent des sociétés sous différents angles en mettant l'accent sur les sociétés non financières. Dans un premier temps, nous nous pencherons sur la position de prêt net et ses principales composantes, soit l'épargne et l'investissement non financier. Nous nous intéresserons également à l'utilisation faite des excédents des entreprises et à l'évolution de la composition de leur financement. En dernier lieu, nous discuterons de la restructuration des bilans des sociétés.

Dégagement d'excédents de sociétés

Les sociétés ont affiché une position de prêt net record de 80,6 milliards de dollars en 2005. La tendance a été amorcée de 1993 à 1996, lorsque quatre excédents d'affilée ont été enregistrés, tandis qu'un seul avait été dégagé au cours des 29 années précédentes. À la suite d'une légère glissade vers une position déficitaire de 1997 à 1999, le secteur s'est redressé et a accumulé d'importants excédents ces six dernières années.

Les positions excédentaires que nous connaissons ont peu de commune mesure avec la situation d'il y a à peine 15 ans. Historiquement, les sociétés ont accusé des déficits, l'acquisition de capital non financier ayant dépassé les fonds autogénérés.

Le secteur a atteint une position déficitaire record de 22,8 milliards de dollars en 1981. La récession profonde de 1981-1982, marquée par des taux d'intérêt nominaux qui ont atteint un sommet historique, était annonciatrice de la

* Cet article est adapté de la publication 13-604-MIF2006050, Division des comptes des revenus et dépenses, (613) 951-9277.

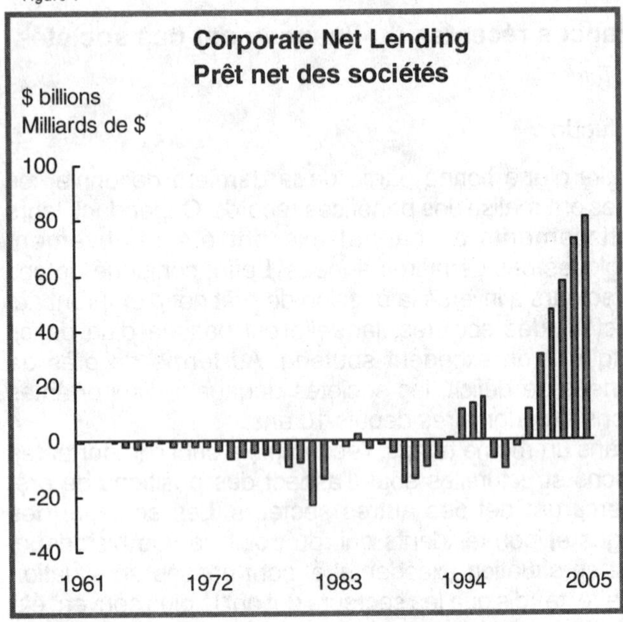

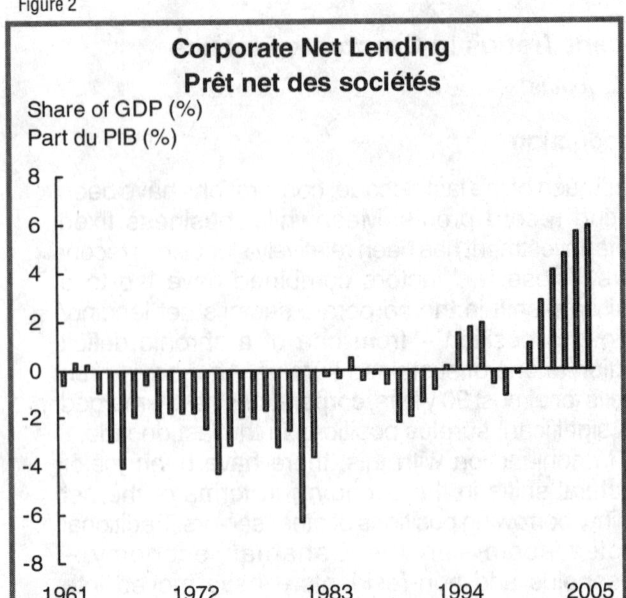

profits, and despite a marked slowdown in fixed capital spending, corporations remained in deficit. The deficit positions persisted for most of that decade through to the next economic downturn that began in mid-1990. However, this was soon to change, as the deficit narrowed through to 1992 and surpluses began to be posted in 1993 for the next few years through 1996. The expansion of the past decade helped drive corporate profits to record levels. Undistributed earnings have increased an annual average of almost 16% since 1995.

The return to a deficit position in the late 1990s was short-lived. In 1997, undistributed corporate profits fell, and non-financial capital acquisition advanced sharply. In 1998, undistributed profits receded further (falling 17%), posting their largest decline since the expansion began in 1993, as North American corporations felt the effects of such events as the plunge in commodity prices and the Asian economic crisis.

However, a sharp rebound in earnings, coupled with a more recent slowdown in capital spending growth, has moved the corporate sector into an expanding surplus position since 2000. The impact of both undistributed earnings and capital expenditure on the evolution of the corporate surplus deficit over time is notable.

Profits drove the surplus

Profits have clearly been the main driver of the corporate net lending surplus for the majority of years over the past decade. Except for a few minor

chute vertigineuse des bénéfices des sociétés et, en dépit d'un ralentissement appréciable des dépenses en capital fixe, les sociétés sont demeurées en situation déficitaire. Cette situation a persisté pendant la plus grande partie de cette décennie, jusqu'à la récession suivante qui a commencé au milieu des années 1990. Toutefois, la situation ne devait pas tarder à se redresser : le déficit s'est rétréci jusqu'en 1992, puis des excédents ont été réalisés en 1993 et pendant les quelques années suivantes, jusqu'en 1996. L'expansion économique de la décennie écoulée a concouru à porter les bénéfices des sociétés à des niveaux sans précédent. En effet, les bénéfices non répartis ont progressé de près de 16 % par an en moyenne depuis 1995.

La position déficitaire de la fin des années 1990 a été de courte durée. En 1997, les bénéfices non répartis des sociétés ont chuté, et l'acquisition de capital non financier s'est fortement accentuée. En 1998, les bénéfices non répartis ont reculé à nouveau (-17 %), soit le plus important recul observé depuis le début de la période de croissance en 1993, tandis que les sociétés nord-américaines encaissaient les contrecoups d'événements tels la dégringolade des prix des produits de base et la crise économique asiatique.

Cela dit, une forte remontée des gains, conjuguée au ralentissement récent de la croissance des dépenses en capital, a placé le secteur des sociétés dans une position excédentaire grandissante depuis 2000. L'incidence tant des bénéfices non répartis que des dépenses en capital sur l'évolution à long terme de la position des excédents/ déficits des entreprises est remarquable.

Les bénéfices sont la cause principale de l'excédent

Les bénéfices ont été le principal facteur à l'origine de l'excédent de prêt net des sociétés pour la majorité des années de la décennie écoulée. Exception faite de quelques

interruptions (for example, the high-tech bust in 2001) corporate earnings have been on a pronounced upward trend since about 1992.

Historically low aggregate dividend payout ratios to other sectors helped boost undistributed earnings to a record high in 2005. Lower dividends paid by corporations to other sectors suggest that shareholders have been disposed to retaining profits in businesses, in favour of alternative returns. Record high market values have contributed to higher wealth positions for respective shareholders.

Figure 3

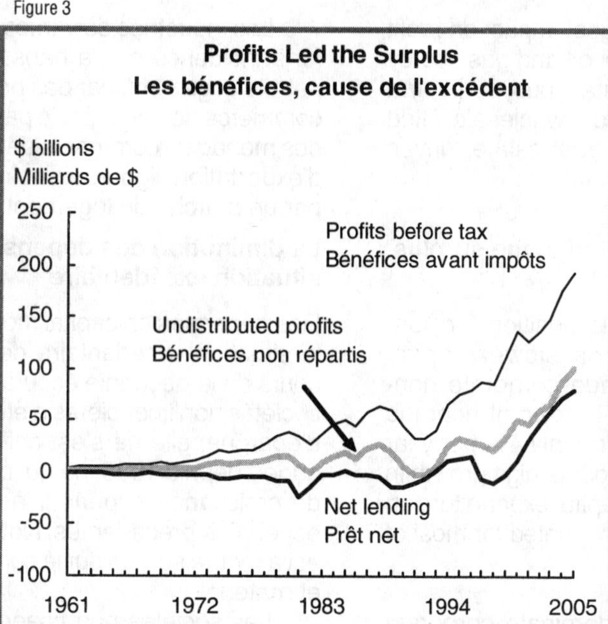

Financial corporations have traditionally been in a small surplus position. By the nature of their business, they do not engage in substantial fixed capital investment. As a result, their expanding surplus in recent years has been largely generated by strong growth in undistributed earnings. The surplus in the financial sector has increased significantly since 2000, led mainly by record profits in the chartered banking and insurance industries.

However, the major shift with respect to the evolution of the surplus has been in the non-financial corporate sector. In 2003, non-financial corporations' surplus overtook that of financial corporations for the first time in 40 years and in 2005 the surplus reached a historical high. Because of this, the focus in the analysis now shifts to private non-financial corporations where the dominant trend in net lending arises, with a $55.8 billion surplus recorded in 2005.

The higher surpluses for non-financial corporations have been the result of significant domestic and foreign demand for Canadian goods and services. The personal sector's record levels of spending have led to increased revenue for corporations. In addition, Canada's booming exports, contributing to a large current account surplus, have filled corporate coffers with plenty of funds from abroad. The downward trend in interest rates has also played a supporting role in improving the bottom line, by helping to reduce business financing costs and facilitating household borrowing.

The growth in net profits before taxes has been widespread across non-financial industries with 15 of 17 industry groups experiencing positive growth between 2001 and 2005. Further, since 1999 positive

courtes interruptions (par exemple, au moment de la débâcle technologique de 2001), les bénéfices des sociétés suivent une tendance haussière prononcée depuis 1992 environ.

Des ratios de distribution de dividendes agrégés, payés à d'autres secteurs, historiquement faibles ont contribué à porter les bénéfices non répartis à un niveau record en 2005. La diminution des dividendes payés par les sociétés à d'autres secteurs laisse entendre que les actionnaires ont été disposés à conserver les bénéfices au sein des entreprises et ont privilégié des sources de rendement autres. Les sommets records atteints en bourse ont contribué à hausser la situation financière des actionnaires.

Historiquement, les sociétés financières ont connu des positions excédentaires modestes. En raison de la nature de leurs activités, elles n'effectuent pas d'importants investissements en capital fixe. Par conséquent, la hausse de leur excédent ces dernières années est principalement due à une forte progression des bénéfices non répartis. Le surplus du secteur financier a augmenté de façon appréciable depuis 2000, surtout sous l'effet de bénéfices record réalisés par les industries des banques à charte et des assurances.

Toutefois, la situation excédentaire a surtout évolué dans le secteur des sociétés non financières. En 2003, l'excédent a rejoint celui des sociétés financières pour la première fois en 40 ans, et a atteint un sommet historique en 2005. Pour cette raison, la présente analyse se concentre maintenant sur les sociétés privées non financières, qui dégagent une forte tendance de prêt net, affichant un excédent de 55,8 milliards de dollars en 2005.

Les excédents accrus des sociétés non financières découlent d'une demande intérieure et étrangère importante de biens et de services canadiens. Les dépenses records des particuliers ont fait augmenter les revenus des sociétés. De plus, l'accroissement rapide des exportations canadiennes qui a contribué à un important excédent du compte courant, a abondamment garni les coffres des sociétés de rentrées de fonds étrangères. La tendance à la baisse des taux d'intérêt a également concouru à bonifier les résultats nets, en réduisant les coûts de financement des entreprises et en facilitant les emprunts des ménages.

Les industries non financières ont pour la plupart vu croître leurs bénéfices nets avant impôts puisque 15 groupes d'industries sur 17 ont affiché une croissance positive de 2001 à 2005. Qui plus est, depuis 1999, bon nombre des industries

net profits before taxes have been widespread among non-financial industries. This suggests that the undistributed earnings are also reasonably diffused by industry.

Select industries with the largest impact on profit growth since 2000 have included: oil and gas, led by record high commodity prices; retail, buoyed by firm domestic demand from households; wholesale, lifted by strong exports markets; and, real estate, driven mainly by a booming housing market.

Slower spending also contributed to the surplus

Another influence on the surplus position for non-financial corporations has been slower capital expenditure. Over the last decade corporate non-financial capital acquisition hasn't grown at near the rate of saving, averaging growth of only 4% per year since 1998, in contrast with the double digit growth in previous decades. In particular, capital expenditure on machinery and equipment has accounted for most of the weakness.

Non-financial corporations dominate corporate capital investment, and investment in fixed capital by private non-financial corporations represents the bulk of total corporate sector non-financial capital acquisition (almost 90% since 1998). Investment in new fixed capital is the dominant component of non-financial capital acquisition, and a significant inverse relationship between new fixed capital investment and net lending/borrowing is evident. This is consistent with the recent role played by investment in the generation of the surplus, since 1998.

How the surplus was used

The generation of a substantial corporate surplus in recent years has reflected the fact that undistributed earnings have exceeded capital investment requirements by a wide margin. This suggests a modification in corporate investment behaviour. It is clear that corporate investment patterns have evolved as the surplus expanded.

A perspective on the surplus can be gleaned by looking at the sources and uses of corporate funds. With internally-generated sources

Figure 4

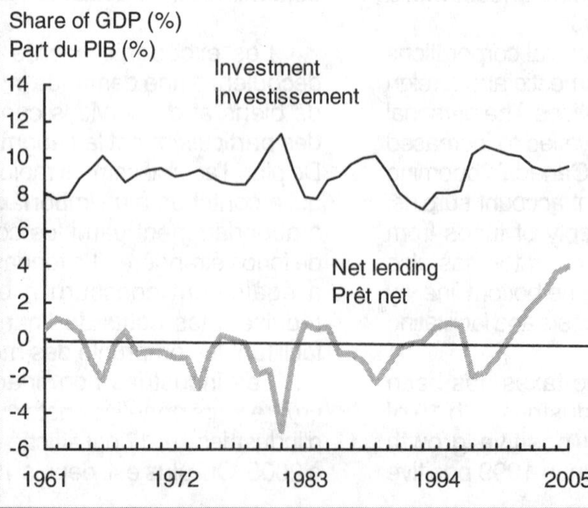

non financières connaissent des bénéfices nets positifs avant impôts. Cela donne à entendre que les bénéfices non répartis sont aussi raisonnablement distribués entre les secteurs.

Les industries suivantes, entre autres, ont exercé la plus forte incidence sur la hausse des bénéfices depuis 2000 : pétrole et gaz, mû par des prix records des produits de base; commerce de détail, porté par la demande intérieure soutenue des ménages; commerce de gros, qui a bénéficié de marchés d'exportation vigoureux; et immobilier, animé principalement par un marché du logement qui bat son plein.

La diminution des dépenses contribue également à la situation excédentaire

Des dépenses en capital moindres sont également cause de la situation excédentaire des sociétés non financières. Au cours de la décennie écoulée, l'acquisition de capital par les sociétés non financières a été largement inférieure à son taux d'épargne; elle ne s'est chiffrée en moyenne qu'à 4 % par année depuis 1998, ce qui contraste nettement avec le taux de croissance supérieur à 10 % enregistré au cours des décennies précédentes. Notamment, l'apathie à ce chapitre est à mettre surtout sur le compte des dépenses en machines et matériel.

Les sociétés non financières sont à l'origine de la plus grande part de l'investissement en capital engagé par les sociétés, et l'investissement en capital fixe effectué par les sociétés privées non financières représente la plus grande masse de l'acquisition totale de capital non financier par le secteur des sociétés (près de 90 % depuis 1998). L'investissement en nouveau capital fixe est l'élément dominant de l'acquisition de capital non financier, et une relation inverse appréciable est à constater entre l'investissement en nouveau capital fixe et le prêt/l'emprunt net. Cela s'inscrit dans la ligne du rôle joué par l'investissement dans la formation de l'excédent depuis 1998.

Comment l'excédent a été utilisé

Le dégagement d'un excédent appréciable des sociétés ces dernières années témoigne du fait que les bénéfices non distribués ont largement dépassé les besoins en investissement de capital. Cela porte à croire à une modification du comportement des sociétés en ce qui a trait à l'investissement. Il ne fait aucun doute que les tendances de l'investissement des entreprises ont évolué alors que l'excédent augmentait.

L'excédent peut être mis en perspective grâce à un examen de la provenance et de l'utilisation des fonds des sociétés. À la suite de la hausse prononcée

of funds up strongly in recent years, uses of funds other than nonfinancial investment have increased in prominence. Since the surplus funds must be used, uses of funds have shifted in favour of various types of financial investments. Specifically, there have been increased investments in various types of financial assets as well as repayment of outstanding debt.

Corporations have directed an increasing amount of funds into financial investments in recent years. Both portfolio and inter-company investment have contributed to notable acquisitions of financial instruments.

Major flows of financial investment have been directed to liquid assets and other portfolio investments since 2000. In particular, currency and bank deposits (domestic and foreign) and various other types of portfolio investments have advanced sharply.

There have been significant new cash flows as profits strengthened and capital spending softened. These increased flows were most significant in 2001-2005. Corporations' currency and bank deposits have increased as a share of both their financial and total investment, and their flows have accounted for an increasing proportion of total deposit flows in the economy. In addition, portfolio investment in debt securities and other financial assets have reflected a partly passive financial investment use of the expanding surplus in recent years.

The last decade has seen a surge in inter-company investment reflecting a boom period in corporate mergers and acquisitions that began in the late 1990s. A significant proportion of inter-company investment was directed abroad. This suggests that corporations have continued to invest in non-financial capital, but perhaps at an increasing rate outside of Canada.

Since 1995, over $256 billion has been invested by non-financial corporations in the form of inter-company investment. This represents almost 32% of total investment in financial assets by non-financial corporations over this period. A principal driver of this growth in inter-company investment by non-financial corporations is direct investment abroad, as the pattern of inter-company investment by non-financial firms is closely correlated with Canadian direct investment abroad (CDIA). Canadian corporations have invested $231 billion in foreign subsidiaries and associated enterprises operating in non-financial industries since 1995. A closer look at CDIA provides further perspective on this. The main years of direct investment mergers and acquisition activity include 1997-1998, and 2000-2001, years in which non-financial firms were

des fonds autogénérés ces dernières années, l'utilisation des fonds – à des fins autres que l'investissement non financier – a pris de l'ampleur. Comme les fonds excédentaires doivent forcément être utilisés, leur utilisation s'est déplacée vers divers types d'investissement financier. Plus particulièrement, les mises de fonds ont augmenté dans diverses catégories d'actif financier, et les entreprises se sont attachées au remboursement de l'encours de la dette.

Les sociétés ont affecté une part grandissante de leurs fonds à l'investissement financier depuis quelques années. Tant l'investissement de portefeuille que l'investissement entre les sociétés ont contribué à des acquisitions appréciables d'instruments financiers.

D'importants flux d'investissement financier ont été affectés à des actifs liquides et à d'autres investissements de portefeuille depuis 2000. Notamment, l'argent liquide et les dépôts bancaires (au pays et à l'étranger) et d'autres catégories d'investissement de portefeuille ont augmenté de façon prononcée.

D'abondants nouveaux flux de liquidités sont à signaler, tandis que progressaient les bénéfices et diminuaient les dépenses en capital. Les hausses des flux de liquidité ont été les plus importantes de 2001 à 2005. L'argent liquide et les dépôts bancaires ont augmenté à la fois en proportion de l'investissement qu'ils constituent et en tant que part de l'investissement total des sociétés, et leurs flux sont à l'origine d'une part grandissante des flux totaux de dépôts dans l'économie. En outre, les placements de portefeuille dans des titres d'emprunt et d'autres éléments d'actif financier constituent, en partie, des investissements financiers passifs témoignant de l'utilisation faite de l'excédent, en hausse ces dernières années.

La dernière décennie a été marquée par la montée de l'investissement entre sociétés, situation qui témoigne de la vague des fusions et d'acquisitions d'entreprises amorcée à la fin des années 1990. Une part importante de l'investissement entre sociétés a été canalisée vers l'étranger. Cela porte à croire que les sociétés ont poursuivi leur investissement en capital non financier, mais l'ont dirigé de plus en plus à l'étranger.

Depuis 1995, les sociétés non financières ont engagé plus de 256 milliards de dollars sous forme d'investissement entre sociétés. Cela représente près de 32 % de la totalité des mises de fonds que les sociétés non financières ont engagées dans des actifs financiers au cours de la période. La montée de l'investissement entre sociétés effectué par les sociétés non financières est attribuable en grande partie à l'investissement direct à l'étranger, comme la tendance de l'investissement entre sociétés engagé par des entreprises non financières est en étroite corrélation avec l'investissement canadien direct à l'étranger (IDCE). À preuve, depuis 1995, les sociétés canadiennes ont investi 231 milliards de dollars dans des filiales étrangères et des entreprises associées ayant des activités dans des secteurs non financiers. Un examen étroit de l'IDCE met la situation en perspective. Les années 1997-1998 et 2000-2001 figurent parmi celles qui sont

beginning to emerge from deficit positions. In recent years, CDIA flows were largely comprised of capital injections into existing affiliates.

Canadian repatriation of domestic foreign held interests – another use of funds – has played a role in the deceleration of foreign direct investment in Canada (FDIC) in recent years (particularly in 2004). Furthermore, the lower levels of FDIC might be related to the sluggish non-financial investment in Canada in recent years.

In aggregate, there has been a notable slowing of demand by non-financial corporations for borrowed funds over the last 10 years. Up to the mid-1990s there was a close correlation between non-financial capital acquisition and borrowing, as corporations raised the majority of their external funds through credit market debt.

Clearly, this is no longer the case. There are two major factors that explain this change. First, the growth in internally-generated funds dampened corporations' recourse to credit markets. This would have been further affected by a softening in capital expenditure in the late 1990s and the early 2000s. Second, the 1990s witnessed strong demand for corporate equities, as net new share issuance overtook borrowing. From 1996 to 2005, net funds raised by corporations were primarily made up of share issues, reflecting strong stock markets. This development was driven, to a large extent, by the effects of significant increased demand for equity investments, in particular by institutional investors and non-residents. This shift in the demand for borrowed funds has become more pronounced in the new millennium.

Figure 5

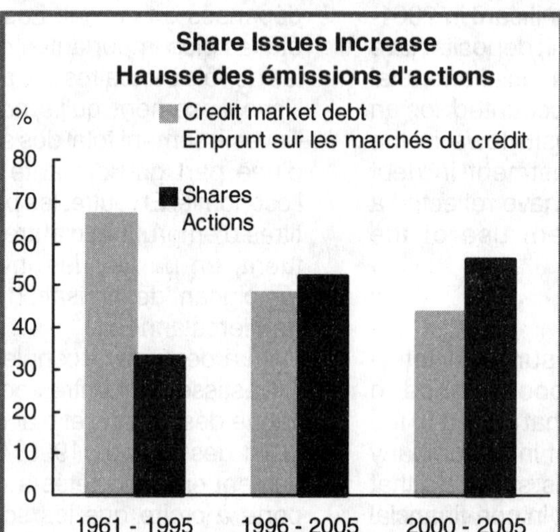

Corporations have been paying down their short-term debt – loans and short-term paper – at a significant clip in recent years, with repayments/retirements exceeding new borrowings in these markets from 2001-2003. This pattern was consistent with reduced demand and the refinancing of short-term debt in favour of longer-term debt instruments, which may have partially reflected corporations' interest rate expectations (as yield curves flattened). The shift in the composition of borrowing in favour of long-term

caractérisées par une activité intense de fusion et d'acquisition par investissement direct. Or, ce sont les années mêmes où les entreprises non financières commençaient tout juste à sortir de leur situation déficitaire. Plus récemment, les flux de l'IDCE étaient surtout constitués d'injections de capitaux dans des sociétés affiliées déjà existantes.

Le rapatriement d'intérêts canadiens sous contrôle étranger – autre utilisation des fonds – a joué un rôle dans la diminution de l'investissement direct étranger au Canada (IDEC) au cours des dernières années (notamment en 2004). Par surcroît, les niveaux réduits d'IDEC ont peut-être un rapport avec l'investissement non financier stagnant qu'a connu le Canada ces dernières années.

Dans l'ensemble, la demande de fonds d'emprunt par les sociétés non financières a sensiblement diminué au cours des 10 dernières années. Jusqu'au milieu des années 1990, l'acquisition de capital non financier et l'emprunt étaient en étroite corrélation, tandis que les sociétés recueillaient la plus grande part de leurs fonds de provenance externe en contractant des emprunts sur les marchés du crédit.

De toute évidence, la situation n'est plus la même. Deux principaux facteurs expliquent le revirement. D'abord, la croissance des fonds autogénérés a freiné le recours des sociétés aux marchés du crédit. Le ralentissement des dépenses en capital à la fin des années 1990 et au début des années 2000 aurait également influé sur la situation. Deuxièmement, les années 1990 ont été marquées par une forte demande d'actions de sociétés, cependant que l'émission nette d'actions rattrapait l'emprunt. De 1996 à 2005, les fonds nets touchés par les sociétés provenaient principalement d'émissions d'actions, situation qui reflète la robustesse des marchés boursiers. La situation était notamment attribuable à la demande sensiblement accrue de titres de participation, surtout de la part des investisseurs institutionnels et des non-résidents. Ce revirement de la demande de fonds d'emprunt s'est accentué au début du nouveau millénaire.

Les sociétés remboursent leur dette à court terme – composée d'emprunts et d'effets à court terme – à vive allure depuis quelques années, si bien que, de 2001 à 2003, le montant des remboursements et des rachats a dépassé celui des nouveaux emprunts sur les marchés concernés. La tendance s'inscrivait dans la ligne de la demande réduite d'emprunts à court terme et du refinancement de l'encours de la dette à court terme au moyen d'instruments d'emprunt à long terme, et elle traduisait peut-être, en partie, les attentes des sociétés vis-à-vis des taux d'intérêt (au moment où les

debt has resulted in almost 3.4 times more long-term than short-term debt being raised since 1995.

Over the last decade, corporate fund raising activity evolved significantly, and at the same time they were experiencing massive growth in saving. The result is that a greater proportion of sources of funds are arising from own funds – saving and share issues – than in the past. In this respect, the growth of equity relative to debt becomes even more pronounced when internally-generated savings or undistributed earnings are taken into account. In the last decade, corporations' sources of funds have mainly been dominated by own funds as opposed to borrowed (other's) funds. Since 2000, over 78 cents of every dollar of net funds raised has been in the form of saving and share issues.

Impact of the surplus

Record profits and slower non-financial investment, coupled with a downward trend in interest rates and strong gains in stock prices, have provided the opportunity for corporations to substantially restructure their balance sheets. This has taken the form of increased liquidity, strengthened inter-company investment abroad, reduced debt levels and a substantial increase in the equity base. In aggregate, corporate balance sheets are in their best shape in decades, and a closer look at the extent of this restructuring is warranted.

The composition of corporate assets has evolved substantially over the last 10 years with financial assets growing from one-third to nearly one-half of all assets. This is supported by increased cash holdings (domestic and foreign deposits) reflecting increased liquidity on the one hand and inter-company investment and changing investment opportunities on the other.

Non-financial corporations have been stockpiling cash over the last decade, with the effect that they hold over 19% of the nation's domestic currency and deposits – a sharp contrast to the situation in the mid 1970s when they held slightly over 5%. Including portfolio investments, it is clear that liquid assets have assumed greater importance over this same period, thus minimizing liquidity risk. Inter-company investment positions have also increased in significance since 1992.

Figure 6

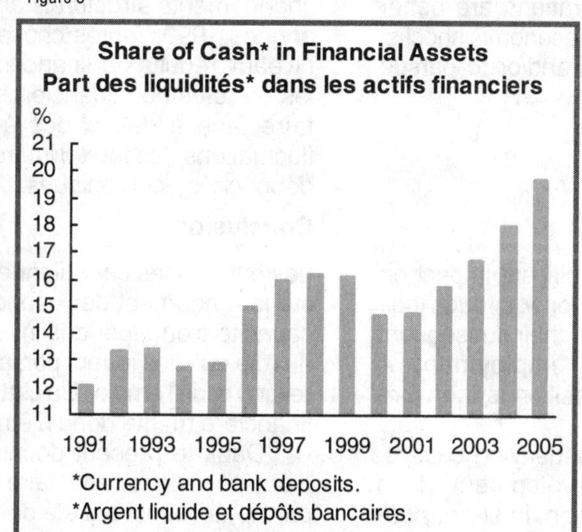

*Currency and bank deposits.
*Argent liquide et dépôts bancaires.

courbes de rendement demeuraient stables). L'évolution de la composition des emprunts en faveur de la dette à long terme a fait que la valeur des emprunts à long terme contractés depuis 1995 est près de 3,4 fois celle des emprunts à court terme.

Au cours de la dernière décennie, les sociétés ont modifié sensiblement leurs activités de financement, au moment même où elles accumulaient des volumes massifs d'épargne. Il s'ensuit que, plus que par le passé, leur financement provient de source interne, sous forme d'épargne et d'émissions d'actions. Dans cette optique, la progression des capitaux propres en regard de l'endettement est encore plus importante si l'épargne et les bénéfices non répartis autogénérés sont pris en compte. Depuis 10 ans, les sociétés ont recouru principalement à leurs propres fonds plutôt qu'à des fonds empruntés (d'autrui). Depuis 2000, plus de 0,78 $ par dollar de fonds nets recueillis proviennent d'épargnes et d'émissions de titres.

Effet de l'excédent

Des bénéfices records et la diminution de l'investissement non financier, conjugués à la tendance baissière des taux d'intérêt et à la forte progression du cours des actions, ont fourni aux sociétés l'occasion de remanier à fond leur bilan. Il s'en est suivi l'augmentation des liquidités, l'intensification de l'investissement entre sociétés à l'étranger, la diminution de l'endettement et une hausse notable des avoirs. Dans l'ensemble, les bilans des sociétés n'ont pas été aussi luisants depuis des décennies, ce qui justifie un examen de l'ampleur des remaniements.

La composition de l'actif des sociétés a sensiblement évolué depuis 10 ans, l'actif financier progressant d'un tiers à près de la moitié de tous les actifs. La situation prend appui sur des encaisses enrichies (dépôts au pays et à l'étranger) qui reflètent, d'une part, la hausse des liquidités et, d'autre part, l'investissement entre sociétés et la mutation des occasions d'investissement.

Les sociétés non financières accumulent de l'argent liquide depuis 10 ans, si bien qu'elles possèdent désormais plus de 19 % de la monnaie nationale et des dépôts – ce qui contraste nettement avec la situation qui caractérisait le milieu des années 1970, auquel moment la donnée correspondante dépassait légèrement 5 %. Il est clair que les actifs liquides, y compris les investissements de portefeuille, ont gagné en importance au cours de la période, ce qui réduit au minimum le risque de liquidité. De plus, l'importance des investissements entre sociétés a aussi augmenté depuis 1992.

The substantially reduced reliance on borrowed funds has contributed in large measure to improved corporate balance sheets. In addition, the slowing growth in credit market debt, combined with the shift in the composition of corporate liabilities in favour of longer term instruments and the easing of interest rates over a number of years, has contributed to both lower leverage and interest burden. This has helped reduce the vulnerability of the sector against a significant rise in short term interest rates.

Figure 7

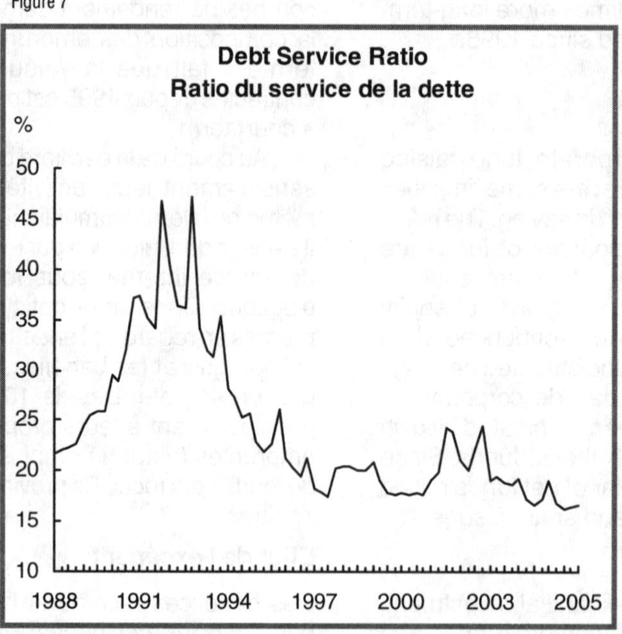

La dépendance sensiblement réduite envers les fonds d'emprunt a contribué dans une large mesure à améliorer les bilans des sociétés. De même, une croissance moindre de l'endettement sur le marché du crédit conjuguée au remaniement de la composition du passif des sociétés en faveur des instruments d'emprunt à long terme, et à la diminution des taux d'intérêt au fil des ans, a contribué à réduire tant le financement par emprunt que les frais d'intérêts. Par conséquent, le secteur n'est pas aussi vulnérable qu'avant à une hausse appréciable des taux d'intérêt à court terme.

Liquidity improves substantially, as leverage continues to ease

Liquidity risk has also been substantially reduced. The liquidity of non-financial firms, as measured by the quick ratio – that is current assets to current liabilities -, has improved markedly. This ratio has now reached a historical high, reflecting as much a substantial increase in liquid assets as a sharp reduction in short term liability growth.

Further, the changing relationship between debt and equity and the strength of internally-generated funds have combined to drive corporate leverage to a 38 year low. The ratio of credit market debt to shares outstanding plus retained earnings has reflected both economic cycles and structural changes beginning in the mid-1990s. All else being equal, lower leverage indicates that non-financial corporations are better equipped to confront unanticipated economic shocks, deal with interest rate fluctuations and/or to pursue new economic opportunities.

Conclusion

Canadian corporations have a significant impact on the performance of the national economy, through their ability to invest on a large scale and their subsequent role in generating income and employment. A significant shift in their financial position is therefore worthy of analysis.

This note has identified the underlying causes, and the major effects, of the development of an expanding corporate surplus position. In short, non-

Les liquidités augmentent fortement, tandis que le financement par emprunt poursuit son déclin

Le risque de liquidité a lui aussi diminué sensiblement. La liquidité des entreprises non financières, mesurée en termes de ratio de liquidité relative – c'est-à-dire le ratio de l'actif à court terme au passif à court terme – s'est remarquablement amélioré. En effet, il a atteint un sommet historique, ce qui témoigne autant d'une hausse marquée des actifs liquides que d'une forte diminution de la croissance du passif à court terme.

En outre, le rapport changeant entre la dette et les capitaux propres et le niveau élevé des fonds autogénérés ont eu pour effet cumulé de porter le financement par emprunt des sociétés à son niveau le plus bas depuis les 38 dernières années. Le ratio de la dette contractée sur le marché du crédit au capital-actions en circulation, augmenté des bénéfices non répartis, témoigne à la fois des cycles économiques et des changements structurels amorcés à compter du milieu des années 1990. Toutes choses étant égales par ailleurs, des niveaux réduits de financement par emprunt indiquent que les sociétés non financières sont en meilleure posture pour faire face à des chocs économiques imprévus et aux fluctuations des taux d'intérêt ou pour exploiter de nouveaux débouchés économiques.

Conclusion

Les entreprises canadiennes ont une incidence appréciable sur le rendement de l'économie nationale en raison de leur capacité d'engager des investissements à grande échelle et du rôle qu'elles jouent par la suite en faveur de la création de revenu et de l'emploi. Un changement important à leur position financière mérite donc d'être analysé.

Dans le présent document, les causes sous-jacentes d'une position excédentaire en expansion des sociétés et ses principaux effets ont été déterminés. En bref, les entreprises

financial corporations have taken advantage of record profits, historically low interest rates and relatively buoyant stock markets to substantially re-structure their balance sheets. It has reached the point where corporate finances, in aggregate, are the healthiest they have been in decades. The ultimate question is what this current situation implies for the economy, looking forward – specifically, with respect to the outlook for investment and economic growth. This is the subject of further research, but a few relevant points are made below.

(i) Corporations finance investment from internally-generated funds and supply funds to the economy

The structural shifts in the composition of sectors' saving and related surplus/deficit positions have been substantial, most notably the generation of substantial corporate saving and surplus as described in this paper. Corporations have been increasingly supplying funds to the rest of the economy, including non-residents.

One issue might be whether there is sufficient saving in the economy to finance investment demand. While a reliance on household saving and funds from abroad have historically been significant, this is not currently the case. In fact, for the last 10 years or so, Canada has continued to generate more than enough funds to finance investment, despite the sharp declines in personal saving and the evolution of a personal sector deficit. The traditional relationship of "households save and corporations invest" has been inverted. Corporate sector saving currently dominates national saving, and exceeds business investment spending needs. One question might be how much of corporate undistributed earnings ultimately accrue to non-residents? Looking at re-invested earnings on foreign direct investment in Canada, there has been a declining trend in the proportion of foreign claims on Canadian business earnings since 2000.

(ii) Slowing of investment in recent years is multi-faceted ...

The slowing of capital expenditure in recent years may be the result of some loosely-related factors. One factor might be the gradual slowing of foreign direct investment in Canada, given the historical post-war significance of foreign subsidiaries in the Canadian economy. A further factor might be the possibility of capital overhangs, where some firms – in particular in the information and communications technologies (ICT) and telecommunication industry – may have over-invested in the late 1990s into the early part of the new millennium. Evolving corporate objectives may

non financières ont misé sur des bénéfices records, des taux d'intérêt historiquement bas et des marchés boursiers relativement vigoureux pour remanier considérablement leurs bilans. À telle enseigne que les finances des sociétés, examinées dans leur ensemble, n'ont pas été aussi robustes depuis des décennies. La question de l'heure est celle de savoir ce que la situation actuelle réserve à l'économie dans une optique prospective – plus particulièrement, en ce qui a trait aux perspectives d'investissement et d'expansion économique. Ces questions appellent en soi des recherches, mais nous abordons ci-dessous quelques points pertinents.

(i) Les sociétés financent leurs investissements à même les fonds autogénérés et consentent un financement à l'économie

La position de l'épargne et la situation connexe de l'excédent et du déficit du secteur a subi un remaniement structurel profond, notamment en ce qui concerne la production d'un important volume d'épargne et d'excédents des sociétés, comme le décrit la présente étude. Les sociétés alimentent de plus en plus en capitaux les autres secteurs de l'économie, celui des non-résidents y compris.

Une question qui vient à l'esprit est celle de savoir s'il y a suffisamment d'épargne dans l'économie pour satisfaire à la demande d'investissement. Si, du point de vue historique, une forte dépendance envers l'épargne des ménages et le financement provenant de l'étranger était constatée, la situation actuelle est toute autre. En effet, depuis 10 ans environ, le Canada produit de façon continue des fonds largement suffisants pour financer l'investissement, malgré le rétrécissement appréciable de l'épargne personnelle et l'évolution du déficit des particuliers. Nous connaissons le contraire du principe selon lequel « les ménages économisent et les entreprises investissent ». À l'heure qu'il est, l'épargne du secteur des sociétés prédomine dans l'épargne nationale, et elle dépasse les besoins des entreprises en dépenses d'investissement. Il y aurait peut-être lieu de se demander quelle part des bénéfices non répartis des sociétés revient, en bout de course, aux non-résidents. En regardant les bénéfices réinvestis sur l'investissement direct étranger au Canada, on remarque une tendance à la baisse de la proportion des créances étrangères sur les bénéfices des sociétés canadiennes depuis 2000.

(ii) Le ralentissement de l'investissement ces dernières années présente plusieurs aspects...

Le ralentissement des dépenses en capital ces dernières années peut être le fait de certains facteurs qui ne sont pas étroitement liés. L'un d'eux pourrait être le ralentissement progressif de l'investissement direct étranger au Canada, eu égard à l'importance historique des filiales étrangères dans l'économie canadienne au cours de la période de l'après-guerre. Un autre facteur susceptible de jouer tient à la possibilité de l'existence de capitaux excédentaires, à savoir, certaines entreprises – surtout dans le secteur des technologies de l'information et des communications et celui des télécommunications – auraient engagé des investissements

also have had some impact on slower capital spending. Investment does not only imply capital expenditure, but can also include various types of financial investment. This can include increased liquidity and/or decreased debt.

Another such investment is the indirect method of adding to a firm's productive capital by acquiring other firms, so as to achieve an overall reduction in operating costs, assume larger market share or to become more vertically or horizontally integrated to take advantage of medium-term opportunities. It could be argued that corporate takeovers are a more efficient means of acquiring capital, so as to avoid excess capacity in the face of fluctuating demand. Increased inter-company investment has been observed in recent years, with a great deal of this investment having taken place abroad. Does this suggest that with globalization firms may be shifting production offshore, attracted by lower costs or emerging markets outside of Canada?

(iii) ... but investment has picked up in 2005

In short, it might be that firms have been waiting for more profitable investment opportunities to arise, given economic uncertainties and the stock market correction of recent years, and thus have been exhibiting increased caution in their domestic capital spending plans. However, this appears to be changing.

Notably, quarterly data for 2005 have shown a firming in business capital expenditure, and there are indications that Canada is in the early stages of an upswing in the investment cycle. If a pick-up in investment is in the cards, it is certainly supported by the relative strength of corporate financial positions in aggregate, as evidenced in this note. An obvious conclusion, at this point, is that Canadian corporations are well positioned to participate in the next investment boom.

Evidence suggests that long upswings in investment are generally preceded by periods of lower corporate leverage and accompanied by increases in corporate leverage. The cycle of strong real business investment in the 1960s (1961-1966) was characterized by historically low corporate leverage and high liquidity; the growth in real business capital spending in the 1968-1974 period was ushered in by relatively low levels of corporate leverage; and, the recovery in business investment after the 1981-1982 recession was precipitated by a sharp drop in debt-to-equity, as was the pick-up in 1993. The only departure with established history is that corporate leverage has continued to slide since 1992, largely due to a strong demand for corporate shares and undistributed earnings growth.

excessifs entre la fin des années 1990 et le début du nouveau millénaire. Par ailleurs, l'évolution des objectifs des sociétés a aussi pu freiner en quelque sorte les dépenses en capital. L'investissement ne signifie pas uniquement des dépenses en capital. En effet, la notion peut englober différents types de mises de fonds, notamment la hausse des liquidités et la diminution de l'endettement.

L'investissement s'étend également à la méthode indirecte qui consiste à accroître le capital productif d'une entreprise par l'acquisition de sociétés, afin de réduire globalement ses frais d'exploitation, d'augmenter sa part de marché à court terme ou d'opérer une intégration verticale ou horizontale afin de profiter d'occasions à moyen terme. D'aucuns pourraient soutenir que la prise de contrôle est un moyen efficient d'acquérir du capital qui permet d'éviter la capacité excédentaire lorsque la demande fluctue. Une autre hausse de l'investissement entre sociétés a été constatée ces dernières années, dont une bonne part a eu lieu à l'étranger. Cela laisse-t-il entendre que, par suite de la mondialisation, des entreprises transfèrent leur production à l'étranger, attirées par de faibles coûts ou des marchés en émergence?

(iii) ... mais l'investissement a repris en 2005

En peu de mots, il se peut que les entreprises aient attendu des occasions d'investissement profitables, compte tenu de la conjoncture incertaine et du rajustement des marchés boursiers des dernières années. Par conséquent, elles font preuve de prudence lorsqu'elles établissent leurs plans de dépenses en capital intérieures. Cela dit, il semble que la situation soit en train de changer.

Fait à noter, les données trimestrielles de 2005 révèlent une reprise des dépenses en capital des entreprises, et des signes portent à croire que le Canada se situe au stade préliminaire d'une remontée du cycle d'investissement. Si une reprise de l'investissement est à prévoir, elle est certainement supportée par la robustesse relative des positions financières des sociétés dans l'ensemble, comme en témoigne le présent document. Il est fondé de conclure, à ce moment, que les sociétés canadiennes sont en bonne posture pour participer au prochain boom de l'investissement.

Des faits probants portent à croire que les longues remontées de l'investissement sont généralement précédées de périodes de faible endettement des entreprises et accompagnées de hausses de l'endettement. Le cycle de fort investissement réel des entreprises des années 1960 (de 1961 à 1966) a été caractérisé par un niveau historiquement faible d'endettement et de forts taux de liquidité. La croissance des dépenses en capital réelles des entreprises de la période de 1968 à 1974 a été annoncée par des niveaux relativement faibles d'endettement. Par ailleurs, la reprise de l'investissement des entreprises au lendemain de la récession de 1981-1982 a été précipitée par une chute rapide du ratio d'endettement, comme l'a été la remontée de 1993. Le seul écart à signaler par rapport aux faits historiques est la glissade régulière de l'endettement des entreprises depuis 1992, à mettre surtout sur le compte d'une forte demande d'actions et de la croissance des bénéfices non répartis.

Source: "Recent Trends in Corporate Finance", from the Statistics Canada publication "Canadian Economic Observer," Catalogue no. 11-010-XIB, April 2006, pages 3.22 to 3.31, URL: http://www.statcan.ca/english/freepub/11-010-XIB/0040611-010-XIB.pdf

Operating Profits by Major Industry

		2005	2006	2004	2005				2006			
				IV	I	II	III	IV	I	II	III	IV
	$'000,000											
Total	*634671*	215,893	231,668	49,136	50,696	52,995	54,597	57,606	56,392	56,807	58,787	59,681
Primary (including oil and gas)	*(634968+26619542+26619582)*	36,734	38,037	7,109	7,579	8,810	9,914	10,430	9,644	9,686	9,736	8,970
Utilities	*635265*	11,412	11,693	751	790	756	721	975	764	726	608	708
Manufacturing	*635463*	42,012	42,290	10,710	10,428	10,255	10,269	11,059	10,473	9,886	10,917	11,014
Construction	*635364*	6,904	9,691	1,518	1,666	1,657	1,676	1,904	1,982	2,212	2,648	2,850
Transportation	*635760*	10,866	11,266	2,336	2,341	2,768	2,839	2,919	2,771	2,759	2,787	2,948
Trade	*(635562+635661)*	12,693	14,889	5,861	6,103	6,243	6,728	7,196	7,191	7,749	7,738	8,157
Finance, insurance and real estate	*(635958+634869+637146)*	115,197	..	24,468	27,852	27,039	29,721	30,586	..	..	..	..
Administrative and support	*636255*	2,984	3,191	711	695	602	787	899	837	731	855	768
Professional and related	*636057*	3,533	3,767	889	783	961	892	897	929	1,032	884	922
Info. and recreation	*(635859+636552)*	8,698	9,014	1,827	2,153	2,342	2,242	1,962	2,052	2,265	2,263	2,434
Accomm. and food	*636651*	1,598	1,214	514	431	420	339	409	367	325	246	275
Education and healthcare	*26619622*	3,626	3,687	915	910	920	908	888	914	928	910	935
Other services	*636750*	1,502	1,503	351	351	355	369	427	380	384	347	392

Source: Quarterly Financial Statistics for Enterprises, (Catalogue no. 61-008-XIE), contact: B. Potter (613-951-2662).
CANSIM table: 187-0002

Quarterly Financial Statistics for Enterprises

2006 and fourth quarter 2006 (preliminary)

Canadian corporations earned record high operating profits of $231.7 billion in 2006, led by solid growth in the wholesale, retail and construction industries. Depository credit intermediaries (mainly chartered banks) also turned in a sizeable profit gain for the year, while manufacturing profits were little changed.

Another record year for profits

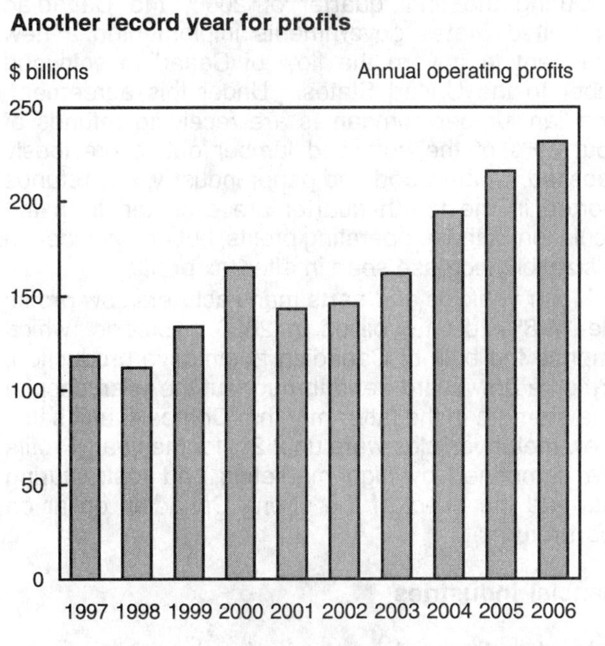

Overall, operating profits increased 7.3% in 2006, down from double-digit growth in the previous two years.

In the fourth quarter, profit growth continued with a 1.5% increase, following a 3.5% gain in the third quarter. Despite the more modest increase, fourth quarter operating profits of $59.7 billion were at record high levels. Profits had previously shown a slight decline over the first two quarters of 2006.

Fourth quarter oil and gas profits weakened, as crude oil prices fell back from their early summer peak. In the manufacturing sector, higher profits of motor vehicle and parts manufacturers were offset by price-led declines in the petroleum refining industry.

In the financial sector, the depository credit intermediaries were the biggest winners for the fourth quarter, while insurance companies reported little overall change in profits.

> ***Note to readers***
>
> *These quarterly financial statistics are based upon a sample survey and represent the activities of all corporations in Canada, except those that are government controlled or not-for-profit. An enterprise can be a single corporation or a family of corporations under common ownership and control for which consolidated financial statements are produced.*
>
> *Operating profits represent the pre-tax profits earned from normal business activities, excluding interest expense on borrowing and valuation adjustments. For non-financial industries, operating profits exclude interest and dividend revenue and capital gains/losses. For financial industries, interest and dividend revenue, capital gains/losses and interest paid on deposits are included in the calculation of operating profits.*
>
> *After-tax profits represent the bottom-line profits earned by corporations.*

Profitable year for retailers and wholesalers

Strong consumer spending propelled operating profits in the retail sector to a record high $14.3 billion, up 20.2% over 2005. Sales jumped 4.5% for the year, as upbeat employment levels, historically low interest rates and high consumer confidence continued to stimulate activity in retail showrooms.

Clothing and general merchandise stores earned $3.9 billion in 2006, up from $2.5 billion in 2005. Furniture, home furnishings and appliance stores earned $1.3 billion, a 41.1% improvement over 2005 profits.

Wholesalers' profits of $16.6 billion were up 15.1% over 2005. The largest gains were seen in wholesalers of motor vehicles (+39.5%), building materials (+25.4%) and machinery and equipment (+22.9%).

Robust activity lifts construction profits in 2006

Operating profits in the construction industry jumped to $9.7 billion in 2006 from $6.9 billion the previous year. Thriving demand for residential and non-residential space in Western Canada lifted the value of building permits to new highs.

Housing starts, as measured by the Canada Mortgage and Housing Corporation, fluctuated throughout the year but showed an annual increase. Engineering and repair construction activity remained strong.

High commodity prices bolster oil and gas and metal mining profits

Oil and gas extraction companies' profits exceeded $31 billion for the first time ever in 2006, up 2.3% over 2005 levels. Crude oil prices peaked in the summer of 2006, but retreated in the latter portion of the year due to high inventories and softening demand. Nonetheless, average crude prices for 2006 were well ahead of 2005, spearheading the gain in annual profits. Natural gas prices were strong early in the year, but fell back considerably as the year wore on.

Mining companies also enjoyed a banner year in 2006, as operating profits jumped 12.0% to $4.7 billion. Strong demand from China and other export markets kept inventories low, propelling non-ferrous metal prices to record highs during the year.

Manufacturing profits little changed in 2006

Operating profits of manufacturers showed little growth in 2006, edging up to $42.3 billion from $42.0 billion in the previous year. Returns on export sales were hampered by the strong Canadian dollar, which peaked around 90 US cents in the spring of 2006, compared to an average of 82.5 US cents in 2005. However, 2006 results may point to a bottoming out of the manufacturing sector, following a 7.0% slide in 2005.

Demand for Canadian goods from the US market was sluggish. The survey of Canadian international merchandise trade recently reported that total exports to the United States registered their first annual decline in three years. However, exports to other countries rose considerably.

Overall manufacturing shipments for 2006 slipped 0.6%, as measured by the Monthly Survey of Manufacturing.

Manufacturers of computers and electronic products were a bright spot, as profits of $2.7 billion reflected a 64.1% increase over 2005 levels. Operating profits have steadily grown since losses were registered in 2002. This industry includes manufacturers of communications equipment and audio and video equipment, which have been in high demand over the past few years.

Primary metal manufacturers reaped the benefit of strong commodity prices and earned $4.3 billion in 2006, a 13.9% gain over 2005 profits.

On the down side, wood and paper companies lost ground in 2006, as profits were trimmed by lower prices, a softer US housing market, high fuel costs and the strong Canadian dollar. Operating profits declined 16.0% to $3.3 billion. Paper producers continued to struggle with shrinking North American newsprint markets.

During the final quarter of 2006, the Canadian and United States governments implemented a new agreement to govern the flow of Canadian softwood lumber to the United States. Under this agreement, Canadian lumber companies are receiving refunds of about 80% of the softwood lumber duties previously deposited. In the wood and paper industry, any refunds reported in the fourth quarter are excluded from the calculation of these operating profits, but are included in the sizeable increase seen in after-tax profits.

Motor vehicles and parts manufacturers saw profits slide 14.8% to $1.5 billion in 2006. Exports, which comprise the bulk of Canadian automotive production, were on a downward trend throughout the year, despite some strength in the latter months. Domestic unit sales of new motor vehicles were up 2.2% for the year. Profits were dampened by high marketing and restructuring costs and the effect of the strong Canadian dollar on export returns.

Financial industries

In the financial sector, the depository credit intermediaries led the way with profits rising 14.3% to $26.4 billion in 2006. Profits were boosted by higher net interest income stemming from growth in mortgage and non-mortgage loans such as credit cards and consumer and corporate loans. Profits also benefited from trading gains derived from equity markets, higher volumes in treasury and investment banking as well as wealth management.

Insurance carriers earned $13.9 billion of operating profits in 2006, up 8.2% over 2005 levels. Both life insurers (+5.9%) and property and casualty insurers (+11.3%) contributed to the profit gains.

Non-depository credit intermediaries' profits rose 9.5% to $7.5 billion.

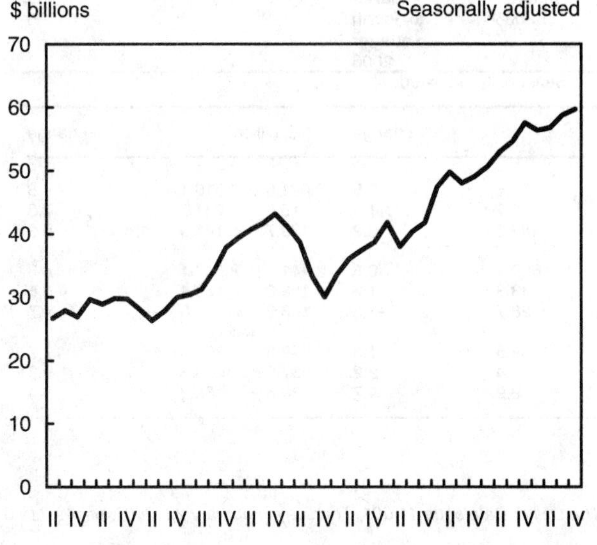

Quarterly growth slows but profits still at record levels

In the fourth quarter, all-industry operating profits increased 1.5% to a record $59.7 billion, following a 3.5% increase in the third quarter. Profits have risen in all but 3 of the past 20 quarters, posting record highs along the way.

In the non-financial sector, gains in 14 of the 17 industries lifted profits by 1.3% to $43.3 billion. The financial sector profits increased 2.2% to $16.4 billion.

The biggest fourth quarter profit swing was in the oil and gas industry, as operating profits declined to $7.2 billion from $8.0 billion in the third quarter. Crude oil prices fell back from the lofty highs of the summer and export demand eased. Natural gas export prices bottomed in October at less than half of the record high prices reaped in the fourth quarter of 2005.

Manufacturing profits edged up 0.9% to $11.0 billion. A price-led decline in petroleum and coal profits was largely offset by higher profits by motor vehicles and parts producers. While domestic and export demand for motor vehicles showed resilience in the fourth quarter, most of the profit increase was due to unusually large restructuring and marketing charges booked in the third quarter.

Wholesalers earned $4.3 billion in fourth quarter profits, up 5.2% from the third quarter. Retailers kept pace as their profits advanced 5.7% to a record high $3.8 billion.

Profits in the transportation and warehousing industry grew by 5.8% to $2.9 billion in the fourth quarter, matching the record highs posted in the final quarter of 2005. Airlines benefited from strong passenger load factors, as travelers eagerly took to the skies. In addition, transportation carriers were helped by lower fuel costs in the fourth quarter.

In the financial sector, the depository credit intermediaries earned $7.2 billion, up from $6.9 billion in the third quarter. Higher revenues were driven by gains in personal and commercial banking as well as efficiencies from some broad restructuring.

Insurance carriers showed little overall change in operating profits for the quarter. Life insurers reported a 2.3% increase in fourth quarter profits to $1.3 billion. Property and casualty insurers' profits slipped 1.3% to $1.8 billion.

Profitability ratios

The operating profit margin increased for a fifth consecutive year in 2006, rising to 8.2% from 8.0% in 2005. However, a sizeable gain in total equity trimmed the 2006 return on average shareholders' equity to 11.2% from 11.5% in 2005. Nonetheless, it remained well above the recent low return of 5.7% earned in 2002.

In the fourth quarter, the operating profit margin edged up to 8.4% from 8.3% in the third quarter. The return on shareholders' equity fell to 10.8% in the fourth quarter from 11.0% in the previous quarter.

Available on CANSIM: tables 187-0001 and 187-0002.

Definitions, data sources and methods: survey number 2501.

The fourth quarter 2006 issue of the *Quarterly Financial Statistics for Enterprises* (61-008-XWE, free) will soon be available.

Financial statistics for enterprises for the first quarter of 2007 will be released on May 24.

For more information or to order data, contact Louise Noel (toll–free 1-888-811-6235; 613-951-2604; *louise.noel@statcan.ca*), Client Services. To enquire about the concepts, methods, or data quality of this release, contact Bill Potter (613-951-2662; *bill.potter@statcan.ca*), Danielle Lafontaine-Sorgo (613-951-2634; *danielle.lafontaine-sorgo@statcan.ca*), or Richard Dornan (613-951-2650; *dornan@statcan.ca*), Industrial Organization and Finance Division.

Quarterly financial statistics for enterprises

	Fourth quarter 2005[r]	Third quarter 2006[r]	Fourth quarter 2006[p]	Third quarter to fourth quarter 2006	2005[r]	2006[p]	2005 to 2006
	Seasonally adjusted						
	$ billions			% change	$ billions		% change
All Industries							
Operating revenue	693.9	711.8	708.6	-0.5	2,691.0	2,816.1	4.6
Operating profit	57.6	58.8	59.7	1.5	215.9	231.7	7.3
After-tax profit	37.3	36.5	36.6	0.2	139.7	146.9	5.2
Non-financial							
Operating revenue	630.3	643.2	639.1	-0.6	2,441.2	2,547.1	4.3
Operating profit	42.5	42.8	43.3	1.3	158.0	168.4	6.6
After-tax profit	27.7	27.1	26.7	-1.3	103.2	108.0	4.7
Financial							
Operating revenue	63.6	68.6	69.5	1.3	249.8	269.0	7.7
Operating profit	15.1	16.0	16.4	2.2	57.9	63.3	9.3
After-tax profit	9.6	9.4	9.9	4.7	36.5	38.9	6.4

r *revised*
p *preliminary*

Source: "Quarterly Financial Statistics for Enterprises", from the Statistics Canada publication "The Daily", Catalogue 11-001, Thursday, February 22, 2007, pages 2 to 5
URL: http://www.statcan.ca/Daily/English/070222/d070222.pdf

MAJOR CANADIAN COMPANIES

Major Companies

Agriculture

Agricore United Ltd.
CabWest Global Place
PO Box 6600, 201 Portage Ave.
Winnipeg, MB R3C 3A7
204-944-5411 Fax: 204-944-5454
infomaster@agricoreunited.com
www.agricoreunited.com
Company Type: Public
Profile: Wholesalers of grain & field beans, & farm supplies; farm product warehousing & storage

Brian Hayward, CEO
Peter Cox, CFO
David Carefoot, Chief Information Officer
Glen Black, Manager, Environment, Safety & Risk

Bennett Environmental Inc.
#208, 1540 Cornwall Rd.
Oakville, ON L6J 7W5
905-339-1540 Fax: 905-339-0016 800-386-1388
info@bennettenv.com
www.bennettenv.com
Ticker Symbol: BEV.TO
Company Type: Public
Profile: The company is engaged in contaminated soil remediation.

Jack Shaw, President/CEO
jshaw@bennett-env.com
Fred Cranston, Chief Financial Officer
fcranston@bennettenv.com
Michael B. McSweeney, Vice-President, Environmental Affairs & Government Relations
mmcsweeney@bennettenv.com

RIDLEY Inc.
17 Speers Rd.
Winnipeg, MB R2J 1M1
204-956-1717 Fax: 204-956-1687
guest@ridleyinc.com
www.ridleyinc.com
Ticker Symbol: RCL
Company Type: Public
Profile: Manufacturers & distributors of formulated animal feeds & animal health products

Robert B. Gallaway, President/CEO
Mike Mitchell, CFO
Larry Fraser, Manager, Information Technology
Garry Connors, Manager, Health & Safety

Saskatchewan Wheat Pool
2625 Victoria Ave.
Regina, SK S4T 7T9
306-569-4411 Fax: 306-569-4708
investor@swp.com
www.swp.com
Ticker Symbol: SWP
Company Type: Public
Profile: Wholesalers of grain & oil seeds, farm product raw materials, farm supplies, nitrogenous fertilizers; Manufacturers of flour & other grain mill products

Mayo Schmidt, President & CEO
Terry Baker, Chairman
Wayne Cheeseman, CFO

Stolt Sea Farm Inc.
#513, 4100 Yonge St.
Toronto, ON M2P 2B5
416-221-0404 Fax: 416-221-4010
info@stoltseafarm.com
www.stoltseafarm.com
Company Type: Private
Profile: Agricultural production & animal aquaculture; Commercial fishing in fish hatcheries & preserves

John Taylor, CEO
James Gracie, President
Joseph Ruffo, Vice-President & Controller
John Larsen, Chief Information Officer

United Farmers of Alberta Co-Operative Limited
PO Box 5350 A, 1016 - 68 Ave. SW
Calgary, AB T2H 2J9
403-258-4500 Fax: 403-258-7630
mbr.relations@ufa.com
www.ufa.net
Company Type: Public
Profile: Wholesalers of farm & garden machinery & equipment, farm supplies, motor vehicle supplies & new parts; Retailing in gasoline service stations

Dallas Thorsteinson, President/CEO
Bill Gantous, CFO
Rob Kellas, Chief Information Officer
Eric Krautheim, Director, Engineering, Environment & Safety

W.G. Thompson & Sons Ltd.
2 Hyland Dr.
Blenheim, ON N0P 1A0
519-676-5411 Fax: 519-676-3185 **Company Type:** Private
Profile: Grain dealers; Multi-crop breeding & research

W.T. Thompson, CEO
D.W. Chapple, Secretary/CFO/Treasurer

Business & Computer Services

724 Solutions Inc.
#201, 20 York Mills Rd.
Toronto, ON M2P 2C2
416-226-2900 Fax: 416-226-4456 www.724.com
Ticker Symbol: SVN
Company Type: Public
Profile: Computer integrated systems design; Prepackaged software; Computer related services

John Sims, CEO
Glenn Barrett, CFO & Sr. Vice-President, Corporate Services

ACD Systems International Inc.
PO Box 36, Saanichton, BC V8M 2C3
250-544-6700 Fax: 250-544-0291
ir@acdsystems.com
www.acdsystems.com
Ticker Symbol: ASA
Company Type: Public
Profile: Image management & technical illustration software

Doug Vandekerkhove, Chair/CEO
Shari Gauthier, Vice-President, Finance
Dianne Escudé, Director, Marketing Communications
David S. Hooper, Chief Technology Officer

ADB Systems International Inc.
#300, 302 The East Mall
Toronto, ON M9B 6C7
416-640-0400 888-287-7467
info@adbsys.com
www.adbsys.com
Ticker Symbol: ADY
Company Type: Public
Profile: Information retrieval services; Computer programming services; Retailing in miscellaneous stores

Jeff Lymburner, CEO
James Moskos, President, ADB Technologies Group
Michael Robb, Director, Finance

Adobe Systems Canada Inc.
785 Carling Ave.
Ottawa, ON K1S 5H4
613-940-3676 Fax: 613-594-8886 866-341-2256
info@adobe.com
www.accelio.com
Company Type: Public
Profile: Imaging, design & document technology software

Bruce Chizen, President/CEO
Murray Demo, CFO & Sr. Vice-President

Apple Canada Inc.
7495 Birchmount Rd.
Markham, ON L3R 5G2
905-513-5800 Fax: 905-477-6305 www.apple.ca
Company Type: Private
Profile: Computer integrated systems design; computer related services

Wendy Hayes, CEO & Director, Sales
Steve Job, President
John Hagias, Vice-President, Finance & Operations
Ayube Rahaman, Manager, Information Systems & Telecommunications
Zandra Zarris, Manager, Facilities

ArtQuest International Alliances Inc.
#290, 2525, boul Daniel-Johnson
Laval, QC H7T 1S9
450-681-1150 Fax: 450-681-1037
info@artquest.ca
www.artquest.ca
Ticker Symbol: AQ
Company Type: Public
Profile: Prepackaged software

Richard Corbo, CEO
Melanie Gareau, Controller
Guy Le Henaff, Chief Technology Officer

ATI Technologies Inc.
1 Commerce Valley Dr. East
Markham, ON L3T 7X6
905-882-2600 Fax: 905-882-2620 www.ati.com
Ticker Symbol: ATY
Company Type: Public
Profile: Computer integrated systems design; Commercial art & graphic design

K.Y. Ho, Chairman/CEO
David Orton, President/COO
Terry Nickerson, CFO & Sr. Vice-President, Finance

Axia NetMedia Corporation
#3300, 450 - 1st St. SW
Calgary, AB T2P 5H1
403-538-4000 Fax: 403-538-4100
info@axia.com
www.axia.com
Ticker Symbol: AXX
Company Type: Public
Profile: Prepackaged software; Computer integrated systems design; Information retrieval services

Art Price, Chair/CEO
Murray Wallace, President
Peter McKeown, CFO
Dave Stack, Manager, Information Technology

BCE Emergis Inc.
#600, 1000, rue de Sérigny
Longueuil, QC J4K 5B1
450-928-6000 Fax: 450-928-6344
866-363-7447www.emergis.com
Ticker Symbol: IFM
Company Type: Public
Profile: Computer processing & data preparation & processing services; Prepackaged software; Computer programming services

François Côté, President/CEO
Robert Comeau, CFO
René Poirier, Chief Technology Officer

Belzberg Technologies Inc.
#3400, 40 King St. West
Toronto, ON M5H 3Y2
416-360-1812 Fax: 416-360-0039 800-823-8631
sales@belzberg.com
www.belzberg.com
Ticker Symbol: BLZ
Company Type: Public
Profile: Computer integrated systems design; Information retrieval services

Belzberg Technologies Inc. (continued)
S.H. Belzberg, Chair/President/CEO & Director
J. Stephen Wilson, CFO & Director

Bioscrypt Inc.
505 Cochrane Dr.
Markham, ON L3R 8E3
905-940-7750 Fax: 905-940-7642
snsales@bioscrypt.com
www.bioscrypt.com
Ticker Symbol: BYT
Company Type: Public
Profile: Security systems services; Patent owners & lessors

Pierre Donaldson, President/CEO
Bruce MacInnis, CFO/Vice-President, Administration & Finance
Colin Soutar, Chief Technology Officer

Burntsand Inc
#201, 300 The East Mall
Toronto, ON M9B 6B7
416-234-3800 Fax: 416-234-3801
info@burntsand.com
www.burntsand.com
Ticker Symbol: BRT
Company Type: Public
Profile: Computer integrated systems design

James Yeates, President/CEO
Blair Baxter, CFO

Calian Technology Ltd.
2 Beaverbrook Rd.
Ottawa, ON K2K 1L1
613-599-8600 Fax: 613-599-8650 877-225-4264
info@calian.com
www.calian.com
Ticker Symbol: CTY
Company Type: Public
Profile: Employment agencies; Help supply services; Management consulting services; Business consulting services

Larry O'Brien, Chair/CEO
Ray Basler, President/COO
Jacqueline Gauthier, CFO
Jerry Johnston, Chief Information Officer

Cedara Software Corp.
6509 Airport Rd.
Mississauga, ON L4V 1S7
905-672-2100 Fax: 905-672-2307 800-724-5970
info@cedara.com
www.cedara.com
Ticker Symbol: CDE
Company Type: Public
Profile: Prepackaged software; Computer integrated systems design; Commercial physical & biological research

Abe Schwartz, CEO
Fraser Sinclair, CFO & Corporate Secretary

Certicom Corp.
5520 Explorer Dr., 4th Fl.
Mississauga, ON L4W 5L1
905-507-4220 Fax: 905-507-4230 800-561-6100
info@certicom.com
www.certicom.com
Company Type: Public
Profile: Manufacturers of computer peripheral equipment; programming services; integrated systems design

Ian McKinnon, President/CEO
Hervé Séguin, CFO
Kevin Tsang, Director, Information Technology
Paula Cowie, Office Manager

Cognos Incorporated
PO Box 9707 T, 3755 Riverside Dr.
Ottawa, ON K1G 4K9
613-738-1440 Fax: 613-738-0002 800-267-2777
ir@cognos.com
www.cognos.com
Ticker Symbol: CSN
Company Type: Public
Profile: Prepackaged software; Computer related services

Ron Zambonini, CEO
Robert G. Ashe, President/COO
Tom Manley, CFO & Sr. Vice-President, Finance & Administration
Rob Collins, Chief Information Officer/Vice-President, Information Services

Compugen Systems Ltd.
25 Leek Cres.
Richmond Hill, ON L4B 4B3
905-707-2000 Fax: 905-707-2020 800-387-5045
info@compugen.com
www.compugen.com
Company Type: Private
Profile: Information technology

Harry Zarek, President/CEO
David Austin, CFO
Dean Reid, Manager, Information Systems

Corel Corporation
1600 Carling Ave.
Ottawa, ON K1Z 8R7
800-772-6735www.corel.com
Company Type: Public
Profile: Provides software solutions to businesses & consumers in over 75 countries to improve their productivity

David Dobson, CEO
Douglas R. McCollam, Chief Financial Officer
Graham Brown, Exec. Vice-President, Software Development

Cossette Communication Group Inc.
#200, 801 Grande Allee Ouest
Québec, QC G1S 1C1
418-647-2727 Fax: 418-647-2564
investor@cossette.com
www.cossette.com
Ticker Symbol: KOS
Company Type: Public
Profile: Company offers a full range of communication services to clients of all sizes

Claude Lessard, Chair/CEO
Richard Hadden, President, Cossette West
Jean Royer, Vice-President/CFO

CryptoLogic Inc.
55 St. Clair Ave. West, 3rd. Fl.
Toronto, ON M4V 2Y7
416-545-1455 Fax: 416-545-1454
investor.relations@cryptologic.com
www.cryptologic.com
Ticker Symbol: CRY
Company Type: Public
Profile: Prepackaged software; Computer programming services; Internet Software Development & Management

Lewis Rose, President/CEO
James A. Ryan, CFO
Nancy Chan-Palmateer, Director, Communications
Michael Starzynski, Chief Technology Officer

Cyberplex Inc.
267 Richmond St. West
Toronto, ON M5V 2Y6
416-597-8889 Fax: 416-597-2345 888-597-8889
investor@cyberplex.com
www.cyberplex.com
Ticker Symbol: CX
Company Type: Public
Profile: Offices of holding companies; Computer integrated systems design; Information retrieval services; Software development

W. Dean Hopkins, CEO & Director
Geoffrey Rotstein, CFO
Peter Bier, Vice-President, Production

Cybersurf Corp.
#300, 1144 - 29 Ave. NE
Calgary, AB T2E 7P1
403-777-2000 Fax: 403-777-2003 888-858-8958
investor.relations@cybersurf.com
www.cybersurf.com
Ticker Symbol: CY
Company Type: Public
Profile: Computer programming services; Information retrieval services; Computer related services

Paul Mercia, President/CEO & Director
Russell Holmes, Controller
Jason Finney, Vice-President, Product Development

DataMirror Corporation
#1100, 3100 Steeles Ave. East
Markham, ON L3R 8T3
905-415-0310 Fax: 905-415-0340 800-362-5955
info@datamirror.com
www.datamirror.com
Ticker Symbol: DMC
Company Type: Public
Profile: Computer programming services; Prepackaged software

Nigel Stokes, President/CEO & Chair
Peter Cauley, CFO
Judy Parkes, Vice-President, Technical Services

The Descartes Systems Group Inc.
120 Randall Dr.
Waterloo, ON N2V 1C6
519-746-8110 Fax: 519-747-0082 800-419-8495
info@descartes.com
www.descartes.com
Ticker Symbol: DSG
Company Type: Public
Profile: Prepackaged software; Computer programming services

Arthur Mescher, CEO
Brandon Nussey, CFO
Chris Jones, Exec. Vice-President, Solutions & Markets

DIEBOLD Company of Canada
6630 Campobello Rd.
Mississauga, ON L5N 2L8
905-817-7600 Fax: 905-813-7380 888-545-9444
infocanada@diebold.com
www.dieboldcanada.com
Company Type: Private
Profile: Information technology & security software

Walden W. O'Dell, Chair/President & CEO, Diebold
Michael J. Hillock, President, Diebold International
Gregory T. Geswein, Sr. Vice-President & CFO

Diversinet Corp.
#1801, 2225 Sheppard Ave. East
Toronto, ON M2J 5C2
416-756-2324 Fax: 416-756-7346 800-357-7050
info@diversinet.com
www.diversinet.com
Company Type: Public
Profile: Computer integrated systems design

Nagy Moustafa, President/CEO
David Hackett, CFO
Atul Parikh, President, DSS Software Technologies

easyhome Ltd.
10239 - 178 St.
Edmonton, AB T5S 1M3
780-930-3000 Fax: 780-481-7426
888-528-3279www.easyhome.ca
Ticker Symbol: RTO
Company Type: Public
Profile: Equipment rental & leasing

David Ingram, President/CEO
S. William Johnson, CFO & Exec. Vice-President

EDS Canada Inc.
#500, 33 Yonge St.
Toronto, ON M5E 1G4
416-814-4500 Fax: 416-814-4600 800-814-9038
infvest@eds.com
www.eds.com
Company Type: Private
Profile: Global technology services company; information technology; business process outsourcing services

John Dowd, President
Peter Watkins, Financial Services Practice & Managing Partner

Eicon Networks Corporation
9800, boul Cavendish
Montréal, QC H4M 2V9
514-745-5500 Fax: 514-745-5588 www.eicon.com
Company Type: Private
Profile: Prepackaged software; computer related services; manufacturers of computer terminals

Nick Jensen, President/CEO
Jean Gagnon, CFO
Andrew Knechtel, Manager, Network

EMJ Data Systems Ltd.
PO Box 1012 Main, Guelph, ON N1H 6N1

519-837-2444 Fax: 519-836-1914 877-365-3282
info@emj.ca
www.emj.ca
Ticker Symbol: EMJ
Company Type: Public
Profile: Wholesalers of computers & peripheral equipment & software; Prepackaged software; Computer related services

James A. Estill, President/CEO
Glen R. Estill, Vice-President/CFO
Mark Tanner, Director, Information Services
Jim Albanese, Chief Technology Officer

Envoy Communications Group Inc.
172 John St.
Toronto, ON M5T 1X5
416-593-9070 Fax: 416-593-4434 866-883-6869
info@envoy.to
www.envoy.to
Ticker Symbol: ECG
Company Type: Public
Profile: Advertising agencies; Commercial art & graphic design; Information retrieval services; Computer related services

Geoffrey B. Genovese, Chair/CEO
J.J. Leeder, Vice-President/CFO
Ash Khan, Director, IT

Epic Data International Inc.
6300 River Rd.
Richmond, BC V6X 1X5
604-273-9146 Fax: 604-273-1830 877-332-3792
info@epicdata.com
www.epicdata.com
Ticker Symbol: EKD
Company Type: Public
Profile: Computer programming services; Prepackaged software

Peter Murphy, President/CEO
James Code, CFO
Leigh Pullen, Chief Information Officer

GT Group Telecom Inc.
#1500, 1066 West Hastings St.
Vancouver, BC V6E 3X1
604-681-6822 Fax: 604-684-0291 www.gt.ca
Ticker Symbol: GTG
Company Type: Public
Profile: Information retrieval services; Telephone communications, except radiotelephone

D.R. Millard, CEO
Tal Bevan, President, Business Operations
S.H. Shoemaker, Exec. Vice-President & CFO

Hartco Corporation
9393, Louis H. Lafontaine
Montréal, QC H1J 1Y8
514-354-3810 Fax: 514-354-2299
information2@hartco.com
www.hartco.com
Ticker Symbol: HCC
Company Type: Public
Profile: Computer integrated systems design; Retails-computer and computer software stores; Retails-miscellaneous retail stores

Harry Hart, Chairman/CEO
Mark Rabinovitch, President, Communication Division
Marc D'Amour, Vice-President & CFO

Hip Interactive Corp.
240 Superior Blvd.
Mississauga, ON L5T 2L2
905-362-3760 Fax: 905-362-1995
jlee@hipinteractive.com
www.hipinteractive.com
Ticker Symbol: HP
Company Type: Public
Profile: Prepackaged software; Retails: hobby, toy, & game shops; Coin-operated amusement devices; Mfrs: miscellaneous publishing; PC & video game distribution

Arindra Singh, President/CEO
Peter Lee, CFO
Michael Vasmani, Chief Information Officer

Hummingbird Ltd.
1 Sparks Ave.
Toronto, ON M2H 2W1
416-496-2200 Fax: 416-496-2207 800-400-6544
support@opentext.com
www.hummingbird.com
Ticker Symbol: HUM
Company Type: Public
Profile: Designer of computer integrated systems; Wholesaler of computers, peripheral equipment & business software

Barry Litwin, President/CEO
Inder P.S. Duggal, CFO/Chief Controller
Alp Hug, Vice-President, Technology Development

Infowave Software Inc.
#200, 4664 Lougheed Hwy.
Burnaby, BC V5C 5T5
604-473-3600 Fax: 604-473-3699 800-463-6928
info@infowave.com
www.infowave.com
Ticker Symbol: IW
Company Type: Public
Profile: Computer programming services; Prepackaged software

George Reznik, CFO
Sal Visca, Chief Technology Officer

Intrinsyc Software Inc.
700 West Pender St., 10th Fl.
Vancouver, BC V6C 1G8
604-801-6461 Fax: 604-801-6417 800-474-7644
invest@intrinsyc.com
www.intrinsyc.com
Ticker Symbol: ICS
Company Type: Public
Profile: Mobility software & services company

Glenda M. Dorchak, Chair/CEO
Chuck Leighton, CFO
Damian Mehers, Chief Software Architect

LGS Group Inc.
#400, 1300, René-Lévesque ouest
Montréal, QC H3G 2W6
514-392-9193 Fax: 514-861-4114 www.lgs.com
Company Type: Private
Profile: Information technology

Jean Bélanger, President/CEO
Zouhair Bahloul, CFO & Vice-President, Finance & Administration
Mario Santerre, Manager, Information Technology

Liquidation World Inc.
3880 - 29 St. NE
Calgary, AB T1Y 6B6
403-250-1222 Fax: 403-291-1306
investorinfo@liquidationworld.com
www.liquidationworld.com
Ticker Symbol: LQW
Company Type: Public
Profile: Business services (various)

Wayne Mantika, President/Co-CEO
Andrew Searby, Exec. Vice President/CFO

MacDonald, Dettwiler & Associates Ltd.
13800 Commerce Pkwy.
Richmond, BC V6V 2J3
604-278-3411 Fax: 604-231-2750
info@mdacorporation.com
www.mda.ca
Ticker Symbol: MDA
Company Type: Public
Profile: Computer integrated systems design; Computer processing & data preparation & processing svcs; Information retrieval services

Daniel E. Friedmann, President/CEO
Anil Wirasekara, Exec. Vice-President/CFO
Peter Louis, Vice-President/General Manager, Information Services
Rick Fox, Manager, Computing & Engineering Services

Mad Catz Canada
2425 Matheson Blvd. East, 7th Fl.
Mississauga, ON L4W 5K4
905-361-2797 Fax: 416-368-7779 www.madcatz.com
Ticker Symbol: MCZ
Company Type: Public
Profile: Distributor & marketer of peripherals for the interactive game industry

Maximizer Software Inc.
1090 West Pender St., 10th Fl.
Vancouver, BC V6E 2N7
604-601-8000 Fax: 604-601-8001
info@maximizer.com
www.maximizer.com
Ticker Symbol: MAX
Company Type: Public
Profile: Prepackaged software

John Caputo, CFO
Tom Bennett, Chief Technical Officer

MDSI Mobile Data Solutions Inc.
10271 Shellbridge Way
Richmond, BC V6X 2W8
604-207-6000 Fax: 604-207-6060 800-294-6374
info@mdsi.ca
www.mdsi-advantex.com
Ticker Symbol: MMD
Company Type: Public
Profile: Computer programming services; Prepackaged software

Erik Dysthe, President/CEO & Chair
Verne Pecho, CFO & Vice-President, Finance & Administration
Oliver Viitamaki, Manager, Information Technology

MedcomSoft Inc.
#900, 1200 Eglinton Ave. East
Toronto, ON M3C 1H9
416-443-8788 Fax: 416-443-9693
info@medcomsoft.com
www.medcomsoft.com
Ticker Symbol: MSF
Company Type: Public
Profile: Computer integrated systems design; Information retrieval services

Sami Aita, Chair/CEO
Nick Clemenzi, Vice-President, Finance
Paul Giampietro, Manager, IT

Mediagrif Interactive Technologies Inc.
#800, 1010, de Sérigny
Longueuil, QC J4K 5G7
450-677-8797 Fax: 450-677-4612
info@mediagrif.com
www.mediagrif.com
Ticker Symbol: MDF
Company Type: Public
Profile: Information retrieval & computer programming services

Denis Gadbois, CEO & Chair
Alain Miquelon, CFO & Vice-President, Corporate Development
Christian Brisson, Vice-President, e-Business Projects

MediSolution Ltd.
110, boul Cremazie ouest, 12e étage
Montréal, QC H2P 1B9
514-850-5000 Fax: 514-850-5005 800-361-4187
paul.roche@medisolution.com
www.medisolution.com
Ticker Symbol: MSH
Company Type: Public
Profile: Healthcare information technology, providing software & services to healthcare customers

Allan D. Lin, President/CEO
Scott J. Boulas, President, U.S. Division
Paul Roche, CFO & Vice-President
Yvan Lafleur, Chief Technology Officer & Vice-President, Development

Mercer Human Resource Consulting LLC
BCE Place
PO Box 501, 161 Bay St.
Toronto, ON M5J 2S5
416-868-2000 Fax: 416-868-7671
866-879-3384www.mercerhr.com
Company Type: Private
Profile: Human resources consulting

Daniel L. McCaw, Chair/CEO
A. McKinney, CFO

Microsoft Canada Co.
1950 Meadowvale Blvd.
Mississauga, ON L5N 8L9
905-568-0434 Fax: 905-568-1527
877-568-2495www.microsoft.ca
Company Type: Private
Profile: Software services & internet technologies

David Hemley, President, Microsoft Corporation

Microtec Enterprises Inc.
4780, rue St-Félix
Saint-Augustin-de-Desmaur, QC G3A 2J9
418-877-2755 Fax: 418-864-7951 866-427-6832
information@microtecsecuri-t.com
www.microtecsecuri-t.com
Ticker Symbol: EMI
Company Type: Public
Profile: Security systems services

Raymond Gilbert, Chair/CFO
Robert Branchaud, President/CEO, Microtec Securi-T Commercial Inc
Michel Gosselin, Exec. Vice-President & CFO
Christian Boutet, Director, IT

Minacs Worldwide Inc.
180 Duncan Mill Rd.
Toronto, ON M3B 1Z6
416-380-3800 Fax: 416-380-3830 888-646-2271
investors@minacs.com
www.minacs.com
Ticker Symbol: MXW
Company Type: Public
Profile: Business process outsourcing solutions in the following areas: contact center solutions, integrated marketing services & program administration

Bruce S. Simmonds, CEO
Bob Cariglia, President/COO
Deb Barrett, Sr. Vice-President/CFO
Keyvan Cohanim, Chief Officer, Sales & Marketing
Eric Greenwood, Sr. Vice-President/Chief Technology Officer

Mindready Solutions Inc.
2800, av Marie-Curie
Montréal, QC H4S 2C2
514-339-1394 Fax: 514-339-1376 877-636-1394
investor@mindready.com
www.mindready.com
Ticker Symbol: MNY
Company Type: Public
Profile: Prepackaged software; Computer integrated systems design

Claude Delage, President/CEO
Marc Lamy, CFO, Finance & Administration

Mitel Networks Corporation
350 Legget Dr.
Kanata, ON K2K 2W7
613-592-2122 Fax: 613-592-4784 www.mitel.com
Ticker Symbol: ZL
Company Type: Private
Profile: Provider of enterprise & small business communications solutions & services

Don Smith, President/CEO
Steve Spooner, CFO

MKS Inc.
410 Albert St.
Waterloo, ON N2L 3V3
519-884-2251 Fax: 519-884-8861 800-265-2797
info@mks.com
www.mks.com
Ticker Symbol: MKX
Company Type: Public
Profile: Computer programming services; Prepackaged software

Philip C. Deck, Chair/CEO
Robert J. Dietrich, CFO

NBS Technologies
#400, 703 Evans Ave.
Toronto, ON M9C 5E9
416-621-1911 Fax: 416-621-8875
info@nbstech.com
www.nbstech.com
Ticker Symbol: MIS
Company Type: Public
Profile: Various business services; Computer integrated systems design; Manufacturers of wireless internet terminals

David Nyland, President/CEO
Michael Galloro, Vice-President, Finance

Nurun Inc.
711, rue de la Commune ouest
Montréal, QC H3C 1X6
514-392-1292 Fax: 514-392-0911 877-696-1292
montreal@nurun.com
www.nurun.com
Ticker Symbol: IFN
Company Type: Public
Profile: Computer integrated systems design; Computer related services

Jacques-Hervé Roubert, President/CEO
Guy Lemieux, CFO
Luc Lalonde, Chief Technology Officer

OnX Enterprise Solutions Inc.
155 Commerce Valley Dr. East
Thornhill, ON L3T 7T2
905-881-4414 Fax: 905-881-6533 800-663-6699
investorrelations@onx.com
www.onx.com
Ticker Symbol: ON
Company Type: Public
Profile: Computer integrated systems design; Information retrieval & Computer related services

Sheldon M. Pollack, CEO
Phillip A. DeLeon, President
Daren G. Selfe, CFO

Open Solutions Canada
#300, 1441 Creekside Dr.
Vancouver, BC V6J 4S7
604-734-7494 Fax: 604-714-2422 800-665-5817
osc-info@opensolutions.com
www.datawest.ca
Ticker Symbol: DS
Company Type: Public
Profile: Offices of holding companies; Computer integrated systems design; Computer related services

D.J. Yea, Chair/CEO
Michael E. Johnson, CFO

Open Text Corporation
275 Frank Tompa Dr.
Waterloo, ON N2L 0A1
519-888-7111 Fax: 519-888-0677 800-499-6544
sales@opentext.com
www.opentext.com
Ticker Symbol: OTC
Company Type: Public
Profile: Prepackaged software; Information retrieval services; Computer integrated systems design

P. Thomas Jenkins, CEO
John Shackelton, President
Alan Hoverd, CFO

Optimal Group Inc.
#1700, 3500, boul de Maisonneuve ouest
Montréal, QC H3Z 3C1
514-738-8885 Fax: 514-738-2284
info@optimalgroup.com
www.optimalgroup.com
Company Type: Public
Profile: Computer integrated systems design; Computer programming services

Neil Wechsler, Co-Chair/CEO/Director
Henry Karp, President/COO/Director
Gary Wechsler, CFO & Treasurer

Optimal Payments
2 Place Alexis Nihon
#700, 3500, boul de Maisonneuve ouest
Montréal, QC H3Z 3C1
514-380-2700 Fax: 514-380-2760
info@optimalpayments.com
www.optimalpayments.com
Ticker Symbol: FIR
Company Type: Public
Profile: Computer processing, data preparation & processing services; Computer facilities management services; Computer integrated systems design

Mitchell A. Garber, President/CEO
Michael Liquornik, Sr. Vice-President/COO
Danny Chazonoff, Sr. Vice-President/Chief Technology Officer

Pason Systems Inc.
6130 - 3 St. SE
Calgary, AB T2H 1K4
403-301-3400 Fax: 403-301-3499
info@pason.com
www.pason.com
Ticker Symbol: PSI
Company Type: Public
Profile: The company is a manufacturer of oil & gas field machinery & equipment. It also provides engineering services.

James Hill, President/CEO
Jim Glasspoole, Chief Financial Officer
David White, Manager, Research & Development

Pivotal CRM / CDC Software
#600, 858 Beatty St.
Vancouver, BC V6B 1C1
604-699-8000 Fax: 604-699-8001 877-748-6825
info@pivotal.com
www.pivotal.com
Ticker Symbol: PVT
Company Type: Public
Profile: The company is engaged in computer integrated systems design.

Eric Musser, President

Professional Computer Consultant Group
#400, 2323 Yonge St.
Toronto, ON M4P 2C9
416-483-0766 Fax: 416-483-8102 800-461-4878
mail@procom.ca
www.procom.ca
Company Type: Private
Profile: Provides IT services to businesses & governments

Frank McCrea, President

Q/Media Services Corporation
13566 Maycrest Way
Richmond, BC V6V 2J7
604-303-6630 Fax: 604-303-6924 800-690-5881
sales@qmedia.ca
www.qmedia.ca
Ticker Symbol: QMS
Company Type: Private
Profile: Prepackaged software; Computer integrated systems design

R.M. Lawrie, President/CEO

Rand Worldwide
5285 Solar Dr.
Mississauga, ON L4W 5B8
905-625-2000 Fax: 905-625-8535
investor@rand.com
www.rand.com
Ticker Symbol: RND
Company Type: Public
Profile: Computer integrated systems design

Frank Baldesarra, President/CEO
Kriss Bush, CFO

Sanchez Computer Associates Inc.
150 York St., 7th Fl.
Toronto, ON M5H 3S5
416-368-7979 Fax: 416-368-7886
info@sanchez.com
www.sanchez.com
Company Type: Private
Profile: Provides integrated software to financial services market

Schlumberger of Canada Ltd.
Eau Clair Place 1
525 - 3rd Ave. SW
Calgary, AB T2P 0G4
403-509-4000 Fax: 403-509-4021 www.slb.com
Company Type: Private
Profile: Supplies products, services & technical solutions to the oil & gas exploration & production industry; Provides information

technology connectivity & security solutions to both the exploration & production industry & to a range of other markets; Provides IT consulting, systems integration, managed services & related products to the oil & gas, telecommunications, energy & utilities, finance, transport & public-sector markets

Catherine Hughes, President & General Manager
Simir Seth, Controllor
Rob Sutherland, Manager, Information Technology
Niel Campbell, Safety Manager

Sierra Systems Group Inc.
#2500, 1177 West Hastings St.
Vancouver, BC V6E 2K3
604-688-1371 Fax: 604-688-6482
davidsmithers@sierrasystems.com
www.sierrasystems.com
Ticker Symbol: SSG
Company Type: Public
Profile: Company is engaged in management consulting, solutions delivery, managed services, justice, health, government & financial services

Iraj Pourian, President/CEO
Warren Beach, CFO & Vice-President
John Broere, Chief Operating Officer

Sonic Solutions
50 West Pearce St.
Richmond Hill, ON L4B 1E3
905-764-7000 Fax: 905-764-7110 866-279-7694
usoemInfo@roxio.com
www.roxio.com
Ticker Symbol: ROXI
Company Type: Public
Profile: Produces digital media software & products

William Christoph Gorog, Chair/CEO
Michael J. Bebel, President/COO, Napster Division
R. Elliot Carpenter, Vice-President/CFO

Sun Microsystems of Canada Inc.
27 Allstate Pkwy., 7th Fl.
Markham, ON L3R 5L7
905-477-6745 Fax: 905-477-9423 www.sun.ca
Company Type: Private
Profile: Provides computing hardware & software; Universal software platform, Java

Andy Canham, President
Li-Kwong Cheah, CFO/Controller
Stéphane Boisvert, Chair/Sr. Vice-President, Client Solutions Organization

SXC Health Solutions, Inc.
555 Industrial Dr.
Milton, ON L9T 5E1
905-876-4741 Fax: 905-878-8869
investors@sxc.com
www.sxc.com
Ticker Symbol: SXC
Company Type: Public
Profile: Provider of healthcare transaction processing services & information technology solutions to the pharmaceutical industry

Gordon S. Glenn, President/CEO
Jeffrey Park, CFO
John Romza, Chief Technology Officer & Sr. Vice-President, Research & Development

TECSYS Inc.
87, rue Prince, 5e étage
Montréal, QC H3C 2M7
514-866-0001 Fax: 514-866-1805 800-922-8649
info@tecsys.com
www.tecsys.com
Ticker Symbol: TCS
Company Type: Public
Profile: Prepackaged software

Peter Brereton, President/Co-CEO
Berty Ho-Wo-Cheong, Vice-President/CFO, Finance & Administration
Robert Colosino, Vice-President, Alliances & Technology Strategy

VOXCOM Incorporated
#102, 4209 - 99 St.
Edmonton, AB T6E 5V7
780-462-1657 Fax: 780-461-8280 800-387-2966
investor.relations@voxcom.com
www.voxcom.com
Ticker Symbol: VOX
Company Type: Public
Profile: Security systems services; Wholesalers of medical, dental, hospital equipment & supplies

Bradley E. Sparrow, President/CEO
Keith Muncy, CFO

Xenos Group Inc.
#201, 95 Mural St.
Richmond Hill, ON L4B 3G2
905-709-1020 Fax: 905-709-1023 888-242-0692
info@xenos.com
www.xenos.com
Ticker Symbol: XNS
Company Type: Public
Profile: Computer programming services; Prepackaged software; Information retrieval services

Stuart J. Butts, Chair/CEO & Director
James T. Farmer, President/COO/Director
Robert Kunihiro, CFO & Vice-President, Finance

Zi Corporation
#2100, 840 - 7 Ave. SW
Calgary, AB T2P 3G2
403-233-8875 Fax: 403-233-8878
info@zicorp.com
www.zicorp.com
Ticker Symbol: ZIC
Company Type: Public
Profile: Offices of holding companies; Prepackaged software

Michael E. Lobsinger, Chair/CEO
Dale Kearns, CFO
Milos Djokovic, COO/Chief Technology Officer

Chemicals

Abbott Laboratories Ltd.
8401, rte Trans-Canada
Saint-Laurent, QC H4S 1Z1
514-832-7000 Fax: 514-832-7800 www.abbott.ca
Company Type: Public
Profile: Manufacturers of pharmaceutical preparations

Marcello Vizio, President
Steve Ramage, Director, Financial Administration
Rosy Bellemare, Director, Information Technology

Acetex Corporation
World Trade Centre
#750, 999 Canada Pl.
Vancouver, BC V6C 3E1
604-688-9600 Fax: 604-688-9620
invest@acetex.com
www.acetex.com
Ticker Symbol: ATX
Company Type: Private
Profile: Manufacturers of various industrial organic chemicals, plastic materials, synthetic resins, & nonvulcanizable elastomers

Brooke N. Wade, Chair/CEO
Kenneth E. Vidalin, President/COO
Lori Bondar, CFO

Agrium Inc.
13131 Lake Fraser Dr. SE
Calgary, AB T2J 7E8
403-225-7000 Fax: 403-225-7609 877-247-4861
environmental@agrium.com
www.agrium.com
Ticker Symbol: AGU
Company Type: Public
Profile: Manufacturers of nitrogenous fertilizers, phosphatic fertilizers, pesticides & agricultural chemicals, & various industrial inorganic chemicals; Chemical & fertilizer mineral mining & quarrying; Potash, soda, & borate minerals mining & quarrying; Retailing in nurseries, lawn & garden supply stores; Wholesalers of farm supplies

Michael M. Wilson, President & CEO
Angela Lekatsas, Vice-President & Controller
Matt Smith, Director, Environment, Health & Safety

Angiotech Pharmaceuticals, Inc.
1618 Stanton St.
Vancouver, BC V6A 1B6
604-221-7676 Fax: 604-221-2330
info@angio.com
www.angiotech.com
Ticker Symbol: ANP
Company Type: Public
Profile: Commercial physical & biological research

William L. Hunter, President/CEO
David M. Hall, CFO
Steve Danic, Director, Information Systems

Apotex Inc., Canada
150 Signet Dr.
Toronto, ON M9L 1T9
416-749-9300 Fax: 416-401-3853 800-268-4623
corpinfo@apotex.com
www.apotex.com
Company Type: Private
Profile: Manufacturers of pharmaceutical preparations

Jack Kay, President/COO
Alex Glassenberg, Vice-President, Finance
Michael Davidson, Chief Information Officer
Fernando Tricta, Director, Medical
Jim Boughs, Director, Health & Safety

Axcan Pharma Inc.
597, boul Laurier
Mont-Saint-Hilaire, QC J3H 6C4
450-467-5138 Fax: 450-464-9979 800-565-3255
axcan@axcan.com
www.axcan.com
Ticker Symbol: AXP
Company Type: Public
Profile: Pharmaceutical company specializing in the field of gastroenterology; Products are marketed in North America & the European Union

Frank Verwiel, President/CEO
Steve Gannon, Sr. Vice-President/CFO
Bruno Proulx, Coordinator, Systems Analysis
Richard Senecal, Director, Production

BASF Canada
100 Milverton Dr., 5th Fl.
Mississauga, ON L5R 4H1
416-675-3611 Fax: 416-674-2588 866-485-2273
noc_canada-webmaster@basf-corp.com
www.basf.ca
Company Type: Private
Profile: Manufacturers of: gum & wood chemicals, paints, lacquers, enamels & allied products, pesticides & agricultural chemicals, prepared feeds & feed ingredients for animals & fowls, industrial organic chemical, synthetic rubber, cyclic crudes, intermediates, organic dyes & pigments; Wholesalers of: chemicals & allied products, paints, agricultural products & nutrition, raw materials, reactants, solvents & catalysts, pigments, plastics, polyurethans, coatings

Robin C. Rotenberg, President
Lloyd Symington, Treasurer/Director, Finance

Baxter Corporation
#700, 4 Robert Speck Pkwy.
Mississauga, ON L4Z 3Y4
905-270-1125 Fax: 905-281-6560 800-387-8399
business_development_canada@baxter.com
www.baxter.ca
Company Type: Private
Profile: Wholesalers of professional equipment & supplies; Manufacturers of pharmaceutical preparations

Barb Leavitt, President
Mary Parniak, Vice-President, Finance
Barbara Dawson, Director, Communications
Jim Porter, Director, Information Technology

Bayer Inc.
77 Belfield Rd.
Toronto, ON M9W 1G6
416-248-0771 800-622-2937
contactbayer@bayer.com
www.bayer.ca
Company Type: Private
Profile: Wholesalers of drugs, drug proprietaries & druggists' sundries, synthetic rubber, chemicals & allied products; Manufacturers of synthetic rubber; agriculture crop engineering

Bayer Inc. (continued)
Phillip Blake, President
Alexander Jahn, Vice-President/CFO
Walter Banas, Health & Safety Officer

Biomira Inc.
2011 - 94 St.
Edmonton, AB T6N 1H1
780-450-3761 Fax: 780-450-4772
ir@biomira.com
www.biomira.com
Ticker Symbol: BRA
Company Type: Public
Profile: Commercial physical & biological research; Manufacturers of biological products; Wholesalers of drugs, drug proprietaries & druggists' sundries

Alex McPherson, President/CEO
Edward A. Taylor, CFO/Vice-President, Finance & Administration

BioMS Medical Corp.
6030 - 88 St.
Edmonton, AB T6E 6G4
780-413-7152 Fax: 780-408-3040 866-701-6603
info@biomsmedical.com
www.biomsmedical.com
Ticker Symbol: MS
Company Type: Public
Profile: Commercial physical & biological research

Kevin Giese, President/CEO & Director
Don Kimak, CFO
Ryan Giese, Director, Corporate Communications

Bioniche Life Sciences Inc.
PO Box 1570, 231 Dundas St. East
Belleville, ON K8N 1E2
613-966-8058 Fax: 613-966-4177
info@bioniche.com
www.bioniche.com
Ticker Symbol: BNC
Company Type: Public
Profile: Manufacturers of pharmaceutical preparations; Commercial physical & biological research

Graeme McRae, President/CEO
Patrick Montpetit, Vice-President/CFO
Lynn Nielsen, Manager, Corporate Communications
Cameron Groome, Exec. Vice-President, Corporate & Strategic Development
Marc Rivière, Sr. Vice-President/Chief Medical Officer

Biovail Corporation
7150 Mississauga Rd.
Mississauga, ON L5N 8M5
905-286-3000 Fax: 905-286-3050
ir@biovail.com
www.biovail.com
Ticker Symbol: BVF
Company Type: Public
Profile: Manufacturers of pharmaceutical preparations; Wholesalers of drugs, drug proprietaries & druggists' sundries; Commercial physical & biological research; Patent owners & lessors

Eugene N. Melnyk, Executive Chair
Douglas J.P. Squires, CEO
Brian H. Crombie, Sr. Vice-President/CFO
Gregory Joseph Szpunar, Sr. Vice-President/Chief Scientific Officer

Cangene Corporation
155 Innovation Dr.
Winnipeg, MB R3T 5Y3
204-275-4200 Fax: 204-269-7003 www.cangene.com
Ticker Symbol: CNJ
Company Type: Public
Profile: Manufacturers of biological products, except diagnostic substances; Commercial physical & biological research

John Langstaff, President/CEO & Director
Alex Glasenberg, CFO/Director
Bill Labossiere Bees, Vice-President, Operations

Cardiome Pharma Corp.
6190 Agronomy Rd., 6th Fl.
Vancouver, BC V6T 1Z3
604-677-6905 Fax: 604-677-6915 800-330-9928
dgraham@cardiome.com
www.cardiome.com
Ticker Symbol: COM
Company Type: Public
Profile: Commercial physical & biological research

Robert Rieder, President/CEO
Doug Janzen, CFO
Alan Ezrin, Chief Scientific Officer

CCL Industries Inc.
#800, 105 Gordon Baker Rd.
Toronto, ON M2H 3P8
416-756-8500 Fax: 416-756-8555
ccl@cclind.com
www.cclind.com
Ticker Symbol: CCL
Company Type: Public
Profile: Manufacturers of specialty packaging for perfumes, cosmetics & other toilet preparations, soap & other detergents, specialty cleaning, polishing & sanitation preparations, coated & laminated paper, metal cans & various fabricated metal products

Donald G. Lang, President/CEO
Steven W. Lancaster, Sr. Vice-President/CFO
Akhil Bhandari, Chief Information Officer & Vice-President, Information Technology
Mary T. Roy, Vice-President, Environmental & Regulatory Services

DRAXIS Health, Inc.
#200, 6870 Goreway Dr.
Mississauga, ON L4V 1P1
905-677-5500 Fax: 905-677-5494 877-441-1984
requestforinfo@draxis.com
www.draxis.com
Ticker Symbol: DAX
Company Type: Public
Profile: Manufacturers of pharmaceutical preparations; Wholesalers of drugs, drug proprietaries & druggists' sundries; Patent owners & lessors; Commercial physical & biological research

Martin Barkin, President/CEO
Mark Oleksiw, CFO
Jerry Ormiston, Exec. Director, Investor Relations

DuPont Canada
PO Box 2200 Streetsville, 7070 Mississauga Rd.
Mississauga, ON L5M 2H3
905-821-3300 Fax: 905-821-5057 800-387-2122
information@can.dupont.com
www.ca.dupont.com
Ticker Symbol: DUP
Company Type: Public
Profile: Manufacturers of various industrial inorganic chemicals, manmade organic fibers & various organic chemicals; Wholesalers of chemicals & allied products

Douglas W. Muzyka, President, DuPont Greater China & Dupont China Holding, Co. Ltd.
William B. White, President
Michael Oxley, CFO
Yanitan G. Ho, Director, Information Technology
Nina Mankovitz, Manager, Safety, Health, Security & Environment

Eli Lilly Canada Inc.
3650 Danforth Ave.
Toronto, ON M1N 2E8
416-694-3221 Fax: 416-694-0487 800-268-4446www.lilly.ca
Company Type: Private
Profile: Manufacturers of pharmaceutical preparations

David Ricks, President & General Manager
Laurel Swartz, Manager, Corporate Communications
Joerg Rustige, Vice-President, Research & Development

GlaxoSmithKline Inc.
7333 Mississauga Rd. North
Mississauga, ON L5N 6L4
905-819-3000 Fax: 905-819-3099 www.gsk.ca
Company Type: Private
Profile: Commercial physical & biological research; Manufacturers of pharmaceutical preparations

Paul Lucas, President/CEO
R. Castonguay, Vice-President, Finance
Savino DiPasquale, Chief Information Officer & Vice-President, Information Technology
Maris Silnis, Manager, Health & Safety

Haemacure Corporation
#430, 2001, rue Université
Montréal, QC H3A 2A6
514-282-3350 Fax: 514-282-3358
info@haemacurecorp.com
www.haemacure.com
Ticker Symbol: HAE
Company Type: Public
Profile: Manufacturers of pharmaceutical preparations; Commercial physical & biological research

Marc Paquin, President/CEO
Lyne Paré, Director, Finance & Administration
Christian Hours, Vice-President & CTO

ICI Canada Inc.
2600 Steeles Ave. West
Concord, ON L4K 3C8
905-738-0080 Fax: 905-738-9723
ici@ici.com
www.ici.com
Company Type: Private
Profile: Manufacturers of various industrial inorganic chemicals, nitrogenous fertilizers, pesticides & agricultural chemicals, paints, varnishes, lacquers, enamels & allied products, explosives, chemicals & various chemical preparations

Vince Rea, Vice-President, Finance
Lee Fortney, Director, Information Technology
Anna Tonaino, Engineer

ID Biomedical Corporation
1630 Waterfront Centre
200 Burrard St.
Vancouver, BC V6C 3L6
604-431-9314 Fax: 604-431-9378
info@idbiomedical.com
www.idbiomedical.com
Ticker Symbol: IDB
Company Type: Public
Profile: Patent owners & lessors; Commercial physical & biological research

Anthony F. Holler, CEO & Director
Todd R. Patrick, President
Staph Bakali, COO

Inex Pharmaceuticals Corporation
#200, 8900 Glenlyon Pkwy.
Burnaby, BC V5J 5J8
604-419-3200 Fax: 604-419-3201
info@inexpharm.com
www.inexpharm.com
Ticker Symbol: IEX
Company Type: Public
Profile: Manufacturers of pharmaceutical preparations, & biological products; commercial & biological research

Timothy Ruane, President/COO
Ian C. Mortimer, CFO/Vice-President, Finance

Inflazyme Pharmaceuticals Ltd.
#425, 5600 Parkwood Way
Richmond, BC V6V 2M2
604-279-8511 Fax: 604-279-8711 800-315-3660
info@inflazyme.com
www.inflazyme.com
Ticker Symbol: IZP
Company Type: Public
Profile: Commercial physical & biological research; Manufacturers of pharmaceutical preparations

Ian McBeath, President/CEO
Michael Liggett, CFO
Sean Millar, Manager, Information Technology

Kronos Canada Inc.
#1610, 2000 McGill College Ave.
Montréal, QC H3A 3H3
514-397-3501 Fax: 514-393-1186 www.kronostio2.com
Company Type: Private
Profile: Manufacturers of titanium dioxide pigments

J. Gravel, President
Antoine Doan, Controller
Gabriel Dionne, Manager, Environment

Labopharm Inc.
480, boul Armand-Frappier
Laval, QC H7V 4B4

450-686-1017 Fax: 450-686-9141 888-686-1017
info@labopharm.com
www.labopharm.com
Ticker Symbol: DDS
Company Type: Public
Profile: Manufacturers of pharmaceutical preparations; Patent owners & lessors

James R. Howard-Tripp, President/CEO
Warren Whitehead, CFO
Marc Hébert, Manager, Information Systems

Merck Frosst Canada Inc.
16711, rte Trans-Canada
Montréal, QC H9H 3L1
514-428-7920 Fax: 514-428-6270 800-567-2594
servicesmf_customer@merck.com
www.merckfrosst.ca
Company Type: Private
Profile: Manufacturers of pharmaceutical preparations

André Marcheterre, President
Kirk Duguid, Vice-President, Finance & Business Development

Methanex Corporation
Waterfront Centre
#1800, 200 Burrard St.
Vancouver, BC V6C 3M1
604-661-2600 Fax: 604-661-2676 800-661-8851
invest@methanex.com
www.methanex.com
Ticker Symbol: MX
Company Type: Public
Profile: Producer & marketer of methanol

Bruce Aitken, President/CEO
Ian Cameron, CFO & Sr. Vice-President, Finance
Chris Cook, Director, Investor Relations
Lorna Young, Director, Corporate Affairs

Migenix
BC Research Bldg.
3650 Westbrook Mall
Vancouver, BC V6S 2L2
604-221-9666 Fax: 604-221-9688
info@migenix.com
www.migenix.com
Ticker Symbol: MBI
Company Type: Public
Profile: Manufacturers of biological products, except diagnostic substances, in vitro & in vivo diagnostic substances; Commercial physical & biological research

James DeMesa, President/CEO
Arthur J. Ayres, CFO & Vice-President, Finance & Administration

Nexia Biotechnologies Inc.
PO Box 187, Montréal, QC H1S 2Z2
514-586-3942 Fax: 514-371-7880 www.nexiabiotech.com
Ticker Symbol: NXB
Company Type: Public
Profile: Testing laboratories; Commercial physical & biological research

William C. Garriock, President/CEO/Chair
Dejan Ristic, CFO

NOVA Chemicals Corporation
PO Box 2518 M, 1000 - 7 Ave. SW
Calgary, AB T2P 5C6
403-750-3600 Fax: 403-269-7410
invest@novachem.com
www.novachem.com
Ticker Symbol: NCX
Company Type: Public
Profile: Manufacturers of plastic materials, synthetic resins, nonvulcanizable elastomers, various industrial organic chemicals, manmade organic fibers, except cellulosic

J.M. Lipton, President/CEO
Larry A. MacDonald, CFO & Sr. Vice-President
John L. Wheeler, Chief Information Officer & Sr. Vice-President

Novartis Pharmaceuticals Canada Inc.
385, boul Bouchard
Montréal, QC H9S 1A9
514-631-6775 Fax: 514-631-1867 www.pharma.ca.novartis.com
Company Type: Private
Profile: Manufacturers of pharmaceutical preparations

Ludwig Hantson, President
Gordon Cummins, Vice-President, Finance
Frances Shanahan, Vice-President, Information Technology
Robert Gauthier, Property Manager

The Nu-Gro Corporation
10 Craig St.
Brantford, ON N3R 7J1
519-757-0077 Fax: 519-757-0010 800-268-2806
finance@nu-gro.ca
www.nu-gro.com
Ticker Symbol: NU
Company Type: Public
Profile: Manufacturers of pesticides & agricultural chemicals, mixing only & nitrogenous fertilizers, minerals & earths, ground or otherwise treated; Wholesalers of farm supplies & various nondurable goods

John Hill, President/CEO
Greg Flanagan, CFO/Secretary
Gerry Haslam, Director, Information Systems
Shannon Bennett, Health & Safety Specialist

Nuvo Research Inc.
#10, 7560 Airport Rd.
Mississauga, ON L4T 4H4
905-673-6980 Fax: 905-673-1842
info@nuvoresearch.com
www.nuvoresearch.com
Ticker Symbol: DMX
Company Type: Public
Profile: Commercial physical & biological research; Manufacturers of pharmaceutical preparations

Heinrich R.K. Guntermann, President/CEO
Grant Britchford, Vice-President/CFO, Finance

Nymox Pharmaceutical Corporation
#306, 9900, boul Cavendish
Montréal, QC H4M 2V2
514-332-3222 Fax: 514-332-2227
info@nymox.com
www.nymox.com
Company Type: Public
Profile: Biopharmaceutical company specializing in research & development of therapeutics & diagnostics for the aging population

Paul Averback, President/CEO & Chair
Roy Wolvin, CFO/Sec.-Treas.
Jack Gemmell, General Counsel

Oncolytics Biotech Inc
#210, 1167 Kensington Cres. NW
Calgary, AB T2N 1X7
403-670-7377 Fax: 403-283-0858
info@oncolyticsbiotech.com
www.oncolyticsbiotech.com
Ticker Symbol: ONC
Company Type: Public
Profile: Researchers & developers of biological products, except diagnostic substances; Commercial physical & biological research

Bradley G. Thompson, PhDPresident/CEO & Chair
Doug Ball, CFO

Orbus Pharma Inc.
20 Konrad Cres.
Markham, ON L3R 8T4
403-235-8300 Fax: 403-248-3306
info@orbus.ca
www.orbus.ca
Ticker Symbol: BVR
Company Type: Public
Profile: Develops & manufactures off-patent generic drugs & drug delivery systems; International provider of environmental management services

Jeffrey W. Renwick, President/CEO
Dennis C. Arsenault, CFO/Vice-President, Finance

Paladin Labs Inc.
#102, 6111, av Royalmount
Montréal, QC H4P 2T4
514-340-1112 Fax: 514-344-4675 888-376-7830
info@paladin-labs.com
www.paladin-labs.com
Ticker Symbol: PLB
Company Type: Public
Profile: Manufacturers of pharmaceutical preparations; Wholesalers of drugs, drug proprietaries & druggists' sundries; Commercial physical & biological research

Jonathan Ross Goodman, President/CEO
Samira Sakhia, CFO

Patheon Inc.
#350, 7070 Mississauga Rd.
Mississauga, ON L5N 7S8
905-821-4001 Fax: 905-812-6709 888-728-4366
patheon@patheon.com
www.patheon.com
Ticker Symbol: PTI
Company Type: Public
Profile: Manufacturers of pharmaceutical preparations; Testing laboratories

Robert C. Tedford, CEO
Nick A. DiPietro, President/COO
Ronald B. Mitchell, CFO/Sr. Vice-President, Finance
Vic Filenko, Manager, Information Technology
Ron Quon, Sr. Vice-President, HR Environment/Health & Safety

PendoPharm Inc.
8580, av de l'Esplanade
Montréal, QC H2P 2R9
514-384-6516 Fax: 514-385-7479 www.pendopharm.com
Ticker Symbol: PIL
Company Type: Public
Profile: Manufacturers of pharmaceutical preparations; Wholesalers of drugs, drug proprietaries & druggists' sundries

Ahmad Doroudian, CEO

PFB Corporation
#270, 3015 - 5th Ave. NE
Calgary, AB T2A 6T8
403-569-4300 Fax: 403-569-4075
mailbox@pfbcorp.com
www.pfbcorp.com
Ticker Symbol: PFB
Company Type: Public
Profile: Manufacturers of plastic materials, synthetic resins, nonvulcanizable elastomers & plastic foam products

Alan Smith, President/CEO & Chair
Bruce M. Carruthers, President & General Manager, Plasti-Fab Division
Stephen P. Hardy, CFO & Vice-President

Pfizer Canada Inc.
17300, rte Trans-Canada
Montréal, QC H9R 2M5
514-695-0500 Fax: 514-426-6831 877-633-2001www.pfizer.ca
Company Type: Private
Profile: Manufacturers of pharmaceutical preparations, prepared feeds & feed ingredients for animals & fowls; Wholesalers of drugs, drug proprietaries & druggists' sundries

Jean-Michel Halton, President/CEO
François Belin, Vice-President, Finance
Guy Lallemand, Vice-President, Government & Public Affairs
Wes Pringle, Vice-President & General Manager, Canada & Caribbean
Daniel Couture, Vice-President, Business Technologies

PPG Canada Inc.
834 Caledonia Rd.
Toronto, ON M6B 3X9
416-789-4105 Fax: 416-789-7966
mshoemaker@ppg.com
www.ppg.com
Company Type: Private
Profile: Manufacturers of paints, varnishes, lacquers, enamels & allied products, plastic materials, synthetic resins, nonvulcanizable elastomers, flat glass & various industrial inorganic chemicals

Mark Shoemaker, CEO & Director, Finance & Human Resources
J.N. Daligadu, Manager, Information Systems
I. Bacchus, Manager, Health & Safety

Procter & Gamble Inc.
PO Box 355 A, 4711 Yonge St.
Toronto, ON M5W 1C5
416-730-4711 Fax: 416-730-4415 800-668-1050www.pg.com
Company Type: Private

Procter & Gamble Inc. (continued)
Profile: Manufacturers of chemicals & chemical preparations, perfumes, cosmetics & other toilet preparations, sanitary paper products, pharmaceutical preparations

Tim Penner, President/CEO
Sandy Argabrite, Director, Finance
Dennis Darby, Director, External Relations
Glenn Dorsey, Vice-President, Technology
Michael Gagnon, Environmental Officer

Procyon BioPharma Inc.
#200, 1650, rte Trans-Canada
Montréal, QC H9P 1H7
514-685-2000 Fax: 514-685-5138
info@procyonbiopharma.com
www.procyonbiopharma.com
Ticker Symbol: PBP
Company Type: Public
Profile: Commercial, physical & biological research

Hans J. Mäder, President/CEO & Chair
Monique Létourneau, CFO & Exec. Vice-President, Finance
Chandra J. Panchal, Sr. Exec. Vice-President, New Technologies
Richard La Rue, Corporate Secretary/Vice-President, Legal Affairs & Human Resources

ProMetic Life Sciences Inc.
8168, rue Montview
Montréal, QC H4P 2L7
514-341-2115 Fax: 514-341-6227
info@prometic.com
www.prometic.com
Ticker Symbol: PLI
Company Type: Public
Profile: Biopharmaceutical company

Pierre Laurin, President/CEO & Chair
André Bédard, COO

QLT Inc.
887 Great Northern Way
Vancouver, BC V5T 4T5
604-707-7000 Fax: 604-707-7001
ir@qltinc.com
www.qltinc.com
Ticker Symbol: QLT
Company Type: Public
Profile: Global biopharmaceutical company; Develops treatments for eye diseases & dermatological & urological conditions

Robert Butchofsky, President/CEO & Director
Cameron Nelson, Vice-President/CFO, Finance
Therese Hayes, Vice-President, Investor Relations & Corporate Communications

Ratiopharm Inc.
#5, 6975 Creditview Rd.
Mississauga, ON L5N 8E9
905-858-9612 Fax: 905-858-9610 800-266-2584
clients@ratiopharm.ca
www.ratiopharm.ca
Company Type: Private
Profile: Manufacturers of pharmaceutical preparations; Wholesalers of drugs, drug proprietaries & druggists' sundries; Commercial physical & biological research

Jean-Guy Goulet, President/CEO

Rohm & Haas Canada Inc.
#A-202, 7900 Tascherau Blvd.
Brossard, QC J4X 1C2
450- 46-6776 Fax: 450-466-7771 www.rohmhass.com
Company Type: Private
Profile: Manufacturers of plastic materials, synthetic resins, nonvulcanizable elastomers, industrial organic chemicals

Raj L. Gupta, CEO
J. Michael Fitzpatrick, President/COO
Jacques M. Croisettiere, CFO & Sr. Vice-President
Gary S. Calabrese, Vice-President/Chief Technology Officer
Phillip G. Lewis, Vice-President/Director, Environmental Health & Safety & Sustainable Development

Schering Canada Inc.
3535, rte Trans-Canada
Montréal, QC H9R 1B4
514-426-7300 Fax: 514-695-7641 www.schering-plough.com
Company Type: Private
Profile: Manufacturers of pharmaceutical preparations; Wholesalers of drugs, drug proprietaries & druggists' sundries; Retailers in drug stores & proprietary stores

Fred Hassan, CEO/Chair
Carlos G. Dourado, President & General Manager
Jack L. Wyszomierski, CFO
Donald R. Lemma, Chief Information Officer
Vivianne Aarestrup, Supervisor, Environment, Health & Safety

ShawCor Ltd.
25 Bethridge Rd.
Toronto, ON M9W 1M7
416-743-7111 Fax: 416-743-9123 www.shawcor.com
Ticker Symbol: SCL
Company Type: Public
Profile: An energy services corporation known for technology-based products & services; Serves the pipeline, exploration & production, petrochemical & industrial markets

William P. Buckley, President/CEO & Director
Gary S. Love, CFO & Vice-President, Finance
Robert E. Steele, Vice-President, Technology
Peter Langdon, Vice-President, Human Resources

Sico Inc.
2505, rue de la Métropole
Longueuil, QC J4G 1E5
514-527-5111 Fax: 514-651-1257 800-463-7426
info@sico.com
www.sico.com
Ticker Symbol: SIC
Company Type: Public
Profile: Manufacturers of paints, varnishes, lacquers, enamels & allied products & inorganic pigments; Wholesalers of paints, varnishes, & supplies

Pierre Dufresne, President/CEO
Jean Ouellet, Vice-President, Finance & Treasurer

Theratechnologies Inc.
2310, boul Alfred-Nobel
Montréal, QC H4S 2A4
514-336-7800 Fax: 514-336-7242 www.theratech.com
Ticker Symbol: TH
Company Type: Public
Profile: Manufacturers of pharmaceutical preparations, in vitro & in vivo diagnostic substances, surgical & medical instruments & apparatus, dental equipment & supplies; Commercial physical & biological research; Wholesalers of drugs, drug proprietaries & druggists' sundries

Yves Rosconi, President/CEO
Luc Tanguay, Sr. Vice-President/CFO, Finance
Chantal Desrochers, Vice-President, Business Development & Commercialization

Vasogen Inc.
2505 Meadowvale Blvd.
Mississauga, ON L5N 5S2
905-817-2000 Fax: 905-569-9231
investor@vasogen.com
www.vasogen.com
Ticker Symbol: VSV
Company Type: Public
Profile: Commercial physical & biological research

David G. Elsley, President/CEO
Christopher Waddick, CFO/Exec. Vice-President
Bernard Lim, Vice-President, Technology
G. Neil, Controller

Communications

Aliant Inc.
PO Box 1430, Saint John, NB E2L 4K2
877-248-3113 Fax: 506-694-2722 866-425-4268
investors@bell.aliant.ca
www.aliant.ca
Ticker Symbol: AIT
Company Type: Public
Profile: Offices of holding companies; Telephone & various other communications services; Computer related services

Jay Forbes, President/CEO
Glen LeBlanc, Sr. Vice-President/CFO
Ivan James Toner, Chief Information Officer, Aliant Telecom
Gary Lund, Chief Technology Officer, Aliant Telecom
Owen Evans, Manager, Safety & Environment, Aliant Telecom

Allstream Corp.
#1600, 200 Wellington St. West
Toronto, ON M5V 3G2
204-225-5687 Fax: 204-949-1244 800-883-2054
brad.woods@mts.ca
www.allstream.com
Ticker Symbol: TEL
Company Type: Public
Profile: Telephone communications; Information retrieval services

Pierre Blouin, CEO
John A. Macdonald, President, Enterprise Solutions
Kelvin A. Shepherd, President, Consumer Markets
Nick Curry, Chief Information Officer

Amtelecom Income Fund
PO Box 1800, 18 Sydenham St. East
Aylmer West, ON N5H 3E7
519-773-8441 Fax: 519-765-3200 800-440-7472
info@amtelecom.ca
www.amtelecom.ca
Ticker Symbol: ATM
Company Type: Public
Profile: Cable & other pay television services; Telephone communications; Internet services

Michael J. Andrews, President/CEO
David Bronicheski, CFO/Corporate Secretary

Astral Media Inc
#1000, 2100, rue Sainte-Catherine ouest
Montréal, QC H3H 2T3
514-939-5000 Fax: 514-939-1515 www.astral.com
Ticker Symbol: ACM
Company Type: Public
Profile: Television broadcasting stations; Cable & other pay television services; Radio broadcasting stations; Outdoor advertising services

Ian Greenberg, President/CEO
Claude Gagnon, Vice-President, Finance
François Duperon, Director, Information Technology

BCE Inc.
#3700, 1000, rue de la Gauchetière ouest
Montréal, QC H3B 4Y7
Fax: 514-786-3970 800-339-6353
investor.relations@bce.ca
www.bce.ca
Ticker Symbol: BCE
Company Type: Public
Profile: Offices of holding companies; Manufacturers of telephone & telegraph apparatus; Radiotelephone & telephone communications; Commercial physical & biological research

Michael J. Sabia, President/CEO & Chair
Siim A. Vanaselja, CFO

Bell Canada
#3700, 1000 rue de la Gauchetière ouest
Montréal, QC H3B 4Y7
514-870-8276 Fax: 514-786-3970 800-339-6353
forum@bell.ca
www.bell.ca
Ticker Symbol: BC
Company Type: Public
Profile: Radiotelephone, telephone, telegraph & other message communications services; Miscellaneous publishing; Special trade electrical work; Electrical & electronic repair shops; Retail stores

Michael Sabia, CEO
Stephen Wetmore, President, National Markets
Siim Vanaselja, CFO
Eugene Roman, Group President, Systems & Technology

Canadian Broadcasting Corporation
PO Box 3220 C, Ottawa, ON K1Y 1E4
613-288-6033 Fax: 613-724-5707
liaison@radio-canada.ca
www.cbc.ca
Company Type: Crown
Profile: Radio & television broadcasting stations; Theatrical producers & miscellaneous services; Motion picture & video tape production

Robert Rabinovitch, President/CEO
Johanne Charbonneau, Vice-President/CFO
Martine Menard, Sr. Director, Corporate Communications

Raymond Carnovale, Vice-President/Chief Technology Officer

Canadian Satellite Communications Inc.
2055 Flavelle Blvd.
Mississauga, ON L5K 1Z8
905-403-2020 Fax: 905-403-2022 800-268-2943
info@cancom.ca
www.cancom.ca
Company Type: Private
Profile: Manages full-service commercial signal distribution network

Peter Bissonette, President

Canbras Communications Corp.
#1240, 1000, rue de la Gauchetière ouest
Montréal, QC H3B 4Y7
514-878-1232 Fax: 514-878-1600
investor.relations@canbras.ca
www.canbras.ca
Ticker Symbol: CBC
Company Type: Public
Profile: Offices of holding companies; Cable & other pay television services; Telephone communications

Howard N. Hendrick, CEO/CFO

CanWest Global Communications Corp.
CanWest Global Place
#3100 , 201 Portage Ave.
Winnipeg, MB R3B 3L7
204-956-2025 Fax: 204-947-9841 www.canwestglobal.com
Ticker Symbol: CGS
Company Type: Public
Profile: Television & radio broadcasting stations; Manufacturers of newspapers: publishing & printing; Motion picture & video tape production & distribution; Information retrieval services; Cable & other pay television services

Leonard J. Asper, President/CEO & Director
John E. Maguire, CFO & Vice-President, Finance
Peter Ashkin, Chief Information Officer

CHUM Limited
299 Queen St. West
Toronto, ON M5V 2Z5
416-591-5757 Fax: 416-591-8457
info@chumlimited.com
www.chumlimited.com
Ticker Symbol: CHM
Company Type: Public
Profile: Radio broadcasting stations; Television broadcasting stations

Jay Switzer, President/CEO
Alan S. Mayne, CFO
Sean Barry, IT Manager

COGECO Cable Inc.
#915, 5 Place Ville Marie
Montreal, QC H3B 2G2
514-874-2600 Fax: 416-263-9394 800-564-6253
service@computershare.com
www.cogecocable.com
Ticker Symbol: CCA
Company Type: Public
Profile: Cable operator provides analogue & digital video & audio services, high-speed Internet access & digital telephony service to residential & commercial customers

Louis Audet, President/CEO
Pierre Gagné, CFO & Vice-President, Finance
Louise St-Pierre, Chief Information Officer & Vice-President
J. François Audet, Vice-President, Telecommunications

COGECO Inc.
#3636, 1, Place Ville-Marie
Montréal, QC H3B 3P2
514-874-2600 Fax: 514-874-2625 www.cogeco.com
Ticker Symbol: CGO
Company Type: Public
Profile: Diversified communications company serves its residential & commercial customers with analogue & digital video & audio services, Internet access, digital telphony, plus television & radio stations

Louis Audet, President/CEO
René Guimond, President/CEO, Cogeco Radio-Télévision
Pierre Gagné, CFO & Vice-President, Finance
Louise St-Pierre, Vice-President/Chief Information Officer

Corus Entertainment Inc.
#1630, 181 Bay St.
Toronto, ON M5J 2T3
416-642-3770 Fax: 416-642-3779 www.corusent.com
Ticker Symbol: CJR
Company Type: Public
Profile: Radio & television broadcasting stations; Cable & other pay television services

John M. Cassaday, President/CEO
Thomas C. Peddie, Sr. Vice-President & CFO
Neil Bhatt, Director, Information Technology

CTV Inc.
Station O
PO Box 9, Scarborough, ON M4A 2M9
416-332-5000 www.ctv.ca
Company Type: Public
Profile: Television broadcasting stations; Motion picture & video tape production

Ivan Fecan, CEO
Robin Fillingham, CFO
Albert Fausts, Director, Media Technology Systems
Nello Corsetti, Manager, Health & Safety

Ericsson Canada Inc.
5255 Satellite Dr.
Mississauga, ON L4W 5E3
905-629-6700 Fax: 905-629-6701 www.ericsson.ca
Company Type: Private
Profile: Provides mobile internet, wireless, IP & data systems, & consulting services

Mark Henderson, President/CEO
Kevin Inglis, Director, Finance, Systems & Operations
Mike Sisto, Vice-President, Network Operations

Glentel Inc.
8501 Commerce Ct.
Burnaby, BC V5A 4N3
604-415-6500 Fax: 604-415-6565 800-453-6835
customer_service@glentel.com
www.glentel.com
Ticker Symbol: GLN
Company Type: Public
Profile: Wireless communications products & services

T.E. Skidmore, President/CEO & Chair
Dale Belsher, CFO
Frank Chay, Manager, Information Technology

Groupe TVA inc
1600, boul de Maisonneuve est
Montréal, QC H2L 4P2
514-598-2808 Fax: 514-598-6085
paul.buron@tva.ca
www.tva.canoe.com
Ticker Symbol: TVA.B
Company Type: Public
Profile: Television broadcasting stations; Motion picture & video tape production & related services

Pierre Dion, President/CEO
Paul Buron, Sr. Vice-President/CFO
Philippe Lapointe, Vice-President, Information & Public Affairs

Look Communications Inc.
#201 Rene Levesque Blvd. E.
Montreal, QC H2K 4P6
514-526-6645 Fax: 514-526-6678 877-296-5665
investorinfo@look.ca
www.look.ca
Ticker Symbol: LKC
Company Type: Public
Profile: Cable & other pay television services; Information retrieval services

Michael Cytrynbaum, Chair
Gerald T. McGoey, CEO

Mamma.com Inc.
388, rue St-Jacques ouest, 9e étage
Montréal, QC H2Y 1S1
514-844-2700 Fax: 514-844-3532 888-844-2372
mamma_marketing@mamma.com
www.mamma.com
Company Type: Public
Profile: Radiotelephone & various communications services

Guy Fauré, President/CEO

Daniel Bertrand, Exec. Vice-President/CFO

Manitoba Telecom Services Inc.
PO Box 6666, 333 Main St, 4th Fl.
Winnipeg, MB R3C 3V6
204-941-8244 Fax: 204-779-5848 888-544-5554
corporate.communications@mtsallstream.com
www.mts.ca
Ticker Symbol: MBT
Company Type: Public
Profile: Connectivity, managed & professional services for businesses across Canada; Wireline voice, data, wireless & MTS TV services for residential & business customers in Manitoba

Pierre Blouin, CEO
Kevin A. Shepherd, President, Consumer Markets
Nick Curry, Vice-President
Wayne S. Demkey, CFO/Exec. Vice-President, Finance
Fred Riddle, Manager, Environment Programs, Wellness, Environment & Disabilit

Newfoundland Capital Corporation Limited
745 Windmill Rd.
Dartmouth, NS B3B 1C2
902-468-7557 Fax: 902-468-7558
ncc@ncc.ca
www.ncc.ca
Ticker Symbol: NCC
Company Type: Public
Profile: Radio broadcasting stations

Robert G. Steele, President & CEO
Scott G.M. Weatherby, CFO
Glendon MacBurnie, Manager, IT

Northwestel Inc.
PO Box 2727 Main, 301 Lambert St.
Whitehorse, YT Y1A 4Y4
867-668-5300 Fax: 867-668-7079 800-773-2121
customerservice@nwtel.ca
www.nwtel.ca
Company Type: Private
Profile: Telephone, telegraph, radiotelephone, cellular & satellite, & other message communications services; Cable television services

Paul Flaherty, President/CEO
Ray Hamelin, CFO
Ray Wells, Vice-President, Corporate

Persona Communications Inc.
PO Box 12155 A, 17 Duffy Pl.
St. John's, NL A1B 4L1
709-754-3775 Fax: 709-754-3883 www.personainc.ca
Ticker Symbol: PSA
Company Type: Public
Profile: Offices of holding companies; Television broadcasting stations; Cable & other pay television services

Dean MacDonald, President/CEO
Paul Hatchet, COO
Bob Day, Director, Technology

Rogers Communications Inc.
333 Bloor St. East, 10th Fl.
Toronto, ON M4W 1G9
416-935-6666 Fax: 416-935-4600
info@rogers.com
www.rogers.com
Ticker Symbol: RCI
Company Type: Public
Profile: Television & radio broadcasting stations; Various communications services; Equipment & videotape rental & leasing; Manufacturers of newspapers & periodicals; Radiotelephone communications

Edward S. Rogers, President/CEO
Ronan D. McGrath, President/Chief Information Officer, Rogers Shared Services
Alan D. Horn, CFO & Vice-President, Finance
Alexander R. Brock, Vice-President, Business Development, RCI Technology

Rogers Wireless Communications Inc.
One Mount Pleasant Rd.
Toronto, ON M4Y 2Y5

investor.relations@rogers.com
www.rogers.com

Rogers Wireless Communications Inc. (continued)
Ticker Symbol: RCM
Company Type: Public
Profile: Telephone & radiotelephone communications; Retailing in miscellaneous stores; Special trade contracting in electrical work

Darryl E. Levy, President, Western Canada
John R. Gossling, CFO & Sr. Vice-President
Robert Berner, Chief Technology Officer & Sr. Vice-President

Saskatchewan Telecommunications Holding Corporation
PO Box 2121, Regina, SK S4P 4C5
306-777-3737 Fax: 306-565-0305
800-727-5835www.sasktel.com
Company Type: Crown
Profile: Telephone, radiotelephone & various other communications services

Robert Watson, President/CEO & Director
Randy Stephanson, CFO
Kym Wittal, Chief Technology Officer
John Meldrum, Vice-President/Corporate Counsel, Regulatory Affairs

Score Media Inc.
1605 Main St. West
Hamilton, ON L8S 1E8
905-522-6146 Fax: 905-522-9744 www.scoremedia.ca
Ticker Symbol: HMG
Company Type: Public
Profile: Cable & other pay television services

John S. Levy, Chair/CEO
Patrick Michaud, Vice-President/CFO

Shaw Communications Inc.
#900, 630 - 3rd Ave. SW
Calgary, AB T2P 4L4
403-750-4500 Fax: 403-750-4501 888-750-7429
angela.haigh@sjrb.ca
www.shaw.ca
Ticker Symbol: SJR
Company Type: Public
Profile: Communications company provides broadband cable television, internet, digital phone, telecommunications services & satellite direct-to-home services

Jim Shaw, CEO
Peter Bissonnette, President
Rhonda Bashnick, Vice-President, Finance
Zoran Stakic, Chief Information Officer
Dennis Steiger, Vice-President, Engineering

Star Choice Communications Inc.
2924 - 11 St. NE
Calgary, AB T2E 2L7
403-538-4320 Fax: 403-538-4380
866-782-7932www.starchoice.com
Company Type: Private
Profile: Cable & other pay television services

Michael Abram, President
Tim McCoy, CFO

Stratos Global Corporation
#210, 2650 Queensview Dr.
Ottawa, ON K2B 8H6
613-230-4544 Fax: 613-230-4212 877-995-9901
investor@stratosglobal.com
www.stratosglobal.com
Ticker Symbol: SGB
Company Type: Public
Profile: Offices of holding companies; Radiotelephone & various other communications services

Carmen L. Lloyd, President/CEO
Richard P. Hakla, Exec. Vice-President & CFO
John M. Mackey, Chief Technology Officer

Télébec
7151, rue Jean-Talon est
Montréal, QC H1M 3N8
Fax: 819-233-6877 888-835-3232
telebec@telebec.com
www.telebec.com
Company Type: Public
Profile: Provides range of integrated telecommunications services in province of Québec

Roche Dubé, President/CEO
Michael Ross, Vice-President, Finance

Telesat Canada
1601 Telesat Ct.
Gloucester, ON K1B 5P4
613-748-0123 Fax: 613-748-8712
info@telesat.ca
www.telesat.ca
Company Type: Private
Profile: Telesat manages satellite communications & systems.

Daniel S. Goldberg, President/CEO
Ted Ignacy, CFO

TELUS Corporation
555 Robson St., 8th Fl.
Vancouver, BC V6B 3K9
604-697-8017 Fax: 604-437-5860
ir@telus.com
www.telus.com
Ticker Symbol: BT
Company Type: Public
Profile: Telephone & radiotelephone communications; Manufacturers of telephone & telegraph apparatus, radio & television broadcasting & communications equipment; Retailing in miscellaneous retail stores

Joseph Grech, Exec. Vice-President, Network Planning & Operations
Darren Entwistle, President/CEO & Director
Robert McFarlane, Exec. Vice-President/CFO
Kevin Salvadori, Exec. Vice-President/CIO, Business Transformations
Eros Spadotto, Exec. Vice-President, Technology Strategy

Construction

Bechtel Canada Inc.
#910, 1500, rue Univesité
Montréal, QC H3A 3S7
514-871-1711 Fax: 514-871-1392 www.bechtel.com
Company Type: Private
Profile: Offices of holding companies; Management & public relations services; Engineering services

Riley Bechtel, Chair/CEO
Adrian Zaccaria, COO/President
Peter Dawson, CFO
Geir Ramleth, Manager, Information Systems & Technology
Susan Kubanis, Manager, Sustainable Development

Bird Construction Company Limited
#206, 5405 Eglinton Ave. West
Toronto, ON M9C 5K6
416-620-7122 Fax: 416-620-1516
toronto.info@bird.ca
www.bird.ca
Ticker Symbol: BDT
Company Type: Public
Profile: General contractors in residential, non-residential & industrial buildings & warehouses

Paul A. Charette, Chair/CEO
Paul R. Raboud, President/COO
Douglas H. Clark, CFO & Secretary

Carma Corporation
7315 - 8 St. NE
Calgary, AB T2E 8A2
403-231-8900 Fax: 403-231-8960
calgaryinfo@carma.ca
www.carma.ca
Company Type: Public
Profile: General contractors in residential buildings, & single family houses; Real estate land subdividers & developers

Alan Norris, President/CEO
Karen Leeds, CFO/Sr. Vice-President

Dominion Construction Company Inc.
#130, 2985 Virtual Way
Vancouver, BC V5M 4X7
604-631-1000 Fax: 604-631-1100
reception@dominionco.com
www.dominionco.com
Company Type: Private
Profile: General contractors in industrial & non-residential buildings & warehouses; Offices located in Vancouver, Calgary, Edmonton, Regina, Saskatoon, Swift Current, Winnipeg & Thunder Bay

Dennis W. Burnham, P.Eng.Chair/CEO
Carl M. Stewart, President
Vance Hackett, Vice-President, Finance

Eastern Construction Company Ltd.
#1100, 505 Consumers Rd.
Toronto, ON M2J 5G2
416-497-7110 Fax: 416-497-7241
info@easternconstruction.com
www.easternconstruction.com
Company Type: Private
Profile: General contractors in industrial & non-residential buildings & warehouses

Frank Decaria, President/CEO
Ron Littlejohns, Vice-President, Finance
Marie MacDonald, Manager, Information Systems

Ellis-Don Construction Ltd.
2045 Oxford St. West
London, ON N5V 2Z7
519-455-6770 Fax: 519-455-2944
jbernhardt@ellisdon.com
www.ellisdon.com
Company Type: Private
Profile: General contractors of industrial buildings & warehouses, residential & non-residential buildings

Geoff Smith, CEO/President
Jim King, CFO
Bruce Fleming, Vice-President/Chief Information Officer
Gerry Murphy, Chief Technology Officer
Kari Lynn Atkinson, Vice-President, Ellis Don Consulting-Health & Safety

Les Entreprises Kiewit ltée
4333, Grande-Allée
Boisbriand, QC J7H 1M7
450-435-5756 Fax: 450-435-6764
kiewit.mtl@kiewit.qc.ca
www.kiewit.qc.ca
Company Type: Private
Profile: Offices of holding companies; Bridge, tunnel, elevated highway & various construction; Water, sewer, pipeline, communications & power line construction; Metal mining services in gold & copper ores; Coal mining services

Louis Chapdelaine, President
Claude Letourneau, CFO
Arnold Morenne, Supervisor, Information Technology
Roger Gagnon, Safety Manager

Finning International Inc.
16830 - 107 Ave.
Edmonton, AB T5P 4C3
780-930-4800 Fax: 780-930-4801
webmaster@finning.ca
www.finning.com
Ticker Symbol: FTT
Company Type: Public
Profile: Wholesalers in construction & mining machinery & equipment, industrial machinery & equipment; Equipment rental & leasing; Repair shops & various related services

Douglas W.G. Whitehead, President/CEO
Jack A. Carthy, President, Power Systems
Michael T. Waites, Exec. Vice-President/CFO

Fluor Canada Ltd.
Sundance Park
55 Sunpark Plaza SE
Calgary, AB T2X 3R4
403-537-4000 Fax: 403-537-4222 www.fluor.com/canada
Company Type: Private
Profile: Engineering, architectural & surveying services; Management & public relations services; Oil & gas field exploration services

Alan L. Boeckmann, Chair/CEO, Fluor Corporation
Lee Richardson, Vice-President, Operations
D. Michael Steuert, Sr. Vice-President/CFO, Fluor Corporation
Lee Tashjian, Vice-President, Corporate Communications, Fluor Corporation

Groupe BMR inc
2375, rue de la Province
Longueuil, QC J4G 1G3

450-463-2441 Fax: 450-463-1766
info@bmr-legroupe.com
www.bmr-legroupe.com
Company Type: Private
Profile: Wholesales brick, stone, lumber, plywood, millwork & related construction materials

Yves Gagnon, President
Jean St-Maurice, Director, Finance
Richard Gatien, Director, Information Technology

Johnson Controls Ltd.
100 Townline Rd.
Tillsonburg, ON N4G 2R7
519-842-5971 Fax: 519-842-3443 www.jci.com
Company Type: Private
Profile: Special trade contracting in plumbing, heating & air-conditioning; Manufacturers of automatic controls regulating environments & appliances

John Barth, President/CEO
Stephen A. Roell, Sr. Vice-President/CFO
Subhash Valanju, Vice-President/Chief Information Officer

Komatsu Canada Ltd.
1725B Sismet Rd
Mississauga, ON L4W 1P9
905-625-6292 Fax: 905-625-3036 www.komatsu.ca
Company Type: Private
Profile: Wholesalers of construction & mining machinery & equipment; Wholesalers of industrial machinery & equipment

Mike Ishida, President/CEO
Verica Simic, Controller

Lockerbie & Hole Inc.
14940-121A Ave.
Edmonton, AB T5V 1A3
780-452-1250 Fax: 780-452-1284 800-417-2329
mail@lockerbiehole.com
www.lockerbiehole.com
Company Type: Private
Profile: Construction services to industrial, municipal, commercial & institutional markets

Darcy J. Trufyn, President/CEO
Gordon Panas, CFO

Macyro Group Inc.
6140, boul Sainte-Anne
L'Ange-Gardien, QC G0A 2K0
418-822-0283 Fax: 418-822-2530
infos@macyro.com
www.macyro.com
Ticker Symbol: MYO
Company Type: Public
Profile: Manufacturers of metal doors, sash, frames, molding & trim

Kevin McCrann, CEO
Jean LeFrançois, CFO

Maple Reinders Constructors Ltd.
2660 Argentia Rd.
Mississauga, ON L5N 5V4
905-821-4844 Fax: 905-821-4822
main@maple.ca
www.maple.ca
Company Type: Private
Profile: Various heavy construction; General contractors in industrial buildings, warehouses & non-residential buildings

Mike Reinders, President/CEO
Eric Van Ginkel, CFO
Kevin Dreyer, Manager, Information Technology

Monarch Development Corporation
#1201, 2025 Sheppard Ave East
Toronto, ON M2J 1V7
416-491-7440 Fax: 416-491-3094
monarch@ca.taylorwoodrow.com
www.monarchgroup.net
Company Type: Private
Profile: Operative builders; General contractors in industrial, non-residential buildings & warehouses; Real estate operators of non-residential buildings; Real estate land subdividers & developers

Brian Johnston, President
Lynn Whelan, Finance/Treasurer/Controller

PCL Constructors Canada Inc.
5400 - 99 St.
Edmonton, AB T6E 3N7
780-435-9711 Fax: 780-436-2247 www.pcl.com
Company Type: Private
Profile: Various heavy construction; General contracting in industrial buildings & warehouses

Paul Douglas, President/COO, PCL Constructors Canada Inc.
Gordon Maron, CFO, PCL Construction Holdings Inc.
Brian Ranger, Manager, Information Systems
Lyonel Neveu, Manager, Safety & Loss Prevention

Steeplejack Industrial Group Inc.
8925 - 62 Ave.
Edmonton, AB T6E 5L2
780-465-9016 Fax: 780-466-8584
request@steeplejack.ca
www.steeplejack.ca
Ticker Symbol: SID
Company Type: Public
Profile: Offices of holding companies; Special trade contractors in plastering, drywall, acoustical & insulation

James I.M. Ross, President/CEO
David S.J. Dawyd, Vice-President/CFO
Jay Pollock, Analyst, Systems

Stuart Olson Construction Ltd.
12836 - 146 St.
Edmonton, AB T5L 2H7
780-452-4260 Fax: 780-455-4178
info@stuartolson.com
www.stuartolson.com
Company Type: Private
Profile: General contractors in residential, non-residential & industrial buildings & warehouses

Al Stowkowy, President/COO
James Saretsky, Vice-President, Finance
Mike Biedul, Director, Information Technology

Winalta Inc.
Kalwin Business Park
26302 Township Rd. 531A
Spruce Grove, AB T7X 3G3
780-960-6900 Fax: 780-960-9523
winalta@winaltainc.com
www.winaltainc.com
Ticker Symbol: WTA
Company Type: Public
Profile: Producer of manufactured CSA certified homes, modular homes, site built homes, industrial project and recreational homes; through its subsidiary, Vanguard Inc., designs, manufactures & wholesales recreational vehicles & industrial oilfield units

James A. Sapara, Chair/CEO
Frank Dixon, COO
Mike Fekete, CFO

Distribution & Retail

A & B Sound Ltd.
13260 Delf Pl.
Richmond, BC V6V 2A2
604-303-2900 Fax: 604-303-2932
webfeedback@absound.ca
www.absound.ca
Company Type: Private
Profile: Retailers of consumer electronics & miscellaneous music & movies

Tim Howley, President/CEO
Katherine Angus, Controller
Craig Dong, Manager, Regional Operations
Jim Matheson, Director, Information Technology

Acklands-Grainger Inc.
90 West Beaver Creek Rd.
Richmond Hill, ON L4B 1E7
905-731-5516 Fax: 905-731-9677
800-668-8989www.acklandsgrainger.com
Company Type: Public
Profile: Provides maintenance, repair & operating products for businesses

Court Carruthers, President
Greg Irving, Vice-President, Finance
Bala Puvitharan, Vice-President, Information Technology

George McClean, General Counsel & Vice-President, Safety & Environment

Alimentation Couche-Tard inc
#200 Tower B, 1600, boul Saint-Martin es
Laval, QC H7G 4S7
450-662-3272 Fax: 450-662-6648 800-361-2612
info@couche-tard.qc.ca
www.couche-tard.qc.ca
Ticker Symbol: ATD
Company Type: Public
Profile: Retailing in grocery stores, gasoline service stations, eating places; Various amusement & recreation services

Alain Bouchard, President/CEO & Chair
Richard Fortin, CFO & Exec. Vice-President

Avon Canada Inc.
5500, aut Transcanadienne
Montréal, QC H9R 1B6
514-695-3371 Fax: 514-630-5439 800-265-2866
questions@avon.com
www.avon.ca
Company Type: Private
Profile: Manufacturers of perfumes, cosmetics & other toilet preparations, costume jewelry & novelties; Retailing in miscellaneous retail stores

Scott Schlackmon, President
Luigi Del Vecchio, Vice-President, Finance
Judith Fyfe, Director, Information Systems
Nicole Gonella, Analyst, Security/Compensation

Black Photo Corporation
371 Gough Rd.
Markham, ON L3R 4B6
905-475-2777 Fax: 905-475-8027 800-668-3826
support@blackphoto.com
www.blackphoto.com
Company Type: Private
Profile: Photograpy equipment & supplies

W.R. Smith, President/CEO
R. Dew, Vice-President & Controller
Roy Short, Director, Information

Calgary Co-Operative Association Ltd.
2735 - 39th Ave. N.E.
Calgary, AB T1Y 7C7
403-219-6025 Fax: 403-299-5445 www.calgarycoop.com
Company Type: Private
Profile: Offers range of retail services in Calgary area, including grocery, pharmacy, petroleum, liquor & travel

Ken McCullough, CEO
Barry Heinrich, Vice-President, Finance & Administration

Canada Safeway Ltd.
1020 - 64 Ave. NE
Calgary, AB T2E 7V8
403-730-3500 Fax: 403-730-3777
800-723-3929www.safeway.com
Company Type: Private
Profile: Manufacturers of fluid milk, bread & other bakery products, various other food preparations; Retailing in grocery stores

Paul Malo, CFO
Chuck Mulvenna, President/COO
David T. Ching, Sr. Vice-President/Chief Information Officer, Safeway Inc.

Canadian Tire Corporation, Limited
PO Box 770 K, 2180 Yonge St.
Toronto, ON M4V 2V8
416-480-3000 Fax: 416-544-7715
investor.relations@cantire.com
www.canadiantire.ca
Ticker Symbol: CTC
Company Type: Public
Profile: Retailers of building materials; Paint, glass & wallpaper stores; Hardware stores; Nurseries, lawn & garden supply stores; Auto & home supply stores; Gasoline service stations; Radio, television & consumer electronics stores; Sporting goods stores & bicycle shops; Hobby, toy & game shops; Insurance agents, brokers & services

Tom Gauld, President/CEO
Mike Arnett, President, Canadian Tire Retail
J. Huw Thomas, Exec. Vice-President/CFO

MAJOR CANADIAN COMPANIES

Canadian Tire Corporation, Limited (continued)
Andrew T. Wnek, Sr. Vice-President, Information Technology & Chief Information Officer
Gail Bebee, Director, Environment, Health & Safety

Cara Operations Limited
6303 Airport Rd.
Mississauga, ON L4V 1R8
905-405-6500
info@cara.com
www.cara.com
Ticker Symbol: CAO
Company Type: Public
Profile: Retail eating places & gift, novelty & souvenir shops, news dealers & newsstands

Gabriel T. Tsampalieros, President/CEO & Director
M. Forsayeth, CFO & Sr. Vice-President
Tony Alleyne, Vice-President, Information Technology
Mark Hennessy, Manager, Health & Safety

Chai-Na-Ta Corp.
#100, 12051 Horseshoe Way
Richmond, BC V7A 4V4
604-272-4118 Fax: 604-272-4113 800-406-7668
info@chainata.com
www.chainata.com
Ticker Symbol: CC
Company Type: Public
Profile: Wholesalers of North American ginseng

W. Zen, Chairman/CEO
W. Wong, CFO/Secretary

Co-op Atlantic
PO Box 750, 123 Halifax St.
Moncton, NB E1C 8N5
506-858-6000 Fax: 506-858-6477 www.co-opsonline.com
Company Type: NA
Profile: Wholesalers of general line groceries, farm supplies, grain & field beans, petroleum & petroleum products, hardware

John Harvie, CEO
Paul-Emile Légère, CFO & Treasurer
Vic Shaw, Vice-President, Information Technology

CoolBrands International Inc.
210 Shields Court
Markham, ON L3R 8V2
905-479-8762 Fax: 905-479-5235
franchising@yogenfruz.com
www.yogenfruz.com
Ticker Symbol: COB
Company Type: Public
Profile: Retailing in eating places; Wholesalers of dairy products, frozen specialties, frozen fruits, fruit juices & vegetables; Manufacturers of ice cream & frozen desserts

David J. Stein, President/Co-CEO
Michael Serruya, Co-Chair
Gary P. Stevens, CFO

Coopérative fédérée de Québec
#200, 9001, boul de L'Acadie
Montréal, QC H4N 3H7
514-384-6450 Fax: 514-384-7176
information@lacoop.coop
www.coopfed.qc.ca
Company Type: NA
Profile: Wholesalers of meats & meat products, fresh fruits & vegetables, dairy products, petroleum & petroleum products

Pierre Gavreau, CEO
Paul Noiseux, CFO/Treasurer

Costco Canada Inc.
415 West Hunt Club
Ottawa, ON K2E 1C5
613-221-2000 Fax: 613-221-2001 www.costco.com
Company Type: Private
Profile: Provides members with discount, bulk retail items

Jim Sinegal, CEO
Joseph P. Portera, President
Ross Hunt, Vice-President, Human Resources & Finance

Empire Company Limited
115 King St.
Stellarton, NS B0K 1S0
902-755-4440 Fax: 902-755-6477
ir-empire@sobeys.com
www.empireco.ca
Ticker Symbol: EMP
Company Type: Public
Profile: Key businesses include food distribution, real estate, theatres & corporate investment activities

Paul D. Sobey, President/CEO & Director
Paul Beesley, Sr. Vice-President, CFO & Sec.

Forzani Group Ltd.
824 - 41 Ave. NE
Calgary, AB T2E 3R3
403-717-1400 Fax: 403-717-1490
cjordan@forzani.com
www.forzanigroup.com
Ticker Symbol: FGL
Company Type: Public
Profile: Retailing in sporting goods stores & bicycle shops, miscellaneous apparel & accessory stores, shoe stores

R. Sartor, CEO
W.D. Gregson, COO & President
Richard Burnet, Vice-President, Finance
Debbie Gillis, Vice-President, Information Technology

Future Shop Ltd.
8800 Glenlyon Pkwy.
Burnaby, BC V5J 5K3
604-435-8223 Fax: 604-412-5280 800-663-2275
service@futureshop.com
www.futureshop.ca
Company Type: Private
Profile: Retailing in radio, television & consumer electronics stores, computer & computer software stores, household appliance stores

Kevin Layden, President/COO
Dan Lagermeier, Exec. Vice-President/CFO

G.E. Shnier Co.
50 Kenview Blvd.
Brampton, ON L6T 5S8
905-789-3755 Fax: 905-789-3757 800-970-2000
info@gesco.ca
www.geshnier.com
Company Type: Private
Profile: Markets floor covering products

E.W.S duDomaine, President/CEO
John Deotto, CFO
Bob Lesiw, Head, Technology

Grand & Toy Ltd.
33 Green Belt Dr.
Don Mills, ON M3C 1M1
416-445-7255 Fax: 416-445-7741
generalinquiries@grandtoy.com
www.grandandtoy.com
Company Type: Private
Profile: Commercial supplier of office supplies, furniture & technology products

Garry Wood, President
Grant Forrest, Vice-President, Finance
John Melodysta, Vice-President, Information Technology

Great Atlantic & Pacific Tea Co. Ltd.
5559 Dundas St. West
Etobicoke, ON M9B 1B9
416-239-7171 Fax: 416-234-6581
877-763-7374www.freshobsessed.com
Company Type: Private
Profile: Offices of holding companies; Retailing in grocery stores

Eric Claus, President/CEO & Chair
G. Gilpin, Sr. Vice-President, Finance
Debra Kinread, Vice-President, Information Services
Keith Lamson, Director, Health & Safety

Groupe BMTC inc
8500, Place Marien
Montréal, QC H1B 5W8
514-648-5757 Fax: 514-881-4056
service.clients@braultetmartineau.com
www.braultetmartineau.com
Ticker Symbol: GBT
Company Type: Public
Profile: Retailing furniture stores, household appliance stores, radio, television, & consumer electronics stores

Yves Des Groseillers, Chair/President & CEO
Gilles Nadeau, Director, Finance

Groupe les Ailes de la Mode inc
50, rue de Lauzon
Boucherville, QC J4B 1E6
450-449-1313 Fax: 450-449-1317
gcharron@bsf.ca
www.bsf.ca
Ticker Symbol: MOD-T
Company Type: Public
Profile: Retailing in women's clothing stores, women's accessory & specialty stores, men's & boys' clothing & accessory stores, children's & infants' wear stores; Manufacturers of: men's & boys' shirts; separate trousers & slacks; women's, misses' & juniors' blouses & shirts; women's, misses' & juniors' dresses; various women's, misses' & juniors' outerwear

Paul Delage Roberge, Chair/President/CEO
Jacques Fournier, Vice-President, Finance & CFO
Jean Boisvert, Vice-President, Management Information Systems

Harry Rosen Inc.
#1600, 77 Bloor St. West
Toronto, ON M5S 1M2
416-935-9200 Fax: 416-515-7067 www.harryrosen.com
Company Type: Private
Profile: Retail menswear

Larry Rosen, Chair & CEO
Peter Stansfield, President/COO
Conrad Frejlich, CFO & Vice-President
Steve Jackson, Director, Information Services

Hart Stores Inc.
9001, boul Louis-H.-Lafontaine
Montréal, QC H1J 2C5
514-354-0101 Fax: 514-354-9493
hartstoresinfo@hartco.com
www.hartstores.com
Ticker Symbol: HIS
Company Type: Public
Profile: Retails-department stores

Michael Hart, President/CEO
Robert Farah, CFO
Sal Pugliese, Director, Information Technology & Internal Systems

Hudson's Bay Company
#500, 401 Bay St.
Toronto, ON M5H 2Y4
416-861-6112 Fax: 416-861-4720 www.hbc.ca
Ticker Symbol: HBC
Company Type: Public
Profile: Retailing in department stores; Short-term business credit institutions; Information retrieval services

George J. Heller, President/CEO & Director
Michael S. Rousseau, Exec. Vice-President/CFO
Gary Davenport, Vice-President & Chief Information Officer
Bob Kolida, Chief Environmental Officer

Hy & Zel's Inc.
7171 Yonge St.
Thornhill, ON L3T 2A9
905-886-7171 Fax: 905-886-9605 www.hyandzels.com
Ticker Symbol: HZI
Company Type: Private
Profile: Retailing in drug stores & proprietary stores, grocery stores & miscellaneous general merchandise stores

Zelick Goldstein, CEO
Larry Cooper, CFO

Indigo Books & Music Inc.
#500, 468 King St. West
Toronto, ON M5V 1L8
416-364-4499 Fax: 416-364-0355 www.chapters.indigo.ca
Ticker Symbol: IDG
Company Type: Public
Profile: Retail book stores

Heather Reisman, Chair/CEO
Jim McGill, CFO
Doug Caldwell, Chief Technology Officer

Indigo Books & Music Online Inc.
#500, 468 King St. W.
Toronto, ON M5V iL8

MAJOR CANADIAN COMPANIES

416-598-8000 Fax: 416-598-5060
800-832-7569www.chapters.indigo.ca
Company Type: Private
Profile: Retail book & music chain

Jim McGill, CFO
Doug Caldwell, Chief Technology Officer

Isle Three Holdings Ltd.
6649 Bulter Cres.
Saanichton, BC V8M 1Z7
250-483-1600 Fax: 250-483-1601 800-667-8280
info@thriftyfoods.com
www.thriftyfoods.com
Company Type: Private
Profile: Retailing in grocery stores & bakeries

Milford Sorensen, President
John Tucker, CFO
Michael Rassenti, Director, Information Technology
Glen Barned, Auditor, Operational Health & Safety

Itochu Canada Ltd
World Trade Centre
#770, 999 Canada Pl.
Vancouver, BC V6C 3E1
604-331-5800 Fax: 604-688-9292 www.itochu.com
Company Type: Private
Profile: Wholesalers of electrical appliances, television & radio sets, commercial equipment, various durable & non-durable goods

Yoshio Akamatsu, President/CEO/Chair

Jean Coutu Group (PJC) Inc.
530, rue Bériault
Longueuil, QC J4G 1S8
450-646-9760 Fax: 450-646-5649 www.jeancoutu.com
Ticker Symbol: PJC
Company Type: Public
Profile: Wholesalers of drugs, drug proprietaries & druggists' sundries; Retailing in drug stores & proprietary stores; Real estate operators of nonresidential buildings; Patent owners & lessors

François Coutu, President/CEO
Carole Bouthillette, Vice-President, Finance
Michel Boucher, Vice-President, Information Systems

Katz Group Canada Ltd.
Bell Tower
#1702, 10104 - 103 Ave.
Edmonton, AB T5J 0H8
780-990-0505 Fax: 780-425-6118 877-378-4100
information@rexall.ca
www.katzgroup.ca
Company Type: Private
Profile: Encompasses more than 1,800 pharmacies across North America; Canadian pharmacies include Rexall Drug Stores, Pharma Plus, Rexall Pharma Plus, Medicine Shoppe Pharmacy, Guardian, I.D.A., Herbies & Meditrust Pharmacy

Andy Giancamilli, CEO
Paul Marcaccio, Chief Financial Officer
Brian McLaughlin, Exec. Vice-President, Human Resources & Corporate Relations
Warren Jeffery, Chief Operating Officer

La Senza Corporation
1604, boul St-Régis
Montréal, QC H9P 1H6
514-684-3651 Fax: 514-421-0381 888-527-3692
ir@lasenza.com
www.lasenza.com
Ticker Symbol: LSZ
Company Type: Public
Profile: Retailing in women's clothing stores, women's accessory & specialty stores, miscellaneous apparel & accessory stores

Irving Teitelbaum, Chair/CEO
Laurence Lewin, President/COO
Anna Palestini, CFO

Leon's Furniture Limited
PO Box 1100 B, 45 Gordon Mackay Rd.
Toronto, ON M9L 2R8
416-243-7880 Fax: 416-243-7890
investors@leons.ca
www.leons.ca
Ticker Symbol: LNF
Company Type: Public
Profile: Retailing in furniture, household appliances, floor covering & miscellaneous stores, radio, television, & consumer electronics

Mark Leon, Vice-Chair/CEO
Terry Leon, President/COO
Dominic Scarangella, Vice-President/CFO
M. Ogilvie, Manager, Information Systems

Liquor Control Board of Ontario
55 Lakeshore Blvd. East
Toronto, ON M5E 1A4
416-365-5900 Fax: 416-864-2596 800-668-5226
infoline@lcbo.com
www.lcbo.com
Company Type: Crown
Profile: Retailers in liquor stores; Testing laboratories

Andrew S. Brandt, Chair/CEO
Alex Browning, Sr. Vice-President, Finance
Hugh Kelly, Sr. Vice-President, Technology
Gerry Ker, Director, Corporate Policy

Loblaw Companies Limited
#1500, 22 St Clair Ave. East
Toronto, ON M4T 2S8
416-922-2500 Fax: 416-922-4395
investor@weston.ca
www.loblaw.com
Ticker Symbol: L
Company Type: Public
Profile: Offices of holding companies; Retailers in grocery stores; Wholesalers in general line groceries

Mark Foote, President & Chief Merchandising Officer
Richard Mayriac, Exec. Vice-President
Galen G. Weston, Exec. Chair
Louise Lacchin, Vice-President, Finance
Walter Kraus, Director, Environmental Affairs

Marubeni Canada Ltd.
#800, 330 Bay St.
Toronto, ON M5H 2S8
416-368-1171 Fax: 416-947-9004 www.marubeni.com
Company Type: Private
Profile: Wholesalers of farm & garden machinery & equipment, automobile & other motor vehicles

Nobuo Katsumata, President/CEO
Susumu Watanabe, Exec. Corporate Officer, Gen. Affairs, Corp. Accounting/Finance & Investor Relat
Toshio Nakagawa, Chief Information Officer
Katsuo Koh, Exec. Deputy President

McKesson Canada Corp.
8625, aut Transcanadienne
Montréal, QC H4S 1Z6
514-725-2100 Fax: 514-745-2300
communication@mckesson.ca
www.mckesson.ca
Company Type: Private
Profile: Wholesalers of drugs, drug proprietaries & druggists' sundries

C. Bussandri, President/CEO
Alain Vachon, CFO
George Attar, Vice-President/Chief Information Officer
Yves Portelance, Vice-President & General Manager, Hospital & Automation Solutions

Metro Inc.
11011, boul Maurice-Duplessis
Montréal, QC H1C 1V6
514-643-1000 Fax: 514-643-1215
finance@metro.ca
www.metro.ca
Ticker Symbol: MRU
Company Type: Public
Profile: Operator of a network of food stores in Ontario & Québec, under the following names: Metro, Metro Plus, Super C, A&P, Dominion, Loeb & Food Basics; Operator of pharmacies under the following banners: Brunet, Clini-Plus, The Pharmacy & Drug Basics

Pierre H. Lessard, President/CEO
Richard Dufresne, Sr. Vice-President/CFO
Jacques Couture, Vice-President, Information Systems
Eric Richer LaFlèche, Exec. Vice-President/COO

Mitsui & Co. (Canada) Ltd.
#1400, 20 Adelaide St. East
Toronto, ON M5C 2T6
416-365-3800 Fax: 416-865-1486 **Company Type:** Private
Profile: Investors; Wholesalers of various nondurable goods, groceries & related products, chemicals & allied products, metals service centers & offices, grain & field beans, farm supplies; Commodity contracts brokers & dealers

Kiyotaka Watanabe, President & CEO
Jorji Okada, CFO

Nevada Bob's International Inc.
#7070, 1 First Canadian Pl.
Toronto, ON M5X 1B1
416-366-2221
corpinfo@nevadabobs.com
www.nevadabobs.com
Ticker Symbol: NBC
Company Type: Public
Profile: Retailing in sporting goods stores & bicycle shops; Patent owners & lessors

Kevin R. Baker, President/CEO & Director
Donald Semenchuk, Director, Information Systems

North West Company Fund
77 Main St.
Winnipeg, MB R3C 2R1
204-943-0881 Fax: 204-934-1455
nwc@northwest.ca
www.northwest.ca
Ticker Symbol: NWF
Company Type: Public
Profile: Open end management investment offices; Retailers in miscellaneous food stores & department stores

Edward S. Kennedy, President/CEO
Léo Charrière, Exec. Vice-President/CFO & Secretary
Gerald Mauthe, Vice-President, Information Services

Olco Petroleum Group Inc.
2775, av Georges Vanier
Montréal, QC H1L 6J7
514-645-6526 Fax: 514-645-8048 800-363-1120
olco@olco.ca
www.olco.ca
Ticker Symbol: OLC
Company Type: Public
Profile: Wholesalers in petroleum bulk stations & terminals, petroleum & petroleum products; Retailers in gasoline service stations

Wilfred Kaneb, Chair/CEO
Mark Kaneb, President/COO & Secretary
Pierre Merineau, Controller
Michel Beaulieu, Supervisor, Construction

Pantorama Industries Inc.
2, rue Lake
Montréal, QC H9B 3H9
514-421-1850 Fax: 514-684-3159
pantoram@netcom.ca
Ticker Symbol: PTA
Company Type: Private
Profile: Retailing in men's & boys' clothing & accessory stores, women's clothing stores & shoe stores

Sydney Aptacker, President/CEO
Ralph Fragomene, Vice-President, Finance & Operations
Hamid Faradel, Director, Information Technology

Parkland Industries LP
#236, 4919 - 59th St.
Red Deer, AB T4N 6C9
403-357-6400 Fax: 403-352-0042
corpinfo@parkland.ca
www.parkland.ca
Ticker Symbol: PKI
Company Type: Public
Profile: Manufacturers of petroleum refining; Wholesalers of petroleum & petroleum products; Retailers in gasoline service stations; Patent owners & lessors

Michael W. Chorlton, President/CEO
John G. Schroeder, Vice-President/CFO
James Carson, Manager, Information Technology
Al Tait, Manager, Health, Safety & Environment

Pet Valu Canada Inc. (continued)

Pet Valu Canada Inc.
130 Royal Crest Ct.
Markham, ON L3R 0A1
905-946-1200 Fax: 905-946-0659 888-254-7824
hr@petvalue.com
www.petvalue.com
Ticker Symbol: PVC
Company Type: Public
Profile: Patent owners & lessors; Retailing in miscellaneous retail stores; Wholesalers of various nondurable goods

Geoffrey F.A. Holt, President/CEO
Dale Winkworth, Exec. Vice-President/CFO
Jagdish Handa, Chief Information Officer

Pharmasave Drugs National Ltd.
6350 - 203rd St.
Langley, BC V2Y 1L9
604-532-2250 Fax: 604-532-2293
info@pharmasave.bc.ca
www.pharmasave.com
Company Type: Private
Profile: Retail pharmacy chain

Terry Blocher, CEO
Judy MacLeod, Director, Accounting & Finance

Provigo Inc.
400, av Sainte-Croix
Saint-Laurent, QC H4N 3L4
514-383-3000 Fax: 514-383-3088 www.provigo.ca
Company Type: Private
Profile: Retailers in grocery stores; Wholesalers in general line groceries; Patent owners & lessors

Bernard J. McDonell, President
Marie Helen Michaud, Manager, Information Technology

Reitmans (Canada) Limited
250, rue Sauvé ouest
Montréal, QC H3L 1Z2
514-384-1140 Fax: 514-385-2664
customerservice@reitmans.com
www.reitmans.com
Ticker Symbol: RET
Company Type: Public
Profile: Retailing in women's clothing stores, children's & infants' wear stores

Kerry Mitchell, President, Penningtons
Douglas M. Deruchie, Vice-President, Finance
Claude Martineau, Chief Information Officer

Richelieu Hardware Ltd.
7900, boul Henri-Bourassa ouest
Montréal, QC H4S 1V4
514-336-4144 Fax: 514-832-4002 866-832-4040
info@richelieu.com
www.richelieu.com
Ticker Symbol: RCH
Company Type: Public
Profile: Wholesalers of hardware, lumber, plywood, millwork, & wood panels; Manufacturers of softwood veneer & plywood

Richard Lord, President/CEO
Georges Albert, Vice-President, Finance

Ritchie Bros. Auctioneers Incorporated
6500 River Rd.
Richmond, BC V6X 4G5
604-273-7564 Fax: 604-273-2102 800-663-1739
info@rbauction.com
www.rbauction.com
Ticker Symbol: RBA
Company Type: Public
Profile: Retailers in miscellaneous retail stores; Various business services

David Ritchie, Chair/CEO
Randall J. Wall, President/COO
Bob Armstrong, Vice-President, Finance
Dale Finlan, Chief Information Officer
Tex Mahler, Manager, Health, Environment & Safety

RONA Inc.
220, ch du Tremblay
Boucherville, QC J4B 8H7
514-599-5100 Fax: 514-599-5110 866-283-2239
investor.relations@rona.ca
www.rona.ca
Company Type: Public
Profile: Wholesalers of hardware, construction materials, lumber, plywood, millwork & wood panels, plumbing/heating equipment & hydronics supplies, farm & garden machinery & equipment

Robert Dutton, President/CEO
Claude Guévin, Exec. Vice-President/CFO
Linda Michaud, Vice-President, Information Technology
Pierre Pelletier, Vice-President, Logistics

Sears Canada Inc.
222 Jarvis St.
Toronto, ON M5B 2B8
416-941-4793 Fax: 416-941-4425
home@sears.ca
www.sears.ca
Ticker Symbol: SCC
Company Type: Public
Profile: Retailers in department stores, catalogue & mail-order houses; Short-term business credit institutions; Repair shops & various related services

Brent Hollister, President/CEO
John T. Butcher, Exec. Vice-President/CFO

Sobeys Inc.
115 King St.
Stellarton, NS B0K 1S0
902-752-8371 Fax: 902-755-6477
investor.relations@sobeys.com
www.sobeys.com
Ticker Symbol: SBY
Company Type: Public
Profile: National grocery retailer & food distributor; Retail banners include Sobey's, IGA extra, IGA & Price Chopper

Bill McEwan, President/CEO
Gary Kerr, President, Operations, Western Region
Bruce Terry, Exec. Vice-President & CFO

Société des alcools du Québec
905, av de Lorimier
Montréal, QC H2K 3V9
514-254-2711 Fax: 514-864-3532 866-873-2020
info@saq.com
www.saq.com
Company Type: Crown
Profile: Regulation, licensing & inspection of miscellaneous commercial sectors

Louis L. Roquet, President/CEO
Gérald Plouffe, First Vice-President, Administration & Finance
Beno(140t Durand, Vice-President, Information Resources

Sodisco-Howden Group Inc.
465, rue McGill, 1e étage
Montréal, QC H2Y 2H4
514-286-8986 Fax: 514-286-2911
info@gshg.com
www.sodisco.com
Ticker Symbol: SOD
Company Type: Public
Profile: Wholesalers of hardware

Jos J. Wintermans, President/CEO
James Shannon, Vice-President/CFO
Norman Hull, Vice-President, Information Systems

Sony of Canada Ltd.
115 Gordon Baker Rd.
Toronto, ON M2H 3R6
416-499-1414 Fax: 416-497-1774
general_enquiries@sony.ca
www.sony.ca
Company Type: Private
Profile: Wholesalers of electrical appliances, television & radio sets, electronic parts & equipment

Douglas D. Wilson, President/COO
Barry Hasler, CFO
Tariq Shameem, Sr. Vice-President, Service & Engineering
Nick Aubry, Manager, Environmental
M. Huntington, Sr. Vice-President, AV/IT Sales

Summit Food Service Distributors Inc.
580 Industrial Rd.
London, ON N5V 1V1
Fax: 519-453-5148 800-265-9267
headoffice@summitfoods.com
www.summitfoods.com
Company Type: Public
Profile: Wholesalers of packaged frozen foods & general line groceries

Jack Battersby, President
Dina Palmer, Controller
Sandy Crellin, Office Manager
Doug Mason, Supervisor, Inventory Control

Toshiba of Canada Ltd.
191 McNabb St.
Markham, ON L3R 8H2
905-470-3500 Fax: 905-470-3509 www.toshiba.ca
Company Type: Private
Profile: Wholesalers of office equipment, computers & peripheral equipment & software, electrical appliances, television & radio sets, electronic parts & equipment, medical, dental, hospital equipment & supplies

M. Kurihara, President
Dan McDonald, Sr. Vice-President/CFO
G. Paynes, Vice-President, Information Systems

Uni-Select Inc.
170, boul Industriel
Boucherville, QC J4B 2X3
450-641-2440 Fax: 450-449-4908 www.uni-select.com
Ticker Symbol: UNS
Company Type: Public
Profile: Wholesalers of motor vehicle supplies & new parts; Retailers in auto & home supply stores

Jacques Landreville, President/CEO
Richard G. Roy, CFO & Vice-President, Administration
David G. Alderson, Vice-President, Management Information Systems
Pierre Chesnay, Secretary & Vice-President, Legal Affairs

United Furniture Warehouse Ltd.
#16930, 114 Ave.
Edmonton, AB T5M 3S2
604-540-8000 Fax: 604-540-4010 www.ufw.com
Company Type: Private
Profile: Warehouse manufacturers-to-public retailers

John Volken, President
Johan Jackobs, Controller

Westfair Foods Ltd.
PO Box 300 M, 3225 - 12 St. NE
Calgary, AB T2P 2H9
403-291-7700 Fax: 403-291-7899 **Ticker Symbol:** WF
Company Type: Public
Profile: Retailing in grocery stores; Wholesalers of general line groceries

John S. Zeller, Exec. Vice-President/CEO

The Winroc Corporation
4949 - 51 St. SE
Calgary, AB T2B 3S7
403-236-5383 Fax: 403-279-0372 www.winroc.com
Company Type: Private
Profile: Wholesalers of construction materials; Retailing in lumber & other building materials dealers

Paul Vanderberg, President/CEO
James Empey, Vice-President, Finance

Electronics & Electrical Equipment

Aastra Technologies Limited
155 Snow Blvd.
Concord, ON L4K 4N9
905-760-4200 Fax: 905-760-4238
investors@aastra.com
www.aastra.com
Ticker Symbol: AAH
Company Type: Public
Profile: Manufacturers of telephone & telegraph apparatus

F.N. Shen, Chair/CEO
A.P. Shen, President/COO
Allan Brett, CFO/Vice-President, Finance
Jamshid Rezar, Chief Information Officer

Bell Canada International Inc.
#1200, 1000 rue de la Gauchetière ouest
Montréal, QC H3B 4Y8
514-392-2384 Fax: 514-392-2266
info@marcnon.qc.ca
www.bci.ca

Ticker Symbol: BI
Company Type: Public
Profile: Manufacturers of telephone & telegraph apparatus; Manufacturers of radio & television broadcasting & communications equipment; Special trade contracting in electrical work

William D. Anderson, Chair/CEO
Howard N. Hendrick, Exec. Vice-President/CFO

Celestica Inc.

1150 Eglinton Ave. East
Toronto, ON M3C 1H7
416-448-5800 Fax: 416-448-4699 888-899-9998
clsir@celestica.com
www.celestica.com
Ticker Symbol: CLS
Company Type: Public
Profile: Manufacturers of various electronic components, printed circuit boards; Wholesalers in electronic parts & equipment

Eugene Polistuk, Chair/CEO
Marv Magee, President/COO
Anthony P. Puppi, Exec. Vice-President/CFO & General Manager, Global Services
Bob Mansbridge, Acting Chief Information Officer
Iaian S. Kennedy, Group Executive, Global Supply Chain & Info Technology
Frank O'Rourke, Manager, Environment, Health & Safety

Cinram International Inc.

2255 Markham Rd.
Scarborough, ON M1B 2W3
416-298-8190 Fax: 416-298-0612
lewritchie@cinram.com
www.cinram.com
Ticker Symbol: CRW
Company Type: Public
Profile: Manufacturers of phonograph records & prerecorded audio tapes & disks; Services allied to motion picture production; Motion picture & video tape distribution

Isidore Philosophe, Chair/CEO & Director
David Hollander, President, European Operations
Lewis Ritchie, CFO/Secretary/Director & Exec. Vice-President, Finance & Administration
Dave Locksley, Director, Information Technology
Henri A. Aboutboul, Director, Waste Management International B.V.

CMC Electronics Inc.

600, boul Dr.-Frederik-Philips
Montréal, QC H4M 2S9
514-748-3148 Fax: 514-748-3100 www.cmcelectronics.ca
Company Type: Private
Profile: Manufacturers of aviation electronics, communications solutions, custom electronic products, CPS OEM products; Marine & land electronics sales & service; Customer support; Calibration

Jean-Pierre Mortreux, President/CEO
Greg Yeldon, CFO
Peter Divorty, Director, Information Technology
Michelle Fournier, Manager, Employee Relations

COM DEV International Ltd.

155 Sheldon Dr.
Cambridge, ON N1R 7H6
519-622-2300 Fax: 519-622-1691
investor.relations@comdev.ca
www.comdev.ca
Ticker Symbol: CDV
Company Type: Public
Profile: Manufacturers of radio & television broadcasting & communications equipment; Wholesalers of electrical appliances, television & radio sets

John Keating, CEO
Mike Pley, President
Gary Calhoun, CFO

Coretec Inc.

8150 Sheppard Ave. East
Toronto, ON M1B 5K2
416-208-2100 www.coretec-inc.com
Ticker Symbol: CYY
Company Type: Public
Profile: Manufacturers of printed circuit boards; Wholesalers of electronic parts & equipment

Paul Colin Langston, President/CEO & Chair
Gareth Parry, Chief Technology Officer
Mark Scruton, Director, Environmental

CSI Wireless Inc.

4110 - 9 St. SE
Calgary, AB T2G 3C4
403-259-3311 Fax: 403-259-8866
info@csi-wireless.com
www.csi-wireless.com
Ticker Symbol: CSY
Company Type: Public
Profile: Manufacturers of radio & television broadcasting & communications equipment, telephone & telegraph apparatus

Stephen A. Verhoeff, President/CEO/Chair & Director
Cameron Olson, Vice-President/CFO, Finance

Cygnal Technologies Corporation

70 Valleywood Dr.
Markham, ON L3R 4T5
905-944-6500 Fax: 905-944-6520 866-429-4625
central@cygnal.ca
www.cygnal.ca
Ticker Symbol: CYN
Company Type: Public
Profile: Manufacturers of radio & television broadcasting & communications equipment

Kieron J. Dowling, President/CEO
Bryan W. Hills, Vice-President, Finance
Eugene Kwong, Director, Technical Services

DALSA Coreco

#142, 7075, place Robert-Joncas
Montréal, QC H4M 2Z2
514-333-1301 Fax: 514-333-1388
investors@coreco.com
www.coreco.com
Ticker Symbol: CRC
Company Type: Public
Profile: Manufacturers of semiconductors & related devices; Manufacturers of printed circuit boards; Computer programming services

Keith A. Reuben, President/CEO
Louis Daigneault, CFO/Vice-President, Finance & Administration

Ghislain Beaupré, Vice-President, Operations, Research & Development
Serge Beaulieu, Director, MIS
Len Van Den Engh, Manager, Quality

Eiger Technology, Inc.

#700, 144 Front St.
Toronto, ON M5J 2L7
416-216-8659 Fax: 416-216-1164
info@eigertechnology.com
www.eigertechnology.com
Ticker Symbol: AXA
Company Type: Public
Profile: Manufacturers of telephone & telegraph apparatus; Computer integrated systems design

Gerry A. Racicot, President/CEO
Keith Attoe, CFO/Secretary

Electrovaya Inc.

2645 Royal Windsor Dr.
Mississauga, ON L5J 1K9
905-855-4610 Fax: 905-822-7953 800-388-2865
customerservice@electrovaya.com
www.electrovaya.com
Ticker Symbol: EFL
Company Type: Public
Profile: Manufacturers of storage batteries

Sankar Das Gupta, President/CEO & Chair
Paul Hart, CFO
Anupam Dhar, Chief Information Officer
James K. Jacobs, Exec. Vice-President/Chief Technology Officer

EXFO Electro-Optical Engineering Inc.

400, av Godin
Québec, QC G1M 2K2
418-683-0211 Fax: 418-683-2170 800-663-3936
info@exfo.com
www.exfo.com
Ticker Symbol: EXF
Company Type: Public
Profile: Manufacturers of opto-eletronics apparatus; Manufactures test & measurement equipment for telecommunication industry; Fibre optic test equipment; Engineering services

Germain Lamonde, President/CEO & Chair
Pierre Plamondon, CFO & Vice-President, Finance
Gregory Schinn, Chief Technology Officer & Director, Research Division

General Electric Canada Inc.

2300 Meadowvale Blvd.
Mississauga, ON L5N 5P9
905-858-5100 Fax: 905-858-5106 www.ge.com/ca/en/
Company Type: Private
Profile: Manufactured products & services include power generation, water processing, aircraft engines, medical imaging, security technology, business & consumer financing, & media content

Elyse Allan, President/CEO
Ferdinando Beccalli, President/CEO, GE Europe
Peter Donovan, Vice-President, Finance
Kim Warburton, Leader, Communications & Public Relations
Roland Hosein, Vice-President, Health, Safety & Environment

Genesis Microchip (Canada) Co.

165 Commerce Valley Dr. West
Thornhill, ON L3T 7V8
905-889-5400 Fax: 905-889-5422
sales-americas@gnss.com
www.gnss.com
Ticker Symbol: GNSS
Company Type: Public
Profile: Manufacturers of semiconductors & related devices; Wholesalers of electronic parts & equipment

Elias Antoun, CEO
Michael E. Healy, CFO & Senior Vice-President, Finance

Gennum Corporation

970 Fraser Dr.
Burlington, ON L7L 5P5
905-632-2996 Fax: 905-632-2055
corporate@gennum.com
www.gennum.com
Ticker Symbol: GND
Company Type: Public
Profile: Manufacturers & marketers of semiconductor components, electrical subsystems & solutions for the global video, audio & data communications markets

Franz J. Fink, President/CEO
Gordon Currie, CFO & Sr. Vice-President, Finance & Administration
J. Giblon, Chief Information Officer

GSW Inc.

#100, 2020 Winston Park Dr.
Oakville, ON L6H 6X7
905-829-1197 Fax: 905-829-0092
info@gswinc.ca
www.gswinc.ca
Ticker Symbol: GSW
Company Type: Public
Profile: Offices of holding companies; Manufacturers of various household appliances, air-conditioning, warm air heating, refrigeration equipment, pumps & pumping equipment, fabricated plate work, various plastics products

Peter M. Sharpe, President/CEO
Dennis Nykoliation, President, GSW Building Products
Jamie Hyde, CFO & Vice-President, Finance
Stephen Gabor, Vice-President, Information Services

Hewlett-Packard (Canada) Ltd.

5150 Spectrum Way
Mississauga, ON L4W 5G1
905-206-4725 Fax: 905-206-4739 www.hp.ca
Company Type: Public
Profile: Provides technology solutions to consumers & businesses; Offers IT infrastructure, personal computing & access devices, global services, imaging & printing for consumers & small & medium businesses

Paul Teaparis, President/CEO
Linda Kitamura, CFO

Hydrogenics Corporation
5985 McLaughlin Rd.
Mississauga, ON L5R 1B8
905-361-3660 Fax: 905-361-3626
investors@hydrogenics.com
www.hydrogenics.com
Ticker Symbol: HYG
Company Type: Public
Profile: Manufacturers of various electrical industrial apparatus, fuel cell systems for power generation; Fuel testing & diagnosis

Pierre Rivard, President/CEO
Lawrence Davis, CFO
Joseph Cargnelli, Chief Technology Officer

L-3 Wescam
649 North Service Rd. West
Burlington, ON L7P 5B9
905-633-4000 Fax: 905-633-4100 800-668-4355
sales@wescam.com
www.wescam.com
Ticker Symbol: WSC
Company Type: Public
Profile: Manufacturers of gyrostabilized imaging turrets, digital & analogue reception & custom fitted system integration

John Dehne, President
Lou Park, CFO/Vice-President, Finance
Steve Tritchew, Chief Technology Officer

Leitch Technology Corporation
25 Syas Rd.
North York, ON M3B 1V7
416-445-9640 Fax: 416-445-0595 800-387-0233
info@leitch.com
www.leitch.com
Ticker Symbol: LTV
Company Type: Public
Profile: Manufacturers of various electronic components for processing high quality audio & video signals

Tim Thorsteinson, President/CEO
David Towes, CFO
John Ouzouis, Director, Information Systems
D. Mance, Chief Technology Officer

Mitec Telecom Inc.
9000, aut Transcanadienne
Montréal, QC H9R 5Z8
514-694-3938 Fax: 514-630-8600
sales@mitectelecom.com
www.mitectelecom.com
Ticker Symbol: MTM
Company Type: Public
Profile: Leading designer & provider of radio frequency products for the telecommunications, satellite communications, defence, as well as a variety of other industries

Keith Findlay, President/CEO
Stefano Bazzocchi, CFO/Exec. Vice-President, Finance

Mobile Knowledge
308 Legget Dr.
Kanata, ON K2K 1Y6
613-287-5020 Fax: 613-287-5021
info@mobile-knowledge.com
www.mobile-knowledge.com
Ticker Symbol: GPS
Company Type: Public
Profile: Manufacturers of various electronic components, computer integrated systems design; Various communications services

David Levy, CEO
Michael Chawner, President/COO
Ross Morgan, CFO
David Schenkel, Chief Technology Officer

MOSAID Technologies Incorporated
11 Hines Rd.
Kanata, ON K2K 2X1
613-599-9539 Fax: 613-591-8148
communications@mosaid.com
www.mosaid.com
Ticker Symbol: MSD
Company Type: Public
Profile: Developer & licensor of semiconductor intellectual property; Supplier of memory test & analysis systems

George J.J. Cwynar, President/CEO
Joseph R. Brown, Vice-President, Finance
Michael Vladescu, Vice-President, Patents

Norsat International Inc.
#110, 4020 Viking Way
Richmond, BC V6V 2N2
604-821-2800 Fax: 604-821-2801
info@norsat.com
www.norsat.com
Ticker Symbol: NII
Company Type: Public
Profile: Manufacturers of radio & television broadcasting & communications equipment; Wholesalers electronic parts & equipment

William Coyne, President/CEO
Constantine McQuade, Controller

Philips Electronics Canada
281 Hillmount Rd.
Markham, ON L6C 2S3
905-201-4100 Fax: 905-887-7921
webmaster@philips.com
www.philips.com
Company Type: Private
Profile: Manufacturers of industrial, institutional & residential electric lighting fixtures, household audio & video equipment, electric housewares & fans; Wholesalers of electronic parts & equipment, medical, dental, hospital equipment & supplies

Iain Burns, President/CEO
John McLindon, CFO & Vice-President, Finance

Research In Motion Limited
295 Phillip St.
Waterloo, ON N2L 3W8
519-888-7465 Fax: 519-888-7884
investor_relations@rim.com
www.rim.net
Ticker Symbol: RIM
Company Type: Public
Profile: Manufacturers of telephone & telegraph apparatus, computer peripheral equipment, mobile commuication devices

James Balsillie, Chair/Co-CEO
Denis Kavelman, CFO

Sierra Wireless, Inc.
13811 Wireless Way
Richmond, BC V6V 3A4
604-231-1100 Fax: 604-231-1109
info@sierrawireless.com
www.sierrawireless.com
Ticker Symbol: SW
Company Type: Public
Profile: Manufacturers of telephone & telegraph apparatus; Wholesalers of electronic parts & equipment, computers & peripheral equipment & software; Prepackaged software

Jason Cohenour, President/CEO
David McLennan, CFO & Secretary
Jim Patrick, Chief Technical Officer

Spectrum Signal Processing Inc.
#300, 2700 Production Way
Burnaby, BC V5A 4X1
604-421-5422 Fax: 604-421-1764 800-663-8986
brent.flichel@spectrumsignal.com
www.spectrumsignal.com
Ticker Symbol: SSY
Company Type: Public
Profile: Designs & manufactures industry-leading high performance signal processing engines & subsystems that acquire, process & transmit signals for wireless signal processing & packet-voice applications

P. Spothelfer, President/CEO
Brent Flichel, CFO & Vice-President, Finance

SR Telecom Inc.
8150, aut Transcanadienne
Montréal, QC H4S 1M5
514-335-1210 Fax: 514-334-7783
investor@srtelecom.com
www.srtelecom.com
Ticker Symbol: SRX
Company Type: Public
Profile: Manufacturers of broadband fixed-access technology & communications equipment; Telecommunications services

Pierre St-Arnaud, President/CEO
David L. Adams, CFO & Vice-President, Finance
Allan Klein, Vice-President, Technology
Michel Gravel, Manager, Maintenance

Teleglobe
1000, rue de la Gauchetière ouest
Montréal, QC H3B 4X5
514-868-7272 Fax: 514-868-7234 www.teleglobe.com
Ticker Symbol: TGO
Company Type: Public
Profile: Offices of holding companies; Manufacturers of radio & television broadcasting & communications equipment, telephone & telegraph apparatus; Telephone, telegraph & other message communications; Computer integrated systems design; Various communications services

Liam Strong, President/CEO
Pierre Duhamel, Exec. Vice-President & CFO
Christian Gervais, Vice-President, Information Technology

TS Telecom Ltd.
180 Amber St.
Markham, ON L3R 3J8
905-470-2282 Fax: 905-470-2273
tsinfo@tstelecom.com
www.tstelecom.com
Ticker Symbol: TOM
Company Type: Public
Profile: Manufacturers of telephone & telegraph apparatus

Ben Chong, President/CEO & Director
Randy Hung, CFO & Director

Tundra Semiconductor Corp.
603 March Rd.
Ottawa, ON K2K 2M5
613-592-0714 Fax: 613-592-1320 800-267-7321
inquire@tundra.com
www.tundra.com
Ticker Symbol: TUN
Company Type: Public
Profile: Manufacturers of semiconductors & related devices; Wholesalers of electronic parts & equipment

Jim Roche, President/CEO
Norm Y. Paquette, CFO
Richard O'Connor, Chief Technology Officer

Turbo Genset Inc.
Power Generation Systems - Canada
#400, 350 Bay St.
Toronto, ON M5H 3V9
208-690-1722
rak@turbogenset.com
www.turbogenset.com
Ticker Symbol: TGN
Company Type: Public
Profile: Offices of holding companies; Manufacturers of motors & generators

Richard Rapuscinski, Manager

Unique Broadband Systems, Inc.
8250 Lawson Rd.
Milton, ON L9T 5C6
905-660-8100 Fax: 905-669-0785
sales@uniquebroadband.com
www.uniquebroadband.com
Ticker Symbol: UBS
Company Type: Public
Profile: Manufacturers of radio & television broadcasting & communications equipment, mobile & fixed wireless communications

Gerald T. McGoey, CEO/Chair
John D. Kennedy, CFO
Alex Dolgonos, Head, Technology
Sherry St. Denis, Manager, Office

Wi-LAN Inc.
#608, 11 Holland Ave.
Ottawa, ON K1Y 4S1
613-688-4900 Fax: 613-688-4894
info@wi-lan.com
www.wi-lan.com
Ticker Symbol: WIN
Company Type: Public
Profile: Manufacturers of electrical machinery, equipment, & supplies, telephone & telegraph apparatus; Wholesalers of electronic parts & equipment; Patent owners & lessors

William Dunbar, President/CEO
Keith Bittner, CFO
Ken Wetherell, Vice-President, Investor Relations

Wireless Matrix Corporation
#102, 1530 - 27th Ave. NE
Calgary, AB T2E 7S6
403-250-3949 Fax: 403-250-8163
invest@wirelessmatrixcorp.com
www.wirelessmatrixcorp.com
Ticker Symbol: WRX
Company Type: Public
Profile: Manufacturers of radio & television broadcasting & communications equipment; Various communications services; Computer programming services

J. Richard Carlson, President/CEO
Maria C. Izurieta, CFO
Bruce Robinson, Chief Technology Officer

Engineering & Management

ADS Inc.
485, des Érables
Saint-Elzéar, QC G0S 2J0
418-387-3383 Fax: 418-387-8853
ads@adsinc.ca
www.adsinc.ca
Ticker Symbol: AAL
Company Type: Public
Profile: Offices of holding companies; Engineering services; General contractors in industrial buildings & warehouses

Paul Drouin, Chair
Guy Drouin, President/CEO
Guy Bérubé, CFO

AEterna Laboratories Inc.
1405 du Parc-Technologique Blvd.
Québec, QC G1P 4P5
418-652-8525 Fax: 418-652-0881
aeterna@aeterna.com
www.aeterna.com
Ticker Symbol: AEL
Company Type: Public
Profile: Commercial physical & biological research

Éric Dupont, Chair
Gilles Gagnon, President/CEO
Dennis Turpin, CFO & Vice-President
Jürgen Engel, COO & Vice-President, Global Resources & Development
Steve Martineau, Head, IT

AMEC Inc.
#700, 2020 Winston Park Dr.
Oakville, ON L6H 6X7
905-829-5400 Fax: 905-829-5625 www.amec.com
Company Type: Private
Profile: Engineering & management services; Heavy construction; Water, sewer, pipeline, communications, power line construct; Refuse systems; Prepackaged software; Real estate, Land subdividers & developers; Manufacturers of general industrial machinery & equipment

Lasse Petterson, President/COO
Grant Ling, CFO
Randy Plener, Director, Safety, Health & Environment

Avcorp Industries Inc.
10025 River Way
Delta, BC V4G 1M7
604-582-1137 Fax: 604-582-2620
info@avcorp.com
www.avcorp.com
Ticker Symbol: AVP
Company Type: Public
Profile: Engineering services; Manufacturers of aircraft parts & auxiliary equipment, aircraft engines & engine parts

Paul Kalil, President/CEO
Ed Merlo, Vice-President, Finance
Helen Aherne, Coordinator, Health & Safety

Cell-Loc Location Technologies Inc.
#220, 3015 - 5th Ave. NE
Calgary, AB T2A 6T8
403-569-5700 Fax: 403-569-5701
investors@cell-loc.com
www.cell-loc.com
Ticker Symbol: CLQ
Company Type: Public
Profile: Commercial physical & biological research; Patent owners & lessors

Michel Fattouche, Chief Technical Officer
Sheldon Reid, President/CEO
Dave Guebert, CFO

CGI Group Inc.
1130, rue Sherbrooke ouest, 5e étage
Montréal, QC H3A 2M8
514-841-3200 Fax: 514-841-3299 www.cgi.com
Ticker Symbol: GIB
Company Type: Public
Profile: Provider of end-to-end information technology & business process services to clients worldwide

Michael E. Roach, President/CEO
Joseph I. Saliba, President, USA & Asia Pacific
David Anderson, Exec. Vice-President/CFO
Doug Wilson, Vice-President, Systems Integration & Consulting

Chromos Molecular Systems Inc.
8081 Lougheed Hwy.
Burnaby, BC V5A 1W9
604-415-7100 Fax: 604-415-7151
info@chromos.com
www.chromos.com
Ticker Symbol: CHR
Company Type: Public
Profile: Commercial physical & biological research

Alistair Duncan, President/CEO
Kathyrn Hayaski, Vice-President, Finance

ConjuChem Inc.
#3950, 225, President Kennedy Ave.
Montréal, QC H2X 3Y8
514-844-5558 Fax: 514-844-1119
ryer@conjuchem.com
www.conjuchem.com
Ticker Symbol: CJC
Company Type: Public
Profile: Commercial physical & biological research

Jacques Lapointe, President/CEO
Lennie Ryer, Vice-President/CFO
Dominique P. Bridon, Chief Technical Officer & Vice-President, Research

Conor Pacific Group Inc.
Four Bentall Centre
PO Box 49224, #3474, 1055 Dunsmuir St.
Vancouver, BC V7X 1L2
604-669-3373 Fax: 604-669-3353
bob.nowack@conorpacific.com
www.conorpacific.com
Ticker Symbol: CPA
Company Type: Public
Profile: Refuse systems

R.E. Nowack, Chair/CEO
Paul Stevenson, Vice-President, Finance

CPI Plastics Group Limited
151 Courtney Park Dr. West
Mississauga, ON L5W 1Y5
905-795-5505 Fax: 416-795-5523 800-663-9097
info@cpiplastics.com
www.cpiplastics.com
Ticker Symbol: CPI
Company Type: Public
Profile: Plastics processor & thermoplastic profile design, engineering & processing

Peter F. Clark, Chair/CEO
Ronald W. Mitchell, President
Daniel J. Ardila, CFO/Vice-President, Finance

CryoCath Technologies Inc.
16771, ch Sainte-Marie
Montréal, QC H9H 5H3
514-694-1212 Fax: 514-694-6279
customerservice@cryocath.com
Ticker Symbol: CYT
Company Type: Public
Profile: Commercial physical & biological research; Manufacturers of surgical & medical instruments & apparatus

Steven G. Arless, President/CEO
Steven R. Gannon, CFO

Cymat Corp.
#6320, 2 Danville Rd.
Mississauga, ON L5T 2L7
905-696-9900 Fax: 905-696-9300
info@cymat.com
www.cymat.com
Ticker Symbol: CYM
Company Type: Public
Profile: Commercial physical & biological research; Patent owners & lessors; Manufacturers of various primary metal products; Wholesalers of metals service centers & offices

Paul Tichauer, President
Richard Rogers, CFO & Corporate Secretary, Corporate Development

Decoma International Inc.
50 Casmir Ct.
Concord, ON L4K 4J5
905-669-2888 Fax: 905-669-5075
info@decoma.com
www.decoma.com
Ticker Symbol: DEC
Company Type: Private
Profile: Engineering services; Manufacturers of motor vehicle parts & accessories, automotive stampings, various plastics products, coating, engraving & allied services

Alan J. Power, President/CEO
Michael E. McCarthy, Exec. Vice-President, Finance
W. Stephen Sloan, Vice-President, Information Technology
John Zymanski, Manager, Environment

Ecopia BioSciences Inc.
7290, rue Frederick-Banting
Montréal, QC H4S 2A1
514-336-2700 Fax: 514-336-8827 888-391-2666
info@ecopiabio.com
www.ecopiabio.com
Ticker Symbol: EIA
Company Type: Public
Profile: Commercial physical & biological research

Pierre Falardeau, President/CEO
Gary Littlejohn, Exec. Vice-President & CFO

Forbes Medi-Tech Inc.
#200, 750 West Pender St.
Vancouver, BC V6C 2T8
604-689-5899 Fax: 604-689-7641
info@forbesmedi.com
www.forbesmedi.com
Ticker Symbol: FMI
Company Type: Public
Profile: Life sciences company focussed on cardiovascular health

Charles A. Butt, President/CEO
Patricia E. Pracher, Acting CFO
Max Ghabel, Manager, Information Technology
John Nestor, Chief Scientific Officer

Freshxtend Technologies Corp.
#104, 334 East Kent Ave.
Vancouver, BC V5X 4N6
604-322-0759 Fax: 604-322-0487 800-269-5269
info@freshxtend.com
www.freshxtend.com
Ticker Symbol: SBT
Company Type: Public
Profile: Patent owners & lessors; Commercial physical & biological research; Retailing florists

Francis H.P. Ko, CEO
Aurora Davidson, CFO

GE Water & Process Technologies
3239 Dundas St. West
Oakville, ON L6M 4B2
905-465-3030 Fax: 905-465-3050 www.zenon.com
Company Type: Private
Profile: ZENON is engaged in commercial physical & biological research. It manufactures various service industry machinery, general industrial machinery & equipment, & water treatment systems.

Jeff Garwood, President/CEO

The Goldfarb Corporation
#100, 18 Spadina Rd.
Toronto, ON M5R 2S7
416-229-2070 Fax: 416-229-5392
info@goldfarbcorp.com
www.goldfarbcorp.com
Ticker Symbol: GDF
Company Type: Public
Profile: Management consulting services; Wholesalers of industrial & personal service paper; General automotive repair shops; Automotive exhaust system repair shops

Martin Goldfarb, President/CEO/Chair & Director
Karen Killeen, CFO

Hatch Ltd.
2800 Speakman Dr.
Mississauga, ON L5K 2R7
905-855-7600 Fax: 905-855-8270
webmaster@hatch.ca
www.hatch.ca
Company Type: Private
Profile: The consulting & technical design firm serves the global mining & metals, energy & infrastructure sectors

Kurt Strobele, President/CEO
Bruce MacDonald, Director, Finance

Helix BioPharma Corp.
#3, 305 Industrial Pkwy. South
Aurora, ON L4G 6X7
905-841-2300 Fax: 905-841-2244
helix@helixbiopharma.com
www.helixbiopharma.com
Ticker Symbol: HBP
Company Type: Public
Profile: Commercial physical & biological research

Donald Segal, President
Frank Michalargias, CFO
Heman Chao, Vice-President, Technology

Hemosol Inc.
2585 Meadowpine Blvd.
Mississauga, ON L5N 8H9
905-286-6200 Fax: 905-286-6300
lhartwell@hemosol.com
www.hemosol.com
Ticker Symbol: HML
Company Type: Public
Profile: Commercial physical & biological research

Lee Hartwell, CEO

Isotechnika Inc.
5120 - 75th St.
Edmonton, AB T6E 6W2
780-487-1600 Fax: 780-484-4105 888-487-9944
investorrelations@isotechnika.com
www.isotechnika.com
Ticker Symbol: ISA
Company Type: Public
Profile: Commercial physical & biological research; Manufacturers of pharmaceutical preparations, in-vitro & in-vivo diagnostic substances

C. Aspeslet, Chief Operating Officer
laspeslet@isotechnika.com
R. Yatscoff, President/CEO
ryatscoff@isotechnika.com
D. Bourgeault, Chief Financial Officer
dbourgeault@isotechnika.com
A.J. Simon, Director, Information Systems
ajsimon@isotechnika.com

Marsulex Inc.
#300, 111 Gordon Baker Rd.
Toronto, ON M2H 3R1
416-496-9655 Fax: 416-496-1874 800-387-5030
investor@marsulex.com
www.marsulex.com
Ticker Symbol: MLX
Company Type: Public
Profile: Refuse systems; Gas cleaning technologies; Desulphurization; Air quality compliance systems

David M. Gee, President/CEO
Edward R. Irwin, CFO

Neurochem Inc.
275, boul Armand-Frappier
Laval, QC H7V 4A7
450-680-4500 Fax: 450-680-4501 877-680-4500
ir@neurochem.com
www.neurochem.com
Ticker Symbol: NRM
Company Type: Public
Profile: Commercial physical & biological research

Francesco Bellini, Chair/President & CEO
Mariano Rodriguez, CFO & Vice-President, Finance
Lise Hébert, Vice-President, Corporate Communications

Stantec Inc.
#200, 10160 - 112th St.
Edmonton, AB T5K 2L6
780-917-7000 Fax: 780-917-7330
corp@stantec.com
www.stantec.com
Ticker Symbol: STN
Company Type: Public
Profile: Engineering services; Management consulting services; Commercial physical & biological research

Anthony P. Franceschini, President/CEO
Donald W. Wilson, Vice-President/CFO

Stressgen Biotechnologies Corporation
#120, 4243 Glanford Ave.
Victoria, BC V8Z 4B9
250-744-2811 Fax: 250-744-3331
800-661-4978www.stressgen.com
Ticker Symbol: SSB
Company Type: Public
Profile: Commercial physical & biological research; Manufacturers of pharmaceutical preparations

D.L. Korpolinski, President/CEO
Greg McKee, CFO & Vice-President, Corporate Development

UMA Group Ltd.
#1700, 1066 West Hastings St.
Vancouver, BC V6E 3X2
604-689-3431 Fax: 604-685-1035
communications@uma.aecom.com
www.uma.aecom.com
Company Type: Private
Profile: Engineering, consulting & management services are provided to the community infrastructure, earth & water, transportation & industrial market sectors

Jim Stewart, President/CEO
Kevin Steinberg, CFO & Vice-President
Marg Latham, Vice-President, Knowledge Management
Tom Wingrove, Sr. Vice-President, Earth & Water

Virtek Vision International Inc.
785 Bridge St.
Waterloo, ON N2V 2K1
519-746-7190 Fax: 519-746-3383
info@virtek.ca
www.virtek.ca
Ticker Symbol: VRK
Company Type: Public
Profile: Virtek is a leading provider of precison laser-based templating, inspection, marking & engraving products & systems integration solutions

Robert G. Sandness, President/CEO & Director
Peter F. Monsberger, CFO & Vice-President, Finance

Westaim Corporation
#1010, 144 - 4th Ave. SW
Calgary, AB T2P 3N4
403-237-7272 Fax: 403-237-6565
info@westaim.com
www.westaim.com
Ticker Symbol: WED
Company Type: Public
Profile: Commercial physical & biological research; Patent owners & lessors

Barry Heck, President/CEO
G.A. (Drew) Fitch, Sr. Vice-President/CFO
Laurie Danielson, Director, Environment, Health & Safety

World Heart Corporation
1 Laser St.
Ottawa, ON K2E 7V1
613-226-4278 Fax: 613-226-4744
investors@worldheart.com
www.worldheart.com
Ticker Symbol: WHT
Company Type: Public
Profile: Medical devices

Roderick M. Bryden, President/CEO
D. Mark Goudie, CFO & Vice-President, Finance
Jal Jassawalla, Chief Technical Officer & Exec. Vice-President

Finance

Accord Financial Corp.
#1803, 77 Bloor St. West
Toronto, ON M5S 1M2
416-961-0007 Fax: 416-961-9443 www.accordfinancial.com
Ticker Symbol: ACD
Company Type: Public
Profile: Offices of holding companies; Short-term business credit institutions, except agricultural

Ken Hitzig, President
Stuart Adair, CFO & Treasurer
Roy Owens, Chief Information Officer

AGF Management Limited
PO Box 50, Toronto-Dominion Centre
Toronto, ON M5K 1E9
905-214-8203 Fax: 905-2q4-8243 800-268-8583
tiger@agf.com
www.agf.com
Ticker Symbol: AGF
Company Type: Public
Profile: Offices of holding companies; Security brokers, dealers, & flotation companies; Services allied with the exchange of securities/commodities; Open-ended management investment offices

Blake C. Goldring, President/CEO
William D. Cameron, Sr. Vice-President & CFO

Allbanc Split Corp.
Scotia Plaza
PO Box 4085 A, 40 King St. West, 26th Fl.
Toronto, ON M5W 2X6
416-945-4171 Fax: 416-863-7425
mc_allbanc@scotiacapital.com
www.scotiamanagedcompanies.com
Ticker Symbol: ABK
Company Type: Public
Profile: Security brokers, dealers, & flotation companies; Unit investment trusts, certificate/closed-end management offices

Brian McChesney, President/CEO & Director
Michael K. Warman, CFO/Secretary & Director

Amisk Inc.
#101, 3633 rue Panet
Jonquière, QC G7X 8T7
418-546-1156 Fax: 418-546-0004
infos@amisk.qc.ca
www.amisk.qc.ca
Ticker Symbol: AS
Company Type: Public
Profile: Miscellaneous business credit institutions

Richard Harvey, President
Robert Taylor, Managing Director

ATB Financial
9888 Jasper Ave. NW
Edmonton, AB T5J 1P1
780-408-7000 Fax: 780-422-4178 800-332-8383
atbinfo@atb.com
www.atb.com
Company Type: Crown
Profile: Provincially chartered banks &/or trust companies

Bob Normand, President/CEO
Jim McKillop, CFO

Bank of Canada
234 Wellington St.
Ottawa, ON K1A 0G9
613-782-8111 Fax: 613-782-7713 800-303-1282
info@bankofcanada.ca
www.bankofcanada.ca
Company Type: Crown
Profile: The Bank of Canada is a federal central bank.

David A. Dodge, Governor
613-782-8383, Fax: 613-782-7003,
ddodge@bankofcanada.ca
Sheila Vokey, Chief Accountant
613-782-8241, Fax: 613-782-7173,
svokey@bankofcanada.ca
John Otterspoor, Director, IT Services
613-782-7571, Fax: 613-782-8933,
jotterspoor@bankofcanada.ca

The Bank of Nova Scotia
Scotia Plaza
44 King St. West
Toronto, ON M5H 1H1
416-866-6161 Fax: 416-866-3750
email@scotiabank.com
www.scotiabank.com
Ticker Symbol: BNS
Company Type: Public
Profile: Federally chartered bank & trust company; Security brokers, dealers, & flotation companies; Mortgage bankers & loan correspondents

Richard E. Waugh, President/CEO
Robert W. Chisholm, President/CEO, Domestic Banking & Wealth Management
Sarabjit S. Marwah, Vice-Chair & Group Treasurer
Margaret J. Mulligan, Exec. Vice-President, Systems & Operations

BMO Financial Group
c/o Corporate Secretary's Department, First Canadi
100 King St. West
Toronto, ON M5X 1A1
416-867-6786 Fax: 416-867-6793
corp.secretary@bmo.com
www.bmo.com
Ticker Symbol: BMO
Company Type: Public
Profile: Federally chartered bank & trust company; Security brokers, dealers, & flotation companies; Mortgage bankers & loan correspondents

F. Anthony Comper, President/CEO
Karen E. Maidment, CFO & Administrative Officer
Lloyd F. Darlington, President & CEO, Technology Solutions

Business Development Bank of Canada
BDC Bldg.
#400, 5, Place Ville Marie
Montréal, QC H3B 5E7
877-232-2269
info@bdc.ca
www.bdc.ca
Ticker Symbol: BDB
Company Type: Crown
Profile: Federal & federally sponsored credit agency; Management consulting services; Business consulting services

Jean-Rene Haldet, President/CEO
Alan Marquis, CFO & Sr. Vice-President, Finance

Canada Mortgage & Housing Corporation
700 Montreal Rd.
Ottawa, ON K1A 0P7
613-748-2000 Fax: 613-748-2098
chic@cmhc-schl.gc.ca
www.cmhc-schl.gc.ca
Company Type: Crown
Profile: Administration of housing programs

Karen Kinsey, President/CEO
Pierre Serré, CFO & Finance

Canadian Imperial Bank of Commerce
Commerce Ct.
Toronto, ON M5L 1A2
416-980-2211 Fax: 416-980-7012 800-465-2422www.cibc.com
Ticker Symbol: CM
Company Type: Public
Profile: Federally chartered bank & trust company; Security brokers, dealers, & flotation companies; Mortgage bankers & loan correspondents

John S. Hunkin, CEO
Tom D. Woods, Sr. Exec. Vice-President/CFO
Michael D. Woeller, Sr. Vice-President & Chief Information Officer

Canadian Western Bank
#2300, 10303 Jasper Ave.
Edmonton, AB T5J 3X6
780-423-8865 Fax: 780-423-8899
InvestorRelations@cwbank.com
www.cwbank.com
Ticker Symbol: CWB
Company Type: Public
Profile: Federally chartered bank

Larry M. Pollock, President/CEO
Tracey C. Ball, CACFO & Sr. Vice-President

Chrysler Financial Canada Inc.
2425 Matheson Blvd. East, 3rd Fl.
Mississauga, ON L4W 5N7
905-629-6000 800-263-6920www.chryslerfinancialcanada.ca
Company Type: Public
Profile: Personal credit & business credit institution

Richard Wardwell, President/CEO & Director

Clarke Inc.
6009 Quinpool Rd., 8th Fl.
Halifax, NS B3K 5J7
902-442-3000 Fax: 902-442-0187 www.clarkeinc.com
Ticker Symbol: CKI; CKI.DB
Company Type: Public
Profile: Clarke Inc. is an activist & catalyst investment company.

George Armoyan, President/CEO
Janet R. Imeson, CFO & Exec. Vice-President, Finance

Clearlink Capital Corporation
2281 North Sheridan Way
Mississauga, ON L5K 2S3
905-855-2500 Fax: 905-855-2725 800-433-5553
mflanagan@clearlink.com
www.clearlink.com
Ticker Symbol: MFP
Company Type: Public
Profile: Miscellaneous business credit institutions

J. Peter Wolfraim, President/CEO
Robert D. Wright, Sr. Vice-President/CFO

Coast Capital Savings Credit Union
15117 - 101 Ave.
Surrey, BC V3R 8P7
604-517-7000 888-517-7000www.coastcapitalsavings.com
Company Type: Private
Profile: Provincially chartered credit union

Lloyd Craig, President/CEO
Hermann G. Bessert, CFO
Sheila Baker, Chief Information Officer

Credit Union Central of British Columbia
1441 Creekside Dr.
Vancouver, BC V6J 4S7
604-734-2511 Fax: 604-737-5085
info@cucbc.com
www.cucbc.com
Company Type: Public
Profile: Provincially chartered credit union

Wayne A. Nygren, President/CEO
Rowland Kelly, Vice-President Finance/CFO, Finance
Mervin Zabinsky, Vice-President, Technology & Payment Services

Credit Union Central of Saskatchewan
PO Box 3030, 2055 Albert St.
Regina, SK S4P 3G8
306-566-1200 Fax: 306-566-1372
communications@cucs.com
www.saskcu.com
Company Type: Private
Profile: Offices of holding companies; Credit unions, provincially chartered

Sid Bildfell, CEO
G. Elwood Harvey, President
Greg Wallace, CFO & Vice-President, Finance
Mark Borgares, Director, IT

Desjardins Trust Inc.
PO Box 34, 1, Complexe Desjardins
Montréal, QC H5B 1E4
514-286-9441 Fax: 514-286-3418
800-361-6840www.desjardins.com
Ticker Symbol: FID
Company Type: Public
Profile: Federally chartered bank & trust company

Hélène Gagné, Vice-President, Communications
Monique F. Leroux, President/CEO
Jean Landry, President/COO
François Gagnon, Sr. Vice-President, Finance
Claude Dupuis, Sr. Vice-President, Technologies

Drug Royalty Corporation Inc.
Royal Bank Plaza, South Tower
PO Box 122, #3120, 200 Bay St.
Toronto, ON M5J 2J3
416-863-1865 Fax: 416-863-5161
info@drugroyalty.com
www.drugroyalty.com
Ticker Symbol: DRI
Company Type: Private
Profile: Patent owners & lessors; Personal credit institutions

Behzad Khosrowshahi, President/CEO
Gordon Winston, Secretary & Exec. Vice-President, Finance

Export Development Canada
151 O'Connor St.
Ottawa, ON K1A 1K3
613-598-2500 Fax: 613-237-2690
investor.relations@edc.ca
www.edc.ca
Company Type: Crown
Profile: Export credit agency; Offers assistance to Canadian exporters & investors to expand their international business

Robert A. Wright, President/CEO
Kevin O'Brien, Sr. Vice-President, Financing
Jim McArdle, Secretary & Sr. Vice-President, Legal Services
Sherry Noble, Sr. Vice-President, Business Solutions & Technology
Arthur FitzGerald, Chief Environmental Advisor

Farm Credit Canada
PO Box 4320, 1800 Hamilton St.
Regina, SK S4P 4L3
306-780-8100 Fax: 306-780-5456 888-332-3301
csc@fcc-fac.ca
www.fcc-fac.ca
Company Type: Crown
Profile: Federal & federally sponsored credit agencies

John J. Ryan, President/CEO
Moyez Somani, Exec. Vice-President/CFO
Kellie Garrett, Vice-President, Knowledge & Reputation
Paul MacDonald, Vice-President, Information Technology

Firm Capital Mortgage Investment Trust
1244 Caledonia Rd.
Toronto, ON M6A 2X5
416-635-0221 Fax: 416-635-1713
mortgages@firmcapital.com
www.firmcapital.com
Ticker Symbol: FC
Company Type: Public
Profile: Real estate investment trusts

Eli Dadouch, President/CEO & Trustee
Jonathan Mair, Sr. Vice-President/CFO & Trustee
Eddie Gilbert, Chief Information Officer

Home Capital Group Inc.
#2300, 145 King St. West
Toronto, ON M5H 1J8
416-360-4663 Fax: 416-363-7611 800-990-7881
inquiry@homecapital.com
www.homecapital.com
Ticker Symbol: HCG.B
Company Type: Public
Profile: A holding company operating through its principal subsidiary, Home Trust Company

Gerald M. Soloway, President/CEO
W. Roy Vincent, Sr. Vice-President/COO
Norn T hacker, Director, Information Technology
Sherry Hatton, Corporate Secretary

HSBC Bank Canada
#100, 885 West Georgia St.
Vancouver, BC V6C 3E9
604-685-1000 Fax: 604-641-3062 888-310-4722
info@hsbc.ca
www.hsbc.ca

HSBC Bank Canada (continued)
Ticker Symbol: HSB
Company Type: Public
Profile: Federally chartered bank & trust company

Lindsay Gordon, President/CEO
Graham McIsaac, CFO
Andy Stacey, Chief Information Officer

Investors Group Inc.
Canada Centre
#1, 447 Portage Ave.
Winnipeg, MB R3C 3B6
204-943-0361 Fax: 204-947-1659 888-746-6344
corpsec@investorsgroup.com
www.investorsgroup.com
Ticker Symbol: IGI
Company Type: Public
Profile: Offices of holding companies; Security brokers, dealers, & flotation company; Open-ended management investment offices; Unit investment trusts, certificate/closed-end management offices; Services allied with the exchange of securities/commodities; Investment advice; Pension, health, & welfare funds

R. Jeffrey Orr, President/CEO
Gregory D. Tretiak, Exec. Vice-President & CFO
Ronald D. Saull, Sr. Vice-President/Chief Information Officer

Laurentian Bank of Canada
Tour Banque Laurentienne
1981, av McGill College
Montréal, QC H3A 3K3
514-284-4500 Fax: 514-284-3396 800-522-1846
mail@laurentianbank.ca
www.laurentianbank.com
Ticker Symbol: LB
Company Type: Public
Profile: Federally chartered bank & trust company; Security brokers, dealers, & flotation company; Miscellaneous business credit institutions

Raymond McManus, President/CEO
Robert Cardinal, Sr. Exec. Vice-President/CFO

MCAN Mortgage Corporation
#400, 200 King St. West
Toronto, ON M5H 3T4
416-591-5214 Fax: 416-598-4142 800-387-4405
mcanexecutive@mcanmortgage.com
www.mcanmortgage.com
Ticker Symbol: MKP
Company Type: Public
Profile: MCAN Mortgage is a mortgage investment corporation.

Blaine Welch, President/CEO
416-591-2726, bwelch@mcanmortgage.com
Tammy Oldenburg, Vice-President/CFO
416-847-3542, toldenburg@mcanmortgage.com
Kevin Dwarte, Coordinator, Business Continuity & Disaster Recovery & AVP, Investments, & Privacy, & Anti-Money Laundering Offices
416-591-2721, kdwarte@mcanmortgage.com
Michael Misener, Vice-President, Investments
416-591-5205, mmisener@mcanmortgage.com

National Bank of Canada
600, rue de la Gauchetière ouest
Montréal, QC H3B 4L2
514-394-5000 Fax: 514-394-8434
investorrelations@nbc.ca
www.nbc.ca
Ticker Symbol: NA
Company Type: Public
Profile: Federally chartered bank & trust company

Réal Raymond, President/CEO
Jean Turmel, President, Financial Markets/Treasury/Investment Banking
Michel Labonté, Sr. Vice-President, Special Projects
Lynn Jeanniot, Vice-President, Marketing & Public Affairs
Jean-Charles Petitclerc, Sr. Vice-President, Information Technology

Royal Bank of Canada
Royal Bank Plaza
PO Box 1, 200 Bay St.
Toronto, ON M5J 2W7
416-842-2000 Fax: 416-955-7800 www.rbc.com
Ticker Symbol: RY
Company Type: Public
Profile: Federally chartered bank & trust company; Security brokers, dealers, & flotation companies; Mortgage bankers & loan correspondents

Gordon M. Nixon, President/CEO
Peter W. Currie, Vice-Chair/CFO
Martin J. Lippert, Chief Information Officer

Sceptre Investment Counsel Limited
26 Wellington St. East, 12th Fl.
Toronto, ON M5E 1W4
416-601-9898 Fax: 416-367-8716
mail@sceptre.ca
www.sceptre.ca
Ticker Symbol: SZ
Company Type: Public
Profile: Investment advice & management

Richard L. Knowles, President/CEO
Betty B. Horton, Sec.-Treas. & Vice-President, Finance

Scotia Mortgage Investment Corporation
Scotia Centre
245 Water St., 2nd Fl.
St. John's, NL A1C 1B5
709-576-7473 Fax: 709-576-7483 **Ticker Symbol:** SMC
Company Type: Public
Profile: Mortgage bankers & loan correspondents

TD Mortgage Investment Corporation
#900, 324 - 8th Ave. SW
Calgary, AB T2P 2Z2
403-292-1077 Fax: 403-292-1834 www.td.com
Ticker Symbol: TDB
Company Type: Public
Profile: Mortgage bankers & loan correspondents

Iain Strump, CEO
Ed Mrozek, CFO
Jane Rooney, Secretary

The Toronto-Dominion Bank
Toronto-Dominion Tower
PO Box 1, 66 Wellington St. West
Toronto, ON M5K 1A2
416-308-9030 Fax: 416-982-5671
tdir@td.com
www.td.com
Ticker Symbol: TD
Company Type: Public
Profile: Federally chartered bank & trust company; Security brokers, dealers, & flotation companies; Mortgage bankers & loan correspondents

W. Edmund Clark, President/CEO, TD Bank Financial Group
Daniel A. Marinangeli, Exec. Vice-President/CFO
John T. Davies, Sr. Vice-President, Information Services
Philip Ginn, Sr. Vice-President, Computing Services
Tanya Bell, Regional Manager, TD Friends of the Environment Foundation (BC, AB, SK, M

Vancouver City Savings Credit Union
PO Box 2120 Terminal, 183 Terminal Ave.
Vancouver, BC V6A 4G2
604-877-7000 888-826-2489www.vancity.com
Company Type: Private
Profile: Provincially chartered credit union

Dave Mowat, CEO
Johan Lemmer, Vice-President, Finance
Rowena Liang, Chief Information Officer & Vice-President, Information Technology

Food, Beverages & Tobacco

A & W Food Services of Canada Inc.
#300, 171 Esplanade West
North Vancouver, BC V7M 3K9
604-988-2141 Fax: 604-988-5531
investorrelations@aw.ca
www.aw.ca
Ticker Symbol: AW.UN
Company Type: Private
Profile: Fast food franchiser

Paul Hollands, CEO
Don Leslie, CFO

Agropur cooperative
510, rue Principale
Granby, QC J2G 7G2
450-375-1991 Fax: 450-375-3987 800-463-7477**Company Type:** NA
Profile: Manufacturers of fluid milk; creamery butter; natural, processed & imitation cheese; dry, condensed & evaporated dairy products; ice cream & frozen desserts

Pierre Claprood, CEO
Robert Gour, President, Fine Cheese Division
Beno(140t Gagnon, CFO
Gilles Chamberland, Vice-President, Management Information Systems
Claude Hade, Project Manager, Environment

Andrés Wines Ltd.
697 South Service Rd.
Grimsby, ON L3M 4E8
905-643-4131 Fax: 905-643-4944
info@andrewpeller.com
www.andreswines.com
Ticker Symbol: ADW
Company Type: Public
Profile: Manufacturers of wines, brandy & brandy spirits; Wholesalers of wines & distilled alcoholic beverages

John E. Peller, President/CEO & Second Vice-Chair
Peter B. Patchet, Exec. Vice-President, Finance & Administration

Arctic Glacier Income Fund
625 Henry Ave.
Winnipeg, MB R3A 0V1
204-772-2473 Fax: 204-783-9857 888-573-9237
info2@arcticglacierinc.com
www.arcticglacierinc.com
Ticker Symbol: AG.UN
Company Type: Public
Profile: Manufacturers of manufactured ice, chemicals & various chemical preparations; Retailers in miscellaneous retail & food stores; Wholesalers of various nondurable goods

Robert J. Nagy, President/CEO
Mike Pyle, President & COO
Keith W. McMahon, Exec. Vice-President/CFO
Hugh A. Adams, Corporate Secretary

Barry Callebaut Canada Inc.
PO Box 398, 2950 rue Nelson
Saint-Hyacinthe, QC J2S 1Y7
450-774-9131 Fax: 450-774-8335
sthyacinthe@barry-callebaut.com
www.barry-callebaut.com
Company Type: Private
Profile: Producers of cocoa & chocolate products

Patrick G. De Maeseneire, CEO
Dieter A. Enkelmann, CFO
Erik Van Assche, Chief Information Officer

Big Rock Brewery Income Trust
5555 - 76 Ave. SE
Calgary, AB T2C 4L8
403-720-3239 Fax: 403-236-7523 800-242-3107
beer@bigrockbeer.com
www.bigrockbeer.com
Ticker Symbol: BR
Company Type: Public
Profile: Manufacturers of malt beverages; Wholesalers of beer & ale

Edward E. McNally, Chair/CEO
Robert J. King, President, Big Rock Brewery Ltd.

Boston Pizza International Inc.
5500 Parkwood Way
Richmond, BC V6V 2M4
604-270-1108 Fax: 604-270-4168 www.bostonpizza.com
Company Type: Public
Profile: Patent owners & lessors; Retail eating places & alcoholic beverage consumption places

Mike Cordoba, President/COO
Mark Powell, Vice-President, Finance
Steve Johnstone, Director, Information Technology

Campbell Soup Company Ltd. of Canada
60 Birmingham St.
Toronto, ON M8V 2B8

MAJOR CANADIAN COMPANIES

416-251-1131 Fax: 416-253-8611
800-575-7687www.campbellsoup.ca
Company Type: Private
Profile: Manufacturers of canned specialties, various food preparations, pickled fruits & vegetables, sauces, seasonings & dressings; Wholesalers of general line groceries

Phillip E. Donne, President
G.J. Arnold, CFO & Vice-President
S. Graham, Director, Research & Development

Canada Bread Company Limited
#1500, 30 St. Clair Ave. W
Toronto, ON M4V 3A2
416-926-2000 Fax: 416-926-2018
Investorrelations@mapleleaf.ca
www.canadabread.ca
Ticker Symbol: CBY
Company Type: Public
Profile: Manufacturers of bread & other bakery products, frozen specialties, frozen bakery products, canned fruits, vegetables, preserves, jams, & jellies, macaroni, spaghetti, vermicelli, & noodles; Wholesalers of packaged frozen foods, groceries & related products

Richard A. Lan, President/CEO
Michael H. Vels, CFO
Lynda J. Kuhn, Vice-President, Public & Investor Relations
Donald J. Wilcox, Vice-President, Technical Services

Cargill Ltd.
PO Box 5900, #300, 240 Graham Ave.
Winnipeg, MB R3C 4C5
204-947-0141 Fax: 204-947-6444 www.cargill.com
Company Type: Private
Profile: Wholesalers of grain & field beans, farm supplies, meat packing plants, sausages & other prepared meat products, prepared feeds & feed ingredients for animals & fowls, nitrogenous fertilizers, phosphatic fertilizers

Kerry Hawkins, President
Julian Hatherell, Treasurer & Vice-President, Finance
Robert Meijer, Director, Public Affairs
Luke Sarrazin, Manager, Health & Safety

Clearly Canadian Beverage Corporation
2267 10th Ave. West
Vancouver, BC V6K 2J1
800-735-7180
consumer.relations@clearly.ca
www.clearly.ca
Ticker Symbol: CLV
Company Type: Public
Profile: Marketer of bottled & carbonated &noncarbonated waters; Patent owners & lessors

Douglas L. Mason, President/CEO

Corby Distilleries Limited
193 Yonge St.
Toronto, ON M5B 1M8
416-369-1859
corbyweb@adsw.com
www.corby.ca
Ticker Symbol: CDL
Company Type: Public
Profile: Manufacturers of distilled & blended liquors, wines, brandy & brandy spirits; Wholesalers wines & distilled alcoholic beverages

Krystyna T. Hoeg, President/CEO
John Nicodemo, Corporate Secretary/CFO & Vice-President, Finance

Cott Corporation
#340, 207 Queens Quay West
Toronto, ON M5J 1A7
416-203-3898 Fax: 416-203-8171
investor_relations@cott.com
www.cott.com
Ticker Symbol: BCB
Company Type: Public
Profile: Manufacturers of retailer branded soft drinks & carbonated waters

John K. Sheppard, President/CEO
Len Watson, Chief Information Officer
Prem Virmani, Vice-President, Technical Services

Dover Industries Limited
4350 Harvester Rd.
Burlington, ON L7L 5S4
905-333-1515 Fax: 905-333-1584
info@dovergrp.com
www.dovergrp.com
Ticker Symbol: DVI
Company Type: Public
Profile: Manufacturers of flour & other grain mill products, cookies & crackers, sanitary food containers, setup paperboard boxes, various plastics products; Wholesalers of groceries & related products, industrial & personal service paper

Howard L. Rowley, President/CEO
Brian J. Short, Sr. Vice-President/CFO

Farmers Co-Operative Dairy Ltd.
745 Hammonds Plains Rd.
Bedford, NS B4B 1A8
902-835-3373 Fax: 902-835-1583 800-565-1626
inquiries@farmersdairy.ns.ca
www.farmersdairy.ca
Company Type: Private
Profile: Produces & distributes dairy & dairy-related products in Atlantic Canada

Dave Collins, Interim President/CEO
Karen McKay, Vice-President, Finance

FPI Limited
PO Box 550, 70 O'Leary Ave.
St. John's, NL A1C 5L1
709-570-0000 Fax: 709-570-0479
fpi@fpil.com
www.fpil.com
Ticker Symbol: FPL
Company Type: Public
Profile: Harvests, processes, sources & markets seafood products

Derrick H. Rowe, CEO
Bernard E. Beckett, CFO & Sec.-Treas.

Gay Lea Foods Co-Operative Ltd.
52 Orbitor Dr.
Mississauga, ON L4W 2G7
905-283-5300 Fax: 416-741-5384 800-268-0508
contact@gayleafoodmembers.com
www.gaylea.com
Company Type: Private
Profile: Manufacturers of fluid milk, creamery butter & dry, condensed & evaporated dairy products; Wholesalers of dairy products, groceries & related products

Andrew MacGillivray, President/CEO
John Rebry, Treasurer & Vice-President, Finance
Michael Barrett, Corporate Secretary & Vice-President, Human Resources & Member Relations

High Liner Foods Incorporated
PO Box 910, 100 Battery Point
Lunenburg, NS B0J 2C0
902-634-8811 Fax: 902-634-4785
info@highlinerfoods.com
www.highlinerfoods.com
Ticker Symbol: HLF
Company Type: Public
Profile: Processor & marketer of prepared, value-added frozen seafood & frozen Italian foods

Henry Earl Demone, President/CEO
Kelly Nelson, CFO & Vice-President, Corporate Services
Peter Burns, Director, Information Services

Humpty Dumpty Snack Foods Inc.
7385 Bren Rd.
Mississauga, ON L4T 1H3
519-893-1460 Fax: 519-893-2772
info@humptydumpty.com
www.humptydumpty.com
Ticker Symbol: SNX
Company Type: Public
Profile: Manufacturers of candy & other confectionery products; Wholesalers of confectionery

Bonita Then, Interim CEO
Lois Norris, CFO & Vice-President, Finance

Imperial Tobacco Canada Limited
3711, rue Saint-Antoine
Montréal, QC H4C 3P6
514-932-6161 Fax: 514-932-3993
www.imperialtobaccocanada.com
Company Type: Private
Profile: Manufacturers of cigarettes, chewing & smoking tobacco & snuff; Wholesalers of tobacco & tobacco products

Benjamin Kemball, President/CEO

Kraft Canada Inc.
95 Moatfield Dr.
Toronto, ON M3B 3L6
416-441-5000 Fax: 416-441-5059
800-323-0768www.kraftcanada.com
Company Type: Private
Profile: Manufacturers of natural, processed & imitation cheese; cereal breakfast foods; canned fruits, vegetables, preserves, jams & jellies; various food preparations; pickled fruits & vegetables, sauces, seasonings, dressings; roasted coffee; chocolate & cocoa products

Betsy D. Holden, President/CEO, Kraft Foods North America, Inc.
Fred Schaeffer, President, Kraft Canada Inc.
James P. Dollive, Sr. Vice-President/CFO, Kraft Foods Inc.

Lassonde Industries Inc.
755, rue Principale
Rougemont, QC J0L 1M0
514-878-1057 Fax: 450-861-9280
info@lassonde.com
www.lassonde.com
Ticker Symbol: LAS
Company Type: Public
Profile: Manufacturers of canned specialties, canned fruits, vegetables, preserves, jams & jellies, pickled fruits & vegetables, sauces, seasonings, dressings, frozen fruits, fruit juices & vegetables, various food preparations; Wholesalers of groceries & related products

Pierre-Paul Lassonde, President/CEO & Chair
Jean Tessier, Treasurer & Vice-President, Finance
Yves Dumont, Vice-President, Research & Development
Pierre Brault, Vice-President, IT

Leading Brands, Inc.
#1800, 1500 West Georgia
Vancouver, BC V6G 2Z6
604-685-5200 Fax: 604-685-5249 866-685-5200
info@lbix.com
www.lbix.com
Company Type: Public
Profile: Manufacturers of bottled & canned soft drinks & carbonated waters; Wholesalers of groceries & related products

Ralph D. McRae, President/CEO & Chair
Donna Higgins, CFO

Magnotta Winery Corporation
271 Chrislea Rd.
Vaughan, ON L4L 8N6
905-738-9463 Fax: 905-738-5551 800-461-9463
mailbox@magnotta.com
www.magnotta.com
Ticker Symbol: MGN
Company Type: Public
Profile: Manufacturers of wines, brandy & brandy spirits, canned fruits, vegetables, preserves, jams & jellies; Retailers in liquor stores; Wholesalers of wines & distilled alcoholic beverages

Gabe Magnotta, CEO/Chair
Rossana Di Zio Magnotta, President
Fulvio DeAngelis, CFO & Director, Finance
Dorothy Arturi, Officer, Health & Safety

Maple Leaf Foods Inc.
#1500, 30 St Clair Ave. West
Toronto, ON M4V 3A2
416-926-2000 Fax: 416-926-2018 www.mapleleaf.ca
Ticker Symbol: MFI
Company Type: Public
Profile: Manufacturers of sausages & other prepared meat products, flour & other grain mill products, prepared feeds & feed ingredients for animals & fowls, poultry slaughtering & processing, animal & marine fats & oils; Retailing in bakeries; Farm product warehousing & storage

Michael H. McCain, President/CEO
Michael H. Vels, Exec. Vice-President/CFO

McCain Foods (Canada)
107 Main St.
Florenceville, NB E7L 1B2
506-392-5541 Fax: 506-392-6062
866-622-2461www.mccain.com
Company Type: Private
Profile: Manufacturers of frozen fruits, fruit juices, vegetables, prepared feeds & feed ingredients for animals & fowls, frozen bakery products; Wholesalers of packaged frozen foods

Dale F. Morrison, President/CEO
David Sanchez, CFO
Anil Rastogi, Chief Information Officer
Larry Derrah, Chief Engineer, Technology
Tom Kaszas, Chief Engineer, Environment

McDonald's Restaurants of Canada Ltd.
1 McDonald's Pl.
Toronto, ON M3C 3L4
416-443-1000 Fax: 416-446-3376
success@mcdonalds.ca
www.mcdonalds.ca
Company Type: Private
Profile: Foodservice company; Owner & operator of over 1,300 restaurants in Canada

Louie W. Mele, President
David J. Hederson, Sr. Vice-President/CFO
David J. Allen, Exec. Vice-President/COO
Jeff Robinson, Vice-President, Operations

Molson Inc.
1555, rue Notre-Dame est
Montréal, QC H2L 2R5
514-597-1786 Fax: 514-598-6969
patricia.dell'elce@molson.com
www.molsoncoors.com
Ticker Symbol: MOL
Company Type: Public
Profile: Offices of holding companies; Manufacturers of malt beverages; Wholesalers of beer & ale; Professional sports clubs & promoters; Various amusement & recreation services

Daniel J. O'Neill, President/CEO
Raynald H. Doin, President, Quebec/Atlantic Region
Brian Burden, CFO & Exec. Vice-President
Gregory L. Wade, Sr. Vice-President, Quality Brewing

Nestlé Canada Inc.
25 Sheppard Ave. West
Toronto, ON M2N 6S8
416-512-9000 Fax: 416-218-2654 800-387-4636
corporateaffairs@ca.nestle.com
www.nestle.ca
Company Type: Private
Profile: 27 facilities in Canada, including manufacturing sites, sales offices & distribution centres, employ 4,000 people; Producer of foods & beverages such as Carnation, Nescafé, Lean Cuisine, Good Start, Nestlé Baby Cereal, Powerbar, Nestlé Pure Life, Nestlé Drumstick, Kit Kat & Purina Beneful

Robert G. (Bob) Leonidas, President/CEO
Doug Holdt, CFO & Sr. Vice-President

Parmalat Canada
405 The West Mall, 10th Fl.
Toronto, ON M9C 5J1
416-626-1973 Fax: 416-620-3123
consumer_inquiry@parmalat.ca
www.parmalat.ca
Company Type: Private
Profile: Manufacturers of fluid milk; creamery butter; cookies & crackers; natural, processed & imitation cheese; canned fruits, vegetable, preserves, jams & jellies; shortening, table oils, margarine & other edible oils

Alnashir (Nash) Lakha, President/CEO

Premium Brands Inc.
7720 Alderbridge Way
Richmond, BC V6X 2A2
604-656-3100 Fax: 604-656-3170
investor@premiumbrandsgroup.com
Ticker Symbol: FFF
Company Type: Public
Profile: Manufacturers of sausages & other prepared meat products; meat packing plants; bread & other bakery products except cookies & crackers; various food preparations; Wholesalers of meats & meat products

Fred Knoedler, Chair/CEO
George Peleologou, President
Will Kalutycz, CFO

Prime Restaurants of Canada Inc.
#600, 10 Kingsbridge Garden Circle
Mississauga, ON L5R 3K6
905-568-0000 Fax: 905-568-0080
marketing@primerestaurants.com
www.primerestaurants.com
Ticker Symbol: EAT.UN
Company Type: Public
Profile: Retail eating & alcoholic beverage consumption places

John Rothschild, CEO
Nick Perpick, President/COO
Peter Park, CFO
Eric Lee, Chief Technology Officer

Quaker Oats Company of Canada Ltd.
14 Hunter St. E.
Peterborough, ON K9J 7B2
705-743-6330 Fax: 705-876-4125
800-267-6287www.quakeroats.ca
Company Type: Private
Profile: Manufacturers of cereal breakfast foods, candy & other confectionery products, bottled & canned soft drinks & carbonated waters; Wholesalers of groceries & related products

Greg Shearson, President/CEO
Mike Jane, CFO

Rothmans Inc.
1500 Don Mills Rd.
Toronto, ON M3B 3L1
416-449-5525 Fax: 416-449-9601
ir@rothmansinc.ca
www.rothmansinc.ca
Ticker Symbol: ROC
Company Type: Public
Profile: Offices of holding companies; Manufacturers of cigarettes, chewing & smoking tobacco & snuff; Wholesalers of tobacco & tobacco products

John R. Barnett, President/CEO & Director
Michael E. Erater, Vice-President & Administration, Finance

Saputo Inc.
6869, boul Métropolitain est
Montréal, QC H1P 1X8
514-328-6662 Fax: 514-328-3094 877-341-8700
saputo@saputo.com
www.saputo.com
Ticker Symbol: SAP
Company Type: Public
Profile: Manufacturers of natural, processed, & imitation cheese, creamery & butter, dry, condensed, & evaporated dairy products; Wholesalers of fresh dairy products

Lino Saputo, Jr., President/CEO
Dino Dello Sbarba, President/COO, Dairy Products (Canada)
Louis-Philippe Carrière, Exec. Vice-President, Finance & Administration
Pierre Leroux, Exec. Vice-President, Human Resources & Corporate Affairs

Schneider Corporation
PO Box 130, 321 Courtland Ave. East
Kitchener, ON N2G 3X8
519-741-5000 Fax: 519-749-7420 www.schneiders.ca
Company Type: Private
Profile: Manufacturers of meat packing, natural & processed & imitation cheese, bread & other bakery products, various food preparations, sausages & other prepared meat products, poultry slaughtering & processing

Douglas W. Dodds, Chair/CEO
Michael Smith, Director, IT
Brad Erhardt, Manager, Environmental Affairs

Scotsburn Co-Operative Services Ltd.
PO Box 340, 4135 Main St.
Scotsburn, NS B0K 1R0
902-485-8023 Fax: 902-485-4013 800-511-6455
consumerservices@scotsburn.com
www.scotsburn.com
Company Type: Private
Profile: Manufacturers of fluid milk, ice cream & frozen desserts; Retailers in hardware stores; Wholesalers in farm supplies & fresh milk dairy products

James M. MacConnell, President/CEO
Jack Wood, Vice-President, Finance
Keith Murdoch, Vice-President, Operations

Sepp's Gourmet Foods Ltd.
529 Annance Ct.
Delta, BC V3M 6Y7
604-524-2540 Fax: 604-524-2941
dcullum@seppsfoods.com
www.seppsfoods.com
Ticker Symbol: SGO
Company Type: Public
Profile: Manufacturers of sausages & other prepared meat products, bread & other bakery products, frozen bakery products; Wholesalers of packaged frozen foods

Tom Poole, President/CEO
James Pratt, CFO/Secretary

Sleeman Breweries Ltd.
551 Clair Rd. West
Guelph, ON N1L 1E9
519-822-1834 Fax: 519-822-0430 800-268-8537
sleemanir@sleeman.ca
www.ale-sleeman.com
Ticker Symbol: ALE
Company Type: Public
Profile: Manufacturers of malt beverages; Wholesalers of beer & ale

John Sleeman, Chair/CEO
Rick Knudson, President/COO
Dan Rogozynski, Secretary/Vice-President, Finance & Administration

Smucker Foods of Canada Co.
80 Whitehall Dr.
Markham, ON L3R 0P3
905-940-9600 Fax: 905-940-6859
800-268-3232www.robinhood.ca
Company Type: Private
Profile: Manufacturer & marketer of food products; Provider of baking mixes flour & condiments to commercial & foodservice customers

Mark Smucker, Managing Director
Jim Nilesen, CFO

Sodexho MS Canada Ltd.
3350 South Service Rd.
Burlington, ON L7N 3M6
905-632-8592 Fax: 905-681-3021
canada@sodexhoCA.com
www.sodexhoca.com
Company Type: Private
Profile: Sodexho MS Canada Ltd. is a provider of outsourced food & facilities management

Garry C. Knox, President
Maarten Galesloot, CFO
Vincent Meehan, Director, Information Systems Technology
Miguel Bruno, Manager, Workers' Compensation

The Spectra Group of Great Restaurants Inc.
1880 West First Ave., 2nd Fl.
Vancouver, BC V6J 1G5
604-714-6500 Fax: 604-730-9155 www.spectragroup.com
Ticker Symbol: SPA
Company Type: Public
Profile: Retailing in eating places, alcoholic beverage drinking places; Patent owners & lessors

Peter Bonner, President/CEO
Richard C. Benmore, CFO

Sun-Rype Products Ltd.
1165 Ethel St.
Kelowna, BC V1Y 2W4
250-860-7973 Fax: 250-762-3611 888-786-7973
info@sunrype.com
www.sunrype.com
Ticker Symbol: SRF
Company Type: Public
Profile: Sun-Rype is a manufacturer & marketer of 100% fruit juices & 100% fruit snacks.

Eric Sorensen, President/CEO
Gary Pearson, CFO & Vice-President, Finance

Unibroue Inc.
80, rue des Carrières
Chambly, QC J3L 2H6

450-658-7658 Fax: 450-658-9195
info@unibroue.com
www.unibroue.com
Ticker Symbol: UBE
Company Type: Public
Profile: Manufacturers of malt beverages

André Dion, President/CEO & Chair
Michel Lacoste, Comptroller
Paul Arnott, Master Brewer

Van Houtte Inc.
8300, 19e av
Montréal, QC H1Z 4J8
514-593-7711 Fax: 514-593-8755 877-593-7722
gbacon@vanhoutte.com
www.vanhoutte.com
Ticker Symbol: VH
Company Type: Public
Profile: Manufacturers of roasted coffee; Wholesalers of groceries & related products; Retailing in miscellaneous food stores; Patent owners & lessors

Jean-Yves Monette, President/CEO
Gérard Geoffrion, CFO & Exec. Vice-President, Finance

Vincor International Inc.
441 Courtneypark Dr. East
Mississauga, ON L5T 2V3
905-564-6900 Fax: 905-564-6909
800-265-9463www.vincorinternational.com
Ticker Symbol: VN
Company Type: Public
Profile: Manufacturers of wines, brandy & brandy spirits; Wholesalers of wines & distilled alcoholic beverages; Retailing in liquor stores; Commercial physical & biological research

Donald L. Triggs, President/CEO
Richard G. Jones, Secretary & Exec. Vice-President, Finance & Administration

Forestry & Paper

3M Canada Company
PO Box 5757 B, 1840 Oxford St. East
London, ON N6A 4T1
519-452-6765 Fax: 519-452-6262 888-364-3577www.3m.ca
Company Type: Private
Profile: Manufacturers of packaging paper & coated & laminated plastics film, adhesives & sealants, photographic equipment & supplies, orthopedic, prosthetic & surgical appliances & supplies

Ian Hardgrove, President/CEO

Abitibi-Consolidated Inc.
#800, 1155, rue Metcalfe
Montréal, QC H3B 5H2
514-875-2160
contact@abitibiconsolidated.com
www.abitibiconsolidated.com
Ticker Symbol: A
Company Type: Public
Profile: Manufacturers in paper mills, pulp mills, logging, sawmills & general planing mills

John W. Weaver, President/CEO
Pierre Rougeau, CFO & Sr. Vice-President, Corporate Development
Blake Maher, Vice-President, Information Technology
Bruno Tremblay, Sr. Vice-President, Technology Services
Francine Dorion, Vice-President, Sustainability & Environment

Ainsworth Lumber Co. Ltd.
Bentall 4
PO Box 49307, #3194, 1055 Dunsmuir St.
Vancouver, BC V7X 1L3
604-661-3200 Fax: 604-661-3201
marketing@ainsworth.ca
www.ainsworth.ca
Ticker Symbol: ANS
Company Type: Public
Profile: Manufacturers in logging, sawmills & general planing mills, hardwood & softwood veneer & plywood, reconstituted wood products, & various other wood products

Brian Ainsworth, Chair/CEO
Allen Ainsworth, President

Arbec Forest Products Inc.
#506, 8000, boul Langelier
Montréal, QC H1P 3K2
514-327-3350 Fax: 514-327-1966
information@uniforet.com
www.uniforet.com
Ticker Symbol: ABR.SV.A
Company Type: Public
Profile: The manufacturer of softwood lumber carries on business through mills in Port-Cartier & in the Péribonka area.

Pierre Moreau, President/CEO
Serge Mercier, Vice-President, Finance & Administration

Canfor Corporation
#100, 1700 - 75 Ave. West
Vancouver, BC V6P 6G2
604-661-5241 Fax: 604-661-5235
info@canfor.ca
www.canfor.com
Ticker Symbol: CFP
Company Type: Public
Profile: Manufacturers in sawmills & general planing mills, logging, pulp mills, paper mills; Forestry services; Wholesalers in lumber, plywood, millwork & wood panels, printing & writing paper; Special product sawmills

James A. Shepherd, President/CEO
Scott Wilson, CFO & Group Vice-President, Finance
Ken O. Higginbotham, Vice-President, Forestry & Environment

Cascades Inc.
PO Box 30, 404, boul Marie-Victorin
Kingsey Falls, QC J0A 1B0
819-363-5100 Fax: 819-363-5155
info@cascades.com
www.cascades.com
Ticker Symbol: CAS
Company Type: Public
Profile: Manufacturers in pulp mills, paper mills; of folding paperboard boxes, paperboard mills, corrugated & solid fiber boxes, sanitary paper products

Alain Lemaire, President/CEO
Mario Plourde, President/COO, Specialty Products
Christian Dubé, CFO & Vice-President
Jean-Luc Bellemare, Vice-President, Information Technologies
Léon Marineau, Vice-President, Environment

Catalyst Paper Corporation
250 Howe St., 16th Fl.
Vancouver, BC V6C 3R8
604-654-4000 Fax: 604-654-4048
contactus@catalystpaper.com
www.catalystpaper.com
Ticker Symbol: CTL
Company Type: Public
Profile: Producer of mechanical printing papers & deinked & market kraft pulp; Owner of Western Canada's largest paper recycling facility

Russell J. Horner, President/CEO
Ralph Leverton, Vice-President/CFO, Finance

Commonwealth Plywood Co. Ltd.
PO Box 90, 15 boul Labelle
Sainte-Thérèse, QC J7E 4H9
450-435-6541 Fax: 450-435-3814
info@commonwealthplywood.com
www.commonwealthplywood.com
Company Type: Private
Profile: Manufacturers of hardwood veneer & plywood, softwood veneer & plywood, millwork; in sawmills & planing mills; wholesales hardwood & softwood lumber, plywood, millwork & wood panels

William T. Caine, President/CEO
J. d'Orazio, Vice-President, Finance

Concert Industries Ltd.
1680 rue Atmec
Gatineau, QC J8P 7G7
819-669-8100 Fax: 819-669-8161
info@concert.ca
www.concert.ca
Ticker Symbol: CNG
Company Type: Public
Profile: Manufacturers sanitary paper products

Domtar Inc.
PO Box 7210 A, 395, boul de Maisonneuve ouest
Montréal, QC H3C 3M1
514-848-5400
ir@domtar.com
www.domtar.com
Ticker Symbol: DTC
Company Type: Public
Profile: Manager of forestland in Canada & the USA; Producer of lumber & other wood products; Manufacturer of business, commercial printing, publication, technical & specialty papers

Raymond Royer, President/CEO
Yves Parent, Chief Technology Officer
Daniel Buron, CFO & Sr. Vice-President
Christian Tardif, , Communications & Government Relations
Richard Garneau, Exec. Vice-President, Operations

Federated Co-Operatives Ltd.
PO Box 1050 Main, 401 - 22 St. East
Saskatoon, SK S7K 0H2
306-244-3311 Fax: 306-244-3403 www.fcl.ca
Company Type: Private
Profile: Manufacturers in sawmills & planing mills, general; of millwork, prepared feeds & feed ingredients for animals & fowls, petroleum refining, dog & cat food; Wholesalers of general-line groceries & hardware; Retailing in lumber & other building materials dealers

Wayne Thompson, CEO
Glen Tully, President
A. Postle, Treasurer & Sr. Vice-President, Finance
Chris Bradshaw, Engineer, Field Services

Goodfellow Inc.
225, rue Goodfellow
Delson, QC J5B 1V5
450-635-6511 Fax: 450-635-3729 800-361-6503
info@goodfellowinc.com
www.goodfellowinc.com
Ticker Symbol: GDL
Company Type: Public
Profile: The company's activities include forest products distribution.

Richard Goodfellow, President/CEO
Fax: 450-638-8123
Pierre Lemoine, Vice-President, Finance
Fax: 450-638-8112, plemoine@goodfellowinc.com

International Forest Products Ltd.
Bentall Tower Four
PO Box 49114, #3500, 1055 Dunsmuir St.
Vancouver, BC V7X 1H7
604-689-6800 Fax: 604-688-0313
info@interfor.com
www.interfor.com
Ticker Symbol: IFP
Company Type: Public
Profile: Manufacturers in sawmills & general planing mills; of logging; special product sawmills; wholesalers of lumber, plywood, millwork & wood panels

Duncan Davies, President/CEO & Director
J.A. Horning, Vice-President/CFO, Finance & Corporate Development
Keith Power, Manager, Information Technology

Kitchen Craft of Canada Ltd.
1180 Springfield Rd.
Winnipeg, MB R2C 2Z2
204-224-3211 Fax: 800-665-3495 800-463-9707
sales@kitchencraft.com
www.kitchencraft.com
Company Type: Private
Profile: Manufacturers of wood kitchen cabinets

Victor Lukic, CEO
D. Litke, Financial Administrator
Bill Rademaker, Manager, Information Systems
Peter Marinelli, Chief Technology Officer
Mark Geiger, Manager, Health & Safety

Kruger Inc.
3285, ch Bedford
Montréal, QC H3S 1G5
514-737-1131 Fax: 514-343-3124
webmaster@kruger.com
www.kruger.com
Company Type: Private

Kruger Inc. (continued)
Profile: Paperboard mills & paper mills; Manufacturers of packaging paper & plastics film, coated & laminated, corrugated & solid fiber boxes

Joseph Kruger II, Chair/CEO
Mario Lecaldare, Exec. Vice-President/CFO
Robert Jobin, Corporate Director, Environmental Services

Masonite International Corporation
1600 Britannia Rd. East
Mississauga, ON L4W 1J2
905-670-6500 Fax: 905-670-6520 800-663-3667
webmaster@masonite.com
www.masonite.com
Ticker Symbol: MHM
Company Type: Private
Profile: Manufacturers of millwork, metal doors, sash, frames, molding & trim; Wholesalers of lumber, plywood, millwork, & wood panels

Philip S. Orsino, President/CEO
Robert V. Tubbesing, CFO & Vice-President
John Przedpelski, Chief Information Officer
Jim Rabe, Vice-President, Environment, Health & Safety

Norwall Group Inc.
1055 Clark Blvd.
Brampton, ON L6T 3W4
905-791-2700 Fax: 905-791-5281
invest@norwallgroup.com
www.norwallgroup.com
Ticker Symbol: NGI
Company Type: Public
Profile: Manufacturer & distributor of residential wallcoverings

James Patton, President/CEO & Vice-Chair
E. Arthur G. Hampson, CFO
Peter Walmsley, Vice-President, Human Resources

PRT Forest Regeneration Income Fund
#101, 1006 Fort St.
Victoria, BC V8V 3K4
250-381-1404 Fax: 250-381-0252 866-553-8733
prt@prtgroup.com
www.prtgroup.com
Ticker Symbol: PRT.UN
Company Type: Private
Profile: PRT produces forest seedlings in nurseries located in Canada & the USA.

John Kitchen, President/CEO
604-687-1404, Fax: 604-683-3137,
john.kitchen@prtgroup.com
Rob Miller, Vice-President/CFO
rob.miller@prtgroup.com
Brett Hill, Manager, Information Systems
brett.hill@prtgroup.com
Herb Markgraf, Vice-President, Business Development
604-687-1404, Fax: 604-683-3137,
herb.markgraf@prtgroup.com

Quebecor Inc.
612, rue Saint-Jacques
Montréal, QC H3C 4M8
514-380-1973
webmaster@quebecor.com
www.quebecor.com
Ticker Symbol: QBR
Company Type: Public
Profile: Offices of holding companies; Manufacturers in pulp & paper mills, sawmills & planing mills; Newspaper, periodical & books: publishing & printing

Pierre Karl Péladeau, President/CEO
Jacques Mallette, CFO & Exec. Vice-President
Luc Lavoie, Exec. Vice-President, Corporate Affairs

Roman Corporation Limited
PO Box 82, #1315, 200 King St. West
Toronto, ON M5H 3T4
416-971-3330 Fax: 416-971-9181
mourantg@romancorp.com
www.romancorp.com
Ticker Symbol: RMN
Company Type: Public
Profile: Offices of holding companies; Manufacturers in paperboard mills; Metal mining of copper & gold ores; Miscellaneous nonmetallic minerals mining & quarrying

Helen Roman-Barber, Chair/CEO
P. Gael Mourant, Vice-President/CFO

Sino-Forest Corporation
#1208, 90 Burnhamthorpe Rd. West
Mississauga, ON L5B 3C3
905-281-8889 Fax: 905-281-3338
info@sinoforest.com
www.sinoforest.com
Ticker Symbol: TRE
Company Type: Public
Profile: Timber tracts; forest nurseries & gathering of forest products; Logging; Wholesalers of lumber, plywood, millwork, wood panels & various durable goods; Manufacturers in sawmills & planing mills

Allen T.Y. Chan, Chair/CEO & Director
Kai Kit Poon, President & Director
David J. Horskey, Sr. Vice-President & CFO
Kee Y. Wong, Vice-Chairman & Director

St. Mary's Paper Ltd.
75 Huron St.
Sault Ste Marie, ON P6A 5P4
705-942-6070 Fax: 705-942-4791 www.stmarys-paper.com
Company Type: Private
Profile: Manufacturers in paper mills

R. Stern, CEO
Gerry Henson, Corporate Controller
Lori Greco, Environmental Officer

Stella-Jones Inc.
4269, rue Ste-Catherine ouest, 7e étage
Montréal, QC H3Z 1P7
514-934-8666 Fax: 514-934-5327
montreal@stella-jones.com
www.stella-jones.com
Ticker Symbol: SJ
Company Type: Public
Profile: Manufacturers of wood preserving products

Brian McManus, President/CEO
George T. Labelle, Vice-President, Finance
Gordon Murray, Vice-President, Environment & Technology

Supremex Inc.
400 Humberline Dr.
Toronto, ON M9W 5T3
416-675-9370 Fax: 416-848-8388
sales@supremex.com
www.supremex.com
Company Type: Private
Profile: Manufacturers of stock & custom envelopes

Charlie MacLean, President
Stéphane Lavigne, Vice-President, Finance & Administration

Taiga Building Products Ltd.
#800, 4710 Kingsway
Burnaby, BC V5H 4M2
604-438-1471 Fax: 604-439-4242 800-663-1470
webmaster@taigabuilding.com
www.taigabuilding.com
Ticker Symbol: TFP
Company Type: Public
Profile: Wholesalers of lumber, plywood, millwork, & wood panels, roofing, siding, & insulation materials, construction materials; Manufacturers of millwork & various wood products

Arkadi Bykhovsky, President/CEO
Ji Yoon, Acting CFO
John Lo, General Manager, Information Systems

Tembec Inc.
#1050, 800, boul René-Lévesque ouest
Montréal, QC H3B 1X9
514-871-0137 Fax: 514-397-0896 www.tembec.ca
Ticker Symbol: TBC
Company Type: Public
Profile: Forest products company with operations in North America & France

James Lopez, President/CEO
Dennis Rounsville, Exec. Vice-President & President, Tembec Forest Products Group
Michel Dumas, CFO & Exec. Vice-President, Finance
Michael D. Danyluk, Chief Information Officer
Jacques Rochon, Vice-President, Information Technology
Mike Martel, Sr. Vice-President, Forest Resource Management

TimberWest Forest Corp.
PO Box 11101, #2300, 1055 West Georgia St.
Vancouver, BC V6E 3P3
604-654-4600 Fax: 604-654-4662
invest@timberwest.com
www.timberwest.com
Ticker Symbol: TWF
Company Type: Public
Profile: Manufacturers of logging; in sawmills & general planing mills; Forestry-timber tracts

Paul J. McElligott, President/CEO
Beverlee Park, CFO & Vice-President, Finance
Virginia Aulin, Vice-President, Public Affairs & Government Relations
Mark Stock, Vice-President, Human Resources & Information Technology

Viceroy Homes Limited
414 Croft St. East
Port Hope, ON L1A 4H1
905-885-8600 Fax: 905-885-8362
infor@viceroy.com
www.viceroy.com
Ticker Symbol: VHL
Company Type: Public
Profile: Manufacturers of prefabricated wood buildings & components, millwork; Wholesalers of construction materials

Gaylord G. Lindal, President/Chair
Bill Simpson, Vice-President, Finance
Carolyn Lewis, Manager, IT
Bev Dealy, Manager, Distribution

West Fraser Timber Co. Ltd.
#501, 858 Beatty St.
Vancouver, BC V6B 1C1
604-895-2700 Fax: 604-681-6061
shareholder@westfraser.com
www.westfrasertimber.ca
Ticker Symbol: WFT
Company Type: Public
Profile: Manufacturers in pulp mills, paper mills, paperboard mills, sawmills & general planing mills; Retailers in hardware stores, lumber & other building materials dealers

Henry H. Ketcham III, President/CEO & Chair
Martti Solin, CFO & Vice-President, Finance
Cindy MacDonald, Manager, Environmental Affairs

Western Forest Products Inc.
435 Trunk Rd., 3rd Fl.
Duncan, BC V9L 2P9
250-748-3711 Fax: 250-748-6045
info@westernforest.com
www.westernforest.com
Ticker Symbol: DOM
Company Type: Public
Profile: Manufacturers in sawmills, planing mills & pulp mills; Wholesalers of lumber, plywood, millwork & wood panels

Duncan Kerr, COO
Reynold Hert, President/CEO
Paul Ireland, Secretary & Vice-President, Finance

Weyerhaeuser Company Limited
925 West Georgia St., 5th Fl.
Vancouver, BC V6C 3L2
604-661-8334 Fax: 604-687-2314 www.weyerhaeuser.com
Ticker Symbol: WYL
Company Type: Public
Profile: Growing & harvesting timber; manufacture, distribution & sale of forest products; real estate construction & development

Steven R. Rogel, President/CEO
Patricia M. Bedient, Sr. Vice-President, Finance & Strategic Planning
Susan M. Mesereau, Chief Information Officer & Sr. Vice-President, Information Technology
George H. Weyerhaeuser Jr., Sr. Vice-President, Technology
Sara S. Kendall, Vice-President, Environmental, Health & Safety

Winpak Ltd.
100 Saulteaux Cres.
Winnipeg, MB R3J 3T3
204-889-1015 Fax: 204-888-7806
info@winpak.com
www.winpak.com
Ticker Symbol: WPK
Company Type: Public

MAJOR CANADIAN COMPANIES

Profile: Manufacturers of sanitary food containers, coated & laminated packaging paper & plastics film

J. Robert Lavery, President/CEO & Director
Murray G. Johnston, CFO & Vice-President
Norman L. Rozek, Vice-President, Technology

Government Administration

British Columbia Lottery Corporation

74 West Seymour St.
Kamloops, BC V2C 1E2
250-828-5500 Fax: 250-828-5631 www.bclc.com
Company Type: Crown
Profile: BC Lottery Corp. is a gaming entertainment company.

Vic Poleschuk, President/CEO
Doug Penrose, Vice-President, Finance & Corporate Services
Kevin Gass, Vice-President, Corporate Communications & Marketing
Scott Norman, Vice-President, Information Technology & Chief Information Officer

Manitoba Lotteries Corporation

830 Empress St.
Winnipeg, MB R3G 3H3
204-957-2500 Fax: 204-957-2621
communications@mlc.mb.ca
www.mlc.mb.ca
Company Type: Crown
Profile: Manitoba Lotteries Corporation owns & operates Club Regent & McPhillips Street Station Casinos in Winnipeg. It also owns & operates the province's Video Lottery Terminal (VLT) network. The corporation is the exclusive supplier of breakopen tickets & bingo paper in Manitoba. The crown company also distributes & sells tickets for lotteries operated by the Western Canada Lottery Corporation & the Interprovincial Lottery Corporation.

Cheryl Eason, Exec. Vice-President/CFO
Susan Olynik, Vice-President, Communications & Public Affairs

Holding & Other Investment

AIC Diversified Canada Split Corp.

1375 Kerns Rd.
Burlington, ON L7R 4X8
905-331-4242 800-263-2144
info@aic.com
www.aic.com
Ticker Symbol: ADC
Company Type: Public
Profile: Unit investment trusts, certificate/closed-end management offices

Michael A. Lee-Chin, Chair/CEO
Vicki Ringelberg, CFO

Algonquin Power Income Fund

2845 Bristol Circle
Oakville, ON L6H 7H7
905-465-4500 Fax: 905-465-4514
apif@algonquinpower.com
www.algonquinpower.com
Ticker Symbol: APF
Company Type: Public
Profile: Non-educational, religious or charitable trusts

Chris K. Jarrat, CEO & Managing Director, Operations
Peter Kampian, CFO
Vito Ciciretto, Chief Operating Officer
David C. Kerr, Managing Director, Environmental Compliance

American Income Trust

PO Box 341, #4500, 77 King St. West
Toronto, ON M5K 1K7
416-304-4440 Fax: 416-304-4441 877-478-2372
info@quadravest.com
www.quadravest.com
Ticker Symbol: USA
Company Type: Public
Profile: Unit investment trusts, certificate/closed-end management offices

Wayne Finch, President/Sec.-Treas. & Chair
Peter F. Cruickshank, CFO

ARC Energy Trust

#2100, 440 - 2nd Ave. SW
Calgary, AB T2P 5E9
403-503-8600 Fax: 403-509-6417 888-272-4900
ir@arcresources.com
www.arcresources.com
Ticker Symbol: AET
Company Type: Public
Profile: Unit investment trusts, certificate/closed-end management offices; Oil royalty traders

John P. Dielwart, President/CEO & Director
Steven W. Sinclair, CFO & Vice-President, Finance

Brascade Resources Inc.

BCE Place
#300, 181 Bay St.
Toronto, ON M5J 2T3
416-363-9491 Fax: 416-365-9642
enquiries@brascancorp.com
www.brascancorp.com
Ticker Symbol: BCA
Company Type: Public
Profile: Offices of holding companies

Edward C. Kress, President/Chair
Lisa W.F. Chu, Vice-President & Controller

Brookfield Asset Management

BCE Place
PO Box 762, #300, 181 Bay St.
Toronto, ON M5J 2T3
416-363-0061 Fax: 416-363-2856 www.brascancorp.com
Ticker Symbol: BNN
Company Type: Public
Profile: Offices of holding companies

George E. Myhal, President/CEO
Brian D. Lawson, Managing Partner, Corporate Finance

Canada Trust Income Investments

c/o TD Asset Management Inc., Canada Trust Tower
161 Bay St., 35th Fl.
Toronto, ON M5J 2T2
416-308-9049 Fax: 416-983-1729 866-888-3383
huck.oon@td.com
www.tdcanadatrust.com
Ticker Symbol: CNN
Company Type: Public
Profile: Unit investment trusts, certificate/closed-end management offices

Steve Geist, President/CEO
Michael Laman, CFO

Canadian Apartment Properties Real Estate Investment

#401, 11 Church St.
Toronto, ON M5E 1W1
416-861-9404 Fax: 416-861-9209
ir@capreit.net
www.capreit.net
Ticker Symbol: CAR
Company Type: Public
Profile: Real estate investment trusts

Thomas Schwartz, President/CEO
Yazdi Bharucha, CFO & Secretary

Canadian Hotel Income Properties Real Estate Investme

Burrard Bldg.
#1600, 1030 West Georgia St.
Vancouver, BC V6E 2Y3
604-646-2447 Fax: 604-646-2404
investor@chipreit.com
www.chipreit.com
Ticker Symbol: HOT
Company Type: Public
Profile: Real estate investment trusts; Hotels & motels; Retailing in eating places

Ed Pitoniak, President/CEO
Kevin E. Grayston, CFO & Exec. Vice-President
Robert Pratt, Sr. Vice-President, Operations
Judy Kan, Vice-President, Real Estate
Sharon MacKay, Vice-President, Human Resource Services
Peter Smolik, Director, Information Technology

Canadian Real Estate Investment Trust

#500, 175 Bloor St.East, North Tower
Toronto, ON M4W 3R8
416-628-7771 Fax: 416-628-7777
info@creit.ca
www.creit.ca
Ticker Symbol: REF
Company Type: Public
Profile: Real estate investment trusts

Stephen E. Johnson, President/CEO
Timothy McSorley, CFO & Vice-President

Canadian Resources Income Trust

Scotia Plaza
PO Box 4085 A, #2600, 40 King St. West
Toronto, ON M5W 2X6
416-863-7144 Fax: 416-863-7425
mc_carit@scotiacapital.com
Ticker Symbol: RTU
Company Type: Public
Profile: Unit investment trusts, certificate/closed-end management offices

Brian D. McChesney, President/CEO, CaRIT Limited
Michael K. Warman, CFO/Secretary, CaRIT Limited

Canadian World Fund Limited

#1601, 110 Yonge St.
Toronto, ON M5C 1T4
416-366-2931 Fax: 416-366-2729 866-443-6097
mma@mmainvestments.com
www.mmainvestments.com
Ticker Symbol: CWF
Company Type: Public
Profile: Unit investment trusts, certificate/closed-end management offices; Global Equity

M.A. Smedley, President & Director
Colin D. Smith, Sec.-Treas.

CanCap Preferred Corporation

#3400, 800, carré Victoria
Montréal, QC H4Z 1E9
514-871-7510 Fax: 514-871-7303 **Ticker Symbol:** CAC
Company Type: Public
Profile: Investors

Vital Proulx, President & Chair
Marc Veilleux, CFO

The Churchill Corporation

12836 - 146th St.
Edmonton, AB T5L 2H7
780-454-3667 Fax: 780-488-0194
inquiries@churchill-cuq.com
www.churchillcorporation.com
Ticker Symbol: CUQ
Company Type: Public
Profile: Offices of holding companies; Management services

J. Norman Rokosh, President/CEO
Daryl Sands, CFO & Vice-President, Finance

Citadel Diversified Investment Trust

#3500, 350 - 7 Ave. SW
Calgary, AB T2P 3N9
403-261-9674 Fax: 403-261-8670 877-261-9674
info@citadelfunds.com
www.citadelfunds.com
Ticker Symbol: CTD
Company Type: Public
Profile: Unit investment trusts, certificate/closed-end mgmt offices

James T. Bruvall, CEO/Director, Citadel Diversified Management Ltd.
Darren K. Duncan, CFO/Director, Citadel Diversified Management Ltd.

Clairvest Group Inc.

#1700, 22 St. Clair Ave. East
Toronto, ON M4T 2S3
416-925-9270 Fax: 416-925-5753
lanar@clairvest.com
www.clairvest.com
Ticker Symbol: CVG
Company Type: Public
Profile: Offices of holding companies

B. Jeffrey Parr, Co-CEO/Managing Director

Clairvest Group Inc. (continued)
Lana Reiken, Corporate Secretary/Vice-President, Finance

Cominar Real Estate Investment Trust
455, rue Marais
Québec, QC G1M 3A2
418-681-8151 Fax: 418-681-2946 866-266-4627
info@cominar.com
www.cominar.com
Ticker Symbol: CUF
Company Type: Public
Profile: Real estate investment trusts

Jules Dallaire, President/CEO/Chair & Trustee
Michel Berthelot, Exec. Vice-President/CFO & Trustee

Counsel Corporation
Scotia Plaza
#3200, 40 King St. West
Toronto, ON M5H 3Y2
416-866-3000 Fax: 416-866-3061
info@counselcorp.com
www.counselcorp.com
Ticker Symbol: CXS
Company Type: Public
Profile: Offices of holding companies

Allan Silber, Chair/CEO
Stephen Weintraub, CFO

Crew Gold Corporation
#411, 837 West Hastings St.
Vancouver, BC V6C 3N6
604-683-7585 Fax: 604-682-0566
enquiries@crewgold.com
www.crewgroup.com
Ticker Symbol: CRU
Company Type: Public
Profile: Offices of holding companies

Jan A. Vestrum, President/CEO & Director
Rupi Khanuja, Acting CFO & Corporate Secretary

Datec Group Ltd.
Scotia 1
#2150, 10060 Jasper Ave.
Edmonton, AB T5J 3R8
780-429-1010 Fax: 780-429-0101 800-299-7823
info@datecgroup.com
www.datecgroup.com
Ticker Symbol: BKI
Company Type: Public
Profile: Offices of holding companies

Michael Ah Koy, Managing Director/CEO
Suray D. Sharma, Interim CFO

Dundee Corporation
1 Adelaide. St. East, 28th Floor
Toronto, ON M5C 2V9
416-863-6990 Fax: 416-363-4536
investor@dundeebancorp.com
www.dundeecorporation.com
Ticker Symbol: DBC
Company Type: Public
Profile: Open-ended management investment offices; Unit investment trusts, certificate/closed-end management offices; Real estate land subdividers & developers

Ned Goodman, President/CEO
Joanne Ferstman, CFO

Dundee Precious Metals Inc.
Royal Bank Plaza, South Tower
#3060, 200 Bay St.
Toronto, ON M5J 2J1
416-365-5191 Fax: 416-365-9080 800-268-8186
info@dundeeprecious.com
www.dundeeprecious.com
Ticker Symbol: DPM
Company Type: Public
Profile: Unit investment trusts, certificate/closed-end management trusts

Jonathan Goodman, President/CEO & Director
Rosanna Gatti, CFO & Vice-President, Finance

Dundee Wealth Management Inc.
Scotia Plaza
40 King St. West, 55th Fl.
Toronto, ON M5H 4A9
416-350-3489 800-301-6745
inquiries@dundeewealth.com
www.dundeewealth.com
Ticker Symbol: DW
Company Type: Public
Profile: Offices of holding companies

Ned Goodman, President/CEO & Chair

Economic Investment Trust Limited
165 University Ave., 10th Fl.
Toronto, ON M5H 3B8
416-947-2578 Fax: 416-868-6199 **Ticker Symbol:** EVT
Company Type: Public
Profile: Unit investment trusts, certificate/closed-end management offices

Duncan N.R. Jackman, Chair
Travis R. Epp, Treasurer

EnerVest Diversified Income Trust
#2800, 700 - 9th Ave. SW
Calgary, AB T2P 3V4
403-571-5550 Fax: 403-571-5554 800-459-3384
info@enervest.com
www.enervest.com
Ticker Symbol: EIT
Company Type: Public
Profile: Unit investment trusts, certificate/closed-end management offices; Real estate investment trusts

Michael L. Streukens, President/CEO, EnerVest Diversified Management Inc.
Dave J. Fischer, CFO, EnerVest Diversified Management Inc.

Fairfax Financial Holdings Limited
#800, 95 Wellington St. West
Toronto, ON M5J 2N7
416-367-4941 Fax: 416-367-4946 www.fairfax.ca
Ticker Symbol: FFH
Company Type: Public
Profile: Offices of holding companies; Life insurance; Accident & health insurance; Fire, marine, & casualty insurance; Insurance agents, brokers, & service

V. Prem Watsa, Chair/CEO
Trevor J. Ambridge, CFO & Vice-President

Forest & Marine Investments Ltd.
#500, 345 Wallace St.
Nanaimo, BC V9R 5B6
250-753-0141 Fax: 250-753-0173 877-772-0022
dhitch@forestandmarine.com
www.forestandmarine.com
Ticker Symbol: FME
Company Type: Public
Profile: Unit investment trusts, certificate/closed-end management offices

John L. Hitchcock, President

Freehold Royalty Trust
#400, 144 - 4th Ave. SW
Calgary, AB T2P 3N4
403-221-0802 Fax: 403-221-0888 888-257-1873
ir@freeholdtrust.com
www.freeholdtrust.com
Ticker Symbol: FRU
Company Type: Public
Profile: Open-ended management investment offices; Oil royalty traders

David J. Sandmeyer, President/CEO
Joseph N. Holowisky, Secretary/CFO & Vice-President, Finance & Administration
Karen C. Taylor, Manager, Investor Relations
William O. Ingram, Vice-President, Production
Michael J. Okrusko, Vice-President, Land

Gendis Inc.
1370 Sony Pl.
Winnipeg, MB R3C 3C3
204-474-5200 Fax: 204-474-5201
finance@gendis.ca
www.gendis.ca
Ticker Symbol: GDS
Company Type: Public
Profile: Offices of holding companies; Management services

Albert D. Cohen, President/CEO/Director
Ernest B. Reinfort, Vice-President, Finance

Global Plus Income Trust
Mulvihill Capital Management
#2600, 121 King St. West
Toronto, ON M5H 3T9
416-681-3900 Fax: 416-681-3901 800-725-7172
hybrid@mulvihill.com
www.mulvihill.com
Ticker Symbol: GIP
Company Type: Public
Profile: Unit investment trusts, certificate/closed-end management offices

John P. Mulvihill, President & Chair, Mulvihill Capital Management
David N. Middleton, CFO & Vice-President, Finance, Mulvihill Capital Management

Global Telecom Split Share Corp.
Standard Life Centre
#2600, 121 King St. West
Toronto, ON M5H 3T9
416-681-3900 Fax: 416-681-3901 800-725-7172
hybrid@mulvihill.com
www.mulvihill.com
Ticker Symbol: GT
Company Type: Public
Profile: Unit investment trusts, certificate/closed-end management offices

John P. Mulvihill, President & Chair, Mulvihill Capital Management
David N. Middleton, CFO & Vice-President, Finance, Mulvihill Capital Management

GLP NT Corporation
BCE Place
PO Box 770, #4440, 181 Bay St.
Toronto, ON M5J 2T3
416-363-9491 Fax: 416-865-1288 **Ticker Symbol:** GP
Company Type: Public
Profile: Offices of holding companies

George E. Myhal, President
Sachin G. Shah, CFO

Great-West Lifeco
100 Osborne St. North
Winnipeg, MB R3C 3A5
204-946-8366 Fax: 204-946-4129
info@gwl.ca
www.greatwestlifeco.com
Ticker Symbol: GWO
Company Type: Public
Profile: Offices of holding companies

William T. McCallum, Co-President/CEO
William W. Lovatt, Vice-President, Finance, Canada
Marlene Klassen, Director, Media & Public Relations

Guardian Capital Group Limited
PO Box 201, #3100, Commerce Ct. West
Toronto, ON M5L 1E8
416-364-8341 Fax: 416-947-0601
sgreiss@guardiancapital.com
Ticker Symbol: GCG
Company Type: Public
Profile: Offices of holding companies; Open-ended management investment offices; Security brokers, dealers & flotation companies; Investment advice

John M. Christodoulou, Chair/CEO
C. Verner Christensen, Vice-President & Secretary, Finance
Sam K. Greiss, Sr. Vice-President, Operations & Corporate Development

Halterm Income Fund
PO Box 1057, Halifax, NS B3J 2X1
902-421-1778 Fax: 902-429-3193
info@halterm.com
www.halterm.com
Ticker Symbol: HAL
Company Type: Public
Profile: Non-charitable, non-educational & non-religious trusts

Doug Rose, President, Halterm Limited
Michael Uberoi, CFO, Halterm Limited

Income Financial Trust
Royal Trust Tower
PO Box 341, #4500, 77 King St. West
Toronto, ON M5K 1K7

416-304-4440 Fax: 416-304-4441 877-478-2372
info@quadravest.com
www.quadravest.com
Ticker Symbol: INC
Company Type: Public
Profile: Unit investment trusts, certificate/closed-end management offices; Investors

Peter F. Cruickshank, CFO, Quadravest Capital Management
S. Wayne Finch, Chair/Chief Investment Officer, Quadravest Capital Management

Labrador Iron Ore Royalty Income Fund
Scotia Plaza
PO Box 4085 A, 40 King St. West, 26th Fl.
Toronto, ON M5W 2X6
416-863-7133 Fax: 416-863-7425 **Ticker Symbol:** LIF
Company Type: Public
Profile: Non-educational, non-religious & non-charitable trusts

Bruce C. Bone, Chair/CEO & Trustee
James C. McCartney, Sec.-Treas. & Trustee

Legacy Hotels Real Estate Investment Trust
TD Centre
PO Box 129, #2000, 100 Wellington St. West
Toronto, ON M5K 1H1
416-860-6100 Fax: 416-860-6101 866-627-0641
investor@legacyhotels.ca
www.legacyhotels.ca
Ticker Symbol: LGY
Company Type: Public
Profile: Real estate investment trusts

Neil J. Labatte, President/CEO
Robert M. Putnam, CFO & Vice-President
Sari L. Diamond, Secretary

MINT Income Fund
Middlefield Group
PO Box 192, First Canadian Pl., 58th Fl.
Toronto, ON M5X 1A6
416-362-0714 Fax: 416-362-7925
invest@middlefield.com
www.middlefield.com
Ticker Symbol: MID
Company Type: Public
Profile: Unit investment trusts, certificate/closed-end management offices

W. Garth Jestley, President/Director, MINT Management Limited
Anthony P. Traub, Sec.-Treas., MINT Management Limited

Morguard Real Estate Investment Trust
#1000, 55 City Centre Dr.
Mississauga, ON L5B 1M3
905-281-4800 Fax: 905-281-4818
investorrelations@morguardreit.com
www.morguardreit.com
Ticker Symbol: MRT
Company Type: Public
Profile: Unit investment trusts, certificate/closed-end management offices

K. Rai Sahi, CEO
Bill Kennedy, President/COO
Carol Taccone, CFO & Vice-President
Jay Camacho, Vice-President, Finance & Administration

Multi-Fund Income Trust
#420, 703-6th Ave.
Calgary, AB M5J 1S9
403-265-6540 Fax: 403-206-7185 888-708-5757
info@multifundtrust.com
www.multifundtrust.com
Ticker Symbol: MFU
Company Type: Public
Profile: Non-educational, non-charitable, & non-religious trusts

John B. Newman, Chair/CEO
Ian D. McPherson, CFO

Mulvihill Capital Management Inc.
Standard Life Centre
#2600, 121 King St. West
Toronto, ON M5H 3T9
416-681-3900 Fax: 416-681-3901 800-725-7172
info@mulvihill.com
www.mulvihill.com
Ticker Symbol: SIX
Company Type: Public
Profile: Unit investment trusts, certificate/closed-end management offices; Investors

John P. Mulvihill, President & Chair
David N. Middleton, CFO & Vice-President, Finance
David Hill, Manager, Information Technology

Mulvihill Premium Canadian Bank Fund
Standard Life Centre
#2600, 121 King St. West
Toronto, ON M5H 3T9
416-681-3900 Fax: 416-681-3901 800-725-7172
info@mulvihill.com
www.mulvihill.com
Ticker Symbol: PIC
Company Type: Public
Profile: Open-ended management investment offices

John P. Mulvihill, President & Secretary
David N. Middleton, CFO

Mulvihill Premium Canadian Fund
Standard Life Centre
#2600, 121 King St. West
Toronto, ON M5H 3T9
416-681-3900 Fax: 416-681-3901 800-725-7172
hybrid@mulvihill.com
www.mulvihill.com
Ticker Symbol: FPI.UN
Company Type: Public
Profile: Unit investment trusts, certificate/closed-end management offices

John P. Mulvihill, President/CEO, Mulvihill Capital Management Inc.

Mulvihill Premium Split Share Fund
Standard Life Centre
#2600, 121 King St. West
Toronto, ON M5H 3T9
416-681-3900 Fax: 416-681-3901 800-725-7172
hybrid@mulvihill.com
www.mulvihill.com
Ticker Symbol: MUH
Company Type: Public
Profile: Open-ended management investment offices

John P. Mulvihill, President & Chair, Mulvihill Capital Management Inc.
David N. Middleton, CFO & Vice-President, Finance

NAL Oil & Gas Trust
NAL Resources Management Limited
#600, 550 - 6th Ave. SW
Calgary, AB T2P 0S2
403-294-3600 Fax: 403-294-3601 888-223-8792
investor.relations@nal.ca
www.nal.ca
Ticker Symbol: NAE.UN
Company Type: Public
Profile: Open-end investment trust; Acquisition, development, production & marketing of oil, natural gas & natural gas liquids generates distributions

Andrew B. Wiswell, President/CEO
awiswell@nal.ca
Keith A. Steeves, CFO & Vice-President, Finance
410-294-3638, Fax: 403-294-3601, ksteeves@nal.ca
Sandra J. Anderson, Assistant Corporate Secretary
403-294-3651, sanderson@nal.ca
Jonathan A. Lexier, Vice-President, Operations
403-515-3427, jlexier@nal.ca

NewGrowth Corp.
Scotia Plaza
PO Box 4085 A, 40 King St. West, 26th Fl.
Toronto, ON M5W 2X6
416-862-3931 Fax: 416-863-7425
mc_newgrowth@scotiacapital.com
www.scotiamanagedcompanies.com
Ticker Symbol: NEW
Company Type: Public
Profile: Unit investment trusts, certificate/closed-end management offices

Robert C. Williams, President/CEO
Michael K. Warman, CFO & Secretary

Northland Power Income Fund
c/o Iroquois Falls Power Management Inc.
30 St Clair Ave. West, 17th Fl.
Toronto, ON M4V 3A2
416-962-6262 Fax: 416-962-6266
info@npifund.com
www.npifund.com
Ticker Symbol: NPI
Company Type: Public
Profile: Open-ended management investment offices; Owner & operator of independent power projects

James C. Temerty, President, Northland Power Inc.
Anthony F. Anderson, CFO, Northland Power Inc.

Northwater Market-Neutral Trust
Bay Wellington Tower, BCE Place
PO Box 794, #4700, 181 Bay St.
Toronto, ON M5J 2T3
416-360-5435 Fax: 416-360-0671 800-422-1867
mpt@northwatercapital.com
www.northwatercapital.com
Ticker Symbol: NMN
Company Type: Public
Profile: Unit investment trusts, certificate/closed-end management offices

David G. Patterson, Chair/CEO, Northwater Fund Management Inc.
Benita M. Warmbold, Treasurer, Northwater Fund Management Inc.
James Sinclair, Secretary, Northwater Fund Management Inc.
David S. Finch, Vice-President
Daniel C.R. Mills, Chief Investment Officer

Oceanex Income Fund
#2550, 630, boul René-Lévesque ouest
Montréal, QC H3B 1S6
514-875-9244 Fax: 514-877-0226
dbelisle@oceanex.com
www.oceanex.com
Ticker Symbol: OAX
Company Type: Public
Profile: Non-educational, non-religious & non-charitable trusts

Peter Henrico, President/CEO, Oceanex Inc.
Daniel Bélisle, Secretary/Vice-President, Finance & Administration

Onex Corporation
PO Box 700, 161 Bay St., 49th Fl.
Toronto, ON M5J 2S1
416-362-7711 Fax: 416-362-5765
info@onex.com
www.onex.com
Ticker Symbol: OCX
Company Type: Public
Profile: Offices of holding companies; Manufacturers of electronic computers, steel works, blast furnaces, coke ovens, rolling mills, motor vehicle parts & accessories; cane sugar refining; Computer facilities management services; Computer integrated systems design; Telephone communications; Retailing in eating places; Motion picture theatres

Gerald W. Schwartz, President/CEO & Chair
Ewout R. Heersink, Managing Director & CFO

Petrofund
#600, 444 - 7th Ave. SW
Calgary, AB T2P 0X8
403-218-8625 Fax: 403-269-5858 866-318-1767
info@petrofund.com
www.petrofund.com
Ticker Symbol: NCF
Company Type: Public
Profile: Open-ended management investment offices; Acquires & manages oil & gas properties

Jeffery E. Errico, President/CEO
Vince P. Moyer, CFO & Sr. Vice-President, Finance
Glen Fischer, Sr. Vice-President, Operations

Power Corporation of Canada
751, carré Victoria
Montréal, QC H2Y 2J3
514-286-7400 Fax: 514-286-7424 www.powercorporation.com
Ticker Symbol: POW
Company Type: Public
Profile: Offices of holding companies

Power Corporation of Canada (continued)
Paul Desmarais Jr., Chair/Co-CEO
Michel Plessis-Bélair, CFO/Vice-Chair
Edward Johnson, Vice-President/General Counsel & Secretary

Power Financial Corporation
751, carré Victoria
Montréal, QC H2Y 2J3
514-286-7400 Fax: 514-286-7424 www.powerfinancial.com
Ticker Symbol: PWF
Company Type: Public
Profile: Offices of holding companies

Robert Gratton, President/CEO
Michel Plessis-Bélair, Exec. Vice-President/CFO
Edward Johnson, Vice-President/General Counsel & Secretary

PrimeWest Energy Trust
#5100, 150 - 6th Ave. SW
Calgary, AB T2P 3Y7
403-234-6600 Fax: 403-699-7269 877-968-7878
investor@primewestenergy.com
www.primewestenergy.com
Ticker Symbol: PWI
Company Type: Public
Profile: Unit investment trusts, certificate/closed-end management offices

Donald A. Garner, President/CEO
Dennis G. Feuchuk, CFO & Vice-President, Finance
George. Kesteven, Manager, Investor Relations

Proprietary Industries Inc.
#227, 200 Barclay Parade SW
Calgary, AB T2P 4R5
403-266-6364 Fax: 403-266-6365
info@proprietaryinc.com
www.proprietaryinc.com
Ticker Symbol: PPI
Company Type: Public
Profile: Offices of holding companies; General contractors of single family houses, residential buildings; Operative builders; Real estate operators of residential mobile home sites; Extraction of crude petroleum, natural gas & natural gas liquids; Metal mining in miscellaneous metal ores

Stephen C. Akerfeldt, President/CEO & Chair
Glenn F. McCowan, CFO
Graham S. Garner, Exec. Vice-President & Corporate Secretary

R Split II Corporation
Scotia Plaza
PO Box 4085 A, 40 King St. West, 26th Fl.
Toronto, ON M5W 2X6
416-945-5353 Fax: 416-863-7425
mc_rsplit2@scotiacapital.com
www.scotiamanagedcompanies.com
Ticker Symbol: RBS
Company Type: Public
Profile: Unit investment trusts, certificate/closed-end management offices; Investors

Brian D. McChesney, President/CEO & Director
Michael K. Warman, CFO/Secretary & Director

Ravensource Fund
Cinnamon Investments
60 Bedford Rd.
Toronto, ON M5R 2K2
416-922-9096 Fax: 416-921-3551 **Company Type:** Public

Rockwater Capital Corporation
Bay Wellington Tower, BCE Place
PO Box 779, #900, 181 Bay St.
Toronto, ON M5J 2T3
416-865-4780 Fax: 416-865-4788 866-775-7704
info@rockwater.ca
www.rockwater.ca
Ticker Symbol: RCC
Company Type: Public
Profile: Investors

William D. Packham, President/CEO
Gordon Weir, CFO
Richard Wyruch, General Counsel/Corporate Secretary

Rogers Sugar Income Fund
4026, rue Notre-Dame est
Montréal, QC H1W 2K3
514-940-4350 Fax: 514-527-1610
infos@rogerssugar.com
www.rogerssugar.com
Ticker Symbol: RSI
Company Type: Public
Profile: Open-ended management investment offices, (refiner, processor, distributor of sugar products)

Pierre G. Côté, President/CEO
Daniel L. Lafrance, CFO/Secretary & Sr. Vice-President, Finance & Procurement

SCI Income Trust
#251, 6900 Airport Rd.
Mississauga, ON L4V 1E8
905-671-1033 Fax: 905-671-0669
sci-investor-relations@simmonscanada.com
www.simmonscanada.com
Ticker Symbol: SMN.UN
Company Type: Public
Profile: Manufacturers of mattresses & foundations

Terry Pace, President/CEO
Gerry Costigan, CFO & Vice-President

Sentry Select Diversified Income Trust
The Exchange Tower
#2850, 130 King St. West
Toronto, ON M5X 1A4
416-861-8729 Fax: 416-364-1197 888-246-6656
info@sentryselect.com
www.sentryselect.com
Ticker Symbol: SDT
Company Type: Public
Profile: Unit investment trusts, certificate/closed-end management offices

John F. Driscoll, President
John Vooglaid, CFO & Vice-President

Senvest Capital Inc.
#1180, 1140, boul Maisonneuve ouest
Montréal, QC H3A 1M8
514-281-8082 Fax: 514-281-0166
georgem@senvest.com
www.senvest.com
Ticker Symbol: SEC
Company Type: Public
Profile: Offices of holding companies

Victor Mashaal, President & Chair
George Malikotsis, CFO
Frank Daniel, Sec.-Treas.

Sonor Investments Limited
PO Box 68, #2020, 130 Adelaide St. West
Toronto, ON M5H 3P5
416-369-1499 Fax: 416-369-0280 **Ticker Symbol:** SNI
Company Type: Public
Profile: Offices of holding companies

Michael R. Gardiner, President/CEO
Michael Gionas, Treasurer
William N. Kinnear, Secretary

Split Yield Corporation
Royal Trust Tower
PO Box 341, #4500, 77 King St. West
Toronto, ON M5K 1K7
416-304-4440 Fax: 416-304-4441 877-478-2372
info@quadravest.com
www.quadravest.com
Ticker Symbol: YLD
Company Type: Public
Profile: Open-ended management investment offices

Peter F. Cruickshank, CFO & Managing Director
Wayne Finch, Chair & Chief Investment Officer

Summit Real Estate Investment Trust
Cambridge Centre, Tower 2
#D-200, 202 Brownlow Ave.
Halifax, NS B3H 1T5
902- - Fax: 902- - 866-786-6481
pdykeman@summitreit.com
www.summitreit.com
Ticker Symbol: SMU
Company Type: Public
Profile: Real estate investment trusts

Louis Maroun, President/CEO & Trustee
Paul Dykeman, CFO & Exec. Vice-President

Superior Plus Income Fund
#2820, 605 - 5th Ave. SW
Calgary, AB T2P 3H5
403-218-2970 Fax: 403-218-2973 866-490-7587
info@superiorplus.ca
www.superiorplus.ca
Ticker Symbol: SPF.UN
Company Type: Public
Profile: Open-end management investment offices; Retails in liquified petroleum gas dealers

Geoffrey N. MacKey, President/CEO
W. Mark Schweitzer, CFO & Exec. Vice-President, Corporate Development
Theresia R. Reisch, Secretary & Manager, Investor Relations

Third Canadian General Investment Trust Limited
#1601, 110 Yonge St.
Toronto, ON M5C 1T4
416-366-2931 Fax: 416-366-2729 866-443-6097
mma@mmainvestments.com
www.mmainvestments.com
Ticker Symbol: THD
Company Type: Public
Profile: Offices of holding companies; Unit investment trusts, certificate/closed-end management offices

Michael A. Smedley, President
Colin D. Smith, Sec.-Treas.

Thirty-Five Split Corp.
Scotia Plaza
PO Box 4085 A, 40 King St. West, 26th Fl.
Toronto, ON M5W 2X6
416-945-4535 Fax: 416-863-7425
mc_thirtyfivesplit@scotiacapital.com
www.scotiamanagedcompanies.com
Ticker Symbol: TFS
Company Type: Public
Profile: Open-ended management investment offices

Brian D. McChesney, President/CEO & Director
Michael K. Warman, CFO/Secretary & Director

Triax Diversified High-Yield Trust
#1400, 95 Wellington St.
Toronto, ON M5J 2N7
416-362-2929 Fax: 416-362-2199 800-407-0287
info@triaxcapital.com
www.triaxcapital.com
Ticker Symbol: TRH
Company Type: Public
Profile: Unit investment trusts, certificate/closed-end management offices

Barry H. Gordon, President/CEO & Director
John R. Mott, CFO

Triax Resource Limited Partnership
#1400, 95 Wellington St.
Toronto, ON M5J 2N7
416-362-2929 Fax: 416-362-2199 800-407-0287
info@triaxcapital.com
www.triaxcapital.com
Ticker Symbol: TRF
Company Type: Public
Profile: Unit investment trusts, certificate/closed-end management offices

Triax Resource Limited Partnership II
#1400, 95 Wellington St.
Toronto, ON M5J2N79
416-362-2929 Fax: 416-362-2199 800-407-0287
info@triaxcapital.com
www.triaxcapital.com
Ticker Symbol: TXL
Company Type: Public
Profile: Unit investment trusts, certificate/closed-end management offices

Barry H. Gordon, President/CEO & Director
John R. Mott, CFO

Trimin Capital Corp.
#1650, 1075 West Georgia St.
Vancouver, BC V6E 3C9
604-688-4693 Fax: 604-688-3419
kkeeney@trimlin.com
Ticker Symbol: TMN
Company Type: Public

Profile: Offices of holding companies

Paul McCurry, Vice-President & Secretary
James D. Meekison, President/CEO
Regina Kuo-Lee, Vice-President, Finance & CFO

United Corporations Limited
165 University Ave., 10th Fl.
Toronto, ON M5H 3B8
416-947-2578 Fax: 416-868-6199 www.ucorp.ca
Ticker Symbol: UNC
Company Type: Public
Profile: Unit investment trusts, certificate/closed-end management offices

Duncan N.R. Jackman, Chair
Travis R. Epp, Treasurer

Utility Corp.
Scotia Plaza
PO Box 4085 A, 40 King St. West, 26th Fl.
Toronto, ON M5W 2X6
416-863-7893 Fax: 416-863-7425
mc_utility@scotiacapital.com
www.scotiamanagedcompanies.com
Ticker Symbol: UTC
Company Type: Public
Profile: Unit investment trusts, certificate/closed-end management offices

Robert C. Williams, President/CEO & Director
Michael K. Warman, CFO/Secretary & Director

Yield Management Group High Income Trust
#2020, 1 Queen St. East
Toronto, ON M5C 2W5
416-364-3711 Fax: 416-955-4877 800-944-9002
hit@ymg.com
www.ymg.com
Ticker Symbol: HIT
Company Type: Public
Profile: Unit investment trusts, certificate/closed-end management offices

Eric Innes, President/CEO, YMG Capital Management Inc.
Elizabeth Jack, CFO
William Kai-Mo Chow, Chief Technology Officer

Insurance

Agriculture Financial Services Corporation
5718 - 56 Ave.
Lacombe, AB T4L 1B1
403-782-8200 Fax: 403-782-4226 800-396-0215
afsc.webmaster@gov.ab.ca
www.afsc.ca
Company Type: Crown
Profile: Fire, marine & casualty insurance; Agricultural services, farm management services

Merle Jacobson, Vice-President, Risk Management
Brad Klak, President & Managing Director
Krish Krishnaswamy, Vice-President, Finance
Rick Bell, Vice-President, Lending

Canada Deposit Insurance Corporation
PO Box 2340 D, 50 O'Connor St., 17th Fl.
Ottawa, ON K1P 5W5
Fax: 613-996-6095 800-461-2342
info@cdic.ca
www.cdic.ca
Company Type: Crown
Profile: Various insurance carriers; Public finance, taxation, & monetary policy

Jean Pierre Sabourin, President/CEO
Tom J. Vice, CFO & Vice-President, Finance & Administration

Co-operators General Insurance Company
Priory Sq.
Guelph, ON N1H 6P8
519-824-4400 Fax: 519-824-0599 800-265-2662
service@cooperators.ca
www.cooperators.ca
Ticker Symbol: CCS
Company Type: Public
Profile: Offices of holding companies; Insurance agents, brokers & service; Insurance in fire, marine, casualty, home, auto, farm, commercial, travel; Wealth management products including mutual funds

Kathy Bardswick, President/CEO
Kevin Daniel, CFO & Sr. Vice-President, Finance
Paul Mlodzik, Vice-President, Marketing & Communications
Kevin Hutchison, Vice-President, Information Systems

The CUMIS Group Limited
PO Box 5065, 151 North Service Rd.
Burlington, ON L7R 4C2
905-632-1221 Fax: 905-632-9412
customer.service@cumis.com
www.cumis.com
Company Type: Private
Profile: Offices of holding companies; Insurance in: life, accident, health, fire, marine & casualty; Pension, health, & welfare funds; Insurance agents, brokers & service

Michael Porter, CEO
Kenneth F. Bolton, CFO
Ian Brady, Chief Information Officer

Cunningham Lindsey Group Inc.
#1000, 70 University Ave.
Toronto, ON M5J 2M4
416-596-8020 Fax: 416-596-6510
corpservices@cl-na.com
www.cunninghamlindsey.com
Ticker Symbol: LIN
Company Type: Public
Profile: Offices of holding companies; Insurance agents, brokers & service

Jan Christiansen, President/CEO
Fax: 416-596-9362, jchristiansen@cl-na.com
Stephen Cottrell, Chief Financial Officer
Fax: 416-596-9362, scottrell@cl-na.com

Desjardins Financial Corporation
PO Box 10500 Desjardins, #2822, 1 complexe Desjardins
Montréal, QC H5B 1J1
514-281-7070 Fax: 514-281-7083
info@desjardins.com
www.desjardins.com
Ticker Symbol: DJN
Company Type: Public
Profile: Offices of holding companies; Life, fire, marine & casualty insurance; Security brokers, dealers & flotation companies; Nondeposit trust facilities; Investment advice

Alban d'Amours, President/CEO, Desjardins Group
Monique F. Leroux, President & CEO, Subsidiaries
Louis-Daniel Gauvin, CFO & Sr. Vice-President
André Chapleau, Manager, Media Relations

Gore Mutual Insurance Company
PO Box 70, 252 Dundas St. North
Cambridge, ON N1R 5T3
519-623-1910 Fax: 800-601-9773
800-265-8600www.goremutual.ca
Company Type: Private
Profile: Fire, marine surety & casualty insurance

Kevin McNeil, President/CEO
Lorne Motton, CFO & Secretary
Barry Kennedy, Vice-President, Marketing
Richard Meertens, Vice-President, Information Technology

The Great-West Life Assurance Company
PO Box 6000, 100 Osborne St. North
Winnipeg, MB R3C 3A5
204-946-1190 Fax: 204-946-4129
800-990-6654www.greatwestlife.com
Ticker Symbol: GWL
Company Type: Public
Profile: Life, accident & health insurance; Hospital & medical service plans; Pension, health & welfare funds; Various insurance carriers

Raymond L. McFeetors, President/CEO
William W. Lovatt, Exec. Vice-President/CFO
Ron Saull, Sr. Vice-President & Chief Information Officer

Hub International Limited
8 Nelson St. West, 6th Fl.
Brampton, ON L6X 4J2
905-459-4000 Fax: 905-459-1401 800-387-2592
dennis.pauls@hubinternational.com
www.hubinternational.com
Ticker Symbol: HBG
Company Type: Public
Profile: Insurance brokerage: property, casualty, life & health, employee benefits, investment & risk management & services

Martin P. Hughes, Chair/CEO
Richard A. Gulliver, President/COO
Dennis J. Pauls, CFO & Vice-President
W. Kirk James, Vice-President/Secretary & General Counsel
Deborah K. Wilson, Chief Technology Officer

Industrial-Alliance Life Insurance Company
PO Box 1907 Terminus, 1080, ch St-Louis
Québec, QC G1K 7M3
418-684-5000 Fax: 418-684-5050 800-463-6236
investors@inalco.com
www.inalco.com
Ticker Symbol: IAG
Company Type: Public
Profile: Offices of holding companies; Life, accident, health, fire, marine & casualty insurance; Security brokers, dealers & flotation companies

Yvon Charest, President/CEO
Yvon Côté, Vice-President & General Manager, Finance & Investments

Insurance Corporation of British Columbia
#517, 151 West Esplanade
North Vancouver, BC V7M 3H9
604-661-2800 800-663-3051www.icbc.com
Company Type: Crown
Profile: Property & casualty insurance

Paul Taylor, President/CEO
Geri Prior, CFO
Keith Stewart, Chief Information Officer

Kingsway Financial Services Inc.
#200, 5310 Explorer Dr.
Mississauga, ON L4W 5H8
905-629-7888 Fax: 905-629-5008
info@kingsway-financial.com
www.kingsway-financial.com
Ticker Symbol: KFS
Company Type: Public
Profile: Offices of holding companies; Fire, marine & casualty insurance

William G. Star, President/CEO & Chair
W. Shaun Jackson, Exec. Vice-President/CFO

London Life Insurance Company
255 Dufferin Ave.
London, ON N6A 4K1
519-432-5281 Fax: 519-435-7679
corporate.information@londonlife.com
www.londonlife.com
Company Type: Public
Profile: Offices of holding companies; Fire, marine & casualty insurance; Pension, health & welfare funds; Insurance agents, brokers & service; Accident & health insurance; Life insurance; Surety insurance

Raymond L. McFeetors, President/CEO
William W. Lovatt, Exec. Vice-President/CFO
Ron Saull, Sr. Vice-President/Chief Information Officer

Manulife Financial Corporation
200 Bloor St. East
Toronto, ON M4W 1E5
416-926-3000 Fax: 416-926-3503 800-795-9767
investor_relations@manulife.com
www.manulife.ca
Ticker Symbol: MFC
Company Type: Public
Profile: Offices of holding companies; Accident & health insurance; Pension, health, & welfare funds; Security brokers, dealers & flotation companies

Bruce Gordon, Sr. Exec. Vice-President, Canada
Dominic D'Alessandro, President/CEO
Peter H. Rubenovitch, CFO & Exec. Vice-President
Diane Bean, Sr. Vice-President, Corporate Human Resources & Communications

MARSH Canada Ltd.
BCE Place
#1400, 161 Bay St.
Toronto, ON M5J 2S4
416-868-2600 Fax: 416-868-2526 www.marsh.ca
Company Type: Private

MARSH Canada Ltd. (continued)
Profile: Provides risk & insurance services, investment management & consulting services

John Chippindale, President/CEO
Jim Abernethy, CFO & Managing Director
Mark Lampert, Sr. Vice-President, Global Technology Services

Optimum Général inc
#1500, 425, boul de Maisonneuve ouest
Montréal, QC H3A 3G5
514-288-8725 Fax: 514-288-0760
direction@optimum-general.com
www.optimum-general.com
Ticker Symbol: OGI
Company Type: Public
Profile: Fire, marine, casualty & surety insurance

Jean-Claude Pagé, Vice-Chair/CEO
David B. Liddle, President/COO
Louis P. Pontbriand, Sr. Vice-President/CFO
Jean-Marie Villemure, Vice-President, Information Technology

Saskatchewan Auto Fund
2260 - 11 Ave.
Regina, SK S4P 0J9
306-775-6900 Fax: 306-347-0089 800-667-8015
sgiinquiries@sgi.sk.ca
www.sgi.sk.ca
Company Type: Crown
Profile: Fire, marine & casualty insurance

Larry Fogg, President
John Dobie, Vice-President, Finance

Sun Life Financial Inc.
150 King St. West
Toronto, ON M5H 1J9
416-979-9966 Fax: 416-585-7892 800-786-5433
investor.relations@sunlife.com
www.sunlife.com
Ticker Symbol: SLF
Company Type: Public
Profile: International financial services; Wealth accumulation & protection products & services to individuals & corporate customers

Donald A. Stewart, Chair/CEO
C. James Prieur, President/COO
Richard P. McKenney, Exec. Vice-President/CFO
John R. Wright, Exec. Vice-President & Chief Information Officer

Western Financial Group Inc.
PO Box 5519, 309 - 1 St. West
High River, AB T1V 1M6
403-652-2663 Fax: 403-652-2661 866-843-9378
info@westernfinancialgroup.net
www.westernfinancialgroup.net
Ticker Symbol: HIA
Company Type: Public
Profile: Offices of holding companies; Insurance agents, brokers & service; Investment advice; Travel agencies

Scott A. Tannas, President/CEO
Catherine A. Rogers, Corporate Secretary/CFO & Sr. Vice-President, Finance & Administration

Machinery

Anchor Lamina Inc.
2590 Ouellette Ave.
Windsor, ON N8X 1L7
519-966-4431 Fax: 519-972-6862 800-265-5007
wineng@anchorlamina.com
www.anchorlamina.com
Company Type: Private
Profile: The company is a manufacturer of special dies & tools, die sets, jigs & fixtures, molds, & fabricated plate work.

Roy Verstraete, President/CEO
Steve Zerio, Vice-President/CFO

Atlas Copco Canada Inc.
#203, 2555, av Dollard
Montréal, QC H8N 3A9
514-366-2626 Fax: 514-366-6430 www.atlascopco.com
Company Type: Private
Profile: International industrial company; Sales, distribution, service & maintenance network

Gunnar Brock, President/CEO
Soheil Chaker, Vice-President, Finance
Larry McIntosh, Manager, Information Systems

ATS Automation Tooling Systems Inc.
PO Box 32100 Preston Centr, 250 Royal Oak Rd.
Cambridge, ON N3H 4R6
519-653-6500 Fax: 519-653-6533
info@atsautomation.com
www.atsautomation.com
Ticker Symbol: ATA
Company Type: Public
Profile: Producers of turn-key automated manufacturing & test systems, precision components, sub-assemblies, & solar power cells & panels

Klaus D. Woerner, President/CEO
Ron J. Jutras, CFO & Secretary
Doug Sawatsky, Chief Information Officer
Mike Cybulski, Chief Technology Officer

Buhler Industries Inc.
1260 Clarence Ave.
Winnipeg, MB R3T 1T2
204-661-8711 Fax: 204-654-2503
info@buhler.com
www.buhler.com
Ticker Symbol: BUI
Company Type: Public
Profile: The company manufactures farm machinery & equipment.

John Buhler, Chair/CEO
204-654-5700
Ossama Abouzeid, President/CFO
204-654-5710
James H. Friesen, CFO & Secretary

CE Franklin Ltd.
#1900, 300 - 5th Ave. SW
Calgary, AB T2P 3C4
403-531-5600 Fax: 403-215-3755 800-345-2858
info@cefranklin.com; ho-calgary@cefrankli
www.cefranklin.com
Ticker Symbol: CFT
Company Type: Public
Profile: Wholesalers of industrial machinery & equipment; Various oil & gas fields services

Michael West, President/CEO
Brent Greenwood, President, Marketing & Supply
Randy Henderson, Vice-President/CFO
Rod Tatham, Manager, Environment, Health & Safety

Collicutt Energy Services Ltd.
7550 Edgar Industrial Dr.
Red Deer, AB T4P 3R2
403-358-3200 Fax: 403-358-3210 888-323-2217
inquiries@collicutt.com
www.collicutt.com
Ticker Symbol: COH
Company Type: Public
Profile: Manufacturers of air & gas compressors; Wholesalers of industrial machinery & equipment; Engineering services; Various oil & gas field services

Steven M. Collicutt, President/CEO
Thomas E. Lewis, CFO & Vice-President, Finance

Enerflex Systems Income Fund
4700 - 47 St. SE
Calgary, AB T2B 3R1
403-236-6800 Fax: 403-236-6816 800-242-8178
info@enerflex.com
www.enerflex.com
Ticker Symbol: EFX
Company Type: Public
Profile: A leading supplier of products & services to the global oil & gas production industry; Provides natural gas compression, power generation & process equipment for either sale or lease, hydrocarbon production & processing facilities, electrical instrumentation & controls services & a comprehensive package of field maintenance & contracting capabilites

Blair Goertzen, President/CEO
Bill Moore, Sr. Vice-President, Operations
Sid Mose, Vice-President, Business Development

Exco Technologies Limited
130 Spy Ct., 2nd Fl.
Markham, ON L3R 5H6
905-477-3065 Fax: 905-477-2449
general@excocorp.com
www.excocorp.com
Ticker Symbol: XTC
Company Type: Public
Profile: Manufacturers of special dies & tools, die sets, jigs & fixtures, molds, cutting tools, mach tool accessories, measuring devices, various industrial & commercial machinery & equipment, motor vehicle parts & accessories

Brian A. Robbins, President/CEO
Lawrence C. Robbins, President, Alu-Die Division
Paul Riganelli, CFO & Vice-President, Finance

Foremost Industries LP
1225 - 64 Ave. NE
Calgary, AB T2E 8P9
403-295-5800 Fax: 403-295-5810 800-661-9190
investorrelations@foremost.ca
www.foremost.ca
Ticker Symbol: FMO.UN
Company Type: Public
Profile: Designs & manufactures heavy-duty, all-terrain wheeled & tracked vehicles, drilling rigs, drill equipment & tooling for applications in oil & gas, mining & mineral exploration, construction, environmental, geo-technical & waterwell drilling worldwide

Pat Breen, President
Mike Dubois, Plant Manager

Groupe Laperrière & Verreault inc
Le Bourg du Fleuve Bldg.
#420, 25, rue Des Forges
Trois-Rivières, QC G9A 6A7
819-371-8265 Fax: 819-373-4439
courrier@glv.com
www.glv.com
Ticker Symbol: GLV
Company Type: Public
Profile: Manufacturers of general industrial machinery & equipment, paper industries machinery; Special trade installation/erection of building equipment

Laurent Verreault, President/CEO & Chair
Richard Verreault, Exec. Vice-President & COO
William Saulnier, CFO & Exec. Vice-President

Husky Injection Molding Systems Ltd.
500 Queen St. South
Bolton, ON L7E 5S5
905-951-5000 Fax: 905-951-5324 888-884-8759
info@husky.ca
www.husky.ca
Ticker Symbol: HKY
Company Type: Public
Profile: Manufacturers of special dies & tools, die sets, jigs & fixtures, molds, machine tools, metal cutting types; Wholesalers of various durable goods

John Galt, President/CEO
Stephen Wilson, CFO & Vice-President, Finance
Bruce Catoen, Vice-President, Automated Systems

IBM Canada Ltd.
3600 Steeles Ave. East
Markham, ON L3R 9Z7
905-316-5000 Fax: 905-316-2535 800-426-4968
canada_int@vnet.ibm.com
www.ibm.com/ca/
Company Type: Private
Profile: Manufacturers of electronic computers, & calculating & accounting machines; Repair shops & various related services; equipment rental & leasing

Dan Fortin, President, IBM Canada Ltd.
John R. Joyce, CFO & Sr. Vice-President

Ingersoll Rand Canada Inc.
1076 Lakeshore Rd. E.
Mississauga, ON L5E 1E4
905-403-1800 Fax: 416-213-4616
IRS&SCanada@irco.com
www.irco.com
Company Type: Private
Profile: Manufacturers of general industrial machinery & equipment, pumps & pumping equipment, various special industry machinery, automatic controls regulating environment & appliances

Agako Nouch, President/CEO

Shawn White, Controller
Raymond Singh, Manager, Information Systems

Luxell Technologies Inc.
2145 Meadowpine Blvd.
Mississauga, ON L5N 6R8
905-363-0325 Fax: 905-363-0336
luxell@luxell.com
www.luxell.com
Ticker Symbol: LUX
Company Type: Public
Profile: Manufacturers of computer terminals

John Wright, President/CEO
Rom Wallace, CFO

McCoy Bros. Inc.
#600, 5241 Calgary Trail NW
Edmonton, AB T6H 5GB
780-453-8451 Fax: 780-453-8756
mccoy@mccoybros.com
www.mccoybros.com
Ticker Symbol: MCB
Company Type: Public
Profile: Manufacturers of oil & gas field machinery & equipment; Retailers in new & used trucks; General truck repair shops

Jim Rakievich, President/CEO
Kerry Brown, Chair & CFO

Pitney Bowes Canada Ltd.
5500 Explorer Dr.
Mississauga, ON L4W 5C7
905-219-3000 Fax: 905-219-3826
866-669-6627www.pitneybowes.ca
Company Type: Private
Profile: Provider of mailstream software, hardware, services & solutions to assist companies manage the flow of mail, documents & packages

Deepak Chopra, President
Michael Moran, Vice-President, Finance
John Lee, Vice-President, Information Technology

Reko International Group Inc.
5390 Brendan Lane
Oldcastle, ON N0R 1L0
519-737-6974 Fax: 519-737-6975
vpf@rekointl.com
www.rekointl.com
Ticker Symbol: REK
Company Type: Public
Profile: Manufacturers of special dies & tools, die sets, molds, jigs & fixtures; Engineering services

Steve M. Reko, President/CEO
Michael Dunn, CFO
Brad Feltham, Administrator, Systems
Joe Sirianni, Administrator, Human Resources

Skyjack Inc.
55 Campbell Rd.
Guelph, ON N1H 1B9
519-837-0888 Fax: 519-837-3102
skyjack@skyjackinc.com
www.skyjackinc.com
Ticker Symbol: SJK
Company Type: Public
Profile: Manufacturers of aerial work platforms

Lloyd Spalding, President

Strongco Income Fund
1640 Enterprise Rd.
Mississauga, ON L4W 4L4
905-565-1899 Fax: 905-565-1907 800-268-7004
info@strongco.com
www.strongco.com
Ticker Symbol: SQP.UN
Company Type: Public
Profile: Strongco is a multi-line equipment distributor in Canada. It sells & rents new & used equipment, provides after-sale customer support (parts & service), & designs, manufactures, sells, installs & services dry bulk material handling equipment. Strongco distributes equipment lines in various territories, including those manufactured by Volvo Construction Equipment North America Inc., Case Corporation, Tigercat Industries, Inc. & Manitowoc Crane Group. It distributes its products through a network of 24 branches and one sales office in Canada & one sales office in the USA. Business segments are equipment distribution & engineered systems.

Robin MacLean, President/CEO
905-565-3802, rmaclean@strongco.com
Robert S. Masaki, Chief Financial Officer, Finance
905-565-3807, bmasaki@strongco.com

SunOpta
2838 Bovaire Dr. West
Norval, ON L0P 1K0
905-455-1990 Fax: 905-455-2529
info@sunopta.com
www.sunopta.com
Ticker Symbol: SOY
Company Type: Public
Profile: Offices of holding companies; Manufacturers of general industrial machinery & equipment; Wholesalers of industrial supplies; Organic & non-GMO

J.N. Kendall, Chair/CEO
Steve Bromley, CFO & Exec. Vice-President
John Dietrich, Treasurer/Controller & Vice-President, Finance

Tesco Corporation
6204 - 6A St. SE
Calgary, AB T2H 2B7
403-692-5700 Fax: 403-692-5710
CABU_Sales@tescocorp.com
www.tescocorp.com
Ticker Symbol: TEO
Company Type: Public
Profile: Manufacturers of oil & gas field machinery & equipment, various electrical industrial apparatus; Various oil & gas fields services; Wholesalers of construction & mining machinery & equipment, electronic parts & equipment

Robert M. Tessari, President/CEO
Bruce Longaker, CFO & Exec. Vice-President, Finance
Quentin Cobb, General Manager, Information Technology
Scotty Boyle, Director, Health, Safety & Environment

Torex Retail North America
#215, 5800 Ambler Dr.
Mississauga, ON L4W 4J4
905-507-4333 Fax: 919-866-1152 **Company Type:** error
Profile: Provider of in-store solutions & support for point-of-sale, back office & e-business products

Toromont Industries Ltd.
PO Box 5511, 3131 Hwy. 7 West
Concord, ON L4K 1B7
416-667-5511 Fax: 416-667-5555
investorrelations@toromont.com
www.toromont.com
Ticker Symbol: TIH
Company Type: Public
Profile: The company is engaged in the sale of specialized equipment & other heavy equipment. Its business segments are the Equipment Group & the Compression Group.

Robert M. Ogilvie, Chair/CEO
rmogilvie@toromont.com
Paul R. Jewer, CFO & Vice-President, Finance
pjewer@toromont.com
Michael P. Cuddy, Vice-President & Chief Information Officer
mcuddy@toromont.com
David C. Wetherald, Vice-President, General Counsel & Corporate Secretary
dwetherald@toromont.com

Wajax Limited
3280 Wharton Way
Mississauga, ON L4X 2C5
905-212-3300 Fax: 905-624-6020
ir@wajax.com
www.wajax.com
Ticker Symbol: WJX
Company Type: Public
Profile: Manufacturers of general industrial machinery & equipment; Forestry services

Neil Manning, President/CEO
John J. Hamilton, CFO & Sr. Vice-President

Westport Innovations Inc.
#101, 1750 West 75th Ave.
Vancouver, BC V6P 6G2
604-718-2000 Fax: 604-718-2001
info@westport.com
www.westport.com
Ticker Symbol: WPT
Company Type: Public
Profile: Develops technologies to allow commercial engine industry to shift from oil-based to gaseous fuels

David R. Demers, CEO
Elaine Wong, CFO & Vice-President, Finance
Michael Gallagher, Dr.President
Patric Ouellette, CTO & Vice-President, Research

Xerox Canada Inc.
5650 Yonge St.
Toronto, ON M2M 4G7
416-229-3769 Fax: 416-229-6826 www.xerox.ca
Company Type: Public
Profile: Manufacturers of various office machines, photographic equipment & supplies; Wholesalers of commercial equipment; Equipment rental & leasing

Anne M. Mulcahy, Chair/CEO
Lawrence Zimmerman, CFO

Manufacturing, Miscellaneous

AirBoss of America Corp.
16441 Yonge St.
Newmarket, ON L3X 2G8
905-751-1188 Fax: 905-751-1101
info@airbossofamerica.com
www.airbossofamerica.com
Ticker Symbol: BOS
Company Type: Public
Profile: The company manufactures natural & synthetic rubber compounds, molded & extruded rubber goods, rubber footwear & rail fastening systems.

R.L. Hagerman, President/CEO
Stephen Richards, CFO & Vice-President, Finance

Amcor PET Packaging—North America
910 Central Pkwy. West
Mississauga, ON L5C 2V5
905-275-1592 Fax: 905-275-3007
brigitte.sigwarth@amcor.com
www.amcor.com
Company Type: Private
Profile: Manufacturers of plastics packaging, rigid plastics & plastube packaging

David Andison, Vice-President & General Manager

ART Advanced Research Technologies Inc.
2300, boul Alfred-Nobel
Montréal, QC H4S 2A4
514-832-0777 Fax: 514-832-0778
info@art.ca
www.art.ca
Ticker Symbol: ARA
Company Type: Public
Profile: Canadian medical device company specializing in optical molecular imaging products

Sébastien Gignac, President/CEO & Director
Jacques Bédard, CFO

Automodular Corporation
#420, 20 Toronto St.
Toronto, ON M5C 2B8
416-861-0662 Fax: 416-861-0063
invest@automodular.com
www.automodular.com
Ticker Symbol: AM
Company Type: Public
Profile: Offices of holding companies; Automotive sub-assembly & sequencing

Michael F. Blair, CEO
Rae E. Wallin, Chair
Christopher S. Nutt, CFO & Vice-President, Finance

Bestar Inc.
4220, rue Villeneuve
Lac-Mégantic, QC G6B 2C3
819-583-1017 Fax: 819-583-5370
bestar@bestar.ca
www.bestar.ca
Ticker Symbol: BES
Company Type: Public

Bestar Inc. (continued)

Profile: Manufacturers of wood household furniture, wood tv, radio, phonograph & sewing machine cabinets; Wholesalers of furniture

Jacques Hertu, CEO
Eric A. Menard, Vice-President, Finance

Brampton Brick Limited

225 Wanless Dr.
Brampton, ON L7A 1E9
905-840-1011 Fax: 905-840-1535
investor.relations@bramptonbrick.com
www.bramptonbrick.com
Ticker Symbol: BBL
Company Type: Public
Profile: Manufacturers of brick & structural clay tile, concrete block & brick; Trucking services; Refuse systems

Jeffrey G. Kerbel, President/CEO
Kenneth J. Mondor, CFO & Vice-President, Finance

BW Technologies Ltd.

2840 - 2 Ave. SE
Calgary, AB T2A 7X9
403-248-9226 Fax: 403-273-3708
info@bwtnet.com
www.gasmonitors.com
Company Type: Public
Profile: Manufacturers of various measuring & controlling devices; Wholesalers of industrial machinery & equipment

Cody Slater, President/CEO
Thomas Jones, CFO & Exec. Vice-President
Barry Moore, Vice-President, Product Development

CAE Inc.

8585, ch de Côte-de-Liesse
Montréal, QC H4T 1G6
514-341-6780 Fax: 514-341-7699
info@cae.com
www.cae.com
Ticker Symbol: CAE
Company Type: Public
Profile: Manufacturers of search, detection, navigation, aeronautical instruments & paper industries machinery; Engineering services; Computer integrated systems design; Repair shops & various related services; Commercial physical & biological research

Robert E. Brown, President/CEO
Alain Raquepas, CFO/Vice-President, Finance

Camco Inc.

PO Box 5345, #300, 5420 North Service Rd.
Burlington, ON L7R 5B6
905-315-2300 Fax: 905-315-2470 888-566-6667
InvestorRelations@mabe.ca
www.geappliances.ca
Ticker Symbol: COC
Company Type: Public
Profile: Manufacturers of household cooking equipment, household refrigerators & home & farm freezers, household laundry equipment, various household appliances; Wholesalers of electrical appliances, television & radio sets

James R. Fleck, President/CEO
Neil G. Gartshore, CFO & Vice-President, Finance
Allan R. Holden, Vice-President, Information Technology
Richard Martel, Vice-President, Technology

CFM Corporation

2695 Meadowvale Blvd.
Mississauga, ON L5N 8A3
905-858-8010 Fax: 905-858-3966 www.cfmcorp.com
Ticker Symbol: CFM
Company Type: Public
Profile: Offices of holding companies; Manufacturers of heating equipment

Larry Robinette, CEO

CGC Inc.

350 Burnhamthorpe Rd. West, 5th Fl.
Mississauga, ON L5B 3J1
905-803-5600 Fax: 905-803-5688
800-565-6607www.cgcinc.com
Company Type: Private
Profile: Manufacturers of gypsum products

Christopher Griffin, President
D. Rick Lowes, Vice-President/CFO & Treasurer

DALSA Corporation

605 McMurray Rd.
Waterloo, ON N2V 2E9
519-886-6000 Fax: 519-886-0185
investor@dalsa.com
www.dalsa.com
Ticker Symbol: DSA
Company Type: Public
Profile: Manufacturers of photographic equipment & supplies

Savvas G. Chamberlain, Chair/CEO
Ralf M. Brooks, President, DALSA Semiconductor
Paul Van Bakel, CFO
Patrick Myles, Director, Corporate Communications

Dorel Industries Inc.

#300, 1255, av Greene
Montréal, QC H3Z 2A4
514-934-3034 Fax: 514-934-9379
info@dorel.com
www.dorel.com
Ticker Symbol: DII
Company Type: Public
Profile: Manufacturers of wood & metal household furniture; Wholesalers of furniture & home furnishings

Martin Schwartz, President/CEO
Jeffrey Schwartz, Exec. Vice-President/CFO & Secretary

Essroc Canada Inc.

PO Box 620, Highway 49 South
Picton, ON K0K 2T0
613-476-3233 Fax: 613-476-8130
info@essroc.com
www.essroc.com
Company Type: Private
Profile: Manufacturers of cement, hydraulic

Fabio Bruchielli, Plant Manager

Imax Corporation

Sheridan Science & Technology Park
2525 Speakman Dr.
Mississauga, ON L5K 1B1
905-403-6500 Fax: 905-403-6450
info@imax.com
www.imax.com
Ticker Symbol: IMX
Company Type: Public
Profile: Manufacturers of photographic equipment & supplies; Motion picture & video tape production & distribution; Motion picture theatres

Richard L. Gelfond, Co-Chair/Co-CEO
Greg Foster, Chair & President, Filmed Entertainment
Francis T. Joyce, CFO
Brian Bonnick, Sr. Vice-President, Technology

INSCAPE Corporation

67 Toll Rd.
Holland Landing, ON L9N 1H2
905-836-7676 Fax: 905-836-6000
info@inscapesolutions.com
www.inscapesolutions.com
Ticker Symbol: INQ
Company Type: Public
Profile: Manufacturers of wood & non-wood office furniture, wood & non-wood office & store fixtures & partitions; Wholesalers of furniture & office equipment

Ram Ramkumar, President/CEO
Rohit Bhardwaj, CFO

IPL Inc.

140, rue Commerciale
Saint-Damien-de-Buckland, QC G0R 2Y0
418-789-2880 Fax: 418-789-2185 800-463-0270
infoipl@ipl-plastics.com
www.ipl-plastics.com
Ticker Symbol: IPI
Company Type: Public
Profile: Manufacturers of unsupported plastics film & sheet, plastics foam products, various plastics products; Wholesalers of various nondurable goods

Serge Bragdon, President/CEO & Director
Fréréic Côté, Vice-President/CFO, Finance
François Béchard, Secretary
Jean-Louis Bodin, Manager, IT
André Bilodeau, Supervisor, Maintenance Personnel

MAAX Corporation

600 Cameron Rd.
Ste-Marie, QC G6E 1B2
Fax: 800-201-8308 888-957-7816
louise.laraouche@maax.com
www.maax.com
Company Type: Private
Profile: Manufacturers of plastic plumbing fixtures, vitreous china plumbing fixtures, bathroom accessories, enameled iron & metal sanitary ware, plumbing fixture fittings & trim, concrete products, wood kitchen cabinets; Wholesalers of plumbing/heating equipment & hydronics supplies, various durable goods

André Héroux, President/CEO
Denis Aubin, CFO & Exec. Vice-President
Michel Tremblay, Corporate Vice-President, Information Technology

Nestlé Purina Pet Care

2500 Royal Windsor Dr.
Mississauga, ON L5J 1K8
905-822-1611 Fax: 905-855-5711 www.purina.ca
Company Type: Private
Profile: Manufacturers & wholesalers of pet foods & various other pet products

Karen Kuwahara, President
Derek Thompson, Director, Financial Planning & Analysis
Georgina Stinton, Specialist, Human Resources, Employment Process & Safety

NovAtel Inc.

1120 - 68 Ave. NE
Calgary, AB T2E 8S5
403-295-4500 Fax: 403-295-4901 800-668-2835
ir@novatel.ca
www.novatel.ca
Company Type: Public
Profile: Provider of precise global positioning & augmentation technologies

Jon Ladd, President/CEO
W. Gartner, CFO & Exec. Vice-President
Pat Fenton, Chief Technology Officer

Owens-Corning Canada Inc.

3450 McNicoll Ave.
Toronto, ON M1V 1Z5
416-292-4000 Fax: 416-412-6719 www.owenscorning.com
Company Type: Private
Profile: Offices of holding companies; Manufacturers of mineral wool, coated fabrics, pressed & blown glass & glassware, manmade organic fibers, & various textile goods

Polyair Inter Pack Inc.

330 Humberline Dr.
Toronto, ON M9W 1R5
416-679-6600 Fax: 416-679-6610 888-765-9247
marketing@polyair.com
www.polyair.com
Ticker Symbol: PPK
Company Type: Public
Profile: Manufacturers of plastic foam products, various plastics products, packaging paper & coated & laminated plastics film; Wholesalers of plastics materials & basic forms & shapes

Henry Schnurbach, President/CEO

Royal Group Technologies Limited

1 Royal Gate Blvd.
Woodbridge, ON L4L 8Z7
905-264-0701 Fax: 905-264-0702
info@royalgrouptech.com
www.royalgrouptech.com
Ticker Symbol: RYG
Company Type: Public
Profile: Manufacturers of various plastics products, plastics plumbing fixtures, plastics pipe, & home improvement products

James Sardo, President/CEO
Robert Lamoureaux, Sr. Vice-President/CFO
Vince Noronha, Manager, Information Technology
Bill Morton, Vice-President, Corporate Purchases

Shermag Inc.

2171, rue King ouest
Sherbrooke, QC J1J 2G1
819-566-1515 Fax: 819-566-7323
info@shermag.com

www.shermag.com
Ticker Symbol: SMG
Company Type: Public
Profile: Manufacturers of wood household furniture, sawmills & general planing mills

Jeff Casselman, President/CEO
Josée Girard, Vice-President, Finance
Christian Melanson, Director, Information Technology
Guy Cardinal, Vice-President, Production

SMED International Inc.
10 SMED Lane SE
Calgary, AB T2C 4T5
403-203-6000 Fax: 403-203-6001 800-661-9163
mo-calg-webmaster@haworth.com
www.smednet.com
Company Type: Private
Profile: Manufacturers of office furniture, office & store fixtures, non-wood partitions, various furniture & fixtures; Wholesalers of commercial equipment; Special trade contracting in plastering, drywall, acoustics & insulation; Retailing in furniture stores

M.F. Smed, Chair, President & CEO
A.R.G Moor, CFO & Exec. Vice-President, Finance

St. Lawrence Cement Group Inc.
1945, boul Graham
Montréal, QC H3R 1H1
514-340-1881 Fax: 514-342-8154
communications@stlawrencecement.com
www.stlawrencecement.com
Ticker Symbol: ST
Company Type: Public
Profile: Offices of holding companies; Manufacturers of cement, hydraulic, concrete block & brick, concrete products, ready-mixed concrete; Crushed & broken stone mining & quarrying; Wholesalers of construction materials; Highway & street construction

Philippe Arto, President/CEO
Dean J. Bergmame, CFO & Vice-President

Tarkett Inc.
1001, rue Yamaska est
Farnham, QC J2N 1J7
450-293-3173 Fax: 450-293-6644 www.domcotarkett.com
Ticker Symbol: DOC
Company Type: Private
Profile: Manufacturers of linoleum, felt-base & other vinyl floorings, hardwood dimension & flooring mills; Wholesalers of home furnishings

Guillaume Laverdure, President/CEO, Residential
Jacques Bénétreau, CFO/Treasurer & Sr. Vice-President, Finance

Teknion Corporation
1150 Flint Rd.
Toronto, ON M3J 2J5
416-661-3370 Fax: 416-661-7970
info.can@teknion.com
www.teknion.com
Ticker Symbol: TKN
Company Type: Public
Profile: Manufacturers of wood & non-wood office furniture, public building & related furniture, wood & non-wood office & store fixtures, partitions, shelving etc.; Wholesalers of furniture

David Feldberg, President/CEO
Scott E. Bond, CFO

Trojan Technologies Inc.
3020 Gore Rd.
London, ON N5V 4T7
519-457-3400 Fax: 519-457-3030
info@trojanuv.com
www.trojanuv.com
Ticker Symbol: TUV
Company Type: Public
Profile: Manufacturers of laboratory analytical instruments & various service industry machinery

Marvin DeVries, President/CEO
Robert Wood, Vice-President, Finance

Mining

Aber Diamond Corporation
PO Box 4569 A, Toronto, ON M5W 4T9
416-362-2237 Fax: 416-362-2230
aber@aber.ca
www.aber.ca
Ticker Symbol: ABZ
Company Type: Public
Profile: Mining & quarrying of miscellaneous nonmetallic minerals

R.A. Gannicott, Chair/CEO
Alice Murphy, CFO & Vice-President

Agnico-Eagle Mines Limited
#500, 145 King St. East
Toronto, ON M5C 2Y7
416-947-1212 Fax: 416-367-4681 888-822-6714
info@agnico-eagle.com
www.agnico-eagle.com
Ticker Symbol: AGE
Company Type: Public
Profile: Metal mining in gold ores

Sean Boyd, President/CEO
David Garofalo, CFO & Vice-President, Finance

AMR Technologies Inc.
#1740, 121 King St. West
Toronto, ON M5H 3T9
416-367-8588 Fax: 416-367-5471
amrinfo@amr-ltd.com
www.amr-ltd.com
Ticker Symbol: AMR
Company Type: Public
Profile: Metal mining in miscellaneous ores; Manufacturing of various industrial inorganic chemicals

Peter Gundy, President/CEO & Chair
G.R. Bedford, CFO & Vice-President, Finance
Alexander Caldwell, Corporate Secretary

Andean American Mining Corp.
#355, 601 West Cordova St.
Vancouver, BC V6B 1G1
604-681-6186 Fax: 604-681-3652
info@andeanamerican.com
www.andeanamerican.com
Ticker Symbol: AAG
Company Type: Public
Profile: Metal mining in gold, silver & copper ores

John Huguet, President/CEO & Chair
Nick DeMare, Corporate Secretary

Argosy Minerals Inc.
20607 Logan Ave.
Langley, BC V3A 7R3
604-530-8436 Fax: 604-530-8423
info@argosyminerals.com
www.argosyminerals.com
Ticker Symbol: AGY
Company Type: Public
Profile: Metal mining in gold & ferroalloy ores

Peter Lloyd, President/Chair
Cecil Bond, CFO & Secretary

Arizona Star Resource Corp.
152
2700 , 401 Bay St.
Toronto, ON M5H 2Y4
416-359-7800 Fax: 416-359-7801
pparisotto@coniston.ca
www.arizonastar.com
Ticker Symbol: AZS
Company Type: Public
Profile: Metal mining gold, copper & miscellaneous metal ores

Paul A. Parisotto, President/CEO & Director
Mark Corra, Vice-President, Finance

Ashton Mining of Canada Inc.
#116, 980 West 1st St.
North Vancouver, BC V7P 3N4
604-983-7750 Fax: 604-987-7107
contact@ashton.ca
www.ashton.ca
Ticker Symbol: ACA
Company Type: Public
Profile: Mining & quarrying of miscellaneous nonmetallic minerals

R.T. Boyd, President/CEO & Director
A. Bitelli, Vice-President, Finance

Atacama Minerals Corp.
#2101, 885 West Georgia St.
Vancouver, BC V6C 3E8
604-689-7842 Fax: 604-689-4250
atacama@namdo.com
www.atacama.com
Ticker Symbol: AAM
Company Type: Public
Profile: Mining & quarrying of potash, soda & borate minerals

R.P. Clark, President/Director
Wanda Lee, CFO

Aur Resources Inc.
#2501, 1 Adelaide St. East
Toronto, ON M5C 2V9
416-362-2614 Fax: 416-367-0427
info@aurresources.com
www.aurresources.com
Ticker Symbol: AUR
Company Type: Public
Profile: Acquisition, exploration, development & mining of mineral properties, with an emphasis on copper

James Gill, President/CEO
John L. Knowles, CFO & Exec. Vice-President, Finance

Aurizon Mines Ltd.
#900, 510 Burrard St.
Vancouver, BC V6C 3A8
604-687-6600 Fax: 604-687-3932
info@aurizon.com
www.aurizon.com
Ticker Symbol: ARZ
Company Type: Public
Profile: Metal mining in gold ores

David Hall, President/CEO & Chair
Ian Walton, Vice-President/CFO & Director

Banro Corporation
First Canadian Place
PO Box 419, #7070, 100 King St. West
Toronto, ON M5X 1E3
416-366-2221 Fax: 416-366-7722
banro@banro.com
www.banro.com
Ticker Symbol: YBE
Company Type: Public
Profile: Metal mining in gold ores

William R. Wilson, President/CEO
Arnold T. Kondrat, Exec. Vice-President

Barrick Gold Corporation
Canada Trust Tower, BCE Place
PO Box 212, #3700, 161 Bay St.
Toronto, ON M5J 2S1
416-861-9911 Fax: 416-861-2492 800-720-7415
investor@barrick.com
www.barrick.com
Ticker Symbol: ABX
Company Type: Public
Profile: Metal mining in gold ores

Gregory C. Wilkins, President/CEO
Jamie C. Sokalsky, CFO & Sr. Vice-President
Richard S. Young, Vice-President, Investor Relations
M. Vincent Borge, Vice-President, Corporate Communications
John T. McDonough, Vice-President, Environment

Bema Gold Corporation
Three Bentall Centre
PO Box 49143, #3100, 595 Burrard St.
Vancouver, BC V7X 1J1
604-681-8371 Fax: 604-681-6209
info@bemagold.com
www.bema.com
Ticker Symbol: BGO
Company Type: Public
Profile: Metal mining in gold ores

Clive T. Johnson, President/CEO & Chair
Mark A. Corra, Vice-President, Finance
Ian MacLean, Manager, Investor Relations
Tom Garagan, Vice-President, Exploration

Breakwater Resources Ltd.
#950, 95 Wellington St. West
Toronto, ON M5J 2N7
416-363-4798 Fax: 416-363-1315
investorinfo@breakwater.ca
www.breakwater.ca
Ticker Symbol: BWR
Company Type: Public
Profile: Mineral resource company acquires, explores, develops & mines base metal & precious metal deposits in the Americas; Zinc mines are located in BC, Honduras & Chile; Langlois mine in Quebec is under development

George Pirie, President/CEO
Dave Langille, CFO & Vice-President, Finance
Jason Stevens, Corporate Secretary & Exec. Vice-President, Legal & Corporate Affairs
Daniel Goffaux, Vice-President, Latin America
Frederick Hermann, Corporate Director, Safety, Health & Training

Caledonia Mining Corporation
#1201 , 67 Yonge St.
Toronto, ON M5E 1JB
416-369-9835 Fax: 416-369-0449
info@caledoniamining.com
www.caledoniamining.com
Ticker Symbol: CAL
Company Type: Public
Profile: Metal mining in copper, gold, silver & ferroalloy ores; Mining & quarrying in miscellaneous nonmetallic minerals

Stefan E. Hayden, President/CEO & Chair
Steven W. Poad, Vice-President, Finance & Administration
F. Christopher Harvey, Director, Technical

Cambior Inc.
#750, 1111, rue Saint-Charles ouest
Longueuil, QC J4K 5G4
450-677-0040 Fax: 450-677-3382
info@cambior.com
www.cambior.com
Ticker Symbol: CBJ
Company Type: Public
Profile: Metal mining in gold & miscellaneous ores

Louis P. Gignac, President/CEO
Bryan A. Coates, CFO & Vice-President, Finance
Robert LaVallière, Manager, Investor Relations & Communications
Serge Vézina, Vice-President, Industrial Engineering & Environment

Cameco Corporation
2121 - 11 St. West
Saskatoon, SK S7M 1J3
306-956-6309 Fax: 306-956-6318
bob_lillie@cameco.com
www.cameco.com
Ticker Symbol: CCO
Company Type: Public
Profile: Metal mining in uranium, radium, vanadium & gold ores

Gerald W. Grandey, President/CEO
David M. Petroff, CFO & Sr. Vice-President, Finance & Administration
Bob Lillie, Manager, Investor Relations
Jamie McIntyre, Director, Sustainable Development & Corporate Relations

Campbell Resources Inc.
#1405, 1155 rue Université
Montréal, QC H3B 3A7
514-875-9033 Fax: 514-875-9764
invest@campbellresources.com
www.campbellresources.com; www.ressourcescampbell.c
Ticker Symbol: CCH
Company Type: Public
Profile: Metal mining in gold & copper ores

André Fortier, President/CEO
Lucie Brun, Chief Administrative Officer & Exec. Vice-President
Louis Archambault, Member, Environmental Committee

Canadian Gold Hunter Corp.
#2101, 885 West Georgia St.
Vancouver, BC V6C 3E8
604-689-7842 Fax: 604-689-4250
goldhunter@namdo.com
www.canadiangoldhunter.com
Ticker Symbol: IC
Company Type: Public
Profile: Metal mining in gold, copper, lead & zinc ores

Richard Bailes, President/CEO
Lukas H. Lundin, Chair
Wanda Lee, CFO

Canadian Salt Company Limited
#700, 755, boul Saint-Jean
Montréal, QC H9R 5M9
514-630-0900 Fax: 514-694-2451
tferrara@windsorsalt.com
www.windsorsalt.com
Company Type: Private
Profile: Chemical & fertilizer mineral mining & quarrying

Wayne Corney, President
François G. Allard, Vice-President, Finance

Continental Minerals Corporation
#1020, 800 West Pender St.
Vancouver, BC V6C 2V6
604-684-6365 Fax: 604-684-8092
info@hdgold.com
www.hdgold.com/kmk/home.asp
Ticker Symbol: KMK
Company Type: Public
Profile: Exploration & mining company; Engaged in the advancement of the Xietongmen Project in Tibet, China

Gerald S. Panneton, President/CEO & Director
J.R. Mason, CFO/Director & Sec.-Treas.

Crystallex International Corporation
#1210, 18 King St. East
Toronto, ON M5C 1C4
416-203-2448 Fax: 416-203-0099 800-738-1577
info@crystallex.com
www.crystallex.com
Ticker Symbol: KRY
Company Type: Public
Profile: Metal mining in gold ores

Todd Bruce, President/CEO
Borden D. Rosiak, CFO
Kenneth G. Thomas, COO

Cumberland Resources Ltd.
One Bentall Centre
PO Box 72, #950, 505 Burrard St.
Vancouver, BC V7X 1M4
604-608-2557 Fax: 604-608-2559
info@cumberlandresources.com
www.cumberlandresources.com
Ticker Symbol: CBD
Company Type: Public
Profile: Metal mining in gold ores

Kerry Curtis, President/CEO
R.A. Evans, CFO

Dynatec Corporation
#200, 9555 Yonge St.
Richmond Hill, ON L4C 9M5
905-780-1980 Fax: 905-780-1990
mutting@dynatec.ca
www.dynatec.ca
Ticker Symbol: DY
Company Type: Public
Profile: Metal mining & metal mining services

Bruce V. Walter, President/CEO
Arnold Klassen, CFO & Vice-President, Finance
Mark Utting, Director, Communications & Investor Relations
Gerald L. Bolton, Vice-President, Metallurgical Technologies
Patrick M. James, Director & Chair, Environmental, Health & Safety Committee

Eldorado Gold Corp.
Bentall 5
#1188, 550 Burrard St.
Vancouver, BC V6C 2B5
604-687-4018 Fax: 604-687-4026 888-353-8166
info@eldoradogold.com
www.eldoradogold.com
Ticker Symbol: ELD
Company Type: Public
Profile: Metal mining in gold ores

Paul N. Wright, President/CEO
Earl W. Price, CFO
Dawn Moss, Corporate Secretary

European Goldfields Ltd.
Financial Plaza
#200, 204 Lambert Street
Whitehorse, YK

info@egoldfields.com
www.egoldfields.com
Ticker Symbol: EGU
Company Type: Public
Profile: Metal mining in gold, silver & copper ores

David Reading, CEO
David Grannell, CFO

European Minerals Corporation
c/o Vanguard Shareholder Solutions Inc.
#1205, 1095 West Pender St.
Vancouver, BC
604-608-0824 Fax: 604-608-0854 866-448-0780
enquiries@eurominerals.com
www.eurominerals.com
Ticker Symbol: EPM.U
Company Type: Public
Profile: Metal mining gold & silver ores; Oil royalty traders

William G. Kennedy, President/CEO & Director
Stephen Gledhill, CFO
Howard Nicholson, Manager

Falconbridge Limited
BCE Place
#200, 181 Bay St.
Toronto, ON M5J 2T3
416-982-7111 Fax: 416-982-7423
invest@falconbridge.com
www.falconbridge.com
Ticker Symbol: FL
Company Type: Public
Profile: Metal mining in ferroalloy, copper, lead, zinc & miscellaneous ores; Manufacturers of various industrial inorganic chemicals

Aaron W. Regent, President/CEO
Michael Doolan, Sr. Vice-President/CFO
Robert Telewiak, Vice-President, Environment

Farallon Resources Ltd.
#1020, 800 West Pender St.
Vancouver, BC V6C 2V6
604-684-6365 Fax: 604-684-8092 800-667-2114
info@hdgold.com
www.hdgold.com
Ticker Symbol: FAN
Company Type: Public
Profile: Metal mining in gold, silver, lead & zinc ores

Dick Whittington, President/CEO
Jeffrey R. Mason, CFO/Secretary & Director

First Quantum Minerals Ltd.
543 Granville St., 8th Fl.
Vancouver, BC V6C 1X8
604-688-6577 Fax: 604-688-3818 800-688-6577
andrew.hancharyk@fqml.com
www.first-quantum.com
Ticker Symbol: FM
Company Type: Public
Profile: Metal mining in gold, copper & ferroalloy ores

Philip K.R. Pascall, Chair/CEO
Clive Newall, President
M.R. Rowley, CFO

Fording Inc.
#1000, 205 - 9th Ave. SE
Calgary, AB T2G 0R3
403-264-1063 Fax: 403-264-7339
investors@fording.ca
www.fording.ca
Ticker Symbol: FDG
Company Type: Public
Profile: Coal mining, bituminous coal & lignite surface mining; Miscellaneous nonmetallic minerals mining & quarrying

Michael Grandin, President/CEO
Ron Millos, CFO
T. Skinner, General Manager, Information Systems
Dermot Lane, Director, Environment & Public Affairs

Gabriel Resources Ltd.
#1501, 110 Yonge St.
Toronto, ON M5C 1T4
416-955-9200 Fax: 416-955-4661
info@gabrielresources.com
www.gabrielresources.com
Ticker Symbol: GBU
Company Type: Public
Profile: Metal mining in gold & silver ores

Alan Hill, President/CEO
Oyvind Hushovd, Chair
Paul Martin, CFO

Goldcorp Inc.
#3400, 666 Burrard St.
Vancouver, BC 86C 2X8
604-696-7300 Fax: 604-696-3001 800-567-6223
info@goldcorp.com
www.goldcorp.com
Ticker Symbol: G
Company Type: Public
Profile: Offices of holding companies; Metal mining in gold ores; Mining & quarrying of potash, soda & borate minerals

Ian W. Telfer, President/CEO
Peter Barnes, Vice-President/CFP

High River Gold Mines Ltd.
#1700, 155 University Ave.
Toronto, ON M5H 3B7
416-947-1440 Fax: 416-360-0010
info@hrg.ca
www.hrg.ca
Ticker Symbol: HRG
Company Type: Public
Profile: Metal mining in gold ores

David V. Mosher, President/CEO
Steven Poad, CFO
Donald A. Whalen, Chair & Vice-President, Marketing

Hudson Bay Mining & Smelting Co. Ltd.
#1906, 201 Portage Ave.
Winnipeg, MB R3B 3L3
204-949-4261 Fax: 204-687-3983 **Company Type:** Private
Profile: Metal mining in gold, silver, copper, ferroalloy, lead, zinc & miscellaneous metal ores

Peter Jones, President/CEO
John L. Knowles, CFO
Wayne Fraser, Director, Environment

IAMGOLD Corporation
PO Box 153, #3200, 401 Bay St.
Toronto, ON M5H 2Y4
416-360-4710 Fax: 416-360-4750 888-464-9999
info@iamgold.com
www.iamgold.com
Ticker Symbol: IMG
Company Type: Public
Profile: The company is engaged in metal mining in gold ores.

William D. Pugliese, Chair
Joseph F. Conway, President/CEO
Grant A. Edey, Chief Financial Officer

Imperial Metals Corporation
#200, 580 Hornby St.
Vancouver, BC V6C 3B6
604-669-8959 Fax: 604-687-4030
info@imperialmetals.com
www.imperialmetals.com
Ticker Symbol: III
Company Type: Public
Profile: Metal mining in copper, gold, silver, lead & zinc ores

Bryan Kynoch, President
Andre Deepwell, CFO/Corporate Secretary

Inco Limited
#1500, 145 King St. West
Toronto, ON M5H 4B7
416-361-7511 Fax: 416-361-7781
inco@inco.com
www.inco.com
Ticker Symbol: N
Company Type: Public
Profile: Metal mining in ferroalloy, copper & gold ores; Manufacturers of primary smelting & refining of nonferrous metals, various industrial inorganic chemicals, secondary smelting & refining of nonferrous metals, nonferrous forgings

Scott M. Hand, Chair/CEO
Peter C. Jones, President/COO
Farokh S. Hakimi, CFO & Exec. Vice-President
Subi Bhandari, Chief Information Officer
William Gordon Bacon, Vice-President, Technology & Engineering
Bruce R. Conard, Vice-President, Environmental & Health Sciences

International Uranium Corporation
Atrium On Bay
#402, 595 Bay St.
Toronto, ON M5G 2C2
416-979-1991 Fax: 416-979-5893
iuc@intluranium.com
www.intluranium.com
Ticker Symbol: IUC
Company Type: Public
Profile: Metal mining in uranium, radium & vanadium ores

Ron F. Hochstein, President/CEO & Director
David C. Frydenlund, Vice-President/CFO/General Counsel/Corporate Secretary & Memb, Environment, Health & Safety Committee
John H. Craig, Member, Environment, Health & Safety Committee

Ivanhoe Mines Ltd.
World Trade Centre
#654, 999 Canada Pl.
Vancouver, BC V6C 3E1
604-688-5755 Fax: 604-682-2060 888-273-9999
info@ivanhoemines.com
www.ivanhoemines.com
Ticker Symbol: IVN
Company Type: Public
Profile: Metal mining in copper, iron, gold, silver, lead & zinc ores

John Macken, President/CEO
Robert M. Friedland, Executive Chairman
Tony Giardini, CFO
Clifford Lawing, Manager, Information Technology

Ivernia Inc.
#300, 44 Victoria St.
Toronto, ON M5C 1Y2
416-867-9298 Fax: 416-867-9384
investor@ivernia.ca
www.ivernia.com
Ticker Symbol: IVW
Company Type: Public
Profile: Offices of holding companies; Metal mining in lead & zinc ores

Alan De'ath, President/CEO/Director

Kinross Gold Corporation
Scotia Plaza
40 King St. West, 52nd Fl.
Toronto, ON M5H 3Y2
416-365-5123 Fax: 416-363-6622 866-561-3636
info@kinross.com
www.kinross.com
Ticker Symbol: K
Company Type: Public
Profile: Metal mining in gold & silver ores

Tye Burt, President/CEO
Thomas Boehlert, Exec. Vice-President & CFO
James Toccacelli, Director, Investor Relations
Wes Hansons, Vice-President, Technical Services
Rick Baker, Vice-President, Health, Safety & Environmental Affairs

LionOre Mining International Ltd.
20 Toronto St., 12th Fl.
Toronto, ON M5C 2B8
416-777-1985 Fax: 416-777-1320
info@lionore.com
www.lionore.com
Ticker Symbol: LIM
Company Type: Public
Profile: Offices of holding companies; Metal mining in gold, ferroalloy & copper ores; Commercial physical & biological research

Colin H. Steyn, President/CEO
Theodore C. Mayers, CFO & Secretary

Major Drilling Group International Inc.
#100, 111 St George St.
Moncton, NB E1C 1T7
506-857-8636 Fax: 506-857-9211 866-264-3986
info@majordrilling.com
www.majordrilling.com
Ticker Symbol: MDI
Company Type: Public
Profile: Metal mining & related services; Various heavy construction

Francis P. McGuire, President/CEO
Michael A. Pavey, CFO
Derick R. Davies, Director, Environmental Health & Safety

Mazarin Inc.
696, rue Monfette est
Thetford Mines, QC G6G 7G9
418-338-3669 Fax: 418-338-0229 **Ticker Symbol:** MAZ
Company Type: Public
Profile: Offices of holding companies; Mining & quarrying of dimension stone & miscellaneous nonmetallic minerals

John LeBoutillier, President/CEO
Mario Simard, CFO

Minefinders Corporation Ltd.
#2288, 1177 West Hastings St.
Vancouver, BC V6E 2K3
604-687-6263 Fax: 604-687-6267 866-687-6263
laney@minefinders.com
www.minefinders.com
Ticker Symbol: MFL
Company Type: Public
Profile: Metal mining in gold & silver ores

Mark H. Bailey, President/CEO
Ronald Simpson, CFO
Thomas Matthews, CTO

Miramar Mining Corporation
#300, 889 Harbourside Dr.
North Vancouver, BC V7P 3S1
604-985-2572 Fax: 604-980-0731 800-663-8780
info@miramarmining.com
www.miramarmining.com
Ticker Symbol: MAE
Company Type: Public
Profile: Metal mining in gold, silver & miscellaneous ores

A.P. Walsh, President/CEO
Elaine Bennett, CFO & Vice-President, Finance
Paulo Coan, Manager, Information Technology
Hugh Wilson, Manager, Environment

Mountain Province Diamonds Inc.
#14, 220 Bay St.
Toronto, ON M5J 2W4
416-361-3562 Fax: 416-603-8565
info@mountainprovince.com
www.mountainprovince.com
Ticker Symbol: MPV
Company Type: Public
Profile: Mining & quarrying of miscellaneous nonmetallic minerals

Patrick Evans, President/CEO & Director
Elizabeth Kirkwood, Chair/CFO & Director

Newmont Mining Corporation of Canada Ltd.
PO Box 2005, #1900, 20 Eglinton Ave. West
Toronto, ON M4R 1K8
416-480-6480 Fax: 416-488-6580 www.newmont.com
Ticker Symbol: NMC
Company Type: Public
Profile: Gold ores metal mining

Pierre Lassonde, President

North American Palladium Ltd.
#2116, 130 Adelaide St. West
Toronto, ON M5H 3P5
416-360-7590 Fax: 416-360-7709
info@napalladium.com
www.napalladium.com
Ticker Symbol: PDL
Company Type: Public
Profile: Metal mining in gold, copper, ferroalloy & miscellaneous metal ores

North American Palladium Ltd. (continued)
André J. Douchane, President/CEO
George D. Faught, CFO & Vice-President, Finance
Mary Batoff, Secretary

Northern Orion Resources Inc.
#250, 1075 West Georgia St.
Vancouver, BC V6E 3C9
604-689-9663 Fax: 604-434-1487 866-608-9970
info@northernorion.com
www.northernorion.com
Ticker Symbol: NNO
Company Type: NA
Profile: Metal mining in copper, gold & silver ores

David Cohen, President/CEO
Brian Montpellier, Vice-President, Project Development
Horng Dih Lee, Vice-President & CFO

Northgate Minerals Corporation
#406, 815 Hornby St.
Vancouver, BC V6Z 2E6
604-681-4004 Fax: 604-681-4003
ngx@northgateminerals.com
www.northgateminerals.com
Ticker Symbol: NGX
Company Type: Public
Profile: Offices of holding companies; Metal mining in gold, copper & miscellaneous metal ores

Kenneth G. Stowe, President/CEO
Jon A. Douglas, CFO & Sr. Vice-President
Harold Bent, Superintendent, Environment

Novicourt Inc.
#200, 181 Bay St.
Toronto, ON M5J 2T3
416-982-7111 Fax: 416-982-7423
boonem@normin.com
Ticker Symbol: NOV
Company Type: Public
Profile: Metal mining in copper, lead & zinc ores

George Jones, President
Michael Boone, Controller & Vice-President, Finance
Stephen Young, Corporate Secretary

Olympus Pacific Minerals Inc.
#500, 10 King St. East
Toronto, ON M5C 1C3
416-572-2525 Fax: 416-572-4202 888-902-5522
info@olympuspacific.com
www.olympuspacific.com
Ticker Symbol: OYM
Company Type: Public
Profile: Production & exploration for gold in Vietnam & SE Asia

Colin Patterson, President
David Seton, CEO & Chairman
Roger Dahn, Vice-President, Exploration
Erik H. Martin, CFO & Corporate Secretary

Pacific Rim Mining Corp.
#410, 625 Howe St.
Vancouver, BC V6C 2T6
604-689-1976 Fax: 604-689-1978 888-775-7097
info@pacrim-mining.com
www.pacrim-mining.com
Ticker Symbol: PMU
Company Type: Public
Profile: Metal mining in gold & silver ores

Thomas C. Shrake, CEO
Catherine McLeod-Seltzer, President
John F. Norman, CFO

Pan American Silver Corp.
#1500, 625 Howe St.
Vancouver, BC V6C 2T6
604-684-1175 Fax: 604-684-0147 800-677-1845
info@panamericansilver.com
www.panamericansilver.com
Ticker Symbol: PAA; PAAS
Company Type: Public
Profile: The company's activities include metal mining of silver, gold, copper, lead & zinc ores.

Ross J. Beaty, Chair
Geoffrey Burns, President/CEO
Robert Doyle, Chief Financial Officer
Alexis Stewart, Director, Corporate & Investor Relations
Michael Steinmann, Sr. Vice-President, Geology & Exploration
Rick Urenda, Director, Safety & Training

Philex Gold Inc.
#1604, 141 Adelaide St. West
Toronto, ON M5H 3L5
416-861-1221 Fax: 416-861-1226
paulak@philexgold.com
www.philexgold.com
Ticker Symbol: PGI
Company Type: Public
Profile: Metal mining in gold & copper ores

Walter W. Brown, President
Paula M. Kember, Vice-President, Finance
Donald C. Ross, Corporate Secretary

Placer Dome Inc.
BCE Place
PO Box 212 Bentall, #3700, 161 Bay St.
Toronto, BC M5J 2S1
416-861-9911 Fax: 416-861-2492 800-720-7415
webmaster@placerdome.com
www.placerdome.com
Ticker Symbol: PDG
Company Type: Public
Profile: Metal mining in gold, silver, copper & ferroalloy ores

Peter W. Tomsett, President/CEO
Lindsay Hall, Exec. Vice-President/CFO
Joseph L. Danni, Vice-President, Corporate Relations
Marilyn P.A. Hames, Vice-President, Research & Technology
Keith D. Ferguson, Vice-President, Safety & Sustainability

Potash Corporation of Saskatchewan Inc.
#500, 122 - 1st Ave. South
Saskatoon, SK S7K 7G3
306-933-8500 Fax: 306-652-2699 800-667-0403
corporaterelations@potashcorp.com
www.potashcorp.com
Ticker Symbol: POT
Company Type: Public
Profile: Potash, soda & borate minerals mining & quarrying; Manufacturers of nitrogenous & phosphatic fertilizers; Wholesalers of farm supplies

William J. Doyle, President/CEO
G. David Delaney, President, PCS Sales
Wayne R. Brownlee, Sr. Vice-President/CFO & Treasurer
Barry E. Humphreys, Sr. Vice-President/Chief Information Officer
Robert A. Jaspar, Sr. Vice-President, Information Technology
Donald R. Roberts, Vice-President, Safety, Health & Environment

Premier Tech Ltd.
1, av Premier
Rivière-du-Loup, QC G5R 6C1
418-867-8883 Fax: 418-862-6642
info@premiertech.com
www.premiertech.com
Ticker Symbol: PTL
Company Type: Public
Profile: Miscellaneous nonmetallic minerals mining & quarrying; Commercial physical & biological research

Bernard Bélanger, Chair/CEO
Jean Belanger, President/COO
Christian Dollo, CFO & Sr. Vice-President
Jean-Pierre Bérubé, Vice-President, Technologies & Infrastructures
Henri Ouellet, President, Premier Tech Environment

Quest Capital Corp.
#300, 570 Granville St.
Vancouver, BC V6C 3P1
604-689-1428 Fax: 604-681-4692 800-318-3094
info@questcapcorp.com
www.questcapcorp.com
Ticker Symbol: QC
Company Type: Public
Profile: Metal mining in gold ores

Brian E. Bayley, President/CEO
Susan M. Neale, CFO

Rex Diamond Mining Corporation
162 Cumberland St.
Toronto, ON M5H 3V5
416-955-9033 Fax: 416-955-0783
info@rexmining.com
www.rexmining.com
Ticker Symbol: RXD
Company Type: Public
Profile: Mining & quarrying of miscellaneous nonmetallic minerals & diamonds; Manufacturers of jewelers' findings & materials, lapidary, jewelry, & precious metal; Retailing in catalogue & mail-order houses

Serge Muller, President/CEO
Ben Holemans, CFO

Richmont Mines Inc.
110, av Principale
Rouyn-Noranda, QC J9X 4P2
819-797-2465 Fax: 819-797-0166
jnormandeau@richmont-mines.com
www.richmont-mines.com
Ticker Symbol: RIC
Company Type: Public
Profile: Metal mining in gold ores

Jean-Guy Rivard, President/CEO
Jean-Yves Laliberté, Vice-President, Finance
Alain Mercier, Manager, Technical Services
Don Seymour, Sr. Mine Coordinator, Operations Newfoundland

Ridgeway Petroleum Corp.
#1080, 700 - 4th Ave. SW
Calgary, AB T2P 3J4
403-266-6362 Fax: 403-262-5294 800-347-0294
rgwpet@telusplanet.net
www.ridgewaypetroleum.com
Ticker Symbol: RGW
Company Type: Public
Profile: Mining & quarrying in miscellaneous nonmetallic minerals

Barry Lasker, President/CEO
J. Bruce Petrie, CFO

Rio Narcea Gold Mines Ltd.
#1210, 181 University Ave.
Toronto, ON M5H 3M7
416-956-7470 Fax: 416-956-7471
info@rngm.com
www.rionarcea.com
Ticker Symbol: RNG
Company Type: Public
Profile: Metal mining in gold ores

Alberto Lavandeira, President
Chris I. von Christierson, CEO
Omar Gomez, CFO
Michelle Roth, Contact, Investor Relations

River Gold Mines Ltd.
#1305, 8 King St. East
Toronto, ON M5C 1B5
416-360-3743 Fax: 416-360-7620
info@rivergoldmine.com
www.rivergoldmine.com
Ticker Symbol: RIV
Company Type: Public
Profile: Metal mining in gold ores

Murray H. Pollitt, President/CEO
Don Orr, CFO
Mike Frost, Director, Safety

SEMAFO Inc.
#375, 750, boul Marcel-Laurin
Montréal, QC H4M 2M4
514-744-4408 Fax: 514-744-2291
info@semafo.com
www.semafo.com
Ticker Symbol: SMF
Company Type: Public
Profile: Metal mining in gold, lead & zinc ores

Benoit La Salle, President/CEO
Martin Milette, CFO

Sherritt International Corporation
1133 Yonge St., 5th Fl.
Toronto, ON M4T 2Y7
416-924-4551 Fax: 416-924-5015 800-704-6698
info@sherritt.com
www.sherritt.com
Ticker Symbol: S
Company Type: Public

MAJOR CANADIAN COMPANIES

Profile: Offices of holding companies; Metal mining in ferroalloy & miscellaneous metal ores; Extraction of crude petroleum, natural gas & natural gas liquids; Manufacturers of nitrogenous fertilizers; Engineering services

Jowdat Waheed, President/CEO
Ernie Lalonde, Vice-President, Investor Relations & Corporate Affairs

Silver Standard Resources Inc.
#1180, 999 West Hastings St.
Vancouver, BC V6C 2W2
604-689-3846 Fax: 604-689-3847 888-338-0046
invest@silverstandard.com
www.silverstandard.com
Ticker Symbol: SSO
Company Type: Public
Profile: Metal mining in gold & silver ores

R.A. Quartermain, President/Director
Ross Mitchell, Vice-President, Finance

Southern Cross Resources Inc.
#820, 26 Wellington St. East
Toronto, ON M5E 1S2
416-350-3657 Fax: 416-363-6806
info@southerncrossres.com
www.southerncrossres.com
Ticker Symbol: SXR
Company Type: Public
Profile: Metal mining in uranium, radium & vanadium ores

Martin Ackland, President
Mark Wheatley, CEO
Oliver Lennox-King, CFO & Chair
Don Falconer, Corporate Secretary & Vice-President, Corporate Development

SouthernEra Resources Limited
PO Box 152, #2700, 401 Bay St.
Toronto, ON M5H 2Y4
416-359-9282 Fax: 416-359-9141
inbox@southernera.com
www.southernera.com
Ticker Symbol: SUF
Company Type: Public
Profile: Mining & quarrying of miscellaneous nonmetallic minerals & miscellaneous metal ores

Alasdair MacPhee, President/CEO
Mark Rosslee, CFO & Sr. Vice-President, Finance
Sally Eyre, Vice-President, Corporate Affairs

Southwestern Resources Corp.
PO Box 10102, #1650, 701 West Georgia St.
Vancouver, BC V7Y 1C6
604-669-2525 Fax: 604-688-5175
info@swgold.com
www.swgold.com
Ticker Symbol: SWG
Company Type: Public
Profile: Metal mining in gold, silver & miscellaneous metal ores; Mining & quarrying of miscellaneous nonmetallic minerals

John G. Paterson, President/CEO & Director
Parkash K. Athwal, CFO & Vice-President, Finance

St. Andrew Goldfields Ltd.
#212, 1540 Cornwall Rd.
Oakville, ON L6J 7W5
905-815-9855 Fax: 905-815-9437 800-463-5139
info@standrewgoldfields.com
www.standrewgoldfields.com
Ticker Symbol: SAS
Company Type: Public
Profile: Metal mining of gold ores

Glenn Laing, President/CEO

Sterlite Gold Ltd.
PO Box 25, 199 Bay St.
Toronto, ON M5L 1A9
416-863-2753 Fax: 416-863-2653
information@sterlitegold.com
www.sterlitegold.com
Ticker Symbol: SGD
Company Type: Public
Profile: Metal mining in gold & ferroalloy ores

Sanjay Dalmia, President/CEO
B.S. Vadivelu, CFO

Tahera Corporation
PO Box 1020 T.D.C., 77 King St. West
Toronto, ON M5K 1P2
416-777-1998 Fax: 416-777-1898 877-777-2004
investor_relations@tahera.com
www.tahera.com
Ticker Symbol: TAH
Company Type: Public
Profile: Miscellaneous nonmetallic minerals mining & quarrying

R. Peter Gillin, Chair/Interim CEO
Andrew Gottwald, Vice-President/CFO, Finance
Grant Ewing, Corporate Secretary & Vice-President, Investor Relations & Corporate Development
Greg Missal, Vice-President, Nunavat Affairs

Taseko Mines Limited
#1020, 800 West Pender St.
Vancouver, BC V6C 2V6
604-684-6365 Fax: 604-684-8092 800-667-2114
info@hdgold.com
www.tasekomines.com
Ticker Symbol: TKO
Company Type: Public
Profile: The company is engaged in metal mining of gold, copper & ferroalloy ores.

Russell. Hallbauer, President/CEO & Director
Jeffrey R. Mason, Secretary/CFO & Director
John McManus, Vice-President, Operations

Teck Cominco Limited
#600, 200 Burrard St.
Vancouver, BC V6C 3L9
604-687-1117 Fax: 604-687-6100
info@teckcominco.com
www.teckcominco.com
Ticker Symbol: TEK
Company Type: Public
Profile: Offices of holding companies; Metal mining in gold, copper, lead, zinc, silver, ferroalloy miscellaneous metal ores; Coal & bituminous coal underground mining

Donald R. Lindsay, President/CEO
John G. Taylor, CFO & Sr. Vice-President, Finance
Tom Merinsky, Director, Investor Relations
Douglas H. Horswill, Sr. Vice-President, Environment & Corporate Affairs

Tenke Mining Corp.
#2101, 885 West Georgia St.
Vancouver, BC V6C 3E8
604-689-7842 Fax: 604-689-4250 888-689-7842
tenke@namdo.com
www.tenke.com
Ticker Symbol: TNK
Company Type: Public
Profile: Metal mining in copper, ferroalloy & gold ores

Paul K. Conibear, President/CEO
Wanda Lee, CFO
Sandy Kansky, Corporate Secretary

Trivalence Mining Corporation
#502, 815 Hornby St.
Vancouver, BC V6Z 2E6
604-684-2401 Fax: 604-684-2407 888-273-3671
tmi@trivalence.com
www.trivalence.com
Ticker Symbol: TMI
Company Type: Public
Profile: Diamond production, exploration & development company, with focus in Africa

Lutfur Rahman Khan, President/CEO
Omair Choudhry, CFO

TVI Pacific Inc.
#2000, 736 - 6th Ave. SW
Calgary, AB T2P 3T7
403-265-4356 Fax: 403-264-7028
tvi-info@tvipacific.com
www.tvipacific.com
Ticker Symbol: TVI
Company Type: Public
Profile: Precious & base metal producer & explorer; contract drilling services in SE Asia & the Philippines

Clifford M. James, President/CEO & Chair
E. John W. Adkins, Vice-President, Finance & Administration

Western Québec Mines Inc.
#1305, 8 King St. East
Toronto, ON M5C 1B5
416-360-3743 Fax: 416-360-7620
info@westernquebecmines.com
www.westernquebecmines.com
Ticker Symbol: WQM
Company Type: Public
Profile: Metal mining in gold ores

Barry Smith, President/Director
Don Orr, CFO

Western Silver Corporation
#1550, 1185 West Georgia St.
Vancouver, BC V6E 4E6
604-684-9497 Fax: 604-688-4670
info@westernsilvercorp.com
www.westernsilvercorp.com
Ticker Symbol: WTC
Company Type: Public
Profile: Metal mining in gold, copper, lead & zinc ores

F. Dale Corman, Chair/CEO
Thomas C. Patton, President/COO
Robert J. Gayton, Vice-President, Finance

Wolfden Resources Inc.
#401, 1113 Jade Ct.
Thunder Bay, ON P7B 6M7
807-346-1668 Fax: 807-345-0284 866-690-9653
info@wolfdenresources.com
www.wolfdenresources.com
Ticker Symbol: WLF
Company Type: Public
Profile: Wolfden resources is a Canadian-based mineral exploration & development company.

Ewan S. Downie, President/CEO
ewan.downie@wolfdenresources.com
John Seaman, Chief Executive Officer
john.seaman@wolfdenresources.com
Steven J. Filipovic, Vice-President, Finance
Naomi Nemeth, Vice-President, Investor Relations

Yamana Resources Inc.
#1102, 150 York St.
Toronto, ON M5H 3S5
416-815-0220 Fax: 416-815-0021
investor@yamana.com
www.yamana.com
Ticker Symbol: YRI
Company Type: Public
Profile: Metal mining: gold & silver ores, & miscellaneous metal ores

Peter Marrone, President & CEO
Charles Main, Vice President, Finance & CFO

Oil & Gas

Akita Drilling Ltd.
#900, 311 - 6 Ave. SW
Calgary, AB T2P 3H2
403-292-7979 Fax: 403-292-7990
akitainfo@akita-drilling.com
www.akita-drilling.com
Ticker Symbol: AKT
Company Type: Public
Profile: Drilling oil & gas wells extraction services

John B. Hlavka, President/CEO
Murray J. Roth, Vice-President, Finance

Apache Canada Ltd.
700 - 9 Ave. SW
Calgary, AB T2P 3V4
403-261-1200 Fax: 403-266-5987 www.apachecorp.com
Company Type: Private
Profile: Crude petroleum & natural gas extraction; oil & gas fields exploration services

Brian Schmidt, President

Badger Income Fund
#2820, 715 - 5th Ave. SW
Calgary, AB T2P 2X6

Badger Income Fund (continued)
403-264-8500 Fax: 403-228-9773
bhollands@badgerinc.com
www.badgerinc.com
Ticker Symbol: BAD
Company Type: Public
Profile: Open-ended trust; North America's largest provider of non-destructive excavating services; traditionally works for contractors & facility owners in the utility & petroleum industries

Tor Wilson, President/CEO
Greg Kelly, CFO/Vice-President, Finance

Baytex Energy Ltd.

Bow Valley Square II
#2200, 205 - 5th Ave. SW
Calgary, AB T2P 2V7
403-269-4282 Fax: 403-205-3845
investor@baytex.ab.ca
www.baytex.ab.ca
Ticker Symbol: BTE
Company Type: Public
Profile: Extraction of crude petroleum, natural gas & natural gas liquids

Raymond T. Chan, President & CEO
W. Derek Aylesworth, CFO

BJ Services Company Canada

4839 - 90 Ave. SE
Calgary, AB T2C 2S8
403-531-5300 Fax: 403-236-8740 www.bjservices.com
Company Type: Private
Profile: Oil & gas field services; Manufacturers of oil & gas field machinery & equipment

Joyce Homeniuk, Controller
Blair Albers, Manager, Canadian Operations
Ross Cumming, Manager, Information Systems
Brad Rieb, Manager, Technical
John Artym, Manager, Health & Safety

BlackRock Ventures Inc.

#2600, 605 - 5 Ave. SW
Calgary, AB T2P 3H5
403-233-2253 Fax: 403-263-0437
info@blackrock-ven.com
www.blackrock-ven.com
Ticker Symbol: BVI
Company Type: Public
Profile: Extraction of crude petroleum & natural gas; Various oil & gas fields services; Mining & quarrying of miscellaneous nonmetallic minerals

John Festival, President
Don Cook, Secretary/CFO & Vice-President, Finance

Bonavista Energy Trust

#700, 311 - 6th Ave. SW
Calgary, AB T2P 3H2
403-213-4300 Fax: 403-262-5184
inv_rel@bonavistaenergy.com
www.bonavistaenergy.com
Ticker Symbol: BNP
Company Type: Public
Profile: Crude petroleum, natural gas & natural gas liquids extraction

Keith MacPhail, President & CEO
R.J. Poelzer, Exec. Vice President & CFO
Henk Spence, Vice-President, Operations

Bow Valley Energy Ltd.

#1200, 333 - 7th Ave. SW
Calgary, AB T2P 2Z1
403-232-0292 Fax: 403-232-8920
bve@bvenergy.com
www.bvenergy.com
Ticker Symbol: BVX
Company Type: Public
Profile: The company is engaged in crude petroleum, natural gas & natural gas liquids extraction.

Robert G. Moffat, President/CEO
Matthew L. Janisch, CFO & Vice-President, Finance
John W. Essex, Vice-President, Operations

Canada Southern Petroleum Ltd.

#250, 706 - 7th Ave. SW
Calgary, AB T2P 0Z1
403-269-7741 Fax: 403-261-5667
info@cansopet.com
www.cansopet.com
Ticker Symbol: CSW
Company Type: Public
Profile: Extraction of crude petroleum, natural gas & natural gas liquids

John MacDonald, President/CEO
Randy Denecky, CFO & Treasurer

Canadex Resources Ltd.

10 Sun Pac Blvd.
Brampton, ON L6S 4R5
905-792-2700 Fax: 905-792-8490
contact@canadex.ca
www.canadex.ca
Ticker Symbol: CDX
Company Type: Public
Profile: Extraction of crude petroleum, natural gas & natural gas liquids; School buses; Local trucking with storage; General warehousing & storage; Truck rental & leasing

John A. Riddell, Chair
Vincent C. McEwan, CFO

Canadian Imperial Venture Corp.

Fortis Bldg.
PO Box 6232, 139 Water St.
St. John's, NL A1C 6J9
709-739-6700 Fax: 709-739-6605
info@canadianimperial.com
www.canadianimperial.com
Ticker Symbol: CQV
Company Type: Public
Profile: Crude petroleum, natural gas & natural gas liquids extraction

Steven M. Millan, President/CEO & Chair
Gerard M. Edwards, CFO

Canadian Natural Resources Limited

#2500, 855 - 2nd St. SW
Calgary, AB T2P 4J8
403-517-7777 Fax: 403-517-7370
investor.relations@cnrl.com
www.cnrl.com
Ticker Symbol: CNQ
Company Type: Public
Profile: Crude petroleum, natural gas & natural gas liquids extraction

Steve W. Laut, President & COO
Douglas A. Proll, CFO & Sr. Vice-President, Finance
Corey B. Bieber, Vice-President, Investor Relations
William R. Clapperton, Vice-President, Regulatory, Stakeholder & Environmental Affairs

Canadian Superior Energy Inc.

#3300, 400 - 3rd Ave. SW
Calgary, AB T2P 4H2
403-294-1411 Fax: 403-216-2374 www.cansup.com
Ticker Symbol: SNG
Company Type: Public
Profile: Extraction of crude petroleum, natural gas & natural gas liquids

Greg Noval, President/CEO
Ross J. Jones, CFO

CCS Income Trust

#2400, 530 - 8th Ave. SW
Calgary, AB T2P 3S8
403-233-7565 Fax: 403-261-5612 www.ccsincometrust.com
Ticker Symbol: CCR
Company Type: Public
Profile: Various oil & gas fields services; Refuse systems

David P. Werklund, President/CEO
Marshall L. McRae, CFO/Corporate Secretary & Vice-President, Finance

Centurion Energy International Inc.

Bow Valley Square II
#1700, 205 - 5th Ave. SW
Calgary, AB T2P 2V7
403-263-6002
info@centurionenergy.com
www.centurionenergy.com
Ticker Symbol: CUX
Company Type: Public
Profile: Extraction of crude petroleum, natural gas & natural gas liquids

Said Arrata, President/CEO
Barry Swan, CFO & Sr. Vice-President, Finance
Tony Anton, COO
Mike Zayat, Officer, Business Development

Compton Petroleum Corporation

East Tower, Fifth Ave. Place
#3300, 425 - 1st St. SW
Calgary, AB T2P 3L8
403-237-9400 Fax: 403-237-9410
investorinfo@comptonpetroleum.com
www.comptonpetroleum.com
Ticker Symbol: CMT
Company Type: Public
Profile: Extraction of crude petroleum, natural gas & natural gas liquids

Ernest G. Sapieha, President/CEO
Norman G. Knecht, CFO & Vice-President, Finance
Wade Mrochuk, Manager, Production

Conoco Canada Resources Limited

PO Box 130 M, 401 - 9 Ave. SW
Calgary, AB T2P 2H7
403-233-4000 Fax: 403-233-5143 www.conocophillips.com
Ticker Symbol: CNK
Company Type: Private
Profile: Extraction of crude petroleum, natural gas & natural gas liquids

Henry W. Sykes, President

Corridor Resources Inc.

#301, 5475 Spring Garden Rd.
Halifax, NS B3J 3T2
902-429-4511 Fax: 902-422-6715
info@corridor.ns.ca
www.corridor.ns.ca
Ticker Symbol: CDH
Company Type: Public
Profile: Extraction of crude petroleum, natural gas & natural gas liquids

Norman W. Miller, President
Brad Perry, CFO
Tom Martel, Chief Geologist

Devon Canada Corporation

#2000, 400 - 3rd Ave. SW
Calgary, AB T2P 4H2
403-232-7100 Fax: 403-232-7221 www.devonenergy.com
Company Type: Public
Profile: Crude petroleum, natural gas & natural gas liquids extraction

John Richels, President/CEO
Paul F. Brereton, Vice-President, Finance
Murray T. Brown, Corporate Secretary/General Counsel

Drillers Technology Corp.

#2920, 715 - 5th Ave. SW
Calgary, AB T2P 2X6
403-261-9877 Fax: 403-213-4860
info@drillerstech.com
www.drillerstech.com
Ticker Symbol: DLR
Company Type: Public
Profile: Extraction services in drilling oil & gas wells

Ronald W. Gnyra, President/CEO
Darcy Campbell, CFO & Vice-President, Finance

Enbridge Inc.

Fifth Ave. Place
#3000, 425 - 1st St. SW
Calgary, AB T2P 3L8
403-231-3900 Fax: 403-231-3920
webmaster@enbridge.com
www.enbridge.com
Ticker Symbol: ENB
Company Type: Public
Profile: Crude & refined petroleum & various pipelines; Natural gas transmission

Patrick D. Daniel, President/CEO
Jim Schultz, President, Enbridge Gas Distribution
Stephen J. Wuori, Group Vice-President/CFO

EnCana Corporation

PO Box 2850, #1800, 855 - 2nd St. SW
Calgary, AB T2P 2S5

403-645-2000 Fax: 403-645-3400
investor.relations@encana.com
www.encana.com
Ticker Symbol: ECA
Company Type: Public
Profile: Crude petroleum, natural gas & natural gas liquids extraction; Crude petroleum pipelines; Natural gas transmission; Gas & other services combined; Wholesalers of petroleum & petroleum products

Randy Eresman, President/CEO
Bill Oliver, President, Mainstream & Marketing
John Watson, CFO & Exec. Vice-President
Brian Ferguson, Exec. Vice-President, Corporate Development

Ensign Resource Service Group Inc.
#900, 400 - 5th Ave. SW
Calgary, AB T2P 0L6
403-262-1361 Fax: 403-262-8215
ir@ensigngroup.com
www.ensigngroup.com
Ticker Symbol: ESI
Company Type: Public
Profile: Exploration services in oil & gas fields; Various oil & gas fields services; Extraction of crude petroleum & natural gas; Extraction services in drilling oil & gas wells

Selby Porter, President
Glenn Dagenais, CFO & Exec. Vice-President, Finance

Enterra Energy Corp.
#2600, 500 - 4th Ave. SW
Calgary, AB T2P 2V6
403-263-0262 Fax: 403-294-1197
info@enterraenergy.com
www.enterraenergy.com
Company Type: Public
Profile: Crude petroleum, natural gas & natural gas liquids extraction

Reg Greenslade, President/CEO
Luc Chartrand, CFO
Debra Armstrong, Environment Co-Ordinator

Esprit Exploration Ltd.
#900, 606 - 4th St. SW
Calgary, AB T2P 1T1
403-213-3700 Fax: 403-213-3710
IR@eee.ca
www.eee.ca
Ticker Symbol: EEE
Company Type: Public
Profile: Crude petroleum, natural gas & natural gas liquids extraction; Refined petroleum & crude petroleum pipelines; Natural gas transmission

Stephen J. Savident, President/CEO
Stephen B. Soules, CFO & Exec. Vice-President

Fairborne Energy Trust
#3500, 450 - 1st St. SW
Calgary, AB T2P 5H1
403-290-7750 Fax: 403-290-7724
info@fairbornetrust.com
www.fairbornetrust.com
Company Type: Public
Profile: Crude petroleum, natural gas & natural gas liquids extraction

Steven R. VanSickle, President/CEO
Aaron Grandberg, CFO & Vice-President, Finance

First Calgary Petroleums Ltd.
#900, 520 - 5th Ave. SW
Calgary, AB T2P 3R7
403-264-6697 Fax: 403-264-3955
info@fcpl.ca
www.fcpl.ca
Ticker Symbol: FCP
Company Type: Public
Profile: Extraction of crude petroleum, natural gas & natural gas liquids

Richard Anderson, President
John van der Welle, CFO, Director & Vice-President, Finance
Roger Whittaker, Vice-President, Exploration

Flint Energy Services Ltd.
#700, 300 - 5th Ave. SW
Calgary, AB T2P 3C4
403-218-7100 Fax: 403-215-5445 877-215-5499
ir@flint-energy.com
www.flintenergy.com
Company Type: Public
Profile: Various oil & gas field services; General contractors in industrial buildings & warehouses; Water, sewer, pipeline, communications, power line construct

W.J. (Bill) Lingard, President/CEO
Terry Freeman, CFO & Secretary

Hunt Oil Company of Canada, Inc.
Transcanada Tower
#3100, 450 First St. SW
Calgary, AB T2P 5H1
403-531-1430 Fax: 403-531-1539
877-444-9295www.huntoil.com
Company Type: Private
Profile: Crude petroleum, natural gas & natural gas liquids extraction

George Ongyerth, President
Mike Tkaczuk, Vice-President, Finance
Charity Paquette, Administrator

Husky Energy Inc.
PO Box 6525 D, 707 - 8 Ave. SW
Calgary, AB T2P 3G7
403-298-6111 Fax: 403-298-7464
investor.relations@huskyenergy.ca
www.huskyenergy.ca
Ticker Symbol: HSE
Company Type: Public
Profile: Crude petroleum, natural gas & natural gas liquids extraction; Petroleum refining; Refined petroleum pipelines; Natural gas transmission; Wholesalers of petroleum & petroleum products, brick, stone & related construction materials; Retailing in gasoline service stations

John C.S. Lau, President/CEO
Neil D. McGee, Vice-President/CFO
Richard M. Alexander, Vice-President, Investor Relations & Communications

Imperial Oil Resources Limited
3535 Research Rd. NW
Calgary, AB T2L 2K8
403-284-7400 Fax: 403-284-7589 www.imperialoil.ca
Ticker Symbol: IMO
Company Type: Private
Profile: Extraction of crude petroleum, natural gas & natural gas liquids; Manufacturers of petroleum refining; Wholesalers of petroleum & petroleum products; Crude petroleum pipelines; Refined petroleum pipelines; Natural gas transmission; Wholesalers of farm supplies; Retailers in gasoline service stations

K.C. Williams, President/CEO

Integrated Production Services Ltd.
#1900, 840 - 7th Ave. SW
Calgary, AB T2P 3G2
403-266-0908 Fax: 403-266-1639 www.ipsadvantage.com
Ticker Symbol: IPL
Company Type: Private
Profile: Various oil & gas fields services

Brian Moore, President/CEO
James M. Hill, CFO

Inter Pipeline Fund
#2600, 237 - 4th Ave. SW
Calgary, AB T2P 4K3
403-290-6000 Fax: 403-290-6090 866-716-7473
investorrelations@interpipelinefund.com
www.interpipelinefund.com
Ticker Symbol: IPL
Company Type: Public
Profile: Services included petroleum transportation, bulk liquid storage & natural gas liquids extraction; Owner & operator of energy infrastructure assets in Western Canada, the United Kingdom, Germany & the Republic of Ireland

David W. Fesyk, President/CEO, Pipeline Management Inc.
William A. van Yzerloo, CFO, Pipeline Management Inc.
David Williams, Vice-President, Operations

Ivanhoe Energy Inc.
#654, 999 Canada Pl.
Vancouver, BC V6C 3E1
604-688-8323 Fax: 604-688-7168
info@ivanhoeenergy.com
www.ivanhoeenergy.com
Ticker Symbol: IE
Company Type: Public
Profile: Extraction of crude petroleum, natural gas & natural gas liquids

Leon Daniel, President/CEO
W. Gordon Lancaster, CFO

Kereco Energy Ltd.
#1100, 530 - 8th Ave. SW
Calgary, AB T2P 3S8
403-290-3400 Fax: 403-290-3447
info@kereco.com
Ticker Symbol: KCH
Company Type: Public
Profile: Crude petroleum, natural gas & natural gas liquids extraction

Grant Fagerheim, President/CEO & Director
Stephen Nikiforuk, Vice-President, Finance

Kick Energy Corporation
#1720, 734 - 7th Ave. SW
Calgary, AB T2P 3P8
403-262-9801 Fax: 403-264-3268
info@kickenergy.com
www.kickenergy.com
Ticker Symbol: KEC
Company Type: Public
Profile: Crude petroleum, natural gas & natural gas liquids extraction

Timothy T. Hunt, President/CEO
Ulla B. Fuss, CFO & Vice-President, Finance
Barry J. Wasyliw, Vice-President, Operations

Kinder Morgan Canada
#2700, 300 - 5th Ave.
Calgary, AB T2P 5J2
403-514-6400 Fax: 403-514-6401 800-535-7219
info@kindermorgan.com
www.kindermorgan.com
Company Type: Public
Profile: Crude petroleum & refined petroleum pipelines

Ian Anderson, President

Nabors Canada LP
#3000, 500 - 4th Ave. SW
Calgary, AB T2P 2V6
403-263-6777 Fax: 403-269-7352 www.nabors.com
Company Type: Private
Profile: Drilling oil & gas wells extraction services

Duane Mather, President/CEO
Lou Doiron, President, Production Services
Edwin Watson, Vice-President, Finance

NAV Energy Trust
#1800, 635 - 8th Ave. SW
Calgary, AB T2P 3W3
403-218-3600 Fax: 403-216-1572
888-414-4144www.navenergytrust.com
Ticker Symbol: NVG
Company Type: Public
Profile: Crude petroleum, natural gas & natural gas liquids extraction

Thomas P. Stan, President/CEO
Janalee Shutiak, CFO & Vice-President

Newalta Income Fund
#1200, 333 - 11th Ave. SW
Calgary, AB T2R 1L9
403-266-6556 Fax: 403-262-7348
info@newalta.com
www.newalta.com
Ticker Symbol: NAL
Company Type: Public
Profile: Industrial waste management company; Recovery of saleable products & recycling; Provision of environmentally sound disposal of solid, nonhazardous industrial waste; Customers are from the forestry, automotive, mining, oil & gas, manufacturing, petrochemical, steel, pulp & paper & transportation industries

Alan P. Cadotte, President/CEO
Ronald L. Sifton, CFO & Sr. Vice-President, Finance

Newalta Income Fund (continued)
Robert Redhead, Exec. Director, Government Affairs
Terry P. Donaleshen, Vice-President, Human Resources & Environment, Health & Safety

Nexen Inc.
801 - 7 Ave. SW
Calgary, AB T2P 3P7
403-699-4000 Fax: 403-699-5776 www.nexeninc.com
Ticker Symbol: NXY
Company Type: Public
Profile: Crude petroleum, natural gas & natural gas liquids extraction; Manufacturers of alkalies & chlorine; Petroleum refining

Charles W. Fischer, President/CEO
Marvin F. Romanow, CFO & Exec. Vice-President

Niko Resources Ltd.
4600 Canterra Tower
#4600, 400 - 3 Ave. SW
Calgary, AB T2P 4H2
403-262-1020 Fax: 403-263-2686
nikocalgary@nikoresources.com
www.nikoresources.com
Ticker Symbol: NKO
Company Type: Public
Profile: Extraction of crude petroleum, natural gas & natural gas liquids

Edward S. Sampson, Chair/President/CEO
Richard Alexander, Vice-President & CFO, Finance

Northrock Resources Ltd.
#3500, 700 - 2nd St. SW
Calgary, AB T2P 2W2
403-213-7600 Fax: 403-232-4650 **Company Type:** Private
Profile: Crude petroleum, natural gas & natural gas liquids extraction

David L. Pearce, President/CEO
John H. Van de Pol, CFO & Sr. Vice-President

Pacific Northern Gas Ltd.
#950, 1185 West Georgia St.
Vancouver, BC V6E 4E6
604-691-5680 Fax: 604-697-6210
info@pacificnortherngas.com
www.pacificnortherngas.com
Ticker Symbol: PNG
Company Type: Public
Profile: Natural gas transmission & distribution

Roy Dyce, President/CEO & Director
Elizabeth A. Fletcher, CFO
Greg Weeres, Vice-President, Engineering & Operations

Paramount Resources Ltd.
Bankers Hall West
#4700, 888 - 3rd St. SW
Calgary, AB T2P 5C5
403-290-3600 Fax: 403-262-7994 www.paramountres.com
Ticker Symbol: POU
Company Type: Public
Profile: Extraction of crude petroleum, natural gas & natural gas liquids; Wholesalers of petroleum & petroleum products

Clay H. Riddell, Chair/CEO
James H.T. Riddell, President/COO
Bernie K. Lee, CFO

Peak Energy Services Trust Ltd.
#1800, 530 - 8th Ave. SW
Calgary, AB T2P 3S8
403-543-7325 Fax: 403-543-7325 800-661-3803
info@pesl.com
www.peak-energy.com
Ticker Symbol: PES
Company Type: Public
Profile: Offices of holding companies; Various oil & gas fields services; Manufacturers of oil & gas field machinery & equipment; Equipment rental & leasing

Christopher E. Haslam, Chair/President/CEO
Matthew J. Huber, CFO
Curtis W. Whitteron, Vice-President, Operations

Pebercan Inc.
#220, 750 Marcel Laurin Blvd.
Saint-Laurent, QC H4M 2M4
514-286-5200 Fax: 514-286-5177
info@pebercan.com
www.pebercan.com
Ticker Symbol: PBC
Company Type: Public
Profile: Extraction of crude petroleum, natural gas & natural gas liquids; Oil & gas field exploration services

Gilles Frachon, President/CEO
Veronique Jallabert, Vice-President, Finance

Pengrowth Energy Trust
BP Centre
#2900, 240 - 4th Ave. SW
Calgary, AB T2P 4H4
403-233-0224 Fax: 403-265-6251 800-223-4122
pengrowth@pengrowth.com
www.pengrowth.com
Ticker Symbol: PGF
Company Type: Public
Profile: Open-ended management investment offices; Extraction of crude petroleum & natural gas

James S. Kinnear, President/CEO
Christopher Webster, CFO
Dean Morrison, Manager, Investor Relations

Penn West Petroleum Ltd.
#2200, 425 - 1st St. SW
Calgary, AB T2P 3L8
403-777-2500 Fax: 403-777-2699 866-693-2707
investor_relations@pennwest.com
www.pennwest.com
Ticker Symbol: PWT
Company Type: Public
Profile: Crude petroleum, natural gas & natural gas liquids extraction; Wholesalers of petroleum & petroleum products

William E. Andrew, President
Gerry J. Elms, Corporate Secretary/Vice-President, Finance
Bryan D. Clake, Vice-President, Corporate Development

Petro-Canada
PO Box 2844, Calgary, AB T2P 3E3
403-296-8000 Fax: 403-296-3030
investor@petro-canada.ca
www.petro-canada.ca
Ticker Symbol: PCZ
Company Type: Public
Profile: Mixed, manufactured, liquified petroleum gas production & distribution; Petroleum refining; Crude petroleum, natural gas & natural gas liquids extraction; Wholesalers of petroleum & petroleum products; Crude & refined petroleum pipelines; Natural gas transmission & distribution; Chemical & fertilizer mineral mining & quarrying; Retailing in gasoline service stations

Ron A. Brenneman, President/CEO
Harry Roberts, CFO & Exec. Vice-President
Neil Camarta, Vice-President, Corporate Planning & Communications
Greta Raymond, Vice-President, Environment, Health, Safety & Security & Corp Responsib

Petrobank Energy & Resources Ltd.
#2600, 240 - 4th Ave. SW
Calgary, AB T2P 4H4
403-750-4400 Fax: 403-266-5794
ir@petrobank.com
www.petrobank.com
Ticker Symbol: PBG
Company Type: Public
Profile: Crude petroleum, natural gas & natural gas liquids extraction

John D. Wright, President/CEO
Chris J. Bloomer, CFO & Vice-President, Heavy Oil
Corey Ruttan, Corporate Finance & Investor Relations

Petrofund Energy Trust
#600, 444 - 7th Ave. SW
Calgary, AB T2P 0X8
403-218-8625 Fax: 403-269-5858
info@petrofund.ca
www.petrofund.ca
Ticker Symbol: PTF
Company Type: Public
Profile: Acquires & manages oil & gas producing properties in western Canada

Jeffery E. Errico, President/CEO
Edward J. Brown, CFO & Vice-President, Finance

Larry Strong, Vice-President, GeoSciences

PEYTO Energy Trust
#2900, 450 - 1st St. SW
Calgary, AB T2P 5H1
403-261-6081 Fax: 403-261-8976
info@peyto.com
www.peyto.com
Ticker Symbol: PEY
Company Type: Public
Profile: Extraction of petroleum & natural gas

Don T. Gray, President/CEO
Kathy Turgeon, Vice-President, Finance
Scott Robinson, Vice-President, Operations

Point North Energy Ltd.
#2810, 605 - 5th Ave. SW
Calgary, AB T2P 3H5
403-269-5803 Fax: 403-264-1336
info@purcellenergy.com
www.purcellenergy.com
Ticker Symbol: PEL
Company Type: Public
Profile: Crude petroleum, natural gas & natural gas liquids extraction

John Emery, President/CEO
Doug Gragham, CFO
Wayne Geddes, Vice-President, Land's Business Development

Precision Drilling Corporation
#4200, 150 - 6th Ave. SW
Calgary, AB T2P 3Y7
403-716-4500 Fax: 403-264-0251
info@precisiondrilling.com
www.precisiondrilling.com
Ticker Symbol: PD
Company Type: Public
Profile: Drilling oil & gas wells extraction services; Various related services; Manufacturers of oil & gas field machinery & equipment

Hank B. Swartout, President/CEO & Chair
Dale E. Tremblay, CFO & Sr. Vice-President, Finance
John R. King, Sr. Vice-President, Energy Services

Progress Energy Ltd.
#1400, 440 - 2nd Ave. SW
Calgary, AB T2P 5E9
403-216-2510 Fax: 403-216-2514 866-216-2510
ir@progressenergy.com
www.progressenergy.com
Ticker Symbol: PGX
Company Type: Public
Profile: Crude petroleum, natural gas & natural gas liquids extraction

Michael R. Culbert, President/CEO
Art MacNichol, CFO/Secretary & Vice-President, Finance
Neil Samis, Vice-President, Production

Provident Energy Trust
#700, 112 - 4th Ave. SW
Calgary, AB T2P 0H3
403-296-2233 Fax: 403-261-6696
info@providentenergy.com
www.providentenergy.com
Ticker Symbol: PVE.UN; PVX
Company Type: Public
Profile: Open-ended energy income trust; Owns & manages an oil & gas production business & a natural gas liquids mid-stream service & marketing business; Energy portfolio located in Western Canada, Southern California & Wyoming

Thomas W. Buchanan, CEO
Randall J. Findlay, President
Mark N. Walker, CFO/Secretary & Vice-President, Finance
Laurie Stretch, Sr. Manager, Investor Relations & Communications

Pulse Data Inc.
#2400, 639 - 5th Ave. SW
Calgary, AB T2P 0M9
403-237-5559 Fax: 403-531-0688 877-460-5559
info@pulsedatainc.com
www.pulsedatainc.com
Ticker Symbol: PSD
Company Type: Public

Profile: Specializing in data ownership through acquisition, marketing & information management, with current focus on the energy sector

Ken MacDonald, President/CEO & Director
Doug Cutts, CFO & Vice-President, Finance

Real Resources Inc.
#700, 555 - 4th Ave. SW
Calgary, AB T2P 3E7
403-262-9077 Fax: 403-262-6403
investor@realres.com
www.realres.com
Ticker Symbol: RER
Company Type: Public
Profile: Crude petroleum, natural gas & natural gas liquids extraction

Lowell E. Jackson, President/CEO
Pamela J. Orr, CFO & Vice-President, Finance
Clay Curry, Field Superintendent

Ryan Energy Technologies Inc.
#3000, 500 - 4th Ave. SW
Calgary, AB T2P 2V6
403-269-5981 Fax: 403-263-2031
info@ryanenergy.com
www.ryanenergy.com
Ticker Symbol: RYN
Company Type: Private
Profile: Drilling oil & gas wells extraction services

R.T. Ryan, CEO
David Simm, Vice-President, Technology Innovation
Mike Judson, Coordinator, Health & Safety, Environment

Shell Canada Limited
PO Box 100 M, 400 - 4 Ave. SW
Calgary, AB T2P 2H5
403-691-3111 Fax: 403-269-8031 800-661-1600
questions@shell.ca
www.shell.ca
Ticker Symbol: SHC
Company Type: Public
Profile: Bitumen & synthetic crude oil, natural gas & natural gas liquids extraction; Wholesalers & retailers of petroleum & petroleum products; Petroleum refining

Clive Mather, President/CEO
Cathy Williams, CFO

Shiningbank Energy Income Fund
#1310, 111 - 5th Ave. SW
Calgary, AB T2P 3Y6
403-268-7477 Fax: 403-268-7499
shiningbank@shiningbank.com
www.shiningbank.com
Ticker Symbol: SHN.UN
Company Type: Public
Profile: Royalty trust purchases, develops & operates producing properties for the benefit of unitholders

David M. Fitzpatrick, President/CEO
Bruce K. Gibson, CFO & Vice-President, Finance
Gregory D. Moore, Chief Operating Officer

Suncor Energy Inc.
PO Box 38, 112 - 4 Ave. SW
Calgary, AB T2P 2V5
403-269-8100 Fax: 403-269-6200 866-786-2671
info@suncormail.com
www.suncor.com
Ticker Symbol: SU
Company Type: Public
Profile: Crude petroleum, natural gas, natural gas liquids, drilling oil & gas wells extraction services; Petroleum refining; Wholesalers of petroleum & petroleum products; Crude petroleum pipelines; Natural gas transmission

R.L. George, President/CEO
Kenneth Alley, CFO & Sr. Vice-President

Syncrude Canada Ltd.
PO Box 4023 Main, 9911 MacDonald Ave.
Fort McMurray, AB T9H 3H5
780-790-5911 Fax: 780-790-6215 800-667-9494
info@syncrude.com
www.syncrude.com
Company Type: Private
Profile: Crude petroleum & natural gas extraction

Charles Ruigrok, CEO
James (Jim) E. Carter, President/COO
Phil Lachambre, CFO & Exec. Vice-President
Donald Thompson, Corporate Secretary & General Manager, Environment, Health & Safety

Talisman Energy Inc.
#3400, 888 - 3rd St. SW
Calgary, AB T2P 5C5
403-237-1234 Fax: 403-237-1902
tlm@talisman-energy.com
www.talisman-energy.com
Ticker Symbol: TLM
Company Type: Public
Profile: Crude petroleum, natural gas & natural gas liquids extraction

James W. Buckee, President/CEO
Michael D. McDonald, CFO/Exec. Vice-President, Finance

Tanganyika Oil Company Ltd.
#2101, 885 West Georgia St.
Vancouver, BC V6C 3E8
604-689-7842 Fax: 604-689-4250
info@tanganyikaoil.com
www.tanganyikaoil.com
Ticker Symbol: TYK
Company Type: Public
Profile: Extraction of crude petroleum, natural gas & natural gas liquids

Gary Guidry, President & CEO
Hazem Farid, Controller & Treasurer
Jean R. Florendo, Corporate Secretary

Taylor NGL Limited Partnership
#2200, 800 - 5th Ave. SW
Calgary, AB T2P 3T6
403-781-8181 Fax: 403-777-1907
info@taylorngl.com
www.taylorngl.com
Ticker Symbol: TAY.UN
Company Type: Public
Profile: Extraction of natural gas liquids; Processing of natural gas

Robert J. Pritchard, President
Barry O'Brien, CFO & Secretary
David Schmunk, COO

Terasen Gas Inc.
16705 Fraser Hwy.
Surrey, BC V3S 2X7
604-576-7000
websupport@terasengas.com
www.terasengas.com
Company Type: Public
Profile: Natural gas transmission & distribution; Gas & other services combined; Refined petroleum pipelines

Thunder Energy Trust
#400, 321 - 6th Ave. SW
Calgary, AB T2P 3H3
403-294-1635 Fax: 403-232-1317
thunder@thunderenergy.com
www.thunderenergy.com
Ticker Symbol: THY
Company Type: Public
Profile: Crude petroleum, natural gas & natural gas liquids extraction

Stuart J. Keck, President/CEO
Brent T. Kirkby, CFO & Vice-President, Finance

Total Energy Services Ltd.
#2410, 520 - 5th Ave. SW
Calgary, AB T2P 3R7
403-216-3939 Fax: 403-234-8731 877-818-6825
investorrelations@totalenergy.ca
www.totalenergy.ca
Ticker Symbol: TOT
Company Type: Public
Profile: Extraction services in drilling of oil & gas wells; Various oil & gas fields services; Local trucking; Equipment rental & leasing; Wholesalers of industrial machinery & equipment

Daniel K. Halyk, CEO
Larry Coston, President/COO
David Hawkins, CFO & Vice-President, Finance

Touchstone Resources Ltd.
PO Box 10356 Pacific Centr, #810, 609 Granville St.
Vancouver, BC V7Y 1G5
604-685-7450 Fax: 604-685-7485
info@touchstonetexas.com
www.touchstonetexas.com
Ticker Symbol: TUT
Company Type: Public
Profile: Extraction of crude petroleum, natural gas & natural gas liquids

Mark Bush, President/CEO

Trans Québec & Maritimes Pipeline Inc.
#525, 6300, av Auteuil
Brossard, QC J4Z 3P2
450-462-5300 Fax: 450-462-5388
otis@gazoductqm.com
www.gazoductqm.com
Company Type: Public
Profile: Natural gas transmission & distribution

Bernard Otis, Acting General Manager
Jean-Marc Rousseau, Financial Manager

TransCanada PipeLines Limited
TransCanada Tower
450 - 1 St. SW
Calgary, AB T2P 5H1
403-920-2000 Fax: 403-920-2200 800-661-3805
investor_relations@transcanada.com
www.transcanada.com
Ticker Symbol: TRP
Company Type: Public
Profile: Natural gas transmission; Natural gas transmission and distribution; Electric services

Harold N. Kvisle, President/CEO
Russell K. Girling, CFO & Exec. Vice-President, Corporate Development
Sarah E. Raiss, Exec. Vice-President, Corporate Services

Trican Well Service Ltd.
#2900, 645 - 7th Ave. SW
Calgary, AB T2P 4G8
403-266-0202 Fax: 403-237-7716 877-587-4226
info@trican.ca
www.trican.ca
Ticker Symbol: TCW
Company Type: Public
Profile: Extraction services in drilling of oil & gas wells; Various oil & gas field services

Murray L. Cobbe, President/CEO
Michael G. Kelly, Corporate Secretary/CFO & Vice-President, Finance
Dale M. Dusterhoft, Vice-President, Technical Services

Trinidad Energy Services Income Trust
#2500, 700 - 9th Ave. SW
Calgary, AB T2P 3V4
403-265-6525 Fax: 403-265-4168
info@trinidaddrilling.com
www.trinidaddrilling.com
Ticker Symbol: TDG.UN
Company Type: Public
Profile: Extraction services in drilling of oil & gas wells

Michael E. Heier, Chair/CEO
Lyle C. Whitmarsh, President
Brent Conway, CFO

TUSK Energy Inc.
#1900, 700 - 4th Ave. SW
Calgary, AB T2P 3J4
403-264-8875 Fax: 403-263-4247
tusk@tusk-energy.com
www.tusk-energy.com
Ticker Symbol: TKE
Company Type: Public
Profile: Crude petroleum, natural gas & natural gas liquids extraction

Norman W. Holton, Chair/CEO
Earl T. Hickok, President/COO
Gordon K. Case, CFO & Vice-President
Darol Turnquist, Vice-President, Exploration
Ed A. Beaman, Vice-President, Production & Operations

Ultramar Ltd.
2200, av McGill College
Montréal, QC H3A 3L3
514-499-6111 Fax: 514-499-6320
publicaffairs@ultramar.ca
www.ultramar.ca
Company Type: Private
Profile: Manufacturers of petroleum refining

Jean Bernier, CEO
Danielle Bradshaw, Manager, Environment
Marcel Dupuis, Vice-President, Finance
Stéphane Trudel, Manager, Information Technology

Union Gas Limited
50 Keil Dr. North
Chatham, ON N7M 5M1
519-352-3100 Fax: 519-436-4566
customerrelations@uniongas.com
www.uniongas.com
Ticker Symbol: UNG
Company Type: Public
Profile: Natural gas transmission & distribution

Gregory L. Ebel, President
Alan N. Harris, Group Vice-President/CFO
M. Richard Birmingham, Vice-President, Regulatory Affairs & Business Services

UPI Inc.
#200, 105 Silvercreek Pkwy. North
Guelph, ON N1H 8M1
519-821-2667 Fax: 519-821-4919
info@upi.on.ca
www.upi-inc.com
Company Type: Private
Profile: Manufacturers of various fuel products; Servicing of equipment

Robert P. Sicard, President/CEO
Clifford Brown, CFO & Vice-President, Finance

UTS Energy Corp.
#1000, 350 - 7th Ave. SW
Calgary, AB T2P 3N9
403-538-7030 Fax: 403-538-7033 866-538-7030www.uts.ca
Ticker Symbol: UTS
Company Type: Public
Profile: Extraction of crude petroleum & natural gas

William Roach, President/CEO
Wayne I. Bobye, Vice-President/CFO
Howard Lutley, Vice-President, Mining & Extraction
Martin Sandell, Vice-President, Engineering
Daryl Wightman, Vice-President, Resource & Business Development

Vermilion Energy Trust
#2800, 400 - 4th Ave. SW
Calgary, AB T2P 0J4
403-269-4884 Fax: 403-264-6306
investor_relations@vermilionenergy.com
www.vermilionenergy.com
Ticker Symbol: VRM
Company Type: Public
Profile: Extraction of crude petroleum, natural gas & natural gas liquids

Lorenzo Donadeo, President/CEO
Curtis Hicks, CFO & Vice-President, Finance
Paul Beique, Director, Investor Relations

Viking Energy Royalty Trust
Calgary Place
#400, 330 - 5th Ave. SW
Calgary, AB T2P 0L4
403-268-3175 Fax: 403-266-0058
vikingin@viking-roy.com
www.vikingenergy.com
Company Type: Private
Profile: Crude petroleum, natural gas & natural gas liquids extraction

John Zachary, President/CEO
Robert Fotheringham, CFO & Vice-President, Finance

Western Oil Sands Inc.
E&Y Tower
#2400, 440 - 2nd Ave. SW
Calgary, AB T2P 5E9
403-233-1700 Fax: 403-296-0122
investorrelations@westernoilsands.com
www.westernoilsands.com
Ticker Symbol: WTO
Company Type: Public
Profile: Various heavy construction; Extraction of crude petroleum & natural gas

James C. Houck, President/CEO & Director
David A. Dyck, CFO & Sr. Vice-President, Finance
Steve D.L. Reynish, Sr. Vice-President, Mining Operations

Zargon Oil & Gas Ltd.
#700, 333 - 5th Ave. SW
Calgary, AB T2P 3B6
403-264-9992 Fax: 403-265-3026
zargon@zargon.ca
www.zargon.ca
Ticker Symbol: ZAR
Company Type: Public
Profile: Crude petroleum, natural gas & natural gas liquids extraction

Craig H. Hansen, President/CEO
Brent C. Heagy, CFO & Vice-President, Finance
Daniel A. Roulston, Vice-President, Operations

ZCL Composites Inc.
6907 - 36 St.
Edmonton, AB T6B 2Z6
780-466-6648 Fax: 780-466-6126 800-661-8265
ir@zcl.com
www.zcl.com
Ticker Symbol: ZCL
Company Type: Public
Profile: Various oil & gas fields products; Manufacturers of fiberglass storage tanks

Venence G. Côté, President/CEO
Tony G. Barlott, Corporate Secretary & Vice-President, Finance

Printing & Publishing

Canadian Bank Note Company, Limited
145 Richmond Rd.
Ottawa, ON K1Z 1A1
613-722-3421 Fax: 613-722-2548
investorrelations@cbnco.com
www.cbnco.com
Ticker Symbol: CBK
Company Type: Public
Profile: Manufacturers of security & commercial printing

Douglas R. Arends, Chair/CEO
Ronald G. Arends, President/COO
Charles R. Lavoie, CFO & Exec. Vice-President
Judy Lonsdale, Director, Corporate Communications

Datamark Systems Group Inc.
2800, av Francis-Hughes
Laval, QC H7L 3Y7
450-663-8716 Fax: 450-663-7720
888-646-8176www.datamark-systems.com
Ticker Symbol: DMK
Company Type: Public
Profile: Manufacturers of manifold business forms, various, gravure & lithographic commercial printing

Jeffrey Zunenshine, President/Co-CEO
Luigi Fuoco, CFO

Hollinger Inc.
10 Toronto St.
Toronto, ON M5C 2B7
416-363-8721 Fax: 416-363-4187 www.hollingerinc.com
Ticker Symbol: HLG
Company Type: Public
Profile: Offices of holding companies; Information retrieval services; Media broadcasting; Publishing & printing of newspapers & periodicals

McGraw-Hill Ryerson Limited
300 Water St.
Whitby, ON L1N 9B6
905-430-5000 Fax: 905-430-5020 800-565-5758
gordond@mcgrawhill.ca
www.mcgrawhill.ca
Ticker Symbol: MHR
Company Type: Public
Profile: Manufacturers of books & miscellaneous publishing

John Dill, President/CEO
Nancy Gerrish, President, School Division
Gordon Dyer, Exec. Vice-President/CFO/Sec.-Treas.
Tim Walthert, Supervisor, Technology
Roy Skinner, Manager, Facilities

MDC Corporation Inc.
45 Hazelton Ave.
Toronto, ON M5R 2E3
416-960-9000 Fax: 416-960-9555 www.mdccorp.com
Ticker Symbol: MDZ
Company Type: Public
Profile: Manufacturers of lithographic & various commercial printing; Retailing in catalogue & mail-order houses; Commercial art & graphic design; Business consulting services; Public relations services; Management consulting services; Management services

Miles S. Nadal, CEO/Chair
Steven Berns, President/CFO

Metro Label Company Ltd.
74 Shorting Rd.
Toronto, ON M1S 3S4
416-292-6600 Fax: 416-332-2371
slal@metrolabel.com
www.invesprint.com
Ticker Symbol: INV
Company Type: Public
Profile: Manufacturers of lithographic, gravure & various other commercial printing, die-cut paper & paperboard & cardboard, labels

Sandeep Lal, Presiden/CEO
Pramod Gupta, CFO

PLM Group Ltd.
210 Duffield Dr.
Markham, ON L6G 1C9
416-848-8500 Fax: 416-848-8501
contact_us@plmgroup.com
www.plmgroup.com
Ticker Symbol: PGL
Company Type: Public
Profile: Manufacturers of lithographic, gravure & various commercial printing

Barry N. Pike, Chair/CEO
David J. Stuart, President/COO
Peter A. Bradley, CFO & Exec. Vice-President

Quebecor World Inc.
612, rue Saint-Jacques
Montréal, QC H3C 4M8
514-954-0101 Fax: 514-954-9624 800-567-7070
webmaster@quebecorworldinc.com
www.quebecorworldinc.com
Ticker Symbol: IQW
Company Type: Public
Profile: Manufacturers of lithographic, gravure & various commercial printing, paper mills & book printing

Pierre Karl Péladeau, President/CEO
Guy Trahan, President, Quebecor World Latin America
Claude Hélie, CFO & Exec. Vice-President
Jacques Mallette, Director, Corporate Communications
David Blair, Sr. Vice-President, Manufacturing, Environment & Technology

The Thomson Corporation
#2706, TD Bank Tower
Toronto, ON M5K 1A1
416-360-8700 Fax: 416-360-8812
generalinfo@thomson.com
www.thomson.com
Ticker Symbol: TOC
Company Type: Public
Profile: Integrated information solutions for business & professional customers; Provides information, software tools & applications to users in the fields of law, tax, accounting, financial services, higher education, reference information, corporate training & assessment, scientific research & healthcare; Seller of electronic databases & services

Richard J. Harrington, President/CEO
R.D. Daleo, Exec. Vice-President/CFO
Michael E. Wilens, Exec. Vice-President & Corporate Chief Technology & Operation

Torstar Corp.
#600, 1 Yonge St.
Toronto, ON M5E 1P9
416-869-4010 Fax: 416-869-4183
torstar@thestar.ca
www.torstar.com/corporate
Ticker Symbol: TS
Company Type: Public
Profile: Publishing & printing of newspapers & books; Various school & educational services

Robert Prichard, President/CEO
Robert J. Steacy, Vice-President, Finance

Real Estate

Anthem Works Ltd.
#500, 1111 Melville St.
Vancouver, BC V6E 2X5
604-689-3040 Fax: 604-689-5642
info@anthemproperties.com
www.anthemproperties.com
Ticker Symbol: ANT
Company Type: Public
Profile: Real estate agents & managers; Real estate land subdividers & developers

Eric H. Carlson, President/CEO
David Ferguson, CFO & Vice-President, Finance

Aspen Properties Ltd.
#1200, 833 - 4th Ave. SW
Calgary, AB T2P 3T5
403-216-2660 Fax: 403-216-2661
apl@aspenpropertiesltd.com
www.aspenpropertiesltd.com
Ticker Symbol: COP
Company Type: Private
Profile: Real estate agents & managers; Real estate land subdividers & developers; Nursing & personal care facilities

R. Scott Hutcheson, President/CEO & Director
Greg Guatto, COO
Veronica Bouvier, Sr. Vice-President, Accounting & Administration

Bentall Capital Limited Partnership
Four Bentall Centre
PO Box 49001, #1800, 1055 Dunsmuir St.
Vancouver, BC V7X 1B1
604-661-5000 Fax: 604-661-5055
info@bentall.com
www.bentall.com
Company Type: Private
Profile: Provides real estate investment management services, property development & merchant banking

Gary Whitelaw, President/CEO
Lawrence Neilson, CFO

Boardwalk Real Estate Income Trust
#200, 1501 - 1st St. SW
Calgary, AB T2R 0W1
403-531-9255 Fax: 403-531-9565
investor@bwalk.com
www.bwalk.com
Ticker Symbol: BEI
Company Type: Public
Profile: Real estate operators of apartment buildings; Real estate real estate agents & managers

Sam Kolias, President/CEO
Roberto A. Geremia, CFO & Sr. Vice-President, Finance
Michael Guyette, Vice-President, Technology

Boston Development Corp.
#211, 3521 - 8th St. East
Saskatoon, SK S7H 0W5
306-955-6012 Fax: 306-955-3446
neil@bostoncorp.com
www.bostoncorp.com
Ticker Symbol: BTN
Company Type: Private
Profile: Real estate operators of apartment buildings

Neil J. Evans, President/CEO
Basil A. Waslen, Secretary/CFO & Vice-President, Finance

BPO Properties Ltd.
Bay Wellington Tower, BCE Place
PO Box 770, #330, 181 Bay St.
Toronto, ON M5J 2T3
416-359-8555 Fax: 416-359-8596
info@bpoproperties.com
www.bpoproperties.com
Ticker Symbol: BPP
Company Type: Public
Profile: Offices of holding companies; Real estate operators of nonresidential buildings

Thomas F. Farley, President/CEO
Craig Laurie, CFO & Sr. Vice-President

British Columbia Buildings Corporation
3350 Douglas St.
Victoria, BC V8Z 3L1
250-952-8500 Fax: 250-952-8295
corpcomm@bcbc.bc.ca
www.bcbc.bc.ca
Company Type: Crown
Profile: Real estate operators of nonresidential buildings; General contractors of nonresidential buildings; Real estate agents & managers; Management services

John Heath, General Manager
Pat Marsh, Acting Controller & CFO

Brookfield Properties Corporation
BCE Pl.
PO Box 770, #330, 181 Bay St.
Toronto, ON M5J 2T3
416-369-2300 Fax: 416-369-2301 www.brookfieldproperties.com
Ticker Symbol: BPO
Company Type: Public
Profile: Real estate operators of nonresidential buildings; Real estate land subdividers & developers

Richard B. Clark, President/CEO
Craig Laurie, CFO & Sr. Vice-President

Cadillac Fairview Corporation Limited
20 Queen St. West, 5th Fl.
Toronto, ON M5H 3R4
416-598-8200 Fax: 416-598-8607 www.cadillacfairview.com
Company Type: Private
Profile: Real estate operators of nonresidential buildings; Real estate agents & managers; Real estate land subdividers & developers

Peter Sharpe, President/CEO
Ian C. MacKellar, CFO & Exec. Vice-President
Scot Adams, Sr. Vice-President/Chief Technology Officer

CML Global Capital Ltd.
#1200, 833 - 4th Ave. SW
Calgary, AB T2P 3T5
403-216-3850 Fax: 403-216-2661
info@cmlglobal.com
www.cmlglobal.com
Ticker Symbol: CNF
Company Type: Public
Profile: Offices of holding companies; Real estate land subdividers & developers; Automobile parking; Security brokers, dealers & flotation companies; Information retrieval services

Elizabeth C. Funk, President/CEO

Dundee Real Estate Investment Trust
State Street Financial Centre
#1600, 30 Adelaide St. East
Toronto, ON M5C 3H1
416-365-3535 Fax: 416-365-6565
info@dundeereit.com
www.dundeereit.com
Ticker Symbol: DUN
Company Type: Public
Profile: Real estate agents & managers; Real estate land subdividers & developers, operators of nonresidential buildings, operators of apartment buildings

Michael J. Cooper, President/CEO
J. Michael Knowlton, CFO & Exec. Vice-President

First Capital Realty Inc.
PO Box 219, #2820, 161 Bay St.
Toronto, ON M5J 2S1
416-504-4114 Fax: 416-941-1655 www.firstcapitalrealty.ca
Ticker Symbol: FCR
Company Type: Public
Profile: Real estate operators of nonresidential buildings

Dori J. Segal, President/CEO
Karen H. Weaver, CFO/Secretary

Genesis Land Development Corp.
2882 - 11 St. NE
Calgary, AB T2E 7S7
403-265-8079 Fax: 403-266-0746
genesis@genesisland.com
www.genesisland.com
Ticker Symbol: GDC
Company Type: Public
Profile: Real estate land subdividers & developers

Gobi Singh, Vice-Chair/President & CEO
Frank Devcich, CFO

Homburg Invest Inc.
#600, 1741 Brunswick St.
Halifax, NS B3J 3X8
902-468-3395 Fax: 902-468-2457 www.homburginvest.com
Ticker Symbol: HII
Company Type: Public
Profile: Real estate operators of nonresidential buildings; Real estate operators of apartment buildings

Richard Homburg, CEO/Chair & Director
James F. Miles, President
Ira D. MacInnis, CFO & Vice-President

Ivanhoe Cambridge
Centre CDP Capital
#C500, 1001, carré Victoria
Montréal, QC H2Z 2B5
514-841-7600 Fax: 514-841-7762 www.ivanhoecambridge.com
Company Type: Private
Profile: Property owners, managers & developers of shopping centres in urban areas

René Tremblay, President/CEO
Gervais Levasseur, CFO & Exec. Vice-President

Madison Pacific Properties Inc.
#305, 1788 West 5th Ave.
Vancouver, BC V6J 1P2
604-732-6540 Fax: 604-732-4427
madpac@telus.net
Ticker Symbol: MPC
Company Type: Public
Profile: Real estate operators of nonresidential buildings; Real estate operators of apartment buildings; Real estate land subdividers & developers

Raymond Heung, President/CEO
Doug Nordan, Vice-President, Development & Investment
Thor Olsen, Vice-President & Secretary

Mainstreet Equity Corp.
#100, 1122 - 8th Ave. SW
Calgary, AB T2P 1J5
403-215-6060 Fax: 403-266-8867
mainstreet@mainst.biz
www.mainst.biz
Ticker Symbol: MEQ
Company Type: Public
Profile: Real estate operators of apartment buildings; Real estate agents & managers

Bob Dhillon, President/CEO
Johnny Lam, CFO

Morguard Corporation
#1000, 55 City Centre Dr.
Mississauga, ON L5B 1M3
905-281-3800 Fax: 905-281-5890 www.morguard.com
Ticker Symbol: MRC
Company Type: Public
Profile: Offices of holding companies; Real estate operators of nonresidential buildings

K. Rai Sahi, Chair/CEO
Donald W. Turple, Chief Financial Officer

Northern Property Real Estate Investment Trust
#110, 6131 - 6th St. SE
Calgary, AB T2H 1L9
403-531-0720 Fax: 403-531-0727
info@npreit.com
www.npreit.com
Ticker Symbol: NPR
Company Type: Public

Northern Property Real Estate Investment Trust (continued)
Profile: Real estate operators of apartment buildings; Real estate operators of dwellings other than apartment buildings & nonresidential buildings; Real estate land subdividers & developers

B. James Britton, President/CEO
Debra Boyle, CFO

Oxford Properties Group Inc.
Oxford Tower
#1100, 130 Adelaide St. West
Toronto, ON M5H 3P5
416-865-8300 Fax: 416-868-3751 www.oxfordproperties.com
Company Type: Private
Profile: Commercial real estate investment firm; Owner & manager of a portfolio of office, retail, industrial & multi-family residential properties across Canada; Holder of interests in real estate assets abroad

Michael Latimer, President/CEO
Anna Kennedy, CFO & Exec. Vice-President

Pacific & Western Credit Corp.
#2002, 140 Fullarton St.
London, ON N6A 5P2
519-645-1919 Fax: 519-645-2060
TelM@pwbank.com
www.pwcorp.com
Ticker Symbol: PWC
Company Type: Public
Profile: Banking & financial services

David R. Taylor, President/CEO
Barry D. Walter, Sr. Vice-President & CFO
Tel Matrundola, Vice-President, Public & Government Relations

Revenue Properties Company Limited
#800, 55 City Centre Dr.
Mississauga, ON L5B 1M3
905-281-3800 Fax: 905-281-5890
pmiatello@revprop.com
www.revprop.com
Ticker Symbol: RPC
Company Type: Public
Profile: Real estate operators of nonresidential buildings, apartment buildings & other dwellings; Land subdividers and developers

Antony K. Stephens, President
Paul A. Miatello, CFO & Secretary

RioCan Real Estate Investment Trust
Exchange Tower
PO Box 378, #700, 130 King St. West
Toronto, ON M5X 1E2
416-866-3033 Fax: 416-866-3020
inquiries@riocan.com
www.riocan.com
Ticker Symbol: REI
Company Type: Public
Profile: Real estate investment trusts; Real estate operators of nonresidential buildings

Edward Sonshine, President/CEO
Robert Wolf, Vice-President/CFO

Sterling Centrecorp Inc.
#703, 123 Edward St.
Toronto, ON M5G 1E2
416-593-4093 Fax: 416-593-0656
info@sterlingcentrecorp.com
www.sterlingcentrecorp.com
Ticker Symbol: SCF
Company Type: Public
Profile: Acquisitions, development, re-development, management, leasing & related services for real estate assets on behalf of its investors, partners & third party clients

David Kosoy, Chair/CEO
Carol Taccone, CFO & Vice-President
Tyson Cloughlin, Manager, Information Technology

TGS North American Real Estate Investment Trust
#200, 1029 - 17 Ave. SW
Calgary, AB T2T 0A9
403-264-4310 Fax: 403-264-9824
investorrelations@tgsreit.com
www.tgsreit.com
Ticker Symbol: NAR
Company Type: Public
Profile: Real estate land subdividers & developers; Real estate operators of nonresidential buildings

Jeffrey Kohn, CEO
Todd R. Cook, CFO

Trizec Canada Inc.
BCE Place
PO Box 800, #3820, 181 Bay St.
Toronto, ON M5J 2T3
416-682-8600 Fax: 416-364-5491 877-239-7200
investor@trizeccanada.com
www.trizeccanada.com
Ticker Symbol: TZH
Company Type: Public
Profile: Offices of holding companies; Real estate operators of nonresidential buildings; Real estate operators of apartment buildings; Real estate land subdividers & developers

Peter Munk, CEO & Chair
Robert B. Wickham, President
Colin J. Chapin, Sr. Vice-President/CFO & Secretary

United Inc.
United Place
#200, 808 - 4 Ave. SW
Calgary, AB T2P 3E8
403-265-6180 Fax: 403-265-6270
inquiriescgy@unitedcommunities.com
www.unitedcommunities.com
Company Type: Private
Profile: Real estate operators of apartment buildings & other dwellings; Land subdividers & developers

Donald J. Douglas, President/CEO
B. Paul Simpson, CFO & Treasurer
Alix M. Halpen, Manager, Marketing

Wall Financial Corporation
#502, 1088 Burrard St.
Vancouver, BC V6Z 2R9
604-893-7131 Fax: 604-893-7179 **Ticker Symbol:** WFC
Company Type: Public
Profile: The corporation is engaged in real estate development and sales.

Bruno Wall, President & Treasurer
Stephanie Gibault, Vice-President, Finance
Darcee Wise, Vice-President, Secretary & Manager, Property

Wilmington Capital Management Inc.
BCE Place
PO Box 762, #300, 181 Bay St.
Toronto, ON M5J 2T3
416-867-9370 Fax: 416-363-2856 www.wilmingtoncapital.com
Ticker Symbol: WCM
Company Type: Public
Profile: Offices of holding companies; Real estate land subdividers & developers

Brian D. Lawson, President/CEO
Lisa W.F. Chu, Sec.-Treas.

Services, Miscellaneous

Alliance Atlantis Communications Inc.
#1500, 121 Bloor St. East
Toronto, ON M4W 3M5
416-967-1174 Fax: 416-960-0971
info@allianceatlantis.com
www.allianceatlantis.com
Ticker Symbol: AAC
Company Type: Public
Profile: Motion picture production & distribution for theatrical release & home entertainment; Operator of cable television channels; Producer & distributor of television entertainment

Phyllis N. Yaffe, CEO
David Lazzarato, Exec. Vice-President/CFO
Andrea Wood, Corporate Secretary & Exec. Vice-President, Business & Legal Affairs

Allied Hotel Properties Inc.
#300, 515 West Pender St.
Vancouver, BC V6B 6H5
604-669-5335 Fax: 604-682-8131
info@alliedhotels.com
www.alliedhotels.com
Ticker Symbol: AHP
Company Type: Public
Profile: Offices of holding companies; Hotels & motels

Peter Y.L. Eng, Chair/CEO
Michael Chan, President
John R. Ellen, Secretary/CFO

Amica Mature Lifestyles Inc.
1111 Melville St., 10th Fl.
Vancouver, BC V6E 3V6
604-608-6777 Fax: 604-608-6717
mail@amica.ca
www.amica.ca
Ticker Symbol: ACC
Company Type: Public
Profile: Residential care; Skilled nursing care facilities; Real estate operators of apartment buildings

Samir A. Manji, President/CEO & Chair
Renzo P. Barazzuol, Corporate Secretary/CFO
Fiona Dutta, Manager, Investor Relations

Arbor Memorial Services Inc.
#211, 2 Jane St.
Toronto, ON M6S 4W8
416-763-4531 Fax: 416-763-0381 www.arbormemorial.com
Ticker Symbol: ABO
Company Type: Public
Profile: Funeral service & crematories; Real estate cemetery subdividers & developers

Richard D. Innes, President/CEO
Brian D. Snowdon, CFO & Vice-President

Berwick Retirement Communities Ltd.
1162 Fort St.
Victoria, BC V8V 3K8
250-385-1505 Fax: 250-385-9851 866-397-5463
mail@berwickrc.com
www.berwickrc.com
Ticker Symbol: BWK
Company Type: Public
Profile: Residential care; Real estate operators of non-apartment building dwellings

Gordon A.C. Denford, President
Sundari Ware, CFO

Boyd Group Inc.
3570 Portage Ave.
Winnipeg, MB R3K 0Z8
204-895-1244 Fax: 204-895-1283
info@boydgroup.com
www.boydgroup.com
Ticker Symbol: BYD
Company Type: Public
Profile: Top, body & upholstery repair & paint shops; General automotive repair shops; Automotive glass replacement shops

Terry Smith, President/CEO
Dan Dott, Vice-President/CFO

Canada Post Corporation
2701 Riverside Dr.
Ottawa, ON K1A 0B1
613-734-8440 Fax: 613-734-6084 866-607-6301
service@canadapost.ca
www.canadapost.ca
Company Type: Crown
Profile: Canadian postal service

André Ouellet, President/CEO
Jacques Côté, Sr. Vice-President/CFO
Roy Keating, Acting General Manager, Computing & Communications

Canadian Commercial Corporation
50 O'Connor St., 11th Floor
Ottawa, ON K1A 0S6
613-996-0034 Fax: 613-995-2121 800-748-8191
info@ccc.ca
www.ccc.ca
Company Type: Crown
Profile: The organization is engaged in the administration of general economic programs.

John McBride, President
jmcbride@ccc.ca
Michel Houle, CFO & Vice-President, Risk & Finance
mhoule@ccc.ca
Marc Whittingham, Vice-President, Strategy & Organizational Development

MAJOR CANADIAN COMPANIES

ClubLink Corporation
15675 Dufferin St.
King City, ON L7B 1K5
905-841-3730 Fax: 905-841-1134
invest@clublink.ca
www.clublink.ca
Ticker Symbol: LNK
Company Type: Public
Profile: Membership sports & recreation clubs; Public golf courses; Hotels & motels; Real estate land subdividers & developers

Robert Poile, President/CEO
Robert Visentin, CFO

CML Healthcare Inc.
6560 Kennedy Rd.
Mississauga, ON L5T 2X4
905-565-0043 Fax: 905-565-1776
lab@canmedlab.com
www.cmlhealthcare.com
Ticker Symbol: CLC
Company Type: Public
Profile: Medical laboratories; Commercial physical & biological research; Management services

John D. Mull, President/CEO & Chair
Tom Weber, CFO

Compass Group Canada
#400, 5560 Explorer Dr.
Mississauga, ON L4W 5M3
905-568-4636
info@compass-canada.com
www.compass-canada.com
Company Type: Private
Profile: Catering & retail eating places

Jack MacDonald, CEO
Steve Kelly, CFO

Extendicare Inc.
3000 Steeles Ave. East
Markham, ON L3R 9W2
905-470-4000 Fax: 905-470-5588
lsilva@extendicare.com
www.extendicare.com
Ticker Symbol: EXE
Company Type: Public
Profile: Offices of holding companies; Nursing, personal care, specialty outpatient, skilled nursing facilities; Home health care services; Management consulting services; Wholesalers of medical, dental, hospital equipment & supplies

Mel Rhinelander, President/CEO
Richard Bertrand, CFO & Vice-President, Finance

Fairmont Hotels & Resorts Inc.
Canadian Pacific Tower
#1600, 100 Wellington St. West
Toronto, ON M5K 1B7
416-874-2600 Fax: 416-874-2601
investor@fairmont.com
www.fairmont.com
Ticker Symbol: FHR
Company Type: Public
Profile: Hotels & motels; Real estate operators of nonresidential buildings

William R. Fatt, CEO
Peter C. Godsoe, Chair
John Carnella, Exec. Vice-President/CFO

FirstService Corporation
#4000, 1140 Bay St.
Toronto, ON M5S 2B4
416-960-9500 Fax: 416-960-5333 www.firstservice.com
Ticker Symbol: FSV
Company Type: Public
Profile: Residential property management; Commercial real estate; Integrated security services; Property improvement services; Business services

Jay S. Hennick, CEO
D. Scott Patterson, President/COO
John B. Friedrichsen, CFO & Sr. Vice-President

Four Seasons Hotels Inc.
1165 Leslie St.
Toronto, ON M3C 2K8
416-449-1750 Fax: 416-441-4374
investors@fourseasons.com
www.fourseasons.com
Ticker Symbol: FSH
Company Type: Public
Profile: Hotels & motels

Isadore Sharp, Chair/CEO
Wolf M. Mengst, President
John Davison, CFO/Exec. Vice-President, Finance
Michael Hwu, Chief Technology Officer/Chief Information Officer

Great Canadian Gaming Corporation
#200, 13775 Commerce Pkwy.
Richmond, BC V6V 2V4
604-303-1000 Fax: 604-279-8605
hblank@gcgaming.com
www.gcgaming.com
Ticker Symbol: GCD
Company Type: Public
Profile: Coin-operated amusement devices; Various amusement & recreation services

Ross J. McLeod, Chair/CEO/Director
Anthony R. Martin, President/COO

Helix Hearing Care of America Corp.
#203, 815 Taylor Creek Dr.
Cumberland, ON K1C 1T1
613-824-1154 Fax: 613-824-1109
info@helixhca.com
www.helixhca.com
Ticker Symbol: HCA
Company Type: Public
Profile: Health care & hearing aids; Offices & clinics of health practitioners

Stephen J. Hansbrough, CEO, HearUSA, Inc.
Gino Chouinard, CFO, HearUSA, Inc.

IMI International Medical Innovations Inc
#300, 4211 Yonge St.
Toronto, ON M2P 2A9
416-222-3449 Fax: 416-222-4533
info@imimedical.com
www.imimedical.com
Ticker Symbol: IMI
Company Type: Public
Profile: Acquires & develops technologies for non-invasive predictive medical products

Brent Norton, President/CEO & Director
R.G. Hosking, CFO & Vice-President
Tim Currie, Director, Business Development
Michael Evelegh, Exec. Vice-President, Clinical & Regulatory Affairs

Intrawest Corporation
#800, 200 Burrard St.
Vancouver, BC V6C 3L6
604-669-9777 Fax: 604-669-0605
intrainfo@intrawest.com
www.intrawest.com
Ticker Symbol: ITW
Company Type: Public
Profile: Hotels & motels; Real estate operators of apartment buildings & nonresidential buildings; Real estate agents & managers; Various amusement & recreation services

Joe S. Houssian, President/CEO & Chair
Daniel O. Jarvis, Chief Corporate Development Officer
Hugh R. Smythe, President, Mountain Operations
John E. Currie, CFO

Lions Gate Entertainment Corp.
#2200, 1055 West Hastings St.
Vancouver, BC V6E 2E9
604-983-5555 Fax: 604-983-5554 877-848-3866
feedback@lgecorp.com
www.lionsgate.com
Ticker Symbol: LGF
Company Type: Public
Profile: Motion picture & video tape production; Services allied to motion picture production; Television broadcasting stations

Jon Feltheimer, CEO
Jim Keegan, CFO

Lorus Therapeutics Inc.
2 Meridian Rd.
Toronto, ON M9W 4Z7
416-798-1200 Fax: 416-798-2200
info@lorusthera.com
www.lorusthera.com
Ticker Symbol: LOR
Company Type: Public
Profile: The organization is engaged in cancer research.

Aiping H. Young, President/CEO
ahyoung@lorusthera.com

Mont Saint-Sauveur International Inc.
350, rue Saint-Denis
Saint-Sauveur, QC J0R 1R3
450-227-4671 Fax: 450-227-2067 800-363-2426
webmaster@montsaintsaveur.com
www.montsaintsaveur.com
Ticker Symbol: MSX
Company Type: Public
Profile: Hotels & motels; Amusement parks; Real estate operators of apartment buildings; Retailing in eating places, alcoholic beverage drinking places & family clothing stores; General contractors of single family houses; Real estate agents & managers

Louis Dufour, Chair/CEO
Chantal Nadeau, President/COO
Louis P. Hébert, Exec. Vice-President, Finance

Peace Arch Entertainment Group Inc.
#650, 1867 Yonge St.
Toronto, ON M4S 1Y5
416-783-8383 Fax: 416-783-8384 888-588-3608
info@peacearch.com
www.peacearch.com
Ticker Symbol: PAE
Company Type: Public
Profile: Offices of holding companies; Motion picture & video tape production

Gary Howsam, President/CEO & Chair
Mara Di Pasquale, CFO/COO

Royal Canadian Mint
320 Sussex Dr.
Ottawa, ON K1A 0G8
613-993-3500 Fax: 613-952-8342 800-267-1871
info@mint.ca
www.rcmint.ca
Company Type: Crown
Profile: Public finance, taxation & monetary policy; Manufacturers of platemaking & related services, primary smelting & refining of nonferrous metals

David Dingwall, President/CEO
Richard Neville, Administrator, Finance
Daniel Blanchette, Manager, Information Technology
Danette Olsheskie, Officer, Occupational Safety

Royal Host Real Estate Investment Trust
#103, 808 - 42 Ave. SE
Calgary, AB T2G 1Y9
403-259-9800 Fax: 403-259-8580
investorinfo@royalhost.com
www.royalhost.com
Ticker Symbol: RYL
Company Type: Public
Profile: Real estate investment trusts; Hotels & motels; Patent owners & lessors

Greg Royer, President/CEO
Wayne King, CFO

Service Corporation International Canada Inc.
United Kingdom Bldg.
#950, 409 Granville St.
Vancouver, BC V6C 1T2
604-806-4100 Fax: 604-806-4111 www.sci-corp.com
Company Type: Private
Profile: Network of funeral homes, crematoria & cemetaries

SMK Speedy International Inc.
#1100, 365 Bloor St. East
Toronto, ON M4W 3M7
416-961-1133 Fax: 416-960-7916 www.speedy.com
Ticker Symbol: SMK
Company Type: Public

SMK Speedy International Inc. (continued)
Profile: Automotive exhaust system repair shops; Automotive repair shops

Dorsy Asplund, President/CEO
Mary Jane Allen, CFO

Société des loteries du Québec
500, rue Sherbrooke ouest
Montréal, QC H3A 3G6
514-282-8000 Fax: 514-873-8999
service_clientele@loto-quebec.com
www.loto-quebec.com
Company Type: Crown
Profile: Oversees games of chance & gambling; Operates & monitors casino, video lottery terminal network

Alain Cousineau, President/CEO & Chair
Gilles Dufour, Sr. Vice-President, Financial Affairs
Pierre Bibeau, Corporate Sr. Vice-President, Communications & Public Affairs

Technicolor Creative Services Canada, Inc.
#300, 2101, rue Sainte-Catherine ouest
Montréal, QC H3H 1M6
514-939-5060 Fax: 514-939-5070 www.technicolor.com
Company Type: Public
Profile: Full port production, transfer, editing, visual effects, lab service & audio

Lanny Raimondo, CEO
Dave Elliott, President, Strategic Relations

TLC Vision Corporation
#100, 5280 Solar Dr.
Mississauga, ON L4W 5M8
800-852-1033 Fax: 905-602-2025 877-852-2020
tlc.info@tlcvision.com
www.tlcvision.com
Ticker Symbol: TLC
Company Type: Public
Profile: Offices & clinics of doctors of medicine

Steve Rasche, CFO
James C. Wachtman, President/CEO
Stephen Kilmer, Director, Investor Relations
Henry Lynn, Exec. Vice-President, Information Systems

Waste Services Inc.
#601, 1122 International Blvd.
Burlington, ON L7L 6Z8
905-319-1237 Fax: 905-319-9050 www.wasteservicesinc.com
Ticker Symbol: WSII
Company Type: Public
Profile: Integrated solid waste services company, providing collection, transfer, landfill disposal & recycling services for commercial, industrial & residential customers

David Sutherland-Yoest, Chair/CEO
Fax: 905-319-6045, dsy@wasteservicesinc.com
Charles A. Wilcox, President/COO
561-237-3400, Fax: 561-237-3491, cwilcox@wasteservicesinc.com
Edwin Johnson, Exec. Vice-President/CFO
561-237-3400, Fax: 561-237-3491, ejohnson@wasteservicesinc.com

Steel & Metal

ADF Group Inc.
300, rue Henry-Bessemer
Terrebonne, QC J6Y 1T3
450-965-1911 Fax: 450-965-8558 800-263-7560
infos@adfgroup.com
www.adfgroup.com
Ticker Symbol: DRX
Company Type: Public
Profile: Manufacturers of fabricated structural metal, steel works, blast furnaces, coke ovens, rolling mills; Engineering services; Wholesalers of metals service centers & offices

Jean Paschini, Chair/CEO
Pierre Paschini, President/COO
Louis Potvin, CFO
Kathleen Ryffranck, Director, Public Relations

Alcan Inc.
1188 Sherbrook St.
Montréal, QC H3A 3G2
514-848-8000 Fax: 514-848-8115
media.relations@alcan.com
www.alcan.com
Ticker Symbol: AL
Company Type: Public
Profile: Manufacturers of aluminum sheet, plate & foil, aluminum rolling & drawing, primary production of aluminum, aluminum foundries, various industrial inorganic chemicals; Metal mining of miscellaneous metal ores

Travis Engen, President/CEO
Michael Hanley, CFO

Algoma Steel Inc.
105 West St.
Sault Ste Marie, ON P6A 7B4
705-945-2351 Fax: 705-945-2203 www.algoma.com
Ticker Symbol: AGA
Company Type: Public
Profile: The company manufactures steel works, blast furnaces, coke ovens, rolling mills, sheet & plate.

Denis Turcotte, President/CEO
Daniel J. Ardila, CFO & Vice-President, Finance

Babcock & Wilcox Canada, Ltd.
581 Coronation Blvd.
Cambridge, ON N1R 5V3
519-621-2130 Fax: 519-622-7352 www.babcock.com/bwc
Company Type: Private
Profile: Manufacturers of fabricated plate work

Richard E. Reimels, President
Ronald E. Van Alstyne, Controller
Chris Sellers, Manager, Public Relations & Communications

Canam Group Inc.
#500, 11505 - 1e av
Saint-Georges, QC G5Y 7X3
418-228-8031 Fax: 418-228-1750
info@canammanac.com
www.canammanac.com
Ticker Symbol: CAM
Company Type: Public
Profile: Manufacturers of fabricated structural metal, strip & bars, building systems, Sandwich Plate System (SPS)

Marcel Dutil, CEO & Chair
Marc Dutil, President/COO
Charles Pinel, CFO & Vice-President

Crown Cork & Seal Canada Inc.
7900 Keele St.
Concord, ON L4K 2A3
905-669-1401 www.crowncork.com
Company Type: Private
Profile: Manufacturers of metal cans, crowns & closures

John W. Conway, President/CEO & Chair
Alan W. Rutherford, CFO & Exec. Vice-President, Finance
Michael F. Dunleavy, Vice-President, Corporate Affairs & Public Relations
James E. Armstrong, Regional Manager, Environment, Health & Safety

Dofasco Inc.
PO Box 2460, 1330 Burlington St. East
Hamilton, ON L8N 3J5
905-544-3761 Fax: 905-545-3236 800-363-2726
general@dofasco.ca
www.dofasco.ca
Ticker Symbol: DFS
Company Type: Public
Profile: Manufacturers of steel works, blast furnaces, coke ovens, rolling mills, cold-rolled steel sheet, strip & bars, steel pipe & tubes

Jacques Chabanier, President/CEO
Walter Bilenki, Vice-President, Finance
Daniel Janczak, Vice-President, Technology

Flex-N-Gate Corporation Canada
538 Blanchard Park Dr.
Tecumseh, ON N8N 2L9
519-727-3931
mchadwick@flexngate.com
www.flex-n-gate.com
Company Type: Private
Profile: Supplier of truck bumpers & accessories

Shahid Khan, President/CEO

Foster Wheeler Ltd.
#450, 7330 Fisher St. SE
Calgary, AB T2H 2H8
403-255-3447 Fax: 403-259-4558
rcampbell@fwfhl.com
www.fwc.com
Company Type: Private
Profile: Manufacturers of fabricated plate work, & general industrial machinery & equipment

Raymond J. Milchovich, President/CEO & Chair

Garneau Inc.
2003 - 5 St.
Nisku, AB T9E 7X4
780-955-2396 Fax: 780-955-7715
darlenek@garneau-inc.com
www.garneau-inc.com
Ticker Symbol: GAR
Company Type: Public
Profile: Manufacturers of coating, engraving & allied services, various fabricated metal products

Glen Garneau, President/CEO & Chair
Frank Deys, CFO
Chris Garneau, Vice-President, Manufacturing

Gerdau Ameristeel Corporation
Hopkins St. South
Whitby, ON L1N 5T1
905-668-3535 Fax: 905-665-3740 www.gerdauameristeel.com
Ticker Symbol: GNA.TO
Company Type: Public
Profile: Manufacturers of steel products, blast furnaces, coke ovens, rolling mills; Wholesalers in metals service centers & offices

Phillip E. Casey, Chair/CEO
Mario Longhi, President
Tom J. Landa, Vice-President/CFO
Mike Christy, Vice-President, Procurement & Logistics
Roger Paiva, Vice-President, Whitby Mill
Matthew C. Yeatman, Vice-President, Canadian Recycling Operations

Groupe Bocenor inc
274, rue Duchesnay
Sainte-Marie, QC G6E 3C2
418-387-7723 Fax: 418-387-3904
corpo@bocenor.com
www.bocenor.com
Ticker Symbol: GBO
Company Type: Public
Profile: Manufacturers of metal doors, sash, frames, molding & trim, millwork, windows; Retail in lumber & other building materials dealers, hardware stores

Dennis Wood, Interim President/CEO
Michel Harvey, Vice-President, Finance

H. Paulin & Co., Limited
55 Milne Ave.
Toronto, ON M1L 4N3
416-694-3351 Fax: 416-694-1869 800-268-4000
paulin@hpaulin.com
www.hpaulin.com
Ticker Symbol: PAP
Company Type: Public
Profile: Manufacturers of bolts, nuts, screws, rivets, washers, valves & pipe fittings, various hardware; Wholesalers of motor vehicle supplies & new parts, industrial supplies; Collection of end cuts & short lengths for recycling

Tim Weatherbie, Chief Technology Officer
Richard C. Paulin, President
Carl Krause, Treasurer

Harris Steel Group Inc.
#404, 4120 Yonge St.
Toronto, ON M2P 2B8
416-590-9549 Fax: 416-590-9560
info@harrissteel.com
www.harrissteel.com
Ticker Symbol: HSG
Company Type: Public
Profile: Fabrication & processing steel training business; installation of steel products

John Harris, Chair/CEO
F. Wesley Colling, President, Harris Rebar

MAJOR CANADIAN COMPANIES

Douglas Deighton, Vice-President/CFO

IPSCO Inc.
PO Box 1670, Armour Rd.
Regina, SK S4P 3C7
306-924-7700 Fax: 306-924-7500
kbrossart@ipsco.com
www.ipsco.com
Ticker Symbol: IPS
Company Type: Public
Profile: Manufacturers of steel pipe & tubes, steel works, blast furnaces, coke ovens, rolling mills; Wholesalers in metals service centers & offices

David Sutherland, President/CEO
Vicki Avril, CFO & Sr. Vice-President
Joseph Russo, Sr. Vice-President/Chief Technical Officer

ITW Canada
120 Travail Rd.
Markham, ON L3S 3J1
800-387-9692
info@itwconstruction.ca
www.itw.com
Company Type: Private
Profile: Offices of holding companies; Manufacturers of various fabricated metal products; Wholesalers of industrial supplies, industrial machinery & equipment, chemicals & allied products

Martinrea International Inc.
30 Aviva Park Dr.
Vaughan, ON L4L 9C7
416-749-0314 Fax: 905-264-2937
info@martinrea.com
www.martinrea.com
Ticker Symbol: MRE
Company Type: Public
Profile: Manufacturers of fabricated structural metal, fabricated plate work, automotive stampings; Engineering services

Fred Jaekel, President/CEO
Natale Rea, President, Automotive Division
Nick Orlando, CFO & Exec. Vice-President

Meridian Technologies Inc.
Centre Tower, Clarica Centre
#2902, 3300 Bloor St. West
Toronto, ON M8X 2X3
416-922-2050 Fax: 416-922-4282 www.meridian-mag.com
Company Type: Private
Profile: Manufacturers of motor vehicle parts & accessories, & magnesium & nonferrous die castings

Paolo Maccario, President/CEO
Patrick Rooke, CFO
Len Miller, Vice-President, Technology

Novamerican Steel Inc.
6001, rue Irwin
Montréal, QC H8N 1A1
514-335-6682 Fax: 514-335-2415
therese_bilodeau@novamerican.ca
www.novamerican.com
Ticker Symbol: TONS
Company Type: Public
Profile: Offices of holding companies; Manufacturers of steel works, blast furnaces, coke ovens, rolling mills, steel pipe & tubes

D. Bryan Jones, CEO/Chair
Scott Jones, President
Christopher H. Pickwoad, CFO & Exec. Vice-President

Prudential Steel Ltd.
#1800, 140 - 4th Ave. SW
Calgary, AB T2P 3N3
403-267-0300 Fax: 403-265-3426 800-661-1050
info@prudentialsteel.com
www.prudentialsteel.com
Ticker Symbol: MAV
Company Type: Public
Profile: Manufacturers of fabricated pipe & pipe fittings; Wholesalers in metals service centres & offices

President Bob, Lee
Fred Rea, Vice-President & CFO
Grant Hennenberg, Supervisor, Safety Services

QIT-Fer & Titane inc
1625, rue Marie-Victorin
Sorel-Tracy, QC J3R 1M6
450-746-3000 Fax: 450-746-4438
info@qit.com
www.qit.com
Company Type: Private
Profile: Manufacturers of steel works, blast furnaces & coke ovens, rolling mills

Pat Fiore, President
Rolland Morier, Vice-President, Finance

Russel Metals Inc.
#210, 1900 Minnesota Ct.
Mississauga, ON L5N 3C9
905-819-7777 Fax: 905-819-7409
info@russelmetals.com
www.russelmetals.com
Ticker Symbol: RUS
Company Type: Public
Profile: Offices of holding companies; Manufacturers of cold-rolled steel sheet, strip & bars; Wholesalers of metals service centers & offices

Edward M. Siegel Jr, President/CEO
Brian R. Hedges, CFO & Exec. Vice-President

Samuel Manu-Tech Inc.
#1500, 185 The West Mall
Toronto, ON M9C 5L5
416-626-2190 Fax: 416-626-5969 www.samuelmanutech.com
Ticker Symbol: SMT
Company Type: Public
Profile: Manufacturer of industrial products including a wide range of steel, plastic & related products

John Morton, President/COO
John D. Amodeo, CFO & Vice-President
Douglas R. Woodward, Vice-President, Information Technology

Slater Steel Inc.
Markborough Place
#202, 6711 Mississauga Rd.
Mississauga, ON L5N 2W3
905-567-1822 Fax: 905-567-0946
info@slatersteel.com
www.slater.com
Ticker Symbol: SSI
Company Type: Private
Profile: Manufacturers of steel works, blast furnaces, coke ovens, rolling mills, cold-rolled steel sheet, strip & bars, metal doors, sash, frames, molding & trim, special dies & tools, die sets, jigs & fixtures, molds

Paul Kelly, President/CEO
Richard P. Rogers, CFO & Sr. Vice-President, Finance

Spectra Premium Industries Inc.
1421, rue Ampère
Boucherville, QC J4B 5Z5
450-641-3090 Fax: 450-641-4570 www.spectrapremium.com
Ticker Symbol: SPD
Company Type: Public
Profile: Manufacturers of fabricated plate work, motor vehicle parts & accessories; Wholesalers in motor vehicle supplies & new parts

Jacques Mombleau, President/CEO
Denis Poirier, CFO & Exec. Vice-President

Stelco Inc.
PO Box 2030, Hamilton, ON L8N 3T1
905-528-2511 Fax: 905-308-7002 800-263-9305
info@stelco.ca
www.stelco.com
Ticker Symbol: STE
Company Type: Public
Profile: Manufacturers of steel works, blast furnaces, coke ovens, rolling mills, hot & cold-rolled steel sheet, bars, steel pipe & tubes, wire & wire products

Rodney B. Mott, President/CEO
J. Kenneth Rutherford, CFO

Timminco Limited
Sun Life Financial Tower
#2401, 150 King St. West
Toronto, ON M5H 1J9
416-364-5171 Fax: 416-364-3451
info@timminco.com
www.timminco.com
Ticker Symbol: TIM
Company Type: Public
Profile: Manufacturers of rolling, drawing & extruding of nonferrous metals, secondary smelting & refining of nonferrous metals; Wholesalers of metals service centers & offices

Charles H. Entrekin, President/CEO
George Chiarucci, CFO & Vice-President, Finance

Tree Island Industries Ltd.
PO Box 50 Main, New Westminster, BC V3L 4Y1
604-524-3744 Fax: 604-523-2362
sales@treeisland.com
www.treeisland.com
Company Type: Private
Profile: Manufacturers of steelwire drawing, steel nails, spikes & miscellaneous fabricated wire products

Theodore A. Leja, President/CEO
Garry Flesher, Vice-President, Finance

Velan Inc.
7007, ch de la Côte-de-Liesse
Montréal, QC H4T 1G2
514-748-7743 Fax: 514-748-8635
sales@velan.com
www.velan.com
Ticker Symbol: VLN
Company Type: Public
Profile: Manufacturers of valves & pipe fittings; Wholesalers of industrial supplies

A.K. Velan, CEO
Tom C. Velan, President
Stephen R. Farrell, CFO & Exec. Vice-President, Finance

Textiles, Apparel & Leather

Algo Group Inc.
5555, rue Cypihot
Montréal, QC H4S 1R3
514-382-1240 Fax: 514-385-0163 www.algo.com
Ticker Symbol: AO
Company Type: Public
Profile: Manufacturers of various men's & boys' clothing, women's, misses' & juniors' dresses, misses' & juniors' suits, skirts, coats & various outerwear; Manufacturers of broadwoven fabric mills, manmade fiber & silk

Dan Elituv, President/CEO & Chair
Sol Chankowsky, CFO & Exec. Vice-President

Beaulieu Canada Company
335, Roxton
Acton Vale, QC J0H 1A0
450-546-5000 Fax: 450-546-5027
800-853-9048www.beaulieucanada.ca
Company Type: Private
Profile: Manufacture & distribution of broadloom carpets

François Bedard, President
Benoit Leclair, Corporate Controller

CFS International Inc.
1951 Leslie St.
Toronto, ON M3B 2M3
416-385-2882 Fax: 416-385-7135
inquiry@ports1961.com
Ticker Symbol: CFY
Company Type: Public
Profile: Manufacturers of: various men's & boys' clothing; women's, misses', & juniors' dresses, suits, skirts & coats; men's & boys' clothing & furnishings; Wholesalers of women's, children's, infants' clothing/accessories, drugs, drug proprietaries & druggists' sundries; Retailing in men's & boys' clothing & accessory stores, & women's clothing stores

Alfred K.T. Chan, President/CEO
Alec Lam, Director, Finance

Consoltex Inc.
8555, rte Transcanadienne
Saint-Laurent, QC H4S 1Z6
514-333-8800 Fax: 514-335-7013 800-736-2743
solutions@consoltex.com
www.consoltex.com
Company Type: Public
Profile: Offices of holding companies; Manufacturers of circular weft, knit fabric mills; Finishers of broadwoven fabrics of manmade fiber & silk; Wholesalers of piece goods, notions & other dry goods

Marcel Thibault, President

Danier Leather Inc.
2650 St Clair Ave. West
Toronto, ON M6N 1M2
416-762-8175 Fax: 416-762-4570 www.danier.com
Ticker Symbol: DL
Company Type: Public
Profile: Manufacturers of leather & sheepskin-lined clothing, leather gloves & mittens, personal leather goods; Retailing luggage & leather goods stores

J. Wortsman, President/CEO
Bryan Tatoff, CFO/Sr. Vice-President & Secretary
Philip Cutter, Chief Information Officer & Vice-President, Information Technology

Gildan Activewear Inc.
725, montée de Liesse
Montréal, QC H4T 1P5
514-735-2023 Fax: 514-735-6810 866-755-2023
info@gildan.com
www.gildan.com
Ticker Symbol: GIL
Company Type: Public
Profile: Manufacturer & marketer of activewear for wholesale in the Canadian, U.S., European & other international markets; Products include T-shirts, placket collar sport shirts & sweatshirts

Glenn J. Chamandy, President/CEO
Laurence G. Sellyn, CFO & Exec. Vice-President, Finance
Gregg Thompson, Exec. Vice-President, Corporate Controller & Chief Informatio
Don Luby, Vice-President, Information Technologies

Intertape Polymer Group Inc.
999 Cavendish Blvd. 2nd Fl.
Montréal, QC H4M 2X5
514-731-7591 Fax: 514-731-5039
info@intertapeipg.com
www.intertapepolymer.com
Ticker Symbol: ITP
Company Type: Public
Profile: Manufacturers of coated fabrics, not rubberized, packaging paper & plastics film, coated & laminated

Melbourne F. Yull, Chair/CEO
Jim Bob Carpenter, President, Woven Products Procurement
Andrew M. Archibald, CFO
James A. Jackson, Vice-President/Chief Information Officer

Le Château Inc.
5695 Ferrier St.
Montreal, QC H4P 1N1
514-738-7000 Fax: 514-738-3670 888-577-7419
comments@lechateau.ca
www.lechateau.ca
Ticker Symbol: CTU
Company Type: Public
Profile: Manufacturers of: women's, misses' & juniors' blouses & shirts, dresses; various men's & boys' clothing; Retailing women's clothing stores, women's accessory & specialty stores, men's & boys' clothing & accessory stores, & shoe stores

Herschel H. Segal, Chair/CEO
Emilia Di Raddo, President & Secretary

Transportation & Travel

Air Canada
7373, boul de la Côte-Vertu ouest
Montréal, QC H4S 1Z3
514-422-5000 Fax: 514-422-5789 www.aircanada.ca
Ticker Symbol: AC
Company Type: Public
Profile: Scheduled air transportation; Travel agencies; Arrangement of transportation of freight & cargo

Lise Fournel, Sr. Vice-President, E-Commerce
Joseph D. Randell, President, Air Canada Jazz
Joshua Koshy, CFO & Exec. Vice-President
Duncan Dee, Sr. Vice-President, Corporate Affairs

Algoma Central Corporation
#600, 63 Church St.
St Catharines, ON L2R 3C4
905-687-7850 Fax: 905-687-7882
gdwight@algonet.com
www.algonet.com
Ticker Symbol: ALC
Company Type: Public
Profile: Offices of holding companies; Freight transportation on the Great Lakes-St. Lawrence Seaway; Real estate operators of nonresidential buildings; Real estate land subdividers & developers; Engineering services; Manufacturers in ship building & repairing

T.S. Dool, President/CEO
G.D. Wight, Vice-President, Finance
Robert Cook, Director, Information Services
Kevin Reid, Director, Safety

AMJ Campbell Inc.
1445 Courtneypark Dr.
Mississauga, ON L5T 2E3
905-795-3785 Fax: 905-670-3787 www.amjcampbell.com
Ticker Symbol: AMJ
Company Type: Public
Profile: Local trucking with storage; Trucking, except local

Bruce Bowser, President/CEO
Richard Smith, CFO

Atlas Cold Storage Income Trust
5255 Yonge St.
Toronto, ON M2N 5P8
416-512-2352 Fax: 416-512-2353 888-642-3333
inquiries@atlascold.com
www.atlascold.com
Ticker Symbol: FZR
Company Type: Public
Profile: Refrigerated warehousing & storage

J. David Williamson, President/CEO
Kevin Glass, Sr. Vice-President & CFO
Robert Lockie, Vice-President, Information Technology Operations

Bombardier Inc.
800, boul René-Lévesque ouest
Montréal, QC H3B 1Y8
514-861-9481 Fax: 514-861-7053 www.bombardier.com
Ticker Symbol: BBD
Company Type: Public
Profile: Manufacturers of railroad equipment, aircraft, aircraft engines & engine parts, aircraft parts & auxiliary equipment, various transportation equipment; Personal credit institutions; Real estate land subdividers & developers

Laurent Beaudoin, Chair/CEO
Pierre Beaudoin, President/COO, Bombardier Aerospace
Pierre Alary, Sr. Vice-President/CFO

British Columbia Railway Company
#400, 221 West Esplanade Ave
North Vancouver, BC V7M 3J3
604-678-4735 Fax: 604-678-4736 www.bcrco.com
Company Type: Crown
Profile: Offices of holding companies; Real estate operators of nonresidential buildings; Real estate agents & managers; Railroads, line-haul operating; Marine cargo handling

Kevin Mahoney, President/CEO
Michael Kaye, CFO & Vice-President, Finance

Canadian National Railway Company
935, rue de la Gauchetière ouest
Montréal, QC H3B 2M9
514-399-0052 Fax: 514-399-5985 www.cn.ca
Ticker Symbol: CNR
Company Type: Public
Profile: Railroads & line-haul operating; Railroad switching & terminal establishments

E. Hunter Harrison, President/CEO
Claude Mongeau, CFO & Exec. Vice-President
Fred Grigsby, Sr. Vice-President & Chief Information Officer
J.V. Raymond Cyr, Chair, Environment, Safety & Security Committee

Canadian Pacific Railway Limited
#500, 401 - 9th Ave. SW
Calgary, AB T2P 4Z4
403-319-7000
investor@cpr.ca
www.cpr.ca
Ticker Symbol: CP
Company Type: Public
Profile: Transcontinental carrier; Rail network operates in Canada & the USA

Fred J. Green, CEO
Michael R. Lambert, Exec. Vice-President/CFO
Allen H. Borak, Vice-President, Information Services

CHC Helicopter Corporation
4740 Agar Dr.
Richmond, BC V7B 1A3
604-276-7500
communications@chc.ca
www.chc.ca
Ticker Symbol: FLY
Company Type: Public
Profile: Nonscheduled & scheduled air transportation; Airports, flying fields & airport terminal services; Vocational schools

Sylvain A. Allard, CEO
Jo Mark Zurel, CFO & Sr. Vice-President

Contrans Income Fund
PO Box 1210, 1179 Ridgeway Rd.
Woodstock, ON N4S 8P6
519-421-4600 Fax: 519-539-9220
info@contrans.ca
www.contrans.ca
Ticker Symbol: CSS
Company Type: Public
Profile: Offices of holding companies; Long-distance trucking

Stan G. Dunford, Chair/CEO
Gregory W. Rumble, President/COO
James S. Clark, CFO & Vice-President, Finance
Kim Barnes, Manager, Management Information Systems

CSL Group Inc.
759, carré Victoria
Montréal, QC H2Y 2K3
514-982-3800 Fax: 514-982-3802
ships@cslmtl.com
www.thecslgroup.ca
Company Type: Private
Profile: Specializes in bulk transportation & self-loading technology

Meredith (Sam) Hayes, President/CEO
Pierre Richard, Vice-President, Finance & Administration

Dynetek Industries Ltd.
4410 - 46 Ave. SE
Calgary, AB T2B 3N7
403-720-0262 Fax: 403-720-0263
invest@dynetek.com
www.dynetek.com
Ticker Symbol: DNK
Company Type: Public
Profile: Manufacturers of cylinders, fuel cell storage systems

Robb D. Thompson, President/CEO
Karen Y. Minton, Vice-President, Finance & Administration

General Motors of Canada Limited
Main Mailing Dept. CA1-002-002
1908 Colonel Sam Dr.
Oshawa, ON L1H 8P7
905-644-5000 Fax: 905-643-830
800-263-3777www.gmcanada.com
Company Type: Private
Profile: Manufacturers of motor vehicles & passenger car bodies, truck & bus bodies, motor vehicle parts & accessories, railroad equipment

Michael Grimaldi, President
Robert-Jan Brabander, Treasurer & Vice-President, Finance
Joyce Sumara, Information Officer
David Paterson, Vice-President, Corporate & Environmental Affairs

Glendale International Corp.
353 Iroquois Shore Rd.
Oakville, ON L6H 1M3
905-844-2870 Fax: 905-844-2907
info@glendaleint.com
www.glendaleint.com
Ticker Symbol: GIN
Company Type: Public
Profile: Manufacturers of motor homes, travel trailers & campers, radio & television broadcasting & communications equipment, printed circuit boards, & various electronic components

Edward C. Hanna, President/CEO & Chair
Philip L. Szabo, Vice-President/CFO & Secretary

Greyhound Canada Transportation Corp.
877 Greyhound Way SW
Calgary, AB T3C 3V8
403-260-0877 Fax: 403-260-0779
canada.info@greyhound.ca
www.greyhound.ca
Company Type: Private
Profile: Intercity & rural bus transportation; travel agencies; courier services

Dave Leach, Sr. Vice President, Canada

Héroux-Devtek inc
Tour est
#658, 1111, rue St-Charles
Longueuil, QC J4K 5G4
450-679-3330 Fax: 450-679-3666
ir@herouxdevtek.com
www.herouxdevtek.com
Ticker Symbol: HRX
Company Type: Public
Profile: Manufacturers of aircraft parts & auxiliary equipment; Wholesalers of transportation equipment & supplies; Airports, flying fields & airport terminal services

Gilles Labbé, President/CEO
Réal Bélanger, CFO & Exec. Vice-President

Honda Canada Inc.
715 Milner Ave.
Toronto, ON M1B 2K8
416-284-8110 Fax: 416-286-1322 888-946-6329www.honda.ca
Company Type: Private
Profile: Manufacturers of motor vehicles & passenger car bodies; Wholesalers of automobiles & other motor vehicles, motor vehicle supplies & new parts

Shigeru Takagi, President/CEO & Secretary
T. Moriya, Vice-President, Finance & Administration

Hyundai Canada Inc.
75 Frontenac Dr.
Markham, ON L3R 6H2
905-948-6712 Fax: 905-477-3820
cr@hyundaicanada.com
www.hyundaicanada.com
Company Type: Private
Profile: Wholesalers of motor vehicle supplies & new parts

Steve Kelleher, President/CEO

Linamar Corporation
287 Speedvale Ave. West
Guelph, ON N1H 1C5
519-836-7550 Fax: 519-836-9175
investorrelations@linamar.com
www.linamar.com
Ticker Symbol: LNR
Company Type: Public
Profile: Manufacturers of motor vehicle parts & accessories, fabricated plate work, carburetors, pistons, piston rings, valves, farm machinery equipment, aircraft parts & auxiliary equipment, pumps & pumping equipment; Wholesalers of farm & garden machinery & equipment

Linda Hasenfratz, President/CEO
Csaba Havasi, Group President, Europe
Peggy Mulligan, CFO/ Exec. Vice-President & Treasurer
Mark Stoddart, Chief Technology Development Officer & Vice-President, Marketing

Logistec Corporation
#1500, 360, rue Saint-Jacques
Montréal, QC H2Y 1P5
514-844-9381 Fax: 514-843-5217
corp@logistec.com
www.logistec.com
Ticker Symbol: LGT
Company Type: Public
Profile: Deep sea foreign transportation of freight; Freight transportation on the Great Lakes & the St. Lawrence Seaway; Marine cargo handling; Various water transportation services; Refuse systems

Madeleine Paquin, President/CEO
Jean-Claude Dugas, Assistant Sec./Treasurer & Vice-President, Finance
Nicole Paquin, Vice-President, Information Systems

Magellan Aerospace Corporation
3160 Derry Rd. East
Mississauga, ON L4T 1A9
905-677-1889 Fax: 905-677-5658
info@aerospace.com
www.magellanaerospace.com
Ticker Symbol: MAL
Company Type: Public
Profile: Manufacturers of aircraft parts & auxiliary equipment, aircraft engines & engine parts

Richard A. Neill, President/CEO
John B. Dekker, Secretary/Vice-President, Finance
Donald C. Lowe, Chair, Risk Management & Environmental Committee

Magna International Inc.
337 Magna Dr.
Aurora, ON L4G 7K1
905-726-2462 Fax: 905-726-7164 www.magnaint.com
Ticker Symbol: MG
Company Type: Public
Profile: Manufacturers of motor vehicle parts & accessories, automotive stampings, various fabricated metal products, motor vehicles & passenger car bodies, vehicular lighting equipment, various fabricated textile products, public building & related furniture; Wholesalers of motor vehicle supplies & new parts; Racing, including track operation; Various amusement & recreation services

Siegfried Wolf, Co-CEO
Vincent J. Galifi, CFO & Exec. Vice-President, Finance

Mazda Canada Inc.
55 Vogell Rd.
Richmond Hill, ON L4B 3K5
905-787-7000 Fax: 905-787-7125 www.mazda.ca
Company Type: Private
Profile: Wholesalers of automobiles & other motor vehicles, motor vehicle supplies & new parts

Mike Benchimol, President
Ted Bartlett, Director, Finance & Administration
Rod Matheson, Manager, Quality Assurance

Mercedes-Benz Canada Inc.
98 Vanderhoof Ave.
Toronto, ON M4G 4C9
800-387-0100www.mercedes-benz.ca
Company Type: Private
Profile: Wholesalers of automobiles & other motor vehicles, motor vehicle supplies & new parts; Retailers in new & used motor vehicle dealers

Marcus W. Breitschwerdt, President/CEO
Harald H. Henn, Vice-President/CFO
John Westcott, Chief Information Officer

Mullen Transportation Inc.
PO Box 87, 1 Maple Leaf Rd.
Aldersyde, AB T0L 0A0
403-652-8888 Fax: 403-601-8301
ir@mullentransportation.com
www.mullen-trans.com
Ticker Symbol: MTL
Company Type: Public
Profile: Offices of holding companies; Long-distance trucking; Local trucking with storage; Various oil & gas fields services

Murray K. Mullen, CEO/Chair
Stephen H. Lockwood, President & Co-CEO
David E. Olsen, CFO & Vice-President, Finance

NAV Canada
PO Box 3411 D, 77 Metcalfe St.
Ottawa, ON K1P 5L6
613-563-5588 Fax: 613-563-3426 800-876-4693
service@navcanada.ca
www.navcanada.ca
Company Type: Public
Profile: Provides, maintains & enhances an air navigation service

John W. Crichton, President/CEO
R.A. (Sandy) Morrison, Chair
William G. Fenton, Treasurer/CFO & Vice-President, Finance
John Morris, Director, Communications
Sidney Koslow, Vice-President/Chief Technology Officer

Northstar Aerospace
105 Bedford Rd.
Toronto, ON M5R 2K4
416-364-5852 Fax: 416-362-5334
www.northstar-aerospace.com
Ticker Symbol: NAS
Company Type: Public
Profile: Manufacturers of motor vehicle parts & accessories, aircraft parts & auxiliary equipment, speed changers, industrial high-speed drives, gears, aircraft engines & engine parts; Airports, flying fields & airport terminal services

Mark Emery, President/CEO
Thomas E. Connerty, CFO

Pratt & Whitney Canada Corp.
1000, boul Marie-Victorin
Longueuil, QC J4G 1A1
450-677-9411 Fax: 450-647-3620
communications@pwc.ca
www.pwc.ca
Company Type: Private
Profile: Manufacturers of aircraft engines & engine parts; Wholesalers of transportation equipment & supplies

Alain M. Bellemare, President
Miguel C. Doyon, Vice-President, Finance
Amal M. Girgis, Chief Information Officer
John Saabas, Exec. Vice-President

Public Storage Canadian Properties
First Canadian Place
#6600, 100 King St. West
Toronto, ON M5X 1B8
866-772-2623
investor@publicstorage.ca
www.publicstoragecanada.com
Ticker Symbol: PUB
Company Type: Public
Profile: General warehousing & storage

David P. Singelyn, President
Vincent R. Chan, Vice-President/Controller

Purolator Courier Ltd.
#100, 5995 Avebury Rd.
Mississauga, ON L5R 3T8
905-712-1251 Fax: 905-712-6696
suggestions@purolator.com
www.purolator.com
Company Type: Private
Profile: Air courier services

Robert C. Johnson, President/CEO
Sheldon Bell, Sr. Vice-President & CFO

Rolls-Royce Canada ltée
9500, ch de la Côte-de-Liesse
Montréal, QC H8T 1A2
514-636-0964 Fax: 514-636-9969 www.rolls-royce.com
Company Type: Private
Profile: Airports, flying fields & airport terminal services; Manufacturers of steam, gas, hydraulic turbines & turbine generator units

Pierre Racine, President/CEO
Stephane Guerin, CFO

Spar Aerospace Limited
Edmonton International Airport
PO Box 9864, Edmonton, AB T5J 2T2
780-890-6300 Fax: 780-890-6652 www.spar.ca
Company Type: Private
Profile: Aviation services: aircraft programs; Component maintenance, repair & operation; Support services

Patrice M. Pelletier, President

Subaru Canada, Inc.
560 Suffolk Ct.
Mississauga, ON L5R 4J7
905-568-4959 Fax: 905-568-8087 www.subaru.ca
Company Type: Private
Profile: Manufacturers & retailers of motor vehicles

Katsuhiro Yokoyama, President/CEO & Chair

ThyssenKrupp Budd Canada Inc.
PO Box 1204, Kitchener, ON N2G 4G8
519-895-1000 Fax: 519-895-0099 **Ticker Symbol:** BUD
Company Type: Private

ThyssenKrupp Budd Canada Inc. (continued)
Profile: Manufacturers of motor vehicle parts & accessories; Wholesalers of motor vehicle supplies & new parts

Micheal Balavich, President
David A. Robinson, CFO & Controller

The Toronto Transit Commission
1900 Yonge St.
Toronto, ON M4S 1Z2
416-393-4000 Fax: 416-482-0478 www.ttc.ca
Company Type: Crown
Profile: Operates & maintains urban transit system: buses, subways, streetcars & trolleys

R. Ducharme, CEO
Mike Roche, CFO
John Cannon, Chief Information Officer

Toyota Canada Inc.
1 Toyota Pl.
Toronto, ON M1H 1H9
416-438-6320 Fax: 416-431-1867 888-869-6828www.toyota.ca
Company Type: Private
Profile: Wholesalers of automobiles & other motor vehicles, motor vehicle supplies & new parts, industrial machinery & equipment

K. Tomikawa, President/CEO
S. Sobatani, Treasurer
Steve Beatty, Vice-President, Public Relations

Transat A.T. Inc.
Place du Parc
#600, 300, rue Léo-Pariseau
Montréal, QC H2X 4C2
514-987-1660 Fax: 514-987-8035
info@transat.com
www.transat.com
Ticker Symbol: TRZ
Company Type: Public
Profile: Offices of holding companies; Air transportation, scheduled; Travel agencies; Airports, flying fields, & airport terminal services; Tour operators

Jean-Marc Eustache, President/CEO
Nelson Gentiletti, CFO & Vice-President, Finance & Administration
Jean-Marc Bélisle, Vice-President/Chief Information Officer

TransForce Income Fund
6600, ch St-François
Montréal, QC H4S 1B7
514-856-7500 Fax: 514-332-9527
administration@transforce.ca
www.transforce.ca
Ticker Symbol: TFI
Company Type: Public
Profile: Long-distance trucking; Local trucking without storage

Alain Bedard, President/CEO & Chair
Salvatore Vitale, CFO

Tri-White Corporation
#1400, 1 University Ave.
Toronto, ON M5J 2P1
416-367-6877 Fax: 416-367-6890 www.tri-white.com
Ticker Symbol: TWH
Company Type: Public
Profile: Local & suburban transit; Local passenger transportation

K. (Rai) Sahi, Chair/CEO
Donald W. Turple, CFO
Beverley Flynn, Corporate Counsel & Secretary

Trimac Corporation
PO Box 3500 M, #1700, 800 - 5th Ave. SW
Calgary, AB T2P 2P9
403-298-5100 Fax: 403-298-5146
info@trimac.com
www.trimac.com
Ticker Symbol: TMA.UN
Company Type: Public
Profile: The company provides services in highway transportation of bulk commodities.

Terry Owen, President/CEO
416-298-5101, Fax: 416-298-5355, tjowen@trimac.com
Ed Malysa, Vice-President/CFO
416-298-5176, Fax: 416-298-5146, emalysa@trimac.com

Vancouver Port Authority
100 The Pointe
999 Canada Pl.
Vancouver, BC V6C 3T4
604-665-9000 Fax: 604-665-9007 888-767-8826
public_affairs@portvancouver.com
www.portvancouver.com
Company Type: Crown
Profile: Marine cargo handling; Regulation & administration of transportation programs

Gordon Houston, President/CEO
Tom Winkler, Sr. Vice-President, Finance
Jim Cox, Vice-President, Infrastructure Development

Vector Aerospace Corporation
#300, 105 Bedford Rd.
Toronto, ON M5R 2K4
416-925-1143 Fax: 416-925-7214
investorinfo@vectoraerospace.ca
www.vectoraerospace.ca
Ticker Symbol: RNO
Company Type: Public
Profile: Manufacturers of aircraft parts & auxiliary equipment; Electrical & electronic repair shops; Various repair shops & related services

Donald Jackson, President/CEO
Randal L. Levine, Sr. Vice-President/CFO & Corporate Secretary

Versacold Income Fund
2115 Commissioner St.
Vancouver, BC V5L 1A6
604-255-4656 Fax: 604-255-4330
info@versacold.com
www.versacold.com
Ticker Symbol: ICE
Company Type: Public
Profile: Refrigerated logistics services: storage & transportation

H. Brent Sugden, Chair/President & CEO
Joel M. Smith, CFO & Exec. Vice-President

VIA Rail Canada Inc.
PO Box 8116 A, #500, 3, Place Ville Marie
Montréal, QC H3C 3N3
514-871-6000 Fax: 514-871-6619 www.viarail.ca
Company Type: Crown
Profile: Railroads, line-haul operating; Local & suburban transit

Paul Côté, President/CEO
J. Roger Paquette, CFO
Paul Raynor, Director, Corporate Communications
Michael Greenberg, Vice-President, Procurement, Real Estate & Environment

Vitran Corporation Inc.
#701, 185 The West Mall
Toronto, ON M9C 5L5
416-596-7664 Fax: 416-596-8039
webmaster@vitran.com
www.vitran.com
Ticker Symbol: VTN
Company Type: Public
Profile: Long-distance trucking; Arrangement of transportation of freight & cargo; General warehousing & storage; Refuse systems

Rick E. Gaetz, President/CEO
Sean P. Washchuk, CFO & Vice-President, Finance

Volvo Cars of Canada Ltd.
175 Gordon Baker Rd.
Toronto, ON M2H 2N7
416-493-3700 Fax: 416-496-0552 800-663-8255
customerservice@volvo.com
www.volvocanada.com
Company Type: Private
Profile: Manufacturers of motor vehicles & passenger car bodies

Paul Cummings, President/CEO
Lisa Graham, Specialist, Public Affairs

Wescast Industries Inc.
150 Savannah Oaks Dr.
Brantford, ON N3T 5L8
519-750-0000 Fax: 519-720-1629
investor.relations@wescast.com
www.wescast.com
Ticker Symbol: WCS
Company Type: Public
Profile: Manufacturers of motor vehicle parts & accessories; Wholesalers of motor vehicle supplies & new parts

Edward G. Frackwiak, Chair/CEO
Dave Dean, Vice-President, Finance

WestJet Airlines Ltd.
5055 - 11 St. NE
Calgary, AB T2E 8N4
403-444-2600 Fax: 403-444-2301
investor_relations@westjet.com
www.westjet.com
Ticker Symbol: WJA
Company Type: Public
Profile: Scheduled air transportation throughout North America

Clive J. Beddoe, President & Chair
Alexander (Sandy) Campbell, CFO/Sr. Vice President, Finance
Russ Hall, Exec. Vice-President, Guest Service & Information Technology

World Point Terminals Inc.
#303, 407 - 8th Ave. SW
Calgary, AB T2P 1E5
403-261-3700 Fax: 403-282-3323 **Ticker Symbol:** WPO
Company Type: Public
Profile: Various transportation services; Special warehousing & storage; Manufacturers of petroleum refining

Bruce N. Calvin, President
Steven G. Twele, CFO

Utilities

AltaGas Services Inc.
#1700, 355 - 4th Ave. SW
Calgary, AB T2P 0J1
403-691-7575 Fax: 403-691-7576 888-890-2715
feedback@altagas.ca
www.altagas.ca
Ticker Symbol: ALA
Company Type: Public
Profile: Natural gas transmission & distribution

David Cornhill, Chair & CEO
Patricia Newson, CFO & Sr. Vice-President, Finance
Don Kitteringham, Manager, Compliance

ATCO Ltd.
#1600, 909 - 11th Ave. SW
Calgary, AB T2R 1N6
403-292-7500 Fax: 403-292-7623
info@atco.com
www.atco.com
Ticker Symbol: ACO
Company Type: Public
Profile: With more than 7,000 employees, the ATCO Group is an Alberta-based corporation actively engaged worldwide in Power Generation, Utilities & Global Enterprises; ATCO Group's core business values include transparency in people & business processes, current achievement, long-term growth with a strong balance sheet & commitment to change with implementaion of best practices

Ronald D. Southern, Chair
Karen M. Watson, Sr. Vice-President & CFO
Siegfried W. Kiefer, Chief Information Officer & Vice-President, Information Technology

Atomic Energy of Canada Limited
2251 Speakman Dr.
Mississauga, ON L5K 1B2
905-823-9040 Fax: 905-823-1290
webmaster@aecl.ca
www.aecl.ca
Company Type: Crown
Profile: Manufacturers of various industrial inorganic chemicals, measuring & controlling devices, special industry machinery; Commercial physical & biological research; Management services; Electric services

Robert Van Adel, President/CEO
Michael Robins, CFO
David F. Torgerson, Sr. Vice-President, Technology

Boralex Inc.
770, rue Sherbrooke ouest
Montréal, QC H3A 1G1

514-284-9890 Fax: 514-284-9895 www.boralex.com
Ticker Symbol: BLX
Company Type: Public
Profile: Electric services

Bernard Lemaire, Chair/CEO
Claude Audet, President/COO
Jean-François Thibodeau, CFO & Vice-President
Mylène Masse, Director, Communications

British Columbia Hydro
6911 Southpoint Dr.
Burnaby, BC V3N 4X8
604-224-9376 Fax: 604-528-3137
800-224-9376www.bchydro.com
Company Type: Crown
Profile: Electric services

Robert G. Elton, President/CEO
Valerie C. Lambert, Treasurer
Robert J. Steele, Chief Information Officer
Glen S. Smyrl, Vice-President, Engineering

Canadian Hydro Developers, Inc.
#500, 1324 - 17th Ave. SW
Calgary, AB T2T 5S8
403-269-9379 Fax: 403-244-7388
canhydro@canhydro.com
www.canhydro.com
Ticker Symbol: KHD
Company Type: Public
Profile: Electric services

John D. Keating, CEO
J. Ross Keating, President/COO
Kent E. Brown, CFO
Kelly Matheson, Vice-President, Environmental Management

Canadian Utilities Limited
#1600, 909 - 11th Ave. SW
Calgary, AB T2R 1N6
403-292-7500 Fax: 403-292-7532 www.canadian-utilities.com
Ticker Symbol: CU
Company Type: Public
Profile: Electric services; Natural gas transmission & distribution

R.D. Southern, Chair
Nancy C. Southern, President/CEO
Karen M. Watson, CFO & Sr. Vice-President

Emera Incorporated
Barrington Tower, Scotia Square
1894 Barrington St.
Halifax, NS B3J 2A8
902-450-0507 Fax: 902-428-6112
investors@emera.com
www.emera.com
Ticker Symbol: EMA
Company Type: Public
Profile: Energy & services company; Operations include 2 regulated electric utilities, hydroelectric facilities & interest in the Maritimes & Northeast Pipeline

Chris Huskilson, President/CEO
Nancy Tower, CFO

EPCOR Power, L.P.
10065 Jasper Ave.
Edmonton, AB T5J 3B1
780-412-4297 Fax: 780-412-3808 866-896-4636
investorinquires@epcorpowerlp.ca
www.epcorpowerlp.ca
Ticker Symbol: TPL
Company Type: Public
Profile: Electric services

Brian T. Vassjo, President
Stuart Lee, CFO

EPCOR Utilities Inc.
10065 Jasper Ave.
Edmonton, AB T5J 3B1
780-412-3414 Fax: 780-412-3096
info@epcor.ca
www.epcor.ca
Company Type: Public
Profile: Provides power & water in Alberta, Ontario, British Columbia & the USA Pacific Northwest

Don J. Lowry, President/CEO

Mark Wiltzen, Sr. Vice-President/CFO
Denise Carpenter, Sr. Vice-President, Public & Government Affairs

Fortis Inc.
Fortis Bldg.
PO Box 8837, #1201, 139 Water St.
St. John's, NL A1B 3T2
709-737-2800 Fax: 709-737-5307
investorrelations@fortisinc.com
www.fortisinc.com
Ticker Symbol: FTS
Company Type: Public
Profile: Offices of holding companies; Electric services; Mortgage bankers & loan correspondents; Real estate operators of nonresidential buildings

H. Stanley Marshall, President/CEO
Barry Perry, CFO/Vice-President, Finance

Gaz Métro inc
1717, rue du Havre
Montréal, QC H2K 2X3
514-598-3444 Fax: 514-598-3144
info@gazmetro.com
www.gazmetro.com
Ticker Symbol: GZM
Company Type: Public
Profile: Offices of holding companies; Natural gas transmission & distribution; Retail in household appliance stores; Equipment rental & leasing

Robert Tessier, President/CEO
Pierre Despars, Vice-President, Finance & Corporate Affairs
Stéphanie-Hélène Leclerc, Contact, Public & Governmental Affairs
E. Morin, Director, Engineering, Geomatics & Technology
J.-P. Noël, Director, Regulatory Matters, Rates & Environment

Gaz Métro Limited Partnership
1717, rue du Havre
Montréal, QC H2K 2X3
514-598-3444 Fax: 514-598-3144 800-361-4005
investors@gazmetro.com
www.gazmetro.com
Ticker Symbol: GZM
Company Type: Public
Profile: Natural gas transmission & distribution; Retailers in household appliance stores; Equipment rental & leasing

Robert Tessier, President/CEO
Pierre Despars, Vice-President, Finance & Corporate Affairs
Geneviève Deschamps, Coordinator, Investor Relations

Great Lakes Hydro Income Fund
#200, 480, boul de la Cité
Gatineau, QC J8T 8R3
819-561-2722 Fax: 819-561-7188
unitholderenquiries@greatlakeshydro.com
www.greatlakeshydro.com
Ticker Symbol: GLH
Company Type: Public
Profile: Electric services; Open-ended management investment offices

Richard Legault, President/CEO
Donald Tremblay, CFO & Vice-President
Shelley Moorhead, Director, Investor Relations & Communications

Hydro One Inc.
483 Bay St., 15th Fl.
Toronto, ON M5G 2P5
416-345-5000 Fax: 416-345-6225
investor.relations@hydroone.com
www.hydroone.com
Company Type: Public
Profile: Electric services

Tom Parkinson, President/CEO
Beth Summers, CFO
Anne Creighton, Director, Corporate Communications
Nairn McQueen, Vice-President, Engineering & Construction Services
Michelle Morrissey O'Ryan, Vice-President, Health, Safety & Environment

Hydro-Québec
75, boul René-Lévesque ouest
Montréal, QC H2Z 1A4
514-289-2211 Fax: 514-289-5773 www.hydroquebec.com
Company Type: Crown
Profile: Electric services

Thierry Vandal, President/CEO
Yves Filion, President, TransÉnergie
Daniel Garant, CFO & Exec. Vice-President, Finance
Marie-José Nadeau, Secretary General/Exec. Vice-President, Corporate Affairs

Manitoba Hydro
PO Box 815 Main, 820 Taylor Ave.
Winnipeg, MB R3C 2P4
204-474-3311 Fax: 204-475-0069
publicaffairs@hydro.mb.ca
www.hydro.mb.ca
Company Type: Crown
Profile: Electric services

Robert B. Brennan, President/CEO
Vince Warden, CFO & Vice-President, Finance & Administration

New Brunswick Power Corporation
PO Box 2000, 515 King St.
Fredericton, NB E3B 4X1
506-458-4444 Fax: 506-458-4000 800-663-6272
questions@nbpower.com
www.nbpower.com
Company Type: Crown
Profile: Electric services

Stewart MacPherson, President/CEO
Sharon MacFarlane, Vice-President, Finance & Information Systems

Newfoundland Power Inc.
PO Box 8910, St. John's, NL A1B 3P6
709-737-5600 Fax: 709-737-5300
contactus@newfoundlandpower.com
www.newfoundlandpower.com
Company Type: Public
Profile: The company is engaged in electric services.

Karl Smith, President/CEO
Bernard Ryan, Director, Environment
Jocelyn Perry, Vice-President, Finance
Peter Collins, Manager, Information Services

Northwest Territories Power Corporation
4 Capital Dr.
Hay River, NT X0E 1G2
867-874-5200 Fax: 867-874-5229
info@ntpc.com
www.ntpc.com
Company Type: Crown
Profile: The following services are offered: electric, water, sewer, pipeline, communications & power line construction.

Leon Courneya, President/CEO
867-874-5245, lcourneya@ntpc.com
Judith Goucher, CFO & Director, Finance
867-874-5234, jgoucher@ntpc.com
John Locke, Director, Information Technology
jlocke@ntpc.com

Nova Scotia Power Incorporated
PO Box 910, #1800, 1894 Barrington St.
Halifax, NS B3J 2W5
902-428-6230 Fax: 902-428-6108
800-428-6230www.nspower.ca
Ticker Symbol: NSI
Company Type: Public
Profile: Electric services

David McD. Mann, President/CEO
Zeda Redden, General Manager, Finance

Ontario Power Generation Inc.
700 University Ave.
Toronto, ON M5G 1X6
416-592-2555 877-592-2555www.opg.com
Company Type: Crown
Profile: Electricity generation company with the principal business of generation & sale of electricity in Ontario

James F. Hankinson, President/CEO
Donn Hanbidge, Chief Financial Officer
Pierre Charlebois, Chief Nuclear Officer
John Murphy, Chief Ethics Officer & Exec. Vice-President, Human Resources

Saskatchewan Power Corporation (continued)

Saskatchewan Power Corporation

2025 Victoria Ave.
Regina, SK S4P 0S1
306-566-2121 Fax: 306-566-2548 888-757-6937
inquiries@saskpower.com
www.saskpower.com
Company Type: Crown
Profile: Electric services

Patricia Youzwa, President/CEO, SaskPower
David Hughes, President, SaskPower International
Bill Jones, CFO & Vice-President, Finance
Eric Rankin, Vice-President & Chief Information Officer
Rick A. Patrick, Vice-President, Planning, Environment & Regulatory Affairs

Toronto Hydro Corporation

14 Carlton St.
Toronto, ON M5B 1K5
416-542-3000 Fax: 416-542-3452
contactus@torontohydro.com
www.torontohydro.com
Company Type: Crown
Profile: Offices of holding companies; Electric services; Natural gas distribution

David S. O'Brien, President/CEO
David Dobbin, President, Toronto Hydro Telecom
Jean-Sebastien Couillard, CFO
Blair H. Peberdy, Vice-President, Communications & Public Affairs
Anthony M. Haines, CAO
Eduardo E. Bresani, Chief Information Officer
Richard Lu, Vice-President, Environment, Health & Safety

TransAlta Corporation

PO Box 1900 M, 110 - 12 Ave. SW
Calgary, AB T2P 2M1
403-267-7110 Fax: 403-267-2590
investor_relations@transalta.com
www.transalta.com
Ticker Symbol: TA
Company Type: Public
Profile: Electric services

Stephen G. Snyder, President/CEO
Ian A. Bourne, CFO & Exec. Vice-President
Gregory Wilson, Sr. Vice-President/Chief Information Officer
Linda Chambers, Exec. Vice-President, Technology

TransAlta Power, L.P.

PO Box 1900 M, 110 - 12 Ave. SW
Calgary, AB T2P 2M1
403-267-7110 Fax: 403-267-2590
investor_relations@transalta.com
www.transalta.com
Ticker Symbol: TPW
Company Type: Public
Profile: Unit investment trusts, certificate/closed-end management offices; Electric services

Ian A. Bourne, President
Marvin J. Waiand, Vice-President & Treasurer

MAJOR CANADIAN COMPANIES

SECTION 7

Government

Included in this section:

Government Quick Reference

Listed in this section are federal, provincial & territorial government contacts (department, address, phone, fax) organized under subjects (e.g. Debt Management, Pensions) for an at-a-glance topical reference. For more in-depth information, refer to specific departments listed following the Government Quick Reference.

Government Listings

Government listings are organized in the following manner:

1. federal government
2. provincial/territorial governments, listed alphabetically by name of province/territory

Government listings are divided into jurisdictional sub-sections beginning with the federal government & followed by the provincial governments in alphabetical order. Each jurisdictional sub-section of the government begins with the office of the prime minister, premier or commissioner, and the executive council, followed by departments, ministries or agencies dealing specifically within the area of finance organized alphabetically. Full detail is given to those ministries or departments that have a strong financial component (e.g. finance, revenue, industry), including relevant acts administered. Departments or ministries that have little or no financial focus, such as environment or culture, are not included.

Federal Budget Earns Solid "B" Grade Say Canada's Chartered Accountants

TORONTO, March 19, 2007 - Reducing the federal debt by $9.2 billion and providing targeted tax relief to those Canadians who most need support earned the Federal Finance Minister a solid "B" grade, Canada's Chartered Accountants said today.

Canada's CAs rated the budget on the three key factors needed to generate strong, long-term economic growth and job creation: debt reduction, controlled spending and broad-based low taxes for businesses and individuals.

"Today's budget earns a solid B because it is a step in the right direction," said Kevin Dancey, FCA, President and CEO of the Canadian Institute of Chartered Accountants. "There are some significant benefits for individual Canadians and businesses in this budget. Yet we are disappointed it does not include broader based tax reductions for individuals and businesses that would help sustain Canada's economic health for future generations."

Canada's CAs are pleased the government is committing $9.2 billion to debt reduction this year and another $6 billion over the next two years. "This will provide the government with the ability to generate significant personal tax savings in future years," said Dancey, adding that Canada's CAs are also pleased by the tax relief provided to seniors, families and low income Canadians and for businesses for new investment in manufacturing and processing equipment.

One of the main reasons we can only grade the budget a B is because program spending is up almost 8% this year and 6% next year. Departmental operating costs are ahead almost 10% this year and this is forecasted to continue next year. This pace of growth is in excess of the rate of inflation and overall economic growth. "This cannot continue," said Dancey. The government must address this situation as soon as possible to bring spending down.

Overall Canada's CAs believe the measures provided in this budget are a step in the right direction. "What is needed now is for the federal government to commit to lowering personal and business taxes even more, and fully commit to controlling program spending," Dancey said, adding that Canada's CAs will continue to look to the federal government for leadership in this area.

The Canadian Institute of Chartered Accountants (CICA), together with the provincial, territorial and Bermuda Institutes/Ordre of Chartered Accountants, represents a membership of approximately 71,000 CAs and 9,500 students in Canada and Bermuda. The CICA conducts research into current business issues and supports the setting of accounting, auditing and assurance standards for business, not-for-profit organizations and government. It issues guidance on control and governance, publishes professional literature, develops continuing education programs and represents the CA profession nationally and internationally.

Budget 2007: Key Highlights

Debt Reduction

- The federal surplus for 2006/07 is ***$9.2 billion.***
- For 2006-07, the Government plans to ***reduce the federal debt by $9.2 billion.*** The Government remains on target to lower the federal debt-to-GDP (gross domestic product) ratio to 25 per cent by 2012-13.
- The debt-to-GDP ratio is expected to be ***25% in 2012-13.***
- The Tax Back Guarantee, which will be legislated with Budget 2007, directs over $1 billion a year in debt interest savings to personal income tax reductions.

Government Program Spending

- Program spending will ***increase by almost 8% this year*** compared to last year. ($175B 05/06, $189B 06/07). Program spending will decrease to 5.6% in 07/08 and 3.6% in 08/09.
- Departmental Operational Costs have ***increased almost 10% over last year,*** and falls to 6.6% for 07/08, and 3.4% in 08/09.
- The government has not brought spending down to the rate of inflation, adjusted for population growth as stated in their election platform. This will only be achieved in 2008/09.

Personal Tax Reductions

Child Tax Credit: A $2,000 child tax credit will provide up to a maximum of $310 per child in tax relief.

GOVERNMENT

For seniors, there is less in terms of new savings in this budget, as pension income splitting was announced last fall.

- New in this budget is the RRSP rollover to a RIF has been pushed back to 71 from 69 years old.
- Pension Income Splitting (no details, still awaiting legislation).
- The age amount increased by $1000 to $5066 from $4066 last fall.

Registered Education Savings Plans:

- Eliminating the $4,000 limit on annual contributions.
- Increasing the lifetime RESP contribution limit from $42,000 to $50,000.
- Increasing the maximum Canada Education Savings Grant annual amount from $400 to $500 and to $1,000 from $800 if there is unused grant room from low contributions made in previous years.

Other Measures introduced in Budget 2007:

- Introducing a new Working Income Tax Benefit of up to $500 for individuals and $1,000 for families. This will reward and strengthen incentives to work for an estimated 1.2 million low-income Canadians, helping them over the "welfare wall."
- Helping parents and others save toward the long-term financial security of persons with severe disabilities with a new Registered Disability Savings Plan.
- Creating an Enabling Accessibility Fund with $45 million over three years to contribute to the cost of improving physical accessibility for persons with disabilities.
- Eliminating the capital gains tax for charitable donations of publicly-listed securities to private foundations.

Lifetime Capital Gains Exemption to $750,000 from $500,000 for small business owners, farmers, fishermen and fisherwomen.

Vehicle Efficiency Incentive (VEI) structure that will cover the full range of passenger vehicles available today. The VEI will have three distinct components and come into effect March 20, 2007:

- A performance-based rebate program offering up to $2,000 for the purchase of a new fuel-efficient vehicle.
- Neutral treatment of a broad range of vehicles with average fuel efficiency that are widely purchased by Canadians.
- A new Green Levy on fuel-inefficient vehicles.

Public Transit Tax Credit:

Budget 2007 proposes to extend the public transit tax credit to include electronic fare cards that are used for at least 32 one-way trips in a monthly period. Transit authorities will need to track and certify usage and cost. Further, the public transit tax credit will be provided where four weekly passes are purchased consecutively.

Corporate Tax Reductions

Budget 2007 proposes to **double the value of goods that may be imported duty- and tax-free by returning Canadian residents after a 48-hour absence, to $400 from $200.**

Budget 2007 proposes **a new investment incentive for Manufacturing & Processing businesses.** For investment in eligible machinery and equipment from now until the end of 2008, businesses engaging in manufacturing or processing will be eligible to **claim accelerated capital cost allowance at a rate of 50 percent on a straight-line basis.** The proposed rate will allow these investments to be written off over a two-year period on average, after taking into account the half-year rule, which treats assets as if they had been purchased in the middle of the year. **This measure will apply to investments in eligible machinery and equipment on or after March 19, 2007, and before 2009 by businesses engaged in manufacturing or processing in Canada of goods for sale or lease.**

Budget 2007 proposes to **extend the exemption to active business income from non-treaty jurisdictions as well as treaty countries,** provided those jurisdictions agree to exchange tax information with Canada.

The existing **Accelerated Capital Cost Allowance will be fully grandfathered for oil sands assets** in project phases that commenced major construction prior to March 19, 2007. For other projects that have not yet begun major construction, in recognition of long project timelines, Budget 2007 will allow companies to maintain the ability to claim ACCA until 2010, with the rate being gradually reduced between 2011 and 2015.

International Tax Fairness Initiative, Budget 2007 proposes to:

- Eliminate the deductibility of interest incurred to invest in business operations abroad.
- Improve our information exchange agreements with other countries.
- Provide more resources to the Canada Revenue Agency to strengthen their audit and enforcement activities.

Aligning Capital Cost Allowance Rates with Useful Life, Budget 2007 proposes to:

- Increase the CCA rate for other non-residential buildings to 6 per cent from 4 per cent.
- Increase the CCA rate for computers to 55 per cent from 45 per cent.
- Increase the CCA rate for natural gas distribution pipelines to 6 per cent from 4 per cent.
- Increase the CCA rate for liquefied natural gas facilities to 8 per cent from 4 per cent.
- (The CCA changes are effective for eligible property acquired on or after March 19, 2007.)

Accountability Issues

The Government's new Expenditure Management System, which will focus on good management and value for money. Under the new system:

- Departments and agencies will manage their programs to clearly defined results, and assess their performance against those results.
- The Treasury Board Secretariat will oversee the quality of these assessments and ensure that departments explicitly address risk as well as cost-effectiveness.
- Building on these assessments, Cabinet will systematically review the funding and relevance of all program spending to ensure that spending is aligned with Canadians' priorities and effectively and efficiently delivers on the Government's responsibilities.
- Cabinet will undertake a rigorous examination of all new spending proposals, taking explicit account of the funding, performance and resource requirements of existing programs in related areas.

The Canadian Institute
of Chartered Accountants
277 Wellington Street West
Toronto, ON M5V 3H2 Canada
Tel: (416) 977-3222
Fax: (416) 977-8585
www.cica.ca

L'Institut Canadien
Des Comptables Agréés
277, rue Wellington Ouest
Toronto, ON M5V 3H2 Canada
Tel: (416) 977-3222
Fax: (416) 977-8585
www.icca.ca

AIM Trimark Investments Federal Budget Analysis 2007

A leader in the timely and thorough preparation of tax information on a range of issues, AIM Trimark has been providing a customized analysis of the federal budget for over a decade. Prepared from within the budget lockup in Ottawa by Jamie Golombek, AIM Trimark's Vice President of Tax & Estate Planning, the 2007 edition selectively focuses on several specific budget elements that will have the biggest impact on your personal finances and investments.

Increasing RRSP Age Limit to 71

Effective immediately, the age limit at which Registered Retirement Savings Plans (RRSPs), Registered Pension Plans (RPPs) and Deferred Profit Sharing Plans (DPSPs) must be converted either into a RRIF or an annuity has been increased to 71 from 69. While this will immediately benefit anyone who turns 69 in 2007, allowing them to defer conversion of their plans by two years, it will also benefit anyone who turns 70 or 71 this year. Specifically, assuming the 70 or 71 year old has RRSP contribution room available, perhaps due to an unused RRSP carryforward that was never used by age 69 or on account of additional earned income (such as employment or rental income) currently being generated, a new RRSP could be opened this year to shelter such contributions from income and provide a tax deduction on a current or future year's tax return.

Alternatively, the 70 or 71 year old could transfer his or her existing RRIF back into an RRSP as long as it is then reconverted back to a RRIF before the end of the year in which he or she turns 71 (i.e., either in 2007 or 2008). Finally, for those who choose not to reconvert their RRIF back to an RRSP, the government announced that it will be waiving the required minimum withdrawals for both this year and next year for RRIF annuitants who turn 70 in 2007 and similarly waiving the minimum withdrawal requirement this year for RRIF annuitants who turn 71 in 2007.

Changes To RESPs

The government has proposed two major changes to the contribution rules for RESPs: the elimination of the $4,000 annual RESP contribution limit and the increase of the lifetime RESP contribution limit to $50,000 from $42,000.

This newfound ability to lump-sum fund an RESP for a child's post-secondary education may outweigh the benefits of collecting the annual Canada Education Savings Grant (CESG), generally equal to 20% per year on eligible contributions. 2 These CESG rules are also changing. The maximum annual RESP contribution that will qualify for the 20% CESG will be increased to $2,500 from $2,000, thereby increasing the maximum annual CESG per beneficiary to $500 from $400. Consequently, if a beneficiary has unused CESGs carried forward from a prior year, by contributing $5,000 in a particular year to an RESP, a total CESG of $1,000 would now be available. Note, however, that the $7,200 lifetime CESG limit is unaffected by this change.

New Child Tax Credit

Last year's federal budget introduced the Universal Child Care Benefit (UCCB), which provided a payment equal to $100 per month per child under the age of six. This year's budget goes a step further in providing tax relief for families with children by introducing a brand new non-refundable child tax credit for parents based on an amount of $2,000 (indexed annually for inflation) for each child under the age of 18. The tax credit is equal to 15.5% of $2,000 or up to $310 per child, effective in 2007. Generally, either parent may claim the credit and any unused portion of the credit unnecessary to reduce a parent's tax payable to zero can be transferred by that parent to a spouse or common-law partner. Note that just like the UCCB, the new child tax credit is available to all parents and is not income-tested.

Registered Disability Savings Plan (RDSP)

The government announced a new program to assist families to save for the long-term financial security of children with disabilities, which will be called the Registered Disability Savings Plan (RDSP), along with a Canada Disability Savings Grant (CDSG) program and Canada Disability Savings Bond (CDSB) program. The new RDSP will be largely based on the rules governing RESPs and will come into force in 2008. Any Canadian resident who is either personally eligible for the disability tax credit (DTC) or is a parent or other legal representative of a disabled person will be eligible to establish an RDSP. The beneficiary of the RDSP will be the disabled person who must have a social insurance number in order to open a plan.

Contributions

As with RESPs, although contributions to an RDSP will not be tax deductible, any earnings or growth on such contributions will accrue tax-free. Contributions can also be withdrawn tax-free and only the deferred growth, along with any CDSGs and CDSBs (discussed below), will be included in the disabled beneficiary's income when ultimately withdrawn from the plan. The lifetime RDSP contribution limit will be $200,000 and, as is now the case

with RESPs, there is no annual contribution limit. In addition, anyone can contribute to the plan up until the end of the year in which the beneficiary turns 59.

CDSGs and CDSBs

To further encourage RDSP contributions, the government will be providing grants, known as CDSGs, at various rates depending on the amounts contributed and the beneficiary's family net income. Specifically, if the family's net income is below $74,357, the government will pay a CDSG of 300% on the first $500 contributed annually and 200% on the next $1,000 contributed. For families with net income above $74,357, the CDSG will be 100% of the first $1,000 contributed annually.

When the beneficiary is under age 18, the "family net income" will generally be the disabled child's family. Once the beneficiary turns 18, however, the definition of "family net income" will be the disabled beneficiary and his or her spouse's or partner's combined net income. The government has imposed a limit of $70,000 on the total amount of CDSGs it will pay on behalf of an RDSP beneficiary. The CDSGs will be paid until the end of the year in which the beneficiary turns 49. For low and modest income families with disabled beneficiaries under age 50, a new CDSB of up to $1,000 will be paid annually (up to a lifetime maximum of $20,000) to the CDSG, regardless of whether or not contributions have been made.

Withdrawals

Payments from an RDSP, which will be subject to an annual maximum withdrawal limit based on the beneficiary's life expectancy and the fair market value of the plan, must begin once the beneficiary reaches age 60.

Unlike RESPs, contributors will not be entitled to a refund of their contributions. Rather, all RDSP contributions, CDSGs and CDSBs must be used to support the beneficiary.

Eligibility for income-tested benefits

Finally, the budget proposes that any amounts paid out of an RDSP will not be taken into account for the purposes of calculating federal income-tested benefits. It will not reduce Old Age Security nor Employment Insurance benefits.

While provinces and territories also provide income support for disabled persons, it remains to be seen whether the provinces will also commit to not disqualifying an RDSP beneficiary from receiving provincial income support because of the withdrawals under the new program.

Other Changes

Donations to private foundations

Last year's federal budget eliminated capital gains tax on donations of publicly-traded securities, including mutual funds, to registered charities and public foundations. To encourage additional charitable donations to private foundations, this year's budget proposes to eliminate capital gains tax on such donations to private foundations as well.

Elementary and secondary school scholarships

The 2006 budget exempted all post-secondary level scholarships and bursaries from tax. This year's budget goes a step further by fully exempting from taxation scholarships and bursaries provided to students to attend elementary and secondary schools.

Spousal amount

For 2007, the basic personal amount, representing the amount of income that an individual can receive before paying personal tax, is set at $8,929. The spousal amount that can be claimed in respect of a spouse or common-law partner is currently set at $7,581 and is reduced on a dollar-for-dollar basis by the dependant's net income above $759.

The budget proposes to remove this so-called "marriage penalty" by increasing the spousal or dependent amount to $8,929, the same level as the basic personal amount, while at the same time eliminating the threshold above which a dependant's net income must be taken into account. Based on the personal tax credit rate of 15.5%, this could result in a maximum benefit of an additional $209 [i.e., ($8,929 - $7,581) x 15.5%].

Capital gains exemption

The budget proposes to increase the lifetime capital gains exemption to $750,000 from $500,000 for capital gains realized on the sale of qualifying small business shares and qualifying farm or fishing property.

Increase of instalment threshold

Under the current rules, individuals who receive income not subject to source deductions such as rental income, investment income, capital gains or self-employment income are required to pay quarterly instalments. Currently, instalments are required if your "net tax owing" is greater than $2,000 ($1,200 for residents of Quebec) in 2007 and was also greater than $2,000 ($1,200) in either 2006 or 2005. The definition of "net tax owing" is complex but essentially refers to the net federal and provincial tax less income tax withheld at source. The 2007 budget proposes to increase this threshold to $3,000 ($1,800 for Quebec residents), effective for the 2008 and future tax years.

No broad-based capital gains tax relief

Perhaps the biggest disappointment with Budget 2007 was that there was no announcement regarding the elimination (or at least the deferral) of capital gains tax on the reinvestment of proceeds within a six-month period. This was something that the Conservatives had promised during last year's election campaign, but have so far failed to deliver. In a similar vein, there was no mention of broad-based income splitting, as some had speculated, nor was there any

update on the status of the "draconian" interest deductibility rules, originally proposed in 2003, but still in draft form.

For more information about this topic, contact your advisor, call us at 1.800.874.6275 or visit our website at www.aimtrimark.com. The information provided is general in nature and is provided with the understanding that it may not be relied upon as, nor considered to be, the rendering of tax, legal, accounting or professional advice. Readers should consult with their own accountants and/or lawyers for advice on the specific circumstances before taking any action. Commissions, trailing commissions, management fees and expenses may all be associated with mutual fund investments. Mutual funds are not guaranteed, their values change frequently and past performance may not be repeated. Please read the prospectus before investing. Copies are available from your financial advisor or from AIM Trimark Investments. + AIM, the chevron logo and all associated trademarks are trademarks of A I M Management Group Inc., used under licence. * Knowing Pays, TRIMARK and all associated trademarks are trademarks of AIM Funds Management Inc. (c) AIM Funds Management Inc., 2007 TEFDBAE(03/07)

Reprinted with permission of AIM Trimark.

AIM Funds Management Inc.
5140 Yonge Street, Suite 900, Toronto, Ontario M2N 6X7
Telephone: 416.590.9855 or 1.800.874.6275
Facsimile: 416.590.9868 or 1.800.631.7008
inquiries@aimtrimark.com
www.aimtrimark.com

GOVERNMENT

Government

Government Quick Reference Guide

ACTS & REGULATIONS

Public Works & Government Services Canada, Place du Portage, Phase III, 11, rue Laurier, Ottawa, K1A 0S5 ON
819-997-6363

Newfoundland & Labrador
Department of Justice, Confederation Bldg., PO Box 8700, St. John's, A1B 4J6 NL
709-729-5942, Fax: 709-729-2129

Nova Scotia
Department of Service Nova Scotia & Municipal Relations, 1505 Barrington St., PO Box 216, Halifax, B3J 2M4 NS
902-424-4141, Fax: 902-424-0581, public-enquiries@gov.ns.ca

Northwest Territories
Department of Justice, PO Box 1320, Yellowknife, X1A 2L9 NT
867-920-6197

Ontario
Ministry of the Attorney General, 720 Bay St., Toronto, M5G 2K1 ON
416-326-2220, Fax: 416-326-4007, 800-518-7901

Prince Edward Island
Office of the Attorney General, PO Box 2000, Charlottetown, C1A 7N8 PE
902-368-5152, Fax: 902-368-4910

Quebec
Publications Québec, 1550D, rue Jean-Talon nord, 1er étage, Québec, G1N 2E5 QC
418-643-5150, Fax: 418-643-6177, 800-463-2100, service.clientele@mrci.gouv.qc.ca

Yukon Territory
Yukon Justice, PO Box 2703, Whitehorse, Y1A 2C6 YT
867-667-8644, Fax: 867-393-6272

AGRICULTURE

See Also: Land Resources

Agriculture & Agri-Food Canada, Sir John Carling Bldg., 930 Carling Ave., Ottawa, K1A 0C5 ON
613-759-1000, Fax: 613-759-6726, info@agr.gc.ca

Alberta
Agriculture Finance Corporation, 5718 - 56 Ave., Lacombe, AB T4L 1B1
403-782-8200, Fax: 403-782-4226, 800-396-0215

Alberta Agriculture, Food & Rural Development, J.G. O'Donoghue Bldg., 7000 - 113 St., Edmonton, T6H 5T6 AB
780-427-2727, Fax: 780-427-2861, 866-882-7677, duke@gov.ab.ca

British Columbia
Ministry of Agriculture & Lands, PO Box 9120 Prov Govt,Victoria, V8W 9B4 BC
250-387-5121, Fax: 250-387-1522

Manitoba
Agricultural Societies, 1129 Queens Ave., Brandon, MB R7A 1L9
204-726-6195, Fax: 204-726-6260

Manitoba Agriculture, Food & Rural Initiatives, Norquay Bldg., 401 York Ave., Winnipeg, R3C 0P8 MB

Food Development Centre, 810 Phillips St., PO Box 1240, Portage la Prairie, MB R1N 3J9
204-239-3150, Fax: 204-239-3180, 800-870-1044

New Brunswick
Department of Agriculture & Aquaculture, PO Box 6000, Fredericton, E3B 5H1 NB
506-453-2666, Fax: 506-453-7170

Prince Edward Island
Department of Agriculture, Fisheries & Aquaculture, Jones Bldg., 11 Kent St., PO Box 2000, Charlottetown, C1A 7N8 PE
902-368-4880, Fax: 902-368-4857

Quebec
Ministère de l'Agriculture, des Pêcheries et de l'Alimentation, 200, ch Sainte-Foy, Québec, G1R 4X6 QC
418-380-2110, 888-222-6272

Saskatchewan
Saskatchewan Agriculture & Food, Walter Scott Bldg., 3085 Albert St., Regina, S4S 0B1 SK
306-787-5140

AGRICULTURE & FOOD

Agriculture & Agri-Food Canada, Sir John Carling Bldg., 930 Carling Ave., Ottawa, K1A 0C5 ON
613-759-1000, Fax: 613-759-6726, info@agr.gc.ca

Alberta
Agriculture Finance Corporation, 5718 - 56 Ave., Lacombe, AB T4L 1B1
403-782-8200, Fax: 403-782-4226, 800-396-0215

Alberta Agriculture, Food & Rural Development, J.G. O'Donoghue Bldg., 7000 - 113 St., Edmonton, T6H 5T6 AB
780-427-2727, Fax: 780-427-2861, 866-882-7677, duke@gov.ab.ca

Farmers' Advocate of Alberta, 7000 - 113 St., 3rd Fl., Edmonton, AB T6H 5T6
780-427-2433, Fax: 780-427-3913

Irrigation Council, Provincial Bldg., 200 - 5 Ave. South, 3rd Fl., PO Bag 3014, Lethbridge, AB T1J 4L1
403-381-5176, Fax: 403-382-4406

British Columbia
Agricultural Land Commission, #133, 4940 Canada Way, Burnaby, BC V5G 4K6
604-660-7000, Fax: 604-660-7033

Ministry of Agriculture & Lands, PO Box 9120 Prov Govt,Victoria, V8W 9B4 BC
250-387-5121, Fax: 250-387-1522

Manitoba
Agricultural Societies, 1129 Queens Ave., Brandon, MB R7A 1L9
204-726-6195, Fax: 204-726-6260

Manitoba Agriculture, Food & Rural Initiatives, Norquay Bldg., 401 York Ave., Winnipeg, R3C 0P8 MB

Farm Lands Ownership Board, #812, Norquay Bldg., 401 York Ave., Winnipeg, MB R3C 0P8
204-945-3149, Fax: 204-945-1489, 800-282-8069, flob@gov.mb.ca

Farm Machinery Board, Norquay Bldg., #812, 401 York Ave., Winnipeg, MB R3C 0P8
204-945-3856

Manitoba Agricultural Services Corporation, #100, 1525 First St. South, Brandon, MB R7A 7A1
204-726-6850, Fax: 204-726-6849, mailbox@mcic.gov.mb.ca

New Brunswick
New Brunswick Crop Insurance Commission, PO Box 6000, Fredericton, NB E3B 5H1
506-453-2185, Fax: 506-453-7406

New Brunswick Farm Products Commission, c/o Department of Agriculture, Fisheries & Aquaculture, PO Box 6000, Fredericton, NB E3B 5H1
506-453-3647, Fax: 506-444-5969

Prince Edward Island
Agricultural Insurance Corporation, 29 Indigo Cres., PO Box 1600, Charlottetown, PE C1A 7N3
902-368-4842, Fax: 902-368-6677

Department of Agriculture, Fisheries & Aquaculture, Jones Bldg., 11 Kent St., PO Box 2000, Charlottetown, C1A 7N8 PE
902-368-4880, Fax: 902-368-4857

Quebec
Ministère de l'Agriculture, des Pêcheries et de l'Alimentation, 200, ch Sainte-Foy, Québec, G1R 4X6 QC
418-380-2110, 888-222-6272

Saskatchewan
Saskatchewan Agriculture & Food, Walter Scott Bldg., 3085 Albert St., Regina, S4S 0B1 SK
306-787-5140

Saskatchewan Crop Insurance Corporation, 484 Prince William Dr., PO Box 3000, Melville, SK S0A 2P0
306-728-7200, Fax: 306-728-7268, customer.service@scic.gov.sk.ca

AIR POLLUTION

See Also: Environment

Nova Scotia
Department of Environment & Labour, 5151 Terminal Rd., 6th Fl., PO Box 697, Halifax, B3J 2T8 NS
902-424-5300, Fax: 902-424-0575

ARCTIC & NORTHERN AFFAIRS

Alberta
Northern Alberta Development Council, #206, Provincial Bldg., 9621 - 96 Ave., PO Bag 900-14, Peace River, T8S 1T4 AB
780-624-6274, Fax: 780-624-6184, nadc.council@gov.ab.ca

British Columbia
Northern Development Initiative Trust, #301, 1268 Fifth Ave., Prince George, BC V2L 3L2
250-561-2525

Northwest Territories
Northwest Territories Business Development & Investment Corporation, #701, 5201 - 50 Ave., Yellowknife, NT X1A 3S9
867-920-6455, Fax: 867-765-0652, bdicinfo@gov.nt.ca

Ontario
Ministry of Northern Development & Mines, 159 Cedar St., Sudbury, P3E 6A5 ON
705-564-0060, Fax: 705-564-7108

Northern Development Division, Roberta Bondar Place, #200, 70 Foster Dr., Sault Ste Marie, P6A 6V8 ON
705-945-5900, Fax: 705-945-5931

Yukon Territory
Yukon Economic Development, PO Box 2703, Whitehorse, Y1A 2C6 YT
867-393-7191, Fax: 867-395-7199, 800-661-0408

ARTS & CULTURE

British Columbia
Ministry of Small Business & Revenue, PO Box 9065 Prov Govt,Victoria, V8W 9E2 BC
250-356-6611, Fax: 250-356-8294

Manitoba
Multiculturalism Secretariat, 213 Notre Dame Ave., 4th Fl., Winnipeg, MB R3B 1N3
204-945-1156, Fax: 204-948-2323

New Brunswick
New Brunswick Film, Assumption Pl., 770 Main St., 16th Fl., PO Box 5001, Moncton, NB E1C 8R3
506-869-6868, Fax: 506-869-6840, nbfilm@gnb.ca

Nova Scotia
Nova Scotia Film Development Corporation, 1724 Granville St., Halifax, NS B3J 1X5
902-424-7177, Fax: 902-424-0617, novascotia.film@ns.sympatico.ca

Ontario
Ontario Northland, 555 Oak St. East, North Bay, ON P1B 8L3
705-472-4500, Fax: 705-476-5598, 800-363-7512, info@ontc.on.ca

Saskatchewan
Saskatchewan Film & Video Classification Board, #500, 1919 Saskatchewan Dr., Regina, SK S4P 4H2
306-787-5550, Fax: 306-787-9779, adwyer@justice.gov.sk.ca

AUDITORS-GENERAL

Auditor General of Canada, 240 Sparks St., Ottawa, K1A 0G6 ON
613-995-3708, Fax: 613-957-0474, communications@oag-bvg.gc.ca

Alberta
Alberta Office of the Auditor General, 9925 - 109 St., 8th Fl., Edmonton, T5K 2J8 AB
780-427-4222, Fax: 780-422-9555

British Columbia
Office of the Auditor General, 8 Bastion Sq., Victoria, V8V 1X4 BC
250-387-6803, Fax: 250-387-1230

Manitoba
Office of the Auditor General, #500, 330 Portage Ave., Winnipeg, R3C 0C4 MB
204-945-3790, Fax: 204-945-2169

New Brunswick
Office of the Auditor General, PO Box 758, Fredericton, E3B 5B4 NB
506-453-2243, Fax: 506-453-3067

Newfoundland & Labrador
Office of the Auditor General, Viking Bldg., 3rd Fl., PO Box 8700, St. John's, A1B 4J6 NL
709-729-2700, Fax: 709-729-5970

Nova Scotia
Office of the Auditor General, #302, 1888 Brunswick St., Halifax, B3J 3J8 NS
902-424-5907, Fax: 902-424-4350

Ontario
Office of the Provincial Auditor, Box 105, #1530, 20 Dundas St. West, 15th Fl., Toronto, M5G 2C2 ON
416-327-2381, Fax: 416-327-9862

Prince Edward Island
Office of the Auditor General, Shaw Bldg., North, 105 Rochford St, 2nd Fl., PO Box 2000, Charlottetown, C1A 7N8 PE
902-368-4520, Fax: 902-368-4598

Quebec
Vérificateur général du Québec, 750, boulevard Charest est, 3e étage, Québec, G1K 9J6 QC
418-691-5900, Fax: 418-644-4460, verificateur.general@vgq.gouv.qc.

Saskatchewan
Provincial Auditor Saskatchewan, #1500, 1920 Broad St., Regina, S4P 3V2 SK
306-787-6398, Fax: 306-787-6383, info@auditor.sk.ca

AUTOMOBILE INSURANCE

See Also: Insurance (Life, Fire Property)

Alberta
Automobile Insurance Rate Board, Terrace Bldg., #200, 9515 - 107 St. NW, Edmonton, AB T5K 2C3
780-427-5428, Fax: 780-644-7771, airb@gov.ab.ca

British Columbia
Insurance Corporation of BC, 151 West Esplanade, North Vancouver, V7M 3H9 BC
604-661-2800

Manitoba
Manitoba Public Insurance, #820, 234 Donald St., PO Box 6300, Winnipeg, R3C 4A4 MB
204-985-7000, Fax: 204-943-9851, 800-665-2410

Nova Scotia
Nova Scotia Insurance Review Board, 5151 Terminal Rd., 2nd Fl., PO Box 2251, Halifax, NS B3J 3C8
902-424-8685, nsirb@gov.ns.ca

Northwest Territories
Department of Finance, PO Box 1320, Yellowknife, X1A 2L9 NT
867-873-0414, Fax: 867-873-7117

Ontario
Financial Services Commission of Ontario, 5160 Yonge St., 17th Fl., Box 85, Toronto, ON M2N 6L9
416-250-7250, Fax: 416-590-7078, 800-668-0128

Saskatchewan
Saskatchewan Government Insurance, 2260 - 11 Ave., Regina, S4P 0J9 SK
306-751-1200, Fax: 306-787-7477

Yukon Territory
Yukon Justice, PO Box 2703, Whitehorse, Y1A 2C6 YT
867-667-8644, Fax: 867-393-6272

BANKING & FINANCIAL INSTITUTIONS

Bank of Canada, 234 Wellington St., Ottawa, K1A 0G9 ON
613-782-8111, Fax: 613-782-8655
Business Development Bank of Canada, #400, 5, Place Ville-Marie, Montréal, H3B 5E7 QC
514-283-5904, Fax: 514-283-2872, 888-463-6232
Canada Deposit Insurance Corporation, 50 O'Connor St., 17th Fl., PO Box 2340 D,Ottawa, K1P 5W5 ON
613-996-2081, Fax: 613-996-6095, info@cdic.ca; info@sadc.ca
Financial Consumer Agency of Canada, 427 Laurier Ave. West, 6th Fl., Ottawa, K1R 1B9 ON
Fax: 613-941-1436, info@fcac-acfc.gc.ca
Office of the Superintendent of Financial Institutions, Kent Square, 255 Albert St., Ottawa, K1A 0H2 ON
613-990-7788, Fax: 613-952-8219, 800-385-8647, extcomm@osfi-bsif.gc.ca

Alberta
ATB Financial, 9888 Jasper Ave., Edmonton, AB T5J 1P1
Credit Union Deposit Guarantee Corporation, 10130 - 103 St., 18th Fl., Edmonton, AB T5J 3N9
780-428-6680, Fax: 780-428-7571, 800-661-0351, mail@cudgc.ab.ca

British Columbia
Ministry of Finance, PO Box 9048 Prov Govt,Victoria, V8W 9E2 BC
250-387-3751, Fax: 250-387-5594
Financial Institutions Commission, #1200, 13450 - 102 Ave., Surrey, BC V3T 5X3
604-953-5300, Fax: 604-953-5301, FICOM@ficombc.ca

Manitoba
Credit Union Deposit Guarantee Corporation, #390, 200 Graham Ave., Winnipeg, MB R3C 4L5
204-942-8480, Fax: 204-947-1723, 800-697-4447, mail@cudgc.com
Financial Institutions Regulation, #1115, 405 Broadway, Winnipeg, R3C 3L6 MB
204-945-2542, Fax: 204-948-2268

New Brunswick
New Brunswick Credit Union Deposit Insurance, PO Box 6000, Fredericton, NB E3B 5H1
506-453-2315, Fax: 506-453-7474

Newfoundland & Labrador
Credit Union Deposit Corporation, PO Box 340, Marystown, NL A0B 2M0
709-279-0170, Fax: 709-279-0177

Northwest Territories
Department of Finance, PO Box 1320, Yellowknife, X1A 2L9 NT
867-873-0414, Fax: 867-873-7117

Nunavut
Nunavut Credit Corporation, PO Box 224, Cape Dorset, NU X0A 0C0

Ontario
Deposit Insurance Corporation of Ontario, #700, 4711 Yonge St., Toronto, ON M2N 6K8
416-325-9444, Fax: 416-325-9722, 800-268-6653
Financial Services Commission of Ontario, 5160 Yonge St., 17th Fl., Box 85, Toronto, ON M2N 6L9
416-250-7250, Fax: 416-590-7078, 800-668-0128

Prince Edward Island
Consumer, Corporate & Insurance Division, Shaw Building, 95 Rochford St., 4th Fl., PO Box 2000, Charlottetown, C1A 7N8 PE
902-368-4550, Fax: 902-368-5283

Quebec
Registraire des entreprises, 800, place D'Youville, Québec, G1R 4Y5 QC
418-528-9074, Fax: 418-646-7329, req@req.gouv.qc.ca

Saskatchewan
Saskatchewan Finance, 2350 Albert St., Regina, S4P 4A6 SK
306-787-6768, Fax: 306-787-6544
Saskatchewan Financial Services Commission, #601, 1919 Saskatchewan Dr., Regina, SK S4P 4H2
306-787-5646, Fax: 306-787-5899

Yukon Territory
Yukon Finance, PO Box 2703, Whitehorse, Y1A 2C6 YT
867-667-5343, Fax: 867-393-6217

BOARDS OF REVIEW

Canadian International Trade Tribunal, Standard Life Centre, 333 Laurier Ave. West, Ottawa, K1A 0G7 ON
613-990-2452, Fax: 613-990-2439

Alberta
Alberta Review Board, J.E. Brownlee Bldg., 10365 - 97 St., 5th Fl., Edmonton, AB T5J 3W7
780-422-5994, Fax: 780-427-1762

British Columbia
British Columbia Review Board, #1203, 865 Hornby St., Vancouver, BC V6Z 2G3
604-660-8789, Fax: 604-660-8809, 877-305-2277

Manitoba
Review Board, 408 York Ave., 2nd Fl., Winnipeg, MB R3C 0P9
204-945-4438, Fax: 204-945-5751

Northwest Territories
Legal Services Board of the Northwest Territories, PO Box 1320, Yellowknife, NT X1A 2L9
867-873-7450, Fax: 867-873-5320, www-jus-tice

Ontario
Ontario Municipal Board & Board of Negotiation, 655 Bay St., 15th Fl., Toronto, ON M5G 1E5
416-326-6800, Fax: 416-326-5370

Saskatchewan
Public & Private Rights Board, 3085 Albert St., 3rd Fl., Regina, SK S4P 3V7
306-787-4071, Fax: 306-787-0088
Saskatchewan Film & Video Classification Board, #500, 1919 Saskatchewan Dr., Regina, SK S4P 4H2
306-787-5550, Fax: 306-787-9779, adwyer@justice.gov.sk.ca
Surface Rights Board of Arbitration, 113 - 2nd Ave. East, PO Box 1597, Kindersley, SK S0L 1S0
306-463-5447, Fax: 306-463-5449, surface@sasktel.net

BUDGET PLANNING

British Columbia
Provincial Treasury, 620 Superior St., Victoria, V8V 1X4 BC
250-387-4541

Nova Scotia
Department of Finance, PO Box 187, Halifax, B3J 2N3 NS
902-424-5554, Fax: 902-424-0635

Northwest Territories
Department of Finance, PO Box 1320, Yellowknife, X1A 2L9 NT
867-873-0414, Fax: 867-873-7117
Financial Management Board Secretariat, 5003 - 49 St., PO Box 1320, Yellowknife, X1A 2L9 NT
867-920-8962, Fax: 867-873-0128

Nunavut
Department of Finance, Bldg. 1079, 1st Fl., PO Box 1000 Stn 360,Iqaluit, X0A 0H0 NU
867-975-5800, Fax: 867-975-5805

Prince Edward Island
Department of the Provincial Treasury, PO Box 2000, Charlottetown, C1A 7N8 PE
902-368-4000, Fax: 902-368-5544

BUSINESS & FINANCE

Atlantic Canada Opportunities Agency, 644 Main St., 3rd Fl., PO Box 6051, Moncton, E1C 9J8 NB
506-851-2271, Fax: 506-851-7403, 800-561-7862
Auditor General of Canada, 240 Sparks St., Ottawa, K1A 0G6 ON
613-995-3708, Fax: 613-957-0474, communications@oag-bvg.gc.ca
Bank of Canada, 234 Wellington St., Ottawa, K1A 0G9 ON
613-782-8111, Fax: 613-782-8655
Business Development Bank of Canada, #400, 5, Place Ville-Marie, Montréal, H3B 5E7 QC
514-283-5904, Fax: 514-283-2872, 888-463-6232
Calgary, Home Oil Tower, #606, 3240 - 8 Ave. SW, Calgary, T2P 2Z2 AB
403-537-9800, Fax: 403-537-9811
Canada Business, 235 Queen St., Ottawa, K1A 0H5 ON
Fax: 613-954-5463, 888-576-4444, cbsc@ic.gc.ca
Canada Deposit Insurance Corporation, 50 O'Connor St., 17th Fl., PO Box 2340 D,Ottawa, K1P 5W5 ON
613-996-2081, Fax: 613-996-6095, info@cdic.ca; info@sadc.ca

Canada Economic Development for Québec Regions, Tour de la Bourse, #3800, 800, Place Victoria, CP 247, Montréal, H4Z 1E8 QC
514-283-6412, Fax: 514-283-3302, 866-385-6412
Canada Investment & Savings, #900, 110 Yonge St., Toronto, ON M5C 1T4
416-952-1252, Fax: 416-952-1270, 800-575-5151, csb@csb.gc.ca
Canada Mortgage & Housing Corporation, 700 Montreal Rd., Ottawa, K1A 0P7 ON
613-748-2000, Fax: 613-748-2098, 800-668-2642
Canada Pension Plan Investment Board, #2700, 1 Queen St. East, PO Box 101, Toronto, M5C 2W5 ON
416-868-4075, Fax: 416-868-4760, 866-557-9510, csr@cppib.ca
Canada Revenue Agency, 555 Mackenzie Ave., 4th Fl., Ottawa, K1A 0L5 ON
613-952-0384
Canadian Commercial Corporation, Clarica Centre, #1100, 50 O'Connor St., Ottawa, K1A 0S6 ON
613-996-0034, Fax: 613-995-2121
Cape Breton Development Fund Corporation, Silicon Island, 70 Crescent St., PO Box 1264, Sydney, NS B1P 6T7
902-564-3600, Fax: 902-564-3825, 800-705-3926
Competition Bureau, Place du Portage, Phase I, 50, rue Victoria, 21e étage, Ottawa, K1A 0C9 ON
613-997-4282, Fax: 613-997-0324, 800-348-5358, compbureau@ic.gc.ca
Competition Tribunal, #600, 90 Sparks St., Ottawa, ON K1P 5B4
613-957-7851, Fax: 613-957-3170, tribunal@ct-tc.gc.ca
Electronic Commerce Branch, 300 Slater St., Ottawa, ON K1A 0C8
613-954-5031, Fax: 613-941-1164, 800-328-6189
Enterprise Cape Breton Corporation, Silicon Island, 70 Crescent St., Sydney, NS B1S 2Z7
902-564-3600, Fax: 902-564-3825, 800-705-3926, ecbcinfo@ecbc.ca
Export Development Canada, 151 O'Connor St., Ottawa, K1A 1K3 ON
613-598-2500, Fax: 613-237-2690, 888-332-3320
Farm Credit Canada, 1800 Hamilton St., PO Box 4320, Regina, S4P 4L3 SK
306-780-8100, Fax: 306-780-5875, 800-387-3232
Finance Canada, L'esplanade Laurier, 140 O'Connor St., Ottawa, K1A 0G5 ON
613-992-1573, Fax: 613-996-8404
Office of the Superintendent of Financial Institutions, Kent Square, 255 Albert St., Ottawa, K1A 0H2 ON
613-990-7788, Fax: 613-952-8219, 800-385-8647, extcomm@osfi-bsif.gc.ca
Financial Transactions & Reports Analysis Centre of Canada, 234 Laurier Ave. West, 24th Fl., Ottawa, ON K1P 1H7
Fax: 613-943-7931, 866-346-8722, guidelines@fintrac.gc.ca
Foreign Affairs & International Trade Canada, 125 Sussex Dr., Ottawa, K1A 0G2 ON
613-944-4000, Fax: 613-996-9709, 800-267-8376
Industry Canada, 235 Queen St., Ottawa, K1A 0H5 ON
613-947-7466, Fax: 613-954-6436
North American Free Trade Agreement (NAFTA) Secretariat, Canadian Section, #705, 90 Sparks St., Ottawa, K1P 5B4 ON
613-992-9388, Fax: 613-992-9392, canada@nafta-sec-alena.org
Public Sector Pension Investment Board, #200, 440 Laurier Ave. West, Ottawa, ON K1R 7X6
613-782-3095, Fax: 613-782-6864, info@investpsp.ca
Royal Canadian Mint, 320 Sussex Dr., Ottawa, K1A 0G8 ON
613-993-3500
Statistics Canada, R.H. Coats Bldg., Tunney's Pasture, 100 Tunney's Pasture Driveway, Ottawa, K1A 0T6 ON
Fax: 877-287-4369, 800-263-1136, infostats@statcan.ca
Treasury Board of Canada, 300 Laurier Ave. West, 10th Fl., Ottawa, K1A 0R5 ON
613-957-2400, Fax: 613-998-9071, 877-636-0656
Western Economic Diversification Canada, Canada Place, #1500, 9700 Jasper Ave. NW, Edmonton, T5J 4H7 AB
780-495-4164, Fax: 780-495-4557, 888-338-9378

Alberta

Agriculture Finance Corporation, 5718 - 56 Ave., Lacombe, AB T4L 1B1
403-782-8200, Fax: 403-782-4226, 800-396-0215
Alberta Capital Finance Authority, 2450 Canadian Western Bank Place, 10303 Jasper Ave., Edmonton, AB T5J 3N6
780-427-9711, Fax: 780-422-2175, webacfa@gov.ab.ca
Alberta Securities Commission, 300 - 5 Ave. SW, 4th Fl., Calgary, AB T2P 3C4
403-297-6454, Fax: 403-297-6156, 877-355-0585, inquiries@seccom.ab.ca
ATB Financial, 9888 Jasper Ave., Edmonton, AB T5J 1P1
Alberta Office of the Auditor General, 9925 - 109 St., 8th Fl., Edmonton, T5K 2J8 AB
780-427-4222, Fax: 780-422-9555
Automobile Insurance Rate Board, Terrace Bldg., #200, 9515 - 107 St. NW, Edmonton, AB T5K 2C3
780-427-5428, Fax: 780-644-7771, airb@gov.ab.ca
Credit Union Deposit Guarantee Corporation, 10130 - 103 St., 18th Fl., Edmonton, AB T5J 3N9
780-428-6680, Fax: 780-428-7571, 800-661-0351, mail@cudgc.ab.ca
Alberta Economic Development, Commerce Place , 6th Fl., 10155 - 102 St., Edmonton, T5J 4L6 AB
780-415-1319, Fax: 780-415-1759
Alberta Finance, Terrace Bldg., 9515 - 107 St., Edmonton, T5K 2C3 AB
780-427-3035, Fax: 780-427-1147
Northern Alberta Development Council, #206, Provincial Bldg., 9621 - 96 Ave., PO Bag 900-14, Peace River, T8S 1T4 AB
780-624-6274, Fax: 780-624-6184, nadc.council@gov.ab.ca

British Columbia

Asia Pacific Foundation of Canada, #666, 999 Canada Place, Vancouver, BC V6C 3E1
604-684-5986, Fax: 604-681-1370, info@asiapacific.ca
Auditor Certification Board, 940 Blanshard St., 2nd Fl., PO Box 9431 Prov Govt, Victoria, BC V8W 9V3
250-356-8658, Fax: 250-356-9422
Office of the Auditor General, 8 Bastion Sq., Victoria, V8V 1X4 BC
250-387-6803, Fax: 250-387-1230
British Columbia Innovation Council, 1188 West Georgia St., 9th Fl., Vancouver, BC V6E 4A2
info@bcinnovationcouncil.com
British Columbia Pension Corporation, 2995 Jutland Rd., PO Box 9460, Victoria, BC V8W 9V8
250-387-8201, Fax: 250-953-0421, 800-663-8823
British Columbia Securities Commission, Pacific Centre, 701 West Georgia St., 12th Fl., PO Box 10142, Vancouver, BC V7Y 1L2
604-899-6500, Fax: 604-899-6506, 800-373-6393, inquiries@bcsc.bc.ca
Crown Corporations Secretariat, PO Box 9300 Prov Govt, Victoria, BC V8W 9N2
250-952-0750, Fax: 250-952-0777
Ministry of Finance, PO Box 9048 Prov Govt,Victoria, V8W 9E2 BC
250-387-3751, Fax: 250-387-5594
Financial Institutions Commission, #1200, 13450 - 102 Ave., Surrey, BC V3T 5X3
604-953-5300, Fax: 604-953-5301, FICOM@ficombc.ca
Insurance Corporation of BC, 151 West Esplanade, North Vancouver, V7M 3H9 BC
604-661-2800
Insurance Council of British Columbia, #300, 1040 West Georgia St., PO Box 7, Vancouver, BC V6E 4H1
604-688-0321, Fax: 604-662-7767, 877-688-0321
International Financial Centre - British Columbia Society, World Trade Centre, #545, 999 Canada Place, Vancouver, BC V6C 3E1
604-683-6626, Fax: 604-683-6646, info@ifcvancouver.com
Public Sector Employers' Council Secretariat, 1215 Broad St., 2nd Fl., Victoria, BC V8W 2A4
250-387-0842, Fax: 250-387-6258
Ministry of Small Business & Revenue, PO Box 9065 Prov Govt,Victoria, V8W 9E2 BC
250-356-6611, Fax: 250-356-8294
Timber Export Advisory Committee, 1520 Blanshard St., 2nd Fl., PO Box 9514 Prov Govt, Victoria, BC V8W 3C8
250-387-8359, Fax: 250-387-5050

Manitoba

Office of the Auditor General, #500, 330 Portage Ave., Winnipeg, R3C 0C4 MB
204-945-3790, Fax: 204-945-2169
Claimant Adviser Office, #200, 330 Portage Ave., Winnipeg, MB R3C 0C4
204-945-7413, Fax: 204-948-3157
Manitoba Competitiveness, Training & Trades, #900, 259 Portage Ave., Winnipeg, R3B 3P4 MB
204-945-2067, Fax: 204-948-2964
Comptroller's Division, #715, 401 York Ave., Winnipeg, R3C 0P8 MB
Credit Union Deposit Guarantee Corporation, #390, 200 Graham Ave., Winnipeg, MB R3C 4L5
204-942-8480, Fax: 204-947-1723, 800-697-4447, mail@cudgc.com
Crown Corporations Council, #1130, 444 St. Mary Ave., Winnipeg, MB R3C 3T1
204-949-5270, Fax: 204-949-5283, crowncc@mts.net
Manitoba Development Corporation, #555, 155 Carlton St., Winnipeg, R3C 3H8 MB
204-945-7626, Fax: 204-945-1193
Federal-Provincial Relations & Research Division, #910, 386 Broadway, Winnipeg, R3C 3R6 MB
Manitoba Finance, #109, Legislative Bldg., Winnipeg, R3C 0V8 MB
204-945-3754, Fax: 204-945-8316, minfin@leg.gov.mb.ca
Manitoba Public Insurance, #820, 234 Donald St., PO Box 6300, Winnipeg, R3C 4A4 MB
204-985-7000, Fax: 204-943-9851, 800-665-2410
Manitoba Intergovernmental Affairs, #301, 450 Broadway, Winnipeg, R3C 0V8 MB
Fax: 204-945-1383, mnia@leg.gov.mb.ca
Manitoba Agricultural Services Corporation, #100, 1525 First St. South, Brandon, MB R7A 7A1
204-726-6850, Fax: 204-726-6849, mailbox@mcic.gov.mb.ca
Manitoba Bureau of Statistics, #824, 155 Carlton St., Winnipeg, R3C 3H9 MB
204-945-2982, Fax: 204-945-0695
Manitoba Securities Commission, #500, 400 St. Mary Ave., Winnipeg, MB R3C 4K5
204-945-2548, Fax: 204-945-0330, 800-655-5244, securities@gov.mb.ca
Pension Commission of Manitoba, #1004, 401 York Ave., Winnipeg, MB R3C 0P8
204-945-2740, Fax: 204-948-2375, pensions@gov.mb.ca
Manitoba Treasury Board, #200, 386 Broadway, Winnipeg, R3C 3R6 MB
204-945-1101, Fax: 204-948-2358

New Brunswick

Office of the Auditor General, PO Box 758, Fredericton, E3B 5B4 NB
506-453-2243, Fax: 506-453-3067
Department of Business New Brunswick, Centennial Bldg., 670 King St., 5th Fl., PO Box 6000, Fredericton, E3B 5H1 NB
506-444-5228, Fax: 506-453-5428
Office of the Comptroller, Centennial Bldg., 670 King St., Fredericton, E3B 5H1 NB
506-453-2565, Fax: 506-453-2917
Department of Finance, 670 King St., PO Box 6000, Fredericton, E3B 5H1 NB
506-453-2451, Fax: 506-444-4724
Lotteries Commission of New Brunswick, PO Box 3000, Fredericton, NB E3B 5G5
506-444-4065, Fax: 506-444-5818
New Brunswick Credit Union Deposit Insurance, PO Box 6000, Fredericton, NB E3B 5H1
506-453-2315, Fax: 506-453-7474
New Brunswick Crop Insurance Commission, PO Box 6000, Fredericton, NB E3B 5H1
506-453-2185, Fax: 506-453-7406
New Brunswick Expropriations Advisory Office, 371 Queen St., Fredericton, NB E3B 1B1
506-453-7771, Fax: 506-453-9600
New Brunswick Farm Products Commission, c/o Department of Agriculture, Fisheries & Aquaculture, PO Box 6000, Fredericton, NB E3B 5H1
506-453-3647, Fax: 506-444-5969
New Brunswick Investment Management Corporation, York Tower, #381, 440 King St., Fredericton, NB E3B 5H8
506-444-5800, Fax: 506-444-5025
New Brunswick Municipal Finance Corporation, #376, 670 King St., PO Box 6000, Fredericton, NB E3B 5H1
506-453-3952, Fax: 506-453-2053
Regional Development Corporation, RDC Bldg., 836 Churchill Row, PO Box 428, Fredericton, E3B 5R4 NB
506-453-2277, Fax: 506-453-7988

Newfoundland & Labrador

Office of the Auditor General, Viking Bldg., 3rd Fl., PO Box 8700, St. John's, A1B 4J6 NL
709-729-2700, Fax: 709-729-5970
Credit Union Deposit Corporation, PO Box 340, Marystown, NL A0B 2M0
709-279-0170, Fax: 709-279-0177

Department of Finance, Confederation Bldg., PO Box 8700, St. John's, A1B 4J6 NL
709-729-6310

Department of Innovation, Trade & Rural Development, PO Box 8700, St. John's, A1B 4J6 NL
709-729-7000, Fax: 709-729-0654, 800-563-2299, itrdinfo@gov.nl.ca

Ireland Business Partnership, PO Box 8700, St. John's, NL A1B 4J6
709-729-1684, Fax: 709-729-2236

Nearshore Atlantic, 84 Elizabeth Ave., 1st Fl., St. John's, NL A1A 1W7
709-772-8324, Fax: 709-757-6284, info@nearshoreatlantic.com

Newfoundland & Labrador Municipal Financing Corporation, Confederation Bldg., PO Box 8700, St. John's, NL A1B 4J6
709-729-6686, Fax: 709-729-2095

Nova Scotia

Office of the Auditor General, #302, 1888 Brunswick St., Halifax, B3J 3J8 NS
902-424-5907, Fax: 902-424-4350

Department of Economic Development, Maritime Centre, 1505 Barrington St., 14th Fl., PO Box 2311, Halifax, B3J 3C8 NS
902-424-0377, Fax: 902-424-0500, comm@gov.ns.ca

Department of Finance, PO Box 187, Halifax, B3J 2N3 NS
902-424-5554, Fax: 902-424-0635

Nova Scotia Business Inc., #701, 1800 Argyle St., PO Box 2374, Halifax, NS B3J 3E4
902-424-6650, Fax: 902-424-5739, nsbi@gov.ns.ca

Nova Scotia Securities Commission, Joseph Howe Bldg., 1690 Hollis St., 2nd Fl., PO Box 458, Halifax, NS B3J 2P8
902-424-7768, Fax: 902-424-4625

Pension Regulation Division, PO Box 2531, Halifax, B3J 3N5 NS
902-424-8915, Fax: 902-424-0662

Northwest Territories

Department of Finance, PO Box 1320, Yellowknife, X1A 2L9 NT
867-873-0414, Fax: 867-873-7117

Financial Management Board Secretariat, 5003 - 49 St., PO Box 1320, Yellowknife, X1A 2L9 NT
867-920-8962, Fax: 867-873-0128

Northwest Territories Business Development & Investment Corporation, #701, 5201 - 50 Ave., Yellowknife, NT X1A 3S9
867-920-6455, Fax: 867-765-0652, bdicinfo@gov.nt.ca

Nunavut

Department of Finance, Bldg. 1079, 1st Fl., PO Box 1000 Stn 360,Iqaluit, X0A 0H0 NU
867-975-5800, Fax: 867-975-5805

Nunavut Legal Registries Division, Brown Bldg., 1st Fl., PO Box 1000 570,Iqaluit, X0A 0H0 NU
867-975-6190, Fax: 867-975-6194

Ontario

Office of the Provincial Auditor, Box 105, #1530, 20 Dundas St. West, 15th Fl., Toronto, M5G 2C2 ON
416-327-2381, Fax: 416-327-9862

Deposit Insurance Corporation of Ontario, #700, 4711 Yonge St., Toronto, ON M2N 6K8
416-325-9444, Fax: 416-325-9722, 800-268-6653

Ministry of Economic Development & Trade, Hearst Block, 900 Bay St., 8th Fl., Toronto, M7A 2E1 ON
416-325-6666, Fax: 416-325-6688

Ministry of Finance, Frost Bldg. South, 7 Queen's Park Cres., 7th Fl., Toronto, M7A 1Y7 ON
416-325-0333, Fax: 416-325-0339

Financial Services Commission of Ontario, 5160 Yonge St., 17th Fl., Box 85, Toronto, ON M2N 6L9
416-250-7250, Fax: 416-590-7078, 800-668-0128

Ministry of Government Services, Ferguson Block, 77 Wellesley St. West, 12th Fl., Toronto, M7A 1N3 ON
416-326-1234

Liquor Control Board of Ontario, 55 Lake Shore Blvd. East, Toronto, ON M5E 1A4
416-864-2570, Fax: 416-864-2476

Ontario Electricity Financial Corporation, #1400, 1 Dundas St. West, Toronto, ON M5G 1Z3
416-325-8000, Fax: 416-325-8005

Ontario Financing Authority, #1400, 1 Dundas St. West, Toronto, ON M5G 1Z3
416-325-8000, Fax: 416-325-8005

Ontario Securities Commission, #1903, 20 Queen St. West, PO Box 55, Toronto, ON M5H 3S8
416-597-0681, Fax: 416-593-8122

Ontario Strategic Infrastructure Financing Authority, 777 Bay St., 9th Fl., Toronto, M5G 2C8 ON
416-212-7132, Fax: 416-212-6452

Stadium Corporation of Ontario Ltd., 33 King St. West, 6th Fl., Oshawa, ON L1H 8H5
Fax: 905-433-6688

Prince Edward Island

Agricultural Insurance Corporation, 29 Indigo Cres., PO Box 1600, Charlottetown, PE C1A 7N3
902-368-4842, Fax: 902-368-6677

Office of the Auditor General, Shaw Bldg., North, 105 Rochford St, 2nd Fl., PO Box 2000, Charlottetown, C1A 7N8 PE
902-368-4520, Fax: 902-368-4598

Department of Development & Technology, Shaw Bldg., 105 Rochford St., 4th & 5th Fl., PO Box 2000, Charlottetown, C1A 7N8 PE
902-368-4242, Fax: 902-368-4224

Prince Edward Island Lending Agency, PO Box 1420, Charlottetown, PE C1A 7N1
902-368-6200, Fax: 902-368-6201

Prince Edward Island Lotteries Commission, Office of the Deputy Provincial Treasurer, 95 Rochford St., PO Box 2000, Charlottetown, PE C1A 7N8
902-368-4053, Fax: 902-368-6575

Department of the Provincial Treasury, PO Box 2000, Charlottetown, C1A 7N8 PE
902-368-4000, Fax: 902-368-5544

Quebec

Ministère des Finances, Édifice Gérard-D.-Lévesque, 12, rue Saint-Louis, 1er étage, Québec, G1R 5L3 QC
418-528-9323, Fax: 418-646-1631, info@finances.gouv.qc.ca

Registraire des entreprises, 800, place D'Youville, Québec, G1R 4Y5 QC
418-528-9074, Fax: 418-646-7329, req@req.gouv.qc.ca

Revenu Québec, 3800, rue de Marly, Québec, G1X 4A5 QC
800-463-2397

Secrétariat du Conseil du trésor, Édifice H, #1.64B, 875, Grande Allée est, 1er étage, Québec, G1R5R8 QC
418-643-5926, Fax: 418-643-7824

Vérificateur général du Québec, 750, boulevard Charest est, 3e étage, Québec, G1K 9J6 QC
418-691-5900, Fax: 418-644-4460, verificateur.general@vgq.gouv.qc.

Saskatchewan

Provincial Auditor Saskatchewan, #1500, 1920 Broad St., Regina, S4P 3V2 SK
306-787-6398, Fax: 306-787-6383, info@auditor.sk.ca

Board of Revenue Commissioners, #480, 2151 Scarth St., Regina, SK S4P 3V7
306-787-6221, Fax: 306-787-1610

Crown Investments Corporation of Saskatchewan, #400, 2400 College Ave., Regina, S4P 1C8 SK
306-787-6851, Fax: 306-787-8125

Saskatchewan Finance, 2350 Albert St., Regina, S4P 4A6 SK
306-787-6768, Fax: 306-787-6544

Saskatchewan Government Insurance, 2260 - 11 Ave., Regina, S4P 0J9 SK
306-751-1200, Fax: 306-787-7477

Saskatchewan Industry & Resources, 2103 - 11th Ave., Regina, S4P 3V7 SK
306-787-2232, Fax: 306-787-2159, 866-727-5427

Saskatchewan Crop Insurance Corporation, 484 Prince William Dr., PO Box 3000, Melville, SK S0A 2P0
306-728-7200, Fax: 306-728-7268, customer.service@scic.gov.sk.ca

Saskatchewan Development Fund Corporation, #300, 2400 College Ave., Regina, SK S4P 1C8
306-787-1645, Fax: 306-787-8030, 800-667-7543

Saskatchewan Financial Services Commission, #601, 1919 Saskatchewan Dr., Regina, SK S4P 4H2
306-787-5646, Fax: 306-787-5899

Saskatchewan Trade & Export Partnership, #320, 1801 Hamilton St., PO Box 1787, Regina, SK S4P 3C6
306-787-9210, Fax: 306-787-6666, 877-313-7244, inquire@sasktrade.sk.ca

Yukon Territory

Yukon Finance, PO Box 2703, Whitehorse, Y1A 2C6 YT
867-667-5343, Fax: 867-393-6217

Yukon Lottery Commission, 312 Wood St., Whitehorse, YT Y1A 2E6
867-633-7890, Fax: 867-668-7561, lotteriesyukon@gov.yk.ca

BUSINESS DEVELOPMENT

See Also: Industry; Science & Technology

Atlantic Canada Opportunities Agency, 644 Main St., 3rd Fl., PO Box 6051, Moncton, E1C 9J8 NB
506-851-2271, Fax: 506-851-7403, 800-561-7862

Business Development Bank of Canada, #400, 5, Place Ville-Marie, Montréal, H3B 5E7 QC
514-283-5904, Fax: 514-283-2872, 888-463-6232

Canada Business, 235 Queen St., Ottawa, K1A 0H5 ON
Fax: 613-954-5463, 888-576-4444, cbsc@ic.gc.ca

Canada Economic Development for Québec Regions, Tour de la Bourse, #3800, 800, Place Victoria, CP 247, Montréal, H4Z 1E8 QC
514-283-6412, Fax: 514-283-3302, 866-385-6412

Cape Breton Development Fund Corporation, Silicon Island, 70 Crescent St., PO Box 1264, Sydney, NS B1P 6T7
902-564-3600, Fax: 902-564-3825, 800-705-3926

Enterprise Cape Breton Corporation, Silicon Island, 70 Crescent St., Sydney, NS B1S 2Z7
902-564-3600, Fax: 902-564-3825, 800-705-3926, ecbcinfo@ecbc.ca

Export Development Canada, 151 O'Connor St., Ottawa, K1A 1K3 ON
613-598-2500, Fax: 613-237-2690, 888-332-3320

Industry Canada, 235 Queen St., Ottawa, K1A 0H5 ON
613-947-7466, Fax: 613-954-6436

Western Economic Diversification Canada, Canada Place, #1500, 9700 Jasper Ave. NW, Edmonton, T5J 4H7 AB
780-495-4164, Fax: 780-495-4557, 888-338-9378

Alberta

Alberta Economic Development Authority, McDougall Centre, 455 - 6 St. SW, Calgary, AB T2P 4E8
403-297-3022, Fax: 403-297-6435

Alberta Economic Development, Commerce Place , 6th Fl., 10155 - 102 St., Edmonton, T5J 4L6 AB
780-415-1319, Fax: 780-415-1759

Northern Alberta Development Council, #206, Provincial Bldg., 9621 - 96 Ave., PO Bag 900-14, Peace River, T8S 1T4 AB
780-624-6274, Fax: 780-624-6184, nadc.council@gov.ab.ca

British Columbia

Asia Pacific Foundation of Canada, #666, 999 Canada Place, Vancouver, BC V6C 3E1
604-684-5986, Fax: 604-681-1370, info@asiapacific.ca

BC Competition Council, 1810 Blanshard St., PO Box 9327 Prov Govt, Victoria, BC V8W 9N3

BC Progress Board, #730, 999 Canada Place, Vancouver, BC V6C 3E1
604-775-1664

British Columbia Innovation Council, 1188 West Georgia St., 9th Fl., Vancouver, BC V6E 4A2
info@bcinnovationcouncil.com

Columbia Basin Trust, #300, 445 - 13 Ave., Castlegar, BC V1N 1G1
250-365-6633, Fax: 250-365-6670, 800-505-8998, cbt@cbt.org

Ministry of Economic Development, PO Box 9324 Prov Govt,Victoria, V8W 9N3 BC

International Financial Centre - British Columbia Society, World Trade Centre, #545, 999 Canada Place, Vancouver, BC V6C 3E1
604-683-6626, Fax: 604-683-6646, info@ifcvancouver.com

Northern Development Initiative Trust, #301, 1268 Fifth Ave., Prince George, BC V2L 3L2
250-561-2525

Ministry of Small Business & Revenue, PO Box 9065 Prov Govt,Victoria, V8W 9E2 BC
250-356-6611, Fax: 250-356-8294

Small Business BC, 601 West Cordova St., Vancouver, BC V6B 1G1
604-775-5525, Fax: 604-775-5520

Manitoba

Manitoba Competitiveness, Training & Trades, #900, 259 Portage Ave., Winnipeg, R3B 3P4 MB
204-945-2067, Fax: 204-948-2964

Manitoba Development Corporation, #555, 155 Carlton St., Winnipeg, R3C 3H8 MB
204-945-7626, Fax: 204-945-1193

New Brunswick

Department of Business New Brunswick, Centennial Bldg., 670 King St., 5th Fl., PO Box 6000, Fredericton, E3B 5H1 NB
506-444-5228, Fax: 506-453-5428

Regional Development Corporation, RDC Bldg., 836 Churchill Row, PO Box 428, Fredericton, E3B 5R4 NB
506-453-2277, Fax: 506-453-7988

Newfoundland & Labrador

Department of Innovation, Trade & Rural Development, PO Box 8700, St. John's, A1B 4J6 NL
709-729-7000, Fax: 709-729-0654, 800-563-2299, itrdinfo@gov.nl.ca

Ireland Business Partnership, PO Box 8700, St. John's, NL A1B 4J6
709-729-1684, Fax: 709-729-2236

Nova Scotia

Department of Economic Development, Maritime Centre, 1505 Barrington St., 14th Fl., PO Box 2311, Halifax, B3J 3C8 NS
902-424-0377, Fax: 902-424-0500, comm@gov.ns.ca

InNOVACorp, #1400, 1801 Hollis St., Halifax, NS B3J 3N4
902-424-8670, Fax: 902-424-4679, 800-565-7051, communications@innovacorp.ca

Nova Scotia Business Inc., #701, 1800 Argyle St., PO Box 2374, Halifax, NS B3J 3E4
902-424-6650, Fax: 902-424-5739, nsbi@gov.ns.ca

Trade Centre Limited, 1800 Argyle St., PO Box 955, Halifax, NS B3J 2V9
902-421-8686, Fax: 902-422-2922

Northwest Territories

Department of Industry, Tourism & Investment, PO Box 1320, Yellowknife, X1A 2L9 NT

Northwest Territories Business Development & Investment Corporation, #701, 5201 - 50 Ave., Yellowknife, NT X1A 3S9
867-920-6455, Fax: 867-765-0652, bdicinfo@gov.nt.ca

Nunavut

Department of Economic Development & Transportation, PO Box 1000 1500,Iqaluit, X0A 0H0 NU
867-975-7800, Fax: 867-975-7870, 888-975-5999, edt@gov.nu.ca

Ontario

Ministry of Economic Development & Trade, Hearst Block, 900 Bay St., 8th Fl., Toronto, M7A 2E1 ON
416-325-6666, Fax: 416-325-6688

Northern Development Division, Roberta Bondar Place, #200, 70 Foster Dr., Sault Ste Marie, P6A 6V8 ON
705-945-5900, Fax: 705-945-5931

Ministry of Research & Innovation, Whitney Block, 99 Wellesley St. West, 1st Fl., Toronto, M7A 1W1 ON
416-325-5181, Fax: 416-314-5599

Prince Edward Island

Department of Development & Technology, Shaw Bldg., 105 Rochford St., 4th & 5th Fl., PO Box 2000, Charlottetown, C1A 7N8 PE
902-368-4242, Fax: 902-368-4224

Quebec

Ministère du Développement économique, de l'Innovation et de l'Exportation, 710, place D'Youville, 3e étage, Québec, G1R 4Y4 QC
418-691-5950, Fax: 418-644-0118, 866-680-1884

Saskatchewan

Saskatchewan Industry & Resources, 2103 - 11th Ave., Regina, S4P 3V7 SK
306-787-2232, Fax: 306-787-2159, 866-727-5427

Saskatchewan Regional Economic & Co-operative Development, 3085 Albert St., Regina, S4S 0B1 SK
306-787-9703, 800-265-2001

Yukon Territory

Yukon Development Corporation, PO Box 2703 D-1,Whitehorse, Y1A 2C6 YT
867-393-7069, Fax: 867-393-7071

Yukon Economic Development, PO Box 2703, Whitehorse, Y1A 2C6 YT
867-393-7191, Fax: 867-395-7199, 800-661-0408

BUSINESS REGULATIONS

Canada Revenue Agency, 555 Mackenzie Ave., 4th Fl., Ottawa, K1A 0L5 ON
613-952-0384

Industry Canada, 235 Queen St., Ottawa, K1A 0H5 ON
613-947-7466, Fax: 613-954-6436

Alberta

Service Alberta & Registries, John E. Brownlee Bldg., 10365 - 97 St., Edmonton, T5J 3W7 AB
780-415-6090

Manitoba

Companies Office, #1010, 405 Broadway, Winnipeg, R3C 3L6 MB
204-945-2500, Fax: 204-945-1459, companies@gov.mb.ca

Nova Scotia

Nova Scotia Business Inc., #701, 1800 Argyle St., PO Box 2374, Halifax, NS B3J 3E4
902-424-6650, Fax: 902-424-5739, nsbi@gov.ns.ca

Northwest Territories

Northwest Territories Business Development & Investment Corporation, #701, 5201 - 50 Ave., Yellowknife, NT X1A 3S9
867-920-6455, Fax: 867-765-0652, bdicinfo@gov.nt.ca

Nunavut

Department of Finance, Bldg. 1079, 1st Fl., PO Box 1000 Stn 360,Iqaluit, X0A 0H0 NU
867-975-5800, Fax: 867-975-5805

Prince Edward Island

Consumer, Corporate & Insurance Division, Shaw Building, 95 Rochford St., 4th Fl., PO Box 2000, Charlottetown, C1A 7N8 PE
902-368-4550, Fax: 902-368-5283

Quebec

Registraire des entreprises, 800, place D'Youville, Québec, G1R 4Y5 QC
418-528-9074, Fax: 418-646-7329, req@req.gouv.qc.ca

BUYING, GOODS & SERVICES

See: Purchasing
This is the Top, QC

CABINETS & EXECUTIVE COUNCILS

See Also: Government (General Information); Parliament

The Canadian Ministry, c/o Information Service, Library of Parliament, Ottawa, K1A 0A9 ON
613-992-4793, Fax: 613-992-1273, 866-599-4999, info@parl.gc.ca

Alberta

Executive Council, Legislature Bldg., 10800 - 97 Ave., Edmonton, T5K 2B6 AB
780-427-2251, Fax: 780-427-1349

British Columbia

Executive Council, #301, Parliament Bldgs., Victoria, V8V 1X4 BC

Manitoba

Executive Council, Legislative Bldg., 450 Broadway, Winnipeg, R3C 0V8 MB

New Brunswick

Executive Council, Centennial Bldg., PO Box 6000, Fredericton, E3B 5H1 NB

Newfoundland & Labrador

Executive Council, Confederation Bldg., PO Box 8700, St. John's, A1B 4J6 NL
709-729-5645

Nova Scotia

Executive Council, One Government Place, PO Box 2125, Halifax, B3J 3B7 NS
902-424-5970, Fax: 902-424-0667

Northwest Territories

Executive Council, PO Box 1320, Yellowknife, X1A 2L9 NT

Nunavut

Executive Council, Legislative Bldg., 2nd Fl., Box 2410, Iqaluit, X0A 0H0 NU
867-975-5090, Fax: 867-975-5095

Ontario

Executive Council, Whitney Block, Queen's Park, 99 Wellesley St. West, 6th Fl., Toronto, M7A 1A1 ON
416-325-5721, Fax: 416-314-1551

Prince Edward Island

Executive Council, Shaw Bldg., PO Box 2000, Charlottetown, C1A 7N8 PE

Quebec

Ministère du Conseil exécutif, 875, Grande Allée est, Québec, G1R 4Y8 QC
418-646-3021, Fax: 418-528-9242

Saskatchewan

Executive Council, Legislative Bldg., 2405 Legislative Dr., Regina, S4S 0B3 SK

Yukon Territory

Executive Council, PO Box 2703, Whitehorse, Y1A 2C6 YT
867-667-5800, Fax: 867-393-6202, 800-040-8 ex, eco@gov.yk.ca

CANADA PENSION PLAN

See: Pensions
This is the Top, QC

CANADIANS & SOCIETY

Foreign Affairs & International Trade Canada, 125 Sussex Dr., Ottawa, K1A 0G2 ON
613-944-4000, Fax: 613-996-9709, 800-267-8376

Government of Canada, 111 Wellington St., PO Box 1103, Ottawa, K1A 0A6 ON

Human Resources & Social Development Canada, Place du Portage, Phase IV, 12th Fl., 140 Promenade du Portage, Gatineau, K1A 0J9 QC
819-994-6313

Office of the Prime Minister (Cons.), Langevin Block, 80 Wellington St., Ottawa, K1A 0A2 ON
613-992-4211, Fax: 613-941-6900, pm@pm.gc.ca

Manitoba

Multiculturalism Secretariat, 213 Notre Dame Ave., 4th Fl., Winnipeg, MB R3B 1N3
204-945-1156, Fax: 204-948-2323

New Brunswick

Regional Development Corporation, RDC Bldg., 836 Churchill Row, PO Box 428, Fredericton, E3B 5R4 NB
506-453-2277, Fax: 506-453-7988

Newfoundland & Labrador

C.A. Pippy Park Commission, PO Box 8861, St. John's, NL A1B 3T2
709-737-3655, Fax: 709-737-3303, 877-477-3655, pippyparkinfo@nf.aibn.com

Nova Scotia

Pay Equity Commission, 5151 Terminal Rd., 7th Fl., PO Box 697, Halifax, NS B3J 2T8
902-424-8596, sherwoop@gov.ns.ca

Department of Service Nova Scotia & Municipal Relations, 1505 Barrington St., PO Box 216, Halifax, B3J 2M4 NS
902-424-4141, Fax: 902-424-0581, public-enquiries@gov.ns.ca

Ontario

Ministry of Government Services, Ferguson Block, 77 Wellesley St. West, 12th Fl., Toronto, M7A 1N3 ON
416-326-1234

Ontario Northland, 555 Oak St. East, North Bay, ON P1B 8L3
705-472-4500, Fax: 705-476-5598, 800-363-7512, info@ontc.on.ca

Quebec

Ministère de l'Emploi et de la Solidarité sociale, 425, rue St-Amable, 4e étage, Québec, G1R 4Z1 QC
418-643-4810, 888-643-4721

Yukon Territory

Yukon Community Services, PO Box 2703, Whitehorse, Y1A 2C6 YT
867-667-5811, Fax: 867-393-6295, 800-661-0408, inquiry@gov.yk.ca

Yukon Human Rights Commission, #201, 211 Hawkins St., Whitehorse, YT Y1A 1X3
867-667-6226, Fax: 867-667-2662, 800-661-0535, humanrights@yhrc.yk.ca

CENSORSHIP (MEDIA)

Saskatchewan

Saskatchewan Film & Video Classification Board, #500, 1919 Saskatchewan Dr., Regina, SK S4P 4H2
306-787-5550, Fax: 306-787-9779, adwyer@justice.gov.sk.ca

COLLECTIONS

See: Finance
This is the Top, QC

COMMUNICATIONS

See: Telecommunications

Chief Information Office, 235 Queen St., Ottawa, ON K1A 0H5
613-954-3574, Fax: 613-941-1938
Communications Research Centre Canada, 3701 Carling Ave., PO Box 11490 H, Ottawa, ON K2H 8S2
613-991-3313, Fax: 613-998-5355, info@crc.ca

COMMUNITY & MUNICIPAL DEVELOPMENT

Atlantic Canada Opportunities Agency, 644 Main St., 3rd Fl., PO Box 6051, Moncton, E1C 9J8 NB
506-851-2271, Fax: 506-851-7403, 800-561-7862
Canada Economic Development for Québec Regions, Tour de la Bourse, #3800, 800, Place Victoria, CP 247, Montréal, H4Z 1E8 QC
514-283-6412, Fax: 514-283-3302, 866-385-6412
Western Economic Diversification Canada, Canada Place, #1500, 9700 Jasper Ave. NW, Edmonton, T5J 4H7 AB
780-495-4164, Fax: 780-495-4557, 888-338-9378

Alberta
Northern Alberta Development Council, #206, Provincial Bldg., 9621 - 96 Ave., PO Bag 900-14, Peace River, T8S 1T4 AB
780-624-6274, Fax: 780-624-6184, nadc.council@gov.ab.ca

Manitoba
Provincial-Municipal Support Services, #508, 800 Portage Ave., Winnipeg, R3G 0N4 MB

New Brunswick
Regional Development Corporation, RDC Bldg., 836 Churchill Row, PO Box 428, Fredericton, E3B 5R4 NB
506-453-2277, Fax: 506-453-7988

Nova Scotia
Department of Service Nova Scotia & Municipal Relations, 1505 Barrington St., PO Box 216, Halifax, B3J 2M4 NS
902-424-4141, Fax: 902-424-0581, public-enquiries@gov.ns.ca

Ontario
Ministry of Municipal Affairs & Housing, 777 Bay St., 17th Fl., Toronto, M5G 2E5 ON
416-585-7041, Fax: 416-585-6227, 866-220-2290

Quebec
Ministère du Développement économique, de l'Innovation et de l'Exportation, 710, place D'Youville, 3e étage, Québec, G1R 4Y4 QC
418-691-5950, Fax: 418-644-0118, 866-680-1884

Saskatchewan
Saskatchewan Regional Economic & Co-operative Development, 3085 Albert St., Regina, S4S 0B1 SK
306-787-9703, 800-265-2001

COMMUNITY FINANCING

Atlantic Canada Opportunities Agency, 644 Main St., 3rd Fl., PO Box 6051, Moncton, E1C 9J8 NB
506-851-2271, Fax: 506-851-7403, 800-561-7862
Business Development Bank of Canada, #400, 5, Place Ville-Marie, Montréal, H3B 5E7 QC
514-283-5904, Fax: 514-283-2872, 888-463-6232
Canada Economic Development for Québec Regions, Tour de la Bourse, #3800, 800, Place Victoria, CP 247, Montréal, H4Z 1E8 QC
514-283-6412, Fax: 514-283-3302, 866-385-6412
Canada Investment & Savings, #900, 110 Yonge St., Toronto, ON M5C 1T4
416-952-1252, Fax: 416-952-1270, 800-575-5151, csb@csb.gc.ca
Finance Canada, L'esplanade Laurier, 140 O'Connor St., Ottawa, K1A 0G5 ON
613-992-1573, Fax: 613-996-8404
Western Economic Diversification Canada, Canada Place, #1500, 9700 Jasper Ave. NW, Edmonton, T5J 4H7 AB
780-495-4164, Fax: 780-495-4557, 888-338-9378

Alberta
Alberta Capital Finance Authority, 2450 Canadian Western Bank Place, 10303 Jasper Ave., Edmonton, AB T5J 3N6
780-427-9711, Fax: 780-422-2175, webacfa@gov.ab.ca

Manitoba
Provincial-Municipal Support Services, #508, 800 Portage Ave., Winnipeg, R3G 0N4 MB

New Brunswick
New Brunswick Municipal Finance Corporation, #376, 670 King St., PO Box 6000, Fredericton, NB E3B 5H1
506-453-3952, Fax: 506-453-2053

Newfoundland & Labrador
Newfoundland & Labrador Municipal Financing Corporation, Confederation Bldg., PO Box 8700, St. John's, NL A1B 4J6
709-729-6686, Fax: 709-729-2095

Nova Scotia
Nova Scotia Municipal Finance Corporation, Maritime Centre, 1723 Hollis St., 7th Fl., PO Box 850 M, Halifax, NS B3J 2V2
902-424-4590, Fax: 902-424-0525

Yukon Territory
Yukon Economic Development, PO Box 2703, Whitehorse, Y1A 2C6 YT
867-393-7191, Fax: 867-395-7199, 800-661-0408

COMMUNITY SERVICES

Alberta
Northern Alberta Development Council, #206, Provincial Bldg., 9621 - 96 Ave., PO Bag 900-14, Peace River, T8S 1T4 AB
780-624-6274, Fax: 780-624-6184, nadc.council@gov.ab.ca

Yukon Territory
Yukon Community Services, PO Box 2703, Whitehorse, Y1A 2C6 YT
867-667-5811, Fax: 867-393-6295, 800-661-0408, inquiry@gov.yk.ca

CONFLICT OF INTEREST

Office of the Ethics Commissioner, 66 Slater St., 22nd Fl., Ottawa, K1A 0A6 ON
613-995-0721, Fax: 613-995-7308

Alberta
Alberta Office of the Ethics Commissioner, #1250, 9925 - 109 St., Edmonton, T5K 2J8 AB
780-422-2273, Fax: 780-422-2261

CONSERVATION & ECOLOGY

See Also: Heritage Resources; Natural Resources

British Columbia
BC Assessment Authority, 1537 Hillside Ave., Victoria, BC V8T 4Y2
250-595-6211, Fax: 250-595-6222, info@bcassessment.ca
Forest Practices Board, 1675 Douglas St., 3rd Fl., PO Box 9905 Prov Govt, Victoria, BC V8W 9R1
250-387-7964, Fax: 250-387-7009, 800-994-5899, fpboard@gov.bc.ca

Saskatchewan
Saskatchewan Assessment Management Agency, #200, 2201 - 11 Ave., Regina, S4P 0J8 SK
306-924-8000, Fax: 306-924-8070, 800-667-7262

CONSTRUCTION

Canada Mortgage & Housing Corporation, 700 Montreal Rd., Ottawa, K1A 0P7 ON
613-748-2000, Fax: 613-748-2098, 800-668-2642

Nova Scotia
Labour Relations Board & Construction Industry Panel, 5151 Terminal Rd.,7th Fl., PO Box 697, Halifax, NS B3J 2T8
902-424-5300, Fax: 902-424-0503

Ontario
Building Code Commission, 777 Bay St., 2nd Fl., Toronto, ON M5G 2E5
416-585-6503, Fax: 416-585-7531
Building Materials Evaluation Commission, 777 Bay St., 2nd Fl., Toronto, ON M5G 2E5
416-585-4234, Fax: 416-585-7531

CONSUMER PROTECTION

See Also: Public Safety
Financial Consumer Agency of Canada, 427 Laurier Ave. West, 6th Fl., Ottawa, K1R 1B9 ON
Fax: 613-941-1436, info@fcac-acfc.gc.ca

Alberta
Consumer Services & Land Titles, Commerce Place, 10155 - 102 St., 3rd Fl., Edmonton, T5J 4L4 AB

Nova Scotia
Department of Service Nova Scotia & Municipal Relations, 1505 Barrington St., PO Box 216, Halifax, B3J 2M4 NS
902-424-4141, Fax: 902-424-0581, public-enquiries@gov.ns.ca

CORONERS

British Columbia
BC Coroner's Service, Metrotower II, #2035, 4720 Kingsway, Burnaby, BC V5H 4N2
604-660-7745, Fax: 604-660-7766

Manitoba
Office of the Chief Medical Examiner, #210, 1 Wesley Ave., Winnipeg, MB R3C 4C6
204-945-2088, Fax: 204-945-2442

Nova Scotia
Nova Scotia Medical Examiner Service, Halifax Insurance Bldg., #701, 5670 Spring Garden Rd., Halifax, NS B3J 1H7
902-424-2722, Fax: 902-424-0607, 888-424-4336

Nunavut
Office of the Chief Coroner, PO Box 1000 590, Iqaluit, NU X0A 0H0

CORRECTIONAL SERVICES

Nunavut
Baffin Correctional Centre, 1550 Federal Rd., PO Box 368, Iqaluit, NU X0A 0H0
867-979-8100, Fax: 867-979-4646

CREDIT COUNSELLING

See: Debt Management
This is the Top, QC

CRIMES COMPENSATION

Manitoba
Compensation for Victims of Crime, 1410 - 405 Broadway, Winnipeg, MB R3C 3L6
204-945-0899, Fax: 204-948-3071

Northwest Territories
Victims Assistance Committee, c/o Community Justice Division, PO Box 1320, Yellowknife, NT X1A 2L9
867-920-6911, Fax: 867-873-0299

Ontario
Criminal Injuries Compensation Board, 439 University Ave., 4th Fl., Toronto, ON M5G 1Y8
416-326-2900, Fax: 416-326-2883, 800-372-7463
Office for Victims of Crime, 700 Bay St., 3rd Fl., Toronto, ON M5G 1Z6
416-326-1682, Fax: 416-326-2343, 887-435-7661

CULTURE & HERITAGE

See: Arts & Culture

Alberta
Alberta International & Intergovernmental Relations, Commerce Place, 10155 - 102 St., 12th Fl., Edmonton, T5J 4G2 AB
780-422-1510, Fax: 780-423-6654

CURRENCY

Bank of Canada, 234 Wellington St., Ottawa, K1A 0G9 ON
613-782-8111, Fax: 613-782-8655
Royal Canadian Mint, 320 Sussex Dr., Ottawa, K1A 0G8 ON
613-993-3500

CUSTOMS

Canada Border Services Agency, 191 Laurier Ave. West, Ottawa, K1A 0L5 ON
613-952-3200

DAIRY INDUSTRY

Manitoba
Manitoba Milk Prices Review Commission, c/o Boards, Commissions & Legislation Branch, #812, 401 York Ave., Winnipeg, MB R3C 0P8
204-945-3854, Fax: 204-948-2844

Prince Edward Island
Department of Agriculture, Fisheries & Aquaculture, Jones Bldg., 11 Kent St., PO Box 2000, Charlottetown, C1A 7N8 PE
902-368-4880, Fax: 902-368-4857

DEBT MANAGEMENT

Finance Canada, L'esplanade Laurier, 140 O'Connor St., Ottawa, K1A 0G5 ON
613-992-1573, Fax: 613-996-8404

British Columbia
Provincial Treasury, 620 Superior St., Victoria, V8V 1X4 BC
250-387-4541

DISCRIMINATION & EMPLOYMENT EQUITY

British Columbia
BC Human Rights Tribunal, #1170, 605 Robson St., Vancouver, BC V6B 5J3
604-775-2000, Fax: 604-775-2020, 888-440-8844

Yukon Territory
Yukon Human Rights Commission, #201, 211 Hawkins St., Whitehorse, YT Y1A 1X3
867-667-6226, Fax: 867-667-2662, 800-661-0535, humanrights@yhrc.yk.ca

DIVORCE

Justice Canada, East Memorial Bldg., 284 Wellington St., Ottawa, K1A 0H8 ON
613-957-4222, Fax: 613-954-0811

DRIVERS' LICENCES

Alberta
Service Alberta & Registries, John E. Brownlee Bldg., 10365 - 97 St., Edmonton, T5J 3W7 AB
780-415-6090

Saskatchewan
Saskatchewan Government Insurance, 2260 - 11 Ave., Regina, S4P 0J9 SK
306-751-1200, Fax: 306-787-7477

Yukon Territory
Driver Control Board, 308 Steele St., PO Box 2703, Whitehorse, YT Y1A 2C6
867-667-3774, Fax: 867-393-6483, dcb@gov.yk.ca

ECONOMIC DEVELOPMENT

See: Business Development
This is the Top, QC

EDUCATION

Alberta
Alberta Teachers' Retirement Fund Board, Barnett House, #600, 11010 - 142 St., Edmonton, AB T5N 2R1
780-451-4166, Fax: 780-452-3547, 800-661-9582, info@atrf.com
Council on Alberta Teaching Standards, 10044 - 108 St., Edmonton, AB T5J 5E6
780-427-2045, Fax: 780-422-4199
Alberta Education, Commerce Place, 10155 - 102 St., 7th Fl., Edmonton, T5J 4L5 AB
780-427-7219, Fax: 780-427-0591

British Columbia
Auditor Certification Board, 940 Blanshard St., 2nd Fl., PO Box 9431 Prov Govt, Victoria, BC V8W 9V3
250-356-8658, Fax: 250-356-9422

EDUCATION & TRAINING

Human Resources & Social Development Canada, Place du Portage, Phase IV, 12th Fl., 140 Promenade du Portage, Gatineau, K1A 0J9 QC
819-994-6313

British Columbia
Ministry of Labour & Citizens' Services, PO Box 9594 Prov Govt,Victoria, V8W 9K4 BC
250-356-1487, Fax: 250-356-1653

Nova Scotia
Department of Environment & Labour, 5151 Terminal Rd., 6th Fl., PO Box 697, Halifax, B3J 2T8 NS
902-424-5300, Fax: 902-424-0575

EMPLOYMENT

Manitoba
Manitoba Labour & Immigration, #317, Legislative Bldg., 450 Broadway, Winnipeg, R3C 0V8 MB
Fax: 204-945-8312, minlab@leg.gov.mb.ca

Northwest Territories
Department of Human Resources, PO Box 1320, Yellowknife, X1A 2L9 NT

Quebec
Ministère de l'Emploi et de la Solidarité sociale, 425, rue St-Amable, 4e étage, Québec, G1R 4Z1 QC
418-643-4810, 888-643-4721

ENERGY

See Also: Natural Resources

Nova Scotia
Canada-Nova Scotia Offshore Petroleum Board, TD Centre, 1791 Barrington St., 6th Fl., Halifax, NS B3J 3K9
902-422-5588, Fax: 902-422-1799, postmaster@cnsopb.ns.ca

Saskatchewan
Saskatchewan Industry & Resources, 2103 - 11th Ave., Regina, S4P 3V7 SK
306-787-2232, Fax: 306-787-2159, 866-727-5427

ENVIRONMENT

Nova Scotia
Department of Environment & Labour, 5151 Terminal Rd., 6th Fl., PO Box 697, Halifax, B3J 2T8 NS
902-424-5300, Fax: 902-424-0575

ENVIRONMENT DEPARTMENTS/MINISTRIES

Nova Scotia
Department of Environment & Labour, 5151 Terminal Rd., 6th Fl., PO Box 697, Halifax, B3J 2T8 NS
902-424-5300, Fax: 902-424-0575

EROSION CONTROL

Saskatchewan
Saskatchewan Agriculture & Food, Walter Scott Bldg., 3085 Albert St., Regina, S4S 0B1 SK
306-787-5140

EXPORT DEVELOPMENT

Business Development Bank of Canada, #400, 5, Place Ville-Marie, Montréal, H3B 5E7 QC
514-283-5904, Fax: 514-283-2872, 888-463-6232
Export Development Canada, 151 O'Connor St., Ottawa, K1A 1K3 ON
613-598-2500, Fax: 613-237-2690, 888-332-3320
Industry Canada, 235 Queen St., Ottawa, K1A 0H5 ON
613-947-7466, Fax: 613-954-6436
Western Economic Diversification Canada, Canada Place, #1500, 9700 Jasper Ave. NW, Edmonton, T5J 4H7 AB
780-495-4164, Fax: 780-495-4557, 888-338-9378

Alberta
Alberta Economic Development, Commerce Place , 6th Fl., 10155 - 102 St., Edmonton, T5J 4L6 AB
780-415-1319, Fax: 780-415-1759

Northwest Territories
Northwest Territories Business Development & Investment Corporation, #701, 5201 - 50 Ave., Yellowknife, NT X1A 3S9
867-920-6455, Fax: 867-765-0652, bdicinfo@gov.nt.ca

Ontario
Ministry of Economic Development & Trade, Hearst Block, 900 Bay St., 8th Fl., Toronto, M7A 2E1 ON
416-325-6666, Fax: 416-325-6688

Saskatchewan
Saskatchewan Industry & Resources, 2103 - 11th Ave., Regina, S4P 3V7 SK
306-787-2232, Fax: 306-787-2159, 866-727-5427
Saskatchewan Trade & Export Partnership, #320, 1801 Hamilton St., PO Box 1787, Regina, SK S4P 3C6
306-787-9210, Fax: 306-787-6666, 877-313-7244, inquire@sasktrade.sk.ca

EXPROPRIATION

Justice Canada, East Memorial Bldg., 284 Wellington St., Ottawa, K1A 0H8 ON
613-957-4222, Fax: 613-954-0811

New Brunswick
New Brunswick Expropriations Advisory Office, 371 Queen St., Fredericton, NB E3B 1B1
506-453-7771, Fax: 506-453-9600

Quebec
Ministère de la Justice, 1200, rte de l'Église, Sainte-Foy, G1V 4M1 QC
418-643-5140, Fax: 418-646-4449, 866-536-5140
Ministère des Transports, 700, boul René-Lévesque est, 27e étage, Québec, G1R 5H1 QC
Fax: 514-643-1269, 888-355-0511, communications@mtq.gouv.qc.ca

Saskatchewan
Public & Private Rights Board, 3085 Albert St., 3rd Fl., Regina, SK S4P 3V7
306-787-4071, Fax: 306-787-0088

FAMILY BENEFITS

See Also: Income Security; Social Services

Quebec
Ministère de l'Emploi et de la Solidarité sociale, 425, rue St-Amable, 4e étage, Québec, G1R 4Z1 QC
418-643-4810, 888-643-4721

FEDERAL-PROVINCIAL AFFAIRS

Alberta
Alberta International & Intergovernmental Relations, Commerce Place, 10155 - 102 St., 12th Fl., Edmonton, T5J 4G2 AB
780-422-1510, Fax: 780-423-6654

Manitoba
Federal-Provincial & International Relations & Trade Division, #42, 450 Broadway, Winnipeg, R3C 0V8 MB

Nunavut
Department of Executive & Intergovernmental Affairs, Box 1000, Iqaluit, X0A 0H0 NU
867-975-6000, Fax: 867-975-6090

Ontario
Ministry of Intergovernmental Affairs & Democratic Renewal Secretariat, 77 Wellesley St. West, Toronto, M7A 1N3 ON
416-325-4800, Fax: 416-325-4787

FILM PRODUCTION & COLLECTIONS

Alberta
Alberta Film Commission, 10155 - 102 St., 5th Fl., Edmonton, AB T5J 4L6
780-422-8584, Fax: 780-422-8582, 888-813-1738

New Brunswick
New Brunswick Film, Assumption Pl., 770 Main St., 16th Fl., PO Box 5001, Moncton, NB E1C 8R3
506-869-6868, Fax: 506-869-6840, nbfilm@gnb.ca

Nova Scotia
Nova Scotia Film Development Corporation, 1724 Granville St., Halifax, NS B3J 1X5
902-424-7177, Fax: 902-424-0617, novascotia.film@ns.sympatico.ca

FINANCE

See Also: Banking & Financial Institutions
Finance Canada, L'esplanade Laurier, 140 O'Connor St., Ottawa, K1A 0G5 ON
613-992-1573, Fax: 613-996-8404

Alberta
Alberta Finance, Terrace Bldg., 9515 - 107 St., Edmonton, T5K 2C3 AB
780-427-3035, Fax: 780-427-1147

British Columbia
Ministry of Finance, PO Box 9048 Prov Govt,Victoria, V8W 9E2 BC
250-387-3751, Fax: 250-387-5594

Manitoba
Manitoba Finance, #109, Legislative Bldg., Winnipeg, R3C 0V8 MB
204-945-3754, Fax: 204-945-8316, minfin@leg.gov.mb.ca

New Brunswick
Department of Finance, 670 King St., PO Box 6000, Fredericton, E3B 5H1 NB
506-453-2451, Fax: 506-444-4724

Newfoundland & Labrador
Department of Finance, Confederation Bldg., PO Box 8700, St. John's, A1B 4J6 NL
709-729-6310

Nova Scotia
Department of Finance, PO Box 187, Halifax, B3J 2N3 NS
902-424-5554, Fax: 902-424-0635

Northwest Territories
Department of Finance, PO Box 1320, Yellowknife, X1A 2L9 NT
867-873-0414, Fax: 867-873-7117

Nunavut
Department of Finance, Bldg. 1079, 1st Fl., PO Box 1000 Stn 360,Iqaluit, X0A 0H0 NU
867-975-5800, Fax: 867-975-5805

Ontario
Ministry of Finance, Frost Bldg. South, 7 Queen's Park Cres., 7th Fl., Toronto, M7A 1Y7 ON
416-325-0333, Fax: 416-325-0339

Prince Edward Island
Department of the Provincial Treasury, PO Box 2000, Charlottetown, C1A 7N8 PE
902-368-4000, Fax: 902-368-5544

Quebec
Ministère des Finances, Édifice Gérard-D.-Lévesque, 12, rue Saint-Louis, 1er étage, Québec, G1R 5L3 QC
418-528-9323, Fax: 418-646-1631, info@finances.gouv.qc.ca

Saskatchewan
Saskatchewan Finance, 2350 Albert St., Regina, S4P 4A6 SK
306-787-6768, Fax: 306-787-6544

Yukon Territory
Yukon Finance, PO Box 2703, Whitehorse, Y1A 2C6 YT
867-667-5343, Fax: 867-393-6217

FINANCING & LOANS

See Also: Investment

Business Development Bank of Canada, #400, 5, Place Ville-Marie, Montréal, H3B 5E7 QC
514-283-5904, Fax: 514-283-2872, 888-463-6232

Canada Mortgage & Housing Corporation, 700 Montreal Rd., Ottawa, K1A 0P7 ON
613-748-2000, Fax: 613-748-2098, 800-668-2642

Farm Credit Canada, 1800 Hamilton St., PO Box 4320, Regina, S4P 4L3 SK
306-780-8100, Fax: 306-780-5875, 800-387-3232

Alberta
Alberta Capital Finance Authority, 2450 Canadian Western Bank Place, 10303 Jasper Ave., Edmonton, AB T5J 3N6
780-427-9711, Fax: 780-422-2175, webacfa@gov.ab.ca

ATB Financial, 9888 Jasper Ave., Edmonton, AB T5J 1P1

British Columbia
International Financial Centre - British Columbia Society, World Trade Centre, #545, 999 Canada Place, Vancouver, BC V6C 3E1
604-683-6626, Fax: 604-683-6646, info@ifcvancouver.com

Provincial Treasury, 620 Superior St., Victoria, V8V 1X4 BC
250-387-4541

Manitoba
Manitoba Agricultural Services Corporation, #100, 1525 First St. South, Brandon, MB R7A 7A1
204-726-6850, Fax: 204-726-6849, mailbox@mcic.gov.mb.ca

New Brunswick
New Brunswick Electric Finance Corporation, #376, 670 King St., PO Box 6000, Fredericton, NB E3B 5H1
506-453-3952, Fax: 506-453-2053

Newfoundland & Labrador
Department of Finance, Confederation Bldg., PO Box 8700, St. John's, A1B 4J6 NL
709-729-6310

Northwest Territories
Department of Industry, Tourism & Investment, PO Box 1320, Yellowknife, X1A 2L9 NT

Nunavut
Nunavut Credit Corporation, PO Box 224, Cape Dorset, NU X0A 0C0

Ontario
Ontario Electricity Financial Corporation, #1400, 1 Dundas St. West, Toronto, ON M5G 1Z3
416-325-8000, Fax: 416-325-8005

Ontario Financing Authority, #1400, 1 Dundas St. West, Toronto, ON M5G 1Z3
416-325-8000, Fax: 416-325-8005

Prince Edward Island
Prince Edward Island Lending Agency, PO Box 1420, Charlottetown, PE C1A 7N1
902-368-6200, Fax: 902-368-6201

Saskatchewan
Saskatchewan Trade & Export Partnership, #320, 1801 Hamilton St., PO Box 1787, Regina, SK S4P 3C6
306-787-9210, Fax: 306-787-6666, 877-313-7244, inquire@sasktrade.sk.ca

Yukon Territory
Yukon Economic Development, PO Box 2703, Whitehorse, Y1A 2C6 YT
867-393-7191, Fax: 867-395-7199, 800-661-0408

FIRE PREVENTION

Manitoba
Office of the Fire Commissioner, #508, 401 York Ave., Winnipeg, MB R3C 0P8
204-945-3322, Fax: 204-948-2089, 800-282-8069, firecomm@gov.mb.ca

FIREARMS

British Columbia
Ministry of the Attorney General, 1001 Douglas St., 10th Fl., PO Box 9282 Prov Govt,Victoria, V8W 9J7 BC
250-356-9596, Fax: 250-387-1753

FISHERIES

British Columbia
Ministry of Agriculture & Lands, PO Box 9120 Prov Govt,Victoria, V8W 9B4 BC
250-387-5121, Fax: 250-387-1522

New Brunswick
Department of Agriculture & Aquaculture, PO Box 6000, Fredericton, E3B 5H1 NB
506-453-2666, Fax: 506-453-7170

Department of Business New Brunswick, Centennial Bldg., 670 King St., 5th Fl., PO Box 6000, Fredericton, E3B 5H1 NB
506-444-5228, Fax: 506-453-5428

Prince Edward Island
Department of Agriculture, Fisheries & Aquaculture, Jones Bldg., 11 Kent St., PO Box 2000, Charlottetown, C1A 7N8 PE
902-368-4880, Fax: 902-368-4857

FISHERIES & WILDLIFE

New Brunswick
Department of Agriculture & Aquaculture, PO Box 6000, Fredericton, E3B 5H1 NB
506-453-2666, Fax: 506-453-7170

Quebec
Ministère de l'Agriculture, des Pêcheries et de l'Alimentation, 200, ch Sainte-Foy, Québec, G1R 4X6 QC
418-380-2110, 888-222-6272

FOREIGN INVESTMENT

See: Investment

This is the Top, QC

FOREST RESOURCES

British Columbia
Ministry of Forests & Range, PO Box 9529 Prov Govt,Victoria, V8W 9C3 BC
250-387-6121, 800-663-7867

FORESTRY & PAPER

British Columbia
Forest Practices Board, 1675 Douglas St., 3rd Fl., PO Box 9905 Prov Govt, Victoria, BC V8W 9R1
250-387-7964, Fax: 250-387-7009, 800-994-5899, fpboard@gov.bc.ca

Ministry of Forests & Range, PO Box 9529 Prov Govt,Victoria, V8W 9C3 BC
250-387-6121, 800-663-7867

Timber Export Advisory Committee, 1520 Blanshard St., 2nd Fl., PO Box 9514 Prov Govt, Victoria, BC V8W 3C8
250-387-8359, Fax: 250-387-5050

GOVERNMENT

Auditor General of Canada, 240 Sparks St., Ottawa, K1A 0G6 ON
613-995-3708, Fax: 613-957-0474, communications@oag-bvg.gc.ca

Bank of Canada, 234 Wellington St., Ottawa, K1A 0G9 ON
613-782-8111, Fax: 613-782-8655

Business Development Bank of Canada, #400, 5, Place Ville-Marie, Montréal, H3B 5E7 QC
514-283-5904, Fax: 514-283-2872, 888-463-6232

Canada Economic Development for Québec Regions, Tour de la Bourse, #3800, 800, Place Victoria, CP 247, Montréal, H4Z 1E8 QC
514-283-6412, Fax: 514-283-3302, 866-385-6412

Canada Revenue Agency, 555 Mackenzie Ave., 4th Fl., Ottawa, K1A 0L5 ON
613-952-0384

Finance Canada, L'esplanade Laurier, 140 O'Connor St., Ottawa, K1A 0G5 ON
613-992-1573, Fax: 613-996-8404

Foreign Affairs & International Trade Canada, 125 Sussex Dr., Ottawa, K1A 0G2 ON
613-944-4000, Fax: 613-996-9709, 800-267-8376

Government of Canada, 111 Wellington St., PO Box 1103, Ottawa, K1A 0A6 ON

House of Commons, Canada, House of Commons, 111 Wellington St., Ottawa, K1A 0A6 ON
866-599-4999

Industry Canada, 235 Queen St., Ottawa, K1A 0H5 ON
613-947-7466, Fax: 613-954-6436

Justice Canada, East Memorial Bldg., 284 Wellington St., Ottawa, K1A 0H8 ON
613-957-4222, Fax: 613-954-0811

North American Free Trade Agreement (NAFTA) Secretariat, Canadian Section, #705, 90 Sparks St., Ottawa, K1P 5B4 ON
613-992-9388, Fax: 613-992-9392, canada@nafta-sec-alena.org

Office of the Prime Minister (Cons.), Langevin Block, 80 Wellington St., Ottawa, K1A 0A2 ON
613-992-4211, Fax: 613-941-6900, pm@pm.gc.ca

Public Works & Government Services Canada, Place du Portage, Phase III, 11, rue Laurier, Ottawa, K1A 0S5 ON
819-997-6363

Royal Canadian Mint, 320 Sussex Dr., Ottawa, K1A 0G8 ON
613-993-3500

Statistics Canada, R.H. Coats Bldg., Tunney's Pasture, 100 Tunney's Pasture Driveway, Ottawa, K1A 0T6 ON
Fax: 877-287-4369, 800-263-1136, infostats@statcan.ca

The Canadian Ministry, c/o Information Service, Library of Parliament, Ottawa, K1A 0A9 ON
613-992-4793, Fax: 613-992-1273, 866-599-4999, info@parl.gc.ca

Treasury Board of Canada, 300 Laurier Ave. West, 10th Fl., Ottawa, K1A 0R5 ON
613-957-2400, Fax: 613-998-9071, 877-636-0656

Alberta
Alberta Pensions Administration Corporation, Park Plaza, 3rd Fl., 10611 - 98 Ave., Edmonton, AB T5K 2P7
780-427-2782, Fax: 780-427-1621, 800-661-8198, apa.info@apa.gov.ab.ca

Alberta Review Board, J.E. Brownlee Bldg., 10365 - 97 St., 5th Fl., Edmonton, AB T5J 3W7
780-422-5994, Fax: 780-427-1762

Alberta Office of the Auditor General, 9925 - 109 St., 8th Fl., Edmonton, T5K 2J8 AB
780-427-4222, Fax: 780-422-9555

Consumer Services & Land Titles, Commerce Place, 10155 - 102 St., 3rd Fl., Edmonton, T5J 4L4 AB

Alberta Office of the Ethics Commissioner, #1250, 9925 - 109 St., Edmonton, T5K 2J8 AB
780-422-2273, Fax: 780-422-2261

Executive Council, Legislature Bldg., 10800 - 97 Ave., Edmonton, T5K 2B6 AB
780-427-2251, Fax: 780-427-1349

Alberta Finance, Terrace Bldg., 9515 - 107 St., Edmonton, T5K 2C3 AB
780-427-3035, Fax: 780-427-1147

Government of Alberta, 9718 - 107 St., Edmonton, T5K 1E4 AB

Alberta International & Intergovernmental Relations, Commerce Place, 10155 - 102 St., 12th Fl., Edmonton, T5J 4G2 AB
780-422-1510, Fax: 780-423-6654

Office of the Premier, Legislature Bldg., #307, 10800 - 97 Ave., Edmonton, T5K 2B6 AB
780-427-2251, Fax: 780-427-1349

British Columbia

Agricultural Land Commission, #133, 4940 Canada Way, Burnaby, BC V5G 4K6
604-660-7000, Fax: 604-660-7033

Office of the Auditor General, 8 Bastion Sq., Victoria, V8V 1X4 BC
250-387-6803, Fax: 250-387-1230

BC Assessment Authority, 1537 Hillside Ave., Victoria, BC V8T 4Y2
250-595-6211, Fax: 250-595-6222, info@bcassessment.ca

Crown Corporations Secretariat, PO Box 9300 Prov Govt, Victoria, BC V8W 9N2
250-952-0750, Fax: 250-952-0777

Executive Council, #301, Parliament Bldgs., Victoria, V8V 1X4 BC

Government of British Columbia, Parliament Bldgs., Victoria, V8V 1X4 BC

Office of the Premier, PO Box 9041 Prov Govt,Victoria, V8W 9E1 BC
250-387-1715, Fax: 250-387-0087, premier@gov.bc.ca

Manitoba

Office of the Auditor General, #500, 330 Portage Ave., Winnipeg, R3C 0C4 MB
204-945-3790, Fax: 204-945-2169

Crown Corporations Council, #1130, 444 St. Mary Ave., Winnipeg, MB R3C 3T1
204-949-5270, Fax: 204-949-5283, crowncc@mts.net

Executive Council, Legislative Bldg., 450 Broadway, Winnipeg, R3C 0V8 MB

Federal-Provincial Relations & Research Division, #910, 386 Broadway, Winnipeg, R3C 3R6 MB

Government of Manitoba, Winnipeg, R3C 0V8 MB

Manitoba Intergovernmental Affairs, #301, 450 Broadway, Winnipeg, R3C 0V8 MB
Fax: 204-945-1383, mnia@leg.gov.mb.ca

Manitoba Civil Service Commission, #935, 155 Carlton St., Winnipeg, MB R3C 3H8
204-945-2332, Fax: 204-945-1486, cschrp@gov.mb.ca

Manitoba Municipal Board, #1144, 363 Broadway, Winnipeg, MB R3C 3N9
204-945-2941, Fax: 204-948-2235

Office of the Premier, Legislative Bldg., #214, 450 Broadway, Winnipeg, R3C 0V8 MB
204-945-3714, Fax: 204-949-1484, premier@leg.gov.mb.ca

Provincial-Municipal Support Services, #508, 800 Portage Ave., Winnipeg, R3G 0N4 MB

Residential Tenancies Commission, #1650, 155 Carlton St., Winnipeg, MB R3C 3H8
204-945-2028, Fax: 204-945-5453, 800-782-8403, rtc@gov.mb.ca

Manitoba Treasury Board, #200, 386 Broadway, Winnipeg, R3C 3R6 MB
204-945-1101, Fax: 204-948-2358

New Brunswick

Office of the Auditor General, PO Box 758, Fredericton, E3B 5B4 NB
506-453-2243, Fax: 506-453-3067

Office of the Comptroller, Centennial Bldg., 670 King St., Fredericton, E3B 5H1 NB
506-453-2565, Fax: 506-453-2917

Executive Council, Centennial Bldg., PO Box 6000, Fredericton, E3B 5H1 NB

Government of New Brunswick, PO Box 6000, Fredericton, E3B 5H1 NB

Office of the Premier, Centennial Bldg., 670 King St., PO Box 6000, Fredericton, E3B 5H1 NB
506-453-2144, Fax: 506-453-7407, premier@gnb.ca

Newfoundland & Labrador

Office of the Auditor General, Viking Bldg., 3rd Fl., PO Box 8700, St. John's, A1B 4J6 NL
709-729-2700, Fax: 709-729-5970

Executive Council, Confederation Bldg., PO Box 8700, St. John's, A1B 4J6 NL
709-729-5645

Government of Newfoundland & Labrador, Confederation Bldg., St. John's, A1B 4J6 NL

Department of Government Services, PO Box 8700, St. John's, A1B 4J6 NL
709-729-4860

Newfoundland & Labrador Municipal Financing Corporation, Confederation Bldg., PO Box 8700, St. John's, NL A1B 4J6
709-729-6686, Fax: 709-729-2095

Office of the Premier, Confederation Bldg., East Block, PO Box 8700, St. John's, A1B 4J6 NL
709-729-3570, Fax: 709-729-5875, premier@gov.nl.ca

Nova Scotia

Office of the Auditor General, #302, 1888 Brunswick St., Halifax, B3J 3J8 NS
902-424-5907, Fax: 902-424-4350

Executive Council, One Government Place, PO Box 2125, Halifax, B3J 3B7 NS
902-424-5970, Fax: 902-424-0667

Government of Nova Scotia, Province House, Halifax, B3J 2T3 NS

Office of the Premier, One Government Place, 1700 Granville St., PO Box 726, Halifax, B3J 2T3 NS
902-424-6600, Fax: 902-424-7648, premier@gov.ns.ca

Department of Service Nova Scotia & Municipal Relations, 1505 Barrington St., PO Box 216, Halifax, B3J 2M4 NS
902-424-4141, Fax: 902-424-0581, public-enquiries@gov.ns.ca

Nova Scotia Treasury & Policy Board, 1700 Granville St., 5th Fl., PO Box 1617, Halifax, B3J 2Y3 NS
902-424-8910, Fax: 902-424-7638, tpbenquiries@gov.ns.ca

Northwest Territories

Executive Council, PO Box 1320, Yellowknife, X1A 2L9 NT

Financial Management Board Secretariat, 5003 - 49 St., PO Box 1320, Yellowknife, X1A 2L9 NT
867-920-8962, Fax: 867-873-0128

Government of the Northwest Territories, PO Box 1320, Yellowknife, X1A 2L9 NT

Office of the Premier, Legislative Assembly Bldg., PO Box 1320, Yellowknife, X1A 2L9 NT
867-669-2311, Fax: 867-873-0385

Nunavut

Department of Executive & Intergovernmental Affairs, Box 1000, Iqaluit, X0A 0H0 NU
867-975-6000, Fax: 867-975-6090

Executive Council, Legislative Bldg., 2nd Fl., Box 2410, Iqaluit, X0A 0H0 NU
867-975-5090, Fax: 867-975-5095

Department of Finance, Bldg. 1079, 1st Fl., PO Box 1000 Stn 360,Iqaluit, X0A 0H0 NU
867-975-5800, Fax: 867-975-5805

Government of the Nunavut Territory, PO Box 1200, Iqaluit, X0A 0H0 NU

Department of Justice, Sivummut, 1st Fl., PO Box 1000 500,Iqaluit, X0A 0H0 NU
867-975-6170, Fax: 867-975-6195

Office of the Premier, Legislative Assembly Bldg., 2nd Fl., PO Box 2410, Iqaluit, X0A 0H0 NU
867-975-5050, Fax: 867-975-5051

Ontario

Office of the Provincial Auditor, Box 105, #1530, 20 Dundas St. West, 15th Fl., Toronto, M5G 2C2 ON
416-327-2381, Fax: 416-327-9862

Executive Council, Whitney Block, Queen's Park, 99 Wellesley St. West, 6th Fl., Toronto, M7A 1A1 ON
416-325-5721, Fax: 416-314-1551

Government of Ontario, Queen's Park, Toronto, M7A 1A2 ON

Ministry of Intergovernmental Affairs & Democratic Renewal Secretariat, 77 Wellesley St. West, Toronto, M7A 1N3 ON
416-325-4800, Fax: 416-325-4787

Ministry of Municipal Affairs & Housing, 777 Bay St., 17th Fl., Toronto, M5G 2E5 ON
416-585-7041, Fax: 416-585-6227, 866-220-2290

Ontario Housing Corporation, 777 Bay St., 2nd Fl., Toronto, ON M5G 2E5

Ontario Northland, 555 Oak St. East, North Bay, ON P1B 8L3
705-472-4500, Fax: 705-476-5598, 800-363-7512, info@ontc.on.ca

Office of the Premier, Legislative Bldg., #281, 1 Queen's Park Cres. South, Toronto, M7A 1A1 ON
416-325-1941, Fax: 416-325-3745, webprem@gov.on.ca

Prince Edward Island

Executive Council, Shaw Bldg., PO Box 2000, Charlottetown, C1A 7N8 PE

Government of Prince Edward Island, Province House, PO Box 2000, Charlottetown, C1A 7N8 PE

Office of the Premier, Shaw Bldg., 95 Rochford St., 5th Fl. South, PO Box 2000, Charlottetown, C1A 7N8 PE
902-368-4400, Fax: 902-368-4416

Department of the Provincial Treasury, PO Box 2000, Charlottetown, C1A 7N8 PE
902-368-4000, Fax: 902-368-5544

Quebec

Ministère du Conseil exécutif, 875, Grande Allée est, Québec, G1R 4Y8 QC
418-646-3021, Fax: 418-528-9242

Ministère du Développement économique, de l'Innovation et de l'Exportation, 710, place D'Youville, 3e étage, Québec, G1R 4Y4 QC
418-691-5950, Fax: 418-644-0118, 866-680-1884

Government of Québec, Hôtel du Parlement, Québec, G1A 1A4 QC

Cabinet du premier ministre, Édifice Honoré-Mercier, 835, boul René-Lévesque est, 3e étage, Québec, G1A 1B4 QC
418-643-5321, Fax: 418-643-3924

Saskatchewan

Provincial Auditor Saskatchewan, #1500, 1920 Broad St., Regina, S4P 3V2 SK
306-787-6398, Fax: 306-787-6383, info@auditor.sk.ca

Board of Revenue Commissioners, #480, 2151 Scarth St., Regina, SK S4P 3V7
306-787-6221, Fax: 306-787-1610

Executive Council, Legislative Bldg., 2405 Legislative Dr., Regina, S4S 0B3 SK

Government of Saskatchewan, Regina, S4S 0B3 SK

Office of the Premier, 226 Legislative Bldg., Regina, S4S 0B3 SK
306-787-9433, Fax: 306-787-0885, premier@gov.sk.ca

Saskatchewan Development Fund Corporation, #300, 2400 College Ave., Regina, SK S4P 1C8
306-787-1645, Fax: 306-787-8030, 800-667-7543

Yukon Territory

Executive Council, PO Box 2703, Whitehorse, Y1A 2C6 YT
867-667-5800, Fax: 867-393-6202, 800-040-8 ex, eco@gov.yk.ca

Government of the Yukon Territory, PO Box 2703, Whitehorse, Y1A 2C6 YT

Office of the Premier, PO Box 2703, Whitehorse, Y1A 2C6 YT
Fax: 867-393-6252

GOVERNMENT (GENERAL INFORMATION)

Auditor General of Canada, 240 Sparks St., Ottawa, K1A 0G6 ON
613-995-3708, Fax: 613-957-0474, communications@oag-bvg.gc.ca

Canada Business, 235 Queen St., Ottawa, K1A 0H5 ON
Fax: 613-954-5463, 888-576-4444, cbsc@ic.gc.ca

Foreign Affairs & International Trade Canada, 125 Sussex Dr., Ottawa, K1A 0G2 ON
613-944-4000, Fax: 613-996-9709, 800-267-8376

House of Commons, Canada, House of Commons, 111 Wellington St., Ottawa, K1A 0A6 ON
866-599-4999

Human Resources & Social Development Canada, Place du Portage, Phase IV, 12th Fl., 140 Promenade du Portage, Gatineau, K1A 0J9 QC
819-994-6313

Industry Canada, 235 Queen St., Ottawa, K1A 0H5 ON
613-947-7466, Fax: 613-954-6436

Office of the Prime Minister (Cons.), Langevin Block, 80 Wellington St., Ottawa, K1A 0A2 ON
613-992-4211, Fax: 613-941-6900, pm@pm.gc.ca

Service Canada, 140, Promenade du Portage, Gatineau, K1A 0J9 QC
800-622-6232

Statistics Canada, R.H. Coats Bldg., Tunney's Pasture, 100 Tunney's Pasture Driveway, Ottawa, K1A 0T6 ON
Fax: 877-287-4369, 800-263-1136, infostats@statcan.ca

Treasury Board of Canada, 300 Laurier Ave. West, 10th Fl., Ottawa, K1A 0R5 ON
613-957-2400, Fax: 613-998-9071, 877-636-0656

Alberta

Alberta Government Services, Commerce Place, 10155 - 102 St., Edmonton, T5J 4L4 AB
780-427-4088, government.services@gov.ab.ca

British Columbia

Service BC, PO Box 9594 Prov Govt,Victoria, V8W 9E2 BC
250-387-6121, 800-663-7867

Newfoundland & Labrador

Department of Government Services, PO Box 8700, St. John's, A1B 4J6 NL
709-729-4860

Nova Scotia
Department of Service Nova Scotia & Municipal Relations, 1505 Barrington St., PO Box 216, Halifax, B3J 2M4 NS
902-424-4141, Fax: 902-424-0581, public-enquiries@gov.ns.ca

Nunavut
Department of Executive & Intergovernmental Affairs, Box 1000, Iqaluit, X0A 0H0 NU
867-975-6000, Fax: 867-975-6090

Quebec
Services Québec, 1056, rue Louis-Alexandre-Taschereau, 4e étage, Québec, G1R 5E6 QC
418-643-1430, 800-363-1363

GOVERNMENT PURCHASING

See: Purchasing
This is the Top, QC

GRANTS & SUBSIDIES

See Also: Student Aid
Atlantic Canada Opportunities Agency, 644 Main St., 3rd Fl., PO Box 6051, Moncton, E1C 9J8 NB
506-851-2271, Fax: 506-851-7403, 800-561-7862
Business Development Bank of Canada, #400, 5, Place Ville-Marie, Montréal, H3B 5E7 QC
514-283-5904, Fax: 514-283-2872, 888-463-6232
Canada Economic Development for Québec Regions, Tour de la Bourse, #3800, 800, Place Victoria, CP 247, Montréal, H4Z 1E8 QC
514-283-6412, Fax: 514-283-3302, 866-385-6412
Canada Mortgage & Housing Corporation, 700 Montreal Rd., Ottawa, K1A 0P7 ON
613-748-2000, Fax: 613-748-2098, 800-668-2642
Western Economic Diversification Canada, Canada Place, #1500, 9700 Jasper Ave. NW, Edmonton, T5J 4H7 AB
780-495-4164, Fax: 780-495-4557, 888-338-9378

Newfoundland & Labrador
Newfoundland & Labrador Municipal Financing Corporation, Confederation Bldg., PO Box 8700, St. John's, NL A1B 4J6
709-729-6686, Fax: 709-729-2095

Nova Scotia
Department of Finance, PO Box 187, Halifax, B3J 2N3 NS
902-424-5554, Fax: 902-424-0635

Prince Edward Island
Department of the Provincial Treasury, PO Box 2000, Charlottetown, C1A 7N8 PE
902-368-4000, Fax: 902-368-5544

Saskatchewan
Saskatchewan Industry & Resources, 2103 - 11th Ave., Regina, S4P 3V7 SK
306-787-2232, Fax: 306-787-2159, 866-727-5427

GUARANTEED INCOME

See: Income Security
This is the Top, QC

HEALTH

Manitoba
Office of the Chief Medical Examiner, #210, 1 Wesley Ave., Winnipeg, MB R3C 4C6
204-945-2088, Fax: 204-945-2442

Nova Scotia
Nova Scotia Medical Examiner Service, Halifax Insurance Bldg., #701, 5670 Spring Garden Rd., Halifax, NS B3J 1H7
902-424-2722, Fax: 902-424-0607, 888-424-4336
Occupational Health & Safety Advisory Council, PO Box 697, Halifax, NS B3J 2T8
902-424-2484, Fax: 902-424-5640
Occupational Health & Safety Appeal Panel, 5151 Terminal Rd., 7th Fl., PO Box 697, Halifax, NS B3J 2T8

Nunavut
Office of the Chief Coroner, PO Box 1000 590, Iqaluit, NU X0A 0H0

HEALTH & SAFETY

Human Resources & Social Development Canada, Place du Portage, Phase IV, 12th Fl., 140 Promenade du Portage, Gatineau, K1A 0J9 QC
819-994-6313

British Columbia
Ministry of Labour & Citizens' Services, PO Box 9594 Prov Govt,Victoria, V8W 9K4 BC
250-356-1487, Fax: 250-356-1653

Manitoba
Advisory Council on Workplace Safety & Health, #200, 401 York Ave., Winnipeg, MB R3C 0P8
204-945-3446, Fax: 204-945-4556
Manitoba Labour & Immigration, #317, Legislative Bldg., 450 Broadway, Winnipeg, R3C 0V8 MB
Fax: 204-945-8312, minlab@leg.gov.mb.ca

Nova Scotia
Department of Environment & Labour, 5151 Terminal Rd., 6th Fl., PO Box 697, Halifax, B3J 2T8 NS
902-424-5300, Fax: 902-424-0575
Occupational Health & Safety Advisory Council, PO Box 697, Halifax, NS B3J 2T8
902-424-2484, Fax: 902-424-5640
Occupational Health & Safety Appeal Panel, 5151 Terminal Rd., 7th Fl., PO Box 697, Halifax, NS B3J 2T8

Ontario
Ministry of Government Services, Ferguson Block, 77 Wellesley St. West, 12th Fl., Toronto, M7A 1N3 ON
416-326-1234

HOUSING

Canada Mortgage & Housing Corporation, 700 Montreal Rd., Ottawa, K1A 0P7 ON
613-748-2000, Fax: 613-748-2098, 800-668-2642

Nova Scotia
Department of Service Nova Scotia & Municipal Relations, 1505 Barrington St., PO Box 216, Halifax, B3J 2M4 NS
902-424-4141, Fax: 902-424-0581, public-enquiries@gov.ns.ca

HUMAN RIGHTS

See Also: Boards of Review

British Columbia
BC Human Rights Tribunal, #1170, 605 Robson St., Vancouver, BC V6B 5J3
604-775-2000, Fax: 604-775-2020, 888-440-8844

Yukon Territory
Yukon Human Rights Commission, #201, 211 Hawkins St., Whitehorse, YT Y1A 1X3
867-667-6226, Fax: 867-667-2662, 800-661-0535, humanrights@yhrc.yk.ca
Yukon Human Rights Panel of Adjudication, #202, 407 Black St., Whitehorse, YT Y1A 2N2
867-667-5412, Fax: 867-633-6952

HYDRO, ELECTRIC POWER

New Brunswick
New Brunswick Electric Finance Corporation, #376, 670 King St., PO Box 6000, Fredericton, NB E3B 5H1
506-453-3952, Fax: 506-453-2053

IMPORTS

See Also: Trade
Canada Border Services Agency, 191 Laurier Ave. West, Ottawa, K1A 0L5 ON
613-952-3200
Canadian International Trade Tribunal, Standard Life Centre, 333 Laurier Ave. West, Ottawa, K1A 0G7 ON
613-990-2452, Fax: 613-990-2439
North American Free Trade Agreement (NAFTA) Secretariat, Canadian Section, #705, 90 Sparks St., Ottawa, K1P 5B4 ON
613-992-9388, Fax: 613-992-9392, canada@nafta-sec-alena.org

Quebec
Revenu Québec, 3800, rue de Marly, Québec, G1X 4A5 QC
800-463-2397

INCOME TAX

See: Taxation
This is the Top, QC

INCORPORATION OF COMPANIES & ASSOCIATIONS

Alberta
Service Alberta & Registries, John E. Brownlee Bldg., 10365 - 97 St., Edmonton, T5J 3W7 AB
780-415-6090

New Brunswick
Service New Brunswick, #200, 82 Westmorland St., PO Box 1998, Fredericton, E3B 5G4 NB
506-457-3581, Fax: 506-453-3043, snb@snb.ca

Nova Scotia
Department of Economic Development, Maritime Centre, 1505 Barrington St., 14th Fl., PO Box 2311, Halifax, B3J 3C8 NS
902-424-0377, Fax: 902-424-0500, comm@gov.ns.ca
Registry of Joint Stock Companies, #8S, Martime Centre, 1505 Barrington St, Halifax, B3J 2Y4 NS
902-424-7742, Fax: 902-424-0523, 800-225-8227, joint-stock@gov.ns.ca

Northwest Territories
Department of Justice, PO Box 1320, Yellowknife, X1A 2L9 NT
867-920-6197

Nunavut
Nunavut Legal Registries Division, Brown Bldg., 1st Fl., PO Box 1000 570,Iqaluit, X0A 0H0 NU
867-975-6190, Fax: 867-975-6194

Prince Edward Island
Consumer, Corporate & Insurance Division, Shaw Building, 95 Rochford St., 4th Fl., PO Box 2000, Charlottetown, C1A 7N8 PE
902-368-4550, Fax: 902-368-5283

Quebec
Registraire des entreprises, 800, place D'Youville, Québec, G1R 4Y5 QC
418-528-9074, Fax: 418-646-7329, req@req.gouv.qc.ca

Yukon Territory
Yukon Community Services, PO Box 2703, Whitehorse, Y1A 2C6 YT
867-667-5811, Fax: 867-393-6295, 800-661-0408, inquiry@gov.yk.ca

INDUSTRY

See Also: Business Development
Agriculture & Agri-Food Canada, Sir John Carling Bldg., 930 Carling Ave., Ottawa, K1A 0C5 ON
613-759-1000, Fax: 613-759-6726, info@agr.gc.ca
Atlantic Canada Opportunities Agency, 644 Main St., 3rd Fl., PO Box 6051, Moncton, E1C 9J8 NB
506-851-2271, Fax: 506-851-7403, 800-561-7862
Canada Mortgage & Housing Corporation, 700 Montreal Rd., Ottawa, K1A 0P7 ON
613-748-2000, Fax: 613-748-2098, 800-668-2642
Canadian International Trade Tribunal, Standard Life Centre, 333 Laurier Ave. West, Ottawa, K1A 0G7 ON
613-990-2452, Fax: 613-990-2439
Canadian Tourism Commission, #1400, 1055 Dunsmuir St., PO Box 49230, Vancouver, BC V7X 1L5
604-638-8300, Fax: 604-638-8425, ctc_feedback@businteractive.com
Cape Breton Development Fund Corporation, Silicon Island, 70 Crescent St., PO Box 1264, Sydney, NS B1P 6T7
902-564-3600, Fax: 902-564-3825, 800-705-3926
Chief Information Office, 235 Queen St., Ottawa, ON K1A 0H5
613-954-3574, Fax: 613-941-1938
Communications Research Centre Canada, 3701 Carling Ave., PO Box 11490 H, Ottawa, ON K2H 8S2
613-991-3313, Fax: 613-998-5355, info@crc.ca
Competition Bureau, Place du Portage, Phase I, 50, rue Victoria, 21e étage, Ottawa, K1A 0C9 ON
613-997-4282, Fax: 613-997-0324, 800-348-5358, compbureau@ic.gc.ca
Competition Tribunal, #600, 90 Sparks St., Ottawa, ON K1P 5B4
613-957-7851, Fax: 613-957-3170, tribunal@ct-tc.gc.ca
Enterprise Cape Breton Corporation, Silicon Island, 70 Crescent St., Sydney, NS B1S 2Z7
902-564-3600, Fax: 902-564-3825, 800-705-3926, ecbcinfo@ecbc.ca
Office of the Ethics Commissioner, 66 Slater St., 22nd Fl., Ottawa, K1A 0A6 ON
613-995-0721, Fax: 613-995-7308

Export Development Canada, 151 O'Connor St., Ottawa, K1A 1K3 ON
613-598-2500, Fax: 613-237-2690, 888-332-3320
Farm Credit Canada, 1800 Hamilton St., PO Box 4320, Regina, S4P 4L3 SK
306-780-8100, Fax: 306-780-5875, 800-387-3232
Office of the Superintendent of Financial Institutions, Kent Square, 255 Albert St., Ottawa, K1A 0H2 ON
613-990-7788, Fax: 613-952-8219, 800-385-8647, extcomm@osfi-bsif.gc.ca
Foreign Affairs & International Trade Canada, 125 Sussex Dr., Ottawa, K1A 0G2 ON
613-944-4000, Fax: 613-996-9709, 800-267-8376
Industry Canada, 235 Queen St., Ottawa, K1A 0H5 ON
613-947-7466, Fax: 613-954-6436
North American Free Trade Agreement (NAFTA) Secretariat, Canadian Section, #705, 90 Sparks St., Ottawa, K1P 5B4 ON
613-992-9388, Fax: 613-992-9392, canada@nafta-sec-alena.org
Western Economic Diversification Canada, Canada Place, #1500, 9700 Jasper Ave. NW, Edmonton, T5J 4H7 AB
780-495-4164, Fax: 780-495-4557, 888-338-9378

Alberta

Agricultural Products Marketing Council, 7000 - 113 St., 3rd Fl., Edmonton, AB T6H 5T6
780-427-2164, Fax: 780-422-9690
Alberta Agriculture, Food & Rural Development, J.G. O'Donoghue Bldg., 7000 - 113 St., Edmonton, T6H 5T6 AB
780-427-2727, Fax: 780-427-2861, 866-882-7677, duke@gov.ab.ca
Alberta Economic Development Authority, McDougall Centre, 455 - 6 St. SW, Calgary, AB T2P 4E8
403-297-3022, Fax: 403-297-6435
Alberta Grain Commission, 7000 - 113 St., 3rd Fl., Edmonton, AB T6H 5T6
780-427-7329, Fax: 780-422-9690
Alberta Economic Development, Commerce Place , 6th Fl., 10155 - 102 St., Edmonton, T5J 4L6 AB
780-415-1319, Fax: 780-415-1759
Farmers' Advocate of Alberta, 7000 - 113 St., 3rd Fl., Edmonton, AB T6H 5T6
780-427-2433, Fax: 780-427-3913
Strategic Tourism Marketing Council, #500, 999 - 8 St. SW, Calgary, AB T2J 1J5
403-297-2700, Fax: 403-297-5068

British Columbia

Agricultural Land Commission, #133, 4940 Canada Way, Burnaby, BC V5G 4K6
604-660-7000, Fax: 604-660-7033
Ministry of Agriculture & Lands, PO Box 9120 Prov Govt,Victoria, V8W 9B4 BC
250-387-5121, Fax: 250-387-1522
British Columbia Farm Industry Review Board, PO Box 9129 Prov Govt, Victoria, BC V8W 9B5
250-356-8945, Fax: 250-356-5731, firb@gov.bc.ca
Ministry of Economic Development, PO Box 9324 Prov Govt,Victoria, V8W 9N3 BC
Financial Institutions Commission, #1200, 13450 - 102 Ave., Surrey, BC V3T 5X3
604-953-5300, Fax: 604-953-5301, FICOM@ficombc.ca
Forest Practices Board, 1675 Douglas St., 3rd Fl., PO Box 9905 Prov Govt, Victoria, BC V8W 9R1
250-387-7964, Fax: 250-387-7009, 800-994-5899, fpboard@gov.bc.ca
Ministry of Forests & Range, PO Box 9529 Prov Govt,Victoria, V8W 9C3 BC
250-387-6121, 800-663-7867
Industry Training Authority, #223, 4600 Kingsway, Burnaby, BC V5H 4L9
604-775-2860, Fax: 604-775-3033, 866-660-6011, ita@gov.bc.ca
Insurance Council of British Columbia, #300, 1040 West Georgia St., PO Box 7, Vancouver, BC V6E 4H1
604-688-0321, Fax: 604-662-7767, 877-688-0321
Ministry of Labour & Citizens' Services, PO Box 9594 Prov Govt,Victoria, V8W 9K4 BC
250-356-1487, Fax: 250-356-1653
Real Estate Council of British Columbia, #900, 750 West Pender St., Vancouver, BC V6C 2T8
604-683-9664, Fax: 604-683-9017, 877-683-9664, info@recbc.ca

Manitoba

Advisory Council on Workplace Safety & Health, #200, 401 York Ave., Winnipeg, MB R3C 0P8
204-945-3446, Fax: 204-945-4556
Agricultural Societies, 1129 Queens Ave., Brandon, MB R7A 1L9
204-726-6195, Fax: 204-726-6260
Manitoba Agriculture, Food & Rural Initiatives, Norquay Bldg., 401 York Ave., Winnipeg, R3C 0P8 MB
Community & Economic Development Committee of Cabinet Secretariat, #648, 155 Carlton St., Winnipeg, R3C 3H8 MB
204-945-8193, Fax: 204-945-8229
Manitoba Competitiveness, Training & Trades, #900, 259 Portage Ave., Winnipeg, R3B 3P4 MB
204-945-2067, Fax: 204-948-2964
Crown Corporations Council, #1130, 444 St. Mary Ave., Winnipeg, MB R3C 3T1
204-949-5270, Fax: 204-949-5283, crowncc@mts.net
Manitoba Development Corporation, #555, 155 Carlton St., Winnipeg, R3C 3H8 MB
204-945-7626, Fax: 204-945-1193
Farm Lands Ownership Board, #812, Norquay Bldg., 401 York Ave., Winnipeg, MB R3C 0P8
204-945-3149, Fax: 204-945-1489, 800-282-8069, flob@gov.mb.ca
Farm Machinery Board, Norquay Bldg., #812, 401 York Ave., Winnipeg, MB R3C 0P8
204-945-3856
Manitoba Labour & Immigration, #317, Legislative Bldg., 450 Broadway, Winnipeg, R3C 0V8 MB
Fax: 204-945-8312, minlab@leg.gov.mb.ca
Manitoba Lotteries Corporation, 830 Empress St., Winnipeg, R3G 3H3 MB
204-957-2500, Fax: 204-957-3991, communications@mlc.mb.ca
Manitoba Agricultural Services Corporation, #100, 1525 First St. South, Brandon, MB R7A 7A1
204-726-6850, Fax: 204-726-6849, mailbox@mcic.gov.mb.ca
Manitoba Bureau of Statistics, #824, 155 Carlton St., Winnipeg, R3C 3H9 MB
204-945-2982, Fax: 204-945-0695
Manitoba Labour Board, A.A. Heaps Bldg., #402, 258 Portage Ave., Winnipeg, MB R3C 0B6
204-945-3783, Fax: 204-945-1296, mlb@gov.mb.ca
Manitoba Minimum Wage Board, 614 - 401 York Ave., Winnipeg, MB R3C 0P8
204-945-4889, Fax: 204-948-2085, mw@gov.mb.ca
Public Utilities Board, #400, 330 Portage Ave., Winnipeg, MB R3C 0C4
204-945-2638, Fax: 204-945-2643, In -Man-itob, publicutilities@gov.mb.ca

New Brunswick

Department of Agriculture & Aquaculture, PO Box 6000, Fredericton, E3B 5H1 NB
506-453-2666, Fax: 506-453-7170
Department of Business New Brunswick, Centennial Bldg., 670 King St., 5th Fl., PO Box 6000, Fredericton, E3B 5H1 NB
506-444-5228, Fax: 506-453-5428
New Brunswick Crop Insurance Commission, PO Box 6000, Fredericton, NB E3B 5H1
506-453-2185, Fax: 506-453-7406
New Brunswick Farm Products Commission, c/o Department of Agriculture, Fisheries & Aquaculture, PO Box 6000, Fredericton, NB E3B 5H1
506-453-3647, Fax: 506-444-5969
New Brunswick Film, Assumption Pl., 770 Main St., 16th Fl., PO Box 5001, Moncton, NB E1C 8R3
506-869-6868, Fax: 506-869-6840, nbfilm@gnb.ca
New Brunswick Industrial Development Board, Business New Brunswick, Centennial Bldg., 670 King St., PO Box 6000, Fredericton, NB E3B 5H1
506-453-4200, Fax: 506-444-4182
New Brunswick Real Estate Association, #1, 22 Durelle St., Fredericton, NB E3C 1N8
506-459-8055, Fax: 506-459-8057, 800-762-1677, nbrea@nbnet.nb.ca
Regional Development Corporation, RDC Bldg., 836 Churchill Row, PO Box 428, Fredericton, E3B 5R4 NB
506-453-2277, Fax: 506-453-7988

Newfoundland & Labrador

Department of Innovation, Trade & Rural Development, PO Box 8700, St. John's, A1B 4J6 NL
709-729-7000, Fax: 709-729-0654, 800-563-2299, itrdinfo@gov.nl.ca
Newfoundland & Labrador Municipal Financing Corporation, Confederation Bldg., PO Box 8700, St. John's, NL A1B 4J6
709-729-6686, Fax: 709-729-2095
Newfoundland Liquor Corporation, 90 Kenmount Rd., PO Box 8750 A, St. John's, NL A1B 3V1
709-724-1100, Fax: 709-754-0529, info@nfliquor.com

Nova Scotia

Canada-Nova Scotia Offshore Petroleum Board, TD Centre, 1791 Barrington St., 6th Fl., Halifax, NS B3J 3K9
902-422-5588, Fax: 902-422-1799, postmaster@cnsopb.ns.ca
Crane Operators Appeal Board, 5151 Terminal Rd., 7th Fl., Halifax, NS B3J 2T8
902-424-8595, Fax: 902-424-0217
Department of Economic Development, Maritime Centre, 1505 Barrington St., 14th Fl., PO Box 2311, Halifax, B3J 3C8 NS
902-424-0377, Fax: 902-424-0500, comm@gov.ns.ca
InNOVACorp, #1400, 1801 Hollis St., Halifax, NS B3J 3N4
902-424-8670, Fax: 902-424-4679, 800-565-7051, communications@innovacorp.ca
Nova Scotia Film Development Corporation, 1724 Granville St., Halifax, NS B3J 1X5
902-424-7177, Fax: 902-424-0617, novascotia.film@ns.sympatico.ca
Trade Centre Limited, 1800 Argyle St., PO Box 955, Halifax, NS B3J 2V9
902-421-8686, Fax: 902-422-2922
Waterfront Development Corporation Ltd., 1751 Lower Water St., 2nd Fl., Halifax, NS B3J 1S5
902-422-6591, Fax: 902-422-7582, info@wdcl.ca

Northwest Territories

Department of Industry, Tourism & Investment, PO Box 1320, Yellowknife, X1A 2L9 NT
Northwest Territories Business Development & Investment Corporation, #701, 5201 - 50 Ave., Yellowknife, NT X1A 3S9
867-920-6455, Fax: 867-765-0652, bdicinfo@gov.nt.ca
Northwest Territories Liquor Commission, #201, 31 Capital Dr., Hay River, NT X0E 1G2
867-874-2100, Fax: 867-874-2180
Northwest Territories Liquor Licensing & Enforcement, #210, 31 Capital Dr., Hay River, NT X0E 1G2
867-874-2906, Fax: 867-874-6011
Northwest Territories Liquor Licensing Board, #210, 31 Capital Dr., Hay River, NT X0E 1G2
867-874-2906, Fax: 867-874-6011, delilah_st-arneault@gov.nt.ca

Nunavut

Department of Economic Development & Transportation, PO Box 1000 1500,Iqaluit, X0A 0H0 NU
867-975-7800, Fax: 867-975-7870, 888-975-5999, edt@gov.nu.ca
Nunavut Liquor Licensing Board, Bag 002, Rankin Inlet, NU X0C 0G0
Fax: 867-645-3327

Ontario

Building Code Commission, 777 Bay St., 2nd Fl., Toronto, ON M5G 2E5
416-585-6503, Fax: 416-585-7531
Building Materials Evaluation Commission, 777 Bay St., 2nd Fl., Toronto, ON M5G 2E5
416-585-4234, Fax: 416-585-7531
Ministry of Economic Development & Trade, Hearst Block, 900 Bay St., 8th Fl., Toronto, M7A 2E1 ON
416-325-6666, Fax: 416-325-6688
Ministry of Government Services, Ferguson Block, 77 Wellesley St. West, 12th Fl., Toronto, M7A 1N3 ON
416-326-1234
Ministry of Municipal Affairs & Housing, 777 Bay St., 17th Fl., Toronto, M5G 2E5 ON
416-585-7041, Fax: 416-585-6227, 866-220-2290
Ministry of Northern Development & Mines, 159 Cedar St., Sudbury, P3E 6A5 ON
705-564-0060, Fax: 705-564-7108

Prince Edward Island

Agricultural Insurance Corporation, 29 Indigo Cres., PO Box 1600, Charlottetown, PE C1A 7N3
902-368-4842, Fax: 902-368-6677
Department of Agriculture, Fisheries & Aquaculture, Jones Bldg., 11 Kent St., PO Box 2000, Charlottetown, C1A 7N8 PE
902-368-4880, Fax: 902-368-4857
Department of Development & Technology, Shaw Bldg., 105 Rochford St., 4th & 5th Fl., PO Box 2000, Charlottetown, C1A

7N8 PE
902-368-4242, Fax: 902-368-4224
Grain Elevator Corporation, PO Box 250, Kensington, PE C0B 1M0
902-836-8935, Fax: 902-836-8926

Quebec
Ministère de l'Agriculture, des Pêcheries et de l'Alimentation, 200, ch Sainte-Foy, Québec, G1R 4X6 QC
418-380-2110, 888-222-6272
Ministère du Développement économique, de l'Innovation et de l'Exportation, 710, place D'Youville, 3e étage, Québec, G1R 4Y4 QC
418-691-5950, Fax: 418-644-0118, 866-680-1884

Saskatchewan
Agri-Food Council, #302, 3085 Albert St., Regina, SK S4S 0B1
306-787-8530, Fax: 306-787-5134
Saskatchewan Agriculture & Food, Walter Scott Bldg., 3085 Albert St., Regina, S4S 0B1 SK
306-787-5140
Crown Investments Corporation of Saskatchewan, #400, 2400 College Ave., Regina, S4P 1C8 SK
306-787-6851, Fax: 306-787-8125
Farm Stress Unit, #329, 3085 Albert St., Regina, SK S4S 0B1
306-787-5196, Fax: 306-798-3042, 800-667-4442, kimhoff@agr.gov.sk.ca
Saskatchewan Industry & Resources, 2103 - 11th Ave., Regina, S4P 3V7 SK
306-787-2232, Fax: 306-787-2159, 866-727-5427
Prairie Agricultural Machinery Institute, Hwy#5, PO Box 1900, Humboldt, SK S0K 2A0
306-682-2555, Fax: 306-682-5080, 800-567-7264, humboldt@pami.ca
Saskatchewan Crop Insurance Corporation, 484 Prince William Dr., PO Box 3000, Melville, SK S0A 2P0
306-728-7200, Fax: 306-728-7268, customer.service@scic.gov.sk.ca
Saskatchewan Lands Appeal Board, #202, 3085 Albert St., Regina, SK S4S 0B1
306-787-4693, Fax: 306-787-1315, dbrooks@agr.gov.sk.ca
Saskatchewan Trade & Export Partnership, #320, 1801 Hamilton St., PO Box 1787, Regina, SK S4P 3C6
306-787-9210, Fax: 306-787-6666, 877-313-7244, inquire@sasktrade.sk.ca

Yukon Territory
Yukon Development Corporation, PO Box 2703 D-1,Whitehorse, Y1A 2C6 YT
867-393-7069, Fax: 867-393-7071
Yukon Economic Development, PO Box 2703, Whitehorse, Y1A 2C6 YT
867-393-7191, Fax: 867-395-7199, 800-661-0408

INDUSTRY & TRADE

Atlantic Canada Opportunities Agency, 644 Main St., 3rd Fl., PO Box 6051, Moncton, E1C 9J8 NB
506-851-2271, Fax: 506-851-7403, 800-561-7862
Business Development Bank of Canada, #400, 5, Place Ville-Marie, Montréal, H3B 5E7 QC
514-283-5904, Fax: 514-283-2872, 888-463-6232
Export Development Canada, 151 O'Connor St., Ottawa, K1A 1K3 ON
613-598-2500, Fax: 613-237-2690, 888-332-3320
Foreign Affairs & International Trade Canada, 125 Sussex Dr., Ottawa, K1A 0G2 ON
613-944-4000, Fax: 613-996-9709, 800-267-8376
Industry Canada, 235 Queen St., Ottawa, K1A 0H5 ON
613-947-7466, Fax: 613-954-6436
Western Economic Diversification Canada, Canada Place, #1500, 9700 Jasper Ave. NW, Edmonton, T5J 4H7 AB
780-495-4164, Fax: 780-495-4557, 888-338-9378

Alberta
Alberta Economic Development Authority, McDougall Centre, 455 - 6 St. SW, Calgary, AB T2P 4E8
403-297-3022, Fax: 403-297-6435
Alberta Economic Development, Commerce Place , 6th Fl., 10155 - 102 St., Edmonton, T5J 4L6 AB
780-415-1319, Fax: 780-415-1759

British Columbia
Timber Export Advisory Committee, 1520 Blanshard St., 2nd Fl., PO Box 9514 Prov Govt, Victoria, BC V8W 3C8
250-387-8359, Fax: 250-387-5050

Manitoba
Manitoba Competitiveness, Training & Trades, #900, 259 Portage Ave., Winnipeg, R3B 3P4 MB
204-945-2067, Fax: 204-948-2964
Federal-Provincial & International Relations & Trade Division, #42, 450 Broadway, Winnipeg, R3C 0V8 MB

New Brunswick
Department of Business New Brunswick, Centennial Bldg., 670 King St., 5th Fl., PO Box 6000, Fredericton, E3B 5H1 NB
506-444-5228, Fax: 506-453-5428
New Brunswick Industrial Development Board, Business New Brunswick, Centennial Bldg., 670 King St., PO Box 6000, Fredericton, NB E3B 5H1
506-453-4200, Fax: 506-444-4182
Regional Development Corporation, RDC Bldg., 836 Churchill Row, PO Box 428, Fredericton, E3B 5R4 NB
506-453-2277, Fax: 506-453-7988

Newfoundland & Labrador
Department of Innovation, Trade & Rural Development, PO Box 8700, St. John's, A1B 4J6 NL
709-729-7000, Fax: 709-729-0654, 800-563-2299, itrdinfo@gov.nl.ca

Nova Scotia
Department of Economic Development, Maritime Centre, 1505 Barrington St., 14th Fl., PO Box 2311, Halifax, B3J 3C8 NS
902-424-0377, Fax: 902-424-0500, comm@gov.ns.ca
Labour Relations Board & Construction Industry Panel, 5151 Terminal Rd.,7th Fl., PO Box 697, Halifax, NS B3J 2T8
902-424-5300, Fax: 902-424-0503
Labour Standards Tribunal, 5151 Terminal Rd., 7th Fl., PO Box 697, Halifax, NS B3J 2T8
902-424-6730, Fax: 902-424-1744
Pay Equity Commission, 5151 Terminal Rd., 7th Fl., PO Box 697, Halifax, NS B3J 2T8
902-424-8596, sherwoop@gov.ns.ca

Northwest Territories
Northwest Territories Business Development & Investment Corporation, #701, 5201 - 50 Ave., Yellowknife, NT X1A 3S9
867-920-6455, Fax: 867-765-0652, bdicinfo@gov.nt.ca

Ontario
Ministry of Economic Development & Trade, Hearst Block, 900 Bay St., 8th Fl., Toronto, M7A 2E1 ON
416-325-6666, Fax: 416-325-6688
Ministry of Northern Development & Mines, 159 Cedar St., Sudbury, P3E 6A5 ON
705-564-0060, Fax: 705-564-7108

Prince Edward Island
Department of Development & Technology, Shaw Bldg., 105 Rochford St., 4th & 5th Fl., PO Box 2000, Charlottetown, C1A 7N8 PE
902-368-4242, Fax: 902-368-4224

Saskatchewan
Saskatchewan Industry & Resources, 2103 - 11th Ave., Regina, S4P 3V7 SK
306-787-2232, Fax: 306-787-2159, 866-727-5427
Saskatchewan Trade & Export Partnership, #320, 1801 Hamilton St., PO Box 1787, Regina, SK S4P 3C6
306-787-9210, Fax: 306-787-6666, 877-313-7244, inquire@sasktrade.sk.ca
Tourism Saskatchewan, 1922 Park St., Regina, SK S4N 7M4
306-787-9600, 877-237-2273

Yukon Territory
Yukon Development Corporation, PO Box 2703 D-1,Whitehorse, Y1A 2C6 YT
867-393-7069, Fax: 867-393-7071

INFORMATION RESOURCES

Industry Canada, 235 Queen St., Ottawa, K1A 0H5 ON
613-947-7466, Fax: 613-954-6436
Public Works & Government Services Canada, Place du Portage, Phase III, 11, rue Laurier, Ottawa, K1A 0S5 ON
819-997-6363
Statistics Canada, R.H. Coats Bldg., Tunney's Pasture, 100 Tunney's Pasture Driveway, Ottawa, K1A 0T6 ON
Fax: 877-287-4369, 800-263-1136, infostats@statcan.ca

New Brunswick
Service New Brunswick, #200, 82 Westmorland St., PO Box 1998, Fredericton, E3B 5G4 NB
506-457-3581, Fax: 506-453-3043, snb@snb.ca

INSURANCE

New Brunswick
New Brunswick Insurance Board, Saint John Mercantile Centre, #600, 55 Union St., Saint John, NB E2L 5B7
506-643-7710, Fax: 506-652-5011, info@bib-canb.org

INSURANCE (LIFE, FIRE, PROPERTY)

See Also: Automobile Insurance; Health Care Insurance
Canada Deposit Insurance Corporation, 50 O'Connor St., 17th Fl., PO Box 2340 D,Ottawa, K1P 5W5 ON
613-996-2081, Fax: 613-996-6095, info@cdic.ca; info@sadc.ca
Office of the Superintendent of Financial Institutions, Kent Square, 255 Albert St., Ottawa, K1A 0H2 ON
613-990-7788, Fax: 613-952-8219, 800-385-8647, extcomm@osfi-bsif.gc.ca

British Columbia
Insurance Council of British Columbia, #300, 1040 West Georgia St., PO Box 7, Vancouver, BC V6E 4H1
604-688-0321, Fax: 604-662-7767, 877-688-0321

Manitoba
Financial Institutions Regulation, #1115, 405 Broadway, Winnipeg, R3C 3L6 MB
204-945-2542, Fax: 204-948-2268
Manitoba Public Insurance, #820, 234 Donald St., PO Box 6300, Winnipeg, R3C 4A4 MB
204-985-7000, Fax: 204-943-9851, 800-665-2410
Manitoba Agricultural Services Corporation, #100, 1525 First St. South, Brandon, MB R7A 7A1
204-726-6850, Fax: 204-726-6849, mailbox@mcic.gov.mb.ca

New Brunswick
New Brunswick Credit Union Deposit Insurance, PO Box 6000, Fredericton, NB E3B 5H1
506-453-2315, Fax: 506-453-7474
New Brunswick Crop Insurance Commission, PO Box 6000, Fredericton, NB E3B 5H1
506-453-2185, Fax: 506-453-7406
New Brunswick Insurance Board, Saint John Mercantile Centre, #600, 55 Union St., Saint John, NB E2L 5B7
506-643-7710, Fax: 506-652-5011, info@bib-canb.org

Nova Scotia
Nova Scotia Insurance Review Board, 5151 Terminal Rd., 2nd Fl., PO Box 2251, Halifax, NS B3J 3C8
902-424-8685, nsirb@gov.ns.ca

Northwest Territories
Department of Finance, PO Box 1320, Yellowknife, X1A 2L9 NT
867-873-0414, Fax: 867-873-7117

Ontario
Deposit Insurance Corporation of Ontario, #700, 4711 Yonge St., Toronto, ON M2N 6K8
416-325-9444, Fax: 416-325-9722, 800-268-6653
Financial Services Commission of Ontario, 5160 Yonge St., 17th Fl., Box 85, Toronto, ON M2N 6L9
416-250-7250, Fax: 416-590-7078, 800-668-0128

Prince Edward Island
Agricultural Insurance Corporation, 29 Indigo Cres., PO Box 1600, Charlottetown, PE C1A 7N3
902-368-4842, Fax: 902-368-6677

Saskatchewan
Saskatchewan Government Insurance, 2260 - 11 Ave., Regina, S4P 0J9 SK
306-751-1200, Fax: 306-787-7477
Saskatchewan Crop Insurance Corporation, 484 Prince William Dr., PO Box 3000, Melville, SK S0A 2P0
306-728-7200, Fax: 306-728-7268, customer.service@scic.gov.sk.ca
Saskatchewan Financial Services Commission, #601, 1919 Saskatchewan Dr., Regina, SK S4P 4H2
306-787-5646, Fax: 306-787-5899

INTELLECTUAL PROPERTY

Canadian Intellectual Property Office, 50, rue Victoria, Gatineau, K1A 0C9 QC
819-997-1936, Fax: 819-953-7620

INTERNATIONAL AFFAIRS

See Also: Trade
Canadian International Trade Tribunal, Standard Life Centre, 333 Laurier Ave. West, Ottawa, K1A 0G7 ON
613-990-2452, Fax: 613-990-2439

Foreign Affairs & International Trade Canada, 125 Sussex Dr., Ottawa, K1A 0G2 ON
613-944-4000, Fax: 613-996-9709, 800-267-8376

Alberta
Alberta International & Intergovernmental Relations, Commerce Place, 10155 - 102 St., 12th Fl., Edmonton, T5J 4G2 AB
780-422-1510, Fax: 780-423-6654

Manitoba
Federal-Provincial & International Relations & Trade Division, #42, 450 Broadway, Winnipeg, R3C 0V8 MB
Manitoba Intergovernmental Affairs, #301, 450 Broadway, Winnipeg, R3C 0V8 MB
Fax: 204-945-1383, mnia@leg.gov.mb.ca

Ontario
Ministry of Intergovernmental Affairs & Democratic Renewal Secretariat, 77 Wellesley St. West, Toronto, M7A 1N3 ON
416-325-4800, Fax: 416-325-4787

INTERNATIONAL TRADE

See: Trade
This is the Top, QC

INVESTMENT

See Also: Business Development; Industry
Canada Economic Development for Québec Regions, Tour de la Bourse, #3800, 800, Place Victoria, CP 247, Montréal, H4Z 1E8 QC
514-283-6412, Fax: 514-283-3302, 866-385-6412
Canada Investment & Savings, #900, 110 Yonge St., Toronto, ON M5C 1T4
416-952-1252, Fax: 416-952-1270, 800-575-5151, csb@csb.gc.ca
Canada Pension Plan Investment Board, #2700, 1 Queen St. East, PO Box 101, Toronto, M5C 2W5 ON
416-868-4075, Fax: 416-868-4760, 866-557-9510, csr@cppib.ca
Finance Canada, L'esplanade Laurier, 140 O'Connor St., Ottawa, K1A 0G5 ON
613-992-1573, Fax: 613-996-8404
Industry Canada, 235 Queen St., Ottawa, K1A 0H5 ON
613-947-7466, Fax: 613-954-6436
Public Sector Pension Investment Board, #200, 440 Laurier Ave. West, Ottawa, ON K1R 7X6
613-782-3095, Fax: 613-782-6864, info@investpsp.ca

British Columbia
Forestry Innovation Investments Ltd., #1200, 1130 West Pender St., Vancouver, BC V6E 4A4
604-685-7507, Fax: 604-685-5373
Marketing, Investment & Trade, #730, 999 Canada Place, Vancouver, V6C 3E1 BC
604-844-1900

Manitoba
Federal-Provincial & International Relations & Trade Division, #42, 450 Broadway, Winnipeg, R3C 0V8 MB

New Brunswick
New Brunswick Investment Management Corporation, York Tower, #381, 440 King St., Fredericton, NB E3B 5H8
506-444-5800, Fax: 506-444-5025

Nova Scotia
InNOVACorp, #1400, 1801 Hollis St., Halifax, NS B3J 3N4
902-424-8670, Fax: 902-424-4679, 800-565-7051, communications@innovacorp.ca

Northwest Territories
Department of Industry, Tourism & Investment, PO Box 1320, Yellowknife, X1A 2L9 NT
Northwest Territories Business Development & Investment Corporation, #701, 5201 - 50 Ave., Yellowknife, NT X1A 3S9
867-920-6455, Fax: 867-765-0652, bdicinfo@gov.nt.ca

JUSTICE DEPARTMENTS

Justice Canada, East Memorial Bldg., 284 Wellington St., Ottawa, K1A 0H8 ON
613-957-4222, Fax: 613-954-0811

Alberta
Alberta Justice & Attorney General, 9833 - 109 St., Edmonton, T5K 2E8 AB
780-427-2745

British Columbia
Ministry of the Attorney General, 1001 Douglas St., 10th Fl., PO Box 9282 Prov Govt,Victoria, V8W 9J7 BC
250-356-9596, Fax: 250-387-1753

Manitoba
Manitoba Justice, 405 Broadway Ave., 5th Fl., Winnipeg, R3C 3L6 MB
204-945-2852, minjus@gov.mb.ca

New Brunswick
Department of Justice & Consumer Affairs, PO Box 6000, Fredericton, E3B 5H1 NB
506-462-5100

Newfoundland & Labrador
Department of Justice, Confederation Bldg., PO Box 8700, St. John's, A1B 4J6 NL
709-729-5942, Fax: 709-729-2129

Nova Scotia
Department of Justice, 5151 Terminal Rd., PO Box 7, Halifax, B3J 2L6 NS
902-424-4222, Fax: 902-424-2809, justweb@gov.ns.ca

Northwest Territories
Department of Justice, PO Box 1320, Yellowknife, X1A 2L9 NT
867-920-6197

Nunavut
Department of Justice, Sivummut, 1st Fl., PO Box 1000 500,Iqaluit, X0A 0H0 NU
867-975-6170, Fax: 867-975-6195

Ontario
Ministry of the Attorney General, 720 Bay St., Toronto, M5G 2K1 ON
416-326-2220, Fax: 416-326-4007, 800-518-7901

Prince Edward Island
Office of the Attorney General, PO Box 2000, Charlottetown, C1A 7N8 PE
902-368-5152, Fax: 902-368-4910

Quebec
Ministère de la Justice, 1200, rte de l'Église, Sainte-Foy, G1V 4M1 QC
418-643-5140, Fax: 418-646-4449, 866-536-5140

Saskatchewan
Saskatchewan Justice, 1874 Scarth St., Regina, S4P 3V7 SK
306-787-7872, Fax: 306-787-3874

Yukon Territory
Yukon Justice, PO Box 2703, Whitehorse, Y1A 2C6 YT
867-667-8644, Fax: 867-393-6272

LABOUR

Human Resources & Social Development Canada, Place du Portage, Phase IV, 12th Fl., 140 Promenade du Portage, Gatineau, K1A 0J9 QC
819-994-6313
Public Service Labour Relations Board, 240 Sparks St., 6th Fl., PO Box 1525 B, Ottawa, ON K1P 5V2
613-990-1800, Fax: 613-990-1849
Workers' Compensation Appeals Tribunal, #1002, 5670 Spring Garden Rd., Halifax, NS B3J 1H6
902-424-2250, Fax: 902-424-2321, 800-274-8281

British Columbia
Employment Standards Tribunal, Oceanic Plaza, #650, 1066 West Hastings St., Vancouver, BC V6E 3X1
604-775-3512, Fax: 604-775-3372, registrar.est@bcest.bc.ca
Ministry of Labour & Citizens' Services, PO Box 9594 Prov Govt,Victoria, V8W 9K4 BC
250-356-1487, Fax: 250-356-1653
Ministry of Labour & Citizens' Services, PO Box 9594 Prov Govt,Victoria, V8W 9K4 BC
250-356-1487, Fax: 250-356-1653
Labour Relations Board, Oceanic Plaza, #600, 1066 West Hastings St., Vancouver, BC V6E 3X1
604-660-1300, Fax: 604-660-1892, information@lrb.bc.ca
Workers' Compensation Appeal Tribunal, #150, 4600 Jacombs Rd., Richmond, BC V6V 3B1
604-664-7800, Fax: 604-664-7898, 800-663-2782

Manitoba
Advisory Council on Workplace Safety & Health, #200, 401 York Ave., Winnipeg, MB R3C 0P8
204-945-3446, Fax: 204-945-4556
Manitoba Labour & Immigration, #317, Legislative Bldg., 450 Broadway, Winnipeg, R3C 0V8 MB
Fax: 204-945-8312, minlab@leg.gov.mb.ca
Manitoba Labour & Immigration, #317, Legislative Bldg., 450 Broadway, Winnipeg, R3C 0V8 MB
Fax: 204-945-8312, minlab@leg.gov.mb.ca
Manitoba Civil Service Commission, #935, 155 Carlton St., Winnipeg, MB R3C 3H8
204-945-2332, Fax: 204-945-1486, cschrp@gov.mb.ca
Manitoba Labour Board, A.A. Heaps Bldg., #402, 258 Portage Ave., Winnipeg, MB R3C 0B6
204-945-3783, Fax: 204-945-1296, mlb@gov.mb.ca
Manitoba Labour Board, A.A. Heaps Bldg., #402, 258 Portage Ave., Winnipeg, MB R3C 0B6
204-945-3783, Fax: 204-945-1296, mlb@gov.mb.ca
Manitoba Minimum Wage Board, 614 - 401 York Ave., Winnipeg, MB R3C 0P8
204-945-4889, Fax: 204-948-2085, mw@gov.mb.ca
Manitoba Minimum Wage Board, 614 - 401 York Ave., Winnipeg, MB R3C 0P8
204-945-4889, Fax: 204-948-2085, mw@gov.mb.ca
Pension Commission of Manitoba, #1004, 401 York Ave., Winnipeg, MB R3C 0P8
204-945-2740, Fax: 204-948-2375, pensions@gov.mb.ca

Nova Scotia
Department of Environment & Labour, 5151 Terminal Rd., 6th Fl., PO Box 697, Halifax, B3J 2T8 NS
902-424-5300, Fax: 902-424-0575
Department of Environment & Labour, 5151 Terminal Rd., 6th Fl., PO Box 697, Halifax, B3J 2T8 NS
902-424-5300, Fax: 902-424-0575
Labour Relations Board & Construction Industry Panel, 5151 Terminal Rd.,7th Fl., PO Box 697, Halifax, NS B3J 2T8
902-424-5300, Fax: 902-424-0503
Labour Relations Board & Construction Industry Panel, 5151 Terminal Rd.,7th Fl., PO Box 697, Halifax, NS B3J 2T8
902-424-5300, Fax: 902-424-0503
Labour Standards Tribunal, 5151 Terminal Rd., 7th Fl., PO Box 697, Halifax, NS B3J 2T8
902-424-6730, Fax: 902-424-1744
Labour Standards Tribunal, 5151 Terminal Rd., 7th Fl., PO Box 697, Halifax, NS B3J 2T8
902-424-6730, Fax: 902-424-1744
Occupational Health & Safety Advisory Council, PO Box 697, Halifax, NS B3J 2T8
902-424-2484, Fax: 902-424-5640
Pay Equity Commission, 5151 Terminal Rd., 7th Fl., PO Box 697, Halifax, NS B3J 2T8
902-424-8596, sherwoop@gov.ns.ca
Workers' Advisers Program, #502, 5670 Spring Garden Rd., PO Box 1063, Halifax, NS B3J 2X1
902-424-5050, Fax: 902-424-0530, 800-774-4712

LAND RESOURCES

See Also: Agriculture; Forest Resources; Parks

Manitoba
Farm Lands Ownership Board, #812, Norquay Bldg., 401 York Ave., Winnipeg, MB R3C 0P8
204-945-3149, Fax: 204-945-1489, 800-282-8069, flob@gov.mb.ca

New Brunswick
Service New Brunswick, #200, 82 Westmorland St., PO Box 1998, Fredericton, E3B 5G4 NB
506-457-3581, Fax: 506-453-3043, snb@snb.ca

Saskatchewan
Saskatchewan Lands Appeal Board, #202, 3085 Albert St., Regina, SK S4S 0B1
306-787-4693, Fax: 306-787-1315, dbrooks@agr.gov.sk.ca

LAND TITLES

See Also: Real Estate

British Columbia
BC Assessment Authority, 1537 Hillside Ave., Victoria, BC V8T 4Y2
250-595-6211, Fax: 250-595-6222, info@bcassessment.ca

New Brunswick
Service New Brunswick, #200, 82 Westmorland St., PO Box 1998, Fredericton, E3B 5G4 NB
506-457-3581, Fax: 506-453-3043, snb@snb.ca

Nunavut
Nunavut Legal Registries Division, Brown Bldg., 1st Fl., PO Box 1000 570,Iqaluit, X0A 0H0 NU
867-975-6190, Fax: 867-975-6194

LANDLORD & TENANT REGULATIONS

Alberta
Alberta Justice & Attorney General, 9833 - 109 St., Edmonton, T5K 2E8 AB
780-427-2745

Ontario
Ontario Rental Housing Tribunal, 777 Bay St., 12th Fl., Toronto, ON M5G 2E5
416-585-7295, Fax: 416-585-6363, 888-332-3234

Saskatchewan
Provincial Mediation Board/Office of the Rentalsman, #120, 2151 Scarth St., Regina, SK S4P 2H8
306-787-2699, Fax: 306-787-5574, 888-215-2222

LANDS & SOILS

Agriculture & Agri-Food Canada, Sir John Carling Bldg., 930 Carling Ave., Ottawa, K1A 0C5 ON
613-759-1000, Fax: 613-759-6726, info@agr.gc.ca

Alberta
Irrigation Council, Provincial Bldg., 200 - 5 Ave. South, 3rd Fl., PO Bag 3014, Lethbridge, AB T1J 4L1
403-381-5176, Fax: 403-382-4406

British Columbia
Forest Practices Board, 1675 Douglas St., 3rd Fl., PO Box 9905 Prov Govt, Victoria, BC V8W 9R1
250-387-7964, Fax: 250-387-7009, 800-994-5899, fpboard@gov.bc.ca
Timber Export Advisory Committee, 1520 Blanshard St., 2nd Fl., PO Box 9514 Prov Govt, Victoria, BC V8W 3C8
250-387-8359, Fax: 250-387-5050

Newfoundland & Labrador
Department of Government Services, PO Box 8700, St. John's, A1B 4J6 NL
709-729-4860

Saskatchewan
Saskatchewan Assessment Management Agency, #200, 2201 - 11 Ave., Regina, S4P 0J8 SK
306-924-8000, Fax: 306-924-8070, 800-667-7262

LAW & JUSTICE

Auditor General of Canada, 240 Sparks St., Ottawa, K1A 0G6 ON
613-995-3708, Fax: 613-957-0474, communications@oag-bvg.gc.ca
Canadian International Trade Tribunal, Standard Life Centre, 333 Laurier Ave. West, Ottawa, K1A 0G7 ON
613-990-2452, Fax: 613-990-2439
Copyright Board of Canada, #800, 56 Sparks St., Ottawa, K1A 0C9 ON
613-952-8621, Fax: 613-952-8630, secretariat@cb-cda.gc.ca
Office of the Ethics Commissioner, 66 Slater St., 22nd Fl., Ottawa, K1A 0A6 ON
613-995-0721, Fax: 613-995-7308
Financial Transactions & Reports Analysis Centre of Canada, 234 Laurier Ave. West, 24th Fl., Ottawa, ON K1P 1H7
Fax: 613-943-7931, 866-346-8722, guidelines@fintrac.gc.ca
Justice Canada, East Memorial Bldg., 284 Wellington St., Ottawa, K1A 0H8 ON
613-957-4222, Fax: 613-954-0811
Workers' Compensation Appeals Tribunal, #1002, 5670 Spring Garden Rd., Halifax, NS B3J 1H6
902-424-2250, Fax: 902-424-2321, 800-274-8281

Alberta
Alberta Review Board, J.E. Brownlee Bldg., 10365 - 97 St., 5th Fl., Edmonton, AB T5J 3W7
780-422-5994, Fax: 780-427-1762
Consumer Services & Land Titles, Commerce Place, 10155 - 102 St., 3rd Fl., Edmonton, T5J 4L4 AB
Alberta Office of the Ethics Commissioner, #1250, 9925 - 109 St., Edmonton, T5K 2J8 AB
780-422-2273, Fax: 780-422-2261
Fatality Review Board, Medical Examiner's Office, 4070 Bowness Rd. NW, Calgary, AB T3B 3R7
403-297-8123, Fax: 403-297-3429
Alberta Justice & Attorney General, 9833 - 109 St., Edmonton, T5K 2E8 AB
780-427-2745

British Columbia
Ministry of the Attorney General, 1001 Douglas St., 10th Fl., PO Box 9282 Prov Govt,Victoria, V8W 9J7 BC
250-356-9596, Fax: 250-387-1753
British Columbia Board of Parole, #303, 960 Quayside Dr., New Westminster, BC V3M 6G2
604-660-8846, Fax: 604-660-2356
British Columbia Review Board, #1203, 865 Hornby St., Vancouver, BC V6Z 2G3
604-660-8789, Fax: 604-660-8809, 877-305-2277
Child & Youth Officer for BC, 1019 Wharf St., PO Box 9207 Prov Govt, Victoria, BC V8W 9J1
250-356-0831, Fax: 250-356-0837, 800-476-3933, cyo@gov.bc.ca
Judicial Council of British Columbia, Pacific Centre, #602, 700 West Georgia St., PO Box 10287, Vancouver, BC V7Y 1E8
604-660-2864, Fax: 604-660-1108
Legal Services Society, #400, 510 Burrard St., Vancouver, BC V6C 3A8
604-601-6000
Office of the Police Complaint Commissioner, 756 Fort St., 3rd Fl., PO Box 9895 Prov Govt, Victoria, BC V8W 9T8
250-356-7458, Fax: 250-356-6503
Public Guardian & Trustee of British Columbia, #700, 808 West Hastings St., Vancouver, BC V6C 3L3
604-660-4444, Fax: 604-660-0374, mail@trustee.bc.ca

Manitoba
Advisory Council on Workplace Safety & Health, #200, 401 York Ave., Winnipeg, MB R3C 0P8
204-945-3446, Fax: 204-945-4556
Office of the Auditor General, #500, 330 Portage Ave., Winnipeg, R3C 0C4 MB
204-945-3790, Fax: 204-945-2169
Automobile Injury Compensation Appeal Commission, #301, 428 Portage Ave..., Winnipeg, MB R3C 0E2
204-945-4155, Fax: 204-948-2402, autoinjury@gov.mb.ca
Compensation for Victims of Crime, 1410 - 405 Broadway, Winnipeg, MB R3C 3L6
204-945-0899, Fax: 204-948-3071
Comptroller's Division, #715, 401 York Ave., Winnipeg, R3C 0P8 MB
Manitoba Justice, 405 Broadway Ave., 5th Fl., Winnipeg, R3C 3L6 MB
204-945-2852, minjus@gov.mb.ca
Law Enforcement Review Agency, #420, 155 Carlton St., Winnipeg, MB R3C 3H8
204-945-8667, Fax: 204-948-1014, lera@gov.mb.ca
Law Reform Commission, #1210, 405 Broadway, Winnipeg, MB R3C 3L6
204-945-2896, Fax: 204-948-2184, lawreform@gov.mb.ca
Legal Aid Manitoba, 402 - 294 Portage Ave., Winnipeg, MB R3C 0B9
204-985-8500, Fax: 204-944-8582, 800-261-2960, info@legalaid.mb.ca
Manitoba Labour Board, A.A. Heaps Bldg., #402, 258 Portage Ave., Winnipeg, MB R3C 0B6
204-945-3783, Fax: 204-945-1296, mlb@gov.mb.ca
Manitoba Liquor Control Commission, 1555 Buffalo Pl., PO Box 1023, Winnipeg, MB R3C 2X1
204-284-2501, Fax: 204-475-7666, info@mlcc.mb.ca
Manitoba Minimum Wage Board, 614 - 401 York Ave., Winnipeg, MB R3C 0P8
204-945-4889, Fax: 204-948-2085, mw@gov.mb.ca
Manitoba Securities Commission, #500, 400 St. Mary Ave., Winnipeg, MB R3C 4K5
204-945-2548, Fax: 204-945-0330, 800-655-5244, securities@gov.mb.ca
Office of the Chief Medical Examiner, #210, 1 Wesley Ave., Winnipeg, MB R3C 4C6
204-945-2088, Fax: 204-945-2442
Office of the Fire Commissioner, #508, 401 York Ave., Winnipeg, MB R3C 0P8
204-945-3322, Fax: 204-948-2089, 800-282-8069, firecomm@gov.mb.ca
Office of the Public Trustee, #500, 155 Carlton St., Winnipeg, MB R3C 5R9
204-945-2700
Residential Tenancies Commission, #1650, 155 Carlton St., Winnipeg, MB R3C 3H8
204-945-2028, Fax: 204-945-5453, 800-782-8403, rtc@gov.mb.ca
Review Board, 408 York Ave., 2nd Fl., Winnipeg, MB R3C 0P9
204-945-4438, Fax: 204-945-5751

New Brunswick
Department of Justice & Consumer Affairs, PO Box 6000, Fredericton, E3B 5H1 NB
506-462-5100
New Brunswick Real Estate Association, #1, 22 Durelle St., Fredericton, NB E3C 1N8
506-459-8055, Fax: 506-459-8057, 800-762-1677, nbrea@nbnet.nb.ca

Newfoundland & Labrador
Department of Justice, Confederation Bldg., PO Box 8700, St. John's, A1B 4J6 NL
709-729-5942, Fax: 709-729-2129
Newfoundland & Labrador Legal Aid Commission, Cormack Bldg., 2 Steers Cove, PO Box 399 C, St. John's, NL A1C 5J9
709-753-7860, Fax: 709-753-6226, 800-563-9911
Royal Newfoundland Constabulary Public Complaints Commission, Bally Rou Place, #E-160, 280 Torbay Rd., St. John's, NL A1A 3W8
709-729-0950, Fax: 709-729-1302

Nova Scotia
Department of Justice, 5151 Terminal Rd., PO Box 7, Halifax, B3J 2L6 NS
902-424-4222, Fax: 902-424-2809, justweb@gov.ns.ca
Labour Relations Board & Construction Industry Panel, 5151 Terminal Rd.,7th Fl., PO Box 697, Halifax, NS B3J 2T8
902-424-5300, Fax: 902-424-0503
Labour Standards Tribunal, 5151 Terminal Rd., 7th Fl., PO Box 697, Halifax, NS B3J 2T8
902-424-6730, Fax: 902-424-1744
Nova Scotia Legal Aid Commission, #102, 137 Chain Lake Dr., Halifax, NS B3S 1B3
902-420-6573, Fax: 902-420-3471, nsla.exec@ns.sympatico.ca
Nova Scotia Medical Examiner Service, Halifax Insurance Bldg., #701, 5670 Spring Garden Rd., Halifax, NS B3J 1H7
902-424-2722, Fax: 902-424-0607, 888-424-4336
Nova Scotia Police Commission, #300, 1601 Lower Water St., PO Box 1573, Halifax, NS B3J 2Y3
902-424-3246, Fax: 902-424-3919, uarb.polcom@gov.ns.ca
Pay Equity Commission, 5151 Terminal Rd., 7th Fl., PO Box 697, Halifax, NS B3J 2T8
902-424-8596, sherwoop@gov.ns.ca

Northwest Territories
Judicial Council, PO Box 188, Yellowknife, NT X1A 2N2
867-873-7105, Fax: 867-873-0287
Department of Justice, PO Box 1320, Yellowknife, X1A 2L9 NT
867-920-6197
Legal Services Board of the Northwest Territories, PO Box 1320, Yellowknife, NT X1A 2L9
867-873-7450, Fax: 867-873-5320, www-jus-tice
Northwest Territories Liquor Commission, #201, 31 Capital Dr., Hay River, NT X0E 1G2
867-874-2100, Fax: 867-874-2180
Northwest Territories Liquor Licensing & Enforcement, #210, 31 Capital Dr., Hay River, NT X0E 1G2
867-874-2906, Fax: 867-874-6011
Northwest Territories Liquor Licensing Board, #210, 31 Capital Dr., Hay River, NT X0E 1G2
867-874-2906, Fax: 867-874-6011, delilah_st-arneault@gov.nt.ca
Victims Assistance Committee, c/o Community Justice Division, PO Box 1320, Yellowknife, NT X1A 2L9
867-920-6911, Fax: 867-873-0299

Nunavut
Baffin Correctional Centre, 1550 Federal Rd., PO Box 368, Iqaluit, NU X0A 0H0
867-979-8100, Fax: 867-979-4646
Department of Justice, Sivummut, 1st Fl., PO Box 1000 500,Iqaluit, X0A 0H0 NU
867-975-6170, Fax: 867-975-6195
Legal Services Board of Nunavut, PO Box 125, Gjoa Haven, NU X0A 0H0
Fax: 867-360-6112
Nunavut Legal Registries Division, Brown Bldg., 1st Fl., PO Box 1000 570,Iqaluit, X0A 0H0 NU
867-975-6190, Fax: 867-975-6194
Nunavut Liquor Licensing Board, Bag 002, Rankin Inlet, NU X0C 0G0
Fax: 867-645-3327
Office of the Chief Coroner, PO Box 1000 590, Iqaluit, NU X0A 0H0

Young Offenders, 1548 Federal Rd., PO Box 1439, Iqaluit, NU X0A 0H0
867-979-4452, Fax: 867-979-5506

Ontario

Assessment Review Board, Eaton Tower, 250 Yonge St., 29th Fl., Toronto, ON M5B 2L7
416-314-6900, Fax: 416-314-3717

Ministry of the Attorney General, 720 Bay St., Toronto, M5G 2K1 ON
416-326-2220, Fax: 416-326-4007, 800-518-7901

Chief Inquiry Officer - Expropriations Act, 720 Bay St., 8th Fl., Toronto, ON M5G 2K1
416-326-4093

Criminal Injuries Compensation Board, 439 University Ave., 4th Fl., Toronto, ON M5G 1Y8
416-326-2900, Fax: 416-326-2883, 800-372-7463

Judicial Appointments Advisory Committee, 720 Bay St., 3rd Fl., Toronto, ON M5G 2K1
416-326-4060, Fax: 416-212-7316

Legal Aid Ontario, #404, 375 University Ave., Toronto, ON M5G 2G1
416-979-1446, Fax: 416-979-8669, 800-668-8258, info@lao.on.ca

Liquor Control Board of Ontario, 55 Lake Shore Blvd. East, Toronto, ON M5E 1A4
416-864-2570, Fax: 416-864-2476

Office for Victims of Crime, 700 Bay St., 3rd Fl., Toronto, ON M5G 1Z6
416-326-1682, Fax: 416-326-2343, 887-435-7661

Ontario Municipal Board & Board of Negotiation, 655 Bay St., 15th Fl., Toronto, ON M5G 1E5
416-326-6800, Fax: 416-326-5370

Prince Edward Island

Office of the Attorney General, PO Box 2000, Charlottetown, C1A 7N8 PE
902-368-5152, Fax: 902-368-4910

Office of the Auditor General, Shaw Bldg., North, 105 Rochford St, 2nd Fl., PO Box 2000, Charlottetown, C1A 7N8 PE
902-368-4520, Fax: 902-368-4598

Quebec

Ministère de la Justice, 1200, rte de l'Église, Sainte-Foy, G1V 4M1 QC
418-643-5140, Fax: 418-646-4449, 866-536-5140

Registraire des entreprises, 800, place D'Youville, Québec, G1R 4Y5 QC
418-528-9074, Fax: 418-646-7329, req@req.gouv.qc.ca

Vérificateur général du Québec, 750, boulevard Charest est, 3e étage, Québec, G1K 9J6 QC
418-691-5900, Fax: 418-644-4460, verificateur.general@vgq.gouv.qc.

Saskatchewan

Agricultural Implements Board, #202, 3085 Albert St., Regina, SK S4S 0B1
306-787-4693, Fax: 306-787-1315

Saskatchewan Justice, 1874 Scarth St., Regina, S4P 3V7 SK
306-787-7872, Fax: 306-787-3874

Law Reform Commission of Saskatchewan, 410 26th St. West, Saskatoon, SK S7L 0H9
306-347-2101

Provincial Mediation Board/Office of the Rentalsman, #120, 2151 Scarth St., Regina, SK S4P 2H8
306-787-2699, Fax: 306-787-5574, 888-215-2222

Public & Private Rights Board, 3085 Albert St., 3rd Fl., Regina, SK S4P 3V7
306-787-4071, Fax: 306-787-0088

Saskatchewan Farm Land Security Board, #207, 3988 Albert St., Regina, SK S4S 3R1
306-787-5047, Fax: 306-787-8599

Saskatchewan Farm Security Programs, #207, 3988 Albert St., Regina, SK S4S 3R1
306-787-5047, Fax: 306-787-8599

Saskatchewan Film & Video Classification Board, #500, 1919 Saskatchewan Dr., Regina, SK S4P 4H2
306-787-5550, Fax: 306-787-9779, adwyer@justice.gov.sk.ca

Saskatchewan Financial Services Commission, #601, 1919 Saskatchewan Dr., Regina, SK S4P 4H2
306-787-5646, Fax: 306-787-5899

Saskatchewan Legal Aid Commission, #502, 201 - 21 St. East, Saskatoon, SK S7K 2H6
306-933-5300, Fax: 306-933-6764, In -Sas-k on, central@legalaid.gov.sk.ca

Saskatchewan Police Commission, 1874 Scarth St., 6th Fl., Regina, SK S4P 3V7
306-787-6518, Fax: 306-787-0136

Saskatchewan Police Complaints Investigator, #600, 1919 Saskatchewan Dr., Regina, SK S4P 4H2
306-787-6519, Fax: 306-787-6528

Surface Rights Board of Arbitration, 113 - 2nd Ave. East, PO Box 1597, Kindersley, SK S0L 1S0
306-463-5447, Fax: 306-463-5449, surface@sasktel.net

Yukon Territory

Driver Control Board, 308 Steele St., PO Box 2703, Whitehorse, YT Y1A 2C6
867-667-3774, Fax: 867-393-6483, dcb@gov.yk.ca

Law Society of Yukon - Discipline Committee, #201, 302 Steele St., Whitehorse, YT Y1A 2C5
867-668-4231, Fax: 867-667-7556, lsy@yknet.yk.ca

Law Society of Yukon - Executive, #202, 302 Steele St., Whitehorse, YT Y1A 2C5
867-668-4231, Fax: 867-667-7556, lsy@yknet.yk.ca

Yukon Human Rights Commission, #201, 211 Hawkins St., Whitehorse, YT Y1A 1X3
867-667-6226, Fax: 867-667-2662, 800-661-0535, humanrights@yhrc.yk.ca

Yukon Human Rights Panel of Adjudication, #202, 407 Black St., Whitehorse, YT Y1A 2N2
867-667-5412, Fax: 867-633-6952

Yukon Judicial Council, PO Box 31222, Whitehorse, YT Y1A 5PT
867-667-5438, Fax: 867-393-6400

Yukon Law Foundation, #202, 302 Steele St., Whitehorse, YT Y1A 2C5
867-668-4231, Fax: 867-667-7556, lsy@yknet.yk.ca

Yukon Legal Services Society/Legal Aid, #203, 2131 - 2nd Ave., Whitehorse, YT Y1A 1C3
867-667-5210, Fax: 867-667-8649, legalaid@yknet.yk.ca

LEGAL & REGULATORY

Nova Scotia

Crane Operators Appeal Board, 5151 Terminal Rd., 7th Fl., Halifax, NS B3J 2T8
902-424-8595, Fax: 902-424-0217

Labour Relations Board & Construction Industry Panel, 5151 Terminal Rd.,7th Fl., PO Box 697, Halifax, NS B3J 2T8
902-424-5300, Fax: 902-424-0503

Labour Standards Tribunal, 5151 Terminal Rd., 7th Fl., PO Box 697, Halifax, NS B3J 2T8
902-424-6730, Fax: 902-424-1744

Occupational Health & Safety Advisory Council, PO Box 697, Halifax, NS B3J 2T8
902-424-2484, Fax: 902-424-5640

Pay Equity Commission, 5151 Terminal Rd., 7th Fl., PO Box 697, Halifax, NS B3J 2T8
902-424-8596, sherwoop@gov.ns.ca

Workers' Advisers Program, #502, 5670 Spring Garden Rd., PO Box 1063, Halifax, NS B3J 2X1
902-424-5050, Fax: 902-424-0530, 800-774-4712

LEGAL AID SERVICES

British Columbia

Legal Services Society, #400, 510 Burrard St., Vancouver, BC V6C 3A8
604-601-6000

Manitoba

Legal Aid Manitoba, 402 - 294 Portage Ave., Winnipeg, MB R3C 0B9
204-985-8500, Fax: 204-944-8582, 800-261-2960, info@legalaid.mb.ca

Newfoundland & Labrador

Newfoundland & Labrador Legal Aid Commission, Cormack Bldg., 2 Steers Cove, PO Box 399 C, St. John's, NL A1C 5J9
709-753-7860, Fax: 709-753-6226, 800-563-9911

Nova Scotia

Nova Scotia Legal Aid Commission, #102, 137 Chain Lake Dr., Halifax, NS B3S 1B3
902-420-6573, Fax: 902-420-3471, nsla.exec@ns.sympatico.ca

Northwest Territories

Legal Services Board of the Northwest Territories, PO Box 1320, Yellowknife, NT X1A 2L9
867-873-7450, Fax: 867-873-5320, www-jus-tice

Ontario

Legal Aid Ontario, #404, 375 University Ave., Toronto, ON M5G 2G1
416-979-1446, Fax: 416-979-8669, 800-668-8258, info@lao.on.ca

Saskatchewan

Saskatchewan Legal Aid Commission, #502, 201 - 21 St. East, Saskatoon, SK S7K 2H6
306-933-5300, Fax: 306-933-6764, In -Sas-k on, central@legalaid.gov.sk.ca

Yukon Territory

Yukon Legal Services Society/Legal Aid, #203, 2131 - 2nd Ave., Whitehorse, YT Y1A 1C3
867-667-5210, Fax: 867-667-8649, legalaid@yknet.yk.ca

LEGISLATIVE ASSEMBLIES/NATIONAL ASSEMBLIES/HO

See Also: uses

House of Commons, Canada, House of Commons, 111 Wellington St., Ottawa, K1A 0A6 ON
866-599-4999

LEISURE CRAFT & VEHICLE REGULATIONS

Alberta

Service Alberta & Registries, John E. Brownlee Bldg., 10365 - 97 St., Edmonton, T5J 3W7 AB
780-415-6090

Quebec

Ministère des Transports, 700, boul René-Lévesque est, 27e étage, Québec, G1R 5H1 QC
Fax: 514-643-1269, 888-355-0511, communications@mtq.gouv.qc.ca

Saskatchewan

Saskatchewan Government Insurance, 2260 - 11 Ave., Regina, S4P 0J9 SK
306-751-1200, Fax: 306-787-7477

LIQUOR CONTROL

See Also: Drugs & Alcohol

Manitoba

Manitoba Liquor Control Commission, 1555 Buffalo Pl., PO Box 1023, Winnipeg, MB R3C 2X1
204-284-2501, Fax: 204-475-7666, info@mlcc.mb.ca

Newfoundland & Labrador

Newfoundland Liquor Corporation, 90 Kenmount Rd., PO Box 8750 A, St. John's, NL A1B 3V1
709-724-1100, Fax: 709-754-0529, info@nfliquor.com

Nova Scotia

Alcohol & Gaming Authority, Alderney Gate, 40 Alderney Dr., PO Box 545, Dartmouth, B2Y 3Y8 NS
902-424-6160, Fax: 902-424-4942, 877-565-0556

Northwest Territories

Northwest Territories Liquor Commission, #201, 31 Capital Dr., Hay River, NT X0E 1G2
867-874-2100, Fax: 867-874-2180

Northwest Territories Liquor Licensing & Enforcement, #210, 31 Capital Dr., Hay River, NT X0E 1G2
867-874-2906, Fax: 867-874-6011

Northwest Territories Liquor Licensing Board, #210, 31 Capital Dr., Hay River, NT X0E 1G2
867-874-2906, Fax: 867-874-6011, delilah_st-arneault@gov.nt.ca

Nunavut

Nunavut Liquor Licensing Board, Bag 002, Rankin Inlet, NU X0C 0G0
Fax: 867-645-3327

Ontario

Liquor Control Board of Ontario, 55 Lake Shore Blvd. East, Toronto, ON M5E 1A4
416-864-2570, Fax: 416-864-2476

LOTTERIES & GAMING

British Columbia

British Columbia Lottery Corporation, 74 West Seymour St., Kamloops, BC V2C 1E2
250-828-5500, Fax: 250-828-5637, consumerservices@bclc.com

Manitoba
Manitoba Lotteries Corporation, 830 Empress St., Winnipeg, R3G 3H3 MB
204-957-2500, Fax: 204-957-3991, communications@mlc.mb.ca
Manitoba Gaming Control Commission, #800, 215 Garry St., Winnipeg, MB R3C 3P3
204-954-9400, 800-782-0363, information@mgcc.mb.ca

New Brunswick
Lotteries Commission of New Brunswick, PO Box 3000, Fredericton, NB E3B 5G5
506-444-4065, Fax: 506-444-5818

Newfoundland & Labrador
Department of Government Services, PO Box 8700, St. John's, A1B 4J6 NL
709-729-4860

Nova Scotia
Alcohol & Gaming Authority, Alderney Gate, 40 Alderney Dr., PO Box 545, Dartmouth, B2Y 3Y8 NS
902-424-6160, Fax: 902-424-4942, 877-565-0556

Ontario
Ontario Lottery & Gaming Corporation, Roberta Bondar Pl., #800, 70 Foster Dr., Sault Ste Marie, ON P6A 6V2

Prince Edward Island
Consumer, Corporate & Insurance Division, Shaw Building, 95 Rochford St., 4th Fl., PO Box 2000, Charlottetown, C1A 7N8 PE
902-368-4550, Fax: 902-368-5283
Prince Edward Island Lotteries Commission, Office of the Deputy Provincial Treasurer, 95 Rochford St., PO Box 2000, Charlottetown, PE C1A 7N8
902-368-4053, Fax: 902-368-6575

Yukon Territory
Yukon Lottery Commission, 312 Wood St., Whitehorse, YT Y1A 2E6
867-633-7890, Fax: 867-668-7561, lotteriesyukon@gov.yk.ca

MERCHANDISING

See: Trade
This is the Top, QC

MINERALS & MINING

Northwest Territories
Department of Industry, Tourism & Investment, PO Box 1320, Yellowknife, X1A 2L9 NT

Ontario
Ministry of Northern Development & Mines, 159 Cedar St., Sudbury, P3E 6A5 ON
705-564-0060, Fax: 705-564-7108

Saskatchewan
Saskatchewan Industry & Resources, 2103 - 11th Ave., Regina, S4P 3V7 SK
306-787-2232, Fax: 306-787-2159, 866-727-5427

MINIMUM WAGES

See Also: Labour

British Columbia
Ministry of Labour & Citizens' Services, PO Box 9594 Prov Govt,Victoria, V8W 9K4 BC
250-356-1487, Fax: 250-356-1653

MULTICULTURALISM

Manitoba
Manitoba Ethnocultural Advisory & Advocacy Council, 215 Notre Dame Ave. 4th Fl., Winnipeg, MB R3B 1N3
204-945-2339, Fax: 204-948-2323, 800-665-8332, meaac@gov.mb.ca
Multiculturalism Secretariat, 213 Notre Dame Ave., 4th Fl., Winnipeg, MB R3B 1N3
204-945-1156, Fax: 204-948-2323

MUNICIPAL & RURAL AFFAIRS

Canada Economic Development for Québec Regions, Tour de la Bourse, #3800, 800, Place Victoria, CP 247, Montréal, H4Z 1E8 QC
514-283-6412, Fax: 514-283-3302, 866-385-6412
Canada Mortgage & Housing Corporation, 700 Montreal Rd., Ottawa, K1A 0P7 ON
613-748-2000, Fax: 613-748-2098, 800-668-2642

Alberta
Alberta Agriculture, Food & Rural Development, J.G. O'Donoghue Bldg., 7000 - 113 St., Edmonton, T6H 5T6 AB
780-427-2727, Fax: 780-427-2861, 866-882-7677, duke@gov.ab.ca
Northern Alberta Development Council, #206, Provincial Bldg., 9621 - 96 Ave., PO Bag 900-14, Peace River, T8S 1T4 AB
780-624-6274, Fax: 780-624-6184, nadc.council@gov.ab.ca

Manitoba
Federal-Provincial & International Relations & Trade Division, #42, 450 Broadway, Winnipeg, R3C 0V8 MB
Manitoba Intergovernmental Affairs, #301, 450 Broadway, Winnipeg, R3C 0V8 MB
Fax: 204-945-1383, mnia@leg.gov.mb.ca
Manitoba Municipal Board, #1144, 363 Broadway, Winnipeg, MB R3C 3N9
204-945-2941, Fax: 204-948-2235

New Brunswick
Regional Development Corporation, RDC Bldg., 836 Churchill Row, PO Box 428, Fredericton, E3B 5R4 NB
506-453-2277, Fax: 506-453-7988

Nova Scotia
Department of Service Nova Scotia & Municipal Relations, 1505 Barrington St., PO Box 216, Halifax, B3J 2M4 NS
902-424-4141, Fax: 902-424-0581, public-enquiries@gov.ns.ca

Ontario
Ministry of Municipal Affairs & Housing, 777 Bay St., 17th Fl., Toronto, M5G 2E5 ON
416-585-7041, Fax: 416-585-6227, 866-220-2290
Ministry of Northern Development & Mines, 159 Cedar St., Sudbury, P3E 6A5 ON
705-564-0060, Fax: 705-564-7108
Northern Development Division, Roberta Bondar Place, #200, 70 Foster Dr., Sault Ste Marie, P6A 6V8 ON
705-945-5900, Fax: 705-945-5931

Quebec
Ministère du Développement économique, de l'Innovation et de l'Exportation, 710, place D'Youville, 3e étage, Québec, G1R 4Y4 QC
418-691-5950, Fax: 418-644-0118, 866-680-1884

Yukon Territory
Yukon Community Services, PO Box 2703, Whitehorse, Y1A 2C6 YT
867-667-5811, Fax: 867-393-6295, 800-661-0408, inquiry@gov.yk.ca

MUNICIPAL AFFAIRS

Manitoba
Manitoba Intergovernmental Affairs, #301, 450 Broadway, Winnipeg, R3C 0V8 MB
Fax: 204-945-1383, mnia@leg.gov.mb.ca
Manitoba Municipal Board, #1144, 363 Broadway, Winnipeg, MB R3C 3N9
204-945-2941, Fax: 204-948-2235
Provincial-Municipal Support Services, #508, 800 Portage Ave., Winnipeg, R3G 0N4 MB

New Brunswick
Regional Development Corporation, RDC Bldg., 836 Churchill Row, PO Box 428, Fredericton, E3B 5R4 NB
506-453-2277, Fax: 506-453-7988

Newfoundland & Labrador
Newfoundland & Labrador Municipal Financing Corporation, Confederation Bldg., PO Box 8700, St. John's, NL A1B 4J6
709-729-6686, Fax: 709-729-2095

Nova Scotia
Nova Scotia Municipal Finance Corporation, Maritime Centre, 1723 Hollis St., 7th Fl., PO Box 850 M, Halifax, NS B3J 2V2
902-424-4590, Fax: 902-424-0525
Department of Service Nova Scotia & Municipal Relations, 1505 Barrington St., PO Box 216, Halifax, B3J 2M4 NS
902-424-4141, Fax: 902-424-0581, public-enquiries@gov.ns.ca

Ontario
Ministry of Municipal Affairs & Housing, 777 Bay St., 17th Fl., Toronto, M5G 2E5 ON
416-585-7041, Fax: 416-585-6227, 866-220-2290

NATIVE PEOPLES & NORTHERN AFFAIRS

Yukon Territory
Yukon Development Corporation, PO Box 2703 D-1,Whitehorse, Y1A 2C6 YT
867-393-7069, Fax: 867-393-7071

NATURAL RESOURCES

British Columbia
Ministry of Forests & Range, PO Box 9529 Prov Govt,Victoria, V8W 9C3 BC
250-387-6121, 800-663-7867

Ontario
Ministry of Northern Development & Mines, 159 Cedar St., Sudbury, P3E 6A5 ON
705-564-0060, Fax: 705-564-7108

Prince Edward Island
Department of Agriculture, Fisheries & Aquaculture, Jones Bldg., 11 Kent St., PO Box 2000, Charlottetown, C1A 7N8 PE
902-368-4880, Fax: 902-368-4857

Saskatchewan
Saskatchewan Industry & Resources, 2103 - 11th Ave., Regina, S4P 3V7 SK
306-787-2232, Fax: 306-787-2159, 866-727-5427

OCCUPATIONAL SAFETY

See Also: Dangerous Goods & Hazardous Materials

British Columbia
Ministry of Labour & Citizens' Services, PO Box 9594 Prov Govt,Victoria, V8W 9K4 BC
250-356-1487, Fax: 250-356-1653

Manitoba
Advisory Council on Workplace Safety & Health, #200, 401 York Ave., Winnipeg, MB R3C 0P8
204-945-3446, Fax: 204-945-4556

Nova Scotia
Occupational Health & Safety Advisory Council, PO Box 697, Halifax, NS B3J 2T8
902-424-2484, Fax: 902-424-5640

OCCUPATIONAL TRAINING

British Columbia
Ministry of Labour & Citizens' Services, PO Box 9594 Prov Govt,Victoria, V8W 9K4 BC
250-356-1487, Fax: 250-356-1653

OIL & NATURAL GAS RESOURCES

See Also: Energy; Natural Resources

Nova Scotia
Canada-Nova Scotia Offshore Petroleum Board, TD Centre, 1791 Barrington St., 6th Fl., Halifax, NS B3J 3K9
902-422-5588, Fax: 902-422-1799, postmaster@cnsopb.ns.ca

PARKS & RECREATION

Manitoba
Manitoba Competitiveness, Training & Trades, #900, 259 Portage Ave., Winnipeg, R3B 3P4 MB
204-945-2067, Fax: 204-948-2964

New Brunswick
Department of Business New Brunswick, Centennial Bldg., 670 King St., 5th Fl., PO Box 6000, Fredericton, E3B 5H1 NB
506-444-5228, Fax: 506-453-5428

Nova Scotia
Department of Economic Development, Maritime Centre, 1505 Barrington St., 14th Fl., PO Box 2311, Halifax, B3J 3C8 NS
902-424-0377, Fax: 902-424-0500, comm@gov.ns.ca

Ontario
Ministry of Economic Development & Trade, Hearst Block, 900 Bay St., 8th Fl., Toronto, M7A 2E1 ON
416-325-6666, Fax: 416-325-6688

Prince Edward Island
Department of Development & Technology, Shaw Bldg., 105 Rochford St., 4th & 5th Fl., PO Box 2000, Charlottetown, C1A 7N8 PE
902-368-4242, Fax: 902-368-4224

Saskatchewan
Tourism Saskatchewan, 1922 Park St., Regina, SK S4N 7M4
306-787-9600, 877-237-2273

PARLIAMENT

See Also: Government (General Information; Protocol (State)
Office of the Prime Minister (Cons.), Langevin Block, 80 Wellington St., Ottawa, K1A 0A2 ON
613-992-4211, Fax: 613-941-6900, pm@pm.gc.ca
The Canadian Ministry, c/o Information Service, Library of Parliament, Ottawa, K1A 0A9 ON
613-992-4793, Fax: 613-992-1273, 866-599-4999, info@parl.gc.ca

PAROLE BOARDS

See Also: Correctional Services

British Columbia
British Columbia Board of Parole, #303, 960 Quayside Dr., New Westminster, BC V3M 6G2
604-660-8846, Fax: 604-660-2356

PATENTS & COPYRIGHT

Copyright Board of Canada, #800, 56 Sparks St., Ottawa, K1A 0C9 ON
613-952-8621, Fax: 613-952-8630, secretariat@cb-cda.gc.ca

PAY EQUITY

Human Resources & Social Development Canada, Place du Portage, Phase IV, 12th Fl., 140 Promenade du Portage, Gatineau, K1A 0J9 QC
819-994-6313

British Columbia
Employment Standards Tribunal, Oceanic Plaza, #650, 1066 West Hastings St., Vancouver, BC V6E 3X1
604-775-3512, Fax: 604-775-3372, registrar.est@bcest.bc.ca
Ministry of Labour & Citizens' Services, PO Box 9594 Prov Govt,Victoria, V8W 9K4 BC
250-356-1487, Fax: 250-356-1653

Nova Scotia
Pay Equity Commission, 5151 Terminal Rd., 7th Fl., PO Box 697, Halifax, NS B3J 2T8
902-424-8596, sherwoop@gov.ns.ca

PENSIONS

Canada Pension Plan Investment Board, #2700, 1 Queen St. East, PO Box 101, Toronto, M5C 2W5 ON
416-868-4075, Fax: 416-868-4760, 866-557-9510, csr@cppib.ca
Finance Canada, L'esplanade Laurier, 140 O'Connor St., Ottawa, K1A 0G5 ON
613-992-1573, Fax: 613-996-8404
Office of the Superintendent of Financial Institutions, Kent Square, 255 Albert St., Ottawa, K1A 0H2 ON
613-990-7788, Fax: 613-952-8219, 800-385-8647, extcomm@osfi-bsif.gc.ca
Public Sector Pension Investment Board, #200, 440 Laurier Ave. West, Ottawa, ON K1R 7X6
613-782-3095, Fax: 613-782-6864, info@investpsp.ca

Alberta
Alberta Pensions Administration Corporation, Park Plaza, 3rd Fl., 10611 - 98 Ave., Edmonton, AB T5K 2P7
780-427-2782, Fax: 780-427-1621, 800-661-8198, apa.info@apa.gov.ab.ca

British Columbia
British Columbia Pension Corporation, 2995 Jutland Rd., PO Box 9460, Victoria, BC V8W 9V8
250-387-8201, Fax: 250-953-0421, 800-663-8823

Manitoba
Pension Commission of Manitoba, #1004, 401 York Ave., Winnipeg, MB R3C 0P8
204-945-2740, Fax: 204-948-2375, pensions@gov.mb.ca

Nova Scotia
Pension Regulation Division, PO Box 2531, Halifax, B3J 3N5 NS
902-424-8915, Fax: 902-424-0662

Ontario
Financial Services Commission of Ontario, 5160 Yonge St., 17th Fl., Box 85, Toronto, ON M2N 6L9
416-250-7250, Fax: 416-590-7078, 800-668-0128

Prince Edward Island
Office of the Attorney General, PO Box 2000, Charlottetown, C1A 7N8 PE
902-368-5152, Fax: 902-368-4910

Saskatchewan
Crown Investments Corporation of Saskatchewan, #400, 2400 College Ave., Regina, S4P 1C8 SK
306-787-6851, Fax: 306-787-8125
Saskatchewan Financial Services Commission, #601, 1919 Saskatchewan Dr., Regina, SK S4P 4H2
306-787-5646, Fax: 306-787-5899

POLICING SERVICES

Manitoba
Manitoba Justice, 405 Broadway Ave., 5th Fl., Winnipeg, R3C 3L6 MB
204-945-2852, minjus@gov.mb.ca
Law Enforcement Review Agency, #420, 155 Carlton St., Winnipeg, MB R3C 3H8
204-945-8667, Fax: 204-948-1014, lera@gov.mb.ca

Newfoundland & Labrador
Royal Newfoundland Constabulary Public Complaints Commission, Bally Rou Place, #E-160, 280 Torbay Rd., St. John's, NL A1A 3W8
709-729-0950, Fax: 709-729-1302

Nova Scotia
Nova Scotia Police Commission, #300, 1601 Lower Water St., PO Box 1573, Halifax, NS B3J 2Y3
902-424-3246, Fax: 902-424-3919, uarb.polcom@gov.ns.ca

Nunavut
Department of Justice, Sivummut, 1st Fl., PO Box 1000 500,Iqaluit, X0A 0H0 NU
867-975-6170, Fax: 867-975-6195

Prince Edward Island
Office of the Attorney General, PO Box 2000, Charlottetown, C1A 7N8 PE
902-368-5152, Fax: 902-368-4910

Saskatchewan
Saskatchewan Police Commission, 1874 Scarth St., 6th Fl., Regina, SK S4P 3V7
306-787-6518, Fax: 306-787-0136
Saskatchewan Police Complaints Investigator, #600, 1919 Saskatchewan Dr., Regina, SK S4P 4H2
306-787-6519, Fax: 306-787-6528

Yukon Territory
Yukon Justice, PO Box 2703, Whitehorse, Y1A 2C6 YT
867-667-8644, Fax: 867-393-6272

POLITICS & SOCIETY

Auditor General of Canada, 240 Sparks St., Ottawa, K1A 0G6 ON
613-995-3708, Fax: 613-957-0474, communications@oag-bvg.gc.ca
Finance Canada, L'esplanade Laurier, 140 O'Connor St., Ottawa, K1A 0G5 ON
613-992-1573, Fax: 613-996-8404
Foreign Affairs & International Trade Canada, 125 Sussex Dr., Ottawa, K1A 0G2 ON
613-944-4000, Fax: 613-996-9709, 800-267-8376
Public Works & Government Services Canada, Place du Portage, Phase III, 11, rue Laurier, Ottawa, K1A 0S5 ON
819-997-6363

Alberta
Alberta International & Intergovernmental Relations, Commerce Place, 10155 - 102 St., 12th Fl., Edmonton, T5J 4G2 AB
780-422-1510, Fax: 780-423-6654

Newfoundland & Labrador
Department of Government Services, PO Box 8700, St. John's, A1B 4J6 NL
709-729-4860

Prince Edward Island
Department of the Provincial Treasury, PO Box 2000, Charlottetown, C1A 7N8 PE
902-368-4000, Fax: 902-368-5544

POPULATION

See Also: Statistics

Statistics Canada, R.H. Coats Bldg., Tunney's Pasture, 100 Tunney's Pasture Driveway, Ottawa, K1A 0T6 ON
Fax: 877-287-4369, 800-263-1136, infostats@statcan.ca

Alberta
Consumer Services & Land Titles, Commerce Place, 10155 - 102 St., 3rd Fl., Edmonton, T5J 4L4 AB

Manitoba
Manitoba Bureau of Statistics, #824, 155 Carlton St., Winnipeg, R3C 3H9 MB
204-945-2982, Fax: 204-945-0695

Nunavut
Department of Executive & Intergovernmental Affairs, Box 1000, Iqaluit, X0A 0H0 NU
867-975-6000, Fax: 867-975-6090

PREMIERS & LEADERS

See Also: Cabinets & Executive Councils; Government (General Info)
Office of the Prime Minister (Cons.), Langevin Block, 80 Wellington St., Ottawa, K1A 0A2 ON
613-992-4211, Fax: 613-941-6900, pm@pm.gc.ca

Alberta
Office of the Premier, Legislature Bldg., #307, 10800 - 97 Ave., Edmonton, T5K 2B6 AB
780-427-2251, Fax: 780-427-1349

British Columbia
Office of the Premier, PO Box 9041 Prov Govt,Victoria, V8W 9E1 BC
250-387-1715, Fax: 250-387-0087, premier@gov.bc.ca

Manitoba
Office of the Premier, Legislative Bldg., #214, 450 Broadway, Winnipeg, R3C 0V8 MB
204-945-3714, Fax: 204-949-1484, premier@leg.gov.mb.ca

New Brunswick
Office of the Premier, Centennial Bldg., 670 King St., PO Box 6000, Fredericton, E3B 5H1 NB
506-453-2144, Fax: 506-453-7407, premier@gnb.ca

Newfoundland & Labrador
Office of the Premier, Confederation Bldg., East Block, PO Box 8700, St. John's, A1B 4J6 NL
709-729-3570, Fax: 709-729-5875, premier@gov.nl.ca

Nova Scotia
Office of the Premier, One Government Place, 1700 Granville St., PO Box 726, Halifax, B3J 2T3 NS
902-424-6600, Fax: 902-424-7648, premier@gov.ns.ca

Northwest Territories
Office of the Premier, Legislative Assembly Bldg., PO Box 1320, Yellowknife, X1A 2L9 NT
867-669-2311, Fax: 867-873-0385

Nunavut
Office of the Premier, Legislative Assembly Bldg., 2nd Fl., PO Box 2410, Iqaluit, X0A 0H0 NU
867-975-5050, Fax: 867-975-5051

Ontario
Office of the Premier, Legislative Bldg., #281, 1 Queen's Park Cres. South, Toronto, M7A 1A1 ON
416-325-1941, Fax: 416-325-3745, webprem@gov.on.ca

Prince Edward Island
Office of the Premier, Shaw Bldg., 95 Rochford St., 5th Fl. South, PO Box 2000, Charlottetown, C1A 7N8 PE
902-368-4400, Fax: 902-368-4416

Quebec
Cabinet du premier ministre, Édifice Honoré-Mercier, 835, boul René-Lévesque est, 3e étage, Québec, G1A 1B4 QC
418-643-5321, Fax: 418-643-3924

Saskatchewan
Office of the Premier, 226 Legislative Bldg., Regina, S4S 0B3 SK
306-787-9433, Fax: 306-787-0885, premier@gov.sk.ca

Yukon Territory
Office of the Premier, PO Box 2703, Whitehorse, Y1A 2C6 YT
Fax: 867-393-6252

PROCUREMENT, GOODS & SERVICES

See: Purchasing
This is the Top, QC

PROPERTY ASSESSMENT

Alberta

Consumer Services & Land Titles, Commerce Place, 10155 - 102 St., 3rd Fl., Edmonton, T5J 4L4 AB

British Columbia

BC Assessment Authority, 1537 Hillside Ave., Victoria, BC V8T 4Y2
250-595-6211, Fax: 250-595-6222, info@bcassessment.ca

Saskatchewan

Saskatchewan Assessment Management Agency, #200, 2201 - 11 Ave., Regina, S4P 0J8 SK
306-924-8000, Fax: 306-924-8070, 800-667-7262

PUBLIC SAFETY

See Also: Occupational Safety

British Columbia

Ministry of Public Safety & Solicitor General, PO Box 9282 Prov Govt,Victoria, V8W 9J7 BC
250-356-6961, Fax: 250-387-1753, 800-663-7867

Northwest Territories

Department of Justice, PO Box 1320, Yellowknife, X1A 2L9 NT
867-920-6197

Nunavut

Department of Justice, Sivummut, 1st Fl., PO Box 1000 500,Iqaluit, X0A 0H0 NU
867-975-6170, Fax: 867-975-6195

PUBLIC SERVICES

Canada Deposit Insurance Corporation, 50 O'Connor St., 17th Fl., PO Box 2340 D,Ottawa, K1P 5W5 ON
613-996-2081, Fax: 613-996-6095, info@cdic.ca; info@sadc.ca

Human Resources & Social Development Canada, Place du Portage, Phase IV, 12th Fl., 140 Promenade du Portage, Gatineau, K1A 0J9 QC
819-994-6313

Public Works & Government Services Canada, Place du Portage, Phase III, 11, rue Laurier, Ottawa, K1A 0S5 ON
819-997-6363

Alberta

Alberta Capital Finance Authority, 2450 Canadian Western Bank Place, 10303 Jasper Ave., Edmonton, AB T5J 3N6
780-427-9711, Fax: 780-422-2175, webacfa@gov.ab.ca

Alberta Pensions Administration Corporation, Park Plaza, 3rd Fl., 10611 - 98 Ave., Edmonton, AB T5K 2P7
780-427-2782, Fax: 780-427-1621, 800-661-8198, apa.info@apa.gov.ab.ca

Northern Alberta Development Council, #206, Provincial Bldg., 9621 - 96 Ave., PO Bag 900-14, Peace River, T8S 1T4 AB
780-624-6274, Fax: 780-624-6184, nadc.council@gov.ab.ca

British Columbia

BC Assessment Authority, 1537 Hillside Ave., Victoria, BC V8T 4Y2
250-595-6211, Fax: 250-595-6222, info@bcassessment.ca

Child & Youth Officer for BC, 1019 Wharf St., PO Box 9207 Prov Govt, Victoria, BC V8W 9J1
250-356-0831, Fax: 250-356-0837, 800-476-3933, cyo@gov.bc.ca

Manitoba

Advisory Council on Workplace Safety & Health, #200, 401 York Ave., Winnipeg, MB R3C 0P8
204-945-3446, Fax: 204-945-4556

Office of the Auditor General, #500, 330 Portage Ave., Winnipeg, R3C 0C4 MB
204-945-3790, Fax: 204-945-2169

Automobile Injury Compensation Appeal Commission, #301, 428 Portage Ave.., Winnipeg, MB R3C 0E2
204-945-4155, Fax: 204-948-2402, autoinjury@gov.mb.ca

Credit Union Deposit Guarantee Corporation, #390, 200 Graham Ave., Winnipeg, MB R3C 4L5
204-942-8480, Fax: 204-947-1723, 800-697-4447, mail@cudgc.com

Manitoba Public Insurance, #820, 234 Donald St., PO Box 6300, Winnipeg, R3C 4A4 MB
204-985-7000, Fax: 204-943-9851, 800-665-2410

Manitoba Justice, 405 Broadway Ave., 5th Fl., Winnipeg, R3C 3L6 MB
204-945-2852, minjus@gov.mb.ca

Manitoba Labour & Immigration, #317, Legislative Bldg., 450 Broadway, Winnipeg, R3C 0V8 MB
Fax: 204-945-8312, minlab@leg.gov.mb.ca

Manitoba Bureau of Statistics, #824, 155 Carlton St., Winnipeg, R3C 3H9 MB
204-945-2982, Fax: 204-945-0695

Manitoba Labour Board, A.A. Heaps Bldg., #402, 258 Portage Ave., Winnipeg, MB R3C 0B6
204-945-3783, Fax: 204-945-1296, mlb@gov.mb.ca

Manitoba Minimum Wage Board, 614 - 401 York Ave., Winnipeg, MB R3C 0P8
204-945-4889, Fax: 204-948-2085, mw@gov.mb.ca

Office of the Fire Commissioner, #508, 401 York Ave., Winnipeg, MB R3C 0P8
204-945-3322, Fax: 204-948-2089, 800-282-8069, firecomm@gov.mb.ca

Provincial-Municipal Support Services, #508, 800 Portage Ave., Winnipeg, R3G 0N4 MB

Public Utilities Board, #400, 330 Portage Ave., Winnipeg, MB R3C 0C4
204-945-2638, Fax: 204-945-2643, In -Man-itob, publicutilities@gov.mb.ca

New Brunswick

New Brunswick Municipal Finance Corporation, #376, 670 King St., PO Box 6000, Fredericton, NB E3B 5H1
506-453-3952, Fax: 506-453-2053

Newfoundland & Labrador

C.A. Pippy Park Commission, PO Box 8861, St. John's, NL A1B 3T2
709-737-3655, Fax: 709-737-3303, 877-477-3655, pippyparkinfo@nf.aibn.com

Department of Government Services, PO Box 8700, St. John's, A1B 4J6 NL
709-729-4860

Newfoundland & Labrador Legal Aid Commission, Cormack Bldg., 2 Steers Cove, PO Box 399 C, St. John's, NL A1C 5J9
709-753-7860, Fax: 709-753-6226, 800-563-9911

Newfoundland Liquor Corporation, 90 Kenmount Rd., PO Box 8750 A, St. John's, NL A1B 3V1
709-724-1100, Fax: 709-754-0529, info@nfliquor.com

Royal Newfoundland Constabulary Public Complaints Commission, Bally Rou Place, #E-160, 280 Torbay Rd., St. John's, NL A1A 3W8
709-729-0950, Fax: 709-729-1302

Nova Scotia

Alcohol & Gaming Authority, Alderney Gate, 40 Alderney Dr., PO Box 545, Dartmouth, B2Y 3Y8 NS
902-424-6160, Fax: 902-424-4942, 877-565-0556

Nova Scotia Legal Aid Commission, #102, 137 Chain Lake Dr., Halifax, NS B3S 1B3
902-420-6573, Fax: 902-420-3471, nsla.exec@ns.sympatico.ca

Nova Scotia Police Commission, #300, 1601 Lower Water St., PO Box 1573, Halifax, NS B3J 2Y3
902-424-3246, Fax: 902-424-3919, uarb.polcom@gov.ns.ca

Workers' Advisers Program, #502, 5670 Spring Garden Rd., PO Box 1063, Halifax, NS B3J 2X1
902-424-5050, Fax: 902-424-0530, 800-774-4712

Northwest Territories

Victims Assistance Committee, c/o Community Justice Division, PO Box 1320, Yellowknife, NT X1A 2L9
867-920-6911, Fax: 867-873-0299

Nunavut

Department of Finance, Bldg. 1079, 1st Fl., PO Box 1000 Stn 360,Iqaluit, X0A 0H0 NU
867-975-5800, Fax: 867-975-5805

Ontario

Ministry of the Attorney General, 720 Bay St., Toronto, M5G 2K1 ON
416-326-2220, Fax: 416-326-4007, 800-518-7901

Deposit Insurance Corporation of Ontario, #700, 4711 Yonge St., Toronto, ON M2N 6K8
416-325-9444, Fax: 416-325-9722, 800-268-6653

Human Rights Tribunal of Ontario, 400 University Ave., 7th Fl., Toronto, ON M7A 1T7
416-314-8419, Fax: 416-314-8743, 800-668-3946, hrto.registrar@jus.gov.on.ca

Ministry of Municipal Affairs & Housing, 777 Bay St., 17th Fl., Toronto, M5G 2E5 ON
416-585-7041, Fax: 416-585-6227, 866-220-2290

Ontario Housing Corporation, 777 Bay St., 2nd Fl., Toronto, ON M5G 2E5

Ontario Rental Housing Tribunal, 777 Bay St., 12th Fl., Toronto, ON M5G 2E5
416-585-7295, Fax: 416-585-6363, 888-332-3234

Prince Edward Island

Office of the Attorney General, PO Box 2000, Charlottetown, C1A 7N8 PE
902-368-5152, Fax: 902-368-4910

Quebec

Ministère de l'Emploi et de la Solidarité sociale, 425, rue St-Amable, 4e étage, Québec, G1R 4Z1 QC
418-643-4810, 888-643-4721

Vérificateur général du Québec, 750, boulevard Charest est, 3e étage, Québec, G1K 9J6 QC
418-691-5900, Fax: 418-644-4460, verificateur.general@vgq.gouv.qc.

Saskatchewan

Saskatchewan Assessment Management Agency, #200, 2201 - 11 Ave., Regina, S4P 0J8 SK
306-924-8000, Fax: 306-924-8070, 800-667-7262

Provincial Auditor Saskatchewan, #1500, 1920 Broad St., Regina, S4P 3V2 SK
306-787-6398, Fax: 306-787-6383, info@auditor.sk.ca

Crown Investments Corporation of Saskatchewan, #400, 2400 College Ave., Regina, S4P 1C8 SK
306-787-6851, Fax: 306-787-8125

Saskatchewan Government Insurance, 2260 - 11 Ave., Regina, S4P 0J9 SK
306-751-1200, Fax: 306-787-7477

Saskatchewan Legal Aid Commission, #502, 201 - 21 St. East, Saskatoon, SK S7K 2H6
306-933-5300, Fax: 306-933-6764, In -Sas-k on, central@legalaid.gov.sk.ca

Yukon Territory

Yukon Community Services, PO Box 2703, Whitehorse, Y1A 2C6 YT
867-667-5811, Fax: 867-393-6295, 800-661-0408, inquiry@gov.yk.ca

Yukon Utilities Board, #19, 1114 - 1st Ave., PO Box 31728, Whitehorse, YT Y1A 6L3
867-667-5058

PUBLIC TRUSTEE

British Columbia

Public Guardian & Trustee of British Columbia, #700, 808 West Hastings St., Vancouver, BC V6C 3L3
604-660-4444, Fax: 604-660-0374, mail@trustee.bc.ca

Manitoba

Office of the Public Trustee, #500, 155 Carlton St., Winnipeg, MB R3C 5R9
204-945-2700

New Brunswick

Department of Justice & Consumer Affairs, PO Box 6000, Fredericton, E3B 5H1 NB
506-462-5100

Newfoundland & Labrador

Department of Justice, Confederation Bldg., PO Box 8700, St. John's, A1B 4J6 NL
709-729-5942, Fax: 709-729-2129

Nova Scotia

Public Trustee Office, #201, 5151 Terminal Rd., PO Box 385, Halifax, NS B3J 2T3
902-424-7760, Fax: 902-424-0616

PUBLIC UTILITIES

Manitoba

Public Utilities Board, #400, 330 Portage Ave., Winnipeg, MB R3C 0C4
204-945-2638, Fax: 204-945-2643, In -Man-itob, publicutilities@gov.mb.ca

Yukon Territory

Yukon Utilities Board, #19, 1114 - 1st Ave., PO Box 31728, Whitehorse, YT Y1A 6L3
867-667-5058

PUBLIC WORKS

Public Works & Government Services Canada, Place du Portage, Phase III, 11, rue Laurier, Ottawa, K1A 0S5 ON
819-997-6363

British Columbia
Ministry of Labour & Citizens' Services, PO Box 9594 Prov Govt,Victoria, V8W 9K4 BC
250-356-1487, Fax: 250-356-1653

Ontario
Ministry of Public Infrastructure Renewal, Mowat Block, 900 Bay St., 6th Fl., Toronto, M7A 1L2 ON
416-325-0424, Fax: 416-325-8851

Quebec
Ministère des Services gouvernementaux, 875, Grande Allée est, Québec, G1R 5R8 QC
418-643-8383

PUBLICATIONS

Public Works & Government Services Canada, Place du Portage, Phase III, 11, rue Laurier, Ottawa, K1A 0S5 ON
819-997-6363

Nova Scotia
Department of Service Nova Scotia & Municipal Relations, 1505 Barrington St., PO Box 216, Halifax, B3J 2M4 NS
902-424-4141, Fax: 902-424-0581, public-enquiries@gov.ns.ca

PURCHASING

British Columbia
Ministry of Labour & Citizens' Services, PO Box 9594 Prov Govt,Victoria, V8W 9K4 BC
250-356-1487, Fax: 250-356-1653

Newfoundland & Labrador
Department of Government Services, PO Box 8700, St. John's, A1B 4J6 NL
709-729-4860

Ontario
Ministry of Public Infrastructure Renewal, Mowat Block, 900 Bay St., 6th Fl., Toronto, M7A 1L2 ON
416-325-0424, Fax: 416-325-8851

Quebec
Centre de services partagés du Québec, 900, place d'Youville, 6e étage, uébec, G1R 0A1 QC
418-643-6080

RAIL TRANSPORTATION

See Also: Transportation

Quebec
Ministère des Transports, 700, boul René-Lévesque est, 27e étage, Québec, G1R 5H1 QC
Fax: 514-643-1269, 888-355-0511, communications@mtq.gouv.qc.ca

REAL ESTATE

See Also: Land Titles
Canada Mortgage & Housing Corporation, 700 Montreal Rd., Ottawa, K1A 0P7 ON
613-748-2000, Fax: 613-748-2098, 800-668-2642

Alberta
Service Alberta & Registries, John E. Brownlee Bldg., 10365 - 97 St., Edmonton, T5J 3W7 AB
780-415-6090

British Columbia
Real Estate Council of British Columbia, #900, 750 West Pender St., Vancouver, BC V6C 2T8
604-683-9664, Fax: 604-683-9017, 877-683-9664, info@recbc.ca

New Brunswick
New Brunswick Real Estate Association, #1, 22 Durelle St., Fredericton, NB E3C 1N8
506-459-8055, Fax: 506-459-8057, 800-762-1677, nbrea@nbnet.nb.ca

Nova Scotia
Department of Service Nova Scotia & Municipal Relations, 1505 Barrington St., PO Box 216, Halifax, B3J 2M4 NS
902-424-4141, Fax: 902-424-0581, public-enquiries@gov.ns.ca

Nunavut
Nunavut Legal Registries Division, Brown Bldg., 1st Fl., PO Box 1000 570,Iqaluit, X0A 0H0 NU
867-975-6190, Fax: 867-975-6194

Ontario
Ontario Realty Corporation, Ferguson Block, 77 Wellesley St. West, 11th Fl., Toronto, ON M7A 2G3
416-327-3937, Fax: 416-327-1906, 877-863-9672

Prince Edward Island
Consumer, Corporate & Insurance Division, Shaw Building, 95 Rochford St., 4th Fl., PO Box 2000, Charlottetown, C1A 7N8 PE
902-368-4550, Fax: 902-368-5283

REAL ESTATE

Ontario
Ontario Realty Corporation, Ferguson Block, 77 Wellesley St. West, 11th Fl., Toronto, ON M7A 2G3
416-327-3937, Fax: 416-327-1906, 877-863-9672

RECREATION

See Also: Tourism & Tourist Information
Canadian Tourism Commission, #1400, 1055 Dunsmuir St., PO Box 49230, Vancouver, BC V7X 1L5
604-638-8300, Fax: 604-638-8425, ctc_feedback@businteractive.com

Alberta
Alberta Economic Development, Commerce Place , 6th Fl., 10155 - 102 St., Edmonton, T5J 4L6 AB
780-415-1319, Fax: 780-415-1759
Strategic Tourism Marketing Council, #500, 999 - 8 St. SW, Calgary, AB T2J 1J5
403-297-2700, Fax: 403-297-5068

British Columbia
BC Olympic & Paralympic Games Secretariat, #860, 1095 West Pender St., Vancouver, BC V6E 2M6
604-660-0914, bcsecretariat@gov.bc.ca
British Columbia Lottery Corporation, 74 West Seymour St., Kamloops, BC V2C 1E2
250-828-5500, Fax: 250-828-5637, consumerservices@bclc.com
Ministry of Small Business & Revenue, PO Box 9065 Prov Govt,Victoria, V8W 9E2 BC
250-356-6611, Fax: 250-356-8294

Manitoba
Manitoba Competitiveness, Training & Trades, #900, 259 Portage Ave., Winnipeg, R3B 3P4 MB
204-945-2067, Fax: 204-948-2964
Manitoba Lotteries Corporation, 830 Empress St., Winnipeg, R3G 3H3 MB
204-957-2500, Fax: 204-957-3991, communications@mlc.mb.ca
Manitoba Horse Racing Commission, PO Box 46086 Westdale, Winnipeg, MB R3R 3S3
204-885-7770, Fax: 204-831-0942, mhrc@manitobahorsecomm.org

New Brunswick
Department of Business New Brunswick, Centennial Bldg., 670 King St., 5th Fl., PO Box 6000, Fredericton, E3B 5H1 NB
506-444-5228, Fax: 506-453-5428
Lotteries Commission of New Brunswick, PO Box 3000, Fredericton, NB E3B 5G5
506-444-4065, Fax: 506-444-5818

Newfoundland & Labrador
C.A. Pippy Park Commission, PO Box 8861, St. John's, NL A1B 3T2
709-737-3655, Fax: 709-737-3303, 877-477-3655, pippyparkinfo@nf.aibn.com

Nova Scotia
Alcohol & Gaming Authority, Alderney Gate, 40 Alderney Dr., PO Box 545, Dartmouth, B2Y 3Y8 NS
902-424-6160, Fax: 902-424-4942, 877-565-0556

Ontario
Ministry of Economic Development & Trade, Hearst Block, 900 Bay St., 8th Fl., Toronto, M7A 2E1 ON
416-325-6666, Fax: 416-325-6688
Ontario Lottery & Gaming Corporation, Roberta Bondar Pl., #800, 70 Foster Dr., Sault Ste Marie, ON P6A 6V2

Prince Edward Island
Department of Development & Technology, Shaw Bldg., 105 Rochford St., 4th & 5th Fl., PO Box 2000, Charlottetown, C1A 7N8 PE
902-368-4242, Fax: 902-368-4224
Prince Edward Island Lotteries Commission, Office of the Deputy Provincial Treasurer, 95 Rochford St., PO Box 2000, Charlottetown, PE C1A 7N8
902-368-4053, Fax: 902-368-6575

Yukon Territory
Yukon Lottery Commission, 312 Wood St., Whitehorse, YT Y1A 2E6
867-633-7890, Fax: 867-668-7561, lotteriesyukon@gov.yk.ca

RESEARCH & DEVELOPMENT

New Brunswick
Service New Brunswick, #200, 82 Westmorland St., PO Box 1998, Fredericton, E3B 5G4 NB
506-457-3581, Fax: 506-453-3043, snb@snb.ca

Newfoundland & Labrador
Department of Innovation, Trade & Rural Development, PO Box 8700, St. John's, A1B 4J6 NL
709-729-7000, Fax: 709-729-0654, 800-563-2299, itrdinfo@gov.nl.ca

Ontario
Ministry of Research & Innovation, Whitney Block, 99 Wellesley St. West, 1st Fl., Toronto, M7A 1W1 ON
416-325-5181, Fax: 416-314-5599

Prince Edward Island
Agricultural Insurance Corporation, 29 Indigo Cres., PO Box 1600, Charlottetown, PE C1A 7N3
902-368-4842, Fax: 902-368-6677

SALES TAX

Legislative Policy & Regulatory Affairs, 123 Slater St., Ottawa, K1A 0L8 ON

Manitoba
Taxation Division, 401 York Ave., 4th Fl., Winnipeg, R3C 0P8 MB

Nova Scotia
Tax Commission, Maritime Centre, 1505 Barrington St., Halifax, B3J 3K5 NS
902-424-5200, Fax: 902-424-0720, 800-670-4357

Northwest Territories
Department of Finance, PO Box 1320, Yellowknife, X1A 2L9 NT
867-873-0414, Fax: 867-873-7117

Nunavut
Department of Finance, Bldg. 1079, 1st Fl., PO Box 1000 Stn 360,Iqaluit, X0A 0H0 NU
867-975-5800, Fax: 867-975-5805

Prince Edward Island
Department of the Provincial Treasury, PO Box 2000, Charlottetown, C1A 7N8 PE
902-368-4000, Fax: 902-368-5544

Quebec
Centre de perception fiscale, 3800, rue de Marly, Secteur 6-4-3, Sainte-Foy, G1X 4A5 QC

SCIENCE & NATURE

Agriculture & Agri-Food Canada, Sir John Carling Bldg., 930 Carling Ave., Ottawa, K1A 0C5 ON
613-759-1000, Fax: 613-759-6726, info@agr.gc.ca
Electronic Commerce Branch, 300 Slater St., Ottawa, ON K1A 0C8
613-954-5031, Fax: 613-941-1164, 800-328-6189

Alberta
Agricultural Products Marketing Council, 7000 - 113 St., 3rd Fl., Edmonton, AB T6H 5T6
780-427-2164, Fax: 780-422-9690
Alberta Agriculture, Food & Rural Development, J.G. O'Donoghue Bldg., 7000 - 113 St., Edmonton, T6H 5T6 AB
780-427-2727, Fax: 780-427-2861, 866-882-7677, duke@gov.ab.ca
Farmers' Advocate of Alberta, 7000 - 113 St., 3rd Fl., Edmonton, AB T6H 5T6
780-427-2433, Fax: 780-427-3913
Irrigation Council, Provincial Bldg., 200 - 5 Ave. South, 3rd Fl., PO Bag 3014, Lethbridge, AB T1J 4L1
403-381-5176, Fax: 403-382-4406

British Columbia
Agricultural Land Commission, #133, 4940 Canada Way, Burnaby, BC V5G 4K6
604-660-7000, Fax: 604-660-7033

Ministry of Agriculture & Lands, PO Box 9120 Prov Govt,Victoria, V8W 9B4 BC
250-387-5121, Fax: 250-387-1522
British Columbia Farm Industry Review Board, PO Box 9129 Prov Govt, Victoria, BC V8W 9B5
250-356-8945, Fax: 250-356-5731, firb@gov.bc.ca
Forest Practices Board, 1675 Douglas St., 3rd Fl., PO Box 9905 Prov Govt, Victoria, BC V8W 9R1
250-387-7964, Fax: 250-387-7009, 800-994-5899, fpboard@gov.bc.ca
Forestry Innovation Investments Ltd., #1200, 1130 West Pender St., Vancouver, BC V6E 4A4
604-685-7507, Fax: 604-685-5373
Ministry of Forests & Range, PO Box 9529 Prov Govt,Victoria, V8W 9C3 BC
250-387-6121, 800-663-7867
Timber Export Advisory Committee, 1520 Blanshard St., 2nd Fl., PO Box 9514 Prov Govt, Victoria, BC V8W 3C8
250-387-8359, Fax: 250-387-5050

Manitoba
Agricultural Societies, 1129 Queens Ave., Brandon, MB R7A 1L9
204-726-6195, Fax: 204-726-6260
Manitoba Agriculture, Food & Rural Initiatives, Norquay Bldg., 401 York Ave., Winnipeg, R3C 0P8 MB
Farm Lands Ownership Board, #812, Norquay Bldg., 401 York Ave., Winnipeg, MB R3C 0P8
204-945-3149, Fax: 204-945-1489, 800-282-8069, flob@gov.mb.ca
Farm Machinery Board, Norquay Bldg., #812, 401 York Ave., Winnipeg, MB R3C 0P8
204-945-3856

New Brunswick
Department of Agriculture & Aquaculture, PO Box 6000, Fredericton, E3B 5H1 NB
506-453-2666, Fax: 506-453-7170
New Brunswick Crop Insurance Commission, PO Box 6000, Fredericton, NB E3B 5H1
506-453-2185, Fax: 506-453-7406
New Brunswick Farm Products Commission, c/o Department of Agriculture, Fisheries & Aquaculture, PO Box 6000, Fredericton, NB E3B 5H1
506-453-3647, Fax: 506-444-5969
Service New Brunswick, #200, 82 Westmorland St., PO Box 1998, Fredericton, E3B 5G4 NB
506-457-3581, Fax: 506-453-3043, snb@snb.ca

Newfoundland & Labrador
C.A. Pippy Park Commission, PO Box 8861, St. John's, NL A1B 3T2
709-737-3655, Fax: 709-737-3303, 877-477-3655, pippyparkinfo@nf.aibn.com
Department of Innovation, Trade & Rural Development, PO Box 8700, St. John's, A1B 4J6 NL
709-729-7000, Fax: 709-729-0654, 800-563-2299, itrdinfo@gov.nl.ca

Nova Scotia
Canada-Nova Scotia Offshore Petroleum Board, TD Centre, 1791 Barrington St., 6th Fl., Halifax, NS B3J 3K9
902-422-5588, Fax: 902-422-1799, postmaster@cnsopb.ns.ca

Ontario
Ministry of Northern Development & Mines, 159 Cedar St., Sudbury, P3E 6A5 ON
705-564-0060, Fax: 705-564-7108

Prince Edward Island
Agricultural Insurance Corporation, 29 Indigo Cres., PO Box 1600, Charlottetown, PE C1A 7N3
902-368-4842, Fax: 902-368-6677
Department of Agriculture, Fisheries & Aquaculture, Jones Bldg., 11 Kent St., PO Box 2000, Charlottetown, C1A 7N8 PE
902-368-4880, Fax: 902-368-4857
Grain Elevator Corporation, PO Box 250, Kensington, PE C0B 1M0
902-836-8935, Fax: 902-836-8926

Quebec
Ministère de l'Agriculture, des Pêcheries et de l'Alimentation, 200, ch Sainte-Foy, Québec, G1R 4X6 QC
418-380-2110, 888-222-6272

Saskatchewan
Agri-Food Council, #302, 3085 Albert St., Regina, SK S4S 0B1
306-787-8530, Fax: 306-787-5134
Agricultural Implements Board, #202, 3085 Albert St., Regina, SK S4S 0B1
306-787-4693, Fax: 306-787-1315
Saskatchewan Agriculture & Food, Walter Scott Bldg., 3085 Albert St., Regina, S4S 0B1 SK
306-787-5140
Farm Stress Unit, #329, 3085 Albert St., Regina, SK S4S 0B1
306-787-5196, Fax: 306-798-3042, 800-667-4442, kimhoff@agr.gov.sk.ca
Prairie Agricultural Machinery Institute, Hwy#5, PO Box 1900, Humboldt, SK S0K 2A0
306-682-2555, Fax: 306-682-5080, 800-567-7264, humboldt@pami.ca
Saskatchewan Regional Economic & Co-operative Development, 3085 Albert St., Regina, S4S 0B1 SK
306-787-9703, 800-265-2001
Saskatchewan Crop Insurance Corporation, 484 Prince William Dr., PO Box 3000, Melville, SK S0A 2P0
306-728-7200, Fax: 306-728-7268, customer.service@scic.gov.sk.ca
Saskatchewan Farm Land Security Board, #207, 3988 Albert St., Regina, SK S4S 3R1
306-787-5047, Fax: 306-787-8599
Saskatchewan Farm Security Programs, #207, 3988 Albert St., Regina, SK S4S 3R1
306-787-5047, Fax: 306-787-8599
Saskatchewan Lands Appeal Board, #202, 3085 Albert St., Regina, SK S4S 0B1
306-787-4693, Fax: 306-787-1315, dbrooks@agr.gov.sk.ca
Surface Rights Board of Arbitration, 113 - 2nd Ave. East, PO Box 1597, Kindersley, SK S0L 1S0
306-463-5447, Fax: 306-463-5449, surface@sasktel.net

Yukon Territory
Yukon Development Corporation, PO Box 2703 D-1,Whitehorse, Y1A 2C6 YT
867-393-7069, Fax: 867-393-7071

SCIENCE & TECHNOLOGY

See Also: Business Development

Nova Scotia
InNOVACorp, #1400, 1801 Hollis St., Halifax, NS B3J 3N4
902-424-8670, Fax: 902-424-4679, 800-565-7051, communications@innovacorp.ca

Ontario
Ministry of Research & Innovation, Whitney Block, 99 Wellesley St. West, 1st Fl., Toronto, M7A 1W1 ON
416-325-5181, Fax: 416-314-5599

SECURITIES ADMINISTRATION

See Also: Finance

Alberta
Alberta Securities Commission, 300 - 5 Ave. SW, 4th Fl., Calgary, AB T2P 3C4
403-297-6454, Fax: 403-297-6156, 877-355-0585, inquiries@seccom.ab.ca

British Columbia
British Columbia Securities Commission, Pacific Centre, 701 West Georgia St., 12th Fl., PO Box 10142, Vancouver, BC V7Y 1L2
604-899-6500, Fax: 604-899-6506, 800-373-6393, inquiries@bcsc.bc.ca

Manitoba
Manitoba Securities Commission, #500, 400 St. Mary Ave., Winnipeg, MB R3C 4K5
204-945-2548, Fax: 204-945-0330, 800-655-5244, securities@gov.mb.ca

New Brunswick
New Brunswick Securities Commission, #300, 85 Charlotte St., Saint John, NB E2L 2J2
506-658-3060, Fax: 506-658-3059, 866-933-2222, information@nbsc-cvmnb.ca

Nova Scotia
Nova Scotia Securities Commission, Joseph Howe Bldg., 1690 Hollis St., 2nd Fl., PO Box 458, Halifax, NS B3J 2P8
902-424-7768, Fax: 902-424-4625

Northwest Territories
Department of Justice, PO Box 1320, Yellowknife, X1A 2L9 NT
867-920-6197

Ontario
Ontario Securities Commission, #1903, 20 Queen St. West, PO Box 55, Toronto, ON M5H 3S8
416-597-0681, Fax: 416-593-8122

Saskatchewan
Saskatchewan Financial Services Commission, #601, 1919 Saskatchewan Dr., Regina, SK S4P 4H2
306-787-5646, Fax: 306-787-5899

SOLICITORS GENERAL

British Columbia
Ministry of Public Safety & Solicitor General, PO Box 9282 Prov Govt,Victoria, V8W 9J7 BC
250-356-6961, Fax: 250-387-1753, 800-663-7867

Manitoba
Manitoba Justice, 405 Broadway Ave., 5th Fl., Winnipeg, R3C 3L6 MB
204-945-2852, minjus@gov.mb.ca

Newfoundland & Labrador
Department of Justice, Confederation Bldg., PO Box 8700, St. John's, A1B 4J6 NL
709-729-5942, Fax: 709-729-2129

Nova Scotia
Department of Justice, 5151 Terminal Rd., PO Box 7, Halifax, B3J 2L6 NS
902-424-4222, Fax: 902-424-2809, justweb@gov.ns.ca

Yukon Territory
Yukon Justice, PO Box 2703, Whitehorse, Y1A 2C6 YT
867-667-8644, Fax: 867-393-6272

STATISTICS

See Also: Vital Statistics
Statistics Canada, R.H. Coats Bldg., Tunney's Pasture, 100 Tunney's Pasture Driveway, Ottawa, K1A 0T6 ON
Fax: 877-287-4369, 800-263-1136, infostats@statcan.ca

Manitoba
Manitoba Bureau of Statistics, #824, 155 Carlton St., Winnipeg, R3C 3H9 MB
204-945-2982, Fax: 204-945-0695

Nunavut
Department of Executive & Intergovernmental Affairs, Box 1000, Iqaluit, X0A 0H0 NU
867-975-6000, Fax: 867-975-6090

STATISTICS (ENVIRONMENTAL)

Statistics Canada, R.H. Coats Bldg., Tunney's Pasture, 100 Tunney's Pasture Driveway, Ottawa, K1A 0T6 ON
Fax: 877-287-4369, 800-263-1136, infostats@statcan.ca

TAXATION

See Also: Sales Tax
Canada Revenue Agency, 555 Mackenzie Ave., 4th Fl., Ottawa, K1A 0L5 ON
613-952-0384

Manitoba
Taxation Division, 401 York Ave., 4th Fl., Winnipeg, R3C 0P8 MB

Nova Scotia
Tax Commission, Maritime Centre, 1505 Barrington St., Halifax, B3J 3K5 NS
902-424-5200, Fax: 902-424-0720, 800-670-4357

Quebec
Centre de perception fiscale, 3800, rue de Marly, Secteur 6-4-3, Sainte-Foy, G1X 4A5 QC

Saskatchewan
Board of Revenue Commissioners, #480, 2151 Scarth St., Regina, SK S4P 3V7
306-787-6221, Fax: 306-787-1610

TELECOMMUNICATIONS

See Also: Broadcasting
Communications Research Centre Canada, 3701 Carling Ave., PO Box 11490 H, Ottawa, ON K2H 8S2
613-991-3313, Fax: 613-998-5355, info@crc.ca

Prince Edward Island
Department of Development & Technology, Shaw Bldg., 105 Rochford St., 4th & 5th Fl., PO Box 2000, Charlottetown, C1A

7N8 PE
902-368-4242, Fax: 902-368-4224

TOURISM & TOURIST INFORMATION

Canadian Tourism Commission, #1400, 1055 Dunsmuir St., PO Box 49230, Vancouver, BC V7X 1L5
604-638-8300, Fax: 604-638-8425, ctc_feedback@businteractive.com

Alberta
Strategic Tourism Marketing Council, #500, 999 - 8 St. SW, Calgary, AB T2J 1J5
403-297-2700, Fax: 403-297-5068

British Columbia
BC Olympic & Paralympic Games Secretariat, #860, 1095 West Pender St., Vancouver, BC V6E 2M6
604-660-0914, bcsecretariat@gov.bc.ca

Northwest Territories
Department of Industry, Tourism & Investment, PO Box 1320, Yellowknife, X1A 2L9 NT

Saskatchewan
Tourism Saskatchewan, 1922 Park St., Regina, SK S4N 7M4
306-787-9600, 877-237-2273

TRADE

See Also: Business Development; Imports
Business Development Bank of Canada, #400, 5, Place Ville-Marie, Montréal, H3B 5E7 QC
514-283-5904, Fax: 514-283-2872, 888-463-6232
Canadian Commercial Corporation, Clarica Centre, #1100, 50 O'Connor St., Ottawa, K1A 0S6 ON
613-996-0034, Fax: 613-995-2121
Canadian International Trade Tribunal, Standard Life Centre, 333 Laurier Ave. West, Ottawa, K1A 0G7 ON
613-990-2452, Fax: 613-990-2439
Export Development Canada, 151 O'Connor St., Ottawa, K1A 1K3 ON
613-598-2500, Fax: 613-237-2690, 888-332-3320
International Trade Canada, 125 Sussex Dr., Ottawa, K1A 0G2 ON
613-944-4000, Fax: 613-996-9709, 800-267-8376
North American Free Trade Agreement (NAFTA) Secretariat, Canadian Section, #705, 90 Sparks St., Ottawa, K1P 5B4 ON
613-992-9388, Fax: 613-992-9392, canada@nafta-sec-alena.org

British Columbia
Asia Pacific Trade Council, #730, 999 Canada Place, Vancouver, BC V6C 3E1
604-775-2100, Fax: 604-775-2070
Marketing, Investment & Trade, #730, 999 Canada Place, Vancouver, V6C 3E1 BC
604-844-1900
Ministry of Small Business & Revenue, PO Box 9065 Prov Govt,Victoria, V8W 9E2 BC
250-356-6611, Fax: 250-356-8294

Manitoba
Manitoba Competitiveness, Training & Trades, #900, 259 Portage Ave., Winnipeg, R3B 3P4 MB
204-945-2067, Fax: 204-948-2964
Federal-Provincial & International Relations & Trade Division, #42, 450 Broadway, Winnipeg, R3C 0V8 MB

New Brunswick
Department of Business New Brunswick, Centennial Bldg., 670 King St., 5th Fl., PO Box 6000, Fredericton, E3B 5H1 NB
506-444-5228, Fax: 506-453-5428

Newfoundland & Labrador
Department of Innovation, Trade & Rural Development, PO Box 8700, St. John's, A1B 4J6 NL
709-729-7000, Fax: 709-729-0654, 800-563-2299, itrdinfo@gov.nl.ca

Nova Scotia
Department of Economic Development, Maritime Centre, 1505 Barrington St., 14th Fl., PO Box 2311, Halifax, B3J 3C8 NS
902-424-0377, Fax: 902-424-0500, comm@gov.ns.ca

Prince Edward Island
Department of Development & Technology, Shaw Bldg., 105 Rochford St., 4th & 5th Fl., PO Box 2000, Charlottetown, C1A 7N8 PE
902-368-4242, Fax: 902-368-4224

Quebec
Ministère du Développement économique, de l'Innovation et de l'Exportation, 710, place D'Youville, 3e étage, Québec, G1R 4Y4 QC
418-691-5950, Fax: 418-644-0118, 866-680-1884

Saskatchewan
Saskatchewan Trade & Export Partnership, #320, 1801 Hamilton St., PO Box 1787, Regina, SK S4P 3C6
306-787-9210, Fax: 306-787-6666, 877-313-7244, inquire@sasktrade.sk.ca

Yukon Territory
Yukon Economic Development, PO Box 2703, Whitehorse, Y1A 2C6 YT
867-393-7191, Fax: 867-395-7199, 800-661-0408

TRANSPORTATION

Alberta
Automobile Insurance Rate Board, Terrace Bldg., #200, 9515 - 107 St. NW, Edmonton, AB T5K 2C3
780-427-5428, Fax: 780-644-7771, airb@gov.ab.ca

British Columbia
BC Ferry Commission, PO Box 1497, Comox, BC V9M 8A2
250-339-2714, Fax: 250-339-2753

Nunavut
Department of Economic Development & Transportation, PO Box 1000 1500,Iqaluit, X0A 0H0 NU
867-975-7800, Fax: 867-975-7870, 888-975-5999, edt@gov.nu.ca

Ontario
Owen Sound Transportation Company Ltd., RR#5, Hwy 6 & 21, Owen Sound, ON N4K 5N7
519-376-8740

Quebec
Ministère des Transports, 700, boul René-Lévesque est, 27e étage, Québec, G1R 5H1 QC
Fax: 514-643-1269, 888-355-0511, communications@mtq.gouv.qc.ca

Yukon Territory
Yukon Community Services, PO Box 2703, Whitehorse, Y1A 2C6 YT
867-667-5811, Fax: 867-393-6295, 800-661-0408, inquiry@gov.yk.ca
Driver Control Board, 308 Steele St., PO Box 2703, Whitehorse, YT Y1A 2C6
867-667-3774, Fax: 867-393-6483, dcb@gov.yk.ca

TREASURY SERVICES

See Also: Finance
Treasury Board of Canada, 300 Laurier Ave. West, 10th Fl., Ottawa, K1A 0R5 ON
613-957-2400, Fax: 613-998-9071, 877-636-0656

British Columbia
Provincial Treasury, 620 Superior St., Victoria, V8V 1X4 BC
250-387-4541

Nova Scotia
Nova Scotia Treasury & Policy Board, 1700 Granville St., 5th Fl., PO Box 1617, Halifax, B3J 2Y3 NS
902-424-8910, Fax: 902-424-7638, tpbenquiries@gov.ns.ca

Nunavut
Department of Finance, Bldg. 1079, 1st Fl., PO Box 1000 Stn 360,Iqaluit, X0A 0H0 NU
867-975-5800, Fax: 867-975-5805

Prince Edward Island
Department of the Provincial Treasury, PO Box 2000, Charlottetown, C1A 7N8 PE
902-368-4000, Fax: 902-368-5544

Quebec
Secrétariat du Conseil du trésor, Édifice H, #1.64B, 875, Grande Allée est, 1er étage, Québec, G1R5R8 QC
418-643-5926, Fax: 418-643-7824

URBAN RENEWAL & DESIGN

See Also: Municipal Affairs

Ontario
Ministry of Municipal Affairs & Housing, 777 Bay St., 17th Fl., Toronto, M5G 2E5 ON
416-585-7041, Fax: 416-585-6227, 866-220-2290

WASTE & GARBAGE

Newfoundland & Labrador
Department of Government Services, PO Box 8700, St. John's, A1B 4J6 NL
709-729-4860

WATER & WASTEWATER

Alberta
Irrigation Council, Provincial Bldg., 200 - 5 Ave. South, 3rd Fl., PO Bag 3014, Lethbridge, AB T1J 4L1
403-381-5176, Fax: 403-382-4406

Nova Scotia
Waterfront Development Corporation Ltd., 1751 Lower Water St., 2nd Fl., Halifax, NS B3J 1S5
902-422-6591, Fax: 902-422-7582, info@wdcl.ca

WOMEN'S ISSUES

See Also: Pay Equity

Manitoba
Manitoba Women's Advisory Council, #301, 155 Carlton St., Winnipeg, MB R3C 3H8
204-945-6281, Fax: 204-945-6511, 800-282-8069, 001women@gov.mb.ca

WORKERS' COMPENSATION

British Columbia
Workers' Compensation Appeal Tribunal, #150, 4600 Jacombs Rd., Richmond, BC V6V 3B1
604-664-7800, Fax: 604-664-7898, 800-663-2782

YOUNG OFFENDERS

Justice Canada, East Memorial Bldg., 284 Wellington St., Ottawa, K1A 0H8 ON
613-957-4222, Fax: 613-954-0811

Alberta
Alberta Justice & Attorney General, 9833 - 109 St., Edmonton, T5K 2E8 AB
780-427-2745

British Columbia
Ministry of the Attorney General, 1001 Douglas St., 10th Fl., PO Box 9282 Prov Govt,Victoria, V8W 9J7 BC
250-356-9596, Fax: 250-387-1753
Child & Youth Officer for BC, 1019 Wharf St., PO Box 9207 Prov Govt, Victoria, BC V8W 9J1
250-356-0831, Fax: 250-356-0837, 800-476-3933, cyo@gov.bc.ca

Nova Scotia
Department of Justice, 5151 Terminal Rd., PO Box 7, Halifax, B3J 2L6 NS
902-424-4222, Fax: 902-424-2809, justweb@gov.ns.ca

Northwest Territories
Department of Justice, PO Box 1320, Yellowknife, X1A 2L9 NT
867-920-6197

Nunavut
Young Offenders, 1548 Federal Rd., PO Box 1439, Iqaluit, NU X0A 0H0
867-979-4452, Fax: 867-979-5506

Ontario
Ministry of the Attorney General, 720 Bay St., Toronto, M5G 2K1 ON
416-326-2220, Fax: 416-326-4007, 800-518-7901

Prince Edward Island
Office of the Attorney General, PO Box 2000, Charlottetown, C1A 7N8 PE
902-368-5152, Fax: 902-368-4910

ZONING

Manitoba
Manitoba Municipal Board, #1144, 363 Broadway, Winnipeg, MB R3C 3N9
204-945-2941, Fax: 204-948-2235,

Government of Canada

Seat of Government:111 Wellington St.
PO Box 1103
Ottawa, ON K1A 0A6
canada.gc.ca
All political authority in Canada is divided between the federal & provincial governments according to the provisions of the Constitution Act, 1867. Local municipalities are a concern of the provinces, & derive their authority from Actsof provincial legislation. The Parliament of Canada consists of the Queen (represented in Canada by the Governor General), an Upper House called the Senate, & an elected House of Commons.

House of Commons, Canada / Chambre des communes

House of Commons
111 Wellington St.
Ottawa, ON K1A 0A6
866-599-4999
www.parl.gc.ca
Speaker of the House, Peter Milliken
Chief Government Whip, Hon. Jay Hill
Chief Opposition Whip, Karen Redman
Bloc Québecois Party Whip, Michel Guimond
613-995-9732
NDP Party Whip, Yvon Godin
613-992-0336, Fax: 613-992-4558, godiny@parl.gc.ca
Clerk of the House, Audrey O'Brien
613-992-2986
Chief Public Service Support Section, Kate Whitridge
613-992-6314

Office of the Prime Minister (Cons.) / Cabinet du Premier ministre

Langevin Block
80 Wellington St.
Ottawa, ON K1A 0A2
613-992-4211
Fax: 613-941-6900
TDD: 613-957-5741pm@pm.gc.ca
pm.gc.ca/
The Prime Minister is the Head of Government in Canada & usually the leader of the party in power in the House of Commons. The Prime Minister recommends the appointment of the Governor General to the monarchy & is responsible forselecting a team of ministers, who are then appointed by the Governor General to the Queen's Privy Council. In addition, he or she also controls the appointment of cabinet ministers, senators, judges & parliamentary secretaries. It is customary thatthe Prime Minister is also appointed to the Imperial Privy Council & is thus titled The Right Honourable. The Prime Minister has the right to dissolve parliament & can therefore control the timing of general elections.

Prime Minister, Rt. Hon. Stephen Harper
613-992-4211, Fax: 613-941-6900, pm@pm.gc.ca
Government House Leader, Hon. Robert D. Nicholson
613-952-4930, Fax: 613-952-4940
Parliamentary Secretary, Sylvie Boucher
Parliamentary Secretary, Jason Kenney
Parliamentary Secretary to the Government House Lead, Tom Lukiwski
National Caucus Chair, Rahim Jaffer
Chief of Staff, Ian Brodie
613-957-5517
Director Communications, Sandra Buckler
613-957-5555
Press Secretary, Carolyn Stewart Olsen
613-957-5547
Director Policy, Mark Cameron
613-957-5575
Director Appointments, Dave Penner
613-957-5569

The Canadian Ministry / The Cabinet

c/o Information Service, Library of Parliament
Ottawa, ON K1A 0A9
613-992-4793
Fax: 613-992-1273
866-599-4999
info@parl.gc.ca
www.parl.gc.ca
The Canadian Ministry, or Cabinet, is the most significant of all federal government committees or councils. Cabinet members are selected & led by the Prime Minister, they must also be or become members of the Queen's Privy Council.Cabinet ministers determine specific policies & are responsible for them in the House of Commons. The Cabinet is responsible for initiating all public bills in the House of Commons, & in some instances can create regulations that have the strength oflaw, termed decisions of the Governor-in-Council. Cabinet meetings are usually closed to the public, allowing members to discuss their opinions on particular policy in secret. Once decided, members usually support all policy uniformly. If a ministeris unable to support the Ministry, he or she is obligated to resign.

Prime Minister, Rt. Hon. Stephen Harper
613-992-4211, Fax: 613-941-6900, harpes@parl.gc.ca
Government House Leader & Minister, Democratic Reform, Hon. Robert D. Nicholson
613-995-1547, Fax: 613-992-7910, nichor@parl.gc.ca
Minister International Trade & Minister, Pacific Gateway & the Vancouver-Whistler Olympics, Hon. David Emerson
613-943-0267, Fax: 613-943-0219, emersd@parl.gc.ca
Minister Labour & Minister, Economic Development Agency of Canada for the Regions of Québec, Hon. Jean-Pierre Blackburn
613-947-2745, Fax: 613-947-2748, blackj@parl.gc.ca
Minister Veteran Affairs, Hon. Greg Thompson
613-995-5550, Fax: 613-995-5226, thompg@parl.gc.ca
Government Senate Leader, Hon. Marjory LeBreton
613-943-0756, Fax: 613-943-1493, lebrem@sen.parl.gc.ca
Minister Citizenship & Immigration, Hon. Monte Solberg
639-992-4516, Fax: 639-992-6181, solbem@parl.gc.ca
Minister Agriculture & Agri-Food & Minister, Canadian Wheat Board, Hon. Chuck Strahl
613-992-2940, Fax: 613-995-5621, strahc@parl.gc.ca
Minister Natural Resources, Hon. Gary Lunn
613-996-1119, Fax: 613-996-0850, lunng@parl.gc.ca
Minister Foreign Affairs & Minister, Atlantic Canada Opportunities Agency, Hon. Peter MacKay
613-992-6022, Fax: 613-992-2337, mackap@parl.gc.ca
Minister Fisheries & Oceans, Hon. Loyola Hearn
613-992-0927, Fax: 613-995-7858, hearnl@parl.gc.ca
Minister Public Safety, Hon. Stockwell Day
613-995-1702, Fax: 613-995-1154, day.s@parl.gc.ca
Minister National Revenue & Minister, Western Economic Diversification, Hon. Carol Skelton
613-995-1551, Fax: 613-943-2010, skeltc@parl.gc.ca
Attorney General & Minister Justice, Hon. Vic Toews
613-992-3128, Fax: 613-995-1049, toewsv@parl.gc.ca
Minister Environment, Hon. Rona Ambrose
613-996-9778, Fax: 613-996-0785, ambror@parl.gc.ca
Minister Human Resources & Social Development, Hon. Diane Finley
613-996-4974, Fax: 613-996-9749, finled@parl.gc.ca
Minister National Defence, Hon. Gordon O'Connor
613-992-1119, Fax: 613-992-1043, oconng@parl.gc.ca
Minister Canadian Heritage & Minister, Status of Women, Hon. Bev Oda
613-992-2792, Fax: 613-992-2794, odab@parl.gc.ca
Minister Indian Affairs & Northern Development & Federal Interlocutor for Métis & Non-Status Indians, Hon. Jim Prentice
613-992-4275, Fax: 613-947-9475, prentj@parl.gc.ca
President Treasury Board, Hon. John Baird
613-996-0984, Fax: 613-996-9880, bairdj@parl.gc.ca
Minister Industry, Hon. Maxime Bernier
613-992-8053, Fax: 613-995-0687, bernim@parl.gc.ca
Minister Transport, Infrastructure & Communities, Hon. Lawrence Cannon
613-992-5516, Fax: 613-992-6802, cannol@parl.gc.ca
Minister Health & Minister, Federal Economic Development Initiative for Northern Ontario, Hon. Tony Clement
613-944-7740, Fax: 613-992-5092, clemet@parl.gc.ca
Minister Finance, Hon. Jim Flaherty
flahej@parl.gc.ca
Minister International Cooperation & Minister, La Francophonie & Official Languages, Hon. Josée Verner
613-996-4151, Fax: 613-954-2269, vernej@parl.gc.ca
Minister Public Works & Government Services, Hon. Mike Fortier
Minister Intergovernmental Affairs & President, Privy Council; Minister for Sport, Hon. Peter Van Loan
Information Service,
613-992-4793, Fax: 613-992-1273, info@parl.gc.ca

Agriculture & Agri-Food Canada / Agriculture et Agro-alimentaire Canada

Sir John Carling Bldg.
930 Carling Ave.
Ottawa, ON K1A 0C5
613-759-1000
Fax: 613-759-6726
TDD: 613-759-7470info@agr.gc.ca
www.agr.ca
Other Communication: Agricultural Farm Policy: www.agr.gc.ca/cb/apf/index_e.php
Responsible for promoting the development, adaptation & competitiveness of the agriculture & agri-food sector through policies, programs & services most appropriately provided by the federal government. Maximizes the sector's contributionto Canadian economic & environmental objectives while providing equitable returns to producers & processors. Develops & implements national policies & programs in support of the agriculture & agri-food sector in a manner that assures a dependablesupply of safe, nutritious food at reasonable prices to consumers. Participates in the development & implementation of federal policies & programs in the areas of socio-economic development, emergency response & international relations. Meetsresponsibilities through the following activities: agricultural research & development, policy & farm economic programs, market & industry services, rural prairie rehabilitation, sustainability & development, & corporate management & services.

Acts Administered:
Advance Payments for Crops Act
Agricultural Marketing Programs Act
Agricultural Products Act
Agricultural Products Co-operative Marketing Act
Agricultural Products Marketing Act
Agricultural Products Standards Act
Animal Pedigree Act
Canada Grain Act
Canadian Dairy Commission Act
Canagrex Dissolution Act (dormant)
Criminal Code, Part VII section 204 (shared responsibility with the Minister of Justice & Attorney General of Canada)
Department of Agriculture & Agri-Food Act
Experimental Farm Stations Act
Farm Debt Mediation Act
Farm Improvement & Marketing Co-operatives Loans Act
Farm Improvement Loans Act
Farm Income Protection Act
Fish Inspection Act
Livestock Feed Assistance Act (dormant)
Prairie Farm Rehabilitation Act
Prairie Grain Advance Payments Act
Western Grain Transition Payments Act
The Minister shares responsibility to Parliament for the following acts:
Department of Foreign Affairs & International Trade Act, Paragraph 10 (2)(e) (shared responsibility with the Minister of
Legislation administered by Agencies outside of AAFC:
Agriculture & Agri-food Administrative Monetary Penalties Act (CFIA)
Canada Agricultural Products Act (CFIA)
Canada Grain Act (CGC)
Canadian Dairy Commission Act (CDC)
Canadian Food Inspection Agency Act (CFIA)
Consumer Packaging & Labelling Act (CFIA)
Farm Credit Canada Act (FCC)
Farm Products Agencies Act (NFPC)
Feeds Act (CFIA)
Fertilizers Act (CFIA)
Fish Inspection Act (CFIA)
Food & Drugs Act (CFIA) (as it relates to food)
Health of Animals Act (CFIA)
Meat Inspection Act (CFIA)
Plant Breeders' Rights Act (CFIA)
Plant Protection Act (CFIA)
Seeds Act (CFIA)
Minister, Hon. Chuck Strahl
613-759-1059, Fax: 613-759-1081
Parliamentary Secretary, David Anderson
613-992-0657
Parliamentary Secretary, Jacques Gourde
613-759-1107
Deputy Minister, Leonard Edwards
613-759-1101

Assoc. Deputy Minister, Christiane Ouimet
613-759-1090, Fax: 613-759-1104
Director General Communication Services & Outreach, Charles Slowey

Associated Agencies, Boards & Commissions:
• Canadian Dairy Commission / Commission canadienne du lait
Listed alphabetically in detail.
• Canadian Food Inspection Agency
Listed alphabetically in detail, this section.
• Canadian Grain Commission / Commission canadienne des grains
Listed alphabetically in detail.
• Farm Credit Canada / Financement agricole Canada
Listed alphabetically in detail.
• National Farm Products Council / Conseil national des produits agricoles
Listed alphabetically in detail.

Deputy Minister's Office / Bureau du sous-ministre

Deputy Minister, Leonard Edwards
613-759-1101, Fax: 613-759-1040
Assoc. Deputy Minister, Christiane Ouimet
613-759-1090, Fax: 613-759-1104
Asst. Deputy Minister National Land & Water Information Service, Susan Till
613-759-1712
Executive Director Rural & Cooperatives Secretariats, Donna Mitchell
613-759-7113
Corporate Secretary Corporate Secretariat, David Swol
613-759-1050
Chief Information Officer, Rita Moritz
613-759-6122
General Counsel & Head Legal Services, Heather Smith
613-759-7879

Farm Financial Programs Branch / Direction générale des programmes de financement agricoles

Administers the Pesticide Risk Reduction & Minor Use Programs, in collaboration with Health Canada's Pest Management Agency. Reduced risk pesticides enhance environmental stewardship, make it easier to compete globally & provide saferfood.

Asst. Deputy Minister, Nada Semaan
613-759-7243
Director General Agriculture Transformation Programs, Clair Gartley
613-759-6842
Director General Business Risk Management Program Development, Danny Foster
613-715-5044
Acting Director General Program Planning, Integration & Management, Tambrae Knapp
613-759-7926
Executive Director Integrated Business Solutions, Jody Aylward
613-759-7333
Executive Director Minor Use Pesticides & Risk Reduction, Bill Boddis
613-759-7431
Acting Executive Director Pest Management Centre, Ken Campbell
613-759-7833
Director Natural Disaster Assessment Analysis, Bill Schissel
613-759-6407

Farm Income Programs Directorate / Direction des programmes de protection du revenu agricole

#600, 200 Graham Ave.
Winnipeg, MB R3C 4N3
Executive Director, Michele Taylor
204-984-5645
Director Finance & Corporate Services, Gavin Wilson
204-984-5106, Fax: 204-984-0374
Director Program Analysis, Reporting & Audit Services, Bill Hurtig
204-984-5125

Atlantic Canada Opportunities Agency (ACOA) / Agence de promotion économique du Canada atlantique (APECA)

644 Main St., 3rd Fl.
PO Box 6051
Moncton, NB E1C 9J8
506-851-2271
Fax: 506-851-7403
800-561-7862
TDD: 506-851-3540www.acoa.ca/
A federal government development agency providing support to entrepreneurs in the Atlantic Region. The goal of the ACOA is to improve the economy of Atlantic Canadian communities, through the successful development of businesses & jobopportunities. The organization helps people set up new, & to expand existing businesses; market Atlantic Canada, nationally & internationally; works together with other federal departments, the provincial governments & private sector within thefour Atlantic provinces to ensure maximum benefit for the region.

Minister, Hon. Peter MacKay
613-941-7241, Fax: 613-941-7844
President, Monique Collette
506-851-6128
Exec. Vice-President, Paul LeBlanc
Acting Vice-President Finance & Corporate Services, Sherril Minns
506-851-6128
Director General Human Resources, Paul Joudrey
506-851-2141
Director General Trade & Investment, Serge Langis
506-851-6240
Director Communications, Stephen Heckbert
613-948-7293
Director Legal Services, Thomas Khattar
506-851-6138
Manager Corporate Services, Maria DiPetta

Regional Offices

New Brunswick
570 Queen St.
PO Box 578
Fredericton, NB E3B 5A6
506-452-3184
Fax: 506-452-3285
800-561-4030
Vice-President, Hermel Vienneau

Newfoundland & Labrador
John Cabot Bldg.
10 Barters' Hill, 11th Fl.
PO Box 1060 C
St. John's, NL A1C 5M5
709-772-2751
Fax: 709-772-2712
800-668-1010
Vice-President, Paul Mills

Nova Scotia
#600, 1801 Hollis St.
PO Box 2284 M
Halifax, NS B3J 3C8
902-426-6743
Fax: 902-426-2054
800-565-1228

Prince Edward Island
100 Sydney St.
PO Box 40
Charlottetown, PE C1A 7K2
902-566-7492
Fax: 902-566-7098
800-871-2596

Auditor General of Canada / Vérificateur Général du Canada

240 Sparks St.
Ottawa, ON K1A 0G6
613-995-3708
Fax: 613-957-0474
communications@oag-bvg.gc.ca
www.oag-bvg.gc.ca/
Established the position of Commissioner of the Environment & Sustainable Development, reporting to the Auditor General, to act as an authority in making the government more environmentally responsible. The Commissioner monitors thedepartmental strategies & action plans, & the status of responses to public petitions. A number of federal departments & agencies are required to prepare sustainable development strategies & update them every three years. The Commissioner monitorsthe extent to which departments have implemented the action plans & met the objectives outlined in their strategies. The Commissioner conducts audits & special studies on the federal government's performance in areas such as climate change, ozonedepletion, management of toxic substances & greening government operations.

Auditor General, Sheila Fraser, FCA
Deputy Auditor General, John Wiersema
613-952-0213
Commissioner of the Environment & Sustainable Develo, Johanne Gélinas
613-952-0213
Asst. Auditor General, Ronald Campbell
613-952-0213
Asst. Auditor General, Nancy Cheng
613-952-0213
Asst. Auditor General, Richard Fiageole
613-952-0213
Asst. Auditor General, Andrew Lennox
613-952-0213
Asst. Auditor General, Hugh McRoberts
613-952-0213
Asst. Auditor General, Lyse Ricard
613-952-0213
Asst. Auditor General, Richard Smith
613-952-0213
Asst. Auditor General, Jean Ste-Marie
613-952-0213
Asst. Auditor General, Douglas Timmins
613-952-0213
Asst. Auditor General, Ronald Thompson
613-952-0213
Sr. Communications Advisor, Sherry Galey
613-952-0123, Fax: 613-957-0474,
sherry.galey@oag-bvg.gc.ca

Regional Offices

Edmonton
Manulife Place
#2460, 10180 - 101 St.
Edmonton, AB T5J 3S4
780-495-2028
Fax: 780-495-2031

Halifax
Centennial Bldg.
#414, 1660 Hollis St.
Halifax, NS B3J 1V7
902-426-9241
Fax: 902-426-8591

Montréal
200, 1060, rue University
Montréal, QC H3B 4V3
514-283-6086
Fax: 514-283-1715

Vancouver
#250, 757 West Hastings St.
Vancouver, BC V6C 1A1
604-666-3596
Fax: 604-666-6162

Bank of Canada / Banque du Canada

234 Wellington St.
Ottawa, ON K1A 0G9
613-782-8111
Fax: 613-782-8655
www.bankofcanada.ca; www.banqueducanada.ca
The Bank is responsible for regulating \credit & currency in the best interests of the economic life of the nation.\ The Bank acts as fiscal agent for the Government of Canada in respect of the management of the public debt of Canada &the Exchange Fund Account. The sole right to issue paper money for circulation in Canada is vested in the Bank of Canada. Reports to government through the Minister of Finance.

Governor, David A. Dodge

Senior Deputy Governor, W. Paul Jenkins
Deputy Governor, Sheryl Kennedy
Deputy Governor, Pierre Duguay
Deputy Governor, David Longworth
Deputy Governor, Tiff Macklem
Special Advisor, Bruce Little
General Counsel & Corporate Secretary, M.L. Jewett
Internal Auditor, D.N. Sullivan
Chief Banking Operations, G.T. Gaetz
Chief Communications, Denis Schuthe
Chief Corporate Services, Sheila Niven
Chief Financial Markets, Donna Howard
Chief Financial Services, S. Vokay
Chief International, Larry Schembri
Chief Monetary & Financial Analysis, A.C. Crawford
Chief Research, M.L.A. Côté
Director Debt Administration, Dale Fleck
Executive Director Pension Plan Review, T. Cugno
Supervisor Public Information, Francine Langevin
613-782-8021

Audit / Vérification

Chief Internal Auditor, D.N. Sullivan
Director, C. Prévost-Vierula
Audit Officer, S. Nadon
Audit Officer, W. Tse

Banking Operations / Opérations bancaires

Chief, G.T. Gaetz
Research Adviser, K.T. McPhail
Chief Curator Currency Museum, P. Berry

Communications Services / Services de communications

Chief, Denis Schuthe
Deputy Chief & Director, Operations, J.M. Catta

Corporate Services / Services de gestion

Chief, Sheila Niven
Deputy Chief, J.M. Gabie

Executive & Legal Services / Services éxécutifs et judiciaires

General Counsel & Corporate Secretary, M.L. Jewett
Director Executive Services, C.G Leighton
Senior Legal Counsel, R.G. Turnbull

Financial Markets / Marchés financiers

Chief, Donna Howard
Deputy Chief Research & Risk Management, C.A. Wilkins
Director, R.W. Morrow
Director, S. Hendry
Director, J. Rudin
Director Montréal Division, M. Tremblay
Director Toronto Division, H.R. MacKinnon

Financial Risk

Adviser Strategic Planning & Risk Management, Janet Cosier
Director, D.M. Zelmer

Financial Services

Chief, S. Vokay
Deputy Chief, R. Wytenburg
Asst. Director Accounting & Internal Control, D. Sinclair
Asst. Director Contracts Management & Procurement, D. Anderson
Asst. Director Management Reporting, A. Guilbault
Adviser Funds Management, W. Speckert
Adviser Research, G. Bauer

International

Chief, Larry Schembri
Deputy Chief, G. Paulin
Research Adviser, J.N. Bailliu
Director Research, D. Coletti
Director Research, R.J.G.R. Lafrance
Director Research, Emerging Markets & International Policy Advice, J.A. Haley

Monetary & Financial Analysis / Études monétaires et financières

Chief, A.C. Crawford
Deputy Chief, D. Maclean
Director Research, W.N. Engert
Director Research, J.M.P. St-Amant
Adviser Research, S. O'Connor

Research / Recherches

Chief, M.L.A. Côté
Deputy Chief, P. Fenton
Research Director, R. Amano
Research Director, S. Kozicki
Research Advisor Current Analysis, G.J. Stuber

Regional Offices

Atlantic Provinces
1583 Hollis St., 5th Fl.
Halifax, NS B3J 1V4
800-303-1282
Senior Regional Representative Economics, David Amirault
Senior Regional Representative Currency, Monique Guérin

British Columbia & Yukon
#2710, 200 Granville St.
Vancouver, BC V6C 1S4
800-303-1282
Senior Regional Representative Economics, Farid Novin
Senior Regional Representative Currency, Lisa Elliott

Ontario
#2000, 150 King St. West
Toronto, ON M5H 1J9
800-303-1282
Senior Regional Representative Economics, Hung-Hay Lau
Senior Regional Representative Currency, Paul de Swart

Prairies Provinces, Nunavut & NWT
#200, 404 - 6 Ave. SW
Calgary, AB T2P 0R9
800-303-1282
Senior Regional Representative Economics, Mark Illing
Senior Regional Representative Currency, Ted Mieszkalski

Québec
#2030, 1501, av McGill College
Montréal, QC H3A 3M8
800-303-1282
Senior Regional Representative Economics, Thérèse Lafléche
Senior Regional Representative Currency, Pierre Laprise

Business Development Bank of Canada (BDC) / Banque de développement du Canada (BDC)

#400, 5, Place Ville-Marie
Montréal, QC H3B 5E7
514-283-5904
Fax: 514-283-2872
888-463-6232
www.bdc.ca
Other Communication: TollFree Fax 1-877-329-9232
Federal crown corporation helping Canadian small business grow. Delivers financial & management services, with a particular focus on the emerging & exporting sectors of the economy. Financial products include micro-business loans, termloans, working capital for growth, working capital for exporters, \Patient Capital\""

President/CEO, Jean-René Halde
Executive Vice-President Financial Services & BDC Consulting Group, André Bourdeau
Executive Vice-President Integrated Risk & Technology Management, Edmée Métivier
Executive Vice-President Investments, Michel Ré
Senior Vice-President Finance & CFO, Alan B. Marquis
Senior Vice-President Human Resources, Mary Karamanos
Vice-President & Treasurer, Clément Albert
Vice-President Audit & Inspection, Richard Morris
Vice-President Legal Affairs & Corporate Secretary, Louise Paradis
Information & Publication Officer, Louise Forest
514-283-3700, Fax: 514-283-7838, louise.forest@bdc.ca

Alberta Branches

Calgary
Barclay Centre
#110, 444 - 7 Ave. SW
Calgary, AB T2P 0X8
403-292-5600
Fax: 403-292-6616
Vice-President & Area Manager, Edward Straw
403-292-5944, edward_straw@bdc.ca

Calgary North
#100, 1935 - 32 Ave. NE
Calgary, AB T2E 7C8
403-292-5590
Fax: 403-292-6651
Branch Manager, Todd Van der Loos

Calgary South
Sovereign Bldg.
#200, 6700 MacLeod Trail SE
Calgary, AB T2H 0L3
403-292-8882
Fax: 403-292-4345
Branch Manager, Travis Kellett
403-292-4346

Edmonton
First Edmonton Place
#200, 10665 Jasper Ave.
Edmonton, AB T5J 3S9
780-495-2277
Fax: 780-495-6616
Vice-President & Area Manager, Steve Zink
780-495-2602, steve.zink@bdc.ca

Edmonton South
Huntington Galleria
#201, 4628 Calgary Trail NW
Edmonton, AB T6H 6A1
Branch Manager, Danny Lidder
780-495-2727, danny.lidder@bdc.ca

Grande Prairie
Windsor Court
#102, 9835 - 101 Ave.
Grande Prairie, AB T8V 5V4
780-532-8875
Fax: 780-539-5130
Branch Manager, Shannon Preus
780-573-5688

Lethbridge
520 - 5 Ave. South
Lethbridge, AB T1J 0T8
403-382-3182
Fax: 403-382-3162
Branch Manager, Grant Kvemshagen
403-382-3002

Red Deer
#107, 4815 - 50 Ave.
Red Deer, AB T4N 4A5
403-340-4255
Fax: 403-340-4243
Customer Service Representative, Judy Gordon
403-340-4263

British Columbia Branches

Campbell River
Georgia Quay
#101, 901 Island Hwy.
Campbell River, BC V9W 2C2
250-286-5820
Fax: 250-286-5830
Manager Business Development, David Thagard

Cranbrook
205 Cranbrook St. North
Cranbrook, BC V1C 3R1
250-417-2200
Fax: 250-417-2213
Account Manager, Sonja Walker
250-417-2222, sonja.walker@bdc.ca

Fort St. John
#7, 10230 - 100 St.
Fort St John, BC V1J 3Y9
250-787-0622
Fax: 250-787-9423
Account Manager Business Development, Karlene Clark
250-787-9137, karlene.clark@bdc.ca

Kamloops
205 Victoria St.
Kamloops, BC V2C 2A1
250-851-4900
Fax: 250-851-4925

Branch Manager, Greg Richard
250-851-4907, greg.richard@bdc.ca

Kelowna
313 Bernard Ave.
Kelowna, BC V1Y 6N6
250-470-4812
Fax: 250-470-4832
Vice-President & Area Manager, Scott Speiser
250-470-4826, scott.speiser@bdc.ca

Langley
#101B, 6424 - 200 St.
Langley, BC V2Y 2T3
250-532-5150
Fax: 250-532-5166
Branch Manager, Rose Swain
604-532-5155, rose.swain@bdc.ca

Nanaimo
#500, 6581 Aulds Rd.
Nanaimo, BC V9T 6J6
250-390-5757
Fax: 250-390-5753
Area Manager, Johann Van Rensburg
250-390-5754

North Vancouver
#6, 221 West Esplanade
North Vancouver, BC V7M 3J3
604-666-7703
Fax: 604-666-1957
Branch Manager, Chris Boissevain
604-666-6007

Prince George
#100, 177 Victoria St.
Prince George, BC V2L 5R8
250-561-5323
Fax: 250-561-5512
Branch Manager, Tom McBride
250-561-5337, tom.mcbride@bdc.ca

Surrey-London Station
#160, 10362 King George Hwy.
Surrey, BC V3T 2W5
604-586-2410
Fax: 604-586-2430
Branch Manager, Jeff Beacom
604-586-2416

Terrace
3233 Emerson St.
PO Box 6
Terrace, BC V8G 5L2
250-615-5300
Fax: 250-615-5320
Area Manager, Rich Toomey
250-615-5317

Vancouver
BDC Tower, One Bentall Centre
#240, 505 Burrard St.
Vancouver, BC V7X 1V3
604-666-5015
Fax: 604-666-1068
Area Manager, Nick Fry
604-666-8210

Victoria
990 Fort St.
Victoria, BC V8V 3K2
250-363-0161
Fax: 250-363-8029
Customer Service Officer, Sherry Gruber
250-363-8014

Manitoba Branches

Brandon
940 Princess Ave.
PO Box 10
Brandon, MB R7A 0P6
204-726-7570
Fax: 204-726-7555
Manager Business Development, Roy Engel
204-726-7576

Winnipeg
#1100, 155 Carlton St.
Winnipeg, MB R3C 3H8
204-983-7900
Fax: 204-983-0870
Vice-President & Area Manager, Kris Smith
204-983-2636

Winnipeg West
#200, 1655 Kenaston Blvd.
Winnipeg, MB R3P 2M4
204-983-6530
Fax: 204-983-6531
Branch Manager, Len Trotter
len.trotter@bdc.ca

New Brunswick Branches

Bathurst
Harbourview Place
#205, 275 Main St.
Bathurst, NB E2A 1A9
506-548-7360
Fax: 506-548-7381
Branch Manager, Vilma Glidden
506-548-7348, vilma.glidden@bdc.ca

Edmundston
Carrefour Assomption
#405, 121, rue de L'Église
Edmundston, NB E3V 3L2
506-739-8311
Fax: 506-735-0019
Account Manager, Joel Pelletier
506-735-3398

Fredericton
The Barker House
#504, 570 Queen St.
PO Box 754
Fredericton, NB E3B 5B4
506-452-3030
Fax: 506-452-2416
Branch Manager, Rodney Carrier
506-452-3062, rodney.carrier@bdc.ca

Moncton
766 Main St.
Moncton, NB E1C 1E6
506-851-6120
Fax: 506-851-6033
Vice-President & Area Manager, Claude Paré
506-851-7601, claude.pare@bdc.ca

Saint John
53 King St.
Saint John, NB E2L 1G5
506-636-4751
Fax: 506-636-3892
Branch Manager, Randal Blackwood
506-636-4590, randal_blackwood@bdc.ca

Newfoundland & Labrador Branches

Corner Brook
Fortis Towers
4 Herald Ave., 1st Fl.
Corner Brook, NL A2H 4B4
709-637-4515
Fax: 709-637-4522
Branch Manager, Bruce Ryan
709-637-4520, bruce.ryan@bdc.ca

Grand Falls-Windsor
42 High St.
PO Box 744
Grand Falls-Windsor, NL A2A 2M4
709-489-2181
Fax: 709-489-6569
Senior Manager Business Development, B. Dale Rideout
709-489-2182, dale.rideout@bdc.ca

St. John's
Atlantic Place
215 Water St.
PO Box 514 C
St. John's, NL A1C 5K4
709-722-5505
Fax: 709-772-2516
Vice-President & Area Manager, Ross W. Miller
709-772-4398, ross.miller@bdc.ca

Northwest Territories & Nunavut Branch

Yellowknife
4912 - 49 St.
Yellowknife, NT X1A 1P3
867-873-3565
Fax: 867-873-3501

Nova Scotia Branches

Halifax
Cogswell Tower, Scotia Square
#1400, 2000 Barrington St.
Halifax, NS B3J 2Z7
902-426-7850
Fax: 902-426-6783
Vice-President & Area Manager, Craig Levangie
902-426-7865, craig.levangie@bdc.ca

Sydney
#117, 225 Charlotte St.
Sydney, NS B1P 1C6
902-564-7700
Fax: 902-564-3975
Vice-President & Area Manager, Craig Levangie
902-426-7865

Truro
622 Prince St.
PO Box 1378
Truro, NS B2N 5N2
902-895-6377
Fax: 902-893-7957
Senior Manager Business Development, Matthew Fraser
902-895-6378, matthew.fraser@bdc.ca

Yarmouth
396 Main St.
PO Box 98
Yarmouth, NS B5A 4B1
902-742-7119
Fax: 902-742-8180
Vice-President & Area Manager, Craig Levangie
902-426-7865

Ontario Branches

Barrie
151 Ferris Lane
PO Box 876
Barrie, ON L4M 4Y6
705-739-0444
Fax: 705-739-0467
Vice-President & Area Manager, Steven R. Holler
705-739-0449

Brampton
52 Queen St. East, Ground Fl.
Brampton, ON L6V 1A2
905-450-1088
Fax: 905-450-7514
Branch Manager, Mark MacKenzie
905-450-7306

Burlington/Halton
#101, 4145 North Service Rd.
Burlington, ON L7L 6A3
905-315-9590
Fax: 905-315-9243
Vice-President & Area Manager, Caroline Cole
905-315-9242

Durham
400 Dundas St. West
Whitby, ON L1N 2M7
905-666-6694
Fax: 905-666-1059
Branch Manager, Margaret Peco
905-666-4558, margaret.peco@bdc.ca

Hamilton
#101, 25 Main St. West
Hamilton, ON L8P 1H1
905-572-2954
Fax: 905-572-4282
Branch Manager, Scott Lewis
905-572-2956

Kenora
227 Second St. South
Kenora, ON P9N 1G1

807-467-3535
Fax: 807-467-3533
Senior Manager Loans, Tony Zuschtok
807-467-3527

Kingston
Plaza 16
16 Bath Rd.
PO Box 265
Kingston, ON K7L 4V8
613-545-8636
Fax: 613-545-3529
Branch Manager, Brett Prikker
613-545-8637

Kitchener-Waterloo
Commerce House Bldg.
#110, 50 Queen St. North, 4th Fl.
Kitchener, ON N2H 6P4
519-571-6676
Fax: 519-571-6685
Branch Manager, Steven Soper
519-571-6677, steven.soper@bdc.ca

London
380 Wellington St.
London, ON N6A 5B5
519-675-3101
Fax: 519-645-5450
Vice-President & District Manager, Glen Ryter
519-675-3108

Markham
3130 Hwy. 7
Markham, ON L3R 5A1
905-305-6867
Fax: 905-305-1969
Branch Manager, Robert Dubé
905-305-8429

Mississauga
#100, 4310 Sherwoodtowne Blvd.
Mississauga, ON L4Z 2G6
905-566-6499
Fax: 905-566-6425
Vice-President & Area Manager, Pat Ghany
pat.ghany@bdc.ca

North Bay
222 McIntyre St. West
North Bay, ON P1B 2Y8
705-495-5700
Fax: 705-495-5707
Senior Manager Loans/Business Development, René De Bernardi
705-495-5702

Ottawa
Manulife Place
55 Metcalfe St., Ground Fl.
Ottawa, ON K1P 6L5
613-995-0234
Fax: 613-995-9045
Customer Service Officer, Desneiges Tambeau
613-943-9471

Peterborough
Peterborough Square Tower
340 George St. North, 4th Fl.
PO Box 1419
Peterborough, ON K9J 7H6
705-750-4800
Fax: 705-750-4808
Branch Manager, Don Anderson
705-750-4802, don.anderson@bdc.ca

Sault Ste Marie
153 Great Northern Rd.
Sault Ste Marie, ON P6B 4Y9
705-941-3030
Fax: 705-941-3040
Manager Business Development, Michele Cooper
705-941-3027

Scarborough
Metro East Corporate Centre
#112, 305 Milner Ave.
Toronto, ON M1B 3V4
416-952-7293
Fax: 416-954-0716
Vice-President & Area Manager, Stéphane Bornais
416-954-0711, stephane.bornais@bdc.ca

St Catharines
#100, 39 Queen St.
PO Box 1193
St Catharines, ON L2R 5G6
905-988-2874
Fax: 905-988-2890
Branch Manager, Sandra Thar
905-988-2877

Stratford
516 Huron St.
Stratford, ON N5A 5T7
519-271-5650
Fax: 519-271-8472
Senior Manager Business Development, Nadine Hayes
519-271-5425

Sudbury
#10, 233 Brady Sq.
Sudbury, ON P3B 4H5
705-670-5482
Fax: 705-670-6387
Vice-President & District Manager, Chuck Smith
705-670-6489, chuck.smith@bdc.ca

Thunder Bay
#102, 1136 Alloy Dr.
Thunder Bay, ON P7B 6M9
807-346-1795
Fax: 807-346-1790
Senior Manager Loans/Business Development, Rod Brescia
807-346-1784

Timmins
#133, 38 Pine St. North
Timmins, ON P4N 6K6
705-267-6416
Fax: 705-268-5437
Manager Business Development, Marc Dinel
705-267-6440

Toronto
#100, 150 King St. West
Toronto, ON M5H 1J9
416-973-0341
Fax: 416-954-5009
Client Services Asst., Neena Don-Liyanage
416-952-6094

Toronto Central
#502, 1120 Finch Ave. West
Toronto, ON M3J 3H7
416-736-3420
Fax: 416-736-3425
Branch Manager, Edmar Selda
416-952-8412

Toronto North
#600, 3901 Hwy. 7 West
Vaughan, ON L4L 8L5
905-264-0623
Fax: 905-264-2122
Branch Manager, Mary Gagliardi
905-264-2106

Windsor
#604, 500 Ouellette Ave.
Windsor, ON N9A 1B3
519-257-6808
Fax: 519-257-6811
Branch Manager, Shaun Rath
519-257-6800

Prince Edward Island Branch

Charlottetown
BDC Place
#230, 119 Kent St.
PO Box 488
Charlottetown, PE C1A 7L1
902-566-7454
Fax: 902-566-7459

Quebec Branches

Chaudière-Appalaches
#100, 1175, boul de la Rive sud
Saint-Romuald, QC G6W 5M6
418-834-5144
Fax: 418-834-1855
Branch Manager, Yanick Dionne
418-834-8160

Chicoutimi
#210, 345, rue des Saguenéens
Chicoutimi, QC G7H 6K9
418-698-5668
Fax: 418-698-5678
Branch Manager, Martin Allard
418-698-5670, martin.allard@bdc.ca

Drummondville
1010, boul René-Lévesque
Drummondville, QC J2C 5W4
819-478-4951
Fax: 819-478-5864
Manager, Chantal Parent
819-478-4179, chantal.parent@bdc.ca

Gatineau
#104, 259, boul St-Joseph
Gatineau, QC J8Y 6T1
819-953-4434
Fax: 819-997-4435
Branch Manager, Pierre St-Jean
819-997-6992

Granby
#302, 155, rue St-Jacques
Granby, QC J2G 9A7
450-372-5202
Fax: 450-372-2423
Senior Manager Loans, Julie Babin
450-372-5238

Laval
#100, 2525, Daniel-Johnson
Laval, QC H7T 1S9
450-973-6868
Fax: 450-973-6860
Vice-President & Area Manager, Alain Gilbert
450-973-6880, alain.gilbert@bdc.ca

Longueuil
#100, 550, ch Chambly
Longueuil, QC J4H 3L8
450-928-4120
Fax: 450-928-4127
Vice-President & Area Manager, France de Gaspé Beaubien
514-928-4500

Lower Laurentians/ Lanaudière
2785, boul Des Plateaux
Terrebonne, QC J6X 4J9
450-964-8778
Fax: 450-964-8773
Branch Manager, Dany Grimard
450-964-8772

Montréal - de Maisonneuve
6068, rue Sherbrooke est
Montréal, QC H1N 1C1
514-283-5858
Fax: 514-496-7535
Branch Manager, Olley Elizabeth
514-283-5887

Montréal - Place Ville-Marie
BDC Bldg.
#500, 5, Place Ville-Marie
Montréal, QC H3B 5E7
514-496-7966
Fax: 514-283-5626
Vice-President & Area Manager, Thierry Limoges
514-496-7953, thierry.limoge@bdc.ca

Pointe-Claire
#110, 755, boul St-Jean
Pointe-Claire, QC H9R 5M9
514-697-8014
Fax: 514-697-3160
Branch Manager, François Carrière
514-697-7882

Québec
1134, Grande-Allée ouest
Sillery, QC G1S 1E5
418-648-3972
Fax: 418-648-5525

Vice-President & Area Manager, Liliane Blais
418-648-5545, liliane.blais@bdc.ca

Rimouski
391, boul Jessop
Rimouski, QC G5L 1M9
418-722-3304
Fax: 418-722-3362
Branch Manager, François Séguin
418-722-3307

Rouyn-Noranda
#301, 139, boul Québec
Rouyn-Noranda, QC J9X 6M8
819-764-6701
Fax: 819-764-5472
Branch Manager, Sylvain Boucher
819-764-2805

Saint-Jerôme
#102, 55, rue Castonguay
Saint-Jérome, QC J7Y 2H9
450-432-7111
Fax: 450-432-8366
Branch Manager, Louise Descoteaux
418-432-7212

Saint-Laurent
#160, 3100, Cote Vertu
Saint-Laurent, QC H4R 2J8
514-496-7500
Fax: 514-496-7510
Vice-President & Area Manager, Martin Roy
450-928-4504

Saint-Leonard
6347, rue Jean-Talon est
Saint-Leonard, QC H1S 3E7
514-251-2818
Fax: 514-251-2758
Branch Manager, Denis Therrien
514-251-8009, denis.therrien@bdc.ca

Sept-Iles
#202B, 701, boul Laure
Sept-Iles, QC G4R 4K9
418-968-1420
Fax: 418-962-2956
Branch Manager, Richard Belley
418-696-5672, richard.belley@bdc.ca

Sherbrooke
2532, rue King ouest
Sherbrooke, QC J1J 2E8
819-564-5700
Fax: 819-564-4276
Branch Manager, Dany Couillard
819-564-4230, dany.couillard@bdc.ca

Trois-Rivières
#150, 1500, rue Royale
Trois-Rivières, QC G9A 6E6
819-371-5215
Fax: 819-371-5220
Branch Manager, Peter O'Grady
819-371-5302, peter.ogrady@bdc.ca.ca

Saskatchewan Branches

Regina
Bank of Canada Bldg.
#320, 2220 - 12 Ave.
Regina, SK S4P 0M8
306-780-6478
Fax: 306-780-7516
Branch Manager, Kurt Carlson
306-780-7340, kurt.carlson@bdc.ca

Saskatoon
Canada Bldg.
135 - 21st St. East, Main Fl.
Saskatoon, SK S7K 0B4
306-975-4822
Fax: 306-975-5955
Branch Manager, Lyndon Holm
306-975-4824, lyndon.holm@bdc.ca

Yukon Branch

Whitehorse
2090A - 2 Ave.
Whitehorse, YT Y1A 1B6
867-633-7510
Fax: 867-667-4058

Canada Border Services Agency (CBSA) / Agence des services frontaliers du Canada (ASFC)

191 Laurier Ave. West
Ottawa, ON K1A 0L5
613-952-3200
www.cbsa-asfc.gc.ca
Other Communication: Border Information Service: 1-800-461-9999
The CBSA's role is to manage the nation's borders by administering & enforcing about 75 domestic laws that govern trade & travel, as well as international agreements & conventions, such as the Convention on International Trade inEndangered Species of Wild Fauna & Flora (CITES).

Acts Administered:
Access to Information Act
Act to Establish the Canada Border Services Agency
Aeronautics Act
Anti-Personnel Mines Convention Implementation Act (through EIPA)
Blue Water Bridge Authority Act
Bretton Woods & Related Agreements Act
Canada Agricultural Products Act
Canada Customs & Revenue Agency Act
Canada Grain Act
Canada Post Corporation Act
Canada Shipping Act
Canada-Chile Free Trade Agreement Implementation Act
Canada-Costa Rica Free Trade Agreement Implementation Act
Canada-Israel Free Trade Agreement Implementation Act
Canada-United States Free Trade Agreement Implementation Act
Canadian Dairy Commission Act
Canadian Environmental Protection Act, 1999
Canadian Food Inspection Agency Act
Canadian International Trade Tribunal Act
Canadian Wheat Board Act
Carriage by Air Act
Chemical Weapons Convention Implementation Act (through EIPA)
Civil International Space Station Agreement Implementation Act
Coastal Fisheries Protection Act
Coasting Trade Act
Consumer Packaging & Labelling Act
Controlled Drug & Substances Act
Convention on International Trade in Endangered Species of Wild Fauna & Flora
Copyright Act
Criminal Code
Cultural Property Export & Import Act
Customs Act
Customs & Excise Offshore Application Act
Customs Tariff Act
Defence Production Act
Department of Health Act
Department of Industry Act
Energy Administration Act
Energy Efficiency Act
Excise Act
Excise Act, 2001
Excise Tax Act
Explosives Act
Export Act
Export & Import of Rough Diamonds Act
Export & Import Permits Act
Federal-Provincial Fiscal Arrangements Act
Feeds Act
Fertilizers Act
Financial Administration Act
Firearms Act
Fish Inspection Act
Fisheries Act
Foods & Drugs Act
Foreign Missions & International Organizations Act
Freshwater Fish Marketing Act
Hazardous Products Act
Health of Animals Act
Immigration & Refugee Protection Act
Importation of Intoxicating Liquors Act
Integrated Circuit Topography Act
International Boundary Commission Act
Manganese-based Fuel Additives Act
Meat Inspection Act
Motor Vehicle Fuel Consumption Standards Act (not in force)
Motor Vehicle Safety Act
National Energy Board Act
Navigable Waters Protection Act
North American Free Trade Agreement Implementation Act
Nuclear Energy Act
Nuclear Safety & Control Act
Pest Control Products Act
Pilotage Act
Plant Breeders' Rights Act
Plant Protection Act
Precious Metals Marking Act
Preclearance Act
Privacy Act
Privileges & Immunities (North Atlantic Organization Act)
Proceeds of Crime (Money Laundering) & Terrorist Financing Act
Quarantine Act
Quebec Harbour, Port Warden Act
Radiation Emitting Devices Act
Radiocommunication Act
Seeds Act
Special Economic Measures Act
Special Import Measures Act
Statistics Act
Telecommunications Act
Textile Labelling Act
Trade-Marks Act
Transportation of Dangerous Goods Act, 1992
United Nations Act
United States Wreckers Act
Visiting Forces Act
Wild Animals & Plant Protection & Regulation of International & Interprovincial Trade Act

Minister, Hon. Stockwell Day
President, Alain Jolicoeur
613-952-3200
Executive Vice-President, Steven Rigby
Vice-President Human Resources, Paul Burkholder
613-948-3180
Vice-President Operations Branch, Barbara Hébert
613-948-4445
Director General Infrastructure & Environmental Operations Directorate, Claude Béland
613-941-7905
Acting Manager Agriculture, Environment & Trade Unit, Wendy Guard
613-954-7138

Admissibility Branch / Admissibilité

Vice-President, Mike Jordan
613-954-7220
Director General Recourse, Steve Bennett
613-688-9504

Border & Compliance Programs / Programmes de l'observation et de la frontière
Director General, Alice Shields
613-946-3036
Director Border Compliance & Monitoring, Craig Turner
613-954-6856
Director Commercial Policy, Bruna Rados
613-952-9488
Director Compliance Management, Jim Clark
613-957-9549
Director Immigration Ports & Border Management, George Boulees
613-954-9936
Director Partnerships, Raymond Bédard
613-954-6856
Director Postal, Courier & Casual Refunds Program, Brian Jones
613-954-6844
Director Travellers, Laurie Bratina
613-954-7507

Trade Programs / Programmes commerciaux
Director General, Suzanne Parent
613-954-7269
Director Consumer Products, Barry Desormeaux
613-954-7369
Director Industrial Products, Caterina Ardito-Toffolo
613-954-7390

Acting Director Origin & Valuation, Brenda Goulet
613-954-7338
Director Tariff Policy, Darwin Satherstrom
613-941-0096

Enforcement Branch / Exécution de la loi

Vice-President, Claudette Deschênes
613-952-2531

Canada Business (CBSC) / Entreprises Canada (CSEC)

235 Queen St.
Ottawa, ON K1A 0H5
Fax: 613-954-5463
888-576-4444
TDD: 800-457-8466cbsc@ic.gc.ca
www.cbsc.org

The CBSC provide a wide range of information on government services, programs & regulations to Canadian business people. The base framework is an organized network of thirteen centres across Canada, one in each province & territory. Thenetwork of CBSC is expanding to include regional access partners in many other communities across Canada. The centres offer various products and services aimed at helping clients obtain quick, accurate & comprehensive business information. Eachcentre exists as a result of cooperative arrangements between federal & provincial governments, & the private sector in some cases. Administration & management of the CBSC varies depending on location between the following federal agencies: WesternEconomic Diversification (WD), Industry Canada, the Canada Economic Development for Quebec Regions (CEDQR) & the Atlantic Canada Opportunities Agency (ACOA).

Acting Executive Director, Marcie Girouard
613-954-3576
Executive Assistant, Diane Lepage
613-941-9275, Fax: 613-954-5463, lepage.diane@ic.gc.ca

Regional Offices

The Business Link Business Service Centre
#100, 10237 - 104 St. NW
Edmonton, AB T5J 1B1
780-422-7722
800-272-9675
buslink@cbsc.ic.gc.ca
www.cbsc.org/alberta
Other Communication: Info-Fax: 780/422-0055

Small Business BC
601 West Cordova St.
Vancouver, BC V6B 1G1
604-775-5525
Fax: 604-775-5520
www.smallbusinessbc.ca
Other Communication: Toll Free Fax: 1-888-417-0442

Canada/Manitoba Business Service Centre
#250, 240 Graham Ave.
PO Box 2609
Winnipeg, MB R3C 4B3
204-984-2272
Fax: 204-983-3852
800-665-2019
manitoba@cbsc.ic.gc.ca
www.cbsc.org/manitoba

Canada/New Brunswick Business Service Centre
570 Queen St.
Fredericton, NB E3B 6Z6
506-444-6140
Fax: 506-444-6172
800-668-1010
TDD: 506-444-6166cbscnb@cbsc.ic.gc.ca
www.cbsc.org/nb

Canada/Newfoundland & Labrador Business Service Centre
90 O'Leary Ave.
PO Box 8687 A
St. John's, NL A1B 3T1
709-772-6022
Fax: 709-772-6090
800-668-1010
info@cbsc.ic.gc.ca
www.cbsc.org/nf/

Canada/NWT Business Service Centre
#701, 5201 - 50 Ave.
Yellowknife, NT X1A 3S9
867-873-7958
Fax: 867-873-0573
800-661-0599
yel@cbsc.ic.gc.ca
www.cbsc.org/nwt

Canada/Nova Scotia Business Service Centre (CNSBSC)
1575 Brunswick St.
Halifax, NS B3J 2G1
902-426-8604
Fax: 902-426-6530
800-668-1010
TDD: 902-426-4188halifax@cbsc.ic.gc.ca
www.cbsc.org/ns

Canada/Nunavut Business Service Centre
Inuksugait Plaza
PO Box 1000 1198
Iqaluit, NU X0A 0H0
867-975-7860
Fax: 867-975-7885
877-499-5199
cnbsc@gov.nu.ca
www.cbsc.org/nunavut
Other Communication: Toll Free Fax: 1-877-499-5299

Canada/Ontario Business Service Centre (COBSC)
151 Yonge St., 9th Fl.
Toronto, ON M5C 2W7
416-775-3456
Fax: 416-954-8597
800-567-2345
ontario@cbsc.ic.gc.ca
www.cbsc.org/ontario

Canada/Prince Edward Island Business Service Centre (CPEIBSC)
75 Fitzroy St.
PO Box 40
Charlottetown, PE C1A 7K2
902-368-0771
Fax: 902-566-7377
800-668-1010
pei@cbsc.ic.gc.ca
www.cbsc.org/pe/

Canada/Saskatchewan Business Service Centre (CSBSC)
#2, 345 Third Ave. South
Saskatoon, SK S7K 1M6
306-956-2323
Fax: 306-956-2328
800-667-4374
saskatooncsbsc@csbc.ic.gc.ca
www.cbsc.org/sask/index.cfm

Canada/Yukon Business Service Centre
#101, 307 Jarvis St.
Whitehorse, YT Y1A 2H3
867-633-6257
Fax: 867-667-2001
800-661-0543
yukon@cbsc.ic.gc.ca
www.cbsc.org/yukon

Info entrepreneurs
380, rue St-Antoine ouest, local 6000
Montréal, QC H2Y 3X7
514-496-4636
Fax: 514-496-5934
800-322-4636
infoentrepreneurs@cbsc.ic.gc.ca
infoentrepreneurs.org
Other Communication: Toll Free Fax: 1-888-417-0442

Canada Deposit Insurance Corporation (CDIC) / Société d'assurance-dépôts du Canada (SADC)

50 O'Connor St., 17th Fl.
PO Box 2340 D
Ottawa, ON K1P 5W5
613-996-2081
Fax: 613-996-6095
info@cdic.ca; info@sadc.ca
www.cdic.ca; www.sadc.ca
Other Communication: Toll Free: 1-800-461-2342 (English); 1-800-461-7232 (French)

CDIC, a Crown corporation established in 1967, ensures eligible deposits in member institutions (banks, trust companies, loan companies & cooperative credit associations) in case a member becomes insolvent. Funding is provided by itsmember institutions through premiums paid on insured deposits. Reports to government through the Minister of Finance. CDIC responsibilities include: providing deposit insurance in case of member failure; contributing to the stability of the Canadianfinancial system.

Chair, Ronald Robertson
President/CEO, Guy Saint-Pierre
Vice-President Insurance & Risk Assessment, Michèle Bourque
Vice-President Corporate Affairs & General Counsel & Corporate Secretary, M. Claudia Morrow
Vice-President Finance & Administration & Chief Financial Officer, Tom Vice
Admin. Coordinator, Lisa Labre
613- -, Fax: 613-947-0435, llabre@cdic.ca

Canada Economic Development for Québec Regions / Développement économique Canada pour les régions du Québec

Tour de la Bourse
#3800, 800, Place Victoria
CP 247
Montréal, QC H4Z 1E8
514-283-6412
Fax: 514-283-3302
866-385-6412
www.dec-ced.gc.ca

Defines federal objectives relating to development opportunities & delivers business assistance programs for small- & medium-sized businesses in Qu,bec for innovation, entrepreneurial & market development purposes. Supports a series ofprograms for appropriate environmental initiatives in various regions of Qu,bec. The agency fosters alliances among the various environmental industry stakeholders including small- & medium-sized enterprises & industrial associations. Goals include astrengthening of existing & new partnerships, & an improvement of access to government programs. The agency also provides a significant amount of support for research & development in areas of environmental technology, demonstration, marketing &transfer projects. Supports initiatives that contribute to making Montr,al an industrial centre of excellence in the environment. Aids small- & medium-sized firms in gaining access to federal procurement process, & encourages training & educationfocusing on business management.

Minister, Hon. Jean-Pierre Blackburn
514-496-1282, Fax: 514-496-5096
President, Michelle d'Auray
514-283-4843, Fax: 514-283-7778
Director General Communications, Gilbert Brunet
514-283-8817, Fax: 514-283-7951
Director Legal Services, Serge Pépin
514-283-2997, Fax: 514-283-1549
Director General Corporate Services, Pierre Bordeleau
514-283-4565, Fax: 514-283-4702
Actig Director Departmental Advisor, Dominique-Line Blondeau
514-283-3824, Fax: 514-283-9679
Chief of Staff & Departmental Advisor, Marie-Josée Reid
514-283-8400, Fax: 514-283-7778
Communications Advisor, Line Maurel
514-283-2026, Fax: 514-283-7951

President's Office / Bureau du présidente

President, Michelle d'Auray
514-283-4843, Fax: 514-283-7778
Director General Communications, Gilbert Brunet
514-283-8817, Fax: 514-283-7951
Director General Human Resources, Finance & Administration, Pierre Bordeleau
514-283-4565, Fax: 514-283-4702

Operations

Vice-President, Manon Brassard
514-283-3510, Fax: 514-283-4547

Director General Business Development & Infrastructure, Gilles Pelletier
514-283-2704, Fax: 514-283-4131
Director General Regional Coordination, Jean-Pierre Thibault
514-283-3628, Fax: 514-283-7491

Policy & Planning / Politiques et planification

Acting Vice-President, Johanne Béchard
514-283-1294, Fax: 514-283-5940
Director General Governmental Affairs, Rita Tremblay
819-997-7716, Fax: 819-997-8519
Acting Director Policy & Programs, Marie-Chantal Girard
514-283-2664, Fax: 514-283-8429
Director General Departmental Performance, Jean-Pierre Lavoie
514-283-7982, Fax: 514-283-0041

Canada Mortgage & Housing Corporation (CMHC) / Société canadienne d'hypothèques et de logement (SCHL)

700 Montreal Rd.
Ottawa, ON K1A 0P7
613-748-2000
Fax: 613-748-2098
800-668-2642
www.cmhc.ca; www.schl.ca
Other Communication: Canadian Housing Information Centre:|613/748-2367

CMHC works closely with a network of professional associations, groups & institutions concerned with regional planning & the residential sector. It prepares various research projects for the examination of relationships between urbanareas, housing & sustainable development issues. Involved in numerous technical research projects addressing interrelationships between housing, energy & resource use. Through its research & information transfer function, CMHC will undertakeinitiatives such as identifying approaches & solutions that lead to more sustainable & healthy communities, examining barriers to potential development of brownfield sites. To assist in meeting Kyoto Accord targets, CMHC will focus on ways to reduceresidential energy consumption in multiple-unit housing, educate consumers on energy-saving changes to homes.

Acts Administered:
CMHC Act
National Housing Act (NHA)
Chair, Dino Chiesa
President/CEO, Karen Kinsley
Vice-President Corporate Services, Berta Zaccardi
Vice-President Insurance, Sharon Matthews
Vice-President Policy & Planning, D.A. Stewart
Acting Vice-President Assisted Housing, Deborah Taylor
Vice-President Human Resources, Melvern Skinner
Vice-President Finance, Pierre Serré
Executive Director CMHC International, Pierre David
Executive Director Communications, Anne Dawson
Executive Director Risk Management & Investments, Gilles Proulx
Executive Director Securization, Anthea English
Senior Communciations Officer, Neil Hrab
613-748-2541, Fax: 613-748-4072, nhrab@cmhc-schl.gc.ca

Regional Business Centres

Atlantic
Barrington Tower, 9th Fl.
1894 Barrington St.
Halifax, NS B3J 2A8
902-426-3530
Fax: 902-426-9991
General Manager, Carolyn Kavanaugh
Marketing & Communications Consultant, Emily Poitras-Benedict
902-426-8127

British Columbia
#200, 1111 West Georgia St.
Vancouver, BC V6E 4S4
604-731-5733
Fax: 604-737-4139
General Manager, Nelson Merizzi
Marketing & Communications Consultant, Tracy Wells
604-737-4162

Ontario
#300, 100 Sheppard Ave. East
Toronto, ON M2N 6Z1
416-221-2642
Fax: 416-218-3310
General Manager, Peter Friedmann
Communications Consultant, Angelina Ritacco
416-218-3332

Alberta, Yukon, NWT & Nunavut
#200, 1000 - 7 Ave. SW
Calgary, AB T2P 5L5
403-515-3000
Fax: 403-515-2930
General Manager, Trevor Gloyn
Senior Consultant Communications & Marketing, Sophie Dupuis
403-515-2986

Québec
1100, boul René-Levesque ouest, 1er étage
Montréal, QC H3B 5J7
514-283-2222
888-772-0772
General Manager, Charles Chenard
Communications & Marketing Consultant, Julie Cohen
514-283-3679

Canada Pension Plan Investment Board / Office d'investissement du Régime de pensions du Canada

#2700, 1 Queen St. East
PO Box 101
Toronto, ON M5C 2W5
416-868-4075
Fax: 416-868-4760
866-557-9510
csr@cppib.ca
www.cppib.ca

The CPP Investment Board is a Crown corporation created as part of 1997 reforms designed to ensure the soundness & sustainability of the CPP. The Board operates under similar investment rules as other pension plans in Canada, whichrequire the prudent management of pension plan assets in the interests of plan contributors & beneficiaries.

President/CEO, David Denison
Vice-President Communications & Stakeholder Relations, Ian Dale
Vice-President & General Counsel & Corporate Secretary, John H. Butler
Vice-President Finance & Administration, Jane Nyman
Vice-President Human Resources, David Wexler
Vice-President Portfolio Design & Risk Management, John H. Ilkiw
Vice-President Private Investments, Mark Wiseman
Vice-President Public Market Investments, Donald M. Raymond
Vice-President Real Estate Investments, Graeme Eadie
Director Capital Markets, Daniel Chiu
Director Corporate Finance, Frank Prong
Director Information Technology, Mike Stone
Director Investment Finance, Henry Kim
Director Investment Research, Thomas Eigl
Director Risk Analysis, Sterling Gunn

Canada Revenue Agency / Agence du revenu du Canada

555 Mackenzie Ave., 4th Fl.
Ottawa, ON K1A 0L5
613-952-0384
www.cra-arc.gc.ca
Other Communication: TIPS (Tax Information Phone Service): 1-800-267-6999~Individual Income Tax Enquiries: 1-800-959-8281~Business/Self-Employed Income Tax Enquiries: 1-

Administers tax laws for the Government of Canada & for most provinces & territories; various social & economic benefit & incentive programs delivered through the tax system.

Acts Administered:
Canada Pension Plan Act, Part I
Customs Act
Customs & Excise Offshore Application Act
Customs Tariff Act
Department of National Revenue Act
Excise Act
Excise Tax Act
Special Import Measures Act
Unemployment Insurance Act, Part III & VII
Minister National Revenue, Hon. Carol Skelton
613-995-2960, Fax: 613-952-6608
Commissioner, Michel Dorais
613-957-3688, Fax: 613-941-4142
Deputy Commissioner, Bill Baker
Asst. Commissioner Human Resources, Lysanne Gauvin
613-954-8200
Asst. Commissioner Information Technology & Chief Information Officer, Patrick Beynon
613-954-8983
Asst. Commissioner Public Affairs, Jean Chartier
613-957-3508
Director General Corporate Audit & Evaluation, Patricia MacDonald
613-957-7522
Communications, Peter Delis
416-512-4135, Fax: 416-512-4097

Appeals Branch / Division des appels

Asst. Commissioner, Jeanne Flemming
613-688-9090
Director General Fariness Provisions & Voluntary Disclosures, Chantal Jalbert
613-688-9134
Acting Director General Program Management & Analysis, Rosaline Frith
613-688-9543
Director General Tax & Charities Appeals, Paul Lynch
613-688-9103
Director CPP/EI Appeals, Natalie Stibernik
613-688-9144

Assessment & Benefit Services / Services des cotisations et de prestations

Asst. Commissioner, Barbara Slater
613-954-6614
Deputy Asst. Commissioner, George Arsenijevic
613-957-7497
Director General Benefit Programs, Elaine Collins
613-957-9338
Director General Business Returns & Payments Processing, Leslie-Ann Scott
613-941-5007
Director General Business Process Development, Dominique Short
613-952-9314
Director General Individual Returns & Payment Processing, Maureen Tapp
613-957-7497
Director Financial Planning & Management Support, Susan Allen
613-954-7303

Compliance Programs Branch / Programmes d'observation de la législation

Asst. Commissioner, Elaine Routledge
613-957-3709
Deputy Asst. Commissioner Audit, John Kowalski
613-957-3585
Director General Audit, Ray MacNeil
613-954-5726
Director General International Tax, Fred O'Riordan
613-952-7472
Director General Investigations, Denis Meunier
613-957-7780
Director General Risk Assessment & Business Management, Martin Leigh
613-954-5126
Director General Scientific Research & Experimental Development, Hèléne Dompierre
613-946-3447

Corporate Strategies & Business Development / Stratégies d'entreprise et croissance des marchés

Asst. Commissioner, Stephen O'Connor
613-952-3660
Director General Corporate Planning, Governance & Measurement, Normand Théberge
613-954-6082
Director General Statistics & Information Management, Michel J. Cloutier
613-957-8706

Director General Strategic Policy, Catherine MacLeod
613-954-6068

Finance & Administration Branch / Finances et administration

Asst. Commissioner & Chief Financial Officer, James Ralston
613-946-1763
Director General Administration, Deirdre Kerr-Perrott
613-688-9270
Director General Financial Administration, Serge Gaudet
613-954-6400
Director General Real Property & Service Integration, Gérald Doucet
613-954-8330
Director General Resource Management, Mary Jane Jackson
613-957-7339
Director General Security, Risk Management & Internal Affairs, Jocelyn Malo
613-688-9500
Acting Director General Strategic Management & Program Support, Filipe Dinis
613-957-7502

Legislative Policy & Regulatory Affairs / Politiques legislatives et affaires réglementaires

123 Slater St.
Ottawa, ON K1A 0L8
Asst. Commissioner, Brian McCauley
613-957-3708
Asst. Deputy Commissioner Tax & Regulatory Affairs, Ed Gauthier
613-952-9198
Director General Charities, Elizabeth Tromp
613-954-0931
Asst. Deputy Commissioner Excise & GST/HST Rulings, Pierre Bertrand
613-998-4398
Director General Registered Plans, Annelisa Gillespie
613-954-0933
Director General Income Tax Rulings, Wayne Adams
613-957-2132
Director General Legislative Policy, Richard Montroy
613-957-2061

Taxpayer Services & Debt Management / Services aux contribuables et gestion des créances

Asst. Commissioner, Guy Proulx
613-954-1269
Director General Business Technology & Solutions, André Potvin
613-957-1863
Director General Revenue Collection Operations, Fred Vivash
613-954-1532
Director General Taxpaper Services, Marj Ogden
613-957-9362

Tax Services Offices

Atlantic Region

Bathurst
201 George St.
PO Box 8888
Bathurst, NB E2A 4L8
Fax: 506-548-9905

Charlottetown
161 St. Peters Rd.
PO Box 8500
Charlottetown, PE C1A 8L3
Fax: 902-566-7197

Halifax
1557 Hollis St.
PO Box 638
Halifax, NS B3J 2T5
Fax: 902-426-7170

Moncton
50 King St.
PO Box 1070
Moncton, NB E1C 4M2
Fax: 506-851-7018

Newfoundland & Labrador
Atlantic Place
165 Duckworth St.
PO Box 12075
St. John's, NL A1B 4R5
709-754-5928

Saint John
126 Prince William St.
Saint John, NB E2L 4H9
Fax: 506-636-5200

St. John's Tax Centre
290 Empire Ave.
St. John's, NL A1B 3Z1
Fax: 709-754-3416

Summerside Tax Centre
275 Pope Rd.
Summerside, PE C1N 6A2
Fax: 902-432-5359

Sydney
47 Dorchester St.
PO Box 1300
Sydney, NS B1P 6K3
Fax: 902-564-3095

Northern Ontario Region

Barrie
81 Mulcaster St.
Barrie, ON L4M 6T7
Fax: 705-721-0056

Belleville
11 Station St.
Belleville, ON K8N 2S3
Fax: 613-969-7845

Kingston
31 Hyperion Ct.
PO Box 2600
Kingston, ON K7L 5P3
Fax: 613-545-3272

Ottawa & Nunavut
333 Laurier Ave. West
Ottawa, ON K1A 0L9
Fax: 613-238-7125

Peterborough
185 King St. West, 5th Fl.
Peterborough, ON K9J 8M3
Fax: 705-876-6422

Sudbury Tax Centre
1050 Notre Dame Ave.
Sudbury, ON P3A 5C1
Fax: 705-671-3994

Thunder Bay
130 South Syndicate Ave.
Thunder Bay, ON P7E 1C7
Fax: 807-622-8512

Pacific Region

Burnaby-Fraser
9737 King George Hwy.
Surrey, BC V3T 5W6
Fax: 604-587-2010

Northern BC & Yukon
280 Victoria St.
Prince George, BC V2L 5N8
Fax: 250-561-7869

Southern Interior
277 Winnipeg St.
Penticton, BC V2A 1N6
Fax: 250-492-8346

Surrey Tax Centre
9755 King George Hwy.
Surrey, BC V3T 5E1
Fax: 604-585-5769

Vancouver
1166 West Pender St.
Vancouver, BC V6E 3H8
Fax: 604-689-7536

Vancouver Island
1415 Vancouver St.
Victoria, BC V8V 3W4
Fax: 250-363-8188

Prairie Region

Edmonton & NWT
#10, 9700 Jasper Ave.
Edmonton, AB T5J 4C8
Fax: 780-495-3533

Lethbridge
#200, 419 - 7 St. South
Lethbridge, AB T1J 4A9
Fax: 403-382-3052

Red Deer
4996 - 49 Ave.
Red Deer, AB T4N 6X2
Fax: 403-341-7053

Regina
1955 Smith St.
Regina, SK S4P 2N9
Fax: 306-757-1412

Saskatoon
340 - 3 Ave. North
Saskatoon, SK S7K 0A8
Fax: 306-652-3211

Calgary
220 - 4 Ave. SE
Calgary, AB T2G 0L1
Fax: 403-264-5843

Winnipeg
325 Broadway
Winnipeg, MB R3C 4T4
Fax: 204-983-2066

Winnipeg Tax Centre
66 Stapon Rd.
Winnipeg, MB R3C 3M2
Fax: 204-984-5164

Southern Ontario Region

Hamilton
55 Bay St.
PO Box 2220
Hamilton, ON L8N 3E1
Fax: 905-546-1615

Kitchener-Waterloo
166 Frederick St.
Kitchener, ON N2G 4N1
Fax: 519-579-4532

London
451 Talbot St.
London, ON N6A 5E5
Fax: 519-645-4029

St Catharines
32 Church St.
PO Box 3038
St Catharines, ON L2R 3B9
Fax: 905-688-5996

Toronto Centre
1 Front St. West
Toronto, ON M5J 2X6
Fax: 416-360-8908

Toronto East
200 Town Centre Court
Toronto, ON M1P 4Y3
Fax: 416-973-5126

Toronto North
#1000, 5001 Yonge St.
Toronto, ON M2N 6R9
Fax: 416-512-2558

Toronto West
5800 Hurontario St.
PO Box 6000
Mississauga, ON L5R 4B4
Fax: 905-566-6182

Windsor
185 Ouellette Ave.
Windsor, ON N9A 5S8
Fax: 519-257-6558

Québec Region

Chicoutimi
#123, 100, rue Lafontaine
Chicoutimi, QC G7H 6X2
Fax: 418-698-6387

Jonquière Tax Centre
2251, boul René-Lévesque
Jonquière, QC G7S 5J1
Fax: 418-548-0846

Laval
3400, av Jean-Béraud
Laval, QC H7T 2Z2
Fax: 514-956-7071

Montérégie-Rive-Sud
3250, boul Lapinière
Brossard, QC J4Z 3T8
Fax: 450-926-7100

Montréal
305, boul René-Lévesque ouest
Montréal, QC H2Z 1A6
Fax: 514-496-1309

Outaouais
1100, boul Maloney ouest
Gatineau, ON K1A 1L4
Fax: 819-994-1103

Québec
165, rue de la Pointe-aux-Lièvres sud
Québec, QC G1K 7L3
Fax: 418-649-6478

Rimouski
#101, 180, av Cathédrale
Rimouski, QC G5L 5H9
Fax: 418-722-3027

Rouyn-Noranda
44, av du Lac
Rouyn-Noranda, QC J9X 6Z9
Fax: 819-797-8366

Shawinigan-Sud Tax Centre
4695, 12e av
Shawinigan-Sud, QC G9N 7S6
Fax: 819-536-7078

Sherbrooke
50, Place de la Cité
CP 1300
Sherbrooke, QC J1H 5L8
Fax: 819-821-8582

Trois-Rivières
#111, 25, rue des Forges
Trois-Rivières, QC G9A 2G4
Fax: 819-371-2744

Canadian Commercial Corporation (CCC) / Corporation commerciale canadienne

Clarica Centre
#1100, 50 O'Connor St.
Ottawa, ON K1A 0S6
613-996-0034
Fax: 613-995-2121
www.ccc.ca
A Crown Corporation mandated to facilitate international trade, particularly in government markets. CCC specializes in international procurement markets for Canadian companies & provides services to help them win, negotiate & manageexport contracts. As prime contractor, CCC offers a government-to-government agreement that simplify customer access to Canadian technology & expertise. CCC contracts have a government guarantee of contract performance.

Minister Responsible, Hon. David Emerson
President, John McBride
613-996-0042, Fax: 613-992-2134
Vice-President Aerospace, Defense & Security, Robert Ryan
613-995-4658
Vice-President Corporate Development, Emechete Onuoha
613-643-4360
Vice-President Risk & Financial Services, Michel Houle
613-992-9638
Administrator Communications, Celine Darmody
613-995-0538, Fax: 613-992-2134, celine.darmody@ccc.ca

Canadian International Trade Tribunal / Tribunal canadien du commerce extérieur

Standard Life Centre
333 Laurier Ave. West
Ottawa, ON K1A 0G7
613-990-2452
Fax: 613-990-2439
www.citt-tcce.gc.ca
The Tribunal is an independent, quasi-judicial body, which carries out both judicial & advisory functions relating to trade remedies for the North American Free Trade Agreement. In this capacity, the Tribunal succeeds the ProcurementReview Board of Canada. Reports to government through the Minister of Finance.

Acts Administered:
Canadian International Trade Tribunal Act
Customs Act
Excise Tax Act
Special Import Measures Act
Chair, Pierre Gosselin
Vice-Chair, Elaine Feldman
Vice-Chair, Serge Fréchette
Secretary, Hèléne Nadeau
Executive Director Research, S. Greig
General Counsel, Reagan Walker
Chief Librarian, Ursula Schultz
613-990-2418, Fax: 613-990-2439, uschultz@citt.gc.ca

Copyright Board of Canada / Commission du droit d'auteur du Canada

#800, 56 Sparks St.
Ottawa, ON K1A 0C9
613-952-8621
Fax: 613-952-8630
secretariat@cb-cda.gc.ca
www.cb-cda.gc.ca
The Board is an economic regulatory body empowered to establish, either mandatorily or at the request of an interested party, the royalties to be paid for the use of copyrighted works, when the administration of such copyright isentrusted to a collective-administration society. The Board also has the right to supervise agreements between users & licensing bodies & issues licences when the copyright owner cannot be located.

Chair, William J. Vancise
Vice-Chair & CEO, Stephen J. Callary
Secretary General, Claude Majeau
General Counsel, Mario Bouchard
613-954-6470
Director Research & Analysis, Gilles McDougall
613-946-4457

Office of the Ethics Commissioner / Bureau du commissaire en éthique

66 Slater St., 22nd Fl.
Ottawa, ON K1A 0A6
613-995-0721
Fax: 613-995-7308
Administers the Conflict of Interest Code for Members of the House of Commons. Also administers the Prime Minister's Conflict of Interest & Post-Employment Code for Public Office Holders as it applies to federal ministers, secretaries ofstate, parliamentary secretaries, full-time Governor-in-Council appointees & ministerial staff.

Ethics Commissioner, Dr. Bernard J. Shapiro
Chief Advisor, Robert Todd
613-996-3132, Fax: 613-995-7308, todd.robert@ic.gc.ca

Export Development Canada (EDC) / Exportation et développement Canada (SEE)

151 O'Connor St.
Ottawa, ON K1A 1K3
613-598-2500
Fax: 613-237-2690
888-332-3320
TDD: 866-574-0451www.edc.ca
A financial services corporation assisting Canadian business to succeed in foreign markets. EDC provides a wide range of financial solutions to exporters across Canada & their customers around the world. The corporation's risk managementservices include: export-credit insurance protecting exporters against losses due to non-payment relating to commercial & political risks; & flexible medium- or long-term financing & guarantees. As a financially self-sustaining Crown corporation, EDCoperates on commercial principles, charging fees & premiums for its products & interest on its loans. EDC is governed by a board of directors composed of representatives from both the private & public sectors, & reports to Parliament through theminister for international trade. An Environmental Review Directive is used to assess the environmental impacts of projects EDC is asked to support. EDC pursues an international multilateral consensus on environmental review practices so that allexporters are subject to the same rules.

Acting President & Chief Operating Officer, Eric Siegel
Chief Environmental Advisor, Arthur Fitzgerald
CFO & Executive Vice-President Finance, Peter Allen
Senior Vice-President Business Solutions & Technology, Sherry Noble
Senior Vice-President Business Development, Benoit Daignault
Senior Vice-President Human Resources, Susanne Laperle
Senior Vice-President Legal Services & Secretary, Jim McArdle
Senior Vice-President Short-Term Financial Services, Pierre Gignac
Communications Advisor, Veronica Prochazka
613-598-3257, Fax: 613-598-3080, vprochazka@edu-see.ca

EDC Regional Offices

Calgary
Home Oil Tower
#606, 3240 - 8 Ave. SW
Calgary, AB T2P 2Z2
403-537-9800
Fax: 403-537-9811

Edmonton
#1000, 10810 - 101 St.
Edmonton, AB T5J 3S4
780-702-5233
Fax: 780-702-5235

Halifax
Purdy's Wharf Tower II
#1410, 1969 Upper Water St.
Halifax, NS B3J 3R7
902-442-5205
Fax: 902-442-5204

London
#1512, 148 Fullarton St.
London, ON N6A 5P3
519-963-5400
Fax: 519-963-5407

Moncton
#400, 735 Main St.
Moncton, NB E1C 1E5
506-851-6066
Fax: 506-851-6406

Montréal
Tour de la Bourse
#4530, 800, Victoria Square
CP 124
Montréal, QC H4Z 1C3
514-908-9200
Fax: 514-878-9891

Québec
#1300, 2875, boul Laurier
Sainte-Foy, QC G1V 2M2
418-266-6130
Fax: 418-266-6131

St. John's
90 O'Leary Ave.
St. John's, NL A1B 2C7
709-772-8808
Fax: 709-772-8693

Toronto
#810, 150 York St.
Toronto, ON M5H 3S5
416-640-7600
Fax: 416-862-1267

Vancouver
#1030, 505 Burrard St.
Vancouver, BC V7X 1M5
604-638-6950
Fax: 604-638-6955

Winnipeg
Commodity Exchange Tower
#2075, 360 Main St.
Winnipeg, MB R3C 3Z3
204-975-5090
Fax: 204-975-5094

Farm Credit Canada / Financement agricole Canada

1800 Hamilton St.
PO Box 4320
Regina, SK S4P 4L3
306-780-8100
Fax: 306-780-5875
800-387-3232
www.fcc-fac.com
Federal Crown corporation reporting to Parliament through the Minister of Agriculture & Agri-Food. Under the Farm Credit Canada Act FCC offers financing to primary producers & agribusiness through 100 offices in rural communities acrossCanada.

President/CEO, John J. Ryan
Executive Vice-President Operations, Greg Stewart
Executive Vice-President & CFO, Moyez Somani
Senior Vice-President Strategy, Knowledge & Reputation, Kellie Garrett
Senior Vice-President & Chief Information Officer, Paul MacDonald
Vice-President & Controller, Rick Hoffman

Finance Canada / Finances Canada

L'esplanade Laurier
140 O'Connor St.
Ottawa, ON K1A 0G5
613-992-1573
Fax: 613-996-8404
TDD: 613-996-0035www.fin.gc.ca
Responsible for providing the federal government with analysis & advice on financial & economic issues. Monitors & researches the performance of the Canadian economy's major factors (output, growth, employment, income, price stability,monetary policy, long-term change). The Department interacts with various other federal departments & agencies to encourage coordination in all federal initiatives with an impact on the economy. Emphasis is placed on consulting with the publicregarding policy directions & options.

Acts Administered:
Bank Act
Bank of Canada Act
Banks & Banking Law Revision Act
Bills of Exchange Act
Bretton Woods & Related Agreements Act
Canada Deposit Insurance Corporation Act
Canada Development Corporation Reorganization Act
Canada Mortgage & Housing Corporation Act
Canada-Newfoundland Atlantic Accord Implementation Act
Canada Pension Plan Act
Canadian International Trade Tribunal Act
Canadian National Railways Capital Revision Act
Canadian National Railways Refunding Act
Canadian National Steamship (West Indies Service) Act
Co-operative Credit Association Act
Currency Act
Customs & Excise Offshore Application Act
Customs Tariff, Debt Servicing & Reduction Account Act
Diplomatic Service (Special) Superannuation Act
Excise Tax Act
Export Credit Insurance Act
Federal Provincial Fiscal Arrangements & Federal Post-Secondary Education & Health Contributions Act
Financial Administration Act
Garnishment Attachment & Pension Diversion Act
Governor General's Retiring Annuity Act
Halifax Relief Commission Pension Continuation Act
Income Tax Act
Income Tax Conventions Interpretation Act
Insurance Companies Canadian & British Act
Insurance Companies Foreign Act
Interest Act
International Development (Financial Institutions) Assistance Act
Investment Companies Act
Loan Companies Act
Members of Parliament Retiring Allowances Act
Newfoundland Additional Finance Assistance Act
Nova Scotia Offshore Retail Sales Tax Act
Office of the Superintendent of Financial Institutions Act
Pension Benefits Standards Act
Prince Edward Island Subsidy Act
Provincial Subsidies Act
Public Service Superannuation Act
Québec Savings Bank Act
Residential Mortgage Financing Act
Small Business Loans Act
Special Import Measures Act
Tax Rental Agreements Act
Trust & Loans Companies Act
Winding Up Act
Minister, Hon. Jim Flaherty
Parliamentary Secretary, Diane Ablonczy
Deputy Minister, Robert A. Wright
Senior Assoc. Deputy Minister, Mark Carney
613-943-2314
Assoc. Deputy Minister, Vacant
Asst. Deputy Minister Economic Development & Corporate Finance, Denis Gauthier
613-992-6401

Associated Agencies, Boards & Commissions:
• Auditor General of Canada / Vérificateur Général du Canada
Listed alphabetically in detail.
• Bank of Canada / Banque du Canada
Listed alphabetically in detail.
• Canada Deposit Insurance Corporation / Société d'assurance-dépôts du Canada
Listed alphabetically in detail.
• Canada Investment & Savings (CI&S) / Placements Épargne Canada (PEC)
#900, 110 Yonge St.
Toronto, ON M5C 1T4
416-952-1252
Fax: 416-952-1270
800-575-5151
csb@csb.gc.ca
www.csb.gc.ca
• Canada Revenue Agency
Listed alphabetically in detail.
• Financial Consumer Agency of Canada / Agence de la consommation en matière financière du Canada
Listed alphabetically in detail.
• Financial Transactions & Reports Analysis Centre of Canada (FINTRAC) / Centre d'analyse des opérations et déclarations financières du Canada (CANAFE)
234 Laurier Ave. West, 24th Fl.
Ottawa, ON K1P 1H7
Fax: 613-943-7931
866-346-8722
guidelines@fintrac.gc.ca
www.fintrac.gc.ca
Created in 2000, FINTRAC is Canada's financial intelligence unit, a specialized agency created to collect, analyze & disclose financial information & intelligence on suspected money laundering & terrorist activities financing.~
• Office of the Superintendent of Financial Institutions / Bureau du surintendant des institutions financières Canada
Listed alphabetically in detail.

Corporate Services Branch / Direction des services ministériels

Provides joint services for the federal Treasury Board Secretariat & Finance Canada.

Asst. Deputy Minister, Coleen Volk
613-995-8487
Executive Director Central Agencies Cluster Internal Services Modernization Project, Nabila Gillett
613-943-2808
Executive Director Finance & Administration, Kelly Gillis
613-992-0554
Executive Director Information Management & Technology, Robert Brodeur
613-992-4306
Executive Director Human Resources Division, Marilyn MacPherson
613-992-1996
Senior Director Internal Audit & Evaluation, Pierre Lacasse
613-992-3805

Consultations & Communications Branch / Direction des consultations et des communications

Asst. Deputy Minister, Allan Darisse
613-992-9194
Director General, Harry Adams
613-992-7763
Director Communications Policy & Strategy, Lucian Blair
613-992-9195
Director Public Affairs & Operations Division, Vacant
613-992-7763

Economic Development & Corporate Finance / Développement économique et finances intégrées

Asst. Deputy Minister, Denis Gauthier
613-992-6401
Director Microeconomic Policy Analysis, Richard Botham
613-992-1011
Director Sectoral Policy Analysis, François Delorme
613-995-4486

Economic & Fiscal Policy Branch / Direction des politiques économique et fiscale

Asst. Deputy Minister, Paul-Henri Lapointe
613-996-0321
Director Economic Analysis & Forecasting Division, Steven James
613-992-4321
Director Economic Studies & Policy Analysis Division, Benoit Robidoux
613-992-4910
Senior Chief Fiscal Policy, Helen Cutts
613-992-6336
Senior Chief Fiscal Policy, Jonathan Will
613-992-6771

Federal Provincial Relations & Social Policy Branch / Direction des relations fédérales, provinciales et de la politique sociale

Asst. Deputy Minister, Barbara Anderson
613-996-0735
Director Federal Provincial Relations, Nancy Horsman
613-992-6786
Director Social Policy, Réal Bouchard
613-996-5083

Financial Sector Policy Branch / Direction de la politique du secteur financier

Asst. Deputy Minister, Frank Swedlove
613-992-4679
Director Financial Markets, Rob Stewart
613-992-9032
Director Financial Sector, Diane Lafleur
613-992-5885
Director Financial Institutions, Gerry Salembier
613-992-1631

International Trade & Finance Branch / Direction des finances et des échanges internationaux

Director General, Alister Smith
613-996-8927
Director International Finance, Peter Cameron
613-996-7902
Director International Trade Policy, Carol Nelder-Corvari
613-996-8650
Director International Policy & Institutions, Vacant
613-992-0763

Law Branch / Direction juridique

Asst. Deputy Minister & Counsel, Yvan Roy
613-996-4667
General Legal Counsel, Werner Heiss
613-995-8724

Tax Policy Branch / Direction de la politique de l'impôt

Asst. Deputy Minister, Bob Hamilton
613-992-1630
Director Business Income Tax Division, Louise Levonian
613-992-1008

Director Intergovernmental Tax Policy Evaluation & Research, Paul Berg-Dick
613-992-6846
Senior Chief Personal Income Tax, Lise Potvin
613-992-6729
Director Sales Tax Division, Jim Daman
613-992-6298
Director Tax Legislation Division, Brian Ernewein
613-992-3045
Chief Resource & Environmental Taxation, James Greene
613-992-0960

Financial Consumer Agency of Canada (FCAC) / Agence de la consommation en matière financière du Canada (ACFC)

427 Laurier Ave. West, 6th Fl.
Ottawa, ON K1R 1B9
Fax: 613-941-1436
info@fcac-acfc.gc.ca
www.fcac-acfc.gc.ca
Other Communication: TollFree: 1-866-461-FCAC (3222) for services in English; 1-866-461-ACFC (2232) for services in French
Created by Parliament in 2001, the Financial Consumer Agency of Canada (FCAC) exists to protect Canada's financial consumers; to make them aware of their rights & responsibilities; & to inform Canadians about the financial products &services available to them. The FCAC ensures that the nearly 500 federally regulated financial institutions respect the consumer provisions in the laws that govern them & monitors the voluntary codes of conduct financial institutions have adopted. Aswell as informing people about their rights as financial consumers, the FCAC provides user-friendly information & easy-to-use tools to help consumers shop around for the best financial product/service for their situation.

Acts Administered:
Bank Act
Co-operative Credit Associations Act
Financial Consumer Agency of Canada Act
Insurance Companies Act
Trust & Loan Companies Act
Commissioner, William G. Knight
613-941-4300
Deputy Commissioner, Jim Callon
613-941-4335
Director Consumer Education & Public Affairs, Susan Murray
613-941-4220
Senior Counsel Legal Services, Stephen Barry
613-941-3910
Teamleader Public Affairs, B. Smith
613-941-4255, Fax: 613-941-1436

Office of the Superintendent of Financial Institutions (OSFI) / Bureau du surintendant des institutions financières Canada

Kent Square
255 Albert St.
Ottawa, ON K1A 0H2
613-990-7788
Fax: 613-952-8219
800-385-8647
extcomm@osfi-bsif.gc.ca
www.osfi-bsif.gc.ca
Responsible for regulating & supervising financial institutions & pension plans under federal jurisdiction. Included under federal jurisdiction are: banks, some insurance companies, trust companies, loan companies, cooperative creditassociations, & fraternal benefit societies. OSFI monitors & examines these institutions & pension plans for solvency, liquidity, & compliance with legislation, regulations & Office guidelines. Provides actuarial services & advice to the Governmentof Canada. Reports to government through the Minister of Finance.

Acting Superintendent, Julie Dickson
Director Security Services, Al Gillich
613-990-9781, Fax: 613-954-4351, agillich@osfi-bsif.gc.ca
Communications Officer, Julie Corbett
613-990-7086, Fax: 613-990-5591, julie.corbett@osfi-bsif.gc.ca

Audit & Consulting Services / Services de vérification et de consultation

Senior Director, Joanne Bagnall
416-973-8935, Fax: 416-954-3169, joanne.bagnall@osfi-bsif.gc.ca

Office of the Chief Actuary / Bureau de l'actuaire en chef

Chief Actuary, Jean-Claude Ménard
613-990-7577, Fax: 613-990-9900, jean-claude.menard@osfi-bsif.gc.c

Corporate Services Sector / Secteur des services intégrés

Asst. Superintendent, Donna D'Angelo Pasteris
613-990-7491, Fax: 613-993-6782, donna.pateris@osfi-bsif.gc.ca
Director Communications & Public Affairs Division, Margaret Pearcy
613-993-0577, Fax: 613-990-5591, margaret.pearcy@osfi-bsif.gc.ca
Senior Director Finance & Informatics Division, Christine Walker
613-993-7426, Fax: 613-990-6328, christine.walker@osfi-bsif.gc.ca
Senior Director Human Resources Division, Gary Walker
613-990-8761, Fax: 613-990-9017, gary.walker@osfi-bsif.gc.ca
Senior Director Project Management, Gordon J. Dunn
416-954-2141
Director Office Management & Technical Services Division, Denis Leroux
613-990-7774, Fax: 613-954-4331, denis.leroux@osfi-bsif.gc.ca
Manager Regulatory Information, Jeff Bee
613-990-6036, Fax: 613-991-6248, jeff.bee@osfi-bsif.gc.ca

Regulation Sector / Secteur de la réglementation

Fax: 613-993-6782
Asst. Superintendent, Julie Dickson
613-990-3667, Fax: 613-993-6525, julie.dickson@osfi-bsif.gc.ca
Director Accounting Policy, Karen Stothers
416-973-0744, Fax: 416-952-0664, karen.stothers@osfi-bsif.gc.ca
Senior Director Actuarial, August Chow
416-973-2056, Fax: 416-959-3167, august.chow@osfi-bsif.gc.ca
Senior Director Capital, Bob Hanna
613-990-7278, Fax: 613-991-6822, bob.hanna@osfi-bsif.gc.ca
Senior Director Compliance, Nick Burbridge
416-973-6117, Fax: 416-954-3169, nicolas.burbridge@osfi-bsif.gc.ca
Senior Director Legislation & Approvals, Patty Evanoff
613-990-9004, Fax: 613-998-6716, patty.evanoff@osfi-bsif.gc.ca
Managing Director International Advisory Group, Kim Norris
613-990-6550, Fax: 613-990-6904, kim.norris@osfi-bsif.gc.ca
General Counsel Legal Services, Alain Prévost
613-990-7787, Fax: 613-952-5031, alain.prevost@csfi-bsif.gc.ca
Director Research, Jerry Goldstein
613-990-8911, Fax: 613-993-6782, gerald.goldstein@osfi-bsif.gc.ca

Supervision Sector / Secteur de la surveillance

Asst. Superintendent, John Doran
416-952-1655, Fax: 416-973-1168, john.doran@osfi-bsif.gc.ca
Senior Director DTI Conglomerate Group, Ted Price
416-973-4385, Fax: 416-954-3167, ted.price@osfi-bsif.gc.ca
Senior Director Financial Institutions Group, Carl Hiralal
416-973-0622, Fax: 416-954-6450
Senior Director Regulatory & Supervisory Practices Division, Naren Sheth
416-973-6118, Fax: 416-952-1662
Senior Managing Director Financial Institution Group, Kent Andrews
416-952-1469, Fax: 416-954-5015, kent.andrews@osfi-bsif.gc.ca
Managing Director Operational Risk & Capital Assessment Services, Abhilash Bhachech
416-973-6654, Fax: 416-952-1663, abhilash.bhachech@osfi-bsif.gc.ca
Managing Director Strategic Initiatives, Pam Hopkins
416-973-6657, Fax: 416-973-1168, pamela.hopkins@osfi-bsif.gc.ca
Managing Director Supervision, Karen Badgerow-Croteau
613-990-7608, Fax: 613-998-5604, karen.badgerow-croteau@osfi-bsif.
Director Capital Markets Division, Jeffrey Kung
416-973-0603, Fax: 416-952-1663, jeffrey.kung@osfi-bsif.gc.ca

Foreign Affairs & International Trade Canada (FAIT) / Affaires étrangères et Commerce international Canada (AECT)

125 Sussex Dr.
Ottawa, ON K1A 0G2
613-944-4000
Fax: 613-996-9709
800-267-8376
www.international.gc.ca
Other Communication: Media Relations: 613/995-1874~
The Departments of Foreign Affairs & International Trade were consolidated into one department, as announced on February 6, 2006.

Acts Administered:
Asia-Pacific Foundation of Canada Act
Bretton Woods Agreements Act
Canadian Commercial Corporation Act
Canadian Institute for International Peace & Security Act
Comprehensive Nuclear Test-Ban Treaty Implementation Act
Cultural Property Export & Import Act
Department of Foreign Affairs & International Trade Act
Diplomatic & Consular Privileges & Immunities Act
Export Development Act
Export & Import Permits Act
Food & Agriculture Organization of the United Nations Act
Forgiveness of Certain Official Development Assistance Debts Act
Fort-Falls Bridge Authority Act
Geneva Conventions Act
High Commissioner of the United Kingdom Act
International Boundary Waters Treaty Act
International Development (Financial Institutions) Continuing Assistance Act
International Development Research Centre Act
Meat Import Act
North American Free Trade Agreement Implementation Act
Northern Pipeline Act
Privileges & Immunities (International Organizations) Act
Privileges & Immunities (North Atlantic Treaty Organization) Act
Prohibition of International Air Services Act
Rainy Lake Watershed Emergency Control Act
Roosevelt-Campobello International Park Commission Act
Skagit River Valley Treaty Implementation Act
State Immunity Act
United Nations Act
Minister Foreign Affairs, Hon. Peter MacKay
613-995-1851, Fax: 613-996-3443
Minister International Trade, Hon. David Emerson
613-992-7332, Fax: 613-996-8924
Information Coordinator Information Services (SXCI), Pat Scharfer
pat.schaefer@dfait-maeci.gc.ca

Foreign Affairs / Affaires étrangères

Parliamentary Secretary, Deepak Obhrai
Deputy Minister, Peter Harder
613-944-4911
Asst. Deputy Minister Human Resources, Gisèle Samson-Verrault
613-996-5369
Legal Advisor, Alan Kessel
613-995-8901

Bilateral Relations / Relations bilatérales

Asst. Deputy Minister, Vacant
Director General Africa, Ian Ferguson
613-944-5989
Director Eastern & Southern Africa, Perry Calderwood
613-944-6585
Director West & Central Africa, Louis Hamel
613-944-4578

GOVERNMENT

Director General Latin America & Caribbean Bureau, Jamal Khokhar
613-996-8435
Director General United States Bureau, Mark Moher
613-944-6900, Fax: 613-995-2603
Director Caribbean, Central America & Andean Region, Christian Lapointe
613-996-0676
Director Brazil, Southern Cone & Inter-American Relations, Sarah Fountain Smith
613-992-2480
Director General East Asia, Ted Lipman
613-995-1097
Director East Asia I, Christie LeClaire
613-995-7575
Director East Asia II, Caroline Chrétien
613-995-1186
Director General South & Southeast Asia Bureau, James Fox
613-992-3372
Director South Asia, Arif Lalani
613-996-0910
Director Southeast Asia & Pacific, Christopher Thornley
613-992-6807
Director General Central, East & South Europe Bureau, Tom MacDonald
613-992-5303
Director Central, European & Eastern Mediterranean, Marta Moszcenska
613-996-6835
Director Eastern Europe & Balkans, Pierre Guimond
613-992-7991
Director General European Union, North & West Europe Bureau, Norbert Kalisch
613-992-8333
Director Northern Europe, John Ausman
613-995-9402
Director Western Europe, Hilary Childs-Adams
613-992-0871
Director European Union, Robert Clark
613-995-6115
Director Middle East, Peter McRae
613-944-5991
Director General Strategy & Services Bureau, Adam Blackwell
613-995-7759
Director General Middle East & North Africa Bureau, Mark E. Bailey
613-944-1144
Director Gulf & Maghreb, Thomas Marr
613-944-6591

Corporate Services Branch / Services aux entreprises
Asst. Deputy Minister, Kathryn McCallion
613-996-7065, Fax: 613-996-4519
Director General Headquarters Administrative Bureau, Christine Perry
613-996-3175
Director General & Chief Information Officer Information Management & Technology, Pierre Sabourin
613-943-1125
Director General Physical Resources Branch, Ian Dawson
613-952-8732, Fax: 613-952-8729

Global Issues / Enjeux mondiaux
Asst. Deputy Minister, David Malone
613-944-2273
Ambassador Circumpolar Affairs, Jack Anawack
613-992-6700
Ambassador Environment, Karen Kraft Sloan
613-944-0784
Director General Economic Policy Bureau, Drew Fagan
613-992-7825
Director General Environment, Energy & Sustainable Development Bureau, Keith Christie
613-944-0886
Director General Human Security & Human Rights, Michael Small
613-944-0325
Director General International Organizations Bureau, Ferry de Kerkhove
613-944-0928

International Security Branch & Political Director / Sécurité international et directeur politique
Asst. Deputy Minister, Jim Wright
613-944-4228
Senior Coordinator International Crime & Terrorism, Adèle Dion
613-944-2906
Director General International Security Bureau, Paul Chaplin
613-992-3402
Director Non-Proliferation, Arms Control & Disarmament, Robert McDougall
613-944-0324
Director Nuclear & Chemical Disarmament Implementation Agency, Marc Vidricaire
613-996-6901
Director Defence & Security Relations Division, Barbara Martin
613-992-7921
Director Global & Security Policy, Janice Attree-Smith
613-944-7646
Director General Security & Intelligence, Dan Livermore
613-992-7400
Director Ambassador for Mine Action, Earl Turcotte
613-995-9282
Director Global Partnership Program, Angela Bogdan
613-944-0308
Director General Secretariat for the Stabilization & Reconstruction Task Force, Ross Hynes
613-995-6689
Director Humanitarian Affairs & Disasters Response Group, Elissa Goldberg
613-996-3908
Director Peacekeeping & Peace Operations Group & Director, Sudan Task Force, Wendy Gilmour
613-992-5457

North America
Asst. Deputy Minister, Peter Boehm
613-944-6183
Director General Consular Affairs Bureau, Robert Desjardins
613-996-0639
Director General North American Bureau, William Crosbie
613-944-6900

International Trade Canada (ITCan) / Commerce international Canada

125 Sussex Dr.
Ottawa, ON K1A 0G2
613-944-4000
Fax: 613-996-9709
800-267-8376

Works to position Canada as a business leader for the 21st century. ITCan helps large & small Canadian companies expand & succeed internationally, promotes Canada as a dynamic place to do business, & negotiates & administers tradeagreements.

Parliamentary Secretary, Helena Guergis
Deputy Minister, Marie-Lucie Morin

Business Development & Chief Trade Commissioner / Développement des affaires et délégué commercial en chef
Provides basic export counselling, information on financial assistance programs to exporters &, in collaboration with the Alliance of Manufacturers & Exporters Canada, offers regional seminars to provide potential exporters with theinformation needed to sell goods & services to foreign governments. Also coordinates the World Information Network (WIN) Exports program for the federal government. Government purchasing by other countries is governed by the General Agreement onTariffs & Trade (GATT) & the North American Free Trade Agreement (NAFTA). International Trade Centres (ITCs) help Canadian exporters organize strategies to take advantage of opportunities in foreign markets. Trade officers at the ITC supplyinformation on international markets, joint ventures, technology transfer projects, trade shows & networking conferences & trade missions abroad. ITC staff are also capable of providing expert advice on developing marketing plans & locatingpotential foreign partners for business opportunities.
Acting Asst. Deputy Minister & Chief Trade Commissioner, Robert Déry
613-944-0504
Director General Market Development Bureau, Richard Lecoq
613-944-2798
Director General Operations & Services, Louise Léger
613-992-8785
Director PEMD & eServices, William Pound
613-996-3024
Executive Assistant, Marjolaine Adam
613-944-3195, Fax: 613-944-3214, marjolaine.adam@international.gc.

Investment, Science & Technology / Secteur de l'investissement, des sciences et de la technologie
Asst. Deputy Minister, John Klassen
613-944-3122
Director General Marketing & Services Bureau, Wally Downswell
613-944-3146
Director General Policy & Partnerships Bureau, Mario Ste-Marie
613-944-3125
Director Science & Technology, Danièle Ayotte
613-995-2224
Sr. Technology Advisor Advanced Materials/Environment, Dr. Hamid Mostaghaci
613-995-7320

Strategic Policy, Communications & Corporate Policy / Politique stratégique, communications et planification ministérielle
Asst. Deputy Minister, Michael Martin
613-944-3122
Chief Economist, John Curtis
613-992-7776
Director General Communications, Danielle Thibault
613-996-2213
Director General Strategic Policy, Randle Wilson
613-992-7979
Director Business & Financial Planning, Charles Larabie

Trade Law / Droit commercial international
Director General Trade Law & General Counsel, Meg Kinnear
613-943-2803

Trade Policy & Negotiations / Politique commercial et négociations
Asst. Deputy Minister, John Gero
613-992-0293, Fax: 613-996-1667
Director General Bilateral Trade Policy, Ian Burney
613-944-9171
Director General Export & Import Controls Bureau, Suzanne McKellips
613-995-2947
Chief Air Negotiator, Nadir Patel

World Markets / Secteur des Marchés mondiaux
Asst. Deputy Minister, Ken Sunquist
613-944-2695
Director General Asia Commercial Relations, Scott Fraser
613-944-1519
Director General Client Relations, Andrée Vary
613-944-0553
Director General International Business Development Policy & Planning, Sara Hradecky
613-996-1745, Fax: 613-996-9265
Director General North American Commercial Relations, Peter McGovern
613-944-0979
Director Emerging Markets, Kathleen MacKay
613-944-2904
Director Europe Commercial Relations, Linda MacDonald
613-992-2099
Director Latin America, Caribbean, Middle East & Africa Commercial Relations, Ron Davidson
613-944-1678
Director Strategic Initiatives, Audri Mukhopadhyay
613-944-0925
Director International Trade Missions, Deborah Gowling
613-944-1233

Human Resources & Social Development Canada (HRSDC) / Ressources humaines et développement social Canada (RHDSC)

Place du Portage, Phase IV, 12th Fl.
140 Promenade du Portage
Gatineau, QC K1A 0J9
819-994-6313
www.hrsdc.gc.ca

The Labour Program promotes a fair, safe, healthy, stable, cooperative & productive work environment, which contributes to the social & economic well-being of all Canadians.

Acts Administered:
Canada Labour Code
Aviation Occupational Safety & Health Regulations
Canada Occupational Health & Safety Regulations
Coal Mines (CBDC) Occupational Safety & Health Regulations
Coal Mining Safety Commission Regulations
Marine Occupational Safety & Health Regulations
Oil & Gas Occupational Safety & Health Regulations
On Board Trains Occupational Safety & Health Regulations
Canada Pension Plan
Canada Student Financial Assistance Act
Canada Student Loans Act

GOVERNMENT

Canadian Centre for Occupational Health & Safety Act
Corporations & Labour Unions Returns Act
Department of Human Resources Development Act
Employment Equity Act
Employment Insurance Act
Fair Wages & Hours of Labour Act
Family Orders & Agreements Enforcement Assistance Act
Federal-Provincial Fiscal Arrangements Act
Government Annuities Act
Government Employees Compensation Act
Labour Adjustment Benefits Act
Merchant Seamen Compensation Act
Non-smokers' Health Act (Transport Canada)
Old Age Security Act
Status of the Artist Act
Unemployment Assistance Act
Vocational Rehabilitation of Disabled Persons Act
Wages Liability Act
Minister, Hon. Diane Finley
819-994-2482, Fax: 819-994-0448
Minister Labour, Hon. Jean-Pierre Blackburn
819-953-5646, Fax: 819-994-5168
Parliamentary Secretary, Lynne Yelich
Deputy Minister, Alan Nymark
819-994-4514
Sr. Assoc. Deputy Minister, Kathy O'Hara
Assoc. Deputy Minister, Hélène Gosselin
Asst. Deputy Minister Employment Programs Policy & Design, Diane Carroll
Acting Senior General Counsel, Mark L. McCombs
Comptroller, Sherry Harrison

Corporate & Public Affairs

Asst. Deputy Minister, Jan Lalonde
819-994-6013
Director General Human Resources, Lucie Allaire
819-994-4015
Director General Strategic & Program Communications, JoAnn Myer
819-953-1308

Service Canada

140, Promenade du Portage
Gatineau, QC K1A 0J9
800-622-6232
TDD: 800-926-9105servicecanada.gc.ca
Delivers government services & benefits through 320 offices throughout the country.

Deputy Head, Hélène Gosselin
Senior Asst. Deputy Minister Service Delivery, Hy Braiter
819-994-6686
Director General E-Channel, Donna Wood
613-947-0900
Director General Investigation & Control, André Hurtubise
819-994-6868

Industry Canada / Industrie Canada

235 Queen St.
Ottawa, ON K1A 0H5
613-947-7466
Fax: 613-954-6436
www.ic.gc.ca
Other Communication: General Enquiries: 613/947-7466; Fax:|613/954-6436~ Strategis: strategis.ic.gc.ca
To help make Canadians more productive & competitive in the global, knowledge-based economy. The department's policies, programs & services help create an economy that: provides more & better-paying jobs for Canadians; supports strongerbusiness growth through sustained improvements in productivity; & gives consumers, businesses & investors confidence that the marketplace is fair, efficient & competitive. To reach its clients, Industry Canada collaborates extensively with partnersat all levels of government & the private sector, & has become a leader in providing leading-edge service products such as the Canada Business Service Centres, & Internet services such as Strategis (strategis.ic.gc.ca) & ExportSource(exportsource.gc.ca). These provide business & individuals with strategic information services 24 hours a day, seven days a week. For clients who prefer personal contact with the department, Industry Canada has regional offices, as well as localservice points located in 50 communities.

Acts Administered:
Agreement on Internal Trade Implementation Act
Bankruptcy & Insolvency Act
Boards of Trade Act
Canada Business Corporations Act
Canada Co-operative Associations Act
Canada Corporations Act
Canada Small Business Financing Act
Canadian Space Agency Act
Canadian Tourism Commission Act
Companies' Creditors Arrangement Act
Department of Industry Act
Departmental Legislation
Electricity & Gas Inspection Act
Radiocommunication Act
Telecommunications Act
Teleglobe Canada Reorganization & Divestiture Act
Telesat Canada Reorganization & Divestiture Act
Marketplace & Trade Regulation
Competition Act
Consumer Packaging & Labelling Act
Government Corporations Operations Act
Telecommunications Legislation
Investment Canada Act
Lobbyists Registration Act
Small Business Loans Act
Winding-up & Restructuring Act
Canadian Intellectual Property Office (CIPO) Legislation
Copyright Act
Industrial Design Act
Integrated Circuit Topography Act
Patent Act
Public Servants Inventions Act
Trade-marks Act
Consumer Legislation
Bills of Exchange Act
Electricity & Gas Inspection Act
Precious Metals Marking Act
Textile Labelling Act
Timber Marking Act
Weights & Measures Act
Registrar General Functions
Public Documents Act
Public Officers Act
Seals Act
Trade Unions Act
Portfolio & Agency Legislation
Business Development Bank of Canada Act
Canada Foundation for Innovation Act (Part I & XI)
Competition Tribunal Act
Copyright Board: Sections 66ff of the Copyright Act
National Research Council Act
Natural Sciences & Engineering Research Council Act
Social Sciences & Humanities Research Council Act
Standards Council of Canada Act
Statistics Act
Largely Inactive or Minimal Involvement
Atlantic Fisheries Restructuring Act
Agricultural & Rural Development Act
Bell Canada Act
Corporations & Labour Unions Returns Act
Pension Fund Societies Act
Regional Development Incentives Act
Special Areas Act
Minister, Hon. Maxime Bernier
613-995-9001, Fax: 613-992-0302, ministre.industrie@ic.gc.ca
Minister Federal Economic Development Initiative for Northern Ontario, Hon. Tony Clement
705-671-0711, Fax: 705-671-0717
Parliamentary Secretary, Colin Carrie
Deputy Minister, Richard Dicerni
Assoc. Deputy Minister, Carole Swan
613-943-7164, Fax: 613-954-3272
Acting Asst. Deputy Minister Comptrollership & Administration, Kevin Lindsey
613-957-9288
Director General Communications & Marketing Branch, Nick Heseltine
613-947-2597, Fax: 613-947-3390, heseltine.nick@ic.gc.ca
Director General Human Resources, Cathy Downes
613-954-5474
Director General Office of Consumer Affairs, Michael Jenkin
613-954-3277
Executive Director Corporate & Portfolio Office, Bill Cleevely
613-954-8911, Fax: 613-957-1990, cleevely.bill@ic.gc.ca

Associated Agencies, Boards & Commissions:

• Canadian Tourism Commission (CTC) / Commission canadienne du Tourisme (CCT)
#1400, 1055 Dunsmuir St.
PO Box 49230
Vancouver, BC V7X 1L5
604-638-8300
Fax: 604-638-8425
ctc_feedback@businteractive.com
www.canadatourism.com
CTC is a unique partnership between tourism business & associations, provincial & territorial governments, & the Government of Canada. The CTC's Board of Directors is a decision-making body composed of 26 members with a wide variety ofskills & knowledge, representing all regions of the country. The CTC's mission is to sustain a vibrant & profitable Canadian tourism industry.

• Cape Breton Development Fund Corporation / Corporation Fonds d'investissement du Cap-Breton
Silicon Island
70 Crescent St.
PO Box 1264
Sydney, NS B1P 6T7
902-564-3600
Fax: 902-564-3825
800-705-3926
www.cbgf.ca
Responsible for the delivery of the economic adjustment fund established by the Governments of Canada & Nova Scotia in the wake of the federal government's decision to close the Cape Breton Development Corporation (Devco). The CBGFcomprises a $86 million contribution from the Government of Canada, & a $12 million contribution from the Government of Nova Scotia.

• Chief Information Office / Secteur de l'agent principal de l'information
235 Queen St.
Ottawa, ON K1A 0H5
613-954-3574
Fax: 613-941-1938
Responsible for information management & information technology (IM/IT) activities for Industry Canada; provides strategic advice & leadership to assist the department in achieving its electronic information & service delivery strategy;champions Industry Canada's Government On-Line agenda; responsible for key leading information & service delivery channels, including *Strategis , the National Secretariat for the Canada Business Service Centres &the Student Connection Program.~*

• Communications Research Centre Canada (CRC) / Centre de recherches sur les communications
3701 Carling Ave.
PO Box 11490 H
Ottawa, ON K2H 8S2
613-991-3313
Fax: 613-998-5355
info@crc.ca
www.crc.ca
Dedicated to advanced communications research & development for over 50 years. Key research areas include radio science, terrestrial wireless systems, satellite communications broadcasting, & broadband network technologies. CRC has a longhistory of technology transfer. CRC operates an Innovation Centre, a technology incubator for small & medium-sized high-tech start-ups, which provides increased access to CRC's technologies, research expertise & unique laboratories & facilities.

• Competition Tribunal / Tribunal de la concurrence
#600, 90 Sparks St.
Ottawa, ON K1P 5B4
613-957-7851
Fax: 613-957-3170
tribunal@ct-tc.gc.ca
www.ct-tc.gc.ca
Hears & decides all applications made under Parts V11.1 & VIII of the Competition Act.

• Electronic Commerce Branch / Direction du commerce électronique
300 Slater St.
Ottawa, ON K1A 0C8
613-954-5031
Fax: 613-941-1164
800-328-6189
e-com.ic.gc.ca

Coordinates the development & implementation of a national electronic commerce strategy. It is responsible for both domestic & international aspects of electronic commerce. The Canadian Electronic Commerce Strategy was announced inSeptember 1998. The Strategy, which was developed in collaboration with provincial & territorial governments, industry & consumer groups, among others, establishes a framework, goals, timetable, & implementation plan for electronic commercedomestically. The Strategy involves coordinating strategic elements that fall within the federal government's responsibilities, including the policy development areas of encryption & privacy.~

• Enterprise Cape Breton Corporation (ECBC) / Société d'expansion du Cap-Breton
Silicon Island
70 Crescent St.
Sydney, NS B1S 2Z7
902-564-3600
Fax: 902-564-3825
800-705-3926
ecbcinfo@ecbc.ca
www.ecbc.ca
Crown corporation established pursuant to Part II of the Government Organization Act, Atlantic Canada, 1987 with a jurisdictional mandate which includes all of Cape Breton Island & a portion of mainland Nova Scotia in & around the Town ofMulgrave. The Corporation is charged with the responsibility for promoting & assisting the financing & development of industry in the region, providing employment outside the coal-producing sector & broadening the base of the local economy.~

• Standards Council of Canada
Listed alphabetically in detail, this section

Competition Bureau / Bureau de la concurrence

Place du Portage, Phase I
50, rue Victoria, 21e étage
Ottawa, ON K1A 0C9
613-997-4282
Fax: 613-997-0324
800-348-5358
TDD: 800-642-3844compbureau@ic.gc.ca
www.competitionbureau.gc.ca
The Competition Bureau is the organization responsible for the enforcement of the Competition Act, the Consumer Packaging & Labelling Act except as it relates to food, the Precious Metals Marking Act & the Textile Labelling Act. TheCompetition Bureau ensures compliance by the business community with legislation administered by the Bureau, & oversees the development of policy & dissemination of information aimed at ensuring optimal compliance levels.

Commissioner, Sherridan Scott
819-997-3304
Senior Deputy Commissioner Mergers, Gaston Jorré
819-994-1863
Deputy Commissioner Civil Matters, André Lafond
819-997-1209, Fax: 819-953-8546, lafond.andre@ic.gc.ca
Acting Deputy Commissioner Compliance & Operations, Johanne Bernard
819-953-7942, Fax: 819-953-3464
Acting Deputy Commissioner Criminal Matters, Richard Taylor
819-997-1208, Fax: 819-997-3835
Deputy Commissioner Fair Business Practices, Raymond Pierce
819-997-1231, Fax: 819-953-4792

Industry Sector / Secteur de l'industrie

Supports & promotes a more innovative & internationally competitive economy through strategic approaches to trade, technology, investment & connectedness by providing detailed sectoral analysis, policy advice & information & services tobusiness.

Asst. Deputy Minister, Tom Wright
613-954-3798, Fax: 613-941-1134
Executive Director Canadian Biotechnology Secretariat, Kim Elmslie
613-946-8926, Fax: 613-941-5533
Director General Industrial Analysis Centre, Chummer Farina
613-954-9633

Aerospace, Defence & Marine Branch / Aérospatiale, defense et la marine

Fax: 613-941-2379
Director General, Leah L. Clark
613-941-8123
Senior Director Marine, Richard Domokos
613-954-3057
Director Aerospace, Martin Sutherland
613-954-3166
Director Defence Industries, Vacant
613-952-2433

Automotive & Industrial Materials Branch / Automobile et matériaux industriels

Director General, Ronald Watkins
613-954-3343, watkins.ron@ic.gc.ca
Director Automotive, Guy Leclaire
613-954-2649
Acting Director Industrial Materials, Gary R. McGee
613-954-5609

Energy & Environment Industries Branch / Énergie et industries environnementales

Director General, Bruce Bowie
613-946-7317
Director Energy Directorate, Glenn MacDonell
613-954-2703

Manufacturing Industries Branch / Industries de la fabrication

Director General, Sara Filbee
613-954-3394
Director Apparel & Textiles, Denise Guèvremont
613-954-4235
Director Forest Industries, Jyostsna Dalvi
613-941-2274
Director Manufacturing Competitiveness, Helen Teeple
613-948-5030

Services Industries Branch / Industries de services

Director General, Alain Beaudoin
613-954-3080
Deputy Director Language Industry Initiative Team, Valérie Sirois
613-954-1854
Deputy Director Olympics Business Development & Tourism Team, Philip Fleming
613-666-5077
Deputy Director Services Industries Team, John Lambie
613-954-2959
Deputy Director SourceCan, David Chase
613-957-9977
Deputy Director Sustainable Cities Initiative, Vacant
613-954-3434

Strategic Policy Sector / Politique stratégique

Acting Director General Micro-Economic Policy Analysis, Richard Roy
613-941-9224
Director General Strategic Policy, Alfred LeBlanc
613-954-3558

Innovation Policy Branch / Politique d'innovation

Director General, Iain Stewart
613-991-9472, Fax: 613-996-7887
Director Knowledge Infrastructure, Feyrouz Kurji
613-990-2773
Director Marketplace Innovation, Peter Boyd
613-991-0037
Director Science & Technology Strategy, Laird Roe
613-998-4417

International & Intergovernmental Affairs Branch / Relations internationales et intergouvernementales

Director General, Frank Vermaeten
613-946-9108, Fax: 613-946-0167
Acting Director Federal Provincial Relations, Michèle Boutin
613-941-0624
Director International Affairs, Simon McInnes
613-954-8895
Director Internal Trade & Outreach, Chris Charette
613-946-7318

Marketplace Frameworks Policy Branch / Politiques-cadres du marchés

Director General, Susan Bincoletto
613-952-0211
Acting Director Corporate & Insolvency Law Policy, Joseph Allen
613-952-0738
Acting Director Intellectual Property Policy, Albert Cloutier
613-952-2527
Acting Director Patent Policy, Douglas Clark
613-952-2118

Small Business Policy / Politique de la petite entreprise

Director General, John Connell
613-954-5489
Director Financing, Peter Webber
613-941-2684
Director Policy & Liaison, Nancy Graham
613-954-3555

Operations Sector / Secteur des opérations

Executive Director Aboriginal Business Canada, Jeff Moore
613-954-5430
Asst. Deputy Minister, Guy Bujold
613-957-4392
Assoc. Asst. Deputy Minister, Rachel Larabie-Lesieur
613-954-3405
Visiting Asst. Deputy Minister Service to Business, Robert Andras
613-952-2664
President Measurement Canada, Alan E. Johnston
613-952-0655
Director General Corporations Canada, Richard G. Shaw
613-941-2837
Director General Operations & Small Business Financing, Mary Pavich
613-954-3449
Director General Policy & Regional Cohesion, Cheryl Grant
613-941-3863
Acting Director General Sectorial Strategies & Services, Martin Zablocki
613-941-2479

Office of the Superintendent of Bankruptcy / Bureau du surintendant des faillites

613-941-1000
Fax: 613-941-2862
Superintendent, Marc Mayrand
613-941-2691, Fax: 613-946-9205
Asst./Deputy Superintendent Programs, Standards & Regulatory Affairs, Joanne Bérubé
613-941-9051

Canadian Intellectual Property Office / Office de la propriété intellectuelle du Canada

50, rue Victoria
Gatineau, QC K1A 0C9
819-997-1936
Fax: 819-953-7620
cip.gc.ca

Justice Canada

East Memorial Bldg.
284 Wellington St.
Ottawa, ON K1A 0H8
613-957-4222
Fax: 613-954-0811
www.justice.gc.ca
Works to ensure that Canada's justice system is as fair, accessible & efficient as possible; helps the federal government to develop policy & to make & reform laws as needed; acts as the government's lawyer, providing legal advice,prosecuting cases under federal law, & representing the government in court. These responsibilities reflect the double role of the Minister of Justice, who is also the Attorney General of Canada: while the Minister is concerned with questions ofpolicy & their relation to the justice system, the Attorney General is the chief law officer of the Crown.

Acts Administered:
Annulment of Marriages (Ontario) Act
Anti-Terroism Act
Canada Evidence Act
Canada Prize Act
Canada-United Kingdom Civil & Commercial Judgments Convention Act
Canadian Bill of Rights
Canadian Human Rights Act
Commercial Arbitration Act
Contraventions Act
Controlled Drugs & Substance Act
Crown Liability & Proceedings Act
Department of Justice Act
Divorce Act
Escheats Act
Extradition Act
Family Orders Agreements Enforcement Assistance Act
Federal Courts Act

Firearms Act
Foreign Enlistment Act
Foreign Extraterritorial Measures Act
Fugitive Offenders Act
Identification of Criminals Act
International Sale of Goods Contracts Convention Act
Interpretation Act
Judges Act
Law Commission of Canada Act
Marriage (Prohibited Degrees) Act
Mutual Legal Assistance in Criminal Matters Act
Official Languages Act
Postal Services Interruption Relief Act
Revised Statutes of Canada, 1985 Act
Security Offences Act
State Immunity Act
Statute Revision Act
Statutory Instruments Act
Supreme Court Act
Tax Court of Canada Act
United Nations Foreign Arbitral Awards Convention Act
Youth Criminal Justice Act
Minister of Justice shares responsibility to Parliament for the following Acts:
Access to Information Act (President of the Treasury Board)
Bills of Lading Act (Minister of Transport)
Criminal Code (Solicitor General & Minister of Agriculture & Agri-Foods)
Garnishment, Attachment Pension Diversion Act (Minister of National Defense, Minister of Finance & Minister of Public Wo
Privacy Act (President of the Treasury Board)
Minister & Attorney General, Hon. Vic Toews
613-992-4621, Fax: 613-990-7255
Parliamentary Secretary, Rob Moore
Deputy Minister & Deputy Attorney General, John Sims
613-957-4998
Assoc. Deputy Minister, William C. McDowell
613-948-8983
Assoc. Deputy Minister, Donna J. Miller
613-948-8990, Other Communications: Winnipeg: 204/983-6029
Assoc. Deputy Minister, Michel Bouchard
613-941-4073
Asst. Deputy Attorney General, Clare Beckton
613-948-8981
Chief General Counsel, Vacant
613-957-4801
Office Coordinator, Pierre Millette
613-946-8920, pierre.millette@justice.gc.ca

Communications Bureau

Director General, Sheila Bird
613-957-4221
Assoc. Director General, Jean Valin
613-957-4215
Director Public Affairs & Outreach, Suesan Saville
613-957-4211

Business & Regulatory Law Portfolio / Portefeuille du droit des affaires et du droit réglementaire

Asst. Deputy Minister, Myles Kirvan
613-947-4944
Senior General Counsel & Director Competition Law, Jeff Richstone
613-953-3884
Senior General Counsel Maritime Law Secretariat, Alfred Popp, Q.C.
613-957-4666, Fax: 613-990-5777

Central Agencies Group / Groupes centraux

Asst. Deputy Minister & Counsel to the Dept. of Finance, Yvan Roy
613-996-4667
Senior General Counsel Treasury Board, Mylène Bouzigon
613-952-3379, Fax: 613-954-5806
Senior Counsel Financial Consumer Agency of Canada, Stephen Barry
613-941-3910
Senior Counsel Finance-General Legal Services, Yvonne Milosevic
613-943-0418
General Counsel Public Service Commission, Gaston Arseneault
613-995-0445
General Counsel Office of the Superintendent of Financial Institutions, Alain Prévost
613-990-7787

Corporate Services / Services à la gestion

Acting Asst. Deputy Minister, Virginia McRae
613-941-7889
Acting Senior General Counsel & Executive Director, Karen Green
613-957-3831
Acting Director Access to Information & Privacy, Suzanne Poirier
613-954-0617, Fax: 613-957-2303
Director General Finance, Administration & Programs, Michael Ivanski
613-946-3854
Director General Human Resources & Professional Development, Camille Therriault-Power
613-941-1867
Chief Information Officer, Simon Labrie
613-941-3444, Fax: 613-941-5201

Tax Law Services / Services du droit fiscal

Asst. Deputy Attorney General, Johanne D'Auray
613-957-4811
Senior General Counsel Canada Revenue Agency, Charles McNab
613-954-5881
Senior General Counsel Revenue Canada, Jean-Marc Raymond
613-954-5881
Senior General Counsel Tax Law Services, Gordon Bourgard
613-952-9810, Fax: 613-941-2293
Senior General Counsel Tax Law Services, Donald G. Gibson
613-957-4883

North American Free Trade Agreement (NAFTA) Secretariat / Secrétariat de l'ALÉNA

Canadian Section
#705, 90 Sparks St.
Ottawa, ON K1P 5B4
613-992-9388
Fax: 613-992-9392
canada@nafta-sec-alena.org
Canadian Secretary, Françoy Raynauld
Deputy Secretary, Daniel Plourde
Records & Information Management Officer, Marie Meunier
613-992-9388

Public Works & Government Services Canada (PWGSC) / Travaux publics et services gouvernementaux

Place du Portage, Phase III
11, rue Laurier
Ottawa, ON K1A 0S5
819-997-6363
TDD: 819-994-5389www.pwgsc.gc.ca

A common service provider to the federal government; employs nearly 12,000 people & delivers services & programs through offices across Canada, as well as in the United States & Europe; provides services in the following areas:accommodation services, compensation, consulting & audit, crown assets disposal, general standards, procurement, public access, publishing, real property services, Receiver General services, Queen's Printer, as well as translation & interpretation.The Department also manages the telecommunications & information management infrastructure of government. It builds & supports government-wide services & systems like the Canada Site on the Internet & the Government Electronic Directory Services,helping connect Canadians with their government.

Acts Administered:
Anti-Personnel Mines Convention Implementation Act
Bridges Act
Canadian Arsenals Limited Divestiture Authorization Act
Defence Production Act
Dry Docks Subsidies Act
Expropriation Act
Federal District Commission to have acquired certain lands, An Act to Confirm the Authority of
Garnishment, Attachment & Pension Diversion Act
Government Property Traffic Act
Ottawa River, Act Respecting Certain Works
Pension Benefits Division Act
Public Works & Government Services Act
Seized Property Management Act
Statutes Act
Surplus Crown Assets Act
Translation Bureau Act
Minister, Hon. Mike Fortier
819-997-5421, Fax: 819-956-8382
Parliamentary Secretary, James Moore
Deputy Minister & Deputy Receiver General, David Marshall
819-956-1706, Fax: 819-956-8280
Assoc. Deputy Minister, Daphne Meredith
Acting Assoc. Deputy Minister, Yvette Aloïsi
819-956-4472
Acting Asst. Deputy Minister Human Resources, Diane Lorenzato
819-956-7548
Senior General Counsel, Ellen Stensholt
819-956-0993
Acting Director General Greening Government Operation, Margaret Kenny
Acting Director General Strategic Transformation, Alex Lakroni
819-934-2522
Chief Risk Officer, Shahid Minto
Director Communications, Jean-Luc Benoît

Associated Agencies, Boards & Commissions:
• Canadian Wheat Board / Commission canadienne du blé
Listed alphabetically in detail.
• Defence Construction Canada / Construction de Défense Canada
Listed alphabetically in detail.

Acquisitions Branch / Direction générale des approvisionnements

Provides departments & agencies with expert assistance at each stage of the supply cycle & offers tools that simplify & accelerate the acquisition of goods & services. It ensures that the government exercises due diligence & maintains theintegrity of the procurement process. It is a primary service provider offering client departments a broad base of procurement solutions aimed at securing best value for their procurement dollar.

Acting Asst. Deputy Minister, Ian Bennett
819-956-1711
Director General Acquisition Renewal Sector, Martin Edmondson
819-956-0901, Fax: 819-956-7475
Director General Commercial Acquisitions & Supply Management Sector, Bruce Fletcher
819-956-0760, Fax: 819-956-4491
Director General Land, Aerospace & Marine Systems & Major Projects, Terry Williston
819-956-0010
Director General Other Commodities, George Butt
819-956-0867
Director General Services & Technology Acquisition Management Sector, Pierre Benoît
819-956-1649, Fax: 819-956-2675
Director General Small & Medium Enterprises, Marshall Moffatt
819-956-8416

MERX
Fax: 613-956-6123
www.merx.com
Other Communication: Suppliers Support: 1-800-964-MERX (6379); Buyers Support: 1-888-738-3005 (Ottawa: 613/737-3796)
Under its contract with the Government of Canada, MERX is the Government Electronic Tendering Service operating an online system that advertises government contracting opportunities to potential bidders. Federal government departmentsmust use MERX for requirements subject to any of the trade agreements. Some are using it as well for other purchases. In addition, several provincial & municipal governments in Canada are using MERX to advertise some of their contractingopportunities.

Audit & Evaluation Branch / Vérification et évaluation

Director General, Linda Anglin
819-956-2971
Director Internal Audit Services Directorate, Basil Orsini
819-956-9396, Fax: 819-956-5868
Director Evaluation Directorate, Tania Mushka
819-956-2978, Fax: 819-956-4488

Consulting & Audit Canada / Conseils et vérification Canada
Tower B, Place de Ville
112 Kent St.
Ottawa, ON K1A 0S5
613-996-0188
CEO, André Auger
Acting Director NCR Operations, Robert Burke
613-947-6078

Corporate Services, Policy & Communications Branch / Services ministériels, politiques et communications
Acting Asst. Deputy Minister, Alain Trépannier
819-956-4056
Acting Director General Communications, Jonathan Massey-Smith
819-956-2304
Acting Director General Corporate Policy & Planning, Jonathan Higdon
819-956-0893
Director General Health, Safety, Security, Emergencies & Administration, Richard Marleau
819-956-3121, Fax: 819-956-4533

Government Information Services Branch / Services d'information du gouvernement
Acting Asst. Deputy Minister, Jane Meyboom-Hardy
613-992-0679
Director General Communications Services, Marc Saint-Pierre
613-992-9218, Fax: 613-998-1450
Director General Consulting Services, Ninon Charlesbois
819-996-0231
Director General Government Services Marketing & Advertising & Exhibitions Program, Paul Fortin
613-996-3004, Fax: 613-992-5980
Director General Industrial Security, Gerry Denault
819-948-1777
Director General Planning & Coordination, René Bolduc
819-943-8425
Director General Public Opinion Research & Advertising Coordination, Laurent Marcoux
613-996-1818, Fax: 613-943-0980
Director General Shared Services Integration, Albert Caro
819-992-3248
Director General Strategic Planning & Transition, David Myer
613-992-2999, Fax: 613-991-1952

Finance, Accounting, Banking & Compensation Branch / Finances, comptabilité, gestion bancaire et rémunération
Responsible for managing the operations of the federal treasury, including issuing Receiver General payments for major government programs as well as maintaining the Accounts of Canada & producing the Government's financial statements.Responsible for providing government-wide accounting & reporting services. Directs the management & delivery of the administration of the public service pension & group insurance plans & maintains accounts for the various pension funds. Focuses inthe financial management & control framework for the Department.

Acting Asst. Deputy Minister Accounting, Banking & Compensation, Renée Jolicoeur
819-956-1936
Acting Asst. Deputy Minister Finance, Mike Hawkes
819-956-7226, Fax: 819-956-5060
Director General Banking & Cash Management, Carol Armatage
819-956-2942, Fax: 819-956-7595
Director General Central Accounting & Reporting, Kim Croucher
819-956-2875, Fax: 819-956-8400
Acting Director General Compensation, Brigitte Fortin
819-956-1936
Acting Director General Financial Operations, Roch Huppé
819-956-1258
Director Cheque Redemption Control Directorate, Gilles Pelletier
418-566-7222, Fax: 418-562-5183
Director Superannuation, Pension Transition & Client Services, Michel Doiron
516-533-5555, Fax: 516-533-5607

Royal Canadian Mint / Monnaie royale canadienne
320 Sussex Dr.
Ottawa, ON K1A 0G8
613-993-3500
www.rcmint.ca
The RCM has two plants located in Ottawa & Winnipeg. Foreign & domestic circulating coinage is manufactured in Winnipeg. The Ottawa facility is responsible for the production of foreign & domestic numismatic products, precious metals &the refining of gold. Reports to government through Public Works & Government Services.

Chair, Max C. Lewis
Acting President/CEO, Marguerite Nadeau
Master of the Mint, Ian E. Bennett
Vice-President & CFO, Richard Neville
613-993-5384
Vice-President Communications, Pam Aung Thin
Acting Vice-President Corporate & Legal Affairs, Lynne Poirier
Chief Operating Officer, Bev Lepine
613-993-0323
Executive Director Foreign Circulation, Peter J. Ho
Executive Director Canadian Circulation, Manon Laplante
Chief Information Officer, Neil Hallum
Director Internal Audit, André Aubrey

Statistics Canada / Statistique Canada
R.H. Coats Bldg., Tunney's Pasture
100 Tunney's Pasture Driveway
Ottawa, ON K1A 0T6
Fax: 877-287-4369
800-263-1136
TDD: 800-363-7629infostats@statcan.ca
www.statscan.ca
Agency of the federal government, headed by the Chief Statistician of Canada which reports to Parliament through the Minister of Industry. As Canada's central statistical agency, it has a mandate to collect, compile, analyse, abstract &publish statistical information relating to the commercial, industrial, financial, social, economic & general activities & condition of the people of Canada; coordinates activities with its federal & provincial partners in the national statisticalsystem to avoid duplication of effort & to ensure the consistency & usefulness of statistics. The agency profiles & measures both social & economic changes in Canada. It presents a comprehensive picture of the national economy through statistics onmanufacturing, agriculture, retail sales, services, prices, productivity changes, trade, transportation, employment & unemployment, & aggregate measures such as gross domestic product. It also presents a comprehensive picture of social conditionsthrough statistics on demography, health, areas.

Acts Administered:
Corporations Returns Act
Statistics Act
Chief Statistician of Canada, Dr. Ivan P. Fellegi
613-951-9757, Fax: 613-951-4842
Departmental Secretary, J. Morin
613-951-9869
Chief Communications Services, Andrée Hébert

Business & Trade Statistics / Statistique du commerce et des entreprises
Director General Economy-Wide Statistics, L.M. Ducharme
613-951-0688
Asst. Chief Statistician, R. Ryan
613-951-9493, Fax: 613-951-3231
Director General Industry Statistics, P. Lys
613-951-4071
Director General Agriculture, Technology & Transportation Statistics Branch, M. Dion
613-951-3528

Management Services Field / Services de gestion
Asst. Chief Statistician, P. Johanis
613-951-9866, Fax: 613-951-5290
Director General Finance, Planning, Audit & Evaluation, C. Falconer
613-951-1440
Director General Human Resources, C. Coffey
613-951-9955
Director Data Access & Control Services, P. Giles
613-951-2891
Manager Corporate Management Information Systems, G. Labelle
613-951-2361

National Accounts & Analytical Studies / Études analytiques et comptes nationaux
Asst. Chief Statistician & Acting Director General, Analytical Studies, P. Smith
613-951-9760, Fax: 613-951-5290
Director General System of National Accounts, K. Wilson
613-951-0439

Treasury Board of Canada / Conseil du Trésor du Canada
300 Laurier Ave. West, 10th Fl.
Ottawa, ON K1A 0R5
613-957-2400
Fax: 613-998-9071
877-636-0656
TDD: 613-957-9090www.tbs-sct.gc.ca
The Treasury Board is a Cabinet Committee of government headed by the President of the Treasury Board. The committee constituting the Treasury Board includes, in addition to the President, the Minister of Finance & four other ministersappointed by the Governor-in-Council. The main role of the Treasury Board is the management of the government's financial, personnel & administrative responsibilities. The Treasury Board derives its authority primarily from the *FinancialAdministration Act & is supported by the Treasury Board Secretariat.*

Acts Administered:
Alternative Fuels Act
Federal Real Property & Federal Immovables Act
President, Hon. John Baird
613-957-2666, Fax: 613-990-2806
Parliamentary Secretary, Pierre Poilievre
Secretary, Wayne Wouters
613-952-1777, Fax: 613-952-6596
Senior Associate Secretary, Robert Fonberg
Comptroller General, Charles-Antoine St-Jean
613-957-7820
Assoc. Secretary, Linda Lizotte-MacPherson
613-941-1843
Asst. Deputy Minister Corporate Services, Coleen Volk
613-995-8487
Asst. Secretary Economic Sector, Helen McDonald
613-957-0556
Asst. Secretary Management Policy & Labour Relations, Hèléne Laurendeau
613-952-3000
Contact Office of the Asst. Deputy Minister, Marina Brisebois
613-992-1483, Fax: 613-947-3643, Brisebois.Marina@fin.gc.ca

Associated Agencies, Boards & Commissions:

• Public Sector Pension Investment Board / Office d'investissement des régimes de pensions du secteur public
#200, 440 Laurier Ave. West
Ottawa, ON K1R 7X6
613-782-3095
Fax: 613-782-6864
info@investpsp.ca
www.investpsp.ca
Crown corporation established by Parliament by the Public Sector Pension Investment Board Act (September 1999). The mandate of PSP Investments is to manage employer & employee contributions made after April 1, 2000 to the federal PublicService, the Canadian Forces & the Royal Canadian Mounted Police pension funds.

• Public Service Human Resources Management Agency of Canada (PSHRMAC) / Agence de gestion des ressources humaines de la fonction publique du Canada (AGRHFPC)
L'esplanade Laurier, West Tower
300 Laurier Ave. West, 5th Fl.
Ottawa, ON K1A 0R3
800-622-6232
TDD: 800-926-9105hr-info-rh@hrma-agrh.gc.ca
Created in 2003 to put in place a new human resources management regime in the public service of Canada.~

• Public Service Labour Relations Board / Commission des relations de travail dans la fonction publique
240 Sparks St., 6th Fl.
PO Box 1525 B
Ottawa, ON K1P 5V2
613-990-1800
Fax: 613-990-1849
www.pslrb-crtfp.gc.ca
Independent, quasi-judicial statutory tribunal responsible for administering the collective bargaining & grievance adjudication systems in the federal Public & Parliamentary Service. Also provides mediation & conflict resolution services,compensation analysis & research services.

Office of the Registrar of Lobbyists
255 Albert St., 10th Fl.
Ottawa, ON K1A 0R5
613-957-2760
Fax: 613-957-3078
Registrar, Michael Nelson
Director, Karen Shepherd

Western Economic Diversification Canada (WD) / Diversification de l'économie de l'Ouest Canada (DEO)

Canada Place
#1500, 9700 Jasper Ave. NW
Edmonton, AB T5J 4H7
780-495-4164
Fax: 780-495-4557
888-338-9378
www.wd.gc.ca
Responsible for promoting economic growth & diversification in the West. By investing in innovation, fostering entrepreneurship & using partnerships to enhance community sustainability, WD is helping to create a more prosperous futurefor western Canadians.Invests in R&D & commercialization in environmental technologies as a focus area for innovation strategies.

Minister, Hon. Carol Skelton
613-954-1110, Fax: 613-957-1155
Deputy Minister, Oryssia Lennie
780-495-5772, Fax: 780-495-6222, Other Communications: Ottawa: 613/952-9382; Fax: 613/954-1044
Director General Corporate Finance & Programs, Jim Saunderson
780-495-4301
Director General Corporate Services, Tim Earle
780-495-3194

Regional Offices

Alberta
Canada Place
#1500, 9700 Jasper Ave. Northwest
Edmonton, AB T5J 4H7
780-495-4164
Fax: 780-495-4557
888-338-9378
Asst. Deputy Minister, Doug Maley
780-495-4168

British Columbia
Price Waterhouse Bldg.
#700, 333 Seymour St.
Vancouver, BC V6B 5G9
604-666-6256
Fax: 604-666-2353
888-338-9378
Asst. Deputy Minister, Ardath Paxton Mann
604-666-6366

Calgary
#400, 639 - 5 Ave. SW
Calgary, AB T2P 0M9
403-292-5458
Fax: 403-292-5487
888-338-9378

Manitoba
The Cargill Bldg.
#712, 240 Graham Ave.
PO Box 777
Winnipeg, MB R3C 2L4
204-983-4472
Fax: 204-983-3852
888-338-9378
Asst. Deputy Minister, Marilyn Kapitany
204-983-5715

Ottawa
#500, 141 Laurier Ave. West
Ottawa, ON K1P 5J3
613-952-2768
Fax: 613-952-9384
Acting Asst. Deputy Minister, Keith Fernandez
613-952-7096

Regina
1925 Rose St., 1st Fl.
Regina, SK S4P 3P1
306-780-8080
Fax: 306-780-8310

Saskatchewan
S.J. Cohen Bldg.
#601, 119 - 4 Ave. South
PO Box 2025
Saskatoon, SK S7K 3S7
306-975-4373
Fax: 306-975-5484
888-338-9378
Asst. Deputy Minister, Daniel Watson
306-975-5858

Government of Alberta

Seat of Government:9718 - 107 St.
Edmonton, AB T5K 1E4
www.gov.ab.ca
The Province of Alberta entered Confederation September 1, 1905. It has an area of 638,232.66 km2, & the StatsCan census population in 2001 was 2,974,807.

Office of the Premier

Legislature Bldg.
#307, 10800 - 97 Ave.
Edmonton, AB T5K 2B6
780-427-2251
Fax: 780-427-1349
www.gov.ab.ca/premier/
Premier, Ed Stelmach
Deputy Premier, Hon. Lyle Oberg
Deputy Minister Executive Council, Ron Hicks
Chief of Staff, Peter Kruselnicki
Deputy Chief of Staff, Gordon Vincent
Director Southern Alberta Office, Rich Jones
403-297-6464
Director Scheduling, Debby Park
Chief Protocol, Betty Anne Spinks
780-422-1542, Fax: 780-422-0786
Director Communications, Marisa Etmanski
780-427-2251
Minister Health & Wellness, Hon. Dave Hancock
780-427-3665
Minister Infrastructure & Transportation, Hon. Luke Ouellette
780-427-2080
Minister Service Alberta, Hon. Lloyd Snelgrove
780-415-4855
Minister International, Intergovernmental & Aboriginal Relations, Hon. Guy Boutilier
780-427-2585
Minister Education, Hon. Ronald Liepert
780-427-5010
Minister Energy, Hon. Mel Knight
780-427-3740
Minister Employment, Immigration & Industry, Hon. Iris Evans
780-415-4800
Minister Environment, Hon. Rob Renner
780-427-2391
Minister Children's Services, Hon. Janis Tarchuk
780-415-4890
Minister Sustainable Resource Development, Hon. Ted Morton
780-415-4815
Minister Municipal Affairs, Hon. Ray Danyluk
780-427-3744
Solicitor General & Minister Public Security, Hon. Fred Lindsay
780-415-9406
Minister Seniors & Community Supports, Hon. Greg Melchin
780-415-9550
Minister Agriculture, Food & Rural Development, Hon. George Groeneveld
780-427-2137
Minister Advanced Education & Technology, Hon. Doug Horner

Executive Council

Legislature Bldg.
10800 - 97 Ave.
Edmonton, AB T5K 2B6
780-427-2251
Fax: 780-427-1349
Acts Administered:
Alberta Bill of Rights
Family Day Act
Queen's Printer Act
Premier & President, Executive Council; Minister Responsible, Public Affairs Bureau, Hon. Ralph Klein
780-427-2251, Fax: 780-427-1349, premier@gov.ab.ca
Minister Finance & Deputy Premier; Chair, Treasury Board, Hon. Shirley McClellan
780-427-8809
Minister Justice & Attorney General, Hon. Ron Stevens
780-427-2339
Minister Health & Wellness, Hon. Iris Evans
780-427-3665
Minister Infrastructure & Transportation, Hon. Ty Lund
780-415-4855
Minister International & Intergovernmental Relations, Hon. Gary G. Mar
780-427-4928
Minister Economic Development, Hon. Clint Dunford
780-427-3162
Minister Education, Hon. Gene Zwozdesky
780-427-5010
Minister Energy, Hon. Greg Melchin
780-427-3440
Minister Human Resources & Employment & Minister Responsible, Personnel Administration Office, Hon. Mike Cardinal
780-415-4800
Minister Environment, Hon. Guy Boutilier
780-427-2391
Minister Children's Services, Hon. Heather Forsyth
780-415-4890
Minister Sustainable Resource Development, Hon. David Coutts
780-415-4815
Minister Aboriginal Affairs & Northern Development, Hon. Pearl Calahasen
780-427-2180, Fax: 780-427-1321
Minister Gaming, Hon. Gordon Graydon
780-415-4894
Minister Municipal Affairs, Hon. Rob Renner
780-427-3744
Minister Restructuring & Government Efficiency, Hon. Luke Ouellette
780-422-7355
Solicitor General & Minister, Public Security, Hon. Harvey Cenaiko
780-415-9406
Minister Seniors & Community Supports, Hon. Yvonne Fritz
780-415-9550
Minister Agriculture, Food & Rural Development, Hon. Doug Horner
780-427-2137
Minister Advanced Education, Hon. Denis Herard
Minister Community Development, Hon. Denis Ducharme
Minister Government Services & Acting Minister, Innovation & Science, Hon. George Vanderburg
Minister Responsible Capital Planning & Assoc. Minister, Infrastructure & Transportation, Hon. Barry McFarland
Administrative Officer, Elaine Usher
780-427-1076, Fax: 780-427-0305, elaine.usher@gov.ab.ca

Alberta Agriculture, Food & Rural Development

J.G. O'Donoghue Bldg.
7000 - 113 St.
Edmonton, AB T6H 5T6
780-427-2727
Fax: 780-427-2861
866-882-7677
duke@gov.ab.ca

www.agric.gov.ab.ca
Other Communication: Publications Office: 780/427-0391, Toll Free: 1-800-292-5697
The Ministry is comprised of the Department of Agriculture, Food & Rural Development; Agriculture Financial Services Corporation; Farmers' Advocate; Irrigation Council; Agricultural Products Marketing Council; & Alberta Grain Commission.Major responsibilities are industry growth, rural sustainability, safety nets, food safety & rural development.The ministry contributes to industry growth through facilitating new product development (primary & value-added food & non-food products),enhanced market access for agriculture & food industry products & improved food industry business services, including access to capital, risk management tools, business & entrepreneurial processes, & enhanced infrastructure.

Acts Administered:
Agricultural Operations Practices Act
Agricultural Pest Act
Pest & Nuisance Control Regulation
Agricultural Services Board Act
Agricultural Societies Act
Agriculture Financial Services Act
Alberta Wheats & Barley Test Market Act
Animal Keepers Act
Animal Protection Act
Bee Act
Brand Act
Crop Liens Priorities Act
Crop Payments Act
Dairy Industry Act
Farm Credit Stability Fund Act
Farm Implement Act
Farm Implement Dealerships Act
Federal-Provincial Farm Assistance Act
Feeder Associations Guarantee Act
Fuel Tax Act
Fur Farms Act & Regulation
Gas Distribution Act
Government Organization Act
Horned Cattle Purchases Act
Irrigation Districts Act
Irrigation Forms Regulation
Irrigation Plebiscite Regulation
Irrigation Seepage Claims Exemption Regulation
Line Fence Act
Livestock Diseases Act
Destruction & Disposal of Dead Animals Regulation
Designated Communicable Diseases Regulation
Livestock Disease Control Regulation
Livestock Market & Assembly Station Regulation
Production Animal Medicine Regulation
Livestock Identification & Brand Inspection Act
Livestock Industry Diversification Act
Livestock & Livestock Products Act
Marketing of Agricultural Products Act
Meat Inspection Act
Natural Gas Rebates Act
Rural Electrification Loan Act
Rural Electrification Long Term Financing Act
Rural Utilities Act
Soil Conservation Act
Stray Animals Act
Weed Control Act
Seed Cleaning Plant Regulations
Weed Designation Regulations
Wheat Board Money Trust Act
Women's Institute Act
Agrologist Act (Human Resources & Employment)
Expropriation Act (Sustainable Resource Development)
Surface Rights Act (Sustainable Resource Development)
Universities Act (Section 64)
Veterinary Profession Act (Human Resources & Employment)
Water Act (Alberta Environment)
Minister, Hon. Doug Horner
780-427-2137, Fax: 780-422-6035
Deputy Minister, Barry Mehr
780-427-2145, Fax: 780-415-6002, barry.mehr@gov.ab.ca
Executive Director Agriculture Information Division, Bard Haddrell
780-427-2727, Fax: 780-427-2861, bard.haddrell@gov.ab.ca
Executive Director Human Resource Services, Holly Stengel
780-422-4623, Fax: 780-427-2794, holly.stengel@gov.ab.ca
Director Communications, Terry Willock
780-422-7099, Fax: 780-427-2861, terry.willock@gov.ab.ca
Division Administrator, Lillian Chan
780-422-0492, Fax: 780-427-2861, lillian.chan@agric.ab.ca

Associated Agencies, Boards & Commissions:
• Agricultural Products Marketing Council
7000 - 113 St., 3rd Fl.
Edmonton, AB T6H 5T6
780-427-2164
Fax: 780-422-9690
www.agric.gov.ab.ca
• Agriculture Finance Corporation (AFSC)
5718 - 56 Ave.
Lacombe, AB T4L 1B1
403-782-8200
Fax: 403-782-4226
800-396-0215
www.afsc.ca
• Alberta Grain Commission
7000 - 113 St., 3rd Fl.
Edmonton, AB T6H 5T6
780-427-7329
Fax: 780-422-9690
www.agric.gov.ab.ca
• Farmers' Advocate of Alberta
7000 - 113 St., 3rd Fl.
Edmonton, AB T6H 5T6
780-427-2433
Fax: 780-427-3913
www1.agric.gov.ab.ca/$department/deptdocs.nss/all/ofa2621
• Irrigation Council
Provincial Bldg.
200 - 5 Ave. South, 3rd Fl., PO Bag 3014
Lethbridge, AB T1J 4L1
403-381-5176
Fax: 403-382-4406
www.agric.gov.ab.ca

Planning & Competitiveness Sector
Asst. Deputy Minister, Colin Jeffares
780-427-1957, Fax: 780-422-6317, colin.jeffares@gov.ab.ca
Director Economics & Competititveness Division, Vacant
780-422-3771, Fax: 780-427-5220
Director Information Technology Services, Lorie Baddock
780-427-2101, Fax: 780-422-4004, lorie.baddock@gov.ab.ca
Director Policy Secretariat, Nithi Govindasamy
780-422-2070, Fax: 780-422-6540, nithi.godindasamy@gov.ab.ca
Director Strategy & Business Planning, Lloyd Andruchow
780-422-9167, Fax: 780-427-5921, lloyd.andruchow@gov.ab.ca

Alberta Office of the Auditor General
9925 - 109 St., 8th Fl.
Edmonton, AB T5K 2J8
780-427-4222
Fax: 780-422-9555
www.oag.ab.ca
Auditor General, Fred J. Dunn, FCA
fdunn@oag.ab.ca
Asst. Auditor General, Jim Hug, CA
jhug@oag.ab.ca
Asst. Auditor General, Merwan Saher, CA
msaher@oag.ab.ca
Asst. Auditor General, Doug Wylie, CMA
dwylie@oag.ab.ca
Asst. Auditor General, Ronda White, CA
rwhite@oag.ab.ca
Communications Coordinator, Lori Trudgeon
780-422-6655, ltrudgeon@oag.ab.ca

Alberta Economic Development
Commerce Place , 6th Fl.
10155 - 102 St.
Edmonton, AB T5J 4L6
780-415-1319
Fax: 780-415-1759
www.aed.gov.ab.ca
Other Communication: www.alberta-canada.com
Alberta Economic Development (AED) works in partnership with the Alberta Economic Development Authority, business, industry associations, other provincial departments & governments to provide information & competitive intelligence,support business, expand trade, production & services. AED maintains a presence in key international regions through a network of nine international offices. The department markets the Alberta Advantage internationally as a desirable location forinvestment or businesses, in addition to marketing the province's exports & company capabilities.

Acts Administered:
Access to the Future Act
Agricultural Societies Act
Alberta Centennial Education Savings Plan Act
Alberta Economic Development Authority Act
Alberta Heritage Scholarship Act
Alberta School Boards Association Act
Apprenticeship & Industry Training Act
Northland School Division Act
Government Organization Act
Post-secondary Learning Act
Private Vocational Schools Act
Remembrance Day Act
School Act
Student Financial Assistance Act
Teachers' Pension Plans Act
Teaching Profession Act
Telecommunications Act
Minister, Hon. Clint Dunford
780-422-3162, Fax: 780-422-6338
Deputy Minister, Rory Campbell
780-427-0662, Fax: 780-427-2852, rory.campbell@gov.ab.ca
Director Corporate Communications, Janice Schroeder
780-427-0528, Fax: 780-427-1529
Senior Communications Manager, Cheryl Mackenzie
780-415-4750, Fax: 780-427-1529
Asst. to the SFO, Rosanna Chung
780-415-8184, Fax: 780-422-9319, rosanna.chung@gov.ab.ca

Associated Agencies, Boards & Commissions:
• Alberta Film Commission
10155 - 102 St., 5th Fl.
Edmonton, AB T5J 4L6
780-422-8584
Fax: 780-422-8582
888-813-1738
• Alberta Economic Development Authority (AEDA)
McDougall Centre
455 - 6 St. SW
Calgary, AB T2P 4E8
403-297-3022
Fax: 403-297-6435
www.alberta-canada.com/aeda/
• Strategic Tourism Marketing Council
#500, 999 - 8 St. SW
Calgary, AB T2J 1J5
403-297-2700
Fax: 403-297-5068
www.travelalberta.com

Business Planning & Knowledge Management
Executive Director, Susan Cribbs
780-422-1290, Fax: 780-422-9319
Manager Business Planning & Performance Measures, Kathleen Blake
780-427-6251, Fax: 780-422-9319
Manager Corporate Issues, Joanna Lamb
780-415-0929, Fax: 780-422-9319
Director Human Resources, Georgina Riddell
780-422-1341, Fax: 780-427-1272

International Offices & Trade Division
Fax: 780-427-0392
Asst. Deputy Minister, Drury Mason
780-427-3325

Advanced Industries
Fax: 403-297-6168
Executive Director, Chris Heseltine
403-297-6377
Senior Trade Director North America & Europe & Team Leader, Heli Carswell
780-427-6386
Team Director North America & Europe, Carmen Killick
780-427-6079
Trade Director North America & Europe, Orest Warchola
780-427-6257
Senior Trade Director Asia & Team Leader, Josephine Choi
403-297-8916
Trade Director Asia, Sylvia Roach
403-297-8919

Agriculture & Food Branch
Fax: 780-422-9746
Executive Director, Jeff Kucharski
780-427-6008
Senior Trade Director Americas & Europe & Team Leader, Penny Mah
780-422-7839
Senior Trade Director Asia & Emerging Markets & Team Leader, John Larson
780-422-7090
Manager Projects & Strategic Information, Doug McMullen
780-427-4249, doug.mcmullen@gov.ab.ca
Trade Director, Jidong Cheng
780-644-2403
Trade Director, Chenier LaSalle
780-422-7195
Trade Director, Rachel Lud
780-422-7102
Trade Director, Angela Lum
780-422-7105
Trade Director, Donna Mauro
780-422-7103
Trade Director, Marcia O'Connor
780-422-1762
Trade Director, Karin Teubert
780-644-4628

Energy Industries & Services
Fax: 780-422-9127
Executive Director, John Cotton
780-422-2789
Senior Trade Director Eastern Hemisphere & Team Leader, Greg Jardine
780-427-6368
Senior Trade Director Western Hemisphere & Team Leader, Benigno Rojas-Moreno
780-427-0794
Trade Director, Norm Morrison
780-427-6421
Manager International Financial Institutions, Shane Jaffer
403-297-6592

International Trade Operations
Executive Director, Stan Fisher
780-427-6628
Financed International Office Liaison, Scott Kennedy
780-427-6239
Mission Planning Coordinator, Doug Cameron
780-427-6702
Strategic Projects, Quinn Goretzky
780-427-6057
Manager Intergovernmental Relations, Hazel Cail
780-427-6256

Industry & Regional Development Division
Fax: 780-422-0626
The Investment & Industry Development is the ministry's investment attraction marketing team as well as an advocate & catalyst for new investment, increased competitiveness, diversification & leading-edge innovation within key Albertamanufacturing & service sectors. The branch partners with private sector & other stakeholders to work on projects to increase competitiveness, opportunities & mitigate logistical & other constraints to development.~The Regional Development Branchencourages economic & business growth in all regions throughout the province. Support is provided to local economic development authorities, municipalities, & other regional stakeholders to facilitate better business decisions & long-term economicviability for their region. The branch consists of a program development unit in Edmonton & a network of ten regional offices. Focus is on key business aspects of information, encouraging development opportunities & networking.

Asst. Deputy Minister, Rick Sloan
780-427-6987
Executive Director Economic Strategy Implementation, Maryann Everett
780-422-9493, Fax: 780-422-0061
Executive Director, Justin Riemer
780-427-6302, Fax: 780-422-2091
Executive Director Regional Development, Rick Siddle
780-427-6656, Fax: 780-422-5804
Alberta Film Commissioner, Dan Chugg
780-422-8581, Fax: 780-422-8582

Policy & Economic Analysis
Fax: 780-422-0061
Executive Director, Duane Pyear
780-427-0850
Director Business Information & Research, Fred McMullan
780-422-1063, Fax: 780-422-0061
Director Information Technology, Carol Lawrence
780-427-0269, Fax: 780-427-4625
Director Policy Coordination, Terry Duffy
780-427-0861, Fax: 780-422-0061
Director Information Management, Brian Payne
780-427-6678, Fax: 780-427-4625

Policy Coordination
Director, Terry Duffy
780-427-0861
Manager Economic Planning, Paul McFadzen
780-422-2743

Office of the Senior Financial Officer
Senior Financial Officer, Anthony Lemphers
780-427-8099, Fax: 780-422-9319
Director Financial Services, Mike Shyluk
780-427-1555, Fax: 780-422-1789

Tourism Marketing & Development Division
Asst. Deputy Minister, Bob Scott
780-415-0892, Fax: 780-427-6454

Tourism Development Branch
Fax: 780-427-0778
The branch facilitates the growth & expansion of tourism by providing a range of information & advisory resources to assist clients of new & expanded tourism projects. Services are organized under three areas, Resource Management &Development, Product Development & Enhancement & Tourism Business Development. The three units of the Branch also undertake industry advocacy roles pertaining to different issues that impact the province's tourism industry.
Executive Director, Louise McGillivray
780-427-6638
Managing Director Travel Alberta, Derek Coke-Kerr
403-297-2700, Fax: 403-297-5068
Director Product & Destination Development, Kevin Crockett
780-427-6676
Director Tourism Business Development Investment, Moe Rehemtulla
780-427-6689
Director Tourism Services, Stephen Hill
780-427-6743, Fax: 780-415-0896

Alberta Education
Commerce Place
10155 - 102 St., 7th Fl.
Edmonton, AB T5J 4L5
780-427-7219
Fax: 780-427-0591
www.education.gov.ab.ca
Responsible for the delivery of basic education programs in Alberta. The Basic Learning Division supports school authorities & learners up to Grade 12 by developing & setting standards, evaluating curriculums, certificating teachers &supporting students with diverse needs.

Acts Administered:
Alberta School Boards Association Act
Government Organization Act, Schedules 4
Northland School Division Act
Private Vocational Schools Act
Remembrance Day Act
School Act
Teaching Profession Act
Minister, Hon. Gene Zwozdesky
780-427-5010, Fax: 780-427-5018, education.minister@gov.ab.ca
Deputy Minister, Keray Henke
780-427-3659, Fax: 780-427-7733, keray.henke@gov.ab.ca
Director Communications, Kathy Telfer
780-422-4495, Fax: 780-427-0591

Associated Agencies, Boards & Commissions:
• Alberta Teachers' Retirement Fund Board
Barnett House
#600, 11010 - 142 St.
Edmonton, AB T5N 2R1
780-451-4166
Fax: 780-452-3547
800-661-9582
info@atrf.com
www.atrf.com
• Council on Alberta Teaching Standards
10044 - 108 St.
Edmonton, AB T5J 5E6
780-427-2045
Fax: 780-422-4199
www.teachingquality.ab.ca

Corporate Services Division
Fax: 780-415-8938
Asst. Deputy Minister, Mat Hanrahan
780-427-2051, Fax: 780-415-8938, mat.hanrahan@gov.ab.ca
Executive Director Finance & Strategic Services Sector, Jeff Olson
780-427-2055, Fax: 780-422-6996, jeff.olson@gov.ab.ca
Director Human Resource Services, John Bergin
780-422-5323, Fax: 780-422-5362, john.bergin@gov.ab.ca

Alberta Office of the Ethics Commissioner
#1250, 9925 - 109 St.
Edmonton, AB T5K 2J8
780-422-2273
Fax: 780-422-2261
www.ethicscommissioner.ab.ca
Acts Administered:
Alberta Conflicts of Interest Act
Alberta Ethics Commissioner, Donald M. Hamilton
Other Communications: EMail: generalinfo@ethicscommissioner.ab.ca
Senior Administrator, Karen South
780-422-2273, ksouth@ethicscommissioner.ab.ca
Senior Adminstrator, Karen South
780-422-2273, ksouth@ethicscommissioner.ab.ca

Alberta Finance
Terrace Bldg.
9515 - 107 St.
Edmonton, AB T5K 2C3
780-427-3035
Fax: 780-427-1147
www.finance.gov.ab.ca
Acts Administered:
Alberta Corporate Tax Act
Alberta Heritage Savings Trust Fund Act
Alberta Income Tax Act
Alberta Personal Income Tax Act
Alberta Municipal Financing Corporation Act
Alberta Securities Commission Reorganization Act
Alberta Stock Savings Plan Act
Alberta Taxpayer Protection Act
Alberta Treasury Branches Act
Appropriation Acts
Balanced Budget & Debt Retirement Act
Civil Services Garnishee Act
Credit Union Act
Employment Pensions Plan Act
Farm Credit Stability Fund Act
Financial Administration Act
Financial Consumers Act
Fiscal Responsibility Act
Government Accountability Act
Government Emergency Guarantee Act
Government Fees & Charges Review Act
Insurance Act
Loan & Trust Corporations Act
Lottery Fund Transfer Act
Members of the Legislative Assembly Pension Plan Act
Municipal Debentures Act
Pari Mutuel Tax Act
Pension Fund Act
Provincial Court Judges Act
Public Sector Pension Plans Act
Securities Act
Small Business Term Assistance Fund Act
Statistics Bureau Act
Telecommunications Act
Minister, Hon. Shirley McClellan
780-427-8809

Deputy Minister Finance, Brian Manning
780-427-4106, Fax: 780-427-0178
Asst. Deputy Minister Pensions, Insurance & Financial Institutions, Dennis Gartner
780-427-9722, Fax: 780-427-1636
Director Communications, Marie Iwanow
780-422-2126
Office Manager, Toni-Lee Johnstone
780-415-8865, Fax: 780-427-1147, toni-lee.johnstone@gov.ab.ca

Associated Agencies, Boards & Commissions:

• Alberta Capital Finance Authority
2450 Canadian Western Bank Place
10303 Jasper Ave.
Edmonton, AB T5J 3N6
780-427-9711
Fax: 780-422-2175
webacfa@gov.ab.ca
www.acfa.gov.ab.ca
To provide local authorities within the Province of Alberta with funding for capital projects at the lowest possible cost, consistent with the viability of the Alberta Capital Finance Authority; a non-profit corporation established in1956 under the authority of the *Alberta Capital Finance Authority Act, Chapter A-14.5, Revised Statutes of Alberta 2000 , as amended.*

• Alberta Pensions Administration Corporation
Park Plaza, 3rd Fl.
10611 - 98 Ave.
Edmonton, AB T5K 2P7
780-427-2782
Fax: 780-427-1621
800-661-8198
apa.info@apa.gov.ab.ca
www.apaco.ab.ca
Responsible for the administration of the Public Sector Pension Plans Act; administering eight statutory pension plans under the direction of five pension boards & the Government of Alberta. The APA provides services to about 500employees, 50,500 pensioners & 130,400 members.

• Alberta Securities Commission
300 - 5 Ave. SW, 4th Fl.
Calgary, AB T2P 3C4
403-297-6454
Fax: 403-297-6156
877-355-0585
inquiries@seccom.ab.ca
www.albertasecurities.com
An industry-funded provincial corporation responsible for regulating Alberta's capital market. The Commission performs its responsibilities under the *Securities Act* .

• ATB Financial
9888 Jasper Ave.
Edmonton, AB T5J 1P1
Offers Albertans financial services on a commercial, non-subsidized basis; provides a wide range of deposit & loan products, including mutual funds, online transactions, ABMs; an arms-length organization that reports to the Minister ofFinance.

• Automobile Insurance Rate Board
Terrace Bldg.
#200, 9515 - 107 St. NW
Edmonton, AB T5K 2C3
780-427-5428
Fax: 780-644-7771
airb@gov.ab.ca
www.airb.gov.ab.ca

• Credit Union Deposit Guarantee Corporation
10130 - 103 St., 18th Fl.
Edmonton, AB T5J 3N9
780-428-6680
Fax: 780-428-7571
800-661-0351
mail@cudgc.ab.ca
www.cudgc.ab.ca
Monitors & regulates the performance of credit unions in Alberta & the compliance of Alberta credit unions with the Credit Union Act. The primary role of the Corporation is to guarantee deposit protection to deposit holders with creditunions in Alberta.

Budget & Management Office

Executive Director Budget & Business Planning, Mike Wevers
780-427-8741
Executive Director Economics & Public Finance, Tony Morehen
780-427-7543, Fax: 780-422-2164
Executive Director Financial Accounting & Standards, Gisele Simard
780-415-9253, Fax: 780-422-2164
Executive Director Performance Measurement, Murray Lyle
780-427-7784
Executive Director Tax Policy & Acting Controller, Nancy Cuelenaere
780-427-8893, Fax: 780-426-4564

Financial Institutions

Deputy Superintendent Financial Institutions & Insurance, James Flett
780-415-4223, Fax: 780-422-2175

Insurance

Deputy Superintendent Insurance & Financial Institutions, Arthur Hagan
780-415-9226

Investment Management

Chief Investment Officer, Jai Parihar
780-427-3089, Fax: 780-425-9153
Director Debt Operations, Dale MacMaster
780-427-7981, Fax: 780-427-9725
Director Equities, Kirby O'Connor
780-422-5625, Fax: 780-427-2992
Director Portfolio Analysis & Research, John Osborne
780-415-0653, Fax: 780-427-5136
Director External Fund Management, David Finstad
780-427-7983, Fax: 780-425-9153

Risk Management & Insurance

Acting Director, Mark Day
780-644-4045
Senior Manager, David Buzzeo
780-644-4041

Strategic & Business Services

Executive Director, Bonnie Lovelace
780-427-3052, Fax: 780-427-0178
Director Human Resource Services, Herb Martin
780-415-9109, Fax: 780-422-0421

Tax & Revenue Administration

Asst. Deputy Minister, Lukas Huisman
780-427-3044
Director Audit, Paul Lefebvre
780-644-4242, Fax: 780-422-2090
Director Business Technology Management, Rick Callaway
780-644-4164, Fax: 780-422-0899
Director Tax Services, Angelina Leung
780-644-4064, Fax: 780-427-5074

Alberta Government Services

Commerce Place
10155 - 102 St.
Edmonton, AB T5J 4L4
780-427-4088
government.services@gov.ab.ca
www.gov.ab.ca/gs
Partners with governments, stakeholders & business to provide a secure, high-quality & innovative gateway to a wide range of registry & related services; facilitate, support, regulate & enforce high standards of consumer protection &business practices; provide information management & privacy support to public bodies administering *Freedom of Information & Protection of Privacy legislation; & support the regulatory review secretariat in its mandate to reduce regulatory redtape & complexity throughout government.*

Acts Administered:
Agricultural & Recreational Land Ownership Act
Business Corporation Act
Cemeteries Act
Cemetery Companies Act
Change of Name Act
Charitable Fund-Raising Act
Companies Act
Condominium Property Act
Cooperatives Act
Cooperative Associations Act
Debtors' Assistance Act
Dower Act
Fair Trading Act
Franchises Act
Freedom of Information & Protection of Privacy Act
Funeral Services Act
Garage Keepers' Lien Act
Government Organization Act, Schedule 11, Schedule 12, s. 2,3 & 4, & Sch.13, s. 2 & 3)
Land Titles Act
Law of Property Act
Marriage Act
Mobile Home Sites Tenancies Act
Motor Vehicle Accident Claims Act, Section 2 & 3
Partnership Act
Personal Information Protection Act
Personal Property Security Act (except Part 5)
Possessory Liens Act
Real Estate Act
Religious Societies' Land Act
Residential Tenancies Act
Societies Act
Surveys Act, Section 5(1)(d) & (2)(b) shared with Alberta Sustainable Development
Traffic Safety Act
Vital Statistics Act
Warehousemen's Lien Act
Woodmen's Lien Act

Minister, Hon. George VanderBurg
Deputy Minister, Robert Bhatia
780-427-0621, Fax: 780-427-0902, government.services@gov.ab.ca
Administrative Assistant Communications, Beth McKinley
780-422-8811, Fax: 780-422-8621, beth.mckinley@gov.ab.ca

Consumer Services & Land Titles

Commerce Place
10155 - 102 St., 3rd Fl.
Edmonton, AB T5J 4L4
Other Communication: Consumer Information Line: 780/427-4088; 1-877-427-4088~
Responsible for consumer services, call centre & land titles.

Asst. Deputy Minister, Laurie Beveridge
780-427-4095, Fax: 780-422-0818
Executive Director Consumer Services, Rob Phillips
780-422-8158, Fax: 780-427-0418
Executive Director Land Titles, Rae Runge
780-427-5166, Fax: 780-422-3105
Director Call Centre, Gary Peckham
780-401-4012, Fax: 780-401-4088

Service Alberta & Registries

John E. Brownlee Bldg.
10365 - 97 St.
Edmonton, AB T5J 3W7
780-415-6090
Other Communication: Registries Info Line: 780/427-7013
Responsible for Service Alberta, motor vehicles, corporate registry, vital statistics & personal property registry.

Asst. Deputy Minister, Wilma Haas
780-415-6092, Fax: 780-422-8151
Acting Executive Director Motor Vehicles & Executive Director, Personal Property Registry, Vital Statistics, Corporate Registry, Doug Morrison
780-427-0108, Fax: 780-415-0469
Executive Director Service Alberta, Marsha Capell
780-427-1075, Fax: 780-416-0469
Executive Director Strategic Partnerships, Laura Cameron
780-427-0937, Fax: 780-422-0665

Capital Projects

Asst. Deputy Minister, Barry Day
780-427-3835, Fax: 780-422-7599
Executive Director Capital Programs, Mike Irving
780-422-7224, Fax: 780-427-5816
Executive Director Program Management, Alan Humphries
780-415-1339, Fax: 780-422-4749
Executive Director Project Delivery, Diane Dalgleish
780-422-0770, Fax: 780-422-9749
Executive Director Technical Services, Tom O'Neill
780-422-7447, Fax: 780-422-7479, tom.oneill@gov.ab.ca
Director Divisional Coordination, Roberta Killips
780-415-0678, Fax: 780-422-7599, roberta.killips@gov.ab.ca

GOVERNMENT

Alberta International & Intergovernmental Relations

Commerce Place
10155 - 102 St., 12th Fl.
Edmonton, AB T5J 4G2
780-422-1510
Fax: 780-423-6654
www.iir.gov.ab.ca

The goal of Alberta's International & Intergovernmental Relations (IIR) ministry is to secure Alberta's future well being & to provide leadership in the management of Alberta's international & intergovernmental relationships. Development& implementation of these strategies & policies require close cooperation with other Alberta ministries, federal, provincial & territorial governments in Canada, as well as strategic partnerships with public & private organizations.The IIR advancesAlberta's interests through intergovernmental negotiations & discussions, coordinating Alberta's strategies relating to international & intergovernmental relations, providing strategic advice & policy analysis, obtaining, disseminating & analyzinginformation on behalf of Alberta's ministries & other clients. The department's key goals are promoting the interests of, & securing benefits for Alberta in Canada, international relations, trade & investment liberalization, domestically &internationally.

Acts Administered:
Constitutional Referendum Act
International Trade & Investment Agreements Implementation Act
Senatorial Selection Act
Statutes Amendment Act, 1995 (Provisions related to the Agreement on Internal Trade)

Minister, Hon. Gary G. Mar
780-427-2585, Fax: 780-422-9023
Deputy Minister, Gerry Bourdeau
780-427-6644, Fax: 780-423-6654, gerry.bourdeau@gov.ab.ca
Director Communications, Carol Chawrun
780-422-2465, carol.chawrun@gov.ab.ca
Executive Director Corporate Services, Lorne Harvey
780-422-2429, Fax: 780-427-0939, lorne.harvey@gov.ab.ca
Administrative Assistant Communications, Deb Broughton
780-422-2462, Fax: 780-423-6654, deb.broughton@gov.ab.ca

International Relations

Fax: 780-427-0699
Asst. Deputy Minister, Wayne Clifford
780-422-2294, wayne.clifford@gov.ab.ca
Executive Director Smithsonian Project, Steve Pritchard
780-427-4897, steve.pritchard@gov.ab.ca
Executive Director U.S. Relations, Marvin Schneider
780-422-2332, marvin.schneider@gov.ab.ca
Director Asia Pacific, Yvette Ng
780-422-2305, yvette.ng@gov.ab.ca
Director Europe, Africa, Middle East & Coordination Services, Vacant
780-422-2359
Assoc. Director Asia Pacific, Kim Mah
780-427-4605, kim.mah@gov.ab.ca
Assoc. Director Coordination, Emly Anderson
780-415-8397, emly.anderson@gov.ab.ca
Assoc. Director AWO, Neelam Chawla
202-448-6273, neelam.chawla@gov.ab.ca
Acting Assoc. Director U.S. Policy Issues, Roisin McCabe
780-422-1935, roisin.mccabe@gov.ab.ca

Trade Policy

Fax: 780-427-0699

The Ministry's Trade Policy section deals with domestic & international trade & investment agreements, negotiations & disputes. It pursues policies that meet Alberta's objectives of reducing trade & investment barriers. The Trade Policysection provides expertise, advice & guidance on agreements such as the Agreement on Internal Trade, the North American Free Trade Agreement, & those developed through the World Trade Organization. These agreements & negotiations cover trade ingoods, agriculture, services, investment, technical barriers & other rules of general application, including dispute settlement.

Acting Alberta Trade Representative, Daryl Hanak
780-422-1339, daryl.hanak@gov.ab.ca
Director Internal Trade, Shawn Robbins
780-422-1129, shawn.robbins@gov.ab.ca
Acting Director Trade-Economic Analysis, Mary Ballantyne
780-422-1133, mary.ballantyne@gov.ab.ca
International Trade Counsel Market Access/Trade Remedies/Technical Barriers, James Doherty
780-422-1137, james.doherty@gov.ab.ca

Alberta Justice & Attorney General

9833 - 109 St.
Edmonton, AB T5K 2E8
780-427-2745
www.justice.gov.ab.ca

To promote safe communities by ensuring access to the courts & other methods of dispute resolution, by providing legal & related strategic services to the Government of Alberta, & by communicating with Albertans about the administrationof justice.

Acts Administered:
Administration of Estates Act
Administrative Procedures Act
Age of Majority Act
Alberta Evidence Act, except Section 9
Alberta Personal Property Bill of Rights
Arbitration Act
Civil Enforcement Act
Commissioners for Oaths Act
Conflicts of Interest Act
Contributory Negligence Act
Court of Appeal Act
Court of Queen's Bench Act
Dangerous Dogs Act
Daylight Saving Time Act
Defamation Act
Devolution of Real Property Act
Domestic Relations Act
Expropriation Act (Sustainable Resource Development)
Extra-provincial Enforcement of Custody Orders Act
Factors Act
Family Relief Act
Fatal Accidents Act
Fatality Inquiries Act
Fraudulent Preferences Act
Frustrated Contracts Act
Government Organization Act, Schedule 9
Guarantees Acknowledgment Act
Innkeepers Act
International Child Abduction Act
International Commercial Arbitration Act
International Conventions Implementation Act
Interpretation Act
Interprovincial Subpoena Act
Intestate Succession Act
Judgement Interest Act
Judicature Act
Jury Act
Justice of the Peace Act
Landlord's Rights on Bankruptcy Act
Languages Act/Loi Linguistique
Legal Profession Act
Legitimacy Act
Limitations Act
Maintenance Enforcement Act
Maintenance Order Act
Married Women's Act
Masters & Servants Act
Matrimonial Property Act
Mechanical Recording of Evidence Act
Minors' Property Act
Notaries Public Act
Oaths of Office Act
Occupiers' Liability Act
Perpetuities Act
Personal Property Security Act, part 5
Petty Trespass Act
Powers of Attorney Act
Proceedings Against the Crown Act
Provincial Court Act
Provincial Court Judges Act
Provincial Offences Procedure Act
Public Inquiries Act
Public Trustee Act
Queen's Counsel Act
Reciprocal Enforcement of Judgements Act
Reciprocal Enforcement of Maintenance Orders Act
Regulations Act
Revised Statutes 1980 Act
Road Building Machinery Equipment Act
Sale of Goods Act
Statute Revision Act
Surrogate Court Act
Survival of Actions Act
Survivorship Act
Tort-Feasors Act
Trespass to Premises Act
Trustee Act
Ultimate Heir Act
Unconscionable Transactions Act
Warehouse Receipts Act
Wills Act
Young Offenders Act

Minister & Attorney General, Hon. Ron Stevens
780-427-2339, Fax: 780-422-6621
Deputy Minister & Deputy Attorney General, Terrence (Terry) J. Matchett, Q.C.
780-427-5032, Fax: 780-422-9639
Executive Director Human Resource Services, Shirley Perras
780-427-9617, Fax: 780-422-9639
Executive Director Maintenance Enforcement Program, Manuel da Costa
780-401-7500, Fax: 780-401-7515
Senior Financial Officer, Shawkat Sabur
780-415-1946, Fax: 780-422-1648
Director Communications, Mark Cooper
780-427-8530
Information Operator, Marion Murdoch
780-427-4978, Fax: 780-427-6821, marion.murdoch@gov.ab.ca

Associated Agencies, Boards & Commissions:
• Alberta Review Board
J.E. Brownlee Bldg.
10365 - 97 St., 5th Fl.
Edmonton, AB T5J 3W7
780-422-5994
Fax: 780-427-1762
• Fatality Review Board
Medical Examiner's Office
4070 Bowness Rd. NW
Calgary, AB T3B 3R7
403-297-8123
Fax: 403-297-3429

Northern Alberta Development Council (NADC)

#206, Provincial Bldg.
9621 - 96 Ave., PO Bag 900-14
Peace River, AB T8S 1T4
780-624-6274
Fax: 780-624-6184
nadc.council@gov.ab.ca
www.nadc.gov.ab.ca

The Northern Alberta Development Council's (NADC) mandate is outlined in the Alberta Act of Legislature. NADC objectives are to identify & implement measures that will advance northern development & advise government on opportunities &issues. Focus is on advancing development of the northern economy. Northern Alberta includes 60% of Alberta's landmass & has 10% of the province's population. It is resource rich, with 90% of Alberta's forests, all of Canada's oil sandsdevelopment, nearly 40% of Alberta's conventional oil & gas activity & 20% of Alberta's agricultural land.

Chair, Ray Danyluk
780-415-9578
Executive Director, Dan Dibbelt
780-624-6277, dan.divvelt@gov.ab.ca
Administrative Team Co-ordinator, Jan Mazurik
780-624-6274, Fax: 780-624-6184, patra.nelson@gov.ab.ca

Northern Development Branch

780-624-6274
Fax: 780-624-6184
Director Projects & Research, Allen Geary
Senior Northern Development Officer, Terry Vulcano
Senior Northern Development Officer, Corinne Huberdeau
Senior Northern Development Officer, Audrey Dewit
Senior Northern Development Officer, Jennifer Bisley
Senior Northern Development Officer, Perry Woodward
Research Officer, Sam Warrior
Research Officer, Kris Rollheiser
Research Officer, Kim Persaud

GOVERNMENT

Alberta Restructuring & Government Efficiency

#319, Legislature Bldg.
10800 - 97 Ave.
Edmonton, AB T5K 2B6
780-422-7355
Fax: 780-422-5279
www.efficiency.gov.ab.ca
Responsible for achieving effectiveness, efficiency, & economy throughout government in the delivery of programs & services to Albertans, & reducing regulations & their complexity. The ministry's four core business functions are:Opportunity & Restructuring Assessment; Business Transformation; Information & Knowledge Management; & Shared Services.

Acts Administered:
Electronic Transactions Act
Government Organization Act
Queen's Printer Act
Minister, Hon. Luke Ouellette
780-422-7355, RGE.Minister@gov.ab.ca
Deputy Minister, Paul Pellis
780-427-1990, Fax: 780-427-4999
Asst. Deputy Minister Financial Services, Brian Fischer
780-427-2214
Asst. Deputy Minister Business Services, Cathyrn Landreth
780-415-8761
Asst. Deputy Minister Technology Services, David Bass
780-427-0033
Executive Director Corporate Human Resources, Linda Moisey
780-427-8352
Director Communications, Lorelei Fiset-Cassidy
780-644-7652, rge.communications@gov.ab.ca
Director Queen's Printer, Sheldon Staszko
780-422-5647

Government of British Columbia

Seat of Government: Parliament Bldgs.
Victoria, BC V8V 1X4
www.gov.bc.ca
The Province of British Columbia entered Confederation July 20, 1871. It has an area of 892,677 km2, & the StatsCan census population in 2001 was 3,907,738.

Office of the Premier

PO Box 9041 Prov Govt
Victoria, BC V8W 9E1
250-387-1715
Fax: 250-387-0087
premier@gov.bc.ca
www.gov.bc.ca/prem
Premier, Hon. Gordon Campbell
Deputy Minister & Cabinet Secretary, Jessica McDonald
250-356-2209
Deputy Minister Strategic Policy, Natural Resources & the Economy, Dana Hayden
250-387-2995
Chief of Staff, Martyn Brown
Deputy Chief of Staff & Executive Assistant to the Premier, Lara Dauphinee
250-387-1715, Other Communications: Fax: 604/775-1600
Deputy Chief of Staff Communications & Research, Steve Vanagas
Deputy Chief of Staff Policy Coordination & Issues Management, Tom Syer
250-387-1715
Press Secretary, Mike Morton

Executive Council

#301, Parliament Bldgs.
Victoria, BC V8V 1X4
www.gov.bc.ca
Premier, Hon. Gordon Campbell
250-387-1715, Fax: 250-387-0087
Minister of State Intergovernmental Relations, Hon. John van Dongen
250-387-1023, Fax: 250-387-1522
Minister Children & Family Development, Hon. Tom Christensen
250-387-1977, Fax: 250-387-3200
Minister Advanced Education & Minister Responsible, Research & Technology, Hon. Murray Coell
250-387-2283, Fax: 250-356-8508
Minister Agriculture & Lands, Hon Pat Bell
250-953-4100, Fax: 250-356-8294
Attorney General & Minister Responsible, Multiculturalism, Hon. Wally Opal
Minister Tourism, Sport & the Arts, Hon. Stan Hagen
250-356-7750, Fax: 250-356-7292
Minister of State Early Childhood Development, Hon. Linda Reid
250-356-7662, Fax: 250-387-9722
Minister Community Services & Minister Responsible, Seniors' & Women's Issues, Hon. Ida Chong
250-387-1223, Fax: 250-387-4312
Minister Economic Development & Minister Responsible, Asia Pacific Initiative & the Olympics, Hon. Colin Hansen
250-953-3547, Fax: 250-356-9587
Minister Education & Deputy Premier & Minister Responsible, Early Learning & Literacy, Hon. Shirley Bond
250-356-2771, Fax: 250-356-3000
Minister Employment & Income Assistance, Hon. Claude Richmond
Minister Energy, Mines & Petroleum Resources, Hon. Richard Neufeld
250-387-5896, Fax: 250-356-2965
Minister of State Mining, Hon. Kevin Kruger
Minister Environment, Hon. Barry Penner
Minister Finance, Hon. Carole Taylor
Minister Forests & Range & Minister Responsible, Housing, Hon. Rich Coleman
250-356-7717, Fax: 250-356-8270
Minister Health, Hon. George Abbott
250-356-9076, Fax: 250-356-8273
Minister Aboriginal Relations & Reconciliation & Government House Leader, Hon. Michael de Jong
250-387-6240, Fax: 250-387-1040
Minister Public Safety & Solicitor General, Hon. John Les
250-356-7411, Fax: 250-356-6376
Minister Small Business & Revenue & Minister Responsible, Deregulation, Hon. Rick Thorpe
250-356-6611, Fax: 250-356-8294
Minister Labour & Citizens' Services, Hon. Olga Ilich
Minister Transportation, Hon. Kevin Falcon
250-387-1978, Fax: 250-356-2290
Minister of State ActNow BC, Hon. Gordon Hogg
Administrative Co-ordinator, Claire Vessey
250-387-5226, Fax: 250-356-7292, claire.vessey@gemsl.gov.bc.ca

Ministry of Agriculture & Lands

PO Box 9120 Prov Govt
Victoria, BC V8W 9B4
250-387-5121
Fax: 250-387-1522
www.gov.bc.ca/al
The ministry is committed to providing the business climate for a competitive & profitable industry providing safe, high quality food for consumers & export markets.

Acts Administered:
Agri-Food Choice & Quality Act
Organic Agricultural Products Certification Regulation
Agricultural Lands Commission
Agricultural Produce Grading Act
Animal Disease Control Act
Bee Act
Boundary Act
British Columbia Wine Act
Cattle (Horned) Act
Environment & Land Use Act
Farm Income Insurance Act
Farm Practices Protection (Right to Farm) Act
Farmers & Womens Institutes Act
Farming & Fishing Industries Development Act
Fisheries Act
Food Products Standards Act
Fur Farm Act
Game Farm Act
Greenbelt Act
Insurance for Crops Act
Land Act
Land Survey Act
Land Surveyors Act
Land Title & Survey Authority
Libby Dam Reservoir Act
Livestock Act
Livestock Identification Act
Livestock Lien Act
Livestock Protection Act
Livestock Public Sale Act
Local Government Act (in part)
Milk Industry Act
Ministry of Agriculture & Food Act
Muskwa-Kechika Management Area Act
Natural Products Marketing (BC) Act
Pharmacists, Pharmacy Operations & Drug Scheduling Act (in part)
Plant Protection Act
Prevention of Cruelty to Animals Act
Private Managed Forest Land Act
Veterinarians Act
Weed Control Act
Wine Act
Minister, Hon. Pat Bell
250-387-1023, Fax: 250-387-1522
Deputy Minister, Larry Pedersen
250-356-1800, Fax: 250-356-8392
Administrative Assistant Communications Branch, Lynne Willoughby
250-356-1687, Fax: 250-387-9105

Associated Agencies, Boards & Commissions:
• Agricultural Land Commission
#133, 4940 Canada Way
Burnaby, BC V5G 4K6
604-660-7000
Fax: 604-660-7033
www.alc.gov.bc.ca
• BC Assessment Authority
1537 Hillside Ave.
Victoria, BC V8T 4Y2
250-595-6211
Fax: 250-595-6222
info@bcassessment.ca
www.bcassessment.bc.ca
BC Assessment Authority produces property assessments that form the basis for local & provincial taxation. The authority also provides information to assist people making real estate decisions. There are 22 field offices in theprovince.
• British Columbia Farm Industry Review Board
PO Box 9129 Prov Govt
Victoria, BC V8W 9B5
250-356-8945
Fax: 250-356-5731
firb@gov.bc.ca

Corporate Services Division

Asst. Deputy Minister, Jacquie Kendall
250-387-9878
Director Corporate Service Delivery, Trish Dohan
250-356-9221
Director Finance & Administration, Denise Bragg
250-356-9220
Director Human Resource & Performance Strategy, Duff McCaghey
250-356-6243

Ministry of the Attorney General

1001 Douglas St., 10th Fl.
PO Box 9282 Prov Govt
Victoria, BC V8W 9J7
250-356-9596
Fax: 250-387-1753
www.gov.bc.ca/ag/
Acts Administered:
Adult Guardianship Act
Age of Majority Act
Attorney General Act
Civil Rights Protection Act
Class Proceedings Act
Commercial Arbitration Act
Commissioner on Resources & Environment Act
Company Act
Conflict of Laws Rules for Trusts Act
Constitution Act
Constitutional Amendment Approval Act
Constitutional Question Act
County Boundary Act
Court Agent Act

Court of Appeal Act
Court Order Enforcement Act
Court Order Interest Act
Court Rules Act
Crown Counsel Act
Crown Franchise Act
Crown Proceeding Act
Debtor Assistance Act
Disciplinary Authority Protection Act
Election Act
Electoral Boundaries Commission Act
Electoral Districts Act
Enforcement of Canadian Judgments Act
Escheat Act
Estate Administration Act
Estates of Missing Persons Act
Evidence Act
Expropriation Act
Family Compensation Act
Family Maintenance Enforcement Act
Family Relations Act
Federal Courts Jurisdiction Act
Financial Disclosure Act
Foreign Arbitral Awards Act
Foreign Money Claims Act
Foresters Act s. 9(2)
Fraudulent Conveyance Act
Fraudulent Preference Act
Frustrated Contract Act
Good Samaritan Act
Holocaust Memorial Day Act
Human Rights Code
Indian Cut-off Lands Dispute
Infants Act
Inquiry Act
Insurance Corporation Divisions 1 & 2 Act
Interjurisdictional Support Order Act
International Commerical Arbitration Act
International Sale of Goods Act
International Trusts Act
Interpretation Act
Judicial Review Procedure Act
Jury Act
Justice Administration Act
Law & Equity Act
Law Reform Commission Act
Legal Profession Act
Legal Services Society Act
Libel & Slander Act
Limitation Act
Lobbyists Registration Act
Members' Conflict of Interest Act
Ministry of Consumer & Corporate Affairs Act
Ministry of Provincial Secretary & Government Services Act
Negligence Act
Nisga'a Final Agreement
Notaries Act
Occupiers Liability Act
Offence Act
Office for Children & Youth Act
Ombudsman Act
Partition of Property Act
Patients Property Act
Perpetuity Act
Power of Appointment Act
Power of Attorney Act
Privacy Act
Probate Recognition Act
Property Law Act
Provincial Court Act
Public Guardian & Trustee Act
Queen's Counsel Act
Recall & Initiative Act
Referendum Act
Regulations Act
Representation Agreement Act
Sechelt Indian Government District Enabling Act
Sheriff Act
Small Claims Act
Statute Revision Act
Statute Uniformity Act
Subpoena (Interprovincial) Act
Supreme Court Act
Survivorship & Presumption of Death Act
Treaty Commission Act
Trespass Act
Trust & Settlement Variation Act
Trustee Act
Trustee (Church Property) Act
Wills Act
Wills Variation Act
Young Offenders (British Columbia) Act

Attorney General, Hon. Wally Oppal
250-387-1866
Deputy Attorney General, Allan Seckel
250-356-0149
Asst. Deputy Minister Management Services, Jim Crone
250-387-5958, Fax: 250-387-0081
Executive Director Information Technology Services, Frank D'Argis
250-356-8787
Executive Director Strategic Planning & Legislative, Carol Anne Rolf
250-387-1773
Director Facilities Service Division, Bourke Findlay
250-356-7159
Director Finance & Administration Division, Deborah Fayad
250-387-6893
Director Investigation, Inspection & Standards, Vaughan Dowie
250-356-8481
Acting Director Strategic Human Resource Services, Marg Sorensen
250-387-5309
Administrative Assistant, Angella Saeger
250-387-2010, Fax: 250-387-1753, angella.seager@gems7.gov.bc.ca

Associated Agencies, Boards & Commissions:

• BC Ferry Commission
PO Box 1497
Comox, BC V9M 8A2
250-339-2714
Fax: 250-339-2753
www.bcferrycommission.com
Regulates British Columbia Ferry Services Inc.; ensures the average level of fares charged does not rise above the price cap set by the Commission; monitors the adherence of the company to the terms of its contract with the province.~

• BC Human Rights Tribunal
#1170, 605 Robson St.
Vancouver, BC V6B 5J3
604-775-2000
Fax: 604-775-2020
888-440-8844
• British Columbia Review Board
#1203, 865 Hornby St.
Vancouver, BC V6Z 2G3
604-660-8789
Fax: 604-660-8809
877-305-2277
www.bcrb.bc.ca
• Child & Youth Officer for BC
1019 Wharf St.
PO Box 9207 Prov Govt
Victoria, BC V8W 9J1
250-356-0831
Fax: 250-356-0837
800-476-3933
cyo@gov.bc.ca
www.gov.bc.ca/cyo
• Elections British Columbia
Listed alphabetically in detail.
• Judicial Council of British Columbia
Pacific Centre
#602, 700 West Georgia St.
PO Box 10287
Vancouver, BC V7Y 1E8
604-660-2864
Fax: 604-660-1108
www.provincialcourt.bc.ca/judicialcouncil
• Legal Services Society
#400, 510 Burrard St.
Vancouver, BC V6C 3A8
604-601-6000
www.lss.bc.ca
• Public Guardian & Trustee of British Columbia
#700, 808 West Hastings St.
Vancouver, BC V6C 3L3
604-660-4444
Fax: 604-660-0374
mail@trustee.bc.ca
www.trustee.bc.ca

Office of the Auditor General

8 Bastion Sq.
Victoria, BC V8V 1X4
250-387-6803
Fax: 250-387-1230
www.bcauditor.com
Acting Auditor General, Arn van Iersel
Deputy Auditor General, Errol S. Price
250-387-6803
Executive Coordinator, Doreen Sullivan
250-356-2627, Fax: 250-387-1230, dsullivan@oag.bc.ca

Local Government

The Department works with a wide range of partners to develop communities with the capacity to manage change & provide quality, affordable service to all British Columbians. The Department offers a range of programs to serve communitiesby facilitating partnerships with local governments & First Nations; developing local government legislation; facilitating community & regional planning, fostering positive inter-governmental relations & resolving differences between localgovernments; providing information & advice to protect the financial viability of & good governance of local governments; &, offering financial support for: communities; infrastructure planning & construction; growth management; & local governmentrestructure.

Asst. Deputy Minister, Dale Wall
250-356-6575, Fax: 250-387-7973
Executive Director Governance & Structure, Gary Paget
250-953-4129
Executive Director Intergovernmental Relations & Planning Division, Alan Osborne
250-387-0089
Executive Director Local Government Policy & Research, Brian Walisser
250-387-4050
Executive Director Infrastructure & Finance, Brenda Gibson
250-387-4067
Deputy Inspector Office of the Inspector of Muncipalities, Dale Wall
250-356-6575

Ministry of Economic Development

PO Box 9324 Prov Govt
Victoria, BC V8W 9N3
www.gov.bc.ca/ecdev
Under the Canada-British Columba Municipal Rural Infrastructure Fund Agreement, signed in June 2006, federal, provincial & local governments will be funding $150 million in infrastructure projects, with at least 60 percent of funding toassist with green local government infrastructure such as water & wastewater systems, public transit, & environmental energy improvements.

Acts Administered:
BC-Alcan Northern Development Fund Act
British Columbia Enterprise Corporation Act
Business Paper Reduction Act
Columbia Basin Trust Act
Economic Development Act
Ministry of International Business & Immigration Act
Northern Development Initiative Trust Act
Minister, Hon. Colin Hansen
250-356-7411, Fax: 250-356-6376
Deputy Minister, Don Fast
250-952-0102
Deputy Minister BC Olympic & Paralympic Winter Games Secretariat, Annette Antoniak
604-660-3425

Associated Agencies, Boards & Commissions:

• Asia Pacific Trade Council
#730, 999 Canada Place
Vancouver, BC V6C 3E1
604-775-2100
Fax: 604-775-2070
www.asiapacifictradecouncil.ca
Makes recommendations to the Premier on opportunities to leverage the Province's unique gateway location in order to maximize commerce to the benefit of British Columbians & Canadians.

• BC Competition Council
1810 Blanshard St.
PO Box 9327 Prov Govt
Victoria, BC V8W 9N3
• BC Olympic & Paralympic Games Secretariat
#860, 1095 West Pender St.
Vancouver, BC V6E 2M6
604-660-0914
bcsecretariat@gov.bc.ca
www.cse.gov.bc.ca/2010secretariat
• BC Progress Board
#730, 999 Canada Place
Vancouver, BC V6C 3E1
604-775-1664
• British Columbia Innovation Council
1188 West Georgia St., 9th Fl.
Vancouver, BC V6E 4A2
info@bcinnovationcouncil.com
www.bcinnovationcouncil.com
• Columbia Basin Trust
#300, 445 - 13 Ave.
Castlegar, BC V1N 1G1
250-365-6633
Fax: 250-365-6670
800-505-8998
cbt@cbt.org
• Industry Training Authority
#223, 4600 Kingsway
Burnaby, BC V5H 4L9
604-775-2860
Fax: 604-775-3033
866-660-6011
ita@gov.bc.ca
www.itabc.ca
• Northern Development Initiative Trust
#301, 1268 Fifth Ave.
Prince George, BC V2L 3L2
250-561-2525
• Small Business BC
601 West Cordova St.
Vancouver, BC V6B 1G1
604-775-5525
Fax: 604-775-5520

Economic Competitiveness

Director Corporate Initiative Branch, Shannon Baskerville
250-952-0367
Director Economic Analysis & Skills Development, Mark Gillis
250-952-0698
Director Infrastructure Development, Kirk Handrahan
250-952-0678
Director Regional Economic Development, Jim Cameron
250-751-7259
Director Trade & Competitiveness, Don White
250-952-0708

Management Services

Asst. Deputy Minister, Doug Callbeck
250-952-0126, Fax: 250-952-0600
Director Finance & Administration, Jennifer Smith
250-952-0174
Director Human Resources Strategic Unit, Brenda Vachon
250-952-0601
Chief Information Officer & Director Information Management, Stewart Symmers
250-952-0229

Marketing, Investment & Trade

#730, 999 Canada Place
Vancouver, BC V6C 3E1
604-844-1900
Asst. Deputy Minister, Soren Harbel
604-775-0005, Fax: 604-775-2070
Director Investment Capital, Vacant
250-952-0190
Director International Relations, Kevin Regan
604-775-2133
Director International Marketing, Troy Machon
604-775-2039
Director Investor Services & Economic Immigration, Ian Mellor
604-775-2183

Ministry of Finance

PO Box 9048 Prov Govt
Victoria, BC V8W 9E2
250-387-3751
Fax: 250-387-5594
www.fin.gov.bc.ca/
Other Communication: ENQUIRY BC: 250/387-6121; 1-800-663-7867
Acts as the government's primary corporate & personal property registrar, banker & money manager; chief accountant; fiscal & economic policy maker, budget & expenditure arm; regulator of B.C. trust companies, credit unions & insurancecompanies; & administrator of public sector pension plans.

Acts Administered:
Auditor General Act
Balanced Budget & Ministerial Accountability Act
BC Railway Act
BC University Loan Act
Bonding Act
Budget Transparency & Accountability Act
Business Corporations Act
Business Number Act
Capital Financing Authority Repeal & Debt Restructuring Act
Community Services Labour Relations Act
Constitution Act, ss. 25-27
Cooperative Association Act
Credit Union Incorporation Act
Creditor Assistance Act
Financial Administration Act
Financial Information Act
Financial Institutions Act
Industrial Development Act
Insurance Act
Insurance (Captive Company) Act
Insurance (Marine) Act
International Financial Business Act
Manufactured Home Act
Medical & Health Care Services Special Account Act
Ministerial Accountability Bases (2004, 2004-2005) Acts
Ministry of Consumer & Corporate Affairs Act, ss. 3-4
Ministry of Intergovernmental Relations Act, s. 3
Miscellaneous Registrations Act, 1992
Mortgage Brokers Act
Mutual Fire Insurance Companies Act
Pacific North Coast Native Cooperative Act
Partnership Act
Pension Agreement Act
Pension Benefits Standards Act
Pension Fund Societies Act
Personal Property Security Act
Ports Property Tax Act
Probate Fee Act
Public Education Labour Relations Act
Public Education Support Staff Collective Bargaining Assistance Act
Public Sector Employers Act
Public Sector Pension Plans Act
Public Works Agreement Act
Real Estate Development Marketing Act
Real Estate Services Act
Repairers Lien Act
Securities (Forged Transfer) Act
Society Act
Special Accounts Appropriation & Control Act
Strata Property Act
Tugboat Worker's Lien Act
Unclaimed Property Act
Warehouse Lien Act
Warehouse Receipt Act
Woodworker Lien Act
Minister, Hon. Carole Taylor
250-387-3751, Fax: 250-387-5594
Deputy Minister, Tamara Vrooman
250-387-3184, Fax: 250-387-9099
Deputy Minister Communications, Linda Morris
250-356-7398
Asst. Deputy Minister Business Partnerships Division, Steve Hollett
250-356-1280
Director Financial & Corporate Sector Policy Branch, Joann Cain
250-387-9090, Fax: 250-387-9093
Associated Agencies, Boards & Commissions:
• Auditor Certification Board
940 Blanshard St., 2nd Fl.
PO Box 9431 Prov Govt
Victoria, BC V8W 9V3
250-356-8658
Fax: 250-356-9422
• Crown Corporations Secretariat
PO Box 9300 Prov Govt
Victoria, BC V8W 9N2
250-952-0750
Fax: 250-952-0777
• Financial Institutions Commission (FICOM)
#1200, 13450 - 102 Ave.
Surrey, BC V3T 5X3
604-953-5300
Fax: 604-953-5301
FICOM@ficombc.ca
www.fic.gov.bc.ca
Maintains public confidence in the financial services sector by effective regulation. FICOM is responsible for administering the following provincial statutes: Credit Union Incorporation Act, Financial Institutions Act, Insurance Act,Insurance (Captive Company) Act, Insurance (Marine) Act, Mortgage Brokers Act, Pension Benefits Standards Act, Real Estate Development Marketing Act, Real Estate Services Act, Strata Property Act.
• Insurance Council of British Columbia
#300, 1040 West Georgia St.
PO Box 7
Vancouver, BC V6E 4H1
604-688-0321
Fax: 604-662-7767
877-688-0321
www.insurancecouncilofbc.com
• Public Sector Employers' Council Secretariat
1215 Broad St., 2nd Fl.
Victoria, BC V8W 2A4
250-387-0842
Fax: 250-387-6258
• Real Estate Council of British Columbia
#900, 750 West Pender St.
Vancouver, BC V6C 2T8
604-683-9664
Fax: 604-683-9017
877-683-9664
info@recbc.ca
www.recbc.ca
A regulatory body established under the *Real Estate Services Act , to protect the public by setting the standards for initial licensing of the province's 16,000 licensees & by improving the standards of practice for continuation oflicensing.*

Office of the Comptroller General

Comptroller General, David Fairbotham
250-387-8543, Fax: 250-356-2001
Acting Executive Director Internal Audit & Advisory Services, Dan Ho
250-387-8167
Acting Director Financial Reporting & Advisory Services, Raj Sihota
250-387-4551
Director Financial Management, Stuart Newton
250-387-0279
Director Payment Review Office, Sheryl Kennedy
250-356-7434

Corporate & Ministry Support Services

Asst. Deputy Minister, Cheryl Wenezenki-Yolland
250-387-8139
Director Financial Services & Administration Branch, Vacant
250-356-7326
Director Strategic Human Resources, Grant Price
250-356-5806
Chief Information Officer, Beau Choo
250-387-8962

Provincial Treasury

620 Superior St.
Victoria, BC V8V 1X4
250-387-4541
Asst. Deputy Minister, Jim Hopkins
250-387-5729
Acting Executive Director Debt Management, Bill Shortreed
250-387-7126

Director Banking & Cash Management, Nick Krischanowsky
250-387-7105, Fax: 250-387-9099
Director Risk Management Branch, Phil Grewar
250-387-0521
Director Information Systems, Bill Moffat
250-356-0650

Ministry of Forests & Range

PO Box 9529 Prov Govt
Victoria, BC V8W 9C3
250-387-6121
800-663-7867
www.gov.bc.ca/for
Other Communication: Vancouver: 604/660-2421
Responsible for protecting & managing the forest resources, focusing on protecting & maintaining the province's forest & range resources. Healthy forests include a diversity of ecosystems that support a full range of forest products,businesses & other opportunities. General responsibilities include compliance, enforcement, forests management, harvest management, reforestation, pest control, fire protection, range land, research, enforcing the Forest & Range Practices Act, timberpricing, allowable annual cut & administration of BC Timber Sales. Goals of the ministry are to maintain healthy forests, a strong forest economy & to ensure a sustainable forest economy. The Mountain Pine Beetle Action Plan (2006-2011) guides alllevels of government, communities, industry & stakeholders in a coordinated response to the infestation. The major boards & commissions are the Forest Appeals Commission & the Forest Practices Board.

Acts Administered:
Forest Act
Advertising, Deposits & Disposition Regulation
Allowable Annual Cut Proportionate Reduction Regulation
Annual Rent Regulation
BC Timber Sales Business Areas Regulation
BC Timber Sales Business Regulation
Christmas Tree Regulation
Community Forest Agreement Regulation
Credit to Stumpage Regulation
Cut Control Regulation
Effective Director Regulation
Forest Accounts Receivable Interest Regulation
Forest Regions Regulation
Free Use Permit Regulation
Innovative Forestry Practices Regulation
Interest Rate Under Various Statutes Regulation
Log Salvage Regulation (Vancouver District)
Manufactured Forest Products Regulation
Minimum Stumpage Rate Regulation
Performance Based Harvesting Regulation
Scaling Regulation
Special Forest Products Regulation
Timber Definition Regulation
Timber Harvesting Contract & Subcontract Regulation
Timber Marketing & Transportation Regulation
Woodlot Licence Regulation
Forest Practices Code of British Columbia Act
Government Actions Regulation
Provincial Forest Use Regulation
Stillwater Pilot Project Regulation
Forest & Range Practises Act
Administrative Remedies Regulation
Administrative Review & Appeal Procedure (Forest Practices) Regulation
Forest Planning & Practices Regulation
Forest Practices Board Regulation
Forest Recreation Regulation
Forest Service Road Use Regulation
Fort St. John Pilot Project Regulation
Invasive Plants Regulation
Range Planning & Practices Regulation
Security for Forest Practice Liabilities Regulation
TFL 49 Pilot Project Regulation
Woodlot Licence Planning & Practices Regulation
Forest Stand Management Fund Act
Forest Stand Management Fund Regulation
Foresters Act
Forestry Revitalization Act, 2003
Manufactured Forest Products Regulation
Ministry of Forests Act
Protected Areas Forests Compensation Act
Range Act
Safety Authority Act
Safety Standards Act
South Moresby Implementation Account Act
Timber Licences Settlement Act
Timber Sale Licence Replacement (Sliammon First Nation) Act
Wildfire Act, 2004

Minister, Hon. Rich Coleman
250-387-6240, Fax: 250-387-1040
Deputy Minister, Doug Konkin
250-356-5012, Fax: 250-953-3687
Asst. Deputy Minister Mountain Pine Beetle Emergency Response Team, Ray Schultz
250-371-3725
Senior Executive Secretary, Andrea G. de Lestard
250-356-5012, Fax: 250-387-7065,
andrea.delestard@gems5.gov.bc.ca

Associated Agencies, Boards & Commissions:
• Forest Practices Board
1675 Douglas St., 3rd Fl.
PO Box 9905 Prov Govt
Victoria, BC V8W 9R1
250-387-7964
Fax: 250-387-7009
800-994-5899
fpboard@gov.bc.ca
www.fpb.gov.bc.ca
• Forestry Innovation Investments Ltd.
#1200, 1130 West Pender St.
Vancouver, BC V6E 4A4
604-685-7507
Fax: 604-685-5373
www.bcfii.ca
• Timber Export Advisory Committee
1520 Blanshard St., 2nd Fl.
PO Box 9514 Prov Govt
Victoria, BC V8W 3C8
250-387-8359
Fax: 250-387-5050

Insurance Corporation of BC

151 West Esplanade
North Vancouver, BC V7M 3H9
604-661-2800
www.icbc.com
President/CEO, Paul Taylor
COO, Bill Goble
Senior Vice-President Marketing & Underwriting, Donnie Wing
Chief Financial Officer, Geri K. Prior
Vice-President Information Services, Keith R. Stewart
Vice-President Human Resources & Corporate Law, Len Posyniak

Ministry of Labour & Citizens' Services

PO Box 9594 Prov Govt
Victoria, BC V8W 9K4
250-356-1487
Fax: 250-356-1653
www.lcs.gov.bc.ca
The ministry's activities include industrial relations, employment standards & the Workers Compensation Act.

Acts Administered:
BC Online Act
British Columbia Buildings Corporation Act
Coastal Forest Industry Dispute Settlement Act
Document Disposal Act
Electronic Transactions Act
Employment Standards Act
Fire & Police Services Collective Bargaining Act
Fishing Collective Bargaining Act
Freedom of Information & Protection of Privacy Act
Health Care Services Collective Agreement Act
Health & Social Services Improvement & Delivery Act
Health Sector Partnerships Agreement Act
Labour Relations Code
Legislative Assembly Allowances & Pension Act
Legislative Assembly Management Committee Act
Legislative Assembly Privilege Act
Legislative Library Act
Legislative Procedure Review Act
Ministry of Labour Act (except in relation to gas, electrical, elevating devices, boiler & pressure vessel safety)
Ministry of Provincial Secretary & Government Services Act
Public Education Flexibility & Choice Act
Public Sector Pension Plans Act
Public Service Benefit Plan Act
Public Service Labour Relations Act
Purchasing Commission Act
Queen's Printer Act
Statistics Act
Workers' Compensation Act

Minister, Hon. Olga Ilich
Deputy Minister, Lori Wanamaker
Chief Information Officer, Dave Nikolejsin
250-387-8509
Executive Director Board Resourcing & Development, Kathryn Dawson
604-775-2084
Executive Director Corporate Planning & Performance, Helen Fletcher
250-387-0864
Director Communications, Graham Currie
250-387-2699, Fax: 250-356-1653

Associated Agencies, Boards & Commissions:
• British Columbia Pension Corporation
2995 Jutland Rd.
PO Box 9460
Victoria, BC V8W 9V8
250-387-8201
Fax: 250-953-0421
800-663-8823
pensionsbc.ca
Formerly Superannuation Commission.
• Employment Standards Tribunal
Oceanic Plaza
#650, 1066 West Hastings St.
Vancouver, BC V6E 3X1
604-775-3512
Fax: 604-775-3372
registrar.est@bcest.bc.ca
www.bcest.bc.ca
• Labour Relations Board
Oceanic Plaza
#600, 1066 West Hastings St.
Vancouver, BC V6E 3X1
604-660-1300
Fax: 604-660-1892
information@lrb.bc.ca
www.lrb.bc.ca
• Workers' Compensation Appeal Tribunal
#150, 4600 Jacombs Rd.
Richmond, BC V6V 3B1
604-664-7800
Fax: 604-664-7898
800-663-2782
www.wcat.bc.ca
• Workers' Compensation Board
Listed alphabetically in detail.

Shared Services BC

CEO, Michael MacDougall
250-952-8578, Fax: 250-952-8299
Asst. Deputy Minister Accommodations & Real Estate Services Customer Service, Trish Shwart
250-952-8013
Asst. Deputy Minister Common Business Services, Richard Poutney
250-356-5846
Asst. Deputy Minister Workplace Technology Services, Elaine McKnight
250-387-0672
Executive Director Business Integration, Wayne Jensen
250-952-8588
Executive Director Business Services & CFO, Patricia Marsh
250-952-8612
Acting Executive Director Corporate Accounting Services, Jill Kot
250-356-9116
Executive Director Product Sales & Services & Queen's Printer, Vern Burkhardt
250-356-5849
Acting Executive Director Strategic Acquisitions & Intellectual Property, Frank Hudson
250-356-0843
Director Purchasing, Chris Duggan
250-387-7316

Service BC
PO Box 9594 Prov Govt
Victoria, BC V8W 9E2
250-387-6121
800-663-7867
Other Communication: Vancouver & outside: 604/660-2421
Asst. Deputy Minister, Lois Fraser
250-387-4823
Executive Director Online Channel Office, David Bacharach
250-953-3679
Executive Director Service Delivery Initiative, Michael Cowley
250-387-8574
Executive Director Service Delivery Options, Bette Jo Hughes
250-356-2031
Executive Director Service Delivery Planning & Business Development, Mark Mackinnon
250-387-1805

BC Stats
250-387-0359
Fax: 250-387-0380
bc.stats@gov.bc.ca
www.bcstats.gov.bc.ca
Director, Don McRae
250-356-2119
Chief Business & Economic Statistics, Lillian Hallin
250-387-0365, Fax: 250-387-0380
Manager Data Services, Paul Gosh
250-387-9221, Fax: 250-387-0329
Manager Population Statistics, David O'Neil
250-387-0335
Acting Manager Surveys & Analysis, Sarah Adams
250-356-0025
Team Leader Labour & Social Statistics, Cathy Stock
250-387-0373

Ministry of Public Safety & Solicitor General
PO Box 9282 Prov Govt
Victoria, BC V8W 9J7
250-356-6961
Fax: 250-387-1753
800-663-7867
www.gov.bc.ca/pssg/
The Ministry of Public Safety & Solicitor General works to maintain & enhance public safety across the province. The portfolio of the ministry includes: corrections; coroners service; law enforcement; crime prevention; victim services;hazard mitigation, emergency management & response; road safety; fire prevention, life safety & property protection; liquor & gaming regulation; consumer protection; & film classification.

Acts Administered:
BC Neurotrauma Fund Contribution Act
Cemetery & Funeral Services Act
Commercial Appeals Commission Act
Commercial Tenancy Act
Commercial Transport Act s.13
Consumer Protection Act
Coroners Act
Correction Act
Cost of Consumer Credit Disclosure Act
Credit Reporting Act
Crime Victim Assistance Act
Criminal Injury Compensation Act
Criminal Records Review Act
Debt Collection Act
Emergency Communications Corporations Act
Emergency Program Act
Fire Services Act
Firearm Act
Flood Relief Act
Food Donor Encouragement Act
Gaming Control Act
Guide Animals Act
Holiday Shopping Regulation Act
Holocaust Memorial Day Act
Insurance Corporation Part I Act
Liquor Control & Licensing Act
Liquor Distribution Act
Local Government Act
Ministry of Consumer & Corporate Affairs Act
Motion Picture Act
Motor Vehicle Act
Parental Responsibility Act
Parole Act
Police Act
Private Investigation & Security Agencies Act
Rent Distress Act
Residential Tenancy Act
Sale of Goods Act
Senior Citizen Automobile Insurance Grant Act
Sex Offender Registry Act
Trade Practice Act
Transport of Dangerous Goods Act
Travel Agents Act
Victim of Crime Act
Video Games Act
Solicitor General, Hon. John Les
250-356-7717, Fax: 250-356-8270
Deputy Solicitor General, David Morhart
250-356-0149
Asst. Deputy Minister & Fire Commissioner, David Hodgins
250-356-9000
Asst. Deputy Minister Management Services, Jim Crone
250-387-5258
Executive Director Information Technology Services, Frank D'Argis
250-356-8787
Director Finance & Administration, Deborah Fayad
250-387-6893
Acting Director Strategic Human Services, Marg Sorensen
250-387-5309
Superintendent Motor Vehicles, Mark Medgyesi
250-387-5692

Associated Agencies, Boards & Commissions:
• BC Coroner's Service
Metrotower II
#2035, 4720 Kingsway
Burnaby, BC V5H 4N2
604-660-7745
Fax: 604-660-7766
www.pssg.gov.bc.ca/coroners/index.htm
• British Columbia Board of Parole
#303, 960 Quayside Dr.
New Westminster, BC V3M 6G2
604-660-8846
Fax: 604-660-2356
• British Columbia Lottery Corporation
74 West Seymour St.
Kamloops, BC V2C 1E2
250-828-5500
Fax: 250-828-5637
consumerservices@bclc.com
www.bclc.com
• Office of the Police Complaint Commissioner
756 Fort St., 3rd Fl.
PO Box 9895 Prov Govt
Victoria, BC V8W 9T8
250-356-7458
Fax: 250-356-6503
www.opcc.bc.ca
Formerly British Columbia Police Commission.

Ministry of Small Business & Revenue
PO Box 9065 Prov Govt
Victoria, BC V8W 9E2
250-356-6611
Fax: 250-356-8294
Acts Administered:
Assessment Act
Assessment Authority Act
Corporation Capital Tax Act
Esquimalt & Nanaimo Railway Belt Tax Act
Home Owner Grant Act
Hotel Room Tax Act
Income Tax Act
Indian Self Government Enabling Act
Insurance Premium Tax Act
International Financial Activity Act
Land Tax Deferment Act
Logging Tax Act
Medicare Protection Act, ss. 5(1) (b), 7 (5), 8 (4), 8.1 & 32
Mining Tax Act
Motor Fuel Tax Act
Petroleum & Natural Gas Act, ss. 74-77
Property Transfer Act
Sechelt Indian Government District Home Owner Grant Act
Socal Service Tax Act
Taxation (Rural Area) Act
Tobacco Tax Act
Tourism Accommodation (Assessment Relief) Act
Acts administered in areas related to revenue management processes only
Forest Act
Forest & Range Practices Act
Forest Practices Code of British Columbia Act
Forest Stand Management Fund Act
Ministry of Forests Act
Mineral Land Tax Act
Mineral Tax Act
Petroleum & Natural Gas Act
Range Act
Range Act
School Act
South Moresby Implementation Account Act
Wildfire Act
Minister, Hon. Rick Thorpe
250-356-6611, Fax: 250-356-6376
Deputy Minister, Robin Ceceri
250-387-6206
Executive Director Policy & Legislation, Sally Chaster
250-356-9149
Executive Director Appeals & Litigation Branch, Janet Baltes
250-387-5785

Associated Agencies, Boards & Commissions:
• Asia Pacific Foundation of Canada
#666, 999 Canada Place
Vancouver, BC V6C 3E1
604-684-5986
Fax: 604-681-1370
info@asiapacific.ca
www.asiapacific.ca
• British Columbia Securities Commission
Pacific Centre
701 West Georgia St., 12th Fl.
PO Box 10142
Vancouver, BC V7Y 1L2
604-899-6500
Fax: 604-899-6506
800-373-6393
inquiries@bcsc.bc.ca
www.bcsc.bc.ca
• International Financial Centre - British Columbia Society (IFC)
World Trade Centre
#545, 999 Canada Place
Vancouver, BC V6C 3E1
604-683-6626
Fax: 604-683-6646
info@ifcvancouver.com
www.ifcbc.com
• Property Assessment Appeal Board
#10, 10551 Shellbridge Way
Richmond, BC V6X 2W9
604-775-1740
Fax: 604-775-1742
888-775-1740
office@paab.bc.ca
www.assessmentappeal.bc.ca

Revenue Programs Division
Asst. Deputy Minister, Elan Symes
250-387-0664, Fax: 250-387-6218
Acting Executive Director Consumer Taxation Programs, Pat Parkinson
604-660-6024
Executive Director Income Taxation Branch, Ian Forman
250-387-3320
Executive Director Property Taxation Branch, Neilane Mayhew
250-387-0532
Director Mineral, Oil & Gas Revenue, Doug Stangeland
250-952-0194

Revenue Services Division
Asst. Deputy Minister, Karen Dellert
250-387-1158
Executive Director Alliance Management Office, Shannon Lundquist
250-387-1510
Director Receivables Management Branch, Dennis Forbes
250-356-8031
Director Forest Revenue Branch, Pat Plunkett
250-356-7400

Strategic Initiatives & Administration Branch
Asst. Deputy Minister, John Powell
250-387-3693, Fax: 250-356-1333
Acting Executive Director Customer Service & Information Branch, Wayne Sparanese
250-356-0670
Acting CIO & Executive Director, Michael Carpenter
250-356-1165
Director Employee Development & Leadership, Elaine Jones
250-387-0595
Director Special Investigations Branch, Walt Charlton
604-775-0733
Director Strategic Planning & Performance Reporting Branch, Donna Selbee
250-356-0044

Small Business & Regulatory Reform
Acting Asst. Deputy Minister, Lindsay Kislock
250-356-1993
Executive Director PST Review & Small Business Roundtable, Simone Decosse
250-387-0661
Executive Director Regulatory Reform, Gail Greenwood
250-387-8709

Government of Manitoba

Seat of Government: Winnipeg, MB R3C 0V8
www.gov.mb.ca
The Province of Manitoba entered Confederation July 15, 1870. It has an area of 547,703.85 km2, & the StatsCan census population in 2001 was 1,119,583.

Office of the Premier
Legislative Bldg.
#214, 450 Broadway
Winnipeg, MB R3C 0V8
204-945-3714
Fax: 204-949-1484
premier@leg.gov.mb.ca
www.gov.mb.ca
Premier, Hon. Gary Doer
204-945-3714
Deputy Premier, Hon. Rosann Wowchuk
Clerk of the Executive Council & Cabinet Secretary, Paul Vogt
204-945-5640, Fax: 204-945-8390
Chief of Staff, Michael Balagus
204-945-5642
Executive Assistant, Bill Bage
204-945-3714
Director Communications, Jonathan Hildebrand
204-945-1494
Director Policy, Jean-Guy Bourgeois
204-945-4721
Administrative Officer, Esther Kotyk
204-945-2421, Fax: 204-948-3820, ekotyk@leg.gov.mb.ca

Executive Council
Legislative Bldg.
450 Broadway
Winnipeg, MB R3C 0V8
Premier & President, Executive Council; Minister, Federal-Provincial Relations, Hon. Gary Doer
204-945-3714, Fax: 204-949-1484, premier@leg.gov.mb.ca
Minister Intergovernmental Affairs, Hon. Steve Ashton
204-945-3788, Fax: 204-945-1383, minia@leg.gov.mb.ca
Minister Justice & Attorney General; Minister Responsible, Manitoba Public Insurance, Manitoba Gaming Control Commission, Hon. David Chomiak
204-945-3728, Fax: 204-945-2517, minjus@leg.gov.mb.ca
Minister Aboriginal & Northern Affairs, Hon. Oscar Lathlin
204-945-3719, Fax: 204-945-8374, minna@leg.gov.mb.ca
Deputy Premier & Minister, Agriculture, Food & Rural Initiatives; Minister Responsible, Co-operative Development, Hon. Rosann Wowchuk
204-945-3722, Fax: 204-945-3470, minagr@leg.gov.mb.ca
Minister Family Services & Housing, Hon. Gord Mackintosh
204-945-4173, Fax: 204-945-5149, minfam@leg.gov.mb.ca
Minister Culture, Heritage & Tourism & Minister Responsible for Sport; Minister Responsible, Voluntary Sector, Hon. Eric Robinson
204-945-3729, Fax: 204-945-5223, mincht@leg.gov.mb.ca
Minister Advanced Education & Literacy, Hon. Diane McGifford
204-945-0825, Fax: 204-948-2216, minaed@leg.gov.mb.ca
Minister Infrastructure & Transportation, Hon. Ron Lemieux
204-945-3723, Fax: 204-945-7610, mininfratran@leg.gov.mb.ca
Minister Finance & Minister Responsible, French Language Services, Civil Service Commission, Manitoba Hydro, Hon. Gregory F. Selinger
204-945-3952, Fax: 204-945-6057, minfin@leg.gov.mb.ca
Minister Competitivesness, Training & Trade & Minister Responsible, Manitoba Liquor Control Commission, Manitoba Lotteries Commission, Hon. Scott Smith
204-945-0067, Fax: 204-945-4882, minctt@leg.gov.mb.ca
Minister Conservation, Hon. Stan Struthers
204-945-3730, Fax: 204-945-3586, mincon@leg.gov.mb.ca
Minister Labour & Immigration & Minister Responsible, Multiculturalism, Status of Women, Hon. Nancy Allan
204-945-4079, Fax: 204-945-8312, minlab@leg.gov.mb.ca
Minister Science, Technology, Energy & Mines, Hon. Jim Rondeau
204-945-5356, Fax: 204-948-2692, minstem@leg.gov.mb.ca
Minister Education, Citizenship & Youth, Hon. Peter Bjornson
204-945-3720, Fax: 204-945-1291, minedu@leg.gov.mb.ca
Minister Water Stewardship, Hon. Christine Melnick
204-945-1133, Fax: 204-948-2864, minwst@leg.gov.mb.ca
Minister Health, Hon. Theresa Oswald
204-945-3731, Fax: 204-945-0441, minhlt@leg.gov.mb.ca
Minister Healthy Living & Minister Responsible, Seniors, Healthy Child Manitoba, Hon. Kerri Irvin-Ross
204-945-1373, Fax: 204-948-2703, minhliv@leg.gov.mb.ca
Administrative Officer, Esther Kotyk
204-945-2421, Fax: 204-948-3420, ekotyk@leg.gov.mb.ca

Manitoba Agriculture, Food & Rural Initiatives
Norquay Bldg.
401 York Ave.
Winnipeg, MB R3C 0P8
www.gov.mb.ca/agriculture/
Acts Administered:
Agricultural Credit Corporation Act
Agricultural Productivity Council Act
Agricultural Producers' Organization Funding Act
Animal Care Act
Animal Diseases Act
Crop Insurance Act
Crown Lands Act, (in part) Sections 6, 7, 10, 12(1), 14, 16, 17, 18, 21, 23, 24 to 28 both inclusive
Dairy Act
Department of Agriculture, Food & Rural Initiatives Act
Family Farm Protection Act
Farm Income Assurance Plans Act
Farm Lands Ownership Act
Farm Machinery & Equipment Act
Farm Practices Protection Act
Fruit & Vegetable Sales Act
Horse Racing Regulation Act
Land Rehabilitation Act
Livestock Industry Diversification Act
Livestock & Livestock Products Act
Margarine Act
Milk Prices Review Act
Natural Products Marketing Act
Noxious Weeds Act
Pesticides & Fertilizers Control Act
Prescribed Spraying Equipment & Controlled Products
Plant Pests & Diseases Act
Seed & Fodder Relief Act
Veterinary Medical Act
Veterinary Science Scholarship Fund Act
Veterinary Services Act
Wildlife Act, (in part) Section 89(e)
Women's Institute Act
Minister, Hon. Rosann Wowchuk
204-945-3722, Fax: 204-945-3470, rwowchuk@leg.gov.mb.ca
Deputy Minister, Barry Todd
204-945-3734, Fax: 204-948-2095
Acting Executive Director Strategic Planning, Maurice Bouvier
204-792-5406

Associated Agencies, Boards & Commissions:

• Agricultural Societies
1129 Queens Ave.
Brandon, MB R7A 1L9
204-726-6195
Fax: 204-726-6260
Promotes improvement in agriculture & development of Manitoba agricultural products. Provide organizational assistance to rural & urban people.

• Farm Lands Ownership Board
#812, Norquay Bldg.
401 York Ave.
Winnipeg, MB R3C 0P8
204-945-3149
Fax: 204-945-1489
800-282-8069
flob@gov.mb.ca
www.gov.mb.ca/agriculture/programs/aaa23s03.html

• Farm Machinery Board
Norquay Bldg.
#812, 401 York Ave.
Winnipeg, MB R3C 0P8
204-945-3856
www.gov.mb.ca/agriculture/programs/aaa14s01.html

• Food Development Centre
810 Phillips St.
PO Box 1240
Portage la Prairie, MB R1N 3J9
204-239-3150
Fax: 204-239-3180
800-870-1044
www.gov.mb.ca/agriculture/fdc
Contract R&D for the value-added agricultural products processing sector.~

• Manitoba Agricultural Services Corporation (MASC)
#100, 1525 First St. South
Brandon, MB R7A 7A1
204-726-6850
Fax: 204-726-6849
mailbox@mcic.gov.mb.ca
Formerly the Manitoba Agricultural Credit Corporation & the Manitoba Crop Insurance Corporation.~

• Manitoba Farm Mediation Board
c/o Boards, Commissions & Legislation Branch
#812, 401 York Ave.
Winnipeg, MB R3C 0P8
204-945-0357
Fax: 204-945-1489
Mediates options to legal action by creditors when farmers cannot meet their obligations.~

• Manitoba Farm Practices Protection Board
c/o Boards, Commissions & Legislation Branch
#812, 401 York Ave.
Winnipeg, MB R3C 0P8
204-945-4495
Fax: 204-948-2844

• Manitoba Farm Products Marketing Council
c/o Boards, Commissions & Legislation Branch
#812, 401 York Ave.
Winnipeg, MB R3C 0P8
204-945-4495
Fax: 204-948-2844

• Manitoba Horse Racing Commission
PO Box 46086 Westdale
Winnipeg, MB R3R 3S3
204-885-7770
Fax: 204-831-0942
mhrc@manitobahorsecomm.org
www.manitobahorsecomm.org
Governs, directs, controls, & regulates horse racing & the operation of all race tracks in Manitoba.~

• Manitoba Milk Prices Review Commission
c/o Boards, Commissions & Legislation Branch
#812, 401 York Ave.
Winnipeg, MB R3C 0P8
204-945-3854
Fax: 204-948-2844

Office of the Auditor General
#500, 330 Portage Ave.
Winnipeg, MB R3C 0C4
204-945-3790
Fax: 204-945-2169

Auditor General, J.W. Singleton
jsingleton@oag.mb.ca
Deputy Auditor General & COO, B. Lysyk
204-945-2686, blysyk@oag.mb.ca
Controller, S. Burton
204-945-0987, sburton@oag.mb.ca

Manitoba Competitiveness, Training & Trades

#900, 259 Portage Ave.
Winnipeg, MB R3B 3P4
204-945-2067
Fax: 204-948-2964
www.gov.mb.ca/itt
Revamped department announced in cabinet shuffle of Sept. 21, 2006. Limited details available. Facilitates private sector job creation by fostering investment & promoting an environment conducive to the sustainable development & growth ofManitoba business & mineral resources.

Acts Administered:
Biofuels Act
Crocus Investment Fund
Design Institute Act
Development Corporations Act
Economic Innovation & Technology Council Act
Electronic Commerce & Information Act (except part 5)
Energy Act
Gas Allocation Act
Gas Pipe Line Act
Greater Winnipeg Gas Distribution Act (S.M. 1988-89, C.40)
Income Tax Act (S. 7.5 & 7.10)
Labour-Sponsored Venture Capital Corporations Act
Manitoba Health Research Council Act
Mines & Minerals Act
Mining & Metallurgy Compensation Act
Oil & Gas Act
Drilling & Production Regulation
Oil & Gas Production Tax Act
Statistics Act
Surface Rights Act
Sustainable Development Act
Minister, Hon. Scott Smith
Deputy Minister, Hugh Eliasson
204-945-4076, Fax: 204-945-1561
Director Finance & Administrative Services, Craig Halwachs
204-945-3675, chalwachs@gov.mb.ca
Director Industry Development Financial Services, Jim Kilgour
204-945-7626, jkilgour@gov.mb.ca
Director Policy, Planning & Coordination, Alan Barber
204-945-8714, abarber@gov.mb.ca
Secretary Community Economic Development Committee, Eugene Kostyra
204-943-8328, ekostyra@gov.mb.ca
Senior Manager Industry Consulting & Marketing Support & Senior Manager, Business Immigration & Investment, David Sprange
204-945-7938, dsprange@gov.mb.ca
Executive Asst., Aura Rodrigues
204-945-2067, Fax: 204-945-1354, arodrigues@gov.mb.ca

Community & Economic Development Committee of Cabinet Secretariat

#648, 155 Carlton St.
Winnipeg, MB R3C 3H8
204-945-8193
Fax: 204-945-8229
Secretary, Eugene Kostyra
204-943-8328, ekostyra@gov.mb.ca
Administrative Officer, Colleen Davies
204-945-0346, codavies@gov.mb.ca

Manitoba Bureau of Statistics

#824, 155 Carlton St.
Winnipeg, MB R3C 3H9
204-945-2982
Fax: 204-945-0695
Chief Statistician, Wilf Falk
204-945-2988, wfalk@mbs.gov.mb.ca

Premier's Economic Advisory Council

#648, 155 Carlton St.
Winnipeg, MB R3C 3N8
204-945-6133
Fax: 204-945-8229
Executive Coordinator, Pat Britton
204-945-5297, pbritton@gov.mb.ca

Small Business Development

#250, 240 Graham Ave.
PO Box 2609
Winnipeg, MB R3C 4B3
204-984-2272
Fax: 204-983-3852
manitoba@cbsc.ic.gc.ca
www.cbsc.org/manitoba
Director, Tony Romeo
204-945-2019
Manager Western Regional Office, Keith Glennie
204-726-6255, Fax: 204-726-6403

Manitoba Development Corporation (MDC)

#555, 155 Carlton St.
Winnipeg, MB R3C 3H8
204-945-7626
Fax: 204-945-1193
General Manager, Jim Kilgour

Manitoba Finance

#109, Legislative Bldg.
Winnipeg, MB R3C 0V8
204-945-3754
Fax: 204-945-8316
minfin@leg.gov.mb.ca
www.gov.mb.ca/finance/
Established in 1969 under authority of the Financial Administration Act. Responsible for central accounting, payroll & financial reporting services for the government, consumer & corporate affairs & central financial control ofcost-shared agreements. The ministry manages government borrowing programs & is responsible for federal-provincial relations.

Acts Administered:
Business Names Registration Act
Business Practices Act
Cemeteries Act
The title to Certain Lands Act (R.S.M. 1990, c.259).
Change of Name Act
Charities Endorsement Act
Commodity Futures Act
Condominium Act
Consumer Protection Act
Cooperatives Act
Corporations Act
Corporation Capital Tax Act
Credit Unions & Caisses Populaires Act
Electronic Commerce & Information Act
Embalmers & Funeral Directors Act
Energy Rate Stabilization Act
Financial Administration Act
Fire Insurance Reserve Fund Act
Fiscal Stabilization Fund Act
Gasoline Tax Act
Health & Post Secondary Education Tax Levy Act
Hospital Capital Financing Authority Act
Housing & Renewal Corporation Act
Hudson's Bay Company Land Register Act
Income Tax Act
Insurance Act
Insurance Corporations Tax Act
Landlord & Tenant Act
Life Leases Act
Manitoba Investment Pool Authority Act
Manitoba Evidence Act (Part II & III)
Manitoba Investment Pool Authority Act
Marriage Act
Mining Claim Tax Act
Mining Tax Act
Mortgage Act (Part III)
Mortgage Dealers Act
Motive Fuel Tax Act
Pari-Mutuel Levy Act
Partnership Act
Personal Investigations Act
Personal Property Security Act
Prearranged Funeral Services Act
Professional Home Economists Act
Property Tax & Insulation Assistance Act
Public Health Act
Bedding, Upholstered & Stuffed Articles Regulation
Public Officers Act
Public Utilities Board Act
Real Estate Brokers Act
Real Property Act
Registry Act
Religious Societies' Lands Act
Residential Tenancies Act
Retail Sales Tax Act
Revenue Act
Succession Duty Act
Securities Act
Special Survey Act
Suitors' Moneys Act
Surveys Act (Part I)
Provincial-Municipal Tax Sharing Act
Tobacco Tax Act
Trade Practises Inquiry Act
Vital Statistics Act
Minister, Hon. Gregory F. Selinger
204-945-3952, Fax: 204-945-6057
Deputy Minister, Ewald Boschmann
204-945-3754, Fax: 204-945-8316
Secretary Treasury Board Secretariat, Tannis Mindell
204-945-4150, Fax: 204-945-4878
Assoc. Secretary Treasury Board, David Woodbury
204-945-4150, Fax: 204-945-4878

Associated Agencies, Boards & Commissions:
• Automobile Injury Compensation Appeal Commission
#301, 428 Portage Ave..
Winnipeg, MB R3C 0E2
204-945-4155
Fax: 204-948-2402
autoinjury@gov.mb.ca
www.gov.mb.ca/cca/autom
• Claimant Adviser Office
#200, 330 Portage Ave.
Winnipeg, MB R3C 0C4
204-945-7413
Fax: 204-948-3157
• Credit Union Deposit Guarantee Corporation
#390, 200 Graham Ave.
Winnipeg, MB R3C 4L5
204-942-8480
Fax: 204-947-1723
800-697-4447
mail@cudgc.com
www.cudgc.com
• Crown Corporations Council
#1130, 444 St. Mary Ave.
Winnipeg, MB R3C 3T1
204-949-5270
Fax: 204-949-5283
crowncc@mts.net
www.crowncc.mb.ca
• Manitoba Securities Commission
#500, 400 St. Mary Ave.
Winnipeg, MB R3C 4K5
204-945-2548
Fax: 204-945-0330
800-655-5244
securities@gov.mb.ca
www.msc.gov.mb.ca
• Public Utilities Board
#400, 330 Portage Ave.
Winnipeg, MB R3C 0C4
204-945-2638
Fax: 204-945-2643
In -Man-itob
publicutilities@gov.mb.ca
• Residential Tenancies Commission
#1650, 155 Carlton St.
Winnipeg, MB R3C 3H8
204-945-2028
Fax: 204-945-5453
800-782-8403
rtc@gov.mb.ca
www.gov.mb.ca/finance/cca/residtc

Administration & Finance Division
Director Finance & Administration, Erroll Kavanagh
204-945-4319
Director Human Resource Services, Melanie Schade
204-945-3001
Director Insurance & Risk Management, John Rislahti
204-945-2482

Comptroller's Division
#715, 401 York Ave.
Winnipeg, MB R3C 0P8
Provides central accounting, payroll & financial reporting services, & central financial control of cost-shared agreements for the government. The division develops government-wide financial systems, policies & procedures, & providespolicy advice for financial & management systems. The division coordinates, develops & maintains departmental data processing systems, & provides direction to the government on the effective use of information systems technology.

Provincial Comptroller, Betty-Anne Pratt
204-945-4919
Director Disbursements & Accounting, Terry Patrick
204-945-1343
Director Internal Audit & Consulting, Jane Holatko
204-945-8110

Consumer & Corporate Affairs Division
Asst. Deputy Minister, Alex Morton
204-945-3742, Fax: 204-945-4009
Executive Director Administration Services, Fred D. Bryans
204-945-2653
Director Claimant Advisor Office, Bob Sample
204-945-8171
Director Consumers Bureau, Nancy Anderson
204-945-4062
Director Information Technology, Zdenek Ondracek
204-945-2659
Director Research & Planning, Ian Anderson
204-945-7892
Director Residential Tenancies Branch, Roger Barsy
204-945-0377, Fax: 204-945-6273

Federal-Provincial Relations & Research Division
#910, 386 Broadway
Winnipeg, MB R3C 3R6
Provides research & analytical support for national/provincial fiscal & economic matters & inter-governmental financial relations. Also administers fiscal arrangements & tax collection agreements with the federal government & tax creditprograms with federal & municipal governments.

Acting Executive Director, Heather Wood
204-945-4120, Fax: 204-945-5051
Director Economic & Fiscal Analysis, Jim Hrichishen
204-945-1468
Director Intergovernmental Finance, Rory Molnar
204-945-1470
Director Taxation Analysis, Stephen Watson
204-945-1473

Taxation Division
401 York Ave., 4th Fl.
Winnipeg, MB R3C 0P8
Director Audit Branch, J.M. Finlay
Director Tax Administration Branch, Brian Forbes
Director Taxation Management & Research, Brad Refvik

Treasury Division
Created as a separate entity in 1976 due to the need for placing greater emphasis on the management of substantial amounts of money, debt & investments. Currency & interest rate risk management programs have been developed due to theincrease in volumes & dollar values. The division assists with the arrangement of financing for municipalities, schools & hospitals.

Asst. Deputy Minister, Gary Gibson
204-945-1184
Director Capital Markets, Ian Hasanally
204-945-6608
Director Treasury & Banking Operations, Scott Wiebe
204-945-6677

Companies Office
#1010, 405 Broadway
Winnipeg, MB R3C 3L6
204-945-2500
Fax: 204-945-1459
companies@gov.mb.ca
companiesoffice.gov.mb.ca
Chief Operating Officer, Myron Pawlowsky
204-945-4206

Financial Institutions Regulation
#1115, 405 Broadway
Winnipeg, MB R3C 3L6
204-945-2542
Fax: 204-948-2268
Other Communication: Insurance: insurance @gov.mb.ca; Cooperatives & Credit Unions: coop-cu@gov.nb.ca
Superintendent Financial Institutions, Jim Scalena
204-945-3911
Deputy Superintendent Insurance, Scott Moore
204-945-1150
Registrar Deposit Taking, Terry Lee
204-945-1003

Administrative Services Division
215 Garry St., 17th Fl.
Winnipeg, MB R3C 3Z1
Fax: 204-945-5115
Asst. Deputy Minister, Paul Rochon
204-945-3887
Director Financial Services, G. Bosma
204-945-2964
Director Information Technology Services, Dan Buhler
204-945-4512
Director Human Resources, Jenny Morris
204-945-5846, Fax: 204-948-3382

Manitoba Intergovernmental Affairs
#301, 450 Broadway
Winnipeg, MB R3C 0V8
Fax: 204-945-1383
mnia@leg.gov.mb.ca
Manitoba Intergovernmental Affairs' mission is to improve the economic, social & environmental well being of Manitoba communities & citizens. The Department serves individuals, local governments, community organizations & businesses.The Department establishes a legislative, financial, planning & policy framework that supports democratic, accountable, effective & financially efficient local government, & the sustainable development of our communities. Programs are aimed atmeeting particular needs for training, on-going advice, technical analysis & funding related to community revitalization & development, infrastructure development, land management, business support & local governance. The Department functions as anadvocate of community needs, a catalyst & co-ordinator of action, promotes & participates in partnerships with private sector & non-government organizations & intergovernmental alliances.

Acts Administered:
Capital Region Partnership Act
City of Winnipeg Charter
Convention Centre Corporation Act
An Act respecting Debts Owing by Municipalities to School Districts
Emergency Measures Act
Emergency 911 Public Safety Answering Point Act
Liquor Control Act
Local Authorities Election Act
Local Government Districts Act
Manitoba Lotteries Corporation Act
Manitoba Trade & Investment Corporation Act
Municipal Act
Municipal Affairs Administration Act
Municipal Assessment Act
Municipal Board Act
Municipal Councils & School Boards Elections Act
Municipal Revenue (Grants & Taxation) (Part 2)
Official Time Act
Planning Act (in part)
Northern Manitoba Planning & Bylaws Regulation
Provincial Land Use Policies Regulation
Subdivision Regulation
Soldiers' Taxation Relief Act
Regional Waste Management Authorities Act
Unconditional Grants Act
Minister, Hon. Steve Ashton
Deputy Minister Intergovernmental Affairs, Marie Elliott
204-945-3787, Fax: 204-945-5255
Chief Financial Services, Brian Johnston
204-945-2199, Fax: 204-945-3769
Administrative Officer, Elizabeth Lawrie
204-945-1856, Fax: 204-945-3769, elawrie@gov.mb.ca

Associated Agencies, Boards & Commissions:
• Manitoba Liquor Control Commission
1555 Buffalo Pl.
PO Box 1023
Winnipeg, MB R3C 2X1
204-284-2501
Fax: 204-475-7666
info@mlcc.mb.ca
www.mlcc.mb.ca
• Manitoba Municipal Board
#1144, 363 Broadway
Winnipeg, MB R3C 3N9
204-945-2941
Fax: 204-948-2235

Provincial-Municipal Support Services
#508, 800 Portage Ave.
Winnipeg, MB R3G 0N4
Asst. Deputy Minister, Laurie Davidson
204-945-2565, Fax: 204-948-2107
Acting Director Municipal Finance & Advisory Services, Denise Carlyle
204-945-1944, Fax: 204-948-2780
Provincial Municipal Assessor Assessment Branch, Mark Boreskie
204-945-2604, Fax: 204-945-1994
Director Information Systems, Larry Phillips
204-945-2585, Fax: 204-945-1994

Federal-Provincial & International Relations & Trade Division
#42, 450 Broadway
Winnipeg, MB R3C 0V8
Deputy Minister, Diane Gray
204-945-5345, Fax: 204-945-1640
Director Federal-Provincial Relations, Kerry McQuarrie-Smith
204-945-5475, Fax: 204-948-3624
Executive Director Manitoba Trade & Investment, Bob Dilay
204-945-8695, Fax: 204-957-1793
Director Canada-US & International Relations, Luci Grechen
204-945-5346, Fax: 204-948-3624
Acting Director International Education, Darcy Rollins
204-945-3335, Fax: 204-945-1793

Urban Strategic Initiatives
#607, 800 Portage Ave.
Winnipeg, MB R3G 0N4
Fax: 204-948-3512
Asst. Deputy Minister, Angela Mathieson
204-945-6117
Director Programs & Policy, Jon Gunn
204-945-3864
Director Winnipeg Partnership Agreement, Vacant
204-984-1806, Fax: 204-983-3844
Coordinator Neighbourhoods Alive!, Bob Dilay
204-945-3379, Fax: 204-945-5059

Manitoba Justice
405 Broadway Ave., 5th Fl.
Winnipeg, MB R3C 3L6
204-945-2852
minjus@gov.mb.ca
www.gov.mb.ca/justice/index.html
Promotes a safe, just & peaceful society supported by a justice system that is fair, effective, trusted & understood by: providing a fair & effective prosecution service; managing offenders in an environment that promotes public safety &rehabilitation; providing mechanisms for timely & peaceful resolution of civil & criminal matters; providing legal advice & services to government; providing programs which assist in protecting & enforcing individual & collective rights; providingsupport & assistance to victims of crime; & promoting effective policing & crime prevention initiatives.

Acts Administered:
Canada-United Kingdom Judgements Enforcement Act
Constitutional Questions Act
Correctional Services Act
Court of Appeal Act
Court of Queens' Bench Act

Court Security Act
Crime Prevention Foundation Act
Crown Attorneys Act
Child Custody Enforcement Act
Department of Justice Act
Discriminatory Business Practices Act
Domestic Violence & Stalking Prevention, Protection & Compensation Act
Enforcement of Judgements Conventions Act
Escheats Act
Executive Government Organization Act (subsection 12(2), only, as Keeper of the Great Seal)
Expropriation Act
Fatality Inquiries Act
Fortified Buildings Act
Helen Betty Osborne Memorial Foundation Act
Human Rights Code
Inter-jurisdictional Support Orders Act
International Commercial Arbitration Act
International Sale of Goods Act
Interprovincial Subpoena Act
Intoxicated Persons Detention Act
Jury Act
Law Enforcement Review Act
Law Fees & Probate Charge Act
Law Reform Commission Act
Legal Aid Services Society of Manitoba Act
Mental Health Act Part 10 & clauses 125(1)(i) & (j)
Minors Intoxicating Substances Control Act
Privacy Act
Private Investigators & Security Guards Act
Proceedings Against the Crown Act
Provincial Police Act
Public Trustee Act
Reciprocal Enforcement of Judgement Act
Regulations Act
Safer Communities & Neighbourhood Act
Sheriffs Act
Summary Convictions Act
Transboundary Pollution Reciprocal Access Act
Uniform Law Conference Commissioners Act
Vacant Property Act
Victims' Bill of Rights

Attorney General & Minister, Hon. David Chomiak
Deputy Minister & Deputy Attorney General, Ron Perozzo
204-945-3739, Fax: 204-945-4133
Asst. Deputy Minister, Vacant
204-945-2873, Fax: 204-948-2392
Executive Director Administration & Finance Division, P. Sinnott
204-945-2880
Web Coordinator & Records/FIPPA Assistant, Melissa Jackson

Associated Agencies, Boards & Commissions:

• Compensation for Victims of Crime
1410 - 405 Broadway
Winnipeg, MB R3C 3L6
204-945-0899
Fax: 204-948-3071
www.gov.mb.ca/justice

• Law Enforcement Review Agency (LERA)
#420, 155 Carlton St.
Winnipeg, MB R3C 3H8
204-945-8667
Fax: 204-948-1014
lera@gov.mb.ca
www.gov.mb.ca/justice/lera

• Law Reform Commission
#1210, 405 Broadway
Winnipeg, MB R3C 3L6
204-945-2896
Fax: 204-948-2184
lawreform@gov.mb.ca
www.gov.mb.ca/justice/mlrc

• Legal Aid Manitoba
402 - 294 Portage Ave.
Winnipeg, MB R3C 0B9
204-985-8500
Fax: 204-944-8582
800-261-2960
TDD: 204-943-1131info@legalaid.mb.ca
www.legalaid.mb.ca

• Manitoba Gaming Control Commission
#800, 215 Garry St.
Winnipeg, MB R3C 3P3
204-954-9400
800-782-0363
information@mgcc.mb.ca
www.mgcc.mb.ca
Other Communication: Toll Free Fax: 1-866-265-0067

• Manitoba Human Rights Commission
Listed alphabetically in detail.

• Office of the Chief Medical Examiner
#210, 1 Wesley Ave.
Winnipeg, MB R3C 4C6
204-945-2088
Fax: 204-945-2442

• Office of the Public Trustee
#500, 155 Carlton St.
Winnipeg, MB R3C 5R9
204-945-2700

• Review Board
408 York Ave., 2nd Fl.
Winnipeg, MB R3C 0P9
204-945-4438
Fax: 204-945-5751

Manitoba Labour & Immigration

#317, Legislative Bldg.
450 Broadway
Winnipeg, MB R3C 0V8
Fax: 204-945-8312
minlab@leg.gov.mb.ca
www.gov.mb.ca/labour
Other Communication: Immigration:
www.immigratemanitoba.com

Acts Administered:

Amusements Act (Part II)
Architects Act
Architects & Engineers Scope of Practice Dispute Settlement Act
Buildings & Mobile Homes Act
Construction Industry Wages Act
Department of Labour & Immigration Act
Electricians' Licence Act
Elevator Act
Employment Services Act
Employment Standards Code
Engineering & Geoscientific Professions Act
Firefighters & Paramedics Arbitration Act
Fires Prevention & Emergency Response Act
Gas & Oil Burner Act
Holocaust Memorial Day Act
Labour Relations Act
Manitoba Ethnocultural Advisory & Advocacy Council Act
Manitoba Immigration Council Act
Manitoba Multiculturalism Act
Manitoba Women's Advisory Council Act
Pay Equity Act
Pension Benefits Act
Power Engineers Act
Remembrance Day Act
Retail Business Holiday Closing Act
Steam & Pressure Plants Act
Workplace Safety & Health Act
Construction Industry Safety Regulation
Fibrosis & Silicosis Regulation
Forestry, Logging & Log Hauling Regulation
Hearing Conservation & Noise Control Regulation
Operation of Mines Regulation
Sanitary & Hygienic Welfare Regulation
Workplace Hazardous Materials Information System Regulation
Workplace Health Hazard Regulation
Workplace Safety & Health Committee Regulation
Workplace Safety Regulation
Minimum Wage & Working Conditions Regulation

Minister, Hon. Nancy Allan
204-945-4079
Deputy Minister, Jeff Parr
204-945-4039, Fax: 204-948-2203
Director Human Resources, Butch Berube

Associated Agencies, Boards & Commissions:

• Advisory Council on Workplace Safety & Health
#200, 401 York Ave.
Winnipeg, MB R3C 0P8
204-945-3446
Fax: 204-945-4556
www.gov.mb.ca/labour/safety/council.html
The Advisory Council on Workplace Safety & Health was established in 1977 under the authority of the Workplace Safety & Health Act. The council reports directly to the Minister of Labour & Immigration. The council advises & makesrecommendations to the Minister of Labour & Immigration concerning general workplace safety & health issues, protection of workers in specific situations & appointment of consultants & advisors.

• Manitoba Civil Service Commission
#935, 155 Carlton St.
Winnipeg, MB R3C 3H8
204-945-2332
Fax: 204-945-1486
cschrp@gov.mb.ca
www.gov.mb.ca/csc/

• Manitoba Ethnocultural Advisory & Advocacy Council
215 Notre Dame Ave. 4th Fl.
Winnipeg, MB R3B 1N3
204-945-2339
Fax: 204-948-2323
800-665-8332
meaac@gov.mb.ca
www.gov.mb.ca/labour/immigrate/multiculturalism/5.html

• Manitoba Labour Board
A.A. Heaps Bldg.
#402, 258 Portage Ave.
Winnipeg, MB R3C 0B6
204-945-3783
Fax: 204-945-1296
mlb@gov.mb.ca
www.gov.mb.ca/labour/labbrd

• Manitoba Minimum Wage Board
614 - 401 York Ave.
Winnipeg, MB R3C 0P8
204-945-4889
Fax: 204-948-2085
mw@gov.mb.ca
www.gov.mb.ca/labour/labmgt/resbr/wages/minwagbd.html

• Manitoba Women's Advisory Council
#301, 155 Carlton St.
Winnipeg, MB R3C 3H8
204-945-6281
Fax: 204-945-6511
800-282-8069
001women@gov.mb.ca

• Multiculturalism Secretariat
213 Notre Dame Ave., 4th Fl.
Winnipeg, MB R3B 1N3
204-945-1156
Fax: 204-948-2323

• Office of the Fire Commissioner
#508, 401 York Ave.
Winnipeg, MB R3C 0P8
204-945-3322
Fax: 204-948-2089
800-282-8069
firecomm@gov.mb.ca
www.firecomm.gov.mb.ca/

• Pension Commission of Manitoba
#1004, 401 York Ave.
Winnipeg, MB R3C 0P8
204-945-2740
Fax: 204-948-2375
pensions@gov.mb.ca
www.gov.mb.ca/labour/pension/index.html

Manitoba Lotteries Corporation

830 Empress St.
Winnipeg, MB R3G 3H3
204-957-2500
Fax: 204-957-3991
communications@mlc.mb.ca
www.mlc.mb.ca/MLC/
President/CEO, Winston Hodgins
Communications Coordinator, Lindsay Sprange
204-957-3930

Manitoba Public Insurance

#820, 234 Donald St.
PO Box 6300
Winnipeg, MB R3C 4A4

204-985-7000
Fax: 204-943-9851
800-665-2410
TDD: 204-985-8832www.mpi.mb.ca
Administers Manitoba's Public Automobile Insurance Program & sells extension auto coverage on a competitive basis.

Minister Responsible, Hon. David Chomiak
President/CEO, Marilyn McLaren
Vice-President Corporate Claims, W.L. Bedard
Vice-President Corporate Insurance Operations, Dan Guimond
Vice-President Corporate Legal & General Counsel & Corporate Secretary, K.M. McCulloch
Vice-President Corporate Resources, Charles Rogers
Vice-President Public Affairs, John Douglas
Vice-President Corporate Information Technology & Chief Information Officer, Clarke Campbell
Vice-President Corporate Finance & CFO & Chief Administration Officer, Barry Galenzoski
Contact Media Relations, Brian Smiley
204-985-7300

Manitoba Treasury Board

#200, 386 Broadway
Winnipeg, MB R3C 3R6
204-945-1101
Fax: 204-948-2358
Minister Responsible, Hon. Gregory F. Selinger
204-945-3952
Secretary to Treasury Board, Tannis Mindell
Asst. Deputy Minister Expenditure Management/Continuous Improvement, Drew Perry
204-945-1088
Asst. Deputy Minister Labour Relations, Gerry Irving
Asst. Deputy Minister Summary Budget & Capital Planning, Kim Sharman
204-945-1095

Government of New Brunswick

Seat of Government:PO Box 6000
Fredericton, NB E3B 5H1
www.gnb.ca
The Province of New Brunswick entered Confederation July 1, 1867. It has an area of 71,569.23 km2, & the StatsCan census population in 2001 was 729,498.

Office of the Premier / Cabinet du Premier ministre

Centennial Bldg.
670 King St.
PO Box 6000
Fredericton, NB E3B 5H1
506-453-2144
Fax: 506-453-7407
premier@gnb.ca
Premier, Hon. Shawn Graham
Chief of Staff, Bernard Thériault
506-453-2144, Fax: 506-453-7407
Correspondence Manager, Linda Landry-Guimond
506-453-2144, Fax: 506-453-7407, linda.landry-guimond@gnb.ca

Executive Council / Conseil exécutif

Centennial Bldg.
PO Box 6000
Fredericton, NB E3B 5H1
Premier & President, Executive Council; Minister, Intergovernmental Affairs; Minister, Wellness, Culture & Sport, Hon. Shawn Graham
Minister Justice & Consumer Affairs & Attorney General, Hon. Thomas J. Burke
Minister Public Safety & Solicitor General, Hon. John Foran
Minister Finance & Minister, Local Government; Minister Responsible, N.B. Liquor Corp., N.B. Investment Management Corp., Lotteries Commis, Hon. Victor Boudreau
Minister Supply & Services & Minister Responsible, Regional Development Corp., Hon. Roly MacIntyre
Minister Transportation, Hon. Denis Landry
Minister Natural Resources, Hon. Donald Arseneault
Minister Energy & Minister Responsible, Efficiency N.B., Hon. Jack Keir
Minister Agriculture & Aquaculture, Hon. Ronald Ouellette
Minister Fisheries, Hon. Rick Doucet
Minister Health, Hon. Michael Murphy
Minister Family & Community Services & Minister Responsible, N.B. Advisory Council on the Status of Women, Hon. Carmel Robichaud
Minister Office of Human Resources & Minister Responsible, Francophonie, Hon. Hédard Albert
Minister Education & Minister Responsible, N.B. Advisory Council on Youth, Hon. Kelly Lamrock
Minister Environment, Hon. Roland Haché
Minister Business New Brunswick & Minister Responsible, Service New Brunswick, Immigration & Repatriation Secretariat, Hon. Greg Byrne
Minister Tourism & Parks, Hon. Stuart Jamieson
Minister of State Seniors & Minister of State, Housing, Hon. Mary Schryer

Department of Agriculture & Aquaculture / Agriculture et Aquaculture

PO Box 6000
Fredericton, NB E3B 5H1
506-453-2666
Fax: 506-453-7170
This Department is to be split into the Department of Agriculture & Aquauculture & the Department of Fisheries, as announced by Premier Graham in October 2006.

Acts Administered:
Agricultural Commodity Price Stabilization Act
Agricultural Land Protection & Development Act
Agricultural Operation Practices Act
Apiary Inspection Act
Aquaculture Act
Crop Insurance Act
Diseases of Animals Act
Farm Income Assurance Act
Fish Processing Act
Fish & Wildlife Act (in part)
Injurious Insect & Pest Act
Inshore Fisheries Representation Act
Livestock Operations Act
Livestock Yard Sales Act
Marshland Reclamation Act
Natural Products Act
New Brunswick Grain Act
Pipeline Act
Plant Health Act
Potato Disease Eradication Act
Poultry Health Protection Act
Sheep Protection Act
Weed Control Act
Women's Institute & Institut féminin Act
Minister Agriculture & Aquaculture, Hon. Ronald Ouellette
Deputy Minister, Byron James
506-453-2450
Officer Communications, Alain Bryar

Associated Agencies, Boards & Commissions:
• New Brunswick Crop Insurance Commission / Commission de l'assurance récolte du Nouveau-Brunswick
PO Box 6000
Fredericton, NB E3B 5H1
506-453-2185
Fax: 506-453-7406
www.gov.nb.ca/afa-apa/50/50001e.htm
• New Brunswick Farm Products Commission / Commission des produits de ferme du Nouveau-Brunswick
c/o Department of Agriculture, Fisheries & Aquaculture
PO Box 6000
Fredericton, NB E3B 5H1
506-453-3647
Fax: 506-444-5969
www.gov.nb.ca/0175/01750001-e/asp

Office of the Auditor General / Bureau du Vérificateur général

PO Box 758
Fredericton, NB E3B 5B4
506-453-2243
Fax: 506-453-3067
www.gnb.ca/oag-bvg/
Auditor General, Michael Ferguson, C.A.
Deputy Auditor General, Kenneth D. Robinson, C.A.
506-453-6751, ken.robinson@gnb.ca
Executive Secretary, Darlene Wield
506-453-2465, darlene.wield@gnb.ca

Department of Business New Brunswick / Entreprises Nouveau-Brunswick

Centennial Bldg.
670 King St., 5th Fl.
PO Box 6000
Fredericton, NB E3B 5H1
506-444-5228
Fax: 506-453-5428
www.gnb.ca/0398/index-e.asp
Responsible for the development & marketing of investment opportunities, job creation & the tourism industry; encourages the growth of small & medium-sized businesses in New Brunswick; improves competitiveness in the global marketplace;assists companies in increasing sales & business in domestic & foreign markets & establishing new markets & export opportunities.

Acts Administered:
Agricultural Associations Act
Economic Development Act
Farm Credit Corporation Assistance Act
Farm Improvement Assistance Loans Act
Farm Machinary Loans Act
Fisheries Development Act
Industrial Relations Act
Livestock Incentives Act
Youth Assistance Act
Minister, Hon. Greg Byrne
Deputy Minister, Éloi Duguay
506-453-5897
Asst. Deputy Minister Corporate Services, Mike McIntosh
506-453-3703, Fax: 506-453-3993, mike.mcintosh@gnb.ca
Executive Director Corporate Services, Gary Jochelman
506-453-3707, gary.jochelman@gnb.ca
Director Red Tape Reduction, Wendy Betts
506-444-4167, wendy.betts@gov.nb.ca
Manager Communications, Sarah Ketcheson
506-444-4983
Secretary, Edith Robichaud-Davis

Associated Agencies, Boards & Commissions:
• New Brunswick Film / Film Nouveau-Brunswick
Assumption Pl.
770 Main St., 16th Fl.
PO Box 5001
Moncton, NB E1C 8R3
506-869-6868
Fax: 506-869-6840
nbfilm@gnb.ca
www.nbfilm.com
Responsible for fostering New Brunswick's film, television & new media industry.

• New Brunswick Industrial Development Board / Conseil de développement industriel du Nouveau-Brunswick
Business New Brunswick, Centennial Bldg.
670 King St.
PO Box 6000
Fredericton, NB E3B 5H1
506-453-4200
Fax: 506-444-4182

Business Development Division / Développement des entreprises

Executive Director Business & Export, Yvon Belliveau
506-453-2727, yvon.belliveau@gnb.ca
Executive Director Export Development, Joanne Walker
506-444-5291, Fax: 506-453-5428, joanne.walker@gnb.ca
Director Financial Programs, John Rosengren
506-453-3929, john.rosengren@gnb.ca
Director Industry Support, Richard Hollies
506-453-2727, Fax: 506-457-7282, richard.hollies@gnb.ca
Director Innovation, Life Sciences & Knowledge Industries, Michel Gauvin
506-453-2794, michel.gauvin@gnb.ca
Director Life Sciences & Institutional Research & Development, Camille Malenfant
506-444-5845, camille.malenfant@gnb.ca

Finance & Support / Finances et support
506-453-2111
Fax: 506-453-7904
Asst. Deputy Minister, Phil Lepage
506-453-2111, phil.lepage@gnb.ca
Executive Director Financial Programs Branch, Deborah McQuade
506-444-4200, Fax: 506-444-4182, debbie.mcquade@gnb.ca
Manager Domestic, Ron Harriott
506-453-2474, Fax: 506-453-7904, ron.harriott@gnb.ca
Manager Greenfield, Bernie Fontaine
bernie.fontaine@gnb.ca
Manager Monitoring, Lyle Green
506-453-2111, lyle.green@gnb.ca

Investment Attraction, Intelligence & Marketing / Attraction des investissements, renseignement et marketing
506-453-3984
Fax: 506-453-3993
Asst. Deputy Minister, Cecil Freeman
506-453-2794, cecil.freeman@gnb.ca
Executive Director Life Sciences, Value Added Resources, Advanced Manufacturing, Roger Y. Cyr
506-453-2402, Fax: 506-444-4277, roger.cyr@gnb.ca
Director Immigration, Tony Lampart
506-453-3981, Fax: 506-444-4277, tony.lampart@gnb.ca

Office of the Comptroller / Bureau du Contrôleur

Centennial Bldg.
670 King St.
Fredericton, NB E3B 5H1
506-453-2565
Fax: 506-453-2917
www.gnb.ca/0087/index-e.asp
Comptroller, Kim MacPherson, C.A.
Director Accounting Services, Janet Gallagher, C.A.
Director Audit & Consulting Services, Stephen Thompson, C.M.A.
Secretary, Jocelyne Macfarlane
506-453-2565

Department of Finance / Finances

670 King St.
PO Box 6000
Fredericton, NB E3B 5H1
506-453-2451
Fax: 506-444-4724
www.gov.nb.ca/finance/index.htm
Central agency of government responsible for managing the financing, revenue & expenses of government, with the identified goal of enhancing the fiscal strength of the province. Core business areas include socio-economic research &analysis, economic, fiscal & financial policy development & advice, treasury & debt management, tax & regulatory program administration, main & supplementary estimate preparation & monitoring, & operational support to the Board of Management.

Acts Administered:
Appropriation Act
Arts Development Trust Fund
Balanced Budget Act
Beaverbrook Art Gallery Act (Section 9)
Beaverbrook Auditorium Act (Section 7)
Environmental Trust Fund (administration of fund)
Equity Tax Credit Act
Financial Administration Act (expect provisions assigned to the Office of the Comptroller or to the Board of Management)
Financial Corporation Capital Tax Act
Fiscal Stabilization Fund
Fishermen's Disaster Fund Act (functions vested in Provincial Secretary-Treasurer)
Fredericton-Moncton Highway Financing Act
Gasoline & Motive Fuel Tax Act
Harmonized Sales Tax Act
Health Care Funding Guarantee Act
Income Tax Act
Loan Act
Municipal Assistance Act (except Section 5, 9 & 10)
Municipalities Act (subsection 19(8) & paragraphs 87.1(b) & (2)(b)
New Brunswick Income Tax Act
Northumberland Strait Crossing Act
Pari-Mutuel Tax Act
Pay Equity Act
Provincial Loans Act
Real Property Tax Act (except Sections 4 & subsection 5 (10))
Real Property Transfer Tax Act
Retirement Plan Benificiaries Act
Revenue Administration Act
Small Business Investment Tax Credit Act
Social Services & Education Tax Act
Special Appropriations Act
Special Retirement Program Act
Sport Development Trust Fund Act (administration of fund)
Statistics Act
Taxpayers Protection Act
Teachers' Pension Act
Tobacco Tax Act
Statutes under the Jurisdiction of the Minister of Finance in the Minister's Capacity as Chairman of the Board of Manage
Auditor General Act (subsections 4(3) & 16(1) & Section 17
Crown Construction Contracts Act
Expenditure Management Act, 1991
Expenditure Management Act, 1992
Financial Administration Act (responsibilties pursuant to subsection 2(2) & Section 6
Member's Pension Act
Members Superannuation Act
Ombudsman Act (pension provision, subsection 2(4))
Provincial Court Act (pension provisions)
Public Service Labour Relations Act (61)
Public Service Superannuation Act
Special Retirement Program Act
Teachers' Pension Act
Statutes under the Jurisdiction of the Minister of Finance & Administered by the Office of the Comptroller
Financial Administration Act (responsibilities pursuant to subsection 2(1))
Statutes under the Jurisdiction of the Minister of Finance & Administered by a Board, Commission or Corporation
Lotteries Act (except provisions related to enforcement by inspectors)
Maritime Provinces Harness Racing Commission Act
New Brunswick Investment Management Corporation Act
New Brunswick Liquor Corporation Act
New Brunswick Municipal Finance Corporation Act
Pay Equity Act
Minister, Hon. Victor Boudreau
Deputy Minister, John Mallory
506-453-2534, Fax: 506-457-4989
Director Communications, Vicky Deschenes
506-453-2451, Fax: 506-457-4989
Admin. Assistant, Liza Bouchard
506-457-6863, Fax: 506-444-4724

Associated Agencies, Boards & Commissions:
• Lotteries Commission of New Brunswick / Commission des loteries du Nouveau-Brunswick
PO Box 3000
Fredericton, NB E3B 5G5
506-444-4065
Fax: 506-444-5818
• New Brunswick Electric Finance Corporation / Corporation financière de l'électricité du N.-B.
#376, 670 King St.
PO Box 6000
Fredericton, NB E3B 5H1
506-453-3952
Fax: 506-453-2053
• New Brunswick Investment Management Corporation / Société de gestion des placements du Nouveau-Brunswick
York Tower
#381, 440 King St.
Fredericton, NB E3B 5H8
506-444-5800
Fax: 506-444-5025
www.nbimc.com
• New Brunswick Municipal Finance Corporation / Corporation de Financement des municipalités du Nouveau-Brunswick
#376, 670 King St.
PO Box 6000
Fredericton, NB E3B 5H1
506-453-3952
Fax: 506-453-2053

Budget & Financial Management / Gestion financière et budgétaire
506-453-2808
Fax: 506-444-4499
Director Board of Management Operations, Keith MacNevin
Director Budget Process, In-Year Monitoring, Troy Mann

Finance & Administration / Finances et administration
Fax: 506-444-4724
Asst. Deputy Minister, James Turgeon
506-457-6863
Director Financial Services, Rick Phillips
506-453-2286
Director Human Resources, Cécile Guérette
506-457-6863
Director Information Management & Technology, Nick Guitard
506-444-5471
Director Policy & Planning, Ann Deveau
506-457-6863

Fiscal Policy / Politiques fiscales
506-453-2097
Fax: 506-453-2281
Executive Director, Peter Kieley
Director Intergovernmental Fiscal Relations, Lucy St-Jean
Director Fiscal Policy & Economics, George Richardson

Revenue & Taxation / Revenu et Impôt
Fax: 506-444-4920
Asst. Deputy Minister, Jean R. Castonguay
506-444-2826
Provincial Tax Commissioner, Rick McCullough
506-444-2826
Director Account Management, Dayle Riva
506-454-4793
Director Audit & Investigation Services, Bill Staples
506-453-2708
Director Strategic Business Initiatives, Calvin MacIntosh
506-444-4065
Director Tax Policy, George McAllister
506-453-6920
Manager Tax Program Monitoring, Information & Interpretation, Andrew Foster
506-453-2404

Treasury / Trésorerie
506-453-3952
Fax: 506-453-2053
Asst. Deputy Minister, John Dicaire
Managing Director Corporate Affairs, Nicole Picot
Managing Director Debt Management, Leonard Lee-White
Managing Director Banking & Cash Management, Roger Jones

Department of Fisheries / Pêches

Research Station
850 Lincoln Rd.
Fredericton, NB E3B 9H8
506-453-2666
Fax: 506-453-7170
Minister, Hon. Rick Doucet
Deputy Minister, James Byron
506-453-2450, Fax: 506-444-5022, byron.james@gnb.ca
Director Communications, Alain Bryar
506-444-4218, Fax: 506-444-5022, alain.bryar@gnb.ca

Department of Justice & Consumer Affairs / Justice et la consommation

PO Box 6000
Fredericton, NB E3B 5H1
506-462-5100
www.gov.nb.ca/justice/index.htm
Formerly Justice & Office of the Attorney General.

Acts Administered:
Absconding Debtors Act
Age of Majority Act
Arbitration Act
Arrest & Examinations Act
Assignments & Preferences Act
Auctioneers Licence Act
Canadian Judgments Act
Charter Compliance Acts
Collection Agencies Act

Commissioners for Taking Affidavits Act
Conflict of Laws Rules for Trusts Act
Consumer Product Warranty & Liability Act
Contributory Negligence Act
Controverted Elections Act
Co-operative Associations Act
Corrupt Practices Inquiries Act
Cost of Credit Disclosure Act
Court Reporters Act
Credit Unions Act
Creditors Relief Act
Criminal Prosecution Expenses Act
Crown Debts Act
Crown Prosecutors Act
Defamation Act
Demise of the Crown Act
Devolution of Estates Act
Direct Sellers Act
Divorce Court Act
Easements Act
Electronic Transactions Act
Entry Warrants Act
Escheats & Forfeitures Act
Evidence Act
Executors & Trustees Act
Expropriation Act
Factors & Agents Act
Family Services Act (Part VII)
Fatal Accidents Act
Federal Courts Jurisdiction Act
Foreign Judgments Act
Frustrated Contracts Act
Garnishee Act
Great Seal Act
Guardianship of Children Act
Habeas Corpus Act
Infirm Persons Act
Innkeepers Act
Inquiries Act
Insurance Act
Interjurisdicational Support Orders Act
International Child Abduction Act
International Commercial Arbitration Act
International Sale of Goods Act
International Trusts Act
International Wills Act
Interpretation Act
Interprovincial Subpoena Act
Judges Disqualification Removal Act
Judicature Act
Jury Act
Landlord & Tenant Act
Law Reform Act
Legal Aid Act
Liens on Goods & Chattels Act
Limitation of Actions Act
Loan & Trust Companies Act
Marital Property Act
Married Woman's Property Act
Mechanics' Lien Act
Memorials & Executions Act
Merger of Supreme & County Courts of New Brunswick Act
Notaries Public Act
Nova Scotia Grants Act
Postal Services Interruption Act
Pre-arranged Funeral Services Act
Premium Tax Act
Presumption of Death Act
Probate Court Act
Proceedings Against the Crown Act
Property Act
Protection of Persons Acting Under Statute Act
Provincial Court Act
Provincial Offences Procedure Act
Provincial Offences Procedure for Young Persons Act
Provision for Dependants Act
Public Records Act
Queen's Counsel & Precedence Act
Queen's Printer Act
Quieting of Titles Act
Real Estate Agents Act
Reciprocal Enforcement of Judgments Act
Reciprocal Recognition & Enforcement of Judgements in Civil & Commerical Matters Act
(An Act Respecting the Convention Between Canada & the United Kingdom of Great Britain & Northern Ireland Providing For
Recording of Evidence by Sound Recording Machine Act
Regulations Act
(An Act Respecting the) Removal of Archaic Terminology from the Acts of New Brunswick
Residential Tenancies Act
Sale of Goods Act
Sale of Lands Publication Act
Sheriffs Act
Small Claims Act
Special Insurance Companies Act
Statute Law Amendment Acts
Statute of Frauds Act
Statute Revision Act
Succession Law Amendment Acts
Support Enforcement Act
Surety Bonds Act
Survival of Actions Act
Survivorship Act
Tortfeasors Act
Trespass Act
Trustees Act
Unconscionable Transactions Relief Act
Wage-Earners Protection Act
Warehouse Receipts Act
Warehouseman's Lien Act
Wills Act
Woodmen's Lien Act

Minister, Hon. Thomas J. Burke
Deputy Minister & Deputy Attorney General, Yvon LeBlanc
Executive Director Administrative Services, Neil Foreman
506-462-5100, neil.foreman@gnb.ca
Director Policy & Planning, Debbie Hackett
506-462-5100, debbie.hackett@gnb.ca
Administrative Secretary, Christine O'Donnell
506-453-6504, Fax: 506-653-8718, christine.odonnell@gnb.ca

Associated Agencies, Boards & Commissions:

• New Brunswick Credit Union Deposit Insurance / Société d'assurance-dépôts des caisses populaires du Nouveau-Brunswick
PO Box 6000
Fredericton, NB E3B 5H1
506-453-2315
Fax: 506-453-7474

• New Brunswick Expropriations Advisory Office / Bureau sur l'expropriation
371 Queen St.
Fredericton, NB E3B 1B1
506-453-7771
Fax: 506-453-9600

• New Brunswick Insurance Board / Commission des assurances du N.-B.
Saint John Mercantile Centre
#600, 55 Union St.
Saint John, NB E2L 5B7
506-643-7710
Fax: 506-652-5011
info@bib-canb.org

• New Brunswick Real Estate Association / Association des agents immobiliers du Nouveau-Brunswick
#1, 22 Durelle St.
Fredericton, NB E3C 1N8
506-459-8055
Fax: 506-459-8057
800-762-1677
nbrea@nbnet.nb.ca
www.nbrea.nb.ca

• New Brunswick Securities Commission / Commission des valeurs mobilières du N.-B.
#300, 85 Charlotte St.
Saint John, NB E2L 2J2
506-658-3060
Fax: 506-658-3059
866-933-2222
information@nbsc-cvmnb.ca

Justice Services / Services judiciaires

Fax: 506-444-2661
Asst. Deputy Minister, Suzanne Bonnell-Burley
506-462-5100, suzanne.bonnell-burley@gnb.ca
Director Credit Unions, Cooperatives & Trust Companies Branch & Director, Examinations, Robert Penney
506-453-2315, Fax: 506-453-7474
Director Insurance, Roderick Mackenzie, Q.C.
506-453-5100, Fax: 506-453-7435, Roderick.Mackenzie@gnb.ca
Director Office of the Rentalsman & Consumer Affairs Branch, Marilyn Evans-Born
506-462-5100, Fax: 506-453-2613, marilyn.born@gnb.ca

Regional Development Corporation (RDC) / Société d'aménagement régional (SAR)

RDC Bldg.
836 Churchill Row
PO Box 428
Fredericton, NB E3B 5R4
506-453-2277
Fax: 506-453-7988
www.gnb.ca/0096/index-e.asp

Head agency for the negotiation & planning processes associated with federal & provincial economic development agreements & arrangements. The RDC makes recommendations to the provincial Cabinet concerning economic developmentopportunities & priorities. Provides ongoing financial & administrative management services for federal & provincial agreements. The delivery of programs & projects is primarily the responsibility of provincial departments. Staff work cooperativelywith other federal & provincial personnel in various activities. The RDC also works with the Atlantic Canada Opportunities Agency on many regional economic development projects & issues in New Brunswick. The Corporation is responsible for theimplementation of the Youth Capital Assistance Program (FYCAP).

Minister Responsible, Hon. Roly MacIntyre
President, Bernard Paulin
506-453-8542
Vice-President Corporate Services & Programs, Doug Holt
506-453-2277, douglas.holt@gnb.ca.ca
Vice-President Development & Special Initiatives, Bill Levesque
506-453-8524, bill.levesque@gnb.ca
Corporate Secretary, Bruce Macfarlane
506-444-4606, bruce.macfarlane@gnb.ca

Service New Brunswick (SNB) / Services Nouveau-Brunswick (SNB)

#200, 82 Westmorland St.
PO Box 1998
Fredericton, NB E3B 5G4
506-457-3581
Fax: 506-453-3043
snb@snb.ca
www.snb.ca
Other Communication: TeleServices: 1-888-762-8600

Chief provider of front-line services to the public, through a network of office locations, online services & teleservices (call centre). Provide one-stop delivery of federal, provincial & municipal government services. Operates the RealProperty Registry, the Personal Property Registry, the Corporate Affairs Registry. Assesses all land, buildings & improvements for property taxation purposes & operates the province's property assessment & taxation system. Maintains New Brunswick'sland information infrastructure.

Acts Administered:

Air Space Act
Assessment Act
Boundaries Confirmation Act
Business Corporation Act
Common Business Identifier Act
Companies Act
Condominium Property Act
Corporations Act
Foreign Resident Corporations Act
Land Titles Act
Limited Partnership Act
Partnership Act
Partnerships & Business Names Registration Act
Personal Property Security Act
Registry Act
Residential Property Tax Relief Act
Service New Brunswick Act
Special Corporate Continuance Act
Standard Forms of Conveyances Act

GOVERNMENT

Surveys Act
Winding-Up Act
Minister Responsible, Hon. Greg Byrne
CEO, Mike McKendy
506-457-3582, Fax: 506-457-7520, mike.mckendy@snb.ca
Vice-President Corporate Services, Carol Macdonald, C.A.
506-457-4805, Fax: 506-444-5239, carol.macdonald@snb.ca
Corporate Legal Counsel Directorate, Claude Poirier
506-869-6389, Fax: 506-869-6523, claude.poirier@snb.ca
Acting Vice-President Operations & Director, Electronic Services, Bernard Arseneau
506-457-4959, Fax: 506-444-3033, bernard.arseneau@snb.ca
General Manager Business Development, Marketing & Sales, David Roberts
506-453-3698, Fax: 506-453-5384, david.roberts@gnb.ca
Executive Director Assessment Services, Bill Morrison
506-453-2658, Fax: 506-453-4005, bill.morrison@snb.ca
Executive Director Strategic Initiatives, Jean Stewart
506-453-7191, Fax: 506-453-3898, jean.stewart@snb.ca
Executive Director Sales, France Hache
506-462-5061, Fax: 506-453-5384, france.hache@snb.ca
Director Administrative Services, David English
506-444-4860, Fax: 506-444-5239, david.english@snb.ca
Director Corporate Affairs, Charles McAllister
506-453-3860, Fax: 506-453-2613, charles.mcallister@snb.ca
Director Vital Statistics, Josée Dubé
506-453-2385, Fax: 506-453-3245, josee.dube@snb.ca
Director Financial Services, Linda Corbett
506-453-3915, Fax: 506-444-5239, linda.corbett@snb.ca
Acting Director Human Resources, Donat Theriault
506-453-8960, Fax: 506-453-3043, donat.theriault@snb.ca
Director Information Technology, Dorothea Foley
506-453-3386, Fax: 506-453-3898, dorothea.foley@snb.ca
Director Business Development, Jeff Trail
506-444-5775, Fax: 506-453-5384, jeff.trail@snb.ca
Director Project Delivery, Darrell Fowler
506-444-5401, Fax: 506-462-2018, darrell.fowler@snb.ca
Director Surveys, Leo-Guy Leblanc
506-453-2353, Fax: 506-453-3898, leo-guy.leblanc@snb.ca
Director Marketing & Communications, Brent Staeben
506-453-6775, Fax: 506-453-5384, brent.staeben@snb.ca
Director Regional Services, Gary Bard
506-643-6200, Fax: 506-658-2156, gary.bard@snb.ca
Director Sales, Gary Wood
506-462-5013, Fax: 506-453-5384, gary.wood@snb.ca
Admin. Support, Audy Furlong
506-444-4922, Fax: 506-453-3935, andy.furlong@snb.ca

Government of Newfoundland & Labrador

Seat of Government: Confederation Bldg.
St. John's, NL A1B 4J6
www.gov.nl.ca
The Province of Newfoundland & Labrador entered Confederation March 31, 1949. It has an area of 371,634.56 km2, & the StatsCan census population in 2001 was 512,930.

Office of the Premier

Confederation Bldg., East Block
PO Box 8700
St. John's, NL A1B 4J6
709-729-3570
Fax: 709-729-5875
premier@gov.nl.ca
www.gov.nl.ca/premier
Premier, Hon. Danny Williams
Chief of Staff, Brian Crawley
709-729-3570
Deputy Minister to the Premier, Ross Reid
709-729-3095
Director Communications, Elizabeth Matthews
709-729-3970, Fax: 709-729-5875

Executive Council

Confederation Bldg.
PO Box 8700
St. John's, NL A1B 4J6
709-729-5645
Premier, Hon. Danny Williams
Minister Natural Resources, Hon. Kathy Dunderdale
Minister Education & Minister Responsible, Status of Women, Hon. Joan Burke
Minister Health & Community Services, Hon. Ross Wiseman
Minister Tourism, Culture & Recreation, Hon. Tom Hedderson
Minister Government Services & Minister Responsible, Government Purchasing Agency, Hon. Dianne Whalen
Minister Municipal Affairs & Registrar General; Minister Responsible, Emergency Preparedness, Hon. Jack Byrne
Minister Fisheries & Aquaculture, Minister Responsible for Aboriginal Affairs, Attorney General, Deputy Premier, Hon. Tom Rideout
Minister Human Resources, Labour & Employment & Minister Responsible, Newfoundland & Labrador Housing, Hon. Shawn Skinner
Minister Innovation, Trade & Rural Development & Minister Responsible, Rural Secretariat, Hon. Trevor Taylor
Minister Finance & President, Treasury Board & Government House Leader, Hon. Loyola Sullivan
Minister Justice, Hon. Tom Osborne
Minister Intergovernmental Affairs, Hon. John Ottenheimer
Minister Environment & Conservation, Hon. Clyde Jackman
Minister Transportation & Works & Minister Responsible, Labrador Affairs, Hon. John Hickey
Minister Business, Hon. Kevin O'Brien
Document Control Officer, Jeanette Fleming
709-729-2921, Fax: 709-729-5218, jfleming@cab.gov.nf.ca

Rural Secretatariat

PO Box 8700
St. John's, NL A1B 4J6
709-729-0168
Fax: 709-729-1673
ruralinfo@gov.nl.ca
www.exec.gov.nl.ca/rural/
Minister Responsible, Hon. Trevor Taylor
Asst. Deputy Minister, Alison Earle
709-729-1611

Cabinet Secretariat

Fax: 709-729-5218
Clerk Executive Council & Secretary to the Cabinet, Robert Thompson
709-729-2853, Fax: 709-729-5218, rthompson@gov.nl.ca
Deputy Clerk Executive Council & Associate Secretary to the Cabinet, Sandra Barnes
709-729-2844, Fax: 709-729-5218
Assistant Secretary Communications, Josephine Cheeseman
709-729-4781, Fax: 709-729-5645
Assistant Secretary Economic Policy, Bill Parrott
709-729-2845, Fax: 709-729-5218
Assistant Secretary Social Policy, Gary Cake
709-729-2850, Fax: 709-729-5218
Acting Director Financial & General Operations, Linda Vaughan
709-729-7337, Fax: 709-729-0435
Director Protocol, David Dempster
709-729-3670, Fax: 709-729-6878

Office of the Chief Information Officer

PO Box 8700
St. John's, NL A1B 4J6
709-729-4000
Fax: 709-729-6767
ocio@gov.nl.ca
Chief Information Officer, Peter Shea

Office of the Auditor General

Viking Bldg., 3rd Fl.
PO Box 8700
St. John's, NL A1B 4J6
709-729-2700
Fax: 709-729-5970
Auditor General, John L. Noseworthy, C.A.
jnoseworthy@gov.nl.ca
Dpeuty Auditor General, Wayne Loveys

Department of Finance

Confederation Bldg.
PO Box 8700
St. John's, NL A1B 4J6
709-729-6310
www.gov.nl.ca/fin/
Other Communication: Tax Inquiries: 709/729-3831
Acts Administered:
Department of Finance Act
Financial Administration Act
Financial Corporations Capital Tax Act
Gasoline Tax Act
Government Money Purchase Pension Plan Act
Health & Post-Secondary Education Tax Act
Horse Racing Regulation & Tax Act
Industrial Development Corporation Act
Insurance Companies Tax Act
Liquor Corporation Act
The Loan Act
The Loan & Guarantee Act, 1957
The Local Authority Guarantee Act, 1957
Members of the House of Assembly Pensions Act
Mining & Mineral Rights Tax Act
Municipal Financing Corporation Act
Pension Benefits Act, 1997
Pensions Funding Act
Public Service Pensions Act, 1991
Retail Sales Tax Act
School Tax Authorities Winding Up Act
Statistics Agency Act
Tax Agreement Act
Taxation of Utilities & Cable Television Companies Act
Teachers' Pensions Act
Tobacco Tax Act
Uniformed Services Pensions Act
Minister & President, Treasury Board, Hon. Loyola Sullivan
709-729-3775
Deputy Minister, Terry Paddon
709-729-2946, Fax: 709-729-2232
Director Financial Administrative Shared Services, Linda Vaughn
709-729-7337, Fax: 709-729-0435
Director Human Resources Development & Shared Services, Elizabeth Horwood
709-729-6435, Fax: 709-729-5421

Associated Agencies, Boards & Commissions:
• C.A. Pippy Park Commission
PO Box 8861
St. John's, NL A1B 3T2
709-737-3655
Fax: 709-737-3303
877-477-3655
pippyparkinfo@nf.aibn.com
www.pippypark.com
• Newfoundland & Labrador Municipal Financing Corporation (NMFC)
Confederation Bldg.
PO Box 8700
St. John's, NL A1B 4J6
709-729-6686
Fax: 709-729-2095
• Newfoundland Liquor Corporation
90 Kenmount Rd.
PO Box 8750 A
St. John's, NL A1B 3V1
709-724-1100
Fax: 709-754-0529
info@nfliquor.com
www.nfliquor.com

Economics & Statistics

Asst. Deputy Minister, Beverley Carter
709-729-0864, Fax: 709-729-0393
Director Economic Research & Analysis, Rod Forsey
709-729-2951, Fax: 709-729-0393
Director Newfoundland Statistics Agency, Alton Hollett
709-729-0158, Fax: 709-729-0393

Financial Planning & Benefits Administration

Asst. Deputy Minister, Donna Brewer
709-729-4581, Fax: 709-729-1746
Director Budgeting, Joan Morris
709-729-4407, Fax: 709-729-2156
Director Insurance, Anthony Lannon
709-729-0502, Fax: 709-729-2156
Director Debt Management, Earl Saunders
709-729-6848, Fax: 709-729-2095
Director Pensions Administration, Maureen McCarthy
709-729-5983, Fax: 709-729-2070

Office of the Comptroller General

Comptroller General, Ronald Williams
709-729-5926, Fax: 709-729-7627
Director Government Accounting, John Martin
709-729-2341, Fax: 709-729-7627
Director Professional Services & Internal Audit, David Hill
709-729-0702, Fax: 709-729-2098

Taxation & Fiscal Policy

Asst. Deputy Minister, Robert Constantine
709-729-2944, Fax: 709-729-2070
Director Fiscal Policy, Christopher Butt
709-729-6714, Fax: 709-729-2070
Director Tax Administration, Bernard Cook
709-729-6307, Fax: 709-729-2277
Director Tax Policy, Jay Griffin
709-729-6847, Fax: 709-729-2070
Director Project Analysis, Brian Hurley
709-729-3669

Department of Government Services

PO Box 8700
St. John's, NL A1B 4J6
709-729-4860
www.gs.gov.nl.ca
Departmental responsibilities include: motor vehicle registration, government service centres, consumer protection, trade practices, vital statistics, lotteries, registries, building accessibility, residential tenancies services,regulation of financial institutions, occupational health & safety, Office of the Queen's Printer, Government Purchasing Agency, permits, licences, approvals & inspections for public health & safety.

Acts Administered:
Accident & Sickness Insurance Act
Architects Act
Automobile Insurance Act
Bank of Nova Scotia Trust Company Act, 1997
Buildings Accessibility Act
Bulk Sales Act
Business Electronic Filing Act
Certified General Accountants Act
Certified Public Accountants Act
Change of Name Act
Chartered Accountants Act
Chartered Accountants & Certified Public Accountants Merger Act
Collections Act
Consumer Protection Act
Condominium Act
Consumer Reporting Agencies Act
Co-operatives Act
Conveyancing Act
Corporations Act
Corporations Guarantee Act
Credit Union Act
Criminal Code
Direct Sellers Act
Electronic Commerce Act
Embalmers & Funeral Director Act
Engineers & Geoscientists Act
Fire Insurance Act
Income Tax Savings Plan Act
Insurance Adjusters, Agents & Brokers Act
Insurance Companies Act
Insurance Contracts Act
Intergovernmental Joint Purchasing Act
Investment Contracts Act
Judgement Recovery (Nfld) Ltd. Act
Life Insurance Act
Limited Partnership Act
Lodgers' Goods Protection Act
Management Accountants Act
Maritime Hospital Service Association Re-Incorporation Act
Mechanics Lien Act
Mortgage Brokers Act
Occupational Health & Safety Act
Asbestos Abatement Regulations
Asbestos Exposure Code Regulations
Mines Safety of Workers Regulations
Occupational Health & Safety Electrical & Fisheries Advisory Committees Regulations
Occupational Health & Safety Regulations
Workplace Hazardous Materials Information System (WHMIS) Regulations
Pension Benefits Act, 1997
Pension Plans Designation of Beneficiaries Act
Perpetuities & Accumulations Act
Personal Property Security Act
Petroleum Products Act
Prepaid Funeral Services Act
Printing Services Act
Private Investigation & Security Services Act
Public Accountancy Act
Public Safety Act
Public Tender Act
Radiation Health & Safety Act
Real Estate Trading Act
Registration of Deeds Act
Residential Tenancies Act, 2000
Sale of Goods Act
Securities Act
Security Interest Registration Act
Solemnization of Marriage Act
Trade Practices Act
Trust & Loan Corporations Licensing Act
Trustee Act
Unconscionable Transactions Relief Act
Unsolicited Goods & Credit Cards Act
Vital Statistics Act
Warehouse Receipts Act
Warehouse's Lien Act
Workplace Health, Safety & Compensation Act
Acts Shared in Part with Other Ministries
Adoptions Act (Health & Community Services)
Building Standards Act (Municipal Affairs)
Child Care Services Act (Health & Community Services)
Child, Youth & Family Services Act (Health & Community Services)
Children's Law Act (Justice)
Communicable Diseases Act (Health & Community Services)
Dangerous Goods Transportation Act (Justice)
Employers' Liability Act (Justice)
Environmental Protection Act (Environment & Conservation)
Fire Prevention Act, 1991 (Municipal Affairs)
Food & Drug Act (Health & Community Services)
Fraudulent Conveyance Act (Justice)
Health & Community Services Act (Health & Community Services)
Highway Traffic Act (Transportation & Works)
Meat Inspection Act (Natural Resources)
Motor Carrier Act (Transportation & Works)
Motorized Snow Vehicles & All-Terrain Vehicles Act (Natural Resources)
Tobacco Act (Federal) (Health & Community Services)
Urban & Rural Planning Act (Municipal Affairs)
Water Resources Act (Environment & Conservation)
Minister, Hon. Dianne Whalen
709-729-4712, Fax: 709-729-4754
Deputy Minister, Sheree MacDonald
709-729-4751, Fax: 709-729-4754
Director Financial Management, Gerry Crocker
709-729-4751, Fax: 709-729-4754
Director Human Resources, Glenn Saunders
709-729-5102, Fax: 709-729-6661
Director Communications, Vanessa Colman-Sadd
709-729-4860, Fax: 709-729-4754
Manager Financial Operations, Wayne Moores
709-729-2041, Fax: 709-729-2609
Manager General Operations, Vacant
709-729-5427, Fax: 709-729-2609
Manager Human Resources, Doug Redmond
709-729-4385, Fax: 709-729-2609
Manager Customer Service, Jim Andrews
709-729-3097, Fax: 709-729-3980, jandrews@gov.nl.ca

Associated Agencies, Boards & Commissions:
• Credit Union Deposit Corporation
PO Box 340
Marystown, NL A0B 2M0
709-279-0170
Fax: 709-279-0177
www.cudgc.nf.net

Consumer & Commercial Affairs Branch

Promotes economic development by assisting businesses & protecting consumers. The branch is responsible for regulating the insurance industry, the securities industries, the trust & loan industry, the credit union industry, the realestate industry, collection agencies, mortgage brokers, automobile dealers, charitable gaming, private investigation agencies, & landlord-tenant relations.

Asst. Deputy Minister, Winston Morris
709-729-2570, Fax: 709-729-4151
Director Commercial Registrations, Doug Laing
709-729-3316, Fax: 709-729-0232
Deputy Registrar Deeds & Personal Property Securities Act, Lorraine Vokey
709-729-5724, Fax: 709-729-0232
Deputy Registrar Lobbyists & Companies, Dean Doyle
709-729-4043, Fax: 709-729-0232
Director Financial Services Regulation, Doug Connolly, C.A.
709-729-2594, Fax: 709-729-3205
Director Trade Practices, Gerard Burke
709-729-2618, Fax: 709-729-6998

Department of Innovation, Trade & Rural Development

PO Box 8700
St. John's, NL A1B 4J6
709-729-7000
Fax: 709-729-0654
800-563-2299
itrdinfo@gov.nl.ca
www.gov.nl.ca/intrd
The department has a number of initiatives to assist businesses in the province or to open in the province.

Acts Administered:
Business Investment Corporation Act
Economic Diversification & Growth Enterprises (EDGE) Act
Industries Act
Research Council Act
Minister, Hon. Trevor Taylor
709-729-4728, Fax: 709-729-0654
Deputy Minister, Cathy Duke
Director Communications, Lynn Evans
709-729-4570, Fax: 709-729-4880
Director Information Management, Ruth Parsons
709-729-1940, Fax: 709-729-4858
Director Policy & Strategic Planning, Andrea Dicks
709-729-4868

Associated Agencies, Boards & Commissions:
• Ireland Business Partnership
PO Box 8700
St. John's, NL A1B 4J6
709-729-1684
Fax: 709-729-2236
A joint public-private partnership with the Government of Ireland to promote business opportunities & educational & cultural exchanges with Newfoundland & Labrador.~

• Nearshore Atlantic
84 Elizabeth Ave., 1st Fl.
St. John's, NL A1A 1W7
709-772-8324
Fax: 709-757-6284
info@nearshoreatlantic.com
www.nearshoreatlantic.com
A public-private partnership between the Government of Newfoundland & Labrador, Aliant & the Newfoundland & Labrador Association of Technical Industries (Nati). The initiative has been developed to promote the Province as a premierdestination for nearshore services in the expanding global IT service delivery model. Nearshore Atlantic is governed by a Steering Committee consisting of representatives of both private & public sectors.

Strategic Industries & Business Development Branch

Asst. Deputy Minister, Philip McCarthy
709-729-4711, Fax: 709-729-4858
Director Strategic Industries Development, Kirk Tilley
709-729-7080, Fax: 709-729-6853
Director Business Analysis, Don Kavanagh
709-729-5066, Fax: 709-729-5936

Trade & Investment Branch

Specializes in assisting provincial businesses develop an export plan to enter new markets, find export business partners & research national & international market opportunities.

Director, Paul Morris
709-729-2781, Fax: 709-729-3208

Director Strategic Partnerships Initiative, Derek Staubitzer
709-729-7043

Department of Justice

Confederation Bldg.
PO Box 8700
St. John's, NL A1B 4J6
709-729-5942
Fax: 709-729-2129
www.gov.nl.ca/just/
Acts Administered:
Adult Corrections Act
Advance Health Care Directives Act
Age of Majority Act
Agreement for Policing the Province Act
American Bases Act, 1941
Apportionment Act
Arbitration Act
Bankers' Books Act
Blind Persons' Rights Act
Canada & United Kingdom Reciprocal Recognition & Enforcement of Judgments Act
Change of Name Act (with Government Services & Lands)
Chattels Real Act
Children's Law Act (with Government Services & Lands)
Commissioners for Oaths Act
Contributory Negligence Act
Criminal Code
Defamation Act
Detention of Intoxicated Persons Act
Divorce Act, 1985 (Canada)
Electoral Boundaries Act
Enduring Powers of Attorney Act
Evidence Act
Exhumation Act
Family Law Act
Family Relief Act
Fatal Accidents Act
Fatalities Investigations Act
Federal Courts Jurisdiction Act
Fraudulent Conveyances Act (with Government Services & Lands)
Freedom of Information Act
Frustrated Contracts Act
Human Rights Code
International Commercial Arbitration Act
International Sale of Goods Act
International Trusts Act
Interpretation Act
Interprovincial Subpoena Act
Intestate Succession Act
Judgement Enforcement Act
Judgment Interest Act
Judicature Act
Jury Act, 1991
Justices Act
Justices & Other Public Authorities Protection Act
Law Reform Commission Act
Law Society Act (1999)
Leaseholds in St. John's Act
Legal Aid Act
Limitations Act
Mentally Disabled Persons' Estates Act
Notaries Public Act
Oaths Act
Oaths of Office Act
Partnership Act
Penitentiary Act (Canada)
Petty Trespass Act
Presumption of Death Act
Prisons Act
Prisons & Reformatories Act (Canada)
Privacy Act
Proceedings Against the Crown Act
Proof of Death Members of Armed Forces Act
Provincial Court Act (1991)
Provincial Offences Act
Public Inquiries Act
Public Investigations Evidence Act
Public Trustee Act
Public Utilities Acquisition of Lands Act
Public Utilities Act
Queen's Counsel Act
Quieting of Titles Act
Reciprocal Enforcement of Judgments Act
Reciprocal Enforcement of Support Orders Act
Recording of Evidence Act
Revised Statutes, 1990 Act
Royal Newfoundland Constabulary Act, 1992
Sheriff's Act, 1991
Small Claims Act
Statutes Act
Statutes Amendment Act
Statutes & Subordinate Legislation Act
Subordinate Legislation Revision & Consolidation Act
Support Orders Enforcement Act (with Social Services)
Survival of Actions Act
Survivorship Act
Unified Family Court Act
Victims of Crime Services Act
Wills Act
Young Offenders Act (Canada - with Social Services)
Young Persons Offences Act(with Social Services)
Minister & Attorney General, Hon. Tom Marshall
709-729-2869
Deputy Minister & Deputy Attorney General, Christopher Curran, Q.C.
709-729-2872
Assoc. Deputy Minister, Donald Burrage
709-729-0288
Acting Asst. Deputy Minister Public Prosecutions, Pam Goulding
709-729-2868
Director Communications, Bill Hickey
709-729-6985
Director Finance & General Operations Division, Theresa Heffernan
709-729-2890
Acting Director Human Resources, Patricia Power
709-729-4256
Director Policy & Strategic Planning, Jackie Lake-Kavanagh
709-729-0543
Chief Medical Examiner, Dr. Simon Avis
709-777-6402
Communications Officer, Heather Donovan
709-729-6985, Fax: 709-729-0469

Associated Agencies, Boards & Commissions:
• Human Rights Commission
Listed alphabetically in detail.
• Newfoundland & Labrador Board of Commissioners of Public Utilities
Listed alphabetically in detail.
• Newfoundland & Labrador Legal Aid Commission
Cormack Bldg.
2 Steers Cove
PO Box 399 C
St. John's, NL A1C 5J9
709-753-7860
Fax: 709-753-6226
800-563-9911
www.gov.nf.ca/just/Other/otherx/legalaid.htm
• Royal Newfoundland Constabulary Public Complaints Commission
Bally Rou Place
#E-160, 280 Torbay Rd.
St. John's, NL A1A 3W8
709-729-0950
Fax: 709-729-1302
www.gov.nl.ca/mcpcc

Government of the Northwest Territories

Seat of Government:PO Box 1320
Yellowknife, NT X1A 2L9
www.gov.nt.ca
The Northwest Territories was reconstituted September 1, 1905. It has an area of 1,004,470 km2, & the StatsCan population in 2001 was 37,360. On April 1, 1999, the Northwest Territories was divided into two new territories: NunavutTerritories and the as yet unnamed territory (known as the Northwest Territories). The Northwest Territories is governed by a fully elected Legislative Assembly of 19 members elected for a four-year term. Government is by consensus rather than partypolitics. The Legislature elects the Premier & a seven-member Executive Council, which is charged with the operation of government & the establishment of program & spending priorities. The Commissioner of the Northwest Territories is appointed by theFederal Government, & serves a role similar to that of a Lieutenant Governor in provincial jurisdictions.

Office of the Premier

Legislative Assembly Bldg.
PO Box 1320
Yellowknife, NT X1A 2L9
867-669-2311
Fax: 867-873-0385
www.premier.gov.nt.ca
Premier, Hon. Joe Handley
Communications Coordinator, Julia Mott
867-669-2304

Executive Council

PO Box 1320
Yellowknife, NT X1A 2L9
Premier & Minister, Executive; Minister, Aboriginal Affairs & Intergovernmental Affairs; Minister Responsible, NWT Housing Corp., Hon. Joe Handley
867-669-2311
Deputy Premier & Minister, Finance; Minister, Health & Social Services; Minister Responsible, Financial Management Board, Hon. Floyd Roland
867-669-2344
Minister Education, Culture & Employment & Minister, HUman Resources; Government House Leader; Minister Responsible, Status of Women, Seniors, Person, Hon. Charles Dent
867-669-2366
Minister Industry, Tourism & Investment & Minister, Justice; Minister Responsible, the Homeless, Hon Brendan Bell
867-669-2388
Minister Environment & Natural Resources & Minister, Municipal & Community Affairs; Minister Responsible, Youth, Hon. Michael McLeod
867-669-2377
Minister Public Works & Services & Minister Responsible, NWT Power Corporation, Workers Compensation Board, Hon. David Krutko
867-669-2399
Executive Press Officer, Drew Williams
867-669-2304, Fax: 867-873-0111,
drew_williams@govt.nt.ca

Department of Finance

PO Box 1320
Yellowknife, NT X1A 2L9
867-873-0414
Fax: 867-873-7117
www.fin.gov.nt.ca
Responsible for obtaining the financial resources to carry on the functions of government & for intergovernmental fiscal negotiations & arrangements. The territorial government has a budget of over $1,055 million (including federalgovernment transfers & grants of $795 million).
Acts Administered:
Borrowing Authorization Act
Central Trust Company Act
Certified General Accountants' Association Act
Financial Agreement Act
Income Tax Act
Income Tax Collection Agreement Questions Act
Institute of Chartered Accountants Act
Insurance Act
Liquor Act
Loan Authorization Act
Northwest Territories Energy Corporation Ltd. Loan Guarantee Act
Payroll Tax Act, 1993
Petroleum Products Tax Act
Property & Assessment Taxation Act
Public Utilities Income Tax Rebates Act
Risk Capital Investment Tax Credit Act
Society of Management Accountants Act
Tobacco Tax Act
Minister, Hon. Floyd Roland
867-669-2344, Fax: 867-873-0481
Deputy Minister, Margaret M. Melhorn
867-873-7117, Fax: 867-873-0414,
margaret_melhorn@gov.nt.ca
Manager Risk Management & Insurance, Lois Grabke

Manager Policy & Planning, Joseph La Ferla
867-920-6364, Fax: 867-873-0414, joseph_laferla@gov.nt.ca
Executive Secretary, Melanie Heppelle
867-873-7117, Fax: 867-873-0414,
melanie_heppelle@gin.gov.nt.ca

Associated Agencies, Boards & Commissions:
• Northwest Territories Liquor Commission
#201, 31 Capital Dr.
Hay River, NT X0E 1G2
867-874-2100
Fax: 867-874-2180
• Northwest Territories Liquor Licensing Board
#210, 31 Capital Dr.
Hay River, NT X0E 1G2
867-874-2906
Fax: 867-874-6011
delilah_st-arneault@gov.nt.ca
• Northwest Territories Liquor Licensing & Enforcement
#210, 31 Capital Dr.
Hay River, NT X0E 1G2
867-874-2906
Fax: 867-874-6011

Finance & Administration
Fax: 867-873-0325
Director, Mel Enge
867-873-7158, mel_enge@gov.nt.ca

Fiscal Policy
Fax: 867-873-0381
Responsible for developing policies & providing research, analysis & recommendations on the fiscal policies of government. The Division also administers the Formula Financing Agreement with Canada & is responsible for intergovernmentalfiscal relations.

Director, John Monroe
867-920-6436, john_monroe@gov.nt.ca
Manager Tax Policy, Vacant
867-920-8891, gerry_gagnon@gov.nt.ca
Manager Fiscal Relations & Economic Policy, Kelly Bluck
867-873-7171, kelly_bluck@gov.nt.ca

Treasury
Fax: 867-873-0325
800-661-0820
Treasury is responsible for managing the government's cash position; conducting banking, borrowing & investment activities; protecting the government's activities & assets from risk of loss by means of appropriate insurance coverage &risk management activities; & regulating insurance companies, agents, brokers & adjusters operating in the NWT.

Director, Doug Doak
867-920-3423, doug_doak@gov.nt.ca

Financial Management Board Secretariat
5003 - 49 St.
PO Box 1320
Yellowknife, NT X1A 2L9
867-920-8962
Fax: 867-873-0128
Manages & controls the government's financial, human & information resources. Provides centralized services.

Minister, Hon. Floyd K. Roland
867-669-2344
Deputy Minister, Mark Cleveland
Director Audit Bureau, Bob Shahi
867-873-7700, Fax: 867-873-0209
Director Budgeting & Evaluation, Terry Pierce
867-920-8689
Director Compensation Services & Labour Relations, Sylvia Haener
867-873-7786, Fax: 867-873-0282
Asst. Comptroller General, John Carter
867-920-3401, Fax: 867-873-0296
Manager Information Management, Fred Ruthven
867-920-8963, Fax: 867-873-0128

Department of Industry, Tourism & Investment (ITI)
PO Box 1320
Yellowknife, NT X1A 2L9
www.iti.gov.nt.ca

Acts Administered:
Agricultural Products Marketing Act
Business Development & Investment Corporation Act
Co-operative Associations Act
Credit Union Act
Freshwater Fish Marketing Act
Herd & Fencing Act
Industry, Tourism & Investment Act
Territorial Parks Act
Minister, Hon. Brendan Bell
867-669-2388
Deputy Minister, Peter Vician
867-920-8048
Asst. Deputy Minister Programs & Operations, Doug Doan
867-873-7115
Asst. Deputy Minister Strategic Initiatives, Vacant
867-920-8691
Director Energy Planning, Dave Nightingale
867-920-3274
Acting Director Investment & Economic Analysis, Garry Singer
867-873-7361
Director Mackenzie Valley Pipeline Office, Tim Coleman
867-874-5405
Director Minerals, Oil & Gas, Deb Archibald
867-920-3214
Director Policy, Legislation & Communications, Sonya Saunders
867-873-7005
Director Shared Services Informatics, Ron Graf
867-920-3327
Director Shared Services, Finance & Administration, Nancy Magrum
867-920-8649
Director Tourism & Parks, Gerry LePrieur
867-873-7902
Chief Geologist, Carolyn Relf
867-669-2635

Associated Agencies, Boards & Commissions:
• Northwest Territories Business Development & Investment Corporation (BDIC)
#701, 5201 - 50 Ave.
Yellowknife, NT X1A 3S9
867-920-6455
Fax: 867-765-0652
bdicinfo@gov.nt.ca
www.bdic.ca
Formerly the Northwest Territories Development Corporation (DEVCORP).

Department of Human Resources
PO Box 1320
Yellowknife, NT X1A 2L9
www.hr.govt.nt.ca
Minister, Hon. Floyd K. Roland
867-669-2344
Deputy Minister, Lynn Elkin
867-920-3399
Director Client Services, Sharilyn Alexander
867-873-7906
Director Employee Relations, Shaleen Woodward
867-873-7786
Manager Policy & Programs, Beth Collins
867-920-8948

Department of Justice
PO Box 1320
Yellowknife, NT X1A 2L9
867-920-6197
www.justice.gov.nt.ca
Minister, Hon. Brendan Bell
867-669-2388
Deputy Minister, Donald Cooper, Q.C.
867-920-6197, donald_cooper@gov.nt.ca
Asst. Deputy Minister & Attorney General, Reg Tolton
867-920-8003
Asst. Deputy Minister & Solicitor General, Bronwyn Watters
867-920-6197
Chief Coroner Coroner's Office, Percy Kinney
867-873-7460
Public Trustee Public Trustee's Office, Larry Pontus
867-873-7464
Director Community Justice, Shirley Kemeys Jones
867-873-7002
Director Finance, Kim Schofield
867-873-7641
Director Legal Division, Karan Shaner
867-920-8605
Director Legal Registries, Gary MacDougall
867-873-7490, gary.macdougall@gov.nt.ca
Director Legislation Division, Mark Aitken, Q.C.
867-873-8777
Director Policy & Planning, Glen Rutland
867-920-6418, Fax: 867-945-8303
Registrar Corporate Registries & Deputy Registrar, Securities, Donald MacDougall
867-920-8984
Registrar Land & Titles & Registrar, Personal Property, Tom Hall
867-920-8986, tom_hall@gov.nt.ca
Coordinator Victims Services, Dawn McInnes
867-920-6911
Executive Secretary, Bev Cameron
867-920-6197, Fax: 867-873-0307, bev_cameron@gov.nt.ca

Associated Agencies, Boards & Commissions:
• Judicial Council
PO Box 188
Yellowknife, NT X1A 2N2
867-873-7105
Fax: 867-873-0287
• Legal Services Board of the Northwest Territories
PO Box 1320
Yellowknife, NT X1A 2L9
867-873-7450
Fax: 867-873-5320
www-jus-tice
www.justice.gov.nt.ca
• Victims Assistance Committee
c/o Community Justice Division
PO Box 1320
Yellowknife, NT X1A 2L9
867-920-6911
Fax: 867-873-0299

Government of Nova Scotia
Seat of Government: Province House
Halifax, NS B3J 2T3
www.gov.ns.ca
The Province of Nova Scotia entered Confederation July 1, 1867. It has an area of 52,840.83 km2, & the StatsCan census population in 2001 was 908,007.

Office of the Premier
One Government Place
1700 Granville St.
PO Box 726
Halifax, NS B3J 2T3
902-424-6600
Fax: 902-424-7648
premier@gov.ns.ca
www.gov.ns.ca/prem/
Premier, Hon. Rodney MacDonald
Deputy Minister, Robert Fowler
902-424-7128, Fax: 902-424-0728
Chief of Staff, Bob Chisholm
Director Communications, Peter Spurway
902-424-4895
Principal Assistant to the Premier & Director, Community Relations, Stephen Greene

Executive Council
One Government Place
PO Box 2125
Halifax, NS B3J 3B7
902-424-5970
Fax: 902-424-0667
Premier & President, Executive Council; Minister, Intergovernmental Affairs, Hon. Rodney MacDonald
Minister Finance & Minister, Aboriginal Affairs; Government House Leader; Minister Responsible, Utility & Review Board, Hon. Michael Baker, Q.C.
Minister Service Nova Scotia & Municipal Relations, Hon. Jamie Muir
Minister Transportation & Public Works & Chair, Treasury & Policy Board; Minister Responsible, Sydney Steel Corporation; Deputy Premier, Hon. Angus MacIsaac

GOVERNMENT

Minister Human Resources & Minister Responsible, Public Service Commission; Minister, Emergency Management, Hon. Ernest Fage
Minister Natural Resources, Hon. David Morse
Minister Health Promotion & Protection & Minister, African Nova Scotian Affairs; Minister, Communications Nova Scotia; Minister, Volunteerism, Hon. Barry Barnet
Minister Economic Development & Minister Responsible, Nova Scotia Business Inc., Hon. Richard Hurlburt
Minister Health & Minister, Acadian Affairs, Hon. Chris A. d'Entremont
Minister Immigration & Chair, Senior Citizens' Secretariat; Minister, Seniors, Hon. Carolyn Bolivar-Getson
Minister Agriculture & Minister Responsible, Maritime Provinces Harness Racing Commission, Hon. Brooke Taylor
Attorney General & Minister Justice & Minister Responsible, Military Relations, Hon. Murray K. Scott
Minister Energy, Hon. Bill Dooks
Minister Fisheries & Aquaculture, Hon. Ron Chisholm
Minister Community Services & Minister Responsible, Disabled Persons Commission, Hon. Judy Streatch
Minister Environment & Labour, Hon. Mark Parent
Minister Tourism, Culture & Heritage, Hon. Len Goucher
Minister Education & Minister Responsible, Youth Secretariat, Hon. Karen Casey
Council Orders Clerk, Carla Kemp
902-424-5970, Fax: 902-424-0667, kempcm@gov.ns.ca

Office of the Auditor General

#302, 1888 Brunswick St.
Halifax, NS B3J 3J8
902-424-5907
Fax: 902-424-4350
www.gov.ns.ca/legi/audg/
Auditor General, Jacques R. Lapointe, B.A., C.A., C.I.A.
lapoinjr@gov.ns.ca
Deputy Auditor General, Claude D. Carter, C.A.
902-424-4396, cartercd@gov.ns.ca
Asst. Auditor General, Elaine M. Morash
902-424-2766, morashem@gov.ns.ca
Asst. Auditor General, Alan D. Horgan, C.A.
902-424-3945, horganal@gov.ns.ca
Administrative Officer, Darleen Langille
902-424-4108, Fax: 902-424-4350, langildm@gov.ns.ca

Department of Economic Development

Maritime Centre
1505 Barrington St., 14th Fl.
PO Box 2311
Halifax, NS B3J 3C8
902-424-0377
Fax: 902-424-0500
comm@gov.ns.ca
www.gov.ns.ca/econ/
The office assists with knowledge management, trade policy, special projects, government relations regarding economic development issues, labour advice, regarding the work force of the future, information on the business climate &assistance on strategic infrastructure. The Office provides assistance with strategic management & rural development regarding the business climate, & services such as the Rural Development Branch, Rural Development Service Locations &Co-operatives Branch, dealing with trade policy negotiations & agreements.

Acts Administered:
Business Development Corporation Act
Cooperation Associations Act
Economic Renewal Agency Act
Industrial Development Act
Industrial Estates Limited Act
Industrial Loan Act
Industrial Property Act
Industry Closing Act
Innovation Corporation Act
Nova Scotia Business Incorporated Act
Nova Scotia Film Development Corporation Act
Regional Community Development Act
Research Foundation Corporation Act
Small Business Development Act
Sydney Steel Corporation Act
Trade Development Authority Act
Venture Corporation Act
Venture Corporation Act - Regulations
Voluntary Planning Act

Minister, Hon. Richard Hurlburt
CEO, Paul Taylor
902-424-2901
Director Communications, Ross McLaren
902-424-4998
Director Community & Rural Development, Neal Conrad
902-424-6014, Fax: 902-424-1263
Director Decision Support, Chris Bryant
902-424-3545, Fax: 902-424-1263
Director Development Initiatives, Andy Hare
902-424-3672
Director Development Initiatives, Marvyn Robar
902-424-3973
Director Policies & Strategies, Andre Massicotte
902-424-5814
Director Procurement, Rick Draper
902-424-4557
Director Strategic Initiatives, Holly Fancy
902-424-2863, Fax: 902-424-0500

Associated Agencies, Boards & Commissions:
• Canada-Nova Scotia Offshore Petroleum Board
TD Centre
1791 Barrington St., 6th Fl.
Halifax, NS B3J 3K9
902-422-5588
Fax: 902-422-1799
postmaster@cnsopb.ns.ca
www.cnsopb.ns.ca
The Canada-Nova Scotia Offshore Petroleum Board (CNSOPB) is responsible for protection of the environment during all phases of offshore petroleum activities, from initial exploration to abandonment. The Board is a Federal Authority underthe Canadian Environmental Assessment Act. The environmental assessment process starts at the Call for Bids stage. At this stage, a strategic or broad environmental assessment is conducted which identifies environmental concerns or issues. Allsubsequent projects, including seismic programs & exploratory wells, must undergo an environmental assessment prior to approval by the CNSOPB. The Board also uses class screenings or generic assessments to streamline the regulatory process. Thesemore in-depth environmental assessments, usually jointly funded by a number of petroleum companies, provide more detailed overviews of potential environmental effects, research priorities & mitigation measure than can be accomplished in a singleproject-specific environmental assessment. A

• InNOVACorp
#1400, 1801 Hollis St.
Halifax, NS B3J 3N4
902-424-8670
Fax: 902-424-4679
800-565-7051
communications@innovacorp.ca
www.innovacorp.ns.ca
A network of critical business resources for the early stage technology entrepreneur. Key services include research & development support, business advice, investment & partnership advice. Focuses on two main growth sectors: life sciences& information technology.

• Nova Scotia Business Inc. (NSBI)
#701, 1800 Argyle St.
PO Box 2374
Halifax, NS B3J 3E4
902-424-6650
Fax: 902-424-5739
nsbi@gov.ns.ca
www.novascotiabusiness.com
• Nova Scotia Film Development Corporation
1724 Granville St.
Halifax, NS B3J 1X5
902-424-7177
Fax: 902-424-0617
novascotia.film@ns.sympatico.ca
www.film.ns.ca
• Trade Centre Limited
1800 Argyle St.
PO Box 955
Halifax, NS B3J 2V9
902-421-8686
Fax: 902-422-2922
www.tradecentrelimited.com
• Waterfront Development Corporation Ltd.
1751 Lower Water St., 2nd Fl.
Halifax, NS B3J 1S5
902-422-6591
Fax: 902-422-7582
info@wdcl.ca
www.wdcl.ca
Coordinates the commercial & recreational development of the downtown waterfront of Halifax & Dartmouth.

Regional/Service Offices

Antigonish
20 St. Andrews St.
Antigonish, NS B2G 2H1
902-863-7539
Fax: 902-863-7477

Amherst
35 Church St.
Amherst, NS B4H 4A1
902-667-3233
Fax: 902-667-2270

Bridgewater
220 North St.
Bridgewater, NS B4V 2V6
902-530-3117
Fax: 902-543-1156

Cape Breton
338 Charlotte St.
Sydney, NS B1P 1C8
902-563-2070
Fax: 902-563-0500

Capital
#11, South Maritime Centre
1505 Barrington St.
Halifax, NS B3J 3K5
902-424-4319
Fax: 902-424-1263

Kentville
#2, 29 Aberdeen St.
Kentville, NS B4N 3X3
902-679-6116
Fax: 902-679-6094

Northeastern
#101, 35 Commercial St.
Truro, NS B2N 3H9
902-893-6212
Fax: 902-893-6108

Southwestern Shore/Valley
103 Water St.
Yarmouth, NS B5A 4P4
902-742-0555
Fax: 902-742-0019

Department of Environment & Labour

5151 Terminal Rd., 6th Fl.
PO Box 697
Halifax, NS B3J 2T8
902-424-5300
Fax: 902-424-0575
www.gov.ns.ca/enla
Responsible for effective & efficient regulatory management for the protection of the environment & the health & safety of Nova Scotians. Almost 70 percent of the department's resources support inspections & monitoring activities. Thedepartment is responsible for air quality, drinking water, workplace safety & fire safety.

Acts Administered:
Amusement Device Safety Act
Building Code Act (Shared with Service Nova Scotia)
Court & Administrative Reform Act
Crane Operators & Power Engineers Act
Credit Union Act
Electrical Installation & Inspection Act
Elevators & Lifts Act
Environment Act
Activities Designation Regulations
Air Quality Regulations
Approvals Procedure Regulations
Asbestos Waste Management Regulations
Dangerous Goods Management Regulations
Emergency Spill Regulations
Environmental Assessment Regulations
Environment Act & Regulations Fees Regulations
Motive Fuel & Fuel Oil Approval Regulations

NS Environmental Assessment Boards Regulation
NS Environmental Trust Regulations
On-Site Services Advisory Board Regulations
On-Site Sewage Disposal Systems Regulations
Ozone Layer Protection Regulations
PCB Management Regulations
Pesticide Regulations
Petroleum Management Regulations
Protected Areas, Water Areas, Designations & Regulations : Bennery Lake, Forbes Lake, French Mill Brook, Hebb, Milipsiga
Round Table Regulations
Solid Waste-Resource Management Regulations
Sulphide Bearing Material Disposal Regulations
Used Oil Regulations
Water and Wastewater Facility Regulations
Well Construction Regulations
Fire Safety Act
Fuel Safety Regulations
Gaming Control Act
Health Act (in part)
Insurance Act
Insurance Premiums Tax Act
Labour Standards Code
Liquor Control Act
Mutual Insurance Companies Act
Occupational Health & Safety Act
Occupational Health & Safety Appeal Panel Regulations
Occupational Safety General Regulations
Underground Mining Regulations
Workplace Hazardous Materials Information System Regulations
Remembrance Day Act
Securities Act
Smoke-free Places Act
Special Places Protection Act (Shared with Tourism, Culture & Heritage)
Steam Boiler & Pressure Vessel Act
Teachers' Collective Bargaining Act
Theaters & Amusements Act
Trade Union Act
Trust & Loan Companies Act
Water Resources Protection Act
Wilderness Areas Protection Act
Workers' Compensation Act
Minister, Hon. Mark Parent
Deputy Minister, William Lahey
902-424-4148
Asst. Deputy Minister, Nancy Vanstone
902-424-3325
Director Communications, Valerie Bellefontaine
902-424-2575, Fax: 902-424-0644, bellefva@gov.ns.ca
Director Policy, Murrin Leim
902-424-5695
Executive Secretary, Lynda Baiden

Associated Agencies, Boards & Commissions:
• Crane Operators Appeal Board
5151 Terminal Rd., 7th Fl.
Halifax, NS B3J 2T8
902-424-8595
Fax: 902-424-0217
www.gov.ns.ca/enla/coab/
• Labour Relations Board & Construction Industry Panel
5151 Terminal Rd.,7th Fl.
PO Box 697
Halifax, NS B3J 2T8
902-424-5300
Fax: 902-424-0503
www.gov.ns.ca/enla/lrb
• Labour Standards Tribunal
5151 Terminal Rd., 7th Fl.
PO Box 697
Halifax, NS B3J 2T8
902-424-6730
Fax: 902-424-1744
www.gov.ns.ca/enla/lst/trib.htm
• Nova Scotia Insurance Review Board
5151 Terminal Rd., 2nd Fl.
PO Box 2251
Halifax, NS B3J 3C8
902-424-8685
nsirb@gov.ns.ca
Other Communication: www.gov.ns.ca/nsirb
• Nova Scotia Securities Commission
Joseph Howe Bldg.
1690 Hollis St., 2nd Fl.
PO Box 458
Halifax, NS B3J 2P8
902-424-7768
Fax: 902-424-4625
www.gov.ns.ca/nssc
• Occupational Health & Safety Advisory Council
PO Box 697
Halifax, NS B3J 2T8
902-424-2484
Fax: 902-424-5640
• Occupational Health & Safety Appeal Panel
5151 Terminal Rd., 7th Fl.
PO Box 697
Halifax, NS B3J 2T8
The Occupational Health & Safety Appeal Panel adjudicates disputes relating to both the technical aspects of health & safety & the protection of individual employees from union & employer reprisals when they have discharged theirresponsibilities under the Occupational Health & Safety Act. The OHS Appeal Panel Office administers & coordinates the process of appeals of orders or decisions made by the executive director of the OHS Division. The OHS Appeal Panel is separate from& independent from the OHS Division.

• Pay Equity Commission
5151 Terminal Rd., 7th Fl.
PO Box 697
Halifax, NS B3J 2T8
902-424-8596
sherwoop@gov.ns.ca
www.gov.ns.ca/enla/pequity/
• Workers' Advisers Program
#502, 5670 Spring Garden Rd.
PO Box 1063
Halifax, NS B3J 2X1
902-424-5050
Fax: 902-424-0530
800-774-4712
www.gov.ns.ca/enla/wap
The Workers' Advisers Program is a legal clinic that is funded by the provincial government offering services to injured workers. Our purpose is to provide legal assistance when an injured worker has been denied Workers' CompensationBoard benefits.

• Workers' Compensation Board of Nova Scotia
Listed alphabetically in detail.

Alcohol & Gaming Authority

Alderney Gate
40 Alderney Dr.
PO Box 545
Dartmouth, NS B2Y 3Y8
902-424-6160
Fax: 902-424-4942
877-565-0556
www.gov.ns.ca/aga
Responsible for licensing & regulating gaming activity, liquor activity, & film classification in Nova Scotia.

Executive Director, Dennis Kerr
902-424-4884, Fax: 902-424-6313, kerrdw@gov.ns.ca
Senior Financial Officer, Bruce Marsh
902-424-3326
Director Investigation & Enforcement, John MacDonald
902-424-6092
Director Licensing & Registration Division, Terry Kelly
902-424-6023, Fax: 902-424-6313, kellytb@gov.ns.ca
Secretary, Tracy James
902-424-4884

Financial Institutions

902-424-6331
Fax: 902-424-1298
The Financial Institutions Division regulates the operations of credit unions, trust & loan companies & insurance companies, agents, brokers & adjusters in the Province. The Division also provides a complaint & enquiry service to thepublic relating to financial institutions & the insurance industry & collects & verifies the insurance premiums tax.

Acting Superintendent, Doug Murphy
902-424-7552
Acting Deputy Superintendent, William Ngu
902-424-2787
Insurance Officer, Jennifer Calder
902-424-4987

Pension Regulation Division

PO Box 2531
Halifax, NS B3J 3N5
902-424-8915
Fax: 902-424-0662
The Pension Regulation Division administers & enforces the Pension Benefits Act to safeguard benefits promised under pension plans. The Division supervises over 470 registered pension plans to ensure the plans are well managed &adequately funded in order to meet their obligations to pension plan members.

Superintendent Pensions, Nancy MacNeil Smith
902-424-4444, macneiln@gov.ns.ca

Department of Finance

PO Box 187
Halifax, NS B3J 2N3
902-424-5554
Fax: 902-424-0635
www.gov.ns.ca/fina/
Acts Administered:
Corporation Capital Tax Act
Equity Tax Credit Act
Halifax-Dartmouth Bridge Commission Act
Home Ownership Savings Plan (Nova Scotia) Act
Homeowners' Incentive Act
Income Tax Act
Members' Retiring Allowances Act
Provincial Finance Act
Public Sector Unpaid Leave Act
Public Service Superannuation Act
Revenue Act
Sales Tax Act
Securities Act
Sydney Steel Corporation Sale Act
Teachers' Pension Act
Minister, Hon. Michael Baker, Q.C.
Deputy Minister, Vicki Harnish
902-424-5774, harnisvl@gov.ns.ca
Asst. Deputy Minister, Liz Cody
902-424-4168, Fax: 902-424-0635, codye@gov.ns.ca
Legal Counsel, Jim Isnor
902-424-3301, isnorj@gov.ns.ca
Director Information Technology, Ken Weston
902-424-0019, westonka@gov.ns.ca
Director Community Counts, Dennis Pilkey
902-424-6816, Fax: 902-424-0635
Administrative Assistant, Debra Shantz
902-424-5553, Fax: 902-424-0635, shantzda@gov.ns.ca

Controller's Branch

Controller, Byron Rafuse
902-424-2424, rafusebg@gov.ns.ca
Director Corporate Internal Audit, Pamela Muir
902-424-6102, Fax: 902-424-3191, muirpg@gov.ns.ca
Director Government Accounting Division, Suzanne Wile
902-424-6543, Fax: 902-424-2777, wilesm@gov.ns.ca
Director Corporate Information Systems, Steve Feindel
902-424-2939, feindesj@gov.ns.ca
Director Payroll Services Division, Shirley Carras
902-424-5567, Fax: 902-424-0590, scarras@gov.ns.ca

Fiscal & Economic Policy Branch

Executive Director, Nancy McInnis-Leek
902-424-4160, Fax: 902-424-0590, nrmsinni@gov.ns.ca
Director Economic & Statistics Division, Fred Bergman
902-424-6129, Fax: 902-424-0714, bergmanf@gov.ns.ca
Director Taxation & Fiscal Policy, Rod MacDougall
902-424-4118, Fax: 902-424-0590, macdourx@gov.ns.ca

Nova Scotia Pension Agency

CEO, John Traves
902-424-5557, travesj@gov.ns.ca
Director Investments, Elizabeth Vandenburg
902-424-1170, Fax: 902-424-4539, vandenbe@gov.ns.ca
Director Pensions, Kim Blinn
902-424-4539, blinnkm@gov.ns.ca

Department of Justice

5151 Terminal Rd.
PO Box 7
Halifax, NS B3J 2L6
902-424-4222
Fax: 902-424-2809
justweb@gov.ns.ca
www.gov.ns.ca/just/

Acts Administered:

Accountant General of the Supreme Court Act
Age of Majority Act
Alimony Act
Alternative Penalty Act
Apportionment Act
Arbitration Act
Architects Act
Assignments & Preferences Act
Barristers & Solicitors Act
Beneficiaries Designation Act
Bills of Lading Act
Canada & the United Kingdom Reciprocal Recognition & Enforcement of Judgments Act
Cape Breton Barristers' Society Act
Change of Name Act
Child Abduction Act
Collection Act
Compensation for Victims of Crime Act
Constables Act
Constables' Protection Act
Constitutional Questions Act
Contributory Negligence Act
Controverted Elections Act
Conveyancing Act
Corporations Miscellaneous Provisions Act
Corrections Act
Costs & Fees Act
Court for Divorce & Matrimonial Causes Act
Court Houses & Lockup Houses Act
Court Officials Act
Court Security Act
Creditors' Relief Act
Defamation Act
Demise of the Crown Act
Descent of Property Act
Elections Act
Engineering Profession Act
Escheats Act
Estate Actions Act
Estreats Act
Evidence Act
Expropriation Act, 1973
Family Court Act
Family Maintenance Act
Family Orders Information Release Act
Fatal Injuries Act
Fatality Inquiries Act
Federal/Provincial Power Act
Floral Emblem Act
Forcible Entry & Detainer Act
Freedom of Information & Protection of Privacy Act
Guardianship Act
House of Assembly Act
Human Rights Act
Incompetent Persons Act
Indigent Debtors Act
Inebriates' Guardianship Act
Interest on Judgements Act
International Commercial Arbitration Act
Interpretation Act
Interprovincial Subpoena Act
Intestate Succession Act
Judicature Act
Judicial Disqualifications Removal Act
Juries Act
Justices of the Peace Act
Land Actions Venue Act
Law Reform Commission Act
Legal Aid Act
Liberty of the Subject Act
Lieutenant Governor & Great Seal Act
Limitation of Actions Act
Maintenance Enforcement Act
Maintenance Orders Enforcement Act
Married Women's Deed Act
Married Women's Property Act
Matrimonial Property Act
Mechanics' Lien Act
Members & Public Employees Disclosure Act
Municipal Conflict of Interest Act
Night Courts Act
Notaries & Commissioners Act
Nova Scotia Tartan Act
Occupiers Liability Act
Official Tree Act
Overholding Tenants Act
Partition Act
Payment into Court Act
Pledging of Service Emblems Act
Police Act
Police Services Act
Powers of Attorney Act
Presumption of Death Act
Private Investigators & Private Guards Act
Probate Act
Proceedings Against the Crown Act
Protection of Property Act
Provincial Bird Act
Provincial Dog Act
Public Inquiries Act
Public Prosecutions Act
Public Service Act
Public Subscriptions Act
Public Trustee Act
Quieting Titles Act
Real Property Act
Real Property Transfer Validation Act
Reciprocal Enforcement of Custody Orders Act
Reciprocal Enforcement of Judgments Orders
Regulations Act
Religious & Charitable Corporations Property Act
Religious Congregations & Societies Act
Remembrance Day Act
Remission of Penalties Act
Residential Tenancies Act
Retail Business Uniform Closing Day Act
Sale of Goods Act
Sale of Land under Execution Act
Salvage Yards Licensing Act
Securities Act
Small Claims Court Act
Solemnization of Marriage Act
Statute Revision Act
Summary Proceedings Act
Supreme & Exchequer Courts of Canada Act
Sureties Act
Survival of Actions Act
Survivorship Act
Taxing Masters Act
Tenancies & Distress for Rent Act
Testators' Family Maintenance Act
Ticket of Leave Act
Time Definition Act
Tortfeasors Act
Trustee Act
Unclaimed Articles Act
Uniform Law Act
Utility & Review Board Act
Variation of Trusts Act
Vendors & Purchasers Act
Victims Rights & Services Act
Volunteer Services Act
Warehouse Receipts Act
Warehousemen's Lien Act
Wills Act
Woodmen's Lien Act
Young Persons Summary Proceedings Act

Minister & Attorney General, Hon. Murray K. Scott
Deputy Minister, Douglas J. Keefe
902-424-4223
Executive Director Information Management, David Deveau
902-424-7782
Director Communications, Richard Perry
902-424-6811
Director Policy, Planning & Research, Bob Purcell
902-424-5341

Associated Agencies, Boards & Commissions:

• Human Rights Commission
Listed alphabetically in detail.

• Nova Scotia Legal Aid Commission
#102, 137 Chain Lake Dr.
Halifax, NS B3S 1B3
902-420-6573
Fax: 902-420-3471
nsla.exec@ns.sympatico.ca
www.gov.ns.ca/just/legad.htm

• Nova Scotia Medical Examiner Service
Halifax Insurance Bldg.
#701, 5670 Spring Garden Rd.
Halifax, NS B3J 1H7
902-424-2722
Fax: 902-424-0607
888-424-4336

• Nova Scotia Police Commission
#300, 1601 Lower Water St.
PO Box 1573
Halifax, NS B3J 2Y3
902-424-3246
Fax: 902-424-3919
uarb.polcom@gov.ns.ca
www.gov.ns.ca/just/polcomm.htm

• Public Trustee Office
#201, 5151 Terminal Rd.
PO Box 385
Halifax, NS B3J 2T3
902-424-7760
Fax: 902-424-0616

• Workers' Compensation Appeals Tribunal
#1002, 5670 Spring Garden Rd.
Halifax, NS B3J 1H6
902-424-2250
Fax: 902-424-2321
800-274-8281
www.gov.ns.ca/wcat/

Department of Service Nova Scotia & Municipal Relations

1505 Barrington St.
PO Box 216
Halifax, NS B3J 2M4
902-424-4141
Fax: 902-424-0581
public-enquiries@gov.ns.ca
www.gov.ns.ca/snsmr
Other Communication: Nova Scotia Business Registry: 1-800-670-4357

Provides leadership in the achievement of effective local government, assessment services, business licensing & registration, vehicle registration & driver licensing, taxation & revenue collection, vital statistics & an integrated landinformation management system to meet the needs of local & provincial agencies & residents of Nova Scotia.

Acts Administered:

Assessment Act
Building Access Act
Business Electronic Filing Act
Cemetery & Funeral Services Act
Change of Name Act
Collection Agencies Act
Communications & Information Act
Companies Act
Condominium Act
Consumer Creditors' Conduct Act
Consumer Protection Act
Consumer Reporting Act
Consumer Services Act
Corporations Registration Act
Direct Sellers' Regulation Act
Embalmers & Funeral Directors Act
Land Registration Act
Limited Partnerships Act
Marketable Titles Act
Mortgage Brokers' & Lenders' Registration Act
Motor Vehicle Act
Municipal Conflict of Interest Act
Municipal Elections Act
Municipal Finance Corporation Act
Municipal Fiscal Year Act
Municipal Government Act
Municipal Grants Act
Municipal Housing Corporations Act
Municipal Loan & Building Fund Act
Off-Highway Vehicles Act

Off-Highway Vehicles Regulations
Snow Vehicles Regulations
Part X of the Bankruptcy & Insolvency Act
Part IV of the Revenue Act for administrative purposes
Partnerships & Business Names Registration Act
Personal Property Security Act
Private Investment Holding Companies Act
Public Accountants Act
Real Estate Trading Act
Registry Act
Rental Property Conversion Act
Residential Tenancies Act
Rural Fire District Act
Sales Tax Act
Shopping Centre Development Act
Societies Act
Solemnization of Marriage Act
Unconscionable Transactions Relief Act
Vital Statistics Act
Minister, Hon. Jamie Muir
Deputy Minister, Greg Keefe
902-424-4100, Fax: 902-424-0581, keefeg@gov.ns.ca
Asst. Deputy Minister, Kevin Malloy
902-424-4559
Director Communications, Susan MacLeod
902-424-6336

Associated Agencies, Boards & Commissions:
• Nova Scotia Municipal Finance Corporation
Maritime Centre
1723 Hollis St., 7th Fl.
PO Box 850 M
Halifax, NS B3J 2V2
902-424-4590
Fax: 902-424-0525
www.gov.ns.ca/nsmfc

Assessment Services
Fax: 902-424-0587
Acting Director, Kathy Gillis
902-424-3955, gilliska@gov.ns.ca
Acting Director Operations, Debi Karrel
902-424-4131
Director Assessment Technology, Rick MacLeod
902-424-3962

Program Management & Corporate Services
Acting Executive Director, Cameron MacNeil
902-424-4417
Director Consumer & Business Policy, Richard Shaffner
902-424-0676
Acting Director Corporate Development, Mike Duda
902-424-4580
Director Human Resources, Janet Lee
902-424-7840

Co-operative Branch
902-893-6190
Fax: 902-893-6108
Inspector, Ron Skibbens

Tax Commission
Maritime Centre
1505 Barrington St.
Halifax, NS B3J 3K5
902-424-5200
Fax: 902-424-0720
800-670-4357
www.gov.ns.ca/snsmr/taxcomm/

Registry of Joint Stock Companies
#8S, Martime Centre
1505 Barrington St
Halifax, NS B3J 2Y4
902-424-7742
Fax: 902-424-0523
800-225-8227
joint-stock@gov.ns.ca
Registrar, Kerry MacLean

Service Delivery
Maritime Centre
1505 Barrington St., 8th Fl. North
PO Box 2734
Halifax, NS B3J 3P7
Executive Director, Graham Poole
902-424-4597

Antigonish
20 St. Andrew's St.
Antigonish, NS B2G 2L4

Bridgewater
77 Dufferin St.
Bridgewater, NS B4V 2W8

Dartmouth
Super Store Mall
650 Portland St.
Dartmouth, NS B2W 6A3

Halifax
West End Mall
6960 Mumford Rd.
Halifax, NS B3L 4P1

Kentville
28 Aberdeen St.
Kentville, NS B4N 2N1

Sydney
Moxam Centre
380 King's Rd.
Sydney, NS B1S 1A8

Truro
#101, 35 Commercial St.
Truro, NS B2N 3H9

Yarmouth
Provincial Bldg.
#127, 10 Starrs Rd.
Yarmouth, NS B5A 2T1

Nova Scotia Treasury & Policy Board
1700 Granville St., 5th Fl.
PO Box 1617
Halifax, NS B3J 2Y3
902-424-8910
Fax: 902-424-7638
tpbenquiries@gov.ns.ca
www.gov.ns.ca/tpb
Advances the priorities of government, aligns government policies & plans with these priorities, & promotes accountability.

Chair, Hon. Angus MacIsaac
Deputy Minister, Robert Fowler
Administrative Asst., Evangeline Williams
902-424-8940, Fax: 902-424-7638, williaev@gov.ns.ca

Government of the Nunavut Territory

Seat of Government:PO Box 1200
Iqaluit, NU X0A 0H0
www.gov.nu.ca
On April 1, 1999, Nunavut Territory was created as part of the Nunavut Land Claims Agreement signed in 1993. It has area of 2,241,918 km2, & the StatsCan population in 2001 was 26,745. Nunavut Territory is governed by a fully electedLegislative Assembly of 19 members elected for a five-year term. Government is by consensus rather than party politics. The Legislature elects the Premier & a seven-member Executive Council, which is charged with the operation of government & theestablishment of program & spending priorities. Nunavut Territory acts under the same conditions as other territories in Canada. For an explanation of the difference between provinces & territories please see the Yukon Territory listing. TheCommissioner of Nunavut Territory is appointed by the Federal Government, & serves a role similar to that of the Lieutenant Governor in provincial jurisdictions.

Office of the Premier
Legislative Assembly Bldg., 2nd Fl.
PO Box 2410
Iqaluit, NU X0A 0H0
867-975-5050
Fax: 867-975-5051
www.gov.nu.ca
Premier, Hon. Paul Okalik
premier@gov.nu.ca
Principal Secretary, Patricia Angnakak
Executive Assistant, Nicole Camphaug
ncamphaug@gov.nu.ca

Executive Council
Legislative Bldg., 2nd Fl.
Box 2410
Iqaluit, NU X0A 0H0
867-975-5090
Fax: 867-975-5095
Premier & Minister, Executive & Intergovernmental Affairs; Minister, Justice, Hon. Paul Okalik
867-975-5050, Fax: 867-975-5051, premier@gov.nu.ca
Deputy Premier & Minister, Community & Government Services, Hon. Levinia Brown
Minister Health & Social Services & Minister Responsible, Status of Women, Hon. Leona Aglukkaq
Minister Economic Development & Transportation & Minister Responsible, Nunavut Housing Corporation; Minister Responsible, Mines, Hon. Olayuk Akesuk
Minister Education & Minister, Energy; Government House Leader; Minister Responsible, Nunavut Arctic College; Minister Responsible, Homeless, Hon. Ed Picco
Minister Finance, Hon David Simailak
Minister Culture, Language, Elders & Youth & Minister, Human Resources, Hon. Louis Tapardjuk
Minister Environment & Minister Responsible, Workers' Compensation Board, Hon. Patterk Netser
Executive Secretary, Leanna Ellsworth
867-975-5050, Fax: 867-975-5051

Department of Economic Development & Transportation
PO Box 1000 1500
Iqaluit, NU X0A 0H0
867-975-7800
Fax: 867-975-7870
888-975-5999
edt@gov.nu.ca
www.edt.gov.nu.ca
Acts Administered:
Agricultural Products Marketing Act
All-Terrain Vehicles Act
All-Terrain Vehicles Regulations
Special All-Terrain Vehicles Fees Regulations
Special All-Terrain Vehicles Helmet Regulations
Economic Development Agreements Act
Motor Vehicles Act
Carrier Fitness Regulations
Exemption of Motor Vehicles Act Regulations
Hours of Service Regulations
Large Vehicle Control Regulations
Motor Vehicle Equipment Regulations
School Bus Regulations
Seasonal Highway Regulations
Nunavut Development Corporation
Public Highways Act
Highway Designation & Classification Regulations
Highway Signs Regulations
Transportation of Dangerous Goods Act
Transportation of Dangerous Goods Regulations
Travel & Tourism Act
Guide Exemption Regulations
Outfitter Regulations
Tourist Establishment Regulations
Travel Development Area Regulations
Minister, Hon. Olayuk Akesuk
Deputy Minister, Alex Campbell
867-975-7829, Fax: 867-975-7880
Director Policy, Planning & Communications, Ed McKenna
867-975-7817, emckenna@gov.nu.ca
Director Finance & Administration, Sherri Rowe
867-975-7801
Director Fisheries & Sealing, Wayne Lynch
867-975-7734, Fax: 867-975-7739
Communications Manager, Eva Michael

Associated Agencies, Boards & Commissions:
• Nunavut Credit Corporation
PO Box 224
Cape Dorset, NU X0A 0C0

Economic Development
Asst. Deputy Minister, Pauloosie Suvega
psuvega@gov.nu.ca
Director Economic Development & Innovation, Paul Lewis
867-473-2661

Director Minerals & Petroleum, Gordon MacKay
867-975-7822

Community Operations

Kitikmeot
PO Box 316
Kugluktuk, NU X0B 0E0
Director, Beatrice Bernhardt
867-982-7459

Kivalliq
PO Box 2
Rankin Inlet, NU X0C 0G0
Director, Metro Solomon
867-645-5067

Qikiqtaaluk
PO Box 389
Pond Inlet, NU X0A 0S0
Director, Malachi Arreak
867-899-7339

Department of Executive & Intergovernmental Affairs

Box 1000
Iqaluit, NU X0A 0H0
867-975-6000
Fax: 867-975-6090
The department provides advice & administrative support to Cabinet & the government, works to ensure that the Nunavut Land Claims Agreement & Nunavut's relationships with other governments in Canada & the circumpolar world are used tosupport common goals. The department compiles & communicates information & evaluates government programs & data.The Intergovernmental Affairs Division is responsible for the management & development of government strategies, policies & initiativesrelating to federal, provincial, territorial, circumpolar & aboriginal affairs. This office participates in preparations for Intergovernmental activities such as the Western & Annual Premiers Conferences, First Ministers meetings & the Social UnionFramework Agreement, the Arctic Council, the Nunavut Implementation Panel & the Clyde River Protocol.
Acts Administered:
Nunavut Power Corporation Assets Transfer Confirmation Act
Public Utilities Act
Public Utilities Regulations
Minister, Hon. Paul Okalik
867-975-5050, Fax: 867-975-5051
Asst. Deputy Minister Planning & Evaluation, Phoebe Hainnu
PHainnu@gov.nu.ca
Deputy Minister & Secretary to Cabinet, John Walsh
Deputy Minister & Secretary to Senior Personnel Secretariat, David Omilgoitak
Asst. Deputy Minister Intergovernmental Affairs, Robert Carson
613-233-9890
Director Aboriginal & Circumpolar Affairs, Letta Cousins
867-975-6036
Director Communications, Nino Wischnewski
867-975-6001
Director Corporate Services, Terry Rogers
875-975-6045
Director Policy, Planning & Evaluation, Rachel Mark
867-975-6029
Director Statistics, Paul Harris
867-473-2693

Department of Finance

Bldg. 1079, 1st Fl.
PO Box 1000 Stn 360
Iqaluit, NU X0A 0H0
867-975-5800
Fax: 867-975-5805
Acts Administered:
Explosives Use Act
Mine Health & Safety Act
Safety Act
Environmental Tobacco Smoke Work Site Reguations
Technical Standards & Safety Act
Worker's Compensation Act
Minister, Hon. David Simailak
867-975-5090, Fax: 867-975-5095
Deputy Minister, Peter Ma
pma@gov.nu.ca
Assoc. Deputy Minister & Comptroller General, Secretary to the Financial Management Board, Bob Vardy
867-975-5803, rvardy@gov.nu.ca
Asst. Deputy Minister, Rosemary Keenainak
Director Compensation & Benefits, Wayne Vincent
867-975-5881, Fax: 867-975-5863, wvincent@gov.nu.ca
Director Corporate Services, Scott Mariott
Director Expenditure Management, Paul Reddy
867-975-5835, Fax: 867-975-6825, preddy@gov.nu.ca
Director Fiscal Policy, Mark Boudreau
Director Government Accounting, Donald Piche
Director Taxation & Risk Management, Peter Tumilty
867-975-5893, Fax: 867-975-5845, ptumilty@gov.nu.ca
Asst. Comptroller General, Gerry O'Donnell
Chief Internal Auditor, Bernie Lodge

Associated Agencies, Boards & Commissions:
• Nunavut Liquor Licensing Board
Bag 002
Rankin Inlet, NU X0C 0G0
Fax: 867-645-3327

Kitikmeot
867-983-4043
Fax: 867-983-4041
Director Regional Financial Services, Sandra Peterson
speterson@gov.nu.ca

Kivalliq
867-645-5019
Fax: 867-645-2243
Director Regional Financial Services, Kerry Angidlik
kangidlik@gov.nu.ca

Qikiqtaaluk
Director Regional Financial Services, Vacant

Department of Justice

Sivummut, 1st Fl.
PO Box 1000 500
Iqaluit, NU X0A 0H0
867-975-6170
Fax: 867-975-6195
Acts Administered:
Engineers, Geologists & Geophysicists Act
Expropriation Act
Land Titles Act
Minister, Hon. Paul Okalik
867-975-5050, Fax: 867-975-5090
Deputy Minister, Markus Weber
867-975-6180
Asst. Deputy Minister, Koovian Flanagan
867-975-6180
Director Policy & Planning, Clara Evalik
867-975-6180, cevalik@gov.nu.ca
Director Corporate Services, Sol Modesto
867-975-6171, smodesto@gov.nu.ca
Associated Agencies, Boards & Commissions:
• Baffin Correctional Centre
1550 Federal Rd.
PO Box 368
Iqaluit, NU X0A 0H0
867-979-8100
Fax: 867-979-4646
• Office of the Chief Coroner
PO Box 1000 590
Iqaluit, NU X0A 0H0
• Legal Services Board of Nunavut
PO Box 125
Gjoa Haven, NU X0A 0H0
Fax: 867-360-6112
• Young Offenders
1548 Federal Rd.
PO Box 1439
Iqaluit, NU X0A 0H0
867-979-4452
Fax: 867-979-5506

Nunavut Legal Registries Division

Brown Bldg., 1st Fl.
PO Box 1000 570
Iqaluit, NU X0A 0H0
867-975-6190
Fax: 867-975-6194
Director, Gary Crowe
gcrowe@gov.nu.ca
Registrar of Legal Registries, Brian Lannan
867-975-6587, blannon@gov.nu.ca
Deputy Registrar Securities & Corporate Registry, Jennifer MacIsaac
jmacisaac@gov.nu.ca

Government of Ontario

Seat of Government: Queen's Park
Toronto, ON M7A 1A2
www.gov.on.ca
The Province of Ontario entered Confederation July 1, 1867. It has an area of 916,733.7 km2, & the StatsCan census population in 2001 was 11,410,046.

Office of the Premier

Legislative Bldg.
#281, 1 Queen's Park Cres. South
Toronto, ON M7A 1A1
416-325-1941
Fax: 416-325-3745
TDD: 416-325-7702webprem@gov.on.ca
www.premier.gov.on.ca/english
Premier, Hon. Dalton McGuinty
416- -, Fax: 416-325-3745
Chief of Staff, Don Guy
416-325-2228
Press Secretary, Chris Morley
416-314-8975
Executive Assistant, Tracey Sobers
416-325-228
Executive Director Communications, Matt Maychak
416-325-5972
Director Caucus Relations, Rod Macdonald
416-325-2250
Director Issues Management & Legislative Affairs, Aaron Lazarus
416-325-8510, Fax: 416-325-1941
Director Operations, John Zerucelli
Director Policy & Stakeholder Relations, Alex Johnston
416-314-2598
Special Assistant, Nadine Rovira
416-325-1619, Fax: 416-325-9895

Executive Council

Whitney Block, Queen's Park
99 Wellesley St. West, 6th Fl.
Toronto, ON M7A 1A1
416-325-5721
Fax: 416-314-1551
Premier & President of the Executive Council; Minister, Research & Innovation, Hon. Dalton McGuinty
premier@gov.on.ca
Minister Community Safety & Correctional Services, Hon. Monte Kwinter
Minister Finance & Chair, Management Board, Hon. Greg Sorbara
Minister Energy, Hon. Dwight Duncan
Minister Transportation, Hon. Donna Cansfield
Minister Public Infrastructure Renewal & Deputy Government House Leader, Hon. David Caplan
Attorney General, Hon. Michael Bryant
Minister Labour, Hon. Steve Peters
Minister Training, Colleges & Universities, Hon. Chris Bentley
Minister Community & Social Services & Minister Responsible, Francophone Affairs; Minister Responsible, Ontarians with Disabilities, Hon. Madeleine Meilleur
Minister Health Promotion, Hon. Jim Watson
Minister Environment, Hon. Laurel Broten
Minister Tourism & Government House Leader; Minister Responsible, Seniors Secretariat, Hon. James Bradley
Minister Natural Resources & Minister Responsible, Aboriginal Affairs Secretariat, Hon. David Ramsay
Minister Government Services, Hon. Gerry Phillips
Minister Northern Development & Mines, Hon. Rick Bartolucci
Minister Municipal Affairs & Housing, Hon. John Gerretsen
Minister Economic Development & Trade & Minister Responsible, Women's Issues, Hon. Sandra Pupatello
Minister Intergovernmental Affairs & Minister Responsible, Democratic Renewal, Hon. Dr. Marie Bountrogianni
Minister Agriculture, Food & Rural Affairs, Hon. Leona Dombrowsky

Minister Health & Long-Term Care & Deputy Premier, Hon. George Smitherman
Minister Children & Youth Services, Hon. Mary Anne Chambers
Minister Small Business & Entrepreneurship, Hon. Harinder Takhar
Minister Citizenship & Immigration, Hon. Mike Colle
Minister Culture, Hon. Caroline Di Cocco
Minister Education, Hon. Kathleen Wynne
Acting Admin. Coordinator, Angelo Matela

Ministry of the Attorney General

720 Bay St.
Toronto, ON M5G 2K1
416-326-2220
Fax: 416-326-4007
800-518-7901
www.attorneygeneral.jus.gov.on.ca
Delivers justice services to Ontarians by: providing effective prosecution services that support community safety & public order, providing criminal, civil & family justice services that are fair, timely & accessible; supporting fairaffordable systems for resolving disputes; supporting victims of crime by strengthening their rights in the justice system; supporting vulnerable people in making property & personal care decisions, on a last resort basis, that promote their dignity& autonomy; & by providing expert legal advice to government.

Acts Administered:
Absconding Debtors Act
Absentees Act
Accumulations Act
Administration of Justice Act
Age of Majority & Accountability Act
Aliens' Real Property Act
Arbitrations Act
Architects Act
Assessment Review Board Act
Bail Act
Barristers Act
Blind Persons' Rights Act
Bulk Sales Act
Business Records Protection Act
Charitable Gifts Act
Chartered Accountants Act
Charities Accounting Act
Children's Law Reform Act
Class Proceedings Act
Commercial Tenancies Act
Commissioners for Taking Affidavits Act
Compensation for Victims of Crime Act
Construction Lien Act
Conveyance & Law of Property Act
Costs of Distress Act
Courts of Justice Act
Creditors' Relief Act
Crown Administration of Estates Act
Crown Agency Act
Crown Attorneys Act
Crown Witnesses Act
Declarations of Death Act
Disorderly Houses Act
Dog Owners' Liability Act
Electronic Commerce Act
Employers & Employees Act
Enforcement of Judgement Conventions Act
Escheats Act
Estates Act
Estates Administration Act
Evidence Act
Execution Act
Expropriation Act
Family Law Act
Fines & Forfeitures Act
Fraudulent Conveyances Act
Frustrated Contracts Act
Habeas Corpus Act
Hospitals & Charitable Institutions Inquiries Act
Hotel Registration of Guests Act
Innkeepers Act
International Commercial Arbitration Act
International Sale of Goods Act
Interpretation Act
Inter-Provincial Summonses Act
Judicial Review Procedure Act
Juries Act
Justices of the Peace Act
Law Society Act
Legal Aid Services Act
Libel & Slander Act
Limitations Act
Mercantile Law Amendment Act
Ministry of the Attorney General Act
Mortgages Act
Negligence Act
Notaries Act
Occupiers' Liability Act
Ombudsman Act
Ontario Law Reform Commission Act
Ontario Lottery & Gaming Corporation Act
Parental Responsibility Act
Partition Act
Pawnbrokers Act
Perpetuities Act
Police Services Act (s. 113)
Powers of Attorney Act
Proceedings Against the Crown Act
Professional Engineers Act
Property & Civil Rights Act
Provincial Offences Act
Public Accountancy Act
Public Authorities' Protection Act
Public Guardian & Trustee Act
Public Inquiries Act
Public Officers Act
Reciprocal Enforcement of Judgements Act
Reciprocal Enforcement of Judgements (U.K.) Act
Regulations Act
Religious Freedom Act
Religious Organizations' Lands Act
Remedies for Organized Crime & Other Unlawful Activities Act
Safe Streets Act
Sale of Goods Act
Settled Estates Act
Short Forms of Leases Act
Solicitors Act
Statute & Regulation Revision Act
Statute of Frauds
Statutes Act
Statutory Powers Procedure Act
Substitute Decisions Act
Succession Law Reform Act
Ticket Speculation Act
Time Act
Transboundary Pollution Reciprocal Access Act
Trespass to Property Act
Trustee Act
Unconscionable Transactions Relief Act
University Expropriation Powers Act
Variation of Trusts Act
Vendors & Purchasers Act
Victims Bill of Rights Act
Victims Right to Proceeds of Crime Act
Wages Act
Warehouse Receipts Act

Attorney General, Hon. Michael Bryant
416-326-4000, Fax: 416-326-4016
Deputy Attorney General, Murray Segal
416-326-2640
Asst. Deputy Minister & Chief Information Officer Justice Technology Services, John DiMarco
416-326-6954, Fax: 416-326-6628
Asst. Deputy Attorney General Policy Division, Mark Leach
416-326-2711
Director Communications, Elie Sadinksy
416-326-2604

Associated Agencies, Boards & Commissions:
• Assessment Review Board
Eaton Tower
250 Yonge St., 29th Fl.
Toronto, ON M5B 2L7
416-314-6900
Fax: 416-314-3717
www.arb.gov.on.ca
• Chief Inquiry Officer - Expropriations Act
720 Bay St., 8th Fl.
Toronto, ON M5G 2K1
416-326-4093
• Criminal Injuries Compensation Board
439 University Ave., 4th Fl.
Toronto, ON M5G 1Y8
416-326-2900
Fax: 416-326-2883
800-372-7463
www.attorneygeneral.jus.gov.on.ca/english/about/vw/cicb.asp
• Human Rights Tribunal of Ontario (ARB)
400 University Ave., 7th Fl.
Toronto, ON M7A 1T7
416-314-8419
Fax: 416-314-8743
800-668-3946
TDD: 416-314-2379hrto.registrar@jus.gov.on.ca
www.hrto.ca
• Judicial Appointments Advisory Committee
720 Bay St., 3rd Fl.
Toronto, ON M5G 2K1
416-326-4060
Fax: 416-212-7316
• Legal Aid Ontario
#404, 375 University Ave.
Toronto, ON M5G 2G1
416-979-1446
Fax: 416-979-8669
800-668-8258
info@lao.on.ca
www.legalaid.on.ca
• Office for Victims of Crime
700 Bay St., 3rd Fl.
Toronto, ON M5G 1Z6
416-326-1682
Fax: 416-326-2343
887-435-7661
• Ontario Human Rights Commission
Listed alphabetically in detail.
• Ontario Municipal Board & Board of Negotiation
655 Bay St., 15th Fl.
Toronto, ON M5G 1E5
416-326-6800
Fax: 416-326-5370
www.omb.gov.on.ca

Corporate Services Management Division

Asst. Deputy Attorney General & Chief Admin. Officer, Stephen Rhodes
416-326-4432, Fax: 416-326-4441
Director Business & Fiscal Planning, David Field
416-326-4020
Director Facilities Management, Judy Stamp
416-326-4033
Director Human Resources Branch, Karen Pashleigh
416-326-3283
Project Lead Anti-Guns & Gangs Violence Strategy, Sandra Hornung
416-212-2084

Civil Remedies for Illicit Activities

77 Wellesley St. West
PO Box 333
Toronto, ON M7A 1N3
416-212-0556
Fax: 416-314-3714
Director, Jeff Simser
416-326-4188

Office of the Provincial Auditor

Box 105
#1530, 20 Dundas St. West, 15th Fl.
Toronto, ON M5G 2C2
416-327-2381
Fax: 416-327-9862
www.auditor.on.ca
Provincial Auditor, Jim McCarter
Deputy Auditor General, Gary Peall
416-327-1658
Director Community, Social Services & Revenue Portfolio, Walter Bordne
416-327-1329
Director Crown Agencies & Transportation Portfolio, John McDowell
416-327-1656
Director Economic Development Portfolio, Gerard Fitzmaurice
416-327-1371

Director Education, Culture & Municipal Affairs Portfolio, Nick Mishchenko
416-327-1657
Director Health & Management Board Secretariat Portfolio, Susan Klein
416-327-1668
Director Justice & Regulatory Portfolio, Andrew Cheung
416-327-1352
Director Public Accounts, Finance & Information Technology Portfolio, Paul Amodeo
416-327-1659
Commissions Coordinator, Andréa Vanasse
416-327-2336, Fax: 416-327-9862,
andrea.vanasse@opa.gov.on.ca

Ministry of Economic Development & Trade

Hearst Block
900 Bay St., 8th Fl.
Toronto, ON M7A 2E1
416-325-6666
Fax: 416-325-6688
www.ontariocanada.com
Promotes economic development & job creation in Ontario by creating a climate for business to prosper & eliminate red tape as well as stimulating trade. This Ministry markets the province as a desirable place to live, work, invest & raisea family. It works with its private sector partners to ensure that its core responsibilities of employment & business development, investment & trade continue to help Ontario businesses compete globally; contribute to a highly-skilled, well-educatedworkforce; & generate prosperity for all Ontarians. In Northern Ontario, the Ministry is represented by the Northern Development Division of the Ministry of Northern Development & Mines.

Acts Administered:
Development Corporations Act
Idea Corporation Act
Ministry of Industry, Trade & Technology Act
Research Foundation Act
Telephone Act
Minister, Hon. Sandra Pupatello
Parliamentary Asst., Jean-Marc Lalonde
Deputy Minister, Fareed Amin
416-325-6927, Fax: 416-325-6999
Information Specialist Communications Branch, Lynda Bond

Industry Division

Asst. Deputy Minister, Bob Seguin
416-325-3668
Director Automotive Programs & Policies, Ken Albright
416-314-2126
Director Economic Development Policy, Leslie Cook
416-325-6806
Director Sector Competitiveness, Fernando Traficante
416-325-6849, Fax: 416-325-6885
Director Trade & International Policy, Katherine McGuire
416-325-6930, Fax: 416-325-6949

Trade & Investment Division

Asst. Deputy Minister, Robin Garrett
416-325-9801
Director International Marketing Centres & Strategic Intelligence, John Monahan
416-314-7274
Director Investment Sales & Services Branch, John Langley
416-325-6758
Director Trade & Investment Marketing, Reed Barrett
416-325-9897

Ministry of Finance

Frost Bldg. South
7 Queen's Park Cres., 7th Fl.
Toronto, ON M7A 1Y7
416-325-0333
Fax: 416-325-0339
www.gov.on.ca/fin
Acts Administered:
Assessment Act
Audit Act
Capital Investment Plan Act, 1993
Commodity Futures Act (responsibility temporarily assigned to Management Board of Cabinet)
Community Small Business Investment Funds Act
Compulsory Automobile Insurance Act
Cooperative Corporations Act
Corporations Tax Act
Credit Unions & Caisses Populaires Act, 1994
Crown Foundations Act, 1996
Employer Health Tax Act
Estate Administration Tax Act, 1998
Financial Administration Act
Financial Services Commission of Ontario Act, 1997
Fuel Tax Act
Gasoline Tax Act
Income Tax Act
Insurance Act
Land Transfer Tax Act
Loan & Trust Corporations Act
Marine Insurance Act
Mining Tax Act
Ministry of Revenue Act
Ministry of Treasury & Economics Act
Mortgage Brokers Act
Motor Vehicle Accident Claims Act
Municipal Property Assessment Corporation Act, 1997
Ontario Credit Union League Limited Act, 1972
Ontario Guaranteed Annual Income Act
Ontario Home Ownership Savings Plan Act
Ontario Loan Act
Pension Benefits Act
Prepaid Hospital & Medical Services Act
Province of Ontario Savings Office Act
Province of Ontario Savings Office Privatization Act, 2002
Provincial Land Tax Act
Public Sector Salary Disclosure Act, 1996
Race Tracks Tax Act
Registered Insurance Brokers Act
Retail Sales Tax Act
Securities Act (responsibility temporarily assigned to Management Board of Cabinet)
Small Business Development Corporations Act
Statistics Act
Succession Duty Act
Supply Act
Tobacco Tax Act
Toronto Futures Exchange Act (responsibility temporarily assigned to Management Board of Cabinet)
Toronto Stock Exchange Act (responsibility temporarily assigned to Management Board of Cabinet)
Unclaimed Intangible Property Act (unproclaimed)
Minister, Hon. Greg Sorbara
Deputy Minister, Colin Andersen
416-325-1590, Fax: 416-325-1595
Acting Asst. Deputy Minister & Chief Information Officer, Marty Gallas
905-433-6890
Director Communications, Diane Flanagan
416-212-0634
Administrator Communications & Corporate Affairs Branch, Georgia Volker
416-325-0325, Fax: 416-325-2334,
georgia.volker@fin.gov.on.ca

Associated Agencies, Boards & Commissions:
• Deposit Insurance Corporation of Ontario
#700, 4711 Yonge St.
Toronto, ON M2N 6K8
416-325-9444
Fax: 416-325-9722
800-268-6653
www.dico.com
• Financial Services Commission of Ontario (FSCO)
5160 Yonge St., 17th Fl., Box 85
Toronto, ON M2N 6L9
416-250-7250
Fax: 416-590-7078
800-668-0128
www.fsco.gov.on.ca
Regulates insurance, pensions plans, credit unions, caisses populaires, mortgage brokers, cooperative corporations & loan & trust companies in Ontario. FSCO provides regulatory services that protect financial services consumers & pensionplan beneficiaries & support a healthy & competitive financial services industry.

• Ontario Electricity Financial Corporation (OEFC)
#1400, 1 Dundas St. West
Toronto, ON M5G 1Z3
416-325-8000
Fax: 416-325-8005
www.oefc.on.ca
• Ontario Financing Authority (OFA)
#1400, 1 Dundas St. West
Toronto, ON M5G 1Z3
416-325-8000
Fax: 416-325-8005
www.ofina.on.ca
• Ontario Securities Commission
#1903, 20 Queen St. West
PO Box 55
Toronto, ON M5H 3S8
416-597-0681
Fax: 416-593-8122
www.osc.gov.on.ca
• Stadium Corporation of Ontario Ltd.
33 King St. West, 6th Fl.
Oshawa, ON L1H 8H5
Fax: 905-433-6688

Office of the Budget & Taxation

416-314-0700
Asst. Deputy Minister, Steve Orsini
416-327-0223
Director Corporate & Commodity Taxation Branch, Ann Langleben
416-327-0222, Fax: 416-325-0438
Director Pension & Income Security Branch, Bruce MacNaughton
416-327-0140, Fax: 416-327-0160
Acting Director Personal Tax Policy & Design, Kostas Plainos
416-327-0246

Corporate & Quality Service Division

905-433-6844
Fax: 905-433-6688
Other Communication: Freedom of Information & Protection of Privacy: 416/325-8370, Toll Free: 1-800-263-7965, Ligne sans frais: 1-800-668-5821
Asst. Deputy Minister & CAO, Len Roozen
416-314-5158
Director Corporate Planning & Finance Branch, Linda Gibney
905-433-5637
Director Human Resources Branch, Laura Bryce
905-433-6049
Director Revenue Operations & Client Services Branch, Pat Doherty
905-433-5880

Office of Economic Policy

Acting Asst. Deputy Minister & Chief Economist, Pat Deutscher
416-325-0840
Acting Director Economic & Revenue Forecasting & Analysis, Brian Lewis
416-325-0754
Director Industrial & Financial Policy Branch, Helen Graham
416-325-0928, Fax: 416-325-1187
Director Labour & Demographic Analysis Branch, Anne Martin
416-325-0801, Fax: 416-325-0841

Fiscal & Financial Policy Division

416-327-2020
Asst. Deputy Minister, John Whitehead
416-325-4569
Director Business Planning & Expenditure Management, Karen Hughes
416-212-0553
Director Fiscal Planning Branch, Terry Hewak
416-327-0165, Fax: 416-327-9115
Acting Director Office of the Provincial Controller, Robert Siddall
416-325-8084, Fax: 416-325-8029
Director Health, Social & Education, Vacant
416-327-0169
Director Resources, Economic Development & Justice, Helen Harper
416-327-2060

Treasury Board Office
Assoc. Deputy Minister, Phil Howell
416-327-2177
Asst. Deputy Minister BPS Supply Chain Secretariat, Dan Wright
416-325-2627, Other Communications: URL: www.fin.gov.on.ca/english/consultations/scm

Acting Asst. Deputy Minister & Chief Internal Audito, Richard Kennedy
416-327-9319
Director Audit Centre for Excellence, Paul Wallis
416-325-4298
Director Enterprise-Wide Audit Service Team, Gary Styba
416-325-8273
Director Finance Audit Service Team - Toronto, Larry Yarmolinksy
416-325-8323
Acting Director Information Technology Audit, John Brans
416-314-3347

Provincial-Local Financial Secretariat

416-325-8796
Asst. Deputy Minister, Sriram Subrahmanyan
416-327-0240
Director Property Tax Legislation & Assessment Policy, Diane Ross
416-327-0266
Director Property Tax Analysis & Municipal Funding Policy, Allan Doheny
416-327-9592
Director Provincial Local Initiatives, Vacant
416-314-2286

Tax Revenue Division

www.trd.fin.gov.on.ca
Asst. Deputy Minister, Marion Crane
905-433-6686, Fax: 905-433-2740
Director Revenue Collections, Dario Savio
905-433-5640
Executive Director Tax Compliance & Regional Operations, Bob Laramy
905-837-5200
Director Corporations Tax, Mark Grimsditch
905-433-6556
Director Income Tax-Related Programs Branch, Richard Gruchala
905-436-4590
Acting Director Motor Fuels & Tobacco Tax Branch, Brad Lawrance
905-433-6329
Director Special Investigations Branch, Peter Deschamps
905-433-6905
Acting Director Tax Appeals Branch & Director, Retail Sales Tax, Pieta Settimi
905-435-2040
Director Strategic Management Services Branch, Nancy Crabbe
905-433-6307

Ministry of Government Services

Ferguson Block
77 Wellesley St. West, 12th Fl.
Toronto, ON M7A 1N3
416-326-1234
www.cbs.gov.on.ca/mcbs/english/welcome.htm
Responsible for the delivery of government services, the government workforce, procurement & technology resources.

Acts Administered:
Alcohol & Gaming Regulation & Public Protection Act
Apportionment Act
Archives Act
Assignments & Preferences Act
Bailiffs Act
Boundaries Act
Bread Sales Act
Business Corporations Act
Business Names Act
Business Practices Act
Business Regulation Reform Act
Cemeteries Act
Certification of Titles Act
Change of Name Act
Collection Agencies Act
Condominium Act
Consumer Protection Act
Consumer Protection Bureau Act
Consumer Reporting Act
Corporations Act
Corporations Information Act
Debt Collectors Act
Discriminatory Business Practices Act
Electricity Act
Electronic Registration Act
Extra-Provincial Corporations Act
Factors Act
Funeral Directors & Establishments Act
Gaming Control Act
Land Registration Reform Act
Land Titles Act
Limited Partnerships Act
Liquor Licence Act
Management Board of Cabinet Act
Loan Brokers Act
Marriage Act
Ministry of Consumer & Commercial Relations Act
Ministry of Consumer & Commercial Relations Red Tape Reduction Act
Motor Vehicle Dealers Act
Motor Vehicle Repair Act
Ontario New Home Warranties Plan Act
Paperback & Periodical Distributors Act
Partnerships Act
Partnerships Registration Act
Personal Property Security Act
Petroleum Products Price Freeze Act
Prearranged Funeral Services Act
Prepaid Services Act
Public Service Act
Racing Commission Act
Real Estate & Business Brokers Act
Repair & Storage Liens Act
Residential Complex Sales Representation Act
Retail Business Holidays Act
Safety & Consumer Statutes Administration Act
Technical Standards & Safety Act, 2000
Travel Industry Act
Vintners Quality Alliance Act
Vital Statistics Act
Wine Content Act
Criminal Code (Canada), s. 207 (administration dealing with lottery licences issued to charitable & religious organizati
Minister, Hon. Gerry Phillips
416-327-2333
Deputy Minister, Michelle DiEmanuele
416-325-1607
Asst. Deputy Minister Corporate Services & CAO, Jane Lee
Asst. Deputy Minister Employee Relations, Gayle Fisher
416-325-1476
Asst. Deputy Minister Human Resource Service Delivery, Donna Marafioti
416-325-7612
Asst. Deputy Minister HR Management & Corporate Policy, Catherine Brown
Asst. Deputy Minister Leadership & Learning, Morag McLean
Asst. Deputy Minister Modernization, Angela Coke
Asst. Deputy Minister Modernization Program Management Office, Patricia Li
Deputy Minister, Michelle DiEmanuele

Deputy Minister's Office & Assoc. Secretary of Cabinet, Centre for Leadership & HR Management & Secretary

416-325-1630
Fax: 416-325-1612
www.mgs.gov.on.ca
Deputy Minister, Michelle Di Emanuele
416-325-1607
Director Communications, Brent Kearse
416-327-2794
Director Operations, Kelly Burke
416-325-3620

Office of the Corporate Chief Information Officer

416-327-3442
Fax: 416-327-3264
Corporate Chief Information & Information Technology Chief Strategist, Service Delivery, Ron McKerlie
416-327-9696
Asst. Deputy Minister E-Ontario Program Management Office, Angela Forest
416-212-6654
Corporate Chief Service Delivery, David Nicholl
416-327-7224
Corporate Chief Strategist, Joan McCalla
416-326-9627
Corporate Chief Technology Officer, Ron Huxter
Chief Information Privacy Officer, Mark Vale
Head Corporate Security, Peter Macaulay

Policy & Consumer Protection Services Division

416-326-8578
Fax: 416-325-6192
Asst. Deputy Minister, Rob Dowler
416-326-2826, Fax: 416-325-6192
Director Consumer Protection, Chris Ferguson
416-326-8598
Director Policy Branch, Barry Goodwin
416-326-8864

Ontario Shared Services

416-326-9300
866-979-9300
Assoc. Deputy Minister, David Hallett
416-212-7550
Asst. Deputy Minister Financial Transaction Services, Roman Zydownyk
416-212-3713
Asst. Deputy Minister HR Transactional Services, Emily Powers
416-212-6731
Asst. Deputy Minister Integrated Financial Information System, David Fulford
416-327-2022
Asst. Deputy Minister Strategy & Enterprise Services, Lois Bain
416-212-6569

Supply Chain Management

www.ppitpb.gov.on.ca/mbs/psb/psb.nsf/english/index.html
Develops & implements an integrated corporate procurement strategy to: leverage & optimize government procurement of goods & services; identify and implement procurement process improvements; enhance procurement controllership; providestrategic advice on large scale procurements; develop innovative policy frameworks to support service delivery through third party service providers.

Asst. Deputy Minister, Neil Sentance
416-327-3536
Director Corporate Procurement Policy, Marion Macdonald
416-327-7508
Director Goods & Services Procurement, Karen Owen
416-325-2206

Ministry of Intergovernmental Affairs & Democratic Renewal Secretariat

77 Wellesley St. West
Toronto, ON M7A 1N3
416-325-4800
Fax: 416-325-4787
www.mia.gov.on.ca
Acts Administered:
Ministry of Intergovernmental Affairs Act
Minister, Hon. Marie Bountrogianni
416-325-1941
Deputy Minister, Matthew Mendelsohn
416-314-9710
Asst. Deputy Minister Canadian Intergovernmental Relations, Michael Kurts
416-325-4804
Asst. Deputy Minister Intergovernmental Policy Coordination, Wendy Noble
416-325-4603
Asst. Deputy Minister International Relations & Chief of Protocol, Roy Norton
416-325-8778
Director Communications, Jennifer Lang
416-212-4965
Asst. to the Deputy Minister, Kathy Overholt
416-325-4783, Fax: 416-325-4787, kathleen.overholt@mia.gov.on.ca

Ministry of Municipal Affairs & Housing

777 Bay St., 17th Fl.
Toronto, ON M5G 2E5
416-585-7041
Fax: 416-585-6227
866-220-2290
www.mah.gov.on.ca
Responsible for providing provincial leadership in defining the framework for governance, finances & management for the local government systems; as well as leadership in the development & administration of the legislative & policyframework for land use planning. It is also responsible for providing the operational,

policy & accountability framework for local government to fund & administer social housing; policy & program instruments to create a competitive marketplace forrental housing; & the regulatory framework for buildings.

Acts Administered:
Barrie Innisfil Annexation Act
Barrie-Vespra Annexation Act
Brantford-Brant Annexation Act
Building Code Act
City of Cornwall Annexation Act
City of Gloucester Act
City of Greater Sudbury Act
City of Hamilton Act
City of Hazeldean-March Act
City of Kawartha Lakes Act
City of London Act
City of Nepean Act
City of Ottawa Act
City of Ottawa Road Closing & Conveyance Validation Act
City of Port Colborne Act
City of Sudbury Hydro-Electric Service Act
City of Thunder Bay Act
City of Thorold Act
City of Timmins-Porcupine Act
City of Toronto Act
City of Toronto Act (No. 2)
Commercial Tenancies Act
Community Economic Development Act
County of Haliburton Act
County of Oxford Act
County of Simcoe Act
Development Charges Act
District Municipality of Muskoka Act
District of Parry Sound Local Government Act
Elderly Person's Housing Aid Act
Geographic Township of Hansen Act
Greater Toronto Services Board Act
Greenbelt Act
Housing Development Act
Local Government Disclosure of Interest Act
London-Middlesex Act
Ministry of Municipal Affairs & Housing Act
Municipal Act
Municipal Affairs Act
Municipal Arbitrations Act
Municipal Conflict of Interest Act
Municipal Corporations Quieting Orders Act
Municipal Elderly Residents' Assistance Act
Municipal Elections Act
Municipal Extra - Territorial Tax Act
Municipal Franchises Act
Municipal Interest & Discount Rates Act
Municipal Private Acts Repeal Act
Municipal & School Tax Credit Assistance Acts
Municipal Subsidies Adjustment Repeal Act
Municipal Tax Assistance Act
Municipal Tax Sales Act
Municipal Unemployment Relief Act
Municipal Water & Sewage Transfer Act
Municipal Works Assistance Act
Municipality of Metropolitan Toronto Act
Municipality of Shuniah Act
North Pickering Development Corporation Act
Oak Ridges Moraine Conservation Act
Oak Ridges Moraine Protection Act, 2001
Designation of the Oak Ridges Moraine Area
Municipalities that are Required to Prepare & Adopt Official Plan Amendments
Oak Ridges Moraine Conservation Plan
Ontario Housing Corporation Act
Ontario Municipal Employees Retirement System Act
Ontario Municipal Support Grants Act
Ontario Planning & Development Act
Ottawa-Carleton Amalgamations & Elections Act
Planning Act
Police Village of St. George Act
Public Utilities Act
Public Utilities Corporations Act
Regional Municipalities Act
Regional Municipality of Durham Act
Regional Municipality of Halton Act
Regional Municipality of Hamilton-Wentworth Act
Regional Municipality of Niagara Act
Regional Municipality of Ottawa-Carleton Act
Regional Municipality of Ottawa-Carleton Land Acquisition Act
Regional Municipality of Peel Act
Regional Municipality of Waterloo Act
Regional Municipality of York Act
Road Access Act
Rural Housing Assistance Act
Sarnia-Lambton Act
Shoreline Property Assistance Act
Snow Roads & Fences Act
Social Housing Reform Act
Statute Labour Act
Tax Sales Confirmation Act
Tenant Protection Act
Territorial Division Act
Tom Longboat Act
Toronto Islands Residential Community Stewardship Act
Town of Haldimand Act
Town of Moosonee Act
Town of Norfolk Act
Town of Wasaga Beach Act
Township of North Plantagenet Act
Township of South Dumfries Act
Wharfs & Harbours Act

Minister, Hon. John Gerretsen
416-585-7000, Fax: 416-585-6470
Deputy Minister, John Burke
416-585-7100, Fax: 416-585-7211
Director Communications, Heather Wright
416-585-6900
Chief Information Officer, Jim Hamilton
416-325-4727
Executive Assistant Communications Branch, Jennifer McDonald
416-585-7105, Fax: 416-585-6227,
jennifer.mcdonald@mah.gov.on.ca

Associated Agencies, Boards & Commissions:

• Building Code Commission
777 Bay St., 2nd Fl.
Toronto, ON M5G 2E5
416-585-6503
Fax: 416-585-7531
www.obc.mah.gov.on.ca
Works with the municipal & building sectors & consumer groups to improve & streamline the building regulatory system. This leads to efficient development & more construction jobs, while protecting public safety. The Branch administersthe Building Code Act (BCA) & the Ontario Building Code (OBC), which govern the construction of new buildings & the renovation & maintenance of existing buildings. It provides enforcement officials & other building code users with advice &information so that they can apply building code requirements more consistently.

• Building Materials Evaluation Commission
777 Bay St., 2nd Fl.
Toronto, ON M5G 2E5
416-585-4234
Fax: 416-585-7531

• Ontario Housing Corporation
777 Bay St., 2nd Fl.
Toronto, ON M5G 2E5

• Ontario Rental Housing Tribunal
777 Bay St., 12th Fl.
Toronto, ON M5G 2E5
416-585-7295
Fax: 416-585-6363
888-332-3234
www.orht.gov.on.ca

Business Management Division

Asst. Deputy Minister, Arnie Temple
416-585-6670, Fax: 416-585-6191
Director Controllership & Financial Planning, Robert Balaban
416-585-7693
Director Corporate Planning, Elspeth Shtern
416-585-7391
Director Organizational Effectiveness, Diane Phillipson
416-585-6742, Fax: 416-585-7195
Director Technology & Business Solutions, Joanne Hiscock
416-585-6830

Local Government Division

Asst. Deputy Minister, Dana Richardson
416-585-6320, Fax: 416-585-6463
Director Municipal Finance, Janet Hope
416-585-6951
Director Municipal Governance Structures, Ralph Walton
416-585-7260
Director Urban Affairs & Stakeholder Relations, Andrew Posluns
416-585-6177

Ministry of Northern Development & Mines (MNDM)

159 Cedar St.
Sudbury, ON P3E 6A5
705-564-0060
Fax: 705-564-7108
www.mndm.gov.on.ca
Other Communication: In Toronto: 416/327-0633, Fax: 416/327-0634

The Ministry of Northern Development & Mines is the only regional ministry within the government & plays a central role in northern affairs. MNDM supports the mineral industry by providing it with valuable information about the province'sgeology. It also delivers & administers Ontario's Mining Act to improve the investment climate for mineral development. The ministry has a two-fold mandate, to promote northern economic development & support mineral sector competitiveness. Theministry is developing an initiative to help Ontario's Far North communities attract environmentally sound development, work with First Nation communities, partner ministries, the federal government, the mineral sector & private sector stakeholdersto create opportunities for residents to help First Nation communities become more self-reliant. The ministry works with the Northern Ontario Heritage Fund Corporation & with the Ontario Northland Transportation Commission to bring much-neededservice improvements to the northeast.

Acts Administered:
Mining Act
Ministry of Northern Development & Mines Act
Northern Services Boards Act
Ontario Mineral Exploration Projects Act
Ontario Northland Transportation Commission Act
Tourism Act

Minister, Hon. Rick Bartolucci
416-327-0633, Fax: 416-327-0665
Deputy Minister, Sue Herbert
416-212-2701
Director Communications Services Branch, Kathy Nosich
416-237-0687, Fax: 416-327-0634, Other Communications: Sudbury: 705/670-7120
Director Corporate Policy Secretariat, Brian Smithies
416-327-8266
Director Legal Services, Andrew Macdonald
416-327-0640

Associated Agencies, Boards & Commissions:

• Ontario Northland
555 Oak St. East
North Bay, ON P1B 8L3
705-472-4500
Fax: 705-476-5598
800-363-7512
info@ontc.on.ca
www.ontc.on.ca

• Owen Sound Transportation Company Ltd.
RR#5, Hwy 6 & 21
Owen Sound, ON N4K 5N7
519-376-8740
www.chicheemaun.com

Corporate Management Division

#705, 159 Cedar St.
Sudbury, ON P3E 6A5
705-564-7444
Fax: 705-564-7447
Asst. Deputy Minister, Don Ignacy
705-564-7448
Director Executive Projects, Indira Singh
807-475-1687
Director Business Planning, Robert Merwin
705-564-7415
Director Human Resources, Cleo Degagne
705-564-7931

Northern Development Division

Roberta Bondar Place
#200, 70 Foster Dr.
Sault Ste Marie, ON P6A 6V8

705-945-5900
Fax: 705-945-5931
Other Communication: Delivery of Government Services: 705/945-5904
Responsible for promoting business, industrial, community & regional economic development & diversification; improving access to social & health services for northerners; planning & coordinating an integrated transportation system to meetprivate & commercial transportation needs at local, regional & provincial levels; coordinating the policies & programs of other ministries to ensure the special needs of northerners are addressed by government.

Acting Asst. Deputy Minister, Cal McDonald
705-945-5901
Executive Director Northern Ontario Heritage Fund Corporation, Aime Dimatteo
705-945-6734
Director Programs, Services & Transportation Branch, Fred Lalonde
705-945-5903
Acting Director Regional Economic Development, Bruce Pollard
705-564-7579
Acting Manager Northern Ontario Grow Bonds Corp., Sharon Tansley
705-564-7115

Ministry of Public Infrastructure Renewal

Mowat Block
900 Bay St., 6th Fl.
Toronto, ON M7A 1L2
416-325-0424
Fax: 416-325-8851
www.pir.gov.on.ca
A central agency responsible for managing infrastructure planning & priority setting. It works with line ministries to ensure that the government's investments deliver the results intended. In addition, the ministry is responsible forcollaborating with line ministries to develop growth management policy through Smart Growth. As well, Public Infrastructure Renewal is accountable for delivering the government's Affordable Housing Program.

Acts Administered:
Places to Grow Act
Growth Plan Areas Regulation
Minister, Hon David Caplan
416-325-2978
Deputy Minister, Carol Layton
416-325-4616
Asst. Deputy Minister Corporate Services, Jeanette Dias D'Souza
416-327-3682
Asst. Deputy Minister Infrastructure Financing & Procurement Division, John McKendrick
416-325-8389
Asst. Deputy Minister Infrastructure Policy & Planning, Paul Evans
416-325-4735
Asst. Deputy Minister Strategic Asset Management Unit, Mahmood Nanji
416-326-4557
Provincial Development Facilitator, Alan Wells
416-325-0255
Director Communications, Cindy Greeniaus
416-212-0687

Associated Agencies, Boards & Commissions:
• Infrastructure Ontario
777 Bay St., 9th Fl.
Toronto, ON M5G 2C8
416-212-7289
Fax: 416-325-4646
Management of complex infrastructure projects identified in the government's mulit-year capital plan as alternative financing & procurement projects.

• Liquor Control Board of Ontario
55 Lake Shore Blvd. East
Toronto, ON M5E 1A4
416-864-2570
Fax: 416-864-2476
www.lcbo.com/
• Ontario Lottery & Gaming Corporation
Roberta Bondar Pl.
#800, 70 Foster Dr.
Sault Ste Marie, ON P6A 6V2
www.OLGC.ca
• Ontario Realty Corporation
Ferguson Block
77 Wellesley St. West, 11th Fl.
Toronto, ON M7A 2G3
416-327-3937
Fax: 416-327-1906
877-863-9672
www.orc.on.ca

Agencies Division

Asst. Deputy Minister, Joyce Barretto
416-325-2070
Director Gaming & Alcohol Policy, Barbara Hewett
416-314-2736
Director Project Development & Agency Liaison, Pat McClellan
416-325-4824
Director Realty Relations, David Cope
416-326-4857
Director Transmission Corridor Program, Barbara Ko
416-327-2840

Ontario Strategic Infrastructure Financing Authority

777 Bay St., 9th Fl.
Toronto, ON M5G 2C8
416-212-7132
Fax: 416-212-6452
www.osifa.on.ca
CEO, Bill Ralph
416-325-8057
Vice-President Community Finance & CFO, Gregg Smyth
416-212-6439
Vice-President Community Relations & Communications, Susan McGovern
416-212-6453

Ministry of Research & Innovation

Whitney Block
99 Wellesley St. West, 1st Fl.
Toronto, ON M7A 1W1
416-325-5181
Fax: 416-314-5599
The Ministry of Research & Innovation works collaboratively across all government ministries to ensure improved coordination & alignment of research, commercialization & innovation activities & to foster a culture of innovation. TheMinistry of Research & Innovation is also committed to engaging all external partners, including the private sector, education & research communities in supporting & delivering on the research & innovation agenda.

Minister, Hon. Dalton J.P. McGuinty
416-325-3903
Deputy Minister, Dr. Alastair Glass
416-325-7517, Fax: 416-325-5927
Chair Ontario Research & Innovation Council, Dr. Adam Chowaniec

Corporate & Agency Services Division

416-325-6486
Fax: 416-325-6392
Acting Asst. Deputy Minister, Diane Frith
416-325-6441
Chair Development Corporations of Ontario, Robert Siddall
416-326-1069
Acting Director Business Planning & Finance, Sheila McGrory
416-327-1137
Director Business Transformation & Organizational Development, Angela Faienza
416-325-7150
Director Human Resources & Facilities Services, Dan Gordon
416-325-6600

Research & Commercialization Division

Asst. Deputy Minister, Tim McTiernan
416-314-8219
Director Commercialization Branch, Bill Mantel
416-314-0670
Director Infrastructure & Innovation Partnerships Branch, Ian Bromley
416-925-0544
Acting Director Research Branch, Allison Barr
416-212-6990

Small & Medium Enterprise Division

Asst. Deputy Minister, Neil Smith
416-212-7793
Director Business & Advisory Services, Bob Marrs
416-325-6522
Director Entrepreneurship, Ann Hoy
416-314-3809
Director Small & Medium Enterprise Policy & Outreach, Rob Swaffield
416-325-4595

Government of Prince Edward Island

Seat of Government: Province House
PO Box 2000
Charlottetown, PE C1A 7N8
www.gov.pe.ca
The Province of Prince Edward Island entered Confederation July 1, 1873. It has an area of 5,660.38 km2, & the StatsCan census population in 2001 was 135,294.

Office of the Premier

Shaw Bldg.
95 Rochford St., 5th Fl. South
PO Box 2000
Charlottetown, PE C1A 7N8
902-368-4400
Fax: 902-368-4416
www.gov.pe.ca/premier/index.php3
Premier, Hon. Patrick Binns
Deputy Minister & Chief of Staff, Peter McQuaid
Executive Assistant & Senior Policy Advisor, Patrick Dorsey
Private Secretary, Cindy Cheverie
Administrative Assistant, Tammy Callaghan

Executive Council

Shaw Bldg.
PO Box 2000
Charlottetown, PE C1A 7N8
www.gov.pe.ca/ec/index.php3
Premier & President, Executive Council; Minister Responsible, Intergovernmental Affairs, Hon. Patrick Binns
902-368-4400, Fax: 902-368-4416, pgbinns@gov.pe.ca
Minister Development & Technology, Hon. Michael F. Currie
902-368-4230, Fax: 902-368-4242, mfcurrie@gov.pe.ca
Provincial Treasurer, Hon. Mitch Murphy
902-368-4050, Fax: 902-368-6575
Minister Health & Minister, Social Services & Seniors, Hon. J. Chester Gillan
902-368-4930, Fax: 902-368-4969, jcgillan@gov.pe.ca
Minister Environment, Energy & Forestry, Hon. Jamie Ballem
902-368-6410, Fax: 902-368-6488, jwballem@gov.pe.ca
Minister Transportation & Public Works, Hon. Gail A. Shea
902-368-5120, Fax: 902-368-5385, gashea@gov.pe.ca
Minister Community & Cultural Affairs, Hon. Elmer MacFadyen
902-368-5250, Fax: 902-368-4121, eemacfadyen@gov.pe.ca
Minister Education & Attorney General, Hon. Mildred Dover
902-368-4610, Fax: 902-368-4699, madover@edu.pe.ca
Minister Tourism, Hon. Philip Brown
902-368-4801, Fax: 902-368-5277, pwbrown@gov.pe.ca
Minister Agriculture, Fisheries & Aquauculture, Hon. Jim Bagnall
902-368-4820, Fax: 902-368-4846, jdbaganll@gov.pe.ca
Clerk, Sandy Stewart
902-368-4300, Fax: 902-368-6118

Department of Agriculture, Fisheries & Aquaculture

Jones Bldg.
11 Kent St.
PO Box 2000
Charlottetown, PE C1A 7N8
902-368-4880
Fax: 902-368-4857
www.gov.pe.ca/af/index.asp
Other Communication: Pest Information Line:|902/368-5658
Promotes the sustainable growth & development of Prince Edward Island's primary industries & improvement of the quality of products, co-administering projects demonstrating practical,

cost-effective soil conservation practices, operates apotato composting program, instituted a pest information hotline to provide information of environmental significance.Financial & technical assistance is being offered to farmers & owners of agricultural & wood land to implement practices to protectthe quality of the Island's soil, water & forest resources & to reduce the risk & use of pesticides. Projects include manure storage, structural soil erosion control, strip cropping, fuel & pesticide storage, deadstock composting, milkhouse wastestorage, developing nutrient management plans & planting trees. Details are also being finalized for a forestry component, which would provide financial & technical assistance to woodlot owners in preparing forest management plans & carry out workidentified in the plans.

Acts Administered:
Agricultural Crop Rotation Act
Agricultural Insurance Act
Agricultural Products Standards Act
Agrologists Act
Animal Health & Protection Act
Artificial Insemination Act
Companion Animal Protection Act
Dairy Industry Act
Dairy Producers Act
Dog Act
Environmental Protection Act (in part)
Farm Machinery Dealers & Vendors Act
Farm Practices Act
Fences & Detention of Stray Livestock Act
Fire Prevention Act
Fish Inspection Act
Fisheries Act
Gasoline Tax Act
Grain Elevators Corporation Act
Livestock Community Auction Sales Act
Natural Products Marketing Act
Occupational Health & Safety Act
Planning Act
Plant Health Act
Poultry & Poultry Products Act
Real Property Assessment Act
Real Property Tax Act
Revenue Tax Axt
Veterinary Profession Act
Weed Control Act
Women's Institute Act

Minister, Hon. Jim Bagnall
Deputy Minister, Wayne Hooper
902-368-4830, Fax: 902-368-4846
Director Corporate & Financial Services, Dianne Bradley
902-368-5741, dcbradley@gov.pe.ca
Communications Officer Communications Section, Wayne S. MacKinnon
902-368-4888, wemackinnon@gov.pe.ca

Associated Agencies, Boards & Commissions:
• Agricultural Insurance Corporation
29 Indigo Cres.
PO Box 1600
Charlottetown, PE C1A 7N3
902-368-4842
Fax: 902-368-6677
• Grain Elevator Corporation
PO Box 250
Kensington, PE C0B 1M0
902-836-8935
Fax: 902-836-8926
• Aquaculture & Fisheries Research Initiative Inc.
902-368-5790
Fax: 902-368-5542
Established to provide industry associations, private businesses, public institutions &/or individual fishers & aquaculturists with increased access to applied & developmental research to address priorities & opportunities in theindustry.~

Office of the Attorney General

PO Box 2000
Charlottetown, PE C1A 7N8
902-368-5152
Fax: 902-368-4910

Acts Administered:
Affidavits Act
Age of Majority Act
Ancient Burial Grounds Act
Appeals Act
Apportionment Act
Arbitration Act
Auctioneers Act
Bailable Proceedings Act
Business Practices Act
Canada-United Kingdom Judgements Recognition Act
Canadian Judgements (Enforcement) Act
Cemeteries Act
Charities Act
Child Status Act
Collection Agencies Act
Commorientes Act
Companies Act
Condominium Act
Consumer Protection Act
Consumer Reporting Act
Contributory Negligence Act
Controverted Elections (Provincial) Act
Cooperative Associations Act
Coroners Act
Correctional Services Act
Court Security Act
Credit Unions Act
Crown Proceedings Act
Custody Jurisdiction & Enforcement Act
Defamation Act
Dependents of a Deceased Person Relief Act
Designation of Beneficiaries under Benefit Plans Act
Direct Sellers Act
Electronic Commerce Act
Electronic Evidence Act
Escheats Act, (jointly with Dept. of Transportation & Public Works)
Evidence Act
Factors Act
Family Law Act
Fatal Accidents Act
Films Act
Foreign Resident Corporations Act
Frauds on Creditors Act
Freedom of Information & Protection of Privacy Act
Frustrated Contracts Act
Garage Keepers' Lien Act
Garnishee Act
Gulf Trust Corporations Act
Habeas Corpus Act
Human Rights Act
Insurance Act
Intercountry Adoption (Hague Convention) Act
Interjurisdictional Support Orders Act
International Commercial Arbitration Act
International Sale of Goods Act
International Trusts Act
Interpretation Act
Investigation of Titles Act
Judgement & Execution Act
Judicial Review Act
Jury Act
Landlord & Tenant Act
Legal Profession Act
Licencing Act
Limited Partnerships Act
Maintenance Enforcement Act
Mechanics' Lien Act
Occupiers' Liability Act
Partnership Act
Perpetuities Act
Personal Property Security Act
Police Act
Powers of Attorney Act
Prearranged Funeral Services Act
Premium Tax Act
Private Investigators & Security Guards Act
Probate Act
Probation Act
Provincial Administrator of Estates Act
Provincial Court Act
Public Accounting & Auditing Act
Public Trustee Act
Quieting Titles Act
Real Estate Trading Act
Real Property Act
Reciprocal Enforcement of Judgements Act
Reciprocal Enforcement of Maintenance Orders Act
Retail Business Holidays Act
Sale of Goods Act
Securities Act
Sheriffs Act
Statute of Frauds
Statute of Limitations
Store Hours Act
Summary Proceedings Act
Supreme Court Act
Supreme Court Reporters Act
Survival of Actions Act
Transboundary Pollution (Reciprocal Access) Act
Trespass to Property Act
Truck Operators' Remuneration Act
Trust & Fiduciary Companies Act
Trustee Act
Unclaimed Articles Act
Unconscionable Transactions Relief Act
Uniformity Commissioners Act
Variation of Trusts Act
Vendors & Purchasers Act
Victims of Crime Act
Victims of Family Violence Act
Volunteers Liability Act
Warehousemen's Liens Act
Winding Up Act
Youth Employment Act
Youth Justice Act

Attorney General, Hon. Mildred A. Dover
902-368-5152, Fax: 902-368-4910, madover@gov.pe.ca
Deputy Attorney General, Edison J. Shea
Policy Advisor Justice Policy, Ellie Reddin
902-368-6619, eereddin@gov.pe.ca
Director Policy & Administration, Kevin Barnes
902-368-4865, Fax: 902-368-5335, kcbarnes@gov.pe.ca

Consumer, Corporate & Insurance Division

Shaw Building
95 Rochford St., 4th Fl.
PO Box 2000
Charlottetown, PE C1A 7N8
902-368-4550
Fax: 902-368-5283
The Consumer Affairs section is responsible for administering Orderly Payment of Debts (OPD), lottery schemes, gun control & film classification, & for handling consumer complaints & inquiries. The Corporations section is responsible forregistering business names, incorporating companies, cooperatives & credit unions, & licensing out-of-province companies, brokers, security sales people & securities sold to the public. The insurance, real estate & public trustee section operatesunder the supervision of the Superintendent of Insurance & is responsible for real estate licenses, insurance legislation, insurance complaints, & collecting premium & fire prevention taxes.

Director, Edison Shea, FCA
902-368-4551, ejshea@gov.pe.ca
Public Trustee, Mark Gallant
902-368-4552
Manager Consumer Affairs, Vacant
Chief Firearms Officer Consumer Affairs, Vivian Haywood
902-368-4585, Fax: 902-368-9189
Superintendent Insurance, Robert Bradley
902-368-6478, rabradley@gov.pe.ca

Securities Office
Registrar, Edison Shea, FCA
902-368-4551
Deputy Registrar, Mark Gallant
902-368-4552

Office of the Auditor General

Shaw Bldg., North
105 Rochford St, 2nd Fl.
PO Box 2000
Charlottetown, PE C1A 7N8
902-368-4520
Fax: 902-368-4598
Auditor General, Colin Younker, C.A.

Department of Development & Technology

Shaw Bldg.
105 Rochford St., 4th & 5th Fl.
PO Box 2000
Charlottetown, PE C1A 7N8

GOVERNMENT

902-368-4242
Fax: 902-368-4224
www.gov.pe.ca/development/index.php3
The ministry is responsible for the creation of jobs for Islanders, assisting Island businesses to remain competitive, promoting entrepreneurial initiative & risk sharing, fostering community economic growth, providing a provincialinfrastructure for sustainable economic development, & aggressively promoting PEI as a favorable place to invest.

Acts Administered:
Area Industrial Commission Act
Business Development Inc. Act, PEI
Employment Development Agency Act
Prince Edward Island Science & Technology Corporation Act
Minister, Hon. Michael F. Currie
902-368-4230, Fax: 902-368-4242, mfcurrie@gov.pe.ca
Acting Deputy Minister, Reagh Hicken
Chief Financial Officer Finance & Administration, Reagh Hicken
902-368-5875, Fax: 902-368-7087, jrhicken@gov.pe.ca
Executive Director Strategy & Issues Management, Kim Jay
902-894-0351, Fax: 902-566-5886, mkjay@gov.pe.ca
Communications Manager, Dennis King
902-368-6574, mdking@gov.pe.ca
Manager Human Resources, Leah Eldershaw
902-368-5876, Fax: 902-368-7087, ljelders@gov.pe.ca

Access PEI

Alberton
Court House
116 Dufferin St.
PO Box 39
Alberton, PE C0B 1B0
902-853-8622
Fax: 902-838-8625

Charlottetown
Highway Safety Bldg.
33 Riverside Dr.
PO Box 2000
Charlottetown, PE C1A 7N8
902-368-5211
Fax: 902-569-7560

Montague
41 Wood Islands Hill
PO Box 1500
Montague, PE C0A 1R0
902-838-0600
Fax: 902-838-0610

O'Leary
45 East Dr.
PO Box 8
O'Leary, PE C0B 1V0
902-859-8801
Fax: 902-859-8709

Souris
Johnny Ross Young Services Centre
15 Green St.
PO Box 550
Souris, PE C0A 2B0
902-687-7050
Fax: 902-687-2026

Summerside
120 Harbour Dr.
Summerside, PE C1N 5L2
902-888-8000
Fax: 902-888-8023

Tignish
103 School St.
PO Box 450
Tignish, PE C0B 2B0
902-882-7351
Fax: 902-882-7362

Wellington
48 Mill Rd.
PO Box 58
Wellington, PE C0B 2E0
902-854-7250
Fax: 902-854-7255

Tourism Development
The Tourism Development Branch is responsible for delivering programs to assist the Island's travel industry, including the development of new tourism products. The Branch co-ordinates the development of major events & infrastructurethrough the Province. It has both an operational & a developmental role. It manages provincial parks & through Golf Links PEI, provincial golf courses.

Director, Ron MacNeill
902-368-5505, Fax: 902-368-4438, rnmacnei@gov.pe.ca
Manager Provincial Parks, Shane Arbing
902-368-4404, Fax: 902-368-5922, sdarbing@gov.pe.ca
Supervisor Visitor Services, Heather Pollard
902-368-4441, Fax: 902-368-4438, hlpollard@gov.pe.ca

Department of the Provincial Treasury
PO Box 2000
Charlottetown, PE C1A 7N8
902-368-4000
Fax: 902-368-5544
www.gov.pe.ca/pt/index.php3
The Department of the Provincial Treasury facilitates the effective & efficient management of government's human & financial resources. The Office of the Comptroller administers the Corporate Procurement Service.

Acts Administered:
Appropriation Act
Civil Service Act
Civil Service Superannuation Act
Deposit Receipt (Winding up) Act
Environment Tax Act
Financial Administration Act
Financial Corporation Capital Tax Act
Gasoline Tax Act
Health Tax Act
Income Tax Act
Lending Agency Act
Loan Act
Lotteries Commission Act
Maritime Province Harness Racing Commission Act
Northumberland Strait Crossing Act
Public Purchasing Act
Public Sector Pay Reduction Act
Queen's Printer Act
Real Property Assessment Act
Real Property Tax Act
Registry Act
Revenue Administration Act
Revenue Tax Act
Supplementary Appropriation Act
Provincial Treasurer, Hon. Mitchell Murphy
902-368-4050
Deputy Provincial Treasurer, Paul R. Jelley
902-368-4053, Fax: 902-368-6575, prjelley@gov.pe.ca
Information Officer, Florine Proud
902-368-4412, Fax: 902-368-5544, fe.proud@gov.pe.ca

Associated Agencies, Boards & Commissions:
• Prince Edward Island Lending Agency
PO Box 1420
Charlottetown, PE C1A 7N1
902-368-6200
Fax: 902-368-6201
• Prince Edward Island Lotteries Commission
Office of the Deputy Provincial Treasurer
95 Rochford St.
PO Box 2000
Charlottetown, PE C1A 7N8
902-368-4053
Fax: 902-368-6575
• Prince Edward Island Public Service Commission
Listed alphabetically in detail.

Office of the Comptroller
902-368-4020
Fax: 902-368-6661
Comptroller, K. Scott Stevens
Acting Manager Procurement, Bob Smith
902-368-4041, Fax: 902-368-5171, bwsmith@gov.pe.ca

Fiscal Management
902-368-5802
Fax: 902-368-4077
Other Communication: Investments: 902/368-4167; Fax: 902/368-4077
Director, Doug Clow
dmclow@gov.pe.ca

Information Services
Director, Vacant
902-368-6324, Fax: 902-368-4736
Manager Document Publishing Centre & Queen's Printer, Beryl Bujosevich
902-368-5190, Fax: 902-368-5168, bjbujosevich@gov.pe.ca
Manager Multimedia Services, Irwin Campbell
902-368-5078, Fax: 902-368-6243, ijcampbell@gov.pe.ca
Manager Strategic Marketing & Design, Sheri Coles
902-368-6326, Fax: 902-569-7543

Information Technology Management Group
902-368-4100
Fax: 902-368-5444
Chief Information Officer, Bill Drost
902-368-4124
Manager Information Systems Delivery, Mike Beamish
902-368-4126, mmbeamish@gov.pe.ca
Manager IT Operations, Keith Larter
902-368-5499, eklarter@gov.pe.ca
Manager Telecommunications, Vacant
902-894-0398

Program Evaluation & Fiscal Relations
902-368-4178
Fax: 902-569-7632
Director, Rick Adams
radams@gov.pe.ca

Taxation & Property Records
Provincial Tax Commissioner, James B. Ramsay
902-368-4075, Fax: 902-368-6584, jbramsay@gov.pe.ca
Registrar Deeds, Glenda Roberts
902-368-4591, Fax: 902-368-4399, garoberts@gov.pe.ca
Manager Audit, Collection & Inspection Services, Mary Hennessey
902-368-4174, Fax: 902-368-6584, mihennessey@gov.pe.ca
Manager Information Technology Services, Trent Crane
902-368-5138, Fax: 902-368-4399, rtcrane@gov.pe.ca
Manager Property Assessment Services, Kevin Dingwell
902-368-4078, Fax: 902-368-6584, ksdingwell@gov.pe.ca
Manager Tax Administration & Client Services, Robert F. Kenny
902-368-5137, Fax: 902-368-6564, rfkenny@gov.pe.ca

Government of Québec
Seat of Government:Hôtel du Parlement
Québec, QC G1A 1A4
www.gouv.qc.ca
The Province of Qu,bec entered Confederation July 1, 1867. It has an area of 1,357,811.73 km2, & the StatsCan census population in 2001 was 7,237,479.

Cabinet du premier ministre / Office of the Premier
Édifice Honoré-Mercier
835, boul René-Lévesque est, 3e étage
Québec, QC G1A 1B4
418-643-5321
Fax: 418-643-3924
www.premier.gouv.qc.ca
Premier ministre/Premier, Hon. Jean J. Charest
Directeur de Cabinet/Chief of Staff, Stéphane Bertrand
Attaché de presse, Hugo D'Amours

Ministère du Conseil exécutif / Executive Council
875, Grande Allée est
Québec, QC G1R 4Y8
418-646-3021
Fax: 418-528-9242
www.mce.gouv.qc.ca
Premier ministre, Hon. Jean J. Charest
418-643-5321, Fax: 418-646-1854
Vice-premier ministre Ministre des Affaires municipales et des Régions, Présidente du Comité ministériel du développement des régions, Nathalie Normandeau
418-691-2050, Fax: 418-643-1795

GOVERNMENT

Présidente Conseil du Trésor & Ministre, Administration gouvernementale, Monique Jérôme-Forget
418-643-5926, Fax: 418-643-7824
Ministre Finances, Michel Audet
418-643-5270, Fax: 418-646-1574
Ministre Relations internationales et responsable de la Francophonie, Monique Gagnon-Tremblay
418-649-2319, Fax: 418-643-4804
Ministre Santé et Services Sociaux, Philippe Couillard
418-266-7171, Fax: 418-266-7197
Ministre Éducation, Loisir et Sport, Jean-Marc Fournier
418-644-0664, Fax: 418-646-7551
Ministre Justice, Yvon Marcoux
418-643-4210, Fax: 418-646-0027
Ministre Développement durable, Environnement et Parcs & Leader-adjoint du gouvernement, Claude Béchard
418-691-5650, Fax: 418-643-8553
Ministre Agriculture, Pêcheries et Alimentation, Yvon Vallières
418-380-2525, Fax: 418-380-2184
Ministre Développement économique, Innovation et Exportation, Raymond Bachand
Ministre Ressources naturelles et Faune, Pierre Corbeil
418-643-7295, Fax: 418-643-4318
Ministre Transports, Michel Després
418-643-6980, Fax: 418-643-2033
Ministre Affaires municipales et Régions, Nathalie Normandeau
418-691-2050, Fax: 418-643-1795
Ministre Culture et Communications, Line Beauchamp
418-380-2310, Fax: 418-380-2311
Ministre responsable Affaires intergouvernementales canadiennes, Francophonie canadienne, Accord sur la comme & Accès à l'information, Benoît Pelletier
418-646-5950, Fax: 418-643-8730
Ministre Revenu, Lawrence S. Bergman
418-652-6835, Fax: 418-643-7379
Ministre Emploi et Solidarité sociale, Michelle Courchesne
418-643-4810, Fax: 418-643-2802
Ministre Tourisme, Françoise Gauthier
418-528-8063, Fax: 418-528-8066
Ministre Famille, Aînés et Condition féminine, Carole Théberge
418-643-2181, Fax: 418-643-2640
Ministre Travail, Laurent Lessard
418-643-5297, Fax: 418-644-0003
Ministre Immigration et Communautés culturelles, Lise Thériault
418-644-2128, Fax: 418-528-0829
Ministre Services gouvernementaux, Henri-François Gautrin
418-528-5590, Fax: 418-643-6535
Ministre déléguée Transports, Julie Boulet
418-643-6980, Fax: 418-643-7606
Ministre délégué Affaires autochtones, Geoffrey Kelley
418-643-4980, Fax: 418-643-4965
Ministre déléguée Protection de la jeunesse et Réadaptation, Margaret F. Delisle
418-266-7181, Fax: 418-266-7199
Whip en chef, Norman MacMillan
Président Caucus, David Whissell
Secrétaire général associé Secrétariat aux affaires autochtones, André Maltais
Responsable de l'information Secrétariat à la communication gouvernementale, Claudette Thorn
418-644-2378, Fax: 418-643-0459, claudette.thorn@cex.gouv.qc.ca

Ministère de l'Agriculture, des Pêcheries et de l'Alimentation (MAPAQ) / Agriculture, Fisheries & Food

200, ch Sainte-Foy
Québec, QC G1R 4X6
418-380-2110
888-222-6272
www.mapaq.gouv.qc.ca
Other Communication: Renseignements: 418/380-2110
Responsible for influencing & maintaining growth in the bio-nutritional industry from a sustainable development perspective; assures the creation & application of policies & programs necessary to developing the agricultural & nutritionalsector as well as fisheries & aquaculture.

Acts Administered:
Code municipal du Québec/Municipal Code of Québec (certain sections)
Loi assurant la reprise des activités de Madelipêche inc.
Loi sur l'acquisition de terres agricoles par des non-résidants/An Act governing the acquisition of farm land by non-res
Loi sur les appellations réservées
Loi sur l'aquaculture commerciale/ An Act respecting commercial aquaculture
Loi sur l'assurance-prêts agricoles et forestiers/An Act respecting farm-loan insurance & forestry-loan insurance
Loi sur l'assurance-récolte/Crop Insurance Act
Loi sur l'assurance-stabilisation des revenus agricoles/An Act respecting farm income stabilization insurance
Loi sur l'école de laiterie et les écoles moyennes d'agriculture/An Act respecting the École de laiterie & intermediate
Loi sur la commercialisation des produits marins/An Act respecting the marketing of marine products
Loi sur la conservation et la mise en valeur de la faune/An Act respecting the conservation & development of wildlife
Loi sur la prévention des maladies de la pomme de terre/An Act respecting prevention of disease in potatoes
Loi sur la protection des animaux pur sang/Thoroughbred Cattle Act
Loi sur la protection des plantes/Plant Protection Act
Loi sur la protection sanitaire des animaux/Animal Health Protection Act
Loi sur la transformation des produits marins/The Marine Products Processing Act
Loi sur le financement de la pêche commerciale/Maritime Fisheries Credit Act
Loi sur le mérite national de la pêche et de l'aquaculture/Fishermen's Merit Act
Loi sur le Mérite national de la restauration et de l'alimentation/Restaurant Merit Act
Loi sur le ministère de l'Agriculture, des Pêcheries et de l'Alimentation/An Act respecting the Ministère de l'Agricultu
Loi sur les abus préjudiciables à l'agriculture/Agricultural Abuses Act
Loi sur les cités et villes/Cities & Towns Act (certain sections)
Loi sur les pêcheries commerciales et la récolte commerciale de végétaux aquatiques
Loi sur les produits agricoles, les produits marins et les aliments/Farm, Food & Fishery Products Act
Loi sur les producteurs agricoles/Farm Producers Act
Loi sur les produits alimentaires/Food Products Act
Loi sur les races animales du Patrimoine agricole du Qu ébec
Loi sur les sociétés agricoles et laitières/An Act respecting farmers' & dairymen's associations
Loi sur les sociétés d'horticulture/Horticultural Societies Act
Loi sur les terres agricoles du domaine de l'État/An Act respecting agricultural lands in the domain of the state
Ordre national du mérite agricole/Agricultural Merit Act
The Charter of the City of Québec (certain sections)
The Charter of the City of Sherbrooke (certain sections)
The Charter of the City of Trois-Rivières (certain sections)

Ministre de l'Agriculture, des Pêcheries et de l'Alimentation Ministre responsable de la région de Chaudière-Appalaches et de la région du Centre-du-Québec, Yvon Vallières
418-380-2525, Fax: 418-380-2184
Sous-ministre, Michel Saint-Pierre
418-380-2136, Fax: 418-380-2171
Sous-ministre associé, Ernest Desrosiers
Secrétaire du ministère, Yvon Bougie
418-380-2136, Fax: 418-380-2171
Directrice Affaires juridiques, Huguette Pagé
418-380-2135, Fax: 418-380-2174
Directrice Communications, Francine Bélanger
418-380-2100, Fax: 418-380-2176
Directeur Planification, Daniel Bouchard
418-380-2100, Fax: 418-380-2171
Prèposée aux Renseignements, Danielle Caux
418-380-2110, Fax: 418-380-2176, info@agr.gouv.qc.ca

Ministère du Développement économique, de l'Innovation et de l'Exportation / Economic Development, Innovation & Export Trade

710, place D'Youville, 3e étage
Québec, QC G1R 4Y4
418-691-5950
Fax: 418-644-0118
866-680-1884
www.mdeie.gouv.qc.ca
Promotes economic & regional development, research for the creation of employment, economic well-being, scientific development & sustainable development. Develops policy to support industrial development, tourism, commerce & cooperatives,to promote resarch, science, technology & innovation in local & regional venues.

Acts Administered:
Loi favorisant l'augmentation du capital des petites et moyennes entreprises/An Act to promote the capitalization of sma
Loi sur Investissement Québec et sur la Financière du Québec/An Act respecting Investissement Québec and La Financière d
Loi sur l'aide au développement des coopérative et des personnes morales sans but lucratif/An Act respecting assistance
Loi sur la Régie des installations olympiques
Loi sur la Société des alcools du Québec/An Act respecting the Société des alcools du Québec
Loi sur la Société du Centre des congrès de Québec
Loi sur la Société du Palais de Congrés de Montréal
Loi sur la Société du parc industriel et portuaire de Bécancour/ An Act respecting the Société du parc industriel et por
Loi sur la Société générale de financement du Québec/ An Act respecting the Société générale de financement du Québec
Loi sur la Société Innovatech du Grand Montréal/An Act respecting the Société Innovatech du Grand Montréal
Loi sur la Société Innovatech du sud du Québec/An Act respecting the Société Innovatech du sud du Québec
Loi sur la Société Innovatech Québec et Chaudière-Appalaches/An Act respecting Société Innovatech Québec et Chaudiére-Ap
Loi sur la Société Innovatech Régions ressources/An Act respecting Société Innovatech Régions ressources
Loi sur le Centre de recherche industriel du Québec/An Act respecting the Centre de recherche industrielle du Québec
Loi sur le ministère des Relations internationales/An Act respecting the Ministère des Relations internationales
Loi sur le ministère du Développement économique et régional et de la Recherche/An Act respecting the Ministère du Dével
Loi sur les concours artistiques, littéraires et scientifiques/An Act respecting artistic, literary and scientific compe
Loi sur les coopératives/Cooperatives Act
Loi sur les heures et les jours d'admission dans les établissements commerciaux/An Act respecting hours and days of admi
Loi sur les matériaux de rembourrage et les articles rembourrés/An Act respecting stuffing and upholstered and stuffed a
Loi sur les sociétés de placement dans l'entreprise québécoise

Ministre, Raymond Bachand
418-691-5650
Sous-ministre, Gilles Demers
418-691-5656, Fax: 418-646-6497
Directeur général Communications et services à la clientèle, André Lachapelle
Directeur Projets économiques, Mario Monette
Directeur de la vérification interne, Jacques Ouimet
418-646-1638, Fax: 418-643-4904
Secrétaire général, Georges Boulet
418-691-5656, Fax: 418-646-6497

Services à la gestion / Management Services

Directeur général, Louis-Gilles Picard
418-691-5963, Fax: 418-528-0392
Directrice Ressources financières, Marlaine Côté
418-691-5971, Fax: 418-528-0392
Directeur Ressources informationnelles, Denis Maheux
418-691-5655, Fax: 418-644-1920
Directrice Ressources humaines, Nicole Lévesque
418-643-0060, Fax: 418-644-5883
Directrice Ressources matérielles, Francine Gosselin
418-643-0040, Fax: 418-528-8416

Affaires économiques régionales / Regional Economic Affairs

Sous-ministre adjoint, Mario Bouchard
418-528-0930, Fax: 418-528-8428
Directeur général adjoint Soutien au développement des entreprises et des régions, Pierre Cauchon
418-528-0930

Directrice Coordination des opérations régionales, Michèle Robert
418-528-0930, Fax: 418-528-8428
Directeur (par intérim) Développement des entreprises, Denis Hébert
418-643-0060, Fax: 418-644-7219
Directrice (par intérim) Programmes et mesures, Lise Mathieu
418-643-0060, Fax: 418-646-3609

Exportation et promotion des investissements / Exports & Investments

Sous-ministre adjoint, François Bouilhac
514-499-2188, Fax: 514-499-2174
Directeur général adjoint, Guy Beaudoin
418-691-5805
Directeur Amérique latine et Antilles, Marcel Gaudreau
418-691-5698, Fax: 418-643-0825
Directeur Amérique du Nord, Pierre Hébert
514-873-1161, Fax: 514-499-2175
Directeur (par intérim) Asie-Pacifique, Afrique et Moyen-Orient, Alain Houde
514-499-2190, Fax: 514-873-1539
Directeur Développement des marchés à l'exportation, Michel Coutu
514-499-2163, Fax: 514-499-3025
Directeur Europe, Jean-Pierre Arsenault
514-499-2185, Fax: 514-873-1540

Industrie et commerce / Industry & Commerce

Sous-ministre adjointe, Madeleine Caron
Directrice Biens de consommation, Marie-Josée Lizotte
418-691-5960, Fax: 418-643-6947
Directeur Chimie, plasturgie, métallurgie et équipements, Clément Drolet
418-691-5976, Fax: 418-644-0519
Directeur Coordination, Normand Beauregard
418-691-5698, Fax: 418-643-6947
Directeur Développement des industries, Mawana Pongo
418-691-5698
Directeur Environnement et services aux entreprises, Gaétan Poiré
418-691-5815, Fax: 418-644-1687
Directeur Équipements de transport, Charles Dieudé
514-499-6535, Fax: 514-864-3755
Directeur Santé et biotechnologies, Roger Marchand
514-499-6534, Fax: 514-864-3755
Directeur Technologies de l'information et des communications, Denis Thériault
418-691-5957, Fax: 418-643-6947

Politique scientifique / Scientific Policy

Sous-ministre adjoint, Jacques Babin
418-646-0590
Directrice Analyse et développement, Julie Grignon
418-646-0943, Fax: 418-646-6889
Directrice Culture scientifique et relève, Monique La Rue
418-646-1197, Fax: 418-528-9248
Directeur (par intérim) Information stratégique et prospective, Réal Pelland
418-643-1852, Fax: 418-646-6288

Politiques et sociétés d'État / Policy & Crown Corporations

Sous-ministre associé, Pierre Cléroux
418-641-5656, Fax: 418-644-3109
Directeur général Politiques régionales et économie sociale, Xavier Fonteneau
418-691-5985, Fax: 418-643-0326
Directeur Analyse des relations économiques extérieures, Jean-Pierre Furlong
418-646-6435, Fax: 418-691-5994
Directeur Analyse économique et projets spéciaux, Germain Hébert
418-691-5698, Fax: 418-646-0814
Directrice Coopératives, Lise Jacob
418-646-6145, Fax: 418-646-6145
Directeur Coordination, Mario Gagné
418-691-5986, Fax: 418-644-3109
Directeur Planification et évaluation, André Viel
418-646-0814, Fax: 418-691-5698
Directeur Politique commerciale, Laurent Cardinal
418-643-4347, Fax: 418-691-5995
Directeur Politiques et Entrepreneurship, Marc Leduc
418-691-5966, Fax: 418-643-0221

Recherche et innovation / Research & Innovation

Sous-ministre adjoint, Georges Archambault
418-873-8370, Fax: 418-873-6409
Directeur Activités internationales, Philippe Éloy
514-873-8245, Fax: 514-873-6392
Directeur (par intérim) Développement de la recherche, Luc Castonguay
418-646-1447, Fax: 418-646-6888
Directeur Financement des infrastructures, Normand Giguère
418-528-6160, Fax: 418-646-6888
Directeur Technologies stratégiques, Gilles Dubé
514-864-2876, Fax: 514-873-1353
Directrice Valorisation et transfert, Dominique Dubuc
418-646-1447, Fax: 418-528-8190

Ministère de l'Emploi et de la Solidarité sociale / Employment & Social Solidarity

425, rue St-Amable, 4e étage
Québec, QC G1R 4Z1
418-643-4810
888-643-4721
www.mess.gouv.qc.ca
Acts Administered:
Loi favorisant le développement de la formation de la main-d'ouvre/An Act to foster the development of manpower training
Loi instituant le Fonds de lutte contre la pauvreté par la réinsertion au travail/An Act to establish a fund to combat p
Loi sur l'Office de la sécurité du revenu des chasseurs et piégeurs cris/An Act respecting income security for Cree hunt
Loi sur la formation et la qualification professionnelles de la main-d'ouvre/An Act respecting manpower vocational train
Loi sur le ministère de l'Emploi et de la Solidarité sociale et instituant la Commission des partenaires du marché du tr
Loi sur le ministère du Conseil exécutif/An Act respecting the Ministère du Conseil exécutif
Loi sur le régime de rentes du Québec/An Act respecting the Québec Pension Plan
Loi sur le soutien du revenu et favorisant l'emploi et la solidarité sociale/An Act respecting income support, employmen
Loi sur les régimes complémentaires de retraite/Supplemental Pension Plans Act
Loi sur les villages nordiques et l'Administration régionale Kativik/An Act respecting Northern villages and the Kativik
Loi visant à lutter contre la pauvreté et l'exclusion sociale/An Act to combat poverty and social exclusion
Ministre de l'Emploi et de la Solidarité sociale, Sam Hamad
418-643-4810, Fax: 418-649-2802
Sous-ministre, François Turenne
418-643-4820, Fax: 418-643-1226
Directeur Bureau du sous-ministre, Laval Tremblay
418-643-4820, Fax: 418-643-1226
Directrice Affaires juridiques, Manuelle Oudar
418-643-4998, Fax: 418-646-8559
Directeur Direction de la vérification interne et des enquêtes administratives, Denis Jacques
418-643-1356, Fax: 418-644-3641
Directeur Ressources humaines, Jacques Pelletier
418-644-0714, Fax: 418-644-4679

Ministère des Finances / Finance

Édifice Gérard-D.-Lévesque
12, rue Saint-Louis, 1er étage
Québec, QC G1R 5L3
418-528-9323
Fax: 418-646-1631
info@finances.gouv.qc.ca
www.finances.gouv.qc.ca
Acts Administered:
Loi sur l'administration financière/Financial Administration Act
Loi sur l'assurance automobile
Loi sur l'assurance-dépôts
Loi sur les assurances
Loi sur l'Autorité des marchés financiers
Loi sur la Caisse de dépôt et placement du Québec
Loi sur les caisses d'entraide économique
Loi concernant certaines caisses d'entraide économique
Loi sur les caisses d'épargne et de crédit
Loi constituant Capital régional et coopératif Desjardins
Loi sur les centres financiers internationaux
Loi sur les compagnies
Loi sur les compagnies de télégraphe et de téléphone
Loi sur les compagnies minières
Loi sur les coopératives de services financiers
Loi sur le courtage immobilier
Loi sur les dépôts et consignations
Loi sur la distribution de produits et services financiers
Loi sur l'équilibre budgétaire
Loi sur l'exercice des activités de bourse au Québec par Nasdaq
Loi sur Financement-Québec
Loi constituant Fondaction, le Fonds de développement de la Confédération des syndicats nationaux pour la coopération et
Loi constituant le Fonds de solidarité des travailleurs du Québec
Loi sur les frais de garantie relatifs aux emprunts des organismes gouvernementaux
Loi sur l'information concernant la rémunération des dirigeants de certaines personnes morales
Loi sur l'Institut de la statistique du Québec
Loi sur le ministère de l'Agriculture, des Pêcheries et de l'Alimentation
Loi sur le ministère des Finances/Act respecting the ministère des Finances
Loi sur le Mouvement Desjardins
Loi sur les pouvoirs spéciaux des personnes morales
Loi sur la réduction du capital-actions de personnes morales de droit public et leurs filiales
Loi sur la Régie de l'assurance maladie du Québec
Loi sur le remplacement de programmes conjoints par un abattement fiscal
Loi sur la Société de financement des infrastructures locales du Québec et modifiant le Code de la Sécurité routière
Loi sur la Société des alcools du Québec
Loi sur la Société des loteries du Québec
Loi concernant la Société nationale du cheval de course
Loi sur les sociétés d'entraide économique
Loi sur les sociétés fiducie et les sociétés d'épargne
Loi concernant les subventions relatives au paiement en capital et intérêts des emprunts des organismes publics ou munic
Loi sur les valeurs mobilières
Ministre des Finances, Monique Jérôme-Forget
418-643-5270, Fax: 418-646-1574
Sous-ministre, Jean Houde
Sous-ministre associé Politiques féd.-prov. et financement, gestion de la dette, Bernard Turgeon
418-643-5738, Fax: 418-646-8616
Sous-ministre adjoint Suivi et prévision de l'économie, et revenus budgétaires, Mario Albert
418-691-2225, Fax: 418-646-6163
Contrôleur Finances et comptabilité gouvernementale, Carole Boisvert
Directeur général Administration, Bob McCollough
Sous-ministre adjoint Consultations et affaires publiques, Pierre Saulnier
Responsable des renseignements aux public, Chantal Labbé
418-528-9323, chantal.labbe@'@finances.gouv.qc.

Droit fiscal et la fiscalité / Fiscal Law & Taxation

Sous-ministre adjoint, Réal Tremblay
418-691-2236, Fax: 418-644-5262
Directeur Impôts des entreprises, P.-J. Bergeron
Directrice Impôts des particuliers, Lyse Gauthier
Directrice Taxes, Lyne Dussault

Financement, gestion de dette et opérations financières / Financing, Debt Management & Financial Transactions

Sous-ministre adjoint, Vacant
Directeur général Opérations bancaires et financières, François Tardif
Directeur général Financement et gestion de la dette, Alain Bélanger
Directeur Contrôle des risques et évaluation de la performance, Carl Lessard
Directrice Documentation financière et Fonds de financement, Nathalie Parenteau
Directrice Financement à long terme, Marie-Claude Desroches
Directeur Gestion de l'encaisse, Renaud Raymond
Directeur Gestion de la dette et del'ingénierie financière, Éric Deschênes
Directeur Opérations de trésorie, Michel Beaudet
Directrice générale Prévisions financières et relations avec les agences de crédit, Odette Hamelin
Directeur Prévisions du service de la dette, Jean-Charles Doucet
Directeur Prévision de la dette et relations avec les agences de crédit, Gino Ouellet
Directeur Relations fédérales-provinciales, Patrick Déry
Directeur Services post-marchés, Pierre Larochelle

Politiques budgétaires et économiques / Budgetary & Economic Policy

Sous-ministre adjoint, Vacant
Directeur général, Brian Girard
Directeur (par intérim) Planification et analyse budgetaire, Richard Massé
Directeur Politiques et organisation financière, Jacques Caron
Directeur Politiques de tarification et finances publiques, Charles Duclos
Directeur Politiques locales et autochtones, Marc Grandisson
Directeur Suivi budgetaire et régimes de retraite, Robert Poirier

Politiques économiques et fiscales / Fiscal & Political Policy

Sous-ministre adjoint, Luc Monty
418-643-8446, Fax: 418-691-2286
Directeur général Politiques aux entreprises, Carl Gauthier
Directeur général Politiques aux particuliers, Vacant
Directeur Développement économique, Bernard Cayouette
Directeur Évaluations fiscales et taxe de vente, Vacant
Directeur Mesures structurantes, Luc Bilodeau
Directeur Politique sociale, Jean-Pierre Simard
Directeur Taxation des particuliers, Gérald Tremblay
Directeur Taxation des entreprises, Éric Ducharme

Politiques relatives aux institutions financières et l'encadrement des personnes morales / Policy Regarding Financial Institutions & Corporations

Sous-ministre adjoint, Richard Boivin
418-646-7563
Directeur général, Maurice Lalancette
Directeur (par intérim) Encadrement des personnes morales et dévelopment du secteur financier, Martin Landry
Directeur Encadrement du secteur financier, Pierre Rhéaume

Sociétés d'État et projets économiques / Crown Corporations & Economic Projects

Sous-ministre adjoint, Yves Lafrance
Directeur général, Vacant
Directeur Projets économiques, Denis Dufresne
Directeur Sociétés d'État, Vacant

Ministère de la Justice / Justice

1200, rte de l'Église
Sainte-Foy, QC G1V 4M1
418-643-5140
Fax: 418-646-4449
866-536-5140
www.justice.gouv.qc.ca
Other Communication: Email: communications.justice@justice.gouv.qc.ca

Acts Administered:
Charte des droits et libertés de la personne/Charter of Human Rights & Freedoms (in part)
Code civil du Québec/Civil Code of Québec
Code de la sécurité routière/Highway Safety Code (in part)
Code de procédure civile/Code of Civil Procedure
Code de procédure pénale/Code of Penal Procedure
Code des professions/Professional Code
Code du travail/Labour Code
Convention des Nations Unies sur les contrats de vente internationale de marchandises/An Act respecting the United Natio
Jugements rendus par la Cour suprême du Canada sur la langue des lois et d'autres actes de nature législative/An Act res
Loi assurant l'application de l'entente sur l'entraide judiciaire entre la France et le Québec/An Act to secure the carr
Loi concernant la loi constitutionnelle de 1982/An Act respecting Constitution Act, 1982
Loi concernant le cadre juridique des technologies de l'information/An Act to establish a Legal framework for informatio
Loi d'interprétation/Interpretation Act
Loi médicale/Medical Act
Loi sur l'acupuncture/An Act respecting Acupuncture
Loi sur l'adoption d'enfants domiciliés en République populaire de Chine/An Act respecting Adoptions of children domicil
Loi sur l'aide aux victimes d'actes criminels/An Act respecting Assistance for victims of crime
Loi sur l'aide juridique/Legal Aid Act
Loi sur l'exécution réciproque d'ordonnances alimentaires/An Act respecting Reciprocal enforcement of maintenance orders
Loi sur l'indemnisation des victimes d'actes criminels/Crime Victims Compensation Act
Loi sur l'optométrie/Optometry Act
Loi sur la chiropratique/Chiropractic Act
Loi sur la denturologie/Denturologists Act
Loi sur la division territoriale/Territorial Division Act (in part)
Loi sur la justice administrative/An Act respecting Administrative Justice
Loi sur la liberté des cultes/Freedom of Worship Act
Loi sur la pharmacie/Pharmacy Act
Loi sur la podiatrie/Podiatry Act
Loi sur la presse/Press Act
Loi sur la protection de la jeunesse/Youth Protection Act (in part)
Loi sur la protection du consommateur/Consumer Protection Act
Loi sur la réforme du cadastre québécois/An Act to promote the Reform of the cadastre in Québec
Loi sur la refonte des lois et des règlements/An Act respecting the Consolidation of the statutes & regulations
Loi sur la Société québécoise d'information juridique/An Act respecting the Société québécoise d'information juridique
Loi sur la transparence et l'éthique en matière de lobbyisme/Lobbying transparency and Ethics Act
Loi sur le barreau/An Act respecting the Barreau
Loi sur le drapeau et les emblèmes du Québec/An Act respecting the Flag and emblems of Québec
Loi sur le ministère de la Justice/An Act respecting the Ministère de la Justice
Loi sur le notariat/Notarial Act
Loi sur le paiement de certaines amendes/An Act respecting the Payment of certain fines
Loi sur le paiement de certains témoins/An Act respecting Payment of certain Crown witnesses
Loi sur le recours collectif/An Act respecting the Class Action
Loi sur le recouvrement de certaines créances/An Act respecting the collection of certain debts
Loi sur le temps réglementaire/Official Time Act
Loi sur les agences des voyages/Travel Agents Act
Loi sur les agronomes/Agrologists Act
Loi sur les architectes/Architects Act
Loi sur les arpenteurs-géomètres/Land Surveyors Act
Loi sur les arrangements préalables de services funéraires et de sépulture/An Act respecting Prearranged funeral service
Loi sur les aspects civils de l'enlèvement internaional et interprovincial d'enfants/An Act respecting Civil aspects of
Loi sur les audioprothésistes/Hearing-aid Acousticians Act
Loi sur les chimistes professionnels/Professional Chemists Act
Loi sur les commissions d'enquête/An Act respecting Public inquiry commissions
Loi sur les comptables agréés/Chartered Accountants Act
Loi sur les cours municipales/An Act respecting the Municipal courts
Loi sur les dentistes/Dental Act
Loi sur les employés publics/Public Officers Act
Loi sur les huissiers de justice/Court Bailiffs Act
Loi sur les infirmières et infirmiers/Nurses Act
Loi sur les ingénieurs/Engineers Act
Loi sur les ingénieurs forestiers/Forest Engineers Act
Loi sur les journaux et autres publications/Newspaper Declaration Act
Loi sur les jurés/Jurors Act
Loi sur les maisons de désordre/Disorderly Houses Act
Loi sur les médecins vétérinaires/Veterinary Surgeons Act
Loi sur les opticiens d'ordonnance/Dispensing Opticians Act
Loi sur les privilèges des magistrats/Magistrate's Privileges Act
Loi sur les règlements/Regulations Act (in part)
Loi sur les renvois à la Cour d'appel/Court of Appeal Reference Act
Loi sur les sages-femmes/Midwives Act
Loi sur les salaires d'officiers de justice/An Act respecting the Salaries of officers of Justice
Loi sur les shérifs/Sheriffs' Act
Loi sur les sténographes/Stenographers' Act
Loi sur les substituts du procureur général/An Act respecting Attorney General's Prosecutors
Loi sur les technologues en radiologie/Radiology Technologists Act
Loi sur les tribunaux judiciaires/Courts of Justice Act
Loi visant à favoriser le civisme/An Act to promote Good citizenship

Ministre de la Justice Ministre de la Sécurité publique, Président du Comité de legislation, Jacques Dupuis
418-643-4210, Fax: 418-646-0027
Sous-ministre, Danièle Montminy
Directeur Cabinet du ministre, Simon Turmel
Directeur Communications, Pierre Régnier
Directrice Bureau du sous-ministre & Directrice, Vérification interne, Andrée Giguère

Registres / Registries

Sous-ministre associé (par intérim), Louise Roy
418-643-8654, Fax: 418-528-9539

Registraire des entreprises

800, place D'Youville
Québec, QC G1R 4Y5
418-528-9074
Fax: 418-646-7329
req@req.gouv.qc.ca
www.req.gouv.qc.ca/default.htm

Acts Administered:
Charte de la Ville de Québec/Charter of Ville de Québec
Code civil du Québec/Civil Code of Québec
Code de procédure civile/Civil Code of Québec
Code du travail/Labour Code
Code municipal du Québec/Municipal Code of Québec
Loi concernant les services de transport par taxi
Loi constituant Capital régional et cooperatif Desjardins
Loi constituant Fondaction, le Fonds de développement de la Confédération des syndicats nationaux pour la coopération et
Loi constituant le Fonds de solidarité des travailleurs du Québec
Loi sur la constitution de certaines Églises/Québec Church Incorporation Act
Loi sur la liquidation des compagnies/Winding Up Act
Loi sur la publicité légale des entreprises individuelles, des sociétés et des personnes morales/An Act respecting the L
Loi sur le courtage immobilier
Loi sur le ministère de la Culture et des Communications
Loi sur le registraire des entreprises/An Act respecting the Entreprise registrar
Loi sur les assurances/Québec Act respecting insurance
Loi sur les cités et villes/Cities & Towns Act
Loi sur les clubs de chasse et de pêche/Québec Fish and Game Clubs Act
Loi sur les clubs de récréation/Québec Amusement Clubs Act
Loi sur les compagnies/Québec Companies Act
Loi sur les compagnies de cimetière/Québec Cemetery Companies Act
Loi sur les compagnies de cimetière catholiques romains/Québec Act respecting Roman Catholic cemetery corporations
Loi sur les compagnies de flottage/Québec Timber-Driving Companies Act
Loi sur les compagnies de gaz, d'eau et d'électricité/Québec Gas, Water and Electricity Companies Act
Loi sur les compagnies de télégraphe et de téléphone/Québec Telegraph and Telephone Companies Act
Loi sur les compagnies minières Québec/Québec Mining Companies Act
Loi sur les coopératives/Québec Cooperatives Act
Loi sur les coopératives de services financiers/Québec Act respecting financial services cooperatives
Loi sur les corporations religieuses/Québec Religious Corporations Act
Loi sur les évêques catholiques romains/Québec Roman Catholic Bishops Act
Loi sur les fabriques/Québec Act respecting fabriques
Loi sur les pouvoirs spéciaux des personnes morales
Loi sur les services de santé et les services sociaux/Québec Act respecting health services & social services
Loi sur les services de santé et les services sociaux pour les autochtones cris/Act respecting health services & social
Loi sur les sociétés agricoles et laitières/Québec Act respecting farmers' and dairymen's associations
Loi sur les sociétés d'horticulture/Québec Horticultural Societies Act
Loi sur les sociétés de fiducie et les sociétés d'épargne/Québec Act respecting trust companies and savings companies
Loi sur les sociétés de transport en commun
Loi sur les sociétés préventives de cruauté envers les animaux/Québec Act respecting societies for the prevention of cru
Loi sur les sociétés nationales de bienfaisance/Qué National Benefit Societies Act
Loi sur les syndicats professionnels/Québec Professional Syndicates Act

Ministre responsable, Lawrence S. Bergman
418-652-6835, Fax: 418-643-7379
Directeur Affaires juridiques et recherche, Pierre Legaré
418-528-9024, Fax: 418-646-2906

Surintendant Bureau du courtage immobilier, Alain Samson
418-528-9726, Fax: 418-643-3336
Directrice des entreprises, Klara de Pokomandy
418-528-9186, Fax: 418-528-5703
Directeur Services administratifs, Pierre Morin
418-528-9074, Fax: 418-646-7329
Registraire des entreprises adjoint (par intérim), Marc Samson
418-643-6850, Fax: 418-528-9584
Directrice (par intérim) Solutions d'affaires, Danielle Dupuis
418-528-9116, Fax: 418-528-6222
Secrétaire, Rémi Dussault
418-528-9072, Fax: 418-528-9584
Agent d'information, Daniel B. Bouchard
418-528-9094, Fax: 418-646-2906,
daniel.b.bouchard@igif.gouv.qc.ca

Revenu Québec / Revenue

3800, rue de Marly
Québec, QC G1X 4A5
800-463-2397
www.revenu.gouv.qc.ca
TVQ/TPS: 418/659-4692; 514/873-4692; 1-800-567-4692
Retenues . la source: 514/873-4530; 418/659-7313; 1-800-413-2277Imptdescorporations:418/659-4155;514/864-629 9;1-800-450-4155Imp""tdesparticuliers:418/659-6299;514/864-6 299;1-800-267-6299""

Acts Administered:
Loi concernant l'application de la Loi sur les impôts/Act respecting the application of the Taxation Act
Loi concernant l'impôt sur le tabac/Tobacco Tax Act
Loi concernant la taxe sur les carburants/Fuel Tax Act
Loi favorisant le développement de la formation de la main-d'ouvre (partiellement)/Act to foster the development of manp
Loi facilitant le paiement des pensions alimentaires/Act to facilitate the payment of support
Loi sur la fiscalité municipale/Act respecting municipal taxation (in part)
Loi sur la Régie de l'assurance maladie du Québec (partiellement)/Act respecting the Régie de l'assurance-maladie du Qué
Loi sur la Société d'habitation du Québec (partiellement)/Act respecting the Société d'habitation du Québec (in part)
Loi sur la taxe d'accise (partiellement)/Excise Tax Act (in part)
Loi sur la taxe de vente du Québec/Act respecting the Québec Sales Tax
Loi sur le ministère du Revenu/Act respecting the Ministère du Revenu
Loi sur le Régime de rentes du Québec (partiellement)/Act respecting the Québec Pension Plan (in part)
Loi sur le remboursement d'impôts fonciers/Act respecting real estate tax refund
Loi sur le soutien du revenu et favorisant l'emploi et la solidarité sociale (partiellement)/Act respecting income suppo
Loi sur les centres financiers internationaux (partiellement)/Act respecting international financial centres (in part)
Loi sur les impôts/Taxation Act
Loi sur les licences/Licenses Act
Loi sur les normes du travail (partiellement)/Act respecting labour standards (in part)
Ministre, Lawrence S. Bergman
418-652-6835, Fax: 418-643-7379
Secrétaire générale Bureau du sous-ministre, Sylvie Carrier
418-652-4915, sylvie.carrier@mrq.gouv.qc.ca

Bureau de la sous-ministre / Office of the Deputy Minister & Secretary General

Fax: 418-643-4962
Sous-ministre, Diane Jean
418-652-6833
Directeur du Bureau & Secrétaire général, Norbert Boudreau
418-652-6834
Directeur Normes et orientations, Marc Samson
418-652-5450
Directeur Traitement des plaintes, Daniel Bourassa
418-652-6159, Fax: 418-652-4036, Other Communications: Fax (sans frais): 1-866-680-1860
Directeur (par intérim) Vérification interne et enquêtes, Pierre Gagné
418-652-6808, Fax: 418-652-4913
Directrice (par intérim) Communications, Chantale Tremblay
418-652-6831, Fax: 418-646-0167

Centre de perception fiscale / Tax Collection

3800, rue de Marly, Secteur 6-4-3
Sainte-Foy, QC G1X 4A5
Responsible for collecting income tax & consumption taxes that are payable under the provincial laws the ministry administers. Implements, for other provincial government departments & agencies, specific social & economic-related programsdeveloped to balance public funds. Relies on the cooperation of agents (to collect & remit consumption taxes) & taxpayers.

Directrice générale, Carole Imbeault
418-577-0011, Fax: 418-577-5085
Directeur régional Québec et Chaudière-Appalaches Capitale-Nationale et autres régions, Marcel Turgeon
418-577-0313, Fax: 418-646-7057
Directrice régionale Outaouais, Claire Garceau
819-779-7321, Fax: 819-779-6085
Directrice régionale Montréal, Lise Hamel
514-415-5012, Fax: 514-285-3820
Directrice régionale Montérégie, Étiennette Morin
450-466-6210, Fax: 450-928-8606
Directeur régional Laval-Laurentides-Lanaudière, Claude Girard
450-967-6466, Fax: 450-967-4761
Directeur Services administratifs et techniques, Richard Demers
418-577-0033, Fax: 418-646-8269

Direction générale de la Législation et des enquêtes / Legislation & Enquiries

418-652-6844
Fax: 418-643-9381
Sous-ministre adjoint, François T. Tremblay
Directrice Loi sur les impôts, Josée Morin
418-652-6836, Fax: 418-643-2699
Directeur Lois sur les taxes et l'administration fiscale, Serge Bouchard
418-652-6837, Fax: 418-643-0953
Directeur Affaires juridiques du Revenu - Ministère de la Justice, Jean-Pierre Bergeron
418-652-6490, Fax: 418-643-8085
Directrice Accès à l'information et protection des renseignements confidentiel, Danielle Corriveau
418-652-5772, Fax: 418-577-5233
Directeur Affaires autochtones, Gaëtan Hallé
418-652-4915, Fax: 418-652-4445
Directrice Services administratifs, Ginette St-Laurent
418-652-6840, Fax: 418-652-6237
Directeur Services informatiques, Raymond Hébert
418-652-4443, Fax: 418-652-6237
Directeur Oppositions - Québec, Denis Morin
418-652-6268, Fax: 418-643-5025
Directrice Oppositions - Montréal, Louise Haspect
514-287-8322, Fax: 514-873-9253
Directeur Principale des enquêtes, Pierre-J. Bouchard
418-652-5195, Fax: 418-528-2049
Directeur Enquêtes et inspections - Québec, Roger Frigon
418-652-5903, Fax: 418-528-2049
Directrice Enquêtes - Montréal, Guylaine Isabelle
514-287-4146, Fax: 514-864-3669
Directeur Enquêtes et dossiers spéciaux - Montréal, Luc Boulanger
514-287-4146, Fax: 514-285-5388
Directeur Enquêtes et projets - Montréal, Daniel Caumartin
514-287-4146, Fax: 514-864-3669
Directeur Direction du contentieux du Revenu - Ministère de la Justice, Paul Veillette
514-287-8213, Fax: 514-873-8992
Directeur Service du contentieux - Québec, André Larivière
418-652-5210, Fax: 418-528-0978
Directeur adjoint Service du contentieux - Montréal, Vacant
514-287-8215, Fax: 514-873-8992

Direction générale de la Planification, de l'administration et de la recherche / Planning, Administration & Research

Sous-ministre adjoint, Raymond Boisvert
418-652-4152, Fax: 418-528-6882
Directeur Systèmes administratifs et soutien à l'organisation, Daniel Pageau
418-652-4764, Fax: 418-528-6882
Directrice Gestion financière, Josette Legrand
418-652-6884, Fax: 418-643-8015
Directrice Ressources matérielles et immobilières, Sylvie St-Pierre
418-652-5549, Fax: 418-643-1347
Chef de service Service de la planification des revenus, Éric Maranda
418-652-4839, Fax: 418-577-5015
Directrice Planification et suivis stratégiques, Lucie Brière
418-652-4707, Fax: 418-577-5040
Directeur général Évaluation des programmes, Yves Bannon
418-652-4657, Fax: 418-528-6882
Directeur général adjoint (par intérim) Recherche fiscale, Gilles Bernard
514-287-6707, Fax: 514-873-0758
Directeur (par intérim) Études économiques, fiscales et statistiques, Daniel Boudreau
418-652-4556, Fax: 418-652-5730
Directrice (par intérim) Gestion de l'information, Marie Blanchard
418-652-6714, Fax: 418-652-5730
Directeur Bureau de la lutte contre l'évasion fiscale, Sami Jabbour
514-287-6707, Fax: 514-873-0758
Directeur général adjoint Ressources humaines & Directeur (par intérim), Développement des personnes de l'organisation, Alain Blouin
418-652-5348, Fax: 418-646-1827
Directeur Conseil et soutien à la gestion - Québec, Robert Moreau
418-652-5392, Fax: 418-652-0240
Directrice Conseil et soutien à la gestion - Montréal, Louise Chartré
514-287-8009, Fax: 514-287-3766
Directeur Paie et avatages sociaux, Pierre St-Hilaire
418-652-4222, Fax: 418-652-0240
Directrice Santé et mieux-être au travail, Doris Bouchard
418-652-6433, Fax: 418-646-9546

Direction générale du Traitement et des Technologies / Treatment & Technology

Sous-ministre adjoint, Denis Garon
418-652-4959, Fax: 418-577-5041
Directrice Planification et soutien à la gestion, Ida Falardeau
418-652-4186, Fax: 418-577-5058
Directeur Solutions informatiques pour les entreprises, Jean-Guy Parent
418-652-5425, Fax: 418-577-5223
Directrice Solutions électroniques et traitements massifs, Suzanne Létourneau
418-652-6575, Fax: 418-577-5226
Directeur Normalisation des communications de masse, Martial Breault
418-652-4722, Fax: 418-646-0167
Directrice Solutions informatiques pour les particuliers, Nicole Méthot
418-652-6738, Fax: 418-646-3461
Directrice Solutions informatiques pour les mandataires, Lyne Lebel
418-652-6868, Fax: 418-577-518
Directeur Traitement infromatique et télécommunications, Denis Gagnon
418-652-5124, Fax: 418-577-5070
Directeur central Traitement, Gaston Boucher
418-652-6226, Fax: 418-646-0713

Direction générale des Particuliers / Individuals Directorate

Sous-ministre adjointe, Mireille Picard
418-652-6807, Fax: 418-652-5049
Directeur Centre d'assistance aux services à la clientèle, Normand Bilodeau
418-689-1400, Fax: 418-689-1420
Directeur Comptabilisation et non-production des déclarations de particuliers, Magdi Abdel-Malak
418-652-4726, Fax: 418-577-5047
Directrice Cotisation des particuliers, Céline Goyette
418-652-5126, Fax: 418-646-1649
Directeur Pensions alimentaires, Michel Stewart
418-652-6704, Fax: 418-646-8270
Directeur Direction régionale - Capitale-Nationale et Est du Québec, Michel Lepage
418-725-6900, Fax: 418-727-3922
Directeur Direction régionale des particuliers - Montréal, Guy Paquin
514-215-3719, Fax: 514-215-3575
Directrice Direction régionale - Centre et Sud du Québec, Christianne Lebleu
819-694-4811, Fax: 819-577-5069

Directrice Direction régionale - Nord et Ouest du Québec, Jacquie Poissant
819-779-6035, Fax: 819-772-3377

Direction générale des Entreprises / Businesses Directorate

Sous-ministre adjointe, Johanne Bergeron
514-287-6216, Fax: 514-285-3848
Directeur Développement des compétences, Dany Pagé
514-287-2020, Fax: 514-864-7242
Directeur Planification et gestion de l'information, Robert Nolin
514-287-3750, Fax: 514-287-6003
Directeur Bureau de Toronto, Marcel Dumont
416-977-6713, Fax: 416-977-9748
Directeur régional Montréal, Pierre Leclerc
514-287-4187, Fax: 514-285-3875
Directeur régional Vérification des entreprises - Centre et Sud du Québec/Nord et Oue, Camélia Attya
514-215-3600, Fax: 514-215-3670, Other Communications: Nord et Ouest: 450/972-2356, Fax: 450/972-2354
Directeur Cotisation des entreprises, Pierre Chevrier
514-287-8126, Fax: 514-285-5374
Directrice régionale Vérification des entreprises - Capitale-Nationale et Est du Québec, Line Paulin
418-652-6811, Fax: 418-643-5050
Directeur principal Services à la clientèle des entreprises, Denis Gendron
514-287-8055, Fax: 514-864-4364

Direction générale des Biens non réclamés / Unclaimed Property Directorate

418-577-0011
Fax: 418-577-5085
Sous-ministre adjointe, Carole Imbeault

Ministère des Services gouvernementaux / Governmental Services

875, Grande Allée est
Québec, QC G1R 5R8
418-643-8383
www.services.gouv.qc.ca
The Department aims are to simplify access to government services, regroup management services & develop e-government.

Acts Administered:
Loi concernant le cadre juridique des technologies de l'information
Loi sur la Société immobilière du Québec
Loi sur le Centre de services partagés du Québec
Loi sur le ministère des Services gouvernementaux
Loi sur le Service des achats du gouvernement
Loi sur les services gouvernementaux aux ministères et organismes publics
Loi sur Services Québec
Ministre des Services gouvernementaux, Monique Jérôme-Forget
418-643-5270, Fax: 418-643-1574
Sous-ministre, Jocelyne Dagenais
Secrétaire générale Secrétariat général et planification, Marielle Charland
418-643-0578, Fax: 418-528-8655
Directeur général Service aérien gouvernemental, Lucien Tremblay
418-528-8383, Fax: 418-871-5313
Affaires publiques et Communications, Hélène Langevin
418-528-7075, helene.langevin@msg.gouv.qc.ca

Centre de services partagés du Québec / Shared Services Centre

900, place d'Youville, 6e étage
uébec, QC G1R 0A1
418-643-6080
www.cspq.gouv.qc.ca
Président-Directeur général, André Trudeau
418-643-6080, Fax: 418-528-2733
Vice-présidente Développement des affaires aux services spécialisées et information, Marlen Carter
418-643-6080, Fax: 418-528-2733

Direction des acquisitions

418-643-5438
Fax: 418-643-9192
888-588-5438
ser.clientele@cspq.gouv.qc.ca
www.cspq.gouv.qc.ca/acquisition/index.asp
Other Communication: Purchasing: www.approvisionnement-quebec.gouv.qc.ca/

Services Québec

1056, rue Louis-Alexandre-Taschereau, 4e étage
Québec, QC G1R 5E6
418-643-1430
800-363-1363
TDD:
514-873-4626www.services.gouv.ac.ca/fr/citoyen/servquebec.as
p
Other Communication: TDD: 1-800-361-9596~Extérieur du Québec: 418-643-1344
Formerly Communications Qu,bec. A new agency whose mandate is to offer Qu,bec citizens & businesses a single window for simplified access to numerous public services.
Présidente-Directrice générale, Francine Martel-Vaillancourt
418-528-9209, Fax: 418-528-9341
Vice-présidente Services aux citoyens et aux régions, Louise Guimond
Vice-présidente Services aux entreprises et au développement, Andrée Blanchet
Directrice générale Communications, Carole Lafond
418-644-2498, Fax: 418-643-2411

Publications Québec

1550D, rue Jean-Talon nord, 1er étage
Québec, QC G1N 2E5
418-643-5150
Fax: 418-643-6177
800-463-2100
service.clientele@mrci.gouv.qc.ca
www.publicationsduquebec.gouv.qc.ca
Other Communication: Toll Free Fax: 1-800-561-3479

Ministère des Transports (MTQ) / Transportation

700, boul René-Lévesque est, 27e étage
Québec, QC G1R 5H1
Fax: 514-643-1269
888-355-0511
communications@mtq.gouv.qc.ca
www.mtq.gouv.qc.ca
Responsible for environmental policy concerning road construction & safety in the province. Responsible for the administration & regulation of dangerous materials transport. Conducts research & development on roads & roadsideenvironments.

Acts Administered:
Code de la sécurité routière/Highway Safety Code
Loi concernant la Compagnie de gestion de Matane inc./Act respecting the Compagnie de gestion de Matane Inc.
Loi concernant les partenariats en matière d'infrastructures de transport/Act respecting transport infrastructure partne
Loi concernant les propriétaires et exploitants de véhicules lourds/Act respecting owners and operators of heavy vehicle
Loi concernant les services de transport par taxi/Act respecting transportation services by taxi
Loi interdisant l'affichage publicitaire le long de certaines voies de circulation/Act to prohibit commercial advertisin
Loi modifiant la Loi sur les transports en matière de camionnage en vrac/Act to amend the Transport Act as regards bulk
Loi sur l'Agence métropolitaine de transport/Act respecting the Agence métropolitaine de transport
Loi sur l'assurance automobile/Automobile Insurance Act
Loi sur l'expropriation/Expropriation Act
Loi sur la publicité au long des routes/Roadside Advertising Act
Loi sur la sécurité du transport terrestre guidé/Act to ensure safety in guided land transportation
Loi sur la Société de l'assurance automobile du Québec/Act respecting the Société de l'assurance automobile du Québec
Loi sur la Société des traversiers du Québec/Act respecting the Société des Traversiers du Québec
Loi sur la Société du port ferroviaire de Baie-Comeau-Hauterive/Act respecting the Société du port ferroviaire de Baie-C
Loi sur la voirie/Act respecting roads
Loi sur le Ministère des Transports/Act respecting the Ministère des Transports
Loi sur les chemins de fer/Railway Act
Loi sur les conseils intermunicipaux de transport dans la région de Montréal/Act respecting intermunicipal boards of tra
Loi sur les sociétés de transport en commun/Act respecting public transit authorities
Loi sur les transports/Transport Act
Loi sur les transports instituant la Commission des transports du Québec/Transport Act established by the Commission des
Loi sur les véhicules hors route/Act respecting off-highway vehicles
Ministre des Transports Ministre responsable de la région de la Mauricie, Michel Després
418-643-6980, Fax: 418-643-2033
Ministre déléguée, Julie Boulet
Sous-ministre, Denys Jean
Sous-ministre associé & Responsable du Bureau de la Capitale-Nationale, Claude Pinault
Sous-ministre adjoint, Michel Lambert
Contact Bureau des sous-ministres ajoints, Françoise Huot
418-643-6740, Fax: 418-643-9836

Secrétariat du Conseil du trésor / Treasury Board

Édifice H
#1.64B, 875, Grande Allée est, 1er étage
Québec, QC G1R5R8
418-643-5926
Fax: 418-643-7824
www.tresor.gouv.qc.ca
Présidente, Monique Jérôme-Forget
418-643-5926, Fax: 418-643-7824
Secrétaire, Luc Meunier
418-643-1977, Fax: 418-643-6494, communication@sct.gouv.qc.ca
Directrice-générale Vérification interne, Hélène Caouette
418-646-6833, Fax: 418-528-6271
Greffier, Serge Martineau
418-528-6108, Fax: 418-643-4877, serge.martineau@sct.gouv.qc.ca
Greffier adjoint, Robert Cavanagh
418-528-6110, Fax: 418-643-4877, robert.cavanagh@sct.gouv.qc.ca
Directeur général Administration, Claude Sicard
418-643-8760, Fax: 418-646-1089
Directrice (par intérim) Communications, Henriette Dumont
418-643-6351, henriette.dumont@sct.gouv.qc.ca

Sous-secrétariat à la modernisation de l'État / Modernizing the State

Secrétaire associée, Sylvie Grondin
Directrice Modernisation, Brigitte Guay
418-643-0805, Fax: 418-528-0527
Directeur Gestion de la performance, Guy Émond
418-528-6203, Fax: 418-643-6034
Directrice Centre d'expertise sur la prestation de services, Jocelyne Sauriol
418-646-0399, Fax: 418-644-2400

Sous-secrétariat aux politiques budgétaires et programmes / Budget Policies & Programs

Secrétaire associé, Gilles Paquin
418-643-1977, Fax: 418-646-4294
Directeur Politiques et opérations budgétaires, Simon-Pierre Falardeau
418-528-6301, Fax: 418-643-4974
Directeur Programmes administratifs, sociaux et de santé, Michèle Bourget
418-528-6513, Fax: 418-643-6569
Directeur Programmes économiques, éducatifs et culturels, Yves Lessard
418-528-6252, Fax: 418-643-7288
Chef de service (par intérim) Programmes administratifs, Jean-François Boudreau
418-528-6314, Fax: 418-643-6569
Chef de service Programmes économiques, Daniel Roy
418-528-6254, Fax: 418-643-7288
Chef de service Programmes éducatifs et culturels, Mario Ste-Croix
418-528-6260, Fax: 418-643-7288
Chef de service Programmes sociaux et de santé, Jean-François Lachine
418-528-6258, Fax: 418-643-6569
Chef de service Opérations de prévisions et de suivi des dépenses, Jacques Fortin
418-528-6303, Fax: 418-643-4974

Sous-secrétariat aux Ressources humaines et aux relations de travail
Secrétaire associé, Gilles Charland
Secrétaire adjoint Politiques de rémunération et des régimes collectifs, Clément D'Astous
Directeur Coordination insectorielle des négociations, Jacques Thibault
418-644-2145, Fax: 418-646-8102
Directeur Gestion de la main-d'oeuvre de la fonction publique, Claude Sicard
Directeur Planification et développement de la main-d'oeuvre, secteur fonction, Jocelyn Poirier
418-528-6638, Fax: 418-644-4938
Directrice Politiques de rémunération et de conditions de travail, Dominique Gauthier
418-528-6406, Fax: 418-643-4588
Directrice Politiques de main-d'oeuvre, Elizabeth Allard
418-528-6460, Fax: 418-646-8131
Directeur Relations de travail, Normand Légaré
418-643-7870, Fax: 418-643-0865
Directeur Santé des personnes et des organisations, Serge Fortin
418-528-6230, Fax: 418-643-7500
Chef de service (par intérim) Actuariat, Françoois Blanchard
418-644-4299, Fax: 418-644-9274
Chef de service Analyse, recherche et comparaison de marché, Marcel Lapointe
418-528-6424, Fax: 418-643-4588
Chef de service Information de gestion, Denis Robitaille

Vérificateur général du Québec / Auditor General

750, boulevard Charest est, 3e étage
Québec, QC G1K 9J6
418-691-5900
Fax: 418-644-4460
verificateur.general@vgq.gouv.qc.
www.vgq.gouv.qc.ca
Vérificateur général, Renaud Lachance
Agente de secrétariat, Louise Parent
louise.parent@vgq.gouv.qc.ca

Government of Saskatchewan

Seat of Government: Regina, SK S4S 0B3
www.gov.sk.ca
The Province of Saskatchewan entered Confederation on September 1, 1905. It has an area of 570,113.47 km2, & the StatsCan census population in 2001 was 978,933.

Office of the Premier

226 Legislative Bldg.
Regina, SK S4S 0B3
306-787-9433
Fax: 306-787-0885
premier@gov.sk.ca
www.gov.sk.ca
Premier, Hon. Lorne Calvert
Deputy Minister, Dan Perrins
Chief of Staff to the Premier, Lois Thacyk
306-787-6254, Fax: 306-787-0883
Executive Director Government Communications, Anna Willey
306-787-2814
Director Community Services, Linda Tiefenbach
306-787-6900
Sr. Admin. Assistant, Kendra Soli
306-787-9433

Executive Council

Legislative Bldg.
2405 Legislative Dr.
Regina, SK S4S 0B3
www.executive.gov.sk.ca
Premier & President, Executive Council, Hon. Lorne Calvert
306-787-0958, Fax: 306-787-0885
Minister Regional Economic & Cooperative Development & Deputy Premier, Hon. Clay Serby
306-787-0623, Fax: 306-787-0399
Minister Highways & Transportation & Minister Responsible, Saskatchewan Transportation Co.; Minister Responsible, Forestry Secretariat, Hon. Eldon Lautermilch
306-787-0394, Fax: 306-798-0263
Minister Advanced Education & Employment & Minister Responsible, Public Service Commission; Minister Responsible, Immigration, Hon. Pat Atkinson
306-787-0110, Fax: 306-798-8050
Minister Industry & Resources & Minister Responsible, Investment Saskatchewan Inc.; Minister Responsible, Information Services Corp. of Saskatchewan, Hon. Eric Cline, Q.C.
306-787-0336, Fax: 306-787-2589
Minister Environment & Minister Responsible, Office of Energy Conservation; Minister Responsible, Saskatchewan Power Corp., Hon. John Nilson, Q.C.
306-787-0613, Fax: 306-787-0395
Minister First Nations & Métis Relations & Minister, Crown Investments Corp. of Saskatchewan, Hon. Maynard Sonntag
306-787-6478, Fax: 306-787-5331
Minister Community Resources & Minister Responsible, Disability Issues, Hon. Buckley Belanger
306-787-7993, Fax: 306-787-0656
Minister Government Relations, Hon. Harry Van Mulligen
306-787-0969, Fax: 306-787-1669
Minister Finance & Minister Responsible, Information Technology; Minister Responsible, SaskEnergy Inc., Hon. Andrew Thomson
306-787-6050, Fax: 306-787-6055
Minister Learning & Minister Responsible, Liquor & Gaming Authority; Minister Responsible, Saskatchewan Telecommunications; Minister Respon, Hon. Debra Higgins
306-787-7137, Fax: 306-787-0237
Minister Agriculture & Food, Hon. Mark Wartman
306-787-1684, Fax: 306-787-0630
Minister Culture, Youth & Recreation & Government House Leader; Provincial Secretary; Minister Responsible, Gaming; Minister Responsible, Saskatchewa, Hon. Glenn Hagel
306-787-1869, Fax: 306-798-2009
Minister Labour & Minister Responsible, Saskatchewan Water Corporation, Hon. David Forbes
306-787-0341, Fax: 306-787-6946
Minister Health, Hon. Len Taylor
306-787-8734, Fax: 306-787-8677
Minister Northern Affairs & Minister Responsible, Status of Women, Hon. Joan Beatty
306-787-0333, Fax: 306-787-1736
Minister Justice & Attorney General, Hon. Frank Quennell, Q.C.
306-787-8824, Fax: 306-787-1232
Minister Healthy Living Services & Minister Responsible, Seniors, Hon. Graham Addley
306-787-4983, Fax: 306-798-0264
Minister Corrections & Public Safety, Hon. Warren McCall
Officer Cabinet Secretariat, Bev Cardinal

Saskatchewan Agriculture & Food

Walter Scott Bldg.
3085 Albert St.
Regina, SK S4S 0B1
306-787-5140
www.agr.gov.sk.ca
Other Communication: SaskAgInfoNet Inc.: www.aginfonet.sk.ca
The mandate of the Department is to foster, in partnership with industry, a commercially viable, self-sufficient & sustainable agricultural sector. The department addresses needs of individual farms, encourages & develops higher valueproduction & processing, promotes the institutional changes required to meet the challenges & opportunities of the future, & co-ordinates assessment of issues that impact rural Saskatchewan. The department is responsible for policy & planning,industry assistance, research & technology, agriculture development & technology transfer, farm stability & adaptation, land management, investment programs, inspection & regulatory management & crop insurance.

Acts Administered:
Agri-Food Act, 2004
Agri-Food Innovation Act
Agricultural Credit Corporation of Saskatchewan Act
Agricultural Equipment Dealerships Act
Agricultural Implements Act
Agricultural Operations Act
Agricultural Safety Net Act
Agricultural Societies Act
Agrologists Act, 1994
Animal Identification Act
Animal Products Act
Animal Protection Act, 1999
Apiaries Act
Cattle Marketing Deductions Act, 1998
Crop Insurance Act
Crop Payments Act
Department of Agriculture, Food & Rural Revitilization Act
Disease of Animal Act
Expropriation (Rehabilitation Projects) Act
Farm Financial Stability Act
Farmers' Counselling & Assistance Act
Farming Communities Land Act
Government Organization Act
Grain Charges Limitation Act
Horned Cattle Purchases Act
Irrigation Act
Land Bank Repeal & Temporary Provisions Act
Leafcutting Beekeepers Registration Act
Line Fence Act
Milk Control Act, 1992
Noxious Weeds Act, 1984
On-farm Quality Assurance Programs Act
Pastures Act
Pest Control Act
Bacterial Ring Rot Control Regulations
Dutch Elm Disease Control Regulations
Pest Control Products (Saskatchewan) Act
Prairie Agricultural Machinery Institute Act, 1999
Provincial Lands Act
Sale or Lease of Certain Lands Act
Saskatchewan 4-H Foundation Act
Saskatchewan Farm Security Act
Saskatchewan Wetland Conservation Corporation Land Regulation
Soil Drifting Control Act
Stray Animals Act
Vegetable, Fruit & Honey Sales Act
Veterinarians Act, 1987
Veterinary Services Act
Minister, Hon. Mark Wartman
306-787-0338, Fax: 306-787-0630
Deputy Minister, Harvey G. Brooks
306-787-5170, Fax: 306-787-2393
Asst. Deputy Minister, Hal Cushon
306-787-8077, hcushon@agr.gov.sk.ca
Asst. Deputy Minister Development, Jacquie Gibney
306-787-5245, jgibney@agr.gov.sk.ca
Director Agri-Business Development, Kari Harvey
306-787-5018, Fax: 306-787-9623
Director Agriculture Research, Abdul Jalil
306-787-5960, Fax: 306-787-2654, ajalil@agr.gov.sk.ca
Director Communications, Scott Brown
306-787-4031, Fax: 306-787-0216, sbrown@agr.gov.sk.ca
Director Corporate Services, Karen Aulie
306-787-5211, Fax: 306-787-0600, kaulie@agr.gov.sk.ca
Director Crop Development, Scott Wright
306-787-4661, Fax: 306-787-0428, swright@agr.gov.sk.ca
Director Financial Programs, David Boehm
306-787-6395, Fax: 306-798-0271, dboehm@agr.gov.sk.ca
Acting Director Inspection & Regulatory Management, Roy White
306-787-6423, Fax: 306-787-1315
Director Lands Administration, Alan Syhlonyk
306-787-5154, Fax: 306-787-5180, asyhlonyk@agr.gov.sk.ca
Director Livestock Development, Greg Haase
306-787-5190, Fax: 306-787-9297, ghaase@agr.gov.sk.ca
Director Market Development & Food, Mitchell Demyen
306-787-8526, Fax: 306-787-0271, mdemyen@agr.gov.sk.ca
Director Policy, Rick Burton
306-787-5134, rburton@agr.gov.sk.ca

Associated Agencies, Boards & Commissions:
• Agri-Food Council
#302, 3085 Albert St.
Regina, SK S4S 0B1
306-787-8530
Fax: 306-787-5134
www.agr.gov.sk.ca/agrifood/
• Agricultural Implements Board
#202, 3085 Albert St.
Regina, SK S4S 0B1

306-787-4693
Fax: 306-787-1315
www.agr.gov.sk.ca/docs/about_us/programs_services/agimplem entsbd0
• Farm Stress Unit
#329, 3085 Albert St.
Regina, SK S4S 0B1
306-787-5196
Fax: 306-798-3042
800-667-4442
kimhoff@agr.gov.sk.ca
www.agr.gov.sk.ca/human_serv/structure/display.asp?id=890
• Prairie Agricultural Machinery Institute
Hwy#5
PO Box 1900
Humboldt, SK S0K 2A0
306-682-2555
Fax: 306-682-5080
800-567-7264
humboldt@pami.ca
www.pami.ca
• Saskatchewan Crop Insurance Corporation
484 Prince William Dr.
PO Box 3000
Melville, SK S0A 2P0
306-728-7200
Fax: 306-728-7268
customer.service@scic.gov.sk.ca
www.saskcropinsurance.com/
The Saskatchewan Crop & Corporation provides crop production insurance to farm businesses in order to manage production risk & to stabilize the farm economy.

• Saskatchewan Lands Appeal Board
#202, 3085 Albert St.
Regina, SK S4S 0B1
306-787-4693
Fax: 306-787-1315
dbrooks@agr.gov.sk.ca
www.agr.gov.sk.ca/docs/about_us/organizational_info/landappea l.as

Saskatchewan Assessment Management Agency (SAMA)

#200, 2201 - 11 Ave.
Regina, SK S4P 0J8
306-924-8000
Fax: 306-924-8070
800-667-7262
www.sama.sk.ca
SAMA is an independent agency with responsibility to develop & maintain the province's assessment policies, standards & procedures, audit assessments, & review & confirm municipal assessment rolls & provide property valuation services tolocal governments (municipalities & school boards).

Chair, Craig Melvin
CEO, Murray Cooney
306-924-8046, Fax: 306-924-8060, murray.cooney@sama.sk.ca
Director Communications, Penny Gingras
306-924-8036, Fax: 306-928-8060

Provincial Auditor Saskatchewan

#1500, 1920 Broad St.
Regina, SK S4P 3V2
306-787-6398
Fax: 306-787-6383
info@auditor.sk.ca
www.auditor.sk.ca
Provincial Auditor, Fred Wendel
306-787-6366
Asst. Provincial Auditor, Brian Atkinson
306-787-6384
Deputy Provincial Auditor Gaming & Insurance, Mobashar Ahmad
306-787-6387
Deputy Provincial Auditor Finance & Crown Corporations, Judy Ferguson
306-787-6372
Deputy Provincial Auditor Health, Mike Heffernan
306-787-6364
Deputy Provincial Auditor Education, Ed Montgomery
306-787-6389
Administrative Assistant, Dawn Watkins
306-787-6398, Fax: 306-787-6383, watkins@auditor.sk.ca

Crown Investments Corporation of Saskatchewan (CIC)

#400, 2400 College Ave.
Regina, SK S4P 1C8
306-787-6851
Fax: 306-787-8125
www.cicorp.sk.ca
Acts as a financial holding company & oversees the operations of commercial Crown corporations. Sponsor for the Capital Pension & Benefits Administration which administers pensions & benefits services to 37 organizations.

Minister Responsible, Hon. Maynard Sonntag
306-787-0894
President/CEO, Ron Styles
306-787-4553
Vice-President & CFO, Blair Swystun
306-787-9085
Vice-President Labour & Aboriginal Issues, Perry Bellegarde
306-787-5908
Vice-President Strategy & Governance, Dale Schmeichel
306-787-3947
Executive Director Capital Pension & Benefits Administration, Ken Klein
306-787-5948
Executive Director Communications, Karen Schmidt
306-787-5889
Executive Director Economic Initiatives, Sheryl Hilash
306-933-7518
Officer Administrator, Del Chorney
306-787-9097, Fax: 306-787-8030, dchorney@cicorp.sk.ca

Saskatchewan Finance

2350 Albert St.
Regina, SK S4P 4A6
306-787-6768
Fax: 306-787-6544
www.gov.sk.ca/finance/
Acts Administered:
Balanced Budget Act
Certified General Accountants Act, 1994
Certified Management Accountants Act
Certified Management Consultants Act
Chartered Accountants Act, 1986
Corporation Capital Tax Act
Federal-Provincial Agreements Act
Financial Administration Act, 1993
Fiscal Stabilization Fund Act
Fuel Tax Act, 2000
Home Energy Loan Act
Income Tax Act
Income Tax Act, 2000
Insurance Premiums Tax Act
Liquor Board Superannuation Act
Liquor Consumption Tax Act
Management Accountants Act
Members of the Legislative Assembly Benefits Act
Motor Vehicle Insurance Premiums Tax Act
Municipal Employees' Pension Act
Municipal Financing Corporation Act
Provincial Auditor Act
Provincial Sales Tax Act
Public Employees Pension Plan Act
Public Service Superannuation Act
Revenue & Financial Services Act
Saskatchewan Development Fund Act
Saskatchewan Pension Annuity Fund Act
Saskatchewan Pension Plan Act
Statistics Act
Superannuation (Supplementary Provisions) Act
Tabling of Documents Act, 1991
Tobacco Tax Act
Workers' Compensation Board Superannuation Act
Minister, Hon. Andrew Thomson
306-787-6060
Deputy Minister, Doug Matthies
Provincial Comptroller, Terry Paton
306-787-9254, Fax: 306-787-9720
Asst. Deputy Minister Public Employees Benefits Agency, Brian L. Smith
306-787-6757, Fax: 306-787-0244
Executive Director Executive Administration, Bill Van Sickle
306-787-6530
Executive Director Personnel Policy Secretariat, Allan Barss
306-787-3101
Director Communications, Mike Woods
306-787-6578
Director Human Resources, Jim Graham
306-787-6531
Director Financial Services, Bill Hoover
306-787-6529
Administrative Assistant, Chantelle Grohs
306-787-6531, Fax: 306-787-6576

Associated Agencies, Boards & Commissions:
• Board of Revenue Commissioners
#480, 2151 Scarth St.
Regina, SK S4P 3V7
306-787-6221
Fax: 306-787-1610
Any write-off or cancellation of monies owing to the Crown is subject to prior approval of the Board of Revenue Commissioners as delegated by the Treasury Board. The Board has the power to hear & determine appeals respecting taxes imposedor assessed pursuant to & by virtue of any taxing enactment & respecting other monies claimed to be due & payable to the Crown where the right of taking appeal to the Board is given by any statute.~

• Saskatchewan Development Fund Corporation
#300, 2400 College Ave.
Regina, SK S4P 1C8
306-787-1645
Fax: 306-787-8030
800-667-7543

Budget Analysis Division

Asst. Deputy Minister Taxation & Intergovernmental Affairs Branch, Kirk McGregor
306-787-6731
Asst. Deputy Minister Treasury Board, Karen Layng
306-787-6780
Executive Director Economic & Fiscal Policy Branch, Joanne Brockman
306-787-6743
Director Performance Management, Raelynn Douglas
306-787-7762

Provincial Comptroller's Division

Provincial Comptroller, Terry Paton
306-787-9254, Fax: 306-787-9720
Executive Director Financial Management, Chris Bayda
306-787-6848
Director Financial Systems, Reg Ronyk
306-787-6709
Director Internal Audit, Gary Jocelyn
306-787-6845

Public Employees Benefits Agency

Asst. Deputy Minister, Brian L. Smith
306-787-6757, Fax: 306-787-0244
Director Benefits Program, Perry Bahr
306-787-3745
Director Communications, John Charlton
306-787-3265
Director Financial Services, Kathy Morgan
306-787-6818
Director Pension Programs, Ann Mackrill
306-787-3239

Revenue Division

Asst. Deputy Minister, Len Rog
306-787-6685, Fax: 306-787-0241
Director Provincial Sales Tax (PST) Branch, Rob Dobson
306-787-7785
Director Revenue Programs Branch, Doug Lambert
306-787-4600
Supervisor Fuel & Tobacco Taxes, Brian Warbey
306-787-7687
Director Audit Branch, Scott Giroux
306-787-7784
Director Revenue Operations Branch, Kelly Laurans
306-787-7788

Treasury & Debt Management Division

Asst. Deputy Minister, Dennis Polowyk
306-787-6753

Executive Director Cash & Debt Management Branch, Margaret Johannsson
306-787-3924
Executive Director Capital Markets Branch, Rae Haverstock
306-787-6773, Fax: 306-787-8493

Saskatchewan Government Insurance (SGI)

2260 - 11 Ave.
Regina, SK S4P 0J9
306-751-1200
Fax: 306-787-7477
www.sgi.sk.ca
Other Communication: Customer Support Unit:
1-888-558-5559~
Minister Responsible, Hon. Glenn Hagel
President/CEO, Jon Schubert
Vice-President Auto Fund, Sherry Wolf
306-751-1646
Vice-President Canadian Operations, John Dobie
306-751-1597
Vice-President Claims, Earl Cameron
306-751-1705
Vice-President Finance & Administration, Don Thompson
306-751-1585
Vice-President Human Resources, Cheryl Barber
306-751-1649
Vice-President Systems, Dwain Wells
306-775-6093
Vice-President Underwriting, Randy Heise
306-751-1653

Saskatchewan Industry & Resources

2103 - 11th Ave.
Regina, SK S4P 3V7
306-787-2232
Fax: 306-787-2159
866-727-5427
www.ir.gov.sk.ca
Lead provincial government agency to spur economic growth & development of the province's resource sector, but is not the only department involved in economic development. The department has a twofold role: to offer direct programs &services to individuals & businesses, & to play a role in coordinating economic development activities among other departments & agencies.The department's goal is to achieve full & responsible development of energy, mineral & forestry resources, towork with businesses & co-operatives to expand the economy by promoting, co-ordinating & implementing policies, strategies & programs that encourage sustainable economic growth.

Acts Administered:
Crown Minerals Act
Department of Economic Development Act, 1993
Department of Energy & Mines Act
Ethanol Fuel Act, 2002
Ethanol Fuel (General) Regulations
Ethanol Fuel (Grant) Regulations
Mineral Resources Act
Seismic Exploration Regulations
Oil & Gas Conservation Act
Oil & Gas Conservation Regulations
Pipelines Act
Minister, Hon. Eric Cline, Q.C.
306-787-9124
Deputy Minister, Bruce Wilson
306-787-2591
Director Public Affairs, Bob Ellis
306-787-8983

Associated Agencies, Boards & Commissions:
• Saskatchewan Trade & Export Partnership (STEP)
#320, 1801 Hamilton St.
PO Box 1787
Regina, SK S4P 3C6
306-787-9210
Fax: 306-787-6666
877-313-7244
inquire@sasktrade.sk.ca
www.sasktrade.sk.ca
Works in partnership with provincial export companies & emerging export companies to maximize commercial success in foreign ventures. STEP provides marketing services using a team of trade professionals, innovative approaches & world-widenetworks. By promoting & developing sales, contracts, projects & referrals, STEP increases exports to existing foreign markets & taps into new markets.

• Tourism Saskatchewan
1922 Park St.
Regina, SK S4N 7M4
306-787-9600
877-237-2273
www.sasktourism.com

Corporate & Financial Services

306-787-1691
Fax: 306-787-8447
Executive Director, Hal Sanders
306-787-3524
Director Administration & Finance Services, Doreen Yurkoski
306-787-1612
Director Audit Services, Ted Pappas
306-787-5343
Director Human Resources, Debbie Brotheridge
306-787-0798
Director Mineral Lands, Doug MacKnight
306-787-2082
Director Planning & Evaluation, Jeff Ritter
306-787-0999
Director Research & Infrastructure Program, Dale Amundson
306-787-7006
Director Revenue Operations, Adeline Skwara
306-787-2830

Industry Development

Fax: 306-787-3989
Asst. Deputy Minister, Debbie Wilkie
306-787-7982
Acting Executive Director Business Development Services, Bill Spring
306-787-2225
Director Competitiveness, Angela Schmidt
306-933-8223
Director Marketing, Pam Bristol
306-787-3880

Resource & Economic Policy

Fax: 306-787-2198
Assoc. Deputy Minister, Glen Veikle
306-787-6717
Executive Director Energy Policy, Trevor Dark
306-787-2469
Director Economic Analysis, David McQuinn
306-787-7983
Director Industrial Policy, Cam Pelzer
306-787-2378
Director Mineral Policy, Jay Fredericks
306-787-3377

Saskatchewan Justice

1874 Scarth St.
Regina, SK S4P 3V7
306-787-7872
Fax: 306-787-3874
www.saskjustice.gov.sk.ca
Acts Administered:
Aboriginal Courtworkers Commission Act
Absconding Debtors Act
Absentee Act
Administration of Estates Act
Adult Guardianship & Co-decision-making Act
Age of Majority Act
Agreements of Sale Cancellation Act
Agricultural Leaseholds Act
Alberta-Saskatchewan Boundary Act, 1939
Arbitration Act, 1992
Assignment of Wages Act
Attachments of Debts Act
Auctioneers Act
Builders' Lien Act
Business Corporations Act
Business Names Registration Act
Canada-United Kingdom Judgements Enforcement Act
Canadian Institute of Management (Saskatchewan Division) Act
Cemeteries Act, 1999
Charitable Fundraising Businesses Act
Children's Law Act, 1997
Choses in Action Act
Class Actions Act
Closing-out Sales Act
Collection Agents Act
Commercial Liens Act
Commissioners for Oaths Act
Companies Act
Companies Winding Up Act
Condominium Property Act, 1993
Constituency Boundaries Act, 1993
Constitutional Questions Act
Consumer & Commercial Affairs Act
Consumer Protection Act
Contributory Negligence Act
Co-operatives Act, 1996
Coroners Act, 1999
Cost of Credit Disclosure Act 2002 (NYP)
Court Jurisdiction & Proceedings Transfer Act
Court of Appeal Act, 2000
Court Officials Act, 1984
Court Reporting Act
Credit Reporting Act
Credit Union Act, 1985
Credit Union Act, 1998
Creditors' Relief Act
Criminal Enterprise Suppression Act
Crown Administration of Estates Act
Crown Employment Contracts Act
Crown Suits (Costs) Act
Department of Justice Act
Dependants' Relief Act, 1996
Devolution of Real Property Act
Direct Sellers Act
Distress Act
Electronic Information & Documents Act, 2000
Enforcement of Canadian Judgements Act, 2002
Enforcement of Foreign Judgements Act
Enforcement of Foreign Arbitral Awards Act, 1996
Enforcement of Judgements Conventions Act (NYP)
Enforcement of Maintenance Orders Act, 1997
Equality of Status of Married Persons Act
Escheats Act
Executions Act
Exemptions Act
Expropriation Act
Expropriation Procedure Act
Factors Act
Family Farm Credit Act
Family Maintenance Act, 1997
Family Property Act
Fatal Accidents Act
Federal Courts Act
Film & Video Classification Act
Foreign Judgments Act
Fraudulent Preferences Act
Freedom of Information & Protection of Privacy Act
Frustrated Contracts Act
Funeral & Cremation Services Act
Guarantee Companies Securities Act
Health Care Directives & Substitute Health Care Decision Makers Act
Home Owners' Protection Act
Homesteads Act, 1989
Hotel Keepers Act
Improvements under Mistake of Title Act
Interjurisdictional Support Orders Act
International Child Abduction Act, 1996
International Commercial Arbitration Act
International Protection of Adults Act (NYP)
International Sale of Goods Act
Interpretation Act, 1995
Interprovincial Subpoena Act
Intestate Succession Act, 1996
Judges' Orders Enforcement Act
Judgments Extension Act
Jury Act, 1998
Justice of the Peace Act, 1988
Land Contracts (Actions) Act
Land Information Services Facilitation Act
Land Titles Act, 2000
Land Surveyors & Professional Surveyors Act
Land Surveys Act, 2000
Landlord & Tenant Act
Language Act
Law Reform Commission Act
Laws Declaratory Act
Legal Aid Act

GOVERNMENT

Legal Profession Act, 1990
Libel & Slander Act
Limitations of Actions Act
Limitation of Actions Act
Limitation of Civil Rights Act
Local Authority Freedom of Information & Protection of Privacy Act
Lord's Day (Saskatchewan) Act
Mandatory Testing & Disclosure (Bodily Substances) Act
Manitoba-Saskatchewan Boundary Act, 1937
Manitoba-Saskatchewan Boundary Act, 1942
Manitoba-Saskatchewan Boundary Act, 1966
Manitoba-Saskatchewan Boundary Act, 1978
Marriage Act, 1995
Marriage Settlement Act
Members' Conflict of Interest Act
Mentally Disordered Persons Act
Mortgage Brokers Act
Motor Dealers Act
Municipal Hail Insurance Act
Names of Homes Act
New Generation Co-operatives Act
Non-profit Corporations Act, 1995
Notaries Public Act
Ombudsman & Children's Advocate Act
Parents' Maintenance Act
Partnership Act
Pawned Property (Recording) Act
Penalties & Forfeitures Act
Pension Benefits Act, 1992
Personal Property Security Act, 1993
Police Act, 1990
Powers of Attorney Act, 2002
Pre-judgement Interest Act
Privacy Act
Private Investigators & Security Guards Act, 1997
Proceedings Against the Crown Act
Professional Corporations Act
Provincial Court Act, 1998
Provincial Mediation Board Act
Public Disclosure Act
Public Guardian & Trustee Act
Public Inquiries Act
Public Officers' Protection Act
Public Utilities Easements Act
Queen's Bench Act, 1998
Queen's Counsel Act
Queen's Printer Act
Real Estate Act
Reciprocal Enforcement of Judgments Act, 1996
Recording of Evidence by Sound Recording Machine Act
Recovery of Possession of Land Act
Referendum & Plebiscite Act
Registered Plan (Retirement Income) Exemption Act
Regulations Act, 1995
Religious Societies Land Act
Residential Tenancies Act
Revised Statutes Act, 1979
Safer Communities & Neighbourhoods Act
Sale of Goods Act
Sale of Training Courses Act
Sales on Consignment Act
Saskatchewan Evidence Act
Saskatchewan Farm Security Act
Saskatchewan Financial Services Commission Act
Saskatchewan Human Rights Code
Saskatchewan Insurance Act
Saskatchewan Northwest Territories Boundary Act, 1966
Securities Act, 1988
Seizure of Criminal Property Act
Slot Machine Act
Small Claims Act, 1997
Summary Offences Procedure Act, 1990
Surface Rights Acquisition & Compensation Act
Survival of Actions Act
Survivorship Act, 1993
Thresher Employees Act
Threshers' Lien Act
Trading Stamp Act
Traffic Safety Court of Saskatchewan Act, 1988
Trust & Loan Corporations Act, 1997
Trustee Act
Trusts Convention Implementation Act
Unconscionable Transactions Relief Act
Variation of Trusts Act
Victims of Crime Act, 1995
Victims of Domestic Violence Act
Wills Act, 1996
Woodmen's Lien Act

Minister & Attorney General, Hon. Frank Quennell, Q.C.
306-787-5353, Fax: 306-787-1232
Deputy Minister & Deputy Attorney General, Doug Moen, Q.C.
306-787-5351, Fax: 306-787-3874
Director Administrative Services, Gordon Sisson
306-787-5472
Executive Director Policy, Planning & Evaluation, Betty Ann Pottruff, Q.C.
306-787-8954
Secretary, Margaret Manz
306-787-5051, Fax: 306-787-3874,
mmanz@justice.gov.sk.ca

Associated Agencies, Boards & Commissions:

• Law Reform Commission of Saskatchewan
410 26th St. West
Saskatoon, SK S7L 0H9
306-347-2101
www.lawreformcommission.sk.ca

• Provincial Mediation Board/Office of the Rentalsman
#120, 2151 Scarth St.
Regina, SK S4P 2H8
306-787-2699
Fax: 306-787-5574
888-215-2222

• Public & Private Rights Board
3085 Albert St., 3rd Fl.
Regina, SK S4P 3V7
306-787-4071
Fax: 306-787-0088

• Saskatchewan Farm Land Security Board
#207, 3988 Albert St.
Regina, SK S4S 3R1
306-787-5047
Fax: 306-787-8599
www.farmland.gov.sk.ca

• Saskatchewan Farm Security Programs
#207, 3988 Albert St.
Regina, SK S4S 3R1
306-787-5047
Fax: 306-787-8599

• Saskatchewan Film & Video Classification Board
#500, 1919 Saskatchewan Dr.
Regina, SK S4P 4H2
306-787-5550
Fax: 306-787-9779
adwyer@justice.gov.sk.ca

• Saskatchewan Financial Services Commission
#601, 1919 Saskatchewan Dr.
Regina, SK S4P 4H2
306-787-5646
Fax: 306-787-5899
www.sfsc.gov.sk.ca

• Saskatchewan Human Rights Commission
Listed alphabetically in detail.

• Saskatchewan Legal Aid Commission
#502, 201 - 21 St. East
Saskatoon, SK S7K 2H6
306-933-5300
Fax: 306-933-6764
In -Sas-k on
central@legalaid.gov.sk.ca
www.legalaid.sk.ca

• Saskatchewan Police Commission
1874 Scarth St., 6th Fl.
Regina, SK S4P 3V7
306-787-6518
Fax: 306-787-0136

• Saskatchewan Police Complaints Investigator
#600, 1919 Saskatchewan Dr.
Regina, SK S4P 4H2
306-787-6519
Fax: 306-787-6528
www.saskjustice.gov.sk.ca/Pol_Complaints/default.shtml

• Surface Rights Board of Arbitration
113 - 2nd Ave. East
PO Box 1597
Kindersley, SK S0L 1S0
306-463-5447
Fax: 306-463-5449
surface@sasktel.net
www.saskjustice.gov.sk.ca/Surface_rights

Saskatchewan Regional Economic & Co-operative Development

3085 Albert St.
Regina, SK S4S 0B1
306-787-9703
800-265-2001
www.recd.gov.sk.ca

Formerly Saskatchewan Rural Development. Coordinate & implements policies, strategies & programs that stimulate & facilitate regional economic development. The Department provides entrepreneurs, small businesses, cooperatives,organizations & communities with services & advice which focus on business information, opportunities, business retention & expansion, & strategic partnerships

Acts Administered:
Economic & Co-operative Development Act
Regional Economic & Co-operative Development Act

Minister, Hon. Clay Serby
306-787-0888
Deputy Minister, Denise Haas
306-787-7518
Director Business Retention & Expansion, Doug Howorko
306-787-2201
Director Co-operative Development, Wayne Thrasher
306-787-0190
Director Investment Programs, John Keeler
306-787-8710
Director Policy & Planning, Dion McGrath
306-787-4483, dmcgrath@agr.gov.sk.ca
Director Program Development & Operations & Acting Director, Regional Programs & Services, Debbie Harrison
306-787-7874

Regional Offices

Estevan
1133 - 4 St.
Estevan, SK S0A 0W6
Fax: 306-637-4510

Moose Jaw
88 Saskatchewan St. East
Moose Jaw, SK S6H 0V4
Fax: 306-694-3500

North Battleford
1202 - 101 St.
North Battleford, SK S9A 1E9
Fax: 306-446-7442

Prince Albert
1084 Central Ave.
Prince Albert, SK S6V 6G1
Fax: 306-922-6499

Regina
1925 Rose St.
Regina, SK S4P 3P1
Fax: 306-787-1620

Saskatoon
345 - 3 Ave. South
Saskatoon, SK S7K 2H6
Fax: 306-933-7692

Swift Current
885 - 6 Ave. NE
Swift Current, SK S9H 2M9
Fax: 306-778-8526

Yorkton
23 Smith St. West
Yorkton, SK S3N 0H9
Fax: 306-786-1417

Government of the Yukon Territory

Seat of Government:PO Box 2703
Whitehorse, YT Y1A 2C6
www.gov.yk.ca

The Yukon was created as a separate territory June 13, 1898. It has an area of 531,843.62 km2, & the StatsCan census population in 2001 was 28,674. A federally appointed commissioner (similar to a provincial lieutenant-governor) overseesfederal interests in the territory, but the day-to-day operation of the government rests with the wholly elected

executive council (cabinet). The territorial legislature has power to make acts on generally all matters of a local nature in theterritory, including the imposition of local taxes, property & civil rights & the administration of justice, education & health & social services. Legislative powers vested in the provinces but not available to the territory include control ofunoccupied Crown land, renewable & non-renewable resources (except wildlife & sport fisheries) & the power to amend the Yukon Act, a federal statute.

Office of the Premier

PO Box 2703
Whitehorse, YT Y1A 2C6
Fax: 867-393-6252
Premier, Hon. Dennis Fentie
867-393-7053
Chief of Staff, Rick Nielsen
867-667-8507
Principal Secretary, Gordon Steele
867-667-5842
Communications Advisor, Peter Carr
867-667-8688

Executive Council

PO Box 2703
Whitehorse, YT Y1A 2C6
867-667-5800
Fax: 867-393-6202
800-040-8 ex
eco@gov.yk.ca

Acts Administered:
Cabinet & Caucus Employees Act
Conflict of Interest Act
Corporate Governance Act
Environmental Assessment Act, 2003
First Nations (Yukon) Self-Government Act
Flag Act
Floral Emblem Act
Government Organisation Act
Intergovernmental Agreements Act
Official Tree Act
Plebiscite Act
Public Inquiries Act
Raven Act
Statistics Act
Waters Act, (shared with Environment & Energy, Mines & Resources)
Yukon Act (Canada)
Yukon Environmental & Socio-Economic Assessment Act
Yukon Land Claim Final Agreements, An Act Approving
Yukon Tartan Act

Premier & Minister, Finance; Minister, Environment, Hon. Dennis Fentie
867-393-7053
Minister Tourism & Culture & Deputy PremMinister Responsible, Women's Directorate, Hon. Elaine Taylor
867-667-8641, Fax: 867-393-6252
Minister Justice, Hon. Marian Horne
Minister Energy, Mines & Resources & Minister, Highways & Public Works; Minister Responsible, Yukon Development Corporation, Yukon Energy Corporation, Hon. Archie Lang
867-667-8643, Fax: 867-393-6252
Minister Community Services & Minister Responsible, Public Service Commission, Hon. Glenn Hart
867-667-8629, Fax: 867-393-7400
Minister Economic Development & Minister Responsible, Yukon Housing Corporation, Yukon Liquor Corporation, Yukon Lottery Commission, Hon. James Kenyon
867-668-8628, Fax: 867-393-7400
Minister Health & Social Services & Minister Responsible, Yukon Workers' Compensation Health Board, Hon. Brad Cathers
867-667-5806
Minister Education, Hon. Patrick Rouble

Executive Council Office

Deputy Minister & Cabinet Secretary, Janet Moodie
867-667-5866
Asst. Deputy Minister Corporate Services, Janet Mann
867-667-5866
Asst. Deputy Minister Land Claims & Implementation Secretariat/First Nations Relations, Karen Armour
867-667-8566
Acting Director Policy & Planning, Karen Hougen-Bell
867-667-8081
Director Aboriginal Languages, Cheryl McLean
867-667-3734, Fax: 867-393-6229
Director Bureau of Statistics, Gerry Ewert
867-667-5963, Fax: 867-393-6203, gerry.ewert@gov.yk.ca
Senior Government Representative Intergovernmental Relations Office, Harley Trudeau
613-234-3206, Fax: 613-563-9602, hstrudeau@sprint.ca
Protocol Officer, Pamela Bangart
867-667-5875, Fax: 867-393-6214, pamela.bangart@gov.yk.ca
Manager Youth Directorate, Judy Thrower
867-667-8213, Fax: 867-393-6341

Yukon Community Services

PO Box 2703
Whitehorse, YT Y1A 2C6
867-667-5811
Fax: 867-393-6295
800-661-0408
TDD: 867-393-7460inquiry@gov.yk.ca
www.community.gov.yk.ca

The main purpose of the department is to serve Yukoners & their communities by providing access to services to strengthen communities. The department focuses on community affairs & municipal relations within government on behalf of Yukoncommunities & acts as a liaison between community groups & government departments.

Acts Administered:
Animal Protection Act (shared with Energy, Mines & Resources)
Area Development Act
Assessment & Taxation Act
Boiler & Pressure Vessels Act
Builder's Lien Act
Building Standards Act
Business Corporation Act
Cemeteries & Burial Sites Act
Certified General Accountants Act
Certified Management Accountants Act
Chartered Accountants Act
Chiropractors Act
Choses in Action Act shared with Department of Justice
Civil Emergency Measures Act
Consumer Protection Act
Cooperative Associations Act
Dental Professions Act
Denture Technicians Act
Dog Act
Electrical Protection Act
Elevator & Fixed Conveyances Act
Emergency Medical Aid Act
Employment Agencies Act
Employment Standards Act
Engineering Profession Act
Factors Act
Fire Prevention Act
First Nation Indemnification (Fire Management) Act
Forest Protection Act shared with Department of Energy, Mines & Resources
Funeral Directors Act
Garage Keepers Lien Act
Gas Burning Devices Act
Gasoline Handling Act
Health Professions Act
Home Owner's Grant Act
Insurance Act
International Commercial Arbitration Act
International Sale of Goods Act
Landlord & Tenant Act
Licensed Practical Nurses Act
Lottery Licensing Act
Medical Profession Act
Miner's Lien Act
Motor Vehicles Act (shared with Highways & Public Works)
Municipal Act
Municipal Finance & Community Grants Act
Municipal Loans Act
Noise Prevention Act
Optometrists Act
Partnership & Business Name Act
Pawnbrokers & Second-Hand Dealers Act
Personal Property Security Act
Pharmacists Act
Private Investigators & Security Guards Act
Public Libraries Act
Real Estate Agents Act
Recreation Act
Registered Nurses Profession Act
Sales of Goods Act
Securities Act
Seniors Property Tax Deferment Act
Societies Act
Subdivision Act
Trustee Act (shared with Economic Development)
Warehouse Keepers Lien Act
Warehouse Receipts Act
Whitehorse Streets & Lanes Ordinance
Yukon Foundation Act

Minister, Hon. Glenn Hart
867-667-8629
Deputy Minister, Marc Tremblay
867-667-5155
Asst. Deputy Minister Corporate Policy & Communications, Dan Boyd
867-667-3224
Director Finance, Systems & Administration, Temes Cherimet
867-667-5311, Fax: 867-393-6264
Director Human Resources, Ellen Zimmerman
867-667-5667, Fax: 867-393-6933
Acting Secretary, Lise Falardeau
867-667-5144, Fax: 867-393-6404, lise.falardeau@gov.yk.ca

Associated Agencies, Boards & Commissions:
• Assessment Appeal Board
867-668-6598
Fax: 867-633-2640
• Driver Control Board
308 Steele St.
PO Box 2703
Whitehorse, YT Y1A 2C6
867-667-3774
Fax: 867-393-6483
dcb@gov.yk.ca
• Yukon Lottery Commission
312 Wood St.
Whitehorse, YT Y1A 2E6
867-633-7890
Fax: 867-668-7561
lotteriesyukon@gov.yk.ca

Consumer & Safety Services

Acting Director, Dale Kozmen
867-667-8290
Registrar Corporate Affairs, Bette Boyd
867-667-5225
Manager Consumer Services, Fiona Charbonneau
867-667-5257
Manager Corporate Affairs & Registrar, Richard Roberts
867-667-5225
Acting Manager Labour Services, Bill Wilcox
867-667-5259
Manager Building Safety, Stan Dueck
867-667-5824
Acting Manager Motor Vehicles, Réjean Babineau
867-667-5313

Protective Services

Asst. Deputy Minister, Dan Boyd
867-667-3224
Director, Ken Colbert
867-456-3904

Yukon Development Corporation (YDC)

PO Box 2703 D-1
Whitehorse, YT Y1A 2C6
867-393-7069
Fax: 867-393-7071

The Yukon Development Corporation (YDC) assists with implementation of energy policies from the Department of Energy, Mines & Resources, by designing & delivering related energy programs. YDC facilitates the generation, production,transmission & distribution of energy in a manner consistent with sustainable development. YDC has investments in electricity & related energy infrastructure & acts as the primary vehicle for delivery of territorial energy programs & services. YDCowns two subsidiary corporations, Yukon Energy Corporation, YEC, & the Energy Solutions Centre Inc., ESC.

YEC is the primary producer & transmitter of electrical energy in the territory & operates under the Yukon Utilities Board & the PublicUtilities Act. ESC provides technical services, promotes efficiency & renewable energy technologies, co-ordinates & delivers federal & territorial energy programs to households, businesses, institutions, First Nation & public governments.

Acts Administered:
Yukon Development Corporation Act
Minister Responsible, Hon. Archie Lang
867-667-8643
CEO, David Morrison
867-393-5400

Yukon Economic Development

PO Box 2703
Whitehorse, YT Y1A 2C6
867-393-7191
Fax: 867-395-7199
800-661-0408
www.economicdevelopment.gov.yk.ca

The Department works with the Yukon business community & with other governments to support business development, trade & investment opportunities, & partnerships for the development of the Yukon economy. It co-ordinates & facilitates theYukon Government's economic development agenda. The Department is focused on creating a positive business climate in Yukon & is committed to First Nation business development in the territory. Economic Development markets Yukon as a great place to dobusiness.

Minister, Hon. Jim Kenyon
867-667-8628
Deputy Minister, Eugene Lysy
867-393-7191
Asst. Deputy Minister, Terry Hayden
867-456-3912
Director Corporate Services, Karen Mason
867-667-5933
Acting Director Strategic Industries, Claire DeRome
867-667-5633
Acting Director Policy, Planning & Research, Andrea Buckley
867-667-5378
Director Business & Trade, Luke Pantin
867-667-8075
Director Regional Economic Development, Kim Cholette
867-456-3929
Assistant to the ADM, Judith Voswinkel
867-667-3180, Fax: 867-393-7191,
judith.voswinkel@gov.uk.ca

Yukon Finance

PO Box 2703
Whitehorse, YT Y1A 2C6
867-667-5343
Fax: 867-393-6217

Acts Administered:
Appropriation Acts
Banking Agency Guarantee Act
Faro Mine Loan Act
Financial Administration Act
Fireweed Fund Act
Fuel Oil Tax Act
Income Tax Act
Insurance Premium Tax Act
Interim Supply Appropriation Acts
Liquor Tax Act
Taxpayer Protection Act
Tobacco Tax Act
Yukon Development Corporation Loan Guarantee Act
Minister, Hon. Dennis Fentie
867-667-8660
Deputy Minister, Bruce McLennan
867-667-3571
Director Finance & Administration, Bill Curtis
867-667-5276

Financial Operations & Revenue Services

Fax: 867-393-6217
Asst. Deputy Minister, David Hrycan
867-667-5355
Director Accounting Services, Miko Miyahara
867-667-5375
Director Financial Systems, Clarke Laprairie
867-667-5278
Director Investments & Debt Services, Lisa Pan
867-667-5346
Director Revenue Services, Karen Johnson
867-667-3074

Fiscal Relations & Management Board Secretariat

Fax: 867-393-6355
Director Budgets, Mark Tubman
867-667-5821
Director Fiscal Relations, Tim Shoniker
867-667-5303
Director Management Board Secretariat, Helen Bebak
867-667-5277

Yukon Justice

PO Box 2703
Whitehorse, YT Y1A 2C6
867-667-8644
Fax: 867-393-6272

Acts Administered:
Age of Majority Act
Arbitration Act
Auxiliary Police Act
Canadian Charter of Rights & Freedoms (Canada) Act
Choices in Action Act
Collection Act
Condominium Act
Conflict of Laws (Traffic Accidents) Act
Constitutional Questions Act
Consumers Protection Act
Continuing Consolidation of Statutes Act
Contributory Negligence Act
Coroners Act
Corrections Act
Court of Appeal Act
Creditor's Relief Act
Crime Prevention & Victim Services Trust Act
Decision Making, Support & Protection to Adults Act, (shared with Health & Social Services
Defamation Act
Department of Justice Act
Dependant's Relief Act
Devolution of Real Property Act
Distress Act
Electronic Evidence Act
Electronic Registration (Dept. of Public Statutes) Act
Enactment Republication Act
Enduring Power of Attorney Act
Estate Administration Act
Evidence Act
Executions Act
Exemptions Act
Expropriation Act
Family Property & Support Act
Family Violence Prevention Act
Fatal Accidents Act
Fine Option Act
Foreign Arbitral Awards Act
Fraudulent Preferences & Conveyances Act
Frustrated Contracts Act
Garnishee Act
Human Rights Act
Human Tissue Gift Act
Interpretation Act
Interprovincial Subpoena Act
Jails Act
Judicature Act
Jury Act
Land Titles Act
Legal Profession Act
Legal Services Society Act
Limitation of Actions Act
Lord's Day Act
Maintenance Enforcement Act
Married Women's Property Act
Mediation Board Act
Notaries Act
Perpetuities Act
Presumption of Death Act
Public Utilities Act
Reciprocal Enforcement of Judgements Act
Reciprocal Enforcement of Judgements UK Act
Reciprocal Enforcement of Maintenance Orders Act
Recording of Evidence Act
Regulations Act
Small Claims Court Act
Spousal Tort Immunity Abolition Act
Summary Convictions Act
Supreme Court Act
Survival of Actions Act
Survivorship Act
Tenants in Common Act
Territorial Court Act
Territorial Court Judiciary Pension Plan
Torture Prohibitation Act
Variation of Trusts Act
Wills Act
Youth Criminal Justice Act (Canada), (shared with Health & Social Services)
Minister, Hon. Marian Horne
Deputy Minister, Dennis Cooley
867-667-5959, Fax: 867-393-6272
Director Finance, Systems & Administration, Brigitte Hunter
867-667-5072, Fax: 867-667-5790
Director Policy, Dan Cable
Executive Assistant to the Deputy Minister, Linda Steinbach
867-667-5959, Fax: 867-393-6272,
linda.steinbach@gov.yk.ca

Associated Agencies, Boards & Commissions:
• Law Society of Yukon - Executive
#202, 302 Steele St.
Whitehorse, YT Y1A 2C5
867-668-4231
Fax: 867-667-7556
lsy@yknet.yk.ca
www.lawsocietyyukon.com
• Law Society of Yukon - Discipline Committee
#201, 302 Steele St.
Whitehorse, YT Y1A 2C5
867-668-4231
Fax: 867-667-7556
lsy@yknet.yk.ca
www.lawsocietyyukon.com
• Yukon Human Rights Commission
#201, 211 Hawkins St.
Whitehorse, YT Y1A 1X3
867-667-6226
Fax: 867-667-2662
800-661-0535
humanrights@yhrc.yk.ca
www.yhrc.yk.ca
• Yukon Human Rights Panel of Adjudication
#202, 407 Black St.
Whitehorse, YT Y1A 2N2
867-667-5412
Fax: 867-633-6952
• Yukon Judicial Council
PO Box 31222
Whitehorse, YT Y1A 5PT
867-667-5438
Fax: 867-393-6400
• Yukon Law Foundation
#202, 302 Steele St.
Whitehorse, YT Y1A 2C5
867-668-4231
Fax: 867-667-7556
lsy@yknet.yk.ca
www.lawsocietyyukon.com
• Yukon Legal Services Society/Legal Aid
#203, 2131 - 2nd Ave.
Whitehorse, YT Y1A 1C3
867-667-5210
Fax: 867-667-8649
legalaid@yknet.yk.ca
www.legalaid.yk.net
Other Communication: 1-800-661-0408, extension 5210 (Yukon only)
• Yukon Utilities Board
#19, 1114 - 1st Ave.
PO Box 31728
Whitehorse, YT Y1A 6L3
867-667-5058

SECTION 8

Associations

Included in this section are Canadian and foreign associations and institutes for bankers, credit unions, trust companies, caisses populaires, accountants, investors, insurance professionals, and consumers.

Listings include all or some of the following information:

- Name of the association, plus the translated name and acronym, if applicable
- The physical address of the association and its communication numbers, including email and URL addresses
- The founding date of the association
- "Also Known As" association name
- Former name
- The number of staff and volunteers
- The annual operating budget
- A profile of qualification for membership, and the number of members
- A list of committees
- A list of awards, grants and scholarships
- The association library or information centre, if applicable
- The serial publications issued by the association
- A breakdown of basic activities carried out by the association
- A list of those organizations affiliated with the association, or to which the association in question belongs
- Upcoming meetings or conferences
- A list of executives and other key personnel involved in running the association
- A basic profile of the group as a whole, usually its mission statement
- A list of branch offices

Listings may also include whether or not the association is a licensing body, whether it rents mailing lists, and what its sources of funding are.

Associations

Aboriginal Financial Officers Association (AFOA)
#301, 1066 Somerset Ave. West, Ottawa ON K1Y 4T3
Tel: 613-722-5543; *Fax:* 613-722-3467
Toll-Free: 866-722-2362
e-mail: info@afoa.ca
URL: www.afoa.ca
Overview: A medium-sized national organization
Chief Officer(s): Marilyn Osecap, Controller; Romeo Crow Chief, Sec.-Treas.
Finances: *Annual Operating Budget:* $500,000-$1.5 Million
Staff: 10 staff member(s)
Membership: 650
Awards: Excellence in Leadership Awards
Publications: AFOA Express, Newsletter, q.
Description: To provide leadership in aboriginal financial management by developing & promoting quality standards, practices, research, certification, & professional development to members & aboriginal organizations

AFOA Alberta
PO Box 1010, Siksika AB T0J 3W0
Tel: 403-734-5446; *Fax:* 403-734-5342
URL: www.afoaab.com
Chief Officer(s): Romeo Crow Chief, President/Executive Director

AFOA Atlantic
c/o 63 Tower Rd., Indian Brook NS B0N 1W0
Chief Officer(s): Richard Sack, Chair

AFOA BC
#060, 1959 Marine Dr., North Vancouver BC V7P 3G1
Tel: 604-988-5564; *Fax:* 604-988-2625
e-mail: exec@afoabc.org
URL: www.afoabc.org
Chief Officer(s): Michael Mearns, Contact

AFOA Manitoba
PO Box 285, Elphinstone MB R0J 0N0
Chief Officer(s): Stephanie Blackbird, President

AFOA NWT
PO Box 819, 5102 - 51st St., 2nd Fl., Yellowknife NT X1A 2N6
Tel: 867-766-3062; *Fax:* 867-766-3063
e-mail: afoa@northwestel.net
Chief Officer(s): Sally Nayally, Office Administrator

AFOA Ontario
Sheshegwaning First Nation, PO Box 14, Sheshegwaning ON P0P 1X0
Tel: 705-283-1245; *Fax:* 705-283-1246
e-mail: afoaontario@ontera.net
URL: www.afoa-on.ca
Chief Officer(s): Robin Malley, Coordinator

AFOA Québec
c/o Assembly of First Nations, 473 Albert St., Ottawa ON K1R 5B4
Tel: 613-241-6789; *Fax:* 613-241-6871
Chief Officer(s): Caroline Garon, President

AFOA Saskatchewan
Concentra Financial, 333 - 3rd Ave. North, Saskatoon SK S2K 2M2
Tel: 306-956-4957; *Fax:* 306-665-1343
Chief Officer(s): Dana Soonias, President

ADR Institute of Canada (ADRIC) / Institut d'arbitrage et de médiation du Canada
#500, 234 Eglinton Ave. East, Toronto ON M4P 1K5
Tel: 416-487-4733; *Fax:* 416-487-4429
Toll-Free: 877-475-4353
e-mail: admin@adrcanada.ca
URL: www.adrcanada.ca
Previous Name: Arbitration & Mediation Institute of Canada Inc.; Canadian Foundation for Dispute Resolution
Overview: A medium-sized national charitable organization founded in 1974
Chief Officer(s): Judy Ballantyne, Executive Director
Finances: *Funding Sources:* Membership fees
Membership: 1,600 arbitrators & mediators, corporations & law firms; *Fees:* Schedule available; *Member Profile:* ADR professionals & corporate users
Activities: ADR Connect; chartered mediators (C.Med.) & chartered arbitrators (C.Arb.) designations
Awards: Lionel J. McGowan Award of Excellence
Publications: Canadian Arbitration & Mediation/Journal d'Arbitrage et de Médiation Canadien, s-a.
Description: To promote the use of arbitration & mediation (ADR - alternative dispute resolution) to settle disputes; to provide information & education on ADR to practitioners, parties, the public, & the business, professional & government communities; to assist those wishing to use ADR through the provision of Arbitration & Mediation Rules, administrative services, & information about the process & member arbitrators & mediators

ADR Atlantic Institute
PO Box 123, Halifax NS B3J 2M4
Tel: 902-435-3084; *Fax:* 902-435-3084
e-mail: apami@attcanada.ca

ADR Institute of Ontario, Inc.
#500, 234 Eglinton Ave. East, Toronto ON M4P 1K5
Tel: 416-487-4447; *Fax:* 416-487-4429
e-mail: admin@adrontario.ca
URL: www.adrontario.ca

ADR Institute of Saskatchewan Inc.
#16, 2700 Montague St., Regina SK S4S 0J9
Tel: 306-596-7275; *Fax:* 306-584-3395
Toll-Free: 866-596-7275
e-mail: admin@adrsaskatchewan.ca
URL: www.adrsaskatchewan.ca

Alberta Arbitration & Mediation Society
Lethbridge Bldg., #605, 10707 - 100th Ave., Edmonton AB T5J 3M1
Tel: 780-433-4881; *Fax:* 780-433-9024
Toll-Free: 800-232-7214
e-mail: aams@aams.ab.ca
URL: www.aams.ab.ca

Arbitration & Mediation Institute of Manitoba Inc.
PO Box 436, RPO Corydon, Winnipeg MB R3M 3V3
Tel: 204-783-0529; *Fax:* 204-897-7191
e-mail: info@amim.mb.ca
URL: www.amim.mb.ca

British Columbia Arbitration & Mediation Institute
#104, 1260 Hornby St., Vancouver BC V6Z 1W2
Tel: 604-736-6614; *Fax:* 604-736-9233
Toll-Free: 877-332-2264
e-mail: info@amibc.org
URL: www.amibc.org

Advanced Card Technology Association of Canada / Association canadienne de la technologie des cartes à mémoire
85 Mullen Dr., Ajax ON L1T 2B3
Tel: 905-426-6360; *Fax:* 905-619-3275
e-mail: info(AT)actcda.com
URL: www.actcda.com
Also Known As: ACT Canada
Overview: A small national organization founded in 1989
Chief Officer(s): Catherine Johnston, CEO & Treasurer
Finances: *Annual Operating Budget:* $100,000-$250,000; *Funding Sources:* Membership dues; seminars; consulting
Staff: 4 staff member(s); 15 volunteer(s)
Membership: 80+; *Fees:* Based on membership level; *Member Profile:* Users, suppliers & parties interested in smart, optical & other advanced card technologies; *Committees:* Membership; Education; Conference; Communication; Marketing
Activities: Teaching; advocacy; consulting; market research; setting international standards; *Speaker Service:* Yes; *Rents Mailing List:* Yes; *Library:* Yes by appointment
Publications: E-Newsletter
Description: To promote the understanding & use of all advanced card technologies across a wide range of applications; to connect users & suppliers; to work with governments, financial institutions & users to advance standards, develop card related policies & prepare the marketplace for a broad based acceptance of advanced cards

Advocis
#209, 390 Queens Quay West, Toronto ON M5V 3A2
Tel: 416-444-5251; *Fax:* 416-444-8031
Toll-Free: 800-563-5822
e-mail: info@advocis.ca
URL: www.advocis.ca
Previous Name: Life Underwriters Association of Canada
Merged from: Canadian Association of Insurance & Financial Advisors; Canadian Association of Financial Planners
Overview: A medium-sized national organization founded in 1906
Chief Officer(s): Steve Howard, President & CEO; Roger McMillan, Chair
Staff: 15 staff member(s)
Membership: 16,000; *Committees:* Governance; Finance
Activities: Advocacy; professional development courses towards the CFP & CLU designations; 50 chapters from coast to coast; *Library:* Yes (Open to Public)
Publications: Forum, Magazine, m., ISSN: 0380-3147, accepts advertising
Description: To represent what our members do best - Advice & Advocacy; to carry on the tradition of effectively representing our members' interests with all levels of government, regulators, & industry, always with the intention of putting the interests of consumers first; *Member of:* Financial Planners Standards Council

Alberta Association of Insolvency & Restructuring Professionals (AAIRP)
#400, 602 - 11 Ave., Edmonton AB T5J 3S9
Tel: 780-428-1671; *Fax:* 780-424-2110
e-mail: tludwig@bdo.ca
URL: www.aairp.com
Previous Name: Alberta Insolvency Practitioners Association
Overview: A small provincial organization
Chief Officer(s): Bruce Alger, President
Description: Non-profit organization that exists to attract, develop and support its members who provide insolvency and restructuring services; *Member of:* Canadian Association of Insolvency & Restructuring Professionals

Alberta Association of Insurance Adjusters (AAIA)
c/o Binns & Associates Adjusters Ltd., 4474 - 97 St., Edmonton AB T6E 5R9
Tel: 780-466-0155
e-mail: info@aaiacalgary.ca
URL: www.aaiacalgary.ca
Overview: A small provincial organization founded in 1952
Chief Officer(s): Luc Chasse FCIP, CRM, President; Arlene Brown CIP, Treasurer
Finances: *Annual Operating Budget:* Less than $50,000
Staff: 10 volunteer(s)
Membership: 200
Publications: AAIA Bulletin

Alberta Independent Insurance Adjusters' Association
c/o Crawford Adjusters Canada, #300, 3115 - 12 St. NE, Calgary AB T2E 7J2
Tel: 403-266-3933; *Fax:* 403-262-4247
e-mail: walter.waugh@crawco.ca
Overview: A small regional organization
Chief Officer(s): Walter J. Waugh BA,CIP, President

Alberta Insolvency Practitioners Association *See* Alberta Association of Insolvency & Restructuring Professionals

Alberta Insurance Council
Toronto Dominion Tower, Edmonton Centre, #901, 10088 - 102nd Ave., Edmonton AB T5J 2Z1
Tel: 780-421-4148; *Fax:* 780-425-5745
e-mail: info@abcouncil.ab.ca
URL: www.abcouncil.ab.ca
Overview: A small provincial organization
Chief Officer(s): Joanne Abram, CEO
Description: Regulatory body responsible for licensing and discipline of insurance agents, brokers and adjusters in the Province of Alberta

Calgary Office
#500, 222 - 58th Ave. SW, Calgary AB T2H 2S3
Tel: 403-233-2929; *Fax:* 403-233-2990
Chief Officer(s): Tom Hampton, COO

L'Alliance des Caisses populaires de l'Ontario limitée (ACPOL)

CP 3500, 1870 Bond St., North Bay ON P1B 4V6
Tél: 705-474-5634; *Téléc:* 705-474-5326
Courriel: support@acpol.com
URL: www.caissealliance.com
Aperçu: *Dimension:* moyenne; *Envergure: provinciale; fondée en 1979*
Membre(s) du bureau directeur: Lucie Moncion, Directrice générale
Membre: 1-99
Activités: *Bibliothèque:* Oui (Bibliothèque publique)
Membre de: Credit Union Central of Canada

American Bankers Association (ABA)

1120 Connecticut Ave. NW, Washington DC 20036 USA
Toll-Free: 800-226-5377
URL: www.aba.com
Overview: A medium-sized national organization
Chief Officer(s): Ed Yingling, President & CEO; Harris H. Simmons, Chair
Description: To represent banks of all sizes on issues of national importance for financial institutions & their customers

Arbitration & Mediation Institute of Canada Inc.; Canadian Foundation for Dispute Resolution ***See*** ADR Institute of Canada

Arbitration & Mediation Institute of Nova Scotia ***See*** ADR Institute of Canada

Les Arbitres Maritimes Associés du Canada ***See*** The Association of Maritime Arbitrators of Canada

Arctic Co-operatives Limited

1645 Inkster Blvd., Winnipeg MB R3C 3K7
Tel: 204-697-1625; *Fax:* 204-697-1880
e-mail: info@ArcticCo-op.com
URL: www.ArcticCo-op.com
Overview: A small provincial organization
Chief Officer(s): Andy Morrison, CEO; Judy Chapman, Manager
Description: To be the vehicle for service to, & cooperation among the multi-purpose Cooperative businesses in Canada's North, by providing leadership & expertise to develop & safeguard the ownership participation of our Member Owners in the business & commerce of their country, to assure control over their own destiny

NWT Regional Office
321C Old Airport Rd., Yellowknife NT X1A 3T3
Tel: 867-873-3481; *Fax:* 867-920-4052

Nunavut Regional Office
1088 Airport Rd., Iqaluit NU X0A 0H0
Tel: 867-979-2448; *Fax:* 867-979-2535

Association canadienne d'assurance nucléaire ***See*** Nuclear Insurance Association of Canada

Association canadienne d'investissement dans des fiducies de revenu ***See*** Canadian Association of Income Trusts Investors

L'Association canadienne d'études fiscales ***See*** Canadian Tax Foundation

Association canadienne de financement et de location ***See*** Canadian Finance & Leasing Association

L'Association canadienne de la paie ***See*** The Canadian Payroll Association

Association canadienne de la technologie des cartes à mémoire ***See*** Advanced Card Technology Association of Canada

Association canadienne des administrateurs de régimes de retraite ***See*** Association of Canadian Pension Management

Association canadienne des agents financiers ***See*** Association of Canadian Financial Officers

Association canadienne des compagnies d'assurance mutuelles ***See*** Canadian Association of Mutual Insurance Companies

Association canadienne des compagnies d'assurances de personnes inc. ***See*** Canadian Life & Health Insurance Association Inc.

Association canadienne des comptables en assurance ***See*** Canadian Insurance Accountants Association

Association canadienne des courtiers de fonds mutuels ***See*** Mutual Fund Dealers Association of Canada

Association canadienne des courtiers en valeurs mobilières ***See*** Investment Dealers Association of Canada

Association Canadienne des Croix Bleue ***See*** Canadian Association of Blue Cross Plans

Association canadienne des experts indépendants ***See*** Canadian Independent Adjusters' Association

Association canadienne des femmes d'assurance ***See*** Canadian Association of Insurance Women

Association canadienne des fonds de revenu ***See*** Canadian Association of Income Funds

Association canadienne des gestionnaires de fonds de retraite ***See*** Pension Investment Association of Canada

Association canadienne des institutions financières en assurance ***See*** Canadian Association of Financial Institutions in Insurance

Association canadienne des marchés des capitaux ***See*** Canadian Capital Markets Association

Association canadienne des paiements ***See*** Canadian Payments Association

Association canadienne des professeurs de comptabilité ***See*** Canadian Academic Accounting Association

Association canadienne des professionnels de l'insolvabilité et de la réorganisation ***See*** Canadian Association of Insolvency & Restructuring Professionals

Association canadienne des professionnels en dons planifiés ***See*** Canadian Association of Gift Planners

Association canadienne des prêteurs sur salaire ***See*** Canadian Payday Loan Association

Association canadienne du capital de risque et d'investissement ***See*** Canada's Venture Capital & Private Equity Association

Association d'assurances des juristes canadiens ***See*** Canadian Lawyers Insurance Association

Association de gestion de trésorerie du Canada ***See*** Treasury Management Association of Canada

Association de planification fiscale et financière (APFF) / Fiscal & Financial Planning Association

#300, 445, boul Saint-Laurent, Montréal QC H2Y 2Y7
Tél: 514-866-2733; *Téléc:* 514-866-0113
Ligne sans frais: 877-866-0113
Courriel: apff@apff.org
URL: www.apff.org
Aperçu: *Dimension:* moyenne; *Envergure: provinciale; Organisme sans but lucratif; fondée en 1976*
Membre(s) du bureau directeur: Daniel Bourgeois, Président et Directeur général; Daniel Gosselin, Président du conseil administration
Finances: *Budget de fonctionnement annuel:* $1.5 Million-$3 Million
Personnel: 14 membre(s) du personnel; 300 bénévole(s)
Membre: 2 000+; *Montant de la cotisation:* 330$; *Critères d'admissibilité/Description:* Fiscaliste et planificateur financiers (avocats, comptable, économistes)
Activités: 5 à 8 colloques d'une journée par année sur des thèmes spécifiques avec publication intégrale des textes de conférences; *Bibliothèque:* Centre d'information
Publications: Flash Fiscal, 20 fois par an, Contenu: Développements fiscaux et mises à jour sur les plus récentes actualités fiscales; Livre du congrès, annuel; Revue de planification fiscale et successorale, trimestriel, publicitéStratège, trimestriel, ISSN: 1203-6625, publicité
Description: Regrouper les personnes intéressées à la planification fiscale successorale et financière; publier et diffuser l'information dans ces domaines; favoriser la recherche

Association de protection des épargnants et investisseurs du Québec (APÉIQ)

82, rue Sherbrooke ouest, Montréal QC H2X 1X3
Tél: 514-286-1155; *Téléc:* 514-286-1154
Aperçu: *Dimension:* moyenne; *Envergure: provinciale; Organisme sans but lucratif; fondée en 1994*
Membre(s) du bureau directeur: Jocelyne Pellerin, Présidente
Personnel: 1 membre(s) du personnel; 9 bénévole(s)
Membre: 1 450; *Montant de la cotisation:* 35 individuel; 250$ institutionnel
Publications: Bulletin de l'APÉIQ, trimestriel, accepts advertising
Description: L'APÉIQ est vouée à la défense des intérêts des épargnants et investisseurs québécois, par la promotion de l'application de meilleures règles de régie d'entreprise dans les sociétés, dont les actions sont cotées en bourse; *Membre de:* International Corporate Governance Network

Association de TED du Canada ***See*** EFILE Association of Canada

Association des analystes financiers de Montréal / Montréal Society of Financial Analysts

CP 155, Succ. Ahuntsic, Montréal QC H3L 3N7
Tél: 514-990-3772; *Téléc:* 514-990-3772
Courriel: info@cfamontreal.org
URL: www.aafm-msfa.org
Aperçu: *Dimension:* petite; *Envergure: locale; fondée en 1950*
Membre(s) du bureau directeur: Michèle Moisan-Girard, Président; Suzie Éthier, Directrice à l'administration
Membre: 1275
Activités: Luncheon presentations; annual events
Description: Faire respecter le code de déontologie et les règles de comportement professionel élaboré par le CFA Institute à l'intention des professionnels de l'industrie de l'analyse financière de manière à assurer la qualité et la perception de notre profession auprès du public. Appuyer ses membres dans leurs efforts de perfectionnement et de formation par le biais de: conférences avec un grand contenu formatif, de nature pratique ou théorique; cours de préparation à l'examen du CFA Institute; la promotion du programme d'accréditation du CFA Institute pour les membres possédant déjà le titre de CFA.

Association des banquiers canadiens ***See*** Canadian Bankers Association

Association des cadres municipaux de Montréal (ACMM)

281, rue St-Paul, Montréal QC H2Y 1H1
Tél: 514-499-1130; *Téléc:* 514-499-1737
Courriel: acmm@acmm.qc.ca
URL: www.acmm.qc.ca/index1.html
Aperçu: *Dimension:* petite; *Envergure: provinciale*
Membre(s) du bureau directeur: Denis Tremblay, Président; Nathalie Deneault, Directrice administrative
Publications: J'Encadre Montréal, Bulletin, trimestriel
Description: A pour objet l'établissement de relations ordonnées entre l'employeur et les membres ainsi que l'étude, la défense et le développement des intérêts économiques sociaux, moraux et professionnels de ces derniers

Association des compagnies financières canadiennes ***See*** Association of Canadian Financial Corporations

Association des comptables généraux accrédités du Nouveau-Brunswick ***See*** Certified General Accountants Association of New Brunswick

Association des conseillers en gestion de portefeuille du Canada ***See*** Investment Counsel Association of Canada

Association des courtiers d'assurances de la Province de Québec ***See*** Chambre de l'assurance de dommages

Association des courtiers d'assurances du Nouveau-Brunswick ***See*** Insurance Brokers Association of New Brunswick

Association des experts en sinistre indépendants du Québec inc (AESIQ)

n/a Les expertises Alain Plourde, 11797, Marie-Anne Lavallee, Montréal QC H3M 3E9
Tél: 514-334-1106; *Téléc:* 514-334-3536
Courriel: alainplourde@hotmail.com
Aperçu: *Dimension:* petite; *Envergure: provinciale; fondée en 1942*
Membre(s) du bureau directeur: Alain Plourde, Président
Finances: *Budget de fonctionnement annuel:* $100,000-$250,000
Personnel: 1 membre(s) du personnel; 8 bénévole(s)
Membre: 300; *Montant de la cotisation:* 215$; *Critères d'admissibilité/Description:* Détenteur d'un certificat d'expert en sinistre du B.S.F.
Publications: Probe, Journal, au 2 mois, accepts advertising
Affiliation(s): Association Canadienne des Experts Indépendants/Canadian Independent Adjusters Association

Association des femmes d'assurance de Montréal (AFAM) / Montréal Association of Insurance Women
a/s Groupe Rosco, 225, av Lindsay, Montréal QC H9P 1C6
Tél: 514-931-7789; *Téléc:* 514-931-2494
Courriel: clarouche@roscodoc.com
URL: www.afam-maiw.com
Aperçu: *Dimension:* petite; *Envergure: locale; fondée en 1963*
Membre(s) du bureau directeur: Catherine Larouche, Présidente
Prix, Bourses: Mildred Jones Award - Insurance Woman of the Year
Description: Promouvoir et coordonner des programmes pratiques et éducatifs afin d'encourager ses membres à rechercher le plus haut niveau de connaissances en matière d'assurance ainsi que dans la conduite des affaires; *Membre de:* Canadian Association of Insurance Women

Association des gestionnaires de risques et d'assurances du Québec (AGRAQ) / Québec Risk & Insurance Management Association
1768, rue de Verbier, Laval QC H7M 5L4
Tél: 450-668-2013; *Téléc:* 450-668-4294
Courriel: agraq@sympatico.ca
URL: quebec.rims.org
Aperçu: *Dimension:* petite; *Envergure: provinciale; fondée en 1950*
Membre(s) du bureau directeur: Michel Turcotte, Président
Activités: *Evénements de sensibilisation:* La Journée gestion des risques, 16 mars
Publications: Info Risque, Journal, trimestriel
Description: Offrir à ses membres, aux membres potentiels et à la communauté de la gestion de risques en général, une tribune professionnelle et éducative qui permet l'échange d'informations et d'idées conformément aux objectifs de RIMS; *Membre de:* Risk & Insurance Management Society

Association des intermédiaires en assurance de personnes du Québec *See* Chambre de la sécurité financière

Association des marchés financiers du Canada *See* Financial Markets Association of Canada

Association des marchés financiers du Canada *See* Canadian Association of Direct Response Insurers

Association for Corporate Growth, Toronto Chapter (ACG)
#1008, 500 Avenue Rd., Toronto ON M4V 2J6
Tel: 416-868-1881; *Fax:* 416-860-0580
e-mail: acgtoronto@baystco.com
URL: www.acg.org/toronto
Also Known As: ACG Toronto
Previous Name: Canadian Association for Corporate Growth
Overview: A medium-sized national organization founded in 1973
Chief Officer(s): Dan Amadori, President; Sue Anderson, Administrator
Finances: *Annual Operating Budget:* Less than $50,000; *Funding Sources:* Membership dues; events
Staff: 1 staff member(s)
Membership: 250; *Fees:* $325; *Member Profile:* Granted on an individual basis only to those involved in corporate growth; approximately 2/3 membership drawn from the industrial & consumer product fields, & the balance from accounting firms, financial intermediaries, & related service businesses; *Committees:* Membership; Marketing & Communications; Program; Social; Sponsorship
Publications: ACG Network, Newsletter, m., Editor: Judith Iacuzzi, ISSN: 1522-4945
Description: To foster sound corporate growth by providing its members with an opportunity to gain new ideas from speakers, seminars & discussions with people working in the field of corporate growth; to develop additional skills & techniques which will contribute to the growth of their respective organizations; to meet other corporate growth professionals who can provide counsel & valuable contacts; *Member of:* Association for Corporate Growth, Chicago USA

Association for Financial Professionals of Canada
#2500, 1 Dundas St. West, Toronto ON M5G 1Z3
Tel: 416-977-5400; *Fax:* 416-595-5032
e-mail: afpc@afponline.ca
URL: www.afponline.ca
Overview: A medium-sized national organization
Chief Officer(s): Robert Horton, Executive Director; Peter Copestake, Chair
Activities: Professional development; certification; networking
Affiliation(s): Society of Canadian Treasurers

L'Association Interac *See* Interac Association

Association nationale des retraités fédéraux *See* Federal Superannuates National Association

Association of Canadian Financial Corporations (ACFC) / Association des compagnies financières canadiennes
Sussex Centre, #401, 50 Burnhamthorpe Rd. West, Mississauga ON L5B 3C2
Tel: 905-949-4920; *Fax:* 905-896-9380
Overview: A medium-sized national organization founded in 1957
Chief Officer(s): Rita Minucci, Corporate Secretary
Finances: *Annual Operating Budget:* $100,000-$250,000; *Funding Sources:* Membership dues
Staff: 1 staff member(s)
Membership: 8; *Fees:* $25,000; $5,000 associate; *Member Profile:* Financial industry; *Committees:* Legal & Legislative; Human Resources; Tax
Description: To represent financial industry; *Member of:* Conseil du Patronat du Québec

Association of Canadian Financial Officers (ACFO) / Association canadienne des agents financiers
#400, 2725 Queensview Dr., Ottawa ON K2B 0A1
Tel: 613-728-0695; *Fax:* 613-761-9568
Toll-Free: 877-728-0695
e-mail: general@acfo-acaf.com
URL: www.acfo-acaf.com
Previous Name: Association of Public Service Financial Administrators (Ind.)/Association des gestionnaires financiers de la fonction publique (Ind.)
Overview: A medium-sized national organization founded in 1989
Chief Officer(s): Jonathan Hood, Vice-President; Robert Loiselle, Vice-President; Arjun Patil, Vice-President; Ann Laroque, Coordinator; Milt Isaacs, Chair; Jim Currier, Executive Vice-President; Raoul Andersen, Vice-President; Tony Bourque, Vice-President
Finances: *Annual Operating Budget:* $250,000-$500,000
Staff: 5 staff member(s)
Membership: 3,000; *Fees:* $28 per month; *Member Profile:* Financial Administrators; *Committees:* Collective Bargaining; Executive; Finance; Honourarium; Nominations; Representative
Activities: *Library:* Yes
Description: To unite in a democratic organization all public service financial administrators for which the association becomes or applies to become a bargaining agent; to serve the welfare of its members through effective collective bargaining with their employers; to obtain for members the best levels of compensation for services rendered to their employers & the best terms & conditions of employment; to protect the rights & interests of all members in all matters upon their employment or upon their relationship with their employers; to seek to maintain high professional standards & promote their professional development; to affiliate as appropriate with other associations, unions or labour organizations for the purpose of enhancing the interests of members in the attainment of their professional & bargaining goals

Association of Canadian Pension Management (ACPM) / Association canadienne des administrateurs de régimes de retraite
#1103, 60 Bloor St. West, Toronto ON M4W 3B8
Tel: 416-964-1260; *Fax:* 416-964-0567
e-mail: acpm@acpm.com
URL: www.acpm.com
Overview: A medium-sized national organization founded in 1976
Chief Officer(s): Stephen Bigsby, Executive Director
Finances: *Annual Operating Budget:* $500,000-$1.5 Million
Staff: 4 staff member(s)
Membership: 750 individual + 25 corporate; *Fees:* Schedule available
Publications: ACPM Newsletter, q.; Penfacts: A Guide to Pensions in Canada, a.
Description: To promote the growth & health of Canada's retirement income system by championing the following principles: clarity in pension legislation; good governance & administration; balanced consideration of stakeholder interests

Association of Certified Fraud Examiners - Toronto Chapter
3266 Yonge St., Box 1408, Toronto ON M4N 3P6
Tel: 416-480-9475; *Fax:* 416-480-1813
e-mail: acfe.toronto@sympatico.ca
URL: www.acfetoronto.com
Overview: A small national organization
Chief Officer(s): Steven Silverberg CA, CFE, President; Astra Williamson CFE, CGA, Vice-President; Penny Hill, Administrator; Bruce Armstrong CA, CFE, Secretary; Tom Eby CA, MBA, Treasurer
Finances: *Annual Operating Budget:* Less than $50,000
Membership: 160; *Fees:* $85

The Association of Maritime Arbitrators of Canada (AMAC) / Les Arbitres Maritimes Associés du Canada
c/o The Shipping Federation of Canada, #326, 300, rue St-Sacrement, Montréal QC H2Y 1X4
Tel: 514-849-2325; *Fax:* 514-849-8774
e-mail: alegars@shipfed.ca
URL: www.amac.ca
Overview: A small national organization founded in 1986
Chief Officer(s): David Colford, President; Anne Legars, Secretary; John D. Hurst, Vice-President; George R. Strathy, Vice-President; Peter L. Wright, Vice-President
Finances: *Annual Operating Budget:* Less than $50,000
Membership: 100-499; *Fees:* $50; *Member Profile:* Shipping, transport & maritime corporations; law firms, surveyors, adjusters & insurers
Description: To promote & provide arbitration facilities for all types of maritime disputes whether in or outside Canada

Association of Municipal Tax Collectors of Ontario
#119, 14845 - 6 Yonge St., Aurora ON L4G 6H8
Tel: 905-725-0019
e-mail: amtco@sympatico.ca
URL: www.amtco.on.ca
Overview: A medium-sized provincial organization
Chief Officer(s): Connie Mesih, President
Membership: 338
Publications: Tax Collectors Journal
Description: To bring those persons in the Municipal field of tax collecting into helpful association with each other so that through improved relations, united effort, participation and involvement promote their professional knowledge and general interests

Association of Public Service Financial Administrators (Ind.)/Association des gestionnaires financiers de la fonction publique (Ind.) *See* Association of Canadian Financial Officers

Association of Women in Finance (AWF)
#102, 211 Columbia St, Vancouver BC V6A 2R5
Tel: 604-662-4401; *Fax:* 604-681-4545
e-mail: ssu@telus.net
URL: womeninfinance.ca/home.htm
Overview: A small provincial organization founded in 1996
Chief Officer(s): Bahar Hafizi, President & Director
Finances: *Annual Operating Budget:* Less than $50,000
Staff: 2 staff member(s)
Membership: 106; *Member Profile:* Women in finance industry in B.C.; *Committees:* PEAK Nominations; PEAK Judging
Activities: Monthly networking events; Aug. & Dec. social; Annual PEAK Awards Gala
Awards: Lifetime Achievement Award; Performance & Excellence Award; Knowledge & Leadership Award
Publications: Update, Newsletter, q.
Description: To promote women in finance-related industries by encouraging their advancement, development & involvement in the business community; to acknowledge accomplished women who have achieved excellence in their field

Association québécoise des professionnels de la réorganisation et de l'insolvabilité (AQPRI) / Québec Association of Insolvency & Restructuring Professionals
a/s Lemieux Nolet Inc., 5020, boul de la Rive-sud, Lévis QC G6V 4Z6
Tél: 418-833-1054; *Téléc:* 418-833-3191
Courriel: mpoirier@lemieuxnolet.ca
Nom précédent: Association québécoise des professionnels d'insolvabilité
Aperçu: *Dimension:* petite; *Envergure: provinciale; fondée en 1980*
Membre(s) du bureau directeur: Martin Poirier CA, CIRP, Président
Finances: *Budget de fonctionnement annuel:* $50,000-$100,000; *Fonds:* Cotisations; séminaires
Membre: 100-499

Activités: *Service de conférenciers:* Oui
Publications: Mot du Président de l'AQPRI, Bulletin, trimestriel
Description: Promouvoir la pratique de l'administration de l'insolvabilité et l'intérêt public en ce domaine; *Membre de:* Canadian Association of Insolvency & Restructuring Professionals

Association québécoise des professionnels d'insolvabilité *See* Association québécoise des professionnels de la réorganisation et de l'insolvabilité

Atlantic Association of Community Business Development Corporations

PO Box 40, 34 England Ave., Mulgrave NS B0E 2G0
Tel: 902-747-2232; *Fax:* 902-747-2019
Toll-Free: 888-303-2232
e-mail: info@cbdc.ca
URL: www.cbdc.ca
Also Known As: Atlantic Association of CBDCs
Overview: A medium-sized regional organization
Membership: 41
Description: Dedicated to the development of small business & job creation; Affiliation(s): Pan Canadian Community Futures Network

Australian Bankers' Association Inc.

56 Pitt St., Level 3, Sydney NSW 2000 Australia
Tel: 61-2-8298-0417; *Fax:* 61-2-8298-0402
e-mail: reception@bankers.asn.au
URL: www.bankers.asn.au
Overview: A medium-sized national organization
Chief Officer(s): David Bell, CEO
Description: To improve the economic well-being of Australians by fostering a banking system recognized as one of the safest, dynamic & most efficient in the world

Autorités canadiennes en valeurs mobilières *See* Canadian Securities Administrators

BC Co-operative Association (BCCA)

#212, 1737 - 3rd Ave. West, Vancouver BC V6J 1K7
Tel: 604-662-3906; *Fax:* 604-662-3968
Toll-Free: 888-494-2944
e-mail: general@bcca.coop
URL: www.bcca.coop
Overview: A medium-sized provincial organization
Chief Officer(s): John Restakis, Executive Director
Finances: *Annual Operating Budget:* $500,000-$1.5 Million
Membership: 55; *Fees:* Sliding scale; *Member Profile:* Co-operatives; credit unions; non profit organizations
Activities: Promotion & development of co-operatives in BC; *Internships:* Yes
Publications: The Co-op Perspective, a., Contents: News & developments concerning co-op issues in BC, Price: Free
Description: To promote & develop the co-operative economy in British Columbia

British Columbia Association of Insolvency & Restructuring Professionals (BCAIRP)

c/o PricewaterhouseCoopers Inc., #700, 250 Howe St., Vancouver BC V6C 3S7
Tel: 604-806-7675; *Fax:* 604-806-7806
e-mail: michael.j.vermette@ca.pwc.com
Previous Name: British Columbia Insolvency Practitioners Association
Overview: A small provincial organization founded in 1979
Chief Officer(s): Michael J. Vermette CA CIRP, President
Staff: 7 volunteer(s)
Membership: 1-99; *Fees:* $85; *Member Profile:* Licensed trustees in bankruptcy
Activities: *Internships:* Yes; *Speaker Service:* Yes
Member of: Canadian Association of Insolvency & Restructuring Professionals; Affiliation(s): Canadian Institute of Chartered Accountants

British Columbia Bailiffs Association

6139 Trapp Ave., Burnaby BC V3N 2V3
Tel: 604-581-4952
e-mail: info@bcbailiffs.ca
URL: www.bcbailiffs.ca
Overview: A small provincial organization
Membership: 1-99; *Member Profile:* Professional bailiffs - recovery & liquidation experts in BC

British Columbia Captive Insurance Association (BCCIA)

PO Box 4228, c/o 900 Howe St., Vancouver BC V6B 3X8
Tel: 604-443-2478; *Fax:* 604-643-5235
e-mail: bill.morgan@aon.ca
URL: www.bccia.com
Overview: A small provincial organization founded in 1992
Chief Officer(s): Donald Rose, Chair; Bill Morgan, Deputy Chair & Treasurer
Finances: *Annual Operating Budget:* Less than $50,000; *Funding Sources:* Membership dues; sustaining contributions
Staff: 5 volunteer(s)
Membership: 40; *Fees:* $100; *Committees:* Professional Development & Promotion; Brochure; Legislative; Website; CRIMS; Conference; Captive Survey
Activities: Professional development services; review of government-proposed legislative changes; recommendations to regulators regarding changes to legislation; *Speaker Service:* Yes; *Rents Mailing List:* Yes
Description: To develop & promote BC as a captive domicile; to provide a forum for the professional development of all members; Affiliation(s): BC Risk Insurance Managers Association; Vancouver International Financial Centre

British Columbia Insolvency Practitioners Association *See* British Columbia Association of Insolvency & Restructuring Professionals

Bureau d'assurance du Canada *See* Insurance Bureau of Canada

Calgary Insurance Women *See* Insurance Professionals of Calgary

Calgary Society of Financial Analysts (CSFA)

4216 - 35th Ave. SW, Calgary AB T3E 1A9
Tel: 403-240-2929; *Fax:* 403-206-0650
e-mail: admin@calgarycfasociety.com
URL: www.calgarycfasociety.com
Overview: A small local organization founded in 1976
Chief Officer(s): Craig Senyk, President; Gabriela Revak, Office Manager
Finances: *Annual Operating Budget:* Less than $50,000
Staff: 1 staff member(s); 20 volunteer(s)
Membership: 700; *Member Profile:* Investment professionals
Activities: *Speaker Service:* Yes
Member of: CFA Institute

Canada's Venture Capital & Private Equity Association (CVCA) / Association canadienne du capital de risque et d'investissement

#200, 234 Eglinton Ave. East, Toronto ON M4P 1K5
Tel: 416-487-0519; *Fax:* 416-487-5899
e-mail: cvca@cvca.ca
URL: www.cvca.ca
Previous Name: Canadian Venture Capital Association
Overview: A small national organization
Chief Officer(s): Rick Nathan, President; Richard M. Rémillard, Executive Director; Kathryn Ryan, Director of Operations
Membership: 150 firms + 750 individuals
Description: To represent the interests of member venture capital firms in dealings with government & the public; to provide research & statistics

Canadian Academic Accounting Association (CAAA) / Association canadienne des professeurs de comptabilité

3997 Chesswood Dr., Toronto ON M3J 2R8
Tel: 416-486-5361; *Fax:* 416-486-6158
e-mail: admin@caaa.ca
URL: www.caaa.ca
Overview: A medium-sized national organization founded in 1976
Chief Officer(s): Glenn Feltham, President; Tim Forristal, Treasurer; Lynda Carson, Secretary; Paul Granatstein, Co-Managing Director; Vittoria Fortunato, Co-Managing Director
Membership: 100-499; *Fees:* $95 individual; $100 institutional; $25 student; *Committees:* Education; Research; Membership; Auditing Exposure Draft Response; Financial Accounting Exposure Draft Response; Management Accounting Exposure Draft Response; Public Sector Accounting & Auditing Exposure Draft Response
Activities: *Rents Mailing List:* Yes
Publications: Canadian Accounting Perspectives, s-a., Editor: Alan Richardson; Canadian Accounting Education & Research News, q., Editor: Esther Deutsch, accepts advertising; Contemporary Accounting Research, q., Editor: Gordon D. Richardson, accepts advertising
Description: To promote excellence in accounting education & research in Canada with particular reference to Canadian post-secondary accounting programs & Canadian issues

Canadian Association for Corporate Growth *See* Association for Corporate Growth, Toronto Chapter

Canadian Association of Blue Cross Plans (CABCP) / Association Canadienne des Croix Bleue

#600, 185 The West Mall, Toronto ON M9C 5P1
Tel: 416-626-1688; *Fax:* 416-626-6645
e-mail: vincent.lesage@ont.bluecross.ca
URL: www.bluecross.ca
Overview: A small national licensing organization founded in 1955
Chief Officer(s): Pierre-Yves Julien, President & CEO; Ron W. Malin, Sec.-Treas.; Vincent Lesage, Executive Director
Membership: 6
Description: To promote, enhance & protect the Association trade marks & trade names across Canada, & to facilitate communication, consensus & cooperation among members, in support of their regional & national growth & development; Affiliation(s): BlueCross BlueShield Association

Canadian Association of Business Valuators *See* Canadian Institute of Chartered Business Valuators

Canadian Association of Community Financial Service Providers *See* Canadian Payday Loan Association

Canadian Association of Direct Response Insurers (CADRI) / Association des marchés financiers du Canada

#301, 250 Consumers Rd., Toronto ON M2J 4V6
Tel: 416-773-0101; *Fax:* 416-495-8723
e-mail: cadri@cadri.com
URL: www.cadri.com
Overview: A medium-sized national organization
Chief Officer(s): Marie Bordeleau, Executive Director
Membership: 200; *Fees:* $150; *Member Profile:* Insurers who are involved in the sales & servicing of property & casualty insurance products in Canada through direct response marketing & distribution

Canadian Association of Financial Institutions in Insurance (CAFII) / Association canadienne des institutions financières en assurance

#255, 55 St. Clair Ave. West, Toronto ON M4V 2Y7
Tel: 416-494-9224; *Fax:* 416-967-6320
e-mail: cafii@cafii.com
URL: www.cafii.com
Overview: A small national organization founded in 1997
Chief Officer(s): Lawrie McGill, Secretary; Neil Skelding, Chair
Description: Dedicated to the development of an open & flexible insurance marketplace that is efficient & effective & allows consumers choice in the purchase of insurance products & services

Canadian Association of Gift Planners (CAGP) / Association canadienne des professionnels en dons planifiés

#201, 325 Dalhousie St., Ottawa ON K1N 7G2
Tel: 613-232-7991; *Fax:* 613-232-7286
Toll-Free: 888-430-9494
e-mail: diane@cagp-acpdp.org
URL: www.cagp-acpdp.org
Overview: A medium-sized national organization founded in 1993
Chief Officer(s): Diane MacDonald, Executive Director
Finances: *Annual Operating Budget:* $250,000-$500,000; *Funding Sources:* Membership fees; conference
Staff: 4 staff member(s); 12 volunteer(s)
Membership: 1,250; *Fees:* $240; *Member Profile:* Gift planners; lawyers; financial planners; accounting; insurance; *Committees:* Communications; Official Languages; Round Tables; Research & Education; Government Relations & Legislation; Ethics & Standards; Nominations; Leave-a-Legacy; Membership; Governance
Activities: Annual conference: comprehensive gift planning course; operates 20 Local Roundtables; workshops; *Awareness Events:* Leave a Legacy Month, May; *Library:* Yes
Awards: Friend of CAGP/Ami de l'ACPDP
Publications: Planner, E-Newsletter, m., 6-M pp.
Description: Advances philanthropy by fostering quality & growth of gift planning; with a vision of integrated philanthropy, enriched communities; se donne pour mission de stimuler l'esprit philantropique et de favoriser l'augmentation, en qualité

et en quantité, des dons planifiés à des oeuvres de bienfaisance; sa vision est enrichir l'esprit philantropique c'est enrichir la collectivitéAffiliation(s): Leave A Legacy

Canadian Association of Income Funds (CAIF) / Association canadienne des fonds de revenu

#301, 250 Consumers Rd., Toronto ON M2J 4V6
Tel: 416-497-5864; *Fax:* 416-495-8723
e-mail: info@caif.ca
URL: www.caif.ca
Overview: A medium-sized national organization
Chief Officer(s): Margaret Lefebvre, Executive Director
Description: To represent & promote the interests of Canadian income funds, publicly listed limited partnerships, income trusts & royalty trusts

Canadian Association of Income Trusts Investors (CAITI) / Association canadienne d'investissement dans des fiducies de revenu

#1062, 1930 Yonge St., Toronto ON M4S 1Z4
Tel: 647-505-2224
e-mail: contact@caiti.info
URL: www.caiti.info
Overview: A small national organization
Chief Officer(s): Brent D. Fullard, President & CEO
Description: Engages in advocacy, accountability & educational efforts regarding the tax treatment of income trusts in Canada; opposes the federal government's "Tax Fairness Plan"

Canadian Association of Independent Credit Counselling Agencies

#204, 6125 Sussex Ave., Burnaby BC V5H 4C1
Tel: 604-435-7800; *Fax:* 604-435-7810
Toll-Free: 800-565-4595
Overview: A small national organization
Chief Officer(s): Bob Fell, President
Finances: *Annual Operating Budget:* $100,000-$250,000
Membership: 6; *Fees:* $100
Description: To maintain a "Code of Ethics" for the independent credit counselling industry; to liaise with appropriate provincial regulatory bodies; to promote & educate consumers & the credit granting industry on our services

Canadian Association of Insolvency & Restructuring Professionals (CAIRP) / Association canadienne des professionnels de l'insolvabilité et de la réorganisation

277 Wellington St. West, Toronto ON M5V 3H2
Tel: 416-204-3242; *Fax:* 416-204-3410
e-mail: info@cairp.ca
URL: www.cairp.ca
Previous Name: Canadian Insolvency Practitioners Association
Overview: A medium-sized national organization founded in 1979
Chief Officer(s): Norman H. Kondo BA, LLB, CIRP (Hon.), President; Sheldon Gordon, Communications Manager
Finances: *Annual Operating Budget:* $500,000-$1.5 Million; *Funding Sources:* Membership dues
Staff: 9 staff member(s)
Membership: 1,441; *Fees:* $210-$610, depending on category; *Member Profile:* Completion of National Insolvency Qualification Program (NIQP) offered jointly by CAIRP & the Superintendent of Bankruptcy; *Committees:* Annual Conference; Board of Directors; Personal Insolvency; Continuing Education; Corporate Practice; Discipline; Executive; Professional Conduct; Professional Standards; Intervention
Activities: Works with the Federal government on joint committees concerning policy, legislation, education programs & Oral Boards for trustee licence candidates; provides its own education programs, continuing education seminars & Rules of Professional Conduct; enacted the Standards of Professional Conduct; *Speaker Service:* Yes
Publications: Chair's Newsletter, q., Editor: Sheldon Gordon; Rebuilding Success
Description: To develop, educate, support & give value to members; to foster the provision of insolvency, business recovery service with integrity, objectivity & competence, in a manner that instils the highest degree of public trust; & advocate for a fair, transparent & effective system of insolvency/business recovery administration throughout Canada; *Member of:* Insol International; Affiliation(s): The Canadian Institute of Chartered Accountants

Canadian Association of Insurance Women / Association canadienne des femmes d'assurance

c/o Valour Triwest Insurance Brokers Ltd., 466 St. Anne's Rd., Winnipeg MB R2M 3E1
Tel: 204-257-4223; *Fax:* 204-255-0498
e-mail: glenda.edwardsen@shawcable.com
URL: www.caiw-acfa.com
Overview: A small national organization founded in 1966
Chief Officer(s): Michèle Malo FCIP, President
Finances: *Annual Operating Budget:* Less than $50,000; *Funding Sources:* Membership dues
Membership: 1,200
Description: To preserve & enhance the value of our member association through education, networking & to foster personal growth

Canadian Association of Mutual Insurance Companies (CAMIC) / Association canadienne des compagnies d'assurance mutuelles

#205, 311 McArthur Ave., Ottawa ON K1L 6P1
Tel: 613-789-6851; *Fax:* 613-789-7665
e-mail: nlafreniere@camic.ca
URL: www.camic.ca
Overview: A small national organization founded in 1980
Chief Officer(s): Normand Lafrenière B.A., M.P.A., President
Finances: *Annual Operating Budget:* $250,000-$500,000; *Funding Sources:* Membership fees; conventions; commissions
Staff: 2 staff member(s)
Membership: 99 corporate; *Fees:* Schedule available; *Member Profile:* Mutual insurance company; mutual reinsurance company or subsidiary of mutual insurance company
Publications: Reflexion, Newsletter, q.
Description: To provide information, research, advocacy to its members in areas of general concerns & to negotiate supply agreements for goods & services of common needs; *Member of:* International Cooperative & Mutual Insurance Federation; National Association of Mutual Insurance Companies

Canadian Bankers Association (CBA) / Association des banquiers canadiens

Commerce Court West, 30th Fl., PO Box 348, 199 Bay St., Toronto ON M5L 1G2
Tel: 416-362-6092; *Fax:* 416-362-7705
Toll-Free: 800-263-0231
e-mail: inform@cba.ca
URL: www.cba.ca
Overview: A large national organization founded in 1893
Chief Officer(s): Karen Michell, Vice-President
Staff: 75 staff member(s)
Membership: 66 organizations; *Member Profile:* Banks incorporated under the Bank Act
Activities: *Library:* Banking Information Centre
Publications: Canadian Banker, Journal, q., accepts advertising, Price: $35
Affiliation(s): Institute of Canadian Bankers

Calgary Office
510 - 5 St. SW, Calgary AB T2P 3S2
Tel: 403-236-1454; *Fax:* 403-218-1810

Montréal Office
Tour Scotia, #1000, 1002, rue Sherbrooke ouest, Montréal QC H3A 3M5
Tel: 514-840-8747; *Fax:* 514-282-7551

Ottawa Office
1421, 50 O'Connor St., Ottawa ON K1P 6L2
Tel: 613-234-4431; *Fax:* 613-234-9803

Vancouver Office
#521, 625 Howe St., Vancouver BC V6C 2T6
Tel: 604-806-3000; *Fax:* 604-806-3011

Canadian Banking Ombudsman *See* Ombudsman for Banking Services & Investments

Canadian Board of Marine Underwriters (CBMU)

6835 Century Ave., 2nd. Fl., Mississauga ON L5N 2L2
Tel: 905-826-4768; *Fax:* 905-826-4873
e-mail: cbmu@cbmu.com
URL: www.cbmu.com
Overview: A medium-sized national organization founded in 1917
Chief Officer(s): Amanda Curtis CAE, Executive Director
Finances: *Annual Operating Budget:* $100,000-$250,000; *Funding Sources:* Membership dues; member service
Staff: 1 staff member(s)
Membership: 26 corporate + 160 associate; *Fees:* $1,000 corporate; $195 associate; *Member Profile:* Marine underwriters; associate - brokers, surveyors, maritime lawyers, government representatives, members of international underwriting boards & others involved in related activities; *Committees:* Underwriting; Claims & Loss Prevention; Legislative; Education; Communications
Publications: The Log, Newsletter, 3 pa, accepts advertising
Description: To procure & disseminate information of interest to marine underwriters & others; to facilitate the exchange of views & ideas which work to improve the marine underwriting industry & marine insurance; to promote & protect the interest of the underwriting community; *Member of:* International Union of Marine Insurers

Canadian Bookkeepers Alliance *See* Canadian Bookkeepers Association

Canadian Bookkeepers Association

695 Rhodes Ave., Toronto ON M4J 4X5
e-mail: info@canadianbookkeepersassociation.com
URL: www.c-b-a.ca
Previous Name: Canadian Bookkeepers Alliance
Overview: A small national organization
Chief Officer(s): Norm Eady, President
Description: To promote, support, provide for & encourage Canadian bookkeepers; to promote & increase the awareness of Bookkeeping in Canada as a professional discipline; to support national, regional & local networking among Canadian Bookkeepers; to provide information on leading-edge procedures, education & technologies that enhance the industry, as well as, the Canadian bookkeeping professional; to support & encourage responsible & accurate bookkeeping practices throughout Canada

Canadian Capital Markets Association (CCMA) / Association canadienne des marchés des capitaux

85 Richmond St. West, 4th Fl., Toronto ON M5H 2C9
Tel: 416-815-2046; *Fax:* 416-365-8700
e-mail: info@ccma-acmc.ca
URL: www.ccma-acmc.ca
Overview: A medium-sized national organization founded in 2000
Chief Officer(s): Toomas Marley, Corporate Secretary
Finances: *Annual Operating Budget:* $500,000-$1.5 Million
Staff: 146 volunteer(s)
Membership: 100-499; *Member Profile:* Key stakeholders of the securities industry, including the regulators
Activities: *Awareness Events:* Annual Conference; Information Sessions
Publications: CCMA Newsletter, Newsletter, q., Contents: Message from the Chair; Update/Progress made on Project Plan; Committee Update; What's New in Canada; What's New in the USA & around the world, Price: free
Description: To identify, analyze & recommend ways to meet the challenges & opportunities facing Canadian & international capital markets; to promote efficient trade matching among Canadian capital market participants

The Canadian Chamber of Commerce / La Chambre de commerce du Canada

#501, 350 Sparks St., Ottawa ON K1R 7S8
Tel: 613-238-4000; *Fax:* 613-238-7643
e-mail: info@chamber.ca
URL: www.chamber.ca
Overview: A large national organization founded in 1925
Chief Officer(s): Nancy Hughes Anthony, President/CEO; Michel Barsalou, Vice-President
Staff: 32 staff member(s)
Membership: Chapters in most cities & towns; 170,000; *Committees:* Environment Committee/Canada-US Sub-Committee on the Environment; Taxation; Economic
Description: To create a climate for competitiveness, profitability & job creation for enterprises of all sizes in all sectors across Canada

Calgary Office
PO Box 38057, Calgary AB T3K 5G9
Tel: 403-271-0595; *Fax:* 403-226-6930

Montréal Office
#709, 1155, rue Université, Montréal QC H3B 3A7
Tel: 514-866-4334; *Fax:* 514-866-7296

Toronto Office
#901, 55 University Ave., Toronto ON M5J 2T3
Tel: 416-868-6415; *Fax:* 416-868-0189

Canadian Co-operative Association (CCA)

#400, 275 Bank St., Ottawa ON K2P 2L6
Tel: 613-238-6711; *Fax:* 613-567-0658
Toll-Free: 866-266-7677
e-mail: info@coopscanada.coop
URL: www.coopscanada.coop
Overview: A large national organization founded in 1987
Chief Officer(s): Carol Hunter, Executive Director; Dave Sikaram, President

Finances: *Funding Sources:* Membership dues; CIDA
Staff: 41 staff member(s)
Membership: 26 organizations cooperatives & credit u; *Committees:* Executive/Audit; International Program; Public Policy
Activities: *Awareness Events:* Co-op Week, Oct.; Credit Union Day, Oct.; *Internships:* Yes; *Library:* Yes
Awards: Lemaire Co-operative Studies Award
Publications: Intersector, E-newlestter, Contents: International affairs digest; Governance Matters, E-newlestter; Concern for Community, E-newlestter, Editor: Brenda Heald
Description: To promote co-operative enterprise; *Member of:* International Cooperative Alliance

Canadian Coalition Against Insurance Fraud (CCAIF) / Coalition canadienne contre la fraude à l'assurance

151 Yonge St., 19th Fl., Toronto ON M5C 2W7
Tel: 416-362-2031; *Fax:* 416-644-4961
e-mail: webmaster@fraudcoalition.org
URL: www.fraudcoalition.org
Overview: A small national organization founded in 1994
Chief Officer(s): Robert Tremblay, Director
Finances: *Funding Sources:* Property & casualty industry
Activities: *Speaker Service:* Yes
Publications: Coalition Notes, Newsletter, m.
Description: To raise awareness about prevention & detection of insurance fraud through a variety of initiatives including strengthened detection & investigation, improved business practices & legislative & regulation change

Canadian Coalition for Good Governance (CCGG)

120 Adelaide St. West, Toronto ON M5H 1T1
Tel: 416-868-3582; *Fax:* 416-367-1954
e-mail: info@ccgg.ca
URL: www.ccgg.ca
Overview: A medium-sized national organization
Chief Officer(s): David Beatty, Managing Director
Description: To improve the performance of publicly traded corporations through the promotion of good governance practices across Canada

Canadian Cooperative Credit Society *See* Credit Union Central of Canada

Canadian Council of Insurance Regulators *See* Financial Services Commission of Ontario

Canadian Credit Institute Educational Foundation

#216C, 219 Dufferin St., Toronto ON M6L 3J1
Tel: 416-572-2615; *Fax:* 416-572-2619
e-mail: generalinformation@creditedu.org
URL: www.creditedu.org/vis_ccief.html
Overview: A small national organization founded in 1967
Chief Officer(s): Geoff Wilkinson, General Manager
Staff: 5 staff member(s)
Description: To provide funding in support of credit initiatives to enhance performance of professionals dedicated to excellence

Canadian Crop Hail Association (CCHA)

c/o Co-op Hail Insurance Co., PO Box 777, 2709 - 13th Ave., Regina SK S4P 3A8
Overview: A small national organization
Chief Officer(s): Nick Gayton, Vice-Chair

Canadian Finance & Leasing Association (CFLA) / Association canadienne de financement et de location

#301, 15 Toronto St., Toronto ON M5C 2E3
Tel: 416-860-1133; *Fax:* 416-860-1140
Toll-Free: 877-213-7373
e-mail: info@cfla-acfl.ca
URL: www.cfla-acfl.ca
Merged from: Canadian Automotive Leasing Association; Equipment Lessors Association of Canada
Overview: A medium-sized national organization founded in 1973
Chief Officer(s): David Powell, President/CEO; Mary Louise Josey CAE, Director; Jason Vandenheyden, Director
Finances: *Annual Operating Budget:* $500,000-$1.5 Million; *Funding Sources:* Membership fees; events fees
Staff: 5 staff member(s); 120 volunteer(s)
Membership: 260; *Member Profile:* Represents the asset-based financing, equipment & vehicle-leasing industry in Canada, ranging from large multinationals to regional financing companies; *Committees:* Accounting; Automotive; Education & Program; Fleet Government Relations; Legal; Membership; Montréal Steering; Taxation; Technology; Vancouver Steering; Finance Working Group
Activities: *Speaker Service:* Yes; *Library:* Resource Centre (Open to Public)
Description: To ensure an environment in Canada where asset-based financing, equipment & vehicle-leasing industry can be profitable

Canadian Foundation for Economic Education (CFEE) / Fondation d'éducation économique

#201, 110 Eglinton Ave. West, Toronto ON M4R 1A3
Tel: 416-968-2236; *Fax:* 416-968-0488
Toll-Free: 888-570-7610
e-mail: mail@cfee.org
URL: www.cfee.org
Overview: A medium-sized national charitable organization founded in 1974
Chief Officer(s): Tim Casgrain, Chair; Gary Rabbior, President
Staff: 5 staff member(s)
Description: To cooperate with educators & representatives of the various sectors of the economy to increase & improve economic education in Canada

Canadian Independent Adjusters' Association (CIAA) / Association canadienne des experts indépendants

5401 Eglinton Ave. West, Toronto ON M9C 5K6
Tel: 416-621-6222; *Fax:* 416-621-7776
Toll-Free: 877-255-5589
e-mail: info@ciaa-adjusters.ca
URL: ciaa-adjusters.ca
Overview: A medium-sized national organization founded in 1953
Chief Officer(s): Patricia M. Battle, Executive Director; J. Miles O. Barber, President; Randy P. LaBrash, Secretary; Brian D. Harris, Treasurer
Finances: *Annual Operating Budget:* $250,000-$500,000; *Funding Sources:* Membership dues
Staff: 3 staff member(s); 25 volunteer(s)
Membership: 1,100 individuals + 122 firms; *Fees:* $200; *Committees:* AESIQ; Advisory; Constitution & Rules; Convention; Discipline; Editorial; Education; FCIAA; Financial; Forms; Legislative; Liaison; Membership & Qualifications; Nominating; Privacy; Public Relations; Ways & Means
Publications: CIAA Claims Manual, a., accepts advertising; The Canadian Independent Adjuster, 5 pa, accepts advertising
Description: To provide leadership for Canada's independent adjusters through advocacy, education & recognized professional standards; to represent the collective interests of independent adjusters to government, industry & the public on a provincial, regional & national level; to provide members with continuing training, education & professional development opportunities; to develop & maintain the highest standards of professionalism through a defined Code of Ethics & fair practice policies; *Member of:* Insurance Institute of Ontario; Insurance Bureau of Canada; Affiliation(s): National Association of Independent Insurance Adjusters (USA); Chartered Institute of Loss Adjustors (UK); International Federation of Adjusting Associations

Canadian Insolvency Practitioners Association *See* Canadian Association of Insolvency & Restructuring Professionals

Canadian Institute of Actuaries (CIA) / Institut canadien des actuaires

#800, 150 Metcalfe St., Ottawa ON K2P 1P1
Tel: 613-236-8196; *Fax:* 613-233-4552
e-mail: secretariat@actuaries.ca
URL: www.actuaries.ca
Overview: A large national organization founded in 1965
Chief Officer(s): Daniel Lapointe, Executive Director; Normand Gendron, President
Finances: *Annual Operating Budget:* $3 Million-$5 Million
Staff: 18 staff member(s); 450 volunteer(s)
Membership: 3,681; *Fees:* $900; *Member Profile:* Actuaries & actuarial students
Activities: Actuaries are responsible for providing certifications required under federal & provincial legislation for insurance companies & employment benefit programs; *Library:* Yes
Publications: Bulletin, Newsletter, 10 pa, Editor: Brenda Warnes, ISSN: 1180-3681
Description: To set educational & professional standards for our members; to operate a review & disciplinary system; to maintain liaison with government authorities & other professions & organizations; to promote research; Affiliation(s): International Actuarial Association; American Academy of Actuaries; Society of Actuaries; Casualty Actuarial Society; Conference of Consulting Actuaries

Canadian Institute of Chartered Accountants (CICA) / Institut canadien des comptables agréés

277 Wellington St. West, Toronto ON M5V 3H2
Tel: 416-977-3222; *Fax:* 416-977-8585
URL: www.cica.ca/
Also Known As: Chartered Accountants of Canada
Overview: A large national licensing organization founded in 1902
Chief Officer(s): David W. Smith FCA, President & CEO; Alain Benedetti FCA, Chair; Nigel F. Byars CA, Executive Vice-President; Douglas N. Baker CA, Vice-Chair
Finances: *Annual Operating Budget:* Greater than $5 Million; *Funding Sources:* Membership fees
Staff: 120 staff member(s)
Membership: 65,000; *Fees:* $395
Activities: *Library:* Studies & Standards Dept. Library
Awards: National Post Annual Reports Awards
Publications: CICA Forum; Risk Alert; CA Magazine, 10 per year, Editor: Christian Bellavance, ISSN: 0317-6878, 100 pp., accepts advertising
Description: To serve the interests of society & the CA profession by providing leadership to uphold the professional integrity, standards & pre-eminence of Canada's chartered accountants nationally & internationally through: enhancing the quality & credibility of financial & other information produced & used in the private & public sectors for measuring & enhancing organizational performance; helping member CAs add value to their customers/employers by providing market information & professional services & products; offering a reliable & respected source of public policy advice & commentary; Affiliation(s): International Accounting Standards Committee; International Federation of Accountants

Canadian Institute of Chartered Business Valuators (CICBV) / L'Institut canadien des experts en évaluation d'entreprises

277 Wellington St. West, Toronto ON M5V 3H2
Tel: 416-204-3396; *Fax:* 416-977-8585
e-mail: admin@cicbv.ca
URL: www.cicbv.ca
Previous Name: Canadian Association of Business Valuators
Overview: A medium-sized national licensing organization founded in 1971
Chief Officer(s): Jeannine M. Brooks FCGA, Executive Vice-President; Laurent Després, President; Mary Jane Andrews, Vice-President; Iseo Pasquali, Sec.-Treas.
Finances: *Annual Operating Budget:* $500,000-$1.5 Million
Staff: 5 staff member(s)
Membership: 1,050; *Fees:* $510; *Member Profile:* Examination & practical experience; *Committees:* Executive; Accreditation/Membership; Education/Continuing Education; Professional Practice; Conference/Workshops; Nominating; Strategic Planning; Research Institute
Activities: Educational programs offered through Atkinson Faculty of York University; grants professional designation CBV (Chartered Business Valuator) or EEE (d'expert en évaluation d'entreprises)
Publications: The Business Valuator, Newsletter, q., ISSN: 0703-1939, accepts advertising; Journal of Business Valuation, Newsletter, a.; Valuation Law Review, Newsletter; Business Valuator Digest, Newsletter
Description: CICBV trains & certifies individuals & grants professional designation to those who have met the Institute's educational & experience requirements; to enhance the long-term value of the CBV designation

Canadian Institute of Chartered Business Planners (CICBP)

Bankers Hall, PO Box 22434, Calgary AB T2P 4J1
e-mail: info@cicbp.ca
URL: www.cicbp.ca
Overview: A small national organization
Description: Dedicated to ensuring excellence in business planning, through training education & certification of its members; committed to protecting the public by developing & enforcing practice standards, codes of ethics & discipline procedures

Canadian Institute of Credit & Financial Management *See* Credit Institute of Canada

Canadian Institute of Financial Planning (CIFPs)

3660 Hurontario St., 8th Fl., Mississauga ON L5B 3C4

ASSOCIATIONS

Toll-Free: 866-933-0233
e-mail: cifps@cifps.ca
URL: www.cifps.ca
Overview: A medium-sized national organization founded in 1979
Chief Officer(s): Keith Costello, President & CEO
Membership: *Member Profile:* Holders of the certified financial planner designation
Activities: Administers Certified Financial Planner (CFP) Educational Program & related continuing education courses; *Library:* Yes
Publications: Planning Ahead, Newsletter, s-a.
Description: To contribute to knowledge of financial planning in Canada through the development of educational programs; Affiliation(s): Investment Funds Institute of Canada; Canadian Association of Financial Planners; Financial Planners Standards Council; Canadian Institute of Financial Planning

Canadian Institute of Mortgage Brokers & Lenders (CIMBL) / Institut canadien des courtiers et des prêteurs hypothécaires
Atria I, #414, 2255 Sheppard Ave. East, Toronto ON M2J 4Y1
Tel: 416-385-2333; *Fax:* 416-385-1177
Toll-Free: 888-442-4625
e-mail: info@cimbl.ca
URL: www.cimbl.ca
Overview: A medium-sized national organization founded in 1994
Chief Officer(s): Michael Ellenzweig, Executive Director; Jim Murphy, Sr. Director
Finances: *Annual Operating Budget:* Greater than $5 Million; *Funding Sources:* Membership dues; conference fees; advertising
Staff: 10 staff member(s); 300 volunteer(s)
Membership: 8,000; *Fees:* $1,950 national lender; $390 provincial lender; $195 mortgage bro; *Member Profile:* Licensed mortgage broker; broker agent; lender & lender employees; mortgage insurer; *Committees:* Education; Nominating; Ethics; Government Relations; Membership; Communications; National Conference; Special Events; Professional Standards
Activities: Accreditation program for mortgage professionals; education & training; conferences; charitable events
Publications: Mortgage, Journal, q., accepts advertising
Description: To provide high-quality service & to protect the consumer

Canadian Institute of Underwriters (CIU)
c/o DKCI Events, #205, 323 Kerr St., Oakville ON L6K 3B6
Tel: 905-842-0239; *Fax:* 905-842-0756
Toll-Free: 877-513-0186
e-mail: inquiries@ciu.ca
URL: www.ciu.ca
Overview: A medium-sized national organization
Chief Officer(s): Michéle Hnatyshen, Chair; Dennis Farronato, Membership Contact; Bill Marschall, Secretary
Finances: *Annual Operating Budget:* $100,000-$250,000
Membership: 682; *Fees:* $100
Activities: Education seminars
Description: To exchange ideas on issues & challenges that face underwriters in the insurance sectors

Canadian Insurance Accountants Association (CIAA) / Association canadienne des comptables en assurance
#310, 2175 Sheppard Ave. East, Toronto ON M2J 1W8
Tel: 416-971-7800; *Fax:* 416-491-1670
e-mail: ciaa@ciaa.org
URL: www.ciaa.org
Overview: A medium-sized national organization founded in 1934
Chief Officer(s): Catherine Fleming, Executive Assistant; Annette Pohle, President
Membership: 600+; *Fees:* $90
Description: To promote study, research & development of management & insurance accounting; to provide professional development; to be a forum for communication with the industry

Canadian Insurance Claims Managers' Association
c/o Insurance Bureau of Canada, #1900, 151 Yonge St., Toronto ON M5C 2W7
Tel: 416-362-2031; *Fax:* 416-644-4965
Overview: A small national organization
Chief Officer(s): Vita Bulovas, Secretary

Canadian Investor Protection Fund (CIPF) / Fonds canadien de protection des épargnants
PO Box 75, #610, 79 Wellington St. West, Toronto ON M5K 1E7
Tel: 416-866-8366; *Fax:* 416-360-8441
Toll-Free: 866-243-6981
e-mail: info@cipf.ca
URL: www.cipf.ca
Previous Name: National Contingency Fund
Overview: A medium-sized national organization founded in 1969
Chief Officer(s): Rozanne E. Reszel FCA, CFA, President & CEO; Michael G. Greenwood, Chair
Finances: *Annual Operating Budget:* $1.5 Million-$3 Million
Staff: 12 staff member(s)
Membership: 214; *Member Profile:* Investment dealers who are members of our sponsoring self-regulatory organizations
Description: To foster a healthy & active capital market in Canada by contributing to the security & confidence of investors who have accounts with members of our sponsoring self-regulatory organizations

Canadian Investor Relations Institute (CIRI) / Institut canadien de relations avec les investisseurs
#201, 1470 Hurontario St., Mississauga ON L5G 3H4
Tel: 905-274-1639; *Fax:* 905-274-7861
e-mail: enquiries@ciri.org
URL: www.ciri.org
Previous Name: National Investor Relations Institute Canada (NIRI Canada)
Overview: A medium-sized national organization founded in 1990
Chief Officer(s): Bob Tait, President/CEO; Mary Blair, Director
Finances: *Annual Operating Budget:* $500,000-$1.5 Million; *Funding Sources:* Membership fees; seminars; annual conference
Staff: 6 staff member(s); 100 volunteer(s)
Membership: 830; *Fees:* $570; *Member Profile:* Investor relations executives with public companies 75%; individuals consulting to publicly-traded companies 14%; vendors 11%; *Committees:* Nominating; Audit; Editorial Board; Resources & Education; Issues; Membership; Marketing
Activities: Chapter programs, seminars, & annual conference; surveys on IR related issues; *Internships:* Yes; *Speaker Service:* Yes; *Rents Mailing List:* Yes; *Library:* Yes (Open to Public)
Publications: Newsline, Newsletter, bi-m., accepts advertising; Standards & Guidance for Disclosure, Newsletter; Board Communications, Newsletter; Shareholder Communications, Newsletter; Compensation Survey, Newsletter; Guide to Developing an IR Program, Newsletter
Description: To advance the practice of investor relations, the professional competency of members & the stature of the profession; *Member of:* International Investor Relations Federation; Canadian Society of Association Executives; Affiliation(s): National Investor Relations Institute

Canadian Lawyers Insurance Association (CLIA) / Association d'assurances des juristes canadiens
#306, 20 Queen St. West, Toronto ON M5H 3R3
Tel: 416-408-5293; *Fax:* 416-408-3721
Toll-Free: 800-268-9484
e-mail: info@clia.ca
URL: www.clia.ca
Overview: A small national organization founded in 1988
Chief Officer(s): Patrick Mahoney, General Manager
Description: To provide a reliable & permanent source of insurance on a non-profit basis; to ensure the availability of reasonably priced & effective excess insurance; to stabilize premiums in both mandatory & excess layers; to ensure premium rates reflect the loss experience of Canadian lawyers

Canadian Life & Health Insurance Association Inc. (CLHIA) / Association canadienne des compagnies d'assurances de personnes inc.
#1700, One Queen St. East, Toronto ON M5C 2X9
Tel: 416-777-2221; *Fax:* 416-777-1895
Toll-Free: 800-268-8099
e-mail: info@clhia.ca
URL: www.clhia.ca
Previous Name: Canadian Life Insurance Association
Overview: A large national organization founded in 1894
Chief Officer(s): Yvon Charest, Chair; Gregory R. Traversy, President; Judy E. Barrie, Sr. Vice-President; Yves Millette, Sr. Vice-President; Angela Albini, Vice-President; Jean-Pierre Bernier, Vice-President & General Counsel; Leslie A. Byrnes, Vice-President; Wendy Hope, Vice-President; James S. Witol, Vice-President; Frank Zinatelli, Vice-President/Associate General Co
Staff: 65 staff member(s)
Membership: 1-99
Activities: *Library:* Research & Information Library by appointment
Publications: Decisions, Newsletter, m., Editor: James Wood, Contents: Analysis of Canadian law pertaining to life insurance, health insurance & pensions, Price: $345
Description: To serve its members in areas of common interest, need, or concern; to ensure that the views & interests of its diverse membership & of the public are equitably addressed; to build consensus among members on issues & concerns of importance to the industry; to promote a legislative & regulatory environment in Canada favourable to the business of its members; & to foster sound & equitable principles in the conduct of the business of its members; *Member of:* Canadian Tax Foundation; Public Policy Forum; Toronto Board of Trade

Montréal Office
#630, 1001, boul de Maisonneuve ouest, Montréal QC H3A 3C8
Tel: 514-845-9004; *Fax:* 514-845-6182

Ottawa Office
#400, 46 Elgin St., Ottawa ON K1P 5K6
Tel: 613-230-0031; *Fax:* 613-230-0297

Canadian Life & Health Insurance OmbudService (CLHIO) / Service de conciliation des assurances de personnes du Canada
#1605A, One Queen St. East, Toronto ON M5C 2X9
Tel: 416-777-9002; *Fax:* 416-777-9750
Toll-Free: 888-295-8112
e-mail: information@clhio.ca
URL: www.clhio.ca
Overview: A medium-sized national organization
Chief Officer(s): Hon. Gilles Loiselle, Chair
Description: An independent service that assists consumers with concerns & complaints about life & health insurance products & services; to provide fair & prompt resolution of problems

Canadian Life Insurance Association ***See*** Canadian Life & Health Insurance Association Inc.

Canadian Mutual Fund Association ***See*** Investment Funds Institute of Canada

Canadian National Association of Real Estate Appraisers
PO Box 157, Qualicum Beach BC V9K 1S7
Toll-Free: 888-399-3366
e-mail: cnarea@cnarea.ca
URL: www.cnarea.ca
Overview: A small national organization
Chief Officer(s): Steven G. Coull, Executive Director; Robert B. Fraser, Sec.-Treas.
Activities: Continuing education for professionals; consumer protection; raising professional standards
Description: Certifies & regulates real property appraisers in Canada; established to provide an effective membership orientated organization of professional real estate appraisers based on their academic qualifications, training, & practical experience; dedicated to raising the standards of the profession, to maintaining the professionalism of its members through continuing education, to advancing the recognition of its members as qualified appraisers, & to protecting the consumer

Canadian Payday Loan Association (CPLA) / Association canadienne des prêteurs sur salaire
#200, 440 Laurier Ave. West, Ottawa ON K1R 7X6
Tel: 613-788-2765; *Fax:* 613-788-2768
e-mail: inquiry@cpla-acps.ca
URL: www.cpla-acps.ca
Previous Name: Canadian Association of Community Financial Service Providers
Overview: A small national organization
Chief Officer(s): R.A. Whitelaw, President & CEO; Norman J.K. Bishop, Secretary
Membership: 40 large, intermediate & small companies; *Member Profile:* Small-sum unsecured short-term credit (payday loan) providers who operate retail outlets across Canada
Description: To represent the interests of the sector to governments & consumers, & to ensure that Association members adhere to national standards of best business practices for the industry

Canadian Payments Association (CPA) / Association canadienne des paiements
#1200, 180 Elgin St., Ottawa ON K2P 2K3

Tel: 613-238-4173; *Fax:* 613-233-3385
e-mail: info@cdnpay.ca
URL: www.cdnpay.ca
Overview: A medium-sized national organization founded in 1980
Chief Officer(s): Guy Legault, President & CEO; Mark S. Ripplinger, Chief Info. Officer & Vice-Pres.
Finances: *Annual Operating Budget:* Greater than $5 Million; *Funding Sources:* Membership dues
Staff: 65 staff member(s)
Membership: 120 financial institutions; *Fees:* Dues based on annual clearing volumes; *Member Profile:* Chartered banks; Bank of Canada; credit unions; caisses populaires; trust companies; other financial institutions
Activities: Bi-annual conference; *Library:* Yes by appointment
Meetings: 2007; Conference, June, Victoria, BC Canada
Publications: Forum, Newsletter, q.; Review, Newsletter
Description: To establish & operate national clearing & settlements systems; to facilitate the interaction of the CPA's systems with others involved in the exchange, clearing & settlement of payments; to facilitate the development of new payment methods & technologies

The Canadian Payroll Association (CPA) / L'Association canadienne de la paie

#1600, 250 Bloor St. East, Toronto ON M4W 1E6
Tel: 416-487-3380; *Fax:* 416-487-3384
Toll-Free: 800-387-4693
e-mail: infoline@payroll.ca
URL: www.payroll.ca
Overview: A large national organization founded in 1978
Chief Officer(s): Patrick Culhane, President & CEO; Wendy McLean, Manager; Wendy Bannon, Atlantic & Ontario Region Contact; Melissa Popadynec, GTA Region Contact; Karen Johnson, Pacific Region Contact; Debbie Aldridge, Prairie Region Contact; Richard Desjardins, Québec Region Contact
Finances: *Annual Operating Budget:* $500,000-$1.5 Million; *Funding Sources:* Membership fees; education program; training sessions
Staff: 23 staff member(s); 212 volunteer(s)
Membership: 10,000+; *Fees:* Schedule available; *Member Profile:* Corporate, Professional & Associate memberships available; *Committees:* Government Relations; Communications; Membership; Programs; Education; Volunteer Management
Activities: CPA Professional Development Series covers all aspects of payroll training, including terminations, taxable benefits, year end reporting & new year requirements; Payroll Management Certificate Program includes Introduction to Payroll, Intermediate Payroll & Advanced Payroll; *Awareness Events:* National Payroll Week, Sept.; *Speaker Service:* Yes; *Library:* Infoline
Publications: Dialogue Magazine, bi-m., 28 pp.
Description: Payroll leadership through advocacy & education

Canadian Property Tax Association, Inc.

#225, 6 Lansing Sq., Toronto ON M2J 1T5
Tel: 416-493-3276; *Fax:* 416-493-3905
e-mail: admin@cpta.org
URL: www.cpta.org
Overview: A medium-sized national organization founded in 1967
Chief Officer(s): Brent Muir, President
Staff: 1 staff member(s)
Membership: 400 individuals + 225 organizations
Publications: Communication Update, Newsletter, bi-m.
Description: Forum for the exchange of ideas & information relating to both commercial & industrial property tax issues arising across Canada

Canadian Research Committee on Taxation (CRCT) / Comité canadien de recherches sur la taxation

#2, 7821, Madeleine Huguenin, Montréal QC H1L 6M6
Tel: 514-352-4231; *Fax:* 514-643-4308
e-mail: fpeddle@sympatico.ca
Overview: A small national charitable organization founded in 1964
Chief Officer(s): Ben Sevack, President; Harry Payne, Sec.-Treas.
Staff: 1 staff member(s)
Membership: 30; *Fees:* $50
Activities: Research on alternative tax policies
Publications: Newsletter, s-a.
Description: To design a framework for genuine tax reform; Affiliation(s): International Union for Land Value Taxation & Free Trade

Canadian Securities Administrators (CSA) / Autorités canadiennes en valeurs mobilières

Tour de la Bourse, #4130, 800, Square Victoria, Montréal QC H4Z 1J2
Tel: 514-864-9510; *Fax:* 514-864-9512
e-mail: csa-acvm-secretariat@lautorite.qc.ca
URL: www.csa-acvm.ca
Overview: A small national organization
Chief Officer(s): Jean St. Gelais, Chair; Ann Leduc, Secretary General
Membership: *Member Profile:* 13 securities regulators across Canada
Description: To give Canada a securities regulatory system that protects investors from unfair, improper or fraudulent practices & fosters fair, efficient & vibrant capital markets, through developing the Canadian Securities Regulatory System (CSRS), a national system of harmonized securities regulation, policy & practice

The Canadian Securities Institute (CSI) / Institut canadien des valeurs mobilières

121 King St. West, 15th Fl., Toronto ON M5H 3T9
Tel: 416-364-9130; *Fax:* 416-359-0486
Toll-Free: 866-866-2601
e-mail: customer_support@csi.ca
URL: www.csi.ca
Overview: A large national organization founded in 1970
Chief Officer(s): Dr. Roberta Wilton, President & CEO
Finances: *Annual Operating Budget:* Greater than $5 Million
Staff: 120 staff member(s); *Committees:* Education
Activities: The Canadian Securities Course, grants CIM, FMA & DMS professional designations as well as Fellow of the Canadian Securities Institute (FCSI); other courses include: Conduct & Practices Handbook, Investment Management Techniques, Portfolio Management Techniques, Professional Financial Planning, Wealth Management Techniques, Derivatives Fundamentals, Options Licensing Course, Futures Licensing Exam, Canadian Commodity Supervisors Exam, Branch Managers Exams, Effective Management Seminar, Partners Directors Senior Officer; *Speaker Service:* Yes
Description: To enhance the knowledge of securities & financial industry professionals & promote knowledge & understanding of investing among the public; Affiliation(s): Investment Dealers Association of Canada; Montreal Exchange; Toronto Stock Exchange; Canadian Venture Exchange

Montréal Office
#600, 1155, rue University, Montréal QC H3B 3A7
Ligne sans frais: 866-866-2601
Membre(s) du bureau directeur: Marc Flynn, Managing Director

Canadian Securities Institute Research Foundation / Fondation de recherche de l'Institut canadien des valeurs mobilières

121 King St. West, 15th Fl., Toronto ON M5H 3T9
Tel: 416-681-2262; *Fax:* 416-359-0486
e-mail: hirwin@csi.ca
URL: www.csifoundation.com
Previous Name: Investor Learning Centre of Canada
Overview: A small national organization founded in 1993
Staff: 10 staff member(s)
Activities: Publications & seminars aimed at the novice investor; publications include: "How to Invest in Canadian Securities", "How to Read Financial Statements", "Investment Terms & Definitions", & "Career Oppoutunities in the Investment Industry"; Intelligent Investing seminar series provides a basic overview of investment principles, stocks, bonds, mutual funds & practical information on how to start investing & plan for retirement; *Library:* ILC Resource Centre
Publications: Investment Facts, Newsletter, Contents: Ongoing series of newsletters introducing the essentials of the investment industry
Description: Encourages, considers & supports realistic & creative ideas for research in issues pertaining to the Canadian capital markets to benefit investors & other participants with a national &/or global perspective; Affiliation(s): Canadian Securities Institute (CSI)

Canadian ShareOwners Association

c/o ShareOwner Magazine Inc., #806, 4 King St. West, Toronto ON M5H 1B5
Tel: 416-595-9600; *Fax:* 416-595-0400
Toll-Free: 800-268-6881
e-mail: customercare@shareowner.com
URL: www.shareowner.com
Overview: A medium-sized national organization founded in 1987
Finances: *Annual Operating Budget:* $500,000-$1.5 Million; *Funding Sources:* Membership dues
Staff: 20 staff member(s)
Membership: 15,000; *Fees:* $99
Activities: Low Cost Investing Program; workshops; *Rents Mailing List:* Yes
Publications: ShareOwner, Magazine, bi-m., ISSN: 0836-0960, accepts advertising, Contents: Investment education; stocks-to-study; market outlook
Description: To provide investors with a strategy for investing in common stocks, through use of the Stock Study Guide software & related publications; *Member of:* World Federation of Investors; Canadian Investor Protection Fund; Investment Dealers Association of Canada; Canadian Depository for Securities Ltd.

Canadian Tax Foundation (CTF) / L'Association canadienne d'études fiscales

#1200, 595 Bay St., Toronto ON M5G 2N5
Tel: 416-599-0283; *Fax:* 416-599-9283
Toll-Free: 877-733-0283
e-mail: mmavroyannis@ctf.ca
URL: www.ctf.ca
Overview: A medium-sized national charitable organization founded in 1945
Chief Officer(s): Stephen R. Richardson LLM, Director & CEO; Douglas S. Ewens Q.C., Chair; Timothy Winter CPA, Treasurer; Norma Forrester, Membership Secretary; Maria Mavroyannis LLM, Director/Secretary
Finances: *Annual Operating Budget:* $3 Million-$5 Million; *Funding Sources:* Membership dues; conferences; book sales; seminars & courses
Staff: 21 staff member(s)
Membership: 8,200 individuals & corporations; *Fees:* $295; $75 academics/students; *Member Profile:* CAs; lawyers; government officials; academics; students
Activities: *Library:* D.J. Sherbaniuk Library (Open to Public)
Awards: Douglas J. Sherbaniuk Distinguished Writing Award; Student - Paper Award Competition
Publications: Canadian Tax Journal, bi-m., Editor: Laurel Amalia, ISSN: 0008-5111, accepts advertising, Contents: Results of research & informed comment on taxation & public finance; current tax cases; international & personal tax planning; corporate reorganizations; US tax developments; statistical fiscal analysis; book reviews, Price: $50/issue; Tax for the Owner-Manager, q.; TaxFind; Canadian Tax Highlights, m., ISSN: 1192-2672, Contents: Tax & public finance information of relevance to small businesses, tax practitioners, corporations & multinationals
Description: Independent tax research organization; to provide both tax-paying public & governments of Canada with benefit of expert, impartial research into current problems of taxation & government finance; to establish the best possible tax system, that is as equitable as possible & that fosters the growth & productivity of the country; Affiliation(s): Canadian Bar Association; Canadian Institute of Chartered Accountants

Association canadienne d'études fiscales
#2935, 1250, boul René-Lévesque ouest, Montréal QC H3B 4W8
Tél: 514-939-6323; *Téléc:* 514-939-7353
Courriel: acef@istar.ca
URL: www.acef.ca
Membre(s) du bureau directeur: Louise Beaugrand-Champagne, Directrice régionale

Canadian Taxpayers Federation (CTF) / Fédération des contribuables canadiens

#105, 438 Victoria Ave. East, Regina SK S4N 0N7
Tel: 306-352-7199; *Fax:* 306-352-7203
URL: www.taxpayer.com
Overview: A large national organization founded in 1989
Chief Officer(s): Ken Azzopardi, CEO
Finances: *Annual Operating Budget:* $3 Million-$5 Million; *Funding Sources:* Membership fees; donations
Staff: 20 staff member(s)
Membership: 83,000; *Fees:* $107 individual
Activities: *Speaker Service:* Yes
Publications: TaxAction, Newsletter, m.; The Taxpayer, Newsletter, bi-m.
Description: To inform taxpayers of government's impact on their economic well-being; to promote responsible fiscal & democratic reforms

CTF - Ottawa
#512, 130 Albert St., Ottawa ON K1P 5G4

Tel: 613-234-6554; *Fax:* 613-234-7748
Toll-Free: 800-265-0442
e-mail: jwilliamson@taxpayer.com
Chief Officer(s): John Williamson, Federal Director

Canadian Taxpayers Federation - Alberta (CTF)
#202, 10621 - 100th Ave., Edmonton AB T5J 0B3
Tel: 780-448-0159; *Fax:* 780-482-1744
Toll-Free: 800-661-0187
e-mail: lwilkie@shawbiz.ca
URL: www.taxpayer.com
Overview: A medium-sized provincial organization
Chief Officer(s): Scott Hennig, Provincial Director
Membership: 50,000 Plus
Publications: The Taxpayer, Magazine, bi-m.
Description: Lower taxes, less waste, more accountability

Canadian Taxpayers Federation - British Columbia (CTF)
#514, 1207 Douglas St., Victoria BC V8W 2E7
Tel: 250-388-3660; *Fax:* 250-388-3680
e-mail: smacintyre@taxpayer.com
URL: www.taxpayer.com
Overview: A medium-sized national organization founded in 1990
Chief Officer(s): Sara MacIntyre, Provincial Director
Finances: *Annual Operating Budget:* $3 Million-$5 Million; *Funding Sources:* Supporter fees
Staff: 2 staff member(s)
Membership: 72,000; *Fees:* $40-110
Activities: *Awareness Events:* Teddy Waste Awards; Gas Tax Honesty Day; *Speaker Service:* Yes
Publications: The Taxpayer, Magazine, 6 pa, Editor: Troy Lanigan, accepts advertising, Price: $110 supporter level
Description: To advocate lower taxes, less waste & accountable government

Canadian Taxpayers Federation - Manitoba (CTF)
#212, 428 Portage Ave., Winnipeg MB R3C 0E2
Tel: 204-982-2150; *Fax:* 204-982-2154
Toll-Free: 800-772-9955
e-mail: abatra@shawbiz.ca
Previous Name: Manitoba Taxpayers Association
Overview: A small provincial organization
Chief Officer(s): Adrienne Batra, Provincial Director
Membership: *Fees:* $100+
Publications: The Taxpayer, Magazine, bi-m.
Description: To promote the responsible & efficient use of tax dollars & to act as a watchdog on government spending

Canadian Taxpayers Federation - Ontario (CTF)
#400, 1235 Bay St., Toronto ON M5R 3K4
Tel: 416-203-0030; *Fax:* 416-203-6030
Overview: A medium-sized provincial organization founded in 1990
Chief Officer(s): Kevin Gaudet, Provincial Director
Finances: *Annual Operating Budget:* $1.5 Million-$3 Million
Staff: 16 staff member(s)
Membership: 83,000
Activities: *Speaker Service:* Yes
Publications: The Taxpayer, Magazine, bi-m.
Description: To act as a watchdog on government spending & to inform taxpayers of governments' impact on the economic well-being; to promote responsible fiscal & democratic reforms; to advocate the common interests of taxpayers; to mobilize taxpayers to exercise their democratic responsibilities; *Member of:* World Taxpayers Association

Canadian Taxpayers Federation - Saskatchewan (CTF)
#105, 438 Victoria Ave. East, Regina SK S4N 0N7
Tel: 306-352-7199; *Fax:* 306-352-7203
Toll-Free: 800-565-1911
e-mail: dmaclean@taxpayer.com
Overview: A medium-sized provincial organization founded in 1989
Chief Officer(s): Dave MacLean, Provincial Director
Finances: *Funding Sources:* Membership fees; donations
Publications: The Taxpayer, Newspaper, bi-m.
Description: To act as a watch dog & to inform taxpayers of government's impact on their economic well-being; to promote responsible fiscal & democratic reforms & to advocate taxpayers' common interests; to motivate & mobilize taxpayers to exercise their democratic responsibilities

Canadian Venture Capital Association ***See*** Canada's Venture Capital & Private Equity Association

Cash Management Association of Canada ***See*** Treasury Management Association of Canada

La Centrale des caisses de crédit du Canada ***See*** Credit Union Central of Canada

Centre d'étude de la pratique d'assurance ***See*** Centre for Study of Insurance Operations

Centre de counselling familial de Cornwall et Comtés unis ***See*** Family Counselling Centre of Cornwall & United Counties

Le Centre Financier International - Montréal ***See*** International Financial Centre - Montréal

Centre for Study of Insurance Operations (CSIO) / Centre d'étude de la pratique d'assurance
#500, 110 Yonge St., Toronto ON M5C 1T4
Tel: 416-360-1773; *Fax:* 416-364-1482
Toll-Free: 800-463-2746
e-mail: generalmanager@csio.com
URL: www.csio.com
Overview: A medium-sized national organization
Chief Officer(s): David Patrick, Interim CEO; Ted Langdon, Operations Manager
Finances: *Annual Operating Budget:* $500,000-$1.5 Million; *Funding Sources:* Membership dues
Staff: 12 staff member(s)
Membership: 55; *Member Profile:* Property casualty insurance companies & independent brokers
Activities: Responsible for overseeing the development, implementation & maintenance of industry standards for EDI, Forms & XML
Publications: Connections, Newsletter, m.
Description: To achieve excellence in the delivery of value added electronic business solutions

Montréal Office - CEPA
#1305, 1155, rue University, Montréal QC H3B 3A7
Tel: 514-393-8200; *Fax:* 514-393-3624
e-mail: jtaverna@csio.com
Chief Officer(s): Josée Taverna, Advisor

Cercle de la finance internationale de Montréal / International Finance Club of Montréal
CP 63123, 40, Place du Commerce, Montréal QC H3E 1V6
Tél: 514-933-1451; *Téléc:* 514-933-1508
Courriel: cfim@cercledelafinance.qc.ca
URL: www.cercledelafinance.qc.ca
Nom précédent: Cercle des banquiers internationaux de Montréal
Aperçu: *Dimension:* petite; *Envergure: internationale; fondée en 1992*
Membre(s) du bureau directeur: Luc St-Arnault, Président
Personnel: 1 bénévole(s)
Membre: 150; *Montant de la cotisation:* 500$ corporatifs; 125$ individuels; 50$ étudiants; *Critères d'admissibilité/Description:* Dirigeants d'institutions et d'organismes financiers à orientation internationale
Activités: *Stagiaires:* Oui; *Listes de destinataires:* Oui
Description: Promouvoir au sein de la communauté financière les activités et les services de ses membres

Cercle des banquiers internationaux de Montréal ***See*** Cercle de la finance internationale de Montréal

Certified General Accountants Association of Canada
#800, 1188 West Georgia St., Vancouver BC V6E 4A2
Tel: 604-669-3555; *Fax:* 604-689-5845
Toll-Free: 800-663-1529
e-mail: public@cga-canada.org
URL: www.cga-online.org/canada
Also Known As: CGA - Canada
Overview: A large national licensing organization founded in 1913
Chief Officer(s): Anthony Ariganello FCGA, CPA, President & CEO
Finances: *Annual Operating Budget:* Greater than $5 Million
Staff: 90 staff member(s)
Membership: 62,000 members + students; *Member Profile:* Complete CGA professional education program; *Committees:* Audit; Curriculum Review Council; Education; Education Advisory Council; Executive; Honours & Awards; International; Planning; Professional Affairs; Public Affairs; Research Foundation; Taxation Policy
Awards: John Leslie Award
Publications: CGA Magazine, m., ISSN: 0318-742X
Description: To establish & monitor standards of skill & competency for members & thereby promote proficiency in accountants; to maintain & advance the profession of accounting & its responsibility to society at large; to ensure the national & international recognition of the CGA designation as a full professional accounting qualification in all respects; to ensure that a high quality education program is available to appropriate candidates who wish to qualify for the CGA designation; to represent views to the federal & provincial governments; to ensure CGAs keep abreast of developments in business & new government regulations; Affiliation(s): International Federation of Accountants; Confederation of Asian & Pacific Accountants; International Accounting Standards Committee; Fédération Internationale des Experts Comptables Francophones; Institute of Chartered Accountants of the Caribbean; Interamerican Accounting Association; International Association of Accounting Education & Research

Certified General Accountants Association of British Columbia
#300, 1867 West Broadway, Vancouver BC V6J 5L4
Tel: 604-732-1211; *Fax:* 604-732-1252
Toll-Free: 800-565-1211
e-mail: info@cga-bc.org
URL: www.cga-bc.org/
Also Known As: CGA - BC
Overview: A medium-sized provincial organization founded in 1951
Chief Officer(s): R.W. Caulfield, Executive Director; Edward Downing, Director
Finances: *Annual Operating Budget:* Greater than $5 Million; *Funding Sources:* Membership dues; student fees
Staff: 65 staff member(s); 100+ volunteer(s)
Membership: 8,000; *Fees:* Annual dues; *Member Profile:* Members are employed in industry, commerce, government & public practice
Publications: Outlook, Magazine, q., ISSN: 1488-2337, accepts advertising, Contents: News & information relating to the accounting profession
Description: To promote the excellence of its members & to advance the accounting profession through education, certification & a dedication to lifelong learning

Certified General Accountants Association of Yukon Territory
PO Box 31536, Whitehorse YT Y1A 6K8
Tel: 867-668-4461; *Fax:* 867-668-8635
Toll-Free: 800-565-1211
e-mail: robert.fendrick@whitehorse.ca
Also Known As: CGA Yukon
Overview: A medium-sized provincial licensing organization
Chief Officer(s): Robert Fendrick CGA, Contact
Finances: *Annual Operating Budget:* Less than $50,000; *Funding Sources:* Membership dues
Staff: 32 volunteer(s)
Membership: 1-99; *Fees:* $100
Activities: *Internships:* Yes; *Speaker Service:* Yes; *Rents Mailing List:* Yes

Certified General Accountants Association of Alberta
#900, 926 - 5 Ave. SW, Calgary AB T2P 0N7
Tel: 403-299-1300; *Fax:* 403-299-1339
Toll-Free: 800-661-1078
URL: www.cga-alberta.org
Also Known As: CGA - Alberta
Overview: A medium-sized provincial organization
Chief Officer(s): John Carpenter FCGA, Executive Director; Sandy Umpherville CGA, Director; Richard Truscott, Director
Staff: 23 staff member(s)
Membership: 1,000-4,999
Activities: *Speaker Service:* Yes

Certified General Accountants Association of the Northwest Territories/Nunavut
PO Box 128, Yellowknife NT X1A 2N1
Tel: 867-873-5620; *Fax:* 867-873-4469
Toll-Free: 888-663-3221
e-mail: office@cga-nwt-nu.org
URL: www.cga-nwt-nu.org
Also Known As: CGA - Northwest Territories/Nunavut
Overview: A medium-sized provincial charitable organization founded in 1977
Finances: *Funding Sources:* Membership & student fees
Staff: 2 staff member(s)

Membership: 100-499; *Fees:* $600; *Member Profile:* CGA designation
Publications: Northern Accounts, Newsletter, q., Contents: Dates & information on activities in NWT/Nunavut

Certified General Accountants Association of Saskatchewan
#114, 3502 Taylor St. East, Saskatoon SK S7H 5H9
Tel: 306-955-4622; *Fax:* 306-373-9219
Toll-Free: 800-667-4754
e-mail: general@cga-saskatchewan.org
URL: www.cga-online.org/sk
Also Known As: CGA - Saskatchewan
Overview: A medium-sized provincial licensing organization founded in 1978
Chief Officer(s): Prabha Vaidyanathan, Executive Director
Finances: *Annual Operating Budget:* $500,000-$1.5 Million; *Funding Sources:* Membership dues; student fees
Staff: 5 staff member(s); 100 volunteer(s)
Membership: 367 active + 14 retired + 30 associates; *Fees:* $730; *Committees:* Audit; Nomination; Bylaws & Ethics; Discipline; Student Appeals; Executive Director Compensation
Activities: CGA Program of Professional Study; mandatory professional development; *Library:* Yes (Open to Public) by appointment
Awards: CGA Canada Awards of Excellence; Three Course Scholarships, Approx. $1,500 each; One Course Scholarships, Approx. $500 each; Students Enrolled in Other Educational Institutions Scholarships; CGA Student Scholarship, $500 tuition; Thompson Professional Publishing Award; Encon Group Inc. Insurance Public Practice Award; Debbi Dillon Memorial Fund, $800; Past Presidents Bursary, $500; General Fund Management Accounting Stream, $500; General Fund Financial Accounting Stream, $500
Publications: CGA Notes, Newsletter, 8 pa, Editor: Larissa Prevost, accepts advertising, Contents: News, technical material, resource information by & about members
Description: To advance & develop the accounting profession & to ensure the highest professional, ethical & educational standards of its members & students

Certified General Accountants Association of Manitoba
4 Donald St. South, Winnipeg MB R3L 2T7
Tel: 204-477-1256; *Fax:* 204-453-7176
Toll-Free: 800-282-8001
e-mail: info@cga-online.org/mb
URL: www.cga-online.org/mb
Also Known As: CGA - Manitoba
Overview: A medium-sized provincial licensing organization founded in 1973
Chief Officer(s): L.W. Hampson FCGA, Executive Director
Finances: *Annual Operating Budget:* $3 Million-$5 Million; *Funding Sources:* Membership dues; services
Staff: 16 staff member(s); 120 volunteer(s)
Membership: 3,100; *Fees:* $695; *Member Profile:* Professional accountants; financial managers
Activities: Certification program; continuing professional education; professional regulation; publications; *Internships:* Yes; *Speaker Service:* Yes; *Library:* Yes
Meetings: 2007; Conference, Oct. 17-20, Brandon, MB Canada
Publications: Newsletter, q.
Member of: International Federation of Accountants

Certified General Accountants Association of Ontario
240 Eglinton Ave. East, Toronto ON M4P 1K8
Tel: 416-322-6520; *Fax:* 416-322-5594
Toll-Free: 800-668-1454
e-mail: info@cga-ontario.org
URL: www.cga-ontario.org
Also Known As: CGA - Ontario
Overview: A large provincial licensing organization founded in 1913
Chief Officer(s): Diane Burgess MBA, CGA, Executive Director/COO
Finances: *Funding Sources:* Membership & tuition fees
Membership: 13,000 CGAs + 8,000 students
Activities: Administers the CGA certification process; provides free accountant referral service to the public; coordinates employment referral service for members & students; produces information booklets for the public free of charge; *Speaker Service:* Yes
Publications: Statements, Newsletter, bi-m.
Description: To control the professional standards, conduct, & discipline of its members & students in Ontario; to provide ongoing professional development & support services

Certified General Accountants Association of New Brunswick / Association des comptables généraux accrédités du Nouveau-Brunswick
#10, 236 St. George St., Moncton NB E1C 1W1
Tel: 506-857-0939; *Fax:* 506-855-0887
e-mail: cganb@nbnet.nb.ca
URL: www.cga-nb.org
Also Known As: CGA - New Brunswick
Overview: A medium-sized provincial organization founded in 1962
Finances: *Funding Sources:* Membership dues
Staff: 2 staff member(s)
Membership: 3 associate + 320 student + 8 senior/lif; *Fees:* Schedule available; *Member Profile:* Certified general accountants; *Committees:* Public Affairs; Member Services; Standards Review; Discipline; Marketing
Activities: *Internships:* Yes
Publications: CGA-NB Newsletter, q., Éditeur: T. Dryden

Certified General Accountants Association of Nova Scotia
PO Box 73, Halifax NS B3J 2L4
Tel: 902-425-4923; *Fax:* 902-425-4983
e-mail: office@cga-ns.org
URL: www.cga-ns.org
Also Known As: CGA - Nova Scotia
Overview: A medium-sized provincial organization founded in 1982
Staff: 1 staff member(s)
Description: To effectively guide & support our diverse membership of future-oriented accountants in order to protect the public that our members serve

Certified General Accountants Association of Prince Edward Island
PO Box 3, #105, 18 Queen St., Charlottetown PE C1A 4A1
Tel: 902-368-7237; *Fax:* 902-368-3627
Toll-Free: 800-463-0163
e-mail: contact@cga-pei.org
URL: www.cga-pei.org
Also Known As: CGA - Prince Edward Island
Overview: A medium-sized provincial organization founded in 1968
Chief Officer(s): Robert Landry CGA, COO; Joanne Smith, Office Administrator
Finances: *Annual Operating Budget:* $50,000-$100,000
Staff: 1 staff member(s); 10 volunteer(s)
Membership: 150 students/members; *Fees:* $630 approx.
Description: To insure its members merit the confidence & trust of all who rely upon their professional knowledge, skill, judgement & integrity

Certified General Accountants Association of Newfoundland & Labrador (CGA-NL)
#201, 294 Freshwater Rd., St. John's NL A1B 1C1
Tel: 709-579-1863; *Fax:* 709-579-0838
Toll-Free: 800-563-2426
e-mail: office@cga-newfoundland.org
URL: www.cga-newfoundland.org
Also Known As: CGA - Newfoundland & Labrador
Overview: A medium-sized provincial licensing organization founded in 1962
Chief Officer(s): Fred Evans CGA, Executive Director
Finances: *Annual Operating Budget:* $100,000-$250,000
Staff: 2 staff member(s); 50 volunteer(s)
Membership: 500; *Fees:* $700; *Member Profile:* Professional accountants; *Committees:* Audit; Education; Ethics & By Laws; Honours/Awards; Local Office; Marketing/Promotion; Member Services; Newsletter/Publication; Practical Experience; Public Practice; Professional Rights; Professional Development; Social/Graduation; Strategic Planning
Activities: Education system which reflects the provincial, national & international scope of accountancy; continuing professional development of members; *Library:* CGA Office Library by appointment
Publications: CGA Nfld. on Balance, Newsletter, q., accepts advertising
Description: To provide highest level of professional accountancy to individuals, business & public sector entities; Affiliation(s): CGA Canada

Ottawa Office
#1201, 350 Sparks St., Ottawa ON K1R 7S8
Tel: 613-789-7771; *Fax:* 613-789-7772
e-mail: ottawa@cga-canada.org

CFA Vancouver
#707, 3061 East Kent Ave. North, Vancouver BC V5S 4P5
Tel: 604-435-9889; *Fax:* 604-434-5695
e-mail: cfavancouver@shaw.ca
URL: www.cfavancouver.com
Previous Name: Vancouver Society of Financial Analysts
Overview: A small local organization
Chief Officer(s): Sheila Hughson, Administrator
Membership: 733
Member of: Association for Investment Management & Research

La Chambre de commerce du Canada *See* The Canadian Chamber of Commerce

Chambre de l'assurance de dommages (CHAD)
999, boul de Maisonneuve ouest, 12e étage, Montréal QC H3A 3L4
Tél: 514-842-2591; *Téléc:* 514-842-3138
Ligne sans frais: 800-361-7288
Courriel: info@chad.qc.ca
URL: www.chad.ca
Nom précédent: Association des courtiers d'assurances de la Province de Québec
Aperçu: *Dimension:* grande; *Envergure: provinciale; Organisme de réglementation; fondée en 1999*
Membre(s) du bureau directeur: Maya Raic, Présidente-Directrice générale; Isabelle Perreault, Directrice des communications
Finances: *Budget de fonctionnement annuel:* $1.5 Million-$3 Million
Personnel: 22 membre(s) du personnel
Membre: à peu près 13 000; *Montant de la cotisation:* 240$; *Critères d'admissibilité/Description:* Agents; courtiers; experts en sinistre
Activités: *Service de conférenciers:* Oui
Publications: ChAD Presse, Journal, au 2 mois, publicité, Contenu: Tendances en assurance, décisions disciplinaires, info sur les lois et règlements, prévention, etc.
Description: Assurer la protection du public en matière d'assurance de dommages et d'expertise en règlement de sinistres; encadrer de façon préventive et disciplinaire la pratique professionnelle des individus et des organisations oeuvrant dans ces domaines

Chambre de la sécurité financière (CSF)
300, rue Léo-Pariseau, 26e étage, Montréal QC H3A 3C6
Tél: 514-282-5777; *Téléc:* 514-282-2225
Ligne sans frais: 800-361-9989
Courriel: renseignements@chambresf.com
URL: www.chambresf.com
Nom précédent: Association des intermédiaires en assurance de personnes du Québec
Aperçu: *Dimension:* moyenne; *Envergure: provinciale; Organisme sans but lucratif*
Membre(s) du bureau directeur: Christine Côté, Directrice
Finances: *Budget de fonctionnement annuel:* Plus de $5 Million
Personnel: 40 membre(s) du personnel; 176 bénévole(s)
Membre: 30 274; *Montant de la cotisation:* 204$ en 2006; 209$ en 2007; *Critères d'admissibilité/Description:* Exerçant dans les disciplines suivantes: l'assurance de personnes; l'assurance collective de personnes; la planification financière; le courtage en épargne collective; le courtage en contrats d'investissement; le courtage en plans de bourses d'études; *Comités:* Comités: Discipline; Réglementation; Gouvernance; Sections; Vérification; Finances; Trésorerie
Activités: Assemblée générale annuelle; camp de formation; *Listes de destinataires:* Oui
Publications: Sécurité financière, Revue, 5 fois par an, Éditeur: Benoît Gagné, ISSN: 0823-8138, publicité, Contenu: Articles d'actualitémot du président; vie régionale; formation continue; protection du public; avis disciplinaires, etc.
Description: Assurer la protection du public en maintenant la discipline et en veillant à la formation et à la déontologie de ses membres

Chartered Accountants' Education Foundation (CAEF)
Manulife Place, #580, 10180 - 101 St., Edmonton AB T5J 4R2
Tel: 780-424-7391; *Fax:* 780-425-8766
Toll-Free: 800-232-9406
e-mail: info@icaa.ab.ca
URL: www.icaa.ab.ca/caef/
Overview: A small provincial organization founded in 1983

Chief Officer(s): Dean Gallimore CA CBV, Chair
Finances: *Annual Operating Budget:* $250,000-$500,000
Staff: 20 volunteer(s)
Description: To promote excellence in university accounting education; Affiliation(s): Institute of Chartered Accountants of Alberta

Chartered Institute of Public Finance & Accountancy (CIPFA)
3 Robert St., London WC2N 6RL United Kingdom
Tel: 44-20-7543-5600; *Fax:* 44-20-7543-5700
e-mail: pressoffice@cipfa.org
URL: www.cipfa.org.uk
Overview: A medium-sized international organization
Chief Officer(s): Clare Rice, Contact
Activities: Launched unique designation program CMA/CPFA with CMA Canada
Description: Leading professional accountancy body in the UK; specializes in the public services

Civil Constables Association of Nova Scotia (CCANS)
#4, 200 Wright Ave., Dartmouth NS B3B 1W5
Tel: 902-423-4389
URL: www.ccans.ca
Overview: A small provincial organization founded in 2002
Chief Officer(s): Rick LeBlanc, President

CMA Canada / La Société des comptables en management
#1400, One Robert Speck Pkwy., Mississauga ON L4Z 3M3
Tel: 905-949-4200; *Fax:* 905-949-0888
Toll-Free: 800-263-7622
e-mail: info@cma-canada.org
URL: www.cma-canada.org
Also Known As: Certified Management Accountants of Canada
Previous Name: Society of Management Accountants of Canada
Overview: A large national organization founded in 1920
Chief Officer(s): Steve F. Vieweg CMA, FCMA, President & CEO; Ronald M. Stoesz CMA, FCMA, Chair
Finances: *Annual Operating Budget:* Greater than $5 Million; *Funding Sources:* Membership dues; business publications; professional development programs
Staff: 158 staff member(s); 300 volunteer(s)
Membership: 44,000; *Fees:* $575 average; *Member Profile:* CMA holders; students
Activities: *Internships:* Yes; *Speaker Service:* Yes
Publications: CMA Management, Magazine, 10 pa, Editor: Kristin Doucet, ISSN: 1490-4225, accepts advertising, Contents: Business magazine produced for senior management professionals, covering business strategies, information technology, career development, risk management, customer & supplier reliationship, e-commerce, organizational management, Price: $48
Description: To optimize the performance of enterprises by driving the continuous development of management accounting & shaping the strategic leadership competencies of CMAs

CMA Canada - Alberta
#1120, 833 - 4th Ave. SW, Calgary AB T2P 3T5
Tel: 403-269-5341; *Fax:* 403-262-5477
Toll-Free: 877-262-2000
e-mail: info@cma-alberta.com
URL: www.cma-alberta.com
Previous Name: Society of Management Accountants of Alberta
Overview: A medium-sized provincial licensing organization founded in 1944
Chief Officer(s): Joy Thomas CMA, FCMA, President & CEO
Finances: *Annual Operating Budget:* $1.5 Million-$3 Million; *Funding Sources:* Membership dues
Staff: 14 staff member(s); 70 volunteer(s)
Membership: 6,100 professional + 465 candidate + 440 students; *Fees:* $677.59 + GST; *Member Profile:* University or college graduate; entrance exam & two-year professional program & 24 months practical experience; *Committees:* Practice Review; Professional Conduct; Hearing; Appeals; Nominating; Registration; Audit
Activities: Careers-on-Line; Continuing Professional Education; CMA Professional Program; *Awareness Events:* CEO of the Future; *Library:* Yes (Open to Public)
Awards: Certified Management Accountants Awards, Maximum of $1,500; up to 5 awards
Publications: Network, Newsletter, 5 pa, Editor: Larissa Innes
Description: To develop & advance the competencies & market relevance of CMAs through accreditation, education, & high standards

CMA Canada - British Columbia (CMABC)
Two Bentall Centre, #1055, 555 Burrard St., Box 269, Vancouver BC V7X 1M8
Tel: 604-687-5891; *Fax:* 604-687-6688
Toll-Free: 800-663-9646
e-mail: cmabc@cmabc.com
URL: www.cmabc.com
Also Known As: Certified Management Accountants of British Columbia
Previous Name: Society of Management Accountants of British Columbia
Overview: A medium-sized provincial licensing organization founded in 1945
Chief Officer(s): Colin Bennett CMA, President & CEO
Finances: *Annual Operating Budget:* $3 Million-$5 Million; *Funding Sources:* Membership dues
Membership: 5,000; *Fees:* $700; *Committees:* Regional BC Chapters
Activities: Professional education; professional development
Publications: CMA Management, Magazine, 10 pa., Editor: Robert Colman
Description: To be pre-eminent in management accounting by ensuring that the body of knowledge is available, by setting & enforcing the standards of competence, ensuring availability of CMAs in the defined territory, & supporting research; to optimize the performance of enterprises by driving the continuous development of financial & strategic management professionals & shaping the strategic leadership competencies of CMAs

CMA Canada - Manitoba
#815, 240 Graham Ave., Winnipeg MB R3C 0J7
Tel: 204-943-1538; *Fax:* 204-947-3308
Toll-Free: 800-841-7148
e-mail: cmamb@cma-canada.org
URL: www.cma-canada.org/Manitoba.asp
Overview: A medium-sized provincial organization founded in 1947
Chief Officer(s): Carleen MacKay CMA, Executive Director
Finances: *Annual Operating Budget:* $500,000-$1.5 Million; *Funding Sources:* Membership
Staff: 6 staff member(s); 70 volunteer(s)
Membership: 1,150; *Fees:* $475; *Member Profile:* Accreditation process including examinations; *Committees:* Education; Member Services; Professional Development; Public Practice
Description: To support members in leading organizations in the application of advanced management practices

CMA Canada - Newfoundland
PO Box 28090, RPO Avalon Mall, St. John's NL A1B 4J8
Tel: 709-726-3652; *Fax:* 709-745-6216
e-mail: cmanl@nl.rogers.com
URL: www.cma-canada.org/newfoundland.asp
Also Known As: Society of Management Accountants of Newfoundland
Overview: A medium-sized provincial licensing organization founded in 1951
Chief Officer(s): Mark A. Bradbury CMA, Executive Director
Finances: *Annual Operating Budget:* $100,000-$250,000
Staff: 1 staff member(s); 12 volunteer(s)
Membership: 100-499

CMA Canada - Northwest Territories & Nunavut
PO Box 512, Yellowknife NT X1A 2N4
Tel: 867-873-2875; *Fax:* 867-920-2503
e-mail: cmanwtn@theedge.ca
URL: www.cma-canada.org/nwt.asp
Overview: A small provincial organization
Chief Officer(s): Michelle Demeule CMA, Executive Director
Membership: 1-99; *Fees:* $550

CMA Canada - Nova Scotia & Bermuda
Sentry Place, #500, 1559 Brunswick St., Halifax NS B3J 2G1
Tel: 902-422-5836; *Fax:* 902-423-1605
Toll-Free: 800-565-7198
e-mail: nforan@cmans.com
URL: www.cmans.com
Also Known As: Society of Management Accountants of Nova Scotia
Overview: A medium-sized provincial organization
Chief Officer(s): Nancy Foran CMA, Director
Finances: *Funding Sources:* Membership fees
Staff: 4 staff member(s); 12 volunteer(s)
Membership: 1,000; *Fees:* $550
Description: To promote standards of excellence in management accounting

CMA Canada - Ontario
#300, 70 University Ave., Toronto ON M5J 2M4
Tel: 416-977-7741; *Fax:* 416-977-6079
Toll-Free: 800-387-2991
e-mail: info@cma-ontario.org
URL: www.cma-ontario.org
Overview: A large provincial licensing organization founded in 1941
Chief Officer(s): David Hipgrave FCMA, P.Eng., President & CEO
Finances: *Annual Operating Budget:* Greater than $5 Million; *Funding Sources:* Membership dues; program fees
Staff: 42 staff member(s); 24 volunteer(s)
Membership: 16,000; *Fees:* $672 certified; $382 candidate; $50 student; *Member Profile:* University degree & practical experience
Activities: Offers management development program; grants exclusive rights to the CMA designation; *Library:* Member Services Centre (Open to Public)
Publications: Ontario Update, Newsletter
Description: To optimize the performance of enterprises by driving the continuous development of management accounting & shaping the strategic competences of CMA's

CMA Canada - Québec
715, square Victoria, 3e étage, Montréal QC H2Y 2H7
Tél: 514-849-1155; *Téléc:* 514-849-9674
Ligne sans frais: 800-263-5390
Courriel: administration@cma-quebec.org
URL: www.cma-quebec.org
Également appelé: Ordre des comptables en management accrédités du Québec
Aperçu: *Dimension:* moyenne; *Envergure: provinciale; Organisme de réglementation; fondée en 1941*
Membre(s) du bureau directeur: François Renauld CMA, Président/Directeur général
Personnel: 26 membre(s) du personnel; 240 bénévole(s)
Membre: 4 200
Activités: *Stagiaires:* Oui; *Listes de destinataires:* Oui
Publications: Elite CMA, Bulletin, 3 fois par an, ISSN: 0847-1568, accepts advertising
Description: Protéger le public en contrôlant la compétence et l'intégrité de ceux et celles qui exercent la profession; favoriser la prééminence de ses membres dans le monde des affaires; assurer une formation de tout premier ordre; l'Ordre joue un rôle primordial dans l'acquisition et l'application du savoir de ses membres; il est responsable de l'émission des permis d'exercice aux candidats qui remplissent les conditions nécessaires, de la garde du tableau des membres, de la surveillance de l'exercice de la profession et du dépistage de la pratique illégale

CMA Canada - Saskatchewan
#202, 1900 Albert St., Regina SK S4P 4K8
Tel: 306-757-9428; *Fax:* 306-347-8580
Toll-Free: 800-667-3535
e-mail: sask@cma-canada.org
URL: www.cma-canada.org/saskatchewan.asp
Overview: A medium-sized provincial licensing organization founded in 1929
Chief Officer(s): Betty Hoffart FCMA, CEO; Susan Stettner CMA, Director of Accreditation
Finances: *Annual Operating Budget:* $500,000-$1.5 Million
Staff: 6 staff member(s)
Membership: 1,000-4,999

CMA Canada - Yukon
c/o Yukon Territorial Govt., Whitehorse YT Y1A 4N6
Tel: 867-667-3074; *Fax:* 867-393-6217
e-mail: karenl.johnson@gov.yk.ca
URL: www.cma-canada.org/yukon.asp
Overview: A small provincial organization founded in 1975
Chief Officer(s): Karen Johnson CMA, Territorial Representative
Description: To promote standards of excellence in management accounting

CMA New Brunswick (CMANB) / La Société des comptables en management du Nouveau-Brunswick
#101, 570 Queen St., Fredericton NB E3B 6Z6
Tel: 506-455-2262; *Fax:* 506-455-2266
Toll-Free: 877-676-2262
e-mail: cmanb@nbnet.nb.ca
URL: www.cmanb.com

Also Known As: The Society of Management Acountants of New Brunswick
Overview: A medium-sized provincial licensing organization founded in 1950
Chief Officer(s): Shelley Pelkey CMA, CEO
Finances: *Annual Operating Budget:* $250,000-$500,000
Staff: 2 staff member(s); 48 volunteer(s)
Membership: 100-499; *Fees:* $620; *Member Profile:* Certified management accountants; *Committees:* Accreditation; professional services; nominations; executive
Activities: Education, accreditation, services to members; *Internships:* Yes
Publications: New Brunswick Update, Newsletter, q., accepts advertising, Contents: News to members, society's activities
Description: Develops professionals & resources to lea the advancement & integration of strategy, accounting & management

Coalition canadienne contre la fraude à l'assurance *See* Canadian Coalition Against Insurance Fraud

Comité canadien de recherches sur la taxation *See* Canadian Research Committee on Taxation

Community Financial Counselling Services (CFCS)
238 Portage Ave., 3rd Fl., Winnipeg MB R3B 0B1
Tel: 204-989-1900; *Fax:* 204-989-1908
e-mail: cfcs@mts.net
URL: www.creditcounsellingcanada.ca/manitoba.html
Previous Name: Credit Counselling Canada - Manitoba
Overview: A small provincial organization
Activities: Credit counselling; debt management; welfare education
Member of: Credit Counselling Canada

Community Futures Development Association of British Columbia
#880, 355 Burrard St., Vancouver BC V6C 2G8
Tel: 604-685-2332; *Fax:* 604-681-6575
e-mail: info@communityfutures.ca
URL: www.communityfutures.ca/provincial/bc/
Overview: A medium-sized provincial organization
Chief Officer(s): Marie Gallant, Managing Director
Description: To create, promote & encourage better understanding, unity, harmony & cooperation amongst the members; to seek, obtain & encourage on behalf of the members the support, recognition & understanding of the public & all levels of government & government agencies or bodies regarding community economic development in British Columbia; to promote, coordinate & facilitate on behalf of the members, community economic development initiatives; to lead the development of the members toward their common vision, through the provision of a system strategic planning, facilities, services & advocacy support; Affiliation(s): Pan Canadian Community Futures Network

Community Futures Network Society of Alberta (CFNSA)
PO Box 184, 115 - 4th Ave. West, Cochrane AB T4C 1A5
Tel: 403-851-9995; *Fax:* 403-851-9905
e-mail: marc@cfnsa.ca
URL: www.cfnsa.ca
Overview: A medium-sized provincial organization
Chief Officer(s): Marc Butikofer, Assistant Executive Director
Activities: Supports 27 Community Futures Development Corporations (CFDCs)
Description: To provide leadership & support for the growth of the Community Futures movement in Alberta; Affiliation(s): Pan Canadian Community Futures Network

Community Futures Partners of Manitoba
#559, 167 Lombard Ave., Winnipeg MB R3B 0V3
Tel: 204-943-2905; *Fax:* 204-956-9363
e-mail: info@cfpm.mb.ca
URL: www.cfpm.mb.ca
Overview: A small provincial organization
Membership: *Member Profile:* Represents 16 Community Futures Development Corporations (CFDCs)
Description: To strengthen rural economies by enabling entrepreneurship & assisting in community economic development; Affiliation(s): Pan Canadian Community Futures Network

Community Futures Partners of Saskatchewan
PO Box 1545, Saskatoon SK S7K 3R3
Tel: 306-260-2390; *Fax:* 306-665-5740
e-mail: office_cfps1@sasktel.net
Overview: A small provincial organization

Conseil de Credit du Canada *See* Credit Counselling Canada

Conseil de recherche en réassurance *See* Reinsurance Research Council

Conseil des experts-comptables de la province de l'Ontario *See* Public Accountants Council for the Province of Ontario

Conseil relatif aux standards des planificateurs financiers *See* Financial Planners Standards Council

Courtiers indépendants en sécurité financière du Canada *See* Independent Financial Brokers of Canada

Credit Counselling Canada (CCC) / Conseil de Credit du Canada
Columbia Sky Train Station Bldg., #330, 435 Columbia St., New Westminster BC V3L 5N8
Tel: 604-527-8999; *Fax:* 604-527-8008
Toll-Free: 888-527-8999
URL: www.creditcounsellingcanada.ca
Overview: A medium-sized national organization founded in 2000
Chief Officer(s): Scott Hannah, Contact
Membership: *Member Profile:* Not-for-profit credit counselling agencies & Orderly Payment of Debt programs from all across Canada
Activities: For credit counselling information in NWT, Nunavut & Yukon contact 1-888-294-0076
Description: To ensure all Canadians have access to not-for-profit credit counselling; to ensure a quality of service is provided to Canadians by member agencies; to advocate on issues relevant to money management & the wise use of credit along with public policy & legislative issues around these; to promote awareness of the existence & availability of non-profit credit counselling; to cultivate positive working relationships with stakeholders

Credit Counselling Canada - Manitoba *See* Community Financial Counselling Servicesy

Credit Counselling Canada - Saskatchewan
#120, 2151 Scarth St., Regina SK S4P 3V7
Tel: 306-787-5387; *Fax:* 306-787-5574
Toll-Free: 888-215-2222
e-mail: tchinn@justice.gov.sk.ca
URL: www.saskjustice.gov.sk.ca/provmediation
Also Known As: Provincial Mediation Board Credit Counselling
Overview: A small provincial organization
Member of: Credit Counselling Canada

Saskatoon
122 - 3rd Ave. North, Saskatoon SK S7K 2H6
Tel: 306-933-6520; *Fax:* 306-933-7030

Credit Counselling London *See* Credit Counselling Thames Valley

Credit Counselling of Regional Niagara
264 Welland Ave., St Catharines ON L2R 2P8
Tel: 905-684-9401; *Fax:* 905-687-9904
Toll-Free: 800-663-3973
e-mail: info@ccrn.ca
URL: www.ccrn.ca
Overview: A small local organization founded in 1975
Chief Officer(s): Bob Lawler, Executive Director
Finances: *Annual Operating Budget:* $250,000-$500,000; *Funding Sources:* United Way
Staff: 9 staff member(s); 10 volunteer(s)
Description: To assist, direct, & educate clients & advocate on their behalf to resolve their financial problems; *Member of:* Ontario Association of Credit Counselling Services

Credit Counselling Service of Durham Region (CCS)
PO Box 26046, #106, 172 King St. East, Oshawa ON L1H 8R4
Tel: 905-579-1951; *Fax:* 905-579-1967
e-mail: ccs@ccsdurhamregion.com
URL: www.ccsdurhamregion.com
Overview: A small regional organization founded in 1971
Chief Officer(s): Sandra Sherk, Executive Director
Finances: *Annual Operating Budget:* $100,000-$250,000; *Funding Sources:* United Way; donations; service fees
Staff: 3 staff member(s)
Membership: 1-99
Activities: *Speaker Service:* Yes
Description: To assist & support individuals & families in Durham Region in finding appropriate solutions to their financial concerns; *Member of:* Credit Counselling Canada; Ontario Association of Credit Counselling Services

Credit Counselling Service of Newfoundland & Labrador
22 Queen's Rd., St. John's NL A1C 2A5
Tel: 709-753-5812; *Fax:* 709-753-3390
e-mail: psweetapple@pccsnf.com
URL: www.debthelpnewfoundland.com
Overview: A small provincial organization
Chief Officer(s): Al Antle, Executive Director
Member of: Credit Counselling Canada; Affiliation(s): Ontario Association of Credit Counselling Services

Corner Brook
PO Box 751, #206, 9 Main St., Corner Brook NL A0H 6G7
Tel: 709-634-7772; *Fax:* 709-634-7790

Credit Counselling Service of Sault Ste Marie
#2, 298 Queen St. East, Sault Ste Marie ON P6A 1Y7
Tel: 705-254-1424; *Fax:* 705-254-2541
e-mail: info@creditcounsellingssm.ca
URL: www.creditcounsellingssm.ca
Overview: A small local organization founded in 1969
Chief Officer(s): Greg Elsby, Executive Director
Finances: *Annual Operating Budget:* $250,000-$500,000
Staff: 8 staff member(s); 13 volunteer(s)
Activities: Personal money management counselling; arrangement of consumer debt repayment programs; credit education
Description: SSM provides personal money management counselling, arrangement of consumer debt repayment programs & the promotion of credit education; *Member of:* United Way; Ontario Association of Credit Counselling Services

Credit Counselling Service of Simcoe County
PO Box 922, 4 Cedar Pointe Dr., #R, Barrie ON L4M 4Y6
Tel: 705-726-2705; *Fax:* 705-726-6830
e-mail: estelle@ccsbarrie.net
URL: www.ccsbarrie.net
Overview: A small local organization
Chief Officer(s): Estelle Forget, Executive Director
Member of: Ontario Association of Credit Counselling Services

Credit Counselling Service of Toronto (CCST)
#810, 45 Sheppard Ave. East, Toronto ON M2N 5W9
Tel: 416-228-3328; *Fax:* 416-228-1164
Toll-Free: 800-267-2272
e-mail: ccsmt@creditcanada.com
URL: www.creditcanada.com
Overview: A small local charitable organization founded in 1965
Chief Officer(s): C.M. Stregger, Executive Director; Ellen Roseman, President & Chair
Finances: *Annual Operating Budget:* $1.5 Million-$3 Million
Staff: 40 staff member(s); 20 volunteer(s)
Membership: 1,500+; *Member Profile:* Non-profit & charitable service
Activities: Credit counselling; debt restructuring; credit education; *Library:* Yes (Open to Public)
Member of: Ontario Association of Credit Counselling Services; Affiliation(s): National Foundation for Consumer Credit

Credit Counselling Services of Alberta Ltd.
Sunrise Square, #225, 602 - 11 Ave. SW, Calgary AB T2R 1J8
Tel: 403-265-2201
Toll-Free: 888-294-0076
e-mail: info@creditcounselling.com
URL: www.creditcounselling.com
Overview: A small provincial organization
Description: Provides confidential consumer money management & debt-counselling services to Albertans; *Member of:* Credit Counselling Canada

CCSA Edmonton
Sun Life Place, #440, 10123 - 99 St., Edmonton AB T5J 3H1
Tel: 780-423-5265

Credit Counselling Services of Atlantic Canada
Fredericton Office, 1149 Smythe St., Fredericton NB E3B 3H4
Fax: 506-453-0564
Toll-Free: 888-753-2227
e-mail: ccsinfo@ccsac.com
URL: www.ccsac.com; www.solveyourdebts.com
Overview: A medium-sized regional organization
Member of: Credit Counselling Canada

New Brunswick - Bathurst
#5, 100 Main St., Bathurst NB E2A 1A4
Fax: 506-548-3445

New Brunswick - Moncton

155 Cornhill St., Moncton NB E1C 6L3
Fax: 506-382-5910
New Brunswick - Saint John
#703, 133 Prince William St., Saint John NB E2L 2B6
Fax: 506-633-6057
Nova Scotia - Halifax
#1003, 6080 Young St., Halifax NS B3K 5L2
Fax: 902-455-0947
Nova Scotia - Kentville
#201, 35 Webster St., Kentville NS B4N 1H4
Fax: 902-678-7495
Nova Scotia - New Glasgow
Aberdeen Mall, #235, 610 East River Rd., New Glasgow NS B2H 3S2
Fax: 902-752-8153
Nova Scotia - Sydney
Cabot House, #305, 500 Kings Rd., Sydney NS B1S 1B1
Fax: 902-564-0448
PEI - Charlottetown
#303, 129 Kent St., Charlottetown PE C1A 1N4
Fax: 902-892-1477

Credit Counselling Services of Cochrane District
#7, 85 Pine St. South, Timmins ON P4N 2K1
Tel: 705-267-5817; *Fax:* 705-264-9767
Toll-Free: 866-267-5817
e-mail: ccsmitch@ntl.sympatico.ca
Overview: A small local organization founded in 1976
Chief Officer(s): Mitch Gauthier, Executive Director
Finances: *Annual Operating Budget:* $50,000-$100,000
Staff: 1 staff member(s)
Description: To assist individuals & families in finding appropriate & satisfactory solutions to their financial problems & to assist them in developing the capacity to manage responsibly their personal financial affairs; *Member of:* Ontario Association of Credit Counselling Services

Credit Counselling Services of Peterborough
#203, 351 Charlotte St., Peterborough ON K9J 2W1
Tel: 705-742-1351; *Fax:* 705-742-2895
Toll-Free: 800-274-1611
e-mail: ccrc@accel.net
URL: www.ccrc-ptbo.com/credit_counselling.html
Overview: A small local organization
Member of: Credit Counselling Canada

Credit Counselling Services of Southwestern Ontario
420 Devonshire Rd., Windsor ON N8Y 4T6
Tel: 519-258-2030; *Fax:* 519-258-9243
e-mail: info@ccswindsor.com
URL: www.ccswindsor.com
Overview: A small local charitable organization
Chief Officer(s): Wendy Dupuis, Executive Director
Staff: 12 staff member(s); 15 volunteer(s)
Membership: 1-99
Activities: *Speaker Service:* Yes
Member of: Credit Counselling Canada; Ontario Association of Credit Counselling Services
Sarnia-Lambton Office
568N Christina St., Unit D, Sarnia ON N7T 5W6
Tel: 519-337-8757; *Fax:* 519-337-8782
e-mail: ccsswo@mnsi.net

Credit Counselling Society of British Columbia
#330, 435 Columbia St., New Westminster BC V3L 5N8
Tel: 604-527-8999; *Fax:* 604-527-8008
Toll-Free: 888-527-8999
e-mail: info@nomoredebts.org
URL: www.nomoredebts.org
Overview: A small provincial organization
Description: To help consumers resolve debt & money problems & gain control over their finances; *Member of:* Credit Counselling Canada
Abbotsford
2420 Montrose Ave., Abbotsford BC V2S 3S9
Fax: 604-527-9611
Toll-Free: 888-527-8999
Kelowna
#230, 1855 Kirschner Rd., Kelowna BC V1Y 4N7
Fax: 280-860-3666
Toll-Free: 888-527-8999
Surrey
#303, 15225 - 104th Ave., Surrey BC V3R 6Y8
Fax: 604-588-6673
Toll-Free: 888-527-8999
Vancouver
#600, 890 West Pender St., Vancouver BC V6C 1J9
Fax: 604-681-9050
Toll-Free: 888-527-8999

Credit Counselling Thames Valley
125 Woodward Ave., London ON N6J 2H1
Tel: 519-433-0159; *Fax:* 519-433-4559
e-mail: info@creditcounsellingthamesvalley.ca
URL: www.creditcounsellingthamesvalley.ca
Previous Name: Credit Counselling London
Overview: A small local organization founded in 1967
Chief Officer(s): Warren Brooke, Executive Director; Andrew Holt, Program Manager
Finances: *Annual Operating Budget:* $250,000-$500,000; *Funding Sources:* Corporate & local donations; fees for some services
Staff: 8 staff member(s); 14 volunteer(s)
Membership: 1-99
Activities: Service Woodstock Tillsonburg, St. Thomas, Clencoe, Strathroy, Parkhill, Lucan, Dorchester
Description: To provide credit counselling service to the people of the City of London & district as a social service in the public interest; to provide debt counselling, both remedial & preventive, &, where appropriate, debt consolidation; to act as an intermediary between debtors & creditors in working out satisfactory arrangements for the orderly payment of debts; *Member of:* Ontario Association of Credit Counselling Services

Credit Institute of Canada (CIC) / L'Institut canadien du crédit
#216C, 219 Dufferin St., Toronto ON M6K 3J1
Tel: 416-572-2615; *Fax:* 416-572-2619
e-mail: geninfo@creditedu.org
URL: www.creditedu.org
Previous Name: Canadian Institute of Credit & Financial Management
Overview: A medium-sized national charitable organization founded in 1928
Chief Officer(s): Yvon Daneau, Chair, President & Dean
Finances: *Annual Operating Budget:* $500,000-$1.5 Million; *Funding Sources:* Membership fees; enrolments; sales
Staff: 5 staff member(s); 100 volunteer(s)
Membership: 1,984 individuals + 948 students; *Fees:* $275
Activities: Educational programs; assists government with legislative proposals; membership programs; *Speaker Service:* Yes; *Rents Mailing List:* Yes; *Library:* Yes (Open to Public) by appointment
Publications: To Your Credit, Newsletter, 3 pa
Description: To be professionals dedicated to excellence in credit management

Credit Union Central Alberta Limited
#350N, 8500 Macleod Trail SE, Calgary AB T2H 2N1
Tel: 403-258-5900; *Fax:* 403-253-7720
e-mail: email@albertacentral.com
URL: www.albertacentral.com
Overview: A small provincial organization
Chief Officer(s): Barry Johnson, Exec. Vice-President
Staff: 330 staff member(s)

Credit Union Central of British Columbia
1441 Creekside Dr., Vancouver BC V6J 4S7
Tel: 604-734-2511; *Fax:* 604-737-5055
Toll-Free: 888-479-4824
e-mail: info@cucbc.com
URL: www.cucbc.com
Overview: A medium-sized provincial organization founded in 1944
Chief Officer(s): Wayne A. Nygren, President/CEO; Daniel Burns, Chair
Staff: 315 staff member(s)

Credit Union Central of Canada (CUCC) / La Centrale des caisses de crédit du Canada
Corporate Office, #500, 300 The East Mall, Toronto ON M9B 6B7
Tel: 416-232-1262; *Fax:* 416-232-9196
Toll-Free: 800-649-0222
e-mail: cucc@cucentral.com
URL: www.cucentral.ca
Previous Name: Canadian Cooperative Credit Society
Overview: A small national organization founded in 1953
Chief Officer(s): David Phillips, President & CEO; Jim Hackett, COO
Finances: *Annual Operating Budget:* Greater than $5 Million
Staff: 51 staff member(s)
Membership: 41; *Fees:* Schedule available; *Member Profile:* Central credit union, cooperative or financial cooperative; *Committees:* Service & Product Development; Legislative Policy; National Technology
Activities: *Library:* Resource Centre (Open to Public)
Awards: Community Economic Development Award
Publications: Briefs, Newsletter, bi-weekly, Editor: Steve Mosey
Description: To lead the development of credit unions in Canada in conjunction with the provincial centrals & other corporate members towards system visions by providing services in the areas of strategic planning, central financial facilities, new product & service offerings, national services, system advocacy & international relations; Affiliation(s): World Council of Credit Unions
Government Affairs
#400, 275 Bank St., Ottawa ON K2P 2L6
Tel: 613-238-6747; *Fax:* 613-238-7283

Credit Union Central of Manitoba
#400, 317 Donald St., Winnipeg MB R3B 2H6
Tel: 204-985-4700; *Fax:* 204-947-5644
URL: www.creditunion.mb.ca
Overview: A small provincial organization
Chief Officer(s): Garth Manness, CEO; John Hamilton, Manager

Credit Union Central of New Brunswick (CUCNB)
663 Pinewood Rd., Riverview NB E1B 5R6
Tel: 506-857-8184; *Fax:* 506-857-9431
Toll-Free: 800-332-3320
e-mail: gerard.adams@cucnb.nb.ca
URL: www.creditunion.nb.ca
Overview: A small provincial organization
Chief Officer(s): Gerard Adams CA, CEO; Tony Baker, President
Staff: 10 staff member(s)
Membership: 25 credit unions
Description: To provide financial, administrative, & development services to the province's credit union movement; to respond to the needs of our members, to represent & promote their interests

Credit Union Central of Newfoundland & Labrador *See* Newfoundland & Labrador Credit Union

Credit Union Central of Nova Scotia
PO Box 9200, 6074 Lady Hammond Rd., Halifax NS B3K 5N3
Tel: 902-453-0680; *Fax:* 902-455-2437
e-mail: info@ns-credit-unions.com
URL: www.ns-credit-unions.com
Overview: A small provincial organization
Chief Officer(s): Bernie O'Neil, President/CEO; Larry Hansen, Manager; David MacLean, Chair

Credit Union Central of Ontario
2810 Matheson Blvd. East, Mississauga ON L4W 4X7
Tel: 905-238-9400; *Fax:* 905-238-8691
Toll-Free: 800-661-6813
e-mail: central@cuco.on.ca
URL: www.cuco.on.ca
Also Known As: Ontario Central
Previous Name: Ontario Credit Union League Ltd.
Overview: A medium-sized provincial organization
Chief Officer(s): Howard Bogach, President & CEO; Sherri Armstrong, Communications Manager
Staff: 130 staff member(s)
Membership: 185 credit unions
Activities: *Internships:* Yes
Publications: Spectrum, Newsletter, bi-m., accepts advertising
Description: To lead & enable the growth & evolution of the credit union system in Ontario; *Member of:* Credit Union Central of Canada

Credit Union Central of Prince Edward Island
PO Box 968, 281 University Ave., Charlottetown PE C1A 7M4
Tel: 902-566-3350; *Fax:* 902-368-3534
e-mail: dturner@cucpei.creditu.net
URL: www.peicreditunions.com
Overview: A medium-sized provincial organization founded in 1936
Chief Officer(s): Gerard T. Dougan, CEO
Finances: *Annual Operating Budget:* $500,000-$1.5 Million
Staff: 10 staff member(s); 11 volunteer(s)
Membership: 1-99
Description: Financial co-operative dedicated to the growth, development & financial stability of Prince Edward Island credit unions

ASSOCIATIONS

Credit Union Central of Saskatchewan
PO Box 3030, 2055 Albert St., Regina SK S4P 3G8
Tel: 306-566-1200; *Fax:* 306-566-1372
e-mail: communications@cucs.com
URL: www.saskcu.com
Also Known As: SaskCentral
Overview: A small provincial organization
Chief Officer(s): Sid Bildfell, CEO; Ian Monteith, Media Contact
Staff: 250 staff member(s)
Membership: 130 credit unions
Activities: Management & consulting services; research & development; monitoring of trends & issues in the financial industry; participation in national organizations
Description: To strengthen relationships & to broaden the range of financial choices available to credit union members & communities

Edmonton CFA Society
Standard Life Centre, PO Box 479, #21, 10405 Jasper Ave., Edmonton AB T5J 3N4
Toll-Free: 866-494-3732
e-mail: info@edmontoncfa.ca
URL: www.membersocieties.org/edmonton/
Also Known As: Edmonton Society of Financial Analysts
Overview: A small local charitable organization founded in 1976
Chief Officer(s): Gabriela Revak, Contact
Finances: *Annual Operating Budget:* $100,000-$250,000
Staff: 8 volunteer(s)
Membership: 100-499; *Member Profile:* CFA holders; investment counselors; pension fund managers; corporate treasury & stockbrokers
Activities: *Speaker Service:* Yes; *Rents Mailing List:* Yes
Publications: CFA, Newsletter, m.
Description: To promote ethical & professional standards within the investment industry; to encourage professional development through the CFA Program; & to facilitate the open exchange of information & opinions

Edmonton Insurance Association (EIA)
#200, 17920 - 100 Ave., Edmonton AB T5S 2H5
Tel: 780-448-0645; *Fax:* 780-448-0877
e-mail: treasurer@edmontoninsuranceassociation.com
URL: www.edmontoninsuranceassociation.com
Previous Name: Insurance Women of Edmonton
Overview: A small local organization
Chief Officer(s): Roxsel Watts, Treasurer
Finances: *Annual Operating Budget:* Less than $50,000
Staff: 8 volunteer(s)
Membership: 50; *Fees:* $50
Description: Non-profit, voluntary association dedicated to promoting education, fellowship and loyalty; *Member of:* Canadian Association of Insurance Women

Efile Agents & Tax Preparers Association of Canada *See* EFILE Association of Canada

EFILE Association of Canada (EAC) / Association de TED du Canada
#200, 1124 Fort St., Victoria BC V8V 3K8
Tel: 250-384-4066; *Fax:* 250-382-0413
Toll-Free: 866-384-4066
e-mail: eacatc@islandnet.com
URL: www.efile.ca
Previous Name: Efile Agents & Tax Preparers Association of Canada
Overview: A medium-sized national organization founded in 1993
Chief Officer(s): Bruce Campbell, Executive Director
Finances: *Annual Operating Budget:* Less than $50,000
Staff: 1 staff member(s)
Membership: 850; *Fees:* $90; *Member Profile:* Prepares tax returns for a fee
Publications: Impact, Newsletter, s-a.
Description: To communicate the wishes & concerns of members to C.R.A. & M.R.Q., & to request remediation; to promote, both to the public & to government, the electronic filing of personal & corporate tax returns & related information; to encourage proficiency in our members, & to assure the public of the integrity of members; to provide members with information & resources

Family Counselling & Support Services (Guelph-Wellington) (FCSS)
109 Surrey St. East, Guelph ON N1H 3P7
Tel: 519-824-2431; *Fax:* 519-824-3598
Toll-Free: 800-307-7078
e-mail: info@familyserviceguelph.on.ca
URL: www.familyserviceguelph.on.ca
Previous Name: Guelph-Wellington Counselling Centre
Overview: A large regional organization founded in 1987
Chief Officer(s): Jack Watkins, Executive Director; Suzanne Longpre, President
Finances: *Annual Operating Budget:* $500,000-$1.5 Million; *Funding Sources:* Provincial government; United Way; fees, grants & contracts
Staff: 25 staff member(s); 20 volunteer(s)
Activities: *Internships:* Yes; *Library:* Yes (Open to Public) by appointment
Description: To support, strengthen & enrich individuals, couples & families in Guelph & Wellington county; to provide dependable & consistent service to a broad range of clients; organized into clinical unit, credit & debt counselling unit, family mediation, developmental services unit, & employee assistance program; *Member of:* Family Service Canada; Family Service Ontario; Ontario Association of Credit Counselling Services

Family Counselling Centre of Brant Inc.
28 Brant Ave., Brantford ON N3T 3G6
Tel: 519-753-4173; *Fax:* 519-753-9287
e-mail: ccs@familycounsellingcentrebrant.com
Previous Name: Family Service Bureau of Brantford & Brant County, Inc.
Overview: A small regional organization founded in 1914
Finances: *Annual Operating Budget:* $500,000-$1.5 Million
Activities: *Speaker Service:* Yes
Publications: Update, Newsletter, 3 pa
Description: To offer professional services to individuals & families in times of need; to facilitate community awareness of issues & information pertinent to individual & family functioning; *Member of:* Ontario Association of Credit Counselling Services

Family Counselling Centre of Cornwall & United Counties / Centre de counselling familial de Cornwall et Comtés unis
26 Montreal Rd., Cornwall ON K6H 1B1
Tel: 613-932-1266; *Fax:* 613-932-5765
e-mail: fccadmin@familycounsellingcentre.ca
Overview: A small local organization founded in 1967
Chief Officer(s): Raymond Houde, Executive Director; William Roddy, President
Finances: *Annual Operating Budget:* $500,000-$1.5 Million
Staff: 8 staff member(s)
Description: Non-profit community based agency providing counselling services to individuals, couples & families to address their concerns through their own strengths & resources; *Member of:* Family Service Ontario; Ontario Association of Credit Counselling Services

Family Service Bureau of Brantford & Brant County, Inc. *See* Family Counselling Centre of Brant Inc.

Family Services Thunder Bay
544 Winnipeg Ave., Thunder Bay ON P7B 3S7
Tel: 807-684-1880; *Fax:* 807-344-3782
Toll-Free: 888-204-2221
e-mail: support@fstb.net
URL: www.fstb.net
Overview: A medium-sized local charitable organization founded in 1967
Chief Officer(s): N. Chamberlain, Executive Director
Finances: *Annual Operating Budget:* $500,000-$1.5 Million; *Funding Sources:* Private; public
Staff: 25 staff member(s); 50 volunteer(s)
Activities: Alcohol & Other Drugs Assessment Program; Credit Counselling Program; Family, Couple & Individual Counselling; Victims of Family Violence Program; Employee Assistance Programs; *Internships:* Yes; *Speaker Service:* Yes
Publications: Solution Source, Newsletter, q., Editor: Colleen Einter, ISSN: 1481-2568, Contents: Solutions to life problems; thematic
Description: Committed to actively participating in the continuum of human services within the district of Thunder Bay; to strengthen & support individuals, couples, families & community through counselling, education & advocacy; *Member of:* Family Service Canada; Family Service Ontario; Ontario Association of Credit Couselling Services

Federal Superannuates National Association (FSNA) / Association nationale des retraités fédéraux
1052 St. Laurent Blvd., Ottawa ON K1K 3B4
Tel: 613-745-2559; *Fax:* 613-745-5457
e-mail: webmaster@fsna.com
URL: www.fsna.com
Overview: A large national organization founded in 1963
Chief Officer(s): Dennis Jackson, National President; Jean-Guy Soulière, Executive Director
Finances: *Annual Operating Budget:* $1.5 Million-$3 Million; *Funding Sources:* Membership fees
Staff: 14 staff member(s); 500 volunteer(s)
Membership: 140,000; *Fees:* $30-40.20; *Member Profile:* Retired federal employees, retired Canadian Forces, retired RCMP & their spouses; *Committees:* Executive; Finance; Membership; Official Languages
Publications: On Guard/En Garde, Newsletter, q., Editor: Francoise Gauthier
Description: To advocate measures beneficial to annuitants & potential annuitants of the Public Service of Canada, the Canadian Forces, the Royal Canadian Mounted Police & other Federal Agencies or bodies deemed appropriate by the Board of Directors

Federation of Canadian Independent Deposit Brokers (FCIDB)
#408-2, 49 High St., Barrie ON L4N 5J4
Tel: 705-730-7599; *Fax:* 705-730-0477
URL: www.fcidb.com
Overview: A large national organization founded in 1987
Chief Officer(s): Mary Rygiel, Vice-President; David J. Newman, President; Clementine A. Peacock, Executive Coordinator
Finances: *Annual Operating Budget:* Less than $50,000
Staff: 1 staff member(s); 12 volunteer(s)
Membership: 116; *Fees:* $100 affiliate; $275 associate/provisional; $550 regular; $750 fi; *Member Profile:* 27 major financial institutions
Description: To represent interests of deposit clients & independent deposit brokers

Federation of Law Societies of Canada / Fédération des ordres professionnels de juristes du Canada
#480, 445, boul Saint-Laurent, Montréal QC H2Y 2Y7
Tel: 514-875-1829; *Fax:* 514-875-6115
e-mail: info@flsc.ca
URL: www.flsc.ca
Overview: A medium-sized national organization founded in 1972
Chief Officer(s): Malcolm Heins, CEO; George D. Hunter, President
Finances: *Annual Operating Budget:* $500,000-$1.5 Million
Staff: 2 staff member(s)
Membership: 14 organizations; *Fees:* Membership assessement based on per capita
Activities: Regulates Canada's 88,500 lawyers & Québec's 3,500 notaries in public interest
Member of: American Bar Association; Union internationale des avocats

Les femmes sur les marchés financiers *See* Women in Capital Markets

Financial Executives Institute Canada *See* Financial Executives International Canada

Financial Executives International Canada (FEIC)
#200, 20 Adelaide St. East, Toronto ON M5C 2T6
Tel: 416-366-3007; *Fax:* 416-366-3008
e-mail: feicanada@feicanada.org
URL: www.fei.org/canada
Also Known As: FEI Canada
Previous Name: Financial Executives Institute Canada
Overview: A medium-sized national organization founded in 1931
Chief Officer(s): Isabel Meharry, President & CEO
Finances: *Annual Operating Budget:* $500,000-$1.5 Million
Staff: 100 volunteer(s)
Membership: 1,700 in 11 chapters; *Fees:* $525; *Member Profile:* Senior financial officers of medium to large organizations; *Committees:* Corporate Reporting; Issues, Policy & Advocacy; Emerging Business Issues
Activities: Networking; communications; personal & professional development; advocacy
Awards: Canada's Chief Financial Officer of the Year
Publications: FE Magazine, Magazine, 10+ pa, Editor: Jeffrey Marshall, ISBN: 0895-4186, accepts advertising, Contents: Independent forum for authoritative views on the problems of business & financial management, Price: $59 USD; FEI Canada Xpress, Magazine, m.
Description: To enhance the professional skills of financial executives; to address national issues affecting the business environment

ASSOCIATIONS

Financial Management Institute of Canada / Institut de la gestion financière
PO Box 613, Stn. B, Ottawa ON K1P 5P7
Tel: 613-569-1158; *Fax:* 613-569-4532
e-mail: national@fmi.ca
URL: www.fmi.ca
Overview: A medium-sized national organization founded in 1962
Chief Officer(s): Joanne Steadman, Administrator; Jean Laporte, President; Derwin Banks, Secretary
Staff: 12 staff member(s)
Membership: 2,000 in 12 chapters; *Member Profile:* Professionals with an interest in sound public sector financial management; from all levels of government, the academic world & private sector firms which serve governments
Publications: FMI Journal, 3 pa, Editor: Bryn Weadon

Financial Markets Association of Canada (FMAC) / Association des marchés financiers du Canada
#301, 250 Consumers Rd., Toronto ON M2J 4V6
Tel: 416-773-0584; *Fax:* 416-495-8723
e-mail: fmac@fmac.ca
URL: www.fmac.ca
Overview: A medium-sized national organization
Chief Officer(s): Evan Steed, President; Gerard Buckley, Secretary
Finances: *Annual Operating Budget:* $50,000-$100,000
Staff: 10 volunteer(s)
Membership: 200; *Fees:* $150
Publications: Newsletter, q.
Description: Industry professionals dealing in foreign exchange, money markets, derivatives, & capital markets; Affiliation(s): Association Cambiste Internationale (ACI)

Financial Planners Standards Council (FPSC) / Conseil relatif aux standards des planificateurs financiers
#1600, 505 University Ave., Toronto ON M5G 1X3
Tel: 416-593-8587; *Fax:* 416-593-6903
Toll-Free: 800-305-9886
e-mail: inform@cfp-ca.org
URL: www.cfp-ca.org
Overview: A medium-sized national licensing organization founded in 1995
Chief Officer(s): Cary List CA, CFP, Acting President & CEO; Peter Volpe CFP, Chair
Staff: 17 staff member(s)
Membership: 15,000-49,999; *Member Profile:* Canadian Institute of Financial Planning; Credit Union Institute of Canada; Canadian Institute of Chartered Accountants; Certified General Accountants Association of Canada; Society of Management Accountants of Canada; The Financial Advisors Association of Canada
Activities: *Speaker Service:* Yes
Publications: CFP Report, Newsletter, q., Editor: Blake Glendenning, Contents: For licensees only
Description: FPSC works to benefit & protect the public by establishing & enforcing uniform standards of education, experience, examination & ethics for Canadians who earn the internationally recognized Certified Financial Planner (CFP) credential

Financial Planning Association (FPA)
#400, 4100 E. Mississippi Ave., Denver CO 80246-3053 USA
Fax: 303-759-0749
Toll-Free: 800-322-4237
URL: www.fpanet.org
Overview: A medium-sized international organization founded in 1969
Chief Officer(s): Marvin W. Tuttle, Jr. CAE, Executive Director & CEO
Finances: *Annual Operating Budget:* Greater than $5 Million
Staff: 72 staff member(s)
Membership: 17,300; *Fees:* $285 USD
Publications: Planning Matters, Newsletter, m.; Journal of Financial Planning, Newsletter, m., Editor: Maurren Peck, accepts advertising, Contents: Articles for & about financial planning & planners
Description: Offers services & resources designed to help the public understand the importance of the financial planning process & the value of objective advice from a CFP professional

Financial Services Commission of Ontario (FSCO)
PO Box 85, 5160 Yonge St., 17th Fl., Toronto ON M2N 6L9
Tel: 416-250-7250; *Fax:* 416-590-7070
Toll-Free: 800-668-0128
e-mail: contactcentre@fsco.gov.on.ca
URL: www.fsco.gov.on.ca
Previous Name: Canadian Council of Insurance Regulators
Overview: A small provincial organization founded in 1998
Chief Officer(s): Bob Christie, CEO/Superintendent
Membership: 13 individual
Activities: *Internships:* Yes; *Library:* Yes
Description: To enhance consumer confidence & public trust in the regulated sectors; to make recommendations to the minister on matters affecting the regulated sectors

Fiscal & Financial Planning Association *See* Association de planification fiscale et financière

Fondation d'éducation économique *See* Canadian Foundation for Economic Education

Fondation de recherche de l'Institut canadien des valeurs mobilières *See* Canadian Securities Institute Research Foundation

Fonds canadien de protection des épargnants *See* Canadian Investor Protection Fund

Forum conjoint des autorités de réglementation du marché financier *See* Joint Forum of Financial Market Regulators

Fédération des caisses Desjardins du Québec (FCDQ)
100, av des Commandeurs, Lévis QC G6V 7N5
Tél: 418-835-8444; *Téléc:* 418-833-4769
Ligne sans frais: 866-866-7000
URL: www.desjardins.com
Nom précédent: Fédération des caisses populaires Desjardins du Québec
Aperçu: *Dimension:* grande; *Envergure: nationale*
Membre(s) du bureau directeur: Bertrand Laferrière, Président/Chef de l'exploitation
Finances: *Budget de fonctionnement annuel:* Plus de $5 Million
Personnel: 2886 membre(s) du personnel
Membre: 500-999
Activités: Institution financière coopérative
Publications: Mes Finances - Ma Caisse, Revue, 5 fois par an, Editor: Micheline Piché, ISSN: 1491-5707, accepts advertising, Price: 6.50$; Partenaires, Revue, 3 fois par an, accepts advertising, Price: 4$; Desjardins Entreprises, Revue, 3 fois par an, Editor: Pierre Goulet, ISSN: 1481-4838, accepts advertising, Price: 6.45$
Description: Est l'entité coopérative responsable de l'orientation, de la coordination et du développement au sein du Mouvement Desjardins; fournit à ses caisses membres divers services dont certains d'ordre technique, financier et administratif; a la responsabilité de l'inspection et de la vérification des caisses ainsi que la conception et développement des systèmes réseaux

Abitibi-Témiscamingue - Nord du Québec
532, 7e rue ouest, Amos QC J9T 3W7
Ligne sans frais: 866-313-8324
Membre(s) du bureau directeur: Richard Lacroix, Vice-président régional

Bas St-Laurent
CP 2000, 681, boul St-Germain ouest, Rimouski QC G5L 7E5
Ligne sans frais: 866-723-4794
Membre(s) du bureau directeur: Richard Dufour, Vice-président régional

Centre du Québec
CP 1000, 2000, boul des Récollets, Trois-Rivières QC G9A 5K3
Tél: 819-374-3594; *Téléc:* 819-374-2486
Membre(s) du bureau directeur: Jacques Dubé, Directeur régional

Côte-Nord
7, Av Marquette 2e étage, Baie-Comeau QC G4Z 1K4
Ligne sans frais: 800-670-8630
Membre(s) du bureau directeur: Jean-Luc Dasté, Vice-président régional

Est de Montréal
#590, 7450, boul les Galeries d'Anjou, Montréal QC H1M 3M3
Ligne sans frais: 800-711-5100
Membre(s) du bureau directeur: Lionel Gauvin, Vice-président régional

Estrie
325, boul Jacques-Cartier sud, Sherbrooke QC J1J 2Z6
Ligne sans frais: 800-567-6110
Membre(s) du bureau directeur: Michel Vachon, Vice-président régional
Activités: *Bibliothèque:* Oui

Gaspésie/Iles-de-la-Madeleine
CP 250, 473, boul Perron, Maria QC G0C 1Y0
Ligne sans frais: 800-463-0625
Membre(s) du bureau directeur: Michel Roussy, Vice-président régional

Kamouraska-Chaudière-Appalaches
#201, 950, rue de la Concorde, Saint-Romuald QC G6W 8A8
Ligne sans frais: 866-835-844
Membre(s) du bureau directeur: Tom Lemieux, Vice-président régional

Lanaudière
CP 500, 275, rue Beaudry nord, Joliette QC J6E 6A7
Ligne sans frais: 800-363-1717
Membre(s) du bureau directeur: Jean Beaudoin, Vice-président régional

Laval-Laurentides
#1310, 2550, boul D.-Johnson, Laval QC H7T 2L1
Ligne sans frais: 800-650-4781
Membre(s) du bureau directeur: Éric Lachaine, Vice-président régional

Mauricie
2000, boul des Récollets, Trois-Rivières QC G9A 5K3
Membre(s) du bureau directeur: Michel Dorais, Vice-président régional

Montréal - Caisses des groupes
7755, boul Louis H. Lafontaine, Montréal QC H1K 4M6
Ligne sans frais: 800-350-4967
Membre(s) du bureau directeur: Serge Dufresne, Premier vice-président; Claude Demers, Directeur conseil régional

Ouest de Montréal
#450, 3333, Côte-Vertu, 4e étage, Montréal QC H4R 2N1
Ligne sans frais: 877-634-6888
Membre(s) du bureau directeur: Denis Dubreuil, Vice-président régional

Ouest du Québec
#107, 420, boul Maloney est, Gatineau QC J8P 1E7
Ligne sans frais: 800-263-8814
Membre(s) du bureau directeur: René Lapointe, Vice-président régional

Québec-Ouest - Rive-Sud
#201, 950, rue de la Concorde, Saint-Romuald QC G6W 8A8
Ligne sans frais: 866-835-8444
Membre(s) du bureau directeur: Raynald Roy, Vice-président régional

Québec-est
#201, 950, rue de la Concorde, Saint-Romuald QC G6W 8A8
Ligne sans frais: 866-835-8444
Membre(s) du bureau directeur: Richard Ferland, Vice-président régional

Richelieu/Yamaska
2175, rue Girouard ouest, Saint-Hyacinthe QC J2S 3A9
Ligne sans frais: 800-363-1003
Membre(s) du bureau directeur: Denis Lafrenière, Vice-président régional

Rive-Sud de Montréal
#300, 1850, rue Panama, Brossard QC J4W 3C6
Ligne sans frais: 800-366-1786
Membre(s) du bureau directeur: Jean-Yves Bédard, Vice-président régional

Saguenay/Lac-Saint-Jean/Charlevoix
50, rue des Roses, Métabetchouan-Lac-a-la-Croix QC G8G 1R6
Ligne sans frais: 800-667-6032
Membre(s) du bureau directeur: Martin Voyer, Vice-président régional

Fédération des caisses populaires Desjardins du Québec *See* Fédération des caisses Desjardins du Québec

Fédération des caisses populaires du Manitoba
185 Provencher Blvd., Winnipeg MB R2H 0G4
Tél: 204-237-8874; *Téléc:* 204-233-5383
Courriel: saintboniface@caisse.biz
URL: www.caissepop.mb.ca
Aperçu: *Dimension:* grande; *Envergure: provinciale; fondée en 1952*
Personnel: 22 membre(s) du personnel; 9 bénévole(s)
Membre: 15,000-49,999; *Critères d'admissibilité/Description:* Résidant ou entreprise du Manitoba
Description: Contribuer à l'essor économique et socio-culturel des manitobains en poursuivant le développement des services et du réseau financiers dont les avoirs sont gérés, administrés et contrôlés par des francophones; Affiliation(s): Mouvement Desjardins

Fédération des contribuables canadiens *See* Canadian Taxpayers Federation

Fédération des ordres professionnels de juristes du Canada *See* Federation of Law Societies of Canada

GAMA International Canada / GAMA International du Canada

350 Bloor St. East, 2nd Fl., Toronto ON M4W 3W8
Tel: 416-444-6291; *Fax:* 416-444-8031
Toll-Free: 866-525-5004
e-mail: info@gamacanada.com
URL: www.gamacanada.com
Previous Name: Managers Association of Financial Advisors of Canada
Overview: A medium-sized national organization founded in 1974
Chief Officer(s): Julianne C. Leith, President
Finances: *Annual Operating Budget:* $250,000-$500,000; *Funding Sources:* Membership dues; corporate sponsorship
Staff: 1 staff member(s)
Membership: 400+; *Fees:* $360; *Member Profile:* Leaders in distribution management in financial services; individuals in activities related to financial services with an interest in management; companies that wish to be sponsors or supporters
Publications: Newsletter, q.; GAMA International, bi-m.
Description: To focus on professional development for leaders involved in the distribution of financial services

GAMA International du Canada *See* GAMA International Canada

General Insurance OmbudService (GIO) / Service de conciliation en assurance de dommages

#701, 10 Milner Business Ct., Toronto ON M1B 3C6
Tel: 416-299-6931; *Fax:* 416-299-4261
Toll-Free: 877-225-0446
e-mail: info@gio-scad.org
URL: www.gio-scad.org
Overview: A medium-sized national organization founded in 2002
Chief Officer(s): Glenn Williamson, Executive Director
Staff: 5 staff member(s)
Description: To assist in resolving differences between home, car & business insurance companies & their customers

The Geneva Association

53 Route de Malagnou, Geneva CH-1208 Switzerland
Tel: 41-22-707-6600; *Fax:* 41-22-736-7536
e-mail: secretariat@genevaassociation.org
URL: www.genevaassociation.org
Also Known As: International Association for the Study of Insurance Economics
Overview: A small international organization
Chief Officer(s): Patrick M. Liedtke, Secretary General & Managing Direct
Membership: 80; *Member Profile:* CEOs of the most important insurance companies in Europe, North America, South America, Asia, Africa & Australia
Description: To research the growing economic importance of world-wide insurance activities in the major sectors of the economy

Groupement des assureurs automobiles (GAA)

#600, 500, rue Sherbrooke ouest, Montréal QC H3A 3C6
Tél: 514-288-6015
Ligne sans frais: 800-361-5131
Courriel: cinfo@gaa.qc.ca
URL: www.gaa.qc.ca
Aperçu: *Dimension:* moyenne; *Envergure: provinciale; fondée en 1978*
Membre(s) du bureau directeur: Brigitte Corbeil, Directeur général
Finances: *Budget de fonctionnement annuel:* $1.5 Million-$3 Million
Personnel: 46 membre(s) du personnel
Membre: 139; *Critères d'admissibilité/Description:* Regroupe tous les assureurs privés autorisés à pratiquer l'assurance automobile au Québec; *Comités:* Assurance Automobile; Finances; Sinistres Automobiles; Statistique Automobile
Activités: *Service de conférenciers:* Oui; *Bibliothèque:* Centre de documentation (Bibliothèque publique)
Publications: Contact Info, Bulletin, mensuel
Description: Administrer, de façon efficace et selon les décisions du conseil d'administration, tous les mandats certifiés au Groupement des assureurs automobiles par la Loi sur l'assurance automobile du Québec; *Membre de:* Chambre de commerce du Québec

Guelph-Wellington Counselling Centre *See* Family Counselling & Support Services (Guelph-Wellington)

Guild of Industrial, Commercial & Institutional Accountants / Guilde des comptables industriels, commerciaux et institutionnels

36 Tandian Ct., Woodbridge ON L4L 8Z9
e-mail: iciaguild@aol.net
URL: www.guildoficia.ca
Also Known As: Guild of ICIA
Overview: A medium-sized national organization founded in 1961
Chief Officer(s): Sara Van Hamme FICIA, President; Dr. Phil Russo FICIA, CGA, Registrar
Finances: *Annual Operating Budget:* Less than $50,000; *Funding Sources:* Membership fees
Staff: 3 staff member(s)
Membership: 500; *Fees:* $125; *Member Profile:* Business accountants, financial managers, taxation specialists, accounting executives; *Committees:* Accrediting; Annual Meeting; Membership
Publications: Guild of ICIA Journal, q., Editor: Phil Rosso, accepts advertising, Contents: Guild's future focus; membership notes; new member listing; tax talks
Description: To promote & support interest in vocational accountancy; to encourage acceptance of modern methods & procedures

Guilde des comptables industriels, commerciaux et institutionnels *See* Guild of Industrial, Commercial & Institutional Accountants

Halton Consumer Credit Counselling Service

PO Box 69523, 235 Lakeshore Rd. East, Oakville ON L6J 7R4
Tel: 905-845-3811; *Fax:* 905-842-1462
e-mail: info@haltonfamilyservices.org
Overview: A small local organization founded in 1975
Chief Officer(s): Nancy J. Brown, Executive Director; Janice Josiak, Councillor; Patty McLean, Councillor
Finances: *Annual Operating Budget:* $100,000-$250,000
Staff: 3 staff member(s)
Affiliation(s): Ontario Association of Family Service Agencies

Hamilton Insurance Women's Association

c/o ING Insurance Company of Canada, #400, 6733 Mississauga Rd., Mississauga ON L5N 6J5
Tel: 905-858-1070; *Fax:* 905-858-2772
Toll-Free: 800-268-4567
Overview: A small local organization
Chief Officer(s): Sandi White, President
Member of: Canadian Association of Insurance Women

Hedge Fund Association Canada

c/o HFA, #900, 2875 NE 191st St., Aventura FL 33180
Tel: 202-478-2000; *Fax:* 202-478-1999
e-mail: info@thehfa.org
URL: www.thehfa.org
Overview: A small national organization founded in 1996
Chief Officer(s): David R. Friedland, President
Member of: International Hedge Fund Association

Independent Financial Brokers of Canada (IFB) / Courtiers indépendants en sécurité financière du Canada

#200, 4284 Village Centre Ct., Mississauga ON L4Z 1S2
Tel: 905-279-2727; *Fax:* 905-276-7295
Toll-Free: 888-654-3333
e-mail: general@ifbc.ca
URL: www.ifbc.ca
Previous Name: Independent Life Insurance Brokers of Canada
Overview: A small national organization founded in 1985
Chief Officer(s): Merlin Chouinard, President; John Whaley, Executive Director; Al Donald, Sec.-Treas.
Finances: *Annual Operating Budget:* $500,000-$1.5 Million; *Funding Sources:* Membership fees; conference registration
Staff: 7 staff member(s); 18 volunteer(s)
Membership: 4,000; *Fees:* $175; *Member Profile:* Independent insurance, mutual fund & other financial service brokers & professionals; *Committees:* Executive; Nominating; Education
Activities: Frequent Educational Summits
Publications: The Independent, Newsletter, q., accepts advertising
Description: To enhance & protect businesses of members; to support consumer choice

Independent Insurance Brokers Association of Alberta (IIBAA)

#1000, 10109 - 106 St., Edmonton AB T5J 3L7
Tel: 780-424-3320; *Fax:* 780-424-7418
Toll-Free: 800-318-0197
e-mail: iibaa@iibaa.com
URL: www.iibaa.com
Overview: A medium-sized provincial organization founded in 1925
Chief Officer(s): Harold Baker, Executive Director; Lorne Rye FCIP, President
Staff: 9 staff member(s)
Membership: 300+
Publications: Alberta Broker, Magazine, bi-m.
Description: To provide members with resources to enhance growth & success

Independent Life Insurance Brokers of Canada *See* Independent Financial Brokers of Canada

Institut canadien de relations avec les investisseurs *See* Canadian Investor Relations Institute

Institut canadien des actuaires *See* Canadian Institute of Actuaries

Institut canadien des comptables agréés *See* Canadian Institute of Chartered Accountants

Institut canadien des courtiers et des prêteurs hypothécaires *See* Canadian Institute of Mortgage Brokers & Lenders

L'Institut canadien des experts en évaluation d'entreprises *See* Canadian Institute of Chartered Business Valuators

Institut canadien des valeurs mobilières *See* The Canadian Securities Institute

L'Institut canadien du crédit *See* Credit Institute of Canada

Institut d'arbitrage et de médiation du Canada *See* ADR Institute of Canada

L'Institut d'assurance de dommages du Québec (IADQ)

#2230, 1200, av McGill College, Montréal QC H3B 4G7
Tél: 514-393-8156; *Téléc:* 514-393-9222
Courriel: iadqmontreal@iadq.qc.ca
URL: www.iadq.qc.ca
Nom précédent: L'Institut d'assurance du Québec
Aperçu: *Dimension:* moyenne; *Envergure: provinciale; Organisme sans but lucratif; fondée en 1927*
Membre(s) du bureau directeur: Lucien Bergeron FPAA, Directeur général
Finances: *Budget de fonctionnement annuel:* $500,000-$1.5 Million
Personnel: 6 membre(s) du personnel
Membre: 6 000; *Montant de la cotisation:* 55$
Activités: Formation professionnelles en assurance de dommages; *Service de conférenciers:* Oui
Publications: L'Informa, Bulletin, 5 fois par an, accepts advertising
Description: Organiser des cours, des séminaires et des conférences; promouvoir le rayonnement des titres professionnels PAA et FPAA d'assurance du Canada (AIAC & FIAC). Organisme sans but lucratif, qui a été mis sur pied par l'industrie de l'assurance de dommages pour donner la formation professionnelle à tous ceux qui oeuvrent dans ce secteur au Québec

Institut d'assurance du Canada *See* Insurance Institute of Canada

L'Institut d'assurance du Québec *See* L'Institut d'assurance de dommages du Québec

Institut de la gestion financière *See* Financial Management Institute of Canada

Institut de médiation et d'arbitrage du Québec (IMAQ)

CP 5455, Succ. B, Montréal QC H3B 4P1
Tél: 514-282-3327; *Téléc:* 514-282-2214
Courriel: info@imaq.org
URL: www.imaq.org
Aperçu: *Dimension:* petite; *Envergure: provinciale; fondée en 1977*
Membre(s) du bureau directeur: Jacques Fortin, Président; Denis F. Gauthier, Vice-président

ASSOCIATIONS

Description: Promouvoir les méthodes alternatives de résolution de conflits (médiation, arbitrage); donner accès par internet à la population et aux entreprises à une banque de médiateurs et d'arbitres accrédités selon leur: spécialité (médiateur ou arbitre), région, langue de communication, catégorie de membre, profession, domaine d'expertise

Institut de prévention des sinistres catastrophiques *See* Institute for Catastrophic Loss Reduction

Institut des banquiers canadiens *See* Institute of Canadian Bankers

Institut des comptables agrées de l'Ontario *See* Institute of Chartered Accountants of Ontario

Institut des comptables agréés du Nouveau-Brunswick *See* New Brunswick Institute of Chartered Accountants

L'Institut des fonds d'investissement du Canada *See* Investment Funds Institute of Canada

Institut québécois de planification financière (IQPF)

#420, 4, place du Commerce, Montréal QC H3E 1J4
Tél: 514-767-4040; *Téléc:* 514-767-2845
Ligne sans frais: 800-640-4050
Courriel: info@iqpf.org
URL: www.iqpf.org
Aperçu: *Dimension:* petite; *Envergure: provinciale; Organisme sans but lucratif; fondée en 1989*
Membre(s) du bureau directeur: André Buteau AVA, Pl.Fin, Président; Jocelyne Houle-LeSarge FCGA, Directrice générale
Finances: *Budget de fonctionnement annuel:* $1.5 Million-$3 Million
Personnel: 18 membre(s) du personnel
Membre: 1 000; *Montant de la cotisation:* 260$; cotisation volontaire; *Critères d'admissibilité/Description:* Planificateur financier; *Comités:* Comité de vérification; Comité pédagogique; Comité des communications et services aux membres
Activités: Formation professionnelle des planificateurs financiers du Québec
Publications: La Cible, Revue, 5 fois par an
Description: Contribuer à la protection et au mieux-être économique des consommateurs québécois, en veillant sur la formation et la qualification des professionnels regroupés en un réseau de planificateurs financiers solidaires d'une approche intégrée de la planification financière

Institute for Catastrophic Loss Reduction (ICLR) / Institut de prévention des sinistres catastrophiques

#210, 20 Richmond St. East, Toronto ON M5C 2R9
Tel: 416-364-8677; *Fax:* 416-364-5889
e-mail: info@iclr.org
URL: www.iclr.org
Overview: A small national licensing organization founded in 1998
Chief Officer(s): Paul Kovacs, Executive Director
Finances: *Annual Operating Budget:* $250,000-$500,000
Membership: 50; *Fees:* $2,000 associate; *Member Profile:* Organizations interested in disaster prevention
Activities: Protecting Kids from Disaster Program; Safety Upgrades for Child Care Centres; *Speaker Service:* Yes
Meetings: 2007; Building Resilient Communities Annual Conference, Nov., Toronto, ON Canada
Description: Reduce the loss of life & property caused by severe weather & earthquakes through the identification & support of sustained actions that improve society's capacity to adapt to, anticipate, mitigate, withstand & recover from natural disasters

London Office
1389 Western Rd., London ON N6A 5B9
Tel: 519-661-3234; *Fax:* 519-661-4273

Institute of Canadian Bankers (ICB) / Institut des banquiers canadiens

Tour Scotia, #1000, 1002, rue Sherbrooke ouest, Montréal QC H3A 3M5
Tel: 514-282-9480; *Fax:* 514-878-4260
Toll-Free: 800-361-7339
e-mail: info@icb.org
URL: www.icb.org
Overview: A medium-sized national organization founded in 1967
Chief Officer(s): Marie Muldowney, Executive Director, ICB
Finances: *Annual Operating Budget:* Greater than $5 Million
Staff: 75 staff member(s)
Membership: 1-99
Activities: Treasury & Risk Management Program; Personal Advisory Services Studies; Corporate/Commercial Services Studies; Management Studies: Financial Services; Skills Development Programs; also administers The Trust Institute; *Library:* Yes (Open to Public)
Publications: Exchange, q.
Description: To be the premier provider of education & training addressing the needs of the financial community

Ontario Regional Office
#1500, 4 King St. West, Toronto ON M5H 1B6
Tel: 416-304-1828; *Fax:* 416-304-1835

Institute of Chartered Accountants of Alberta

Manulife Place, #580, 10180 - 101 St., Edmonton AB T5J 4R2
Tel: 780-424-7391; *Fax:* 780-425-8766
Toll-Free: 800-232-9406
e-mail: info@icaa.ab.ca
URL: www.icaa.ab.ca
Overview: A medium-sized provincial organization
Chief Officer(s): Jane Halford FCA, CEO & Executive Director; Ross Harris FCA, President
Finances: *Annual Operating Budget:* Greater than $5 Million
Membership: 5,000-14,999
Publications: CA Monthly Statement, Newsletter
Description: To serve the public trust by upholding CA regulations & code of ethics; to provide continuous professional development to Alberta's nearly 9,500 CAs & CA students

Institute of Chartered Accountants of British Columbia (ICABC)

One Bentall Centre, #500, 505 Burrard St., Box 22, Vancouver BC V7X 1M4
Tel: 604-681-3264; *Fax:* 604-681-1523
Toll-Free: 800-663-2677
e-mail: rees@ica.bc.ca
URL: www.ica.bc.ca
Overview: A large provincial licensing organization founded in 1905
Chief Officer(s): Richard Rees FCA, CEO; Sandy Parcher, Manager
Finances: *Annual Operating Budget:* Greater than $5 Million; *Funding Sources:* Membership dues
Staff: 37 staff member(s); 400 volunteer(s)
Membership: 8,400; *Fees:* $495; *Member Profile:* 30-month service term & successful completion of national uniform final exam (UFE)
Activities: *Speaker Service:* Yes
Publications: Beyond Numbers, Magazine, 10 pa, Editor: Michelle MacRae, accepts advertising
Description: To protect & serve the public, our members & students by providing exceptional education, regulation & member services programs so that chartered accountants may provide the highest quality of professional services; Affiliation(s): All provincial CA institutes in Canada & Bermuda

Institute of Chartered Accountants of Manitoba (ICAM)

#500, 161 Portage Ave. East, Winnipeg MB R3B 0Y4
Tel: 204-942-8248; *Fax:* 204-943-7119
Toll-Free: 888-942-8248
e-mail: icam@icam.mb.ca
URL: www.icam.mb.ca
Also Known As: Chartered Accountants of Manitoba
Overview: A medium-sized provincial licensing organization founded in 1886
Chief Officer(s): Gary Hannaford FCA, CEO; Dianne Laidler CMA, Director of Administration
Finances: *Funding Sources:* Membership dues; practitioner & user fees
Staff: 9 staff member(s)
Membership: 2,700; 300 students
Activities: Practice advisory; professional development; employment services; CA assistance
Publications: Folio; MB Check-Up
Description: To continue to be the leading professional accounting organization in Manitoba; to protect the public interest; to provide exceptional services & programs which members value

Institute of Chartered Accountants of Newfoundland (ICAN)

PO Box 21130, 95 Bonaventure Ave., St. John's NL A1A 5B2
Tel: 709-753-7566; *Fax:* 709-753-3609
e-mail: kharnum@ican.nfld.net
URL: www.ican.nfld.net
Also Known As: CA Newfoundland
Overview: A medium-sized provincial organization founded in 1949
Chief Officer(s): Karen Harnum, Executive Assistant
Staff: 2 staff member(s); 150 volunteer(s)
Membership: 576
Activities: *Library:* Yes by appointment
Publications: ICAN News, Newsletter, 3 pa, accepts advertising
Description: To serve the interests of society & the membership by providing leadership to uphold the professional integrity, standards & preeminence of Newfoundland & Labrador's Chartered Accountants

Institute of Chartered Accountants of Nova Scotia (ICANS)

#1101, 1791 Barrington St., Halifax NS B3J 3L1
Tel: 902-425-3291; *Fax:* 902-423-4505
e-mail: icans@icans.ns.ca
URL: www.icans.ns.ca
Overview: A medium-sized provincial licensing organization founded in 1900
Chief Officer(s): Gordon D. Moore CA, President; Donald M. Flinn, Vice-President
Finances: *Annual Operating Budget:* $500,000-$1.5 Million
Staff: 6 staff member(s)
Membership: 1,000-4,999
Publications: E-Scan, Newsletter, m.; Practitioner's View, Newsletter, q.
Description: To protect & serve the public & our members by providing exceptional services & resources within a well regulated profession

Institute of Chartered Accountants of Ontario (ICAO) / Institut des comptables agrées de l'Ontario

69 Bloor St. East, Toronto ON M4W 1B3
Tel: 416-962-1841; *Fax:* 416-962-8900
Toll-Free: 800-387-0735
e-mail: custserv@icao.on.ca
URL: www.icao.on.ca
Overview: A medium-sized provincial licensing organization founded in 1879
Chief Officer(s): Brian A. Hunt FCA, President & CEO; Tom Warner, Vice-President & Registrar; Peter Varley, Vice-President
Finances: *Annual Operating Budget:* Greater than $5 Million; *Funding Sources:* Membership fees; CA education & professional development programs
Staff: 96 staff member(s); 400 volunteer(s)
Membership: 31,743 chartered accountants + 3,500 CA; *Member Profile:* CA designation
Activities: CA Golf Day for Children's Charities
Awards: Award of Outstanding Merit
Publications: CheckMark, Newsletter, q., accepts advertising
Description: Ensures that chartered accountants are the recognized leading business professionals, who add credibility to information; *Member of:* Ontario Chamber of Commerce; Metro Toronto Board of Trade

Institute of Chartered Accountants of Prince Edward Island

PO Box 301, Charlottetown PE C1A 7K7
Tel: 902-894-4290; *Fax:* 902-894-4791
URL: www.icapei.com
Overview: A medium-sized provincial licensing organization founded in 1921
Chief Officer(s): Albert M. Ferris FCA, Executive Director; Terry Soloman CA, President
Finances: *Annual Operating Budget:* $100,000-$250,000
Membership: 100-499
Activities: *Internships:* Yes

Institute of Chartered Accountants of Saskatchewan

#830, 1801 Hamilton St., Regina SK S4P 4B4
Tel: 306-359-1010; *Fax:* 306-569-8288
Toll-Free: 800-268-3793
e-mail: inst.ca@icas.sk.ca
URL: www.icas.sk.ca
Overview: A medium-sized provincial licensing organization
Chief Officer(s): Nola Dianne Joorisity CMA, FCA, CEO
Membership: 1,600
Publications: Horizons, Newsletter, q.

Institute of Chartered Accountants of the Northwest Territories & Nunavut (ICANWT)

c/o Indian & Northern Affairs Canada, PO Box 2433, Yellowknife NT X1A 2P8
Tel: 867-873-3680; *Fax:* 867-920-4135
URL: www.icanwt.nt.ca

Overview: A small provincial organization
Chief Officer(s): Mike Huvenaars CA, President
Staff: 7 volunteer(s)

Insurance Agents Association of Manitoba *See* Insurance Brokers Association of Manitoba

Insurance Brokers Association of British Columbia (IBABC)
#1300, 1095 West Pender St., Vancouver BC V6E 2M6
Tel: 604-606-8000; *Fax:* 604-683-7831
URL: www.ibabc.org
Overview: A small provincial organization founded in 1920
Chief Officer(s): Charles (Chuck) Byrne CIP, Executive Director; Trudy Lancelyn, Deputy Executive Director
Finances: *Annual Operating Budget:* $500,000-$1.5 Million
Staff: 12 staff member(s)
Membership: 750 corporate; *Committees:* ICBC; IBC; BIP; Membership Services
Activities: Licensing courses; continuing education
Publications: BC Broker, Magazine, bi-m., Editor: Trudy Lancelyn, ISSN: 0841-7660, accepts advertising, Contents: Information of interest to property/casualty insurance agents in BC, Price: $35
Description: To promote the member insurance broker as the premiere distributor of general insurance products & services in British Columbia

Insurance Brokers Association of Manitoba (IBAM)
#205, 530 Kenaston Blvd., Winnipeg MB R3N 1Z4
Tel: 204-488-1857; *Fax:* 204-489-0316
Toll-Free: 800-204-5649
e-mail: info@ibam.mb.ca
URL: www.ibam.mb.ca
Previous Name: Insurance Agents Association of Manitoba
Overview: A medium-sized provincial organization founded in 1951
Chief Officer(s): Irwin Kumka CRM, President
Finances: *Funding Sources:* Membership dues
Staff: 4 staff member(s)
Membership: 1,200; *Member Profile:* Independent property & casualty insurance brokers in Manitoba
Publications: The Manitoba Broker, Magazine, q.
Description: To promote insurance brokers as the primary providers of insurance products & services in Manitoba

Insurance Brokers Association of New Brunswick (IBANB) / Association des courtiers d'assurances du Nouveau-Brunswick
#3, 590 Brunswick St., Fredericton NB E3B 5G2
Tel: 506-450-2898; *Fax:* 506-450-1494
e-mail: ibanb@ibanb.org
URL: www.ibanb.org
Overview: A small provincial organization
Chief Officer(s): Linda M. Dawe FIIC, CAIB, CEO; Danny Harrigan, President
Finances: *Annual Operating Budget:* $100,000-$250,000
Staff: 3 staff member(s); 12 volunteer(s)
Membership: 80
Publications: The Atlantic Insurance Broker, Newsletter, q., accepts advertising
Description: Championing the professional, independent insurance broker system in New Brunswick

Insurance Brokers Association of Newfoundland (IBAN)
Chimo Bldg., PO Box 275, 151 Crosbie Rd., Level 3, Mount Pearl NL A1N 2C3
Tel: 709-726-4450; *Fax:* 709-754-4399
e-mail: iban@nfld.net
URL: www.iban.ca
Overview: A small regional organization
Chief Officer(s): Carol Hedd CIP, Administrative Assistant
Staff: 1 staff member(s); 15 volunteer(s)
Membership: 772
Description: Association of insurance brokers in Newfoundland. Insurance brokers work on clients behalf to secure the best coverage in the market from federally regulated insurance companies

Insurance Brokers Association of Nova Scotia (IBANS)
2 Lakeside Park Dr., #9C, Halifax NS B3T 1L7
Tel: 902-876-0526; *Fax:* 902-876-0527
e-mail: info@ibans.com
URL: www.ibans.com
Overview: A small provincial organization founded in 1949
Chief Officer(s): Stephen Greene, Executive Director
Staff: 3 staff member(s); 12 volunteer(s)
Membership: 800+; *Member Profile:* Independent property & casualty insurance brokers in Nova Scotia; *Committees:* Public Affairs/Liaison; Professional Development; Member Services; Technology
Publications: Atlantic Broker, Magazine
Description: To promote the independent insurance broker as the premiere distribution vehicle of property & casualty insurance products & other related insurance services in Nova Scotia

Insurance Brokers Association of Ontario (IBAO)
90 Eglinton Ave. East, 2nd Fl., Toronto ON M4P 2Y3
Tel: 416-488-7422; *Fax:* 416-488-7526
Toll-Free: 800-268-8845
e-mail: contact@ibao.com
URL: www.ibao.org
Overview: A medium-sized provincial organization founded in 1920
Chief Officer(s): Randy Carroll, COO
Finances: *Annual Operating Budget:* $1.5 Million-$3 Million
Staff: 11 staff member(s)
Membership: 707 institutional members; 8,700 individ; *Member Profile:* Registered insurance brokers
Publications: IBAO News, Newsletter, m.
Description: To preserve & enhance the value & integrity of the independent broker insurance distribution system & to be recognized as an invaluable resource to & by member brokers

Insurance Brokers Association of Prince Edward Island
c/o Hyndman & Co. Limited, 57 Queen St., Charlottetown PE C1A 4B1
Tel: 902-566-4244; *Fax:* 902-368-2936
e-mail: hyndmaninsurance@anchorgroup.com
Overview: A small provincial organization

Insurance Brokers Association of Saskatchewan (IBAS)
#310, 2631 - 28 Ave., Regina SK S4S 6X3
Tel: 306-525-5900; *Fax:* 306-569-3018
e-mail: IBASinfo@ibas.sk.ca
URL: www.ibas.sk.ca
Overview: A medium-sized provincial organization
Chief Officer(s): Ernie Gaschler, Executive Director
Staff: 5 staff member(s); 14 volunteer(s)
Membership: 380; *Member Profile:* Independent insurance brokerages
Activities: Information; licensing courses & education programs
Publications: IBAS Newsletter, q.; Saskatchewan Insurance Directory, a.
Description: To promote & preserve the independent insurance brokerage system as a secure, knowledgeable, cost-effective, customer-oriented, professional method of insurance delivery; *Member of:* Insurance Brokers Association of Canada

Insurance Brokers' Association of Québec - Assembly *See* Regroupement des cabinets de courtage d'assurance du Québec

Insurance Bureau of Canada (IBC) / Bureau d'assurance du Canada
#1900, 151 Yonge St., Toronto ON M5C 2W7
Tel: 416-362-2031; *Fax:* 416-361-5952
Toll-Free: 800-387-2880
e-mail: consumercentre@ibc.ca
URL: www.ibc.ca
Previous Name: Insurance Council of Canada
Overview: A medium-sized national organization founded in 1964
Chief Officer(s): Stan Griffin, President & CEO; Igal Mayer, Chair
Membership: 200
Activities: *Speaker Service:* Yes; *Library:* Yes (Open to Public) by appointment
Publications: Facts of the General Insurance Industry in Canada, a.; Perspective, q., Price: Free to selected audience; Financial Affairs, q.; Regulatory Affairs, q.
Description: To foster a healthy property & casualty insurance marketplace & strenghten the ability of our members to serve the needs of Canada's insurance consumers; to advocate public policies that foster a healthy insurance marketplace; to facilitate communication, seek consensus & when in a unique position to do so, undertake industry solutions to common insurance industry concerns

Atlantic Canada Office
#1706, 1969 Upper Water St., Halifax NS B3J 3B7
Tel: 902-429-2730; *Fax:* 902-420-0157
Toll-Free: 800-565-7189
Chief Officer(s): Don Forgeron, Regional Vice-President

British Columbia & Yukon Office
#1010, 510 Burrard St., Vancouver BC V6C 3A8
Tel: 604-684-3635; *Fax:* 604-684-6235
Toll-Free: 877-772-3777
Chief Officer(s): Lindsay Olson, Regional Vice-President

Insurance Information Division
Atria II, #1100, 2235 Sheppard Ave. East, Atria II, Toronto ON M2J 5B5
Tel: 416-445-5912; *Fax:* 416-449-9357
Toll-Free: 800-761-6703
Also Known As: Insurance Information Centre of Canada
Chief Officer(s): Terri MacLean, Executive Vice-President

Member of: Canadian Council of Motor Transport Administrators; Society of Automotive Engineers; American Statistical Association

Ontario Office
#1900, 151 Yonge St., Toronto ON M5C 2W7
Tel: 416-362-2031; *Fax:* 416-644-4961
Toll-Free: 800-387-2880
Chief Officer(s): Mark Yakabuski, Vice-President

Ottawa Office
#808, 155 Queen St., Ottawa ON K1P 6L1
Tel: 613-236-5043; *Fax:* 613-236-5208
Chief Officer(s): Mark Yakabuski, Vice-President

Prairies, Northwest Territories & Nunavut
#401, 10722 - 103 Ave., Edmonton AB T5J 5G6
Tel: 780-423-2212; *Fax:* 780-423-4796
Toll-Free: 800-377-6378
Chief Officer(s): Jim Rivait, Regional Vice-President

Québec Office
Tour de la Bourse, CP 336, #2410, 800, Place-Victoria, Montréal QC H4Z 0A2
Tél: 514-288-1563; *Téléc:* 514-288-0753
Ligne sans frais: 877-288-4321
Membre(s) du bureau directeur: Brigitte Corbeil, Directrice générale

Insurance Council of British Columbia
Box 7, #300, 1040 West Georgia St., Vancouver BC V6E 4H1
Tel: 604-688-0321; *Fax:* 604-662-7767
Toll-Free: 877-688-0321
URL: www.insurancecouncilofbc.com
Overview: A medium-sized provincial licensing organization founded in 1930
Chief Officer(s): Gerald Matier, Executive Director
Finances: *Annual Operating Budget:* $1.5 Million-$3 Million
Staff: 27 staff member(s)
Description: Has the authority to license insurance agents, salespersons, and adjusters, and to investigate and discipline licensees. The Council is accountable to the provincial government and reports to the Minister of Finance

Insurance Council of Canada *See* Insurance Bureau of Canada

Insurance Council of Manitoba (ICM)
#466, 167 Lombard Ave., Winnipeg MB R3B 0T6
Tel: 204-988-6800; *Fax:* 204-988-6801
e-mail: contactus@icm.mb.ca
URL: www.icm.mb.ca
Overview: A small provincial licensing organization founded in 1992
Chief Officer(s): Lois Broder, General Manager
Staff: 6 staff member(s)
Membership: 5,000-14,999
Description: The Council's role is to administer the regulatory legislation governing insurance agents/brokers operating in Manitoba

Insurance Councils of Saskatchewan
#310, 2631 - 28 Ave., Regina SK S4S 6X3
Tel: 306-347-0862; *Fax:* 306-569-3018
URL: www.skcouncil.sk.ca
Also Known As: General Insurance Council of Sakatchewan; Life Insurance Council of Saskatchewan, Hail Insurance Council of Saskatchewan
Overview: A small provincial licensing organization founded in 1986
Chief Officer(s): Ernie Gaschler, Administrator
Membership: 5,000-14,999
Publications: Bulletin, s-a.

Insurance Institute of British Columbia (IIBC)
#410, 800 Pender St. West, Vancouver BC V6C 2V6
Tel: 604-681-5491; *Fax:* 604-681-5479
Toll-Free: 888-681-5491
e-mail: genmail@iibc.org
URL: www.iibc.org
Overview: A medium-sized provincial organization
Chief Officer(s): Danielle Bolduc, General Manager; John Dickinson, President
Staff: 3 staff member(s)
Membership: 3,012
Publications: Newsletter, 3 pa

Insurance Institute of Canada (IIC) / Institut d'assurance du Canada
18 King St. East, 6th Fl., Toronto ON M5C 1C4
Tel: 416-362-8586; *Fax:* 416-362-4239
e-mail: genmail@iic-iac.org
URL: www.iic-iac.org
Overview: A large national licensing organization founded in 1952
Chief Officer(s): Peter G. Hohman MBA, FCIP, CAE, President & CEO
Finances: *Annual Operating Budget:* Greater than $5 Million; *Funding Sources:* Fees for services & voluntary corporate subscriptions
Staff: 28 staff member(s); 100 volunteer(s)
Membership: 150 corporate + 11,000 FCIPs & CIPs + 6,; *Fees:* $50; $95 CIP Society; *Member Profile:* Employed in property/casualty insurance industry; *Committees:* Academic Council; Professionals' Council; Executive
Activities: Offers education programs through local institutes (Chartered Insurance Professionals Program - CIP) & through participating Canadian universities, including the University of Toronto, School of Continuing Studies (Fellowship Program - FCIP), parent organization of the Chartered Insurance Professional Society; *Internships:* Yes; *Speaker Service:* Yes; *Library:* Yes
Publications: I.Q., Newsletter, q.; Pulse, Newsletter, s-a.; Exam Statistics, Newsletter, a.; Eduquorum, Newsletter, a.
Description: To design, develop & deliver insurance educational programs & texts; to prepare examinations & award diplomas; to provide a graduate society; to develop career information on behalf of the property/casualty insurance industry; *Member of:* Institute for Global Insurance Education; Affiliation(s): Insurance Institute of America; Chartered Insurance Institute; Australian Insurance Institute; Insurance Institute of India; Insurance Institute of Malaysia

Insurance Institute of Manitoba (IIM)
#533, 167 Lombard Ave., Winnipeg MB R3B 0V3
Tel: 204-956-1702; *Fax:* 204-956-0758
e-mail: iimmail@insuranceinstitute.ca
URL: www.insuranceinstitute.ca
Overview: A medium-sized provincial organization founded in 1923
Chief Officer(s): Keith Phillips, President; Erin Lubinski, Manager
Finances: *Annual Operating Budget:* $100,000-$250,000; *Funding Sources:* Evening classes; seminars
Staff: 2 staff member(s)
Membership: 1,033; *Fees:* $35
Publications: Insurance Omnibus, Newsletter, 3 pa

Insurance Institute of New Brunswick (IINB)
25 Hedgewood Dr., Moncton NB E1E 2W4
Tel: 506-386-5896; *Fax:* 506-386-1130
e-mail: IINBmail@insuranceinstitute.ca
Overview: A medium-sized provincial organization founded in 1952
Chief Officer(s): Darrel Coates CIP, President; Gillianne King, Manager
Membership: 500-999

Insurance Institute of Newfoundland Inc. (IIN)
117 Ropewalk St., 3rd Fl., St. John's NL A1E 4P1
Tel: 709-754-4398; *Fax:* 709-754-4399
e-mail: iin@nfld.com
Overview: A medium-sized provincial organization founded in 1956
Chief Officer(s): Darrell Swain, President
Finances: *Annual Operating Budget:* $50,000-$100,000
Staff: 1 staff member(s); 5 volunteer(s)
Membership: 400
Activities: *Speaker Service:* Yes; *Library:* Yes

Insurance Institute of Northern Alberta (IINA)
Oxford Tower, #1104, 10235 - 101 St., Edmonton AB T5J 3G1
Tel: 780-424-1268; *Fax:* 780-420-1940
e-mail: iinamail@insuranceinstitute.ca
URL: www.iina.ca
Overview: A medium-sized local charitable organization
Chief Officer(s): Cheryl Lee, Manager
Finances: *Annual Operating Budget:* $100,000-$250,000
Staff: 2 staff member(s); 12 volunteer(s)
Membership: 2,300; *Fees:* $50; *Committees:* Education; Seminars; Operations; CIP Society
Activities: Seminars; fundraising; social events
Publications: e-Newsletter, m.
Description: The function of the Insurance Institute of Northern Alberta is to provide and to carry out the principal aim of the Insurance Institute of Canada, i.e. establish and maintain a uniform standard of education for the general Insurance Business throughout Canada; Affiliation(s): CIP Society of Canada

Insurance Institute of Nova Scotia (IINS)
c/o A.P. Reid Insurance, #250, 100 Main St., Dartmouth NS B2X 1R5
Tel: 902-829-2326; *Fax:* 902-829-3061
e-mail: ins.inst@ns.sympatico.ca
Overview: A medium-sized provincial organization founded in 1953
Chief Officer(s): Jennifer Simpson, General Manager
Finances: *Annual Operating Budget:* $100,000-$250,000
Staff: 9 volunteer(s)
Membership: 1,200; *Fees:* $50
Publications: Atlantic Update, Newsletter, q.

Insurance Institute of Ontario (IIO)
18 King St. East, 16th Fl., Toronto ON M5C 1C4
Tel: 416-362-8586; *Fax:* 416-362-8081
Toll-Free: 866-362-8585
e-mail: iiomail@insuranceinstitute.ca
URL: www.insuranceinstitute.ca
Overview: A medium-sized provincial organization founded in 1899
Chief Officer(s): Paul Feron CIP, President; Peter Hohman MBA, FCIP, ICD.D, General Manager; Kathryn Bettridge CIP, CRM, Manager
Finances: *Funding Sources:* Membership dues; fees for services
Staff: 14 staff member(s); 100 volunteer(s)
Membership: 16,116; 9,047 GTA; *Fees:* $65; *Committees:* Seminars; Communication; Special Events; Faculty; Library
Activities: *Speaker Service:* Yes; *Library:* Yes (Open to Public)
Publications: In Ontario, Newsletter, q., ISSN: 0848-1342
Description: To deliver insurance education programs to the membership, & to supplement them with other educational programs; to promote careers & graduates; to maintain a reference library; to organize appropriate social functions for the membership

Insurance Institute of Prince Edward Island (IIPEI)
51 University Ave., Charlottetown PE C1A 4K8
Tel: 902-892-1692; *Fax:* 902-368-7305
e-mail: iipeimail@insuranceinstitute.ca
Overview: A small provincial organization founded in 1960
Chief Officer(s): Duffy Bill CIP, President
Finances: *Funding Sources:* Membership fees; seminar fees
Membership: 100-499; *Fees:* $25
Activities: Courses; seminars

Insurance Institute of Saskatchewan (IIS)
#310, 2631 - 28 Ave., Regina SK S4S 6X3
Tel: 306-525-5900; *Fax:* 306-569-3018
Toll-Free: 800-733-0933
e-mail: iis@ibas.sk.ca
URL: www.ibas.sk.ca
Overview: A medium-sized provincial organization
Chief Officer(s): Ernie Gaschler, Executive Director; Michael Van Dorpe, President
Finances: *Annual Operating Budget:* $50,000-$100,000
Staff: 4 staff member(s); 10 volunteer(s)
Membership: 840
Publications: Newsletter, q.

Insurance Institute of Southern Alberta (IISA)
#1110, 833 - 4 Ave. SW, Calgary AB T2P 3T5
Tel: 403-266-3427; *Fax:* 403-269-3199
e-mail: ksager@insuranceinstitute.ca
URL: www.iisalberta.org
Overview: A medium-sized regional organization founded in 1954
Chief Officer(s): Janis Losie, General Manager; Leah Strader-Goled FCIP, President
Finances: *Annual Operating Budget:* $100,000-$250,000; *Funding Sources:* Membership dues; industry
Staff: 2 staff member(s)
Membership: 3,540; *Fees:* $50; *Committees:* Education; Professional; Seminars; Newsletter
Description: To advance the efficiency, expertise & ability of people employed in the insurance & financial services business

Insurance Professionals of Calgary
Bankers Hall, PO Box 22297, Calgary AB T2P 4J1
Tel: 403-663-2807; *Fax:* 403-263-1839
e-mail: info@ipcalgary.ca
URL: www.ipcalgary.ca
Previous Name: Calgary Insurance Women
Overview: A small local organization
Chief Officer(s): Tara Lynn Talsma, President; Marlene Dickson, 1st Vice-President; Keira McDonagh, 2nd Vice-President
Description: Association of individuals employed in the insurance industry or related service providers; *Member of:* Canadian Association of Insurance Women

Insurance Women of Edmonton *See* Edmonton Insurance Association

Insurance Women's Association of Manitoba *See* Manitoba Association of Insurance Professionals

Insurance Women's Association of Western Manitoba
PO Box 325, Wawanesa MB R0K 2G0
Tel: 204-824-6237; *Fax:* 204-824-2140
e-mail: jchalanchuk@wawanesa.com
URL: www.caiw-acfa.com/iwawm/
Overview: A medium-sized regional organization founded in 1988
Chief Officer(s): Joyce Chalanchuk, President
Finances: *Annual Operating Budget:* Less than $50,000
Staff: 30 volunteer(s)
Membership: 30; *Fees:* $45 individual; *Member Profile:* Those employed in the insurance industry
Activities: Monthly meeetings; seminars; golf tournament, Aug.; Wine & Cheese, April; *Awareness Events:* Insurance Information Week
Publications: Prairie Press, Newsletter, m., Editor: Cindy Cassils, accepts advertising
Description: To encourage & foster education programs for members; to foster & cultivate good fellowship & loyalty among members; to make members more responsive to requirements of the Canadian insurance industry as a whole; Affiliation(s): Canadian Association of Insurance Women

Interac Association / L'Association Interac
PO Box 109, #1905, 121 King St. West, Toronto ON M5H 3T9
Tel: 416-362-8550
e-mail: info@interac.org
URL: www.interac.org
Overview: A medium-sized national organization founded in 1984
Chief Officer(s): Tina Romano, Manager
Membership: 115 organizations; *Member Profile:* Banks; trust companies; credit unions; caisses populaires; technology & payment related companies
Activities: Responsible for the development of a national network of two shared electronic financial services: Shared Cash Dispensing Service at automated banking machines, & Interac Direct Payment Services, a national debit service
Description: To keep Interac services a well used, trusted & reliable method for electronic commerce in Canada

Interamerican Association of Securities Commissions & Similar Agencies *See* International Organization of Securities Commissions

International Federation of Accountants (IFAC)
545 Fifth Ave., 14th Fl., New York NY 10017 USA
Tel: 212-286-9344; *Fax:* 212-286-9570
e-mail: stphenwalker@ifac.org
URL: www.ifac.org
Overview: A medium-sized international organization founded in 1977
Chief Officer(s): Ferm¡n del Valle, President; Stephen Walker, Contact

Staff: 12 staff member(s)
Membership: 155; *Member Profile:* National accountancy bodies; *Committees:* International Auditing Practices; Ethics; Education; Public Sector; Financial & Management Accounting; Information Technology; Membership; Task Forces
Activities: Task Forces: Anti-Corruption; GATS; Legal Liability; Quality Assurance; Small & Medium Enterprise; Structure & Organization
Publications: IFAC News & Views, Newsletter; IFAC Quarterly, Newsletter
Description: Worldwide development & enhancement of an accountancy profession with harmonized standards, able to provide services of consistently high quality in the public interest; Affiliation(s): Canadian Institute of Chartered Accountants; Certified General Accountants Association of Canada; Society of Management Accountants of Canada

International Finance Club of Montréal *See* Cercle de la finance internationale de Montréal

International Financial Centre - Montréal (IFC) / Le Centre Financier International - Montréal
404, rue St-Dizier, Montréal QC H2Y 3T3
Tel: 514-287-1540; *Fax:* 514-287-1694
e-mail: info@cfimontreal.com
URL: www.cfimontreal.com
Also Known As: CFI Montréal
Overview: A small local organization founded in 1986
Chief Officer(s): Jacques Girard, CEO
Staff: 5 staff member(s)
Description: To facilitate the establishment, development & preservation in the Montréal City region of companies specializing in international financial transactions

International Fiscal Association
PO Box 1570, Kingston ON K7L 5C8
Tel: 613-531-8292; *Fax:* 613-531-0626
e-mail: office@ifacanada.org
URL: www.ifacanada.org
Also Known As: IFA Canada
Overview: A small national organization
Chief Officer(s): Elizabeth Hooper, Administrative Director
Membership: 850; *Fees:* $135 + GST
Description: To study & advance international & comparative law in regard to public finance, specifically international & comparative fiscal law & the financial & economic aspects of taxation; Affiliation(s): International Fiscal Association

International Organization of Securities Commissions (IOSCO) / Organisation internationale des commissions de valeurs
C/Oquendo 12, Madrid 28006 Spain
Tel: 34-91-417-55-49; *Fax:* 34-91-555-93-68
e-mail: mail@oicv.iosco.org
URL: www.iosco.org
Previous Name: Interamerican Association of Securities Commissions & Similar Agencies
Overview: A large international organization founded in 1983
Chief Officer(s): Philippe Richard, Secretary General
Finances: *Annual Operating Budget:* $500,000-$1.5 Million; *Funding Sources:* Membership dues
Staff: 8 staff member(s)
Membership: 180; *Fees:* 8.300 euro; *Member Profile:* Ordinary - securities commission or similar governmental agency, self-regulatory organization when there is no governmental regulatory agency; Associate - association that assembles the public regulatory bodies having jurisdiction in subdivisions of a country, when the national regulatory body is already a member or any other regulatory body, with exception of a self-regulatory body, recommended by the Executive Committee; Affiliate - international organization with universal or regional scope or organization recommended by the Executive Committee & recommended self-regulatory organizations; *Committees:* Executive; Technical Committee on International Transactions; Emerging Markets; Consultative (Self-Regulatory Organizations); Interamerican Regional; European Regional; Asia-Pacific Regional; Africa-Middle East Regional
Activities: On-the-job training program; IOSCO Educational Program
Publications: Annual Report
Description: To cooperate together to ensure a better regulation of the markets, on both the domestic & international level, in order to maintain just & efficient securities markets; to exchange information in order to promote development of domestic markets; to unite efforts to establish standards & effective surveillance of international securities transactions; to provide mutual assistance to ensure the integrity of the markets by rigorous application of standards & by effective enforcement against offences

Investment Counsel Association of Canada (ICAC) / Association des conseillers en gestion de portefeuille du Canada
#1602, 110 Yonge St., Toronto ON M5C 1T4
Tel: 416-504-1118; *Fax:* 416-504-1117
e-mail: icacinfo@investmentcounsel.org
URL: www.investmentcounsel.org
Overview: A medium-sized provincial organization founded in 1952
Chief Officer(s): F. Gwyer Moore, President; Cheryl Matthews, Administrator
Finances: *Annual Operating Budget:* $100,000-$250,000; *Funding Sources:* Membership fees
Staff: 2 staff member(s); 14 volunteer(s)
Membership: 64 firms; *Fees:* Scale based on assets managed; *Member Profile:* Registration as Investment Counsel &/or portfolio manager, 70% minimum of total income from investment management fees; securities underwriting firm or securities dealer affiliation subject to certain conditions; *Committees:* Industry Regulations; Tax; Member Services; Public Relations
Activities: *Speaker Service:* Yes; *Rents Mailing List:* Yes
Publications: Member Letter, s-a.
Description: To advocate the highest standards of portfolio management in the interest of investors served by members

Investment Dealers Association of Canada (IDA) / Association canadienne des courtiers en valeurs mobilières
#1600, 121 King St. West, Toronto ON M5H 3T9
Tel: 416-364-6133; *Fax:* 416-364-0753
e-mail: publicaffairs@ida.ca
URL: www.ida.ca
Overview: A large national licensing organization founded in 1916
Chief Officer(s): Joseph J. Oliver, President & CEO; Ronald Lloyd, Chair
Finances: *Funding Sources:* Membership fees
Staff: 235 staff member(s)
Membership: 190 firms; *Fees:* Based on revenue & capital formula; *Member Profile:* Registered investment dealers who meet the terms of IDA by-law #2; *Committees:* Audit; Capital Markets; Chair's Consultative Council; Corporate Finance; Discount Brokers; Executive; Financial Administrators Section; National Advisory; Nominating; Pension; Regional Dealers; Retail Sales; Futures; Equity Trading; Executive
Publications: IDA Report, q.; Provincial Economic Outlooks, a.; Quarterly Review of Equity New Issues & Trading; Economic Indicator Card, 3 pa; Higher-Yielding Debt Issuance; Securities Industry Performance, q.; Bulletins; Trends in Secondary Debt Trading; Securities Industry & Capital Markets Developments
Description: To protect investors & enhance the efficiency & competitiveness of the Canadian capital markets; *Member of:* International Organization of Securities Commissions; International Councils of Securities Associations

Calgary Office
#2300, 355 - 4 Ave. SW, Calgary AB T2P 0J1
Tel: 403-262-6393; *Fax:* 403-265-4603
e-mail: prairie@ida.ca

Halifax Office
TD Centre, #1620, 1791 Barrington St., Halifax NS B3J 3K9
Tel: 902-423-8800; *Fax:* 902-423-0629
e-mail: atlantic@ida.ca

Montréal Office
#2802, 1, Place Ville-Marie, Montréal QC H3B 4R4
Tél: 514-878-2854; *Téléc:* 514-878-3860
Courriel: quebec@ida.ca

Vancouver Office
PO Box 11614, #1325, 650 West Georgia St., Vancouver BC V6B 4N9
Tel: 604-683-6222; *Fax:* 604-683-3491
e-mail: pacific@ida.ca

Investment Funds Institute of Canada (IFIC) / L'Institut des fonds d'investissement du Canada
11 King St. West, 4th Fl., Toronto ON M5H 4C7
Tel: 416-363-2150; *Fax:* 416-861-9937
Toll-Free: 866-347-1961
URL: www.ific.ca
Previous Name: Canadian Mutual Fund Association
Overview: A medium-sized national organization founded in 1962
Chief Officer(s): Joanne De Laurentiis, President/CEO; Brenda Vince, Chair
Finances: *Annual Operating Budget:* Greater than $5 Million; *Funding Sources:* Membership dues
Staff: 30 staff member(s)
Membership: 175 organizations; *Fees:* Schedule available; *Member Profile:* Mutual fund companies; retail distributors & affiliate members
Activities: Representation & advocacy; member services; investor education; *Library:* Yes (Open to Public)
Publications: Industry Guidelines; Annual Report
Description: To preserve & enhance the integrity of our industry; to ensure the continuing confidence of the millions of Canadians who own mutual funds; to advance the mutual fund industry

Bureau au Québec
#1800, 1010, rue Sherbrooke ouest, Montréal QC H3A 2R7
Tel: 514-985-7025; *Fax:* 514-985-5113

Investment Industry Association of Canada (IIAC)
#1600, 11 King St. West, Toronto ON M5H 4C7
Tel: 416-364-2754; *Fax:* 416-364-4861
e-mail: publicaffairs@iiac.ca
URL: www.iiac.ca
Overview: A small national organization founded in 2006
Chief Officer(s): William Hatanaka, Chair

Investment Property Owners Association of Nova Scotia Ltd. (IPOANS)
#603, 5121 Sackville St., Halifax NS B3J 1K1
Tel: 902-425-3572; *Fax:* 902-422-0700
e-mail: association@ipoans.ns.ca
URL: www.ipoans.ns.ca
Overview: A medium-sized provincial organization founded in 1979
Chief Officer(s): Rex Maclaine, Executive Director
Finances: *Annual Operating Budget:* $50,000-$100,000; *Funding Sources:* Membership fees; education
Staff: 2 staff member(s)
Membership: 400; *Fees:* $300; *Member Profile:* Must own or operate rental/commercial property; *Committees:* Education; Legislative; Membership; Public Relations
Activities: Lobbying; legislative task forces; Certified Management Program discounts; property management advice; *Speaker Service:* Yes; *Rents Mailing List:* Yes
Publications: The Property Reporter, Newsletter, bi-m., accepts advertising
Description: To protect, enhance & contribute to the ability of rental housing owners & operators to profit from their investments; to provide educational programs for members; to serve as an information centre; *Member of:* Canadian Society of Association Executives; Canadian Federation of Apartment Associations; Affiliation(s): National Apartment Association

Investor Learning Centre of Canada *See* Canadian Securities Institute Research Foundation

Investors Association of Canada (IAC)
#2103, 1 King St. West, Toronto ON M5H 1A1
e-mail: contact@iac.ca
URL: www.iac.ca
Overview: A medium-sized national organization founded in 1986
Chief Officer(s): Chuck Chakrapani, Chair
Staff: 1 staff member(s)
Membership: 4,000 individual
Activities: *Internships:* Yes; *Speaker Service:* Yes; *Rents Mailing List:* Yes
Publications: Money Digest, Online Newsletter, m.

Joint Forum of Financial Market Regulators / Forum conjoint des autorités de réglementation du marché financier
c/o Joint Forum, 5160 Yonge St., 17th Fl., Box 85, Toronto ON M2N 6L9
Tel: 416-226-7773; *Fax:* 416-590-7070
e-mail: capsa-acor@fsco.gov.on.ca
URL: www.jointforum.ca/JF-WWWSite/index.htm
Overview: A small national organization founded in 1999
Chief Officer(s): Robert Gates, Contact
Activities: National coordination of securities, insurance & pension regulators
Description: Established as a mechanism through which pension, securities and insurance regulators could co-ordinate, harmonize and streamline the regulation of financial products and services in Canada

ASSOCIATIONS

K3C Community Counselling Centres
417 Bagot St., Kingston ON K7K 3C1
Tel: 613-549-7850; *Fax:* 613-544-8138
e-mail: kccc@k3c.org
URL: www.k3c.org
Previous Name: Kingston Community Counselling Centre
Overview: A medium-sized regional organization
Member of: Ontario Association of Credit Counselling Services
Brockville Credit Counselling
438 Laurier Blvd., Brockville ON K6V 7J6
Fax: 613-544-8138
Toll-Free: 800-379-5556
Credit Counselling Service of Eastern Ontario
#209, 1300 Carling Ave., Ottawa ON K1Z 7L2
Tel: 613-728-2041; *Fax:* 613-722-5609
Toll-Free: 866-202-0425
e-mail: ccseo@k3c.org
Chief Officer(s): David I. Thompson, Executive Director
Staff: 7 staff member(s)
Member of: Ontario Association of Credit Counselling Services
Quinte Region Credit Counselling Service
237B Coleman St., Belleville ON K8P 3H8
Tel: 613-966-3556; *Fax:* 613-966-6092
e-mail: grccs@k3c.org

Kingston Community Counselling Centre ***See*** K3C Community Counselling Centres

Life Underwriters Association of Canada ***See*** Advocis

London Insurance Professionals Association
c/o Preferred Insurance Group, 217 Wharncliffe Rd. South, London ON N6J 2L2
Tel: 519-661-0200; *Fax:* 519-661-0972
e-mail: mhooper@preferred-ins.com
Overview: A small local organization
Chief Officer(s): Mary Hooper, President
Member of: Canadian Association of Insurance Women

Managers Association of Financial Advisors of Canada ***See*** GAMA International Canada

Manitoba Association of Insolvency & Restructuring Professionals (MAIRP)
c/o KPMG Inc., #2000, 1 Lombard Pl., Winnipeg MB R3B 0X3
Tel: 204-957-1770; *Fax:* 204-957-0808
e-mail: lryback@kpmg.ca
Previous Name: Manitoba Insolvency Association
Overview: A small provincial organization
Chief Officer(s): Laura Ryback CA CIRP, President
Member of: Canadian Association of Insolvency & Restructuring Professionals

Manitoba Association of Insurance Professionals (MAIP)
c/o Valour Tri-West Insurance Brokers Ltd., 466 St. Anne's Rd., Winnipeg MB R2M 3E1
Tel: 204-257-4223; *Fax:* 204-255-0498
e-mail: maip@caiw-acfa.com
URL: www.caiw-acfa.com/maip/
Previous Name: Insurance Women's Association of Manitoba
Overview: A small provincial organization founded in 1966
Chief Officer(s): Shirley MacKenzie, President
Description: To preserve and enhance the value of its members through education, networking, and to foster personal growth; *Member of:* Canadian Association of Insurance Women

Manitoba Cooperative Association
#400, 317 Donald St., Winnipeg MB R3B 2H6
Tel: 204-989-5930; *Fax:* 204-949-0217
e-mail: vera@mbcai.coop
URL: www.coopcouncil.mb.ca
Also Known As: Manitoba Cooperative Council Inc.
Overview: A medium-sized provincial organization
Staff: 1 staff member(s)
Description: To promote a united, growing & influential co-operative movement through focussed, collective energies & resources

Manitoba Insolvency Association ***See*** Manitoba Association of Insolvency & Restructuring Professionals

Manitoba Taxpayers Association ***See*** Canadian Taxpayers Federation - Manitoba

Market Regulation Services Inc. / Services de réglementation du marché inc.
PO Box 939, #900, 145 King St. West, Toronto ON M5H 1J8
Tel: 416-646-7200; *Fax:* 416-646-7265
Toll-Free: 866-214-7200
e-mail: inquiries@rs.ca
URL: www.rs.ca
Also Known As: RS
Overview: A small national organization
Chief Officer(s): Tom Atkinson, President & CEO
Staff: 11 volunteer(s)
Activities: Provides independent regulation services to the TSE & the Canadian Venture Exchange
Description: To develop, administer, surveil & enforce the universal market integrity rules applicable to trading in the Canadian securities market in a neutral, cost-effective, service-oriented & responsive manner

Montréal Association of Insurance Women ***See*** Association des femmes d'assurance de Montréal

Montréal Society of Financial Analysts ***See*** Association des analystes financiers de Montréal

Mouvement des caisses populaires acadiennes
Place de l'Acadie, CP 5554, 295, boul St-Pierre ouest, Caraquet NB E1W 1B7
Tél: 506-726-4000; *Téléc:* 506-726-4001
Courriel: info@acadie.net
URL: www.acadie.com
Aperçu: *Dimension:* moyenne; *Envergure: provinciale; fondée en 1945*
Membre(s) du bureau directeur: Yves Duguay, Directeur
Personnel: 86 membre(s) du personnel; 790 bénévole(s)
Description: Améliorer la qualité de vie de ceux et celles qui y adhèrent tout en contribuant à l'autosuffisance socio-économique de la collectivité acadienne du Nouveau-Brunswick, dans le respect de son identité linguistique et ses valeurs coopératives

Mutual Fund Dealers Association of Canada (MFDA) / Association canadienne des courtiers de fonds mutuels
#1000, 121 King St. West, Toronto ON M5H 3T9
Tel: 416-361-6332
Toll-Free: 888-466-6332
URL: www.mfda.ca
Overview: A large national organization founded in 1998
Chief Officer(s): Larry M. Waite, President & CEO
Description: To enhance investor protection & strengthen public confidence in the Canadian mutual fund industry
Pacific Regional Office
PO Box 11614, #1325, 650 West Georgia St., Vancouver BC V6B 4N9
Tel: 604-694-8840
Chief Officer(s): Wendy Royle, Vice-President
Prairie Regional Office
#2330, 355 - 4th Ave. SW, Calgary AB T2P 0J1
Tel: 403-266-8826; *Fax:* 403-266-8858
Chief Officer(s): John Smeeton, Vice-President

National Contingency Fund ***See*** Canadian Investor Protection Fund

National Insurance Buyers Association; American Society of Insurance Management ***See*** Risk & Insurance Management Society Inc.

National Investor Relations Institute Canada (NIRI Canada) ***See*** Canadian Investor Relations Institute

Native Investment & Trade Association (NITA)
6520 Salish Dr., Vancouver BC V6N 2C7
Tel: 604-275-6670; *Fax:* 604-275-0307
Toll-Free: 800-337-7743
e-mail: nita@express.ca
URL: www.native-invest-trade.com
Overview: A small national licensing organization founded in 1989
Chief Officer(s): Calvin Helin, President
Finances: *Annual Operating Budget:* $250,000-$500,000; *Funding Sources:* Registration fees
Staff: 10 staff member(s); 2 volunteer(s)
Activities: *Library:* NITA Resource Library
Description: To promote, establish & maintain trade/investment opportunities in Native communities; encourages free enterprise solutions to economic & social problems confronting Native communities, but remains sensitive to their special cultural heritage, needs, requirements; views non-governmental business involvement with First Nations as a vital step towards greater self-reliance; fosters business ventures with high employment potential; promotes projects with potential for sustainable economic growth; conducts research into innovative approaches to economic development of Native communities

New Brunswick & Prince Edward Island Independent Adjusters' Association
c/o Crawford Adjusters Canada, 468 Bowlen St., Fredericton NB E3A 2T4
Tel: 506-452-1909; *Fax:* 506-452-1910
e-mail: troy.quigley@crawco.ca
Overview: A small provincial organization
Chief Officer(s): Troy A.P. Quigley BBA, CIP, Regional President
Member of: Canadian Independent Adjusters' Association

New Brunswick Association of CBDCs
360 Parkside Dr., Bathurst NB E2A 1N4
Tel: 506-548-2406; *Fax:* 506-546-2661
e-mail: jennifer.henry@cbdc.ca
Overview: A medium-sized provincial organization
Chief Officer(s): Jennifer Henry, Executive Director
Membership: 10 CBDCs
Affiliation(s): Pan Canadian Community Futures Network

New Brunswick Institute of Chartered Accountants (NBICA) / Institut des comptables agréés du Nouveau-Brunswick
93 Prince William St., 4th Fl., Saint John NB E2L 2B2
Tel: 506-634-1588; *Fax:* 506-634-1015
e-mail: nbica@nb.aibn.com
URL: www.nbica.org
Overview: A medium-sized provincial organization founded in 1916
Chief Officer(s): J. Blackier LLB, CA, Executive Director
Finances: *Annual Operating Budget:* $3 Million-$5 Million
Staff: 3 staff member(s); 110 volunteer(s)
Membership: 1,000-4,999
Activities: *Speaker Service:* Yes; *Library:* Yes
Publications: Interim Report, Newsletter, q., Editor: Kathy Wills, accepts advertising
Description: To serve members, students & the interests of the public with integrity, objectivity & a commitment to excellence; to promote & increase the knowledge, skills & proficiency of members & students; to regulate the discipline & professional conduct of members & students; to require public practitioners to carry minimum levels of professional liability insurance; to have lay representatives sit on Council; to conduct practice inspection of its public practitioners

Newfoundland & Labrador Association of Insolvency & Restructuring Professionals
c/o Janes & Noseworthy Ltd., #201, 516 Topsail Rd., St. John's NL A1E 2C5
Tel: 709-364-8148; *Fax:* 709-368-2146
e-mail: davidhowe@jnl.nf.ca
Previous Name: Newfoundland & Labrador Insolvency Association
Overview: A small provincial organization
Chief Officer(s): David A. Howe CMA, CA CIRP, President
Finances: *Annual Operating Budget:* Less than $50,000
Membership: *Fees:* $25
Member of: Canadian Association of Insolvency & Restructuring Professionals

Newfoundland & Labrador Credit Union
341 Freshwater Rd., 2nd Fl., St. John's NL A1B 1C4
Toll-Free: 800-563-3300
URL: www.nlcu.com
Previous Name: Credit Union Central of Newfoundland & Labrador
Overview: A medium-sized provincial organization founded in 1977
Chief Officer(s): Allison Chaytor-Loveys, CEO; Glenn Bolger, COO; Elizabeth Duff, CFO; Michael Boland, President
Finances: *Annual Operating Budget:* $100,000-$250,000
Staff: 3 staff member(s); 10 volunteer(s)
Membership: 10
Description: We are committed to every owner achieving personal financial success as they define it by: listening, providing complete & accurate information; providing sound advice & personalized solutions, providing access to financial & related services as owners' needs dictate, when owners' needs dictate, where owners' needs dictate

Newfoundland & Labrador Independent Adjusters' Association
c/o Crawford Adjusters Canada, Chimo Bldg., #310, 44 Torbay Rd., St. John's NL A1A 2G4
Tel: 709-753-6351; *Fax:* 709-753-6129
e-mail: neil.lacey@crawco.ca
Overview: A small regional organization
Chief Officer(s): Neil Lacey CIP, Regional President

Newfoundland & Labrador Insolvency Association ***See*** Newfoundland & Labrador Association of Insolvency & Restructuring Professionals

Newfoundland-Labrador Federation of Cooperatives
Cooperators Bldg., Crosbie Place, PO Box 13369, Stn. A, St. John's NL A1B 4B7
Tel: 709-726-9431; *Fax:* 709-726-9433
e-mail: info@nlfc.nf.ca
URL: www.nlfc.nf.ca
Overview: A medium-sized provincial organization
Chief Officer(s): Glen Fitzpatrick, Managing Director
Description: Represents the collective interests of the co-operative business sector in the province; promotes the co-operative business model & supports the growth & development of co-op enterprises; provides information & advice for people considering the formation of a co-operative; advisory support services for newly developing co-operatives; assistance for existing co-operatives; support services including research, project planning, training government relations & co-op programs for youth; service delivery is undertaken in partnerships with existing co-ops, community development agencies, industry associations & government

Northwestern Ontario Insurance Professionals
c/o The Standard, PO Box 2890, 319 - 2nd St. South, Kenora ON P9N 3X8
Tel: 807-468-3333; *Fax:* 807-468-4289
e-mail: llacroix@thestandardonline.com
Overview: A small regional organization
Chief Officer(s): Linda LaCroix, Director
Member of: Canadian Association of Insurance Women

Nova Scotia Association of Insolvency & Restructuring Professionals (NSAIRP)
c/o PricewaterhouseCoopers Inc., #600, 1809 Barrington St., Halifax NS B3J 3K8
Tel: 902-491-7400; *Fax:* 902-422-1166
e-mail: david.a.boyd@ca.pwc.com
Previous Name: Nova Scotia Insolvency Association
Overview: A small provincial organization
Chief Officer(s): David A. Boyd CA CIRP, President
Member of: Canadian Association of Insolvency & Restructuring Professionals

Nova Scotia Independent Adjusters' Association
c/o Crawford Adjusters Canada, #290, 3 Spectacle Lake Dr., Dartmouth NS B3B 1W8
Tel: 902-468-7787; *Fax:* 902-468-5822
e-mail: ian.saunders@crawco.ca
Overview: A small regional organization
Chief Officer(s): Ian Saunders AIIC, President

Nova Scotia Insolvency Association ***See*** Nova Scotia Association of Insolvency & Restructuring Professionals

Nuclear Insurance Association of Canada (NIAC) / Association canadienne d'assurance nucléaire
90 Allstate Pkwy., Markham ON L3R 6H3
Tel: 905-474-7356; *Fax:* 905-474-1567
Overview: A small national organization founded in 1958
Chief Officer(s): Dermot P. Murphy M.B.A., F.I.I.C., C.R.M., Manager
Staff: 3 staff member(s)
Description: To administer insurance to companies who require nuclear insurance (liability &/or property insurance); *Member of:* Canadian Nuclear Association

Ombudsman des services bancaires et d'investissement ***See*** Ombudsman for Banking Services & Investments

Ombudsman for Banking Services & Investments (OBSI) / Ombudsman des services bancaires et d'investissement
PO Box 896, Stn. Adelaide, Toronto ON M5C 2K3
Tel: 416-287-2877; *Fax:* 416-225-4722
Toll-Free: 888-451-4519
e-mail: ombudsman@obsi.ca
URL: www.obsi.ca
Previous Name: Canadian Banking Ombudsman
Overview: A medium-sized national organization founded in 1996
Chief Officer(s): David Agnew, Ombudsman & CEO; Peggy-Anne Brown, Chair
Finances: *Annual Operating Budget:* $1.5 Million-$3 Million
Staff: 20 staff member(s)
Membership: 500; *Member Profile:* Retail & commercial banks; investment dealers; mutual fund dealers; fund companies
Activities: Complaints — bank & bank-owned investment dealer & insurance companies; *Speaker Service:* Yes
Publications: Annual Report
Description: To investigate complaints from individuals & small businesses about banking services; to provide impartial & prompt resolution of complaints, based on fairness & good business & banking practices

Ontario Association of Community Futures Development Corporations (OACFDC)
300 South Edgeware Rd., St Thomas ON N5P 4L1
Tel: 519-633-2326; *Fax:* 519-633-3563
Toll-Free: 888-633-2326
e-mail: info@oacfdc.com
URL: www.ontcfdc.com
Overview: A medium-sized provincial organization founded in 1994
Chief Officer(s): Diana Jedig CAE, Executive Director
Finances: *Annual Operating Budget:* $250,000-$500,000
Staff: 3 staff member(s); 9 volunteer(s)
Membership: 61; *Fees:* $700 individual; $350 associates
Description: To promote amongst members, best practices of community development in order to maintain & enhance economic & employment growth; Affiliation(s): Pan Canadian Community Futures Network

Ontario Association of Credit Counselling Services (OACCS)
PO Box 189, Grimsby ON L3M 4G3
Tel: 905-945-5644; *Fax:* 905-945-4680
Toll-Free: 888-746-3328
e-mail: oaccs@indebt.org
URL: www.indebt.org
Overview: A medium-sized provincial charitable organization founded in 1975
Finances: *Annual Operating Budget:* $100,000-$250,000; *Funding Sources:* Member agency fees
Staff: 3 staff member(s); 25 volunteer(s)
Membership: 26 agencies; *Fees:* % of operating budget
Activities: *Speaker Service:* Yes
Publications: Connections, Newsletter, q., ISSN: 1183-3556
Description: To represent member agencies & provide them with a forum for the pursuit of common interests in order to support, strengthen & enhance not-for-profit credit counselling services; to enhance the quality & availability of not-for-profit credit counselling

Ontario Association of Insolvency & Restructuring Professionals (OAIRP)
c/o D. & A. MacLeod Company Ltd., 343 O'Connor St., Ottawa ON K2P 1V9
Tel: 613-236-9111; *Fax:* 613-236-6766
e-mail: suttons@macleod.ca
Previous Name: Ontario Insolvency Practitioners Association
Overview: A small provincial organization
Chief Officer(s): Allen W. MacLeod CA CIRP, CIRP, President
Activities: *Rents Mailing List:* Yes
Member of: Canadian Association of Insolvency & Restructuring Professionals

Ontario Bailiffs Association
#203, 262 Queen St. East, Sault Ste Marie ON P6A 1Y7
Toll-Free: 888-622-9909
e-mail: oba@shaw.ca
URL: www.ontariobailiff.ca
Overview: A small provincial organization
Chief Officer(s): Rick Latour, President; Craig Danford, Treasurer
Description: Association of recovery and liquidation experts located throughout Ontario

Ontario Co-operative Association
#101, 450 Speedvale Ave. West, Guelph ON N1H 7Y6
Tel: 519-763-8271; *Fax:* 519-763-7239
Toll-Free: 888-745-5521
e-mail: info@ontario.coop
URL: www.ontario.coop
Overview: A small provincial organization founded in 1979
Chief Officer(s): Denyse Guy, Executive Director
Membership: *Member Profile:* Agriculture, finance, insurance, consumer, supply & services cooperatives
Member of: The Ontario Rural Council; Foundation for Rural Living; Agricultural Adaptation Council; Association of Co-operative Education

Ontario Credit Union League Ltd. ***See*** Credit Union Central of Ontario

Ontario Independent Insurance Adjusters' Association
c/o Crawford Adjusters Canada, #6, 39 Parkside Dr., Newmarket ON L3Y 8J9
Tel: 905-898-0008; *Fax:* 905-898-1705
e-mail: mary.charman@crawco
Overview: A small provincial organization
Chief Officer(s): Mary Charman CIP, President

Ontario Insolvency Practitioners Association ***See*** Ontario Association of Insolvency & Restructuring Professionals

Ontario Insurance Adjusters Association (OIAA)
29 De Jong Dr., Mississauga ON L5M 1B9
Tel: 905-542-0576; *Fax:* 905-542-1301
Toll-Free: 888-259-1555
e-mail: manager@oiaa.com
URL: www.oiaa.com
Overview: A medium-sized provincial organization founded in 1930
Chief Officer(s): Jackie Johnston-Schnurr, Business Manager
Finances: *Annual Operating Budget:* $500,000-$1.5 Million
Staff: 1 staff member(s); 21 volunteer(s)
Membership: 1,800; *Fees:* $40; *Member Profile:* Insurance adjusters actively adjusting claims
Publications: Without Prejudice, Magazine, m., accepts advertising, Contents: Insurance adjusting related articles

Ontario Mutual Insurance Association
PO Box 3187, 1305 Bishop St. North, Cambridge ON N3H 4S6
e-mail: information@omia.com
URL: www.omia.com
Overview: A small provincial organization
Membership: *Member Profile:* Mutual insurance companies that provide home, auto, business & farm insurance

Ordre des CGA du Québec
#1800, 500, Place D'Armes, Montréal QC H2Y 2W2
Tél: 514-861-1823; *Téléc:* 514-861-7661
Ligne sans frais: 800-463-0163
Courriel: ordre@cga-quebec.org
URL: www.cga-online.org/qc
Également appelé: CGA - Québec
Nom précédent: Ordre des comptables généraux licenciés du Québec
Aperçu: *Dimension:* grande; *Envergure: nationale; Organisme sans but lucratif; Organisme de réglementation; fondée en 1908*
Membre(s) du bureau directeur: Danielle Blanchard, Président-Directeur général; Roger Sirard, Chargée des communications
Finances: *Budget de fonctionnement annuel:* $3 Million-$5 Million
Personnel: 26 membre(s) du personnel
Membre: 7 440 membres + 2 100 candidats et étudiants; *Montant de la cotisation:* 573.85$ membre; 195.25$ candidat; *Critères d'admissibilité/Description:* Réussir 4 examens + stage de deux ans; *Comités:* Affaires publiques; Appel des étudiants; Associations étudiantes; Discipline; FiscalitéHonneurs; Inspection professionnelle; Planification stratégique; Pratique professionnelle; Consultatif des présidents de l'Ordre; Présidents de section; Programmes professionnels; Révision des plaintes; Vérification
Activités: *Bibliothèque:* Oui (Bibliothèque publique)
Publications: Performance CGA Express, 6 fois par an, Éditeur: Nadine Bourgeois, Contenu: Mot du président; titres des articles que l'on retrouve sur le site Internet de l'Ordre
Description: Assurer la protection du public; contrôler l'exercice de la profession par ses membres

Ordre des comptables agréés du Québec (OCAQ)
680, rue Sherbrooke ouest, 18e étage, Montréal QC H3A 2S3
Tél: 514-288-3256; *Téléc:* 514-843-8375
Ligne sans frais: 800-363-4688
Courriel: info@ocaq.qc.ca
URL: www.ocaq.qc.ca

Aperçu: *Dimension:* grande; *Envergure: provinciale; fondée en 1880*
Membre(s) du bureau directeur: Daniel McMahon FCA, Président/Secrétaire général; Christine Montamant MBA, CA, Directrice
Finances: *Budget de fonctionnement annuel:* Plus de $5 Million
Personnel: 65 membre(s) du personnel; 300 bénévole(s)
Membre: 2 000 étudiants + 16 600 membres; *Montant de la cotisation:* 1,126$ praticiens; 908$ non-praticiens; *Critères d'admissibilité/Description:* Détenir DESS, réussir examen final uniforme et completer un stage de 2 ans dans un cabinet d'expert-comptables; *Comités:* Activité de formation continue; Administrations municipales; Arbitrage des comptes des membres; Assurances; CA en affaires et en industrie; Coopératives; Discipline; Étude des exposés-sondages; Examen; Expertise de la profession; FiscalitéFonds d'indemnisation; Formation professionnelle; Inspection professionnelle; Institutions d'enseignement; Relève; Révision des plaintes; Spécialisation; Terminologie française
Activités: Formation professionnelle; formation continue; inspection professionnelle; *Stagiaires:* Oui; *Bibliothèque:* Centre de documentation (Bibliothèque publique) rendez-vous
Publications: InfoOCA, Bulletin, hebdomadaire, Editor: Sebastien Langevin, accepts advertising; Répertoire de cours, Bulletin, annuel
Description: Protection du public; dépister l'exercice illégal de la comptabilité publique; s'assurer de la formation adéquate des membres; *Membre de:* Conseil interprofessionel du Québec

Ordre des comptables généraux licenciés du Québec *See* Ordre des CGA du Québec

Organisation internationale des commissions de valeurs *See* International Organization of Securities Commissions

Pacific Independent Insurance Adjusters' Association

c/o Crawford Adjusters Canada, #22, 3318 Oak St., Victoria BC V8X 1R1
Tel: 250-360-0304; *Fax:* 250-360-0310
e-mail: gary.saward@crawco.ca
Overview: A small provincial organization
Chief Officer(s): Gary Sawada CIP, President

Pension Investment Association of Canada (PIAC) / Association canadienne des gestionnaires de fonds de retraite

39 River St., Toronto ON M5A 3P1
Tel: 416-640-0264; *Fax:* 416-646-9460
e-mail: info@piacweb.org
URL: www.piacweb.org
Overview: A medium-sized national organization founded in 1977
Chief Officer(s): Peter Waite CAE, Executive Director
Finances: *Annual Operating Budget:* $250,000-$500,000; *Funding Sources:* Membership fees
Staff: 2 staff member(s); 45 volunteer(s)
Membership: 221; *Fees:* Schedule available; *Member Profile:* Pension fund employees who have investment responsibilities at their respective pension funds/organizations; *Committees:* Executive; Government Relations; Corporate Governance; Industry Practices; Membership; Editorial Advisory
Awards: Chuck Harvie Award; Terry Staples Award
Publications: Communique, Newsletter, q., accepts advertising, Contents: News & updates; articles on investment issues relevant to pension funds
Description: To promote the financial security of pension fund beneficiaries through sound investment policy & practices

Petroleum Accountants Society of Canada (PASC)

PO Box 4520, Stn. C, #400, 1040 - 7 Ave. SW, Calgary AB T2T 5N3
Tel: 403-262-4744; *Fax:* 403-244-2340
e-mail: pasc04@petroleumaccountants.com
URL: www.petroleumaccountants.com
Overview: A medium-sized national organization founded in 1950
Chief Officer(s): Douglas Baine, President; Matthew Breadner, Vice-President; Gail Quartly, Treasurer
Finances: *Annual Operating Budget:* $50,000-$100,000; *Funding Sources:* Membership dues
Staff: 1 staff member(s); 70 volunteer(s)
Membership: 400; *Fees:* $75; *Member Profile:* Accounting, auditing, finance or economics employees with organizations associated with the petroleum or natural gas industry; *Committees:* Education; Electronic Data Exchange; Financial Accounting Research; Joint Audit Data Exchange User Group; Joint Interest Research; Joint Venture Audit; Joint Interest Billing Exchange User Group; Material & Inventory; Revenue Research
Activities: Education, standards & information; *Library:* Yes (Open to Public) by appointment
Description: To contribute to the long term success of the Canadian petroleum industry by staying abreast of the constantly changing needs of the industry & striving to satisfy those needs; *Member of:* Council of Petroleum Societies of North America

Provincial Association of CBDCs

PO Box 14064, Stn Manuels, Conception Bay South NL A1W 3A6
Tel: 709-834-8343; *Fax:* 709-834-8363
Toll-Free: 888-303-2232
URL: www.cbdc.nf.ca
Overview: A small provincial organization
Affiliation(s): Pan Canadian Community Futures Network

Public Accountants Council for the Province of Ontario / Conseil des experts-comptables de la province de l'Ontario

#901, 1200 Bay St., Toronto ON M5R 2A5
Tel: 416-920-1444; *Fax:* 416-920-1917
Toll-Free: 800-387-2154
e-mail: info@pacont.org
URL: www.pacont.org
Also Known As: Public Accountants Council
Overview: A medium-sized provincial licensing organization founded in 1950
Finances: *Annual Operating Budget:* $1.5 Million-$3 Million; *Funding Sources:* Licence fees
Staff: 4 staff member(s); 17 volunteer(s)
Membership: 3; *Member Profile:* Institute of Chartered Accountants of Ontario; Certified General Accountants of Ontario; Society of Management Accountants of Ontario; *Committees:* Finance; Audit; Governance; Unauthorized Practice
Activities: *Internships:* Yes; *Speaker Service:* Yes; *Rents Mailing List:* Yes

Québec Association of Insolvency & Restructuring Professionals *See* Association québécoise des professionnels de la réorganisation et de l'insolvabilité

Québec Risk & Insurance Management Association *See* Association des gestionnaires de risques et d'assurances du Québec

RBC Fondation *See* RBC Foundation

RBC Foundation / RBC Fondation

Royal Bank Plaza, South Tower, #950, 200 Bay St., Toronto ON M5J 2J5
Tel: 416-974-5151; *Fax:* 416-955-7800
URL: www.rbc.com/community/donations/index.html
Previous Name: Royal Bank of Canada Charitable Foundation
Overview: A medium-sized national organization founded in 1993
Chief Officer(s): Gayle Longley, National Donations Manager
Finances: *Funding Sources:* RBC Financial Group
Publications: Donations & Sponsorships, Brochure, a.

Regina Association of Insurance Women

c/o Jordan Insurance Ltd., 1842 Victoria Ave. East, Regina SK S4N 7K3
Tel: 306-522-8528; *Fax:* 306-347-1087
Overview: A small local organization
Chief Officer(s): Susan Ewart, President
Member of: Canadian Association of Insurance Women

Registered Insurance Brokers of Ontario (RIBO)

PO Box 45, #1200, 401 Bay St., Toronto ON M5H 2Y4
Tel: 416-365-1900; *Fax:* 416-365-7664
Toll-Free: 800-265-3097
e-mail: jeff@ribo.com
URL: www.ribo.com
Overview: A medium-sized provincial organization founded in 1981
Chief Officer(s): Jeffrey A. Bear, CEO; Bonnie Warder, President
Staff: 23 staff member(s)
Description: RIBO regulates the licensing, professional competence, ethical conduct, & insurance related financial obligations of all independent general insurance brokers in the province

Regroupement des cabinets de courtage d'assurance du Québec (RCCAQ) / Insurance Brokers' Association of Québec - Assembly

#139, 955, rue D'Assigny, Longueuil QC J4K 5C3
Tél: 450-674-6258; *Téléc:* 450-674-3609
Ligne sans frais: 800-516-6258
Courriel: info@rccaq.com
URL: www.rccaq.com
Aperçu: *Dimension:* petite; *Envergure: provinciale; Organisme sans but lucratif; fondée en 1973*
Membre(s) du bureau directeur: Louis Gagnon, Président; Claude Brosseau, Vice-président
Finances: *Budget de fonctionnement annuel:* $1.5 Million-$3 Million
Personnel: 7 membre(s) du personnel; 30 bénévole(s)
Membre: 850 cabinets; 3 300 courtiers; *Montant de la cotisation:* Variable, en fonction du profil du cabinet; *Critères d'admissibilité/Description:* Courtier d'assurance de dommages, propriétaire
Activités: *Stagiaires:* Oui; *Listes de destinataires:* Oui
Publications: Informateur, Bulletin, 2 fois par mois; Liaison, Bulletin, 6 fois par an, accepts advertising
Description: Promouvoir les intérêts socio-économiques des membres

Reinsurance Research Council (RRC) / Conseil de recherche en réassurance

#7, 296 Jarvis St., Toronto ON M5B 2C5
Tel: 416-968-0183; *Fax:* 416-968-6818
e-mail: mail@rrccanada.org
URL: www.rrccanada.org
Overview: A small national organization founded in 1973
Chief Officer(s): Anthony Laycock, General Manager
Finances: *Funding Sources:* Membership dues
Staff: 1 staff member(s)
Membership: 26 corporate; *Member Profile:* Licenced re-insurers
Description: Represents the majority of professional reinsurers registered in Canada; conducts research into all lines of property/casualty reinsurance, presents the views of its members where appropriate, & provides liaison with governments, the primary insurance market, & other interested parties

Réseau des SADC du Québec (SADC)

#530, 979, av de Bourgogne, Québec QC G1W 2L4
Tél: 418-658-1530; *Téléc:* 418-658-9900
Courriel: sadc@ciril.qc.ca
URL: www.reseau-sadc.qc.ca
Également appelé: Sociétés d'aide au développement des collectivités
Aperçu: *Dimension:* moyenne; *Envergure: provinciale; Organisme sans but lucratif; fondée en 1995*
Membre(s) du bureau directeur: Hélène Deslauriers, Directrice générale
Finances: *Budget de fonctionnement annuel:* Moins de $50,000
Personnel: 400 membre(s) du personnel; 1350 bénévole(s)
Membre: 67; *Critères d'admissibilité/Description:* Sociétés d'investissement (financement d'entreprises et accompagnement personnalisé)
Description: Soutenir les efforts de regroupement des SADC (Sociétés d'aide au développement des collectivités) et des CAE (Centres d'aide aux entreprises) du Québec; il veille à leurs intérêts et procure des services qui facilitent le développement de ses membres; au cours des années, les SADC et CAE sont devenus de véritables experts en développement local et régional

Risk & Insurance Management Society Inc. (RIMS)

c/o Wasser Resources, 42 Arlstan Dr., Toronto ON M3H 4V9
Tel: 416-638-1645
e-mail: bwasser@sympatico.ca
URL: www.rims.org/canada
Also Known As: RIMS Canada
Previous Name: National Insurance Buyers Association; American Society of Insurance Management
Overview: A large international organization founded in 1950
Chief Officer(s): Bonnie Wasser, Canadian Consultant; Glen Frederick, Chair
Finances: *Annual Operating Budget:* $50,000-$100,000; *Funding Sources:* Membership fees; conferences
Staff: 1 staff member(s); 10 volunteer(s)
Membership: 7,800 individuals + 4,500 organizations; 11 chapters across Canada; *Fees:* US$415 + chapter fees; *Committees:* Canadian Chapters; Conference Programming; Education; Employee Benefits Legislation; Environmental;

Government Affairs; Health & Safety; International; Membership & Chapter Services; Public Affairs; Risk Management Industry Liaison; Risk Management Roundtable; Student Involvement
Activities: Offers education program through the University of Toronto, School of Continuing Education (Canadian Risk Management Diploma Program - CRM); courses also offered through Carleton University, McGill University, Simon Fraser University, the University of Calgary & University of Manitoba; advanced course through Institute of Risk Management (FRM); Cost of Risk Survey; RIMSNET - electronic news & information service; monitors government activities & legislation; combats hampering legislation
Awards: Don Stuart Award; Fred Bossons Award; Institute of Risk Management Award; Insurance Institute of Canada Fellowship Award; University of Calgary Scholarship Award
Publications: RIMSCAN, Newsletter, q., Contents: For Canadian chapters; RIMSCOPE, Newsletter, q., Contents: Activities undertaken by officers, committee members & staff; Risk Management, Newsletter, m., accepts advertising, Contents: Risk analysis, funding techniques, loss prevention, employee benefits planning, legislative & regulatory developments
Description: To advance the theory & practice of risk management by promoting the awareness, understanding & application of risk management & by developing competency & influence of risk managers; to position risk management as a discipline vital to the protection & utilization of human & financial resources; *Member of:* RIMS New York; Affiliation(s): International Federation of Risk & Insurance Management Associations

BC RIMA
PO Box 1000, 524 Yates St., Victoria BC V8W 2S6
Tel: 250-360-3036; *Fax:* 250-360-3023
URL: britishcolumbia.rims.org
Chief Officer(s): Chris Grelson, Contact

Canadian Capital Chapter
3755 Riverside Dr., Ottawa ON K1G 4K9
Tel: 613-738-1338; *Fax:* 613-738-7003
URL: canadiancapital.rims.org
Chief Officer(s): Valerie Martin, Contact

Manitoba Chapter (MaRIMS)
Norquay Bldg., #417, 401 York Ave., Winnipeg MB R3C 0P8
Tel: 204-945-2482; *Fax:* 204-948-2452
URL: manitoba.rims.org
Chief Officer(s): John Rislahti, Contact

Maritime Chapter
PO Box 5777, 300 Union St., Saint John NB E2L 4M3
Tel: 506-633-3270; *Fax:* 506-634-2446
URL: maritime.rims.org
Chief Officer(s): Adib Samaan, Contact

Newfoundland & Labrador Chapter (NALRIMS)
PO Box 8910, 55 Kenmount Rd., St. John's NL A1B 3P6
Tel: 709-737-5664; *Fax:* 709-737-2892
URL: newfoundlandlabrador.rims.org
Chief Officer(s): Pat Ryan, Contact

Northern Alberta Risk & Insurance Management Society (NARIMS)
Admin. Bldg., Northlands Park, 116 Ave. & 73 St., Edmonton AB T5J 2N5
Tel: 780-471-7372; *Fax:* 780-471-8195
e-mail: bpeter@northlands.com
URL: northernalberta.rims.org
Chief Officer(s): Barbara Peter, Contact

Ontario Chapter (ORIMS)
c/o Sun Life Financial Inc., 150 King St. West, Toronto ON M5H 1J9
Tel: 416-204-3862; *Fax:* 416-979-4808
URL: ontario.rims.org
Chief Officer(s): Niver Rubenyan, Contact

Saskatchewan Chapter (SaskRIMS)
c/o Saskferco Products Inc., PO Box 39, Belle Plaine SK S0G 0G0
Tel: 306-345-4228; *Fax:* 306-345-2353
URL: saskatchewan.rims.org
Chief Officer(s): Gordon Dolney, Contact

Southern Alberta Risk & Insurance Management Society (SARIMS)
c/o City of Calgary, PO Box 2100, Stn. M, Calgary AB T2P 2M5
Tel: 403-268-5405; *Fax:* 403-268-8257
URL: southernalberta.rims.org
Chief Officer(s): Phil Corbeil, Contact

Royal Bank of Canada Charitable Foundation *See* RBC Foundation

CAE Basses-Laurentides inc.
#104, 55, rue Castonguay, Saint-Jérome QC J7Y 2H9
Tél: 450-432-4455; *Téléc:* 450-432-4897
Courriel: info@caebl.ca
URL: www.caebl.ca
Membre(s) du bureau directeur: Louis Chauvette, Directeur général

CAE Beauce-Chaudière inc
551-B, boul Renault, Beauceville QC G5X 1N3
Tél: 418-774-2022; *Téléc:* 418-774-2024
Courriel: caebci@sogetel.net
Membre(s) du bureau directeur: Rémy Poulin, Directeur général

CAE Haute-Montérégie
Parc industriel E.L. Farrar, 700, rue Lucien-Beaudin, Saint-Jean-sur-Richelieu QC J2X 5M3
Tél: 450-357-9800; *Téléc:* 450-357-9583
Courriel: info@caehm.com
URL: www.caehm.com
Membre(s) du bureau directeur: Édouard Bonaldo, Directeur général

CAE Haute-Yamaska et région inc.
166, rue Boivin, Granby QC J2G 2J7
Tél: 450-378-2294; *Téléc:* 450-378-7370
Courriel: info@caehyr.com
URL: www.caehyr.com
Membre(s) du bureau directeur: Roland Choinière, Directeur général

CAE Memphrémagog inc
Place du Moulinier, #206, 101, rue du Moulin, Magog QC J1X 4A1
Tél: 819-843-4342; *Téléc:* 819-843-4393
Courriel: cae_memphremagog@ciril.qc.ca
Membre(s) du bureau directeur: Louise Paradis, Directrice générale

CAE Montmagny-L'Islet
191, ch des Poirier, Montmagny QC G5V 4L2
Tél: 418-248-4815; *Téléc:* 418-248-4836
Courriel: cae_montmagny@ciril.qc.ca
Membre(s) du bureau directeur: Gilles Boulet, Directeur général

CAE Val-St-François
745, rue Gouin, Richmond QC J0B 2H0
Tél: 819-826-6571; *Téléc:* 819-826-6281
Courriel: info@caevsf.com
URL: www.caevsf.com
Membre(s) du bureau directeur: Bertrand Ménard, Directeur général

CAE de la Rive-Sud inc.
#203, 230 rue Brébeuf, Beloeil QC J3G 5P3
Tél: 450-446-3650; *Téléc:* 450-446-3806
Courriel: caers@videotron.ca
URL: www.caers.ca
Membre(s) du bureau directeur: Michel Aubin, Directeur général

CAE des 3 Rivières
#300, 370, rue des Forges, Trois-Rivières QC G9A 2H1
Tél: 819-378-6000; *Téléc:* 819-378-2019
Courriel: cae_3rivieres@ciril.qc.ca; cae@cae3r.com
URL: www.cae3r.com
Membre(s) du bureau directeur: Jacinthe Gosselin, Directrice générale

Eeyou Economic Group
CP 39, 58, rue Pine, Waswanipi QC J0Y 3C0
Tél: 819-753-2560; *Téléc:* 819-753-2568
Courriel: chriscooper@waswanipi.net
URL: www.waswanipi.com
Membre(s) du bureau directeur: Christopher Cooper, Directeur général

Fondel Drummond
136, rue Lindsay, Drummondville QC J2C 1N6
Tél: 819-474-6477; *Téléc:* 819-474-5944
Courriel: emayrand@fondeldrummond.ca
URL: www.fondeldrummond.ca
Membre(s) du bureau directeur: Errold Mayrand, Directeur général

Nunavik Investment Corporation
CP 789, Kuujjuaq QC J0M 1C0
Tél: 819-964-1872; *Téléc:* 819-964-1497
Courriel: ekauki@tamaani.ca
Membre(s) du bureau directeur: Jonathan Grenier, Directeur général

SADC Abitibi-Ouest
#202, 80, 12e av est, La Sarre QC J9Z 3K6
Tél: 819-333-3113; *Téléc:* 819-333-3132
Courriel: sadc_abitibi@ciril.qc.ca
URL: www.sadcao.com
Membre(s) du bureau directeur: Thérèse Grenier, Directrice générale

SADC Achigan-Montcalm inc.
104, rue St-Jacques, Saint-Jacques QC J0K 2R0
Tél: 450-839-9218; *Téléc:* 450-839-7036
Courriel: info@sadc.org
URL: www.sadc.org
Membre(s) du bureau directeur: Claude Chartier, Directeur général

SADC Arthabaska-Érable inc.
#101, 975, boul Industriel est., Victoriaville QC G6T 1T8
Tél: 819-758-1501; *Téléc:* 819-758-7971
Courriel: sadc_ae@ciril.qc.ca
URL: www.reseau-sadc.qc.ca/arth-erable
Membre(s) du bureau directeur: Jean-François Girard, Directeur général
Personnel: 5 membre(s) du personnel; 9 bénévole(s)
Affiliation(s): Développement économique Canada

SADC Baie-des-Chaleurs
#201, 152-A, boul Perron ouest, New Richmond QC G0C 2B0
Tél: 418-392-5014; *Téléc:* 418-392-5425
Courriel: sadc_chaleurs@ciril.qc.ca
URL: www.sadcbc.ca
Membre(s) du bureau directeur: Lyne Lebrasseur, Directrice générale

SADC Barraute-Senneterre-Quévillon inc
CP 308, 674, 11e Avenue, Senneterre QC J0Y 2M0
Tél: 819-737-2211; *Téléc:* 819-737-8888
Courriel: sadc_bsq@ciril.qc.ca
URL: www.reseau-sadc.qc.ca/sadcbsq
Membre(s) du bureau directeur: Marc Hardy, Directeur général

SADC Bellechasse-Etchemins
CP 158, 494-B, rue Principale, Standon QC G0R 4L0
Tél: 418-642-2844; *Téléc:* 418-642-5316
Courriel: info@sadcbe.qc.ca
URL: www.sadcbe.qc.ca
Membre(s) du bureau directeur: Mélanie Simard, Directrice générale

SADC Centre-de-la-Mauricie
812, ave des Cèdres, Shawinigan QC G9N 1P2
Tél: 819-537-5107; *Téléc:* 819-537-5109
Courriel: info@sadccm.ca
URL: www.sadccm.ca
Membre(s) du bureau directeur: Simon Charlebois, Directeur général

SADC Chibougamau-Chapais inc
#1, 600, 3e rue, Chibougamau QC G8P 1P1
Tél: 418-748-6477; *Téléc:* 418-748-6160
Courriel: sadc_chibougamau@ciril.qc.ca
URL: www.reseau_sadc.qc.ca/chibchap
Membre(s) du bureau directeur: Annie Potvin, Directrice générale

SADC Côte-Nord inc
#205, 456, av Arnaud, Sept-Iles QC G4R 3B1
Tél: 418-962-7233; *Téléc:* 418-968-5513
Ligne sans frais: 877-962-7233
Courriel: sadciles@globetrotter.net
URL: www.sadccote-nord.org
Membre(s) du bureau directeur: Patsy Keays, Directrice générale

SADC Harricana inc.
550, 1re av ouest, Amos QC J9T 1V3
Tél: 819-732-8311; *Téléc:* 819-732-2240
Courriel: sadc_harricana@ciril.qc.ca
URL: www.sadc-harricana.qc.ca
Membre(s) du bureau directeur: Jocelyne Bédard, Directrice générale

SADC Haute-Côte-Nord inc.
#200, 459, rte 138, Les Escoumins QC G0T 1K0
Tél: 418-233-3495; *Téléc:* 418-233-2485
Courriel: sadchcn@ciril.qc.ca
URL: www.sadccote-nord.org
Membre(s) du bureau directeur: Léna St-Pierre, Directrice générale

SADC Kamouraska
#2, 900, 6e ave, La Pocatière QC G0R 1Z0
Tél: 418-856-3482; *Téléc:* 418-856-5053
Courriel: sadc_kamouraska@ciril.qc.ca
URL: www.kamouraska.com
Membre(s) du bureau directeur: Brigitte Pouliot, Directrice générale

ASSOCIATIONS

SADC La Mitis
#101, 1534, boul Jacques-Cartier, Mont-Joli QC G5H 2V8
Tél: 418-775-4619; *Téléc:* 418-775-5504
Courriel: sadc_mitis@ciril.qc.ca
URL: www.reseau-sadc.qc.ca/mitis
Membre(s) du bureau directeur: Benoît Thériault, Directeur général
SADC Lac-Saint-Jean Ouest inc.
#102, 915, boul St-Joseph, Roberval QC G8H 2M1
Tél: 418-275-2531; *Téléc:* 418-275-5787
Courriel: sadc@sadclacstjeanouest.com
URL: www.sadclacstjeanouest.com
Membre(s) du bureau directeur: Serge Desgagné, Directeur général
SADC Lac-Saint-Jean-Est inc.
625, Bergeron ouest, Alma QC G8B 1V3
Tél: 418-668-3148; *Téléc:* 418-668-6977
Courriel: info@sadclacstjean.qc.ca
URL: www.sadc.lacstjean.qc.ca
Membre(s) du bureau directeur: Daniel Deschênes, Directeur général
SADC Manicouagan
#301, 67 Place LaSalle, Baie-Comeau QC G4Z 1K1
Tél: 418-296-6956; *Téléc:* 418-296-5176
Courriel: sadcmanic@bc.cgocable.ca
URL: www.sadccote-nord.org
Membre(s) du bureau directeur: Marie-Claire Larose, Directrice générale
SADC Maria-Chapdelaine
#200, 201, boul des Pères, Dolbeau-Mistassini QC G8L 5K6
Tél: 418-276-0405; *Téléc:* 418-276-0623
Courriel: sadc@sadcmaria.qc.ca; sadc_maria-chapdelaine@ciril.qc.ca
URL: www.sadcmaria.qc.ca
Membre(s) du bureau directeur: Mario Bussière, Directeur général
SADC Matagami
CP 910, 180, place du Commerce, Matagami QC J0Y 2A0
Tél: 819-739-2155; *Téléc:* 819-739-4271
URL: www.sadcdematagami.qc.ca
Membre(s) du bureau directeur: François Cossette, Directeur général
SADC Matapédia inc.
#401, 123, rue Desbiens, 4e étage, Amqui QC G5J 3P9
Tél: 418-629-4474; *Téléc:* 418-629-5530
Courriel: sadc_amqui@ciril.qc.ca
URL: www.reseau-sadc.qc.ca/matapedia
Membre(s) du bureau directeur: Guy Côté, Directeur général
SADC Matawinie inc.
1080, rte 343, Saint-Alphonse-Rodriguez QC J0K 1W0
Tél: 450-883-0717; *Téléc:* 450-883-2006
Courriel: sadc_matawinie@ciril.qc.ca
URL: www.matawinie.qc.ca
Membre(s) du bureau directeur: Jacques Girardin, Directeur général
SADC Nicolet-Bécancour inc.
#102, 19205, boul des Acadiens, Bécancour QC G9H 1M5
Tél: 819-233-3315; *Téléc:* 819-233-3338
Courriel: sadc_nicolet@ciril.qc.ca
URL: www.sadcnicoletbecancour.ca
Membre(s) du bureau directeur: Johanne Gauthier, Directrice générale
SADC Pontiac CFDC
CP 425, 1409, rte 148, Campbell's Bay QC J0X 1K0
Tél: 819-648-2186; *Téléc:* 819-648-2226
Courriel: sadc@commercepontiac.ca
URL: www.commercepontiac.ca
Membre(s) du bureau directeur: Louise Donaldson, Directrice générale
SADC Portneuf
299, 1re av, Portneuf QC G0A 2Y0
Tél: 418-286-4422; *Téléc:* 418-286-3737
Courriel: sadc_portneuf@ciril.qc.ca
URL: www.sadcportneuf.qc.ca
Membre(s) du bureau directeur: Guy Beaulieu, Directeur général
SADC Vallée de la Batiscan
54, rue Goulet, Saint-Stanislas QC G0X 3E0
Tél: 418-328-4200; *Téléc:* 418-328-4201
Courriel: sadc_batiscan@ciril.qc.ca; sadcvb@globetrotter.net
URL: www.reseau-sadc.qc.ca/vallee-batiscan
Membre(s) du bureau directeur: Gilles Mercure, Directeur général
SADC Vallée-de-l'Or
#201, 40, place Hammond, Val-d'Or QC J9P 3A9
Tél: 819-874-3676; *Téléc:* 819-874-3670
Courriel: sadc_valdor@ciril.qc.ca; sadcvdo@lino.com
URL: www.reseau-sadc.qc.ca/sadcvdo
Membre(s) du bureau directeur: Francis Dumais, Directeur général
SADC Vallée-de-la-Gatineau
#210, 100, rue Principale sud, Maniwaki QC J9E 3L4
Tél: 819-449-1551; *Téléc:* 819-449-7431
Ligne sans frais: 866-449-1551
Courriel: sadc@ireseau.com
URL: www.sadc-vg.ca
Membre(s) du bureau directeur: Pierre Monette, Directeur général
SADC d'Antoine-Labelle
#4, 636 rue de la Madone, Mont-Laurier QC J9L 1S9
Tél: 819-623-3300; *Téléc:* 819-623-7300
Courriel: info@sadcal.com
URL: www.sadcal.com
Membre(s) du bureau directeur: Miguel Gauthier, Directeur général
SADC de Autray-Joliette
#500, 550, rue Montcalm, Berthierville QC J0K 1A0
Tél: 450-836-0990; *Téléc:* 450-836-2001
Ligne sans frais: 877-777-0990
Courriel: info@sadc-autray.qc.ca
URL: www.sadc-autray.qc.ca
Membre(s) du bureau directeur: Jocelyn de Grandpré, Directeur général
SADC de Charlevoix
#208, 11, rue Saint-Jean-Baptiste, Baie-Saint-Paul QC G3Z 1M1
Tél: 418-435-4033; *Téléc:* 418-435-4050
Courriel: sadc_charlevoix@ciril.qc.ca
URL: www.charlevoix.qc.ca/sadc
Membre(s) du bureau directeur: Jean Gilbert, Directeur général
SADC de Gaspé
CP 5012, #200, 15, rue Adams, Gaspé QC G4X 1E5
Tél: 418-368-2906; *Téléc:* 418-368-3927
Courriel: sadc_gaspe@ciril.qc.ca
URL: www.reseau-sadc.qc.ca/gaspe
Membre(s) du bureau directeur: Mario Cotton, Directeur général
SADC de Gaspé-Nord
Édifice des Monts, 10G, boul Sainte-Anne ouest, 1er étage, Sainte-Anne-des-Monts QC G4V 1P3
Tél: 418-763-5355; *Téléc:* 418-763-2933
Courriel: sadc_gaspenord@ciril.qc.ca
URL: www.reseau-sadc.qc.ca/gaspenord
Membre(s) du bureau directeur: Richard Marin, Directeur général
SADC de Lotbinière
238, rte 269, Saint-Patrice-de-Beaurivage QC G0S 1B0
Tél: 418-596-3300; *Téléc:* 418-596-3303
Ligne sans frais: 866-596-3300
Courriel: sadc_lotbiniere@ciril.qc.ca
URL: www.sadclotbiniere.qc.ca
Membre(s) du bureau directeur: Sonia Forbes, Directrice générale
SADC de Papineau
565, av de Buckingham, Gatineau QC J8L 2H2
Tél: 819-986-1747; *Téléc:* 819-281-0303
Ligne sans frais: 888-986-7232
Courriel: sadc_papineau@ciril.qc.ca
URL: www.sadcpapineau.ca
Membre(s) du bureau directeur: Michel Lavergne, Directeur général
SADC de Rouyn-Noranda
161, av Murdoch, Rouyn-Noranda QC J9X 1E3
Tél: 819-797-6068; *Téléc:* 819-797-0096
Courriel: sadc_rouyn@ciril.qc.ca
URL: www.sadcrn.ca
Membre(s) du bureau directeur: Denis Jodouin, Directeur général
SADC de Témiscouata
3-A rue Hôtel-de-Ville, Notre-Dame-du-Lac QC G0L 1X0
Tél: 418-899-0808; *Téléc:* 418-899-0808
Courriel: sadc_temiscouata@ciril.qc.ca
URL: www.mrctemiscouata.qc.ca/sadc
Membre(s) du bureau directeur: Gaston Rousseau, Directeur général
SADC de l'Amiante
#201, 754, rue Notre-Dame nord, Thetford Mines QC G6G 2S7
Tél: 418-338-4531; *Téléc:* 418-338-9256
Courriel: sadc_amiante@ciril.qc.ca
URL: www.sadcamiante.com
Membre(s) du bureau directeur: Luce Dubois, Directrice générale
SADC de la MRC de Maskinongé
651, boul Saint-Laurent est, Louiseville QC J5V 1J1
Tél: 819-228-5921; *Téléc:* 819-228-0497
Courriel: sadcmask@cgocable.ca
URL: www.sadcmaskinonge.qc.ca
Membre(s) du bureau directeur: Doris Scott, Directrice générale
SADC de la MRC de Rivière-du-Loup
#201, 646, rue Lafontaine, Rivière-du-Loup QC G5R 3C8
Tél: 418-867-4272; *Téléc:* 418-867-8060
Courriel: sadc@mrc-rdl.qc.ca
URL: www.sadcmrcriviereduloup.ca
Membre(s) du bureau directeur: Gilles Goulet, Directeur général
SADC de la Neigette inc.
671, rte des Pionniers, Rimouski QC G0K 1J0
Tél: 418-735-2514; *Téléc:* 418-735-5854
Courriel: sadc_neigette@ciril.qc.ca
URL: www.reseau-sadc.qc.ca/neigette
Membre(s) du bureau directeur: Yvan Collin, Directeur général
SADC de la région d'Acton inc.
#101, 1545, rue Peerless, Acton Vale QC J0H 1A0
Tél: 450-546-3239; *Téléc:* 450-546-3619
Courriel: sadcacton@cooptel.qc.ca
URL: www.sadcacton.qc.ca
Membre(s) du bureau directeur: Line Robillard, Directrice générale
SADC de la région de Matane
#312, 235, av St-Jérôme, Matane QC G4W 3A7
Tél: 418-562-3171; *Téléc:* 418-562-1259
Courriel: sadc_matane@ciril.qc.ca
URL: www.sadc-matane.qc.ca
Membre(s) du bureau directeur: Annie Fournier, Directrice générale
SADC des Basques inc.
CP 970, 400-3, rue Jean Rioux, Trois-Pistoles QC G0L 4K0
Tél: 418-851-3172; *Téléc:* 418-851-3171
Courriel: sadc_basques@ciril.qc.ca
URL: www.reseau-sadc.qc.ca/sadcbasques
Membre(s) du bureau directeur: Alain Doucet, Directeur général
SADC des Iles-de-la-Madeleine
CP 940, #203, 735, ch Principal, Cap-aux-Meules QC G4T 1G8
Tél: 418-986-4601; *Téléc:* 418-986-4874
Courriel: sadc_iles@ciril.qc.ca
URL: www.sadcim.qc.ca
Membre(s) du bureau directeur: Lucien Landry, Directeur général
SADC des Laurentides
#230, 1332, boul Sainte-Adéle, Sainte-Adèle QC J8B 2N5
Tél: 450-229-3001; *Téléc:* 450-229-6928
Ligne sans frais: 888-229-3001
Courriel: info@sadclaurentides.org
URL: www.sadclaurentides.org
Membre(s) du bureau directeur: Josée Quevillon, Directrice générale
SADC du Bas-Richelieu
#2, 50, rue du Roi, Sorel-Tracy QC J3P 4M7
Tél: 450-746-5595; *Téléc:* 450-746-1803
Courriel: sadc@bellnet.ca
URL: www.soreltracyregion.net/sadc
Membre(s) du bureau directeur: Sylvie Pouliot, Directrice générale
SADC du Fjord inc
3031, rue Mgr. Dufour, La Baie QC G7B 1E8
Tél: 418-544-2885; *Téléc:* 418-544-0303
Courriel: courrier@sadcdufjord.qc.ca
URL: www.sadcdufjord.qc.ca
Membre(s) du bureau directeur: André Nepton, Directeur général
SADC du Haut-Saguenay
328, rue Gagnon, Saint-Ambroise QC G7P 2R1
Tél: 418-672-6333; *Téléc:* 418-672-4882
Courriel: sadc@videotron.ca
URL: www.sadchs.qc.ca
Membre(s) du bureau directeur: André Boily, Directeur général
SADC du Haut-Saint-François

47, rue Angus nord, East Angus QC J0B 1R0
Tél: 819-832-2447; *Téléc:* 819-832-1831
Ligne sans frais: 877-473-7232
Courriel: sadc_haut-saint-francois@ciril.qc.ca
URL: www.sadchsf.qc.ca
Membre(s) du bureau directeur: Danielle Simard, Directrice générale
SADC du Haut-Saint-Maurice inc
290, rue St. Joseph, La Tuque QC G9X 3Z8
Tél: 819-523-4227; *Téléc:* 819-523-5722
Courriel: info-sadchsm@ciril.qc.ca
URL: www.reseau-sadc.qc.ca/sadchsm
Membre(s) du bureau directeur: Julie Pelletier, Directrice générale
SADC du Rocher-Percé
CP 186, 129, boul René-Lévesque ouest, Chandler QC G0C 1K0
Tél: 418-689-5699; *Téléc:* 418-689-5556
Courriel: sadc_rocher-perce@ciril.qc.ca
URL: www.reseau-sadc.qc.ca/perce
Membre(s) du bureau directeur: Andreé Roy, Directrice générale
SADC du Témiscamingue
7B, rue des Oblats nord, Ville-Marie QC J9V 1H9
Tél: 819-629-3355; *Téléc:* 819-629-2793
Courriel: sadc_temiscamingue@ciril.qc.ca
URL: www.temiscamingue.net/sdt
Membre(s) du bureau directeur: Guy Trépanier, Directeur général
SADC région d'Asbestos
309, Chassé, Asbestos QC J1T 2B4
Tél: 819-879-7147; *Téléc:* 819-879-5188
Courriel: sadc_asbestos@ciril.qc.ca; sadc@mrcasbestos.com
URL: www.sadcasbestos.com
Membre(s) du bureau directeur: Marc Grimard, Directeur général
SADC région de Coaticook
#140, 38, rue Child, Coaticook QC J1A 2B0
Tél: 819-849-3053; *Téléc:* 819-849-7393
Courriel: sadccoat@videotron.ca
URL: www.regioncoaticook.qc.ca/sadc
Membre(s) du bureau directeur: Michel Dassylva, Directeur général
SADC région de Mégantic
5137, rue Frontenac, Lac-Mégantic QC G6B 1H2
Tél: 819-583-5332; *Téléc:* 819-583-5957
Courriel: sadc_megantic@ciril.qc.ca
URL: www.sadcmegantic.ca
Membre(s) du bureau directeur: Ginette Isabel, Directrice générale

Saint John Association of Insurance Professionals
c/o Plant Hope Adjusters Ltd., 33 Charlotte St., Saint John NB E2L 2H3
Tel: 506-632-1980; *Fax:* 506-632-1829
e-mail: maryanne@planthope.com
Overview: A small local organization
Chief Officer(s): Mary Anne LeBlanc AIIC, Director
Member of: Canadian Association of Insurance Women

Saskatchewan Association of Insolvency & Restructuring Professionals (SAIRP)
c/o Cameron Okolita Inc., #650, 2220 - 12th Ave., Regina SK S4P 0M8
Tel: 306-359-7131; *Fax:* 306-359-7144
e-mail: j.okolita@sasktel.net
Previous Name: Saskatchewan Insolvency Practitioners Association
Overview: A small provincial organization
Chief Officer(s): Joseph Andrew Okolita CA CIRP, President
Member of: Canadian Association of Insolvency & Restructuring Professionals

Saskatchewan Co-operative Association
#301, 201 - 21st St. East, Saskatoon SK S7K 0B8
Tel: 306-244-3702; *Fax:* 306-244-2165
e-mail: sca@sask.coop
URL: www.sask.coop
Overview: A medium-sized provincial organization
Chief Officer(s): Warren Crossman, Executive Director
Description: Provincial coalition of co-operatives, including credit unions, that collaborates to support and promote the co-operative model for community and economic development

Saskatchewan Independent Insurance Adjusters' Association
c/o Crawford Adjusters Canada, #210, 227 Primrose Dr., Saskatoon SK S7K 5E4
Tel: 306-931-1999; *Fax:* 306-931-2212
e-mail: tom.rixon@crawco.ca
Overview: A small provincial organization
Chief Officer(s): Thomas James Rixon, President

Saskatchewan Insolvency Practitioners Association *See* Saskatchewan Association of Insolvency & Restructuring Professionals

Saskatchewan Municipal Hail Insurance Association (SMHI)
2100 Cornwall St., Regina SK S4P 2K7
Tel: 306-569-1852; *Fax:* 306-522-3717
Toll-Free: 877-414-7644
e-mail: smhi@smhi.ca
URL: www.smhi.ca
Overview: A medium-sized provincial organization founded in 1917
Chief Officer(s): Murray Otterson, CEO; Rodney Schoettler, COO
Finances: *Annual Operating Budget:* Greater than $5 Million
Staff: 100 staff member(s)
Description: To provide spot-loss hail insurance coverage to Saskatchewan grain farmers at cost

Service budgétaire et communautaire d'Alma inc.
CP 594, 415, rue Collard ouest, Alma QC G8B 5W1
Tél: 418-668-2148; *Téléc:* 418-668-2048
Courriel: sbc.alma@globetrotter.net
URL: http://membres.lycos.fr/sbalma/
Aperçu: *Dimension:* petite; *Envergure: régionale; Organisme sans but lucratif; fondée en 1977*
Membre(s) du bureau directeur: Thérèse Gagnon, Coordonnatrice
Finances: *Budget de fonctionnement annuel:* Moins de $50,000
Personnel: 2 membre(s) du personnel; 40 bénévole(s)
Membre: 100-499; *Comités:* Prêts; Promotion; Recherche
Activités: Cours de budget et consommation; consultation budgétaire individuelle; fonds d'épargne et de prêt populaire; *Bibliothèque:* Centre de documentation au service budgétaire (Bibliothèque publique)
Publications: Budget conjoint, Document, Contenu: Méthode budgétaire au prorata des revenus destinés aux couples dont les 2 conjoints ont des revenus, afin que ceux-ci contribuent aux dépenses communes selon leurs revenus respectifs, Prix: 7$
Description: Aider les individus et les familles à faibles et moyens revenus, à résoudre leur difficultés financières et les problèmes qui en découlent; prévenir l'endettement; informer les consommateurs et les consommatrices sur les lois et sur leurs droits; travailler sur différentes problématiques au niveau des habitudes de consommation et de leurs conséquences sur le budget, la santé, l'organisation familiale, etc.

Service budgétaire et communautaire de Chicoutimi inc (SBC)
2422, rue Roussel, Chicoutimi QC G7G 1X6
Tél: 418-549-7597; *Téléc:* 418-549-1325
Courriel: sbc@vl.videotron.ca
Aperçu: *Dimension:* petite; *Envergure: locale; Organisme sans but lucratif; fondée en 1980*
Membre(s) du bureau directeur: Marlène Proulx, Personne ressource; Ginette Dutil, Personne ressource
Finances: *Budget de fonctionnement annuel:* $100,000-$250,000
Personnel: 5 membre(s) du personnel; 35 bénévole(s)
Membre: 1-99
Description: Aider les personnes dans leurs difficultés financières et aux prises avec les problèmes sociaux qui en découlent

Service de conciliation des assurances de personnes du Canada *See* Canadian Life & Health Insurance OmbudService

Service de conciliation en assurance de dommages *See* General Insurance OmbudService

Services de réglementation du marché inc. *See* Market Regulation Services Inc.

Social Investment Organization (SIO)
184 Pearl St., 2nd Fl., Toronto ON M4J 5B9
Tel: 416-461-6042; *Fax:* 416-461-2481
e-mail: info@socialinvestment.ca
URL: www.socialinvestment.ca
Also Known As: Canadian Association for Socially Responsible Investment
Overview: A medium-sized national organization founded in 1989
Chief Officer(s): Eugene Ellmen, Executive Director
Finances: *Annual Operating Budget:* $250,000-$500,000
Staff: 2 staff member(s); 20 volunteer(s)
Membership: 400; *Fees:* $2,500 associate; $250 professional; *Member Profile:* Asset management companies; investment fund companies; financial advisors; investors
Activities: *Internships:* Yes; *Speaker Service:* Yes; *Rents Mailing List:* Yes
Publications: SIO Forum Newsletter, q.; Asset Manager Report; Industry Bulletin, a.
Description: To take a leadership role in coordinating the SRI agenda in Canada; to raise public awareness of SRI in Canada; to reach out to other groups interested in SRI; to provide information on SRI to our members & the public

Society of Management Accountants of Alberta *See* CMA Canada - Alberta

Society of Management Accountants of British Columbia *See* CMA Canada - British Columbia

Society of Management Accountants of Canada *See* CMA Canada

The Society of Professional Accountants of Canada / La Société des comptables professionnels du Canada
#1007, 250 Consumers Rd., Toronto ON M2J 4V6
Tel: 416-350-8145; *Fax:* 416-350-8146
Toll-Free: 877-515-4447
e-mail: registrar@professionalaccountant.org
URL: www.professionalaccountant.org
Overview: A medium-sized national organization founded in 1978
Chief Officer(s): W.O. Nichols RPA, President
Finances: *Annual Operating Budget:* $50,000-$100,000
Membership: 300; *Fees:* $250; *Member Profile:* Individuals who have completed successfully mandatory accreditation examinations, adhered to the code of ethics, & provided evidence of at least three years of practical experience in accountancy
Activities: Professional development; employment referral service
Publications: Professional Accountant, s-a., Editor: W.O. Nicols
Description: To provide ongoing education & to set qualifying standards, to ensure the professional competence of its members in the practice of accountancy

Society of Public Insurance Administrators of Ontario (SPIAO)
c/o Town of Oakville, PO Box 310, Oakville ON L6J 5A6
Tel: 905-845-6601; *Fax:* 905-815-2019
Overview: A small provincial organization founded in 1977
Chief Officer(s): B. Angevaare, Treasurer
Finances: *Annual Operating Budget:* Less than $50,000
Staff: 6 volunteer(s)
Membership: 70 individual; *Fees:* $50; *Member Profile:* Must work for any of three levels of government, board of education, public utility, conservation authority or public housing authority
Activities: 2 one-day & 1 two-day workshops per year
Description: To exchange knowledge & pursue matters dealing with risk & insurance management; to promote cooperation among all local government bodies which have interests in the field of risk & insurance management; to encourage development of educational training programs; to collect & disperse information

La Société des comptables en management *See* CMA Canada

La Société des comptables en management du Nouveau-Brunswick *See* CMA New Brunswick

La Société des comptables professionnels du Canada *See* The Society of Professional Accountants of Canada

1000 Islands Credit Counselling Service
PO Box 191, 105 Strowger Blvd., Brockville ON K6V 5V2
Tel: 613-498-2111; *Fax:* 613-498-2116
Toll-Free: 800-926-0777
e-mail: info@eecentre.com
URL: eecentre.com
Overview: A small local organization founded in 1986
Chief Officer(s): Sherri Simzer, Executive Director

Finances: *Annual Operating Budget:* $500,000-$1.5 Million
Staff: 13 staff member(s); 10 volunteer(s)
Activities: *Speaker Service:* Yes; *Library:* Yes (Open to Public)
Member of: Youth Volunteer Corp. Canada; Ontario Association of Youth Employment Centres; Ontario Association of Credit Counselling Services

Toronto CFA Society

#1700, 80 Richmond St. West, Toronto ON M5H 2A4
Tel: 416-366-5755; *Fax:* 416-366-6716
URL: www.torontocfa.ca
Also Known As: Toronto Chartered Financial Analyst Society
Previous Name: Toronto Society of Financial Analysts
Overview: A small local organization
Chief Officer(s): Christine Cavanagh, Executive Director
Staff: 3 staff member(s)
Membership: 5,500
Description: To lead the investment profession in our local community by setting the highest standards of education, integrity & professional excellence; Affiliation(s): CFA Institute

Toronto Insurance Women's Association (TIWA)

PO Box 861, 31 Adelaide St. East, Toronto ON M5C 2K1
Tel: 416-359-8739
e-mail: dfsabour@mroc.com
URL: www.tiwa.org
Overview: A small local organization founded in 1960
Chief Officer(s): Dalia Sabour, President
Staff: 10 volunteer(s)
Membership: 150; *Fees:* $60
Publications: TIWA Topics, Newsletter, m., accepts advertising
Description: To educate and assist its members in reaching their potential both professionally and personally, promote the spirit of friendship and service in the industry, and encourage and foster high ethical standards in business and social relations; *Member of:* Canadian Association of Insurance Women

Toronto Society of Financial Analysts ***See*** Toronto CFA Society

Toronto Venture Group (TVG)

Heritage Bldg., MaRS Centre, #120B, 101 College St., Toronto ON M5G 1L7
Tel: 416-673-8480; *Fax:* 416-673-8480
e-mail: tvginfo@tvg.org
URL: www.tvg.org
Overview: A small local organization founded in 1990
Chief Officer(s): Erica Seibert, Executive Director
Finances: *Funding Sources:* Admission fees; subscriptions; corporate membership
Staff: 4 staff member(s)

Treasury Management Association of Canada (TMAC) / Association de gestion de trésorerie du Canada

#1010, 8 King St. East, Toronto ON M5C 1B5
Tel: 416-367-8500; *Fax:* 416-367-3240
Toll-Free: 800-449-8622
e-mail: info@tmac.ca
URL: www.tmac.ca
Previous Name: Cash Management Association of Canada
Overview: A medium-sized national organization founded in 1982
Chief Officer(s): Blair McRobie, Executive Director; Mike Whiston, President; Riina Koppel, Manager of Administration; Belinda Espley, Director; Rose Ficco, Coordinator; Jennifer Robb, Coordinator
Finances: *Annual Operating Budget:* $1.5 Million-$3 Million; *Funding Sources:* Seminars; conferences; membership fees
Staff: 5 staff member(s); 50+ volunteer(s)
Membership: 1,400; *Fees:* Schedule available; *Member Profile:* Employed in treasury management position; *Committees:* Nominating; Audit
Activities: The premier resource for the advancement of the treasury & finance profession; *Library:* National Resource Centre
Meetings: 2007; Cash & Treasury Management Conference, Oct.
Publications: The Canadian Treasurer, Magazine, bi-m., Editor: Bruce McDougall, Price: $40
Description: To provide forum for members to develop expertise in treasury management; to promote cooperation between suppliers & users of treasury management services; to maintain standards of professionalism within field of treasury management; *Member of:* International Group of Treasury Associations; Affiliation(s): Canadian Institute of Chartered Accountants; Society of Management Accountants; Certified General Accountants; Canadian Payments Association; Association of Canadian Pension Management; International Group of Treasury Associations; Financial Executive Institute

Vancouver Society of Financial Analysts ***See*** CFA Vancouver

Vehicle Information Centre of Canada ***See*** Insurance Bureau of Canada

Women in Capital Markets (WCM) / Les femmes sur les marchés financiers

#301, 250 Consumers Rd., Toronto ON M2J 4V6
Tel: 416-502-3614; *Fax:* 416-495-8723
e-mail: wcm@wcm.ca
URL: www.wcm.ca
Overview: A small national organization founded in 1995
Chief Officer(s): Marina deSouza, Executive Director; Jacqueline Szeto, President
Finances: *Annual Operating Budget:* $100,000-$250,000; *Funding Sources:* Founding firms; sponsors; membership dues
Staff: 2 staff member(s); 100 volunteer(s)
Membership: 500+; *Fees:* $150 full; $100 associate; $25 student; *Member Profile:* Full - 4 yrs. experience in capital markets or 2 yrs. with advanced degree in a business or professional designation; Associate - non-voting; Student; *Committees:* Programming; Education & Outreach; Scholarship; Marketing; Vinifera Wine Lovers Gala
Activities: Education & outreach; mentorship program; *Internships:* Yes; *Speaker Service:* Yes; *Rents Mailing List:* Yes
Publications: Newsletter, s-a., Contents: For members only
Description: To enable capital markets professionals to reach their greatest potential for success; to advance woment within Canadian financial services

World Council of Credit Unions, Inc. (WOCCU)

PO Box 2982, 5710 Mineral Point Rd., Madison WI 53701-2982 USA
Tel: 608-231-7130; *Fax:* 608-238-8020
Toll-Free: 800-356-2644
e-mail: mail@woccu.org
URL: www.woccu.org
Overview: A large international organization founded in 1971
Chief Officer(s): Pete Crear, CEO; Brian Branch, COO; Gary Plank, Chair; Grzegorz Bierecki, Secretary
Finances: *Annual Operating Budget:* Greater than $5 Million; *Funding Sources:* Membership dues; grants
Staff: 59 staff member(s)
Membership: 50,000 Plus; *Member Profile:* Represents the largest credit union cooperative network in the world, over 40,000 credit unions in more than 90 countries in which 136 million people are served by credit unions
Activities: Information; education; advocacy; leadership & technical services; Global Credit Union Network, an international clearinghouse for credit unions, offers affiliated credit unions access to resources produced by other members, electronically links credit union movements & leaders together from across the globe; *Awareness Events:* International Credit Union Day, 3rd Thursday in Oct.; *Internships:* Yes; *Library:* Information Resource Centre (Open to Public)
Awards: Distinguished Service Award
Publications: Credit Union World, Magazine, q., Editor: Kimberly Johnston, accepts advertising, Contents: Updates, global trends, economic & commerce issues, development spotlights, & activities of the international credit union movement
Description: To promote the sustainable growth & expansion of credit unions & financial cooperatives worldwide; to provide technical assistance & trade association services to members; Affiliation(s): Credit Union Central of Canada; International Cooperative Banking Assoc.; Assoc. of British Credit Unions Ltd.; Assoc. of Asian Confederation of Credit Unions; Caribbean Confederation of Credit Unions; Confederacion Latinoamericana de Cooperativas de Ahorro y Credito; Credit Union National Association; CUNA Caribbean Insurance Society Ltd; CUNA Mutual Group; Credit Union Services Corp. (Australia) Ltd.; ECCU Assurance Company Ltd.; Irish League of Credit Unions; International Raiffeisen Union; National Assoc. of Cooperative Savings & Credit Unions; National Credit Union Federation of Korea

SECTION 9

Publications

Included in this section are leading publications serving the Canadian business and finance industries.

Publications

Business & Finance

Advisor's Edge
One Mount Pleasant Rd., Toronto, ON M4Y 2Y5
416-764-3859, Fax: 416-764-3943,
service@advisor.ca
www.advisor.ca
Owned by: Rogers Publishing Ltd.
Circulation: 40,000
Frequency: 12 times a year
Profile:: Advisor's Edge magazine is an independent Canadian publication focused solely on the information needs of Canadian retail financial advisors (brokers, financial planners, insurance specialists, mutual fund salespeople and bank-based consultants). With a strong emphasis on practice management, the magazine helps advisors stay on top of industry trends, investment insurance products and strategies, as well as marketing and client relationship best practices

Deanne N. Gage, Editor

Affaires Plus Magazine
1100, boul René-Lévesque 24e étage, Montréal, QC H3B 4X9
514-392-9000, Fax: 514-392-4726,
aplus@transcontiental.ca
www.lesaffaires.com
Owned by: Transcontinental Media Inc.
Circulation: 88 806
Frequency: 12 fois par an; français
Profile:: Créé en 1978, le magazine Affaires PLUS est le magazine d'affaires au plus fort tirage et au plus fort lectorat au Québec. C'est aussi la plus personnelle des publications d'affaires de Médias Transcontinental. Le magazine est bâti autour de trois axes: mon argent, ma carrière, ma vie, qui déterminent à la fois le positionnement et le contenu d'Affaires PLUS

Daniel Germain, Rédacteur en chef

Alberta Insurance Directory
PO Box Terminal, 661 Market Hill, Vancouver, BC V5Z 4B5
604-874-1001, Fax: 604-874-3922,
manager@insurancewest.ca
www.insurancewest.ca
Owned by: Insurancewest Media Ltd.
Circulation: 1,555
Frequency: Annually
Profile:: The directory, started in 1982, is considered the recognized reference authority. It contains full, accurate and up-to-date listings in Alberta of 600 general insurance broker offices, 100 independent adjusting offices, 280 general and life insurer offices, and 50 insurance association and government-related offices. In addition, 2700 senior insurance personnel are listed and cross-referenced; 100 trades and suppliers also included. The 230-page coil-bound book is used primarily by general insurance brokers, adjusters and insurers in Alberta.

Bill Earle, Publisher & Editor

Alberta Venture
10259 - 105 St., Edmonton, AB T5J 1E3
780-990-0839, Fax: 780-425-4921, 866-227-4276
admin@albertaventure.com
www.albertaventure.com
Circulation: 40,800
Frequency: 10 times a year
Profile:: Alberta Venture is the only province-wide magazine that keeps you informed about Alberta's business community. Covers trends, issues, people and events that set the pace for Canada's fastest growing economy

Ruth Kelly, Editor

Atlantic Business Magazine
PO Box C, 197 Water St., St. John's, NL A1C 6E7
709-726-9300, Fax: 709-726-3013,
www.atlanticbusinessmagazine.com
Circulation: 33,000
Frequency: 6 times a year
Profile:: Founded in 1989, Atlantic Business Magazine is an independently owned, bi-monthly glossy publication that covers all areas of business within the four Atlantic provinces.

Hubert Hutton, Publisher

The Atlantic Co-operator
Atlantic Co-operative Publishers, 123 Halifax St., Moncton, NB E1C 8N5
506-858-6617, Fax: 506-858-6615,
editor@theatlanticco-opoerator.coop
www.theatlanticco-operator.coop
Circulation: 17,500 English; 3,500 French
Frequency: 9 times a year; English & French
Profile:: The Atlantic Co-operator is a monthly newspaper covering all aspects of co-operation values and principles in Atlantic Canada and around the world. We are published 9 times a year in both French and English by the Atlantic Co-operative Publishers and distributed throughout Atlantic Canada and les Iles-de-la-Madeleine, in Québec.

Jennifer MacLeod, Publisher

Atlantic Restaurant News
905-206-0150, Fax: 905-206-9972, 800-201-8596
www.can-restaurantnews.com
Owned by: Ishcom Publications Ltd.
Circulation: 5,500
Frequency: 6 times a year
Steve Isherwood, Publisher

Avantages
#800, 1200, ave McGill College, Montréal, QC H3B 4G7
514-843-2510, Fax: 514-843-2182,
www.revueavantages.ca
Owned by: Rogers Publishing Ltd.
Circulation: 5 159
Frequency: 8 fois par an; français
Profile:: Avantages is a French-language pension and benefits publication produced to meet the needs of the Quebec marketplace. Avantages provides information and analysis on pensions, benefits, healthcare and investments to key decision-makers who manage employer-sponsored pension and benefits plans in Quebec

Paul O. Williams, Publisher

Aviation Business Directory - Eastern Directory
250-658-6575, Fax: 250-658-6576, 800-656-7598
sales@canadianaviatormagazine.com
www.aviatormag.com
Former Name: Ontario - Aviation Business Directory
Owned by: Pilot Press Ltd.
Frequency: annual
Jack Scholfield, Publisher

Aviation Business Directory - Western Directory
250-658-6575, Fax: 250-658-6576, 800-656-7598
sales@canadianaviatormagazine.com
www.aviationbusinessdirectories.com
Former Name: BC & Yukon - Aviation Business Directory
Owned by: Pilot Press Ltd.
Frequency: annual
Mark Yelic, Publisher

Backbone Magazine
c/o Publimedia Communications Inc., 300 Beaver Rd., North Vancouver, BC V7N 3H6
905-918-0567, Fax: 604-986-5309,
info@backbonemag.com
www.backbonemag.com
Circulation: 115,000
Frequency: 6 times per year
Profile:: Backbone magazine's aim is to provide business people with a tangible tool to enhance the way they do business in Canada's New Economy

Steve Dietrich, Publisher

Le Banquier/Canadian Banker
Canadian Bankers Association, CP , Commerce Ct. West, 30th Fl., Toronto, ON M5L 1G2
416-362-6092, Fax: 416-362-7705,
cbacallcentre@cba.ca
www.cba.ca
Circulation: 8 400
Frequency: 4 fois par an; français/anglais
Profile:: Canadian Banker and Le Banquier are published four times annually by the Canadian Bankers Association. The magazines aim to keep their readers informed about the broad trends and changes in banking and the financial-services industry

Bar & Beverage Business
204-954-2085, Fax: 204-954-2057,
mp@mercury.mb.ca
www.barandbeverage.com
Owned by: Mercury Publications Ltd.
Circulation: 17,063
Frequency: 6 times a year
Frank Yeo, Publisher

The Bay Street Bull
#208, 80 Park Lawn Rd., Toronto, ON M8Y 3H8
416-252-4356, Fax: 416-252-0838,
info@thebaystreetbull.com
www.thebaystreetbull.com
Profile:: Magazine for men and women who make up Canada's leading business community

Stephen Petherbridge, Publisher

The BC Broker
PO Box Terminal, 661 Market Hill, Vancouver, BC V5Z 4B5
604-874-1001, Fax: 604-874-3922,
manager@insurancewest.ca
www.insurancewest.ca
Owned by: Insurancewest Media Ltd.
Circulation: 3,500
Frequency: 6 times a year
Profile:: The official publication of the Insurance Brokers Association of British Columbia (IBABC), the magazine is published six times a year - February, April, June, August, October and December. Circulation is 3500 of which 2600 is to member insurance brokers, the balance going to insurance companies, adjusters and suppliers to the industry. The BC Broker is an ideal medium for advertisers who wish to reach a target audience of all or part of the B.C. general insurance industry market. Not only does its circulation cover virtually all the key decision makers, it is also widely recognized as the best provincial insurance publication in Canada.

Bill Earle, Publisher & Managing Editor

BC Restaurant News
British Columbia Restaurant & Foodservices Association, #140, 475 West Georgia St., Vancouver, BC V6B 4M9
604-773-7883, Fax: 604-669-6175,
www.bcrfa.com
Frequency: 8 times a year
Jason McRobbie, Editor

BCBusiness Magazine
4180 Lougheed Hwy. 4th Fl., Burnaby, BC V5C 6A7
604-299-7311, Fax: 604-299-9188, 800-663-0518
ttjaden@canadawide.com
www.bcbusinessmagazine.com
Owned by: Canada Wide Magazines & Communications Ltd.
Circulation: 26,000
Frequency: Monthly; ISSN: 0849-481X
Profile:: An authoritative voice on the province's business scene, BCBusiness goes beyond the headlines to give readers valuable, relevant insights into today's trends and issues

Bonnie Irving, Editor

Benefits & Pensions Monitor
#501, 245 Fairview Mall Dr., Toronto, ON M2J 4T1
416-494-1066, Fax: 416-494-2536,
info@powershift.ca
www.bpmmagazine.com
Circulation: 22,850
Frequency: 12 times a year

Benefits & Pensions Monitor (continued)

Profile:: Benefits and Pensions Monitor is published eight times a year. Benefits and Pensions Monitor had to be different from the other industry magazine to succeed. It had to provide a unique editorial focus on issues that affect the industry. Monitor delivers. Today, Monitor has the industry's highest audited circulation.

John McLaine, Publisher

Benefits Canada

One Mount Pleasant Rd. 12th Floor, Toronto, ON M4Y 2Y5
416-764-3915, Fax: 416-764-3938,
paulb.williams@rci.rogers.com
www.benefitscanada.com
Owned by: Rogers Media Inc.
Circulation: 17,000
Frequency: 12 times a year; English & French
Profile:: Provides information and analysis on pensions, benefits, healthcare and investments to key decision-makers who manage employer-sponsored pension and benefits plans. The publication targets the plan sponsor community, particularly those employers with more than 500 employees

Paul Williams, Publisher

Bike Trade Canada

#703, 317 Adelaide St. West, Toronto, ON M5V 1P9
416-977-2100, Fax: 416-977-9200, 866-977-3325
info@pedalmag.com
www.pedalmag.com
Circulation: 5,000
Frequency: 3 times a year
Benjamin A. Sadavoy, Publisher & Editor

BIZ Magazine

1074 Cooke Blvd, Hamilton, ON L7T 4A8
905-522-6117, Fax: 905-529-2242,
info@townmedia.ca
Former Name: BIZ Hamilton/Halton Business Report; Hamilton Business Report
Owned by: Town Media Inc., a division of Osprey Media Group
Circulation: 24,000
Frequency: 4 times a year
Profile:: Business publication in the Hamilton/Burlington region, with award-winning features, profiles, real-life photography and controversial opinions

Arend Kirsten, Editor

The Bottom Line

#700, 123 Commerce Valley Dr. East, Markham, ON L3T 7W8
905-415-5804, Fax: 905-479-3758,
tbl@butterworths.ca
www.thebottomlinenews.com
Owned by: LexisNexis Canada Ltd.
Circulation: 30,428
Frequency: 16 times a year
Profile:: The Bottom Line is an independent and specialized business periodical that keeps accredited professional accountants, financial managers, and consultants abreast of news, trends, and technology within the industry

Michael Lewis, Editor

British Columbia Insurance Directory

PO Box Terminal, 661 Market Hill, Vancouver, BC V5Z 4B5
604-874-1001, Fax: 604-874-3922,
manager@insurancewest.ca
www.insurancewest.ca
Owned by: Insurancewest Media Ltd.
Circulation: 2,563
Frequency: Annually, Apr.
Profile:: The directory, started in 1964, is considered the recognized reference authority. It contains full, accurate and up-to-date listings in B.C. of 950 general insurance broker offices, 160 independent adjusting offices, 250 general and life insurer offices, and 60 insurance association and government-related offices. In addition, 5000 senior insurance personnel are listed and cross-referenced; 200 trades and suppliers also included. The 340-page coil-bound book is used primarily by general insurance brokers, adjusters and insurers in B.C.

Bill Earle, Editor & Publisher

Broadcast Dialogue

18 Turtle Path, Site 1, Box 150, Brechin, ON L0K 1B0
705-484-0752,
broadcastdialogue@rogers.com
www.broadcastdialogue.com
Circulation: 7,200
Howard Christensen, Publisher

The Bruce County Marketplace

PO Box , 910 Queen St., Kincardine, ON N2Z 2Y9
519-396-9142, Fax: 519-396-3555, 877-396-9142
marketplace@bmts.com
Circulation: 13,000
Frequency: 12 times a year
James Pannell, Publisher

Business Bulletin

Mississauga Board of Trade, #701, 77 City Centre Dr., Mississauga, ON L5B 1M5
905-273-6151, Fax: 905-273-4937,
info@mbot.com
www.mbot.com
Circulation: 22,000
Frequency: 11 times a year
Profile:: Business Bulletin has been replaced by the mbot magazine. mbot magazine is our dynamic business resource and reference tool. It provides an array of practical articles and advice that address the issues, news and trends important to businesses of all sizes and scopes in Mississauga as well as companies located outside the City. mbot magazine replaces our tabloid-style newspaper Business Bulletin.

Bill Dzugan, Coordinator

Business Central Magazine

#304, 4820 Gaetz Ave., Red Deer, AB T4N 4A4
403-309-5587, Fax: 403-346-3044
Circulation: 5,000
Frequency: 6 times a year
Donald C. Sylvester, Publisher & Editor

Business Examiner - North

777B Poplar St., Nanaimo, BC V9S 2H7
250-754-8344, Fax: 250-754-8304, 800-332-7355
merv@businessexaminer.net
www.businessexaminer.net
Circulation: 14,000
Frequency: Monthly
Steve Weatherbee, Editor

Business Examiner - South Island Edition

818 Broughton St., Victoria, BC V8W 1E4
250-381-3926, Fax: 250-381-5606,
www.businessexaminer.net
Circulation: 14,400
Frequency: 24 times a year
Bill MacAdam, Publisher

The Business Executive

#220, 466 Speers Rd., Oakville, ON L6K 3W9
905-845-8300, Fax: 905-845-9086,
wpeters@busexec.com
www.busexec.com
Also Known As: Southern & Southwestern Ontario's Business Publication
Circulation: 30,000
Frequency: 12 times a year
Profile:: The Business Executive is Southern Ontario's only business-to-business newspaper published on a monthly basis. The Business Executive is divided into sections to allow the readers to pick and choose subjects of most interest to them. Some of the sections include: Real Estate & Construction, Finance, Business News, People and Lifestyles, Computers and Technology, International Trade & Travel.

Thomas Peters, Publisher

Business in Calgary

#1025, 101 - 6th Ave. SW, Calgary, AB T2P 3P4
403-264-3270, Fax: 403-264-3276, 800-465-0322
info@businessincalgary.com
www.businessincalgary.com
Circulation: 30,735
Frequency: Monthly
Profile:: A monthly publication dedicated to producing intelligent, colorful articles about the people, trends and events that make Calgary a prominent business centre in the west.

Carnie Leard, Editor

Business in Vancouver

102 East 4th St., Vancouver, BC V5T 1G2
604-688-2398, Fax: 604-688-1963,
www.biv.com
Circulation: 16,000
Frequency: Weekly, Tue.
Profile:: Business in Vancouver is an award-winning weekly newspaper serving Greater Vancouver since 1989. Targeted at business decision-makers, it provides local business news and information every Tuesday and reaches more than 62,000+ readers a week.

Tom Siba, Publisher

Business London

PO Box , London, ON, ON N5Y 4X3
519-472-7601, Fax: 519-473-7859,
editorial@businesslondon.ca
www.businesslondon.ca
Former Name: London Business Magazine
Owned by: Bowes Publishers Ltd.
Circulation: 12,000
Frequency: Monthly
Profile:: The Magazine provides unparalleled behind-the-scenes coverage, chronicling companies on the move and putting faces to faceless events.

Gord Delamont, Publisher

Business Niagara Magazine

159 York St., St Catharines, ON L2R 6E9
905-682-4509, Fax: 905-682-8219,
www.bizniagara.com
Circulation: 20,000
Profile:: Released bi-monthly by Osprey Media Group Inc., Business Niagara Magazine reaches over 20,000 registered businesses and is geared to everyone from a one-person operation to a large publicly traded organization.

Mishka Balsom, Publisher

Business Trends

1383 Confederation St., Sarnia, ON N7S 5P1
519-336-1100, Fax: 519-336-1833,
businesstrends@cogeco.net
www.sarniabusinesstrends.com
Circulation: 6,300
Frequency: 12 times a year
Profile:: Covers business trends in the Sarnia area

Gord Bowes, Editor

Business Voice

1300 Hollis St., Halifax, NS B3J 1T6
902-420-9943, Fax: 902-429-9058,
publishers@metroguide.ca
www.metroguidepublishing.ca/bv.php
Owned by: Metro Guide Publishing
Circulation: 7,500
Frequency: 10 times a year
Profile:: Business Voice is Halifax's leading business magazine, offering unrivalled access to Metro's decision-makers. Business Voice is the official voice of the Halifax Chamber of Commerce: 95% of members read most or every issue. It keeps readers updated on Chamber policies and activities, plus develop-ments in the business community

Sheila Blair, Publisher

BusinessWoman Canada Magazine

PO Box , Barrie, ON L4N 0B3
705-722-9692, Fax: 705-722-7268, 877-251-7226
Circulation: 20,000
Frequency: 4 times a year
Donna Messer, Editor

Businest

CP A, 217, av Léonidas, Rimouski, QC G5L 9G6
514-866-3131, Fax: 514-866-3030, 800-361-7262
reseau@hebdos-select.qc.ca
www.reseauselect.com
Circulation: 20 100
Frequency: Mensuel; français
Profile:: Publication qui couvre de domaine des affaires, et dessert les professionnels, les entreprises et les gens d'affaires le territoire de La Pocatière aux les-de-la-Madeleine, et la Côte-Nord

Pierre Michaud, Rédacteur-en-chef

CA Magazine

277 Wellington St. West, Toronto, ON M5V 3H2
416-977-3222, Fax: 416-204-3409,
CAmagazine@cica.ca
www.camagazine.com
Circulation: 72,500

Frequency: 10 times a year; English & French
Profile:: CAmagazine is published by the Canadian Institute of Chartered Accountants (CICA) ten times a year. Articles about careers in chartered accounting are featured while current issues are discussed and explained. The magazine also deals with a wide variety of business topics from the Chartered Accountant's perspective

Christian Bellavance, Editor-in-chief

Canada Japan Journal
Japan Advertising Ltd., #410, 1199 West Pender St., Vancouver, BC V6E 2R1
604-688-2486, Fax: 604-688-1487, 888-245-2549
japanad@telus.net
www.canadajournal.com
Former Name: Canada Japan Business Journal
Circulation: 15,750
Frequency: Monthly; Japanese
Taka Aoki, Editor

Canada Journal
KLR Communications, 44 Cameron Cres., Toronto, ON M4G 1Z8
416-487-0166, Fax: 416-487-2452,
info@canadajournal.ca
www.canadajournal.ca
Circulation: 27,000
Frequency: bi-weekly; German
Klaus Ruland, Publisher/Editor

Canadian Advertising Rates & Data
416-764-2000, Fax: 416-764-1709, 800-268-9119
www.cardonline.ca
Owned by: Rogers Publishing Ltd.
Circulation: 2,100
Frequency: Monthly
Artemis Hall, Managing Manager

Canadian Apparel Magazine
Canadian Apparel Federation, #504, 124 O'Connor St., Ottawa, ON K1P 5M9
613-231-3220, Fax: 613-231-2305, 800-661-1187
info@apparel.ca
www.apparel.ca
Circulation: 25,466
Frequency: 6 times a year
Bob Kirke, Publisher

Canadian Appraiser / L'Évaluateur Canadien
#3C, 2020 Portage Ave., Winnipeg, MB R3J 0K4
204-985-9780, Fax: 204-985-9795,
info@kelman.ca
www.kelman.ca
Circulation: 5,961
Frequency: 4 times a year
Craig Kelman, Editor

Canadian Association Publishers
PO Box , 230 Markham Rd., Scarborough, ON M1J 3N7
416-955-1550, Fax: 416-955-1391,
info@capmagazines.ca
www.capmagazines.ca
Circulation: 30,650
Frequency: Semi-annual
Profile:: Business Resources Canada is Canada's premier Small Business Resource Directory for Owners and Entrepreneurs. Published quarterly, Business Resources Canada, with its combined directory and magazine format, guides and inspires Canadians who are starting or growing a business as their career.

Kelly Chase, Production

Canadian Business
One Mount Pleasant Rd. 11th Floor, Toronto, ON M4Y 2Y5
416-764-1200, Fax: 416-764-1404,
adsales@canadianbusiness.com
www.canadianbusiness.com/canadian_business_ magazine
Owned by: Rogers Publishing Ltd.
Circulation: 84,000
Frequency: 24 times a year; ISSN: 0008-3100
Profile:: Canadian Business, Canada's best-selling business magazine, captures the attention of Canada's business leaders with topical, timely stories that matter to corporate managers and executives. Written for an audience with an orientation to the future, its compelling insight inspires readers to capitalize on change

Joe Chidley, Editor

Canadian Business Franchise/L'entreprise
c/o Kenilworth Media Inc., #710, 15 Wertheim Ct., Richmond Hill, BC L4B 3H7
905-771-7333, Fax: 905-771-7336, 800-409-8688
info@kenilworth.com
www.cgb.ca
Frequency: Bi-monthly
Profile:: Canadian Business Franchise Magazine is a bi-monthly publication that features articles on franchise advice from bankers, lawyers and franchise specialists. The magazine is in its eleventh year of production and is the best selling Franchise magazine in Canada

Colin Bradbury, Publisher & Editor

Canadian Direct Marketing News
#302, 137 Main St. North, Markham, ON L3P 1Y2
905-201-6600, Fax: 905-201-6601, 800-688-1838
home@dmn.ca
www.dmn.ca
Circulation: 8,058
Frequency: Monthly, plus annual directory of suppliers & annual directories The List of Lists...The DM Industry Sourcebook & the Canadian Call Centre Industry Directory
Ron Glen, Editor

Canadian German Trade
#1500, 480 University Ave., Toronto, ON M5G 1V2
416-598-3355, Fax: 416-598-1840,
info@germanchamber.ca
www.germanchamber.ca
Circulation: 2,500
Frequency: 6 times a year
Profile:: Covers news concerning the Canadian and German economy, special articles which are of interest to the Canadian and German business community, as well as updated economic datanews concerning the Canadian and German economy, special articles which are of interest to the Canadian and German business community, as well as updated economic data

Sonya Deevy, Contact

Canadian Insurance
416-599-0772, Fax: 416-599-0867,
info@cdnins.com
www.cdnins.com
Owned by: Stone & Cox Ltd.
Circulation: 11,600
Frequency: Monthly
Profile:: Canadian Insurance magazine provides leading coverage of the news, events and trends that shape the p&c insurance industry. Focus is on the issues of claims management, information technology; global & commercial risks, reinsurance, loss prevention, adjusters, risk management, brokers & underwriters, environment, and financial services

Barbara Aarsteinsen, Editor

Canadian Insurance Claims Directory
#700, 10 St Mary St., Toronto, ON M4Y 2W8
416-978-2239, Fax: 416-978-4738, 800-565-9523
publishing@utpress.untoronto.ca
www.utppublishing.com
Owned by: University of Toronto Press Inc.
Circulation: 1,500
Frequency: Annually, May
Profile:: This directory is published yearly to facilitate the forwarding of insurance claims throughout Canada and the United States. Its subscribers are adjusters, firms specializing in counsel to the insurance industry, insurance companies, and industrial and government offices. Listed are a total of 1600 independent adjusting offices, which offer dependable service to claims forwarders, as well as some 100 insurance counsel, who are experienced in insurance defense litigation.

Gwen Peroni, Editor

Canadian Investment Review
One Mount Pleasant Ave., 12th Fl., Toronto, ON M4Y 2Y5
416-764-3867, Fax: 416-764-3934,
www.investmentreview.com
Owned by: Rogers Publishing Ltd.
Frequency: 4 times a year
Profile:: Canada's leading forum for academics, institutional investors and industry practitioners to exchange ideas on the capital markets, investment and economic theory, and the related sociology and demographics.

Caroline Cakebread, Editor

The Canadian Manager
Canadian Institute of Management, 15 Collier St., Lower Level, Barrie, ON L4M 1G5
705-725-8926, Fax: 705-725-8196, 800-387-5774
office@cim.ca
www.cim.ca
Circulation: 4,500
Frequency: 4 times a year
Profile:: The Canadian Manager is published 4 times per year by the Canadian Institute of Management, with a readership over 12,000 (approx.)

Anna Victoria Wong, Editor/Manager

Canadian MoneySaver
PO Box , 5540 Loyalist Pkwy., Bath, ON K0H 1G0
613-352-7448, Fax: 613-352-7700,
moneyinfo@canadianmoneysaver.ca
www.canadianmoneysaver.ca
Circulation: 69,700
Frequency: 9 times a year
Profile:: Canadian MoneySaver is an acclaimed investment advisory with a recognized reputation for providing a trustworthy and down-to-earth service since 1981. Canadian MoneySaver publishes monthly with three double issues (July/August, November/December and March/April).

Dale Ennis

Canadian Shareowner Magazine
#806, 4 King St. West, Toronto, ON M5H 1B6
416-595-9600, Fax: 416-595-0400, 800-268-6881
magazine@ShareOwner.com
www.shareowner.com
Circulation: 20,876
Frequency: 6 times a year; ISSN: 0836-0960
Profile:: Periodical offering a proprietary Stock Selection Guide to find stocks in which subscribers ought to consider investing

John T. Bart, Publisher & Editor

The Canadian Taxpayer
416-609-8000, Fax: 416-298-5082, 800-387-5164
carswell.orders@thomson.com
www.carswell.com
Owned by: Carswell
Circulation: 1,000
Frequency: 24 times per year
Profile:: The Taxpayer is the flagship publication of the Canadian Taxpayers Federation (CTF). It is published six times a year and contains comprehensive updates on CTF happenings and accomplishments around the country. It features articles written by CTF researchers and spokespersons. Guest editorial writers also contribute to this publication.

Robert Freeman, Vice-President

Canadian Treasurer
c/o Treasury Management Association of Canada, #1010, 8 King St. East, Toronto, ON M5C 1B5
416-367-8500, Fax: 416-367-3240, 800-449-8622
info@tmac.ca
www.tmac.ca
Circulation: 5,313
Frequency: 6 times a year
Profile:: TMAC's bimonthly magazine, Canadian Treasurer, brings directly to you the latest trends in treasury management. Canadian Treasurer reaches treasury professionals of major corporate and government organizations throughout Canada. It is also distributed to other organizations within the Canadian financial community, the U.S. and around the world. Circulation includes the top 1,000 companies in Canada.

Bruce McDougall, Managing Editor

Canadian Underwriter
#800, 12 Concorde Pl., Toronto, ON M3C 4J2
Fax: 416-510-6809, 800-268-7742
www.cdnunderwriter.com
Owned by: Business Information Group
Circulation: 10,061
Frequency: Monthly; also Rehabilitation & Medical Services Guide, Litigation Services Guide, Insurance Marketer, Annual Statistical Issue, Ontario Insurance Directory
Profile:: Canadian Underwriter is a professional Insurance and Risk Management magazine covering all aspects of Canada's property and casualty Insurance Market. Covers all the insurance news and insight into the issues, events and people

Canadian Underwriter (continued)

affecting this $30 billion market. Reporting on all sectors of the market, including: brokers; insurers; reinsurance; claims; risk management; associations; legislation; legal; technology; insurer statistical review and all other related Insurance topics

David Gambrill, Editor

CCN Matthews Media Directories

48 Yonge St., 8 Fl., Toronto, ON M5E 1G6
416-362-0885, Fax: 416-955-0705, 888-299-0338
info@ccnmatthews.com
www.ccnmatthews.com
Other information: Toll Free Fax: 1-800-363-9296
Former Name: Matthews Media Directories
Elizabeth Fowler, Research Manager

Central Nova Business News

Advocate Print & Publishing Ltd., PO Box , 181 Brown's Point Rd., Pictou, NS B0K 1H0
902-893-0375, Fax: 902-893-1353
Circulation: 1,500
Frequency: Monthly
Profile:: The official Publication of the Truro and District Chamber of Commerce

Jason Warren, Editor

CGA Magazine

#800, 1188 Georgia St. West, Vancouver, BC V6E 4A2
604-669-3555, Fax: 604-689-5845, 800-663-1529
jward@cga-canada.org
www.cga-online.org/canada
Circulation: 60,000
Frequency: 6 times a year; English & French
Profile:: CGA Magazine profiles current issues relevant to professional accountancy and discusses news and trends in the business and regulatory environment. Printed 6 times a year, this glossy publication is distributed to 68,000 CGA students, members, and leaders in the business, government, education and regulatory communities.

Barbara Cameron, Publisher

China's Wired!

#400, 1235 Bay St., Toronto, ON M5R 3K4
416-966-9391, Fax: 416-699-1165,
www.flyingarmchair.com
Frequency: 12 times a year (internet)
Profile:: China's Wired! Your Guide to the Internet in China, is the first book written on the Internet and its use and potential in the People's Republic of China. China's Wired! is designed to be the Internet guide on the PRC for investors and entrepreneurs

The Chronicle of Healthcare Marketing

905-273-9116, Fax: 905-273-4322, 866-633-4766
health@chronicle.org
www.chronicle.ca
Owned by: Chronicle Information Resources Ltd.
Circulation: 2,159
Frequency: 9 times a year
Mitchell Shannon, Publisher

CMA Management Magazine

c/o Society of Management Accountants of Canada, Miss. Exec., #1400, One Robert Speck Pkwy., Mississauga, ON L4Z 3M3
905-949-4200, Fax: 905-949-0888, 800-263-7622
info@cma-canada.org
www.managementmag.com
Former Name: CMA Magazine
Circulation: 48,000
Frequency: 9 times a year; English & French
Profile:: Management is an outstanding business magazine specifically tailored to help you make informed business decisions and give you a strategic advantage. It provides effective, practical solutions to your most pressing business challenges. It features the latest trends in management strategies with sharp, fresh editorial and attention-grabbing design.

David Fletcher, Publisher

CNS Cabling Networking Systems

416-510-6755, Fax: 416-510-5134, 800-268-7742
vpetsis@cablingsystems.com
www.cablingsystems.com
Former Name: Cabling Systems
Owned by: Business Information Group
Circulation: 10,313
Frequency: 6 times a year

Vaios Petsis, Publisher

Commerce & Industry

1740 Wellington Ave., Winnipeg, MB R3H 0E8
204-954-2085, Fax: 204-954-2057,
mp@mercury.mb.ca
www.mercury.mb.ca
Owned by: Mercury Publications Ltd.
Circulation: 18,154
Frequency: 6 times a year
Profile:: A national publication focused on the industrial, manufacturing, resource, transportation and construction sectors. Each issue offers a large variety of sector analysis, in-depth company profiles and reports on key areas of interest to the magazine's target audience.

Al Kaglik, National Account Manager

Commerce News

Edmonton Chamber of Commerce, #700, 9990 Jasper Ave., Edmonton, AB T5J 1P7
780-426-4620, Fax: 780-424-7946,
info@edmontonchamber.com
www.edmontonchamber.com
Also Known As: Edmonton Chamber News
Circulation: 36,000
Frequency: 11 times a year
Profile:: Published by the Edmonton Chamber of Commerce, reaches an estimated audience of over 150,000 business readers per issue. It is direct mailed eleven times per year to every Chamber member and subscriber (4,500 copies), to all Edmonton area businesses, government and association leaders around the region, and to all Alberta Chambers of Commerce (25,500 copies).

Martin Salloum, Publisher

Contact

Canadian Professional Sales Assn., #800, 310 Front St., Toronto, ON M5V 3B5
416-408-2685, Fax: 416-408-2684,
www.cpsa.com
Circulation: 37,125
Frequency: 6 times a year
Bernadette Johnson, Editor

Conventions Meetings Canada

416-764-1635, Fax: 416-764-1419,
sdempsey@rmpublishing.com
www.meetingscanada.com
Owned by: Rogers Publishing Ltd.
Circulation: 10,586
Frequency: Annually
Stephen Dempsey, Publisher

Corporate Ethics Monitor

Lawrence Plaza, PO Box , Toronto, ON M6A 3B7
416-783-6776, Fax: 416-783-7386,
info@ethicscan.ca
www.ethicscan.ca
Circulation: 400
Frequency: Bi-monthly
Profile:: Each sixteen page issue of the bi-monthly Corporate Ethics Monitor ($297 Canadian for one year, $456 CDN for foreign subscriptions) is laden with articles and stories that deal with recognizing and enhancing ethics in the workplace. Expect to find original research, timely articles, provocative perspectives, and practical ideas. The reporting on comparative business practices reflects dozens of hours of interviews, data base retrieval, fact checking and preparation of tables, charts and profiles. All this, plus insightful articles from regular columnists, an OPEN FORUM for executives, a Face to Face debate section, and lively book reviews.

Defined Benefit Monitor

#501, 245 Fairview Mall Dr., Toronto, ON M2J 4T1
Frequency: 2 times a year
John McLaine, Publisher

Defined Contribution Monitor

#501, 245 Fairview Maill Dr., Toronto, ON M2J 4T1
Frequency: 2 times a year
John McLaine, Publisher

Direct Marketing News

#302, 137 Main St. North, Markham, ON L3P 1Y2
905-201-6600, Fax: 905-201-6601,
www.dmn.ca
Ron Glen, Editor

EDGE

#302, 55 World Town Centre Ct., Scarborough, ON M1P 4X4
416-290-0240, 800-387-5312
info@itbusiness.ca
www.itbusiness.ca
Former Name: Info Systems Executive
Owned by: Transcontinental ITBusiness Group
Circulation: 16,640
Frequency: 12 times a year
Profile:: EDGE (Executives in a Digital Global Economy) is a non-technical, monthly magazine for CEOs, CFOs, CIOs and other senior executives who want to know how information technology can be used to transform their business. Through a combination of case studies, executive profiles and a look at best practices, EDGE not only demystifies IT, it shows how organizations can achieve competitive advantage.

Martin Slofstra, Editor

Entreprendre

Editions Qualité Performante inc., #660, 1600, boul St-Martin est, Laval, QC H7G 4R8
450-669-8373, Fax: 450-669-9078, 800-479-1777
message@entreprendre.ca
www.entreprendre.ca
Circulation: 45 000
Frequency: 10 fois par an; français
Profile:: Le magazine Entreprendre rejoint un auditoire exceptionnel de décideurs du monde des affaires. Outil d'information qui développe des références et éclaire la nature profonde de l'entrepreneurship au Québec

Edmond Bourque, Publisher

Ethnic Media & Markets

416-764-1606, Fax: 416-764-1709,
www.cardonline.ca
Owned by: Rogers Media Inc.
Circulation: 1,500
Frequency: 2 times a year
Bruce Richards, Publisher

Exchange Magazine for Business

#10, 160 Frobisher Dr., Waterloo, ON N2V 2B1
519-886-0298, Fax: 519-886-6409,
editor@exchangemagazine.com
www.exchangemagazine.com
Circulation: 17,500
Frequency: 8 times a year
Profile:: Covers business news in the Kitchener-Waterloo area

Jon Rohr, Editor-in-chief

Finance et Investissement

514-392-9000, Fax: 514-392-4726, 800-361-5479
www.finance-investissement.com
Owned by: Transcontinental Media Inc.
Circulation: 18,000
Frequency: 14 times a year
Profile:: Depuis son lancement en novembre 1999, le journal Finance et Investissement est devenu la source d'information privilégiée des représentants en épargne collective, des conseillers en valeurs mobilières, des conseillers en sécurité financière et des planificateurs financiers

Sylvain Bedard, Publisher

Financial Post Business

#300, 1450 Don Mills Rd., Toronto, ON M3B 3R5
416-383-2300, Fax: 416-386-2836,
editorial@nationalpostbusiness.com
www.nationalpostbusiness.com
Former Name: National Post Business
Circulation: 289,000
Frequency: 12 times a year
Brian Banks, Editor

FlashFinance

#100, 321, rue de la Commune, Montréal, QC H2Y 2E1
514-289-9595, Fax: 514-289-9527,
flash@flashfinance.ca
www.flashfinance.ca
Circulation: 2 000
Frequency: Weekly
Profile:: Outil privilégié d'information du monde de l'assurance et de la finance, FlashFinance.ca joint des milliers de dirigeants de compagnies d'assurance, de propriétaires de cabinets, de directeurs de courtage, et de conseillers financiers

Serge Therrien, Publisher

Forum
c/o Advocis, 350 Bloor St. East, 2nd Fl., Toronto, ON M4W 3W8
416-444-5251, Fax: 416-444-8031,
info@advocis.ca
www.advocis.ca
Former Name: CAIFA Forum
Circulation: 18,100
Frequency: 12 times a year
Peter Wilmshurst, Publisher

The FP Survey of Industrials
Financial Post Data Group, 1450 Don Mills Rd., 2nd Fl., Toronto, ON M3B 2X7
416-442-2121, Fax: 416-442-2968,
fpdg@canwest.com
Former Name: The Financial Post Survey of Industrials
Circulation: 3,870
Frequency: Annually, Aug.
Profile:: Financial and operational information on publicly traded Canadian companies

Franchise Canada Magazine
Canadian Franchise Association, #116, 5399 Eglinton Ave. West, Toronto, ON M9C 5K6
416-695-2896, Fax: 416-695-1950, 800-665-4232
info@cfa.ca
www.cfa.ca
Circulation: 6,000
Frequency: 6 times a year
Profile:: A bi-monthly magazine geared at entrepreneurs interested in acquiring a franchise. Franchise Canada Magazine will contain top-notch editorial from leading authorities in the industry as well as countless tips on how to establish a successful franchise.

John Scofield, Editor

General Insurance Register
416-599-0772, Fax: 416-599-0867,
info@cdnins.com
www.cdnins.com
Owned by: Stone & Cox Ltd.
Circulation: 5,500
Frequency: Annually, Jan.
Profile:: Lists insurance Adjusters, Appraisers, Legal firms in Canada; Consultants, Engineering, Investigation, Rehabilitation, Replacement, Restoration and other services companies; also lists Brokers, Intermediaries and Managing Agents

J. Wyndham, Publisher & Editor

Gestion
3000, ch de la Côte-Sainte-Catherine, Montréal, QC H3T 2A7
514-340-6677, Fax: 514-340-6975,
revue.gestion@hec.ca
revue.hec.ca/gestion
Circulation: 3 500
Frequency: 4 fois par an; français
Profile:: La Revue Gestion a pour but de favoriser la diffusion des connaissances dans tous les domaines de la gestion en français. Particulièrement populaire au Québec, la revue est également lue dans d'autres régions francophones. Offre à ses lecteurs des articles inédits présentant les dernières recherches, des analyses critiques, des synthèses et des réflexions originales dans le domaine de la gestion en Amérique du nord

Michel Vézina, Rédacteur-en-chef

Guide to Canadian Healthcare Facilities
c/o Canadian Healthcare Association, 17 York St., Ottawa, ON K1N 9J6
613-241-8005, Fax: 613-241-9481,
custserv@cha.ca
www.cha.ca
Former Name: Canadian Hospital Association Buyer's Guide
Also Known As: The Guide
Circulation: 1,300
Frequency: annual
Eleanor Sawyer, Director

Halton Business Times
#1, 5040 Mainway, Burlington, ON L7L 7G5
905-632-4444, Fax: 905-632-9162,
thepost@worldchat.com
Circulation: 12,000
Frequency: 12 times a year
Ian Oliver, Publisher

Huronia Business Times
Kozlov Centre, #243, 400 Bayfield St., Barrie, ON L4M 5A1
705-728-3090, Fax: 705-734-9600,
businesstimes@simcoe.com
www.huroniabusinesstimes.com
Circulation: 12,000
Frequency: 12 times a year
Profile:: Purchased by Metroland Business Publications in September of 1998, Huronia Business Times, and its sister publication the Mississauga Business Times, was formerly owned by North Island Publishing from 1992-1998. Metroland also publishes five other Business Times newspapers in southern Ontario

Martin Melbourne, Editor

Imprint Canada
#16, 190 Marycroft Ave., Woodbridge, ON L4L 5Y2
905-856-2600, Fax: 905-856-2667, 877-895-7022
feedback@imprintcanada.com
www.imprintcanada.com
Circulation: 6,700
Tony Muccilli, Publisher

In Business Windsor
1775 Sprucewood, La Salle, ON N9J 1X7
519-250-2880, Fax: 519-250-2881,
gbaxter@inbusinesswindsor.com
www.inbusinesswindsor.com
Circulation: 10,500
Frequency: 12 times a year
Profile:: Monthly publication which highlights business news in the Windsor area

Jenine Fry, Associate Editor

Info-ACAIQ
Association des courtiers et agents immobilier du Québec, #300, 6300, rue Auteuil, Brossard, QC J4Z 3P2
450-676-4800, Fax: 450-676-7801, 800-440-5110
info@acaiq.com
www.acaiq.com
Former Name: ACAIQ Magazine
Circulation: 16 000
Profile:: L'Info ACAIQ est le journal des professionnels du courtage immobilier du Québec. Il couvre divers sujets relatifs à l'application de la Loi sur le courtage immobilier, aux règlements de la profession, au marché immobilier en plus de questions d'ordre juridique et déontologique reliées à la pratique du courtage immobilier

Infopresse
514-842-5873, Fax: 514-842-2422,
redaction@infopresse.com
www.infopresse.com
Owned by: Éditions Infopresse inc.
Circulation: 7 500
Frequency: 10 fois par an
Charles Grandmont, Rédacteur-en-chef

The Insurance Journal
#100, 321 Rue de la Commune West, Montreal, QC H2Y 2E1
514-289-9595, Fax: 514-289-9527,
idesk@insurance-journal.ca
www.insurance-journal.ca
Owned by: Les Editions du Journal de l'Assurance
Circulation: 15 500
Frequency: 10 times a year
Profile:: The Insurance Journal targets financial advisors, life insurance producers, financial planners, and general insurance brokers in Canada. The magazine publishes news and examines trends in the development of insurance and financial products, such as group and individual insurance, disability insurance, mutual funds, segregated funds, health care management, and information technology. Published 10 times per year.

Serge Therrien, Publisher

Insurancewest
PO Box Terminal, 661 Market Hill, Vancouver, BC V5Z 4B5
604-874-1001, Fax: 604-874-3922,
manager@insurancewest.ca
www.insurancewest.ca
Owned by: Insurancewest Media Ltd.
Circulation: 6,000
Frequency: 6 times a year
Profile:: Launched in 1996, this bi-monthly magazine (formerly a quarterly) circulates to 6000 in Canada's four western provinces - virtually every insurance industry decision-maker in the west. Insurancewest is about insurance people and companies

Bill Earle, Publisher & Editor

Investment Executive
#100, 25 Sheppard Ave. West, Toronto, ON M2N 6S7
416-733-7600, Fax: 416-218-3544,
twilmott@investmentexecutive.com
www.investmentexecutive.com
Circulation: 50,200
Frequency: 16 times a year
Profile:: Investment Executive is Canada's national newspaper for financial service industry professionals. Investment Executive is published 16 times a year and reaches more than 120,000 financial advisors. Investment Executive has gained the respect of its readers by offering intelligent, informed coverage of the financial services industry and providing insightful information for advisors on topics as diverse as mutual funds, investment research, technology, estate planning, tax, building relationships with clients and developing products and services for the client of the future.

Tessa Wilmott, Editor-in-chief

Investor's Digest of Canada
#700, 133 Richmond St. West, Toronto, ON M5H 3M8
416-869-1177, Fax: 416-869-0616, 800-504-8846
customers@mplcomm.com
www.adviceforinvestors.com
Also Known As: The Digest
Circulation: 42,912
Frequency: 24 times a year
Profile:: Devoted to uncovering profitable opportunities in every area of investing, using the insights of Canada's leading investment professionals

Michael Popovich, Editor

Italcommerce
Italian Chamber of Commerce in Canada, #1150, 550, rue Sherbrooke ouest, Montréal, QC H3A 1B9
514-844-4249, Fax: 514-844-4875, 800-263-4372
info.montreal@italchambers.net
www.italchamber.qc.ca
Frequency: 3 times a year; French, English & Italian
Profile:: A pour mission de promouvoir et soutenir les échanges commerciaux entre le Québec, le Canada et l'Italie. Le magazine est diffusé au Canada, en Italie ainsi que dans 60 autres pays où on retrouve des chambres de commerce italiennes

Pasquale Iacobacci, Managing Editor

ITBusiness Report
#302, 55 Town Ct., Scarborough, ON M1P 4X4
416-290-0240,
info@itbusiness.ca
www.itbusiness.ca
Former Name: eBusiness Journal
Owned by: Transcontinental ITBusiness Group
Circulation: 20,000
Frequency: 12 times a year
Profile:: Covers Canada's IT industry: the key players, the important issues, the decision-making processes. Provides informative, incisive and unbiased coverage examining Canadian case studies, news stories and applications. It provides an overview of trends and technologies, and looks at Canadian product availability and costs

Joe Tersigni, Publisher

Ivey Business Journal
c/o Richard Ivey School of Business, University of Western O, London, ON N6A 3K7
519-661-3208, Fax: 519-661-3882,
www.iveybusinessjournal.com
Circulation: 12,013
Frequency: 6 times a year; ISSN: 1481-8248
Profile:: For more than 70 years, the Ivey Business Journal has delivered incisive, practical articles about managing. Covers articles about e-business, managing uncertainty, knowledge management, marketing, strategy and other topics that managers need to know more about to steer their firms to success

Ed Pearce, Publisher

Le Journal de l'Assurance
#100, 321, Rue de la Commune West, Montreal, QC H2Y 2E1
514-289-9595, Fax: 514-289-9527

PUBLICATIONS

Le Journal de l'Assurance (continued)

Owned by: Les Editions du Journal de l'Assurance
Circulation: 26 000
Frequency: 10 times a year; français; ISSN: 1198-4678
Profile:: Journal de l'assurance is a French-language news magazine that targets life insurance producers, general insurance brokers, financial planners, and financial advisors in Quebec

Serge Therrien, Éditeur

Journal Économique de Québec
#900, 1265, boul Charest ouest, Québec, QC G1N 4V4
418-686-6400, Fax: 418-868-1086, 888-293-0999
redacjeq@transcontinental.ca
Circulation: 19 000
Frequency: Hebdomadaire
Yvon Giroux, Rédacteur-en-chef

Kootenay Business Magazine
250-426-7253, Fax: 250-426-4125, 800-663-8555
info@kpimedia.com
www.kootenaybiz.com
Owned by: Koocanusa Publications Inc.
Circulation: 9,400
Frequency: 6 times a year
Profile:: Kootenay Business magazine is free to businesses within the Kootenay/ Columbia/ Boundary/ Revelstoke area

Keith Powell, Publisher

L'Opportuniste
450, 2e av, Sainte-Marie, QC G6E 1B6
418-387-6969, Fax: 418-387-5223, 877-387-6969
redactionopp@dynamiques.com
www.dynamiques.com
Frequency: Mensuel

Les Affaires
1100, boul René-Lévesque ouest 24e étage, Montréal, QC H3B 4X9
514-392-9000, Fax: 514-392-1586, 800-361-5479
lesaffaires.redaction@transcontinental.ca
www.lesaffaires.com
Owned by: Transcontinental Media Inc.
Circulation: 90 000
Frequency: 52 fois par an; français; aussi Affaires 500, PME, Affaires plus (10 fois par an, 93 288)
Profile:: Principal journal d'affaires de langue française au Canada, fondé en 1928. Ce tabloïd tout en couleur para(140t le samedi et a un tirage de 88 000 exemplaires, surtout vendus au Québec. Il est publié par les Publications Transcontinental Inc. Il est reconnu pour sa couverture des grandes sociétés canadiennes, des petites et moyennes entreprises québécoises, de l'économie canadienne et des affaires publiques. La moitié de son contenu est consacrée aux finances personnelles et aux placements avec diverses pages spécialisées, des tableaux et des graphiques

Jean-Paul Gagné, Éditeur

Le lien économique
#2, 500, rue Somerset ouest, Ottawa, ON K1R 5J8
613-858-1336, Fax: 613-234-1148,
sara,grenier@lieneconomique.com
Circulation: 13 500
Frequency: 6 fois par an
Profile:: Le Lien économique est lu par des décideurs de tous les secteurs de l'économie: Propriétaires et gestionnaires d'entreprises dans tous les secteurs d'activité commerciale : manufactures, institutions financières, services de santé, vente au détail, services et haute technologie

Réjean Grenier, Éditeur et rédacteur en chef

Magazine PME
1100, boul René-Lévesque 24e étage, Montréal, QC H3B 4X9
514-392-9000, Fax: 514-392-2026
Owned by: Transcontinental Media Inc.
Circulation: 35 922
Frequency: 10 fois par an; français
Profile:: Couvre les petites et moyennes entreprises au Québec

Marie Quinty, Rédactrice en chef

The Manitoba Broker
#3C, 2020 Portage Ave., Winnipeg, MB R3J 0K4
204-985-9785, Fax: 204-985-9795,
info@kelman.mb.ca
Circulation: 1,300
Frequency: 4 times a year
Profile:: Has timely industry releated articles by feature writers and advertisements of interest to Manitoba brokers

Terry Ross, Editor-in-chief

Manitoba Business Magazine
#508, 294 Portage Ave., Winnipeg, MB R3C 0B9
204-943-2931, Fax: 204-943-2942, 888-477-4620
mbm@mts.net
www.manitobabusinessmagazine.com
Circulation: 8,000
Frequency: 10 times a year
Ritchie Gage, Editor

Marketing Magazine
416-596-5853, Fax: 416-596-3482,
www.marketingmag.ca
Owned by: Rogers Publishing Ltd.
Circulation: 10,187
Frequency: Weekly
Richard Elliott, Executive Publisher

mbot Magazine
Mississauga Board of Trade, 701-77 City Dr., Mississauga, ON L5B 1M5
905-273-6151, Fax: 905-273-4937,
info@mbot.com
www.mbot.com
Circulation: 5,000
Frequency: 11 times a year
Sheryl McKean, President & CEO

Meeting Places
BIV Media Group, #500, 1155 West Pender St., Vancouver, BC V6E 2P4
604-688-2398, Fax: 604-688-6058
Circulation: 13,000
Paul Harris, Editor

Meetings & Incentive Travel (M&IT)
416-764-1635, Fax: 416-764-1419
Owned by: Rogers Publishing Ltd.
Circulation: 10,764
Frequency: 6 times a year
Steven Dempsey, Publisher

Mississauga Business Times
3145 Wolfedale Rd., Mississauga, ON L5C 3A9
905-273-8111, Fax: 905-273-8219,
www.mississauganews.com
Circulation: 40,000
Frequency: Monthly
Profile:: The News is a perennial newspaper award winner, including best newspaper in Ontario and Canada, on several occasions. The Mississauga News is delivered three times a week to houses.

Rick Drennan, Editor

Monday Report on Retailers
One Mount Pleasant Rd., 7th Fl., Toronto, ON M4Y 2Y5
416-764-1463, Fax: 416-764-1711,
www.mondayreport.ca
Owned by: Rogers Publishing Ltd.
Frequency: Weekly
Profile:: Canada's premier information resource for people seeking in-depth, up-to-date data on the retail, food service and shopping centre industries in Canada

Don Douloff, Managing Editor

MoneySense
One Mount Pleasant Rd., 11th Fl., Toronto, ON M4Y 2Y5
416-764-1400, Fax: 416-764-1404,
adsales@moneysense.com
www.canadianbusiness.com/moneysense_magazine
Owned by: Rogers Media Inc.
Circulation: 106,600
Frequency: 6 times a year
Profile:: MoneySense is Canada's leading personal finance magazine. Each issue contains insightful and informative columns and articles to help you make the most of your money. MoneySense magazine is published seven times a year by Rogers Media.

Ian McGugan, Editor

The National List of Advertisers
416-467-1621, Fax: 416-596-5158,
mala.singh@cardonline.rogers.com
www.cardonline.ca
Owned by: Rogers Publishing Ltd.
Circulation: 1,467
Frequency: Annually, Dec.
Bruce Richards, Publisher

National Post Business, FP 500
#300, 1450 Don Mills Rd., Toronto, ON M3B 3R5
416-383-2300, Fax: 416-386-2836, 800-668-7678
feedback@canada.com
www.nationalpostbusiness.com
Former Name: National Post 500; The Financial Post 500
Circulation: 289,000
Frequency: Annually, June
Profile:: Ranking of Canada's largest corporations

Brian Banks, Editor

Network Cabling
905-727-0077, Fax: 905-727-0017,
www.networkcabling.ca
Former Name: Structured Cabling
Owned by: CLB Media Inc.
Circulation: 9,200
Frequency: 6 times a year
Peter Young

North Country Business
PO Box , Bracebridge, ON P1L 1T6
705-646-1314, Fax: 705-645-6424,
info@muskokamagazine.com
http://ospreymediagroup.com
Circulation: 5,259
Frequency: 12 times a year
Donald Smith, Publisher

Northern Ontario Business
Laurentian Publishing Co., 158 Elgin St., Sudbury, ON P3E 3N5
705-673-5705, Fax: 705-673-9542, 800-757-2766
info@nob.on.ca
www.northernontariobusiness.com
Circulation: 10,000
Frequency: Monthly
Profile:: Northern Ontario Business is printed every month and is the only publication devoted to the region's business community

Patricia Mills, Publisher

Northwest Business Magazine
Dakota Design & Advertising Ltd., 3907 - 3A St. NE, Bay 114, Calgary, AB T2E 6S7
403-250-1128, Fax: 403-250-1194,
dakotade@telusplanet.net
Circulation: 15,000
Frequency: 10 times a year
Profile:: Regional business magazine that focuses on developments affecting the resource sectors in Northern BC, Alberta, Northwest Territories

Kathryn Engel, Editor

Nova Scotia Business Journal
Transontinental Specialty Publications, #609, 1888 Brunswick St., Halifax, NS B3J 3J8
902-468-8027, Fax: 902-468-1775,
info@transcontinental.ca
www.novascotiabusinessjournal.com
Circulation: 15,000
Frequency: Monthly
Profile:: This established business-to-business journal, published 12 times a year, features coverage of premier events, local success stories, issues affecting Nova Scotia's many business sectors, and sought-after special features.

Scott Higgins, Editor

Office@Home
PO Box , Bowen Island, BC V0N 1G0
604-947-2275, Fax: 604-947-0633,
officeathome@dowco.com
Frequency: 4 times a year
Dave Sharrock, Publisher

Okanagan Business Magazine
Byrne Publishing Group Inc., #10, 1753 Dolphin Ave., Kelowna, BC V1Y 8A6
250-861-5399, Fax: 250-868-3040, 888-311-1119
info@okanaganlife.com
www.okanaganlife.com
Circulation: 25,000

Frequency: 10 times a year
Profile:: Okanagan Life captures the essence of life and lifestyles in the Okanagan with informative and entertaining stories on Okanagan food and wine, Okanagan travel, Valley music and entertainment, Okanagan real estate, fashion trends, Okanagan personalities, Okanagan business profiles, community activism, and much more. Okanagan Life Magazine is distributed to 24,460 Okanagan Valley homes, businesses, newsstands and subscribers making it the only city or regional magazine in North America to match or exceed the circulation of the region's largest daily newspaper.

Paul Byrne, Publisher

Ontario Industrial Magazine
#1159, 1011 Upper Middle Rd. East, Oakville, ON L6H 5Z9
416-446-1404, Fax: 416-446-0502, 800-624-2776
sales@oim-online.com
www.oim-online.com
Circulation: 20,000
Frequency: Monthly
Profile:: OIM provides the very latest information about manufacturing technology, material handling products, industrial equipment & services, financial management and general business news

Keith Laverty, Publisher

Ontario Insurance Directory
#800, 12 Concorde Place, Toronto, ON M3C 4J2
416-442-2122, Fax: 416-442-2191, 800-668-2374
Owned by: Business Information Group
Circulation: 3,500
Frequency: Annually, Dec.
Profile:: Personal address and telephone book dedicated solely to the Ontario insurance industry

Steve Wilson, Senior Publisher

Ottawa Business Journal
Transcontinental Media, #30, 5300 Canotek Rd., Ottawa, ON K1J 8R7
613-744-4800, Fax: 613-744-8232,
obj@transcontinental.ca
www.ottawabusinessjournal.com
Circulation: 16,300
Frequency: 51 times a year
Profile:: Ottawa Business Journal is the leading source of local business news and information for Canada's national capital region. Every Monday, the newspaper provides authoritative and in-depth news coverage on the sectors that comprise Ottawa's vibrant business scene, ranging from technology to commercial real estate and corporate finance to hospitality.

Michael Curran, Publisher

Partners, Italy & Canada
Italian Chamber of Commerce of Toronto, #1502, 80 Richmond St. West, Toronto, ON M5H 2A4
416-789-7169, Fax: 416-789-7160,
info.toronto@italchambers.net
www.italchambers.ca
Circulation: 12,000
Frequency: 4 times a year
Profile:: partners is the official publication of the Italian Chamber of Commerce of Toronto. Published quarterly, the magazine features editorials and special reports written by international experts and tackles themes such as business ethics, design, multiculturalism, foreign trade, arts and entertainment. Through interviews and company profiles, partners is the voice of the Canadian, Italian and international business community.

Corrado Paina, Editor-in-chief

Pensez-y bien!
Les Éditions EJS, 13, ch du Pied-de-Roi, Lac Beaufort, QC G0A 2C0
418-686-1940, Fax: 418-871-0972,
info@ejs.qc.ca
www.ejs.qc.ca
Circulation: 150 000
Frequency: 4 fois par an; français
Profile:: Les articles présentent et expliquent les services et les produits financiers

France Bégin, Éditeur

Photo Life Buyers' Guide
185, rue St-Paul, Québec, QC G1K 3W2
800-905-7468
sales@photolife.com
www.photolife.com
Other information: Toll Free Fax: 1-800-664-2739
Former Name: National Photo Buyers' Guide
Circulation: 65,000
Frequency: Annual
Xavier Bonaconsi, Editor

Port of Halifax
902-420-9943, Fax: 902-429-9058,
publishers@metroguide.ca
www.portofhalifaxmagazine.com
Owned by: Metro Guide Publishing
Circulation: 20,000
Profile:: Port of Halifax Magazine features information about the Port of Halifax along with stories of interest to the international shipping community

Sheila Blair, Publisher

Professionally Speaking / Pour parler profession
Ontario College of Teachers, 121 Bloor St. East, Toronto, ON M4W 3M5
416-961-8800, Fax: 416-961-8822, 888-534-2222
ps@oct.ca
www.oct.ca
Circulation: 218,570
Frequency: 4 times a year
Richard Lewko, Publisher

Profit: The Magazine for Canadian Entrepreneurs
One Mount Pleasant Rd., 11th Fl., Toronto, ON M4Y 2Y5
416-764-1402, Fax: 416-764-1404,
www.canadianbusiness.com
Owned by: Rogers Media Inc.
Circulation: 102,600
Frequency: 6 times a year; ISSN: 1183-1324
Profile:: Published six times per year and boasting circulation of 101,000 and readership of 373,000, PROFIT delivers the highest composition of business decision-makers and managers / owner / professionals amongst all PMB measured English-language magazines in Canada

Deborah Rosser, Publisher

Progress
Penthouse, #1201, 1660 Hollis St., Halifax, NS B3J 1V7
902-494-0999, Fax: 902-494-0997,
progress@progresscorp.com
www.progresscorp.com
Former Name: Atlantic Progress
Circulation: 26,513
Frequency: 10 times a year; ISSN: 0046-6735
Pamela Scott Crace, Editor

Publication Profiles
416- -, Fax: 416-764-1709, 800-265-3561
mala.singh@cardonline.rogers.com
www.cardonline.ca
Owned by: Rogers Media Inc.
Circulation: 1,432
Frequency: Annually, Apr.
Bruce Richards, Publisher

Québec Enterprise
#200, 5, Place du Commerce, Ile des Soeurs, Montréal, QC H3E 1M8
514-842-5492, Fax: 514-842-5375, 866-303-5492
magazine@quebecenterprise.com
www.quebecentreprise.com
Circulation: 25,000
Frequency: 5 fois par an; français
Profile:: Magazine d'affaires couvrant les activités industrielles de toutes les régions du Québec

Daniel Boisvert, Président-éditeur

Québec Franchise & Occasions d'Affaires
CP , Youville, QC H2P 2V2
514-383-0034, Fax: 514-383-0057,
info@quebec-franchise.qc.ca
www.quebec-franchise.qc.ca
Former Name: Québec Franchise & Microfranchise
Circulation: 10 000 copies
Frequency: 6 times a year, French, 25% English
Profile:: Spécialisé dans la franchise et les opportunités d'affaires au Québec et au Canada

Jacques Desforges, Editor

Québec inc
#100, 321, rue de la Commune ouest, Montréal, QC H2Y 2E1
514-289-9595, Fax: 514-289-9527,
quebecinc@quebecinc.ca
www.quebecinc.ca/
Former Name: Magazine Finance
Circulation: 33 231
Frequency: 8 fois par an
Profile:: Magazine pour gens d'affaires du Québec

Claude Breton, Rédacteur en chef

Real Estate News
1400 Don Mills Rd., Toronto, ON M3B 3N1
416-443-8113, Fax: 416-443-9185,
ren@thestar.ca
www.toronto.com/realestatenews
Circulation: 99,442
Frequency: Weekly
Mirella Torchia, General Manager

Real Estate Victoria
Monday Publications, 818 Broughton St., Victoria, BC V8W 1E2
250-381-3926, Fax: 250-381-5606,
rev@revweekly.com
www.revweekly.com
Circulation: 20,000
Frequency: Weekly
Glenda Turner, Publisher

REM: Canada's Magazine for Real Estate Professionals
House Magazine Inc., 808 Coxwell Ave., Toronto, ON M4C 3E4
416-425-3504, Fax: 416-406-0882,
www.remonline.com
Also Known As: Real Estate Marketing
Circulation: 50,000
Frequency: 12 times a year
Heino Molls, Publisher

Report on Business Magazine (ROB)
c/o The Globe and Mail, 444 Front St. West, Toronto, ON M5V 2S9
416-585-5000, Fax: 416-585-3327,
newsroom@globeandmail.com
www.theglobeandmail.com
Frequency: 11 times a year
Profile:: Canada's premier business magazine is distributed nationwide with The Globe and Mail to targeted circulation. The thought-provoking and important business stories reach an influential and educated audience. As a pro-business, pro-Canada and pro-reader magazine, it charts the path of business like no other publication in this country

Philip Crawley, Publisher

Revue Commerce
1100, boul René-Lévesque ouest, 24e étage, Montréal, QC H3B 4X9
514-392-9000, Fax: 514-392-2026,
www.lesaffaires.com/publications/commerce.fr.html
Owned by: Transcontinental Media Inc.
Circulation: 37,766
Frequency: Mensuel; français; ISSN: 0380-9811
Profile:: Magazine d'actualité qui couvre le monde des affaires

Diane Bérar, Rédactrice en chef

Sales Promotion
905-634-2100, Fax: 905-634-2238,
www.sp-mag.com
Owned by: CLB Media Inc.
Circulation: 14,000
Frequency: 6 times a year
Jackie Roth, Publisher

Silver Screen
383 Lawrence Ave. West, Toronto, ON M5M 1B9
416-488-3393, Fax: 416-488-5217,
malcolm@msilver.com
www.msilver.com
Circulation: 1,800
Malcolm Silver, Publisher

SOHO Business Report
439A Marmont St., Coquitlam, BC V3K 4S4
604-936-5815, Fax: 604-936-5805, 888-963-5815
info@SOHObusinessreport.com
www.sohobusinessreport.com
Former Name: Home Business Report

SOHO Business Report (continued)
Circulation: 40,000
Frequency: 4 times a year
Profile:: SOHO Business Report is a quarterly magazine begun in 1989, when the SOHO-based business phenomenon was just a "blip" on the screen of public consciousness. It originated in Abbotsford, British Columbia, Canada from the home of founding publisher Barbara Mowat. Starting as a small newsletter, it first started as The B.C. Home Business Report, and was designed to help link home-based businesses across the province, providing the lone entrepreneur with practical tips and sensible advice on running their business. The newsletter was in demand, and soon other regional editions followed in Alberta and Ontario. Then in 1994, Home Business Report went national. After all these years, it was time for the magazine to enter its teenage growth spurt and the SOHO Business Report emerged as a celebration of over a decade and a half of helping entrepreneurs

Chad Thiessen, Publisher

Sounding Board
World Trade Center, #400, 999 Canada Pl., Vancouver, BC V6C 3E1
604-681-2111, Fax: 604-681-0437,
contactus@boardoftrade.com
www.boardoftrade.com
Circulation: 12,000
Frequency: 10 times a year
Profile:: As the official monthly publication of The Vancouver Board of Trade, the Sounding Board newspaper provides analysis and discussion of regional and national issues facing the business community. The paper has a primary circulation of 12,000 and a conservatively estimated total readership of 30,000. Sounding Board is published 10 times per year by The Board, Vancouver's chamber of commerce.

Darcy Rezac, Editor-in-chief

Strategy
416-408-2300, Fax: 416-408-0870,
cmacdonald@brunico.com
www.strategymag.com
Owned by: Brunico Communications
Circulation: 13,152
Frequency: 12 times a year
Claire MacDonald, Associate Publisher

Thompson's World Insurance News
PO Box , Waterloo, ON N2J 4S1
519-579-2500, Fax: 519-745-7321,
mpub@sympatico.ca
www.thompsonsnews.com
Frequency: Weekly
Profile:: Canada's only independent weekly for p&c insurance professionals, has been the industry's most trusted news source for more than a decade

Mark Publicover, Managing Editor

Thunder Bay Business
1145 Barton Street, Thunder Bay, ON P7B 5N3
807-623-2348, Fax: 807-623-7515,
nspinc@tbaytel.net
www.thunderbaybusiness.ca
Owned by: North Superior Publishing Inc.
Circulation: 5,000
Frequency: Monthly
Profile:: Northwestern Ontario business publication

Scott Sumner, Publisher & Editor

Toronto Business Magazine
11966 Woodbine Ave., Gormley, ON L0H 1G0
905-887-5048, Fax: 905-887-0764
Circulation: 48,085
Frequency: 6 times a year
Janet Gardiner, Publisher

The Toronto Stock Exchange Daily Record
130 King St. West, 3rd Fl., Toronto, ON M5X 1J2
416-947-4655, Fax: 416-814-8811
Circulation: 1,000
Frequency: Daily
Profile:: Toronto Stock Exchange publishes the names of conditionally approved companies in the Daily Record, a daily TSX publication

Catherine McGravey, Publisher & Editor

The Toronto Stock Exchange Monthly Review
130 King St., 3rd Fl., Toronto, ON M5X 1J2
416-947-4655, Fax: 416-814-8811
Also Known As: TSE Review
Circulation: 2,000
Frequency: 12 times a year
Profile:: Monthly bulletin containing market information for companies traded on the Toronto Stock Exchange

Catherine McGravey, Publisher & Editor

Trade & Commerce
1700 Church Ave., Winnipeg, MB R2X 3A2
204-632-2606, Fax: 204-694-3040,
tcommerce@wpgsun.com
www.tradeandcom.com
Circulation: 10,000
Frequency: 4 times a year
Profile:: Trade & Commerce magazine produces annual "Market Surveys" on all Canadian provinces and territories, that review overall economic performance and highlight investment and growth opportunities in specific communities. Each of the year's five issues also profiles leading companies operating within the surveyed regions. The Access Americas section features attractive U.S. and international locations for Canadian business and industrial expansion. Distributed nationally to top managers in Canada fastest growing companies

George Mitchell, Publisher

Western & Eastern Canada - Aviation Business Directory
reception@oppublishing.com
Former Name: Québec & Atlantic Provinces - Aviation Business Directory
Owned by: OP Publishing Ltd.
Frequency: annual
Katherine Kjaer, Manager

The Western Investor
Business in Vancouver Media Group, #501, 1155 West Pender St., Vancouver, BC V6E 2P4
604-669-8500, Fax: 604-669-2154,
www.westerninvestor.com
Circulation: 16,000
Frequency: Monthly
Cheryl Carter, Publisher

YorkU
York University, West Office Bldg., 4700 Keele St., Toronto, ON M3J 1P3
416-736-5058, Fax: 416-736-5681,
editor@yorku.ca
www.yorku.ca/yorku
Circulation: 180,000 alumni editions
Frequency: 5 times a year; includes 3 for alumni
Profile:: YorkU is the magazine of York University

Berton Woodward, Publications Director

SECTION 10

Indexes

Included in this section:

Alphabetical Entry Index

A

B

C

D

E

F

G

H

K

L

M

N

O

P

Q

R

S

T

U

V

W

X

Y

Z

Geographic Index

GEOGRAPHIC INDEX

Camrose

Canmore

Carbon

Claresholm

Cochrane

Drayton Valley

Drumheller

Eckville

Edmonton

British Columbia

GEOGRAPHIC INDEX

Vernon

Victoria

West Vancouver

White Rock

Williams Lake

Manitoba

Altona

Arborg

Ashern

Austin

Boissevain

Brandon

Carman

Cypress River

Dauphin

Erickson

Eriksdale

Ethelbert

Flin Flon

Grandview

Grunthal

Headingley

Island Lake

Minnedosa

Morden

Morris

Neepawa

Niverville

Oakbank

New Brunswick

Bathurst

Blackville

Burnt Church

Campbellton

Caraquet

Dieppe

Edmundston

Florenceville

Fredericton

Hampton

Miramichi

Moncton

Petitcodiac

Rexton

Riverview

Saint John

Shediac

St. Stephen

Stanley

Sussex

Woodstock

Newfoundland & Labrador

Channel-Port-aux-Basques

Conception Bay South

Corner Brook

Creston

Doyles

Gander

Grand Bank

Grand Falls-Windsor

Grand-Falls-Windsor

L'Anse au Loup

Marystown

Mount Pearl

Plum Point

St John's

St. John's

GEOGRAPHIC INDEX

Prince Edward Island

Saskatchewan

Yukon Territory

Executive Name Index

A

B

EXECUTIVE NAME INDEX

EXECUTIVE NAME INDEX

EXECUTIVE NAME INDEX

EXECUTIVE NAME INDEX

C

EXECUTIVE NAME INDEX

D

EXECUTIVE NAME INDEX

EXECUTIVE NAME INDEX

EXECUTIVE NAME INDEX

E

F

EXECUTIVE NAME INDEX

EXECUTIVE NAME INDEX

Q

EXECUTIVE NAME INDEX

S

EXECUTIVE NAME INDEX

EXECUTIVE NAME INDEX

T

EXECUTIVE NAME INDEX

U

V

EXECUTIVE NAME INDEX

W

EXECUTIVE NAME INDEX

EXECUTIVE NAME INDEX

EXECUTIVE NAME INDEX

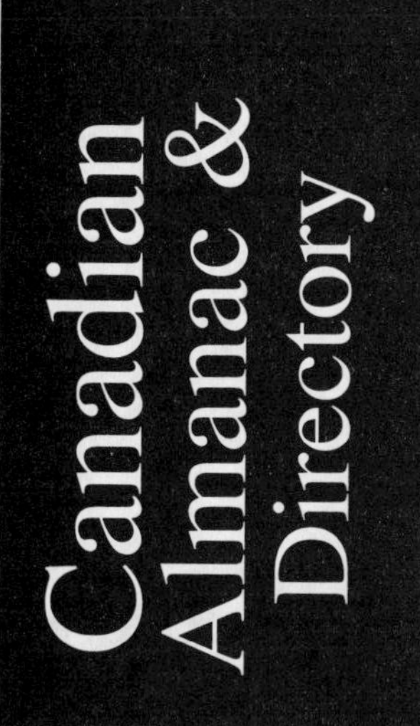

THE DEFINITIVE RESOURCE FOR FACTS AND FIGURES ON CANADA

The Canadian Almanac & Directory is the most complete source of Canadian information available – cultural, professional and financial institutions, legislative, governmental, judicial and educational systems.

Canada's authoritative sourcebook for almost 160 years, the Canadian Almanac & Directory is both a directory and guide that gives you access to almost 100,000 names and addresses of contacts throughout the network of Canadian institutions. However, this is not just a list of organizations. Also included are valuable facts such as profiles, populations, affiliates, publications – thoroughly indexed and easy to find.

This essential Canadian resource delivers quality information that has been verified and organized for easy retrieval. For critical contacts throughout Canada; for any number of business projects; for that once-in-a-while critical fact; the Canadian Almanac & Directory will help you find the leads that you didn't know existed – quickly and easily!

A wealth of general information provides national statistics on population, employment, CPI, imports and exports, etc. Images of national awards are presented with Canadian symbols, flags, emblems and Canadian Parliamentary leaders. Forms of address, order of precedence, postal information, weights, measures and distances and other useful charts are incorporated. Complete almanac information includes perpetual calendar, astronomical information, star charts, time zones and a five-year holiday planner.

With almost 160 years of editorial know-how, the Canadian Almanac & Directory has been developed to suit every kind of user need and is enhanced and verified regularly. Reliable information is critical to this best-selling publication's success – editorial professionals revise roughly 40% of the information annually. If you only want one source for Canadian information, this is it.

Print or online - Quick access to all the information you need!

Available in hardcover print or electronically via the Web, the Canadian Almanac & Directory provides instant access to the people you need and the facts you want every time. Canadian Almanac & Directory print edition is verified and updated annually. Regular ongoing changes are added to the Web version on a monthly basis. The Web version allows you to narrow your search by using index fields such as name or type of organization, subject, location, contact name or title, and postal code.

Create your own contact lists! Online subscribers have the option to pay a little more to instantly generate their own contact lists and export them into spreadsheets for further use. A great alternative to high cost list broker services.

It's 10 directories in one!

Organizations – Key Canadian associations in business, professions, labour, government and general interest.

Federal / Provincial Government – Officials in every department, plus listings for the Royal Family, the Commonwealth and a complete Diplomatic Directory.

Municipal Government – All Canadian cities and metro regions, together with the smallest hamlets in every province. No need for separate volumes.

Arts and Culture – Art galleries, archives, museums, zoos and performing arts.

Communications and Information Management – Newspaper, radio, TV, magazine and Internet organizations, book publishers and libraries.

Business & Finance – Stock exchanges, banks, credit unions, insurance companies, mutual fund managers and other financial institutions. Also included are accounting firms and major Canadian company listings with top officers.

Health and Medical – Hospitals, nursing homes, long-term care, health centres, regional health authorities and boards, and other care facilities with executive contacts.

Education – School boards, private schools, native schools, colleges, universities and other post-secondary educational institutions and government information.

Legal – All the judicial districts with courts and judges, plus 5,500 of the nation's law firms.

Almanac and Miscellany – Canadian statistics along with postal, transport and general information, forms of address, astronomical charts, Canadian honours and awards.

For more information please contact Grey House Publishing Canada by Tel.: 1-866-433-4739 or (416) 644-6479, Fax: (416) 644-1904 or via E-mail: info@greyhouse.ca • www.greyhouse.ca

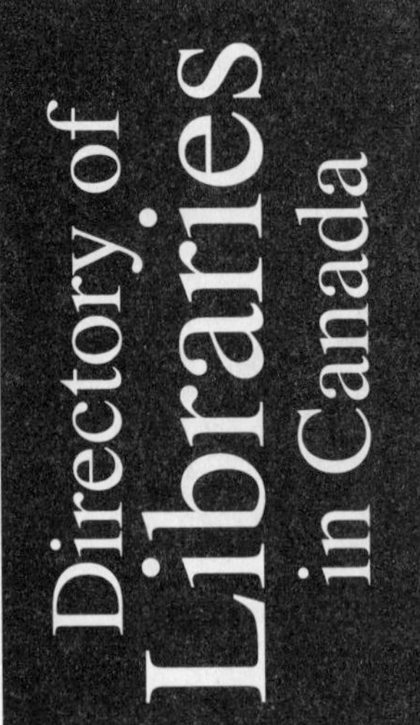

GAIN ACCESS TO COMPLETE AND DETAILED INFORMATION ON CANADIAN LIBRARIES

The Directory of Libraries in Canada brings together information from across the entire Canadian library sector, including libraries and branch libraries, educational libraries, regional systems, resource centres, archives, related periodicals, library schools and programs, provincial and governmental agencies, and associations.

The nation's leading library directory for 20 years, the Directory of Libraries in Canada gives you access to almost 10,000 names and addresses of contacts in Canadian institutions. Also included are valuable details such as library symbol, number of staff, operating systems, library type and acquisitions budget, hours of operation – thoroughly indexed and easy to find.

Available in print and online, the Directory of Libraries in Canada delivers quality information that has been verified and organized for easy retrieval. Five easy-to-use indexes assist you in navigating the print edition while the online version utilizes multiple index fields that help you get results.

Packed with over 800 pages of information the Grey House Canada editorial staff have gone to great lengths to ensure that what's included in this valuable resource is useful, reliable and current. This is your connection to the library industry in Canada.

Instant access to Canadian library sector information

For publishers, advocacy groups, computer hardware suppliers, Internet service providers and other diverse groups that provide products and services to the library community; associations that need to maintain a current list of library resources in Canada; research departments, students and government agencies that require information about the types of services and programs available at various research institutions; the Directory of Libraries in Canada will help you find the information you need – quickly and easily.

Expert search options available with online version...

The Directory of Libraries in Canada provides instant access to the people you need and the facts you want every time. The print edition is verified and updated annually and regular ongoing changes are added to the Web version on a monthly basis.

Available on Grey House Canada's CIRC interface, you can choose between Expert and Quick search to pinpoint information. Designed for both novice and advanced researchers, you can conduct simple text searches as well as powerful Boolean searches, plus you can narrow your search by using index fields such as name or type of institution, headquarters, location, area code, contact name or title, and postal code. You can also build on a previous search by highlighting words in the record and searching laterally throughout the database, and the mark record function permits you to view, print, e-mail or export up to 25 selected records.

Create your own contact lists! Online subscribers have the option to pay a little more to instantly generate their own contact lists and export them into spreadsheets for further use. A great alternative to high cost list broker services.

The Directory of Libraries in Canada gives you all the essentials for each institution:

- name, address, contact information and key personnel, number of staff;
- collection information, type of library, acquisitions budget, subject area, special collections;
- user services, number of branches, hours of operation, ILL information, photocopy and microform facilities, for-fee research, Internet access;
- systems information, details on electronic access, operating and online systems, Internet and e-mail software, Internet connectivity, access to electronic resources;
- additional information including associations, publications and regional systems.

With almost 60% of the data changing annually it has never been more important to have the latest version of the Directory of Libraries in Canada.

For more information please contact Grey House Publishing Canada by Tel.: 1-866-433-4739 or (416) 644-6479, Fax: (416) 644-1904 or via E-mail: info@greyhouse.ca • www.greyhouse.ca

Canadian Environmental Directory

THE ONLY COMPLETE GUIDE TO THE BUSINESS OF ENVIRONMENTAL MANAGEMENT

The Canadian Environmental Directory provides comprehensive details on government offices and programs, information sources, product and service firms and trade fairs that pertain to the business of environmental management.

The Canadian Environmental Directory provides information on every aspect of the environment industry in unprecedented detail. All information is fully indexed and cross-referenced for easy use. The directory features current information on all key contacts in Canada's environmental industry including:

Directory of Products and Services – contains detailed listings for companies producing and selling products and services in the environmental sector. Includes EcoLogo™ companies, and companies certified to ISO standards.

Environmental Associations – over 2,000 Canadian industrial, commercial and professional associations, registered charities and environmental interest groups.

Chronology of Environmental Events - a one-year summary of environmental events, providing an overview of regulatory trends, company contracts, critical decisions and major events.

Law Firms – an inclusive list of Canadian firms with lawyers specializing in environmental law. Locate lawyers by region, select by specialization or size, and contact them directly.

Special Libraries and Resource Centres – listings for almost 1,000 special libraries and resource centres across Canada, including specialized collections.

Major Canadian Companies – private, public and crown corporation listings complete with environmental contacts or the CEO/President, as well as a brief description of the business.

Federal and Provincial Government – information for every department and agency influencing environmental initiatives and purchasing policies.

Environmental Trade Representatives - provides contact information for those responsible for developing trade in the environmental sector in foreign countries. - information to assist organizations with the development of business ties in foreign markets.

Municipal and Local Governments – facts, figures and contact information for cities, towns and regional areas.

Conferences, Seminars and Tradeshows – events, shows and meetings planned for 2006 and years following including location, sponsor, contact and number of attendees where applicable.

Valuable indexing and sourcing tools to aid your search!

Main Index - Key words and subject classifications.

Quick Reference to Government - Find federal/provincial contacts instantly with an at-a-glance index of environmental topics.

Associations - Complete subject and key word index to environmental associations everywhere, plus an acronym index.

Directory of Products and Services - Indexed by the industry's best product/service classifications PLUS a separate geographic index for sources in your region. All companies listed alphabetically.

Tabs - Main sections are tabbed for easy look-up. Headnotes on each page make it easy to locate the data you need.

Print or online - Quick access to all the information you need!

Available in hardcover print or electronically via the Web, the Canadian Environmental Directory provides instant access to the people you need and the facts you want every time. The Canadian Environmental Directory is verified and updated annually. Regular ongoing changes are added to the Web version on a monthly basis.

The Web version allows you to narrow your search by using index fields such as name or type of organization, subject, location, contact name or title and postal code.

Create your own contact lists! Online subscribers have the option to pay a little more to instantly generate their own contact lists and export them into spreadsheets for further use. A great alternative to high cost list broker services.

For more information please contact Grey House Publishing Canada by Tel.: 1-866-433-4739 or (416) 644-6476, Fax: (416) 644-1904 or via E-mail: info@greyhouse.ca • www.greyhouse.ca

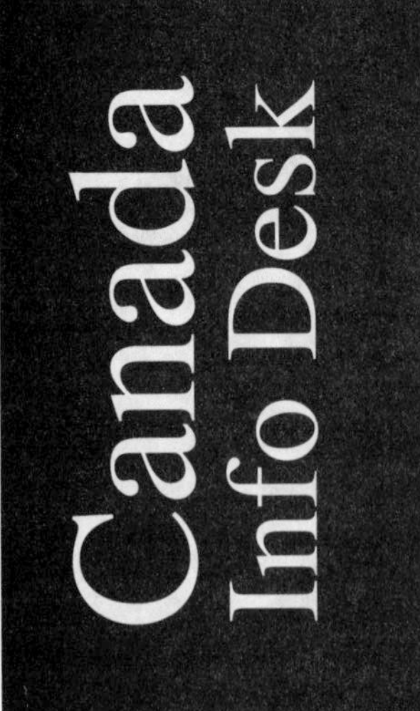

Canada Info Desk integrates Grey House Canada's best-selling directories into a single online Canadian resource – making it the most comprehensive directory database in Canada. The easy-to-use Web interface gives users instant access to thousands of organizations, contacts, facts and figures about Canadian business, government and society. No other single source offers as in-depth and diverse array of Canadian information.

Subscribers can search based on more general record categorization, including:

- arts and culture
- business and finance
- communication and information
- Canadians and society
- education
- environment
- government
- health
- industry
- labour
- law and justice
- public services
- recreation
- religion
- science and nature
- transportation

Start your search here

Canada Info Desk is your comprehensive quick reference guide to Canada. It can be found on the desks and shelves of Canada's finest libraries and institutions. Professional researchers can search by fielded data to pinpoint information on the spot. Students can quickly track down organizations or people, locate addresses, analyze activities or even job hunt using the extensive listings. Invaluable to business professionals, Canada Info Desk is an excellent tool to pinpoint contacts or prospects, identify partner groups, search for promotional opportunities and export custom lists in seconds.

Design your own custom lists, why wait?

Save time and money with this unique and valuable resource. Canada Info Desk database gives you the option to define and extract your own lists in seconds. Whether you need contact, mail or e-mail lists, Canada Info Desk can pull together the information quickly and export it in a variety of formats. It is your key to the who's who of government, business, law, associations, media, education... quality information where you need it most, your desktop.

Innovative interface with enhanced functionality

Canada Info Desk gives users the ability to limit their search many different ways including the original database source, subject category and location. Researchers can choose between a complex Expert Search or a simple Quick Search depending on their familiarity with search technology.

Key advantages of Canada Info Desk:

- seamlessly cross-database search all database content or content subsets
- generate and export customized lists for contact data, marketing, or research collection
- regular ongoing changes are added to the Web version on a monthly basis.
- conduct a quick search with fields common to all databases, or build a complex Boolean expert search query
- customize results by searching for records that are head offices, have e-mail, phone, fax or Web sites, promote conferences, produce publications, or are mailing list compliant
- highlight words to laterally search within results
- save time by saving search results for future reference
- mark records in the results list or full record and then view, print, e-mail or export
- link directly to Web sites or e-mail addresses

With Canada Info Desk, subscribers can set their own search parameters based on a list of over 30 fields. Fields include organization name, contact name or title, address or location, postal code range, sector specific information based on the type of organization, plus full text searching of the entire record.

For more information please contact Grey House Publishing Canada by Tel.: 1-866-433-4739 or (416) 644-6479, Fax: (416) 644-1904 or via E-mail: info@greyhouse.ca • www.greyhouse.ca

Grey House Canada maintains substantial databases of contacts in many Canadian institutions. Our editors compile and update listings on a regular basis for the publications listed here. Lists can be compiled from many different criteria to closely target your needs.

Grey House Canada Custom Mailing Lists:

- **Associations** - the most extensive list of Canadian Associations available, featuring all professional, trade and business organizations together with not-for profit groups.
- **Arts & Culture** - the definitive source of key prospects in various Canadian arts and cultural outlets.
- **Education** - the most comprehensive list of educational institutions and organizations in Canada.
- **Health Care / Hospitals** - includes all major medical facilities with chief executive.
- **Lawyers** - key prospects for a number of direct mail offers.
- **Media** - the definitive source of key prospects in various Canadian media outlets, offering the top business managers/publishers.
- **Environmental** - a complete profile of the Canadian Environmental scene constantly revised for the annual Canadian Environmental Directory.
- **Financial Services** - a list of key contacts from the full range of Canada's financial services industry.
- **Government Key Contacts** - a list of key Government contacts, maintained by the Canadian Almanac & Directory, Canada's standard institutional reference for over 150 years.
- **Libraries** - the most unique and complete list of special and public libraries available.
- **Major Canadian Companies** - listings of Canada's largest private, public and crown corporations with major key contacts of the top business decision-makers.

Availability

Lists are available on CD, mailing labels and via e-mail. They are provided on a one time use basis or for a one year lease. Use the contact information below to request a quotation on lists, tailormade to suit your needs.

For more information please contact Grey House Publishing Canada by Tel.: 1-866-433-4739 or (416) 644-6476, Fax: (416) 644-1904 or via E-mail: info@greyhouse.ca • www.greyhouse.ca

INFORMATION FORM

PHOTOCOPY THIS FORM FOR CONVENIENCE

CHANGE TO LISTING

PAGE NUMBER: DIRECTORY:

NAME OF ORGANIZATION:

PLEASE CHANGE OUR LISTING TO REFLECT THE FOLLOWING:

NEW LISTING:

WE ARE NOT REPRESENTED IN THE DIRECTORY. HERE IS THE INFORMATION ON OUR ASSOCIATION/ORGANIZATION/ GOVERNMENT BODY: (*Please examine the guidelines in the front of the directory and the entries of similar organizations for an indication of how best to present your data*).

WE WOULD LIKE TO SEE MORE INFORMATION ON:

MAIL INFORMATION TO:
GREY HOUSE PUBLISHING CANADA
20 VICTORIA ST.
TORONTO, ONTARIO
M5C 2N8

E-MAIL TO:
INFO@GREYHOUSE.CA

FAX INFORMATION TO:
THE EDITOR,
FINANCIAL SERVICES
CANADA DIRECTORY
(416) 644-1904

DIRECTORIES ORDER FORM

QTY	TITLE	HARDCOVER PRINT	ONLINE
	CANADIAN ALMANAC & DIRECTORY 2007	$300.00	*Call for quote*
	FINANCIAL SERVICES CANADA 2007/2008	$325.00	*Call for quote*
	CANADIAN ENVIRONMENTAL DIRECTORY 2007	$325.00	*Call for quote*
	ASSOCIATIONS CANADA 2007	$325.00	*Call for quote*
	DIRECTORY OF LIBRARIES IN CANADA 2006/2007	$225.00	*Call for quote*
	GOVERNMENTS CANADA *(updated monthly)*	*NA*	*Call for quote*
	CANADA INFO DESK *(updated monthly)*	*NA*	*Call for quote*

PLEASE NOTE.
Prices are stated in Canadian dollars. All prices are subject to change without notice. NA = Not Available
To purchase print directories online visit our Web site - www.greyhouse.ca
Orders shipped outside Canada are charged in US dollars.

COMMENTS:

METHOD OF PAYMENT:

❑ **CHEQUE/MONEY ORDER**
Please make cheque/money order payable to Grey House Publishing Canada for total amount including applicable taxes. (Please call to confirm total)

❑ **CREDIT CARD**

❑ VISA ❑ AMEX ❑ Mastercard

CARD NUMBER

EXPIRY DATE

SIGNATURE

❑ **BILL MY COMPANY/ORGANIZATION**

PO# IF APPLICABLE

SHIP TO:

NAME

TITLE/DEPT.

ORGANIZATION

ADDRESS

CITY

PROV POSTAL CODE

BUSINESS PHONE FAX NUMBER

E-MAIL

❑ **STANDING ORDER PLAN**
Please book my standing order for future annual print editions.
With an automatic renewal, I'll save 10% off subsequent orders.

APPLICABLE TAXES
6% GST applies to Ontario, Quebec, Manitoba, Saskatchewan, Alberta, British Columbia. An additional 8% PST applies to Ontario. 14% HST applies to all Atlantic Provinces.

SHIPPING & HANDLING
$12.00 for a single directory, $4.00 each additional directory (Canadian & US Orders).

International Orders - Call for rates. Subject to customs duty tax at customer expense.

20 Victoria Street
Toronto, Ontario M5C 2N8

PHONE
(866) 433-4739

FAX
(416) 644-1904

E-MAIL
info@greyhouse.ca